NEW JERSEY
CODE OF CRIMINAL JUSTICE AND MOTOR VEHICLE LAWS

With Related
Statutes and Court Rules

2010 EDITION

As Amended Through Chapter 3 of the 2010 Laws

WEST®

A Thomson Reuters business

Mat#40835365

© 2010 Thomson Reuters

ISBN 978–0–314–90155–2

PREFACE

This Pamphlet is designed to provide the reader with a convenient easy-to-use Criminal and Motor Vehicle Laws reference tool. It contains the complete text of New Jersey's Criminal Code, Title 2C, and Motor Vehicle Code, Title 39. In addition, related subject matter provisions selected from Title 2A, Administration of Civil and Criminal Justice, Title 2B, Court Organization and Civil Code, Title 4, Agriculture and Domestic Animals, Title 9, Children-Juvenile and Domestic Relations Courts, Title 13, Conservation and Development, Title 15, Corporations, Title 21, Explosives and Fireworks, Title 24, Food and Drugs, Title 26, Health and Vital Statistics, Title 27, Highways, Title 33, Intoxicating Liquors, Title 40A, Municipalities and Counties, Title 48, Public Utilities, Title 53, State Police, Title 56, Trade Names, Trade-Marks, and Unfair Trade Practices, and Title 58, Waters and Water Supply have also been included.

Rules of Court, including rules governing general application, criminal practice and practice in the chancery division, family part and the municipal courts, are current with orders received through April 16, 2010.

A combined index to all laws and court rules contained herein is set forth at the end of the pamphlet.

For other laws, annotations to the judicial construction and application of the criminal laws, detailed historical notes explaining legislative changes in the laws, references to law review commentaries, and many other informative features and aids to research, the user should examine West's New Jersey Statutes Annotated.

Laws included are through Chapter 3 of the 2010 First Annual Session of the 214th Legislature.

For the text of subsequently enacted legislation, see New Jersey Session Law Service.

WEST

May, 2010

*

PREFACE

This Pamphlet is designed to provide the reader with a convenient easy-to-use Criminal and Motor Vehicle Laws reference tool. It contains the complete text of New Jersey's Criminal Code, Title 2C, and Motor Vehicle Code, Title 39. In addition, related subject matter provisions selected from Title 2A, Administration of Civil and Criminal Justice, Title 2B, Court Organization and Civil Code, Title 4, Agriculture and Domestic Animals, Title 9, Children-Juvenile and Domestic Relations Courts, Title 13, Conservation and Development, Title 15, Corporations, Title 21, Explosives and Fireworks, Title 24, Food and Drugs, Title 26, Health and Vital Statistics, Title 27, Highways, Title 33, Intoxicating Liquors, Title 40A, Municipalities and Counties, Title 48, Public Utilities, Title 53, State Police, Title 56, Trade Names, Trade-Marks, and Unfair Trade Practices, and Title 58, Waters and Water Supply have also been included.

Rules of Court including rules governing general application, criminal practice and practice in the chancery division, family part and the municipal court, are current with orders received through April 16, 2010.

A combined index to all laws and court rules contained herein is set forth at the end of the pamphlet.

For other laws, annotations to the judicial construction and application of the criminal laws, detailed historical notes explaining legislative changes in the laws, references to law review commentaries, and many other informative features and aids to research, the user should examine West's New Jersey Statutes Annotated.

Laws included are through Chapter 3 of the 2010 First Annual Session of the 214th Legislature.

For the text of subsequently enacted legislation, see New Jersey Session Law Service.

WEST

May 2010

III

RELATED PRODUCTS FROM WEST

NEW JERSEY PRACTICE SERIES

Court Rules Annotated
John H. Klock

Court Rules Annotated—Evidence Rules
John H. Klock

Court Rules Annotated—Trial Lawyer's Manual
John H. Klock

Civil Practice Forms
James H. Walzer

Wills and Administration
Alfred C. Clapp and Dorothy G. Black

Family Law and Practice with Forms
Susan Reach Winters and Thomas D. Baldwin

Real Estate Law and Practice with Forms
Henry Walentowicz and Matthew Slowinski

Legal Forms
James H. Walzer

Municipal Court Practice
Robert Ramsey

Municipal Court Practice Manual
Robert Ramsey

Employment Law
Marvin M. Goldstein and Stanley L. Goodman

Skills and Methods

Landlord and Tenant Law
Raymond I. Korona

Motor Vehicle Law and Practice
Robert Ramsey

New Jersey Drunk Driving Law
Robert Ramsey

Motor Vehicle Law and Practice Forms
Robert Rubinstein

Uniform Commercial Code Forms
Samuel N. Reiken

Law of Mortgages with Forms
Myron Weinstein

Criminal Practice and Procedure
Leonard N. Arnold

V

RELATED PRODUCTS

Criminal Law
Gerald D. Miller

Local Government Law
Michael A. Pane

Land Use Law
David J. Frizell

Administrative Law and Practice
Steven L. Lefelt, Anthony Miragliotta and Patricia Prunty

Workers' Compensation Law
Jon L. Gelman

Appellate Practice and Procedure
Edward A. Zunz, Jr. and Edwin Chociey

Construction Law
Robert S. Peckar

Discovery
S. Robert Allcorn

State and Local Taxation
David E. Crabtree

Debtor–Creditor Law and Practice
Michael D. Sirota and Michael S. Meisel

Elder Law—Guardianships and Conservatorships
Sharon Rivenson Mark

Elder Law—New Jersey Medicaid Laws and Regulations
Sharon Rivenson Mark

New Jersey Attorney and Judicial Discipline
Robert Ramsey

Civil Trial Handbook
William S. Greenburg and John Flaherty

Title 39—New Jersey Motor Vehicle Code Annotated
Robert Ramsey

Arrest, Search and Seizure Review
Robert Ramsey

Business Law Deskbook
Brent A. Olson, Kristina K. Pappa and Elga A. Goodman

Elements of Action
James H. Walzer

Insurance Codes Annotated
Robert Ramsey

––––––––––

New Jersey Digest
New Jersey Digest Law Finder

RELATED PRODUCTS

New Jersey Reports
New Jersey Rules of Court, State and Federal
New Jersey Statutes Annotated
New Jersey Statutes Compact Edition
New Jersey Tax Court Reports
New Jersey Business Organizations Law
New Jersey Code of Criminal Justice and Motor Vehicle Laws
New Jersey Education Law
New Jersey Estate and Probate Law
New Jersey Family Law
Guralnick's New Jersey Family Law Annotated

———————

Westlaw®
WestCheck.com™
West CD–ROM Libraries™
KeyCite®

———————

Many of these products are also available on CD–ROM and online via Westlaw.
To order any of these New Jersey practice tools, call your West Representative or **1–800–328–9352**.

NEED RESEARCH HELP?

You can get quality research results with free help—call the West Reference Attorneys when you have questions concerning Westlaw or West Publications at **1–800–REF–ATTY** (1–800–733–2889).

INTERNET ACCESS

Contact the West Editorial Department directly with your questions and suggestions by e-mail at west.editor@thomson.com. Visit West's home page at west.thomson.com.

*

WESTLAW ELECTRONIC
RESEARCH GUIDE

Westlaw—Expanding the Reach of Your Library

Westlaw, West's online legal research service, provides you with the same quality and integrity that you have come to expect from West books. In addition, you have quick, easy access to West's vast collection of statutes, case law materials, public records, news and business information, and other legal and nonlegal resources. West's editorial enhancements, such as case headnotes and topic and key numbers, enable you to move quickly and easily between West print resources and Westlaw for your legal research.

Accessing Databases Using the Westlaw Directory

You can use the Westlaw Directory to view all the databases on Westlaw, as well as to link to detailed information about each database. To access the Westlaw Directory, click **Directory** at the top of any Westlaw page. Browse the directory by clicking the links for the headings or subheadings in the right frame. Click a database name to access a database. You can also type all or part of a database name in the *Search for a database* text box in the left frame and click **Go**. A list of databases is displayed. To access a database, click its name.

Retrieving a Specific Document

If you know the citation of a document, use the Find service on Westlaw to quickly retrieve the document. Click **Find&Print** at the top of any Westlaw page to display the Find a Document page. Type the citation in the *Find this document by citation* text box in the left frame and click **Go**.

Find templates are available for federal and state case law, the U.S. Constitution and state constitutions, federal and state statutes and regulations, and many other materials. If you are unsure of the correct citation format, simply type the publication abbreviation in the *Find this document by citation* text box and click **Go**. A fill-in-the-blank template is displayed. For example, to display a Find template for a state's statutes, type **xx st** (where xx is a state's two-letter postal abbreviation).

To retrieve a specific case when you know one or more parties' names, click **Find&Print**. Then click **Find a Case by Party Name** in the left frame. The Find a Case by Party Name search template is displayed.

Checking Citations in KeyCite®

KeyCite is the citation research service on Westlaw. KeyCite information is available for every case in West's® National Reporter System® and more than 1 million unpublished cases; federal statutes and regulations; statutes from all 50 states; administrative decisions from selected federal agencies; regulations and administrative decisions from selected states; and other materials.

You can use KeyCite to determine whether a case, statute, regulation, or administrative decision is good law. You can also use KeyCite to retrieve citing references to a document, including cases, administrative materials, secondary sources, and briefs and other court documents. KeyCite history for a statute includes citations to recent session laws that amend or repeal the section and proposed legislation.

WESTLAW GUIDE

Click **KeyCite** at the top of any Westlaw page to get a detailed explanation of the KeyCite status flags and depth of treatment stars. Depth of treatment stars help you focus on the most important citing references.

The KeyCite Alert service allows you to monitor the status of a case, statute, regulation, or administrative decision and sends you updates when its KeyCite result (i.e., history or citing references) changes.

United States Code Annotated® **(USCA**®**)**

The USCA contains the official text of the U.S. Code along with annotations that include notes of decisions, historical notes, research references, and cross-references.

State Statutes

Annotated state statutes are available for all 50 states and the District of Columbia.

Links Tab

When you are viewing a statute, the Links tab in the left frame allows you to view information related to the statute, including cases that cite the statute, legislative history, and prior versions of the statute.

- **Legislative History**

    Legislative history for federal statutes provides you with public laws, *Congressional Record* documents, committee reports, bill drafts, congressional testimony, congressional bills, and presidential messages. Legislative history for state statutes, available for 36 states and the District of Columbia, provides you with committee reports, legislative journals, transcripts of legislative proceedings, records of legislators' votes, and governors' messages.

- **Graphical Statutes**®

    This feature allows you to track changes to a statute in an easy-to-read graphical display, which includes enacting public laws, relevant legislative history materials, and prior versions.

- **Versions**

    You can view prior versions of the USCA and selected state statutes that were effective on a specific date.

- **50 State Surveys**

    These surveys allow you to see how a particular legal topic has been addressed by comparable state statutes in any of the 50 states and the District of Columbia.

RegulationsPlus®

USCA® sections are linked to related **Code of Federal Regulations (CFR)** provisions to allow seamless viewing between the two Codes. Additional features include a full-service CFR Index of more than 1 million references created by West attorney-editors, arranged by topic and linked directly to CFR sections, plus CFR Notes of Decisions, linked to the caselaw and to West Key Numbers and Topics.

ResultsPlus®

After you run a search in a statutes database, Westlaw automatically creates a ResultsPlus list of additional documents and West topic and key numbers that have a high statistical likelihood of matching the concepts in your search. Click a document title in the list to view the full text of the document.

WESTLAW GUIDE

Additional Information

Westlaw is available on the Web at westlaw.com.

For search assistance, call the West Reference Attorneys at 1–800–REF–ATTY (1–800–733–2889).

For technical assistance, call West Customer Technical Support at 1–800–WESTLAW (1–800–937–8529).

*

TABLE OF CONTENTS

		Page
Preface		III

TITLE 2C.   CODE OF CRIMINAL JUSTICE

Subtitle 1.   General Provisions

Chapter		Page
1.	Preliminary	1
2.	General Principles of Liability	7
3.	General Principles of Justification	12
4.	Responsibility	16
5.	Inchoate Crimes	20
6.	Bail	23
7.	Registration and Notification of Release of Certain Offenders	23
8 to 10.	[Reserved]	31

Subtitle 2.   Definition of Specific Offenses

PART 1.   OFFENSES INVOLVING DANGER TO THE PERSON

11.	Criminal Homicide	32
11A.	Human Cloning	36
12.	Assault; Reckless Endangering; Threats	36
13.	Kidnapping and Related Offenses: Coercion	42
14.	Sexual Offenses	47
15.	Robbery	51
16.	Bias Crimes	51

PART 2.   OFFENSES AGAINST PROPERTY

17.	Arson, Criminal Mischief, and Other Property Destruction	52
18.	Burglary and Other Criminal Intrusion	56
19.	[Reenacted as Chapter 15 of Title 2C by P.L.1979, c. 178]	57
20.	Theft and Related Offenses	57
21.	Forgery and Fraudulent Practices	73
22.	Human Remains	99
23.	[Reserved]	100

PART 3.   OFFENSES AGAINST OTHERS

24.	Offenses Against the Family, Children and Incompetents	100
25.	Domestic Violence	102
26.	[Reserved]	113

XIII

TABLE OF CONTENTS

Chapter		Page

PART 4. OFFENSES AGAINST PUBLIC ADMINISTRATION

27.	Bribery and Corrupt Influence	113
28.	Perjury and Other Falsification in Official Matters	116
29.	Obstructing Governmental Operations: Escape	119
30.	Misconduct in Office: Abuse of Office	124
31.	[Reserved]	127
32.	[Reserved]	127

PART 5. OFFENSES AGAINST PUBLIC ORDER, HEALTH AND DECENCY

33.	Riot, Disorderly Conduct, and Related Offenses	127
34.	Public Indecency	138
35.	Controlled Dangerous Substances	142
35A.	Anti–Drug Profiteering	170
35B.	Drug Dealer Liability	173
36.	Drug Paraphernalia	177
36A.	Conditional Discharge for Certain First Offenders	180
37.	Gambling Offenses	181
38.	September 11th, 2001 Anti-Terrorism Act	184
39.	Firearms, Other Dangerous Weapons and Instruments of Crime	188
40.	Other Offenses Relating to Public Safety	203
40A.	Miscellaneous	208

PART 6. OFFENSES INVOLVING ORGANIZED CRIME
AND ORGANIZED CRIME ACTIVITIES

| 41. | Racketeering | 209 |
| 42. | [Reserved] | 214 |

Subtitle 3. Sentencing

43.	Authorized Disposition of Offenders	215
44.	Authority of Court in Sentencing	235
45.	Suspension of Sentence; Probation	244
46.	Fines and Restitution	246
47.	Adult Diagnostic and Treatment Center	251
48.	Criminal Disposition Commission	256
48A.	Criminal Sentencing and Disposition Commission	257
49.	Capital Punishment	258
50.	[Reserved]	258
51.	Loss and Restoration of Rights Incident to Conviction of an Offense	258
52.	Expungement of Records	262
53 to 57.	[Reserved]	268
58.	Licensing and Other Provisions Relating to Firearms	268
59 to 61.	[Reserved]	284
62.	Willful Nonsupport	284
63.	[Reserved]	285

TABLE OF CONTENTS

Chapter		Page
64.	Forfeiture	285
65.	Disposition of Stolen Property and Documentary Exhibits	287
66.	Attachment, Freezing of Terrorist Funds	288
67 to 97.	[Reserved]	290
98.	Repealers, Allocations and Effective Date	290
99 to 103.	[Reserved]	294
104.	Material Witnesses	294

TITLE 39.   MOTOR VEHICLES AND TRAFFIC REGULATIONS

Subtitle 1.   Motor Vehicle and Traffic Laws

1.	Definitions	297
2.	Department of Motor Vehicles	301
2A.	New Jersey Motor Vehicle Commission	307
3.	Motor Vehicles	323
3A.	Additional Equipment Regulations	458
3B.	School Buses, Equipment and Regulations	458
3C.	Snowmobiles	464
4.	Traffic Regulation	482
5.	Enforcement and Procedure	578
5A.	Application of Subtitle to Highways Owned by Public or Semipublic Corporations	593
5B.	Transportation of Dangerous Articles on Highway	594
5C.	Motor Vehicle Racing on Highways	598
5D.	Interstate Compact; Drivers Licenses	598
5E.	Transportation of Bulk Commodities [Repealed]	601
5F.	Nonresident Violator Compact	601
5G.	Limousine Operation and Enforcement	605

Subtitle 2.   Other Laws Regulating Motor Vehicles

6.	Financial Responsibility	608
6A.	Compulsory Automobile Liability Insurance—No Fault Provisions	627
6B.	Compulsory Motor Vehicle Insurance	651
7.	Service of Process Upon Nonresidents	652
8.	Inspection of Motor Vehicles	654
9.	Hours of Duty of Operators of Certain Motor Vehicles	686
10.	Purchase, Sale and Transfer of Motor Vehicles	687
10A.	Abandoned and Unclaimed Motor Vehicles	700
10B.	Motor Vehicle Component Parts	703
11.	Junk Yards	706
12.	Driving Schools	708
13.	Auto Body Repair Facilities	712

TABLE OF CONTENTS

TITLE 2A.   ADMINISTRATION OF CIVIL AND CRIMINAL JUSTICE

Subtitle 1.   The Courts

Chapter   Page
4A. Family Court, selected provisions 717

Subtitle 9.   Evidence, Witnesses and Public Hearings

84A. Rules of Evidence 748
     New Jersey Rules of Evidence 763

Subtitle 10.   Crimes

93. Bribery and Corruption, selected provisions 814
102. Embezzlement, Conversion and Misappropriation, selected provisions 814
123. Manufacture, Sale, Etc., of Certain Articles, selected provisions ... 817
149. Unauthorized Use of Voting Machines or Electrical Voting Systems in Legislative or Public Bodies 821

Subtitle 11.   Criminal Procedure

152. Definitions, Construction and General Provisions................ 822
153. Rewards for Apprehension of Persons Accused of Crime 823
154. Peace Officers.. 824
155. Uniform Fresh Pursuit Law 825
156. Uniform Act on Intrastate Fresh Pursuit 826
156A. Wiretapping, Etc.. 827
157. County Detectives and Investigators 841
158. County Prosecutors.. 845
158A. Public Defender 849
159A. Interstate Agreement on Detainers........................... 853
160. Extradition 857
161. Preliminary Proceedings in General 863
161A. Personal Searches 863
162. Bail and Recognizances 865
163. Trial 868
164. Sentence and Imprisonment, selected provisions............... 868
166. Costs and Fines 869
166A. Reimbursement to Counties for Criminal Prosecution Expenses... 870
167. Executive Clemency 870
168. Probation and Parole 872
168A. Rehabilitated Convicted Offenders 884

Subtitle 12.   Disorderly Persons

169. General Provisions 890
170. Disorderly Persons Generally, selected provisions.............. 890

TITLE 2B.   COURT ORGANIZATION AND CIVIL CODE

12. Municipal Courts.. 895
19. Comprehensive Enforcement Program Fund 903

TABLE OF CONTENTS

Chapter		Page
20.	Qualification and Selection of Jurors	906
21.	County Grand Juries	909
22.	State Grand Juries	910
23.	Petit Jurors	912
25.	Municipal Prosecutors	914

TITLE 4.   AGRICULTURE AND DOMESTIC ANIMALS

22.	Prevention of Cruelty to Animals	919

TITLE 9.   CHILDREN—JUVENILE AND DOMESTIC RELATIONS COURTS

Subtitle 3.   Protective Welfare Laws

6.	Abandonment, Abuse, Cruelty and Neglect	925

TITLE 13.   CONSERVATION AND DEVELOPMENT—PARKS AND RESERVATIONS

1E.	Solid Waste Management	953
9.	State Forest Fire Service	957

TITLE 15.   CORPORATIONS AND ASSOCIATIONS NOT FOR PROFIT

4.	Detective Associations	959
Appendix.	New Jersey Detective Associations	959

TITLE 21.   EXPLOSIVES AND FIREWORKS

Subtitle 1.   Explosives

1A.	Explosives Act	961
1B.	Liquefied Petroleum Gases	968
1C.	Model Rockets	972

Subtitle 2.   Fireworks

2.	Manufacture, Storage and Transportation	974
3.	Sale and Public Display	978

TITLE 24.   FOOD AND DRUGS

Subtitle 3.   Narcotic Drugs and Other Dangerous Substances

21.	Dangerous Substances Control Law	981

TITLE 26.   HEALTH AND VITAL STATISTICS

2C.	Air Pollution Control	997
2D.	Radiation Protection	998

TABLE OF CONTENTS

Chapter   **Page**

TITLE 27. HIGHWAYS

Subtitle 2. Public Roads and Highways in General

5. Advertising Along Highways 1001
5I. Unattended Dumpsters 1002
5J. Archaeological Findings 1003
5K. Scenic and Historic Highways 1003

Subtitle 3. State Highways

7. Acquisition, Construction and Maintenance by the State 1004

Subtitle 5. County and Municipal Roads

19. County Bridges and Viaducts 1005

Subtitle 6. Turnpikes

23. New Jersey Turnpike Authority 1006

TITLE 33. INTOXICATING LIQUORS

1. Alcoholic Beverage Law 1037
2. Stills and Distilling Apparatus 1090
3. Other Laws Relating to Intoxicating Liquors 1091
4. Commission on Alcoholism and Promotion of Temperance 1092

APPENDIX to CHAPTER 1 OF THE NEW JERSEY ADMINISTRATIVE CODE

TITLE 13. LAW AND PUBLIC SAFETY

2. Division of Alcoholic Beverage Control 1093

TITLE 40A. MUNICIPALITIES AND COUNTIES

14. Fire and Police 1119

TITLE 48. PUBLIC UTILITIES

13A. Solid Waste Collection and Disposal 1121

TITLE 53. STATE POLICE

1. Organization and Personnel 1123
2. Powers and Duties 1136
3. Housing, Equipment, and Expenses 1136

TITLE 56. TRADE NAMES, TRADE—MARKS AND UNFAIR TRADE PRACTICES

9. Antitrust Act 1139

TABLE OF CONTENTS

TITLE 58. WATERS AND WATER SUPPLY

Chapter   **Page**
10.   Pollution of Waters 1145
10A. Water Pollution Control 1146

NEW JERSEY RULES OF COURT

Rules of General Application 1153
Rules Governing Criminal Practice 1295
Rules Governing Practice in the Chancery Division, Family Part 1345
Rules Governing Practice in the Municipal Courts 1361

COMBINED INDEX

(Page I–1)

*

TITLE 2C

THE NEW JERSEY CODE OF CRIMINAL JUSTICE

Subtitle
1. General Provisions.

Subtitle
2. Definition of Specific Offenses.
3. Sentencing.

SUBTITLE 1

GENERAL PROVISIONS

Chapter
1. Preliminary.
2. General Principles of Liability.
3. General Principles of Justification.
4. Responsibility.
5. Inchoate Crimes.
6. Bail.
7. Registration and Notification of release of Certain Offenders.
8 to 10. [Reserved].

CHAPTER 1

PRELIMINARY

Section

2C:1–1. Short title; rules of construction.
2C:1–2. Purposes; principles of construction.
2C:1–3. Territorial applicability.
2C:1–4. Classes of offenses.
2C:1–5. Abolition of common law crimes; all offenses defined by statute; application of general provisions of the code; limitation of local government laws.
2C:1–6. Time limitations.
2C:1–8. Method of prosecution when conduct constitutes more than one offense.
2C:1–9. When prosecution barred by former prosecution for the same offense.
2C:1–10. When prosecution barred by former prosecution for different offense.
2C:1–11. Former prosecution in another jurisdiction: when a bar.
2C:1–12. Former prosecution before court lacking jurisdiction or when fraudulently procured by the defendant.
2C:1–13. Proof beyond a reasonable doubt; affirmative defenses; burden of proving fact when not an element of an offense.
2C:1–14. General definitions.

2C:1–1. Short title; rules of construction

a. This Title shall be known and may be cited as the "New Jersey Code of Criminal Justice."

b. Except as provided in subsections c. and d. of this section, the code does not apply to offenses committed prior to its effective date and prosecutions and dispositions for such offenses shall be governed by the prior law, which is continued in effect for that purpose, as if this code were not in force. For the purposes of this section, an offense was committed after the effective date of the code if any of the elements of the offenses occurred subsequent thereto.

c. In any case pending on or initiated after the effective date of the code involving an offense committed prior to such date:

(1) The procedural provisions of the code shall govern, insofar as they are justly applicable and their application does not introduce confusion or delay;

(2) The court, with the consent of the defendant, may impose sentence under the provisions of the code applicable to the offense and the offender.

(3) The court shall, if the offense committed is no longer an offense under the provisions of the code, dismiss such prosecution.

d. (1) The provisions of the code governing the treatment and the release or discharge of prisoners, probationers and parolees shall apply to persons under sentence for offenses committed prior to the effective date of the code, except that the minimum or maximum period of their detention or supervision shall in no case be increased.

(2) Any person who is under sentence of imprisonment on the effective date of the code for an offense committed prior to the effective date which has been eliminated by the code or who has been sentenced to a maximum term of imprisonment for an offense committed prior to the effective date which exceeds the maximum established by the code for such an offense and who, on said effective date, has not had his sentence suspended or been paroled or discharged, may move to have his sentence reviewed by the sentencing court and the court may impose a new sentence, for good cause shown as though the person had been convicted under

the code, except that no period of detention or supervision shall be increased as a result of such resentencing.

e. The provisions of the code not inconsistent with those of prior laws shall be construed as a continuation of such laws.

f. The classification and arrangement of the several sections of the code have been made for the purpose of convenience, reference and orderly arrangement, and therefore no implication or presumption of a legislative construction is to be drawn therefrom.

g. In the construction of the code, or any part thereof, no outline or analysis of the contents of said title or of any subtitle, chapter, article or section, no cross-reference or cross-reference note and no headnote or source note to any section shall be deemed to be a part of the code.

h. If said title or any subtitle, chapter, article or section of the code, or any provision thereof, shall be declared to be unconstitutional, invalid or inoperative in whole or in part, by a court of competent jurisdiction, such title, subtitle, chapter, article, section or provision shall, to the extent that it is not unconstitutional, invalid or inoperative, be enforced and effectuated, and no such determination shall be deemed to invalidate or make ineffectual the remaining provisions of the title, or of any subtitle, chapter, article or section of the code.

L.1978, c. 95, § 2C:1–1, eff. Sept. 1, 1979. Amended by L.1979, c. 178, § 1, eff. Sept. 1, 1979.

2C:1–2. Purposes; principles of construction

a. The general purposes of the provisions governing the definition of offenses are:

(1) To forbid, prevent, and condemn conduct that unjustifiably and inexcusably inflicts or threatens serious harm to individual or public interests;

(2) To insure the public safety by preventing the commission of offenses through the deterrent influence of the sentences authorized, the rehabilitation of those convicted, and their confinement when required in the interests of public protection;

(3) To subject to public control persons whose conduct indicates that they are disposed to commit offenses;

(4) To give fair warning of the nature of the conduct proscribed and of the sentences authorized upon conviction;

(5) To differentiate on reasonable grounds between serious and minor offenses; and

(6) To define adequately the act and mental state which constitute each offense, and limit the condemnation of conduct as criminal when it is without fault.

b. The general purposes of the provisions governing the sentencing of offenders are:

(1) To prevent and condemn the commission of offenses;

(2) To promote the correction and rehabilitation of offenders;

(3) To insure the public safety by preventing the commission of offenses through the deterrent influence of sentences imposed and the confinement of offenders when required in the interest of public protection;

(4) To safeguard offenders against excessive, disproportionate or arbitrary punishment;

(5) To give fair warning of the nature of the sentences that may be imposed on conviction of an offense;

(6) To differentiate among offenders with a view to a just individualization in their treatment;

(7) To advance the use of generally accepted scientific methods and knowledge in sentencing offenders; and

(8) To promote restitution to victims.

c. The provisions of the code shall be construed according to the fair import of their terms but when the language is susceptible of differing constructions it shall be interpreted to further the general purposes stated in this section and the special purposes of the particular provision involved. The discretionary powers conferred by the code shall be exercised in accordance with the criteria stated in the code and, insofar as such criteria are not decisive, to further the general purposes stated in this section.

d. Nothing contained in this code shall limit the right of a defendant and, subject only to the Federal and State constitutions, the right of the State to appeal or seek leave to appeal pursuant to law and Rules of Court.

L.1978, c. 95, § 2C:1–2, eff. Sept. 1, 1979. Amended by L.1979, c. 178, § 2, eff. Sept. 1, 1979; L.1991, c. 329, § 1, eff. Dec. 23, 1991.

2C:1–3. Territorial applicability

a. Except as otherwise provided in this section, a person may be convicted under the law of this State of an offense committed by his own conduct or the conduct of another for which he is legally accountable if:

(1) Either the conduct which is an element of the offense or the result which is such an element occurs within this State;

(2) Conduct occurring outside the State is sufficient under the law of this State to constitute an attempt to commit a crime within the State;

(3) Conduct occurring outside the State is sufficient under the law of this State to constitute a conspiracy to commit an offense within the State and an overt act in furtherance of such conspiracy occurs within the State;

(4) Conduct occurring within the State establishes complicity in the commission of, or an attempt, or conspiracy to commit, an offense in another jurisdiction which also is an offense under the law of this State;

(5) The offense consists of the omission to perform a legal duty imposed by the law of this State with respect to domicile, residence or a relationship to a person, thing or transaction in the State; or

(6) The offense is based on a statute of this State which expressly prohibits conduct outside the State, when the conduct bears a reasonable relation to a legitimate interest of this State and the actor knows or should know that his conduct is likely to affect that interest.

b. Subsection a.(1) does not apply when either causing a specified result or a purpose to cause or danger of causing such a result is an element of an offense and the result occurs or is designed or likely to occur only in another jurisdiction where the conduct charged would not constitute an offense, unless a legislative purpose plainly appears to declare the conduct criminal regardless of the place of the result.

c. Except as provided in subsection g., subsection a. (1) does not apply when causing a particular result is an element of an offense and the result is caused by conduct occurring outside the State which would not constitute an offense if the result had occurred there, unless the actor purposely or knowingly caused the result within the State.

d. When the offense is homicide, either the death of the victim or the bodily impact causing death constitutes a "result," within the meaning of subsection a.(1) and if the body of a homicide victim is found within the State, it may be inferred that such result occurred within the State.

e. This State includes the land and water, including the waters set forth in N.J.S.40A:13–2 and the air space above such land and water with respect to which the State has legislative jurisdiction. It also includes any territory made subject to the criminal jurisdiction of this State by compacts between it and another state or between it and the Federal Government.

f. Notwithstanding that territorial jurisdiction may be found under this section, the court may dismiss, hold in abeyance for up to six months, or, with the permission of the defendant, place on the inactive list a criminal prosecution under the law of this State where it appears that such action is in the interests of justice because the defendant is being prosecuted for an offense based on the same conduct in another jurisdiction and this State's interest will be adequately served by a prosecution in the other jurisdiction.

g. When the result which is an element of an offense consists of inflicting a harm upon a resident of this State or depriving a resident of this State of a benefit, the result occurs within this State, even if the conduct occurs wholly outside this State and any property that was affected by the offense was located outside this State.

L.1978, c. 95, § 2C:1–3, eff. Sept. 1, 1979. Amended by L.2003, c. 184, § 1, eff. Sept. 25, 2003.

2C:1–4. Classes of offenses

a. An offense defined by this code or by any other statute of this State, for which a sentence of imprisonment in excess of 6 months is authorized, constitutes a crime within the meaning of the Constitution of this State. Crimes are designated in this code as being of the first, second, third or fourth degree.

b. An offense is a disorderly persons offense if it is so designated in this code or in a statute other than this code. An offense is a petty disorderly persons offense if it is so designated in this code or in a statute other than this code. Disorderly persons offenses and petty disorderly persons offenses are petty offenses and are not crimes within the meaning of the Constitution of this State. There shall be no right to indictment by a grand jury nor any right to trial by jury on such offenses. Conviction of such offenses shall not give rise to any disability or legal disadvantage based on conviction of a crime.

c. An offense defined by any statute of this State other than this code shall be classified as provided in this section or in section 2C:43–1 and, except as provided in section 2C:1–5b and chapter 43, the sentence that may be imposed upon conviction thereof shall hereafter be governed by this code. Insofar as any provision outside the code declares an offense to be a misdemeanor when such offense specifically provides a maximum penalty of 6 months' imprisonment or less, whether or not in combination with a fine, such provision shall constitute a disorderly persons offense.

d. Subject to the provisions of section 2C:43–1, reference in any statute, rule, or regulation outside the code to the term "high misdemeanor" shall mean crimes of the first, second, or third degree and reference to the term "misdemeanor" shall mean all crimes.

L.1978, c. 95, § 2C:1–4, eff. Sept. 1, 1979. Amended by L.1979, c. 178, § 3, eff. Sept. 1, 1979; L.1981, c. 290, § 1, eff. Sept. 24, 1981.

2C:1–5. Abolition of common law crimes; all offenses defined by statute; application of general provisions of the code; limitation of local government laws

a. Common law crimes are abolished and no conduct constitutes an offense unless the offense is defined by this code or another statute of this State.

b. The provisions of subtitle 1 of the code [1] are applicable to offenses defined by other statutes. The provisions of subtitle 3 [2] are applicable to offenses defined by other statutes but the maximum penalties applicable to such offenses, if specifically provided in the statute defining such offenses, shall be as provided therein, rather than as provided in this code, except that if the non-code offense is a misdemeanor with a maximum penalty of more than 18 months imprisonment, the provisions of section 2C:43–1b shall apply.

c. This section does not affect the power to punish for contempt, either summarily or after indictment, or to employ any sanction authorized by law for the enforcement of an order or a civil judgment or decree.

d. Notwithstanding any other provision of law, the local governmental units of this State may neither enact nor enforce any ordinance or other local law or regulation conflicting with, or preempted by, any provision of this code or with any policy of this State expressed by this code, whether that policy be expressed by inclusion of a provision in the code or by exclusion of that subject from the code.

L.1978, c. 95, § 2C:1–5, eff. Sept. 1, 1979. Amended by L.1979, c. 178, § 4, eff. Sept. 1, 1979.

1 Chapters 1 to 10 of Title 2C.
2 Chapters 43 to 104 of Title 2C.

2C:1–6. Time limitations

a. (1) A prosecution for any offense set forth in N.J.S.2C:11–3, N.J.S.2C:11–4, N.J.S.2C:14–2 or sections 1 through 5 of P.L.2002, c. 26 (C.2C:38–1 through C.2C:38–5) may be commenced at any time.

(2) A prosecution for any offense set forth in N.J.S.2C:17–2, section 9 of P.L.1970, c. 39 (C.13:1E–9), section 20 of P.L.1989, c. 34 (C.13:1E–48.20), section 19 of P.L.1954, c. 212 (C.26:2C–19), section 10 of P.L.1984, c. 173 (C.34:5A–41), or section 10 of P.L.1977, c. 74 (C.58:10A–10) may be commenced at any time.

b. Except as otherwise provided in this section, prosecutions for other offenses are subject to the following periods of limitations:

(1) A prosecution for a crime must be commenced within five years after it is committed;

(2) A prosecution for a disorderly persons offense or petty disorderly persons offense must be commenced within one year after it is committed;

(3) A prosecution for any offense set forth in N.J.S.2C:27–2, N.J.S.2C:27–4, N.J.S.2C:27–6, N.J.S.2C:27–7, N.J.S.2C:29–4, N.J.S.2C:30–2, N.J.S.2C:30–3, or any attempt or conspiracy to commit such an offense, must be commenced within seven years after the commission of the offense;

(4) A prosecution for an offense set forth in N.J.S.2C:14–3 or N.J.S.2C:24–4, when the victim at the time of the offense is below the age of 18 years, must be commenced within five years of the victim's attaining the age of 18 or within two years of the discovery of the offense by the victim, whichever is later;

(5) (Deleted by amendment, P.L.2007, c. 131).

c. An offense is committed either when every element occurs or, if a legislative purpose to prohibit a continuing course of conduct plainly appears, at the time when the course of conduct or the defendant's complicity therein is terminated. Time starts to run on the day after the offense is committed, except that when the prosecution is supported by physical evidence that identifies the actor by means of DNA testing or fingerprint analysis, time does not start to run until the State is in possession of both the physical evidence and the DNA or fingerprint evidence necessary to establish the identification of the actor by means of comparison to the physical evidence.

d. A prosecution is commenced for a crime when an indictment is found and for a nonindictable offense when a warrant or other process is issued, provided that such warrant or process is executed without unreasonable delay. Nothing contained in this section, however, shall be deemed to prohibit the downgrading of an offense at any time if the prosecution of the greater offense was commenced within the statute of limitations applicable to the greater offense.

e. The period of limitation does not run during any time when a prosecution against the accused for the same conduct is pending in this State.

f. The limitations in this section shall not apply to any person fleeing from justice.

g. Except as otherwise provided in this code, no civil action shall be brought pursuant to this code more than five years after such action accrues.

L.1978, c. 95, § 2C:1–6, eff. Sept. 1, 1979. Amended by L.1979, c. 178, § 5, eff. Sept. 1, 1979; L.1980, c. 105, § 1, eff. Sept. 11, 1980; L.1986, c. 166, § 1, eff. Dec. 3, 1986; L.1988, c. 68, § 1, eff. July 20, 1988; L.1989, c. 228, § 1, eff. Dec. 29, 1989; L.1994, c. 53, § 1, eff. June 24, 1994; L.1996, c. 22, § 1, eff. May 1, 1996; L.1997, c. 325, § 1, eff. Jan. 8, 1998; L.2001, c. 308, § 1, eff. Jan. 3, 2002; L.2002, c. 26, § 7, eff. June 18, 2002; L.2007, c. 131, § 1, eff. Aug. 6, 2007.

2C:1–7. Blank

2C:1–8. Method of prosecution when conduct constitutes more than one offense

a. **Prosecution for multiple offenses; limitation on convictions.** When the same conduct of a defendant may establish the commission of more than one offense, the defendant may be prosecuted for each such offense. He may not, however, be convicted of more than one offense if:

(1) One offense is included in the other, as defined in subsection d. of this section;

(2) One offense consists only of a conspiracy or other form of preparation to commit the other;

(3) Inconsistent findings of fact are required to establish the commission of the offenses; or

(4) The offenses differ only in that one is defined to prohibit a designated kind of conduct generally and the other to prohibit a specific instance of such conduct. The provisions of this paragraph (4) of subsection a. of this section or any other provision of law notwithstanding, no State tax offense defined in Title 54 of the Revised Statutes or Title 54A of the New Jersey Statutes, as amended and supplemented, shall be construed to preclude a prosecution for any offense defined in this code.

A determination barring multiple convictions shall be made by the court after verdict or finding of guilt.

b. Limitation on separate trials for multiple offenses. Except as provided in subsection c. of this section, a defendant shall not be subject to separate trials for multiple criminal offenses based on the same conduct or arising from the same episode, if such offenses are known to the appropriate prosecuting officer at the time of the commencement of the first trial and are within the jurisdiction and venue of a single court.

c. Authority of court to order separate trials. When a defendant is charged with two or more criminal offenses based on the same conduct or arising from the same episode, the court may order any such charges to be tried separately in accordance with the Rules of Court.

d. Conviction of included offense permitted. A defendant may be convicted of an offense included in an offense charged whether or not the included offense is an indictable offense. An offense is so included when:

(1) It is established by proof of the same or less than all the facts required to establish the commission of the offense charged; or

(2) It consists of an attempt or conspiracy to commit the offense charged or to commit an offense otherwise included therein; or

(3) It differs from the offense charged only in the respect that a less serious injury or risk of injury to the same person, property or public interest or a lesser kind of culpability suffices to establish its commission.

e. Submission of included offense to jury. The court shall not charge the jury with respect to an included offense unless there is a rational basis for a verdict convicting the defendant of the included offense. *L.1978, c. 95, § 2C:1–8, eff. Sept. 1, 1979. Amended by L.1979, c. 178, § 6, eff. Sept. 1, 1979; L.1981, c. 290, § 2, eff. Sept. 24, 1981; L.1987, c. 76, § 30, eff. Dec. 9, 1987.*

2C:1–9. When prosecution barred by former prosecution for the same offense

A prosecution of a defendant for a violation of the same provision of the statutes based upon the same facts as a former prosecution is barred by such former prosecution under the following circumstances:

a. The former prosecution resulted in an acquittal by a finding of not guilty by the trier of fact or in a determination that there was insufficient evidence to warrant a conviction. A finding of guilty of a lesser included offense is an acquittal of the greater inclusive offense, although the conviction is subsequently set aside.

b. The former prosecution was terminated, after the complaint had been filed or the indictment found, by a final order or judgment for the defendant, which has not been set aside, reversed, or vacated and which necessarily required a determination inconsistent with a fact or a legal proposition that must be established for conviction of the offense. This subsection shall not apply to an order or judgment quashing an indictment prior to trial.

c. The former prosecution resulted in a conviction. There is a conviction if the prosecution resulted in a judgment of conviction which has not been reversed or vacated, a verdict of guilty which has not been set aside and which is capable of supporting a judgment, or a plea of guilty accepted by the court. In the latter two cases failure to enter judgment must be for a reason other than a motion of the defendant.

d. The former prosecution was improperly terminated. Except as provided in this subsection, there is an improper termination of a prosecution if the termination is for reasons not amounting to an acquittal, and it takes place after the jury was impaneled and sworn or, in a trial before a court without a jury, after the first witness was sworn but before findings were rendered by the trier of facts. Termination under any of the following circumstances is not improper:

(1) The defendant consents to the termination or waives, by motion to dismiss or otherwise, his right to object to the termination.

(2) The trial court finds that the termination is necessary because of the failure of the jury to agree upon a verdict after a reasonable time for deliberation has been allowed.

(3) The trial court finds that the termination is required by a sufficient legal reason and a manifest or absolute or overriding necessity.

L.1978, c. 95, § 2C:1–9, eff. Sept. 1, 1979.

2C:1–10. When prosecution barred by former prosecution for different offense

A prosecution of a defendant for a violation of a different provision of the statutes or based on different facts than a former prosecution is barred by such former prosecution under the following circumstances:

a. The former prosecution resulted in an acquittal or in a conviction as defined in section 2C:1–9 and the subsequent prosecution is for:

(1) Any offense of which the defendant could have been convicted on the first prosecution; or

(2) Any offense for which the defendant should have been tried on the first prosecution under section 2C:1–8 unless the court ordered a separate trial of the charge of such offense; or

(3) The same conduct, unless (a) the offense of which the defendant was formerly convicted or acquitted and the offense for which he is subsequently prosecuted each requires proof of a fact not required by the other and the law defining each of such offenses is intended to prevent a substantially different harm or

evil, or (b) the second offense was not consummated when the former trial began.

b. The former prosecution was terminated, after the complaint was filed or the indictment found, by an acquittal or by a final order or judgment for the defendant which has not been set aside, reversed or vacated and which acquittal, final order or judgment necessarily required a determination inconsistent with a fact which must be established for conviction of the second offense.

c. The former prosecution was improperly terminated, as improper termination is defined in section 2C:1–9, and the subsequent prosecution is for an offense of which the defendant could have been convicted had the former prosecution not been improperly terminated.

d. Nothing in this section shall bar the disposition of a nonindictable complaint after disposition of an indictable offense except as required by the Federal and State constitutions.

L.1978, c. 95, § 2C:1–10, eff. Sept. 1, 1979. Amended by L.1981, c. 290, § 3, eff. Sept. 24, 1981.

2C:1–11. Former prosecution in another jurisdiction: when a bar

When conduct constitutes an offense within the concurrent jurisdiction of this State and of the United States, a prosecution in the District Court of the United States is a bar to a subsequent prosecution in this State under the following circumstances:

a. The first prosecution resulted in an acquittal or in a conviction, or in an improper termination as defined in section 2C:1–9 and the subsequent prosecution is based on the same conduct, unless (1) the offense of which the defendant was formerly convicted or acquitted and the offense for which he is subsequently prosecuted each requires proof of a fact not required by the other and the law defining each of such offenses is intended to prevent a substantially different harm or evil or (2) the offense for which the defendant is subsequently prosecuted is intended to prevent a substantially more serious harm or evil than the offense of which he was formerly convicted or acquitted or (3) the second offense was not consummated when the former trial began; or

b. The former prosecution was terminated, after the information was filed or the indictment found, by an acquittal or by a final order or judgment for the defendant which has not been set aside, reversed or vacated and which acquittal, final order or judgment necessarily required a determination inconsistent with a fact which must be established for conviction of the offense of which the defendant is subsequently prosecuted.

L.1978, c. 95, § 2C:1–11, eff. Sept. 1, 1979.

2C:1–12. Former prosecution before court lacking jurisdiction or when fraudulently procured by the defendant

A prosecution is not a bar within the meaning of sections 2C:1–9, 10 and 11 under any of the following circumstances:

a. The former prosecution was before a court which lacked jurisdiction over the defendant or the offense tried in that court; or

b. The former prosecution was procured by the defendant without the knowledge of the appropriate prosecuting officer; or

c. The former prosecution resulted in a judgment of conviction which was held invalid in a subsequent proceeding on a petition for post-conviction relief or similar process, except that any bar as to reprosecution for a greater inclusive offense created by section 2C:1–9a. shall apply.

L.1978, c. 95, § 2C:1–12, eff. Sept. 1, 1979.

2C:1–13. Proof beyond a reasonable doubt; affirmative defenses; burden of proving fact when not an element of an offense

a. No person may be convicted of an offense unless each element of such offense is proved beyond a reasonable doubt. In the absence of such proof, the innocence of the defendant is assumed.

b. Subsection a. of this section does not:

(1) Require the disproof of an affirmative defense unless and until there is evidence supporting such defense; or

(2) Apply to any defense which the code or another statute requires the defendant to prove by a preponderance of evidence or such other standard as specified in this code.

c. A defense is affirmative, within the meaning of subsection b.(1) of this section, when:

(1) It arises under a section of the code which so provides; or

(2) It relates to an offense defined by a statute other than the code and such statute so provides; or

d. When the application of the code depends upon the finding of a fact which is not an element of an offense, unless the code otherwise provides:

(1) The burden of proving the fact is on the prosecution or defendant, depending on whose interest or contention will be furthered if the finding should be made; and

(2) The fact must be proved to the satisfaction of the court or jury, as the case may be.

e. When the code or other statute defining an offense establishes a presumption with respect to any fact which is an element of an offense, it has the meaning accorded it by the law of evidence.

f. In any civil action commenced pursuant to any provision of this code the burden of proof shall be by a preponderance of the evidence.

L.1978, c. 95, § 2C:1–13, eff. Sept. 1, 1979. Amended by L.1979, c. 178, § 7, eff. Sept. 1, 1979.

2C:1–14. General definitions

In this code, unless a different meaning plainly is required:

a. "Statute" includes the Constitution and a local law or ordinance of a political subdivision of the State;

b. "Act" or "action" means a bodily movement whether voluntary or involuntary;

c. "Omission" means a failure to act;

d. "Conduct" means an action or omission and its accompanying state of mind, or, where relevant, a series of acts and omissions;

e. "Actor" includes, where relevant, a person guilty of an omission;

f. "Acted" includes, where relevant, "omitted to act";

g. "Person," "he," and "actor" include any natural person and, where relevant, a corporation or an unincorporated association;

h. "Element of an offense" means (1) such conduct or (2) such attendant circumstances or (3) such a result of conduct as

(a) Is included in the description of the forbidden conduct in the definition of the offense;

(b) Establishes the required kind of culpability;

(c) Negatives an excuse or justification for such conduct;

(d) Negatives a defense under the statute of limitations; or

(e) Establishes jurisdiction or venue;

i. "Material element of an offense" means an element that does not relate exclusively to the statute of limitations, jurisdiction, venue or to any other matter similarly unconnected with (1) the harm or evil, incident to conduct, sought to be prevented by the law defining the offense, or (2) the existence of a justification or excuse for such conduct;

j. "Reasonably believes" or "reasonable belief" designates a belief the holding of which does not make the actor reckless or criminally negligent;

k. "Offense" means a crime, a disorderly persons offense or a petty disorderly persons offense unless a particular section in this code is intended to apply to less than all three;

l. (Deleted by amendment, P.L.1991, c. 91).

m. "Amount involved," "benefit," and other terms of value. Where it is necessary in this act to determine value, for purposes of fixing the degree of an offense, that value shall be the fair market value at the time and place of the operative act.

n. "Motor vehicle" shall have the meaning provided in R. S.39:1–1.

o. "Unlawful taking of a motor vehicle" means conduct prohibited under N.J.S.2C:20–10 when the means of conveyance taken, operated or controlled is a motor vehicle.

p. "Research facility" means any building, laboratory, institution, organization, school, or person engaged in research, testing, educational or experimental activities, or any commercial or academic enterprise that uses warm-blooded or cold-blooded animals for food or fiber production, agriculture, research, testing, experimentation or education. A research facility includes, but is not limited to, any enclosure, separately secured yard, pad, pond, vehicle, building structure or premises or separately secured portion thereof.

q. "Communication" means any form of communication made by any means, including, but not limited to, any verbal or written communication, communications conveyed by any electronic communication device, which includes but is not limited to, a wire, radio, electromagnetic, photoelectric or photo-optical system, telephone, including a cordless, cellular or digital telephone, computer, video recorder, fax machine, pager, or any other means of transmitting voice or data and communications made by sign or gesture.

r. "School" means a public or nonpublic elementary or secondary school within this State offering education in grades K through 12, or any combination thereof, at which a child may legally fulfill compulsory school attendance requirements.

L.1978, c. 95, § 2C:1–14, eff. Sept. 1, 1979. Amended by L.1979, c. 178, § 8, eff. Sept. 1, 1979; L.1991, c. 91, § 142, eff. April 9, 1991; L.1993, c. 219, § 1, eff. Aug. 2, 1993; L.1995, c. 20, § 1, eff. Jan. 25, 1995; L.2001, c. 220, § 1, eff. Aug. 24, 2001; L.2006, c. 78, § 1, eff. Aug. 2, 2006.

CHAPTER 2

GENERAL PRINCIPLES OF LIABILITY

Section

2C:2–1.   Requirement of voluntary act; omission as basis of liability; possession as an act.

2C:2–2.   General requirements of culpability.

2C:2–3.   Causal relationship between conduct and result; divergence between result designed, contemplated or risked and actual result.

2C:2–4.   Ignorance or mistake.

2C:2–5.   Defenses generally.

2C:2–6.   Liability for conduct of another; complicity.

2C:2–7.   Liability of corporations and persons acting, or under a duty to act, in their behalf.

2C:2–8.   Intoxication.

2C:2–9.   Duress.

2C:2–10.   Consent.

2C:2–11.   De minimis infractions.

Section
2C:2–12. Entrapment.

2C:2–1. Requirement of voluntary act; omission as basis of liability; possession as an act

a. A person is not guilty of an offense unless his liability is based on conduct which includes a voluntary act or the omission to perform an act of which he is physically capable. A bodily movement that is not a product of the effort or determination of the actor, either conscious or habitual, is not a voluntary act within the meaning of this section.

b. Liability for the commission of an offense may not be based on an omission unaccompanied by action unless:

(1) The omission is expressly made sufficient by the law defining the offense; or

(2) A duty to perform the omitted act is otherwise imposed by law, including but not limited to, laws such as the "Uniform Fire Safety Act," P.L.1983, c. 383 (C.52:27D–192 et seq.), the "State Uniform Construction Code Act," P.L.1975, c. 217 (C.52:27D–119 et seq.), or any other law intended to protect the public safety or any rule or regulation promulgated thereunder.

c. Possession is an act, within the meaning of this section, if the possessor knowingly procured or received the thing possessed or was aware of his control thereof for a sufficient period to have been able to terminate his possession.

L.1978, c. 95, § 2C:2–1, eff. Sept. 1, 1979. Amended by L.1997, c. 180, § 1, eff. Aug. 1, 1997.

2C:2–2. General requirements of culpability

a. **Minimum requirements of culpability.** Except as provided in subsection c.(3) of this section, a person is not guilty of an offense unless he acted purposely, knowingly, recklessly or negligently, as the law may require, with respect to each material element of the offense.

b. **Kinds of culpability defined.**

(1) *Purposely.* A person acts purposely with respect to the nature of his conduct or a result thereof if it is his conscious object to engage in conduct of that nature or to cause such a result. A person acts purposely with respect to attendant circumstances if he is aware of the existence of such circumstances or he believes or hopes that they exist. "With purpose," "designed," "with design" or equivalent terms have the same meaning.

(2) *Knowingly.* A person acts knowingly with respect to the nature of his conduct or the attendant circumstances if he is aware that his conduct is of that nature, or that such circumstances exist, or he is aware of a high probability of their existence. A person acts knowingly with respect to a result of his conduct if he is aware that it is practically certain that his conduct will cause such a result. "Knowing," "with knowledge" or equivalent terms have the same meaning.

(3) *Recklessly.* A person acts recklessly with respect to a material element of an offense when he consciously disregards a substantial and unjustifiable risk that the material element exists or will result from his conduct. The risk must be of such a nature and degree that, considering the nature and purpose of the actor's conduct and the circumstances known to him, its disregard involves a gross deviation from the standard of conduct that a reasonable person would observe in the actor's situation. "Recklessness," "with recklessness" or equivalent terms have the same meaning.

(4) *Negligently.* A person acts negligently with respect to a material element of an offense when he should be aware of a substantial and unjustifiable risk that the material element exists or will result from his conduct. The risk must be of such a nature and degree that the actor's failure to perceive it, considering the nature and purpose of his conduct and the circumstances known to him, involves a gross deviation from the standard of care that a reasonable person would observe in the actor's situation. "Negligently" or "negligence" when used in this code, shall refer to the standard set forth in this section and not to the standards applied in civil cases.

c. **Construction of statutes with respect to culpability requirements.**

(1) Prescribed culpability requirement applies to all material elements. When the law defining an offense prescribes the kind of culpability that is sufficient for the commission of an offense, without distinguishing among the material elements thereof, such provision shall apply to all the material elements of the offense, unless a contrary purpose plainly appears.

(2) Substitutes for kinds of culpability. When the law provides that a particular kind of culpability suffices to establish an element of an offense such element is also established if a person acts with higher kind of culpability.

(3) Construction of statutes not stating culpability requirement. Although no culpable mental state is expressly designated in a statute defining an offense, a culpable mental state may nevertheless be required for the commission of such offense, or with respect to some or all of the material elements thereof, if the proscribed conduct necessarily involves such culpable mental state. A statute defining a crime, unless clearly indicating a legislative intent to impose strict liability, should be construed as defining a crime with the culpability defined in paragraph b.(2) of this section. This provision applies to offenses defined both within and outside of this code.

d. **Culpability as to illegality of conduct.** Neither knowledge nor recklessness nor negligence as to whether conduct constitutes an offense or as to the existence, meaning or application of the law determining the elements of an offense is an element of such offense, unless the definition of the offense or the code so provides.

e. Culpability as determinant of grade of offense. When the grade or degree of an offense depends on whether the offense is committed purposely, knowingly, recklessly or criminally negligently, its grade or degree shall be the lowest for which the determinative kind of culpability is established with respect to any material element of the offense.

L.1978, c. 95, § 2C:2–2, eff. Sept. 1, 1979. Amended by L.1981, c. 290, § 4, eff. Sept. 24, 1981.

2C:2–3. Causal relationship between conduct and result; divergence between result designed, contemplated or risked and actual result

a. Conduct is the cause of a result when:

(1) It is an antecedent but for which the result in question would not have occurred; and

(2) The relationship between the conduct and result satisfies any additional causal requirements imposed by the code or by the law defining the offense.

b. When the offense requires that the defendant purposely or knowingly cause a particular result, the actual result must be within the design or contemplation, as the case may be, of the actor, or, if not, the actual result must involve the same kind of injury or harm as that designed or contemplated and not be too remote, accidental in its occurrence, or dependent on another's volitional act to have a just bearing on the actor's liability or on the gravity of his offense.

c. When the offense requires that the defendant recklessly or criminally negligently cause a particular result, the actual result must be within the risk of which the actor is aware or, in the case of criminal negligence, of which he should be aware, or, if not, the actual result must involve the same kind of injury or harm as the probable result and must not be too remote, accidental in its occurrence, or dependent on another's volitional act to have a just bearing on the actor's liability or on the gravity of his offense.

d. A defendant shall not be relieved of responsibility for causing a result if the only difference between what actually occurred and what was designed, contemplated or risked is that a different person or property was injured or affected or that a less serious or less extensive injury or harm occurred.

e. When causing a particular result is a material element of an offense for which absolute liability is imposed by law, the element is not established unless the actual result is a probable consequence of the actor's conduct.

L.1978, c. 95, § 2C:2–3, eff. Sept. 1, 1979.

2C:2–4. Ignorance or mistake

a. Ignorance or mistake as to a matter of fact or law is a defense if the defendant reasonably arrived at the conclusion underlying the mistake and:

(1) It negatives the culpable mental state required to establish the offense; or

(2) The law provides that the state of mind established by such ignorance or mistake constitutes a defense.

b. Although ignorance or mistake would otherwise afford a defense to the offense charged, the defense is not available if the defendant would be guilty of another offense had the situation been as he supposed. In such case, however, the ignorance or mistake of the defendant shall reduce the grade and degree of the offense of which he may be convicted to those of the offense of which he would be guilty had the situation been as he supposed.

c. A belief that conduct does not legally constitute an offense is a defense to a prosecution for that offense based upon such conduct when:

(1) The statute defining the offense is not known to the actor and has not been published or otherwise reasonably made available prior to the conduct alleged; or

(2) The actor acts in reasonable reliance upon an official statement of the law, afterward determined to be invalid or erroneous, contained in (a) a statute, (b) judicial decision, opinion, judgment, or rule, (c) an administrative order or grant of permission, or (d) an official interpretation of the public officer or body charged by law with responsibility for the interpretation, administration or enforcement of the law defining the offense; or

(3) The actor otherwise diligently pursues all means available to ascertain the meaning and application of the offense to his conduct and honestly and in good faith concludes his conduct is not an offense in circumstances in which a law-abiding and prudent person would also so conclude.

The defendant must prove a defense arising under subsection c. of this section by clear and convincing evidence.

L.1978, c. 95, § 2C:2–4, eff. Sept. 1, 1979.

2C:2–5. Defenses generally

Conduct which would otherwise be an offense is excused or alleviated by reason of any defense now provided by law for which neither the code nor other statutory law defining the offense provides exceptions or defenses dealing with the specific situation involved and a legislative purpose to exclude the defense claimed does not otherwise plainly appear.

L.1978, c. 95, § 2C:2–5, eff. Sept. 1, 1979.

2C:2–6. Liability for conduct of another; complicity

a. A person is guilty of an offense if it is committed by his own conduct or by the conduct of another person for which he is legally accountable, or both.

b. A person is legally accountable for the conduct of another person when:

(1) Acting with the kind of culpability that is sufficient for the commission of the offense, he causes an innocent or irresponsible person to engage in such conduct;

(2) He is made accountable for the conduct of such other person by the code or by the law defining the offense;

(3) He is an accomplice of such other person in the commission of an offense; or

(4) He is engaged in a conspiracy with such other person.

c. A person is an accomplice of another person in the commission of an offense if:

(1) With the purpose of promoting or facilitating the commission of the offense; he

(a) Solicits such other person to commit it;

(b) Aids or agrees or attempts to aid such other person in planning or committing it; or

(c) Having a legal duty to prevent the commission of the offense, fails to make proper effort so to do; or

(2) His conduct is expressly declared by law to establish his complicity.

d. A person who is legally incapable of committing a particular offense himself may be guilty thereof if it is committed by another person for whose conduct he is legally accountable, unless such liability is inconsistent with the purpose of the provision establishing his incapacity.

e. Unless otherwise provided by the code or by the law defining the offense, a person is not an accomplice in an offense committed by another person if:

(1) He is a victim of that offense;

(2) The offense is so defined that his conduct is inevitably incident to its commission; or

(3) He terminates his complicity under circumstances manifesting a complete and voluntary renunciation as defined in section 2C:5–1 d. prior to the commission of the offense. Termination by renunciation is an affirmative defense which the defendant must prove by a preponderance of evidence.

f. An accomplice may be convicted on proof of the commission of the offense and of his complicity therein, though the person claimed to have committed the offense has not been prosecuted or convicted or has been convicted of a different offense or degree of offense or has an immunity to prosecution or conviction or has been acquitted.

L.1978, c. 95, § 2C:2–6, eff. Sept. 1, 1979.

2C:2–7. Liability of corporations and persons acting, or under a duty to act, in their behalf

a. A corporation may be convicted of the commission of an offense if:

(1) The conduct constituting the offense is engaged in by an agent of the corporation while acting within the scope of his employment and in behalf of the corporation unless the offense is one defined by a statute which indicates a legislative purpose not to impose criminal liability on corporations. If the law governing the offense designates the agents for whose conduct the corporation is accountable or the circumstances under which it is accountable, such provisions shall apply;

(2) The offense consists of an omission to discharge a specific duty of affirmative performance imposed on corporations by law; or

(3) The conduct constituting the offense is engaged in, authorized, solicited, requested, commanded, or recklessly tolerated by the board of directors or by a high managerial agent acting within the scope of his employment and in behalf of the corporation.

b. As used in this section:

(1) "Corporation" does not include an entity organized as or by a governmental agency for the execution of a governmental program;

(2) "Agent" means any director, officer, servant, employee or other person authorized to act in behalf of the corporation;

(3) "High managerial agent" means an officer of a corporation or any other agent of a corporation having duties of such responsibility that his conduct may fairly be assumed to represent the policy of the corporation.

c. In any prosecution of a corporation for the commission of an offense included within the terms of subsection a. (1) of this section, other than an offense for which absolute liability has been imposed, it shall be a defense if the defendant proves by a preponderance of evidence that the high managerial agent having supervisory responsibility over the subject matter of the offense employed due diligence to prevent its commission. This paragraph shall not apply if it is plainly inconsistent with the legislative purpose in defining the particular offense.

d. Nothing in this section imposing liability upon a corporation shall be construed as limiting the liability for an offense of an individual by reason of his being an agent of the corporation.

L.1978, c. 95, § 2C:2–7, eff. Sept. 1, 1979.

2C:2–8. Intoxication

a. Except as provided in subsection d. of this section, intoxication of the actor is not a defense unless it negatives an element of the offense.

b. When recklessness establishes an element of the offense, if the actor, due to self-induced intoxication, is unaware of a risk of which he would have been aware had he been sober, such unawareness is immaterial.

c. Intoxication does not, in itself, constitute mental disease within the meaning of chapter 4.[1]

d.   Intoxication which (1) is not self-induced or (2) is pathological is an affirmative defense if by reason of such intoxication the actor at the time of his conduct did not know the nature and quality of the act he was doing, or if he did know it, that he did not know what he was doing was wrong.   Intoxication under this subsection must be proved by clear and convincing evidence.

e.   Definitions.   In this section unless a different meaning plainly is required:

(1)   "Intoxication" means a disturbance of mental or physical capacities resulting from the introduction of substances into the body;

(2)   "Self-induced intoxication" means intoxication caused by substances which the actor knowingly introduces into his body, the tendency of which to cause intoxication he knows or ought to know, unless he introduces them pursuant to medical advice or under such circumstances as would afford a defense to a charge of crime;

(3)   "Pathological intoxication" means intoxication grossly excessive in degree, given the amount of the intoxicant, to which the actor does not know he is susceptible.

L.1978, c. 95, § 2C:2–8, eff. Sept. 1, 1979.   Amended by L.1983, c. 306, § 1, eff. Aug. 26, 1983.

1 N.J.S.A. § 2C:4–1 et seq.

2C:2–9.   Duress

a.   Subject to subsection b. of this section, it is an affirmative defense that the actor engaged in the conduct charged to constitute an offense because he was coerced to do so by the use of, or a threat to use, unlawful force against his person or the person of another, which a person of reasonable firmness in his situation would have been unable to resist.

b.   The defense provided by this section is unavailable if the actor recklessly placed himself in a situation in which it was probable that he would be subjected to duress.   The defense is also unavailable if he was criminally negligent in placing himself in such a situation, whenever criminal negligence suffices to establish culpability for the offense charged.   In a prosecution for murder, the defense is only available to reduce the degree of the crime to manslaughter.

c.   It is not a defense that a woman acted on the command of her husband, unless she acted under such coercion as would establish a defense under this section.   The presumption that a woman, acting in the presence of her husband, is coerced is abolished.

L.1978, c. 95, § 2C:2–9, eff. Sept. 1, 1979.

2C:2–10.   Consent

a.   In general.   The consent of the victim to conduct charged to constitute an offense or to the result thereof is a defense if such consent negatives an element of the offense or precludes the infliction of the harm or evil sought to be prevented by the law defining the offense.

b.   Consent to bodily harm.   When conduct is charged to constitute an offense because it causes or threatens bodily harm, consent to such conduct or to the infliction of such harm is a defense if:

(1)   The bodily harm consented to or threatened by the conduct consented to is not serious;   or

(2)   The conduct and the harm are reasonably foreseeable hazards of joint participation in a concerted activity of a kind not forbidden by law;   or

(3)   The consent establishes a justification for the conduct under chapter 3 of the code.

c.   Ineffective consent.   Unless otherwise provided by the code or by the law defining the offense, assent does not constitute consent if:

(1)   It is given by a person who is legally incompetent to authorize the conduct charged to constitute the offense;   or

(2)   It is given by a person who by reason of youth, mental disease or defect or intoxication is manifestly unable or known by the actor to be unable to make a reasonable judgment as to the nature of harmfulness of the conduct charged to constitute an offense;   or

(3)   It is induced by force, duress or deception of a kind sought to be prevented by the law defining the offense.

L.1978, c. 95, § 2C:2–10, eff. Sept. 1, 1979.

2C:2–11.   De minimis infractions

The assignment judge may dismiss a prosecution if, having regard to the nature of the conduct charged to constitute an offense and the nature of the attendant circumstances, it finds that the defendant's conduct:

a.   Was within a customary license or tolerance, neither expressly negated by the person whose interest was infringed nor inconsistent with the purpose of the law defining the offense;

b.   Did not actually cause or threaten the harm or evil sought to be prevented by the law defining the offense or did so only to an extent too trivial to warrant the condemnation of conviction;   or

c.   Presents such other extenuations that it cannot reasonably be regarded as envisaged by the Legislature in forbidding the offense.   The assignment judge shall not dismiss a prosecution under this section without giving the prosecutor notice and an opportunity to be heard.   The prosecutor shall have a right to appeal any such dismissal.

L.1978, c. 95, § 2C:2–11, eff. Sept. 1, 1979.

2C:2–12.   Entrapment

a.   A public law enforcement official or a person engaged in cooperation with such an official or one acting as an agent of a public law enforcement official perpetrates an entrapment if for the purpose of obtaining evidence of the commission of an offense, he induces or encourages and, as a direct result, causes another person to engage in conduct constituting such offense by either:

(1) Making knowingly false representations designed to induce the belief that such conduct is not prohibited; or

(2) Employing methods of persuasion or inducement which create a substantial risk that such an offense will be committed by persons other than those who are ready to commit it.

b. Except as provided in subsection c. of this section, a person prosecuted for an offense shall be acquitted if he proves by a preponderance of evidence that his conduct occurred in response to an entrapment. The issue of entrapment shall be tried by the trier of fact.

c. The defense afforded by this section is unavailable when causing or threatening bodily injury is an element of the offense charged and the prosecution is based on conduct causing or threatening such injury to a person other than the person perpetrating the entrapment.

L.1978, c. 95, § 2C:2–12, eff. Sept. 1, 1979. Amended by L.1979, c. 178, § 9, eff. Sept. 1, 1979.

CHAPTER 3

GENERAL PRINCIPLES OF JUSTIFICATION

Section
2C:3–1.   Justification an affirmative defense; civil remedies unaffected.
2C:3–2.   Necessity and other justifications in general.
2C:3–3.   Execution of public duty.
2C:3–4.   Use of force in self-protection.
2C:3–5.   Use of force for the protection of other persons.
2C:3–6.   Use of force in defense of premises or personal property.
2C:3–7.   Use of force in law enforcement.
2C:3–8.   Use of force by persons with special responsibility for care, discipline or safety of others.
2C:3–9.   Mistake of law as to unlawfulness of force or legality of arrest; reckless or negligent use of excessive but otherwise justifiable force; reckless or negligent injury or risk of injury to innocent persons.
2C:3–10.   Justification in property crimes.
2C:3–11.   Definitions.

2C:3–1. Justification an affirmative defense; civil remedies unaffected

a. In any prosecution based on conduct which is justifiable under this chapter, justification is an affirmative defense.

b. The fact that conduct is justifiable under this chapter does not abolish or impair any remedy for such conduct which is available in any civil action.

L.1978, c. 95, § 2C:3–1, eff. Sept. 1, 1979.

2C:3–2. Necessity and other justifications in general

a. Necessity. Conduct which would otherwise be an offense is justifiable by reason of necessity to the extent permitted by law and as to which neither the code nor other statutory law defining the offense provides exceptions or defenses dealing with the specific situation involved and a legislative purpose to exclude the justification claimed does not otherwise plainly appear.

b. Other justifications in general. Conduct which would otherwise be an offense is justifiable by reason of any defense of justification provided by law for which neither the code nor other statutory law defining the offense provides exceptions or defenses dealing with the specific situation involved and a legislative purpose to exclude the justification claimed does not otherwise plainly appear.

L.1978, c. 95, § 2C:3–2, eff. Sept. 1, 1979.

2C:3–3. Execution of public duty

a. Except as provided in subsection b. of this section, conduct is justifiable when it is required or authorized by:

(1) The law defining the duties or functions of a public officer or the assistance to be rendered to such officer in the performance of his duties;

(2) The law governing the execution of legal process;

(3) The judgment or order of a competent court or tribunal;

(4) The law governing the armed services or the lawful conduct of war; or

(5) Any other provision of law imposing a public duty.

b. The other sections of this chapter apply to:

(1) The use of force upon or toward the person of another for any of the purposes dealt with in such sections; and

(2) The use of deadly force for any purpose, unless the use of such force is otherwise expressly authorized by law.

c. The justification afforded by subsection a. of this section applies:

(1) When the actor reasonably believes his conduct to be required or authorized by the judgment or direction of a competent court or tribunal or in the lawful execution of legal process, notwithstanding lack of jurisdiction of the court or defect in the legal process; and

(2) When the actor reasonably believes his conduct to be required or authorized to assist a public officer in the performance of his duties, notwithstanding that the officer exceeded his legal authority.

L.1978, c. 95, § 2C:3–3, eff. Sept. 1, 1979.

2C:3–4.   Use of force in self-protection.

a.   Use of force justifiable for protection of the person.   Subject to the provisions of this section and of section 2C:3–9, the use of force upon or toward another person is justifiable when the actor reasonably believes that such force is immediately necessary for the purpose of protecting himself against the use of unlawful force by such other person on the present occasion.

b.   Limitations on justifying necessity for use of force.

(1) The use of force is not justifiable under this section:

(a) To resist an arrest which the actor knows is being made by a peace officer in the performance of his duties, although the arrest is unlawful, unless the peace officer employs unlawful force to effect such arrest; or

(b) To resist force used by the occupier or possessor of property or by another person on his behalf, where the actor knows that the person using the force is doing so under a claim of right to protect the property, except that this limitation shall not apply if:

(i) The actor is a public officer acting in the performance of his duties or a person lawfully assisting him therein or a person making or assisting in a lawful arrest;

(ii) The actor has been unlawfully dispossessed of the property and is making a reentry or recaption justified by section 2C:3–6; or

(iii) The actor reasonably believes that such force is necessary to protect himself against death or serious bodily harm.

(2) The use of deadly force is not justifiable under this section unless the actor reasonably believes that such force is necessary to protect himself against death or serious bodily harm; nor is it justifiable if:

(a) The actor, with the purpose of causing death or serious bodily harm, provoked the use of force against himself in the same encounter; or

(b) The actor knows that he can avoid the necessity of using such force with complete safety by retreating or by surrendering possession of a thing to a person asserting a claim of right thereto or by complying with a demand that he abstain from any action which he has no duty to take, except that:

(i) The actor is not obliged to retreat from his dwelling, unless he was the initial aggressor; and

(ii) A public officer justified in using force in the performance of his duties or a person justified in using force in his assistance or a person justified in using force in making an arrest or preventing an escape is not obliged to desist from efforts to perform such duty, effect such arrest or prevent such escape because of resistance or threatened resistance by or on behalf of the person against whom such action is directed.

(3) Except as required by paragraphs (1) and (2) of this subsection, a person employing protective force may estimate the necessity of using force when the force is used, without retreating, surrendering possession, doing any other act which he has no legal duty to do or abstaining from any lawful action.

c.   (1) Notwithstanding   the   provisions   of N.J.S.2C:3–5, N.J.S.2C:3–9, or this section, the use of force or deadly force upon or toward an intruder who is unlawfully in a dwelling is justifiable when the actor reasonably believes that the force is immediately necessary for the purpose of protecting himself or other persons in the dwelling against the use of unlawful force by the intruder on the present occasion.

(2) A reasonable belief exists when the actor, to protect himself or a third person, was in his own dwelling at the time of the offense or was privileged to be thereon and the encounter between the actor and intruder was sudden and unexpected, compelling the actor to act instantly and:

(a) The actor reasonably believed that the intruder would inflict personal injury upon the actor or others in the dwelling; or

(b) The actor demanded that the intruder disarm, surrender or withdraw, and the intruder refused to do so.

(3) An actor employing protective force may estimate the necessity of using force when the force is used, without retreating, surrendering possession, withdrawing or doing any other act which he has no legal duty to do or abstaining from any lawful action.

L.1978, c. 95, § 2C:3–4, eff. Sept. 1, 1979.   Amended by L.1987, c. 120, § 1, eff. May 15, 1987; L.1999, c. 73, § 1, eff. April 30, 1999.

2C:3–5.   Use of force for the protection of other persons

a.   Subject to the provisions of this section and of section 2C:3–9, the use of force upon or toward the person of another is justifiable to protect a third person when:

(1) The actor would be justified under section 2C:3–4 in using such force to protect himself against the injury he believes to be threatened to the person whom he seeks to protect; and

(2) Under the circumstances as the actor reasonably believes them to be, the person whom he seeks to protect would be justified in using such protective force; and

(3) The actor reasonably believes that his intervention is necessary for the protection of such other person.

b.   Notwithstanding subsection a. of this section:

(1) When the actor would be obliged under section 2C:3–4 b. (2)(b) to retreat or take other action he is not obliged to do so before using force for the protection of

another person, unless he knows that he can thereby secure the complete safety of such other person, and

(2) When the person whom the actor seeks to protect would be obliged under section 2C:3–4 b. (2)(b) to retreat or take similar action if he knew that he could obtain complete safety by so doing, the actor is obliged to try to cause him to do so before using force in his protection if the actor knows that he can obtain complete safety in that way; and

(3) Neither the actor nor the person whom he seeks to protect is obliged to retreat when in the other's dwelling to any greater extent than in his own.

L.1978, c. 95, § 2C:3–5, eff. Sept. 1, 1979.

2C:3–6.   Use of force in defense of premises or personal property

a.   Use of force in defense of premises. Subject to the provisions of this section and of section 2C:3–9, the use of force upon or toward the person of another is justifiable when the actor is in possession or control of premises or is licensed or privileged to be thereon and he reasonably believes such force necessary to prevent or terminate what he reasonably believes to be the commission or attempted commission of a criminal trespass by such other person in or upon such premises.

b.   Limitations on justifiable use of force in defense of premises.

(1) Request to desist. The use of force is justifiable under this section only if the actor first requests the person against whom such force is used to desist from his interference with the property, unless the actor reasonably believes that:

(a) Such request would be useless;

(b) It would be dangerous to himself or another person to make the request; or

(c) Substantial harm will be done to the physical condition of the property which is sought to be protected before the request can effectively be made.

(2) Exclusion of trespasser. The use of force is not justifiable under this section if the actor knows that the exclusion of the trespasser will expose him to substantial danger of serious bodily harm.

(3) Use of deadly force. The use of deadly force is not justifiable under subsection a. of this section unless the actor reasonably believes that:

(a) The person against whom the force is used is attempting to dispossess him of his dwelling otherwise than under a claim of right to its possession; or

(b) The person against whom the force is used is attempting to commit or consummate arson, burglary, robbery or other criminal theft or property destruction; except that

(c) Deadly force does not become justifiable under subparagraphs (a) and (b) of this subsection unless the actor reasonably believes that:

(i) The person against whom it is employed has employed or threatened deadly force against or in the presence of the actor; or

(ii) The use of force other than deadly force to terminate or prevent the commission or the consummation of the crime would expose the actor or another in his presence to substantial danger of bodily harm. An actor within a dwelling shall be presumed to have a reasonable belief in the existence of the danger. The State must rebut this presumption by proof beyond a reasonable doubt.

c.   Use of force in defense of personal property. Subject to the provisions of subsection d. of this section and of section 2C:3–9, the use of force upon or toward the person of another is justifiable when the actor reasonably believes it necessary to prevent what he reasonably believes to be an attempt by such other person to commit theft, criminal mischief or other criminal interference with personal property in his possession or in the possession of another for whose protection he acts.

d.   Limitations on justifiable use of force in defense of personal property.

(1) Request to desist and exclusion of trespasser. The limitations of subsection b. (1) and (2) of this section apply to subsection c. of this section.

(2) Use of deadly force. The use of deadly force in defense of personal property is not justified unless justified under another provision of this chapter.

L.1978, c. 95, § 2C:3–6, eff. Sept. 1, 1979. Amended by L.1987, c. 120, § 2, eff. May 15, 1987.

2C:3–7.   Use of force in law enforcement

a.   Use of force justifiable to effect an arrest. Subject to the provisions of this section and of section 2C:3–9, the use of force upon or toward the person of another is justifiable when the actor is making or assisting in making an arrest and the actor reasonably believes that such force is immediately necessary to effect a lawful arrest.

b.   Limitations on the use of force.

(1) The use of force is not justifiable under this section unless:

(a) The actor makes known the purpose of the arrest or reasonably believes that it is otherwise known by or cannot reasonably be made known to the person to be arrested; and

(b) When the arrest is made under a warrant, the warrant is valid or reasonably believed by the actor to be valid.

(2) The use of deadly force is not justifiable under this section unless:

(a) The actor effecting the arrest is authorized to act as a peace officer or has been summoned by and is assisting a person whom he reasonably believes to be authorized to act as a peace officer; and

(b) The actor reasonably believes that the force employed creates no substantial risk of injury to innocent persons; and

(c) The actor reasonably believes that the crime for which the arrest is made was homicide, kidnapping, an offense under 2C:14–2 or 2C:14–3, arson, robbery, burglary of a dwelling, or an attempt to commit one of these crimes; and

(d) The actor reasonably believes:

(i) There is an imminent threat of deadly force to himself or a third party; or

(ii) The use of deadly force is necessary to thwart the commission of a crime as set forth in subparagraph (c) of this paragraph; or

(iii) The use of deadly force is necessary to prevent an escape.

c. Use of force to prevent escape from custody. The use of force to prevent the escape of an arrested person from custody is justifiable when the force could, under subsections a. and b. of this section, have been employed to effect the arrest under which the person is in custody. A correction officer or other person authorized to act as a peace officer is, however, justified in using any force including deadly force, which he reasonably believes to be immediately necessary to prevent the escape of a person committed to a jail, prison, or other institution for the detention of persons charged with or convicted of an offense so long as the actor believes that the force employed creates no substantial risk of injury to innocent persons.

d. Use of force by private person assisting an unlawful arrest.

(1) A private person who is summoned by a peace officer to assist in effecting an unlawful arrest is justified in using any force which he would be justified in using if the arrest were lawful, provided that he does not believe the arrest is unlawful.

(2) A private person who assists another private person in effecting an unlawful arrest, or who, not being summoned, assists a peace officer in effecting an unlawful arrest, is justified in using any force which he would be justified in using if the arrest were lawful, provided that (a) he reasonably believes the arrest is lawful, and (b) the arrest would be lawful if the facts were as he believes them to be and such belief is reasonable.

e. Use of force to prevent suicide or the commission of a crime. The use of force upon or toward the person of another is justifiable when the actor reasonably believes that such force is immediately necessary to prevent such other person from committing suicide, inflicting serious bodily harm upon himself, committing or consummating the commission of a crime involving or threatening bodily harm, damage to or loss of property or a breach of the peace, except that:

(1) Any limitations imposed by the other provisions of this chapter on the justifiable use of force in self-

protection, for the protection of others, the protection of property, the effectuation of an arrest or the prevention of an escape from custody shall apply notwithstanding the criminality of the conduct against which such force is used; and

(2) The use of deadly force is not in any event justifiable under this subsection unless the actor reasonably believes that it is likely that the person whom he seeks to prevent from committing a crime will endanger human life or inflict serious bodily harm upon another unless the commission or the consummation of the crime is prevented and that the use of such force presents no substantial risk of injury to innocent persons.

L.1978, c. 95, § 2C:3–7, eff. Sept. 1, 1979. Amended by L.1979, c. 178, § 10, eff. Sept. 1, 1979; L.1981, c. 290, § 5, eff. Sept. 24, 1981.

2C:3–8. Use of force by persons with special responsibility for care, discipline or safety of others

The use of force upon or toward the person of another is justifiable as permitted by law or as would be a defense in a civil action based thereon where the actor has been vested or entrusted with special responsibility for the care, supervision, discipline or safety of another or of others and the force is used for the purpose of and, subject to section 2C:3–9(b), to the extent necessary to further that responsibility, unless:

a. The code or the law defining the offense deals with the specific situation involved; or

b. A legislative purpose to exclude the justification claimed otherwise plainly appears; or

c. Deadly force is used, in which case such force must be otherwise justifiable under the provisions of this chapter.

L.1978, c. 95, § 2C:3–8, eff. Sept. 1, 1979.

2C:3–9. Mistake of law as to unlawfulness of force or legality of arrest; reckless or negligent use of excessive but otherwise justifiable force; reckless or negligent injury or risk of injury to innocent persons

a. The justification afforded by sections 2C:3–4 to 2C:3–7 is unavailable when:

(1) The actor's belief in the unlawfulness of the force or conduct against which he employs protective force or his belief in the lawfulness of an arrest which he endeavors to effect by force is erroneous; and

(2) His error is due to ignorance or mistake as to the provisions of the code, any other provisions of the criminal law or the law governing the legality of an arrest or search.

b. (Deleted by amendment, P.L.1981, c. 290.)

c. When the actor is justified under sections 2C:3–3 to 2C:3–8 in using force upon or toward the person of another but he recklessly or negligently injures or creates a risk of injury to innocent persons, the justification afforded by those sections is unavailable in a prosecution for such recklessness or negligence towards innocent persons.

L.1978, c. 95, § 2C:3–9, eff. Sept. 1, 1979. Amended by L.1981, c. 290, § 6, eff. Sept. 24, 1981.

2C:3–10. Justification in property crimes

Conduct involving the appropriation, seizure or destruction of, damage to, intrusion on, or interference with, property is justifiable under circumstances which would establish a defense of privilege in a civil action based thereon, unless:

a. The code or the law defining the offense deals with the specific situation involved; or

b. A legislative purpose to exclude the justification claimed otherwise plainly appears.

L.1978, c. 95, § 2C:3–10, eff. Sept. 1, 1979.

2C:3–11. Definitions

In this chapter, unless a different meaning plainly is required: a. " Unlawful force" means force, including confinement, which is employed without the consent of the person against whom it is directed and the employment of which constitutes an offense or actionable tort or would constitute such offense or tort except for a defense (such as the absence of intent, negligence, or mental capacity; duress, youth, or diplomatic status) not amounting to a privilege to use the force. Assent constitutes consent, within the meaning of this section, whether or not it otherwise is legally effective, except assent to the infliction of death or serious bodily harm.

b. "Deadly force" means force which the actor uses with the purpose of causing or which he knows to create a substantial risk of causing death or serious bodily harm. Purposely firing a firearm in the direction of another person or at a vehicle, building or structure in which another person is believed to be constitutes deadly force unless the firearm is loaded with less-lethal ammunition and fired by a law enforcement officer in the performance of the officer's official duties. A threat to cause death or serious bodily harm, by the production of a weapon or otherwise, so long as the actor's purpose is limited to creating an apprehension that he will use deadly force if necessary, does not constitute deadly force.

c. "Dwelling" means any building or structure, though movable or temporary, or a portion thereof, which is for the time being the actor's home or place of lodging except that, as used in 2C:3–7, the building or structure need not be the actor's own home or place of lodging.

d. "Serious bodily harm" means bodily harm which creates a substantial risk of death or which causes serious, permanent disfigurement or protracted loss or impairment of the function of any bodily member or organ or which results from aggravated sexual assault or sexual assault.

e. "Bodily harm" means physical pain, or temporary disfigurement, or impairment of physical condition.

f. "Less–lethal ammunition" means ammunition approved by the Attorney General which is designed to stun, temporarily incapacitate or cause temporary discomfort to a person without penetrating the person's body. The term shall also include ammunition approved by the Attorney General which is designed to gain access to a building or structure and is used for that purpose.

L.1978, c. 95, § 2C:3–11, eff. Sept. 1, 1979. Amended by L.1979, c. 178, § 11, eff. Sept. 1, 1979; L.1981, c. 290, § 7, eff. Sept. 24, 1981; L.1987, c. 120, § 3, eff. May 15, 1987; L.2005, c. 250, § 1, eff. Jan. 4, 2006.

CHAPTER 4

RESPONSIBILITY

Section
2C:4–1.   Insanity defense.
2C:4–2.   Evidence of mental disease or defect admissible when relevant to element of the offense.
2C:4–3.   Requirement of notice.
2C:4–4.   Mental incompetence excluding fitness to proceed.
2C:4–5.   Psychiatric or psychological examination of defendant with respect to fitness to proceed.
2C:4–6.   Determination of fitness to proceed; effect of finding of unfitness; proceedings if fitness is regained; post–commitment hearing.
2C:4–7.   Disposition.
2C:4–8.   Commitment of a person by reason of insanity.
2C:4–9.   Release of persons committed by reason of insanity.
2C:4–10.   Statements for purposes of examination or treatment inadmissible except on issue of mental condition.
2C:4–11.   Immaturity excluding criminal conviction; transfer of proceedings to family court.

2C:4–1. Insanity defense

A person is not criminally responsible for conduct if at the time of such conduct he was laboring under such a defect of reason, from disease of the mind as not to know the nature and quality of the act he was doing, or if he did know it, that he did not know what he was doing was wrong. Insanity is an affirmative defense which must be proved by a preponderance of the evidence.

L.1978, c. 95, § 2C:4–1, eff. Sept. 1, 1979. Amended by L.1979, c. 178, § 11A, eff. Sept. 1, 1979.

2C:4–2. Evidence of mental disease or defect admissible when relevant to element of the offense

Evidence that the defendant suffered from a mental disease or defect is admissible whenever it is relevant to prove that the defendant did not have a state of mind which is an element of the offense. In the absence of such evidence, it may be presumed that the defendant had no mental disease or defect which would negate a state of mind which is an element of the offense.

L.1978, c. 95, § 2C:4–2, eff. Sept. 1, 1979. Amended by L.1979, c. 178, § 11B, eff. Sept. 1, 1979; L.1981, c. 290, § 8, eff. Sept. 24, 1981; L.1990, c. 63, § 1, eff. July 7, 1990.

2C:4–3. Requirement of notice

a. If a defendant intends to claim insanity pursuant to section 2C:4–1 or the absence of a requisite state of mind pursuant to section 2C:4–2, he shall serve notice of such intention upon the prosecuting attorney in accordance with the Rules of Court.

b. When a defendant is acquitted on the ground of insanity, the verdict and judgment shall so state.

L.1978, c. 95, § 2C:4–3, eff. Sept. 1, 1979. Amended by L.1979, c. 178, § 12, eff. Sept. 1, 1979.

2C:4–4. Mental incompetence excluding fitness to proceed

a. No person who lacks capacity to understand the proceedings against him or to assist in his own defense shall be tried, convicted or sentenced for the commission of an offense so long as such incapacity endures.

b. A person shall be considered mentally competent to stand trial on criminal charges if the proofs shall establish:

(1) That the defendant has the mental capacity to appreciate his presence in relation to time, place and things; and

(2) That his elementary mental processes are such that he comprehends:

(a) That he is in a court of justice charged with a criminal offense;

(b) That there is a judge on the bench;

(c) That there is a prosecutor present who will try to convict him of a criminal charge;

(d) That he has a lawyer who will undertake to defend him against that charge;

(e) That he will be expected to tell to the best of his mental ability the facts surrounding him at the time and place where the alleged violation was committed if he chooses to testify and understands the right not to testify;

(f) That there is or may be a jury present to pass upon evidence adduced as to guilt or innocence of such charge or, that if he should choose to enter into plea negotiations or to plead guilty, that he comprehend the consequences of a guilty plea and that he be able to knowingly, intelligently, and voluntarily waive those rights which are waived upon such entry of a guilty plea; and

(g) That he has the ability to participate in an adequate presentation of his defense.

L.1978, c. 95, § 2C:4–4, eff. Sept. 1, 1979. Amended by L.1979, c. 178, § 13, eff. Sept. 1, 1979.

2C:4–5. Psychiatric or psychological examination of defendant with respect to fitness to proceed

a. Whenever there is reason to doubt the defendant's fitness to proceed, the court may on motion by the prosecutor, the defendant or on its own motion, appoint at least one qualified psychiatrist or licensed psychologist to examine and report upon the mental condition of the defendant. The psychiatrist or licensed psychologist so appointed shall be either:

(1) From a list agreed to by the court, the prosecutor and the defendant; or

(2) Agreed to by the court, prosecutor and defendant.

Alternatively, the court may order examination of a defendant for fitness to proceed by the Department of Human Services. The department shall provide or arrange for examination of the defendant at a jail, prison or psychiatric hospital. However, to ensure that a defendant is not unnecessarily hospitalized for the purpose of the examination, a defendant shall not be admitted to a State psychiatric hospital for an examination regarding his fitness to proceed unless a qualified psychiatrist or licensed psychologist designated by the commissioner determines that hospitalization is clinically necessary to perform the examination. Whenever the qualified psychiatrist or licensed psychologist determines that hospitalization is clinically necessary to perform the examination, the court shall order the defendant to be committed to the custody of the Commissioner of Human Services for placement in a State psychiatric hospital designated for that purpose for a period not exceeding 30 days.

A qualified psychiatrist or licensed psychologist retained by the defendant or by the prosecutor shall, if requested, be permitted to examine a defendant who has been admitted to a State psychiatric hospital.

b. The report of the examination shall include at least the following: (1) a description of the nature of the examination; (2) a diagnosis of the mental condition of the defendant; (3) an opinion as to the defendant's capacity to understand the proceedings against him and to assist in his own defense. The person or persons conducting the examination may ask questions respecting the crime charged when such questions are necessary to enable formation of an opinion as to a relevant issue, however, the evidentiary character of any inculpatory statement shall be limited expressly to the question of competency and shall not be admissible on the issue of guilt.

c. If the examination cannot be conducted by reason of the unwillingness of the defendant to participate therein, the report shall so state and shall include, if possible, an opinion as to whether such unwillingness of the defendant was the result of mental incompetence. Upon the filing of such a report, the court may permit examination without cooperation, may appoint a different psychiatrist or licensed psychologist, or may commit the defendant for observation for a period not exceeding 30 days except on good cause shown, or exclude or limit testimony by the defense psychiatrist or licensed psychologist.

d. The report of the examination shall be sent by the psychiatrist or licensed psychologist to the court, the prosecutor and counsel for the defendant.

L.1978, c. 95, § 2C:4–5, eff. Sept. 1, 1979. Amended by L.1979, c. 178, § 13A, eff. Sept. 1, 1979; L.1997, c. 77, § 1, eff. April 24, 1997; L.1998, c. 111, § 1, eff. Oct. 17, 1998.

2C:4–6. Determination of fitness to proceed; effect of finding of unfitness; proceedings if fitness is regained; post–commitment hearing

a. When the issue of the defendant's fitness to proceed is raised, the issue shall be determined by the court. If neither the prosecutor nor counsel for the defendant contests the finding of the report filed pursuant to section 2C:4–5, the court may make the determination on the basis of such report. If the finding is contested or if there is no report, the court shall hold a hearing on the issue. If the report is received in evidence upon such hearing, either party shall have the right to summon and examine the psychiatrists or licensed psychologists who joined in the report and to offer evidence upon the issue.

b. If the court determines that the defendant lacks fitness to proceed, the proceeding against him shall be suspended, except as provided in subsection c. of this section. At this time, the court may commit him to the custody of the Commissioner of Human Services to be placed in an appropriate institution if it is found that the defendant is so dangerous to himself or others as to require institutionalization, or it shall proceed to determine whether placement in an outpatient setting or release is appropriate; provided, however, that no commitment to any institution shall be in excess of such period of time during which it can be determined whether it is substantially probable that the defendant could regain his competence within the foreseeable future.

If the court determines that the defendant is fit to proceed, but suffers from mental illness, as defined in section 2 of P.L.1987, c. 116 (C.30:4–27.2), that does not require institutionalization, the court shall order the defendant to be provided appropriate treatment in the jail or prison in which the defendant is incarcerated. Where the defendant is incarcerated in a county correctional facility, the county shall provide or arrange for this treatment. The Department of Corrections shall reimburse the county for the reasonable costs of treatment, as determined by the Commissioner of Corrections, provided that the county has submitted to the commissioner such documentation and verification as the commissioner shall require.

c. If the defendant has not regained his fitness to proceed within three months, the court shall hold a hearing on the issue of whether the charges against him shall be dismissed with prejudice or held in abeyance.

The hearing shall be held only upon notice to the prosecutor and with an opportunity for the prosecutor to be heard. When the charges are not dismissed, each defendant's case shall be specifically reviewed by the court at six-month intervals until an order is made by the court that the defendant stand trial or that the charges be dismissed.

There shall be a presumption that charges against a defendant who is not competent to proceed shall be held in abeyance. The presumption can be overcome only if the court determines, using the factors set forth in this subsection, that continuing the criminal prosecution under the particular circumstances of the case would constitute a constitutionally significant injury to the defendant attributable to undue delay in being brought to trial.

In determining whether the charges shall be held in abeyance or dismissed, the court shall weigh the following factors: the defendant's prospects for regaining competency; the period of time during which the defendant has remained incompetent; the nature and extent of the defendant's institutionalization; the nature and gravity of the crimes charged; the effects of delay on the prosecution; the effects of delay on the defendant, including any likelihood of prejudice to the defendant in the trial arising out of the delay; and the public interest in prosecuting the charges.

d. When the court, on its own motion or upon application of the commissioner, his designee or either party, determines after a hearing, if a hearing is requested, that the defendant has regained fitness to proceed, the proceedings shall be resumed.

e. (Deleted by amendment, P.L.1996, c. 133).

f. The fact that the defendant is unfit to proceed does not preclude determination of any legal objection to the prosecution which is susceptible of fair determination prior to trial and without the personal participation of the defendant.

L.1978, c. 95, § 2C:4–6, eff. Sept. 1, 1979. Amended by L.1979, c. 178, § 13B, eff. Sept. 1, 1979; L.1996, c. 133, § 1, eff. Dec. 5, 1996; L.1997, c. 77, § 2, eff. April 24, 1997; L.1999, c. 16, § 1.

2C:4–7. Disposition

If a defendant is acquitted by reason of insanity the court shall dispose of the case as provided for in section 2C:4–8 of this chapter.

L.1978, c. 95, § 2C:4–7, eff. Sept. 1, 1979.

2C:4–8. Commitment of a person by reason of insanity

a. After acquittal by reason of insanity, the court shall order that the defendant undergo a psychiatric examination by a psychiatrist of the prosecutor's choice. If the examination cannot take place because of the unwillingness of the defendant to participate, the court shall proceed as in section 2C:4–5c. The defendant, pursuant to this section, may also be examined by a psychiatrist of his own choice.

b. The court shall dispose of the defendant in the following manner:

(1) If the court finds that the defendant may be released without danger to the community or himself without supervision, the court shall so release the defendant; or

(2) If the court finds that the defendant may be released without danger to the community or to himself under supervision or under conditions, the court shall so order; or

(3) If the court finds that the defendant cannot be released with or without supervision or conditions without posing a danger to the community or to himself, it shall commit the defendant to a mental health facility approved for this purpose by the Commissioner of Human Services to be treated as a person civilly committed. In all proceedings conducted pursuant to this section and pursuant to section N.J.S. 2C:4–6 concerning a defendant who lacks the fitness to proceed, including any periodic review proceeding, the prosecuting attorney shall have the right to appear and be heard. The defendant's continued commitment, under the law governing civil commitment, shall be established by a preponderance of the evidence, during the maximum period of imprisonment that could have been imposed, as an ordinary term of imprisonment, for any charge on which the defendant has been acquitted by reason of insanity. Expiration of that maximum period of imprisonment shall be calculated by crediting the defendant with any time spent in confinement for the charge or charges on which the defendant has been acquitted by reason of insanity.

c. No person committed under this section shall be confined within any penal or correctional institution or any part thereof.

L.1978, c. 95, § 2C:4–8, eff. Sept. 1, 1979. Amended by L.1979, c. 178, § 15, eff. Sept. 1, 1979; L.1981, c. 290, § 9, eff. Sept. 24, 1981; L.1996, c. 133, § 2, eff. Dec. 5, 1996.

2C:4–9. Release of persons committed by reason of insanity

a. If a person has been committed pursuant to section 2C:4–8 or section 2C:4–6 and if the commissioner, or his designee, or the superintendent of the institution to which the person has been committed, is of the view that a person committed to his custody, pursuant to section 2C:4–8 or section 2C:4–6, may be discharged or released on condition without danger to himself or to others, or that he may be transferred to a less restrictive setting for treatment, the commissioner or superintendent shall make application for the discharge or release of such person in a report to the court by which such person was committed and shall transmit a copy of such application and report to the prosecutor, the court, and defense counsel. The court may, in its discretion, appoint at least two qualified psychiatrists, neither of whom may be on the staff of the hospital to which the defendant had been committed, to examine such person and to report within 30 days, or such longer period as the court determines to be necessary for the purpose, their opinion as to his mental condition.

b. The court shall hold a hearing to determine whether the committed person may be safely discharged, released on condition without danger to himself or others, or treated as in civil commitment. The hearing shall be held upon notice to the prosecutor and with the prosecutor's opportunity to be heard. Any such hearing shall be deemed a civil proceeding. According to the determination of the court upon the hearing, the court shall proceed as in section 2C:4–8b. (1), (2) or (3).

c. A committed person may make application for his discharge or release to the court by which he was committed, and the procedure to be followed upon such application shall be the same as that prescribed above in the case of an application by the commissioner.

d. Each defendant's case shall be specifically reviewed as provided by the law governing civil commitment.

L.1978, c. 95, § 2C:4–9, eff. Sept. 1, 1979. Amended by L.1979, c. 178, § 16, eff. Sept. 1, 1979; L.1996, c. 133, § 3, eff. Dec. 5, 1996.

2C:4–10. Statements for purposes of examination or treatment inadmissible except on issue of mental condition

A statement made by a person subjected to psychiatric or psychological examination or treatment pursuant to section 2C:4–5, 2C:4–6 or 2C:4–9 for the purposes of such examination or treatment shall not be admissible in evidence against him in any criminal proceeding on any issue other than that of his mental condition but it shall be admissible upon that issue, whether or not it would otherwise be deemed a privileged communication. When such a statement constitutes an admission of guilt of the crime charged or of an element thereof, it shall only be admissible where it appears at trial that conversations with the examining psychiatrist or licensed psychologist were necessary to enable him to form an opinion as to a matter in issue.

L.1978, c. 95, § 2C:4–10, eff. Sept. 1, 1979. Amended by L.1997, c. 77, § 3, eff. April 24, 1997.

2C:4–11. Immaturity excluding criminal conviction; transfer of proceedings to family court

a. A person shall not be tried for or convicted of an offense if:

(1) At the time of the conduct charged to constitute the offense he was less than 14 years of age, in which case the family court shall have exclusive jurisdiction unless pursuant to section 8 of the "New Jersey Code of Juvenile Justice"[1] the juvenile has demanded indictment and trial by jury; or

(2) At the time of the conduct charged to constitute the offense he was 14, 15, 16 or 17 years of age, unless:

(a) The family court has no jurisdiction over him;

(b) The family court has, pursuant to section 7 of "New Jersey Code of Juvenile Justice,"[2] entered an order waiving jurisdiction and referring the case to the county prosecutor for the institution of criminal proceedings against him;

(c) The juvenile has, pursuant to section 8 of the "New Jersey Code of Juvenile Justice," demanded indictment and trial by jury.

b. No court shall have jurisdiction to try and convict a person of an offense if criminal proceedings against him are barred by subsection a. of this section. When it appears that a person charged with the commission of an offense may be of such an age that proceedings may be barred under subsection a. of this section, the court shall hold a hearing thereon, and the burden shall be on such person to establish to the satisfaction of the court that the proceeding is barred upon such grounds. If the court determines that the proceeding is barred, custody of the person charged shall be surrendered to the family court and the case, including all papers and processes relating thereto shall be transferred.

L.1978, c. 95, § 2C:4–11, eff. Sept. 1, 1979. Amended by L.1982, c. 77, § 32, eff. Dec. 31, 1983.

[1] N.J.S.A. § 2A:4A–27.
[2] N.J.S.A. § 2A:4A–26.

CHAPTER 5

INCHOATE CRIMES

Section
2C:5–1. Criminal attempt.
2C:5–2. Conspiracy.
2C:5–3. Incapacity, irresponsibility or immunity of party to conspiracy.
2C:5–4. Grading of criminal attempt and conspiracy; mitigation in cases of lesser danger.
2C:5–5. Burglar's tools.
2C:5–6. Motor vehicle master keys.
2C:5–7. Key to lock in or on real property owned or leased by state.

2C:5–1. Criminal attempt

a. **Definition of attempt.** A person is guilty of an attempt to commit a crime if, acting with the kind of culpability otherwise required for commission of the crime, he:

(1) Purposely engages in conduct which would constitute the crime if the attendant circumstances were as a reasonable person would believe them to be;

(2) When causing a particular result is an element of the crime, does or omits to do anything with the purpose of causing such result without further conduct on his part; or

(3) Purposely does or omits to do anything which, under the circumstances as a reasonable person would believe them to be, is an act or omission constituting a substantial step in a course of conduct planned to culminate in his commission of the crime.

b. **Conduct which may be held substantial step under subsection a. (3).** Conduct shall not be held to constitute a substantial step under subsection a. (3) of this section unless it is strongly corroborative of the actor's criminal purpose.

c. **Conduct designed to aid another in commission of a crime.** A person who engages in conduct designed to aid another to commit a crime which would establish his complicity under section 2C:2–6 if the crime were committed by such other person, is guilty of an attempt to commit the crime, although the crime is not committed or attempted by such other person.

d. **Renunciation of criminal purpose.** When the actor's conduct would otherwise constitute an attempt under subsection a. (2) or (3) of this section, it is an affirmative defense which he must prove by a preponderance of the evidence that he abandoned his effort to commit the crime or otherwise prevented its commission, under circumstances manifesting a complete and voluntary renunciation of his criminal purpose. The establishment of such defense does not, however, affect the liability of an accomplice who did not join in such abandonment or prevention.

Within the meaning of this chapter, renunciation of criminal purpose is not voluntary if it is motivated, in whole or in part, by circumstances, not present or apparent at the inception of the actor's course of conduct, which increase the probability of detection or apprehension or which make more difficult the accomplishment of the criminal purpose. Renunciation is not complete if it is motivated by a decision to postpone the criminal conduct until a more advantageous time or to transfer the criminal effort to another but similar objective or victim. Renunciation is also not complete if mere abandonment is insufficient to accomplish avoidance of the offense in which case the defendant must have taken further and affirmative steps that prevented the commission thereof.

L.1978, c. 95, § 2C:5–1, eff. Sept. 1, 1979.

2C:5–2. Conspiracy

a. Definition of conspiracy. A person is guilty of conspiracy with another person or persons to commit a crime if with the purpose of promoting or facilitating its commission he:

(1) Agrees with such other person or persons that they or one or more of them will engage in conduct which constitutes such crime or an attempt or solicitation to commit such crime; or

(2) Agrees to aid such other person or persons in the planning or commission of such crime or of an attempt or solicitation to commit such crime.

b. Scope of conspiratorial relationship. If a person guilty of conspiracy, as defined by subsection a. of this section, knows that a person with whom he conspires to commit a crime has conspired with another person or persons to commit the same crime, he is guilty of conspiring with such other person or persons, whether or not he knows their identity, to commit such crime.

c. Conspiracy with multiple objectives. If a person conspires to commit a number of crimes, he is guilty of only one conspiracy so long as such multiple crimes are the object of the same agreement or continuous conspiratorial relationship. It shall not be a defense to a charge under this section that one or more of the objectives of the conspiracy was not criminal; provided that one or more of its objectives or the means of promoting or facilitating an objective of the conspiracy is criminal.

d. Overt act. No person may be convicted of conspiracy to commit a crime other than a crime of the first or second degree or distribution or possession with intent to distribute a controlled dangerous substance or controlled substance analog as defined in chapter 35 of this title, unless an overt act in pursuance of such conspiracy is proved to have been done by him or by a person with whom he conspired.

e. Renunciation of purpose. It is an affirmative defense which the actor must prove by a preponderance of the evidence that he, after conspiring to commit a crime, informed the authority of the existence of the conspiracy and his participation therein, and thwarted or caused to be thwarted the commission of any offense in furtherance of the conspiracy, under circumstances manifesting a complete and voluntary renunciation of criminal purpose as defined in N.J.S.2C:5–1d.; provided, however, that an attempt as defined in N.J.S.2C:5–1 shall not be considered an offense for purposes of renunciation under this subsection.

f. Duration of conspiracy. For the purpose of N.J.S.2C:1–6d.:

(1) Conspiracy is a continuing course of conduct which terminates when the crime or crimes which are its object are committed or the agreement that they be committed is abandoned by the defendant and by those with whom he conspired; and

(2) Such abandonment is presumed with respect to a crime other than one of the first or second degree if neither the defendant nor anyone with whom he conspired does any overt act in pursuance of the conspiracy during the applicable period of limitation; and

(3) If an individual abandons the agreement, the conspiracy is terminated as to him only if and when he advises those with whom he conspired of his abandonment or he informs the law enforcement authorities of the existence of the conspiracy and of his participation therein.

g. Leader of organized crime. A person is a leader of organized crime if he purposefully conspires with others as an organizer, supervisor, manager or financier to commit a continuing series of crimes which constitute a pattern of racketeering activity under the provisions of N.J.S. 2C:41–1, provided, however, that notwithstanding 2C:1–8a. (2), a conviction of leader of organized crime shall not merge with the conviction of any other crime which constitutes racketeering activity under 2C:41–1. As used in this section, "financier" means a person who provides money, credit or a thing of value with the purpose or knowledge that it will be used to finance or support the operations of a conspiracy to commit a series of crimes which constitute a pattern of racketeering activity, including but not limited to the purchase of materials to be used in the commission of crimes, buying or renting housing or vehicles, purchasing transportation for members of the conspiracy or otherwise facilitating the commission of crimes which constitute a pattern of racketeering activity.

L.1978, c. 95, § 2C:5–2, eff. Sept. 1, 1979. Amended by L.1979, c. 178, § 17, eff. Sept. 1, 1979; L.1981, c. 167, § 3, eff. June 15, 1981; L.1981, c. 290, § 10, eff. Sept. 24, 1981; L.1981, c. 511, § 1, eff. Jan. 12, 1982; L.1987, c. 106, § 4; L.2002, c. 26, § 8, eff. June 18, 2002.

2C:5–3. Incapacity, irresponsibility or immunity of party to conspiracy

a. In general. Except as provided in subsection b. of this section, it is immaterial to the liability of a person who conspires with another to commit a crime that:

(1) He or the person with whom he conspires does not occupy a particular position or have a particular characteristic which is an element of such crime, if he believes that one of them does; or

(2) The person with whom he conspires is irresponsible or has an immunity to prosecution or conviction for the commission of the crime.

b. Exceptions to subsection a.: Victims, behavior inevitably incident to the commission of the crime. It is a defense to a charge of conspiracy to commit a crime that if the object of the conspiracy were achieved, the person charged would not be guilty of a crime under the law defining the crime or as an accomplice under section 2C:2–6e. (1) or (2).

L.1978, c. 95, § 2C:5–3, eff. Sept. 1, 1979.

2C:5–4. Grading of criminal attempt and conspiracy; mitigation in cases of lesser danger

a. Grading. Except as provided in subsections c. and d., an attempt or conspiracy to commit a crime of the first degree is a crime of the second degree; except that an attempt or conspiracy to commit murder or terrorism is a crime of the first degree,provided, however, that if the person attempted or conspired to murder five or more persons, the person shall be sentenced by the court to a term of 30 years, during which the person shall not be eligible for parole, or to a specific term of years which shall be between 30 years and life imprisonment, of which the person shall serve not less than 30 years before eligibility for parole. Otherwise an attempt is a crime of the same degree as the most serious crime which is attempted, and conspiracy is a crime of the same degree as the most serious crime which is the object of the conspiracy; provided that, leader of organized crime is a crime of the second degree. An attempt or conspiracy to commit an offense defined by a statute outside the code shall be graded as a crime of the same degree as the offense is graded pursuant to N.J.S.2C:1–4 and N.J.S.2C:43–1.

b. Mitigation. The court may impose sentence for a crime of a lower grade or degree if neither the particular conduct charged nor the defendant presents a public danger warranting the grading provided for such crime under subsection a. because:

(1) The criminal attempt or conspiracy charged is so inherently unlikely to result or culminate in the commission of a crime; or

(2) The conspiracy, as to the particular defendant charged, is so peripherally related to the main unlawful enterprise.

c. Notwithstanding the provisions of subsection a. of this section, conspiracy to commit a crime set forth in subsection a., b., or d. of N.J.S.2C:17–1 where the structure which was the target of the crime was a church, synagogue, temple or other place of public worship is a crime of the first degree.

d. Notwithstanding the provisions of subsection a. of this section, conspiracy to commit a crime as set forth in P.L.1994, c. 121 (C.2C:21–23 et seq.) is a crime of the same degree as the most serious crime that was conspired to be committed.

L.1978, c. 95, § 2C:5–4, eff. Sept. 1, 1979. Amended by L.1979, c. 178, § 18, eff. Sept. 1, 1979; L.1981, c. 167, § 4, eff. June 15, 1981; L.1981, c. 290, § 11, eff. Sept. 24, 1981; L.1981, c. 511, § 2, eff. Jan. 12, 1982; L.1986, c. 190, § 1, eff. Dec. 17, 1986; L.1997, c. 34, § 1, eff. March 7, 1997; L.1999, c. 25, § 2, eff. Feb. 16, 1999; L.2002, c. 26, § 9, eff. June 18, 2002.

2C:5–5. Burglar's tools

a. Any person who manufactures or possesses any engine, machine, tool or implement adapted, designed or commonly used for committing or facilitating any offense in chapter 20 of this Title or offenses involving forcible entry into premises

(1) Knowing the same to be so adapted or designed or commonly used; and

(2) With either a purpose so to use or employ it, or with a purpose to provide it to some person who he knows has such a purpose to use or employ it, is guilty of an offense.

b. Any person who publishes plans or instructions dealing with the manufacture or use of any burglar tools as defined above, with the intent that such publication be used for committing or facilitating any offense in chapter 20 of this Title or offenses involving forcible entry into premises is guilty of an offense.

The offense under a. or b. of this section is a crime of the fourth degree if the defendant manufactured such instrument or implements or published such plans or instructions; otherwise it is a disorderly persons offense.

L.1978, c. 95, § 2C:5–5, eff. Sept. 1, 1979. Amended by L.1979, c. 178, § 18A, eff. Sept. 1, 1979; L.1992, c. 198, § 1, eff. Dec. 23, 1992.

2C:5–6. Motor vehicle master keys

a. Any person who knowingly possesses a motor vehicle master key or device designed to operate a lock or locks on motor vehicles or to start a motor vehicle without an ignition key is guilty of a crime of the fourth degree.

b. Any person who offers or advertises for sale, sells or gives to any person other than those excepted in subsection c. a motor vehicle master key or device designed to operate a lock or locks on a motor vehicle or to start a motor vehicle without an ignition key is guilty of a crime of the fourth degree.

c. Subsection a. shall not apply to a law enforcement officer, constable, locksmith or dealer, distributor or manufacturer of motor vehicles or motor vehicle locks, a garage keeper, or a person engaged in the business of lending on the security of motor vehicles, or in the business of acquiring by purchase evidence of debt secured by interests in motor vehicles, and his employees and agents.

L.1978, c. 95, § 2C:5–6, eff. Sept. 1, 1979.

2C:5–7. Key to lock in or on real property owned or leased by state

Any person who knowingly uses, distributes, manufactures, duplicates or possesses a key designed to be used in a lock in or on real property owned or leased by the State without conforming to the rules and regulations established according to section 2 of this act [1] is guilty of a disorderly persons offense.

L.1981, c. 248, § 1, eff. Feb. 2, 1982.

[1] N.J.S.A. § 52:27B–56a.

CHAPTER 6

BAIL

Section
2C:6–1.   Persons accused of minor offenses.

2C:6–1.   Persons accused of minor offenses

No person charged with a crime of the fourth degree, a disorderly persons offense or a petty disorderly persons offense shall be required to deposit bail in an amount exceeding $2,500.00, unless the court finds that the person presents a serious threat to the physical safety of potential evidence or of persons involved in circumstances surrounding the alleged offense or unless the court finds bail of that amount will not reasonably assure the appearance of the defendant as required. The court may for good cause shown impose a higher bail; the court shall specifically place on the record its reasons for imposing bail in an amount exceeding $2,500.00.

L.1983, c. 423, § 1, eff. Jan. 5, 1984.

CHAPTER 7

REGISTRATION AND NOTIFICATION OF RELEASE OF CERTAIN OFFENDERS

Section
2C:7–1.   Legislative findings and declaration.
2C:7–2.   Registration of sex offenders; definitions.
2C:7–2.1.   Address verification prior to release.
2C:7–3.   Notice of obligation to register as sex offender.
2C:7–4.   Registration forms; contents; transmission of form.
2C:7–5.   Records; access; immunity.
2C:7–6.   Notification of community of intent of sex offender released from correctional facility or adjudicated delinquent to reside in municipality.
2C:7–7.   Chief law enforcement officer to provide notification to community.
2C:7–8.   Notification guidelines; identification of factors relevant to risk of re-offense.
2C:7–9.   Immunity from civil and criminal liability for providing or failing to provide relevant information.
2C:7–10.   Notification concerning other dangerous circumstances unaffected.
2C:7–11.   Notification advisory council established; qualifications of members.
2C:7–12.   Legislative findings.
2C:7–13.   Information in central registry to be made available on the Internet.
2C:7–14.   Duties of the Attorney General.
2C:7–15.   Failure to investigate or disclose any information from the registry.
2C:7–16.   Use of disclosed information.
2C:7–17.   Provisions are severable.
2C:7–18.   Internet Registry Advisory Council.
2C:7–19.   Short title.
2C:7–20.   Legislative findings and declarations; implementation and consistent application of Megan's Law across the State.
2C:7–21.   Comprehensive study.

Section
2C:7–22.   "Excluded sex offender" defined; "youth serving organization" defined.
2C:7–23.   Prohibitions upon sex offender participation in any youth serving organization; exceptions.

2C:7–1.   Legislative findings and declaration

The Legislature finds and declares:

a.   The danger of recidivism posed by sex offenders and offenders who commit other predatory acts against children, and the dangers posed by persons who prey on others as a result of mental illness, require a system of registration that will permit law enforcement officials to identify and alert the public when necessary for the public safety.

b.   A system of registration of sex offenders and offenders who commit other predatory acts against children will provide law enforcement with additional information critical to preventing and promptly resolving incidents involving sexual abuse and missing persons.

L.1994, c. 133, § 1, eff. Oct. 31, 1994.

2C:7–2   Registration of sex offenders; definitions

a.   (1) A person who has been convicted, adjudicated delinquent or found not guilty by reason of insanity for commission of a sex offense as defined in subsection b. of this section shall register as provided in subsections c. and d. of this section.

(2) A person who in another jurisdiction is required to register as a sex offender and (a) is enrolled on a full-time or part-time basis in any public or private educational institution in this State, including any secondary school, trade or professional institution, institution of higher education or other post-secondary school, or (b) is employed or carries on a vocation in this State, on either a full-time or a part-time basis, with or without compensation, for more than 14 consecutive days or for an aggregate period exceeding 30 days in a calendar year, shall register in this State as provided in subsections c. and d. of this section.

(3) A person who fails to register as required under this act [1] shall be guilty of a crime of the third degree.

b.   For the purposes of this act a sex offense shall include the following:

(1) Aggravated sexual assault, sexual assault, aggravated criminal sexual contact, kidnapping pursuant to paragraph (2) of subsection c. of N.J.S.2C:13–1 or an attempt to commit any of these crimes if the court found that the offender's conduct was characterized by a pattern of repetitive, compulsive behavior, regardless of the date of the commission of the offense or the date of conviction;

(2) A conviction, adjudication of delinquency, or acquittal by reason of insanity for aggravated sexual assault; sexual assault; aggravated criminal sexual contact; kidnapping pursuant to paragraph (2) of subsec-

tion c. of N.J.S.2C:13–1; endangering the welfare of a child by engaging in sexual conduct which would impair or debauch the morals of the child pursuant to subsection a. of N.J.S.2C:24–4; endangering the welfare of a child pursuant to paragraph (3) or (4) or subparagraph (a) of paragraph (5) of subsection b. of N.J.S.2C:24–4; luring or enticing pursuant to section 1 of P.L.1993, c. 291 (C.2C:13–6); criminal sexual contact pursuant to N.J.S.2C:14–3b. if the victim is a minor; kidnapping pursuant to N.J.S.2C:13–1, criminal restraint pursuant to N.J.S.2C:13–2, or false imprisonment pursuant to N.J.S.2C:13–3 if the victim is a minor and the offender is not the parent of the victim; knowingly promoting prostitution of a child pursuant to paragraph (3) or paragraph (4) of subsection b. of N.J.S.2C:34–1; or an attempt to commit any of these enumerated offenses if the conviction, adjudication of delinquency or acquittal by reason of insanity is entered on or after the effective date of this act [2] or the offender is serving a sentence of incarceration, probation, parole or other form of community supervision as a result of the offense or is confined following acquittal by reason of insanity or as a result of civil commitment on the effective date of this act;

(3) A conviction, adjudication of delinquency or acquittal by reason of insanity for an offense similar to any offense enumerated in paragraph (2) or a sentence on the basis of criteria similar to the criteria set forth in paragraph (1) of this subsection entered or imposed under the laws of the United States, this State or another state.

c. A person required to register under the provisions of this act shall do so on forms to be provided by the designated registering agency as follows:

(1) A person who is required to register and who is under supervision in the community on probation, parole, furlough, work release, or a similar program, shall register at the time the person is placed under supervision or no later than 120 days after the effective date of this act, whichever is later, in accordance with procedures established by the Department of Corrections, the Department of Human Services, the Juvenile Justice Commission established pursuant to section 2 of P.L.1995, c. 284 (C.52:17B–170) or the Administrative Office of the Courts, whichever is responsible for supervision;

(2) A person confined in a correctional or juvenile facility or involuntarily committed who is required to register shall register prior to release in accordance with procedures established by the Department of Corrections, the Department of Human Services or the Juvenile Justice Commission and, within 48 hours of release, shall also register with the chief law enforcement officer of the municipality in which the person resides or, if the municipality does not have a local police force, the Superintendent of State Police;

(3) A person moving to or returning to this State from another jurisdiction shall register with the chief law enforcement officer of the municipality in which the

person will reside or, if the municipality does not have a local police force, the Superintendent of State Police within 120 days of the effective date of this act or 10 days of first residing in or returning to a municipality in this State, whichever is later;

(4) A person required to register on the basis of a conviction prior to the effective date who is not confined or under supervision on the effective date of this act shall register within 120 days of the effective date of this act with the chief law enforcement officer of the municipality in which the person will reside or, if the municipality does not have a local police force, the Superintendent of State Police;

(5) A person who in another jurisdiction is required to register as a sex offender and who is enrolled on a full-time or part-time basis in any public or private educational institution in this State, including any secondary school, trade or professional institution, institution of higher education or other post-secondary school shall, within ten days of commencing attendance at such educational institution, register with the chief law enforcement officer of the municipality in which the educational institution is located or, if the municipality does not have a local police force, the Superintendent of State Police;

(6) A person who in another jurisdiction is required to register as a sex offender and who is employed or carries on a vocation in this State, on either a full-time or a part-time basis, with or without compensation, for more than 14 consecutive days or for an aggregate period exceeding 30 days in a calendar year, shall, within ten days after commencing such employment or vocation, register with the chief law enforcement officer of the municipality in which the employer is located or where the vocation is carried on, as the case may be, or, if the municipality does not have a local police force, the Superintendent of State Police;

(7) In addition to any other registration requirements set forth in this section, a person required to register under this act who is enrolled at, employed by or carries on a vocation at an institution of higher education or other post-secondary school in this State shall, within ten days after commencing such attendance, employment or vocation, register with the law enforcement unit of the educational institution, if the institution has such a unit.

d. (1) Upon a change of address, a person shall notify the law enforcement agency with which the person is registered and shall re-register with the appropriate law enforcement agency no less than 10 days before he intends to first reside at his new address. Upon a change of employment or school enrollment status, a person shall notify the appropriate law enforcement agency no later than five days after any such change. A person who fails to notify the appropriate law enforcement agency of a change of address or status in accordance with this subsection is guilty of a crime of the fourth degree.

(2) A person required to register under this act [3] shall provide the appropriate law enforcement agency

with information as to whether the person has routine access to or use of a computer or any other device with Internet capability. A person who fails to notify the appropriate law enforcement agency of such information or of a change in the person's access to or use of a computer or other device with Internet capability or who provides false information concerning the person's access to or use of a computer or any other device with Internet capability is guilty of a crime of the fourth degree.

e. A person required to register under paragraph (1) of subsection b. of this section or under paragraph (3) of subsection b. due to a sentence imposed on the basis of criteria similar to the criteria set forth in paragraph (1) of subsection b. shall verify his address with the appropriate law enforcement agency every 90 days in a manner prescribed by the Attorney General. A person required to register under paragraph (2) of subsection b. of this section or under paragraph (3) of subsection b. on the basis of a conviction for an offense similar to an offense enumerated in paragraph (2) of subsection b. shall verify his address annually in a manner prescribed by the Attorney General. One year after the effective date of this act, the Attorney General shall review, evaluate and, if warranted, modify pursuant to the "Administrative Procedure Act," P.L.1968, c. 410 (C.52:14B–1 et seq.) the verification requirement. Any person who knowingly provides false information concerning his place of residence or who fails to verify his address with the appropriate law enforcement agency or other entity, as prescribed by the Attorney General in accordance with this subsection, is guilty of a crime of the fourth degree.

f. Except as provided in subsection g. of this section, a person required to register under this act may make application to the Superior Court of this State to terminate the obligation upon proof that the person has not committed an offense within 15 years following conviction or release from a correctional facility for any term of imprisonment imposed, whichever is later, and is not likely to pose a threat to the safety of others.

g. A person required to register under this section who has been convicted of, adjudicated delinquent, or acquitted by reason of insanity for more than one sex offense as defined in subsection b. of this section or who has been convicted of, adjudicated delinquent, or acquitted by reason of insanity for aggravated sexual assault pursuant to subsection a. of N.J.S.2C:14–2 or sexual assault pursuant to paragraph (1) of subsection c. of N.J.S.2C:14–2 is not eligible under subsection f. of this section to make application to the Superior Court of this State to terminate the registration obligation.

L.1994, c. 133, § 2, eff. Oct. 31, 1994. Amended by L.1995, c. 280, § 18, eff. Dec. 15, 1995; L.2001, c. 392, § 1, eff. Jan. 8, 2002; L.2003, c. 34, § 1, eff. July 1, 2003; L.2003, c. 219, § 1, eff. April 8, 2004; L.2003, c. 220, § 1, eff. April 8, 2004; L.2007, c. 19, § 1, eff. March 1, 2007; L.2007, c. 219, § 2, eff. Feb. 25, 2008.

[1] N.J.S.A. § 2C:7–1 et seq.
[2] L.1994, c. 133, eff. Oct. 31, 1994.
[3] L.2007, c. 219.

2C:7–2.1   Address verification prior to release

a. No person confined in a correctional or juvenile facility or involuntarily committed who is required to register under the provisions of P.L.1994, c. 133 (C.2C:7–1 et seq.) shall be released from that confinement prior to expiration of sentence or termination from supervision or of custody, as the case may be, until the address set forth on his form of registration as his proposed place of residence has been verified as valid in accordance with procedures established by the Attorney General, which shall include provisions governing written notification of appropriate State and local officials. The address verification shall take place prior to the scheduled date of release and shall be provided to the department to which the individual is confined or committed or the commission, as appropriate. Nothing in this section shall be construed to require a person to be held in confinement or involuntary commitment beyond the date of expiration of that person's sentence, termination from supervision, or judicially ordered termination of custody, as the case may be.

b. No person under supervision in the community on probation, parole, furlough, work release or any similar program who is required to register under the provisions of P.L.1994, c. 133 (C.2C:7–1 et seq.) shall be released from that supervision until the address set forth on his form of registration as his proposed place of residence has been verified as valid. The address verification shall take place prior to the scheduled date of release.

L.2007, c. 19, § 2, eff. March 1, 2007.

2C:7–3.   Notice of obligation to register as sex offender

Notice of the obligation to register shall be provided as follows:

(1) A court imposing a sentence, disposition or order of commitment following acquittal by reason of insanity shall notify the defendant of the obligation to register pursuant to section 2 of this act.[1]

(2) The Department of Corrections, the Administrative Office of the Courts, the Juvenile Justice Commission established pursuant to section 2 of P.L.1995, c. 284 (C. 52:17B–170) and the Department of Human Services shall (a) establish procedures for notifying persons under their supervision of the obligation to register pursuant to this act and (b) establish procedures for registration by persons with the appropriate law enforcement agency who are under supervision in the community on probation, parole, furlough, work release or similar program outside the facility, and registration with the appropriate law enforcement agency of persons who are released from the facility in which they are confined without supervision.

(3) The Division of Motor Vehicles in the Department of Law and Public Safety shall provide notice of the obligation to register pursuant to this section in connection with each application for a license to operate a motor vehicle and each application for an

identification card issued pursuant to section 2 of P.L.1980, c. 47 (C. 39:3–29.3).

(4) The Attorney General shall cause notice of the obligation to register to be published in a manner reasonably calculated to reach the general public within 30 days of the effective date of this act.

L.1994, c. 133, § 3, eff. Oct. 31, 1994. Amended by L.1995, c. 280, § 19, eff. Dec. 15, 1995.

1 N.J.S.A. § 2C:7–2.

2C:7–4. Registration forms; contents; transmission of form

a. Within 60 days of the effective date of this act, the Superintendent of State Police, with the approval of the Attorney General, shall prepare the form of registration statement as required in subsection b. of this section and shall provide such forms to each organized full-time municipal police department, the Department of Corrections, the Administrative Office of the Courts and the Department of Human Services. In addition, the Superintendent of State Police shall make such forms available to the Juvenile Justice Commission established pursuant to section 2 of P.L.1995, c. 284 (C.52:17B–170).

b. The form of registration required by this act shall include:

(1) A statement in writing signed by the person required to register acknowledging that the person has been advised of the duty to register and reregister imposed by this act and including the person's name, social security number, age, race, sex, date of birth, height, weight, hair and eye color, address of legal residence, address of any current temporary residence, date and place of employment; and any anticipated or current school enrollment, including but not limited to enrollment at or employment by any institution of higher education;

(2) Date and place of each conviction, adjudication or acquittal by reason of insanity, indictment number, fingerprints, and a brief description of the crime or crimes for which registration is required; and

(3) Any other information that the Attorney General deems necessary to assess risk of future commission of a crime, including criminal and corrections records, non-privileged personnel, treatment, and abuse registry records, and evidentiary genetic markers when available.

c. Within three days of receipt of a registration pursuant to subsection c. of section 2 of this act,[1] the registering agency shall forward the statement and any other required information to the prosecutor who shall, as soon as practicable, transmit the form of registration to the Superintendent of State Police, and, if the registrant will reside in a different county, to the prosecutor of the county in which the person will reside. The prosecutor of the county in which the person will reside shall transmit the form of registration to the law

enforcement agency responsible for the municipality in which the person will reside and other appropriate law enforcement agencies. The superintendent shall promptly transmit the conviction data and fingerprints to the Federal Bureau of Investigation.

d. The Superintendent of State Police shall maintain a central registry of registrations provided pursuant to this act.

L.1994, c. 133, § 4, eff. Oct. 31, 1994. Amended by L.1995, c. 280, § 20, eff. Dec. 15, 1995; L.2003, c. 34, § 2, eff. July 1, 2003.

1 N.J.S.A. § 2C:7–2.

2C:7–5. Records; access; immunity

a. Records maintained pursuant to this act shall be open to any law enforcement agency in this State, the United States or any other state and may be released to the Division of Youth and Family Services in the Department of Children and Families for use in carrying out its responsibilities under law. Law enforcement agencies in this State shall be authorized to release relevant and necessary information regarding sex offenders to the public when the release of the information is necessary for public protection in accordance with the provisions of P.L.1994, c. 128 (C.2C:7–6 et seq.).

b. An elected public official, public employee, or public agency is immune from civil liability for damages for any discretionary decision to release relevant and necessary information, unless it is shown that the official, employee, or agency acted with gross negligence or in bad faith. The immunity provided under this section applies to the release of relevant information to other employees or officials or to the general public.

c. Nothing in this act shall be deemed to impose any liability upon or to give rise to a cause of action against any public official, public employee, or public agency for failing to release information as authorized in subsection d. of this section.

d. Nothing in this section shall be construed to prevent law enforcement officers from notifying members of the public exposed to danger of any persons that pose a danger under circumstances that are not enumerated in this act.

L.1994, c. 133, § 5, eff. Oct. 31, 1994. Amended by L.2006, c. 6, § 1, eff. April 11, 2006; L.2006, c. 47, § 23, eff. July 1, 2006.

2C:7–6. Notification of community of intent of sex offender released from correctional facility or adjudicated delinquent to reside in municipality

Within 45 days after receiving notification pursuant to section 1 of P.L.1994, c. 135 (C. 30:4–123.53a) that an inmate convicted of or adjudicated delinquent for a sex offense as defined in section 2 of P.L.1994 c. 133 (C. 2C:7–2) is to be released from incarceration and after receipt of registration as required therein, the chief law enforcement officer of the municipality where the inmate intends to reside shall provide notification in accordance with the provisions of section 3 of this act [1] of that inmate's release to the community. If the municipality does not have a police force, the Superintendent of State Police shall provide notification.

L.1994, c. 128, § 1, eff. Oct. 31, 1994.

[1] N.J.S.A. § 2C:7–8.

2C:7–7. Chief law enforcement officer to provide notification to community

After receipt of notification and registration pursuant to P.L.1994, c. 133 (C. 2C:7–1 et seq.) that a person required to register pursuant to that act intends to change his address, the chief law enforcement officer of the municipality to which the person is relocating shall provide notification of that relocation to the community pursuant to section 3 of this act.[1] If the municipality does not have a police force, the Superintendent of State Police shall provide notification.

L.1994, c. 128, § 2, eff. Oct. 31, 1994.

[1] N.J.S.A. § 2C:7–8.

2C:7–8. Notification guidelines; identification of factors relevant to risk of re-offense

a. After consultation with members of the advisory council established pursuant to section 6 of this act [1] and within 60 days of the effective date, the Attorney General shall promulgate guidelines and procedures for the notification required pursuant to the provisions of this act. The guidelines shall identify factors relevant to risk of re-offense and shall provide for three levels of notification depending upon the degree of the risk of re-offense.

b. Factors relevant to risk of re-offense shall include, but not be limited to, the following:

(1) Conditions of release that minimize risk of re-offense, including but not limited to whether the offender is under supervision of probation or parole; receiving counseling, therapy or treatment; or residing in a home situation that provides guidance and supervision;

(2) Physical conditions that minimize risk of re-offense, including but not limited to advanced age or debilitating illness;

(3) Criminal history factors indicative of high risk of re-offense, including:

(a) Whether the offender's conduct was found to be characterized by repetitive and compulsive behavior;

(b) Whether the offender served the maximum term;

(c) Whether the offender committed the sex offense against a child;

(4) Other criminal history factors to be considered in determining risk, including:

(a) The relationship between the offender and the victim;

(b) Whether the offense involved the use of a weapon, violence, or infliction of serious bodily injury;

(c) The number, date and nature of prior offenses;

(5) Whether psychological or psychiatric profiles indicate a risk of recidivism;

(6) The offender's response to treatment;

(7) Recent behavior, including behavior while confined or while under supervision in the community as well as behavior in the community following service of sentence; and

(8) Recent threats against persons or expressions of intent to commit additional crimes.

c. The regulations shall provide for three levels of notification depending upon the risk of re-offense by the offender as follows:

(1) If risk of re-offense is low, law enforcement agencies likely to encounter the person registered shall be notified;

(2) If risk of re-offense is moderate, organizations in the community including schools, religious and youth organizations shall be notified in accordance with the Attorney General's guidelines, in addition to the notice required by paragraph (1) of this subsection;

(3) If risk of re-offense is high, the public shall be notified through means in accordance with the Attorney General's guidelines designed to reach members of the public likely to encounter the person registered, in addition to the notice required by paragraphs (1) and (2) of this subsection.

d. In order to promote uniform application of the notification guidelines required by this section, the Attorney General shall develop procedures for evaluation of the risk of re-offense and implementation of community notification. These procedures shall require, but not be limited to, the following:

(1) The county prosecutor of the county where the person was convicted and the county prosecutor of the county where the registered person will reside, together with any law enforcement officials that either deems appropriate, shall assess the risk of re-offense by the registered person;

(2) The county prosecutor of the county in which the registered person will reside, after consultation with local law enforcement officials, shall determine the means of providing notification.

e. The Attorney General's guidelines shall provide for the manner in which records of notification provided pursuant to this act shall be maintained and disclosed.

L.1994, c. 128, § 3, eff. Oct. 31, 1994.

[1] N.J.S.A. § 2C:7–11.

2C:7–9. Immunity from civil and criminal liability for providing or failing to provide relevant information

Notwithstanding any other provision of law to the contrary, any person who provides or fails to provide information relevant to the procedures set forth in this act shall not be liable in any civil or criminal action. Nothing herein shall be deemed to grant any such immunity to any person for his willful or wanton act of commission or omission.

L.1994, c. 128, § 4, eff. Oct. 31, 1994.

2C:7–10.   Notification concerning other dangerous circumstances unaffected

Nothing in this act shall be construed to prevent law enforcement officers from providing community notification concerning any person who poses a danger under circumstances that are not provided for in this act.

L.1994, c. 128, § 5, eff. Oct. 31, 1994.

2C:7–11.   Notification advisory council established; qualifications of members

A notification advisory council is established to consult with and provide recommendations to the Attorney General concerning the guidelines to be promulgated pursuant to section 3 of this act.[1] The council shall consist of 12 persons who, by experience or training, have a personal interest or professional expertise in law enforcement, crime prevention, victim advocacy, criminology, psychology, parole, public education or community relations. The members of the council shall be appointed in the following manner: four shall be appointed by the Governor, of whom no more than two shall be of the same political party; four shall be appointed by the President of the Senate, of whom no more than two shall be of the same political party; and four shall be appointed by the Speaker of the General Assembly, of whom no more than two shall be of the same political party. Any vacancies occurring in the membership shall be filled in the same manner as the original appointments.

One year after the effective date of this act, the Attorney General and the council shall conduct a comprehensive review of the guidelines to determine whether any changes or revisions should be promulgated. Upon completion of that review and the submission of any recommendations thereon, the council shall expire.

L.1994, c. 128, § 6, eff. Oct. 31, 1994.

[1] N.J.S.A. § 2C:7–8.

2C:7–12.   Legislative findings

The Legislature finds and declares that the public safety will be enhanced by making information about certain sex offenders contained in the sex offender central registry established pursuant to section 4 of P.L.1994, c. 133 (C.2C:7–4) available to the public through the Internet. Knowledge of whether a person is a convicted sex offender at risk of re-offense could be a significant factor in protecting oneself and one's family members, or those in care of a group or community organization, from recidivist acts by the offender. The technology afforded by the Internet would make this information readily accessible to parents and private entities, enabling them to undertake appropriate remedial precautions to prevent or avoid placing potential victims at risk. Public access to registry information is intended solely for the protection of the public, and is not intended to impose additional criminal punishment upon any convicted sex offender.

The Legislature further finds and declares that, in some instances, countervailing interests support a legislative determination to exclude from the Internet registry the registration information of certain sex offenders. For example, the interest in facilitating rehabilitation of juveniles who have been adjudicated delinquent for the commission of one sex offense, but who do not present a relatively high risk of re-offense, justifies the decision to limit public access to information about such juveniles through the Internet. Other instances where the Legislature has determined that making sex offender registry information available to the general public through the Internet would not necessarily serve the public safety purposes of the law include moderate risk offenders whose sole sex offense involved incest or consensual sex. However, in such cases, the legislature deems it appropriate and consistent with the public safety purposes of the law to provide a process that permits inclusion of information about these individuals in the Internet registry where public access would be warranted, based on the relative risk posed by the particular offender.

L.2001, c. 167, § 1, eff. July 23, 2001, operative Jan. 1, 2002.

2C:7–13.   Information in central registry to be made available on the Internet

a.   Pursuant to the provisions of this section, the Superintendent of State Police shall develop and maintain a system for making certain information in the central registry established pursuant to subsection d. of section 4 of P.L.1994, c. 133 (C.2C:7–4) publicly available by means of electronic Internet technology.

b.   The public may, without limitation, obtain access to the Internet registry to view an individual registration record, any part of, or the entire Internet registry concerning all offenders whose risk of re-offense is high or for whom the court has ordered notification in accordance with paragraph (3) of subsection c. of section 3 of P.L.1994, c. 128 (C.2C:7–8), regardless of the age of the offender.

c.   Except as provided in subsection d. of this section, the public may, without limitation, obtain access to the Internet registry to view an individual registration record, any part of, or the entire Internet registry concerning offenders whose risk of re-offense is moderate and for whom the court has ordered notification in accordance with paragraph (2) of subsection c. of section 3 of P.L.1994, c. 128 (C.2C:7–8).

d.   The individual registration record of an offender whose risk of re-offense has been determined to be moderate and for whom the court has ordered notification in accordance with paragraph (2) of subsection c. of section 3 of P.L.1994, c. 128 (C.2C:7–8) shall not be made available to the public on the Internet registry if the sole sex offense committed by the offender which renders him subject to the requirements of P.L.1994, c. 133 (C.2C:7–1 et seq.) is one of the following:

(1) An adjudication of delinquency for any sex offense as defined in subsection b. of section 2 of P.L.1994, c. 133 (C.2C:7–2);

(2) A conviction or acquittal by reason of insanity for a violation of N.J.S.2C:14–2 or N.J.S.2C:14–3 under circumstances in which the offender was related to the victim by blood or affinity to the third degree or was a resource family parent, a guardian, or stood in loco parentis within the household; or

(3) A conviction or acquittal by reason of insanity for a violation of N.J.S.2C:14–2 or N.J.S.2C:14–3 in any case in which the victim assented to the commission of the offense but by reason of age was not capable of giving lawful consent.

For purposes of this subsection, "sole sex offense" means a single conviction, adjudication of guilty or acquittal by reason of insanity, as the case may be, for a sex offense which involved no more than one victim, no more than one occurrence or, in the case of an offense which meets the criteria of paragraph (2) of this subsection, members of no more than a single household.

e. Notwithstanding the provisions of paragraph d. of this subsection, the individual registration record of an offender to whom an exception enumerated in paragraph (1), (2) or (3) of subsection d. of this section applies shall be made available to the public on the Internet registry if the State establishes by clear and convincing evidence that, given the particular facts and circumstances of the offense and the characteristics and propensities of the offender, the risk to the general public posed by the offender is substantially similar to that posed by offenders whose risk of re-offense is moderate and who do not qualify under the enumerated exceptions.

f. The individual registration records of offenders whose risk of re-offense is low or of offenders whose risk of re-offense is moderate but for whom the court has not ordered notification in accordance with paragraph (2) of subsection c. of section 3 of P.L.1994, c. 128 (C.2C:7–8) shall not be available to the public on the Internet registry.

g. The information concerning a registered offender to be made publicly available on the Internet shall include: the offender's name and any aliases the offender has used or under which the offender may be or may have been known; any sex offense as defined in subsection b. of section 2 of P.L.1994, c. 133 (C.2C:7–2) for which the offender was convicted, adjudicated delinquent or acquitted by reason of insanity, as the case may be; the date and location of disposition; a brief description of any such offense, including the victim's gender and indication of whether the victim was less than 18 years old or less than 13 years old; a general description of the offender's modus operandi, if any; the determination of whether the risk of re-offense by the offender is moderate or high; the offender's age, race, sex, date of birth, height, weight, hair, eye color and any distinguishing scars or tattoos; a photograph of the offender and the date on which the photograph was entered into the registry; the make, model, color, year and license plate number of any vehicle operated by the offender; and the street address, zip code, municipality and county in which the offender resides.

L.2001, c. 167, § 2, eff. July 23, 2001, operative Jan. 1, 2002. Amended by L.2004, c. 130, § 12, eff. Aug. 27, 2004; L.2004, c. 151, § 1, eff. Sept. 14, 2004.

2C:7–14. Duties of the Attorney General

The Attorney General shall:

a. Ensure that the Internet registry contains warnings that any person who uses the information contained therein to threaten, intimidate or harass another, or who otherwise misuses that information may be criminally prosecuted;

b. Ensure that the Internet registry contains an explanation of its limitations, including statements advising that a positive identification of an offender whose registration record has been made available may be confirmed only by fingerprints; that some information contained in the registry may be outdated or inaccurate; and that the Internet registry is not a comprehensive listing of every person who has ever committed a sex offense in New Jersey;

c. Strive to ensure the information contained in the Internet registry is accurate, and that the data therein is revised and updated as appropriate in a timely and efficient manner; and

d. Provide in the Internet registry information designed to inform and educate the public about sex offenders and the operation of Megan's Law, as well as pertinent and appropriate information concerning crime prevention and personal safety, with appropriate links to relevant web sites operated by the State of New Jersey.

L.2001, c. 167, § 3, eff. July 23, 2001, operative Jan. 1, 2002.

2C:7–15. Failure to investigate or disclose any information from the registry

No action shall be brought against any person for failure to investigate or disclose any information from the registry that is compiled or made available to the citizens of this State pursuant to P.L.2001, c. 167 (C.2C:7–12 et seq.).

L.2001, c. 167, § 4, eff. July 23, 2001, operative Jan. 1, 2002.

2C:7–16. Use of disclosed information

a. Any information disclosed pursuant to this act may be used in any manner by any person or by any public, governmental or private entity, organization or official, or any agent thereof, for any lawful purpose consistent with the enhancement of public safety.

b. Any person who uses information disclosed pursuant to this act to commit a crime shall be guilty of a crime of the third degree. Any person who uses information disclosed pursuant to this act to commit a disorderly persons or petty disorderly persons offense shall be guilty of a disorderly persons offense and shall be fined not less than $500 or more than $1,000, in addition to any other penalty or fine imposed.

c. Except as authorized under any other provision of law, use of any of the information disclosed pursuant to this act for the purpose of applying for, obtaining, or denying any of the following, is prohibited:

(1) Health insurance;

(2) Insurance;

(3) Loans;

(4) Credit;

(5) Education, scholarships, or fellowships;

(6) Benefits, privileges, or services provided by any business establishment, unless for a purpose consistent with the enhancement of public safety; or

(7) Housing or accommodations.

d. Whenever there is reasonable cause to believe that any person or group of persons is engaged in a pattern or practice of misuse of the information disclosed pursuant to this act, the Attorney General, or any county or municipal prosecutor having jurisdiction, or any person aggrieved by the misuse of that information is authorized to bring a civil action in the appropriate court requesting preventive relief, including an application for a permanent or temporary injunction, restraining order, or other order against the person or group of persons responsible for the pattern or practice of misuse. The foregoing remedies shall be independent of and in addition to any other remedies or procedures that may be available under other provisions of law.

e. Evidence that a person obtained information about an offender from the Internet registry within one year prior to committing a criminal offense against that offender shall give rise to an inference that the person used information in violation of subsection b. of this section.

L.2001, c. 167, § 5, eff. July 23, 2001, operative Jan. 1, 2002.

2C:7–17. Provisions are severable

The provisions of this act shall be deemed to be severable, and if any phrase, clause, sentence, word or provision of this act is declared to be unconstitutional, invalid or inoperative in whole or in part, or the applicability thereof to any person is held invalid, by a court of competent jurisdiction, the remainder of this act shall not thereby be deemed to be unconstitutional, invalid or inoperative and, to the extent it is not declared unconstitutional, invalid or inoperative, shall be effectuated and enforced.

L.2001, c. 167, § 6, eff. July 23, 2001, operative Jan. 1, 2002.

2C:7–18. Internet Registry Advisory Council

An Internet Registry Advisory Council is established to consult with and provide recommendations to the Attorney General concerning the making of sex offender registration records available to the public on the Internet. The council shall consist of nine persons who, by experience or training, have a personal interest or professional expertise in law enforcement, crime prevention, victim advocacy, criminology, psychology, parole, public education or community relations. The members of the council shall be appointed in the following manner: three shall be appointed by the Governor, of whom no more than two shall be of the same political party; three shall be appointed by the President of the Senate, of whom no more than two shall be of the same political party; and three shall be appointed by the Speaker of the General Assembly, of whom no more than two shall be of the same political party. Any vacancies occurring in the membership shall be filled in the same manner as the original appointments. The council shall hold at least two meetings per year to review the implementation and operations of the Internet registry.

L.2001, c. 167, § 7, eff. July 23, 2001, operative Jan. 1, 2002.

2C:7–19. Short title

This act and the system of registration and community notification provided pursuant to P. L.1994, c. 133 and P.L.1994, c. 128 (C.2C:7–1 through 11) shall be known and may be cited as "Megan's Law."

L.2001, c. 167, § 8, eff. July 23, 2001, operative Jan. 1, 2002.

2C:7–20. Legislative findings and declarations; implementation and consistent application of Megan's Law across the State

The Legislature finds and declares that New Jersey enacted the groundbreaking legislation known as Megan's Law in 1994 to warn citizens that a dangerous sex offender had moved into their neighborhood. At that time more than a decade ago, the law created the most comprehensive system of sex offender registration and community notification in the nation. Subsequently, the Legislature enacted the law establishing the sex offender Internet registry, utilizing modern technology to afford even greater access to information concerning dangerous sex offenders and make that information readily accessible to the public.

Recently, however, questions have been raised concerning the implementation of Megan's Law, and whether the law is not consistently applied in the 21 counties. Published reports indicate that there are great variations among the counties in the number of sex offenders whose registration information is published on the Internet. In addition, many municipalities have limited where sex offenders may reside, or banned residency by them altogether. It also has been observed that sex offenders seem to be relocating at a higher rate to certain areas of the State, suggesting that the law is being implemented differently in some areas. Since the evidence indicates that Megan's Law is being applied inconsistently across the State, the Legislature finds that a study should be undertaken to identify the causes of these inconsistencies and to recommend procedures to make the law's application more uniform and equitable.

L.2007, c. 227, § 1, eff. April 1, 2008.

2C:7–21. Comprehensive study

a. The Violence Institute of the University of Medicine and Dentistry of New Jersey shall undertake a comprehensive study of the implementation and application of Megan's Law. Specifically, the institute shall examine the implementation and application of P.L. 1994, c. 133 (C.2C:7–1 et al.), which requires registration by sex offenders and P.L.1994, c. 128 (C.2C:7–6 et seq.), which requires community notification for certain sex offenders.

b. The study shall evaluate the current procedures utilized by the county prosecutors and the courts in determining a sex offender's tier designation and implementing community notification. In evaluating these procedures, the study shall examine the disposition of all sex offenders who have registered and have been assigned a tier rating since the enactment of Megan's Law. The study shall make recommendations regarding the standardization of procedures for evaluating the risk of re-offense, assigning tier designations, implementing community notification, and ensuring uniform application of the Attorney General's guidelines by law enforcement in providing community notification. In addition, the study shall examine the use of the Internet registry in providing information to the public about sex offenders. Specifically, the study shall review the implementation of P.L.2001, c. 167 (C.2C:7–12 et seq.) and determine whether the Internet registry has accomplished its mission to inform the public of dangerous sex offenders, or if geographic inconsistencies have mitigated its effectiveness. Finally, the study shall examine whether a central agency should be charged with the administration of Megan's Law and the determination as to which offenders appear on the Internet registry.

L.2007, c. 227, § 2, eff. April 1, 2008.

2C:7–22. "Excluded sex offender" defined; "youth serving organization" defined

As used in this act:

"Excluded sex offender" means a person who has been convicted, adjudicated delinquent or found not guilty by reason of insanity for the commission of a sex offense, as defined in subsection b. of section 2 of P.L.1994, c. 133 (C.2C:7–2), which involves a victim under 18 years of age.

"Youth serving organization" means a sports team, league, athletic association or any other corporation, association or organization, excluding public and non-public schools, which provides recreational, educational, cultural, social, charitable or other activities or services to persons under 18 years of age.

L.2009, c. 139, § 1, eff. Oct. 19, 2009.

2C:7–23. Prohibitions upon sex offender participation in any youth serving organization; exceptions

a. Except as otherwise provided in subsection e. of this section, it shall be unlawful for an excluded sex offender to hold a position or otherwise participate, in a paid or unpaid capacity, in a youth serving organization.

b. A person who violates subsection a. of this section is guilty of a crime of the third degree.

c. A person who knowingly hires, engages or appoints an excluded sex offender to serve in a youth serving organization in violation of subsection a. of this section is guilty of a crime of the fourth degree.

d. The provisions of this act shall not apply to participation by an excluded sex offender under 18 years of age in a youth serving organization which provides rehabilitative or other services to juvenile sex offenders.

e. It shall not be a violation of subsection a. of this section for an excluded sex offender to serve in a youth serving organization if the excluded sex offender is under Parole Board supervision and the Parole Board has given express written permission for the excluded sex offender to hold a position or otherwise participate in that particular youth serving organization.

f. Nothing herein shall be construed to authorize an excluded sex offender, as defined in section 1 of P.L.2009, c. 139 (C.2C:7–22), to hold a position or otherwise participate, in a paid or unpaid capacity, in a youth serving organization or any other entity from which the excluded sex offender is otherwise statutorily disqualified.

L.2009, c. 139, § 2, eff. Oct. 19, 2009.

CHAPTERS 8 to 10

[RESERVED]

SUBTITLE 2

DEFINITION OF SPECIFIC OFFENSES

Part

1. Offenses Involving Danger to the Person.
2. Offenses Against Property.
3. Offenses Against Others.
4. Offenses Against Public Administration.
5. Offenses Against Public Order, Health and Decency.
6. Offenses Involving Organized Crime and Organized Crime Activities.

PART 1

OFFENSES INVOLVING DANGER TO THE PERSON

Chapter

11. Criminal Homicide.
11A. [Human Cloning].
12. Assault; Reckless Endangering; Threats.
13. Kidnapping and related Offenses: Coercion.
14. Sexual Offenses.
15. Robbery.
16. Bias Crimes.

CHAPTER 11

CRIMINAL HOMICIDE

Section

2C:11–1.   Definitions.
2C:11–2.   Criminal homicide.
2C:11–2.1. Elapse of time between assault and death, prosecution for criminal homicide.
2C:11–3.   Murder.
2C:11–3a.   Rules pertaining to display of certain photographs.
2C:11–3b.   Resentencing of inmates sentenced to death.
2C:11–3c.   Restitution to surviving relatives.
2C:11–4.   Manslaughter.
2C:11–5.   Death by vehicular homicide.
2C:11–5.1. Leaving the scene of a motor vehicle accident.
2C:11–6.   Aiding suicide.

2C:11–1. Definitions

In chapters 11 through 15, unless a different meaning plainly is required:

a. "Bodily injury" means physical pain, illness or any impairment of physical condition;

b. "Serious bodily injury" means bodily injury which creates a substantial risk of death or which causes serious, permanent disfigurement, or protracted loss or impairment of the function of any bodily member or organ;

c. "Deadly weapon" means any firearm or other weapon, device, instrument, material or substance, whether animate or inanimate, which in the manner it is used or is intended to be used, is known to be capable of producing death or serious bodily injury or which in the manner it is fashioned would lead the victim reasonably to believe it to be capable of producing death or serious bodily injury;

d. "Significant bodily injury" means bodily injury which creates a temporary loss of the function of any bodily member or organ or temporary loss of any one of the five senses.

L.1978, c. 95, § 2C:11–1, eff. Sept. 1, 1979. Amended by L.1979, c. 178, § 19, eff. Sept. 1, 1979; L.1981, c. 384, § 1, eff. Jan. 4, 1982; L.1995, c. 307, § 1, eff. Jan. 5, 1996.

2C:11–2. Criminal homicide

a. A person is guilty of criminal homicide if he purposely, knowingly, recklessly or, under the circumstances set forth in section 2C:11–5, causes the death of another human being.

b. Criminal homicide is murder, manslaughter or death by auto.

L.1978, c. 95, § 2C:11–2, eff. Sept. 1, 1979. Amended by L.1979, c. 178, § 20, eff. Sept. 1, 1979.

2C:11–2.1. Elapse of time between assault and death, prosecution for criminal homicide

The length of time which has elapsed between the initial assault and the death of the victim shall not be a bar to prosecution of the actor for criminal homicide.

L.1979, c. 363, § 1, eff. Feb. 1, 1980.

2C:11–3. Murder

a. Except as provided in N.J.S.2C:11–4, criminal homicide constitutes murder when:

(1) The actor purposely causes death or serious bodily injury resulting in death; or

(2) The actor knowingly causes death or serious bodily injury resulting in death; or

(3) It is committed when the actor, acting either alone or with one or more other persons, is engaged in the commission of, or an attempt to commit, or flight after committing or attempting to commit robbery, sexual assault, arson, burglary, kidnapping, carjacking, criminal escape or terrorism pursuant to section 2 of P.L.2002, c. 26 (C.2C:38–2), and in the course of such crime or of immediate flight therefrom, any person causes the death of a person other than one of the participants; except that in any prosecution under this subsection, in which the defendant was not the only

participant in the underlying crime, it is an affirmative defense that the defendant:

(a) Did not commit the homicidal act or in any way solicit, request, command, importune, cause or aid the commission thereof; and

(b) Was not armed with a deadly weapon, or any instrument, article or substance readily capable of causing death or serious physical injury and of a sort not ordinarily carried in public places by law-abiding persons; and

(c) Had no reasonable ground to believe that any other participant was armed with such a weapon, instrument, article or substance; and

(d) Had no reasonable ground to believe that any other participant intended to engage in conduct likely to result in death or serious physical injury.

b. (1) Murder is a crime of the first degree but a person convicted of murder shall be sentenced, except as provided in paragraphs (2), (3) and (4) of this subsection, by the court to a term of 30 years, during which the person shall not be eligible for parole, or be sentenced to a specific term of years which shall be between 30 years and life imprisonment of which the person shall serve 30 years before being eligible for parole.

(2) If the victim was a law enforcement officer and was murdered while performing his official duties or was murdered because of his status as a law enforcement officer, the person convicted of that murder shall be sentenced by the court to a term of life imprisonment, during which the person shall not be eligible for parole.

(3) A person convicted of murder shall be sentenced to a term of life imprisonment without eligibility for parole if the murder was committed under all of the following circumstances:

(a) The victim is less than 14 years old; and

(b) The act is committed in the course of the commission, whether alone or with one or more persons, of a violation of N.J.S.2C:14–2 or N.J.S.2C:14–3.

(4) Any person convicted under subsection a.(1) or (2) who committed the homicidal act by his own conduct; or who as an accomplice procured the commission of the offense by payment or promise of payment of anything of pecuniary value; or who, as a leader of a narcotics trafficking network as defined in N.J.S.2C:35–3 and in furtherance of a conspiracy enumerated in N.J.S.2C:35–3, commanded or by threat or promise solicited the commission of the offense, or, if the murder occurred during the commission of the crime of terrorism, any person who committed the crime of terrorism, shall be sentenced by the court to life imprisonment without eligibility for parole, which sentence shall be served in a maximum security prison, if a jury finds beyond a reasonable doubt that any of the following aggravating factors exist:

(a) The defendant has been convicted, at any time, of another murder. For purposes of this section, a conviction shall be deemed final when sentence is imposed and may be used as an aggravating factor regardless of whether it is on appeal;

(b) In the commission of the murder, the defendant purposely or knowingly created a grave risk of death to another person in addition to the victim;

(c) The murder was outrageously or wantonly vile, horrible or inhuman in that it involved torture, depravity of mind, or an aggravated assault to the victim;

(d) The defendant committed the murder as consideration for the receipt, or in expectation of the receipt of anything of pecuniary value;

(e) The defendant procured the commission of the murder by payment or promise of payment of anything of pecuniary value;

(f) The murder was committed for the purpose of escaping detection, apprehension, trial, punishment or confinement for another offense committed by the defendant or another;

(g) The murder was committed while the defendant was engaged in the commission of, or an attempt to commit, or flight after committing or attempting to commit murder, robbery, sexual assault, arson, burglary, kidnapping, carjacking or the crime of contempt in violation of subsection b. of N.J.S.2C:29–9;

(h) The defendant murdered a public servant, as defined in N.J.S.2C:27–1, while the victim was engaged in the performance of his official duties, or because of the victim's status as a public servant;

(i) The defendant: (i) as a leader of a narcotics trafficking network as defined in N.J.S.2C:35–3 and in furtherance of a conspiracy enumerated in N.J.S.2C:35–3, committed, commanded or by threat or promise solicited the commission of the murder or (ii) committed the murder at the direction of a leader of a narcotics trafficking network as defined in N.J.S.2C:35–3 in furtherance of a conspiracy enumerated in N.J.S.2C:35–3;

(j) The homicidal act that the defendant committed or procured was in violation of paragraph (1) of subsection a. of N.J.S.2C:17–2;

(k) The victim was less than 14 years old; or

(*l*) The murder was committed during the commission of, or an attempt to commit, or flight after committing or attempting to commit, terrorism pursuant to section 2 of P.L.2002, c. 26 (C.2C:38–2).

(5) A juvenile who has been tried as an adult and convicted of murder shall be sentenced pursuant to paragraph (1), (2) or (3) of this subsection.

c. (Deleted by amendment, P.L.2007, c. 204).

d. (Deleted by amendment, P.L.2007, c. 204).

e. (Deleted by amendment, P.L.2007, c. 204).

f. (Deleted by amendment, P.L.2007, c. 204).

g. (Deleted by amendment, P.L.2007, c. 204).

h. (Deleted by amendment, P.L.2007, c. 204).

i. For purposes of this section the term "homicidal act" shall mean conduct that causes death or serious bodily injury resulting in death.

j. In a sentencing proceeding conducted pursuant to this section, the display of a photograph of the victim taken before the homicide shall be permitted.

L.1978, c. 95, § 2C:11–3, eff. Sept. 1, 1979. Amended by L.1979, c. 178, § 21, eff. Sept. 1, 1979; L.1981, c. 290, § 12, eff. Sept. 24, 1981; L.1982, c. 111, § 1, eff. Aug. 6, 1982; L.1985, c. 178, § 2, eff. June 10, 1985; L.1985, c. 478, § 1, eff. Jan. 17, 1986; L.1992, c. 5, § 1, eff. May 12, 1992; L.1992, c. 76, § 1, eff. July 31, 1992; L.1993, c. 27, § 1, eff. Jan. 26, 1993; L.1993, c. 111, § 1, eff. May 5, 1993; L.1993, c. 206, § 1, eff. July 28, 1993; L.1994, c. 132, § 1, eff. Oct. 31, 1994; L.1995, c. 123, § 1, eff. June 19, 1995; L.1996, c. 115, § 1, eff. Jan. 9, 1997; L.1997, c. 60, § 1, eff. April 3, 1997; L.1998, c. 25, § 1, eff. June 12, 1998; L.1999, c. 209, § 1, eff. Sept. 17, 1999; L.1999, c. 294, § 1, eff. Dec. 23, 1999; L.2000, c. 88, § 1, eff. Aug. 22, 2000; L.2002, c. 26, § 10, eff. June 18, 2002; L.2007, c. 204, § 1, eff. Dec. 17, 2007.

2C:11–3a. Rules pertaining to display of certain photographs

The Supreme Court may adopt court rules pertaining to the display of a photograph of a homicide victim in court as permitted in N.J.S.2C:11–3 concerning murder and in section 3 of P.L.1985, c. 249 (C.52:4B–36) concerning other homicide prosecutions. These court rules may include, but shall not be limited to, the following matters to ensure uniformity in all homicide prosecutions:

a. the size of the photograph;

b. the duration of the display;

c. the location of the photograph in the courtroom.

L.1999, c. 294, § 3, eff. Dec. 23, 1999.

2C:11–3b. Resentencing of inmates sentenced to death

An inmate sentenced to death prior to the date of the enactment of this act,[1] upon motion to the sentencing court and waiver of any further appeals related to sentencing, shall be resentenced to a term of life imprisonment during which the defendant shall not be eligible for parole. Such sentence shall be served in a maximum security prison.

Any such motion to the sentencing court shall be made within 60 days of the enactment of this act. If the motion is not made within 60 days the inmate shall remain under the sentence of death previously imposed by the sentencing court.

L.2007, c. 204, § 2, eff. Dec. 17, 2007.

[1] L.2007, c. 204, approved Dec. 17, 2007.

2C:11–3c. Restitution to surviving relatives

In addition to the provisions of any other law requiring restitution, a person convicted of murder pursuant to N.J.S.2C:11–3 shall be required to pay restitution to the nearest surviving relative of the victim. The court shall determine the amount and duration of the restitution pursuant to N.J.S.2C:43–3 and the provisions of chapter 46 of Title 2C of the New Jersey Statutes.

L.2007, c. 204, § 3, eff. Dec. 17, 2007.

2C:11–4. Manslaughter

a. Criminal homicide constitutes aggravated manslaughter when:

(1) The actor recklessly causes death under circumstances manifesting extreme indifference to human life; or

(2) The actor causes the death of another person while fleeing or attempting to elude a law enforcement officer in violation of subsection b. of N.J.S.2C:29–2. Notwithstanding the provision of any other law to the contrary, the actor shall be strictly liable for a violation of this paragraph upon proof of a violation of subsection b. of N.J.S.2C:29–2 which resulted in the death of another person. As used in this paragraph, "actor" shall not include a passenger in a motor vehicle.

b. Criminal homicide constitutes manslaughter when:

(1) It is committed recklessly; or

(2) A homicide which would otherwise be murder under section 2C:11–3 is committed in the heat of passion resulting from a reasonable provocation.

c. Aggravated manslaughter under paragraph (1) of subsection a. of this section is a crime of the first degree and upon conviction thereof a person may, notwithstanding the provisions of paragraph (1) of subsection a. of N.J.S.2C:43–6, be sentenced to an ordinary term of imprisonment between 10 and 30 years. Aggravated manslaughter under paragraph (2) of subsection a. of this section is a crime of the first degree. Manslaughter is a crime of the second degree.

L.1978, c. 95, § 2C:11–4, eff. Sept. 1, 1979. Amended by L.1979, c. 178, § 21A, eff. Sept. 1, 1979; L.1981, c. 290, § 13, eff. Sept. 24, 1981; L.1986, c. 172, § 1, eff. Dec. 8, 1986; L.1991, c. 341, § 1. eff. Jan. 7, 1992; L.2001, c. 412, § 1, eff. Jan. 8, 2002.

2C:11–5. Death by vehicular homicide

a. Criminal homicide constitutes vehicular homicide when it is caused by driving a vehicle or vessel recklessly.

Proof that the defendant fell asleep while driving or was driving after having been without sleep for a period in excess of 24 consecutive hours may give rise to an inference that the defendant was driving recklessly. Proof that the defendant was driving while intoxicated in violation of R.S.39:4–50 or was operating a vessel under the influence of alcohol or drugs in violation of section 3 of P.L.1952, c. 157 (C.12:7–46) shall give rise to an inference that the defendant was driving recklessly. Nothing in this section shall be construed to in any way limit the conduct or conditions that may be found to constitute driving a vehicle or vessel recklessly.

b. Except as provided in paragraph (3) of this subsection, vehicular homicide is a crime of the second degree.

(1) If the defendant was operating the auto or vessel while under the influence of any intoxicating liquor, narcotic, hallucinogenic or habit-producing drug, or with a blood alcohol concentration at or above the prohibited level as prescribed in R.S.39:4–50, or if the defendant was operating the auto or vessel while his driver's license or reciprocity privilege was suspended or revoked for any violation of R.S.39:4–50, section 2 of P.L.1981, c. 512 (C.39:4–50.4a), by the Director of the Division of Motor Vehicles pursuant to P.L.1982, c. 85 (C.39:5–30a et seq.), or by the court for a violation of R.S.39:4–96, the defendant shall be sentenced to a term of imprisonment by the court. The term of imprisonment shall include the imposition of a minimum term. The minimum term shall be fixed at, or between, one-third and one-half of the sentence imposed by the court or three years, whichever is greater, during which the defendant shall be ineligible for parole.

(2) The court shall not impose a mandatory sentence pursuant to paragraph (1) of this subsection unless the grounds therefor have been established at a hearing. At the hearing, which may occur at the time of sentencing, the prosecutor shall establish by a preponderance of the evidence that the defendant was operating the auto or vessel while under the influence of any intoxicating liquor, narcotic, hallucinogenic or habit-producing drug, or with a blood alcohol concentration at or above the level prescribed in R.S.39:4–50 or that the defendant was operating the auto or vessel while his driver's license or reciprocity privilege was suspended or revoked for any violation of R.S.39:4–50, section 2 of P.L.1981, c. 512 (C.39:4–50.4a), by the Director of the Division of Motor Vehicles pursuant to P.L.1982, c. 85 (C.39:5–30a et seq.), or by the court for a violation of R.S.39:4–96. In making its findings, the court shall take judicial notice of any evidence, testimony or information adduced at the trial, plea hearing, or other court proceedings and shall also consider the presentence report and any other relevant information.

(3) Vehicular homicide is a crime of the first degree if the defendant was operating the auto or vessel while in violation of R.S.39:4–50 or section 2 of P.L.1981, c. 512 (C.39:4–50.4a) while:

(a) on any school property used for school purposes which is owned by or leased to any elementary or secondary school or school board, or within 1,000 feet of such school property;

(b) driving through a school crossing as defined in R.S.39:1–1 if the municipality, by ordinance or resolution, has designated the school crossing as such; or

(c) driving through a school crossing as defined in R.S.39:1–1 knowing that juveniles are present if the municipality has not designated the school crossing as such by ordinance or resolution.

A map or true copy of a map depicting the location and boundaries of the area on or within 1,000 feet of any property used for school purposes which is owned by or leased to any elementary or secondary school or school board produced pursuant to section 1 of P.L. 1987, c. 101 (C.2C:35–7) may be used in a prosecution under subparagraph (a) of this paragraph.

It shall be no defense to a prosecution for a violation of subparagraph (a) or (b) of this paragraph that the defendant was unaware that the prohibited conduct took place while on or within 1,000 feet of any school property or while driving through a school crossing. Nor shall it be a defense to a prosecution under subparagraph (a) or (b) of this paragraph that no juveniles were present on the school property or crossing zone at the time of the offense or that the school was not in session.

(4) If the defendant was operating the auto or vessel in violation of R.S.39:4–50 or section 2 of P.L.1981, c. 512 (C.39:4–50.4a), the defendant's license to operate a motor vehicle shall be suspended for a period of between five years and life, which period shall commence upon completion of any prison sentence imposed upon that person.

c. For good cause shown, the court may, in accepting a plea of guilty under this section, order that such plea not be evidential in any civil proceeding.

d. Nothing herein shall be deemed to preclude, if the evidence so warrants, an indictment and conviction for aggravated manslaughter under the provisions of subsection a. of N.J.S.2C:11–4.

As used in this section, "auto or vessel" means all means of conveyance propelled otherwise than by muscular power.

e. Any person who violates paragraph (3) of subsection b. of this section shall forfeit the auto or vessel used in the commission of the offense, unless the defendant can establish at a hearing, which may occur at the time of sentencing, by a preponderance of the evidence that such forfeiture would constitute a serious hardship to the family of the defendant that outweighs the need to deter such conduct by the defendant and others. In making its findings, the court shall take judicial notice of any evidence, testimony or information adduced at the trial, plea hearing, or other court proceedings and shall also consider the presentence report and any other relevant information. Forfeiture pursuant to this subsection shall be in addition to, and not in lieu of, civil forfeiture pursuant to chapter 64 of this title.

L.1978, c. 95, § 2C:11–5, eff. Sept. 1, 1979. Amended by L.1981, c. 312, § 1, eff. Dec. 3, 1981; L.1983, c. 39, § 1, eff. Jan. 26, 1983; L.1984, c. 212, § 1, eff. Dec. 13, 1984; L.1985, c. 97, § 1, eff. March 27, 1985; L.1988, c. 75, § 1, eff. Aug. 1, 1988; L.1989, c. 211, § 1, eff. Dec. 29, 1989; L.1991, c. 237, § 1, eff. Aug. 2, 1991; L.1995, c. 285, § 1, eff. Dec. 15, 1995; L.1999, c. 185, § 1; L.2003, c. 143, § 1, eff. Aug. 5, 2003.

2C:11–5.1. Leaving the scene of a motor vehicle accident

A motor vehicle operator who knows he is involved in an accident and knowingly leaves the scene of that accident under circumstances that violate the provisions of R.S.39:4–129 shall be guilty of a crime of the second degree if the accident results in the death of another person.

If the evidence so warrants, nothing in this section shall be deemed to preclude an indictment and conviction for aggravated manslaughter under the provisions of N.J.S.2C:11–4 or vehicular homicide under the provisions of N.J.S.2C:11–5.

Notwithstanding the provisions of N.J.S.2C:1–8 or any other provisions of law, a conviction arising under this section shall not merge with a conviction for aggravated manslaughter under the provisions of N.J.S.2C:11–4 or for vehicular homicide under the provisions of N.J.S.2C:11–5 and a separate sentence shall be imposed upon each such conviction.

Notwithstanding the provisions of N.J.S.2C:44–5 or any other provisions of law, when the court imposes multiple sentences of imprisonment for more than one offense, those sentences shall run consecutively.

For the purposes of this section, neither knowledge of the death nor knowledge of the violation are elements of the offense and it shall not be a defense that the operator of the motor vehicle was unaware of the death or of the provisions of R.S.39:4–129.

L.1997, c. 111, § 1, eff. June 4, 1997. Amended by L.2003, c. 55, § 2, eff. June 1, 2003; L.2007, c. 83, § 1, eff. May 4, 2007.

2C:11–6. Aiding suicide

A person who purposely aids another to commit suicide is guilty of a crime of the second degree if his conduct causes such suicide or an attempted suicide, and otherwise of a crime of the fourth degree.

L.1978, c. 95, § 2C:11–6, eff. Sept. 1, 1979.

CHAPTER 11A

[HUMAN CLONING]

Chapter heading editorially supplied

Section
2C:11A–1.   Human cloning; first degree crime; definition.

2C:11A–1. Human cloning; first degree crime; definition

A person who knowingly engages or assists, directly or indirectly, in the cloning of a human being is guilty of a crime of the first degree.

As used in this section, "cloning of a human being" means the replication of a human individual by cultivating a cell with genetic material through the egg, embryo, fetal and newborn stages into a new human individual.

L.2003, c. 203, § 3, eff. Jan. 2, 2004.

CHAPTER 12

ASSAULT; RECKLESS ENDANGERING; THREATS

Section
2C:12–1.   Assault.
2C:12–1.1.   Leaving the scene of a motor vehicle accident.
2C:12–1.2.   Endangering an injured victim.
2C:12–2.   Recklessly endangering another person.
2C:12–3.   Terroristic threats.
2C:12–4 to 2C:12–9.   Repealed.
2C:12–10.   Stalking.
2C:12–10.1.   Stalking conviction to operate as application for permanent restraining order; hearing; dissolution of order; notice; violations.
2C:12–10.2.   Stalking of children and persons with mental defect; restraining order.
2C:12–11.   Disarming law enforcement or corrections officer.
2C:12–12.   Definitions.
2C:12–13.   Throwing bodily fluid at certain enumerated law enforcement employees.

2C:12–1. Assault

a. **Simple assault.** A person is guilty of assault if he:

(1) Attempts to cause or purposely, knowingly or recklessly causes bodily injury to another; or

(2) Negligently causes bodily injury to another with a deadly weapon; or

(3) Attempts by physical menace to put another in fear of imminent serious bodily injury.

Simple assault is a disorderly persons offense unless committed in a fight or scuffle entered into by mutual consent, in which case it is a petty disorderly persons offense.

b. **Aggravated assault.** A person is guilty of aggravated assault if he:

(1) Attempts to cause serious bodily injury to another, or causes such injury purposely or knowingly or under circumstances manifesting extreme indifference to the value of human life recklessly causes such injury; or

(2) Attempts to cause or purposely or knowingly causes bodily injury to another with a deadly weapon; or

(3) Recklessly causes bodily injury to another with a deadly weapon; or

(4) Knowingly under circumstances manifesting extreme indifference to the value of human life points a firearm, as defined in section 2C:39–1f., at or in the direction of another, whether or not the actor believes it to be loaded; or

(5) Commits a simple assault as defined in subsection a. (1), (2) or (3) of this section upon:

(a) Any law enforcement officer acting in the performance of his duties while in uniform or exhibiting evidence of his authority or because of his status as a law enforcement officer; or

(b) Any paid or volunteer fireman acting in the performance of his duties while in uniform or otherwise clearly identifiable as being engaged in the performance of the duties of a fireman; or

(c) Any person engaged in emergency first-aid or medical services acting in the performance of his duties while in uniform or otherwise clearly identifiable as being engaged in the performance of emergency first-aid or medical services; or

(d) Any school board member, school administrator, teacher, school bus driver or other employee of a public or nonpublic school or school board while clearly identifiable as being engaged in the performance of his duties or because of his status as a member or employee of a public or nonpublic school or school board or any school bus driver employed by an operator under contract to a public or nonpublic school or school board while clearly identifiable as being engaged in the performance of his duties or because of his status as a school bus driver; or

(e) Any employee of the Division of Youth and Family Services while clearly identifiable as being engaged in the performance of his duties or because of his status as an employee of the division; or

(f) Any justice of the Supreme Court, judge of the Superior Court, judge of the Tax Court or municipal judge while clearly identifiable as being engaged in the performance of judicial duties or because of his status as a member of the judiciary; or

(g) Any operator of a motorbus or the operator's supervisor or any employee of a rail passenger service while clearly identifiable as being engaged in the performance of his duties or because of his status as an operator of a motorbus or as the operator's supervisor or as an employee of a rail passenger service; or

(h) Any Department of Corrections employee, county corrections officer, juvenile corrections officer, State juvenile facility employee, juvenile detention staff member, juvenile detention officer, probation officer or any sheriff, undersheriff, or sheriff's officer acting in the performance of his duties while in uniform or exhibiting evidence of his authority; or

(i) Any employee, including any person employed under contract, of a utility company as defined in section 2 of P.L.1971, c. 224 (C.2A:42–86) or a cable television company subject to the provisions of the "Cable Television Act," P.L.1972, c. 186 (C.48:5A–1 et seq.) while clearly identifiable as being engaged in the performance of his duties in regard to connecting, disconnecting or repairing or attempting to connect, disconnect or repair any gas, electric or water utility, or cable television or telecommunication service; or

(6) Causes bodily injury to another person while fleeing or attempting to elude a law enforcement officer in violation of subsection b. of N.J.S.2C:29–2 or while operating a motor vehicle in violation of subsection c. of N.J.S.2C:20–10. Notwithstanding any other provision of law to the contrary, a person shall be strictly liable for a violation of this subsection upon proof of a violation of subsection b. of N.J.S.2C:29–2 or while operating a motor vehicle in violation of subsection c. of N.J.S.2C:20–10 which resulted in bodily injury to another person; or

(7) Attempts to cause significant bodily injury to another or causes significant bodily injury purposely or knowingly or, under circumstances manifesting extreme indifference to the value of human life recklessly causes such significant bodily injury; or

(8) Causes bodily injury by knowingly or purposely starting a fire or causing an explosion in violation of N.J.S.2C:17–1 which results in bodily injury to any emergency services personnel involved in fire suppression activities, rendering emergency medical services resulting from the fire or explosion or rescue operations, or rendering any necessary assistance at the scene of the fire or explosion, including any bodily injury sustained while responding to the scene of a reported fire or explosion. For purposes of this subsection, "emergency services personnel" shall include, but not be limited to, any paid or volunteer fireman, any person engaged in emergency first-aid or medical services and any law enforcement officer. Notwithstanding any other provision of law to the contrary, a person shall be strictly liable for a violation of this paragraph upon proof of a violation of N.J.S.2C:17–1 which resulted in bodily injury to any emergency services personnel; or

(9) Knowingly, under circumstances manifesting extreme indifference to the value of human life, points or displays a firearm, as defined in subsection f. of N.J.S.2C:39–1, at or in the direction of a law enforcement officer; or

(10) Knowingly points, displays or uses an imitation firearm, as defined in subsection f. of N.J.S.2C:39–1, at or in the direction of a law enforcement officer with the purpose to intimidate, threaten or attempt to put the officer in fear of bodily injury or for any unlawful purpose; or

(11) Uses or activates a laser sighting system or device, or a system or device which, in the manner used, would cause a reasonable person to believe that it is a laser sighting system or device, against a law enforcement officer acting in the performance of his duties while in uniform or exhibiting evidence of his authority. As used in this paragraph, "laser sighting system or

device" means any system or device that is integrated with or affixed to a firearm and emits a laser light beam that is used to assist in the sight alignment or aiming of the firearm.

Aggravated assault under subsections b. (1) and b. (6) is a crime of the second degree; under subsections b. (2), b. (7), b. (9) and b. (10) is a crime of the third degree; under subsections b. (3) and b. (4) is a crime of the fourth degree; and under subsection b. (5) is a crime of the third degree if the victim suffers bodily injury, otherwise it is a crime of the fourth degree. Aggravated assault under subsection b.(8) is a crime of the third degree if the victim suffers bodily injury; if the victim suffers significant bodily injury or serious bodily injury it is a crime of the second degree. Aggravated assault under subsection b.(11) is a crime of the third degree.

c. (1) A person is guilty of assault by auto or vessel when the person drives a vehicle or vessel recklessly and causes either serious bodily injury or bodily injury to another. Assault by auto or vessel is a crime of the fourth degree if serious bodily injury results and is a disorderly persons offense if bodily injury results.

(2) Assault by auto or vessel is a crime of the third degree if the person drives the vehicle while in violation of R.S.39:4–50 or section 2 of P.L.1981, c. 512 (C.39:4–50.4a) and serious bodily injury results and is a crime of the fourth degree if the person drives the vehicle while in violation of R.S.39:4–50 or section 2 of P.L.1981, c. 512 (C.39:4–50.4a) and bodily injury results.

(3) Assault by auto or vessel is a crime of the second degree if serious bodily injury results from the defendant operating the auto or vessel while in violation of R.S.39:4–50 or section 2 of P.L.1981, c. 512 (C.39:4–50.4a) while:

(a) on any school property used for school purposes which is owned by or leased to any elementary or secondary school or school board, or within 1,000 feet of such school property;

(b) driving through a school crossing as defined in R.S.39:1–1 if the municipality, by ordinance or resolution, has designated the school crossing as such; or

(c) driving through a school crossing as defined in R.S.39:1–1 knowing that juveniles are present if the municipality has not designated the school crossing as such by ordinance or resolution.

Assault by auto or vessel is a crime of the third degree if bodily injury results from the defendant operating the auto or vessel in violation of this paragraph.

A map or true copy of a map depicting the location and boundaries of the area on or within 1,000 feet of any property used for school purposes which is owned by or leased to any elementary or secondary school or school board produced pursuant to section 1 of P.L. 1987, c. 101 (C.2C:35–7) may be used in a prosecution under subparagraph (a) of paragraph (3) of this section.

It shall be no defense to a prosecution for a violation of subparagraph (a) or (b) of paragraph (3) of this subsection that the defendant was unaware that the prohibited conduct took place while on or within 1,000 feet of any school property or while driving through a school crossing. Nor shall it be a defense to a prosecution under subparagraph (a) or (b) of paragraph (3) of this subsection that no juveniles were present on the school property or crossing zone at the time of the offense or that the school was not in session.

As used in this section, "vessel" means a means of conveyance for travel on water and propelled otherwise than by muscular power.

d. A person who is employed by a facility as defined in section 2 of P.L.1977, c. 239 (C.52:27G–2) who commits a simple assault as defined in paragraph (1) or (2) of subsection a. of this section upon an institutionalized elderly person as defined in section 2 of P.L.1977, c. 239 (C.52:27G–2) is guilty of a crime of the fourth degree.

e. (Deleted by amendment, P.L.2001, c. 443).

f. A person who commits a simple assault as defined in paragraph (1), (2) or (3) of subsection a. of this section in the presence of a child under 16 years of age at a school or community sponsored youth sports event is guilty of a crime of the fourth degree. The defendant shall be strictly liable upon proof that the offense occurred, in fact, in the presence of a child under 16 years of age. It shall not be a defense that the defendant did not know that the child was present or reasonably believed that the child was 16 years of age or older. The provisions of this subsection shall not be construed to create any liability on the part of a participant in a youth sports event or to abrogate any immunity or defense available to a participant in a youth sports event. As used in this act, "school or community sponsored youth sports event "means a competition, practice or instructional event involving one or more interscholastic sports teams or youth sports teams organized pursuant to a nonprofit or similar charter or which are member teams in a youth league organized by or affiliated with a county or municipal recreation department and shall not include collegiate, semi-professional or professional sporting events.

L.1978, c. 95, § 2C:12–1, eff. Sept. 1, 1979. Amended by L.1979, c. 178, § 22, eff. Sept. 1, 1979; L.1981, c. 290, § 14, eff. Sept. 24, 1981; L.1983, c. 101, § 1, eff. March 14, 1983; L.1985, c. 97, § 2, eff. March 27, 1985; L.1985, c. 444, § 1, eff. Jan. 13, 1986; L.1990, c. 87, § 1, eff. Aug. 9, 1990; L.1991, c. 237, § 2, eff. Aug. 2, 1991; L.1991, c. 341, § 2, eff. Jan. 7, 1992; L.1993, c. 219, § 2, eff. Aug. 2, 1993; L.1995, c. 6, § 1, eff. Jan. 10, 1995; L.1995, c. 181, § 1, eff. July 24, 1995; L.1995, c. 211, § 1, eff. Aug. 14, 1995; L.1995, c. 307, § 2, eff. Jan. 5, 1996; L.1997, c. 42, § 1, eff. March 27, 1997; L.1997, c. 119, § 1, eff. June 18, 1997; L.1999, c. 77, § 1, eff. April 30, 1999; L.1999, c. 185, § 2; L.1999, c. 281, § 1; L.1999, c. 381, § 1, eff. Jan. 14, 2000; L.2001, c. 215, § 1, eff. Aug. 20, 2001; L.2001, c. 443, § 2, eff. Jan. 11, 2002; L.2002, c. 53, § 1, eff. Aug. 3, 2002; L.2003, c. 218, § 1, eff. Jan. 9, 2004; L.2005, c. 2, § 1, eff. Jan. 19, 2005; L.2006, c. 78, § 2, eff. Aug. 2, 2006.

2C:12–1.1. Leaving the scene of a motor vehicle accident

A motor vehicle operator who knows he is involved in an accident and knowingly leaves the scene of that accident under circumstances that violate the provisions of R.S.39:4–129 shall be guilty of a crime of the third degree if the accident results in serious bodily injury to another person. The presumption of nonimprisonment set forth in N.J.S.2C:44–1 shall not apply to persons convicted under the provisions of this section.

If the evidence so warrants, nothing in this section shall be deemed to preclude an indictment and conviction for aggravated assault or assault by auto under the provisions of N.J.S.2C:12–1.

Notwithstanding the provisions of N.J.S.2C:1–8 or any other provisions of law, a conviction arising under this section shall not merge with a conviction for aggravated assault or assault by auto under the provisions of N.J.S.2C:12–1 and a separate sentence shall be imposed upon each conviction.

Notwithstanding the provisions of N.J.S.2C:44–5 or any other provisions of law, whenever in the case of such multiple convictions the court imposes multiple sentences of imprisonment for more than one offense, those sentences shall run consecutively.

For the purposes of this section, neither knowledge of the serious bodily injury nor knowledge of the violation are elements of the offense and it shall not be a defense that the driver of the motor vehicle was unaware of the serious bodily injury or provisions of R.S.39:4–129.

L.1997, c. 111, § 2, eff. June 4, 1997. Amended by L.2003, c. 55, § 3, eff. June 1, 2003; L.2007, c. 83, § 2, eff. May 4, 2007.

2C:12–1.2. Endangering an injured victim

a. A person is guilty of endangering an injured victim if he causes bodily injury to any person or solicits, aids, encourages, or attempts or agrees to aid another, who causes bodily injury to any person, and leaves the scene of the injury knowing or reasonably believing that the injured person is physically helpless, mentally incapacitated or otherwise unable to care for himself.

b. As used in this section, the following definitions shall apply:

(1) "Physically helpless" means the condition in which a person is unconscious, unable to flee, or physically unable to summon assistance;

(2) "Mentally incapacitated" means that condition in which a person is rendered temporarily or permanently incapable of understanding or controlling one's conduct, or of appraising or controlling one's condition, which incapacity shall include but is not limited to an inability to comprehend one's own peril;

(3) "Bodily injury" shall have the meaning set forth in N.J.S.2C:11–1.

c. It is an affirmative defense to prosecution for a violation of this section that the defendant summoned medical treatment for the victim or knew that medical treatment had been summoned by another person, and protected the victim from further injury or harm until emergency assistance personnel arrived. This affirmative defense shall be proved by the defendant by a preponderance of the evidence.

d. A person who violates the provisions of this section shall be guilty of a crime of the third degree. Notwithstanding the provisions of N.J.S.2C:1–8 or any other provision of law, a conviction arising under this subsection shall not merge with a conviction of the crime that rendered the person physically helpless or mentally incapacitated, nor shall such other conviction merge with a conviction under this section. Notwithstanding the provisions of N.J.S.2C:44–5 or any other provision of law, the sentence imposed pursuant to this section shall be ordered to be served consecutively to that imposed for any conviction of the crime that rendered the person physically helpless or mentally incapacitated.

e. Nothing herein shall be deemed to preclude, if the evidence so warrants, an indictment and conviction for murder, manslaughter, assault or any other offense.

L.2000, c. 174, § 1, eff. Jan. 8, 2001.

2C:12–2. Recklessly endangering another person

a. A person who purposely or knowingly does any act, including putting up a false light, which results in the loss or destruction of a vessel commits a crime of the third degree.

b. A person commits a crime of the fourth degree if he:

(1) Manufactures or sells a golf ball containing acid or corrosive fluid substance; or

(2) Purposely or knowingly offers, gives or entices any person to take or accept any treat, candy, gift, food, drink or other substance that is intended to be consumed which is poisonous, intoxicating, anesthetizing, tranquilizing, disorienting, deleterious or harmful to the health or welfare of such person, without the knowledge of the other person as to the identity and effect of the substance, except that it is a crime of the third degree if the actor violates the provisions of this paragraph with the purpose to commit or facilitate the commission of another criminal offense.

Notwithstanding the term of imprisonment provided under N.J.S. 2C:43–6, and the provisions of subsection e. of N.J.S.2C:44–1, if a person is convicted of a crime of the fourth degree under paragraph (2) of this subsection, the sentence imposed shall include a fixed minimum sentence of not less than six months during which the defendant shall not be eligible for parole. If a person is convicted of a crime of the third degree under paragraph (2) of this subsection, the sentence imposed shall include a fixed minimum sentence of not less than eighteen months during which the defendant shall not be eligible for parole. The court may not suspend or make any other noncustodial disposition of that person. Notwithstanding the provisions of N.J.S.2C:1–8 or any other provision of law, a conviction arising under this subsection shall not merge with a conviction for any offense that the defendant intended to commit or facilitate, when the defendant violated the provisions of this section, nor shall any such other conviction merge with a conviction under this section. Notwithstanding the provisions of N.J.S.2C:44–5 or any other provision of law, the sentence for a crime of the third degree imposed pursuant to this paragraph shall be ordered to be served consecutively to that imposed for a conviction of the offense that the defendant intended to commit or facilitate when the defendant violated the provisions of this subsection.

L.1978, c. 95, § 2C:12–2, eff. Sept. 1, 1979. Amended by L.1982, c. 160, § 1, eff. Oct. 28, 1982; L.1999, c. 335, § 1, eff. Jan. 10, 2000.

2C:12–3. Terroristic threats

a. A person is guilty of a crime of the third degree if he threatens to commit any crime of violence with the purpose to terrorize another or to cause evacuation of a building, place of assembly, or facility of public transportation, or otherwise to cause serious public inconvenience, or in reckless disregard of the risk of causing such terror or inconvenience. A violation of this subsection is a crime of the second degree if it occurs during a declared period of national, State or county emergency. The actor shall be strictly liable upon proof that the crime occurred, in fact, during a declared period of national, State or county emergency. It shall not be a defense that the actor did not know that there was a declared period of emergency at the time the crime occurred.

b. A person is guilty of a crime of the third degree if he threatens to kill another with the purpose to put him in imminent fear of death under circumstances reasonably causing the victim to believe the immediacy of the threat and the likelihood that it will be carried out.

L.1978, c. 95, § 2C:12–3, eff. Sept. 1, 1979; L.1981, c. 290, § 15, eff. Sept. 24, 1981. Amended by L.2002, c. 26, § 11, eff. June 18, 2002.

2C:12–4 to 2C:12–9. Repealed by L.1981, c. 426, § 18, eff. April 9, 1982

2C:12–10. Stalking

a. As used in this act:

(1) "Course of conduct" means repeatedly maintaining a visual or physical proximity to a person; directly, indirectly, or through third parties, by any action, method, device, or means, following, monitoring, observing, surveilling, threatening, or communicating to or about, a person, or interfering with a person's property; repeatedly committing harassment against a person; or repeatedly conveying, or causing to be conveyed, verbal or written threats or threats conveyed by any other means of communication or threats implied by conduct or a combination thereof directed at or toward a person.

(2) "Repeatedly" means on two or more occasions.

(3) "Emotional distress" means significant mental suffering or distress.

(4) "Cause a reasonable person to fear" means to cause fear which a reasonable victim, similarly situated, would have under the circumstances.

b. A person is guilty of stalking, a crime of the fourth degree, if he purposefully or knowingly engages in a course of conduct directed at a specific person that would cause a reasonable person to fear for his safety or the safety of a third person or suffer other emotional distress.

c. A person is guilty of a crime of the third degree if he commits the crime of stalking in violation of an existing court order prohibiting the behavior.

d. A person who commits a second or subsequent offense of stalking against the same victim is guilty of a crime of the third degree.

e. A person is guilty of a crime of the third degree if he commits the crime of stalking while serving a term of imprisonment or while on parole or probation as the result of a conviction for any indictable offense under the laws of this State, any other state or the United States.

f. This act shall not apply to conduct which occurs during organized group picketing.

L.1992, c. 209, § 1, eff. Jan. 5, 1993. Amended by L.1996, c. 39, § 1, eff. June 20, 1996; L.1998, c. 17, § 3, eff. May 6, 1998; L.1999, c. 47, § 1, eff. March 12, 1999; L.2001, c. 220, § 2, eff. Aug. 24, 2001; L.2009, c. 28, § 1, eff. March 21, 2009.

2C:12–10.1. Stalking conviction to operate as application for permanent restraining order; hearing; dissolution of order; notice; violations

a. A judgment of conviction for stalking shall operate as an application for a permanent restraining order limiting the contact of the defendant and the victim who was stalked.

b. A hearing shall be held on the application for a permanent restraining order at the time of the verdict or plea of guilty unless the victim requests otherwise. This hearing shall be in Superior Court. A permanent restraining order may grant the following specific relief:

(1) An order restraining the defendant from entering the residence, property, school, or place of employment of the victim and requiring the defendant to stay away from any specified place that is named in the order and is frequented regularly by the victim.

(2) An order restraining the defendant from making contact with the victim, including an order forbidding the defendant from personally or through an agent initiating any communication likely to cause annoyance or alarm including, but not limited to, personal, written,

or telephone contact, or contact via electronic device, with the victim, the victim's employers, employees, or fellow workers, or others with whom communication would be likely to cause annoyance or alarm to the victim. As used in this paragraph, "communication" shall have the same meaning as defined in subsection q. of N.J.S. 2C:1–14.

c. The permanent restraining order entered by the court subsequent to a conviction for stalking as provided in this act may be dissolved upon the application of the stalking victim to the court which granted the order.

d. Notice of permanent restraining orders issued pursuant to this act shall be sent by the clerk of the court or other person designated by the court to the appropriate chiefs of police, members of the State Police and any other appropriate law enforcement agency or court.

e. Any permanent restraining order issued pursuant to this act shall be in effect throughout the State, and shall be enforced by all law enforcement officers.

f. A violation by the defendant of an order issued pursuant to this act shall constitute an offense under subsection a. of N.J.S.2C:29–9 and each order shall so state. Violations of these orders may be enforced in a civil or criminal action initiated by the stalking victim or by the court, on its own motion, pursuant to applicable court rules. Nothing in this act shall preclude the filing of a criminal complaint for stalking based on the same act which is the basis for the violation of the permanent restraining order.

L.1996, c. 39, § 3, eff. June 20, 1996. Amended by L.2009, c. 232, § 1, eff. March 17, 2010.

2C:12–10.2. Stalking of children and persons with mental defect; restraining order

a. In any case involving an allegation of stalking where the victim is a child under the age of 18 years or is developmentally disabled as defined in section 3 of P.L.1977, c. 200 (C.5:5–44.4) or where the victim is 18 years of age or older and is mentally defective as defined in N.J.S. 2C:14–1, the court may issue a temporary restraining order against the defendant which limits the contact of the defendant and the victim.

b. The provisions of subsection a. of this section are in addition to, and not in lieu of, the provisions of section 3 of P.L.1996, c. 39 (C.2C:12–10.1) which provide that a judgment of conviction for stalking shall operate as an application for a permanent restraining order limiting the contact of the defendant and the victim.

c. The parent or guardian of the child or the person described in subsection a. of this section may file a complaint with the Superior Court in conformity with the rules of court seeking a temporary restraining order against a person alleged to have committed stalking against the child or the person described in subsection a. of this section. The parent or guardian may seek emergency, ex parte relief. A decision shall be made by the judge regarding the emergency relief forthwith. If it appears that the child or the person described in subsection a. of this section is in danger of being stalked by the defendant, the judge shall issue a temporary restraining order pursuant to subsection e. of this section.

d. A conviction of stalking shall not be a prerequisite for the grant of a temporary restraining order under this act.

e. A temporary restraining order issued under this act shall limit the contact of the defendant and the child or the person described in subsection a. of this section who was stalked and in addition may grant all other relief specified in section 3 of P.L.1996, c. 39 (C.2C:12–10.1).

f. A hearing shall be held in the Superior Court within 10 days of the issuance of any temporary restraining order which was issued on an emergency, ex parte basis. A copy of the complaint shall be served on the defendant in conformity with the rules of court. At the hearing the standard for continuing the temporary restraining order shall be by a preponderance of the evidence.

g. If the court rules that the temporary restraining order shall be continued, the order shall remain in effect until either:

(1) the defendant is convicted of stalking, in which case the court shall hold a hearing on the issue of whether a permanent restraining order shall be entered pursuant to section 3 of P.L.1996, c. 39 (C.2C:12–10.1); or

(2) the victim's parent or guardian or, in the case of a victim who has reached the age of 18, the victim, requests that the restraining order be dismissed and the court finds just cause to do so.

L.1999, c. 47, § 2, eff. March 12, 1999.

2C:12–11. Disarming law enforcement or corrections officer

a. A person who knowingly takes or attempts to exercise unlawful control over a firearm or other weapon in the possession of a law enforcement or corrections officer when that officer is acting in the performance of his duties, and either is in uniform or exhibits evidence of his authority, is guilty of a crime of the second degree.

b. A person violating the provisions of subsection a. of this section shall be guilty of a crime of the first degree if:

(1) The person fires or discharges the firearm;

(2) The person uses or threatens to use the firearm or weapon against the officer or any other person; or

(3) The officer or another person suffers serious bodily injury.

L.1996, c. 14, § 1, eff. April 11, 1996.

2C:12–12. Definitions

As used in this act:

"Bodily fluid" means saliva, blood, urine, feces, seminal fluid or any other bodily fluid.

"Department of Corrections employee" means any corrections officer, parole officer or other employee of the New Jersey Department of Corrections and any person under contract to provide services to the department.

L.1997, c. 182, § 1, eff. Aug. 1, 1997.

2C:12–13. Throwing bodily fluid at certain enumerated law enforcement employees

A person who throws a bodily fluid at a Department of Corrections employee, county corrections officer, juvenile corrections officer, State juvenile facility employee, juvenile detention staff member, probation officer, any sheriff, undersheriff or sheriff's officer or any municipal, county or State law enforcement officer while in the performance of his duties or otherwise purposely subjects such employee to contact with a bodily fluid commits an aggravated assault. If the victim suffers bodily injury, this shall be a crime of the third degree. Otherwise, this shall be a crime of the fourth degree. A term of imprisonment imposed for this offense shall run consecutively to any term of imprisonment currently being served and to any other term imposed for another offense committed at the time of the assault. Nothing herein shall be deemed to preclude, if the evidence so warrants, an indictment and conviction for a violation or attempted violation of chapter 11 of Title 2C of the New Jersey Statutes or subsection b. of N.J.S.2C:12–1 or any other provision of the criminal laws.

L.1997, c. 182, § 2, eff. Aug. 1, 1997. Amended by L.1999, c. 429, § 1, eff. Jan. 18, 2000; L.2003, c. 283, § 1, eff. Jan. 14, 2004.

CHAPTER 13

KIDNAPPING AND RELATED OFFENSES: COERCION

Section
2C:13–1.   Kidnapping.
2C:13–2.   Criminal restraint.
2C:13–3.   False imprisonment.
2C:13–4.   Interference with custody.
2C:13–5.   Criminal coercion.
2C:13–6.   Luring, enticing child by various means, attempts; crime of second degree; subsequent offense, mandatory imprisonment.
2C:13–7.   Luring or enticing adult by electronic or any other means to commit criminal offense with or against person lured or enticed or against any other person; crime of third degree; definition; merger of convictions; separate sentences.
2C:13–8.   Human trafficking.

2C:13–1. Kidnapping

a. Holding for ransom, reward or as a hostage. A person is guilty of kidnapping if he unlawfully removes another from the place where he is found or if he unlawfully confines another with the purpose of holding that person for ransom or reward or as a shield or hostage.

b. Holding for other purposes. A person is guilty of kidnapping if he unlawfully removes another from his place of residence or business, or a substantial distance from the vicinity where he is found, or if he unlawfully confines another for a substantial period, with any of the following purposes:

(1) To facilitate commission of any crime or flight thereafter;

(2) To inflict bodily injury on or to terrorize the victim or another;

(3) To interfere with the performance of any governmental or political function; or

(4) To permanently deprive a parent, guardian or other lawful custodian of custody of the victim.

c. Grading of kidnapping. (1) Except as provided in paragraph (2) of this subsection, kidnapping is a crime of the first degree and upon conviction thereof, a person may, notwithstanding the provisions of paragraph (1) of subsection a. of N.J.S.2C:43–6, be sentenced to an ordinary term of imprisonment between 15 and 30 years. If the actor releases the victim unharmed and in a safe place prior to apprehension, it is a crime of the second degree.

(2) Kidnapping is a crime of the first degree and upon conviction thereof, an actor shall be sentenced to a term of imprisonment by the court, if the victim of the kidnapping is less than 16 years of age and if during the kidnapping:

(a) A crime under N.J.S.2C:14–2 or subsection a. of N.J.S.2C:14–3 is committed against the victim;

(b) A crime under subsection b. of N.J.S.2C:24–4 is committed against the victim; or

(c) The actor sells or delivers the victim to another person for pecuniary gain other than in circumstances which lead to the return of the victim to a parent, guardian or other person responsible for the general supervision of the victim.

Notwithstanding the provisions of paragraph (1) of subsection a. of N.J.S. 2C:43–6, the term of imprisonment imposed under this paragraph shall be either a term of 25 years during which the actor shall not be eligible for parole, or a specific term between 25 years and life imprisonment, of which the actor shall serve 25 years before being eligible for parole; provided, however, that the crime of kidnapping under this paragraph and underlying aggravating crimes listed in subparagraph (a), (b) or (c) of this paragraph shall merge for purposes of sentencing. If the actor is convicted of the criminal homicide of a victim of a kidnapping under the provisions of chapter 11, any sentence imposed under provisions of this paragraph shall be served consecutively to any sentence imposed pursuant to the provisions of chapter 11.

d. "Unlawful" removal or confinement. A removal or confinement is unlawful within the meaning of this section and of sections 2C:13–2 and 2C:13–3, if it is accomplished by force, threat or deception, or, in the case of a person who is under the age of 14 or is incompetent, if it is accomplished without the consent of a parent, guardian or other person responsible for general supervision of his welfare.

e. It is an affirmative defense to a prosecution under paragraph (4) of subsection b. of this section, which must be proved by clear and convincing evidence, that:

(1) The actor reasonably believed that the action was necessary to preserve the victim from imminent danger to his welfare. However, no defense shall be available pursuant to this subsection if the actor does not, as soon as reasonably practicable but in no event more than 24 hours after taking a victim under his protection, give notice of the victim's location to the police department of the municipality where the victim resided, the office of the county prosecutor in the county where the victim resided, or the Division of Youth and Family Services in the Department of Children and Families;

(2) The actor reasonably believed that the taking or detaining of the victim was consented to by a parent, or by an authorized State agency; or

(3) The victim, being at the time of the taking or concealment not less than 14 years old, was taken away at his own volition by his parent and without purpose to commit a criminal offense with or against the victim.

f. It is an affirmative defense to a prosecution under paragraph (4) of subsection b. of this section that a parent having the right of custody reasonably believed he was fleeing from imminent physical danger from the other parent, provided that the parent having custody, as soon as reasonably practicable:

(1) Gives notice of the victim's location to the police department of the municipality where the victim resided, the office of the county prosecutor in the county where the victim resided, or the Division of Youth and Family Services in the Department of Children and Families; or

(2) Commences an action affecting custody in an appropriate court.

g. As used in subsections e. and f. of this section, "parent" means a parent, guardian or other lawful custodian of a victim.

L.1978, c. 95, § 2C:13–1, eff. Sept. 1, 1979. Amended by L.1979, c. 178, § 23, eff. Sept. 1, 1979; L.1986, c. 172, § 2, eff. Dec. 8, 1986; L.1999, c. 190, § 1, eff. Aug. 31, 1999; L.2006, c. 47, § 24, eff. July 1, 2006.

2C:13–2. Criminal restraint

A person commits a crime of the third degree if he knowingly:

a. Restrains another unlawfully in circumstances exposing the other to risk of serious bodily injury; or

b. Holds another in a condition of involuntary servitude.

The creation by the actor of circumstances resulting in a belief by another that he must remain in a particular location shall for purposes of this section be deemed to be a holding in a condition of involuntary servitude.

In any prosecution under subsection b., it is an affirmative defense that the person held was a child less than 18 years old and the actor was a relative or legal guardian of such child and his sole purpose was to assume control of such child.

L.1978, c. 95, § 2C:13–2, eff. Sept. 1, 1979.

2C:13–3. False imprisonment

A person commits a disorderly persons offense if he knowingly restrains another unlawfully so as to interfere substantially with his liberty. In any prosecution under this section, it is an affirmative defense that the person restrained was a child less than 18 years old and that the actor was a relative or legal guardian of such child and that his sole purpose was to assume control of such child.

L.1978, c. 95, § 2C:13–3, eff. Sept. 1, 1979. Amended by L.1979, c. 178, § 24, eff. Sept. 1, 1979.

2C:13–4. Interference with custody

a. Custody of children. A person, including a parent, guardian or other lawful custodian, is guilty of interference with custody if he:

(1) Takes or detains a minor child with the purpose of concealing the minor child and thereby depriving the child's other parent of custody or parenting time with the minor child; or

(2) After being served with process or having actual knowledge of an action affecting marriage or custody but prior to the issuance of a temporary or final order determining custody and parenting time rights to a minor child, takes, detains, entices or conceals the child within or outside the State for the purpose of depriving the child's other parent of custody or parenting time, or to evade the jurisdiction of the courts of this State; or

(3) After being served with process or having actual knowledge of an action affecting the protective services needs of a child pursuant to Title 9 of the Revised Statutes in an action affecting custody, but prior to the issuance of a temporary or final order determining custody rights of a minor child, takes, detains, entices or conceals the child within or outside the State for the purpose of evading the jurisdiction of the courts of this State; or

(4) After the issuance of a temporary or final order specifying custody, joint custody rights or parenting time, takes, detains, entices or conceals a minor child from the other parent in violation of the custody or parenting time order.

Interference with custody is a crime of the second degree if the child is taken, detained, enticed or concealed: (i) outside the United States or (ii) for more than 24 hours. Otherwise, interference with custody is a crime of the third degree but the presumption of non-imprisonment set forth in subsection e. of N.J.S.2C:44–1 for a first offense of a crime of the third degree shall not apply.

b. Custody of committed persons. A person is guilty of a crime of the fourth degree if he knowingly takes or entices any committed person away from lawful custody when he is not privileged to do so. "Committed person" means, in addition to anyone committed under judicial warrant, any orphan, neglected or delinquent child, mentally defective or insane person, or other dependent or incompetent person entrusted to another's custody by or through a recognized social agency or otherwise by authority of law.

c. It is an affirmative defense to a prosecution under subsection a. of this section, which must be proved by clear and convincing evidence, that:

(1) The actor reasonably believed that the action was necessary to preserve the child from imminent danger to his welfare. However, no defense shall be available pursuant to this subsection if the actor does not, as soon as reasonably practicable but in no event more than 24 hours after taking a child under his protection, give notice of the child's location to the police department of the municipality where the child resided, the office of the county prosecutor in the county where the child resided, or the Division of Youth and Family Services in the Department of Children and Families;

(2) The actor reasonably believed that the taking or detaining of the minor child was consented to by the other parent, or by an authorized State agency; or

(3) The child, being at the time of the taking or concealment not less than 14 years old, was taken away at his own volition and without purpose to commit a criminal offense with or against the child.

d. It is an affirmative defense to a prosecution under subsection a. of this section that a parent having the right of custody reasonably believed he was fleeing from imminent physical danger from the other parent, provided that the parent having custody, as soon as reasonably practicable:

(1) Gives notice of the child's location to the police department of the municipality where the child resided, the office of the county prosecutor in the county where the child resided, or the Division of Youth and Family Services in the Department of Children and Families; or

(2) Commences an action affecting custody in an appropriate court.

e. The offenses enumerated in this section are continuous in nature and continue for so long as the child is concealed or detained.

f. (1) In addition to any other disposition provided by law, a person convicted under subsection a. of this section shall make restitution of all reasonable expenses and costs, including reasonable counsel fees, incurred by the other parent in securing the child's return.

(2) In imposing sentence under subsection a. of this section the court shall consider, in addition to the factors enumerated in chapter 44 of Title 2C of the New Jersey Statutes:

(a) Whether the person returned the child voluntarily; and

(b) The length of time the child was concealed or detained.

g. As used in this section, "parent" means a parent, guardian or other lawful custodian of a minor child.

L.1978, c. 95, § 2C:13–4, eff. Sept. 1, 1979. Amended by L.1979, c. 178, § 25, eff. Sept. 1, 1979; L.1982, c. 199, § 1, eff. Dec. 13, 1982; L.1990, c. 104, § 1, eff. Nov. 14, 1990; L.1997, c. 299, § 7, eff. Jan. 8, 1998; L.1999, c. 190, § 2, eff. Aug. 31, 1999; L.2006, c. 47, § 25, eff. July 1, 2006.

2C:13–5. Criminal coercion

a. **Offense defined.** A person is guilty of criminal coercion if, with purpose unlawfully to restrict another's freedom of action to engage or refrain from engaging in conduct, he threatens to:

(1) Inflict bodily injury on anyone or commit any other offense;

(2) Accuse anyone of an offense;

(3) Expose any secret which would tend to subject any person to hatred, contempt or ridicule, or to impair his credit or business repute;

(4) Take or withhold action as an official, or cause an official to take or withhold action;

(5) Bring about or continue a strike, boycott or other collective action, except that such a threat shall not be deemed coercive when the restriction compelled is demanded in the course of negotiation for the benefit of the group in whose interest the actor acts;

(6) Testify or provide information or withhold testimony or information with respect to another's legal claim or defense; or

(7) Perform any other act which would not in itself substantially benefit the actor but which is calculated to substantially harm another person with respect to his health, safety, business, calling, career, financial condition, reputation or personal relationships.

It is an affirmative defense to prosecution based on paragraphs (2), (3), (4), (6) and (7) that the actor believed the accusation or secret to be true or the proposed official action justified and that his purpose was limited to compelling the other to behave in a way reasonably related to the circumstances which were the subject of the accusation, exposure or proposed official action, as by desisting from further misbehavior, making good a wrong done, or refraining from taking any action or responsibility for which the actor believes the other disqualified.

b. Grading. Criminal coercion is a crime of the fourth degree unless the threat is to commit a crime more serious than one of the fourth degree or the actor's purpose is criminal, in which cases the offense is a crime of the third degree.

L.1978, c. 95, § 2C:13–5, eff. Sept. 1, 1979.

2C:13–6 Luring, enticing child by various means, attempts; crime of second degree; subsequent offense, mandatory imprisonment.

a. A person commits a crime of the second degree if he attempts, via electronic or any other means, to lure or entice a child or one who he reasonably believes to be a child into a motor vehicle, structure or isolated area, or to meet or appear at any other place, with a purpose to commit a criminal offense with or against the child.

b. As used in this section:

"Child" means a person less than 18 years old.

"Electronic means" includes, but is not limited to, the Internet, which shall have the meaning set forth in N.J.S.2C:24–4.

"Structure" means any building, room, ship, vessel or airplane and also means any place adapted for overnight accommodation of persons, or for carrying on business therein, whether or not a person is actually present.

c. Nothing herein shall be deemed to preclude, if the evidence so warrants, an indictment and conviction for attempted kidnapping under the provisions of N.J.S.2C:13–1.

d. A person convicted of a second or subsequent offense under this section shall be sentenced to a term of imprisonment. Notwithstanding the provisions of subsection a. of N.J.S.2C:43–6, the term of imprisonment shall include, unless the person is sentenced pursuant to the provisions of N.J.S.2C:43–7, a mandatory minimum term of one-third to one-half of the sentence imposed, or three years, whichever is greater, during which time the defendant shall not be eligible for parole. If the person is sentenced pursuant to N.J.S.2C:43–7, the court shall impose a minimum term of one-third to one-half of the sentence imposed, or five years, whichever is greater. The court may not suspend or make any other non-custodial disposition of any person sentenced as a second or subsequent offender pursuant to this section.

For the purposes of this section, an offense is considered a second or subsequent offense if the actor has at any time been convicted pursuant to this section, or under any similar statute of the United States, this State or any other state for an offense that is substantially equivalent to this section.

e. A person convicted of an offense under this section who has previously been convicted of a violation of N.J.S.2C:14–2, subsection a. of N.J.S.2C:14–3 or N.J.S.2C:24–4 shall be sentenced to a term of imprisonment. Notwithstanding the provisions of subsection a. of N.J.S.2C:43–6, the term of imprisonment shall include, unless the person is sentenced pursuant to the provisions of N.J.S.2C:43–7, a mandatory minimum term of five years, during which time the defendant shall not be eligible for parole. The court may not suspend or make any other non-custodial disposition of any person sentenced pursuant to this section.

For the purposes of this subsection, an offense is considered a previous conviction of N.J.S.2C:14–2, subsection a. of N.J.S.2C:14–3 or N.J.S.2C:24–4 if the actor has at any time been convicted under any of these sections or under any similar statute of the United States, this State or any other state for an offense that is substantially equivalent to any of these sections.

f. Notwithstanding the provisions of N.J.S.2C:1–8 or any other law, a conviction under this section shall not merge with a conviction of any other criminal offense, nor shall such other conviction merge with a conviction under this section, and the court shall impose separate sentences upon each violation of this section and any other criminal offense. The court may not suspend or make any other non-custodial disposition of any person sentenced pursuant to this section.

L.1993, c. 291, § 1, eff. Dec. 21, 1993. Amended by L.1994, c. 91, § 1, eff. Aug. 9, 1994; L.1999, c. 277, § 1, eff. Dec. 3, 1999; L.2001, c. 233, § 1, eff. Aug. 27, 2001; L.2003, c. 229, § 1, eff. Jan. 9, 2004; L.2007, c. 273, § 1, eff. Jan. 13, 2008.

2C:13–7. Luring or enticing adult by electronic or any other means to commit criminal offense with or against person lured or enticed or against any other person; crime of third degree; definition; merger of convictions; separate sentences

a. A person commits a crime of the third degree if he attempts, via electronic or any other means, to lure or entice a person into a motor vehicle, structure or isolated area, or to meet or appear at any place, with a purpose to commit a criminal offense with or against the person lured or enticed or against any other person.

b. As used in this section:

"Electronic means" includes, but is not limited to, the Internet, which shall have the meaning set forth in N.J.S.2C:24–4.

"Structure" shall have the meaning set forth in P.L.1993, c. 291 (C.2C:13–6).

c. Nothing herein shall be deemed to preclude, if the evidence so warrants, an indictment and conviction for attempted kidnapping under the provisions of N.J.S.2C:13–1 or for any other crime or offense.

d. A person convicted of a second or subsequent offense under this section shall be sentenced to a term of imprisonment. Notwithstanding the provisions of subsection a. of N.J.S.2C:43–6, the term of imprisonment shall include, unless the person is sentenced pursuant to the provisions of N.J.S.2C:43–7, a mandatory minimum term of one-third to one-half of the sentence imposed, or one year, whichever is greater, during which time the defendant shall not be eligible for parole. If the person is sentenced pursuant to N.J.S.2C:43–7, the court shall impose a minimum term of one-third to one-half of the sentence imposed, or five years, whichever is greater. The court may not suspend or make any other non-custodial disposition of any person sentenced as a second or subsequent offender pursuant to this section.

For the purposes of this section, an offense is considered a second or subsequent offense if the actor has at any time been convicted pursuant to this section, or under any similar statute of the United States, this State or any other state for an offense that is substantially equivalent to this section.

e. A person convicted of an offense under this section who has previously been convicted of a violation of N.J.S.2C:14–2, subsection a. of N.J.S.2C:14–3 or N.J.S.2C:24–4 shall be sentenced to a term of imprisonment. Notwithstanding the provisions of subsection a. of N.J.S.2C:43–6, the term of imprisonment shall include, unless the person is sentenced pursuant to the provisions of N.J.S.2C:43–7, a mandatory minimum term of three years, during which time the defendant shall not be eligible for parole. The court may not suspend or make any other non-custodial disposition of any person sentenced pursuant to this section.

For the purposes of this subsection, an offense is considered a previous conviction of N.J.S.2C:14–2, subsection a. of N.J.S.2C:14–3 or N.J.S.2C:24–4 if the actor has at any time been convicted under any of these sections or under any similar statute of the United States, this State or any other state for an offense that is substantially equivalent to any of these sections.

f. Notwithstanding the provisions of N.J.S.2C:1–8 or any other law, a conviction under this section shall not merge with a conviction of any other criminal offense, nor shall such other conviction merge with a conviction under this section, and the court shall impose separate sentences upon each violation of this section and any other criminal offense. The court may not suspend or make any other non-custodial disposition of any person sentenced pursuant to this section.

L.2005, c. 1, § 1, eff. Jan. 18, 2005. Amended by L.2007, c. 273, § 2, eff. Jan. 13, 2008.

2C:13–8. Human trafficking

a. A person commits the crime of human trafficking if he:

(1) knowingly holds, recruits, lures, entices, harbors, transports, provides or obtains, by any means, another, to engage in sexual activity as defined in paragraph (2) of subsection a. of N.J.S.2C:34–1 or to provide labor or services:

(a) by threats of serious bodily harm or physical restraint against the person or any other person;

(b) by means of any scheme, plan or pattern intended to cause the person to believe that the person or any other person would suffer serious bodily harm or physical restraint;

(c) by committing a violation of N.J.S.2C:13–5 against the person; or

(d) by destroying, concealing, removing, confiscating, or possessing any passport, immigration-related document as defined in section 1 of P.L.1997, c. 1 (C.2C:21–31), or other document issued by a governmental agency to any person which could be used as a means of verifying the person's identity or age or any other personal identifying information; or

(e) by means of the abuse or threatened abuse of the law or legal process; or

(2) receives anything of value from participation as an organizer, supervisor, financier or manager in a scheme or course of conduct which violates paragraph (1) of this subsection.

b. An offense under this section constitutes a crime of the first degree.

c. It is an affirmative defense to prosecution for a violation of this section that, during the time of the alleged commission of the offense of human trafficking created by this section, the defendant was a victim of human trafficking.

d. Notwithstanding the provisions of N.J.S.2C:43–6, the term of imprisonment imposed for a crime of the first degree under paragraph (2) of subsection a. shall be either a term of 20 years during which the actor shall not be eligible for parole, or a specific term between 20 years and life imprisonment, of which the actor shall serve 20 years before being eligible for parole.

e. In addition to any other disposition authorized by law, any person who violates the provisions of this section shall be sentenced to make restitution to any victim. The court shall award to the victim restitution which is the greater of:

(1) the gross income or value to the defendant of the victim's labor or services; or

(2) the value of the victim's labor or services as determined by the "New Jersey Prevailing Wage Act," P.L.1963, c. 150 (C.34:11–56.25 et seq.), the " New Jersey State Wage and Hour Law," P.L.1966, c. 113 (C.34:11–56a et seq.), the Seasonal Farm Labor Act,

P.L.1945, c. 71 (C.34:9A–1 et seq.), the laws concerning the regulation of child labor in chapter 2 of Title 34 of the Revised Statutes, or any other applicable State law, and the "Fair Labor Standards Act of 1938," 29 U.S.C. s.201 et seq. or any other applicable federal law. *L.2005, c. 77, § 1, eff. April 26, 2005.*

CHAPTER 14
SEXUAL OFFENSES

Section
2C:14–1.   Definitions.
2C:14–2.   Sexual assault.
2C:14–2.1.   Right of victim to consult with prosecuting authority.
2C:14–3.   Criminal sexual contact.
2C:14–4.   Lewdness.
2C:14–5.   Provisions generally applicable to Chapter 14.
2C:14–6.   Sentencing.
2C:14–7.   Admissibility of evidence.
2C:14–8.   Juveniles in need of supervision (J.I.N.S.) law not affected.
2C:14–9.   Observation of sexual contact; reproduction or disclosure of images of sexual contact; dressing rooms; defenses.
2C:14–10.   Penalties assessed against sex offenders; amounts; "Sex Crime Victim Treatment Fund".
2C:14–11.   Sex offense defined; victim defined.
2C:14–12.   Conditional release from custody; contents of order; confidentiality of victim's location.

2C:14–1. Definitions

The following definitions apply to this chapter:

a. "Actor" means a person accused of an offense proscribed under this act;

b. "Victim" means a person alleging to have been subjected to offenses proscribed by this act;

c. "Sexual penetration" means vaginal intercourse, cunnilingus, fellatio or anal intercourse between persons or insertion of the hand, finger or object into the anus or vagina either by the actor or upon the actor's instruction. The depth of insertion shall not be relevant as to the question of commission of the crime;

d. "Sexual contact" means an intentional touching by the victim or actor, either directly or through clothing, of the victim's or actor's intimate parts for the purpose of degrading or humiliating the victim or sexually arousing or sexually gratifying the actor. Sexual contact of the actor with himself must be in view of the victim whom the actor knows to be present;

e. "Intimate parts" means the following body parts: sexual organs, genital area, anal area, inner thigh, groin, buttock or breast of a person;

f. "Severe personal injury" means severe bodily injury, disfigurement, disease, incapacitating mental anguish or chronic pain;

g. "Physically helpless" means that condition in which a person is unconscious or is physically unable to flee or is physically unable to communicate unwillingness to act;

h. "Mentally defective" means that condition in which a person suffers from a mental disease or defect which renders that person temporarily or permanently incapable of understanding the nature of his conduct, including, but not limited to, being incapable of providing consent;

i. "Mentally incapacitated" means that condition in which a person is rendered temporarily incapable of understanding or controlling his conduct due to the influence of a narcotic, anesthetic, intoxicant, or other substance administered to that person without his prior knowledge or consent, or due to any other act committed upon that person which rendered that person incapable of appraising or controlling his conduct;

j. "Coercion" as used in this chapter shall refer to those acts which are defined as criminal coercion in section 2C:13–5(1), (2), (3), (4), (6) and (7).

L.1978, c. 95, § 2C:14–1, eff. Sept. 1, 1979. Amended by L.1983, c. 249, § 1, eff. July 7, 1983; L.1989, c. 228, § 2, eff. Dec. 29, 1989.

2C:14–2. Sexual assault

a. An actor is guilty of aggravated sexual assault if he commits an act of sexual penetration with another person under any one of the following circumstances:

(1) The victim is less than 13 years old;

(2) The victim is at least 13 but less than 16 years old; and

(a) The actor is related to the victim by blood or affinity to the third degree, or

(b) The actor has supervisory or disciplinary power over the victim by virtue of the actor's legal, professional, or occupational status, or

(c) The actor is a resource family parent, a guardian, or stands in loco parentis within the household;

(3) The act is committed during the commission, or attempted commission, whether alone or with one or more other persons, of robbery, kidnapping, homicide, aggravated assault on another, burglary, arson or criminal escape;

(4) The actor is armed with a weapon or any object fashioned in such a manner as to lead the victim to reasonably believe it to be a weapon and threatens by word or gesture to use the weapon or object;

(5) The actor is aided or abetted by one or more other persons and the actor uses physical force or coercion;

(6) The actor uses physical force or coercion and severe personal injury is sustained by the victim;

(7) The victim is one whom the actor knew or should have known was physically helpless, mentally defective or mentally incapacitated.

Aggravated sexual assault is a crime of the first degree.

b. An actor is guilty of sexual assault if he commits an act of sexual contact with a victim who is less than 13 years old and the actor is at least four years older than the victim.

c. An actor is guilty of sexual assault if he commits an act of sexual penetration with another person under any one of the following circumstances:

(1) The actor uses physical force or coercion, but the victim does not sustain severe personal injury;

(2) The victim is on probation or parole, or is detained in a hospital, prison or other institution and the actor has supervisory or disciplinary power over the victim by virtue of the actor's legal, professional or occupational status;

(3) The victim is at least 16 but less than 18 years old and:

(a) The actor is related to the victim by blood or affinity to the third degree; or

(b) The actor has supervisory or disciplinary power of any nature or in any capacity over the victim; or

(c) The actor is a resource family parent, a guardian, or stands in loco parentis within the household;

(4) The victim is at least 13 but less than 16 years old and the actor is at least four years older than the victim.

Sexual assault is a crime of the second degree.

L.1978, c. 95, § 2C:14–2, eff. Sept. 1, 1979. Amended by L.1979, c. 178, § 26, eff. Sept. 1, 1979; L.1983, c. 249, § 2, eff. July 7, 1983; L.1989, c. 228, § 3, eff. Dec. 29, 1989; L.1997, c. 194, § 1, eff. Aug. 8, 1997; L.2001, c. 60, § 1, eff. April 19, 2001; L.2004, c. 130, § 13, eff. Aug. 27, 2004.

2C:14–2.1. Right of victim to consult with prosecuting authority

Whenever there is a prosecution for a violation of N.J.S.A.2C: 14–2, the victim of the sexual assault shall be provided an opportunity to consult with the prosecuting authority prior to the conclusion of any plea negotiations.

Nothing contained herein shall be construed to alter or limit the authority or discretion of the prosecutor to enter into any plea agreement which the prosecutor deems appropriate.

L.2003, c. 137, § 1, eff. Aug. 1, 2003.

2C:14–3. Criminal sexual contact

a. An actor is guilty of aggravated criminal sexual contact if he commits an act of sexual contact with the victim under any of the circumstances set forth in 2C:14–2a. (2) through (7).

Aggravated criminal sexual contact is a crime of the third degree.

b. An actor is guilty of criminal sexual contact if he commits an act of sexual contact with the victim under any of the circumstances set forth in section 2C:14–2c. (1) through (4).

Criminal sexual contact is a crime of the fourth degree.

L.1978, c. 95, § 2C:14–3, eff. Sept. 1, 1979. Amended by L.1979, c. 178, § 27, eff. Sept. 1, 1979; L.1997, c. 194, § 2, eff. Aug. 8, 1997.

2C:14–4. Lewdness

a. A person commits a disorderly persons offense if he does any flagrantly lewd and offensive act which he knows or reasonably expects is likely to be observed by other nonconsenting persons who would be affronted or alarmed.

b. A person commits a crime of the fourth degree if:

(1) He exposes his intimate parts for the purpose of arousing or gratifying the sexual desire of the actor or of any other person under circumstances where the actor knows or reasonably expects he is likely to be observed by a child who is less than 13 years of age where the actor is at least four years older than the child.

(2) He exposes his intimate parts for the purpose of arousing or gratifying the sexual desire of the actor or of any other person under circumstances where the actor knows or reasonably expects he is likely to be observed by a person who because of mental disease or defect is unable to understand the sexual nature of the actor's conduct.

c. As used in this section:

"lewd acts" shall include the exposing of the genitals for the purpose of arousing or gratifying the sexual desire of the actor or of any other person.

L.1978, c. 95, § 2C:14–4, eff. Sept. 1, 1979. Amended by L.1992, c. 8, § 1, eff. May 13, 1992.

2C:14–5. Provisions generally applicable to Chapter 14

a. The prosecutor shall not be required to offer proof that the victim resisted, or resisted to the utmost, or reasonably resisted the sexual assault in any offense proscribed by this chapter.

b. No actor shall be presumed to be incapable of committing a crime under this chapter because of age or impotency or marriage to the victim.

c. It shall be no defense to a prosecution for a crime under this chapter that the actor believed the victim to be above the age stated for the offense, even if such a mistaken belief was reasonable.

L.1978, c. 95, § 2C:14–5, eff. Sept. 1, 1979.

2C:14–6. Sentencing

If a person is convicted of a second or subsequent offense under sections 2C:14–2 or 2C:14–3a., the sentence imposed under those sections for the second or subsequent offense shall, unless the person is sentenced pursuant to the provisions of 2C:43–7, include a fixed minimum sentence of not less than 5 years during which the defendant shall not be eligible for parole. The court may not suspend or make any other non-custodial disposition of any person sentenced as a second or subsequent offender pursuant to this section. For the purpose of this section an offense is considered a second or subsequent offense, if the actor has at any time been convicted under sections 2C:14–2 or 2C:14–3a. or under any similar statute of the United States, this state, or any other state for an offense that is substantially equivalent to sections 2C:14–2 or 2C:14–3a.

L.1978, c. 95, § 2C:14–6, eff. Sept. 1, 1979.

2C:14–7. Admissibility of evidence

a. In prosecutions for aggravated sexual assault, sexual assault, aggravated criminal sexual contact, criminal sexual contact, endangering the welfare of a child in violation of N.J.S. 2C:24–4 or the fourth degree crime of lewdness in violation of subsection b. of N.J.S. 2C:14–4, evidence of the victim's previous sexual conduct shall not be admitted nor reference made to it in the presence of the jury except as provided in this section. When the defendant seeks to admit such evidence for any purpose, the defendant must apply for an order of the court before the trial or preliminary hearing, except that the court may allow the motion to be made during trial if the court determines that the evidence is newly discovered and could not have been obtained earlier through the exercise of due diligence. After the application is made, the court shall conduct a hearing in camera to determine the admissibility of the evidence. If the court finds that evidence offered by the defendant regarding the sexual conduct of the victim is relevant and highly material and meets the requirements of subsections c. and d. of this section and that the probative value of the evidence offered substantially outweighs its collateral nature or the probability that its admission will create undue prejudice, confusion of the issues, or unwarranted invasion of the privacy of the victim, the court shall enter an order setting forth with specificity what evidence may be introduced and the nature of the questions which shall be permitted, and the reasons why the court finds that such evidence satisfies the standards contained in this section. The defendant may then offer evidence under the order of the court.

b. In the absence of clear and convincing proof to the contrary, evidence of the victim's sexual conduct occurring more than one year before the date of the offense charged is presumed to be inadmissible under this section.

c. Evidence of previous sexual conduct with persons other than the defendant which is offered by any lay or expert witness shall not be considered relevant unless it is material to proving the source of semen, pregnancy or disease.

d. Evidence of the victim's previous sexual conduct with the defendant shall be considered relevant if it is probative of whether a reasonable person, knowing what the defendant knew at the time of the alleged offense, would have believed that the alleged victim freely and affirmatively permitted the sexual behavior complained of.

e. Evidence of the manner in which the victim was dressed at the time an offense was committed shall not be admitted unless such evidence is determined by the court to be relevant and admissible in the interest of justice, after an offer of proof by the proponent of such evidence outside the hearing of the jury or at such hearing as the court may require, and a statement by the court of its findings of fact essential to its determination. A statement by the court of its findings shall also be included in the record.

f. For the purposes of this section, "sexual conduct" shall mean any conduct or behavior relating to sexual activities of the victim, including but not limited to previous or subsequent experience of sexual penetration or sexual contact, use of contraceptives, sexual activities reflected in gynecological records, living arrangement and life style.

L.1978, c. 95, § 2C:14–7, eff. Sept. 1, 1979. Amended by L.1988, c. 69, § 1, eff. July 20, 1988; L.1994, c. 95, § 1, eff. Aug. 11, 1994; L.1995, c. 237, § 1, eff. Aug. 29, 1995.

2C:14–8. Juveniles in need of supervision (J.I.N.S.) law not affected

Nothing in this chapter shall be deemed to limit the jurisdiction of the court under P.L.1973, c. 306 (C. 2A:4–42 et seq.).

L.1979, c. 178, § 27A, eff. Sept. 1, 1979.

2C:14–9. Observation of sexual contact; reproduction or disclosure of images of sexual contact; dressing rooms; defenses

a. An actor commits a crime of the fourth degree if, knowing that he is not licensed or privileged to do so, and under circumstances in which a reasonable person would know that another may expose intimate parts or may engage in sexual penetration or sexual contact, he observes another person without that person's consent and under circumstances in which a reasonable person would not expect to be observed.

b. An actor commits a crime of the third degree if, knowing that he is not licensed or privileged to do so, he photographs, films, videotapes, records, or otherwise reproduces in any manner, the image of another person whose intimate parts are exposed or who is engaged in an act of sexual penetration or sexual contact, without that person's consent and under circumstances in which a reasonable person would not expect to be observed.

c. An actor commits a crime of the third degree if, knowing that he is not licensed or privileged to do so, he discloses any photograph, film, videotape, recording or any other reproduction of the image of another person whose intimate parts are exposed or who is engaged in an act of sexual penetration or sexual contact, unless that person has consented to such disclosure. For purposes of this subsection, "disclose" means sell, manufacture, give, provide, lend, trade, mail, deliver, transfer, publish, distribute, circulate, disseminate, present, exhibit, advertise or offer. Notwithstanding the provisions of subsection b. of N.J.S.2C:43–3, a fine not to exceed $30,000 may be imposed for a violation of this subsection.

d. It is an affirmative defense to a crime under this section that:

(1) the actor posted or otherwise provided prior notice to the person of the actor's intent to engage in the conduct specified in subsection a., b., or c., and

(2) the actor acted with a lawful purpose.

e. (1) It shall not be a violation of subsection a. or b. to observe another person in the access way, foyer or entrance to a fitting room or dressing room operated by a retail establishment or to photograph, film, videotape, record or otherwise reproduce the image of such person, if the actor conspicuously posts at the entrance to the fitting room or dressing room prior notice of his intent to make the observations, photographs, films, videotapes, recordings or other reproductions.

(2) It shall be a violation of subsection c. to disclose in any manner any such photograph, film, videotape or recording of another person using a fitting room or dressing room except under the following circumstances:

(a) to law enforcement officers in connection with a criminal prosecution;

(b) pursuant to subpoena or court order for use in a legal proceeding; or

(c) to a co-worker, manager or supervisor acting within the scope of his employment.

f. It shall be a violation of subsection a. or b. to observe another person in a private dressing stall of a fitting room or dressing room operated by a retail establishment or to photograph, film, videotape, record or otherwise reproduce the image of another person in a private dressing stall of a fitting room or dressing room.

g. For purposes of this act, a law enforcement officer, or a corrections officer or guard in a correctional facility or jail, who is engaged in the official performance of his duties shall be deemed to be licensed or privileged to make and to disclose observations, photographs, films, videotapes, recordings or any other reproductions.

h. Notwithstanding the provisions of N.J.S.2C:1–8 or any other provisions of law, a conviction arising under subsection b. of this section shall not merge with a conviction under subsection c. of this section, nor shall

a conviction under subsection c. merge with a conviction under subsection b.

L.2003, c. 206, § 1, eff. Jan. 8, 2004.

2C:14–10. Penalties assessed against sex offenders; amounts; "Sex Crime Victim Treatment Fund"

a. In addition to any fine, fee, assessment or penalty authorized under the provisions of Title 2C of the New Jersey Statutes, a person convicted of a sex offense, as defined in section 2 of P.L.1994, c. 133 (C.2C:7–2), shall be assessed a penalty for each such offense not to exceed:

(1) $2,000, when the conviction is a crime of the first degree;

(2) $1,000, when the conviction is a crime of the second degree;

(3) $750, when the conviction is a crime of the third degree; and

(4) $500, when the conviction is a crime of the fourth degree.

b. All penalties provided for in this section shall be collected as provided for collection of fines and restitutions in section 3 of P.L.1979, c. 396 (C.2C:46–4), and shall be forwarded to the Department of the Treasury as provided in subsection c. of this section.

c. All moneys collected pursuant to this section shall be forwarded to the Department of the Treasury to be deposited in the "Sex Crime Victim Treatment Fund" established in the State Treasury by section 2 of P.L.2005, c. 73 (C.52:4B–43.2).

L.2005, c. 73, § 1, eff. April 26, 2005.

2C:14–11. Sex offense defined; victim defined

As used in this act:

"Sex offense" means a sex offense as defined in subsection b. of section 2 of P.L.1994, c. 133 (C.2C:7–2).

"Victim" means a "victim" as defined in N.J.S.2C:14–1.

L.2007, c. 133, § 1, eff. Aug. 6, 2007.

2C:14–12. Conditional release from custody; contents of order; confidentiality of victim's location

a. When a defendant charged with a sex offense is released from custody before trial on bail or personal recognizance, the court authorizing the release may, as a condition of release, issue an order prohibiting the defendant from having any contact with the victim including, but not limited to, restraining the defendant from entering the victim's residence, place of employment or business, or school, and from harassing or stalking the victim or the victim's relatives in any way.

b. The written court order releasing the defendant shall contain the court's directives specifically restricting the defendant's ability to have contact with the victim or the victim's friends, co-workers or relatives. The clerk of the court or other person designated by the court shall provide a copy of this order to the victim forthwith.

c. The victim's location shall remain confidential and shall not appear on any documents or records to which the defendant has access.

L.2007, c. 133, § 2, eff. Aug. 6, 2007.

CHAPTER 15

ROBBERY

Section
2C:15–1.   Robbery.
2C:15–2.   Carjacking.

2C:15–1. Robbery

a. **Robbery defined.** A person is guilty of robbery if, in the course of committing a theft, he:

(1) Inflicts bodily injury or uses force upon another; or

(2) Threatens another with or purposely puts him in fear of immediate bodily injury; or

(3) Commits or threatens immediately to commit any crime of the first or second degree.

An act shall be deemed to be included in the phrase "in the course of committing a theft" if it occurs in an attempt to commit theft or in immediate flight after the attempt or commission.

b. **Grading.** Robbery is a crime of the second degree, except that it is a crime of the first degree if in the course of committing the theft the actor attempts to kill anyone, or purposely inflicts or attempts to inflict serious bodily injury, or is armed with, or uses or threatens the immediate use of a deadly weapon.

L.1979, c. 178, § 28, eff. Sept. 1, 1979. Amended by L.1981, c. 22, § 1, eff. Feb. 6, 1981.

2C:15–2. Carjacking

a. **Carjacking defined.** A person is guilty of carjacking if in the course of committing an unlawful taking of a motor vehicle, as defined in R.S.39:1–1, or in an attempt to commit an unlawful taking of a motor vehicle he:

(1) inflicts bodily injury or uses force upon an occupant or person in possession or control of a motor vehicle;

(2) threatens an occupant or person in control with, or purposely or knowingly puts an occupant or person in control of the motor vehicle in fear of, immediate bodily injury;

(3) commits or threatens immediately to commit any crime of the first or second degree; or

(4) operates or causes said vehicle to be operated with the person who was in possession or control or was an occupant of the motor vehicle at the time of the taking remaining in the vehicle.

An act shall be deemed to be "in the course of committing an unlawful taking of a motor vehicle" if it occurs during an attempt to commit the unlawful taking of a motor vehicle or during an immediate flight after the attempt or commission.

b. **Grading.** Carjacking is a crime of the first degree and upon conviction thereof a person may, notwithstanding the provisions of paragraph (1) of subsection a. of N.J.S.2C:43–6, be sentenced to an ordinary term of imprisonment between 10 and 30 years. A person convicted of carjacking shall be sentenced to a term of imprisonment and that term of imprisonment shall include the imposition of a minimum term of at least five years during which the defendant shall be ineligible for parole.

L.1993, c. 221, § 1, eff. Aug. 4, 1993.

CHAPTER 16

BIAS CRIMES

Section
2C:16–1.   Bias intimidation.

2C:16–1. Bias intimidation

a. A person is guilty of the crime of bias intimidation if he commits, attempts to commit, conspires with another to commit, or threatens the immediate commission of an offense specified in chapters 11 through 18 of Title 2C of the New Jersey Statutes; N.J.S.2C:33–4; N.J.S.2C:39–3; N.J.S.2C:39–4 or N.J.S.2C:39–5,

(1) with a purpose to intimidate an individual or group of individuals because of race, color, religion, gender, disability, sexual orientation, gender identity or expression, national origin, or ethnicity; or

(2) knowing that the conduct constituting the offense would cause an individual or group of individuals to be intimidated because of race, color, religion, gender, disability, sexual orientation, gender identity or expression, national origin, or ethnicity; or

(3) under circumstances that caused any victim of the underlying offense to be intimidated and the victim, considering the manner in which the offense was committed, reasonably believed either that (a) the offense was committed with a purpose to intimidate the victim or any person or entity in whose welfare the victim is interested because of race, color, religion, gender, disability, sexual orientation, gender identity or expression, national origin, or ethnicity, or (b) the victim or the victim's property was selected to be the target of the offense because of the victim's race, color, religion, gender, disability, sexual orientation, gender identity or expression, national origin, or ethnicity.

b. Permissive inference concerning selection of targeted person or property. Proof that the target of the underlying offense was selected by the defendant, or by another acting in concert with the defendant, because of race, color, religion, gender, disability, sexual orientation, gender identity or expression, national origin, or ethnicity shall give rise to a permissive inference by the trier of fact that the defendant acted with a purpose to intimidate an individual or group of individuals because of race, color, religion, gender, disability, sexual orientation, gender identity or expression, national origin, or ethnicity.

c. Grading. Bias intimidation is a crime of the fourth degree if the underlying offense referred to in subsection a. is a disorderly persons offense or petty disorderly persons offense. Otherwise, bias intimidation is a crime one degree higher than the most serious underlying crime referred to in subsection a., except that where the underlying crime is a crime of the first degree, bias intimidation is a first-degree crime and the defendant upon conviction thereof may, notwithstanding the provisions of paragraph (1) of subsection a. of N.J.S.2C:43–6, be sentenced to an ordinary term of imprisonment between 15 years and 30 years, with a presumptive term of 20 years.

d. Gender exemption in sexual offense prosecutions. It shall not be a violation of subsection a. if the underlying criminal offense is a violation of chapter 14 of Title 2C of the New Jersey Statutes and the circumstance specified in paragraph (1), (2) or (3) of subsection a. of this section is based solely upon the gender of the victim.

e. Merger. Notwithstanding the provisions of N.J.S.2C:1–8 or any other provision of law, a conviction for bias intimidation shall not merge with a conviction of any of the underlying offenses referred to in subsection a. of this section, nor shall any conviction for such underlying offense merge with a conviction for bias intimidation. The court shall impose separate sentences upon a conviction for bias intimidation and a conviction of any underlying offense.

f. Additional Penalties. In addition to any fine imposed pursuant to N. J.S.2C:43–3 or any term of imprisonment imposed pursuant to N.J.S.2C:43–6, a court may order a person convicted of bias intimidation to one or more of the following:

(1) complete a class or program on sensitivity to diverse communities, or other similar training in the area of civil rights;

(2) complete a counseling program intended to reduce the tendency toward violent and antisocial behavior; and

(3) make payments or other compensation to a community-based program or local agency that provides services to victims of bias intimidation.

g. As used in this section "gender identity or expression" means having or being perceived as having

a gender related identity or expression whether or not stereotypically associated with a person's assigned sex at birth.

h. It shall not be a defense to a prosecution for a crime under this section that the defendant was mistaken as to the race, color, religion, gender, disability, sexual orientation, gender identity or expression, national origin, or ethnicity of the victim.

L.2001, c. 443, § 1, eff. Jan. 11, 2002. Amended by L.2007, c. 303, § 1, eff. March 13, 2008.

PART 2

OFFENSES AGAINST PROPERTY

Chapter
17. Arson, Criminal Mischief, and Other Property Destruction.
18. Burglary and Other Criminal Intrusion.
19. [Reenacted as Chapter 15 of Title 2C by P.L.1979, c. 178].
20. Theft and related Offenses.
21. Forgery and Fraudulent Practices.
22. Human Remains.
23. [Reserved].

CHAPTER 17

ARSON, CRIMINAL MISCHIEF, AND OTHER PROPERTY DESTRUCTION

Section
2C:17–1.   Arson and related offenses.
2C:17–2.   Causing or risking widespread injury or damage.
2C:17–3.   Criminal mischief.
2C:17–3.1.   Defacement, removal or injury to official traffic signs or signals.
2C:17–4, 2C:17–5.   Repealed.
2C:17–6.   Motor vehicles; removal or alteration of identification number or mark; possession; penalty.
2C:17–7.   Nuclear electric generating plant; damaging or tampering with equipment with intent to release radiation; penalty.
2C:17–8.   Nuclear electric generating plant; damaging or tampering with equipment which results in death; crime of first degree.
2C:17–9.   Nuclear electric generating plant; damaging or tampering with equipment which results in injury; crime of second degree.

2C:17–1.   Arson and related offenses

a. Aggravated arson. A person is guilty of aggravated arson, a crime of the second degree, if he starts a fire or causes an explosion, whether on his own property or another's:

(1) Thereby purposely or knowingly placing another person in danger of death or bodily injury; or

(2) With the purpose of destroying a building or structure of another; or

(3) With the purpose of collecting insurance for the destruction or damage to such property under circum-

(3) Fencing or other enclosure manifestly designed to exclude intruders.

c. **Peering into windows or other openings of dwelling places.** A person commits a crime of the fourth degree if, knowing that he is not licensed or privileged to do so, he peers into a window or other opening of a dwelling or other structure adapted for overnight accommodation for the purpose of invading the privacy of another person and under circumstances in which a reasonable person in the dwelling or other structure would not expect to be observed.

d. **Defenses.** It is an affirmative defense to prosecution under this section that:

(1) A structure involved in an offense under subsection a. was abandoned;

(2) The structure was at the time open to members of the public and the actor complied with all lawful conditions imposed on access to or remaining in the structure; or

(3) The actor reasonably believed that the owner of the structure, or other person empowered to license access thereto, would have licensed him to enter or remain, or, in the case of subsection c. of this section, to peer.

L.1978, c. 95, § 2C:18–3, eff. Sept. 1, 1979. Amended by L.1980, c. 112, § 3, eff. Sept. 19, 1980; L.1994, c. 90, § 1, eff. Aug. 9, 1994; L.1995, c. 20, § 4, eff. Jan. 25, 1995; L.1997, c. 15, § 1, eff. Jan. 31, 1997; L.2005, c. 100, § 1, eff. June 15, 2005; L.2009, c. 283, § 3, eff. Jan. 17, 2010.

2C:18–4. Lands defined

As used in this act, "lands" means agricultural or horticultural lands devoted to the production for sale of plants and animals useful to man, encompassing plowed or tilled fields, standing crops or their residues, cranberry bogs and appurtenant dams, dikes, canals, ditches and pump houses, including impoundments, man-made reservoirs and the adjacent shorelines thereto, orchards, nurseries, and lands with a maintained fence for the purpose of restraining domestic livestock. "Lands" shall also include lands in agricultural use, as defined in section 3 of P.L.1983, c. 32 (C. 4:1C–13), where public notice prohibiting trespass is given by actual communication to the actor, conspicuous posting, or fencing or other enclosure manifestly designed to exclude intruders.

L.1983, c. 522, § 1, eff. Jan. 17, 1984.

2C:18–5. Knowingly or recklessly operating motor vehicle or riding horseback on lands of another without written permission, or damaging or injuring tangible property

It is an offense under this act to:

a. Knowingly or recklessly operate a motorized vehicle or to ride horseback upon the lands of another without obtaining and in possession of the written permission of the owner, occupant, or lessee thereof.

b. Knowingly or recklessly damage or injure any tangible property, including, but not limited to, any fence, building, feedstocks, crops, live trees, or any domestic animals, located on the lands of another. L.1983, c. 522, § 2, eff. Jan. 17, 1984.

2C:18–6. Offenses; penalties; restitution

a. An offense pursuant to section 2 of this act [1] is a crime of the third degree if the actor causes pecuniary loss of $2,000.00 or more; a crime of the fourth degree if the actor causes pecuniary loss in excess of $500.00 but less than $2,000.00; and a disorderly persons offense if he causes pecuniary loss of $500.00 or less.

b. The provisions of N.J.S. 2C:43–3 to the contrary notwithstanding, in addition to any other sentence which the court may impose, a person convicted of an offense under this act shall be sentenced to make restitution, and to pay a fine of not less than $500.00 if the offense is a crime of the third degree; to pay a fine of not less than $200.00 if the offense is a crime of the fourth degree; and to pay a fine of not less than $100.00 when the conviction is of a disorderly persons offense. L.1983, c. 522, § 3, eff. Jan. 17, 1984.

[1] N.J.S.A. § 2C:18–5.

CHAPTER 19

[REENACTED AS CHAPTER 15 OF TITLE 2C BY P.L.1979, c. 178]

2C:19–1. Reenacted by L.1979, c. 178, §§ 28, 32 as § 2C:15–1

CHAPTER 20

THEFT AND RELATED OFFENSES

I. GENERAL PROVISIONS

Section
2C:20–1.   Definitions.
2C:20–1.1.   Access devices; defacement, removal, alteration, destruction; presumption.
2C:20–2.   Consolidation of theft offenses; grading; provisions applicable to theft generally.
2C:20–2.1.   Automobile theft; additional penalties; suspension or postponement of license.
2C:20–2.2.   Assessment for fair market value of stolen automobile in excess of $7,500.
2C:20–2.3.   Removal of headstones and other markers from grave sites; criminal and other penalties.
2C:20–3.   Theft by unlawful taking or disposition.
2C:20–4.   Theft by deception.
2C:20–5.   Theft by extortion.
2C:20–6.   Theft of property lost, mislaid, or delivered by mistake.
2C:20–7.   Receiving stolen property.
2C:20–7.1.   Fencing.
2C:20–7.2.   Theft of scrap metal.

Section

2C:20–8.   Theft of services.

2C:20–9.   Theft by failure to make required disposition of property received.

2C:20–10. Unlawful taking of means of conveyance.

2C:20–11. Shoplifting.

2C:20–11.1. Guidelines for uniform prosecution.

2C:20–11.2. Leaders of organized retail theft enterprises; penalties.

2C:20–12. Library material and library facility defined.

2C:20–13. Library materials; purposeful concealment; prima facie presumption.

2C:20–14. Taking person into custody for probable cause for belief of willfully concealing library material; arrest without warrant; probable cause for belief of theft; immunity from liability.

2C:20–15. Sign; posting.

2C:20–16. Maintaining facility for sale of stolen automobiles or their parts.

2C:20–17. Employment of juvenile to commit automobile theft.

2C:20–18. Leader of auto theft trafficking network.

2C:20–19. Reserved.

2C:20–20. Civil actions.

2C:20–21. Injunctive relief by state; other persons.

2C:20–22. Estoppel.

II.   COMPUTER–RELATED CRIMES

2C:20–23. Definitions.

2C:20–24. Value of property or services.

2C:20–25. Computer-related theft.

2C:20–26 to 2C:20–30.   Repealed.

2C:20–31. Disclosure of data from wrongful access; no assessable damage; degree of crime.

2C:20–32. Repealed.

2C:20–33. Copy or alteration of program or software with value of $1,000 or less.

2C:20–34. Situs of offense.

2C:20–35. Definitions.

2C:20–36. Prohibited transactions involving food stamp coupons or ATP card of $150 or more; crime of the fourth degree.

2C:20–37. Prohibited transactions involving food stamp coupons or ATP card of less than $150; disorderly persons offense.

I.   GENERAL PROVISIONS

2C:20–1.   Definitions.

In chapters 20 and 21, unless a different meaning plainly is required:

a.   "Deprive" means: (1) to withhold or cause to be withheld property of another permanently or for so extended a period as to appropriate a substantial portion of its economic value, or with purpose to restore only upon payment of reward or other compensation; or (2) to dispose or cause disposal of the property so as to make it unlikely that the owner will recover it.

b.   "Fiduciary" means an executor, general administrator of an intestate, administrator with the will annexed, substituted administrator, guardian, substituted guardian, trustee under any trust, express, implied, resulting or constructive, substituted trustee, executor, conservator, curator, receiver, trustee in bankruptcy, assignee for the benefit of creditors, partner, agent or officer of a corporation, public or private, temporary administrator, administrator, administrator pendente lite, administrator ad prosequendum, administrator ad litem or other person acting in a similar capacity.

c.   "Financial institution" means a bank, insurance company, credit union, savings and loan association, investment trust or other organization held out to the public as a place of deposit of funds or medium of savings or collective investment.

d.   "Government" means the United States, any state, county, municipality, or other political unit, or any department, agency or subdivision of any of the foregoing, or any corporation or other association carrying out the functions of government.

e.   "Movable property" means property the location of which can be changed, including things growing on, affixed to, or found in land, and documents, although the rights represented thereby have no physical location. "Immovable property" is all other property.

f.   "Obtain" means: (1) in relation to property, to bring about a transfer or purported transfer of a legal interest in the property, whether to the obtainer or another; or (2) in relation to labor or service, to secure performance thereof.

g.   "Property" means anything of value, including real estate, tangible and intangible personal property, trade secrets, contract rights, choses in action and other interests in or claims to wealth, admission or transportation tickets, captured or domestic animals, food and drink, electric, gas, steam or other power, financial instruments, information, data, and computer software, in either human readable or computer readable form, copies or originals.

h.   "Property of another" includes property in which any person other than the actor has an interest which the actor is not privileged to infringe, regardless of the fact that the actor also has an interest in the property and regardless of the fact that the other person might be precluded from civil recovery because the property was used in an unlawful transaction or was subject to forfeiture as contraband. Property in possession of the actor shall not be deemed property of another who has only a security interest therein, even if legal title is in the creditor pursuant to a conditional sales contract or other security agreement.

i.   "Trade secret" means the whole or any portion or phase of any scientific or technical information, design, process, procedure, formula or improvement which is secret and of value. A trade secret shall be presumed to be secret when the owner thereof takes measures to prevent it from becoming available to persons other than those selected by the owner to have access thereto for limited purposes.

j.   "Dealer in property" means a person who buys and sells property as a business.

k. "Traffic" means:

(1) To sell, transfer, distribute, dispense or otherwise dispose of property to another person; or

(2) To buy, receive, possess, or obtain control of or use property, with intent to sell, transfer, distribute, dispense or otherwise dispose of such property to another person.

l. "Broken succession of title" means lack of regular documents of purchase and transfer by any seller except the manufacturer of the subject property, or possession of documents of purchase and transfer by any buyer without corresponding documents of sale and transfer in possession of seller, or possession of documents of sale and transfer by seller without corresponding documents of purchase and transfer in possession of any buyer.

m. "Person" includes any individual or entity or enterprise, as defined herein, holding or capable of holding a legal or beneficial interest in property.

n. "Anything of value" means any direct or indirect gain or advantage to any person.

o. "Interest in property which has been stolen" means title or right of possession to such property.

p. "Stolen property" means property that has been the subject of any unlawful taking.

q. "Enterprise" includes any individual, sole proprietorship, partnership, corporation, business trust, association, or other legal entity, and any union or group of individuals associated in fact, although not a legal entity, and it includes illicit as well as licit enterprises and governmental as well as other entities.

r. "Attorney General" includes the Attorney General of New Jersey, his assistants and deputies. The term shall also include a county prosecutor or his designated assistant prosecutor, if a county prosecutor is expressly authorized in writing by the Attorney General to carry out the powers conferred on the Attorney General by this chapter.

s. "Access device" means property consisting of any telephone calling card number, credit card number, account number, mobile identification number, electronic serial number, personal identification number, or any other data intended to control or limit access to telecommunications or other computer networks in either human readable or computer readable form, either copy or original, that can be used to obtain telephone service. Access device also means property consisting of a card, code or other means of access to an account held by a financial institution, or any combination thereof, that may be used by the account holder for the purpose of initiating electronic fund transfers.

t. "Defaced access device" means any access device, in either human readable or computer readable form, either copy or original, which has been removed, erased, defaced, altered, destroyed, covered or otherwise changed in any manner from its original configuration.

u. "Domestic companion animal" means any animal commonly referred to as a pet or one that has been bought, bred, raised or otherwise acquired, in accordance with local ordinances and State and federal law for the primary purpose of providing companionship to the owner, rather than for business or agricultural purposes.

v. "Personal identifying information" means any name, number or other information that may be used, alone or in conjunction with any other information, to identify a specific individual and includes, but is not limited to, the name, address, telephone number, date of birth, social security number, official State issued identification number, employer or taxpayer number, place of employment, employee identification number, demand deposit account number, savings account number, credit card number, mother's maiden name, unique biometric data, such as fingerprint, voice print, retina or iris image or other unique physical representation, or unique electronic identification number, address or routing code of the individual.

L.1978, c. 95, § 2C:20–1, eff. Sept. 1, 1979. Amended by L.1981, c. 167, § 5, eff. June 15, 1981; L.1984, c. 184, § 1, eff. March 14, 1985; L.1997, c. 6, § 1, eff. Jan. 24, 1997; L.1998, c. 100, § 1, eff. Sept. 9, 1998; L.2002, c. 85, § 1, eff. Oct. 16, 2002; L.2004, c. 11, § 1, eff. May 5, 2004.

2C:20–1.1. Access devices; defacement, removal, alteration, destruction; presumption

In any prosecution for an offense enumerated in chapter 20 of Title 2C of the New Jersey Statutes involving a defaced access device, any removal, erasure, defacement, alteration, destruction, covering or other change in such access device from its original configuration performed by any person other than an authorized manufacturer of, or service provider to access devices shall be presumed to be for an unlawful purpose.

L.1997, c. 6, § 6, eff. Jan. 24, 1997.

2C:20–2. Consolidation of theft offenses; grading; provisions applicable to theft generally

a. Consolidation of Theft and Computer Criminal Activity Offenses. Conduct denominated theft or computer criminal activity in this chapter constitutes a single offense, but each episode or transaction may be the subject of a separate prosecution and conviction. A charge of theft or computer criminal activity may be supported by evidence that it was committed in any manner that would be theft or computer criminal activity under this chapter, notwithstanding the specification of a different manner in the indictment or accusation, subject only to the power of the court to ensure fair trial by granting a bill of particulars, discovery, a continuance, or other appropriate relief where the conduct of the defense would be prejudiced by lack of fair notice or by surprise.

b. Grading of theft offenses.

(1) Theft constitutes a crime of the second degree if:

(a) The amount involved is $75,000.00 or more;

(b) The property is taken by extortion;

(c) The property stolen is a controlled dangerous substance or controlled substance analog as defined in N.J.S.2C:35–2 and the quantity is in excess of one kilogram;

(d) The property stolen is a person's benefits under federal or State law, or from any other source, which the Department of Human Services or an agency acting on its behalf has budgeted for the person's health care and the amount involved is $75,000.00 or more; or

(e) The property stolen is human remains or any part thereof; except that, if the human remains are stolen by deception or falsification of a document by which a gift of all or part of a human body may be made pursuant to P.L.2008, c. 50 (C.26:6–77 et al.), the theft constitutes a crime of the first degree.

(2) Theft constitutes a crime of the third degree if:

(a) The amount involved exceeds $500.00 but is less than $75,000.00;

(b) The property stolen is a firearm, motor vehicle, vessel, boat, horse, domestic companion animal or airplane;

(c) The property stolen is a controlled dangerous substance or controlled substance analog as defined in N.J.S.2C:35–2 and the amount involved is less than $75,000.00 or is undetermined and the quantity is one kilogram or less;

(d) It is from the person of the victim;

(e) It is in breach of an obligation by a person in his capacity as a fiduciary;

(f) It is by threat not amounting to extortion;

(g) It is of a public record, writing or instrument kept, filed or deposited according to law with or in the keeping of any public office or public servant;

(h) The property stolen is a person's benefits under federal or State law, or from any other source, which the Department of Human Services or an agency acting on its behalf has budgeted for the person's health care and the amount involved is less than $75,000.00;

(i) The property stolen is any real or personal property related to, necessary for, or derived from research, regardless of value, including, but not limited to, any sample, specimens and components thereof, research subject, including any warm-blooded or cold-blooded animals being used for research or intended for use in research, supplies, records, data or test results, prototypes or equipment, as well as any proprietary information or other type of information related to research;

(j) The property stolen is a New Jersey Prescription Blank as referred to in R.S.45:14–14;

(k) The property stolen consists of an access device or a defaced access device; or

(l) The property stolen consists of anhydrous ammonia and the actor intends it to be used to manufacture methamphetamine.

(3) Theft constitutes a crime of the fourth degree if the amount involved is at least $200.00 but does not exceed $500.00. If the amount involved was less than $200.00 the offense constitutes a disorderly persons offense.

(4) The amount involved in a theft or computer criminal activity shall be determined by the trier of fact. The amount shall include, but shall not be limited to, the amount of any State tax avoided, evaded or otherwise unpaid, improperly retained or disposed of. Amounts involved in thefts or computer criminal activities committed pursuant to one scheme or course of conduct, whether from the same person or several persons, may be aggregated in determining the grade of the offense.

c. Claim of right. It is an affirmative defense to prosecution for theft that the actor:

(1) Was unaware that the property or service was that of another;

(2) Acted under an honest claim of right to the property or service involved or that he had a right to acquire or dispose of it as he did; or

(3) Took property exposed for sale, intending to purchase and pay for it promptly, or reasonably believing that the owner, if present, would have consented.

d. Theft from spouse. It is no defense that theft or computer criminal activity was from or committed against the actor's spouse, except that misappropriation of household and personal effects, or other property normally accessible to both spouses, is theft or computer criminal activity only if it occurs after the parties have ceased living together.

L.1978, c. 95, § 2C:20–2, eff. Sept. 1, 1979. Amended by L.1979, c. 178, § 33, eff. Sept. 1, 1979; L.1981, c. 167, § 6, eff. June 15, 1981; L.1987, c. 76, § 31, eff. Dec. 9, 1987; L.1987, c. 106, § 5; L.1993, c. 219, § 3, eff. Aug. 2, 1993; L.1993, c. 363, § 1, eff. Jan. 4, 1994; L.1995, c. 20, § 5, eff. Jan. 25, 1995; L.1996, c. 154, § 9, eff. Jan. 6, 1997; L.1997, c. 6, § 2, eff. Jan. 24, 1997; L.1998, c. 100, § 2, eff. Sept. 9, 1998; L.1999, c. 95, § 2, eff. May 3, 1999; L.2003, c. 39, § 7, eff. April 14, 2003; L.2005, c. 207, § 4, eff. Nov. 22, 2005; L.2007, c. 36, § 2, eff. Jan. 29, 2007; L.2008, c. 50, § 21, eff. July 22, 2008.

2C:20–2.1. Automobile theft; additional penalties; suspension or postponement of license

a. In addition to any other disposition authorized by law, a person convicted under the provisions of this chapter of theft or unlawful taking of a motor vehicle shall be subject:

(1) For the first offense, to a penalty of $500.00 and to the suspension or postponement of the person's license to operate a motor vehicle over the highways of this State for a period of one year.

(2) For a second offense, to a penalty of $750.00 and to the suspension or postponement of the person's license to operate a motor vehicle over the highways of this State for a period of two years.

(3) For a third or subsequent offense, to a penalty of $1,000.00, and to the suspension or postponement of the person's license to operate a motor vehicle over the highways of this State for 10 years.

b. The suspension or postponement of the person's license to operate a motor vehicle pursuant to subsection a. of this section shall commence on the day the sentence is imposed. In the case of any person who at the time of the imposition of sentence is less than 17 years of age, the period of the suspension of driving privileges authorized herein, including a suspension of the privilege of operating a motorized bicycle, shall commence on the day the sentence is imposed and shall run for a period as fixed by the court of one year for a first offense, two years for a second offense or 10 years for a third offense calculated from the day after the day the person reaches the age of 17 years. If the driving privilege of any person is under revocation, suspension, or postponement for a violation of any provision of this Title or Title 39 of the Revised Statutes at the time of any conviction or adjudication of delinquency for a violation of any offense defined in this chapter or chapter 36 of this Title, the revocation, suspension, or postponement period imposed herein shall commence as of the date of termination of the existing revocation, suspension, or postponement.

Upon conviction the court shall collect forthwith the New Jersey driver's licenses of the person and forward such license or licenses to the Director of the Division of Motor Vehicles along with a report indicating the first and last day of the suspension or postponement period imposed by the court pursuant to this section. If the court is for any reason unable to collect the license or licenses of the person, the court shall cause a report of the conviction or adjudication of delinquency to be filed with the director. That report shall include the complete name, address, date of birth, eye color, and sex of the person and shall indicate the first and last day of the suspension or postponement period imposed by the court pursuant to this section. The court shall inform the person orally and in writing that if the person is convicted of personally operating a motor vehicle during the period of license suspension or postponement imposed pursuant to this section the person shall, upon conviction, be subject to the penalties set forth in R.S. 39:3–40. A person shall be required to acknowledge receipt of the written notice in writing. Failure to receive a written notice or failure to acknowledge in writing the receipt of a written notice shall not be a defense to a subsequent charge of a violation of R.S. 39:3–40. If the person is the holder of a driver's license

from another jurisdiction, the court shall not collect the license but shall notify the director who shall notify the appropriate officials in the licensing jurisdiction. The court shall, however, in accordance with the provisions of this section, revoke the person's non-resident driving privileges in this State.

c. All penalties provided for in this section shall be collected as provided for the collection of fines and restitutions in section 3 of P.L.1979, c. 396 (C.2C:46–4), and shall be distributed in accordance with the provisions of N.J.S. 2C:64–6 as if the collected monies were the proceeds of property forfeited pursuant to the provisions of chapter 64. However, the distributed monies are to be used for law enforcement activities related to auto theft.

L.1991, c. 83, § 1, eff. April 2, 1991. Amended by L.1993, c. 219, § 4, eff. Aug. 2, 1993.

2C:20–2.2. Assessment for fair market value of stolen automobile in excess of $7,500

Notwithstanding the provisions of N.J.S. 2C:43–3, if the fair market value of the automobile and its contents at the time it was stolen exceeds $7,500.00 and the automobile is not recovered, the court may sentence the defendant to pay a fine for that higher amount.

L.1991, c. 83, § 2, eff. April 2, 1991.

2C:20–2.3. Removal of headstones and other markers from grave sites; criminal and other penalties

a. A person is guilty of theft if he unlawfully removes a headstone, headstone marker, flag or flag holder from a grave site or exercises control over a headstone, headstone marker, flag or flag holder without license or privilege to do so under circumstances which would cause a reasonable person to believe that the object was unlawfully removed. For purposes of this section, "flag" includes, but is not limited to, the American flag.

b. Notwithstanding the provisions of N.J.S.2C:43–3 and in addition to any other fine or penalty imposed, a person who commits theft in violation of subsection a. of this section shall be liable to a fine of up to $1,000 for each headstone, headstone marker, flag or flag holder that the person removed or over which the person exercised control.

c. In addition to imposing any other appropriate penalties established for a crime pursuant to Title 2C of the New Jersey Statutes, the court shall impose a term of community service of up to 30 days.

L.2007, c. 321, § 1, eff. Jan. 13, 2008.

2C:20–3. Theft by unlawful taking or disposition

a. **Movable property.** A person is guilty of theft if he unlawfully takes, or exercises unlawful control over, movable property of another with purpose to deprive him thereof.

b. Immovable property. A person is guilty of theft if he unlawfully transfers any interest in immovable property of another with purpose to benefit himself or another not entitled thereto.

L.1978, c. 95, § 2C:20–3, eff. Sept. 1, 1979.

2C:20–4. Theft by deception

A person is guilty of theft if he purposely obtains property of another by deception. A person deceives if he purposely:

a. Creates or reinforces a false impression, including false impressions as to law, value, intention or other state of mind, and including, but not limited to, a false impression that the person is soliciting or collecting funds for a charitable purpose; but deception as to a person's intention to perform a promise shall not be inferred from the fact alone that he did not subsequently perform the promise;

b. Prevents another from acquiring information which would affect his judgment of a transaction; or

c. Fails to correct a false impression which the deceiver previously created or reinforced, or which the deceiver knows to be influencing another to whom he stands in a fiduciary or confidential relationship.

The term "deceive" does not, however, include falsity as to matters having no pecuniary significance, or puffing or exaggeration by statements unlikely to deceive ordinary persons in the group addressed.

L.1978, c. 95, § 2C:20–4, eff. Sept. 1, 1979. Amended by L.2003, c. 43, § 1, eff. April 16, 2003.

2C:20–5. Theft by extortion

A person is guilty of theft by extortion if he purposely and unlawfully obtains property of another by extortion. A person extorts if he purposely threatens to:

a. Inflict bodily injury on or physically confine or restrain anyone or commit any other criminal offense;

b. Accuse anyone of an offense or cause charges of an offense to be instituted against any person;

c. Expose or publicize any secret or any asserted fact, whether true or false, tending to subject any person to hatred, contempt or ridicule, or to impair his credit or business repute;

d. Take or withhold action as an official, or cause an official to take or withhold action;

e. Bring about or continue a strike, boycott or other collective action, if the property is not demanded or received for the benefit of the group in whose interest the actor purports to act;

f. Testify or provide information or withhold testimony or information with respect to another's legal claim or defense; or

g. Inflict any other harm which would not substantially benefit the actor but which is calculated to materially harm another person.

It is an affirmative defense to prosecution based on paragraphs b, c, d or f that the property obtained was honestly claimed as restitution or indemnification for harm done in the circumstances or as lawful compensation for property or services.

L.1978, c. 95, § 2C:20–5, eff. Sept. 1, 1979. Amended by L.1979, c. 178, § 34, eff. Sept. 1, 1979.

2C:20–6. Theft of property lost, mislaid, or delivered by mistake

A person who comes into control of property of another that he knows to have been lost, mislaid, or delivered under a mistake as to the nature or amount of the property or the identity of the recipient is guilty of theft if, knowing the identity of the owner and with purpose to deprive said owner thereof, he converts the property to his own use.

L.1978, c. 95, § 2C:20–6, eff. Sept. 1, 1979.

2C:20–7. Receiving stolen property

a. Receiving. A person is guilty of theft if he knowingly receives or brings into this State movable property of another knowing that it has been stolen, or believing that it is probably stolen. It is an affirmative defense that the property was received with purpose to restore it to the owner. "Receiving" means acquiring possession, control or title, or lending on the security of the property.

b. Presumption of knowledge. The requisite knowledge or belief is presumed in the case of a person who:

(1) Is found in possession or control of two or more items of property stolen on two or more separate occasions; or

(2) Has received stolen property in another transaction within the year preceding the transaction charged; or

(3) Being a person in the business of buying or selling property of the sort received, acquires the property without having ascertained by reasonable inquiry that the person from whom he obtained it had a legal right to possess and dispose of it; or

(4) Is found in possession of two or more defaced access devices.

L.1978, c. 95, § 2C:20–7, eff. Sept. 1, 1979. Amended by L.1979, c. 178, § 35, eff. Sept. 1, 1979; L.1981, c. 290, § 19, eff. Sept. 24, 1981; L.1997, c. 6, § 3, eff. Jan. 24, 1997.

2C:20–7.1. Fencing

a. Possession of altered property. Any dealer in property who knew or should have known that the identifying features such as serial numbers and permanently affixed labels of property in his possession have been removed or altered without the consent of the manufacturer is guilty of possession of altered property. It is a defense to a prosecution under this subsection that a person lawfully possesses the usual indicia of ownership in addition to mere possession.

b. Dealing in stolen property. A person is guilty of dealing in stolen property if he traffics in, or initiates, organizes, plans, finances, directs, manages or supervises trafficking in stolen property.

c. The value of the property involved in the violation of this section shall be determined by the trier of fact. The value of the property involved in the violation of this section may be aggregated in determining the grade of the offense where the acts or conduct constituting a violation were committed pursuant to one scheme or course of conduct, whether from the same person or several persons.

d. It is an affirmative defense to a prosecution under this section that the actor:

(1) Was unaware that the property or service was that of another;

(2) Acted under an honest claim of right to the property or service involved or that he had a right to acquire or dispose of it as he did.

e. In addition to the presumptions contained in N.J.S. 2C:20-7b. the following presumptions are available in the prosecution for a fencing offense:

(1) Proof of the purchase or sale of property at a price substantially below its fair market value, unless satisfactorily explained, gives rise to an inference that the person buying or selling the property knew that it had been stolen;

(2) Proof of the purchase or sale of property by a dealer in that property, out of the regular course of business, or without the usual indicia of ownership other than mere possession, or the property or the job lot of which it is a part was bought, received, possessed or controlled in broken succession of title, so that it cannot be traced, by appropriate documents, in unbroken succession to the manufacturer, in all cases where the regular course of business reasonably indicates records of purchase, transfer or sale, unless satisfactorily explained, gives rise to an inference that the person buying or selling the property knew that it had been stolen; and

(3) Proof that a person buying or selling property of the sort received obtained such property without having ascertained by reasonable inquiry that the person from whom he obtained it had a legal right to possess or control it gives rise to an inference that such person knew that it had been stolen.

L.1981, c. 167, § 7, eff. June 15, 1981.

2C:20-7.2. Theft of scrap metal

Each State, county, and municipal police department may, upon receiving reliable information that scrap metal has been stolen, promptly notify scrap metal businesses of the theft and provide such businesses with information to identify the stolen scrap metal, to effectuate the purposes of P.L.2009, c. 8 (C.45:28-1 et al.).

L.2009, c. 8, § 3, eff. Aug. 1, 2009.

2C:20-8. Theft of services

a. A person is guilty of theft if he purposely obtains services which he knows are available only for compensation, by deception or threat, or by false token, slug, or other means, including but not limited to mechanical or electronic devices or through fraudulent statements, to avoid payment for the service. "Services" include labor or professional service; transportation, telephone, telecommunications, electric, water, gas, cable television, or other public service; accommodation in hotels, restaurants or elsewhere; entertainment; admission to exhibitions; use of vehicles or other movable property. Where compensation for service is ordinarily paid immediately upon the rendering of such service, as in the case of hotels and restaurants, absconding without payment or offer to pay gives rise to a presumption that the service was obtained by deception as to intention to pay.

b. A person commits theft if, having control over the disposition of services of another, to which he is not entitled, he knowingly diverts such services to his own benefit or to the benefit of another not entitled thereto.

c. Any person who, without permission and for the purpose of obtaining electric current, gas or water with intent to defraud any vendor of electricity, gas or water or a person who is furnished by a vendor with electric current, gas or water:

(1) Connects or causes to be connected by wire or any other device with the wires, cables or conductors of any such vendor or any other person; or

(2) Connects or disconnects the meters, pipes or conduits of such vendor or any other person or in any other manner tampers or interferes with such meters, pipes or conduits, or connects with such meters, pipes or conduits by pipes, conduits or other instruments—is guilty of a disorderly persons offense.

The existence of any of the conditions with reference to meters, pipes, conduits or attachments, described in this subsection, is presumptive evidence that the person to whom gas, electricity or water is at the time being furnished by or through such meters, pipes, conduits or attachments has, with intent to defraud, created or caused to be created with reference to such meters, pipes, conduits or attachments, the condition so existing; provided, however, that the presumption shall not apply to any person so furnished with gas, electricity or water for less than 31 days or until there has been at least one meter reading.

A violation of this subsection shall be deemed to be a continuing offense as long as the conditions described in this subsection exist.

d. Any person who, without permission or authority, connects or causes to be connected by wires or other devices, any meter erected or set up for the purpose of registering or recording the amount of electric current supplied to any customer by any vendor of electricity within this State, or changes or shunts the wiring leading to or from any such meter, or by any device, appliance or means whatsoever tampers with any such meter so that the meter will not measure or record the full amount of electric current supplied to such customer, is guilty of a disorderly persons offense.

The existence of any of the conditions with reference to meters or attachments described in this subsection is presumptive evidence that the person to whom electricity is at the time being furnished by or through such meters or attachments has, with intent to defraud, created or caused to be created with reference to such meters or attachments, the condition so existing; provided, however, that the presumption shall not apply to any person so furnished with electricity for less than 31 days or until there has been at least one meter reading.

A violation of this subsection shall be deemed to be a continuing offense as long as the conditions described in this subsection exist.

e. Any person who, with intent to obtain cable television service without payment, in whole or in part, of the lawful charges therefor, or with intent to deprive another of the lawful receipt of such service, damages, cuts, tampers with, installs, taps or makes any connection with, or who displaces, removes, injures or destroys any wire, cable, conduit, apparatus or equipment of a cable television company operating a CATV system; or who, without authority of a cable television company, intentionally prevents, obstructs or delays, by any means or contrivance, the sending, transmission, conveyance, distribution or receipt of programming material carried by equipment of the cable television company operating a CATV system, is a disorderly person.

The existence of any of the conditions with reference to wires, cables, conduits, apparatus or equipment described in this subsection is presumptive evidence that the person to whom cable television service is at the time being furnished has, with intent to obtain cable television service without authorization or compensation or to otherwise defraud, created or caused to be created the condition so existing.

f. Any person who purposely or knowingly manufactures, constructs, sells, offers for sale, distributes or installs any equipment, device or instrument designed or intended to facilitate the interception, decoding or receipt of any cable television service with intent to obtain such service and avoid the lawful payment of the charges therefor to the provider, in whole or in part, is a disorderly person.

Any communications paraphernalia prohibited under this subsection shall be subject to forfeiture and may be seized by the State or any law enforcement officer in accordance with the provisions of N.J.S. 2C:64–1 et seq.

g. Any person who purposely or knowingly maintains or possesses any equipment, device or instrument of the type described in subsection f. of this section or maintains or possesses any equipment, device or instrument actually used to facilitate the interception, decoding or receipt of any cable television service with intent to obtain such service and avoid the lawful payment, in whole or in part, of the charges therefor to the provider, is a disorderly person.

Any communications paraphernalia prohibited under this subsection shall be subject to forfeiture and may be seized by the State or any law enforcement officer in accordance with the provisions of N.J.S. 2C:64–1 et seq.

h. Any person who, with the intent of depriving a telephone company of its lawful charges therefor, purposely or knowingly makes use of any telecommunications service by means of the unauthorized use of any electronic or mechanical device or connection, or by the unauthorized use of billing information, or by the use of a computer, computer equipment or computer software, or by the use of misidentifying or misleading information given to a representative of the telephone company is guilty of a crime of the third degree.

The existence of any of the conditions with reference to electronic or mechanical devices, computers, computer equipment or computer software described in this subsection is presumptive evidence that the person to whom telecommunications service is at the time being furnished has, with intent to obtain telecommunications service without authorization or compensation or to otherwise defraud, created or caused to be created the condition so existing.

i. Any person who purposely or knowingly manufactures, constructs, sells, offers for sale, distributes, installs, or otherwise provides any service, equipment, device, computer, computer equipment, computer software or instrument designed or intended to facilitate the receipt of any telecommunications service and avoid the lawful payment of the charges therefor to the provider, in whole or in part, is guilty of a crime of the third degree.

Any communications paraphernalia, computer, computer equipment or computer software prohibited under this subsection shall be subject to forfeiture and may be seized by the State or any law enforcement officer in accordance with the provisions of N.J.S. 2C:64–1 et seq.

j. Any person who purposely or knowingly maintains or possesses any equipment, device, computer, computer equipment, computer software or instrument of the type described in subsection i. of this section, or maintains or possesses any equipment, device, computer, computer equipment, computer software or instrument actually used to facilitate the receipt of any telecommunications service with intent to obtain such service and avoid the lawful payment, in whole or in part, of the charges therefor to the provider, is guilty of a crime of the third degree.

Any communications paraphernalia, computer, computer equipment or computer software prohibited under this subsection shall be subject to forfeiture and may be seized by the State or any law enforcement officer in accordance with the provisions of N.J.S. 2C:64–1 et seq.

k. In addition to any other disposition authorized by law, and notwithstanding the provisions of N.J.S. 2C:43–3, every person who violates this section shall be sentenced to make restitution to the vendor and to pay a minimum fine of $500.00 for each offense. In determining the amount of restitution, the court shall consider the costs expended by the vendor, including but not limited to the repair and replacement of damaged equipment, the cost of the services unlawfully obtained, investigation expenses, and attorney fees.

l. The presumptions of evidence applicable to offenses defined in subsections c., d., e. and h. of this section shall also apply in any prosecution for theft of services brought pursuant to the provisions of subsection a. or b. of this section.

L.1978, c. 95, § 2C:20–8, eff. Sept. 1, 1979. Amended by L.1983, c. 15, § 1, eff. Jan. 20, 1983; L.1985, c. 10, § 1, eff. Jan. 16, 1985; L.1989, c. 112, § 1, eff. June 29, 1989; L.1997, c. 6, § 4, eff. Jan. 24, 1997.

2C:20–9. Theft by failure to make required disposition of property received

A person who purposely obtains or retains property upon agreement or subject to a known legal obligation to make specified payment or other disposition, whether from such property or its proceeds or from his own property to be reserved in equivalent amount, is guilty of theft if he deals with the property obtained as his own and fails to make the required payment or disposition. The foregoing applies notwithstanding that it may be impossible to identify particular property as belonging to the victim at the time of the actor's failure to make the required payment or disposition. An officer or employee of the government or of a financial institution is presumed: (a) to know any legal obligation relevant to his criminal liability under this section, and (b) to have dealt with the property as his own if he fails to pay or account upon lawful demand, or if an audit reveals a shortage or falsification of accounts. The fact that any payment or other disposition was made with a subsequently dishonored negotiable instrument shall constitute prima facie evidence of the actor's failure to make the required payment or disposition, and the trier of fact may draw a permissive inference therefrom that the actor did not intend to make the required payment or other disposition.

L.1978, c. 95, § 2C:20–9, eff. Sept. 1, 1979. Amended by L.1987, c. 76, § 32, eff. Dec. 9, 1987.

2C:20–10. Unlawful taking of means of conveyance

a. A person commits a disorderly persons offense if, with purpose to withhold temporarily from the owner, he takes, operates, or exercises control over any means of conveyance, other than a motor vehicle, without consent of the owner or other person authorized to give consent. "Means of conveyance" includes but is not limited to motor vehicles, bicycles, motorized bicycles, boats, horses, vessels, surfboards, rafts, skimobiles, airplanes, trains, trams and trailers. It is an affirmative defense to prosecution under subsections a., b. and c. of this section that the actor reasonably believed that the owner or any other person authorized to give consent would have consented to the operation had he known of it.

b. A person commits a crime of the fourth degree if, with purpose to withhold temporarily from the owner, he takes, operates or exercises control over a motor vehicle without the consent of the owner or other person authorized to give consent.

c. A person commits a crime of the third degree if, with purpose to withhold temporarily from the owner, he takes, operates or exercises control over a motor vehicle without the consent of the owner or other person authorized to give consent and operates the motor vehicle in a manner that creates a risk of injury to any person or a risk of damage to property.

d. A person commits a crime of the fourth degree if he enters and rides in a motor vehicle knowing that the motor vehicle has been taken or is being operated without the consent of the owner or other person authorized to consent.

L.1978, c. 95, § 2C:20–10, eff. Sept. 1, 1979. Amended by L.1979, c. 178, § 35A, eff. Sept. 1, 1979; L.1993, c. 134, § 1, eff. June 3, 1993.

2C:20–11. Shoplifting

a. **Definitions.** The following definitions apply to this section:

(1) "Shopping cart" means those push carts of the type or types which are commonly provided by grocery stores, drug stores or other retail mercantile establishments for the use of the public in transporting commodities in stores and markets and, incidentally, from the stores to a place outside the store;

(2) "Store or other retail mercantile establishment" means a place where merchandise is displayed, held, stored or sold or offered to the public for sale;

(3) "Merchandise" means any goods, chattels, foodstuffs or wares of any type and description, regardless of the value thereof;

(4) "Merchant" means any owner or operator of any store or other retail mercantile establishment, or any agent, servant, employee, lessee, consignee, officer, director, franchisee or independent contractor of such owner or proprietor;

(5) "Person" means any individual or individuals, including an agent, servant or employee of a merchant where the facts of the situation so require;

(6) "Conceal" means to conceal merchandise so that, although there may be some notice of its presence, it is not visible through ordinary observation;

(7) "Full retail value" means the merchant's stated or advertised price of the merchandise;

(8) "Premises of a store or retail mercantile establishment" means and includes but is not limited to, the retail mercantile establishment; any common use areas in shopping centers and all parking areas set aside by a merchant or on behalf of a merchant for the parking of vehicles for the convenience of the patrons of such retail mercantile establishment;

(9) "Under–ring" means to cause the cash register or other sale recording device to reflect less than the full retail value of the merchandise;

(10) "Antishoplifting or inventory control device countermeasure" means any item or device which is designed, manufactured, modified, or altered to defeat any antishoplifting or inventory control device;

(11) "Organized retail theft enterprise" means any association of two or more persons who engage in the conduct of or are associated for the purpose of effectuating the transfer or sale of shoplifted merchandise.

b. Shoplifting. Shoplifting shall consist of any one or more of the following acts:

(1) For any person purposely to take possession of, carry away, transfer or cause to be carried away or transferred, any merchandise displayed, held, stored or offered for sale by any store or other retail mercantile establishment with the intention of depriving the merchant of the possession, use or benefit of such merchandise or converting the same to the use of such person without paying to the merchant the full retail value thereof.

(2) For any person purposely to conceal upon his person or otherwise any merchandise offered for sale by any store or other retail mercantile establishment with the intention of depriving the merchant of the processes, use or benefit of such merchandise or converting the same to the use of such person without paying to the merchant the value thereof.

(3) For any person purposely to alter, transfer or remove any label, price tag or marking indicia of value or any other markings which aid in determining value affixed to any merchandise displayed, held, stored or offered for sale by any store or other retail mercantile establishment and to attempt to purchase such merchandise personally or in consort with another at less than the full retail value with the intention of depriving the merchant of all or some part of the value thereof.

(4) For any person purposely to transfer any merchandise displayed, held, stored or offered for sale by any store or other retail merchandise establishment from the container in or on which the same shall be displayed to any other container with intent to deprive the merchant of all or some part of the retail value thereof.

(5) For any person purposely to under-ring with the intention of depriving the merchant of the full retail value thereof.

(6) For any person purposely to remove a shopping cart from the premises of a store or other retail mercantile establishment without the consent of the merchant given at the time of such removal with the intention of permanently depriving the merchant of the possession, use or benefit of such cart.

c. Gradation. (1) Shoplifting constitutes a crime of the second degree under subsection b. of this section if the full retail value of the merchandise is $75,000 or more, or the offense is committed in furtherance of or in conjunction with an organized retail theft enterprise and the full retail value of the merchandise is $1,000 or more.

(2) Shoplifting constitutes a crime of the third degree under subsection b. of this section if the full retail value of the merchandise exceeds $500 but is less than $75,000, or the offense is committed in furtherance of or in conjunction with an organized retail theft enterprise and the full retail value of the merchandise is less than $1,000.

(3) Shoplifting constitutes a crime of the fourth degree under subsection b. of this section if the full retail value of the merchandise is at least $200 but does not exceed $500.

(4) Shoplifting is a disorderly persons offense under subsection b. of this section if the full retail value of the merchandise is less than $200.

The value of the merchandise involved in a violation of this section may be aggregated in determining the grade of the offense where the acts or conduct constituting a violation were committed pursuant to one scheme or course of conduct, whether from the same person or several persons, or were committed in furtherance of or in conjunction with an organized retail theft enterprise.

Additionally, notwithstanding the term of imprisonment provided in N.J.S.2C:43–6 or 2C:43–8, any person convicted of a shoplifting offense shall be sentenced to perform community service as follows: for a first offense, at least ten days of community service; for a second offense, at least 15 days of community service; and for a third or subsequent offense, a maximum of 25 days of community service and any person convicted of a third or subsequent shoplifting offense shall serve a minimum term of imprisonment of not less than 90 days.

d. Presumptions. Any person purposely concealing unpurchased merchandise of any store or other retail mercantile establishment, either on the premises or outside the premises of such store or other retail mercantile establishment, shall be prima facie presumed to have so concealed such merchandise with the intention of depriving the merchant of the possession, use or benefit of such merchandise without paying the full retail value thereof, and the finding of such merchandise concealed upon the person or among the belongings of such person shall be prima facie evidence of purposeful concealment; and if such person conceals, or causes to be concealed, such merchandise upon the person or among the belongings of another, the finding of the same shall also be prima facie evidence of willful concealment on the part of the person so concealing such merchandise.

e. A law enforcement officer, or a special officer, or a merchant, who has probable cause for believing that a person has willfully concealed unpurchased merchandise and that he can recover the merchandise by taking the person into custody, may, for the purpose of attempting to effect recovery thereof, take the person into custody and detain him in a reasonable manner for not more than a reasonable time, and the taking into custody by a law enforcement officer or special officer or merchant shall not render such person criminally or civilly liable in any manner or to any extent whatsoever.

Any law enforcement officer may arrest without warrant any person he has probable cause for believing has committed the offense of shoplifting as defined in this section.

A merchant who causes the arrest of a person for shoplifting, as provided for in this section, shall not be criminally or civilly liable in any manner or to any extent whatsoever where the merchant has probable cause for believing that the person arrested committed the offense of shoplifting.

f. Any person who possesses or uses any antishoplifting or inventory control device countermeasure within any store or other retail mercantile establishment is guilty of a disorderly persons offense.

L.1978, c. 95, § 2C:20–11, eff. Sept. 1, 1979. Amended by L.1979, c. 178, § 35B, eff. Sept. 1, 1979; L.1997, c. 319, § 1, eff. Jan. 8, 1998; L.2000, c. 16, § 1, eff. April 28, 2000; L.2006, c. 56, § 1, eff. Aug. 2, 2006.

2C:20–11.1. Guidelines for uniform prosecution

The Attorney General shall develop, no later than the 120th day after the effective date of this act, guidelines to ensure that the prosecution of shoplifting offenses is conducted in a uniform manner throughout the State.

L.2000, c. 16, § 2, eff. April 28, 2000.

2C:20–11.2. Leaders of organized retail theft enterprises; penalties

A person is a leader of an organized retail theft enterprise if he conspires with others as an organizer, supervisor, financier or manager, to engage for profit in a scheme or course of conduct to effectuate the transfer or sale of shoplifted merchandise. Leader of organized retail theft enterprise is a crime of the second degree. Notwithstanding the provisions of subsection a. of N.J.S.2C:43–3, the court may impose a fine not to exceed $250,000 or five times the retail value of the merchandise seized at the time of the arrest, whichever is greater.

Notwithstanding the provisions of N.J.S.2C:1–8, a conviction of leader of organized retail theft enterprise shall not merge with the conviction for any offense

which is the object of the conspiracy. Nothing contained in this section shall prohibit the court from imposing an extended term pursuant to N.J.S.2C:43–7; nor shall this section be construed in any way to preclude or limit the prosecution or conviction of any person for conspiracy under N.J.S.2C:5–2, or any prosecution or conviction for any other offense.

It shall not be necessary in any prosecution under this section for the State to prove that any intended profit was actually realized. The trier of fact may infer that a particular scheme or course of conduct was undertaken for profit from all of the attending circumstances, including but not limited to the number of persons involved in the scheme or course of conduct, the actor's net worth and his expenditures in relation to his legitimate sources of income, the amount of merchandise involved, or the amount of cash or currency involved.

It shall not be a defense to a prosecution under this section that any shoplifted merchandise was brought into or transported in this State solely for ultimate distribution in another jurisdiction; nor shall it be a defense that any profit was intended to be made in another jurisdiction.

L.2006, c. 56, § 2, eff. Aug. 2, 2006.

2C:20–12. Library material and library facility defined

The following definitions apply to sections 2 through 4 of this act [1] as they relate to the theft of library material:

a. "Library material" means any material, regardless of physical form or characteristics, or any part thereof, belonging to, on loan to, or otherwise in the custody of a library facility;

b. "Library facility" means any public library, any library of an educational, historical, or charitable institution, organization or society, or any museum.

L.1985, c. 373, § 1, eff. Nov. 26, 1985.

    [1] N.J.S.A. §§ 2C:20–13 to 2C:20–15.

2C:20–13. Library materials; purposeful concealment; prima facie presumption

Any person who purposely conceals, on or off the premises of the library facility, upon his person or among his belongings, or upon the person or among the belongings of another, any library material shall be prima facie presumed to have concealed the material for the purpose of depriving the library facility of its use or benefit.

L.1985, c. 373, § 2, eff. Nov. 26, 1985.

2C:20–14. Taking person into custody for probable cause for belief of willfully concealing library material; arrest without warrant; probable cause for belief of theft; immunity from liability

a. A law enforcement officer, a special officer, or an employee of a library facility who has probable cause for believing that a person has willfully concealed library material and that he can recover the material by taking the person into custody, may, for the purpose of attempting to recover the material, take the person into custody and detain him in a reasonable manner for a reasonable time. Taking the person into custody shall not render the law enforcement officer, the special officer, or the employee of a library facility civilly or criminally liable.

b. Any law enforcement officer who has probable cause for believing that a person has committed the offense of theft of library material may arrest the person without warrant.

c. An employee of a library facility who causes the arrest of a person for theft of library material, as provided for in this act, shall not be civilly or criminally liable where the employee has probable cause for believing that the person arrested committed the offense of theft of library material.

L.1985, c. 373, § 3, eff. Nov. 26, 1985.

2C:20–15. Sign; posting

All library facilities shall post at their primary entrances and exits a conspicuous sign to read as follows: IN ORDER TO PREVENT THE THEFT OF BOOKS AND LIBRARY MATERIAL, STATE LAW AUTHORIZES THE DETENTION FOR A REASONABLE PERIOD OF ANY PERSON USING THESE FACILITIES WHO IS SUSPECTED OF COMMITTING A THEFT OF LIBRARY MATERIAL.

L.1985, c. 373, § 4, eff. Nov. 26, 1985.

2C:20–16. Maintaining facility for sale of stolen automobiles or their parts

a. A person who knowingly maintains or operates any premises, place or facility used for the remodeling, repainting, or separating of automobile parts for resale of any stolen automobile is guilty of a crime of the second degree.

b. Notwithstanding any provision of law to the contrary, any person convicted of a violation of this section shall forthwith forfeit his right to operate a motor vehicle in this State for a period to be fixed by the court at not less than three nor more than five years. The court shall cause a report of the conviction to be filed with the Director of the Division of Motor Vehicles.

L.1991, c. 80, § 1, eff. April 2, 1991.

2C:20–17. Employment of juvenile to commit automobile theft

a. A person who is at least 18 years of age who knowingly uses, solicits, directs, hires or employs a person who is in fact 17 years of age or younger to commit theft of an automobile is guilty of a crime of the second degree. Notwithstanding the provisions of N.J.S. 2C:1–8, a conviction under this section shall not merge with a conviction for theft of an automobile.

Nothing contained in this act shall prohibit the court from imposing an extended term pursuant to N.J.S. 2C:43–7; nor shall this act be construed in any way to preclude or limit the prosecution or conviction of any person for conspiracy under N.J.S. 2C:5–2, or any prosecution or conviction for any other offense.

b. It shall be no defense to a prosecution under this section that the actor mistakenly believed that the person which the actor used, solicited, directed, hired or employed was older than 17 years of age, even if such mistaken belief was reasonable.

L.1991, c. 81, § 1, eff. April 2, 1991.

2C:20–18. Leader of auto theft trafficking network

A person is a leader of an auto theft trafficking network if he conspires with others as an organizer, supervisor, financier or manager, to engage for profit in a scheme or course of conduct to unlawfully take, dispose of, distribute, bring into or transport in this State automobiles as stolen property. Leader of auto theft trafficking network is a crime of the second degree. Notwithstanding the provisions of subsection a. of N.J.S. 2C:43–3, the court may impose a fine not to exceed $250,000.00 or five times the retail value of the automobiles seized at the time of the arrest, whichever is greater.

Notwithstanding the provisions of N.J.S. 2C:1–8, a conviction of leader of auto theft trafficking network shall not merge with the conviction for any offense which is the object of the conspiracy. Nothing contained in this act shall prohibit the court from imposing an extended term pursuant to N.J.S. 2C:43–7; nor shall this act be construed in any way to preclude or limit the prosecution or conviction of any person for conspiracy under N.J.S. 2C:5–2, or any prosecution or conviction for any other offense.

It shall not be necessary in any prosecution under this act for the State to prove that any intended profit was actually realized. The trier of fact may infer that a particular scheme or course of conduct was undertaken for profit from all of the attending circumstances, including but not limited to the number of persons involved in the scheme or course of conduct, the actor's net worth and his expenditures in relation to his legitimate sources of income, the number of automobiles involved, or the amount of cash or currency involved.

It shall not be a defense to a prosecution under this act that the automobile was brought into or transported in this State solely for ultimate distribution in another jurisdiction; nor shall it be a defense that any profit was intended to be made in another jurisdiction.

L.1991, c. 82, § 1, eff. April 2, 1991.

2C:20–19. Reserved

2C:20–20. Civil actions

a. Any person damaged in his business or property by reason of a violation of section 7 of this amendatory and supplementary act [1] may sue therefor in any appropriate court and shall recover threefold any damages he sustains and the cost of the suit, including a reasonable attorney's fee, costs of investigation and litigation.

b. (1) All persons who have possessed or obtained control of stolen property are liable as principals and may be sued jointly or severally, whether or not possession or control was joint.

(2) Any person held liable for possession or control of stolen property under chapter 20 of Title 2C of the New Jersey Statutes shall have standing to bring a civil action for contribution from any person who possessed or exercised control over the stolen property and who knew, had reason to know, or was reckless with regard to the risk that it was stolen.

c. Any action for damages under chapter 20 of Title 2C of the New Jersey Statutes shall be maintained in the Superior Court sitting without a jury.

L.1981, c. 167, § 8, eff. June 15, 1981. Amended by L.1991, c. 91, § 143, eff. April 9, 1991.

  [1] N.J.S.A. § 2C:20–7.1.

2C:20–21. Injunctive relief by state; other persons

a. In addition to any other action or proceeding authorized by law, the Attorney General or a person alleging injury or loss, may bring an action in the Superior Court to enjoin violations of chapter 20 of Title 2C of the New Jersey Statutes, or to enjoin any acts in furtherance thereof. The Superior Court, in any action brought pursuant to this section, shall, after making due provision for the rights of innocent persons such as prior lienholders or other valid lienholders whose rights are prior to those of the State, grant relief as may be appropriate in the circumstances, including but not limited to:

(1) Ordering any defendant to divest himself of any interest in any enterprise, including real estate;

(2) Imposing reasonable restrictions upon the future activities or investments of any defendant, including but not limited to, prohibiting any defendant from engaging in the same type of endeavor as the enterprise in which he was engaged in violation of chapter 20 of Title 2C of the New Jersey Statutes; or

(3) Ordering the dissolution or reorganization of any enterprise; or

(4) Ordering the suspension or revocation of any license, permit, or prior approval granted to any enterprise by any department or agency of the State; or

(5) Ordering the forfeiture of the charter of a corporation organized under the laws of this State or the revocation of a certificate authorizing a foreign corporation to conduct business within this State, upon finding that the board of directors or a managerial agent acting on behalf of the corporation, in conducting the affairs of the corporation, has authorized or engaged in conduct in violation of chapter 20 of Title 2C of the New Jersey Statutes and that, for the prevention of future criminal activity, the public interest requires the charter of the corporation forfeited and the corporation dissolved or the certificate revoked.

b. In any action the Attorney General or injured person shall move as soon as practicable for a hearing and determination. Pending final determination, the Superior Court may enter temporary orders, including restraints and prohibitions, or take other actions as are in the interest of justice.

L.1981, c. 167, § 9, eff. June 15, 1981.

2C:20–22. Estoppel

A final judgment rendered in favor of the Attorney General or other person in any criminal action, or proceeding under chapter 20 of Title 2C of the New Jersey Statutes, shall estop the defendant in the action or proceeding in any subsequent civil action or proceeding under chapter 20 of Title 2C of the New Jersey Statutes as to all matters as to which the judgment in the action or proceeding would be an estoppel as between the parties to it.

L.1981, c. 167, § 10, eff. June 15, 1981.

II. COMPUTER–RELATED CRIMES

2C:20–23. Definitions

As used in this act:

a. "Access" means to instruct, communicate with, store data in, retrieve data from, or otherwise make use of any resources of a computer, computer storage medium, computer system, or computer network.

b. "Computer" means an electronic, magnetic, optical, electrochemical or other high speed data processing device or another similar device capable of executing a computer program, including arithmetic, logic, memory, data storage or input-output operations and includes all computer equipment connected to such a device, computer system or computer network, but shall not include an automated typewriter or typesetter or a portable, hand-held calculator.

c. "Computer equipment" means any equipment or devices, including all input, output, processing, storage, software, or communications facilities, intended to interface with the computer.

d. "Computer network" means the interconnection of communication lines, including microwave or other means of electronic communications, with a computer through remote terminals, or a complex consisting of two or more interconnected computers, and shall include the Internet.

e. "Computer program" means a series of instructions or statements executable on a computer, which directs the computer system in a manner to produce a desired result.

f. "Computer software" means a set of computer programs, data, procedures, and associated documentation concerned with the operation of a computer system.

g. "Computer system" means a set of interconnected computer equipment intended to operate as a cohesive system.

h. "Data" means information, facts, concepts, or instructions contained in a computer, computer storage medium, computer system, or computer network. It shall also include, but not be limited to, any alphanumeric, hexadecimal, octal or binary code.

i. "Data base" means a collection of data.

j. "Financial instrument" includes but is not limited to a check, draft, warrant, money order, note, certificate of deposit, letter of credit, bill of exchange, credit or debit card, transaction authorization mechanism, marketable security and any computer representation of these items.

k. "Services" includes but is not limited to the use of a computer system, computer network, computer programs, data prepared for computer use and data contained within a computer system or computer network.

l. "Personal identifying information" shall have the meaning set forth in subsection a. of N.J.S.2C:21–17, and shall also include passwords and other codes that permit access to any data, data base, computer, computer storage medium, computer program, computer software, computer equipment, computer system or computer network, where access is intended to be secure, restricted or limited.

m. "Internet" means the international computer network of both federal and non-federal interoperable packet switched data networks.

n. "Alter," "damage" or " destroy" shall include, but not be limited to, any change or impairment to the integrity or availability of any data or other information, data base, computer program, computer software, computer equipment, computer, computer storage medium, computer system, or computer network by any means including introduction of a computer contaminant.

o. "User of computer services" shall include, but not be limited to, any person, business, computer, computer network, computer system, computer equipment or any other device which makes use of any resources of a computer, computer network, computer system, computer storage medium, computer equipment, data or data base.

p. "Computer contaminant" means any set of computer instructions that are designed to alter, damage, destroy, record or transmit information within a computer, computer system or computer network without the authorization of the owner of the information.

They include, but are not limited to, a group of computer instructions commonly called viruses or worms, that are self-replicating or self-propagating and are designed to contaminate other computer programs or computer data, consume computer resources, alter, damage, destroy, record or transmit data or in some other fashion usurp the normal operation of the computer, computer program, computer operations, computer services or computer network.

q. "Authorization" means permission, authority or consent given by a person who possesses lawful authority to grant such permission, authority or consent to another person to access, operate, use, obtain, take, copy, alter, damage or destroy a computer, computer network, computer system, computer equipment, computer software, computer program, computer storage medium, or data. An actor has authorization if a reasonable person would believe that the act was authorized.

L.1984, c. 184, § 2, eff. March 14, 1985. Amended by L.2003, c. 39, § 1, eff. April 14, 2003.

2C:20–24. Value of property or services

For the purposes of this act, the value of any property or services, including the use of computer time, shall be their fair market value, if it is determined that a willing buyer and willing seller exist. Value shall include the cost of repair or remediation of any damage caused by an unlawful act and the gross revenue from any lost business opportunity caused by the unlawful act. The value of any lost business opportunity may be determined by comparison to gross revenue generated before the unlawful act that resulted in the lost business opportunity. Value shall include, but not be limited to, the cost of generating or obtaining data and storing it within a computer or computer system.

L.1984, c. 184, § 3, eff. March 14, 1985. Amended by L.2003, c. 39, § 2, eff. April 14, 2003.

2C:20–25. Computer-related theft

A person is guilty of computer criminal activity if the person purposely or knowingly and without authorization, or in excess of authorization:

a. Accesses any data, data base, computer storage medium, computer program, computer software, computer equipment, computer, computer system or computer network;

b. Alters, damages or destroys any data, data base, computer, computer storage medium, computer program, computer software, computer system or computer network, or denies, disrupts or impairs computer services, including access to any part of the Internet, that are available to any other user of the computer services;

c. Accesses or attempts to access any data, data base, computer, computer storage medium, computer program, computer software, computer equipment, computer system or computer network for the purpose of executing a scheme to defraud, or to obtain services, property, personal identifying information, or money, from the owner of a computer or any third party;

d.　(Deleted by amendment, P.L.2003, c.39).

e.　Obtains, takes, copies or uses any data, data base, computer program, computer software, personal identifying information, or other information stored in a computer, computer network, computer system, computer equipment or computer storage medium; or

f.　Accesses and recklessly alters, damages or destroys any data, data base, computer, computer storage medium, computer program, computer software, computer equipment, computer system or computer network.

g.　A violation of subsection a. of this section is a crime of the third degree. A violation of subsection b. is a crime of the second degree. A violation of subsection c. is a crime of the third degree, except that it is a crime of the second degree if the value of the services, property, personal identifying information, or money obtained or sought to be obtained exceeds $ 5,000. A violation of subsection e. is a crime of the third degree, except that it is a crime of the second degree if the data, data base, computer program, computer software, or information:

(1) is or contains personal identifying information, medical diagnoses, treatments or other medical information concerning an identifiable person;

(2) is or contains governmental records or other information that is protected from disclosure by law, court order or rule of court; or

(3) has a value exceeding $5,000.

A violation of subsection f. is a crime of the fourth degree, except that it is a crime of the third degree if the value of the damage exceeds $5,000.

A violation of any subsection of this section is a crime of the first degree if the offense results in:

(1) a substantial interruption or impairment of public communication, transportation, supply of water, gas or power, or other public service. The term "substantial interruption or impairment" shall mean such interruption or impairment that:

(a) affects 10 or more structures or habitations;

(b) lasts for two or more hours; or

(c) creates a risk of death or significant bodily injury to any person;

(2) damages or loss in excess of $250,000; or

(3) significant bodily injury to any person.

Every sentence of imprisonment for a crime of the first degree committed in violation of this section shall include a minimum term of one-third to one-half of the sentence imposed, during which term the defendant shall not be eligible for parole.

h.　Every sentence imposed upon a conviction pursuant to this section shall, if the victim is a government agency, include a period of imprisonment. The period of imprisonment shall include a minimum term of one-third to one-half of the sentence imposed, during which term the defendant shall not be eligible for parole. The victim shall be deemed to be a government agency if a computer, computer network, computer storage medium, computer system, computer equipment, computer program, computer software, computer data or data base that is a subject of the crime is owned, operated or maintained by or on behalf of a governmental agency or unit of State or local government or a public authority. The defendant shall be strictly liable under this subsection and it shall not be a defense that the defendant did not know or intend that the victim was a government agency, or that the defendant intended that there be other victims of the crime.

A violation of any subsection of this section shall be a distinct offense from a violation of any other subsection of this section, and a conviction for a violation of any subsection of this section shall not merge with a conviction for a violation of any other subsection of this section or section 10 of P.L.1984, c. 184 (C.2C:20–31), or for conspiring or attempting to violate any subsection of this section or section 10 of P.L.1984, c. 184 (C.2C:20–31), and a separate sentence shall be imposed for each such conviction.

When a violation of any subsection of this section involves an offense committed against a person under 18 years of age, the violation shall constitute an aggravating circumstance to be considered by the court when determining the appropriate sentence to be imposed.

L.1984, c. 184, § 4, eff. March 14, 1985. Amended by L.2003, c. 39, § 3, eff. April 14, 2003.

2C:20–26 to 2C:20–30.　Repealed by L.2003, c. 39, § 9, eff. April 14, 2003

2C:20–31.　Disclosure of data from wrongful access; no assessable damage; degree of crime

a.　A person is guilty of a crime of the third degree if the person purposely or knowingly and without authorization, or in excess of authorization, accesses any data, data base, computer, computer storage medium, computer software, computer equipment, computer system and knowingly or recklessly discloses or causes to be disclosed any data, data base, computer software, computer programs or personal identifying information.

b.　A person is guilty of a crime of the second degree if the person purposely or knowingly and without authorization, or in excess of authorization, accesses any data, data base, computer, computer storage medium, computer software, computer equipment, computer system or computer network and purposely or knowingly discloses or causes to be disclosed any data, data base, computer software, computer program or other information that is protected from disclosure by any law, court order or rule of court. Every sentence imposed upon a conviction pursuant to this subsection shall include a period of imprisonment. The period of imprisonment shall include a minimum term of one-third to one-half of the sentence imposed, during which term the defendant shall not be eligible for parole.

L.1984, c. 184, § 10, eff. March 14, 1985. Amended by L.2003, c. 39, § 4, eff. April 14, 2003.

2C:20–32.   **Repealed by L.2003, c. 39, § 9, eff. April 14, 2003**

2C:20–33.   **Copy or alteration of program or software with value of $1,000 or less**

It is an affirmative defense to a prosecution pursuant to subsection e. of section 4 of P.L.1984, c. 184 (C.2C:20–25), which shall be proved by clear and convincing evidence, that the actor obtained, copied or accessed a computer program or computer software that had a retail value of less than $1, 000 and the actor did not disseminate or disclose the program or software to any other person.

L.1984, c. 184, § 12, eff. March 14, 1985. Amended by L.2003, c. 39, § 5, eff. April 14, 2003.

2C:20–34.   **Situs of offense**

For the purpose of prosecution under this act, and in addition to determining the situs of the offense pursuant to the provisions of N.J.S.2C:1–3, the situs of an offense of computer criminal activity shall also be the location of the computer, computer storage medium, computer program, computer software, computer equipment, computer system or computer network which is accessed, or where the computer, computer storage medium, computer program, computer software, computer equipment, computer system, computer network or other device used in the offense is situated, or where the actual damage occurs.

L.1984, c. 184, § 13, eff. March 14, 1985. Amended by L.2003, c. 39, § 6, eff. April 14, 2003.

2C:20–35.   **Definitions**

As used in this act:

"ATP card" means a document issued by a State or federal agency, to a certified household, to show the food stamp allotment a household is authorized to receive on presentation.

"Benefit card" means a card used or intended for use to access Work First New Jersey, food stamp or other benefits as determined by the Commissioner of Human Services under the electronic benefit distribution system established pursuant to the "Public Assistance Electronic Benefit Distribution System Act," P.L.1985, c. 501 (C.44:10–5.1 et seq.) and continued pursuant to P.L. 1997, c. 37 (C.44:10–71 et al.).

"Department" means the Department of Human Services.

"Food stamp coupon" means any coupon or stamp used or intended for use in the purchase of food pursuant to the federal food stamp program authorized by Title XIII of the "Food and Agriculture Act of 1977," Pub.L.95–113 (7 U.S.C. s.2011 et seq.), or the New Jersey Supplementary Food Stamp Program established pursuant to P.L.1998, c. 32 (C.44:10–79 et al.).

L.1993, c. 13, § 1, eff. Jan. 15, 1993. Amended by L.1995, c. 215, § 1, eff. Aug. 14, 1995; L.1997, c. 37, § 8, eff. March 24, 1997; L.1998, c. 32, § 7, eff. July 1, 1998.

2C:20–36.   **Prohibited transactions involving food stamp coupons or ATP card of $150 or more; crime of the fourth degree**

If the face value of food stamp coupons or an ATP card or benefit card is equal to or greater than $150, an individual shall be guilty of a crime of the fourth degree if he purposely or knowingly and without authorization:

a. Receives or uses the proceeds of food stamp coupons or an ATP card or benefit card for which he has not applied or has not been approved by the department to use;

b. Engages in any transaction to convert food stamp coupons or an ATP card or benefit card to other property contrary to federal and State government rules and regulations governing the Work First New Jersey program, the federal food stamp program, the New Jersey Supplementary Food Stamp Program, or any other program included in the electronic benefit distribution system; or

c. Transfers food stamp coupons or an ATP card or benefit card to another person who is not lawfully entitled or approved by the department to use the coupons or ATP card or benefit card.

L.1993, c. 13, § 2, eff. Jan. 15, 1993. Amended by L.1995, c. 215, § 2, eff. Aug. 14, 1995; L.1997, c. 37, § 9, eff. March 24, 1997; L.1998, c. 32, § 8, eff. July 1, 1998.

2C:20–37.   **Prohibited transactions involving food stamp coupons or ATP card of less than $150; disorderly persons offense**

If the face value of food stamp coupons or an ATP card or benefit card is less than $150, an individual shall be guilty of a disorderly persons offense if he purposely or knowingly and without authorization:

a. Receives or uses the proceeds of food stamp coupons or an ATP card or benefit card for which he has not applied or has not been approved, by the department, to use;

b. Engages in any transaction to convert food stamp coupons or an ATP card or benefit card to other property contrary to federal and State government rules and regulations governing the Work First New Jersey program, the federal food stamp program, the New Jersey Supplementary Food Stamp Program, or any other program included in the electronic benefit distribution system; or

c. Transfers food stamp coupons or an ATP card or benefit card to another person who is not lawfully entitled or approved, by the department, to use the coupons or ATP card or benefit card.

L.1993, c. 13, § 3, eff. Jan. 15, 1993. Amended by L.1995, c. 215, § 3, eff. Aug. 14, 1995; L.1997, c. 37, § 10, eff. March 24, 1997; L.1998, c. 32, § 9, eff. July 1, 1998.

CHAPTER 21

FORGERY AND FRAUDULENT PRACTICES

Section
2C:21–1.   Forgery and related offenses.
2C:21–2.   Criminal simulation.
2C:21–2.1.   Driver's license, birth certificate or other document issued by governmental agency to verify identity or age; simulation.
2C:21–2.2.   Law enforcement agency badges; unauthorized sale, purchase, gift, or loan.
2C:21-2.3.   Motor vehicle insurance identification card; production or sale.
2C:21-2.4.   Possession of forged or altered receipts, universal product code labels, or checks.
2C:21–3.   Frauds relating to public records and recordable instruments.
2C:21–4.   Falsifying or tampering with records.
2C:21–4.1.   Purposeful destruction, alteration or falsification of record relating to care of medical or surgical or podiatric patient in order to deceive or mislead.
2C:21–4.2.   Definitions relating to health care claims fraud.
2C:21–4.3.   Health care claims fraud; elements; penalties; evidence.
2C:21–4.4.   Legislative findings.
2C:21–4.5.   Definitions.
2C:21–4.6.   Insurance fraud.
2C:21–4.7.   Insurance fraud detection reward program.
2C:21–4.8.   Penalties for vehicle title fraud.
2C:21–5.   Bad checks.
2C:21–6.   Credit cards.
2C:21–6.1.   Payment cards; fraudulent use of scanning and other electronic devices; definitions.
2C:21–7.   Deceptive business practices.
2C:21–7.1.   Repealed.
2C:21–7.2.   Definitions.
2C:21–7.3.   False representation by oral or written statement to make person believe non-kosher food or food product is kosher; presumptive evidence; defense.
2C:21–7.4.   Disorderly persons offenses.
2C:21–8.   Misrepresentation of mileage of motor vehicle.
2C:21–8.1.   Definition; determination of degree of offense.
2C:21–9.   Misconduct by corporate official.
2C:21–10.   Commercial bribery and breach of duty to act disinterestedly.
2C:21–11.   Rigging publicly exhibited contest.
2C:21–12.   Defrauding secured creditors.
2C:21–13.   Fraud in insolvency.
2C:21–14.   Receiving deposits in a failing financial institution.
2C:21–15.   Misapplication of entrusted property and property of government or financial institution.
2C:21–16.   Securing execution of documents by deception.
2C:21–17.   Impersonation; theft of identity; crime.
2C:21–17.1.   Victim restitution for personal identification information offenses.
2C:21–17.2.   False driver's license, birth certificate or document issued by government agency; use of personal identifying information of another.
2C:21–17.3.   Fraudulent use, distribution, manufacture, possession of items containing personal identifying information of another.
2C:21–17.4.   Action for damages resulting from use of personal identifying information; standard of proof; other remedies.
2C:21–17.5.   Consumer reporting agencies; deletion of information resulting from unlawful use of personal identifying information.
2C:21–17.6.   Victim of identity theft; report to law enforcement agency.
2C:21–18.   Slugs.
2C:21–19.   Wrongful credit practices and related offenses.
2C:21–20.   Unauthorized practice of medicine and surgery or podiatric medicine.
2C:21–20.1.   Unauthorized practice of acupuncture.
2C:21–21.   New Jersey Anti–Piracy Act.
2C:21–22.   Unauthorized practice of law; disorderly persons offense.
2C:21–22.1.   Definitions.
2C:21–23.   Legislative findings and declaration.
2C:21–24.   Definitions.
2C:21–25.   Money laundering and illegal investment; crime.
2C:21–26.   Knowledge of criminal activity.
2C:21–27.   Degrees of offense; penalties; nonmerger.
2C:21–27.1.   Criteria for imposition of anti-money laundering profiteering penalty.
2C:21–27.2.   Calculation of anti-money laundering profiteering penalty.
2C:21–27.3.   Revocation or reduction of penalty assessment.
2C:21–27.4.   Payment schedule.
2C:21–27.5.   Relation to other dispositions.
2C:21–27.6.   Collection and distribution.
2C:21–28.   Attorney general authorized to bring civil action.
2C:21–29.   Investigative interrogatories.
2C:21–30.   Practice of dentistry without a license; crime of the third degree.
2C:21–31.   Unauthorized practice of immigration law.
2C:21–32.   Trademark counterfeiting; definitions; offenses.
2C:21–33.   Electrical contracting without business permit.
2C:21–34.   False claim for payment of government contract.
2C:21–35.   Sale or transfer of a public utility employee identification badge; criminal penalties for fraudulently or falsely exhibiting, displaying or uttering badge documents.
2C:21–36.   Purchase of used secondhand jewelry; requirements for resale; exclusions.
2C:21–37.   Duty of purchaser purchasing with the intent of reselling jewelry to certain businesses.
2C:21–38.   Presumption of knowledge or belief.
2C:21–39.   Duty of purchaser to report suspicious circumstances.
2C:21–40.   Immunity from civil liability.
2C:21–41.   Rules and regulations.

2C:21–1. Forgery and related offenses

a. Forgery. A person is guilty of forgery if, with purpose to defraud or injure anyone, or with knowledge that he is facilitating a fraud or injury to be perpetrated by anyone, the actor:

(1) Alters or changes any writing of another without his authorization;

(2) Makes, completes, executes, authenticates, issues or transfers any writing so that it purports to be the act of another who did not authorize that act or of a fictitious person, or to have been executed at a time or place or in a numbered sequence other than was in fact the case, or to be a copy of an original when no such original existed; or

(3) Utters any writing which he knows to be forged in a manner specified in paragraph (1) or (2).

"Writing" includes printing or any other method of recording information, money, coins, tokens, stamps, seals, credit cards, badges, trademarks, access devices, and other symbols of value, right, privilege, or identification, including retail sales receipts, universal product code (UPC) labels and checks. This section shall apply without limitation to forged, copied or imitated checks.

As used in this section, "information" includes, but is not limited to, personal identifying information as defined in subsection v. of N.J.S.2C:20–1.

b. Grading of forgery. Forgery is a crime of the third degree if the writing is or purports to be part of an issue of money, securities, postage or revenue stamps, or other instruments, certificates or licenses issued by the government, New Jersey Prescription Blanks as referred to in R.S.45:14–14, or part of an issue of stock, bonds or other instruments representing interest in or claims against any property or enterprise, personal identifying information or an access device. Forgery is a crime of the third degree if the writing is or purports to be a check. Forgery is a crime of the third degree if the writing is or purports to be 15 or more forged or altered retail sales receipts or universal product code labels.

Otherwise forgery is a crime of the fourth degree.

c. Possession of forgery devices. A person is guilty of possession of forgery devices, a crime of the third degree, when with purpose to use, or to aid or permit another to use the same for purposes of forging written instruments, including access devices and personal identifying information, he makes or possesses any device, apparatus, equipment, computer, computer equipment, computer software or article specially designed or adapted to such use.

L.1978, c. 95, § 2C:21–1, eff. Sept. 1, 1979. Amended by L.1981, c. 290, § 20, eff. Sept. 24, 1981; L.1996, c. 154, § 10, eff. Jan. 6, 1997; L.1997, c. 6, § 5, eff. Jan. 24, 1997; L.2001, c. 110, § 1, eff. June 21, 2001; L.2002, c. 85, § 2, eff. Oct. 16, 2002.

2C:21–2. Criminal simulation

A person commits a crime of the fourth degree if, with purpose to defraud anyone or with knowledge that he is facilitating a fraud to be perpetrated by anyone, he makes, alters or utters any object so that it appears to have value because of antiquity, rarity, source, or authorship which it does not possess.

L.1978, c. 95, § 2C:21–2, eff. Sept. 1, 1979.

2C:21–2.1. Driver's license, birth certificate or other document issued by governmental agency to verify identity or age; simulation

a. A person who knowingly sells, offers or exposes for sale, or otherwise transfers, or possesses with the intent to sell, offer or expose for sale, or otherwise transfer, a document, printed form or other writing which falsely purports to be a driver's license, birth certificate or other document issued by a governmental agency and which could be used as a means of verifying a person's identity or age or any other personal identifying information is guilty of a crime of the second degree.

b. A person who knowingly makes, or possesses devices or materials to make, a document or other writing which falsely purports to be a driver's license, birth certificate or other document issued by a governmental agency and which could be used as a means of verifying a person's identity or age or any other personal identifying information is guilty of a crime of the second degree.

c. A person who knowingly exhibits, displays or utters a document or other writing which falsely purports to be a driver's license, birth certificate or other document issued by a governmental agency and which could be used as a means of verifying a person's identity or age or any other personal identifying information is guilty of a crime of the third degree. A violation of N.J.S.2C:28–7, constituting a disorderly persons offense, section 1 of P.L.1979, c. 264 (C.2C:33–15), R.S.33:1–81 or section 6 of P.L.1968, c. 313 (C.33:1–81.7) in a case where the person uses the personal identifying information of another to illegally purchase an alcoholic beverage or for using the personal identifying information of another to misrepresent his age for the purpose of obtaining tobacco or other consumer product denied to persons under 18 years of age shall not constitute an offense under this subsection if the actor received only that benefit or service and did not perpetrate or attempt to perpetrate any additional injury or fraud on another.

d. A person who knowingly possesses a document or other writing which falsely purports to be a driver's license, birth certificate or other document issued by a governmental agency and which could be used as a means of verifying a person's identity or age or any other personal identifying information is guilty of a crime of the fourth degree. A violation of N.J.S.2C:28–7, constituting a disorderly persons offense, section 1 of P.L.1979, c. 264 (C.2C:33–15), R.S.33:1–81 or section 6 of P.L.1968, c. 313 (C.33:1–81. 7) in a case where the person uses the personal identifying information of another to illegally purchase an alcoholic beverage or for using the personal identifying information of another to misrepresent his age for the purpose of obtaining tobacco or other consumer product denied to persons under 18 years of age shall not constitute an offense under this subsection if the actor received only that benefit or service and did not perpetrate or attempt to perpetrate any additional injury or fraud on another.

e. In addition to any other disposition authorized by this Title, the provisions of section 24 of P.L.1982, c. 77 (C.2A:4A–43), or any other statute indicating the dispositions that may be ordered for an adjudication of delinquency, and, notwithstanding the provisions of subsection c. of N.J.S.2C:43–2, every person convicted of or adjudicated delinquent for a violation of any offense defined in this section shall forthwith forfeit his right to operate a motor vehicle over the highways of this State for a period to be fixed by the court at not less than six months or more than two years which shall commence on the day the sentence is imposed. In the case of any person who at the time of the imposition of the sentence is less than 17 years of age, the period of the suspension of driving privileges authorized herein, including a suspension of the privilege of operating a motorized bicycle, shall commence on the day the sentence is imposed and shall run for a period as fixed by the court of not less than six months or more than two years after the day the person reaches the age of 17 years. If the driving privilege of any person is under revocation, suspension, or postponement for a violation of any provision of this Title or Title 39 of the Revised Statutes at the time of any conviction or adjudication of delinquency for a violation of any offense defined in this chapter or chapter 36 of this Title, the revocation, suspension, or postponement period imposed herein shall commence as of the date of termination of the existing revocation, suspension or postponement.

The court before whom any person is convicted of or adjudicated delinquent for a violation of any offense defined in this section shall collect forthwith the New Jersey driver's license or licenses of that person and forward the license or licenses to the Chief Administrator of the New Jersey Motor Vehicle Commission along with a report indicating the first and last day of the suspension or postponement period imposed by the court pursuant to this section. If the court is for any reason unable to collect the license or licenses of the person, the court shall cause a report of the conviction or adjudication of delinquency to be filed with the director. The report shall include the complete name, address, date of birth, eye color and sex of the person and shall indicate the first and last day of the suspension or postponement period imposed by the court pursuant to this section. The court shall inform the person orally and in writing that if the person is convicted of personally operating a motor vehicle during the period of license suspension or postponement imposed pursuant to this section, the person shall, upon conviction, be subject to the penalties set forth in R.S.39:3–40. A person shall be required to acknowledge receipt of the written notice in writing. Failure to receive a written notice or failure to acknowledge in writing the receipt of a written notice shall not be a defense to a subsequent

charge of a violation of R.S.39:3–40. If the person is the holder of a driver's license from another jurisdiction, the court shall not collect the license, but shall notify forthwith the director who shall notify the appropriate officials in that licensing jurisdiction. The court shall, however, in accordance with the provisions of this section, revoke the person's non-resident driving privileges in this State.

In addition to any other condition imposed, a court, in its discretion, may suspend, revoke or postpone the driving privileges of a person admitted to supervisory treatment under N.J.S.2C:36A–1 or N.J.S.2C:43–12 without a plea of guilty or finding of guilt.

L.1983, c. 565, § 1, eff. Jan. 17, 1984. Amended by L.1999, c. 28, § 14, eff. Feb. 25, 1999; L.2002, c. 85, § 3, eff. Oct. 16, 2002; L.2003, c. 184, § 2, eff. Sept. 25, 2003; L.2005, c. 224, § 1, eff. Sept. 22, 2005.

2C:21–2.2. Law enforcement agency badges; unauthorized sale, purchase, gift, or loan

It shall be a disorderly persons offense to:

a. Sell a law enforcement agency badge, the prescribed form of which is presently in use or has been in use in New Jersey during any of the five years preceding the sale, to a person other than a member of a law enforcement agency who presents a letter authorizing the purchase, signed by the commanding officer of that law enforcement agency;

b. Purchase a law enforcement agency badge, described in subsection a. of this section, unless the purchaser is a member of a law enforcement agency who presents a letter authorizing the purchase, signed by the commanding officer of that law enforcement agency; or

c. Give or lend a law enforcement agency badge described in subsection a. of this section, unless the person to whom a badge was given or loaned is a member of a law enforcement agency who presents a letter authorizing the transfer, signed by the commanding officer of that law enforcement agency.

L.1987, c. 29, § 1, eff. Jan. 27, 1987.

2C:21–2.3. Motor vehicle insurance identification card; production or sale

a. A person who knowingly produces, sells, offers or exposes for sale a document, printed form or other writing which simulates a motor vehicle insurance identification card is guilty of a crime of the third degree. In addition to any other penalty imposed, a person convicted under this section shall be ordered by the court to perform community service for a period of 30 days.

b. A person who exhibits or displays to a law enforcement officer or a person conducting a motor vehicle inspection pursuant to chapter 8 of Title 39 of the Revised Statutes a falsely made, forged, altered, counterfeited or simulated motor vehicle insurance identification card, knowing that the insurance identification card was falsely made, forged, altered, counterfeited or simulated, commits a crime of the fourth degree.

c. A person who possesses a falsely made, forged, altered, counterfeited or simulated motor vehicle insurance identification card, knowing that the insurance identification card was falsely made, forged, altered, counterfeited or simulated, commits a disorderly persons offense.

L.1997, c. 385, § 2, eff. March 1, 1998. Amended by L.2001, c. 124, § 1, eff. June 26, 2001.

2C:21-2.4. Possession of forged or altered receipts, universal product code labels, or checks

a. Except as provided in subsection b. of this section, any person who knowingly possesses a forged or altered retail sales receipt, universal product code (UPC) label or check for the purpose of defrauding a retail merchant shall be guilty of a disorderly persons offense.

b. Any person who knowingly possesses 15 or more forged or altered retail sales receipts, universal product code labels or checks for the purpose of defrauding a retail merchant shall be guilty of a crime of the fourth degree.

L.2001, c. 110, § 2, eff. June 21, 2001.

2C:21–3. Frauds relating to public records and recordable instruments

a. Fraudulent destruction, removal or concealment of recordable instruments. A person commits a crime of the third degree if, with purpose to deceive or injure anyone, he destroys, removes or conceals any will, deed, mortgage, security instrument or other writing for which the law provides public recording.

b. Offering a false instrument for filing. A person is guilty of a disorderly persons offense when, knowing that a written instrument contains a false statement or false information, he offers or presents it to a public office or public servant with knowledge or belief that it will be filed with, registered or recorded in or otherwise become a part of the records of such public office or public servant.

L.1978, c. 95, § 2C:21–3, eff. Sept. 1, 1979.

2C:21–4. Falsifying or tampering with records

a. Except as provided in subsection b. of this section, a person commits a crime of the fourth degree if he falsifies, destroys, removes, conceals any writing or record, or utters any writing or record knowing that it contains a false statement or information, with purpose to deceive or injure anyone or to conceal any wrongdoing.

b. Issuing a false financial statement. A person is guilty of issuing a false financial statement, a crime of the third degree, when, with purpose to deceive or

injure anyone or to conceal any wrongdoing; he by oath or affirmation:

(1) Knowingly makes or utters a written instrument which purports to describe the financial condition or ability to pay of some person and which is inaccurate in some substantial respect; or

(2) Represents in writing that a written instrument purporting to describe a person's financial condition or ability to pay as of a prior date is accurate with respect to such person's current financial condition or ability to pay, whereas, he knows it is substantially inaccurate in that respect.

L.1978, c. 95, § 2C:21–4, eff. Sept. 1, 1979. Amended by L.1981, c. 290, § 21, eff. Sept. 24, 1981.

2C:21–4.1. Purposeful destruction, alteration or falsification of record relating to care of medical or surgical or podiatric patient in order to deceive or mislead

A person is guilty of a crime of the fourth degree if he purposefully destroys, alters or falsifies any record relating to the care of a medical or surgical or podiatric patient in order to deceive or mislead any person as to information, including, but not limited to, a diagnosis, test, medication, treatment or medical or psychological history, concerning the patient.

L.1989, c. 300, § 15, eff. Jan. 12, 1990.

2C:21–4.2. Definitions relating to health care claims fraud

As used in this act:

"Health care claims fraud" means making, or causing to be made, a false, fictitious, fraudulent, or misleading statement of material fact in, or omitting a material fact from, or causing a material fact to be omitted from, any record, bill, claim or other document, in writing, electronically or in any other form, that a person attempts to submit, submits, causes to be submitted, or attempts to cause to be submitted for payment or reimbursement for health care services.

"Practitioner" means a person licensed in this State to practice medicine and surgery, chiropractic, podiatric medicine, dentistry, optometry, psychology, pharmacy, nursing, physical therapy, or law; any other person licensed, registered or certified by any State agency to practice a profession or occupation in the State of New Jersey or any person similarly licensed, registered, or certified in another jurisdiction.

L.1997, c. 353, § 2, eff. Jan. 15, 1998. Amended by L.2005, c. 259, § 20, eff. Jan. 4, 2006.

2C:21–4.3. Health care claims fraud; elements; penalties; evidence

a. A practitioner is guilty of a crime of the second degree if that person knowingly commits health care claims fraud in the course of providing professional services. In addition to all other criminal penalties allowed by law, a person convicted under this subsection may be subject to a fine of up to five times the pecuniary benefit obtained or sought to be obtained.

b. A practitioner is guilty of a crime of the third degree if that person recklessly commits health care claims fraud in the course of providing professional services. In addition to all other criminal penalties allowed by law, a person convicted under this subsection may be subject to a fine of up to five times the pecuniary benefit obtained or sought to be obtained.

c. A person, who is not a practitioner subject to the provisions of subsection a. or b. of this section, is guilty of a crime of the third degree if that person knowingly commits health care claims fraud. A person, who is not a practitioner subject to the provisions of subsection a. or b. of this section, is guilty of a crime of the second degree if that person knowingly commits five or more acts of health care claims fraud and the aggregate pecuniary benefit obtained or sought to be obtained is at least $1,000. In addition to all other criminal penalties allowed by law, a person convicted under this subsection may be subject to a fine of up to five times the pecuniary benefit obtained or sought to be obtained.

d. A person, who is not a practitioner subject to the provisions of subsection a. or b. of this section, is guilty of a crime of the fourth degree if that person recklessly commits health care claims fraud. In addition to all other criminal penalties allowed by law, a person convicted under this subsection may be subject to a fine of up to five times the pecuniary benefit obtained or sought to be obtained.

e. Each act of health care claims fraud shall constitute an additional, separate and distinct offense, except that five or more separate acts may be aggregated for the purpose of establishing liability pursuant to subsection c. of this section. Multiple acts of health care claims fraud which are contained in a single record, bill, claim, application, payment, affidavit, certification or other document shall each constitute an additional, separate and distinct offense for purposes of this section.

f. (1) The falsity, fictitiousness, fraudulence or misleading nature of a statement may be inferred by the trier of fact in the case of a practitioner who attempts to submit, submits, causes to be submitted, or attempts to cause to be submitted, any record, bill, claim or other document for treatment or procedure without the practitioner, or an associate of the practitioner, having performed an assessment of the physical or mental condition of the patient or client necessary to determine the appropriate course of treatment.

(2) The falsity, fictitiousness, fraudulence or misleading nature of a statement may be inferred by the trier of fact in the case of a person who attempts to submit, submits, causes to be submitted, or attempts to cause to be submitted any record, bill, claim or other document for more treatments or procedures than can be per-

formed during the time in which the treatments or procedures were represented to have been performed.

(3) Proof that a practitioner has signed or initialed a record, bill, claim or other document gives rise to an inference that the practitioner has read and reviewed that record, bill, claim or other document.

g. In order to promote the uniform enforcement of this act, the Attorney General shall develop health care claims fraud prosecution guidelines and disseminate them to the county prosecutors within 120 days of the effective date of this act.

h. For the purposes of this section, a person acts recklessly with respect to a material element of an offense when he consciously disregards a substantial and unjustifiable risk that the material element exists or will result from his conduct. The risk must be of such a nature and degree that, considering the nature and purpose of the actor's conduct and the circumstances known to him, its disregard involves a gross deviation from the standard of conduct that a reasonable person would observe in the actor's situation.

i. (1) Nothing in this act shall preclude an indictment and conviction for any other offense defined by the laws of this State.

(2) Nothing in this act shall preclude an assignment judge from dismissing a prosecution of health care claims fraud if the assignment judge determines, pursuant to N.J.S.2C:2–11, the conduct charged to be a de minimis infraction.

L.1997, c. 353, § 3, eff. Jan. 15, 1998. Amended by L.2003, c. 89, § 75, eff. June 9, 2003.

2C:21–4.4. Legislative findings

With respect to sections 72 through 74 of P.L.2003, c.89 (C.17:33A–32 through C.17:33A–34),[1] the Legislature finds and declares:

a. Insurance fraud is inimical to public safety, welfare and order within the State of New Jersey. Insurance fraud is pervasive and expensive, costing consumers and businesses millions of dollars in direct and indirect losses each year. Insurance fraud increases insurance premiums, to the detriment of individual policyholders, small businesses, large corporations and governmental entities. All New Jerseyans ultimately bear the societal burdens and costs caused by those who commit insurance fraud.

b. The problem of insurance fraud must be confronted aggressively by facilitating the detection, investigation and prosecution of such misconduct, as well as by reducing its occurrence and achieving deterrence through the implementation of measures that more precisely target specific conduct constituting insurance fraud.

c. To enable more efficient prosecution of criminally culpable persons who knowingly commit or assist or conspire with others in committing fraud against insurance companies, it is necessary to establish a crime of "insurance fraud" to directly and comprehensively criminalize this type of harmful conduct, with substantial criminal penalties to punish wrongdoers and to appropriately deter others from such illicit activity.

d. In addition to criminal penalties, in order to maintain the public trust and ensure the integrity of professional licensees and certificate-holders who by virtue of their professions are involved in insurance transactions, it is appropriate to provide civil remedial provisions governing license or certificate forfeiture and suspension tailored to this new crime of insurance fraud and other criminal insurance-related activities.

e. To enhance the State's ability to detect insurance fraud, which will lead to more productive investigations and, ultimately, more successful criminal prosecutions, it is appropriate to provide members of the public with significant incentives to come forward when they may have reasonable suspicions or knowledge of a person or persons committing insurance fraud. The establishment of an Insurance Fraud Detection Reward Program will enable the Insurance Fraud Prosecutor to obtain information which may lead to the arrest, prosecution and conviction of persons or entities who have committed insurance-related fraud.

L.2003, c. 89, § 71, eff. June 9, 2003.

[1]Reallocated at N.J.S.A. 2C:21–4.5 to 2C:21–4.7.

Historical and Statutory Notes

L.2003, c. 89, § 86, approved June 9, 2003, provides:

"This act shall take effect immediately, except that section 38 [17:33B–25] shall take effect on January 1, 2004, section 45 [39:6A–3.3] shall take effect on the earlier of the 120th day next following enactment or the adoption of regulations by the Commissioner of Banking and Insurance to implement that section, section 65 [17:29A–39] shall take effect upon the adoption of regulations by the Commissioner of Banking and Insurance, sections 83 [17:17–10] and 84 [17:33B–30] shall take effect on January 1, 2007, and section 79 [39:3–29.1a] shall take effect on 365th day next following enactment."

2C:21–4.5. Definitions

As used in sections 73 and 74 of P.L.2003, c.89 (C.17:33A–33; 17:33A–34),[1] unless the context otherwise requires, the following words and terms shall have the following meanings:

"Insurance company" means any person, company, corporation, unincorporated association, partnership, professional corporation, agency of government and any other entity authorized or permitted to do business in New Jersey, subject to regulation by the State, or incorporated or organized under the laws of any other state of the United States or of any foreign nation or of any province or territory thereof, to indemnify another against loss, damage, risk or liability arising from a contingent or unknown event. "Insurance company" includes, but is not limited to, an insurance company as that term is defined in section 3 of P.L.1983, c. 320 (C.17:33A–3), self-insurer, re-insurer, reciprocal exchange, inter-insurer, hospital, medical or health service corporation, health maintenance organization, surety,

assigned risk plan, joint insurance fund, and any other entity legally engaged in the business of insurance as authorized or permitted by the State of New Jersey, including but not limited to any such entity incorporated or organized under the laws of any other state of the United States or of any foreign nation or of any province or territory thereof.

"Insurance policy" means the instrument, in writing, electronically or in any other form, in which are set forth the terms of any certificate of insurance, binder of coverage, contract of insurance or contract of re-insurance, issued by an insurance company, including, but not limited to, a State-assigned risk plan, plan of indemnity protection provided by or on behalf of a joint insurance fund or benefit plan, motor club service plan, or guaranty bond, surety bond, cash bond or any other alternative to insurance authorized or permitted by the State of New Jersey.

"Insurance transaction" means a transaction by, between, or among (1) an insurance company and (2) an insured, claimant, applicant for insurance, public adjuster, insurance professional, practitioner as defined by section 2 of P.L.1997, c. 353 (C.2C:21–4.2), attorney, or any person who acts on behalf of any of the foregoing for the purpose of obtaining insurance or reinsurance, calculating insurance premiums, submitting a claim, negotiating or adjusting a claim, or otherwise obtaining insurance, self insurance, or reinsurance, or obtaining the benefits or annuities thereof or therefrom.

"Premium finance transaction" means a transaction involving or related to insurance premium financing which is subject to the "Insurance Premium Finance Company Act," P.L.1968, c. 221 (C.17:16D–1 et seq.).

L.2003, c. 89, § 72, eff. June 9, 2003.

[1]Reallocated at N.J.S.A. 2C:21–4.6 and 2C:21–4.7.

Historical and Statutory Notes

L.2003, c. 89, § 86, approved June 9, 2003, provides:

"This act shall take effect immediately, except that section 38 [17:33B–25] shall take effect on January 1, 2004, section 45 [39:6A–3.3] shall take effect on the earlier of the 120th day next following enactment or the adoption of regulations by the Commissioner of Banking and Insurance to implement that section, section 65 [17:29A–39] shall take effect upon the adoption of regulations by the Commissioner of Banking and Insurance, sections 83 [17:17–10] and 84 [17:33B–30] shall take effect on January 1, 2007, and section 79 [39:3–29.1a] shall take effect on 365th day next following enactment."

2C:21–4.6. Insurance fraud

a. A person is guilty of the crime of insurance fraud if that person knowingly makes, or causes to be made, a false, fictitious, fraudulent, or misleading statement of material fact in, or omits a material fact from, or causes a material fact to be omitted from, any record, bill, claim or other document, in writing, electronically, orally or in any other form, that a person attempts to submit, submits, causes to be submitted, or attempts to cause to be submitted as part of, in support of or opposition to or in connection with: (1) a claim for payment, reimbursement or other benefit pursuant to an insurance policy, or from an insurance company or the "Unsatisfied Claim and Judgment Fund Law," P.L.1952, c. 174 (C.39:6–61 et seq.); (2) an application to obtain or renew an insurance policy; (3) any payment made or to be made in accordance with the terms of an insurance policy or premium finance transaction; or (4) an affidavit, certification, record or other document used in any insurance or premium finance transaction.

b. Insurance fraud constitutes a crime of the second degree if the person knowingly commits five or more acts of insurance fraud, including acts of health care claims fraud pursuant to section 2 of P.L.1997, c. 353 (C.2C:21–4.2) and if the aggregate value of property, services or other benefit wrongfully obtained or sought to be obtained is at least $1,000. Otherwise, insurance fraud is a crime of the third degree. Each act of insurance fraud shall constitute an additional, separate and distinct offense, except that five or more separate acts may be aggregated for the purpose of establishing liability pursuant to this subsection. Multiple acts of insurance fraud which are contained in a single record, bill, claim, application, payment, affidavit, certification or other document shall each constitute an additional, separate and distinct offense for purposes of this subsection.

c. Proof that a person has signed or initialed an application, bill, claim, affidavit, certification, record or other document may give rise to an inference that the person has read and reviewed the application, bill, claim, affidavit, certification, record or other document.

d. In order to promote the uniform enforcement of this act, the Attorney General shall develop insurance fraud prosecution guidelines and disseminate them to county prosecutors within 180 days of the effective date of this act.

e. Nothing in this act shall preclude an indictment and conviction for any other offense defined by the laws of this State.

f. Nothing in this act shall preclude an assignment judge from dismissing a prosecution of insurance fraud if the assignment judge determines, pursuant to N.J.S.2C:2–11, the conduct charged to be a de minimis infraction.

L.2003, c. 89, § 73, eff. June 9, 2003.

2C:21–4.7. Insurance fraud detection reward program

a. There is established within the Office of the Insurance Fraud Prosecutor an Insurance Fraud Detection Reward Program, to be funded from surcharges imposed pursuant to section 53 of P.L.2002, c. 34 (C.17:33A–5.1) and supplemented as necessary and appropriate by amounts budgeted for the operation of the office.

b. A member of the public who has knowledge of or who believes that an act of health care claims fraud, insurance fraud or any other criminal offense involving or related to an insurance transaction is being or has

been committed may provide the Insurance Fraud Prosecutor with a report or information pertinent to that knowledge or belief and may provide additional information that the Insurance Fraud Prosecutor requests.

c. The Insurance Fraud Prosecutor shall maintain a 24–hour toll-free insurance fraud hotline to receive information from members of the public who have knowledge of or who believe that an act of health care claims fraud, insurance fraud or any other criminal offense involving or related to an insurance transaction is being or has been committed.

d. The Attorney General, through the Insurance Fraud Prosecutor, is authorized to pay a reward of up to $25,000 to persons providing information leading to the arrest, prosecution and conviction of persons or entities who have committed health care claims fraud, insurance fraud or any other criminal offense related to an insurance transaction. Only a single reward amount may be paid by the Insurance Fraud Prosecutor for claims arising out of the same transaction or occurrence, regardless of the number of persons arrested, prosecuted and convicted and regardless of the number of persons submitting claims for the reward. The reward may be divided and disbursed among more than one person in amounts determined by the Insurance Fraud Prosecutor, in accordance with the provisions of this subsection. The decision of the Insurance Fraud Prosecutor as to the person or persons entitled to the reward shall be final unless the reward recipients shall disagree, in which event, the matter shall be referred to the Attorney General whose decision shall be final and shall not be subject to judicial review.

e. Any person acting in good faith who provides information in accordance with subsection b. of this section shall have immunity from any liability, civil or criminal, that might otherwise be incurred or imposed as a result of such act.

f. The Attorney General shall promulgate and adopt rules and regulations which set forth the reward program application and approval process, including the criteria against which claims shall be evaluated, the basis for determining specific reward amounts, and the manner of reward disbursement. Applications for rewards authorized by this section must be submitted in accordance with rules established by the Attorney General.

L.2003, c. 89, § 74, eff. June 9, 2003.

Historical and Statutory Notes

L.2003, c. 89, § 86, approved June 9, 2003, provides:

"This act shall take effect immediately, except that section 38 [17:33B–25] shall take effect on January 1, 2004, section 45 [39:6A–3.3] shall take effect on the earlier of the 120th day next following enactment or the adoption of regulations by the Commissioner of Banking and Insurance to implement that section, section 65 [17:29A–39] shall take effect upon the adoption of regulations by the Commissioner of Banking and Insurance, sections 83 [17:17–10] and 84 [17:33B–30] shall take effect on January 1, 2007, and section 79 [39:3–29.1a] shall take effect on 365th day next following enactment."

2C:21–4.8. Penalties for vehicle title fraud

a. A person who purposely or knowingly violates a provision of chapter 10 of Title 39 of the Revised Statutes, for which a specific penalty is not provided in that chapter or this section, shall be guilty of a crime of the fourth degree.

b. A person who purposely or knowingly commits the following violations of chapter 10 of Title 39 of the Revised Statutes shall be guilty of a crime of the third degree:

(1) Makes a misrepresentation or false statement in any title papers or other papers submitted to the Chief Administrator of the New Jersey Motor Vehicle Commission in connection therewith;

(2) Purchases, receives or obtains a motor vehicle on a title paper in violation of chapter 10 of Title 39 of the Revised Statutes;

(3) Forges, changes or counterfeits a part of title papers;

(4) Misrepresents a number placed on a motor vehicle by the manufacturer, or in any other manner misrepresents the description of a motor vehicle; or

(5) Uses title papers on or for a wrong motor vehicle, with intent to evade or violate the requirements of chapter 10 of Title 39 of the Revised Statutes.

L.2003, c. 217, § 2, eff. Jan. 9, 2004.

2C:21–5. Bad checks

A person who issues or passes a check or similar sight order for the payment of money, knowing that it will not be honored by the drawee, commits an offense as provided for in subsection c. of this section. For the purposes of this section as well as in any prosecution for theft committed by means of a bad check, an issuer is presumed to know that the check or money order (other than a post-dated check or order) would not be paid, if:

a. The issuer had no account with the drawee at the time the check or order was issued; or

b. Payment was refused by the drawee for lack of funds, or due to a closed account, after a deposit by the payee into a bank for collection or after presentation to the drawee within 46 days after issue, and the issuer failed to make good within 10 days after receiving notice of that refusal or after notice has been sent to the issuer's last known address. Notice of refusal may be given to the issuer orally or in writing in any reasonable manner by any person.

c. An offense under this section is:

(1) a crime of the second degree if the check or money order is $75,000.00 or more;

(2) a crime of the third degree if the check or money order is $1,000.00 or more but is less than $75,000.00;

(3) a crime of the fourth degree if the check or money order is $200.00 or more but is less than $1,000.00;

(4) a disorderly persons offense if the check or money order is less than $200.00.

L.1978, c. 95, § 2C:21–5, eff. Sept. 1, 1979. Amended by L.1981, c. 290, § 22, eff. Sept. 24, 1981; L.2002, c. 65, § 1, eff. Aug. 14, 2002.

2C:21–6. Credit cards

a. **Definitions.** As used in this section:

(1) "Cardholder" means the person or organization named on the face of a credit card to whom or for whose benefit the credit card is issued by an issuer.

(2) "Credit card" means any tangible or intangible instrument or device issued with or without fee by an issuer that can be used, alone or in connection with another means of account access, in obtaining money, goods, services or anything else of value on credit, including credit cards, credit plates, account numbers, or any other means of account access.

(3) "Expired credit card" means a credit card which is no longer valid because the term shown either on it or on documentation provided to the cardholder by the issuer has elapsed.

(4) "Issuer" means the business organization or financial institution which issues a credit card or its duly authorized agent.

(5) "Receives" or "receiving" means acquiring possession or control or accepting a credit card as security for a loan.

(6) "Revoked credit card" means a credit card which is no longer valid because permission to use it has been suspended or terminated by the issuer.

b. **False statements made in procuring issuance of credit card.** A person who makes or causes to be made, either directly or indirectly, any false statement in writing, knowing it to be false and with intent that it be relied on, respecting his identity or that of any other person, firm or corporation, or his financial condition or that of any other person, firm or corporation, for the purpose of procuring the issuance of a credit card is guilty of a crime of the fourth degree.

c. **Credit card theft.**

(1) A person who takes or obtains a credit card from the person, possession, custody or control of another without the cardholder's consent or who, with knowledge that it has been so taken, receives the credit card with intent to use it or to sell it, or to transfer it to a person other than the issuer or the cardholder is guilty of a crime of the fourth degree. Taking a credit card without consent includes obtaining it by any conduct defined and prescribed in Chapter 20 of this title, Theft and Related Offenses.

A person who has in his possession or under his control (a) credit cards issued in the names of two or more other persons or, (b) two or more stolen credit cards is presumed to have violated this paragraph.

(2) A person who receives a credit card that he knows to have been lost, mislaid, or delivered under a mistake as to the identity or address of the cardholder, and who retains possession with intent to use it or to sell it or to transfer it to a person other than the issuer or the cardholder is guilty of a crime of the fourth degree.

(3) A person other than the issuer who sells a credit card or a person who buys a credit card from a person other than the issuer is guilty of a crime of the fourth degree.

(4) A person who, with intent to defraud the issuer, a person or organization providing money, goods, services or anything else of value, or any other person, obtains control over a credit card as security for debt is guilty of a crime of the fourth degree.

(5) A person who, with intent to defraud a purported issuer, a person or organization providing money, goods, services or anything else of value, or any other person, falsely makes or falsely embosses a purported credit card or utters such a credit card is guilty of a third degree offense. A person other than the purported issuer who possesses two or more credit cards which are falsely made or falsely embossed is presumed to have violated this paragraph. A person "falsely makes" a credit card when he makes or draws, in whole or in part, a device or instrument which purports to be the credit card of a named issuer but which is not such a credit card because the issuer did not authorize the making or drawing, or alters a credit card which was validly issued. A person "falsely embosses" a credit card when, without the authorization of the named issuer, he completes a credit card by adding any of the matter, other than the signature of the cardholder, which an issuer requires to appear on the credit card before it can be used by a cardholder.

(6) A person other than the cardholder or a person authorized by him who, with intent to defraud the issuer, or a person or organization providing money, goods, services or anything else of value, or any other person, signs a credit card, is guilty of a crime of the fourth degree. A person who possesses two or more credit cards which are so signed is presumed to have violated this paragraph.

d. Intent of cardholder to defraud; penalties; knowledge of revocation. A person, who, with intent to defraud the issuer, a person or organization providing money, goods, services or anything else of value, or any other person, (1) uses for the purpose of obtaining money, goods, services or anything else of value a credit card obtained or retained in violation of subsection c. of this section or a credit card which he knows is forged, expired or revoked, or (2) obtains money, goods, services or anything else of value by representing without the consent of the cardholder that he is the holder of a specified card or by representing that he is the holder of a card and such card has not in fact been

issued, is guilty of a crime of the third degree. Knowledge of revocation shall be presumed to have been received by a cardholder four days after it has been mailed to him at the address set forth on the credit card or at his last known address by registered or certified mail, return receipt requested, and, if the address is more than 500 miles from the place of mailing, by air mail. If the address is located outside the United States, Puerto Rico, the Virgin Islands, the Canal Zone and Canada, notice shall be presumed to have been received 10 days after mailing by registered or certified mail.

e. Intent to defraud by person authorized to furnish money, goods, or services; penalties.

(1) A person who is authorized by an issuer to furnish money, goods, services or anything else of value upon presentation of a credit card by the cardholder, or any agent or employees of such person, who, with intent to defraud the issuer or the cardholder, furnishes money, goods, services or anything else of value upon presentation of a credit card obtained or retained in violation of subsection c. of this section or a credit card which he knows is forged, expired or revoked violates this paragraph and is guilty of a crime of the third degree.

(2) A person who is authorized by an issuer to furnish money, goods, services or anything else of value upon presentation of a credit card by the cardholder, fails to furnish money, goods, services or anything else of value which he represents in writing to the issuer that he has furnished is guilty of a crime of the fourth degree.

f. Incomplete credit cards; intent to complete without consent. A person other than the cardholder possessing two or more incomplete credit cards, with intent to complete them without the consent of the issuer or a person possessing, with knowledge of its character, machinery, plates or any other contrivance designed to reproduce instruments purporting to be the credit cards of an issuer who has not consented to the preparation of such credit cards, is guilty of a crime of the third degree. A credit card is "incomplete" if part of the matter other than the signature of the cardholder, which an issuer requires to appear on the credit card, before it can be used by a cardholder, has not yet been stamped, embossed, imprinted or written on it.

g. Receiving anything of value knowing or believing that it was obtained in violation of subsection d. of N.J.S. 2C:21–6. A person who receives money, goods, services or anything else of value obtained in violation of subsection d. of this section, knowing or believing that it was so obtained is guilty of a crime of the fourth degree. A person who obtains, at a discount price a ticket issued by an airline, railroad, steamship or other transportation company which was acquired in violation of subsection d. of this section without reasonable inquiry to ascertain that the person from whom it was obtained had a legal right to possess it shall be presumed to know that such ticket was acquired under circumstances constituting a violation of subsection d. of this section.

h. Fraudulent use of credit cards.

A person who knowingly uses any counterfeit, fictitious, altered, forged, lost, stolen or fraudulently obtained credit card to obtain money, goods or services, or anything else of value; or who, with unlawful or fraudulent intent, furnishes, acquires, or uses any actual or fictitious credit card, whether alone or together with names of credit cardholders, or other information pertaining to a credit card account in any form, is guilty of a crime of the third degree.

L.1978, c. 95, § 2C:21–6, eff. Sept. 1, 1979. Amended by L.1979, c. 178, § 36, eff. Sept. 1, 1979; L.1984, c. 119, § 1, eff. Aug. 8, 1984; L.1991, c. 122, § 1, eff. April 25, 1991.

2C:21–6.1. Payment cards; fraudulent use of scanning and other electronic devices; definitions

a. Definitions. As used in this section:

(1) "Merchant" means any owner or operator of any store or other retail mercantile establishment, or any agent, servant, employee, lessee, consignee, officer, director, franchisee or independent contractor of such owner or proprietor.

(2) "Payment card" means a credit card, charge card, debit card or any other card that is issued to an authorized card user and that allows the user to obtain, purchase, or receive goods, services, money or anything of value from a merchant.

(3) "Reencoder" means an electronic device that places encoded information from the magnetic strip or stripe of a payment card onto the magnetic strip or stripe of a different payment card or any electronic medium that allows a transaction to occur.

(4) "Scanning device" means a scanner, skimmer, reader or any other electronic device that is used to access, read, scan, obtain, memorize or store, temporarily or permanently, information encoded on the magnetic strip or stripe of a payment card.

b. It shall be a crime of the third degree for a person, with the intent to defraud an authorized user of a payment card, the issuer of the authorized user's payment card or a merchant, to use:

(1) a scanning device to access, read, obtain, memorize or store, temporarily or permanently, information encoded on the magnetic strip or stripe of a payment card, without the permission of the authorized user of the payment card; or

(2) a reencoder to place information encoded on the magnetic strip or stripe of a payment card onto the magnetic strip or stripe of a different card or any electronic medium that allows a transaction to occur without the permission of the authorized user of the card from which the information is being reencoded.

c. It shall be a crime of the fourth degree for a person to knowingly possess with intent to commit a violation of paragraph (1) or (2) of subsection b. of this section any device, apparatus, equipment, software, article, material, good, property or supply that is specifically designed or adapted for use as or in a scanning device or reencoder.

L.2005, c. 225, § 1, eff. Sept. 22, 2005.

2C:21–7. Deceptive business practices

A person commits an offense if in the course of business he:

a. Uses or possesses for use a false weight or measure, or any other device for falsely determining or recording any quality or quantity;

b. Sells, offers or exposes for sale, or delivers less than the represented quantity of any commodity or service;

c. Takes or attempts to take more than the represented quantity of any commodity or service when as buyer he furnishes the weight or measure;

d. Sells, offers or exposes for sale adulterated or mislabeled commodities;

e. Makes a false or misleading statement in any advertisement addressed to the public or to a substantial segment thereof for the purpose of promoting the purchase or sale of property or services;

f. Deleted by amendment (P.L.1981, c. 290).

g. Deleted by amendment (P.L.1981, c. 290).

h. Makes a false or misleading written statement for the purpose of obtaining property or credit; or

i. Makes a false or misleading written statement for the purpose of promoting the sale of securities, or omits information required by law to be disclosed in written documents relating to securities.

The offense is a crime of the fourth degree if subsection h. or i. is violated. Otherwise it is a disorderly persons offense.

It is an affirmative defense to prosecution under this section if the defendant proves by a preponderance of the evidence that his conduct was not knowingly or recklessly deceptive.

"Adulterated" means varying from the standard of composition or quality prescribed by or pursuant to any statute providing criminal penalties for such variance, or set by established commercial usage. "Mislabeled" means varying from the standard of truth or disclosure in labeling prescribed by or pursuant to any statute providing criminal penalties for such variance, or set by established commercial usage.

L.1978, c. 95, § 2C:21–7, eff. Sept. 1, 1979. Amended by L.1979, c. 178, § 36A, eff. Sept. 1, 1979; L.1981, c. 290, § 23A, eff. Sept. 24, 1981.

2C:21–7.1. Repealed by L.1988, c. 154, § 4, eff. Feb. 12, 1989

2C:21–7.2. Definitions

As used in this act:

a. "Advertise" means engaging in promotional activities including, but not limited to, newspaper, radio and television advertising; the distribution of fliers and circulars; and the display of window and interior signs.

b. "Food," "food product," or "food commodity" means any food, food product or food preparation, whether raw or prepared for human consumption, and whether in a solid or liquid state, including, but not limited to, any meat, meat product or meat preparation; any milk, milk product or milk preparation; and any alcoholic or non-alcoholic beverage.

c. "Food commodity in package form" means a food commodity put up or packaged in any manner in advance of sale in units suitable for retail sale and which is not intended for consumption at the point of manufacture.

d. "Kosher" means prepared under and maintained in strict compliance with the laws and customs of the Orthodox Jewish religion and includes foods prepared for the festival of Passover and represented to be "kosher for Passover."

L.1988, c. 154, § 1, eff. Feb. 12, 1987.

2C:21–7.3. False representation by oral or written statement to make person believe non-kosher food or food product is kosher; presumptive evidence; defense

a. A false representation prohibited by this act shall include any oral or written statement that directly or indirectly tends to deceive or otherwise lead a reasonable individual to believe that a non-kosher food or food product is kosher.

b. The presence of any non-kosher food or food product in any place of business that advertises or represents itself in any manner as selling, offering for sale, preparing or serving kosher food or food products only, is presumptive evidence that the person in possession offers the same for sale in violation of this act.

c. It shall be a complete defense to a prosecution under this act that the defendant relied in good faith upon the representations of a slaughterhouse, manufacturer, processor, packer or distributor, or any person or organization which certifies or represents any food or food product at issue to be kosher, kosher for Passover, or as having been prepared under or sanctioned by Orthodox Jewish religious requirements.

L.1988, c. 154, § 2, eff. Feb. 12, 1989.

2C:21–7.4. Disorderly persons offenses

A person commits a disorderly persons offense if in the course of business he:

a. (1) Falsely represents any food sold, prepared, served or offered for sale to be kosher or kosher for Passover;

(2) Removes or destroys, or causes to be removed or destroyed, the original means of identification affixed to food commodities to indicate that same are kosher or kosher for Passover, except that this paragraph shall not be construed to prevent the removal of the identification if the commodity is offered for sale as non-kosher; or

(3) Sells, disposes of or has in his possession for the purpose of resale as kosher any food commodity to which a slaughterhouse plumba, mark, stamp, tag, brand, label or other means of identification has been fraudulently attached.

b. (1) Labels or identifies a food commodity in package form to be kosher or kosher for Passover or possesses such labels or means of identification, unless he is the manufacturer or packer of the food commodity in package form;

(2) Labels or identifies an article of food not in package form to be kosher or kosher for Passover or possesses such labels or other means of identification, unless he is the manufacturer of the article of food;

(3) Falsely labels any food commodity in package form as kosher or kosher for Passover by having or permitting to be inscribed on it, in any language, the words "kosher" or "kosher for Passover," "parve," "glatt," or any other words or symbols which would tend to deceive or otherwise lead a reasonable individual to believe that the commodity is kosher or kosher for Passover; or

(4) Labels any food commodity in package form by having or permitting to be inscribed on it the words "kosher-style," "kosher-type," "Jewish," or "Jewish-style," unless the product label also displays the word "non-kosher" in letters at least as large and in close proximity.

c. (1) Sells, offers for sale, prepares, or serves in or from the same place of business both unpackaged non-kosher food and unpackaged food he represents to be kosher unless he posts a window sign at the entrance of his establishment which states in block letters at least four inches in height: "Kosher and Non-Kosher Foods Sold Here," or "Kosher and Non-Kosher Foods Served Here," or a statement of similar import; or

(2) Employs any Hebrew word or symbol in any advertising of any food offered for sale or place of business in which food is prepared, whether for on-premise or off-premises consumption, unless the advertisement also sets forth in conjunction therewith and in English, the words "We Sell Kosher Food Only," "We Sell Both Kosher and Non-Kosher Foods," or words of similar import, in letters of at least the same size as the characters used in Hebrew. For the purpose of this paragraph, "Hebrew symbol" means any Hebrew word,

or letter, or any symbol, emblem, sign, insignia, or other mark that simulates a Hebrew word or letter.

d. (1) Displays for sale in the same show window or other location on or in his place of business, both unpackaged food represented to be kosher and unpackaged non-kosher food unless he:

(a) displays over the kosher and non-kosher food signs that read, in clearly visible block letters, "kosher food" and "non-kosher food," respectively, or, as to the display of meat alone, "kosher meat" and "non-kosher meat," respectively;

(b) separates the kosher food products from the non-kosher food products by keeping the products in separate display cabinets, or by segregating kosher items from non-kosher items by use of clearly visible dividers; and

(c) slices or otherwise prepares the kosher food products for sale with utensils used solely for kosher food items;

(2) Prepares or serves any food as kosher whether for consumption in his place of business or elsewhere if in the same place of business he also prepares or serves non-kosher food, unless he:

(a) uses and maintains separate and distinctly labeled or marked dishes and utensils for each type of food; and

(b) includes in clearly visible block letters the statement "Kosher and Non-Kosher Foods Prepared and Sold Here" in each menu or sign used or posted on the premise or distributed or advertised off the premises;

(3) Sells or has in his possession for the purpose of resale as kosher any food commodity not having affixed thereto the original slaughterhouse plumba, mark, stamp, tag, brand, label or other means of identification employed to indicate that the food commodity is kosher or kosher for Passover; or

(4) Sells or offers for sale, as kosher, any fresh meat or poultry that is identified as "soaked and salted," unless (a) the product has in fact been soaked and salted in a manner which makes it kosher; and (b) the product is marked "soaked and salted" on the package label or, if the product is not packaged, on a sign prominently displayed in conjunction with the product. For the purpose of this paragraph, "fresh meat or poultry" shall mean meat and poultry that has not been processed except for salting and soaking.

L.1988, c. 154, § 3, eff. Feb. 12, 1989.

2C:21–8. Misrepresentation of mileage of motor vehicle

A person commits a disorderly persons offense when he sells, exchanges, offers for sale or exchange or exposes for sale or exchange a used motor vehicle on which he has changed or disconnected the mileage registering instrument on the vehicle to show a lesser mileage reading than that actually recorded on the vehicle or on the instrument with purpose to misrepresent the mileage of the vehicle. This provision shall not prevent the servicing, repair or replacement of a mileage registering instrument which by reason of normal wear or through damage requires service, repair or replacement if the instrument is then set at zero or at the actual previously recorded mileage.

In addition to the penalty authorized for violation of this section, the Director of the Division of Motor Vehicles may, after notice and hearing, revoke the license of any motor vehicle dealer as defined in R.S. 39:1–1 so convicted.

L.1978, c. 95, § 2C:21–8, eff. Sept. 1, 1979.

2C:21–8.1. Definition; determination of degree of offense

a. As used in chapter 21, unless a different meaning plainly is required:

"Benefit derived" means the loss resulting from the offense or any gain or advantage to the actor, or coconspirators, or any person in whom the actor is interested, whichever is greater, whether loss, gain or advantage takes the form of money, property, commercial interests or anything else the primary significance of which is economic gain.

b. The benefit derived or resulting harm in violation of chapter 21 shall be determined by the trier of fact. The benefit derived or resulting harm pursuant to one scheme or course of conduct, whether in relation to the same person or several persons, may be aggregated in determining the degree of the offense.

L.1981, c. 290, § 23, eff. Sept. 24, 1981.

2C:21–9. Misconduct by corporate official

A person is guilty of a crime when:

a. Being a director of a corporation, he knowingly with purpose to defraud, concurs in any vote or act of the directors of such corporation, or any of them, which has the purpose of:

(1) Making a dividend except in the manner provided by law;

(2) Dividing, withdrawing or in any manner paying to any stockholder any part of the capital stock of the corporation except in the manner provided by law;

(3) Discounting or receiving any note or other evidence of debt in payment of an installment of capital stock actually called in and required to be paid, or with purpose of providing the means of making such payment;

(4) Receiving or discounting any note or other evidence of debt with purpose of enabling any stockholder to withdraw any part of the money paid in by him on his stock; or

(5) Applying any portion of the funds of such corporation, directly or indirectly, to the purchase of shares of its own stock, except in the manner provided by law; or

b. Being a director or officer of a corporation, he, with purpose to defraud:

(1) Issues, participates in issuing, or concurs in a vote to issue any increase of its capital stock beyond the amount of the capital stock thereof, duly authorized by or in pursuance of law; or

(2) Sells, or agrees to sell, or is directly interested in the sale of any share of stock of such corporation, or in any agreement to sell the same, unless at the time of such sale or agreement he is an actual owner of such share, provided that the foregoing shall not apply to a sale by or on behalf of an underwriter or dealer in connection with a bona fide public offering of shares of stock of such corporation.

c. He purposely or knowingly uses, controls or operates a corporation for the furtherance or promotion of any criminal object.

If the benefit derived from a violation of this section is $75,000.00, or more, the offender is guilty of a crime of the second degree. If the benefit derived exceeds $1,000.00, but is less than $75,000.00, the offender is guilty of a crime of the third degree. If the benefit derived is $1,000.00, or less, the offender is guilty of a crime of the fourth degree.

L.1978, c. 95, § 2C:21–9, eff. Sept. 1, 1979. Amended by L.1979, c. 178, § 37, eff. Sept. 1, 1979; L.1981, c. 290, § 24, eff. Sept. 24, 1981.

2C:21–10. Commercial bribery and breach of duty to act disinterestedly

a. A person commits a crime if he solicits, accepts or agrees to accept any benefit as consideration for knowingly violating or agreeing to violate a duty of fidelity to which he is subject as:

(1) An agent, partner or employee of another;

(2) A trustee, guardian, or other fiduciary;

(3) A lawyer, physician, accountant, appraiser, or other professional adviser or informant;

(4) An officer, director, manager or other participant in the direction of the affairs of an incorporated or unincorporated association;

(5) A labor official, including any duly appointed representative of a labor organization or any duly appointed trustee or representative of an employee welfare trust fund; or

(6) An arbitrator or other purportedly disinterested adjudicator or referee.

b. A person who holds himself out to the public as being engaged in the business of making disinterested selection, appraisal, or criticism of commodities, real properties or services commits a crime if he solicits, accepts or agrees to accept any benefit to influence his selection, appraisal or criticism.

c. A person commits a crime if he confers, or offers or agrees to confer, any benefit the acceptance of which would be criminal under this section.

d. If the benefit offered, conferred, agreed to be conferred, solicited, accepted or agreed to be accepted in violation of this section is $75,000.00 or more, the offender is guilty of a crime of the second degree. If the benefit exceeds $1,000.00, but is less than $75,000.00, the offender is guilty of a crime of the third degree. If the benefit is $1,000.00 or less, the offender is guilty of a crime of the fourth degree.

L.1978, c. 95, § 2C:21–10, eff. Sept. 1, 1979. Amended by L.1979, c. 178, § 38, eff. Sept. 1, 1979; L.1986, c. 129, § 1, eff. Oct. 20, 1986.

2C:21–11. Rigging publicly exhibited contest

a. A person commits a crime if, with purpose to prevent a publicly exhibited contest from being conducted in accordance with the rules and usages which govern it, he:

(1) Confers or offers or agrees to confer any benefit upon, or threatens any injury to a participant, official or other person associated with the contest or exhibition; or

(2) Tampers with any person, animal or thing.

b. Soliciting or accepting benefit for rigging. A person commits a crime if he knowingly solicits, accepts or agrees to accept any benefit the giving of which would be criminal under subsection a.

c. If the benefit offered, conferred, agreed to be conferred, solicited, accepted or agreed to be accepted in violation of subsections a. and b. of this section is $75,000.00 or more, the offender is guilty of a crime of the second degree. If the benefit exceeds $1,000.00, but is less than $75,000.00, the offender is guilty of a crime of the third degree. If the benefit is $1,000.00 or less, the offender is guilty of a crime of the fourth degree.

d. Failure to report solicitation for rigging. A person commits a disorderly persons offense if he fails to report, with reasonable promptness, a solicitation to accept any benefit or to do any tampering, the giving or doing of which would be criminal under subsection a.

e. Participation in rigged contest. A person commits a crime of the fourth degree if he knowingly engages in, sponsors, produces, judges, or otherwise participates in a publicly exhibited contest knowing that the contest is being conducted in violation of subsection a. of this section.

L.1978, c. 95, § 2C:21–11, eff. Sept. 1, 1979. Amended by L.1979, c. 178, § 39, eff. Sept. 1, 1979; L.1986, c. 129, § 2, eff. Oct. 20, 1986.

2C:21–12. Defrauding secured creditors

A person is guilty of a crime of the fourth degree when he destroys, removes, conceals, encumbers, transfers or otherwise deals with property subject to a security interest with purpose to hinder enforcement of that interest.

L.1978, c. 95, § 2C:21–12, eff. Sept. 1, 1979.

2C:21–13. Fraud in insolvency

A person commits a crime if, knowing that proceedings have been or are about to be instituted for the appointment of a receiver or other person entitled to administer property for the benefit of creditors, or that any other composition or liquidation for the benefit of creditors has been or is about to be made, he:

a. Destroys, removes, conceals, encumbers, transfers, or otherwise deals with any property or obtains any substantial part of or interest in the debtor's estate with purpose to defeat or obstruct the claim of any creditor, or otherwise to obstruct the operation of any law relating to administration of property for the benefit of creditors;

b. Knowingly falsifies any writing or record relating to the property; or

c. Knowingly misrepresents or refuses to disclose to a receiver or other person entitled to administer property for the benefit of creditors, the existence, amount or location of the property, or any other information which the actor could be legally required to furnish in relation to such administration.

If the benefit derived from a violation of this section is $75,000.00, or more, the offender is guilty of a crime of the second degree. If the benefit derived exceeds $1,000.00, but is less than $75,000.00, the offender is guilty of a crime of the third degree. If the benefit derived is $1,000.00, or less, the offender is guilty of a crime of the fourth degree.

L.1978, c. 95, § 2C:21–13, eff. Sept. 1, 1979. Amended by L.1979, c. 178, § 40, eff. Sept. 1, 1979.

2C:21–14. Receiving deposits in a failing financial institution

An officer, manager or other person directing or participating in the direction of a financial institution commits a crime of the fourth degree if he receives or permits the receipt of a deposit, premium payment or other investment in the institution knowing that:

a. Due to financial difficulties the institution is about to suspend operations or go into receivership or reorganization; and

b. The person making the deposit or other payment is unaware of the precarious situation of the institution.

L.1978, c. 95, § 2C:21–14, eff. Sept. 1, 1979.

2C:21–15. Misapplication of entrusted property and property of government or financial institution

A person commits a crime if he applies or disposes of property that has been entrusted to him as a fiduciary, or property belonging to or required to be withheld for the benefit of the government or of a financial institution in a manner which he knows is unlawful and

involves substantial risk of loss or detriment to the owner of the property or to a person for whose benefit the property was entrusted whether or not the actor has derived a pecuniary benefit. "Fiduciary" includes trustee, guardian, executor, administrator, receiver and any person carrying on fiduciary functions on behalf of a corporation or other organization which is a fiduciary.

If the benefit derived from a violation of this section is $75,000.00, or more, the offender is guilty of a crime of the second degree. If the benefit derived exceeds $1,000.00, but is less than $75,000.00, the offender is guilty of a crime of the third degree. If the benefit derived is $1,000.00, or less, the offender is guilty of a crime of the fourth degree.

For the purposes of this section, the term "benefit derived" shall include but shall not be limited to the amount of any tax avoided, evaded or otherwise unpaid or improperly retained or disposed of.

L.1978, c. 95, § 2C:21–15, eff. Sept. 1, 1979. Amended by L.1979, c. 178, § 41, eff. Sept. 1, 1979; L.1987, c. 76, § 33, eff. Dec. 9, 1987.

2C:21–16. Securing execution of documents by deception

A person commits a crime of the fourth degree if by deception as to the contents of the instrument, he causes or induces another to execute any instrument affecting, purporting to affect, or likely to affect the pecuniary interest of any person.

L.1978, c. 95, § 2C:21–16, eff. Sept. 1, 1979.

2C:21–17. Impersonation; theft of identity; crime

a. A person is guilty of an offense if the person:

(1) Impersonates another or assumes a false identity and does an act in such assumed character or false identity for the purpose of obtaining a benefit for himself or another or to injure or defraud another;

(2) Pretends to be a representative of some person or organization and does an act in such pretended capacity for the purpose of obtaining a benefit for himself or another or to injure or defraud another;

(3) Impersonates another, assumes a false identity or makes a false or misleading statement regarding the identity of any person, in an oral or written application for services, for the purpose of obtaining services;

(4) Obtains any personal identifying information pertaining to another person and uses that information, or assists another person in using the information, in order to assume the identity of or represent himself as another person, without that person's authorization and with the purpose to fraudulently obtain or attempt to obtain a benefit or services, or avoid the payment of debt or other legal obligation or avoid prosecution for a crime by using the name of the other person; or

(5) Impersonates another, assumes a false identity or makes a false or misleading statement, in the course of making an oral or written application for services, with

the purpose of avoiding payment for prior services. Purpose to avoid payment for prior services may be presumed upon proof that the person has not made full payment for prior services and has impersonated another, assumed a false identity or made a false or misleading statement regarding the identity of any person in the course of making oral or written application for services.

As used in this section:

"Benefit" means, but is not limited to, any property, any pecuniary amount, any services, any pecuniary amount sought to be avoided or any injury or harm perpetrated on another where there is no pecuniary value.

b.   (Deleted by amendment, P.L.2005, c. 224).

c.   A person who violates subsection a. of this section is guilty of a crime as follows:

(1) If the actor obtains a benefit or deprives another of a benefit in an amount less than $500 and the offense involves the identity of one victim, the actor shall be guilty of a crime of the fourth degree except that a second or subsequent conviction for such an offense constitutes a crime of the third degree; or

(2) If the actor obtains a benefit or deprives another of a benefit in an amount of at least $500 but less than $75,000, or the offense involves the identity of at least two but less than five victims, the actor shall be guilty of a crime of the third degree; or

(3) If the actor obtains a benefit or deprives another of a benefit in the amount of $75,000 or more, or the offense involves the identity of five or more victims, the actor shall be guilty of a crime of the second degree.

d.   A violation of N.J.S.2C:28–7, constituting a disorderly persons offense, section 1 of P.L.1979, c. 264 (C.2C:33–15), R.S.33:1–81 or section 6 of P.L.1968, c. 313 (C.33:1–81.7) in a case where the person uses the personal identifying information of another to illegally purchase an alcoholic beverage or for using the personal identifying information of another to misrepresent his age for the purpose of obtaining tobacco or other consumer product denied to persons under 18 years of age shall not constitute an offense under this section if the actor received only that benefit or service and did not perpetrate or attempt to perpetrate any additional injury or fraud on another.

e.   The sentencing court shall issue such orders as are necessary to correct any public record or government document that contains false information as a result of a theft of identity. The sentencing court may provide restitution to the victim in accordance with the provisions of section 4 of P.L.2002, c. 85 (C.2C:21–17.1).

L.1978, c. 95, § 2C:21–17, eff. Sept. 1, 1979. Amended by L.1995, c. 417, § 1, eff. Jan. 10, 1996; L.1999, c. 117, § 1, eff. May 21, 1999; L.2002, c. 85, § 5, eff. Oct. 16, 2002; L.2003, c. 184, § 3, eff. Sept. 25, 2003; L.2005, c. 224, § 2, eff. Sept. 22, 2005.

2C:21–17.1. Victim restitution for personal identification information offenses

Restitution to a victim of an offense under N.J.S.2C:21–1, section 1 of P.L.1983, c. 565 (C.2C:21–2.1), N.J.S.2C:21–17, section 5 of P.L.2003, c. 184 (C.2C:21–17.2) or section 6 of P.L. 2003, c. 184 (C.2C:21–17.3) when the offense concerns personal identifying information may include costs incurred by the victim:

a.   in clearing the credit history or credit rating of the victim; or

b.   in connection with any civil or administrative proceeding to satisfy any debt, lien, or other obligation of the victim arising as a result of the actions of the defendant.

L.2002, c. 85, § 4, eff. Oct. 16, 2002. Amended by L.2005, c. 224, § 3, eff. Sept. 22, 2005.

2C:21–17.2. False driver's license, birth certificate or document issued by government agency; use of personal identifying information of another

a.   A person is guilty of a crime of the second degree if, in obtaining or attempting to obtain a driver's license, birth certificate or other document issued by a governmental agency which could be used as a means of verifying a person's identity, age or any other personal identifying information, that person knowingly exhibits, displays or utters a document or other writing which falsely purports to be a driver's license, birth certificate or other document issued by a governmental agency or which belongs or pertains to a person other than the person who possesses the document.

b.   Notwithstanding the provisions of N.J.S.2C:1–8 or any other law, a conviction under this section shall not merge with a conviction of any other criminal offense, nor shall such other conviction merge with a conviction under this section, and the court shall impose separate sentences upon each violation of this section and any other criminal offense.

c.   A violation of N.J.S.2C:28–7, constituting a disorderly persons offense, section 1 of P.L.1979, c. 264 (C.2C:33–15), R.S.33:1–81 or section 6 of P.L.1968, c. 313 (C.33:1–81.7) in a case where the person uses the personal identifying information of another to illegally purchase an alcoholic beverage or for using the personal identifying information of another to misrepresent his age for the purpose of obtaining tobacco or other consumer product denied to persons under 18 years of age shall not constitute an offense under this section if the actor received only that benefit or service and did not perpetrate or attempt to perpetrate any additional injury or fraud on another.

L.2003, c. 184, § 5, eff. Sept. 25, 2003. Amended by L.2005, c. 224, § 4, eff. Sept. 22, 2005.

2C:21–17.3. Fraudulent use, distribution, manufacture, possession of items containing personal identifying information of another

a. A person who knowingly distributes, manufactures or possesses any item containing personal identifying information pertaining to another person, without that person's authorization, and with knowledge that the actor is facilitating a fraud or injury to be perpetrated by anyone is guilty of a crime of the fourth degree.

b. (1) If the person distributes, manufactures or possesses 20 or more items containing personal identifying information pertaining to another person, or five or more items containing personal information pertaining to five or more separate persons, without authorization, and with knowledge that the actor is facilitating a fraud or injury to be perpetrated by anyone the person is guilty of a crime of the third degree.

(2) If the person distributes, manufactures or possesses 50 or more items containing personal identifying information pertaining to another person, or ten or more items containing personal identifying information pertaining to five or more separate persons, without authorization, and with knowledge that the actor is facilitating a fraud or injury to be perpetrated by anyone the person is guilty of a crime of the second degree.

c. Distribution, manufacture or possession of 20 or more items containing personal identifying information pertaining to another person or of items containing personal identifying information pertaining to five or more separate persons without authorization shall create an inference that the items were distributed, manufactured or possessed with knowledge that the actor is facilitating a fraud or injury to be perpetrated by anyone.

d. As used in this section:

"Distribute" means, but is not limited to, any sale, purchase, transfer, gift, delivery, or provision to another, regardless of whether the distribution was for compensation.

"Item" means a writing or document, whether issued by a governmental agency or made by any business or person, recorded by any method that contains personal identifying information. Item includes, but is not limited to, an access device, book, check, paper, card, instrument, or information stored in electronic form by way of e-mail or otherwise, on any computer, computer storage medium, computer program, computer software, computer equipment, computer system or computer network or any part thereof, or by other mechanical or electronic device such as cellular telephone, pager or other electronic device capable of storing information.

L.2003, c. 184, § 6, eff. Sept. 25, 2003.

2C:21–17.4. Action for damages resulting from use of personal identifying information; standard of proof; other remedies

a. Any person who suffers any ascertainable loss of moneys or property, real or personal, as a result of the use of that person's personal identifying information, in violation of N.J.S.2C:21–1, section 1 of P.L.1983, c. 565 (2C:21–2.1), N.J.S.2C:21–17, section 5 of P.L.2003, c. 184 (C.2C:21–17.2) or section 6 of P.L.2003, c. 184 (C.2C:21–17.3), may bring an action in any court of competent jurisdiction. In any action under this section the court shall, in addition to any other appropriate legal or equitable relief, award damages in an amount three times the value of all costs incurred by the victim as a result of the person's criminal activity. These costs may include, but are not limited to, those incurred by the victim in clearing his credit history or credit rating, or those incurred in connection with any civil or administrative proceeding to satisfy any debt, lien, or other obligation of the victim arising as a result of the actions of the defendant. The victim may also recover those costs incurred for attorneys' fees, court costs and any out-of-pocket losses. A financial institution, insurance company, bonding association or business that suffers direct financial loss as a result of the offense shall also be entitled to damages, but damages to natural persons shall be fully satisfied prior to any payment to a financial institution, insurance company, bonding association or business.

b. The standard of proof in actions brought under this section is a preponderance of the evidence, and the fact that a prosecution for a violation of N.J.S.2C:21–1, section 1 of P.L.1983, c. 565 (2C:21–2.1) or N.J.S.2C:21–17 is not instituted or, where instituted, terminates without a conviction shall not preclude an action pursuant to this section. A final judgment rendered in favor of the State in any criminal proceeding shall estop the defendant from denying the same conduct in any civil action brought pursuant to this section.

c. The cause of action authorized by this section shall be in addition to and not in lieu of any forfeiture or any other action, injunctive relief or any other remedy available at law, except that where the defendant is convicted of a violation of this act, the court in the criminal action, upon the application of the Attorney General or the prosecutor, shall in addition to any other disposition authorized by this Title sentence the defendant to pay restitution in an amount equal to the costs incurred by the victim as a result of the defendant's criminal activity, regardless of whether a civil action has been instituted. These costs may include, but are not limited to those incurred by the victim in clearing his credit history or credit rating; those incurred in connection with any civil or administrative proceeding to satisfy any debt, lien, or other obligation of the victim arising as a result of the actions of the defendant; or those incurred for attorneys' fees, court costs and any out-of-pocket losses. A financial institution, insurance company, bonding association or business that suffers direct financial loss as a result of the offense shall also be entitled to restitution, but restitution to natural persons shall be fully satisfied prior to any payment to a financial institution, insurance company, bonding association or business.

L.2003, c. 184, § 7, eff. Sept. 25, 2003. Amended by L.2005, c. 224, § 5, eff. Sept. 22, 2005.

2C:21–17.5. Consumer reporting agencies; deletion of information resulting from unlawful use of personal identifying information

a. On motion of a person who has been the victim of a violation of N.J. S.2C:21–1, section 1 of P.L.1983, c. 565 (C.2C:21–2.1), N.J.S.2C:21–17, section 5 of P.L. 2003, c. 184 (C.2C:21–17.2) or section 6 of P.L.2003, c. 184 (C.2C:21–17.3), or on its own motion, the court may, without a hearing, grant an order directing all consumer reporting agencies doing business within the State of New Jersey to delete those items of information from the victim's file that were the result of the unlawful use of the victim's personal identifying information. The consumer reporting agency shall thereafter, provide the victim with a copy of the corrected credit history report at no charge.

b. Following any deletion of information pursuant to this section, the consumer reporting agency shall, at the request of the victim, furnish notification that the item has been deleted, to any person specifically designated by the victim who has within two years prior thereto received a consumer report for employment purposes, or within one year prior thereto received a consumer report for any other purpose, which contained the deleted or disputed information.

L.2003, c. 184, § 8, eff. Sept. 25, 2003. Amended by L.2005, c. 224, § 6, eff. Sept. 22, 2005.

2C:21–17.6. Victim of identity theft; report to law enforcement agency

a. A person who reasonably believes or reasonably suspects that he has been the victim of identity theft in violation of N.J.S. 2C:21–1, section 1 of P.L.1983, c. 565 (C.2C:21–2.1) or N.J.S.2C:21–17 may contact the local law enforcement agency in the jurisdiction where he resides, which shall take a police report of the matter and provide the complainant with a copy of that report. Notwithstanding the fact that jurisdiction may lie elsewhere for investigation and prosecution of a crime of identity theft, the local law enforcement agency shall take the complaint and provide the complainant with a copy of the complaint and may refer the complaint to a law enforcement agency in that different jurisdiction.

b. Nothing in this section shall interfere with the discretion of a local law enforcement agency to allocate resources for investigations of crimes. A complaint filed under this section is not required to be counted as an open case for purposes such as compiling open case statistics.

L.2005, c. 226, § 3, eff. Sept. 22, 2005.

2C:21–18. Slugs

A person is guilty of a disorderly persons offense when, other than under such circumstances as would constitute a violation of any of the provisions of the "Casino Control Act" (P.L.1977, c.110):[1]

(1) He inserts or deposits a slug, key, tool, instrument, explosive or device in a coin, currency or credit card activated machine with purpose to defraud; or

(2) He makes, possesses or disposes of a slug, key, tool, instrument, explosive or device or a drawing, print or mold of a key, tool, instrument, explosive or device with purpose to enable a person to insert or deposit it in a coin, currency or credit card activated machine.

"Slug" means an object or article which, by virtue of its size, shape or any other quality is capable of being inserted or deposited in a coin, currency or credit card activated machine as an improper substitute for money.

L.1978, c. 95, § 2C:21–18, eff. Sept. 1, 1979. Amended by L.1979, c. 176, § 1, eff. Sept. 1, 1979; L.1989, c. 33, § 1, eff. March 3, 1989.

[1] N.J.S.A. § 5:12–1 et seq.

2C:21–19. Wrongful credit practices and related offenses

a. **Criminal usury.** A person is guilty of criminal usury when not being authorized or permitted by law to do so, he:

(1) Loans or agrees to loan, directly or indirectly, any money or other property at a rate exceeding the maximum rate permitted by law; or

(2) Takes, agrees to take, or receives any money or other property as interest on the loan or on the forbearance of any money or other interest in excess of the maximum rate permitted by law.

For the purposes of this section and notwithstanding any law of this State which permits as a maximum interest rate a rate or rates agreed to by the parties of the transaction, any loan or forbearance with an interest rate which exceeds 30% per annum shall not be a rate authorized or permitted by law, except if the loan or forbearance is made to a corporation, limited liability company or limited liability partnership any rate not in excess of 50% per annum shall be a rate authorized or permitted by law.

Criminal usury is a crime of the second degree if the rate of interest on any loan made to any person exceeds 50% per annum or the equivalent rate for a longer or shorter period. It is a crime of the third degree if the interest rate on any loan made to any person except a corporation, limited liability company or limited liability partnership does not exceed 50% per annum but the amount of the loan or forbearance exceeds $1,000.00.

Otherwise, making a loan to any person in violation of subsections a.(1) and a.(2) of this section is a disorderly persons offense.

b. Business of criminal usury. Any person who knowingly engages in the business of making loans or forbearances in violation of subsection a. of this section is guilty of a crime of the second degree and, notwithstanding the provisions of N.J.S. 2C:43–3, shall be subject to a fine of not more than $250,000.00 and any other appropriate disposition authorized by N.J.S. 2C:43–2b.

c. Possession of usurious loan records. A person is guilty of a crime of the third degree when, with knowledge of the nature thereof, he possesses any writing, paper instrument or article used to record criminally usurious transactions prohibited by subsection a. of this section.

d. Unlawful collection practices. A person is guilty of a disorderly persons offense when, with purpose to enforce a claim or judgment for money or property, he sends, mails or delivers to another person a notice, document or other instrument which has no judicial or official sanction and which in its format or appearance simulates a summons, complaint, court order or process or an insignia, seal or printed form of a federal, State or local government or an instrumentality thereof, or is otherwise calculated to induce a belief that such notice, document or instrument has a judicial or official sanction.

e. Making a false statement of credit terms. A person is guilty of a disorderly persons offense when he understates or fails to state the interest rate, or makes a false or inaccurate or incomplete statement of any other credit terms.

f. Debt adjusters. Any person who shall act or offer to act as a debt adjuster without a license as required by P.L.1979, c. 16 (C.17:16G–1 et seq.), unless exempt from licensure pursuant to that act, shall be guilty of a crime of the fourth degree.

L.1978, c. 95, § 2C:21–19, eff. Sept. 1, 1979. Amended by L.1979, c. 178, § 42, eff. Sept. 1, 1979; L.1981, c. 104, § 1, eff. March 31, 1981; L.1981, c. 290, § 25, eff. Sept. 24, 1981; L.1986, c. 184, § 6, eff. Dec. 10, 1986; L.1997, c. 426, § 2, eff. Jan. 19, 1998; L.2009, c. 173, § 2, eff. Jan. 11, 2010.

2C:21–20. Unauthorized practice of medicine and surgery or podiatric medicine

A person is guilty of a crime of the third degree if he knowingly does not possess a license or permit to practice medicine and surgery or podiatric medicine, or knowingly has had the license or permit suspended, revoked or otherwise limited by an order entered by the State Board of Medical Examiners, and he:

a. engages in that practice;

b. exceeds the scope of practice permitted by the board order;

c. holds himself out to the public or any person as being eligible to engage in that practice;

d. engages in any activity for which such license or permit is a necessary prerequisite, including, but not limited to, the ordering of controlled dangerous substances or prescription legend drugs from a distributor or manufacturer; or

e. practices medicine or surgery or podiatric medicine under a false or assumed name or falsely impersonates another person licensed by the board.

L.1989, c. 300, § 14, eff. Jan. 12, 1990. Amended by L.2005, c. 259, § 21, eff. Jan. 4, 2006.

2C:21–20.1. Unauthorized practice of acupuncture

A person is guilty of a crime of the third degree if he does not possess a license to practice acupuncture, or his license is suspended, revoked or otherwise limited by an order entered by the Acupuncture Examining Board, and, so knowing, he:

a. engages in that practice;

b. exceeds the scope of practice permitted by the board order;

c. holds himself out to the public or any person as being licensed to engage in that practice;

d. engages in any activity for which a license is a necessary prerequisite; or

e. practices acupuncture under a false or assumed name or falsely impersonates another person licensed by the board.

L.2009, c. 56, § 16, eff. Nov. 2, 2009.

2C:21–21. New Jersey Anti–Piracy Act

a. This act shall be known and may be cited as the "New Jersey Anti–Piracy Act."

b. As used in this act:

(1) "Sound recording" means any phonograph record, disc, tape, film, wire, cartridge, cassette, player piano roll or similar material object from which sounds can be reproduced either directly or with the aid of a machine.

(2) "Owner" means (a) the person who owns the sounds fixed in any master sound recording on which the original sounds were fixed and from which transferred recorded sounds are directly or indirectly derived; or (b) the person who owns the rights to record or authorize the recording of a live performance.

(3) "Audiovisual work" means any work that consists of a series of related images which are intrinsically intended to be shown by the use of machines or devices such as projectors, viewers, or electronic equipment, together with accompanying sounds, if any, regardless of the nature of the material object, such as film or tape, in which the work is embodied. "Audiovisual work" includes but is not limited to a motion picture.

(4) "Audiovisual recording function" means the capability of a device to record or transmit a motion picture or any part thereof by means of any technology.

(5) "Facility" means any theater, screening room, indoor or outdoor screening venue, auditorium, ballroom or other premises where motion pictures are publicly exhibited but does not include a library or retail establishment.

c. A person commits an offense who:

(1) Knowingly transfers, without the consent of the owner, any sounds recorded on a sound recording with intent to sell the sound recording onto which the sounds are transferred or to use the sound recording to promote the sale of any product, provided, however, that this paragraph shall only apply to sound recordings initially fixed prior to February 15, 1972.

(2) Knowingly transports, advertises, sells, resells, rents, or offers for rental, sale or resale, any sound recording or audiovisual work that the person knows has been produced in violation of this act.

(3) Knowingly manufactures or transfers, directly or indirectly by any means, or records or fixes a sound recording or audiovisual work, with the intent to sell or distribute for commercial advantage or private financial gain, a live performance with the knowledge that the live performance has been recorded or fixed without the consent of the owner of the live performance.

(4) For commercial advantage or private financial gain, knowingly advertises or offers for sale, resale or rental, or sells, resells, rents or transports, a sound recording or audiovisual work or possesses with intent to advertise, sell, resell, rent or transport any sound recording or audiovisual work, the label, cover, box or jacket of which does not clearly and conspicuously disclose the true name and address of the manufacturer, and, in the case of a sound recording, the name of the actual performer or group.

(5) Knowingly operates an audiovisual recording function of a device in a facility while a motion picture is being exhibited, for the purpose of recording the motion picture, without the consent of both the licensor of the motion picture and the owner or lessee of the facility.

d. Notwithstanding the provisions of subsection b. of N.J.S.2C:43–3:

(1) Any offense set forth in this act which involves at least 1,000 unlawful sound recordings or at least 65 audiovisual works within any 180–day period shall be punishable as a crime of the third degree and a fine of up to $250,000 may be imposed.

(2) Any offense which involves more than 100 but less than 1,000 unlawful sound recordings or more than 7 but less than 65 unlawful audiovisual works within any 180–day period shall be punishable as a crime of the third degree and a fine of up to $150,000 may be imposed.

(3) Any offense punishable under the provisions of this act not described in paragraph (1) or (2) of this subsection shall be punishable for the first offense as a crime of the fourth degree and a fine of up to $25,000 may be imposed. For a second and subsequent offense pursuant to this paragraph, a person shall be guilty of a crime of the third degree. A fine of up to $50,000 may be imposed for a second offense pursuant to this paragraph and a fine of up to $100,000 for a third and subsequent offense may be imposed.

e. All unlawful sound recordings and audiovisual works and any equipment or components used in violation of the provisions of this act shall be subject to forfeiture in accordance with the procedures set forth in chapter 64 of Title 2C of the New Jersey Statutes.

f. The provisions of this act shall not apply to:

(1) Any broadcaster who, in connection with or as part of a radio or television broadcast transmission, or for the purposes of archival preservation, transfers any sounds or images recorded on a sound recording or audiovisual work.

(2) Any person who, in his own home, for his own personal use, and without deriving any profit, transfers any sounds or images recorded on a sound recording or audiovisual work.

(3) Any law enforcement officer who, while engaged in the official performance of his duties, transfers any sounds or images recorded on a sound recording or audiovisual work.

g. A law enforcement officer, an owner or lessee of a facility where a motion picture or a live performance is being exhibited, the authorized agent or employee of the owner or lessee, the licensor of the motion picture or the live performance or the authorized agent or employee of the licensor, who has probable cause for believing that a person has operated an audiovisual recording function of a device in violation of this section and that he can recover the recording by taking the person into custody, may, for the purpose of attempting to effect recovery thereof, take the person into custody and detain him in a reasonable manner for not more than a reasonable time, and the taking into custody by a law enforcement officer, owner, lessee, licensor, authorized agent or employee shall not render such person criminally or civilly liable in any manner or to any extent whatsoever.

Any law enforcement officer may arrest without warrant any person he has probable cause for believing has operated an audiovisual recording function of a device in violation of this section.

An owner or lessee of a facility, the authorized agent or employee of the owner or lessee, the licensor of the motion picture or the live performance or the authorized agent or employee of the licensor who causes the arrest of a person for operating an audiovisual recording function of a device in violation of this section, shall not be criminally or civilly liable in any manner or to any extent whatsoever where the owner, lessee, licensor, authorized agent or employee has probable cause for believing that the person arrested committed the offense.

L.1991, c. 125, § 1, eff. June 24, 1991. Amended by L.2004, c. 144, § 1, eff. Sept. 10, 2004.

2C:21–22. Unauthorized practice of law; disorderly persons offense

a. A person is guilty of a disorderly persons offense if the person knowingly engages in the unauthorized practice of law.

b. A person is guilty of a crime of the fourth degree if the person knowingly engages in the unauthorized practice of law and:

(1) Creates or reinforces a false impression that the person is licensed to engage in the practice of law; or

(2) Derives a benefit; or

(3) In fact causes injury to another.

c. For the purposes of this section, the phrase "in fact" indicates strict liability.

L.1994, c. 47, § 1, eff. June 23, 1994.

2C:21–22.1. Definitions

a. As used in this section:

"Provider" means an attorney, a health care professional, an owner or operator of a health care practice or facility, any person who creates the impression that he or his practice or facility can provide legal or health care services, or any person employed or acting on behalf of any of the aforementioned persons.

"Public media" means telephone directories, professional directories, newspapers and other periodicals, radio and television, billboards and mailed or electronically transmitted written communications that do not involve in-person contact with a specific prospective client, patient or customer.

"Runner" means a person who, for a pecuniary benefit, procures or attempts to procure a client, patient or customer at the direction of, request of or in cooperation with a provider whose purpose is to seek to obtain benefits under a contract of insurance or assert a claim against an insured or an insurance carrier for providing services to the client, patient or customer, or to obtain benefits under or assert a claim against a State or federal health care benefits program or prescription drug assistance program. "Runner" shall not include a person who procures or attempts to procure clients, patients or customers for a provider through public media or a person who refers clients, patients or customers to a provider as otherwise authorized by law.

b. A person is guilty of a crime of the third degree if that person knowingly acts as a runner or uses, solicits, directs, hires or employs another to act as a runner.

c. Notwithstanding the provisions of subsection e. of N.J.S.2C:44–1, the court shall deal with a person who has been convicted of a violation of this section by imposing a sentence of imprisonment unless, having regard to the character and condition of the person, the court is of the opinion that imprisonment would be a serious injustice which overrides the need to deter such conduct by others. If the court imposes a noncustodial or probationary sentence, such sentence shall not become final for 10 days in order to permit the appeal of such sentence by the prosecution. Nothing in this section shall preclude an indictment and conviction for any other offense defined by the laws of this State.

L.1999, c. 162, § 1, eff. July 12, 1999. Amended by L.2007, c. 58, § 12, eff. March 16, 2007.

2C:21–23. Legislative findings and declaration

The Legislature hereby finds and declares to be the public policy of this State, the following:

a. By enactment of the "Criminal Justice Act of 1970," P.L.1970, c. 74 (C. 52:17B–97 et seq.), the legislature recognized that the existence of organized crime and organized crime type activities present a serious threat to the political, social and economic institutions of this State.

b. By enactment of P.L.1981, c. 167 (C. 2C:41–1 et al.), the Legislature recognized the need to impose strict civil and criminal sanctions upon those whose activity is inimical to the general health, welfare and prosperity of this State, including, but not limited to, those who drain money from the economy by illegal conduct and then undertake the operation of otherwise legitimate businesses with the proceeds of illegal conduct.

c. By enactment of the "Comprehensive Drug Reform Act of 1987," P.L.1987, c. 106 (C. 2C:35–1 et seq.), the Legislature recognized the need to punish the more culpable drug offenders with strict, consistently imposed criminal sanctions. The Legislature intended a greater culpability for those who profit from the illegal trafficking of drugs and expressed an intent that such individuals be dealt with swiftly and sternly.

d. Despite the impressive efforts and gains of our law enforcement agencies, individuals still profit financially from illegal organized criminal activities and illegal trafficking of drugs, and they continue to pose a serious and pervasive threat to the health, safety and welfare of the citizens of this State while, at the same time, converting their illegally obtained profits into "legitimate" funds with the assistance of other individuals.

e. The increased trafficking in drugs and other organized criminal activities have strengthened the money laundering industry which takes illegally acquired income and makes that money appear to be legitimate. In order to safeguard the public interest and stop the conversion of ill-gotten criminal profits, effective criminal and civil sanctions are needed to deter and punish those who are converting the illegal profits, those who are providing a method of hiding the true source of the funds, and those who facilitate such activities. It is in the public interest to make such conduct subject to strict criminal and civil penalties because of a need to deter individuals and business entities from assisting in the "legitimizing" of proceeds of illegal activity. To allow individuals or business entities to avoid responsibility for their criminal assistance in money laundering is clearly inimical to the public good.

L.1994, c. 121, § 1, eff. Oct. 26, 1994.

2C:21–24. Definitions

As used in this act:

"Attorney General" includes the Attorney General of the State of New Jersey and the Attorney General's assistants and deputies. The term also shall include a county prosecutor or the county prosecutor's designated assistant prosecutor if a county prosecutor is expressly authorized in writing by the Attorney General pursuant to this act.

"Derived from" means obtained directly or indirectly from, maintained by or realized through.

"Person" means any corporation, unincorporated association or any other entity or enterprise, as defined in subsection q. of N.J.S. 2C:20–1, which is capable of holding a legal or beneficial interest in property.

"Property" means anything of value, as defined in subsection g. of N.J.S. 2C:20–1, and includes any benefit or interest without reduction for expenses incurred for acquisition, maintenance or any other purpose.

L.1994, c. 121, § 2, eff. Oct. 26, 1994.

2C:21–25. Money laundering and illegal investment; crime

A person is guilty of a crime if the person:

a. transports or possesses property known or which a reasonable person would believe to be derived from criminal activity; or

b. engages in a transaction involving property known or which a reasonable person would believe to be derived from criminal activity

(1) with the intent to facilitate or promote the criminal activity; or

(2) knowing that the transaction is designed in whole or in part:

(a) to conceal or disguise the nature, location, source, ownership or control of the property derived from criminal activity; or

(b) to avoid a transaction reporting requirement under the laws of this State or any other state or of the United States; or

c. directs, organizes, finances, plans, manages, supervises, or controls the transportation of or transac-

tions in property known or which a reasonable person would believe to be derived from criminal activity.

d. For the purposes of this act, property is known to be derived from criminal activity if the person knows that the property involved represents proceeds from some form, though not necessarily which form, of criminal activity. Among the factors that the finder of fact may consider in determining that a transaction has been designed to avoid a transaction reporting requirement shall be whether the person, acting alone or with others, conducted one or more transactions in currency, in any amount, at one or more financial institutions, on one or more days, in any manner. The phrase "in any manner" includes the breaking down of a single sum of currency exceeding the transaction reporting requirement into smaller sums, including sums at or below the transaction reporting requirement, or the conduct of a transaction, or series of currency transactions, including transactions at or below the transaction reporting requirement. The transaction or transactions need not exceed the transaction reporting threshold at any single financial institution on any single day in order to demonstrate a violation of subparagraph (b) of paragraph (2) of subsection b. of this section.

e. A person is guilty of a crime if, with the purpose to evade a transaction reporting requirement of this State or of 31 U.S.C. § 5311 et seq. or 31 C.F.R. § 103 et seq., or any rules or regulations adopted under those chapters and sections, he:

(1) causes or attempts to cause a financial institution, including a foreign or domestic money transmitter or an authorized delegate thereof, casino, check casher, person engaged in a trade or business or any other individual or entity required by State or federal law to file a report regarding currency transactions or suspicious transactions to fail to file a report; or

(2) causes or attempts to cause a financial institution, including a foreign or domestic money transmitter or an authorized delegate thereof, casino, check casher, person engaged in a trade or business or any other individual or entity required by State or federal law to file a report regarding currency transactions or suspicious transactions to file a report that contains a material omission or misstatement of fact; or

(3) structures or assists in structuring, or attempts to structure or assist in structuring any transaction with one or more financial institutions, including foreign or domestic money transmitters or an authorized delegate thereof, casinos, check cashers, persons engaged in a trade or business or any other individuals or entities required by State or federal law to file a report regarding currency transactions or suspicious transactions. "Structure" or "structuring" means that a person, acting alone, or in conjunction with, or on behalf of, other persons, conducts or attempts to conduct one or more transactions in currency, in any amount, at one or more financial institutions, on one or more days, in any manner, for the purpose of evading currency transaction

reporting requirements provided by State or federal law. "In any manner" includes, but is not limited to, the breaking down into smaller sums of a single sum of currency meeting or exceeding that which is necessary to trigger a currency reporting requirement or the conduct of a transaction, or series of currency transactions, at or below the reporting requirement. The transaction or transactions need not exceed the reporting threshold at any single financial institution on any single day in order to meet the definition of "structure" or "structuring" provided in this paragraph.

L.1994, c. 121, § 3, eff. Oct. 26, 1994. Amended by L.1999, c. 25, § 3, eff. Feb. 16, 1999; L.2002, c. 26, § 14, eff. June 18, 2002.

2C:21–26. Knowledge of criminal activity

For the purposes of section 3 of this act,[1] the requisite knowledge may be inferred where the property is transported or possessed in a fashion inconsistent with the ordinary or usual means of transportation or possession of such property and where the property is discovered in the absence of any documentation or other indicia of legitimate origin or right to such property.

L.1994, c. 121, § 4, eff. Oct. 26, 1994.

[1] N.J.S.A. § 2C:21–25.

2C:21–27. Degrees of offense; penalties; nonmerger

a. The offense defined in subsections a. b. and c. of section 3 of P.L. 1994, c. 121 (C.2C:21–25) constitutes a crime of the first degree if the amount involved is $500,000.00 or more. If the amount involved is at least $75,000.00 but less than $500,000.00 the offense constitutes a crime of the second degree; otherwise, the offense constitutes a crime of the third degree. The offense defined in subsection e. of section 3 of P.L.1994, c. 121 (C.2C:21–25) constitutes a crime of the third degree. Notwithstanding the provisions of N.J.S.2C:43–3, the court may also impose a fine up to $500,000.00. The amount involved in a prosecution for violation of this section shall be determined by the trier of fact. Amounts involved in transactions conducted pursuant to one scheme or course of conduct may be aggregated in determining the degree of the offense. Notwithstanding the provisions of paragraph (1) of subsection a. of N.J.S.2C:43–6, a person convicted of a crime of the first degree pursuant to the provisions of this subsection shall be sentenced to a term of imprisonment that shall include the imposition of a minimum term which shall be fixed at, or between, one-third and one-half of the sentence imposed, during which time the defendant shall not be eligible for parole.

b. In addition to any other dispositions authorized by this Title, upon conviction of a violation of this section, the court may sentence the defendant to pay an amount as calculated pursuant to subsection a. of section 6 of P.L.1994, c. 121 (C.2C:21–28).

c. Notwithstanding N.J.S.2C:1–8 or any other provision of law, a conviction of an offense defined in this section shall not merge with the conviction of any other offense constituting the criminal activity involved or from which the property was derived, and a conviction of any offense constituting the criminal activity involved or from which the property was derived shall not merge with a conviction of an offense defined in section 3 of P.L.1994, c. 121 (C.2C:21–25), and the sentence imposed upon a conviction of any offense defined in section 3 of P.L.1994, c. 121 (C.2C:21–25) shall be ordered to be served consecutively to that imposed for a conviction of any offense constituting the criminal activity involved or from which the property was derived. Nothing in P.L.1994, c. 121 (C.2C:21–23 et seq.) shall be construed in any way to preclude or limit a prosecution or conviction for any other offense defined in this Title or any other criminal law of this State.

L.1994, c. 121, § 5, eff. Oct. 26, 1994. Amended by L.1999, c. 25, § 4, eff. Feb. 16, 1999; L.2002, c. 26, § 15, eff. June 18, 2002.

2C:21–27.1. Criteria for imposition of anti-money laundering profiteering penalty

In addition to any other disposition authorized by this title, including but not limited to any fines which may be imposed pursuant to the provisions of N.J.S.2C:43–3, where a person has been convicted of a crime defined in P.L.1994, c. 121 (C.2C:21–23 et seq.) or an attempt or conspiracy to commit such a crime, the court shall, upon the application of the prosecutor, sentence the person to pay a monetary penalty in an amount determined pursuant to section 9 of P.L.1999, c. 25 (C.2C:21–27.2), provided the court finds at a hearing, which may occur at the time of sentencing, that the prosecutor has established by a preponderance of the evidence that the defendant was convicted of a violation of P.L.1994, c. 121 (C.2C:21–23 et seq.).

L.1999, c. 25, § 8, eff. Feb. 16, 1999.

2C:21–27.2. Calculation of anti-money laundering profiteering penalty

Where, pursuant to section 8 of P.L.1999, c. 25 (C.2C:21–27.1) the prosecutor has established by a preponderance of the evidence that the defendant was convicted of a violation of P.L.1994, c. 121 (C.2C:21–23 et seq.), the court shall assess a monetary penalty as follows:

a. $500,000.00 in the case of a crime of the first degree; $250,000.00 in the case of a crime of the second degree; $75,000.00 in the case of a crime of the third degree; or

b. an amount equal to three times the value of any property involved in a money laundering activity in violation of P.L.1994, c. 121 (C.2C:21–23 et seq.).

c. Where the prosecution requests that the court assess a penalty in an amount calculated pursuant to subsection b. of this section, the prosecutor shall have the burden of establishing by a preponderance of the evidence the appropriate amount of the penalty to be assessed pursuant to that subsection. In making its finding, the court shall take judicial notice of any evidence, testimony or information adduced at trial, plea hearing or other court proceedings and shall also consider the presentence report and other relevant information, including expert opinion in the form of live testimony or by affidavit. The court's findings shall be incorporated in the record, and such findings shall not be subject to modification by an appellate court except upon a showing that the finding was totally lacking support in the record or was arbitrary and capricious.

L.1999, c. 25, § 9, eff. Feb. 16, 1999.

2C:21–27.3. Revocation or reduction of penalty assessment

The court shall not revoke or reduce a penalty imposed pursuant to section 9 of P.L.1999, c. 25 (C.2C:21–27.2). An anti-money laundering profiteering penalty imposed pursuant to section 9 of P.L.1999, c. 25 (C.2C:21–27.2) shall not be deemed a fine for purposes of N.J.S.2C:46–3.

L.1999, c. 25, § 10, eff. Feb. 16, 1999.

2C:21–27.4. Payment schedule

The court may, for good cause shown, and subject to the provisions of this section, grant permission for the payment of an anti-money laundering profiteering penalty assessed pursuant to section 9 of P.L.1999, c. 25 (C.2C:21–27.2) to be made within a specified period of time or in specified installments, provided however that the payment schedule fixed by the court shall require the defendant to pay the anti-money laundering profiteering penalty in the shortest period of time consistent with the nature and extent of his assets and his ability to pay, and further provided that the prosecutor shall be afforded the opportunity to present evidence or information concerning the nature, extent and location of the defendant's assets or interests in property which are or might be subject to levy and execution. In such event, the court may only grant permission for the payment to be made within a specified period of time or installments with respect to that portion of the assessed penalty which would not be satisfied by the liquidation of property which is or may be subject to levy and execution, unless the court finds that the immediate liquidation of such property would result in undue hardship to innocent persons. If no permission to make payment within a specified period of time or in installments is embodied in the sentence, the entire penalty shall be payable forthwith.

L.1999, c. 25, § 11, eff. Feb. 16, 1999.

2C:21–27.5. Relation to other dispositions

a. An anti-money laundering profiteering penalty assessed pursuant to section 9 of P.L.1999, c. 25 (C.2C:21–27.2) shall be imposed and paid in addition to any penalty, fine, fee or order for restitution which may be imposed.

b. An anti-money laundering profiteering penalty imposed pursuant to section 9 of P.L.1999, c. 25 (C.2C:21–27.2) shall be in addition to and not in lieu of any forfeiture or other cause of action instituted pursuant to chapter 41 or 64 of Title 2C of the New Jersey Statutes, and nothing in this chapter shall be construed in any way to preclude, preempt or limit any such cause of action. A defendant shall not be entitled to receive credit toward the payment of an anti-money laundering profiteering penalty imposed pursuant to section 9 of P.L.1999, c. 25 (C.2C:21–27.2) for the value of property forfeited, or subject to forfeiture, pursuant to the provisions of chapter 41 or 64 of Title 2C of the New Jersey Statutes.

L.1999, c. 25, § 12, eff. Feb. 16, 1999.

2C:21–27.6. Collection and distribution

All anti-money laundering profiteering penalties assessed pursuant to section 9 of P.L.1999, c. 25 (C.2C:21–27.2) shall be docketed and collected as provided for the collection of fines, penalties, fees and restitution in chapter 46 of Title 2C of the New Jersey Statutes. The Attorney General or prosecutor may prosecute an action to collect any anti-money laundering profiteering penalties imposed pursuant to section 9 of P.L.1999, c. 25 (C.2C:21–27.2). All anti-money laundering profiteering penalties assessed pursuant to section 9 of P.L.1999, c. 25 (C.2C:21–27.2) shall be disposed of, distributed, appropriated and used as if the collected penalties were the proceeds of property forfeited pursuant to chapter 64 of Title 2C of the New Jersey Statutes.

L.1999, c. 25, § 13, eff. Feb. 16, 1999.

2C:21–28. Attorney general authorized to bring civil action

a. The Attorney General may institute a civil action against any person who violates section 3 of this act,[1] and may recover a judgment against all persons who violate this section, jointly and severally, for damages in an amount equal to three times the value of all property involved in the criminal activity, together with costs incurred for resources and personnel used in the investigation and litigation of both criminal and civil proceedings. The standard of proof in actions brought under this subsection is a preponderance of the evidence, and the fact that a prosecution for a violation of this act is not instituted or, where instituted, terminates without a conviction shall not preclude an action pursuant to this subsection. A final judgment rendered in favor of the State in any criminal proceedings shall estop the defendant from denying the same conduct in any civil action brought pursuant to this subsection.

b. The cause of action authorized by this section shall be in addition to and not in lieu of any forfeiture or any other action, injunctive relief or any other remedy available at law, except that where the defendant is convicted of a violation of this act, the court in the criminal action, upon the application of the Attorney General or the prosecutor, may in addition to any other disposition authorized by this Title, sentence the defendant to pay an amount equal to the damages calculated pursuant to the provisions of this subsection, whether or not a civil action has been instituted.

c. Notwithstanding any other provision of law, all monies collected pursuant to any judgment recovered or order issued pursuant to this section shall first be allocated to the payment of any State tax, penalty and interest due and owing to the State as a result of the conduct which is the basis for the action. Monies collected shall be allocated next in accordance with the provisions of N.J.S. 2C:64–6 as if collected pursuant to chapter 64 of Title 2C, in an amount equal to the amount of all property involved in the criminal activity plus the costs incurred for resources and personnel used in the investigation and litigation. The remainder of the monies collected shall be allocated to the General Fund of the State.

L.1994, c. 121, § 6, eff. Oct. 26, 1994.

1 N.J.S.A. § 2C:21–25.

2C:21–29. Investigative interrogatories

a. Whenever the Attorney General, by the Attorney General's own inquiry or as the result of a complaint, determines that there exists reasonable suspicion that a violation of this act is occurring, has occurred or is about to occur, or, whenever the Attorney General believes it to be in the public interest that an investigation be made, the Attorney General may, prior to the institution of any criminal or civil action, issue in writing and cause to be served upon any person investigative interrogatories requiring the person to answer and produce material for examination.

b. Any investigative interrogatories issued pursuant to this subsection and all procedures related to such interrogatories shall comply with the provisions of N.J.S. 2C:41–5.

L.1994, c. 121, § 7, eff. Oct. 26, 1994.

2C:21–30. Practice of dentistry without a license; crime of the third degree

A person is guilty of a crime of the third degree if he knowingly does not possess a license to practice dentistry or knowingly has had the license suspended, revoked or otherwise limited by an order entered by the New Jersey State Board of Dentistry, and he:

a. engages in that practice;

b. exceeds the scope of practice permitted by a board order;

c. holds himself out to the public or any person as being eligible to engage in that practice;

d. engages in any activity for which such license is a necessary prerequisite, including, but not limited to, the ordering of controlled dangerous substances or pre-scription legend drugs from a distributor or manufacturer; or

e. practices dentistry under a false or assumed name or falsely impersonates another person licensed by the board.

L.1995, c. 124, § 1, eff. June 19, 1995.

2C:21–31. Unauthorized practice of immigration law

a. As used in this section:

(1) "Immigration consultant" means any person rendering services for a fee, including the completion of forms and applications, to another person in furtherance of that person's desire to determine or modify his status in an immigration or naturalization matter under federal law.

(2) "Immigration or naturalization matter" means any matter which involves any law, action, filing or proceeding related to a person's immigration or citizenship status in the United States.

(3) "Immigration-related document" means any birth certificate or marriage certificate; any document issued by the government of the United States, any foreign country, any state, or any other public entity relating to a person's immigration or naturalization status.

b. Any immigration consultant not licensed as an attorney or counselor at law who:

(1) Engages in this State in the practice of law; or

(2) Holds himself out to the public, either alone or together with, by or through another person, whether such other person is licensed as an attorney or counselor at law or not, as engaging in or entitled to engage in the practice of law, or as rendering legal service or advice, or as furnishing attorneys or counsel, in any immigration or naturalization matter; or

(3) Assumes, uses or advertises the title of lawyer or attorney at law, or equivalent terms, in the English language or any other language, is guilty of a crime of the fourth degree.

c. Any person who knowingly retains possession of another person's immigration-related document for more than a reasonable time after the person who owns the document has submitted a written request for the document's return is guilty of a crime of the fourth degree.

d. Nothing in this section shall be construed to prohibit a person accredited as a representative by federal law pursuant to 8 CFR 292.2 from providing immigration services.

L.1997, c. 1, § 1, eff. April 24, 1997.

2C:21–32. Trademark counterfeiting; definitions; offenses

a. This act shall be known and may be cited as the "New Jersey Trademark Counterfeiting Act."

b. As used in this act:

(1) "Counterfeit mark" means a spurious mark that is identical with or substantially indistinguishable from a genuine mark that is registered on the principal register in the United States Patent and Trademark Office or registered in the New Jersey Secretary of State's office or a spurious mark that is identical with or substantially indistinguishable from the words, names, symbols, emblems, signs, insignias or any combination thereof, of the United States Olympic Committee or the International Olympic Committee; and that is used or is intended to be used on, or in conjunction with, goods or services for which the genuine mark is registered and in use.

(2) "Retail value" means the counterfeiter's regular selling price for the item or service bearing or identified by the counterfeit mark. In the case of items bearing a counterfeit mark which are components of a finished product, the retail value shall be the counterfeiter's regular selling price of the finished product on or in which the component would be utilized.

c. A person commits the offense of counterfeiting who, with the intent to deceive or defraud some other person, knowingly manufactures, uses, displays, advertises, distributes, offers for sale, sells, or possesses with intent to sell or distribute within, or in conjunction with commercial activities within New Jersey, any item, or services, bearing, or identified by, a counterfeit mark.

A person who has in his possession or under his control more than 25 items bearing a counterfeit mark shall be presumed to have violated this section.

d. (1) An offense set forth in this act shall be punishable as a crime of the fourth degree if:

the offense involves fewer than 100 items bearing a counterfeit mark;

the offense involves a total retail value of less than $1,000.00 for all items bearing, or services identified by, a counterfeit mark; or

the offense involves a first conviction under this act.

(2) An offense set forth in this act shall be punishable as a crime of the third degree if:

the offense involves 100 or more but fewer than 1,000 items bearing a counterfeit mark;

the offense involves a total retail value of $1,000.00 or more but less than $15,000.00 of all items bearing, or services identified by, a counterfeit mark; or

the offense involves a second conviction under this act.

(3) An offense set forth in this act shall be punishable as a crime of the second degree if:

the offense involves 1,000 or more items bearing a counterfeit mark;

the offense involves a total retail value of $15,000.00 or more of all items bearing, or services identified by a counterfeit mark; or

the offense involves a third or subsequent conviction under this act.

In addition, any person convicted under this act, notwithstanding the provisions of N.J.S.2C:43–3, shall be fined by the court an amount up to threefold the retail value of the items or services involved, providing that the fine imposed shall not exceed the following amounts: for a crime of the fourth degree, $100,000.00; for a crime of the third degree, $250,000.00; and for a crime of the second degree, $500,000.00.

e. All items bearing a counterfeit mark, and all personal property, including but not limited to, any items, objects, tools, machines, equipment, instrumentalities or vehicles of any kind, employed or used in connection with a violation of this act, shall be subject to forfeiture in accordance with the procedures set forth in chapter 64 of Title 2C of the New Jersey Statutes.

f. For purposes of this act:

(1) the quantity or retail value of items or services shall include the aggregate quantity or retail value of all items bearing, or services identified by, every counterfeit mark the defendant manufactures, uses, displays, advertises, distributes, offers for sale, sells or possesses;

(2) any State or federal certificate of registration of any intellectual property shall be prima facie evidence of the facts stated therein.

g. Conviction for an offense under this act does not preclude the defendant's liability for the civil remedy available pursuant to section 2 of P.L.1987, c. 454 (C.56:3–13.16).

L.1997, c. 57, § 1, eff. April 1, 1997. Amended by L.1999, c. 313, § 1, eff. Jan. 4, 2000.

2C:21–33. Electrical contracting without business permit

a. A person is guilty of a crime of the fourth degree if that person knowingly engages in the business of electrical contracting without having a business permit issued by the Board of Examiners of Electrical Contractors and:

(1) Creates or reinforces a false impression that the person is licensed as an electrical contractor or possesses a business permit; or

(2) Derives a benefit, the value of which is more than incidental; or

(3) In fact causes injury to another.

b. For the purposes of this section, the phrase "in fact" indicates strict liability.

L.1998, c. 151, § 1, eff. Jan. 12, 1999.

2C:21–34. False claim for payment of government contract

a. A person commits a crime if the person knowingly submits to the government any claim for payment for performance of a government contract knowing such claim to be false, fictitious, or fraudulent. If the claim submitted is for $25,000.00 or above, the offender is guilty of a crime of the second degree. If the claim exceeds $2,500.00, but is less than $25,000. 00, the offender is guilty of a crime of the third degree. If the claim is for $2,500.00 or less, the offender is guilty of a crime of the fourth degree.

b. A person commits a crime if the person knowingly makes a material representation that is false in connection with the negotiation, award or performance of a government contract. If the contract amount is for $25,000. 00 or above, the offender is guilty of a crime of the second degree. If the contract amount exceeds $2,500.00, but is less than $25,000.00, the offender is guilty of a crime of the third degree. If the contract amount is for $2,500.00 or less, the offender is guilty of a crime of the fourth degree.

c. An employer commits a crime if the employer knowingly pays one or more employees employed in public work subject to the provisions of P.L.1963, c. 150 (C.34:11–56.25 et seq.) at a rate less than the rate required pursuant to that act. If the contract amount is for $75,000.00 or above, the employer is guilty of a crime of the second degree; if the contract amount exceeds $2,500.00, but is less than $75,000.00, the employer is guilty of a crime of the third degree; and if the contract amount is for $2,500.00 or less, the employer is guilty of a crime of the fourth degree. In addition, the employer shall be deemed to have caused loss to the employees in the amount by which the employees were underpaid and shall be subject to the provisions of N.J.S.2C:43–3 regarding fines and restitution to victims and be subject to other pertinent provisions of Title 2C of the New Jersey Statutes, including, but not limited to, N.J.S.2C:43–4, 2C:43–6 and 2C:44–1.

L.1999, c. 440, § 97. Amended by L.2003, c. 276, § 2, eff. Jan. 14, 2004.

2C:21–35. Sale or transfer of a public utility employee identification badge; criminal penalties for fraudulently or falsely exhibiting, displaying or uttering badge documents

a. A person who knowingly sells, offers or exposes for sale, or otherwise transfers, or possesses with the intent to sell, offer or expose for sale, or otherwise transfer, a document, printed form or other writing which falsely purports to be a public utility employee identification badge as required under the provisions of P.L.1977, c. 35 (C.48:3–42 et seq.) which could be used as a means of verifying a person's identity as a public utility employee is guilty of a crime of the second degree.

b. A person who knowingly makes, or possesses devices or materials to make, a document or other writing which falsely purports to be a public utility employee identification badge as required under the provisions of P.L.1977, c. 35 (C.48:3–42 et seq.) which could be used as a means of verifying a person's identity

as a public utility employee is guilty of a crime of the second degree.

c. A person who knowingly exhibits, displays or utters a document or other writing which falsely purports to be a public utility employee identification badge as required under the provisions of P.L.1977, c. 35 (C.48:3–42 et seq.) which could be used as a means of verifying a person's identity as a public utility employee is guilty of a crime of the third degree.

d. A person who knowingly possesses a document or other writing which falsely purports to be a public utility employee identification badge as required under the provisions of P.L.1977, c. 35 (C.48:3–42 et seq.) which could be used as a means of verifying a person's identity as a public utility employee is guilty of a crime of the fourth degree.

L.2007, c. 232, § 2, eff. Jan. 3, 2008.

2C:21–36. Purchase of used secondhand jewelry; requirements for resale; exclusions

No person engaged in the business of retailing, wholesaling, or smelting jewelry who purchases any article of used or secondhand jewelry shall sell or offer to sell that used or secondhand jewelry, unless that person:

a. Maintains, for five years, a record of the name, address and telephone number of the person from whom it was purchased and:

(1) a descriptive list of any used jewelry purchased from that seller, including any identifying characteristics of that jewelry; or

(2) photographs of any used jewelry purchased from that seller;

b. Verifies the identity of the person selling the jewelry by requesting and examining a photograph-bearing, valid State or federal issued driver's license or other government issued form of identification bearing a photograph;

c. Delivers, on a weekly basis, to the police department having jurisdiction in the location of that person's place of business a copy of the record of all used jewelry purchased by that person during the preceding week;

d. Maintains in his possession any used jewelry purchased for not less than three business days following the delivery of the record of the purchase of that jewelry to the police department, as required by subsection c. of this section; and

e. Maintains, for five years, a copy of any list provided by an individual pursuant to section 2 of P.L.2009, c. 214 (C.2C:21–37).

Nothing in this section shall be construed to apply to pawnbrokers licensed and regulated pursuant to the pawnbroking law, R.S.45:22–1 et seq., or sales made through an Internet website. Nothing in this section shall be construed to apply to a person engaged in retail, provided the sale of jewelry is not his primary business and further provided the person does not engage in the purchase of used or secondhand jewelry on more than three days in a calendar year.

L.2009, c. 214, § 1, eff. May 1, 2010.

2C:21–37. Duty of purchaser purchasing with the intent of reselling jewelry to certain businesses

Any individual who purchases used or secondhand jewelry from another individual with the intent of selling that jewelry to a person engaged in the business of retailing, wholesaling, or smelting jewelry shall:

a. Maintain, for five years, a record of the sale of that jewelry, including, but not limited to, the date the jewelry is sold; name of the person engaged in the business of retailing, wholesaling, or smelting jewelry to whom it is sold; and an itemized, descriptive list of that jewelry; and

b. Provide an itemized, descriptive list of the jewelry sold to the person engaged in the business of retailing, wholesaling, or smelting jewelry at the time of sale.

L.2009, c. 214, § 2, eff. May 1, 2010.

2C:21–38. Presumption of knowledge or belief

The requisite knowledge or belief for a violation of N.J.S.2C:20–7 is presumed in the case of a person subject to the provisions of section 1 or 2 of P.L.2009, c. 214 (C.2C:21–36 or C.2C:21–37) who purchases any article of used or secondhand jewelry and fails to comply with the requirements of section 1 or 2 of P.L.2009, c. 214 (C.2C:21–36 or C.2C:21–37), as applicable.

L.2009, c. 214, § 3, eff. May 1, 2010.

2C:21–39. Duty of purchaser to report suspicious circumstances

Any person who purchases any article of used or secondhand jewelry shall immediately report to an appropriate law enforcement agency any delivery or sale of used jewelry under circumstances that would cause a reasonable person to believe the used jewelry was probably stolen or otherwise inappropriately obtained.

L.2009, c. 214, § 4, eff. May 1, 2010.

2C:21–40. Immunity from civil liability

Notwithstanding any provision of the law to the contrary, any person who reports information to a law enforcement official or agency concerning the suspect sale of used jewelry shall be immune from any civil liability on account of the report, unless such person has acted in bad faith or with malicious purpose.

L.2009, c. 214, § 5, eff. May 1, 2010.

2C:21–41. Rules and regulations

The Attorney General shall promulgate regulations pursuant to the "Administrative Procedure Act," P.L.

1968, c. 410 (C.52:14B–1 et seq.), necessary to effectuate the provisions of this act.

L.2009, c. 214, § 6, eff. May 1, 2010.

CHAPTER 22

HUMAN REMAINS

Section
2C:22–1.   Desecration of human remains.
2C:22–2.   Sale or purchase of human body or body part intended for donation; prohibition; falsification or alteration to documents for donation; criminal penalties.

2C:22–1. Desecration of human remains

a. A person commits a crime of the second degree if he:

(1) Unlawfully disturbs, moves or conceals human remains;

(2) Unlawfully desecrates, damages or destroys human remains; or

(3) Commits an act of sexual penetration or sexual contact, as defined in N.J.S.2C:14–1, upon human remains.

b. A person commits a crime of the third degree if he purposely or knowingly fails to dispose of human remains in a manner required by law.

c. As used in this act, "human remains" means the body of a deceased person or the dismembered part of a body of a living person but does not include cremated remains.

d. Nothing in this section shall be construed to apply to any act performed in accordance with law, including but not limited to the "State Medical Examiner Act," P.L.1967, c. 234 (C.52:17B–78 et al.); the "Mortuary Science Act," P.L.1952, c. 340 (C.45:7–32 et seq.); the provisions of chapters 6 and 7 of Title 26 of the Revised Statutes concerning disposal of dead bodies and cremation; the "New Jersey Cemetery Act," N.J.S.8A:1–1 et seq.; a criminal investigation conducted by a law enforcement authority; or an order of a court of competent jurisdiction or other appropriate legal authority. Nothing in this section shall be construed to criminalize any good faith action involving interment or disinterment which disturbs, moves, conceals, desecrates, damages or destroys human remains.

L.2002, c. 127, § 1, eff. Dec. 20, 2002.

2C:22–2. Sale or purchase of human body or body part intended for donation; prohibition; falsification or alteration to documents for donation; criminal penalties

a. A person who knowingly, for valuable consideration, purchases or sells a part for transplantation or therapy, if removal of a part from a donor is intended to occur after the donor's death, is guilty of a crime of the third degree and, notwithstanding the provisions of N.J.S.2C:43–3, shall be subject to a fine of not more than $50,000, as well as the term of imprisonment provided under N.J.S.2C:43–6, or both.

Nothing in this subsection shall be construed to prohibit a person from charging a reasonable amount for the removal, processing, disposal, preservation, quality control, storage, transportation, or implantation of a part.

b. A person who intentionally falsifies, forges, conceals, defaces, or obliterates a document by which a gift of all or part of a human body may be made pursuant to P.L.2008, c. 50 (C.26:6–77 et al.), an amendment or revocation of such a document, or any death record or document of medical or social history pertaining to the body or part of the donor, or a refusal to make a gift, in order to obtain a financial benefit or gain, is guilty of a crime of the second degree and, notwithstanding the provisions of N.J.S.2C:43–3, shall be subject to a fine of not more than $50,000, as well as the term of imprisonment provided under N.J.S.2C:43–6, or both.

c. As used in this section, the terms "decedent," "donor," "part," and "person" have the meaning ascribed to them in section 2 of P.L.2008, c. 50 (C.26:6–78).

L.2007, c. 36, § 1, eff. Jan. 29, 2007. Amended by L.2008, c. 50, § 22, eff. July 22, 2008.

CHAPTER 23

[RESERVED]

PART 3

OFFENSES AGAINST OTHERS

Chapter
24. Offenses Against the Family, Children and Incompetents.
25. Domestic Violence.
26. [Reserved].

CHAPTER 24

OFFENSES AGAINST THE FAMILY, CHILDREN AND INCOMPETENTS

Section
2C:24–1. Bigamy.
2C:24–2, 2C:24–3. Blank.
2C:24–4. Endangering welfare of children.
2C:24–5. Willful nonsupport.
2C:24–6. Unlawful adoptions.
2C:24–7. Endangering the welfare of an incompetent person.
2C:24–8. Endangering welfare of elderly or disabled.
2C:24–9. Employing a juvenile in commission of a crime.

2C:24–1. Bigamy

a. **Bigamy.** A married person is guilty of bigamy, a disorderly persons offense, if he contracts or purports to contract another marriage, unless at the time of the subsequent marriage:

(1) The actor believes that the prior spouse is dead;

(2) The actor and the prior spouse have been living apart for 5 consecutive years throughout which the prior spouse was not known by the actor to be alive;

(3) A court has entered a judgment purporting to terminate or annul any prior disqualifying marriage, and the actor does not know that judgment to be invalid; or

(4) The actor reasonably believes that he is legally eligible to remarry.

b. **Other party to bigamous marriage.** A person is guilty of bigamy if he contracts or purports to contract marriage with another knowing that the other is thereby committing bigamy.

L.1978, c. 95, § 2C:24–1, eff. Sept. 1, 1979.

2C:24–2, 2C:24–3. Blank

2C:24–4. Endangering welfare of children

a. Any person having a legal duty for the care of a child or who has assumed responsibility for the care of a child who engages in sexual conduct which would impair or debauch the morals of the child, or who causes the child harm that would make the child an abused or neglected child as defined in R.S.9:6–1, R.S.9:6–3 and P.L.1974, c. 119, s.1 (C.9:6–8.21) is guilty of a crime of the second degree. Any other person who engages in conduct or who causes harm as described in this subsection to a child under the age of 16 is guilty of a crime of the third degree.

b. (1) As used in this subsection:

"Child" means any person under 16 years of age.

"Internet" means the international computer network of both federal and non-federal interoperable packet switched data networks.

"Prohibited sexual act" means

(a) Sexual intercourse; or

(b) Anal intercourse; or

(c) Masturbation; or

(d) Bestiality; or

(e) Sadism; or

(f) Masochism; or

(g) Fellatio; or

(h) Cunnilingus;

(i) Nudity, if depicted for the purpose of sexual stimulation or gratification of any person who may view such depiction; or

(j) Any act of sexual penetration or sexual contact as defined in N.J.S.2C:14–1.

"Reproduction" means, but is not limited to, computer generated images.

(2) (Deleted by amendment, P.L.2001, c. 291).

(3) A person commits a crime of the second degree if he causes or permits a child to engage in a prohibited sexual act or in the simulation of such an act if the person knows, has reason to know or intends that the prohibited act may be photographed, filmed, reproduced, or reconstructed in any manner, including on the Internet, or may be part of an exhibition or performance. If the person is a parent, guardian or other person legally charged with the care or custody of the child, the person shall be guilty of a crime of the first degree.

(4) Any person who photographs or films a child in a prohibited sexual act or in the simulation of such an act or who uses any device, including a computer, to reproduce or reconstruct the image of a child in a prohibited sexual act or in the simulation of such an act is guilty of a crime of the second degree.

(5) (a) Any person who knowingly receives for the purpose of selling or who knowingly sells, procures, manufactures, gives, provides, lends, trades, mails, delivers, transfers, publishes, distributes, circulates, disseminates, presents, exhibits, advertises, offers or agrees to offer, through any means, including the Internet, any photograph, film, videotape, computer program or file, video game or any other reproduction or reconstruction which depicts a child engaging in a prohibited sexual act or in the simulation of such an act, is guilty of a crime of the second degree.

(b) Any person who knowingly possesses or knowingly views any photograph, film, videotape, computer program or file, video game or any other reproduction or reconstruction which depicts a child engaging in a prohibited sexual act or in the simulation of such an act, including on the Internet, is guilty of a crime of the fourth degree.

(6) For purposes of this subsection, a person who is depicted as or presents the appearance of being under the age of 16 in any photograph, film, videotape, computer program or file, video game or any other reproduction or reconstruction shall be rebuttably presumed to be under the age of 16. If the child who is depicted as engaging in, or who is caused to engage in, a prohibited sexual act or simulation of a prohibited sexual act is under the age of 16, the actor shall be strictly liable and it shall not be a defense that the actor did not know that the child was under the age of 16, nor shall it be a defense that the actor believed that the child was 16 years of age or older, even if such a mistaken belief was reasonable.

L.1978, c. 95, § 2C:24–4, eff. Sept. 1, 1979. Amended by L.1979, c. 178, § 46, eff. Sept. 1, 1979; L.1983, c. 494, § 1, eff. Jan. 17, 1984; L.1992, c. 2, § 1, eff. April 2, 1992; L.1992, c. 6, § 1, eff. May 13, 1992; L.1995, c. 109, § 1, eff. June 1, 1995; L.1998, c. 126, § 1, eff. May 1, 1999; L.2001, c. 291, § 1, eff. Dec. 28, 2001, retroactive to May 1, 1999.

2C:24–5. Willful nonsupport

A person commits a crime of the fourth degree if he willfully fails to provide support which he can provide and which he knows he is legally obliged to provide to a spouse, child or other dependent. In addition to the sentence authorized by the code, the court may proceed under section 2C:62–1.

L.1978, c. 95, § 2C:24–5, eff. Sept. 1, 1979.

2C:24–6. Unlawful adoptions

Unlawful adoptions shall be governed by the provisions of Title 9 of the Revised Statutes.

L.1978, c. 95, § 2C:24–6, eff. Sept. 1, 1979. Amended by L.1979, c. 178, § 46A, eff. Sept. 1, 1979.

2C:24–7. Endangering the welfare of an incompetent person

A person is guilty of a disorderly persons offense when he knowingly acts in a manner likely to be injurious to the physical, mental or moral welfare of a person who is unable to care for himself because of mental disease or defect.

L.1978, c. 95, § 2C:24–7, eff. Sept. 1, 1979.

2C:24–8. Endangering welfare of elderly or disabled

a. A person having a legal duty to care for or who has assumed continuing responsibility for the care of a person 60 years of age or older or a disabled adult, who abandons the elderly person or disabled adult or unreasonably neglects to do or fails to permit to be done any act necessary for the physical or mental health of the elderly person or disabled adult, is guilty of a crime of the third degree. For purposes of this section "abandon" means the willful desertion or forsaking of an elderly person or disabled adult.

b. A person shall not be considered to commit an offense under this section for the sole reason that he provides or permits to be provided nonmedical remedial treatment by spiritual means through prayer alone in lieu of medical care, in accordance with the tenets and practices of the elderly person's or disabled adult's established religious tradition, to an elderly person or disabled adult to whom he has a legal duty to care for or has assumed responsibility for the care of.

c. Nothing in this section shall be construed to preclude or limit the prosecution or conviction for any other offense defined in this code or in any other law of this State.

L.1989, c. 23, § 1, eff. Feb. 6, 1989. Amended by L.1999, c. 8, § 1, eff. Jan. 25, 1999.

2C:24–9. Employing a juvenile in commission of a crime

a. Except as provided in P.L.1991, c. 81 (C.2C:20–17) and N.J.S.2C:35–6, any person who is at least 18 years of age who knowingly uses, solicits, directs, hires, employs or conspires with a person who is in fact 17 years of age or younger to commit a criminal offense is guilty of a crime.

b. An offense under this section constitutes a crime of the fourth degree if the underlying offense is a disorderly persons offense. Otherwise, an offense under this section shall be classified one degree higher than the underlying offense.

c. Notwithstanding the provisions of N.J.S.2C:1–8, a conviction under this section shall not merge with a conviction for the underlying offense. Nor shall a conviction for the underlying offense merge with a conviction under this section. Nothing contained in this act shall prohibit the court from imposing an extended term of imprisonment pursuant to 2C:43–7; nor shall this be construed to preclude or limit a prosecution or conviction of any person for conspiracy under N.J.S.2C:5–2, or any prosecution or conviction for any offense.

d. It shall be no defense to a prosecution under this act that the actor mistakenly believed that the person which the actor used, solicited, directed, hired or employed was 18 years of age or older, even if such mistaken belief was reasonable.

L.1998, c. 102, § 1, eff. Sept. 9, 1998.

CHAPTER 25

DOMESTIC VIOLENCE

Section
2C:25–1 to 2C:25–16.   Repealed.
2C:25–17.   Prevention of Domestic Violence Act of 1991; short title.
2C:25–18.   Legislative findings and declaration.
2C:25–19.   Definitions.
2C:25–20.   Training course and curriculum; domestic crisis teams.
2C:25–21.   Arrest; criminal complaint; seizure of weapons.
2C:25–21.1.   Rules and regulations.
2C:25–22.   Immunity from civil liability.
2C:25–23.   Notice provided to victims; contents.
2C:25–24.   Domestic violence offense report; contents; annual report by superintendent of state police.
2C:25–25.   Criminal complaint; effect of dissolution of marriage, civil proceedings, or leaving residence; waiver of disclosure of victim's location.
2C:25–26.   Release from custody before trial; restraining orders; confidentiality of victim's location; bail.
2C:25–26.1.   Notification of victim of release of defendant charged with crime involving domestic violence.
2C:25–27.   Conditions of sentence.
2C:25–28.   Complaint by victim; emergency relief; temporary restraining orders; service of process.
2C:25–28.1.   In-house restraining orders prohibited.
2C:25–29.   Hearing; factors considered; orders for relief.
2C:25–29.1.   Civil penalty.
2C:25–29.2.   Penalties collected to be deposited in Domestic Violence Victims' Fund.
2C:25–29.3.   Rules of Court.
Section
2C:25–29.4.   Surcharge on penalty for domestic violence.
2C:25–30.   Violation of order; contempt proceedings; subsequent offenses.
2C:25–31.   Contempt of order; arrest and custody of defendant.
2C:25–32.   Lack of probable cause for arrest for contempt; advice and assistance to victim.
2C:25–33.   Uniform record of applications for relief; information included; confidentiality.
2C:25–34.   Domestic violence restraining orders; central registry.
2C:25–35.   Rules of Court.

2C:25–1 to 2C:25–16. Repealed by L.1991, c. 261, § 20, eff. Nov. 12, 1991

2C:25–17. Prevention of Domestic Violence Act of 1991; short title

This act shall be known and may be cited as the "Prevention of Domestic Violence Act of 1991."

L.1991, c. 261, § 1, eff. Nov. 12, 1991.

2C:25–18. Legislative findings and declaration

The Legislature finds and declares that domestic violence is a serious crime against society; that there are thousands of persons in this State who are regularly beaten, tortured and in some cases even killed by their spouses or cohabitants; that a significant number of women who are assaulted are pregnant; that victims of domestic violence come from all social and economic backgrounds and ethnic groups; that there is a positive correlation between spousal abuse and child abuse; and that children, even when they are not themselves physically assaulted, suffer deep and lasting emotional effects from exposure to domestic violence. It is therefore, the intent of the Legislature to assure the victims of domestic violence the maximum protection from abuse the law can provide.

The Legislature further finds and declares that the health and welfare of some of its most vulnerable citizens, the elderly and disabled, are at risk because of incidents of reported and unreported domestic violence, abuse and neglect which are known to include acts which victimize the elderly and disabled emotionally, psychologically, physically and financially; because of age, disabilities or infirmities, this group of citizens frequently must rely on the aid and support of others; while the institutionalized elderly are protected under P.L.1977, c. 239 (C. 52:27G–1 et seq.), elderly and disabled adults in noninstitutionalized or community settings may find themselves victimized by family members or others upon whom they feel compelled to depend.

The Legislature further finds and declares that violence against the elderly and disabled, including criminal neglect of the elderly and disabled under section 1 of P.L.1989, c. 23 (C. 2C:24–8), must be recognized and addressed on an equal basis as violence against spouses and children in order to fulfill our responsibility as a society to protect those who are less able to protect themselves.

The Legislature further finds and declares that even though many of the existing criminal statutes are applicable to acts of domestic violence, previous societal attitudes concerning domestic violence have affected the response of our law enforcement and judicial systems, resulting in these acts receiving different treatment from similar crimes when they occur in a domestic context. The Legislature finds that battered adults presently experience substantial difficulty in gaining access to protection from the judicial system, particularly due to that system's inability to generate a prompt response in an emergency situation.

It is the intent of the Legislature to stress that the primary duty of a law enforcement officer when responding to a domestic violence call is to enforce the laws allegedly violated and to protect the victim. Further, it is the responsibility of the courts to protect victims of violence that occurs in a family or family-like setting by providing access to both emergent and long-term civil and criminal remedies and sanctions, and by ordering those remedies and sanctions that are available to assure the safety of the victims and the public. To that end, the Legislature encourages the training of all police and judicial personnel in the procedures and enforcement of this act, and about the social and psychological context in which domestic violence occurs; and it further encourages the broad application of the remedies available under this act in the civil and criminal courts of this State. It is further intended that the official response to domestic violence shall communicate the attitude that violent behavior will not be excused or tolerated, and shall make clear the fact that the existing criminal laws and civil remedies created under this act will be enforced without regard to the fact that the violence grows out of a domestic situation.

L.1991, c. 261, § 2, eff. Nov. 12, 1991.

2C:25–19. Definitions

As used in this act:

a. "Domestic violence" means the occurrence of one or more of the following acts inflicted upon a person protected under this act by an adult or an emancipated minor:

(1) Homicide N.J.S. 2C:11–1 et seq.

(2) Assault N.J.S. 2C:12–1

(3) Terroristic threats N.J.S. 2C:12–3

(4) Kidnapping N.J.S. 2C:13–1

(5) Criminal restraint N.J.S. 2C:13–2

(6) False imprisonment N.J.S. 2C:13–3

(7) Sexual assault N.J.S. 2C:14–2

(8) Criminal sexual contact N.J.S. 2C:14–3

(9) Lewdness N.J.S. 2C:14–4

(10) Criminal mischief N.J.S. 2C:17–3

(11) Burglary N.J.S. 2C:18–2

(12) Criminal trespass N.J.S. 2C:18–3

(13) Harassment N.J.S. 2C:33–4

(14) Stalking P.L.1992, c. 209 (C. 2C:12–10)

When one or more of these acts is inflicted by an unemancipated minor upon a person protected under this act, the occurrence shall not constitute "domestic violence," but may be the basis for the filing of a petition or complaint pursuant to the provisions of section 11 of P.L.1982, c. 77 (C. 2A:4A–30).

b. "Law enforcement agency" means a department, division, bureau, commission, board or other authority of the State or of any political subdivision thereof which employs law enforcement officers.

c. "Law enforcement officer" means a person whose public duties include the power to act as an officer for the detection, apprehension, arrest and conviction of offenders against the laws of this State.

d. "Victim of domestic violence" means a person protected under this act and shall include any person who is 18 years of age or older or who is an emancipated minor and who has been subjected to domestic violence by a spouse, former spouse, or any other person who is a present or former household member. "Victim of domestic violence" also includes any person, regardless of age, who has been subjected to domestic violence by a person with whom the victim has a child in common, or with whom the victim anticipates having a child in common, if one of the parties is pregnant. "Victim of domestic violence" also includes any person who has been subjected to domestic violence by a person with whom the victim has had a dating relationship.

e. "Emancipated minor" means a person who is under 18 years of age but who has been married, has entered military service, has a child or is pregnant or has been previously declared by a court or an administrative agency to be emancipated.

L.1991, c. 261, § 3, eff. Nov. 12, 1991. Amended by L.1994, c. 93, § 1, eff. Aug. 11, 1994; L.1994, c. 94, § 1, eff. Aug. 11, 1994.

2C:25–20. Training course and curriculum; domestic crisis teams

a. (1) The Division of Criminal Justice shall develop and approve a training course and curriculum on the handling, investigation and response procedures concerning reports of domestic violence and abuse and neglect of the elderly and disabled. This training course and curriculum shall be reviewed at least every two years and modified by the Division of Criminal Justice from time to time as need may require. The Division of Criminal Justice shall distribute the curriculum to all local police agencies.

(2) The Attorney General shall be responsible for ensuring that all law enforcement officers attend initial training within 90 days of appointment or transfer and

annual inservice training of at least four hours as described in this section.

b. (1) The Administrative Office of the Courts shall develop and approve a training course and a curriculum on the handling, investigation and response procedures concerning allegations of domestic violence. This training course shall be reviewed at least every two years and modified by the Administrative Office of the Courts from time to time as need may require.

(2) The Administrative Director of the Courts shall be responsible for ensuring that all judges and judicial personnel attend initial training within 90 days of appointment or transfer and annual inservice training as described in this section.

(3) The Division of Criminal Justice and the Administrative Office of the Courts shall provide that all training on the handling of domestic violence matters shall include information concerning the impact of domestic violence on society, the dynamics of domestic violence, the statutory and case law concerning domestic violence, the necessary elements of a protection order, policies and procedures as promulgated or ordered by the Attorney General or the Supreme Court, and the use of available community resources, support services, available sanctions and treatment options. Law enforcement agencies shall: (1) establish domestic crisis teams or participate in established domestic crisis teams, and (2) shall train individual officers in methods of dealing with domestic violence and neglect and abuse of the elderly and disabled. The teams may include social workers, clergy or other persons trained in counseling, crisis intervention or in the treatment of domestic violence and neglect and abuse of the elderly and disabled victims.

L.1991, c. 261, § 4, eff. Nov. 12, 1991. Amended by L.1994, c. 93, § 2, eff. Aug. 11, 1994; L.1999, c. 289, § 1; L.1999, c. 433, § 1, eff. Jan. 18, 2000.

2C:25–21. Arrest; criminal complaint; seizure of weapons

a. When a person claims to be a victim of domestic violence, and where a law enforcement officer responding to the incident finds probable cause to believe that domestic violence has occurred, the law enforcement officer shall arrest the person who is alleged to be the person who subjected the victim to domestic violence and shall sign a criminal complaint if:

(1) The victim exhibits signs of injury caused by an act of domestic violence;

(2) A warrant is in effect;

(3) There is probable cause to believe that the person has violated N.J.S. 2C:29–9, and there is probable cause to believe that the person has been served with the order alleged to have been violated. If the victim does not have a copy of a purported order, the officer may verify the existence of an order with the appropriate law enforcement agency; or

(4) There is probable cause to believe that a weapon as defined in N.J.S.2C:39–1 has been involved in the commission of an act of domestic violence.

b. A law enforcement officer may arrest a person; or may sign a criminal complaint against that person, or may do both, where there is probable cause to believe that an act of domestic violence has been committed, but where none of the conditions in subsection a. of this section applies.

c. (1) As used in this section, the word "exhibits" is to be liberally construed to mean any indication that a victim has suffered bodily injury, which shall include physical pain or any impairment of physical condition. Where the victim exhibits no visible sign of injury, but states that an injury has occurred, the officer should consider other relevant factors in determining whether there is probable cause to make an arrest.

(2) In determining which party in a domestic violence incident is the victim where both parties exhibit signs of injury, the officer should consider the comparative extent of the injuries, the history of domestic violence between the parties, if any, and any other relevant factors.

(3) No victim shall be denied relief or arrested or charged under this act with an offense because the victim used reasonable force in self defense against domestic violence by an attacker.

d. (1) In addition to a law enforcement officer's authority to seize any weapon that is contraband, evidence or an instrumentality of crime, a law enforcement officer who has probable cause to believe that an act of domestic violence has been committed shall:

(a) question persons present to determine whether there are weapons on the premises; and

(b) upon observing or learning that a weapon is present on the premises, seize any weapon that the officer reasonably believes would expose the victim to a risk of serious bodily injury. If a law enforcement officer seizes any firearm pursuant to this paragraph, the officer shall also seize any firearm purchaser identification card or permit to purchase a handgun issued to the person accused of the act of domestic violence.

(2) A law enforcement officer shall deliver all weapons, firearms purchaser identification cards and permits to purchase a handgun seized pursuant to this section to the county prosecutor and shall append an inventory of all seized items to the domestic violence report.

(3) Weapons seized in accordance with the "Prevention of Domestic Violence Act of 1991", P.L.1991, c. 261(C.2C:25–17 et seq.) shall be returned to the owner except upon order of the Superior Court. The prosecutor who has possession of the seized weapons may, upon notice to the owner, petition a judge of the Family Part of the Superior Court, Chancery Division, within 45 days of seizure, to obtain title to the seized weapons, or to revoke any and all permits, licenses and other

authorizations for the use, possession, or ownership of such weapons pursuant to the law governing such use, possession, or ownership, or may object to the return of the weapons on such grounds as are provided for the initial rejection or later revocation of the authorizations, or on the grounds that the owner is unfit or that the owner poses a threat to the public in general or a person or persons in particular.

A hearing shall be held and a record made thereof within 45 days of the notice provided above. No formal pleading and no filing fee shall be required as a preliminary to such hearing. The hearing shall be summary in nature. Appeals from the results of the hearing shall be to the Superior Court, Appellate Division, in accordance with the law.

If the prosecutor does not institute an action within 45 days of seizure, the seized weapons shall be returned to the owner.

After the hearing the court shall order the return of the firearms, weapons and any authorization papers relating to the seized weapons to the owner if the court determines the owner is not subject to any of the disabilities set forth in N.J.S.2C:58–3c. and finds that the complaint has been dismissed at the request of the complainant and the prosecutor determines that there is insufficient probable cause to indict; or if the defendant is found not guilty of the charges; or if the court determines that the domestic violence situation no longer exists. Nothing in this act shall impair the right of the State to retain evidence pending a criminal prosecution. Nor shall any provision of this act be construed to limit the authority of the State or a law enforcement officer to seize, retain or forfeit property pursuant to chapter 64 of Title 2C of the New Jersey Statutes.

If, after the hearing, the court determines that the weapons are not to be returned to the owner, the court may:

(a) With respect to weapons other than firearms, order the prosecutor to dispose of the weapons if the owner does not arrange for the transfer or sale of the weapons to an appropriate person within 60 days; or

(b) Order the revocation of the owner's firearms purchaser identification card or any permit, license or authorization, in which case the court shall order the owner to surrender any firearm seized and all other firearms possessed to the prosecutor and shall order the prosecutor to dispose of the firearms if the owner does not arrange for the sale of the firearms to a registered dealer of the firearms within 60 days; or

(c) Order such other relief as it may deem appropriate. When the court orders the weapons forfeited to the State or the prosecutor is required to dispose of the weapons, the prosecutor shall dispose of the property as provided in N.J.S.2C:64–6.

(4) A civil suit may be brought to enjoin a wrongful failure to return a seized firearm where the prosecutor refuses to return the weapon after receiving a written request to do so and notice of the owner's intent to bring a civil action pursuant to this section. Failure of the prosecutor to comply with the provisions of this act shall entitle the prevailing party in the civil suit to reasonable costs, including attorney's fees, provided that the court finds that the prosecutor failed to act in good faith in retaining the seized weapon.

(5) No law enforcement officer or agency shall be held liable in any civil action brought by any person for failing to learn of, locate or seize a weapon pursuant to this act, or for returning a seized weapon to its owner.

L.1991, c. 261, § 5, eff. Nov. 12, 1991. Amended by L.2003, c. 277, § 1, eff. Jan. 14, 2004.

2C:25–21.1. Rules and regulations

The Attorney General may adopt, pursuant to the "Administrative Procedure Act," P.L.1968, c. 410 (C.52:14B–1 et seq.), rules and regulations necessary and appropriate to implement this act.

L.2003, c. 277, § 6, eff. Jan. 14, 2004.

2C:25–22. Immunity from civil liability

A law enforcement officer or a member of a domestic crisis team or any person who, in good faith, reports a possible incident of domestic violence to the police shall not be held liable in any civil action brought by any party for an arrest based on probable cause, enforcement in good faith of a court order, or any other act or omission in good faith under this act.

L.1991, c. 261, § 6, eff. Nov. 12, 1991. Amended by L.1994, c. 94, § 2, eff. Aug. 11, 1994.

2C:25–23. Notice provided to victims; contents

A law enforcement officer shall disseminate and explain to the victim the following notice, which shall be written in both English and Spanish:

"You have the right to go to court to get an order called a temporary restraining order, also called a TRO, which may protect you from more abuse by your attacker. The officer who handed you this card can tell you how to get a TRO.

The kinds of things a judge can order in a TRO may include:

(1) That your attacker is temporarily forbidden from entering the home you live in;

(2) That your attacker is temporarily forbidden from having contact with you or your relatives;

(3) That your attacker is temporarily forbidden from bothering you at work;

(4) That your attacker has to pay temporary child support or support for you;

(5) That you be given temporary custody of your children;

(6) That your attacker pay you back any money you have to spend for medical treatment or repairs because of the violence. There are other things the court can order, and the court clerk will explain the procedure to you and will help you fill out the papers for a TRO.

You also have the right to file a criminal complaint against your attacker. The police officer who gave you this paper will tell you how to file a criminal complaint.

On weekends, holidays and other times when the courts are closed, you still have a right to get a TRO. The police officer who gave you this paper can help you get in touch with a judge who can give you a TRO."
L.1991, c. 261, § 7, eff. Nov. 12, 1991.

2C:25–24. Domestic violence offense report; contents; annual report by superintendent of state police

a. It shall be the duty of a law enforcement officer who responds to a domestic violence call to complete a domestic violence offense report. All information contained in the domestic violence offense report shall be forwarded to the appropriate county bureau of identification and to the State bureau of records and identification in the Division of State Police in the Department of Law and Public Safety. A copy of the domestic violence offense report shall be forwarded to the municipal court where the offense was committed unless the case has been transferred to the Superior Court.

b. The domestic violence offense report shall be on a form prescribed by the supervisor of the State bureau of records and identification which shall include, but not be limited to, the following information:

(1) The relationship of the parties;

(2) The sex of the parties;

(3) The time and date of the incident;

(4) The number of domestic violence calls investigated;

(5) Whether children were involved, or whether the alleged act of domestic violence had been committed in the presence of children;

(6) The type and extent of abuse;

(7) The number and type of weapons involved;

(8) The action taken by the law enforcement officer;

(9) The existence of any prior court orders issued pursuant to this act concerning the parties;

(10) The number of domestic violence calls alleging a violation of a domestic violence restraining order;

(11) The number of arrests for a violation of a domestic violence order; and

(12) Any other data that may be necessary for a complete analysis of all circumstances leading to the alleged incident of domestic violence.

c. It shall be the duty of the Superintendent of the State Police with the assistance of the Division of Systems and Communications in the Department of Law and Public Safety to compile and report annually to the Governor, the Legislature and the Advisory Council on Domestic Violence on the tabulated data from the domestic violence offense reports, classified by county.
L.1991, c. 261, § 8, eff. Nov. 12, 1991. Amended by L.1999, c. 119, § 2, eff. June 9, 1999.

2C:25–25. Criminal complaint; effect of dissolution of marriage, civil proceedings, or leaving residence; waiver of disclosure of victim's location

The court in a criminal complaint arising from a domestic violence incident:

a. Shall not dismiss any charge or delay disposition of a case because of concurrent dissolution of a marriage, other civil proceedings, or because the victim has left the residence to avoid further incidents of domestic violence;

b. Shall not require proof that either party is seeking a dissolution of a marriage prior to institution of criminal proceedings;

c. Shall waive any requirement that the victim's location be disclosed to any person.
L.1991, c. 261, § 9, eff. Nov. 12, 1991.

2C:25–26. Release from custody before trial; restraining orders; confidentiality of victim's location; bail

a. When a defendant charged with a crime or offense involving domestic violence is released from custody before trial on bail or personal recognizance, the court authorizing the release may as a condition of release issue an order prohibiting the defendant from having any contact with the victim including, but not limited to, restraining the defendant from entering the victim's residence, place of employment or business, or school, and from harassing or stalking the victim or victim's relatives in any way. The court may enter an order prohibiting the defendant from possessing any firearm or other weapon enumerated in subsection r. of N.J.S.2C:39–1 and ordering the search for and seizure of any such weapon at any location where the judge has reasonable cause to believe the weapon is located. The judge shall state with specificity the reasons for and scope of the search and seizure authorized by the order.

b. The written court order releasing the defendant shall contain the court's directives specifically restricting the defendant's ability to have contact with the victim or the victim's friends, co-workers or relatives. The clerk of the court or other person designated by the court shall provide a copy of this order to the victim forthwith.

c. The victim's location shall remain confidential and shall not appear on any documents or records to which the defendant has access.

d. Before bail is set, the defendant's prior record shall be considered by the court. The court shall also conduct a search of the domestic violence central registry. Bail shall be set as soon as is feasible, but in all cases within 24 hours of arrest.

e. Once bail is set it shall not be reduced without prior notice to the county prosecutor and the victim. Bail shall not be reduced by a judge other than the judge who originally ordered bail, unless the reasons for the amount of the original bail are available to the judge who reduces the bail and are set forth in the record.

f. A victim shall not be prohibited from applying for, and a court shall not be prohibited from issuing, temporary restraints pursuant to this act because the victim has charged any person with commission of a criminal act.

L.1991, c. 261, § 10, eff. Nov. 12, 1991. Amended by L.1994, c. 94, § 3, eff. Aug. 11, 1994; L.1999, c. 421, § 2, eff. Jan. 18, 2000.

2C:25–26.1. Notification of victim of release of defendant charged with crime involving domestic violence

Notwithstanding any other provision of law to the contrary, whenever a defendant charged with a crime or an offense involving domestic violence is released from custody the prosecuting agency shall notify the victim.

L.1994, c. 137, § 1, eff. Oct. 31, 1994.

2C:25–27. Conditions of sentence

When a defendant is found guilty of a crime or offense involving domestic violence and a condition of sentence restricts the defendant's ability to have contact with the victim, that condition shall be recorded in an order of the court and a written copy of that order shall be provided to the victim by the clerk of the court or other person designated by the court. In addition to restricting a defendant's ability to have contact with the victim, the court may require the defendant to receive professional counseling from either a private source or a source appointed by the court, and if the court so orders, the court shall require the defendant to provide documentation of attendance at the professional counseling. In any case where the court order contains a requirement that the defendant receive professional counseling, no application by the defendant to dissolve the restraining order shall be granted unless, in addition to any other provisions required by law or conditions ordered by the court, the defendant has completed all required attendance at such counseling.

L.1991, c. 261, § 11, eff. Nov. 12, 1991. Amended by L.1999, c. 236, § 1, eff. Oct. 13, 1999.

2C:25–28. Complaint by victim; emergency relief; temporary restraining orders; service of process

a. A victim may file a complaint alleging the commission of an act of domestic violence with the Family Part of the Chancery Division of the Superior Court in conformity with the Rules of Court. The court shall not dismiss any complaint or delay disposition of a case because the victim has left the residence to avoid further incidents of domestic violence. Filing a com-

plaint pursuant to this section shall not prevent the filing of a criminal complaint for the same act.

On weekends, holidays and other times when the court is closed, a victim may file a complaint before a judge of the Family Part of the Chancery Division of the Superior Court or a municipal court judge who shall be assigned to accept complaints and issue emergency, ex parte relief in the form of temporary restraining orders pursuant to this act.

A plaintiff may apply for relief under this section in a court having jurisdiction over the place where the alleged act of domestic violence occurred, where the defendant resides, or where the plaintiff resides or is sheltered, and the court shall follow the same procedures applicable to other emergency applications. Criminal complaints filed pursuant to this act shall be investigated and prosecuted in the jurisdiction where the offense is alleged to have occurred. Contempt complaints filed pursuant to N.J.S.2C:29–9 shall be prosecuted in the county where the contempt is alleged to have been committed and a copy of the contempt complaint shall be forwarded to the court that issued the order alleged to have been violated.

b. The court shall waive any requirement that the petitioner's place of residence appear on the complaint.

c. The clerk of the court, or other person designated by the court, shall assist the parties in completing any forms necessary for the filing of a summons, complaint, answer or other pleading.

d. Summons and complaint forms shall be readily available at the clerk's office, at the municipal courts and at municipal and State police stations.

e. As soon as the domestic violence complaint is filed, both the victim and the abuser shall be advised of any programs or services available for advice and counseling.

f. A plaintiff may seek emergency, ex parte relief in the nature of a temporary restraining order. A municipal court judge or a judge of the Family Part of the Chancery Division of the Superior Court may enter an ex parte order when necessary to protect the life, health or well-being of a victim on whose behalf the relief is sought.

g. If it appears that the plaintiff is in danger of domestic violence, the judge shall, upon consideration of the plaintiff's domestic violence complaint, order emergency ex parte relief, in the nature of a temporary restraining order. A decision shall be made by the judge regarding the emergency relief forthwith.

h. A judge may issue a temporary restraining order upon sworn testimony or complaint of an applicant who is not physically present, pursuant to court rules, or by a person who represents a person who is physically or mentally incapable of filing personally. A temporary restraining order may be issued if the judge is satisfied that exigent circumstances exist sufficient to excuse the failure of the applicant to appear personally and that sufficient grounds for granting the application have been shown.

i. An order for emergency, ex parte relief shall be granted upon good cause shown and shall remain in effect until a judge of the Family Part issues a further order. Any temporary order hereunder is immediately appealable for a plenary hearing de novo not on the record before any judge of the Family Part of the county in which the plaintiff resides or is sheltered if that judge issued the temporary order or has access to the reasons for the issuance of the temporary order and sets forth in the record the reasons for the modification or dissolution. The denial of a temporary restraining order by a municipal court judge and subsequent administrative dismissal of the complaint shall not bar the victim from refiling a complaint in the Family Part based on the same incident and receiving an emergency, ex parte hearing de novo not on the record before a Family Part judge, and every denial of relief by a municipal court judge shall so state.

j. Emergency relief may include forbidding the defendant from returning to the scene of the domestic violence, forbidding the defendant from possessing any firearm or other weapon enumerated in subsection r. of N.J.S.2C:39–1, ordering the search for and seizure of any such weapon at any location where the judge has reasonable cause to believe the weapon is located and the seizure of any firearms purchaser identification card or permit to purchase a handgun issued to the defendant and any other appropriate relief. The judge shall state with specificity the reasons for and scope of the search and seizure authorized by the order. The provisions of this subsection prohibiting a defendant from possessing a firearm or other weapon shall not apply to any law enforcement officer while actually on duty, or to any member of the Armed Forces of the United States or member of the National Guard while actually on duty or traveling to or from an authorized place of duty.

k. The judge may permit the defendant to return to the scene of the domestic violence to pick up personal belongings and effects but shall, in the order granting relief, restrict the time and duration of such permission and provide for police supervision of such visit.

l. An order granting emergency relief, together with the complaint or complaints, shall immediately be forwarded to the appropriate law enforcement agency for service on the defendant, and to the police of the municipality in which the plaintiff resides or is sheltered, and shall immediately be served upon the defendant by the police, except that an order issued during regular court hours may be forwarded to the sheriff for immediate service upon the defendant in accordance with the Rules of Court. If personal service cannot be effected upon the defendant, the court may order other appropriate substituted service. At no time shall the plaintiff be asked or required to serve any order on the defendant.

m. (Deleted by amendment, P.L.1994, c. 94.)

n. Notice of temporary restraining orders issued pursuant to this section shall be sent by the clerk of the court or other person designated by the court to the appropriate chiefs of police, members of the State Police and any other appropriate law enforcement agency or court.

o. (Deleted by amendment, P.L.1994, c. 94.)

p. Any temporary or permanent restraining order issued pursuant to this act shall be in effect throughout the State, and shall be enforced by all law enforcement officers.

q. Prior to the issuance of any temporary or permanent restraining order issued pursuant to this section, the court shall order that a search be made of the domestic violence central registry with regard to the defendant's record.

L.1991, c. 261, § 12, eff. Nov. 12, 1991. Amended by L.1994, c. 94, § 4, eff. Aug. 11, 1994; L.1999, c. 421, § 3, eff. Jan. 18, 2000; L.2003, c. 277, § 5, eff. Jan. 14, 2004.

2C:25–28.1. In-house restraining orders prohibited

Notwithstanding any provision of P.L.1991, c. 261 (C.2C:25–17 et seq.) to the contrary, no order issued by the Family Part of the Chancery Division of the Superior Court pursuant to section 12 or section 13 of P.L.1991, c. 261 (C.2C:25–28 or 2C:25–29) regarding emergency, temporary or final relief shall include an in-house restraining order which permits the victim and the defendant to occupy the same premises but limits the defendant's use of that premises.

L.1995, c. 242, § 2, eff. Sept. 1, 1995.

2C:25–29. Hearing; factors considered; orders for relief

a. A hearing shall be held in the Family Part of the Chancery Division of the Superior Court within 10 days of the filing of a complaint pursuant to section 12 of P.L.1991, c. 261 (C.2C:25–28) in the county where the ex parte restraints were ordered, unless good cause is shown for the hearing to be held elsewhere. A copy of the complaint shall be served on the defendant in conformity with the Rules of Court. If a criminal complaint arising out of the same incident which is the subject matter of a complaint brought under P.L.1981, c. 426 (C.2C:25–1 et seq.) or P.L.1991, c. 261 (C.2C:25–17 et seq.) has been filed, testimony given by the plaintiff or defendant in the domestic violence matter shall not be used in the simultaneous or subsequent criminal proceeding against the defendant, other than domestic violence contempt matters and where it would otherwise be admissible hearsay under the rules of evidence that govern where a party is unavailable. At the hearing the standard for proving the allegations in the complaint shall be by a preponderance of the evidence. The court shall consider but not be limited to the following factors:

(1) The previous history of domestic violence between the plaintiff and defendant, including threats, harassment and physical abuse;

(2) The existence of immediate danger to person or property;

(3) The financial circumstances of the plaintiff and defendant;

(4) The best interests of the victim and any child;

(5) In determining custody and parenting time the protection of the victim's safety; and

(6) The existence of a verifiable order of protection from another jurisdiction.

An order issued under this act shall only restrain or provide damages payable from a person against whom a complaint has been filed under this act and only after a finding or an admission is made that an act of domestic violence was committed by that person. The issue of whether or not a violation of this act occurred, including an act of contempt under this act, shall not be subject to mediation or negotiation in any form. In addition, where a temporary or final order has been issued pursuant to this act, no party shall be ordered to participate in mediation on the issue of custody or parenting time.

b. In proceedings in which complaints for restraining orders have been filed, the court shall grant any relief necessary to prevent further abuse. In addition to any other provisions, any restraining order issued by the court shall bar the defendant from purchasing, owning, possessing or controlling a firearm and from receiving or retaining a firearms purchaser identification card or permit to purchase a handgun pursuant to N.J.S.2C:58–3 during the period in which the restraining order is in effect or two years whichever is greater,except that this provision shall not apply to any law enforcement officer while actually on duty, or to any member of the Armed Forces of the United States or member of the National Guard while actually on duty or traveling to or from an authorized place of duty. At the hearing the judge of the Family Part of the Chancery Division of the Superior Court may issue an order granting any or all of the following relief:

(1) An order restraining the defendant from subjecting the victim to domestic violence, as defined in this act.

(2) An order granting exclusive possession to the plaintiff of the residence or household regardless of whether the residence or household is jointly or solely owned by the parties or jointly or solely leased by the parties. This order shall not in any manner affect title or interest to any real property held by either party or both jointly. If it is not possible for the victim to remain in the residence, the court may order the defendant to pay the victim's rent at a residence other than the one previously shared by the parties if the defendant is found to have a duty to support the victim and the victim requires alternative housing.

(3) An order providing for parenting time. The order shall protect the safety and well-being of the plaintiff and minor children and shall specify the place and frequency of parenting time. Parenting time arrangements shall not compromise any other remedy provided by the court by requiring or encouraging contact between the plaintiff and defendant. Orders for parenting time may include a designation of a place of parenting time away from the plaintiff, the participation of a third party, or supervised parenting time.

(a) The court shall consider a request by a custodial parent who has been subjected to domestic violence by a person with parenting time rights to a child in the parent's custody for an investigation or evaluation by the appropriate agency to assess the risk of harm to the child prior to the entry of a parenting time order. Any denial of such a request must be on the record and shall only be made if the judge finds the request to be arbitrary or capricious.

(b) The court shall consider suspension of the parenting time order and hold an emergency hearing upon an application made by the plaintiff certifying under oath that the defendant's access to the child pursuant to the parenting time order has threatened the safety and well-being of the child.

(4) An order requiring the defendant to pay to the victim monetary compensation for losses suffered as a direct result of the act of domestic violence. The order may require the defendant to pay the victim directly, to reimburse the Victims of Crime Compensation Board for any and all compensation paid by the Victims of Crime Compensation Board directly to or on behalf of the victim, and may require that the defendant reimburse any parties that may have compensated the victim, as the court may determine. Compensatory losses shall include, but not be limited to, loss of earnings or other support, including child or spousal support, out-of-pocket losses for injuries sustained, cost of repair or replacement of real or personal property damaged or destroyed or taken by the defendant, cost of counseling for the victim, moving or other travel expenses, reasonable attorney's fees, court costs, and compensation for pain and suffering. Where appropriate, punitive damages may be awarded in addition to compensatory damages.

(5) An order requiring the defendant to receive professional domestic violence counseling from either a private source or a source appointed by the court and, in that event, requiring the defendant to provide the court at specified intervals with documentation of attendance at the professional counseling. The court may order the defendant to pay for the professional counseling. No application by the defendant to dissolve a final order which contains a requirement for attendance at professional counseling pursuant to this paragraph shall be granted by the court unless, in addition to any other provisions required by law or conditions ordered by the court, the defendant has completed all required attendance at such counseling.

(6) An order restraining the defendant from entering the residence, property, school, or place of employment of the victim or of other family or household members of the victim and requiring the defendant to stay away from any specified place that is named in the order and is frequented regularly by the victim or other family or household members.

(7) An order restraining the defendant from making contact with the plaintiff or others, including an order forbidding the defendant from personally or through an agent initiating any communication likely to cause annoyance or alarm including, but not limited to, personal, written, or telephone contact with the victim or other family members, or their employers, employees, or fellow workers, or others with whom communication would be likely to cause annoyance or alarm to the victim.

(8) An order requiring that the defendant make or continue to make rent or mortgage payments on the residence occupied by the victim if the defendant is found to have a duty to support the victim or other dependent household members; provided that this issue has not been resolved or is not being litigated between the parties in another action.

(9) An order granting either party temporary possession of specified personal property, such as an automobile, checkbook, documentation of health insurance, an identification document, a key, and other personal effects.

(10) An order awarding emergency monetary relief, including emergency support for minor children, to the victim and other dependents, if any. An ongoing obligation of support shall be determined at a later date pursuant to applicable law.

(11) An order awarding temporary custody of a minor child. The court shall presume that the best interests of the child are served by an award of custody to the non-abusive parent.

(12) An order requiring that a law enforcement officer accompany either party to the residence or any shared business premises to supervise the removal of personal belongings in order to ensure the personal safety of the plaintiff when a restraining order has been issued. This order shall be restricted in duration.

(13) (Deleted by amendment, P.L.1995, c. 242).

(14) An order granting any other appropriate relief for the plaintiff and dependent children, provided that the plaintiff consents to such relief, including relief requested by the plaintiff at the final hearing, whether or not the plaintiff requested such relief at the time of the granting of the initial emergency order.

(15) An order that requires that the defendant report to the intake unit of the Family Part of the Chancery Division of the Superior Court for monitoring of any other provision of the order.

(16) In addition to the order required by this subsection prohibiting the defendant from possessing any firearm,the court may also issue an order prohibiting the defendant from possessing any other weapon enumerated in subsection r. of N.J.S.2C:39–1 and ordering the search for and seizure of any firearm or other weapon at any location where the judge has reasonable cause to believe the weapon is located. The judge shall state with specificity the reasons for and scope of the search and seizure authorized by the order.

(17) An order prohibiting the defendant from stalking or following, or threatening to harm, to stalk or to follow, the complainant or any other person named in the order in a manner that, taken in the context of past actions of the defendant, would put the complainant in reasonable fear that the defendant would cause the death or injury of the complainant or any other person. Behavior prohibited under this act includes, but is not limited to, behavior prohibited under the provisions of P.L.1992, c. 209 (C.2C:12–10).

(18) An order requiring the defendant to undergo a psychiatric evaluation.

c. Notice of orders issued pursuant to this section shall be sent by the clerk of the Family Part of the Chancery Division of the Superior Court or other person designated by the court to the appropriate chiefs of police, members of the State Police and any other appropriate law enforcement agency.

d. Upon good cause shown, any final order may be dissolved or modified upon application to the Family Part of the Chancery Division of the Superior Court, but only if the judge who dissolves or modifies the order is the same judge who entered the order, or has available a complete record of the hearing or hearings on which the order was based.

e. Prior to the issuance of any order pursuant to this section, the court shall order that a search be made of the domestic violence central registry.

L.1991, c. 261, § 13, eff. Nov. 12, 1991. Amended by L.1994, c. 94, § 5, eff. Aug. 11, 1994; L.1994, c. 137, § 2, eff. Oct. 31, 1994; L.1995, c. 242, § 1, eff. Sept. 1, 1995; L.1997, c. 299, § 8, eff. Jan. 8, 1998; L.1999, c. 236, § 2, eff. Oct. 13, 1999; L.1999, c. 421, § 4, eff. Jan. 18, 2000; L.2003, c. 277, § 2, eff. Jan. 14, 2004.

2C:25–29.1. Civil penalty

In addition to any other disposition, any person found by the court in a final hearing pursuant to section 13 of P.L.1991, c. 261 (C.2C: 25–29) to have committed an act of domestic violence shall be ordered by the court to pay a civil penalty of at least $50, but not to exceed $500. In imposing this civil penalty, the court shall take into consideration the nature and degree of injury suffered by the victim. The court may waive the penalty in cases of extreme financial hardship.

L.2001, c. 195, § 1, eff. Jan. 29, 2002.

2C:25–29.2. Penalties collected to be deposited in Domestic Violence Victims' Fund

All civil penalties imposed pursuant to section 1 of P.L.2001, c. 195 (C.2C:25–29.1 et al.) shall be collected as provided by the Rules of Court. All moneys collected shall be forwarded to the Domestic Violence Victims' Fund established pursuant to section 3 of P.L.2001, c. 195 (C.30:14–15).

L.2001, c. 195, § 2, eff. Jan. 29, 2002.

2C:25–29.3. Rules of Court

The Supreme Court may promulgate Rules of Court to effectuate the purposes of this act.

L.2001, c. 195, § 4, eff. Aug. 2, 2001.

2C:25–29.4. Surcharge on penalty for domestic violence

In addition to any other penalty, fine or charge imposed pursuant to law, a person convicted of an act of domestic violence, as that term is defined by subsection a. of section 3 of P.L.1991, c. 261 (C.2C:25–19), shall be subject to a surcharge in the amount of $100 payable to the Treasurer of the State of New Jersey for use by the Department of Human Services to fund grants for domestic violence prevention, training and assessment.

L.2002, c. 34, § 50, eff. July 1, 2002.

2C:25–30. Violation of order; contempt proceedings; subsequent offenses

Except as provided below, a violation by the defendant of an order issued pursuant to this act shall constitute an offense under subsection b. of N.J.S. 2C:29–9 and each order shall so state. All contempt proceedings conducted pursuant to N.J.S. 2C:29–9 involving domestic violence orders, other than those constituting indictable offenses, shall be heard by the Family Part of the Chancery Division of the Superior Court. All contempt proceedings brought pursuant to P.L.1991, c. 261 (C. 2C:25–17 et seq.) shall be subject to any rules or guidelines established by the Supreme Court to guarantee the prompt disposition of criminal matters. Additionally, and notwithstanding the term of imprisonment provided in N.J.S. 2C:43–8, any person convicted of a second or subsequent nonindictable domestic violence contempt offense shall serve a minimum term of not less than 30 days. Orders entered pursuant to paragraphs (3), (4), (5), (8) and (9) of subsection b. of section 13 of this act [1] shall be excluded from enforcement under subsection b. of N.J.S. 2C:29–9; however, violations of these orders may be enforced in a civil or criminal action initiated by the plaintiff or by the court, on its own motion, pursuant to applicable court rules.

L.1991, c. 261, § 14, eff. Nov. 12, 1991. Amended by L.1994, c. 93, § 3, eff. Aug. 11, 1994; L.1994, c. 94, § 6, eff. Aug. 11, 1994.

[1] Section 2C:25–29.

2C:25–31. Contempt of order; arrest and custody of defendant

Where a law enforcement officer finds that there is probable cause that a defendant has committed contempt of an order entered pursuant to the provisions of P.L.1981, c. 426 (C.2C:25–1 et seq.) or P.L.1991, c. 261 (C.2C:25–17 et seq.), the defendant shall be arrested and taken into custody by a law enforcement officer. The law enforcement officer shall follow these procedures:

The law enforcement officer shall transport the defendant to the police station or such other place as the law enforcement officer shall determine is proper. The law enforcement officer shall:

a. Conduct a search of the domestic violence central registry and sign a complaint concerning the incident which gave rise to the contempt charge;

b. Telephone or communicate in person or by facsimile with the appropriate judge assigned pursuant to this act and request bail be set on the contempt charge;

c. If the defendant is unable to meet the bail set, take the necessary steps to insure that the defendant shall be incarcerated at police headquarters or at the county jail; and

d. During regular court hours, the defendant shall have bail set by a Superior Court judge that day. On weekends, holidays and other times when the court is closed, the officer shall arrange to have the clerk of the Family Part notified on the next working day of the new complaint, the amount of bail, the defendant's whereabouts and all other necessary details. In addition, if a municipal court judge set the bail, the arresting officer shall notify the clerk of that municipal court of this information.

L.1991, c. 261, § 15, eff. Nov. 12, 1991. Amended by L.1994, c. 94, § 7, eff. Aug. 11, 1994; L.1999, c. 421, § 5, eff. Jan. 18, 2000.

2C:25–32. Lack of probable cause for arrest for contempt; advice and assistance to victim

Where a person alleges that a defendant has committed contempt of an order entered pursuant to the provisions of P.L.1981, c. 426 (C.2C:25–1 et seq.) or P.L.1991, c. 261, but where a law enforcement officer has found that there is not probable cause sufficient to arrest the defendant, the law enforcement officer shall advise the complainant of the procedure for completing and signing a criminal complaint alleging a violation of N.J.S. 2C:29–9. During regular court hours, the assistance of the clerk of the Family Part of the Chancery Division of the Superior Court shall be made available to such complainants. Nothing in this section shall be construed to prevent the court from granting any other emergency relief it deems necessary.

L.1991, c. 261, § 16, eff. Nov. 12, 1991.

2C:25–33. Uniform record of applications for relief; information included; confidentiality

a. The Administrative Office of the Courts shall, with the assistance of the Attorney General and the county prosecutors, maintain a uniform record of all applications for relief pursuant to sections 9, 10, 11, 12, and 13 of P.L.1991, c. 261 (C.2C:25–25, C.2C:25–26, C.2C:25–27, C.2C:25–28, and C.2C:25–29). The record shall include the following information:

(1) The number of criminal and civil complaints filed in all municipal courts and the Superior Court;

(2) The sex of the parties;

(3) The relationship of the parties;

(4) The relief sought or the offense charged, or both;

(5) The nature of the relief granted or penalty imposed, or both, including, but not limited to, the following:

(a) custody;

(b) child support;

(c) the specific restraints ordered;

(d) any requirements or conditions imposed pursuant to paragraphs (1) through (18) of subsection b. of section 13 of P.L.1991, c. 261 (C.2C:25–29), including but not limited to professional counseling or psychiatric evaluations;

(6) The effective date of each order issued; and

(7) In the case of a civil action in which no permanent restraints are entered, or in the case of a criminal matter that does not proceed to trial, the reason or reasons for the disposition.

It shall be the duty of the Director of the Administrative Office of the Courts to compile and report annually to the Governor, the Legislature and the Advisory Council on Domestic Violence on the data tabulated from the records of these orders.

All records maintained pursuant to this act shall be confidential and shall not be made available to any individual or institution except as otherwise provided by law.

b. In addition to the provisions of subsection a. of this section, the Administrative Office of the Courts shall, with the assistance of the Attorney General and the county prosecutors, create and maintain uniform forms to record sentencing, bail conditions and dismissals. The forms shall be used by the Superior Court and by every municipal court to record any order in a case brought pursuant to this act. Such recording shall include but not be limited to, the specific restraints ordered, any requirements or conditions imposed on the defendant, and any conditions of bail.

L.1991, c. 261, § 17, eff. Nov. 12, 1991. Amended by L.1994, c. 94, § 8, eff. Aug. 11, 1994; L.1999, c. 119, § 1, eff. June 9, 1999; L.1999, c. 421, § 6, eff. Jan. 18, 2000.

2C:25–34. Domestic violence restraining orders; central registry

The Administrative Office of the Courts shall establish and maintain a central registry of all persons who have had domestic violence restraining orders entered against them, all persons who have been charged with a crime or offense involving domestic violence, and all persons who have been charged with a violation of a court order involving domestic violence. All records made pursuant to this section shall be kept confidential and shall be released only to:

a. A public agency authorized to investigate a report of domestic violence;

b. A police or other law enforcement agency investigating a report of domestic violence, or conducting a background investigation involving a person's application for a firearm permit or employment as a police or law enforcement officer or for any other purpose authorized by law or the Supreme Court of the State of New Jersey;

c. A court, upon its finding that access to such records may be necessary for determination of an issue before the court;

d. A surrogate, in that person's official capacity as deputy clerk of the Superior Court, in order to prepare documents that may be necessary for a court to determine an issue in an adoption proceeding; or

e. The Division of Youth and Family Services in the Department of Children and Families when the division is conducting a background investigation involving:

(1) an allegation of child abuse or neglect, to include any adult member of the same household as the individual who is the subject of the abuse or neglect allegation; or

(2) an out-of-home placement for a child being placed by the Division of Youth and Family Services, to include any adult member of the prospective placement household.

Any individual, agency, surrogate or court which receives from the Administrative Office of the Courts the records referred to in this section shall keep such records and reports, or parts thereof, confidential and shall not disseminate or disclose such records and reports, or parts thereof; provided that nothing in this section shall prohibit a receiving individual, agency, surrogate or court from disclosing records and reports, or parts thereof, in a manner consistent with and in furtherance of the purpose for which the records and reports or parts thereof were received.

Any individual who disseminates or discloses a record or report, or parts thereof, of the central registry, for a purpose other than investigating a report of domestic violence, conducting a background investigation involving a person's application for a firearm permit or employment as a police or law enforcement officer, making a determination of an issue before the court, conducting a background investigation as specified in subsection e. of this section, or for any other purpose other than that which is authorized by law or the Supreme Court of the State of New Jersey, shall be guilty of a crime of the fourth degree.

L.1999, c. 421, § 1, eff. Jan. 18, 2000. Amended by L.2003, c. 286, § 1, eff. Jan. 14, 2004; L.2006, c. 47, § 26, eff. July 1, 2006.

2C:25–35. Rules of Court

The Supreme Court of New Jersey may adopt Rules of Court appropriate or necessary to effectuate the purposes of this act.

L.1999, c. 421, § 7, eff. Jan. 18, 2000.

CHAPTER 26

[RESERVED]

PART 4

OFFENSES AGAINST PUBLIC ADMINISTRATION

Chapter
27. **Bribery and Corrupt Influence.**
28. **Perjury and Other Falsification in Official Matters.**
29. **Obstructing Governmental Operations; Escape.**
30. **Misconduct in Office: Abuse of Office.**
31, 32. **[Reserved].**

CHAPTER 27

BRIBERY AND CORRUPT INFLUENCE

Section
2C:27–1.   Definitions.
2C:27–2.   Bribery in official and political matters.
2C:27–3.   Threats and other improper influence in official and political matters.
2C:27–4.   Repealed.
2C:27–5.   Retaliation for past official action.
2C:27–6.   Repealed.
2C:27–7.   Repealed.
2C:27–8.   Repealed.
2C:27–9.   Public servant transacting business with certain persons.
2C:27–10. Acceptance or receipt of unlawful benefit by public servant for official behavior.
2C:27–11. Offer of unlawful benefit to public servant for official behavior.
2C:27–12. Corruption of public resources.

2C:27–1.   Definitions

In chapters 27 through 30, unless a different meaning plainly is required:

a. "Benefit" means gain or advantage, or anything regarded by the beneficiary as gain or advantage, including a pecuniary benefit or a benefit to any other person or entity in whose welfare he is interested;

b. "Government" includes any branch, subdivision or agency of the government of the State or any locality within it;

c. "Harm" means loss, disadvantage or injury, or anything so regarded by the person affected, including loss, disadvantage or injury to any other person or entity in whose welfare he is interested;

d. "Official proceeding" means a proceeding heard or which may be heard before any legislative, judicial, administrative or other governmental agency, arbitration proceeding, or official authorized to take evidence under oath, including any arbitrator, referee, hearing examiner, commissioner, notary or other person taking testimony or deposition in connection with any such proceeding;

e. "Party official" means a person who holds an elective or appointive post in a political party in the United States by virtue of which he directs or conducts, or participates in directing or conducting party affairs at any level of responsibility;

f. "Pecuniary benefit" is benefit in the form of money, property, commercial interests or anything else the primary significance of which is economic gain;

g. "Public servant" means any officer or employee of government, including legislators and judges, and any person participating as juror, advisor, consultant or otherwise, in performing a governmental function, but the term does not include witnesses;

h. "Administrative proceeding" means any proceeding, other than a judicial proceeding, the outcome of which is required to be based on a record or documentation prescribed by law, or in which law or regulation is particularized in application to individuals;

i. "Statement" means any representation, but includes a representation of opinion, belief or other state of mind only if the representation clearly relates to state of mind apart from or in addition to any facts which are the subject of the representation.

L.1978, c. 95, § 2C:27–1, eff. Sept. 1, 1979. Amended by L.1979, c. 178, § 47, eff. Sept. 1, 1979.

2C:27–2.   Bribery in official and political matters

A person is guilty of bribery if he directly or indirectly offers, confers or agrees to confer upon another, or solicits, accepts or agrees to accept from another:

a. Any benefit as consideration for a decision, opinion, recommendation, vote or exercise of discretion of a public servant, party official or voter on any public issue or in any public election; or

b. Any benefit as consideration for a decision, vote, recommendation or exercise of official discretion in a judicial or administrative proceeding; or

c. Any benefit as consideration for a violation of an official duty of a public servant or party official; or

d. Any benefit as consideration for the performance of official duties.

For the purposes of this section "benefit as consideration" shall be deemed to mean any benefit not authorized by law.

It is no defense to prosecution under this section that a person whom the actor sought to influence was not qualified to act in the desired way whether because he had not yet assumed office, or lacked jurisdiction, or for any other reason.

In any prosecution under this section of an actor who offered, conferred or agreed to confer, or who solicited, accepted or agreed to accept a benefit, it is no defense that he did so as a result of conduct by another constituting theft by extortion or coercion or an attempt to commit either of those crimes.

Any offense proscribed by this section is a crime of the second degree. If the benefit offered, conferred, agreed to be conferred, solicited, accepted or agreed to be accepted is of the value of $200.00 or less, any offense proscribed by this section is a crime of the third degree.

L.1978, c. 95, § 2C:27–2, eff. Sept. 1, 1979. Amended by L.1979, c. 178, § 48, eff. Sept. 1, 1979.

2C:27–3. Threats and other improper influence in official and political matters

a. Offenses defined. A person commits an offense if he directly or indirectly:

(1) Threatens unlawful harm to any person with purpose to influence a decision, opinion, recommendation, vote or exercise of discretion of a public servant, party official or voter on any public issue or in any public election; or

(2) Threatens harm to any public servant with purpose to influence a decision, opinion, recommendation, vote or exercise of discretion in a judicial or administrative proceeding; or

(3) Threatens harm to any public servant or party official with purpose to influence him to violate his official duty.

It is no defense to prosecution under this section that a person whom the actor sought to influence was not qualified to act in the desired way, whether because he had not yet assumed office or lacked jurisdiction, or for any other reason.

b. Grading. An offense under this section is a crime of the third degree.

L.1978, c. 95, § 2C:27–3, eff. Sept. 1, 1979. Amended by L.1979, c. 178, § 49, eff. Sept. 1, 1979.

2C:27–4. Repealed by L.2003, c. 255, § 7, eff. January 14, 2004

2C:27–5. Retaliation for past official action

A person commits a crime of the fourth degree if he harms another by any unlawful act with purpose to retaliate for or on account of the service of another as a public servant.

L.1978, c. 95, § 2C:27–5, eff. Sept. 1, 1979.

2C:27–6. Repealed by L.2003, c. 255, § 7, eff. January 14, 2004

2C:27–7. Repealed by L.1999, c. 440, § 108

2C:27–8. Repealed by L.1979, c. 178, § 147, eff. Sept. 1, 1979

2C:27–9. Public servant transacting business with certain persons

A public servant commits a crime of the fourth degree if, while performing his official functions on behalf of a governmental entity, the public servant knowingly transacts any business with himself, a member of his immediate family, or a business organization in which the public servant or an immediate family member has an interest. For purposes of this section, an interest in a business organization shall not include aggregate familial ownership or control of one percent or less of an interest in the capital or equity of the business organization. A public servant shall not be guilty of an offense under this section if the public servant's performance of official functions would not affect the public servant, family member or business organization differently than such performance would affect the public generally, or would not affect the public servant, family member or business organization, as a member of a business, profession, occupation or group, differently than such performance would affect any other member of such business, profession, occupation or group.

L.1999, c. 440, § 100.

2C:27–10. Acceptance or receipt of unlawful benefit by public servant for official behavior

a. A public servant commits a crime if, under color of office and in connection with any official act performed or to be performed by the public servant, the public servant directly or indirectly, knowingly solicits, accepts or agrees to accept any benefit, whether the benefit inures to the public servant or another person, to influence the performance of an official duty or to commit a violation of an official duty.

b. A public servant commits a crime if, under color of office and in connection with any official act performed or to be performed by the public servant, the public servant directly or indirectly, knowingly receives any benefit, whether the benefit inures to the public servant or another person, to influence the performance of an official duty or to commit a violation of an official duty.

c. In addition to the definition set forth in N.J.S. 2C:27–1, " benefit" as used in this act includes any benefit from or by reason of a contract or agreement for goods, property or services if the contract or agreement is awarded, made or paid by the branch, subdivision, or agency of the government that employs the public servant.

d.　The provisions of this section shall not apply to:

(1) Fees prescribed by law to be received by a public servant or any other benefit to which the public servant is otherwise legally entitled if these fees or benefits are received in the manner legally prescribed and not bartered for another benefit to influence the performance of an official duty or to commit a violation of an official duty;

(2) Gifts or other benefits conferred on account of kinship or other personal, professional or business relationship independent of the official status of the recipient if these gifts or benefits are within otherwise legally permissible limits and are not bartered for another benefit to influence the performance of an official duty or to commit a violation of an official duty; or

(3) Trivial benefits the receipt of which involve no risk that the public servant would perform official duties in a biased or partial manner.

e.　An offense proscribed by this section is a crime of the second degree. If the benefit solicited, accepted, agreed to be accepted or received is of a value of $200.00 or less, any offense proscribed by this section is a crime of the third degree.

L.2003, c. 255, § 5, eff. Jan. 14, 2004.

2C:27–11.　Offer of unlawful benefit to public servant for official behavior

a.　A person commits a crime if the person offers, confers or agrees to confer any benefit, whether the benefit inures to the public servant or another person, to influence a public servant in the performance of an official duty or to commit a violation of an official duty.

b.　A person commits a crime if the person, directly or indirectly, confers or agrees to confer any benefit not allowed by law to a public servant.

c.　In addition to the definition set forth in N.J.S. 2C:27–1, " benefit" as used in this act includes any benefit from or by reason of a contract or agreement for goods, property or services if the contract or agreement is awarded, made or paid by the branch, subdivision, or agency of the government that employs the public servant.

d.　The provisions of this section shall not apply to:

(1) Fees prescribed by law to be received by a public servant or any other benefit to which the public servant is otherwise legally entitled if these fees or benefits are received in the manner legally prescribed and not bartered for another benefit to influence the performance of an official duty or to commit a violation of an official duty;

(2) Gifts or other benefits conferred on account of kinship or other personal, professional or business relationship independent of the official status of the recipient if these gifts or benefits are within otherwise legally permissible limits and are not bartered for another benefit to influence the performance of an official duty or to commit a violation of an official duty; or

(3) Trivial benefits the receipt of which involve no risk that the public servant would perform official duties in a biased or partial manner.

e.　(1) An offense proscribed by subsection a. of this section is a crime of the second degree. If the benefit solicited, accepted or agreed to be accepted is of a value of $200.00 or less, any offense proscribed by subsection a. of this section is a crime of the third degree.

(2) An offense proscribed by subsection b. of this section is a crime of the third degree. If the gift or other benefit is of a value of $200.00 or less, an offense proscribed by subsection b. of this section is a crime of the fourth degree.

L.2003, c. 255, § 6, eff. Jan. 14, 2004.

2C:27–12.　Corruption of public resources

a.　A person commits the crime of corruption of public resources if, with respect to a public resource which is subject to an obligation to be used for a specified purpose or purposes, the person knowingly uses or makes disposition of that public resource or any portion thereof for an unauthorized purpose.

(1) If the public resource involved is subject to an obligation to be used to perform or facilitate the performance of a governmental function or public service, corruption of public resources constitutes a crime of the first degree if the amount or value of the public resource involved is $500,000 or more; the offense constitutes a crime of the second degree if the amount or value involved is $75,000 or more but is less than $500,000; and the offense constitutes a crime of the third degree if the amount or value involved is less than $75,000.

(2) If the public resource involved is not subject to an obligation to be used for a purpose to perform or facilitate the performance of a governmental function or public service, corruption of public resources constitutes a crime of the second degree if the amount or value of the public resource involved is $500,000 or more; the offense constitutes a crime of the third degree if the amount or value involved is $75,000 or more but is less than $500,000; and the offense constitutes a crime of the fourth degree if the amount or value involved is less than $75,000.

b.　Except as otherwise provided in section 97 of P.L.1999, c. 440 (C.2C:21–34), a person commits a crime if he makes a material representation that is false to a government agency, officer or employee (1) with the purpose to obtain or retain a public resource, or (2) with the purpose to mislead or deceive any person as to the use or disposition of a public resource. This offense constitutes a crime of the second degree if the amount or value of the public resource involved is $500,000 or more; the offense constitutes a crime of the third degree if the amount or value involved is $75,000 or more but is less than $500,000; and the offense constitutes a crime of the fourth degree if the amount or value involved is less than $75,000.

c. For purposes of this section, "public resource" means any funds or property provided by the government, or a person acting on behalf of the government, which shall include but is not limited to: (1) money or the equivalent of money paid by the government directly or indirectly to or on behalf of a person or his employer; (2) transfer by the government of an asset of value for less than fair market price; (3) fees, costs, rents, insurance or bond premiums, loans, interest rates or other obligations that would normally be required in the execution of the contract, that are paid, reduced, charged at less than fair market value, waived, or forgiven by the government; (4) money loaned by the government that is to be repaid on a contingent basis; (5) money loaned by an entity based upon or in accordance with a guarantee provided by the government; (6) grants awarded by the government or an entity acting on behalf of the government; and (7) credits that are applied by the government against repayment obligations to the government. For purposes of this section, a purpose is unauthorized if it is not the specified purpose or purposes for which a public resource is obligated to be used, and the government agency having supervision of or jurisdiction over the person or public resource has not given its approval for such use.

d. Each act of corruption of public resources shall constitute an additional, separate and distinct offense, except that the amounts or values of public resources used for an unauthorized purpose in separate acts of corruption of public resources may be aggregated for the purpose of establishing liability pursuant to this section.

e. Proof that a person made a false statement, prepared a false report or if the government agency having supervision of or jurisdiction over the person or public resource required a report to be prepared, failed to prepare a report concerning the conduct that is the subject of the prosecution, shall give rise to an inference that the actor knew that the public resource was used for an unauthorized purpose.

f. Nothing in this act shall preclude an indictment and conviction for any other offense defined by the laws of this State.

g. Nothing in this act shall preclude an assignment judge from dismissing a prosecution under this section if the assignment judge determines, pursuant to N.J.S.2C:2–11, the conduct charged to be a de minimis infraction.

L.2007, c. 158, § 1, eff. Sept. 4, 2007.

CHAPTER 28

PERJURY AND OTHER FALSIFICATION IN OFFICIAL MATTERS

Section
2C:28–1.   Perjury.
2C:28–2.   False swearing.
2C:28–3.   Unsworn falsification to authorities.
2C:28–4.   False reports to law enforcement authorities.
2C:28–5.   Tampering with witnesses and informants; retaliation against them; bribery of witnesses or informants.
2C:28–5.1. Defendants and witnesses; protective orders; contents.
2C:28–5.2. Violation of protective orders; penalties.
2C:28–5.3. Movants for protective orders.
2C:28–5.4. Hearing; findings.
2C:28–5.5. Protective orders interfering with case preparation.
2C:28–6.   Tampering with or fabricating physical evidence.
2C:28–7.   Tampering with public records or information.
2C:28–8.   Impersonating a public servant or law enforcement officer.

2C:28–1. Perjury

a. **Offense defined.** A person is guilty of perjury, a crime of the third degree, if in any official proceeding he makes a false statement under oath or equivalent affirmation, or swears or affirms the truth of a statement previously made, when the statement is material and he does not believe it to be true.

b. **Materiality.** Falsification is material, regardless of the admissibility of the statement under rules of evidence, if it could have affected the course or outcome of the proceeding or the disposition of the matter. It is no defense that the declarant mistakenly believed the falsification to be immaterial. Whether a falsification is material is a question of law.

c. **Irregularities no defense.** It is not a defense to prosecution under this section that the oath or affirmation was administered or taken in an irregular manner. A document purporting to be made upon oath or affirmation at any time when the actor presents it as being so verified shall be deemed to have been duly sworn or affirmed.

d. **Retraction.** It is an affirmative defense under this section that the actor retracted the falsification in the course of the proceeding or matter in which it was made prior to the termination of the proceeding or matter without having caused irreparable harm to any party.

e. **Corroboration.** No person shall be convicted of an offense under this section where proof of falsity rests solely upon contradiction by testimony of a single person other than the defendant.

L.1978, c. 95, § 2C:28–1, eff. Sept. 1, 1979. Amended by L.1979, c. 178, § 54, eff. Sept. 1, 1979.

2C:28–2. False swearing

a. False swearing. A person who makes a false statement under oath or equivalent affirmation, or swears or affirms the truth of such a statement previously made, when he does not believe the statement to be true, is guilty of a crime of the fourth degree.

b. Perjury provisions applicable. Subsections c. and d. of section 2C:28–1 apply to the present section.

c. Inconsistent statements. Where the defendant made inconsistent statements under oath or equivalent affirmation, both having been made within the period of the statute of limitations, the prosecution may proceed by setting forth the inconsistent statements in a single count alleging in the alternative that one or the other was false and not believed by the defendant. In such case it shall not be necessary for the prosecution to prove which statement was false but only that one or the other was false and not believed by the defendant to be true.

L.1978, c. 95, § 2C:28–2, eff. Sept. 1, 1979. Amended by L.1979, c. 178, § 55, eff. Sept. 1, 1979.

2C:28–3. Unsworn falsification to authorities

a. Statements "Under Penalty." A person commits a crime of the fourth degree if he makes a written false statement which he does not believe to be true, on or pursuant to a form bearing notice, authorized by law, to the effect that false statements made therein are punishable.

b. In general. A person commits a disorderly persons offense if, with purpose to mislead a public servant in performing his function, he:

(1) Makes any written false statement which he does not believe to be true;

(2) Purposely creates a false impression in a written application for any pecuniary or other benefit, by omitting information necessary to prevent statements therein from being misleading;

(3) Submits or invites reliance on any writing which he knows to be forged, altered or otherwise lacking in authenticity; or

(4) Submits or invites reliance on any sample, specimen, map, boundary-mark, or other object which he knows to be false.

c. Perjury provisions applicable. Subsections c. and d. of section 2C:28–1 and subsection c. of 2C:28–2 apply to the present section.

L.1978, c. 95, § 2C:28–3, eff. Sept. 1, 1979. Amended by L.1981, c. 290, § 26, eff. Sept. 24, 1981.

2C:28–4. False reports to law enforcement authorities

a. Falsely incriminating another. A person who knowingly gives or causes to be given false information to any law enforcement officer with purpose to implicate another commits a crime of the fourth degree.

b. Fictitious reports. A person commits a disorderly persons offense if he:

(1) Reports or causes to be reported to law enforcement authorities an offense or other incident within their concern knowing that it did not occur; or

(2) Pretends to furnish or causes to be furnished such authorities with information relating to an offense or incident when he knows he has no information relating to such offense or incident.

L.1978, c. 95, § 2C:28–4, eff. Sept. 1, 1979.

2C:28–5. Tampering with witnesses and informants; retaliation against them; bribery of witnesses or informants

a. Tampering. A person commits an offense if, believing that an official proceeding or investigation is pending or about to be instituted or has been instituted, he knowingly engages in conduct which a reasonable person would believe would cause a witness or informant to:

(1) Testify or inform falsely;

(2) Withhold any testimony, information, document or thing;

(3) Elude legal process summoning him to testify or supply evidence;

(4) Absent himself from any proceeding or investigation to which he has been legally summoned; or

(5) Otherwise obstruct, delay, prevent or impede an official proceeding or investigation.

Witness tampering is a crime of the first degree if the conduct occurs in connection with an official proceeding or investigation involving any crime enumerated in subsection d. of section 2 of P.L.1997, c. 117 (C.2C:43–7.2) and the actor employs force or threat of force. Witness tampering is a crime of the second degree if the actor employs force or threat of force. Otherwise it is a crime of the third degree. Privileged communications may not be used as evidence in any prosecution for violations of paragraph (2), (3) , (4) or (5).

b. Retaliation against witness or informant. A person commits an offense if he harms another by an unlawful act with purpose to retaliate for or on account of the service of another as a witness or informant. The offense is a crime of the second degree if the actor employs force or threat of force. Otherwise it is a crime of the third degree.

c. Witness or informant taking bribe. A person commits a crime of the third degree if he solicits, accepts or agrees to accept any benefit in consideration of his doing any of the things specified in subsection a. (1) through (5) of this section.

d. Bribery of a witness or informant. A person commits a crime of the second degree if he directly or indirectly offers, confers or agrees to confer upon a witness or informant any benefit in consideration of the witness or informant doing any of the things specified in subsection a. (1) through (5) of this section.

e. Notwithstanding the provisions of N.J.S.2C:1–8, N.J.S.2C:44–5 or any other provision of law, a conviction arising under this section shall not merge with a conviction of an offense that was the subject of the official proceeding or investigation and the sentence imposed pursuant to this section shall be ordered to be served consecutively to that imposed for any such conviction.

L.1978, c. 95, § 2C:28–5, eff. Sept. 1, 1979. Amended by L.1981, c. 290, § 27, eff. Sept. 24, 1981; L.1991, c. 33, § 1, eff. Feb. 25, 1991; L.2008, c. 81, § 1, eff. Sept. 10, 2008.

2C:28–5.1. Defendants and witnesses; protective orders; contents

If a court having jurisdiction under any criminal matter finds that the defendant in that criminal action or any other person connected in any way with the action has violated or is likely to violate N.J.S. 2C:28–5, N.J.S. 2C:29–3 or N.J.S. 2C:29–4 in regard to the pending offense, or that the defendant or other person has injured or intimidated or is threatening to injure or intimidate any witness in the pending offense or member of the witness' family with purpose to affect the testimony of the witness, the court may issue a protective order providing:

a. That the defendant or other person not violate any provision of N.J.S. 2C:28–5, N.J.S. 2C:29–3, or N.J.S. 2C:29–4;

b. That the defendant or other person maintain a prescribed geographic distance from any specified witness or victim;

c. That the defendant or other person have no communication with any specified witness or victim, except through an attorney under any reasonable restrictions which the court may impose.

L.1985, c. 250, § 1, eff. July 31, 1985.

2C:28–5.2. Violation of protective orders; penalties

Any person violating any order made pursuant to section 1 of this act may be subject to any of the following penalties:

a. He may be charged with any substantive offense defined in N.J.S. 2C:28–5, N.J.S. 2C:29–3, or N.J.S. 2C:29–4 when violation of an order constitutes violation of any provision of those statutes;

b. He may be charged with contempt of the court that made the order. No finding of contempt shall be a bar to prosecution for a substantive offense; and any sentence for a conviction of contempt may be served consecutively to any sentence imposed for the underlying substantive offense. If the court does not impose a consecutive sentence, the court shall state on the record the reason for not imposing a consecutive sentence.

L.1985, c. 250, § 2, eff. July 31, 1985.

2C:28–5.3. Movants for protective orders

A motion for an order as provided by section 1 of this act [1] may be made by the prosecuting authority, the defendant, or by any witness.

L.1985, c. 250, § 3, eff. July 31, 1985.

   [1] N.J.S.A. § 2C:28–5.1.

2C:28–5.4. Hearing; findings

No order may be issued under this act unless the court's findings are made upon a preponderance of evidence adduced at a hearing. The rules of evidence shall not be applicable to any such hearing.

L.1985, c. 250, § 4, eff. July 31, 1985.

2C:28–5.5. Protective orders interfering with case preparation

No order shall be entered under this act which interferes with the preparation of the underlying criminal case by the defendant or by his attorney, if any.

L.1985, c. 250, § 5, eff. July 31, 1985.

2C:28–6. Tampering with or fabricating physical evidence

A person commits a crime of the fourth degree if, believing that an official proceeding or investigation is pending or about to be instituted, he:

(1) Alters, destroys, conceals or removes any article, object, record, document or other thing of physical substance with purpose to impair its verity or availability in such proceeding or investigation; or

(2) Makes, devises, prepares, presents, offers or uses any article, object, record, document or other thing of physical substance knowing it to be false and with purpose to mislead a public servant who is engaged in such proceeding or investigation.

L.1978, c. 95, § 2C:28–6, eff. Sept. 1, 1979.

2C:28–7. Tampering with public records or information

a. Offense defined. A person commits an offense if he:

(1) Knowingly makes a false entry in, or false alteration of, any record, document or thing belonging to, or received or kept by, the government for information or record, or required by law to be kept by others for information of the government;

(2) Makes, presents, offers for filing, or uses any record, document or thing knowing it to be false, and with purpose that it be taken as a genuine part of information or records referred to in paragraph (1); or

(3) Purposely and unlawfully destroys, conceals, removes, mutilates, or otherwise impairs the verity or availability of any such record, document or thing.

b. Grading. An offense under subsection a. is a disorderly persons offense unless the actor's purpose is to defraud or injure anyone, in which case the offense is a crime of the third degree.

c. A person commits a crime of the fourth degree if he purposely and unlawfully alters, destroys, conceals, removes or disables any camera or other monitoring device including any videotape, film or other medium used to record sound or images that is installed in a patrol vehicle.

L.1978, c. 95, § 2C:28–7, eff. Sept. 1, 1979. Amended by L.2001, c. 219, § 1, eff. Aug. 24, 2001.

2C:28–8. Impersonating a public servant or law enforcement officer

a. Except as provided in subsection b. of this section, a person commits a disorderly persons offense if he falsely pretends to hold a position in the public service with purpose to induce another to submit to such pretended official authority or otherwise to act in reliance upon that pretense.

b. A person commits a crime of the fourth degree if he falsely pretends to hold a position as an officer or member or employee or agent of any organization or association of law enforcement officers with purpose to induce another to submit to such pretended official authority or otherwise to act in reliance upon that pretense.

L.1978, c. 95, § 2C:28–8, eff. Sept. 1, 1979. Amended by L.2000, c. 110, § 1, eff. Sept. 8, 2000.

CHAPTER 29

OBSTRUCTING GOVERNMENTAL OPERATIONS; ESCAPE

Section
2C:29–1.   Obstructing administration of law or other governmental function.
2C:29–2.   Resisting arrest; eluding officer.
2C:29–3.   Hindering apprehension or prosecution.
2C:29–3.1. Purposeful infliction of harm on animal owned or used by law enforcement agency or interference with law enforcement officer using such animal; "search and rescue dog" defined.
2C:29–4.   Compounding.
2C:29–5.   Escape.
2C:29–6.   Implements for escape; other contraband.
2C:29–7.   Bail jumping; default in required appearance.
2C:29–8.   Corrupting or influencing a jury.
2C:29–8.1. Negotiation for, solicitation for, or acceptance of contract for literary expression or presentation with or by jurors during criminal proceeding.
2C:29–9.   Contempt.
2C:29–10. Electronic communication devices within correctional or detention facilities.

2C:29–1. Obstructing administration of law or other governmental function

a. A person commits an offense if he purposely obstructs, impairs or perverts the administration of law or other governmental function or prevents or attempts to prevent a public servant from lawfully performing an official function by means of flight, intimidation, force, violence, or physical interference or obstacle, or by means of any independently unlawful act. This section does not apply to failure to perform a legal duty other than an official duty, or any other means of avoiding compliance with law without affirmative interference with governmental functions.

b. An offense under this section is a crime of the fourth degree if the actor obstructs the detection or investigation of a crime or the prosecution of a person for a crime, otherwise it is a disorderly persons offense.

L.1978, c. 95, § 2C:29–1, eff. Sept. 1, 1979. Amended by L.1986, c. 34, § 1, eff. June 23, 1986; L.2000, c. 18, § 1, eff. April 28, 2000.

2C:29–2. Resisting arrest; eluding officer

a. (1) Except as provided in paragraph (3), a person is guilty of a disorderly persons offense if he purposely prevents or attempts to prevent a law enforcement officer from effecting an arrest. (2) Except as provided in paragraph (3), a person is guilty of a crime of the fourth degree if he, by flight, purposely prevents or attempts to prevent a law enforcement officer from effecting an arrest. (3) An offense under paragraph (1) or (2) of subsection a. is a crime of the third degree if the person:

(a) Uses or threatens to use physical force or violence against the law enforcement officer or another; or

(b) Uses any other means to create a substantial risk of causing physical injury to the public servant or another.

It is not a defense to a prosecution under this subsection that the law enforcement officer was acting unlawfully in making the arrest, provided he was acting under color of his official authority and provided the law enforcement officer announces his intention to arrest prior to the resistance.

b. Any person, while operating a motor vehicle on any street or highway in this State or any vessel, as defined pursuant to section 2 of P.L.1995, c. 401 (C.12:7–71), on the waters of this State, who knowingly flees or attempts to elude any police or law enforcement officer after having received any signal from such officer to bring the vehicle or vessel to a full stop commits a crime of the third degree; except that, a person is guilty of a crime of the second degree if the flight or attempt to elude creates a risk of death or injury to any person. For purposes of this subsection, there shall be a permissive inference that the flight or attempt to elude creates a risk of death or injury to any person if the person's conduct involves a violation of chapter 4 of Title 39 or chapter 7 of Title 12 of the Revised Statutes. In addition to the penalty prescribed under this subsection or any other section of law, the court shall order the suspension of that person's driver's license, or privilege to operate a vessel, whichever is appropriate, for a period of not less than six months or more than two years.

In the case of a person who is at the time of the imposition of sentence less than 17 years of age, the period of the suspension of driving privileges authorized herein, including a suspension of the privilege of operating a motorized bicycle, shall commence on the day the sentence is imposed and shall run for a period as fixed by the court. If the driving or vessel operating privilege of any person is under revocation, suspension, or postponement for a violation of any provision of this Title or Title 39 of the Revised Statutes at the time of any conviction or adjudication of delinquency for a violation of any offense defined in this chapter or chapter 36 of this Title, the revocation, suspension, or postponement period imposed herein shall commence as of the date of termination of the existing revocation, suspension, or postponement.

Upon conviction the court shall collect forthwith the New Jersey driver's licenses of the person and forward such license or licenses to the Director of the Division of Motor Vehicles along with a report indicating the first and last day of the suspension or postponement period imposed by the court pursuant to this section. If the court is for any reason unable to collect the license or licenses of the person, the court shall cause a report of the conviction or adjudication of delinquency to be filed with the director. That report shall include the complete name, address, date of birth, eye color, and sex of the person and shall indicate the first and last day of the suspension or postponement period imposed by the court pursuant to this section. The court shall inform the person orally and in writing that if the person is convicted of personally operating a motor vehicle or a vessel, whichever is appropriate, during the period of license suspension or postponement imposed pursuant to this section the person shall, upon conviction, be subject to the penalties set forth in R.S.39:3–40 or section 14 of P.L.1995, c. 401 (C.12:7–83), whichever is appropriate. A person shall be required to acknowledge receipt of the written notice in writing. Failure to receive a written notice or failure to acknowledge in writing the receipt of a written notice shall not be a defense to a subsequent charge of violation of R.S.39:3–40 or section 14 of P.L.1995, c. 401 (C.12:7–83), whichever is appropriate. If the person is the holder of a driver's or vessel operator's license from another jurisdiction, the court shall not collect the license but shall notify the director who shall notify the appropriate officials in the licensing jurisdiction. The court shall, however, in accordance with the provisions of this section, revoke the person's non-resident driving or vessel operating privileges, whichever is appropriate, in this State.

For the purposes of this subsection, it shall be a rebuttable presumption that the owner of a vehicle or vessel was the operator of the vehicle or vessel at the time of the offense.

L.1978, c. 95, § 2C:29–2, eff. Sept. 1, 1979. Amended by L.1979, c. 178, § 57, eff. Sept. 1, 1979; L.1981, c. 290, § 28, eff. Sept. 24, 1981; L.1989, c. 84, § 1, eff. May 31, 1989; L.1991, c. 341, § 3, eff. Jan. 7, 1992; L.1993, c. 219, § 5, eff. Aug. 2, 1993; L.1995, c. 401, § 54, eff. July 1, 1996; L.2000, c. 18, § 2, eff. April 28, 2000.

2C:29–3.   Hindering apprehension or prosecution

a. A person commits an offense if, with purpose to hinder the detention, apprehension, investigation, prosecution, conviction or punishment of another for an offense or violation of Title 39 of the Revised Statutes or a violation of chapter 33A of Title 17 of the Revised Statutes he:

(1) Harbors or conceals the other;

(2) Provides or aids in providing a weapon, money, transportation, disguise or other means of avoiding discovery or apprehension or effecting escape;

(3) Suppresses, by way of concealment or destruction, any evidence of the crime, or tampers with a witness, informant, document or other source of information, regardless of its admissibility in evidence, which might aid in the discovery or apprehension of such person or in the lodging of a charge against him;

(4) Warns the other of impending discovery or apprehension, except that this paragraph does not apply to a warning given in connection with an effort to bring another into compliance with law;

(5) Prevents or obstructs, by means of force, intimidation or deception, anyone from performing an act which might aid in the discovery or apprehension of such person or in the lodging of a charge against him;

(6) Aids such person to protect or expeditiously profit from an advantage derived from such crime; or

(7) Gives false information to a law enforcement officer or a civil State investigator assigned to the Office of the Insurance Fraud Prosecutor established by section 32 of P.L.1998, c. 21 (C.17:33A–16).

An offense under paragraph (5) of subsection a. of this section is a crime of the second degree, unless the actor is a spouse, domestic partner, partner in a civil union, parent or child to the person aided who is the victim of the offense, in which case the offense is a crime of the fourth degree. Otherwise, the offense is a crime of the third degree if the conduct which the actor knows has been charged or is liable to be charged against the person aided would constitute a crime of the second degree or greater, unless the actor is a spouse, domestic partner, partner in a civil union, parent or child of the person aided, in which case the offense is a crime of the fourth degree. The offense is a crime of the fourth degree if such conduct would constitute a crime of the third degree. Otherwise it is a disorderly persons offense.

b.   A person commits an offense if, with purpose to hinder his own detention, apprehension, investigation, prosecution, conviction or punishment for an offense or violation of Title 39 of the Revised Statutes or a violation of chapter 33A of Title 17 of the Revised Statutes, he:

(1) Suppresses, by way of concealment or destruction, any evidence of the crime or tampers with a document or other source of information, regardless of its admissibility in evidence, which might aid in his discovery or apprehension or in the lodging of a charge against him; or

(2) Prevents or obstructs by means of force or intimidation anyone from performing an act which might aid in his discovery or apprehension or in the lodging of a charge against him; or

(3) Prevents or obstructs by means of force, intimidation or deception any witness or informant from providing testimony or information, regardless of its admissibility, which might aid in his discovery or apprehension or in the lodging of a charge against him; or

(4) Gives false information to a law enforcement officer or a civil State investigator assigned to the Office of the Insurance Fraud Prosecutor established by section 32 of P.L.1998, c. 21 (C.17:33A–16).

An offense under paragraph (3) of subsection b. of this section is a crime of the second degree. Otherwise, the offense is a crime of the third degree if the conduct which the actor knows has been charged or is liable to be charged against him would constitute a crime of the second degree or greater. The offense is a crime of the fourth degree if such conduct would constitute a crime of the third degree. Otherwise it is a disorderly persons offense.

L.1978, c. 95, § 2C:29–3, eff. Sept. 1, 1979. Amended by L.1981, c. 290, § 29, eff. Sept. 24, 1981; L.1999, c. 297, § 1, eff. Dec. 23, 1999; L.2008, c. 81, § 2, eff. Sept. 10, 2008.

2C:29–3.1.   Purposeful infliction of harm on animal owned or used by law enforcement agency or interference with law enforcement officer using such animal; "search and rescue dog" defined

Any person who purposely kills a dog, horse or other animal owned or used by a law enforcement agency or a search and rescue dog shall be guilty of a crime of the third degree. Any person who purposely maims or otherwise inflicts harm upon a dog, horse or other animal owned or used by a law enforcement agency or a search and rescue dog shall be guilty of a crime of the fourth degree. Any person who interferes with any law enforcement officer using an animal in the performance of his official duties commits a disorderly persons offense, subject to a sentence of six months' imprisonment, some or all of which may be community service, restitution and a $1,000.00 fine.

As used in this section, "search and rescue dog" means any dog trained or being trained for the purpose

of search and rescue that is owned by an independent handler or member of a search and rescue team, and used in conjunction with local law enforcement or emergency services organizations for the purpose of locating missing persons or evidence of arson.

L.1983, c. 261, § 1, eff. July 7, 1983. Amended by L.1999, c. 14, § 1, eff. Feb. 3, 1999; L.2005, c. 24, § 1, eff. Jan. 26, 2005.

2C:29–4.   Compounding

A person commits a crime if he accepts or agrees to accept any pecuniary benefit in consideration of refraining from reporting to law enforcement authorities the commission or suspected commission of any offense or information relating to an offense or from seeking prosecution of an offense. A person commits a crime if he confers or agrees to confer any pecuniary benefit in consideration of the other person agreeing to refrain from any such reporting or seeking prosecution. It is an affirmative defense to prosecution under this section that the pecuniary benefit did not exceed an amount which the actor reasonably believed to be due as restitution or indemnification for harm caused by the offense. An offense proscribed by this section is a crime of the second degree. If the thing of value accepted, agreed to be accepted, conferred or agreed to be conferred is any benefit of $200.00 or less, an offense proscribed by this section is a crime of the third degree.

L.1978, c. 95, § 2C:29–4, eff. Sept. 1, 1979. Amended by L.1979, c. 178, § 58, eff. Sept. 1, 1979.

2C:29–5.   Escape

a.   Escape.   A person commits an offense if he without lawful authority removes himself from official detention or fails to return to official detention following temporary leave granted for a specific purpose or limited period. "Official detention" means arrest, detention in any facility for custody of persons under charge or conviction of a crime or offense, or committed pursuant to chapter 4 of this Title, or alleged or found to be delinquent, detention for extradition or deportation, or any other detention for law enforcement purposes; but "official detention" does not include supervision of probation or parole, or constraint incidental to release on bail.

b.   Absconding from parole.   A person subject to parole commits a crime of the third degree if the person goes into hiding or leaves the State with a purpose of avoiding supervision. As used in this subsection, "parole" includes participation in the Intensive Supervision Program (ISP) established pursuant to the Rules Governing the Courts of the State of New Jersey. Abandoning a place of residence without the prior permission of or notice to the appropriate supervising authority shall constitute prima facie evidence that the person intended to avoid such supervision.

c.   Permitting or facilitating escape.   A public servant concerned in detention commits an offense if he knowingly or recklessly permits an escape. Any person who knowingly causes or facilitates an escape commits an offense.

d. Effect of legal irregularity in detention. Irregularity in bringing about or maintaining detention, or lack of jurisdiction of the committing or detaining authority, shall not be a defense to prosecution under this section if the escape is from a prison or other custodial facility or from detention pursuant to commitment by official proceedings. In the case of other detentions, irregularity or lack of jurisdiction shall be a defense only if:

(1) The escape involved no substantial risk of harm to the person or property of anyone other than the detainee; or

(2) The detaining authority did not act in good faith under color of law.

e. Grading of offenses. An offense under subsection a. or c. of this section is a crime of the second degree where the actor employs force, threat, deadly weapon or other dangerous instrumentality to effect the escape. Otherwise it is a crime of the third degree.
L.1978, c. 95, § 2C:29–5, eff. Sept. 1, 1979. Amended by L.1979, c. 178, § 58A, eff. Sept. 1, 1979; L.1981, c. 290, § 30, eff. Sept. 24, 1981; L.1991, c. 34, § 1, eff. Feb. 25, 1991.

2C:29–6. Implements for escape; other contraband

a. Escape implements. (1) A person commits an offense if he knowingly and unlawfully introduces within an institution for commitment of persons under N.J.S. 2C:4–8 or a detention facility, or knowingly and unlawfully provides an inmate with any weapon, tool, instrument, document or other thing which may be useful for escape. The offense is a crime of the second degree and shall be punished by a minimum term of imprisonment, which shall be fixed at no less than three years if the item is a weapon as defined by N.J.S. 2C:39–1(r). Otherwise it is a crime of the third degree.

(2) An inmate of an institution or facility defined by paragraph (1) of subsection a. of this section commits an offense if he knowingly and unlawfully procures, makes, or otherwise provides himself with, or has in his possession, any such implement of escape. The offense is a crime of the second degree and shall be punished by a minimum term of imprisonment, which shall be fixed at no less than three years if the item is a weapon as defined by N.J.S. 2C:39–1(r). Otherwise it is a crime of the third degree.

"Unlawfully" means surreptitiously or contrary to law, regulation or order of the detaining authority.

b. Other contraband. A person commits a petty disorderly persons offense if he provides an inmate with any other thing which the actor knows or should know it is unlawful for the inmate to possess.
L.1978, c. 95, § 2C:29–6, eff. Sept. 1, 1979. Amended by L.1979, c. 178, § 59, eff. Sept. 1, 1979; L.1981, c. 290, § 31, eff. Sept. 24, 1981; L.1981, c. 511, § 3, eff. Jan. 12, 1982; L.1983, c. 87, § 1, eff. March 3, 1983.

2C:29–7. Bail jumping; default in required appearance

A person set at liberty by court order, with or without bail, or who has been issued a summons, upon condition that he will subsequently appear at a specified time and place in connection with any offense or any violation of law punishable by a period of incarceration, commits an offense if, without lawful excuse, he fails to appear at that time and place. It is an affirmative defense for the defendant to prove, by a preponderance of evidence, that he did not knowingly fail to appear. The offense constitutes a crime of the third degree where the required appearance was to answer to a charge of a crime of the third degree or greater, or for disposition of any such charge and the actor took flight or went into hiding to avoid apprehension, trial or punishment. The offense constitutes a crime of the fourth degree where the required appearance was otherwise to answer to a charge of crime or for disposition of such charge. The offense constitutes a disorderly persons offense or a petty disorderly persons offense, respectively, when the required appearance was to answer a charge of such an offense or for disposition of any such charge. Where the bail imposed or summons issued is in connection with any other violation of law, the failure to appear shall be a disorderly persons offense.

This section does not apply to obligations to appear incident to release under suspended sentence or on probation or parole. Nothing herein shall interfere with or prevent the exercise by any court of this State of its power to punish for contempt.
L.1978, c. 95, § 2C:29–7, eff. Sept. 1, 1979. Amended by L.1981, c. 290, § 32, eff. Sept. 24, 1981.

2C:29–8. Corrupting or influencing a jury

Any person who, directly or indirectly, corrupts, influences or attempts to corrupt or influence a jury or juror to be more favorable to the one side than to the other by promises, persuasions, entreaties, threats, letters, money, entertainment or other sinister means; or any person who employs any unfair or fraudulent practice, art or contrivance to obtain a verdict, or attempts to instruct a jury or juror beforehand at any place or time, or in any manner or way, except in open court at the trial of the cause, by the strength of the evidence, the arguments of the parties or their counsel, or the opinion or charge of the court is guilty of a crime.

a. Corrupting or influencing a jury is a crime of the first degree if the conduct occurs in connection with an official proceeding involving any of the following crimes, as enumerated in subsection d. of section 2 of P.L.1997, c.117 (C.2C:43–7.2), and the actor employs force or threat of force:

(1) N.J.S.2C:11–3, murder;

(2) N.J.S.2C:11–4, aggravated manslaughter or manslaughter;

(3) N.J.S.2C:11–5, vehicular homicide;

(4) subsection b. of N.J.S.2C:12–1, aggravated assault;

(5) subsection b. of section 1 of P.L.1996, c.14 (C.2C:12–11), disarming a law enforcement officer;

(6) N.J.S.2C:13–1, kidnapping;

(7) subsection a. of N.J.S.2C:14–2, aggravated sexual assault;

(8) subsection b. of N.J.S.2C:14–2 and paragraph (1) of subsection c. of N.J.S.2C:14–2, sexual assault;

(9) N.J.S.2C:15–1, robbery;

(10) section 1 of P.L.1993, c.221 (C.2C:15–2), carjacking;

(11) paragraph (1) of subsection a. of N.J.S.2C:17–1, aggravated arson;

(12) N.J.S.2C:18–2, burglary;

(13) subsection a. of N.J.S.2C:20–5, extortion;

(14) subsection b. of section 1 of P.L.1997, c.185 (C.2C:35–4.1), booby traps in manufacturing or distribution facilities;

(15) N.J.S.2C:35–9, strict liability for drug induced deaths;

(16) section 2 of P.L.2002, c.26 (C.2C:38–2), terrorism;

(17) section 3 of P.L.2002, c.26 (C.2C:38–3), producing or possessing chemical weapons, biological agents or nuclear or radiological devices; or

(18) N.J.S.2C:41–2, racketeering, when it is a crime of the first degree.

b. Corrupting or influencing a jury is a crime of the second degree if the actor employs force or threat of force and the conduct occurs in connection with an action which does not involve any of the crimes enumerated in subsection a. of this section.

c. Otherwise, corrupting or influencing a jury is a crime of the third degree, provided, however, that the presumption of nonimprisonment set forth in subsection e. of 2C:44–1 for persons who have not previously been convicted of an offense shall not apply.

L.1981, c. 290, § 33, eff. Sept. 24, 1981. Amended by L.1986, c. 140, § 1, eff. Nov. 6, 1986; L.2009, c. 169, § 1, eff. Jan. 9, 2010.

2C:29–8.1. Negotiation for, solicitation for, or acceptance of contract for literary expression or presentation with or by jurors during criminal proceeding

a. Any person impaneled as a petit or grand juror in any criminal action in this State who, before the rendering of a verdict, entry of a plea, or the termination of service as a grand juror, solicits, negotiates, accepts, or agrees to accept a contract for a movie, book, magazine article, other literary expression, recording, radio or television presentation, or live entertainment or presentation of any kind which would depict his service as a juror is guilty of a crime of the fourth degree.

b. Any person who offers, negotiates, confers, or agrees to confer a contract for a movie, book, magazine article, other literary expression, recording, radio or television presentation, or live entertainment or presentation of any kind which would depict the juror's service, to any person impaneled as a petit or grand juror in any criminal action in this State, during the term of service of the juror, is guilty of a crime of the fourth degree. *L.1989, c. 22, § 1, eff. Feb. 6, 1989.*

2C:29–9. Contempt

a. A person is guilty of a crime of the fourth degree if he purposely or knowingly disobeys a judicial order or protective order, pursuant to section 1 of P.L.1985, c. 250 (C.2C:28–5.1), or hinders, obstructs or impedes the effectuation of a judicial order or the exercise of jurisdiction over any person, thing or controversy by a court, administrative body or investigative entity.

b. Except as provided below, a person is guilty of a crime of the fourth degree if that person purposely or knowingly violates any provision in an order entered under the provisions of the "Prevention of Domestic Violence Act of 1991," P.L.1991, c. 261 (C.2C:25–17 et al.) or an order entered under the provisions of a substantially similar statute under the laws of another state or the United States when the conduct which constitutes the violation could also constitute a crime or a disorderly persons offense. In all other cases a person is guilty of a disorderly persons offense if that person knowingly violates an order entered under the provisions of this act or an order entered under the provisions of a substantially similar statute under the laws of another state or the United States. Orders entered pursuant to paragraphs (3), (4), (5), (8) and (9) of subsection b. of section 13 of P.L.1991, c. 261 (C.2C:25–29) or substantially similar orders entered under the laws of another state or the United States shall be excluded from the provisions of this subsection.

As used in this subsection, "state" means a state of the United States, the District of Columbia, Puerto Rico, the United States Virgin Islands, or any territory or insular possession subject to the jurisdiction of the United States. The term includes an Indian tribe or band, or Alaskan native village, which is recognized by a federal law or formally acknowledged by a state.

L.1981, c. 290, § 34, eff. Sept. 24, 1981. Amended by L.1987, c. 356, § 9, eff. Apr. 4, 1988; L.1988, c. 28, § 3, eff. June 6, 1988; L.1991, c. 261, § 18, eff. Nov. 12, 1991; L.2005, c. 333, § 1, eff. Jan. 12, 2006; L.2008, c. 81, § 3, eff. Sept. 10, 2008.

2C:29–10. Electronic communication devices within correctional or detention facilities

a. For the purposes of this section:

"County correctional facility" means any prison or other secure facility managed and operated by any county of this State in which adult offenders are incarcerated.

"County juvenile detention facility" means any secure juvenile facility managed and operated by any county of this State.

"Secure juvenile facility" means the New Jersey Training School for Boys, the Juvenile Medium Security Facility, and any other secure juvenile facility managed and operated by the Juvenile Justice Commission.

"State correctional facility" means a State prison or other penal institution.

b. A person who possesses or uses an electronic communication device or a battery or device to recharge an electronic communication device while confined to a State correctional facility, secure juvenile facility, county correctional facility, or county juvenile detention facility is guilty of a crime of the third degree.

c. A person, other than an employee or a contract employee of the Department of Corrections, the Juvenile Justice Commission, a county correctional facility, or a county juvenile detention facility who knowingly sells, transfers, assigns, provides, or otherwise gives an electronic communication device to a person who is confined in a State correctional facility, secure juvenile facility, county correctional facility, or county juvenile detention facility is guilty of a crime of the third degree.

d. An employee or a contract employee of the Department of Corrections, the Juvenile Justice Commission, a county correctional facility, or a county juvenile detention facility who knowingly sells, transfers, assigns, provides, or otherwise gives an electronic communication device to a person who is confined in a State correctional facility, secure juvenile facility, county correctional facility, or county juvenile detention facility is guilty of a crime of the second degree.

L.2007, c. 127, § 1, eff. Aug. 6, 2007.

CHAPTER 30

MISCONDUCT IN OFFICE: ABUSE OF OFFICE

Section
2C:30–1. Repealed.
2C:30–2. Official misconduct.
2C:30–3. Speculating or wagering on official action or information.
2C:30–4. Disbursement of public moneys or incurrence of obligations in excess of appropriation and limit of expenditure.
2C:30–5. Legislative findings.
2C:30–6. Official deprivation of civil rights.
2C:30–7. Pattern of official misconduct.
2C:30–8. Public corruption profiteering penalty.

2C:30–1. Repealed by L.1979, c. 178, § 147, eff. Sept. 1, 1979

2C:30–2. Official misconduct

A public servant is guilty of official misconduct when, with purpose to obtain a benefit for himself or another or to injure or to deprive another of a benefit:

a. He commits an act relating to his office but constituting an unauthorized exercise of his official functions, knowing that such act is unauthorized or he is committing such act in an unauthorized manner; or

b. He knowingly refrains from performing a duty which is imposed upon him by law or is clearly inherent in the nature of his office.

Official misconduct is a crime of the second degree. If the benefit obtained or sought to be obtained, or of which another is deprived or sought to be deprived, is of a value of $200.00 or less, the offense of official misconduct is a crime of the third degree.

L.1978, c. 95, § 2C:30–2, eff. Sept. 1, 1979. Amended by L.1979, c. 178, § 61, eff. Sept. 1, 1979.

2C:30–3. Speculating or wagering on official action or information

A person commits a crime if, in contemplation of official action by himself or by a governmental unit with which he is or has been associated, or in reliance on information to which he has or has had access in an official capacity and which has not been made public, he:

a. Acquires a pecuniary interest in any property, transaction or enterprise which may be affected by such information or official; or

b. Speculates or wagers on the basis of such information or official action; or

c. Aids another to do any of the foregoing, while in office or after leaving office with a purpose of using such information.

An offense proscribed by this section is a crime of the second degree. If the benefit acquired or sought to be acquired is of a value of $200.00 or less, an offense proscribed by this section is a crime of the third degree.

L.1978, c. 95, § 2C:30–3, eff. Sept. 1, 1979. Amended by L.1979, c. 178, § 62, eff. Sept. 1, 1979.

2C:30–4. Disbursement of public moneys or incurrence of obligations in excess of appropriation and limit of expenditure

A person or member of a board or body charged with or having the control of a State office, division, department or institution or a member of a county or municipal governing body or a member of a board of education, commits a crime of the fourth degree if he purposely and knowingly:

a. Disburses, orders or votes for the disbursement of public moneys, in excess of the appropriation for that office, division, department, institution, board or body; or

b. Incurs obligations in excess of the appropriation and limit of expenditure provided by law for that office, division, department, institution, board or body.

Nothing contained in this section shall be construed to prevent a board of education from keeping open the public schools.

L.1989, c. 131, § 1, eff. Aug. 2, 1989.

2C:30–5. Legislative findings

The Legislature finds and declares that:

a. Public confidence in the institutions of government is undermined when an official engages in any form of misconduct involving the official's office.

b. Such misconduct, and the corresponding damage to the public confidence, impairs the ability of government to function properly, fosters mistrust and engenders disrespect for government and public servants.

c. A particular concern arises when a law enforcement official, duly entrusted to protect the public safety and impartially enforce the laws, abuses that trust by unlawfully depriving persons of their civil rights, especially in the context of racial profiling.

d. It is important to ensure that law enforcement officers are prohibited from using racial characteristics or color, either alone or in conjunction with other composite characteristics such as a generalized vehicle description or the age of the driver or passengers, as the basis for initiating an investigative stop.

e. Existing laws must be amended to provide a greater deterrent to this type of conduct, as well as to enhance other provisions of the law targeting official misconduct.

f. Accordingly, it is in the public interest to strengthen our laws that define and punish acts of official misconduct by members of law enforcement and other public servants.

L.2003, c. 31, § 1, eff. March 14, 2003.

2C:30–6. Official deprivation of civil rights

a. A public servant acting or purporting to act in an official capacity commits the crime of official deprivation of civil rights if, knowing that his conduct is unlawful, and acting with the purpose to intimidate or discriminate against an individual or group of individuals because of race, color, religion, gender, handicap, sexual orientation or ethnicity, the public servant: (1) subjects another to unlawful arrest or detention, including, but not limited to, motor vehicle investigative stops, search, seizure, dispossession, assessment, lien or other infringement of personal or property rights; or (2) denies or impedes another in the lawful exercise or enjoyment of any right, privilege, power or immunity.

b. (1) Except as provided in paragraphs (2) and (3) of this subsection, a public servant who violates the provisions of subsection a. of this section is guilty of a crime of the third degree.

(2) If bodily injury results from depriving a person of a right or privilege in violation of subsection a. of this section, the public servant is guilty of a crime of the second degree.

(3) If, during the course of violating the provisions of this section, a public servant commits or attempts or conspires to commit murder, manslaughter, kidnapping or aggravated sexual assault against a person who is being deprived of a right or privilege in violation of subsection a. of this section, the public servant is guilty of a crime of the first degree.

c. Notwithstanding the provisions of N.J.S.2C:1–8 or any other law, a conviction of official deprivation of civil rights under this section shall not merge with a conviction of any other criminal offense, nor shall such other conviction merge with a conviction under this section, and the court shall impose separate sentences upon each violation of this section and any other criminal offense.

d. Proof that a public servant made a false statement, prepared a false report, or, if the agency that employs the public servant, the Attorney General or the county prosecutor having supervisory authority over the agency required a report to be prepared, failed to prepare a report concerning the conduct that is the subject of the prosecution, shall give rise to an inference that the actor knew his conduct was unlawful.

e. For purposes of this section, an act is unlawful if it violates the Constitution of the United States or the Constitution of this State, or if it constitutes a criminal offense under the laws of this State.

L.2003, c. 31, § 2, eff. March 14, 2003.

2C:30–7. Pattern of official misconduct

a. A person commits the crime of pattern of official misconduct if he commits two or more acts that violate the provisions of N.J.S.2C:30–2 or section 2 of P.L.2003, c. 31 (C.2C:30–6). It shall not be a defense that the violations were not part of a common plan or scheme, or did not have similar methods of commission.

b. Pattern of official misconduct is a crime of the second degree if one of the acts committed by the defendant is a first or second degree crime; otherwise, it is a crime of the third degree, provided, however, that the presumption of nonimprisonment set forth in subsection e. of N.J.S.2C:44–1 for persons who have not previously been convicted of an offense shall not apply. Notwithstanding the provisions of N.J.S.2C:1–8 or any other law, a conviction of pattern of official misconduct shall not merge with a conviction of official misconduct, official deprivation of civil rights, or any other criminal offense, nor shall such other conviction merge with a conviction under this section, and the court shall impose separate sentences upon each violation of N.J.S.2C:30–2 and sections 2 and 3 of P.L.2003, c. 31 (C.2C:30–6 and C.2C:30–7).

L.2003, c. 31, § 3, eff. March 14, 2003.

2C:30–8. Public corruption profiteering penalty

a. This act shall be known and may be cited as the "Public Corruption Profiteering Penalty Act."

b. In addition to any other disposition authorized by the court, including but not limited to any fines, penalties or assessments which may be imposed pursuant to the provisions of Title 2C of the New Jersey Statutes where a person has been convicted of a crime enumerated in subsection c. of this section or an attempt or conspiracy to commit such crime, the court shall, upon the application of the Attorney General or the county prosecutor, impose a public corruption profiteering penalty in an amount determined pursuant to this section; provided that the trier of fact has found beyond a reasonable doubt that the defendant is guilty of a crime or an attempt or conspiracy to commit a crime involving the negotiation, award, performance or payment of a local, county or State contract as enumerated in subsection c. of this section.

c. The public corruption profiteering penalty set forth in this section may be imposed when a person is convicted of a crime or an attempt or conspiracy to commit a crime involving the negotiation, award, performance or payment of a local, county or State contract, including, but not limited to:

(1) a violation of any of the provisions of chapter 21 of Title 2C of the New Jersey Statutes;

(2) a violation of any of the provisions of chapter 27 of Title 2C of the New Jersey Statutes;

(3) a violation of any of the provisions of chapter 28 of Title 2C of the New Jersey Statutes;

(4) a violation of any of the provisions of chapter 29 of Title 2C of the New Jersey Statutes; or

(5) a violation of any of the provisions of chapter 30 of Title 2C of the New Jersey Statutes.

d. Where the defendant was convicted of any of the crimes enumerated in subsection c. of this section, the court shall assess a public corruption profiteering penalty as follows:

(1) $500,000 in the case of a crime of the first degree; $250,000 in the case of a crime of the second degree; $75,000 in the case of a crime of the third degree; or

(2) an amount equal to three times the value of any property involved in any of the crimes enumerated in subsection c. of this section.

e. Where the prosecution requests that the court assess a public corruption profiteering penalty in an amount calculated pursuant to this section, the court shall take judicial notice of any evidence, testimony or information adduced at trial, plea hearing or other court proceedings and shall also consider the presentence report and other relevant information, including expert opinion in the form of live testimony or by affidavit. The court's findings shall be incorporated in the record, and such findings shall not be subject to modification by an appellate court except upon a showing that the finding was totally lacking support in the record or was arbitrary and capricious.

f. The court shall not revoke or reduce the public corruption profiteering penalty imposed pursuant to this section. A public corruption profiteering penalty imposed pursuant to this section shall not be deemed a fine for purposes of N.J.S.2C:46–3.

g. The court may, for good cause shown, and subject to the provisions of this section, grant permission for the payment of a public corruption profiteering penalty imposed pursuant to this section to be made within a specified period of time or in specified installments, provided however that the payment schedule fixed by the court shall require the defendant to pay the penalty in the shortest period of time consistent with the nature and extent of his assets and his ability to pay, and further provided that the Attorney General or the county prosecutor shall be afforded the opportunity to present evidence or information concerning the nature, extent and location of the defendant's assets or interests in property which are or might be subject to levy and execution. In such event, the court may only grant permission for the payment to be made within a specified period of time or installments with respect to that portion of the assessed penalty which would not be satisfied by the liquidation of property which is or may be subject to levy and execution, unless the court finds that the immediate liquidation of such property would result in undue hardship to innocent persons. If no permission to make payment within a specified period of time or in installments is embodied in the sentence, the entire penalty shall be payable forthwith.

h. A public corruption profiteering penalty assessed pursuant to this section shall be imposed and paid in addition to any penalty, fine, fee or order for restitution which may be imposed pursuant to Title 2C of the New Jersey Statutes.

i. A public corruption profiteering penalty imposed pursuant to this section shall be in addition to and not in lieu of any forfeiture or other cause of action instituted pursuant to chapter 41 or 64 of Title 2C of the New Jersey Statutes, and nothing in this section shall be construed in any way to preclude, preempt or limit any such cause of action. A defendant shall not be entitled to receive credit toward the payment of a public corruption profiteering penalty imposed pursuant to this section for the value of property forfeited, or subject to forfeiture, pursuant to the provisions of chapter 41 or 64 of Title 2C of the New Jersey Statutes.

j. All public corruption profiteering penalties imposed pursuant to this section shall be docketed and collected as provided for the collection of fines, penalties, fees and restitution in chapter 46 of Title 2C of the New Jersey Statutes. The Attorney General or the county prosecutor may prosecute an action to collect any public corruption profiteering penalties imposed pursuant to this section. All public corruption profiteering penalties assessed pursuant to this section shall be disposed of, distributed, appropriated and used as if the collected penalties were the proceeds of property forfeited pursuant to chapter 64 of Title 2C of the New Jersey Statutes.

L.2007, c. 159, § 1, eff. Sept. 4, 2007.

CHAPTERS 31, 32

[RESERVED]

PART 5

OFFENSES AGAINST PUBLIC ORDER, HEALTH AND DECENCY

Chapter
33.   Riot, Disorderly Conduct, and related Offenses.
34.   Public Indecency.
35.   Controlled Dangerous Substances.
35A.   Anti–Drug Profiteering.
35B.   Drug Dealer Liability.
36.   Drug Paraphernalia.
36A.   Conditional Discharge for Certain First Offenders.
37.   Gambling Offenses.
38.   September 11TH, 2001 Anti–Terrorism Act.
39.   Firearms, Other Dangerous Weapons and Instruments of Crime.
40.   Other Offenses relating to Public Safety.
40A.   Miscellaneous.

CHAPTER 33

RIOT, DISORDERLY CONDUCT, AND RELATED OFFENSES

Section
2C:33–1.   Riot; failure to disperse.
2C:33–2.   Disorderly conduct.
2C:33–2.1.   Loitering for purpose of illegally using, possessing or selling controlled substance.
2C:33–3.   False public alarms.
2C:33–3.1.   Juvenile's right to operate a motor vehicle; suspension or postponement.
2C:33–3.2.   Penalty.
2C:33–4.   Harassment.
2C:33–5, 2C:33–6.   Blank.
2C:33–7.   Obstructing highways and other public passages.
2C:33–8.   Disrupting meetings and processions.
2C:33–8.1.   Demonstrations at funerals; definitions.
2C:33–9.   Desecration of venerated objects.
2C:33–10.   Causing fear of unlawful bodily violence, crime of third degree; act of graffiti, additional penalty.
2C:33–11.   Defacement of private property, crime of fourth degree; act of graffiti, additional penalty.
2C:33–11.1. Disorderly persons offense; forcible entry and detainer.
2C:33–12.   Maintaining a nuisance.
2C:33–12.1. Abating nuisance.
2C:33–12.2. Sexually oriented businesses.
2C:33–13.   Smoking in public.
2C:33–13.1. Sale or provision of cigarettes or electronic smoking devices to persons under 19 years of age.

Section
2C:33–14.   Interference with transportation.
2C:33–14.1. Vandalizing railroad warning signals or protection devices.
2C:33–15.   Possession or consumption of alcoholic beverage in public place or motor vehicle by person under legal age.
2C:33–16.   Alcoholic beverages; bringing or possession on school property by person of legal age; penalty.
2C:33–17.   Offer or service of alcoholic beverage to underage person; disorderly persons; exceptions.
2C:33–18.   Repealed.
2C:33–19.   Bringing or possessing remotely activated paging device by student on property used for school purposes without express written permission of school board; disorderly persons offense.
2C:33–20.   Use of remotely activated paging device while engaged in commission of or attempt to commit or flight after committing controlled dangerous substances or drug paraphernalia violation.
2C:33–21.   Use of information intercepted from police, fire or emergency medical communications system.
2C:33–22.   Possession of radio capable of receiving transmission from police, fire or emergency medical communication system.
2C:33–23.   Radar devices used to monitor vehicular speed not considered police, fire or emergency medical communications system.
2C:33–23.1. Unlicensed radio transmissions of energy; prohibitions.
2C:33–23.2. Penalty for unlicensed radio transmissions of energy.
2C:33–24.   Definitions.
2C:33–25.   Exhibition of warning sign required for sale of spray paint; violations, penalties.
2C:33–26.   Sale of motor vehicle on Sunday.
2C:33–27.   Consumption of alcohol in restaurants.
2C:33–28.   Soliciting or recruiting gang members; sentence.
2C:33–29.   Gang criminality; definition; grading.
2C:33–30.   Promotion of organized street crime.

2C:33–1. Riot; failure to disperse

a. Riot. A person is guilty of riot if he participates with four or more others in a course of disorderly conduct as defined in section 2C:33–2a:

(1) With purpose to commit or facilitate the commission of a crime;

(2) With purpose to prevent or coerce official action; or

(3) When he or any other participant, known to him, uses or plans to use a firearm or other deadly weapon.

Riot if committed under circumstances set forth in paragraph (3) is a crime of the third degree. Otherwise riot is a crime of the fourth degree.

b. Failure of disorderly persons to disperse upon official order. Where five or more persons are participating in a course of disorderly conduct as defined in section 2C:33–2 a. likely to cause substantial harm, a peace officer or other public servant engaged in executing or enforcing the law may order the participants and others in the immediate vicinity to disperse. A person who refuses or knowingly fails to obey such an order commits a disorderly persons offense.

L.1978, c. 95, § 2C:33–1, eff. Sept. 1, 1979. Amended by L.1979, c. 178, § 63, eff. Sept. 1, 1979; L.1981, c. 290, § 35, eff. Sept. 24, 1981.

2C:33–2. Disorderly conduct

a. Improper behavior. A person is guilty of a petty disorderly persons offense, if with purpose to cause public inconvenience, annoyance or alarm, or recklessly creating a risk thereof he

(1) Engages in fighting or threatening, or in violent or tumultuous behavior; or

(2) Creates a hazardous or physically dangerous condition by any act which serves no legitimate purpose of the actor.

b. Offensive language. A person is guilty of a petty disorderly persons offense if, in a public place, and with purpose to offend the sensibilities of a hearer or in reckless disregard of the probability of so doing, he addresses unreasonably loud and offensively coarse or abusive language, given the circumstances of the person present and the setting of the utterance, to any person present.

"Public" means affecting or likely to affect persons in a place to which the public or a substantial group has access; among the places included are highways, transport facilities, schools, prisons, apartment houses, places of business or amusement, or any neighborhood.

L.1978, c. 95, § 2C:33–2, eff. Sept. 1, 1979.

2C:33–2.1. Loitering for purpose of illegally using, possessing or selling controlled substance

a. As used in this section:

"Public place" means any place to which the public has access, including but not limited to a public street, road, thoroughfare, sidewalk, bridge, alley, plaza, park, recreation or shopping area, public transportation facility, vehicle used for public transportation, parking lot, public library or any other public building, structure or area.

b. A person, whether on foot or in a motor vehicle, commits a disorderly persons offense if (1) he wanders, remains or prowls in a public place with the purpose of unlawfully obtaining or distributing a controlled dangerous substance or controlled substance analog; and (2) engages in conduct that, under the circumstances, manifests a purpose to obtain or distribute a controlled dangerous substance or controlled substance analog.

c. Conduct that may, where warranted under the circumstances, be deemed adequate to manifest a purpose to obtain or distribute a controlled dangerous substance or controlled substance analog includes, but is not limited to, conduct such as the following:

(1) Repeatedly beckoning to or stopping pedestrians or motorists in a public place;

(2) Repeatedly passing objects to or receiving objects from pedestrians or motorists in a public place;

(3) Repeatedly circling in a public place in a motor vehicle and on one or more occasions passing any object to or receiving any object from a person in a public place.

d. The element of the offense described in paragraph (1) of subsection b. of this section may not be established solely by proof that the actor engaged in the conduct that is used to satisfy the element described in paragraph (2) of subsection b. of this section.

L.1991, c. 383, § 1, eff. March 16, 1992.

2C:33–3. False public alarms

a. Except as provided in subsection b. or c. of this section, a person is guilty of a crime of the third degree if he initiates or circulates a report or warning of an impending fire, explosion, bombing, crime, catastrophe or emergency knowing that the report or warning is false or baseless and that it is likely to cause evacuation of a building, place of assembly, or facility of public transport, or to cause public inconvenience or alarm. A person is guilty of a crime of the third degree if he knowingly causes such false alarm to be transmitted to or within any organization, official or volunteer, for dealing with emergencies involving danger to life or property.

b. A person is guilty of a crime of the second degree if in addition to the report or warning initiated, circulated or transmitted under subsection a. of this section, he places or causes to be placed any false or facsimile bomb in a building, place of assembly, or facility of public transport or in a place likely to cause public inconvenience or alarm. A violation of this subsection is a crime of the first degree if it occurs during a declared period of national, State or county emergency.

c. A person is guilty of a crime of the second degree if a violation of subsection a. of this section in fact results in serious bodily injury to another person or occurs during a declared period of national, State or county emergency. A person is guilty of a crime of the first degree if a violation of subsection a. of this section in fact results in death.

d. For the purposes of this section, "in fact" means that strict liability is imposed. It shall not be a defense that the death or serious bodily injury was not a foreseeable consequence of the person's acts or that the death or serious bodily injury was caused by the actions of another person or by circumstances beyond the control of the actor. The actor shall be strictly liable upon proof that the crime occurred during a declared period of national, State or county emergency. It shall not be a defense that the actor did not know that there was a declared period of emergency at the time the crime occurred.

e.   A person is guilty of a crime of the fourth degree if the person knowingly places a call to a 9–1–1 emergency telephone system without purpose of reporting the need for 9–1–1 service.

L.1978, c. 95, § 2C:33–3, eff. Sept. 1, 1979.   Amended by L.1987, c. 6, § 1, eff. Feb. 19, 1987; L.1994, c. 115, § 1, eff. Oct. 12, 1994; L.1996, c. 63, § 1, eff. July 12, 1996; L.1999, c. 195, § 1, eff. Aug. 31, 1999; L.2002, c. 26, § 16, eff. June 18, 2002.

2C:33–3.1.   Juvenile's right to operate a motor vehicle; suspension or postponement

a.   In the case of a juvenile adjudicated delinquent for a violation of N.J.S. 2C:33–3 the court shall suspend or postpone the juvenile's right to operate a motor vehicle including a motorized bicycle for a period of six months, in addition to any other disposition ordered by the court under section 24 of P.L.1982, c. 77 (C.2A:4A–43).   In the case of a person who at the time of the disposition is less than 17 years of age, the period of the suspension of driving privileges authorized herein, including a suspension of the privilege of operating a motorized bicycle, shall commence on the day the disposition is imposed and shall run for a period of six months after the day the person reaches the age of 17 years.

b.   In addition to any other sentence imposed by the court under this code, the court shall suspend or postpone a person's right to operate a motor vehicle including a motorized bicycle for any person who is convicted under N.J.S.2C:33–3 and is less than 21 years of age at the time of the conviction.   The period of the suspension of driving privileges authorized herein, including a suspension of the privilege of operating a motorized bicycle, shall commence on the day the sentence is imposed and shall run for a period of six months.

c.   If the driving privilege of any person is under revocation, suspension, or postponement for a violation of any provision of this Title or Title 39 of the Revised Statutes at the time of any adjudication of delinquency for a violation of N.J.S.2C:33–3 or a conviction under N.J.S.2C:33–3, the revocation, suspension, or postponement period imposed herein shall commence as of the date of termination of the existing revocation, suspension, or postponement.

d.   The court before whom any person is convicted or adjudicated delinquent for a violation of N.J.S.2C:33–3 shall collect forthwith the New Jersey driver's license or licenses of the person and forward such license or licenses to the Director of the Division of Motor Vehicles along with a report indicating the first and last day of the suspension or postponement period imposed by the court pursuant to this section.   If the court is for any reason unable to collect the license or licenses of the person, the court shall cause a report of the conviction or adjudication of delinquency to be filed with the director.   That report shall include the complete name, address, date of birth, eye color, and sex of the person and shall indicate the first and last day of the suspension or postponement period imposed by the court pursuant to this section.   The court shall inform the person orally and in writing that if the person is convicted of personally operating a motor vehicle during the period of license suspension or postponement imposed pursuant to this section the person shall, upon conviction, be subject to the penalties set forth in R.S.39:3–40.   A person shall be required to acknowledge receipt of the written notice in writing.   Failure to receive a written notice or failure to acknowledge in writing the receipt of a written notice shall not be a defense to a subsequent charge of violation of R.S.39:3–40.   If the person is the holder of a driver's license from another jurisdiction, the court shall not collect the license but shall notify the director who shall notify the appropriate officials in the licensing jurisdiction.   The court shall, however, in accordance with the provisions of this section, revoke the person's non-resident driving privileges in this State.

L.1999, c. 195, § 2, eff. Aug. 31, 1999.

2C:33–3.2.   Penalty

Any person who violates the provisions of N.J.S.2C:33–3 shall be liable for a civil penalty of not less than $2,000 or actual costs incurred by or resulting from the law enforcement and emergency services response to the false alarm, whichever is higher.   Any monies collected pursuant to this section shall be made payable to the municipality or other entity providing the law enforcement or emergency services response to the false alarm.   "Emergency services" includes, but is not limited to, paid or volunteer fire fighters, paramedics, members of an ambulance team, rescue squad or mobile intensive care unit.

L.1999, c. 195, § 3, eff. Aug. 31, 1999.   Amended by L.2002, c. 26, § 17, eff. June 18, 2002.

2C:33–4.   Harassment

Except as provided in subsection e., a person commits a petty disorderly persons offense if, with purpose to harass another, he:

a.   Makes, or causes to be made, a communication or communications anonymously or at extremely inconvenient hours, or in offensively coarse language, or any other manner likely to cause annoyance or alarm;

b.   Subjects another to striking, kicking, shoving, or other offensive touching, or threatens to do so; or

c.   Engages in any other course of alarming conduct or of repeatedly committed acts with purpose to alarm or seriously annoy such other person.

A communication under subsection a. may be deemed to have been made either at the place where it originated or at the place where it was received.

d.   (Deleted by amendment, P.L.2001, c. 443).

e.   A person commits a crime of the fourth degree if, in committing an offense under this section, he was serving a term of imprisonment or was on parole or probation as the result of a conviction of any indictable offense under the laws of this State, any other state or the United States.

L.1978, c. 95, § 2C:33–4, eff. Sept. 1, 1979. Amended by L.1983, c. 334, § 1, eff. Sept. 2, 1983; L.1990, c. 87, § 2, eff. Aug. 9, 1990; L.1995, c. 211, § 2, eff. Aug. 14, 1995; L.1998, c. 17, § 4, eff. May 6, 1998; L.2001, c. 443, § 3, eff. Jan. 11, 2002.

2C:33–5, 2C:33–6. Blank

2C:33–7. Obstructing highways and other public passages

a. A person, who, having no legal privilege to do so, purposely or recklessly obstructs any highway or other public passage whether alone or with others, commits a petty disorderly persons offense. "Obstructs" means renders impassable without unreasonable inconvenience or hazard. No person shall be deemed guilty of recklessly obstructing in violation of this subsection solely because of a gathering of persons to hear him speak or otherwise communicate, or solely because of being a member of such a gathering.

b. A person in a gathering commits a petty disorderly persons offense if he refuses to obey a reasonable official request or order to move:

(1) To prevent obstruction of a highway or other public passage; or

(2) To maintain public safety by dispersing those gathered in dangerous proximity to a fire or other hazard.

An order to move, addressed to a person whose speech or other lawful behavior attracts an obstructing audience, shall not be deemed reasonable if the obstruction can be readily remedied by police control of the size or location of the gathering.

L.1978, c. 95, § 2C:33–7, eff. Sept. 1, 1979.

2C:33–8. Disrupting meetings and processions

A person commits a disorderly persons offense if, with purpose to prevent or disrupt a lawful meeting, procession or gathering, he does an act tending to obstruct or interfere with it physically.

L.1978, c. 95, § 2C:33–8, eff. Sept. 1, 1979.

2C:33–8.1. Demonstrations at funerals; definitions

a. As used in this act:

"funeral" means the ceremonies, processions and memorial services held in connection with the burial or cremation of the dead; and

"demonstration" includes the following:

(1) any picketing or similar conduct,

(2) any oration, speech, use of sound amplification equipment or device, or similar conduct that is not part of a funeral,

(3) the display of any placard, banner, flag, or similar device, unless such a display is part of a funeral, or

(4) the distribution of any handbill, pamphlet, leaflet, or other written or printed matter other than a program distributed as part of a funeral.

b. A person is guilty of disrupting a funeral if, during the period beginning one hour prior to the scheduled commencement of a funeral, and until one hour following the actual completion of the funeral, with the purpose of causing inconvenience, annoyance or alarm to the funeral or its participants, or of recklessly creating the risk thereof, the person knowingly:

(1) obstructs, hinders, impedes or blocks another person's entry to or exit from the funeral, the funeral procession, the funeral home, church, synagogue, temple or other place of public worship or other location at which a funeral takes place as part of demonstration activities, or

(2) engages in demonstration activities within 500 feet of the funeral, the funeral procession, the funeral home, church, synagogue, temple or other place of public worship or other location at which a funeral takes place and makes or assists in the making of noise, diversions, or threatening gestures, or engages in any other disruptive conduct, that disrupts or tends to disrupt the peace or good order of the funeral.

c. Disrupting a funeral is a disorderly persons offense.

L.2006, c. 93, § 2, eff. Aug. 21, 2006.

2C:33–9. Desecration of venerated objects

A person commits a disorderly persons offense if he purposely desecrates any public monument, insignia, symbol, or structure, or place of worship or burial. "Desecrate" means defacing, damaging or polluting.

L.1978, c. 95, § 2C:33–9, eff. Sept. 1, 1979.

2C:33–10. Causing fear of unlawful bodily violence, crime of third degree; act of graffiti, additional penalty

A person is guilty of a crime of the third degree if he purposely, knowingly or recklessly puts or attempts to put another in fear of bodily violence by placing on private property of another a symbol, an object, a characterization, an appellation or graffiti that exposes another to threats of violence. A person shall not be guilty of an attempt unless his actions cause a serious and imminent likelihood of causing fear of unlawful bodily violence.

A person convicted of an offense under this section that involves an act of graffiti may, in addition to any other penalty imposed by the court, be required either to pay to the owner of the damaged property monetary restitution in the amount of the pecuniary damage caused by the act of graffiti or to perform community service, which shall include removing the graffiti from the property, if appropriate. If community service is ordered, it shall be for either not less than 20 days nor less than the number of days necessary to remove the graffiti from the property.

L.1981, c. 282, § 1, eff. Sept. 10, 1981. Amended by L.1995, c. 211, § 4, eff. Aug. 14, 1995; L.1995, c. 251, § 2, eff. Dec. 12, 1995.

2C:33–11. Defacement of private property, crime of fourth degree; act of graffiti, additional penalty

A person is guilty of a crime of the fourth degree if he purposely defaces or damages, without authorization of the owner or tenant, any private premises or property primarily used for religious, educational, residential, memorial, charitable, or cemetery purposes, or for assembly by persons for purpose of exercising any right guaranteed by law or by the Constitution of this State or of the United States by placing thereon a symbol, an object, a characterization, an appellation, or graffiti that exposes another to threat of violence.

A person convicted of an offense under this section that involves an act of graffiti may, in addition to any other penalty imposed by the court, be required either to pay to the owner of the damaged property monetary restitution in the amount of pecuniary damage caused by the act of graffiti or to perform community service, which shall include removing the graffiti from the property, if appropriate. If community service is ordered, it shall be for either not less than 20 days or not less than the number of days necessary to remove the graffiti from the property.

L.1981, c. 282, § 2, eff. Sept. 10, 1981. Amended by L.1995, c. 211, § 5, eff. Aug. 14, 1995; L.1995, c. 251, § 3, eff. Dec. 12, 1995.

2C:33–11.1. Disorderly persons offense; forcible entry and detainer

a. A person commits a disorderly persons offense if, after being warned by a law enforcement or other public official of the illegality of that action, the person (1) takes possession of residential real property or effectuates a forcible entry or detainer of residential real property without lawful execution of a warrant for possession in accordance with the provisions of section 2 of P.L.1974, c. 47 (C.2A:42–10.16) or without the consent of the occupant solely in possession of the residential real property; or (2) refuses to restore immediately to exclusive possession and occupancy any such occupant so displaced. Legal occupants unlawfully displaced shall be entitled without delay to reenter and reoccupy the premises, and shall not be considered trespassers or chargeable with any offense, provided that a law enforcement officer is present at the time of reentry. It shall be the duty of such officer to prevent the landlord or any other persons from obstructing or hindering the reentry and reoccupancy of the dwelling by the displaced occupant.

As used in this section, "forcible entry and detainer" means to enter upon or into any real property and detain and hold that property by:

(1) any kind of violence including threatening to kill or injure the party in possession;

(2) words, circumstances or actions which have a clear intention to incite fear or apprehension or danger in the party in possession;

(3) putting outside of the residential premises the personal effects or furniture of the party in possession;

(4) entering peaceably and then, by force or threats, turning the party out of possession;

(5) padlocking or otherwise changing locks to the property;

(6) shutting off, or causing to be shut off, vital services such as, but not limited to, heat, electricity or water, in an effort to regain possession; or by

(7) any means other than compliance with lawful eviction procedures pursuant to section 2 of P.L.1974, c. 47 (C.2A:42–10.16), as established through possession of a lawfully prepared and valid "Execution of Warrant."

b. A person who is convicted of an offense under this section more than once within a five-year period is guilty of a crime of the fourth degree.

L.2005, c. 319, § 3, eff. Jan. 12, 2006.

2C:33–12. Maintaining a nuisance

A person is guilty of maintaining a nuisance when:

a. By conduct either unlawful in itself or unreasonable under all the circumstances, he knowingly or recklessly creates or maintains a condition which endangers the safety or health of a considerable number of persons;

b. He knowingly conducts or maintains any premises, place or resort where persons gather for purposes of engaging in unlawful conduct; or

c. He knowingly conducts or maintains any premises, place or resort as a house of prostitution or as a place where obscene material, as defined in N.J.S. 2C:34–2 and N.J.S. 2C:34–3, is sold, photographed, manufactured, exhibited or otherwise prepared or shown, in violation of N.J.S. 2C:34–2, N.J.S. 2C:34–3, and N.J.S. 2C:34–4.

A person is guilty of a disorderly persons offense if the person is convicted under subsection a. or b. of this section. A person is guilty of a crime of the fourth degree if the person is convicted under subsection c. of this section.

Upon conviction under this section, in addition to the sentence authorized by this code, the court may proceed as set forth in section 2C:33–12.1.

L.1978, c. 95, § 2C:33–12, eff. Sept. 1, 1979. Amended by L.1979, c. 178, § 64, eff. Sept. 1, 1979; L.1982, c. 233, § 1, eff. Jan. 7, 1983; L.1983, c. 234, § 1, eff. June 30, 1983.

2C:33–12.1. Abating nuisance

a. In addition to the penalty imposed in case of conviction under N.J.S. 2C:33–12 or under section 2 of P.L.1995, c.167 (C. 2C:33–12.2), the court may order the immediate abatement of the nuisance, and for that purpose may order the seizure and forfeiture or destruction of any chattels, liquors, obscene material or other personal property which may be found in such building or place, and which the court is satisfied from the evidence were possessed or used with a purpose of maintaining the nuisance. Any such forfeiture shall be in the name and to the use of the State of New Jersey, and the court shall direct the forfeited property to be sold at public sale, the proceeds to be paid to the treasurer of the county wherein conviction was had.

b. If the owner of any building or place is found guilty of maintaining a nuisance, the court may order that the building or place where the nuisance was maintained be closed and not used for a period not exceeding one year from the date of the conviction. *L.1979, c. 178, § 66, eff. Sept. 1, 1979. Amended by L.1982, c. 233, § 2, eff. Jan. 7, 1983; L.1983, c. 234, § 2, eff. June 30, 1983; L.1995, c. 167, § 1, eff. Sept. 3, 1995.*

2C:33–12.2. Sexually oriented businesses

a. As used in this act:

(1) "Sexually oriented business" means:

(a) A commercial establishment which as one of its principal business purposes offers for sale, rental, or display any of the following:

Books, magazines, periodicals or other printed material, or photographs, films, motion pictures, video cassettes, slides or other visual representations which depict or describe a "specified sexual activity" or "specified anatomical area"; or still or motion picture machines, projectors or other image-producing devices which show images to one person per machine at any one time, and where the images so displayed are characterized by the depiction of a "specified sexual activity" or "specified anatomical area"; or instruments, devices, or paraphernalia which are designed for use in connection with a "specified sexual activity"; or

(b) A commercial establishment which regularly features live performances characterized by the exposure of a "specified anatomical area" or by a "specified sexual activity," or which regularly shows films, motion pictures, video cassettes, slides, or other photographic representations which depict or describe a "specified sexual activity" or "specified anatomical area";

(2) "Person" means an individual, proprietorship, partnership, corporation, association, or other legal entity.

(3) "Specified anatomical area" means:

(a) Less than completely and opaquely covered human genitals, pubic region, buttock or female breasts below a point immediately above the top of the areola; or

(b) Human male genitals in a discernibly turgid state, even if covered.

(4) "Specified sexual activity" means:

(a) The fondling or other erotic touching of covered or uncovered human genitals, pubic region, buttock or female breast; or

(b) Any actual or simulated act of human masturbation, sexual intercourse or deviate sexual intercourse.

b. In addition to any activities proscribed by the provisions of N.J.S. 2C:33–12, a person is guilty of maintaining a nuisance when the person owns or operates a sexually oriented business which offers for public use booths, screens, enclosures or other devices which facilitate sexual activity by patrons.

c. Notwithstanding any other provision of law, a municipality shall have the power to determine restrictions, if any, on the hours of operation of sexually oriented businesses.

d. A person who violates this act is guilty of a crime of the fourth degree.

L.1995, c. 167, § 2, eff. Sept. 3, 1995.

2C:33–13. Smoking in public

a. Any person who smokes or carries lighted tobacco in or upon any bus or other public conveyance, except group charter buses, specially marked railroad smoking cars, limousines or livery services, and, when the driver is the only person in the vehicle, autocabs, is a petty disorderly person. For the purposes of this section, "bus" includes school buses and other vehicles owned or contracted for by the governing body, board or individual of a nonpublic school, a public or private college, university, or professional training school, or a board of education of a school district, that are used to transport students to and from school and school-related activities; and the prohibition on smoking or carrying lighted tobacco shall apply even if students are not present in the vehicle.

b. Any person who smokes or carries lighted tobacco in any public place, including but not limited to places of public accommodation, where such smoking is prohibited by municipal ordinance under authority of R.S.40:48–1 and 40:48–2 or by the owner or person responsible for the operation of the public place, and when adequate notice of such prohibition has been conspicuously posted, is guilty of a petty disorderly persons offense. Notwithstanding the provisions of

2C:43–3, the maximum fine which can be imposed for violation of this section is $200.

c.   The provisions of this section shall supersede any other statute and any rule or regulation adopted pursuant to law.

L.1978, c. 95, § 2C:33–13, eff. Sept. 1, 1979.   Amended by L.1979, c. 178, § 66A, eff. Sept. 1, 1979;   L.1985, c. 187, § 1, eff. July 12, 1985;   L.2003, c. 233, § 1, eff. Jan. 9, 2004.

2C:33–13.1.   Sale or provision of cigarettes or electronic smoking devices to persons under 19 years of age

a.   A person who sells or gives to a person under 19 years of age any cigarettes made of tobacco or of any other matter or substance which can be smoked, or any cigarette paper or tobacco in any form, including smokeless tobacco, or any electronic smoking device that can be used to deliver nicotine or other substances to the person inhaling from the device, including, but not limited to, an electronic cigarette, cigar, cigarillo, or pipe, or any cartridge or other component of the device or related product, including an employee of a retail dealer licensee under P.L.1948, c. 65 (C.54:40A–1 et seq.) who actually sells or otherwise provides a tobacco product or electronic smoking device to a person under 19 years of age, shall be punished by a fine as provided for a petty disorderly persons offense.   A person who has been previously punished under this section and who commits another offense under it may be punishable by a fine of twice that provided for a petty disorderly persons offense.

b.   The establishment of all of the following shall constitute a defense to any prosecution brought pursuant to subsection a. of this section:

(1)   that the purchaser or recipient of the tobacco product or electronic smoking device falsely represented, by producing either a driver's license or non-driver identification card issued by the New Jersey Motor Vehicle Commission, a similar card issued pursuant to the laws of another state or the federal government of Canada, or a photographic identification card issued by a county clerk, that the purchaser or recipient was of legal age to purchase or receive the tobacco product or electronic smoking device;

(2)   that the appearance of the purchaser or recipient of the tobacco product or electronic smoking device was such that an ordinary prudent person would believe the purchaser or recipient to be of legal age to purchase or receive the tobacco product or electronic smoking device; and

(3)   that the sale or distribution of the tobacco product or electronic smoking device was made in good faith, relying upon the production of the identification set forth in paragraph (1) of this subsection, the appearance of the purchaser or recipient, and in the reasonable belief that the purchaser or recipient was of legal age to purchase or receive the tobacco product or electronic smoking device.

c.   A penalty imposed pursuant to this section shall be in addition to any penalty that may be imposed pursuant to section 1 of P.L.2000, c. 87 (C.2A:170–51.4).
L.1999, c. 90, § 3, eff. May 3, 1999.   Amended by L.2000, c. 87, § 4, eff. Aug. 14, 2000;   L.2005, c. 384, § 5, eff. April 15, 2006;   L.2009, c. 182, § 4, eff. March 12, 2010.

2C:33–14.   Interference with transportation

a.   Interference with Transportation.   A person is guilty of interference with transportation if the person purposely or knowingly:

(1)   casts, shoots or throws anything at, against or into any vehicle, including, but not limited to, a bus, light rail vehicle, railroad locomotive, railroad car, jitney, trolley car, subway car, ferry, airplane, or other facility of transportation; or

(2)   casts, shoots, throws or otherwise places any stick, stone, object or other substance upon any street railway track, trolley track or railroad track; or

(3)   endangers or obstructs the safe operation of motor vehicles by casting, shooting, throwing or otherwise placing any stick, stone, object or other substance upon any highway or roadway; or

(4)   unlawfully climbs into or upon any light rail vehicle, railroad locomotive or railroad car, either in motion or standing on the track of any railroad company in this State; or

(5)   unlawfully disrupts, delays or prevents the operation of any vehicle, including, but not limited to, a bus, light rail vehicle, railroad locomotive, train, bus, jitney, trolley, subway, airplane or any other facility of transportation.   The term "unlawfully disrupts, delays or prevents the operation of" does not include non-violent conduct growing out of a labor dispute as defined in N.J.S.2A:15–58; or

(6)   endangers or obstructs the safe operation of motor vehicles by using a traffic control preemption device to interfere with or impair the operation of a traffic control signal as defined in R.S.39:1–1; or

(7)   shines, points or focuses a laser lighting device beam, directly or indirectly, upon a person operating any vehicle, including, but not limited to, a bus, light rail vehicle, railroad locomotive, railroad car, jitney, trolley car, subway car, ferry, airplane, or other facility of transportation.   As used in this paragraph, "laser lighting device" means a device which emits a laser beam that is designed to be used by the operator as a pointer or highlighter to indicate, mark or identify a specific position, place, item or object.

As used in this subsection, "traffic control preemption device" means an infrared transmitter or other device which transmits an infrared beam, radio wave or other signal designed to change, alter, or disrupt in any manner the normal operation of a traffic control signal.

b.   Interference with transportation is a disorderly persons offense.

c. Interference with transportation is a crime of the fourth degree if the person purposely, knowingly or recklessly causes bodily injury to another person or causes pecuniary loss in excess of $500 but less than $2,000.

d. Interference with transportation is a crime of the third degree if the person purposely, knowingly or recklessly causes significant bodily injury to another person or causes pecuniary loss of $2,000 or more, or if the person purposely or knowingly creates a risk of significant bodily injury to another person.

e. Interference with transportation is a crime of the second degree if the person purposely, knowingly or recklessly causes serious bodily injury to another person.

L.1978, c. 95, § 2C:33–14, eff. Sept. 1, 1979. Amended by L.2001, c. 413, § 2, eff. Jan. 8, 2002; L.2005, c. 96, § 1, eff. Sept. 1, 2005; L.2007, c. 145, § 1, eff. Aug. 21, 2007.

2C:33–14.1. Vandalizing railroad warning signals or protection devices

a. Any person who purposely, knowingly or recklessly defaces, damages, obstructs, removes or otherwise impairs the operation of any railroad crossing warning signal or protection device, including, but not limited to safety gates, electric bell, electric sign or any other alarm or protection system authorized by the Commissioner of Transportation, which is required under the provisions of R.S.48:12–54 or R.S.48:2–29, or any other railroad property or equipment, other than administrative buildings, offices or equipment, shall, for a first offense, be guilty of a crime of the fourth degree; however, if the defacement, damage, obstruction, removal or impediment of the crossing warning signal or protection device, property or equipment recklessly causes bodily injury or pecuniary loss of $2000 or more, the actor is guilty of a crime of the third degree, or if it recklessly causes a death or serious bodily injury, the actor is guilty of a crime of the second degree.

b. A person convicted of a violation of this section that involves an act of graffiti may, in addition to any other penalty imposed by the court, be required to pay to the owner of the damaged property monetary restitution in the amount of the pecuniary damage caused by the act of graffiti and to perform community service, which shall include removing the graffiti from the property, if appropriate. If community service is ordered, it shall be for either not less than 20 days or not less than the number of days necessary to remove the graffiti from the property. As used in this section, "act of graffiti" means the drawing, painting or making of any mark or inscription on public or private real or personal property without the permission of the owner.

L.1991, c. 335, § 1, eff. Jan. 6, 1992. Amended by L.1998, c. 54, § 2, eff. July 10, 1998; L.2001, c. 413, § 3, eff. Jan. 8, 2002.

2C:33–15. Possession or consumption of alcoholic beverage in public place or motor vehicle by person under legal age

a. Any person under the legal age to purchase alcoholic beverages who knowingly possesses without legal authority or who knowingly consumes any alcoholic beverage in any school, public conveyance, public place, or place of public assembly, or motor vehicle, is guilty of a disorderly persons offense, and shall be fined not less than $500.00.

b. Whenever this offense is committed in a motor vehicle, the court shall, in addition to the sentence authorized for the offense, suspend or postpone for six months the driving privilege of the defendant. Upon the conviction of any person under this section, the court shall forward a report to the New Jersey Motor Vehicle Commission stating the first and last day of the suspension or postponement period imposed by the court pursuant to this section. If a person at the time of the imposition of a sentence is less than 17 years of age, the period of license postponement, including a suspension or postponement of the privilege of operating a motorized bicycle, shall commence on the day the sentence is imposed and shall run for a period of six months after the person reaches the age of 17 years.

If a person at the time of the imposition of a sentence has a valid driver's license issued by this State, the court shall immediately collect the license and forward it to the commission along with the report. If for any reason the license cannot be collected, the court shall include in the report the complete name, address, date of birth, eye color, and sex of the person as well as the first and last date of the license suspension period imposed by the court.

The court shall inform the person orally and in writing that if the person is convicted of operating a motor vehicle during the period of license suspension or postponement, the person shall be subject to the penalties set forth in R.S.39:3–40. A person shall be required to acknowledge receipt of the written notice in writing. Failure to receive a written notice or failure to acknowledge in writing the receipt of a written notice shall not be a defense to a subsequent charge of a violation of R.S.39:3–40.

If the person convicted under this section is not a New Jersey resident, the court shall suspend or postpone, as appropriate, the non-resident driving privilege of the person based on the age of the person and submit to the commission the required report. The court shall not collect the license of a non-resident convicted under this section. Upon receipt of a report by the court, the commission shall notify the appropriate officials in the licensing jurisdiction of the suspension or postponement.

c. In addition to the general penalty prescribed for a disorderly persons offense, the court may require any person who violates this act to participate in an alcohol education or treatment program, authorized by the

Department of Health and Senior Services, for a period not to exceed the maximum period of confinement prescribed by law for the offense for which the individual has been convicted.

d. Nothing in this act shall apply to possession of alcoholic beverages by any such person while actually engaged in the performance of employment pursuant to an employment permit issued by the Director of the Division of Alcoholic Beverage Control, or for a bona fide hotel or restaurant, in accordance with the provisions of R.S.33:1–26, or while actively engaged in the preparation of food while enrolled in a culinary arts or hotel management program at a county vocational school or post secondary educational institution.

e. The provisions of section 3 of P.L.1991, c. 169 (C.33:1–81.1a) shall apply to a parent, guardian or other person with legal custody of a person under 18 years of age who is found to be in violation of this section.

f. An underage person and one or two other persons shall be immune from prosecution under this section if:

(1) one of the underage persons called 9–1–1 and reported that another underage person was in need of medical assistance due to alcohol consumption;

(2) the underage person who called 9–1–1 and, if applicable, one or two other persons acting in concert with the underage person who called 9–1–1 provided each of their names to the 9–1–1 operator;

(3) the underage person was the first person to make the 9–1–1 report; and

(4) the underage person and, if applicable, one or two other persons acting in concert with the underage person who made the 9–1–1 call remained on the scene with the person under the legal age in need of medical assistance until assistance arrived and cooperated with medical assistance and law enforcement personnel on the scene.

The underage person who received medical assistance also shall be immune from prosecution under this section.

L.1979, c. 264, § 1, eff. Sept. 1, 1979. Amended by L.1991, c. 169, § 2, eff. June 19, 1991; L.1997, c. 161, § 1, eff. July 10, 1997; L.2009, c. 133, § 1, eff. Oct. 1, 2009.

2C:33–16. Alcoholic beverages; bringing or possession on school property by person of legal age; penalty

Any person of legal age to purchase alcoholic beverages, who knowingly and without the express written permission of the school board, its delegated authority, or any school principal, brings or possesses any alcoholic beverages on any property used for school purposes which is owned by any school or school board, is guilty of a disorderly persons offense.

L.1981, c. 197, § 1, eff. July 9, 1981.

2C:33–17. Offer or service of alcoholic beverage to underage person; disorderly persons; exceptions

a. Anyone who purposely or knowingly offers or serves or makes available an alcoholic beverage to a person under the legal age for consuming alcoholic beverages or entices or encourages that person to drink an alcoholic beverage is a disorderly person.

This subsection shall not apply to a parent or guardian of the person under legal age for consuming alcoholic beverages if the parent or guardian is of the legal age to consume alcoholic beverages or to a religious observance, ceremony or rite. This subsection shall also not apply to any person in his home who is of the legal age to consume alcoholic beverages who offers or serves or makes available an alcoholic beverage to a person under the legal age for consuming alcoholic beverages or entices that person to drink an alcoholic beverage in the presence of and with the permission of the parent or guardian of the person under the legal age for consuming alcoholic beverages if the parent or guardian is of the legal age to consume alcoholic beverages.

b. A person who makes real property owned, leased or managed by him available to, or leaves that property in the care of, another person with the purpose that alcoholic beverages will be made available for consumption by, or will be consumed by, persons who are under the legal age for consuming alcoholic beverages is guilty of a disorderly persons offense.

This subsection shall not apply if:

(1) the real property is licensed or required to be licensed by the Division of Alcoholic Beverage Control in accordance with the provisions of R.S. 33:1–1 et seq.;

(2) the person making the property available, or leaving it in the care of another person, is of the legal age to consume alcoholic beverages and is the parent or guardian of the person who consumes alcoholic beverages while under the legal age for consuming alcoholic beverages; or

(3) the alcoholic beverages are consumed by a person under the legal age for consuming alcoholic beverages during a religious observance, ceremony or rite.

L.1985, c. 311, § 1, eff. Aug. 28, 1985. Amended by L.1995, c. 31, § 1, eff. Feb. 23, 1995.

2C:33–18. Repealed by L.1996, c. 94, § 2, eff. July 26, 1996

2C:33–19. Bringing or possessing remotely activated paging device by student on property used for school purposes without express written permission of school board; disorderly persons offense

No person enrolled as a student of an elementary or secondary school, knowingly and without the express written permission of the school board, its delegated authority, or any school principal, shall bring or possess any remotely activated paging device on any property used for school purposes, at any time and regardless of whether school is in session or other persons are present. A violation of this section shall be a disorderly persons offense. No permission to bring or possess any remotely activated paging device on school property shall be granted unless and until a student shall have established to the satisfaction of the school authorities a reasonable basis for the possession of the device on school property.

This section shall not apply to any student who is an active member in good standing of a volunteer fire company or first aid, ambulance or rescue squad provided that (1) the student is required to respond to an emergency and (2) a copy of the statement by the chief executive officer of the volunteer fire company or first aid, ambulance or rescue squad authorizing the possession of the paging device is in the possession of the student at all times while that student is in possession of the remotely activated paging device. *L.1989, c. 232, § 2, eff. Dec. 29, 1989. Amended by L.1996, c. 94, § 1, eff. July 26, 1996.*

2C:33–20. Use of remotely activated paging device while engaged in commission of or attempt to commit or flight after committing controlled dangerous substances or drug paraphernalia violation

A person is guilty of a crime of the fourth degree if he uses a remotely activated paging device while engaged in the commission of, or an attempt to commit, or flight after committing or attempting to commit any crime or offense enumerated in chapter 35 or 36 of Title 2C of the New Jersey Statutes.

L.1989, c. 232, § 3, eff. Dec. 29, 1989.

2C:33–21. Use of information intercepted from police, fire or emergency medical communications system

Any person who intercepts any message or transmission made on or over any police, fire or emergency medical communications system, or any person who is the recipient of information so intercepted, and who uses the information obtained thereby to facilitate the commission of or the attempt to commit a crime or a violation of any law of this State, or uses the same in a manner which interferes with the discharge of police or firefighting operations or provision of medical services by first aid, rescue or ambulance squad personnel, shall be guilty of a crime of the fourth degree.

L.1991, c. 432, § 1, eff. Jan. 18, 1992. Amended by L.1999, c. 317, § 1, eff. Jan. 6, 2000.

2C:33–22. Possession of radio capable of receiving transmission from police, fire or emergency medical communication system

Any person who, while in the course of committing or attempting to commit a crime, including the immediate flight therefrom, possesses or controls a radio capable of receiving any message or transmission made on or over any police, fire or emergency medical communica-

tions system, shall be guilty of a crime of the fourth degree.

L.1991, c. 432, § 2, eff. Jan. 18, 1992.

2C:33–23. Radar devices used to monitor vehicular speed not considered police, fire or emergency medical communications system

For purposes of P.L.1991, c. 432 (C.2C:33–21 et seq.), the term "police, fire or emergency medical communications system" shall not include radar devices used to monitor vehicular speed.

L.1991, c. 432, § 3, eff. Jan. 18, 1992.

2C:33–23.1. Unlicensed radio transmissions of energy; prohibitions

A person shall not:

a. Make, or cause to be made, a radio transmission of energy in this State unless the person obtains a license, or an exemption from licensure, from the Federal Communications Commission pursuant to 47 U.S.C. § 301, or other applicable federal law or regulation; or

b. Do any act to cause an unlicensed radio transmission of energy or interference with a public or commercial radio station licensed by the Federal Communications Commission or to enable the radio transmission of energy or interference to occur.

c. As used in this section, "radio transmission of energy" has the same meaning given that term under 47 U.S.C. s.153.

L.2005, c. 293, § 1, eff. April 9, 2006.

2C:33–23.2. Penalty for unlicensed radio transmissions of energy

A person who violates the provisions of this act is guilty of a crime of the fourth degree.

L.2005, c. 293, § 2, eff. April 9, 2006.

2C:33–24. Definitions

As used in this chapter:

a. "Act of graffiti" means the drawing, painting or making any mark or inscription on public or private real or personal property without the permission of the owner.

b. "Spray paint" means any paint or pigmented substance that is in an aerosol or similar spray container.

L.1995, c. 251, § 7, eff. Dec. 12, 1995.

2C:33–25. Exhibition of warning sign required for sale of spray paint; violations, penalties

No person shall knowingly sell or offer for sale to the general public any spray paint unless a sign is exhibited, either where the product is displayed or where it is paid for, warning that in New Jersey an act of graffiti committed by a juvenile may carry a penalty of a one-year driver's license suspension for a first offense and a two year suspension for a second offense, and that an act of graffiti committed by either an adult or a juvenile may carry a penalty of restitution or 20 days' community service.

A person who knowingly violates this section shall be fined $50 for the first offense and $100 for a second or subsequent offense.

L.1995, c. 251, § 8, eff. Dec. 12, 1995.

2C:33–26. Sale of motor vehicle on Sunday

A person who engages in the business of buying, selling or exchanging motor vehicles or who opens a place of business and attempts to engage in such conduct on a Sunday commits a disorderly persons offense. The first offense is punishable by a fine not to exceed $100.00 or imprisonment for a period of not more than 10 days or both; the second offense is punishable by a fine not to exceed $500 or imprisonment for a period of not more than 30 days or both; the third or each subsequent offense is punishable by a fine of $750.00 or imprisonment for a period of six months or both. If the person is a licensed dealer in new or used motor vehicles in this State, under the provisions of chapter 10, Title 39 of the Revised Statutes, the person shall also be subject to suspension or revocation of his dealer's license to engage in the business of buying, selling or exchanging in motor vehicles in this State as provided in Title 39, chapter 10, section 10, section 20, for violation of this statute. Nothing contained in this section shall be construed to prohibit a person from accepting a deposit to secure the sale of a recreational vehicle, as defined in section 1 of P.L.1999, c. 284 (C.54:4–1.18), at an off-site sale authorized pursuant to section 2 of P.L.2005, c. 351 (C.39:10–19.2), on a Sunday.

L.1999, c. 90, § 4, eff. May 3, 1999. Amended by L.2005, c. 351, § 5, eff. Aug. 1, 2006.

2C:33–27. Consumption of alcohol in restaurants

a. No person who owns or operates a restaurant, dining room or other public place where food or liquid refreshments are sold or served to the general public, and for which premises a license or permit authorizing the sale of alcoholic beverages for on-premises consumption has not been issued:

(1) Shall allow the consumption of alcoholic beverages, other than wine or a malt alcoholic beverage, in a portion of the premises which is open to the public; or

(2) Shall charge any admission fee or cover, corkage or service charge or advertise inside or outside of such premises that patrons may bring and consume their own wine or malt alcoholic beverages in a portion of the premises which is open to the public.

(3) Shall allow the consumption of wine or malt alcoholic beverages at times or by persons to whom the service or consumption or alcoholic beverages on li-

censed premises is prohibited by State or municipal law or regulation.

b. Nothing in this act shall restrict the right of a municipality or an owner or operator of a restaurant, dining room or other public place where food or liquid refreshments are sold or served to the general public from prohibiting the consumption of alcoholic beverages on those premises.

c. A person who violates any provision of this act is a disorderly person, and the court, in addition to the sentence imposed for the disorderly person violation, may by its judgment bar the owner or operator from allowing consumption of wine or malt alcoholic beverages in his premises as authorized by this act.

L.1999, c. 90, § 5, eff. May 3, 1999.

2C:33–28. Soliciting or recruiting gang members; sentence

a. An actor who solicits or recruits another to join or actively participate in a criminal street gang with the knowledge or purpose that the person who is solicited or recruited will promote, further, assist, plan, aid, agree, or attempt to aid in the commission of criminal conduct by a member of a criminal street gang commits a crime of the fourth degree. For purposes of this section, the actor shall have the requisite knowledge or purpose if he knows that the person who is solicited or recruited will engage in some form, though not necessarily which form, of criminal activity. "Criminal street gang" shall have the meaning set forth in subsection h. of N.J.S.2C:44–3.

b. An actor who, in the course of violating subsection a. of this section, threatens another with bodily injury on two or more separate occasions within a 30–day period commits a crime of the third degree.

c. An actor who, in the course of violating subsection a. of this section, inflicts significant bodily injury upon another commits a crime of the second degree.

d. Any defendant convicted of soliciting, recruiting, coercing or threatening a person under 18 years of age in violation of subsection a. or b. of this section shall be guilty of a crime of the second degree.

e. An actor who violates subsection a. of this section while under official detention commits a crime of the second degree. As used in this subsection, "official detention" means detention in any facility for custody of persons under charge or conviction of a crime or offense, or committed pursuant to chapter 4 of this Title, [1] or alleged or found to be delinquent; detention for extradition or deportation; mandatory commitment to a residential treatment facility imposed as a condition of special probation pursuant to subsection d. of N.J.S.2C:35–14; or any other detention for law enforcement purposes. "Official detention" also includes supervision of probation or parole, or constraint incidental to release on bail. Notwithstanding the provisions of N.J.S.2C:44–5 or any other provision of law, the court shall order that the sentence imposed upon a violation of this section be served consecutively to the period or periods of detention the actor was serving at the time of the violation.

f. Any defendant convicted of soliciting, recruiting, coercing or threatening a person under 18 years of age in violation of subsection c. or e. of this section shall be sentenced by the court to an extended term of imprisonment as set forth in subsection a. of N.J.S.2C:43–7.

Notwithstanding the provisions of N.J.S.2C:1–8, N.J.S.2C:44–5 or any other provision of law, a conviction arising under this section shall not merge with a conviction for any criminal offense that the actor committed while involved in criminal street gang related activity, as defined in subsection h. of N.J.S.2C:44–3, nor shall the conviction for any such offense merge with a conviction pursuant to this section and the sentence imposed upon a violation of this section shall be ordered to be served consecutively to that imposed upon any other such conviction.

L.1999, c. 160, § 1, eff. July 8, 1999. Amended by L.2007, c. 234, § 1, eff. Jan. 3, 2008.

   [1] N.J.S.A. § 2C:4–1 et seq.

2C:33–29. Gang criminality; definition; grading

a. A person is guilty of the crime of gang criminality if, while knowingly involved in criminal street gang activity, he commits, attempts to commit, or conspires to commit, whether as a principal or an accomplice, any crime specified in chapters 11 through 18, 20, 33, 35 or 37 of Title 2C of the New Jersey Statutes; N.J.S.2C:34–1; N.J.S.2C:39–3; N.J.S.2C:39–4; section 1 of P.L.1998, c. 26 (C.2C:39–4.1); N.J.S.2C:39–5; or N.J.S.2C:39–9. A crime is committed while involved in a criminal street gang related activity if the crime was committed for the benefit of, at the direction of, or in association with a criminal street gang.

"Criminal street gang" means three or more persons associated in fact. Individuals are associated in fact if: (1) two of the following seven criteria that indicate criminal street gang membership apply: (a) self-proclamation; (b) witness testimony or official statement; (c) written or electronic correspondence; (d) paraphernalia or photographs; (e) tattoos; (f) clothing or colors; (g) any other indicia of street gang activity; and (2) individually or in combination with other members of a criminal street gang, while engaging in gang related activity, have committed or conspired or attempted to commit, within the preceding five years from the date of the present offense, excluding any period of imprisonment, one or more offenses on separate occasions of robbery, carjacking, aggravated assault, assault, aggravated sexual assault, sexual assault, arson, burglary, kidnapping, extortion, tampering with witnesses and informants or a violation of chapter 11, section 3, 4, 5, 6, or 7 of chapter 35 or chapter 39 of Title 2C of the New Jersey Statutes.

b. Grading. Gang criminality is a crime of one degree higher than the most serious underlying crime

referred to in subsection a. of this section, except that where the underlying crime is a crime of the first degree, gang criminality is a first degree crime and the defendant, upon conviction, and notwithstanding the provisions of paragraph (1) of subsection a. of N.J.S.2C:43–6, shall be sentenced to an ordinary term of imprisonment between 15 and 30 years. A sentence imposed upon conviction of the crime of gang criminality shall be ordered to be served consecutively to the sentence imposed upon conviction of any underlying offense referred to in subsection a. of this section.

L.2007, c. 341, § 1, eff. Jan. 13, 2008.

2C:33–30. Promotion of organized street crime

a. A person promotes organized street crime if he conspires with others as an organizer, supervisor, financier or manager to commit any crime specified in chapters 11 through 18, 20, 33, 35, or 37 of Title 2C of the New Jersey Statutes; N.J.S.2C:34–1; N.J.S.2C:39–3; N.J.S.2C:39–4; section 1 of P.L.1998, c. 26 (C.2C:39–4.1); N.J.S.2C:39–5; or N.J.S.2C:39–9.

b. Grading. Promotion of organized street crime is a crime of one degree higher than the most serious underlying crime referred to in subsection a. of this section, except that where the underlying offense is a crime of the first degree, promotion of organized street crime is a first degree crime and the defendant, upon conviction, and notwithstanding the provisions of paragraph (1) of subsection a of N.J.S.2C:43–6, shall be sentenced to an ordinary term of imprisonment between 15 and 30 years. A sentence imposed upon conviction of the crime of promotion of organized street crime shall be ordered to be served consecutively to the sentence imposed upon conviction of any underlying offense referred to in subsection a. of this section.

L.2007, c. 341, § 2, eff. Jan. 13, 2008.

CHAPTER 34

PUBLIC INDECENCY

Section
2C:34–1.   Prostitution and related offenses.
2C:34–1.1.   Loitering for the purpose of engaging in prostitution.
2C:34–2.   Obscenity for persons 18 years of age or older.
2C:34–3.   Obscenity for persons under 18.
2C:34–3.1.   Retailer defined.
2C:34–3.2.   Display by retailer of obscene material at height of less than five feet or without blinder or cover; authorization for ordinance to prohibit.
2C:34–4.   Public communication of obscenity.
2C:34–5.   Diseased person committing an act of sexual penetration.
2C:34–6.   Additional definitions.
2C:34–7.   Sexually oriented businesses; restrictions on location and display of signs; perimeter buffer requirements.

2C:34–1. Prostitution and related offenses

a. As used in this section:

(1) "Prostitution" is sexual activity with another person in exchange for something of economic value, or the offer or acceptance of an offer to engage in sexual activity in exchange for something of economic value.

(2) "Sexual activity" includes, but is not limited to, sexual intercourse, including genital-genital, oral-genital, anal-genital, and oral-anal contact, whether between persons of the same or opposite sex; masturbation; touching of the genitals, buttocks, or female breasts; sadistic or masochistic abuse and other deviate sexual relations.

(3) "House of prostitution" is any place where prostitution or promotion of prostitution is regularly carried on by one person under the control, management or supervision of another.

(4) "Promoting prostitution" is:

(a) Owning, controlling, managing, supervising or otherwise keeping, alone or in association with another, a house of prostitution or a prostitution business;

(b) Procuring an inmate for a house of prostitution or place in a house of prostitution for one who would be an inmate;

(c) Encouraging, inducing, or otherwise purposely causing another to become or remain a prostitute;

(d) Soliciting a person to patronize a prostitute;

(e) Procuring a prostitute for a patron;

(f) Transporting a person into or within this State with purpose to promote that person's engaging in prostitution, or procuring or paying for transportation with that purpose; or

(g) Knowingly leasing or otherwise permitting a place controlled by the actor, alone or in association with others, to be regularly used for prostitution or promotion of prostitution, or failure to make a reasonable effort to abate such use by ejecting the tenant, notifying law enforcement authorities, or other legally available means.

b. A person commits an offense if:

(1) The actor engages in prostitution;

(2) The actor promotes prostitution;

(3) The actor knowingly promotes prostitution of a child under 18 whether or not the actor mistakenly believed that the child was 18 years of age or older, even if such mistaken belief was reasonable;

(4) The actor knowingly promotes prostitution of the actor's child, ward, or any other person for whose care the actor is responsible;

(5) The actor compels another to engage in or promote prostitution;

(6) The actor promotes prostitution of the actor's spouse; or

(7) The actor knowingly engages in prostitution with a person under the age of 18, or if the actor enters into or remains in a house of prostitution for the purpose of engaging in sexual activity with a child under the age of 18, or if the actor solicits or requests a child under the age of 18 to engage in sexual activity. It shall be no defense to a prosecution under this paragraph that the actor mistakenly believed that the child was 18 years of age or older, even if such mistaken belief was reasonable.

c. Grading of offenses under subsection b.

(1) An offense under subsection b. constitutes a crime of the second degree if the offense falls within paragraph (3) or (4) of that subsection.

(2) An offense under subsection b. constitutes a crime of the third degree if the offense falls within paragraph (5), (6) or (7) of that subsection.

(3) An offense under paragraph (2) of subsection b. constitutes a crime of the third degree if the conduct falls within subparagraph (a), (b), or (c) of paragraph (4) of subsection a. Otherwise the offense is a crime of the fourth degree.

(4) An offense under subsection b. constitutes a disorderly persons offense if the offense falls within paragraph (1) of that subsection except that a second or subsequent conviction for such an offense constitutes a crime of the fourth degree. In addition, where a motor vehicle was used in the commission of any offense under paragraph (1) of subsection b. the court shall suspend for six months the driving privilege of any such offender who has a valid driver's license issued by this State. Upon conviction, the court shall immediately collect the offender's driver's license and shall forward it, along with a report stating the first and last day of the suspension imposed pursuant to this paragraph, to the New Jersey Motor Vehicle Commission.

d. Presumption from living off prostitutes. A person, other than the prostitute or the prostitute's minor child or other legal dependent incapable of self-support, who is supported in whole or substantial part by the proceeds of prostitution is presumed to be knowingly promoting prostitution.

e. It is an affirmative defense to prosecution for a violation of this section that, during the time of the alleged commission of the offense, the defendant was a victim of human trafficking pursuant to section 1 of P.L.2005, c. 77 (C.2C:13–8).

L.1978, c. 95, § 2C:34–1, eff. Sept. 1, 1979. Amended by L.1991, c. 211, § 1, eff. Sept. 21, 1991; L.1997, c. 93, § 1, eff. May 8, 1997; L.1999, c. 9, § 1, eff. Jan. 25, 1999; L.2005, c. 77, § 2, eff. April 26, 2005.

2C:34–1.1. Loitering for the purpose of engaging in prostitution.

a. As used in this section, "public place" means any place to which the public has access, including but not limited to any public street, sidewalk, bridge, alley, plaza, park, boardwalk, driveway, parking lot or transportation facility, public library or the doorways and entrance ways to any building which fronts on any of the aforesaid places, or a motor vehicle in or on any such place.

b. A person commits a disorderly persons offense if he:

(1) wanders, remains or prowls in a public place with the purpose of engaging in prostitution or promoting prostitution as defined in N.J.S. 2C:34–1; and

(2) engages in conduct that, under the circumstances, manifests a purpose to engage in prostitution or promoting prostitution as defined in N.J.S. 2C:34–1.

c. Conduct that may, where warranted under the circumstances, be deemed adequate to manifest a purpose to engage in prostitution or promoting prostitution includes, but is not limited to, conduct such as the following:

(1) Repeatedly beckoning to or stopping pedestrians or motorists in a public place;

(2) Repeatedly attempting to stop, or repeatedly attempting to engage passers-by in conversation;

(3) Repeatedly stopping or attempting to stop motor vehicles.

d. The element described in paragraph (1) of subsection b. of this section may not be established solely by proof that the actor engaged in the conduct that is used to satisfy the element described in paragraph (2) of subsection b. of this section.

L.1997, c. 93, § 3, eff. May 8, 1997.

2C:34–2. Obscenity for persons 18 years of age or older

a. Definitions for purpose of this section:

(1) "Obscene material" means any description, narrative account, display, or depiction of sexual activity or anatomical area contained in, or consisting of, a picture or other representation, publication, sound recording, live performance, or film, which by means of posing, composition, format or animated sensual details:

(a) Depicts or describes in a patently offensive way, ultimate sexual acts, normal or perverted, actual or simulated, masturbation, excretory functions, or lewd exhibition of the genitals,

(b) Lacks serious literary, artistic, political, or scientific value, when taken as a whole, and

(c) Is a part of a work, which to the average person applying contemporary community standards, has a dominant theme taken as a whole, which appeals to the prurient interest.

(2) "Exhibit" means the sale of admission to view obscene material.

b. A person who sells, distributes, rents or exhibits obscene material to a person 18 years of age or older

commits a crime of the fourth degree. Sale of obscene material shall be deemed to include any form of transaction which results in the admission to a display or depiction of obscene material or temporary or permanent access to any obscene material.

Nothing contained herein or in section 3 of P.L.1995, c. 230 (C. 2C:34–7) shall be construed to prohibit a municipality from adopting as a part of its zoning ordinances an ordinance permitting the sale, distribution, rental or exhibition of obscene material in which event such sale, distribution, rental or exhibition shall be deemed legal.

L.1978, c. 95, § 2C:34–2, eff. Sept. 1, 1979. Amended by L.1982, c. 211, § 1, eff. Dec. 23, 1982; L.1989, c. 54, § 1, eff. April 14, 1989; L.1995, c. 230, § 1, eff. Sept. 15, 1995.

2C:34–3. Obscenity for persons under 18

a. Definitions for purposes of this section:

(1) "Obscene material" means any description, narrative account, display, depiction of a specified anatomical area or specified sexual activity contained in, or consisting of, a picture or other representation, publication, sound recording, live performance or film, which by means of posing, composition, format or animated sensual details, emits sensuality with sufficient impact to concentrate prurient interest on the area or activity.

(2) "Obscene film" means any motion picture film or preview or trailer to a film, not including newsreels portraying actual current events or pictorial news of the day, in which a scene, taken by itself:

(a) Depicts a specified anatomical area or specified sexual activity, or the simulation of a specified sexual activity, or verbalization concerning a specified sexual activity; and

(b) Emits sensuality sufficient, in terms of the duration and impact of the depiction, to appeal to prurient interest.

(3) "Specified anatomical area" means:

(a) Less than completely and opaquely covered human genitals, pubic region, buttock or female breasts below a point immediately above the top of the areola; or

(b) Human male genitals in a discernibly turgid state, even if covered.

(4) "Specified sexual activity" means:

(a) Human genitals in a state of sexual stimulation or arousal; or

(b) Any act of human masturbation, sexual intercourse or deviate sexual intercourse; or

(c) Fondling or other erotic touching of covered or uncovered human genitals, pubic region, buttock or female breast.

(5) "Knowingly" means:

(a) Having knowledge of the character and content of the material or film described herein; or

(b) Having failed to exercise reasonable inspection which would disclose its character and content.

(6) "Exhibit" means the sale of admission to view obscene material.

(7) "Show" means cause or allow to be seen.

b. Promoting obscene material.

(1) A person who knowingly sells, distributes, rents or exhibits to a person under 18 years of age obscene material is guilty of a crime of the third degree.

(2) A person who knowingly shows obscene material to a person under 18 years of age with the knowledge or purpose to arouse, gratify or stimulate himself or another is guilty of a crime of the third degree if the person showing the obscene material is at least four years older than the person under 18 years of age viewing the material.

c. Admitting to exhibition of obscene film.

(1) Any person who knowingly admits a person under 18 years of age to a theatre then exhibiting an obscene film is guilty of a crime of the third degree.

(2) A person who knowingly shows an obscene film to a person under 18 years of age with the knowledge or purpose to arouse, gratify or stimulate himself or another is guilty of a crime of the third degree if the person showing the obscene film is at least four years older than the person under 18 years of age viewing the film.

d. Presumption of knowledge and age.

The requisite knowledge with regard to the character and content of the film or material and of the age of the person is presumed in the case of an actor who sells, distributes, rents, exhibits or shows obscene material to a person under 18 years of age or admits to a film obscene for a person under 18 years of age a person who is under 18 years of age.

e. Defenses.

(1) It is an affirmative defense to a prosecution under subsections b. and c. which the defendant must prove by a preponderance of evidence that:

(a) The person under age 18 falsely represented in or by writing that he was age 18 or over;

(b) The person's appearance was such that an individual of ordinary prudence would believe him to be age 18 or over; and

(c) The sale, distribution, rental, showing or exhibition to or admission of the person was made in good faith relying upon such written representation and appearance and in the reasonable belief that he was actually age 18 or over.

(2) It is an affirmative defense to a prosecution under subsection c. that the defendant is an employee in a motion picture theatre who has no financial interest in that motion picture theatre other than his wages and has no decision-making authority or responsibility with respect to the selection of the motion picture show which is exhibited.

L.1978, c. 95, § 2C:34–3, eff. Sept. 1, 1979. Amended by L.1989, c. 54, § 2, eff. April 14, 1989; L.1999, c. 227, § 1.

2C:34–3.1. Retailer defined

"Retailer," as used in this act,[1] means any person who operates a store, newsstand, booth, concession or similar business with unimpeded access for persons under 18 years old, who is in the business of making sales of periodicals or other publications at retail containing pictures, drawings or photographs.

L.1988, c. 17, § 1, eff. June 1, 1988.

[1] N.J.S.A. §§ 2C:34–3.1, 2C:34–3.2.

2C:34–3.2. Display by retailer of obscene material at height of less than five feet or without blinder or cover; authorization for ordinance to prohibit

A municipality may enact an ordinance making it a petty disorderly persons offense for a retailer to display or permit to be displayed at his business premises any obscene material as defined in N.J.S. 2C:34–3, at a height of less than 5 feet or without a blinder or other covering placed or printed on the front of the material displayed. Any such ordinance shall contain a provision stating that public display of the obscene material shall constitute presumptive evidence that the retailer knowingly made or permitted the display.

L.1988, c. 17, § 2, eff. June 1, 1988.

2C:34–4. Public communication of obscenity

a. "Publicly communicate" means to display, post, exhibit, give away or vocalize material in such a way that its character and content may be readily and distinctly perceived by the public by normal unaided vision or hearing when viewing or hearing it in, on or from a public street, road, thoroughfare, recreation or shopping center or area, public transportation facility or vehicle used for public transportation.

b. A person who knowingly publicly communicates obscene material, as defined in section 2C:34–3 or causes or permits it to be publicly communicated on property he owns or leases or operates is guilty of a crime of the fourth degree.

c. Public communication of obscene material shall constitute presumptive evidence that the defendant made the communication or caused or permitted it to be made knowingly.

L.1978, c. 95, § 2C:34–4, eff. Sept. 1, 1979.

2C:34–5. Diseased person committing an act of sexual penetration.

a. A person is guilty of a crime of the fourth degree who, knowing that he or she is infected with a venereal disease such as chancroid, gonorrhea, syphilis, herpes virus, or any of the varieties or stages of such diseases, commits an act of sexual penetration without the informed consent of the other person.

b. A person is guilty of a crime of the third degree who, knowing that he or she is infected with human immune deficiency virus (HIV) or any other related virus identified as a probable causative agent of acquired immune deficiency syndrome (AIDS), commits an act of sexual penetration without the informed consent of the other person.

L.1978, c. 95, § 2C:34–5, eff. Sept. 1, 1979. Amended by L.1979, c. 178, § 68, eff. Sept. 1, 1979; L.1997, c. 201, § 1, eff. Aug. 14, 1997.

2C:34–6. Additional definitions

As used in sections 2 and 3 of this act:[1]

a. "Sexually oriented business" means:

(1) A commercial establishment which as one of its principal business purposes offers for sale, rental, or display any of the following:

Books, magazines, periodicals or other printed material, or photographs, films, motion pictures, video cassettes, slides or other visual representations which depict or describe a "specified sexual activity" or "specified anatomical area"; or still or motion picture machines, projectors or other image-producing devices which show images to one person per machine at any one time, and where the images so displayed are characterized by the depiction of a "specified sexual activity" or "specified anatomical area"; or instruments, devices, or paraphernalia which are designed for use in connection with a "specified sexual activity"; or

(2) A commercial establishment which regularly features live performances characterized by the exposure of a "specified anatomical area" or by a "specified sexual activity," or which regularly shows films, motion pictures, video cassettes, slides, or other photographic representations which depict or describe a "specified sexual activity" or "specified anatomical area".

b. "Person" means an individual, proprietorship, partnership, corporation, association, or other legal entity.

c. "Specified anatomical area" means:

(1) Less than completely and opaquely covered human genitals, pubic region, buttock or female breasts below a point immediately above the top of the areola; or

(2) Human male genitals in a discernibly turgid state, even if covered.

d. "Specified sexual activity" means:

(1) The fondling or other erotic touching of covered or uncovered human genitals, pubic region, buttock or female breast; or

(2) Any actual or simulated act of human masturbation, sexual intercourse or deviate sexual intercourse.

L.1995, c. 230, § 2, eff. Sept. 15, 1995.

[1] N.J.S.A. §§ 2C:34–6 and 2C:34–7.

2C:34–7. Sexually oriented businesses; restrictions on location and display of signs; perimeter buffer requirements

a. Except as provided in a municipal zoning ordinance adopted pursuant to N.J.S.2C:34–2, no person shall operate a sexually oriented business within 1,000 feet of any existing sexually oriented business, or any church, synagogue, temple or other place of public worship, or any elementary or secondary school or any school bus stop, or any municipal or county playground or place of public resort and recreation, or any hospital or any child care center, or within 1,000 feet of any area zoned for residential use. This subsection shall not apply to a sexually oriented business already lawfully operating on the effective date of this act where another sexually oriented business, an elementary or secondary school or school bus stop, or any municipal or county playground or place of public resort and recreation, or any hospital or any child care center, is subsequently established within 1,000 feet, or a residential district or residential lot is subsequently established within 1,000 feet.

b. Every sexually oriented business shall be surrounded by a perimeter buffer of at least 50 feet in width with plantings, fence, or other physical divider along the outside of the perimeter sufficient to impede the view of the interior of the premises in which the business is located. The municipality may, by ordinance, require the perimeter buffer to meet additional requirements or standards. This subsection shall not apply to a sexually oriented business already lawfully operating on the effective date of this act.

c. No sexually oriented business shall display more than two exterior signs, consisting of one identification sign and one sign giving notice that the premises are off limits to minors. The identification sign shall be no more than 40 square feet in size.

d. A person who violates this section is guilty of a crime of the fourth degree.

L.1995, c. 230, § 3, eff. Sept. 15, 1995. Amended by L.1999, c. 41, § 1, eff. March 12, 1999.

CHAPTER 35

CONTROLLED DANGEROUS SUBSTANCES

Section

2C:35–1.	Short title.
2C:35–1.1.	Declaration of policy and legislative findings.
2C:35–1.2.	References to Controlled Dangerous Substances Act and chapters 35 and 36 in Code of Criminal Justice.
2C:35–2.	Definitions.
2C:35–2.1.	Repealed.

Section

2C:35–3.	Leader of narcotics trafficking network.
2C:35–4.	Maintaining or operating a controlled dangerous substance production facility.
2C:35–4.1.	Booby traps in manufacturing or distribution facilities; fortified premises.
2C:35–5.	Manufacturing, distributing or dispensing.
2C:35–5.1.	Repealed.
2C:35–5.2.	Manufacture, distribution, or possession of gamma hydroxybutyrate.
2C:35–5.3.	Manufacture, distribution, or possession of flunitrazepam.
2C:35–5.4.	Short title.
2C:35–5.5.	Legislative findings.
2C:35–5.6.	Definitions.
2C:35–5.7.	Restraining orders; certain released persons.
2C:35–5.8.	Violation of order; sanctions.
2C:35–5.9.	Restraining order upon request and submission of a certification.
2C:35–5.10.	Discretion in seeking restraining order.
2C:35–5.11.	Fines imposed for possession or distribution of certain drugs.
2C:35–6.	Employing a juvenile in a drug distribution scheme.
2C:35–7.	Distributing, dispensing or possessing controlled dangerous substance or controlled substance analog on or within 1,000 feet of school property or bus; penalty; defenses; approved or revised map; prima facie evidence; official record.
2C:35–7a.	Review of sentence for violation of drug-free school zones provisions.
2C:35–7.1.	Distributing, dispensing or possession controlled substances; proximity to public housing facilities, parks or buildings.
2C:35–8.	Distribution to persons under age 18; enhanced punishment.
2C:35–9.	Strict liability for drug-induced deaths.
2C:35–10.	Possession, use or being under the influence, or failure to make lawful disposition.
2C:35–10.1.	Repealed.
2C:35–10.2.	Obtaining or possessing gamma hydroxybutyrate without a prescription.
2C:35–10.3.	Obtaining or possession flunitrazepam without a prescription.
2C:35–10.4.	Toxic chemicals.
2C:35–10.5.	Distribution or possession of prescription legend drugs; authorized dosage units; violations; exceptions.
2C:35–11.	Imitation controlled dangerous substances; distribution, possession, manufacture, etc.; penalties.
2C:35–12.	Waiver of mandatory minimum and extended terms.
2C:35–13.	Obtaining by fraud.
2C:35–14.	Rehabilitation program for drug and alcohol dependent persons subject to a presumption of incarceration or a mandatory minimum period of parole ineligibility; special probation; mandatory commitment to residential treatment facilities; sentencing considerations.
2C:35–15.	Mandatory drug enforcement and demand reduction penalties; collection; disposition; suspension.
2C:35–16.	Forfeiture or postponement of driving privileges.

Section

2C:35–16.1.	Conviction of drug related offense taking place upon leased residential premises; notice to owner of premises or agent.
2C:35–17.	Exception to physician-patient privilege.
2C:35–18.	Exemption; burden of proof.
2C:35–18.	Exemption; burden of proof.
2C:35–19.	Laboratory certificates; use; admission into evidence; objections.
2C:35–20.	Forensic laboratory fees.
2C:35–21.	Seizure in violation of chapter; pretrial destruction of bulk seizures of controlled dangerous substances.
2C:35–22.	Severability.
2C:35–23.	Pending cases.
2C:35–24.	Possession of certain prescription drugs.
2C:35–25.	Restrictions on retail sales of ephedrine products; disorderly persons offense; exceptions.
2C:35–26.	Reporting loss of ephedrine products to law enforcement authorities.
2C:35–27.	Possession of certain amounts of ephedrine products to give rise to permissive inference of purpose to create methamphetamine.
2C:35–28.	Unlawful possession of precursor with intent to manufacture methamphetamine; crime of second degree.
2C:35–29.	Industrial use chemicals; exclusion from definition of controlled substance under certain conditions.

2C:35–1. Short title

This act shall be known and may be cited as the "Comprehensive Drug Reform Act of 1987."

L.1987, c. 106, § 1, operative July 9, 1987.

2C:35–1.1. Declaration of policy and legislative findings

The Legislature hereby finds and declares to be the public policy of this State, the following:

a. By enactment of the "New Jersey Code of Criminal Justice," N.J.S. 2C:1–1 et seq., the Legislature recognized the need for the comprehensive reevaluation, revision, consolidation and codification of our criminal laws, and the need to ensure a uniform, consistent and predictable system for the sentencing of convicted offenders, focusing principally on the seriousness and degree of dangerousness inherent in a particular offense. In enacting the sentencing provisions of the penal code, the Legislature recognized that the imposition of a uniform, consistent and predictable sentence for a given offense is an essential prerequisite to any rational deterrent scheme designed ultimately to reduce the incidence of crime.

b. Despite the impressive efforts and gains of our law enforcement agencies, the unlawful use, manufacture and distribution of controlled dangerous substances continues to pose a serious and pervasive threat to the health, safety and welfare of the citizens of this State. New Jersey continues to experience an unacceptably high rate of drug-related crime, and continues to serve as a conduit for the illegal trafficking of drugs to and from other jurisdictions. In addition to the harm suffered by the victims of drug abuse and drug-related crime, the incidence of such offenses is directly related to the rate of other violent and non-violent crimes, including murder, assault, robbery, theft, burglary and organized criminal activities. For this reason, enhanced and coordinated efforts designed specifically to curtail drug-related offenses will lead inexorably to a reduction in the rate of crime generally, and is [1] therefore decidedly in the public interest.

c. In order to be effective, the battle against drug abuse and drug-related crime must be waged aggressively at every level along the drug distribution chain, but in particular, our criminal laws must target for expedited prosecution and enhanced punishment those repeat drug offenders and upper echelon members of organized narcotics trafficking networks who pose the greatest danger to society. In order to ensure the most efficient and effective dedication of limited investigative, prosecutorial, judicial and correctional resources, it is the policy of this State to distinguish between drug offenders based on the seriousness of the offense, considering principally the nature, quantity and purity of the controlled substance involved, and the role of the actor in the overall drug distribution network. It is the intention of the Legislature to provide for the strict punishment, deterrence and incapacitation of the most culpable and dangerous drug offenders, and to facilitate where feasible the rehabilitation of drug dependent persons so as ultimately to reduce the demand for illegal controlled dangerous substances and the incidence of drug-related crime. It is also the policy of this State to afford special protection to children from the perils of drug trafficking, to ensure that all schools and areas adjacent to schools are kept free from drug distribution activities, and to provide especially stern punishment for those drug offenders who operate on or near schools and school buses, who distribute to juveniles, or who employ juveniles in a drug distribution scheme. In addition, our criminal laws and sentencing practices must be reexamined and amended so as to minimize pretrial delay, thereby to ensure the prompt disposition of all drug-related criminal charges and the prompt imposition of fair and certain punishment.

d. Under the current drug laws, there are inadequate sentencing guidelines with which consistently to identify the most serious offenders and offenses and to guard against sentencing disparity and the resulting depreciation of the deterrent thrust of the criminal law. In order to protect the public interest, and so as to deter, disrupt and eliminate the operation of organized drug trafficking networks, it is necessary to undertake a comprehensive reexamination of our controlled dangerous substances laws, procedures and sentencing practices. The transfer of the provisions of the "New Jersey Controlled Dangerous Substances Act," P.L.1970, c. 226 (C. 24:21–1 et seq.) into the penal code which is accomplished herein, along with the amendments and supplements thereto, will better ensure that the most

culpable drug offenders will be subject to swift prosecutions and strict, consistently imposed criminal sanctions.

L.1987, c. 106, § 1, operative July 9, 1987.

[1] So in original. Probably should read "are".

2C:35–1.2. References to Controlled Dangerous Substances Act and chapters 35 and 36 in Code of Criminal Justice

Whenever in any law, rule or regulation, reference is made to the "New Jersey Controlled Dangerous Substances Act," P.L.1970, c. 226 (C. 24:21–1 et seq.) or any part thereof, the same shall mean and refer to the appropriate chapter, section or provision of the "New Jersey Code of Criminal Justice" as amended and supplemented herein. Similarly, any reference to chapter 35 or 36 in the "New Jersey Code of Criminal Justice" shall be deemed to incorporate P.L.1970, c. 226 (C. 24:21–1 et seq.) or any other predecessor statute.

L.1987, c. 106, § 24, operative July 9, 1987.

2C:35–2. Definitions

As used in this chapter:

"Administer" means the direct application of a controlled dangerous substance or controlled substance analog, whether by injection, inhalation, ingestion, or any other means, to the body of a patient or research subject by: (1) a practitioner (or, in his presence, by his lawfully authorized agent), or(2) the patient or research subject at the lawful direction and in the presence of the practitioner.

"Agent" means an authorized person who acts on behalf of or at the direction of a manufacturer, distributor, or dispenser but does not include a common or contract carrier, public warehouseman, or employee thereof.

"Controlled dangerous substance" means a drug, substance, or immediate precursor in Schedules I through V, any substance the distribution of which is specifically prohibited in N.J.S.2C:35–3, in section 3 of P.L.1997, c. 194 (C.2C:35–5.2) or in section 5 of P.L.1997,c. 194 (C.2C:35–5.3) and any drug or substance which, when ingested, is metabolized or otherwise becomes a controlled dangerous substance in the human body. When any statute refers to controlled dangerous substances, or to a specific controlled dangerous substance, it shall also be deemed to refer to any drug or substance which, when ingested, is metabolized or otherwise becomes a controlled dangerous substance or the specific controlled dangerous substance, and to any substance that is an immediate precursor of a controlled dangerous substance or the specific controlled dangerous substance. The term shall not include distilled spirits, wine, malt beverages, as those terms are defined or used in R.S.33:1–1 et seq., or tobacco and tobacco products. The term, wherever it appears in any law or administrative regulation of this State, shall include controlled substance analogs.

"Controlled substance analog" means a substance that has a chemical structure substantially similar to that of a controlled dangerous substance and that was specifically designed to produce an effect substantially similar to that of a controlled dangerous substance. The term shall not include a substance manufactured or distributed in conformance with the provisions of an approved new drug application or an exemption for investigational use within the meaning of section 505 of the "Federal Food, Drug and Cosmetic Act," 52 Stat. 1052 (21 U.S.C. s.355).

"Counterfeit substance" means a controlled dangerous substance or controlled substance analog which, or the container or labeling of which, without authorization, bears the trademark, trade name, or other identifying mark, imprint, number or device, or any likeness thereof, of a manufacturer, distributor, or dispenser other than the person or persons who in fact manufactured, distributed or dispensed such substance and which thereby falsely purports or is represented to be the product of, or to have been distributed by, such other manufacturer, distributor, or dispenser.

"Deliver" or "delivery" means the actual, constructive, or attempted transfer from one person to another of a controlled dangerous substance or controlled substance analog, whether or not there is an agency relationship.

"Dispense" means to deliver a controlled dangerous substance or controlled substance analog to an ultimate user or research subject by or pursuant to the lawful order of a practitioner, including the prescribing, administering, packaging, labeling, or compounding necessary to prepare the substance for that delivery. "Dispenser" means a practitioner who dispenses.

"Distribute" means to deliver other than by administering or dispensing a controlled dangerous substance or controlled substance analog. "Distributor" means a person who distributes.

"Drugs" means (a) substances recognized in the official United States Pharmacopoeia, official Homeopathic Pharmacopoeia of the United States, or official National Formulary, or any supplement to any of them; and (b) substances intended for use in the diagnosis, cure, mitigation, treatment, or prevention of disease in man or other animals; and (c) substances (other than food) intended to affect the structure or any function of the body of man or other animals; and (d) substances intended for use as a component of any article specified in subsections (a), (b) and (c) of this section; but does not include devices or their components, parts or accessories.

"Drug or alcohol dependent person" means a person who as a result of using a controlled dangerous substance or controlled substance analog or alcohol has been in a state of psychic or physical dependence, or both, arising from the use of that controlled dangerous substance or controlled substance analog or alcohol on a continuous or repetitive basis. Drug or alcohol dependence is characterized by behavioral and other responses, including but not limited to a strong compulsion to take the substance on a recurring basis in order to experience its psychic effects, or to avoid the discomfort of its absence.

"Hashish" means the resin extracted from any part of the plant Genus Cannabis L. and any compound, manufacture, salt, derivative, mixture, or preparation of such resin.

"Manufacture" means the production, preparation, propagation, compounding, conversion or processing of a controlled dangerous substance or controlled substance analog, either directly or by extraction from substances of natural origin, or independently by means of chemical synthesis, or by a combination of extraction and chemical synthesis, and includes any packaging or repackaging of the substance or labeling or relabeling of its container, except that this term does not include the preparation or compounding of a controlled dangerous substance or controlled substance analog by an individual for his own use or the preparation, compounding, packaging, or labeling of a controlled dangerous substance: (1) by a practitioner as an incident to his administering or dispensing of a controlled dangerous substance or controlled substance analog in the course of his professional practice, or (2) by a practitioner (or under his supervision) for the purpose of, or as an incident to, research, teaching, or chemical analysis and not for sale.

"Marijuana" means all parts of the plant Genus Cannabis L., whether growing or not; the seeds thereof, and every compound, manufacture, salt, derivative, mixture, or preparation of such plant or its seeds, except those containing resin extracted from such plant; but shall not include the mature stalks of such plant, fiber produced from such stalks, oil or cake made from the seeds of such plant, any other compound, manufacture, salt, derivative, mixture, or preparation of such mature stalks, fiber, oil, or cake, or the sterilized seed of such plant which is incapable of germination.

"Narcotic drug" means any of the following, whether produced directly or indirectly by extraction from substances of vegetable origin, or independently by means of chemical synthesis, or by a combination of extraction and chemical synthesis:

(a) Opium, coca leaves, and opiates;

(b) A compound, manufacture, salt, derivative, or preparation of opium, coca leaves, or opiates;

(c) A substance (and any compound, manufacture, salt, derivative, or preparation thereof) which is chemically identical with any of the substances referred to in subsections (a) and (b), except that the words "narcotic drug" as used in this act shall not include decocainized coca leaves or extracts of coca leaves, which extracts do not contain cocaine or ecogine.

"Opiate" means any dangerous substance having an addiction-forming or addiction-sustaining liability similar to morphine or being capable of conversion into a drug having such addiction-forming or addiction-sustaining liability. It does not include, unless specifically designated as controlled pursuant to the provisions of section 3 of P.L.1970, c. 226 (C.24:21–3), the dextrorotatory isomer of 3–methoxy–n–methylmorphinan and its salts (dextromethorphan). It does include its racemic and levorotatory forms.

"Opium poppy" means the plant of the species Papaver somniferum L., except the seeds thereof.

"Person" means any corporation, association, partnership, trust, other institution or entity or one or more individuals.

"Plant" means an organism having leaves and a readily observable root formation, including, but not limited to, a cutting having roots, a rootball or root hairs.

"Poppy straw" means all parts, except the seeds, of the opium poppy, after mowing.

"Practitioner" means a physician, dentist, veterinarian, scientific investigator, laboratory, pharmacy, hospital or other person licensed, registered, or otherwise permitted to distribute, dispense, conduct research with respect to, or administer a controlled dangerous substance or controlled substance analog in the course of professional practice or research in this State.

(a) "Physician" means a physician authorized by law to practice medicine in this or any other state and any other person authorized by law to treat sick and injured human beings in this or any other state.

(b) "Veterinarian" means a veterinarian authorized by law to practice veterinary medicine in this State.

(c) "Dentist" means a dentist authorized by law to practice dentistry in this State.

(d) "Hospital" means any federal institution, or any institution for the care and treatment of the sick and injured, operated or approved by the appropriate State department as proper to be entrusted with the custody and professional use of controlled dangerous substances or controlled substance analogs.

(e) "Laboratory" means a laboratory to be entrusted with the custody of narcotic drugs and the use of controlled dangerous substances or controlled substance analogs for scientific, experimental and medical purposes and for purposes of instruction approved by the State Department of Health and Senior Services.

"Production" includes the manufacture, planting, cultivation, growing, or harvesting of a controlled dangerous substance or controlled substance analog.

"Immediate precursor" means a substance which the State Department of Health and Senior Services has found to be and by regulation designates as being the principal compound commonly used or produced primarily for use, and which is an immediate chemical intermediary used or likely to be used in the manufacture of a controlled dangerous substance or controlled

substance analog, the control of which is necessary to prevent, curtail, or limit such manufacture.

"Residential treatment facility" means any facility licensed and approved by the Department of Health and Senior Services and which is approved by any county probation department for the inpatient treatment and rehabilitation of drug or alcohol dependent persons.

"Schedules I, II, III, IV, and V" are the schedules set forth in sections 5 through 8 of P.L.1970, c. 226 (C.24:21–5 through 24:21–8) and in section 4 of P.L. 1971, c. 3 (C.24:21–8.1) and as modified by any regulations issued by the Commissioner of Health and Senior Services pursuant to his authority as provided in section 3 of P.L.1970, c. 226 (C.24:21–3).

"State" means the State of New Jersey.

"Ultimate user" means a person who lawfully possesses a controlled dangerous substance or controlled substance analog for his own use or for the use of a member of his household or for administration to an animal owned by him or by a member of his household.

"Prescription legend drug" means any drug which under federal or State law requires dispensing by prescription or order of a licensed physician, veterinarian or dentist and is required to bear the statement "Rx only" or similar wording indicating that such drug may be sold or dispensed only upon the prescription of a licensed medical practitioner and is not a controlled dangerous substance or stramonium preparation.

"Stramonium preparation" means a substance prepared from any part of the stramonium plant in the form of a powder, pipe mixture, cigarette, or any other form with or without other ingredients.

"Stramonium plant" means the plant Datura Stramonium Linne, including Datura Tatula Linne.

L.1987, c. 106, § 1, operative July 9, 1987. Amended by L.1997, c. 186, § 1, eff. Aug. 4, 1997; L.1999, c. 90, § 1, eff. May 3, 1999; L.1999, c. 186, § 1, eff. Aug. 19, 1999; L.1999, c. 376, § 1, eff. Jan. 14, 2000; L.2005, c. 205, § 1, eff. Aug. 24, 2005.

2C:35–2.1.   **Repealed by L.1992, c. 71, § 3, eff. July 30, 1992**

2C:35–3.   **Leader of narcotics trafficking network**

As used in this section:

"Financier" means a person who, with the intent to derive a profit, provides money or credit or other thing of value in order to purchase a controlled dangerous substance or an immediate precursor, or otherwise to finance the operations of a drug trafficking network.

A person is a leader of a narcotics trafficking network if he conspires with two or more other persons in a scheme or course of conduct to unlawfully manufacture, distribute, dispense, bring into or transport in this State methamphetamine, lysergic acid diethylamide, phencyclidine, gamma hydroxybutyrate, flunitrazepam or any controlled dangerous substance classified in Schedule I or II, or any controlled substance analog thereof as a financier, or as an organizer, supervisor or manager of at least one other person.

Leader of narcotics trafficking network is a crime of the first degree and upon conviction thereof, except as may be provided by N.J.S.2C:35–12, a person shall be sentenced to an ordinary term of life imprisonment during which the person must serve 25 years before being eligible for parole. Notwithstanding the provisions of subsection a. of N.J.S.2C:43–3, the court may also impose a fine not to exceed $750,000.00 or five times the street value of the controlled dangerous substance, controlled substance analog, gamma hydroxybutyrate or flunitrazepam involved, whichever is greater.

Notwithstanding the provisions of N.J.S.2C:1–8, a conviction of leader of narcotics trafficking network shall not merge with the conviction for any offense which is the object of the conspiracy. Nothing contained in this section shall prohibit the court from imposing an extended term pursuant to N.J.S.2C:43–7; nor shall this section be construed in any way to preclude or limit the prosecution or conviction of any person for conspiracy under N.J.S.2C:5–2, or any prosecution or conviction under N.J.S.2C:35–4 (maintaining or operating a CDS production facility), N.J.S.2C:35–5 (manufacturing, distributing or dispensing), N.J.S.2C:35–6 (employing a juvenile in a drug distribution scheme), N.J.S.2C:35–9 (strict liability for drug induced death), N.J.S.2C:41–2 (racketeering activities) or subsection g. of N.J.S.2C:5–2 (leader of organized crime).

It shall not be necessary in any prosecution under this section for the State to prove that any intended profit was actually realized. The trier of fact may infer that a particular scheme or course of conduct was undertaken for profit from all of the attendant circumstances, including but not limited to the number of persons involved in the scheme or course of conduct, the actor's net worth and his expenditures in relation to his legitimate sources of income, the amount or purity of the specified controlled dangerous substance, controlled substance analog, gamma hydroxybutyrate or flunitrazepam involved, or the amount of cash or currency involved.

It shall not be a defense to a prosecution under this section that such controlled dangerous substance, controlled substance analog, gamma hydroxybutyrate or flunitrazepam was brought into or transported in this State solely for ultimate distribution or dispensing in another jurisdiction; nor shall it be a defense that any profit was intended to be made in another jurisdiction.

It shall not be a defense that the defendant was subject to the supervision or management of another, nor that another person or persons were also leaders of the narcotics trafficking network.

L.1987, c. 106, § 1, operative July 9, 1987. Amended by L.1997, c. 181, § 1, eff. Aug. 1, 1997; L.1997, c. 343, § 1, eff. Jan. 12, 1998; L.1999, c. 133, § 1, eff. June 25, 1999.

2C:35–4. Maintaining or operating a controlled dangerous substance production facility

Except as authorized by P.L.1970, c. 226 (C.24:21–1 et seq.), any person who knowingly maintains or operates any premises, place or facility used for the manufacture of methamphetamine, lysergic acid diethylamide, phencyclidine, gamma hydroxybutyrate, flunitrazepam, marijuana in an amount greater than five pounds or ten plants or any substance listed in Schedule I or II, or the analog of any such substance, or any person who knowingly aids, promotes, finances or otherwise participates in the maintenance or operations of such premises, place or facility, is guilty of a crime of the first degree and shall, except as provided in N.J.S.2C:35–12, be sentenced to a term of imprisonment which shall include the imposition of a minimum term which shall be fixed at, or between, one-third and one-half of the sentence imposed, during which the defendant shall be ineligible for parole. Notwithstanding the provisions of subsection a. of N.J.S.2C:43–3, the court may also impose a fine not to exceed $750,000.00 or five times the street value of all controlled dangerous substances, controlled substance analogs, gamma hydroxybutyrate or flunitrazepam at any time manufactured or stored at such premises, place or facility, whichever is greater.

L.1987, c. 106, § 1, operative July 9, 1987. Amended by L.1988, c. 44, § 1, eff. June 28, 1988; L.1997, c. 181, § 2, eff. Aug. 1, 1997; L.1997, c. 186, § 2, eff. Aug. 4, 1997; L.1999, c. 133, § 2, eff. June 25, 1999.

2C:35–4.1. Booby traps in manufacturing or distribution facilities; fortified premises

a. As used in this section:

(1) "Booby trap" means any concealed or camouflaged device designed or reasonably likely to cause bodily injury when triggered by the action of a person entering a property or building or any portion thereof, or moving on the property or in the building, or by the action of another person. The term includes, but is not limited to, firearms, ammunition or destructive devices activated by a trip wire or other triggering mechanism, sharpened stakes, traps, and lines or wires with hooks, weights or other objects attached.

(2) "Structure" means any building, room, ship, vessel or airplane and also means any place adapted for overnight accommodation of persons, or for carrying on business therein, whether or not the person is actually present.

b. Any person who knowingly assembles, maintains, places or causes to be placed a booby trap on property used for the manufacture, distribution, dispensing, or possession or control with intent to manufacture, distribute or dispense, controlled dangerous substances in violation of this chapter shall be guilty of a crime of the second degree. If the booby trap causes bodily injury to any person, the defendant shall be guilty of a crime of the first degree.

It shall not be a defense that the device was inoperable or was not actually triggered, or that its existence or location was known to a law enforcement officer or another person.

c. Any person who fortifies or maintains in a fortified condition a structure for the manufacture, distribution, dispensing or possession or control with intent to manufacture, distribute or dispense, controlled dangerous substances, or who violates section 3, 4, 5, 6 or 7 of chapter 35 in a structure which he owns, leases, occupies or controls, and which has been fortified, is guilty of a crime of the third degree. A structure has been fortified if steel doors, wooden planking, cross bars, alarm systems, dogs, lookouts or any other means are employed to prevent, impede, delay or provide warning of the entry into a structure or any part of a structure by law enforcement officers.

d. A booby trap or fortification is maintained if it remains on property or in a structure while the property or structure is owned, occupied, controlled or used by the defendant.

e. Nothing herein shall be deemed to preclude, if the evidence so warrants, an indictment and conviction for a violation of chapters 11, 12, 17, and 39 of this title, or any other law. Notwithstanding the provisions of N.J.S.2C:1–8, N.J.S.2C:44–5 or any other provisions of law, a conviction arising under this section shall not merge with a conviction for a violation of any section of chapter 35 of Title 2C of the New Jersey Statutes, or for conspiring or attempting to violate any section of chapter 35 of Title 2C of the New Jersey Statutes, and the sentence imposed upon a violation of this section shall be ordered to be served consecutively to that imposed for any other conviction arising under any section of chapter 35 of Title 2C of the New Jersey Statutes or for conspiracy or attempt to violate any section of chapter 35 of Title 2C of the New Jersey Statutes, unless the court, in consideration of the character and circumstances of the defendant, finds that imposition of consecutive sentences would be a serious injustice which overrides the need to deter such conduct by others. If the court does not impose a consecutive sentence, the sentence shall not become final for 10 days in order to permit the appeal of such sentence by the prosecution.

L.1997, c. 185, § 1, eff. Aug. 4, 1997.

2C:35–5. Manufacturing, distributing or dispensing

a. Except as authorized by P.L.1970, c. 226 (C.24:21–1 et seq.), it shall be unlawful for any person knowingly or purposely:

(1) To manufacture, distribute or dispense, or to possess or have under his control with intent to manufacture, distribute or dispense, a controlled dangerous substance or controlled substance analog; or

(2) To create, distribute, or possess or have under his control with intent to distribute, a counterfeit controlled dangerous substance.

b. Any person who violates subsection a. with respect to:

(1) Heroin, or its analog, or coca leaves and any salt, compound, derivative, or preparation of coca leaves, and any salt, compound, derivative, or preparation thereof which is chemically equivalent or identical with any of these substances, or analogs, except that the substances shall not include decocainized coca leaves or extractions which do not contain cocaine or ecogine, or 3,4–methylenedioxymethamphetamine or 3,4–methylenedioxyamphetamine, in a quantity of five ounces or more including any adulterants or dilutants is guilty of a crime of the first degree. The defendant shall, except as provided in N.J.S.2C:35–12, be sentenced to a term of imprisonment by the court. The term of imprisonment shall include the imposition of a minimum term which shall be fixed at, or between, one-third and one-half of the sentence imposed, during which the defendant shall be ineligible for parole. Notwithstanding the provisions of subsection a. of N.J.S.2C:43–3, a fine of up to $500,000.00 may be imposed;

(2) A substance referred to in paragraph (1) of this subsection, in a quantity of one-half ounce or more but less than five ounces, including any adulterants or dilutants is guilty of a crime of the second degree;

(3) A substance referred to in paragraph (1) of this subsection in a quantity less than one-half ounce including any adulterants or dilutants is guilty of a crime of the third degree except that, notwithstanding the provisions of subsection b. of N.J.S.2C:43–3, a fine of up to $75,000.00 may be imposed;

(4) A substance classified as a narcotic drug in Schedule I or II other than those specifically covered in this section, or the analog of any such substance, in a quantity of one ounce or more including any adulterants or dilutants is guilty of a crime of the second degree;

(5) A substance classified as a narcotic drug in Schedule I or II other than those specifically covered in this section, or the analog of any such substance, in a quantity of less than one ounce including any adulterants or dilutants is guilty of a crime of the third degree except that, notwithstanding the provisions of subsection b. of N.J.S.2C:43–3, a fine of up to $75,000.00 may be imposed;

(6) Lysergic acid diethylamide, or its analog, in a quantity of 100 milligrams or more including any adulterants or dilutants, or phencyclidine, or its analog, in a quantity of 10 grams or more including any adulterants or dilutants, is guilty of a crime of the first degree. Except as provided in N.J.S.2C:35–12, the court shall impose a term of imprisonment which shall include the imposition of a minimum term, fixed at, or

between, one-third and one-half of the sentence imposed by the court, during which the defendant shall be ineligible for parole. Notwithstanding the provisions of subsection a. of N.J.S.2C:43–3, a fine of up to $500,000.00 may be imposed;

(7) Lysergic acid diethylamide, or its analog, in a quantity of less than 100 milligrams including any adulterants or dilutants, or where the amount is undetermined, or phencyclidine, or its analog, in a quantity of less than 10 grams including any adulterants or dilutants, or where the amount is undetermined, is guilty of a crime of the second degree;

(8) Methamphetamine, or its analog, or phenyl–2–propanone (P2P), in a quantity of five ounces or more including any adulterants or dilutants is guilty of a crime of the first degree. Notwithstanding the provisions of subsection a. of N.J.S.2C:43–3, a fine of up to $300,000.00 may be imposed;

(9) (a) Methamphetamine, or its analog, or phenyl–2–propanone (P2P), in a quantity of one-half ounce or more but less than five ounces including any adulterants or dilutants is guilty of a crime of the second degree;

(b) Methamphetamine, or its analog, or phenyl–2–propanone (P2P), in a quantity of less than one-half ounce including any adulterants or dilutants is guilty of a crime of the third degree except that notwithstanding the provisions of subsection b. of N.J.S.2C:43–3, a fine of up to $75,000.00 may be imposed;

(10) (a) Marijuana in a quantity of 25 pounds or more including any adulterants or dilutants, or 50 or more marijuana plants, regardless of weight, or hashish in a quantity of five pounds or more including any adulterants or dilutants, is guilty of a crime of the first degree. Notwithstanding the provisions of subsection a. of N.J.S.2C:43–3, a fine of up to $300,000.00 may be imposed;

(b) Marijuana in a quantity of five pounds or more but less than 25 pounds including any adulterants or dilutants, or 10 or more but fewer than 50 marijuana plants, regardless of weight, or hashish in a quantity of one pound or more but less than five pounds, including any adulterants and dilutants, is guilty of a crime of the second degree;

(11) Marijuana in a quantity of one ounce or more but less than five pounds including any adulterants or dilutants, or hashish in a quantity of five grams or more but less than one pound including any adulterants or dilutants, is guilty of a crime of the third degree except that, notwithstanding the provisions of subsection b. of N.J.S.2C:43–3, a fine of up to $25,000.00 may be imposed;

(12) Marijuana in a quantity of less than one ounce including any adulterants or dilutants, or hashish in a quantity of less than five grams including any adulter-

ants or dilutants, is guilty of a crime of the fourth degree;

(13) Any other controlled dangerous substance classified in Schedule I, II, III or IV, or its analog, is guilty of a crime of the third degree, except that, notwithstanding the provisions of subsection b. of N.J.S.2C:43–3, a fine of up to $25,000.00 may be imposed; or

(14) Any Schedule V substance, or its analog, is guilty of a crime of the fourth degree except that, notwithstanding the provisions of subsection b. of N.J.S.2C:43–3, a fine of up to $25,000.00 may be imposed.

c. Where the degree of the offense for violation of this section depends on the quantity of the substance, the quantity involved shall be determined by the trier of fact. Where the indictment or accusation so provides, the quantity involved in individual acts of manufacturing, distribution, dispensing or possessing with intent to distribute may be aggregated in determining the grade of the offense, whether distribution or dispensing is to the same person or several persons, provided that each individual act of manufacturing, distribution, dispensing or possession with intent to distribute was committed within the applicable statute of limitations.

L.1987, c. 106, § 1, operative July 9, 1987. Amended by L.1988, c. 44, § 2, eff. June 28, 1988; L.1997, c. 181, § 3, eff. Aug. 1, 1997; L.1997, c. 186, § 3, eff. Aug. 4, 1997; L.2000, c. 55, § 1, eff. July 3, 2000; L.2000, c. 136, § 1, eff. Nov. 1, 2000.

2C:35–5.1. Repealed by L.1992, c. 71, § 3, eff. July 30, 1992

2C:35–5.2. Manufacture, distribution, or possession of gamma hydroxybutyrate

a. Except as authorized by P.L.1970, c. 226 (C.24:21–1 et seq.), it shall be a crime of the second degree for any person knowingly or purposely to manufacture, distribute or dispense, or to possess or have under his control with intent to manufacture, distribute or dispense gamma hydroxybutyrate.

b. Notwithstanding the provisions of N.J.S.2C:43–3 or any other law, a fine of up to $150,000.00 may be imposed upon a person who violates this section. *L.1997, c. 194, § 3, eff. Aug. 8, 1997.*

2C:35–5.3. Manufacture, distribution, or possession of flunitrazepam

a. Except as authorized by P.L.1970, c. 226 (C.24:21–1 et seq.), it is unlawful for any person knowingly or purposely to manufacture, distribute or dispense, or to possess or have under his control with intent to manufacture, distribute or dispense flunitrazepam.

b. A person who violates subsection a. of this section with respect to flunitrazepam in a quantity of one gram or more is guilty of a crime of the first degree and, notwithstanding the provisions of N.J.S.2C:43–3 or any other law, a fine of up to $250,000.00 may be imposed upon the person.

c. A person who violates subsection a. of this section with respect to flunitrazepam in a quantity of less than one gram is guilty of a crime of the second degree and, notwithstanding the provisions of N.J.S.2C:43–3 or any other law, a fine of up to $150,000.00 may be imposed upon the person.

L.1997, c. 194, § 5, eff. Aug. 8, 1997.

2C:35–5.4. Short title

This act shall be known and may be cited as the "Drug Offender Restraining Order Act of 1999."

L.1999, c. 334, § 1, eff. Jan. 10, 2000.

2C:35–5.5. Legislative findings

The Legislature hereby finds and declares to be the public policy of this State, the following:

a. By the enactment of the "Comprehensive Drug Reform Act of 1987," N.J.S.2C:35–1 et seq., the Legislature recognized that the unlawful manufacture, distribution, possession and use of controlled dangerous substances poses a serious and pervasive threat to the health, safety and welfare of the citizens of this State.

b. In particular, the unlawful manufacture and distribution of controlled dangerous substances can undermine the quality of life enjoyed by all persons who live or work in a neighborhood where such unlawful activity occurs.

c. Persons who engage in unlawful drug activity serve as negative role models for the young, enlist others to join in illicit enterprises, attract violent criminals who prey upon the innocent, and drive away law-abiding citizens, thus having an adverse impact upon legitimate businesses.

d. Displacing those who engage in the unlawful manufacture and distribution of controlled dangerous substances from the situs of their offenses will disrupt drug trafficking by forcing offenders to abandon familiar and comfortable surroundings and requiring them to rely on more cumbersome techniques for conducting street-level transactions. Restraining orders will also protect the public by separating drug offenders from their known markets for sales and purchases of controlled dangerous substances.

L.1999, c. 334, § 2, eff. Jan. 10, 2000.

2C:35–5.6. Definitions

Definitions.

As used in this act:

a. "Person" means any person charged with or convicted of a criminal offense or any juvenile charged with delinquency or adjudicated delinquent for an act which, if committed by an adult, would be a criminal offense.

b. "Place" includes any premises, residence, business establishment, location or specified area including all buildings and all appurtenant land, in which or at which a criminal offense occurred or is alleged to have occurred or is affected by the criminal offense with which the person is charged. "Place" does not include public rail, bus or air transportation lines or limited access highways which do not allow pedestrian access.

c. "Criminal offense" means:

(1) any of the following: N.J.S.2C:35–3, N.J.S.2C:35–4, N.J.S.2C: 35–5, N.J.S.2C:35–6, N.J.S.2C:35–8, N.J.S.2C:35–9, P. L.1997, c. 185 (C.2C: 35–4.1), section 3 or 5 of P.L.1997, c. 194 (C.2C:35–5. 2 or C.2C:35–5.3), P.L.1987, c. 101 (C.2C:35–7) or P.L. 1997, c. 327 (C.2C:35–7.1), or

(2) the unlawful possession or use of an assault firearm as defined in subsection w. of N.J.S.2C:39–1.

L.1999, c. 334, § 3, eff. Jan. 10, 2000. Amended by L.2001, c. 365, § 1, eff. May 7, 2002.

2C:35–5.7. Restraining orders; certain released persons

a. When a person is charged with a criminal offense on a warrant and the person is released from custody before trial on bail or personal recognizance, the court, upon application of a law enforcement officer or prosecuting attorney pursuant to section 3 of P.L.2001, c. 365 (C.2C:35–5.9) and except as provided in subsection e. of this section, shall as a condition of release issue an order prohibiting the person from entering any place defined by subsection b. of section 3 of P.L.1999, c. 334 (C.2C:35–5.6), including a buffer zone surrounding the place or modifications as provided by subsection f. of this section.

b. When a person is charged with a criminal offense on a summons, the court, upon application of a law enforcement officer or prosecuting attorney pursuant to section 3 of P.L.2001, c. 365 (C.2C:35–5.9) and except as provided in subsection e. of this section, shall, at the time of the defendant's first appearance, issue an order prohibiting the person from entering any place defined by subsection b. of section 3 of P.L.1999, c. 334 (C.2C:35–5.6), including a buffer zone surrounding the place or modifications as provided by subsection f. of this section.

c. When a person is charged with a criminal offense on a juvenile delinquency complaint and is released from custody at a detention hearing pursuant to section 19 of P.L.1982, c. 77 (C.2A:4A–38), the court, upon application of a law enforcement officer or prosecuting attorney pursuant to section 3 of P.L.2001, c. 365 (C.2C:35–5.9) and except as provided in subsection e. of this section, shall issue an order prohibiting the person from entering any place defined by subsection b. of section 3 of P.L.1999, c. 334 (C.2C:35–5.6), including a buffer zone surrounding the place or modifications as provided by subsection f. of this section.

d. When a person is charged with a criminal offense on a juvenile delinquency complaint and is released without being detained pursuant to section 15 or 16 of P.L.1982, c. 77 (C.2A:4A–34 or C.2A:4A–35), the law enforcement officer or prosecuting attorney shall prepare an application pursuant to section 3 of P.L.2001, c. 365 (C.2C:35–5.9) for filing on the next court day.

The law enforcement officer releasing the juvenile shall serve the juvenile and his parent or guardian with written notice that an order shall be issued by the Family Part of the Superior Court on the next court day prohibiting the juvenile from entering any place defined by subsection b. of section 3 of P.L.1999, c. 334 (C.2C:35–5.6), including a buffer zone surrounding the place or modifications as provided by subsection f. of this section.

The court shall issue such order on the first court day following the release of the juvenile. If the restraints contained in the court order differ from the restraints contained in the notice, the order shall not be effective until the third court day following the issuance of the order. The juvenile may apply to the court to stay or modify the order on the grounds set forth in subsection e. of this section.

e. The court may forego issuing a restraining order for which application has been made pursuant to section 3 of P.L.2001, c. 365 (C.2C:35–5.9) only if the defendant establishes by clear and convincing evidence that:

(1) the defendant lawfully resides at or has legitimate business on or near the place, or otherwise legitimately needs to enter the place. In such an event, the court shall not issue an order pursuant to this section unless the court is clearly convinced that the need to bar the person from the place in order to protect the public safety and the rights, safety and health of the residents and persons working in the place outweighs the person's interest in returning to the place. If the balance of the interests of the person and the public so warrants, the court may issue an order imposing conditions upon the person's entry at, upon or near the place; or

(2) the issuance of an order would cause undue hardship to innocent persons and would constitute a serious injustice which overrides the need to protect the rights, safety and health of persons residing in or having business in the place.

f. A restraining order issued pursuant to subsection a., b., c., d. or h. of this section shall describe the place from which the person has been barred and any conditions upon the person's entry into the place, with sufficient specificity to enable the person to guide his conduct accordingly and to enable a law enforcement officer to enforce the order. The order shall also prohibit the person from entering an area of up to 500 feet surrounding the place, unless the court rules that a different buffer zone would better effectuate the purposes of this act. In the discretion of the court, the order may contain modifications to permit the person to enter the area during specified times for specified purposes, such as attending school during regular school hours. When appropriate, the court may append to the order a map depicting the place. The person shall be given a copy of the restraining order and any appended map and shall acknowledge in writing the receipt thereof.

g. (1) The court shall provide notice of the restraining order to the local law enforcement agency where the arrest occurred and to the county prosecutor.

(2) Notwithstanding the provisions of section 1 of P.L.1982, c. 79 (C.2A:4A–60), prior to the person's conviction or adjudication of delinquency for a criminal offense, the local law enforcement agency may post a copy of any orders issued pursuant to this section, or an equivalent notice containing the terms of the order, upon one or more of the principal entrances of the place or in any other conspicuous location. Such posting shall be for the purpose of informing the public, and the failure to post a copy of the order shall in no way excuse any violation of the order.

(3) Notwithstanding the provisions of section 1 of P.L.1982, c. 79 (C.2A:4A–60), prior to the person's conviction or adjudication of delinquency for a criminal offense, any law enforcement agency may publish a copy of any orders issued pursuant to this section, or an equivalent notice containing the terms of the order, in a newspaper circulating in the area of the restraining order. Such publication shall be for the purpose of informing the public, and the failure to publish a copy of the order shall in no way excuse any violation of the order.

(4) Notwithstanding the provisions of section 1 of P.L.1982, c. 79 (C.2A:4A–60), prior to the person's conviction or adjudication of delinquency for a criminal offense, any law enforcement agency may distribute copies of any orders issued pursuant to this section, or an equivalent notice containing the terms of the order, to residents or businesses located within the area delineated in the order or, in the case of a school or any government-owned property, to the appropriate administrator, or to any tenant association representing the residents of the affected area. Such distribution shall be for the purpose of informing the public, and the failure to publish a copy of the order shall in no way excuse any violation of the order.

h. When a person is convicted of or adjudicated delinquent for any criminal offense, the court, upon application of a law enforcement officer or prosecuting attorney pursuant to section 3 of P.L.2001, c. 365 (C.2C:35–5. 9) and except as provided in subsection e. of this section, shall, by separate order or within the judgment of conviction, issue an order prohibiting the person from entering any place defined by subsection b. of section 3 of P.L.1999, c. 334 (C.2C:35–5.6), including a buffer zone surrounding the place or modifications as provided by subsection f. of this section. Upon the person's conviction or adjudication of delinquency for a criminal offense, a law enforcement agency, in addition to posting, publishing, and distributing the order or an equivalent notice pursuant to paragraphs (2), (3) and (4) of subsection g. of this section, may also post, publish and distribute a photograph of the person.

i. When a juvenile has been adjudicated delinquent for an act which, if committed by an adult, would be a criminal offense, in addition to an order required by subsection h. of this section or any other disposition authorized by law, the court may order the juvenile and any parent, guardian or any family member over whom the court has jurisdiction to take such actions or obey such restraints as may be necessary to facilitate the rehabilitation of the juvenile or to protect public safety or to safeguard or enforce the rights of residents of the place. The court may commit the juvenile to the care and responsibility of the Department of Children and Families until such time as the juvenile reaches the age of 18 or until the order of removal and restraint expires, whichever first occurs, or to such alternative residential placement as is practicable.

j. An order issued pursuant to subsection a., b., c. or d. of this section shall remain in effect until the case has been adjudicated or dismissed, or for not less than two years, whichever is less. An order issued pursuant to subsection h. of this section shall remain in effect for such period of time as shall be fixed by the court but not longer than the maximum term of imprisonment or incarceration allowed by law for the underlying offense or offenses. When the court issues a restraining order pursuant to subsection h. of this section and the person is also sentenced to any form of probationary supervision or participation in the Intensive Supervision Program, the court shall make continuing compliance with the order an express condition of probation or the Intensive Supervision Program. When the person has been sentenced to a term of incarceration, continuing compliance with the terms and conditions of the order shall be made an express condition of the person's release from confinement or incarceration on parole. At the time of sentencing or, in the case of a juvenile, at the time of disposition of the juvenile case, the court shall advise the defendant that the restraining order shall include a fixed time period in accordance with this subsection and shall include that provision in the judgment of conviction, dispositional order, separate order or order vacating an existing restraining order, to the law enforcement agency that made the arrest and to the county prosecutor.

k. All applications to stay or modify an order issued pursuant to this act, including an order originally issued in municipal court, shall be made in the Superior Court. The court shall immediately notify the county prosecutor in writing whenever an application is made to stay or modify an order issued pursuant to this act. If the court does not issue a restraining order, the sentence imposed by the court for a criminal offense as defined in subsection b. of this section shall not become final for ten days in order to permit the appeal of the court's findings by the prosecution.

l. Nothing in this section shall be construed in any way to limit the authority of the court to take such other actions or to issue such orders as may be necessary to protect the public safety or to safeguard or enforce the rights of others with respect to the place.

m. Notwithstanding any other provision of this section, the court may permit the person to return to the place to obtain personal belongings and effects and, by court order, may restrict the time and duration and provide for police supervision of such a visit.

L.1999, c. 334, § 4, eff. Jan. 10, 2000. Amended by L.2001, c. 365, § 2, eff. May 7, 2002; L.2004, c. 130, § 14, eff. Aug. 27, 2004; L.2006, c. 47, § 27, eff. July 1, 2006.

2C:35–5.8. Violation of order; sanctions

Violation of any order issued pursuant to this act shall subject the person to civil contempt, criminal contempt, revocation of bail, probation or parole, or any combination of these sanctions and any other sanctions authorized by law. A law enforcement officer may arrest an adult or take into custody a juvenile when an officer has probable cause to believe that the person has violated the terms of any removal and restraining order issued pursuant to section 4 of P.L.1999, c. 334 (C.2C: 35–5.7).

L.1999, c. 334, § 5, eff. Jan. 10, 2000.

2C:35–5.9. Restraining order upon request and submission of a certification

The court shall issue a restraining order pursuant to P.L.1999, c. 334 (C. 2C:35–5.4 et seq.) only upon request by a law enforcement officer or prosecuting attorney and submission of a certification describing the location of the offense.

L.2001, c. 365, § 3, eff. May 7, 2002.

2C:35–5.10. Discretion in seeking restraining order

A law enforcement officer or prosecuting attorney shall have discretion to not seek a restraining order pursuant to P.L.1999, c. 334 (C.2C:35–5.4 et seq.) if the defendant is charged with an offense resulting from the stop of a motor vehicle, if the defendant was using public transportation, or if the provisions of paragraph (1) or (2) of subsection e. of section 4 of P.L.1999, c. 334 (C.2C:35–5.7) are applicable.

L.2001, c. 365, § 4, eff. May 7, 2002.

2C:35–5.11. Fines imposed for possession or distribution of certain drugs

Any person who possesses, distributes, dispenses or has under his control with intent to distribute or dispense   3,4–methylenedioxymethamphetamine, 3,4–methylenedioxyamphetamine,   gammabutyrolactone, gamma hydroxybutyrate or flunitrazepam, or a controlled substance analog of any of these substances, shall, notwithstanding the provisions of any other law, be subject to a drug enforcement and demand reduction penalty of twice the amount otherwise applicable to the offense.

L.2003, c. 37, § 1, eff. April 4, 2003.

2C:35–6. Employing a juvenile in a drug distribution scheme

Any person being at least 18 years of age who knowingly uses, solicits, directs, hires or employs a person 17 years of age or younger to violate N.J.S.2C:35–4 or subsection a. of N.J.S.2C:35–5, is guilty of a crime of the second degree and shall, except as provided in N.J.S.2C:35–12, be sentenced to a term of imprisonment which shall include the imposition of a minimum term which shall be fixed at, or between, one-third and one-half of the sentence imposed, or five years, whichever is greater, during which the defendant shall be ineligible for parole. Notwithstanding the provisions of subsection a. of N.J.S.2C:43–3, the court may also impose a fine not to exceed $500,000.00 or five times the street value of the controlled dangerous substance or controlled substance analog involved, whichever is greater.

It shall be no defense to a prosecution under this section that the actor mistakenly believed that the person which the actor used, solicited, directed, hired or employed was 18 years of age or older, even if such mistaken belief was reasonable.

Nothing in this section shall be construed to preclude or limit a prosecution or conviction for a violation of any offense defined in this chapter pursuant to N.J.S.2C:2–6 or any other provision of law governing an actor's liability for the conduct of another, and, notwithstanding the provisions of N.J.S.2C:1–8 or any other provision of law, a conviction arising under this section shall not merge with a conviction for a violation of N.J.S.2C:35–3 (leader of narcotics trafficking network), N.J.S.2C:35–4 (maintaining or operating a CDS production facility), N.J.S.2C:35–5 (manufacturing, distributing or dispensing), or N.J.S.2C:35–9 (strict liability for drug induced death).

L.1987, c. 106, § 1, operative July 9, 1987. Amended by L.1997, c. 181, § 4, eff. Aug. 1, 1997.

2C:35–7. Distributing, dispensing or possessing controlled dangerous substance or controlled substance analog on or within 1,000 feet of school property or bus; penalty; defenses; approved or revised map; prima facie evidence; official record

a. Any person who violates subsection a. of N.J.S.2C:35–5 by distributing, dispensing or possessing with intent to distribute a controlled dangerous substance or controlled substance analog while on any school property used for school purposes which is owned by or leased to any elementary or secondary school or school board, or within 1,000 feet of such school property or a school bus, or while on any school bus, is guilty of a crime of the third degree and shall, except as provided in N.J.S.2C:35–12, be sentenced by the court to a term of imprisonment. Where the violation involves less than one ounce of marijuana, the term of imprisonment shall include the imposition of a minimum term which shall be fixed at, or between, one-third and one-half of the sentence imposed, or one year, whichever is greater, during which the defendant shall be ineligible for parole. In all other cases, the term of imprisonment shall include the imposition of a minimum term which shall be fixed at, or between, one-third and one-half of the sentence imposed, or three years, whichever is greater, during which the defendant shall be ineligible for parole. Notwithstanding the provisions of subsection b. of N.J.S.2C:43–3, a fine of up to $150,000 may also be imposed upon any conviction for a violation of this section.

b. (1) Notwithstanding the provisions of N.J.S.2C:35–12 or subsection a. of this section, the court may waive or reduce the minimum term of parole ineligibility required under subsection a. of this section or place the defendant on probation pursuant to paragraph (2) of subsection b. of N.J.S.2C:43–2. In making this determination, the court shall consider:

(a) the extent of the defendant's prior criminal record and the seriousness of the offenses for which the defendant has been convicted;

(b) the specific location of the present offense in relation to the school property, including distance from the school and the reasonable likelihood of exposing children to drug-related activities at that location;

(c) whether school was in session at the time of the offense; and

(d) whether children were present at or in the immediate vicinity of the location when the offense took place.

(2) The court shall not waive or reduce the minimum term of parole ineligibility or sentence the defendant to probation if it finds that:

(a) the offense took place while on any school property used for school purposes which is owned by or leased to any elementary or secondary school or school board, or while on any school bus; or

(b) the defendant in the course of committing the offense used or threatened violence or was in possession of a firearm.

If the court at sentencing elects not to impose a minimum term of imprisonment and parole ineligibility pursuant to this subsection, imposes a term of parole ineligibility less than the minimum term prescribed in subsection a. of this section, or places the defendant on probation for a violation of subsection a. of this section, the sentence shall not become final for 10 days in order to permit the prosecution to appeal the court's finding and the sentence imposed. The Attorney General shall develop guidelines to ensure the uniform exercise of discretion in making determinations regarding whether to appeal a decision to waive or reduce the minimum term of parole ineligibility or place the defendant on probation.

Nothing in this subsection shall be construed to establish a basis for overcoming a presumption of imprisonment authorized or required by subsection d. of N.J.S.2C:44–1, or a basis for not imposing a term of imprisonment or term of parole ineligibility authorized or required to be imposed pursuant to subsection f. of N.J.S.2C:43–6 or upon conviction for a crime other than the offense set forth in this subsection.

c. Notwithstanding the provisions of N.J.S.2C:1–8 or any other provisions of law, a conviction arising under this section shall not merge with a conviction for a violation of subsection a. of N.J.S.2C:35–5 (manufacturing, distributing or dispensing) or N.J.S.2C:35–6 (employing a juvenile in a drug distribution scheme).

d. It shall be no defense to a prosecution for a violation of this section that the actor was unaware that the prohibited conduct took place while on or within 1,000 feet of any school property. Nor shall it be a defense to a prosecution under this section, or under any other provision of this title, that no juveniles were present on the school property at the time of the offense or that the school was not in session.

e. It is an affirmative defense to prosecution for a violation of this section that the prohibited conduct took place entirely within a private residence, that no person 17 years of age or younger was present in such private residence at any time during the commission of the offense, and that the prohibited conduct did not involve distributing, dispensing or possessing with the intent to distribute or dispense any controlled dangerous substance or controlled substance analog for profit. The affirmative defense established in this section shall be proved by the defendant by a preponderance of the evidence. Nothing herein shall be construed to establish an affirmative defense with respect to a prosecution for an offense defined in any other section of this chapter.

f. In a prosecution under this section, a map produced or reproduced by any municipal or county engineer for the purpose of depicting the location and boundaries of the area on or within 1,000 feet of any property used for school purposes which is owned by or leased to any elementary or secondary school or school board, or a true copy of such a map, shall, upon proper authentication, be admissible and shall constitute prima facie evidence of the location and boundaries of those areas, provided that the governing body of the municipality or county has adopted a resolution or ordinance approving the map as official finding and record of the location and boundaries of the area or areas on or within 1,000 feet of the school property. Any map approved pursuant to this section may be changed from time to time by the governing body of the municipality or county. The original of every map approved or revised pursuant to this section, or a true copy thereof, shall be filed with the clerk of the municipality or county, and shall be maintained as an official record of the municipality or county. Nothing in this section shall be construed to preclude the prosecution from introduc-

ing or relying upon any other evidence or testimony to establish any element of this offense; nor shall this section be construed to preclude the use or admissibility of any map or diagram other than one which has been approved by the governing body of a municipality or county, provided that the map or diagram is otherwise admissible pursuant to the Rules of Evidence.

L.1987, c. 101, § 1, eff. April 15, 1987, operative April 23, 1987. Amended by L.1988, c. 44, § 3, eff. June 28, 1988; L.1997, c. 181, § 5, eff. Aug. 1, 1997; L.2009, c. 192, § 1, eff. Jan. 12, 2010.

2C:35–7a. Review of sentence for violation of drug-free school zones provisions

Notwithstanding any court rule limiting the time period within which a motion to reduce or change a sentence may be filed, any person who, on the effective date of this act, is serving a mandatory minimum sentence as provided by section 1 of P.L.1987, c. 101 (C.2C:35–7) and who has not had his sentence suspended or been paroled or discharged may move to have his sentence reviewed by the court. If the court finds that the sentence under review does not serve the interests of justice, the judge may re-sentence the defendant pursuant to subsection b. of section 1 of P.L.1987, c. 101 (C.2C:35–7). In determining whether the sentence under review serves the interests of justice, the court shall consider all relevant circumstances, including whether the defendant pleaded guilty pursuant to a negotiated agreement, and whether the prosecution has agreed to dismiss one or more charges which, upon conviction, would have subjected the defendant to the presumption of imprisonment under subsection d. of N.J.S.2C:44–1. The determination by the court shall not be subject to appeal.

L.2009, c. 192, § 2, eff. Jan. 12, 2010.

2C:35–7.1. Distributing, dispensing or possession controlled substances; proximity to public housing facilities, parks or buildings

a. Any person who violates subsection a. of N.J.S.2C:35–5 by distributing, dispensing or possessing with intent to distribute a controlled dangerous substance or controlled substance analog while in, on or within 500 feet of the real property comprising a public housing facility, a public park, or a public building is guilty of a crime of the second degree, except that it is a crime of the third degree if the violation involved less than one ounce of marijuana.

b. It shall be no defense to a prosecution for violation of this section that the actor was unaware that the prohibited conduct took place while on or within 500 feet of a public housing facility, a public park, or a public building.

c. Notwithstanding the provisions of N.J.S.2C:1–8 or any other provisions of law, a conviction arising under this section shall not merge with a conviction for a violation of subsection a. of N.J.S.2C:35–5 (manufacturing, distributing or dispensing) or N.J.S.2C:35–6 (employing a juvenile in a drug distribution scheme). Nothing in this section shall be construed to preclude or limit a prosecution or conviction for a violation of N.J.S.2C:35–7 or any other offense defined in this chapter.

d. It is an affirmative defense to prosecution for a violation of this section that the prohibited conduct did not involve distributing, dispensing or possessing with the intent to distribute or dispense any controlled dangerous substance or controlled substance analog for profit, and that the prohibited conduct did not involve distribution to a person 17 years of age or younger. The affirmative defense established in this section shall be proved by the defendant by a preponderance of the evidence. Nothing herein shall be construed to establish an affirmative defense with respect to a prosecution for an offense defined in any other section of this chapter.

e. In a prosecution under this section, a map produced or reproduced by any municipal or county engineer for the purpose of depicting the location and boundaries of the area on or within 500 feet of a public housing facility which is owned by or leased to a housing authority according to the "Local Redevelopment and Housing Law," P.L.1992, c. 79 (C.40A:12A–1 et seq.), the area in or within 500 feet of a public park, or the area in or within 500 feet of a public building, or a true copy of such a map, shall, upon proper authentication, be admissible and shall constitute prima facie evidence of the location and boundaries of those areas, provided that the governing body of the municipality or county has adopted a resolution or ordinance approving the map as official finding and record of the location and boundaries of the area or areas on or within 500 feet of a public housing facility, a public park, or a public building. Any map approved pursuant to this section may be changed from time to time by the governing body of the municipality or county. The original of every map approved or revised pursuant to this section, or a true copy thereof, shall be filed with the clerk of the municipality or county, and shall be maintained as an official record of the municipality or county. Nothing in this section shall be construed to preclude the prosecution from introducing or relying upon any other evidence or testimony to establish any element of this offense; nor shall this section be construed to preclude the use or admissibility of any map or diagram other than one which has been approved by the governing body of a municipality or county, provided that the map or diagram is otherwise admissible pursuant to the Rules of Evidence.

f. As used in this act:

"Public housing facility" means any dwelling, complex of dwellings, accommodation, building, structure or facility and real property of any nature appurtenant thereto and used in connection therewith, which is owned by or leased to a local housing authority in accordance with the "Local Redevelopment and Housing Law," P.L.1992, c. 79 (C.40A:12A–1 et seq.) for the purpose of providing living accommodations to persons of low income.

"Public park" means a park, recreation facility or area or playground owned or controlled by a State, county or local government unit.

"Public building" means any publicly owned or leased library or museum.

L.1997, c. 327, § 1, eff. Jan. 9, 1998.

2C:35–8. Distribution to persons under age 18; enhanced punishment

Upon the application of the prosecuting attorney, any person being at least 18 years of age who has been convicted for violating subsection a. of N.J.S. 2C:35–5 or section 1 of P.L.1987, c. 101 (C. 2C:35–7) by distributing a controlled dangerous substance or controlled substance analog to a pregnant female or a person 17 years of age or younger shall, except as provided in N.J.S. 2C:35–12, be subject to twice the term of imprisonment, fine and penalty, including twice the term of parole ineligibility, if any, authorized or required to be imposed by subsection b. of N.J.S. 2C:35–5 or section 1 of P.L.1987, c. 101 (C. 2C:35–7) or any other provision of this title. In addition, the presumption of non-imprisonment for certain offenders set forth in subsection e. of N.J.S. 2C:44–1 shall not apply to any person subject to enhanced punishment pursuant to this section.

The court shall not impose more than one enhanced sentence pursuant to this section. If the defendant is convicted of more than one offense which is otherwise subject to enhanced punishment pursuant to this section, the court shall impose enhanced punishment based upon the most serious such offense for which the defendant was convicted, or, where applicable, the offense which mandates the imposition of the longest term of parole ineligibility. Notwithstanding the provisions of paragraph (2) of subsection a. of 2C:44–5, nothing herein shall prevent the court from also imposing an extended term pursuant to subsection f. of N.J.S. 2C:43–6. The court shall not impose an enhanced sentence pursuant to this section unless the prosecutor has established the ground therefor by a preponderance of the evidence at a hearing, which may occur at the time of sentencing. In making its finding, the court shall take judicial notice of any evidence, testimony or information adduced at the trial, plea hearing or other court proceedings, and shall also consider the presentence report and any other relevant information. It shall not be relevant to the imposition of enhanced punishment pursuant to this section that the defendant mistakenly believed that the recipient of the substance was 18 years of age or older, even if the mistaken belief was reasonable. Nor shall it be relevant to the imposition of enhanced punishment pursuant to this section that the defendant did not know that the recipient was pregnant.

L.1987, c. 106, § 1, operative July 9, 1987. Amended by L.1988, c. 44, § 4, eff. June 28, 1988.

2C:35–9.   Strict liability for drug-induced deaths

a. Any person who manufactures, distributes or dispenses methamphetamine, lysergic acid diethylamide, phencyclidine or any other controlled dangerous substance classified in Schedules I or II, or any controlled substance analog thereof, in violation of subsection a. of N.J.S. 2C:35–5, is strictly liable for a death which results from the injection, inhalation or ingestion of that substance, and is guilty of a crime of the first degree.

b. The provisions of N.J.S. 2C:2–3 (governing the causal relationship between conduct and result) shall not apply in a prosecution under this section. For purposes of this offense, the defendant's act of manufacturing, distributing or dispensing a substance is the cause of a death when:

(1) The injection, inhalation or ingestion of the substance is an antecedent but for which the death would not have occurred; and

(2) The death was not:

(a) too remote in its occurrence as to have a just bearing on the defendant's liability; or

(b) too dependent upon conduct of another person which was unrelated to the injection, inhalation or ingestion of the substance or its effect as to have a just bearing on the defendant's liability.

c. It shall not be a defense to a prosecution under this section that the decedent contributed to his own death by his purposeful, knowing, reckless or negligent injection, inhalation or ingestion of the substance, or by his consenting to the administration of the substance by another.

d. Nothing in this section shall be construed to preclude or limit any prosecution for homicide. Notwithstanding the provisions of N.J.S. 2C:1–8 or any other provision of law, a conviction arising under this section shall not merge with a conviction for leader of narcotics trafficking network, maintaining or operating a controlled dangerous substance production facility, or for unlawfully manufacturing, distributing, dispensing or possessing with intent to manufacture, distribute or dispense the controlled dangerous substance or controlled substance analog which resulted in the death.

L.1987, c. 106, § 1, operative July 9, 1987.

2C:35–10.   Possession, use or being under the influence, or failure to make lawful disposition

a. It is unlawful for any person, knowingly or purposely, to obtain, or to possess, actually or constructively, a controlled dangerous substance or controlled substance analog, unless the substance was obtained directly, or pursuant to a valid prescription or order form from a practitioner, while acting in the course of his professional practice, or except as otherwise authorized by P.L.1970, c. 226 (C.24:21–1 et seq.). Any person who violates this section with respect to:

(1) A controlled dangerous substance, or its analog, classified in Schedule I, II, III or IV other than those specifically covered in this section, is guilty of a crime of the third degree except that, notwithstanding the provisions of subsection b. of N.J.S.2C:43–3, a fine of up to $35,000.00 may be imposed;

(2) Any controlled dangerous substance, or its analog, classified in Schedule V, is guilty of a crime of the fourth degree except that, notwithstanding the provisions of subsection b. of N.J.S.2C:43–3, a fine of up to $15,000.00 may be imposed;

(3) Possession of more than 50 grams of marijuana, including any adulterants or dilutants, or more than five grams of hashish is guilty of a crime of the fourth degree, except that, notwithstanding the provisions of subsection b. of N.J.S.2C:43–3, a fine of up to $25,000.00 may be imposed; or

(4) Possession of 50 grams or less of marijuana, including any adulterants or dilutants, or five grams or less of hashish is a disorderly person.

Any person who commits any offense defined in this section while on any property used for school purposes which is owned by or leased to any elementary or secondary school or school board, or within 1,000 feet of any such school property or a school bus, or while on any school bus, and who is not sentenced to a term of imprisonment, shall, in addition to any other sentence which the court may impose, be required to perform not less than 100 hours of community service.

b. Any person who uses or who is under the influence of any controlled dangerous substance, or its analog, for a purpose other than the treatment of sickness or injury as lawfully prescribed or administered by a physician is a disorderly person.

In a prosecution under this subsection, it shall not be necessary for the State to prove that the accused did use or was under the influence of any specific drug, but it shall be sufficient for a conviction under this subsection for the State to prove that the accused did use or was under the influence of some controlled dangerous substance, counterfeit controlled dangerous substance, or controlled substance analog, by proving that the accused did manifest physical and physiological symptoms or reactions caused by the use of any controlled dangerous substance or controlled substance analog.

c. Any person who knowingly obtains or possesses a controlled dangerous substance or controlled substance analog in violation of subsection a. of this section and who fails to voluntarily deliver the substance to the nearest law enforcement officer is guilty of a disorderly persons offense. Nothing in this subsection shall be construed to preclude a prosecution or conviction for any other offense defined in this title or any other statute.

L.1987, c. 106, § 1, operative July 9, 1987. Amended by L.1988, c. 44, § 5, eff. June 28, 1988; L.1997, c. 181, § 6, eff. Aug. 1, 1997.

2C:35–10.1. Repealed by L.1992, c. 71, § 3, eff. July 30, 1992

2C:35–10.2. Obtaining or possessing gamma hydroxy-butyrate without a prescription

a. It is a crime of the third degree for any person, knowingly or purposely, to obtain, or to possess, gamma hydroxybutyrate unless the substance was obtained directly, or pursuant to a valid prescription or order form from a practitioner, while acting in the course of his professional practice, or except as otherwise authorized by P.L.1970, c. 226 (C.24:21–1 et seq.).

b. Notwithstanding the provisions of N.J.S.2C:43–3 or any other law, a fine of up to $100,000.00 may be imposed upon a person who violates this section.
L.1997, c. 194, § 4, eff. Aug. 8, 1997.

2C:35–10.3. Obtaining or possession flunitrazepam without a prescription

a. It is a crime of the third degree for any person, knowingly or purposely, to obtain, or to possess, flunitrazepam, unless the substance was obtained directly, or pursuant to a valid prescription or order form from a practitioner, while acting in the course of his professional practice, or except as otherwise authorized by P.L. 1970, c. 226 (C.24:21–1 et seq.).

b. Notwithstanding the provisions of N.J.S.2C:43–3 or any other law, a fine of up to $100,000.00 may be imposed upon a person who violates this section.
L.1997, c. 194, § 6, eff. Aug. 8, 1997.

2C:35–10.4. Toxic chemicals

a. As used in this section the term "toxic chemical" means any chemical or substance having the property of releasing toxic fumes. "Toxic chemical" includes, but is not limited to, acetone, acetate, benzene, butyl alcohol, ethyl alcohol, ethylene dichloride, isopropyl alcohol, methyl alcohol, methyl ethyl ketone, nitrous oxide, pentachlorophenol, petroleum ether, toluol, toluene and any glue, cement, adhesive, paint remover or other substance containing a chemical capable of releasing vapors or fumes causing a condition of intoxication, inebriation, excitement, stupefaction, or dulling of the brain or nervous system.

b. A person commits a disorderly persons offense if the person:

(1) inhales the fumes of any toxic chemical for the purpose of causing a condition of intoxication; or

(2) possesses any toxic chemical for the purpose of causing a condition of intoxication.

This subsection shall not apply to the possession and use of nitrous oxide or any material containing nitrous oxide for the purpose of medical, surgical, or dental care by a person duly licensed to administer nitrous oxide.

c. A person commits a fourth degree offense if the person sells, or offers to sell, any substance containing a toxic chemical knowing that the intended use of the product is to cause a condition of intoxication, or knowing that the product does not include an additive required by the Commissioner of the State Department of Health and Senior Services to discourage the inhalation of vapors of toxic chemicals for the purpose of causing a condition of intoxication. This subsection does not apply to adhesives manufactured only for industrial application or to the sale of nitrous oxide or any material containing nitrous oxide lawfully distributed pursuant to sections 1 though 6 of P.L.1982, c. 127 (C.24:6G–1 et seq.).
L.1999, c. 90, § 7, eff. May 3, 1999. Amended by L.2007, c. 31, § 1, eff. Jan. 29, 2007.

2C:35–10.5. Distribution or possession of prescription legend drugs; authorized dosage units; violations; exceptions

a. A person who knowingly:

(1) distributes a prescription legend drug or stramonium preparation in an amount of four or fewer dosage units unless lawfully prescribed or administered by a licensed physician, veterinarian, dentist or other practitioner authorized by law to prescribe medication is a disorderly person;

(2) distributes for pecuniary gain or possesses or has under his control with intent to distribute for pecuniary gain a prescription legend drug or stramonium preparation in an amount of four or fewer dosage units unless lawfully prescribed or administered by a licensed physician, veterinarian, dentist or other practitioner authorized by law to prescribe medication is guilty of a crime of the fourth degree;

(3) distributes or possesses or has under his control with intent to distribute a prescription legend drug or stramonium preparation in an amount of at least five but fewer than 100 dosage units unless lawfully prescribed or administered by a licensed physician, veterinarian, dentist or other practitioner authorized by law to prescribe medication is guilty of a crime of the third degree. Notwithstanding the provisions of subsection b. of N.J. S.2C:43–3, a fine of up to $200,000 may be imposed; or

(4) distributes or possesses or has under his control with intent to distribute a prescription legend drug or stramonium preparation in an amount of 100 or more dosage units unless lawfully prescribed or administered by a licensed physician, veterinarian, dentist or other practitioner authorized by law to prescribe medication is guilty of a crime of the second degree. Notwithstanding the provisions of subsection b. of N.J.S.2C:43–3, a fine of up to $300,000 may be imposed.

Notwithstanding the above, a violation of paragraph (1) or (3) of this subsection shall be deemed a de minimis infraction subject to dismissal pursuant to N.J.S. 2C:2–11 if the person demonstrates that the conduct involved no more than six dosage units distributed within a 24–hour period, that the prescription legend drug or stramonium preparation was lawfully prescribed for or administered to that person by a licensed physician, veterinarian, dentist or other practitioner authorized by law to prescribe medication, and that the person intended for the amount he distributed to be solely for the recipient's personal use.

b. A person who uses any prescription legend drug or stramonium preparation for a purpose other than treatment of sickness or injury as lawfully prescribed or administered by a licensed physician, veterinarian, dentist or other practitioner authorized by law to prescribe medication is a disorderly person.

c. A defendant may be convicted for a violation of subsection b. if the State proves that the defendant manifested symptoms or reactions caused by the use of prescription legend drugs or stramonium preparation. The State need not prove which specific prescription legend drug or stramonium preparation the defendant used.

d. A person who obtains or attempts to obtain possession of a prescription legend drug or stramonium preparation by forgery or deception is guilty of a crime of the fourth degree. Nothing in this section shall be deemed to preclude or limit a prosecution for theft as defined in chapter 20 of Title C of the New Jersey Statutes.

e. A person who knowingly possesses, actually or constructively:

(1) a prescription legend drug or stramonium preparation in an amount of four or fewer dosage units unless lawfully prescribed or administered by a licensed physician, veterinarian, dentist or other practitioner authorized by law to prescribe medication is a disorderly person; or

(2) a prescription legend drug or stramonium preparation in an amount of five or more dosage units unless lawfully prescribed or administered by a licensed physician, veterinarian, dentist or other practitioner authorized by law to prescribe medication is guilty of a crime of the fourth degree.

Notwithstanding the above, a violation of this subsection shall be deemed a de minimis infraction subject to dismissal pursuant to N.J.S. 2C:2–11 if the person demonstrates that he unlawfully received no more than six dosage units within a 24-hour period, that the prescription legend drug or stramonium preparation was lawfully prescribed for or administered to the person from whom he had received it, and that the person possessed the prescription legend drug or stramonium preparation for solely for his personal use.

f. Where the degree of the offense for violation of this section depends on the number of dosage units of the prescription legend drug or stramonium preparation, the number of dosage units involved shall be determined by the trier of fact. Where the indictment or accusation so provides, the number of dosage units involved in individual acts of distribution or possession

with intent to distribute may be aggregated in determining the grade of the offense, whether distribution is to the same person or several persons, provided that each individual act of distribution or possession with intent to distribute was committed within the applicable statute of limitations.

g. Subsections a. and e. of this section shall not apply to: a licensed pharmacy, licensed pharmacist, researcher, wholesaler, distributor, manufacturer, warehouseman or his representative acting within the line and scope of his employment; a physician, veterinarian, dentist or other practitioner authorized by law to prescribe medication; a nurse acting under the direction of a physician; or a common carrier or messenger when transporting such prescription legend drug or stramonium preparation in the same unbroken package in which the prescription legend drug or stramonium preparation was delivered to him for transportation. *L.1999, c. 90, § 8, eff. May 3, 1999. Amended by L.2005, c. 205, § 2, eff. Aug. 24, 2005.*

2C:35–11. Imitation controlled dangerous substances; distribution, possession, manufacture, etc.; penalties

a. It is unlawful for any person to distribute or to possess or have under his control with intent to distribute any substance which is not a controlled dangerous substance or controlled substance analog:

(1) Upon the express or implied representation to the recipient that the substance is a controlled dangerous substance or controlled substance analog; or

(2) Upon the express or implied representation to the recipient that the substance is of such nature, appearance or effect that the recipient will be able to distribute or use the substance as a controlled dangerous substance or controlled substance analog; or

(3) Under circumstances which would lead a reasonable person to believe that the substance is a controlled dangerous substance or controlled substance analog.

Any of the following shall constitute prima facie evidence of such circumstances:

(a) The substance was packaged in a manner normally used for the unlawful distribution of controlled dangerous substances or controlled substance analogs.

(b) The distribution or attempted distribution of the substance was accompanied by an exchange of or demand for money or other thing as consideration for the substance, and the value of the consideration exceeded the reasonable value of the substance.

(c) The physical appearance of the substance is substantially the same as that of a specific controlled dangerous substance or controlled substance analog.

b. It is unlawful for any person to manufacture, compound, encapsulate, package or imprint any substance which is not a controlled dangerous substance, controlled substance analog or any combination of such substances, other than a prescription drug, with the purpose that it resemble or duplicate the physical appearance of the finished form, package, label or imprint of a controlled dangerous substance or controlled substance analog.

c. In any prosecution under this section, it shall not be a defense that the defendant mistakenly believed a substance to be a controlled dangerous substance or controlled substance analog.

d. A violation of this section is a crime of the third degree, except that, notwithstanding the provisions of subsection b. of N.J.S.2C:43–3, a fine of up to $200,000.00 may be imposed.

e. The provisions of this section shall not be applicable to (1) practitioners or agents, servants and employees of practitioners dispensing or administering noncontrolled substances to patients on behalf of practitioners in the normal course of their business or professional practice; and (2) persons who manufacture, process, package, distribute or sell noncontrolled substances to practitioners for use as placebos in the normal course of their business, professional practice or research or for use in Federal Food and Drug Administration investigational new drug trials.

L.1987, c. 106, § 1, operative July 9, 1987. Amended by L.1997, c. 181, § 7, eff. Aug. 1, 1997.

2C:35–12. Waiver of mandatory minimum and extended terms

Whenever an offense defined in this chapter specifies a mandatory sentence of imprisonment which includes a minimum term during which the defendant shall be ineligible for parole, a mandatory extended term which includes a period of parole ineligibility, or an anti-drug profiteering penalty pursuant to section 2 of P.L. 1997, c. 187 (N.J.S.2C:35A–1 et seq.), the court upon conviction shall impose the mandatory sentence or anti-drug profiteering penalty unless the defendant has pleaded guilty pursuant to a negotiated agreement or, in cases resulting in trial, the defendant and the prosecution have entered into a post-conviction agreement, which provides for a lesser sentence, period of parole ineligibility or anti-drug profiteering penalty. The negotiated plea or post-conviction agreement may provide for a specified term of imprisonment within the range of ordinary or extended sentences authorized by law, a specified period of parole ineligibility, a specified fine, a specified anti-drug profiteering penalty, or other disposition. In that event, the court at sentencing shall not impose a lesser term of imprisonment, lesser period of parole ineligibility, lesser fine or lesser anti-drug profiteering penalty than that expressly provided for under the terms of the plea or post-conviction agreement.

L.1987, c. 106, § 1, operative July 9, 1987. Amended by L.1997, c. 187, § 1, eff. Aug. 4, 1997.

2C:35–13. Obtaining by fraud

It shall be unlawful for any person to acquire or obtain possession of a controlled dangerous substance or controlled substance analog by misrepresentation, fraud, forgery, deception or subterfuge. It shall be unlawful for any person to acquire or obtain possession of a forged or fraudulent certificate of destruction required pursuant to N.J.S.2C:35–21. A violation of this section shall be a crime of the third degree except that, notwithstanding the provisions of subsection b. of N.J.S.2C:43–3, a fine of up to $50,000.00 may be imposed. Nothing in this section shall be deemed to preclude or limit a prosecution for theft as defined in chapter 20 of this title.

L.1987, c. 106, § 1, operative July 9, 1987. Amended by L.1997, c. 181, § 8, eff. Aug. 1, 1997.

2C:35–14. Rehabilitation program for drug and alcohol dependent persons subject to a presumption of incarceration or a mandatory minimum period of parole ineligibility; special probation; mandatory commitment to residential treatment facilities; sentencing considerations

a. Any person who is ineligible for probation due to a conviction for a crime which is subject to a presumption of incarceration or a mandatory minimum period of parole ineligibility may be sentenced to a term of special probation in accordance with this section, and may not apply for drug and alcohol treatment pursuant to N.J.S.2C:45–1. Nothing in this section shall be construed to prohibit a person who is eligible for probation in accordance with N.J.S.2C:45–1 due to a conviction for an offense which is not subject to a presumption of incarceration or a mandatory minimum period of parole ineligibility from applying for drug or alcohol treatment as a condition of probation pursuant to N.J.S.2C:45–1. Notwithstanding the presumption of incarceration pursuant to the provisions of subsection d. of N.J.S.2C:44–1, and except as provided in subsection c. of this section, whenever a drug or alcohol dependent person who is subject to sentencing under this section is convicted of or adjudicated delinquent for an offense, other than one described in subsection b. of this section, the court, upon notice to the prosecutor, may, on motion of the person, or on the court's own motion, place the person on special probation, which shall be for a term of five years, provided that the court finds on the record that:

(1) the person has undergone a professional diagnostic assessment to determine whether and to what extent the person is drug or alcohol dependent and would benefit from treatment; and

(2) the person is a drug or alcohol dependent person within the meaning of N.J.S.2C:35–2 and was drug or alcohol dependent at the time of the commission of the present offense; and

(3) the present offense was committed while the person was under the influence of a controlled dangerous substance, controlled substance analog or alcohol or was committed to acquire property or monies in order to support the person's drug or alcohol dependency; and

(4) substance abuse treatment and monitoring will serve to benefit the person by addressing his drug or alcohol dependency and will thereby reduce the likelihood that the person will thereafter commit another offense; and

(5) the person did not possess a firearm at the time of the present offense and did not possess a firearm at the time of any pending criminal charge; and

(6) the person has not been previously convicted on two or more separate occasions of crimes of the first or second degree, other than those listed in paragraph (7); or the person has not been previously convicted on two or more separate occasions, where one of the offenses is a crime of the third degree, other than crimes defined in N.J.S.2C:35–10, and one of the offenses is a crime of the first or second degree; and

(7) the person has not been previously convicted or adjudicated delinquent for, and does not have a pending charge of murder, aggravated manslaughter, manslaughter, robbery, kidnapping, aggravated assault, aggravated sexual assault or sexual assault, or a similar crime under the laws of any other state or the United States; and

(8) a suitable treatment facility licensed and approved by the Division of Addiction Services in the Department of Human Services is able and has agreed to provide appropriate treatment services in accordance with the requirements of this section; and

(9) no danger to the community will result from the person being placed on special probation pursuant to this section.

In determining whether to sentence the person pursuant to this section, the court shall consider all relevant circumstances, and shall take judicial notice of any evidence, testimony or information adduced at the trial, plea hearing or other court proceedings, and shall also consider the presentence report and the results of the professional diagnostic assessment to determine whether and to what extent the person is drug or alcohol dependent and would benefit from treatment.

As a condition of special probation, the court shall order the person to enter a residential treatment program at a facility licensed and approved by the Division of Addiction Services in the Department of Human Services or a program of nonresidential treatment by a licensed and approved treatment provider, to comply with program rules and the requirements of the course of treatment, to cooperate fully with the treatment provider, and to comply with such other reasonable terms and conditions as may be required by the court or by law, pursuant to N.J.S.2C:45–1, and which shall include periodic urine testing for drug or alcohol usage throughout the period of special probation. In determining whether to order the person to participate in a nonresidential rather than a residential treatment program, the court shall follow the procedure set forth in subsection j. of this section. Subject to the requirements of subsection d. of this section, the conditions of special probation may include different methods and levels of community-based or residential supervision.

b. A person shall not be eligible for special probation pursuant to this section if the person is convicted of or adjudicated delinquent for:

(1) a crime of the first degree;

(2) a crime of the first or second degree enumerated in subsection d. of section 2 of P.L.1997, c. 117 (C.2C:43–7.2);

(3) a crime, other than that defined in section 1 of P.L.1987, c. 101 (C.2C:35–7), for which a mandatory minimum period of incarceration is prescribed under chapter 35 of this Title or any other law; or

(4) an offense that involved the distribution or the conspiracy or attempt to distribute a controlled dangerous substance or controlled substance analog to a juvenile near or on school property.

c. A person who is subject to sentencing under this section in accordance with subsection a. shall not be eligible for a sentence of special probation pursuant to this section if:

(1) the person has been:

(a) convicted of or adjudicated delinquent for an offense under section 1 of P.L.1987, c. 101 (C.2C:35–7), subsection b. of section 1 of P.L. 1997, c. 185 (C.2C:35–4.1), or any crime for which there exists a presumption of imprisonment pursuant to subsection d. of N.J.S.2C:44–1 or any other statute;

(b) previously convicted of an offense under subsection a. of N.J.S.2C:35–5 or a similar offense under any other law of this State, any other state or the United States; or

(c) previously convicted on two or more separate occasions of crimes of the third degree, other than crimes defined in N.J.S.2C:35–10; and

(2) the prosecutor objects to the person being placed on special probation. The court shall not place a person on special probation over the prosecutor's objection except upon a finding by the court of a gross and patent abuse of prosecutorial discretion. If the court makes a finding of a gross and patent abuse of prosecutorial discretion and imposes a sentence of special probation notwithstanding the objection of the prosecutor, the sentence of special probation imposed pursuant to this section shall not become final for 10 days in order to permit the appeal of such sentence by the prosecution.

d. Except as otherwise provided in subsection j. of this section, a person convicted of or adjudicated delinquent for a crime of the second degree or of a violation of section 1 of P.L.1987, c. 101 (C.2C:35–7), or who previously has been convicted of or adjudicated delinquent for an offense under subsection a. of N.J.S.2C:35–5 or a similar offense under any other law of this State, any other state or the United States, who is placed on special probation under this section shall be committed to the custody of a residential treatment facility licensed and approved by the Division of Addiction Services in the Department of Human Services. Subject to the authority of the court to temporarily suspend imposition of all or any portion of the term of commitment to a residential treatment facility pursuant to subsection j. of this section, the person shall be committed to the residential treatment facility immediately, unless the facility cannot accommodate the person, in which case the person shall be incarcerated to await commitment to the residential treatment facility. The term of such commitment shall be for a minimum of six months, or until the court, upon recommendation of the treatment provider, determines that the person has successfully completed the residential treatment program, whichever is later, except that no person shall remain in the custody of a residential treatment facility pursuant to this section for a period in excess of five years. Upon successful completion of the required residential treatment program, the person shall complete the period of special probation, as authorized by subsection a. of this section, with credit for time served for any imprisonment served as a condition of probation and credit for each day during which the person satisfactorily complied with the terms and conditions of special probation while committed pursuant to this section to a residential treatment facility. Except as otherwise provided in subsection l. of this section, the person shall not be eligible for early discharge of special probation pursuant to N.J.S.2C:45–2, or any other provision of the law. The court, in determining the number of credits for time spent in residential treatment, shall consider the recommendations of the treatment provider. A person placed into a residential treatment facility pursuant to this section shall be deemed to be subject to official detention for the purposes of N.J.S.2C:29–5 (escape).

e. The probation department or other appropriate agency designated by the court to monitor or supervise the person's special probation shall report periodically to the court as to the person's progress in treatment and compliance with court-imposed terms and conditions. The treatment provider shall promptly report to the probation department or other appropriate agency all significant failures by the person to comply with any court imposed term or condition of special probation or any requirements of the course of treatment, including but not limited to a positive drug or alcohol test or the unexcused failure to attend any session or activity, and shall immediately report any act that would constitute an escape. The probation department or other appropriate agency shall immediately notify the court and the prosecutor in the event that the person refuses to submit to a periodic drug or alcohol test or for any reason terminates his participation in the course of treatment, or commits any act that would constitute an escape.

f. (1) Upon a first violation of any term or condition of the special probation authorized by this section or of any requirements of the course of treatment, the court in its discretion may permanently revoke the person's special probation.

(2) Upon a second or subsequent violation of any term or condition of the special probation authorized by this section or of any requirements of the course of treatment, the court shall, subject only to the provisions of subsection g. of this section, permanently revoke the person's special probation unless the court finds on the record that there is a substantial likelihood that the person will successfully complete the treatment program if permitted to continue on special probation, and the court is clearly convinced, considering the nature and seriousness of the violations, that no danger to the community will result from permitting the person to continue on special probation pursuant to this section. The court's determination to permit the person to continue on special probation following a second or subsequent violation pursuant to this paragraph may be appealed by the prosecution.

(3) In making its determination whether to revoke special probation, and whether to overcome the presumption of revocation established in paragraph (2) of this subsection, the court shall consider the nature and seriousness of the present infraction and any past infractions in relation to the person's overall progress in the course of treatment, and shall also consider the recommendations of the treatment provider. The court shall give added weight to the treatment provider's recommendation that the person's special probation be permanently revoked, or to the treatment provider's opinion that the person is not amenable to treatment or is not likely to complete the treatment program successfully.

(4) If the court permanently revokes the person's special probation pursuant to this subsection, the court shall impose any sentence that might have been imposed, or that would have been required to be imposed, originally for the offense for which the person was convicted or adjudicated delinquent. The court shall conduct a de novo review of any aggravating and mitigating factors present at the time of both original sentencing and resentencing. If the court determines or is required pursuant to any other provision of this chapter or any other law to impose a term of imprisonment, the person shall receive credit for any time served in custody pursuant to N. J.S.2C:45–1 or while awaiting placement in a treatment facility pursuant to this section, and for each day during which the person satisfactorily complied with the terms and conditions of special probation while committed pursuant to this section to a residential treatment facility. The court, in determining the number of credits for time spent in a residential treatment facility, shall consider the recommendations of the treatment provider.

(5) Following a violation, if the court permits the person to continue on special probation pursuant to this section, the court shall order the person to comply with such additional terms and conditions, including but not limited to more frequent drug or alcohol testing, as are

necessary to deter and promptly detect any further violation.

(6) Notwithstanding any other provision of this subsection, if the person at any time refuses to undergo urine testing for drug or alcohol usage as provided in subsection a. of this section, the court shall, subject only to the provisions of subsection g. of this section, permanently revoke the person's special probation. Notwithstanding any other provision of this section, if the person at any time while committed to the custody of a residential treatment facility pursuant to this section commits an act that would constitute an escape, the court shall forthwith permanently revoke the person's special probation.

(7) An action for a violation under this section may be brought by a probation officer or prosecutor or on the court's own motion. Failure to complete successfully the required treatment program shall constitute a violation of the person's special probation. A person who fails to comply with the terms of his special probation pursuant to this section and is thereafter sentenced to imprisonment in accordance with this subsection shall thereafter be ineligible for entry into the Intensive Supervision Program, provided however that this provision shall not affect the person's eligibility for entry into the Intensive Supervision Program for a subsequent conviction.

g. When a person on special probation is subject to a presumption of revocation on a second or subsequent violation pursuant to paragraph (2) of subsection f. of this section, or when the person refuses to undergo drug or alcohol testing pursuant to paragraph (6) of subsection f. of this section, the court may, in lieu of permanently revoking the person's special probation, impose a term of incarceration for a period of not less than 30 days nor more than six months, after which the person's term of special probation pursuant to this section may be reinstated. In determining whether to order a period of incarceration in lieu of permanent revocation pursuant to this subsection, the court shall consider the recommendations of the treatment provider with respect to the likelihood that such confinement would serve to motivate the person to make satisfactory progress in treatment once special probation is reinstated. This disposition may occur only once with respect to any person unless the court is clearly convinced that there are compelling and extraordinary reasons to justify reimposing this disposition with respect to the person. Any such determination by the court to reimpose this disposition may be appealed by the prosecution. Nothing in this subsection shall be construed to limit the authority of the court at any time during the period of special probation to order a person on special probation who is not subject to a presumption of revocation pursuant to paragraph (2) of subsection f. of this section to be incarcerated over the course of a weekend, or for any other reasonable period of time, when the court in its discretion determines that

such incarceration would help to motivate the person to make satisfactory progress in treatment.

h. The court, as a condition of its order, and after considering the person's financial resources, shall require the person to pay that portion of the costs associated with his participation in any rehabilitation program, nonresidential treatment program or period of residential treatment imposed pursuant to this section which, in the opinion of the court, is consistent with the person's ability to pay, taking into account the court's authority to order payment or reimbursement to be made over time and in installments.

i. The court shall impose, as a condition of the special probation, any fine, penalty, fee or restitution applicable to the offense for which the person was convicted or adjudicated delinquent.

j. Where the court finds that a person has satisfied all of the eligibility criteria for special probation and would otherwise be required to be committed to the custody of a residential treatment facility pursuant to the provisions of subsection d. of this section, the court may temporarily suspend imposition of all or any portion of the term of commitment to a residential treatment facility and may instead order the person to enter a nonresidential treatment program, provided that the court finds on the record that:

(1) the person conducting the diagnostic assessment required pursuant to paragraph (1) of subsection a. of this section has recommended in writing that the proposed course of nonresidential treatment services is clinically appropriate and adequate to address the person's treatment needs; and

(2) no danger to the community would result from the person participating in the proposed course of nonresidential treatment services; and

(3) a suitable treatment provider is able and has agreed to provide clinically appropriate nonresidential treatment services.

If the prosecutor objects to the court's decision to suspend the commitment of the person to a residential treatment facility pursuant to this subsection, the sentence of special probation imposed pursuant to this section shall not become final for ten days in order to permit the appeal by the prosecution of the court's decision.

After a period of six months of nonresidential treatment, if the court, considering all available information including but not limited to the recommendation of the treatment provider, finds that the person has made satisfactory progress in treatment and that there is a substantial likelihood that the person will successfully complete the nonresidential treatment program and period of special probation, the court, on notice to the prosecutor, may permanently suspend the commitment of the person to the custody of a residential treatment program, in which event the special monitoring provisions set forth in subsection k. of this section shall no longer apply.

Nothing in this subsection shall be construed to limit the authority of the court at any time during the term of special probation to order the person to be committed to a residential or nonresidential treatment facility if the court determines that such treatment is clinically appropriate and necessary to address the person's present treatment needs.

k. (1) When the court temporarily suspends the commitment of the person to a residential treatment facility pursuant to subsection j. of this section, the court shall, in addition to ordering participation in a prescribed course of nonresidential treatment and any other appropriate terms or conditions authorized or required by law, order the person to undergo urine testing for drug or alcohol use not less than once per week unless otherwise ordered by the court. The court-ordered testing shall be conducted by the probation department or the treatment provider. The results of all tests shall be reported promptly to the court and to the prosecutor. In addition, the court shall impose appropriate curfews or other restrictions on the person's movements, and may order the person to wear electronic monitoring devices to enforce such curfews or other restrictions as a condition of special probation.

(2) The probation department or other appropriate agency shall immediately notify the court and the prosecutor in the event that the person fails or refuses to submit to a drug or alcohol test, knowingly defrauds the administration of a drug test, terminates his participation in the course of treatment, or commits any act that would constitute absconding from parole. If the person at any time while entered in a nonresidential treatment program pursuant to subsection j. of this section knowingly defrauds the administration of a drug test, goes into hiding or leaves the State with a purpose of avoiding supervision, the court shall permanently revoke the person's special probation.

l. If the court finds that the person has made exemplary progress in the course of treatment, the court may, upon recommendation of the person's supervising probation officer or on the court's own motion, and upon notice to the prosecutor, grant early discharge from a term of special probation provided that the person: (1) has satisfactorily completed the treatment program ordered by the court; (2) has served at least two years of special probation; (3) did not commit a substantial violation of any term or condition of special probation, including but not limited to a positive urine test, within the preceding 12 months; and (4) is not likely to relapse or commit an offense if probation supervision and related services are discontinued.

L.1987, c. 106, § 1, operative July 9, 1987. Amended by L.1999, c. 376, § 2, eff. Jan. 14, 2000; L.2001, c. 129, § 2, eff. June 29, 2001; L.2008, c. 15, § 1, eff. Aug. 1, 2008.

2C:35–15.   Mandatory drug enforcement and demand reduction penalties; collection; disposition; suspension

a. (1) In addition to any disposition authorized by this title, the provisions of section 24 of P.L.1982, c. 77 (C.2A:4A–43), or any other statute indicating the dispositions that can be ordered for an adjudication of delinquency, every person convicted of or adjudicated delinquent for a violation of any offense defined in this chapter or chapter 36 of this title shall be assessed for each such offense a penalty fixed at:

(a) $3,000.00 in the case of a crime of the first degree;

(b) $2,000.00 in the case of a crime of the second degree;

(c) $1,000.00 in the case of a crime of the third degree;

(d) $750.00 in the case of a crime of the fourth degree;

(e) $500.00 in the case of a disorderly persons or petty disorderly persons offense.

(2) A person being sentenced for more than one offense set forth in subsection a. of this section who is neither placed in supervisory treatment pursuant to this section nor ordered to perform reformative service pursuant to subsection f. of this section may, in the discretion of the court, be assessed a single penalty applicable to the highest degree offense for which the person is convicted or adjudicated delinquent, if the court finds that the defendant has established the following:

(a) the imposition of multiple penalties would constitute a serious hardship that outweighs the need to deter the defendant from future criminal activity; and

(b) the imposition of a single penalty would foster the defendant's rehabilitation.

Every person placed in supervisory treatment pursuant to the provisions of N.J.S.2C:36A–1 or N.J.S.2C:43–12 for a violation of any offense defined in this chapter or chapter 36 of this title shall be assessed the penalty prescribed herein and applicable to the degree of the offense charged, except that the court shall not impose more than one such penalty regardless of the number of offenses charged. If the person is charged with more than one offense, the court shall impose as a condition of supervisory treatment the penalty applicable to the highest degree offense for which the person is charged.

All penalties provided for in this section shall be in addition to and not in lieu of any fine authorized by law or required to be imposed pursuant to the provisions of N.J.S.2C:35–12.

b. All penalties provided for in this section shall be collected as provided for collection of fines and restitutions in section 3 of P.L.1979, c. 396 (C.2C:46–4), and shall be forwarded to the Department of the Treasury as provided in subsection c. of this section.

c. All moneys collected pursuant to this section shall be forwarded to the Department of the Treasury to be deposited in a nonlapsing revolving fund to be known as the "Drug Enforcement and Demand Reduction Fund." Moneys in the fund shall be appropriated by the Legislature on an annual basis for the purposes of funding in the following order of priority: (1) the Alliance to Prevent Alcoholism and Drug Abuse and its administration by the Governor's Council on Alcoholism and Drug Abuse; (2) the "Alcoholism and Drug Abuse Program for the Deaf, Hard of Hearing and Disabled" established pursuant to section 2 of P.L.1995, c. 318 (C.26:2B–37); (3) the "Partnership for a Drug Free New Jersey," the State affiliate of the "Partnership for a Drug Free America"; and (4) other alcohol and drug abuse programs.

Moneys appropriated for the purpose of funding the "Alcoholism and Drug Abuse Program for the Deaf, Hard of Hearing and Disabled" shall not be used to supplant moneys that are available to the Department of Health and Senior Services as of the effective date of P.L.1995, c. 318 (C.26:2B–36 et al.), and that would otherwise have been made available to provide alcoholism and drug abuse services for the deaf, hard of hearing and disabled, nor shall the moneys be used for the administrative costs of the program.

d. (Deleted by amendment, P.L.1991, c. 329).

e. The court may suspend the collection of a penalty imposed pursuant to this section; provided the person is ordered by the court to participate in a drug or alcohol rehabilitation program approved by the court; and further provided that the person agrees to pay for all or some portion of the costs associated with the rehabilitation program. In this case, the collection of a penalty imposed pursuant to this section shall be suspended during the person's participation in the approved, court-ordered rehabilitation program. Upon successful completion of the program, as determined by the court upon the recommendation of the treatment provider, the person may apply to the court to reduce the penalty imposed pursuant to this section by any amount actually paid by the person for his participation in the program. The court shall not reduce the penalty pursuant to this subsection unless the person establishes to the satisfaction of the court that he has successfully completed the rehabilitation program. If the person's participation is for any reason terminated before his successful completion of the rehabilitation program, collection of the entire penalty imposed pursuant to this section shall be enforced. Nothing in this section shall be deemed to affect or suspend any other criminal sanctions imposed pursuant to this chapter or chapter 36 of this title.

f. A person required to pay a penalty under this section may propose to the court and the prosecutor a plan to perform reformative service in lieu of payment of up to one-half of the penalty amount imposed under this section. The reformative service plan option shall not be available if the provisions of paragraph (2) of subsection a. of this section apply or if the person is placed in supervisory treatment pursuant to the provisions of N.J.S.2C:36A–1 or N.J.S.2C:43–12. For purposes of this section, "reformative service" shall include training, education or work, in which regular attendance and participation is required, supervised, and recorded, and which would assist in the defendant's rehabilitation and reintegration. "Reformative service" shall include, but not be limited to, substance abuse treatment or services, other therapeutic treatment, educational or vocational services, employment training or services, family counseling, service to the community and volunteer work. For the purposes of this section, an application to participate in a court-administered alcohol and drug rehabilitation program shall have the same effect as the submission of a reformative service plan to the court.

The court, in its discretion, shall determine whether to accept the plan, after considering the position of the prosecutor, the plan's appropriateness and practicality, the defendant's ability to pay and the effect of the proposed service on the defendant's rehabilitation and reintegration into society. The court shall determine the amount of the credit that would be applied against the penalty upon successful completion of the reformative service, not to exceed one-half of the amount assessed, except that the court may, in the case of an extreme financial hardship, waive additional amounts of the penalty owed by a person who has completed a court administered alcohol and drug rehabilitation program if necessary to aid the person's rehabilitation and reintegration into society. The court shall not apply the credit against the penalty unless the person establishes to the satisfaction of the court that he has successfully completed the reformative service. If the person's participation is for any reason terminated before his successful completion of the reformative service, collection of the entire penalty imposed pursuant to this section shall be enforced. Nothing in this subsection shall be deemed to affect or suspend any other criminal sanctions imposed pursuant to this chapter or chapter 36 of this title.

Any reformative service ordered pursuant to this section shall be in addition to and not in lieu of any community service imposed by the court or otherwise required by law. Nothing in this section shall limit the court's authority to order a person to participate in any activity, program or treatment in addition to those proposed in a reformative service plan.

L.1987, c. 106, § 1, operative July 9, 1987. Amended by L.1988, c. 44, § 6, eff. June 28, 1988; L.1989, c. 51, § 16; L.1991, c. 329, § 14, eff. Dec. 23, 1991; L.1995, c. 318, § 5, eff. Jan. 5, 1996; L.1997, c. 174, § 1, eff. July 30, 1997; L.1999, c. 376, § 3, eff. Jan. 14, 2000; L.2007, c. 297, § 1, eff. April 14, 2008; L.2008, c. 15, § 2, eff. Aug. 1, 2008.

2C:35–16. Forfeiture or postponement of driving privileges

a. In addition to any disposition authorized by this title, the provisions of section 24 of P.L.1982, c. 77 (C.2A:4A–43), or any other statute indicating the dispositions that can be ordered for an adjudication of delinquency, and notwithstanding the provisions of subsection c. of N.J.S. 2C:43–2, a person convicted of or adjudicated delinquent for a violation of any offense defined in this chapter or chapter 36 of this title shall forthwith forfeit his right to operate a motor vehicle over the highways of this State for a period to be fixed by the court at not less than six months or more than two years which shall commence on the day the sentence is imposed unless the court finds compelling circumstances warranting an exception. For the purposes of this section, compelling circumstances warranting an exception exist if the forfeiture of the person's right to operate a motor vehicle over the highways of this State will result in extreme hardship and alternative means of transportation are not available. In the case of a person who at the time of the imposition of sentence is less than 17 years of age, the period of any suspension of driving privileges authorized herein, including a suspension of the privilege of operating a motorized bicycle, shall commence on the day the sentence is imposed and shall run for a period as fixed by the court of not less than six months or more than two years after the day the person reaches the age of 17 years. If the driving privilege of any person is under revocation, suspension, or postponement for a violation of any provision of this title or Title 39 of the Revised Statutes at the time of any conviction or adjudication of delinquency for a violation of any offense defined in this chapter or chapter 36 of this title, any revocation, suspension, or postponement period imposed herein shall commence as of the date of termination of the existing revocation, suspension, or postponement.

b. If forfeiture or postponement of driving privileges is ordered by the court pursuant to subsection a. of this section, the court shall collect forthwith the New Jersey driver's license or licenses of the person and forward such license or licenses to the Chief Administrator of the New Jersey Motor Vehicle Commission along with a report indicating the first and last day of the suspension or postponement period imposed by the court pursuant to this section. If the court is for any reason unable to collect the license or licenses of the person, the court shall cause a report of the conviction or adjudication of delinquency to be filed with the Chief Administrator. That report shall include the complete name, address, date of birth, eye color, and sex of the person and shall indicate the first and last day of the suspension or postponement period imposed by the court pursuant to this section. The court shall inform the person orally and in writing that if the person is convicted of personally operating a motor vehicle during the period of license suspension or postponement imposed pursuant to this section, the person shall, upon conviction, be subject to the penalties set forth in R.S.39:3–40. A person shall be required to acknowledge receipt of the written notice in writing. Failure to receive a written notice or failure to acknowledge in writing the receipt of a written notice shall not be a defense to a subsequent charge of a violation of R.S.39:3–40. If the person is the holder of a driver's license from another jurisdiction, the court shall not collect the license but shall notify forthwith the Chief Administrator who shall notify the appropriate officials in the licensing jurisdiction. The court shall, however, in accordance with the provisions of this section, revoke the person's non-resident driving privilege in this State.

c. In addition to any other condition imposed, a court may in its discretion suspend, revoke or postpone in accordance with the provisions of this section the driving privileges of a person admitted to supervisory treatment under N.J.S.2C:36A–1 or N.J.S.2C:43–12 without a plea of guilty or finding of guilt.

d. After sentencing and upon notice to the prosecutor, a person subject to suspension or postponement of driving privileges under this section may seek revocation of the remaining portion of any suspension or postponement based on compelling circumstances warranting an exception that were not raised at the time of sentencing. The court may revoke the suspension or postponement if it finds compelling circumstances.

L.1987, c. 106, § 1, operative July 9, 1987. Amended by L.1988, c. 44, § 7, eff. June 28, 1988; L.2005, c. 343, § 1, eff. Jan. 12, 2006; L.2008, c. 84, § 2, eff. Sept. 10, 2008.

2C:35–16.1. Conviction of drug related offense taking place upon leased residential premises; notice to owner of premises or agent

The court in which any conviction is had or any plea of guilty entered to a charge of an offense under the "Comprehensive Drug Reform Act of 1987," N.J.S. 2C:35–1 et al., involving the use, possession, manufacture, dispensing or distribution of a controlled dangerous substance, controlled dangerous substance analog or drug paraphernalia, or in which any adjudication of juvenile delinquency is made on the basis of an act which if committed by an adult would constitute such an offense, shall ascertain whether the offense or act took place upon leased residential premises in which the defendant was a resident at the time of the offense or act, and upon ascertaining that it did so occur shall cause notice of the conviction, plea or adjudication to be forthwith transmitted to the owner of those premises or his appropriate agent.

L.1989, c. 294, § 3, eff. Jan. 12, 1990.

2C:35–17. Exception to physician-patient privilege

Information communicated to a practitioner in an effort unlawfully to obtain or procure the administration of a controlled dangerous substance or controlled substance analog shall not be a privileged communication.

L.1987, c. 106, § 1, operative July 9, 1987.

2C:35–18. Exemption; burden of proof

Text of section effective until July 1, 2010.

a. If conduct is authorized by the provisions of P.L. 1970, c. 226 (C. 24:21–1 et seq.), that authorization shall, subject to the provisions of this section, constitute an exemption from criminal liability under this chapter or chapter 36, and the absence of such authorization shall not be construed to be an element of any offense in this chapter or chapter 36. It is an affirmative defense to any criminal action arising under this chapter or chapter 36 that the defendant is the authorized holder of an appropriate registration or order form or is otherwise exempted or excepted from criminal liability by virtue of any provision of P.L. 1970, c. 226 (C. 24:21–1 et seq.). The affirmative defense established herein shall be proved by the defendant by a preponderance of the evidence. It shall not be necessary for the State to negate any exemption set forth in this act or in any provision of Title 24 of the Revised Statutes in any complaint, information, indictment or other pleading or in any trial, hearing or other proceeding under this act.

b. No liability shall be imposed by virtue of this chapter or chapter 36 upon any duly authorized State officer, engaged in the enforcement of any law or municipal ordinance relating to controlled dangerous substances or controlled substance analogs.

L.1987, c. 106, § 1, operative July 9, 1987. Amended by L.1988, c. 44, § 8, eff. June 28, 1988.

2C:35–18. Exemption; burden of proof

Text of section effective on July 1, 2010.

a. If conduct is authorized by the provisions of P.L.1970, c. 226 (C.24:21–1 et seq.) or P.L.2009, c. 307 (C.24:6I–1 et al.), that authorization shall, subject to the provisions of this section, constitute an exemption from criminal liability under this chapter or chapter 36, and the absence of such authorization shall not be construed to be an element of any offense in this chapter or chapter 36. It is an affirmative defense to any criminal action arising under this chapter or chapter 36 that the defendant is the authorized holder of an appropriate registration, permit or order form or is otherwise exempted or excepted from criminal liability by virtue of any provision of P.L.1970, c 226 (C.24:21–1 et seq.) or P.L.2009, c. 307 (C.24:6I–1 et al.). The affirmative defense established herein shall be proved by the defendant by a preponderance of the evidence. It shall not be necessary for the State to negate any exemption set forth in this act or in any provision of Title 24 of the Revised Statutes in any complaint, information, indictment or other pleading or in any trial, hearing or other proceeding under this act.

b. No liability shall be imposed by virtue of this chapter or chapter 36 upon any duly authorized State officer, engaged in the enforcement of any law or municipal ordinance relating to controlled dangerous substances or controlled substance analogs.

L.1987, c. 106, § 1, operative July 9, 1987. Amended by L.1988, c. 44, § 8, eff. June 28, 1988; L.2009, c. 307, § 12, eff. July 1, 2010.

2C:35–19. Laboratory certificates; use; admission into evidence; objections

a. The Attorney General of New Jersey may designate State Forensic Laboratories. These laboratories shall be staffed by employees of this State or any of the State's political subdivisions. In a proceeding for a violation of the provisions of chapters 35 and 36 of this title or any other statute concerning controlled dangerous substances or controlled dangerous substance analogs, a law enforcement agency may submit to one of these laboratories any substance, including, but not limited to, any substance believed to be a controlled dangerous substance or controlled substance analog thereof, or any poisons, drugs or medicines or human body tissues or fluids. The laboratory shall analyze these substances.

b. Upon the request of any law enforcement agency, the laboratory employee performing the analysis shall prepare a certificate. This employee shall sign the certificate under oath and shall include in the certificate an attestation as to the result of the analysis. The presentation of this certificate to a court by any party to a proceeding shall be evidence that all of the requirements and provisions of this section have been complied with. This certificate shall be sworn to before a notary public or other person empowered by law to take oaths and shall contain a statement establishing the following: the type of analysis performed; the result achieved; any conclusions reached based upon that result; that the subscriber is the person who performed the analysis and made the conclusions; the subscriber's training or experience to perform the analysis; and the nature and condition of the equipment used. When properly executed, the certificate shall, subject to subsection c. of this section and notwithstanding any other provision of law, be admissible evidence of the composition, quality, and quantity of the substance submitted to the laboratory for analysis, and the court shall take judicial notice of the signature of the person performing the analysis and of the fact that he is that person.

c. Whenever a party intends to proffer in a criminal or quasi-criminal proceeding, a certificate executed pursuant to this section, notice of an intent to proffer that certificate and all reports relating to the analysis in question, including a copy of the certificate, shall be conveyed to the opposing party or parties at least 20 days before the proceeding begins. An opposing party who intends to object to the admission into evidence of a certificate shall give notice of objection and the grounds for the objection within 10 days upon receiving the adversary's notice of intent to proffer the certificate. Whenever a notice of objection is filed, admissibility of the certificate shall be determined not later than two days before the beginning of the trial. A proffered certificate shall be admitted in evidence unless it appears from the notice of objection and specific grounds for that objection that the composition, quality, or quantity of the substance submitted to the laboratory for analysis will be contested at trial. A failure to comply with the time limitations regarding the notice of objection required by this section shall constitute a waiver of any objections to the admission of the certificate. The time limitations set forth in this section shall not be relaxed except upon a showing of good cause.

L.1987, c. 106, § 1, operative July 9, 1987. Amended by L.1988, c. 44, § 9, eff. June 28, 1988.

2C:35–20. Forensic laboratory fees

a. In addition to any disposition made pursuant to the provisions of N.J.S. 2C:43–2, any person convicted of an offense under this chapter shall be assessed a criminal laboratory analysis fee of $50.00 for each offense for which he was convicted. Any person who is placed in supervisory treatment pursuant to N.J.S. 2C:36A–1 or N.J.S. 2C:43–12 shall be assessed a criminal laboratory analysis fee of $50.00 for each such offense for which he was charged.

b. In addition to any other disposition made pursuant to the provisions of section 24 of P.L. 1982, c. 77 (C. 2A:4A–43) or any other statute indicating the dispositions that can be ordered for adjudications of delinquency, any juvenile adjudicated delinquent for a violation of this chapter shall be assessed a laboratory analysis fee of $25.00 for each adjudication.

c. All criminal laboratory analysis fees provided for in this section shall be collected as provided for the collection of fines and restitutions in section 3 of P.L. 1979, c. 396 (C. 2C:46–4), and shall be forwarded to the appropriate forensic laboratory fund as provided in subsection d. of this section.

d. Forensic laboratory funds shall be established as follows:

(1) Any county or municipality which maintains a publicly funded forensic laboratory that regularly employs at least one forensic chemist or scientist engaged in the analysis of controlled dangerous substances may establish a forensic laboratory fund within the office of the county or municipal treasurer.

(2) Any other county or municipality which has agreed by contract to pay or reimburse the entire salary of at least one forensic chemist or scientist employed by a laboratory designated as a State Forensic Laboratory pursuant to N.J.S. 2C:35–19, may establish a forensic laboratory fund within the office of the county or municipal treasurer.

(3) A separate account shall be established in the State Treasury and shall be designated the "State Forensic Laboratory Fund."

e. The analysis fee provided for in subsections a. and b. of this section shall be forwarded to the office of the treasurer of the county or municipality that performed the laboratory analysis if that county or municipality has established a forensic laboratory fund or, to the State forensic laboratory fund if the analysis was performed by a laboratory operated by the State. If the county or municipality has not established a forensic laboratory fund, then the analysis fee shall be forwarded to the State forensic laboratory fund within the State Treasury. If the analysis was performed by a forensic chemist or scientist whose salary was paid or reimbursed by a county or municipality pursuant to a contract, the analysis fee shall be forwarded to the appropriate forensic laboratory fund established pursuant to paragraph (2) of subsection d. of this section unless the contract provides for a different means of allocating and distributing forensic laboratory fees, in which event the terms of the contract may determine the amounts to be forwarded to each forensic laboratory fund. The county or municipal treasurer and State Treasurer may retain an amount of the total of all collected analysis fees equal to the administrative costs incurred pursuant to carrying out their respective responsibilities under this section.

f. Moneys deposited in the county or municipal forensic laboratory fund created pursuant to paragraph (1) of subsection d. of this section shall be in addition to any allocations pursuant to existing law and shall be designated for the exclusive use of the county or municipal forensic laboratory. These uses may include, but are not limited to, the following:

(1) costs incurred in providing analyses for controlled substances in connection with criminal investigations conducted within this State;

(2) purchase and maintenance of equipment for use in performing analyses; and

(3) continuing education, training and scientific development of forensic scientists regularly employed by these laboratories.

g. Moneys deposited in the State forensic laboratory fund created pursuant to paragraph (3) of subsection d. of this section shall be used by State forensic laboratories that the Attorney General designates pursuant to N.J.S. 2C:35–19, and the Division of State Police in the Department of Law and Public Safety. These moneys shall be in addition to any allocations pursuant to existing law and shall be designated for the exclusive use of State forensic facilities. These uses may include those enumerated in subsection f. of this section.

L.1987, c. 106, § 1, operative July 9, 1987. Amended by L.1988, c. 14, § 1, eff. April 7, 1988; L.1988, c. 44, § 10, eff. June 28, 1988.

2C:35–21. Seizure in violation of chapter; pretrial destruction of bulk seizures of controlled dangerous substances

Any controlled dangerous substance or controlled substance analog seized in violation of this chapter shall be subject to the forfeiture provisions of chapter 64 of this title. In any case involving a bulk seizure of a controlled dangerous substance or a controlled substance analog, a prosecuting authority, upon notice to defense counsel, may apply to the trial court for an order to destroy all or some portion of the seized substance. The State, county or municipal forensic laboratory that analyzes the substance shall make a photographic record thereof.

In the event that the defendant objects to the application to destroy all or some portion of the controlled dangerous substance or controlled substance analog, defense counsel shall within 20 days of receiving notice from the prosecuting authority serve notice of objection upon the trial judge and the prosecuting authority. The notice of objection shall include the reasons therefor. Failure to comply with the time limitations regarding the notice of objection required by this section shall constitute a waiver of any objections to the destruction of all or some portion of the substance.

The decision to order the destruction of the substance shall be vested in the sound discretion of the trial court. Prior to the issuance of any order authorizing the destruction of all or some portion of the controlled dangerous substance or controlled substance analog, and subject to reasonable supervision by laboratory or agency personnel, defense counsel shall be afforded an opportunity to inspect or test the substance.

The State, county or municipal forensic laboratory authorized to destroy all or some portion of the controlled dangerous substance or controlled substance analog shall file with the court a certificate under oath attesting to the date on which the substance was destroyed, the quantity of the substance destroyed, and the method used to destroy the substance.

Notwithstanding any other provision of law, the photographic record made in accordance with the provisions of this section, upon proper authentication, may be introduced as evidence in any court.

L.1987, c. 106, § 1, operative July 9, 1987. Amended by L.1988, c. 44, § 11, eff. June 28, 1988.

2C:35-22. Severability

If any one or more sections, clauses, sentences or parts of this chapter shall for any reason be questioned in any court, and shall be adjudged unconstitutional or invalid, the judgment shall not affect, impair or invalidate the remaining provisions thereof, but shall be confined in its operation to the specific provisions so held unconstitutional or invalid.

L.1987, c. 106, § 1, operative July 9, 1987.

2C:35-23. Pending cases

a. Except as provided in subsections b. and c. of this section, any violation of a provision of P.L.1970, c. 226 (C. 24:21-1 et seq.) which is amended or deleted by this act, and which violation was committed prior to the effective date of this chapter, shall be governed by the prior law, which is continued in effect for that purpose, as if this act were not in force.

b. Any offense defined in this act and committed on or after the effective date shall be governed by the provisions of this act. For the purposes of this section, an offense was committed after the effective date of this act if any of the elements of the offense occurred subsequent thereto.

c. In any case pending on or initiated after the effective date of this act involving an offense defined herein and committed prior to such date:

(1) N.J.S. 2C:35-19 and N.J.S. 2C:35-21 shall govern, insofar as they are justly applicable and their application does not introduce confusion or delay;

(2) The court, with the consent of the defendant, may impose sentence under the provisions of this chapter applicable to the offense and the offender;

(3) A defendant who, on the effective date of this act, has not made application for supervisory treatment under section 27 of P.L.1970, c. 226 (C. 24:21-27) shall not be eligible for supervisory treatment except pursuant to the provisions of 2C:43-12 and as provided in Chapter 36A of this title.

L.1987, c. 106, § 1, operative July 9, 1987.

2C:35-24. Possession of certain prescription drugs

A person who possesses a controlled dangerous substance that was prescribed or dispensed lawfully may possess it only in the container in which it was dispensed; except that the person may possess no more than a 10-day supply in other than the original container if the person produces, upon the request of a law enforcement officer, the name and address of the practitioner who prescribed the substance or the pharmacist who dispensed it. A person who violates this section is a disorderly person.

L.1999, c. 90, § 9, eff. May 3, 1999.

2C:35-25. Restrictions on retail sales of ephedrine products; disorderly persons offense; exceptions

a. Except as provided in subsection d. of this section, no person shall sell, offer for sale or purchase in any single retail transaction more than:

(1) three packages, or any number of packages that contain a total of nine grams, of any drug containing a sole active ingredient of ephedrine, pseudoephedrine, phenylpropanolamine, or any of their salts, optical isomers or salts of optical isomers, or

(2) three packages of any combination drug containing, as one of its active ingredients, ephedrine, pseudoephedrine, phenylpropanolamine, or any of their salts, optical isomers or salts of optical isomers, or any number of packages of such combination drug that contain a total of nine grams of ephedrine, pseudoephedrine, phenylpropanolamine, or any of their salts, optical isomers or salts of optical isomers.

b. As used in this section, "drug" has the meaning as defined in R.S.24:1–1.

c. A violation of this section is a disorderly persons offense.

d. This act shall not apply to a drug lawfully prescribed or administered by a licensed physician, veterinarian or dentist.

L.2005, c. 207, § 1, eff. Nov. 22, 2005.

2C:35–26. Reporting loss of ephedrine products to law enforcement authorities

Every pharmacy, store and other retail mercantile establishment shall promptly communicate to local law enforcement authorities the confirmed report of, or actual knowledge of, a loss of 30 or more grams of any drug containing a sole active ingredient of ephedrine, pseudoephedrine, phenylpropanolamine, or any of their salts, optical isomers or salts of optical isomers. As used in this section, "store or other retail mercantile establishment" means a place where merchandise is displayed, held, stored or sold or offered to the public for sale.

L.2005, c. 207, § 2, eff. Nov. 22, 2005.

2C:35–27. Possession of certain amounts of ephedrine products to give rise to permissive inference of purpose to create methamphetamine

Proof that a person has in his possession more than 30 grams or 10 packages of any drug containing a sole active ingredient of ephedrine, pseudoephedrine, phenylpropanolamine, or any of their salts, optical isomers or salts of optical isomers; or more than 30 grams or 10 packages of any combination drug containing, as one of its active ingredients, ephedrine, pseudoephedrine, phenylpropanolamine, or any of their salts, optical isomers or salts of optical isomers, shall give rise to a permissive inference by the trier of fact that the person acted with a purpose to create methamphetamine.

L.2005, c. 207, § 3, eff. Nov. 22, 2005.

2C:35–28. Unlawful possession of precursor with intent to manufacture methamphetamine; crime of second degree

a. Except as authorized by P.L.1970, c. 226 (C.24:21–1 et seq.), a person is guilty of the crime of unlawful possession of a precursor if the person knowingly or purposely possesses anhydrous ammonia with intent to unlawfully manufacture methamphetamine or any of its analogs.

b. Except as authorized by P.L.1970, c. 226 (C.24:21–1 et seq.), a person is guilty of the crime of unlawful possession of a precursor if the person knowingly or purposely possesses phenylalanine with intent to unlawfully manufacture methamphetamine or amphetamine or any of their analogs.

c. Except as authorized by P.L.1970, c. 226 (C.24:21–1 et seq.), a person is guilty of the crime of

unlawful possession of a precursor if the person knowingly or purposely possesses, with intent to manufacture a controlled dangerous substance or controlled substance analog, any of the following:

(1) carbamide (urea) and propanedioc and malonic acid or its derivatives;

(2) ergot or an ergot derivative and diethylamine or dimethyl-formamide or diethylamide;

(3) phenylacetone (1–phenyl–2 propanone);

(4) pentazocine and methyliodid;

(5) phenylacetonitrile and dichlorodiethyl methylamine or dichlorodiethyl benzylamine;

(6) diephenylacetonitrile and dimethylaminoisopropyl chloride;

(7) piperidine and cyclohexanone and bromobenzene and lithium or magnesium; or

(8) 2, 5–dimethoxy benzaldehyde and nitroethane and a reducing agent.

d. (1) Except as authorized by P.L.1970, c. 226 (C.24:21–1 et seq.), a person is guilty of the crime of unlawful possession of a precursor if the person, with intent to unlawfully manufacture methamphetamine, knowingly or purposely possesses ephedrine (including its salts, isomers or salts of isomers), norpseudoephedrine (including its salts, isomers or salts of isomers), n-methylephedrine (including its salts, isomers or salts of isomers), n-methylpseudoephedrine (including its salts, isomers or salts of isomers), or pseudoephedrine (including its salts, isomers or salts of isomers).

(2) Proof that a person in possession of any of the substances enumerated in paragraph (1) of this subsection at the same time also possesses any of the following substances shall give rise to a permissive inference by the trier of fact that the person acted with intent to unlawfully manufacture methamphetamine:

(a) amorphous (red) phosphorus or white phosphorus;

(b) hydroiodic acid;

(c) anhydrous ammonia;

(d) sodium;or

(e) lithium.

Unlawful possession of a precursor in violation of this section is a crime of the second degree.

L.2005, c. 207, § 5, eff. Nov. 22, 2005.

2C:35–29. Industrial use chemicals; exclusion from definition of controlled substance under certain conditions

a. For the purposes of this section:

"Finished product" means a product: (1) that does not contain an industrial use chemical or from which an industrial chemical cannot be readily extracted or readily synthesized and (2) which is not sold for human consumption.

"Industrial distribution" means any process or operation necessary for distributing an industrial product, including, but not limited to, wholesaling, delivery or transport, and storage.

"Industrial product" means a non-drug, non-controlled finished product that is not for human consumption.

"Industrial use chemical" means gamma butyrolactone or 1,4–butanedoil.

"Industrial use chemical manufacturer" means a person who: (1) is involved in the manufacture of an industrial chemical for use in the manufacture of an industrial product; (2) provides that industrial use chemical to an industrial use chemical distributor or a manufacturer of an industrial product; and (3) is in compliance with any requirements to register with the United States Drug Enforcement Administration as a List I Chemical registrant.

"Industrial use chemical distributor" means a person who: (1) is involved in the industrial distribution of an industrial use chemical; and (2) is in compliance with any requirements to register with the United States Drug Enforcement Administration as a List I Chemical registrant.

"Manufacturer of an industrial product" means a person who is involved in any process or operation necessary for manufacturing an industrial product in which that person acquires an industrial use chemical from an industrial use chemical manufacturer or an industrial use chemical distributor and who possesses that substance solely for use in the manufacture of an industrial product.

b.   An industrial use chemical shall not be deemed a controlled dangerous substance within the meaning of N.J.S.2C:35–2 when that substance is in the possession of:

(1) An industrial use chemical manufacturer;

(2) An industrial use chemical distributor;

(3) A manufacturer of an industrial product; or

(4) A person possessing a finished product.

c.   This section shall not apply to:

(1) An industrial use chemical manufacturer who sells, delivers or otherwise distributes an industrial use chemical to a person who is not an industrial use chemical distributor or a manufacturer of an industrial product;

(2) An industrial use chemical distributor who sells, delivers or otherwise distributes an industrial use chemical to a person who is not an industrial use chemical distributor or a manufacturer of an industrial product;

(3) A person who extracts or synthesizes an industrial use chemical from a finished product or a person who extracts or synthesizes an industrial use chemical from any product or material, unless that extraction or synthesis is authorized by law; or

(4) A person whose possession of an industrial use chemical is not in compliance with the provisions of subsection b. of this section or whose possession of that substance is not specifically authorized by law.

d.   (1) There shall be a permissive inference that a person to whom an industrial use chemical is sold, delivered or otherwise distributed in a quantity of 10 gallons or less is not an industrial use chemical distributor or a manufacturer of an industrial product.

(2) There shall be a permissive inference that a person who possesses an industrial use chemical in a quantity of one gallon or less is not an industrial use chemical manufacturer, an industrial use chemical distributor, a manufacturer of an industrial product or a person possessing a finished product, and is a person whose possession of the industrial use chemical is not specifically authorized by law.

(3) The inferences established in paragraphs (1) and (2) of this subsection shall not apply to the distribution or possession of sample quantities for the purpose of conducting chemical research, chemical quality assurance testing or industrial product or applications development.

L.2007, c. 152, § 1, eff. Dec. 1, 2007.

CHAPTER 35A

ANTI–DRUG PROFITEERING

Section
2C:35A–1.   Short title.
2C:35A–2.   Declaration of policy and legislative findings.
2C:35A–3.   Criteria for imposition of anti-drug profiteering penalty.
2C:35A–4.   Calculation of anti-drug profiteering penalty.
2C:35A–5.   Revocation or reduction of penalty assessment.
2C:35A–6.   Payment schedule.
2C:35A–7.   Relation to other dispositions.
2C:35A–8.   Collection and distribution.

2C:35A–1.   Short title

This act shall be known and may be cited as the "Anti–Drug Profiteering Act."

L.1997, c. 187, § 2, eff. Aug. 4, 1997.

2C:35A–2.   Declaration of policy and legislative findings

The Legislature hereby finds and declares the following:

a.   Persons who engage in drug trafficking activities for profit are a form of professional criminal, and deserve enhanced punishment that is specially adapted to remove the economic incentives inherent in such criminal activities.

b. It shall be the overriding objective of the provisions of this chapter to eliminate to the greatest extent possible the economic incentives inherent in commercial drug distribution activities at all levels within the drug distribution chain. In order to accomplish this objective, it is appropriate to impose stern economic sanctions in the form of monetary penalties against certain convicted drug offenders. So as to ensure that such economic sanctions are specially adapted and proportionate to the true nature, extent and profitability of the specific criminal activities involved, such monetary penalties should in appropriate cases be based upon a multiple of the street level value of all the illicit substances involved. The use of such a mechanism for calculating an appropriate monetary penalty will help to offset and overcome the perception of some drug offenders, and especially those who are well insulated within a drug trafficking network, that they face only a comparatively low risk of immediate detection and punishment. The Legislature, by adoption of the "Comprehensive Drug Reform Act," N.J.S.2C:35–1 et al., recognized the utility of such a mechanism by providing for the imposition of discretionary cash fines which may be based upon three, or in some cases five, times the street value of the illicit drugs involved.

c. The imposition of monetary penalties pursuant to this act is intended to serve as an adjunct to forfeiture actions, which are designed to deprive offenders of the proceeds of their criminal activities and of all property used in furtherance of or to facilitate such illegal activities. While the seizure and forfeiture of property in accordance with the provisions of chapters 41 and 64 of this Title and P.L.1994, c. 121 (money laundering) remain a critically important means by which to reduce the economic incentive inherent in drug trafficking activities, in many instances, given the efforts undertaken by offenders to conceal and disguise assets and to resort to complex financial transactions and money laundering schemes, it has become increasingly difficult for law enforcement agencies to establish to the required degree of certainty that a given asset or interest in property is subject to forfeiture. Accordingly, it is necessary and appropriate to impose an in personam debt against the defendant which may be satisfied by proceeding against any asset or interest in property belonging to the defendant, whether or not such property can be directly or indirectly linked to criminal activity.

d. In order to ensure the maximum deterrent effect of imposing such specially adapted economic sanctions as are required pursuant to the provisions of this act, it shall be the policy of this State to enforce the judgment and to collect the entire debt, or the greatest possible portion thereof, as soon as is feasible following the imposition of the penalty, taking full advantage, where necessary, of this State's long arm jurisdiction and the full faith and credit clause of the Constitution of the United States.

L.1997, c. 187, § 2, eff. Aug. 4, 1997.

2C:35A–3. Criteria for imposition of anti-drug profiteering penalty.

a. In addition to any other disposition authorized by this title, including but not limited to any fines which may be imposed pursuant to the provisions of N.J.S.2C:43–3 and except as may be provided by section 5 of this chapter, where a person has been convicted of a crime defined in chapter 35 or 36 of this Title or any crime involving criminal street gang related activity as defined in subsection h. of N.J.S.2C:44–3 or an attempt or conspiracy to commit such a crime, the court shall, upon the application of the prosecutor, sentence the person to pay a monetary penalty in an amount determined pursuant to section 4 of this chapter, provided the court finds at a hearing, which may occur at the time of sentencing, that the prosecutor has established by a preponderance of the evidence one or more of the grounds specified in this section. The findings of the court shall be incorporated in the record, and in making its findings, the court shall take judicial notice of any evidence, testimony or information adduced at the trial, plea hearing or other court proceedings and shall also consider the presentence report and any other relevant information.

b. Any of the following shall constitute grounds for imposing an Anti–Drug Profiteering Penalty:

(1) The defendant was convicted of: (a) a violation of N.J.S.2C:35–3 (leader of narcotics trafficking network), or (b) a violation of subsection g. of N.J.S.2C:5–2 (leader of organized crime), or (c) an offense defined in chapter 41 of this Title (racketeering) which involved the manufacture, distribution, possession with intent to distribute or transportation of any controlled dangerous substance or controlled substance analog.

(2) The defendant is a drug profiteer. A defendant is a drug profiteer when the conduct constituting the crime shows that the person has knowingly engaged in the illegal manufacture, distribution or transportation of any controlled dangerous substance, controlled substance analog or drug paraphernalia as a substantial source of livelihood. In making its determination, the court may consider all of the attending circumstances, including but not limited to the defendant's role in the criminal activity, the nature, amount and purity of the substance involved, the amount of cash or currency involved, the extent and accumulation of the defendant's assets during the course of the criminal activity and the defendant's net worth and his expenditures in relation to his legitimate sources of income.

(3) The defendant is a wholesale drug distributor. (a) A defendant is a wholesale drug distributor when the conduct constituting the crime involves the manufacture, distribution or intended or attempted distribution of a controlled dangerous substance or controlled substance analog to any other person for pecuniary gain, knowing, believing, or under circumstances where it reasonably could be assumed that such other person would in turn distribute the substance to another or

others for pecuniary gain. It shall not be necessary for the prosecution to establish to whom the substance was distributed or intended or attempted to be distributed, and the court may draw all reasonable inferences from the nature of the defendant's conduct and the substance involved that such other person, while not specifically identified, would in turn distribute the substance to another or others for pecuniary gain. In making its determination, the court shall consider all of the attending circumstances, including but not limited to the defendant's role in the criminal activity, the nature, amount and purity of the substance involved, and the likelihood that a substance of such purity would be intended to be distributed directly to the ultimate consumer of the substance.

(b) Notwithstanding that the prosecutor has established that the defendant is a wholesale drug distributor within the meaning of this paragraph, the court shall not impose an anti-drug profiteering penalty on that ground if the defendant establishes by a preponderance of the evidence at the hearing that his participation in the conduct constituting the crime was limited solely to operating a conveyance used to transport a controlled dangerous substance or controlled substance analog, or loading or unloading the substance into such a conveyance or storage facility. Nothing in this paragraph shall be construed to establish a basis for not imposing a penalty where the prosecutor has established any other ground or grounds specified in this section for the imposition of an anti-drug profiteering penalty.

(4) The defendant is a professional drug distributor. A professional drug distributor is a person who has at any time, for pecuniary gain, unlawfully distributed a controlled dangerous substance, controlled substance analog or drug paraphernalia to three or more different persons, or on five or more separate occasions regardless of the number of persons to whom the substance or paraphernalia was distributed.

(5) The defendant was involved in criminal street gang related activity.

c. In making its determination, the court may rely upon expert opinion in the form of live testimony or by affidavit, or by such other means as the court deems appropriate.

d. For the purposes of this chapter, an act is undertaken for pecuniary gain if it involves or contemplates the transfer of anything of value in exchange for a controlled dangerous substance, controlled substance analog or drug paraphernalia, provided that the thing of value received or intended to be received in exchange for the substance or paraphernalia is or was reasonably believed to be of a higher value than that expended by the defendant or by any other person with whom the actor is acting in concert, to acquire or manufacture the substance or paraphernalia. It shall also include any act which would constitute a violation of subsection a. of N.J.S.2C:35–5, N.J.S.2C:35–11, N.J.S.2C:36–3 or any other crime for which the actor was paid or expected to

be paid in return for performing such act, or from which the actor received a benefit for himself or another or injured another or deprived another of a benefit. There shall be a rebuttable presumption at the hearing that any manufacturing, distribution or possession with intent to distribute which contemplates or involves the payment or exchange of anything of value constitutes an act undertaken for pecuniary gain. It shall not be necessary for the prosecution to establish that any intended profit or payment was actually received; nor shall it be relevant that the act, payment in return for such act or the transfer of anything of value in exchange for the substance or paraphernalia, occurred or was intended to occur in another jurisdiction.

L.1997, c. 187, § 2, eff. Aug. 4, 1997. Amended by L.1999, c. 160, § 2, eff. July 8, 1999.

2C:35A–4. Calculation of anti-drug profiteering penalty.

a. Where the prosecutor has established one or more grounds for imposing an Anti–Drug Profiteering Penalty pursuant to section 3 of this chapter, the court shall assess a monetary penalty as follows:

(1) $200,000.00 in the case of a crime of the first degree; $100,000.00 in the case of a crime of the second degree; $50,000.00 in the case of a crime of the third degree; $25,000.00 in the case of a crime of the fourth degree;

(2) an amount equal to three times the street value of all controlled dangerous substances or controlled substance analogs involved, or three times the market value of all drug paraphernalia involved, if this amount is greater than that provided in paragraph (1) of this subsection; or

(3) an amount equal to three times the value of any benefit illegally obtained by the actor for himself or another, or any injury to or benefit deprived of another.

b. When the court is for any reason unable to determine the amount of the penalty pursuant to paragraph (2) of subsection a., the court shall assess a penalty in the amount appropriate to the degree of the offense as provided in paragraph (1) of subsection a.

c. In determining the street value of the substance involved or the market value of drug paraphernalia involved, the court shall take into account all amounts of the substance or paraphernalia reasonably believed to have been involved in the course of the criminal activity in which the defendant knowingly participated, and it shall not be relevant for the purposes of this section that some of those amounts or paraphernalia were involved in acts or transactions which occurred, or which were intended to occur, in another jurisdiction.

d. Where the prosecution requests that the court assess a penalty in an amount calculated pursuant to paragraph (2) or (3) of subsection a., the prosecutor shall have the burden of establishing by a preponderance of the evidence the appropriate amount of the penalty to be assessed pursuant to that paragraph. In making its finding, the court shall take judicial notice of any evidence, testimony or information adduced at trial, plea hearing or other court proceedings and shall also consider the presentence report and other relevant information, including expert opinion in the form of live testimony or by affidavit. The court's findings shall be incorporated in the record, and such findings shall not be subject to modification by an appellate court except upon a showing that the finding was totally lacking support in the record or was arbitrary and capricious.

L.1997, c. 187, § 2, eff. Aug. 4, 1997. Amended by L.1999, c. 160, § 3, eff. July 8, 1999.

2C:35A–5. Revocation or reduction of penalty assessment

The court shall not revoke or reduce a penalty imposed pursuant to this chapter except in accordance with the provisions of N.J.S.2C:35–12. An anti-drug profiteering penalty imposed pursuant to this chapter shall not be deemed a fine for purposes of N.J.S.2C:46–3.

L.1997, c. 187, § 2, eff. Aug. 4, 1997.

2C:35A–6. Payment schedule

The court may, for good cause shown, and subject to the provisions of this section, grant permission for the payment of a penalty assessed pursuant to this chapter to be made within a specified period of time or in specified installments, provided however that the payment schedule fixed by the court shall require the defendant to pay the penalty in the shortest period of time consistent with the nature and extent of his assets and his ability to pay, and further provided that the prosecutor shall be afforded the opportunity to present evidence or information concerning the nature, extent and location of the defendant's assets or interests in property which are or might be subject to levy and execution. In such event, the court may only grant permission for the payment to be made within a specified period of time or installments with respect to that portion of the assessed penalty which would not be satisfied by the liquidation of property which is or may be subject to levy and execution, unless the court finds that the immediate liquidation of such property would result in undue hardship to innocent persons. If no permission to make payment within a specified period of time or in installments is embodied in the sentence, the entire penalty shall be payable forthwith.

L.1997, c. 187, § 2, eff. Aug. 4, 1997.

2C:35A–7. Relation to other dispositions

a. An anti-drug profiteering penalty assessed pursuant to this chapter shall be imposed and paid in addition to any penalty required to be imposed pursuant to N.J.S.2C:35–15 and N.J.S.2C:43–3.1, any fee required to be imposed pursuant to N.J.S. 2C:35–20, and any other fine, penalty, fee or order for restitution which may be imposed.

b. An anti-drug profiteering penalty imposed pursuant to this chapter shall be in addition to and not in lieu of any forfeiture or other cause of action instituted pursuant to chapter 41 or 64 of this Title, and nothing in this chapter shall be construed in any way to preclude, preempt or limit any such cause of action. A defendant shall not be entitled to receive credit toward the payment of a penalty imposed pursuant to this chapter for the value of property forfeited, or subject to forfeiture, pursuant to the provisions of chapters 41 and 64 of this Title.

L.1997, c. 187, § 2, eff. Aug. 4, 1997.

2C:35A–8. Collection and distribution

All penalties assessed pursuant to this chapter shall be docketed and collected as provided for collection of fines, penalties and restitution in chapter 46 of this Title. The Attorney General or prosecutor may prosecute an action to collect penalties imposed pursuant to this chapter. All penalties assessed pursuant to this chapter shall be disposed of, distributed, appropriated and used as if the collected penalties were the proceeds of property forfeited pursuant to chapter 64 of this Title.

L.1997, c. 187, § 2, eff. Aug. 4, 1997.

CHAPTER 35B

DRUG DEALER LIABILITY

Section
2C:35B–1.   Short title.
2C:35B–2.   Legislative findings.
2C:35B–3.   Definitions.
2C:35B–4.   Liability; damages.
2C:35B–5.   Plaintiff; recovery.
2C:35B–6.   Cause of action.
2C:35B–7.   Third party; damages; public agency.
2C:35B–8.   Controlled dangerous substances; marketing; liability.
2C:35B–9.   Plaintiffs; joinder.
2C:35B–10.   Comparative responsibility.
2C:35B–11.   Liability; contribution.
2C:35B–12.   Liability; burden of proof .
2C:35B–13.   Potential award; attachment order.
2C:35B–14.   Cause of action; accrual; statute of limitations.
2C:35B–15.   Cause of action; stay.
2C:35B–16.   Judgment; satisfaction.
2C:35B–17.   Retroactivity.

2C:35B–1. Short title

This act shall be known and may be cited as the "Drug Dealer Liability Act."

L.2001, c. 114, § 1, eff. June 26, 2001.

2C:35B–2. Legislative findings

The Legislature finds and declares:

a. Although the criminal justice system is an important weapon in the battle against controlled dangerous substances, the civil justice system can and must also be used. The civil justice system can provide an avenue of compensation for those who have suffered harm as a result of the marketing and distribution of controlled dangerous substances. The persons who have joined the marketing of controlled dangerous substances should bear the cost of the harm caused by that market in the community.

b. The threat of liability under this act serves as an additional deterrent to a recognizable segment of the network for marketing controlled dangerous substances. Because of this threat, a person who has assets unrelated to the sale of controlled dangerous substances, who markets controlled dangerous substances at the workplace, who encourages friends to become users, is likely to decide that the added cost of entering the market is not worth the benefit. This is particularly true for a first-time, casual dealer who has not yet made substantial profits.

c. This act is intended to provide a mechanism whereby the costs of the injuries caused by illegal drug use will be borne by those who benefit from illegal drug dealing.

d. This act imposes liability against all participants in the marketing of controlled dangerous substances, including small dealers, particularly those in the workplace, who are not usually the focus of criminal investigations. Small dealers increase the number of users and ultimately are the people who become large dealers. It is these small dealers who are most likely to be deterred by the threat of liability.

L.2001, c. 114, § 2, eff. June 26, 2001.

2C:35B–3. Definitions

As used in this act:

a. "Marketing of controlled dangerous substances" means the illegal distributing, dispensing, or possessing with intent to distribute, a specified controlled dangerous substance.

b. "Individual user of controlled dangerous substance" means the individual whose illegal use of a specified controlled dangerous substance is the basis of an action brought under this act.

c. "Level 1 offense" means:

(1) possessing with intent to distribute less than four ounces of a specified controlled dangerous substance as defined in this section;

(2) distributing or dispensing less than one ounce of a specified controlled dangerous substance as defined in this section;

(3) possessing with intent to distribute 25 or more but less than 50 marijuana plants;

(4) possessing with intent to distribute less than four pounds of marijuana, or

(5) distributing or dispensing more than 28.5 grams of marijuana.

d. "Level 2 offense" means:

(1) possessing with intent to distribute four ounces or more but less than eight ounces of a specified controlled dangerous substance as defined in this section;

(2) distributing or dispensing one ounce or more but less than two ounces of a specified controlled dangerous substance as defined in this section;

(3) possessing with intent to distribute 50 or more but less than 75 marijuana plants;

(4) possessing with intent to distribute four pounds or more but less than eight pounds of marijuana, or

(5) distributing or dispensing more than one pound but less than five pounds of marijuana.

e. "Level 3 offense" means:

(1) possessing with intent to distribute eight ounces or more but less than 16 ounces of a specified controlled dangerous substance as defined in this section;

(2) distributing or dispensing two ounces or more but less than four ounces of a specified controlled dangerous substance as defined in this section;

(3) possessing with intent to distribute 75 or more but less than 100 marijuana plants;

(4) possessing with intent to distribute eight pounds or more but less than 16 pounds of marijuana, or

(5) distributing or dispensing more than five pounds but less than 10 pounds of marijuana.

f. "Level 4 offense" means:

(1) possessing with intent to distribute 16 ounces or more of a specified controlled dangerous substance as defined in this section;

(2) distributing or dispensing four ounces or more of a specified controlled dangerous substance as defined in this section;

(3) possessing with intent to distribute 100 or more marijuana plants;

(4) possessing with intent to distribute 16 pounds or more of marijuana, or

(5) distributing or dispensing more than 10 pounds of marijuana.

g. "Participate in the illegal marketing of controlled dangerous substances" means to transport, import into this State, distribute, dispense, sell, possess with intent to distribute, or offer to distribute a controlled dangerous substance, in violation of any of the provisions of chapter 35 of Title 2C of the New Jersey Statutes. "Participate in the marketing of controlled dangerous substances" does not include the purchase or receipt of a controlled dangerous substance for personal use only.

h. "Person" means any natural person, association, partnership, corporation or other entity.

i. "Period of illegal use" means, in relation to the individual user of a controlled dangerous substance, the time of the individual's first illegal use of a controlled dangerous substance to the accrual of the cause of action.

j. "Place of illegal activity" means, in relation to the individual user of a specified controlled dangerous substance, each county in which the individual illegally possess or uses a specified controlled dangerous substance.

k. "Place of participation" means, in relation to a defendant in an action brought under this act, each county in which the defendant participates in the marketing of controlled dangerous substances.

l. "Specified controlled dangerous substance" means heroin, cocaine, lysergic acid diethylamide, phencyclidine, methamphetamine, phenyl–2–propanone (P2P) and any other controlled dangerous substance specified under the provisions of N.J.S.2C:35–5 as being unlawful to manufacture, distribute, or dispense, or to possess or have under a person's control with intent to manufacture, distribute or dispense.

L.2001, c. 114, § 3, eff. June 26, 2001.

2C:35B–4. Liability; damages

A person who knowingly participates in the illegal marketing of controlled dangerous substances within this State is liable for damages, as provided in this act, for injury resulting from an individual's illegal use of a controlled dangerous substance.

L.2001, c. 114, § 4, eff. June 26, 2001.

2C:35B–5. Plaintiff; recovery

a. Any of the following persons may bring an action for damages caused by an individual's illegal use of a controlled dangerous substance:

(1) A parent, legal guardian, child, spouse, or sibling of the controlled dangerous substance user.

(2) An individual who was exposed to a controlled dangerous substance in utero.

(3) An employer of the controlled dangerous substance user.

(4) A medical facility, insurer, employer, or other nongovernmental entity that funded a drug treatment program or employee assistance program for the controlled dangerous substance user or that otherwise expended money on behalf of the controlled dangerous substance user.

(5) A person injured as a result of the reckless or negligent actions of an individual user of a controlled dangerous substance.

No public entity, and no public agency other than a public hospital, shall have a cause of action under this act.

b. A person entitled to bring an action under this act may seek damages against:

(1) A person who illegally distributed or dispensed a controlled dangerous substance to the individual user of the controlled dangerous substance; or

(2) A person who knowingly participated in the illegal marketing of controlled dangerous substances, if all of the following apply:

(a) The defendant's place of participation is situated in the same county as the individual user's place of illegal activity;

(b) The defendant participated in the marketing of the same type of controlled dangerous substances as those used by the individual user;

(c) The defendant was previously convicted of an offense in the State of New Jersey for that type of controlled dangerous substance; and

(d) The defendant participated in the marketing of controlled dangerous substances at any time during the period the individual user unlawfully used the controlled dangerous substance.

c. A person entitled to bring an action under this section may recover all of the following damages:

(1) Economic damages, including, but not limited to, the cost of treatment and rehabilitation, medical expenses, loss of economic or educational potential, lose of productivity, absenteeism, support expenses, accidents or injury, and any other pecuniary loss proximately caused by the use of a controlled dangerous substance.

(2) Noneconomic damages, including but not limited to physical and emotional pain, suffering, physical impairment, physical impairment, emotional distress, disfigurement, loss of enjoyment, loss of companionship, services and consortium, and other nonpecuniary losses proximately caused by an individual's use of a controlled dangerous substance.

(3) Punitive damages.

(4) Reasonable attorney fees.

(5) Costs of suit, including, but not limited to, reasonable expenses for expert testimony.

L.2001, c. 114, § 5, eff. June 26, 2001.

2C:35B–6. Cause of action

a. An individual user of a controlled dangerous substance may bring an action for damages caused by the use of a controlled dangerous substance only if all of the following conditions are met:

(1) The individual personally discloses to narcotics enforcement authorities all of the information known to the individual regarding all that individual's sources of controlled dangerous substances.

(2) The individual has not used a controlled dangerous substance within the 30 days before filing the action.

(3) The individual continues to remain free of the use of an illegal controlled substance throughout the pendency of the action.

b. An individual user entitled to bring an action under this section may seek damages only from a person who transported, imported into this State, distributed, dispensed, sold, possessed with intent to distribute, or offered to distribute, in violation of any of the provisions of chapter 35 of Title 2C of the New Jersey Statutes, the controlled dangerous substance actually used by the individual user of a controlled dangerous substance.

c. An individual user entitled to bring an action under this section may recover only the following damages:

(1) Economic damages, including, but not limited to, the cost of treatment, rehabilitation and medical expenses, loss of economic or educational potential, loss of productivity, absenteeism, accidents or injury, and any other pecuniary loss proximately caused by the person's use of a controlled dangerous substance.

(2) Reasonable attorney fees.

(3) Costs of suit, including, but not limited to, reasonable expenses for expert testimony.

L.2001, c. 114, § 6, eff. June 26, 2001.

2C:35B–7. Third party; damages; public agency

a. A third party shall not pay damages awarded under this act, or provide a defense or money for a defense, on behalf of an insured under a contract of insurance or indemnification.

b. A cause of action authorized pursuant to this act may not be assigned, either expressly, by subrogation, or by any other means, directly or indirectly, to any public or publicly funded agency or institution.

L.2001, c. 114, § 7, eff. June 26, 2001.

2C:35B–8. Controlled dangerous substances; marketing; liability

A person whose participation in the marketing of controlled dangerous substances is grounds for liability pursuant to this act shall be rebuttably presumed to be liable for damages incurred by the plaintiff in the following percentages:

a. For a level 1 offense, 25 percent of the damages;

b. For a level 2 offense, 50 percent of the damages;

c. For a level 3 offense, 75 percent of the damages; and

d. For a level 4 offense, 100 percent of the damages.

L.2001, c. 114, § 8, eff. June 26, 2001.

2C:35B–9. Plaintiffs; joinder

a. Two or more persons may join in one action under this act as plaintiffs if their respective actions have at least one market for controlled dangerous substances in common and if any portion of the period of use of a controlled dangerous substance overlaps with the period of use of a controlled dangerous substance for every other plaintiff.

b. Two or more persons may be joined in one action under this act as defendants if those persons are liable to at least one plaintiff.

L.2001, c. 114, § 9, eff. June 26, 2001.

2C:35B–10. Comparative responsibility

a. An action by an individual user of a controlled dangerous substance is governed by the principles of comparative responsibility. Comparative responsibility attributed to an individual user does not bar the user's recovery but diminishes the award of damages proportionately, according to the measure of responsibility attributed to the user. The burden of proving comparative responsibility is on the defendant, who shall prove comparative responsibility by clear and convincing evidence.

b. Comparative responsibility shall not be attributed to a plaintiff who is not an individual user of a controlled substance, unless that plaintiff knowingly gave the individual user money for the purchase of the controlled dangerous substance.

L.2001, c. 114, § 10, eff. June 26, 2001.

2C:35B–11. Liability; contribution

A person subject to liability under this act has a right of action for contribution against another person subject to liability under this act. Contribution may be enforced either in the original action or by a separate action brought for that purpose. A plaintiff may seek recovery in accordance with this act and other laws against a person whom a defendant has asserted a right of contribution.

L.2001, c. 114, § 11, eff. June 26, 2001.

2C:35B–12. Liability; burden of proof

a. Proof of liability in an action brought under this act shall be shown by clear and convincing evidence.

b. A person against whom recovery is sought who has been convicted of a violation of N.J.S.2C:35–5, Manufacturing, Distributing or Dispensing, or an equivalent offense under federal law or the law of any other state, is estopped from denying illegal participation in the market for controlled dangerous substances. If such conviction was based upon the same type of controlled dangerous substance as that used by the individual user, the conviction also constitutes prima facie evidence of the person's participation in the marketing of controlled dangerous substance user pursuant to this act.

c. The absence of a criminal conviction for a violation of N.J.S.2C:35–5 or an equivalent offense under federal law or the law of any other state does not bar recovery by a plaintiff bringing suit pursuant to subsection b. of section 5 of this act.

L.2001, c. 114, § 12, eff. June 26, 2001.

2C:35B–13. Potential award; attachment order

A plaintiff under this act may request an ex parte prejudgment attachment order from the court against all assets of a defendant sufficient to satisfy a potential award. Any claim of the State authorized pursuant to chapter 35A and 64 of Title 2C of the New Jersey Statutes shall have priority over an order issued pursuant to this section.

L.2001, c. 114, § 13, eff. June 26, 2001.

2C:35B–14. Cause of action; accrual; statute of limitations

a. A cause of action accrues under this act when a person has reason to know of the harm from use of a controlled dangerous substance that is the basis for the cause of action and has reason to know that the use of a controlled dangerous substance is the cause of the harm.

b. Except as provided in subsection a. of this section, a claim under this act shall not be brought more than one year after the defendant distributes, dispenses, or possesses with intent to distribute, the controlled dangerous substance or more than one year after the defendant is convicted of a crime involving controlled dangerous substances, whichever is the later.

L.2001, c. 114, § 14, eff. June 26, 2001.

2C:35B–15. Cause of action; stay

On motion by a governmental agency involved in an investigation or prosecution involving a controlled dangerous substance, an action brought under this act shall be stayed until the completion of any underlying criminal investigation or prosecution.

L.2001, c. 114, § 15, eff. June 26, 2001.

2C:35B–16. Judgment; satisfaction

Any judgment resulting from a cause of action brought pursuant to this act shall be satisfied only after the satisfaction of any assessment, fine, fee, penalty or restitution imposed by law and enumerated in section 13 of P.L. 1991, c. 329 (C.2C:46–4.1).

L.2001, c. 114, § 16, eff. June 26, 2001.

2C:35B–17. Retroactivity

No cause of action shall arise based on any act by a defendant which occurred prior to the effective date of this act.

L.2001, c. 114, § 17, eff. June 26, 2001.

CHAPTER 36

DRUG PARAPHERNALIA

Section
2C:36–1.   Drug paraphernalia, defined; determination.
2C:36–2.   Use or possession with intent to use; disorderly persons offense.
2C:36–3.   Distribute, dispense or possession with intent to distribute or manufacture; crime of fourth degree.
2C:36–4.   Advertising to promote sale; crime of fourth degree.
2C:36–5.   Delivering drug paraphernalia to person under 18 years of age; crime of third degree.
2C:36–6.   Possession or distribution of hypodermic syringe or needle.
2C:36–6a.   Exemption for participants in sterile syringe access program.
2C:36–6.1.   Discarding hypodermic needle or syringe.
2C:36–7.   Seizure in violation of chapter.
2C:36–8.   Severability.
2C:36–9.   Pending cases.
2C:36–10.   Defraud the administration of a drug test, defined; crime of third and fourth degree.

2C:36–1. Drug paraphernalia, defined; determination

As used in this act, [1] "drug paraphernalia" means all equipment, products and materials of any kind which are used or intended for use in planting, propagating, cultivating, growing, harvesting, manufacturing, compounding, converting, producing, processing, preparing, testing, analyzing, packaging, repackaging, storing, containing, concealing, ingesting, inhaling, or otherwise introducing into the human body a controlled dangerous substance , controlled substance analog or toxic chemical in violation of the provisions of chapter 35 of this title. It shall include, but not be limited to: a. kits used or intended for use in planting, propagating, cultivating, growing or harvesting of any species of plant which is a controlled dangerous substance or from which a controlled dangerous substance can be derived; b. kits used or intended for use in manufacturing, compounding, converting, producing, processing, or preparing controlled dangerous substances or controlled substance analogs; c. isomerization devices used or intended for use in increasing the potency of any species of plant which is a controlled dangerous substance; d. testing equipment used or intended for use identifying, or in analyzing the strength, effectiveness or purity of controlled dangerous substances or controlled substance analogs; e. scales and balances used or intended for use in weighing or measuring controlled dangerous substances or controlled substance analogs; f. dilutants and adulterants, such as quinine hydrochloride, mannitol, mannite, dextrose and lactose, used or intended for use in cutting controlled dangerous substances or controlled substance analogs; g. separation gins and sifters used or intended for use in removing twigs and seeds from, or in otherwise cleaning or refining, marihuana; h. blenders, bowls, containers, spoons and mixing devices used or intended for use in compounding controlled dangerous substances or controlled substance analogs; i. capsules, balloons, envelopes and other containers used or intended for use in packaging small quantities of controlled dangerous substances or controlled substance analogs; j. containers and other objects used or intended for use in storing or concealing controlled dangerous substances, controlled substance analogs or toxic chemicals; k. objects used or intended for use in ingesting, inhaling, or otherwise introducing marihuana, cocaine, hashish, hashish oil, nitrous oxide or the fumes of a toxic chemical into the human body, such as (1) metal, wooden, acrylic, glass, stone, plastic, or ceramic pipes with or without screens, permanent screens, hashish heads, or punctured metal bowls; (2) water pipes; (3) carburetion tubes and devices; (4) smoking and carburetion masks; (5) roach clips, meaning objects used to hold burning material, such as a marihuana cigarette, that has become too small or too short to be held in the hand; (6) miniature cocaine spoons, and cocaine vials; (7) chamber pipes; (8) carburetor pipes; (9) electric pipes; (10) air-driven pipes; (11) chillums; (12) bongs; (13) ice pipes or chillers; (14) compressed gas containers, such as tanks, cartridges or canisters, that contain food grade or pharmaceutical grade nitrous oxide as a principal ingredient; (15) chargers or charging bottles, meaning metal, ceramic or plastic devices that contain an interior pin that may be used to expel compressed gas from a cartridge or canister; and (16) tubes, balloons, bags, fabrics, bottles or other containers used to concentrate or hold in suspension a toxic chemical or the fumes of a toxic chemical.

In determining whether or not an object is drug paraphernalia, the trier of fact, in addition to or as part of the proofs, may consider the following factors: a. statements by an owner or by anyone in control of the object concerning its use; b. the proximity of the object of illegally possessed controlled dangerous substances, controlled substance analogs or toxic chemicals; c. the existence of any residue of illegally possessed controlled dangerous substances, controlled substance analogs or toxic chemicals on the object; d. direct or circumstantial evidence of the intent of an owner, or of anyone in control of the object, to deliver it to persons whom he knows intend to use the object to facilitate a violation of this act; the innocence of an owner, or of anyone in control of the object, as to a direct violation of this act shall not prevent a finding that the object is intended for use as drug paraphernalia; e. instructions, oral or written, provided with the object concerning its use; f. descriptive materials accompanying the object which explain or depict its use; g. national or local advertising whose purpose the person knows or should know is to promote the sale of objects intended for use as drug paraphernalia; h. the manner in which the object is displayed for sale; i. the existence and scope of legitimate uses for the object in the community; and j. expert testimony concerning its use.

L.1987, c. 106, § 2, operative July 9, 1987. Amended by L.2007, c. 31, § 2, eff. Jan. 29, 2007.

  ¹ L.1987, c. 106.

2C:36–2. Use or possession with intent to use; disorderly persons offense

It shall be unlawful for any person to use, or to possess with intent to use, drug paraphernalia to plant, propagate, cultivate, grow, harvest, manufacture, compound, convert, produce, process, prepare, test, analyze, pack, repack, store, contain, conceal, ingest, inhale, or otherwise introduce into the human body a controlled dangerous substance, controlled substance analog or toxic chemical in violation of the provisions of chapter 35 of this title. Any person who violates this section is guilty of a disorderly persons offense.

L.1987, c. 106, § 2, operative July 9, 1987. Amended by L.2007, c. 31, § 3, eff. Jan. 29, 2007.

2C:36–3. Distribute, dispense or possession with intent to distribute or manufacture; crime of fourth degree

It shall be unlawful for any person to distribute or dispense, or possess with intent to distribute or dispense, or manufacture with intent to distribute or dispense, drug paraphernalia, knowing that it will be used to plant, propagate, cultivate, grow, harvest, manufacture, compound, convert, produce, process, prepare, test, analyze, pack, repack, store, contain, conceal, ingest, inhale or otherwise introduce into the human body a controlled dangerous substance, controlled substance analog or toxic chemical in violation of the provisions of chapter 35 of this title. Any person who violates this section commits a crime of the fourth degree.

L.1987, c. 106, § 2, operative July 9, 1987. Amended by L.2007, c. 31, § 4, eff. Jan. 29, 2007.

2C:36–4. Advertising to promote sale; crime of fourth degree

It shall be unlawful for any person to place in any newspaper, magazine, handbill, or other publication any advertisement, knowing that the purpose of the advertisement in whole or in part, is to promote the sale of objects intended for use as drug paraphernalia. Any person who violates this section commits a crime of the fourth degree.

L.1987, c. 106, § 2, operative July 9, 1987.

2C:36–5. Delivering drug paraphernalia to person under 18 years of age; crime of third degree

Any person 18 years of age or over who violates N.J.S. 2C:36–3 by delivering drug paraphernalia to a person under 18 years of age commits a crime of the third degree.

L.1987, c. 106, § 2, operative July 9, 1987.

2C:36–6. Possession or distribution of hypodermic syringe or needle

a. Except as authorized by subsection b., c. or other law, it shall be unlawful for a person to have under his control or possess with intent to use a hypodermic syringe, hypodermic needle or any other instrument adapted for the use of a controlled dangerous substance or a controlled substance analog as defined in chapter 35 of Title 2C of the New Jersey Statutes or to sell, furnish or give to any person such syringe, needle or instrument. Any person who violates this section is guilty of a disorderly persons offense.

b. A person is authorized to possess and use a hypodermic needle or hypodermic syringe if the person obtains the hypodermic syringe or hypodermic needle by a valid prescription issued by a licensed physician, dentist or veterinarian and uses it for its authorized purpose. No prescription for a hypodermic syringe, hypodermic needle or any other instrument adapted for the use of controlled dangerous substances by subcutaneous injections shall be valid for more than one year from date of issuance.

c. Subsection a. does not apply to a duly licensed physician, dentist, veterinarian, undertaker, nurse, podiatrist, registered pharmacist, or a hospital, sanitarium, clinical laboratory or any other medical institution, or a state or a governmental agency, or a regular dealer in medical, dental or surgical supplies, or a resident physician or intern of a hospital, sanitarium or other medical institution.

L.1987, c. 106, § 2, operative July 9, 1987. Amended by L.1999, c. 90, § 2, eff. May 3, 1999.

2C:36–6a. Exemption for participants in sterile syringe access program

The possession of a hypodermic syringe or needle by a consumer who participates in, or an employee or volunteer of, a sterile syringe access program established pursuant to sections 3 and 4 of P.L.2006, c. 99 (C.26:5C–27 and C.26:5C–28) shall not constitute an offense pursuant to N.J.S.2C:36–1 et seq. This provision shall extend to a hypodermic syringe or needle that contains a residual amount of a controlled dangerous substance or controlled substance analog.

L.2006, c. 99, § 8, eff. Dec. 19, 2006.

2C:36–6.1. Discarding hypodermic needle or syringe

a. A person commits a petty disorderly persons offense if:

(1) the person discards, in a place accessible to other persons, a hypodermic needle or syringe without destroying the hypodermic needle or syringe; or

(2) he is the owner, lessee or person in control of real property and, knowing that needles and syringes in an intact condition have been discarded or abandoned on his real property, allows them to remain.

b. A hypodermic needle is destroyed if the needle is broken from the hub or mangled. A syringe is destroyed if the nipple of the barrel is broken from the barrel, or the plunger and barrel are melted. Alternatively, a hypodermic needle or syringe is destroyed if it is discarded as a single unit, without recapping, into a rigid container and the container is destroyed by grinding or crushing in a compactor, or by burning in an incinerator approved by the Department of Environmental Protection, or by another method approved by the Department of Health and Senior Services.

L.1999, c. 90, § 6, eff. May 3, 1999.

2C:36–7. Seizure in violation of chapter

Any drug paraphernalia, hypodermic syringe or needle seized in violation of this chapter shall be subject to the forfeiture provisions of Chapter 64 of this title.

L.1987, c. 106, § 2, operative July 9, 1987.

2C:36–8. Severability

If any provision of this chapter or the application thereof to any person or circumstance are [1] held invalid, the invalidity shall not affect other provisions or applications of the sections which can be given effect without the invalid provision or application, and to this end the provisions of this chapter are severable.

L.1987, c. 106, § 2, operative July 9, 1987.

[1] So in original. Probably should read "is".

2C:36–9. Pending cases

Notwithstanding any other provision of this act, the provisions of P.L.1970, c. 226 (C. 24:21–1 et seq.) shall remain in full force and effect as to any offense committed prior to the effective date of this act.

L.1987, c. 106, § 2, operative July 9, 1987.

2C:36–10. Defraud the administration of a drug test, defined; crime of third and fourth degree

a. As used in this act, "defraud the administration of a drug test" means to submit a substance that purports to be from a person other than its actual source, or purports to have been excreted or collected at a time other than when it was actually excreted or collected, or to otherwise engage in conduct intended to produce a false or misleading outcome of a test for the presence of a chemical, drug or controlled dangerous substance, or a metabolite of a drug or controlled dangerous substance, in the human body. It shall specifically include, but shall not be limited to, the furnishing of urine with the purpose that the urine be submitted for urinalysis as a true specimen of a person.

b. Any person who offers for sale or rental, or who manufactures, sells, transfers, or gives to any person, any instrument, tool, device or substance adapted, designed or commonly used to defraud the administration of a drug test, is guilty of a crime of the third degree.

c. Any person who knowingly defrauds the administration of a drug test that is administered as a condition of employment or continued employment as a law enforcement officer, corrections officer, school bus driver, operator of a motorbus, employee of a rail passenger service, firefighter, provider of emergency first-aid or medical services, or any other occupation that requires the administration of a drug test as a condition of employment or continued employment by law, rule or regulation of the State or a local agency, public authority, or the federal government, is guilty of a crime of the third degree.

d. Any person who knowingly defrauds the administration of a drug test that is administered as a condition of monitoring a person on bail, in custody or on parole, probation or pretrial intervention, or any other form of supervision administered in connection with a criminal offense or juvenile delinquency matter, is guilty of a crime of the third degree.

e. Any person who knowingly possesses any instrument, product, tool, device or substance adapted, designed or commonly used to defraud the administration of a drug test is guilty of a crime of the fourth degree.

f. Any person who knowingly defrauds the administration of a drug test which is administered as a condition of any employment or continued employment not specified in subsection c. of this section is guilty of a crime of the fourth degree.

L.2002, c. 60, § 1, eff. Aug. 3, 2002.

CHAPTER 36A

CONDITIONAL DISCHARGE FOR CERTAIN FIRST OFFENDERS

Section
2C:36A–1. Conditional discharge for certain first offenses; expunging of records.

2C:36A–1. Conditional discharge for certain first offenses; expunging of records

a. Whenever any person who has not previously been convicted of any offense under section 20 of P.L.1970, c. 226 (C.24:21–20), or a disorderly persons or petty disorderly persons offense defined in chapter 35 or 36 of this title or, subsequent to the effective date of this title, under any law of the United States, this State or any other state relating to marijuana, or stimulant, depressant, or hallucinogenic drugs, is charged with or convicted of any disorderly persons offense or petty disorderly persons offense under chapter 35 or 36 of this title, the court upon notice to the prosecutor and subject to subsection c. of this section, may on motion of the defendant or the court:

(1) Suspend further proceedings and with the consent of the person after reference to the State Bureau of Identification criminal history record information files, place him under supervisory treatment upon such reasonable terms and conditions as it may require; or

(2) After plea of guilty or finding of guilty, and without entering a judgment of conviction, and with the consent of the person after proper reference to the State Bureau of Identification criminal history record information files, place him on supervisory treatment upon reasonable terms and conditions as it may require, or as otherwise provided by law.

b. In no event shall the court require as a term or condition of supervisory treatment under this section, referral to any residential treatment facility for a period exceeding the maximum period of confinement prescribed by law for the offense for which the individual has been charged or convicted, nor shall any term of supervisory treatment imposed under this subsection exceed a period of three years. If a person is placed under supervisory treatment under this section after a plea of guilty or finding of guilt, the court as a term and condition of supervisory treatment shall suspend the person's driving privileges for a period to be fixed by the court at not less than six months or more than two years unless the court finds compelling circumstances warranting an exception. For the purposes of this subsection, compelling circumstances warranting an exception exist if the suspension of the person's driving privileges will result in extreme hardship and alternative means of transportation are not available. In the case of a person who at the time of placement under supervisory treatment under this section is less than 17 years of age, the period of suspension of driving privileges authorized herein, including a suspension of the privilege of operating a motorized bicycle, shall commence on the day the person is placed on supervisory treatment and shall run for a period as fixed by the court of not less than six months or more than two years after the day the person reaches the age of 17 years.

If the driving privilege of a person is under revocation, suspension, or postponement for a violation of this title or Title 39 of the Revised Statutes at the time of the person's placement on supervisory treatment under this section, the revocation, suspension or postponement period imposed herein shall commence as of the date of the termination of the existing revocation, suspension or postponement. The court which places a person on supervisory treatment under this section shall collect and forward the person's driver's license to the New Jersey Motor Vehicle Commission and file an appropriate report with the commission in accordance with the procedure set forth in N.J.S.2C:35–16. The court shall also inform the person of the penalties for operating a motor vehicle during the period of license suspension or postponement as required in N.J.S.2C:35–16.

Upon violation of a term or condition of supervisory treatment the court may enter a judgment of conviction and proceed as otherwise provided, or where there has been no plea of guilty or finding of guilty, resume proceedings. Upon fulfillment of the terms and conditions of supervisory treatment the court shall terminate the supervisory treatment and dismiss the proceedings against him. Termination of supervisory treatment and dismissal under this section shall be without court adjudication of guilt and shall not be deemed a conviction for purposes of disqualifications or disabilities, if any, imposed by law upon conviction of a crime or disorderly persons offense but shall be reported by the clerk of the court to the State Bureau of Identification criminal history record information files. Termination of supervisory treatment and dismissal under this section may occur only once with respect to any person. Imposition of supervisory treatment under this section shall not be deemed a conviction for the purposes of determining whether a second or subsequent offense has occurred under section 29 of P.L.1970, c. 226 (C.24:21–29), chapter 35 or 36 of this title or any law of this State.

c.   Proceedings under this section shall not be available to any defendant unless the court in its discretion concludes that:

(1) The defendant's continued presence in the community, or in a civil treatment center or program, will not pose a danger to the community; or

(2) That the terms and conditions of supervisory treatment will be adequate to protect the public and will benefit the defendant by serving to correct any dependence on or use of controlled substances which he may manifest; and

(3) The person has not previously received supervisory treatment under section 27 of P.L.1970, c. 226 (C.24:21–27), N.J.S.2C:43–12, or the provisions of this chapter.

d.   A person seeking conditional discharge pursuant to this section shall pay to the court a fee of $75. The court shall forward all money collected under this subsection to the treasurer of the county in which the court is located. This money shall be used to defray the cost of juror compensation within that county. A person may apply for a waiver of this fee, by reason of poverty, pursuant to the Rules Governing the Courts of the State of New Jersey. Of the moneys collected under this subsection, $30 of each fee shall be deposited in the temporary reserve fund created by section 25 of P.L.1993, c. 275.[1] After December 31, 1994, the $75 fee shall be paid to the court, for use by the State.

L.1987, c. 106, § 3, operative July 9, 1987. Amended by L.1988, c. 44, § 12, eff. June 28, 1988; L.1993, c. 275, § 14, eff. Jan. 5, 1994; L.2008, c. 84, § 1, eff. Sept. 10, 2008.

[1] Temporary and executed.

CHAPTER 37

GAMBLING OFFENSES

Section
2C:37–1.   Definitions.
2C:37–2.   Promoting gambling.
2C:37–3.   Possession of gambling records.
2C:37–4.   Maintenance of a gambling resort.
2C:37–4.1.   Shipboard gambling; applicability.
2C:37–5.   Gambling offenses; presumption.
2C:37–6.   Lottery offenses; no defense.
2C:37–6.1.   Lottery equipment or advice for out of state
                  utilization; manufacture, sale and transport;

Section
                  inapplicability of law providing penalty or dis-
                  ability.
2C:37–7.   Possession of a gambling device.
2C:37–8.   Gambling offenses; jurisdiction.
2C:37–9.   Nonapplicability.

2C:37–1. Definitions

The following definitions apply to this chapter and to chapter 64:

a. "Contest of chance" means any contest, game, pool, gaming scheme or gaming device in which the outcome depends in a material degree upon an element of chance, notwithstanding that skill of the contestants or some other persons may also be a factor therein.

b. "Gambling" means staking or risking something of value upon the outcome of a contest of chance or a future contingent event not under the actor's control or influence, upon an agreement or understanding that he will receive something of value in the event of a certain outcome.

c. "Player" means a person who engages in any form of gambling solely as a contestant or bettor, without receiving or becoming entitled to receive any profit therefrom other than personal gambling winnings, and without otherwise rendering any material assistance to the establishment, conduct or operation of the particular gambling activity. A person who gambles at a social game of chance on equal terms with the other participants therein does not thereby render material assistance to the establishment, conduct or operation of such game if he performs, without fee or remuneration, acts directed toward the arrangement or facilitation of the game, such as inviting persons to play, permitting the use of premises therefor or supplying cards or other equipment used therein. A person who engages in "bookmaking" as defined in this section is not a "player."

d. "Something of value" means any money or property, any token, object or article exchangeable for money or property, or any form of credit or promise directly or indirectly contemplating transfer of money or property or of any interest therein, or involving extension of a service, entertainment or a privilege of playing at a game or scheme without charge. This definition, however, does not include any form of promise involving extension of a privilege of playing at a game without charge on a mechanical or electronic amusement device, other than a slot machine as an award for the attainment of a certain score on that device.

e. "Gambling device" means any device, machine, paraphernalia or equipment which is used or usable in the playing phases of any gambling activity, whether such activity consists of gambling between persons or gambling by a person involving the playing of a machine. Notwithstanding the foregoing, lottery tickets, policy slips and other items used in the playing phases of lottery and policy schemes are not gambling devices.

f. "Slot machine" means any mechanical, electrical or other device, contrivance or machine which, upon insertion of a coin, token or similar object therein, or upon payment of any consideration whatsoever, is available to play or operate, the play or operation of which, whether by reason of the skill of the operator or application of the element of chance, or both, may deliver or entitle the person playing or operating the machine to receive cash or tokens to be exchanged for cash, whether the payoff is made automatically from the machine or in any other manner whatsoever. A device so constructed, or readily adaptable or convertible to such use, is no less a slot machine because it is not in working order or because some mechanical act of manipulation or repair is required to accomplish its adaptation, conversion or workability.

g. "Bookmaking" means advancing gambling activity by unlawfully accepting bets from members of the public upon the outcome of future contingent events as a business.

h. "Lottery" means an unlawful gambling scheme in which (a) the players pay or agree to pay something of value for chances, represented and differentiated by numbers or by combinations of numbers or by some other media, one or more of which chances are to be designated the winning ones; and (b) the winning chances are to be determined by a drawing or by some other method based upon the element of chance; and (c) the holders of the winning chances are to receive something of value.

i. "Policy" or "the numbers game" means a form of lottery in which the winning chances or plays are not determined upon the basis of a drawing or other act on the part of persons conducting or connected with the scheme, but upon the basis of the outcome or outcomes of a future contingent event or events otherwise unrelated to the particular scheme.

j. "Gambling resort" means a place to which persons may resort for engaging in gambling activity.

k. "Unlawful" means not specifically authorized by law.

L.1978, c. 95, § 2C:37-1, eff. Sept. 1, 1979. Amended by L.1979, c. 176, § 4, eff. Sept. 1, 1979; L.1982, c. 60, § 1, eff. July 8, 1982.

2C:37-2. Promoting gambling

a. Promoting Gambling Defined. A person is guilty of promoting gambling when he knowingly:

(1) Accepts or receives money or other property, pursuant to an agreement or understanding with any person whereby he participates or will participate in the proceeds of gambling activity; or

(2) Engages in conduct, which materially aids any form of gambling activity. Such conduct includes but is not limited to conduct directed toward the creation or establishment of the particular game, contest, scheme, device or activity involved, toward the acquisition or maintenance of premises, paraphernalia, equipment or apparatus therefor, toward the solicitation or inducement of persons to participate therein, toward the actual conduct of the playing phases thereof, toward the arrangement of any of its financial or recording phases, or toward any other phase of its operation.

b. Grading. A person who violates the provisions of subsection a. by:

(1) Engaging in bookmaking to the extent he receives or accepts in any one day more than five bets totaling more than $1,000.00; or

(2) Receiving, in connection with a lottery or policy scheme or enterprise (a) money or written records from a person other than a player whose chances or plays are represented by such money or records, or (b) more than $100.00 in any one day of money played in such scheme or enterprise, is guilty of a crime of the third degree and notwithstanding the provisions of section 2C:43-3 shall be subject to a fine of not more than $35,000.00 and any other appropriate disposition authorized by N.J.S.2C:43-2b.

A person who violates the provisions of subsection a. by engaging in bookmaking to the extent he receives or accepts three or more bets in any two–week period is guilty of a crime of the fourth degree and notwithstanding the provisions of section 2C:43-3 shall be subject to a fine of not more than $25,000.00 and any other appropriate disposition authorized by N.J.S.2C:43-2b. Otherwise, promoting gambling is a disorderly persons offense and notwithstanding the provisions of section 2C:43-3 shall be subject to a fine of not more than $10,000.00 and any other appropriate disposition authorized by N.J.S.2C:43-2b.

c. It is a defense to a prosecution under subsection a. that the person participated only as a player. It shall be the burden of the defendant to prove by clear and convincing evidence his status as such player.

L.1978, c. 95, § 2C:37-2, eff. Sept. 1, 1979. Amended by L.1979, c. 178, § 69, eff. Sept. 1, 1979; L.1997, c. 181, § 9, eff. Aug. 1, 1997.

2C:37-3. Possession of gambling records

a. A person is guilty of possession of gambling records when, with knowledge of the contents thereof, he possesses any writing, paper, instrument or article:

(1) Of a kind commonly used in the operation or promotion of a bookmaking scheme or enterprise, including any paper or paper product in sheet form chemically converted to nitrocellulose having explosive characteristics as well as any water soluble paper or paper derivative in sheet form; or

(2) Of a kind commonly used in the operation, promotion or playing of a lottery or policy scheme or enterprise.

b. Defenses.

(1) It is a defense to a prosecution under subsection a. (2) which must be proven by the defendant by clear and convincing evidence that the writing, paper, instrument or article possessed by the defendant constituted, reflected or represented plays, bets or chances of the defendant himself in a number not exceeding 10.

(2) It is a defense to a prosecution under subsection a. which must be proven by the defendant by clear and convincing evidence that the writing, paper, instrument or article possessed by the defendant was neither used nor intended to be used in the operation or promotion of a bookmaking scheme or enterprise, or in the operation, promotion or playing of a lottery or policy scheme or enterprise.

c. Grading. Possession of gambling records is a crime of the third degree and notwithstanding the provisions of section 2C:43–3 shall be subject to a fine of not more than $35,000.00 and any other appropriate disposition authorized by N.J.S.2C:43–2b. when the writing, paper, instrument or article:

(1) In a bookmaking scheme or enterprise, constitute, reflect or represent more than five bets totaling more than $1,000.00; or

(2) In the case of a lottery or policy scheme or enterprise, constitute, reflect or represent more than one hundred plays or chances therein.

Otherwise, possession of gambling records is a disorderly persons offense and notwithstanding the provisions of section 2C:43–3 shall be subject to a fine of not more than $20,000.00 and any other appropriate disposition authorized by N.J.S.2C:43–2b.

L.1978, c. 95, § 2C:37–3, eff. Sept. 1, 1979. Amended by L.1979, c. 178, § 70, eff. Sept. 1, 1979; L.1997, c. 181, § 10, eff. Aug. 1, 1997.

2C:37–4. Maintenance of a gambling resort

a. A person is guilty of a crime of the fourth degree if, having substantial proprietary or other authoritative control over premises which are being used with his knowledge for purposes of activities prohibited by N.J.S.2C:37–2 and N.J.S.2C:37–3, he permits such to occur or continue or makes no effort to prevent its occurrence or continuation and he accepts or receives money or other property pursuant to an agreement or understanding with any person whereby he participates or will participate in the proceeds of such gambling activity on such premises and notwithstanding the provisions of section 2C:43–3 shall be subject to a fine of not more than $25,000.00 and any other appropriate disposition authorized by N.J.S.2C:43–2b.

b. A person is guilty of a crime of the fourth degree if, having substantial proprietary or other authoritative control over premises open to the general public which are being used with his knowledge for purposes of gambling activity, he permits such to occur or continue or makes no effort to prevent its occurrence or continuation and notwithstanding the provisions of section 2C:43–3 shall be subject to a fine of not more than

$25,000.00 and any other appropriate disposition authorized by N.J.S.2C:43–2b.

L.1978, c. 95, § 2C:37–4, eff. Sept. 1, 1979. Amended by L.1979, c. 178, § 71, eff. Sept. 1, 1979; L.1997, c. 181, § 11, eff. Aug. 1, 1997.

2C:37–4.1. Shipboard gambling; applicability

a. A person is guilty of shipboard gambling when the person:

(1) knowingly causes, engages in or permits any gambling activity prohibited under N.J.S.2C:37–2, 2C:37–3 or 2C:37–4 to be conducted on a vessel that embarks from any point within the State, and disembarks at the same or another point within the State, whether the gambling activity is conducted within or without the waters of the State; or

(2) manages, supervises, controls, operates or owns any vessel that embarks from any point within the State, and disembarks at the same or another point within the State, during which time the person knowingly causes or permits any gambling activity prohibited under this chapter, whether the gambling activity is conducted within or without the waters of the State.

b. Any person who violates the provisions of subsection a. of this section is guilty of a crime of the same degree as the most serious crime that was committed in violation of N.J.S.2C:37–2, 2C:37–3 or 2C:37–4, as appropriate.

c. This section shall not apply to gambling activity conducted on United States-flagged or foreign-flagged vessels during travel from a foreign nation or another state or possession of the United States up to the point of first entry into New Jersey waters or during travel to a foreign nation or another state or possession of the United States from the point of departure from New Jersey waters, provided that nothing herein shall preclude prosecution for any other offense under this chapter.

L.1999, c. 263, § 1, eff. Oct. 26, 1999.

2C:37–5. Gambling offenses; presumption

In any prosecution under this article in which it is necessary to prove the occurrence of a sporting event, a published report of its occurrence in any daily newspaper, magazine or other periodically printed publication of general circulation shall be admissible in evidence and shall constitute presumptive proof of the occurrence of such event.

L.1978, c. 95, § 2C:37–5, eff. Sept. 1, 1979.

2C:37–6. Lottery offenses; no defense

Any offense defined in this article which consists of the commission of acts relating to a lottery is no less criminal because the lottery itself is drawn or conducted without the State. This section shall not apply to any person who has in his possession or custody any paper, document, slip or memorandum of a lottery which is authorized, sponsored and operated by any state of the United States, provided that the paper, document, slip or memorandum was purchased by the holder thereof in the State wherein such lottery was authorized, sponsored and operated.

L.1978, c. 95, § 2C:37–6, eff. Sept. 1, 1979.

2C:37–6.1. Lottery equipment or advice for out of state utilization; manufacture, sale and transport; inapplicability of law providing penalty or disability

No law providing any penalty or disability for the sale of lottery tickets or any acts done in connection with a lottery shall apply to the rendering of consultation or advice in connection with a lottery, or the manufacturing, processing, selling, possessing or transporting of equipment, tickets or materials, for use or designed for use in a lottery, if such lottery is (a) conducted by a state of the United States and such equipment, tickets or materials are for shipment out of this State to addresses within such state, or (b) not violative of the laws of a foreign country in which it is conducted or intended to be conducted and such equipment, tickets or materials are for shipment to foreign countries to persons or entities that can lawfully use such materials. For purposes of this section, "foreign country" means any empire, country, dominion, colony or protectorate, or any subdivision or subdivisions thereof (other than the United States and its possessions).

L.1979, c. 129, § 2, eff. Sept. 1, 1979.

2C:37–7. Possession of a gambling device

A person except a player is guilty of possession of a gambling device when, with knowledge of the character thereof, he manufactures, sells, transports, places or possesses, or conducts or negotiates any transaction affecting or designed to affect ownership, custody or use of:

    a.   A slot machine; or

    b.   Any other gambling device, believing that the same is to be used in the advancement of unlawful gambling activity.

Possession of a gambling device other than under such circumstances as would constitute a violation of section 116 of the "Casino Control Act" (P.L.1977, c. 110; C. 5:12–1 et seq.) is a disorderly persons offense; provided, however, that possession of not more than one gambling device other than a slot machine for social use within the home shall not be an offense under this section; and provided further, however, that possession of one or more antique slot machines shall not be an offense under this section or under section 116 of the "Casino Control Act" (P.L.1977, c. 110; C. 5:12–1 et seq.). As used in this section, "antique slot machine" means a slot machine which was manufactured prior to 1941. Nothing herein contained shall be construed to

authorize the use of an antique slot machine for any unlawful purpose or for gaming.

L.1978, c. 95, § 2C:37–7, eff. Sept. 1, 1979. Amended by L.1979, c. 176, § 2, eff. Sept. 1, 1979.

2C:37–8. Gambling offenses; jurisdiction

All offenses under this chapter shall be prosecuted in the Superior Court.

L.1978, c. 95, § 2C:37–8, eff. Sept. 1, 1979. Amended by L.1979, c. 178, § 72, eff. Sept. 1, 1979.

2C:37–9. Nonapplicability

Nothing in this chapter shall be construed to prohibit any activity authorized by the "Casino Control Act" (P.L.1977, c. 110; C. 5:12–1 et seq.), or to supersede any provision of said act.

L.1978, c. 95, § 2C:37–9, eff. Sept. 1, 1979. Amended by L.1979, c. 176, § 3, eff. Sept. 1, 1979.

CHAPTER 38

SEPTEMBER 11TH, 2001 ANTI–TERRORISM ACT

Section
2C:38–1.   Short title.
2C:38–2.   Terrorism; other crimes; definitions; sentence.
2C:38–3.   Producing or possessing chemical weapons, biological agents or nuclear or radiological devices; definitions; sentence.
2C:38–4.   Hindering apprehension, detention or prosecution of another for terrorism.
2C:38–5.   Soliciting or providing material support or resources for terrorism; definitions.

2C:38–1. Short title

Sections 1 through 5 of this act shall be known and may be cited as the "September 11th, 2001 Anti–Terrorism Act."

L.2002, c. 26, § 1, eff. June 18, 2002.

2C:38–2. Terrorism; other crimes; definitions; sentence

    a.   A person is guilty of the crime of terrorism if he commits or attempts, conspires or threatens to commit any crime enumerated in subsection c. of this section with the purpose:

    (1) to promote an act of terror; or

    (2) to terrorize five or more persons; or

    (3) to influence the policy or affect the conduct of government by terror; or

    (4) to cause by an act of terror the impairment or interruption of public communications, public transportation, public or private buildings, common carriers, public utilities or other public services.

    b.   Terrorism is a crime of the first degree.

(1) Notwithstanding any other provision of law to the contrary, any person convicted under this section shall be sentenced to a term of 30 years, during which the person shall not be eligible for parole, or to a specific term of years which shall be between 30 years and life imprisonment, of which the person shall serve not less than 30 years before being eligible for parole.

(2) If a violation of this section results in death, the person shall be sentenced to a term of life imprisonment, during which time the person shall not be eligible for parole.

c. The crimes encompassed by this section are: murder pursuant to N.J.S.2C:11–3; aggravated manslaughter or manslaughter pursuant to N.J.S.2C:11–4; vehicular homicide pursuant to N.J.S.2C:11–5; aggravated assault pursuant to subsection b. of N.J.S.2C:12–1; disarming a law enforcement officer pursuant to section 1 of P.L.1996, c. 14 (C.2C:12–11); kidnapping pursuant to N.J.S.2C:13–1; criminal restraint pursuant to N.J.S.2C:13–2; robbery pursuant to N.J.S.2C:15–1; carjacking pursuant to section 1 of P.L.1993, c. 221 (C.2C:15–2); aggravated arson or arson pursuant to N.J.S.2C:17–1; causing or risking widespread injury or damage pursuant to N.J.S.2C:17–2; damage to nuclear plant with the purpose to cause or threat to cause release of radiation pursuant to section 1 of P.L.1983, c. 480 (C.2C:17–7); damage to nuclear plant resulting in death by radiation pursuant to section 2 of P.L.1983, c. 480 (C.2C:17–8); damage to nuclear plant resulting in injury by radiation pursuant to section 3 of P.L.1983, c. 480 (C.2C:17–9); producing or possessing chemical weapons, biological agents or nuclear or radiological devices pursuant to section 3 of P.L.2002, c. 26 (C.2C:38–3); burglary pursuant to N.J.S.2C:18–2; possession of prohibited weapons and devices pursuant to N.J.S.2C:39–3; possession of weapons for unlawful purposes pursuant to N.J.S.2C:39–4; unlawful possession of weapons pursuant to N.J.S.2C:39–5; weapons training for illegal activities pursuant to section 1 of P.L.1983, c. 229 (C.2C:39–14); racketeering pursuant to N.J.S.2C:41–1 et seq.; and any other crime involving a risk of death or serious bodily injury to any person.

d. Definitions. For the purposes of this section:

"Government" means the United States, any State, county, municipality, or other political unit, or any department, agency or subdivision of any of the foregoing, or any corporation or other association carrying out the functions of government.

"Serious bodily injury" means bodily injury which creates a substantial risk of death or which causes serious, permanent disfigurement, or protracted loss or impairment of the function of any bodily member or organ.

"Terror" means the menace or fear of death or serious bodily injury.

"Terrorize" means to convey the menace or fear of death or serious bodily injury by words or actions.

e. A prosecution pursuant to this section may be brought by the Attorney General, his assistants and deputies within the Division of Criminal Justice, or by a county prosecutor or a designated assistant prosecutor if the county prosecutor is expressly authorized in writing by the Attorney General to prosecute a violation of this section.

f. Notwithstanding the provisions of N.J.S.2C:1–8 or any other provision of law, a conviction of terrorism under this section shall not merge with a conviction of any other offense, nor shall such other conviction merge with a conviction under this section, and the court shall impose separate sentences upon each violation of this section and any other offense.

g. Nothing contained in this section shall be deemed to preclude, if the evidence so warrants, an indictment and conviction for murder under the provisions of N.J.S.2C:11–3 or any other offense.

L.2002, c. 26, § 2, eff. June 18, 2002.

2C:38–3. Producing or possessing chemical weapons, biological agents or nuclear or radiological devices; definitions; sentence

a. A person who, purposely or knowingly, unlawfully develops, produces, otherwise acquires, transfers, receives, stockpiles, retains, owns, possesses or uses, or threatens to use, any chemical weapon, biological agent, toxin, vector or delivery system for use as a weapon, or nuclear or radiological device commits a crime of the first degree, except that:

(1) Notwithstanding any other provision of law to the contrary, any person convicted under this subsection shall be sentenced to a term of 30 years, during which the person shall not be eligible for parole, or to a specific term of years which shall be between 30 years and life imprisonment, of which the person shall serve not less than 30 years before being eligible for parole.

(2) If a violation of this section results in death, the person shall be sentenced to a term of life imprisonment, during which time the person shall not be eligible for parole.

b. Any manufacturer, distributor, transferor, possessor or user of any toxic chemical, biological agent, toxin or vector, or radioactive material that is related to a lawful industrial, agricultural, research, medical, pharmaceutical or other activity, who recklessly allows an unauthorized individual to obtain access to the toxic chemical or biological agent, toxin or vector or radioactive material, commits a crime of the second degree and, notwithstanding the provisions of subsection a. of N.J.S.2C:43–3, shall be subject to a fine of up to $250,000 for each violation.

c. For the purposes of this section:

(1) "Chemical weapon" means:

(a) a toxic chemical and its precursors, except where intended for a lawful purpose as long as the type and quantity is consistent with such a purpose. "Chemical weapon" shall include, but not be limited to:

(i) nerve agents, including GA (Tabun) cyanide irreversible inhibitor, Sarin (GB), GB (Soman) fluorine, reversible "slow aging," GF, and VX sulfur, irreversible;

(ii) choking agents, including Phosgene (CG) and Diphosgene (DP);

(iii) blood agents, including Hydrogen Cyanide (AC), Cyanogen Chloride (CK), and Arsine (SA); and

(iv) blister agents, including mustards (H, HD {sulfur mustard}, HN–1, HN–2, HN–3 {nitrogen mustard}), arsenicals, such as Lewisite (L), and urticants, including CX; and

(v) incapacitating agents, including BZ; or

(b) a munition or device specifically designed to cause death or other harm through the toxic properties of those chemical weapons defined in subparagraph (a) of paragraph (1) of subsection c. of this section, which would be released as a result of the employment of such munition or device; or

(c) any equipment specifically designed for use directly in connection with the employment of munitions or devices specified in subparagraph (b) of paragraph (1) of subsection c. of this section.

(2) "Biological agent" means any microorganism, virus, bacteria, rickettsiae, fungi, toxin, infectious substance or biological product that may be engineered as a result of biotechnology, or any naturally occurring or bioengineered component of any such microorganism, virus, bacteria, rickettsiae, fungi, infectious substance or biological product, capable of causing:

(a) death, disease, or other biological malfunction in a human, an animal, a plant, or another living organism; or

(b) deterioration of food, water, equipment, supplies, or material of any kind; or

(c) deleterious alteration of the environment.

"Biological agent" shall include, but not be limited to: viruses, including Crimean–Congo hemorrhagic fever virus, eastern equine encephalitis virus, ebola viruses, equine morbilli virus, lassa fever virus, Marburg virus, Rift Valley fever virus, South American hemorrhagic fever viruses (Junin, Machupo, Sabia, Flexal, Guanarito), tick-borne encephalitis complex viruses, variola major virus (smallpox virus), Venezuelan equine encephalitis virus, viruses causing hantavirus pulmonary syndrome, and yellow fever virus; bacteria including Bacillus anthracis (commonly known as anthrax), Brucella abortus, Brucella melitensis, Brucella suis, Burkholderia (pseudomonas) mallei, Burkholderia (pseudomonas) pseudomallei, Clostridium botulinum, Francisella tularensis, Yersinia pestis (commonly known as plague); rickettsiae, including Coxiella burnetii, Rickettsia prowazekii and Rickettsia rickettsii; Coccidioides immitis fungus; and toxins, including abrin, aflatoxins, Botulinum toxins, Clostridium per-ringes epsilon toxin, conotoxins, diacetoxyscirpenol, ricin, saxitoxin, shigatoxin, Staphylococcal enterotoxins, tetrodotoxins and T–2 toxin.

(3) "Toxin" means the toxic material of plants, animals, microorganisms, viruses, fungi, or infectious substances, or a recombinant molecule, whatever its origin or method of production, including:

(a) any poisonous substance or biological product that may be engineered as a result of biotechnology or produced by a living organism; or

(b) any poisonous isomer or biological product, homolog, or derivative of such a substance.

(4) "Vector" means a living organism or molecule, including a recombinant molecule, or biological product that may be engineered as a result of biotechnology, capable of carrying a biological agent or toxin to a host.

(5) "Nuclear or radiological device" includes: (a) any nuclear device which is an explosive device designed to cause a nuclear yield; (b) a radiological dispersal device which is an explosive device used to spread radioactive material; or (c) a simple radiological dispersal device which is any act, container or any other device used to release radiological material for use as a weapon.

(6) "Delivery system" means any apparatus, equipment, device, or means of delivery specifically designed to deliver or disseminate a biological agent, toxin or vector.

(7) "For use as a weapon" means all situations in which the circumstances indicate that the person intended to employ an item's ready capacity of lethal use or of inflicting serious bodily injury.

d. This section shall not apply to the development, production, acquisition, transfer, receipt, possession or use of any toxic chemical, biological agent, toxin or vector that is related to a lawful industrial, agricultural, research, medical, pharmaceutical, or other activity.

e. This section shall not apply to any device whose possession is otherwise lawful pursuant to N.J.S.2C:39–6.

f. Nothing contained in this section shall be deemed to preclude, if the evidence so warrants, an indictment and conviction for murder under the provisions of N.J.S.2C:11–3 or any other offense.

L.2002, c. 26, § 3, eff. June 18, 2002.

2C:38–4. Hindering apprehension, detention or prosecution of another for terrorism

a. A person commits a crime if, with the purpose to hinder the detention, apprehension, investigation, prosecution, conviction or punishment of another for the crime of terrorism, he:

(1) Harbors or conceals the other;

(2) Provides or aids in providing a weapon, money, transportation, disguise or other means of avoiding discovery or apprehension or effecting escape;

(3) Suppresses, by way of concealment or destruction, any evidence of the crime, or tampers with a witness, informant, document or other source of information, regardless of its admissibility in evidence, which might aid in the discovery or apprehension of such person or in the lodging of a charge against him;

(4) Warns the other of impending discovery or apprehension, except that this paragraph does not apply to a warning given in connection with an effort to bring another into compliance with law;

(5) Prevents or obstructs, by means of force, intimidation or deception, anyone from performing an act which might aid in the discovery or apprehension of such person or in the lodging of a charge against him;

(6) Aids such person to protect or expeditiously profit from an advantage derived from such crime; or

(7) Gives false information to a law enforcement officer.

b. A violation of subsection a. of this section is a crime of the first degree if the crime of terrorism resulted in death. Otherwise, it is a crime of the second degree.

L.2002, c. 26, § 4, eff. June 18, 2002.

2C:38–5. Soliciting or providing material support or resources for terrorism; definitions

a. As used in this section:

"Charitable organization" means: (1) any person determined by the federal Internal Revenue Service to be a tax exempt organization pursuant to section 501(c)(3) of the Internal Revenue Code of 1986, 26 U.S.C. s.501(c)(3); or

(2) any person who is, or holds himself out to be, established for any benevolent, philanthropic, humane, social welfare, public health, or other eleemosynary purpose, or for the benefit of law enforcement personnel, firefighters or other persons who protect the public safety, or any person who in any manner employs a charitable appeal as the basis of any solicitation, or an appeal which has a tendency to suggest there is a charitable purpose to any such solicitation.

"Charitable purpose" means: (1) any purpose described in section 501(c)(3) of the Internal Revenue Code of 1986, 26 U.S.C. s.501(c)(3); or (2) any benevolent, philanthropic, humane, social welfare, public health, or other eleemosynary objective, or an objective that benefits law enforcement personnel, firefighters, or other persons who protect the public safety.

"Material support or resources" means: (1) services or assistance with knowledge or purpose that the services or assistance will be used in preparing for or carrying out an act of terrorism in violation of section 2 of P.L.2002, c. 26 (C.2C:38–2);

(2) currency, financial securities or other monetary instruments, financial services, lodging, training, safehouses, false documentation or identification, communications equipment, facilities, weapons, lethal substances, explosives, personnel, including but not limited to persons recruited to participate directly or indirectly in a terrorist organization, transportation and other physical assets or anything of value; or

(3) any chemical weapon, or any biological agent, toxin, vector or delivery system for use as a weapon, or any nuclear or radiological device, as defined in subsection c. of section 3 of P.L.2002, c. 26 (C.2C:38–3).

"Professional fund raiser" means any person who for compensation performs for a charitable organization any service in connection with which contributions are or will be solicited in this State by that compensated person or by any compensated person he employs, procures, or engages, directly or indirectly to solicit contributions. A bona fide salaried officer, employee, or volunteer of a charitable organization shall not be deemed to be a professional fund raiser. No attorney, accountant or banker who advises a person to make a charitable contribution during the course of rendering professional services to that person shall be deemed, as a result of that advice, to be a professional fund raiser.

b. (1) It shall be unlawful for any person, charitable organization or professional fund raiser to solicit, transport or otherwise provide material support or resources with the purpose or knowledge that such material support or resources will be used, in whole or in part, to aid, plan, prepare or carry out an act of terrorism in violation of section 2 of P.L.2002, c. 26 (C.2C:38–2) or with the purpose or knowledge that such material support or resources are to be given, in whole or in part, to a person or an organization that has committed or has the purpose to commit or has threatened to commit an act of terrorism in violation of section 2 of P.L.2002, c. 26 (C.2C:38–2).

(2) It shall be unlawful for any person, charitable organization or professional fund raiser to solicit, transport or otherwise provide material support or resources to or on behalf of a person or an organization that is designated as a foreign terrorist organization by the United States Secretary of State pursuant to 8 U.S.C. s.1189. It shall not be a defense to a prosecution for a violation of this section that the actor did not know that the person or organization is designated as a foreign terrorist organization.

c. A person who violates the provisions of subsection b. of this section shall be guilty of a crime of the first degree if the act of terrorism in violation of section 2 of P.L.2002, c. 26 (C.2C:38–2) results in death. Otherwise, it is a crime of the second degree.

L.2002, c. 26, § 5, eff. June 18, 2002. Amended by L.2003, c. 50, § 1, eff. April 23, 2003.

CHAPTER 39

FIREARMS, OTHER DANGEROUS WEAPONS AND INSTRUMENTS OF CRIME

Section
2C:39–1. Definitions.
2C:39–2. Presumptions.
2C:39–3. Prohibited weapons and devices.
2C:39–4. Possession of weapons for unlawful purposes.
2C:39–4.1. Possession of weapons during commission of certain crimes; penalties.
2C:39–5. Unlawful possession of weapons.
2C:39–6. Exemptions.
2C:39–6.1. Expired.
2C:39–7. Certain persons not to have weapons.
2C:39–9. Manufacture, transport, disposition and defacement of weapons and dangerous instruments and appliances.
2C:39–9.1. Sale of knife with blade length over 5 inches or overall length over 10 inches to person under 18.
2C:39–9.2. Sale of handcuffs to person under age 18; disorderly persons offense.
2C:39–10. Violation of the regulatory provisions relating to firearms; false representation in applications.
2C:39–11. Pawnbrokers; loaning on firearms.
2C:39–12. Voluntary surrender.
2C:39–13. Unlawful use of body vests.
2C:39–14. Training, practice or instruction in use, application or making of firearm, explosive device or technique capable of causing injury for illegal activity.
2C:39–15. Offer to sell machine gun, semi–automatic rifle or assault firearm by advertisement in newspaper without statement of necessity of license.
2C:39–16. Leader of firearms trafficking network; crime of the first degree.

2C:39–1. Definitions

The following definitions apply to this chapter and to chapter 58:

a. "Antique firearm" means any rifle or shotgun and "antique cannon" means a destructive device defined in paragraph (3) of subsection c. of this section, if the rifle, shotgun or destructive device, as the case may be, is incapable of being fired or discharged, or which does not fire fixed ammunition, regardless of date of manufacture, or was manufactured before 1898 for which cartridge ammunition is not commercially available, and is possessed as a curiosity or ornament or for its historical significance or value.

b. "Deface" means to remove, deface, cover, alter or destroy the name of the maker, model designation, manufacturer's serial number or any other distinguishing identification mark or number on any firearm.

c. "Destructive device" means any device, instrument or object designed to explode or produce uncontrolled combustion, including (1) any explosive or incendiary bomb, mine or grenade; (2) any rocket having a propellant charge of more than four ounces or any missile having an explosive or incendiary charge of

more than one-quarter of an ounce; (3) any weapon capable of firing a projectile of a caliber greater than 60 caliber, except a shotgun or shotgun ammunition generally recognized as suitable for sporting purposes; (4) any Molotov cocktail or other device consisting of a breakable container containing flammable liquid and having a wick or similar device capable of being ignited. The term does not include any device manufactured for the purpose of illumination, distress signaling, line-throwing, safety or similar purposes.

d. "Dispose of" means to give, give away, lease, loan, keep for sale, offer, offer for sale, sell, transfer, or otherwise transfer possession.

e. "Explosive" means any chemical compound or mixture that is commonly used or is possessed for the purpose of producing an explosion and which contains any oxidizing and combustible materials or other ingredients in such proportions, quantities or packing that an ignition by fire, by friction, by concussion or by detonation of any part of the compound or mixture may cause such a sudden generation of highly heated gases that the resultant gaseous pressures are capable of producing destructive effects on contiguous objects. The term shall not include small arms ammunition, or explosives in the form prescribed by the official United States Pharmacopoeia.

f. "Firearm" means any handgun, rifle, shotgun, machine gun, automatic or semi-automatic rifle, or any gun, device or instrument in the nature of a weapon from which may be fired or ejected any solid projectable ball, slug, pellet, missile or bullet, or any gas, vapor or other noxious thing, by means of a cartridge or shell or by the action of an explosive or the igniting of flammable or explosive substances. It shall also include, without limitation, any firearm which is in the nature of an air gun, spring gun or pistol or other weapon of a similar nature in which the propelling force is a spring, elastic band, carbon dioxide, compressed or other gas or vapor, air or compressed air, or is ignited by compressed air, and ejecting a bullet or missile smaller than three-eighths of an inch in diameter, with sufficient force to injure a person.

g. "Firearm silencer" means any instrument, attachment, weapon or appliance for causing the firing of any gun, revolver, pistol or other firearm to be silent, or intended to lessen or muffle the noise of the firing of any gun, revolver, pistol or other firearm.

h. "Gravity knife" means any knife which has a blade which is released from the handle or sheath thereof by the force of gravity or the application of centrifugal force.

i. "Machine gun" means any firearm, mechanism or instrument not requiring that the trigger be pressed for each shot and having a reservoir, belt or other means of storing and carrying ammunition which can be loaded into the firearm, mechanism or instrument and fired therefrom.

j. "Manufacturer" means any person who receives or obtains raw materials or parts and processes them into firearms or finished parts of firearms, except a person who exclusively processes grips, stocks and other nonmetal parts of firearms. The term does not include a person who repairs existing firearms or receives new and used raw materials or parts solely for the repair of existing firearms.

k. "Handgun" means any pistol, revolver or other firearm originally designed or manufactured to be fired by the use of a single hand.

l. "Retail dealer" means any person including a gunsmith, except a manufacturer or a wholesale dealer, who sells, transfers or assigns for a fee or profit any firearm or parts of firearms or ammunition which he has purchased or obtained with the intention, or for the purpose, of reselling or reassigning to persons who are reasonably understood to be the ultimate consumers, and includes any person who is engaged in the business of repairing firearms or who sells any firearm to satisfy a debt secured by the pledge of a firearm.

m. "Rifle" means any firearm designed to be fired from the shoulder and using the energy of the explosive in a fixed metallic cartridge to fire a single projectile through a rifled bore for each single pull of the trigger.

n. "Shotgun" means any firearm designed to be fired from the shoulder and using the energy of the explosive in a fixed shotgun shell to fire through a smooth bore either a number of ball shots or a single projectile for each pull of the trigger, or any firearm designed to be fired from the shoulder which does not fire fixed ammunition.

o. "Sawed-off shotgun" means any shotgun having a barrel or barrels of less than 18 inches in length measured from the breech to the muzzle, or a rifle having a barrel or barrels of less than 16 inches in length measured from the breech to the muzzle, or any firearm made from a rifle or a shotgun, whether by alteration, or otherwise, if such firearm as modified has an overall length of less than 26 inches.

p. "Switchblade knife" means any knife or similar device which has a blade which opens automatically by hand pressure applied to a button, spring or other device in the handle of the knife.

q. "Superintendent" means the Superintendent of the State Police.

r. "Weapon" means anything readily capable of lethal use or of inflicting serious bodily injury. The term includes, but is not limited to, all (1) firearms, even though not loaded or lacking a clip or other component to render them immediately operable; (2) components which can be readily assembled into a weapon; (3) gravity knives, switchblade knives, daggers, dirks, stilettos, or other dangerous knives, billies, blackjacks, bludgeons, metal knuckles, sandclubs, slingshots, cesti or similar leather bands studded with metal filings or razor blades imbedded in wood; and (4) stun guns; and any

weapon or other device which projects, releases, or emits tear gas or any other substance intended to produce temporary physical discomfort or permanent injury through being vaporized or otherwise dispensed in the air.

s. "Wholesale dealer" means any person, except a manufacturer, who sells, transfers, or assigns firearms, or parts of firearms, to persons who are reasonably understood not to be the ultimate consumers, and includes persons who receive finished parts of firearms and assemble them into completed or partially completed firearms, in furtherance of such purpose, except that it shall not include those persons dealing exclusively in grips, stocks and other nonmetal parts of firearms.

t. "Stun gun" means any weapon or other device which emits an electrical charge or current intended to temporarily or permanently disable a person.

u. "Ballistic knife" means any weapon or other device capable of lethal use and which can propel a knife blade.

v. "Imitation firearm" means an object or device reasonably capable of being mistaken for a firearm.

w. "Assault firearm" means:

(1) The following firearms:

Algimec AGM1 type

Any shotgun with a revolving cylinder such as the "Street Sweeper" or "Striker 12"

Armalite AR–180 type

Australian Automatic Arms SAR

Avtomat Kalashnikov type semi-automatic firearms

Beretta AR–70 and BM59 semi-automatic firearms

Bushmaster Assault Rifle

Calico M–900 Assault carbine and M–900

CETME G3

Chartered Industries of Singapore SR–88 type

Colt AR–15 and CAR–15 series

Daewoo K–1, K–2, Max 1 and Max 2, AR 100 types

Demro TAC–1 carbine type

Encom MP–9 and MP–45 carbine types

FAMAS MAS223 types

FN–FAL, FN–LAR, or FN–FNC type semi-automatic firearms

Franchi SPAS 12 and LAW 12 shotguns

G3SA type

Galil type Heckler and Koch HK91, HK93, HK94, MP5, PSG–1

Intratec TEC 9 and 22 semi-automatic firearms

M1 carbine type

M14S type

MAC 10, MAC 11, MAC 11–9mm carbine type firearms

PJK M–68 carbine type

Plainfield Machine Company Carbine

Ruger K–Mini–14/5F and Mini–14/5RF

SIG AMT, SIG 550SP, SIG 551SP, SIG PE–57 types

SKS with detachable magazine type

Spectre Auto carbine type

Springfield Armory BM59 and SAR–48 type

Sterling MK–6, MK–7 and SAR types

Steyr A.U.G. semi-automatic firearms

USAS 12 semi-automatic type shotgun

Uzi type semi-automatic firearms

Valmet M62, M71S, M76, or M78 type semi-automatic firearms

Weaver Arm Nighthawk.

(2) Any firearm manufactured under any designation which is substantially identical to any of the firearms listed above.

(3) A semi-automatic shotgun with either a magazine capacity exceeding six rounds, a pistol grip, or a folding stock.

(4) A semi-automatic rifle with a fixed magazine capacity exceeding 15 rounds.

(5) A part or combination of parts designed or intended to convert a firearm into an assault firearm, or any combination of parts from which an assault firearm may be readily assembled if those parts are in the possession or under the control of the same person.

x. "Semi-automatic" means a firearm which fires a single projectile for each single pull of the trigger and is self-reloading or automatically chambers a round, cartridge, or bullet.

y. "Large capacity ammunition magazine" means a box, drum, tube or other container which is capable of holding more than 15 rounds of ammunition to be fed continuously and directly therefrom into a semi-automatic firearm.

z. "Pistol grip" means a well-defined handle, similar to that found on a handgun, that protrudes conspicuously beneath the action of the weapon, and which permits the shotgun to be held and fired with one hand.

aa. "Antique handgun" means a handgun manufactured before 1898, or a replica thereof, which is recognized as being historical in nature or of historical significance and either (1) utilizes a match, friction, flint, or percussion ignition, or which utilizes a pin-fire cartridge in which the pin is part of the cartridge or (2) does not fire fixed ammunition or for which cartridge ammunition is not commercially available.

bb. "Trigger lock" means a commercially available device approved by the Superintendent of State Police which is operated with a key or combination lock that prevents a firearm from being discharged while the device is attached to the firearm. It may include, but need not be limited to, devices that obstruct the barrel or cylinder of the firearm, as well as devices that immobilize the trigger.

cc. "Trigger locking device" means a device that, if installed on a firearm and secured by means of a key or mechanically, electronically or electromechanically operated combination lock, prevents the firearm from being discharged without first deactivating or removing the device by means of a key or mechanically, electronically or electromechanically operated combination lock.

dd. "Personalized handgun" means a handgun which incorporates within its design, and as part of its original manufacture, technology which automatically limits its operational use and which cannot be readily deactivated, so that it may only be fired by an authorized or recognized user. The technology limiting the handgun's operational use may include, but not be limited to: radio frequency tagging, touch memory, remote control, fingerprint, magnetic encoding and other automatic user identification systems utilizing biometric, mechanical or electronic systems. No make or model of a handgun shall be deemed to be a "personalized handgun" unless the Attorney General has determined, through testing or other reasonable means, that the handgun meets any reliability standards that the manufacturer may require for its commercially available handguns that are not personalized or, if the manufacturer has no such reliability standards, the handgun meets the reliability standards generally used in the industry for commercially available handguns.

L.1978, c. 95, § 2C:39–1, eff. Sept. 1, 1979. Amended by L.1981, c. 363, § 1, eff. Dec. 30, 1981; L.1983, c. 479, § 1, eff. Jan. 12, 1984; L.1985, c. 360, § 1, eff. Nov. 12, 1985; L.1987, c. 228, § 1, eff. July 30, 1987; L.1989, c. 120, § 1, eff. Aug. 1, 1989; L.1990, c. 32, § 1, eff. May 30, 1990; L.1999, c. 233, § 1; L.1999, c. 255, § 1, eff. Oct. 15, 1999; L.2002, c. 130, § 5, eff. Dec. 23, 2002.

2C:39–2. Presumptions

a. **Possession of firearms, weapons, destructive devices, silencers, or explosives in a vehicle.** When a firearm, weapon, destructive device, silencer, or explosive described in this chapter is found in a vehicle, it is presumed to be in the possession of the occupant if there is but one. If there is more than one occupant in the vehicle, it shall be presumed to be in the possession of all, except under the following circumstances:

(1) When it is found upon the person of one of the occupants, it shall be presumed to be in the possession of that occupant alone;

(2) When the vehicle is not a stolen one and the weapon or other instrument is found out of view in a glove compartment, trunk or other enclosed customary depository, it shall be presumed to be in the possession

of the occupant or occupants who own or have authority to operate the vehicle; and

(3) When the vehicle is a taxicab and a weapon or other instrument is found in the passenger's portion of the vehicle, it shall be presumed to be in the possession of all the passengers, if there are any, and if not, in the possession of the driver.

b. Licenses and permits. When the legality of a person's conduct under this chapter depends on his possession of a license or permit or on his having registered with or given notice to a particular person or agency, it shall be presumed that he does not possess such a license or permit or has not registered or given the required notice, until he establishes the contrary.

L.1978, c. 95, § 2C:39–2, eff. Sept. 1, 1979. Amended by L.1979, c. 179, § 1, eff. Sept. 1, 1979.

2C:39–3. Prohibited weapons and devices

a. Destructive devices. Any person who knowingly has in his possession any destructive device is guilty of a crime of the third degree.

b. Sawed-off shotguns. Any person who knowingly has in his possession any sawed-off shotgun is guilty of a crime of the third degree.

c. Silencers. Any person who knowingly has in his possession any firearm silencer is guilty of a crime of the fourth degree.

d. Defaced firearms. Any person who knowingly has in his possession any firearm which has been defaced, except an antique firearm or an antique handgun, is guilty of a crime of the fourth degree.

e. Certain weapons. Any person who knowingly has in his possession any gravity knife, switchblade knife, dagger, dirk, stiletto, billy, blackjack, metal knuckle, sandclub, slingshot, cestus or similar leather band studded with metal filings or razor blades imbedded in wood, ballistic knife, without any explainable lawful purpose, is guilty of a crime of the fourth degree.

f. Dum-dum or body armor penetrating bullets. (1) Any person, other than a law enforcement officer or persons engaged in activities pursuant to subsection f. of N.J.S.2C:39–6, who knowingly has in his possession any hollow nose or dum-dum bullet, or (2) any person, other than a collector of firearms or ammunition as curios or relics as defined in Title 18, United States Code, section 921 (a) (13) and has in his possession a valid Collector of Curios and Relics License issued by the Bureau of Alcohol, Tobacco and Firearms, who knowingly has in his possession any body armor breaching or penetrating ammunition, which means: (a) ammunition primarily designed for use in a handgun, and (b) which is comprised of a bullet whose core or jacket, if the jacket is thicker than .025 of an inch, is made of tungsten carbide, or hard bronze, or other material which is harder than a rating of 72 or greater on the Rockwell B. Hardness Scale, and (c) is therefore capable of breaching or penetrating body armor, is guilty of a crime of the fourth degree. For purposes of this section, a collector may possess not more than three examples of each distinctive variation of the ammunition described above. A distinctive variation includes a different head stamp, composition, design, or color.

g. Exceptions. (1) Nothing in subsection a., b., c., d., e., f., j. or k. of this section shall apply to any member of the Armed Forces of the United States or the National Guard, or except as otherwise provided, to any law enforcement officer while actually on duty or traveling to or from an authorized place of duty, provided that his possession of the prohibited weapon or device has been duly authorized under the applicable laws, regulations or military or law enforcement orders. Nothing in subsection h. of this section shall apply to any law enforcement officer who is exempted from the provisions of that subsection by the Attorney General. Nothing in this section shall apply to the possession of any weapon or device by a law enforcement officer who has confiscated, seized or otherwise taken possession of said weapon or device as evidence of the commission of a crime or because he believed it to be possessed illegally by the person from whom it was taken, provided that said law enforcement officer promptly notifies his superiors of his possession of such prohibited weapon or device.

(2) a. Nothing in subsection f. (1) shall be construed to prevent a person from keeping such ammunition at his dwelling, premises or other land owned or possessed by him, or from carrying such ammunition from the place of purchase to said dwelling or land, nor shall subsection f. (1) be construed to prevent any licensed retail or wholesale firearms dealer from possessing such ammunition at its licensed premises, provided that the seller of any such ammunition shall maintain a record of the name, age and place of residence of any purchaser who is not a licensed dealer, together with the date of sale and quantity of ammunition sold.

b. Nothing in subsection f. (1) shall be construed to prevent a designated employee or designated licensed agent for a nuclear power plant under the license of the Nuclear Regulatory Commission from possessing hollow nose ammunition while in the actual performance of his official duties, if the federal licensee certifies that the designated employee or designated licensed agent is assigned to perform site protection, guard, armed response or armed escort duties and is appropriately trained and qualified, as prescribed by federal regulation, to perform those duties.

(3) Nothing in paragraph (2) of subsection f. or in subsection j. shall be construed to prevent any licensed retail or wholesale firearms dealer from possessing that ammunition or large capacity ammunition magazine at its licensed premises for sale or disposition to another licensed dealer, the Armed Forces of the United States or the National Guard, or to a law enforcement agency, provided that the seller maintains a record of any sale or disposition to a law enforcement agency. The record shall include the name of the purchasing agency,

together with written authorization of the chief of police or highest ranking official of the agency, the name and rank of the purchasing law enforcement officer, if applicable, and the date, time and amount of ammunition sold or otherwise disposed. A copy of this record shall be forwarded by the seller to the Superintendent of the Division of State Police within 48 hours of the sale or disposition.

(4) Nothing in subsection a. of this section shall be construed to apply to antique cannons as exempted in subsection d. of N.J.S.2C:39–6.

(5) Nothing in subsection c. of this section shall be construed to apply to any person who is specifically identified in a special deer management permit issued by the Division of Fish and Wildlife to utilize a firearm silencer as part of an alternative deer control method implemented in accordance with a special deer management permit issued pursuant to section 4 of P.L.2000, c. 46 (C.23:4–42.6), while the person is in the actual performance of the permitted alternative deer control method and while going to and from the place where the permitted alternative deer control method is being utilized. This exception shall not, however, otherwise apply to any person to authorize the purchase or possession of a firearm silencer.

h. Stun guns. Any person who knowingly has in his possession any stun gun is guilty of a crime of the fourth degree.

i. Nothing in subsection e. of this section shall be construed to prevent any guard in the employ of a private security company, who is licensed to carry a firearm, from the possession of a nightstick when in the actual performance of his official duties, provided that he has satisfactorily completed a training course approved by the Police Training Commission in the use of a nightstick.

j. Any person who knowingly has in his possession a large capacity ammunition magazine is guilty of a crime of the fourth degree unless the person has registered an assault firearm pursuant to section 11 of P.L.1990, c. 32 (C.2C:58–12) and the magazine is maintained and used in connection with participation in competitive shooting matches sanctioned by the Director of Civilian Marksmanship of the United States Department of the Army.

k. Handcuffs. Any person who knowingly has in his possession handcuffs as defined in P.L.1991, c. 437 (C.2C:39–9.2), under circumstances not manifestly appropriate for such lawful uses as handcuffs may have, is guilty of a disorderly persons offense. A law enforcement officer shall confiscate handcuffs possessed in violation of the law.

L.1978, c. 95, § 2C:39–3, eff. Sept. 1, 1979. Amended by L.1979, c. 179, § 2, eff. Sept. 1, 1979; L.1983, c. 58, § 1, eff. Feb. 7, 1983; L.1983, c. 479, § 2, eff. Jan. 12, 1984; L.1985, c. 360, § 2, eff. Nov. 12, 1985; L.1987, c. 228, § 2, eff. July 30, 1987; L.1989, c. 11, § 1, eff. Feb. 1, 1989; L.1990, c. 32, § 10, eff. May 30, 1990; L.1991, c. 437, § 1, eff. Jan. 18, 1992; L.1999, c. 233, § 2; L.2000, c. 46, § 5, eff. June 30, 2000; L.2003, c. 168, § 1, eff. Sept. 3, 2003.

2C:39–4. Possession of weapons for unlawful purposes

a. Firearms. (1) Any person who has in his possession any firearm with a purpose to use it unlawfully against the person or property of another is guilty of a crime of the second degree.

(2) Any person who possesses, receives or transfers a community gun is guilty of a crime of the second degree and shall be sentenced to a term of imprisonment by the court. The term of imprisonment shall include the imposition of a minimum term. The minimum term shall be fixed at one-half of the sentence imposed by the court or three years, whichever is greater and during which the defendant shall be ineligible for parole. As used in this paragraph, "community gun" means a firearm that is transferred among, between or within any association of two or more persons who, while possessing that firearm, engage in criminal activity or use it unlawfully against the person or property of another.

b. Explosives. Any person who has in his possession or carries any explosive substance with a purpose to use it unlawfully against the person or property of another is guilty of a crime of the second degree.

c. Destructive devices. Any person who has in his possession any destructive device with a purpose to use it unlawfully against the person or property of another is guilty of a crime of the second degree.

d. Other weapons. Any person who has in his possession any weapon, except a firearm, with a purpose to use it unlawfully against the person or property of another is guilty of a crime of the third degree.

e. Imitation firearms. Any person who has in his possession an imitation firearm under circumstances that would lead an observer to reasonably believe that it is possessed for an unlawful purpose is guilty of a crime of the fourth degree.

L.1978, c. 95, § 2C:39–4, eff. Sept. 7, 1979. Amended by L.1979, § 179, § 3, eff. Sept. 1, 1979; L.1989, c. 120, § 2, eff. Aug. 1, 1989; L.2007, c. 24, § 1, eff. Jan. 26, 2007.

2C:39–4.1. Possession of weapons during commission of certain crimes; penalties

a. Any person who has in his possession any firearm while in the course of committing, attempting to commit, or conspiring to commit a violation of N.J.S.2C:35–3, N.J.S. 2C:35–4, N.J.S.2C:35–5, section 3 or section 5 of P.L.1997, c. 194 (C.2C:35–5.2 or 2C:35–5.3), N.J.S.2C:35–6, section 1 of P.L.1987, c. 101 (C.2C:35–7), section 1 of P.L.1997, c. 327 (C.2C:35–7.1), N.J.S.2C:35–11 or N.J.S.2C:16–1 is guilty of a crime of the second degree.

b. Any person who has in his possession any weapon, except a firearm, with a purpose to use such weapon unlawfully against the person or property of another, while in the course of committing, attempting to commit, or conspiring to commit a violation of

N.J.S.2C:35–3, N.J.S.2C:35–4, N.J.S.2C:35–5, section 3 or 5 of P.L.1997, c. 194 (C.2C:35–5.2 or 2C:35–5.3), N.J.S.2C:35–6, section 1 of P.L.1987, c. 101 (C.2C:35–7), section 1 of P.L.1997,c.327 (C.2C:35–7.1), N.J.S.2C:35–11 or N.J.S.2C:16–1 is guilty of a crime of the second degree.

c. Any person who has in his possession any weapon, except a firearm, under circumstances not manifestly appropriate for such lawful uses as the weapon may have, while in the course of committing, attempting to commit, or conspiring to commit a violation of N.J.S.2C:35–3, N.J.S.2C:35–4, N.J.S.2C:35–5, section 3 or section 5 of P.L. 1997, c. 194 (C.2C:35–5.2 or 2C:35–5.3), N.J.S.2C:35–6, section 1 of P.L.1987, c. 101 (C.2C:35–7), section 1 of P.L.1997,c.327(C.2C:35–7.1), N.J.S.2C:35–11 or N.J.S.2C:16–1 is guilty of a crime of the second degree.

d. Notwithstanding the provisions of N.J.S.2C:1–8 or any other provision of law, a conviction arising under this section shall not merge with a conviction for a violation of any of the sections of chapter 35 or chapter 16 referred to in this section nor shall any conviction under those sections merge with a conviction under this section. Notwithstanding the provisions of N.J.S.2C:44–5 or any other provision of law, the sentence imposed upon a violation of this section shall be ordered to be served consecutively to that imposed for any conviction for a violation of any of the sections of chapter 35 or chapter 16 referred to in this section or a conviction for conspiracy or attempt to violate any of those sections.

e. Nothing herein shall be deemed to preclude, if the evidence so warrants, an indictment and conviction for a violation of N.J.S.2C:39–4 or N. J.S.2C:39–5 or any other provision of law.

f. Nothing herein shall prevent the court from also imposing enhanced punishments, pursuant to N.J.S.2C:35–8, section 2 of P.L.1997, c. 117 (C.2C:43–7.2), or any other provision of law, or an extended term.

L.1998, c. 26, § 1, eff. June 24, 1998. Amended by L.2001, c. 443, § 4, eff. Jan. 11, 2002.

2C:39–5. Unlawful possession of weapons

a. Machine guns. Any person who knowingly has in his possession a machine gun or any instrument or device adaptable for use as a machine gun, without being licensed to do so as provided in N.J.S.2C:58–5, is guilty of a crime of the second degree.

b. Handguns. Any person who knowingly has in his possession any handgun, including any antique handgun, without first having obtained a permit to carry the same as provided in N.J.S.2C:58–4, is guilty of a crime of the third degree if the handgun is in the nature of an air gun, spring gun or pistol or other weapon of a similar nature in which the propelling force is a spring, elastic band, carbon dioxide, compressed or other gas or vapor, air or compressed air, or is ignited by compressed air, and ejecting a bullet or missile smaller than three-eighths of an inch in diameter, with sufficient force to injure a person. Otherwise it is a crime of the second degree.

c. Rifles and shotguns. (1) Any person who knowingly has in his possession any rifle or shotgun without having first obtained a firearms purchaser identification card in accordance with the provisions of N.J.S.2C:58–3, is guilty of a crime of the third degree.

(2) Unless otherwise permitted by law, any person who knowingly has in his possession any loaded rifle or shotgun is guilty of a crime of the third degree.

d. Other weapons. Any person who knowingly has in his possession any other weapon under circumstances not manifestly appropriate for such lawful uses as it may have is guilty of a crime of the fourth degree.

e. Firearms or other weapons in educational institutions.

(1) Any person who knowingly has in his possession any firearm in or upon any part of the buildings or grounds of any school, college, university or other educational institution, without the written authorization of the governing officer of the institution, is guilty of a crime of the third degree, irrespective of whether he possesses a valid permit to carry the firearm or a valid firearms purchaser identification card.

(2) Any person who knowingly possesses any weapon enumerated in paragraphs (3) and (4) of subsection r. of N.J.S.2C:39–1 or any components which can readily be assembled into a firearm or other weapon enumerated in subsection r. of N.J.S.2C:39–1 or any other weapon under circumstances not manifestly appropriate for such lawful use as it may have, while in or upon any part of the buildings or grounds of any school, college, university or other educational institution without the written authorization of the governing officer of the institution is guilty of a crime of the fourth degree.

(3) Any person who knowingly has in his possession any imitation firearm in or upon any part of the buildings or grounds of any school, college, university or other educational institution, without the written authorization of the governing officer of the institution, or while on any school bus is a disorderly person, irrespective of whether he possesses a valid permit to carry a firearm or a valid firearms purchaser identification card.

f. Assault firearms. Any person who knowingly has in his possession an assault firearm is guilty of a crime of the second degree except if the assault firearm is licensed pursuant to N.J.S.2C:58–5; registered pursuant to section 11 of P.L.1990, c. 32 (C.2C:58–12); or rendered inoperable pursuant to section 12 of P.L.1990, c. 32 (C.2C:58–13).

g. (1) The temporary possession of a handgun, rifle or shotgun by a person receiving, possessing, carrying or using the handgun, rifle, or shotgun under the provisions of section 1 of P.L.1992, c. 74 (C.2C:58–3.1) shall not be considered unlawful possession under the provisions of subsection b. or c. of this section.

(2) The temporary possession of a firearm by a person receiving, possessing, carrying or using the firearm under the provisions of section 1 of P.L.1997, c. 375 (C.2C:58–3.2) shall not be considered unlawful possession under the provisions of this section.

h. A person who is convicted of a crime under subsection a., b. or f. of this section shall be ineligible for participation in any program of intensive supervision; provided, however, that this provision shall not apply to a crime under subsection b. involving only a handgun which is in the nature of an air gun, spring gun or pistol or other weapon of a similar nature in which the propelling force is a spring, elastic band, carbon dioxide, compressed or other gas or vapor, air or compressed air, or is ignited by compressed air, and ejecting a bullet or missile smaller than three-eighths of an inch in diameter, with sufficient force to injure a person.

i. A person convicted of violating subsection a., b. or f. of this section shall be sentenced by the court to a term of imprisonment, which shall include the imposition of a minimum term during which the defendant shall be ineligible for parole, if the court finds that the aggravating circumstance set forth in paragraph (5) of subsection a. of N.J.S.2C:44–1 applies. The minimum term of parole ineligibility shall be fixed at five years. The sentencing court shall make a finding on the record as to whether the aggravating circumstance set forth in paragraph (5) of subsection a. of N.J.S.2C:44–1 applies, and the court shall presume that there is a substantial likelihood that the defendant is involved in organized criminal activity if there is a substantial likelihood that the defendant is a member of an organization or group that engages in criminal activity. The prosecution at the sentencing hearing shall have the initial burden of producing evidence or information concerning the defendant's membership in such an organization or group.

L.1978, c. 95, § 2C:39–5, eff. Sept. 1, 1979. Amended by L.1979, c. 179, § 4, eff. Sept. 1, 1979; L.1990, c. 32, § 2, eff. May 30, 1990; L.1992, c. 74, § 2, eff. July 31, 1992; L.1992, c. 94, § 1, eff. Sept. 9, 1992; L.1995, c. 389, § 1, eff. Jan. 10, 1996; L.1997, c. 375, § 2, eff. Jan. 19, 1998; L.2007, c. 284, § 1, eff. Jan. 13, 2008; L.2009, c. 13, § 1, eff. Feb. 2, 2009.

2C:39–6. Exemptions

a. Provided a person complies with the requirements of subsection j. of this section, N.J.S.2C:39–5 does not apply to:

(1) Members of the Armed Forces of the United States or of the National Guard while actually on duty, or while traveling between places of duty and carrying authorized weapons in the manner prescribed by the appropriate military authorities;

(2) Federal law enforcement officers, and any other federal officers and employees required to carry firearms in the performance of their official duties;

(3) Members of the State Police and, under conditions prescribed by the superintendent, members of the Marine Law Enforcement Bureau of the Division of State Police;

(4) A sheriff, undersheriff, sheriff's officer, county prosecutor, assistant prosecutor, prosecutor's detective or investigator, deputy attorney general or State investigator employed by the Division of Criminal Justice of the Department of Law and Public Safety, investigator employed by the State Commission of Investigation, inspector of the Alcoholic Beverage Control Enforcement Bureau of the Division of State Police in the Department of Law and Public Safety authorized to carry such weapons by the Superintendent of State Police, State park police officer, or State conservation officer;

(5) Except as hereinafter provided, a prison or jail warden of any penal institution in this State or his deputies, or an employee of the Department of Corrections engaged in the interstate transportation of convicted offenders, while in the performance of his duties, and when required to possess the weapon by his superior officer, or a corrections officer or keeper of a penal institution in this State at all times while in the State of New Jersey, provided he annually passes an examination approved by the superintendent testing his proficiency in the handling of firearms;

(6) A civilian employee of the United States Government under the supervision of the commanding officer of any post, camp, station, base or other military or naval installation located in this State who is required, in the performance of his official duties, to carry firearms, and who is authorized to carry such firearms by said commanding officer, while in the actual performance of his official duties;

(7)(a) A regularly employed member, including a detective, of the police department of any county or municipality, or of any State, interstate, municipal or county park police force or boulevard police force, at all times while in the State of New Jersey;

(b) A special law enforcement officer authorized to carry a weapon as provided in subsection b. of section 7 of P.L.1985, c. 439 (C.40A:14–146.14);

(c) An airport security officer or a special law enforcement officer appointed by the governing body of any county or municipality, except as provided in subsection (b) of this section, or by the commission, board or other body having control of a county park or airport or boulevard police force, while engaged in the actual performance of his official duties and when specifically authorized by the governing body to carry weapons;

(8) A full-time, paid member of a paid or part-paid fire department or force of any municipality who is

assigned full-time or part-time to an arson investigation unit created pursuant to section 1 of P.L.1981, c. 409 (C.40A:14–7.1) or to the county arson investigation unit in the county prosecutor's office, while either engaged in the actual performance of arson investigation duties or while actually on call to perform arson investigation duties and when specifically authorized by the governing body or the county prosecutor, as the case may be, to carry weapons. Prior to being permitted to carry a firearm, such a member shall take and successfully complete a firearms training course administered by the Police Training Commission pursuant to P.L.1961, c. 56 (C.52:17B–66 et seq.), and shall annually qualify in the use of a revolver or similar weapon prior to being permitted to carry a firearm;

(9) A juvenile corrections officer in the employment of the Juvenile Justice Commission established pursuant to section 2 of P.L.1995, c. 284 (C.52:17B–170) subject to the regulations promulgated by the commission;

(10) A designated employee or designated licensed agent for a nuclear power plant under license of the Nuclear Regulatory Commission, while in the actual performance of his official duties, if the federal licensee certifies that the designated employee or designated licensed agent is assigned to perform site protection, guard, armed response or armed escort duties and is appropriately trained and qualified, as prescribed by federal regulation, to perform those duties. Any firearm utilized by an employee or agent for a nuclear power plant pursuant to this paragraph shall be returned each day at the end of the employee's or agent's authorized official duties to the employee's or agent's supervisor. All firearms returned each day pursuant to this paragraph shall be stored in locked containers located in a secure area;

(11) A county corrections officer at all times while in the State of New Jersey, provided he annually passes an examination approved by the superintendent testing his proficiency in the handling of firearms.

b. Subsections a., b. and c. of N.J.S.2C:39–5 do not apply to:

(1) A law enforcement officer employed by a governmental agency outside of the State of New Jersey while actually engaged in his official duties, provided, however, that he has first notified the superintendent or the chief law enforcement officer of the municipality or the prosecutor of the county in which he is engaged; or

(2) A licensed dealer in firearms and his registered employees during the course of their normal business while traveling to and from their place of business and other places for the purpose of demonstration, exhibition or delivery in connection with a sale, provided, however, that the weapon is carried in the manner specified in subsection g. of this section.

c. Provided a person complies with the requirements of subsection j. of this section, subsections b. and c. of N.J.S.2C:39–5 do not apply to:

(1) A special agent of the Division of Taxation who has passed an examination in an approved police training program testing proficiency in the handling of any firearm which he may be required to carry, while in the actual performance of his official duties and while going to or from his place of duty, or any other police officer, while in the actual performance of his official duties;

(2) A State deputy conservation officer or a full-time employee of the Division of Parks and Forestry having the power of arrest and authorized to carry weapons, while in the actual performance of his official duties;

(3) (Deleted by amendment, P.L.1986, c. 150.)

(4) A court attendant serving as such under appointment by the sheriff of the county or by the judge of any municipal court or other court of this State, while in the actual performance of his official duties;

(5) A guard in the employ of any railway express company, banking or building and loan or savings and loan institution of this State, while in the actual performance of his official duties;

(6) A member of a legally recognized military organization while actually under orders or while going to or from the prescribed place of meeting and carrying the weapons prescribed for drill, exercise or parade;

(7) A humane law enforcement officer of the New Jersey Society for the Prevention of Cruelty to Animals or of a county society for the prevention of cruelty to animals, while in the actual performance of his duties;

(8) An employee of a public utilities corporation actually engaged in the transportation of explosives;

(9) A railway policeman, except a transit police officer of the New Jersey Transit Police Department, at all times while in the State of New Jersey, provided that he has passed an approved police academy training program consisting of at least 280 hours. The training program shall include, but need not be limited to, the handling of firearms, community relations, and juvenile relations;

(10) A campus police officer appointed under P.L. 1970, c. 211 (C.18A:6–4.2 et seq.) at all times. Prior to being permitted to carry a firearm, a campus police officer shall take and successfully complete a firearms training course administered by the Police Training Commission, pursuant to P.L.1961, c. 56 (C.52:17B–66 et seq.), and shall annually qualify in the use of a revolver or similar weapon prior to being permitted to carry a firearm;

(11) (Deleted by amendment, P.L.2003, c. 168).

(12) A transit police officer of the New Jersey Transit Police Department, at all times while in the State of New Jersey, provided the officer has satisfied the training requirements of the Police Training Commission, pursuant to subsection c. of section 2 of P.L.1989, c. 291 (C.27:25–15.1);

(13) A parole officer employed by the State Parole Board at all times. Prior to being permitted to carry a firearm, a parole officer shall take and successfully complete a basic course for regular police officer training administered by the Police Training Commission, pursuant to P.L.1961, c. 56 (C.52:17B–66 et seq.), and shall annually qualify in the use of a revolver or similar weapon prior to being permitted to carry a firearm;

(14) A Human Services police officer at all times while in the State of New Jersey, as authorized by the Commissioner of Human Services;

(15) A person or employee of any person who, pursuant to and as required by a contract with a governmental entity, supervises or transports persons charged with or convicted of an offense;

(16) A housing authority police officer appointed under P.L.1997, c. 210 (C.40A:14–146.19 et al.) at all times while in the State of New Jersey; or

(17) A probation officer assigned to the "Probation Officer Community Safety Unit" created by section 2 of P.L.2001, c. 362 (C.2B:10A–2) while in the actual performance of the probation officer's official duties. Prior to being permitted to carry a firearm, a probation officer shall take and successfully complete a basic course for regular police officer training administered by the Police Training Commission, pursuant to P.L. 1961, c. 56 (C.52:17B–66 et seq.), and shall annually qualify in the use of a revolver or similar weapon prior to being permitted to carry a firearm.

d. (1) Subsections c. and d. of N.J.S.2C:39–5 do not apply to antique firearms, provided that such antique firearms are unloaded or are being fired for the purposes of exhibition or demonstration at an authorized target range or in such other manner as has been approved in writing by the chief law enforcement officer of the municipality in which the exhibition or demonstration is held, or if not held on property under the control of a particular municipality, the superintendent.

(2) Subsection a. of N.J.S.2C:39–3 and subsection d. of N.J.S.2C:39–5 do not apply to an antique cannon that is capable of being fired but that is unloaded and immobile, provided that the antique cannon is possessed by (a) a scholastic institution, a museum, a municipality, a county or the State, or (b) a person who obtained a firearms purchaser identification card as specified in N.J.S.2C:58–3.

(3) Subsection a. of N.J.S.2C:39–3 and subsection d. of N.J.S.2C:39–5 do not apply to an unloaded antique cannon that is being transported by one eligible to possess it, in compliance with regulations the superintendent may promulgate, between its permanent location and place of purchase or repair.

(4) Subsection a. of N.J.S.2C:39–3 and subsection d. of N.J.S.2C:39–5 do not apply to antique cannons that are being loaded or fired by one eligible to possess an antique cannon, for purposes of exhibition or demon-

stration at an authorized target range or in the manner as has been approved in writing by the chief law enforcement officer of the municipality in which the exhibition or demonstration is held, or if not held on property under the control of a particular municipality, the superintendent, provided that performer has given at least 30 days' notice to the superintendent.

(5) Subsection a. of N.J.S.2C:39–3 and subsection d. of N.J.S.2C:39–5 do not apply to the transportation of unloaded antique cannons directly to or from exhibitions or demonstrations authorized under paragraph (4) of subsection d. of this section, provided that the transportation is in compliance with safety regulations the superintendent may promulgate. Nor do those subsections apply to transportation directly to or from exhibitions or demonstrations authorized under the law of another jurisdiction, provided that the superintendent has been given 30 days' notice and that the transportation is in compliance with safety regulations the superintendent may promulgate.

e. Nothing in subsections b., c. and d. of N.J.S.2C:39–5 shall be construed to prevent a person keeping or carrying about his place of business, residence, premises or other land owned or possessed by him, any firearm, or from carrying the same, in the manner specified in subsection g. of this section, from any place of purchase to his residence or place of business, between his dwelling and his place of business, between one place of business or residence and another when moving, or between his dwelling or place of business and place where such firearms are repaired, for the purpose of repair. For the purposes of this section, a place of business shall be deemed to be a fixed location.

f. Nothing in subsections b., c. and d. of N.J.S.2C:39–5 shall be construed to prevent:

(1) A member of any rifle or pistol club organized in accordance with the rules prescribed by the National Board for the Promotion of Rifle Practice, in going to or from a place of target practice, carrying such firearms as are necessary for said target practice, provided that the club has filed a copy of its charter with the superintendent and annually submits a list of its members to the superintendent and provided further that the firearms are carried in the manner specified in subsection g. of this section;

(2) A person carrying a firearm or knife in the woods or fields or upon the waters of this State for the purpose of hunting, target practice or fishing, provided that the firearm or knife is legal and appropriate for hunting or fishing purposes in this State and he has in his possession a valid hunting license, or, with respect to fresh water fishing, a valid fishing license;

(3) A person transporting any firearm or knife while traveling:

(a) Directly to or from any place for the purpose of hunting or fishing, provided the person has in his possession a valid hunting or fishing license; or

(b) Directly to or from any target range, or other authorized place for the purpose of practice, match, target, trap or skeet shooting exhibitions, provided in all cases that during the course of the travel all firearms are carried in the manner specified in subsection g. of this section and the person has complied with all the provisions and requirements of Title 23 of the Revised Statutes and any amendments thereto and all rules and regulations promulgated thereunder; or

(c) In the case of a firearm, directly to or from any exhibition or display of firearms which is sponsored by any law enforcement agency, any rifle or pistol club, or any firearms collectors club, for the purpose of displaying the firearms to the public or to the members of the organization or club, provided, however, that not less than 30 days prior to the exhibition or display, notice of the exhibition or display shall be given to the Superintendent of the State Police by the sponsoring organization or club, and the sponsor has complied with such reasonable safety regulations as the superintendent may promulgate. Any firearms transported pursuant to this section shall be transported in the manner specified in subsection g. of this section;

(4) A person from keeping or carrying about a private or commercial aircraft or any boat, or from transporting to or from such vessel for the purpose of installation or repair a visual distress signaling device approved by the United States Coast Guard.

g. All weapons being transported under paragraph (2) of subsection b., subsection e., or paragraph (1) or (3) of subsection f. of this section shall be carried unloaded and contained in a closed and fastened case, gunbox, securely tied package, or locked in the trunk of the automobile in which it is being transported, and in the course of travel shall include only such deviations as are reasonably necessary under the circumstances.

h. Nothing in subsection d. of N.J.S.2C:39–5 shall be construed to prevent any employee of a public utility, as defined in R.S.48:2–13, doing business in this State or any United States Postal Service employee, while in the actual performance of duties which specifically require regular and frequent visits to private premises, from possessing, carrying or using any device which projects, releases or emits any substance specified as being noninjurious to canines or other animals by the Commissioner of Health and Senior Services and which immobilizes only on a temporary basis and produces only temporary physical discomfort through being vaporized or otherwise dispensed in the air for the sole purpose of repelling canine or other animal attacks.

The device shall be used solely to repel only those canine or other animal attacks when the canines or other animals are not restrained in a fashion sufficient to allow the employee to properly perform his duties.

Any device used pursuant to this act shall be selected from a list of products, which consist of active and inert ingredients, permitted by the Commissioner of Health and Senior Services.

i. Nothing in N.J.S.2C:39–5 shall be construed to prevent any person who is 18 years of age or older and who has not been convicted of a felony, from possession for the purpose of personal self-defense of one pocket-sized device which contains and releases not more than three-quarters of an ounce of chemical substance not ordinarily capable of lethal use or of inflicting serious bodily injury, but rather, is intended to produce temporary physical discomfort or disability through being vaporized or otherwise dispensed in the air. Any person in possession of any device in violation of this subsection shall be deemed and adjudged to be a disorderly person, and upon conviction thereof, shall be punished by a fine of not less than $100.00.

j. A person shall qualify for an exemption from the provisions of N.J.S.2C:39–5, as specified under subsections a. and c. of this section, if the person has satisfactorily completed a firearms training course approved by the Police Training Commission.

Such exempt person shall not possess or carry a firearm until the person has satisfactorily completed a firearms training course and shall annually qualify in the use of a revolver or similar weapon. For purposes of this subsection, a "firearms training course" means a course of instruction in the safe use, maintenance and storage of firearms which is approved by the Police Training Commission. The commission shall approve a firearms training course if the requirements of the course are substantially equivalent to the requirements for firearms training provided by police training courses which are certified under section 6 of P.L.1961, c. 56 (C.52:17B–71). A person who is specified in paragraph (1), (2), (3) or (6) of subsection a. of this section shall be exempt from the requirements of this subsection.

k. Nothing in subsection d. of N.J.S.2C:39–5 shall be construed to prevent any financial institution, or any duly authorized personnel of the institution, from possessing, carrying or using for the protection of money or property, any device which projects, releases or emits tear gas or other substances intended to produce temporary physical discomfort or temporary identification.

l. Nothing in subsection b. of N.J.S.2C:39–5 shall be construed to prevent a law enforcement officer who retired in good standing, including a retirement because of a disability pursuant to section 6 of P.L.1944, c. 255 (C.43:16A–6), section 7 of P.L.1944, c. 255 (C.43:16A–7), section 1 of P.L.1989, c. 103 (C.43:16A–6.1) or any substantially similar statute governing the disability retirement of federal law enforcement officers, provided the officer was a regularly employed, full-time law enforcement officer for an aggregate of four or more years prior to his disability retirement and further provided that the disability which constituted the basis for the officer's retirement did not involve a certification that the officer was mentally incapacitated for the performance of his usual law enforcement duties and any other available duty in the department which his employer was willing to assign to him or does not subject that retired officer to any of the disabilities set forth in subsection c. of N.J.S.2C:58–3 which would disqualify the retired officer from possessing or carrying a firearm, who semi-annually qualifies in the use of the handgun he is permitted to carry in accordance with the requirements and procedures established by the Attorney General pursuant to subsection j. of this section and pays the actual costs associated with those semi-annual qualifications, who is 75 years of age or younger, and who was regularly employed as a full-time member of the State Police; a full-time member of an interstate police force; a full-time member of a county or municipal police department in this State; a full-time member of a State law enforcement agency; a full-time sheriff, undersheriff or sheriff's officer of a county of this State; a full-time State or county corrections officer; a full-time county park police officer; a full-time county prosecutor's detective or investigator; a full-time federal law enforcement officer; or is a qualified retired law enforcement officer as used in the federal "Law Enforcement Officers Safety Act of 2004," Pub.L. 108–277, domiciled in this State from carrying a handgun in the same manner as law enforcement officers exempted under paragraph (7) of subsection a. of this section under the conditions provided herein:

(1) The retired law enforcement officer shall make application in writing to the Superintendent of State Police for approval to carry a handgun for one year. An application for annual renewal shall be submitted in the same manner.

(2) Upon receipt of the written application of the retired law enforcement officer, the superintendent shall request a verification of service from the chief law enforcement officer of the organization in which the retired officer was last regularly employed as a full-time law enforcement officer prior to retiring. The verification of service shall include:

(a) The name and address of the retired officer;

(b) The date that the retired officer was hired and the date that the officer retired;

(c) A list of all handguns known to be registered to that officer;

(d) A statement that, to the reasonable knowledge of the chief law enforcement officer, the retired officer is not subject to any of the restrictions set forth in subsection c. of N.J.S.2C:58–3; and

(e) A statement that the officer retired in good standing.

(3) If the superintendent approves a retired officer's application or reapplication to carry a handgun pursuant to the provisions of this subsection, the superintendent shall notify in writing the chief law enforcement officer of the municipality wherein that retired officer resides. In the event the retired officer resides in a municipality which has no chief law enforcement officer

or law enforcement agency, the superintendent shall maintain a record of the approval.

(4) The superintendent shall issue to an approved retired officer an identification card permitting the retired officer to carry a handgun pursuant to this subsection. This identification card shall be valid for one year from the date of issuance and shall be valid throughout the State. The identification card shall not be transferable to any other person. The identification card shall be carried at all times on the person of the retired officer while the retired officer is carrying a handgun. The retired officer shall produce the identification card for review on the demand of any law enforcement officer or authority.

(5) Any person aggrieved by the denial of the superintendent of approval for a permit to carry a handgun pursuant to this subsection may request a hearing in the Superior Court of New Jersey in the county in which he resides by filing a written request for such a hearing within 30 days of the denial. Copies of the request shall be served upon the superintendent and the county prosecutor. The hearing shall be held within 30 days of the filing of the request, and no formal pleading or filing fee shall be required. Appeals from the determination of such a hearing shall be in accordance with law and the rules governing the courts of this State.

(6) A judge of the Superior Court may revoke a retired officer's privilege to carry a handgun pursuant to this subsection for good cause shown on the application of any interested person. A person who becomes subject to any of the disabilities set forth in subsection c. of N.J.S.2C:58–3 shall surrender, as prescribed by the superintendent, his identification card issued under paragraph (4) of this subsection to the chief law enforcement officer of the municipality wherein he resides or the superintendent, and shall be permanently disqualified to carry a handgun under this subsection.

(7) The superintendent may charge a reasonable application fee to retired officers to offset any costs associated with administering the application process set forth in this subsection.

m. Nothing in subsection d. of N.J.S.2C:39–5 shall be construed to prevent duly authorized personnel of the New Jersey Division of Fish and Wildlife, while in the actual performance of duties, from possessing, transporting or using any device that projects, releases or emits any substance specified as being non-injurious to wildlife by the Director of the Division of Animal Health in the Department of Agriculture, and which may immobilize wildlife and produces only temporary physical discomfort through being vaporized or otherwise dispensed in the air for the purpose of repelling bear or other animal attacks or for the aversive conditioning of wildlife.

n. Nothing in subsection b., c., d. or e. of N.J.S.2C:39–5 shall be construed to prevent duly authorized personnel of the New Jersey Division of Fish and Wildlife, while in the actual performance of duties, from possessing, transporting or using hand held pistol-like devices, rifles or shotguns that launch pyrotechnic missiles for the sole purpose of frightening, hazing or aversive conditioning of nuisance or depredating wild-life; from possessing, transporting or using rifles, pistols or similar devices for the sole purpose of chemically immobilizing wild or non-domestic animals; or, provided the duly authorized person complies with the requirements of subsection j. of this section, from possessing, transporting or using rifles or shotguns, upon completion of a Police Training Commission approved training course, in order to dispatch injured or dangerous animals or for non-lethal use for the purpose of frightening, hazing or aversive conditioning of nuisance or depredating wildlife.

L.1978, c. 95, § 2C:39–6, eff. Sept. 1, 1979. Amended by L.1979, c. 179, § 5, eff. Sept. 1, 1979; L.1979, c. 332, § 8, eff. Jan. 21, 1980; L.1981, c. 108, § 1, eff. April 2, 1981; L.1981, c. 219, § 1, eff. July 20, 1981; L.1981, c. 294, § 1, eff. Oct. 9, 1981; L.1981, c. 409, § 2, eff. Jan. 7, 1982; L.1981, c. 480, § 1, eff. Jan. 12, 1982; L.1981, c. 511, § 4, eff. Jan. 12, 1982; L.1982, c. 154, § 1, eff. Oct. 26, 1982; L.1982, c. 173, § 1, eff. Nov. 12, 1982; L.1983, c. 479, § 3, eff. Jan. 12, 1984; L.1983, c. 552, § 1, eff. Jan. 17, 1984; L.1985, c. 76, § 8, eff. March 14, 1985; L.1985, c. 150, § 1, eff. April 25, 1985; L.1985, c. 324, § 1; L.1985, c. 376, § 1, eff. Nov. 26, 1985; L.1985, c. 439, § 13, eff. Oct. 1, 1986; L.1986, c. 150, § 7, eff. Feb. 12, 1987; L.1987, c. 139, § 1, eff. June 9, 1987; L.1987, c. 172, § 1, eff. July 9, 1987; L.1989, c. 291, § 4, eff. Feb. 11, 1990; L.1991, c. 327, § 2, eff. Dec. 20, 1991; L.1991, c. 386, § 3, eff. March 16, 1992; L.1992, c. 94, § 2, eff. Sept. 9, 1992; L.1993, c. 246, § 2, eff. Aug. 9, 1993; L.1995, c. 273, § 2, eff. Dec. 8, 1995; L.1995, c. 280, § 21, eff. Dec. 15, 1995; L.1997, c. 67, § 1, eff. April 8, 1997; L.1997, c. 210, § 6, eff. Aug. 18, 1997; L.1997, c. 393, § 1, eff. Jan. 19, 1998; L.2001, c. 79, § 15; L.2001, c. 362, § 4, eff. Jan. 7, 2002; L.2003, c. 168, § 2, eff. Sept. 3, 2003; L.2005, c. 216, § 1, eff. Nov. 1, 2005; L.2005, c. 372, § 14, eff. Jan. 12, 2006; L.2007, c. 313, § 1, eff. March 1, 2008; L.2007, c. 314, § 1, eff. April 1, 2008.

Validity

Subsection (c)(17) of § 2C:39–6 was held unconstitutional by the Supreme Court of New Jersey in the case of In the Matter of P.L.2001, Chapter 362, In re P.L. 2001, Chapter 362, 186 N.J. 368, 895 A.2d 1128 (2006).

2C:39–6.1. Expired

2C:39–7. Certain persons not to have weapons

a. Except as provided in subsection b. of this section, any person, having been convicted in this State or elsewhere of the crime of aggravated assault, arson, burglary, escape, extortion, homicide, kidnapping, robbery, aggravated sexual assault, sexual assault, bias intimidation in violation of N.J.S.2C:16–1 or endangering the welfare of a child pursuant to N.J.S.2C:24–4, whether or not armed with or having in his possession any weapon enumerated in subsection r. of N.J.S.2C:39–1, or any person convicted of a crime

pursuant to the provisions of N.J.S.2C:39–3, N.J.S.2C:39–4 or N.J. S.2C:39–9, or any person who has ever been committed for a mental disorder to any hospital, mental institution or sanitarium unless he possesses a certificate of a medical doctor or psychiatrist licensed to practice in New Jersey or other satisfactory proof that he is no longer suffering from a mental disorder which interferes with or handicaps him in the handling of a firearm, or any person who has been convicted of other than a disorderly persons or petty disorderly persons offense for the unlawful use, possession or sale of a controlled dangerous substance as defined in N.J.S.2C:35–2 who purchases, owns, possesses or controls any of the said weapons is guilty of a crime of the fourth degree.

b. (1) A person having been convicted in this State or elsewhere of the crime of aggravated assault, arson, burglary, escape, extortion, homicide, kidnapping, robbery, aggravated sexual assault, sexual assault, bias intimidation in violation of N.J.S.2C:16–1, endangering the welfare of a child pursuant to N.J.S.2C:24–4, stalking pursuant to P.L.1992, c. 209 (C.2C:12–10) or a crime involving domestic violence as defined in section 3 of P.L.1991, c. 261 (C.2C:25–19), whether or not armed with or having in his possession a weapon enumerated in subsection r. of N.J.S.2C: 39–1, or a person having been convicted of a crime pursuant to the provisions of N.J.S.2C:35–3 through N.J.S.2C:35–6, inclusive; section 1 of P.L.1987, c. 101 (C.2C:35–7); N.J.S.2C:35–11; N.J.S.2C:39–3; N.J.S.2C:39–4; or N.J.S.2C:39–9 who purchases, owns, possesses or controls a firearm is guilty of a crime of the second degree and upon conviction thereof, the person shall be sentenced to a term of imprisonment by the court. The term of imprisonment shall include the imposition of a minimum term, which shall be fixed at five years, during which the defendant shall be ineligible for parole. If the defendant is sentenced to an extended term of imprisonment pursuant to N.J.S.2C:43–7, the extended term of imprisonment shall include the imposition of a minimum term, which shall be fixed at, or between, one-third and one-half of the sentence imposed by the court or five years, whichever is greater, during which the defendant shall be ineligible for parole.

(2) A person having been convicted in this State or elsewhere of a disorderly persons offense involving domestic violence,whether or not armed with or having in his possession a weapon enumerated in subsection r. of N.J.S. 2C:39–1, who purchases, owns, possesses or controls a firearm is guilty of a crime of the third degree.

(3) A person whose firearm is seized pursuant to the "Prevention of Domestic Violence Act of 1991," P.L. 1991, c. 261 (C.2C:25–17 et seq.) and whose firearm has not been returned, or who is subject to a court order prohibiting the possession of firearms issued pursuant to the "Prevention of Domestic Violence Act of 1991," P.L.1991, c.261 (C.2C:25–17 et seq.) who purchases, owns, possesses or controls a firearm is guilty of a crime

of the third degree, except that the provisions of this paragraph shall not apply to any law enforcement officer while actually on duty, or to any member of the Armed Forces of the United States or member of the National Guard while actually on duty or traveling to or from an authorized place of duty.

c. Whenever any person shall have been convicted in another state, territory, commonwealth or other jurisdiction of the United States, or any country in the world, in a court of competent jurisdiction, of a crime which in said other jurisdiction or country is comparable to one of the crimes enumerated in subsection a. or b. of this section, then that person shall be subject to the provisions of this section.

L.1979, c. 179, § 6, eff. Sept. 1, 1979. Amended by L.1987, c. 106, § 6; L.1991, c. 436, § 1, eff. Jan. 18, 1992; L.1992, c. 74, § 3, eff. July 31, 1992; L.1995, c. 114, § 1, eff. June 2, 1995; L.2001, c. 216, § 1, eff. Aug. 21, 2001; L.2001, c. 443, § 5, eff. Jan. 11, 2002; L.2003, c. 277, § 3, eff. Jan. 14, 2004.

2C:39–8. Blank

2C:39–9. Manufacture, transport, disposition and defacement of weapons and dangerous instruments and appliances

a. Machine guns. Any person who manufactures, causes to be manufactured, transports, ships, sells or disposes of any machine gun without being registered or licensed to do so as provided in chapter 58 is guilty of a crime of the third degree.

b. Sawed-off shotguns. Any person who manufactures, causes to be manufactured, transports, ships, sells or disposes of any sawed-off shotgun is guilty of a crime of the third degree.

c. Firearm silencers. Any person who manufactures, causes to be manufactured, transports, ships, sells or disposes of any firearm silencer is guilty of a crime of the fourth degree.

d. Weapons. Any person who manufactures, causes to be manufactured, transports, ships, sells or disposes of any weapon, including gravity knives, switchblade knives, ballistic knives, daggers, dirks, stilettos, billies, blackjacks, metal knuckles, sandclubs, slingshots, cesti or similar leather bands studded with metal filings, or, except as otherwise provided in subsection i. of this section, in the case of firearms if he is not licensed or registered to do so as provided in chapter 58, is guilty of a crime of the fourth degree. Any person who manufactures, causes to be manufactured, transports, ships, sells or disposes of any weapon or other device which projects, releases or emits tear gas or other substances intended to produce temporary physical discomfort or permanent injury through being vaporized or otherwise dispensed in the air, which is intended to be used for any purpose other than for authorized military or law enforcement purposes by duly authorized military or law enforcement personnel or the device is for the purpose of personal self-defense, is pocket-sized and

contains not more than three-quarters of an ounce of chemical substance not ordinarily capable of lethal use or of inflicting serious bodily injury, or other than to be used by any person permitted to possess such weapon or device under the provisions of subsection d. of N.J.S. 2C:39–5, which is intended for use by financial and other business institutions as part of an integrated security system, placed at fixed locations, for the protection of money and property, by the duly authorized personnel of those institutions, is guilty of a crime of the fourth degree.

e. Defaced firearms. Any person who defaces any firearm is guilty of a crime of the third degree. Any person who knowingly buys, receives, disposes of or conceals a defaced firearm, except an antique firearm or an antique handgun, is guilty of a crime of the fourth degree.

f. (1) Any person who manufactures, causes to be manufactured, transports, ships, sells, or disposes of any bullet, which is primarily designed for use in a handgun, and which is comprised of a bullet whose core or jacket, if the jacket is thicker than .025 of an inch, is made of tungsten carbide, or hard bronze, or other material which is harder than a rating of 72 or greater on the Rockwell B. Hardness Scale, and is therefore capable of breaching or penetrating body armor and which is intended to be used for any purpose other than for authorized military or law enforcement purposes by duly authorized military or law enforcement personnel, is guilty of a crime of the fourth degree.

(2) Nothing in this subsection shall be construed to prevent a licensed collector of ammunition as defined in paragraph (2) of subsection f. of N.J.S.2C:39–3 from transporting the bullets defined in paragraph (1) of this subsection from (a) any licensed retail or wholesale firearms dealer's place of business to the collector's dwelling, premises, or other land owned or possessed by him, or (b) to or from the collector's dwelling, premises or other land owned or possessed by him to any gun show for the purposes of display, sale, trade, or transfer between collectors, or (c) to or from the collector's dwelling, premises or other land owned or possessed by him to any rifle or pistol club organized in accordance with the rules prescribed by the National Board for the Promotion of Rifle Practice; provided that the club has filed a copy of its charter with the superintendent of the State Police and annually submits a list of its members to the superintendent, and provided further that the ammunition being transported shall be carried not loaded in any firearm and contained in a closed and fastened case, gun box, or locked in the trunk of the automobile in which it is being transported, and the course of travel shall include only such deviations as are reasonably necessary under the circumstances.

g. Assault firearms. Any person who manufactures, causes to be manufactured, transports, ships, sells or disposes of an assault firearm without being registered or licensed to do so pursuant to N.J.S.2C:58–1 et seq. is guilty of a crime of the third degree.

h.   Large capacity ammunition magazines.   Any person who manufactures, causes to be manufactured, transports, ships, sells or disposes of a large capacity ammunition magazine which is intended to be used for any purpose other than for authorized military or law enforcement purposes by duly authorized military or law enforcement personnel is guilty of a crime of the fourth degree.

i.   Transporting firearms into this State for an unlawful sale or transfer.   Any person who knowingly transports, ships or otherwise brings into this State any firearm for the purpose of unlawfully selling, transferring, giving, assigning or otherwise disposing of that firearm to another individual is guilty of a crime of the second degree.   The temporary transfer of a firearm while hunting or target shooting, the transfer of any firearm that uses air or carbon dioxide to expel a projectile, or the transfer of an antique firearm shall not constitute a violation of this subsection.

L.1978, c. 95, § 2C:39–9, eff. Sept. 1, 1979.   Amended by L.1979, c. 179, § 7, eff. Sept. 1, 1979; L.1980, c. 108, § 1, eff. Sept. 11, 1980; L.1981, c. 480, § 2, eff. Jan. 12, 1982; L.1983, c. 58, § 2, eff. Feb. 7, 1983; L.1987, c. 228, § 3, eff. July 30, 1987; L.1990, c. 32, § 3, eff. May 30, 1990; L.1999, c. 233, § 3; L.2007, c. 298, § 1, eff. April 1, 2008.

2C:39–9.1.   Sale of knife with blade length over 5 inches or overall length over 10 inches to person under 18

A person who sells any hunting, fishing, combat or survival knife having a blade length of five inches or more or an overall length of 10 inches or more to a person under 18 years of age commits a crime of the fourth degree; except that the establishment by a preponderance of the evidence of all of the following facts by a person making the sale shall constitute an affirmative defense to any prosecution therefor: a. that the purchaser falsely represented his age by producing a driver's license bearing a photograph of the licensee, or by producing a photographic identification card issued pursuant to section 2 of P.L.1980, c. 47 (C.39:3–29.3), or by producing a similar card purporting to be a valid identification card indicating that he was 18 years of age or older, and b. that the appearance of the purchaser was such that an ordinary prudent person would believe him to be 18 years of age or older, and c. that the sale was made in good faith relying upon the indicators of age listed in a. and b. above.

L.1987, c. 228, § 4, eff. July 30, 1987.   Amended by L.2003, c. 175, § 2, eff. Sept. 10, 2003.

2C:39–9.2.   Sale of handcuffs to person under age 18; disorderly persons offense

A person who sells handcuffs to a person under 18 years of age is guilty of a disorderly persons offense.   A law enforcement officer shall confiscate handcuffs sold in violation of the law.   As used in this section, "handcuffs" mean a device, conventionally used for law enforcement purposes, that can be tightened and locked about the wrists for the purpose of restraining a person's movement.

L.1991, c. 437, § 2, eff. Jan. 18, 1992.

2C:39–10.   Violation of the regulatory provisions relating to firearms;   false representation in applications

a.   (1) Except as otherwise provided in paragraph (2) of this subsection, any person who knowingly violates the regulatory provisions relating to manufacturing or wholesaling of firearms (section 2C:58–1), retailing of firearms (section 2C:58–2), permits to purchase certain firearms (section 2C:58–3), permits to carry certain firearms (section 2C:58–4), licenses to procure machine guns or assault firearms (section 2C:58–5), or incendiary or tracer ammunition (section 2C:58–10), except acts which are punishable under section 2C:39–5 or section 2C:39–9, is guilty of a crime of the fourth degree.

(2) A licensed dealer who knowingly violates the provisions of subparagraph (d) of paragraph (5) of subsection a. of N.J.S.2C:58–2 is a disorderly person.

b.   Any person who knowingly violates the regulatory provisions relating to notifying the authorities of possessing certain items of explosives (section 2C:58–7), or of certain wounds (section 2C:58–8) is a disorderly person.

c.   Any person who gives or causes to be given any false information, or signs a fictitious name or address, in applying for a firearms purchaser identification card, a permit to purchase a handgun, a permit to carry a handgun, a permit to possess a machine gun, a permit to possess an assault firearm, or in completing the certificate or any other instrument required by law in purchasing or otherwise acquiring delivery of any rifle, shotgun, handgun, machine gun, or assault firearm or any other firearm, is guilty of a crime of the third degree.

d.   Any person who gives or causes to be given any false information in registering an assault firearm pursuant to section 11 of P.L.1990, c. 32 (C.2C:58–12) or in certifying that an assault firearm was rendered inoperable pursuant to section 12 of P.L.1990, c. 32 (C.2C:58–13) commits a crime of the fourth degree.

e.   Any person who knowingly sells, gives, transfers, assigns or otherwise disposes of a firearm to a person who is under the age of 18 years, except as permitted in section 14 of P.L.1979, c. 179 (C.2C:58–6.1), is guilty of a crime of the third degree.   Notwithstanding any other provision of law to the contrary, the sentence imposed for a conviction under this subsection shall include a mandatory minimum three–year term of imprisonment, during which the defendant shall be ineligible for parole.

f.   Unless the recipient is authorized to possess the handgun in connection with the performance of official duties under the provisions of N. J.S.2C:39–6, any person who knowingly sells, gives, transfers, assigns or otherwise disposes of a handgun to a person who is under the age of 21 years, except as permitted in section 14 of P.L.1979, c. 179 (C.2C:58–6.1), is guilty of a crime of the third degree.

g. Any person who knowingly gives or causes to be given any false information or knowingly engages in any other fraudulent conduct in applying for an exemption to purchase more than one handgun in a 30–day period in violation of the provisions of section 4 of P.L.2009, c. 186 (C.2C:58–3.4) shall be guilty of a crime of the third degree. The presumption of nonimprisonment set forth in N.J.S.2C:44–1 shall not apply to persons convicted under the provisions of this subsection.

L.1978, c. 95, § 2C:39–10, eff. Sept. 1, 1979. Amended by L.1979, c. 179, § 8, eff. Sept. 1, 1979; L.1990, c. 32, § 4, eff. May 30, 1990; L.1993, c. 49, § 1, eff. Feb. 18, 1993; L.1999, c. 233, § 4; L.2000, c. 145, § 2; L.2009, c. 186, § 3, eff. Jan. 12, 2010.

2C:39–11. Pawnbrokers; loaning on firearms

a. Any pawnbroker who sells, offers to sell or to lend or to give away any weapon, destructive device or explosive is guilty of a crime of the third degree.

b. Any person who loans money, the security for which is any handgun, rifle or shotgun is guilty of a disorderly persons offense.

L.1978, c. 95, § 2C:39–11, eff. Sept. 1, 1979. Amended by L.1979, c. 179, § 9, eff. Sept. 1, 1979.

2C:39–12. Voluntary surrender

No person shall be convicted of an offense under this chapter for possessing any firearms, weapons, destructive devices, silencers or explosives, if after giving written notice of his intention to do so, including the proposed date and time of surrender, he voluntarily surrendered the weapon, device, instrument or substance in question to the superintendent or to the chief of police in the municipality in which he resides, provided that the required notice is received by the superintendent or chief of police before any charges have been made or complaints filed against such person for the unlawful possession of the weapon, device, instrument or substance in question and before any investigation has been commenced by any law enforcement agency concerning the unlawful possession. Nothing in this section shall be construed as granting immunity from prosecution for any crime or offense except that of the unlawful possession of such weapons, devices, instruments or substances surrendered as herein provided.

L.1978, c. 95, § 2C:39–12, eff. Sept. 1, 1979.

2C:39–13. Unlawful use of body vests

Unlawful use of body vests. A person is guilty of a crime if he uses or wears a body vest while engaged in the commission of, or an attempt to commit, or flight after committing or attempting to commit murder, manslaughter, robbery, sexual assault, burglary, kidnap-ing, criminal escape or assault under N.J.S. 2C:12–1b. Use or wearing a body vest while engaged in the commission of, or an attempt to commit, or flight after committing or attempting to commit a crime of the first degree is a crime of the second degree. Otherwise it is a crime of the third degree.

As used in this section, "body vest" means bullet-resistant body armor which is intended to provide ballistic and trauma protection.

L.1983, c. 152, § 1, eff. April 22, 1983. Amended by L.1999, c. 306, § 1, eff. Jan. 4, 2000.

2C:39–14. Training, practice or instruction in use, application or making of firearm, explosive device or technique capable of causing injury for illegal activity

a. Any person who teaches or demonstrates to any other person the use, application, or making of any firearm, explosive or destructive device, or technique capable of causing injury or death to a person, knowing or having reason to know or intending that it will be employed for use in, or in furtherance of, an illegal activity is guilty of a crime of the second degree.

b. Any person who assembles with one or more persons for the purpose of training with, practicing with, or being instructed in the use of any firearm, explosive or destructive device, or technique capable of causing injury or death to a person, intending to unlawfully employ it for use in, or in furtherance of, an illegal activity is guilty of a crime of the second degree.

L.1983, c. 229, § 1, eff. June 29, 1983. Amended by L.1988, c. 76, § 1, eff. Aug. 1, 1988.

2C:39–15. Offer to sell machine gun, semi–automatic rifle or assault firearm by advertisement in newspaper without statement of necessity of license

Any person who offers to sell a machine gun, semi-automatic rifle, or assault firearm by means of an advertisement published in a newspaper circulating within this State, which advertisement does not specify that the purchaser shall hold a valid license to purchase and possess a machine gun or assault firearm, or a valid firearms identification card to purchase and possess an automatic or semi-automatic rifle, is a disorderly person.

L.1983, c. 515, § 1, eff. Jan. 17, 1984. Amended by L.1990, c. 32, § 5, eff. May 30, 1990.

2C:39–16. Leader of firearms trafficking network; crime of the first degree

A person is a leader of a firearms trafficking network if he conspires with others as an organizer, supervisor, financier or manager, to engage for profit in a scheme or course of conduct to unlawfully manufacture, transport, ship, sell or dispose of any firearm. Leader of firearms trafficking network is a crime of the first degree.

As used in this section: "leader of a firearms trafficking network" means a person who occupies a position of authority or control over other persons in a scheme or organization of illegal firearms manufacturing, transporting, shipping or selling and who exercises that authority or control over others involved in the scheme or organization.

Notwithstanding the provisions of subsection a. of N.J.S. 2C:43–3, the court may also impose a fine not to exceed $500,000.00 or five times the value of the firearms involved, whichever is greater.

Notwithstanding the provisions of N.J.S. 2C:1–8, a conviction of leader of firearms trafficking network shall not merge with the conviction for any offense which is the object of the conspiracy. Nothing contained in this section shall prohibit the court from imposing an extended term pursuant to N.J.S. 2C:43–7; nor shall this section be construed in any way to preclude or limit the prosecution or conviction of any person for conspiracy under N.J.S. 2C:5–2, or any prosecution or conviction for weapons offenses under the provisions of chapter 39 of Title 2C of the New Jersey Statutes, N.J.S. 2C:41–2 (racketeering activities) or subsection g. of N.J.S. 2C:5–2 (leader of organized crime).

It shall not be necessary in any prosecution under this section for the State to prove that any intended profit was actually realized. The trier of fact may infer that a particular scheme or course of conduct was undertaken for profit from all of the attendant circumstances, including but not limited to the number of persons involved in the scheme or course of conduct, the actor's net worth and his expenditures in relation to his legitimate sources of income, the amount of firearms involved, or the amount of cash or currency involved.

It shall not be a defense to a prosecution under this section that the firearms were brought into or transported in this State solely for ultimate distribution or dispensing in another jurisdiction; nor shall it be a defense that any profit was intended to be made in another jurisdiction.

L.1995, c. 405, § 1, eff. Jan. 10, 1996.

CHAPTER 40

OTHER OFFENSES RELATING TO PUBLIC SAFETY

Section
2C:40–1.   Creating a hazard.
2C:40–2.   Refusing to yield a party line.
2C:40–3.   Hazing; aggravated hazing.
2C:40–4.   Consent not available as defense to hazing.
2C:40–5.   Conduct constituting offense may be prosecuted under other provisions of Title 2C.
2C:40–6.   Definitions.
2C:40–7.   Portable, oil-burning heating devices; certificate of evaluation by test of safety prior to sale, offer for sale or use.
2C:40–8.   Label cautioning and informing user.
2C:40–9.   Inclusion of instructions concerning proper and safe maintenance and operation.
2C:40–10.   Construction requirements.

Section
2C:40–11.   Automatic safety shut-off device or design feature to eliminate fire hazard in event of tipover.
2C:40–12.   Carbon monoxide limitations.
2C:40–13.   Posting of sign at point of sale or display of prohibition of use in multiple dwellings or in residences in certain municipalities.
2C:40–14.   Regulations.
2C:40–15.   Violations; petty disorderly persons offense.
2C:40–16.   Definitions.
2C:40–17.   Tampering with cosmetic, drug, or food product; third degree crime; exception.
2C:40–18.   Knowing violation or failure to perform duty imposed by law intended to protect public safety.
2C:40–19.   Placing or inserting writing in or on consumer product.
2C:40–20.   Markers used to designate boundary lines; visibility required to avoid injury; exception.
2C:40–21.   Tattooing and body piercing of minors.
2C:40–22.   Driving without a license or when a license is suspended or revoked by listed governmental authorities; additional penalties for causing injury or death; causal relationship provisions inapplicable.
2C:40–23.   Information required to produce devices to operate motor vehicle locks.
2C:40–24.   Possession of traffic control preemption device; exceptions; civil penalty.
2C:40–25.   Persons permitted to dispense contact lenses; violation; penalties.
2C:40–26.   Driving while license is suspended or revoked; degree of crime; minimum sentence.

2C:40–1.   Creating a hazard

A person is guilty of a disorderly persons offense when:

a. He maintains, stores or displays unattended in a place other than a permanently enclosed building or discards in any public or private place, including any junkyard, where it might attract children, a container which has a compartment of more than one and one-half cubic feet capacity and a door or lid which locks or fastens automatically when closed and which cannot easily be opened from the inside, he fails to remove the door, lid, locking or fastening device;

b. Being the owner or otherwise having possession of property upon which an abandoned well or cesspool is located, he fails to cover the same with suitable protective construction; or

c. He discards or abandons in any public or private place accessible to children, whether or not such children are trespassers, any intact television picture tube, or being the owner, lessee or manager of such place, knowingly permits such abandoned or discarded television picture tube to remain there in such condition.

L.1978, c. 95, § 2C:40–1, eff. Sept. 1, 1979.

2C:40–2. Refusing to yield a party line

A person is guilty of a disorderly persons offense when, being informed that a party line is needed for an emergency call, he refuses immediately to relinquish such line.

"Party line" means a subscriber's line telephone circuit, consisting of two or more main telephone stations connected therewith, each station with a distinctive ring or telephone number.

"Emergency call" means a telephone call to a police or fire department or for medical aid or ambulance service, necessitated by a situation in which human life or property is in jeopardy and prompt summoning of aid is essential.

L.1978, c. 95, § 2C:40–2, eff. Sept. 1, 1979.

2C:40–3. Hazing; aggravated hazing

a. A person is guilty of hazing, a disorderly persons offense, if, in connection with initiation of applicants to or members of a student or fraternal organization, he knowingly or recklessly organizes, promotes, facilitates or engages in any conduct, other than competitive athletic events, which places or may place another person in danger of bodily injury.

b. A person is guilty of aggravated hazing, a crime of the fourth degree, if he commits an act prohibited in subsection a. which results in serious bodily injury to another person.

L.1980, c. 169, § 1, eff. Dec. 18, 1980.

2C:40–4. Consent not available as defense to hazing

Notwithstanding any other provision of Title 2C of the New Jersey Statutes to the contrary, consent shall not be available as a defense to a prosecution under this Act.

L.1980, c. 169, § 2, eff. Dec. 18, 1980.

2C:40–5. Conduct constituting offense may be prosecuted under other provisions of Title 2C

Conduct constituting an offense under this Act may, at the discretion of the prosecuting attorney, be prosecuted under any other applicable provision of Title 2C of the New Jersey Statutes.

L.1980, c. 169, § 3, eff. Dec. 18, 1980.

2C:40–6. Definitions

As used in this act:

a. "Portable, oil-burning heating device" means any self-contained, self-supporting, oil-fueled heater not connected to a flue, equipped with an integral reservoir, and designed to be carried from one location to another.

b. "Oil" means any liquid fuel with a flash point of greater than 100 degrees Fahrenheit, including but not limited to kerosene.

L.1983, c. 438, § 1, eff. July 7, 1984.

2C:40–7. Portable, oil-burning heating devices; certificate of evaluation by test of safety prior to sale, offer for sale or use

A portable, oil-burning heating device shall not be sold, offered for sale, or used in this State unless a nationally recognized testing or inspection agency, such as but not limited to Underwriters' Laboratory, Inc.:

a. Has evaluated the portable, oil-burning heating device with respect to reasonably foreseeable hazards to life and property that it might cause;

b. Has found the portable, oil-burning heating device to be reasonably safe for its specific purpose;

c. Has shown the particular model of the portable, oil-burning heating device on a list of devices that have been evaluated according to the requirements of subsection a. of this section and found to be safe according to the requirements of subsection b. of this section;

d. Has accompanied the portable, oil-burning heating device with a certificate or with the mark, name, or symbol of the agency as an indication that it has been evaluated according to the requirements of subsection a. of this section, found safe according to the requirements of subsection b. of this section, and listed according to the requirements of subsection c. of this section. The certificate or the mark, name, or symbol of the agency must accompany the portable, oil-burning heating device at all times when it is sold, offered for sale, or used in this State.

L.1983, c. 438, § 2, eff. July 7, 1984.

2C:40–8. Label cautioning and informing user

A portable, oil-burning heating device shall not be sold, offered for sale, or used in this State unless a label is affixed to the device cautioning and informing the user concerning:

a. The amount and source of ventilation that is adequate when the device is in operation;

b. The type of fuel that should be used in the device;

c. The steps that should be followed in order to refuel the device safely;

d. The proper placement and handling of the device when it is in operation to prevent fire, burns, and other safety hazards;

e. The proper procedures for lighting the device and regulating and extinguishing the flame.

L.1983, c. 438, § 3, eff. July 7, 1984.

2C:40–9. Inclusion of instructions concerning proper and safe maintenance and operation

No portable, oil-burning heating device shall be sold or offered for sale in this State unless it is accompanied by instructions concerning its proper and safe maintenance and operation.

L.1983, c. 438, § 4, eff. July 7, 1984.

2C:40–10. Construction requirements

No portable, oil-burning heating device shall be sold, offered for sale, or used in this State unless it is constructed with a low center of gravity and a minimum tipping angle of 33 degrees from the vertical with an empty reservoir.

L.1983, c. 438, § 5, eff. July 7, 1984.

2C:40–11. Automatic safety shut-off device or design feature to eliminate fire hazard in event of tipover

No portable, oil-burning heating device shall be sold, offered for sale, or used in this State unless equipped with an automatic safety shut-off device or inherent design feature that eliminates fire hazards in the event of tipover.

L.1983, c. 438, § 6, eff. July 7, 1984.

2C:40–12. Carbon monoxide limitations

No portable, oil-burning heating device which, when operated according to the instructions that must accompany the heater as required by section 4 of this act,[1] produces carbon monoxide at a rate that creates a hazard shall be sold, offered for sale, or used in this State.

L.1983, c. 438, § 7, eff. July 7, 1984.

[1] N.J.S.A. § 2C:40–9.

2C:40–13. Posting of sign at point of sale or display of prohibition of use in multiple dwellings or in residences in certain municipalities

No portable, oil-burning heating device shall be sold or offered for sale in this State unless a conspicuous sign is posted at the point of sale and the point of display notifying a purchaser or potential purchaser that portable, oil-burning heating devices are prohibited for use in multiple dwellings in the State by regulations adopted pursuant to the "Hotel and Multiple Dwelling Law," P.L.1967, c. 76 (C. 55:13A–1 et seq.) and that certain municipalities in the State have adopted housing codes prohibiting the use of portable, oil-burning heating devices in residences within the municipality.

L.1983, c. 438, § 8, eff. July 7, 1984.

2C:40–14. Regulations

Pursuant to the "Administrative Procedure Act," P.L.1968, c. 410 (C. 52:14B–1 et seq.), the Commissioner of the Department of Community Affairs shall adopt regulations for the implementation and enforcement of this act.

L.1983, c. 438, § 9, eff. July 7, 1984.

2C:40–15. Violations; petty disorderly persons offense

Any person who sells, offers for sale or uses any portable, kerosene-burning heating device in violation of the provisions of this act is guilty of a petty disorderly persons offense. Each sale of a heater in violation of this act constitutes a separate offense.

L.1983, c. 438, § 10, eff. July 7, 1984.

2C:40–16. Definitions

As used in this act:

a. "Cosmetic" means any substance or other device which is used for the treatment of the skin, hair or nails.

b. "Drug" means any over-the-counter or prescribed medicine.

c. "Food product" means anything sold for human consumption, and includes tobacco products.

d. "Tamper" means to adulterate a cosmetic, drug or food product by adding any poisonous, deleterious or noxious substance or diluent which may be injurious or detrimental to a person's health. "Tamper" includes the addition of any substance or diluent or both to a prescribed drug resulting in a reduction or increase of the strength of that drug without so being ordered by the prescriber. Any change in the strength of the prescribed drug must be noted on the medication or prescription label and if not so noted the drug shall be considered to have been tampered with and mislabeled.

L.1987, c. 421, § 1. Amended by L.2007, c. 69, § 1, eff. April 30, 2007.

2C:40–17. Tampering with cosmetic, drug, or food product; third degree crime; exception

a. Except as provided in subsection b. of this section, a person who knowingly tampers with a cosmetic, drug or food product is guilty of a crime of the third degree, except that nothing herein shall be deemed to preclude a charge for a greater crime under any other provision of Title 2C of the New Jersey Statutes.

b. A health care professional or his agent who is authorized to prescribe, dispense or administer medication who knowingly tampers with medicine prescribed for a person is guilty of a crime of the second degree, except that nothing herein shall be deemed to preclude a charge for a greater crime under any other provision of Title 2C of the New Jersey Statutes.

c. Notwithstanding the provisions of paragraph (2) of subsection a. of N.J.S.2C:43–6, any sentence imposed upon a health care professional or his agent pursuant to subsection b. of this section shall include a term of imprisonment. The court may not suspend or make any other noncustodial disposition of a person sentenced pursuant to the provisions of this subsection.

L.1987, c. 421, § 2. Amended by L.2007, c. 69, § 2, eff. April 30, 2007.

2C:40–18. Knowing violation or failure to perform duty imposed by law intended to protect public safety

a. A person is guilty of a crime of the second degree if the person knowingly violates a law intended to protect the public health and safety or knowingly fails to perform a duty imposed by a law intended to protect the public health and safety and recklessly causes death.

b. A person is guilty of a crime of the third degree if the person knowingly violates a law intended to protect the public health and safety or knowingly fails to perform a duty imposed by a law intended to protect the public health and safety and recklessly causes serious bodily injury.

c. A person is guilty of a crime of the fourth degree if the person knowingly violates a law intended to protect the public health and safety or knowingly fails to perform a duty imposed by a law intended to protect the public health and safety and recklessly causes significant bodily injury.

L.1997, c. 180, § 2, eff. Aug. 1, 1997.

2C:40–19. Placing or inserting writing in or on consumer product

a. Except as provided in subsection b. of this section, any person who stamps, prints, places or inserts any writing in or on a consumer product offered for sale or the box, package or other container containing the product is guilty of a disorderly persons offense.

b. This act shall not apply in any case where the owner or manager of the premises where the product is stored or sold; the product manufacturer; the authorized distributor or the retailer of the product consents to the placing or inserting of the writing.

c. As used in this act:

(1) "Writing" means any form of representation or communication, including handbills, notices or advertising, that contains letters, words or pictorial representations;

(2) "Consumer product" includes but is not limited to any cosmetic, drug or food product as defined in section 1 of P.L.1987, c. 421 (C.2C:40–16) or any article, product or commodity which is customarily produced or distributed for use by individuals.

L.2000, c. 153, § 1, eff. Nov. 13, 2000.

2C:40–20. Markers used to designate boundary lines; visibility required to avoid injury; exception

A person who uses any type of device, including but not limited to wire or cable, that is not a fence but is installed at a height under 10 feet from the ground, to indicate boundary lines or otherwise to divide, partition or segregate portions of real property, if the device is not readily visible or marked in such a way as to make it readily visible to persons who are pedestrians, equestrians, bicyclists or drivers of off-the- road vehicles and poses a risk of causing significant bodily injury to such persons, shall be guilty of a crime of the fourth degree. However, this section is not intended to apply to markers set by a licensed land surveyor, pursuant to existing statute.

L.2001, c. 36, § 2, eff. March 23, 2001.

2C:40–21. Tattooing and body piercing of minors

A person commits a disorderly persons offense if he knowingly tattoos or engages in body piercing of a minor under the age of 18 years without first having obtained the written permission of the minor's parent or legal guardian or, if neither exists, a person who stands in place of a parent.

L.2001, c. 190, § 1, eff. Nov. 28, 2001.

2C:40–22. Driving without a license or when a license is suspended or revoked by listed governmental authorities; additional penalties for causing injury or death; causal relationship provisions inapplicable

a. A person who, while operating a motor vehicle in violation of R.S.39:3–40 or while the person's driver's license is suspended or revoked in any other State, the District of Columbia or the United States Territories of American Samoa, Guam, Puerto Rico or the Virgin Islands, or by another country, or without ever having been issued a driver's license by this or any other State, the District of Columbia or the United States Territories of American Samoa, Guam, Puerto Rico or the Virgin Islands, or by another country, is involved in a motor vehicle accident resulting in the death of another person, shall be guilty of a crime of the third degree, in addition to any other penalties applicable under R.S.39:3–40 or any other provision of law. Upon conviction, the person's driver's license or reciprocity privilege shall be suspended for an additional period of one year, in addition to any suspension applicable under R.S.39:3–40 and shall be consecutive to any existing suspension or revocation. If the person did not have a driver's license at the time the accident occurred, the person shall be disqualified from obtaining a driver's license in this State for a period of one year. The additional period of suspension, revocation or disqualification shall commence upon the completion of any term of imprisonment.

b. A person who, while operating a motor vehicle in violation of R.S.39:3–40 or while the person's driver's license is suspended or revoked in any other State, the District of Columbia or the United States Territories of American Samoa, Guam, Puerto Rico or the Virgin Islands, or by another country, or without ever having been issued a driver's license by this or any other State, the District of Columbia or the United States Territories of American Samoa, Guam, Puerto Rico or the Virgin Islands, or by another country, is involved in a motor vehicle accident resulting in serious bodily injury, as defined in N.J.S.2C:11–1, to another person shall be guilty of a crime of the fourth degree, in addition to any other penalties applicable under R.S.39:3–40 or any other provision of law. Upon conviction, the person's driver's license or reciprocity privilege shall be suspended for an additional period of one year, in addition to any suspension applicable under R.S.39:3–40, and shall be consecutive to any existing suspension or revocation. If the person did not have a driver's license at the time the motor vehicle accident occurred, the person shall be disqualified from obtaining a driver's license in this State for a period of one year. The additional period of suspension, revocation or disqualification shall commence upon the completion of any term of imprisonment.

c. The provisions of N.J.S.2C:2–3 governing the causal relationship between conduct and result shall not apply in a prosecution under this section. For purposes of this offense, the defendant's act of operating a motor vehicle while his driver's license or reciprocity privilege has been suspended or revoked or who operates a motor vehicle without being licensed to do so is the cause of death or injury when:

(1) The operation of the motor vehicle is an antecedent but for which the death or injury would not have occurred; and

(2) The death or injury was not:

(a) too remote in its occurrence as to have a just bearing on the defendant's liability; or

(b) too dependent upon the conduct of another person which was unrelated to the defendant's operation of a motor vehicle as to have a just bearing on the defendant's liability.

d. It shall not be a defense to a prosecution under this section that the decedent contributed to his own death or injury by reckless or negligent conduct or operation of a motor vehicle.

e. Nothing in this section shall be construed to preclude or limit any prosecution for homicide.

L.2001, c. 213, § 2, eff. Aug. 20, 2001. Amended by L.2005, c. 230, § 1, eff. Sept. 22, 2005.

2C:40–23. Information required to produce devices to operate motor vehicle locks

a. No person shall produce and deliver an ignition key or other device designed to operate a lock or locks on a motor vehicle or start a motor vehicle to any person on the basis of a motor vehicle identification number without obtaining and making a record of:

(1) proof that the person requesting the ignition key or other device is the owner or lessee of the vehicle, or is a member of the same household as the owner or lessee of the vehicle, and which, at a minimum, shall include one of the following: a valid motor vehicle registration certificate, a valid insurance identification card, a valid insurance policy or a certificate of ownership; and

(2) identification of the person requesting the ignition key or other device, which identification shall include a photograph of the person.

b. The records made pursuant to the requirements of subsection a. of this section shall be retained for five years.

c. Nothing in this act shall be construed to deny a lessor or lienholder lawful access to a motor vehicle.

d. A person who violates any provision of this act shall be guilty of a disorderly persons offense, except that notwithstanding the provisions of subsection c. of N.J.S.2C:43–3, a fine of not more than $2,000 may be imposed.

L.2003, c. 170, § 1, eff. Sept. 3, 2003.

2C:40–24. Possession of traffic control preemption device; exceptions; civil penalty

a. As used in this section:

"Traffic control preemption device" means an infrared transmitter or other device which transmits an infrared beam, radio wave or other signal designed to change, alter, or disrupt in any manner the normal operation of a traffic control signal.

b. It shall be unlawful for any person to knowingly possess a traffic control preemption device.

c. The provisions of this section shall not apply to (1) emergency services personnel which shall include, but not be limited to, any paid or volunteer fireman, any person engaged in emergency first-aid or medical services and any law enforcement officer, while in the actual performance of that person's official duties, or (2) an employee or agent of a traffic control preemption device manufacturer or retailer in the course of his employment in providing, selling, manufacturing, or transporting a traffic control preemption device to emergency services personnel listed in this subsection.

d. Any person violating the provisions of this section shall be subject to a civil penalty of up to $5,000. Any such civil penalty imposed may be collected with costs in a summary proceeding pursuant to the "Penalty Enforcement Law of 1999," P.L.1999, c. 274 (C.2A:58–10 et seq.). The Superior Court and the municipal court shall have jurisdiction to enforce the provisions of the "Penalty Enforcement Law of 1999" in connection with this section.

L.2005, c. 96, § 2, eff. Sept. 1, 2005.

2C:40–25. Persons permitted to dispense contact lenses; violation; penalties

a. No person shall dispense contact lenses in this State unless he is a licensed ophthalmic dispenser or person licensed to practice medicine or optometry in this State. For the purposes of this act, "contact lenses" shall include contact lenses without power, sometimes referred to as "plano" lenses.

b. Any person who dispenses contact lenses in violation of the provisions of this section is guilty of a crime in the fourth degree, provided, however, that the court shall:

(1) impose a fine of not less than $1,000 for a first offense;

(2) impose a fine of not less than $5,000 and require the performance of 40 hours of community service for a second offense; and

(3) impose a fine of not less than $10,000 and require the performance of 100 hours of community service for a third and each subsequent offense.

c. Upon conviction of a person under this section, the court shall authorize the appropriate law enforcement agency or officer to seize and destroy all contact lenses held or owned by, or under the control of, the convicted person, with the exception of any contact lenses which have been prescribed for his personal use and dispensed by a licensed ophthalmic dispenser or person licensed to practice medicine or optometry in this State.

d. Notwithstanding any other provision of law to the contrary, half of the fines imposed and collected under authority of law for any violation of this section shall be forwarded by the judge to whom the same have been paid to the financial officer of the county or municipality, as designated by the governing body of the respective county or municipality, for all violations occurring within their jurisdictions, provided the complaining witness was a law enforcement officer or other official of the county or municipality.

L.2005, c. 262, § 3, eff. April 1, 2006.

2C:40–26. Driving while license is suspended or revoked; degree of crime; minimum sentence

Section effective on August 1, 2011.

a. It shall be a crime of the fourth degree to operate a motor vehicle during the period of license suspension in violation of R.S.39:3–40, if the actor's license was suspended or revoked for a first violation of R.S. 39:4–50 or section 2 of P.L.1981, c. 512 (C.39:4–50.4a) and the actor had previously been convicted of violating R.S.39:3–40 while under suspension for that first offense. A person convicted of an offense under this subsection shall be sentenced by the court to a term of imprisonment.

b. It shall be a crime of the fourth degree to operate a motor vehicle during the period of license suspension in violation of R.S.39:3–40, if the actor's license was suspended or revoked for a second or subsequent violation of R.S.39:4–50 or section 2 of P.L.1981, c. 512 (C.39:4–50.4a). A person convicted of an offense under this subsection shall be sentenced by the court to a term of imprisonment.

c. Notwithstanding the term of imprisonment provided under N.J.S.2C:43–6 and the provisions of subsection e. of N.J.S.2C:44–1, if a person is convicted of a crime under this section the sentence imposed shall include a fixed minimum sentence of not less than 180 days during which the defendant shall not be eligible for parole.

L.2009, c. 333, § 1, eff. Aug. 1, 2011.

CHAPTER 40A

MISCELLANEOUS

Section
2C:40A–1. Employer requiring lie detector test.
2C:40A–2. Violation of contract to pay employees.
2C:40A–3. Wrongful discharge of employee.
2C:40A–4. Certain professionals prohibited from contacting accident or disaster victims for 30 days.
2C:40A–5. Sanctions for violations.

2C:40A–1. Employer requiring lie detector test

Any person who as an employer shall influence, request or require an employee or prospective employee to take or submit to a lie detector test as a condition of employment or continued employment, commits a disorderly persons offense. The provisions of this section shall not apply if: (1) the employer is authorized to manufacture, distribute or dispense controlled dangerous substances pursuant to the provisions of the "New Jersey Controlled Dangerous Substances Act," P.L.1970, c. 226 (C. 24:21–1 et seq.); (2) the employee or prospective employee is or will be directly involved in the manufacture, distribution, or dispensing of, or has or will have access to, legally distributed controlled dangerous substances; and (3) the test, which shall cover a period of time no greater than 5 years preceding the test, and except as provided in this section, shall be limited to the work of the employee or prospective employee and the individual's improper handling, use or illegal sale of legally distributed controlled dangerous substances. The test may include standard baseline questions necessary and for the sole purpose of establishing a normal test pattern. Any employee or prospective employee who is required to take a lie detector test as a precondition of employment or continued employment shall have the right to be represented by legal counsel. A copy of the report containing the results of a lie detector test shall be in writing and be provided, upon request, to the individual who has taken the test. Information obtained from the test shall not be released to any other employer or person. The employee or prospective employee shall be informed of his right to present to the employer the results of an independently administered second lie detector examination prior to any personnel decision being made in his behalf by the employer.

L.1981, c. 290, § 36, eff. Sept. 24, 1981. Amended by L.1983, c. 463, § 1, eff. Jan. 12, 1984.

2C:40A–2. Violation of contract to pay employees

a. An employer who has agreed with an employee or with a bargaining agent for employees to pay wages, compensation or benefits to or for the benefit of employees commits a disorderly persons offense if the employer:

(1) fails to pay wages when due; or

(2) fails to pay compensation or benefits within 30 days after due.

b. If a corporate employer violates subsection a., any officer or employee of the corporation who is responsible for the violation commits a disorderly persons offense.

L.1999, c. 90, § 10, eff. May 3, 1999.

2C:40A–3. Wrongful discharge of employee

a. An employer who discharges an employee or takes any other disciplinary action against the employee because the employee's earnings have been subjected to garnishment commits a disorderly persons offense.

b. An employer who discharges an employee or takes any other disciplinary action in violation of this section shall re-employ any employee discharged, and shall compensate any employee for any damages resulting from the discharge or disciplinary action.

c. The term "earnings" means any form of compensation payable for personal services, regardless of whether the payment is denominated as wages, salary, commission, bonus, income from trust funds, profits, or otherwise, and includes periodic payments pursuant to a pension or retirement program.

L.1999, c. 90, § 11, eff. May 3, 1999.

2C:40A–4. Certain professionals prohibited from contacting accident or disaster victims for 30 days

a. No person shall solicit professional employment from an accident or disaster victim or an accident or disaster victim's relative concerning an action for personal injury or wrongful death involving that accident or disaster victim for a period of 30 days after the date on which the accident or disaster occurred.

b. Subsection a. of this section shall not apply if the accident or disaster victim, or his relative, as the case may be, had a previous professional business relationship with the professional.

c. Subsection a. of this section shall not apply to recommendations or referrals by past or present clients or patients, friends, relatives or other individuals relying on the reputation of the professional, provided the recommendation or referral is not made for value.

d. Subsection a. of this section shall not apply to any solicitation through advertising which is not directed to the victim or victims of a specific accident or disaster.

e. Subsection a. of this section shall not apply to emergency medical care.

f. For the purposes of this section:

"Professional employment" means services rendered by a physician, chiropractor or other health care professional.

"Solicit" means to contact a person with a request or plea, which is made in person, by telephone or other electronic medium.

g. A person who violates the provisions of this section, and who acts with intent to accept money or something of value for his services, shall be guilty of a crime of the third degree.

L.1999, c. 325, § 1.

2C:40A–5. Sanctions for violations

In addition to any other sanction that may be imposed by the Supreme Court, an attorney who violates the Rules of Professional Conduct promulgated by the Supreme Court of New Jersey by contacting an accident or disaster victim or an accident or disaster victim's relative, using means other than written communication, to solicit professional employment on the attorney's own behalf, and who acts with intent to accept money or something of value for his services, shall be guilty of a crime of the third degree.

L.1999, c. 325, § 2.

PART 6

OFFENSES INVOLVING ORGANIZED CRIME AND ORGANIZED CRIME ACTIVITIES

Chapter
41. Racketeering.
42. [Reserved].

CHAPTER 41

RACKETEERING

Section
2C:41–1.   Definitions.
2C:41–1.1.   Declaration of policy and legislative findings.
2C:41–2.   Prohibited activities.
2C:41–3.   Criminal penalties.
2C:41–4.   Civil remedies.
2C:41–5.   Investigative interrogatories.
2C:41–6.   Liberal construction.
2C:41–6.1.   Remedies cumulative.
2C:41–6.2.   Severability.

2C:41–1. Definitions

For purposes of this section and N.J.S.2C:41–2 through N.J.S.2C:41–6:

a. "Racketeering activity" means (1) any of the following crimes which are crimes under the laws of New Jersey or are equivalent crimes under the laws of any other jurisdiction:

  (a) murder

  (b) kidnapping

  (c) gambling

  (d) promoting prostitution

  (e) obscenity

  (f) robbery

  (g) bribery

  (h) extortion

(i) criminal usury

(j) violations of Title 33 of the Revised Statutes

(k) violations of Title 54A of the New Jersey Statutes and Title 54 of the Revised Statutes

(*l*) arson

(m) burglary

(n) theft and all crimes defined in chapter 20 of Title 2C of the New Jersey Statutes

(*o*) forgery and fraudulent practices and all crimes defined in chapter 21 of Title 2C of the New Jersey Statutes

(p) fraud in the offering, sale or purchase of securities

(q) alteration of motor vehicle identification numbers

(r) unlawful manufacture, purchase, use or transfer of firearms

(s) unlawful possession or use of destructive devices or explosives

(t) violation of sections 112 through 116 inclusive of the "Casino Control Act," P.L.1977, c. 110 (C.5:12–112 through 5:12–116)

(u) violation of N.J.S.2C:35–4, N.J.S.2C:35–5 or N.J.S.2C:35–6 and all crimes involving illegal distribution of a controlled dangerous substance or controlled substance analog, except possession of less than one ounce of marijuana

(v) violation of subsection b. of N.J.S.2C:24–4 except for subparagraph (b) of paragraph (5) of subsection b.

(w) violation of section 1 of P.L.1995, c. 405 (C.2C:39–16), leader of firearms trafficking network

(x) violation of section 1 of P.L.1983, c. 229 (C.2C:39–14), weapons training for illegal activities

(y) violation of section 2 of P.L.2002, c. 26 (C.2C:38–2), terrorism

(z) violation of section 1 of P.L.2005,c.77 (C.2C:13–8), human trafficking

(aa) violation of N.J.S.2C:12–1 requiring purposeful or knowing conduct

(bb) violation of N.J.S.2C:12–3, terroristic threats.

(2) any conduct defined as "racketeering activity" under Title 18, U.S.C.s.1961(1)(A), (B) and (D).

b. "Person" includes any individual or entity or enterprise as defined herein holding or capable of holding a legal or beneficial interest in property.

c. "Enterprise" includes any individual, sole proprietorship, partnership, corporation, business or charitable trust, association, or other legal entity, any union or group of individuals associated in fact although not a legal entity, and it includes illicit as well as licit enterprises and governmental as well as other entities.

d. "Pattern of racketeering activity" requires:

(1) Engaging in at least two incidents of racketeering conduct one of which shall have occurred after the effective date of this act and the last of which shall have occurred within 10 years (excluding any period of imprisonment) after a prior incident of racketeering activity; and

(2) A showing that the incidents of racketeering activity embrace criminal conduct that has either the same or similar purposes, results, participants or victims or methods of commission or are otherwise interrelated by distinguishing characteristics and are not isolated incidents.

e. "Unlawful debt" means a debt:

(1) Which was incurred or contracted in gambling activity which was in violation of the law of the United States, a state or political subdivision thereof; or

(2) Which is unenforceable under state or federal law in whole or in part as to principal or interest because of the laws relating to usury.

f. "Documentary material" includes any book, paper, document, writing, drawing, graph, chart, photograph, phonorecord, magnetic or recording or video tape, computer printout, other data compilation from which information can be obtained or from which information can be translated into useable form or other tangible item.

g. "Attorney General" includes the Attorney General of New Jersey, his assistants and deputies. The term shall also include a county prosecutor or his designated assistant prosecutor if a county prosecutor is expressly authorized in writing by the Attorney General to carry out the powers conferred on the Attorney General by this chapter.

h. "Trade or commerce" shall include all economic activity involving or relating to any commodity or service.

L.1981, c. 167, § 2, eff. June 15, 1981. Amended by L.1987, c. 106, § 7; L.1995, c. 110, § 1, eff. June 1, 1995; L.1999, c. 25, § 5, eff. Feb. 16, 1999; L.2002, c. 26, § 18, eff. June 18, 2002; L.2005, c. 77, § 3, eff. April 26, 2005; L.2007, c. 341, § 4, eff. Jan. 13, 2008.

2C:41–1.1. Declaration of policy and legislative findings

The Legislature hereby finds and declares to be the public policy of this State, the following:

a. By enactment of the "Criminal Justice Act of 1970," P.L.1970, c. 74 (C. 52:17B–97 et seq.), the Legislature recognized that the existence of organized crime and organized crime type activities presents a serious threat to the political, social and economic institutions of this State.

b. Despite the impressive gains of our law enforcement agencies, organized crime and similar activities in this State are still a highly sophisticated, diversified and widespread activity that annually drains millions of dollars from this State's economy by unlawful conduct and the illegal use of force, fraud and corruption. In recent years, that organized crime and organized criminal type activity has spread to the operation of otherwise legitimate businesses.

c. In order to safeguard the public interest, effective criminal and civil sanctions are needed to prevent, disrupt and eliminate the infiltration of organized crime type activities which are substantial in nature into the legitimate trade or commerce of this State. It is, therefore, in the public interest to provide that activity which is inimical to the general health, welfare and prosperity of the State and its inhabitants be made subject to strict civil and criminal sanctions.

L.1981, c. 167, § 1, eff. June 15, 1981.

2C:41–2. Prohibited activities

a. It shall be unlawful for any person who has received any income derived, directly or indirectly, from a pattern of racketeering activity or through collection of an unlawful debt in which he has participated as a principal within the meaning of N.J.S. 2C:2–6 to use or invest, directly or indirectly, any part of the income, or the proceeds of the income, in acquisition of any interest in, or the establishment or operation of any enterprise which is engaged in or the activities of which affect trade or commerce. A purchase of securities on the open market for purposes of investment, and without the intention of controlling or participating in the control of the issuer or of assisting another to do so, shall not be unlawful under this section, provided that the sum total of the securities of the issuer held by the purchaser, the members of his family, and his or their accomplices in any pattern of racketeering activity or in the collection of an unlawful debt does not amount in the aggregate to 1% of the outstanding securities of any one class, or does not, either in law or in fact, empower the holders thereof to elect one or more directors of the issuer, provided further, that if, in any proceeding involving an alleged investment in violation of this section, it is established that over half of the defendant's aggregate income for a period of 2 or more years immediately preceding the investment was derived from a pattern of racketeering activity, a rebuttable presumption shall arise that the investment included income derived from a pattern of racketeering activity.

b. It shall be unlawful for any person through a pattern of racketeering activity or through collection of an unlawful debt to acquire or maintain, directly or indirectly, any interest in or control of any enterprise which is engaged in or activities of which affect trade or commerce.

c. It shall be unlawful for any person employed by or associated with any enterprise engaged in or activities of which affect trade or commerce to conduct or participate, directly or indirectly, in the conduct of the enterprise's affairs through a pattern of racketeering activity or collection of unlawful debt.

d. It shall be unlawful for any person to conspire as defined by N.J.S. 2C:5–2, to violate any of the provisions of this section.

L.1981, c. 167, § 2, eff. June 15, 1981.

2C:41–3. Criminal penalties

a. Any person who violates any provision of N.J.S.2C:41–2 in connection with a pattern of racketeering activity which involves a crime of violence, a crime of the first degree or the use of firearms shall be guilty of a crime of the first degree. All other violations of N.J.S.2C:41–2 shall be crimes of the second degree.

b. In addition, such persons shall forfeit to the entity funding the prosecuting agency involved the following:

(1) Any interest including money or anything of value he has acquired or maintained in violation of this chapter and

(2) Any interest in, security of, claim against, or property or contractual right of any kind affording a source of influence over any enterprise which he has established, acquired, maintained, operated, controlled, conducted, or participated in the conduct of, in violation of this chapter.

c. In any action brought by the Attorney General under this section, the Superior Court shall have jurisdiction to enter such restraining orders or prohibitions, or to take such other actions, including, but not limited to, the acceptance of satisfactory performance bonds, in connection with any property or other interests subject to forfeiture under this section, as it shall deem proper.

d. Upon conviction of a person under this section, the court shall authorize the Attorney General to seize all property or other interest declared forfeited under this section, subject to the rights of innocent persons such as any prior lienholders or other valid lienholders, upon such other terms and conditions as the court shall deem proper. If a property right or other interest is not exercisable or transferable for value by the Attorney General, it shall expire, and shall not revert to the convicted person.

e. The Attorney General shall dispose of all such property as soon as commercially feasible, making due provision for the rights of innocent persons.

f. When an offense charged may result in a criminal forfeiture, the indictment shall allege the extent of the interest or property subject to forfeiture. If the indictment alleges that an interest or property is subject to criminal forfeiture, a special verdict shall be returned as to the extent of the interest or property subject to forfeiture, if any.

L.1981, c. 167, § 2, eff. June 15, 1981. Amended by L.1999, c. 25, § 6, eff. Feb. 16, 1999.

2C:41–4. Civil remedies

a. The Superior Court, making due provision for the rights of innocent persons, shall have jurisdiction to prevent and restrain the acts or conduct which constitute violations of N.J.S. 2C:41–2, by issuing appropriate orders, including, but not limited to:

(1) Ordering any person to divest himself of any interest, direct or indirect, in any enterprise;

(2) Imposing reasonable restrictions on the future activities or investments of any person, including but not limited to, prohibiting any person from engaging in the same type of endeavor as the enterprise found to be in violation of N.J.S. 2C:41–2;

(3) Ordering the dissolution or reorganization of any enterprise;

(4) Ordering the denial, suspension or revocation of the charter of any corporation organized under the laws of this State and to deny, suspend or revoke the license of any foreign corporation authorized to do business in the State of New Jersey;

(5) Ordering the denial, suspension or revocation of the license or permit granted to any enterprise by any department or agency of the State of New Jersey;

(6) Entering a cease and desist order which specifies the acts or conduct which is to be discontinued, altered or implemented by any person;

(7) Ordering the restitution of any moneys or property unlawfully obtained or retained by any person found to be in violation of N.J.S. 2C:41–2;

(8) Assessing civil monetary penalties against any person who has violated N.J.S. 2C:41–2 to deter future violations, provided that the court shall, upon making a finding on the record as to the gain any such person has acquired or maintained through the violation, assess such penalties in an amount not to exceed three times the amount of the gain; and

(9) Ordering any person to forfeit to the State any interest he has acquired or maintained in violation of this chapter and any interest in, security of, claim against, or property or contractual right of any kind affording a source of influence over any enterprises he has established, operated, controlled, conducted, or participated in the conduct of, in violation of this chapter. Forfeiture under this subsection shall be in accordance with chapter 64 of Title 2C of the New Jersey Statutes. The interest which shall be subject to forfeiture shall be as defined by this section and as defined by N.J.S. 2C:64–1a.;

(10) Imposing any or all of the foregoing sanctions in combination with each other.

b. The Attorney General may institute proceedings in Superior Court for violations of N.J.S. 2C:41–2. In any action brought under this section, the court shall proceed as soon as practicable to the hearing and determination thereof. Pending final determination thereof, the court may at any time enter restraining orders or prohibitions, or take other actions, including the acceptance of satisfactory performance bonds, as it shall deem proper.

c. Any person damaged in his business or property by reason of a violation of N.J.S. 2C:41–2 may sue therefor in any appropriate court and shall recover threefold any damages he sustains and the cost of the suit, including a reasonable attorney's fee, costs of investigation and litigation.

d. A final judgment rendered in favor of the State in any criminal proceeding brought under this chapter shall estop the defendant from denying the essential allegations of the criminal offense in any subsequent civil proceeding.

L.1981, c. 167, § 2, eff. June 15, 1981.

2C:41–5. Investigative interrogatories

a. Whenever the Attorney General determines that there exists a reasonable suspicion that any person or enterprise may have information or be in possession, custody, or control of any documentary materials relevant to an investigation under this chapter, or whenever the Attorney General believes it to be in the public interest that an investigation be made pursuant to this chapter, he may, prior to the institution of a civil or criminal proceeding thereon, issue in writing, and cause to be served upon the person, an investigative interrogatory requiring him to answer and produce material for examination.

b. Each interrogatory shall:

(1) State the nature of the conduct constituting the alleged violation which is under investigation and the provision of law applicable thereto;

(2) Advise the person that he has the right to discuss the interrogatory with legal counsel prior to returning it to the Attorney General or prior to making material available as provided hereinafter in subsection f. and that he has the right to file in Superior Court a petition to modify or set aside the interrogatory pursuant to subsection j. hereinafter;

(3) Describe the class or classes of documentary material to be produced thereunder with such specificity and certainty as to permit the material to be fairly identified;

(4) Prescribe a return date which will provide a reasonable period of time within which answers may be made and material so demanded may be assembled and made available for inspection and copying or reproduction as provided hereinafter in subsection f.

c. No interrogatory shall:

(1) Contain any requirement which would be held to be unreasonable if contained in a subpena duces tecum issued in aid of a grand jury investigation; or

(2) Require the production of any documentary evidence which would be otherwise privileged from disclosure if demanded by a subpena duces tecum issued in aid of a grand jury investigation.

d. Service of any interrogatory filed under this section may be made upon a person by:

(1) Delivering a duly executed copy thereof to any partner, executive officer, managing agent, or general agent thereof, or to any agent thereof authorized by appointment or by law to receive service of process on behalf of the person, or upon any individual person; or

(2) Delivering a duly executed copy thereof to the principal office or place of business of the person to be served; or

(3) Depositing a copy in the United States mail, by registered or certified mail duly addressed to the person at his principal office or place of business.

e. A verified return by the individual serving any interrogatory, setting forth the manner of service shall be prima facie proof of service. In the case of service by registered or certified mail, the return shall be accompanied by the return post office receipt of delivery of the interrogatory.

f. Any person upon whom any interrogatory issued under this section has been duly served which requires the production of materials shall make the material available for inspection and copying or reproduction to the Attorney General at the principal place of business of that person in the State of New Jersey or at such other place as the Attorney General and the person thereafter may agree and prescribe in writing, on the return date specified in the interrogatory or on a later date as the Attorney General may prescribe in writing. Upon written agreement between the person and the Attorney General, copies may be substituted for all or any part of the original materials. The Attorney General may cause the preparation of any copies of documentary material as may be required for official use by the Attorney General.

No material produced pursuant to this section shall be available for examination, without the consent of the person who produced the material, by an individual other than the Attorney General or any person retained by the Attorney General in connection with the enforcement of this act. Under reasonable terms and conditions as the Attorney General shall prescribe, documentary material while in his possession shall be available for examination by the person who produced the material or any duly authorized representatives of the person.

In any case or proceeding involving any alleged violation of this chapter, the Attorney General may present before any court or Grand Jury, any such documentary material in his possession pursuant to this section subject to any protective order deemed proper by the Superior Court.

Any person who shall disclose to any person other than the Attorney General or a person retained by the Attorney General as set forth above, the name of any person who receives an investigative interrogatory or any information obtained pursuant thereto, except in proceedings involving an alleged violation of this chapter and except as so directed by the Attorney General shall be guilty of a crime of the fourth degree.

g. Upon completion of:

(1) The review and investigation for which any documentary material was produced under this section, and

(2) Any case or proceeding arising from the investigation, the Attorney General shall return to the person who produced the material all the material other than copies thereof made by the Attorney General pursuant to this section which has not passed into the control of any court or grand jury through the introduction thereof into the record of the case or proceeding.

h. When any documentary material has been produced by any person under this section for use in any racketeering investigation, and no case or proceeding arising therefrom has been instituted within 2 years after completion of the examination and analysis of all evidence assembled in the course of the investigation, the person shall be entitled, upon written demand made upon the Attorney General, to the return of all documentary material other than copies thereof made pursuant to this section so produced by the person.

i. Whenever any person fails to comply with any investigative interrogatory duly served upon him under this section or whenever satisfactory copying or reproduction of any material cannot be done and the person refuses to surrender the material, the Attorney General may file in the Superior Court a petition for an order of the court for the enforcement of this section.

j. At any time before the return date specified in the interrogatory, such person may file in the Superior Court a petition for an order modifying or setting aside the interrogatory. The time allowed for compliance of the interrogatory, in whole or in part as deemed proper and ordered by the court, shall not run during the pendency of such petition in the court. The petition shall specify each ground upon which the petitioner relies in seeking relief, and may be based upon any failure of the interrogatory to comply with the provisions of this section or upon any constitutional or other legal right or privilege of the petitioner. In such proceeding the Attorney General shall establish the existence of an investigation pursuant to this chapter and the nature and subject matter of the investigation.

L.1981, c. 167, § 2, eff. June 15, 1981.

2C:41–6. Liberal construction

The provisions of subsections a., c., d., e., and h. of 2C:41–1; 2C:41–2; subsections b., c., d., e., and f. of 2C:41–3; and 2C:41–4 shall be liberally construed to effectuate the remedial purposes of this chapter.

L.1981, c. 167, § 2, eff. June 15, 1981.

2C:41–6.1. Remedies cumulative

The remedies provided in this act shall be cumulative with each other and other remedies at law.

L.1981, c. 167, § 11, eff. June 15, 1981.

2C:41–6.2. Severability

If any one or more sections, clauses, sentences or parts of this act shall for any reason be questioned in any court, and shall be adjudged unconstitutional or invalid, such judgment shall not affect, impair or invalidate the remaining provisions thereof, but shall be confined in its operation to the specific provisions so held unconstitutional or invalid.

L.1981, c. 167, § 12, eff. June 15, 1981.

CHAPTER 42

[RESERVED]

SUBTITLE 3

SENTENCING

Chapter
43. Authorized Disposition of Offenders.
44. Authority of Court in Sentencing.
45. Suspension of Sentence; Probation.
46. Fines and Restitution.
47. Adult Diagnostic and Treatment Center.
48. Criminal Disposition Commission [Repealed].
48A. Criminal Sentencing and Disposition Commission.
49. Capital Punishment.
50. [Reserved].
51. Loss and Restoration of Rights Incident to Conviction of an Offense.
52. Expungement of Records.
53 to 57. [Reserved].
58. Licensing and Other Provisions relating to Firearms.
59 to 61. [Reserved].
62. Willful Nonsupport.
63. [Reserved].
64. Forfeiture.
65. Disposition of Stolen Property and Documentary Exhibits.
66. Attachment, Freezing of Terrorist Funds.
67 to 97. [Reserved].
98. Repealers, Allocations and Effective Date.
99 to 103. [Reserved].
104. Material Witnesses.

CHAPTER 43

AUTHORIZED DISPOSITION OF OFFENDERS

Section
2C:43–1. Degrees of crimes.
2C:43–2. Sentence in accordance with code; authorized dispositions.
2C:43–2.1. Motor vehicle theft or unlawful taking; restitution.
2C:43–2.2. AIDS and HIV infection testing of certain persons convicted of, indicted for or formally charged with acts constituting sexual assault or aggravated sexual assault; reimbursement; notification; counseling; confidentiality; immunity of testers; construction of section.
2C:43–2.3. AIDS and HIV infection testing ordered by court under certain circumstances.
2C:43–3. Fines and restitution.
2C:43–3.1. Additional assessments; collection and disposition by victims of crime compensation board.
2C:43–3.2. Assessments; amounts collected deposited in safe neighborhoods services fund.
2C:43–3.3. Additional fines deposited in law enforcement officers training and equipment fund.
2C:43–3.4. Restitution for extradition costs incurred by law enforcement entities.
2C:43–3.5. Additional penalties.
2C:43–3.6. Penalties.
2C:43–3.7. Surcharge on penalty for sexual assault.

Section
2C:43–3.8. Additional assessment for certain computer-related criminal activities; Computer Crime Prevention Fund.
2C:43–4. Penalties against corporations; forfeiture of corporate charter or revocation of certificate authorizing foreign corporation to do business in the state.
2C:43–5. Young adult offenders.
2C:43–5.1. Offenders enrolled in secondary education at time of criminal charge, adjudication or conviction; written notice to the school; confidentiality.
2C:43–6. Sentence of imprisonment for crime; ordinary terms; mandatory terms.
2C:43–6.1. Person under minimum mandatory sentence for possession of firearm with intent to use against property of another; review of sentence; imposition of other sentence.
2C:43–6.2. Conviction of certain offenses while armed for first time; reduction of mandatory minimum term.
2C:43–6.3. Person serving mandatory minimum term; motion to have sentence reviewed.
2C:43–6.4. Special sentence of community supervision for life imposed on persons convicted of certain sexual offense.
2C:43–6.5. Offenses by public officers or employees; mandatory minimum term of imprisonment for crimes that involve or touch upon the public office or employment.
2C:43–6.6. Internet access; court's authority to place conditions and restrictions for certain sex offenders.
2C:43–6.7. Effective date; application of act.
2C:43–7. Sentence of imprisonment for crime; extended terms.
2C:43–7.1. Persistent offenders; sentencing.
2C:43–7.2. Eligibility for parole; persons convicted of certain violent crimes.
2C:43–8. Sentence of imprisonment for disorderly persons offenses and petty disorderly persons offenses.
2C:43–8.1. Termination of right to occupy or visit seasonally leased premises.
2C:43–9. Release of all offenders; length of recommitment and reparole after revocation of parole.
2C:43–10. Place of imprisonment; beginning sentences; transfers.
2C:43–11. Conduct precluding admission to intensive supervision programs; objections to admission.
2C:43–12. Statewide pretrial intervention program; admission criteria; time for referral; denial and appeal; program monitoring.
2C:43–13. Supervisory treatment procedure.
2C:43–14. Authority of supreme court.
2C:43–15. Presentation of proposed rules at judicial conference.
2C:43–16. Public announcement of proposed rules; delivery of copies.
2C:43–17. Effective date of rules; rules subject to cancellation by joint resolution.

215

Section

2C:43–18. Change or cancellation of rules by statute or adoption of subsequent rules.

2C:43–19. Adoption of rules at such time, or with such effective date, or without presentation at judicial conference, as may be provided in joint resolution.

2C:43–20. Reduction or elimination of time during which rules may be canceled by joint resolution.

2C:43–21. Index and reports.

2C:43–22. Disclaimer.

2C:43–1. Degrees of crimes

a. Crimes defined by this code are classified, for the purpose of sentence, into four degrees, as follows:

(1) Crimes of the first degree;

(2) Crimes of the second degree;

(3) Crimes of the third degree; and

(4) Crimes of the fourth degree.

A crime is of the first, second, third or fourth degree when it is so designated by the code. An offense, declared to be a crime, without specification of degree, is of the fourth degree.

b. Notwithstanding any other provision of law, a crime defined by any statute of this State other than this code and designated as a high misdemeanor shall constitute for the purpose of sentence a crime of the third degree. Except as provided in sections 2C:1–4c. and 2C:1–5b. and notwithstanding any other provision of law, a crime defined by any statute of this State other than this code and designated as a misdemeanor shall constitute for the purpose of sentence a crime of the fourth degree.

L.1978, c. 95, § 2C:43–1, eff. Sept. 1, 1979. Amended by L.1979, c. 178, § 81, eff. Sept. 1, 1979; L.1987, c. 106, § 8, operative July 9, 1987.

2C:43–2. Sentence in accordance with code; authorized dispositions

a. Except as otherwise provided by this code, all persons convicted of an offense or offenses shall be sentenced in accordance with this chapter.

b. Except as provided in subsection a. of this section and subject to the applicable provisions of the code, the court may suspend the imposition of sentence on a person who has been convicted of an offense, or may sentence him as follows:

(1) To pay a fine or make restitution authorized by N.J.S.2C:43–3 or P.L.1997, c. 253 (C.2C:43–3.4 et al.); or

(2) Except as provided in subsection g. of this section, to be placed on probation and, in the case of a person convicted of a crime, to imprisonment for a term fixed by the court not exceeding 364 days to be served as a condition of probation, or in the case of a person convicted of a disorderly persons offense, to imprisonment for a term fixed by the court not exceeding 90 days to be served as a condition of probation; or

(3) To imprisonment for a term authorized by sections 2C:11–3, 2C:43–5, 2C:43–6, 2C:43–7, and 2C:43–8 or 2C:44–5; or

(4) To pay a fine, make restitution and probation, or fine, restitution and imprisonment; or

(5) To release under supervision in the community or to require the performance of community-related service; or

(6) To a halfway house or other residential facility in the community, including agencies which are not operated by the Department of Human Services; or

(7) To imprisonment at night or on weekends with liberty to work or to participate in training or educational programs.

c. Instead of or in addition to any disposition made according to this section, the court may postpone, suspend, or revoke for a period not to exceed two years the driver's license, registration certificate, or both of any person convicted of a crime, disorderly persons offense, or petty disorderly persons offense in the course of which a motor vehicle was used. In imposing this disposition and in deciding the duration of the postponement, suspension, or revocation, the court shall consider the severity of the crime or offense and the potential effect of the loss of driving privileges on the person's ability to be rehabilitated. Any postponement, suspension, or revocation shall be imposed consecutively with any custodial sentence.

d. This chapter does not deprive the court of any authority conferred by law to decree a forfeiture of property, suspend or cancel a license, remove a person from office, or impose any other civil penalty. Such a judgment or order may be included in the sentence.

e. The court shall state on the record the reasons for imposing the sentence, including its findings pursuant to the criteria for withholding or imposing imprisonment or fines under sections 2C:44–1 to 2C:44–3, where imprisonment is imposed, consideration of the defendant's eligibility for release under the law governing parole and the factual basis supporting its findings of particular aggravating or mitigating factors affecting sentence.

f. The court shall explain the parole laws as they apply to the sentence and shall state:

(1) the approximate period of time in years and months the defendant will serve in custody before parole eligibility;

(2) the jail credits or the amount of time the defendant has already served;

(3) that the defendant may be entitled to good time and work credits; and

(4) that the defendant may be eligible for participation in the Intensive Supervision Program.

g. Notwithstanding the provisions of paragraph (2) of subsection b. of this section, a court imposing sentence on a defendant who has been convicted of any offense enumerated in subsection a. of section 2 of P.L.1994, c. 130 (C.2C:43–6.4) may not sentence the defendant to be placed on probation.

L.1978, c. 95, § 2C:43–2, eff. Sept. 1, 1979. Amended by L.1979, c. 178, § 82, eff. Sept. 1, 1979; L.1981, c. 269, § 2, eff. Aug. 24, 1981; L.1983, c. 124, § 1, eff. April 5, 1983; L.1987, c. 106, § 9, operative July 9, 1987; L.1994, c. 155, § 1, eff. Jan. 8, 1995; L.1997, c. 253, § 1, eff. Sept. 12, 1997; L.2003, c. 267, § 5, eff. Jan. 14, 2004.

2C:43–2.1. Motor vehicle theft or unlawful taking; restitution

A person who is convicted of an offense involving the theft or unlawful taking of a motor vehicle, in addition to any other fine, penalty, or restitution which may be imposed by law, is liable to the owner of the motor vehicle for any reasonable and necessary expense incurred by the owner in recovering the motor vehicle and for any damage to the motor vehicle prior to its recovery by the owner. In the sentencing proceedings on the offense, the owner may submit evidence of expenses incurred and damages sustained. The court shall make a finding of the amount of expenses incurred and damages sustained, and if the record does not contain sufficient evidence to support such a finding, the court may conduct a hearing upon the issue. The court shall order the person convicted of the offense to make restitution to the owner in the amount of the expenses and damages found by the court. The court shall file a copy of the order with the clerk of the Superior Court who shall enter upon his record of docketed judgments the name of the convicted person as judgment debtor, and of the owner as judgment creditor, a statement that the restitution is ordered under this section, the amount of the restitution, and the date of the order. This entry shall have the same force as a judgment docketed in the Superior Court.

L.1983, c. 411, § 1, eff. Jan. 4, 1984.

2C:43–2.2. AIDS and HIV infection testing of certain persons convicted of, indicted for or formally charged with acts constituting sexual assault or aggravated sexual assault; reimbursement; notification; counseling; confidentiality; immunity of testers; construction of section

a. In addition to any other disposition made pursuant to law, a court shall order a person convicted of, indicted for or formally charged with, or a juvenile charged with delinquency or adjudicated delinquent for an act which if committed by an adult would constitute, aggravated sexual assault or sexual assault as defined in subsection a. or c. of N.J.S. 2C:14–2 to submit to an approved serological test for acquired immune deficiency syndrome (AIDS) or infection with the human immunodeficiency virus (HIV) or any other related virus identified as a probable causative agent of AIDS.

The court shall issue such an order only upon the request of the victim and upon application of the prosecutor made at the time of indictment, charge, conviction or adjudication of delinquency. The person or juvenile shall be ordered by the court to submit to such repeat or confirmatory tests as may be medically necessary.

As used in this section, "formal charge" includes a proceeding by accusation in the event that the defendant has waived the right to an indictment.

b. A court order issued pursuant to subsection a. of this section shall require testing to be performed as soon as practicable by the Commissioner of the Department of Corrections pursuant to authority granted to the commissioner by sections 6 and 10 of P.L.1976, c. 98 (C. 30:1B–6 and 30:1B–10), by a provider of health care, at a health facility licensed pursuant to section 12 of P.L.1971, c. 136 (C. 26:2H–12) or the Juvenile Justice Commission established pursuant to section 2 of P.L. 1995, c. 284 (C. 52:17B–170). The order shall also require that the results of the test be reported to the offender and to the appropriate Office of Victim–Witness Advocacy.

c. The Office of Victim–Witness Advocacy, established pursuant to section 5 of P.L.1985, c. 404 (C. 52:4B–43), shall reimburse the Department of Corrections , Department of Health or the Juvenile Justice Commission for the direct costs incurred by these departments for any tests ordered by a court pursuant to subsection a. of this section. Reimbursement shall be made following a request from the department.

d. In addition to any other disposition authorized, a court may order an offender at the time of sentencing to reimburse the State for the costs of the tests ordered by subsection a. of this section.

e. Upon receipt of the result of a test ordered pursuant to subsection a. of this section, the Office of Victim–Witness Advocacy shall provide the victim with appropriate counseling, referral for counseling and if appropriate, referral for health care. The office shall notify the victim or make appropriate arrangements for the victim to be notified of the test result.

f. The result of a test ordered pursuant to subsection a. of this section shall be confidential and employees of the Department of Corrections, the Juvenile Justice Commission, the Office of Victim–Witness Advocacy, a health care provider, health care facility or counseling service shall not disclose the result of a test performed pursuant to this section except as authorized herein or as otherwise authorized by law or court order. The provisions of this section shall not be deemed to prohibit disclosure of a test result to the person tested.

g. Persons who perform tests ordered pursuant to subsection a. of this section in accordance with accepted medical standards for the performance of such tests shall be immune from civil and criminal liability arising from their conduct.

h. This section shall not be construed to preclude or limit any other testing for acquired immune deficiency syndrome (AIDS) or infection with the human immuno-deficiency virus (HIV) or any other related virus identified as a probable causative agent of AIDS which is otherwise permitted by statute, court rule or common law.

L.1993, c. 364, § 4, eff. Jan. 4, 1994. Amended by L.1995, c. 280, § 22, eff. Dec. 15, 1995.

2C:43–2.3. AIDS and HIV infection testing ordered by court under certain circumstances

a. In addition to any other disposition made pursuant to law, a court shall order a person convicted of, indicted for or formally charged with a criminal offense, a disorderly persons offense or a petty disorderly persons offense, to submit to an approved serological test for acquired immune deficiency syndrome (AIDS) or infection with the human immunodeficiency virus (HIV) or any other related virus identified as a probable causative agent of AIDS if:

(1) in the course of the commission of the offense, including the immediate flight thereafter or during any investigation or arrest related to that offense, a law enforcement officer, the victim or other person suffered a prick from a hypodermic needle, provided there is probable cause to believe that the defendant is an intravenous user of controlled dangerous substances; or

(2) in the course of the commission of the offense, including the immediate flight thereafter or during any investigation or arrest related to that offense, a law enforcement officer, the victim or other person had contact with the defendant which involved or was likely to involve the transmission of bodily fluids.

The court may order a person to submit to an approved serological test for AIDS or infection with the HIV or any other related virus identified as a probable causative agent of AIDS if in the course of the performance of any other law enforcement duties, a law enforcement officer suffers a prick from a hypodermic needle, provided that there is probable cause to believe that the defendant is an intravenous user of controlled dangerous substances, or had contact with the defendant which involved or was likely to involve the transmission of bodily fluids. The court shall issue such an order only upon the request of the law enforcement officer, victim of the offense or other affected person made at the time of indictment, charge or conviction. If a county prosecutor declines to make such an application within 72 hours of being requested to do so by the law enforcement officer, the law enforcement officer may appeal to the Division of Criminal Justice in the Department of Law and Public Safety for that officer to bring the application. The person shall be ordered by the court to submit to such repeat or confirmatory tests as may be medically necessary.

As used in this section, "formal charge" includes a proceeding by accusation in the event that the defendant has waived the right to an indictment.

b. A court order issued pursuant to subsection a. of this section shall require testing to be performed as soon as practicable by the Commissioner of the Department of Corrections pursuant to authority granted to the commissioner by sections 6 and 10 of P.L.1976, c. 98 (C. 30:1B–6 and 30:1B–10) or by a provider of health care or at a health care facility licensed pursuant to section 12 of P.L.1971, c. 136 (C. 26:2H–12). The order shall also require that the results of the test be reported to the offender, the appropriate Office of Victim–Witness Advocacy if a victim of an offense is tested, and the affected law enforcement officer. Upon receipt of the result of a test ordered pursuant to subsection a. of this section, the Office of Victim–Witness Advocacy shall provide the victim with appropriate counseling, referral for counseling and if appropriate, referral for health care. The office shall notify the victim or make appropriate arrangements for the victim to be notified of the test result.

c. In addition to any other disposition authorized, a court may order an offender at the time of sentencing to reimburse the State for the costs of the tests ordered pursuant to subsection a. of this section.

d. The result of a test ordered pursuant to subsection a. of this section shall be confidential and health care providers and employees of the Department of Corrections, the Office of Victim–Witness Advocacy, a health care facility or counseling service shall not disclose the result of a test performed pursuant to this section except as authorized herein or as otherwise authorized by law or court order. The provisions of this section shall not be deemed to prohibit disclosure of a test result to the person tested.

e. Persons who perform tests ordered pursuant to subsection a. of this section in accordance with accepted medical standards for the performance of such tests shall be immune from civil and criminal liability arising from their conduct.

f. This section shall not be construed to preclude or limit any other testing for AIDS or infection with the HIV or any other related virus identified as a probable causative agent of AIDS which is otherwise permitted by statute, court rule or common law.

L.1996, c. 115, § 7, eff. Jan. 9, 1997.

2C:43–3. Fines and restitution

A person who has been convicted of an offense may be sentenced to pay a fine, to make restitution, or both, such fine not to exceed:

a. (1) $200,000.00 when the conviction is of a crime of the first degree;

(2) $150,000.00 when the conviction is of a crime of the second degree;

b. (1) $15,000.00 when the conviction is of a crime of the third degree;

(2) $10,000.00 when the conviction is of a crime of the fourth degree;

c. $1,000.00, when the conviction is of a disorderly persons offense;

d. $500.00, when the conviction is of a petty disorderly persons offense;

e. Any higher amount equal to double the pecuniary gain to the offender or loss to the victim caused by the conduct constituting the offense by the offender. In such case the court shall make a finding as to the amount of the gain or loss, and if the record does not contain sufficient evidence to support such a finding the court may conduct a hearing upon the issue. For purposes of this section the term "gain" means the amount of money or the value of property derived by the offender and "loss" means the amount of value separated from the victim or the amount of any payment owed to the victim and avoided or evaded and includes any reasonable and necessary expense incurred by the owner in recovering or replacing lost, stolen or damaged property, or recovering any payment avoided or evaded, and, with respect to property of a research facility, includes the cost of repeating an interrupted or invalidated experiment or loss of profits. The term "victim" shall mean a person who suffers a personal physical or psychological injury or death or incurs loss of or injury to personal or real property as a result of a crime committed against that person, or in the case of a homicide, the nearest relative of the victim. The terms "gain" and "loss" shall also mean, where appropriate, the amount of any tax, fee, penalty and interest avoided, evaded, or otherwise unpaid or improperly retained or disposed of;

f. Any higher amount specifically authorized by another section of this code or any other statute;

g. Up to twice the amounts authorized in subsection a., b., c. or d. of this section, in the case of a second or subsequent conviction of any tax offense defined in Title 54 of the Revised Statutes or Title 54A of the New Jersey Statutes, as amended and supplemented, or of any offense defined in chapter 20 or 21 of this code;

h. In the case of violations of chapter 35, any higher amount equal to three times the street value of the controlled dangerous substance or controlled substance analog. The street value for purposes of this section shall be determined pursuant to subsection e. of N.J.S.2C:44–2.

The restitution ordered paid to the victim shall not exceed the victim's loss, except that in any case involving the failure to pay any State tax, the amount of restitution to the State shall be the full amount of the tax avoided or evaded, including full civil penalties and interest as provided by law. In any case where the victim of the offense is any department or division of State government, the court shall order restitution to the victim. Any restitution imposed on a person shall be in addition to any fine which may be imposed pursuant to this section.

L.1978, c. 95, § 2C:43–3, Sept. 1, 1979. Amended by L.1979, c. 178, § 83, eff. Sept. 1, 1979; L.1981, c. 290, § 37, eff. Sept. 24, 1981; L.1987, c. 76, § 34, eff. Dec. 9, 1987; L.1987, c. 106, § 10, operative July 9, 1987; L.1991, c. 329, § 2, eff. Dec. 23, 1991; L.1995, c. 20, § 6, eff. Jan. 25, 1995; L.1995, c. 417, § 2, eff. Jan. 10, 1996; L.1997, c. 181, § 12, eff. Aug. 1, 1997.

2C:43–3.1. Additional assessments; collection and disposition by victims of crime compensation board

a. (1) In addition to any disposition made pursuant to the provisions of N.J.S. 2C:43–2, any person convicted of a crime of violence, theft of an automobile pursuant to N.J.S. 2C:20–2, eluding a law enforcement officer pursuant to subsection b. of N.J.S. 2C:29–2 or unlawful taking of a motor vehicle pursuant to subsection b., c. or d. of N.J.S. 2C:20–10 shall be assessed at least $100.00, but not to exceed $10,000.00 for each such crime for which he was convicted which resulted in the injury or death of another person. In imposing this assessment, the court shall consider factors such as the severity of the crime, the defendant's criminal record, defendant's ability to pay and the economic impact of the assessment on the defendant's dependents.

(2)(a) In addition to any other disposition made pursuant to the provisions of N.J.S. 2C:43–2 or any other statute imposing sentences for crimes, any person convicted of any disorderly persons offense, any petty disorderly persons offense, or any crime not resulting in the injury or death of any other person shall be assessed $50.00 for each such offense or crime for which he was convicted.

(b) In addition to any other disposition made pursuant to the provisions of section 24 of P.L.1982, c. 77 (C. 2A:4A–43) or any other statute indicating the dispositions that can be ordered for adjudications of delinquency, any juvenile adjudicated delinquent, according to the definition of "delinquency" established in section 4 of P.L.1982, c. 77 (C. 2A:4A–23), shall be assessed at least $30.00 for each such adjudication, but not to exceed the amount which could be assessed pursuant to paragraph (1) or paragraph (2)(a) of subsection a. of this section if the offense was committed by an adult.

(c) In addition to any other assessment imposed pursuant to the provisions of R.S. 39:4–50, the provisions of section 12 of P.L.1990, c. 103 (C.39:3–10.20) relating to a violation of section 5 of P.L.1990, c. 103 (C.39:3–10.13), the provisions of section 19 of P.L.1954, c. 236 (C. 12:7–34.19) or the provisions of section 3 of P.L.1952, c. 157 (C.12:7–46), any person convicted of operating a motor vehicle, commercial motor vehicle or vessel while under the influence of liquor or drugs shall be assessed $50.00.

(d) In addition to any term or condition that may be included in an agreement for supervisory treatment pursuant to N.J.S. 2C:43–13 or imposed as a term or condition of conditional discharge pursuant to N.J.S. 2C:36A–1, a participant in either program shall be required to pay an assessment of $50.00.

(3) All assessments provided for in this section shall be collected as provided in section 3 of P.L.1979, c. 396 (C. 2C:46–4) and the court shall so order at the time of sentencing. When a defendant who is sentenced to incarceration in a State correctional facility has not, at the time of sentencing, paid an assessment for the crime for which he is being sentenced or an assessment imposed for a previous crime, the court shall specifically order the Department of Corrections to collect the assessment during the period of incarceration and to deduct the assessment from any income the inmate receives as a result of labor performed at the institution or on any work release program or from any personal account established in the institution for the benefit of the inmate. All moneys collected, whether in part or in full payment of any assessment imposed pursuant to this section, shall be forwarded monthly by the parties responsible for collection, together with a monthly accounting on forms prescribed by the Victims of Crime Compensation Board pursuant to section 19 of P.L. 1991, c. 329 (C. 52:4B–8.1), to the Victims of Crime Compensation Board.

(4) The Victims of Crime Compensation Board shall forward monthly all moneys received from assessments collected pursuant to this section to the State Treasury for deposit as follows:

(a) Of moneys collected on assessments imposed pursuant to paragraph a.(1):

(i) the first $72.00 collected for deposit in the Victims of Crime Compensation Board Account,

(ii) the next $3.00 collected for deposit in the Criminal Disposition and Revenue Collection Fund,

(iii) the next $25.00 collected for deposit in the Victim Witness Advocacy Fund, and

(iv) moneys collected in excess of $100.00 for deposit in the Victims of Crime Compensation Board Account;

(b) Of moneys collected on assessments imposed pursuant to paragraph a.(2)(a), (c) or (d):

(i) the first $39.00 collected for deposit in the Victims of Crime Compensation Board Account,

(ii) the next $3.00 collected for deposit in the Criminal Disposition and Revenue Collection Fund, and

(iii) the next $8.00 collected for deposit in the Victim and Witness Advocacy Fund;

(c) Of moneys collected on assessments imposed pursuant to paragraph a.(2)(b):

(i) the first $17.00 for deposit in the Victims of Crime Compensation Board Account, and

(ii) the next $3.00 collected for deposit in the Criminal Disposition and Revenue Collection Fund, and

(iii) the next $10.00 for deposit in the Victim and Witness Advocacy Fund, and

(iv) moneys collected in excess of $30.00 for deposit in the Victims of Crime Compensation Board Account.

(5) The Victims of Crime Compensation Board shall provide the Attorney General with a monthly accounting of moneys received, deposited and identified as receivable, on forms prescribed pursuant to section 19 of P.L.1991, c. 329 (C. 52:4B–8.1).

(6)(a) The Victims of Crime Compensation Board Account shall be a separate, nonlapsing, revolving account that shall be administered by the Victims of Crime Compensation Board. All moneys deposited in that Account shall be used in satisfying claims pursuant to the provisions of the "Criminal Injuries Compensation Act of 1971," P.L.1971, c. 317 (C. 52:4B–1 et seq.) and for related administrative costs.

(b) The Criminal Disposition and Revenue Collection Fund shall be a separate, nonlapsing, revolving account that shall be administered by the Victims of Crime Compensation Board. All moneys deposited in that Fund shall be used as provided in section 19 of P.L.1991, c. 329 (C. 52:4B–8.1).

(c) The Victim and Witness Advocacy Fund shall be a separate, nonlapsing, revolving fund and shall be administered by the Division of Criminal Justice, Department of Law and Public Safety and all moneys deposited in that Fund pursuant to this section shall be used for the benefit of victims and witnesses of crime as provided in section 20 of P.L.1991, c. 329 (C. 52:4B–43.1) and for related administrative costs.

b. (Deleted by amendment, P.L.1991, c. 329).

c. (Deleted by amendment, P.L.1991, c. 329).

d. (Deleted by amendment, P.L.1991, c. 329).

L.1979, c. 396, § 2, eff. Feb. 6, 1980. Amended by L.1982, c. 164, § 1, eff. Jan. 30, 1983; L.1985, c. 251, § 1, eff. July 31, 1985; L.1985, c. 406, § 1, eff. Jan. 9, 1986; L.1987, c. 106, § 11, operative July 9, 1987; L.1990, c. 64, § 1; L.1991, c. 329, § 3, eff. Dec. 23, 1991; L.1995, c. 135, § 1, eff. June 26, 1995.

2C:43–3.2. Assessments; amounts collected deposited in safe neighborhoods services fund

a. (1) In addition to any other fine, fee or assessment imposed, any person convicted of a crime, disorderly or petty disorderly persons offense or violation of R.S. 39:4–50 shall be assessed $75 for each conviction.

(2) In addition to any term or condition that may be included in an agreement for supervisory treatment pursuant to N.J.S. 2C:43–13 or imposed as a term or condition of conditional discharge pursuant to section 3 of P.L.1987, c. 106 (C. 2C:36A–1), a participant in either program shall be required to pay an assessment of $75.

b. All assessments provided for in this section shall be collected as provided for collection of fines and restitutions in section 3 of P.L.1979, c. 396 (C. 2C:46–4) and shall be forwarded to the Department of the Treasury as provided in subsection c. of this section.

c. All money collected pursuant to this section shall be forwarded to the Department of the Treasury to be deposited into the Safe Neighborhoods Services Fund created by section 5 of this act.[1]

L.1993, c. 220, § 11, eff. Aug. 2, 1993.

[1] N.J.S.A. § 52:17B–163.

2C:43–3.3. Additional fines deposited in law enforcement officers training and equipment fund

a. In addition to any disposition made pursuant to the provisions of Title 2C of the New Jersey Statutes, any person convicted of a crime shall be assessed a penalty of $30.

b. In addition to any other disposition made pursuant to the provisions of section 24 of P.L.1982, c. 77 (C. 2A:4A–43) or any other statute indicating the dispositions that may be ordered for adjudications of delinquency, a juvenile adjudicated delinquent for an offense which if committed by an adult would be a crime shall be assessed a penalty of $15.

c. The penalties assessed under subsections a. and b. of this section shall be collected as provided for the collection of fines and restitution in section 3 of P.L.1979, c. 396 (C. 2C:46–4) and forwarded to the State Treasury for deposit in a separate account to be known as the "Law Enforcement Officers Training and Equipment Fund." The penalty assessed in this section shall be collected only after a penalty assessed in section 2 of P.L.1979, c. 396 (C. 2C:43–3.1) and any restitution ordered is collected.

The fund shall be used to support the development and provision of basic and in-service training courses for law enforcement officers by police training schools approved pursuant to P.L.1961, c. 56 (C. 52:17B–66 et seq.). In addition, the fund shall also be used to enable police training schools to purchase equipment needed for the training of law enforcement officers. Distributions from the fund shall only be made directly to such approved schools.

d. The Police Training Commission in the Department of Law and Public Safety shall be responsible for the administration and distribution of the fund pursuant to its authority under section 6 of P.L.1961, c. 56 (C. 52:17B–71).

e. An adult prisoner of a State correctional institution who does not pay the penalty imposed pursuant to this section shall have the penalty deducted from any income the inmate receives as a result of labor performed at the institution or any type of work release program. If any person, including an inmate, fails to pay the penalty imposed pursuant to this section, the court may order the suspension of the person's driver's license or nonresident reciprocity privilege, or prohibit the person from receiving or obtaining a license until the assessment is paid. The court shall notify the Director of the Division of Motor Vehicles of such an action. Prior to any action being taken pursuant to this subsection, the person shall be given notice and a hearing before the court to contest the charge of the failure to pay the assessment.

L.1996, c. 115, § 9, eff. Jan. 9, 1997.

2C:43–3.4. Restitution for extradition costs incurred by law enforcement entities

In addition to any fine or restitution authorized by N.J.S.2C:43–3, the court may sentence a defendant to make restitution for costs incurred by any law enforcement entity in extraditing the defendant from another jurisdiction if the court finds that, at the time of the extradition, the defendant was located in the other jurisdiction in order to avoid prosecution for a crime committed in this State or service of a criminal sentence imposed by a court of this State.

L.1997, c. 253, § 4, eff. Sept. 12, 1997.

2C:43–3.5. Additional penalties

a. In addition to any term or condition that may be included in an agreement for supervisory treatment pursuant to N.J.S.2C:43–13 or imposed as a term or condition of conditional discharge pursuant to N.J.S.2C:36A–1 for a violation of any offense defined in chapter 35 or 36 of Title 2C of the New Jersey Statutes, each participant shall be assessed a penalty of $50 for each adjudication or conviction.

b. All penalties provided by this section shall be collected as provided for collection of fines and restitutions in section 3 of P.L.1979, c. 396 (C.2C:46–4) and shall be forwarded to the Department of the Treasury as provided in subsection c. of this section.

c. All monies collected pursuant to this section shall be forwarded to the Department of the Treasury to be deposited in the "Drug Abuse Education Fund" established pursuant to section 1 of P.L.1999, c. 12 (C.54A: 9–25.12).

d. Monies in the fund shall be appropriated by the Legislature on an annual basis in the manner and for the purposes prescribed by section 2 of P.L.1999, c. 12 (C.54A:9–25.13).

L.1999, c. 295, § 1, eff. Dec. 23, 1999.

2C:43–3.6. Penalties

a. In addition to any fine, fee, assessment or penalty authorized under the provisions of Title 2C of the New Jersey Statutes, a person convicted of a sex offense, as defined in section 2 of P.L.1994, c. 133 (C.2C:7–2), shall be assessed a penalty of $800 for each such offense.

b. All penalties provided for in this section, collected as provided for the collection of fines and restitutions in section 3 of P.L.1979, c. 396 (C.2C:46–4), shall be forwarded to the Department of the Treasury to be deposited in the "Statewide Sexual Assault Nurse

Examiner Program Fund" established pursuant to section 12 of P.L.2001, c. 81 (C.52:4B–59).

L.2001, c. 81, § 11, eff. May 4, 2001.

2C:43–3.7. Surcharge on penalty for sexual assault

In addition to any other penalty, fine or charge imposed pursuant to law, a person convicted of an act of aggravated sexual assault or sexual assault under N.J.S.2C:14–2, or aggravated criminal sexual contact or criminal sexual contact under N.J.S.2C:14–3, shall be subject to a surcharge in the amount of $100 payable to the Treasurer of the State of New Jersey for use by the Department of Community Affairs to fund programs and grants for the prevention of violence against women.

L.2002, c. 34, § 51, eff. July 1, 2002.

2C:43–3.8. Additional assessment for certain computer-related criminal activities; Computer Crime Prevention Fund

a. In addition to any disposition authorized by this Title, the provisions of section 24 of P.L.1982, c. 77 (C.2A:4A–43), or any other statute indicating the dispositions that can be ordered for an adjudication of delinquency, every person convicted of or adjudicated delinquent for a violation of subparagraph (b) of paragraph (5) of subsection b. of N.J.S.2C:24–4, N.J.S.2C:34–3, or an offense involving computer criminal activity in violation of any provision of chapter 20 of this title shall be assessed for each such offense a penalty fixed at:

(a) $2,000 in the case of a crime of the first degree;

(b) $1,000 in the case of a crime of the second degree;

(c) $750 in the case of a crime of the third degree;

(d) $500 in the case of a crime of the fourth degree;

(e) $250 in the case of a disorderly persons or petty disorderly persons offense.

b. All penalties provided for in this section shall be collected as provided for collection of fines and restitutions in section 3 of P.L.1979, c. 396 (C.2C:46–4), and shall be forwarded to the Department of the Treasury as provided in subsection c. of this section.

c. All moneys collected pursuant to this section shall be forwarded to the Department of the Treasury to be deposited in a nonlapsing revolving fund to be known as the "Computer Crime Prevention Fund." Moneys in the fund shall be appropriated by the Legislature to the Department of Law and Public Safety on an annual basis for the purposes of investigating and prosecuting computer-related crime, and funding continuing educational programs on high technology crimes and the 24–hour toll-free computer crime hotline telephone service established pursuant to section 3 of P.L.1998, c. 134 (C.52:17B–193) and publicizing thereof, as well as other programs designed to enhance public awareness of computer-related crime, including but not limited to use of the Internet to facilitate sexual predatory acts, cyber-stalking and cyberbullying, online child pornography, threats of violence in schools or other institutions, Internet fraud, and unauthorized intrusions into computer systems.

d. There is created in the Department of Treasury a non-lapsing fund entitled the "Computer Crime Prevention Fund." The fund shall be the depository for assessments collected pursuant to subsection a. of this section, to be appropriated and used in accordance with the purposes set forth in subsection c. of this section.

L.2009, c. 143, § 1, eff. Oct. 19, 2009.

2C:43–4. Penalties against corporations; forfeiture of corporate charter or revocation of certificate authorizing foreign corporation to do business in the state

a. The court may suspend the imposition of sentence of a corporation which has been convicted of an offense or may sentence it to pay a fine of up to three times the fine provided for in N.J.S. 2C:43–3 in addition to any restitution required by N.J.S. 2C:44–2.

b. When a corporation is convicted of an offense or a high managerial agent of a corporation, as defined in N.J.S. 2C:2–7 is convicted of an offense committed in conducting the affairs of the corporation, the court may request the Attorney General to institute appropriate proceedings to dissolve the corporation, forfeit its charter, revoke any franchises held by it, or to revoke the certificate authorizing the corporation to conduct business in this State.

L.1978, c. 95, § 2C:43–4, eff. Sept. 1, 1979. Amended by L.1991, c. 329, § 4, eff. Dec. 23, 1991.

2C:43–5. Young adult offenders

Any person who, at the time of sentencing, is less than 26 years of age and who has been convicted of a crime may be sentenced to an indeterminate term at the Youth Correctional Institution Complex, in accordance with R.S. 30:4–146 et seq., in the case of men, and to the Correctional Institution for Women, in accordance with R.S. 30:4–153 et seq., in the case of women, instead of the sentences otherwise authorized by the code. This section shall not apply to any person less than 26 years of age at the time of sentencing who qualifies for a mandatory minimum term of imprisonment without eligibility for parole, pursuant to subsection c. of N.J.S. 2C:43–6; however, notwithstanding the provisions of subsection c. of N.J.S. 2C:43–6, the mandatory minimum term may be served at the Youth Correctional Institution Complex or the Correctional Institution for Women.

L.1978, c. 95, § 2C:43–5, eff. Sept. 1, 1979. Amended by L.1979, c. 178, § 84, eff. Sept. 1, 1979; L.1983, c. 92, § 1, eff. March 11, 1983.

2C:43–5.1. Offenders enrolled in secondary education at time of criminal charge, adjudication or conviction; written notice to the school; confidentiality

At the time of a criminal charge, adjudication of delinquency, or conviction of any student who is 18 years of age or older and is enrolled in secondary school, the law enforcement or prosecuting agency shall provide written notice to the school principal of the identity of that student, the offense charged, the adjudication, and the conviction if:

a. The offense occurred on school property or a school bus, occurred at a school-sponsored function or was committed against an employee or official of the school;

b. The student was taken into custody as a result of information or evidence provided by school officials; or

c. The offense constitutes a crime, and the offense:

(1) resulted in death or serious bodily injury or involved an attempt or conspiracy to cause death or serious bodily injury;

(2) involved the unlawful use or possession of a firearm or other weapon;

(3) involved the unlawful manufacture, distribution or possession with intent to distribute a controlled dangerous substance or controlled substance analog;

(4) was committed with a purpose to intimidate an individual or group of individuals because of race, color, religion, sexual orientation or ethnicity; or

(5) is a crime of the first, second, or third degree.

Information provided to the principal pursuant to this subsection shall be maintained by the school and shall be treated as confidential but may be made available to such members of the staff and faculty of the school as the principal deems appropriate for maintaining order, safety or discipline in the school or for planning programs relevant to a student's educational and social development.

L.2009, c. 157, § 1, eff. Nov. 20, 2009.

2C:43–6. Sentence of imprisonment for crime; ordinary terms; mandatory terms

a. Except as otherwise provided, a person who has been convicted of a crime may be sentenced to imprisonment, as follows:

(1) In the case of a crime of the first degree, for a specific term of years which shall be fixed by the court and shall be between 10 years and 20 years;

(2) In the case of a crime of the second degree, for a specific term of years which shall be fixed by the court and shall be between five years and 10 years;

(3) In the case of a crime of the third degree, for a specific term of years which shall be fixed by the court and shall be between three years and five years;

(4) In the case of a crime of the fourth degree, for a specific term which shall be fixed by the court and shall not exceed 18 months.

b. As part of a sentence for any crime, where the court is clearly convinced that the aggravating factors substantially outweigh the mitigating factors, as set forth in subsections a. and b. of 2C:44–1, or the court finds that the aggravating factor set forth in paragraph (5) of subsection a. of N.J.S.2C:44–1 applies, the court may fix a minimum term not to exceed one-half of the term set pursuant to subsection a., or one-half of the term set pursuant to a maximum period of incarceration for a crime set forth in any statute other than this code, during which the defendant shall not be eligible for parole; provided that no defendant shall be eligible for parole at a date earlier than otherwise provided by the law governing parole.

c. A person who has been convicted under subsection b. or d. of N.J.S.2C:39–3, subsection a. of N.J.S.2C:39–4, subsection a. of section 1 of P.L.1998, c. 26 (C.2C:39–4.1), subsection a., b. or c. of N.J.S.2C:39–5, subsection a. or paragraph (2) or (3) of subsection b. of section 6 of P.L.1979, c. 179 (C.2C:39–7), or subsection a., b., e. or g. of N.J.S.2C:39–9, or of a crime under any of the following sections: 2C:11–3, 2C:11–4, 2C:12–1b., 2C:13–1, 2C:14–2a., 2C:14–3a., 2C:15–1, 2C:18–2, 2C:29–5, who, while in the course of committing or attempting to commit the crime, including the immediate flight therefrom, used or was in possession of a firearm as defined in 2C:39–1f., shall be sentenced to a term of imprisonment by the court. The term of imprisonment shall include the imposition of a minimum term. The minimum term shall be fixed at, or between, one-third and one-half of the sentence imposed by the court or three years, whichever is greater, or 18 months in the case of a fourth degree crime, during which the defendant shall be ineligible for parole.

The minimum terms established by this section shall not prevent the court from imposing presumptive terms of imprisonment pursuant to 2C:44–1f. (1) except in cases of crimes of the fourth degree.

A person who has been convicted of an offense enumerated by this subsection and who used or possessed a firearm during its commission, attempted commission or flight therefrom and who has been previously convicted of an offense involving the use or possession of a firearm as defined in 2C:44–3d., shall be sentenced by the court to an extended term as authorized by 2C:43–7c., notwithstanding that extended terms are ordinarily discretionary with the court.

d. The court shall not impose a mandatory sentence pursuant to subsection c. of this section, 2C:43–7c. or 2C:44–3d., unless the ground therefor has been established at a hearing. At the hearing, which may occur at the time of sentencing, the prosecutor shall establish by a preponderance of the evidence that the weapon used or possessed was a firearm. In making its finding, the court shall take judicial notice of any evidence, testimony or information adduced at the trial, plea hearing, or other court proceedings and shall also consider the presentence report and any other relevant information.

e. A person convicted of a third or subsequent offense involving State taxes under N.J.S.2C:20–9, N.J.S.2C:21–15, any other provision of this code, or under any of the provisions of Title 54 of the Revised Statutes, or Title 54A of the New Jersey Statutes, as amended and supplemented, shall be sentenced to a term of imprisonment by the court. This shall not preclude an application for and imposition of an extended term of imprisonment under N.J.S.2C:44–3 if the provisions of that section are applicable to the offender.

f. A person convicted of manufacturing, distributing, dispensing or possessing with intent to distribute any dangerous substance or controlled substance analog under N.J.S.2C:35–5, of maintaining or operating a controlled dangerous substance production facility under N.J.S.2C:35–4, of employing a juvenile in a drug distribution scheme under N.J.S.2C:35–6, leader of a narcotics trafficking network under N.J.S.2C:35–3, or of distributing, dispensing or possessing with intent to distribute on or near school property or buses under section 1 of P.L.1987, c. 101 (C.2C:35–7), who has been previously convicted of manufacturing, distributing, dispensing or possessing with intent to distribute a controlled dangerous substance or controlled substance analog, shall upon application of the prosecuting attorney be sentenced by the court to an extended term as authorized by subsection c. of N.J.S.2C:43–7, notwithstanding that extended terms are ordinarily discretionary with the court. The term of imprisonment shall, except as may be provided in N.J.S.2C:35–12, include the imposition of a minimum term. The minimum term shall be fixed at, or between, one-third and one-half of the sentence imposed by the court or three years, whichever is greater, not less than seven years if the person is convicted of a violation of N.J.S.2C:35–6, or 18 months in the case of a fourth degree crime, during which the defendant shall be ineligible for parole.

The court shall not impose an extended term pursuant to this subsection unless the ground therefor has been established at a hearing. At the hearing, which may occur at the time of sentencing, the prosecutor shall establish the ground therefor by a preponderance of the evidence. In making its finding, the court shall take judicial notice of any evidence, testimony or information adduced at the trial, plea hearing, or other court proceedings and shall also consider the presentence report and any other relevant information.

For the purpose of this subsection, a previous conviction exists where the actor has at any time been convicted under chapter 35 of this title or Title 24 of the Revised Statutes or under any similar statute of the United States, this State, or any other state for an offense that is substantially equivalent to N.J.S.2C:35–3,

N.J.S.2C:35–4, N.J.S.2C:35–5, N.J.S.2C:35–6 or section 1 of P.L.1987, c. 101 (C.2C:35–7).

g. Any person who has been convicted under subsection a. of N.J.S.2C: 39–4 or of a crime under any of the following sections: N.J.S.2C:11–3, N.J.S.2C:11–4, N.J.S.2C:12–1b., N.J.S.2C:13–1, N.J.S.2C:14–2a., N.J.S.2C:14–3a., N.J.S.2C:15–1, N.J.S.2C:18–2, N.J.S.2C: 29–5, N.J.S.2C:35–5 who, while in the course of committing or attempting to commit the crime, including the immediate flight therefrom, used or was in possession of a machine gun or assault firearm shall be sentenced to a term of imprisonment by the court. The term of imprisonment shall include the imposition of a minimum term. The minimum term shall be fixed at 10 years for a crime of the first or second degree, five years for a crime of the third degree, or 18 months in the case of a fourth degree crime, during which the defendant shall be ineligible for parole.

The minimum terms established by this section shall not prevent the court from imposing presumptive terms of imprisonment pursuant to paragraph (1) of subsection f. of N.J.S.2C:44–1 for crimes of the first degree.

A person who has been convicted of an offense enumerated in this subsection and who used or possessed a machine gun or assault firearm during its commission, attempted commission or flight therefrom and who has been previously convicted of an offense involving the use or possession of any firearm as defined in subsection d. of N.J.S.2C:44–3, shall be sentenced by the court to an extended term as authorized by subsection d. of N.J.S.2C:43–7, notwithstanding that extended terms are ordinarily discretionary with the court.

h. The court shall not impose a mandatory sentence pursuant to subsection g. of this section, subsection d. of N.J.S.2C:43–7 or N.J.S.2C:44–3, unless the ground therefor has been established at a hearing. At the hearing, which may occur at the time of sentencing, the prosecutor shall establish by a preponderance of the evidence that the weapon used or possessed was a machine gun or assault firearm. In making its finding, the court shall take judicial notice of any evidence, testimony or information adduced at the trial, plea hearing, or other court proceedings and shall also consider the presentence report and any other relevant information.

i. A person who has been convicted under paragraph (6) of subsection b. of 2C:12–1 of causing bodily injury while eluding shall be sentenced to a term of imprisonment by the court. The term of imprisonment shall include the imposition of a minimum term. The minimum term shall be fixed at, or between one-third and one-half of the sentence imposed by the court. The minimum term established by this subsection shall not prevent the court from imposing a presumptive term of imprisonment pursuant to paragraph (1) of subsection f. of 2C:44–1.

L.1978, c. 95, § 2C:43–6, eff. Sept. 1, 1979. Amended by L.1979, c. 178, § 85, eff. Sept. 1, 1979; L.1981, c. 31, § 1, eff. Feb. 12, 1981; L.1981, c. 290, § 38, eff. Sept. 24, 1981; L.1981, c. 569, § 1, eff. Jan. 18, 1982; L.1982, c. 119, § 1, eff. Aug. 31, 1982; L.1987, c. 76, § 35, eff. Dec. 9, 1987; L.1987, c. 106, § 12, operative July 9, 1987; L.1988, c. 44, § 13, eff. June 28, 1988; L.1990, c. 32, § 6, eff. May 30, 1990; L.1993, c. 219, § 6, eff. Aug. 2, 1993; L.2007, c. 341, § 5, eff. Jan. 13, 2008.

2C:43–6.1. Person under minimum mandatory sentence for possession of firearm with intent to use against property of another; review of sentence; imposition of other sentence

Any person who, on the effective date of this amendatory and supplementary act, is serving a minimum mandatory sentence as provided for by N.J.S. 2C:43–6c. solely as a result of his conviction under subsection a. of N.J.S. 2C:39–4 for the possession of a firearm with intent to use it against the property of another, and has not had his sentence suspended or been paroled or discharged, may move to have his sentence reviewed by the sentencing court. For good cause shown, the court may impose any sentence which would have otherwise been available for such person.

L.1982, c. 119, § 2, eff. Aug. 31, 1982.

2C:43–6.2. Conviction of certain offenses while armed for first time; reduction of mandatory minimum term

On a motion by the prosecutor made to the assignment judge that the imposition of a mandatory minimum term of imprisonment under (a) subsection c. of N.J.S. 2C:43–6 for a defendant who has not previously been convicted of an offense under that subsection, or (b) subsection e. of N.J.S. 2C:39–10 for a defendant who has not previously been convicted of an offense under chapter 39 of Title 2C of the New Jersey Statutes, does not serve the interests of justice, the assignment judge shall place the defendant on probation pursuant to paragraph (2) of subsection b. of N.J.S. 2C:43–2 or reduce to one year the mandatory minimum term of imprisonment during which the defendant will be ineligible for parole. The sentencing court may also refer a case of a defendant who has not previously been convicted of an offense under that subsection to the assignment judge, with the approval of the prosecutor, if the sentencing court believes that the interests of justice would not be served by the imposition of a mandatory minimum term.

L.1989, c. 53, § 1, eff. April 14, 1989. Amended by L.1993, c. 49, § 2, eff. Feb. 18, 1993.

2C:43–6.3. Person serving mandatory minimum term; motion to have sentence reviewed

Any person who, on the effective date of this act, is serving a mandatory minimum sentence as provided for by subsection c. of N.J.S. 2C:43–6, who has not been previously convicted under that subsection, and has not had his sentence suspended or been paroled or discharged, may move to have his sentence reviewed by the assignment judge for the sentencing court. If the prosecutor agrees that the sentence under review does not serve the interests of justice, the judge shall reduce the mandatory minimum term of imprisonment without parole eligibility to one year or place the person on probation pursuant to paragraph (2) of subsection b. of N.J.S. 2C:43–2.

L.1989, c. 53, § 2, eff. April 14, 1989.

2C:43–6.4. Special sentence of community supervision for life imposed on persons convicted of certain sexual offense

a. Notwithstanding any provision of law to the contrary, a judge imposing sentence on a person who has been convicted of aggravated sexual assault, sexual assault, aggravated criminal sexual contact, kidnapping pursuant to paragraph (2) of subsection c. of N.J.S.2C:13–1, endangering the welfare of a child by engaging in sexual conduct which would impair or debauch the morals of the child pursuant to subsection a. of N.J.S.2C:24–4, endangering the welfare of a child pursuant to paragraph (3) of subsection b. of N.J.S.2C:24–4, luring or an attempt to commit any of these offenses shall include, in addition to any sentence authorized by this Code, a special sentence of parole supervision for life.

b. The special sentence of parole supervision for life required by this section shall commence immediately upon the defendant's release from incarceration. If the defendant is serving a sentence of incarceration for another offense at the time he completes the custodial portion of the sentence imposed on the present offense, the special sentence of parole supervision for life shall not commence until the defendant is actually released from incarceration for the other offense. Persons serving a special sentence of parole supervision for life shall remain in the legal custody of the Commissioner of Corrections, shall be supervised by the Division of Parole of the State Parole Board, shall be subject to the provisions and conditions set forth in subsection c. of section 3 of P.L.1997, c. 117 (C.30:4–123.51b) and sections 15 through 19 and 21 of P.L.1979, c. 441 (C.30:4–123.59 through 30:4–123.63 and 30:4–123.65), and shall be subject to conditions appropriate to protect the public and foster rehabilitation. Such conditions may include the requirement that the person comply with the conditions set forth in subsection f. of this section concerning use of a computer or other device with access to the Internet. If the defendant violates a condition of a special sentence of parole supervision for life, the defendant shall be subject to the provisions of sections 16 through 19 and 21 of P.L.1979, c. 441 (C.30:4–123.60 through 30:4–123.63 and 30:4–123.65), and for the purpose of calculating the limitation on time served pursuant to section 21 of P.L.1979, c. 441 (C.30:4–123.65) the custodial term imposed upon the defendant related to the special sentence of parole supervision for life shall be deemed to be a term of life imprisonment. When the court suspends the imposition of sentence on a defendant who has been convicted of any offense enumerated in subsection a. of this section, the court may not suspend imposition of the special sentence of parole supervision for life, which shall commence immediately, with the Division of Parole of the State Parole Board maintaining supervision over that defendant, including the defendant's compliance with any conditions imposed by the court pursuant to N.J.S.2C:45–1, in accordance with the provisions of this subsection. Nothing contained in this subsection shall prevent the court from at any time proceeding under the provisions of N.J.S.2C:45–1 through 2C:45–4 against any such defendant for a violation of any conditions imposed by the court when it suspended imposition of sentence, or prevent the Division of Parole from proceeding under the provisions of sections 16 through 19 and 21 of P.L.1979, c. 441 (C. 30:4–123.60 through 30:4–123.63 and C.30:4–123.65) against any such defendant for a violation of any conditions of the special sentence of parole supervision for life, including the conditions imposed by the court pursuant to N.J.S.2C:45–1.

In any such proceeding by the Division of Parole, the provisions of subsection c. of section 3 of P.L.1997, c. 117 (C.30:4–123.51b) authorizing revocation and return to prison shall be applicable to such a defendant, notwithstanding that the defendant may not have been sentenced to or served any portion of a custodial term for conviction of an offense enumerated in subsection a. of this section.

c. A person sentenced to a term of parole supervision for life may petition the Superior Court for release from that parole supervision. The judge may grant a petition for release from a special sentence of parole supervision for life only upon proof by clear and convincing evidence that the person has not committed a crime for 15 years since the last conviction or release from incarceration, whichever is later, and that the person is not likely to pose a threat to the safety of others if released from parole supervision. Notwithstanding the provisions of section 22 of P.L.1979, c. 441 (C.30:4–123.66), a person sentenced to a term of parole supervision for life may be released from that parole supervision term only by court order as provided in this subsection.

d. A person who violates a condition of a special sentence imposed pursuant to this section without good cause is guilty of a crime of the fourth degree. Notwithstanding any other law to the contrary, a person sentenced pursuant to this subsection shall be sentenced to a term of imprisonment, unless the court is clearly convinced that the interests of justice so far outweigh the need to deter this conduct and the interest in public safety that a sentence to imprisonment would be a manifest injustice. Nothing in this subsection shall preclude subjecting a person who violates any condition

of a special sentence of parole supervision for life to the provisions of sections 16 through 19 and 21 of P.L.1979, c. 441 (C.30:4–123.60 through 30:4–123.63 and C.30:4–123.65) pursuant to the provisions of subsection c. of section 3 of P.L.1997, c. 117 (C.30:4–123.51b).

e. A person who, while serving a special sentence of parole supervision for life imposed pursuant to this section, commits a violation of N.J.S.2C:11–3, N.J.S.2C:11–4, N.J.S.2C:11–5, subsection b. of N.J.S.2C:12–1, N.J.S.2C:13–1, section 1 of P.L.1983, c.291 (C.2C:13–6), N.J.S.2C:14–2, N.J.S.2C:14–3, N.J.S.2C:24–4, N. J.S.2C:18–2 when the offense is a crime of the second degree, or subsection a. of N.J.S.2C:39–4 shall be sentenced to an extended term of imprisonment as set forth in N.J.S.2C:43–7, which term shall, notwithstanding the provisions of N.J.S.2C:43–7 or any other law, be served in its entirety prior to the person's resumption of the term of parole supervision for life.

f. The special sentence of parole supervision for life required by this section may include any of the following Internet access conditions:

(1) Prohibit the person from accessing or using a computer or any other device with Internet capability without the prior written approval of the court except the person may use a computer or any other device with Internet capability in connection with that person's employment or search for employment with the prior approval of the person's parole officer;

(2) Require the person to submit to periodic unannounced examinations of the person's computer or any other device with Internet capability by a parole officer, law enforcement officer or assigned computer or information technology specialist, including the retrieval and copying of all data from the computer or device and any internal or external peripherals and removal of such information, equipment or device to conduct a more thorough inspection;

(3) Require the person to submit to the installation on the person's computer or device with Internet capability, at the person's expense, one or more hardware or software systems to monitor the Internet use; and

(4) Require the person to submit to any other appropriate restrictions concerning the person's use or access of a computer or any other device with Internet capability.

L.1994, c. 130, § 2, eff. Oct. 31, 1994. Amended by L.2003, c. 267, § 1, eff. Jan. 14, 2004; L.2007, c. 219, § 3, eff. Feb. 25, 2008.

2C:43–6.5. Offenses by public officers or employees; mandatory minimum term of imprisonment for crimes that involve or touch upon the public office or employment

a. Notwithstanding the provisions of subsection a. of N.J.S.2C:43–6 and except as otherwise provided in subsection c. of this section, a person who serves or has served as a public officer or employee under the government of this State, or any political subdivision thereof, who is convicted of a crime that involves or touches such office or employment as set forth in subsection b. of this section, shall be sentenced to a mandatory minimum term of imprisonment without eligibility for parole as follows: for a crime of the fourth degree, the mandatory minimum term shall be one year; for a crime of the third degree, two years; for a crime of the second degree, five years; and for a crime of the first degree, 10 years; unless the provisions of any other law provide for a higher mandatory minimum term. As used in this subsection, "a crime that involves or touches such office or employment" means that the crime was related directly to the person's performance in, or circumstances flowing from, the specific public office or employment held by the person.

b.   Subsection a. of this section applies to a conviction of any of the following crimes:

(1) Paragraph (4) of subsection a. of N.J.S.2C:13–5, criminal coercion;

(2) N.J.S.2C:20–4, theft by deception, if the amount involved exceeds $10,000;

(3) Subsection d. of N.J.S.2C:20–5, theft by extortion;

(4) N.J.S.2C:20–9, theft by failure to make required disposition of property received, if the amount involved exceeds $10,000;

(5) N.J.S.2C:21–10, commercial bribery;

(6) Section 3 of P.L.1994, c. 121 (C.2C:21–25), money laundering;

(7) Section 97 of P.L.1999, c. 440 (C.2C:21–34), false contract payment claims;

(8) N.J.S.2C:27–2, bribery in official matters;

(9) N.J.S.2C:27–3, threats and other improper influence in official and political matters;

(10) Section 100 of P.L.1999, c. 440 (C.2C:27–9), unlawful official business transaction where interest is involved;

(11) Section 5 of P.L.2003, c. 255 (C.2C:27–10), acceptance or receipt of unlawful benefit by public servant for official behavior;

(12) Section 6 of P.L.2003, c. 255 (C.2C:27–11), offer of unlawful benefit to public servant for official behavior;

(13) N.J.S.2C:28–1, perjury;

(14) N.J.S.2C:28–5, tampering with witnesses;

(15) N.J.S.2C:28–7, tampering with public records or information;

(16) N.J.S.2C:29–4, compounding;

(17) N.J.S.2C:30–2, official misconduct;

(18) N.J.S.2C:30–3, speculating or wagering on official action or information; or

(19) Section 3 of P.L.2003, c. 31 (C.2C:30–7), pattern of official misconduct.

c.   (1) On motion by the prosecutor stating that the defendant has provided substantial assistance in a criminal investigation or prosecution of another person, the court may waive or reduce the mandatory minimum term of imprisonment required by subsection a. of this section.   The appropriate waiver or reduction shall be determined by the court for reasons stated that may include, but are not limited to, consideration of the following:

(i) the court's evaluation of the significance and usefulness of the defendant's assistance, giving substantial weight to the prosecutor's evaluation of the assistance rendered;

(ii) the truthfulness, completeness, and reliability of any information or testimony provided by the defendant;

(iii) the nature and extent of the defendant's assistance;

(iv) any injury suffered, or any danger or risk of injury to the defendant or his family resulting from his assistance;

(v) the timeliness of the defendant's assistance.

In making such a determination, the court shall give substantial weight to the prosecutor's evaluation of the extent of the defendant's assistance, particularly where the extent and value of the assistance are difficult to ascertain.

(2) If the court finds by clear and convincing evidence that extraordinary circumstances exist such that imposition of a mandatory minimum term would be a serious injustice which overrides the need to deter such conduct in others, the court may waive or reduce the mandatory minimum term of imprisonment required by subsection a. of this section.   In making any such finding, the court must state with specificity its reasons for waiving or reducing the mandatory minimum sentence that would otherwise apply.

(3) If, pursuant to paragraph (1) or (2) of this subsection, the court waives or reduces the mandatory minimum term required by subsection a. of this section, such sentence shall not become final for 10 days in order to permit the appeal of the sentence by the prosecution.

d.   (1) A prosecutor shall not recommend the admission into or consent to the referral to a pretrial intervention program of a person who serves or has served as a public officer or employee under the government of this State, or any political subdivision thereof, who is charged with a crime that involves or touches such office or employment as set forth in subsection b. of this section, without the prior approval of the Attorney General.

(2) A person who serves or has served as a public officer or employee under the government of this State,

or any political subdivision thereof, who is convicted of a crime that involves or touches such office or employment as set forth in subsection b. of this section shall be ineligible for participation in any program of intensive supervision during any period of parole ineligibility.

e. The Attorney General shall develop guidelines to ensure the uniform exercise of discretion in making determinations regarding the waiver or reduction of a mandatory minimum term of imprisonment pursuant to paragraph (1) of subsection c. of this section and participation in a pretrial intervention program pursuant to paragraph (1) of subsection d. of this section.

L.2007, c. 49, § 6, eff. April 14, 2007.

2C:43–6.6. Internet access; court's authority to place conditions and restrictions for certain sex offenders

a. In the case of a person who has been convicted, adjudicated delinquent or found not guilty by reason of insanity for the commission of a sex offense as defined in subsection b. of section 2 of P.L.1994, c. 133 (C.2C:7–2), and who is required to register as provided in subsections c. and d. of section 2 of P.L.1994, c. 133 (C.2C:7–2), or who is serving a special sentence of community or parole supervision for life as provided in section 2 of P.L.1994, c. 130 (C.2C:43–6.4), or who has been convicted, adjudicated delinquent or found not guilty by reason of insanity for a violation of N.J.S.2C:34–3, and where the trier of fact makes a finding that a computer or any other device with Internet capability was used to facilitate the commission of the crime the court shall, in addition to any other disposition, order the following Internet access conditions:

(1) Prohibit the person from accessing or using a computer or any other device with Internet capability without the prior written approval of the court except, if such person is on probation or parole, the person may use a computer or any other device with Internet capability in connection with that person's employment or search for employment with the prior approval of the person's probation or parole officer;

(2) Require the person to submit to periodic unannounced examinations of the person's computer or any other device with Internet capability by a probation officer, parole officer, law enforcement officer or assigned computer or information technology specialist, including the retrieval and copying of all data from the computer or device and any internal or external peripherals and removal of such information, equipment or device to conduct a more thorough inspection;

(3) Require the person to submit to the installation on the person's computer or device with Internet capability, at the person's expense, one or more hardware or software systems to monitor the Internet use; and

(4) Require the person to submit to any other appropriate restrictions concerning the person's use or access of a computer or any other device with Internet capability.

b. A person who fails to comply with the Internet access conditions set forth in this section shall be guilty of a crime of the fourth degree.

c. The appropriate agency heads shall promulgate guidelines which set forth standards to guide agency action in regard to the specific Internet access conditions which may be imposed on a person pursuant to the provisions of this act.[1]

d. The Attorney General or the County Prosecutor may petition the court to impose restrictions pursuant to this section upon any person who is required to register as provided in section 2 of P.L.1994, c. 133 (C.2C:7–2) for a sex offense set forth in paragraph (3) of subsection b. of section 2 of P.L.1994, c. 133 (C.2C:7–2).

L.2007, c. 219, § 1, eff. Feb. 25, 2008.

[1] L.2007, c. 219.

2C:43–6.7. Effective date; application of act

This act[1] shall take effect on the 60th day following enactment and shall apply to any person who commits an offense subject to sentencing under section 1 of this act[2] after the effective date of this act and to any person who is under probation or parole supervision, including community or parole supervision for life, on the effective date of this act.

L.2007, c. 219, § 7, eff. Feb. 25, 2008.

[1] L.2007, c. 219, approved December 27, 2007, eff. Feb. 25, 2008.
[2] N.J.S.A. § 26:43–6.6.

2C:43–7. Sentence of imprisonment for crime; extended terms

a. In the cases designated in section 2C:44–3, a person who has been convicted of a crime may be sentenced, and in the cases designated in subsection e. of section 2 of P.L.1994, c. 130 (C.2C:43–6.4), in subsection b. of section 2 of P.L.1995, c. 126 (C.2C:43–7.1) and in the cases designated in section 1 of P.L.1997, c. 410 (C.2C:44–5.1), a person who has been convicted of a crime shall be sentenced, to an extended term of imprisonment, as follows:

(1) In case of aggravated manslaughter sentenced under subsection c. of N. J.S.2C:11–4; or kidnapping when sentenced as a crime of the first degree under paragraph (1) of subsection c. of 2C:13–1; or aggravated sexual assault if the person is eligible for an extended term pursuant to the provisions of subsection g. of N.J.S.2C:44–3 for a specific term of years which shall be between 30 years and life imprisonment;

(2) Except for the crime of murder and except as provided in paragraph (1) of this subsection, in the case of a crime of the first degree, for a specific term of years which shall be fixed by the court and shall be between 20 years and life imprisonment;

(3) In the case of a crime of the second degree, for a term which shall be fixed by the court between 10 and 20 years;

(4) In the case of a crime of the third degree, for a term which shall be fixed by the court between five and 10 years;

(5) In the case of a crime of the fourth degree pursuant to 2C:43–6c, 2C:43–6g and 2C:44–3d for a term of five years, and in the case of a crime of the fourth degree pursuant to any other provision of law for a term which shall be fixed by the court between three and five years;

(6) In the case of the crime of murder, for a specific term of years which shall be fixed by the court between 35 years and life imprisonment, of which the defendant shall serve 35 years before being eligible for parole;

(7) In the case of kidnapping under paragraph (2) of subsection c. of 2C:13–1, for a specific term of years which shall be fixed by the court between 30 years and life imprisonment, of which the defendant shall serve 30 years before being eligible for parole.

b.   As part of a sentence for an extended term and notwithstanding the provisions of 2C:43–9, the court may fix a minimum term not to exceed one-half of the term set pursuant to subsection a. during which the defendant shall not be eligible for parole or a term of 25 years during which time the defendant shall not be eligible for parole where the sentence imposed was life imprisonment; provided that no defendant shall be eligible for parole at a date earlier than otherwise provided by the law governing parole.

c.   In the case of a person sentenced to an extended term pursuant to 2C:43–6c, 2C:43–6f and 2C:44–3d, the court shall impose a sentence within the ranges permitted by 2C:43–7a(2), (3), (4) or (5) according to the degree or nature of the crime for which the defendant is being sentenced, which sentence shall include a minimum term which shall, except as may be specifically provided by N.J.S.2C:43–6f, be fixed at or between one-third and one-half of the sentence imposed by the court or five years, whichever is greater, during which the defendant shall not be eligible for parole. Where the sentence imposed is life imprisonment, the court shall impose a minimum term of 25 years during which the defendant shall not be eligible for parole, except that where the term of life imprisonment is imposed on a person convicted for a violation of N.J.S.2C:35–3, the term of parole ineligibility shall be 30 years.

d.   In the case of a person sentenced to an extended term pursuant to N.J.S.2C:43–6g, the court shall impose a sentence within the ranges permitted by N.J.S.2C:43–7a(2), (3), (4) or (5) according to the degree or nature of the crime for which the defendant is being sentenced, which sentence shall include a minimum term which shall be fixed at 15 years for a crime of the first or second degree, eight years for a crime of the third degree, or five years for a crime of the fourth degree during which the defendant shall not be eligible

for parole. Where the sentence imposed is life imprisonment, the court shall impose a minimum term of 25 years during which the defendant shall not be eligible for parole, except that where the term of life imprisonment is imposed on a person convicted of a violation of N.J.S.2C:35–3, the term of parole eligibility shall be 30 years.

L.1978, c. 95, § 2C:43–7, eff. Sept. 1, 1979. Amended by L.1979, c. 178, § 86, eff. Sept. 1, 1979; L.1981, c. 31, § 2, eff. Feb. 12, 1981; L.1982, c. 111, § 2, eff. Aug. 6, 1982; L.1986, c. 172, § 3, eff. Dec. 8, 1986; L.1987, c. 106, § 13, operative July 9, 1987; L.1988, c. 44, § 14, eff. June 28, 1988; L.1990, c. 32, § 7, eff. May 30, 1990; L.1990, c. 87, § 3, eff. Aug. 9, 1990; L.1994, c. 127, § 1, eff. Oct. 31, 1994; L.1994, c. 130, § 3, eff. Oct. 31, 1994; L.1995, c. 126, § 3, eff. June 22, 1995; L.1997, c. 410, § 2, eff. Jan. 19, 1998; L.2001, c. 443, § 6, eff. Jan. 11, 2002; L.2003, c. 267, § 4, eff. Jan. 14, 2004.

2C:43–7.1.   Persistent offenders; sentencing

a.   Life Imprisonment Without Parole.   A person convicted of a crime under any of the following: N.J.S.2C:11–3; subsection a. of N.J.S.2C:11–4; a crime of the first degree under N.J.S.2C:13–1, paragraphs (3) through (6) of subsection a. of N.J.S.2C:14–2; N.J.S.2C:15–1; or section 1 of P.L.1993, c. 221 (C.2C:15–2), who has been convicted of two or more crimes that were committed on prior and separate occasions, regardless of the dates of the convictions, under any of the foregoing sections or under any similar statute of the United States, this State, or any other state for a crime that is substantially equivalent to a crime under any of the foregoing sections, shall be sentenced to a term of life imprisonment by the court, with no eligibility for parole.

b.   Extended Term for Repeat Violent Offenders.   A person shall be sentenced to an extended term of imprisonment pursuant to N.J.S.2C:43–7 if:

(1) The person is convicted of any of the following crimes: a crime of the second degree under N.J.S.2C:11–4; a crime of the second or third degree under subsection b. of N.J.S.2C:12–1; a crime of the second degree under N.J.S.2C:13–1; a crime under N.J.S.2C:14–3 for aggravated criminal sexual contact under any of the circumstances set forth in paragraphs (3) through (6) of subsection a. of N.J.S.2C:14–2; a crime of the second degree under N.J.S.2C:15–1; a crime of the second degree under N.J.S.2C:18–2; or a crime of the second degree under N.J.S.2C:39–4 for possession of a weapon with the purpose of using it unlawfully against the person of another, and the person has been convicted of any of the foregoing crimes or any of the crimes enumerated in subsection a. of this section or under any similar statute of the United States, this State, or any other state for a crime that is substantially equivalent to a crime enumerated in this subsection or in subsection a. of this section committed on two or more prior and separate occasions regardless of the dates of the convictions; or

(2) The person is convicted of a crime enumerated in subsection a. of this section, does not have two or more prior convictions that require sentencing under subsection a. and has two or more prior convictions that would require sentencing under paragraph (1) of this subsection if the person had been convicted of a crime enumerated in paragraph (1).

c. The provisions of this section shall not apply unless the prior convictions are for crimes committed on separate occasions and unless the crime for which the defendant is being sentenced was committed either within 10 years of the date of the defendant's last release from confinement for commission of any crime or within 10 years of the date of the commission of the most recent of the crimes for which the defendant has a prior conviction.

d. The court shall not impose a sentence of imprisonment pursuant to this section, unless the ground therefor has been established at a hearing after the conviction of the defendant and on written notice to the defendant of the ground proposed. The defendant shall have the right to hear and controvert the evidence against him and to offer evidence upon the issue. Prior convictions shall be defined and proven in accordance with N.J.S.2C:44–4.

e. For purposes of this section, a term of life shall mean the natural life of a person sentenced pursuant to this section. Except that a defendant who is at least 70 years of age and who has served at least 35 years in prison pursuant to a sentence imposed under this section shall be released on parole if the full Parole Board determines that the defendant is not a danger to the safety of any other person or the community.

L.1995, c. 126, § 2, eff. June 22, 1995. Amended by L.2003, c. 48, § 1, eff. April 23, 2003.

2C:43–7.2. Eligibility for parole; persons convicted of certain violent crimes

a. A court imposing a sentence of incarceration for a crime of the first or second degree enumerated in subsection d. of this section shall fix a minimum term of 85% of the sentence imposed, during which the defendant shall not be eligible for parole.

b. The minimum term required by subsection a. of this section shall be fixed as a part of every sentence of incarceration imposed upon every conviction of a crime enumerated in subsection d. of this section, whether the sentence of incarceration is determined pursuant to N.J.S.2C:43–6, N.J.S. 2C:43–7, N.J.S.2C:11–3 or any other provision of law, and shall be calculated based upon the sentence of incarceration actually imposed. The provisions of subsection a. of this section shall not be construed or applied to reduce the time that must be served before eligibility for parole by an inmate sentenced to a mandatory minimum period of incarceration. Solely for the purpose of calculating the minimum term of parole ineligibility pursuant to subsection

a. of this section, a sentence of life imprisonment shall be deemed to be 75 years.

c. Notwithstanding any other provision of law to the contrary and in addition to any other sentence imposed, a court imposing a minimum period of parole ineligibility of 85 percent of the sentence pursuant to this section shall also impose a five-year term of parole supervision if the defendant is being sentenced for a crime of the first degree, or a three-year term of parole supervision if the defendant is being sentenced for a crime of the second degree. The term of parole supervision shall commence upon the completion of the sentence of incarceration imposed by the court pursuant to subsection a. of this section unless the defendant is serving a sentence of incarceration for another crime at the time he completes the sentence of incarceration imposed pursuant to subsection a., in which case the term of parole supervision shall commence immediately upon the defendant's release from incarceration. During the term of parole supervision the defendant shall remain in release status in the community in the legal custody of the Commissioner of the Department of Corrections and shall be supervised by the State Parole Board as if on parole and shall be subject to the provisions and conditions of section 3 of P.L.1997, c. 117 (C.30:4–123.51b).

d. The court shall impose sentence pursuant to subsection a. of this section upon conviction of the following crimes or an attempt or conspiracy to commit any of these crimes:

(1) N.J.S.2C:11–3, murder;

(2) N.J.S.2C:11–4, aggravated manslaughter or manslaughter;

(3) N.J.S.2C:11–5, vehicular homicide;

(4) subsection b. of N.J.S.2C:12–1, aggravated assault;

(5) subsection b. of section 1 of P.L. 1996, c. 14 (2C:12–11), disarming a law enforcement officer;

(6) N.J.S.2C:13–1, kidnapping;

(7) subsection a. of N.J.S.2C:14–2, aggravated sexual assault;

(8) subsection b. of N.J.S.2C:14–2 and paragraph (1) of subsection c. of N.J.S.2C:14–2, sexual assault;

(9) N.J.S.2C:15–1, robbery;

(10) section 1 of P.L.1993, c. 221 (C.2C:15–2), carjacking;

(11) paragraph (1) of subsection a. of N.J.S.2C:17–1, aggravated arson;

(12) N.J.S.2C:18–2, burglary;

(13) subsection a. of N.J.S.2C:20–5, extortion;

(14) subsection b. of section 1 of P.L.1997, c. 185 (C.2C:35–4.1), booby traps in manufacturing or distribution facilities;

(15) N.J.S.2C:35–9, strict liability for drug induced deaths;

(16) section 2 of P.L.2002, c. 26 (C.2C:38–2), terrorism;

(17) section 3 of P.L.2002, c. 26 (C.2C:38–3), producing or possessing chemical weapons, biological agents or nuclear or radiological devices; or

(18) N.J.S.2C:41–2, racketeering, when it is a crime of the first degree.

e. (Deleted by amendment, P.L.2001, c. 129).

L.1997, c. 117, § 2, eff. June 9, 1997. Amended by L.2001, c. 79, § 16; L.2001, c. 129, § 1, eff. June 29, 2001; L.2002, c. 26, § 19, eff. June 18, 2002; L.2007, c. 341, § 6, eff. Jan. 13, 2008.

2C:43–8. Sentence of imprisonment for disorderly persons offenses and petty disorderly persons offenses

A person who has been convicted of a disorderly persons offense or a petty disorderly persons offense may be sentenced to imprisonment for a definite term which shall be fixed by the court and shall not exceed 6 months in the case of a disorderly persons offense or 30 days in the case of a petty disorderly persons offense.

L.1978, c. 95, § 2C:43–8, eff. Sept. 1, 1979.

2C:43–8.1. Termination of right to occupy or visit seasonally leased premises

In addition to any other disposition authorized by law, if a person is convicted of a disorderly persons offense, a petty disorderly persons offense or a violation of a municipal ordinance and the offense or violation occurred at or involved the use of a seasonally leased premises, the court may order the termination of that person's right to occupy or visit the seasonally leased premises for a period not to exceed 125 days.

As used in this section, "seasonally leased premises" means premises leased as a residence for a period of less than 125 consecutive days. The term "seasonally leased premises" shall not include any structure provided by an employer on the employer's property which is used as living quarters for seasonal, temporary or migrant workers nor shall it include any premises used as the principal residence of a tenant pursuant to the terms of a month to month or week to week lease.

L.1992, c. 29, § 1, eff. June 29, 1992.

2C:43–9. Release of all offenders; length of recommitment and reparole after revocation of parole

Release of offenders on parole, recommitment and reparole after revocation shall be governed by the "Parole Act of 1979," P.L.1979, c. 441 (C. 30:4–123.45 et seq.).

L.1978, c. 95, § 2C:43–9, eff. Sept. 1, 1979. Amended by L.1979, c. 178, § 86A, eff. Sept. 1, 1979; L.1981, c. 290, § 39, eff. Sept. 24, 1981.

2C:43–10. Place of imprisonment; beginning sentences; transfers

a. Sentences for terms of 1 year or longer. Except as provided in section 2C:43–5 and in subsection b. of this section, when a person is sentenced to imprisonment for any term of 1 year or greater, the court shall commit him to the custody of the Commissioner of the Department of Corrections for the term of his sentence and until released in accordance with law.

b. County institution. In any county in which a county penitentiary or a county workhouse is located, a person sentenced to imprisonment for a return not exceeding 18 months may be committed to the penitentiary or workhouse of such county.

c. Sentences for terms of less than 1 year. When a person is sentenced to imprisonment for a term of less than 1 year, the court shall commit him either to the common jail of the county, the county workhouse or the county penitentiary for the term of his sentence and until released in accordance with law. In counties of the first class having a workhouse or penitentiary, however, no sentence exceeding 6 months shall be to the common jail of the county.

d. Aggregation of sentences when a person is sentenced to more than one term of imprisonment, and the sentences are to be consecutive, the terms shall be aggregated for the purpose of determining the place of imprisonment under subsections a., b. or c. of this section.

e. Duties of sheriff and keeper on sentence to State Prison. In all cases where the defendant, upon conviction, is sentenced by the court to imprisonment, for any term of 1 year or greater, the sheriff of the county or his lawful deputy shall, within 15 days transport him to the State Prison and there deliver him into the custody of the Commissioner of the Department of Corrections together with a copy of the sentence of the court ordering such imprisonment certified by the clerk of the court where the conviction was had, a copy of the court's statement of reasons for the sentence, and a copy of the presentence report or any presentence information used by the judge in determining sentence.

In every case at least 48 hours, exclusive of Sundays and legal holidays, shall elapse between the time of sentence and removal to the State Prison.

f. Beginning sentences in county institutions. Every person sentenced to the county workhouse or penitentiary shall be transferred to and confined therein within 10 days after the sentence.

g. Transfer of persons sentenced to county jail, penitentiary or workhouse from one to another thereof. Every person sentenced to imprisonment in a county jail, penitentiary or workhouse may upon the application of the board of chosen freeholders of such county and by order of the Superior Court, be transferred from any one of such county penal institutions to any other thereof. No such transfer or retransfer shall in any way affect the term of the original sentence of the person so transferred or retransferred.

L.1978, c. 95, § 2C:43–10, eff. Sept. 1, 1979. Amended by L.1979, c. 178, § 87, eff. Sept. 1, 1979.

2C:43–11. Conduct precluding admission to intensive supervision programs; objections to admission

a. No custodial sentence imposed pursuant to Chapter 43, 44 or 45 of Title 2C [1] shall be changed to permit entry into any program of intensive supervision established pursuant to the Rules Governing the Courts of the State of New Jersey if the inmate:

(1) Is serving a sentence for a conviction of any crime of the first degree; or

(2) Is serving a sentence for a conviction of any offense in which the sentencing court found that there is a substantial likelihood that the defendant is involved in organized criminal activity pursuant to N.J.S.2C:44–1a.(5); or

(3) Is serving any statutorily mandated parole ineligibility, or any parole ineligibility imposed by the court pursuant to subsection b. of N.J.S. 2C:43–6 or section 6 of P.L.2007, c. 49 (C.2C:43–6.5); or

(4) (Deleted by amendment, P.L.2008, c. 30)

(5) Has previously been convicted of a crime of the first degree, or of any offense in any other jurisdiction which, if committed in New Jersey, would constitute a crime of the first degree and the inmate was released from incarceration on the first degree offense within five years of the commission of the offense for which the inmate is applying for intensive supervision.

Nothing in this subsection shall be construed to preclude the program of intensive supervision from imposing more restrictive standards for admission.

b. Unless the inmate is within nine months of parole eligibility and has served at least six months of the sentence, no custodial sentence of an inmate serving a sentence for conviction of any crime of the second degree shall be changed to permit entry into any program of intensive supervision established pursuant to the Rules Governing the Courts of the State of New Jersey, if, within 20 days of receipt of notice of the inmate's application, the county prosecutor or Attorney General objects in writing.

c. If an inmate's application for a change of custodial sentence to permit entry into any program of intensive supervision established pursuant to the Rules Governing the Courts of the State of New Jersey is granted over the objection of the county prosecutor or the Attorney General, the order shall not become final for 20 days or until reconsideration by the Intensive Supervision Resentencing Panel in order to permit the county prosecutor or the Attorney General to appear personally or in writing, with notice to defense counsel, to request reconsideration of the application approval.

d. A victim of the offense for which the inmate was sentenced shall have the right to make a written statement or to appear at a proceeding regarding the application for a change of custodial sentence imposed pursuant to Chapter 43, 44 or 45 of Title 2C for entry into any program of intensive supervision established pursuant to the Rules Governing the Courts of the State of New Jersey.

L.1993, c. 123, § 2. Amended by L.2007, c. 49, § 8, eff. April 14, 2007; L.2008, c. 30, § 1, eff. June 30, 2008.

[1] N.J.S.A. §§ 2C:43–1 et seq.; 2C:44–1 et seq.; 2C:45–1 et seq.

2C:43–12. Statewide pretrial intervention program; admission criteria; time for referral; denial and appeal; program monitoring

a. **Public policy.** The purpose of sections 2C:43–12 through 2C:43–22 of this chapter is to effectuate a Statewide program of Pretrial Intervention. It is the policy of the State of New Jersey that supervisory treatment should ordinarily be limited to persons who have not previously been convicted of any criminal offense under the laws of New Jersey, or under any criminal law of the United States, or any other state when supervisory treatment would:

(1) Provide applicants, on an equal basis, with opportunities to avoid ordinary prosecution by receiving early rehabilitative services or supervision, when such services or supervision can reasonably be expected to deter future criminal behavior by an applicant, and when there is apparent causal connection between the offense charged and the rehabilitative or supervisory need, without which cause both the alleged offense and the need to prosecute might not have occurred; or

(2) Provide an alternative to prosecution for applicants who might be harmed by the imposition of criminal sanctions as presently administered, when such an alternative can be expected to serve as sufficient sanction to deter criminal conduct; or

(3) Provide a mechanism for permitting the least burdensome form of prosecution possible for defendants charged with "victimless" offenses, other than defendants who were public officers or employees charged with offenses that involved or touched their office or employment; or

(4) Provide assistance to criminal calendars in order to focus expenditure of criminal justice resources on matters involving serious criminality and severe correctional problems; or

(5) Provide deterrence of future criminal or disorderly behavior by an applicant in a program of supervisory treatment.

b. Admission of an applicant into a program of supervisory treatment shall be measured according to the applicant's amenability to correction, responsiveness to rehabilitation and the nature of the offense. There shall be a presumption against admission into a program of supervisory treatment for a defendant who was a public officer or employee whose offense involved or touched upon his public office or employment.

c. The decision and reasons therefor made by the designated judges (or assignment judges), prosecutors and program directors in granting or denying applications for supervisory treatment, in recommending and ordering termination from the program or dismissal of charges, in all cases shall be reduced to writing and disclosed to the applicant.

d. If an applicant desires to challenge the decision of the prosecutor or program director not to recommend enrollment in a program of supervisory treatment the proceedings prescribed under section 14 shall be followed.

e. **Referral.** At any time prior to trial but after the filing of a criminal complaint, or the filing of an accusation or the return of an indictment, with the consent of the prosecutor and upon written recommendation of the program director, the assignment judge or a judge designated by him may postpone all further proceedings against an applicant and refer said applicant to a program of supervisory treatment approved by the Supreme Court. Prosecutors and program directors shall consider in formulating their recommendation of an applicant's participation in a supervisory treatment program, among others, the following criteria:

(1) The nature of the offense;

(2) The facts of the case;

(3) The motivation and age of the defendant;

(4) The desire of the complainant or victim to forego prosecution;

(5) The existence of personal problems and character traits which may be related to the applicant's crime and for which services are unavailable within the criminal justice system, or which may be provided more effectively through supervisory treatment and the probability that the causes of criminal behavior can be controlled by proper treatment;

(6) The likelihood that the applicant's crime is related to a condition or situation that would be conducive to change through his participation in supervisory treatment;

(7) The needs and interests of the victim and society;

(8) The extent to which the applicant's crime constitutes part of a continuing pattern of anti-social behavior;

(9) The applicant's record of criminal and penal violations and the extent to which he may present a substantial danger to others;

(10) Whether or not the crime is of an assaultive or violent nature, whether in the criminal act itself or in the possible injurious consequences of such behavior;

(11) Consideration of whether or not prosecution would exacerbate the social problem that led to the applicant's criminal act;

(12) The history of the use of physical violence toward others;

(13) Any involvement of the applicant with organized crime;

(14) Whether or not the crime is of such a nature that the value of supervisory treatment would be outweighed by the public need for prosecution;

(15) Whether or not the applicant's involvement with other people in the crime charged or in other crime is such that the interest of the State would be best served by processing his case through traditional criminal justice system procedures;

(16) Whether or not the applicant's participation in pretrial intervention will adversely affect the prosecution of codefendants; and

(17) Whether or not the harm done to society by abandoning criminal prosecution would outweigh the benefits to society from channeling an offender into a supervisory treatment program.

f. **Review of Supervisory Treatment Applications; Procedure Upon Denial.** Each applicant for supervisory treatment shall be entitled to full and fair consideration of his application. If an application is denied, the program director or the prosecutor shall precisely state his findings and conclusion which shall include the facts upon which the application is based and the reasons offered for the denial. If the applicant desires to challenge the decision of a program director not to recommend, or of a prosecutor not to consent to, enrollment into a supervisory treatment program, a motion shall be filed before the designated judge (or assignment judge) authorized pursuant to the rules of court to enter orders.

g. **Limitations.** Supervisory treatment may occur only once with respect to any defendant and any person who has previously received supervisory treatment under section 27 of P.L.1970, c. 226 (C.24:21–27), shall not be eligible for supervisory treatment under this section. However, supervisory treatment, as provided herein, shall be available to a defendant irrespective of whether the defendant contests his guilt of the charge or charges against him.

h. **Termination.** Termination of supervisory treatment under this section shall be immediately reported to the assignment judge of the county who shall forward such information to the Administrative Director of the Courts.

i. **Appointment of Program Directors; Authorized Referrals.** Programs of supervisory treatment and appointment of the program directors require approval by the Supreme Court with the consent of the assignment judge and prosecutor. Referrals of participants from supervisory treatment programs may be to any public or private office or agency, including but not limited to, programs within the probation service of the court, offering counseling or any other social service likely to aid in the rehabilitation of the participant and to deter the commission of other offenses.

j. Health Care Professional Licensing Board Notification. The program director shall promptly notify the State Board of Medical Examiners when a State licensed physician or podiatrist has been enrolled in a supervisory treatment program after he has been charged with an offense involving drugs or alcohol.
L.1978, c. 95, § 2C:43–12, eff. Sept. 1, 1979. Amended by L.1979, c. 178, § 88, eff. Sept. 1, 1979; L.1987, c. 106, § 14, operative July 9, 1987; L.1989, c. 300, § 22, eff. Jan. 12, 1990; L.2007, c. 49, § 9, eff. April 14, 2007.

2C:43–13. Supervisory treatment procedure

a. Agreement. The terms and duration of the supervisory treatment shall be set forth in writing, signed by the prosecutor and agreed to and signed by the participant. Payment of the assessment required by section 2 of P.L.1979, c. 396 (C. 2C:43–3.1) shall be included as a term of the agreement. If the participant is represented by counsel, defense counsel shall also sign the agreement. Each order of supervisory treatment shall be filed with the county clerk.

b. Charges. During a period of supervisory treatment the charge or charges on which the participant is undergoing supervisory treatment shall be held in an inactive status pending termination of the supervisory treatment pursuant to subsection d. or e. of this section.

c. Period of treatment. Supervisory treatment may be for such period, as determined by the designated judge or the assignment judge, not to exceed three years, provided, however, that the period of supervisory treatment may be shortened or terminated as the program director may determine with the consent of the prosecutor and the approval of the court.

d. Dismissal. Upon completion of supervisory treatment, and with the consent of the prosecutor, the complaint, indictment or accusation against the participant may be dismissed with prejudice.

e. Violation of conditions. Upon violation of the conditions of supervisory treatment, the court shall determine, after summary hearing, whether said violation warrants the participant's dismissal from the supervisory treatment program or modification of the conditions of continued participation in that or another supervisory treatment program. Upon dismissal of the participant from the supervisory treatment program, the charges against the participant may be reactivated and the prosecutor may proceed as though no supervisory treatment had been commenced.

f. Evidence. No statement or other disclosure by a participant undergoing supervisory treatment made or disclosed to the person designated to provide such supervisory treatment shall be disclosed, at any time, to the prosecutor in connection with the charge or charges against the participant, nor shall any such statement or disclosure be admitted as evidence in any civil or criminal proceeding against the participant. Nothing provided herein, however, shall prevent the person providing supervisory treatment from informing the prosecutor, or the court, upon request or otherwise as to whether or not the participant is satisfactorily responding to supervisory treatment.

g. Delay. No participant agreeing to undergo supervisory treatment shall be permitted to complain of a lack of speedy trial for any delay caused by the commencement of supervisory treatment.

A person applying for admission to a program of supervisory treatment shall pay to the court a fee of $75.00. The court shall forward all money collected under this subsection to the treasurer of the county in which the court is located. This money shall be used to defray the cost of juror compensation within that county. A person may apply for a waiver of this fee, by reason of poverty, pursuant to the Rules Governing the Courts of the State of New Jersey. Of the moneys collected under this subsection, $30.00 of each application fee shall be deposited in the temporary reserve fund created by section 25 of P.L.1993, c. 275.[1] After December 31, 1994, the $75.00 fee shall be paid to the court, for use by the State.
L.1978, c. 95, § 2C:43–13, eff. Sept. 1, 1979. Amended by L.1979, c. 178, § 89, eff. Sept. 1, 1979; L.1988, c. 44, § 15, eff. June 28, 1988; L.1991, c. 329, § 5, eff. Dec. 23, 1991; L.1993, c. 275, § 15, eff. Jan. 5, 1994.

[1] Temporary and executed.

2C:43–14. Authority of supreme court

The Supreme Court may adopt rules dealing with Supervisory Treatment in accordance with procedures herein set forth.
L.1978, c. 95, § 2C:43–14, eff. Sept. 1, 1979.

2C:43–15. Presentation of proposed rules at judicial conference

The subject matter and a tentative draft of a rule or rules proposed to be adopted pursuant to this chapter shall be entered upon the agenda and discussed at a Judicial Conference whose membership shall at least include delegates from the Supreme Court, the Appellate Division of the Superior Court, the judges of the Superior Court, the judges of the municipal courts, the surrogates, the State Bar Association, the county bar associations, the Senate and General Assembly, the Attorney General, the county prosecutors, the law schools of this State, and members of the public.
L.1978, c. 95, § 2C:43–15, eff. Sept. 1, 1979. Amended by L.1979, c. 178, § 90, eff. Sept. 1, 1979; L.1991, c. 91, § 145, eff. April 9, 1991.

2C:43–16. Public announcement of proposed rules; delivery of copies

The proposed rule or rules shall be publicly announced by the Supreme Court on September 15 next following such Judicial Conference (or, if such day be a Saturday, Sunday or legal holiday, on the first day thereafter that is not), and the court shall, on the same day, cause true copies thereof to be delivered to the President of the Senate, the Speaker of the General Assembly, and the Governor.

L.1978, c. 95, § 2C:43–16, eff. Sept. 1, 1979.

2C:43–17. Effective date of rules; rules subject to cancellation by joint resolution

The rule or rules so announced and delivered shall take effect on July 1 next following; provided, however, that all such rules shall remain subject to cancellation at any time up to such effective date by joint resolution to that effect adopted by the Senate and General Assembly and signed by the Governor.

L.1978, c. 95, § 2C:43–17, eff. Sept. 1, 1979.

2C:43–18. Change or cancellation of rules by statute or adoption of subsequent rules

Any rule or rules so proposed or adopted shall be subject to change or cancellation at any time by statute or by a subsequent rule adopted pursuant to this chapter.

L.1978, c. 95, § 2C:43–18, eff. Sept. 1, 1979. Amended by L.1979, c. 178, § 91, eff. Sept. 1, 1979.

2C:43–19. Adoption of rules at such time, or with such effective date, or without presentation at judicial conference, as may be provided in joint resolution

By joint resolution adopted by the Senate and General Assembly and signed by the Governor with respect to a particular rule or rules therein specified the Supreme Court may adopt such rule or rules at such time or times, or with such effective date, or without presentation at a Judicial Conference, as may be provided in the joint resolution.

L.1978, c. 95, § 2C:43–19, eff. Sept. 1, 1979.

2C:43–20. Reduction or elimination of time during which rules may be canceled by joint resolution

By joint resolution adopted by the Senate and General Assembly and signed by the Governor with respect to a particular rule or rules therein specified, the period of time as provided in 2C:43–17 during which the same may be canceled by joint resolution may be reduced or eliminated.

L.1978, c. 95, § 2C:43–20, eff. Sept. 1, 1979.

2C:43–21. Index and reports

a. Index. The Administrative Director of the Courts shall establish and maintain an index of cases in which applications for supervisory treatment have been made and such index shall indicate the dispositions of those applications.

b. Reports. At the termination of the year in which this chapter takes effect and at the termination of each calendar year thereafter, for a period of 5 years, the assignment judge for each county shall report the results of the rehabilitative effort prescribed in this act to the Administrative Director of the Courts. The report shall include a description of offenses for which supervisory treatment was prescribed, the type of treatment to which defendants were assigned, the number and types of criminal acts, if any, committed by persons during their period of supervisory treatment, the number of persons successfully completing supervisory treatment and against whom charges were dismissed, and, where possible, the number and types of criminal acts, if any, committed by such persons subsequent to successful completion of supervisory treatment.

c. Evaluation. The Administrative Director of the Courts shall, from time to time as he deems necessary, or upon request from the Legislature, evaluate the program of supervisory treatment on the basis of reports made to him by county and municipal prosecutors. He shall submit his evaluation, together with special findings and recommendations to the Legislature.

d. No order of expungement or sealing shall affect any entry in the index or any registry of such information established by the Administrative Office of the Courts.

L.1978, c. 95, § 2C:43–21, eff. Sept. 1, 1979. Amended by L.1979, c. 178, § 92, eff. Sept. 1, 1979.

2C:43–22. Disclaimer

Nothing contained in this act is intended to supersede, repeal or modify the authority granted and procedure prescribed under section 27 of P.L.1970, c. 226 (C. 24:21–27).[1]

L.1978, c. 95, § 2C:43–22, eff. Sept. 1, 1979.

[1] C. 24:21–27 was repealed by L.1987, c. 106, § 25, operative July 9, 1987. See, now, § 2C:35–23.

CHAPTER 44

AUTHORITY OF COURT IN SENTENCING

Section

2C:44–1.	Criteria for withholding or imposing sentence of imprisonment.
2C:44–2.	Criteria for imposing fines and restitution.
2C:44–3.	Criteria for sentence of extended term of imprisonment.
2C:44–4.	Definition of prior conviction; conviction in another jurisdiction; proof of prior conviction.
2C:44–5.1.	Crimes committed while released on bail; sentence enhancement.
2C:44–6.	Procedure on sentence; presentence investigation and report.
2C:44–6.1.	Inmate's liability for cost of psychological evaluation.
2C:44–6.2.	Incarceration of sole caretakers of minor children; assumption of responsibility for care of children.
2C:44–6.3.	Cases requiring referral to Division of Youth and Family Services; definition.
2C:44–6.4.	Adoption of Rules of Court.

Section
2C:44–7. Appellate review of actions of sentencing court.
2C:44–8. Continuation of prior "no contact" order or condition of bail release; additional conditions relating to contact with victim.

2C:44–1. Criteria for withholding or imposing sentence of imprisonment

a. In determining the appropriate sentence to be imposed on a person who has been convicted of an offense, the court shall consider the following aggravating circumstances:

(1) The nature and circumstances of the offense, and the role of the actor therein, including whether or not it was committed in an especially heinous, cruel, or depraved manner;

(2) The gravity and seriousness of harm inflicted on the victim, including whether or not the defendant knew or reasonably should have known that the victim of the offense was particularly vulnerable or incapable of resistance due to advanced age, ill-health, or extreme youth, or was for any other reason substantially incapable of exercising normal physical or mental power of resistance;

(3) The risk that the defendant will commit another offense;

(4) A lesser sentence will depreciate the seriousness of the defendant's offense because it involved a breach of the public trust under chapters 27 and 30, or the defendant took advantage of a position of trust or confidence to commit the offense;

(5) There is a substantial likelihood that the defendant is involved in organized criminal activity;

(6) The extent of the defendant's prior criminal record and the seriousness of the offenses of which he has been convicted;

(7) The defendant committed the offense pursuant to an agreement that he either pay or be paid for the commission of the offense and the pecuniary incentive was beyond that inherent in the offense itself;

(8) The defendant committed the offense against a police or other law enforcement officer, correctional employee or fireman, acting in the performance of his duties while in uniform or exhibiting evidence of his authority; the defendant committed the offense because of the status of the victim as a public servant; or the defendant committed the offense against a sports official, athletic coach or manager, acting in or immediately following the performance of his duties or because of the person's status as a sports official, coach or manager;

(9) The need for deterring the defendant and others from violating the law;

(10) The offense involved fraudulent or deceptive practices committed against any department or division of State government;

(11) The imposition of a fine, penalty or order of restitution without also imposing a term of imprisonment would be perceived by the defendant or others merely as part of the cost of doing business, or as an acceptable contingent business or operating expense associated with the initial decision to resort to unlawful practices;

(12) The defendant committed the offense against a person who he knew or should have known was 60 years of age or older, or disabled; and

(13) The defendant, while in the course of committing or attempting to commit the crime, including the immediate flight therefrom, used or was in possession of a stolen motor vehicle.

b. In determining the appropriate sentence to be imposed on a person who has been convicted of an offense, the court may properly consider the following mitigating circumstances:

(1) The defendant's conduct neither caused nor threatened serious harm;

(2) The defendant did not contemplate that his conduct would cause or threaten serious harm;

(3) The defendant acted under a strong provocation;

(4) There were substantial grounds tending to excuse or justify the defendant's conduct, though failing to establish a defense;

(5) The victim of the defendant's conduct induced or facilitated its commission;

(6) The defendant has compensated or will compensate the victim of his conduct for the damage or injury that he sustained, or will participate in a program of community service;

(7) The defendant has no history of prior delinquency or criminal activity or has led a law-abiding life for a substantial period of time before the commission of the present offense;

(8) The defendant's conduct was the result of circumstances unlikely to recur;

(9) The character and attitude of the defendant indicate that he is unlikely to commit another offense;

(10) The defendant is particularly likely to respond affirmatively to probationary treatment;

(11) The imprisonment of the defendant would entail excessive hardship to himself or his dependents;

(12) The willingness of the defendant to cooperate with law enforcement authorities;

(13) The conduct of a youthful defendant was substantially influenced by another person more mature than the defendant.

c. (1) A plea of guilty by a defendant or failure to so plead shall not be considered in withholding or imposing a sentence of imprisonment.

(2) When imposing a sentence of imprisonment the court shall consider the defendant's eligibility for release under the law governing parole, including time credits awarded pursuant to Title 30 of the Revised Statutes, in determining the appropriate term of imprisonment.

d. Presumption of imprisonment. The court shall deal with a person who has been convicted of a crime of the first or second degree, or a crime of the third degree where the court finds that the aggravating factor in paragraph (5) of subsection a. applies, by imposing a sentence of imprisonment unless, having regard to the character and condition of the defendant, it is of the opinion that his imprisonment would be a serious injustice which overrides the need to deter such conduct by others. Notwithstanding the provisions of subsection e. of this section, the court shall deal with a person who has been convicted of theft of a motor vehicle or of the unlawful taking of a motor vehicle and who has previously been convicted of either offense by imposing a sentence of imprisonment unless, having regard to the character and condition of the defendant, it is of the opinion that his imprisonment would be a serious injustice which overrides the need to deter such conduct by others.

e. The court shall deal with a person convicted of an offense other than a crime of the first or second degree, who has not previously been convicted of an offense, without imposing a sentence of imprisonment unless, having regard to the nature and circumstances of the offense and the history, character and condition of the defendant, it is of the opinion that his imprisonment is necessary for the protection of the public under the criteria set forth in subsection a., except that this subsection shall not apply if the person is convicted of any of the following crimes of the third degree: theft of a motor vehicle; unlawful taking of a motor vehicle; eluding; if the person is convicted of a crime of the third degree constituting use of a false government document in violation of subsection c. of section 1 of P.L.1983, c. 565 (C.2C:21–2.1); if the person is convicted of a crime of the third degree constituting distribution, manufacture or possession of an item containing personal identifying information in violation of subsection b. of section 6 of P.L.2003, c. 184 (C.2C:21–17.3); if the person is convicted of a crime of the third or fourth degree constituting bias intimidation in violation of N.J.S.2C:16–1; or if the person is convicted of a crime of the third degree under section 2 of P.L.1997, c. 111 (C.2C:12–1.1); or if the person is convicted of a crime of the third or fourth degree under the provisions of section 1 or 2 of P.L.2007, c.341 (C.2C:33–29 or C.2C:33–30).

f. Presumptive Sentences. (1) Except for the crime of murder, unless the preponderance of aggravating or mitigating factors, as set forth in subsections a. and b., weighs in favor of a higher or lower term within the limits provided in N.J.S.2C:43–6, when a court deter-

mines that a sentence of imprisonment is warranted, it shall impose sentence as follows:

(a) To a term of 20 years for aggravated manslaughter or kidnapping pursuant to paragraph (1) of subsection c. of N.J.S.2C:13–1 when the offense constitutes a crime of the first degree;

(b) Except as provided in paragraph (a) of this subsection to a term of 15 years for a crime of the first degree;

(c) To a term of seven years for a crime of the second degree;

(d) To a term of four years for a crime of the third degree; and

(e) To a term of nine months for a crime of the fourth degree.

In imposing a minimum term pursuant to 2C:43–6b., the sentencing court shall specifically place on the record the aggravating factors set forth in this section which justify the imposition of a minimum term.

Unless the preponderance of mitigating factors set forth in subsection b. weighs in favor of a lower term within the limits authorized, sentences imposed pursuant to 2C:43–7a.(1) shall have a presumptive term of life imprisonment. Unless the preponderance of aggravating and mitigating factors set forth in subsections a. and b. weighs in favor of a higher or lower term within the limits authorized, sentences imposed pursuant to 2C:43–7a.(2) shall have a presumptive term of 50 years' imprisonment; sentences imposed pursuant to 2C:43–7a.(3) shall have a presumptive term of 15 years' imprisonment; and sentences imposed pursuant to 2C:43–7a.(4) shall have a presumptive term of seven years' imprisonment.

In imposing a minimum term pursuant to 2C:43–7b., the sentencing court shall specifically place on the record the aggravating factors set forth in this section which justify the imposition of a minimum term.

(2) In cases of convictions for crimes of the first or second degree where the court is clearly convinced that the mitigating factors substantially outweigh the aggravating factors and where the interest of justice demands, the court may sentence the defendant to a term appropriate to a crime of one degree lower than that of the crime for which he was convicted. If the court does impose sentence pursuant to this paragraph, or if the court imposes a noncustodial or probationary sentence upon conviction for a crime of the first or second degree, such sentence shall not become final for 10 days in order to permit the appeal of such sentence by the prosecution.

g. Imposition of Noncustodial Sentences in Certain Cases. If the court, in considering the aggravating factors set forth in subsection a., finds the aggravating factor in paragraph a.(2), a.(5), or a.(12) and does not impose a custodial sentence, the court shall specifically place on the record the mitigating factors which justify the imposition of a noncustodial sentence.

h. Except as provided in section 2 of P.L.1993, c. 123 (C.2C:43–11), the presumption of imprisonment as provided in subsection d. of this section shall not preclude the admission of a person to the Intensive Supervision Program, established pursuant to the Rules Governing the Courts of the State of New Jersey.

L.1978, c. 95, § 2C:44–1, eff. Sept. 1, 1979. Amended by L.1979, c. 178, § 93, eff. Sept. 1, 1979; L.1981, c. 290, § 40, eff. Sept. 24, 1981; L.1983, c. 317, § 1, eff. Aug. 29, 1983; L.1986, c. 172, § 4, eff. Dec. 8, 1986; L.1987, c. 76, § 36, eff. Dec. 9, 1987; L.1989, c. 23, § 4, eff. Feb. 6, 1989; L.1993, c. 123, § 1, eff. May 28, 1993; L.1993, c. 132, § 1, eff. June 3, 1993; L.1993, c. 135, § 1, eff. June 3, 1993; L.1995, c. 6, § 2, eff. Jan. 10, 1995; L.2001, c. 443, § 7, eff. Jan. 11, 2002; L.2003, c. 55, § 4, eff. June 1, 2003; L.2003, c. 184, § 4, eff. Sept. 25, 2003; L.2007, c. 83, § 3, eff. May 4, 2007; L.2007, c. 341, § 7, eff. Jan. 13, 2008.

2C:44–2. Criteria for imposing fines and restitution

a. The court may sentence a defendant to pay a fine in addition to a sentence of imprisonment or probation if:

(1) The defendant has derived a pecuniary gain from the offense or the court is of opinion that a fine is specially adapted to deterrence of the type of offense involved or to the correction of the offender;

(2) The defendant is able, or given a fair opportunity to do so, will be able to pay the fine; and

(3) The fine will not prevent the defendant from making restitution to the victim of the offense.

b. The court shall sentence a defendant to pay restitution in addition to a sentence of imprisonment or probation that may be imposed if:

(1) The victim, or in the case of a homicide, the nearest relative of the victim, suffered a loss; and

(2) The defendant is able to pay or, given a fair opportunity, will be able to pay restitution.

c. (1) In determining the amount and method of payment of a fine, the court shall take into account the financial resources of the defendant and the nature of the burden that its payment will impose.

(2) In determining the amount and method of payment of restitution, the court shall take into account all financial resources of the defendant, including the defendant's likely future earnings, and shall set the amount of restitution so as to provide the victim with the fullest compensation for loss that is consistent with the defendant's ability to pay. The court shall not reduce a restitution award by any amount that the victim has received from the Violent Crimes Compensation Board, but shall order the defendant to pay any restitution ordered for a loss previously compensated by the Board to the Violent Crimes Compensation Board.

If restitution to more than one person is set at the same time, the court shall set priorities of payment.

d. Nonpayment. When a defendant is sentenced to pay a fine or make restitution, or both, the court shall not impose at the same time an alternative sentence to be served in the event that the fine or restitution is not paid. The response of the court to nonpayment shall be determined only after the fine or restitution has not been paid, as provided in section 2C:46–2.

e. Whenever the maximum potential fine which may be imposed on a conviction for an offense defined in the "Comprehensive Drug Reform Act of 1986," N.J.S. 2C:35–1 et al. depends on the street value of the controlled dangerous substance or controlled substance analog involved and the court intends to impose a fine in excess of the maximum ordinary fine applicable to the offense for which defendant was convicted, and where the fine has not been agreed to pursuant to the provisions of N.J.S. 2C:35–12, the court at the time of sentence shall determine the street value at the time and place of the offense based on the amount and purity of the controlled dangerous substance or controlled substance analog involved. The sentencing court's finding as to the street value may be based on expert opinion in the form of live testimony or by affidavit, or by such other means as the court deems appropriate. The court's finding as to street value shall not be subject to modification by an appellate court except upon a showing that the finding was totally lacking in support on the record or was arbitrary or capricious.

f. The ordering of restitution pursuant to this section shall not operate as a bar to the seeking of civil recovery by the victim based on the incident underlying the criminal conviction. Restitution ordered under this section is to be in addition to any civil remedy which a victim may possess, but any amount due the victim under any civil remedy shall be reduced by the amount ordered under this section to the extent necessary to avoid double compensation for the same loss, and the initial restitution judgment shall remain in full force and effect.

L.1978, c. 95, § 2C:44–2, eff. Sept. 1, 1979. Amended by L.1979, c. 178, § 94, eff. Sept. 1, 1979; L.1987, c. 106, § 15, operative July 9, 1987; L.1991, c. 329, § 6, eff. Dec. 23, 1991.

2C:44–3. Criteria for sentence of extended term of imprisonment

The court may, upon application of the prosecuting attorney, sentence a person who has been convicted of a crime of the first, second or third degree to an extended term of imprisonment if it finds one or more of the grounds specified in subsection a., b., c., or f. of this section. If the grounds specified in subsection d. are found, and the person is being sentenced for commission of any of the offenses enumerated in N.J.S.2C:43–6c. or N.J.S.2C:43–6g., the court shall sentence the defendant to an extended term as required by N.J.S.2C:43–6c. or N.J.S.2C:43–6g., and application by the prosecutor shall not be required. The court shall, upon application of the prosecuting attorney, sentence a person who has been convicted of a crime under N.J.S.2C:14–2 or N.J.S.2C:14–3 to an extended term of imprisonment if the grounds specified in subsection g. of this section are found. The court shall, upon application of the prosecuting attorney, sentence a person to an extended term if the imposition of such term is required pursuant to the provisions of section 2 of P.L.1994, c. 130 (C.2C:43–6.4). The finding of the court shall be incorporated in the record.

a. The defendant has been convicted of a crime of the first, second or third degree and is a persistent offender. A persistent offender is a person who at the time of the commission of the crime is 21 years of age or over, who has been previously convicted on at least two separate occasions of two crimes, committed at different times, when he was at least 18 years of age, if the latest in time of these crimes or the date of the defendant's last release from confinement, whichever is later, is within 10 years of the date of the crime for which the defendant is being sentenced.

b. The defendant has been convicted of a crime of the first, second or third degree and is a professional criminal. A professional criminal is a person who committed a crime as part of a continuing criminal activity in concert with two or more persons, and the circumstances of the crime show he has knowingly devoted himself to criminal activity as a major source of livelihood.

c. The defendant has been convicted of a crime of the first, second or third degree and committed the crime as consideration for the receipt, or in expectation of the receipt, of anything of pecuniary value the amount of which was unrelated to the proceeds of the crime or he procured the commission of the offense by payment or promise of payment of anything of pecuniary value.

d. Second offender with a firearm. The defendant is at least 18 years of age and has been previously convicted of any of the following crimes: 2C:11–3, 2C:11–4, 2C:12–1b., 2C:13–1, 2C:14–2a., 2C:14–3a., 2C:15–1, 2C:18–2, 2C:29–5, 2C:39–4a., or has been previously convicted of an offense under Title 2A of the New Jersey Statutes or under any statute of the United States or any other state which is substantially equivalent to the offenses enumerated in this subsection and he used or possessed a firearm, as defined in 2C:39–1f., in the course of committing or attempting to commit any of these crimes, including the immediate flight therefrom.

e. (Deleted by amendment, P.L.2001, c. 443).

f. The defendant has been convicted of a crime under any of the following sections: N.J.S.2C:11–4, N.J.S.2C:12–1b., N.J.S.2C:13–1, N.J.S.2C:14–2a., N.J.S.2C:14–3a., N.J.S.2C:15–1, N.J.S.2C:18–2, N.J.S.2C:29–2b., N.J.S.2C:29–5, N.J.S.2C:35–5, and in the course of committing or attempting to commit the crime, including the immediate flight therefrom, the defendant used or was in possession of a stolen motor vehicle.

g. The defendant has been convicted of a crime under N.J.S.2C:14–2 or N.J. S.2C:14–3 involving violence or the threat of violence and the victim of the crime was 16 years of age or less.

For purposes of this subsection, a crime involves violence or the threat of violence if the victim sustains serious bodily injury as defined in subsection b. of N.J.S.2C:11–1, or the actor is armed with and uses a deadly weapon or threatens by word or gesture to use a deadly weapon as defined in subsection c. of N.J.S.2C:11–1, or threatens to inflict serious bodily injury.

h. (Deleted by amendment, P.L.2007, c. 341).

L.1978, c. 95, § 2C:44–3, eff. Sept. 1, 1979. Amended by L.1979, c. 178, § 95, eff. Sept. 1, 1979; L.1981, c. 31, § 3, eff. Feb. 12, 1981; L.1990, c. 32, § 8, eff. May 30, 1990; L.1990, c. 87, § 4, eff. Aug. 9, 1990; L.1993, c. 132, § 2, eff. June 3, 1993; L.1994, c. 127, § 2, eff. Oct. 31, 1994; L.1994, c. 130, § 4, eff. Oct. 31, 1994; L.1995, c. 211, § 3, eff. Aug. 14, 1995; L.1997, c. 120, § 1, eff. June 20, 1997; L.1999, c. 160, § 4, eff. July 8, 1999; L.2001, c. 443, § 8, eff. Jan. 11, 2002; L.2007, c. 341, § 8, eff. Jan. 13, 2008.

2C:44–4. Definition of prior conviction; conviction in another jurisdiction; proof of prior conviction

a. Prior conviction of an offense. An adjudication by a court of competent jurisdiction that the defendant committed an offense constitutes a prior conviction.

b. Prior conviction of a crime. An adjudication by a court of competent jurisdiction that the defendant committed a crime constitutes a prior conviction, although sentence or the execution thereof was suspended, provided that the time to appeal has expired and that the defendant was not pardoned on the ground of innocence.

c. Prior conviction in another jurisdiction. A conviction in another jurisdiction shall constitute a prior conviction of a crime if a sentence of imprisonment in excess of 6 months was authorized under the law of the other jurisdiction.

d. Proof of prior conviction. Any prior conviction may be proved by any evidence, including fingerprint records made in connection with arrest, conviction or imprisonment, that reasonably satisfies the court that the defendant was convicted.

L.1978, c. 95, § 2C:44–4, eff. Sept. 1, 1979. Amended by L.1979, c. 178, § 96, eff. Sept. 1, 1979.

2C:44–5. Multiple sentences; concurrent and consecutive terms

a. Sentences of imprisonment for more than one offense. When multiple sentences of imprisonment are imposed on a defendant for more than one offense, including an offense for which a previous suspended sentence or sentence of probation has been revoked, such multiple sentences shall run concurrently or consecutively as the court determines at the time of sentence, except that:

(1) The aggregate of consecutive terms to a county institution shall not exceed 18 months; and

(2) Not more than one sentence for an extended term shall be imposed.

There shall be no overall outer limit on the cumulation of consecutive sentences for multiple offenses.

b. Sentences of imprisonment imposed at different times. When a defendant who has previously been sentenced to imprisonment is subsequently sentenced to another term for an offense committed prior to the former sentence, other than an offense committed while in custody:

(1) The multiple sentences imposed shall so far as possible conform to subsection a. of this section; and

(2) Whether the court determines that the terms shall run concurrently or consecutively, the defendant shall be credited with time served in imprisonment on the prior sentence in determining the permissible aggregate length of the term or terms remaining to be served; and

(3) When a new sentence is imposed on a prisoner who is on parole, the balance of the parole term on the former sentence shall not be deemed to run during the period of the new imprisonment unless the court determines otherwise at the time of sentencing.

c. Sentence of imprisonment for offense committed while on parole. When a defendant is sentenced to imprisonment for an offense committed while on parole in this State, such term of imprisonment and any period of reimprisonment that the parole board may require the defendant to serve upon the revocation of his parole shall run consecutively unless the court orders these sentences to run concurrently.

d. Multiple sentences of imprisonment in other cases. Except as otherwise provided in this section, multiple terms of imprisonment shall run concurrently or consecutively as the court determines when the second or subsequent sentence is imposed.

e. Calculation of concurrent and consecutive terms of imprisonment.

(1) When terms of imprisonment run concurrently, the shorter terms merge in and are satisfied by discharge of the longest term.

(2) When terms of imprisonment run consecutively, the terms are added to arrive at an aggregate term to be served equal to the sum of all terms.

f. Suspension of sentence or probation and imprisonment; multiple terms of suspension and probation. When a defendant is sentenced for more than one offense or a defendant already under sentence is sentenced for another offense committed prior to the former sentence:

(1) The court shall not sentence to probation a defendant who is under sentence of imprisonment, except as authorized by paragraph (2) of subsection b. of N.J.S.2C:43–2;

(2) Multiple periods of suspension or probation shall run consecutively, unless the court orders these sentences to run concurrently from the date of the first such disposition;

(3) When a sentence of imprisonment in excess of one year is imposed, the service of such sentence shall satisfy a suspended sentence on another count or prior suspended sentence or sentence to probation, unless the suspended sentence or probation has been violated in which case any imprisonment for the violation shall run consecutively; and

(4) When a sentence of imprisonment of one year or less is imposed, the period of a suspended sentence on another count or a prior suspended sentence or sentence to probation shall run during the period of such imprisonment, unless the suspended sentence or probation has been violated in which case any imprisonment for the violation shall run consecutively.

g. Offense committed while under suspension of sentence or probation. When a defendant is convicted of an offense committed while under suspension of sentence or on probation and such suspension or probation is not revoked:

(1) If the defendant is sentenced to imprisonment in excess of one year, the service of such sentence shall not satisfy the prior suspended sentence or sentence to probation, unless the court determines otherwise at the time of sentencing;

(2) If the defendant is sentenced to imprisonment of one year or less, the period of the suspension or probation shall not run during the period of such imprisonment; and

(3) If sentence is suspended or the defendant is sentenced to probation, the period of such suspension or probation shall run concurrently with or consecutively to the remainder of the prior periods, as the court determines at the time of sentence.

h. Offense committed while released pending disposition of a previous offense. When a defendant is sentenced to imprisonment for an offense committed while released, with or without bail, pending disposition of a previous offense, the term of imprisonment shall run consecutively to any sentence of imprisonment imposed for the previous offense, unless the court, in consideration of the character and conditions of the defendant, finds that imposition of consecutive sentences would be a serious injustice which overrides the need to deter such conduct by others.

i. Sentence of imprisonment for assault on corrections employee. Any term of imprisonment imposed on an inmate of a State or county correctional facility for an assault on a Department of Corrections employee, an employee of a county correctional facility, an employee of a State juvenile facility or a county juvenile detention facility, a county sheriff's department employee or any State, county or municipal law enforcement officer while in the performance of his duties shall run consecutively to any term of imprisonment currently being served and to any other term imposed for any other offense committed at the time of the assault.

L.1978, c. 95, § 2C:44–5, eff. Sept. 1, 1979. Amended by L.1979, c. 178, § 97, eff. Sept. 1, 1979; L.1983, c. 462, § 1, eff. Jan. 12, 1984; L.1993, c. 160, § 1, eff. June 29, 1993; L.1993, c. 223, § 1, eff. Aug. 5, 1993; L.2001, c. 16, § 1, eff. Jan. 29, 2001.

2C:44–5.1. Crimes committed while released on bail; sentence enhancement

a. A person who has been convicted under subsection a. of N.J.S.2C:39–4 of possession of a firearm with intent to use it unlawfully against the person of another; or a crime under N.J.S.2C:11–3; N.J.S.2C:11–4; N.J.S.2C:13–1; subsection a. of N.J.S.2C:14–2; subsection a. of N.J.S.2C:14–3; N.J.S.2C:15–1; N.J.S.2C:18–2 if the burglary is a crime of the second degree or the structure was adapted for overnight accommodation of persons; or a crime of the first, second or third degree under subsection b. of N.J.S.2C:12–1; shall be sentenced to an extended term of imprisonment pursuant to the provisions of N.J.S.2C:43–7 and shall be subject to double the fine authorized for that crime under the provisions of N.J.S.2C:43–3 if, at the time of the commission of the crime, the defendant was released on bail or on his own recognizance for one of the enumerated crimes and was convicted of that crime.

b. The court shall not impose a sentence of imprisonment pursuant to this section unless the ground therefor has been established at a hearing after the conviction of the defendant and on written notice to the defendant of the ground proposed. The defendant shall have the right to hear and controvert the evidence against the defendant and to offer evidence upon the issue.

L.1997, c. 410, § 1, eff. Jan. 19, 1998.

2C:44–6. Procedure on sentence; presentence investigation and report

a. The court shall not impose sentence without first ordering a presentence investigation of the defendant and according due consideration to a written report of such investigation when required by the Rules of Court. The court may order a presentence investigation in any other case.

b. The presentence investigation shall include an analysis of the circumstances attending the commission of the offense, the defendant's history of delinquency or criminality, family situation, financial resources, including whether or not the defendant is an enrollee or covered person under a health insurance contract, policy or plan, debts, including any amount owed for a fine, assessment or restitution ordered in accordance with the provisions of Title 2C, any obligation of child support including any child support delinquencies, employment history, personal habits, the disposition of any charge made against any codefendants, the defendant's history of civil commitment, any disposition which arose out of charges suspended pursuant to N.J.S.2C:4–6 including the records of the disposition of those charges and any acquittal by reason of insanity pursuant to N.J.S.2C:4–1, and any other matters that the probation officer deems relevant or the court directs to be included. The defendant shall disclose any information concerning any history of civil commitment. The report shall also include a medical history of the defendant and a complete psychological evaluation of the defendant in any case in which the defendant is being sentenced for a first or second degree crime involving violence and:

(1) the defendant has a prior acquittal by reason of insanity pursuant to N.J.S.2C:4–1 or had charges suspended pursuant to N.J.S.2C:4–6; or

(2) the defendant has a prior conviction for murder pursuant to N.J.S.2C:11–3, aggravated sexual assault or sexual assault pursuant to N.J.S. 2C:14–2, kidnapping pursuant to N.J.S.2C:13–1, endangering the welfare of a child which would constitute a crime of the second degree pursuant to N.J.S.2C:24–4, or stalking which would constitute a crime of the third degree pursuant to section 1 of P.L.1992, c. 209 (C.2C:12–10); or

(3) the defendant has a prior diagnosis of psychosis.

The court, in its discretion and considering all the appropriate circumstances, may waive the medical history and psychological examination in any case in which a term of imprisonment including a period of parole ineligibility is imposed. In any case involving a conviction of N.J.S.2C:24–4, endangering the welfare of a child; N.J.S.2C:18–3, criminal trespass, where the trespass was committed in a school building or on school property; section 1 of P.L.1993, c. 291 (C.2C:13–6), attempting to lure or entice a child with purpose to commit a criminal offense; section 1 of P.L.1992, c. 209 (C.2C:12–10), stalking; or N.J.S.2C:13–1, kidnapping, where the victim of the offense is a child under the age of 18, the investigation shall include a report on the defendant's mental condition.

The presentence report shall also include a report on any compensation paid by the Victims of Crime Compensation Office as a result of the commission of the offense and, in any case where the victim chooses to provide one, a statement by the victim of the offense for which the defendant is being sentenced. The statement may include the nature and extent of any physical harm or psychological or emotional harm or trauma suffered by the victim, the extent of any loss to include loss of earnings or ability to work suffered by the victim and the effect of the crime upon the victim's family. The probation department shall notify the victim or nearest relative of a homicide victim of his right to make a statement for inclusion in the presentence report if the victim or relative so desires. Any such statement shall be made within 20 days of notification by the probation department.

The presentence report shall specifically include an assessment of the gravity and seriousness of harm inflicted on the victim, including whether or not the defendant knew or reasonably should have known that the victim of the offense was particularly vulnerable or incapable of resistance due to advanced age, disability, ill-health, or extreme youth, or was for any other reason substantially incapable of exercising normal physical or mental power of resistance.

c. If, after the presentence investigation, the court desires additional information concerning an offender convicted of an offense before imposing sentence, it may order any additional psychological or medical testing of the defendant.

d. Disclosure of any presentence investigation report or psychiatric examination report shall be in accordance with law and the Rules of Court, except that information concerning the defendant's financial resources shall be made available upon request to the Victims of Crime Compensation Office or to any officer authorized under the provisions of section 3 of P.L. 1979, c. 396 (C.2C:46–4) to collect payment on an assessment, restitution or fine and that information concerning the defendant's coverage under any health insurance contract, policy or plan shall be made available, as appropriate to the Commissioner of Corrections and to the chief administrative officer of a county jail in accordance with the provisions of P.L.1995, c. 254 (C.30:7E–1 et al.).

e. The court shall not impose a sentence of imprisonment for an extended term unless the ground therefor has been established at a hearing after the conviction of the defendant and on written notice to him of the ground proposed. The defendant shall have the right to hear and controvert the evidence against him and to offer evidence upon the issue.

f. (Deleted by amendment, P.L.1986, c. 85).

L.1978, c. 95, § 2C:44–6, eff. Sept. 1, 1979. Amended by L.1981, c. 481, § 1, eff. March 13, 1982; L.1983, c. 317, § 2, eff. Aug. 29, 1983; L.1986, c. 85, § 1, eff. Aug. 14, 1986; L.1991, c. 329, § 7, eff. Dec. 23, 1991; L.1994, c. 92, § 1, eff. Aug. 9, 1994; L.1995, c. 254, § 7, eff. March 1, 1996; L.1996, c. 39, § 2, eff. June 20, 1996; L.1997, c. 216, § 2, eff. Aug. 19, 1997; L.2009, c. 328, § 2, eff. May 1, 2010.

2C:44–6.1. Inmate's liability for cost of psychological evaluation

a. A defendant who is required to submit to a psychological evaluation pursuant to the provisions of N.J.S.2C:44–6 shall be liable for the cost of such evaluation. If the defendant is an enrollee or a covered person under a health insurance contract, policy or plan, the Administrative Office of the Courts shall file a claim

with the health insurance contract, policy or plan for a reimbursement of the costs of the psychological evaluation. The claim shall be filed in accordance with the rules and regulations promulgated pursuant to subsection b. of this section. The reimbursement authorized under this section shall be payable to the Administrative Office of the Courts and shall be used exclusively for the purpose of defraying the costs incurred for the psychological evaluation.

b. The Commissioner of the Department of Banking and Insurance, in accordance with the provisions of the "Administrative Procedure Act," P.L.1968, c. 410 (C.52:14B–1 et seq.), shall promulgate rules and regulations to effectuate the purposes of this section.

c. In the event that a defendant is not covered under a health insurance contract, policy or plan, or if the defendant's insurance contract, policy or plan does not fully cover the costs of the psychological evaluation, a lien may be filed for any unpaid amounts due and payable on any and all property and income to which the defendant shall have or may acquire an interest. Any lien filed shall be in accordance with the rules and regulations promulgated pursuant to subsection b. of this section.

L.1997, c. 216, § 4, eff. Aug. 19, 1997.

2C:44–6.2. Incarceration of sole caretakers of minor children; assumption of responsibility for care of children

a. In any case in which a person has been convicted of a crime for which the person will be incarcerated, the court shall order, as part of the presentence investigation required pursuant to N.J.S.2C:44–6, that a determination be made as to whether the person is the sole caretaker of a minor child and, if so, who will assume responsibility for the child's care and custody during the period the person is incarcerated.

b. If the determination is made that the person is the sole caretaker of the child, the presentence investigation shall also include:

(1) verification that the person who will be responsible for the child's care and custody during the period of incarceration has agreed to assume responsibility for the child's care and custody;

(2) an inquiry as to the willingness of the person to assume responsibility for the child's care and custody during the period of incarceration; and

(3) a PROMIS/GAVEL network check, juvenile central registry check and domestic violence central registry check on the person who will be responsible for the child's care and custody during the period of incarceration and on any adult and juvenile over 12 years of age in the person's household.

c. The court shall provide the information compiled pursuant to subsection b. of this section, from the presentence investigation, to the Division of Youth and

Family Services in the Department of Children and Families.

L.2003, c. 301, § 1. Amended by L.2006, c. 47, § 28, eff. July 1, 2006.

2C:44–6.3. Cases requiring referral to Division of Youth and Family Services; definition

a.   In any case in which a person has been convicted of a crime enumerated in subsection b. of this section and:

(1) the victim of the crime was either a person under the age of 18 at the time of the commission of the crime, or a person defined in paragraph (9) of subsection b. of this section; and

(2) the person convicted of the crime resides in a household with other minor children or is a parent of a minor child, the court, based on an interview with the defendant, shall make a referral to the Division of Youth and Family Services in the Department of Children and Families and provide the division with the name and address of the person convicted of the crime, information on the person's criminal history and the name and address of each child referred to in paragraph (2) of this subsection.

b.   For purposes of this section, "crime" includes any of the following:

(1) murder pursuant to N.J.S.2C:11–3 or manslaughter pursuant to N.J.S.2C:11–4;

(2) simple assault or aggravated assault pursuant to N.J.S.2C:12–1;

(3) stalking   pursuant   to   P.L.1992,   c.   209 (C.2C:12–10);

(4) terrorist threats pursuant to N.J.S.2C:12–3;

(5) kidnapping and related offenses including criminal restraint; false imprisonment; interference with custody; criminal coercion; or enticing a child into a motor vehicle, structure, or isolated area pursuant to N.J.S.2C:13–1 through 2C:13–6;

(6) sexual assault, criminal sexual contact or lewdness pursuant to N.J.S. 2C:14–2 through N.J.S.2C:14–4;

(7) arson pursuant to N.J.S.2C:17–1, or causing or risking widespread injury or damage which would constitute a crime of the second degree pursuant to N.J.S.2C:17–2;

(8) a crime against a child, including endangering the welfare of a child and child pornography pursuant to N.J.S.2C:24–4; or child abuse, neglect, or abandonment pursuant to R.S.9:6–3;

(9) endangering the welfare of an incompetent person pursuant to N.J.S.2C:24–7 or endangering the welfare of an elderly or disabled person pursuant to N.J.S.2C:24–8;

(10) domestic violence pursuant to P.L.1991, c. 261 (C.2C:25–17 et seq.); or

(11) an attempt or conspiracy to commit an offense listed in paragraphs (1) through (10) of this subsection.

L.2003, c. 301, § 3. Amended by L.2006, c. 47, § 29, eff. July 1, 2006.

2C:44–6.4. Adoption of Rules of Court

The Supreme Court of the State of New Jersey may adopt Rules of Court appropriate or necessary to effectuate the purposes of sections 1 and 3 of this act.

L.2003, c. 301, § 5, eff. April 13, 2004.

2C:44–7. Appellate review of actions of sentencing court

Any action taken by the court in imposing sentence shall be subject to review by an appellate court. The court shall specifically have the authority to review findings of fact by the sentencing court in support of its findings of aggravating and mitigating circumstances and to modify the defendant's sentence upon his application where such findings are not fairly supported on the record before the trial court.

L.1978, c. 95, § 2C:44–7, eff. Sept. 1, 1979.

2C:44–8. Continuation of prior "no contact" order or condition of bail release; additional conditions relating to contact with victim

When a defendant is found guilty of a sex offense, the court may, at the time of sentencing and in addition to any other disposition authorized by law, order the continuation of a prior order or condition of bail that restricts the defendant's contact with the victim, or enter an order imposing such restrictions at the time of sentencing.

In addition to restricting a defendant's contact with the victim, the court may enter an order:

a.   restraining the defendant from entering the residence, property, school, or place of employment of the victim or of other family or household members of the victim and requiring the defendant to stay away from any specified place that is named in the order and is frequented regularly by the victim or other family or household members;

b.   restraining the defendant from making contact with the plaintiff or others, including an order forbidding the defendant from personally or through an agent initiating any communication likely to cause annoyance or alarm including, but not limited to, personal, written, or telephone contact with the victim or other family members, or their employers, employees, or fellow workers, or others with whom communication would be likely to cause annoyance or alarm to the victim;

c.   prohibiting the defendant from stalking or following, or threatening to harm, to stalk or to follow, the complainant or any other person named in the order in a manner that, taken in the context of past actions of the defendant, would put the complainant in reasonable fear that the defendant would cause the death or injury of the complainant or any other person. Behavior prohibited under this act includes, but is not limited to, behavior prohibited under the provisions of P.L.1992, c. 209 (C.2C:12–10);

d. providing for any other appropriate restraints necessary to protect the victim.

L.2007, c. 133, § 3, eff. Aug. 6, 2007.

CHAPTER 45

SUSPENSION OF SENTENCE; PROBATION

Section

2C:45–1.   Conditions of suspension or probation.
2C:45–2.   Period of suspension or probation; modification of conditions; discharge of defendant.
2C:45–3.   Summons or arrest of defendant under suspended sentence or on probation; commitment without bail; revocation and resentence.
2C:45–4.   Notice and hearing on revocation or modification of conditions of suspension or probation.

2C:45–1. Conditions of suspension or probation

a. When the court suspends the imposition of sentence on a person who has been convicted of an offense or sentences him to be placed on probation, it shall attach such reasonable conditions, authorized by this section, as it deems necessary to insure that he will lead a law-abiding life or is likely to assist him to do so. These conditions may be set forth in a set of standardized conditions promulgated by the county probation department and approved by the court.

b. The court, as a condition of its order, may require the defendant:

(1) To support his dependents and meet his family responsibilities;

(2) To find and continue in gainful employment;

(3) To undergo available medical or psychiatric treatment and to enter and remain in a specified institution, when required for that purpose;

(4) To pursue a prescribed secular course of study or vocational training;

(5) To attend or reside in a facility established for the instruction, recreation or residence of persons on probation;

(6) To refrain from frequenting unlawful or disreputable places or consorting with disreputable persons;

(7) Not to have in his possession any firearm or other dangerous weapon unless granted written permission;

(8) (Deleted by amendment, P.L.1991, c. 329);

(9) To remain within the jurisdiction of the court and to notify the court or the probation officer of any change in his address or his employment;

(10) To report as directed to the court or the probation officer, to permit the officer to visit his home, and to answer all reasonable inquiries by the probation officer;

(11) To pay a fine;

(12) To satisfy any other conditions reasonably related to the rehabilitation of the defendant and not unduly restrictive of his liberty or incompatible with his freedom of conscience;

(13) To require the performance of community-related service; and

(14) To be subject to Internet access conditions pursuant to paragraph (2) of subsection d. of this section.

In addition to any condition of probation, the court may enter an order prohibiting a defendant who is convicted of a sex offense from having any contact with the victim including, but not limited to, entering the victim's residence, place of employment or business, or school, and from harassing or stalking the victim or victim's relatives in any way, and may order other protective relief as provided in section 2 of P.L.2007, c. 133 (C.2C:14–12).

c. The court, as a condition of its order, shall require the defendant to pay any assessments required by section 2 of P.L.1979, c. 396 (C.2C:43–3.1) and shall, consistent with the applicable provisions of N.J.S.2C:43–3, N.J.S. 2C:43–4 and N.J.S.2C:44–2 or section 1 of P.L.1983, c. 411 (C.2C:43–2.1) require the defendant to make restitution.

d. (1) In addition to any condition imposed pursuant to subsection b. or c., the court shall order a person placed on probation to pay a fee, not exceeding $25.00 per month for the probationary term, to probation services for use by the State, except as provided in subsection g. of this section. This fee may be waived in cases of indigency upon application by the chief probation officer to the sentencing court.

(2) In addition to any conditions imposed pursuant to subsection b. or c., the court may order a person who has been convicted or adjudicated delinquent of a sex offense as defined in subsection b. of section 2 of P.L.1994, c. 133 (C.2C:7–2), and who is required to register as provided in subsections c. and d. of section 2 of P.L.1994, c. 133 (C.2C:7–2), or who has been convicted or adjudicated delinquent for a violation of N.J.S.2C:34–3 to be subject to any of the following Internet access conditions:

(a) Prohibit the person from accessing or using a computer or any other device with Internet capability without the prior written approval of the court, except the person may use a computer or any other device with Internet capability in connection with that person's employment or search for employment with the prior approval of the person's probation officer;

(b) Require the person to submit to periodic unannounced examinations of the person's computer or any other device with Internet capability by a probation officer, law enforcement officer or assigned computer or information technology specialist, including the retrieval and copying of all data from the computer or device and any internal or external peripherals and removal of such information, equipment or device to conduct a more thorough inspection;

(c) Require the person to submit to the installation on the person's computer or device with Internet capability, at the person's expense, one or more hardware or software systems to monitor the Internet use; and

(d) Require the person to submit to any other appropriate restrictions concerning the person's use or access of a computer or any other device with Internet capability.

e. When the court sentences a person who has been convicted of a crime to be placed on probation, it may require him to serve a term of imprisonment not exceeding 364 days as an additional condition of its order. When the court sentences a person convicted of a disorderly persons offense to be placed on probation, it may require him to serve a term of imprisonment not exceeding 90 days as an additional condition of its order. In imposing a term of imprisonment pursuant to this subsection, the sentencing court shall specifically place on the record the reasons which justify the sentence imposed. The term of imprisonment imposed hereunder shall be treated as part of the sentence, and in the event of a sentence of imprisonment upon the revocation of probation, the term of imprisonment served hereunder shall be credited toward service of such subsequent sentence. A term of imprisonment imposed under this section shall be governed by the "Parole Act of 1979," P.L.1979, c. 441 (C.30:4–123.45 et al.).

Whenever a person is serving a term of parole as a result of a sentence of incarceration imposed as a condition of probation, supervision over that person shall be maintained pursuant to the provisions of the law governing parole. Upon termination of the period of parole supervision provided by law, the county probation department shall assume responsibility for supervision of the person under sentence of probation. Nothing contained in this section shall prevent the sentencing court from at any time proceeding under the provisions of this chapter against any person for a violation of probation.

f. The defendant shall be given a copy of the terms of his probation or suspension of sentence and any requirements imposed pursuant to this section, stated with sufficient specificity to enable him to guide himself accordingly. The defendant shall acknowledge, in writing, his receipt of these documents and his consent to their terms.

g. Of the moneys collected under the provisions of subsection d. of this section, $15.00 of each monthly fee collected before January 1, 1995 shall be deposited in the temporary reserve fund created by section 25 of P.L.1993, c. 275, [1] and $10.00 of each shall be deposited into a "Community Service Supervision Fund" which shall be established by each county. The moneys in the "Community Service Supervision Fund" shall be expended only in accordance with the provisions of State law as shall be enacted to provide for expenditures from this fund for the purpose of supervising and monitoring probationers performing community service to ensure, by whatever means necessary and appropriate, that probationers are performing the community service ordered by the court and that the performance is in the manner and under the terms ordered by the court. *L.1978, c. 95, § 2C:45–1, eff. Sept. 1, 1979. Amended by L.1979, c. 178, § 98, eff. Sept. 1, 1979; L.1979, c. 180, § 1, eff. Sept. 1, 1979; L.1983, c. 124, § 2, eff. April 5, 1983; L.1991, c. 329, § 8, eff. Dec. 23, 1991; L.1993, c. 275, § 16, eff. Jan. 5, 1994; L.2007, c. 133, § 4, eff. Aug. 6, 2007; L.2007, c. 219, § 4, eff. Feb. 25, 2008.*

[1] Temporary and executed.

2C:45–2. Period of suspension or probation; modification of conditions; discharge of defendant

a. When the court has suspended imposition of sentence or has sentenced a defendant to be placed on probation, the period of the suspension shall be fixed by the court at not to exceed the maximum term which could have been imposed or more than 5 years whichever is lesser. The period of probation shall be fixed by the court at not less than 1 year nor more than 5 years. The court, on application of a probation officer or of the defendant, or on its own motion, may discharge the defendant at any time.

b. During the period of the suspension or probation, the court, on application of a probation officer or of the defendant, or on its own motion, may (1) modify the requirements imposed on the defendants; or (2) add further requirements authorized by N.J.S.2C:45–1. The court shall eliminate any requirement that imposes an unreasonable burden on the defendant.

c. Upon the termination of the period of suspension or probation or the earlier discharge of the defendant, the defendant shall be relieved of any obligations imposed by the order of the court and shall have satisfied his sentence for the offense unless the defendant has failed:

(1) to fulfill conditions imposed pursuant to paragraph b. (11) of N.J.S.2C:45–1, in which event the court may order that the probationary period be extended for an additional period not to exceed that authorized by subsection a. of this section; or

(2) to fulfill the conditions imposed pursuant to subsection c. of N.J.S.2C:45–1, in which event the court shall order that the probationary period be extended for an additional period not to exceed that authorized by subsection a. of this section.

The extension may be entered by the court without the defendant's personal appearance if the defendant agrees to the extension.

Notwithstanding any provision in this section to the contrary, any order of the court prohibiting contact with a victim imposed on a defendant convicted of a sex offense shall continue in effect following the termination of probation supervision until further order of the court.

L.1978, c. 95, § 2C:45–2, eff. Sept. 1, 1979. Amended by L.1979, c. 180, § 2, eff. Sept. 1, 1979; L.1991, c. 329, § 9, eff. Dec. 23, 1991; L.2007, c. 133, § 5, eff. Aug. 6, 2007.

2C:45–3. Summons or arrest of defendant under suspended sentence or on probation; commitment without bail; revocation and resentence

a. At any time before the discharge of the defendant or the termination of the period of suspension or probation:

(1) The court may summon the defendant to appear before it or may issue a warrant for his arrest;

(2) A probation officer or peace officer, upon request of the chief probation officer or otherwise having probable cause to believe that the defendant has failed to comply with a requirement imposed as a condition of the order or that he has committed another offense, may arrest him without a warrant;

(3) The court, if there is probable cause to believe that the defendant has committed another offense or if he has been held to answer therefor, may commit him without bail, pending a determination of the charge by the court having jurisdiction thereof;

(4) The court, if satisfied that the defendant has inexcusably failed to comply with a substantial requirement imposed as a condition of the order or if he has been convicted of another offense, may revoke the suspension or probation and sentence or resentence the defendant, as provided in this section. No revocation of suspension or probation shall be based on failure to pay a fine or make restitution, unless the failure was willful.

b. When the court revokes a suspension or probation, it may impose on the defendant any sentence that might have been imposed originally for the offense of which he was convicted.

c. The commencement of a probation revocation proceeding shall toll the probationary period until termination of such proceedings. In the event that the court does not find a violation of probation, this subsection shall not operate to toll the probationary period.

L.1978, c. 95, § 2C:45–3, eff. Sept. 1, 1979. Amended by L.1979, c. 178, § 99, eff. Sept. 1, 1979; L.1979, c. 180, § 3, eff. Sept. 1, 1979; L.1981, c. 290, § 41, eff. Sept. 24, 1981.

2C:45–4. Notice and hearing on revocation or modification of conditions of suspension or probation

The court shall not revoke a suspension of sentence or probation or delete, add or modify conditions of probation except after a hearing upon written notice to the defendant of the grounds on which such action is proposed. The defendant shall have the right to hear and controvert the evidence against him, to offer evidence in his defense, and to be represented by counsel.

L.1978, c. 95, § 2C:45–4, eff. Sept. 1, 1979.

CHAPTER 46

FINES AND RESTITUTION

Section
2C:46–1. Time and Method of Payment; Disposition of Funds.
2C:46–1.1. Courts computerized collection fund; corrections computerized collection fund.
2C:46–1.2. Rules of court; rules and regulations.
2C:46–2. Consequences of nonpayment; summary collection.
2C:46–3. Revocation of fine.
2C:46–4. Fines, assessments and restitution; collection; disposition.
2C:46–4.1. Application of moneys collected in satisfaction of additional assessments, fines or restitution.
2C:46–5. Chapter not to affect fines and restitution imposed under Title 39 or in proceedings in superior court, chancery division, family part.

2C:46–1. Time and Method of Payment; Disposition of Funds.

a. When a defendant is sentenced to pay an assessment pursuant to section 2 of P.L.1979, c. 396 (C.2C:43–3.1), a fine, a penalty imposed pursuant to N.J.S.2C:35–15, a forensic laboratory fee imposed pursuant to N.J.S.2C:35–20, a penalty imposed pursuant to section 1 of P.L.1999, c. 295 (C.2C:43–3.5), a penalty imposed pursuant to section 11 of P.L.2001, c. 81 (C.2C:43–3.6), a penalty imposed pursuant to section 1 of P.L.2005, c. 73 (C.2C:14–10) or to make restitution, the court may grant permission for the payment to be made within a specified period of time or in specified installments. If no such permission is embodied in the sentence, the assessment, fine, penalty, fee or restitution shall be payable forthwith, and the court shall file a copy of the judgment of conviction with the Clerk of the Superior Court who shall enter the following information upon the record of docketed judgments:

(1) the name of the convicted person as judgment debtor;

(2) the amount of the assessment imposed pursuant to section 2 of P.L.1979, c. 396 (C.2C:43–3.1) and the Victims of Crime Compensation Board as a judgment creditor in that amount;

(3) the amount of any restitution ordered and the name of any persons entitled to receive payment as judgment creditors in the amount and according to the priority set by the court;

(4) the amount of any fine and the governmental entity entitled to receive payment pursuant to section 3 of P.L.1979, c. 396 (C.2C:46–4);

(5) the amount of the mandatory Drug Enforcement and Demand Reduction penalty imposed;

(6) the amount of the forensic laboratory fee imposed;

(7) the amount of the penalty imposed pursuant to section 1 of P.L.1999, c. 295 (C.2C:43–3.5);

(8) the date of the order;

(9) the amount of the penalty imposed pursuant to section 11 of P.L.2001, c. 81 (C.2C:43–3.6); and

(10) the amount of the penalty imposed pursuant to section 1 of P.L.2005, c. 73 (C.2C:14–10).

b. (1) When a defendant sentenced to pay an assessment imposed pursuant to section 2 of P.L.1979, c. 396 (C.2C:43–3.1), a fine, a penalty imposed pursuant to N.J.S.2C:35–15, a forensic laboratory fee imposed pursuant to N.J.S.2C:35–20, a penalty imposed pursuant to section 1 of P.L.1999, c. 295 (C.2C:43–3.5), a penalty imposed pursuant to section 11 of P.L.2001, c. 81 (C.2C:43–3.6), a penalty imposed pursuant to section 1 of P.L.2005, c. 73 (C.2C:14–10) or to make restitution is also sentenced to probation, the court shall make continuing payment of installments on the assessment and restitution a condition of probation, and may make continuing payment of installments on the fine, the mandatory Drug Enforcement and Demand Reduction penalty, the mandatory penalty pursuant to section 1 of P.L.1999, c. 295 (C.2C:43–3.5), the penalty pursuant to section 11 of P.L.2001, c. 81 (C.2C: 43–3.6), the mandatory penalty pursuant to section 1 of P.L.2005, c. 73 (C.2C:14–10) or the forensic laboratory fee a condition of probation.

(2) When a defendant sentenced to pay an assessment imposed pursuant to section 2 of P.L.1979, c. 396 (C.2C:43–3.1), a fine, a penalty imposed pursuant to N.J.S.2C:35–15, a forensic laboratory fee imposed pursuant to N.J.S.2C:35–20, a penalty imposed pursuant to section 1 of P.L.1999, c. 295 (C.2C:43–3.5), a penalty imposed pursuant to section 11 of P.L.2001, c. 81 (C.2C:43–3.6), a penalty imposed pursuant to section 1 of P.L.2005, c. 73 (C.2C:14–10) or to make restitution is also sentenced to a custodial term in a State correctional facility, the court may require the defendant to pay installments on the assessment, penalty, fee, fine and restitution.

c. The defendant shall pay an assessment imposed pursuant to section 2 of P.L.1979, c. 396 (C.2C:43–3.1), restitution, penalty, fee or fine or any installment thereof to the officer entitled by law to collect the payment. In the event of default in payment, such agency shall take appropriate action for its collection.

d. (1) When, in connection with a sentence of probation, a defendant is sentenced to pay an assessment imposed pursuant to section 2 of P.L.1979, c. 396 (C.2C:43–3.1), a fine, a penalty imposed pursuant to N.J.S.2C:35–15, a forensic laboratory fee imposed pursuant to N.J.S.2C:35–20, a penalty imposed pursuant to section 1 of P.L.1999, c. 295 (C.2C:43–3.5), a penalty imposed pursuant to section 11 of P.L.2001, c. 81 (C.2C:43–3.6), a penalty imposed pursuant to section 1 of P.L.2005, c. 73 (C.2C:14–10) or to make restitution, the defendant, in addition, shall be sentenced to pay a transaction fee on each occasion that the defendant makes a payment or an installment payment, until the defendant has paid the full amount he is sentenced to pay. All other individuals making payments on court ordered financial obligations through the probation division shall also pay a transaction fee on each payment or installment payment. The Administrative Office of the Courts shall promulgate a transaction fee schedule for use in connection with installment payments made pursuant to this paragraph; provided, however, the transaction fee on an installment payment shall not exceed $2.00.

(2) When, in connection with a custodial sentence in a State correctional institution, a defendant is sentenced to pay an assessment imposed pursuant to section 2 of P.L.1979, c. 396 (C.2C:43–3.1), a fine, a penalty imposed pursuant to N.J.S.2C:35–15, a forensic laboratory fee imposed pursuant to N.J.S.2C:35–20, a penalty imposed pursuant to section 1 of P.L.1999, c. 295 (C.2C:43–3.5), a penalty imposed pursuant to section 11 of P.L.2001, c. 81 (C.2C:43–3.6), a penalty imposed pursuant to section 1 of P.L.2005, c. 73 (C.2C:14–10) or to make restitution, the defendant, in addition, shall be sentenced to pay a transaction fee on each occasion that the defendant makes a payment or an installment payment until the defendant has paid the full amount he is sentenced to pay. The Department of Corrections shall promulgate a transaction fee schedule for use in connection with installment payments made pursuant to this paragraph; provided, however, the transaction fee on an installment payment shall not exceed $1.00.

L.1978, c. 95, § 2C:46–1, eff. Sept. 1, 1979. Amended by L.1985, c. 252, § 1, eff. July 31, 1985; L.1991, c. 329, § 10, eff. Dec. 23, 1991; L.1992, c. 169, § 1, eff. Feb. 1, 1993; L.1995, c. 9, § 10, eff. March 13, 1995; L.1999, c. 295, § 2, eff. Dec. 23, 1999; L.2001, c. 81, § 13, eff. May 4, 2001; L.2005, c. 73, § 3, eff. April 26, 2005.

2C:46–1.1. Courts computerized collection fund; corrections computerized collection fund

a. Transaction fees collected pursuant to paragraph (1) of subsection d. of N.J.S. 2C:46–1 shall be deposited in the Courts Computerized Collection Fund, which is hereby established as a separate fund in the General Fund, to be administered by the Administrative Office of the Courts and dedicated to the development, establishment, operation and maintenance of a computerized system for use by the Administrative Office of the Courts in developing, implementing, operating and improving the judiciary's component of the uniform system for tracking and collecting assessments, restitutions, penalties, fees and fines imposed in accordance with the provisions of Title 2C of the New Jersey Statutes, as required by section 19 of P.L.1991, c. 329 (C. 52:4B–8.1).

b. Transaction fees collected pursuant to paragraph (2) of subsection d. of N.J.S. 2C:46–1 shall be deposited in the Corrections Computerized Collection Fund, which is hereby established as a separate fund in the General Fund, to be administered by the Department of Corrections and dedicated to the development, establishment, operation and maintenance of a computerized system for use by the Department of Corrections in developing, implementing, operating and improving the Department's component of the uniform system for tracking and collecting assessments, restitutions, penalties, fees and fines imposed in accordance with the provisions of Title 2C of the New Jersey Statutes, as required by section 19 of P.L.1991, c. 329 (C. 52:4B–8.1).

L.1992, c. 169, § 2, eff. Feb. 1, 1993.

2C:46–1.2. Rules of court; rules and regulations

a. The Supreme Court of New Jersey may issue Rules of Court to effectuate the purposes of this act.

b. The Commissioner of the Department of Corrections shall promulgate rules and regulations, pursuant to the "Administrative Procedures Act," P.L.1968, c. 410 (C. 52:14B–1 et seq.), necessary to effectuate the purposes of this act.

L.1992, c. 169, § 3, eff. Feb. 1, 1993.

2C:46–2. Consequences of nonpayment; summary collection

a. When a defendant sentenced to pay an assessment imposed pursuant to section 2 of P.L.1979, c. 396 (C.2C:43–3.1), a penalty imposed pursuant to section 11 of P.L.2001, c. 81 (C.2C:43–3.6), a penalty imposed pursuant to section 1 of P.L.2005, c. 73 (C.2C:14–10), monthly probation fee, fine, a penalty imposed pursuant to section 1 of P.L.1999, c. 295 (C.2C:43–3.5), other court imposed financial penalties or to make restitution defaults in the payment thereof or of any installment, upon the motion of the person authorized by law to collect the payment, the motion of the prosecutor, the motion of the victim entitled to payment of restitution, the motion of the Victims of Crime Compensation Board, the motion of the State or county Office of Victim and Witness Advocacy or upon its own motion, the court shall recall him, or issue a summons or a warrant of arrest for his appearance. The court shall afford the person notice and an opportunity to be heard on the issue of default. Failure to make any payment when due shall be considered a default. The standard of proof shall be by a preponderance of the evidence, and the burden of establishing good cause for a default shall be on the person who has defaulted.

(1) If the court finds that the person has defaulted without good cause, the court shall:

(a) Order the suspension of the driver's license or the nonresident reciprocity driving privilege of the person; and

(b) Prohibit the person from obtaining a driver's license or exercising reciprocity driving privileges until the person has made all past due payments; and

(c) Notify the Chief Administrator of the New Jersey Motor Vehicle Commission of the action taken; and

(d) Take such other actions as may be authorized by law.

(2) If the court finds that the person defaulted on payment of a court imposed financial obligation without good cause and finds that the default was willful, the court may, in addition to the action required by paragraph (1) of this subsection a., impose a term of imprisonment or participation in a labor assistance program or enforced community service to achieve the objective of the court imposed financial obligation. These options shall not reduce the amount owed by the person in default. The term of imprisonment or enforced community service or participation in a labor assistance program in such case shall be specified in the order of commitment. It need not be equated with any particular dollar amount but, in the case of a fine it shall not exceed one day for each $20.00 of the fine nor 40 days if the fine was imposed upon conviction of a disorderly persons offense nor 25 days for a petty disorderly persons offense nor one year in any other case, whichever is the shorter period. In no case shall the total period of imprisonment in the case of a disorderly persons offense for both the sentence of imprisonment and for failure to pay a fine exceed six months.

(3) Except where incarceration is ordered pursuant to paragraph (2) of this subsection a., if the court finds that the person has defaulted the court shall take appropriate action to modify or establish a reasonable schedule for payment, and, in the case of a fine, if the court finds that the circumstances that warranted the fine have changed or that it would be unjust to require payment, the court may revoke or suspend the fine or the unpaid portion of the fine.

(4) When failure to pay an assessment imposed pursuant to section 2 of P.L.1979, c. 396 (C.2C:43–3.1), monthly probation fee, restitution, a penalty imposed pursuant to section 1 of P.L.1999, c. 295 (C.2C:43–3.5), a penalty imposed pursuant to section 11 of P.L.2001, c. 81 (C.2C:43–3.6), a penalty imposed pursuant to section 1 of P.L.2005, c. 73 (C.2C:14–10), or other financial penalties or to perform enforced community service or to participate in a labor assistance program is determined to be willful, the failure to do so shall be considered to be contumacious.

(5) When a fine, assessment imposed pursuant to section 2 of P.L.1979, c. 396 (C.2C:43–3.1), other financial penalty or restitution is imposed on a corporation, it is the duty of the person or persons authorized to make disbursements from the assets of the corporation or association to pay it from such assets and their failure so to do may be held to be contumacious.

b. Upon any default in the payment of a fine, assessment imposed pursuant to section 2 of P.L.1979, c. 396 (C.2C:43–3.1), monthly probation fee, a penalty imposed pursuant to section 1 of P.L.1999, c. 295 (C.2C:43–3.5), a penalty imposed pursuant to section 11 of P.L.2001, c. 81 (C.2C:43–3.6), a penalty imposed pursuant to section 1 of P.L.2005, c. 73 (C.2C:14–10), other financial penalties, restitution, or any installment thereof, execution may be levied and such other measures may be taken for collection of it or the unpaid balance thereof as are authorized for the collection of an unpaid civil judgment entered against the defendant in an action on a debt.

c. Upon any default in the payment of restitution or any installment thereof, the victim entitled to the payment may institute summary collection proceedings authorized by subsection b. of this section.

d. Upon any default in the payment of an assessment imposed pursuant to section 2 of P.L.1979, c. 396 (C.2C:43–3.1) or any installment thereof, the Victims of Crime Compensation Board or the party responsible for collection may institute summary collection proceedings authorized by subsection b. of this section.

e. When a defendant sentenced to make restitution to a public entity other than the Victims of Crime Compensation Board, defaults in the payment thereof or any installment, the court may, in lieu of other modification of the sentence, order the defendant to perform work in a labor assistance program or enforced community service program.

f. If a defendant ordered to participate in a labor assistance program or enforced community service program fails to report for work or to perform the assigned work, the comprehensive enforcement hearing officer may revoke the work order and impose any sentence permitted as a consequence of the original conviction.

g. If a defendant ordered to participate in a labor assistance program or an enforced community service program pays all outstanding assessments, the comprehensive enforcement hearing officer may review the work order, and modify the same to reflect the objective of the sentence.

h. As used in this section:

(1) "Comprehensive enforcement program" means the program established pursuant to the "Comprehensive Enforcement Program Fund Act," P.L.1995, c. 9 (C.2B:19–1 et seq.).

(2) The terms "labor assistance program" and "enforced community service" have the same meaning as those terms are defined in section 5 of the "Compre-

hensive Enforcement Program Fund Act," P.L.1995, c. 9 (C.2B:19–5).

(3) "Public entity" means the State, any county, municipality, district, public authority, public agency and any other political subdivision or public body in the State.

L.1978, c. 95, § 2C:46–2, eff. Sept. 1, 1979. Amended by L.1985, c. 252, § 2, eff. July 31, 1985; L.1991, c. 329, § 11, eff. Dec. 23, 1991; L.1993, c. 275, § 17, eff. Jan. 5, 1994; L.1995, c. 9, § 11, eff. Jan. 12, 1995; L.1999, c. 295, § 3, eff. Dec. 23, 1999; L.2001, c. 81, § 14, eff. May 4, 2001; L.2005, c. 73, § 4, eff. April 26, 2005.

2C:46–3. Revocation of fine

A defendant who has been sentenced to pay a fine may at any time petition the court which sentenced him for a revocation of the fine or of any unpaid portion thereof. If it appears to the satisfaction of the court that the circumstances which warranted the imposition of the fine have changed, or that it would otherwise be unjust to require payment, the court may revoke the fine or the unpaid portion thereof in whole or in part.

L.1978, c. 95, § 2C:46–3, eff. Sept. 1, 1979.

2C:46–4. Fines, assessments and restitution; collection; disposition

a. All fines, assessments imposed pursuant to section 2 of P.L.1979, c. 396 (C.2C:43–3.1), all penalties imposed pursuant to section 1 of P.L.1999, c. 295 (C.2C:43–3.5), all penalties imposed pursuant to section 11 of P.L.2001, c. 81 (C.2C:43–3.6), all penalties imposed pursuant to section 1 of P.L.2005, c. 73 (C.2C:14–10), all penalties imposed pursuant to section 1 of P.L.2009, c. 143 (C.2C:43–3.8) and restitution shall be collected as follows:

(1) All fines, assessments imposed pursuant to section 2 of P.L.1979, c. 396 (C.2C:43–3.1), all penalties imposed pursuant to section 1 of P.L.1999, c. 295 (C.2C:43–3.5), all penalties imposed pursuant to section 11 of P.L.2001, c. 81 (C.2C:43–3.6), all penalties imposed pursuant to section 1 of P.L.2005, c. 73 (C.2C:14–10), all penalties imposed pursuant to section 1 of P.L.2009, c. 143 (C.2C:43–3.8) and restitution imposed by the Superior Court or otherwise imposed at the county level, shall be collected by the county probation division except when such fine, assessment or restitution is imposed in conjunction with a custodial sentence to a State correctional facility or in conjunction with a term of incarceration imposed pursuant to section 25 of P.L.1982, c. 77 (C.2A:4A–44) in which event such fine, assessment or restitution shall be collected by the Department of Corrections or the Juvenile Justice Commission established pursuant to section 2 of P.L.1995, c. 284 (C.52:17B–170). An adult prisoner of a State correctional institution or a juvenile serving a term of incarceration imposed pursuant to section 25 of P.L.1982, c. 77 (C.2A:4A–44) who has not paid an assessment imposed pursuant to section 2 of P.L.1979, c. 396 (C.2C:43–3.1), a penalty imposed

pursuant to section 1 of P.L.1999, c. 295 (C.2C:43–3.5), a penalty imposed pursuant to section 1 of P.L.2005, c. 73 (C.2C:14–10), a penalty imposed pursuant to section 1 of P.L.2009, c. 143 (C.2C:43–3.8) or restitution shall have the assessment, penalty, fine or restitution deducted from any income the inmate receives as a result of labor performed at the institution or on any type of work release program or, pursuant to regulations promulgated by the Commissioner of the Department of Corrections or the Juvenile Justice Commission, from any personal account established in the institution for the benefit of the inmate.

(2) All fines, assessments imposed pursuant to section 2 of P.L.1979, c. 396 (C.2C:43–3.1), any penalty imposed pursuant to section 1 of P.L.1999, c. 295 (C.2C:43–3.5) and restitution imposed by a municipal court shall be collected by the municipal court administrator except if such fine, assessments imposed pursuant to section 2 of P.L.1979, c. 396 (C.2C:43–3.1), or restitution is ordered as a condition of probation in which event it shall be collected by the county probation division.

b. Except as provided in subsection c. with respect to fines imposed on appeals following convictions in municipal courts and except as provided in subsection i. with respect to restitution imposed under the provisions of P.L.1997, c. 253 (C.2C:43–3.4 et al.), all fines imposed by the Superior Court or otherwise imposed at the county level, shall be paid over by the officer entitled to collect same to:

(1) The county treasurer with respect to fines imposed on defendants who are sentenced to and serve a custodial term, including a term as a condition of probation, in the county jail, workhouse or penitentiary except where such county sentence is served concurrently with a sentence to a State institution; or

(2) The State Treasurer with respect to all other fines.

c. All fines imposed by municipal courts, except a central municipal court established pursuant to N.J.S.2B:12–1 on defendants convicted of crimes, disorderly persons offenses and petty disorderly persons offenses, and all fines imposed following conviction on appeal therefrom, and all forfeitures of bail shall be paid over by the officer entitled to collect same to the treasury of the municipality wherein the municipal court is located.

In the case of an intermunicipal court, fines shall be paid into the municipal treasury of the municipality in which the offense was committed, and costs, fees, and forfeitures of bail shall be apportioned among the several municipalities to which the court's jurisdiction extends according to the ratios of the municipalities' contributions to the total expense of maintaining the court.

In the case of a central municipal court, established by a county pursuant to N.J.S.2B:12–1, all costs, fines, fees and forfeitures of bail shall be paid into the county

treasury of the county where the central municipal court is located.

d. All assessments imposed pursuant to section 2 of P.L.1979, c. 396 (C.2C:43–3.1) shall be forwarded and deposited as provided in that section.

e. All mandatory Drug Enforcement and Demand Reduction penalties imposed pursuant to N.J.S.2C:35–15 shall be forwarded and deposited as provided for in that section.

f. All forensic laboratory fees assessed pursuant to N.J.S.2C:35–20 shall be forwarded and deposited as provided for in that section.

g. All restitution ordered to be paid to the Victims of Crime Compensation Agency pursuant to N.J.S.2C:44–2 shall be forwarded to the agency for deposit in the Victims of Crime Compensation Agency Account.

h. All assessments imposed pursuant to section 11 of P.L.1993, c. 220 (C.2C:43–3.2) shall be forwarded and deposited as provided in that section.

i. All restitution imposed on defendants under the provisions of P.L.1997, c. 253 (C.2C:43–3.4 et al.) for costs incurred by a law enforcement entity in extraditing the defendant from another jurisdiction shall be paid over by the officer entitled to collect same to the law enforcement entities which participated in the extradition of the defendant.

j. All penalties imposed pursuant to section 1 of P.L.1999, c. 295 (C.2C:43–3.5) shall be forwarded and deposited as provided in that section.

k. All penalties imposed pursuant to section 11 of P.L.2001, c. 81 (C.2C:43–3.6) shall be forwarded and deposited as provided in that section.

l. All mandatory penalties imposed pursuant to section 1 of P.L.2005, c. 73 (C.2C:14–10) shall be forwarded and deposited as provided in that section.

m. All mandatory Computer Crime Prevention penalties imposed pursuant to section 1 of P.L.2009, c. 143 (C.2C:43–3.8) shall be forwarded and deposited as provided in that section.

L.1979, c. 396, § 3, eff. Feb. 6, 1980. Amended by L.1981, c. 224, § 1, eff. July 20, 1981; L.1983, c. 73, § 1, eff. Feb. 24, 1983; L.1991, c. 91, § 146, eff. April 9, 1991; L.1991, c. 329, § 12, eff. Dec. 23, 1991; L.1993, c. 220, § 12, eff. Aug. 2, 1993; L.1995, c. 281, § 2, eff. Dec. 15, 1995; L.1996, c. 95, § 17, eff. Oct. 24, 1996; L.1997, c. 253, § 2, eff. Sept. 12, 1997; L.1999, c. 295, § 4, eff. Dec. 23, 1999; L.2001, c. 81, § 15, eff. May 4, 2001; L.2005, c. 73, § 5, eff. April 26, 2005; L.2009, c. 143, § 2, eff. Oct. 19, 2009.

2C:46–4.1. Application of moneys collected in satisfaction of additional assessments, fines or restitution

Moneys that are collected in satisfaction of any assessment imposed pursuant to section 2 of P.L.1979, c. 396 (C.2C:43–3.1), or in satisfaction of restitution or fines imposed in accordance with the provisions of Title 2C of the New Jersey Statutes or with the provisions of section 24 of P.L.1982, c. 77 (C.2A:4A–43), shall be applied in the following order:

a. first, in satisfaction of all assessments imposed pursuant to section 2 of P.L.1979, c. 396 (C.2C:43–3.1);

b. second, except as provided in subsection f. of this section, in satisfaction of any restitution ordered;

c. third, in satisfaction of all assessments imposed pursuant to section 11 of P.L.1993, c. 220 (C.2C:43–3.2);

d. fourth, in satisfaction of any forensic laboratory fee assessed pursuant to N.J.S.2C:35–20;

e. fifth, in satisfaction of any mandatory Drug Enforcement and Demand Reduction penalty assessed pursuant to N.J.S.2C:35–15;

f. sixth, in satisfaction of any anti-drug profiteering penalty imposed pursuant to N.J.S.2C:35A–1 et seq.;

g. seventh, in satisfaction of any anti-money laundering profiteering penalty imposed pursuant to section 9 of P.L.1999, c. 25 (C.2C:21–27.2);

h. eighth, in satisfaction of restitution for any extradition costs imposed pursuant to section 4 of P.L.1997, c. 253 (C.2C:43–3.4);

i. ninth, in satisfaction of any penalty imposed pursuant to section 1 of P.L.1999, c. 295 (C.2C:43–3.5);

j. tenth, in satisfaction of any penalty imposed pursuant to section 11 of P.L.2001, c. 81 (C.2C:43–3.6);

k. eleventh, in satisfaction of the mandatory penalty imposed pursuant to section 1 of P.L.2005, c. 73 (C.2C:14–10);

l. twelfth, in satisfaction of any mandatory Computer Crime Prevention penalty assessed pursuant to section 1 of P.L.2009, c. 143 (C.2C:43–3.8); and

m. in satisfaction of any fine.

L.1991, c. 329, § 13, eff. Dec. 23, 1991. Amended by L.1993, c. 220, § 13, eff. Aug. 2, 1993; L.1995, c. 281, § 3, eff. Dec. 15, 1995; L.1997, c. 187, § 3, eff. Aug. 4, 1997; L.1997, c. 253, § 3, eff. Sept. 12, 1997; L.1999, c. 25, § 7, eff. Feb. 16, 1999; L.1999, c. 295, § 5, eff. Dec. 23, 1999; L.2001, c. 81, § 16, eff. May 4, 2001; L.2005, c. 73, § 6, eff. April 26, 2005; L.2009, c. 143, § 3, eff. Oct. 19, 2009.

2C:46–5. Chapter not to affect fines and restitution imposed under Title 39 or in proceedings in superior court, chancery division, family part

Except as expressly provided, this chapter shall not affect fines and restitutions imposed under Title 39 of the Revised Statutes or in proceedings in the Superior Court, Chancery Division, Family Part, which shall remain as heretofore.

L.1979, c. 396, § 4, eff. Feb. 6, 1980. Amended by L.1991, c. 91, § 147, eff. April 9, 1991; L.1991, c. 329, § 15, eff. Dec. 23, 1991.

CHAPTER 47

ADULT DIAGNOSTIC AND TREATMENT CENTER

Section
2C:47–1. Referral to adult diagnostic and treatment center; commitment; examination.
2C:47–2. Report on Examination.
2C:47–3. Disposition.
2C:47–4. Repealed.
2C:47–4.1. Failure of inmate to cooperate or participate; inmates no longer amenable to treatment; transfers out of the Adult Diagnostic and Treatment Center; requests for reinstatement.
2C:47–4.2. Female inmates in sex offender treatment programs subject to same conditions as males.
2C:47–5. Parole.
2C:47–5.1. Revocation of parole; psychological examination; amenability to and willingness to participate in sex offender treatment.
2C:47–6. Repealed.
2C:47–7. Cost of maintenance.
2C:47–8. Eligibility for good behavior credits for repetitive and compulsive sex offenders dependent upon full cooperation with treatment during confinement.
2C:47–9. Sex offenders; study of recidivism of inmates released from Adult Diagnostic and Treatment Center.
2C:47–10. Receipt, possession or distribution of sexually oriented material.

2C:47–1. Referral to adult diagnostic and treatment center; commitment; examination

Whenever a person is convicted of the offense of aggravated sexual assault, sexual assault, aggravated criminal sexual contact, kidnapping pursuant to paragraph (2) of subsection c. of N.J.S.2C:13–1, endangering the welfare of a child by engaging in sexual conduct which would impair or debauch the morals of the child pursuant to subsection a. of N.J.S.2C:24–4, endangering the welfare of a child pursuant to paragraph (4) of subsection b. of N.J.S.2C:24–4, or an attempt to commit any such crime, the judge shall order the Department of Corrections to complete a psychological examination of the offender, except the judge shall not require a psychological examination if the offender is to be sentenced to a term of life imprisonment without eligibility for parole. The examination shall include a determination of whether the offender's conduct was characterized by a pattern of repetitive, compulsive behavior and, if it was, a further determination of the offender's amenability to sex offender treatment and willingness to participate in such treatment. The court's order shall contain a determination of the offender's legal settlement in accordance with subdivision D of article 3 of chapter 4 of Title 30 of the Revised Statutes.

L.1978, c. 95, § 2C:47–1, eff. Sept. 1, 1979. Amended by L.1979, c. 178, § 101, eff. Sept. 1, 1979; L.1994, c. 130, § 5, eff. Oct. 31, 1994; L.1998, c. 72, § 1, eff. Dec. 1, 1998.

2C:47–2. Report on Examination

The Department of Corrections shall conduct the psychological examination required pursuant to N.J.S.2C:47–1 within 30 days after it receives the Presentence Report. Upon completion of the psychological examination, the Department of Corrections shall send to the court a written report of the results of the examination,including a determination of whether the offender's conduct was characterized by a pattern of repetitive, compulsive behavior and, if it was, a further determination of the offender's amenability to sex offender treatment and willingness to participate in such treatment.

L.1978, c. 95, § 2C:47–2, eff. Sept. 1, 1979. Amended by L.1979, c. 178, § 102, eff. Sept. 1, 1979; L.1998, c. 72, § 2, eff. Dec. 1, 1998.

2C:47–3. Disposition

a. If the report of the examination reveals that the offender's conduct was characterized by a pattern of repetitive, compulsive behavior and further reveals that the offender is amenable to sex offender treatment and is willing to participate in such treatment, the court shall determine whether the offender's conduct was so characterized and whether the offender is amenable to sex offender treatment and is willing to participate in such treatment and shall record its findings on the judgment of conviction.

b. If the court finds that the offender's conduct was characterized by a pattern of repetitive, compulsive behavior and that the offender is amenable to sex offender treatment and is willing to participate in such treatment, the court shall, upon the recommendation of the Department of Corrections, sentence the offender to a term of incarceration to be served in the custody of the commissioner at the Adult Diagnostic and Treatment Center for sex offender treatment as provided in subsection h. of this section, or place the offender on probation with the requirement, as a condition of probation, that he receive outpatient psychological or psychiatric treatment as prescribed.

c. A sentence of incarceration or probation imposed pursuant to subsection b. or f. of this section shall be set in accordance with chapters 43, 44 and 45 of this Title.

d. The court shall impose sentence in accordance with chapters 43, 44 and 45 of this Title and not as provided in subsection b. of this section

if it shall appear from the report of the examination made of the offender pursuant to section N.J.S.2C:47–1 that the offender's conduct was not characterized by a pattern of repetitive, compulsive behavior

or that the offender is not amenable to sex offender treatment. Notwithstanding the provisions of R.S.30:4–140 or R.S.30:4–92 or any other law, a sentence imposed pursuant to this subsection on an offender who is not amenable to sex offender treatment shall not be reduced by commutation time for good behavior or credits for diligent application to work and other institutional assignments.

e. (Deleted by amendment, P.L.1998, c. 72).

f. If the court finds that the offender's conduct was characterized by a pattern of repetitive, compulsive behavior and that the offender is amenable to sex offender treatment, but that the offender is not willing to participate in such treatment, the court shall sentence the offender to a term of incarceration to be served in a facility designated by the commissioner pursuant to section 2 of P.L.1969, c. 22 (C.30:4–91.2). The offender shall become primarily eligible for parole in accordance with the provisions of N.J.S.2C:47–5; provided, however, no offender shall become primarily eligible for parole prior to the expiration of any judicial or statutory mandatory minimum term. An offender who meets the criteria of this subsection may, on a biennial basis, request to be transferred to the Adult Diagnostic and Treatment Center. Within 90 days after receiving a request for a transfer, the Department of Corrections shall conduct a psychological examination. If, upon the completion of a psychological examination, the Department of Corrections determines that the offender is amenable to sex offender treatment and is willing to participate in such treatment, the commissioner may order the offender to be transferred to the Adult Diagnostic and Treatment Center.

g. Notwithstanding the provisions of R.S.30:4–140 or R.S.30:4–92 or any other law, a sentence imposed pursuant to subsection f. of this section shall not be reduced by commutation time for good behavior or credits for diligent application to work and other institutional assignments for any year or fractional part of a year that the offender is confined in a facility other than the Adult Diagnostic and Treatment Center; provided, however, if the offender is at any time transferred to the Adult Diagnostic and Treatment Center pursuant to subsection f. of this section, the sentence imposed on the offender shall be reduced by commutation time for good behavior and credits for diligent application to work and other institutional assignments for any year or fractional part of a year that the offender is incarcerated at the Adult Diagnostic and Treatment Center following the date of such transfer.

h. An offender sentenced to a term of incarceration pursuant to subsection b. of this section shall be confined as follows:

(1) If the court imposes a sentence of seven years or less, the Department of Corrections shall confine the offender to the Adult Diagnostic and Treatment Center as soon as practicable after the date of sentence.

(2) If the court imposes a sentence of more than seven years, the Department of Corrections shall confine the offender in a facility designated by the commissioner pursuant to section 2 of P.L.1969, c. 22 (C.30:4–91.2). At least 30 days prior to the date which precedes the expiration date of the offender's sentence by five years, including any reductions for commutation

time for good behavior and credits for diligent application to work and other institutional assignments, the Department of Corrections shall complete a psychological examination of the offender to determine the offender's amenability to sex offender treatment and willingness to participate in such treatment; provided, however, no such examination shall be required if less than two years has elapsed since the Department of Corrections completed a psychological examination pursuant to N.J.S.2C:47–1. If the report of the examination reveals that the offender is amenable to sex offender treatment and is willing to participate in such treatment, the offender shall be transferred to the Adult Diagnostic and Treatment Center as soon as practicable. If the report of the examination reveals that the offender is not amenable to sex offender treatment, the offender shall not be transferred to the Adult Diagnostic and Treatment Center. If the report of the examination reveals that the offender is amenable to sex offender treatment but is not willing to participate in such treatment, the offender shall not be transferred to the Adult Diagnostic and Treatment Center. An offender may, on a biennial basis, request to be transferred to the Adult Diagnostic and Treatment Center. Within 90 days after receiving a request for a transfer, the Department of Corrections shall conduct a psychological examination. If, upon the completion of a psychological examination, the Department of Corrections determines that the offender is amenable to sex offender treatment and is willing to participate in such treatment, the commissioner shall order the offender to be transferred to the Adult Diagnostic and Treatment Center as soon as practicable.

(3) If a sentence is imposed pursuant to section 2 of P.L.1997, c. 117 (C.2C:43–7.2) or if any other judicial or statutory mandatory minimum term of more than seven years is imposed, the offender shall be confined in a facility designated by the commissioner pursuant to section 2 of P.L.1969, c. 22 (C.30:4–91.2). At least 30 days prior to the date which precedes the expiration date of the mandatory minimum term by five years, the Department of Corrections shall complete a psychological examination of the offender to determine the offender's amenability to sex offender treatment and willingness to participate in such treatment; provided, however, no such examination shall be required if less than two years has elapsed since the Department of Corrections completed a psychological examination pursuant to N.J.S.2C:47–1. If the report of the examination reveals that the offender is amenable to sex offender treatment and is willing to participate in such treatment, the offender shall be transferred to the Adult Diagnostic and Treatment Center as soon as practicable. If the report of the examination reveals that the offender is not amenable to sex offender treatment, the offender shall not be transferred to the Adult Diagnostic and Treatment Center. If the report of the examination reveals that the offender is amenable to sex offender treatment, but is not willing to participate in such treatment, the offender shall not be transferred to

the Adult Diagnostic and Treatment Center. An offender may, on a biennial basis, request to be transferred to the Adult Diagnostic and Treatment Center. Within 90 days after receiving a request for a transfer, the Department of Corrections shall conduct a psychological examination. If upon completion of a psychological examination the Department of Corrections determines that the offender is amenable to sex offender treatment and is willing to participate in such treatment, the commissioner shall order the offender to be transferred to the Adult Diagnostic and Treatment Center as soon as practicable.

i. Notwithstanding the provisions of R.S. 30:4–140 or R.S. 30:4–92 or any other law, a sentence imposed pursuant to subsection b. of this section shall not be reduced by commutation time for good behavior or credits for diligent application to work and other institutional assignments for any year or fractional part of a year from the date the Department of Corrections determines, as a result of a psychological evaluation conducted pursuant to paragraph (2) or (3) of subsection h. of this section, that the offender is not amenable to sex offender treatment or not willing to participate in such treatment; provided, however, if the offender is subsequently determined by the Department of Corrections to be amenable to sex offender treatment and willing to participate in such treatment and is transferred to the Adult Diagnostic and Treatment Center, the sentence imposed on the offender shall be reduced by commutation time for good behavior and credits for diligent application to work and other institutional assignments for any year or fractional part of a year that the offender is incarcerated at the Adult Diagnostic and Treatment Center following the date of such transfer.

j. An offender who is sentenced to a term of life imprisonment without eligibility for parole shall not be confined in the Adult Diagnostic and Treatment Center but shall be confined in a facility designated by the commissioner pursuant to section 2 of P.L. 1969, c. 22 (C.30:4–91.2).

k. The commissioner shall be required to provide for the treatment of a sex offender sentenced pursuant to N.J.S.2C:47–1 et seq. only when the offender is incarcerated in the Adult Diagnostic and Treatment Center. This requirement shall not apply when the offender is incarcerated in another facility.

L.1978, c. 95, § 2C:47–3, eff. Sept. 1, 1979. Amended by L.1979, c. 178, § 103, eff. Sept. 1, 1979; L.1994, c. 130, § 6, eff. Oct. 31, 1994; L.1994, c. 134, § 2, eff. Oct. 31, 1994; L.1998, c. 72, § 3, eff. Dec. 1, 1998.

2C:47–4. Repealed by L.1998, c. 72, § 8, eff. Dec. 1, 1998

2C:47–4.1. Failure of inmate to cooperate or participate; inmates no longer amenable to treatment; transfers out of the Adult Diagnostic and Treatment Center; requests for reinstatement

a. The commissioner shall order the transfer out of the Adult Diagnostic and Treatment Center of any offender serving a life sentence without eligibility for parole and any offender not participating in or cooperating with the sex offender treatment provided in the Adult Diagnostic and Treatment Center and any offender who is determined by the Department of Corrections to be no longer amenable to sex offender treatment.

b. Any offender transferred out of the Adult Diagnostic and Treatment Center for failure to participate in or cooperate with the sex offender treatment provided there or because of a determination by the Department of Corrections that the offender is no longer amenable to sex offender treatment may, on a biennial basis, request to be transferred back to the Adult Diagnostic and Treatment Center. Within 90 days after receiving a request for a transfer, the Department of Corrections shall conduct a psychological examination. If, upon completion of a psychological examination, the Department of Corrections determines that the offender is amenable to sex offender treatment and is willing to participate in and cooperate with such treatment, the commissioner shall order the offender to be transferred back to the Adult Diagnostic and Treatment Center.

c. Notwithstanding the provisions of R.S.30:4–140 or R.S.30:4–92 or any other law, a sentence imposed on an offender transferred pursuant to subsection a. of this section shall not be reduced by commutation time for good behavior or credits for diligent application to work and other institutional assignments for any year or fractional part of a year following the date of the transfer; provided, however, if the offender is at any time thereafter transferred back to the Adult Diagnostic and Treatment Center pursuant to subsection b. of this section, the sentence imposed on such offender shall be reduced by commutation time for good behavior and credits for diligent application to work and other institutional assignments for any year or fractional part of a year that such offender is incarcerated at the Adult Diagnostic and Treatment Center following the date of such transfer.

L.1998, c. 72, § 6, eff. Dec. 1, 1998.

2C:47–4.2. Female inmates in sex offender treatment programs subject to same conditions as males

An offender sentenced in accordance with the provisions of this chapter who is female shall be confined in a facility designated by the commissioner pursuant to section 2 of P.L.1969, c. 22 (C.30:4–91.2), but otherwise shall be subject to the same statutes and rules and regulations as an offender sentenced in accordance with the provisions of this chapter who is male. All statutory references to the Adult Diagnostic and Treatment Center shall be deemed, when applied to a female sentenced in accordance with the provisions of this chapter, to refer to the sex offender treatment program at the facility designated by the commissioner.

L.1998, c. 72, § 7, eff. Dec. 1, 1998.

2C:47–5. Parole

a. Any offender committed to confinement under the terms of this chapter shall become eligible for parole consideration upon referral to the State Parole Board of the offender's case by a special classification review board appointed by the commissioner. The referral shall be based on the determination by the special classification review board that the offender has achieved a satisfactory level of progress in sex offender treatment. The offender shall be released on parole unless the State Parole Board determines that the information supplied in the report filed pursuant to section 10 of P.L.1979, c. 441 (C. 30:4–123.54) or developed or produced at a hearing held pursuant to section 11 of P.L.1979, c. 441 (C.30:4–123.55) indicates by a preponderance of the evidence that the offender has failed to cooperate in his or her own rehabilitation or that there is a reasonable expectation that the offender will violate conditions of parole imposed pursuant to section 15 of P.L.1979, c. 441 (C.30:4–123.59) if released on parole at that time.

b. (Deleted by amendment, P.L.1998, c. 73).

c. Any offender paroled pursuant to this section shall be subject to the provisions of Title 30 of the Revised Statutes governing parole and the regulations promulgated pursuant thereto.

d. When an offender confined under the terms of this chapter has not been paroled in accordance with subsection a. of this section and is scheduled for release, not less than 90 days prior to the date of the offender's scheduled release the Chief Executive Officer shall:

(1) Notify the Attorney General and the prosecutor of the county from which the offender was committed of the scheduled release;

(2) Provide the Attorney General and the county prosecutor with the officer's opinion as to whether the offender may be "in need of involuntary commitment" within the meaning of section 2 of P.L. 1987, c. 116 (C. 30:4–27.2) and as to whether the person may be a "sexually violent predator" within the meaning of section 3 of P.L.1998, c. 71 (C.30:4–27.26); and

(3) Without regard to classification as confidential pursuant to regulations of the State Parole Board or the Department of Corrections, provide the Attorney General and county prosecutor with all reports, records and assessments relevant to determining whether the offender is "in need of involuntary commitment" and whether the person is a "sexually violent predator." All information received shall be deemed confidential and shall be disclosed only as provided in section 4 of P.L.1994, c. 134 (C.30:4–82.4).

e. Upon receipt of the notice, advice and information required by subsection d. of this section, the Attorney General or county prosecutor shall proceed as provided in section 4 of P.L.1994, c.134 (C.30:4–82.4) or section 5 of P.L.1998, c. 71 (C.30:4–27.28), as appropriate.

f.　(Deleted by amendment, P.L.1998, c. 73).

L.1978, c. 95, § 2C:47–5, eff. Sept. 1, 1979. Amended by L.1994, c. 134, § 3, eff. Oct. 31, 1994; L.1997, c. 60, § 2; L.1998, c. 71, § 16, eff. Aug. 12, 1999; L.1998, c. 73, § 1, eff. Dec. 1, 1998.

2C:47–5.1. Revocation of parole; psychological examination; amenability to and willingness to participate in sex offender treatment

a.　Whenever the parole of an offender committed to confinement under the terms of this chapter is revoked by the State Parole Board, the Department of Corrections shall, within 90 days of the date of revocation of parole, complete a psychological examination of the offender to determine whether the violation of the conditions of parole reflects emotional or behavioral problems as a sex offender that cause the offender to be incapable of making any acceptable social adjustment in the community and, if so, to determine further the offender's amenability to sex offender treatment and, if amenable, the offender's willingness to participate in such treatment. Not more than 30 days after the date of the examination, the Department of Corrections shall provide a written report of the results to the State Parole Board.

b.　The offender shall be confined in the Adult Diagnostic and Treatment Center if the report of the examination conducted pursuant to subsection a. of this section reveals that the offender's violation of the conditions of parole reflects emotional or behavioral problems as a sex offender that cause the offender to be incapable of making any acceptable social adjustment in the community and further reveals that the offender is amenable to sex offender treatment and is willing to participate in such treatment. The offender shall be eligible for parole pursuant to the provisions of subsection a. of N.J.S.2C:47–5.

c.　The offender shall be confined in a facility designated by the commissioner pursuant to section 2 of P.L.1969, c. 22 (C.30:4–91.2) if the report of the examination conducted pursuant to subsection a. of this section reveals that the offender's violation of the conditions of parole reflects emotional or behavioral problems as a sex offender that cause the offender to be incapable of making any acceptable social adjustment in the community and further reveals that the offender is amenable to sex offender treatment, but is not willing to participate in such treatment. The offender shall be eligible for parole pursuant to the provisions of subsection a. of N.J.S.2C:47–5.

d.　(1) The offender shall be confined in a facility designated by the commissioner pursuant to section 2 of P.L.1969, c. 22 (C.30:4–91.2) if the report of the examination conducted pursuant to subsection a. of this section reveals that the offender's violation of the conditions of parole:

(a) does not reflect emotional or behavioral problems as a sex offender; or

(b) reflects emotional or behavioral problems as a sex offender that cause the offender to be incapable of making any acceptable social adjustment in the community and further reveals that the offender is not amenable to sex offender treatment.

(2) An offender confined pursuant to the provisions of paragraph (1) of this subsection shall be eligible for parole pursuant to the provisions of Title 30 of the Revised Statutes. However, a parole eligibility date established by the State Parole Board pursuant to section 20 of P.L.1979, c. 441 (C.30:4–123.64) or a future parole eligibility date established by the State Parole Board pursuant to section 12 of P.L.1979, c. 441 (C.30:4–123.56) shall not be reduced by commutation time for good behavior pursuant to R.S. 30:4–140 or credits for diligent application to work and other institutional assignments pursuant to R.S.30:4–92.

e.　Notwithstanding the provisions of R.S.30:4–92, the balance of the sentence of an offender confined pursuant to subsection c. or subparagraph (b) of paragraph (1) of subsection d. of this section shall not be reduced by credits for diligent application to work and other institutional assignments; provided, however, if the offender is at any time transferred to the Adult Diagnostic and Treatment Center pursuant to subsection f. of this section the balance of the sentence shall be reduced by credits for diligent application to work and other institutional assignments earned by the offender during confinement in the Adult Diagnostic and Treatment Center.

f.　If an offender is confined pursuant to subsection c. or subparagraph (b) of paragraph (1) of subsection d. of this section, the offender may, on a biennial basis, request to be transferred to the Adult Diagnostic and Treatment Center. Within 90 days after receiving a request for a transfer, the Department of Corrections shall conduct a psychological examination. If, upon the completion of a psychological examination, the Department of Corrections determines that the offender is amenable to sex offender treatment and is willing to participate in such treatment, the commissioner shall order the offender to be transferred to the Adult Diagnostic and Treatment Center as soon as practicable. When an offender previously determined not to be amenable to sex offender treatment is transferred to the Adult Diagnostic and Treatment Center, the offender shall be eligible for parole pursuant to the provisions of subsection a. of N.J.S.2C:47–5.

L.1998, c. 73, § 3, eff. Dec. 1, 1998.

2C:47–6. Repealed by L.1979, c. 178, § 147, eff. Sept. 1, 1979

2C:47–7. Cost of maintenance

The Commissioner shall determine and fix the per capita cost of examining and maintaining any offender upon order of the court pursuant to N.J.S.2C:47–1 and shall furnish a copy of the order to the county treasurer of the county in which the offender has a legal settlement as determined in that order, and upon certification of the amount due, the governing body of the county shall make provisions for payment of one-half of the cost thereof to the Adult Diagnostic and Treatment Center, the remaining one-half to be borne by the State. If the order contains a determination that the offender has no legal settlement in any county, the entire cost shall be borne by the State.

L.1978, c. 95, § 2C:47–7, eff. Sept. 1, 1979. Amended by L.1979, c. 178, § 104, eff. Sept. 1, 1979; L.1998, c. 72, § 4, eff. Dec. 1, 1998.

2C:47–8. Eligibility for good behavior credits for repetitive and compulsive sex offenders dependent upon full cooperation with treatment during confinement

Notwithstanding the provisions of section 7 of P.L. 1979, c. 441 (C.30:4–123.51), R.S.30:4–140, R.S.30:4–92 or any other law, a term of imprisonment imposed on a person confined to the Adult Diagnostic and Treatment Center pursuant to the provisions of chapter 47 of this Title shall not be reduced by progressive time credits or credits for diligent application to work and other institutional assignments for any year or fractional part of a year if the person failed to fully cooperate with all treatment offered to him during that time period. This section shall not prohibit the reduction of a person's term of imprisonment by such credits if the person is entitled to the credits pursuant to the provisions of subsection g. of N.J.S.2C:47–3.

L.1994, c. 129, § 1, eff. Oct. 31, 1994. Amended by L.1998, c. 72, § 5, eff. Dec. 1, 1998.

2C:47–9. Sex offenders; study of recidivism of inmates released from Adult Diagnostic and Treatment Center

a. The Commissioner of Corrections shall establish a program to record and analyze the recidivism of all inmates who are released from the Adult Diagnostic and Treatment Center, whether on parole or upon the completion of their maximum sentences. The purpose of this program shall be to assist in measuring the effectiveness of the center in providing specialized treatment to repetitive and compulsive sex offenders pursuant to N.J.S.2C:47–3.

b. The program shall record the arrests for all offenses committed by releasees for a period of five years following their release and any convictions resulting from these arrests. These data shall be analyzed to determine whether the rates and nature of rearrests and convictions differ according to the criminal histories and personal characteristics of releasees, the treatment they received at the Adult Diagnostic and Treatment Center, length of sentence, conditions of parole, and such other factors as may be relevant to the purposes of this act.

c. The program shall also perform a comparative analysis of the recidivism rates and patterns of releasees from the Adult Diagnostic and Treatment Center with those of persons released from this State's general prison population and with sex offenders released in other jurisdictions with specialized programs for the treatment of sex offenders.

d. The department shall prepare and disseminate to the Governor and the Legislature reports documenting the program's findings, along with any recommendations it may have for legislation to improve the effectiveness of treatment offered by the Adult Diagnostic and Treatment Center.

L.1997, c. 266, § 1, eff. Dec. 22, 1997.

2C:47–10. Receipt, possession or distribution of sexually oriented material

a. As used in this act, "sexually oriented material" means any description, narrative account, display, or depiction of sexual activity or associated anatomical area contained in, or consisting of, a picture or other representation, publication, sound recording, live performance, or film.

b. An inmate sentenced to a period of confinement in the Adult Diagnostic Treatment Center shall not receive, possess, distribute or exhibit within the center sexually oriented material, as defined in subsection a. of this section. Upon the discovery of any such material within the center, the commissioner shall provide for its removal and destruction, subject to a departmental appeal procedure for the withholding or removal of such material from the inmate's possession.

c. The commissioner shall request an inmate sentenced to confinement in the center to acknowledge in writing the requirements of this act prior to the enforcement of its provisions. Any inmate who violates the provisions of subsection b. of this section shall be subject to on-the-spot sanctions pursuant to rules and regulations adopted by the commissioner.

d. A person who sells or offers for sale the material prohibited in subsection b. either for purposes of possession or viewing or who receives, possesses, distributes or exhibits any text, photograph, film, video or any other reproduction or reconstruction which depicts a person under 18 years of age engaging in a prohibited sexual act or in the simulation of such an act as defined in section 2 of P.L.1992, c. 7 (C.2A:30B–2), within the center shall be considered to have committed an inmate prohibited act and be subject to sanctions pursuant to rules and regulations adopted by the commissioner.

L.1997, c. 422, § 1, eff. June 1, 1998.

CHAPTER 48

CRIMINAL DISPOSITION COMMISSION [REPEALED]

2C:48–1 to 2C:48–4. Repealed by L.2009, c. 81, § 5, eff. July 2, 2009

CHAPTER 48A

CRIMINAL SENTENCING AND DISPOSITION COMMISSION

Section
2C:48A–1.   Criminal Sentencing and Disposition Commis-
                  sion; establishment; membership and term of
                  office.
2C:48A–2.   Review and recommendations relating to criminal
                  sentencing; report to the Governor and the
                  Legislature.
2C:48A–3.   Designation as legislative commission.
2C:48A–4.   Date to issue report; annual report.

2C:48A–1. Criminal Sentencing and Disposition Commission; establishment; membership and term of office

a. There is hereby created a commission to be known as the "Criminal Sentencing and Disposition Commission" to consist of 13 members as follows: the Attorney General, or his designee; the Public Defender, or his designee; the Chief Justice, or a designee of the Chief Justice who may be a retired judge with experience in the Criminal Division of the Superior Court; the Commissioner of the Department of Corrections, or his designee; the Chairman of the State Parole Board, or his designee; the President of the New Jersey County Prosecutors Association, or his designee; the President of the New Jersey Bar Association, or his designee; one public member appointed by the Senate President; one public member appointed by the Senate Minority Leader; one public member appointed by the Speaker of the General Assembly; one public member appointed by the Assembly Minority Leader; and two public members appointed by the Governor, not more than one of whom shall be of the same political party. In selecting the public members, the Senate President, the Senate Minority Leader, the Speaker of the General Assembly, the Assembly Minority Leader and the Governor should seek to include persons who have experience, training, or academic background in victims' rights advocacy, corrections, judicial administration or criminal law. The public members appointed by the Governor shall include one representative of a police organization.

Public members shall serve for a term of three years from their date of appointment and until their successors are appointed and qualified. Any vacancy in the membership of the commission shall be filled by appointment in the same manner as the original appointment. Vacancies resulting from causes other than by expiration of term shall be filled for the unexpired term only.

b. The commission shall organize as soon as possible after the appointment of its members. The Senate President and the Speaker of the General Assembly shall appoint one of the public members to serve as chair and the Minority Leader of the Senate and the Minority Leader of the Assembly shall appoint one of the public members to serve as vice-chair.

c. The members of the commission shall serve without compensation, but shall be eligible for reimbursement for necessary and reasonable expenses incurred in the performance of their official duties within the limits of funds appropriated or otherwise made available to the commission for its purposes.

d. The Office of Legislative Services shall provide staffing for the work of the commission. At the request of the commission all State entities shall, as soon as practicable, provide the commission with any available information concerning sentencing. In addition, the commission shall be entitled to accept the assistance and services of such employees of any State, county, or municipal department, board, bureau, commission, or agency as may be made available to it and to employ such legal, stenographic, technical, and clerical assistance and incur such expenses as may be necessary in order to perform its duties within the limits of funds appropriated or otherwise made available to it for its purposes.

L.2009, c. 81, § 1, eff. July 2, 2009.

2C:48A–2. Review and recommendations relating to criminal sentencing; report to the Governor and the Legislature

a. It shall be the duty of the commission to conduct a thorough review of the criminal sentencing provisions of New Jersey law for consideration of possible recommendations for revisions to the laws governing the criminal justice system. These recommendations shall be developed with the goal of providing a rational, just and proportionate sentencing scheme that achieves to the greatest extent possible public safety, offender accountability, crime reduction and prevention, and offender rehabilitation while promoting the efficient use of the State's resources. Additionally, the commission shall consider issues regarding disparity in the criminal justice process, including but not limited to racial and ethnic disparity issues. The recommendations shall be based on the available statistical data as well as any other relevant information.

b. As provided in section 4 of P.L.2009, c. 81 (C.2C:48A–4), the commission shall submit to the Governor and the Legislature reports containing its recommendations consistent with these purposes. The commission's reports shall include, but need not be limited to, recommendations regarding:

(1) An assessment of the current sentencing provisions under New Jersey law, and a consideration as to whether the sentencing options available to courts are sufficient or should be expanded in some manner to provide a greater range of sentencing options;

(2) A review of judicial discretion available under the Criminal Code, considering the appropriateness of existing mandatory minimum sentencing and whether it

would be beneficial to enhance, reduce or retain the current level of judicial discretion;

(3) A recommendation as to whether determinate sentencing should be extended to all criminal offenses, or to additional criminal offenses under New Jersey law;

(4) A recommendation as to appropriate limits and conditions on terms of supervised release, including whether there should be a mechanism for changing the length of a term of supervised release after its imposition and whether there should be supervised release for offenders who serve their maximum sentence;

(5) A projection of the impact, if any, on the size of New Jersey's correctional and supervised offender populations of the implementation of each measure proposed by the commission;

(6) A recommendation for intermediate, alternative or additional sanctions that should be made available in the New Jersey criminal justice system, including proposals for alternatives to incarceration for suitable offenders, the estimated cost of such programs, and recommendations for rules or principles to guide a judge's imposition of such sanctions as part of a criminal sentence; and

(7) A review of disparity issues in the criminal justice process, including but not limited to racial and ethnic disparity issues, whether evidenced in sentencing outcomes or at earlier stages of the criminal process, such as but not limited to charging and plea decisions, and recommend appropriate revisions or other means to address any such issues.

L.2009, c. 81, § 2, eff. July 2, 2009.

2C:48A–3. Designation as legislative commission

The commission shall constitute a commission of the Legislature in accordance with the provisions of Article IV, Section V, paragraph 2 of the New Jersey Constitution.

L.2009, c. 81, § 3, eff. July 2, 2009.

2C:48A–4. Date to issue report; annual report

The commission shall issue a report of its findings and recommendations to the Governor and the Legislature within one year of organization of the commission and each year thereafter.

L.2009, c. 81, § 4, eff. July 2, 2009.

CHAPTER 49

CAPITAL PUNISHMENT

Section
2C:49–1 to 2C:49–12. Repealed.

2C:49–1 to 2C:49–12. Repealed by L.2007, c. 204, § 7, eff. Dec. 17, 2007

CHAPTER 50

[RESERVED]

CHAPTER 51

LOSS AND RESTORATION OF RIGHTS INCIDENT TO CONVICTION OF AN OFFENSE

Section
2C:51–1. Basis of disqualification or disability.
2C:51–2. Forfeiture of public office, position or employment under certain circumstances; order of forfeiture.
2C:51–2.1. Forfeiture or disqualification from public office, position or employment.
2C:51–3. Voting and jury service.
2C:51–4. Repealed.
2C:51–5. Practitioners convicted of health care claims fraud.

2C:51–1. Basis of disqualification or disability

a. No person shall suffer any legal disqualification or disability because of his conviction of an offense or his sentence on such conviction, unless the disqualification or disability involves the deprivation of a right or privilege which is:

(1) Necessarily incident to execution of the sentence of the court;

(2) Provided by the Constitution or the code;

(3) Provided by a statute other than the code, when the conviction is of an offense defined by such statute; or

(4) Provided by the judgment, order or regulation of a court, agency or official exercising a jurisdiction conferred by law, or by the statute defining such jurisdiction, when the commission of the offense or the conviction or the sentence is reasonably related to the competency of the individual to exercise the right or privilege of which he is deprived.

b. Proof of a conviction as relevant evidence upon the trial or determination of any issue, or for the purpose of impeaching the convicted person as a witness is not a disqualification or disability within the meaning of this chapter.

L.1978, c. 95, § 2C:51–1, eff. Sept. 1, 1979.

2C:51–2. Forfeiture of public office, position or employment under certain circumstances; order of forfeiture

a. A person holding any public office, position, or employment, elective or appointive, under the government of this State or any agency or political subdivision thereof, who is convicted of an offense shall forfeit such office , position or employment if:

(1) He is convicted under the laws of this State of an offense involving dishonesty or of a crime of the third

degree or above or under the laws of another state or of the United States of an offense or a crime which, if committed in this State, would be such an offense or crime;

(2) He is convicted of an offense involving or touching such office, position or employment; or

(3) The Constitution so provides.

As used in this subsection, "involving or touching such office, position or employment" means that the offense was related directly to the person's performance in, or circumstances flowing from, the specific public office, position or employment held by the person.

b. A court of this State shall enter an order of forfeiture pursuant to subsection a.:

(1) Immediately upon a finding of guilt by the trier of fact or a plea of guilty entered in any court of this State unless the court, for good cause shown, orders a stay of such forfeiture pending a hearing on the merits at the time of sentencing; or

(2) Upon application of the county prosecutor or the Attorney General, when the forfeiture is based upon a conviction of an offense under the laws of another state or of the United States. An order of forfeiture pursuant to this paragraph shall be deemed to have taken effect on the date the person was found guilty by the trier of fact or pled guilty to the offense.

c. No court shall grant a stay of an order of forfeiture pending appeal of a conviction or forfeiture order unless the court is clearly convinced that there is a substantial likelihood of success on the merits. If the conviction be reversed or the order of forfeiture be overturned, he shall be restored, if feasible, to his office, position or employment with all the rights, emoluments and salary thereof from the date of forfeiture.

Any official action taken by the convicted person on or after the date as of which a forfeiture of the person's office shall take effect shall, during a period of 60 days following the date on which an order of forfeiture shall have been issued hereunder, be voidable by the person's successor in office or, if the office of the person was that of member of the governing body of a county, municipality or independent authority, by that governing body.

d. In addition to the punishment prescribed for the offense, and the forfeiture set forth in subsection a. of N.J.S.2C:51–2, any person convicted of an offense involving or touching on his public office, position or employment shall be forever disqualified from holding any office or position of honor, trust or profit under this State or any of its administrative or political subdivisions. As used in this subsection, "involving or touching on his public office, position or employment" means that the offense was related directly to the person's performance in, or circumstances flowing from, the specific public office, position or employment held by the person.

e. Any forfeiture or disqualification under subsection a., b. or d. which is based upon a conviction of a disorderly persons or petty disorderly persons offense may be waived by the court upon application of the county prosecutor or the Attorney General and for good cause shown.

f. Except as may otherwise be ordered by the Attorney General as the public need may require, any person convicted of an offense under section 97 of P.L.1999, c. 440 (C.2C:21–34), N.J.S. 2C:27–2, N.J.S. 2C:27–3, N.J.S. 2C:27–5, section 100 of P.L.1999, c. 440 (C.2C:27–9), section 5 of P.L.2003, c. 255 (C.2C:27–10), section 6 of P.L.2003, c. 255 (C.2C:27–11), N.J.S. 2C:29–4, N.J.S. 2C:30–2, or N.J.S. 2C:30–3 of this Title shall be ineligible, either directly or indirectly, to submit a bid, enter into any contract, or to conduct any business with any board, agency, authority, department, commission, public corporation, or other body of this State, of this or one or more other states, or of one or more political subdivisions of this State for a period of, but not more than, 10 years from the date of conviction for a crime of the second degree, or five years from the date of conviction for a crime of the third degree. It is the purpose of this subsection to bar any individual convicted of any of the above enumerated offenses and any business, including any corporation, partnership, association or proprietorship in which such individual is a principal, or with respect to which such individual owns, directly or indirectly, or controls 5% or more of the stock or other equity interest of such business, from conducting business with public entities.

The State Treasurer shall keep and maintain a list of all corporations barred from conducting such business pursuant to this section.

g. In any case in which the issue of forfeiture is not raised in a court of this State at the time of a finding of guilt, entry of guilty plea or sentencing, a forfeiture of public office, position or employment required by this section may be ordered by a court of this State upon application of the county prosecutor or the Attorney General or upon application of the public officer or public entity having authority to remove the person convicted from his public office, position or employment. The fact that a court has declined to order forfeiture shall not preclude the public officer or public entity having authority to remove the person convicted from seeking to remove or suspend the person from his office, position or employment on the ground that the conduct giving rise to the conviction demonstrates that the person is unfit to hold the office, position or employment.

L.1978, c. 95, § 2C:51–2, eff. Sept. 1, 1979. Amended by L.1979, c. 388, § 3, eff. Feb. 5, 1980; L.1981, c. 290, § 42, eff. Sept. 24, 1981; L.1981, c. 356, § 1, eff. Dec. 26, 1981; L.1987, c. 427, § 1, eff. Jan. 14, 1988; L.1995, c. 250, § 1, eff. Sept. 12, 1995; L.2003, c. 145, § 1, eff. Aug. 15, 2003; L.2007, c. 49, § 5, eff. April 14, 2007.

2C:51–2.1. Forfeiture or disqualification from public office, position or employment

This act shall apply as follows:

a. Any person who forfeited or was disqualified from holding any public office, position, or employment, elective or appointive, under the government of this State or any agency or political subdivision thereof, by a court of competent jurisdiction, prior to the effective date of this act shall continue to be disqualified or continue to forfeit such office, position or employment.

b. Any person holding any public office, position, or employment, elective or appointive, under the government of this State or any agency or political subdivision thereof, on the effective date of this act, shall be subject to disqualification or forfeiture of that public office, position, or employment only pursuant to N.J.S.2C:51–2 and not pursuant to a statute other than the criminal code.

L.2003, c. 145, § 3, eff. Aug. 15, 2003.

2C:51–3. Voting and jury service

A person who is convicted of a crime shall be disqualified

a. From voting in any primary, municipal, special or general election as determined by the provisions of R.S. 19:4–1; and

b. From serving as a juror as determined by the provisions of N.J.S. 2A:69–1.[1]

L.1978, c. 95, § 2C:51–3, eff. Sept. 1, 1979. Amended by L.1979, c. 178, § 106, eff. Sept. 1, 1979.

[1] Repealed by L.1995, c. 44, § 2.

2C:51–4. Repealed by L.1979, c. 178, § 147, eff. Sept. 1, 1979

2C:51–5. Practitioners convicted of health care claims fraud

a. (1) A practitioner convicted of health care claims fraud pursuant to subsection a. of section 3 of P.L.1997, c. 353 (C.2C:21–4.3) or a substantially similar crime under the laws of another state or the United States shall forfeit his license and be forever barred from the practice of the profession unless the court finds that such license forfeiture would be a serious injustice which overrides the need to deter such conduct by others and in such case the court shall determine an appropriate period of license suspension which shall be for a period of not less than one year. If the court does not permanently forfeit such license pursuant to this paragraph, the sentence shall not become final for 10 days in order to permit the appeal of such sentence by the prosecution.

(2) Upon a first conviction of health care claims fraud pursuant to subsection b. of section 3 of P.L.1997, c. 353 (C.2C:21–4.3) or a substantially similar crime under the laws of another state or the United States, a practitioner shall have his license suspended and be barred from the practice of the profession for a period of at least one year.

(3) Upon a second conviction of health care claims fraud pursuant to subsection b. of section 3 of P.L.1997, c. 353 (C.2C:21–4.3) or a substantially similar crime under the laws of another state or the United States, a practitioner shall forfeit his license and be forever barred from the practice of the profession.

(4) A person convicted of second degree insurance fraud pursuant to section 73 of P.L.2003, c.89 (C.2C:21–4.6) or a substantially similar crime under the laws of another state or the United States who holds a license or certificate of authority or qualification to engage in the practice of a profession, occupation, trade, or vocation or business, including but not limited to a practitioner as defined in section 2 of P.L.1997, c. 353 (C.2C:21–4.2), shall forfeit that license or certificate and be forever barred from the practice of that profession, occupation, trade, vocation or business if the act or acts of insurance fraud were related to or performed while engaged in the practice of that profession, occupation, trade, vocation or business, unless the court finds that such license or certificate forfeiture would be a serious injustice which overrides the need to deter such conduct by others and in that case the court shall determine an appropriate period of license or certificate suspension which shall be for a period of not less than one year. If the court does not permanently forfeit such license or certificate pursuant to this paragraph, the sentence shall not become final for 10 days in order to permit the appeal of that sentence by the prosecution.

(5) A person convicted of third degree insurance fraud pursuant to section 73 of P.L.2003, c.89 (C.2C:21–4.6) or a substantially similar crime under the laws of another state or the United States who holds a license or certificate of authority or qualification to engage in the practice of a profession, occupation, trade, vocation or business, including but not limited to a practitioner as defined in section 2 of P.L.1997, c. 353 (C.2C:21–4.2), shall have his license or certificate suspended and be barred from the practice of that profession, occupation, trade, vocation or business for a period of at least one year if the act or acts of insurance fraud were related to or performed while engaged in the practice of that profession, occupation, trade, vocation or business.

(6) Upon a second conviction of third degree insurance fraud pursuant to section 73 of P.L.2003, c.89 (C.2C:21–4.6) or a substantially similar crime under the laws of another state or the United States which meets the criteria of paragraph (2) of this subsection, a person shall forfeit his license or certificate and be forever barred from the practice of that profession, occupation, trade, vocation or business.

(7) Upon application of the county prosecutor or the Attorney General, a person convicted of any crime of the second degree or above enumerated in chapter 20

or 21 of Title 2C of the New Jersey Statutes or a substantially similar crime under the laws of another state or the United States who holds a license or certificate or authority or qualification to engage in the practice of a profession, occupation, trade, vocation or business, including a practitioner as defined in section 2 of P.L.1997, c. 353 (C.2C:21–4.2), shall forfeit such license or certificate and be forever barred from the practice of that profession, occupation, trade, vocation or business if the act or acts underlying the conviction involved or were related to an insurance transaction as defined in section 72 of P.L.2003, c.89 (C.2C:21–4.5) and touched upon or were performed while engaged in the practice of that profession, occupation, trade, vocation or business, unless the court finds that the license or certificate forfeiture would be a serious injustice which overrides the need to deter such conduct by others and in that case the court shall determine an appropriate period of license or certificate suspension which shall be for a period of not less than one year. If the court does not permanently forfeit that license or certificate pursuant to this paragraph, the sentence shall not become final for 10 days in order to permit the appeal of that sentence by the prosecution.

(8) Upon application of the county prosecutor or the Attorney General, a person convicted of any crime of the third degree enumerated in chapter 20 or 21 of Title 2C of the New Jersey Statutes or a substantially similar crime under the laws of another state or the United States who holds a license or certificate of authority or qualification to engage in the practice of a profession, occupation, trade, vocation or business, including but not limited to a practitioner as defined in section 2 of P.L.1997, c. 353 (C.2C:21–4.2), shall have his license or certificate suspended and be barred from the practice of that profession, occupation, trade, vocation or business for a period of at least one year if the act or acts underlying the conviction involved or were related to an insurance transaction as defined in section 72 of P.L. 2003, c.89 (C.2C:21–4.5) and touched upon or were performed while engaged in the practice of that profession, occupation, trade, vocation or business.

b. A court of this State shall enter an order of license or certificate forfeiture or suspension pursuant to subsection a. of this section:

(1) Immediately upon a finding of guilt by the trier of fact or a plea of guilty entered in any court of this State; or

(2) Upon application of the county prosecutor or the Attorney General, when the license or certificate forfeiture or suspension is made pursuant to paragraph (4) of subsection a. of this section or is based upon a conviction of an offense under the laws of another state or of the United States. An order of license or certificate forfeiture or suspension pursuant to this paragraph shall be effective as of the date the person is found guilty by the trier of fact or pleads guilty to the offense.

This application may also be made in the alternative by the Attorney General to the appropriate licensing agency.

The court shall provide notice of the forfeiture or suspension to the appropriate licensing agency within 10 days of the date an order of forfeiture or suspension is entered.

c. No court shall grant a stay of an order of license or certificate forfeiture or suspension pending appeal of a conviction or forfeiture or suspension order unless the court is clearly convinced that there is a substantial likelihood of success on the merits. If the conviction is reversed or the order of license or certificate forfeiture or suspension is overturned, the court shall provide notice of reinstatement to the appropriate licensing agency within 10 days of the date of the order of reinstatement. The license or certificate shall be restored, in accordance with applicable procedures, unless the appropriate licensing agency determines to suspend or revoke the license or certificate.

d. In any case in which the issue of license or certificate forfeiture or suspension is not raised in a court of this State at the time of a finding of guilt, entry of a guilty plea or sentencing, a license or certificate forfeiture or suspension required by this section may be ordered by a court or by the appropriate licensing agency of this State upon application of the county prosecutor or the Attorney General or upon application of the appropriate licensing agency having authority to revoke or suspend the professional's license or certificate. The fact that a court has declined to order license or certificate forfeiture or suspension shall not preclude the appropriate licensing agency having authority to revoke or suspend the professional's license or certificate from seeking to do so on the ground that the conduct giving rise to the conviction demonstrates that the person is unfit to hold the license or certificate or is otherwise liable for an offense as specified in section 8 of P.L.1978, c. 73 (C.45:1–21).

e. If the Supreme Court of the State of New Jersey issues Rules of Court pursuant to this act, the Supreme Court may revoke the license to practice law of any attorney who has been convicted, under the laws of this State, of health care claims fraud pursuant to section 3 of P.L.1997, c. 353 (C.2C:21–4.3), or an offense which, if committed in this State, would constitute health care claims fraud, insurance fraud pursuant to section 73 of P.L.2003, c.89 (C.2C:21–4.6), or an offense which, if committed in this State, would constitute insurance fraud.

f. Nothing in this section shall be construed to prevent or limit the appropriate licensing agency or any other party from taking any other action permitted by law against the practitioner.

L.1997, c. 353, § 4, eff. Jan. 15, 1998. Amended by L.2003, c. 89, § 76, eff. June 9, 2003.

CHAPTER 52

EXPUNGEMENT OF RECORDS

Section
2C:52–1.   Definition of expungement.
2C:52–2.   Indictable offenses.
2C:52–3.   Disorderly persons offenses and petty disorderly persons offenses.
2C:52–4.   Ordinances.
2C:52–4.1. Juvenile delinquent; expungement of adjudications and charges.
2C:52–5.   Expungement of records of young drug offenders.
2C:52–6.   Arrests not resulting in conviction.
2C:52–7.   Petition for expungement.
2C:52–8.   Statements to accompany petition.
2C:52–9.   Order fixing time for hearing.
2C:52–10.   Service of petition and documents.
2C:52–11.   Order directing expungement where no objection prior to hearing.
2C:52–12.   Denial of relief although no objection entered.
2C:52–13.   When hearing on petition for expungement shall not be held.
2C:52–14.   Grounds for denial of relief.
2C:52–15.   Records to be removed; control.
2C:52–16.   Expunged record including names of persons other than petitioner.
2C:52–17.   Use of expunged records by agencies on pending petition for expungement.
2C:52–18.   Supplying information to violent crimes compensation board.
2C:52–19.   Order of superior court permitting inspection of records or release of information; limitations.
2C:52–20.   Use of expunged records in conjunction with supervisory treatment or diversion programs.
2C:52–21.   Use of expunged records in conjunction with setting bail, presentence report or sentencing.
2C:52–22.   Use of expunged records by parole board.
2C:52–23.   Use of expunged records by department of corrections.
2C:52–24.   County prosecutor's obligation to ascertain propriety of petition.
2C:52–25.   Retroactive application.
2C:52–26.   Vacating of orders of sealing; time; basis.
2C:52–27.   Effect of expungement.
2C:52–27.1. Practitioners convicted of health care claims fraud; rescission of debarment order.
2C:52–28.   Motor vehicle offenses.
2C:52–29.   Fee.
2C:52–30.   Disclosure of expungement order.
2C:52–31.   Limitation.
2C:52–32.   Construction.

2C:52–1. Definition of expungement

a. Except as otherwise provided in this chapter, expungement shall mean the extraction and isolation of all records on file within any court, detention or correctional facility, law enforcement or criminal justice agency concerning a person's detection, apprehension, arrest, detention, trial or disposition of an offense within the criminal justice system.

b. Expunged records shall include complaints, warrants, arrests, commitments, processing records, finger-prints, photographs, index cards, "rap sheets" and judicial docket records.

L.1979, c. 178, § 108, eff. Sept. 1, 1979.

2C:52–2. Indictable offenses

a. In all cases, except as herein provided, wherein a person has been convicted of a crime under the laws of this State and who has not been convicted of any prior or subsequent crime, whether within this State or any other jurisdiction, and has not been adjudged a disorderly person or petty disorderly person on more than two occasions may, after the expiration of a period of 10 years from the date of his conviction, payment of fine, satisfactory completion of probation or parole, or release from incarceration, whichever is later, present a duly verified petition as provided in section 2C:52–7 to the Superior Court in the county in which the conviction was entered praying that such conviction and all records and information pertaining thereto be expunged.

Notwithstanding the provisions of the preceding paragraph, a petition may be filed and presented, and the court may grant an expungement pursuant to this section, although less than 10 years has expired in accordance with the requirements of the preceding paragraph where the court finds:

(1) less than 10 years has expired from the satisfaction of a fine, but the 10–year time requirement is otherwise satisfied, and the court finds that the person substantially complied with any payment plan ordered pursuant to N.J.S.2C:46–1 et seq., or could not do so due to compelling circumstances affecting his ability to satisfy the fine; or

(2) at least five years has expired from the date of his conviction, payment of fine, satisfactory completion of probation or parole, or release from incarceration, whichever is later; the person has not been convicted of a crime, disorderly persons offense, or petty disorderly persons offense since the time of the conviction; and the court finds in its discretion that expungement is in the public interest, giving due consideration to the nature of the offense, and the applicant's character and conduct since conviction.

In determining whether compelling circumstances exist for the purposes of paragraph (1) of this subsection, a court may consider the amount of the fine or fines imposed, the person's age at the time of the offense, the person's financial condition and other relevant circumstances regarding the person's ability to pay.

Although subsequent convictions for no more than two disorderly or petty disorderly offenses shall not be an absolute bar to relief, the nature of those conviction or convictions and the circumstances surrounding them shall be considered by the court and may be a basis for denial of relief if they or either of them constitute a continuation of the type of unlawful activity embodied in the criminal conviction for which expungement is sought.

b. Records of conviction pursuant to statutes repealed by this Code for the crimes of murder, manslaughter, treason, anarchy, kidnapping, rape, forcible sodomy, arson, perjury, false swearing, robbery, embracery, or a conspiracy or any attempt to commit any of the foregoing, or aiding, assisting or concealing persons accused of the foregoing crimes, shall not be expunged.

Records of conviction for the following crimes specified in the New Jersey Code of Criminal Justice shall not be subject to expungement: Section 2C:11–1 et seq. (Criminal Homicide), except death by auto as specified in section 2C:11–5; section 2C:13–1 (Kidnapping); section 2C:13–6 (Luring or Enticing); section 1 of P.L.2005, c. 77 (C.2C:13–8) (Human Trafficking); section 2C:14–2 (Aggravated Sexual Assault); section 2C:14–3a (Aggravated Criminal Sexual Contact); if the victim is a minor, section 2C:14–3b (Criminal Sexual Contact); if the victim is a minor and the offender is not the parent of the victim, section 2C:13–2 (Criminal Restraint) or section 2C:13–3 (False Imprisonment); section 2C:15–1 (Robbery); section 2C:17–1 (Arson and Related Offenses); section 2C:24–4a. (Endangering the welfare of a child by engaging in sexual conduct which would impair or debauch the morals of the child); section 2C:24–4b(4) (Endangering the welfare of a child); section 2C:24–4b. (3) (Causing or permitting a child to engage in a prohibited sexual act); section 2C:24:4b.(5)(a)[1] (Selling or manufacturing child pornography); section 2C:28–1 (Perjury); section 2C:28–2 (False Swearing); section 2C:34–1b.(4) (Knowingly promoting the prostitution of the actor's child); section 2 of P.L.2002, c. 26 (C.2C:38–2) (Terrorism); subsection a. of section 3 of P.L.2002, c. 26 (C.2C:38–3) (Producing or Possessing Chemical Weapons, Biological Agents or Nuclear or Radiological Devices); and conspiracies or attempts to commit such crimes.

Records of conviction for any crime committed by a person holding any public office, position or employment, elective or appointive, under the government of this State or any agency or political subdivision thereof and any conspiracy or attempt to commit such a crime shall not be subject to expungement if the crime involved or touched such office, position or employment.

c. In the case of conviction for the sale or distribution of a controlled dangerous substance or possession thereof with intent to sell, expungement shall be denied except where the crimes involve:

(1) Marijuana, where the total quantity sold, distributed or possessed with intent to sell was 25 grams or less;

(2) Hashish, where the total quantity sold, distributed or possessed with intent to sell was five grams or less; or

(3) Any controlled dangerous substance provided that the conviction is of the third or fourth degree, where the court finds that expungement is consistent with the public interest, giving due consideration to the

nature of the offense and the petitioner's character and conduct since conviction.

d. In the case of a State licensed physician or podiatrist convicted of an offense involving drugs or alcohol or pursuant to section 14 or 15 of P.L. 1989, c. 300 (C.2C:21–20 or 2C:21–4.1), the court shall notify the State Board of Medical Examiners upon receipt of a petition for expungement of the conviction and records and information pertaining thereto.

L.1979, c. 178, § 109, eff. Sept. 1, 1979. Amended by L.1989, c. 300, § 23, eff. Jan. 12, 1990; L.1993, c. 301, § 1, eff. Dec. 23, 1993; L.1994, c. 133, § 6, eff. Oct. 31, 1994; L.2009, c. 188, § 1, eff. March 13, 2010.

1 Probably should read section 2C:24–4 b.(5)(a).

2C:52–3. Disorderly persons offenses and petty disorderly persons offenses

Any person convicted of a disorderly persons offense or petty disorderly persons offense under the laws of this State who has not been convicted of any prior or subsequent crime, whether within this State or any other jurisdiction, or of another three disorderly persons or petty disorderly persons offenses, may, after the expiration of a period of 5 years from the date of his conviction, payment of fine, satisfactory completion of probation or release from incarceration, whichever is later, present a duly verified petition as provided in section 2C:52–7 hereof to the Superior Court in the county in which the conviction was entered praying that such conviction and all records and information pertaining thereto be expunged.

L.1979, c. 178, § 110, eff. Sept. 1, 1979. Amended by L.1981, c. 290, § 43, eff. Sept. 24, 1981.

2C:52–4. Ordinances

In all cases wherein a person has been found guilty of violating a municipal ordinance of any governmental entity of this State and who has not been convicted of any prior or subsequent crime, whether within this State or any other jurisdiction, and who has not been adjudged a disorderly person or petty disorderly person on more than two occasions, may, after the expiration of a period of 2 years from the date of his conviction, payment of fine, satisfactory completion of probation or release from incarceration, whichever is later, present a duly verified petition as provided in section 2C:52–7 herein to the Superior Court in the county in which the violation occurred praying that such conviction and all records and information pertaining thereto be expunged.

L.1979, c. 178, § 111, eff. Sept. 1, 1979.

2C:52–4.1. Juvenile delinquent; expungement of adjudications and charges

a. Any person adjudged a juvenile delinquent may have such adjudication expunged as follows:

(1) Pursuant to N.J.S.2C:52–2, if the act committed by the juvenile would have constituted a crime if committed by an adult;

(2) Pursuant to N.J.S.2C:52–3, if the act committed by the juvenile would have constituted a disorderly or petty disorderly persons offense if committed by an adult; or

(3) Pursuant to N.J.S.2C:52–4, if the act committed by the juvenile would have constituted an ordinance violation if committed by an adult.

For purposes of expungement, any act which resulted in a juvenile being adjudged a delinquent shall be classified as if that act had been committed by an adult.

b. Additionally, any person who has been adjudged a juvenile delinquent may have his entire record of delinquency adjudications expunged if:

(1) Five years have elapsed since the final discharge of the person from legal custody or supervision or 5 years have elapsed after the entry of any other court order not involving custody or supervision, except that periods of post-incarceration supervision pursuant to section 25 of P.L.1982, c. 77 (C.2A:4A–44), shall not be considered in calculating the five-year period for purposes of this paragraph;

(2) He has not been convicted of a crime, or a disorderly or petty disorderly persons offense, or adjudged a delinquent, or in need of supervision, during the 5 years prior to the filing of the petition, and no proceeding or complaint is pending seeking such a conviction or adjudication, except that periods of post-incarceration supervision pursuant to section 25 of P.L.1982, c. 77 (C.2A:4A–44), shall not be considered in calculating the five-year period for purposes of this paragraph;

(3) He was never adjudged a juvenile delinquent on the basis of an act which if committed by an adult would constitute a crime not subject to expungement under N.J.S.2C:52–2;

(4) He has never had an adult conviction expunged; and

(5) He has never had adult criminal charges dismissed following completion of a supervisory treatment or other diversion program.

c. Any person who has been charged with an act of delinquency and against whom proceedings were dismissed may have the filing of those charges expunged pursuant to the provisions of N.J.S.2C:52–6.

L.1980, c. 163, § 1, eff. Jan. 10, 1981. Amended by L.1981, c. 290, § 44, eff. Sept. 24, 1981; L.2009, c. 188, § 2, eff. March 13, 2010.

2C:52–5. Expungement of records of young drug offenders

Notwithstanding the provisions of sections 2C:52–2 and 2C:52–3, after a period of not less than one year following conviction, termination of probation or parole

or discharge from custody, whichever is later, any person convicted of an offense under chapters 35 or 36 of this title for the possession or use of a controlled dangerous substance, convicted of violating P.L.1955, c. 277, § 3 (C. 2A:170–77.5),[1] or convicted of violating P.L.1962, c. 113, § 1 (C. 2A:170–77.8), and who at the time of the offense was 21 years of age or younger, may apply to the Superior Court in the county wherein the matter was disposed of for the expungement of such person's conviction and all records pertaining thereto. The relief of expungement under this section shall be granted only if said person has not, prior to the time of hearing, violated any of the conditions of his probation or parole, albeit subsequent to discharge from probation or parole, has not been convicted of any previous or subsequent criminal act or any subsequent or previous violation of chapters 35 or 36 of this title or of P.L.1955, c. 277, § 3 (C. 2A:170–77.5) or of P.L.1962, c. 113, § 1 (C. 2A:170–77.8), or who has not had a prior or subsequent criminal matter dismissed because of acceptance into a supervisory treatment or other diversion program.

This section shall not apply to any person who has been convicted of the sale or distribution of a controlled dangerous substance or possession with the intent to sell any controlled dangerous substance except:

(1) Marihuana, where the total sold, distributed or possessed with intent to sell was 25 grams or less, or

(2) Hashish, where the total amount sold, distributed or possessed with intent to sell was 5 grams or less.

L.1979, c. 178, § 112, eff. Sept. 1, 1979. Amended by L.1987, c. 106, § 16, eff. July 9, 1987.

1 Repealed; see, now, N.J.S.A. § 24:21–51.

2C:52–6. Arrests not resulting in conviction

a. In all cases, except as herein provided, wherein a person has been arrested or held to answer for a crime, disorderly persons offense, petty disorderly persons offense or municipal ordinance violation under the laws of this State or of any governmental entity thereof and against whom proceedings were dismissed, or who was acquitted, or who was discharged without a conviction or finding of guilt, may at any time following the disposition of proceedings, present a duly verified petition as provided in section 2C:52–7 to the Superior Court in the county in which the disposition occurred praying that records of such arrest and all records and information pertaining thereto be expunged.

b. Any person who has had charges dismissed against him pursuant to P.L.1970, c. 226, § 27 (C. 24:21–27)[1] or pursuant to a program of supervisory treatment, shall be barred from the relief provided in this section until 6 months after the entry of the order of dismissal.

c. Any person who has been arrested or held to answer for a crime shall be barred from the relief provided in this section where the dismissal, discharge, or acquittal resulted from a determination that the person was insane or lacked the mental capacity to commit the crime charged.

L.1979, c. 178, § 113, eff. Sept. 1, 1979.

1 Repealed; see, now, N.J.S.A. § 2C:36A–1.

2C:52–7. Petition for expungement

Every petition for expungement filed pursuant to this chapter shall be verified and include:

a. Petitioner's date of birth.

b. Petitioner's date of arrest.

c. The statute or statutes and offense or offenses for which petitioner was arrested and of which petitioner was convicted.

d. The original indictment, summons or complaint number.

e. Petitioner's date of conviction, or date of disposition of the matter if no conviction resulted.

f. The court's disposition of the matter and the punishment imposed, if any.

L.1979, c. 178, § 114, eff. Sept. 1, 1979.

2C:52–8. Statements to accompany petition

There shall be attached to a petition for expungement:

a. A statement with the affidavit or verification that there are no disorderly persons, petty disorderly persons or criminal charges pending against the petitioner at the time of filing of the petition for expungement.

b. In those instances where the petitioner is seeking the expungement of a criminal conviction, a statement with affidavit or verification that he has never been granted expungement, sealing or similar relief regarding a criminal conviction by any court in this State or other state or by any Federal court. "Sealing" refers to the relief previously granted pursuant to P.L.1973, c. 191 (C. 2A:85–15 et seq.) 1.

c. In those instances where a person has received a dismissal of a criminal charge because of acceptance into a supervisory treatment or any other diversion program, a statement with affidavit or verification setting forth the nature of the original charge, the court of disposition and date of disposition.

L.1979, c. 178, § 115, eff. Sept. 1, 1979.

1 Repealed; see, now, N.J.S.A. § 2C:52–1 et seq.

2C:52–9. Order fixing time for hearing

Upon the filing of a petition for relief pursuant to this chapter, the court shall, by order, fix a time not less than 35 nor more than 60 days thereafter for hearing of the matter.

L.1979, c. 178, § 116, eff. Sept. 1, 1979.

2C:52–10. Service of petition and documents

A copy of each petition, together with a copy of all supporting documents, shall be served pursuant to the rules of court upon the Superintendent of State Police; the Attorney General; the county prosecutor of the county wherein the court is located; the chief of police or other executive head of the police department of the municipality wherein the offense was committed; the chief law enforcement officer of any other law enforcement agency of this State which participated in the arrest of the individual; the superintendent or warden of any institution in which the petitioner was confined; and, if a disposition was made by a municipal court, upon the magistrate of that court. Service shall be made within 5 days from the date of the order setting the date for the hearing upon the matter.

L.1979, c. 178, § 117, eff. Sept. 1, 1979.

2C:52–11. Order directing expungement where no objection prior to hearing

If, prior to the hearing, there is no objection from those law enforcement agencies notified or from those offices or agencies which are required to be served under 2C:52–10, and no reason, as provided in section 2C:52–14, appears to the contrary, the court may, without a hearing, grant an order directing the clerk of the court and all relevant criminal justice and law enforcement agencies to expunge records of said disposition including evidence of arrest, detention, conviction and proceedings related thereto.

L.1979, c. 178, § 118, eff. Sept. 1, 1979.

2C:52–12. Denial of relief although no objection entered

In the event that none of the persons or agencies required to be noticed under 2C:52–10 has entered any objection to the relief being sought, the court may nevertheless deny the relief sought if it concludes that petitioner is not entitled to relief for the reasons provided in section 2C:52–14.

L.1979, c. 178, § 119, eff. Sept. 1, 1979.

2C:52–13. When hearing on petition for expungement shall not be held

No petition for relief made pursuant to this section shall be heard by any court if the petitioner, at the time of filing or date of hearing, has a charge or charges pending against him which allege the commission of a crime, disorderly persons offense or petty disorderly persons offense. Such petition shall not be heard until such times as all pending criminal and or disorderly persons charges are adjudicated to finality.

L.1979, c. 178, § 120, eff. Sept. 1, 1979.

2C:52–14. Grounds for denial of relief

A petition for expungement filed pursuant to this chapter shall be denied when:

a. Any statutory prerequisite, including any provision of this chapter, is not fulfilled or there is any other statutory basis for denying relief.

b. The need for the availability of the records outweighs the desirability of having a person freed from any disabilities as otherwise provided in this chapter. An application may be denied under this subsection only following objection of a party given notice pursuant to 2C:52–10 and the burden of asserting such grounds shall be on the objector, except that in regard to expungement sought for third or fourth degree drug offenses pursuant to paragraph (3) of subsection c. of N.J.S. 2C:52–2, the court shall consider whether this factor applies regardless of whether any party objects on this basis.

c. In connection with a petition under section 2C:52–6, the acquittal, discharge or dismissal of charges resulted from a plea bargaining agreement involving the conviction of other charges. This bar, however, shall not apply once the conviction is itself expunged.

d. The arrest or conviction sought to be expunged is, at the time of hearing, the subject matter of civil litigation between the petitioner or his legal representative and the State, any governmental entity thereof or any State agency and the representatives or employees of any such body.

e. A person has had a previous criminal conviction expunged regardless of the lapse of time between the prior expungement, or sealing under prior law, and the present petition. This provision shall not apply:

(1) When the person is seeking the expungement of a municipal ordinance violation or,

(2) When the person is seeking the expungement of records pursuant to section 2C:52–6.

f. The person seeking the relief of expungement of a conviction for a disorderly persons, petty disorderly persons, or criminal offense has prior to or subsequent to said conviction been granted the dismissal of criminal charges following completion of a supervisory treatment or other diversion program.

L.1979, c. 178, § 121, eff. Sept. 1, 1979. Amended by L.2009, c. 188, § 3, eff. March 13, 2010.

2C:52–15. Records to be removed; control

If an order of expungement of records of arrest or conviction under this chapter is granted by the court, all the records specified in said order shall be removed from the files of the agencies which have been noticed of the pendency of petitioner's motion and which are, by the provisions of this chapter, entitled to notice, and shall be placed in the control of a person who has been designated by the head of each such agency which, at the time of the hearing, possesses said records. That designated person shall, except as otherwise provided in this chapter, insure that such records or the information contained therein are not released for any reason and are not utilized or referred to for any purpose. In

response to requests for information or records of the person who was arrested or convicted, all noticed officers, departments and agencies shall reply, with respect to the arrest, conviction or related proceedings which are the subject of the order, that there is no record information.

L.1979, c. 178, § 122, eff. Sept. 1, 1979.

2C:52–16. Expunged record including names of persons other than petitioner

Any record or file which is maintained by a judicial or law enforcement agency, or agency in the criminal justice system, which is the subject of an order of expungement which includes the name or names of persons other than that of the petitioner need not be isolated from the general files of the agency retaining same if the other persons named in said record or file have not been granted an order of expungement of said record, provided that a copy of the record shall be given to the person designated in 2C:52–15 and the original shall remain in the agency's general files with the petitioner's name and other personal identifiers obliterated and deleted.

L.1979, c. 178, § 123, eff. Sept. 1, 1979.

2C:52–17. Use of expunged records by agencies on pending petition for expungement

Expunged records may be used by the agencies that possess same to ascertain whether a person has had prior conviction expunged, or sealed under prior law, when the agency possessing the record is noticed of a pending petition for the expungement of a conviction. Any such agency may supply information to the court wherein the motion is pending and to the other parties who are entitled to notice pursuant to 2C:52–10.

L.1979, c. 178, § 124, eff. Sept. 1, 1979.

2C:52–18. Supplying information to violent crimes compensation board

Information contained in expunged records may be supplied to the Violent Crimes Compensation Board, in conjunction with any claim which has been filed with said board.

L.1979, c. 178, § 125, eff. Sept. 1, 1979.

2C:52–19. Order of superior court permitting inspection of records or release of information; limitations

Inspection of the files and records, or release of the information contained therein, which are the subject of an order of expungement, or sealing under prior law, may be permitted by the Superior Court upon motion for good cause shown and compelling need based on specific facts. The motion or any order granted pursuant thereto shall specify the person or persons to whom the records and information are to be shown and the purpose for which they are to be utilized. Leave to inspect shall be granted by the court only in those instances where the subject matter of the records of arrest or conviction is the object of litigation or judicial proceedings. Such records may not be inspected or utilized in any subsequent civil or criminal proceeding for the purposes of impeachment or otherwise but may be used for purposes of sentencing on a subsequent offense after guilt has been established.

L.1979, c. 178, § 126, eff. Sept. 1, 1979.

2C:52–20. Use of expunged records in conjunction with supervisory treatment or diversion programs

Expunged records may be used by any judge in determining whether to grant or deny the person's application for acceptance into a supervisory treatment or diversion program for subsequent charges. Any expunged records which are possessed by any law enforcement agency may be supplied to the Attorney General, any county prosecutor or judge of this State when same are requested and are to be used for the purpose of determining whether or not to accept a person into a supervisory treatment or diversion program for subsequent charges.

L.1979, c. 178, § 127, eff. Sept. 1, 1979.

2C:52–21. Use of expunged records in conjunction with setting bail, presentence report or sentencing

Expunged records, or sealed records under prior law, of prior arrests or convictions shall be provided to any judge, county prosecutor, probation department or the Attorney General when same are requested for use in conjunction with a bail hearing or for the preparation of a presentence report or for purpose of sentencing.

L.1979, c. 178, § 128, eff. Sept. 1, 1979.

2C:52–22. Use of expunged records by parole board

Expunged records, or sealed records under prior law, of prior disorderly persons, petty disorderly persons and criminal convictions shall be provided to the Parole Board when same are requested for the purpose of evaluating the granting of parole to the person who is the subject of said records. Such sealed or expunged records may be used by the Parole Board in the same manner and given the same weight in its considerations as if the records had not been expunged or sealed.

L.1979, c. 178, § 129, eff. Sept. 1, 1979.

2C:52–23. Use of expunged records by department of corrections

Expunged records, and records sealed under prior law, shall be provided to the Department of Corrections for its use solely in the classification, evaluation and assignment to correctional and penal institutions of persons placed in its custody.

L.1979, c. 178, § 130, eff. Sept. 1, 1979.

2C:52–24. County prosecutor's obligation to ascertain propriety of petition

Notwithstanding the notice requirements provided herein, it shall be the obligation of the county prosecu-tor of the county wherein any petition for expungement is filed to verify the accuracy of the allegations con-tained in the petition for expungement and to bring to the court's attention any facts which may be a bar to, or which may make inappropriate the granting of, such relief. If no disabling, adverse or relevant information is ascertained other than that as included in the petitioner's affidavit, such facts shall be communicated by the prosecutor to the hearing judge.

L.1979, c. 178, § 131, eff. Sept. 1, 1979.

2C:52–25. Retroactive application

This chapter shall apply to arrests and convictions which occurred prior to, and which occur subsequent to, the effective date of this act.

L.1979, c. 178, § 132, eff. Sept. 1, 1979.

2C:52–26. Vacating of orders of sealing; time; basis

If, within 5 years of the entry of an expungement order, any party to whom notice is required to be given pursuant to section 2C:52–10 notifies the court which issued the order that at the time of the petition or hearing there were criminal, disorderly persons or petty disorderly persons charges pending against the person to whom the court granted such order, which charges were not revealed to the court at the time of hearing of the original motion or that there was some other statutory disqualification, said court shall vacate the expungement order in question and reconsider the original motion in conjunction with the previously undisclosed information.

L.1979, c. 178, § 133, eff. Sept. 1, 1979.

2C:52–27. Effect of expungement

Unless otherwise provided by law, if an order of expungement is granted, the arrest, conviction and any proceedings related thereto shall be deemed not to have occurred, and the petitioner may answer any questions relating to their occurrence accordingly, except as follows:

a. The fact of an expungement, sealing or similar relief shall be disclosed as provided in section 2C:52–8b.

b. The fact of an expungement of prior charges which were dismissed because of the person's accep-tance into and successful completion of a supervisory treatment or other diversion program shall be disclosed by said person to any judge who is determining the propriety of accepting said person into a supervisory treatment or other diversion program for subsequent criminal charges; and

c. Information divulged on expunged records shall be revealed by a petitioner seeking employment within the judicial branch or with a law enforcement or corrections agency and such information shall continue to provide a disability as otherwise provided by law.

L.1979, c. 178, § 134, eff. Sept. 1, 1979. Amended by L.1981, c. 290, § 45, eff. Sept. 24, 1981.

2C:52–27.1. Practitioners convicted of health care claims fraud; rescission of debarment order

a. If an order of expungement of records of conviction under the provisions of chapter 52 of Title 2C of the New Jersey Statutes is granted by the court to a person convicted of health care claims fraud in which the court had ordered the offender's professional license or certificate be forfeited and the person be forever barred from the practice of the profession, occupation, trade, vocation or business pursuant to subsection a. of section 4 of P.L.1997, c. 353 (C.2C:51–5), the person may petition the court for an order to rescind the court's order of debarment if the person can demonstrate that the person is sufficiently rehabilitated.

b. If an order to rescind the court's order of debarment is granted, the person granted the order may apply to be licensed or certified to practice the profession, occupation, trade, vocation or business from which the offender was barred.

L.1997, c. 353, § 5, eff. Jan. 15, 1998. Amended by L.2003, c. 89, § 77, eff. June 9, 2003.

2C:52–28. Motor vehicle offenses

Nothing contained in this chapter shall apply to arrests or conviction for motor vehicle offenses contained in Title 39.

L.1979, c. 178, § 135, eff. Sept. 1, 1979.

2C:52–29. Fee

Any person who files an application pursuant to this chapter shall pay to the State Treasurer a fee of $30.00 to defer administrative costs in processing an application hereunder.

L.1979, c. 178, § 136, eff. Sept. 1, 1979.

2C:52–30. Disclosure of expungement order

Except as otherwise provided in this chapter, any person who reveals to another the existence of an arrest, conviction or related legal proceeding with knowledge that the records and information pertaining thereto have been expunged or sealed is a disorderly person. Notwithstanding the provisions of section 2C:43–3, the maximum fine which can be imposed for violation of this section is $200.00.

L.1979, c. 178, § 137, eff. Sept. 1, 1979.

2C:52–31. Limitation

Nothing provided in this chapter shall be interpreted to permit the expungement of records contained in the Controlled Dangerous Substances Registry created pursuant to P.L.1970, c. 227 (C. 26:2G–17 et seq.),[1] or the registry created by the Administrative Office of the Courts pursuant to section 2C:43–21.

L.1979, c. 178, § 138, eff. Sept. 1, 1979.

1 Repealed by L.1984, c. 91, § 4.

2C:52–32. Construction

This chapter shall be construed with the primary objective of providing relief to the one-time offender who has led a life of rectitude and disassociated himself with unlawful activity, but not to create a system whereby periodic violators of the law or those who associate themselves with criminal activity have a regular means of expunging their police and criminal records.

L.1979, c. 178, § 139, eff. Sept. 1, 1979.

CHAPTERS 53 to 57

[RESERVED]

CHAPTER 58

LICENSING AND OTHER PROVISIONS RELATING TO FIREARMS

Section

2C:58–1. Registration of manufacturers and wholesale dealers of firearms.
2C:58–2. Retailing of firearms.
2C:58–2.1. Guidelines.
2C:58–2.2. Legislative findings; personalized handguns.
2C:58–2.3. Retail sales availability; production model.
2C:58–2.4. List of personalized handguns that may be sold.
2C:58–2.5. Sales; commission to qualify use by law enforcement; penalty.
2C:58–2.6. Rules and regulations.
2C:58–3. Purchase of firearms.
2C:58–3.1. Temporary transfer of firearms; duration; presence of owner or dealer.
2C:58–3.2. Transfer of firearm; participation in training courses.
2C:58–3.3. Handgun ammunition sales and transfers.
2C:58–3.4. Exemption from restrictions on the purchase of handguns; applicant certification; denial; appeal.
2C:58–4. Permits to carry handguns.
2C:58–4.1. Employee of armored car company; application; letter from chief executive officer.
2C:58–5. Licenses to possess and carry machine guns and assault firearms.
2C:58–6. Repealed.
2C:58–6.1. Possession of firearms by minors; exceptions.
2C:58–7. Persons possessing explosives or destructive devices to notify police.
2C:58–8. Certain wounds and injuries to be reported.
2C:58–9. Certain convictions to be reported.
2C:58–10. Incendiary or tracer ammunition.
2C:58–11. Repealed.
2C:58–12. Assault firearms; registration; death of registrant; civil liability for use in crime.
2C:58–13. One year period to transfer, render inoperable, or surrender assault firearm in lieu of registration.
2C:58–14. Report by Attorney General to Legislature regarding assault firearms.
2C:58–15. Access by minors to loaded firearm; disorderly persons offense; exceptions.
2C:58–16. Warning to purchasers of criminal liability for leaving loaded firearm within access by minor.
2C:58–17. KeepSafe program.

Section
2C:58–18.   Effectiveness report.
2C:58–19.   Lost or stolen firearms; report to law enforcement officials; civil penalties.

2C:58–1. Registration of manufacturers and wholesale dealers of firearms

a. Registration. Every manufacturer and wholesale dealer of firearms shall register with the superintendent as provided in this section. No person shall engage in the business of, or act as a manufacturer or wholesale dealer of firearms, or manufacture or sell at wholesale any firearm, until he has so registered.

Applications for registration shall be made on such forms as shall be prescribed by the superintendent, and the applicant shall furnish such information and other particulars as may be prescribed by law or by any rules or regulations promulgated by the superintendent. Each application for registration or renewal shall be accompanied by a fee of $150.00.

The superintendent shall prescribe standards and qualifications for the registration of manufacturers and wholesalers of firearms, for the protection of the public safety, health and welfare. He shall refuse to register any applicant for registration unless he is satisfied that the applicant can be permitted to engage in business as a manufacturer or wholesale dealer of firearms without any danger to the public safety, health or welfare.

The superintendent shall issue a certificate of registration to every person registered under this section, and such certificate shall be valid for a period of 3 years from the date of issuance.

b. Wholesale dealer's agent. Every registered wholesale dealer of firearms shall cause each of his agents or employees actively engaged in the purchase or sale of firearms to be licensed with the superintendent as a wholesale dealer's agent. Applications for agents' licenses shall be submitted on such forms as shall be prescribed by the superintendent, and shall be signed by the registered wholesale dealer and by the agent. Each application shall be accompanied by a fee of $5.00, and each license shall be valid for so long as the agent or employee remains in the employ of the wholesale dealer and the wholesale dealer remains validly registered under this section. The superintendent shall prescribe standards and qualifications for licensed wholesale dealers' agents, for the protection of the public safety, health and welfare.

c. Revocation of certificate of registration or license. The superintendent may, after reasonable notice to all affected parties and a hearing if requested, revoke any certificate of registration or agent's license if he finds that the registered or licensed person is no longer engaged in the business of manufacturing or wholesaling firearms in this State or that he can no longer be permitted to carry on such business without endangering the public safety, health or welfare. A certificate or license may be canceled at any time at the request of the registered or licensed person.

d. Appeals. Any person aggrieved by the refusal of the superintendent to register him as a manufacturer or wholesale dealer or a wholesale dealer's agent, or by revocation of his certificate or license, may appeal to the Appellate Division of the Superior Court.

e. Records of sales. Every manufacturer and wholesale dealer shall keep a detailed record of each firearm sold by him. The record shall include the date of sale, the name and address of the purchaser, a description of each firearm and the serial number thereof. The records shall be available for inspection at all reasonable times by any law enforcement officer. *L.1978, c. 95, § 2C:58–1, eff. Sept. 1, 1979.*

2C:58–2. Retailing of firearms

a. Licensing of retail dealers and their employees. No retail dealer of firearms nor any employee of a retail dealer shall sell or expose for sale, or possess with the intent of selling, any firearm unless licensed to do so as hereinafter provided. The superintendent shall prescribe standards and qualifications for retail dealers of firearms and their employees for the protection of the public safety, health and welfare.

Applications shall be made in the form prescribed by the superintendent, accompanied by a fee of $50 payable to the superintendent, and shall be made to a judge of the Superior Court in the county where the applicant maintains his place of business. The judge shall grant a license to an applicant if he finds that the applicant meets the standards and qualifications established by the superintendent and that the applicant can be permitted to engage in business as a retail dealer of firearms or employee thereof without any danger to the public safety, health and welfare. Each license shall be valid for a period of three years from the date of issuance, and shall authorize the holder to sell firearms at retail in a specified municipality.

In addition, every retail dealer shall pay a fee of $5 for each employee actively engaged in the sale or purchase of firearms. The superintendent shall issue a license for each employee for whom said fee has been paid, which license shall be valid for so long as the employee remains in the employ of said retail dealer.

No license shall be granted to any retail dealer under the age of 21 years or to any employee of a retail dealer under the age of 18 or to any person who could not qualify to obtain a permit to purchase a handgun or a firearms purchaser identification card, or to any corporation, partnership or other business organization in which the actual or equitable controlling interest is held or possessed by such an ineligible person.

All licenses shall be granted subject to the following conditions, for breach of any of which the license shall be subject to revocation on the application of any law enforcement officer and after notice and hearing by the issuing court:

(1) The business shall be carried on only in the building or buildings designated in the license, provided that repairs may be made by the dealer or his employees outside of such premises.

(2) The license or a copy certified by the issuing authority shall be displayed at all times in a conspicuous place on the business premises where it can be easily read.

(3) No firearm or imitation thereof shall be placed in any window or in any other part of the premises where it can be readily seen from the outside.

(4) No rifle or shotgun, except antique rifles or shotguns, shall be delivered to any person unless such person possesses and exhibits a valid firearms purchaser identification card and furnishes the seller, on the form prescribed by the superintendent, a certification signed by him setting forth his name, permanent address, firearms purchaser identification card number and such other information as the superintendent may by rule or regulation require. The certification shall be retained by the dealer and shall be made available for inspection by any law enforcement officer at any reasonable time.

(5) No handgun shall be delivered to any person unless:

(a) Such person possesses and exhibits a valid permit to purchase a firearm and at least seven days have elapsed since the date of application for the permit;

(b) The person is personally known to the seller or presents evidence of his identity;

(c) The handgun is unloaded and securely wrapped;

(d) Except as otherwise provided in subparagraph (e) of this paragraph, the handgun is accompanied by a trigger lock or a locked case, gun box, container or other secure facility; provided, however, this provision shall not apply to antique handguns. The exemption afforded under this subparagraph for antique handguns shall be narrowly construed, limited solely to the requirements set forth herein and shall not be deemed to afford or authorize any other exemption from the regulatory provisions governing firearms set forth in chapter 39 and chapter 58 of Title 2C of the New Jersey Statutes; and

(e) On and after the first day of the sixth month following the date on which the list of personalized handguns is prepared and delivered pursuant to section 3 of P.L.2002, c. 130 (C.2C:58–2.4), the handgun is identified as a personalized handgun and included on that list or is an antique handgun. The provisions of subparagraph (d) of this section shall not apply to the delivery of a personalized handgun.

(6) The dealer shall keep a true record of every handgun sold, given or otherwise delivered or disposed of, in accordance with the provisions of subsections b. through e. of this section and the record shall note whether a trigger lock, locked case, gun box, container

or other secure facility was delivered along with the handgun.

(7) A dealer shall not knowingly deliver more than one handgun to any person within any 30–day period. This limitation shall not apply to:

(a) a federal, State, or local law enforcement officer or agency purchasing handguns for use by officers in the actual performance of their law enforcement duties;

(b) a collector of handguns as curios or relics as defined in Title 18, United States Code, section 921 (a) (13) who has in his possession a valid Collector of Curios and Relics License issued by the federal Bureau of Alcohol, Tobacco, Firearms and Explosives;

(c) transfers of handguns among licensed retail dealers, registered wholesale dealers and registered manufacturers;

(d) any transaction where the person has purchased a handgun from a licensed retail dealer and has returned that handgun to the dealer in exchange for another handgun within 30 days of the original transaction, provided the retail dealer reports the exchange transaction to the superintendent; or

(e) any transaction where the superintendent issues an exemption from the prohibition in this subsection pursuant to the provisions of section 4 of P.L.2009, c. 186 (C.2C:58–3.4).

b. Records. Every person engaged in the retail business of selling, leasing or otherwise transferring a handgun, as a retail dealer or otherwise, shall keep a register in which shall be entered the time of the sale, lease or other transfer, the date thereof, the name, age, date of birth, complexion, occupation, residence and a physical description including distinguishing physical characteristics, if any, of the purchaser, lessee or transferee, the name and permanent home address of the person making the sale, lease or transfer, the place of the transaction, and the make, model, manufacturer's number, caliber and other marks of identification on such handgun and such other information as the superintendent shall deem necessary for the proper enforcement of this chapter. The register shall be retained by the dealer and shall be made available at all reasonable hours for inspection by any law enforcement officer.

c. Forms of register. The superintendent shall prepare the form of the register as described in subsection b. of this section and furnish the same in triplicate to each person licensed to be engaged in the business of selling, leasing or otherwise transferring firearms.

d. Signatures in register. The purchaser, lessee or transferee of any handgun shall sign, and the dealer shall require him to sign his name to the register, in triplicate, and the person making the sale, lease or transfer shall affix his name, in triplicate, as a witness to the signature. The signatures shall constitute a representation of the accuracy of the information contained in the register.

e. Copies of register entries; delivery to chief of police or county clerk. Within five days of the date of the sale, assignment or transfer, the dealer shall deliver or mail by certified mail, return receipt requested, legible copies of the register forms to the office of the chief of police of the municipality in which the purchaser resides, or to the office of the captain of the precinct of the municipality in which the purchaser resides, and to the superintendent. If hand delivered a receipt shall be given to the dealer therefor.

Where a sale, assignment or transfer is made to a purchaser who resides in a municipality having no chief of police, the dealer shall, within five days of the transaction, mail a duplicate copy of the register sheet to the clerk of the county within which the purchaser resides.

L.1978, c. 95, § 2C:58–2, eff. Sept. 1, 1979. Amended by L.1979, c. 179, § 10, eff. Sept. 1, 1979; L.1999, c. 233, § 5; L.2002, c. 130, § 6, eff. Dec. 23, 2002; L.2009, c. 104, § 1, eff. Jan. 1, 2010; L.2009, c. 168, § 1, eff. Jan. 3, 2010; L.2009, c. 186, § 1, eff. Jan. 12, 2010.

2C:58–2.1. Guidelines

The Superintendent of State Police, in consultation with the Attorney General, shall promulgate guidelines to effectuate the purposes of P.L.1999, c. 233.

L.1999, c. 233, § 6.

2C:58–2.2. Legislative findings; personalized handguns

a. The Legislature finds:

New Jersey's commitment to firearms safety is unrivaled anywhere in the nation;

New Jersey was the first state to require retail dealers to include, as part of every handgun sale, either a State Police approved trigger lock or a locked case, gun box, container or other secure facility;

To encourage all firearms owners to practice safe storage, the State has waived all sales taxes on trigger locks, firearms lock-boxes and vaults and, under the "KeepSafe" program, offers an instant $5 rebate to all retail firearms purchasers who buy a compatible trigger locking device along with their firearm;

New Jersey was the first state to require all firearms dealers to prominently display State-provided firearms information and safety warnings;

New Jersey was one of the first states to make parents and guardians statutorily responsible for unwittingly or carelessly permitting minors under their control to gain access to loaded firearms;

New Jersey statutorily prohibits anyone under the age of 18 years from purchasing or otherwise acquiring a firearm and permits such minors to possess or carry a firearm only in a very limited number of strictly defined situations and under the direct supervision of a qualified parent, guardian or instructor;

To enforce this strict regulatory scheme, New Jersey imposes harsh penalties, including a mandatory minimum prison term of three years, on anyone who knowingly sells, transfers or gives a firearm to a person under the age of 18 years; and

New Jersey was the first state to allocate, as part of its annual Appropriations Act, moneys dedicated exclusively for the development of personal handgun technology, and the amount so allocated, $1,000,000, was one-fifth the total amount the federal government allocated toward the development of this important firearms safety technology in the same fiscal year.

b. The Legislature, therefore, declares:

It is within the public interest, and vital to the safety of our families and children, for New Jersey to take the bold and innovative step of fostering the development of personalized handguns by firearms manufacturers. To accomplish this objective, the Legislature determines that it should enact legislation designed to further enhance firearms safety by requiring that, within a specified period of time after the date on which these new personalized handguns are deemed to be available for retail sales purposes, no other type of handgun shall be sold or offered for sale by any registered or licensed firearms dealer in this State.

L.2002, c. 130, § 1, eff. Dec. 23, 2002.

2C:58–2.3. Retail sales availability; production model

a. On the first day of the sixth month following the effective date of P.L.2002, c. 130 (C.2C:58–2.2 et al.), the Attorney General shall report to the Governor and the Legislature as to the availability of personalized handguns for retail sales purposes. If the Attorney General determines that personalized handguns are not available for retail sales purposes, the Attorney General, every six months thereafter, shall report to the Governor and the Legislature as to the availability of personalized handguns for retail sales purposes until such time as the Attorney General shall deem that personalized handguns are available for retail sales purposes and so report to the Governor and the Legislature. In making this determination, the Attorney General may consult with any other neutral and detached public or private entity that may have useful information and expertise to assist in determining whether, through performance and other relevant indicators, a handgun meets the statutory definition of a personalized handgun set forth in N.J.S.2C:39–1.

b. For the purposes of this section, personalized handguns shall be deemed to be available for retail sales purposes if at least one manufacturer has delivered at least one production model of a personalized handgun to a registered or licensed wholesale or retail dealer in New Jersey or any other state. As used in this subsection, the term "production model" shall mean a handgun which is the product of a regular manufacturing process that produces multiple copies of the same handgun model, and shall not include a prototype or other unique specimen that is offered for sale.

L.2002, c. 130, § 2, eff. Dec. 23, 2002.

2C:58–2.4. List of personalized handguns that may be sold

a. On the first day of the 24th month following the date on which the Attorney General reports that personalized handguns are available for retail sales purposes pursuant to section 2 of P.L.2002, c. 130 (C.2C:58–2.3), the Attorney General shall direct the Superintendent of State Police to promulgate a list of personalized handguns that may be sold in the State. This list shall identify those handguns by manufacturer, model and caliber.

b. The list required under subsection a. of this section shall be prepared within six months of the Attorney General's directive to the superintendent and a copy thereof made available to registered and licensed firearms dealers in this State. Whenever a handgun is determined to meet the statutory definition of a personalized handgun as set forth in N.J.S.2C:39–1, the Attorney General shall report that determination in writing to the Governor and the Legislature within 60 days. The superintendent shall promptly amend and supplement the list to include handguns which meet the statutory definition of a personalized handgun as set forth in N.J.S.2C:39–1 or to remove previously listed handguns, if appropriate. Registered and licensed retail firearms dealers in this State shall be notified forthwith of any such changes in the list. The notice shall be given in a manner prescribed by rule and regulation. The Attorney General shall promulgate rules and regulations establishing a process for handgun manufacturers to demonstrate that their handguns meet the statutory definition of a personalized handgun set forth in N.J.S.2C:39–1 and request that their handgun be added to this list. These rules and regulations may require that the handgun manufacturer: (1) deliver a handgun or handguns to the Attorney General or his designee for testing; (2) pay a reasonable application fee; and (3) pay any reasonable costs incurred in, or associated with, the testing and independent scientific analysis of the handgun, including any analysis of the technology the manufacturer has incorporated within the handgun's design to limit its operational use, that is conducted to determine whether the handgun meets the statutory definition of a personalized handgun set forth in N.J.S.2C:39–1.

L.2002, c. 130, § 3, eff. Dec. 23, 2002.

2C:58–2.5. Sales; commission to qualify use by law enforcement; penalty

a. On and after the first day of the sixth month following the preparation and delivery of the list of personalized handguns which may be sold in the State pursuant to section 3 of P.L.2002, c. 130 (C.2C:58–2.4), no person registered or licensed by the superintendent

as a manufacturer, wholesale dealer of firearms, retail dealer of firearms or agent or employee of a wholesale or retail dealer of firearms pursuant to the provisions of N.J.S.2C:58–1 or N.J.S.2C:58–2 shall transport into this State, sell, expose for sale, possess with the intent of selling, assign or otherwise transfer any handgun unless it is a personalized handgun or an antique handgun.

b. The provisions of this section shall not apply to handguns to be sold, transferred, assigned and delivered for official use to: (1) State and local law enforcement officers of this State; (2) federal law enforcement officers and any other federal officers and employees required to carry firearms in the performance of their official duties and (3) members of the Armed Forces of the United States or of the National Guard.

c. The provisions of this section also shall not apply to handguns to be sold, transferred, assigned and delivered solely for use in competitive shooting matches sanctioned by the Civilian Marksmanship Program, the International Olympic Committee or USA Shooting. The Attorney General may promulgate rules and regulations governing the scope and application of the exemption afforded under this section. The Attorney General, by rule and regulation, may require, at a minimum, that a person acquiring a handgun pursuant to this section submit valid proof of participation in these sanctioned shooting matches.

d. No later than 30 days after the preparation and delivery of the list of personalized handguns which may be sold in the State pursuant to section 3 of P.L.2002, c. 130 (C.2C:58–2.4), there shall be established a seven-member commission in the Department of Law and Public Safety that shall meet at least once a year to determine whether personalized handguns qualify for use by State and local law enforcement officers. The Governor shall appoint the following six members of the commission: a county sheriff; a county law enforcement officer; a county prosecutor; one local law enforcement officer who shall be an active member of the New Jersey Fraternal Order of Police; one local law enforcement officer who shall be an active member of the New Jersey State Policemen's Benevolent Association; and an experienced firearms instructor qualified to teach a firearms training course approved by the Police Training Commission. The seventh member of the commission shall be the Superintendent of State Police.

The commission shall issue a report to the Attorney General upon its determination that personalized handguns qualify for use by State and local law enforcement officers. In making this determination, the commission shall consider any advantages and disadvantages to using these weapons in the performance of the official duties of law enforcement officers and shall give due regard to the safety of law enforcement officers and others. The commission shall expire thereafter. The Attorney General shall be authorized to promulgate rules and regulations that apply the provisions of this section to handguns to be sold, transferred, assigned and delivered for official use to State and local law enforcement officers upon a determination by the commission that personalized handguns qualify for use by State and local law enforcement officers.

e. A person who knowingly violates the provisions of this section is guilty of a crime of the fourth degree. *L.2002, c. 130, § 4, eff. Dec. 23, 2002.*

2C:58–2.6. Rules and regulations

The Attorney General, in accordance with the provisions of the "Administrative Procedure Act," P.L.1968, c. 410 (C. 52: 14B–1 et seq.), shall promulgate rules and regulations to effectuate the purposes of this act. *L.2002, c. 130, § 7, eff. Dec. 23, 2002.*

2C:58–3.   Purchase of firearms

a. Permit to purchase a handgun. No person shall sell, give, transfer, assign or otherwise dispose of, nor receive, purchase, or otherwise acquire a handgun unless the purchaser, assignee, donee, receiver or holder is licensed as a dealer under this chapter or has first secured a permit to purchase a handgun as provided by this section.

b. Firearms purchaser identification card. No person shall sell, give, transfer, assign or otherwise dispose of nor receive, purchase or otherwise acquire an antique cannon or a rifle or shotgun, other than an antique rifle or shotgun, unless the purchaser, assignee, donee, receiver or holder is licensed as a dealer under this chapter or possesses a valid firearms purchaser identification card, and first exhibits said card to the seller, donor, transferor or assignor, and unless the purchaser, assignee, donee, receiver or holder signs a written certification, on a form prescribed by the superintendent, which shall indicate that he presently complies with the requirements of subsection c. of this section and shall contain his name, address and firearms purchaser identification card number or dealer's registration number. The said certification shall be retained by the seller, as provided in paragraph (4) of subsection a. of N.J.S.2C:58–2, or, in the case of a person who is not a dealer, it may be filed with the chief of police of the municipality in which he resides or with the superintendent.

c. Who may obtain. No person of good character and good repute in the community in which he lives, and who is not subject to any of the disabilities set forth in this section or other sections of this chapter, shall be denied a permit to purchase a handgun or a firearms purchaser identification card, except as hereinafter set forth. No handgun purchase permit or firearms purchaser identification card shall be issued:

(1) To any person who has been convicted of any crime, or a disorderly persons offense involving an act of domestic violence as defined in section 3 of P.L.1991, c. 261 (C.2C:25–19), whether or not armed with or possessing a weapon at the time of such offense;

(2) To any drug dependent person as defined in section 2 of P.L.1970, c. 226 (C.24:21–2), to any person who is confined for a mental disorder to a hospital, mental institution or sanitarium, or to any person who is presently an habitual drunkard;

(3) To any person who suffers from a physical defect or disease which would make it unsafe for him to handle firearms, to any person who has ever been confined for a mental disorder, or to any alcoholic unless any of the foregoing persons produces a certificate of a medical doctor or psychiatrist licensed in New Jersey, or other satisfactory proof, that he is no longer suffering from that particular disability in such a manner that would interfere with or handicap him in the handling of firearms; to any person who knowingly falsifies any information on the application form for a handgun purchase permit or firearms purchaser identification card;

(4) To any person under the age of 18 years for a firearms purchaser identification card and to any person under the age of 21 years for a permit to purchase a handgun;

(5) To any person where the issuance would not be in the interest of the public health, safety or welfare;

(6) To any person who is subject to a restraining order issued pursuant to the "Prevention of Domestic Violence Act of 1991," P.L.1991, c. 261 (C.2C:25–17 et seq.) prohibiting the person from possessing any firearm;

(7) To any person who as a juvenile was adjudicated delinquent for an offense which, if committed by an adult, would constitute a crime and the offense involved the unlawful use or possession of a weapon, explosive or destructive device or is enumerated in subsection d. of section 2 of P.L.1997, c. 117 (C.2C:43–7.2); or

(8) To any person whose firearm is seized pursuant to the "Prevention of Domestic Violence Act of 1991," P.L.1991, c. 261 (C.2C:25–17 et seq.) and whose firearm has not been returned.

d. Issuance. The chief of police of an organized full–time police department of the municipality where the applicant resides or the superintendent, in all other cases, shall upon application, issue to any person qualified under the provisions of subsection c. of this section a permit to purchase a handgun or a firearms purchaser identification card.

Any person aggrieved by the denial of a permit or identification card may request a hearing in the Superior Court of the county in which he resides if he is a resident of New Jersey or in the Superior Court of the county in which his application was filed if he is a nonresident. The request for a hearing shall be made in writing within 30 days of the denial of the application for a permit or identification card. The applicant shall serve a copy of his request for a hearing upon the chief of police of the municipality in which he resides, if he is a resident of New Jersey, and upon the superintendent in all cases. The hearing shall be held and a record made thereof within 30 days of the receipt of the application for such hearing by the judge of the Superior Court. No formal pleading and no filing fee shall be required as a preliminary to such hearing. Appeals from the results of such hearing shall be in accordance with law.

e. Applications. Applications for permits to purchase a handgun and for firearms purchaser identification cards shall be in the form prescribed by the superintendent and shall set forth the name, residence, place of business, age, date of birth, occupation, sex and physical description, including distinguishing physical characteristics, if any, of the applicant, and shall state whether the applicant is a citizen, whether he is an alcoholic, habitual drunkard, drug dependent person as defined in section 2 of P.L.1970, c. 226 (C.24:21–2), whether he has ever been confined or committed to a mental institution or hospital for treatment or observation of a mental or psychiatric condition on a temporary, interim or permanent basis, giving the name and location of the institution or hospital and the dates of such confinement or commitment, whether he has been attended, treated or observed by any doctor or psychiatrist or at any hospital or mental institution on an inpatient or outpatient basis for any mental or psychiatric condition, giving the name and location of the doctor, psychiatrist, hospital or institution and the dates of such occurrence, whether he presently or ever has been a member of any organization which advocates or approves the commission of acts of force and violence to overthrow the Government of the United States or of this State, or which seeks to deny others their rights under the Constitution of either the United States or the State of New Jersey, whether he has ever been convicted of a crime or disorderly persons offense, whether the person is subject to a restraining order issued pursuant to the "Prevention of Domestic Violence Act of 1991," P.L.1991, c. 261 (C.2C:25–17 et seq.) prohibiting the person from possessing any firearm, and such other information as the superintendent shall deem necessary for the proper enforcement of this chapter. For the purpose of complying with this subsection, the applicant shall waive any statutory or other right of confidentiality relating to institutional confinement. The application shall be signed by the applicant and shall contain as references the names and addresses of two reputable citizens personally acquainted with him.

Application blanks shall be obtainable from the superintendent, from any other officer authorized to grant such permit or identification card, and from licensed retail dealers.

The chief police officer or the superintendent shall obtain the fingerprints of the applicant and shall have them compared with any and all records of fingerprints in the municipality and county in which the applicant resides and also the records of the State Bureau of Identification and the Federal Bureau of Investigation,

provided that an applicant for a handgun purchase permit who possesses a valid firearms purchaser identification card, or who has previously obtained a handgun purchase permit from the same licensing authority for which he was previously fingerprinted, and who provides other reasonably satisfactory proof of his identity, need not be fingerprinted again; however, the chief police officer or the superintendent shall proceed to investigate the application to determine whether or not the applicant has become subject to any of the disabilities set forth in this chapter.

f. Granting of permit or identification card; fee; term; renewal; revocation. The application for the permit to purchase a handgun together with a fee of $2, or the application for the firearms purchaser identification card together with a fee of $5, shall be delivered or forwarded to the licensing authority who shall investigate the same and, unless good cause for the denial thereof appears, shall grant the permit or the identification card, or both, if application has been made therefor, within 30 days from the date of receipt of the application for residents of this State and within 45 days for nonresident applicants. A permit to purchase a handgun shall be valid for a period of 90 days from the date of issuance and may be renewed by the issuing authority for good cause for an additional 90 days. A firearms purchaser identification card shall be valid until such time as the holder becomes subject to any of the disabilities set forth in subsection c. of this section, whereupon the card shall be void and shall be returned within five days by the holder to the superintendent, who shall then advise the licensing authority. Failure of the holder to return the firearms purchaser identification card to the superintendent within the said five days shall be an offense under subsection a. of N.J.S.2C:39–10. Any firearms purchaser identification card may be revoked by the Superior Court of the county wherein the card was issued, after hearing upon notice, upon a finding that the holder thereof no longer qualifies for the issuance of such permit. The county prosecutor of any county, the chief police officer of any municipality or any citizen may apply to such court at any time for the revocation of such card.

There shall be no conditions or requirements added to the form or content of the application, or required by the licensing authority for the issuance of a permit or identification card, other than those that are specifically set forth in this chapter.

g. Disposition of fees. All fees for permits shall be paid to the State Treasury if the permit is issued by the superintendent, to the municipality if issued by the chief of police, and to the county treasurer if issued by the judge of the Superior Court.

h. Form of permit; quadruplicate; disposition of copies. The permit shall be in the form prescribed by the superintendent and shall be issued to the applicant in quadruplicate. Prior to the time he receives the handgun from the seller, the applicant shall deliver to the seller the permit in quadruplicate and the seller shall complete all of the information required on the form. Within five days of the date of the sale, the seller shall forward the original copy to the superintendent and the second copy to the chief of police of the municipality in which the purchaser resides, except that in a municipality having no chief of police, such copy shall be forwarded to the superintendent. The third copy shall then be returned to the purchaser with the pistol or revolver and the fourth copy shall be kept by the seller as a permanent record.

i. Restriction on number of firearms person may purchase. Only one handgun shall be purchased or delivered on each permit and no more than one handgun shall be purchased within any 30–day period, but this limitation shall not apply to:

(1) a federal, State or local law enforcement officer or agency purchasing handguns for use by officers in the actual performance of their law enforcement duties;

(2) a collector of handguns as curios or relics as defined in Title 18, United States Code, section 921 (a) (13) who has in his possession a valid Collector of Curios and Relics License issued by the federal Bureau of Alcohol, Tobacco, Firearms and Explosives;

(3) transfers of handguns among licensed retail dealers, registered wholesale dealers and registered manufacturers;

(4) transfers of handguns from any person to a licensed retail dealer or a registered wholesale dealer or registered manufacturer;

(5) any transaction where the person has purchased a handgun from a licensed retail dealer and has returned that handgun to the dealer in exchange for another handgun within 30 days of the original transaction, provided the retail dealer reports the exchange transaction to the superintendent; or

(6) any transaction where the superintendent issues an exemption from the prohibition in this subsection pursuant to the provisions of section 4 of P.L.2009, c. 186 (C.2C:58–3.4).

The provisions of this subsection shall not be construed to afford or authorize any other exemption from the regulatory provisions governing firearms set forth in chapter 39 and chapter 58 of Title 2C of the New Jersey Statutes.

A person shall not be restricted as to the number of rifles or shotguns he may purchase, provided he possesses a valid firearms purchaser identification card and provided further that he signs the certification required in subsection b. of this section for each transaction.

j. Firearms passing to heirs or legatees. Notwithstanding any other provision of this section concerning the transfer, receipt or acquisition of a firearm, a permit to purchase or a firearms purchaser identification card shall not be required for the passing of a firearm upon the death of an owner thereof to his heir or legatee, whether the same be by testamentary bequest or by the laws of intestacy. The person who shall so receive, or acquire said firearm shall, however, be subject to all other provisions of this chapter. If the heir or legatee of such firearm does not qualify to possess or carry it, he may retain ownership of the firearm for the purpose of sale for a period not exceeding 180 days, or for such further limited period as may be approved by the chief law enforcement officer of the municipality in which the heir or legatee resides or the superintendent, provided that such firearm is in the custody of the chief law enforcement officer of the municipality or the superintendent during such period.

k. Sawed–off shotguns. Nothing in this section shall be construed to authorize the purchase or possession of any sawed–off shotgun.

l. Nothing in this section and in N.J.S.2C:58–2 shall apply to the sale or purchase of a visual distress signalling device approved by the United States Coast Guard, solely for possession on a private or commercial aircraft or any boat; provided, however, that no person under the age of 18 years shall purchase nor shall any person sell to a person under the age of 18 years such a visual distress signalling device.

L.1978, c. 95, § 2C:58–3, eff. Sept. 1, 1979. Amended by L.1979, c. 179, § 11, eff. Sept. 1, 1979; L.1981, c. 363, § 2, eff. Dec. 30, 1981; L.1982, c. 173, § 2, eff. Nov. 12, 1982; L.1983, c. 479, § 4, eff. Jan. 12, 1984; L.1991, c. 261, § 19, eff. Nov. 12, 1991; L.2000, c. 145, § 1; L.2001, c. 3, § 1, eff. Jan. 16, 2001; L.2003, c. 73, § 1, eff. May 5, 2003; L.2003, c. 277, § 4, eff. Jan. 14, 2004; L.2009, c. 104, § 2, eff. Jan. 1, 2010; L.2009, c. 168, § 2, eff. Jan. 3, 2010; L.2009, c. 186, § 2, eff. Jan. 12, 2010.

2C:58–3.1. Temporary transfer of firearms; duration; presence of owner or dealer

a. Notwithstanding the provisions of N.J.S.2C:39–9, N.J.S.2C:58–2, N.J. S.2C:58–3 or any other statute to the contrary concerning the transfer or disposition of firearms, the legal owner, or a dealer licensed under N.J.S.2C:58–2, may temporarily transfer a handgun, rifle or shotgun to another person who is 18 years of age or older, whether or not the person receiving the firearm holds a firearms purchaser identification card or a permit to carry a handgun. The person to whom a handgun, rifle or shotgun is temporarily transferred by the legal owner of the firearm or a licensed dealer may receive, possess, carry and use that handgun, rifle or shotgun, if the transfer is made upon a firing range operated by a licensed dealer, by a law enforcement agency, a legally recognized military organization or a rifle or pistol club which has filed a copy of its charter with the superintendent and annually submits to the superintendent a list of its members and if the firearm is received, possessed, carried and used for the sole purpose of target practice, trap or skeet shooting, or competition upon that firing range or instruction and training at any location.

A transfer under this subsection shall be for not more than eight consecutive hours in any 24–hour period and may be made for a set fee or an hourly charge.

The firearm shall be handled and used by the person to whom it is temporarily transferred only in the actual presence or under the direct supervision of the legal owner of the firearm, the dealer who transferred the firearm or any other person competent to supervise the handling and use of firearms and authorized to act for that purpose by the legal owner or licensed dealer. The legal owner of the firearm or the licensed dealer shall be on the premises or the property of the firing range during the entire time that the firearm is in the possession of the person to whom it is temporarily transferred.

The term "legal owner" as used in this subsection means a natural person and does not include an organization, commercial enterprise, or a licensed manufacturer, wholesaler or dealer of firearms.

b. Notwithstanding the provisions of N.J.S.2C:39–9, N.J.S.2C:58–2, N.J.S.2C:58–3 or any other statute to the contrary concerning the transfer and disposition of firearms, a legal owner of a shotgun or a rifle may temporarily transfer that firearm to another person who is 18 years of age or older, whether or not the person receiving the firearm holds a firearms purchaser identification card. The person to whom a shotgun or rifle is temporarily transferred by the legal owner may receive, possess, carry and use that shotgun or rifle in the woods or fields or upon the waters of this State for the purposes of hunting if the transfer is made in the woods or fields or upon the waters of this State, the shotgun or rifle is legal and appropriate for hunting and the person to whom the firearm is temporarily transferred possesses a valid license to hunt with a firearm, and a valid rifle permit if the firearm is a rifle, obtained in accordance with the provisions of chapter 3 of Title 23 of the Revised Statutes.

The transfer of a firearm under this subsection shall be for not more than eight consecutive hours in any 24–hour period and no fee shall be charged for the transfer.

The legal owner of the firearm which is temporarily transferred shall remain in the actual presence or in the vicinity of the person to whom it was transferred during the entire time that the firearm is in that person's possession.

The term "legal owner" as used in this subsection means a natural person and does not include an organization, commercial enterprise, or a licensed manufacturer, wholesaler or dealer of firearms.

c. No firearm shall be temporarily transferred or received under the provisions of subsections a. or b. of this section for the purposes described in section 1 of P.L.1983, c. 229 (C.2C:39–14).

d. An owner or dealer shall not transfer a firearm to any person pursuant to the provisions of this section if the owner or dealer knows the person does not meet the qualifications set forth in subsection c. of N.J.S.2C:58–3 for obtaining or holding a firearms purchaser identification card or a handgun purchase permit. A person shall not receive, possess, carry or use a firearm pursuant to the provisions of this section if the person knows he does not meet the qualifications set forth in subsection c. of N.J.S.2C:58–3 for obtaining or holding a firearms purchaser identification card or a handgun purchase permit.

L.1992, c. 74, § 1, eff. July 31, 1992. Amended by L.2000, c. 145, § 4, eff. Jan. 1, 2001.

2C:58–3.2. Transfer of firearm; participation in training courses

a. Notwithstanding the provisions of N.J.S.2C:39–9, N.J.S.2C:58–2, N.J.S.2C:58–3 or any other statute to the contrary, a person who is certified as an instructor in the use, handling and maintenance of firearms by the Police Training Commission, the Division of Fish, Game and Wildlife and the State Park Service in the Department of Environmental Protection, the Director of Civilian Marksmanship of the United States Department of the Army or by a recognized rifle or pistol association that certifies instructors may transfer a firearm temporarily in accordance with the terms of this section to a person participating in a training course for the use, handling and maintenance of firearms by the Police Training Commission, the Division of Fish, Game and Wildlife, the Director of Civilian Marksmanship or by a recognized rifle or pistol association that certifies instructors. The person to whom a firearm is transferred by a certified instructor in accordance with the terms of this section may receive, possess, carry and use the firearm temporarily during the sessions of the course for the purpose of training and participating in the course.

b. A transfer of a firearm under this section may be made only if:

(1) the transfer is made upon a firearms range or, if the firearm is unloaded, in an area designated and appropriate for the training;

(2) the transfer is made during the sessions of the firearms course for the sole purpose of participating in the course;

(3) the transfer is made for not more than eight consecutive hours in any 24–hour period; and

(4) the transferred firearm is used and handled only in the actual presence and under the direct supervision of the instructor.

c. The transfer permitted by this section may be made whether or not the person participating in the course holds a firearms license, firearms purchaser identification card or a handgun purchase permit. However, an instructor shall not knowingly transfer a firearm under the terms of this section to a person who does not meet the qualifications set forth in subsection c. of N.J.S.2C:58–3 for obtaining or holding a firearms purchaser identification card or a handgun purchase permit, and a person who knows that he does not meet such qualifications shall not receive the transferred firearm under the terms of this section.

d. No firearm shall be transferred or received under the provisions of this section for purposes described in section 1 of P.L.1983, c. 229 (C.2C:39–14).

L.1997, c. 375, § 1, eff. Jan. 19, 1998.

2C:58–3.3. Handgun ammunition sales and transfers

a. As used in this act,[1] "handgun ammunition" means ammunition specifically designed to be used only in a handgun. "Handgun ammunition" shall not include blank ammunition, air gun pellets, flare gun ammunition, nail gun ammunition, paint ball ammunition, or any non-fixed ammunition.

b. No person shall sell, give, transfer, assign or otherwise dispose of, or receive, purchase, or otherwise acquire handgun ammunition unless the purchaser, assignee, donee, receiver or holder is licensed as a manufacturer, wholesaler, or dealer under this chapter or is the holder of and possesses a valid firearms purchaser identification card, a valid copy of a permit to purchase a handgun, or a valid permit to carry a handgun and first exhibits such card or permit to the seller, donor, transferor or assignor.

c. No person shall sell, give, transfer, assign or otherwise dispose of handgun ammunition to a person who is under 21 years of age.

d. The provisions of this section shall not apply to a collector of firearms or ammunition as curios or relics who purchases, receives, acquires, possesses, or transfers handgun ammunition which is recognized as being historical in nature or of historical significance.

e. A person who violates this section shall be guilty of a crime of the fourth degree, except that nothing contained herein shall be construed to prohibit the sale, transfer, assignment or disposition of handgun ammunition to or the purchase, receipt or acceptance of ammunition by a law enforcement agency or law enforcement official for law enforcement purposes.

f. Nothing in this section shall be construed to prohibit the transfer of ammunition for use in a lawfully transferred firearm in accordance with the provisions of section 1 of P.L.1992, c. 74 (C.2C:58–3.1), section 1 of P.L.1997, c. 375 (C.2C:58–3.2) or section 14 of P.L.1979, c. 179 (C.2C:58–6.1).

g. Nothing in this section shall be construed to prohibit the sale of a de minimis amount of handgun ammunition at a firearms range operated by a licensed dealer; a law enforcement agency; a legally recognized military organization; or a rifle or pistol club which has filed a copy of its charter with the superintendent for immediate use at that range.

L.2007, c. 318, § 1, eff. April 1, 2008.

1 L.2007, c. 318 (N.J.S.A. § 2C:58–3.3).

2C:58–3.4. Exemption from restrictions on the purchase of handguns; applicant certification; denial; appeal

a. The superintendent may grant an exemption from the restriction on the purchase of handguns set forth in subsection i. of N.J.S.2C:58–3 if the applicant demonstrates to the satisfaction of the superintendent that the applicant's request meets one of the following conditions:

(1) The application is to purchase multiple handguns from a person who obtained the handguns through inheritance or intestacy;

(2) The applicant is a collector of handguns and has a need to purchase or otherwise receive multiple handguns in the same transaction or within a 30–day period in furtherance of the applicant's collecting activities. As used in this paragraph, "need" shall include, but not be limited to, situations where there is a reasonable likelihood that the additional handguns sought to be purchased would not be readily available after the 30–day period, that it would not be feasible or practical to purchase the handguns separately, or that prohibiting the purchase of more than one handgun within a 30–day period would have a materially adverse impact on the applicant's ability to enhance his collection. As used in this paragraph, "collector" shall include any person who devotes time and attention to acquiring firearms for the enhancement of the person's collection: as curios; for inheritance; for historical, investment, training and competitive, recreational, educational, scientific, or defensive purposes; or any or other lawful related purpose. If an applicant is a member of an organized gun club; firearms competitors organization; firearms collectors organization; or any other organization dedicated to the acquisition, preservation, or use of firearms for historical, investment, training and competitive, recreational, educational, scientific, or defensive purposes, or any other lawful related purpose, such membership shall be considered in determining whether the applicant qualifies as a collector; or

(3) The applicant participates in sanctioned handgun shooting competitions and needs to purchase or otherwise receive multiple handguns in a single transaction or within a 30–day period, and the need is related to the applicant's competitive shooting activities, including use in or training for sanctioned competitions.

b. The applicant shall certify, on a form prescribed by the superintendent, the specific exemption sought and the particular handguns to be purchased. This form shall be submitted to the superintendent at the same time as the permit to purchase a handgun, along with any pertinent documentation supporting the need for an exemption. If the information concerning the particular handguns to be purchased is not available when the form is submitted, that information shall be provided to the superintendent as soon as practicable thereafter. The superintendent shall consider the veracity, accuracy, and completeness of the information provided in determining whether the applicant meets the requirements for an exemption pursuant to this section. In considering whether an applicant qualifies as a collector under paragraph (2) of subsection a. of this section, the superintendent shall not consider the number of guns in the applicant's collection. In considering an exemption sought under paragraph (2) of subsection a. of this section, the superintendent shall not consider the merit or validity of the applicant's collecting activities.

The superintendent shall not grant an exemption if he finds a reasonable likelihood that the public safety would be endangered by granting the exemption, including but not limited to instances where the applicant may be purchasing a handgun to give, sell or distribute to a person who would not qualify to purchase or otherwise acquire a handgun under the provisions of this chapter.

The exemptions set forth in this section shall not be construed and are not intended to authorize multiple handgun purchases where the sole justification set forth by the applicant is that the seller offers a discount for the purchase of more than one handgun.

c. Any person aggrieved by the denial of a request for an exemption pursuant to this paragraph may request a hearing in the Superior Court. The request for a hearing shall be made within 30 days of the denial of the application for an exemption. The applicant shall serve a copy of his request for a hearing upon the superintendent. The hearing shall be held and a record made thereof within 30 days of the receipt for the application for such a hearing by the judge of the Superior Court. The judge shall grant the request for the exemption if the judge finds that the denial of the applicant's request was an abuse of discretion, arbitrary or capricious, or a misapplication of the requirements for an exemption as a matter of law.

d. Notwithstanding the provisions of the "Administrative Procedure Act," P.L.1968, c. 410 (C.52:14B–1 et seq.), the superintendent may adopt, immediately upon filing with the Office of Administrative Law, such temporary regulations as the superintendent deems necessary to implement the provisions of P.L.2009, c. 186 (C.2C:58–3.4 et al.). The regulations so adopted shall be effective for a period not to exceed 270 days from the date of the filing, but in no case shall those regulations be in effect one year after the effective date of P.L.2009, c. 186 (C.2C:58–3.4 et al.). The regulations may thereafter be amended, adopted or readopted by the superintendent as the superintendent deems necessary in accordance with the requirements of the "Administrative Procedure Act."

L.2009, c. 186, § 4, eff. Jan. 12, 2010.

2C:58–4. Permits to carry handguns

a. **Scope and duration of authority.** Any person who holds a valid permit to carry a handgun issued pursuant to this section shall be authorized to carry a handgun in all parts of this State, except as prohibited by section 2C:39–5e. One permit shall be sufficient for all handguns owned by the holder thereof, but the permit shall apply only to a handgun carried by the actual and legal holder of the permit.

All permits to carry handguns shall expire 2 years from the date of issuance or, in the case of an employee of an armored car company, upon termination of his employment by the company occurring prior thereto whichever is earlier in time, and they may thereafter be renewed every 2 years in the same manner and subject to the same conditions as in the case of original applications.

b. **Application forms.** All applications for permits to carry handguns, and all applications for renewal of such permits, shall be made on the forms prescribed by the superintendent. Each application shall set forth the full name, date of birth, sex, residence, occupation, place of business or employment, and physical description of the applicant, and such other information as the superintendent may prescribe for the determination of the applicant's eligibility for a permit and for the proper enforcement of this chapter. The application shall be signed by the applicant under oath, and shall be indorsed by three reputable persons who have known the applicant for at least 3 years preceding the date of application, and who shall certify thereon that the applicant is a person of good moral character and behavior.

c. **Investigation and approval.** Each application shall in the first instance be submitted to the chief police officer of the municipality in which the applicant resides, or to the superintendent, (1) if the applicant is an employee of an armored car company, or (2) if there is no chief police officer in the municipality where the applicant resides, or (3) if the applicant does not reside in this State. The chief police officer, or the superintendent, as the case may be, shall cause the fingerprints of the applicant to be taken and compared with any and all records maintained by the municipality, the county in which it is located, the State Bureau of Identification and the Federal Bureau of Identification. He shall also determine and record a complete description of each handgun the applicant intends to carry.

No application shall be approved by the chief police officer or the superintendent unless the applicant demonstrates that he is not subject to any of the disabilities set forth in 2C:58–3c., that he is thoroughly familiar with the safe handling and use of handguns, and that he has a justifiable need to carry a handgun. If the application is not approved by the chief police officer or the superintendent within 60 days of filing, it shall be deemed to have been approved, unless the applicant agrees to an extension of time in writing.

d. **Issuance by Superior Court; fee.** If the application has been approved by the chief police officer or the superintendent, as the case may be, the applicant shall forthwith present it to the Superior Court of the county in which the applicant resides, or to the Superior Court in any county where he intends to carry a handgun, in the case of a nonresident or employee of an armored car company. The court shall issue the permit to the applicant if, but only if, it is satisfied that the applicant is a person of good character who is not subject to any of the disabilities set forth in section 2C:58–3c., that he is thoroughly familiar with the safe handling and use of handguns, and that he has a justifiable need to carry a handgun. The court may at its discretion issue a limited-type permit which would restrict the applicant as to the types of handguns he may carry and where and for what purposes such handguns may be carried. At the time of issuance, the applicant shall pay to the county clerk of the county where the permit was issued a permit fee of $20.00.

e. Appeals from denial of applications. Any person aggrieved by the denial by the chief police officer or the superintendent of approval for a permit to carry a handgun may request a hearing in the Superior Court of the county in which he resides or in any county in which he intends to carry a handgun, in the case of a nonresident, by filing a written request for such a hearing within 30 days of the denial. Copies of the request shall be served upon the superintendent, the county prosecutor and the chief police officer of the municipality where the applicant resides, if he is a resident of this State. The hearing shall be held within 30 days of the filing of the request, and no formal pleading or filing fee shall be required. Appeals from the determination at such a hearing shall be in accordance with law and the rules governing the courts of this State.

If the superintendent or chief police officer approves an application and the Superior Court denies the application and refuses to issue a permit, the applicant may appeal such denial in accordance with law and the rules governing the courts of this State.

f. Revocation of permits. Any permit issued under this section shall be void at such time as the holder thereof becomes subject to any of the disabilities set forth in section 2C:58–3c., and the holder of such a void permit shall immediately surrender the permit to the superintendent who shall give notice to the licensing authority.

Any permit may be revoked by the Superior Court, after hearing upon notice to the holder, if the court finds that the holder is no longer qualified for the issuance of such a permit. The county prosecutor of any county, the chief police officer of any municipality, the superintendent or any citizen may apply to the court at any time for the revocation of any permit issued pursuant to this section.

L.1978, c. 95, § 2C:58–4, eff. Sept. 1, 1979. Amended by L.1979, c. 179, § 12, eff. Sept. 1, 1979; L.1981, c. 135, § 1, eff. June 1, 1981.

2C:58–4.1. Employee of armored car company; application; letter from chief executive officer

In addition to the requirements of N.J.S. 2C:58–4 any application to carry a handgun by an employee of an armored car company shall be accompanied by a letter from the chief executive officer of the armored car company verifying employment of the applicant; endorsing approval of the application; and agreeing to notify the superintendent forthwith upon the termination of the employee [1] of any person to whom a permit is issued and to obtain from the employee the permit which shall thereupon be surrendered to the superintendent.

L.1981, c. 135, § 2, eff. June 1, 1981.

[1] So in original. Probably should be "employment".

2C:58–5. Licenses to possess and carry machine guns and assault firearms

a. Any person who desires to purchase, possess and carry a machine gun or assault firearm in this State may apply for a license to do so by filing in the Superior Court in the county in which he resides, or conducts his business if a nonresident, a written application setting forth in detail his reasons for desiring such a license. The Superior Court shall refer the application to the county prosecutor for investigation and recommendation. A copy of the prosecutor's report, together with a copy of the notice of the hearing on the application, shall be served upon the superintendent and the chief police officer of every municipality in which the applicant intends to carry the machine gun or assault firearm, unless, for good cause shown, the court orders notice to be given wholly or in part by publication.

b. No license shall be issued to any person who would not qualify for a permit to carry a handgun under section 2C:58–4, and no license shall be issued unless the court finds that the public safety and welfare so require. Any person aggrieved by the decision of the court in granting or denying an application, including the applicant, the prosecutor, or any law enforcement officer entitled to notice under subsection a. who appeared in opposition to the application, may appeal said decision in accordance with law and the rules governing the courts of this State.

c. Upon the issuance of any license under this section, true copies of such license shall be filed with the superintendent and the chief police officer of the municipality where the licensee resides or has his place of business.

d. In issuing any license under this section, the court shall attach thereto such conditions and limitations as it deems to be in the public interest. Unless otherwise provided by court order at the time of issuance, each license shall expire one year from the date of issuance, and may be renewed in the same manner and under the same conditions as apply to original applications.

e. Any license may be revoked by the Superior Court, after a hearing upon notice to the holder thereof, if the court finds that the holder is no longer qualified for the issuance of such a license or that revocation is necessary for the public safety and welfare. Any citizen may apply to the court for revocation of a license issued under this section.

f. A filing fee of $75.00 shall be required for each application filed pursuant to the provisions of this section. Of this filing fee, $25.00 shall be forwarded to the State Treasury for deposit in the account used by the Violent Crimes Compensation Board in satisfying claims and for related administrative costs pursuant to the provisions of the "Criminal Injuries Compensation Act of 1971," P.L.1971, c. 317 (C.52:4B–1 et seq.).

g. Any license granted pursuant to the provisions of this section shall expire two years from the date of issuance and may be renewed in the same manner and under the same conditions as apply to original applications. If the holder of a license dies, the holder's heirs or estate shall have 90 days to dispose of that firearm as provided in section 12 of P.L.1990, c. 32 (C. 2C:58–13).

h. If an assault firearm licensed pursuant to the provisions of this section is used in the commission of a crime, the holder of the license for that assault firearm shall be civilly liable for any damages resulting from that crime. The liability imposed by this subsection shall not apply if the assault firearm used in the commission of the crime was stolen and the license holder reported the theft of the firearm to law enforcement authorities within 24 hours of the license holder's knowledge of the theft.

i. Nothing in P.L.1990 c. 32 (C. 2C:58–12 et al.) shall be construed to abridge any exemptions provided under N.J.S.2C:39–6.

L.1978, c. 95, § 2C:58–5, eff. Sept. 1, 1979. Amended by L.1979, c. 179, § 13, eff. Sept. 1, 1979; L.1990, c. 32, § 9, eff. May 30, 1990.

2C:58–6. Repealed by L.1979, c. 178, § 147, eff. Sept. 1, 1979

2C:58–6.1. Possession of firearms by minors; exceptions

a. No person under the age of 18 years shall purchase, barter or otherwise acquire a firearm and no person under the age of 21 years shall purchase, barter or otherwise acquire a handgun, unless the person is authorized to possess the handgun in connection with the performance of official duties under the provisions of N.J.S.2C:39–6.

b. No person under the age of 18 years shall possess, carry, fire or use a firearm except as provided under paragraphs (1), (2), (3) and (4) of this subsection; and, unless authorized in connection with the performance of official duties under the provisions of N.J.S.2C:39–6, no person under the age of 21 years shall possess, carry, fire or use a handgun except under the following circumstances:

(1) In the actual presence or under the direct supervision of his father, mother or guardian, or some other person who holds a permit to carry a handgun or a firearms purchaser identification card, as the case may be; or

(2) For the purpose of military drill under the auspices of a legally recognized military organization and under competent supervision; or

(3) For the purpose of competition or target practice in and upon a firing range approved by the governing body of the municipality in which the range is located or the National Rifle Association and which is under competent supervision at the time of such supervision or target practice or instruction and training at any location; or

(4) For the purpose of hunting during the regularly designated hunting season, provided that he possesses a valid hunting license and has successfully completed a hunter's safety course taught by a qualified instructor or conservation officer and possesses a certificate indicating the successful completion of such a course.

c. A person who violates this section shall be guilty of a crime of the fourth degree. For purposes of this section the fact that the act would not constitute a crime if committed by an adult shall not be deemed to prohibit or require waiver of family court jurisdiction pursuant to N.J.S.2C: 4–11 or to preclude a finding of delinquency under the "New Jersey Code of Juvenile Justice," P.L.1982, c. 77 (C.2A:4A–20 et seq.), P.L.1982, c. 79 (C.2A:4A–60 et seq.), P.L.1982, c. 80 (C.2A:4A–76 et seq.) and P.L.1982, c. 81 (C.2A:4A–70 et seq.).

L.1979, c. 179, § 14, eff. Sept. 1, 1979. Amended by L.1980, c. 52, § 1, eff. June 27, 1980; L.2000, c. 145, § 3, eff. Jan. 1, 2001.

2C:58–7. Persons possessing explosives or destructive devices to notify police

a. Any person who becomes the possessor of any explosive, destructive device, or ammunition therefor, which is or may be loaded or otherwise dangerous, except such as is possessed for any lawful commercial or other purpose in connection with which the use of explosives is authorized or as is authorized in subsection d. of N.J.S. 2C:39–6, shall within 15 days notify the police authorities of the municipality in which he resides or the State Police that the same is in his possession and shall present the same to them for inspection.

b. When any such ammunition, explosive or destructive device is presented for inspection it shall be inspected to ascertain whether or not it is loaded or of a dangerous character, and if it is found to be loaded or of dangerous character, it shall be destroyed or be unloaded or so processed as to remove its dangerous character before being returned to the possessor.

c. Any police officer having reasonable cause to believe that any person is possessed of any such ammunition, explosive, or destructive device shall investigate, under a proper search warrant when necessary, and shall seize the same for the purpose of inspection, unloading, processing or destruction, as provided in this section, and the same shall not be returned to the possessor thereof until it has been unloaded or so processed.

L.1978, c. 95, § 2C:58–7, eff. Sept. 1, 1979. Amended by L.1983, c. 479, § 5, eff. Jan. 12, 1984.

2C:58–8. Certain wounds and injuries to be reported

a. Every case of a wound, burn or any other injury arising from or caused by a firearm, destructive device, explosive or weapon shall be reported at once to the police authorities of the municipality where the person reporting is located or to the State Police by the physician consulted, attending or treating the case or the manager, superintendent or other person in charge, whenever such case is presented for treatment or treated in a hospital, sanitarium or other institution. This subsection shall not, however, apply to wounds, burns or injuries received by a member of the armed forces of the United States or the State of New Jersey while engaged in the actual performance of duty.

b. Every case which contains the criteria defined in this subsection shall be reported at once to the police authorities of the municipality where the person reporting is located, or to the Division of State Police, by the physician consulted, attending, or treating the injury, or by the manager, superintendent, or other person in charge, whenever such case is presented for treatment or treated in a hospital, sanitarium or any other institution, facility, or office where medical care is provided. This subsection shall not apply to injuries received by a member of the armed forces of the United States or the State of New Jersey while engaged in the actual performance of duty.

The defined criteria shall consist of a flame burn injury accompanied by one or more of the following factors:

(1) A fire accelerant was used in the incident causing the injury and the presence of an accelerant creates a reasonable suspicion that the patient committed arson in violation of N.J.S.2C:17–1.

(2) Treatment for the injury was sought after an unreasonable delay of time.

(3) Changes or discrepancies in the account of the patient or accompanying person concerning the cause of the injury which creates a reasonable suspicion that the patient committed arson in violation of N.J.S.2C:17–1.

(4) Voluntary statement by the patient or accompanying person that the patient was injured during the commission of arson in violation of N.J.S.2C:17–1.

(5) Voluntary statement by the patient or accompanying person that the patient was injured during a suicide attempt or the commission of criminal homicide in violation of N.J.S.2C:11–1.

(6) Voluntary statement by the patient or accompanying person that the patient has exhibited fire setting behavior prior to the injury or has received counseling for such behavior.

(7) Any other factor determined by the bureau of fire safety in the Department of Community Affairs from information in the burn patient arson registry established under section 4 of P.L.1991, c. 433 (C. 52:27D–25d3) to typify a patient whose injuries were caused during the commission of arson in violation of N.J.S.2C:17–1.

L.1978, c. 95, § 2C:58–8, eff. Sept. 1, 1979. Amended by L.1991, c. 433, § 1, eff. April 17, 1992.

2C:58–9. Certain convictions to be reported

Every conviction under any provision of chapter 39 of this code of a person who is not a citizen of the United States, shall be certified to the proper officer of the United States Government by the county prosecutor of the county in which such conviction was had, or by the Attorney General or his representative.

L.1978, c. 95, § 2C:58–9, eff. Sept. 1, 1979.

2C:58–10. Incendiary or tracer ammunition

No incendiary or tracer type ammunition shall be discharged anywhere in this State except for law enforcement purposes by law enforcement officers in the course of their official duties or by members of legally recognized military organizations during the actual course of their official duties in or upon military establishments or ranges constructed or maintained for such purposes. Nonincendiary shotgun tracer ammunition may, however, be used on a trap or skeet field for target purposes. Nothing in this section shall prohibit the carrying or possession for distress signal purposes of a visual distress signalling device approved by the United States Coast Guard aboard a private or commercial aircraft or any boat.

L.1978, c. 95, § 2C:58–10, eff. Sept. 1, 1979. Amended by L.1982, c. 173, § 3, eff. Nov. 12, 1982.

2C:58–11. Repealed by L.1979, c. 178, § 147, eff. Sept. 1, 1979

2C:58–12. Assault firearms; registration; death of registrant; civil liability for use in crime

a. Within 90 days of the effective date of P.L.1990, c. 32 (C. 2C:58–12 et al.), the Attorney General shall promulgate a list by trade name of any assault firearm which the Attorney General determines is an assault firearm which is used for legitimate target-shooting purposes. This list shall include, but need not be limited to, the Colt AR–15 and any other assault firearm used in competitive shooting matches sanctioned by the Director of Civilian Marksmanship of the United States Department of the Army.

b. The owner of an assault firearm purchased on or before May 1, 1990 which is on the list of assault firearms determined by the Attorney General to be legitimate for target-shooting purposes shall have one year from the effective date of P.L.1990, c. 32 (C.

2C:58–12 et al.) to register that firearm. In order to register an assault firearm, the owner shall:

(1) Complete an assault firearm registration statement, in the form to be prescribed by the Superintendent of the State Police;

(2) Pay a registration fee of $50.00 per each assault firearm;

(3) Produce for inspection a valid firearms purchaser identification card, a valid permit to carry handguns, or a copy of the permit to purchase a handgun which was used to purchase the assault firearm which is being registered; and

(4) Submit valid proof that the person is a member of a rifle or pistol club in existence prior to the effective date of P.L.1990, c. 32 (C. 2C:58–12 et al.).

Membership in a rifle or pistol club shall not be considered valid unless the person joined the club no later than 210 days after the effective date of P.L.1990, c. 32 (C. 2C:58–12 et al.) and unless the rifle or pistol club files its charter with the Superintendent no later than 180 days following the effective date of P.L.1990, c. 32 (C. 2C:58–12 et al.). The rifle or pistol club charter shall contain the name and address of the club's headquarters and the name of the club's officers.

The information to be provided in the registration statement shall include, but shall not be limited to: the name and address of the registrant; the number or numbers on the registrant's firearms purchaser identification card, permit to carry handguns, or permit to purchase a handgun; the name, address, and telephone number of the rifle or pistol club in which the registrant is a member; and the make, model, and serial number of the assault firearm being registered. Each registration statement shall be signed by the registrant, and the signature shall constitute a representation of the accuracy of the information contained in the registration statement.

c. For an applicant who resides in a municipality with an organized full-time police department, the registration shall take place at the main office of the police department. For all other applicants, the registration shall take place at any State Police station.

d. Within 60 days of the effective date of P.L.1990, c. 32 (C. 2C:58–12 et al.), the Superintendent shall prepare the form of registration statement as described in subsection b. of this section and shall provide a suitable supply of statements to each organized full-time municipal police department and each State Police station.

e. One copy of the completed assault firearms registration statement shall be returned to the registrant, a second copy shall be sent to the Superintendent, and, if the registration takes place at a municipal police department, a third copy shall be retained by that municipal police department.

f. If the owner of an assault firearm which has been registered pursuant to this section dies, the owner's heirs or estate shall have 90 days to dispose of that firearm in accordance with section 12 of P.L.1990, c. 32 (C.2C:58–13).

g. If an assault firearm registered pursuant to the provisions of this section is used in the commission of a crime, the registrant of that assault firearm shall be civilly liable for any damages resulting from that crime. The liability imposed by this subsection shall not apply if the assault firearm used in the commission of the crime was stolen and the registrant reported the theft of the firearm to law enforcement authorities within 24 hours of the registrant's knowledge of the theft.

h. Of the registration fee required pursuant to subsection b. of this section, $20.00 shall be forwarded to the State Treasury for deposit in the account used by the Violent Crimes Compensation Board in satisfying claims and for related administrative costs pursuant to the provisions of the "Criminal Injuries Compensation Act of 1971," P.L.1971, c. 317 (C.52:4B–1 et seq.).

L.1990, c. 32, § 11, eff. May 30, 1990.

2C:58–13. One year period to transfer, render inoperable, or surrender assault firearm in lieu of registration

a. Any person who legally owns an assault firearm on the effective date of this act and who is unable to register or chooses not to register the firearm pursuant to section 11 of P.L.1990, c. 32 (C.2C:58–12) may retain possession of that firearm for a period not to exceed one year from the effective date of this act. During this time period, the owner of the assault firearm shall either:

(1) Transfer the assault firearm to any person or firm lawfully entitled to own or possess such firearm;

(2) Render the assault firearm inoperable; or

(3) Voluntarily surrender the assault firearm pursuant to the provisions of N.J.S.2C:39–12.

b. If the owner of an assault firearm elects to render the firearm inoperable, the owner shall file a certification on a form prescribed by the Superintendent of the State Police indicating the date on which the firearm was rendered inoperable. This certification shall be filed with either the chief law enforcement officer of the municipality in which the owner resides or, in the case of an owner who resides outside this State but stores or possesses an assault firearm in this State, with the Superintendent of the State Police.

c. As used in this section, "inoperable" means that the firearm is altered in such a manner that it cannot be immediately fired and that the owner or possessor of the firearm does not possess or have control over the parts necessary to make the firearm operable.

L.1990, c. 32, § 12, eff. May 30, 1990.

2C:58–14. Report by Attorney General to Legislature regarding assault firearms

Within 180 days of the enactment of P.L.1990, c. 32 (C. 2C:58–12 et al.), and annually thereafter, the Attorney General shall present a report to the Legislature which includes the types and quantities of firearms surrendered or rendered inoperable pursuant to section 12 of this act [1] and the number and types of criminal offenses involving assault firearms and any recommendations, including additions or deletions to the inventory of assault firearms delineated in N.J.S.2C:39–1, which the Attorney General believes should be considered by the Legislature.

L.1990, c. 32, § 13, eff. May 30, 1990.

[1] N.J.S.A. § 2C:58–13.

2C:58–15. Access by minors to loaded firearm; disorderly persons offense; exceptions

a. A person who knows or reasonably should know that a minor is likely to gain access to a loaded firearm at a premises under the person's control commits a disorderly persons offense if a minor gains access to the firearm, unless the person:

(1) Stores the firearm in a securely locked box or container;

(2) Stores the firearm in a location which a reasonable person would believe to be secure; or

(3) Secures the firearm with a trigger lock.

b. This section shall not apply:

(1) To activities authorized by section 14 of P.L.1979, c. 179 (C. 2C:58–6.1), concerning the lawful use of a firearm by a minor; or

(2) Under circumstances where a minor obtained a firearm as a result of an unlawful entry by any person.

c. As used in this act, "minor" means a person under the age of 16.

L.1991, c. 397, § 1, eff. Jan. 17, 1992.

2C:58–16. Warning to purchasers of criminal liability for leaving loaded firearm within access by minor

a. Upon the retail sale or transfer of any firearm, the retail dealer or his employee shall deliver to the purchaser or transferee the following written warning, printed in block letters not less than one-fourth of an inch in height:

"IT IS A CRIMINAL OFFENSE, PUNISHABLE BY A FINE AND IMPRISONMENT, FOR AN ADULT TO LEAVE A LOADED FIREARM WITHIN EASY ACCESS OF A MINOR."

b. Every wholesale and retail dealer of firearms shall conspicuously post at each purchase counter the following warning, printed in block letters not less than one inch in height:

"IT IS A CRIMINAL OFFENSE TO LEAVE A LOADED FIREARM WITHIN EASY ACCESS OF A MINOR."

c. Violation of this section by any retail or wholesale dealer of firearms is a petty disorderly persons offense.

L.1991, c. 397, § 2, eff. Jan. 17, 1992.

2C:58–17. KeepSafe program

a. There is established a "KeepSafe" program to encourage and stimulate the safe storage of firearms in the State of New Jersey by providing instant rebates to firearms purchasers who purchase trigger locking devices.

Under the program, a person who purchases a firearm from a retail dealer licensed under the provisions of N.J.S.2C:58–2 shall be eligible for a $5 instant rebate when a compatible trigger locking device is purchased along with that firearm. The licensed retail dealer shall deduct the rebate from the price of the compatible locking device in order to reduce by $5 the cost of the device for the purchaser.

b. The Superintendent of State Police, in conjunction with the Attorney General, shall adopt guidelines in accordance with the Administrative Procedure Act, P.L.1968, c. 410 (C.52:14B–1 et seq.), to effectuate the purposes of this act.

In addition, the superintendent shall prepare and deliver to each licensed retail firearms dealer in the State the forms necessary to record and report participation in the program. The forms, which shall set forth the name, address, telephone number, State tax number and State license number of the retail firearms dealer, the name of the firearms purchaser and his firearms purchaser identification card number or permit to purchase a handgun number, the make and model number of the compatible trigger locking device purchased and the date of the sale, shall be in duplicate. One copy shall be retained by the retail dealer for his records. The other shall be submitted to the Attorney General for reimbursement. The reimbursement copies shall be submitted monthly at a time prescribed by the superintendent. The submitting retail dealer shall be entitled to a reimbursement of $5 for each trigger locking device sold as part of the KeepSafe program. To help defray any administrative costs, each participating retail dealer shall receive, in addition to the reimbursement, $0.50 for each valid reimbursement copy submitted.

The superintendent also shall provide each licensed retail firearms dealer with a sign to be prominently displayed at a conspicuous place on the dealer's business premises where firearms are offered for sale. The sign shall state substantially the following:

"KEEP NEW JERSEY FIREARMS SAFE.

TO ENCOURAGE NEW JERSEY GUN OWNERS TO STORE THEIR FIREARMS SAFELY, THE STATE IS OFFERING A $5 INSTANT REBATE WHEN YOU PURCHASE A COM-

PATIBLE TRIGGER LOCK ALONG WITH YOUR FIREARM.

REMEMBER—THE USE OF A TRIGGER LOCK IS ONLY ONE ASPECT OF RESPONSIBLE FIREARM STORAGE. FIREARMS SHOULD BE STORED, UNLOADED AND LOCKED IN A LOCATION THAT IS BOTH SEPARATE FROM THEIR AMMUNITION AND INACCESSIBLE TO CHILDREN.

NEW JERSEY'S FAMILIES AND CHILDREN ARE PRECIOUS—KEEP THEM SAFE!!"

L.1999, c. 255, § 2, eff. Oct. 15, 1999.

2C:58–18. Effectiveness report

On the first day of the thirteenth month following the effective date of this act, the superintendent shall submit a report on the effectiveness of the KeepSafe program to the Governor and Legislature. In addition to those matters the superintendent deems appropriate and necessary, the report shall include the superintendent's assessment of whether the program should be expanded to include sales of trigger locking devices which are not part of firearm purchases.

L.1999, c. 255, § 3, eff. Oct. 15, 1999.

2C:58–19. Lost or stolen firearms; report to law enforcement officials; civil penalties

The legal owner of a firearm, upon discovering that the firearm is lost or stolen, shall report the loss or theft within 36 hours to the chief law enforcement officer of the municipality in which the loss or theft occurred or, if the municipality does not have a local police force, to the Superintendent of State Police.

A person who violates the provisions of this section shall be liable to a civil penalty of not less than $500 for a first offense, and not less than $1,000 for any second or subsequent offense. The civil penalty shall be collected pursuant to the "Penalty Enforcement Law of 1999," P.L.1999, c. 274 (C.2A:58–10 et seq.).

L.2007, c. 299, § 1, eff. Jan. 13, 2008.

CHAPTERS 59 to 61

[RESERVED]

CHAPTER 62

WILLFUL NONSUPPORT

Section
2C:62–1. Support orders for willful nonsupport.

2C:62–1. Support orders for willful nonsupport

a. Order for support pendente lite. At any time after a sworn complaint is made charging an offense under section 2C:24–5 and before trial, the court may enter such temporary order as may seem just, providing for the support of the spouse or children, or both,

pendente lite, and may punish a violation of such order as for contempt.

b. Order for future support; release on recognizance conditioned on obeying order; periodic service of sentence. Before trial, with the consent of the defendant, or after conviction, instead of imposing the penalty provided for violation of section 2C:24–5, or in addition thereto, the court, having regard to the circumstances and the financial ability or earning capacity of the defendant, may make an order, which shall be subject to change by the court from time to time as circumstances may require, directing the defendant to pay a sum certain periodically to the spouse, or to the guardian or custodian of the minor child or children, or to an organization or individual approved by the court as trustee. The court may release the defendant from custody on probation, upon his or her entering into a recognizance, with or without surety, in such sum as the court may order and approve. The condition of the recognizance shall be such that if the defendant shall personally appear in court whenever ordered to do so, and shall comply with the terms of the order, or of any modification thereof, the recognizance shall be void, otherwise it will remain in full force and effect. The court may, in addition to or in place of any order under this section, order and direct that any sentence of imprisonment be served periodically, instead of consecutively, during periods of time between Friday at 6 p.m. and Monday at 8 a.m. or at other times or on other days, whenever the court determines the existence of proper circumstances and that the ends of justice will be served thereby. Any person so imprisoned shall be given credit for each day or fraction of a day to the nearest hour actually served.

c. Violation of order. If the court be satisfied by information and due proof under oath that the defendant has violated the terms of the order, it may forthwith proceed with the trial of the defendant under the original charge, or sentence the defendant under the original conviction or plea of guilty, or enforce the suspended sentence or punish for contempt, as the case may be. In case of forfeiture of a recognizance, and the enforcement thereof by execution, the sum recovered may, in the discretion of the court, be paid in whole or part to the spouse, or to the guardian, custodian or trustee of such minor child or children.

d. Proof of marriage; husband and wife as witness. No other or greater evidence shall be required to prove the marriage of such husband and wife, or that the defendant is the father or mother of such child or children, than is required in a civil action. In no prosecution under this chapter shall any existing statute or rule of law prohibiting the disclosure of confidential communications between husband and wife apply, and both husband and wife shall be competent and compellable witnesses to testify against each other as to any and all relevant matters, including the fact of the marriage and the parentage of the child or children.

e. Place of residence confers jurisdiction of offense. The place of residence at the time of the desertion of the spouse, child or children, under the provisions of this chapter, shall confer jurisdiction of the offense set forth therein, upon the county, county district, or juvenile and domestic relations court having territorial jurisdiction of the place of such residence, until the deserted party shall establish a legal residence in some other county or State.

L.1978, c. 95, § 2C:62–1, eff. Sept. 1, 1979.

CHAPTER 63

[RESERVED]

CHAPTER 64

FORFEITURE

Section
2C:64–1. Property subject to forfeiture.
2C:64–2. Forfeiture procedures; prima facie contraband.
2C:64–3. Forfeiture procedures.
2C:64–4. Seized property; evidentiary use.
2C:64–5. Seized property; rights of owners and others holding interests.
2C:64–6. Disposal of forfeited property.
2C:64–7. Vesting of title in forfeited property.
2C:64–8. Seized property; statute of limitations on claims.
2C:64–9. Forfeited weapons with military value; donation to National Guard Militia Museum.

2C:64–1. Property subject to forfeiture

a. Any interest in the following shall be subject to forfeiture and no property right shall exist in them:

(1) Controlled dangerous substances, firearms which are unlawfully possessed, carried, acquired or used, illegally possessed gambling devices, untaxed cigarettes, untaxed special fuel, unlawful sound recordings and audiovisual works and items bearing a counterfeit mark. These shall be designated prima facie contraband.

(2) All property which has been, or is intended to be, utilized in furtherance of an unlawful activity, including, but not limited to, conveyances intended to facilitate the perpetration of illegal acts, or buildings or premises maintained for the purpose of committing offenses against the State.

(3) Property which has become or is intended to become an integral part of illegal activity, including, but not limited to, money which is earmarked for use as financing for an illegal gambling enterprise.

(4) Proceeds of illegal activities, including, but not limited to, property or money obtained as a result of the sale of prima facie contraband as defined by subsection a. (1), proceeds of illegal gambling, prostitution, bribery and extortion.

b. Any article subject to forfeiture under this chapter may be seized by the State or any law enforcement officer as evidence pending a criminal prosecution pursuant to section 2C:64–4 or, when no criminal proceeding is instituted, upon process issued by any court of competent jurisdiction over the property, except that seizure without such process may be made when not inconsistent with the Constitution of this State or the United States, and when

(1) The article is prima facie contraband; or

(2) The property subject to seizure poses an immediate threat to the public health, safety or welfare.

c. For the purposes of this section:

"Items bearing a counterfeit mark" means items bearing a counterfeit mark as defined in N.J.S.2C:21–32.

"Unlawful sound recordings and audiovisual works" means sound recordings and audiovisual works as those terms are defined in N.J.S.2C:21–21 which were produced in violation of N.J.S.2C:21–21.

"Untaxed special fuel" means diesel fuel, No. 2 fuel oil and kerosene on which the motor fuel tax imposed pursuant to R.S.54:39–1 et seq. is not paid that is delivered, possessed, sold or transferred in this State in a manner not authorized pursuant to R.S.54:39–1 et seq. or P.L. 1938, c. 163 (C.56:6–1 et seq.).

L.1978, c. 95, § 2C:64–1, eff. Sept. 1, 1979. Amended by L.1979, c. 344, § 1, eff. Jan. 23, 1980; L.1981, c. 290, § 46, eff. Sept. 24, 1981; L.1992, c. 23, § 70, eff. July 1, 1992; L.2004, c. 150, § 3, eff. Sept. 14, 2004.

2C:64–2. Forfeiture procedures; prima facie contraband

Except as provided in N.J.S. 2C:35–21, prima facie contraband shall be retained by the State until entry of judgment or dismissal of the criminal proceeding, if any, arising out of the seizure. Thereafter, prima facie contraband shall be forfeited to the entity funding the prosecuting agency involved, subject to the rights of owners and others holding interests pursuant to section 2C:64–5.

L. 1978, c. 95, § 2C:64–2, eff. Sept. 1, 1979. Amended by L. 1979, c. 344, § 2, eff. Jan. 23, 1980; L. 1981, c. 290, § 47, eff. Sept. 24, 1981; L.1987, c. 106, § 17.

2C:64–3. Forfeiture procedures

a. Whenever any property other than prima facie contraband is subject to forfeiture under this chapter, such forfeiture may be enforced by a civil action, instituted within 90 days of the seizure and commenced by the State and against the property sought to be forfeited.

b. The complaint shall be verified on oath or affirmation. It shall describe with reasonable particularity the property that is the subject matter of the action and shall contain allegations setting forth the reason or reasons the article sought to be or which has been seized is contraband.

c. Notice of the action shall be given to any person known to have a property interest in the article. In addition, the notice requirements of the Rules of Court for an in rem action shall be followed.

d. The claimant of the property that is the subject of an action under this chapter shall file and serve his claim in the form of an answer in accordance with the Rules of Court. The answer shall be verified on oath or affirmation, and shall state the interest in the property by virtue of which the claimant demands its restitution and the right to defend the action. If the claim is made in behalf of the person entitled to possession by an agent, bailee or attorney, it shall state that he is duly authorized to make the claim.

e. If no answer is filed and served within the applicable time, the property seized shall be disposed of pursuant to N.J.S.2C:64–6.

f. If an answer is filed, the Superior or county district court shall set the matter down for a summary hearing as soon as practicable. Upon application of the State or claimant, if he be a defendant in a criminal proceeding arising out of the seizure, the Superior or county district court may stay proceedings in the forfeiture action until the criminal proceedings have been concluded by an entry of final judgment.

g. Any person with a property interest in the seized property, other than a defendant who is being prosecuted in connection with the seizure of property may secure its release pending the forfeiture action unless the article is dangerous to the public health, safety and welfare or the State can demonstrate that the property will probably be lost or destroyed if released or employed in subsequent criminal activity. Any person with such a property interest other than a defendant who is being prosecuted, prior to the release of said property shall post a bond with the court in the amount of the market value of the seized item.

h. The prosecuting agency with approval of the entity funding such agency, or any other entity, with the approval of the prosecuting agency, where the other entity's law enforcement agency participated in the surveillance, investigation or arrest which is the subject of the forfeiture action, may apply to the Superior Court for an order permitting use of seized property, pending the disposition of the forfeiture action provided, however, that such property shall be used solely for law enforcement purposes. Approval shall be liberally granted but shall be conditioned upon the filing of a bond in an amount equal to the market value of the item seized or a written guarantee of payment for property which may be subject to return, replacement or compensation as to reasonable value in the event that the forfeiture is refused or only partial extinguishment of property rights is ordered by the court.

i. If the property is of such nature that substantial difficulty may result in preserving its value during the pendency of the forfeiture action, the Superior or county district court may appoint a trustee to protect the interests of all parties involved in the action.

j. Evidence of a conviction of a criminal offense in which seized property was either used or provided an integral part of the State's proofs in the prosecution shall be considered in the forfeiture proceeding as creating a rebuttable presumption that the property was utilized in furtherance of an unlawful activity.

L.1978, c. 95, § 2C:64–3, eff. Sept. 1, 1979. Amended by L.1979, c. 344, § 3, eff. Jan. 23, 1980; L.1981, c. 290, § 48, eff. Sept. 24, 1981; L.1989, c. 279, § 1, eff. Jan. 11, 1990.

2C:64–4. Seized property; evidentiary use

a. Nothing in this chapter shall impair the right of the State to retain evidence pending a criminal prosecution.

b. The fact that a prosecution involving seized property terminates without a conviction does not preclude forfeiture proceedings against the property pursuant to this chapter.

L.1978, c. 95, § 2C:64–4, eff. Sept. 1, 1979. Amended by L.1979, c. 344, § 4, eff. Jan. 23, 1980; L.1981, c. 290, § 49, eff. Sept. 24, 1981.

2C:64–5. Seized property; rights of owners and others holding interests

a. No forfeiture under this chapter shall affect the rights of any lessor in the ordinary course of business or any person holding a perfected security interest in property subject to seizure unless it shall appear that such person had knowledge of or consented to any act or omission upon which the right of forfeiture is based. Such rights are only to the extent of interest in the seized property and at the option of the entity funding the prosecuting agency involved may be extinguished by appropriate payment.

b. Property seized under this chapter shall not be subject to forfeiture if the owner of the property establishes by a preponderance of the evidence that the owner was not involved in or aware of the unlawful activity and that the owner had done all that could reasonably be expected to prevent the proscribed use of the property by an agent. A person who uses or possesses property with the consent or knowledge of the owner is deemed to be the agent of the owner for purposes of this chapter.

c. Property seized under this chapter shall not be subject to forfeiture if the property is seized while entrusted to a person by the owner or the agent of the owner when the property has been entrusted to the person for repairs, restoration or other services to be performed on the property, and that person, without the owner's knowledge or consent, uses the property for unlawful purposes.

L.1978, c. 95, § 2C:64–5, eff. Sept. 1, 1979. Amended by L.1979, c. 344, § 5, eff. Jan. 23, 1980; L.1981, c. 290, § 50, eff. Sept. 24, 1981; L.1986, c. 79, § 1, eff. Aug. 6, 1986.

2C:64–6. Disposal of forfeited property

a. Property which has been forfeited shall be destroyed if it can serve no lawful purpose or it presents a danger to the public health, safety or welfare. All other forfeited property or any proceeds resulting from the forfeiture and all money seized pursuant to this chapter shall become the property of the entity funding the prosecuting agency involved and shall be disposed of, distributed, appropriated and used in accordance with the provisions of this chapter.

The prosecutor or the Attorney General, whichever is prosecuting the case, shall divide the forfeited property, any proceeds resulting from the forfeiture or any money seized pursuant to this chapter with any other entity where the other entity's law enforcement agency participated in the surveillance, investigation, arrest or prosecution resulting in the forfeiture, in proportion to the other entity's contribution to the surveillance, investigation, arrest or prosecution resulting in the forfeiture, as determined in the discretion of the prosecutor or the Attorney General, whichever is prosecuting the case. Notwithstanding any other provision of law, such forfeited property and proceeds shall be used solely for law enforcement purposes, and shall be designated for the exclusive use of the law enforcement agency which contributed to the surveillance, investigation, arrest or prosecution resulting in the forfeiture.

The Attorney General is authorized to promulgate rules and regulations to implement and enforce the provisions of this act.

b. For a period of two years from the date of enactment of P.L.1993, c. 227 (C. 26:4–100.13 et al.), 10% of the proceeds obtained by the Attorney General under the provisions of subsection a. of this section shall be deposited into the Hepatitis Inoculation Fund established pursuant to section 2 of P.L.1993, c. 227 (C. 26:4–100.13).

c. Beginning two years from the date of enactment of P.L.1993, c. 227 (C. 26:4–100.13 et al.) and in subsequent years, 5% of the proceeds obtained by the Attorney General under the provisions of subsection a. of this section shall be deposited into the Hepatitis Inoculation Fund established pursuant to Section 2 of P.L.1993, c. 227 (C. 26:4–100.13).

L.1978, c. 95, § 2C:64–6, eff. Sept. 1, 1979. Amended by L.1979, c. 344, § 6, eff. Jan. 23, 1980; L.1985, c. 110, § 1, eff. April 9, 1985; L.1986, c. 135, § 1, eff. Dec. 1, 1986; L.1993, c. 227, § 1, eff. Aug. 6, 1993.

2C:64–7. Vesting of title in forfeited property

Title to property forfeited under this chapter shall vest in the entity funding the prosecuting agency involved at the time the item was utilized illegally, or, in the case of proceeds, when received.

If another entity's law enforcement agency has participated in the surveillance, investigation, arrest or prosecution resulting in the forfeiture, then the prosecutor or the Attorney General, whichever is prosecuting the case, shall vest title to forfeited property, including motor vehicles, by dividing the forfeited property with the other entity in proportion to the other entity's contribution to the surveillance, investigation, arrest or prosecution resulting in the forfeiture, as determined in the discretion of the prosecutor or the Attorney General. If the property, including motor vehicles, cannot be divided as required by this section, then the prosecutor or the Attorney General, whichever is prosecuting the case, shall sell the property, including motor vehicles, and the proceeds of the sale shall be divided with the other entity in proportion to the other entity's contribution to the surveillance, investigation, arrest or prosecution resulting in the forfeiture, as determined in the discretion of the prosecutor or the Attorney General.

L.1978, c. 95, § 2C:64–7, eff. Sept. 1, 1979. Amended by L.1979, c. 344, § 7, eff. Jan. 23, 1980; L.1985, c. 110, § 2, eff. April 9, 1985; L.1986, c. 135, § 2, eff. Dec. 1, 1986.

2C:64–8. Seized property; statute of limitations on claims

Any person who could not with due diligence have discovered that property which he owns was seized as contraband may file a claim for its return or the value thereof at the time of seizure within 3 years of the seizure if he can demonstrate that he did not consent to, and had no knowledge of its unlawful use. If the property has been sold, the claimant receives a claim against proceeds.

L.1978, c. 95, § 2C:64–8, eff. Sept. 1, 1979. Amended by L.1979, c. 344, § 8, eff. Jan. 23, 1980.

2C:64–9. Forfeited weapons with military value; donation to National Guard Militia Museum

Any weapon with present or historical military value that has been forfeited pursuant to the provisions of chapter 64 of Title 2C of the New Jersey Statutes may be donated to the National Guard Militia Museum of New Jersey at Sea Girt by the law enforcement agency retaining it.

L.1981, c. 112, § 1, eff. April 2, 1981.

CHAPTER 65

DISPOSITION OF STOLEN PROPERTY AND DOCUMENTARY EXHIBITS

Section
2C:65–1. Procedure to be followed by law enforcement agencies when stolen property is taken into custody.

Section

2C:65–2.   Release of stolen property prior to final determina-
           tion of proceeding.

2C:65–3.   Disposition of stolen property after final determina-
           tion of proceeding.

2C:65–4.   Disposition of documentary exhibits.

2C:65–1. Procedure to be followed by law enforcement agencies when stolen property is taken into custody

When any article of property alleged to be stolen comes into the custody of a law enforcement agency, that agency shall enter in a suitable book a description of that article and shall attach a number to each article, and make a corresponding entry thereof. The agency shall also make and retain a complete photographic record of the property. The photographic record, upon proper authentication, may be introduced as evidence in any court in lieu of the property.

L.1979, c. 178, § 140, eff. Sept. 1, 1979.

2C:65–2. Release of stolen property prior to final determination of proceeding

a. A law enforcement agency, upon satisfactory proof of ownership of property held pursuant to this section, and upon presentation of proper personal identification, may release the property to the person presenting such proof pursuant to the provisions of subsection b. The release shall be without prejudice to the State or to the person from whom custody of the property was taken or to any person who may have a claim against the property. Any such delivery shall be noted in the book required by 2C:65–1. The person to whom the property is delivered shall sign a sworn declaration of ownership which shall be retained by the agency.

b. Nothing in this section shall prohibit a law enforcement agency from immediately returning property to its rightful owner where the agency is satisfied that there is no colorable dispute as to ownership; provided, however, that where the law enforcement agency has reason to believe that there is a dispute concerning ownership of property, or if the person from whom custody of the property was taken shall claim ownership, or if any other person shall claim ownership, the property shall not be released to any person claiming it until a hearing has been held pursuant to subsection c.

c. The court having jurisdiction over the case in which the stolen property is involved, upon application by the person from whom possession was taken, or the person claiming ownership, shall review the matter and order the property to be delivered to the person claiming ownership, or to be retained by the law enforcement agency upon a finding that the person claiming ownership of the property is not entitled thereto.

L.1979, c. 178, § 140, eff. Sept. 1, 1979. Amended by L.1981, c. 290, § 51, eff. Sept. 24, 1981.

2C:65–3. Disposition of stolen property after final determination of proceeding

a. After final determination of any action or proceeding, the court, on application of the person claiming ownership, or an agent designated in writing by the person, may order all property, other than documentary exhibits, to be delivered to the person.

b. After the expiration of 6 months from the final determination of the action, if the person entitled to the property is unknown, or fails to apply, the court in which the case was tried, upon application of the law enforcement agency in possession of the property, shall make an order specifying what property may be released from the custody of the agency without prejudice to the State. Upon receipt of the order, the clerk of the court shall transfer the property for disposal at public sale to the State, county or municipality, whichever was the prosecuting authority. The property shall not be transferred where it consists of money or currency, but it shall be deposited immediately in the general fund of either the State, county or municipality.

L.1979, c. 178, § 140, eff. Sept. 1, 1979.

2C:65–4. Disposition of documentary exhibits

No exhibit shall be destroyed or otherwise disposed of until 60 days after the clerk of the court has posted a notice conspicuously in three places in the county, referring to the order for the disposition, describing briefly the exhibit, and indicating the date after which the exhibit will be destroyed or otherwise disposed of.

L.1979, c. 178, § 140, eff. Sept. 1, 1979.

CHAPTER 66

ATTACHMENT, FREEZING OF TERRORIST FUNDS

Section

2C:66–1.   Definitions.
2C:66–2.   Attorney General application.
2C:66–3.   Attachment order.
2C:66–4.   Financial institution duties.
2C:66–5.   Hearing to contest freezing of funds; release of
            funds.
2C:66–6.   Disposition of funds.
2C:66–7.   Time limit; expiration.
2C:66–8.   Notice of attachment order.
2C:66–9.   Rights of financial institutions.
2C:66–10.   Liability of financial institutions.
2C:66–11.   Construction with other laws.

2C:66–1. Definitions

a. As used in this act:

"Financial institution" means a state or federally chartered bank, savings bank or savings and loan association or any other financial services company or provider, including, but not limited to, broker- dealers, investment companies, money market and mutual funds, credit unions and insurers.

b. Upon application by the Attorney General, a court may issue an attachment order directing a financial institution to freeze some or all of the funds or assets deposited with or held by the financial institution by or on behalf of an account holder when there exists a reasonable suspicion that the account holder has committed or is about to commit the crime of terrorism in violation of section 2 of P.L.2002, c. 26 (C.2C:38–2) or soliciting or providing material support or resources for terrorism in violation of section 5 of P.L.2002, c. 26 (C.2C:38–5).

L.2003, c. 22, § 1, eff. Feb. 27, 2003.

2C:66–2. Attorney General application

The application of the Attorney General required by this act shall contain:

a. a statement of the approximate financial loss caused by the account holder in the commission of the crime of terrorism in violation of section 2 of P.L.2002, c 26 (C.2C:38–2) or soliciting or providing material support or resources for terrorism in violation of section 5 of P.L.2002, c. 26 (C.2C:38–5);

b. a statement of facts relied upon by the Attorney General, including the details of the particular offense that is about to be committed or that has been committed; and

c. identification of the account holder's name and financial institution account number.

L.2003, c. 22, § 2, eff. Feb. 27, 2003.

2C:66–3. Attachment order

If the court finds that:

a. there exists a reasonable suspicion that the account holder has committed or is about to commit the crime of terrorism in violation of section 2 of P.L.2002, c. 26 (C.2C:38–2) or the crime of soliciting or providing material support or resources for terrorism in violation of section 5 of P.L.2002, c. 26 (C.2C:38–5);

b. the accounts of the account holder are specifically identified; and

c. it is necessary to freeze the account holder's funds or assets to ensure eventual restitution to victims of the alleged offense, the court may order the financial institution to freeze all or part of the account holder's deposited funds or assets so that the funds or assets may not be withdrawn or disposed of until further order of the court.

As part of the consideration of an application in which there is no corroborative evidence offered, the judge shall inquire in camera as to the identity of any informants or any other additional information concerning the basis upon which the Attorney General has applied for the attachment order which the judge finds relevant in order to determine if there exists a reasonable suspicion pursuant to this act.

L.2003, c. 22, § 3, eff. Feb. 27, 2003.

2C:66–4. Financial institution duties

Upon receipt of the order authorized by this act, a financial institution shall not permit any funds or assets that were frozen by the order to be withdrawn or disposed of until further order of the court.

L.2003, c. 22, § 4, eff. Feb. 27, 2003.

2C:66–5. Hearing to contest freezing of funds; release of funds

a. The account holder may, upon notice and motion, have a hearing to contest the freezing of funds or assets and to seek the release of all or part of them.

b. The account holder is entitled to an order releasing all or part of the funds or assets by showing:

(1) that the account holder has posted a bond or other adequate surety, guaranteeing that, upon conviction, adequate funds or assets will be available to pay complete restitution to victims of the alleged offense;

(2) that there does not exist a reasonable suspicion that the account holder has committed or is about to commit the alleged offense;

(3) that the amount of funds or assets frozen is more than is necessary to pay complete restitution to all victims of the alleged offense; or

(4) that the funds or assets should be returned in the interests of justice.

c. It is not grounds for the release of funds or assets that the particular accounts frozen do not contain funds or assets that were proceeds from or used in the commission of the crime of terrorism in violation of section 2 of P.L.2002, c. 26 (C.2C:38–2) or soliciting or providing material support or resources for terrorism in violation of section 5 of P.L.2002, c. 26 (C.2C:38–5).

L.2003, c. 22, § 5, eff. Feb. 27, 2003.

2C:66–6. Disposition of funds

a. The court may order the financial institution to remit all or part of the frozen funds or assets to the court.

b. If the account holder is acquitted or the charges are dismissed with prejudice, the court shall issue an order releasing the freeze on the funds or assets.

c. If the account holder is not acquitted or the charges are not dismissed, the frozen funds or assets shall become the property of the State and shall be used to provide restitution to victims of terrorism, to fund State law enforcement anti-terrorism programs and activities and for other law enforcement purposes.

L.2003, c. 22, § 6, eff. Feb. 27, 2003.

2C:66–7. Time limit; expiration

The freeze permitted by this act expires 24 months after the date of the court's initial attachment order

unless the time limit is extended by the court in writing upon a showing of good cause by the Attorney General.
L.2003, c. 22, § 7, eff. Feb. 27, 2003.

2C:66–8. Notice of attachment order

Within ten days after a court issues an attachment order under this act, the Attorney General shall send a copy of the order to the account holder's last known address or to the account holder's attorney, if known.
L.2003, c. 22, § 8, eff. Feb. 27, 2003.

2C:66–9. Rights of financial institutions

A financial institution that is directed to block, freeze or encumber an account pursuant to this act shall be entitled during the period that the account is blocked, frozen or encumbered to exercise any right or remedy with respect to the account as provided by law, or in the deposit agreement and rules or regulations of the financial institution applicable to the account. The provision of this act shall not be construed to preclude a financial institution from exercising its right of set-off or to charge back or recoup a deposit to an account.
L.2003, c. 22, § 9, eff. Feb. 27, 2003.

2C:66–10. Liability of financial institutions

Notwithstanding any other law to the contrary, a financial institution shall not be liable to any person for blocking, freezing, encumbering or refusing to release any funds or assets held by the financial institution in response to an order issued by a court, or for any other action taken by the financial institution in good faith to comply with the requirements of this act. A financial institution shall not be required to give notice to an account holder or customer that the financial institution has taken any action pursuant to this act and shall not be liable for failure to provide the notice.
L.2003, c. 22, § 10, eff. Feb. 27, 2003.

2C:66–11. Construction with other laws

Nothing contained in this act shall be construed to abrogate or affect the status, force or operation of the forfeiture provisions of the "New Jersey Code of Criminal Justice," N.J.S.2C:64–1 et seq., or any other provision of law.
L.2003, c. 22, § 11, eff. Feb. 27, 2003.

CHAPTERS 67 to 97

[RESERVED]

CHAPTER 98

REPEALERS, ALLOCATIONS AND EFFECTIVE DATE

Section
2C:98–1. Construction.
2C:98–2. Repealer.
2C:98–3. Allocations.
2C:98–4. Effective date.

2C:98–1. Construction

The provisions of R.S. 1:1–8 and R.S. 1:1–11 to 1:1–21, both inclusive, shall be applicable to the enactment and operation of said Title 2C. The enactment of this law shall not, due to the repeal set forth in section 2C:98–2:

a. Be deemed to revive any common law right or remedy abolished by any sections, acts or parts of acts repealed thereby; or

b. Affect any right now vested in any person pursuant to the provisions of those sections, acts or parts of acts, nor any remedy where an action or proceeding thereunder has heretofore been instituted and is pending on the effective date of said repeal.
L.1978, c. 95, § 2C:98–1, eff. Sept. 1, 1979.

2C:98–2. Repealer

All acts and parts of acts inconsistent with this act are hereby superseded and repealed, and without limiting the general effect of this act in superseding and repealing acts so inconsistent herewith, the following sections, acts and parts of acts, together with all amendments and supplements thereto, are specifically repealed:

New Jersey Statutes sections:

2A:85–1 to 2A:85–5 both inclusive;

2A:85–6 to 2A:85–14 both inclusive;

2A:86–1 to 2A:88–1 both inclusive;

2A:89–1 to 2A:90–3 both inclusive;

2A:91–1 to 2A:94–3 both inclusive;

2A:95–1 and 2A:95–2;

2A:96–1 to 2A:96–4 both inclusive;

2A:97–1 to 2A:98–2 both inclusive;

2A:99–1 and 2A:99–2;

2A:100–1 to 2A:102–12 both inclusive;

2A:103–1 to 2A:104–12 both inclusive;

2A:105–1 to 2A:105–4 both inclusive;

2A:106–1 to 2A:108–8 both inclusive;

2A:109–1 to 2A:111–21 both inclusive;

2A:111–22 to 2A:111–24 both inclusive;

2A:112–1 to 2A:115–1 both inclusive;

2A:115–2;

2A:115–3;

2A:115–4 and 2A:115–5;

2A:116–1 to 2A:119–5 both inclusive;

2A:119–6 to 2A:119–8 both inclusive;

2A:119–9;

2A:120–1 to 2A:121–5 both inclusive;

2A:122–1 to 2A:122–9 both inclusive;

2A:123–1 and 2A:123–2;

2A:124–1 to 2A:127–3 both inclusive;

2A:128–1 to 2A:134–1 both inclusive;

2A:135–1 to 2A:145–1 both inclusive;

2A:146–2 to 2A:148–22 both inclusive;

2A:150–1;

2A:151–1 to 2A:151–9 both inclusive;

2A:151–12;

2A:151–14 to 2A:151–28 both inclusive;

2A:151–31 to 2A:151–41 both inclusive;

2A:151–42 to 2A:151–44 both inclusive;

2A:151–45 to 2A:151–57 both inclusive;

2A:151–58 to 2A:151–61 both inclusive;

2A:152–5 to 2A:152–9 both inclusive;

2A:152–10 and 2A:152–11;

2A:152–14;

2A:159–1 to 2A:159–3 both inclusive;

2A:163–2;

2A:163–3;

2A:164–2 to 2A:164–13 both inclusive;

2A:164–14 to 2A:164–23 both inclusive;

2A:164–25 to 2A:164–28 both inclusive;

2A:165–1 to 2A:165–12 both inclusive;

2A:166–1 to 2A:166–7 both inclusive;

2A:166–11;

2A:166–14 to 2A:166–16 both inclusive;

2A:167–1 to 2A:167–3 both inclusive;

2A:168–1 to 2A:168–4 both inclusive;

2A:169–1 and 2A:169–2; 2A:169–4 to 2A:169–10 both inclusive;

2A:170–1 to 2A:170–3 both inclusive;

2A:170–4 to 2A:170–7 both inclusive;

2A:170–9 to 2A:170–11 both inclusive;

2A:170–14;

2A:170–16 to 2A:170–19 both inclusive;

2A:170–21 and 2A:170–25;

2A:170–26 to 2A:170–30 both inclusive;

2A:170–31;

2A:170–32 to 2A:170–41 both inclusive;

2A:170–42 to 2A:170–44 both inclusive;

2A:170–46 to 2A:170–49 both inclusive;

2A:170–53;

2A:170–55 to 2A:170–64 both inclusive;

2A:170–65 to 2A:170–67 both inclusive;

2A:170–68 and 2A:170–69;

2A:170–70 to 2A:170–76 both inclusive;

2A:170–86 to 2A:170–90 both inclusive;

2A:170–93 to 2A:170–96 both inclusive;

2A:171–1;

2A:171–2;

2A:171–4 and 2A:171–5;

2A:171–6 to 2A:171–12 both inclusive;

Pamphlet Laws:

Laws of 1971, c. 450 (C. 2A:85–5.1);

Laws of 1973, c. 191 (C. 2A:85–15 to C. 2A:85–23 both inclusive);

Laws of 1964, c. 74 (C. 2A:88A–1);

Laws of 1962, c. 39 (C. 2A:90–4);

Laws of 1971, c. 314 (C. 2A:94–4);

Laws of 1954, c. 219 (C. 2A:95–3);

Laws of 1961, c. 53 (C. 2A:98–3 and C. 2A:98–4);

Laws of 1960, c. 177 (C. 2A:99A–1 to C. 2A:99A–4 both inclusive);

Laws of 1970, c. 131 (C. 2A:99B–1);

Laws of 1959, c. 98 (C. 2A:102–12.1);

Laws of 1964, c. 265 (C. 2A:104–13 and C. 2A:104–14);

Laws of 1968, c. 83 (C. 2A:105–5);

Laws of 1964, c. 179 (C. 2A:111–21.1);

Laws of 1952, c. 332 (C. 2A:111–25 to C. 2A:111–27 both inclusive);

Laws of 1954, c. 58 (C. 2A:111–28 to C. 2A:111–31 both inclusive);

Laws of 1960, c. 62 (C. 2A:111–32 and C. 2A:111–33);

Laws of 1964, c. 294 (C. 2A:111–34 to C. 2A:111–36 both inclusive);

Laws of 1968, c. 253 (C. 2A:111–37 and C. 2A:111–38);

Laws of 1968, c. 260 (C. 2A:111–39);

Laws of 1968, c. 300 (C. 2A:111–40 to C. 2A:111–51 both inclusive);

Laws of 1962, c. 165 (C. 2A:115–1.1);

Laws of 1971, c. 449 (C. 2A:115–1.1a and C. 2A:115–1.1b);

Laws of 1971, c. 446 (C. 2A:115–1.6 to C. 2A:115–1.12 both inclusive);

Laws of 1971, c. 447 (C. 2A:115–2.1 to C. 2A:115–2.4 both inclusive);

Laws of 1971, c. 448 (C. 2A:115–2.5 to C. 2A:115–2.9 both inclusive);

Laws of 1953, c. 392 (C. 2A:115–3.1);

Laws of 1962, c. 166 (C. 2A:115–3.3 and C. 2A:115–3.5 to C. 2A:115–3.10 both inclusive);

Laws of 1971, c. 376 (C. 2A:116–6);

Laws of 1965, c. 52 (C. 2A:119–5.1 to C. 2A:119–5.5 both inclusive);

Laws of 1962, c. 201 (C. 2A:119–8.1);

Laws of 1968, c. 349 (C. 2A:119A–1 to C. 2A:119A–4 both inclusive);

Laws of 1961, c. 39 (C. 2A:121–6);

Laws of 1971, c. 87 (C. 2A:122–9.1 and C. 2A:122–9.2);

Laws of 1960, c. 5 (C. 2A:122–10);

Laws of 1960, c. 69 (C. 2A:122–11);

Laws of 1967, c. 72 (C. 2A:122–12);

Laws of 1964, c. 86 (C. 2A:127–5);

Laws of 1957, c. 49 (C. 2A:148–22.1);

Laws of 1967, c. 182 (C. 2A:149A–1);

Laws of 1968, c. 395 (C. 2A:149A–2 and C. 2A:149A–3);

Laws of 1968, c. 147 (C. 2A:151–10.1);

Laws of 1969, c. 157 (C. 2A:151–41.1 and C. 2A:151–41.2);

Laws of 1966, c. 60 (C. 2A:151–44.1 and C. 2A:151–44.2);

Laws of 1966, c. 60 (C. 2A:151–57.1 and C. 2A:151–57.2);

Laws of 1952, c. 5 (C. 2A:151–62 and C. 2A:151–63);

Laws of 1962, c. 160 (C. 2A:152–9.1 to C. 2A:152–9.5 both inclusive);

Laws of 1952, c. 212 (C. 2A:152–15 and C. 2A:152–16);

Laws of 1952, c. 74 (C. 2A:159–4);

Laws of 1968, c. 279 (C. 2A:169–11);

Laws of 1971, c. 315 (C. 2A:170–3.1 to C. 2A:170–3.3 both inclusive);

Laws of 1955, c. 105 (C. 2A:170–20.8);

Laws of 1953, c. 67 (C. 2A:170–25.2);

Laws of 1954, c. 147 (C. 2A:170–25.3);

Laws of 1955, c. 213 (C. 2A:170–25.4);

Laws of 1955, c. 250 (C. 2A:170–25.5);

Laws of 1959, c. 194 (C. 2A:170–25.7);

Laws of 1964, c. 178 (C. 2A:170–25.8);

Laws of 1966, c. 150 (C. 2A:170–25.14 and C. 2A:170–25.15);

Laws of 1970, c. 133 (C. 2A:170–25.16);

Laws of 1973, c. 258 (C. 2A:170–25.18 to C. 2A:170–25.20 both inclusive);

Laws of 1972, c. 159 (C. 2A:170–30.1);

Laws of 1956, c. 185 (C. 2A:170–31.1);

Laws of 1972, c. 160 (C. 2A:170–41.1);

Laws of 1956, c. 195 (C. 2A:170–50.1 to C. 2A:170–50.3 both inclusive);

Laws of 1965, c. 184, sections 3 to 5 (C. 2A:170–50.4 to C. 2A:170–50.6 both inclusive);

Laws of 1957, c. 203 (C. 2A:170–54.1);

Laws of 1968, c. 324 (C. 2A:170–54.2);

Laws of 1953, c. 68 (C. 2A:170–64.1);

Laws of 1961, c. 139 (C. 2A:170–64.2);

Laws of 1954, c. 16 (C. 2A:170–67.1);

Laws of 1954, c. 137 (C. 2A:170–69.1);

Laws of 1958, c. 170 (C. 2A:170–69.1a and C. 2A:170–69.1b);

Laws of 1955, c. 245, sections 2 and 3 (C. 2A:170–69.2 and C. 2A:170–69.3);

Laws of 1964, c. 53 (C. 2A:170–69.4 to C. 2A:170–69.6 both inclusive);

Laws of 1968, c. 288 (C. 2A:170–69.7 and C. 2A:170–69.8);

Laws of 1962, c. 178 (C. 2A:170–97 to C. 2A:170–101 both inclusive);

Laws of 1968, c. 256 (C. 2A:170–102 and C. 2A:170–103);

Laws of 1958, c. 138 (C. 2A:171–5.1 to C. 2A:171–5.7 both inclusive).

L.1978, c. 95, § 2C:98–2, eff. Sept. 1, 1979. Amended by L.1979, c. 178, § 145, eff. Sept. 1, 1979.

2C:98–3. Allocations

Pending enactment of acts to revise, repeal or to compile the same in Title 2C of the New Jersey Statutes, the following sections, acts or parts of acts, together with all amendments and supplements thereto, shall remain in full force and effect for use, administration and enforcement as heretofore:

New Jersey Statutes sections:

2A:127–4;

2A:149–1;

2A:151–10 and 2A:151–11;[1]

2A:152–1;

2A:152–2;

2A:152–3;

2A:152–4;

2A:152–12;

2A:152–13;

2A:153–1 to 2A:153–3 both inclusive;

2A:154–1 to 2A:154–3 both inclusive;

2A:155–1 to 2A:156–4 both inclusive;

2A:157–1 to 2A:158–1 both inclusive;[2]

2A:158–2 to 2A:158–10 both inclusive;

2A:158–13;

2A:158–15;

2A:158–16;

2A:158–18;

2A:158–19 and 2A:158–20;

2A:160–1 to 2A:162–8 both inclusive;

2A:163–1;

2A:164–1;

2A:164–24;

2A:166–8 to 2A:166–10 both inclusive;[3]

2A:166–12 and 2A:166–13;

2A:166–17 to 2A:166–19 both inclusive;[4]

2A:167–4 to 2A:167–12 both inclusive;

2A:168–5 to 2A:168–17 both inclusive;

2A:169–3;

2A:170–20;

2A:170–51;

2A:170–77;

2A:170–78 to 2A:170–85 both inclusive;

2A:170–91 and 2A:170–92;

Pamphlet Laws:

Laws of 1952, c. 121 (C. 2A:96–5);

Laws of 1966, c. 12 (C. 2A:96–5.1);

Laws of 1957, c. 182 (C. 2A:102–13 to C. 2A:102–17 both inclusive);

Laws of 1952, c. 95 (C. 2A:108–9);

Laws of 1953, c. 267 (C. 2A:123–3 to C. 2A:123–15 both inclusive);

Laws of 1971, c. 412 (C. 2A:150A–1 to C. 2A:150A–5 both inclusive);

Laws of 1973, c. 354 (C. 2A:150A–6);

Laws of 1956, c. 134 (C. 2A:152–17 to C. 2A:152–19 both inclusive);

Laws of 1968, c. 427 (C. 2A:154–4);

Laws of 1967, c. 171 (C. 2A:153–4);

Laws of 1968, c. 409 (C. 2A:156A–1 to C. 2A:156A–26);

Laws of 1970, c. 6 (C. 2A:158–1.1 and C. 2A:158–1.2);

Laws of 1970, c. 6 (C. 2A:158–15.1 and C. 2A:158–15.2);

Laws of 1957, c. 128 (C. 2A:158–16.1);

Laws of 1953, c. 307 (C. 2A:158–18.1 and C. 2A:158–18.2);

Laws of 1964, c. 168 (C. 2A:158–21);

Laws of 1967, c. 43 (C. 2A:158A–1 to C. 2A:158A–5 both inclusive);

Laws of 1974, c. 33 (C. 2A:158A–5.1 and C. 2A:158A–5.2);

Laws of 1967, c. 43 (C. 2A:158A–6 to C. 2A:158A–20 both inclusive);

Laws of 1967, c. 43 (C. 2A:158A–22);

Laws of 1968, c. 371 (C. 2A:158A–23 to C. 2A:158A–25 both inclusive);

Laws of 1958, c. 12 (C. 2A:159A–1 to 2A:159A–15 both inclusive);

Laws of 1952, c. 163 (C. 2A:162–9 and C. 2A:162–10);

Laws of 1960, c. 24 (C. 2A:166A–1 to 2A:166A–4 both inclusive);

Laws of 1953, c. 83 (C. 2A:168–18 to C. 2A:168–25 both inclusive);

Laws of 1968, c. 282 (C. 2A:168A–1 to C. 2A:168A–3 both inclusive);

Laws of 1954, c. 181 (C. 2A:170–20.1 to C. 2A:170–20.4 both inclusive);

Laws of 1956, c. 230 (C. 2A:170–20.9 and C. 2A:170–20.10);

Laws of 1975, c. 183 (C. 2A:170–20.11 and C. 2A:170–20.12);

Laws of 1952, c. 106 (C. 2A:170–25.1);

Laws of 1965, c. 41 (C. 2A:170–25.9 to C. 2A:170–25.13 both inclusive);

Laws of 1972, c. 143 (C. 2A:170–25.17);

Laws of 1955, c. 48 (C. 2A:170–77.2);

Laws of 1962, c. 174 (C. 2A:170–77.2a and C. 2A:170–77.2b);

Laws of 1955, c. 277 (C. 2A:170–77.3 to C. 2A:170–77.7 both inclusive);[5]

Laws of 1962, c. 113 (C. 2A:170–77.8 to C. 2A:170–77.11 both inclusive);

Laws of 1964, c. 230 (C. 2A:170–77.12 to C. 2A:170–77.14 both inclusive);

Laws of 1966, c. 314 (C. 2A:170–77.15);

Laws of 1977, c. 215 (C. 2A:170–77.16 to C. 2A:170–77.18 both inclusive);

Laws of 1966, c. 114 (C. 2A:170–90.1 and C. 2A:170–90.2);[6]

Laws of 1975, c. 182 (C. 2A:170–90.3 to C. 2A:170–90.5 both inclusive);

Laws of 1955, c. 254 (C. 2A:171–1.1 and C. 2A:171–1.2);

Laws of 1959, c. 119 (C. 2A:171–5.8 to C. 2A:171–5.18 both inclusive).

L.1978, c. 95, § 2C:98–3, eff. Sept. 1, 1979. Amended by L.1979, c. 178, § 146, eff. Sept. 1, 1979.

[1] Repealed in 1979.
[2] N.J.S.A. §§ 2A:157–7 and 2A:157–14 repealed in 1981.
[3] N.J.S.A. § 2A:166–10 repealed in 1979.
[4] N.J.S.A. § 2A:166–19 repealed in 1979.
[5] Repealed in 1980.
[6] N.J.S.A. § 2A:170–90.1 repealed in 1981.

2C:98–4. Effective date

This act shall take effect the first day of the thirteenth month following enactment.

L.1978, c. 95, § 2C:98–4, eff. Sept. 1, 1979.

CHAPTERS 99 to 103

[RESERVED]

CHAPTER 104

MATERIAL WITNESSES

Section
2C:104–1. Definitions.

Section
2C:104–2. Application for material witness order.
2C:104–3. Order to appear.
2C:104–4. Arrest with warrant.
2C:104–5. Arrest without warrant.
2C:104–6. Material witness hearing.
2C:104–7. Conditions of release; confinement.
2C:104–8. Deposition.
2C:104–9. Orders appealable.

2C:104–1. Definitions

a. A material witness is a person who has information material to the prosecution or defense of a crime.

b. A material witness order is a court order fixing conditions necessary to secure the appearance of a person who is unlikely to respond to a subpoena and who has information material to the prosecution or defense of a pending indictment, accusation or complaint for a crime or a criminal investigation before a grand jury.

L.1994, c. 126, § 1, eff. Oct. 26, 1994.

2C:104–2. Application for material witness order

a. The Attorney General, county prosecutor or defendant in a criminal action may apply to a judge of the Superior Court for an order compelling a person to appear at a material witness hearing, if there is probable cause to believe that: (1) the person has information material to the prosecution or defense of a pending indictment, accusation or complaint for a crime or a criminal investigation before a grand jury and (2) the person is unlikely to respond to a subpoena. The application may be accompanied by an application for an arrest warrant when there is probable cause to believe that the person will not appear at the material witness hearing unless arrested.

b. The application shall include a copy of any pending indictment, complaint or accusation and an affidavit containing: (1) the name and address of the person alleged to be a material witness, (2) a summary of the facts believed to be known by the alleged material witness and the relevance to the criminal action or investigation, (3) a summary of the facts supporting the belief that the person possesses information material to the pending criminal action or investigation, and (4) a summary of the facts supporting the claim that the alleged material witness is unlikely to respond to a subpoena.

c. If the application requests an arrest warrant, the affidavit shall set forth why immediate arrest is necessary.

L.1994, c. 126, § 1, eff. Oct. 26, 1994.

2C:104–3. Order to appear

a. If there is probable cause to believe that a material witness order may issue against the person named in the application, the judge may order the person to appear at a hearing to determine whether the person should be adjudged a material witness.

b. The order and a copy of the application shall be served personally upon the alleged material witness at least 48 hours before the hearing, unless the judge adjusts the time period for good cause, and shall advise the person of:

(1) the time and place of the hearing; and

(2) the right to be represented by an attorney and to have an attorney appointed if the person cannot afford one.

L.1994, c. 126, § 1, eff. Oct. 26, 1994.

2C:104–4. Arrest with warrant

a. If there is clear and convincing evidence that the person named in the application will not be available as a witness unless immediately arrested, the judge may issue an arrest warrant. The arrest warrant shall require that the person be brought before the court immediately after arrest. If the arrest does not take place during regular court hours, the person shall be brought to the emergency-duty Superior Court judge.

b. The judge shall inform the person of:

(1) the reason for arrest;

(2) the time and place of the hearing to determine whether the person is a material witness; and

(3) the right to an attorney and to have an attorney appointed if the person cannot afford one.

c. The judge shall set conditions for release, or if there is clear and convincing evidence that the person will not be available as a witness unless confined, the judge may order the person confined until the material witness hearing which shall take place within 48 hours of the arrest.

L.1994, c. 126, § 1, eff. Oct. 26, 1994.

2C:104–5. Arrest without warrant

a. A law enforcement officer may arrest an alleged material witness without a warrant only if the arrest occurs prior to the filing of an indictment, accusation or complaint for a crime or the initiation of a criminal investigation before a grand jury, and if the officer has probable cause to believe that:

(1) a crime has been committed;

(2) the alleged material witness has information material to the prosecution of that crime;

(3) the alleged material witness will refuse to cooperate with the officer in the investigation of that crime; and

(4) the delay necessary to obtain an arrest warrant or order to appear would result in the unavailability of the alleged material witness.

b. Following the warrantless arrest of an alleged material witness, the law enforcement officer shall bring the person immediately before a judge. If court is not in session, the officer shall immediately bring the person before the emergency-duty Superior Court judge. The judge shall determine whether there is probable cause to believe that the person is a material witness of a crime and, if an indictment, accusation or complaint for that crime has not issued or if a grand jury has not commenced a criminal investigation of that crime, the judge shall determine whether there is probable cause to believe that, within 48 hours of the arrest, an indictment, accusation or complaint will issue or a grand jury investigation will commence. The judge then shall proceed as if an application for a warrant has been made under N.J.S. 2C:104–4.

L.1994, c. 126, § 1, eff. Oct. 26, 1994.

2C:104–6. Material witness hearing

a. At the material witness hearing, the following rights shall be afforded to the person:

(1) the right to be represented by an attorney and to have an attorney appointed if the person cannot afford one;

(2) the right to be heard and to present witnesses and evidence;

(3) the right to have all of the evidence considered by the court in support of the application; and

(4) the right to confront and cross-examine witnesses.

b. If the judge finds that there is probable cause to believe that the person is unlikely to respond to a subpoena and has information material to the prosecution or defense of a pending indictment, accusation or complaint for a crime, or a criminal investigation before a grand jury, the judge shall determine that the person is a material witness and may set the conditions of release of the material witness.

c. If the judge finds by clear and convincing evidence that confinement is the only method that will secure the appearance of the material witness, the judge may order the confinement of the material witness.

d. The judge shall set forth the facts and reasons in support of the material witness order on the record.

L.1994, c. 126, § 1, eff. Oct. 26, 1994.

2C:104–7. Conditions of release; confinement

a. A confined person shall not be held in jail or prison, but shall be lodged in comfortable quarters and served ordinary food.

b. The conditions of release for a material witness or for a person held on an application for a material witness order shall be the least restrictive to effectuate the appearance of the material witness. A judge may:

(1) place the witness in the custody of a designated person or organization agreeing to supervise the person;

(2) restrict the travel of the person;

(3) require the person to report;

(4) set bail; or

(5) impose other reasonable restrictions on the material witness.

c. A person confined shall be paid $40.00 per day, and when the interests of justice require, the judge may order additional payment not exceeding the actual financial loss resulting from the confinement. The party obtaining the material witness order bears the cost of confinement and payment unless the party is indigent.

L.1994, c. 126, § 1, eff. Oct. 26, 1994.

2C:104–8. Deposition

A material witness may apply to the Superior Court for an order directing that a deposition be taken to preserve the witness's testimony. After the deposition is taken, the judge shall vacate the terms of confinement contained in the material witness order and impose the least restrictive conditions to secure the appearance of the material witness.

L.1994, c. 126, § 1, eff. Oct. 26, 1994.

2C:104–9. Orders appealable

A material witness order shall constitute a final order for purposes of appeal, but, on motion of the material witness, may be reconsidered at any time by the court which entered the order.

L.1994, c. 126, § 1, eff. Oct. 26, 1994.

TITLE 39

MOTOR VEHICLES AND TRAFFIC REGULATION

Subtitle
1. Motor Vehicle and Traffic Laws.
2. Other Laws Regulating Motor Vehicles.

SUBTITLE 1

MOTOR VEHICLE AND TRAFFIC LAWS

Chapter
1. Definitions.
2. Department of Motor Vehicles.
2A. New Jersey Motor Vehicle Commission.
3. Motor Vehicles.
3A. Additional Equipment Regulations.
3B. School Buses, Equipment and Regulations.
3C. Snowmobiles, All-Terrain Vehicles and Dirt Bikes.
4. Traffic Regulation.
5. Enforcement and Procedure.
5A. Application of Subtitle to Highways Owned by Public or Semipublic Corporations.
5B. Transportation of Dangerous Articles on Highway.
5C. Motor Vehicle Racing on Highways.
5D. Interstate Compact; Drivers Licenses.
5E. Transportation of Bulk Commodities [Repealed].
5F. Nonresident Violator Compact.
5G. Limousine Operation and Enforcement.

CHAPTER 1

DEFINITIONS

Section
39:1–1. Words and phrases defined.

39:1–1. Words and phrases defined

As used in this subtitle, unless other meaning is clearly apparent from the language or context, or unless inconsistent with the manifest intention of the Legislature:

"Alley" means a public highway wherein the roadway does not exceed 12 feet in width.

"Authorized emergency vehicles" means vehicles of the fire department, police vehicles and such ambulances and other vehicles as are approved by the chief administrator when operated in response to an emergency call.

"Automobile" includes all motor vehicles except motorcycles.

"Berm" means that portion of the highway exclusive of roadway and shoulder, bordering the shoulder but not to be used for vehicular travel.

"Business district" means that portion of a highway and the territory contiguous thereto, where within any 600 feet along such highway there are buildings in use for business or industrial purposes, including but not limited to hotels, banks, office buildings, railroad stations, and public buildings which occupy at least 300 feet of frontage on one side or 300 feet collectively on both sides of the roadway.

"Car pool" means two or more persons commuting on a daily basis to and from work by means of a vehicle with a seating capacity of nine passengers or less.

"Chief Administrator" or "Administrator" means the Chief Administrator of the New Jersey Motor Vehicle Commission.

"Commercial motor vehicle" includes every type of motor-driven vehicle used for commercial purposes on the highways, such as the transportation of goods, wares and merchandise, excepting such vehicles as are run only upon rails or tracks and vehicles of the passenger car type used for touring purposes or the carrying of farm products and milk, as the case may be.

"Commission" means the New Jersey Motor Vehicle Commission established by section 4 of P.L.2003, c. 13 (C.39:2A–4).

"Commissioner" means the Commissioner of Transportation of this State.

"Commuter van" means a motor vehicle having a seating capacity of not less than seven nor more than 15 adult passengers, in which seven or more persons commute on a daily basis to and from work and which vehicle may also be operated by the driver or other designated persons for their personal use.

"Crosswalk" means that part of a highway at an intersection, either marked or unmarked existing at each approach of every roadway intersection, included within the connections of the lateral lines of the sidewalks on opposite sides of the highway measured from the curbs or, in the absence of curbs, from the edges of the shoulder, or, if none, from the edges of the roadway; also, any portion of a highway at an intersection or elsewhere distinctly indicated for pedestrian crossing by lines or other marking on the surface.

"Curb extension" or "bulbout" means a horizontal extension of the sidewalk into the street which results in a narrower roadway section.

"Dealer" includes every person actively engaged in the business of buying, selling or exchanging motor vehicles or motorcycles and who has an established place of business.

"Deputy Chief Administrator" means the deputy chief administrator of the commission.

"Driver" means the rider or driver of a horse, bicycle or motorcycle or the driver or operator of a motor vehicle, unless otherwise specified.

"Explosives" means any chemical compound or mechanical mixture that is commonly used or intended for the purpose of producing an explosion and which contains any oxidizing and combustive units or other ingredients in such proportions, quantities or packing that an ignition by fire, friction, by concussion, by percussion, or by detonator of any part of the compound or mixture may cause such a sudden generation of highly heated gases that the resultant gaseous pressures are capable of producing destructive effects on contiguous objects or of destroying life or limb.

"Farm tractor" means every motor vehicle designed and used primarily as a farm implement for drawing plows, mowing machines, and other implements of husbandry.

"Flammable liquid" means any liquid having a flash point below 200 degrees Fahrenheit, and a vapor pressure not exceeding 40 pounds.

"Gross weight" means the combined weight of a vehicle and a load thereon.

"High occupancy vehicle" or "HOV" means a vehicle which is used to transport two or more persons and shall include public transportation, car pool, van pool, and other vehicles as determined by regulation of the Department of Transportation.

"Highway" means the entire width between the boundary lines of every way publicly maintained when any part thereof is open to the use of the public for purposes of vehicular travel.

"Horse" includes mules and all other domestic animals used as draught animals or beasts of burden.

"Inside lane" means the lane nearest the center line of the roadway.

"Intersection" means the area embraced within the prolongation of the lateral curb lines or, if none, the lateral boundary lines of two or more highways which join one another at an angle, whether or not one such highway crosses another.

"Laned roadway" means a roadway which is divided into two or more clearly marked lanes for vehicular traffic.

"Leased limousine" means any limousine subject to regulation in the State which:

a. Is offered for rental or lease, without a driver, to be operated by a limousine service as the lessee, for the purpose of carrying passengers for hire; and

b. Is leased or rented for a period of one year or more following registration.

"Leased motor vehicle" means any motor vehicle subject to registration in this State which:

a. Is offered for rental or lease, without a driver, to be operated by the lessee, his agent or servant, for purposes other than the transportation of passengers for hire; and

b. Is leased or rented for a period of one year or more following registration.

"Limited-access highway" means every highway, street, or roadway in respect to which owners or occupants of abutting lands and other persons have no legal right of access to or from the same except at such points only and in such manner as may be determined by the public authority having jurisdiction over such highway, street, or roadway; and includes any highway designated as a "freeway" or "parkway" by authority of law.

"Local authorities" means every county, municipal and other local board or body having authority to adopt local police regulations under the Constitution and laws of this State, including every county governing body with relation to county roads.

"Low-speed vehicle" means a four-wheeled low-speed vehicle, as defined in 49 CFR s. 571.3(b), whose attainable speed is more than 20 miles per hour but not more than 25 miles per hour on a paved level surface and which is not powered by gasoline or diesel fuel and complies with federal safety standards as set forth in 49 CFR s. 571.500.

"Magistrate" means any municipal court and the Superior Court, and any officer having the powers of a committing magistrate and the chief administrator.

"Manufacturer" means a person engaged in the business of manufacturing or assembling motor vehicles, who will, under normal business conditions during the year, manufacture or assemble at least 10 new motor vehicles.

"Metal tire" means every tire the surface of which in contact with the highway is wholly or partly of metal or other hard nonresilient material.

"Mid-block crosswalk" means a crosswalk located away from an intersection, distinctly indicated by lines or markings on the surface.

"Motorized bicycle" means a pedal bicycle having a helper motor characterized in that either the maximum piston displacement is less than 50 cc. or said motor is rated at no more than 1.5 brake horsepower or is powered by an electric drive motor and said bicycle is capable of a maximum speed of no more than 25 miles per hour on a flat surface.

"Motorcycle" includes motorcycles, motor bikes, bicycles with motor attached and all motor-operated vehicles of the bicycle or tricycle type, except motorized bicycles as defined in this section, whether the motive power be a part thereof or attached thereto and having a saddle or seat with driver sitting astride or upon it or a platform on which the driver stands.

"Motor-drawn vehicle" includes trailers, semitrailers, or any other type of vehicle drawn by a motor-driven vehicle.

"Motor vehicle" includes all vehicles propelled otherwise than by muscular power, excepting such vehicles as run only upon rails or tracks and motorized bicycles.

"Motorized scooter" means a miniature motor vehicle and includes, but is not limited to, pocket bikes, super pocket bikes, scooters, mini-scooters, sport scooters, mini choppers, mini motorcycles, motorized skateboards and other vehicles with motors not manufactured in compliance with Federal Motor Vehicle Safety Standards and which have no permanent Federal Safety Certification stickers affixed to the vehicle by the original manufacturer. This term shall not include: electric personal assistive mobility devices, motorized bicycles or low-speed vehicles; or motorized wheelchairs, mobility scooters or similar mobility assisting devices used by persons with physical disabilities, or persons whose ambulatory mobility has been impaired by age or illness.

"Motorized skateboard" means a skateboard that is propelled otherwise than by muscular power.

"Motorized wheelchair" means any motor-driven wheelchair utilized to increase the independent mobility, in the activities of daily living, of an individual who has limited or no ambulation abilities, and includes mobility scooters manufactured specifically for such purposes and designed primarily for indoor use.

"Noncommercial truck" means every motor vehicle designed primarily for transportation of property, and which is not a "commercial vehicle."

"Official traffic control devices" means all signs, signals, markings, and devices not inconsistent with this subtitle placed or erected by authority of a public body or official having jurisdiction for the purpose of regulating, warning, or guiding traffic.

"Omnibus" includes all motor vehicles used for the transportation of passengers for hire, except commuter vans and vehicles used in ridesharing arrangements and school buses, if the same are not otherwise used in the transportation of passengers for hire.

"Operator" means a person who is in actual physical control of a vehicle or street car.

"Outside lane" means the lane nearest the curb or outer edge of the roadway.

"Owner" means a person who holds the legal title of a vehicle, or if a vehicle is the subject of an agreement for the conditional sale or lease thereof with the right of purchase upon performance of the conditions stated in the agreement and with an immediate right of possession vested in the conditional vendee or lessee, or if a mortgagor of a vehicle is entitled to possession, then the conditional vendee, lessee or mortgagor shall be deemed the owner for the purpose of this subtitle.

"Parking" means the standing or waiting on a street, road or highway of a vehicle not actually engaged in receiving or discharging passengers or merchandise, unless in obedience to traffic regulations or traffic signs or signals.

"Passenger automobile" means all automobiles used and designed for the transportation of passengers, other than omnibuses and school buses.

"Pedestrian" means a person afoot.

"Person" includes natural persons, firms, copartnerships, associations, and corporations.

"Pneumatic tire" means every tire in which compressed air is designed to support the load.

"Pole trailer" means every vehicle without motive power designed to be drawn by another vehicle and attached to the towing vehicle by means of a reach, or pole, or by being boomed or otherwise secured to the towing vehicle, and ordinarily used for transporting long or irregularly shaped loads, such as poles, pipes, or structural members capable, generally, of sustaining themselves as beams between the supporting connections.

"Private road or driveway" means every road or driveway not open to the use of the public for purposes of vehicular travel.

"Railroad train" means a steam engine, electric or other motor, with or without cars coupled thereto, operated upon rails, except street cars.

"Recreation vehicle" means a self-propelled or towed vehicle equipped to serve as temporary living quarters for recreational, camping or travel purposes and used solely as a family or personal conveyance.

"Residence district" means that portion of a highway and the territory contiguous thereto, not comprising a business district, where within any 600 feet along such highway there are buildings in use for business or residential purposes which occupy 300 feet or more of frontage on at least one side of the highway.

"Ridesharing" means the transportation of persons in a motor vehicle, with a maximum carrying capacity of not more than 15 passengers, including the driver, where such transportation is incidental to the purpose of the driver. The term shall include such ridesharing arrangements known as car pools and van pools.

"Right-of-way" means the privilege of the immediate use of the highway.

"Road tractor" means every motor vehicle designed and used for drawing other vehicles and not so constructed as to carry any load thereon either independently or any part of the weight of a vehicle or load so drawn.

"Roadway" means that portion of a highway improved, designed, or ordinarily used for vehicular travel, exclusive of the berm or shoulder. In the event a highway includes two or more separate roadways, the term "roadway" as used herein shall refer to any such roadway separately, but not to all such roadways, collectively.

"Safety zone" means the area or space officially set aside within a highway for the exclusive use of pedestrians, which is so plainly marked or indicated by proper signs as to be plainly visible at all times while set apart as a safety zone.

"School bus" means every motor vehicle operated by, or under contract with, a public or governmental agency, or religious or other charitable organization or corporation, or privately operated for the transportation of children to or from school for secular or religious education, which complies with the regulations of the New Jersey Motor Vehicle Commission affecting school buses, including "School Vehicle Type I" and "School Vehicle Type II" as defined below:

"School Vehicle Type I" means any vehicle designed to transport 16 or more passengers, including the driver, used to transport enrolled children, and adults only when serving as chaperones, to or from a school, school connected activity, day camp, summer day camp, summer residence camp, nursery school, child care center, preschool center or other similar places of education. Such vehicle shall comply with the regulations of the New Jersey Motor Vehicle Commission and either the Department of Education or the Department of Human Services, whichever is the appropriate supervising agency.

"School Vehicle Type II" means any vehicle designed to transport less than 16 passengers, including the driver, used to transport enrolled children, and adults only when serving as chaperones, to or from a school, school connected activity, day camp, summer day camp, summer residence camp, nursery school, child care center, preschool center or other similar places of education. Such vehicle shall comply with the regulations of the New Jersey Motor Vehicle Commission and either the Department of Education or the Department of Human Services, whichever is the appropriate supervising agency.

"School zone" means that portion of a highway which is either contiguous to territory occupied by a school building or is where school crossings are established in the vicinity of a school, upon which are maintained appropriate "school signs" in accordance with specifications adopted by the chief administrator and in accordance with law.

"School crossing" means that portion of a highway where school children are required to cross the highway in the vicinity of a school.

"Semitrailer" means every vehicle with or without motive power, other than a pole trailer, designed for carrying persons or property and for being drawn by a motor vehicle and so constructed that some part of its weight and that of its load rests upon or is carried by another vehicle.

"Shipper" means any person who shall deliver, or cause to be delivered, any commodity, produce or article for transportation as the contents or load of a commercial motor vehicle. In the case of a sealed ocean container, "shipper" shall not be construed to include any person whose activities with respect to the shipment are limited to the solicitation or negotiation of the sale, resale, or exchange of the commodity, produce or article within that container.

"Shoulder" means that portion of the highway, exclusive of and bordering the roadway, designed for emergency use but not ordinarily to be used for vehicular travel.

"Sidewalk" means that portion of a highway intended for the use of pedestrians, between the curb line or the lateral line of a shoulder, or if none, the lateral line of the roadway and the adjacent right-of-way line.

"Sign." See "Official traffic control devices."

"Slow-moving vehicle" means a vehicle run at a speed less than the maximum speed then and there permissible.

"Solid tire" means every tire of rubber or other resilient material which does not depend upon compressed air for the support of the load.

"Street" means the same as highway.

"Street car" means a car other than a railroad train, for transporting persons or property and operated upon rails principally within a municipality.

"Stop," when required, means complete cessation from movement.

"Stopping or standing," when prohibited, means any cessation of movement of a vehicle, whether occupied or not, except when necessary to avoid conflict with other traffic or in compliance with the directions of a police officer or traffic control sign or signal.

"Suburban business or residential district" means that portion of highway and the territory contiguous thereto, where within any 1,320 feet along that highway there is land in use for business or residential purposes and that land occupies more than 660 feet of frontage on one side or collectively more than 660 feet of frontage on both sides of that roadway.

"Through highway" means every highway or portion thereof at the entrances to which vehicular traffic from intersecting highways is required by law to stop before entering or crossing the same and when stop signs are erected as provided in this chapter.

"Trackless trolley" means every motor vehicle which is propelled by electric power obtained from overhead trolley wires but not operated upon rails.

"Traffic" means pedestrians, ridden or herded animals, vehicles, street cars, and other conveyances either singly, or together, while using any highway for purposes of travel.

"Traffic control signal" means a device, whether manually, electrically, mechanically, or otherwise controlled, by which traffic is alternately directed to stop and to proceed.

"Trailer" means every vehicle with or without motive power, other than a pole trailer, designed for carrying persons or property and for being drawn by a motor vehicle and so constructed that no part of its weight rests upon the towing vehicle.

"Truck" means every motor vehicle designed, used, or maintained primarily for the transportation of property.

"Truck tractor" means every motor vehicle designed and used primarily for drawing other vehicles and not so constructed as to carry a load other than a part of the weight of the vehicle and load so drawn.

"Van pooling" means seven or more persons commuting on a daily basis to and from work by means of a vehicle with a seating arrangement designed to carry seven to 15 adult passengers.

"Vehicle" means every device in, upon or by which a person or property is or may be transported upon a highway, excepting devices moved by human power or used exclusively upon stationary rails or tracks or motorized bicycles.

Amended by L.1951, c. 25, § 1; L.1953, c. 36, § 1; L.1955, c. 8, § 1, eff. March 1, 1956; L.1956, c. 132, § 1; L.1965, c. 226, § 1, eff. Jan. 10, 1966; L.1967, c. 238, § 1, eff. Jan. 1, 1968; L.1968, c. 439, § 1; L.1974, c. 162, § 1, eff. Dec. 2, 1974; L.1975, c. 250, § 1, eff. Oct. 31, 1975; L.1977, c. 267, § 1; L.1981, c. 139, § 1; L.1981, c. 413, § 7, eff. Jan. 7, 1982; L.1982, c. 87, § 1, eff. July 23, 1982; L.1984, c. 33, § 1, eff. May 19, 1984; L.1992, c. 32, § 14, eff. June 30, 1992; L.1993, c. 12, § 1, eff. Jan. 15, 1993; L.1993, c. 125, § 1; L.1993, c. 315, § 1, eff. Dec. 23, 1993; L.1995, c. 397, § 1, eff. Jan. 10, 1996; L.2001, c. 416, § 3, eff. Jan. 8, 2002; L.2003, c. 13, § 36; L.2005, c. 147, § 1; L.2005, c. 158, § 5, eff. July 19, 2005; L.2005, c. 159, § 1, eff. July 19, 2005; L.2005, c. 273, § 1, eff. April 6, 2006; L.2009, c. 107, § 1, eff. Aug. 6, 2009.

Historical and Statutory Notes

L.2003, c. 13, § 127, approved Jan. 28, 2003, provides:

"Sections 1, 2, 3, 12, 38, 109, 110 and 121 shall take effect immediately, sections 105, 106, 107, 108, and 120 shall take effect on July 1, 2003 and the remainder of this act shall take effect on the date the Commissioner of Transportation certifies to the Governor (hereinafter the "date of certification") that a majority of the members of the commission have been appointed or are in office and that all necessary anticipatory actions have been accomplished, provided, that the amount of revenues received pursuant to sections 109 and 110 prior to the date of certification are hereby appropriated to the division. Upon the date of certification, all such collected revenue shall be revenue of the commission. The Commissioner of Transportation, the Director of the Division of Motor Vehicles and the commission may take such anticipatory administrative action in advance as shall be necessary for the implementation of the act."

CHAPTER 2

DEPARTMENT OF MOTOR VEHICLES

Section
39:2–1.　Department continued.
39:2–2.　Director of division of motor vehicles; appointment; term; salary; bond; oath.
39:2–3.　Powers and duties of commissioner generally; collection of data; contracts; disbursements.
39:2–3.1.　Repealed.
39:2–3.2.　Procedure for simultaneous application for driver's license and registration to vote.
39:2–3.3.　Definitions.
39:2–3.4.　Disclosure of personal information.
39:2–3.5.　Violations; criminal penalties.
39:2–3.6.　Violations; civil penalties.
39:2–3.7.　Obtaining personal information.
39:2–3.8.　Electronic processing; regulations.
39:2–4.　Deputy director; powers; bond; oath.
39:2–5.　Repealed.
39:2–6 to 39:2–9.　Repealed.
39:2–9.1.　Abolishment of positions of chief inspector, deputy chief inspector, inspector and special inspector.
39:2–9.2.　Reemployment rights.
39:2–9.3.　Appointment to state police.
39:2–9.4.　Qualifications of appointee.
39:2–9.5.　Transfer of pension contributions and reserves.
39:2–9.6.　Construction of act to preserve rights of tenure, civil service, pension or retirements.
39:2–9.7.　State Agency Transfer Act; application to act.
39:2–9.8.　Construction of act.
39:2–10.　Records and seal; authentication of documents.
39:2–11.　Office facilities and supplies.
39:2–12.　Repealed.
39:2–13.　Medical advisory panel.
39:2–14.　Appointments; term; reimbursement for expenses.
39:2–15.　Duties; recommendations; adoption by division.
39:2–16.　Nonliability for civil damages as a result of providing reports, records, etc.

39:2–1.　Department continued

The department of motor vehicles,[1] created and established by an act entitled "A supplement to an act entitled 'An act defining motor vehicles and providing for the registration of the same and the licensing of the drivers thereof; fixing rules regulating the use and speed of motor vehicles; fixing the amount of license and registration fees; prescribing and regulating process and the service thereof and proceedings for the violation of the provisions of the act and penalties for said violations,' approved April eighth, one thousand nine hundred and twenty-one," passed March twenty-fourth, one thousand nine hundred and twenty-six (L.1926, c. 147, p. 228), as amended and supplemented is continued. The department shall have full charge of the registration and regulation of all motor vehicles as provided by L.1921, c. 208, p. 643, entitled "An act defining motor vehicles and providing for the registration of the same and the licensing of the drivers thereof; fixing rules regulating the use and speed of motor vehicles; fixing the amount of license and registration fees; prescribing and regulating process and the service thereof and proceedings for the violation of the provisions of the act and penalties for said violations", effective January first, one thousand nine hundred and twenty-two, and the amendments and supplements thereto. The department shall also have such other duties and powers as are described in said L.1921, c. 208, p. 643, or as may hereafter be provided by law.

¹ Now New Jersey Motor Vehicle Commission, see N.J.S.A. § 39:2A–4.

39:2–2. Director of division of motor vehicles; appointment; term; salary; bond; oath

The division shall be administered by the Director of the Division of Motor Vehicles.

The director shall be appointed by the Governor with the advice and consent of the Senate and shall serve at the pleasure of the Governor during the Governor's term of office and until the director's successor is appointed and has qualified.

The director shall receive such salary as shall be provided by law.

The director shall give bond, conditioned for the faithful discharge of his duties, in the sum of $50,000.00, which bond shall be approved by a justice of the supreme court or a judge of the superior court, and shall be filed with the State Treasurer.

The director shall take an oath before one of the supreme court justices or superior court judges, in form similar to that now required by the State Treasurer, which oath shall be filed with the Secretary of State.

Amended by L.1944, c. 44, p. 100, § 1; L.1953, c. 36, p. 617, § 2; L.1962, c. 65, § 8, eff. July 1, 1962; L.1971, c. 105, § 1, eff. April 16, 1971; L.1975, c. 97, § 1, eff. May 20, 1975.

39:2–3. Powers and duties of commissioner generally; collection of data; contracts; disbursements

The commission shall:

a. Have all the powers and perform all the duties conferred or imposed upon it by this Title;

b. Have charge and supervision of the administration and enforcement of this Title and attend to the enforcement thereof, and for the purpose of enforcement may communicate with the police departments and police officers in the state;

c. Collect such data with respect to the proper restrictions to be placed upon motor vehicles and their use upon the public roads, turnpikes and thoroughfares as shall seem for the public good;

d. Execute all contracts entered into by the commission and approve all bills for disbursement of money under any provision of this chapter and chapter 3 of this title (R.S. 39:3–1 et seq.), which bills shall be paid by the State Treasurer upon the warrant of the comptroller out of any appropriation regularly made therefor.

Amended by L.2003, c. 13, § 42 (contingent effective date).

39:2–3.1. Repealed by L.1994, c. 182, § 45

39:2–3.2. Procedure for simultaneous application for driver's license and registration to vote

a. The Secretary of State, with the assistance and concurrence of the Director of the Division of Motor Vehicles, shall formulate a means of permitting a person to simultaneously apply for a motor vehicle driver's license and to register to vote which satisfies both the requirements necessary to receive a license to operate a motor vehicle, pursuant to R.S.39:3–10, and to be permitted to register to vote, pursuant to R.S.19:4–1.

The Division of Motor Vehicles, upon receipt of a completed voter registration application under this section, shall stamp or otherwise mark the lower right hand corner of the document with the date on which it was so received and forward the document to the Secretary of State no later than the 10th day following the date of acceptance.

b. Each application for voter registration which is received by the Division of Motor Vehicles shall be considered and processed as the replacement for any pre-existing voter registration of the applicant.

c. Each change of address notification submitted to the Director of the Division of Motor Vehicles for the purpose of maintaining current information on a person's motor vehicle license shall be reported to the Secretary of State no later than the 10th day following its receipt by the Division of Motor Vehicles and shall serve as notification for the change of address process, unless the registrant indicates that the change of address is not for voter registration purposes.

L.1994, c. 182, § 24.

39:2–3.3. Definitions

As used in this act:

"Director" means the Director of the Division of Motor Vehicles in the Department of Transportation.

"Division" means the Division of Motor Vehicles in the Department of Transportation.

"Motor vehicle record" means any record that pertains to a motor vehicle operator's permit, driver's license, motor vehicle title, motor vehicle registration, or identification card issued by the Division of Motor Vehicles.

"Person" means an individual, organization or entity, but does not include the State or a political subdivision thereof.

"Personal information" means information that identifies an individual, including an individual's photograph; social security number; driver identification number; name; address other than the five-digit zip code; telephone number; and medical or disability information, but does not include information on vehicular accidents, driving violations, and driver's status. *L.1997, c. 188, § 1, eff. Aug. 5, 1997.*

39:2–3.4. Disclosure of personal information

a. Notwithstanding the provisions of P.L.1963, c. 73 (C.47:1A–1 et seq.) or any other law to the contrary, except as provided in this act, the Motor Vehicle Commission and any officer, employee or contractor thereof shall not knowingly disclose or otherwise make available to any person personal information about any individual obtained by the commission in connection with a motor vehicle record.

b. A person requesting a motor vehicle record including personal information shall produce proper identification and shall complete and submit a written request form provided by the chief administrator for the commission's approval. The written request form shall bear notice that the making of false statements therein is punishable and shall include, but not be limited to, the requestor's name and address; the requestor's driver's license number or corporate identification number; the requestor's reason for requesting the record; the driver's license number or the name, address and birth date of the person whose driver record is requested; the license plate number or VIN number of the vehicle for which a record is requested; any additional information determined by the chief administrator to be appropriate and the requestor's certification as to the truth of the foregoing statements. Prior to the approval of the written request form, the commission may also require the requestor to submit documentary evidence supporting the reason for the request.

In lieu of completing a written request form for each record requested, the commission may permit a person to complete and submit for approval of the chief administrator or the chief administrator's designee, on a case by case basis, a written application form for participation in a public information program on an ongoing basis. The written application form shall bear notice that the making of false statements therein is punishable and shall include, but not be limited to, the applicant's name, address and telephone number; the nature of the applicant's business activity; a description of each of the applicant's intended uses of the information contained in the motor vehicle records to be requested; the number of employees with access to the information; the name, title and signature of the authorized company representative; and any additional information determined by the chief administrator to be appropriate. The chief administrator may also require the applicant to submit a copy of its business credentials, such as license to do business or certificate of incorporation. Prior to approval by the chief administrator or the chief administrator's designee, the applicant shall certify in writing as to the truth of all statements contained in the completed application form.

c. Personal information shall be disclosed for use in connection with matters of motor vehicle or driver safety and theft; motor vehicle emissions; motor vehicle product alterations, recalls or advisories; performance monitoring of motor vehicles and dealers by motor vehicle manufacturers; and removal of non-owner records from the original owner records of motor vehicle manufacturers to carry out the purposes of the Automobile Information Disclosure Act, Pub.L.85–506, the Motor Vehicle Information and Cost Saving Act, Pub. L.92–513, the National Traffic and Motor Vehicle Safety Act of 1966, Pub.L.89–563, the Anti–Car Theft Act of 1992, Pub.L.102–519, and the Clean Air Act, Pub.L.88–206, and may be disclosed as follows:

(1) For use by any government agency, including any court or law enforcement agency in carrying out its functions, or any private person or entity acting on behalf of a federal, State or local agency in carrying out its functions.

(2) For use in connection with matters of motor vehicle or driver safety and theft; motor vehicle emissions; motor vehicle product alterations, recalls, or advisories; performance monitoring of motor vehicles, motor vehicle parts and dealers; motor vehicle market research activities, including survey research; and the removal of non-owner records from the original owner records of motor vehicle manufacturers.

(3) For use in the normal course of business by a legitimate business or its agents, employees or contractors, but only:

(a) to verify the accuracy of personal information submitted by the individual to the business or its agents, employees, or contractors; and

(b) if such information as so submitted is not correct or is no longer correct, to obtain the correct information, but only for the purposes of preventing fraud by, pursuing legal remedies against, or recovering on a debt or security interest against the individual.

(4) For use in connection with any civil, criminal, administrative or arbitral proceeding in any federal, State or local court or agency or before any self-regulatory body, including service of process, investigation in anticipation of litigation, and the execution or enforcement of judgments and orders, or pursuant to an order of a federal, State or local court.

(5) For use in educational initiatives, research activities, and for use in producing statistical reports, so long

as the personal information is not published, redisclosed, or used to contact individuals and, in the case of educational initiatives, only to organ procurement organizations as aggregated, non-identifying information.

(6) For use by any insurer or insurance support organization, or by a self-insured entity, or its agents, employees, or contractors, in connection with claims investigation activities, antifraud activities, rating or underwriting.

(7) For use in providing notice to the owners of towed or impounded vehicles.

(8) For use by an employer or its agent or insurer to obtain or verify information relating to a holder of a commercial driver's license that is required under the "Commercial Motor Vehicle Safety Act," 49 U.S.C.App.s.2710 et seq.

(9) For use in connection with the operation of private toll transportation facilities.

(10) For use by any requestor, if the requestor demonstrates it has obtained the notarized written consent of the individual to whom the information pertains.

(11) For product and service mail communications from automotive-related manufacturers, dealers and businesses, if the commission has implemented methods and procedures to ensure that:

(a) individuals are provided an opportunity, in a clear and conspicuous manner, to prohibit such uses; and

(b) product and service mail communications from automotive-related manufacturers, dealers and businesses will not be directed at individuals who exercise their option under subparagraph (a) of this paragraph.

(12) For use by an organ procurement organization designated pursuant to 42 U.S.C. s.1320b–8 to serve in the State of New Jersey, or any donor registry established by any such organization, exclusively for the purposes of determining, verifying, and recording organ and tissue donor designation and identity. For these purposes, an organ procurement organization shall have electronic access at all times, without exception, to real-time organ donor designation and identification information. An organ procurement organization may also have information for research activities, pursuant to paragraph (5) of subsection c. of this section.

d. As provided by the federal "Drivers' Privacy Protection Act of 1994," Pub.L.103–322, a person authorized to receive personal information under paragraphs (1) through (10) of subsection c. of this section may resell or redisclose the personal information only for a use permitted by paragraphs (1) through (10) of subsection c. of this section subject to regulation by the commission. A person authorized to receive personal information under paragraph (11) of subsection c. of this section may resell or redisclose the personal information pursuant to paragraph (11) of subsection c. of this section subject to regulation by the commission.

An organization authorized to receive personal information under paragraph (12) of subsection c. of this section may redisclose the personal information only for the purposes set forth in that paragraph.

e. As provided by the federal "Drivers' Privacy Protection Act of 1994," Pub.L.103–322, a person authorized to receive personal information under this section who resells or rediscloses personal information covered by the provisions of this act shall keep for a period of five years records identifying each person or entity that receives information and the permitted purpose for which the information will be used and shall make such records available to the commission upon request. Any person who receives, from any source, personal information from a motor vehicle record shall release or disclose that information only in accordance with this act.

f. The release of personal information under this section shall not include an individual's social security number except in accordance with applicable State or federal law.

L.1997, c. 188, § 2, eff. Aug. 5, 1997. Amended by L.2007, c. 80, § 2, eff. Sept. 1, 2007; L.2008, c. 48, § 12, eff. July 22, 2008.

39:2–3.5. Violations; criminal penalties

A person who knowingly obtains or discloses personal information from a motor vehicle record for any use not permitted under section 2 of P.L.1997, c.188 (C.39:2–3.4) is guilty of a crime of the fourth degree.

L.1997, c.188, § 3, eff. Aug. 5, 1997.

39:2–3.6. Violations; civil penalties

a. A person who knowingly obtains, discloses or uses personal information from a motor vehicle record for a purpose not permitted under this act shall be liable to the individual to whom the information pertains, who may bring a civil action in the Superior Court.

b. The court may award:

(1) actual damages, but not less than liquidated damages in the amount of $2,500;

(2) punitive damages upon proof of willful or reckless disregard of the law;

(3) reasonable attorney's fees and other litigation costs reasonably incurred; and

(4) such other preliminary and equitable relief as the court determines to be appropriate.

L.1997, c. 188, § 4, eff. Aug. 5, 1997.

39:2–3.7. Obtaining personal information

Nothing in this act shall be construed as authorizing the division to obtain personal information, except as provided in subsection b. of section 2 of this act.

L.1997, c. 188, § 5, eff. Aug. 5, 1997.

39:2–3.8. Electronic processing; regulations

a. Whenever any law, rule or regulation requires or permits documents or information to be prepared by or submitted to the Division of Motor Vehicles in the Department of Transportation, the director may permit the documents or information to be prepared by or submitted to the division in electronic or digital form, or processed electronically. In no event shall an individual be required to submit documents or information only in electronic or digital form; nor shall documents or information be made available to an individual only in electronic or digital form. Submission in electronic or digital form may be permitted pursuant to this section notwithstanding that any law, rule or regulation requires documents or information to be written or to be submitted in writing, specifies that documents or information be signed, certified, verified or witnessed, or otherwise explicitly or implicitly requires the preparation or submission of documents or information on paper or in written form. As used in this subsection, "individual" means a natural person.

b. The director, after consultation with the State Records Committee in the Department of State, shall adopt, pursuant to the "Administrative Procedure Act," P.L.1968, c. 410 (C.52:14B–1 et seq.), regulations specifying how the signature, verification, certification, witnessing or other formal requirements shall be met with respect to documents or information permitted to be prepared or submitted in electronic or digital form pursuant to this section and specifying such additional safeguards as the director deems necessary to protect the privacy, and prevent improper access to or disclosure, of any personal information as defined in section 1 of P.L.1997, c. 188 (C.39:2–3.3) that may be transmitted in an electronic or digital form, or processed electronically. Regulations adopted pursuant to this subsection may permit the use of digital signature technology for the signing of documents and other appropriate purposes.

L.1999, c. 149, § 1, eff. June 28, 1999.

39:2–4. Deputy director; powers; bond; oath

The director shall appoint a deputy director for a term to correspond with his term of office. He shall assist the director in the administration and enforcement of this subtitle and have all the powers of the director when deputized by the director in the performance of such duties as the director may assign to him. He shall receive such compensation as shall be approved by the director and the president of the Civil Service Commission subject to availability of funds.

The deputy director shall give bond, conditioned for the faithful discharge of his duties, in the sum of $50,000.00, which bond shall be approved by a judge of the Superior Court and filed with the State Treasurer. He shall also take an oath of office before a judge of the Superior Court, in form similar to that now required of the State Treasurer, which oath shall be filed with the Secretary of State.

Amended by L.1953, c. 36, p. 618, § 3; L.1962, c. 65, § 9, eff. July 1, 1962.

39:2–5. Repealed by L.2003, c. 13, § 126

39:2–6 to 39:2–9. Repealed by L.1983, c. 403, § 45, eff. Dec. 23, 1983

39:2–9.1. Abolishment of positions of chief inspector, deputy chief inspector, inspector and special inspector

The positions in the Division of Motor Vehicles designated chief inspector, deputy chief inspector, inspector and special inspector are abolished.

L.1983, c. 403, § 1, eff. Dec. 23, 1983.

39:2–9.2. Reemployment rights

A person employed in a position designated as chief inspector, deputy chief inspector, inspector, special inspector or equivalent Civil Service classifications shall have the following reemployment rights:

a. The person may be appointed, at his request and at the discretion of the superintendent of the Division of State Police, as a member of the State Police; or

b. The person shall be reemployed by the State of New Jersey, as provided by the laws governing Civil Service.

L.1983, c. 403, § 2, eff. Dec. 23, 1983.

39:2–9.3. Appointment to state police

a. An appointment to the State Police under this act shall be in accordance with R.S. 53:1–8, except that upon satisfactory conclusion of the two-year appointment period specified in R.S. 53:1–8, the person appointed shall serve continuously as a member of the State Police during good behavior, notwithstanding the requirements of R.S. 53:1–8.1.

b. A person appointed to the State Police under this act shall be ranked, approximately equivalent to his current salary range and step therein, by the superintendent, as adjusted by the State Treasurer, the President of the Civil Service Commission and the Director of the Division of Budget and Accounting.

c. For the purposes of internal management only, the seniority of a person appointed to the State Police under this act shall be determined by the superintendent.

d. No person appointed to the State Police under this act shall retain any entitlement upon retirement from the State Police to receive a lump sum payment as supplemental compensation for each full day of earned and unused accumulated sick leave, as authorized by section 1 of P.L.1973, c. 130 (C. 11:14–9).[1]

L.1983, c. 403, § 3, eff. Dec. 23, 1983.

[1] Repealed; see, now, § 11A:6–16.

39:2–9.4. Qualifications of appointee

Notwithstanding the provisions of R.S. 53:1–9, the Superintendent of the Division of State Police may establish the qualifications of a person appointed to the State Police under this act.

L.1983, c. 403, § 4, eff. Dec. 23, 1983.

39:2–9.5. Transfer of pension contributions and reserves

The Boards of Trustees of the Police and Firemen's Retirement System and the Public Employees' Retirement System shall cause to be made any transfer of pension contributions and reserves to the State Police Retirement System of New Jersey necessary to implement the provisions of this act.

L.1983, c. 403, § 42, eff. Dec. 23, 1983.

39:2–9.6. Construction of act to preserve rights of tenure, civil service, pension or retirements

Except as otherwise provided in this act, nothing in this act shall be construed to deprive a person of tenure rights or of a right or protection under the laws concerning Civil Service, pension or retirement.

L.1983, c. 403, § 43, eff. Dec. 23, 1983.

39:2–9.7. State Agency Transfer Act; application to act

All of the provisions of this act, except as otherwise provided herein, shall be carried out in accordance with the "State Agency Transfer Act," P.L. 1971, c. 375 (C. 52:14D–1 et seq.).

L.1983, c. 403, § 44, eff. Dec. 23, 1983.

39:2–9.8. Construction of act

The provisions of this act are not intended, nor shall they be construed or used, as a basis to privatize existing services or programs, or in any manner reduce the number of State employees performing driver testing duties in the Division of Motor Vehicles.

L.2001, c. 420, § 12, eff. Jan. 8, 2002.

39:2–10. Records and seal; authentication of documents

The director shall keep a record of all his official acts, shall preserve copies of all decisions, rules and orders made by him and shall adopt an official seal. Copies of any act, rule, order or decision made by him and of any paper filed in his office may be authenticated under such seal, at a cost not to exceed $5.00 for each authentication, and when so authenticated shall be evidence the same as the original.

Amended by L.1975, c. 180, § 1, eff. Jan. 1, 1976.

39:2–11. Office facilities and supplies

The state house commission shall provide suitable quarters for the department and shall furnish all necessary supplies and equipment for the proper enforcement of this subtitle.

39:2–12. Repealed by L.2003, c. 13, § 126

39:2–13. Medical advisory panel

There is hereby created in the Division of Motor Vehicles a special study and advisory panel to be known as the Medical Advisory Panel consisting of physicians licensed to practice medicine and surgery (including physicians specialty-board certified in internal medicine, psychiatry, neurology, physical medicine, and ophthalmology), licensed optometrists, and officials of the division supervising motor vehicle driver licensing.

L.1977, c. 26, § 1, eff. Feb. 24, 1977. Amended by L.1980, c. 37, § 2, eff. June 19, 1980.

39:2–14. Appointments; term; reimbursement for expenses

The members of the panel shall be appointed by the Governor upon recommendations by the director and shall be in such number as the Governor and director shall deem appropriate. In recommending the physician and optometrist members, the director shall seek the advice and recommendations of the Medical Society of New Jersey with respect to the physician members, and the New Jersey Optometric Association with respect to the optometrist member or members. The panel and the members thereof shall serve at the pleasure of the Governor. They shall receive no compensation for their services but shall be reimbursed for the reasonable expenses actually incurred in the performance of their duties as approved by the director.

L.1977, c. 26, § 2, eff. Feb. 24, 1977.

39:2–15. Duties; recommendations; adoption by division

The Medical Advisory Panel shall study and review all medical criteria and vision standards applicable to the licensing of motor vehicle drivers by the division and recommend such additions and revisions thereof as it shall deem necessary and appropriate. Any such recommended additions and revisions may be adopted by the division on a trial basis to determine the necessity and validity thereof.

The director may from time to time require panel members to give testimony at administrative hearings concerning applicants and licensees who may suffer from medical, vision, psychiatric, psychological or characterological disorders relating to a person's ability to safely operate a motor vehicle.

L.1977, c. 26, § 3, eff. Feb. 24, 1977. Amended by L.1980, c. 37, § 3, eff. June 19, 1980.

39:2–16. Nonliability for civil damages as a result of providing reports, records, etc.

No member of the Medical Advisory Panel, the Director of the Division of Motor Vehicles or his employees, or any physician or optometrist licensed to practice in this State shall be liable for any civil damages as a result of providing any reports, records, examinations, opinions or recommendations pursuant to the act to which this act is a supplement.

L.1980, c. 173, § 1, eff. Dec. 29, 1980.

CHAPTER 2A

NEW JERSEY MOTOR VEHICLE COMMISSION

Section
39:2A–1.   Short title.
39:2A–2.   Legislative findings.
39:2A–3.   Definitions.
39:2A–4.   New Jersey Motor Vehicle Commission.
39:2A–5.   Employees of commission.
39:2A–6.   Civil service credit; private employees.
39:2A–7.   Probationary period.
39:2A–8.   Salary.
39:2A–9.   Competitive testing.
39:2A–10.   Deputy chief administrator; powers and duties.
39:2A–11.   Appointing authority.
39:2A–12.   Composition of board; chair; appointment and terms of office of members; designation of persons to act for members; vacancies.
39:2A–13.   Powers and duties of board.
39:2A–14.   Member elections.
39:2A–15.   Compensation.
39:2A–16.   Meetings.
39:2A–17.   Minutes.
39:2A–18.   Conflicts of interest.
39:2A–19.   Removal.
39:2A–20.   Authorized payments.
39:2A–21.   Rules and regulations.
39:2A–22.   Annual report.
39:2A–23.   Civil liability.
39:2A–24.   Immunity.
39:2A–25.   Legal representation.
39:2A–26.   Advisory council.
39:2A–27.   Agency facilities.
39:2A–28.   Additional powers and duties of board.
39:2A–29.   Authorized actions.
39:2A–30.   Motor Vehicles Affordability & Fairness Task Force.
39:2A–31.   Taxes and assessments.
39:2A–32.   Fingerprinting of employees; criminal history background check.
39:2A–33.   Contracts for ancillary services and advertising; rules and regulations.
39:2A–34.   Reorganization plans; inconsistencies superceded.
39:2A–35.   Commercial Business Unit; functions, powers and duties transferred to commission.
39:2A–36.   Service charges; revenue.
39:2A–36.1. Increased fees and surcharges; factors to be considered.
39:2A–37.   Fees and revenue.
39:2A–38.   Additional vehicle registration fees; security surcharge.
39:2A–39.   Revenues exempt.
39:2A–40.   Inconsistent acts superceded.
39:2A–41.   Severability.
Section
39:2A–42.   Promotional payment incentives to collect certain surcharges levied; deposit into the Motor Vehicle Surcharges Revenue Fund.

39:2A–1. Short title

Sections 1 through 30, 32 through 35, 40, 41, 105, 109, 110 and 120 through 123[1] of this act shall be known and may be cited as "The Motor Vehicle Security and Customer Service Act."

L.2003, c. 13, § 1, eff. Jan. 28, 2003.

[1] N.J.S.A. §§ 39:2A–1 to 39:2A–41; 39:3–10.17a; 39:3–37.1.

39:2A–2. Legislative findings

The Legislature finds and declares that:

a. The Division of Motor Vehicle Services (DMV) is one of the State's principal customer service agencies with regular and direct contact with virtually every citizen;

b. The DMV has over 15 million contacts a year with the public, including 39 million transactions, more than any other State agency;

c. The DMV has responsibility for issuing and certifying motor vehicle driver's licenses, ensuring the proper registration of motor vehicles, as well as conducting safety and emissions inspections of motor vehicles;

d. The public expects courteous, efficient and accessible service from government agencies, including the DMV;

e. The DMV's failed security systems are contributing to a growing national problem of identity theft that is costing New Jersey and the nation millions of dollars each week;

f. In the past, the DMV has been unable to deal with fraud and corruption because of inadequate funding, training, security, internal controls and oversight;

g. The DMV must improve its security system and equipment, and its fraud detection, training and monitoring so that fraudulent driver's licenses, such as those used in the furtherance of terroristic activities, will be eliminated;

h. Internal audits and controls and investigations are also needed to detect patterns of fraud, theft, corruption, identity theft and mismanagement in the issuance of driver's licenses, registrations, and titles because DMV documents must be more resistant to compromise;

i. Criminals have used counterfeit passports, Social Security cards, county identification cards, pay stubs and W–2 forms to obtain fraudulent driver's licenses and identification cards in furtherance of identity-theft schemes;

j. Proper identification must be required at all phases of the licensing and driver testing process to assure that only those persons qualified to legally obtain licenses do so;

k. It is essential that DMV records be matched with Social Security Administration records in order to verify the validity of Social Security numbers in DMV databases;

l. Cameras, armed security guards, panic buttons, alarms, safety upgrades, card access systems and door replacements are needed in order to prevent fraud;

m. Employees or agents of the DMV should be required to undergo background checks and fingerprinting;

n. Cleaning crews and maintenance workers at DMV facilities must be supervised by DMV employees to ensure the security of DMV records;

o. In a time of rapidly changing information technology and Internet communications, the DMV lacks an information technology plan to bring it to the 21st Century and still operates on a decades-old computer network with patchwork hardware, antiquated software and obsolete display terminals that lack processing abilities;

p. Previous DMV efforts to implement complex technological mandates have failed, due to bureaucratic mismanagement, inefficient planning and inadequate oversight, as characterized by reports of the State Commission of Investigation;

q. The DMV has become a reactive agency, struggling to keep up with the demands of newly legislated responsibilities, and without the necessary resources to prevent fraud and corruption at its front-line agencies and without the ability to provide even adequate service to its six million customers;

r. The DMV needs a strategic business plan, which is a key to the operation of an agency, and must work within the confines of such plan in an effort to adopt best practices, improve customer service and gain back the confidence of New Jersey citizens and the Legislature;

s. The DMV's privatization of some of its agencies in July 1995 has created poor, disjointed and confused service delivery without consistency among the agencies in terms of policies and procedures, which has led to confusion and frustration in the minds of New Jersey citizens;

t. The DMV privatization has also resulted in poorly paid employees who have received inadequate benefits, resulting in a high turnover rate at DMV agencies;

u. A major benefit to a State-operated DMV system is the ability to centralize anti-fraud policies and procedures;

v. Historically, the privately-operated local motor vehicle agencies have been plagued with long lines, poor customer service and inadequate business practices that have routinely caused network delays and failures for hours at a time;

w. The DMV would be in a better position to plan for long-term improvements, replacements and daily operations if it had a dedicated and consistent source of funding;

x. In order to address the various problems with the DMV, a "FIX DMV Commission" was formed on April 25, 2002, by Governor's Executive Order Number 19 to conduct a comprehensive review of the DMV and to make recommendations on the restructuring and reorganization of the agency;

y. The "FIX DMV Commission" has reported that the DMV is in crisis and has recommended that a New Jersey Motor Vehicle Commission be formed in, but not of, the Department of Transportation to replace the current New Jersey Division of Motor Vehicles with the purposes of: (1) identifying and regulating drivers and motor vehicles to deter unlawful and unsafe acts; (2) identifying and correcting vehicle defects and limiting the amount of vehicle-produced air pollution; (3) focusing on and responding to customer service and security issues; and (4) effectuating change by bringing greater attention and resources to the needs of the organization;

z. It is therefore in the public interest to create a New Jersey Motor Vehicle Commission, the duties of which would include, but not be limited to: (1) addressing the multitude of functions assigned to it while curtailing fraudulent and criminal activities that present threats to the State's security system; (2) following a multi-year strategic business plan that is constantly reviewed and updated, thus avoiding the need for the cyclical reforms that have characterized its history; and (3) conducting operations on a fiscal year budget, controlling fees sufficient to fund the budget, adopting regulations regarding processes and fees; and implementing an annual strategic business plan.

L.2003, c. 13, § 2, eff. Jan. 28, 2003.

39:2A–3. Definitions

As used in this act:

"Agency" or "motor vehicle agency" means that enterprise run by an agent designated by the commission to be the commission's agent for the registering of motor vehicles, issuing registration certificates and licensing of drivers, as provided in R.S.39:3–3 and R.S.39:10–25.

"Agent" or "Motor Vehicle Agent" means a person designated as agent in R.S.39:3–3 and R.S.39:10–25.

"Board" means the board established by section 12 of P.L.2003, c. 13 (C.39:2A–12).

"Chair" means the chair of the board.

"Chief Administrator" or "administrator" means the chief administrator of the commission.

"Commission" means the New Jersey Motor Vehicle Commission established and created by section 4 of P.L.2003, c. 13 (C.39:2A–4).

"Commissioner" means the Commissioner of Transportation of this State.

"Department" means the Department of Transportation of this State.

"Deputy Chief Administrator" or "deputy administrator" means the deputy chief administrator of the commission and all references in any law, rule, regulation or order to the Deputy Director of the division shall mean and refer to the deputy administrator.

"Director" means the Director of the Division of Motor Vehicles.

"Division" or "DMV" means the Division of Motor Vehicles in the Department of Transportation.

"Service charge" means an amount charged by the commission for services rendered, which includes all new fees and surcharges, increases in existing fees and surcharges, and such amounts as provided in section 105 of P.L.2003, c. 13 (C.39:2A–36). Service charges are revenue of the commission and are not subject to appropriation as Direct State Services by the Legislature.

L.2003, c. 13, § 3, eff. Jan. 28, 2003. Amended by L.2007, c. 335, § 1, eff. Feb. 12, 2008.

39:2A–4.　New Jersey Motor Vehicle Commission

a.　There is hereby established a body corporate and politic, with corporate succession, to be known as the "New Jersey Motor Vehicle Commission." The commission shall be established in the Executive Branch of the State Government and for the purposes of complying with the provisions of Article V, Section IV, paragraph 1 of the New Jersey Constitution, the commission is allocated, in but not of, the Department of Transportation, but notwithstanding this allocation, the commission shall be independent of any supervision and control by the department or by any board or officer thereof. The commission is hereby constituted as an instrumentality of the State exercising public and essential governmental functions, and the exercise by the commission of the powers conferred by this act shall be deemed and held to be an essential governmental function of the State.

b.　The Division of Motor Vehicles, transferred to the Department of Transportation pursuant to Reorganization Plan No. 002–1995, is abolished as a division in the Department of Transportation, and all of its functions, powers and duties, except as herein otherwise provided, are transferred to, and are continued in the commission and shall be exercised by the chief administrator of the commission. Unless otherwise specified in this act, this transfer shall be subject to the provisions of the "State Agency Transfer Act," P.L.1971, c. 375 (C.52:14D–1 et seq.). All records, equipment and other personal property, appropriations, and any unexpended balances of funds appropriated or otherwise available to the division, shall be transferred to the commission pursuant to the "State Agency Transfer Act."

c.　Whenever any law, rule, regulation, order, contract, tariff, document, reorganization plan, judicial, or administrative proceeding or otherwise thereunder, refers to the Division of Motor Vehicles in the Department of Law and Public Safety or in the Department of Transportation, or to the director thereof, the reference shall mean and refer to the commission, unless otherwise stated in this act.

d.　Regulations adopted by the division shall continue with full force and effect until amended or repealed pursuant to law.

e.　The commission shall operate on a fiscal year budget cycle.

f.　The commission shall continue in existence until dissolved by act of the Legislature. However, any dissolution of the commission shall be on condition that the commission has no debts, contractual duties or obligations outstanding, or that provision has been made for the payment, discharge or retirement of these debts, contractual duties or obligations. Upon any dissolution of the commission, all property, rights, funds and assets thereof shall pass to and become vested in the State.

L.2003, c. 13, § 4 (contingent effective date).

Historical and Statutory Notes

L.2003, c. 13, § 127, approved Jan. 28, 2003, provides:

"Sections 1, 2, 3, 12, 38, 109, 110 and 121 shall take effect immediately, sections 105, 106, 107, 108, and 120 shall take effect on July 1, 2003 and the remainder of this act shall take effect on the date the Commissioner of Transportation certifies to the Governor (hereinafter the "date of certification") that a majority of the members of the commission have been appointed or are in office and that all necessary anticipatory actions have been accomplished, provided, that the amount of revenues received pursuant to sections 109 and 110 prior to the date of certification are hereby appropriated to the division. Upon the date of certification, all such collected revenue shall be revenue of the commission. The Commissioner of Transportation, the Director of the Division of Motor Vehicles and the commission may take such anticipatory administrative action in advance as shall be necessary for the implementation of the act."

39:2A–5.　Employees of commission

a.　Upon the abolishment of the division, all career service employees serving in the division on that date shall be employees of the commission and shall be transferred to the commission pursuant to the "State Agency Transfer Act," P.L.1971, c. 375 (C.52:14D–1 et seq.) and shall retain their present career service employment status and their collective bargaining status, including all rights of tenure, retirement, pension, disability, leave of absence, or similar benefits. Future employees of the commission shall be hired consistent with the provisions of Title 11A of the New Jersey Statutes and the rules promulgated thereunder.

b. Upon action of the commission, all agency employees shall become employees of the commission. Such employees shall be assigned to appropriate titles by the Civil Service Commission. Those private motor vehicle agency employees who were employed by the agency on or before January 1, 2003 and who are assigned to career service titles upon employment with the commission shall, upon completion of the special probationary period described in section 7 of P.L.2003, c. 13 (C.39:2A–7), attain permanent, regular appointments in their respective titles. No special probationary period shall be required for those who have previously completed a probationary period during their previous State service employment. Except for managerial and confidential employees as defined by the "New Jersey Employer—Employee Relations Act," P.L.1941, c. 100 (C.34:13A–1 et seq.), such employees shall be covered under the State of New Jersey's collective bargaining agreements and shall obtain all employment and collective bargaining rights consistent therewith.

c. Officers and employees of the commission shall be enrolled in the Public Employees' Retirement System and shall be eligible to participate in the State Health Benefits Program established pursuant to the "New Jersey State Health Benefits Program Act," P.L.1961, c. 49 (C.52:14–17.25 et seq.).

L.2003, c. 13, § 5. Amended by L.2008, c. 29, § 93, eff. June 30, 2008.

39:2A–6. Civil service credit; private employees

a. Notwithstanding the provisions of Title 11A of the New Jersey Statutes and rules promulgated thereunder to the contrary, employees of a private motor vehicle agency who were employed with that agency immediately after serving in the division prior to its privatization, shall, upon returning to State service as employees of the commission, receive civil service seniority credit for all years of employment service retroactive to the date upon which they commenced State employment prior to employment with the private motor vehicle agency. These employees shall also receive civil service seniority credit for all years of employment with the private motor vehicle agency as if the employment were total and continuous.

b. Employees employed by the private motor vehicle agency who enter State service as employees of the commission but who have no prior State service shall receive civil service seniority credit for all years of employment with the private motor vehicle agency.

c. Civil service seniority credit for all employees referred to in subsections a. and b. of this section shall only be used to determine seniority credit for layoff and promotional purposes and accrual of paid leave.

d. Accumulated sick and vacation leave for employees entering or returning to State service as provided in subsections a. and b. of this section shall be transferred and credited to their State leave accounts immediately upon their return to State service.

L.2003, c. 13, § 6 (contingent effective date).

Historical and Statutory Notes

L.2003, c. 13, § 127, approved Jan. 28, 2003, provides:

"Sections 1, 2, 3, 12, 38, 109, 110 and 121 shall take effect immediately, sections 105, 106, 107, 108, and 120 shall take effect on July 1, 2003 and the remainder of this act shall take effect on the date the Commissioner of Transportation certifies to the Governor (hereinafter the "date of certification") that a majority of the members of the commission have been appointed or are in office and that all necessary anticipatory actions have been accomplished, provided, that the amount of revenues received pursuant to sections 109 and 110 prior to the date of certification are hereby appropriated to the division. Upon the date of certification, all such collected revenue shall be revenue of the commission. The Commissioner of Transportation, the Director of the Division of Motor Vehicles and the commission may take such anticipatory administrative action in advance as shall be necessary for the implementation of the act."

39:2A–7. Probationary period

Notwithstanding the provisions of Title 11A of the New Jersey Statutes and the rules promulgated thereunder to the contrary, all employees entering or returning to State service other than those on a Special Reemployment List as employees of the commission following employment with a private motor vehicle agency, who have been employed with the private motor vehicle agency on or before January 1, 2003, and assigned to the career service shall be subject to a special probationary period unless they have already completed a probationary period during their previous State service employment. The special probationary period shall have a duration of six months from the date that the employees enter or return to State service as employees of the commission. Each employee's work performance shall be evaluated to determine whether the employee can satisfactorily perform the duties of the title to which the employee is appointed and progress reports shall be provided to the employee as provided by the rules of the Civil Service Commission. An employee who is determined to have satisfactorily performed the duties of the employee's career service title shall attain permanent status in that title at the conclusion of the special probationary period. An employee who is determined not to have satisfactorily performed the duties of that title during or at the conclusion of the special probationary period shall be immediately separated from State service and shall not have any right of appeal regarding the separation to the Civil Service Commission.

L.2003, c. 13, § 7. Amended by L.2008, c. 29, § 94, eff. June 30, 2008.

39:2A–8. Salary

Notwithstanding the provisions of Title 11A of the New Jersey Statutes and the rules promulgated thereunder to the contrary, the employees entering or returning to State service as employees of the commission in career service titles following employment with a private motor vehicle agency, shall receive a salary commensurate with total years of service as determined by the commission in the salary range assigned to the career service titles to which they have received an appointment.

L.2003, c. 13, § 8 (contingent effective date).

Historical and Statutory Notes

L.2003, c. 13, § 127, approved Jan. 28, 2003, provides:

"Sections 1, 2, 3, 12, 38, 109, 110 and 121 shall take effect immediately, sections 105, 106, 107, 108, and 120 shall take effect on July 1, 2003 and the remainder of this act shall take effect on the date the Commissioner of Transportation certifies to the Governor (hereinafter the "date of certification") that a majority of the members of the commission have been appointed or are in office and that all necessary anticipatory actions have been accomplished, provided, that the amount of revenues received pursuant to sections 109 and 110 prior to the date of certification are hereby appropriated to the division. Upon the date of certification, all such collected revenue shall be revenue of the commission. The Commissioner of Transportation, the Director of the Division of Motor Vehicles and the commission may take such anticipatory administrative action in advance as shall be necessary for the implementation of the act."

39:2A–9. Competitive testing

a. Notwithstanding the provisions of Title 11A of the New Jersey Statutes and the rules promulgated thereunder to the contrary, employees entering State service other than those on a Special Reemployment List as employees of the commission in career service titles following employment after January 1, 2003 with a private motor vehicle agency shall be considered provisional employees subject to competitive testing.

b. Notwithstanding the provisions of Title 11A of the New Jersey Statutes and the rules promulgated thereunder, employees entering State service as provided in subsection a. of this section shall not be subject to displacement by persons on preexisting Special Reemployment Lists. Special Reemployment Lists for applicable titles shall be used only to fill vacant positions in the commission.

L.2003, c. 13, § 9 (contingent effective date).

Historical and Statutory Notes

L.2003, c. 13, § 127, approved Jan. 28, 2003, provides:

"Sections 1, 2, 3, 12, 38, 109, 110 and 121 shall take effect immediately, sections 105, 106, 107, 108, and 120 shall take effect on July 1, 2003 and the remainder of this act shall take effect on the date the Commissioner of Transportation certifies to the Governor (hereinafter the "date of certification") that a majority of the members of the commission have been appointed or are in office and that all necessary anticipatory actions have been accomplished, provided, that the amount of revenues received pursuant to sections 109 and 110 prior to the date of certification are hereby appropriated to the division. Upon the date of certification, all such collected revenue shall be revenue of the commission. The Commissioner of Transportation, the Director of the Division of Motor Vehicles and

the commission may take such anticipatory administrative action in advance as shall be necessary for the implementation of the act."

39:2A–10. Deputy chief administrator; powers and duties

The Deputy Chief Administrator shall assist the chief administrator in the day-to-day administration of the commission and shall have all of the powers and duties of the chief administrator, as authorized and assigned by the chief administrator.

The deputy chief administrator shall carry out all of the chief administrator's duties and responsibilities during the chief administrator's absence, disqualification or inability to serve, and shall perform such other duties and responsibilities as the chief administrator shall determine and assign. If a vacancy occurs in the office of the chief administrator for any reason, the deputy chief administrator shall become acting chief administrator to serve until a successor is appointed in accordance with section 13 of P.L.2003, c. 13 (C.39:2A–12). The deputy chief administrator shall serve at the pleasure of the chief administrator and shall receive such salary as fixed by the chief administrator in accordance with the table of organization. The deputy chief administrator shall be in the State unclassified service.

L.2003, c. 13, § 10. Amended by L.2009, c. 298, § 1, eff. Jan. 17, 2010.

39:2A–11. Appointing authority

Except as otherwise provided by law, the administrator shall be considered the "appointing authority" for the commission within the contemplation of the civil service laws and the table of organization. The administrator may delegate such appointing authority to the deputy administrator as he deems necessary.

L.2003, c. 13, § 11 (contingent effective date).

Historical and Statutory Notes

L.2003, c. 13, § 127, approved Jan. 28, 2003, provides:

"Sections 1, 2, 3, 12, 38, 109, 110 and 121 shall take effect immediately, sections 105, 106, 107, 108, and 120 shall take effect on July 1, 2003 and the remainder of this act shall take effect on the date the Commissioner of Transportation certifies to the Governor (hereinafter the "date of certification") that a majority of the members of the commission have been appointed or are in office and that all necessary anticipatory actions have been accomplished, provided, that the amount of revenues received pursuant to sections 109 and 110 prior to the date of certification are hereby appropriated to the division. Upon the date of certification, all such collected revenue shall be revenue of the commission. The Commissioner of Transportation, the Director of the Division of Motor Vehicles and the commission may take such anticipatory administrative action in advance as shall be necessary for the implementation of the act."

39:2A–12. Composition of board; chair; appointment and terms of office of members; designation of persons to act for members; vacancies

a. Except as otherwise provided by law, the commission shall be governed by a board which shall consist of the following eight members:

(1) The Commissioner of Transportation, who shall serve as an ex officio voting member;

(2) The State Attorney General, who shall serve as an ex officio voting member;

(3) The Chair of the board who shall be a nonvoting member and who shall also be the person appointed and serving as the chief administrator. The chief administrator shall be appointed by the Governor with the advice and consent of the Senate. The chief administrator shall serve at the pleasure of the Governor during the Governor's term of office, and shall receive such salary as shall be fixed by the Governor which is not greater than the salary of a cabinet-level official of the State. Prior to nomination, the Governor shall cause the Attorney General to conduct an inquiry into the nominee's background, financial stability, integrity and responsibility and reputation for good character, honesty and integrity. The person appointed and serving as chief administrator shall devote full time to the performance of the duties of that position. The chief administrator shall be in the State unclassified service;

(4) The State Treasurer, who shall serve as an ex officio voting member; and

(5) Four public members who shall be appointed by the Governor with the advice and consent of the Senate, not more than two of whom shall be of the same political party. The public members shall be voting members and serve for a term of four years. These members shall be New Jersey residents who shall provide appropriate geographic representation from throughout the State and who shall have experience and familiarity with public safety, customer service, security, or business operations. At least one member shall reside in a northern county (Bergen, Essex, Hudson, Morris, Passaic, Union, Sussex and Warren), at least one member shall reside in a central county (Hunterdon, Mercer, Middlesex, Monmouth and Somerset); and at least one member shall reside in a southern county (Atlantic, Burlington, Camden, Cape May, Cumberland, Gloucester, Ocean and Salem).

b. Appointments of public members to the board shall be for terms of four years, except that in filling each vacancy, among the several public members, that first arises by expiration of the respective terms of those members following the effective date of P.L.2007, c. 335 (C.39:2A–36.1 et al.),[1] appointments shall be for terms as follows: one member for four years, one member for three years, one member for two years, and one member for one year. A public member may be appointed for any number of successive terms. The board may elect a secretary and a treasurer, who need

not be members, and the same person may be elected to serve both as secretary and treasurer.

c. Each ex officio member of the board may designate two employees of the member's department or agency, who may represent the member at meetings of the board. A designee may lawfully vote and otherwise act on behalf of the member. The designation shall be in writing delivered to the board and shall continue in effect until revoked or amended by writing delivered to the board.

d. Each public member shall continue in office after the expiration of the member's term until a successor is appointed and qualified. The successor shall be appointed in like manner for the unexpired term only.

e. A vacancy in the membership of the board occurring other than by expiration of term shall be filled in the same manner as the original appointment, but for the unexpired term only.

L.2003, c. 13, § 12, eff. Jan. 28, 2003. Amended by L.2007, c. 335, § 2, eff. Feb. 12, 2008; L.2009, c. 298, § 2, eff. Jan. 17, 2010.

[1] L.2007, c. 335, eff. Feb. 12, 2008.

39:2A–13. Powers and duties of board

a. In addition to any powers and duties conferred upon it elsewhere in this act, the board shall be authorized to:

(1) Make, amend and repeal bylaws not inconsistent with State and federal law;

(2) Adopt an official seal;

(3) Maintain an office at such place or places within the State as it may designate;

(4) Apply for and accept grants from the State or federal government, or any agency thereof, or grants, gifts or other contributions from any foundation, corporation, association or individual, or any private source, and comply with the terms, conditions and limitations thereof, as necessary and proper to carry out the purposes of this act;

(5) Delegate to the chief administrator and any other officers of the commission such powers and duties as necessary and proper to carry out the purposes of this act;

(6) Operate, lease, license or contract in such manner as to produce revenue for the commission, as provided in this act, including engaging in advertising services pursuant to section 35 of P.L.2003, c. 13 (C.39:2A–33);

(7) Accept and use any funds available to the commission;

(8) Enter into agreements or contracts to pay for goods from and services rendered by any public or private entity, and receive payment for services rendered to any public or private entity, including advertis-

ing services provided pursuant to section 35 of P.L.2003, c. 13 (C.39:2A–33); and

(9) Enter into agreements or contracts, execute any and all instruments, and do and perform acts or things necessary, convenient or desirable for the purposes of the commission, or to carry out any power expressly or implicitly given in this act.

b. The board is further authorized to:

(1) Review and approve a statement of the vision, mission, and goals of the commission, as submitted by the chief administrator;

(2) Review and approve the strategic business plan of the commission which shall include the commission's long-term objectives, policies, and programs, including a facilities improvement and management plan and a table of organization, as submitted by the chief administrator;

(3) Review and approve the annual budget of the commission as submitted by the chief administrator and ensure that projected revenues and service charges are sufficient to adequately fund the commission both in the short and long-term;

(4) Receive reports and recommendations from any advisory council created pursuant to section 26 of P.L.2003, c. 13 (C.39:2A–26) and provide policy direction related thereto to the chief administrator;

(5) Review and recommend all capital purchases and construction projects undertaken by the commission;

(6) Review any proposed bill, joint resolution or concurrent resolution introduced in either House of the Legislature which establishes or modifies any motor vehicle statute or regulation in this State. Such a review shall include, but not be limited to, an analysis of the fiscal impact of the bill or resolution on the commission and any comments upon or recommendations concerning the legislation including rejection, modification or approval. Additionally, the board shall suggest alternatives to the legislation which it deems may be appropriate; and

(7) Recommend to the Governor and the Legislature any statutory changes it deems appropriate, including, but not limited to, any revisions to fees or service charges or changes to programs, in order to insure the proper functioning and operation of the commission.

c. Except as provided in this section and section 21 of P.L.2003, c. 13 (C.39:2A–21), all administrative functions, powers and duties of the commission may be exercised by the chief administrator and any reference to the commission in any law, rule or regulation may for this purpose be deemed to refer to the chief administrator.

L.2003, c. 13, § 13. Amended by L.2007, c. 335, § 3, eff. Feb. 12, 2008; L.2009, c. 298, § 3, eff. Jan. 17, 2010.

39:2A–14. Member elections

The board shall elect annually, by a majority of the full membership of the board, one of its members, other than the Chair, to serve as Vice–Chair for the ensuing year. The Vice–Chair shall hold office until January 1 next ensuing. The Vice–Chair, acting in the capacity of presiding officer, shall carry out all of the responsibilities of the Chair of the board during the Chair's absence, disqualification, or inability to serve.

L.2003, c. 13, § 14. Amended by L.2007, c. 335, § 4, eff. Feb. 12, 2008.

39:2A–15. Compensation

Members other than those serving ex officio shall serve without compensation, but the board shall reimburse board members for actual expenses necessarily incurred in the discharge of their duties.

L.2003, c. 13, § 15. Amended by L.2007, c. 335, § 5, eff. Feb. 12, 2008.

39:2A–16. Meetings

a. The board shall meet every other month or at more frequent times at the discretion of the Chair or as a majority of the board shall decide. Meetings of the board shall be held at such times and places as the Chair may deem necessary and convenient.

b. The meetings shall be subject to the provisions of the "Senator Byron M. Baer Open Public Meetings Act," P.L.1975, c. 231 (C.10:4–6 et seq.).

c. Any other law, rule or regulation to the contrary notwithstanding, the board shall take all necessary steps to ensure that all interested persons are given adequate notice of board meetings and the agenda of such meetings, through the utilization of media engaged in the dissemination of information.

d. The powers of the board shall be vested in the members thereof. Four members of the board shall constitute a quorum at any meeting. Actions may be taken and motions and resolutions adopted by the board by the affirmative vote of at least four voting members. No vacancy in the membership of the board shall impair the right of a quorum to exercise all the rights and perform all the duties of the board.

L.2003, c. 13, § 16. Amended by L.2007, c. 335, § 6, eff. Feb. 12, 2008.

39:2A–17. Minutes

A true copy of the minutes of every meeting of the board shall be delivered by and under the certification of the secretary of the board, without delay, to the Governor. No action taken at the meeting shall have force or effect until 10 days, Saturdays, Sundays, and public holidays excepted, after the minutes are delivered, unless during the 10–day period the Governor approves the minutes, in which case the action shall become effective upon approval. If, in that 10–day period, the Governor returns copies of the minutes with a veto of any action taken by the board or any member, the action shall be null and void and of no effect.

L.2003, c. 13, § 17. Amended by L.2007, c. 335, § 7, eff. Feb. 12, 2008.

39:2A–18. Conflicts of interest

Members of the board shall be subject to the provisions of the "New Jersey Conflicts of Interest Law," P.L.1971, c. 182 (C.52:13D–12 et seq.).

L.2003, c. 13, § 18. Amended by L.2007, c. 335, § 8, eff. Feb. 12, 2008.

39:2A–19. Removal

Each appointed member of the board may be removed from office by the Governor for cause, after a public hearing and may be suspended by the Governor pending the completion of the hearing. Before assuming the duties of board membership, each member shall take and subscribe an oath to perform the duties of the office faithfully, impartially and justly to the best of the member's ability. A record of the oaths shall be filed in the office of the Secretary of State.

L.2003, c. 13, § 19. Amended by L.2007, c. 335, § 9, eff. Feb. 12, 2008.

39:2A–20. Authorized payments

The commission may, in acceptance of payment of any fees, fines, penalties, surcharges, service charges or other charges, authorize the use of a credit or debit card or any other electronic payment device.

L.2003, c. 13, § 20 (contingent effective date).

Historical and Statutory Notes

L.2003, c. 13, § 127, approved Jan. 28, 2003, provides:

"Sections 1, 2, 3, 12, 38, 109, 110 and 121 shall take effect immediately, sections 105, 106, 107, 108, and 120 shall take effect on July 1, 2003 and the remainder of this act shall take effect on the date the Commissioner of Transportation certifies to the Governor (hereinafter the "date of certification") that a majority of the members of the commission have been appointed or are in office and that all necessary anticipatory actions have been accomplished, provided, that the amount of revenues received pursuant to sections 109 and 110 prior to the date of certification are hereby appropriated to the division. Upon the date of certification, all such collected revenue shall be revenue of the commission. The Commissioner of Transportation, the Director of the Division of Motor Vehicles and the commission may take such anticipatory administrative action in advance as shall be necessary for the implementation of the act."

39:2A–21. Rules and regulations

The board shall adopt all rules and regulations in accordance with the " Administrative Procedure Act," P.L.1968, c. 410 (C.52:14B–1 et seq.) for the proper functioning of the commission, and as necessary to effectuate the purposes of this act, except for those relating to the internal governance of the commission adopted by the administrator. Current rules and regulations of the division shall remain in full force and

effect until such time as they are repealed or amended by the board or in accordance with any other law.

L.2003, c. 13, § 21. Amended by L.2007, c. 335, § 10, eff. Feb. 12, 2008.

39:2A–22. Annual report

a. On or before January 31 of each year, the commission shall file with the Governor, the presiding officer of each House of the Legislature, and the Senate Transportation Committee and the Assembly Transportation and Public Works Committee, or their successors, a report setting forth the operational, capital and financial expenditures of the previous year, and the operational, capital, and financial plan, and the table of organization and staffing plan, for the current year.

The commission shall include in this report the latest audited annual financial statement. In this statement, the commission shall disclose all revenues remitted to the commission and provide a detailed listing of the various categories in which it receives revenue, including any surplus revenue from the prior year.

The commission shall also include in the report an assessment of the service provided by the commission. The assessment shall include information or data or both relating to security improvements, annual transactions performed, customer wait times, and criminal complaints.

b. The commission shall cause a financial audit of its books and accounts to be made at least once each year by certified public accountants and a copy thereof shall be filed with the State Treasurer.

c. (Deleted by amendment, P.L.2007, c. 335).

L.2003, c. 13, § 22. Amended by L.2007, c. 335, § 11, eff. Feb. 12, 2008.

39:2A–23. Civil liability

Members of the board and officers and employees of the commission shall not be liable in an action for damages to any person for any action taken or recommendation made within the scope of their employment as a member, officer or employee if the action or recommendation was taken or made without malice. The members of the board shall be indemnified and their defense of any action provided for in the same manner and to the same extent as employees of the State under the "New Jersey Tort Claims Act," P.L. 1972, c. 45 (N.J.S.59:1–1 et seq.) on account of acts or omissions in the scope of their employment.

L.2003, c. 13, § 23. Amended by L.2007, c. 335, § 12, eff. Feb. 12, 2008.

39:2A–24. Immunity

As the commission is a State agency, all absolute and qualified immunities and defenses provided to public entities and public employees by the "New Jersey Tort Claims Act," P.L.1972, c. 45 (N.J.S.59:1–1 et seq.), the "New Jersey Contractual Liability Act," P.L.1972, c. 45

(N.J.S.59:13–1 et seq.), and any other law shall apply to all interests held and activities performed by the commission and its employees pursuant to this act.

L.2003, c. 13, § 24 (contingent effective date).

Historical and Statutory Notes

L.2003, c. 13, § 127, approved Jan. 28, 2003, provides:

"Sections 1, 2, 3, 12, 38, 109, 110 and 121 shall take effect immediately, sections 105, 106, 107, 108, and 120 shall take effect on July 1, 2003 and the remainder of this act shall take effect on the date the Commissioner of Transportation certifies to the Governor (hereinafter the "date of certification") that a majority of the members of the commission have been appointed or are in office and that all necessary anticipatory actions have been accomplished, provided, that the amount of revenues received pursuant to sections 109 and 110 prior to the date of certification are hereby appropriated to the division. Upon the date of certification, all such collected revenue shall be revenue of the commission. The Commissioner of Transportation, the Director of the Division of Motor Vehicles and the commission may take such anticipatory administrative action in advance as shall be necessary for the implementation of the act."

39:2A–25. Legal representation

The Attorney General shall provide legal representation to the commission and its employees to the same extent as representation is provided to other State agencies and their employees.

L.2003, c. 13, § 25 (contingent effective date).

Historical and Statutory Notes

L.2003, c. 13, § 127, approved Jan. 28, 2003, provides:

"Sections 1, 2, 3, 12, 38, 109, 110 and 121 shall take effect immediately, sections 105, 106, 107, 108, and 120 shall take effect on July 1, 2003 and the remainder of this act shall take effect on the date the Commissioner of Transportation certifies to the Governor (hereinafter the "date of certification") that a majority of the members of the commission have been appointed or are in office and that all necessary anticipatory actions have been accomplished, provided, that the amount of revenues received pursuant to sections 109 and 110 prior to the date of certification are hereby appropriated to the division. Upon the date of certification, all such collected revenue shall be revenue of the commission. The Commissioner of Transportation, the Director of the Division of Motor Vehicles and the commission may take such anticipatory administrative action in advance as shall be necessary for the implementation of the act."

39:2A–26. Advisory council

There is created within the commission one advisory council, which shall provide the board with advice, technical expertise, information, guidance, and recommendations in the area of security and privacy. The board shall designate the appropriate State and local government representatives, interest group representatives, technical experts, and constituent representatives as appropriate to serve on the council. Federal government representatives and representatives of national organizations shall be asked to serve, and if willing, may be designated by the board to serve. All council members shall be designated by board action. The Chair, or the Chair's designee, shall serve on the council. The council shall meet and report to the board as frequently as the board requests. The council is as follows:

    a.   (Deleted by amendment, P.L.2009, c. 298).

    b.   (Deleted by amendment, P.L.2009, c. 298).

    c.   The Security and Privacy Advisory Council, which shall: advise the board as to how to effectively maintain the commission's system and business processes in the securest manner; help the board to address the commission's most serious security breaches; advise as to new or modified programs needed to achieve heightened security; and recommend methods to curtail fraudulent and criminal activities that present threats to the State's security as well as measures to protect the privacy of driver information, including but not limited to the Driver's Privacy Protection Act of 1994, Pub.L. 103–322.

    d.   (Deleted by amendment, P.L.2009, c. 298).

    e.   (Deleted by amendment, P.L.2009, c. 298).

In addition to the council created above, the chief administrator may create and establish as necessary within the commission any other advisory council to examine issues affecting or identified by the commission. The members of such councils shall be designated, serve, meet and report to the board as provided for the members of the council created above. The Chair or Chair's designee shall serve on each council. The Safety Advisory Council, the Customer Service Advisory Council, the Business Advisory Council, and the Technology Advisory Council are abolished.

L.2003, c. 13, § 26. Amended by L.2007, c. 335, § 13, eff. Feb. 12, 2008; L.2009, c. 298, § 4, eff. Jan. 17, 2010.

39:2A–27. Agency facilities

The administrator is directed to immediately commence a study on the location and adequacy of agency facilities. Special attention shall be paid to siting agencies which are accessible to transit and parking facilities. The study shall examine the affordability and practicality of using smaller satellite offices. The study shall reexamine the location and number of the commission's regional service centers. The study shall reevaluate the core business practices used in the administration of motor vehicle services and so report to the commission.

L.2003, c. 13, § 27 (contingent effective date).

Historical and Statutory Notes

L.2003, c. 13, § 127, approved Jan. 28, 2003, provides:

"Sections 1, 2, 3, 12, 38, 109, 110 and 121 shall take effect immediately, sections 105, 106, 107, 108, and 120 shall take effect on July 1, 2003 and the remainder of this act shall take effect on the date the Commissioner of Transportation certifies to the Governor (hereinafter the "date of certification") that a majority of the members of the commission have been appointed or are in office and that all necessary anticipatory actions have been accomplished, provided, that the amount of revenues received pursuant to sections 109 and 110 prior to the date of certification are hereby appropriated to the division. Upon the date of certification, all such collected revenue shall be revenue of the commission. The Commissioner of Transportation, the Director of the Division of Motor Vehicles and the commission may take such anticipatory administrative action in advance as shall be necessary for the implementation of the act."

39:2A–28. Additional powers and duties of board

In addition to any powers and duties otherwise imposed by this act, the administrator shall have general responsibility for the implementation of this act, and shall, without limitation:

a. Perform, exercise and discharge the functions, powers and duties of the commission through such offices as may be established by this act or otherwise by law;

b. Administer and organize the work of the commission in such organizational units, and from time to time alter the plan of organization as deemed expedient, as necessary for the secure, efficient and effective operation of the commission;

c. Appoint, remove and fix the compensation of subordinate officers and other personnel employed by the commission in accordance with the commission's table of organization, except as herein otherwise specifically provided;

d. Appoint, remove, and fix the compensation and terms of employment of the deputy administrator, who shall serve in the State unclassified service, in accordance with the commission's table of organization;

e. Organize and maintain an administrative office and employ therein such secretarial, clerical and other assistants in the commission as the internal operations of the commission may require;

f. Formulate and adopt rules and regulations for the efficient conduct of the work and general administration of the commission, its officers and employees;

g. Prepare an annual budget, and submit it to the board;

h. Prepare annually, a strategic business plan and submit it to the board, including a facilities improvement and management plan and a table of organization;

i. Institute or cause to be instituted such legal proceedings or processes as may be necessary to properly enforce and give effect to any of the powers or duties of the administrator;

j. Report as the Governor shall from time to time request or as may be required by law;

k. Collect all fees, fines, penalties, surcharges, service charges and other charges imposed by this act and the regulations issued pursuant thereto or pursuant to law;

l. Develop and maintain a master list of all assets;

m. Oversee the implementation of the facilities improvement and management plan, in consultation with the State Treasurer; and

n. Perform such other functions as may be prescribed in this act or by any other law or by the board.
L.2003, c. 13, § 28. Amended by L.2007, c. 335, § 14, eff. Feb. 12, 2008.

39:2A–29. Authorized actions

The administrator, and the deputy administrator under the direction of the administrator, shall have as their immediate goal the improvement of the safety and security of the State's motor vehicle licensing, registration, titling and inspection system and to this end are authorized to:

a. Make technological improvements, including the modernization of software and hardware, the addition of surveillance cameras, alarms, and access systems, and the utilization of biometrics;

b. Increase the number of audit staff, security guards, and other security-related employees;

c. Improve training and monitoring procedures;

d. Utilize document imaging from the field;

e. Integrate the New Jersey title database with the National Motor Vehicle Title Information System;

f. Improve license plate management, including an automated inventory system and reissuance program;

g. Acquire the ability to access State vital statistics data to immediately update driver's license information;

h. Implement additional proofs of identity verification for a non-driver identification card, driver's license, permits, and registrations;

i. Implement card access systems, clear visibility barriers and door replacements where needed;

j. Replace the written driver's license knowledge test with an online test;

k. Increase the use of credit or debit cards or any other electronic payment device;

l. Increase the use of scanned documents;

m. Match motor vehicle records with Social Security records to verify Social Security numbers in the motor vehicle database, to the extent allowable; and

n. Seek the assistance of the Immigration and Naturalization Service to verify authenticity of motor vehicle applicants and their eligibility for documents.
L.2003, c. 13, § 29 (contingent effective date).

Historical and Statutory Notes

L.2003, c. 13, § 127, approved Jan. 28, 2003, provides:

"Sections 1, 2, 3, 12, 38, 109, 110 and 121 shall take effect immediately, sections 105, 106, 107, 108, and 120 shall take effect on July 1, 2003 and the remainder of this act shall take effect on the date the Commissioner of Transportation certifies to the Governor (hereinafter the "date of certification") that a majority of the members of the commission have been appointed or are in office and that all necessary anticipatory actions have been accomplished, provided, that the amount of revenues received pursuant to sections 109 and 110 prior to the date of certification are hereby appropriated to the division. Upon the date of certification, all such collected revenue shall be revenue of the commission. The Commissioner of Transportation, the Director of the Division of Motor Vehicles and the commission may take such anticipatory administrative action in advance as shall be necessary for the implementation of the act."

39:2A–30. Motor Vehicles Affordability & Fairness Task Force

a. There is created a task force to be known as the "Motor Vehicles Affordability & Fairness Task Force" to study the impact of the current point system and non-driving related suspension of driving privileges, in particular, the Merit Rating Plan Surcharges, on the driving public and make recommendations for the reform of the surcharge suspension program to increase motorist safety. In addition, the task force shall examine "The Parking Offenses Adjudication Act," P.L.1985, c. 14 (C.39:4–139.2 et seq.) and municipal court processes related thereto, as well as court actions on surcharge assessments and license suspensions related to nonpayment of fines or tickets as well as motor vehicle moving violations.

b. The task force shall consist of 19 members as follows: the Commissioner of Transportation, ex officio, or a designated representative; the Chair of the New Jersey Motor Vehicle Commission, ex officio or a designated representative; a representative of the Administrative Office of the Courts; the Director of the Office of Highway Traffic Safety, in the Department of Law and Public Safety, ex officio, or a designated representative; the Director of the Division of Insurance in the Department of Banking and Insurance, ex officio, or a designated representative; the Chairperson of the State Employment and Training Commission, ex officio or a designated representative; and nine public members, to be appointed by the Governor, among whom shall be included a representative of the New Jersey Highway Traffic Safety Policy Advisory Council, a representative of a not-for-profit highway safety organization, a representative of the automobile retailers industry, a representative of the automobile insurance industry, a regular operator of a motor vehicle weighing in excess of twenty-six thousand pounds, one law enforcement officer engaged in highway patrol, a representative from the New Jersey State League of Municipalities, a representative from the New Jersey Institute for Social Justice and a representative of a New Jersey based chapter of the American Automobile Association. The Speaker of the General Assembly and the President of the Senate shall each appoint two members who may be public members or members of the Legislature. No more than two of the legislative appointees shall be from the same political party. Legislative appointees shall serve during the legislative term of the appointing authority.

c. The members of the task force shall serve without compensation, but may be reimbursed for necessary expenses incurred in the performance of their duties.

d. The task force shall organize as soon as may be practicable after the appointment of a majority of its members and shall select a chairperson from among the members. The members shall select a secretary, who need not be a member of the task force.

e. The task force shall meet at the call of the chairperson.

f. The task force shall be entitled to call to its assistance and avail itself of the services of the employees of any State department, board, bureau, commission or agency, as it may require and as may be available for its purposes, and to employ stenographic and clerical assistance and incur traveling and other miscellaneous expenses as may be necessary in order to perform its duties, within the limits of funds appropriated or otherwise made available to it for its purposes.

g. The task force shall study and develop recommendations concerning the following issues, including but not limited to:

(1) the rapid growth in the number of driver's license suspensions;

(2) identification and regulation of drivers to deter unlawful and unsafe acts;

(3) establishment of a mechanism to assist low-income residents that are hard pressed to secure the restoration of driving privileges;

(4) reform of the parking ticket suspension system and "The Parking Offenses Adjudication Act"; and

(5) increasing the collection of outstanding surcharges.

h. The study shall include, but not be limited to, investigating issues of motor vehicle safety, insurance, finance, and socioeconomic conditions. The task force shall review and analyze studies examining the social impacts of driver's license and registration suspensions. The task force shall also review and analyze studies and statistics regarding surcharges and suspensions to develop recommendations for reform.

i. The task force shall develop recommendations for public and private strategies and recommendations for legislative or regulatory action, if deemed appropriate, to address these issues. The recommendations shall include suggestions for the development of public information campaigns to educate and inform motorists about driver's license and registration suspensions, and methods of lessening financial and social burdens on motorists.

j. The task force's recommendations shall be aimed at developing and implementing an amnesty policy and a reform of the surcharge suspension. The task force shall review the impact of suspension of driving privileges upon businesses and individuals dependent upon having a valid driver's license for gainful employment and to conduct commerce in this State.

k. The task force shall prepare and submit a final report containing its findings and recommendations, including any recommendations for legislative or regulatory action that it deems appropriate, no later than one year after the task force organizes, to the Governor, the President of the Senate and the Speaker of the General Assembly, and the members of the Senate Transportation Committee and the Assembly Transportation Committee, or their successors.

l. Upon the submission of the final report the task force shall dissolve. Any and all materials, records, work products or other property of the task force shall become property of the commission.

L.2003, c. 13, § 30.

Historical and Statutory Notes

L.2003, c. 13, § 127, approved Jan. 28, 2003, provides:

"Sections 1, 2, 3, 12, 38, 109, 110 and 121 shall take effect immediately, sections 105, 106, 107, 108, and 120 shall take effect on July 1, 2003 and the remainder of this act shall take effect on the date the Commissioner of Transportation certifies to the Governor (hereinafter the "date of certification") that a majority of the members of the commission have been appointed or are in office and that all necessary anticipatory actions have been accomplished, provided, that the amount of revenues received pursuant to sections 109 and 110 prior to the date of certification are hereby appropriated to the division. Upon the date of certification, all such collected revenue shall be revenue of the commission. The Commissioner of Transportation, the Director of the Division of Motor Vehicles and the commission may take such anticipatory administrative action in advance as shall be necessary for the implementation of the act."

39:2A–31. Taxes and assessments

The exercise of the powers granted by this act will be in all respects for the benefit of the people of the State, for the increase of their commerce and prosperity, and for the improvement of their health and living conditions, and as the operation and maintenance of facilities and assets by the commission will constitute the performance of essential governmental functions, the commission shall not be required to pay any taxes or assessments upon any facility and assets or any property acquired or used by the commission under the provisions of this act or upon the income therefrom, and any facility and assets and any property acquired or used by the commission under the provisions of this act and the income therefrom shall be exempt from taxation.

L.2003, c. 13, § 32 (contingent effective date).

Historical and Statutory Notes

L.2003, c. 13, § 127, approved Jan. 28, 2003, provides:

"Sections 1, 2, 3, 12, 38, 109, 110 and 121 shall take effect immediately, sections 105, 106, 107, 108, and 120 shall take effect on July 1, 2003 and the remainder of this act shall take effect on the date the Commissioner of Transportation certifies to the Governor (hereinafter the "date of certification") that a majority of the members of the commission have been

appointed or are in office and that all necessary anticipatory actions have been accomplished, provided, that the amount of revenues received pursuant to sections 109 and 110 prior to the date of certification are hereby appropriated to the division. Upon the date of certification, all such collected revenue shall be revenue of the commission. The Commissioner of Transportation, the Director of the Division of Motor Vehicles and the commission may take such anticipatory administrative action in advance as shall be necessary for the implementation of the act."

39:2A–32. Fingerprinting of employees; criminal history background check

a. The commission shall require the fingerprinting of all prospective employees, employees of the commission, and employees of the agents of the commission, for purposes of determining employment eligibility in any title or capacity that is either directly or indirectly involved in the issuance or processing of driver's licenses, permits, business licenses, identification cards, driving records, or vehicle registrations and titles, and of all independent contractors and their employees who work on a motor vehicle premises or have access to motor vehicle records or documents. The commission is hereby authorized to exchange fingerprint data with, and receive criminal history record information from, the Federal Bureau of Investigation and the Division of State Police, consistent with the provisions of Pub. L.92–544, for use in determining employment eligibility.

b. The commission may, as deemed necessary by the commission, receive the results of periodic follow-ups of criminal history record checks of all employees of the commission and employees of its agents, for purposes of determining continuing employment eligibility in any title or capacity that is either directly or indirectly involved in the issuance or processing of driver's licenses, identification cards, driving records, or vehicle registrations and titles.

c. If the information from the criminal history record background check discloses that a prospective or current employee has a record of criminal history, the commission shall review the information with respect to the type and date of the criminal offense to determine if the person is qualified for employment with the commission. Criminal offenses which shall disqualify an individual from employment include, but are not limited to, any crime or offense, whether committed in New Jersey or in another jurisdiction, which in New Jersey would constitute murder, assault with intent to murder, espionage, treason, rape, kidnaping, unlawful possession of an explosive or weapon, extortion, armed robbery, distribution of or intent to distribute a controlled substance, possession of a controlled substance, willful destruction of property, burglary, theft, fraud, forgery, terrorism, solicitation of money or resources for a terrorist organization and aggravated assault.

d. Notwithstanding the provisions of subsection b. or c. of this section, an individual shall not be disqualified from employment or service under this act on the basis of any conviction disclosed by a criminal record check performed pursuant to this act without an opportunity to challenge the accuracy of the disqualifying criminal history record.

e. An individual who has been disqualified under the provisions of this act shall be entitled to reapply for the position if the disqualifying conviction is reversed.

f. Notwithstanding the provisions of subsection b. or c. of this section, an individual shall not be disqualified from employment or service on the basis of any conviction disclosed by a criminal history record background check performed pursuant to this act if the individual has affirmatively demonstrated to the administrator, clear and convincing evidence of the individual's rehabilitation. In determining whether an individual has affirmatively demonstrated rehabilitation, the following factors shall be considered:

(1) the nature and responsibility of the position which the applicant would hold, has held or currently holds, as the case may be;

(2) the nature and seriousness of the offense;

(3) the circumstances under which the offense occurred;

(4) the date of the offense;

(5) the age of the applicant when the offense was committed;

(6) whether the offense was an isolated or repeated incident;

(7) any social conditions which may have contributed to the offense; and

(8) any evidence of rehabilitation, including good conduct in prison or in the community, counseling or psychiatric treatment received, acquisition of additional academic or vocational schooling, successful participation in correctional work-release programs, or the recommendation of those who have had the applicant under their supervision.

L.2003, c. 13, § 33 (contingent effective date).

Historical and Statutory Notes

L.2003, c. 13, § 127, approved Jan. 28, 2003, provides:

"Sections 1, 2, 3, 12, 38, 109, 110 and 121 shall take effect immediately, sections 105, 106, 107, 108, and 120 shall take effect on July 1, 2003 and the remainder of this act shall take effect on the date the Commissioner of Transportation certifies to the Governor (hereinafter the "date of certification") that a majority of the members of the commission have been appointed or are in office and that all necessary anticipatory actions have been accomplished, provided, that the amount of revenues received pursuant to sections 109 and 110 prior to the date of certification are hereby appropriated to the division. Upon the date of certification, all such collected revenue shall be revenue of the commission. The Commissioner of Transportation, the Director of the Division of Motor Vehicles and the commission may take such anticipatory administrative action in advance as shall be necessary for the implementation of the act."

39:2A–33. Contracts for ancillary services and advertising; rules and regulations

a. The commission may contract for ancillary services at facilities used by the commission, including but not limited to food and beverage concessions, service concessions that would be beneficial to its customers, and information services that would be of interest or informative to its customers, such as television displays, public service displays, and the like.

b. In entering into a contract pursuant to subsection a. of this section, the commission shall award a contract on the basis of competitive public bids or proposals to the responsible bidder or proposer whose bid or proposal is determined to be in the best interest of the State, price and other factors considered.

c. The commission may also sell, lease, or otherwise contract for advertising in or on its equipment or facilities, in any mailing it conducts, or in any publication it produces, including, but not limited to, the New Jersey Driver Manual distributed pursuant to R.S.39:3–41.

d. The commission is authorized to receive funds from contracts entered into pursuant to subsections a. and c. of this section and shall have the right to use the same. The revenue shall not be subject to appropriation as Direct State Services by the Legislature. In addition, this revenue shall not be restricted from use by the commission in any manner except as provided by law. This revenue shall be used in the furtherance of commission purposes. This revenue shall be considered revenue of the commission and shall not be subject to the calculation of proportional revenue remitted to the commission pursuant to section 105 of P.L.2003, c. 13 (C.39:2A–36).

e. In accordance with the "Administrative Procedure Act," P.L.1968, c. 401 (C.52:14B–1 et seq.), the commission shall promulgate rules and regulations necessary to effectuate the purposes of this section, including, but not limited to, the criteria for determining the appropriateness of any advertising and the suitability of any advertising message.

L.2003, c. 13, § 35. Amended by L.2009, c. 298, § 5, eff. Jan. 17, 2010.

39:2A–34. Reorganization plans; inconsistencies superceded

To the extent that Reorganization Plans Nos. 002–1995 and 005–1998 are inconsistent with any provisions of this act, they are superseded to the extent of such inconsistencies and any reference in such Plans to the Division of Motor Vehicles in the Department of Transportation shall mean and refer to the commission.

L.2003, c. 13, § 40 (contingent effective date).

Historical and Statutory Notes

L.2003, c. 13, § 127, approved Jan. 28, 2003, provides:

"Sections 1, 2, 3, 12, 38, 109, 110 and 121 shall take effect immediately, sections 105, 106, 107, 108, and 120 shall take effect on July 1, 2003 and the remainder of this act shall take effect on the date the Commissioner of Transportation certifies to the Governor (hereinafter the "date of certification") that a majority of the members of the commission have been appointed or are in office and that all necessary anticipatory actions have been accomplished, provided, that the amount of revenues received pursuant to sections 109 and 110 prior to the date of certification are hereby appropriated to the division. Upon the date of certification, all such collected revenue shall be revenue of the commission. The Commissioner of Transportation, the Director of the Division of Motor Vehicles and the commission may take such anticipatory administrative action in advance as shall be necessary for the implementation of the act."

39:2A–35. Commercial Business Unit; functions, powers and duties transferred to commission

The Commercial Bus Unit in the Department of Transportation, together with all of its functions, powers and duties is transferred to and vested in the commission. This transfer shall be subject to the provisions of the "State Agency Transfer Act," P.L.1971, c. 375 (C.52:14D–1 et seq.). All career service employees who serve in the Commercial Bus Unit shall be employees of the commission and shall retain their present civil service employment status and their collective bargaining status, including all rights of tenure, retirement pension, disability, leave of absence, or similar benefits. All records, property appropriations, and any unexpended balance of funds appropriated or otherwise available to the Commercial Bus Unit, shall be transferred to the commission pursuant to the "State Agency Transfer Act."

L.2003, c. 13, § 41 (contingent effective date).

Historical and Statutory Notes

L.2003, c. 13, § 127, approved Jan. 28, 2003, provides:

"Sections 1, 2, 3, 12, 38, 109, 110 and 121 shall take effect immediately, sections 105, 106, 107, 108, and 120 shall take effect on July 1, 2003 and the remainder of this act shall take effect on the date the Commissioner of Transportation certifies to the Governor (hereinafter the "date of certification") that a majority of the members of the commission have been appointed or are in office and that all necessary anticipatory actions have been accomplished, provided, that the amount of revenues received pursuant to sections 109 and 110 prior to the date of certification are hereby appropriated to the division. Upon the date of certification, all such collected revenue shall be revenue of the commission. The Commissioner of Transportation, the Director of the Division of Motor Vehicles and the commission may take such anticipatory administrative action in advance as shall be necessary for the implementation of the act."

39:2A–36. Service charges; revenue

a. The first $200,000,000 of fees and surcharges thereon collected pursuant to the following statutes shall be considered service charges which are revenues to be remitted to the New Jersey Motor Vehicle Commission and the remainder shall be remitted to the General Fund, provided that if the total amount of such fees and surcharges collected, as verified by the relevant fiscal year New Jersey Comprehensive Annual Financial Report, produce more or less revenue than the sum of $200,000,000 and the amount anticipated in the fiscal year 2004 Appropriations Act for those statutes, then the $200,000,000 in revenue from those service charges to the commission shall be increased or lowered proportionately:

Section 4 of P.L.1995, c. 401 (C.12:7–73); section 24 of P.L.1984, c. 152 (C.12:7A–24); section 28 of P.L. 1984, c. 152 (C.12:7A–28); section 1 of P.L.1983, c. 65 (C.17:29A–33); section 6 of P.L.1983, c. 65 (C.17:29A–35); section 9 of P.L.1998, c. 108 (C.27:5F–42); R.S.39:2–10; section 1 of P.L.1969, c. 301 (C.39:3–4b); section 2 of P.L.1969, c. 301 (C.39:3–4c); R.S.39:3–8; section 2 of P.L.1968, c. 439 (C.39:3–8.1); section 1 of P.L.1992, c. 87 (C.39:3–8.2); R.S.39:3–10; section 23 of P.L. 1975, c. 180 (C.39:3–10a); section 1 of P.L.1977, c. 23 (C.39:3–10b); section 1 of P.L.1979, c. 261 (C.39:3–10f); section 22 of P.L.1990, c. 103 (C.39:3–10.30); R.S.39:3–13; R.S.39:3–18; R.S.39:3–19; section 2 of P.L.1974, c. 162 (C.39:3–19.2); section 12 of P.L.1979, c. 224 (C.39:3–19.5); R.S.39:3–20; section 1 of P.L.1973, c. 319 (C.39:3–20.1); R.S.39:3–21; R.S.39:3–24; R.S.39:3–25; R.S.39:3–26; section 2 of P.L.1964, c. 195 (C.39:3–27.4); section 2 of P.L.1968, c. 247 (C.39:3–27.6); section 2 of P.L.1977, c. 369 (C.39:3–27.9); section 2 of P. L.1979, c. 457 (C.39:3–27.16); section 2 of P.L.1981, c. 139 (C.39:3–27.19); R.S.39:3–28; R.S.39:3–30; R.S.39:3–31; section 1 of P.L.1961, c. 77 (C.39:3–31.1); R.S.39:3–32; section 1 of P.L.1999, c. 192 (C.39:3–33a); section 1 of P.L.2001, c. 35 (C.39:3–33b); section 2 of P.L.1959, c. 56 (C.39:3–33.4); section 4 of P.L.1959, c. 56 (C.39:3–33.6); R.S.39:3–36; section 1 of P.L.1979, c. 314 (C.39:3–54.14); section 2 of P. L.1999, c. 308 (C.39:3–75.2); R.S.39:3–84; section 2 of P.L.1999, c. 396 (C.39:3–84.7); section 3 of P.L.1973, c. 307 (C.39:3C–3); section 10 of P.L. 1983, c. 105 (C.39:4–14.3j); section 23 of P.L.1983, c. 105 (C.39:4–14. 3w); R.S.39:4–26; R.S.39:4–30; section 11 of P.L.1985, c. 14 (C.39:4–139.12); section 1 of P.L. 1972, c. 38 (C.39:5–30.4); section 31 of P.L.1994, c. 60 (C.39:5–36.1); section 20 of P.L.1952, c. 173 (C.39:6–42); section 2 of P.L.1983, c. 141 (C.39:6B–3); R.S.39:7–3; section 3 of P.L.1975, c. 156 (C.39:8–11); section 8 of P.L.1975, c. 156 (C.39:8–16); section 9 of P.L.1975, c. 156 (C.39:8–17); section 15 of P.L.1975, c. 156 (C.39:8–23); section 5 of P.L.1995, c. 112 (C.39:8–45); section 7 of P.L.1995, c. 112 (C.39:8–47); section 12 of P.L.1995, c. 112 (C.39:8–52); section 11 of P.L.1995, c. 157 (C.39:8–69); section 13 of P.L.1995, c. 112 (C.39:8–53); section 14 of P.L. 1995, c. 112 (C.39:8–54); R.S.39:10–11; R. S.39:10–12; R.S.39:10–14; R.S.39:10–16; R.S.39:10–19; R.S.39:10–25; section 5 of P.L.1983, c. 323 (C.39:10–35); section 8 of P.L.1983, c. 455 (C.39:10A–15); R.S.39:11–8; section 2 of P.L.1951, c. 216 (C.39:12–2); section 5 of P.L.1951, c. 216

(C.39:12–5); and section 2 of P.L.1983, c. 360 (C.39:13–2).

Proportional revenues remitted to the commission for the fiscal years beginning July 1, 2004 and thereafter shall have the same proportion as the proportional revenues remitted to the commission for the fiscal year beginning July 1, 2003, and this calculation shall not be impacted by the acceleration of revenue attributable to new passenger automobile registrations implemented pursuant to P.L.2004, c. 64.

b. In addition to the proportionately increased or lowered revenue provided for in subsection a. of this section, the commission shall receive 100 percent of the revenues collected from any new service charge and 100 percent of the increased revenues collected from any existing service charge increased by law or regulation. Any new or increased service charge shall not be included in the calculation of the proportional revenue remitted to the commission.

c. In addition to the revenues provided for in subsections a. and b. of this section, all fees collected pursuant to Chapter 3 of Title 39 of the Revised Statutes required to defray the costs of the commission with respect to producing, issuing, renewing, and publicizing license plates, or related computer programming shall be considered revenues of the commission notwithstanding any other provision of law.

d. Revenues of the commission shall not be subject to appropriation as direct State services by the Legislature. In addition, the revenues of the commission shall not be restricted from use by the commission in any manner except as provided by law. Revenues of the commission may be used in the furtherance of any purpose of the commission or as otherwise provided for by law.

L.2003, c. 13, § 105, eff. July 1, 2003. Amended by L.2004, c. 64, § 5, eff. June 30, 2004; L.2007, c. 335, § 15, eff. Feb. 12, 2008.

39:2A–36.1. Increased fees and surcharges; factors to be considered

a. On and after the effective date of P.L.2007, c. 335 (C.39:2A–36.1 et al.),[1] the board may, by regulation adopted pursuant to the "Administrative Procedure Act," P.L.1968, c. 410 (C.52:14B–1 et seq.), increase fees and surcharges collected pursuant to the following statutes, notwithstanding any law, rule, or regulation to the contrary:

Section 4 of P.L.1995, c. 401 (C.12:7–73); section 24 of P.L.1984, c. 152 (C.12:7A–24); section 28 of P.L. 1984, c. 152 (C.12:7A–28); section 1 of P.L.1983, c. 65 (C.17:29A–33); section 6 of P.L.1983, c. 65 (C.17:29A–35); section 9 of P.L.1998, c. 108 (C.27:5F–42); R.S.39:2–10; section 1 of P.L.1969, c. 301 (C.39:3–4b); section 2 of P.L.1969, c. 301 (C.39:3–4c); section 2 of P.L.1968, c. 439 (C.39:3–8.1); section 1 of P.L.1992, c. 87 (C.39:3–8.2); section 23 of P.L.1975, c. 180 (C.39:3–10a); section 1 of P.L.1977, c.

23 (C.39:3–10b); section 1 of P.L.1979, c. 261 (C.39:3–10f); section 22 of P.L.1990, c. 103 (C.39:3–10.30); R.S.39:3–13; R.S.39:3–18; R.S.39:3–19; section 2 of P.L.1974, c. 162 (C.39:3–19.2); section 12 of P.L.1979, c. 224 (C.39:3–19.5); R.S.39:3–20; section 1 of P. L.1973, c. 319 (C.39:3–20.1); R.S.39:3–21; R.S.39:3–24; R.S.39:3–25; R.S. 39:3–26; section 2 of P.L.1964, c. 195 (C.39:3–27.4); section 2 of P.L.1968, c. 247 (C.39:3–27.6); section 2 of P.L.1977, c. 369 (C.39:3–27.9); section 2 of P.L.1979, c. 457 (C.39:3–27.16); section 2 of P.L.1981, c. 139 (C.39:3–27.19); R.S.39:3–28; R.S.39:3–30; R.S.39:3–31; section 1 of P.L.1961, c. 77 (C.39:3–31.1); R.S.39:3–32; section 1 of P.L. 1999, c. 192 (C.39:3–33a); section 1 of P.L.2001, c. 35 (C.39:3–33b); section 2 of P.L.1959, c. 56 (C.39:3–33.4); section 4 of P.L.1959, c. 56 (C.39:3–33.6); R.S.39:3–36; section 1 of P.L.1979, c. 314 (C.39:3–54.14); section 2 of P.L.1999, c. 308 (C.39:3–75.2); R.S.39:3–84; section 2 of P.L.1999, c. 396 (C.39:3–84.7); section 3 of P.L.1973, c. 307 (C.39:3C–3); section 10 of P.L. 1983, c. 105 (C.39:4–14.3j); section 23 of P.L.1983, c. 105 (C.39:4–14.3w); R.S.39:4–26; R.S.39:4–30; section 11 of P.L.1985, c. 14 (C.39:4–139.12); section 1 of P.L. 1972, c. 38 (C.39:5–30.4); section 31 of P.L.1994, c. 60 (C.39:5–36.1); section 20 of P.L.1952, c. 173 (C.39:6–42); section 2 of P.L.1983, c. 141 (C.39:6B–3); R.S.39:7–3; section 3 of P.L.1975, c. 156 (C.39:8–11); section 8 of P.L.1975, c. 156 (C.39:8–16); section 9 of P.L.1975, c. 156 (C.39:8–17); section 15 of P.L.1975, c. 156 (C.39:8–23); section 5 of P.L.1995, c. 112 (C.39:8–45); section 7 of P.L.1995, c. 112 (C.39:8–47); section 12 of P.L.1995, c. 112 (C.39:8–52); section 11 of P.L.1995, c. 157 (C.39:8–69); section 13 of P.L. 1995, c. 112 (C.39:8–53); section 14 of P.L. 1995, c. 112 (C.39:8–54); R.S. 39:10–11; R.S.39:10–12; R.S.39:10–14; R.S.39:10–16; R.S.39:10–19; R.S.39:10–25; section 5 of P.L.1983, c. 323 (C.39:10–35); section 8 of P.L.1983, c. 455 (C.39:10A–15); R.S.39:11–8; section 2 of P.L.1951, c. 216 (C.39:12–2); section 5 of P.L.1951, c. 216 (C.39:12–5); and section 2 of P. L.1983, c. 360 (C.39:13–2).

b. (1) In determining an appropriate increase of any fee or surcharge pursuant to subsection a. of this section, the board shall consider at least the following factors: (a) the year in which the fee or surcharge was last increased; (b) the actual costs to the State of New Jersey for administering any transaction, process, filing, registration, inspection, audit, or any license, permit, or other document issuance, for which the fee or surcharge is collected; and (c) the annual percentage increase in the Consumer Price Index or other similar relevant index.

No fee or surcharge set forth in this section shall be increased by regulation more than once during any five-year period, and no such fee or surcharge shall be increased beyond an amount that exceeds the actual costs to the State of New Jersey for administering any transaction, process, filing, registration, inspection, audit, or any license, permit, or other document issuance, for which the fee or surcharge is collected.

(2) All increases in a fee or surcharge after the first increase shall also be subject to the following limitation: the increase shall not exceed the cumulative annual percentage increase in the Consumer Price Index for the five fiscal years prior to the date of the proposed subsequent increase.

(3) All increases in fees or surcharges imposed by regulation proposed to be adopted in a calendar year shall be consolidated in one single regulatory proposal in that calendar year.

(4) As used in this section, the "Consumer Price Index" means the consumer price index for all urban consumers in the New York City and Philadelphia areas as reported by the Department of Labor or successor index.

c. Pursuant to subsection b. of section 105 of P.L.2003, c. 13 (C.39:2A–36), 100 percent of the increased revenues collected from such increase shall be remitted to the commission.

L.2007, c. 335, § 16, eff. Feb. 12, 2008.

1 L.2007, c. 335, eff. Feb. 12, 2008.

39:2A–37. Fees and revenue

Notwithstanding any other provision of law, all fees established pursuant to P.L. 2001, c. 391 shall take effect on the enactment of P.L.2003, c. 13 (C. 39:2A–1 et al.). The $6 digitized picture fee shall be charged regardless of whether the license or identification card displays a picture, and shall be revenues of the commission for use in the furtherance of any commission purpose. This fee shall be considered revenues of the commission and shall not be subject to the calculation of proportional revenue remitted to the commission pursuant to section 105 of P.L.2003, c. 13 (C.39:2A–36).

Revenues of the commission shall not be subject to appropriation as direct State services by the Legislature. In addition, the revenues of the commission shall not be restricted from use by the commission in any manner except as provided by law. Revenues of the commission may be used in the furtherance of any purpose of the commission or as otherwise provided for in law.

L.2003, c. 13, § 109, eff. Jan. 28, 2003.

Historical and Statutory Notes

L.2003, c. 13, § 127, approved Jan. 28, 2003, provides:

"Sections 1, 2, 3, 12, 38, 109, 110 and 121 shall take effect immediately, sections 105, 106, 107, 108, and 120 shall take effect on July 1, 2003 and the remainder of this act shall take effect on the date the Commissioner of Transportation certifies to the Governor (hereinafter the "date of certification") that a majority of the members of the commission have been appointed or are in office and that all necessary anticipatory actions have been accomplished, provided, that the amount of revenues received pursuant to sections 109 and 110 prior to the date of certification are hereby appropriated to the division.

Upon the date of certification, all such collected revenue shall be revenue of the commission. The Commissioner of Transportation, the Director of the Division of Motor Vehicles and the commission may take such anticipatory administrative action in advance as shall be necessary for the implementation of the act."

39:2A–38. Additional vehicle registration fees; security surcharge

In addition to the vehicle registration fees imposed pursuant to the provisions of chapters 3, 4, and 8 of Title 39 of the Revised Statutes, the commission shall impose and collect an additional $7 for each new and renewal vehicle registration as a security surcharge, which surcharge shall take effect on the enactment of P.L.2003, c. 13 (C.39:2A–1 et al.). The security surcharges collected pursuant to this section shall be revenues of the commission and shall not be subject to the calculation of proportional revenue remitted to the commission pursuant to section 105 of P.L.2003, c. 13 (C.39:2A–36). The security surcharge shall not be imposed on the registration of passenger vehicles registered to persons possessing a valid handicapped person identification card issued pursuant to section 2 of P.L.1949, c. 280 (C.39:4–205) or to persons aged 65 years of age or older at the time of registration or registration renewal. Revenues of the commission shall not be subject to appropriation as direct State services by the Legislature. In addition, the revenues of the commission shall not be restricted from use by the commission in any manner except as provided by law. Revenues of the commission may be used in the furtherance of any purpose of the commission or as otherwise provided for in law.

L.2003, c. 13, § 110, eff. Jan. 28, 2003. Amended by L.2007, c. 335, § 17, eff. Feb. 12, 2008.

39:2A–39. Revenues exempt

All monies paid to the commission pursuant to section 1 of P.L.1952, c. 176 (C.39:6–58) are revenues of the commission and shall not be subject to the calculation of proportional revenues remitted to the commission pursuant to section 105 of P.L.2003, c. 13 (C.39:2A–36).

L.2003, c. 13, § 120, eff. July 1, 2003.

Historical and Statutory Notes

L.2003, c. 13, § 127, approved Jan. 28, 2003, provides:

"Sections 1, 2, 3, 12, 38, 109, 110 and 121 shall take effect immediately, sections 105, 106, 107, 108, and 120 shall take effect on July 1, 2003 and the remainder of this act shall take effect on the date the Commissioner of Transportation certifies to the Governor (hereinafter the "date of certification") that a majority of the members of the commission have been appointed or are in office and that all necessary anticipatory actions have been accomplished, provided, that the amount of revenues received pursuant to sections 109 and 110 prior to the date of certification are hereby appropriated to the division. Upon the date of certification, all such collected revenue shall be revenue of the commission. The Commissioner of Transportation, the Director of the Division of Motor Vehicles and the commission may take such anticipatory administrative action in advance as shall be necessary for the implementation of the act."

39:2A–40. Inconsistent acts superceded

All acts and parts of acts inconsistent with any of the provisions of this act are superseded to the extent of such inconsistencies.

L.2003, c. 13, § 122 (contingent effective date).

Historical and Statutory Notes

L.2003, c. 13, § 127, approved Jan. 28, 2003, provides:

"Sections 1, 2, 3, 12, 38, 109, 110 and 121 shall take effect immediately, sections 105, 106, 107, 108, and 120 shall take effect on July 1, 2003 and the remainder of this act shall take effect on the date the Commissioner of Transportation certifies to the Governor (hereinafter the "date of certification") that a majority of the members of the commission have been appointed or are in office and that all necessary anticipatory actions have been accomplished, provided, that the amount of revenues received pursuant to sections 109 and 110 prior to the date of certification are hereby appropriated to the division. Upon the date of certification, all such collected revenue shall be revenue of the commission. The Commissioner of Transportation, the Director of the Division of Motor Vehicles and the commission may take such anticipatory administrative action in advance as shall be necessary for the implementation of the act."

39:2A–41. Severability

The provisions of this act shall be deemed to be severable, and if any phrase, clause, sentence or provision of this act is declared to be unconstitutional or the applicability thereof to any person is held invalid, the remainder of this act shall not thereby be deemed to be unconstitutional or invalid.

This act shall be liberally construed to obtain the objectives and effect the purposes thereof.

L.2003, c. 13, § 123 (contingent effective date).

Historical and Statutory Notes

L.2003, c. 13, § 127, approved Jan. 28, 2003, provides:

"Sections 1, 2, 3, 12, 38, 109, 110 and 121 shall take effect immediately, sections 105, 106, 107, 108, and 120 shall take effect on July 1, 2003 and the remainder of this act shall take effect on the date the Commissioner of Transportation certifies to the Governor (hereinafter the "date of certification") that a majority of the members of the commission have been appointed or are in office and that all necessary anticipatory actions have been accomplished, provided, that the amount of revenues received pursuant to sections 109 and 110 prior to the date of certification are hereby appropriated to the division. Upon the date of certification, all such collected revenue shall be revenue of the commission. The Commissioner of Transportation, the Director of the Division of Motor Vehicles and the commission may take such anticipatory administrative action in advance as shall be necessary for the implementation of the act."

39:2A–42. Promotional payment incentives to collect certain surcharges levied; deposit into the Motor Vehicle Surcharges Revenue Fund

a. Notwithstanding the provisions of any other law to the contrary, no later than six months from the date of enactment of this act, and periodically thereafter, the Chief Administrator of the New Jersey Motor Vehicle Commission shall establish promotional payment incentives and shall offer such incentives to any driver who has failed to pay any motor vehicle surcharges levied pursuant to paragraph (1) or paragraph (3) of subsection b. of section 6 of P.L.1983, c. 65 (C.17:29A–35) or who has been authorized by the chief administrator to pay a surcharge levied pursuant to paragraph (1) or paragraph (3) of subsection b. of section 6 of P.L.1983, c. 65 (C.17:29A–35) on an installment basis. The promotional payment incentives afforded under this subsection shall not apply to surcharges levied pursuant to paragraph (2) of subsection b. of section 6 of P.L.1983, c. 65 (C.17:29A–35) nor shall any driver who has any outstanding surcharges levied pursuant to that paragraph be eligible to participate in any promotional payment incentives established by the chief administrator.

Promotional payment incentives may include, but need not be limited to, waivers of down payments necessary to satisfy any surcharge suspension, waivers of interest for the payment of the full principal amount of any surcharges owed to the chief administrator, or any other incentive that the chief administrator establishes.

b. All monies collected pursuant to the provisions of this section shall be remitted to the "Motor Vehicle Surcharges Revenue Fund," established pursuant to section 6 of P.L.2004, c. 70 (C.34:1B–21.28).

L.2009, c. 224, § 2, eff. Jan. 16, 2010.

CHAPTER 3

MOTOR VEHICLES

ARTICLE 1. CONSTRUCTION OF CHAPTER

Section
39:3–1. Certain vehicles excepted from chapter.
39:3–2. Motor vehicles used on rural mail routes not commercial cars.

ARTICLE 2. REGISTRATION AND LICENSING

39:3–3. Registration and licensing agents; fees.
39:3–4. Registration of automobiles and motorcycles; application; registration certificates; expiration; issuance; violations.
39:3–4a. Temporary registration of motor vehicle in another state by resident of New Jersey.
39:3–4b. Temporary registration.
39:3–4c. Rules and regulations over temporary registration requirements; issuance; duration of license; insurance.
39:3–4d. "Geographical district" defined.
39:3–4e. Rules and regulations; information by insurers.

Section

39:3–4f.   Motor vehicle with registration in foreign country; time limit on operation after import.

39:3–4.1.   Licensing motor vehicles for transportation of passengers for hire.

39:3–5.   Registration refused.

39:3–5.1.   Registration of vehicles subject to federal heavy vehicle use tax.

39:3–6.   Repealed.

39:3–6.1.   Definitions.

39:3–6.2.   Authority of director to make arrangements, agreements or declarations.

39:3–6.3.   Registration in another jurisdiction of vehicles located or operated from base in such jurisdiction.

39:3–6.4.   Repealed.

39:3–6.5.   Exemptions, benefits and privileges; examination of laws and requirements of other jurisdictions.

39:3–6.6.   Leased vehicles.

39:3–6.7.   Vehicles registered in jurisdiction where no agreement, arrangement or declaration is in effect; commercial vehicles.

39:3–6.8.   Repealed.

39:3–6.9.   Written agreements, arrangements or declarations required; filing.

39:3–6.10. Suspension or cancellation of exemptions, benefits, or privileges.

39:3–6.11. Definitions; apportioned vehicles.

39:3–6.12. International registration plan.

39:3–6.13. Registration of apportioned vehicles.

39:3–6.14. Registration and administrative fees.

39:3–6.15. Preservation of operational records.

39:3–6.16. Temporary registration.

39:3–6.17. Violations; fines.

39:3–6.18. Motor carrier audits of operational accounts.

39:3–6.19. Supersedure over other laws and agreements.

39:3–6.20. Disbursement of fees; proportional registration distributive fund.

39:3–6.21. Reciprocity privileges.

39:3–7.   Power of attorney given by nonresident; service of process.

39:3–8.   Fees for registration of passenger automobiles; license of semitrailers and trailers.

39:3–8.1.   Noncommercial trucks; license; application for registration.

39:3–8.2.   Collection of fees for certain program funds.

39:3–8.3.   Definitions.

39:3–8.4.   Additional fees on certain passenger automobiles.

39:3–9.   Repealed.

39:3–9a.   Endorsement of legal name in own handwriting on driver's license; notice of change of name; violation; penalty.

39:3–9b.   Application or renewal of driver's license; street address of place of residence or business.

39:3–9c.   Adoption of rules and regulations.

39:3–10.   Driver's licenses; examination; surrender of current license; classifications; issuance; license periods; renewals; denial of license; penalties.

39:3–10a.   Restoration of suspended or revoked license or registration; fee.

39:3–10b.   Initial license; two year probationary basis.

39:3–10c.   Vision screening every ten years.

39:3–10d.   Implementation of vision reexamination.

Section

39:3–10e.   Involvement in two or more accidents within 6 months with assessment of points; reexamination.

39:3–10f.   Color photograph driver licenses; "valid without photo" license.

39:3–10f1. Verification of authenticity.

39:3–10f2. Release or disclosure of pictures.

39:3–10f3. Rules and regulations.

39:3–10f4. Fee for digitized picture.

39:3–10f5. Secure Driver's License Fund.

39:3–10g.   Repealed.

39:3–10h.   Nonalterable construction of license.

39:3–10i.   Repealed.

39:3–10j.   Legislative findings and declarations concerning exemptions from licensing requirements set forth in the Commercial Motor Vehicle Safety Act of 1986.

39:3–10k.   Farmers and designated drivers of volunteer fire companies and National Guard; exempt from licensing provisions of Commercial Motor Vehicle Safety Act of 1986.

39:3–10l.   Rules and regulations.

39:3–10m.   Applicants for license and license renewal to be offered opportunity to register to vote.

39:3–10n.   Chief administrator; discretion to issue temporary driver's licenses to New Jersey licensees serving in the military.

39:3–10.1. Driver of motor vehicle or trackless trolley with capacity over six passengers; special license.

39:3–10.1a. School bus drivers; examination for presence of controlled dangerous substance.

39:3–10.2, 39:3–10.3. Repealed.

39:3–10.4. Report to director by physicians of persons subject to epileptiform seizures.

39:3–10.5. Report by drivers' license applicants subject to epileptiform seizures.

39:3–10.6. Procedure for evaluation and screening of persons subject to epileptiform seizures.

39:3–10.7. Confidentiality of reports of persons subject to epileptiform seizures.

39:3–10.8. Violations of provisions requiring reports of persons subject to epileptiform seizures.

39:3–10.9. Short title.

39:3–10.10. Purpose of act.

39:3–10.11. Definitions.

39:3–10.11a. Drivers of vehicles related to provision of funeral services; medical examination required.

39:3–10.12. Tests for commercial driver license.

39:3–10.13. Operation of commercial motor vehicle while under influence of alcohol or controlled substance.

39:3–10.14. Requests to Commercial Driver License Information System for driving record of applicant; provision of information to other licensing authorities; notification of issuance of license.

39:3–10.15. Notification of traffic violations, disqualification or suspension.

39:3–10.16. Denial, suspension or revocation of commercial driver license by director.

39:3–10.17. Licensee to be domiciled in State.

39:3–10.17a. Commercial drivers license applicants; fingerprinting and background checks.

39:3–10.18. Possession of valid commercial driver license with applicable endorsements required; operation of vehicle during period of refusal,

Section

suspension, revocation, prohibition, disqualification, or out of service order; penalties.

39:3–10.19. Operation of commercial vehicle in this State by person with waiver of requirements or license issued by other jurisdiction.

39:3–10.20. Suspension or revocation of commercial driver license by chief administrator; notification to Commercial Driver License Information System.

39:3–10.21. Administration of commercial driver testing.

39:3–10.22. Waiver of skills test.

39:3–10.23. Processing of applicants; time and place of testing.

39:3–10.24. Consent to taking samples of breath; record of test; independent test; prohibition of use of force; refusal to submit to test; penalties.

39:3–10.25. Chemical analyses of breath; uniform form for reports of analyses.

39:3–10.26. Operator of commercial vehicle restricted to one license; penalty for violation.

39:3–10.27. Rules and regulations.

39:3–10.28. Agreements, arrangements, or declarations to carry out provisions of act.

39:3–10.29. Waiver of provisions.

39:3–10.30. Fees; duration of examination of learner's permit; testing opportunities; expiration of commercial driver license.

39:3–10.31. Waiver of road test for completion of motorcycle safety education course.

39:3–10.32. Violations; disorderly persons offense.

39:3–10.33. Request for medical review or retesting of certain motor vehicle operators; confirmation of notices.

39:3–11. Driver's license with restrictions or conditions; violations; punishment.

39:3–11a. Hearing impaired persons; special driver's license; fee.

39:3–11b. Rules and regulations.

39:3–11.1. License to persons 16 years of age to drive motor vehicles in agricultural pursuits.

39:3–11.2. Discretion as to granting license; consent of parent or guardian.

39:3–11.3. Rules and regulations.

39:3–11.4. Repealed.

39:3–11.5. Persons in military or naval service or discharged or released therefrom; "in time of emergency" defined.

39:3–12. Illegal securing of driver's license; punishment.

39:3–12.1. Application for renewal of registration or license.

39:3–12.2. Organ donor under the "Uniform Anatomical Gift Act"; designation; real-time electronic access to donor list.

39:3–12.3. Donate Life NJ Registry; development and establishment of on-line database; monetary donations to fund.

39:3–12.4. Drivers license or ID card registration or renewal; donations to Donate Life NJ Registry via on-line portal.

39:3–12.5. Federal or private grants for development and implementation of registry; receipt and expenditure of funds.

39:3–13. Examination and special learner's permit; scope and effect; fees.

39:3–13. Examination and special learner's permit; scope and effect; fees.

Section

39:3–13a. Written examination administered in high school; student with cognitive difficulty; grading.

39:3–13b. Minor's driving record; parent or guardian's request for information.

39:3–13b. Minor's driving record; parent or guardian's request for information.

39:3–13.1. Special learner's permit; place of keeping.

39:3–13.1. Special learner's permit; place of keeping.

39:3–13.2. Scope and effect of special learner's permit.

39:3–13.2a. Special learner's permit; duration.

39:3–13.2a. Special learner's permit; duration.

39:3–13.3. Application for special permit.

39:3–13.4. Examination for driver's license.

39:3–13.4. Examination for driver's license.

39:3–13.5. Repealed.

39:3–13.6. Evaluation and report regarding new driver performance.

39:3–13.7. Adoption of rules and regulations.

39:3–13.8. Specific violations of certain permits or licenses.

39:3–13.8. Specific violations of certain permits or licenses.

39:3–13.9. Public education campaign.

39:3–14. Official drivers licensed free; special certificate; termination and surrender.

39:3–15. Operation of motor vehicle by nonresident; touring privileges; seasonal permits; violations; fines.

39:3–15.1. Rules and regulations; forms.

39:3–16. Authority of commissioner; suspension of touring privileges.

39:3–17. Touring privileges of nonresident chauffeurs or drivers.

39:3–17.1. Continuation of nonresident driving rights after becoming resident; vehicle registration after certain date; criminal penalties; repeat offenses.

39:3–18. General registration; "D" or temporary plates; fees.

39:3–19. Omnibus registration; fees; markers; application for registration.

39:3–19.1. Penalty for violating omnibus registration requirements.

39:3–19.2. School vehicles; fees; exemptions.

39:3–19.3. Inapplicability of act to certain buses and vehicles.

39:3–19.4. Vehicle used for summer day or residence camps; inspection; liability insurance coverage.

39:3–19.5. Autocab, limousine or livery service; special registration plates; fees.

39:3–19.6. Fee for operating period from October 1 through September 30 for passenger limousines.

39:3–20. Commercial motor vehicles other than omnibuses and motor–drawn vehicles; registration year; fees; gross weight; definition; violations; penalties.

39:3–20.1. Empty trucks, tractors, trailers and semitrailers; "in-transit empty" registration plates; fees.

39:3–20.2. Misuse of "in-transit empty" registration; penalty.

39:3–20.3. Operation of commercial motor vehicle exceeding gross weight limit on registration certificate unlawful; penalties.

39:3–20.4. Highway Safety Fund established.

39:3–21. Motorcycle registration; fee.

Section

39:3–22.	Repealed.
39:3–22a.	Reduction of fees on or after October 1.
39:3–22.1.	Persons in military or naval service; refund of registration fees; application.
39:3–22.2.	Warrant for refund.
39:3–23.	Rubber tires or tires of approved material required.
39:3–23.1.	Approval of tires of material other than rubber.
39:3–24.	Farm tractors and traction equipment; motor vehicles used as farm machinery or farm implements; registration; operation; fee.
39:3–24.1.	Repealed.
39:3–25.	License plates for farmers' trucks; fee; expiration.
39:3–26.	Traction or tractor well-drill machines or well-drilling equipment; trucks with powered feed impregnating machines; fee.
39:3–26.1.	Self-propelled unregistered vehicle used solely on private property; highway crossing permit.
39:3–26.2.	Application; issuance; contents.
39:3–26.3.	Unauthorized use of highway by unregistered vehicles; penalty.
39:3–26.4.	Fees; refund; duration of permit; renewal.
39:3–26.5.	Death, bodily injury or property damage involving vehicle on public highway; application of Motor Vehicle Security-Responsibility Law.
39:3–27.	Free registration of certain vehicles; expiration; transfer to other motor vehicle.
39:3–27.1.	Free registration of vehicles owned by resident blind or disabled veterans or holder of Medal of Honor.
39:3–27.2.	Special registration for passenger automobiles used in connection with convention, pageant or parade.
39:3–27.3.	Definitions.
39:3–27.4.	Registration of historic motor vehicles.
39:3–27.5.	Amateur radio call letter registration plates.
39:3–27.6.	Application; form; fee.
39:3–27.7.	Revocation or expiration; notification of director.
39:3–27.8.	Special license plate; fire department, first aid or rescue squad; member, spouse, parent or business firm.
39:3–27.9.	Issuance; proof of membership; fees.
39:3–27.10.	Termination of association; return of special plate.
39:3–27.11.	Unauthorized uses.
39:3–27.12.	Violations; fine.
39:3–27.13.	Member of national guard; special license plate; fee.
39:3–27.14.	Rules and regulations.
39:3–27.15.	Disabled veteran; special license plate.
39:3–27.16.	Issuance; fee.
39:3–27.17.	Unauthorized use; prohibition.
39:3–27.18.	Violations; fine.
39:3–27.19.	Commuter vans; registration certificate and plates; fee.
39:3–27.20.	Termination of use; surrender of special plate.
39:3–27.21.	Unauthorized use of special plate.
39:3–27.22.	Violations; fine.
39:3–27.23.	Rules and regulations.
39:3–27.24.	P.O.W. license plates; fees.
39:3–27.25.	Rules and regulations.
39:3–27.26.	Repealed.

Section

39:3–27.27.	Street rod license plates; fees; display of National Street Rod Association safety inspection sticker; violations; fine.
39:3–27.28.	Disposition of fees.
39:3–27.29.	Officers and elected officials of counties; special license plates.
39:3–27.30.	Issuance; fees.
39:3–27.31.	Surrender on leaving office.
39:3–27.32.	Disposition of fees.
39:3–27.33.	Members of military reserve unit; special license plates.
39:3–27.34.	Rules and regulations.
39:3–27.35.	Special organization vehicle registration plates for members of nonprofit community, alumni or service organizations; issuance.
39:3–27.36.	Conditions for issuance.
39:3–27.37.	Authority for final decision of approval of organization.
39:3–27.38.	Right to suspend approval.
39:3–27.39.	Rules and regulations.
39:3–27.40.	Effect on existing laws and regulations.
39:3–27.41.	Surviving spouse of purple heart veteran; retention of special organization vehicle registration plates.
39:3–27.42.	Special license plates issued to mayor or chief executive; fee; surrender of plates; violation.
39:3–27.43.	Active members of Military Order of Purple Heart authorized to affix approved emblem to license plate.
39:3–27.44.	Rules and regulations; use; design; placement on license plates.
39:3–27.45.	Special license plates for Silver Star medal recipients; retention of plate by surviving spouse; rules and regulations.
39:3–27.46.	Special license plates for Combat Infantryman Badge recipients; fee; retention of plate by surviving spouse; rules and regulations.
39:3–27.47.	Definitions.
39:3–27.48.	Coastal protection license plates; design.
39:3–27.49.	Application for coastal protection license plates; fees.
39:3–27.50.	Coastal Protection Trust Fund; use of monies collected; special emergency reserve account; use of monies.
39:3–27.51.	Fees used to reimburse division for costs.
39:3–27.52.	Appropriations from fund.
39:3–27.53.	Notification of availability of coastal protection license plates.
39:3–27.54.	Interagency memorandum of agreement.
39:3–27.55.	Animal welfare license plates; application.
39:3–27.56.	Fees to be deposited in Animal Population Control Fund.
39:3–27.57.	Notification of availability of animal welfare license plates.
39:3–27.58.	Interagency memorandum of agreement.
39:3–27.59.	Emergency medical technician-ambulance license plates; application; fees.
39:3–27.60.	Fees for special license plates to cover costs of implementation.
39:3–27.61.	Definitions.
39:3–27.62.	Olympic license plates authorized.
39:3–27.63.	Application and fee for olympic license plate.
39:3–27.64.	Garden state games trust fund created.
39:3–27.65.	Garden state games trust fund; allocation of funds.
39:3–27.66.	Notice of availability of olympic license plates.

Section

39:3–27.67. Issuance of Battleship U.S.S. New Jersey license plates.

39:3–27.68. Application; fees.

39:3–27.69. Battleship New Jersey Memorial Fund.

39:3–27.70. Use of license plate fees.

39:3–27.71. Notification of motorists.

39:3–27.72. Definitions.

39:3–27.73. Historic preservation license plates; slogans and emblems displayed.

39:3–27.74. Application; fee; additional fee with registration.

39:3–27.75. Historic Preservation License Plate Fund; fees deposited.

39:3–27.76. Reimbursement for costs incurred by historic preservation license plate program; average cost per license plate.

39:3–27.77. Notice to motorists of availability of license plates.

39:3–27.78. Interagency memorandum of agreement.

39:3–27.79. Shade tree and community forest preservation license plates.

39:3–27.80. Application for shade tree and community forest preservation license plate.

39:3–27.81. Shade tree and community forest preservation license plate fund.

39:3–27.82. Use of license plate fees; reimbursement for costs related to issuance of plates.

39:3–27.83. Methods used to notify motorists of availability of license plates.

39:3–27.84. Interagency memorandum of agreement.

39:3–27.85. Pinelands preservation license plates; application fee; use of proceeds.

39:3–27.86. Issuance of Barnegat Bay Decoy and Baymen's Museum license plates.

39:3–27.87. Application for license plates; fees.

39:3–27.88. Reimbursement of division for certain costs; annual certification of cost per license plate; discontinuance if cost exceeds application fee.

39:3–27.89. Notification of motorists; availability of special plates.

39:3-27.90. Conquer cancer license plates; application; fees.

39:3–27.91. Definitions.

39:3–27.92. Liberty State Park license plates; issuance; description.

39:3–27.93. Liberty State Park license plates; application; fees.

39:3–27.94. Liberty State Park License Plate Fund established.

39:3–27.95. Liberty State Park License Plate Fund; amounts deposited.

39:3–27.96. Liberty State Park license plates; notice of eligibility.

39:3–27.97. Interagency memorandum of agreement.

39:3–27.98. License plates; submarine veterans emblem.

39:3–27.99. Rules and regulations; submarine veteran license plate emblems.

39:3–27.100. Meadowlands conservation license plates.

39:3–27.101. Application and fee.

39:3–27.102. Fees; deposited in trust.

39:3–27.103. Division of Motor Vehicles; reimbursement of costs.

39:3–27.104. Availability of license plates; notification to motorists.

39:3–27.105. Interagency agreement.

39:3–27.106. Navy Cross license plates; description; fees.

Section

39:3–27.107. Deborah Heart and Lung Center license plates.

39:3–27.108. Application.

39:3–27.109. Deborah Hospital Foundation Fund.

39:3–27.110. Center contributions.

39:3–27.111. Fees; reimbursement.

39:3–27.112. Notification to eligible motorists.

39:3–27.113. Memorandum of agreement.

39:3–27.114. Special registration plates; municipal mayor.

39:3–27.115. Special registration plates; former members of New Jersey State Legislature.

39:3–27.116. "Promote Agriculture" license plates.

39:3–27.117. Fees.

39:3–27.118. Funding.

39:3–27.119. Use of fees collected.

39:3–27.120. Average cost per license plate.

39:3–27.121. Notification of eligible motorists.

39:3–27.122. Procedure for carrying out provisions of this act.

39:3–27.123. Design; fees; cost; notification of eligible motorists.

39:3–27.124. Monies contributed; law enforcement memorial license plates.

39:3–27.125. Funds annually appropriated; reimbursements.

39:3–27.126. Procedures for carrying out provisions of act.

39:3–27.127. "Be An Organ Donor" special license plates.

39:3–27.128. Contributions to offset initial costs.

39:3–27.129. Notice to motorists; procedures.

39:3–27.130. Certification of average cost; discontinuance of issuance.

39:3–27.131. Rewards for Justice License Plate Fund.

39:3–27.132. United We Stand license plates.

39:3–27.133. Application for United We Stand license plates; fee.

39:3–27.134. Funding.

39:3–27.135. Contribution to fund.

39:3–27.136. Use of funds.

39:3–27.137. Notification of eligible motorists.

39:3–27.138. Memorandum of agreement; procedures.

39:3–27.139. Rules and regulations.

39:3–28. Licenses and registrations indexed; certified copies of applications as evidence; destruction of applications and copies.

39:3–29. License, registration certificate and insurance identification card; possession; exhibit upon request; violations; fine; defense.

39:3–29.1. Insurance identification cards; rules and regulations.

39:3–29.1a. Failure to provide proof of insurance; impoundment and sale of vehicle.

39:3–29.2. Short title.

39:3–29.3. Qualifications; data; signature and verification.

39:3–29.4. Standard license form; color; "For Identification Only".

39:3–29.5. Duration of card; renewal; fee.

39:3–29.6. Duplicate card.

39:3–29.7. Fees.

39:3–29.8. Prohibited acts.

39:3–29.9. Rules and regulations.

39:3–29.10. Violation of provisions.

39:3–30. Transfer of ownership or destruction of motor vehicle; use on another motor vehicle; death of registered owner; joint registration.

39:3–30.1. Registration in names of husband and wife; title; presumption; procedure upon death.

39:3–30.1a. Affidavit that registrants husband and wife.

39:3–30.2. Rights of creditors; construction against waiver of inheritance tax requirements.

Section

39:3–30.3. Operation of motor vehicles registered in name of decedent.
39:3–31. Duplicate certificates and licenses; fees.
39:3–31.1. Duplicate certificate for use by members of family; fee.
39:3–32. Loss, destruction or defacement of license plates; reissuance or replacement of surrendered plates; replacement fees.
39:3–33. Identification mark or marks; display; registration plate inserts; issuance; requirements; use of fictitious numbers or plate with advertisement; violations; penalties.
39:3–33a. Additional application fees.
39:3–33b. Personalized, courtesy or specialty license plates; second set.
39:3–33.1. Veterans buying motor vehicles from United States; temporary identification markers.
39:3–33.2. License plates; words "Garden State" to be imprinted.
39:3–33.3. Special identifying marks; issuance of plates.
39:3–33.4. Additional fees for courtesy and personalized identifying marks.
39:3–33.5. Restrictions upon issuance.
39:3–33.5a. Issuance of courtesy marks.
39:3–33.6. Disposition of funds.
39:3–33.7. Rules and regulations.
39:3–33.8. Effective date.
39:3–33.9. Reflectorized registration plates; phase-in program; reflectorized license plate selection commission; additional annual fee; duration; rules and regulations; annual progress report.
39:3–33.10. Special wildlife conservation license plates; fees; establishment of Wildlife Conservation Fund.
39:3–33.11. Renewal fee for wildlife conservation license plates.
39:3–34. Application for certificate or license during suspension, revocation or prohibition period forbidden.
39:3–35. Lending or using registration certificate or plates on other vehicle prohibited; fine.
39:3–36. Notice of change of address; penalty for failure.
39:3–37. Falsifying application, examination or waiver certificate; knowingly sell, loan or give identification document to unqualified person; punishment; revocation of registration or license.
39:3–37.1. Use of license or vehicle by unlicensed driver prohibited.
39:3–38. Counterfeiting or using other markers; placement of forged or counterfeit plate on motor vehicle; revocation of license; fine.
39:3–38.1 to 39:3–39. Repealed.
39:3–40. Driving when license refused, suspended, revoked or prohibited; motor vehicle license revoked; punishment.
39:3–40. Driving when license refused, suspended, revoked or prohibited; motor vehicle license revoked; punishment.
39:3–40.1. Revocation of registration certificate and plates.
39:3–40.2. Issuance of temporary registration certificate and plates to spouse, child, dependent or legal guardian of violator or to owner or lessee of vehicle.
39:3–40.3. Impoundment of motor vehicle subject to registration restriction.

Section

39:3–40.4. Sale or transfer of vehicle subject to registration restrictions.
39:3–40.5. Rules and regulations.
39:3–40.6. Release of impounded vehicle; proof of insurance.
39:3–41. Driver's manual; distribution.
39:3–41.1. Driver's manual; distribution of remaining copies before reprinting.
39:3–42. Compliance with chapter sufficient.

ARTICLE 3. EQUIPMENT

39:3–43. Powers of commissioner.
39:3–44. Scope and effect.
39:3–45. Certain vehicles excepted.
39:3–46. Words and phrases defined.
39:3–47. Certain acts forbidden.
39:3–48. Visibility.
39:3–49. Headlamps.
39:3–50. Color of lights, permits; cancellation or revocation of permits.
39:3–51. Auxiliary driving lamps.
39:3–52. Additional lighting equipment.
39:3–53. Spot lamps.
39:3–54. Special restrictions on lamps, emergency warning lighting.
39:3–54.1 to 39:3–54.6. Repealed.
39:3–54.7. Members of certain organizations; display of emergency warning lights.
39:3–54.8. Time of operation.
39:3–54.9. Specifications.
39:3–54.10. Placement on motor vehicle.
39:3–54.11. Display of emergency warning lights; identification cards.
39:3–54.12. Rights of motor vehicle with emergency warning lights in operation.
39:3–54.13. Violations; penalty.
39:3–54.14. Special identification lights; vehicles of licensed private detective businesses; permits; penalty for violation.
39:3–54.15. Red emergency warning lights and/or siren on motor vehicles owned by current volunteer fire chief or first assistant chief or chief officer of first aid or rescue squad.
39:3–54.16. Placement of red emergency warning lights.
39:3–54.17. Placement of sirens.
39:3–54.18. Identification cards for chief or first assistant chief; issuance; purpose.
39:3–54.19. Operation of motor vehicles with red emergency warning lights or sirens; yielding right of way.
39:3–54.20. Unlawful use of red emergency warning lights or sirens; penalty.
39:3–54.21. Use of amber warning lights by United States Postal Service employees.
39:3–54.22. Permit to display emergency warning lights; application to County Emergency Management Coordinator.
39:3–54.23. Permit to display emergency warning lights; application to Municipal Emergency Management Coordinator.
39:3–54.24. Amber warning lights for use by an authorized public utility company employee; permit authorizing display; fees; approved operation.
39:3–54.25. Magnetic sign with utility logo affixed on to vehicle; authorized display.

Section

39:3–54.26. Violation of authorized use of amber warning lights or magnetic sign; penalties.

39:3–55. Alternate road lighting equipment.

39:3–56. Number of driving lamps required or permitted.

39:3–57. Single-beam road lighting.

39:3–58. Multiple-beam road lighting.

39:3–59. Beam indicator lights.

39:3–60. Use of multiple-beam road lighting equipment.

39:3–61. Lamps and reflectors required on particular vehicles.

39:3–61.1. Mounting of lamps and reflectors.

39:3–61.2. Combination of lighting devices and reflectors; prohibited combinations.

39:3–61.3. Stop lamps; construction, placement and use.

39:3–61.4. Overhang loads; placement and use of red lamps and flags.

39:3–62. Lamps on parked vehicles.

39:3–63. Regulations governing lamps, turn signals and reflectors; promulgation by commissioner.

39:3–64. Vehicular traffic hazard warning signals.

39:3–64.1. Itinerant vendors' vehicle.

39:3–64.2. Signaling system; flashing simultaneously.

39:3–64.3. Signals to flash simultaneously when stopped for purpose of transacting business.

39:3–64.4. Rules and regulations.

39:3–65. Lamps on other vehicles and equipment.

39:3–66. Maintenance of lamps, reflectors, etc.

39:3–66.1. Repealed.

39:3–66.2. Punishment for violation.

39:3–67. Brake equipment required.

39:3–68. Brake performance.

39:3–68.1. Towing vehicle and towed vehicle defined.

39:3–68.2. Emergency stopping system for vehicles using compressed air at wheels for application of service brakes; requirement.

39:3–69. Horns and audible warning devices.

39:3–70. Mufflers.

39:3–70. Mufflers.

39:3–70.1. Air pollution control; tests.

39:3–70.2. Idling and operation of motor vehicles and school buses; emission of smoke and other air contaminants; penalties; exceptions.

39:3–70.2. Idling and operation of motor vehicles and school buses; emission of smoke and other air contaminants; penalties; exceptions.

39:3–71. Mirrors.

39:3–71.1. Backup monitoring device or rear cross-view mirrors.

39:3–72. Tire equipment.

39:3–73. Tire-chains.

39:3–74. Windshields must be unobstructed and equipped with cleaners.

39:3–75. Safety glass.

39:3–75.1. Regular transport of persons with medical conditions; application for windshield treatment.

39:3–75.2. Rules and regulations.

39:3–75.3. Violations and penalties.

39:3–76. Dangerous exhaust gases.

39:3–76.1. Use of sign "Press" on motor vehicle.

39:3–76.2. Safety belts or restraining devices.

39:3–76.2a. Child passenger restraint system; use; failure to use not contributory negligence; inadmissibility in evidence.

39:3–76.2b. Repealed.

39:3–76.2c. Informational material.

39:3–76.2d. Fines; suspension of fine.

Section

39:3–76.2e. Short title.

39:3–76.2f. Seat belt usage by drivers and passengers required.

39:3–76.2g. Exceptions to seat belt usage requirements.

39:3–76.2h. Personal injury or death actions; effect of act.

39:3–76.2i. Repealed.

39:3–76.2j. Violations; fines.

39:3–76.2k. Informational booklet; availability to public.

39:3–76.2l. Wheelchair passengers; restraint and securement systems in passenger vehicles.

39:3–76.2m. Violations; fines.

39:3–76.2n. Offense level for violation of seat belt laws; fines for back seat violations.

39:3–76.3. Motorcycles; height of handle bar grips.

39:3–76.3a. Motorcycle operation; conformance to federal standards; NHTSA certification.

39:3–76.4. Muffler systems for motorcycles.

39:3–76.5. Permanent seat; passengers; seat, handholds and footrests; helmets; method of riding; violations; penalties.

39:3–76.6. Rules and regulations; motorcycle equipment.

39:3–76.7. Protective helmet of proper size to be worn by operator and passenger; points not assessed for violations.

39:3–76.8. Goggles or face shield to be worn by motorcycle operator.

39:3–76.9. Wind screen; goggles or face shield not necessary.

39:3–76.10. Sale of helmets, goggles or face shields; type and specifications approved by director.

39:3–77. Selling or using unapproved devices or equipment.

39:3–77.1. Use of national school bus chrome paint on motor vehicles.

39:3–77.2. Motor vehicles to which persons admitted to purchase merchandise or view exhibit; exit door.

39:3–78. Construction of article.

39:3–79. Fine for violating article.

39:3–79.1. Devices to prevent throwing of dirt on windshields of following vehicles.

39:3–79.2. Violations.

39:3–79.3. Effective date.

39:3–79.4. Motor vehicle powered by compressed or liquified gaseous fuel; identification with diamond shaped label; fee.

39:3–79.5. Diamond shaped label; requirements; rules and regulations on placement and appearance.

39:3–79.6. Inspection for compliance with provisions of act.

39:3–79.7. Failure to comply; penalties.

39:3–79.8. Prohibition of supplying fuel to vehicle without label; violations; penalty.

39:3–79.9. Publicity of provisions of act.

39:3–79.10. Intermodal chassis; definitions.

39:3–79.11. Intermodal equipment provider; violations.

39:3–79.12. Systematic maintenance check program for intermodal chassis; requirements; reports.

39:3–79.13. Identification of out–of–service intermodal chassis; tags; repair of defects.

39:3–79.14. Events triggering full SMC eight–point inspection.

39:3–79.15. Qualifications of SMC inspectors.

39:3–79.16. Driver request for repair or replacement of intermodal chassis; driver compensation; complaint; penalty.

39:3–79.17. Maintenance of records.

Section
39:3–79.18.   Intermodal equipment providers; registration; annual certification; audits; compliance and penalty.
39:3–79.19.   Roadside inspection; summons, complaint or violation report.
39:3–79.20.   Interference with motor carrier or driver, intermodal equipment provider or SMC inspector; penalty.
39:3–79.21.   Intermodal chassis; rules and regulations.
39:3–79.22.   Omnibus owner or operators without a certificate of public convenience and necessity; additional fine.
39:3–79.23.   Omnibus Safety Enforcement Fund within the Department of Treasury; deposit and utilization of funds.
39:3–79.24.   Omnibus Safety Enforcement Fund within the Motor Vehicle Commission; deposit and utilization of funds.

ARTICLE 4.   TIRES AND LOADS

39:3–80.   Rubber tires or tires of approved material required; penalties.
39:3–81.   Sale, possession or use of tires of type approved by director; regulations; penalties.
39:3–82.   Tires on commercial vehicles, tractors and motor-drawn vehicles; distribution of load; fine for violation of section.
39:3–83.   Repealed.

ARTICLE 5.   DIMENSIONS AND WEIGHT

39:3–84.   Dimensional restrictions; outside width; height; overall length; weight; special written permit for exceptions.
39:3–84a.   Repealed.
39:3–84.1.   Application of weight limitations.
39:3–84.2.   Repeal.
39:3–84.3.   Violations as to weights and measurements of vehicles.
39:3–84.4.   Damage to highways or structures by overweight vehicles; liability.
39:3–84.5.   Partial invalidity.
39:3–84.6.   Definitions.
39:3–84.7.   Issuance of distinctive markers.
39:3–84.8.   Tow truck registration; application contents.
39:3–84.9.   Repealed.
39:3–84.10.   Suspension, revocation or refusal of registration.
39:3–84.11.   Proper display of license plates or markers.
39:3–84.12.   Preemption of certain political subdivision actions.
39:3–84.13.   Violations; fines.
39:3–84.14.   Rules and regulations.
39:3–85.   Repealed.

ARTICLE 6.   REPORTS OF THEFT, ETC.

39:3–85.1.   Stolen motor vehicles or registration plates; notification of police.
39:3–85.2.   Report to Superintendent of State Police and Commissioner of Motor Vehicles.
39:3–85.3.   Record of stolen motor vehicles and registration plates.
39:3–85.4.   Partial invalidity.
39:3–85.5.   Program to combat theft of motor vehicles; establishment; consent agreement; decal.

Section
39:3–85.6.   Authority of law enforcement officer to stop vehicle displaying decal.
39:3–85.7.   Form of consent agreement.
39:3–85.8.   Recording of participants in program.
39:3–85.9.   Fees for consent forms and decals.
39:3–85.10.   Rules and regulations.

ARTICLE 7.   GENERAL PENALTIES

39:3–86.   Penalty where no specific penalty provided.

ARTICLE 8.   APPROPRIATIONS

39:3–87.   Expenditure of receipts, apportionment.

ARTICLE 1.   CONSTRUCTION OF CHAPTER

39:3–1.   Certain vehicles excepted from chapter

Automobile fire engines and such self-propelling vehicles as are used neither for the conveyance of persons for hire, pleasure or business, nor for the transportation of freights, such as steam road rollers and traction engines are excepted from the provisions of this chapter.

39:3–2.   Motor vehicles used on rural mail routes not commercial cars

Motor vehicles not of the commercial type may be used in the delivery of mail on rural free delivery routes and shall not be classed or considered as commercial cars.

ARTICLE 2.   REGISTRATION AND LICENSING

39:3–3.   Registration and licensing agents; fees

A Motor Vehicle Agent (hereinafter "agent") shall administer and ensure the efficient operations of a local commission office. The board shall designate at least one person in each county to be its agent for the registering of motor vehicles, issuing registration certificates and licensing of drivers, subject to the requirements of this subtitle and to any rules and regulations the board imposes. The agent shall so act until the agent's authority is revoked by the board. All moneys received by such agents for registrations and licenses granted under the provisions of this chapter shall forthwith be deposited as received with the State Treasurer. Notwithstanding any provision of law to the contrary, all current agent contracts shall remain in effect until their expiration. Until the agent contract expires, the fee allowed the agent for registration certificates issued by him and for every license granted by him shall be fixed by the board on the basis of the registration or license fees collected by the agent. The board may limit the fee so paid to a maximum. Such fee shall be paid to the agent by the State Treasurer upon the voucher of the commission in the same manner as other State expenses are paid until the agent contract expires. At such time as the agent becomes a State employee, the agent shall receive a salary as fixed by the administrator in accordance with the commission table of organization. Future agent appointments shall be in the State unclassified service and the agents shall serve at the pleasure of the administrator. To determine suitability for appointment, all agents shall undergo a background check prior to appointment based upon an examination of State, federal and financial records. No person shall be appointed as an agent who has contributed $1,000 or more to any gubernatorial or State party committee in any one year during the five years preceding appointment. All agents appointed pursuant to this section shall be qualified by education and experience to administer and ensure the efficient operation of a local commission office. As used in this section, education and experience shall include a background in law enforcement, security services, customer relations or services; business administration, finance or management; or public administration or finance.

Amended by L.1955, c. 8, p. 41, § 2; L.1959, c. 145, p. 587, § 1; L.2003, c. 13, § 43; L.2007, c. 335, § 18, eff. Feb. 12, 2008.

39:3–4. Registration of automobiles and motorcycles; application; registration certificates; expiration; issuance; violations

Except as hereinafter provided, every resident of this State and every nonresident whose automobile or motorcycle shall be driven in this State shall, before using such vehicle on the public highways, register the same, and no automobile or motorcycle shall be driven unless so registered.

Such registration shall be made in the following manner: An application in writing, signed by the applicant or by an agent or officer, in case the applicant is a corporation, shall be made to the chief administrator or the chief administrator's agent, on forms prepared and supplied by the chief administrator, containing the name, street address of the residence or the business of the owner, mailing address, if different from the street address of the owner's residence or business, and age of the owner, together with a description of the character of the automobile or motorcycle, including the name of the maker and the vehicle identification number, or the manufacturer's number or the number assigned by the chief administrator if the vehicle does not have a vehicle identification number, and any other statement that may be required by the chief administrator. A post office box shall appear on the application only as part of a mailing address that is submitted by the owner, agent or officer, as the case may be, in addition to the street address of the applicant's residence or business; provided, however, the chief administrator, upon application, shall permit a person who was a victim of a violation of N.J.S.2C:12–10, N.J.S.2C:14–2, or N.J.S.2C:25–17 et seq., or who the chief administrator otherwise determines to have good cause, to use as a mailing address a post office box, an address other than the applicant's address or other contact point. An owner whose last address appears on the records of the division as a post office box shall change his address on

his application for renewal to the street address of his residence or business and, if different from his street address, his mailing address unless the chief administrator has determined, pursuant to this section, that the owner may use a post office box, an address other than the owner's address or other contact point as a mailing address. The application shall contain the name of the insurer of the vehicle and the policy number. If the vehicle is a leased motor vehicle, the application shall make note of that fact and shall include along with the name and street address of the lessor the name, street address and driver license number of the lessee.

Thereupon the chief administrator shall have the power to grant a registration certificate to the owner of any motor vehicle, if over 17 years of age, application for the registration having been properly made and the fee therefor paid, and the vehicle being of a type that complies with the requirements of this title. The form and contents of the registration certificate to be issued shall be determined by the chief administrator.

If the vehicle is a leased motor vehicle, the registration certificate shall, in addition to containing the name and street address of the lessor, identify the vehicle as a leased motor vehicle.

The chief administrator shall maintain a record of all registration certificates issued, and of the contents thereof.

Every registration shall expire and the registration certificate thereof become void on the last day of the twelfth calendar month following the calendar month in which the certificate was issued; provided, however, that the chief administrator may, at his discretion, require registrations which shall expire, and issue certificates thereof which shall become void, on a date fixed by him, which date shall not be sooner than three months nor later than 26 months after the date of issuance of such certificates, and the fees for such registrations, including any other fees or charges collected in connection with the registration fee, shall be fixed by the chief administrator in amounts proportionately less or greater than the fees established by law. The chief administrator may fix the expiration date for registration certificates at a date other than 12 months if the chief administrator determines that the change is necessary, appropriate or convenient in order to aid in implementing the vehicle inspection requirements of chapter 8 of Title 39 or for other good cause. The chief administrator may, for good cause extend a registration beyond the expiration date that appears upon the registration certificate for periods not to exceed 12 additional months. The chief administrator may extend the expiration date of a registration without payment of a proportionate fee when the chief administrator determines that such extension is necessary for good cause. If any registration is so extended, the owner shall pay upon renewal the full registration fee for the period fixed by the chief administrator as if no extension had been granted.

Notwithstanding any other provision of law to the contrary, every registration for new passenger automobiles shall expire and the registration certificate shall become void on the last day of the 48th calendar month following the calendar month in which the certificate was initially issued. On and after February 1, 2005, the provisions of this paragraph shall not apply to new passenger automobiles purchased by a rental company for use as rental passenger automobiles. As used in this paragraph, "rental company" means a person engaged in the business of renting motor vehicles; and "rental passenger automobile" means a passenger automobile that is rented without a driver and used in the transportation of persons or property other than commercial freight.

If the new passenger automobile being registered is a leased passenger automobile, the registration shall expire in accordance with the term of the lease. If the term of the lease extends beyond one or more 12–month periods by one or more months, the registration period shall be based upon the full year into which one or more of the months extend; provided, however, the registration period for a leased automobile shall not exceed 48–months.

Following the 48–month period of the initial registration of a new passenger automobile, the subsequent registration shall expire, and the registration certificate shall become void, on the last day of the 12th calendar month following the calendar month in which the certificate was next issued.

All motorcycles for which registrations have been issued prior to the effective date of P.L.1989, c. 167 and which are scheduled to expire between November 1 and March 31 shall, upon renewal, be issued registrations by the chief administrator which shall expire on a date fixed by him, but in no case shall that expiration date be earlier than April 30 nor later than October 31. The fees for the renewal of the motorcycle registrations authorized under this paragraph shall be fixed by the chief administrator in an amount proportionately less or greater than the fee established by R.S.39:3–21.

Application forms for all renewals of registrations for passenger automobiles shall be sent to the last addresses of owners of motor vehicles and motorcycles, as they appear on the records of the division.

No person owning or having control over any unregistered vehicle shall permit the same to be parked or to stand on a public highway.

Any police officer is authorized to remove any unregistered vehicle from the public highway to a storage space or garage, and the expense involved in such removal and storing of the vehicle shall be borne by the owner of the vehicle, except that the expense shall be borne by the lessee of a leased vehicle.

Any person violating the provisions of this section shall be subject to a fine not exceeding $100, except that for the misstatement of any fact in the application required to be made to the chief administrator, the person making such statement or omitting the statement that the motor vehicle is to be used as a leased motor vehicle when that is the case shall be subject to the penalties provided in R.S.39:3–37.

The chief administrator may extend the expiration date of a registration certificate without payment of a proportionate fee when the chief administrator determines that such extension is necessary, appropriate or convenient to the implementation of vehicle inspection requirements. If any registration certificate is so extended, the owner shall pay upon renewal the full registration fee for the period fixed by the chief administrator as if no extension had been granted.

The New Jersey Motor Vehicle Commission shall make a reasonable effort to notify any lessor whose name and address is on file with the commission, or any other lessor the commission may determine it is necessary to notify, of the requirements of this amendatory act.

A lessor doing business in this State shall notify in writing the lessee of a motor vehicle registered pursuant to this Title of any change in its policies or procedures affecting the registration of the motor vehicle.

Amended by L.1938, c. 66, p. 171, § 1; L.1940, c. 246, p. 939, § 1; L.1944, c. 5, p. 15, § 1; L.1949, c. 275, p. 847, § 1; L.1952, c. 45, p. 363, § 1; L.1954, c. 172, p. 679, § 1; L.1955, c. 8, p. 41, § 3; L.1957, c. 107, p. 209, § 1; L.1968, c. 321, § 1, eff. July 1, 1969; L.1969, c. 103, § 1, eff. July 1, 1969; L.1972, c. 205, § 1, eff. Dec. 26, 1972; L.1983, c. 403, § 6, eff. Dec. 23, 1983; L.1989, c. 167, § 2, eff. Aug. 14, 1990; L.1989, c. 326, § 1, eff. Feb. 1, 1991; L.1993, c. 125, § 2, eff. Dec. 1, 1994; L.1995, c. 112, § 27, eff. June 2, 1995; L.1997, c. 189, § 1, eff. Aug. 5, 1997; L.2003, c. 204, § 3, eff. Jan. 6, 2004; L.2003, c. 212, § 1, eff. Jan. 9, 2004; L.2004, c. 64, § 1, eff. June 30, 2004.

Historical and Statutory Notes

L.2004, c. 64, § 6, approved June 30, 2004, provides:

"This act shall take effect immediately; provided, however, the Chief Administrator of the Motor Vehicle Commission may, for good cause, delay the implementation of the provisions of this act for a period not to extend beyond October 1, 2004."

L.1993, c. 125, § 3, approved June 1, 1993, provides:

"This act shall take effect on the first day of the 18th month following enactment [eff. Dec. 1, 1994] and shall apply only to registration certificates or renewals of such certificates applied for and issued after the effective date."

39:3–4a. Temporary registration of motor vehicle in another state by resident of New Jersey

Notwithstanding the provisions of Revised Statutes 39:3–4 every resident of this State who acquires and temporarily registers a motor vehicle in another State may operate such vehicle or cause such vehicle to be operated on the public highways of this State for a period not in excess of the unexpired term of such temporary registration in another State.

L.1967, c. 38, § 1, eff. April 27, 1967.

39:3–4b. Temporary registration

Any nonresident purchasing an automobile in the State while enroute to another State or Federal district from a licensed dealer may register the same in New Jersey on a temporary basis.

Such temporary registration shall be made in the following manner: An application in writing, signed by the applicant or by an agent or officer in case the applicant is a corporation, shall be made to the director or his lawful agent, on forms prepared and supplied by the director, containing the name, address and age of the owner, together with a description of the character of the automobile, including the name of the maker and the manufacturer's number or the motor number, or both, and any other statement that may be required by the director. If the vehicle is insured by motor vehicle liability insurance as provided for in section 3 of chapter 173 of the laws of 1952,[1] the applicant must file an accompanying certificate, issued by the insurance carrier. An application shall contain the name of the insurer of said vehicle and the policy number.

In the event that such insurance is terminated, the insurer shall notify the director within 30 days, following such termination.

Thereupon the director or licensed dealer shall have the power to grant a temporary registration certificate and temporary plates to the owner of any automobile, if over 17 years of age, either directly or through any licensed motor vehicle dealer who is not within the geographical district, application for the temporary registration having been properly made and the fee therefor paid, and the vehicle being of a type that complies with the requirements of this subtitle. The form and contents of the temporary registration certificate to be issued shall be prescribed by the director. The director shall maintain a record of all temporary registration certificates issued, and of the contents thereof.

Every temporary registration shall expire and the certificate thereof become void on the twentieth day following the date on which the certificate was issued; no temporary registration shall be renewed, except as a permanent registration pursuant to section 39:3–4 of the Revised Statutes, and after payment of the fees prescribed therein.

The director shall issue temporary registration certificates for the 20 day registration period, which shall be effective immediately.

Any person violating the provisions of this section shall be subject to a fine not exceeding $100.00, except that for the misstatement of any fact in the application required to be made by the director, the person making such statement shall be subject to the penalties provided in section 39:3–37 of this Title.

L.1969, c. 301, § 1.

[1] N.J.S.A. § 39:6–25.

39:3–4c. Rules and regulations over temporary registration requirements; issuance; duration of license; insurance

The chief administrator may prescribe rules and regulations governing the issuance of temporary registration certificates and temporary plates by motor vehicle dealers, motorized bicycle dealers, and the Motor Vehicle Commission and may require security in sufficient amount to guarantee payment of all fees and moneys to the State of New Jersey and, upon a finding that any abuse has been practiced by any licensed motor vehicle or motorized bicycle dealer, the chief administrator shall have the right to suspend such dealer's privilege or franchise to issue such temporary registration certificates and plates. Temporary registration certificates for vehicles to be permanently registered in New Jersey shall be valid for a period of 30 days. In the event permanent registration has been delayed by reason of a lost title certificate or failure of a lien holder to timely turn over a certificate of title, a second temporary registration certificate may be issued. A licensed motor vehicle or motorized bicycle dealer shall make a record in the form and manner prescribed by the chief administrator for each such second temporary registration certificate issued and shall pay an enhanced fee to be determined by the chief administrator for each such registration issued. Each licensed motor vehicle or motorized bicycle dealer shall annually determine the fees to be paid pursuant to this section and shall remit annually under certification the amount due to the Motor Vehicle Commission.

No temporary registration certificate shall be issued by a licensed dealer hereunder unless such licensed dealer has confirmed that the vehicle for which the temporary registration is to be issued is insured in accordance with the requirements of the "Motor Vehicle Security–Responsibility Law," P.L.1952,c.173 (C.39:6–23 et seq.), whether by a policy in the name of the purchaser or an endorsement to a policy in the name of the licensed dealer, provided, however, no permanent registration shall be issued unless a policy in the name of the purchaser or someone in the purchaser's household is confirmed.

A temporary registration certificate issued hereunder may be issued by any employee authorized by a licensed dealer to do so; however, the licensee shall be liable for the acts of any such authorized person in issuing temporary registrations, whether the particular unlawful acts were authorized or unauthorized.

L.1969, c. 301, § 2. Amended by L.1983, c. 105, § 5; L.2007, c. 335, § 19, eff. July 11, 2008.

39:3–4d. "Geographical district" defined

"Geographical district" shall be defined as within a 5 mile radius of a motor vehicle agency or agent designated pursuant to section 39:3–3 of the Revised Statutes.

L.1969, c. 301, § 3.

39:3–4e. Rules and regulations; information by insurers

The director, after consultation with the Commissioner of Insurance, is hereby empowered to prescribe, adopt, promulgate, rescind and enforce rules and regulations requiring insurers to provide all information with respect to the issuance, renewal, cancellation, nonrenewal and termination of insurance as the director may deem necessary to assist the division in enforcement of the provisions of this Title relating to insurance coverage for motor vehicles.

L.1972, c. 205, § 2, eff. Dec. 26, 1972.

39:3–4f. Motor vehicle with registration in foreign country; time limit on operation after import

A resident owner of any motor vehicle which has been registered in accordance with the laws respecting the registration of motor vehicles in a foreign country may operate the motor vehicle in this State for 20 days after the owner imports the motor vehicle into this State in the same manner and to the same extent as though the motor vehicle was registered in this State, provided the registration number is conspicuously displayed on the motor vehicle.

L.1989, c. 210, § 1, eff. Dec. 29, 1989.

39:3–4.1. Licensing motor vehicles for transportation of passengers for hire

As used in this section the term "motor vehicle" is hereby defined as meaning any motor vehicle propelled otherwise than by muscular power (except such vehicles as run only on rails or tracks exclusively) carrying passengers for hire of any kind over the highways in this State, except (1) taxicabs, (2) hotel buses, (3) autobuses with a carrying capacity of not more than six passengers now or hereafter operated under municipal consent upon a route established wholly within the limits of a single municipality, which route does not in whole or in part parallel upon the same street the line of any street railway or traction railway or any other autobus line and (4) vehicles used in ridesharing arrangements.

No motor vehicle as herein defined shall be licensed by the commissioner until the applicant for such license shall first obtain a certificate from the Board of Public Utilities, that such motor vehicle conforms to the rules, regulations and specifications of the Board of Public Utilities, as to construction and safety devices of such motor vehicle; but all motor vehicles as herein defined and approved by the Board of Public Utilities, prior to June 6, 1936, shall not require the further approval of such board as a condition precedent to the issuance of such license.

Amended by L.1981, c. 413, § 8, eff. Jan. 7, 1982.

39:3–5. Registration refused

The director may refuse registration in the case of any automobile, commercial motor vehicle, trailer, semitrailer, tractor or omnibus that shall not comply with the requirements of this title or that shall seem to him unsuitable for use on the roads and highways of this State. The director shall deny registration to any motor vehicle that has failed to comply with applicable inspection requirements of chapter 8 of Title 39, or of any rules and regulations adopted pursuant thereto, within the time limits established by the director and to any vehicle subject to the inspection jurisdiction of the Department of Transportation that has failed to comply with the applicable inspection requirements of Titles 27 and 48 of the Revised Statutes or of any rules and regulations adopted pursuant thereto. The director may suspend or revoke the registration reciprocity privilege of any motor vehicle that has failed to undergo inspection in accordance with chapter 8 of Title 39 or that is subject to the inspection jurisdiction of the Department of Transportation and has failed to undergo inspection in accordance with the requirements of Titles 27 and 48 of the Revised Statutes or of any rules and regulations adopted pursuant thereto.

Amended by L.1995, c. 112, § 28, eff. June 2, 1995.

39:3–5.1. Registration of vehicles subject to federal heavy vehicle use tax

The Director of the Division of Motor Vehicles shall refuse registration of a vehicle which is subject to the federal heavy vehicle use tax if the applicant has failed to furnish proof of payment, in the form prescribed by the United States Secretary of the Treasury, that the federal heavy vehicle use tax imposed by section 4481 of the Internal Revenue Code of 1954 (26 U.S.C. § 4481) has been paid.

L.1985, c. 387, § 1, eff. Dec. 19, 1985.

39:3–6. Repealed by L.1995, c. 157, § 38

39:3–6.1. Definitions

As used in this act unless other meaning is clearly apparent from the language or context, or unless inconsistent with the manifest intention of the Legislature:

"Commercial vehicle" means any vehicle which is operated in interstate commerce and used for the transportation of persons for hire, compensation or profit, or designed or used primarily for the transportation of property.

"Jurisdiction" means and includes a State, territory or possession of the United States, the District of Columbia, the Commonwealth of Puerto Rico, a foreign country and a state or province of a foreign country.

"Properly registered," as applied to place of registration, means:

(a) The jurisdiction where the person registering the vehicle has his legal residence, or

(b) In the case of a commercial vehicle, the jurisdiction in which it is registered if the commercial enterprise in which such vehicle is used has a place of business therein and, if the vehicle is most frequently dispatched, garaged, serviced, maintained, operated or otherwise controlled in or from such place of business and, the vehicle has been assigned to such place of business, or

(c) In the case of a commercial vehicle, the jurisdiction where, because of an agreement or arrangement between two or more jurisdictions, or pursuant to a declaration, the vehicle has been registered as required by that jurisdiction.

In case of doubt or dispute as to the proper place of registration of a vehicle, the division shall make the final determination, but in making such determination, the division may confer with departments of the other jurisdictions affected.

"Fleet" means one or more commercial vehicles.

The words "division," "motor vehicle," "person," "vehicle," and "owner" shall each have the meanings ascribed to them respectively by R.S. 39:1–1.

The director shall promulgate regulations, after public hearing, establishing definitions of other words and terms as may be necessary for the administration of this act.

L.1969, c. 119, § 3, eff. July 1, 1969. Amended by L.1995, c. 157, § 33.

Historical and Statutory Notes

L.1995, c. 157, § 39, approved June 30, 1995, provides:

"This act shall take effect immediately [June 30, 1995] and shall apply to interstate commercial registrations that are valid on or after July 1, 1995."

39:3–6.2. Authority of director to make arrangements, agreements or declarations

The director shall have the authority to execute or make arrangements, agreements or declarations to carry out the provisions of this act.

The director may enter into an agreement or arrangement with the duly authorized representatives of other jurisdictions, granting to vehicles or to owners of vehicles which are properly registered or licensed in such jurisdictions, and for which evidence of compliance is supplied, benefits, privileges and exemptions from the payment, wholly or partially, of any taxes, fees, or other charges imposed upon such vehicles or owners with respect to the operation or ownership of such vehicles under the laws of this State. Such an agreement or arrangement shall provide that vehicles properly registered or licensed in this State, when operated upon highways of such other jurisdiction, shall receive exemptions, benefits and privileges of a similar kind or to a similar degree as are extended to vehicles properly registered or licensed in such jurisdiction when operated in this State. Each such agreement or arrangement shall, in the judgment of the director be in the best interest of this State and the citizens thereof and shall be fair and equitable to this State and the citizens thereof, and all of the same shall be determined on the basis and recognition of the benefits which accrue to the

economy of this State from the uninterrupted flow of commerce.

L.1969, c. 119, § 4, eff. July 1, 1969.

39:3–6.3. Registration in another jurisdiction of vehicles located or operated from base in such jurisdiction

An agreement or arrangement entered into, or a declaration issued under the authority of this act may contain provisions authorizing the registration or licensing in another jurisdiction of vehicles located in or operated from a base in such other jurisdiction which vehicles otherwise would be required to be registered or licensed in this State; and in such event the exemptions, benefits and privileges extended by such agreement, arrangement or declaration shall apply to such vehicles, when properly licensed or registered in such base jurisdiction.

L.1969, c. 119, § 5, eff. July 1, 1969.

39:3–6.4. Repealed by L.1995, c. 157, § 38

39:3–6.5. Exemptions, benefits and privileges; examination of laws and requirements of other jurisdictions

In the absence of an agreement or arrangement with another jurisdiction, the director may examine the laws and requirements of such jurisdiction and declare the extent and nature of exemptions, benefits and privileges to be extended to vehicles properly registered or licensed in such other jurisdiction, or to the owners of such vehicles, which shall, in the judgment of the director be in the best interest of this State and the citizens thereof, and which shall be fair and equitable to this State and the citizens thereof, and all of the same shall be determined on the basis and recognition of the benefits which accrue to the economy of this State from the uninterrupted flow of commerce.

L.1969, c. 119, § 7, eff. July 1, 1969.

39:3–6.6. Leased vehicles

An agreement or arrangement entered into, or a declaration issued under the authority of this act, may contain provisions under which a leased vehicle properly registered by the lessor thereof may be entitled, subject to terms and conditions stated therein, to the exemptions, benefits and privileges extended by such agreement, arrangement or declaration.

L.1969, c. 119, § 8, eff. July 1, 1969.

39:3–6.7. Vehicles registered in jurisdiction where no agreement, arrangement or declaration is in effect; commercial vehicles

After July 1, 1969 if no agreement, arrangement or declaration is in effect with respect to another jurisdiction as authorized by this act, any vehicle properly registered or licensed in such other jurisdiction, and for which evidence of compliance is supplied, shall receive, when operated in this State, the same exemptions, benefits and privileges granted by such other jurisdiction to vehicles properly registered in this State. Reciprocity extended under this section shall apply to commercial vehicles only when engaged exclusively in interstate commerce, except as to a foreign registered trailer or semitrailer in intrastate commerce when hauled by a truck, road tractor, or truck tractor registered with the director in conformity with Revised Statutes 39:3–20.

L.1969, c. 119, § 9, eff. July 1, 1969.

39:3–6.8. Repealed by L.1995, c. 157, § 38

39:3–6.9. Written agreements, arrangements or declarations required; filing

All agreements, arrangements or declarations, or amendments thereto, shall be in writing and shall be filed in the office of the director. A copy of each agreement, arrangement or declaration, or amendment thereto, shall be filed by the director in the office of the Secretary of State within 10 days after execution, or the effective date of the instrument whichever is later.

L.1969, c. 119, § 11, eff. July 1, 1969.

39:3–6.10. Suspension or cancellation of exemptions, benefits, or privileges

Agreements, arrangements or declarations made under the authority of this act may include provisions authorizing the director to suspend or cancel the exemptions, benefits, or privileges granted thereunder to a person who violates any of the conditions or terms of such agreements, arrangements or declarations or who violates the laws of this State relating to motor vehicles, or regulations lawfully promulgated thereunder.

L.1969, c. 119, § 12, eff. July 1, 1969.

39:3–6.11. Definitions; apportioned vehicles

As used in this act:

"Apportioned vehicle" means any vehicle used or intended for use in two or more member jurisdictions that register vehicles; is used for the transportation of persons for hire or is designed, used, or maintained for transportation of persons for hire or is designed, used, or maintained for transportation of property; and has a declared gross weight in excess of 26,000 pounds, or has three or more axles regardless of weight, or is used in combination when the gross vehicle weight of such combination exceeds 26,000 pounds; except that recreation vehicles, vehicles displaying restricted plates, city pick-up and delivery vehicles, buses used in transportation of chartered parties, and government-owned vehicles are not apportioned vehicles.

"Base jurisdiction" means, for the purpose of fleet registration, the jurisdiction where the registrant has an established place of business, where mileage is accrued by the fleet vehicles and where operational records for the vehicles are maintained or can be made available.

"Fleet" means one or more apportioned vehicles.

"In-jurisdiction miles" means the total number of miles operated by a fleet of apportioned vehicles in a jurisdiction during the preceding year. Mileage of New Jersey registered vehicles accrued in jurisdictions that are not member jurisdictions shall be counted as in-jurisdiction miles operated in New Jersey.

"International Registration Plan" means a registration reciprocity agreement among the signatory states of the United States and provinces of Canada providing the payment of registration fees on the basis of fleet miles operated in each jurisdiction.

"Interstate operations" means apportioned vehicle movement between or through two or more jurisdictions.

"Jurisdiction" means a state, territory or possession of the United States, the District of Columbia, the Commonwealth of Puerto Rico or a state, province or territory of a country.

"Member jurisdiction" means a jurisdiction which is a party to the International Registration Plan.

"Motor carrier audit" means a physical examination of a motor carrier's operational records including source documentation to verify fleet mileage and accuracy of the carrier's record keeping system.

"Negotiable title" means a title issued by a jurisdiction that documents ownership of a vehicle and can be used to transfer ownership.

"Operational records" means documents supporting miles traveled in each jurisdiction and total miles travelled, such as, but not limited to fuel reports, trip sheets, and logs.

"Owner" means a person, business firm, or corporation holding the negotiable title to a vehicle or in whom the legal right of possession or control of the vehicle is vested.

"Preceding year" means the period of twelve consecutive months immediately before July 1 of the year preceding the commencement of the registration year for which apportioned registration is sought.

"Reciprocity" means that an apportioned vehicle properly registered in New Jersey shall be exempt from further registration requirements by any other member jurisdictions.

"Reciprocity agreement" means the agreement, arrangement or understanding governing the reciprocal grant of rights and privileges to vehicles that are based in and properly registered under the applicable laws of the jurisdiction that are parties to the International Registration Plan.

"Registrant" means a person, business firm, or corporation in whose name a vehicle or fleet of vehicles is registered.

"Registration year" means the 12–month period when the registration plates issued by the base jurisdiction are valid according to the laws of the base jurisdiction.

"Restricted plate" means a registration plate that has restrictions of time, geographic area, mileage or commodities or persons which may be hauled, such as a dealer plate or a farm plate.

"Total miles" means the total number of miles accumulated in all jurisdictions during the preceding year by all vehicles of the fleet while they were a part of the fleet. Mileage accumulated by the fleet that did not engage in interstate operations shall not be included in total miles.

L.1995, c. 157, § 21.

39:3–6.12. International registration plan

a. The Director of the Division of Motor Vehicles, on behalf of the State of New Jersey, may enter into and become a member of the International Registration Plan. Such plan may provide, but shall not be limited to, the following:

(1) the grant of full reciprocity, in accordance with the plan, to apportioned vehicles not based in New Jersey which are operated in interstate commerce in exchange for equivalent reciprocity for New Jersey-based apportioned vehicles;

(2) the exchange of audits of operational records or owners of fleets of apportioned vehicles with jurisdictions participating in the plan; and

(3) Provisions for the orderly administration of the plan, including the collection and disbursement of proportional registration fees, cooperative enforcement activities and the free exchange of information.

b. The director shall adopt rules and regulations in accordance with the provisions of the "Administrative Procedure Act," P.L.1968, c. 410 (C. 52:14B–1 et seq.), to implement the provisions of the International Registration Plan.

c. The director may, by contract, agreement or otherwise, or by appointment as a motor vehicle agent or by licensing, authorize a private corporation, organization or association to register apportioned vehicles and to maintain and perform motor carrier audits of the records necessary for participation in the International Registration Plan on behalf of the Division of Motor Vehicles.

L.1995, c. 157, § 22.

39:3–6.13. Registration of apportioned vehicles

a. The Division of Motor Vehicles or its designee shall register all apportioned vehicles within its jurisdiction upon application and payment of registration fees and upon proof of proper insurance and proof of filing of Federal Form 2290 pursuant to the federal highway motor vehicle use tax, 26 U.S.C. § 4481 et seq. A registration certificate shall be issued for each vehicle that is registered and that certificate shall identify the vehicle for which it is issued and shall list the jurisdic-

tions in which the vehicle has been apportioned, the weight of the vehicle and the fee classification of the vehicle. The registration card shall be carried in or upon the vehicle for which it has been issued at all times.

b. Any registration issued for an apportioned vehicle pursuant to this section may be suspended, cancelled or revoked by the Division of Motor Vehicles in the event of the registrant's falsification of information, misstatement of fact, failure to pay fees, or failure to maintain the vehicle in accordance with standards set by the Federal Department of Transportation.

L.1995, c. 157, § 23.

39:3–6.14. Registration and administrative fees

a. The registration fee for an apportioned vehicle shall be determined by the number of in-jurisdiction miles an apportioned vehicle drives in the State of New Jersey and in each of the jurisdictions in which it is authorized to travel by its registration. The formula used for the registration fee shall be in accord with the International Registration Plan and shall be set forth in regulation.

b. In addition to the registration fee, the commission shall set by regulation an administrative fee which will be collected from each registrant to subsidize the cost of the administration of the program.

c. The administrative fee collected pursuant to this act shall be forwarded to the State Treasurer and be deposited into the Commercial Vehicle Enforcement Fund established pursuant to section 17 of this act.[1]

L.1995, c. 157, § 24. Amended by L.2003, c. 13, § 100 (contingent effective date).

[1] N.J.S.A. § 39:8–75.

Historical and Statutory Notes

L.2003, c. 13, § 127, approved Jan. 28, 2003, provides:

"Sections 1, 2, 3, 12, 38, 109, 110 and 121 shall take effect immediately, sections 105, 106, 107, 108, and 120 shall take effect on July 1, 2003 and the remainder of this act shall take effect on the date the Commissioner of Transportation certifies to the Governor (hereinafter the "date of certification") that a majority of the members of the commission have been appointed or are in office and that all necessary anticipatory actions have been accomplished, provided, that the amount of revenues received pursuant to sections 109 and 110 prior to the date of certification are hereby appropriated to the division. Upon the date of certification, all such collected revenue shall be revenue of the commission. The Commissioner of Transportation, the Director of the Division of Motor Vehicles and the commission may take such anticipatory administrative action in advance as shall be necessary for the implementation of the act."

39:3–6.15. Preservation of operational records

a. A registrant whose application for apportioned registration has been accepted shall preserve its operational records for a period of three years after the close of the registration year. Such records shall be made available to the Division of Motor Vehicles or its designee upon request for an audit as to the accuracy of computation, payments and assessments for deficiencies or allowances for credit during the normal business hours of the day.

b. If a registrant fails to make records available to the Division of Motor Vehicles or its designee upon proper request or if a registrant fails to maintain operational records from which true liability can be determined, the Director of the Division of Motor Vehicles has the discretion to:

(1) suspend, revoke or cancel the registration.

(2) assess liability based upon the director's estimate of the actual miles traveled by the registrant in each jurisdiction; and

(3) take whatever action is reasonably necessary to advance the purposes of the International Registration Plan.

c. At the option of the carrier, on-board recording devices that are pre-approved by the director may be used in lieu of, or in addition to, handwritten trip reports for apportioned registration record keeping purposes.

L.1995, c. 157, § 25.

39:3–6.16. Temporary registration

a. The Director of the Division of Motor Vehicles may issue temporary registration credentials for any vehicle or combination of vehicles that could be lawfully operated in the jurisdiction if full registration or apportioned registration were obtained.

b. A person desiring a temporary registration certificate shall make application therefor on forms provided by the division. Every application shall be accompanied by the fee established by regulation.

c. The temporary registration shall be carried in the cab of the vehicle for which the permit is issued and shall not be valid for more than 72 hours.

L.1995, c. 157, § 26.

39:3–6.17. Violations; fines

A person who violates any provision of sections 21 through 26 of this act [1] shall be subject to a fine of $500 for each offense. Such fine shall be forwarded by the judge to whom the same has been paid to the State Treasurer for deposit into the State General Fund.

L.1995, c. 157, § 27.

[1] N.J.S.A. §§ 39:8–79 to 39–8–84.

39:3–6.18. Motor carrier audits of operational accounts

The Division of Motor Vehicles or its designee shall perform motor carrier audits of the operational records of carrier accounts registered in New Jersey in accordance with the International Registration Plan Agreement and, upon the completion of any such audit, shall notify each jurisdiction in which the registrant is apportioned of the accuracy of the records of the registrant.

L.1995, c. 157, § 28.

39:3–6.19. Supersedure over other laws and agreements

a. Registration of apportioned vehicles under this act and the State's participation in the International Registration Plan supersedes all other statutes, acts, and reciprocal agreements covering in whole or in part any of the matters covered by this act.

b. The State's participation in the International Registration Plan shall not affect any reciprocal or other agreement, arrangement or understanding the State has with any non-member jurisdiction.

L.1995, c. 157, § 29.

39:3–6.20. Disbursement of fees; proportional registration distributive fund

a. The Division of Motor Vehicles shall distribute the registration fees collected for participating jurisdictions in accordance with the International Registration Program Agreement.

b. There is created within the State Treasury a special account to be known as the "Proportional Registration Distributive Fund" into which all fees collected for other jurisdictions shall be deposited and held in trust until distributed pursuant to subsection a. of this section.

c. Funds collected for other jurisdictions pursuant to the International Registration Plan shall not be considered funds of the State of New Jersey and shall not be appropriated for purposes other than distribution pursuant to subsection a. of this section.

L.1995, c. 157, § 30.

39:3–6.21. Reciprocity privileges

After July 1, 1995, if no agreement, arrangement or declaration is in effect with respect to another jurisdiction as authorized by this act, any vehicle properly registered or licensed in such other jurisdiction, and for which evidence of compliance is supplied, shall receive, when operated in this State, the same exemptions, benefits, and privileges granted by such other jurisdiction to vehicles properly registered in this State. Reciprocity extended under this section shall apply to commercial vehicles only when engaged exclusively in interstate commerce, except as to a foreign registered trailer or semi-trailer in intrastate commerce when hauled by a truck, road tractor, or truck tractor registered with the director in conformity with R.S. 39:3–20.

L.1995, c. 157, § 31.

39:3–7. Power of attorney given by nonresident; service of process

Each owner, required by this subtitle to register his motor vehicle or motor cycle, who has a residence outside of the state shall file with the commissioner a duly executed instrument, constituting the commissioner and his successors in office his true and lawful attorney upon whom all original process in any action or legal proceeding against him, caused by the operation of his registered motor vehicle or motor cycle in this state, may be served, and shall agree therein that any original process against him which is so served shall have the same force and effect as if served on himself in this state. Service of the process shall be made by leaving a copy thereof in the commissioner's office with a service fee of two dollars, to be taxed on the plaintiff's costs of suit. The commissioner shall forthwith notify such owner of the service by registered letter directed to him at the post-office address stated in his application for registration.

39:3–8. Fees for registration of passenger automobiles; license of semitrailers and trailers

The applicant for registration for any passenger automobile manufactured in any model year prior to the 1971 model year shall pay to the chief administrator for each registration a fee of $14 for each such vehicle having a manufacturer's shipping weight of less than 2,700 pounds, a fee of $23 for each such vehicle having a manufacturer's shipping weight of 2,700 pounds or more, but not greater than 3,800 pounds, and a fee of $44 for each vehicle having a manufacturer's shipping weight in excess of 3,800 pounds; provided, however, an applicant who has been issued a handicapped person identification card pursuant to section 2 of P.L.1949, c. 280 (C.39:4–205) and is registering a private passenger van manufactured in any model year prior to the 1971 model year which has been equipped with a wheelchair lift for the handicapped, or any other specially designed mechanical device for the handicapped as designated by the chief administrator that specifically requires installation only in a private passenger van because of the device's dimensions, operating characteristics or manufacturer's installation requirements, shall pay a fee of $14 for that vehicle. The applicant for registration for any passenger automobile manufactured in model year 1971 and thereafter, except as determined hereinafter, shall pay to the chief administrator for each registration a fee of $17 for each such vehicle having a manufacturer's shipping weight of less than 2,700 pounds, a fee of $28 for each such vehicle having a manufacturer's shipping weight of 2,700 pounds or more, but not greater than 3,800 pounds, and a fee of $51 for each such vehicle having a manufacturer's shipping weight in excess of 3,800 pounds; provided, however, an applicant who has been issued a handicapped person identification card pursuant to section 2 of P.L.1949, c. 280 (C.39:4–205) and is registering a private passenger van manufactured in model year 1971 or thereafter, except as determined hereinafter, which has been equipped with a wheelchair lift for the handicapped, or any other specially designed mechanical device for the handicapped as designated by the chief administrator that specifically requires installation only in a private passen-

ger van because of the device's dimensions, operating characteristics or manufacturer's installation requirements, shall pay a fee of $17 for that vehicle. The applicant for registration for any 1980 or thereafter model year passenger automobile registered on or after March 1, 1979 shall pay to the chief administrator for each registration a fee of $25 for each such vehicle having a manufacturer's shipping weight not greater than 3,500 pounds and a fee of $50 for each vehicle having a manufacturer's shipping weight in excess of 3,500 pounds; provided, however, an applicant who has been issued a handicapped person identification card pursuant to section 2 of P.L.1949, c. 280 (C.39:4–205) and is registering any 1980 or thereafter model year private passenger van which has been equipped with a wheelchair lift for the handicapped, or any other specially designed mechanical device for the handicapped as designated by the chief administrator that specifically requires installation only in a private passenger van because of the device's dimensions, operating characteristics or manufacturer's installation requirements, shall pay a fee of $25 for that vehicle. Notwithstanding any other provision of law to the contrary, the applicant for registration for any new passenger automobile, for which the registration will expire on the last day of the 48th calendar month following the calendar month in which it was first issued, or for the term of the lease if the new passenger automobile is a leased motor vehicle subject to an extended registration period pursuant to R.S.39:3–4, shall prepay to the chief administrator the full amount due for the 48–month term, or the full amount due based upon the term of the lease if the new passenger automobile is a leased motor vehicle, upon the initial registration. The portion of that prepayment that is dedicated to specific purposes in accordance with section 110 of P.L.2003, c. 13 (C.39:2A–38) and subsections a. and b. of section 1 of P.L.1992, c. 87 (C.39:3–8.2) shall be deposited in their respective dedicated accounts. The chief administrator shall determine manufacturer's shipping weight and model year for each passenger automobile on the basis of the information contained in the certificate of origin, the application for registration or for renewal of registration, or the records of the division, or any or all of these; and any case in which the manufacturer's shipping weight of any particular passenger automobile is unavailable, or in doubt or dispute, the chief administrator may require that such automobile be weighed on a scale designated by him, and such actual weight shall be considered the manufacturer's shipping weight for the purposes of this section; but in all cases the chief administrator's determination of the manufacturer's shipping weight of any such automobile shall be final. The applicant for registration for passenger automobile shall also pay to the chief administrator the inspection fee fixed in R.S.39:8–2 in addition to the fees described hereinabove.

The chief administrator may also license private utility and house type semitrailers and trailers with a gross load not in excess of 2,000 pounds at a fee of $4.00

per annum and all other such utility and house-type semitrailers and trailers at $9.00 per annum. Application for such registration shall be made on a blank to be furnished by the commission and the application shall contain a statement to the effect that the vehicle so registered will not be used for the commercial transportation of goods, wares and merchandise, or for hire.

Except as provided in R.S.39:3–84 for recreation vehicles, no private utility or house type semitrailer or trailer with an outside width of more than 96 inches, a maximum height of 13 feet 6 inches, a maximum length for a single vehicle of more than 35 feet, a maximum length for a semitrailer and its towing vehicle of more than 45 feet, and a maximum length for a trailer and its towing vehicle of more than 50 feet, shall be operated on any highway in this State, except that a vehicle exceeding the above limitations may be operated when a special permit so to operate is secured in advance from the chief administrator. A house type semitrailer or trailer with an outside width of no more than 16 feet shall be entitled to operate with such a special permit if the vehicle is a manufactured home on a transportation system that is designed in accordance with the "Manufactured Home Construction and Safety Standards," 24 CFR part 3280.901 et seq., promulgated by the United States Department of Housing and Urban Development, as amended and supplemented, provided that the operator complies with the provisions of this Title and the rules and regulations issued thereunder. If such a vehicle has an outside width of more than 16 feet, it shall be entitled to operate with such a special permit if it is transported on a commercial type low-bed trailer, semitrailer or properly registered dolly wheels pursuant to rules and regulations established by the chief administrator. The application for such permit shall be accompanied by a fee fixed by the chief administrator. A special permit issued by the chief administrator shall be in the possession of the operator of the vehicle for which such permit was issued. In computing any dimensions of a vehicle, for the purposes of this section, there shall not be included in the dimensional limitations safety equipment such as mirrors or lights, provided such appliances do not exceed the overall limitations established by the chief administrator by rule or regulation.

Amended by L.1953, c. 256, p. 1753, § 1; L.1955, c. 8, p. 43, § 4; L.1963, c. 49, § 1, eff. May 27, 1963; L.1968, c. 130, § 1, eff. Aug. 1, 1968; L.1975, c. 180, § 2, eff. Jan. 1, 1976; L.1976, c. 43, § 1; L.1979, c. 3, § 1, eff. March 1, 1979; L.1995, c. 397, § 2, eff. Jan. 10, 1996; L.1998, c. 135, § 1, eff. Dec. 3, 1998; L.1999, c. 392, § 1, eff. Jan. 18, 2000; L.2004, c. 64, § 2, eff. June 30, 2004.

39:3–8.1. Noncommercial trucks; license; application for registration

The director may license noncommercial trucks at the same weight fees set forth in Revised Statutes 39:3–20; provided, however, applicants for registration who have been issued handicapped person identification cards pursuant to section 2 of P.L.1949, c. 280 (C.39:4–205)

and are registering a noncommercial truck which has been equipped with a wheelchair lift for the handicapped, or any other specially designed mechanical device for the handicapped as designated by the director that specifically requires installation only in a noncommercial truck or van because of the device's dimensions, operating characteristics or manufacturer's installation requirements, shall pay the same weight fees set forth in R.S.39:3–8 for similarly modified passenger automobiles of the same model year. Application for such registration shall be made on a form to be furnished by the division and the application shall contain a statement to the effect that the vehicle so registered will not be used for the commercial transportation of goods, wares and merchandise, or for hire, and that vehicles so registered will not contain any advertising, signs, lettering, names or addresses on its exterior, excepting trademarks and labels of the manufacturer and dealer.

L.1968, c. 439, § 2. Amended by L.1999, c. 392, § 2, eff. Jan. 18, 2000.

39:3–8.2. Collection of fees for certain program funds

a. In addition to the motor vehicle registration fees imposed pursuant to the provisions of chapter 3 of Title 39 of the Revised Statutes, the chief administrator shall impose and collect an additional fee of $3 to be deposited in the New Jersey Emergency Medical Service Helicopter Response Program Fund created pursuant to section 2 of P.L.1992, c. 87 (C.26:2K–36.1).

b. In addition to the motor vehicle registration fees imposed pursuant to the provisions of chapter 3 of Title 39 of the Revised Statutes, the chief administrator shall impose and collect an additional fee of $.50 to be deposited in the Traumatic Brain Injury Fund established pursuant to section 5 of P.L.2001, c. 332 (C.30:6F–5).

c. In addition to the motor vehicle registration fees imposed pursuant to the provisions of chapter 3 of Title 39 of the Revised Statutes, the chief administrator shall impose and collect an additional fee of $1, which shall be deposited to a separate account dedicated for the funding of new State Police trooper classes. The Legislature shall annually appropriate the balance of the separate account to the Department of Law and Public Safety for the Division of State Police for the funding of new State Police trooper classes.

L.1992, c. 87, § 1, eff. Nov. 1, 1992. Amended by L.2001, c. 332, § 9, eff. Jan. 5, 2002; L.2005, c. 311, § 1, eff. July 1, 2006.

39:3–8.3. Definitions

As used in this act:

"Environmental Protection Administration average fuel efficiency rating" means the fuel efficiency rating for a particular motor vehicle calculated by adding together the Environmental Protection Administration's city and highway miles per gallon rating for that motor vehicle and dividing the resulting sum by two.

"Lease price" means the capitalized cost as stated in the agreement between a lessor and a lessee.

"Sales price" means the gross selling price appearing on a contract of sale.

L.2006, c. 39, § 1, eff. July 8, 2006.

39:3–8.4. Additional fees on certain passenger automobiles

a. In addition to the motor vehicle registration fees imposed pursuant to the provisions of chapter 3 of Title 39 of the Revised Statutes, the chief administrator shall, as a condition for the issuance and filing of a certificate of ownership pursuant to R.S.39:10–11, impose and collect an additional fee for any new passenger automobile having:

(1) A sales price or lease price of $45,000 or more, prior to any credit or offset of that sales price or lease price resulting from any rebate or trade-in which lowers the price of the passenger automobile to less than $45,000, or

(2) An Environmental Protection Administration average fuel efficiency rating of less than 19 miles per gallon.

b. The additional fee authorized under subsection a. of this section shall be determined by multiplying the sales price or lease price for the new passenger automobile, prior to any credit or offset for any rebate or trade-in, by 0.4 percent. The fee imposed under this section shall be separately stated on any bill, receipt, invoice or similar document provided to the purchaser and shall not be subject to the retail sales taxes imposed under the provisions of the "Sales and Use Tax Act," P.L. 1966, c. 30 (C.54: 32B–1 et seq.).

c. In the case of a new passenger automobile purchased or leased in New Jersey, the fee shall be collected by the person required to collect the retail sales tax imposed on that motor vehicle pursuant to subsection a. of section 3 of P.L.1966, c.30 (C.54:32B–3). That person shall be personally liable for collecting, reporting and remitting the fee in a manner prescribed by the chief administrator.

In the case of a new passenger automobile purchased or leased in a jurisdiction other than New Jersey, the fee and any forms required by the chief administrator shall be remitted directly to the chief administrator. If the seller or lessor of the new passenger automobile in that other jurisdiction is required to collect the retail sales tax imposed on that motor vehicle pursuant to subsection a. of section 3 of P.L.1966, c. 30 (C.54: 32B–3) and is authorized to apply for the issuance and filing of a certificate of ownership pursuant to R.S.39:10–11, that seller or lessor may collect, report and remit the fee in a manner prescribed by the chief administrator.

d. The fee authorized under this section shall not be imposed on the sale or lease of any new passenger automobile having a sale price or lease price, as the case may be, over $45,000 that:

(1) Has an Environmental Protection Administration average fuel efficiency rating of 40 or more miles per gallon; or

(2) Is certified as a zero emission vehicle by the Commissioner of Environmental Protection pursuant to the provisions of P.L.2003, c. 266 (C.26:2C–8.15 et al.).

e. The chief administrator, in accordance with the provisions of the "Administrative Procedure Act," P.L. 1968, c. 410 (C.52:14B–1 et seq.), shall promulgate rules and regulations to effectuate the purposes of this act.

L.2006, c. 39, § 2, eff. July 8, 2006.

39:3–9. Repealed by L.1955, c. 8, p. 49, § 12

39:3–9a. Endorsement of legal name in own handwriting on driver's license; notice of change of name; violation; penalty

Each driver's license issued pursuant to R.S.39:3–10 shall have the legal name of the licensee endorsed thereon in his own handwriting. For purposes of this section, legal name shall mean the name recorded on a birth certificate unless otherwise changed by marriage, divorce or order of court. The director may require that only the legal name be recorded on the driver's license. A person who has been issued a driver's license pursuant to R.S.39:3–10 whose name is changed due to marriage, divorce or by order of court shall notify the director of the change in name within two weeks after the change is made.

A person who fails to notify the Director of the Division of Motor Vehicles of a change in name as required in this section shall be subject to a fine. A person who is fined under this section for a violation of this section shall not be subject to a surcharge under the New Jersey Merit Rating Plan as provided in section 6 of P.L.1983, c. 65 (C.17:29A–35).

For the purposes of this section, a digitized signature image shall constitute a licensee's signature in his own handwriting. A digitized signature image is an electronic representation of a person's written signature.

L.1987, c. 20, § 2, eff. Jan. 27, 1987. Amended by L.1988, c. 8, § 1, eff. April 4, 1988; L.1999, c. 28, § 1, eff. Jan. 1, 2000.

Historical and Statutory Notes

L.2001, c. 391, § 17, approved Jan. 8, 2002, provides:

"Notwithstanding the provisions of P.L.1999, c. 28 (C.39:3–10f1 et al.) to the contrary, the Director of the Division of Motor Vehicles may delay the implementation of the provisions of that act, other than those set forth in section 14 thereof, until the 60th day after the director certifies to the Commissioner of Transportation that the division is prepared to issue drivers' licenses with digitized pictures of licensees, but such implementing date shall be not later than January 1, 2003. The director shall make every effort to provide the certification required for P. L.1999, c. 28 to be implemented as soon as practicable."

39:3–9b. Application or renewal of driver's license; street address of place of residence or business

Each application for a driver's license, or a renewal thereof, required by R.S.39:3–10 shall contain the street address of the place of residence or business of the licensee at the time of application or renewal. A post office box shall appear on a driver's license application only as part of a mailing address that is submitted by the licensee in addition to the street address of the licensee's residence or business; provided, however, the director, upon application, shall permit a person who was a victim of a violation of N.J.S.2C:12–10, N.J.S.2C:14–2, or N.J.S.2C:25–17 et seq., or who the director otherwise determines to have good cause, to use as a mailing address a post office box, an address other than the applicant's address or other contact point. A licensee whose last address appears on the records of the division as a post office box shall change the address on the application for renewal to the street address of the licensee's residence or business and, if different from the street address, his mailing address unless the director has determined, pursuant to this section, that the licensee may use a post office box, an address other than the licensee's address or other contact point as a mailing address.

L.1989, c. 326, § 2, eff. Feb. 1, 1991. Amended by L.1997, c. 189, § 2, eff. Aug. 5, 1997.

39:3–9c. Adoption of rules and regulations

Pursuant to the provisions of the "Administrative Procedure Act," P.L.1968, c. 410 (C.52:14B–1 et seq.), the director, in consultation with the Attorney General, may promulgate rules and regulations to effectuate the purposes of P.L.1997, c.189.

L.1997, c. 189, § 3, eff. Aug. 5, 1997.

39:3–10. Driver's licenses; examination; surrender of current license; classifications; issuance; license periods; renewals; denial of license; penalties

No person shall drive a motor vehicle on a public highway in this State unless the person is under supervision while participating in a behind-the-wheel driving course pursuant to section 6 of P.L.1977, c. 25 (C.39:3–13.2a) or is in possession of a validated permit, or a probationary or basic driver's license issued to him in accordance with this article.

No person under 18 years of age shall be issued a basic license to drive motor vehicles, nor shall a person be issued a validated permit, including a validated examination permit, until he has passed a satisfactory examination and other requirements as to his ability as an operator. The examination shall include a test of the applicant's vision, his ability to understand traffic control devices, his knowledge of safe driving practices and of the effects that ingestion of alcohol or drugs has on a person's ability to operate a motor vehicle, his knowledge of such portions of the mechanism of motor vehicles as is necessary to insure the safe operation of a vehicle of the kind or kinds indicated by the applicant

and of the laws and ordinary usages of the road. No person shall sit for an examination for any permit without exhibiting photo identification deemed acceptable by the commission, unless that person is a high school student participating in a course of driving education approved by the State Department of Education and conducted in a public, parochial or private school of this State, pursuant to section 1 of P.L.1950, c. 127 (C.39:3–13.1). The commission may waive the written law knowledge examination for any person 18 years of age or older possessing a valid driver's license issued by any other state, the District of Columbia or the United States Territories of American Samoa, Guam, Puerto Rico or the Virgin Islands. The commission shall be required to provide that person with a booklet that highlights those motor vehicle laws unique to New Jersey. A road test shall be required for a probationary license and serve as a demonstration of the applicant's ability to operate a vehicle of the class designated. No person shall sit for a road test unless that person exhibits photo identification deemed acceptable by the commission. A high school student who has completed a course of behind-the-wheel automobile driving education approved by the State Department of Education and conducted in a public, parochial or private school of this State, who has been issued a special learner's permit pursuant to section 1 of P.L.1950, c. 127 (C.39:3–13.1) prior to January 1, 2003, shall not be required to exhibit photo identification in order to sit for a road test. The commission may waive the road test for any person 18 years of age or older possessing a valid driver's license issued by any other state, the District of Columbia or the United States Territories of American Samoa, Guam, Puerto Rico or the Virgin Islands. The road test shall be given on public streets, where practicable and feasible, but may be preceded by an off-street screening process to assess basic skills. The commission shall approve locations for the road test which pose no more than a minimal risk of injury to the applicant, the examiner and other motorists. No new locations for the road test shall be approved unless the test can be given on public streets.

The commission shall issue a basic driver's license to operate a motor vehicle other than a motorcycle to a person over 18 years of age who previously has not been licensed to drive a motor vehicle in this State or another jurisdiction only if that person has: (1) operated a passenger automobile in compliance with the requirements of this title for not less than one year, not including any period of suspension or postponement, from the date of issuance of a probationary license pursuant to section 4 of P.L.1950, c. 127 (C.39:3–13.4); (2) not been assessed more than two motor vehicle points; (3) not been convicted in the previous year for a violation of R.S.39:4–50, section 2 of P.L.1981, c. 512 (C.39:4–50.4a), P.L.1992, c. 189 (C.39:4–50.14), R.S.39:4–129, N.J.S.2C:11–5, subsection c. of N.J.S.2C:12–1, or any other motor vehicle-related violation the commission determines to be significant and applicable pursuant to regulation; and (4) passed an examination of his ability to operate a motor vehicle pursuant to this section.

The commission shall expand the driver's license examination by 20%. The additional questions to be added shall consist solely of questions developed in conjunction with the State Department of Health and Senior Services concerning the use of alcohol or drugs as related to highway safety. The commission shall develop in conjunction with the State Department of Health and Senior Services supplements to the driver's manual which shall include information necessary to answer any question on the driver's license examination concerning alcohol or drugs as related to highway safety.

Up to 20 questions may be added to the examination on subjects to be determined by the commission that are of particular relevance to youthful drivers, after consultation with the Director of the Office of Highway Traffic Safety.

The commission shall expand the driver's license examination to include a question asking whether the applicant is aware of the provisions of the "Revised Uniform Anatomical Gift Act," P.L.2008, c. 50 (C.26:6–77 et al.) and the procedure for indicating on the driver's license the intention to make a donation of body organs or tissues pursuant to P.L.1978, c. 181 (C.39:3–12.2).

Any person applying for a driver's license to operate a motor vehicle or motorized bicycle in this State shall surrender to the commission any current driver's license issued to him by another state or jurisdiction upon his receipt of a driver's license for this State. The commission shall refuse to issue a driver's license if the applicant fails to comply with this provision. An applicant for a permit or license who is less than 18 years of age, and who holds a permit or license for a passenger automobile issued by another state or country that is valid or has expired within a time period designated by the commission, shall be subject to the permit and license requirements and penalties applicable to State permit and license applicants who are of the same age; except that if the other state or country has permit or license standards substantially similar to those of this State, the credentials of the other state or country shall be acceptable.

The commission shall create classified licensing of drivers covering the following classifications:

a. Motorcycles, except that for the purposes of this section, motorcycle shall not include any three-wheeled motor vehicle equipped with a single cab with glazing enclosing the occupant, seats similar to those of a passenger vehicle or truck, seat belts and automotive steering.

b. Omnibuses as classified by R.S.39:3–10.1 and school buses classified under N.J.S.18A:39–1 et seq.

c. (Deleted by amendment, P.L.1999, c. 28).

d. All motor vehicles not included in classifications a. and b. A license issued pursuant to this classification d. shall be referred to as the "basic driver's license."

Every applicant for a license under classification b. shall be a holder of a basic driver's license. Any issuance of a license under classification b. shall be by endorsement on the basic driver's license.

A driver's license for motorcycles may be issued separately, but if issued to the holder of a basic driver's license, it shall be by endorsement on the basic driver's license.

The commission, upon payment of the lawful fee and after it or a person authorized by it has examined the applicant and is satisfied of the applicant's ability as an operator, may, in its discretion, issue a license to the applicant to drive a motor vehicle. The license shall authorize him to drive any registered vehicle, of the kind or kinds indicated, and shall expire, except as otherwise provided, on the last day of the 48th calendar month following the calendar month in which such license was issued.

The commission may, at its discretion and for good cause shown, issue licenses which shall expire on a date fixed by it. If the commission issues a license to a person who has demonstrated authorization to be present in the United States for a period of time shorter than the standard period of the license, the commission shall fix the expiration date of the license at a date based on the period in which the person is authorized to be present in the United States under federal immigration laws. The commission may renew such a license only if it is demonstrated that the person's continued presence in the United States is authorized under federal law. The fee for licenses with expiration dates fixed by the commission shall be fixed by the commission in amounts proportionately less or greater than the fee herein established.

The required fee for a license for the 48–month period shall be as follows:

Motorcycle license or endorsement: $18.

Omnibus or school bus endorsement: $18.

Basic driver's license: $18.

The commission shall waive the payment of fees for issuance of omnibus endorsements whenever an applicant establishes to the commission's satisfaction that said applicant will use the omnibus endorsement exclusively for operating omnibuses owned by a nonprofit organization duly incorporated under Title 15 or 16 of the Revised Statutes or Title 15A of the New Jersey Statutes.

The commission shall issue licenses for the following license period on and after the first day of the calendar month immediately preceding the commencement of such period, such licenses to be effective immediately.

All applications for renewals of licenses shall be made in a manner prescribed by the commission and in accordance with procedures established by it.

The commission in its discretion may refuse to grant a permit or license to drive motor vehicles to a person who is, in its estimation, not a proper person to be granted such a permit or license, but no defect of the applicant shall debar him from receiving a permit or license unless it can be shown by tests approved by the commission that the defect incapacitates him from safely operating a motor vehicle.

In addition to requiring an applicant for a driver's license to submit satisfactory proof of identity and age, the commission also shall require the applicant to provide, as a condition for obtaining a permit and license, satisfactory proof that the applicant's presence in the United States is authorized under federal law.

If the commission has reasonable cause to suspect that any document presented by an applicant as proof of identity, age or legal residency is altered, false or otherwise invalid, the commission shall refuse to grant the permit or license until such time as the document may be verified by the issuing agency to the commission's satisfaction.

A person violating this section shall be subject to a fine not exceeding $500 or imprisonment in the county jail for not more than 60 days, but if that person has never been licensed to drive in this State or any other jurisdiction, he shall be subject to a fine of not less than $200 and, in addition, the court shall issue an order to the commission requiring the commission to refuse to issue a license to operate a motor vehicle to the person for a period of not less than 180 days. The penalties provided for by this paragraph shall not be applicable in cases where failure to have actual possession of the operator's license is due to an administrative or technical error by the commission.

Nothing in this section shall be construed to alter or extend the expiration of any license issued prior to the date this amendatory and supplementary act becomes operative.

Amended by L.1938, c. 66, p. 173, § 3; L.1953, c. 72, p. 986, § 1; L.1955, c. 8, p. 44, § 5; L.1955, c. 76, p. 242, § 1; L.1957, c. 108, p. 211, § 1; L.1964, c. 118, § 1, eff. Jan. 1, 1965; L.1968, c. 130, § 2, eff. Aug. 1, 1968; L.1977 c. 25, § 1, eff. Feb. 24, 1977; L.1979, c. 97, § 1, eff. May 24, 1979; L.1979, c. 261, § 5; L.1980, c. 105, § 7, eff. Sept. 11, 1980; L.1981, c. 322, § 2, eff. Dec. 9, 1981; L.1982, c. 45, § 1, eff. Sept. 1, 1982; L.1983, c. 162, § 1; L.1983, c. 163, § 1, eff. May 2, 1983; L.1983, c. 403, § 7, eff. Dec. 23, 1983; L.1984, c. 33, § 2; L.1985, c. 264, § 2, eff. July 31, 1985; L.1987, c. 20, § 1, eff. Jan. 27, 1987; L.1988, c. 8, § 2, eff. April 4, 1988; L.1991, c. 452, § 7, eff. July 1, 1992; L.1992, c. 110, § 1, eff. Sept. 25, 1992; L.1993, c. 34, § 1, eff. Jan. 29, 1993; L.1998, c. 108, § 1, eff. Jan. 1, 2001; L.1999, c. 28, § 2, eff. Jan. 1, 2000; L.2001, c. 391, § 2, eff. Jan. 8, 2002; L.2001, c. 420, § 3, eff. Jan. 8, 2002; L.2003, c. 13, § 37; L.2008, c. 50, § 24, eff. July 22, 2008; L.2009, c. 38, § 1, eff. May 1, 2010.

39:3–10a. Restoration of suspended or revoked license or registration; fee

The chief administrator shall charge a fee of $100 for the restoration of any license which has been suspended or revoked by reason of the licensee's violation of any law or regulation and for the restoration of vehicle registrations that have been suspended pursuant to any law. The chief administrator may promulgate such regulations hereunder as he may deem necessary.

L.1975, c. 180, § 23, eff. Jan. 1, 1976. Amended by L.1982, c. 53, § 1, eff. July 1, 1982; L.1994, c. 60, § 14, eff. July 1, 1994; L.2002, c. 34, § 14, eff. July 1, 2002; L.2007, c. 283, § 2, eff. July 1, 2008.

39:3–10b. Initial license; two year probationary basis

An applicant for a motorcycle license, but not for a motorcycle endorsement to a basic license, who previously has never been licensed to drive a motor vehicle in this, or any other state, shall, during the permit period, be subject to the applicable restrictions and penalties for examination permit holders as provided under R.S.39:3–13. Until the provisions of P.L.1998, c. 108, as amended by P.L.2001, c. 420, are fully implemented, all holders of permits issued pursuant to R.S.39:3–13 and section 6 of P.L.1977, c. 25 (C.39:3–13.2a) shall be subject to a probationary driver program for the two-year period immediately following the issuance of the permits. This two-year period shall not be altered if the permit holder obtains a probationary driver's license pursuant to section 4 of P.L.1950, c. 127 (C.39:3–13.4). All holders of permits issued on or after the date of full implementation of P.L. 1998, c. 108, as amended by P.L.2001, c. 420, shall not be subject to this section.

L.1977, c. 23, § 1. Amended by L.1998, c. 108, § 2, eff. Jan. 1, 2001; L.2001, c. 420, § 4, eff. Jan. 8, 2002; L.2009, c. 38, § 2, eff. May 1, 2010.

Historical and Statutory Notes

L.2001, c. 420, § 13, approved Jan. 8, 2002, provides:

"This act shall take effect immediately and shall apply to any applicant for an initial special learner's permit or examination permit on or after the effective date of this act."

39:3–10c. Vision screening every ten years

The division shall require every licensed driver to take and successfully pass a screening of his vision at least once every 10 years as a condition for the renewal of his driver's license and of any endorsement thereon.

The vision screening may be certified by the division or by any licensed optometrist or ophthalmologist, licensed ophthalmic dispenser or by any person licensed to practice medicine and surgery. If the screening shows a need for corrective eyeglasses or any other corrective action, the renewal of the applicant's license shall be conditioned upon his compliance with such need. The division may require a road test of any applicant to determine the adequacy of, or the applicant's adaptation to the required corrective action.

The division shall, by regulation, prescribe minimum standards with respect to the equipment to be used for screenings.

L.1977, c. 28, § 1, eff. Feb. 24, 1977. Amended by L.1979, c. 446, § 1, eff. Feb. 22, 1980; L.1989, c. 15, § 1, eff. Feb. 1, 1989.

39:3–10d. Implementation of vision reexamination

To implement the reexamination program provided for by this act and to establish it on a current basis, the division shall reexamine approximately 10% of all of the State's licensed drivers in each year during the first 10 years following the date this act becomes operative. Once reexamined during said 10-year period, no licensed driver shall be again reexamined pursuant to the provisions of this act sooner than 10 years thereafter.

L.1977, c. 28, § 2, eff. Feb. 24, 1977.

39:3–10e. Involvement in two or more accidents within 6 months with assessment of points; reexamination

The holder of any motor vehicle driver's license who is involved, within any 6-month period, in two or more motor vehicle accidents resulting in death or in personal injury or damage to property of any one person in excess of $500.00 required to be reported to police pursuant to R.S. 39:4–130, and against whom there has been assessed motor vehicle points for each such accident, shall on notice to be given by the Division of Motor Vehicles, be required to submit to reexamination and successful passage of an examination of his ability as an operator and a test of his vision, by the division or by any licensed optometrist or ophthalmologist.

Failure to pass the examination or test required by this act shall be justification for the revocation and refusal to renew the holder's driver's license.

L.1979, c. 136, § 1, eff. July 6, 1979. Amended by L.1983, c. 193, § 2, eff. May 24, 1983.

39:3–10f. Color photograph driver licenses; "valid without photo" license

In addition to the requirements for the form and content of a motor vehicle driver's license under R.S.39:3–10 and a probationary license issued under section 4 of P.L.1950, c. 127 (C.39:3–13.4), on and after the operative date of P.L.2001, c. 391 (C.39:3–10f4 et al.), each initial New Jersey license, each renewal of a New Jersey driver's license, and each probationary license shall have a digitized color picture of the licensee. All licenses issued on and after January 1, 2000 shall be valid for a period of 48 calendar months. However, the chief administrator may, at his discretion, issue licenses and endorsements which shall expire on a date fixed by him. The fee for such licenses or endorsements shall be fixed in amounts proportionately less or greater than the fee otherwise established. Notwithstanding the provisions of this section to the contrary, a person 70 years of age or older may elect to have a license issued for a period of two or four years, which election may not be altered by the chief adminis-

trator. The fee for the two-year license shall be $9, in addition to the fee for a digitized picture established in section 4 of P.L.2001, c. 391 (C.39:3–10f4). The chief administrator may, for good cause extend a license and any endorsement thereon beyond their expiration dates for periods not to exceed 12 additional months. The chief administrator may extend the expiration date of a license and any endorsement thereon without payment of a proportionate fee when the chief administrator determines that such extension is necessary for good cause. If any license and endorsements thereon are so extended, the licensee shall pay upon renewal the full license fee for the period fixed by the chief administrator as if no extension had been granted.

Each initial motor vehicle license issued to a person under the age of 21 after the effective date of P.L.1999, c. 28 shall be conspicuously distinct, through the use of color and design, from the driver's licenses issued to persons 21 years of age or older. The chief administrator, in consultation with the Superintendent of State Police, shall determine the color and the manner in which the license is designed to achieve this result. The license shall also bear the words "UNDER 21" in a conspicuous manner. The chief administrator shall provide that upon attaining the age of 21, a licensee shall be issued a replacement driver's license or a new license, as appropriate. The fee for a replacement license shall be $5 in addition to the digitized picture fee.

As conditions for the renewal of a driver's license, the chief administrator shall provide that the picture of a licensee be updated except that the chief administrator may elect to use a stored picture to renew a license for a period not exceeding four additional years for $18 in addition to the digitized picture fee.

Whenever a person has reconstructive or cosmetic surgery which significantly alters the person's facial features, the person shall notify the chief administrator who may require the picture of the licensee to be updated, for $5 in addition to the digitized picture fee.

Nothing in this section shall be construed to alter or change any expiration date on any New Jersey driver's license issued prior to the operative date of P.L.2001, c. 391 (C.39:3–10f4 et al.) and, unless a licensee's driving privileges are otherwise suspended or revoked, except as provided in R.S.39:3–10, that license shall remain valid until that expiration date.

Specific use of the driver's license and any information stored or encoded, electronically or otherwise, in relation thereto shall be in accordance with P.L.1997, c. 188 (C.39:2–3.3 et seq.) and the federal Driver's Privacy Protection Act of 1994, Pub. L.103–322. Notwithstanding the provisions of any other law to the contrary, the digitized picture or any access thereto or any use thereof shall not be sold, leased or exchanged for value.

To replace a photo-license issued prior to the effective date of this act for a licensee who is temporarily out of this State, the chief administrator may issue a "valid without picture" picture license for the unexpired term of the license.

L.1979, c. 261, § 1. Amended by L.1981, c. 322, § 1, eff. Dec. 9, 1981; L.1985, c. 264, § 1, eff. July 31, 1985; L.1990, c. 103, § 26, eff. Nov. 9, 1990; L.1999, c. 28, § 3, eff. Jan. 1, 2000; L.2001, c. 391, § 3, eff. Jan. 8, 2002; L.2003, c. 204, § 1, eff. Jan. 6, 2004; L.2009, c. 38, § 3, eff. May 1, 2010.

Historical and Statutory Notes

L.2001, c. 391, §§ 17, 18, approved Jan. 8, 2002, provide:

"17. Notwithstanding the provisions of P.L.1999, c. 28 (C.39:3–10f1 et al.) to the contrary, the Director of the Division of Motor Vehicles may delay the implementation of the provisions of that act, other than those set forth in section 14 thereof, until the 60th day after the director certifies to the Commissioner of Transportation that the division is prepared to issue drivers' licenses with digitized pictures of licensees, but such implementing date shall be not later than January 1, 2003. The director shall make every effort to provide the certification required for P. L.1999, c. 28 to be implemented as soon as practicable.

"18. This act shall take effect immediately, except that sections 3, 5, 6, 8, 9, 10, 11, and the required fees for the 48–month license added to R.S. 39:3–10 by section 2 of this act shall remain inoperative until the 60th day after the Director of the Division of Motor Vehicles in the Department of Transportation certifies to the Commissioner of Transportation that the division is prepared to issue drivers' licenses with digitized pictures of licensees, but such operative date shall be no later than January 1, 2003."

39:3–10f1. Verification of authenticity

Nothing in this act shall be construed as requiring any county or municipal law enforcement agency to acquire or use any electronic reader or other device in order to verify the authenticity of a driver's license issued pursuant to the provisions of this act, unless the cost of acquiring and using such devices is paid for by the State of New Jersey.

L.1999, c. 28, § 15, eff. Jan. 1, 2000.

39:3–10f2. Release or disclosure of pictures

Notwithstanding the provisions of P.L.1963, c. 73 (C.47:1A–1 et seq.) or any other law to the contrary, a licensee's picture shall not be released or otherwise disclosed by the director, except, subject to the approval of the director, for use by a governmental agency, including any court or law enforcement agency in carrying out its functions, or, subject to the approval of the director, for use by any private person or entity acting on behalf of a federal, State or local agency in carrying out its functions.

L.1999, c. 28, § 16, eff. Jan. 1, 2000.

Historical and Statutory Notes

L.2001, c. 391, § 17, approved Jan. 8, 2002, provides:

"Notwithstanding the provisions of P.L.1999, c. 28 (C.39:3–10f1 et al.) to the contrary, the Director of the Division of Motor Vehicles may delay the implementation of the provisions of that act, other than those set forth in section

14 thereof, until the 60th day after the director certifies to the Commissioner of Transportation that the division is prepared to issue drivers' licenses with digitized pictures of licensees, but such implementing date shall be not later than January 1, 2003. The director shall make every effort to provide the certification required for P. L.1999, c. 28 to be implemented as soon as practicable."

39:3–10f3. Rules and regulations

The Director of the Division of Motor Vehicles, in accordance with the provisions of the "Administrative Procedure Act," P.L.1968, c. 410 (C.52:14B–1 et seq.), may promulgate rules and regulations to effectuate the purposes of this act.

L.1999, c. 28, § 17, eff. Jan. 1, 2000.

Historical and Statutory Notes

L.2001, c. 391, § 17, approved Jan. 8, 2002, provides:

"Notwithstanding the provisions of P.L.1999, c. 28 (C.39:3–10f1 et al.) to the contrary, the Director of the Division of Motor Vehicles may delay the implementation of the provisions of that act, other than those set forth in section 14 thereof, until the 60th day after the director certifies to the Commissioner of Transportation that the division is prepared to issue drivers' licenses with digitized pictures of licensees, but such implementing date shall be not later than January 1, 2003. The director shall make every effort to provide the certification required for P. L.1999, c. 28 to be implemented as soon as practicable."

39:3–10f4. Fee for digitized picture

The fee for a digitized picture shall be $6 for each license, renewal or duplicate thereof, and shall be in addition to the fee presently authorized for the issuance of a driver's license pursuant to R.S.39:3–10.

L.2001, c. 391, § 4, eff. Jan. 8, 2002.

Historical and Statutory Notes

L.2001, c. 391, § 18, approved Jan. 8, 2002, provides:

"This act shall take effect immediately, except that sections 3, 5, 6, 8, 9, 10, 11, and the required fees for the 48–month license added to R.S. 39:3–10 by section 2 of this act shall remain inoperative until the 60th day after the Director of the Division of Motor Vehicles in the Department of Transportation certifies to the Commissioner of Transportation that the division is prepared to issue drivers' licenses with digitized pictures of licensees, but such operative date shall be no later than January 1, 2003."

39:3–10f5. Secure Driver's License Fund

a. Revenues from the fees collected for the digitized picture provided for in this act shall be revenues of the commission upon enactment of P.L.2003, c. 13 (C.39:2A–1 et seq.) and used for the purposes of the commission.

b. (Deleted by amendment, P.L.2003, c. 13)

c. Any revenue credited to the fund shall remain in the fund exclusively for the purposes of the commission.

L.2001, c. 391, § 15, eff. Jan. 8, 2002. Amended by L.2003, c. 13, § 38, eff. Jan. 28, 2003.

Historical and Statutory Notes

L.2003, c. 13, § 127, approved Jan. 28, 2003, provides:

"Sections 1, 2, 3, 12, 38, 109, 110 and 121 shall take effect immediately, sections 105, 106, 107, 108, and 120 shall take effect on July 1, 2003 and the remainder of this act shall take effect on the date the Commissioner of Transportation certifies to the Governor (hereinafter the "date of certification") that a majority of the members of the commission have been appointed or are in office and that all necessary anticipatory actions have been accomplished, provided, that the amount of revenues received pursuant to sections 109 and 110 prior to the date of certification are hereby appropriated to the division. Upon the date of certification, all such collected revenue shall be revenue of the commission. The Commissioner of Transportation, the Director of the Division of Motor Vehicles and the commission may take such anticipatory administrative action in advance as shall be necessary for the implementation of the act."

39:3–10g. Repealed by L.1999, c. 28, § 18, eff. Jan. 1, 2000

39:3–10h. Nonalterable construction of license

The director shall provide for the use of a process or processes in the issuance of licenses with digitized color pictures that prevent, to the extent possible, the alteration, delamination, duplication, counterfeiting, photographing, forging or other modification of the license and prevent the superimposition of a digitized color picture other than the authorized original on such license. The director shall provide that material used for, and the manufacturing process, of, the license shall prevent, to the greatest extent possible, any alteration, delamination, duplication, counterfeiting, photographing, forging or other modification of the license. A license that consists of a composite material that does not use lamination and offers at least the same level of security as that required by the director for noncomposite material may fulfill the requirements of this section. The director may provide for the electronic storage of the licensee's motor vehicle information, including the licensee's digitized picture and digitized signature, in a bar code, magnetic stripe or database. In addition, the director shall provide that the license include features to ensure the security and integrity of the license. Any information encoded in a bar code or magnetic stripe on the license shall be limited to the following: name, address, municipality of residence, state, zip code of residence, date of birth, under 21 until xx/xx/xx (date of licensee's 21st birthday), gender, color of eyes, height, driver's license number, date of issuance, expiration date, document type, class, endorsements and restrictions, organ donor status, identification of issuer, license fee, transaction number, and the licensee's digitized picture and digitized signature. Any information encoded in a bar code or magnetic stripe on the license shall be displayed on the driver's license, which may be done in abbreviated form.

L.1979, c. 261, § 3. Amended by L.1999, c. 28, § 4, eff. Jan. 1, 2000; L.2001, c. 391, § 5, eff. Jan. 8, 2002.

Historical and Statutory Notes

L.2001, c. 391, §§ 17, 18 approved Jan. 8, 2002, provide:

"17. Notwithstanding the provisions of P.L.1999, c. 28 (C.39:3–10f1 et al.) to the contrary, the Director of the Division of Motor Vehicles may delay the implementation of the provisions of that act, other than those set forth in section 14 thereof, until the 60th day after the director certifies to the Commissioner of Transportation that the division is prepared to issue drivers' licenses with digitized pictures of licensees, but such implementing date shall be not later than January 1, 2003. The director shall make every effort to provide the certification required for P. L.1999, c. 28 to be implemented as soon as practicable.

"18. This act shall take effect immediately, except that sections 3, 5, 6, 8, 9, 10, 11, and the required fees for the 48–month license added to R.S. 39:3–10 by section 2 of this act shall remain inoperative until the 60th day after the Director of the Division of Motor Vehicles in the Department of Transportation certifies to the Commissioner of Transportation that the division is prepared to issue drivers' licenses with digitized pictures of licensees, but such operative date shall be no later than January 1, 2003."

39:3–10i. Repealed by L.1981, c. 322, § 3, eff. Dec. 9, 1981

39:3–10j. Legislative findings and declarations concerning exemptions from licensing requirements set forth in the Commercial Motor Vehicle Safety Act of 1986

The Legislature finds that:

a. On September 20, 1988, the Secretary of the United States Department of Transportation granted the states of this nation the authority to exempt certain drivers from the licensing provisions of the "Commercial Motor Vehicle Safety Act of 1986," Pub.L.99–570 (49 U.S.C. § 2701 et seq.).

b. The "Commercial Motor Vehicle Safety Act of 1986" requires a commercial driver's license for anyone who operates a vehicle that has a gross weight rating in excess of 26,000 pounds, carries 15 or more passengers or transports hazardous materials.

c. While that act's objectives to regulate and improve the traffic safety of the commercial trucking industry are laudable, it could have an unintended, and largely adverse, impact upon certain non-commercial drivers.

d. Unless the State of New Jersey, in accordance with the Secretary of the United States Department of Transportation's directive, exercises its exemption authority, certain operators of firefighting apparatus, operators of emergency or rescue equipment operated for the purposes of a first aid, ambulance or rescue squad or for disaster control, non-civilian operators of military vehicles owned or operated by the United States Department of Defense or the National Guard, and farmers operating farm vehicles will be obligated to secure commercial driver's licenses under that act.

e. There appears to be no significant evidence that the operators of firefighting apparatus, operators of emergency or rescue equipment operated for the purposes of a first aid, ambulance or rescue squad or for disaster control, non-civilian operators of military vehicles owned or operated by the United States Department of Defense or the National Guard, or farmers operating farm vehicles in and about their regular agricultural activities pose or have created any safety hazards on the public highways which would warrant their being licensed under the provisions of the "Commercial Motor Vehicle Safety Act of 1986."

The Legislature, therefore, declares that it is altogether fitting and proper to authorize, in accordance with the directives issued by the Secretary of the United States Department of Transportation, that the designated operators of firefighting apparatus, operators of emergency or rescue equipment operated for the purposes of a first aid, ambulance or rescue squad or for disaster control, non-civilian operators of military vehicles owned and operated by the United States Department of Defense or the National Guard, and operators of farm vehicles under certain circumstances be exempted from the licensing requirements set forth in the "Commercial Motor Vehicle Safety Act of 1986."

L.1989, c. 164, § 1, eff. Aug. 11, 1989. Amended by L.1990, c. 103, § 36, eff. Nov. 9, 1990; L.1991, c. 11, § 1, eff. Jan. 24, 1991; L.1991, c. 126, § 1, eff. April 25, 1991; L.1997, c. 269, § 1, eff. Dec. 22, 1997.

39:3–10k. Farmers and designated drivers of volunteer fire companies and National Guard; exempt from licensing provisions of Commercial Motor Vehicle Safety Act of 1986

Unless otherwise required by federal law or regulation, and subject to any rules and regulations promulgated pursuant to the provisions of this act, no (1) designated operator of firefighting apparatus, (2) non-civilian operator of a military vehicle owned or operated by the United States Department of Defense or the National Guard, (3) operator of a farm vehicle controlled and operated by a farmer, used to transport agricultural products, farm machinery or farm supplies to or from a farm, operated within 150 miles of a person's farm, and not used in the operation of a common or contract motor carrier, or (4) operator of emergency or rescue equipment operated for the purposes of a first aid, ambulance or rescue squad or for disaster control, shall be subject to the licensing provisions of the "Commercial Motor Vehicle Safety Act of 1986," Pub.L.99–570 (49 U.S.C. § 2701 et seq.).

Notwithstanding the provisions of this section, a waiver shall not be granted if the granting of the waiver would place the State in a position of not being in substantial compliance with the requirements of the federal act.

L.1989, c. 164, § 2, eff. Aug. 11, 1989. Amended by L.1990, c. 105, § 37, eff. Nov. 9, 1990; L.1991, c. 11, § 2, eff. Jan. 24, 1991; L.1991, c. 126, § 2, eff. April 25, 1991; L.1997, c. 269, § 2, eff. Dec. 22, 1997.

39:3–10l. Rules and regulations

The Director of the Division of Motor Vehicles in the Department of Law and Public Safety, pursuant to the provisions of the "Administrative Procedure Act," P.L. 1968, c. 410 (C. 52:14B–1 et seq.), shall promulgate rules and regulations, which are in accordance with the directive issued by the Secretary of the United States Department of Transportation on September 20, 1988, to effectuate the purposes of this act.

L.1989, c. 164, § 3, eff. Aug. 11, 1989.

39:3–10m. Applicants for license and license renewal to be offered opportunity to register to vote

Notwithstanding any law, rule or regulation to the contrary, each applicant for a State motor vehicle driver's license application, including any application for a renewal thereof, submitted to an agent of the Division of Motor Vehicles in the Department of Law and Public Safety shall be offered an opportunity to register to vote.

L.1994, c. 182, § 23.

39:3–10n. Chief administrator; discretion to issue temporary driver's licenses to New Jersey licensees serving in the military

Notwithstanding the provisions of any law to the contrary, the chief administrator may, at the chief administrator's discretion, issue a temporary driver's license that is valid without a digitized color picture of the licensee to New Jersey licensees who are serving in the military outside the State or who temporarily are residents of another state or foreign country.

The form and content of a temporary license issued under this section shall be prescribed by the chief administrator; shall bear the words "TEMPORARY LICENSE" in a conspicuous manner; and shall be valid for a period not to exceed 12 calendar months.

If the temporary licensee is under the age of 21 years, the temporary license shall bear the words "UNDER 21" in a conspicuous manner.

An applicant for a temporary driver's license shall submit such satisfactory proof of identity and age as the chief administrator shall require.

L.2003, c. 204, § 5, eff. Jan. 6, 2004.

39:3–10.1. Driver of motor vehicle or trackless trolley with capacity over six passengers; special license

No person shall drive any motor vehicle or trackless trolley with a capacity of more than six passengers used for the transportation of passengers for hire or for the transportation of passengers to or from summer day camps or summer residence camps or any bus as defined by the director used for the transportation of passengers, except vehicles used in ride-sharing arrangements, taxicabs, motor vehicles with a capacity of more than six passengers, which are owned and operated directly by businesses engaged in the practice of mortuary science when those vehicles are used exclusively for providing transportation related to the provision of funeral services and which shall not be used in that capacity at any time to pick up or discharge passengers to any airline terminal, train station or other transportation center or for any purpose not directly related to the provision of funeral services or any bus used to transport children to and from school pursuant to N.J.S.18A:39–1 et seq. or when being used by a private school to transport children to and from school, unless specially licensed so to do by the chief administrator or in the case of a nonresident, licensed pursuant to the laws of his resident state with respect to the licensing of bus drivers. Such license shall not be granted by the chief administrator until the applicant therefor is at least 18 years of age and has passed a satisfactory examination in ascertainment of his driving ability and familiarity with the mechanism of said vehicle and has presented evidence, satisfactory to the chief administrator of his previous experience (including proof that he has had at least three years of driving experience), good character and physical fitness. Said license shall be effective until suspended or revoked by the director; provided, the special licensee is also the holder of a license as provided for in R.S.39:3–10.

Every holder of a special license issued pursuant to this section shall furnish to the chief administrator satisfactory evidence of continuing physical fitness, good character and experience at the time of application renewal or such other time as the chief administrator may require, and in such form as the chief administrator may require. In addition, any person applying for a special license pursuant to this section for the transporting of children to and from schools, pursuant to N.J.S.18A:39–1 et seq., shall comply with the provisions of section 6 of P.L.1989, c. 104 (C.18A:39–19.1).

The chief administrator may suspend or revoke a license granted under authority of this section for a violation of any of the provisions of this subtitle, or on other reasonable grounds, or where, in his opinion, the licensee is either physically or morally unfit to retain the same. Notwithstanding the provisions of any law to the contrary the chief administrator shall, upon notice of disqualification from the Commissioner of Education pursuant to section 6 of P.L.1989, c. 104 (C.18A:39–19.1), immediately revoke the special license granted under authority of this section without the necessity of a further hearing.

The chief administrator may make such rules and regulations as he may deem necessary to carry out the provisions of this section.

Amended by L.1938, c. 49, p. 143, § 1; L.1938, c. 66, p. 174, § 4; L.1951, c. 218, p. 782, § 1; L.1955, c. 23, p. 76, § 1; L.1965, c. 119, § 5; L.1975, c. 180, § 3, eff. Jan. 1, 1976; L.1975, c. 284, § 1, eff. Jan. 1, 1977; L.1977, c. 25, § 2, eff. Feb. 24, 1977; L.1979, c. 147, § 1, eff. July 16, 1979; L.1981, c. 413, § 9, eff. Jan. 7, 1982; L.1985, c. 246, § 1; L.1989, c. 104, § 5, eff. July 1, 1989; L.1990, c. 103, § 27, eff. Nov. 9, 1990; L.2004, c. 124, § 1, eff. Sept. 15, 2004.

39:3–10.1a. School bus drivers; examination for presence of controlled dangerous substance

All drivers of buses or other vehicles used by a board of education or by a private school for the transportation of pupils to and from school shall, in addition to any exam required by law, submit to a medical exam for the presence of alcohol, narcotics or habit-producing drugs within the scope of the "New Jersey Controlled Dangerous Substances Act" (P.L.1970, c. 226, C. 24:21–1 et seq.).

L.1975, c. 284, § 2, eff. Jan. 1, 1977.

39:3–10.2, 39:3–10.3. Repealed by L.1973, c. 108, § 1, eff. May 2, 1973

39:3–10.4. Report to director by physicians of persons subject to epileptiform seizures

Each physician treating any person 16 years of age or older for recurrent convulsive seizures or for recurrent periods of unconsciousness or for impairment or loss of motor coordination due to conditions such as, but not limited to, epilepsy in any of its forms, when such conditions persist or recur despite medical treatments, shall, within 24 hours after his determination of such fact, report the same to the Director of the Division of Motor Vehicles. The director, in consultation with the State Commissioner of Health, shall prescribe and furnish the forms on which such reports shall be made.

L.1970, c. 195, § 1, eff. Sept. 4, 1970.

39:3–10.5. Report by drivers' license applicants subject to epileptiform seizures

Each person subject to recurrent convulsive seizures or recurrent periods of unconsciousness or impairment or loss of motor coordination due to conditions such as, but not limited to, epilepsy in any of its forms, shall at the time of his initial application for a driver's license or any subsequent application for a renewal thereof or at such other time as prescribed by the Director of the Division of Motor Vehicles, report the existence of such conditions to the Director of the Division of Motor Vehicles in a manner to be prescribed by the director.

L.1970, c. 195, § 2, eff. Sept. 4, 1970.

39:3–10.6. Procedure for evaluation and screening of persons subject to epileptiform seizures

In order to be assured that no person is unwarrantedly denied the privilege of operating a motor vehicle in this State because of reports submitted under the provisions of this act, the Director of the Division of Motor Vehicles, in consultation with the State Commissioner of Health, shall establish a procedure for evaluation and screening of cases so reported.

L.1970, c. 195, § 3, eff. Sept. 4, 1970.

39:3–10.7. Confidentiality of reports of persons subject to epileptiform seizures

Reports submitted pursuant to the provisions of this act shall be for the information of the Director of the Division of Motor Vehicles in enforcing State motor vehicle laws and shall be kept in the confidence of the Division of Motor Vehicles and shall not be revealed or used by the division in any manner or any circumstances except for the purpose of determining the eligibility of any person to operate a motor vehicle on the highways of this State.

L.1970, c. 195, § 4, eff. Sept. 4, 1970.

39:3–10.8. Violations of provisions requiring reports of persons subject to epileptiform seizures

Any person who is guilty of a violation of section 1 of this act[1] shall be subject to a fine of $50.00 for each violation. Any person who is guilty of a violation of section 2 of this act[2] shall be subject to a fine of $50.00 and, in the discretion of the Director of the Division of Motor Vehicles, to suspension or revocation of his driving privileges in accordance with the procedures prescribed by R.S. 39:5–30.

L.1970, c. 195, § 5, eff. Sept. 4, 1970.

[1] N.J.S.A. § 39:3–10.4.
[2] N.J.S.A. § 39:3–10.5.

39:3–10.9. Short title

This act shall be known and may be cited as the "New Jersey Commercial Driver License Act."

L.1990, c. 103, § 1, eff. Nov. 9, 1990.

39:3–10.10. Purpose of act

The purpose of this act is to reduce or prevent commercial motor vehicle accidents, fatalities, and injuries by strengthening licensing and testing standards for drivers of commercial motor vehicles, and by disqualifying those drivers who have committed certain serious traffic violations or other specified offenses. This act is also designed to substantially conform the laws of this State to the requirements and standards established under the federal "Commercial Motor Vehicle Safety Act of 1986," Pub.L. 99–570 (49 U.S.C. § 2701 et seq.) and the regulations promulgated pursuant to that federal law. This act is a remedial law and shall be liberally construed to promote the public health, safety, and welfare.

L.1990, c. 103, § 2, eff. Nov. 9, 1990.

39:3–10.11. Definitions

For purposes of this act, a term shall have the meaning set forth in R. S.39:1–1 unless another meaning for the term is set forth in this act, or unless another meaning is clearly apparent from the language or context of this act, or unless the meaning for the term set forth in R.S.39:1–1 is inconsistent with the manifest intent of the Legislature in this act.

For purposes of this act:

"Alcohol concentration" means:

a. The number of grams of alcohol per 100 milliliters of blood; or

b. The number of grams of alcohol per 210 liters of breath.

"Commercial driver license" or "CDL" means a license issued in accordance with this act to a person authorizing the person to operate a certain class of commercial motor vehicle.

"Commercial Driver License Information System" or "CDLIS" means the information system established pursuant to the federal "Commercial Motor Vehicle Safety Act of 1986," Pub.L.99–570 (49 U.S.C. s.2701 et seq.) to serve as a clearinghouse for locating information related to the licensing and identification of commercial motor vehicle drivers.

"Commercial motor vehicle" or "CMV" means a motor vehicle or combination of motor vehicles used or designed to transport passengers or property:

a. If the vehicle has a gross vehicle weight rating of 26,001 or more pounds or displays a gross vehicle weight rating of 26,001 or more pounds;

b. If the vehicle has a gross combination weight rating of 26,001 or more pounds inclusive of a towed unit with a gross vehicle weight rating of more than 10,000 pounds;

c. If the vehicle is designed to transport 16 or more passengers including the driver;

d. If the vehicle is designed to transport eight or more but less than 16 persons, including the driver, and is used to transport such persons for hire on a daily basis to and from places of employment;

e. If the vehicle is transporting or used in the transportation of hazardous materials and is required to be placarded in accordance with Subpart F. of 49 C.F.R. s.172, or the vehicle displays a hazardous material placard; or

f. If the vehicle is operated by, or under contract with, a public or governmental agency, or religious or other charitable organization or corporation, or is privately operated, and is used for the transportation of children to or from a school, school connected activity, day camp, summer day camp, summer residence camp, nursery school, child care center, preschool center or other similar places of education.

The chief administrator may, by regulation, include within this definition such other motor vehicles or combination of motor vehicles as he deems appropriate.

This term shall not include recreation vehicles.

This term shall not include motor vehicles designed to transport eight or more but less than sixteen persons, including the driver, which are owned and operated directly by businesses engaged in the practice of mortuary science when those vehicles are used exclusively for providing transportation related to the provision of funeral services and which shall not be used in that capacity at any time to pick up or discharge passengers to any airline terminal, train station or other transportation center, or for any purpose not directly related to the provision of funeral services.

"Controlled substance" means any substance so classified under subsection (6) of section 102 of the "Controlled Substances Act" (21 U.S.C. s.802), and includes all substances listed on Schedules I through V of 21 C.F.R. s.1308, or under P.L.1970, c. 226 (C.24:21–1 et seq.) as they may be revised from time to time. The term, wherever it appears in this act or administrative regulation promulgated pursuant to this act, shall include controlled substance analogs.

"Controlled substance analog" means a substance that has a chemical structure substantially similar to that of a controlled dangerous substance and that was specifically designed to produce an effect substantially similar to that of a controlled dangerous substance. The term shall not include a substance manufactured or distributed in conformance with the provisions of an approved new drug application or an exemption for investigational use within the meaning of section 505 of the Federal Food, Drug and Cosmetic Act (21 U.S.C. s.355).

"Conviction" means a final adjudication that a violation has occurred, a final judgment on a verdict, a finding of guilt in a tribunal of original jurisdiction, or a conviction following a plea of guilty, non vult or nolo contendere accepted by a court. It also includes an unvacated forfeiture of bail, bond or collateral deposited to secure the person's appearance in court, or the payment of a fine or court costs, or violation of a condition of release without bail, regardless of whether the penalty is rebated, suspended, or probated.

"Disqualification" means either:

a. The suspension, revocation, cancellation, or any other withdrawal by a state of a person's privilege to operate a commercial motor vehicle;

b. A determination by the Federal Motor Carrier Safety Administration under the rules of practice for motor carrier safety contained in 49 C.F.R. s.386, that a person is no longer qualified to operate a commercial motor vehicle under 49 C.F.R. s.391; or

c. The loss of qualification which automatically follows conviction of an offense listed in 49 C.F.R.s. 383.51.

"Domicile" means that state where a person has a true, fixed, and permanent home and principal residence and to which the person intends to return whenever the person is absent.

"Driver license" means a license issued by this State or any other jurisdiction to a person authorizing the person to operate a motor vehicle.

"Endorsement" means an authorization to a commercial driver license required to permit the holder of the license to operate certain types of commercial motor vehicles.

"Felony" means any offense under any federal law or the law of a state, including this State, that is punishable by death or imprisonment for a term exceeding one year. The term includes, but is not limited to, "crimes" as that term is defined in N.J.S.2C:1–1 et seq.

"Foreign jurisdiction" means any jurisdiction other than a state of the United States.

"Gross vehicle weight rating" or "GVWR" means the value specified by a manufacturer as the loaded weight of a single or a combination (articulated) vehicle, or the registered gross weight, whichever is greater. The GVWR of a combination (articulated) vehicle, commonly referred to as the "gross combination weight rating" or "GCWR," is the GVWR of the power unit plus the GVWR of the towed unit or units. In the absence of a value specified for the towed unit or units by the manufacturer, the GVWR of a combination (articulated) vehicle is the GVWR of the power unit plus the total weight of the towed unit, including the loads on them.

"Hazardous material" means a substance or material determined by the Secretary of the United States Department of Transportation to be capable of posing an unreasonable risk to health, safety, and property when transported in commerce and so designated pursuant to the provisions of the "Hazardous Materials Transportation Act" (49 U.S.C. s.1801 et seq.).

"Motor vehicle" includes all vehicles propelled otherwise than by muscular power, except such vehicles as run only upon rails or tracks. The term "motor vehicle" includes motorized bicycles.

"Non-commercial motor vehicle" means a motor vehicle or combination of motor vehicles other than a "commercial motor vehicle" as defined in this section.

"Out-of-service order" means a declaration by an authorized enforcement officer of a federal, state, Canadian, Mexican, or local jurisdiction that a driver, a commercial motor vehicle, or a motor carrier operation is out-of-service pursuant to 49 C.F.R. s.386.72, 392.5., 395.13, 396.9, or any compatible law or the North American Uniform Out-of-Service Criteria.

"Recreation vehicle" means a self-propelled or towed vehicle equipped to serve as temporary living quarters for recreational, camping, or travel purposes and is used solely as a family or personal conveyance.

"Representative vehicle" means a motor vehicle which represents the type of motor vehicle that a commercial driver license applicant operates or expects to operate.

"Serious traffic violation" means conviction for one of the following offenses committed while operating a commercial motor vehicle:

a. Excessive speeding, involving any single offense for a speed of 15 miles per hour or more above the speed limit;

b. Reckless driving, as defined by state or local law or regulation, including, but not limited to, offenses of driving a commercial motor vehicle in willful or wanton disregard of the safety of persons or property, including violations of R.S.39:4–96;

c. Improper or erratic traffic lane changes;

d. Following a vehicle ahead too closely, including violations of R.S.39:4–89;

e. A violation, arising in connection with a fatal accident, of state or local law relating to motor vehicle traffic control, other than a parking violation;

f. Any other violation of a state or local law relating to motor vehicle traffic control determined by the Secretary of the United States Department of Transportation in 49 C.F.R. s.383.5 to be a serious traffic violation;

g. Driving a commercial motor vehicle without a commercial driver license in the driver's possession; or

h. Driving a commercial motor vehicle without the proper class of commercial driver license or endorsements for the specific vehicle group being operated or for the passengers or type of cargo being transported.

This term shall not include vehicle weight or defect violations.

"State" means a state of the United States or the District of Columbia.

"Tank vehicle" means any commercial motor vehicle that is designed to transport any liquid or gaseous material within a tank that is either permanently or temporarily attached to the vehicle or the chassis. Such vehicles include, but are not limited to, cargo tanks and portable tanks as defined by the director. However, this definition does not include portable tanks having a rated capacity under 1,000 gallons.

"Vehicle group" means a class or type of vehicle with certain operating characteristics.

L.1990, c. 103, § 3, eff. Nov. 9, 1990. Amended by L.2004, c. 124, § 2; L.2005, c. 147, § 2, eff. Sept. 30, 2005; L.2009, c. 271, § 1, eff. Jan. 17, 2010.

39:3–10.11a. Drivers of vehicles related to provision of funeral services; medical examination required

Notwithstanding the exemption of motor vehicles which are owned directly by businesses engaged in the practice of mortuary science from the provisions of P.L.1990, c. 103(C.39:3–10.9 et seq.), pursuant to section 3 of P.L.1990, c. 103 (C.39:3–10.11) as amended by section 2 of P.L.2004, c. 124, the driver or operator of such a motor vehicle shall fulfill all of the requirements of a medical examination required of those holding a

commercial driver license as provided under 49 C.F.R. s.391.41 et seq.

L.2004, c. 124, § 3, eff. Sept. 15, 2004.

39:3–10.12. Tests for commercial driver license

a. Notwithstanding any other provision of law to the contrary, the chief administrator shall adopt and administer a classified licensing system and a program for testing and ensuring the fitness of persons to operate commercial motor vehicles in accordance with the minimum federal standards established under the federal "Commercial Motor Vehicle Safety Act of 1986," Pub. L. 99–570 (49 U.S.C. s. 2701 et seq.) and the regulations promulgated pursuant to that law. The chief administrator shall not issue a commercial driver license to a person unless that person passes a knowledge and skills test for the operation of a commercial motor vehicle which complies with the federal standards. The chief administrator may issue commercial driver examination or learner's permits, subject to such conditions and restrictions as deemed necessary, to carry out the provisions of this act.

b. A knowledge and skills test shall not be required by the chief administrator for the renewal of a commercial driver license issued pursuant to the provisions of this act. However, a knowledge and skills test may be required for (1) the renewal of an endorsement permitting the operation of vehicles required to be placarded for hazardous materials, (2) for the renewal or reissuance of a commercial driver license if the license was suspended or revoked under section 12 of this act during the last license period preceding the renewal or reissuance, or (3) for the renewal or reissuance of a license which had not been renewed for a period of three or more years.

c. Upon the request of an applicant for a commercial driver license, the chief administrator shall administer to the applicant oral knowledge tests for the commercial driver license and any endorsements if the applicant supplies sufficient proof or otherwise demonstrates to the satisfaction of the chief administrator his inability to comprehend a written test. The chief administrator shall provide an English and Spanish version of the knowledge tests for a commercial driver license and for any endorsements and shall be authorized to provide versions in such other languages as he, in his discretion, may deem appropriate.

d. A person who satisfactorily completes the knowledge tests required by this act for a commercial driver license and any endorsement shall not be required under R.S.39:3–10, R.S.39:3–10.1, or any other section in Title 39 of the Revised Statutes to take any other knowledge test for the operation of a commercial motor vehicle.

e. (Deleted by amendment, P.L.2005, c. 147).

f. For the purposes of an application for a commercial driver license by a person who has never held a license issued under the provisions of this act, a person who satisfactorily completes the knowledge test for the commercial driver license but not the test for an endorsement, or a person who satisfactorily completes the knowledge test for an endorsement but not the test for the commercial driver license, shall not be required to retake that test which was satisfactorily completed.

g. No provision in this act, or in any manual, test, or administrative procedure developed to implement the provisions of this act, shall be deemed to expand the requirements for commercial motor vehicle operators concerning pre-trip inspection, after-trip inspection and inspection during a trip as such requirements are set forth in federal law or regulation. This subsection, however, shall not be deemed to limit the authority of the chief administrator, or the authority of any State department or agency, to promulgate, pursuant to other provisions of State law, standards and procedures on vehicle inspections which are consistent with federal law and regulation.

h. Classified licensing of drivers of school buses shall be by endorsement on the commercial driver licenses issued pursuant to P.L.1990, c. 103 (C.39:3–10.9 et seq.).

L.1990, c. 103, § 4, eff. Nov. 9, 1990. Amended by L.2005, c. 147, § 3, eff. Sept. 30, 2005.

39:3–10.13. Operation of commercial motor vehicle while under influence of alcohol or controlled substance

Notwithstanding any other provision of law to the contrary, a person shall not operate a commercial motor vehicle in this State with an alcohol concentration of 0.04% or more, or while under the influence of a controlled substance.

L.1990, c. 103, § 5.

39:3–10.14. Requests to Commercial Driver License Information System for driving record of applicant; provision of information to other licensing authorities; notification of issuance of license

a. Before issuing a commercial driver license to an applicant, the chief administrator shall notify the Commercial Driver License Information System of the proposed issuance and shall request driving record information from the Commercial Driver License Information System, the National Driver Register, and from any other state which has issued a commercial driver license, non-commercial motor vehicle driver license or basic driver license to the applicant to determine whether the applicant has a commercial driver license, non-commercial motor vehicle driver license or basic driver license issued by another state, whether the applicant's driving privilege has been suspended, revoked, cancelled, or whether the applicant has been disqualified from operating a commercial motor vehicle.

The chief administrator also shall provide driving record and other information to the licensing authority of any other state, or province or territory of Canada,

which requests such information in connection with a commercial driver license. The chief administrator may charge such fees as are deemed appropriate to cover the costs of providing information, except that no fee shall be charged if the other jurisdiction does not charge this State for similar requests.

b. Within 10 days after the issuance of a commercial driver license, the chief administrator shall notify the Commercial Driver License Information System of that fact, providing all information required to ensure identification of the licensee.

L.1990, c. 103, § 6, eff. Nov. 9, 1990. Amended by L.2005, c. 147, § 4, eff. Sept. 30, 2005.

39:3–10.15. Notification of traffic violations, disqualification or suspension

Within 10 days after receiving a report of the conviction of a holder of a commercial driver license for any violation of state law related to motor vehicle traffic control committed in a vehicle, other than a parking violation, or a report of the conviction of a person who is not the holder of a commercial driver license for any violation of state law related to motor vehicle traffic control committed in a commercial vehicle, other than a parking violation, or after the disqualification of the holder of a commercial driver license or suspension of privileges for a period of 60 days or more, the commission shall notify the driver licensing authority in the licensing state, if other than this State, and the Commercial Driver License Information System of the conviction, suspension, or disqualification. The notification shall include all information the chief administrator deems necessary.

L.1990, c. 103, § 7, eff. Nov. 9, 1990. Amended by L.2005, c. 147, § 5, eff. Sept. 30, 2005.

39:3–10.16. Denial, suspension or revocation of commercial driver license by director

The director, in his discretion, may refuse to grant a commercial driver license to a person who is, in his estimation, not a proper person to be granted such a license, but no defect of the applicant shall bar him from receiving a license unless it can be shown by tests approved by the director that the defect incapacitates him from safely operating a commercial motor vehicle.

The director may suspend or revoke a license to operate a commercial motor vehicle, may prohibit a person from obtaining such a license, or may suspend or revoke the reciprocity privilege of a person for a violation of any provision of Title 39 of the Revised Statutes or for any other reasonable grounds, after due notice in writing of such proposed suspension, revocation, or prohibition and the grounds thereof.

L.1990, c. 103, § 8, eff. Nov. 9, 1990.

39:3–10.17.   Licensee to be domiciled in State

The director shall issue a commercial driver license only to a person who operates or will operate a commercial motor vehicle and is domiciled in this State.

A person shall apply to the director within 30 days after establishing domicile in this State for the transfer of a commercial driver license from the state in which the person was previously domiciled.

L.1990, c. 103, § 9, eff. Nov. 9, 1990.

39:3–10.17a.   Commercial drivers license applicants; fingerprinting and background checks

a.   The commission shall require the fingerprinting of all applicants for commercial driver's licenses with a hazardous material endorsement, a tank vehicle endorsement or both, at the initial application and upon renewal, in order to determine eligibility for those endorsements.   The commission is hereby authorized to exchange fingerprint data with, and receive criminal history record information from the Federal Bureau of Investigation and the Division of State Police, consistent with the provisions of Pub.L.92–544, for use in determining eligibility.   The commission shall require any person who, prior to the date of enactment of this act, has been issued a commercial driver's license with a hazardous material endorsement, a tanker vehicle endorsement or both, to undergo a criminal history record background check as a condition to continue to hold, use and renew such an endorsement.   No criminal history record check shall be performed without the applicant's written consent.   The applicant shall bear the cost for the criminal history record check, including all costs for administering and processing the check. Failure or refusal to submit a disclosure and fingerprints will result in an automatic disqualification.

b.   Upon receipt of the criminal history record information, the commission shall notify the applicant, in writing, of the applicant's qualification or disqualification for a commercial driver's license with a hazardous material endorsement, a tank vehicle endorsement or both.   If the applicant is disqualified, the basis for the disqualification shall be identified in the written notice to the applicant.

c.   The applicant shall have 30 days from the postmarked date of the written notice of disqualification to challenge the accuracy of the criminal history record information.   If no challenge is filed or if the determination of the accuracy of the criminal history record information upholds the disqualification, the applicant's disqualification for a commercial driver's license, with a hazardous material endorsement, a tank vehicle endorsement or both will stand.

d.   The commission, in a manner not inconsistent with appropriate federal requirements, shall provide by regulation the grounds upon which an applicant may be disqualified.

L.2003, c. 13, § 34 (contingent effective date).

39:3–10.18.   Possession of valid commercial driver license with applicable endorsements required; operation of vehicle during period of refusal, suspension, revocation, prohibition, disqualification, or out of service order;   penalties

a.   (1) (Deleted by amendment, P.L.2005, c. 147).

(2) On and after April 1, 1992, and except when operating under a valid commercial driver examination or learner's permit and accompanied by the holder of a commercial driver license valid for the class or type of vehicle being operated, a person shall not operate a commercial motor vehicle unless the person has been issued and is in possession of a valid commercial driver license and applicable endorsements for the class and type of vehicle being operated.   A person shall not operate a commercial motor vehicle if the person is restricted from operating a commercial vehicle of that class or type.

(3) A person violating this subsection shall be fined not less than $250 or more than $500, or imprisoned for not more than 60 days, or both.   If that person has never been licensed to operate a commercial motor vehicle in this State or any other jurisdiction, the chief administrator shall refuse to issue a license to operate a commercial motor vehicle to that person for a period of 180 days from the date of the conviction.   This penalty shall not be applicable in cases where failure to have actual possession of the commercial driver license is due to an administrative or technical error by the commission.   If a person charged with a failure to have possession of a valid commercial driver license can exhibit the license to the judge of the court before whom he is summoned to answer to a charge and the license was valid on the day the person was charged, the judge may dismiss the charge.   However, the judge may impose court costs.

b.   (1) A person who has been refused a commercial driver license, whose commercial motor vehicle driving privilege or any endorsement has been suspended or revoked, who has been prohibited or disqualified from operating a commercial motor vehicle, who is subject to an out-of-service order, or whose driving privilege is suspended or revoked, shall not operate a commercial motor vehicle during the period of refusal, suspension, revocation, prohibition, or disqualification, or during the period of the out-of-service order.

(2) A person who violates this subsection shall, upon conviction, be fined not less than $500 or more than $5,000 for each offense, or imprisoned for a term of not more than 90 days, or both;   provided, however, a person who operates a commercial motor vehicle during the period of an out-of-service order shall, upon conviction, be fined $2,500 and may be imprisoned for a term of not more than 90 days.   A person who operates a commercial motor vehicle during the period of an out-of-service order shall, upon a second or subsequent conviction of this subsection, be fined $5,000 and may be imprisoned for a term of not more than 90 days.   If a

person is involved in an accident resulting in personal injury to another person while operating a commercial motor vehicle in violation of this subsection, the court shall impose both a period of imprisonment for 90 days and a fine of $5,000.

(3) An employer shall not knowingly allow, require, permit or authorize a driver to operate a commercial motor vehicle during the period of refusal, suspension, revocation, prohibition, disqualification, or during the period of the out-of-service order. An employer who is convicted of a violation of this subsection shall be subject to a fine of not less than $2,750 or more than $25,000.

In addition, the commercial motor vehicle driving privilege of a person convicted under this subsection shall be suspended in accordance with section 12 of this act.[1]

L.1990, c. 103, § 10, eff. Nov. 9, 1990. Amended by L.2005, c. 147, § 6, eff. Sept. 30, 2005; L.2009, c. 271, § 2, eff. Jan. 17, 2010.

 [1] N.J.S.A. § 39:3–10.20.

39:3–10.19. Operation of commercial vehicle in this State by person with waiver of requirements or license issued by other jurisdiction

Notwithstanding any other law to the contrary, a person may operate a commercial motor vehicle in this State if the person has received a waiver of the commercial driver license requirements from the Secretary of the United States Department of Transportation or the licensing authority of any other state, has a commercial driver license issued by any state in accordance with minimum federal standards for the issuance of commercial motor vehicle driver licenses, or has a commercial driver license issued by any other jurisdiction in accordance with minimum standards which are substantially similar to the standards in the federal "Commercial Motor Vehicle Safety Act of 1986," Pub.L. 99–570 (49 U.S.C. § 2701 et seq.) and this act. This section shall apply only if the person's driving privilege is not suspended or revoked or cancelled in this State or in the jurisdiction that issued the commercial driver license, and the person is not disqualified from operating a commercial motor vehicle, or subject to an "out of service" order.

L.1990, c. 103, § 11, eff. Nov. 9, 1990.

39:3–10.20. Suspension or revocation of commercial driver license by chief administrator; notification to Commercial Driver License Information System

a. In addition to the imposition of any other penalty provided by law, the chief administrator shall suspend for not less than one year nor more than three years the commercial motor vehicle driving privilege of a person convicted for a first violation of:

(1) R.S.39:4–50 if the motor vehicle was a commercial motor vehicle or section 5 of this act.

(2) R.S.39:4–129 if the motor vehicle was a commercial motor vehicle operated by the person.

(3) Using a commercial motor vehicle in the commission of any "crime" as defined in subsection a., c., or d. of N.J.S.2C:1–4.

(4) Refusal to submit to a chemical test under section 2 of P.L.1966, c. 142 (C.39:4–50.2) or section 16 of this act if the motor vehicle was a commercial motor vehicle.

(5) Paragraph (1) of subsection b. of section 10 of this act.

(6) A violation, arising in connection with a fatal accident, of State or local law relating to motor vehicle traffic control, other than a parking violation, regardless of whether the motor vehicle operated by the person was a commercial motor vehicle or a non-commercial motor vehicle.

b. If a first violation of any of the violations specified in subsection a. of this section takes place while transporting hazardous material or takes place in a vehicle displaying a hazardous material placard, the chief administrator shall suspend the commercial motor vehicle driving privilege of the person for three years.

c. Subject to the provisions of subsection d. of this section, the chief administrator shall revoke for life the commercial motor vehicle driving privilege of a person for a second or subsequent violation of any of the offenses specified in subsections a. and j. of this section or any combination of those offenses arising from two or more separate incidents.

d. The chief administrator may issue rules and regulations establishing guidelines, including conditions under which a revocation of commercial motor vehicle driving privilege for life under subsection c. may be reduced to a period of not less than 10 years.

e. Notwithstanding any other provision of law to the contrary, the chief administrator shall revoke for life the commercial motor vehicle driving privilege of a person who uses a commercial motor vehicle or a non-commercial motor vehicle in the commission of a crime involving the manufacture, distribution, or dispensing of a controlled substance or controlled substance analog, or possession with intent to manufacture, distribute, or dispense a controlled substance or controlled substance analog. A revocation under this subsection shall not be subject to reduction in accordance with subsection d. of this section.

f. (1) The chief administrator shall suspend the commercial motor vehicle driving privilege of a person for a period of not less than 60 days if the person is convicted of a serious traffic violation, other than a violation arising in connection with a fatal accident as set forth in paragraph (6) of subsection a. of this section, and that conviction constitutes the second serious traffic violation committed in a commercial motor vehicle or non-commercial motor vehicle in this or any other state arising from separate incidents occurring within a three-year period. The chief administrator shall suspend the commercial motor vehicle driving privilege for 120 days if the conviction constitutes the third or subsequent serious traffic violation, other than a violation arising in connection with a fatal accident as set forth in paragraph (6) of subsection a. of this section, committed in a commercial motor vehicle or non-commercial motor vehicle in this or any other state arising from separate incidents occurring within a three-year period.

(2) The chief administrator shall suspend the commercial motor vehicle driving privilege of a person for a period of not less than 60 days if the person is convicted of a violation of R.S.39:4–128; section 68 of P.L.1951, c. 23 (C.39:4–127.1); or section 10 of P.L.2005, c. 147 (C.39:4–128.11). The chief administrator shall suspend the commercial motor vehicle driving privilege for not less than 120 days if the conviction constitutes the second violation of R.S.39:4–128; section 68 of P.L. 1951, c. 23 (C.39:4–127. 1); section 10 of P.L.2005, c. 147 (C.39:4–128.11) or any combination of such violations in this or any other state arising from separate incidents occurring within a three-year period. The chief administrator shall suspend the commercial motor vehicle driving privilege for not less than one year if the conviction constitutes the third or subsequent violation of R.S.39:4–128; section 68 of P.L.1951, c. 23 (C.39:4–127.1); section 10 of P.L.2005, c. 147 (C.39:4–128.11) or any combination of such violations in this or any other state arising from separate incidents occurring within the past three years.

(3) The chief administrator shall suspend the commercial motor vehicle driving privilege of a person for a period of not less than 180 days or more than one year if the person is convicted of violating a driver, commercial motor vehicle, or motor carrier operation out-of-service order while driving a commercial motor vehicle transporting nonhazardous materials. The chief administrator shall suspend the commercial motor vehicle driving privilege of a person for a period of not less than two years or more than five years if the conviction constitutes the second conviction in a separate incident in this or any other state within a 10–year period of violating a driver, commercial motor vehicle, or motor carrier operation out-of-service order while driving a commercial motor vehicle transporting nonhazardous materials. The chief administrator shall suspend the commercial motor vehicle driving privilege for a person for a period of not less than three years or more than five years if the conviction constitutes the third or subsequent conviction in a separate incident in this or any other state within a 10–year period of violating a driver, commercial motor vehicle, or motor carrier operation out-of-service order while driving a commercial motor vehicle transporting nonhazardous materials.

(4) The chief administrator shall suspend the commercial motor vehicle driving privilege of a person for a period of not less than 180 days or more than two years if the person is convicted of violating a driver, commercial motor vehicle, or motor carrier operation out-of-

service order while driving a commercial motor vehicle transporting hazardous materials required to be placarded under Subpart F of 49 C.F.R.s.172, or while operating a vehicle designed to transport 16 or more passengers, including the driver. The chief administrator shall suspend the commercial motor vehicle driving privilege of a person for a period of not less than three years or more than five years if the conviction constitutes a second or subsequent conviction in a separate incident within a 10–year period in this or any other state of violating a driver, commercial motor vehicle, or motor carrier operation out-of-service order while driving a commercial motor vehicle transporting hazardous materials required to be placarded under Subpart F of 49 C.F.R. s.172, or while operating a vehicle designed to transport 16 or more passengers, including the driver.

g. A court shall make a report to the chief administrator within three days in such form as the chief administrator may require concerning conviction for violation of P.L.1990, c. 103 (C.39:3–10.9 et seq.). The chief administrator shall notify the Commercial Driver License Information System of the suspension, revocation, or cancellation. In the case of non-residents, the chief administrator also shall notify the licensing authority of the state which issued the commercial driver license or the state where the person is domiciled. The chief administrator shall provide these notices within 10 days after the suspension, revocation, cancellation, or disqualification.

h. The chief administrator shall in accordance with this section suspend a commercial motor vehicle driving privilege of a person holding, or required to hold, a commercial driver license issued by this State if the person is convicted in another state or foreign jurisdiction of an offense of a substantially similar nature to the offenses specified in subsection a., e., f., g., h., i. or j. of this section. For purposes of this section, a violation such as driving while intoxicated, driving under the influence, or driving while ability is impaired shall be considered substantially similar offenses. For purposes of this section, a violation committed in another state but substantially similar to those enumerated in subsection a., e., f., g., h., i. or j. of this section committed in this State shall be included.

i. Notwithstanding any other provision of law to the contrary, a conviction under this section, or section 5 or 16 of this act, shall not merge with a conviction for a violation of R.S.39:4–50 or section 2 of P.L.1966, c. 142 (C.39:4–50.2).

j. In addition to any other penalty provided by law, the chief administrator shall suspend for one year the commercial motor vehicle driving privilege of a person for a first violation of:

(1) R.S.39:4–50 while operating a non-commercial motor vehicle;

(2) R.S.39:4–129 while operating a non-commercial motor vehicle;

(3) Refusing to submit to a chemical test under section 2 of P.L.1966, c. 142 (C.39:4–50.2) while operating a non-commercial motor vehicle; or

(4) Using a non-commercial motor vehicle in the commission of any "crime" as defined in subsection a., c., or d. of N.J.S.2C:1–4.

k.   The chief administrator shall in accordance with this section suspend the commercial motor vehicle driving privilege of a person holding, or required to hold, a commercial driver license issued by this State if that person has been disqualified from operating a commercial motor vehicle by the Federal Motor Carrier Safety Administration pursuant to 49 C.F.R. s.383.52 because that person's driving has been determined to constitute an imminent hazard.

l.   The Motor Vehicle Commission shall maintain records of accidents, convictions, and disqualification for persons holding, or required to hold, a commercial driver license in accordance with 49 C.F.R. s.384.225 and the AAMVAnet, Inc.'s "Commercial Driver License Information System State Procedures," as amended and supplemented.

m.   Any driver who is found to be in violation of the provisions of paragraph (a) or (b) of 49 C.F.R. s.392.5, relating to the use of alcohol, being under the influence of alcohol, having any measured alcohol concentration or detected presence of alcohol, or possessing alcohol, shall be placed out-of-service immediately for a period of 24 hours.

L.1990, c. 103, § 12.   Amended by L.2005, c. 147, § 7, eff. Sept. 30, 2005; L.2009, c. 271, § 3, eff. Jan. 17, 2010.

39:3–10.21.   Administration of commercial driver testing

The director may, by contract, by appointment as a motor vehicle agent, or by licensing, authorize any necessary persons, including but not limited to an agency of this or another state, an employer, a private driver training facility or other private institution, or a department, agency or instrumentality of local government to administer the knowledge or skills tests for a commercial driver license or endorsement. The director shall adopt such regulations as deemed necessary to establish, oversee and regulate the administration of commercial motor vehicle driver testing by third parties including establishment of maximum fees that may be charged. The maximum fee for a skills test administered by a third party shall be set at an amount equal to the cost to the State for administering such testing.

The director may limit the number of persons licensed to administer examinations and may suspend or revoke an authorization on any reasonable ground. The director may terminate third party testing at any time. A person authorized to administer examinations by appointment as a motor vehicle agent shall so act until this authority is revoked by the director.

An examiner administering a skills test shall not be held accountable for any violation of Title 39 of the Revised Statutes committed by the person being tested.

L.1990, c. 103, § 13, eff. Nov. 9, 1990.

39:3–10.22.   Waiver of skills test

The chief administrator shall waive the skills test for a commercial driver license applicant who demonstrates that he meets the requirements for a waiver under the federal "Commercial Motor Vehicle Safety Act of 1986," Pub. L. 99–570 (49 U.S.C. s. 2701 et seq.), as those requirements are set forth in 49 C.F.R. s.383.77.

L.1990, c. 103, § 14, eff. Nov. 9, 1990.   Amended by L.2005, c. 147, § 8, eff. Sept. 30, 2005.

39:3–10.23.   Processing of applicants; time and place of testing

a.   The director may take such steps as are necessary to provide for the efficient, timely and orderly processing of persons required to obtain commercial driver licenses under this act. The director may require persons to take the skills test for the commercial driver license or for an endorsement at the time and place selected by the director. The director may require those persons who fail to satisfactorily complete a knowledge test for the commercial driver license or an endorsement on the initial attempt to take those knowledge tests for a second or subsequent time at a time and place selected by the director.

b.   If the director determines that persons required to obtain commercial driver licenses and endorsements by April 1, 1992 are not voluntarily and in a timely manner scheduling with the division a date, time and location for the taking of the knowledge tests or are failing to appear as scheduled, the director may for the timely processing of all such persons require each person to appear for the initial taking of the knowledge tests on a date and at a time and location selected by the director.

L.1990, c. 103, § 15, eff. Nov. 9, 1990.

39:3–10.24.   Consent to taking samples of breath; record of test; independent test; prohibition of use of force; refusal to submit to test; penalties

a.   A person who operates a commercial motor vehicle on a public road, street, or highway, or quasi-public area in this State, shall be deemed to have given his consent to the taking of samples of his breath for the purposes of making chemical tests to determine alcohol concentration; provided, however, that the taking of samples shall be made in accordance with the provisions of this act and at the request of a police officer who has reasonable grounds to believe that the person has been operating a commercial motor vehicle with an alcohol concentration of 0.04% or more.

b.   A record of the taking of such a sample, disclosing the date and time thereof, as well as the result of a chemical test, shall be made and a copy thereof, upon request, shall be furnished or made available to the person so tested.

c. In addition to the samples taken and tests made at the direction of a police officer hereunder, the person tested shall be permitted to have such samples taken and chemical tests of his breath, urine, or blood made by a person or physician of his own selection.

d. The police officer shall inform the person tested of his rights under subsections b. and c. of this section.

e. No chemical test, as provided in this section, or specimen necessary thereto, may be made or taken forcibly and against physical resistance thereto by the defendant. The police officer shall, however, inform the person arrested of the consequences of refusing to submit to such test including the penalties under section 12 of this act [1]. A standard statement, prepared by the director, shall be read by the police officer to the person.

f. The court shall revoke for six months the right to operate any motor vehicle of any person who, after being arrested for a violation of section 5 of this act,[2] shall refuse to submit to the chemical test provided for in this section when requested to do so, unless the refusal was in connection with a subsequent offense under this section, section 5 of this act, R.S. 39:4–50 or section 2 of P.L.1981, c. 512 (C. 39:4–50.4a), in which case the revocation period shall be for 2 years. In addition, a court shall impose the penalties provided in section 12 of this act.

The court shall determine by a preponderance of the evidence whether the arresting officer had probable cause to believe that the person had been operating or was in actual physical control of a commercial motor vehicle on the public highways or quasi-public areas of this State with an alcohol concentration at 0.04% or more, whether the person was placed under arrest, whether he refused to submit to the test upon request of the officer, and if these elements of the violation are not established, no conviction shall issue. In addition to any other requirements provided by law, a person whose driving privilege is revoked for refusing to submit to a chemical test shall satisfy the requirements of a program of alcohol education or rehabilitation pursuant to the provisions of R.S. 39:4–50. The revocation shall be independent of any revocation imposed by virtue of a conviction under the provisions of R.S. 39:4–50 or section 12 of this act.

In addition to imposing a revocation under this subsection, a court shall impose a fine of not less than $250 or more than $500.

L.1990, c. 103, § 16.

[1] N.J.S.A. § 39:3–10.20.
[2] N.J.S.A. § 39:3–10.13.

39:3–10.25. Chemical analyses of breath; uniform form for reports of analyses

Chemical analyses of an arrested person's breath, to be considered valid under the provisions of this act, shall have been performed according to methods approved by the Attorney General, and by a person certified for this purpose by the Attorney General. The Attorney General is authorized to approve satisfactory techniques or methods, to ascertain the qualifications and competence of individuals to conduct analyses, and to make certifications of such individuals, which certifications shall be subject to termination or revocation at the discretion of the Attorney General. The Attorney General shall prescribe a uniform form for reports of the chemical analysis of breath to be used by law enforcement officers and others acting in accordance with the provisions of this act. Each chief of police, in the case of forms distributed to law enforcement officers and others in his municipality, or the other officer, board, or official having charge or control of the police department where there is no chief, and the Director of the Division of Motor Vehicles and the Superintendent of State Police, in the case of such forms distributed to law enforcement officers and other personnel in their divisions, shall be responsible for the furnishing and proper disposition of such uniform forms. Each responsible party shall prepare or cause to be prepared the records and reports relating to the uniform forms and their disposition in the manner and at the times prescribed by the Attorney General. Unless otherwise provided by the Attorney General, the approval of methods and techniques, the certification of persons and the prescription of forms of reports pursuant to section 3 of P.L.1966, c. 142 (C. 39:4–50.3) shall constitute approval, certification or prescription, as the case may be, for purposes of this section.

L.1990, c. 103, § 17, eff. Nov. 9, 1990.

39:3–10.26. Operator of commercial vehicle restricted to one license; penalty for violation

A person who operates a commercial motor vehicle shall not have more than one driver license.

A person convicted of a violation of this section shall be subject for each offense to a fine of not more than $5,000, or imprisoned for a term of not more than 90 days, or both.

L.1990, c. 103, § 18.

39:3–10.27. Rules and regulations

The director may adopt any rules and regulations, in accordance with the provisions of the "Administrative Procedure Act," P.L.1968, c. 410 (C. 52:14B–1 et seq.), necessary to carry out the provisions of this act, including the regulations necessary to place this State in substantial compliance with the requirements of the federal "Commercial Motor Vehicle Safety Act of

1986," Pub.L. 99–570 (49 U.S.C. § 2701 et seq.) and the regulations promulgated pursuant to that federal law. *L.1990, c. 103, § 19, eff. Nov. 9, 1990.*

39:3–10.28. Agreements, arrangements, or declarations to carry out provisions of act

The director may enter into or make agreements, arrangements, or declarations to carry out the provisions of this act. The director may also enter into an agreement or arrangement with the duly authorized representative of another state, the federal government, or province concerning licensing or testing of commercial motor vehicle operators, the exchange of information concerning operators, and their operating history. Such arrangements shall, in the judgment of the director, be in the best interest of this State and its citizens, keeping in mind the public safety benefits that flow to this State from a nationwide system for regulating commercial motor vehicle operators. *L.1990, c. 103, § 20, eff. Nov. 9, 1990.*

39:3–10.29. Waiver of provisions

Notwithstanding any other provision of law to the contrary, the director may waive, in whole or in part, after notice and an opportunity for comment, application of any provision of this act or any regulation promulgated pursuant to this act with respect to a class of persons or class of commercial motor vehicles if the director determines that such waiver is not contrary to the public interest and does not diminish the safe operation of commercial motor vehicles. A waiver under this section shall be published in the New Jersey Register, together with reasons for the waiver. A waiver shall not be granted if the granting of the waiver is likely to or will place the State in the position of not being in substantial compliance with the requirements set forth in the "Commercial Motor Vehicle Safety Act of 1986," Pub.L. 99–570 (49 U.S.C. § 2701 et seq.). The director may make such applications as he deems appropriate to the Secretary of the United States Department of Transportation to obtain any waiver permitted under federal law. *L.1990, c. 103, § 21, eff. Nov. 9, 1990.*

39:3–10.30. Fees; duration of examination of learner's permit; testing opportunities; expiration of commercial driver license

Notwithstanding the provisions of R.S.39:3–14 or any other sections of law which permit or require the issuance of a driver's license without charge, the required fee for a commercial driver license examination or learner's permit shall be $35. A permit issued before April 1, 1992 shall be valid for a period of two years from the date of issuance, unless another time period is established for such permits in federal regulations promulgated by the Secretary of the United States Department of Transportation. The permit holder shall have unlimited testing opportunities consistent with the scheduling obligations of the Division of Motor

Vehicles and the need to provide testing opportunities to all persons affected by this act. For an examination or learner's permit issued on or after April 1, 1992, the director may limit the permit's validity to a specific length of time or number of testing opportunities.

After the issuance of a commercial driver license, the examination or learner's permit fee for an additional endorsement or license class shall be $10 per endorsement or class.

In addition to fees for a basic driver license and any non-commercial endorsement and renewals thereof, the required fee for a 48–month licensing period shall be $18 for each commercial driver license and renewal thereof and $2 for each endorsement and renewal thereof. In addition, the director shall charge a fee of $6 for a digitized picture of the licensee.

The commercial driver license shall expire on the last day of the 48th calendar month following the calendar month in which the license was issued. However, the director may, at his discretion, issue licenses and endorsements which shall expire on a date fixed by him. The fee for such licenses or endorsements shall be fixed in amounts proportionately less or greater than the fee otherwise established.

Nothing in this section shall be construed to alter or change any expiration date on any New Jersey commercial driver license issued prior to the operative date of P.L.2001, c. 391 (C.39:3–10 et al.) and, unless a licensee's driving privileges are otherwise suspended or revoked, except as provided in R.S.39:3–10, the license shall remain valid until its expiration date. *L.1990, c. 103, § 22, eff. Nov. 9, 1990. Amended by L.1999, c. 28, § 5, eff. Jan. 1, 2000; L.2001, c. 391, § 6, eff. Jan. 8, 2002.*

39:3–10.31. Waiver of road test for completion of motorcycle safety education course

The Director of the Division of Motor Vehicles may waive the road test portion of the examinations required for a motorcycle license or endorsement under R.S.39:3–10 for the holder of an examination permit who has successfully completed a motorcycle safety education course established under the provisions of section 1 of P.L.1991, c. 452 (C. 27:5F–36). *L.1991, c. 452, § 6, eff. July 1, 1992.*

39:3–10.32. Violations; disorderly persons offense

In addition to any other penalty provided by law, a school bus driver who violates section 5 of P.L.1990, c. 103 (C.39:3–10.13) or section 16 of P.L.1990, c. 103 (C.39:3–10.24) while transporting school children shall be guilty of a disorderly persons offense.

Notwithstanding any other provision of law to the contrary, a conviction under this section shall not merge with a conviction for a violation of R.S.39:4–50, section 2 of P.L.1981, c. 512 (C.39:4–50.4a), section 5 of

P.L.1990, c. 103 (C.39:3–10.13) or section 16 of P.L. 1990, c. 103 (C.39:3–10. 24).

L.2003, c. 66, § 6, eff. Nov. 1, 2003.

39:3–10.33. Request for medical review or retesting of certain motor vehicle operators; confirmation of notices

a. Whenever a person contacts the New Jersey Motor Vehicle Commission requesting that a family member be given a medical review or be retested to determine whether that family member is capable of safely operating a motor vehicle in this State, upon a request by the person who contacted the commission, the commission shall send confirmation that a notice has been sent regarding a medical review or retesting of the family member to the person who contacted the commission.

b. Whenever the commission is required to send a subsequent notice regarding a medical review or retesting in order to determine whether such a family member is capable of safely operating a motor vehicle in this State because there was no response to the first such notice, upon a request by the person who contacted the commission, the commission shall send a confirmation of that subsequent notice to the person who originally contacted the commission.

L.2005, c. 255, § 1, eff. Jan. 4, 2006.

39:3–11. Driver's license with restrictions or conditions; violations; punishment

Whenever, in the interest of public safety, the director determines that good cause appears therefor he may, in issuing any driver's license, impose thereon: (a) any reasonable restrictions and conditions in light of the applicant's physical condition and driving ability including conditions with respect to the type of, or special control devices required on, a motor vehicle which such applicant may operate; and (b) such other reasonable conditions or restrictions applicable to the applicant as the director may ascertain by tests approved by him to be appropriate to assure the safe operation of a motor vehicle by such applicant.

It shall be unlawful for any person to whom a conditional or restricted driver's license has been issued to operate a motor vehicle in violation of any of the conditions or restrictions upon such license.

Any person to whom a conditional or restricted driver's license has been issued who operates a motor vehicle in violation of any of the conditions or restrictions upon such license shall be subject to a fine not exceeding one hundred dollars ($100.00) or imprisonment for a term not exceeding thirty days, or both.

Amended by L.1953, c. 73, p. 987, § 1.

39:3–11a. Hearing impaired persons; special driver's license; fee

Upon application by any person with a hearing loss of a pure tone average of 41 dB or greater, verified by an otorhinolaryngologist (ENT) or by an audiologist clinically certified by the American Speech, Language, and Hearing Association, the Director of the Division of Motor Vehicles shall issue to the applicant a special driver's license bearing either the international symbol of the deaf or a numerical code designating hearing-impairment, whichever shall be specified by the applicant. The design of the special driver's license shall be approved by the Director of the Division of Motor Vehicles. No fee over and above the required fee for a driver's license shall be imposed for the special driver's license.

L.1983, c. 493, § 1, eff. July 16, 1984.

39:3–11b. Rules and regulations

Pursuant to the "Administrative Procedure Act," P.L. 1968, c. 410 (C. 52:14B–1 et seq.), the Director of the Division of Motor Vehicles shall promulgate rules and regulations to effectuate the purposes of this act.

L.1983, c. 493, § 2, eff. July 16, 1984.

39:3–11.1. License to persons 16 years of age to drive motor vehicles in agricultural pursuits

Any person, under seventeen years of age and not under sixteen years of age, may be licensed to drive motor vehicles in agricultural pursuits as herein limited; provided such person has passed an examination satisfactory to the chief administrator as to his ability as an operator. The chief administrator, upon payment of the lawful fee and after he or a person authorized by him has examined the applicant and is satisfied of the applicant's ability as an operator, may, in his discretion, license the applicant to drive any motor vehicle which is registered under the provisions of R.S.39:3–24 and R.S.39:3–25. The holder of an agricultural permit or license shall be subject to the applicable requirements, restrictions and penalties for special learner's permit holders provided under section 6 of P.L.1977, c. 25 (C.39:3–13.2a). Such registration shall expire on March thirty-first of each year terminating the period for which such license is issued. The annual license fee for such license shall be one dollar ($1.00), and is for the limited use herein provided, and is not to be used in the operation of any other vehicle and shall have the name of the licensee endorsed thereon in his own handwriting. The holder of an agricultural license shall be entitled to a probationary driver's license upon attaining the age of 17 years and shall be subject to applicable restrictions and penalties in section 4 of P.L.1950, c. 127 (C.39:3–13.4) as they pertain to a probationary driver's license holder.

L.1942, c. 324, p. 1162, § 1. Amended by L.1983, c. 403, § 8, eff. Dec. 23, 1983; L.2001, c. 420, § 5, eff. Jan. 8, 2002; L.2009, c. 38, § 4, eff. May 1, 2010.

39:3–11.2.   **Discretion as to granting license; consent of parent or guardian**

The commissioner, in his discretion, may refuse to grant such a license to a person who is, in his estimation, not a proper person to be granted such license. No such license shall be granted by the commissioner unless a parent of, guardian of, or some person who stands in the place of parents to such person shall consent, in writing, that such license be granted.

L.1942, c. 324, p. 1163, § 2.

39:3–11.3.   **Rules and regulations**

The commissioner may make rules and regulations to effectuate the purpose of this act.

L.1942, c. 324, p. 1163, § 3.

39:3–11.4.   **Repealed by L.1953, c. 127, p. 1325, § 1**

39:3–11.5.   **Persons in military or naval service or discharged or released therefrom; "in time of emergency" defined**

Any person, who is the holder of a valid license to drive a motor vehicle at the time he or she enters the active military or naval service of the United States, in time of war or time of emergency, may continue to exercise the driving privilege therein conferred until the expiration of 180 days after the termination of the war or emergency, or for a period of 3 months from the date of his or her discharge or release from such service under conditions other than dishonorable, without payment of any fee therefor to the Director of the Division of Motor Vehicles; provided, however, no such person shall exercise said privilege except when attired in official military uniform or when having in his or her possession evidence of his or her said discharge or release or of his or her active military status or assignment.

As used herein the term "in time of emergency" shall mean and include any time after June 23, 1950, and prior to the termination, suspension or revocation of the proclamation of the existence of a national emergency issued by the President of the United States on December 16, 1950, or termination of the existence of such national emergency by appropriate action of the President or Congress of the United States, and shall also mean and include any time after December 31, 1960, and prior to the date of the termination of the warlike conditions in the southeast Asia area by appropriate action of the President or Congress of the United States.

L.1943, c. 98, p. 321, § 1. Amended by L.1944, c. 38, p. 94, § 1; L.1946, c. 3, p. 16, § 1; L.1953, c. 106, p. 1286, § 1; L.1970, c. 332, § 1, eff. Dec. 29, 1970.

39:3–12.   **Illegal securing of driver's license; punishment**

No applicant for a driver's license shall employ or procure the employment of another person to take the license examination for him, and no person shall take a driver's license examination in the name of or in the place of the applicant. No person shall procure or attempt to procure a driver's license without taking the examination therefor as herein provided, nor shall a person procure or attempt to procure a driver's license for another who has not taken an examination therefor.

A person who violates any provision of this section shall be subject to a fine of not less than two hundred dollars nor more than five hundred dollars, or imprisonment for not less than thirty days nor more than ninety days, or both, at the discretion of the court.

39:3–12.1.   **Application for renewal of registration or license**

Any owner of a passenger automobile or motorcycle, or licensed driver may, if he so desires, apply directly to any agent of the director, as heretofore, for renewal of his registration or license, or both, as the case may be.

L.1955, c. 8, p. 46, § 6.

39:3–12.2.   **Organ donor under the "Uniform Anatomical Gift Act"; designation; real-time electronic access to donor list**

a. The Chief Administrator of the New Jersey Motor Vehicle Commission shall provide with every new license, renewal license, identification card or renewal identification card the opportunity for each person pursuant to the provisions of the "Revised Uniform Anatomical Gift Act," P.L.2008, c. 50 (C.26:6–77 et al.), to designate that the person shall donate all or any organs or tissues for the purposes of transplantation or therapy.

b. The designation indicating that a person is a donor pursuant to subsection a. of this section shall be done in accordance with procedures prescribed by the chief administrator. The designation shall be displayed in print in a conspicuous form and manner on the license or identification card, and electronically, by substantially the following statement: "ORGAN DONOR" and shall constitute sufficient legal authority for the removal of organs or tissues for the purposes of transplantation or therapy upon the death of the licensee or identification cardholder. The designation shall be removed in accordance with procedures prescribed by the chief administrator.

c. (Deleted by amendment, P.L.1999, c. 28).

d. (Deleted by amendment, P.L.2007, c. 80).

e. The chief administrator, in consultation with those organ procurement organizations designated pursuant to 42 U.S.C. s.1320b–8 to serve in the State of New Jersey, shall establish and provide an annual education program for agency employees and personnel. The program shall focus on the benefits associated with organ and tissue donations, the scope and operation of New Jersey's donor program, and how the agency's employees and personnel can effectively inform the public about the donor program and can best assist those wishing to participate in the donor program, including use of the Donate Life NJ Registry, established pursuant to P.L.2008, c. 48 (C.26:6-66 et al.).

f. The chief administrator shall electronically record and store all organ donor designations and identification information, and shall provide the organ procurement organizations designated pursuant to 42 U.S.C. s.1320b–8 to serve in the State of New Jersey with real-time electronic access to the organ donor designation information collected pursuant to subsection a. of this section. An organ procurement organization designated pursuant to 42 U.S.C. s.1320b–8 to serve in the State of New Jersey, or any donor registry established by any such organization, shall have real-time electronic access to those organ donor designations and identification at all times, without exception, for the purposes of verifying organ and tissue donation status and identity. For these purposes, the federally designated organ procurement organization shall have electronic access to each recorded donor's name, address, date of birth, gender, color of eyes, height, and driver's license number. Upon request, the chief administrator shall provide a copy of the donor's original driver's license application.

g. Those organ procurement organizations designated pursuant to 42 U.S.C. s.1320b–8 to serve in the State of New Jersey may contract with a third party, in consultation with the chief administrator, to assess, develop, and implement any system set-up necessary to support the initial and ongoing electronic access by those organizations to the donor designation and identification information required to be made available in accordance with the provisions of this section; however, the organ procurement organizations shall not be required to incur an aggregate cost in excess of $50,000 for the purposes of this subsection.

L.1978, c. 181, § 1. Amended by L.1999, c. 28, § 6, eff. Jan. 1, 2000; L.2007, c. 80, § 1, eff. Sept. 1, 2007; L.2008, c. 48, § 13; L.2008, c. 50, § 25, eff. July 22, 2008.

39:3–12.3. Donate Life NJ Registry; development and establishment of on-line database; monetary donations to fund

a. (1) Within nine months after the effective date of P.L.2008, c. 48 (C.26:6–66 et al.), the Chief Administrator of the New Jersey Motor Vehicle Commission shall insure access by residents to an Internet-based interface that promotes organ and tissue donation and enables residents 18 years of age or older to register as donors and have their decisions immediately integrated into the current database maintained by the commission. The database shall include only affirmative donation decisions.

(2) Within one year of the effective date of P.L.2008, c. 48 (C.26:6–66 et al.), the commission shall establish a system which allows New Jersey holders of driver's licenses or personal identification cards who do not have access to the Internet-based interface to add their

donor designation to the Donate Life NJ Registry by submitting a paper form to the commission.

Registration shall be provided at no cost to the registrant.

b. The database and Internet-based interface established in this section shall be known as the Donate Life NJ Registry.

c. The form and content of the Internet-based interface shall be designed in collaboration with the organ procurement organizations designated pursuant to 42 U.S.C. s.1320b–8 to serve in the State of New Jersey.

d. Donor information entered into the registry shall supersede any prior conflicting information provided to the registry or on the individual's driver's license or identification card, and pursuant to section 2 of P.L. 1969, c. 161 (C.26:6–58) and section 1 of P.L.1987, c. 244 (C.26:6–58.1) or any subsequent statute adopted pursuant thereto, registration by a donor shall constitute sufficient authorization to donate organ and tissues for transplantation and therapy and authorization of another person shall not be necessary to effectuate the gift.

e. Within one year of the effective date of P.L.2008, c. 48 (C.26:6–66 et al.), the Donate Life NJ Registry and the official website of the commission shall provide links through which individuals may make voluntary contributions of $1.00 or more to the Organ and Tissue Donor Awareness Education Fund established by P.L.1999, c. 386 (C.54A:9–25.17 et seq.). Such opportunities shall include both electronic and paper contributions. The links shall be provided in connection with the issuance of licenses, personal identification cards, and the registration of motor vehicles.

L.2008, c. 48, § 7, eff. July 22, 2008.

39:3–12.4. Drivers license or ID card registration or renewal; donations to Donate Life NJ Registry via on-line portal

a. Beginning five years after the effective date of P.L.2008, c. 48 (C.26:6–66 et al.), no driver's license or personal identification card shall be issued or renewed unless the applicant first addresses the issue of donation through an on-line portal connected to the Donate Life NJ Registry or at New Jersey Motor Vehicle Commission agencies and regional service centers. This section shall not apply to applicants for provisional licenses or personal identification cards who are under the age of 18.

b. The portal shall be accessible to applicants seven days per week, 24 hours per day, and shall provide for adequate security to protect an individual's privacy. The form and content of the portal shall be designed in collaboration with the organ procurement organizations designated pursuant to 42 U.S.C. s.1320b–8 to serve in the State of New Jersey.

c. The portal shall require a resident who has not registered as an organ donor, and who seeks a driver's license or identification card or seeks renewal thereof, to either: (1) register as an organ donor through the Donate Life NJ Registry; or (2) review information about the life-saving potential of organ and tissue donation, and the consequences when an individual does not make a decision to become an organ donor and does not register or otherwise record a designated decision-maker.

In addition to promoting organ and tissue donation, the portal shall provide information about the procedure for designating a decision-maker.

d.   Any information technology system adopted by the commission after the effective date of P.L.2008, c. 48 (C.26:6–66 et al.) shall accommodate the inclusion of donor information into the database and the on-going operation of the Donate Life NJ Registry.

L.2008, c. 48, § 8, eff. July 22, 2008.

39:3–12.5. Federal or private grants for development and implementation of registry; receipt and expenditure of funds

a.   For purposes of the development and implementation of the Donate Life NJ Registry, the New Jersey Motor Vehicle Commission shall collaborate with the organ procurement organizations designated pursuant to 42 U.S.C. s.1320b–8 to serve in the State of New Jersey in applying for any federal or private grants recommended by the organ procurement organizations.

b.   The Chief Administrator of the commission shall collaborate with the organ procurement organizations designated pursuant to 42 U.S.C. s.1320b–8 to serve in the State of New Jersey to identify, and if appropriate, apply for and accept on behalf of the State any relevant grants from the federal government or any agency thereof, or from any foundation, corporation, association or individual.   Any money so received may be expended by the commission, subject to any limitations imposed in such grants to effect any of the purposes of the commission upon warrant of the Director of the Division of Budget and Accounting of the Department of the Treasury on vouchers certified and approved by the director.   The power herein granted shall be in addition to and shall in no way limit the authority granted to the chief administrator by other existing law.

c.   The commission, and the Departments of Human Services, Health and Senior Services, and Law and Public Safety may collaborate with the organ procurement organizations designated to serve in the State of New Jersey in applying for any federal or private grants recommended by the organ procurement organizations.

L.2008, c. 48, § 9, eff. July 22, 2008.

39:3–13. Examination and special learner's permit; scope and effect; fees

The chief administrator may, in his discretion, issue to a person over 17 years of age an examination permit, under the hand and seal of the chief administrator, allowing such person, for the purpose of fitting himself to become a licensed driver, to operate a designated class of motor vehicles other than passenger automobiles and motorcycles of persons licensed to operate motorcycles only for a specified period of not more than 90 days, while in the company and under the supervision of a driver licensed to operate such designated class of motor vehicles.

The chief administrator, in his discretion, may issue for a specified period of not less than one year a passenger automobile or motorcycle-only examination permit to a person over 17 years of age regardless of whether a person has completed a course of behind-the-wheel automobile driving education pursuant to section 1 of P.L.1950, c. 127 (C.39:3–13.1).   An examination permit applicant who is under 18 years of age shall obtain the signature of a parent or guardian for submission to the commission on a form prescribed by the chief administrator.   The chief administrator shall postpone for six months the driving privileges of any person who submits a fraudulent signature for a parent or guardian.

For six months immediately following the validation of an examination permit, and until the holder passes the road test, the holder who is less than 21 years of age shall operate the passenger automobile or motorcycle only when accompanied by, and under the supervision of, a New Jersey licensed driver who is at least 21 years of age and has been licensed to drive a passenger automobile or motorcycle, as the case may be, for not less than three years.   The holder of an examination permit who is at least 21 years of age shall operate the passenger automobile or motorcycle for the first three months under such supervision and until the holder passes the road test.   The supervising driver of the passenger automobile shall sit in the front seat of the vehicle.   Whenever operating a vehicle while in possession of an examination permit, the holder of the permit shall operate the passenger automobile with only one additional passenger in the vehicle excluding dependents of the permit holder, except that this passenger restriction shall not apply when the permit holder is at least 21 years of age or when the permit holder is accompanied by a parent or guardian.   Further, the holder of the permit who is less than 21 years of age shall not drive during the hours between 11:01 p.m. and 5 a.m.; provided, however, that this condition may be waived for an emergency which, in the judgment of local police, is of sufficient severity and magnitude to substantially endanger the health, safety, welfare, or property of a person, or for any bona fide employment or religion-related activity if the employer or appropriate religious authority provides written verification of such activity in a manner provided for by the chief administrator.   The holder of the examination permit shall not use any hand-held or hands-free interactive wireless communication device, except in an emergency, while operating a moving passenger automobile on a public road or highway.   "Use" shall include, but not be limited to, talking or listening on any hand-held or hands-free interactive wireless communication device or operating its keys, buttons, or other controls. The passenger automobile permit holder shall ensure that all occupants of the vehicle are secured in a properly adjusted and fastened seat belt or child restraint system.

The chief administrator shall provide the holder of an examination permit with two removable, transferable, highly visible, reflective decals indicating that the driver of the vehicle may be the holder of an examination permit. The decals shall be designed by the chief administrator, in consultation with the Division of Highway Traffic Safety in the Department of Law and Public Safety. The chief administrator may charge a fee for the decals not to exceed the actual cost of producing and distributing the decals. The decals shall be displayed in a manner prescribed by the chief administrator, in consultation with the Division of Highway Traffic Safety in the Department of Law and Public Safety, and shall be clearly visible to law enforcement officers. The holder of an examination permit shall not operate a vehicle unless the decals are displayed. The decal shall be removed once the driver's examination permit period has ended.

When notified by a court of competent jurisdiction that an examination permit holder has been convicted of a violation which causes the permit holder to accumulate more than two motor vehicle points or has been convicted of a violation of R.S.39:4–50; section 2 of P.L.1981, c. 512 (C.39:4–50.4a); P.L.1992, c. 189 (C.39:4–50.14); R.S.39:4–129; N.J.S.2C:11–5; subsection c. of N.J.S.2C:12–1; or any other motor vehicle-related law the chief administrator deems significant and applicable pursuant to regulation, in addition to any other penalty that may be imposed, the chief administrator shall, without the exercise of discretion or a hearing, suspend the examination permit holder's examination permit for 90 days. The chief administrator shall restore the permit following the term of the permit suspension if the permit holder satisfactorily completes a remedial training course of not less than four hours which may be given by the commission, a driving school licensed by the chief administrator pursuant to section 2 of P.L.1951, c. 216 (C.39:12–2), or any Statewide safety organization approved by the chief administrator. The course shall be subject to oversight by the commission according to its guidelines. The permit holder shall also remit a course fee prior to the commencement of the course. The chief administrator also shall postpone without the exercise of discretion or a hearing the issuance of a basic license for 90 days if the chief administrator is notified by a court of competent jurisdiction that the examination permit holder, after completion of the remedial training course, has been convicted of any motor vehicle violation which results in the imposition of any motor vehicle points or has been convicted of a violation of R.S.39:4–50; section 2 of P.L.1981, c. 512 (C.39:4–50.4a); P.L.1992, c. 182 (C.39:4–50.14); R.S.39:4–129; N.J.S.2C:11–5, subsection c. of N.J.S.2C:12–1 or any other motor vehicle-related law the chief administrator deems significant and applicable pursuant to regulation. When the chief administrator is notified by a court of competent

jurisdiction that an examination permit holder has been convicted of any alcohol or drug-related offense unrelated to the operation of a motor vehicle and is not otherwise subject to any other suspension penalty therefor, the chief administrator shall, without the exercise of discretion or a hearing, suspend the examination permit for six months.

An examination permit for a motorcycle or a commercial motor vehicle issued to a handicapped person, as determined by the New Jersey Motor Vehicle Commission after consultation with the Department of Education, shall be valid for nine months or until the completion of the road test portion of his license examination, whichever period is shorter.

Each permit shall be sufficient license for the person to operate such designated class of motor vehicles in this State during the period specified, while in the company of and under the control of a driver licensed by this State to operate such designated class of motor vehicles, or, in the case of a commercial driver license permit, while in the company of and under the control of a holder of a valid commercial driver license for the appropriate license class and with the appropriate endorsements issued by this or any other state. Such person, as well as the licensed driver, except for a motor vehicle examiner administering a driving skills test, shall be held accountable for all violations of this subtitle committed by such person while in the presence of the licensed driver. In addition to requiring an applicant for an examination permit to submit satisfactory proof of identity and age, the chief administrator also shall require the applicant to provide, as a condition for obtaining the permit, satisfactory proof that the applicant's presence in the United States is authorized under federal law. If the chief administrator has reasonable cause to suspect that any document presented by an applicant as proof of identity, age, or legal residency is altered, false, or otherwise invalid, the chief administrator shall refuse to grant the permit until such time as the document may be verified by the issuing agency to the chief administrator's satisfaction.

The holder of an examination permit shall be required to take a road test in order to obtain a probationary license. No road test for any person who has been issued an examination permit to operate a passenger vehicle shall be given unless the person has met the requirements of this section. No road test for a probationary license shall be given unless the applicant has first secured an examination permit and no such road test shall be scheduled for an applicant who has secured an examination permit for a passenger vehicle or a motorcycle for which an endorsement is not required until at least six months for an applicant under 21 years of age or three months for an applicant 21 years of age or older shall have elapsed following the validation of the examination permit for practice driving or, in the case of an examination permit for other vehicles, until 20 days have elapsed. In the case of an omnibus endorsement or school bus, no road test shall be scheduled until at least 10 days shall have elapsed. Every applicant for an examination permit to qualify for an omnibus endorsement or an articulated vehicle endorsement shall be a holder of a valid basic driver's license.

The required fees for special learner's permits and examination permits shall be as follows:

Basic driver's license . . . . up to $10

Motorcycle license or endorsement . . . . $ 5

Omnibus or school bus endorsement. $25

The chief administrator shall waive the payment of fees for issuance of examination permits for omnibus endorsements whenever the applicant establishes to the chief administrator's satisfaction that said applicant will use the omnibus endorsement exclusively for operating omnibuses owned by a nonprofit organization duly incorporated under Title 15 or 16 of the Revised Statutes or Title 15A of the New Jersey Statutes.

The specified period for which a permit is issued may be extended for not more than an additional 60 days, without payment of an added fee, upon application made by the holder thereof, where the holder has applied to take the examination for a driver's license prior to the expiration of the original period for which the permit was issued and the chief administrator was unable to schedule an examination during said period.

As a condition for the issuance of an examination permit under this section, the chief administrator shall secure a digitized picture of the applicant. The picture shall be stored in a manner prescribed by the chief administrator and may be displayed on the examination permit.

The chief administrator may require that whenever a person to whom an examination permit has been issued has reconstructive or cosmetic surgery which significantly alters the person's facial features, the person shall notify the chief administrator who may require the picture of the person to be updated.

Specific use of the examination permit and any information stored or encoded, electronically or otherwise, in relation thereto shall be in accordance with P.L.1997, c. 188 (C.39:2–3.3 et seq.) and the federal Driver's Privacy Protection Act of 1994, Pub. L.103–322. Notwithstanding the provisions of any other law to the contrary, the digitized picture or any access thereto or any use thereof shall not be sold, leased or exchanged for value.

Amended by L.1947, c. 247, p. 921, § 1; 1955, c. 8, p. 46, § 7; L.1965, c. 58, § 1; L.1967, c. 238, § 2, eff. Jan. 1, 1968; L.1968, c. 130, § 3, eff. Aug. 1, 1968; L.1975, c. 180, § 4, eff. Jan. 1, 1976; L.1977, c. 25, § 3, eff. Feb. 24, 1977; L.1979, c. 97, § 2, eff. May 24, 1979; L.1979, c. 360, § 1, eff. Feb. 1, 1980; L.1980 c. 105, § 8, eff. Sept. 11, 1980; L.1986, c. 23, § 1, eff. June 3, 1986; L.1990, c. 103, § 28, eff. Nov. 9, 1990; L.1993, c. 34, § 2, eff. Jan. 29, 1993; L.1998, c. 108, § 3, eff. Jan. 1, 2001; L.2001, c. 391, § 12, eff. Jan. 8, 2002; L.2001, c. 420, § 6, eff. Jan. 8, 2002; L.2003, c. 204, § 4, eff. Jan. 6, 2004; L.2009, c. 37, § 2, eff. May 1, 2010; L.2009, c. 38, § 5, eff. May 1, 2010.

39:3–13a. Written examination administered in high school; student with cognitive difficulty; grading

Whenever the director authorizes a written examination to be administered in a high school as part of a driver education program and accepts the results thereof in satisfaction of any written examination requirement imposed pursuant to R.S. 39:3–10, he shall allow the examination to be read by a certified driver education instructor or special education teacher to any student who has been diagnosed by a local child study team, pursuant to N.J.S. 18A:46–5, as having a deficiency in reading, perception, or other cognitive difficulty associated with any learning disability, with the student recording his responses on the appropriate answer sheet. The director may make rules and regulations necessary to carry out the provisions of this section.

L.1982, c. 188, § 1, eff. Dec. 1, 1982.

39:3–13b. Minor's driving record; parent or guardian's request for information

Upon request, the Motor Vehicle Commission shall provide the parent or guardian of a special learner's permit holder, an examination permit holder, or a probationary license holder under 18 years of age with information pertaining to the driving privilege status and any vehicular accident or violation information on the minor's driving record. When requesting this information about the minor's driving record, the parent or guardian shall be required to provide the parent or guardian's name, date of birth, address, and driver's license number as well as the name, date of birth, address, and driver's license number of the permit or probationary license holder.

L.2007, c. 285, § 1, eff. Jan. 13, 2008. Amended by L.2009, c. 38, § 6, eff. May 1, 2010.

39:3–13.1. Special learner's permit; place of keeping

The Chief Administrator of the New Jersey Motor Vehicle Commission may issue to a person over 16 years of age a special learner's permit, under the hand and seal of the chief administrator, allowing such person, for the purpose of preparing himself to qualify for a probationary license for a passenger automobile by operating a dual pedal controlled motor vehicle while taking a required course of behind-the-wheel automobile driving education approved by the State Department of Education and conducted in a public, parochial or private school of this State or a course of behind-the-wheel automobile driving instruction conducted by a drivers' school duly licensed pursuant to the provisions of P.L.1951, c. 216 (C.39:12–1 et seq.). The special learner's permit shall be issued in lieu of the examination permit provided for in R.S. 39:3–13. In addition to requiring an applicant for a permit to submit satisfactory proof of identity and age, the chief administrator also shall require the applicant to provide, as a condition for obtaining a permit, satisfactory proof that the applicant's presence in the United States is authorized under federal law. If the chief administrator has reasonable cause to suspect that any document presented by an applicant as proof of identity, age or legal residency is altered, false or otherwise invalid, the chief administrator shall refuse to grant the permit until such time as the document may be verified by the issuing agency to the chief administrator's satisfaction.

The special learner's permit described above, when issued to a person taking a course of behind-the-wheel driving education conducted in a public, parochial or private school, shall be retained in the office of the school principal at all times except during such time as the person to whom the permit is issued is undergoing behind-the-wheel automobile driving instruction. The chief administrator may make such rules and regulations as he may deem necessary to carry out the provisions of this section.

L.1950, c. 127, p. 237, § 1. Amended by L.1951, c. 7, p. 27, § 1; L.1975, c. 129, § 1, eff. June 27, 1975; L.1977, c. 25, § 4, eff. Feb. 24, 1977; L.1993, c. 34, § 3, eff. Jan. 29, 1993; L.1998, c. 108, § 4, eff. Jan. 1, 2001; L.2001, c. 391, § 13, eff. Jan. 8, 2002; L.2003, c. 204, § 2, eff. Jan. 6, 2004; L.2009, c. 38, § 7, eff. May 1, 2010.

39:3–13.2. Scope and effect of special learner's permit

The special permit shall be sufficient license for the person to operate a dual pedal controlled motor vehicle in this State during the period specified, while in the company of and under the control of a teacher, certified by the State Department of Education as authorized to instruct in an approved behind-the-wheel automobile driving education course or a duly licensed instructor of a drivers' school, or while in the company of a representative of the Division of Motor Vehicles for the purpose of submitting to examination for a driver's license. Such person, as well as the said teacher or instructor, shall be held accountable for all violations of subtitle 1 of Title 39 of the Revised Statutes[1] and any supplements thereto committed by such person while in the presence of the teacher or instructor.

L.1950, c. 127, p. 237, § 2. Amended by L.1977, c. 25, § 5, eff. Feb. 24, 1977.

[1] N.J.S.A. §§ 39:1–1 to 39:5F–30.

39:3–13.2a. Special learner's permit; duration

a. Any person to whom a special learner's permit has been issued pursuant to section 1 of P.L.1950, c. 127 (C.39:3–13.1), upon successful completion of a State approved written examination, eye examination and an approved minimum six-hour behind-the-wheel driving course, shall be entitled to retain the special learner's permit in his own possession. The special learner's permit shall be validated by the commission for the purpose of driving a motor vehicle on a public highway in this State after the holder has successfully met the necessary examination requirements, and upon the successful completion of a behind-the-wheel driving course. Such person may operate a motor vehicle of the class for which a basic driver's license is required except during the hours between 11:01 p.m. and 5:00

a.m. while in the company and under the supervision, from the front passenger seat, of a licensed motor vehicle driver of this State who is over 21 years of age and has been licensed to drive a passenger automobile for at least three years. Such special permit shall be valid until such person's seventeenth birthday or until he qualifies for a probationary license. Except during an instructional period of a behind-the-wheel driving course, the holder of a special permit shall operate a passenger automobile with only the following passengers: (1) the supervising passenger; (2) any parent, guardian, or dependent of the special permit holder; and (3) one additional passenger. The holder of the special learner's permit shall not use any hand-held or hands-free interactive wireless communication device, except in an emergency, while operating a moving passenger automobile on a public road or highway. "Use" shall include, but not be limited to, talking or listening on any hand-held or hands-free interactive wireless communication device or operating its keys, buttons, or other controls. All occupants of the automobile shall be secured in a properly adjusted and fastened seat belt or child restraint system.

The chief administrator shall provide the holder of a special learner's permit with two removable, transferable, highly visible, reflective decals indicating that the driver of the vehicle may be the holder of a special learner's permit. The decals shall be designed by the chief administrator, in consultation with the Division of Highway Traffic Safety in the Department of Law and Public Safety. The chief administrator may charge a fee for the decals not to exceed the actual cost of producing and distributing the decals. The decals shall be displayed in a manner prescribed by the chief administrator, in consultation with the Division of Highway Traffic Safety in the Department of Law and Public Safety, and shall be clearly visible to law enforcement officers. The holder of a special learner's permit shall not operate a vehicle unless the decals are displayed. The decal shall be removed once the driver's special learner's permit period has ended.

b. When notified by a court of competent jurisdiction that a special learner's permit holder has been convicted of a violation which causes the permit holder to accumulate more than two motor vehicle points or has been convicted of a violation of R.S.39:4–50; section 2 of P.L.1981, c. 512 (C.39:4–50.4a); P.L.1992, c. 189 (C.39:4–50.14); R.S.39:4–129; N.J.S.2C:11–5; subsection c. of N.J.S.2C:12–1; or any other motor vehicle-related law the chief administrator determines to be significant and applicable pursuant to regulation, and in addition to any other penalty that may be imposed, the chief administrator shall, without the exercise of discretion or a hearing, suspend the holder's special learner's permit for 90 days. The chief administrator shall restore the permit following the term of the permit suspension if the permit holder, regardless of age, satisfactorily completes a remedial training course of not less than four hours which may be given by the commission, a driving school licensed by the chief administrator pursuant to section 2 of P.L.1951, c. 216 (C.39:12–2), or any Statewide safety organization approved by the chief administrator. The course shall be administered pursuant to rules and regulations promulgated by the chief administrator and subject to oversight by the commission. The authority of the chief administrator to suspend, revoke, or deny issuance of an initial or renewal license to operate a driving school or an instructor's license, and to assess fines, pursuant to P.L.1951, c. 216 (C.39:12–1 et seq.) shall apply to any violations related to the administration of a remedial training course. The permit holder shall also remit a course fee prior to the commencement of the course. If, after completion of the remedial training course, the chief administrator is notified by a court of competent jurisdiction that the special learner's permit holder has been convicted of any motor vehicle violation which results in the imposition of any motor vehicle points or has been convicted of a violation of R.S.39:4–50; section 2 of P.L.1981, c. 512 (C.39:4–50.4a); P.L.1992, c. 189 (C.39:4–50.14); R.S.39:4–129; N.J.S.2C:11–5; subsection c. of N.J.S.2C:12–1; or any other motor vehicle-related law the chief administrator deems significant and applicable pursuant to regulation, the chief administrator, without the exercise of discretion or a hearing, shall also postpone the issuance of a basic license for 90 days. When the chief administrator is notified by a court of competent jurisdiction that a special learner's permit holder has been convicted of any alcohol or drug-related offense unrelated to the operation of a motor vehicle and he is not otherwise subject to any other suspension penalty therefor, the chief administrator shall, without the exercise of discretion or a hearing, suspend the special learner's permit for six months.

L.1977, c. 25, § 6, eff. Feb. 24, 1977. Amended by L.1979, c. 13, § 1, eff. Feb. 8, 1979; L.1981, c. 80, § 1, eff. March 25, 1981; L.1983, c. 497, § 1, eff. Jan. 17, 1984; L.1993, c. 287, § 1, eff. Dec. 16, 1993; L.1998, c. 108, § 5, eff. Jan. 1, 2001; L.2001, c. 420, § 7, eff. Jan. 8, 2002; L.2009, c. 37, § 1, eff. May 1, 2010; L.2009, c. 38, § 8, eff. May 1, 2010.

39:3–13.3.   Application for special permit

No special permit shall be issued unless the person applying therefor shall present a written application for the same, bearing a certification by the principal of the school indicating that the person is enrolled in an approved behind-the-wheel driving education course in the school of which he is principal or by the person operating a duly licensed drivers' school indicating that the person has contracted to take a course of behind-the-wheel automobile driving instruction offered by the school and shall pay a sum of up to $10 as determined by the director to an agent of the Division of Motor Vehicles, which sum shall be turned over by the agent to the director, and by him remitted with the other funds collected in his division to the State Treasurer, in accordance with law. A special learner's permit to operate a passenger automobile shall not be issued to

any person younger than 18 years of age without the signature of a parent or guardian. The signature shall be submitted to the division on a form prescribed by the director. The director shall postpone for six months the driving privileges of any person who submits a fraudulent signature for a parent or guardian.

L.1950, c. 127, p. 237, § 3. Amended by L.1977, c. 25, § 7, eff. Feb. 24, 1977; L.1998, c. 108, § 6, eff. Jan. 1, 2001.

39:3–13.4.   Examination for driver's license

a.   The holder of a special learner's permit shall be entitled to a probationary driver's license (1) upon attaining the age of 17 years, (2) upon the satisfactory completion of an approved behind-the-wheel driver training course as indicated upon the face of the special permit over the signature of the principal of the school or the person operating the driving school in which the course was conducted, (3) upon the completion of six months' driving experience with a validated special learner's permit in compliance with the provisions of section 6 of P.L.1977, c. 25 (C.39:3–13.2a), and (4) upon passing the road test pursuant to R.S.39:3–10.

b.   The holder of a probationary license shall be permitted to operate the passenger automobile with only one additional passenger in the vehicle besides any dependent of the probationary license holder, except that this passenger restriction shall not apply when the holder of the probationary license is at least 21 years of age or the probationary license holder is accompanied by a parent or guardian. Further, the holder of the probationary license who is under 21 years of age shall not drive during the hours between 11:01 p.m. and 5 a.m.; provided however, that this condition may be waived for an emergency which, in the judgment of local police, is of sufficient severity and magnitude to substantially endanger the health, safety, welfare, or property of a person or for any bona fide employment or religion-related activity if the employer or appropriate religious authority provides written verification of such activity in a manner provided for by the chief administrator.

c.   The holder of the probationary license shall not use any hand-held or hands-free interactive wireless communication device, except in an emergency, while operating a moving passenger automobile on a public road or highway. "Use" shall include, but not be limited to, talking or listening on any hand-held or hands-free interactive wireless communication device or operating its keys, buttons, or other controls. In addition, the holder of the probationary license shall ensure that all occupants of the vehicle are secured in a properly adjusted and fastened seat belt or child restraint system.

d.   In addition to any other penalties provided under law, the holder of a probationary license who accumulates more than two motor vehicle points or is convicted of a violation of R.S.39:4–50; section 2 of P.L.1981, c. 512 (C.39:4–50.4a); P.L.1992, c. 189 (C.39:4–50.14);

R.S. 39:4–129; N.J.S.2C:11–5; subsection c. of N.J.S.2C:12–1; or any other motor vehicle law the chief administrator deems to be significant and applicable pursuant to regulation shall, for the first violation, be required to satisfactorily complete a remedial training course of not less than four hours which may be given by the commission, a driving school licensed by the chief administrator pursuant to section 2 of P.L.1951, c. 216 (C.39:12–2), or any Statewide safety organization approved by the chief administrator. The course shall be administered pursuant to rules and regulations promulgated by the chief administrator and subject to oversight by the commission. The authority of the chief administrator to suspend, revoke, or deny issuance of an initial or renewal license to operate a driving school or an instructor's license, and to assess fines, pursuant to P.L.1951, c. 216 (C.39:12–1 et seq.) shall apply to any violations related to the administration of a remedial training course. The license holder shall also remit a course fee prior to the commencement of the course.

e. When notified by a court of competent jurisdiction that a probationary license holder has been convicted of a second or subsequent violation, in addition to any other penalties provided under law, the chief administrator shall, without the exercise of discretion or a hearing, suspend the probationary license for three months, and shall postpone eligibility for a basic license for an equivalent period. In addition, when the chief administrator is notified by a court of competent jurisdiction that a probationary license holder has been convicted of any alcohol or drug-related offense unrelated to the operation of a motor vehicle, and he is not otherwise subject to any other suspension penalty therefor, the chief administrator shall, without the exercise of discretion or a hearing, suspend the probationary license for six months.

f. The chief administrator shall provide the holder of a provisional license with two removable, transferable, highly visible, reflective decals indicating that the driver of the vehicle may be the holder of a provisional license. The decals shall be designed by the chief administrator, in consultation with the Division of Highway Traffic Safety in the Department of Law and Public Safety. The chief administrator may charge a fee for the decals not to exceed the actual cost of producing and distributing the decals. The decals shall be displayed in a manner prescribed by the chief administrator, in consultation with the Division of Highway Traffic Safety in the Department of Law and Public Safety, and shall be clearly visible to law enforcement officers. The holder of a provisional license shall not operate a vehicle unless the decals are displayed. The decal shall be removed once the driver's provisional license period has ended.

g. A probationary license may be sent by mail and shall be clearly identifiable and distinguishable in appearance from a basic license by any name, mark, color,

or device deemed appropriate by the chief administrator.

L.1950, c. 127, p. 238, § 4. Amended by L.1951, c. 7, p. 28, § 2; L.1977, c. 25, § 8, eff. Feb. 24, 1977; L.1998, c. 108, § 7, eff. Jan. 1, 2001; L.2001, c. 420, § 8, eff. Jan. 8, 2002; L.2009, c. 37, § 3, eff. May 1, 2010; L.2009, c. 38, § 9, eff. May 1, 2010.

39:3–13.5. Repealed by L.1990, c. 103, § 38, eff. Nov. 9, 1990

39:3–13.6. Evaluation and report regarding new driver performance

The Division of Motor Vehicles shall monitor the performance of new drivers of passenger automobiles and, in conjunction with the Office of Highway Traffic Safety, report to the Governor and the Legislature evaluating the operation and effectiveness of this act. The Division of Motor Vehicles shall detail the disbursement of monies from the Driver Education Fund in the report. The division and the office shall make any recommendations necessary to better effectuate the provisions of this act.

L.1998, c. 108, § 11, eff. Jan. 1, 2001.

39:3–13.7. Adoption of rules and regulations

The Director of the Division of Motor Vehicles and the Director of the Office of Highway Traffic Safety shall adopt, pursuant to the "Administrative Procedure Act," P.L.1968, c. 410 (C.52:14B–1 et seq.), any rules and regulations each determines to be necessary to effectuate their respective responsibilities under this act.

L.1998, c. 108, § 12, eff. Jan. 1, 2001.

39:3–13.8. Specific violations of certain permits or licenses

A fine of $100 shall be imposed for violating the following conditions of a special learner's permit, an examination permit or a probationary driver's license:

a. supervision requirements for permit holders;

b. passenger restrictions;

c. hours of operation;

d. seat belt requirements;

e. hand-held or hands-free interactive wireless communication device use restrictions;

f. any other violation of the conditions of a permit or probationary license as the chief administrator may designate; or

g. decal requirements.

L.2001, c. 420, § 11, eff. Jan. 8, 2002. Amended by L.2009, c. 37, § 4, eff. May 1, 2010; L.2009, c. 38, § 10, eff. May 1, 2010.

39:3–13.9. Public education campaign

The Division of Highway Traffic Safety in the Department of Law and Public Safety shall develop and undertake a public education campaign to inform the public about the provisions of this act.[1]

L.2009, c. 38, § 11, eff. May 1, 2010.

   1 L.2009, c. 38 (N.J.S.A. § 39:3–10 et al.).

39:3–14. Official drivers licensed free; special certificate; termination and surrender

Every driver operating a state, county or city owned motor vehicle or motorcycle exclusively for the use of the state, county or city shall be licensed to do so without charge by the commissioner in accordance with this chapter. A special certificate, to be prescribed and furnished by the commissioner, shall be issued to him. The license so granted shall, unless otherwise revoked, terminate upon the licensee's ceasing to be an employee of the state, county or city, and it shall, upon demand made therefor by the commissioner, be surrendered.

39:3–15. Operation of motor vehicle by nonresident; touring privileges; seasonal permits; violations; fines

A nonresident owner of any motor vehicle or motor-drawn vehicle which has been registered in accordance with the laws respecting the registration of motor vehicles of the jurisdiction in which the nonresident resides, and which has conspicuously displayed thereon the registration number thereof, may, without complying with the provisions of this subtitle with respect to registration and equipment, operate or permit the operation of such vehicle in this State during such portion of the entire year as the free operation of a similar type of vehicle belonging to a resident of this State and registered in compliance with the laws of this State, and whose registration number is conspicuously displayed thereon, is permitted in the jurisdiction of the nonresident; provided that such vehicle is not:

(a) Used for the transportation of persons for hire, compensation or profit, or

(b) Regularly operated in carrying on business within this State,

(c) Designed, used or maintained primarily for the transportation of property.

The foregoing shall not apply to a vehicle leased by an owner engaged in the business of leasing such vehicles.

Any vehicle properly registered in, and having conspicuously displayed on it the registration number issued by, another jurisdiction may be operated on the highways of this State without complying with the provisions of this subtitle with respect to registration during such portion of the entire year as the director shall determine to be the normal period of seasonal employment in agricultural pursuits, provided a special permit is obtained from the director for such operation, which may be issued to any applicant who satisfies the director that he is engaged in such employment, and upon the payment of a fee of $1.00.

Except as otherwise provided by reciprocity agreement or arrangement entered into by the director, or by a declaration issued by him, the privilege of operation in this State of motor vehicles or motor-drawn vehicles belonging to nonresidents extended by this act shall not permit the intrastate operation of any truck, road tractor, truck tractor or trailer and semitrailer of the commercial type, except that a trailer or semitrailer duly registered in another jurisdiction is extended the privilege of intrastate operation when being drawn by a truck, road tractor, or truck tractor registered in accordance with the provisions of Revised Statutes 39:3–20 and provided that the gross weight of the combination of vehicles, including load, does not exceed the maximum weight allowed by the registration certificate of the drawing vehicle registered in this State. The owner or driver of any vehicle used in intrastate operations not permitted by this section shall be subject to fine in accordance with the following schedule:

   a.   a 2-axle truck, a fine of $288.00;

   b.   a 3-axle truck, a fine of $381.50;

   c.   a 3-axle combination of vehicles, a fine of $475.00;

   d.   a combination of vehicles with more than 3 axles, a fine of $687.50; and

   e.   a commercial motor vehicle having 3 or more axles and a gross weight over 40,000 pounds but not exceeding 70,000 pounds, the owner or driver of which is actually engaged in construction work or in the business of supplying material, transporting material, or using such vehicle for construction work, a fine of $1,120.00.

Amended by L.1938, c. 66, p. 175, § 5, eff. Oct. 1, 1938; L.1938, c. 332, p. 845, § 1, eff. June 14, 1938; L.1939, c. 79, p. 132, § 1; L.1956, c. 97, p. 200, § 1; L.1957, c. 132, p. 514, § 1; L.1966, c. 209, § 1; L.1967, c. 144, § 1, eff. July 7, 1967; L.1969, c. 119, § 2, eff. July 1, 1969; L.1982, c. 217, § 1, eff. Dec. 29, 1982.

39:3–15.1. Rules and regulations; forms

The director may prescribe and provide forms and make such rules and regulations as are necessary to effectuate the purposes of this amendatory act.[1]

L.1956, c. 97, p. 201, § 2.

   1 N.J.S.A. § 39:3–15 and this section.

39:3–16. Authority of commissioner; suspension of touring privileges

The commissioner shall enforce the provisions of sections 39:3–12, 39:3–13 and 39:3–15 to 39:3–17 of this Title, and shall have the power to suspend the operating privilege of all, a class, or a part of any class of motor vehicles and motor-drawn vehicles registered in another State, Territory, Federal district of the United States or province of the Dominion of Canada, or foreign country, when, in his judgment, any such State, Territory, Federal district or foreign country prohibits the free operation therein of a class or part of any class of motor vehicles or motor-drawn vehicles belonging to residents of this State and which have been properly registered in accordance with the laws of this State. The commissioner shall also have power to suspend, for violation of any of the provisions of this subtitle, or on other reasonable grounds, the operating privilege of any motor vehicle or motor-drawn vehicle belonging to a nonresident. In suspending any such operating privilege, the commissioner shall notify the official or body performing the registration duty in the State, Territory, Federal district of the United States or province of the Dominion of Canada, or foreign country, in which the nonresident resides of such action, give public notice of the same and cause the police authorities to be notified. If any such motor vehicle or motor-drawn vehicle whose operating privilege has been suspended shall thereafter be driven in this State, such driving shall constitute a violation of section 39:3–4 of this Title, and the driver of any such vehicle shall be subject to the penalty prescribed in said section 39:3–4.

Amended by L.1939, c. 79, p. 132, § 2.

39:3–17. Touring privileges of nonresident chauffeurs or drivers

The touring privileges allowed by R.S. 39:3–15 are also extended to any nonresident chauffeur or driver who has complied with the law of his resident state, or country, with respect to the licensing of drivers or chauffeurs. No such nonresident shall operate a motor vehicle registered under the laws of this State unless he is seventeen years of age or over. No nonresident shall be permitted to avail himself of the right of driving a New Jersey registered vehicle under his reciprocity privilege unless he is a holder of a driver's license from the state, or country, in which he resides. A nonresident shall, at all times while operating a motor vehicle in this State under this reciprocity provision, have in his possession the registration certificate of the car which he shall be then operating and his driver's license, and shall exhibit them to a police officer or judge who, in the performance of the duties of his office, shall request the same. Any person violating the provisions of this section shall be subject to a fine not exceeding five hundred dollars, or to imprisonment in the county jail for not more than sixty days.

Amended by L.1939, c. 79, p. 133, § 3; L.1983, c. 403, § 9, eff. Dec. 23, 1983.

39:3–17.1. Continuation of nonresident driving rights after becoming resident; vehicle registration after certain date; criminal penalties; repeat offenses

a. Except as provided in section 9 of P.L.1990, c. 103 (C.39:3–10.17), any person who becomes a resident of this State and who immediately prior thereto was authorized to operate and drive a motor vehicle or motor vehicles in this State as a nonresident pursuant to R.S.39:3–15 and R.S.39:3–17, shall not lose his right to so operate and drive such motor vehicle or motor

vehicles by becoming a resident of this State, but such right shall continue to be in full force and effect for 60 days, unless a longer period of reciprocity is otherwise provided by law, after the establishment of his residence in this State in the same manner and to the same extent as though he were a nonresident. The chief administrator shall not issue a driver's license to a person who is entitled to operate a motor vehicle in this State under a reciprocity privilege granted by any law.

b. Any person who becomes a resident of this State and who immediately prior thereto was authorized to operate and drive a motor vehicle or motor vehicles in this State as a nonresident pursuant to R.S.39:3–15 and R.S.39:3–17, shall register any vehicle operated on the public highways of this State within 60 days of so becoming a resident of New Jersey, pursuant to R.S.39:3–4 or section 2 of P.L.1968, c. 439 (C.39:3–8.1).

c. Any person who violates subsection b. of this section is subject to a fine of not more than $250 for a first offense and not more than $500 for a second or subsequent offense.

d. Any person who violates subsection b. of this section a third or subsequent time shall have the vehicle impounded by the law enforcing agency for not less than 96 hours. The vehicle shall only be released to the registered owner upon proof of registration and insurance and payment of all reasonable towing and storage fees.

If the owner of an impounded vehicle fails to claim the impounded vehicle by midnight of the 30th day following the day on which the vehicle was impounded, that vehicle may be sold at auction. Notice of the sale shall be given by the impounding entity by certified mail to the owner of the vehicle, if the owner's name and address are known, and to the lienholder, if the lienholder's name and address are known, and by publication in a form prescribed by the chief administrator by one insertion, at least five days before the date of the sale, in one or more newspapers published in this State and circulating in the municipality in which the vehicle is impounded.

At any time prior to the sale of an impounded vehicle, the owner or other person entitled to the vehicle may reclaim possession upon showing proof of registration and insurance and paying all costs associated with the impound, and reasonable towing and storage fees.

The owner-lessor of an impounded vehicle shall be entitled to reclaim possession without payment or proof of insurance and the lessee shall be liable for all outstanding costs associated with the impoundment, towing, and storage of the vehicle.

e. Any proceeds obtained from the sale of a vehicle at public auction pursuant to subsection d. of this section in excess of the amount owed to the impounding entity for the reasonable costs of towing and storage and any other costs associated with the impoundment of the vehicle shall be returned to the owner of that vehicle, if his name and address are known.

L.1955, c. 53, p. 179, § 1.   Amended by L.1990, c. 103, § 29, eff. Nov. 9, 1990; L.1993, c. 34, § 4, eff. Jan. 29, 1993; L.2007, c. 178, § 1, eff. Sept. 27, 2007.

39:3–18. General registration; "D" or temporary plates; fees

A manufacturer of motor vehicles, motor-drawn vehicles, motor vehicle bodies, motorized bicycles, or motorcycles doing business in this State may, with regard to motor or motor-drawn vehicles, motorized bicycles, or motorcycles owned or controlled by him, obtain general registration and registration plates therefor of the style and kind provided for in this subtitle, with the letter "D" stated thereon. Such plates can be placed on any vehicle or cycle owned or controlled by such manufacturer, but only if it is operated only for shop, demonstration or delivery purposes.

A bona fide converter of commercial motor vehicles, motor-drawn vehicles or motor vehicle chassis doing business in this State may, with regard to motor or motor-drawn vehicles owned or controlled by him, obtain general registration and registration plates therefor of the style and kind provided for in this subtitle, with the letter "D" stated thereon. Such plates can be placed on any vehicles owned or controlled by such converter, but only if such vehicles are operated for shop, demonstration or delivery purposes.

A bona fide dealer in motor vehicles, motor-drawn vehicles or motorcycles doing business in this State and having a license to do business as such issued by the chief administrator may, with regard to motor or motor-drawn vehicles or cycles owned by him, obtain general registration and registration plates therefor of the style and kind provided for in this subtitle, with the letter "D" stated thereon. Such plates shall only be placed on any vehicle or cycle owned by such dealer; and provided, such vehicle is not used for hire. Such vehicles may be assigned to dealership principals or employees for product familiarization or compensation purposes, and may be used for any lawful purpose, including personal use, and personal use by persons authorized by those dealership employees or principals. Any person who shall be convicted of a violation of this paragraph shall be subject to a fine not exceeding $1000.

A bona fide dealer in motorized bicycles, as defined in R.S. 39:1–1, who has an established place of business in this State, may, with regard to motorized bicycles owned by him, obtain general registration and registration plates therefor of the style and kind provided for in this subtitle, with the letter "D" stated thereon. The plates can be placed on a motorized bicycle by the dealer, but only if the motorized bicycle is operated only for shop, demonstration, or delivery purposes.

Any person engaged in the business of financing the purchase of motor or motor-drawn vehicles or motorized bicycles or lending money thereon may, with regard to motor or motor-drawn vehicles or motorized bicycles owned or controlled by him, obtain general registration and registration plates therefor of the style and kind provided for in this subtitle, with the word "temporary" stated thereon. Such plates can be placed on any such vehicle only when it is being transported from the place where it has been kept by the purchaser or borrower to the place where it is to be kept by the repossessor, or when the repossessor desires to operate it for the purpose of demonstration for sale.

Any corporation engaged in the business of insuring motor vehicles, motorized bicycles, or motor-drawn vehicles against theft may, with regard to vehicles owned or controlled by it, obtain general registration and registration plates therefor of the style and kind provided for in this subtitle, with the word "temporary" stated thereon. Such plates can be placed on any such vehicle, if ownership or control thereof has been obtained by virtue of the terms of an insurance against theft contract made by such corporation, and only when the vehicle is to be transported for delivery to the owner thereof from the place where it has been abandoned by or seized from a thief.

Any person, partnership or corporation engaged in the business of transporting motor or motor-drawn vehicles or motorized bicycles from the place of manufacture for delivery to dealers may, with regard to such vehicles, obtain general registration and registration plates therefor of the kind and style provided for in this subtitle, with the word "temporary" stated thereon, but only if the chief administrator is satisfied as to the financial responsibility of such person, partnership or corporation to meet any claim for damages arising out of any automobile accident and satisfactory evidence of such responsibility has been filed with him.

Any person engaged in the business of renting or leasing motor vehicles, motorized bicycles, or motor-drawn vehicles may, with regard to said motor vehicles, motorized bicycles, or motor-drawn vehicles owned by him, obtain general registration and registration plates therefor, provided for in this subtitle, with the word "temporary" stated thereon. Said registration plates may be placed on any motor vehicle, motorized bicycle, or motor-drawn vehicle owned by such person while said vehicle is not individually registered and not in use as a rented or leased vehicle.

A bona fide dealer in "nonconventional" type motor vehicles, as defined in R.S. 39:10–2, who has an established place of business in this State, may, with regard to "nonconventional" type motor vehicles owned by him, obtain general registration and registration plates therefor of the style and kind provided for in this subtitle, with the letter "D" stated thereon. Such plates can be placed on any "nonconventional" type motor vehicle by such dealer, but only if such "nonconventional" type motor vehicle is operated only for shop, demonstration or delivery purposes.

Any person, partnership or corporation engaged in the business of conducting a wholesale automobile auction block in this State for duly licensed dealers only, at least once each week, may, with regard to vehicles controlled by it, obtain general registration and registration plates therefor of the style and kind provided for in this subtitle, with the word "temporary" stated thereon. Such plates can be placed on any vehicle controlled by the auction block, which is to be transported from the place where stored by the owner to the auction block. Such plates may not be displayed on a vehicle sold at the auction block for delivery to the purchaser. Application for such plates shall be approved only if the chief administrator is satisfied as to the financial responsibility of such person, partnership or corporation to meet any claim for damages arising out of any automobile accident and satisfactory proof of such responsibility has been filed with him.

Registration plates issued pursuant to this section shall be a single plate and shall be issued in sets of five and shall bear the letter "D" or the word "temporary" and shall bear a number corresponding to the number on the certificate of registration. The single registration plate shall be displayed in accordance with the provisions of R.S. 39:3–33.

The annual fee for the issuance of a certificate of registration, four duplicates thereof and one set of five single "D" or "temporary" plates bearing a number corresponding to the number on the certificate of registration shall be $100.00; but the annual fee for the issuance of a certificate of registration for motorcycles or motorized bicycles, two duplicates thereof and one set of three single "D" plates bearing a number on the certificate of registration shall be $20.00.

Following the effective date of P.L.2007, c. 335 (C.39:2A–36.1 et al.), the chief administrator may, as a condition for the issuance of general registration and registration plates, require security in an amount deemed sufficient by the chief administrator to secure the prompt return of such plates to the Motor Vehicle Commission when the use and possession of such plates by any person or entity previously entitled to the plates pursuant to this section is no longer necessary or proper in the determination of the chief administrator. Any security amount held by the Motor Vehicle Commission as security for any returned plates shall be refunded to the person or entity to whom the plates were issued.

Amended by L.1951, c. 4, § 1; L.1962, c. 164, § 1; L.1963, c. 34, § 1; L.1965, c. 71, § 1; L.1968, c. 130, § 4, eff. Aug. 1, 1968; L.1969, c. 254, § 1, eff. Jan. 1, 1970; L.1973, c. 65, § 1, eff. March 22, 1973; L.1983, c. 105, § 1, eff. June 11, 1984; L.2007, c. 335, § 20, eff. Feb. 12, 2008.

39:3–19. Omnibus registration; fees; markers; application for registration

For each vehicle used as an omnibus for the transportation of passengers for hire the applicant for the registration thereof shall pay an annual fee as follows:

$30.00 for each vehicle having a seating capacity of 18 passengers or less;

$48.00 for each vehicle having a seating capacity of not less than 19 nor more than 30 passengers;

$48.00 for vehicles having a seating capacity of more than 30 passengers and an additional fee of $3.00 for each passenger measured by the seating capacity in excess of 30 passengers.

Whenever the number of regular route passengers carried by an applicant in the previous calendar year represents 75% or more of the combined number of passengers carried on regular route, casino, special and charter bus operations during that year, then such applicant shall pay $10.00 per annum for the registration of each vehicle used as an omnibus for the transportation of passengers for hire in lieu of the annual fees hereinbefore prescribed. In addition, any applicant who is operating regular route bus service under a contract with the New Jersey Transit Corporation pursuant to P.L.1979, c. 150 (C. 27:25–1 et seq.), shall pay $10.00 per annum for the registration of each vehicle used as an omnibus for the transportation of passengers for hire in lieu of the annual fees hereinbefore prescribed and without regard to the aforementioned 75% requirement.

Applicants seeking to register a vehicle for the reduced fee shall first obtain a letter from the Department of Transportation certifying that the number of regular route passengers carried by the applicant in the previous calendar year represents 75% or more of the combined number of passengers carried on regular route, casino, special and charter bus operations during that year, or in the case of applicants operating under contract with the New Jersey Transit Corporation pursuant to P.L.1979, c. 150 (C. 27:25–1 et seq.) shall obtain a letter from the corporation certifying that they are under such a contract. Applicants shall present the appropriate letters of certification with their applications for omnibus registration to the Director of the Division of Motor Vehicles.

The director shall provide identification marks of the general style and kind provided for motor vehicle registrations, assigning a number to each identification mark, and before each number the letter "O" shall be placed.

Every applicant for omnibus registration shall make application, setting forth the fact that he is in the business of transporting passengers for hire; and the director, if satisfied of the correctness of the statements made in such application, may issue a registration certificate for omnibus license.

Nothing in this section shall prohibit the use by an omnibus operator of any automobile duly licensed by him as owner.

Amended by L.1951, c. 5, p. 25, § 1; L.1968, c. 130, § 5, eff. Aug. 1, 1968; L.1972, c. 211, § 1; L.1987, c. 445, § 4, eff. Jan. 19, 1988.

39:3–19.1. Penalty for violating omnibus registration requirements

Any person owning or operating a motor vehicle who shall use his motor vehicle for transportation of passengers for hire, without having an omnibus registration as provided for in section 39:3–19 of this title, shall be subject to a fine of $250 for a first offense, and the unregistered motor vehicle so used may be impounded. Any offender who shall be convicted of a second or any subsequent offense of the same violation shall be subject to a fine of $500, and the unregistered motor vehicle so used may be impounded.

Any police officer is authorized to remove any such unregistered motor vehicle from the public highway to a storage space or garage, and the expense involved in such removal and storing of the vehicle shall be borne by the owner of the vehicle, except that the expense shall be borne by the lessee of a leased vehicle.

In addition to and independent of any fine or other penalty provided for under law, the court shall impose a fine of $150 on any driver or operator of an omnibus, convicted of a violation of this section, who does not have a certificate of public convenience and necessity as required pursuant to R.S.48:4–3. The State Treasurer shall annually deposit the monies collected from the fines imposed pursuant to this paragraph to the "Omnibus Safety Enforcement Fund" established pursuant to section 4 of P.L.2007, c. 40 (C.39:3–79.23). The fine described herein shall not be deemed a fine, penalty, or forfeiture pursuant to R.S.39:5–41.

Amended by L.2007, c. 40, § 1, eff. July 1, 2007.

39:3–19.2. School vehicles; fees; exemptions

The Director of Motor Vehicles shall have the authority to issue upon application therefor a license plate for school vehicles marked "School Vehicle Type I" or "School Vehicle Type II" as the application may indicate is warranted in accordance with the definition of these vehicles contained in R.S. 39:1–1. Except as otherwise provided in this section, every registration for a school vehicle shall expire and the certificate thereof shall become void on the last day of the eleventh calendar month following the month in which the certificate was issued.

School vehicles for which school vehicle registrations had been issued prior to the effective date of this act and which expire June 30, 1982 shall be issued registrations which, in the director's discretion, shall expire on a date to be fixed by him, which date shall not be sooner than 4 months nor later than 16 months following the date of issuance of the registration. The fees for such registrations shall be fixed by the director in amounts proportionately less or greater than the fees established by this section.

No fee shall be charged the United States Government, the State of New Jersey, a local school district, a regional school district, or a county vocational or technical school upon application for a Type I or Type II school vehicle license plate.

All other applicants for license plates herein authorized of the "School Vehicle Type I" kind shall pay an annual registration fee of $140.00. All other applicants for license plates herein authorized of the "School Vehicle Type II" shall pay an annual registration fee of $40.00.

L.1974, c. 162, § 2, eff. Dec. 2, 1974. Amended by L.1975, c. 180, § 5, eff. Jan. 1, 1976; L.1981, c. 554, § 2, eff. Jan. 12, 1982.

39:3–19.3. Inapplicability of act to certain buses and vehicles

The provisions of this act shall not apply to buses used in common carrier line service and school transportation service whose owner meets the qualifications prescribed in R.S. 39:3–19 or to any vehicle with a seating capacity of 16 or less which is solely used to transport children to or from summer day camps or summer residence camps from May 15 to September 15 of any year.

L.1974, c. 162, § 3, eff. Dec. 2, 1974. Amended by L.1980, c. 115, § 1, eff. Sept. 19, 1980.

39:3–19.4. Vehicle used for summer day or residence camps; inspection; liability insurance coverage

Notwithstanding the provisions of section 2 of P.L. 1974, c. 162 (C. 39:3–19.2) or of any other law, any vehicle with a seating capacity of 16 or less which is used to transport children to or from summer day camps or summer residence camps from May 15 to September 15 shall be inspected by the Division of Motor Vehicles prior to May 15 of any year in which the vehicle is to be used for those purposes for compliance with the minimum standards for small vehicles which have been adopted by the Department of Education and shall be covered by motor vehicle liability insurance coverage insuring against loss resulting from liability imposed by law for bodily injury or death sustained by any person arising out of the ownership, maintenance, operation or use of said vehicle wherein such coverage shall be at least in: a. an amount or limit of $300,000.00, exclusive of interest and costs, on account of injury to, or death of, one person, in any one accident; and b. an amount or limit, subject to such limit for any one person so injured or killed, of $500,000.00, exclusive of interest and costs, on account of injury to or death of, more than one person, in any one accident.

L.1979, c. 147, § 2, eff. July 16, 1979. Amended by L.1980, c. 115, § 2, eff. Sept. 19, 1980.

39:3–19.5. Autocab, limousine or livery service; special registration plates; fees

a. Upon the application of any person who owns a limousine service, the Director of the Division of Motor Vehicles shall issue special registration plates bearing the word "limousine" in addition to the registration number and other markings or identification otherwise prescribed by law.

b. The special registration plates authorized by this act shall be issued upon proof, satisfactory to the director, that the applicant has complied with the provisions of article 2 of chapter 16 of Title 48 of the Revised Statutes.

c. The fee for such special registration plates shall be $10.00 in addition to the fees otherwise prescribed by law for the registration of such motor vehicles.

L.1979, c. 224, § 12, eff. Oct. 12, 1979. Amended by L.1999, c. 356, § 19.

39:3–19.6. Fee for operating period from October 1 through September 30 for passenger limousines

a. On or before October 1, 2003 and on or before each October 1 thereafter, or in the case of persons commencing transporting passengers after that date at least 10 business days before the commencement of transporting, a fee shall be due and payable pursuant to this section for the operating period from October 1 through September 30 for each limousine, as that term is defined pursuant to R.S.48:16–13, and any other vehicle for hire that is used to transport passengers, from or to a location in New Jersey if such vehicle is not registered in New Jersey. If the only use of the limousine or other vehicle for hire during the operating period is the transporting of passengers to or from an airport located in this State, the fee shall be $100; in all other cases, the fee shall be $250.

b. Upon payment of the fee pursuant to subsection a. of this section, the Chief Administrator of the New Jersey Motor Vehicle Commission shall issue a "for hire" permit, which permit shall be displayed in the vehicle at all times while the vehicle is within the State, in a manner prescribed by the Chief Administrator.

c. Failure to display the "for hire" permit is a motor vehicle violation, punishable by a fine of up to $350 in addition to any other penalty otherwise authorized for motor vehicle violations. Failure to pay the fee due under this section is a separate motor vehicle violation and shall be punishable by a fine of not less than $350, in addition to any other penalty authorized for motor vehicle violations. A vehicle failing to display a "for hire" permit may be impounded by a law enforcement agency, its agent, or any other appropriate authority, which may charge the owner or operator fees for the costs of towing and impoundment.

d. The Chief Administrator is authorized to promulgate rules and regulations necessary to effectuate the purposes of this section, including, but not limited to, regulations concerning the assessment of motor vehicle violation points for violation of the provisions of this section and fee collection and remittance methods and procedures, in accordance with the "Administrative Procedure Act," P.L.1968, c. 410 (C.52:14B–1 et seq.), and prescribe forms to administer the provisions of this section. Notwithstanding the provisions of P.L.1968, c.

410 to the contrary, the Chief Administrator may adopt immediately upon filing with the Office of Administrative Law such regulations as the Chief Administrator deems necessary to implement the provisions of this section, which regulations shall be effective for a period not to exceed 180 days from the date of the filing. The regulations may thereafter be amended, adopted or readopted by the Chief Administrator as the Chief Administrator deems necessary in accordance with the requirements of P.L.1968, c. 410.

L.2003, c. 117, § 43, eff. July 1, 2003.

39:3–20. Commercial motor vehicles other than omnibuses and motor–drawn vehicles; registration year; fees; gross weight; definition; violations; penalties

For the purpose of this section, gross weight means the weight of the vehicle or combination of vehicles, including load or contents.

a. The chief administrator is authorized to issue registrations for commercial motor vehicles other than omnibuses or motor–drawn vehicles upon application therefor and payment of a fee based on the gross weight of the vehicle, including the gross weight of all vehicles in any combination of vehicles of which the commercial motor vehicle is the drawing vehicle. The gross weight of a disabled commercial vehicle or combination of disabled commercial vehicles being removed from a highway shall not be included in the calculation of the registration fee for the drawing vehicle.

Except as otherwise provided in this subsection, every registration for a commercial motor vehicle other than an omnibus or motor–drawn vehicle shall expire and the certificate thereof shall become void on the last day of the twelfth calendar month following the month in which the certificate was issued; provided, however, that the chief administrator may require registrations which shall expire, and issue certificates thereof which shall become void, on a date fixed by the chief administrator, which shall not be sooner than three months or later than 26 months after the date of issuance of such certificates, and the fees for such registrations or registration applications, including any other fees or charges collected in connection with the registration fee, shall be fixed by the chief administrator in amounts proportionately less or greater than the fees established by law. The chief administrator may fix the expiration date for registration certificates at a date other than 12 months if the chief administrator determines that such change is necessary, appropriate or convenient in order to aid in implementing the vehicle inspection requirements of chapter 8 of Title 39 or for other good cause. The minimum registration fee shall be as follows:

(1) In the case of vehicles other than trucks transporting ready-mixed concrete, asphalt, stone, sand, gravel, clay and cleanfill:

For vehicles not in excess of 5,000 pounds, $53.50.

For vehicles in excess of 5,000 pounds and not in excess of 10,000 pounds, $53.50 plus $11.50 for each 1,000 pounds or portion thereof in excess of 5,000 pounds.

For vehicles in excess of 10,000 pounds and not in excess of 18,000 pounds, $53.50 plus $13.50 for each 1,000 pounds or portion thereof in excess of 5,000 pounds.

For vehicles in excess of 18,000 pounds and not in excess of 50,000 pounds, $53.50 plus $14.50 for each 1,000 pounds or portion thereof in excess of 5,000 pounds.

For vehicles in excess of 50,000 pounds, $53.50 plus $15.50 for each 1,000 pounds or portion thereof in excess of 5,000 pounds; and

(2) In the case of trucks transporting ready-mixed concrete, asphalt, stone, sand, gravel, clay and cleanfill:

For vehicles not in excess of 5,000 pounds, $53.50.

For vehicles in excess of 5,000 pounds and not in excess of 18,000 pounds, $53.50 plus $11.50 for each 1,000 pounds or portion thereof in excess of 5,000 pounds.

For vehicles in excess of 18,000 pounds and not in excess of 50,000 pounds, $53.50 plus $12.50 for each 1,000 pounds or portion thereof in excess of 5,000 pounds.

For vehicles in excess of 50,000 pounds, $53.50 plus $13.50 for each 1,000 pounds or portion thereof in excess of 5,000 pounds.

b. The chief administrator is also authorized to issue registrations for commercial motor vehicles having three or more axles and a gross weight over 40,000 pounds but not exceeding 70,000 pounds, upon application therefor and proof to the satisfaction of the chief administrator that the applicant is actually engaged in construction work or in the business of supplying material, transporting material, or using such registered vehicle for construction work.

Except as otherwise provided in this subsection, every registration for these commercial motor vehicles shall expire and the certificate thereof shall become void on the last day of the twelfth calendar month following the month in which the certificate was issued; provided, however, that the chief administrator may require registrations which shall expire, and issue certificates thereof which shall become void on a date fixed by the chief administrator, which shall not be sooner than three months or later than 26 months after the date of issuance of such certificates, and the fees for such registrations or registration applications, including any other fees or charges collected in connection with the registration fee, shall be fixed by the chief administrator in amounts proportionately less or greater than the fees established by law. The chief administrator may fix the expiration date for registration certificates at a date other than 12 months if the chief administrator deter-

mines that such change is necessary, appropriate or convenient in order to aid in implementing the vehicle inspection requirements of chapter 8 of Title 39 or for other good cause.

The registration fee shall be $22.50 for each 1,000 pounds or portion thereof.

For purposes of calculating this fee, weight means the gross weight, including the gross weight of all vehicles in any combination of which such commercial motor vehicle is the drawing vehicle.

Such commercial motor vehicle shall be operated in compliance with the speed limitations of Title 39 of the Revised Statutes and shall not be operated at a speed greater than 45 miles per hour when one or more of its axles has a load which exceeds the limitations prescribed in R.S.39:3–84.

c. The chief administrator is also authorized to issue registrations for each of the following solid waste vehicles: two–axle vehicles having a gross weight not exceeding 42,000 pounds; tandem three-axle and four-axle vehicles having a gross weight not exceeding 60,000 pounds; four–axle tractor-trailer combination vehicles having a gross weight not exceeding 60,000 pounds. Registration is based upon application to the chief administrator and proof to his satisfaction that the applicant is actually engaged in the performance of solid waste disposal or collection functions and holds a certificate of convenience and necessity therefor issued by the Department of Environmental Protection.

Except as otherwise provided in this subsection, every registration for a solid waste vehicle shall expire and the certificate thereof shall become void on the last day of the twelfth calendar month following the month in which the certificate was issued.

The registration fee shall be $50 plus $11.50 for each 1,000 pounds or portion thereof in excess of 5,000 pounds.

d. The chief administrator is also authorized to issue registrations for commercial motor-drawn vehicles upon application therefor. The registration year for commercial motor-drawn vehicles shall be April 1 to the following March 31 and the fee therefor shall be $18 for each such vehicle.

At the discretion of the chief administrator, an applicant for registration for a commercial motor-drawn vehicle may be provided the option of registering such vehicle for a period of four years. In the event that the applicant for registration exercises the four-year option, a fee of $64 for each such vehicle shall be paid to the chief administrator in advance.

If any commercial motor-drawn vehicle registered for a four-year period is sold or withdrawn from use on the highways, the chief administrator may, upon surrender of the vehicle registration and plate, refund $16 for each full year of unused prepaid registration.

e. It shall be unlawful for any vehicle or combination of vehicles registered under this act, having a gross weight, including load or contents, in excess of the gross weight provided on the registration certificate to be operated on the highways of this State.

The owner, lessee, bailee or any one of the aforesaid of a vehicle or combination of vehicles, including load or contents, found or operated on any public road, street or highway or on any public or quasi-public property in this State with a gross weight of that vehicle or combination of vehicles, including load or contents, in excess of the weight limitation permitted by the certificate of registration for the vehicle or combination of vehicles, pursuant to the provisions of this section, shall be assessed a penalty of $500 plus an amount equal to $100 for each 1,000 pounds or fractional portion of 1,000 pounds of weight in excess of the weight limitation permitted by the certificate of registration for that vehicle or combination of vehicles. A vehicle or combination of vehicles for which there is no valid certificate of registration is deemed to have been registered for zero pounds for the purposes of the enforcement of this act, in addition to any other violation of this Title, but is not deemed to be lawfully or validly registered pursuant to the provisions of this Title.

This section shall not be construed to supersede or repeal the provisions of section 39:3–84, 39:4–75, or 39:4–76 of this Title.

f. Of the registration fees collected by the chief administrator pursuant to this section for vehicles with gross vehicle weights in excess of 5,000 pounds, an amount equal to $3 per 1,000 pounds or portion thereof in excess of 5,000 pounds for each registration shall be forwarded to the State Treasurer for deposit in the Commercial Vehicle Enforcement Fund established pursuant to section 17 of P.L.1995, c. 157 (C.39:8–75). Moneys in the fund shall be used by the Department of Law and Public Safety and the Department of Transportation for enforcement of laws and regulations governing commercial motor vehicles.

Amended by L.1946, c. 46, p. 103, § 1; L.1950, c. 142, p. 279, § 1; L.1960, c. 12, p. 30, § 1; L.1961, c. 113, p. 700, § 1; L.1962, c. 155, § 1; L.1963, c. 166, § 1; L.1966, c. 209, § 2, eff. April 1, 1967; L.1968, c. 130, § 6, eff. Aug. 1, 1968; L.1972, c. 55, § 1, eff. July 1, 1972; L.1973, c. 138, § 1, eff. May 17, 1973; L.1973, c. 373, § 1, eff. Jan. 7, 1974; L.1975, c. 92, § 2, eff. May 8, 1975; L.1975, c. 180, § 6, eff. Jan. 1, 1976; L.1977, c. 51, § 1; L.1979, c. 162, § 1, eff. July 19, 1979; L.1981, c. 554, § 1, eff. Jan. 12, 1982; L.1983, c. 349, § 1; L.1984, c. 73, § 32, eff. July 10, 1984; L.1994, c. 60, § 32, eff. July 1, 1994; L.1995, c. 112, § 29, eff. June 2, 1995; L.1995, c. 157, § 34; L.1997, c. 313, § 1, eff. April 1, 1998; L.2002, c. 34, § 13, eff. July 1, 2002; L.2005, c. 214, § 1, eff. Feb. 1, 2006.

39:3–20.1. Empty trucks, tractors, trailers and semi-trailers; "in-transit empty" registration plates; fees

In addition to the motor vehicle registration provisions authorized pursuant to this chapter, the director may issue, upon application on a form prescribed by him, a registration certificate and registration plates for trucks, tractors, trailers and semitrailers that are empty and being transported from one terminal to another, or from the place of sale to the registrant's terminal or place of business, or are empty and being transported for the purpose of having additional equipment added or lettering affixed.

The director may issue, upon application on the form prescribed by the director, a registration certificate and registration plates for mobile and manufactured homes being transported from the place of manufacture to the registrant's terminal or place of business, or being transported for the purpose of delivering the mobile or manufactured home to a final point of delivery.

The annual fee for the issuance of each set of such plates shall be $25.00. Such plates are to be in the form prescribed by the director and shall be marked in a manner to indicate the vehicle is "in-transit empty."

L.1973, c. 319, § 1, eff. Dec. 18, 1973. Amended by L.1998, c. 135, § 2, eff. Dec. 3, 1998.

39:3–20.2. Misuse of "in-transit empty" registration; penalty

The penalty for misuse of the registration provisions of section 1 shall be a fine of no less than $25.00 nor more than $100.00 and suspension or revocation of the privilege.

L.1973, c. 319, § 2, eff. Dec. 18, 1973.

39:3–20.3. Operation of commercial motor vehicle exceeding gross weight limit on registration certificate unlawful; penalties

It shall be unlawful for any vehicle or combination of vehicles registered as a commercial motor vehicle by another state or jurisdiction to operate on the highways of this State if it has a gross weight, including load or contents, which is in excess of the gross weight limit permitted on the registration certificate issued for it by that other state or jurisdiction.

The owner, lessee or bailee of any vehicle or combination of vehicles that is found or operated on any public road, street or highway or on any public or quasi-public property in this State with a gross weight in excess of the weight limitation permitted by the certificate of registration issued for it by that other state or jurisdiction shall be assessed a penalty of $500 plus an amount equal to $100 for each 1,000 pounds or fractional portion of 1,000 pounds of weight in excess of the weight limitation permitted by that certificate of registration.

For the purposes of enforcement, a vehicle or combination of vehicles for which there is no valid certificate of registration shall be deemed to have been registered for zero pounds.

All fines, penalties and forfeitures imposed and collected in the enforcement of this section shall be forwarded by the person to whom they are paid to the State Treasurer, who shall annually deposit those moneys in the "Highway Safety Fund" established pursuant to section 5 of P.L.2003, c. 131 (C.39:3–20.4).

L.2003, c. 131, § 4, eff. Feb. 15, 2004.

39:3–20.4. Highway Safety Fund established

There is established in the General Fund a separate, nonlapsing, dedicated account to be known as the "Highway Safety Fund." All fines, penalties and forfeitures imposed and collected as a result of the enforcement of section 4 of P.L.2003, c. 131 (C.39:3–20.3) and 50 percent of all fines and penalties imposed and collected in enforcement of section 5 of P.L.1983, c. 401 (C.39:5B–29), and the increase from the doubling of fines imposed and collected pursuant to section 1 of P.L.1993, c. 332 (C.39: 4–203.5) in designated safe corridor areas shall be forwarded to the State Treasurer for deposit into the Highway Safety Fund account. The fund shall be administered by the Department of Transportation which shall establish a grant program to fund local law enforcement agencies for special enforcement efforts associated with this act. The department shall annually, in conjunction with the Division of State Police, submit a report on the results of the safe corridor areas and a list of highway safety projects and programs paid for by the fund within the past year to the Senate Transportation Committee and the Assembly Transportation Committee, the President and minority leader of the Senate, and the Speaker and the minority leader of the General Assembly. The moneys in the account shall be used exclusively for highway safety projects and programs, including education, enforcement, capital improvements and such other related measures and undertakings as the Department of Transportation and the Division of State Police may deem appropriate to foster highway safety.

L.2003, c. 131, § 5, eff. Feb. 15, 2004.

39:3–21. Motorcycle registration; fee

The applicant for registration for a motorcycle shall pay to the commission for each registration a fee of $10.00.

Amended by L.1968, c. 130, § 7, eff. Aug. 1, 1968; L.2003, c. 13, § 101 (contingent effective date).

39:3–22. Repealed by L.1971, c. 215, § 1, eff. June 17, 1971

39:3–22a. Reduction of fees on or after October 1

If application is made for the registration of a motor vehicle, other than a passenger automobile or motorcycle, or for the registration of a commercial motor or motor-drawn vehicle, or an omnibus, on or after October 1 in a registration year beginning April 1 and ending the following March 31, the applicant shall pay only one-half of the registration fee provided for in the class to which such vehicle belongs.

L.1973, c. 90, § 1, eff. April 24, 1973. Amended by L.1975, c. 180, § 7, eff. Jan. 1, 1976; L.1977, c. 51, § 2.

39:3–22.1. Persons in military or naval service; refund of registration fees; application

Any person, who has entered or shall enter into active service in any branch of the naval or military forces of the United States and who has or shall have registered his motor vehicle in this State for any registration period, shall be entitled to a refund on the registration fee paid for such vehicle for the number of full months remaining of the registration period for which the vehicle will not be operated on the public highways of this or any other state; provided, that such person makes written application to the director for such refund, under oath, in such form as the director shall require and surrenders the certificate of registration and license plates of such motor vehicle.

L.1944, c. 228, p. 771, § 1. Amended by L.1995, c. 112, § 30, eff. June 2, 1995.

39:3–22.2. Warrant for refund

Upon approval by the commissioner of such application and the surrender of such certificate of registration and license plates, the State Comptroller shall draw his warrant upon the State Treasurer for the amount of such claim in favor of such claimant, and such warrant shall be paid from the moneys collected from motor vehicle registrations.

L.1944, c. 228, p. 771, § 2.

39:3–23. Rubber tires or tires of approved material required

No automobile, commercial vehicle, trailer, semitrailer or tractor shall be registered by the commissioner unless the same are equipped with rubber tires or tires of a material other than rubber which have been approved by the commissioner, on all wheels.

Amended by L.1942, c. 227, p. 608, § 1.

39:3–23.1. Approval of tires of material other than rubber

The commission may in its discretion approve the use of any particular type of tire, of a material other than rubber, on vehicles operated upon the highways of this State, if it finds the said tire will not damage the public highways and that the use of said tire is not likely to be hazardous to the public safety.

L.1942, c. 227, p. 609, § 3. Amended by L.2003, c. 13, § 102 (contingent effective date).

39:3–24. Farm tractors and traction equipment; motor vehicles used as farm machinery or farm implements; registration; operation; fee

(a) The director shall register farm tractors and traction equipment used for farm operation to travel upon the public highways. The fee for such registration shall be $5 per annum, whether the registration is issued for the yearly period or only a portion thereof. Such traction equipment or farm tractors may draw farm machinery and implements while in transit from one farm to another without additional registration therefor.

(b) The director may register motor vehicles, not for hire, used exclusively as farm machinery or farm implements, to travel upon the public highways, from one farm, or portion thereof, to another farm, or portion thereof, both owned or managed by the registered owner of the vehicle or vehicles. The fee for such registration shall be $5 per annum, whether the registration is issued for a yearly period or only a portion thereof. Any vehicle so registered and any truck registered pursuant to the provisions of 39:3–25 of this Title may draw not more than one vehicle used exclusively on the farm and a vehicle so drawn need not be registered. A vehicle registered pursuant to this section or to R.S. 39:3–25 may be used under contract with a municipality to remove snow upon a public highway.

(c) No vehicle registered pursuant to this section shall be operated on a public highway at any time from sunset to sunrise, except a vehicle being operated under contract with a municipality to remove snow. Every such vehicle when operated on a public highway shall have means adequate to control the movement of and to stop and hold such vehicle on any up or down grade and shall be operated in accordance with uniform rules and regulations prescribed by the Director of the Division of Motor Vehicles. Such rules and regulations shall specify the coverings that may be used on the wheels of such vehicles, the days, hours and conditions under which such vehicles can be operated, the circumstance under which escort vehicles shall be required, the distance that may be traveled upon the public highways and such vehicle equipment or other requirements or restrictions as may be necessary to protect the safety of the users of the public highways.

Motor vehicles, not for hire, which are used exclusively as farm tractors, traction equipment, farm machinery or farm implements which cannot be operated at a speed in excess of 20 miles per hour shall not be required to be registered under this section.

Amended by L.1938, c. 66, p. 176, § 7; L.1947, c. 317, p. 1041, § 1; L.1961, c. 71, p. 597, § 2; L.1963, c. 128, § 1, eff. July 1, 1963; L.1968, c. 130, § 8, eff. Aug. 1, 1968; L.1994, c. 60, § 16, eff. July 1, 1994; L.1996, c. 31, § 1, eff. June 6, 1996; L.1996, c. 119, § 1, eff. Oct. 30, 1996.

39:3–24.1. Repealed by L.1961, c. 71, p. 598, § 3, eff. June 3, 1961

39:3–25. License plates for farmers' trucks; fee; expiration

In addition to the motor vehicle licenses authorized to be issued pursuant to the provisions of this chapter, the administrator shall issue, upon application therefor, a license plate for trucks marked "farmer," which shall be issued upon evidence satisfactory to the administrator that the applicant is a farmer and is actually engaged in the growing, raising and producing of farm products as an occupation. License plates issued under authority of this section shall be placed upon motor trucks engaged in the carrying or transportation of farm products, and farm supplies, and not engaged in hauling for hire, except for a truck being operated under contract with a municipality to remove snow.

Applicants for license plates herein authorized shall pay a registration fee of $25 plus $4.25 for each 1,000 pounds or portion thereof in excess of 5,000 pounds. If the registration cycle established by the administrator is for more or less than 11 months, applicants shall pay amounts proportionately less or greater than the fees established by law.

Except as otherwise provided in this section, every registration for a farm truck shall expire and the certificate thereof shall become void on the last day of the eleventh calendar month following the month in which the certificate was issued; except that the administrator may require registrations which shall expire, and issue certificates thereof which shall become void, on a date fixed by the administrator, which shall not be sooner than three months or later than 26 months after the date of issuance of such certificates, and the fees for such registrations, including any other fees or charges collected in connection with the registration fee, shall be fixed by the administrator in amounts proportionately less or greater than the fees established by law. The administrator may fix the expiration date for registration certificates at a date other than 11 months if the administrator determines that such change is necessary, appropriate or convenient in order to aid in implementing the vehicle inspection requirements of chapter 8 of Title 39 or for other good cause.

The term "farmer" as used in this section means any person engaged in the commercial raising, growing and producing of farm products on a farm not less than five acres in area; the term "farm products" means any crop, livestock or fur products; and the term "farm supplies" means any farm- related supply or repair item.

Amended by L.1963, c. 193, § 1; L.1981, c. 554, § 3, eff. Jan. 12, 1982; L.1984, c. 73, § 33, eff. July 10, 1984; L.1995, c. 112, § 31, eff. June 2, 1995; L.1996, c. 119, § 2, eff. Oct. 30, 1996; L.2005, c. 76, § 1, eff. July 1, 2005.

39:3–26. Traction or tractor well-drill machines or well-drilling equipment; trucks with powered feed impregnating machines; fee

In addition to the motor vehicle licenses authorized to be issued pursuant to the provisions of this chapter, the commissioner is authorized and empowered to license traction or tractor well-drill machines or well-drilling equipment, however mounted, whether or not such vehicles be equipped with rubber tires, and to license any truck equipped with rubber tires which has permanently affixed thereto a powered feed impregnating machine, which license shall permit such vehicles to travel upon the public highways of this State in accordance with the provisions of this chapter. The fee for such license shall be three dollars ($3.00) per annum, whether such license shall be issued for the yearly period or only for portion thereof.

Amended by L.1938, c. 66, p. 176, § 8; L.1945, c. 265, p. 797, § 1.

39:3–26.1. Self-propelled unregistered vehicle used solely on private property; highway crossing permit

Any self-propelled vehicle or vehicles which are used or intended to be used solely upon the private property of one person, and which would otherwise be required to be registered under this title in order to operate upon a public highway, may be allowed, subject to the provisions of this act, to cross a public highway for the purpose of gaining access from one portion of such private property to another, without the necessity of complying with the registration requirements of this title, upon issuance of a crossing permit by the director and subject to compliance with the terms and conditions of such permit.

L.1973, c. 6, § 1, eff. Jan. 16, 1973.

39:3–26.2. Application; issuance; contents

a. A property owner wishing a crossing permit under the terms of this act shall make application to the director, setting forth the number and types of vehicles which may cross the public highway, the anticipated frequency of crossings, and the proposed location or locations of such crossings, and shall supply such further information as the director may deem necessary, in such form and detail as the director shall require.

b. After receipt of the application and of the required fee, and having determined to his satisfaction that the proposed crossings may be permitted without danger of damage to the highway or hazard to the public traveling along such highway, the director shall issue a crossing permit, which shall specify:

(1) the vehicle or vehicles, or type or types of vehicles permitted to cross;

(2) the location or locations of the crossing or crossings permitted, provided that the width of any such crossing zone be no greater than 150 feet;

(3) any warning signs or other safety devices or precautions, and their location with respect to the location of the crossing or crossings, which are to be erected and maintained by the holder of the permit at his expense, and which are deemed necessary for safety;

(4) any safety devices or other equipment, including lights to be installed and used upon vehicles making the crossing;

(5) any restrictions upon the time of day at which such crossings may be made; and

(6) any other terms and conditions which the director deems necessary in order to secure the safety of the public or to protect the highway from damage.

L.1973, c. 6, § 2, eff. Jan. 16, 1973.

39:3–26.3. Unauthorized use of highway by unregistered vehicles; penalty

In addition to subjecting the holder of a crossing permit to the penalty provided for operation of an unregistered vehicle upon a highway, the director shall revoke the crossing permit of any person who operates or permits the operation of an unregistered vehicle upon a highway other than as authorized by the crossing permit. No person shall operate such vehicle upon a highway as authorized by the crossing permit unless he shall possess a valid New Jersey driver's license for the class of vehicle being operated.

L.1973, c. 6, § 3, eff. Jan. 16, 1973.

39:3–26.4. Fees; refund; duration of permit; renewal

a. Each applicant for a crossing permit under this act shall accompany his application with a fee based on the gross weight of vehicle and load for each vehicle which he proposes to operate under the permit, in accordance with the following schedule:

4,000 pounds or less	$ 5.00
4,001 to 8,000 pounds	8.00
8,001 to 12,000 pounds	12.00
12,001 to 16,000 pounds	16.00
16,001 to 20,000 pounds	20.00
20,001 pounds or more	25.00

In the event that the permit is denied or the number of permitted vehicles is reduced by the director, the fee or the amount thereof which is in excess of the amount indicated by the number of vehicles permitted shall be refunded.

b. A permit under this act shall be in effect for 1 year from the date of issuance and shall be renewable annually upon payment of the fee prescribed in subsection a. of this section. The director may refuse to renew or modify the terms of the permit upon renewal if he finds that the safety of the public or the proper maintenance of the highway so requires.

L.1973, c. 6, § 4, eff. Jan. 16, 1973.

39:3–26.5. Death, bodily injury or property damage involving vehicle on public highway; application of Motor Vehicle Security-Responsibility Law

In the event of death, bodily injury or property damage arising in connection with the operation of any vehicle while on a public highway and with respect to which a crossing permit under this act has been issued, the operator, permit holder and owner of the vehicle (if he be other than the permit holder) shall be subject to the provisions of the "Motor Vehicle Security-Responsibility Law" (L.1952, c. 173, C. 39:6–23 et seq.). Any circumstances which would authorize or require the director to suspend the registration of a registered vehicle pursuant to said law shall also be deemed to authorize or require the revocation of a permit issued pursuant to this act; and in such case the permit shall be revoked in its entirety and not with respect only to a particular vehicle or vehicles.

L.1973, c. 6, § 5, eff. Jan. 16, 1973.

39:3–27. Free registration of certain vehicles; expiration; transfer to other motor vehicle

No fee shall be charged for the registration of motor vehicles not used for pleasure or hire, owned by the United States, the State of New Jersey, a municipality, county, Regional Air Pollution Control Agency, Passaic Valley Sewerage Commissioners, North Jersey District Water Supply Commission, a county improvement authority created under the "county improvement authorities law" (P.L.1960, c. 183),[1] a local school district, a regional school district, a county vocational or technical school, a duly authorized volunteer fire department, a duly authorized volunteer first aid, rescue or emergency squad, any duly recognized auxiliary or reserve police organization of any municipality, hospital, humane society, and anticruelty society in this State, New Jersey wing of the Civil Air Patrol incorporated by the Act of July 1946 (Public Law 476–79th Congress),[2] the American Red Cross, chartered local councils in New Jersey of the Boy Scouts of America or the Girl Scouts of the United States of America, chartered local councils in New Jersey of the Boys' Clubs of America or the Girls' Clubs of America, or chartered local organizations of the Police Athletic League or for the registration of ambulances owned by any nonprofit organization. These vehicles shall be registered and display number plates as provided in this title or the director may, in his discretion, issue special registration certificates and special number plates for any of these motor vehicles which shall be valid for such motor vehicle for a period fixed by the director which may correspond with the inspection expiration date applicable to such vehicles, which date shall not be later than 26 months after the date of issuance of such certificates. Upon the expiration or nonrenewal of any special registration the registration certificate and special number marker shall be returned to the director; provided, however, upon proper application to the director the special registration and special number marker may be transferred to another motor vehicle acquired by the owner to whom the special registration and marker were issued.

Amended by L.1951, c. 217, p. 781, § 1; L.1952, c. 226, p. 768, § 1; L.1955, c. 24, p. 77, § 1; L.1959, c. 89, p. 220, § 1; L.1960, c. 96, p. 583, § 1; L.1970, c. 34, § 1, eff. April 24, 1970; L.1971, c. 462, § 1, eff. Feb. 29, 1972; L.1973, c. 51, § 1, eff. March 2, 1973; L.1977, c. 359, § 1, eff. Jan. 31, 1978; L.1983, c. 106, § 1, eff. March 14, 1983; L.1983, c. 228, § 1, eff. June 29, 1983; L.1995, c. 112, § 32, eff. June 2, 1995.

[1] N.J.S.A. §§ 40:37A–44 to 40:37A–91.
[2] 36 U.S.C.A. §§ 201 to 208.

39:3–27.1. Free registration of vehicles owned by resident blind or disabled veterans or holder of Medal of Honor

No fee shall be charged for the registration, in any year or years, of one motor vehicle of passenger type, which is not to be used for hire, owned by any resident of the State of New Jersey, individually or jointly with a spouse;

(1) who is eligible for compensation pursuant to R.S. 38:18–1, 38:18–2 and 38:18–3,

(2) who has qualified or shall qualify under the provisions of Public Law 663–79th Congress of the United States of America (August 8, 1946)[1] or of Public Law 187—82nd Congress of the United States of America (October 20, 1951)[2] or who is a veteran of World War I with service-connected disabilities of the kind set forth in said Public Laws, and who is the holder of a current driver's license issued by this State, if such motor vehicle is equipped with such special attachments and devices as the Director of the Division of Motor Vehicles in the Department of Law and Public Safety may deem necessary to provide for the safe operation thereof by such person, or

(3) who is the holder of the Congressional Medal of Honor, which registration shall be evidenced by distinctive license plates of a design approved by the Director of the Division of Motor Vehicles.

L.1948, c. 28, p. 89, § 1. Amended by L.1951, c. 13, p. 39, § 1; L.1952, c. 73, p. 402, § 1; L.1953, c. 59, p. 969, § 1; L.1956, c. 49, p. 100, § 1; L.1972, c. 144, § 1, eff. Aug. 31, 1972; L.1979, c. 122, § 1, eff. July 3, 1979.

[1] Act of Congress of Aug. 8, 1946, c. 870, 60 Stat. 910, making additional appropriations for the fiscal year 1947, made an appropriation to the Administrator of Veterans' Affairs for the purpose of providing an automobile or other conveyance for each veteran of World War II entitled to compensation for the loss, or loss of use, of one or both legs at or above the ankle under the laws administered by the Veterans' Administration. See U.S.Code Cong. Service 1946, p. 879. (2 U.S.C.A. § 60a [omitted])
[2] Act of Congress Oct. 20, 1951, c. 532, 65 Stat. 574, authorized payments by the Administrator of Veterans' Affairs on the purchase of automobiles or other conveyances by certain disabled veterans. See U.S.Code Cong. Service 1951, p. 592. (See 38 U.S.C.A. § 1901 et seq.)

39:3–27.2. Special registration for passenger automobiles used in connection with convention, pageant or parade

Whenever, in connection with any convention, conference, meeting, pageant, parade, celebration or similar function held in this State, a manufacturer or dealer desires to make passenger automobiles available for such function, the said manufacturer or dealer may request the director, in writing, to issue special registrations for such vehicles. The director may, in his discretion, issue such special registrations and prescribe the form and contents thereof. A fee of $1.00 shall be charged and paid for each such special registration. Such special registrations shall be valid for the term specified therein, by the director, which term shall be for the duration of the function plus a number of days, not exceeding 10 days in all, preceding or following the commencement and termination of the function, or either, or both. Upon request of the applicant for any such special registration the director may, in his discretion, issue special license plates to accompany each such special registration upon the payment to him in addition to said fee of $1.00 an amount equal to the estimated actual cost to the division of manufacturing and handling such special license plates. The design, form and contents of each such special license plate shall be prescribed by the director.

L.1958, c. 120, p. 600, § 1.

39:3–27.3. Definitions

As used in this act:

"Historic motor vehicle" shall mean any motor vehicle which is at least 25 years old and which is owned as a collector's item and used solely for exhibition and educational purposes by the owner;

"Director" shall mean the Director of Motor Vehicles.

L.1964, c. 195, § 1.

39:3–27.4. Registration of historic motor vehicles

Any owner of an historic motor vehicle who is a resident of this State may register such motor vehicle under the provisions of this act. Application for registering an historic vehicle shall be on forms prescribed by the director. Upon proper application and payment of the prescribed fee, the director shall issue a special nonconventional registration and special license plate for each historic motor vehicle registered in this State. Such registration and license plate shall be valid during the period of time that the vehicle is owned by the registrant. The fee for such registration and license plate shall be $25.00. The license plate shall bear the word "historic" and shall be of such design and colors as the director may determine. Notwithstanding the provisions of R.S.39:3–33 or any other law to the contrary, an owner of a vehicle registered as an historic vehicle, or any vehicle manufactured before 1945, shall not be required to display more than one special license plate issued for that vehicle, which plate shall be displayed on the rear of the vehicle.

L.1964, c. 195, § 2. Amended by L.1999, c. 305, § 1, eff. Jan. 4, 2000.

39:3–27.5. Amateur radio call letter registration plates

The Director of the Division of Motor Vehicles shall cause to be issued to applicants who hold amateur radio licenses issued by the Federal Communications Commission, registration plates for motor vehicles owned or leased by the applicants bearing the term "amateur radio" and the amateur radio call letters of the respective applicants. The director, upon request, shall cause to be issued duplicate plates, with such marks as the director may deem appropriate to distinguish them from

the original plates, for any additional motor vehicle which an applicant may register.

L.1968, c. 247, § 1, eff. July 1, 1968. Amended by L.1977, c. 398, § 1, eff. Feb. 23, 1978; L.2001, c. 280, § 1, eff. Jan. 27, 2002.

39:3–27.6. Application; form; fee

Application for registration of such motor vehicles and for the issuance of such amateur radio call letter registration plates shall be made in such form and accompanied by such proof as the director shall prescribe. An additional fee of $15 shall be paid for the issuance or replacement of any such plates.

L.1968, c. 247, § 2, eff. July 1, 1968. Amended by L.2001, c. 280, § 2, eff. Jan. 27, 2002.

39:3–27.7. Revocation or expiration; notification of director

Upon revocation or expiration of the amateur radio station license the motor vehicle registrant within 15 days after said revocation or expiration shall notify the director thereof. The director shall issue new registration and registration plates in lieu of such amateur radio call letter registration plates and shall charge the usual fee for the issuance of lost registration plates. If the holder of such amateur radio station call letter registration plates shall fail to notify the director as set forth herein, the director may revoke said motor vehicle registration.

L.1968, c. 247, § 3, eff. July 1, 1968.

39:3–27.8. Special license plate; fire department, first aid or rescue squad; member, spouse, parent or business firm

Upon the application of any person who is a compensated, partially compensated or volunteer member of any fire department in this State, the director may issue for a motor vehicle owned or leased by such person, or owned by the spouse or parent thereof, or owned by a business firm of which such person is the principal owner or stockholder a license plate bearing a Maltese Cross and the letters "F.D." The design and color for such plate shall be approved by the director.

Upon the application of any person who is a compensated, partially compensated or volunteer member of any first aid or rescue squad in this State, the director may issue for a motor vehicle owned or leased by such person, or owned by the spouse or parent thereof, or owned by a business firm of which such person is the principal owner or stockholder a special license plate. The design for such plate shall be approved by the director.

L.1977, c. 369, § 1. Amended by L.1979, c. 447, § 1, eff. July 1, 1980; L.1983, c. 74, § 1, eff. Feb. 24, 1983.

39:3–27.9. Issuance; proof of membership; fees

The special plate authorized by this act may be issued upon proof, satisfactory to the director, that the applicant is presently a bona fide member of a fire fighting department or first aid or rescue squad in this State. The fee for such plate shall be $15.00 in addition to the fees otherwise prescribed by law for the registration of such motor vehicle.

L.1977, c. 369, § 2. Amended by L.1979, c. 447, § 2, eff. July 1, 1980.

39:3–27.10. Termination of association; return of special plate

Any person lawfully in possession of such special plate who resigns, is removed or otherwise terminates or is terminated from his association with such fire department or first aid or rescue squad, shall return such special plate to the division within 15 days.

L.1977, c. 369, § 2. Amended by L.1979, c. 447, § 3, eff. July 1, 1980.

39:3–27.11. Unauthorized uses

No person shall lend the special plate for use on a motor vehicle other than the vehicle for which issued, or use the same for a motor vehicle other than the vehicle for which issued.

L.1977, c. 369, § 4.

39:3–27.12. Violations; fine

Any person violating any of the provisions of this act shall be fined not less than $25.00 nor more than $50.00.

L.1977, c. 369, § 5.

39:3–27.13. Member of national guard; special license plate; fee

a. Upon the application of any person who is an active member of the New Jersey National Guard, or former active member who has been honorably separated from the New Jersey National Guard, as certified in either case by the Adjutant General, New Jersey Department of Defense, the Director of the Division of Motor Vehicles shall issue for the motor vehicle owned by such person special registration plates, of a design and at a fee to be prescribed by the director, identifying the holder as a member or former member of the "Air National Guard" or "Army National Guard," as the case may be, in addition to the registration number and other markings or identification otherwise prescribed by law.

b. The director shall permit any person who is an active member of the New Jersey National Guard with special National Guard registration plates to affix a National Guard "Minuteman" emblem, of a design approved by the director and the Adjutant General, New Jersey Department of Defense, to their registration plates in a manner approved by the director.

L.1979, c. 456, § 1. Amended by L.1983, c. 132, § 1, eff. Oct. 10, 1983; L.1985, c. 488, § 1, eff. Jan. 17, 1986.

39:3–27.14. Rules and regulations

The Director of the Division of Motor Vehicles and the Adjutant General of the State Department of Defense shall promulgate and adopt interdepartmental rules and regulations governing the issuance and use of such registration plates, the design and affixation of the Minuteman emblem, and providing for their surrender by persons who cease to be members of the New Jersey National Guard for reasons other than honorable separation.

L.1979, c. 456, § 2. Amended by L.1983, c. 132, § 2; L.1984, c. 181, § 34, eff. Nov. 14, 1984; L.1985, c. 488, § 2, eff. Jan. 17, 1986.

39:3–27.15. Disabled veteran; special license plate

Upon the application of any disabled veteran eligible to operate a motor vehicle in this State under the provision of R.S.39:3–10, the Director of the Division of Motor Vehicles may issue for a motor vehicle owned or leased by such a person a license plate bearing the term "Disabled Vet" and registration numbers to be selected from the following registration numbers which shall be reserved for disabled veterans: D V 1 through D V 9999 and 1 D V through 9999 D V. The plate shall resemble the following illustration:

NEW JERSEY
DV1
DISABLED VET

For the purposes of this section, "disabled veteran" shall mean any citizen and resident of this State now or hereafter honorably discharged or released under honorable circumstances from active service in any branch of the Armed Forces of the United States and who has been or shall be declared by the United States Veterans Administration, or its successor, to have a service-connected disability.

L.1979, c. 457, § 1, eff. Aug. 22, 1980. Amended by L.1997, c. 159, § 1, eff. July 3, 1997.

39:3–27.16. Issuance; fee

The special plates authorized by this act may be issued upon proof, satisfactory to the director, that the applicant is a disabled veteran. The fee for such plates shall be $15.00 in addition to any other fees otherwise prescribed by law for the registration of such motor vehicle.

L.1979, c. 457, § 2, eff. Aug. 22, 1980.

39:3–27.17. Unauthorized use; prohibition

No person shall lend the special plates for use on a motor vehicle other than the vehicle for which issued, or use the same for a motor vehicle other than the vehicle for which issued.

L.1979, c. 457, § 3, eff. Aug. 22, 1980.

39:3–27.18. Violations; fine

Any person who violates any of the provisions of this act shall be fined not less than $25.00 nor more than $50.00.

L.1979, c. 457, § 4, eff. Aug. 22, 1980.

39:3–27.19. Commuter vans; registration certificate and plates; fee

The Director of the Division of Motor Vehicles may issue, upon application on a form prepared by him, a registration certificate and registration plates for commuter vans as the application may indicate is warranted in accordance with the definition of these vehicles contained in R.S. 39:1–1 for the registration period as fixed by the director.

For each vehicle used as a commuter van the applicant for the registration thereof shall pay an annual fee of $50 or, if the registration is not annual, the fee shall be fixed by the director in an amount proportionately less or greater than $50 and proportionately less or greater than any other fees or charges imposed by law and collected in connection with the registration fee.

The director shall design a plate to identify a vehicle as a commuter van.

L.1981, c. 139, § 2. Amended by L.1995, c. 112, § 33, eff. June 2, 1995.

39:3–27.20. Termination of use; surrender of special plate

Upon the termination of service of any vehicle used as a commuter van, the owner of the van shall return such special plate to the Division of Motor Vehicles within 10 days.

L.1981, c. 139, § 3.

39:3–27.21. Unauthorized use of special plate

No person shall lend the special plate for use on a motor vehicle other than the vehicle for which issued, or use the same for a motor vehicle other than the vehicle for which issued.

L.1981, c. 139, § 4.

39:3–27.22. Violations; fine

The fine for violating this act is not less than $25.00 nor more than $50.00.

L.1981, c. 139, § 5.

39:3–27.23. Rules and regulations

After consultation with the Department of Energy, the director is authorized to promulgate rules and regulations necessary to effectuate the purposes of this act.

L.1981, c. 139, § 6.

39:3–27.24. P.O.W. license plates; fees

Upon the application of any person who served in the armed forces of the United States and who was held as a prisoner of war by an enemy of the United States during any armed conflict, as certified by the Department of Military and Veterans' Affairs, the Director of the Division of Motor Vehicles shall issue for the motor vehicle owned by such person special plates bearing the letters "P.O.W.," in addition to the registration number and other markings or identification otherwise prescribed by law. There shall be no cost to the applicant for these special plates. The applicant is required to pay the fees otherwise prescribed by law for the registration of motor vehicles.

The surviving spouse of a former prisoner of war who is eligible to operate a motor vehicle in this State under the provision of R.S. 39:3–10 may retain the special license plates obtained by the deceased spouse pursuant to this section for display on a motor vehicle registered to the surviving spouse under the provision of R.S. 39:3–4.

L.1981, c. 236, § 1. Amended by L.1983, c. 56, § 1, eff. Feb. 4, 1983; L.1989, c. 117, § 1, eff. June 29, 1989.

39:3–27.25. Rules and regulations

The Director of the Division of Motor Vehicles and the Adjutant General of the Department of Military and Veterans' Affairs shall promulgate and adopt rules and regulations governing the issuance and use of such registration plates.

L.1981, c. 236, § 2. Amended by L.1989, c. 117, § 2, eff. June 29, 1989.

39:3–27.26. Repealed by L.1983, c. 56, § 2, eff. Feb. 4, 1983

39:3–27.27. Street rod license plates; fees; display of National Street Rod Association safety inspection sticker; violations; fine

a. The owner of a modified antique automobile manufactured before 1949, referred to as a "street rod," which is registered in this State, may apply to the Director of the Division of Motor Vehicles for a special license plate to be displayed in place of the standard license plate.

The special plate shall be issued upon proof that the street rod is registered in a New Jersey street rod club which is fully affiliated with the National Street Rod Association, Inc. The plate shall be issued for the applicant's use only for the registered vehicle and upon a transfer of title he shall surrender the plate to the director.

b. The special plate shall bear the words "street rod" and shall be of a design approved by the director. The fee for the plate shall be $15.00 in addition to the fees otherwise prescribed by law for the registration of the motor vehicle.

c. A person issued the special plate, in addition to the prescribed inspection sticker, shall display a valid National Street Rod Association safety inspection sticker on the vehicle.

d. The fine for violating this act is not less than $25.00 nor more than $50.00.

L.1981, c. 240, § 1.

39:3–27.28. Disposition of fees

All fees collected as provided for herein are hereby appropriated to the Division of Motor Vehicles to fund the additional costs incurred in making such plates available.

L.1981, c. 240, § 2.

39:3–27.29. Officers and elected officials of counties; special license plates

Upon the application of any person who is a member of the board of chosen freeholders in, or surrogate, county clerk, county register of deeds and mortgages, elected county executive, sheriff, or any other officer of any county, the Director of the Division of Motor Vehicles shall issue for the motor vehicle owned or leased by such person special registration plates bearing the word "freeholder, surrogate, county clerk, county register of deeds and mortgages, elected county executive, or sheriff," or such other title designation as may be appropriate, in addition to the registration number and other markings or identification otherwise prescribed by law.

These registration plates shall be imprinted with three letters and a numeral.

L.1981, c. 401, § 1, eff. Jan. 6, 1982. Amended by L.1991, c. 146, § 1, eff. May 28, 1991.

39:3–27.30. Issuance; fees

The motor vehicle registration plates authorized by this act shall be issued upon proof, satisfactory to the director, that the vehicle for which the plates are issued is owned or leased by a freeholder, surrogate, county clerk, county register of deeds and mortgages, elected county executive, sheriff or other county officer. The fee for such plates shall be $15.00 in addition to the fees otherwise prescribed by law for the registration of motor vehicles.

L.1981, c. 401, § 2, eff. Jan. 6, 1982. Amended by L.1991, c. 146, § 2, eff. May 28, 1991.

39:3–27.31. Surrender on leaving office

Said special registration plates shall be surrendered to the Division of Motor Vehicles within 30 days after leaving said office.

L.1981, c. 401, § 3, eff. Jan. 6, 1982. Amended by L.1991, c. 146, § 3, eff. May 28, 1991.

39:3–27.32. Disposition of fees

The fees established hereinabove are appropriated to the Division of Motor Vehicles to fund the additional costs incurred in making such plates available.

L.1981, c. 401, § 4, eff. Jan. 6, 1982.

39:3–27.33. Members of military reserve unit; special license plates

Upon the application of any person who is a resident of this State and who is an active member of a military reserve unit, as certified by the appropriate military authority, the director shall issue for the motor vehicle owned by the person special registration plates, of a design to be approved by the director and at a fee to be prescribed by the director, identifying the holder as a member of a military reserve unit, in addition to the registration number and other markings or identification otherwise prescribed by law.

L.1983, c. 165, § 1, eff. Oct. 30, 1983.

39:3–27.34. Rules and regulations

The director shall promulgate rules and regulations governing the issuance and use of these registration plates and providing for their surrender by persons who cease to be either members of a military reserve unit or residents of this State.

L.1983, c. 165, § 2.

39:3–27.35. Special organization vehicle registration plates for members of nonprofit community, alumni or service organizations; issuance

A person who is a member in good standing of a nonprofit community, alumni or service organization in the State approved by the director pursuant to the provisions of this act may be issued special organization vehicle registration plates to be displayed on motor vehicles owned or leased by that person in place of standard registration plates.

L.1987, c. 374, § 1, eff. July 1, 1988. Amended by L.1989, c. 49, § 1, eff. March 14, 1989.

39:3–27.36. Conditions for issuance

Special organization vehicle registration plates shall be issued subject to the following conditions:

a. Each organization shall appoint an organization representative who will act as a liaison between the organization and the division.

b. The representative shall, upon application on behalf of any member, provide a copy of the charter of the organization to the division which shall indicate the organization's lawful purpose and shall also provide proof of its nonprofit status.

c. The representative shall submit an organization Certification of Membership when requested by the division and, once the organization and a registration plate arrangement under subsection d. are approved, forward a fee of no more than $75.00 as determined by the director for each set of special organization vehicle registration plates, in addition to fees otherwise prescribed by law, for these plates. The Certification of Membership shall be printed at the organization's expense and contain the organization's official letterhead, the signature of the organization's representative, the names and addresses of organization members requesting special organization vehicle registration plates, and the present registration plate numbers of the vehicles of the members.

d. The representative also shall submit to the division the name or initials the organization wishes to be placed at the bottom of the plate and a logotype. The use and arrangement of the name, initials, or logotype of the organization on the registration plates shall be in the sole discretion of the director.

e. Special organization vehicle registration plates shall not be provided to any commercially registered vehicle or any motorcycle.

f. The initial order for plates shall be for no less than 500 members of the organization in good standing and shall be accompanied by the fees prescribed by the director, except that the initial order for plates submitted by a service organization shall be for no less than 175 members.

L.1987, c. 374, § 2, eff. July 1, 1988. Amended by L.1989, c. 49, § 2, eff. March 14, 1989.

39:3–27.37. Authority for final decision of approval of organization

The director shall have the authority to make the final decision as to whether or not an organization is approved for the issuance of special organization vehicle registration plates to its members notwithstanding the organization's compliance with section 2 of P.L. 1987, c. 374 (C. 39:3–27.36).

L.1987, c. 374, § 3, eff. July 1, 1988.

39:3–27.38. Right to suspend approval

The director shall have the right to suspend approval of any organization granted permission to obtain special organization vehicle registration plates on behalf of its members if the organization:

a. No longer qualifies according to the provisions of this act; or

b. Has perpetrated a fraud against the Division of Motor Vehicles in obtaining special plates for its members.

L.1987, c. 374, § 4, eff. July 1, 1988.

39:3–27.39. Rules and regulations

Pursuant to the "Administrative Procedure Act," P.L.1968, c. 410 (C. 52:14B–1 et seq.), the director may adopt rules and regulations governing the design, issuance and use of these vehicle registration plates including the nature of the documentation to be used as proof of nonprofit status, definitions of community, alumni,

and service organizations, and procedures for the return of special organization vehicle registration plates from persons who are no longer members in the approved organization or who have been convicted of any violation pursuant to P.L.1959, c. 56 (C. 39:3–33.5).

L.1987, c. 374, § 5, eff. Jan. 7, 1988.

39:3–27.40. Effect on existing laws and regulations

Notwithstanding the provisions of this act, laws and regulations which are in existence as of the effective date of this act and which provide for the issuance of specific types of special registration plates shall remain operative.

L.1987, c. 374, § 6, eff. July 1, 1988.

39:3–27.41. Surviving spouse of purple heart veteran; retention of special organization vehicle registration plates

The surviving spouse of a purple heart veteran who is eligible to operate a motor vehicle in this State under the provision of R.S. 39:3–10 may retain the special organization vehicle registration plates obtained by the deceased spouse pursuant to P.L.1987, c. 374 (C. 39:3–27.35 et seq.) for display on a motor vehicle registered to the surviving spouse under the provision of R.S. 39:3–4.

L.1989, c. 117, § 3, eff. June 29, 1989.

39:3–27.42. Special license plates issued to mayor or chief executive; fee; surrender of plates; violation

a. Upon the application of any person who is the mayor or chief executive of a municipality in this State, the Director of the Division of Motor Vehicles shall issue special registration plates bearing the word "mayor" in addition to the registration number and other markings or identification prescribed by law for display on a motor vehicle owned or leased by the applicant. Only one set of special registration plates shall be issued to an applicant. The special plates shall be displayed only on the vehicle for which they were issued.

b. The special registration plates authorized by this section shall be issued upon proof to the director in the form of a notarized letter from the clerk of the municipality in which the applicant is the mayor or chief executive verifying that the applicant is the mayor or chief executive.

c. The fee for the motor vehicle registration plates issued under this section shall be $25.00, in addition to the fees otherwise prescribed by law for the registration of motor vehicles. The fees collected for the issuance of these special plates shall be appropriated to the Division of Motor Vehicles to fund the additional costs incurred for the issuance of the plates.

d. A person possessing special registration plates issued under this section who ceases to be the mayor or chief executive of a municipality shall surrender the plates to the director within 30 days after leaving office. If the special registration plates are not surrendered to the director within 30 days, the director may revoke the registration of the motor vehicle for which the special plates were issued.

e. A person who violates a provision of this section shall be fined $50.00.

f. The Director of the Division of Motor Vehicles shall promulgate rules and regulations pursuant to the "Administrative Procedure Act," P.L.1968, c. 410 (C. 52:14B–1 et seq.) necessary to effectuate the purpose of this act.

L.1991, c. 168, § 1, eff. Dec. 16, 1991.

39:3–27.43. Active members of Military Order of Purple Heart authorized to affix approved emblem to license plate

A person who is an active member of the Military Order of the Purple Heart may affix a purple heart emblem which has been approved by the Director of the Division of Motor Vehicles to a license plate issued for a motor vehicle owned or leased by that member.

L.1991, c. 232, § 1.

39:3–27.44. Rules and regulations; use; design; placement on license plates

The Director of the Division of Motor Vehicles shall promulgate rules and regulations governing the use, design, materials and placement of purple heart emblems on license plates issued for motor vehicles owned or leased by active members of the Military Order of the Purple Heart.

L.1991, c. 232, § 2.

39:3–27.45. Special license plates for Silver Star medal recipients; retention of plate by surviving spouse; rules and regulations

a. Upon application of any person who is the holder of a Silver Star medal as certified on the applicant's DD–214 form or on a Certificate of Release or Discharge from Active Duty, the director shall issue, for the motor vehicle owned or leased by the person, distinctive plates bearing a design approved by the director in addition to the registration number and other markings or identification prescribed by law. The plates shall bear the words "Silver Star" and depict the Silver Star emblem. There shall be no cost to the applicant for these special plates other than the fees otherwise prescribed by law for the registration of motor vehicles.

b. The surviving spouse of a former holder of the Silver Star who is eligible to operate a motor vehicle in this State under the provision of R.S.39:3–10 may retain the special license plates obtained by the deceased spouse pursuant to this section for display on a motor vehicle registered to the surviving spouse under the provisions of R.S.39:3–4.

c. The director shall promulgate rules and regulations governing the issuance and use of these registration plates.

d. A person who is issued a Silver Star special plate may affix a silver star insignia which has been approved by the director to the license plate. The director shall promulgate rules and regulations governing the use, design, materials and placement of an insignia on the Silver Star special license plate.

L.1992, c. 154, § 1, eff. April 1, 1993. Amended by L.1999, c. 127, § 1, eff. Dec. 25, 1999.

39:3–27.46. Special license plates for Combat Infantryman Badge recipients; fee; retention of plate by surviving spouse; rules and regulations

a. Upon application of any person who is the holder of a Combat Infantryman Badge, as certified on the applicant's DD–214 form or on a Certificate of Release or Discharge from Active Duty, the director shall issue, for the motor vehicle owned or leased by the person, distinctive plates bearing a design approved by the director in addition to the registration number and other markings or identification prescribed by law. The plates shall bear the words "Combat Infantryman Badge" and depict the Combat Infantryman Badge emblem. The fee for these plates shall be $15 in addition to the fees otherwise prescribed by law for the registration of motor vehicles.

b. The surviving spouse of a former holder of the Combat Infantryman Badge who is eligible to operate a motor vehicle in this State under the provisions of R.S. 39:3–10 may retain the special license plates obtained by the deceased spouse pursuant to this section for display on a motor vehicle registered to the surviving spouse under the provisions of R.S. 39:3–4.

c. The director shall promulgate rules and regulations governing the issuance and use of these registration plates.

L.1993, c. 72, § 1, eff. Aug. 1, 1993.

39:3–27.47. Definitions

As used in this act:

"Commissioner" means the Commissioner of Environmental Protection and Energy;

"Department" means the Department of Environmental Protection and Energy;

"Director" means the Director of the Division of Motor Vehicles in the Department of Law and Public Safety;

"Division" means the Division of Motor Vehicles in the Department of Law and Public Safety;

"Fund" means the "Coastal Protection Trust Fund" created pursuant to section 4 of this act.[1]

L.1993, c. 168, § 1, eff. Dec. 29, 1993.

1 N.J.S.A. § 39:3–27.50.

39:3–27.48. Coastal protection license plates; design

The Director of the Division of Motor Vehicles shall, upon proper application therefor, issue coastal protection license plates for any motor vehicle owned or leased and registered in the State. In addition to the registration number and other markings or identification otherwise prescribed by law, a coastal protection license plate shall display words or a slogan and an emblem indicating support for, or an interest in, the protection of the coastal resources of this State. The words or slogan and emblem shall be chosen by the director; however, the director shall solicit, in conjunction with the Legislature, input from the general public on the design of the plate and shall review the submissions prior to choosing the design. Issuance of coastal protection license plates in accordance with this section shall be subject to the limitations of section 3 of P.L.1959, c. 56 (C. 39:3–33.5) and other applicable requirements of chapter 3 of Title 39 of the Revised Statutes, except as hereinafter otherwise specifically provided.

L.1993, c. 168, § 2, eff. Dec. 29, 1993.

39:3–27.49. Application for coastal protection license plates; fees

a. Application for issuance of a coastal protection license plate shall be made to the division on forms and in a manner as may be prescribed by the director. In order to be deemed complete, an application shall be accompanied by a fee of $50, which fee shall be in addition to the fee for the renewal of the registration certificate, payable to the division.

b. The annual fee for the registration certificate of a motor vehicle that has been issued a coastal protection license plate pursuant to the provisions of this act shall include in each year subsequent to the year of issuance a coastal protection license plate fee in the amount of $10, which fee shall be in addition to the fee for the renewal of the registration certificate, collected by the division and deposited into the Coastal Protection Trust Fund created pursuant to section 4 of this act.[1]

L.1993, c. 168, § 3, eff. Dec. 29, 1993.

[1] N.J.S.A. § 39:3–27.50.

39:3–27.50. Coastal Protection Trust Fund; use of monies collected; special emergency reserve account; use of monies

a. There is created in the Department of the Treasury a special non-lapsing fund to be known as the "Coastal Protection Trust Fund." There shall be deposited in the fund the amount collected from all license plate fees collected pursuant to section 3 of this act,[1] less the amounts necessary to reimburse the division for administrative costs pursuant to section 5 of this act.[2] Except as otherwise provided in subsection b. of this section, moneys deposited in the fund shall be dedicated to the purposes set forth in section 6 of this act.[3] Moneys deposited in the fund shall be held in interest-bearing accounts in public depositories as defined pursuant to section 1 of P.L.1970, c. 236 (C. 17:9–41), and may be invested or reinvested in such securities as are approved by the State Treasurer.

Interest or other income earned on moneys deposited into the fund, and any moneys which may be appropriated or otherwise become available for the purposes of the fund, shall be credited to and deposited in the fund for use as set forth in this act.

b. There is created within the "Coastal Protection Trust Fund" a special emergency reserve account, to which shall annually be credited the amount of license plate fees collected in excess of $1,000,000 during the year. The commissioner may, pursuant to specific appropriations made by law, use moneys deposited in the special emergency reserve account to:

(1) finance shore protection projects of an emergency nature in the event of storm, stress of weather or similar act of God; and

(2) provide for the cleanup of discharges of pollutants or contaminants discharged into the ocean waters of this State.

L.1993, c. 168, § 4, eff. Dec. 29, 1993.

[1] N.J.S.A. § 39:3–27.49.
[2] N.J.S.A. § 39:3–27.51.
[3] N.J.S.A. § 39:3–27.52.

39:3–27.51. Fees used to reimburse division for costs

a. Prior to the deposit of license plate fees collected pursuant to section 3 of this act [1] into the fund, amounts thereof as are necessary shall be used to reimburse the division for all costs reasonably and actually incurred, as stipulated by the director, for:

(1) producing, issuing, renewing, and publicizing the availability of coastal protection license plates; and

(2) any initial fees, in an amount not to exceed $150,000, collected from the issuance of coastal protection license plates to be allocated to the division to pay the cost of any computer programming changes that may be necessary to implement the coastal protection license plate program established by this act.

b. The director shall annually certify to the commissioner the average cost per license plate incurred in the immediately preceding year by the division in producing, issuing, renewing, and publicizing the availability of coastal protection license plates. The annual certification of the average cost per license plate shall be approved by the Joint Budget Oversight Committee, or its successor.

c. In the event that the average cost per license plate as certified by the director and approved by the Joint Budget Oversight Committee, or its successor, is greater than the $50 application fee established in subsection a. of section 3 of this act in two consecutive fiscal years, the director may discontinue the issuance of coastal protection license plates.

L.1993, c. 168, § 5, eff. Dec. 29, 1993.

[1] N.J.S.A. § 39:3–27.49.

39:3–27.52. Appropriations from fund

a. The Governor shall include in the annual budget recommendations to the Legislature pursuant to section 11 of article 3 of P.L.1944, c. 112 (C. 52:27B–20), a recommendation for an appropriation from the fund for the purposes set forth in this section. The Legislature shall annually appropriate to the department from the first $1,000,000 in license plate fees collected pursuant to section 3 of this act [1] and deposited in the fund:

(1) An amount not to exceed $600,000 for the cost of any program of the department, or conducted in cooperation with the Department of Corrections that utilizes prisoners to clean up or maintain beaches or shores;

(2) An amount not to exceed $200,000 for the cost of providing aircraft overflights for monitoring, surveillance and enforcement activities of the Cooperative Coastal Monitoring Program established by the department;

(3) An amount not to exceed $150,000 for establishment of a program of grants for the construction of sewage pump-out devices for marine sanitation devices and portable toilet emptying receptacles at public or private marinas or boatyards in furtherance of the provisions of P.L.1988, c. 117 (C. 58:10A–56 et seq.); and

(4) An amount not to exceed $50,000 to implement the provisions of the "New Jersey Adopt a Beach Act," P.L.1992, c. 213 (C. 13:19–22 et seq.).

b. If an amount less than $1,000,000 is collected from license plate fees pursuant to section 3 of this act in any given year, the amounts provided in paragraph (1) through paragraph (4), inclusive, of this subsection shall be reduced proportionately, and no amounts shall be credited to the special emergency reserve account created pursuant to subsection b. of section 4 of this act.

L.1993, c. 168, § 6, eff. Dec. 29, 1993.

[1] N.J.S.A. § 39:3–27.49.

39:3–27.53. Notification of availability of coastal protection license plates

The director shall notify eligible motorists of the opportunity to obtain coastal protection license plates by including a notice with all motor vehicle registration renewals, and by posting appropriate posters or signs in all division facilities and offices, as may be provided by the department. The notices, posters, and signs shall be designed by the commissioner. The designs shall be subject to the approval of the director, and the commissioner shall supply the division with the notices, posters, and signs to be circulated or posted by that division.

L.1993, c. 168, § 7, eff. Dec. 29, 1993.

39:3–27.54. Interagency memorandum of agreement

The commissioner, the director, and the State Treasurer shall develop and enter into an interagency memorandum of agreement setting forth the proce-

dures to be followed by the department and the division in carrying out their respective responsibilities under this act.

L.1993, c. 168, § 8, eff. Dec. 29, 1993.

39:3–27.55. Animal welfare license plates; application

a. Upon proper application, the Director of the Division of Motor Vehicles may issue animal welfare license plates for a motor vehicle owned or leased and registered in the State. In addition to the registration number and other markings or identification otherwise prescribed by law, an animal welfare license plate shall display words or a slogan and an emblem indicating support for, or interest in, animal welfare. The words or slogan and emblem shall be selected by the director. Issuance of animal welfare license plates in accordance with this subsection shall be subject to the limitations of section 3 of P.L.1959, c. 56 (C. 39:3–33.5) and other applicable requirements of chapter 3 of Title 39 of the Revised Statutes, except as hereinafter specifically provided.

b. Application for issuance of an animal welfare license plate shall be made to the director on forms and in a manner as may be prescribed by the director. In order to be deemed complete, an application shall be accompanied by a fee of $50, payable to the Division of Motor Vehicles, which shall be in addition to the fee otherwise prescribed by law for the registration of motor vehicles. The annual renewal fee for the registration certificate of a motor vehicle for which an animal welfare license plate has been issued shall include, in each year subsequent to the year of issuance, an animal welfare license plate fee in the amount of $10, which shall be in addition to the fee for the renewal of the registration certificate.

L.1993, c. 184, § 1, eff. Jan. 6, 1994.

39:3–27.56. Fees to be deposited in Animal Population Control Fund

Moneys from the application and renewal fees collected by the Division of Motor Vehicles for animal welfare license plates shall be deposited in the Animal Population Control Fund established in the Department of Health pursuant to P.L.1983, c. 172 (C. 4:19A–1 et al.), and used for the purposes of that act, except that an amount not to exceed $100,000 of the fees first collected from the issuance of these plates shall be allocated to the Division of Motor Vehicles to defray the administrative costs necessary to implement the provisions of this act.

L.1993, c. 184, § 2, eff. Jan. 6, 1994.

39:3–27.57. Notification of availability of animal welfare license plates

The director shall notify eligible motorists of the opportunity to obtain animal welfare license plates by including a notice with all motor vehicle registration renewals, and by posting appropriate posters or signs in all division facilities and offices. The notices, posters and signs shall be designed by the Commissioner of Health, in consultation with advocacy groups having an interest in animal welfare and animal population control, subject to the approval of the director. The Department of Health shall supply the division with the notices, posters, and signs to be circulated or posted by the division.

L.1993, c. 184, § 3, eff. Jan. 6, 1994.

39:3–27.58. Interagency memorandum of agreement

The Commissioner of Health and the director shall enter into an interagency memorandum of agreement setting forth the procedures to be followed by the Department of Health and the Division of Motor Vehicles in carrying out their respective responsibilities under this act.

L.1993, c. 184, § 4, eff. Jan. 6, 1994.

39:3–27.59. Emergency medical technician-ambulance license plates; application; fees

a. Upon application by a person who has been certified by the Commissioner of Health as an Emergency Medical Technician–Ambulance, the Director of the Division of Motor Vehicles shall issue for the motor vehicle owned or leased by the applicant special vehicle registration plates bearing the letters "EMT–A." The plates shall also include the vehicle registration number and other markings or identification prescribed by law, including the "Tree of Life" insignia for an Emergency Medical Technician–Ambulance in a design approved by the director. Only one set of special registration plates shall be issued to an applicant. The special plates shall be displayed only on the vehicle for which they were issued.

b. The special vehicle registration plates authorized by this section shall be issued upon proof satisfactory to the director that the applicant meets the condition specified in subsection a. of this section. A person who has been issued special vehicle registration plates under this section shall return the special plates when that person no longer meets the qualification in subsection a. of this section.

c. The fee for the motor vehicle registration plates issued under this section shall be $25, in addition to the fees otherwise prescribed by law for the registration of motor vehicles.

d. A person who violates a provision of this section shall be fined $50.

e. The director may adopt rules and regulations pursuant to the "Administrative Procedure Act," P.L. 1968, c. 410 (C. 52:14B–1 et seq.), governing the issuance and use of the special vehicle registration plates authorized by this section.

L.1994, c. 29, § 1, eff. Sept. 1, 1994.

39:3–27.60. Fees for special license plates to cover costs of implementation

The director shall retain from the fees collected pursuant to subsection c. of section 1 of this act [1] such sums as are necessary to provide for all costs incurred by the division in the implementation of this act as certified by the director.

L.1994, c. 29, § 2, eff. Sept. 1, 1994.
[1] N.J.S.A. § 39:3–27.59.

39:3–27.61. Definitions

As used in this act:

"Director" means the Director of the Division of Motor Vehicles in the Department of Law and Public Safety;

"Division" means the Division of Motor Vehicles in the Department of Law and Public Safety;

"Fund" means the fund created pursuant to section 4 of this act.[1]

L.1995, c. 176, § 1, eff. Jan. 6, 1996.
[1] N.J.S.A. § 39:3–27.64.

39:3–27.62. Olympic license plates authorized

The director shall, upon proper application therefor, issue United States Olympic license plates, for any motor vehicle owned or leased and registered in the State. In addition to the registration number and other markings or identification otherwise prescribed by law, a United States Olympic license plate shall display the official United States Olympic Committee logo and wording which indicates support for the advancement of excellence in amateur athletic competition in this State. The wording, design and color scheme of the plate shall be chosen by the director.

L.1995, c. 176, § 2, eff. Jan. 6, 1996.

39:3–27.63. Application and fee for olympic license plate

Application for issuance of a United States Olympic license plate shall be made to the division on forms and in a manner as may be prescribed by the director. In order to be deemed complete, an application shall be accompanied by a fee of $50, in addition to any other fees required by law for the registration of the motor vehicle.

An annual fee of $10 shall be charged for the renewal of a United States Olympic license plate in addition to any other fees required by law. Applicants for a United States Olympic license plate shall be advised of the annual $10 renewal fee at the time of initial application.

L.1995, c. 176, § 3, eff. Jan. 6, 1996.

39:3–27.64. Garden state games trust fund created

There is created in the Department of the Treasury a special non-lapsing fund to be known as the "Garden State Games Trust Fund." There shall be deposited in the fund the $50 application fee and the $10 renewal fee collected pursuant to section 3 of this act.[1] Moneys deposited in the fund shall be dedicated to the purposes set forth in section 5 of this act.[2] Moneys deposited in the fund shall be held in interest-bearing accounts in public depositories as defined pursuant to section 1 of P.L.1970, c. 236 (C. 17:9–41), and may be invested or reinvested in such securities as are approved by the State Treasurer. Interest or other income earned on moneys deposited into the fund, and any moneys which may be appropriated or otherwise become available for the purposes of the fund, shall be credited to and deposited in the fund for use as set forth in this act.

L.1995, c. 176, § 4, eff. Jan. 6, 1996.

[1] N.J.S.A. § 39:3–27.63.
[2] N.J.S.A. § 39:3–27.65.

39:3–27.65. Garden state games trust fund; allocation of funds

Moneys deposited in the fund shall be allocated as follows:

a. Prior to the deposit of license plate fees collected pursuant to section 4 of this act[1] into the fund, the division shall be reimbursed for all costs reasonably and actually incurred as stipulated by the director for:

(1) producing, issuing, renewing and publicizing the availability of United States Olympic license plates; and

(2) any initial fees collected from the issuance of United States Olympic license plates shall be allocated to the division to pay the cost of any computer programming changes that may be necessary to implement the United States Olympic license plate program established by this act.

b. The director shall annually certify the average cost per license plate incurred in the immediately preceding year by the division in producing, issuing, renewing and publicizing the availability of United States Olympic license plates. The annual certification of the average cost per license plate shall be approved by the Joint Budget Oversight Committee, or its successor.

c. In the event that the average cost per license plate as certified by the director and approved by the Joint Budget Oversight Committee, or its successor, is greater than the $50 application fee established in section 3 of this act[2] in two consecutive fiscal years, the director may discontinue the issuance of United States Olympic license plates.

d. The moneys remaining in the fund shall be provided in equal amounts to the Garden State Games, for New Jersey's sports festival for amateur athletes, and the United States Olympic Committee.

L.1995, c. 176, § 5, eff. Jan. 6, 1996.

[1] N.J.S.A. § 39:3–27.64.
[2] N.J.S.A. § 39:3–27.63.

39:3–27.66. Notice of availability of olympic license plates

The director shall notify eligible motorists of the opportunity to obtain United States Olympic license plates by including a notice with all motor vehicle registration renewals, and by posting appropriate posters or signs in all division facilities and offices.

L.1995, c. 176, § 6, eff. Jan. 6, 1996.

39:3–27.67. Issuance of Battleship U.S.S. New Jersey license plates

The Chief Administrator of the Motor Vehicle Commission shall, upon proper application therefor, issue Battleship U.S.S. New Jersey license plates for any motor vehicle owned or leased and registered in the State. In addition to the registration number and other markings of identification otherwise prescribed by law, the plate shall display a depiction of a battleship and wording which either recognizes the U.S.S. New Jersey's role in U.S. naval history or indicates support for the restoration, and maintenance of the U.S.S. New Jersey. The wording, design and color scheme of the plate shall be chosen by the chief administrator.

L.1995, c. 252, § 1, eff. April 1, 1996. Amended by L.2007, c. 262, § 1, eff. Jan. 13, 2008.

39:3–27.68. Application; fees

Application for a Battleship U.S.S. New Jersey license plate shall be made to the Division of Motor Vehicles on forms and in a manner prescribed by the director and shall be accompanied by a fee of $50, which shall be in addition to all fees otherwise required by law for the registration of the motor vehicle. The annual renewal of a registration certificate of a motor vehicle that has been issued a Battleship U.S.S. New Jersey license plate shall be accompanied by an additional fee of $15. The $50 application fee and $15 renewal fee shall be deposited by the division in the Battleship New Jersey Memorial Fund created pursuant to section 3 of this act.[1]

L.1995, c. 252, § 2, eff. April 1, 1996.

[1] N.J.S.A. § 39:3–27.69.

39:3–27.69. Battleship New Jersey Memorial Fund

There is created in the Department of the Treasury a special non-lapsing fund to be known as the "Battleship New Jersey Memorial Fund." There shall be deposited into the fund the additional application and renewal fees collected pursuant to section 2 of P.L.1995, c. 252 (C.39:3–27.68) and any interest earned thereon, less the amounts necessary to reimburse the division for administrative costs pursuant to section 4 of P.L.1995, c. 252 (C.39:3–27.70). Monies deposited in the fund shall be annually appropriated to the Home Port Alliance to support the restoration, maintenance and operation of the Battleship U.S.S. New Jersey.

L.1995, c. 252, § 3, eff. April 1, 1996. Amended by L.2007, c. 262, § 2, eff. Jan. 13, 2008.

39:3–27.70.   Use of license plate fees

a.   Prior to the deposit of license plate fees collected pursuant to section 2 of this act [1] into the fund, amounts thereof as are necessary shall be used to reimburse the division for costs reasonably and actually incurred as stipulated by the director for producing, issuing, renewing, and publicizing the availability of Battleship U.S.S. New Jersey license plates, including the cost of any initial computer programming changes.

b.   The director annually shall certify to the State Treasurer the average cost per license plate incurred in the immediately preceding year by the division in producing, issuing, renewing, and publicizing the availability of Battleship U.S.S. New Jersey license plates. The annual certification of the average cost per license plate shall be approved by the Joint Budget Oversight Committee, or its successor.

c.   In the event that the average cost per license plate as certified by the director and approved by the Joint Budget Oversight Committee, or its successor, is greater than the $50 application fee established in section 2 of this act in two consecutive fiscal years, the director may discontinue the issuance of Battleship U.S.S. New Jersey license plates.

L.1995, c. 252, § 4, eff. April 1, 1996.

[1] N.J.S.A. § 39:3–27.68.

39:3–27.71.   Notification of motorists

The chief administrator shall notify eligible motorists of the opportunity to obtain Battleship U.S.S. New Jersey license plates by including a notice with all motor vehicle registration renewals and by posting appropriate posters or signs in all commission facilities and offices. The notices, posters, and signs shall be designed by the commission.

L.1995, c. 252, § 5, eff. April 1, 1996.   Amended by L.2007, c. 262, § 3, eff. Jan. 13, 2008.

39:3–27.72.   Definitions

As used in P.L.1995, c. 368 (C.39:3–27.72 et seq.):

"Department" means the Department of State;

"Director" means the Director of the Division of Motor Vehicles in the Department of Transportation;

"Division" means the Division of Motor Vehicles in the Department of Transportation;

"Fund" means the "Historic Preservation License Plate Fund" created pursuant to section 4 of P.L.1995, c. 368 (C.39:3–27.75);

"Historic resources" means the historic resources in New Jersey, and shall include, but need not necessarily be limited to, buildings, sites, and structures listed in or eligible for listing in the New Jersey Register of Historic Places, and museums and library collections related to New Jersey history; and

"Secretary" means the Secretary of State.

L.1995, c. 368, § 1, eff. July 3, 1996.   Amended by L.1999, c. 152, § 52, eff. June 30, 1999.

39:3–27.73.   Historic preservation license plates; slogans and emblems displayed

The Director of the Division of Motor Vehicles shall, upon proper application therefor, issue historic preservation license plates for any motor vehicle owned or leased and registered in the State.   In addition to the registration number and other markings or identification otherwise prescribed by law, an historic preservation license plate shall display words or a slogan and an emblem indicating support for, or an interest in, historic preservation.   The words or slogan and emblem shall be chosen by the director in consultation with the Historic Preservation License Plate Advisory Committee established pursuant to subsection a. of section 4 of this act;[1] however, the director shall solicit, in conjunction with the Legislature, input from the general public on the design of the plate and shall review the submissions prior to choosing the design.   Issuance of historic preservation license plates in accordance with this section shall be subject to the provisions of chapter 3 of Title 39 of the Revised Statutes, except as hereinafter otherwise specifically provided.

L.1995, c. 368, § 2, eff. July 3, 1996.

[1] N.J.S.A. § 39:3–27.75.

39:3–27.74.   Application; fee; additional fee with registration

a.   Application for issuance of an historic preservation license plate shall be made to the division on forms and in a manner as may be prescribed by the director. In order to be deemed complete, an application shall be accompanied by a fee of $50 payable to the division, which fee shall be in addition to all fees otherwise required by law for the registration of the motor vehicle.

b.   The annual fee for the registration certificate of a motor vehicle that has been issued an historic preservation license plate pursuant to the provisions of this act shall include in each year subsequent to the year of issuance a fee in the amount of $10, which fee shall be in addition to all fees otherwise required by law for the renewal of the registration of the motor vehicle and shall be collected by the division and deposited in the Historic Preservation License Plate Fund created pursuant to section 4 of this act.[1]

L.1995, c. 368, § 3, eff. July 3, 1996.

[1] N.J.S.A. § 39:39:3–27.75.

39:3–27.75.   Historic Preservation License Plate Fund; fees deposited

a.   There is created in the Department of Community Affairs a special non-lapsing fund to be known as the "Historic Preservation License Plate Fund."   The fund shall be administered by the New Jersey Historic Trust. There shall be deposited in the fund the amount collected from all license plate fees collected pursuant to section 3 of P.L. 1995, c. 368 (C.39:3–27.74), less the amounts necessary to reimburse the division for administrative costs pursuant to section 5 of P.L.1995, c. 368 (C.39:3–27.76). Moneys deposited in the fund shall be dedicated to (1) the awarding of grants to State agencies, local government units, and qualifying tax-exempt nonprofit organizations to meet costs related to the physical preservation of, development of interpretive and educational programming for, or operation of New Jersey's historic resources pursuant to the criteria established by the New Jersey Heritage Tourism Task Force in the heritage tourism master plan prepared and submitted by the New Jersey Heritage Tourism Task Force; and (2) the payment of expenses incurred by the New Jersey Heritage Tourism Task Force up to $135,000 in implementing the provisions of P.L.2006, c. 60. Approval of any grants shall be made by the New Jersey Historic Trust pursuant to its guidelines.

b. Moneys deposited in the fund shall be held in interest-bearing accounts in public depositories as defined pursuant to section 1 of P.L.1970, c. 236 (C.17:9–41), and may be invested or reinvested in such securities as are approved by the State Treasurer. Interest or other income earned on moneys deposited in the fund, and any moneys which may be appropriated or otherwise become available for the purposes of the fund, shall be credited to and deposited in the fund for use as set forth in P.L.1995, c. 368 (C.39:3–27.72 et seq.).

L.1995, c. 368, § 4, eff. July 3, 1996. Amended by L.1999, c. 152, § 53, eff. June 30, 1999; L.2006, c. 60, § 7, eff. Aug. 2, 2006.

39:3–27.76. Reimbursement for costs incurred by historic preservation license plate program; average cost per license plate

a. Prior to the deposit of license plate fees collected pursuant to section 3 of P.L.1995, c. 368 (C.39:3–27.74) into the fund, amounts thereof as are necessary shall be used to reimburse the division for all costs reasonably and actually incurred, as stipulated by the director, for:

(1) producing, issuing, renewing, and publicizing the availability of historic preservation license plates; and

(2) any initial computer programming changes that may be necessary to implement the historic preservation license plate program established by P.L.1995, c. 368 (C.39:3–27.72 et seq.).

b. The director shall annually certify to the secretary the average cost per license plate incurred in the immediately preceding year by the division in producing, issuing, renewing, and publicizing the availability of historic preservation license plates. The annual certification of the average cost per license plate shall be approved by the Joint Budget Oversight Committee, or its successor.

c. In the event that the average cost per license plate as certified by the director and approved by the

Joint Budget Oversight Committee, or its successor, is greater than the $50 application fee established in subsection a. of section 3 of P.L.1995, c. 368 (C.39:3–27.74) in two consecutive fiscal years, the director may discontinue the issuance of historic preservation license plates.

L.1995, c. 368, § 5, eff. July 3, 1996. Amended by L.1999, c. 152, § 54, eff. June 30, 1999.

39:3–27.77. Notice to motorists of availability of license plates

The director shall notify eligible motorists of the opportunity to obtain historic preservation license plates by including a notice with all motor vehicle registration renewals, and by posting appropriate posters or signs in all division facilities and offices, as may be provided by the department. The notices, posters, and signs shall be designed by the New Jersey Historic Trust with the approval of the secretary. The designs shall be subject to the approval of the director, and the secretary shall supply the division with the notices, posters, and signs to be circulated or posted by that division.

L.1995, c. 368, § 6, eff. July 3, 1996. Amended by L.1999, c. 152, § 55, eff. June 30, 1999; L.2006, c. 60, § 8, eff. Aug. 2, 2006.

39:3–27.78. Interagency memorandum of agreement

The secretary, the New Jersey Historic Trust, the director, and the State Treasurer shall develop and enter into an interagency memorandum of agreement setting forth the procedures to be followed by the departments, the New Jersey Historic Trust, and the division in carrying out their respective responsibilities under P.L.1995, c. 368 (C.39:3–27.72 et seq.).

L.1995, c. 368, § 7, eff. July 3, 1996. Amended by L.1999, c. 152, § 56, eff. June 30, 1999; L.2006, c. 60, § 9, eff. Aug. 2, 2006.

39:3–27.79. Shade tree and community forest preservation license plates

The Director of the Division of Motor Vehicles in the Department of Transportation shall, upon proper application therefor, issue shade tree and community forest preservation license plates for any motor vehicle, including a commercial motor vehicle issued a registration or license plate pursuant to R.S.39:3–20, owned or leased and registered in the State. In addition to the registration number and other markings or identification otherwise prescribed by law, a shade tree and community forest preservation license plate shall display words or a slogan and an emblem indicating support for, or an interest in, shade tree and community forest preservation except for a shade tree and community forest preservation license plate issued to a commercial motor vehicle which, in addition to the registration number and other markings prescribed by law, shall display an emblem indicating an interest in shade tree and community forest preservation in New Jersey. The words or slogan and emblem shall be chosen by the director; however, the director shall solicit, in conjunction with the Legislature, input from the general public on the design of the plate and shall review the submissions prior to choosing the design. Issuance of shade tree and community forest preservation license plates in accordance with this section shall be subject to the provisions of chapter 3 of Title 39 of the Revised Statutes, except as hereinafter otherwise specifically provided.

L.1996, c. 135, § 10, eff. June 3, 1997. Amended by L.2001, c. 436, § 1, eff. July 1, 2001.

39:3–27.80. Application for shade tree and community forest preservation license plate

a. Application for issuance of a shade tree and community forest preservation license plate shall be made to the Division of Motor Vehicles on forms and in a manner as may be prescribed by the director. In order to be deemed complete, an application shall be accompanied by a fee of $50 payable to the Division of Motor Vehicles, which fee shall be in addition to all fees otherwise required by law for the registration of the motor vehicle.

b. The annual fee for the registration certificate of a motor vehicle that has been issued a shade tree and community forest preservation license plate pursuant to the provisions of P.L.1996, c. 135 (C. 13:1L–17.1 et al.) shall include in each year subsequent to the year of issuance a fee in the amount of $10, which fee shall be in addition to all fees otherwise required by law for the renewal of the registration of the motor vehicle and shall be collected by the Division of Motor Vehicles and deposited in the Shade Tree and Community Forest Preservation License Plate Fund created pursuant to section 12 of P.L.1996, c. 135 (C. 39:3–27.81).

L.1996, c. 135, § 11, eff. June 3, 1997.

39:3–27.81. Shade tree and community forest preservation license plate fund

a. There is created in the Department of Environmental Protection a special non-lapsing fund to be known as the "Shade Tree and Community Forest Preservation License Plate Fund." There shall be deposited in the fund the amount collected from all license plate fees collected pursuant to section 11 of P.L.1996, c. 135 (C. 39:3–27.80), less the amounts necessary to reimburse the Division of Motor Vehicles for all costs authorized pursuant to section 13 of P.L.1996, c. 135 (C. 39:3–27.82). Monies deposited in the fund shall be dedicated for support and funding of projects and programs concerned with shade tree and community forest preservation, including but not limited to the awarding of grants for such purposes to municipal shade tree commissions created pursuant to R.S. 40:64–1 et seq., county shade tree commissions created pursuant to R.S. 40:37–1 et seq., municipalities, and counties. Monies in the fund may also be awarded as grants to local governments and shade tree commissions pursuant to subsection c. of section 4 of P.L.1996,

c. 135 (C. 13:1L–17.4). Monies deposited in the fund shall be held in interest-bearing accounts in public depositories as defined pursuant to section 1 of P.L. 1970, c. 236 (C. 17:9–41), and may be invested or reinvested in such securities as are approved by the State Treasurer. Interest or other income earned on monies deposited in the fund, and any monies which may be appropriated or otherwise become available for the purposes of the fund, shall be credited to and deposited in the fund for use as set forth in P.L.1996, c. 135 (C. 13:1L–17.1 et al.).

b. The Division of Parks and Forestry in the Department of Environmental Protection shall administer the fund and the distribution of grants pursuant to this section. The Division of Parks and Forestry shall, by rule or regulation adopted pursuant to the "Administrative Procedure Act," P.L.1968, c. 410 (C.52:14B–1 et seq.), establish qualifications for determining grant eligibility, criteria for ranking grant applications, and standards and authorized purposes for the use of such grants.

L.1996, c. 135, § 12, eff. June 3, 1997.

39:3–27.82. Use of license plate fees; reimbursement for costs related to issuance of plates

a. Prior to the deposit of license plate fees collected pursuant to section 11 of P.L.1996, c. 135 (C. 39:3–27.80) into the fund, amounts thereof as are necessary shall be used to reimburse the Division of Motor Vehicles for all costs reasonably and actually incurred, as stipulated by the director, for:

(1) producing, issuing, renewing, and publicizing the availability of shade tree and community forest preservation license plates; and

(2) any initial computer programming changes that may be necessary to implement the shade tree and community forest preservation license plate program established by P.L.1996, c. 135 (C.39:3–27.79 et al.).

b. The Director of the Division of Motor Vehicles shall annually certify to the Commissioner of Environmental Protection the average cost per license plate incurred in the immediately preceding year by the Division of Motor Vehicles in producing, issuing, renewing, and publicizing the availability of shade tree and community forest preservation license plates. The annual certification of the average cost per license plate shall be approved by the Joint Budget Oversight Committee, or its successor.

c. In the event that the average cost per license plate as certified by the director and approved by the Joint Budget Oversight Committee, or its successor, is greater than the $50 application fee established in subsection a. of section 11 of P.L.1996, c. 135 (C. 39:3–27.80) in two consecutive fiscal years, the director may discontinue the issuance of shade tree and community forest preservation license plates.

L.1996, c. 135, § 13, eff. June 3, 1997.

39:3–27.83. Methods used to notify motorists of availability of license plates

The Director of the Division of Motor Vehicles shall notify eligible motorists of the opportunity to obtain shade tree and community forest preservation license plates by including a notice with all motor vehicle registration renewals, and by posting appropriate posters or signs in all facilities and offices of the Division of Motor Vehicles. The notices, posters, and signs shall be designed by the Commissioner of Environmental Protection. The designs shall be subject to the approval of the director, and the Commissioner of Environmental Protection shall supply the Division of Motor Vehicles with the notices, posters, and signs to be circulated or posted by that division.

L.1996, c. 135, § 14, eff. June 3, 1997.

39:3–27.84. Interagency memorandum of agreement

The Commissioner of Environmental Protection, the Director of the Division of Motor Vehicles, and the State Treasurer shall develop and enter into an interagency memorandum of agreement setting forth the procedures to be followed by the departments and the Division of Motor Vehicles in carrying out their respective responsibilities under P.L.1996, c. 135 (C. 13:1L–17.1 et al.).

L.1996, c. 135, § 15, eff. Dec. 5, 1996.

39:3–27.85. Pinelands preservation license plates; application fee; use of proceeds

a. The director may issue for a motor vehicle registered in this State special license plates bearing, in addition to the registration number and other markings or identification otherwise prescribed by law, words and an emblem indicating support for, or an interest in, Pinelands preservation. The license plate shall be designed by the director, in consultation with the Pinelands Commission created by section 4 of P.L.1979, c. 111 (C. 13:18A–4). Issuance of Pinelands preservation license plates shall be subject to all applicable requirements of chapter 3 of Title 39 of the Revised Statutes, except as hereinafter otherwise specifically provided.

b. The director shall collect a $50 application fee for the Pinelands preservation license plate in addition to the fees otherwise prescribed by law for the registration of the motor vehicle. The director shall collect annually subsequent to the year of issuance of the license plate a $10 fee for the license plate in addition to the fees otherwise prescribed by law for the registration of the motor vehicle. The additional fees required by this subsection shall be deposited into the Pinelands Preservation Fund, established pursuant to section 2 of P.L.1996, c. 147 (C. 13:18A–55).

c. The director shall annually certify to the State Treasurer the average cost per license plate incurred in the immediately preceding year by the Division of Motor Vehicles in producing, issuing, renewing, making computer programming changes in connection with and publicizing the Pinelands preservation license plates. On a quarterly basis, the State Treasurer shall transfer a sum equal to the division's cost in connection with the Pinelands preservation license plates from the Pinelands Preservation Fund, established pursuant to section 2 of P.L.1996, c. 147 (C. 13:18A–55), to the division. The annual certification of the average cost per license plate shall be approved by the Joint Budget Oversight Committee, or its successor.

d. In the event that the average cost per license plate as certified by the director and approved by the Joint Budget Oversight Committee, or its successor, is greater than the $50 application fee established in subsection b. of this section in two consecutive fiscal years, the director may discontinue the issuance of Pinelands preservation license plates.

e. The Pinelands Commission and the director shall develop and enter into an interagency memorandum of agreement on procedures to be followed to carry out their respective responsibilities under this act.

L.1996, c. 147, § 1, eff. June 18, 1997.

39:3–27.86. Issuance of Barnegat Bay Decoy and Baymen's Museum license plates

The Director of the Division of Motor Vehicles shall, upon proper application therefor, issue Barnegat Bay Decoy and Baymen's Museum license plates or such other maritime history or marine life preservation project license plates as the Department of Environmental Protection selects pursuant to section 4 of this act [1] for any motor vehicle owned or leased and registered in the State. In addition to the registration number and other markings or identification otherwise prescribed by law, the license plate shall display words or a slogan and an emblem indicating support for, or an interest in, the Barnegat Bay Decoy and Baymen's Museum or a maritime history or marine life preservation project selected by the department pursuant to section 4 of this act. The words or slogan and emblem shall be chosen by the director, who shall solicit, in conjunction with the Legislature, input from the general public on the design of the plate and shall review the submissions prior to choosing the design. Issuance of special license plates in accordance with this section shall be subject to the provisions of chapter 3 of Title 39 of the Revised Statutes, except as hereinafter otherwise specifically provided.

L.1997, c. 74, § 3, eff. Oct. 14, 1997.

[1] N.J.S.A. § 13:11A–2.

39:3–27.87. Application for license plates; fees

a. Application for issuance of a license plate authorized pursuant to section 3 of this act [1] shall be made to the division on forms and in a manner as may be prescribed by the director. In order to be deemed complete, an application shall be accompanied by a fee of $50 payable to the division, which fee shall be in addition to all fees otherwise required by law for the registration of the motor vehicle.

b. The annual fee for the registration certificate of a motor vehicle that has been issued a license plate authorized in section 3 of this act, pursuant to the provisions of this act, shall include in each year subsequent to the year of issuance a Barnegat Bay Decoy and Baymen's Museum license plate fee or a maritime history or marine life preservation project license plate fee in the amount of $10, which fee shall be in addition to all fees otherwise required by law for the renewal of the registration of the motor vehicle and shall be collected by the division and, as provided in section 6 of this act, deposited into the respective accounts created pursuant to section 6 of this act.[2]

L.1997, c. 74, § 5, eff. Oct. 14, 1997.

[1] N.J.S.A. § 39:3–27.86.
[2] N.J.S.A. § 13:11A–3.

39:3–27.88. Reimbursement of division for certain costs; annual certification of cost per license plate; discontinuance if cost exceeds application fee

a. Prior to the deposit of license plate fees collected pursuant to section 5 of this act[1] into the accounts, amounts thereof as are necessary shall be used to reimburse the division for all costs reasonably and actually incurred, as stipulated by the director, for producing, issuing, renewing, making computer programming changes in connection with and publicizing the availability of Barnegat Bay Decoy and Baymen's Museum and other maritime history or marine life preservation project license plates.

b. The director shall annually certify to the commissioner the average cost per license plate incurred in the immediately preceding year by the division in producing, issuing, renewing, making computer programming changes in connection with and publicizing the availability of Barnegat Bay Decoy and Baymen's Museum and other maritime history or marine life preservation project license plates. The annual certification of the average cost per license plate shall be approved by the Joint Budget Oversight Committee, or its successor.

c. In the event that the average cost per license plate as certified by the director and approved by the Joint Budget Oversight Committee, or its successor, is greater than the $50 application fee established in subsection a. of section 5 of this act in two consecutive fiscal years, the director may discontinue the issuance of Barnegat Bay Decoy and Baymen's Museum and other maritime history or marine life preservation project license plates.

L.1997, c. 74, § 7, eff. Oct. 14, 1997.

[1] N.J.S.A. § 39:3–27.87.

39:3–27.89. Notification of motorists; availability of special plates

The director shall notify eligible motorists of the opportunity to obtain special license plates authorized in section 3 of this act[1] by including a notice with all motor vehicle registration renewals, and by posting appropriate posters or signs in all division facilities and offices, as may be provided by the department. The notices, posters, and signs shall be designed by the commissioner. The designs shall be subject to the approval of the director, and the commissioner shall supply the division with the notices, posters, and signs to be circulated or posted by that division.

L.1997, c. 74, § 9, eff. Oct. 14, 1997.

[1] N.J.S.A. § 39:3–27.86.

39:3–27.90. Conquer cancer license plates; application; fees

a. The Director of the Division of Motor Vehicles may issue for a motor vehicle owned or leased and registered in the State special license plates bearing, in addition to the registration number and other markings or identification otherwise prescribed by law, the slogan "Conquer Cancer." These plates may include an emblem, to be designed by the Commissioner of Health and approved by the Director of the Division of Motor Vehicles, indicating support for, or an interest in, finding new methods of treating and preventing cancer.

b. Application for issuance of a "Conquer Cancer" license plate shall be made to the director on such forms and in such manner as may be prescribed by the director. The director shall collect for each set of plates issued an application fee of $50, and an annual renewal fee of $10, in addition to the fees otherwise prescribed by law for the registration of motor vehicles.

c. Monies collected from all fees for "Conquer Cancer" license plates shall be deposited in the Cancer Research Fund, established in the Department of Health pursuant to section 5 of P.L.1982, c. 40 (C. 54:40A–37.1). Any monetary donation made available to the State to support the provisions of this bill shall be deposited in the Cancer Research Fund for use as set forth in this section. Interest or other income earned on monies deposited under this act into the Cancer Research Fund shall be credited to the fund for use as set forth in this section. Funds shall be utilized by the New Jersey State Commission on Cancer Research: (1) first to reimburse the Division of Motor Vehicles for all costs, including those costs associated with computer programing changes, incurred in producing, issuing, renewing and publicizing the availability of "Conquer Cancer" license plates; (2) to reimburse the Department of Health for the design and printing of notices, posters and signs to be utilized by the Division of Motor Vehicles; and (3) for approved research projects as defined in section 3 of P.L.1983, c. 6 (C. 52:9U–3).

d. The director shall annually certify to the Commissioner of Health the average cost per license plate incurred in the immediately preceding year by the Division of Motor Vehicles in producing, issuing, renewing and publicizing the availability of "Conquer Cancer" license plates. The commissioner shall annually report the Department of Health's costs and the division's costs to the Office of Management and Budget.

e. The director shall notify eligible motorists of the opportunity to obtain "Conquer Cancer" license plates by including a notice with all motor vehicle registration renewals, and by posting appropriate posters or signs in all division facilities and offices, as may be provided by the Department of Health. The notices, posters and signs shall be designed by the Commissioner of Health after consulting with the New Jersey State Commission on Cancer Research. The designs shall be subject to the approval of the director. The Department of Health shall supply the division with the notices, posters and signs to be circulated or posted by the division.

f. The Commissioner of Health, the New Jersey State Commission on Cancer Research, and the director shall develop and enter into an interagency memorandum of agreement setting forth the procedures to be followed by the Department of Health, the commission and the division in carrying out their respective responsibilities under this act.

g. In the event that the average cost per license plate, as certified by the director and approved by the Joint Budget Oversight Committee, or its successor, is greater than the $50 application fee established in subsection b. of this section in two consecutive fiscal years, the director may discontinue the issuance of the "Conquer Cancer" license plate.

L.1997, c. 92, § 1, eff. December 1, 1997.

39:3–27.91. Definitions

As used in this act:

"Commissioner" means the Commissioner of Environmental Protection;

"Department" means the Department of Environmental Protection;

"Director" means the Director of the Division of Motor Vehicles in the Department of Transportation;

"Division" means the Division of Motor Vehicles in the Department of Transportation;

"Fund" means the "Liberty State Park License Plate Fund" created pursuant to section 4 of this act.

L.1997, c. 195, § 1.

39:3–27.92. Liberty State Park license plates; issuance; description

The Director of the Division of Motor Vehicles shall, upon proper application therefor, issue Liberty State Park license plates for any motor vehicle owned or leased and registered in the State. In addition to the registration number and other markings or identification otherwise prescribed by law, a Liberty State Park license plate shall display words or a slogan and an emblem indicating support for, or an interest in, Liberty State Park. The words or slogan and emblem shall be chosen by the director; however, the director shall

solicit, in conjunction with the Legislature, input from the general public on the design of the plate and shall review the submissions prior to choosing the design. Issuance of Liberty State Park license plates in accordance with this section shall be subject to the provisions of chapter 3 of Title 39 of the Revised Statutes, except as hereinafter otherwise specifically provided.

L.1997, c. 195, § 2.

39:3–27.93. Liberty State Park license plates; application; fees

a. Application for issuance of a Liberty State Park license plate shall be made to the division on forms and in a manner as may be prescribed by the director. In order to be deemed complete, an application shall be accompanied by a fee of $50 payable to the division, which fee shall be in addition to all fees otherwise required by law for the registration of the motor vehicle.

b. The annual fee for the registration certificate of a motor vehicle that has been issued a Liberty State Park license plate pursuant to the provisions of this act shall include in each year subsequent to the year of issuance a fee in the amount of $10, which fee shall be in addition to all fees otherwise required by law for the renewal of the registration of the motor vehicle and shall be collected by the division and deposited in the Liberty State Park License Plate Fund created pursuant to section 4 of this act.

L.1997, c. 195, § 3.

39:3–27.94. Liberty State Park License Plate Fund established

There is created in the Department of Environmental Protection a special non-lapsing fund to be known as the "Liberty State Park License Plate Fund." There shall be deposited in the fund the amount collected from all license plate fees collected pursuant to section 3 of this act, less the amounts necessary to reimburse the division for administrative costs pursuant to section 5 of this act. Monies deposited in the fund shall be dedicated for support and funding of projects and programs at Liberty State Park. Monies deposited in the fund shall be held in interest-bearing accounts in public depositories as defined pursuant to section 1 of P.L.1970, c. 236 (C.17:9–41), and may be invested or reinvested in such securities as are approved by the State Treasurer. Interest or other income earned on monies deposited in the fund, and any monies which may be appropriated or otherwise become available for the purposes of the fund, shall be credited to and deposited in the fund for use as set forth in this act.

L.1997, c. 195, § 4.

39:3–27.95. Liberty State Park License Plate Fund; amounts deposited

a. Prior to the deposit of license plate fees collected pursuant to section 3 of this act into the fund, amounts thereof as are necessary shall be used to reimburse the division for all costs reasonably and actually incurred, as stipulated by the director, for:

(1) producing, issuing, renewing, and publicizing the availability of Liberty State Park license plates; and

(2) any initial fees, in an amount conferred as necessary to the commissioner, collected from the issuance of Liberty State Park license plates to be allocated to the division to pay the cost of any computer programming changes that may be necessary to implement the Liberty State Park license plate program established by this act.

b. The director shall annually certify to the commissioner the average cost per license plate incurred in the immediately preceding year by the division in producing, issuing, renewing, and publicizing the availability of Liberty State Park license plates. The annual certification of the average cost per license plate shall be approved by the Joint Budget Oversight Committee, or its successor.

c. In the event that the average cost per license plate as certified by the director and approved by the Joint Budget Oversight Committee, or its successor, is greater than the $50 application fee established in subsection a. of section 3 of this act in two consecutive fiscal years, the director may discontinue the issuance of Liberty State Park license plates.

L.1997, c. 195, § 5.

39:3–27.96. Liberty State Park license plates; notice of eligibility

The director shall notify eligible motorists of the opportunity to obtain Liberty State Park license plates by including a notice with all motor vehicle registration renewals, and by posting appropriate posters or signs in all division facilities and offices, as may be provided by the department. The notices, posters, and signs shall be designed by the commissioner. The designs shall be subject to the approval of the director, and the commissioner shall supply the division with the notices, posters, and signs to be circulated or posted by that division.

L.1997, c. 195, § 6.

39:3–27.97. Interagency memorandum of agreement

The commissioner, the director, and the State Treasurer shall develop and enter into an interagency memorandum of agreement setting forth the procedures to be followed by the departments and the division in carrying out their respective responsibilities under this act.

L.1997, c. 195, § 7.

39:3–27.98. License plates; submarine veterans emblem

a. A person who is an active member of the United States Submarine Veterans may affix a submarine veterans emblem which has been approved by the Director of the Division of Motor Vehicles to a license plate issued to that submarine veteran pursuant to the provisions of P.L.1987, c. 374 (C.39:27.35 et seq.) for a motor vehicle owned or leased by that member.

b. The surviving spouse of a person authorized to display an emblem pursuant to subsection a. of this section may display the emblem on a motor vehicle owned or leased by the surviving spouse.

L.1997, c. 289, § 1.

39:3–27.99. Rules and regulations; submarine veteran license plate emblems

The Director of the Division of Motor Vehicles may promulgate rules and regulations governing the use, design, materials and placement of submarine veterans emblems on license plates issued for motor vehicles owned or leased by active members of the United States Submarine Veterans.

L.1997, c. 289, § 2, eff. Jan. 8, 1998.

39:3–27.100. Meadowlands conservation license plates

The Director of the Division of Motor Vehicles in the Department of Transportation shall, upon proper application therefor, issue Meadowlands conservation license plates for any motor vehicle owned or leased and registered in the State. In addition to the registration number and other markings or identification otherwise prescribed by law, a Meadowlands conservation license plate shall display words or a slogan and an emblem indicating support for, or an interest in, conservation of the Hackensack meadowlands and the Hackensack river watershed. The words or slogan and emblem shall be chosen by the director; however, the director shall solicit, in conjunction with the Legislature, input on the design of the plate from the general public and from the board of trustees of the Meadowlands Conservation Trust created pursuant to section 4 of P.L.1999, c. 31 (C.13:17–90), and shall review the submissions prior to choosing the design. Issuance of Meadowlands conservation license plates in accordance with this section shall be subject to the provisions of chapter 3 of Title 39 of the Revised Statutes, except as hereinafter otherwise specifically provided.

L.1999, c. 31, § 9, eff. Aug. 29, 1999.

39:3–27.101. Application and fee

a. Application for issuance of a Meadowlands conservation license plate shall be made to the Division of Motor Vehicles on forms and in a manner as may be prescribed by the director. In order to be deemed complete, an application shall be accompanied by a fee of $50 payable to the Division of Motor Vehicles, which fee shall be in addition to all fees otherwise required by law for the registration of the motor vehicle.

b. The annual fee for the registration certificate of a motor vehicle that has been issued a Meadowlands conservation license plate pursuant to the provisions of sections 9 through 14 of P.L.1999, c. 31 (C.39:3–27.100 through C.39:3–27.105) shall include in each year subsequent to the year of issuance a fee in the amount of $10, which fee shall be in addition to all fees otherwise required by law for the renewal of the registration of the motor vehicle and shall be collected by the Division of Motor Vehicles and remitted to the Meadowlands Conservation Trust created pursuant to section 3 of P.L.1999, c. 31 (C.13:17–89) for deposit in the Meadowlands Conservation Trust Fund created pursuant to section 6 of P.L.1999, c. 31 (C.13:17–92).

L.1999, c. 31, § 10, eff. Aug. 29, 1999.

39:3–27.102. Fees; deposited in trust

There shall be deposited in the Meadowlands Conservation Trust Fund created pursuant to section 6 of P.L.1999, c. 31 (C.13:17–92) the amount collected from all license plate fees collected pursuant to section 10 of P.L.1999, c. 31 (C.39:3–27.101), less the amounts necessary to reimburse the Division of Motor Vehicles for all costs authorized pursuant to section 12 of P.L.1999, c. 31 (C.39:3–27.103).

L.1999, c. 31, § 11, eff. Aug. 29, 1999.

39:3–27.103. Division of Motor Vehicles; reimbursement of costs

a. Prior to the deposit of license plate fees collected pursuant to section 10 of P.L.1999, c. 31 (C.39:3–27.101) into the Meadowlands Conservation Trust Fund created pursuant to section 6 of P.L.1999, c. 31 (C.13:17–92), amounts thereof as are necessary shall be used to reimburse the Division of Motor Vehicles for all costs reasonably and actually incurred, as stipulated by the director, for:

(1) producing, issuing, renewing, and publicizing the availability of Meadowlands conservation license plates; and

(2) any initial computer programming changes that may be necessary to implement the Meadowlands conservation license plate program established pursuant to sections 9 through 14 of P.L.1999, c. 31 (C.39:3–27.100 through C.39:3–27.105).

b. The Director of the Division of Motor Vehicles shall annually certify to the board of trustees of the Meadowlands Conservation Trust created pursuant to section 4 of P.L.1999, c. 31 (C.13:17–90) the average cost per license plate incurred in the immediately preceding year by the Division of Motor Vehicles in producing, issuing, renewing, and publicizing the availability of Meadowlands conservation license plates. The annual certification of the average cost per license plate shall be approved by the Joint Budget Oversight Committee or its successor.

c. In the event that the average cost per license plate as certified by the director and approved by the Joint Budget Oversight Committee, or its successor, is greater than the $50 application fee established in subsection a. of section 10 of P.L.1999, c. 31 (C.39:3–27.101) in two consecutive fiscal years, the

director may discontinue the issuance of Meadowlands conservation license plates.

L.1999, c. 31, § 12, eff. Aug. 29, 1999.

39:3–27.104. Availability of license plates; notification to motorists

The Director of the Division of Motor Vehicles shall notify eligible motorists of the opportunity to obtain Meadowlands conservation license plates by including a notice with all motor vehicle registration renewals, and by posting appropriate posters or signs in all facilities and offices of the Division of Motor Vehicles. The notices, posters, and signs shall be designed by the board of trustees of the Meadowlands Conservation Trust created pursuant to section 4 of P.L.1999, c. 31 (C.13:17–90). The designs shall be subject to the approval of the director, and the board of trustees of the Meadowlands Conservation Trust shall supply the Division of Motor Vehicles with the notices, posters, and signs to be circulated or posted by that division.

L.1999, c. 31, § 13, eff. Aug. 29, 1999.

39:3–27.105. Interagency agreement

The board of trustees of the Meadowlands Conservation Trust created pursuant to section 4 of P.L.1999, c. 31 (C.13:17–90), the Director of the Division of Motor Vehicles, and the State Treasurer shall develop and enter into an interagency memorandum of agreement setting forth the procedures to be followed by those parties in carrying out their respective responsibilities under sections 9 through 14 of P.L.1999, c. 31 (C.39:3–27.100 through C.39:3–27.105).

L.1999, c. 31, § 14, eff. Aug. 29, 1999.

39:3–27.106. Navy Cross license plates; description; fees

a. Upon application of any person who is the holder of a Navy Cross as certified on the applicant's DD–214 form or on a Certificate of Release or Discharge from Active Duty, the director shall issue, for the motor vehicle owned or leased by the person, distinctive plates bearing a design approved by the director, in addition to the registration number and other markings or identification prescribed by law. The plates shall bear the words "Navy Cross" and depict the Navy Cross emblem.

b. There shall be a fee of $15 to the applicant for these special plates in addition to the fees otherwise prescribed by law for the registration of motor vehicles. The director shall retain from the fees collected such sums as are necessary to provide for all costs incurred by the division in producing and issuing Navy Cross license plates.

c. The surviving spouse of a deceased recipient of the Navy Cross who is eligible to operate a motor vehicle in this State under the provisions of R.S.39:3–10 may retain the special license plates obtained by the deceased spouse pursuant to this section for display on a motor vehicle registered to the surviving spouse under the provisions of R.S.39:3–4.

d.   The director may promulgate rules and regulations governing the issuance and use of these special license plates.

L.1999, c. 56, § 1.

39:3–27.107.   Deborah Heart and Lung Center license plates

The Director of the Division of Motor Vehicles shall, upon proper application therefor, issue Deborah Heart and Lung Center license plates for any motor vehicle owned or leased and registered in the State. In addition to the registration number and other markings prescribed by law, a Deborah Heart and Lung Center license plate shall display words or a slogan and an emblem indicating support for, or interest in, the Deborah Heart and Lung Center. The license plate shall be designed by the director, in consultation with the Deborah Hospital Foundation's Board of Directors. Issuance of the Deborah Heart and Lung Center license plates in accordance with this section shall be subject to the provisions of chapter 3 of Title 39 of the Revised Statutes, except as hereinafter otherwise specifically provided.

L.1999, c. 354, § 1.

39:3–27.108.   Application

An application for issuance of a Deborah Heart and Lung Center license plate shall be accompanied by a fee of $50, in addition to the fees otherwise required by law for the registration of the motor vehicle. An application for the renewal of the plates shall be accompanied by an additional fee of $10. The additional application and renewal fees shall be deposited in the Deborah Hospital Foundation Fund created pursuant to section 3 of this act.

L.1999, c. 354, § 2.

39:3–27.109.   Deborah Hospital Foundation Fund

a.   There is created in the Department of the Treasury a non- lapsing, interest-bearing fund to be known as the "Deborah Hospital Foundation Fund." There shall be deposited in the fund the amount collected from the application and renewal fees collected pursuant to section 2 of this act, after reimbursement of the division for its actual costs in administering this act,and the amount remaining from the monies contributed by the Deborah Heart and Lung Center pursuant to section 4 of this act.

b.   Monies deposited in the fund shall be used by the Deborah Hospital Foundation to fund programs and services for persons served by the Deborah Heart and Lung Center in New Jersey. Monies deposited in the fund shall be held in interest-bearing accounts in public depositories as defined pursuant to section 1 of P.L. 1970, c. 236 (C.17:9–41), and may be invested or reinvested in such securities as are approved by the State Treasurer. Interest or other income earned on monies deposited into the fund, and any monies which may be appropriated or otherwise become available for the purposes of the fund, shall be credited to and deposited in the fund for use as set forth in this act.

c.   Monies in the Deborah Hospital Foundation Fund shall be withdrawn by the State Treasurer and disbursed to the Deborah Hospital Foundation in Browns Mills, New Jersey, upon request of the foundation pursuant to a voucher system to be established by the State Treasurer. The foundation shall indicate on each voucher request the purpose to which the monies disbursed shall be applied.

d.   The State Treasurer shall provide an annual report to the Deborah Hospital Foundation on the status of the funds, and the foundation shall provide an annual report to the State Treasurer documenting expenditures by the center of monies from the fund.

L.1999, c. 354, § 3.

39:3–27.110.   Center contributions

The Deborah Heart and Lung Center shall contribute monies in an amount to be determined by the director, not to exceed $50,000, to be used to offset the initial costs incurred by the division pursuant to section 5 of this act. Any amount remaining after the payment of the initial costs shall be deposited in the "Deborah Hospital Foundation Fund," created pursuant to section 3 of this act.

L.1999, c. 354, § 4.

39:3–27.111.   Fees; reimbursement

a.   Prior to the deposit of the fees collected pursuant to section 2 of this act into the Deborah Hospital Foundation Fund, such amounts thereof as are necessary shall first be used to reimburse the Deborah Heart and Lung Center, up to the amount contributed by the Center pursuant to section 4 of this act, and then to reimburse the division for all costs reasonably and actually incurred, as stipulated by the director, for:

(1) producing, issuing, renewing, and publicizing the availability of Deborah Heart and Lung Center license plates; and

(2) any initial computer programming fees that may be necessary to implement the Deborah Heart and Lung Center license plate program established by this act.

b.   The director shall annually certify the average cost per license plate incurred in the immediately preceding year by the division in producing, issuing, renewing and publicizing the availability of Deborah Heart and Lung Center license plates.

c.   In the event that the average cost per license plate, as certified by the director and approved by the Joint Budget Oversight Committee, or its successor, is greater than the $50 application fee established in section 2 of this act in two consecutive fiscal years, the director may discontinue the issuance of Deborah Heart and Lung Center license plates.

L.1999, c. 354, § 5.

39:3–27.112. Notification to eligible motorists

The director shall notify eligible motorists of the opportunity to obtain Deborah Heart and Lung Center license plates by including a notice with all motor vehicle registration renewals, and by posting appropriate posters or signs in all division facilities and offices. The notices, posters, and signs shall be designed by the director after consultation with the Deborah Hospital Foundation's Board of Directors.

L.1999, c. 354, § 6.

39:3–27.113. Memorandum of agreement

The director and the Trustees of the Deborah Heart and Lung Center shall enter into a memorandum of agreement setting forth the procedures to be followed by the division and the trustees in carrying out the provisions of this act.

L.1999, c. 354, § 7.

39:3–27.114. Special registration plates; municipal mayor

a. Upon the application of a person who has served as a municipal mayor for one term or longer but who presently does not occupy that position, the Director of the Division of Motor Vehicles shall issue special registration plates for a motor vehicle owned or leased by that person. The plates shall be of a design approved by the director and shall convey appropriate recognition of the person's service as a mayor, in addition to containing the markings or identification otherwise required by law.

b. In addition to the fees otherwise prescribed by law for the registration of motor vehicles, an application for these special plates shall be accompanied by a fee of $50 which shall be retained by the Division of Motor Vehicles to defray the cost of producing and distributing the plates. The application also shall be accompanied by proof, in a form specified by the director, that the applicant served as mayor of a municipality in this State for at least one term.

L.1999, c. 374, § 1.

39:3–27.115. Special registration plates; former members of New Jersey State Legislature

a. Upon the application of a former member of the New Jersey State Legislature, the Director of the Division of Motor Vehicles shall issue special registration plates for a motor vehicle owned or leased by the former member. The plates shall identify the holder as a " Senate–Former Member" or "General Assembly–Former Member"; provided however, if the former member served in both the General Assembly and the Senate, the former member shall receive plates identifying him as a former member of the Senate. The plates

also shall contain the Shield of the State of New Jersey, in addition to the registration number and other markings or identification otherwise prescribed by law. The identifying characters displayed on the license plate shall be in a form as to adapt to the size of the license plate. The director shall design the special plates, subject to approval by the President of the Senate and Speaker of the General Assembly.

b. In addition to the fees otherwise prescribed by law for the registration of motor vehicles, an application for these special plates shall be accompanied by a fee of $50, which shall be retained by the Division of Motor Vehicles, to defray the cost of producing and distributing the plates. The application also shall be accompanied by proof, in a form specified by the director, that the applicant served as a member of the New Jersey General Assembly or State Senate.

L.1999, c. 374, § 2.

39:3–27.116. "Promote Agriculture" license plates

The Director of the Division of Motor Vehicles shall, upon proper application therefor, issue "Promote Agriculture" license plates for any motor vehicle owned or leased and registered in the State. Under this act, any motor vehicle shall include, in addition to passenger motor vehicles, all commercial, farm use and farm vehicles issued registration or license plates pursuant to R.S.39:3–20, R.S.39:3–24 or R.S.39:3–25. In addition to the registration number and other markings prescribed by law, a "Promote Agriculture" license plate shall display the words "Garden State" and an emblem indicating interest in agriculture in New Jersey except for a " Promote Agriculture" license plate issued to a commercial, farm use or farm vehicle which, in addition to the registration number and other markings prescribed by law, shall display an emblem indicating interest in agriculture in New Jersey. The license plate shall be designed by the director, in consultation with the New Jersey Farm Bureau. Issuance of the "Promote Agriculture" license plates in accordance with this section shall be subject to the provisions of chapter 3 of Title 39 of the Revised Statutes, except as hereinafter otherwise specifically provided.

L.2001, c. 13, § 1, eff. July 28, 2001.

39:3–27.117. Fees

An application for issuance of a "Promote Agriculture" license plate shall be accompanied by a fee of $20, in addition to the fees otherwise required by law for the registration of the motor vehicle.

L.2001, c. 13, § 2 (contingent effective date).

39:3–27.118. Funding

The New Jersey Farm Bureau, representing agricultural interests statewide, shall contribute monies in an amount to be determined by the director, not to exceed $50,000, to be used to offset the initial costs incurred by the division for producing, issuing, renewing, and publicizing the availability of "Promote Agriculture" license plates and for any initial computer programming fees that may be necessary to implement the " Promote Agriculture" license plate program. Any amount remaining after the payment of the initial costs shall be returned to the New Jersey Farm Bureau.

L.2001, c. 13, § 3 (contingent effective date).

39:3–27.119. Use of fees collected

The additional application fees collected pursuant to section 2 of this act shall first be used to reimburse the New Jersey Farm Bureau, up to the amount contributed by the Bureau pursuant to section 3 of this act, and then shall be retained by the director to reimburse the division for costs incurred in producing, issuing, renewing, and publicizing the availability of "Promote Agriculture" license plates.

L.2001, c. 13, § 4 (contingent effective date).

39:3–27.120. Average cost per license plate

a. The director shall annually certify the average cost per license plate incurred in the immediately preceding year by the division in producing and publicizing the availability of the "Promote Agriculture" license plates.

b. In the event that the average cost per license plate, as certified by the director and approved by the Joint Budget Oversight Committee, or its successor, is greater than the application fee established in section 2 of in two consecutive fiscal years, the director may increase the fee for a " Promote Agriculture" license plate to an amount which, as certified by the director and approved by the Joint Budget Oversight Committee, or its successor, is no greater than the average cost per license plate or·the director may discontinue the issuance of the "Promote Agriculture" license plate.

L.2001, c. 13, § 5 (contingent effective date).

39:3–27.121. Notification of eligible motorists

The director shall notify eligible motorists of the opportunity to obtain "Promote Agriculture" license plates by including a notice with all motor vehicle registration renewals, and by posting appropriate posters or signs in all division facilities and offices. The notices, posters, and signs shall be designed by the director after consultation with the New Jersey Farm Bureau.

L.2001, c. 13, § 6 (contingent effective date).

39:3–27.122. Procedure for carrying out provisions of this act

The director and the Executive Director of the New Jersey Farm Bureau shall enter into a memorandum of agreement setting forth the procedures to be followed by the division and the executive director in carrying out the provisions of this act.

L.2001, c. 13, § 7 (contingent effective date).

39:3–27.123. Design; fees; cost; notification of eligible motorists

a. The Director of the Division of Motor Vehicles may issue for a motor vehicle owned or leased and registered in the State special license plates bearing, in addition to the registration number and other markings or identification otherwise prescribed by law, an appropriate slogan and an emblem, to be designed by the Superintendent of State Police, in consultation with the State Police Benevolent Association, the State Fraternal Order of Police and the staff of the National Law Enforcement Officers Memorial Fund, Inc., and approved by the Director of the Division of Motor Vehicles. These design features shall commemorate and honor law enforcement officers killed in the line of duty in New Jersey.

b. Application for issuance of law enforcement officer memorial license plates shall be made to the director on such forms and in such manner as may be prescribed by the director. The director shall collect for each set of plates issued an application fee of $50, and an annual renewal fee of $10, in addition to the fees otherwise prescribed by law for the registration of motor vehicles.

c. Monies collected from all fees for law enforcement officer memorial license plates shall be deposited in a special account to be known as the "Law Enforcement Officer Memorial Fund" to be established in the Department of the Treasury. Other funds made available to the State to support the provisions of this act shall be deposited in this fund for use as set forth in this act. Interest or other income earned on monies deposited into the fund shall be credited to the fund for use as set forth in this act.

d. The director shall annually certify to the Commissioner of Transportation the average cost per license plate incurred in the immediately preceding year by the Division of Motor Vehicles in producing, issuing, renewing and publicizing the availability of law enforcement officer memorial license plates. The Commissioner of Transportation shall annually report to the Director of the Division of Budget and Accounting in the Department of the Treasury the costs incurred by the Department of Transportation and the Division of Motor Vehicles to implement the provisions of this section.

e. The director shall notify eligible motorists of the opportunity to obtain law enforcement officer memorial license plates by including a notice with all motor vehicle registration renewals, and by posting appropriate posters or signs in all division facilities and offices. The notices, posters and signs shall be designed by the Superintendent of State Police after consulting with the State Police Benevolent Association, the State Fraternal Order of Police and the staff of the National Law Enforcement Officers Memorial Fund, Inc. The designs shall be subject to the approval of the director. The Superintendent shall supply the division with the notices, posters and signs to be circulated or posted by the division.

f. In the event that the average cost per license plate, as certified by the director and approved by the Joint Budget Oversight Committee, or its successor, is greater than the $50 application fee established in subsection b. of this section in two consecutive fiscal years, the director may discontinue the issuance of the law enforcement officer memorial license plate.

L.2001, c. 41, § 2, eff. March 27, 2001.

39:3–27.124. Monies contributed; law enforcement memorial license plates

The State Police Benevolent Association, the State Fraternal Order of Police, and the National Law Enforcement Officers Memorial Fund, Inc. shall contribute monies in an amount to be determined by the director, not to exceed an aggregate amount of $50,000, to be used to offset the initial costs incurred by the division for producing, issuing, renewing, and publicizing the availability of special license plates that commemorate and honor law enforcement officers killed in the line of duty in New Jersey. To help offset the initial costs incurred by the division for the special license plates authorized by this act, other law enforcement organizations and donors may assist by contributing monies to any of the three organizations listed herein. Any amount remaining after the payment of the initial costs shall be returned to the three contributing organizations.

L.2001, c. 41, § 3, eff. March 27, 2001.

39:3–27.125. Funds annually appropriated; reimbursements

Funds from the Law Enforcement Officer Memorial Fund shall be annually appropriated first to reimburse the amount contributed by those organizations pursuant to section 3 of this act, and then:

a. to reimburse the Division of Motor Vehicles for all costs, including those costs associated with computer programming changes, incurred in producing, issuing, renewing and publicizing the availability of law enforcement officer memorial license plates;

b. to reimburse the Department of Transportation for the design and printing of notices, posters and signs to be utilized by the Division of Motor Vehicles; and

c. for the establishment of a scholarship program for the children of law enforcement officers killed in the line of duty pursuant to section 5 of this act.

L.2001, c. 41, § 4, eff. March 27, 2001.

39:3–27.126. Procedures for carrying out provisions of act

The director and the organizations contributing monies pursuant to section 3 of this act shall enter into a memorandum of agreement setting forth the procedures to be followed by the division and the contributing organizations in carrying out the provisions of this act.

L.2001, c. 41, § 8, eff. March 27, 2001.

39:3–27.127. "Be An Organ Donor" special license plates

a. The Director of the Division of Motor Vehicles may issue for a motor vehicle owned or leased and registered in the State special license plates bearing, in addition to the marking or identification otherwise required by law, the slogan "Be An Organ Donor." These plates shall be designed by the director, in consultation with the New Jersey Transplant Association, to educate the public about the urgent need for organ donation and the life saving benefits of organ transplants. Opportunity for comment on the design of the plates shall be afforded to the organ procurement organizations designated by the federal government to provide services in this State.

b. Application for issuance of "Be An Organ Donor" license plates shall be made to the director on such forms and in such manner as may be prescribed by the director. The director shall collect for each set of plates issued an application fee of $50 and an annual renewal fee of $10, in addition to the fees otherwise prescribed by law for the registration of motor vehicles.

c. Monies collected from the additional application and renewal fees for organ donor license plates shall be deposited in the Organ and Tissue Donor Awareness Education Fund established by P.L.1999, c. 386 (C.54A:9–25.17 et seq.).

These monies shall be allocated from the fund in the following order of priority:

(1) to reimburse the amount of contributions provided pursuant to section 2 of this act;

(2) to reimburse the Division of Motor Vehicles for any additional costs, including computer programming changes, incurred in producing, issuing, reviewing and publicizing the availability of organ donor license plates; and

(3) for the purposes of the fund as designated in section 2 of P.L.1999, c. 386 (C.54A:9–25.18).

L.2001, c. 164, § 1, eff. Oct. 1, 2001.

39:3–27.128. Contributions to offset initial costs

The New Jersey Transplant Association shall contribute an amount to be determined by the director, not to exceed a total of $50,000, to be used to offset the initial costs incurred by the division for producing, issuing, renewing, and publicizing the availability of special organ donor license plates. To help offset the initial costs incurred by the division for the special license plates authorized by this act, other concerned organizations and individual donors may assist by contributing monies to the association for this purpose. Any amount remaining after the payment of the initial costs shall be returned to the contributors.

L.2001, c. 164, § 2, eff. Oct. 1, 2001.

39:3–27.129. Notice to motorists; procedures

a. The director shall notify eligible motorists of the opportunity to obtain organ donor license plates by including a notice with all motor vehicle registration renewals, and by posting appropriate posters or signs in all division facilities and offices. The notices, posters and signs shall be designed by the director after consulting with the New Jersey Transplant Association.

b. The Commissioner of Transportation, the State Treasurer, and the director shall develop and enter into an interagency memorandum of agreement setting forth the procedures to be followed by the departments and the division in carrying out their respective responsibilities under this act.

L.2001, c. 164, § 3, eff. Oct. 1, 2001.

39:3–27.130. Certification of average cost; discontinuance of issuance

a. The director shall annually certify to the Commissioner of Transportation the average cost per license plate incurred in the immediately preceding year by the Division of Motor Vehicles in producing, issuing, renewing and publicizing the availability of organ donor license plates. The annual certification of the average cost per license plate shall be approved by the Joint Budget Oversight Committee.

b. In the event that the average cost per license plate, as certified by the director and approved by the Joint Budget Oversight Committee, or its successor, is greater than the $50 application fee established in section 1 of this act in two consecutive fiscal years, the director may discontinue the issuance of the organ donor license plates.

L.2001, c. 164, § 4, eff. Oct. 1, 2001.

39:3–27.131. Rewards for Justice License Plate Fund

As used in this act, "fund" means the "Rewards for Justice License Plate Fund" created pursuant to section 4 of this act.

L.2002, c. 52, § 1, eff. Dec. 1, 2002.

39:3–27.132. United We Stand license plates

The Director of the Division of Motor Vehicles shall, upon proper application therefor, issue United We Stand license plates for any motor vehicle owned or leased and registered in the State. In addition to the registration number and other markings or identification otherwise prescribed by law, the license plate shall display the words "United We Stand" in addition to an American flag. The colors red, white and blue shall be appropriately displayed on the license plate. Issuance of the United We Stand license plates in accordance with this section shall be subject to the provisions of

chapter 3 of Title 39 of the Revised Statutes, except as hereinafter otherwise specifically provided.

L.2002, c. 52, § 2, eff. Dec. 1, 2002.

39:3–27.133. Application for United We Stand license plates; fee

a. Application for issuance of a United We Stand license plate shall be made to the division on forms and in a manner as may be prescribed by the director. In order to be deemed complete, an application shall be accompanied by a fee of $50 payable to the division, which fee shall be in addition to all fees otherwise required by law for the registration of the motor vehicle.

b. The annual fee for the registration certificate of a motor vehicle that has been issued a United We Stand license plate pursuant to the provisions of this act shall include, in each year subsequent to the year of issuance, a fee in the amount of $10, which fee shall be in addition to all fees otherwise required by law for the renewal of the registration of the motor vehicle, and shall be collected by the division and deposited in the Rewards for Justice License Plate Fund created pursuant to section 4 of this act.

L.2002, c. 52, § 3, eff. Dec. 1, 2002.

39:3–27.134. Funding

There is created in the Department of Transportation a special non- lapsing fund to be known as the "Rewards for Justice License Plate Fund." There shall be deposited in the fund the amounts collected from license plate fees pursuant to section 3 of this act, less the amounts necessary to reimburse the division for administrative costs pursuant to section 5 of this act. Monies deposited in the fund shall be distributed, at the discretion of the Commissioner of Transportation, either into the Rewards for Justice Fund, established by a private non-profit organization, all of which shall be contributed to the United States State Department's Rewards for Justice Program or directly to the Rewards for Justice Program. Prior to distribution, monies deposited in the fund shall be held in interest-bearing accounts in public depositories as defined pursuant to section 1 of P.L.1970, c. 236 (C.17:9–41), and may be invested or reinvested in such securities as are approved by the State Treasurer. Interest or other income earned on monies deposited in the fund, and any monies which may be appropriated or otherwise become available for the purposes of the fund, shall be credited to and deposited in the fund for use as set forth in this act.

L.2002, c. 52, § 4, eff. Dec. 1, 2002.

39:3–27.135. Contribution to fund

The Rewards for Justice Fund shall contribute monies in an amount to be determined by the director, not to exceed $50,000, to be used to offset the initial costs incurred by the division pursuant to section 6 of this act.

Any amount remaining after the payment of the initial costs shall be deposited in the fund.

L.2002, c. 52, § 5, eff. Dec. 1, 2002.

39:3–27.136. Use of funds

a. Prior to the deposit of license plate fees collected pursuant to section 3 of this act into the fund, amounts thereof as are necessary shall be used to reimburse the Rewards for Justice Fund, up to the amount contributed by the Rewards for Justice Fund pursuant to section 5 of this act, and then to reimburse the division for all costs reasonably and actually incurred, as stipulated by the director, for:

(1) producing, issuing, renewing, and publicizing the availability of United We Stand license plates; and

(2) from the initial fees, any computer programming changes that may be necessary to implement the United We Stand license plate program established by this act.

b. The director shall annually certify to the commissioner the average cost per license plate incurred in the immediately preceding year by the division in producing, issuing, renewing, and publicizing the availability of United We Stand license plates. The annual certification of the average cost per license plate shall be approved by the Joint Budget Oversight Committee, or its successor.

c. In the event that the average cost per license plate as certified by the director and approved by the Joint Budget Oversight Committee, or its successor, is greater than the $50 application fee established in subsection a. of section 3 of this act in two consecutive fiscal years, the director may discontinue the issuance of United We Stand license plates.

L.2002, c. 52, § 6, eff. Dec. 1, 2002.

39:3–27.137. Notification of eligible motorists

The director shall notify eligible motorists of the opportunity to obtain United We Stand license plates by including a notice with all motor vehicle registration renewals, and by posting appropriate posters or signs in all division facilities and offices. The notices, posters, and signs shall be designed by the director.

L.2002, c. 52, § 7, eff. Dec. 1, 2002.

39:3–27.138. Memorandum of agreement; procedures

The director and officials of the Rewards for Justice Fund shall enter into a memorandum of agreement setting forth the procedures to be followed by the division and the Rewards for Justice Fund in carrying out the provisions of this act.

L.2002, c. 52, § 8, eff. Dec. 1, 2002.

39:3–27.139. Rules and regulations

Pursuant to the "Administrative Procedure Act," P.L.1968, c. 410 (C.52:14B–1 et seq.), the director may promulgate rules and regulations to effectuate the provisions of this act.

L.2002, c. 52, § 9, eff. Dec. 1, 2002.

39:3–28. Licenses and registrations indexed; certified copies of applications as evidence; destruction of applications and copies

The director shall cause all applications for registration and drivers' licenses to be indexed, and any original application or copy thereof certified to be a true copy under the hand of the director shall be received as evidence in any court to prove the facts contained therein. For each uncertified copy so issued the director shall collect a fee of $8 and for each certified copy so issued the director shall collect a fee of $10. The indexing and copying of these applications shall meet the standards and requirements established in regulation by the Secretary of State for the maintenance and preservation of records.

The director may destroy all records of registration certificates or drivers' licenses and their indices after having made copies of such records in accordance with standards and requirements established in regulation by the Secretary of State for the maintenance and preservation of records. Such copies made in accordance with standards and requirements established in regulation by the Secretary of State for the maintenance and preservation of records may be destroyed when they have been on file in the office of the director for a period of three years after the date of expiration of the registration certificates and drivers' licenses.

Amended by L.1950, c. 165, p. 354, § 1; L.1952, c. 59, p. 378, § 1; L.1953, c. 295, p. 1834, § 1; L.1975, c. 180, § 8, eff. Jan. 1, 1976; L.1994, c. 60, § 17, eff. July 1, 1994; L.2001, c. 276, § 1, eff. Dec. 26, 2001.

39:3–29. License, registration certificate and insurance identification card; possession; exhibit upon request; violations; fine; defense

The driver's license, the registration certificate of a motor vehicle and an insurance identification card shall be in the possession of the driver or operator at all times when he is in charge of a motor vehicle on the highways of this State.

The driver or operator shall exhibit his driver's license and an insurance identification card, and the holder of a registration certificate or the operator or driver of a motor vehicle for which a registration certificate has been issued, whether or not the holder, driver or operator is a resident of this State, shall also exhibit the registration certificate, when requested so to do by a police officer or judge, while in the performance of the duties of his office, and shall write his name in the presence of the officer, so that the officer may thereby determine the identity of the licensee and at the same time determine the correctness of the registration certificate, as it relates to the registration number and number plates of the motor vehicle for which it was issued; and the correctness of the evidence of a policy of insurance, as it relates to the coverage of the motor vehicle for which it was issued.

Any person violating this section shall be subject to a fine of $150, except that if the person is a driver or operator of an omnibus, as defined pursuant to R.S.39:1–1, the amount of the fine shall be $250. Of the amount of any such fine collected pursuant to this paragraph, $25 shall be deposited in the Uninsured Motorist Prevention Fund established by section 2 of P.L.1983, c. 141 (C.39:6B–3).

If a person charged with a violation of this section can exhibit his driver's license, insurance identification card and registration certificate, which were valid on the day he was charged, to the judge of the municipal court before whom he is summoned to answer to the charge, such judge may dismiss the charge. However, the judge may impose court costs.

In addition to and independent of any fine or other penalty provided for under law, the court shall impose a fine of $150 on any driver or operator of an omnibus, convicted of a violation of this section, who does not have a certificate of public convenience and necessity as required pursuant to R.S.48:4–3. The State Treasurer shall annually deposit the monies collected from the fines imposed pursuant to this paragraph to the "Omnibus Safety Enforcement Fund" established pursuant to section 4 of P.L.2007, c. 40 (C.39:3–79.23). The fine described herein shall not be deemed a fine, penalty, or forfeiture pursuant to R.S.39:5–41.

Amended by L.1972, c. 200, § 1, eff. Dec. 26, 1972; L.1981, c. 242, § 1, eff. Aug. 3, 1981; L.1983, c. 403, § 10, eff. Dec. 23, 1983; L.2003, c. 89, § 78, eff. June 9, 2003; L.2007, c. 40, § 2, eff. July 1, 2007.

39:3–29.1. Insurance identification cards; rules and regulations

The Commissioner of Banking and Insurance shall, after consultation with the Director of the New Jersey Motor Vehicle Commission, promulgate rules and regulations concerning the issuance, design and content of the insurance identification cards required by this act.

The rules and regulations shall contain provisions designed to deter and detect counterfeit or fraudulent insurance identification cards.

L.1972, c. 200, § 2, eff. Dec. 26, 1972. Amended by L.2003, c. 89, § 70, eff. June 9, 2003.

39:3–29.1a. Failure to provide proof of insurance; impoundment and sale of vehicle

a. Upon the issuance of a summons for failing to possess or exhibit an insurance identification card in violation of R.S.39:3–29, the violator or registrant shall have 24 hours from the time of the citation to provide the issuing law enforcement agency with the insurance identification card, or other satisfactory proof of insurance. Failure to provide the insurance identification card or other satisfactory proof of insurance within the 24 hour time frame shall result in the issuance of a

warrant for the immediate impoundment of the vehicle that was being operated when the summons was issued. A motor vehicle impounded pursuant to the provisions of this subsection shall be removed to a storage space or garage. The registrant shall be responsible for the cost of the removal and storage of the impounded motor vehicle.

b. (1) If the registrant fails to claim a motor vehicle impounded pursuant to subsection a. of this section and pay the reasonable costs of removal and storage by midnight of the 30th day following impoundment, along with a fine of $100 to cover the administrative costs of the municipality wherein the violation occurred, and after a hearing, the municipality may sell the motor vehicle at public auction. The municipality shall give notice of the sale by certified mail to the registrant of the motor vehicle and to the holder of any security interest filed with the New Jersey Motor Vehicle Commission, and by publication in a form to be prescribed by the director by one insertion, at least five days before the date of the sale, in one or more newspapers published in this State and circulating in the municipality in which the motor vehicle has been impounded.

(2) At any time prior to the sale, the registrant or other person entitled to the motor vehicle may reclaim possession of it upon providing satisfactory proof of motor vehicle liability insurance coverage and payment of the reasonable costs of removal and storage of the motor vehicle and any outstanding fines or penalties; provided, however, if the other person entitled to the motor vehicle is a lessor or the holder of a lien on the motor vehicle, he may reclaim the motor vehicle without payment. In such cases, the registrant shall be liable for all outstanding costs, fines and penalties, and the municipality shall have a lien against the property and income of that registrant for the total amount of those outstanding costs, fines and penalties.

(3) Any proceeds obtained from the sale of a motor vehicle at public auction pursuant to paragraph (1) of this subsection in excess of the amount owed to the municipality for the reasonable costs of removal and storage of the motor vehicle and any outstanding fines or penalties shall be returned to the registrant of the vehicle.

L.2003, c. 89, § 79, eff. June 8, 2004.

39:3–29.2. Short title

This act shall be known and may be cited as the "Identification Cards for Nondrivers' Act."

L.1980, c. 47, § 1. Amended by L.1989, c. 52, § 1.

39:3–29.3. Qualifications; data; signature and verification

The Division of Motor Vehicles shall issue an identification card to any resident of the State who is 17 years of age or older and who is not the holder of a valid learner's permit or a valid driver's license. The identification card shall attest to the true name, correct age, and other identifying data as certified by the applicant for such identification card. Every application for an identification card shall be signed and verified by the applicant and shall be supported by such documentary evidence of the age and identity, or blindness, disability, or handicap, of such person as the division may require. In addition to requiring an applicant for an identification card to submit satisfactory proof of identity and age, the director also shall require the applicant to provide, as a condition for obtaining the card, satisfactory proof that the applicant's presence in the United States is authorized under federal law. If the director has reasonable cause to suspect that any document presented by an applicant as proof of identity, age or legal residency is altered, false or otherwise invalid, the director shall refuse to grant the identification card until such time as the document may be verified by the issuing agency to the director's satisfaction.

L.1980, c. 47, § 2. Amended by L.1989, c. 52, § 2; L.1990, c. 30, § 2, eff. May 24, 1990; L.1993, c. 34, § 5, eff. Jan. 29, 1993; L.2001, c. 391, § 14, eff. Jan. 8, 2002.

39:3–29.4. Standard license form; color; "For Identification Only"

Every identification card authorized by section 2 of this act[1] shall bear a color picture of the person to whom it is issued and shall be issued upon the standard license form prescribed by the Division of Motor Vehicles for color picture drivers' licenses, except that the card shall prominently contain the words "For Identification Only."

L.1980, c. 47, § 3. Amended by L.1989, c. 52, § 3; L.1999, c. 28, § 7, eff. Jan. 1, 2000.

[1] Section 39:3-29.3.

39:3–29.5. Duration of card; renewal; fee

a. Except as provided in subsection b. of this section, each original identification card authorized by section 2 of this act[1] shall, unless canceled earlier, be valid for 48 calendar months from its date of issuance, and shall be renewable upon the request of the bearer of the card, pursuant to terms of license renewal established by the Division of Motor Vehicles, and upon payment of a fee as required by section 6 of this act.[2] An identification card issued pursuant to this act to an applicant who is blind, disabled, or handicapped shall be valid for the life of the holder unless canceled by the holder. Cards issued prior to October 16, 1989 and valid upon the effective date of this amendatory act shall be valid for the life of the holder unless canceled by the holder. Cards issued to blind, disabled or handicapped persons between October 16, 1989 and the effective date of this amendatory act, and which are valid on the effective date of this act, shall be made valid for the life of the holder unless canceled by the holder, upon presentation of proof that the blindness, disability, or handicap existed at the time of the original application. The director is authorized to require

periodic verification of information included on any identification card issued for or valid for the life of the holder. Nothing in this section shall be construed to alter or change any expiration date on any New Jersey identification card issued prior to the operative date of P.L.2001, c. 391 (C.39:3–10f4 et al.) and any such identification card shall remain valid until its expiration date.

b. If the director issues an identification card to a person who has demonstrated authorization to be present in the United States for a period of time shorter than the standard periods of such cards, the director shall fix the expiration date of the identification card at a date based on the period in which the person is authorized to be present in the United States under federal immigration laws. The director may renew such an identification card only if it is demonstrated that the person's continued presence in the United States is authorized under federal law.

L.1980, c. 47, § 4. Amended by L.1989, c. 52, § 4; L.1990, c. 30, § 1, eff. May 24, 1990; L.1993, c. 34, § 6, eff. Jan. 29, 1993; L.1999, c. 28, § 8, eff. Jan. 1, 2000; L.2001, c. 391, § 7, eff. Jan. 8, 2002.

[1] Section 39:3–29.3.
[2] Section 39:3–29.7.

39:3–29.6. Duplicate card

In the event an identification card issued under section 2 of this act[1] is lost, destroyed or mutilated, a new name or address is acquired, or there is some other change in the information contained on the identification card, the person to whom it was issued may obtain a duplicate upon furnishing satisfactory proof of such fact to the division and upon payment of a fee as established in section 6 of this act.[2] Any person who loses an identification card and who, after obtaining a duplicate, finds the original card, shall immediately surrender the original card to the division. The same documentary evidence shall be furnished for a duplicate as for an original identification card.

L.1980, c. 47, § 5.

[1] N.J.S.A. § 39:3–29.3.
[2] N.J.S.A. § 39:3–29.7.

39:3–29.7. Fees

The Division of Motor Vehicles shall charge fees as follows:

Identification Card, Original	$18
Identification Card, Duplicate	$5
Identification Card, Renewal	$18
Digitized picture	$6, in addition to the fees required above

L.1980, c. 47, § 6. Amended by L.1989, c. 52, § 5; L.1999, c. 28, § 9, eff. Jan. 1, 2000; L.2001, c. 391, § 8, eff. Jan. 8, 2002.

39:3–29.8. Prohibited acts

It shall be unlawful for any person:

a. To display or cause or permit to be displayed or have in his possession any canceled, fictitious, fraudulently altered, or fraudulently obtained identification card;

b. To lend his identification card to any other person or knowingly permit the use thereof by another;

c. To display or represent any identification card not issued to him as being his card;

d. To permit any unlawful use of an identification card issued to him;

e. To do any act forbidden or fail to perform any act required by this act in reference to identification cards;

f. To photograph, photostat, duplicate, or in any way reproduce any identification card or facsimile thereof in such a manner that it could be mistaken for a valid identification card, or to display or have in his possession any such photograph, photostat, duplicate, reproduction, or facsimile unless authorized by the provisions of this act;

g. To alter any identification card in any manner not authorized by this act.

L.1980, c. 47, § 7.

39:3–29.9. Rules and regulations

The Director of the Division of Motor Vehicles shall promulgate, pursuant to the "Administrative Procedure Act," P.L.1968, c. 410 (C. 52:14B–1 et seq.), such rules and regulations as he considers necessary to effectuate the purposes of this act.

L.1980, c. 47, § 8.

39:3–29.10. Violation of provisions

Any person who violates any of the provisions of this act is a disorderly person.

L.1980, c. 47, § 9.

39:3–30. Transfer of ownership or destruction of motor vehicle; use on another motor vehicle; death of registered owner; joint registration

Upon the transfer of ownership or the destruction of any motor vehicle or vehicle its registration shall become void. If the motor vehicle or vehicle is sold the original owner shall remove the license plates therefrom, and surrender them to the division in a manner specified by the director if such plates are not transferred to another vehicle pursuant to this section.

The original owner may, by proper sworn application on a form to be furnished by the division, register another motor vehicle for the unexpired portion of the registration period of the original vehicle. A person applying to use the unexpired portion of a registration under this section shall pay a fee of $4.50 if the vehicle is of a weight or other classification equal with or less than the one originally registered, and shall pay a fee of $4.50 and the difference between the fee originally paid and that due if the new motor vehicle is properly registerable in a higher class. Unless the original license plates have been destroyed, the owner shall be assigned the license number previously issued to him and shall receive a new registration certificate. If the original license plates have been destroyed, replacement of the plates will be made under the provisions of R.S. 39:3–32.

The surviving husband, wife, child or children of a deceased registered owner of any motor vehicle in whom title thereto shall vest by virtue of the terms of the will of such deceased owner, or otherwise, shall, upon application to the director, and upon the payment of a fee of $4.50, be entitled to have the registration of such vehicle transferred to his or her name.

The registered owner of any motor vehicle shall, upon application to the director, and payment of a fee of $4.50, be entitled to have the vehicle registered jointly in the name of the registered owner and the spouse of said owner. The registration certificate and certificate of ownership shall be amended accordingly without the payment of any additional fee.

Amended by L.1955, c. 8, p. 47, § 9; L.1963, c. 34, § 2; L.1976, c. 43, § 2; L.1978, c. 96, § 1, eff. Aug. 14, 1978; L.1995, c. 112, § 34, eff. June 2, 1995.

39:3–30.1. Registration in names of husband and wife; title; presumption; procedure upon death

In the event that a motor vehicle is registered in the names of 2 individuals who are husband and wife title shall be presumed to vest in both persons with right of survivorship. In the event of the death of either, a new certificate of ownership and registration certificate may be granted to the survivor upon proof of such death and surrender of the certificate of ownership signed by said survivor and without the necessity of a Short Certificate, Surrogate's Affidavit or other evidence of administration.

L.1964, c. 41, § 2. Amended by L.1965, c. 183, § 1, eff. Nov. 29, 1965.

39:3–30.1a. Affidavit that registrants husband and wife

The Division of Motor Vehicles shall accept as proof that the registrants were husband and wife on the date of death, an affidavit to that effect, executed by the survivor, the form of which affidavit shall be prescribed by the Director of the Division of Motor Vehicles.

L.1965, c. 183, § 2, eff. Nov. 29, 1965.

39:3–30.2. Rights of creditors; construction against waiver of inheritance tax requirements

This act shall not impair the rights of any creditor of the decedent nor shall it be construed to waive the requirements of the laws of the State of New Jersey relating to Transfer Inheritance Tax.

L.1964, c. 41, § 2.

39:3–30.3. Operation of motor vehicles registered in name of decedent

Any motor vehicles registered in the name of any decedent may be operated, upon the public highways of this State, by a duly licensed driver who is, or is authorized to drive the same by, the surviving spouse or other member of the family of said decedent, under and by virtue of the registration certificate of such motor vehicle issued to such decedent, for a period of not exceeding 30 days after the death of such decedent.

L.1964, c. 163, § 1.

39:3–31. Duplicate certificates and licenses; fees

The chief administrator, upon presentation of a statement duly sworn to, stating that the original registration certificate or original motorized bicycle registration certificate has been destroyed, lost or stolen, may, if he is satisfied that the facts as set forth in the statement are substantially true, issue a duplicate or amended registration certificate or motorized bicycle registration certificate to the original holder thereof, upon the payment to the chief administrator of a fee of $5 for each duplicate or amended registration certificate or motorized bicycle registration certificate so issued. The chief administrator, upon presentation of a statement, duly sworn to, stating that the original driver's license has been destroyed, lost or stolen, or requesting a new color picture, may, if he is satisfied that the facts as set forth in the statement are substantially true, issue a duplicate driver's license to the original holder thereof, upon payment to the chief administrator of a fee of $5 in addition to the digitized picture fee. Notwithstanding any other provision of law to the contrary, the fee for a duplicate or amended registration certificate for any new passenger automobile required to be registered for a 48–month term or for any new passenger automobile leased for a term of more than 12 months pursuant to R.S.39:3–4, shall be $11.

Amended by L.1961, c. 77, p. 617, § 2, eff. Jan. 1, 1962; L.1968, c. 130, § 9, eff. Aug. 1, 1968; L.1983, c. 105, § 2; L.1994, c. 60, § 18, eff. July 1, 1994; L.1999, c. 28, § 10, eff. Jan. 1, 2000; L.2001, c. 391, § 9, eff. Jan. 8, 2002; L.2004, c. 64, § 3, eff. June 30, 2004.

39:3–31.1. Duplicate certificate for use by members of family; fee

The Chief Administrator of the New Jersey Motor Vehicle Commission, upon presentation of a statement by the holder of an original registration certificate that he requires a duplicate registration certificate for use by members of his family, shall issue a duplicate original registration certificate to the holder of the original registration certificate upon the payment to the chief administrator of a fee of $5. Notwithstanding any other provision of law to the contrary, the fee for a duplicate

registration certificate for any new passenger automobile required to be registered for a 48–month term or for any new passenger automobile leased for a term of more than 12 months pursuant to R.S.39:3–4, shall be $11.

Any such duplicate original registration certificate may be used in the same manner and for the same purpose as the original registration certificate but may be used only by the holder of the original registration certificate or a member of his family. Any reference to the original registration certificate in the chapter to which this act is supplementary or in Title 39 of the Revised Statutes as amended and supplemented shall be deemed to include any and all duplicate original registration certificates issued pursuant to this act and, in the event that the holder of the original registration certificate shall be required to surrender the same by virtue of the provisions of any law, he shall also be required to surrender the duplicate original registration certificate if he shall have had such duplicate original registration certificate issued to him. The chief administrator shall make and promulgate such rules and regulations as may be necessary to effectuate the purposes of this act.

This section shall also apply to registration certificates for motorized bicycles.

L.1961, c. 77, p. 616, § 1. Amended by L.1968, c. 130, § 10, eff. Aug. 1, 1968; L.1983, c. 105, § 6; L.1994, c. 60, § 19, eff. July 1, 1994; L.2004, c. 64, § 4, eff. June 30, 2004.

39:3–32. Loss, destruction or defacement of license plates; reissuance or replacement of surrendered plates; replacement fees

If one or both license plates or one or both inserts are lost, destroyed, or so defaced that the numbers thereon are illegible, the owner of the motor vehicle for which the same were issued shall apply to the director or his representative for new plates or inserts within 24 hours of the discovery of such loss, destruction, or deface- ment. The application shall be made upon a form furnished by the division, on which the loss, defacement or destruction of the plate or plates, insert or inserts shall be set forth. The application, except as hereinaf- ter provided, shall be accompanied by a fee fixed by the director, the amount of which fee shall equal, as nearly as possible, the cost to the division of replacing the plates or inserts. Thereupon the division may cancel the original registration and shall issue to the applicant new plates or new inserts, as the case may be, and a new registration certificate, if necessary.

Every replacement by reason of defacement shall be by a license plate or plates of the same identifying characters as those on the plate or plates replaced.

When a person has surrendered license plates to the director pursuant to any law or regulation, the director may charge a fee under this section for the reissuance of the plates surrendered or the issuance of new plates, as determined by the director, in an amount set by regulation but equal, as nearly as possible, to the cost incurred by the division in reissuing or replacing the plates.

Amended by L.1951, c. 61, p. 415, § 1; L.1952, c. 46, p. 364, § 1; L.1955, c. 8, p. 48, § 10; L.1956, c. 137, p. 559, § 1; L.1994, c. 60, § 20, eff. July 1, 1994.

39:3–33. Identification mark or marks; display; registration plate inserts; issuance; requirements; use of fictitious numbers or plate with advertisement; violations; penalties

The owner of an automobile which is driven on the public highways of this State shall display not less than 12 inches nor more than 48 inches from the ground in a horizontal position, and in such a way as not to swing, an identification mark or marks to be furnished by the division; provided, that if two marks are issued they shall be displayed on the front and rear of the vehicle; and provided, further, that if only one mark is issued it shall be displayed on the rear of the vehicle; and provided, further, that the rear identification mark may be displayed more than 48 inches from the ground on tank trucks, trailers and other commercial vehicles carrying inflammable liquids and on sanitation vehicles which are used to collect, transport and dispose of garbage, solid wastes and refuse. Motorcycles shall also display an identification mark or marks; provided, that if two marks are issued they shall be displayed on the front and rear of the motorcycle; and provided, further, that if only one mark is issued it shall be displayed on the rear of the motorcycle.

The identification mark or marks shall contain the number of the registration certificate of the vehicle and shall be of such design and material as prescribed pursuant to section 2 of P.L.1989, c. 202 (C. 39:3–33.9). All identification marks shall be kept clear and distinct and free from grease, dust or other blurring matter, so as to be plainly visible at all times of the day and night.

No person shall drive a motor vehicle which has a license plate frame or identification marker holder that conceals or otherwise obscures any part of any marking imprinted upon the vehicle's registration plate or any part of any insert which the director, as hereinafter provided, issues to be inserted in and attached to that registration plate or marker.

The director is authorized and empowered to issue registration plate inserts, to be inserted in and attached to the registration plates or markers described herein. They may be issued in the place of new registration plates or markers; and inscribed thereon, in numerals, shall be the year in which registration of the vehicle has been granted.

No person shall drive a motor vehicle the owner of which has not complied with the provisions of this subtitle concerning the proper registration and identification thereof, nor drive a motor vehicle which displays a fictitious number, or a number other than that designated for the motor vehicle in its registration certificate. During the period of time between the application for motor vehicle registration and the receipt of registration plates from the division, no person shall affix a plate or marker for the purpose of advertisement in the position on a motor vehicle normally reserved for the display of the registration plates required by this section if the plate or marker is designed with a combination of letters, numbers, colors, or words to resemble the registration plates required by this section.

A person convicted of displaying a fictitious number, as prohibited herein, shall be subject to a fine not exceeding $500.00 or imprisonment in the county jail for not more than 60 days.

A person violating any other provision of this section shall be subject to a fine not exceeding $100.00. In default of the payment thereof, there shall be imposed an imprisonment in the county jail for a period not exceeding 10 days. A person convicted of a second offense of the same violation may be fined in double the amount herein prescribed for the first offense and may, in default of the payment thereof, be punished by imprisonment in the county jail for a period not exceeding 20 days. These penalties shall not apply to the display of a fictitious number.

Amended by L.1943, c. 173, p. 493, § 1; L.1952, c. 46, p. 365, § 2; L.1968, c. 363, § 1, eff. Dec. 26, 1968; L.1973, c. 164, § 1, eff. June 7, 1973; L.1981, c. 133, § 1, eff. May 4, 1981; L.1983, c. 428, § 1, eff. Jan. 5, 1984; L.1989, c. 132, § 1; L.1989, c. 202, § 1, eff. Dec. 8, 1989.

39:3–33a. Additional application fees

Whenever the Division of Motor Vehicles is authorized to charge an additional application fee for the issuance of a personalized, courtesy or special license plate, the division shall charge that additional application fee only upon the initial issuance of the plate. If a personalized, courtesy or special plate is issued to a lessee in a motor vehicle leasing agreement, upon termination of the lease the lessee may apply to the director to have the plate reissued to another motor vehicle leased or owned by the lessee upon payment of a fee of $4.50. If a personalized, courtesy or special license plate is issued to an owner of a motor vehicle, the owner may apply to the director to have the plate reissued to another motor vehicle leased or owned by the owner upon payment of a fee of $4.50. Nothing in this section shall be construed as prohibiting the division from charging, at the time of annual registration renewal, the payment of the additional fee which has been required under any other section of law for a special license plate.

L.1999, c. 192, § 1, eff. Sept. 1, 2000.

39:3–33b. Personalized, courtesy or specialty license plates; second set

a. The lessee in a motor vehicle leasing agreement or the owner of a motor vehicle who obtains a base set of personalized, courtesy or special license plates with special identifying marks may obtain and use subsequent sets in a series for use upon other motor vehicles if they are owned or leased from the same or different lessor by that person, provided that there is sufficient space for the series' subscript.

b. The fees for the subsequent sets in a series shall be prescribed by the director.

c. The administrator may promulgate rules and regulations to effectuate the purposes of this act.

L.2001, c. 35, § 1, eff. March 18, 2002. Amended by L.2004, c. 91, § 1, eff. July 9, 2004.

39:3–33.1. Veterans buying motor vehicles from United States; temporary identification markers

Any person who served in the active military or naval service of the United States, and who has been discharged or released from such service under conditions other than dishonorable, and who purchases a motor vehicle from the War Assets Corporation or any other agency of the United States Government authorized to sell surplus property and has obtained from such corporation or agency a certificate of identification and a temporary identification marker which shall be displayed on such vehicle in accordance with the requirements of section 39:3–33 of the Revised Statutes, may operate such motor vehicle from the place of purchase to any place within the State for the purpose of registering such motor vehicle, without violating any of the provisions of section 39:3–4 of the Revised Statutes.

L.1946, c. 45, p. 102, § 1.

39:3–33.2. License plates; words "Garden State" to be imprinted

The Director of the Division of Motor Vehicles in the Department of Law and Public Safety shall, upon the occasion of the next and each subsequent general issue of passenger car motor vehicle registration license plates, cause to be imprinted thereon in addition to other markings which he shall prescribe, the words "Garden State."

L.1954, c. 221, p. 834, § 1.

39:3–33.3. Special identifying marks; issuance of plates

The Director of the Division of Motor Vehicles is hereby authorized to issue, upon application, registration plates of a particular identifying mark or marks to be displayed as provided in section 39:3–33 of the Revised Statutes, composed of such combination of letters and figures, in accordance with the identification system as may be requested in such application provided that the particular identifying mark so requested is not then issued to and held by some other person or otherwise reserved by the director.

L.1959, c. 56, p. 164, § 1.

39:3–33.4. Additional fees for courtesy and personalized identifying marks

The director is authorized to charge an additional fee for the issuance of such particular identifying mark in such amount as he may fix from time to time but not in excess of $30 for identifying marks defined by the director to be courtesy marks, and not in excess of $100 for identifying marks defined by the director to be personalized marks, and the amount of such fee shall accompany the application.

L.1959, c. 56, p. 164, § 2. Amended by L.1975, c. 180, § 9, eff. Jan. 1, 1976; L.1994, c. 60, § 21, eff. July 1, 1994.

39:3–33.5. Restrictions upon issuance

Except as provided for courtesy marks in section 2 of P.L.2000, c. 15 (C.39:3–33.5a), no particular identifying mark or special organization license plate issued pursuant to P.L.1987, c. 374 (C.39:3–27.35) may be issued to any applicant who:

(a) for the 10–year period next preceding the date of application for a particular identifying mark or special organization license plate has been convicted of a violation of either section 39:4–50, or section 39:4–96 of this Title or section 2 of P.L.1966, c. 142 (C.39:4–50.2) or has been convicted of a violation of a law of a substantially similar nature in another jurisdiction; or

(b) has been convicted of a violation of N.J.S.2C:11–5; or

(c) for the two year period next preceding his application for a particular identifying mark or a special organization license plate has had his driving privileges in this State or in another jurisdiction revoked or suspended for any reason whatsoever.

L.1959, c. 56, p. 164, § 3. Amended by L.2000, c. 15, § 1, eff. April 24, 2000.

39:3–33.5a. Issuance of courtesy marks

No courtesy mark may be issued to any applicant who:

a. has been convicted of a violation of either section 39:4–50, or section 39:4–96 of this Title or section 2 of P.L.1966, c. 142 (C.39:4–50.2) or has been convicted of a violation of a law of a substantially similar nature in another jurisdiction; or

b. has been convicted of a violation of N.J.S.2C:11–5; or

c. for the two year period next preceding his application for a courtesy mark has had his driving privileges in this State or in another jurisdiction revoked or suspended for any reason whatsoever.

L.2000, c. 15, § 2, eff. April 24, 2000.

39:3–33.6. Disposition of funds

For a period commencing with the effective date of this act and terminating upon the completion of the first full fiscal year thereafter, all moneys received by the director pursuant to this act shall be forthwith deposited as received with the State Treasurer, and the expenses of administration incurred by the director in carrying out the provisions of this act, during the aforementioned period are hereby appropriated to such purposes and shall be disbursed by the State Treasurer out of such funds in the same manner as other State expenses are paid. Upon the termination of the first full fiscal year after the effective date of this act, any excess of the moneys deposited with the State Treasurer as heretofore provided and over the amount of the expenses of administration during the period heretofore set forth, shall become a part of the General State Fund, and all moneys received thereafter by the director pursuant to this act, shall become a part of the General State Fund.

L.1959, c. 56, p. 165, § 4.

39:3–33.7.　Rules and regulations

The Director of the Division of Motor Vehicles shall promulgate rules and regulations for effectuating the purposes of this act.

L.1959, c. 56, p. 165, § 5.

39:3–33.8.　Effective date

This act shall take effect July 1, 1959.

L.1959, c. 56, p. 165, § 6.

39:3–33.9.　Reflectorized registration plates; phase-in program; reflectorized license plate selection commission; additional annual fee; duration; rules and regulations; annual progress report

a.　The chief administrator of the New Jersey Motor Vehicle Commission shall implement a phase-in program for the issuance of reflectorized motor vehicle registration plates in this State, the planning of which shall begin immediately for the issuance which shall begin on the first day of the seventh month following the report of the Reflectorized License Plate Selection Commission established pursuant to this section of this 1989 amendatory and supplementary act, P.L.1989, c. 202 (C.39:3–33.9), except that the commission shall first use any existing supplies of nonreflectorized plates which it orders prior to the commencement of the issuance. The purpose of the issuance shall be to change the color scheme and style of the registration plates in use prior to the beginning of the issuance in order to provide for greater contrast between the background of the plate and the lettering and to ensure that all plates are fully treated with a reflectorized material designed to increase their nighttime visibility and legibility. The color scheme and style of the new plates shall be selected by the Reflectorized License Plate Selection Commission. The markings on the plates shall be in accordance with specifications prescribed by the chief administrator.

For a period of six years commencing on the first day of the seventh month following enactment of this 1989 amendatory and supplementary act, P.L. 1989, c. 202

(C.39:3–33.9 et al.), the commission may charge in addition to an annual motor vehicle registration fee, an additional annual fee not to exceed $0.40 for the costs of the issuance of reflectorized motor vehicle registration plates in this State.

b.　The chief administrator of the New Jersey Motor Vehicle Commission shall promulgate rules and regulations pursuant to the "Administrative Procedure Act," P.L.1968, c. 410 (C.52:14B–1 et seq.) in order to effectuate the purposes of this act.

c.　The chief administrator shall submit an annual progress report on the planning and implementation of the reflectorized motor vehicle registration plate phase-in program to the Governor and members of the Legislature with the first report to be submitted one year after enactment of this 1989 amendatory and supplementary act. The annual report submitted after the fourth year of implementation shall contain a recommendation as to the advisability and feasibility of a general recall of all plates of an earlier design that are still in use at the completion of the phase-in program. This report shall also contain the chief administrator's recommendation of a funding source for the ongoing costs associated with the continued issuance of reflectorized plates. The last report shall be submitted after the completion of the phase-in program.

L.1989, c. 202, § 2, eff. Dec. 8, 1989. Amended by L.2007, c. 39, § 5, eff. Jan. 29, 2007.

39:3–33.10.　Special wildlife conservation license plates; fees; establishment of Wildlife Conservation Fund

a.　The Director of the Division of Motor Vehicles may issue for a motor vehicle owned or leased and registered in the State, wildlife conservation license plates bearing, in addition to the registration number and other markings or identification otherwise prescribed by law, words or a slogan and an emblem, to be designed by the Commissioner of Environmental Protection and approved by the Director of the Division of Motor Vehicles, indicating support for, or an interest in, wildlife conservation. Issuance of wildlife conservation license plates in accordance with this subsection shall be subject to the provisions of chapter 3 of Title 39 of the Revised Statutes,[1] except as hereinafter otherwise specifically provided.

b.　Application for issuance of a wildlife conservation license plate shall be made to the Director of the Division of Motor Vehicles on such forms and in such manner as may be prescribed by the director. In order to be deemed complete, an application shall be accompanied by a fee of $50, payable to the Director of the Division of Motor Vehicles. The $50 fee for a wildlife conservation license plate shall be in addition to the fees otherwise prescribed by law for the registration of motor vehicles. Monies collected from the fees for wildlife conservation license plates shall be deposited into a non-lapsing, interest-bearing "Wildlife Conservation Fund," which is herewith established in the Division of Fish, Game and Wildlife. Interest or other income earned on monies deposited into the Wildlife Conservation Fund shall be credited to the fund for use as set forth in this section for other monies in the fund.

c. Except as provided in section 1 of P.L.1995, c. 241 (C. 39:3–33.11), monies in the Wildlife Conservation Fund shall be utilized by the Division of Fish, Game and Wildlife: (1) to reimburse the Division of Motor Vehicles for all costs incurred by that division, as stipulated by the director of that division, in producing, issuing, and publicizing the availability of wildlife conservation license plates; and (2) for endangered and nongame species conservation, including effectuating the purposes of "The Endangered and Nongame Species Conservation Act," P.L.1973, c. 309 (C. 23:2A–1 et seq.). The Director of the Division of Motor Vehicles shall annually certify to the Director of the Division of Fish, Game and Wildlife the average cost per license plate incurred in the immediately preceding year by the Division of Motor Vehicles in producing, issuing, and publicizing the availability of wildlife conservation license plates.

d. The Director of the Division of Motor Vehicles shall notify eligible motorists of the opportunity to obtain wildlife conservation license plates by including a notice with all motor vehicle registration renewals, and by posting appropriate posters or signs in all division facilities and offices, as may be provided by the Division of Fish, Game and Wildlife. The notices, posters, and signs shall be designed by the Commissioner of Environmental Protection. The designs shall be subject to the approval of the Director of the Division of Motor Vehicles, and the Director of the Division of Fish, Game and Wildlife shall supply the Division of Motor Vehicles with the notices, posters, and signs to be circulated or posted by that division.

e. The directors of the Division of Fish, Game and Wildlife and the Division of Motor Vehicles shall develop and enter into an interagency memorandum of agreement setting forth the procedures to be followed by the two divisions in carrying out their respective responsibilities under this act.

L.1993, c. 119, § 1, eff. Nov. 20, 1993. Amended by L.1995, c. 241, § 2, eff. Nov. 27, 1995.

1 N.J.S.A. § 39:3–1 et seq.

39:3–33.11. Renewal fee for wildlife conservation license plates

The annual renewal fee for the registration certificate of a motor vehicle for which a wildlife conservation license plate has been issued shall include, in each year subsequent to the year of issuance, a wildlife conservation license plate renewal fee in the amount of $10, which shall be in addition to the fee for the renewal of the registration certificate, and which shall be collected by the Division of Motor Vehicles.

For each $10 wildlife conservation license plate renewal fee collected, the Division of Motor Vehicles shall deposit:

a. $3 thereof into a non-lapsing, interest-bearing "Marine Mammal Stranding Center Fund" to be established in the Department of the Treasury. Interest or other income earned on monies deposited into the Marine Mammal Stranding Center Fund shall be credited to the fund for use as set forth in this subsection for other monies in that fund. Monies in the Marine Mammal Stranding Center Fund shall be withdrawn by the State Treasurer and disbursed to the Marine Mammal Stranding Center in Brigantine, New Jersey, upon request of the center pursuant to a voucher system to be established by the State Treasurer. The center shall indicate on each voucher request the purpose to which the monies disbursed shall be applied. Monies disbursed from the fund to the center shall be utilized by the center in support of its work pertaining to the rescue, treatment, rehabilitation, and conservation of marine mammals and marine reptiles, and toward meeting the costs of related research and public education activities, and may be applied toward the costs of personnel and the purchase and maintenance of equipment and supplies for such purposes. The State Treasurer shall provide an annual report to the Marine Mammal Stranding Center on the status of the fund, and the center shall provide an annual report to the State Treasurer documenting expenditures by the center of monies from the fund; and

b. $7 thereof into the Wildlife Conservation Fund established pursuant to subsection b. of section 1 of P.L.1993, c. 119 (C. 39:3–33.10), of which:

(1) $5 shall be utilized by the Division of Fish, Game and Wildlife for the purpose only of funding research, information and data collection and dissemination, population and habitat studies, environmental education, and conservation activities pertaining to endangered and non-game wildlife, and which may include the funding of full-time or part-time personnel and the purchase and maintenance of equipment and supplies dedicated to that purpose; and

(2) $2 shall be made available to the Division of Fish, Game and Wildlife for the purpose only of providing funding grants to endangered and non-game wildlife conservation projects proposed by non-profit organizations.

The Division of Fish, Game and Wildlife shall adopt, pursuant to the "Administrative Procedure Act," P.L. 1968, c. 410 (C. 52:14B–1 et seq.), rules and regulations which set forth the criteria for awarding grants pursuant to paragraph (2) of this subsection.

c. Any person whose application for issuance of a wildlife conservation license plate has been received by the State prior to the effective date of P.L.1995, c. 241, or is received within 30 days thereafter, shall be permanently exempt from payment of the $10 annual wildlife conservation license plate renewal fee required pursuant to this section for that wildlife conservation license plate unless the person waives the exemption on a form therefor to be provided by the Division of Motor Vehicles at the time of renewal of the registration certificate for the motor vehicle.

L.1995, c. 241, § 1, eff. Nov. 27, 1995.

39:3–34. Application for certificate or license during suspension, revocation or prohibition period forbidden

No person whose registration certificate or driving privilege, including any privilege to operate a commercial motor vehicle as defined in P.L.1990, c. 103 (C.39:3–10.9 et al.), has been suspended or revoked, or who has been prohibited or disqualified from obtaining a driver's license or registration certificate, shall apply to the director for a registration certificate or license, or a learner's permit, as the case may be, during the period of the suspension, revocation, or prohibition. A person who violates this section shall be subject to a fine of not more than $500 or imprisonment for not more than three months, or both, at the discretion of the court.

Amended by L.1942, c. 313, p. 1147, § 1; L.1945, c. 222, p. 727, § 1; L.1990, c. 103, § 30, eff. Nov. 9, 1990.

39:3–35. Lending or using registration certificate or plates on other vehicle prohibited; fine

No person shall lend the registration certificate or registration plates for use on a motor vehicle other than the vehicle for which issued, or use the same for a motor vehicle other than the vehicle for which issued.

Any person who violates this section shall be fined not less than twenty-five nor more than fifty dollars.

39:3–36. Notice of change of address; penalty for failure

a. A licensed operator shall notify the chief administrator of any change in residence within one week after the change is made. Notice shall be in such form and shall contain such information as the chief administrator may require. Upon notification, and payment of a fee of $5 for the license in addition to the digitized picture fee, the chief administrator shall provide the licensed operator with a new license.

The registered owner of a motor vehicle or a motorized bicycle shall notify the chief administrator of any change in residence within one week after the change is made. Notice shall be in such form and shall contain such information as the chief administrator may require. Upon notification, and payment of a fee of $5, the chief administrator shall provide the registered owner with a new registration certificate.

A person who violates this section shall be subject to a penalty of not more than $25.

b. The chief administrator shall establish a public awareness campaign to inform the general public about the importance of maintaining a current address with the commission.

Amended by L.1983, c. 105, § 3; L.1990, c. 103, § 31, eff. Nov. 9, 1990; L.1999, c. 28, § 11, eff. Jan. 1, 2000; L.2001, c. 391, § 10, eff. Jan. 8, 2002; L.2007, c. 281, § 2, eff. July 1, 2008.

39:3–37. Falsifying application, examination or waiver certificate; knowingly sell, loan or give identification document to unqualified person; punishment; revocation of registration or license

A person who gives a fictitious name or address or makes any other intentional misstatement of a material fact in an application for registration of a motor vehicle, an application for a waiver pursuant to section 15 of P.L.1995, c. 112 (C. 39:8–55) of the emission standards requirement, or an application for a driver's license or in a preliminary application, examination or proceeding, or a person who knowingly sells, loans or gives an identification document to another person for the purpose of aiding that person to obtain a driver's license, registration certificate or waiver certificate for which that person is not qualified, shall be subject to a fine of not less than $200 or more than $500, or imprisonment for not more than six months or both, at the discretion of the court. The director shall, upon proper evidence not limited to a conviction, revoke the registration of the motor vehicle or driver's license of a person who violates this section for a period of not less than six months or more than two years.

Amended by L.1968, c. 323, § 9; L.1969, c. 113, § 2, eff. June 26, 1969; L.1978, c. 174, § 1, eff. Dec. 28, 1978; L.1989, c. 298, § 1, eff. Jan. 12, 1990; L.1995, c. 112, § 35, eff. June 2, 1995.

39:3–37.1. Use of license or vehicle by unlicensed driver prohibited

a. A person who has been issued a driver's license shall not lend that driver's license for use by another person.

b. A person who owns, leases or otherwise has control or custody of a motor vehicle registered under the provisions of this title shall not allow that motor vehicle to be operated by an unlicensed driver.

c. The penalty for a violation of this section shall be a fine of not less than $200 or more than $500, imprisonment for not more than 15 days, or both.

L.2003, c. 13, § 121, eff. Jan. 28, 2003.

39:3–38. Counterfeiting or using other markers; placement of forged or counterfeit plate on motor vehicle; revocation of license; fine

No person shall counterfeit a number plate or marker or make a substitute or temporary marker, under penalty of revocation of such person's driver's license for a period not to exceed 6 months, or a fine of not less than $50.00 nor more than $100.00.

No person shall use a marker other than the one issued to him by the commissioner, except as provided in R.S. 39:3–15, under penalty of a fine of not less than $25.00 nor more than $50.00.

No person shall cause to be placed a forged or counterfeit license plate on any motor vehicle, under penalty of revocation of such person's driver's license for a period not to exceed 6 months, or a fine of not less than $50.00 nor more than $100.00, or both.

Amended by L.1979, c. 173, § 1, eff. Aug. 27, 1979.

39:3–38.1 to 39:3–39. Repealed by L.1999, c. 28, § 18, eff. Jan. 1, 2000

39:3–40. Driving when license refused, suspended, revoked or prohibited; motor vehicle license revoked; punishment

Text of section effective until August 1, 2011.

No person to whom a driver's license has been refused or whose driver's license or reciprocity privilege has been suspended or revoked, or who has been prohibited from obtaining a driver's license, shall personally operate a motor vehicle during the period of refusal, suspension, revocation, or prohibition.

No person whose motor vehicle registration has been revoked shall operate or permit the operation of such motor vehicle during the period of such revocation.

Except as provided in subsections i. and j. of this section, a person violating this section shall be subject to the following penalties:

a. Upon conviction for a first offense, a fine of $500.00 and, if that offense involves the operation of a motor vehicle during a period when the violator's driver's license is suspended for a violation of R.S.39:4–50 or section 2 of P.L.1981, c. 512 (C.39:4–50.4a), revocation of the violator's motor vehicle registration privilege in accordance with the provisions of sections 2 through 6 of P.L.1995, c. 286 (C.39:3–40.1 through C.39:3–40.5);

b. Upon conviction for a second offense, a fine of $750.00, imprisonment in the county jail for at least one but not more than five days and, if the second offense involves the operation of a motor vehicle during a period when the violator's driver's license is suspended and that second offense occurs within five years of a conviction for that same offense, revocation of the violator's motor vehicle registration privilege in accordance with the provisions of sections 2 through 6 of P.L.1995, c. 286 (C.39:3–40.1 through C.39:3–40.5);

c. Upon conviction for a third offense or subsequent offense, a fine of $1,000.00 and imprisonment in the county jail for 10 days. If the third or a subsequent offense involves the operation of a motor vehicle during a period when the violator's driver's license is suspended and the third or subsequent offense occurs within five years of a conviction for the same offense, revocation of the violator's motor vehicle registration privilege

in accordance with the provisions of sections 2 through 6 of P.L.1995, c. 286 (C.39:3–40.1 through C.39:3–40.5);

d. Upon conviction, the court shall impose or extend a period of suspension not to exceed six months;

e. Upon conviction, the court shall impose a period of imprisonment for not less than 45 days or more than 180 days, if while operating a vehicle in violation of this section a person is involved in an accident resulting in bodily injury to another person;

f. (1) In addition to any penalty imposed under the provisions of subsections a. through e. of this section, any person violating this section while under suspension issued pursuant to section 2 of P.L.1972, c. 197 (C.39:6B–2), upon conviction, shall be fined $500.00, shall have his license to operate a motor vehicle suspended for an additional period of not less than one year nor more than two years, and may be imprisoned in the county jail for not more than 90 days.

(2) In addition to any penalty imposed under the provisions of subsections a. through e. of this section and paragraph (1) of this subsection, any person violating this section under suspension issued pursuant to R.S.39:4–50, section 2 of P.L.1981, c. 512 (C.39:4–50.4a) or P.L. 1982, c. 85 (C.39:5–30a et seq.), shall be fined $500, shall have his license to operate a motor vehicle suspended for an additional period of not less than one year or more than two years, and shall be imprisoned in the county jail for not less than 10 days or more than 90 days.

(3) In addition to any penalty imposed under the provisions of subsections a. through e. of this section and paragraphs (1) and (2) of this subsection, a person shall have his license to operate a motor vehicle suspended for an additional period of not less than one year or more than two years, which period shall commence upon the completion of any prison sentence imposed upon that person, shall be fined $500 and shall be imprisoned for a period of 60 to 90 days for a first offense, imprisoned for a period of 120 to 150 days for a second offense, and imprisoned for 180 days for a third or subsequent offense, for operating a motor vehicle while in violation of paragraph (2) of this subsection while:

(a) on any school property used for school purposes which is owned by or leased to any elementary or secondary school or school board, or within 1,000 feet of such school property;

(b) driving through a school crossing as defined in R.S.39:1–1 if the municipality, by ordinance or resolution, has designated the school crossing as such; or

(c) driving through a school crossing as defined in R.S.39:1–1 knowing that juveniles are present if the municipality has not designated the school crossing as such by ordinance or resolution.

A map or true copy of a map depicting the location and boundaries of the area on or within 1,000 feet of any property used for school purposes which is owned by or leased to any elementary or secondary school or school board produced pursuant to section 1 of P.L.

1987, c. 101 (C.2C:35–7) may be used in a prosecution under subparagraph (a) of this paragraph.

It shall not be relevant to the imposition of sentence pursuant to subparagraph (a) or (b) of this paragraph that the defendant was unaware that the prohibited conduct took place while on or within 1,000 feet of any school property or while driving through a school crossing. Nor shall it be relevant to the imposition of sentence that no juveniles were present on the school property or crossing zone at the time of the offense or that the school was not in session;

g.   (Deleted by amendment, P.L. 2009, c. 224);

h.   A person who owns or leases a motor vehicle and permits another to operate the motor vehicle commits a violation and is subject to suspension of his license to operate a motor vehicle and to revocation of registration pursuant to sections 2 through 6 of P.L.1995, c. 286 (C.39:3–40.1 through C.39:3–40.5) if the person:

(1) Knows that the operator's license to operate a motor vehicle has been suspended for a violation of R.S.39:4–50 or section 2 of P.L.1981, c. 512 (C. 39:4–50.4a); or

(2) Knows that the operator's license to operate a motor vehicle is suspended and that the operator has been convicted, within the past five years, of operating a vehicle while the person's license was suspended or revoked;

i.   If the violator's driver's license to operate a motor vehicle has been suspended pursuant to section 9 of P.L.1985, c. 14 (C.39:4–139.10) or for failure to comply with a time payment order, the violator shall be subject to a maximum fine of $100 upon proof that the violator has paid all fines and other assessments related to the parking violation that were the subject of the Order of Suspension, or if the violator makes sufficient payments to become current with respect to payment obligations under the time payment order;

j.   If a person is convicted for a second or subsequent violation of this section and the second or subsequent offense involves a motor vehicle moving violation, the term of imprisonment for the second or subsequent offense shall be 10 days longer than the term of imprisonment imposed for the previous offense.

For the purposes of this subsection, a "motor vehicle moving violation" means any violation of the motor vehicle laws of this State for which motor vehicle points are assessed by the chief administrator pursuant to section 1 of P.L.1982, c. 43 (C.39:5–30.5).

Amended by L.1941, c. 344, p. 902, § 1; L.1945, c. 222, p. 727, § 2; L.1947, c. 25, p. 79, § 1; L.1964, c. 9, § 1; L.1968, c. 323, § 10; L.1981, c. 38, § 1, eff. Feb. 12, 1981; L.1982, c. 45, § 2; L.1983, c. 90, § 1, eff. March 11, 1983; L.1986, c. 38, § 1, eff. June 25, 1986; L.1992, c. 203, § 1, eff. Dec. 24, 1992; L.1994, c. 64, § 2, eff. June 30, 1994; L.1995, c. 286, § 1, eff. June 1, 1996; L.1999, c. 185, § 3; L.1999, c. 423, § 3, eff. Jan. 18, 2000; L.2001, c. 213, § 1, eff. Aug. 20, 2001; L.2002, c. 28, § 1, eff. June 24, 2002; L.2007, c. 187, § 1, eff. Jan. 1, 2008; L.2009, c. 224, § 1, eff. Jan. 16, 2010.

39:3–40. Driving when license refused, suspended, revoked or prohibited; motor vehicle license revoked; punishment

Text of section effective on August 1, 2011.

No person to whom a driver's license has been refused or whose driver's license or reciprocity privilege has been suspended or revoked, or who has been prohibited from obtaining a driver's license, shall personally operate a motor vehicle during the period of refusal, suspension, revocation, or prohibition.

No person whose motor vehicle registration has been revoked shall operate or permit the operation of such motor vehicle during the period of such revocation.

Except as provided in subsections i. and j. of this section, a person violating this section shall be subject to the following penalties:

a.   Upon conviction for a first offense, a fine of $500.00 and, if that offense involves the operation of a motor vehicle during a period when the violator's driver's license is suspended for a violation of R.S.39:4–50 or section 2 of P.L.1981, c. 512 (C.39:4–50.4a), revocation of the violator's motor vehicle registration privilege in accordance with the provisions of sections 2 through 6 of P.L.1995, c. 286 (C.39:3–40.1 through C.39:3–40.5);

b.   Upon conviction for a second offense, a fine of $750.00, imprisonment in the county jail for at least one but not more than five days and, if the second offense involves the operation of a motor vehicle during a period when the violator's driver's license is suspended and that second offense occurs within five years of a conviction for that same offense, revocation of the violator's motor vehicle registration privilege in accordance with the provisions of sections 2 through 6 of P.L.1995, c. 286 (C.39:3–40.1 through C.39:3–40.5);

c.   Upon conviction for a third offense or subsequent offense, a fine of $1,000.00 and imprisonment in the county jail for 10 days. If the third or a subsequent offense involves the operation of a motor vehicle during a period when the violator's driver's license is suspended and the third or subsequent offense occurs within five years of a conviction for the same offense, revocation of the violator's motor vehicle registration privilege in accordance with the provisions of sections 2 through 6 of P.L.1995, c. 286 (C.39:3–40.1 through C.39:3–40.5);

d.   Upon conviction, the court shall impose or extend a period of suspension not to exceed six months;

e.   Upon conviction, the court shall impose a period of imprisonment for not less than 45 days or more than 180 days, if while operating a vehicle in violation of this section a person is involved in an accident resulting in bodily injury to another person;

f.   (1) In addition to any penalty imposed under the provisions of subsections a. through e. of this section, any person violating this section while under suspension issued pursuant to section 2 of P.L.1972, c. 197 (C.39:6B–2), upon conviction, shall be fined $500.00, shall have his license to operate a motor vehicle suspended for an additional period of not less than one year nor more than two years, and may be imprisoned in the county jail for not more than 90 days.

(2) In addition to any penalty imposed under the provisions of subsections a. through e. of this section and paragraph (1) of this subsection, any person violating this section under suspension issued pursuant to R.S.39:4–50, section 2 of P.L.1981, c. 512 (C.39:4–50.4a) or P.L. 1982, c. 85 (C.39:5–30a et seq.), shall be fined $500, shall have his license to operate a motor vehicle suspended for an additional period of not less than one year or more than two years, and shall be imprisoned in the county jail for not less than 10 days or more than 90 days.

(3) In addition to any penalty imposed under the provisions of subsections a. through e. of this section and paragraphs (1) and (2) of this subsection, a person shall have his license to operate a motor vehicle suspended for an additional period of not less than one year or more than two years, which period shall commence upon the completion of any prison sentence imposed upon that person, shall be fined $500 and shall be imprisoned for a period of 60 to 90 days for a first offense, imprisoned for a period of 120 to 150 days for a second offense, and imprisoned for 180 days for a third or subsequent offense, for operating a motor vehicle while in violation of paragraph (2) of this subsection while:

(a) on any school property used for school purposes which is owned by or leased to any elementary or secondary school or school board, or within 1,000 feet of such school property;

(b) driving through a school crossing as defined in R.S.39:1–1 if the municipality, by ordinance or resolution, has designated the school crossing as such; or

(c) driving through a school crossing as defined in R.S.39:1–1 knowing that juveniles are present if the municipality has not designated the school crossing as such by ordinance or resolution.

A map or true copy of a map depicting the location and boundaries of the area on or within 1,000 feet of any property used for school purposes which is owned by or leased to any elementary or secondary school or school board produced pursuant to section 1 of P.L. 1987, c. 101 (C.2C:35–7) may be used in a prosecution under subparagraph (a) of this paragraph.

It shall not be relevant to the imposition of sentence pursuant to subparagraph (a) or (b) of this paragraph that the defendant was unaware that the prohibited conduct took place while on or within 1,000 feet of any school property or while driving through a school crossing. Nor shall it be relevant to the imposition of sentence that no juveniles were present on the school property or crossing zone at the time of the offense or that the school was not in session;

g. (Deleted by amendment, P.L. 2009, c. 224);

h. A person who owns or leases a motor vehicle and permits another to operate the motor vehicle commits a violation and is subject to suspension of his license to operate a motor vehicle and to revocation of registration pursuant to sections 2 through 6 of P.L.1995, c. 286 (C.39:3–40.1 through C.39:3–40.5) if the person:

(1) Knows that the operator's license or reciprocity privilege to operate a motor vehicle has been suspended for a violation of R.S.39:4–50 or section 2 of P.L.1981, c. 512 (C.39:4–50.4a); or

(2) Knows that the operator's license or reciprocity privilege to operate a motor vehicle is suspended and that the operator has been convicted, within the past five years, of operating a vehicle while the person's license was suspended or revoked.

In any case where a person who owns or leases a motor vehicle knows that the operator's license or reciprocity privilege of the person he permits to operate the motor vehicle is suspended or revoked for any violation of R.S.39:4–50 or section 2 of P.L.1981, c. 512 (C.39:4–50.4a), the person also shall be subject to the following penalties: for a first or second offense, a fine of $1,000, imprisonment for not more than 15 days, or both; and for a third or subsequent offense, a fine of $1,000, imprisonment for not more than 15 days, or both, and forfeiture of the right to operate a motor vehicle over the highways of this State for a period of 90 days;

i. If the violator's driver's license to operate a motor vehicle has been suspended pursuant to section 9 of P.L.1985, c. 14 (C.39:4–139.10) or for failure to comply with a time payment order, the violator shall be subject to a maximum fine of $100 upon proof that the violator has paid all fines and other assessments related to the parking violation that were the subject of the Order of Suspension, or if the violator makes sufficient payments to become current with respect to payment obligations under the time payment order;

j. If a person is convicted for a second or subsequent violation of this section and the second or subsequent offense involves a motor vehicle moving violation, the term of imprisonment for the second or subsequent offense shall be 10 days longer than the term of imprisonment imposed for the previous offense.

For the purposes of this subsection, a "motor vehicle moving violation" means any violation of the motor vehicle laws of this State for which motor vehicle points are assessed by the chief administrator pursuant to section 1 of P.L.1982, c. 43 (C.39:5–30.5).

Amended by L.1941, c. 344, p. 902, § 1; L.1945, c. 222, p. 727, § 2; L.1947, c. 25, p. 79, § 1; L.1964, c. 9, § 1; L.1968, c. 323, § 10; L.1981, c. 38, § 1, eff. Feb. 12, 1981; L.1982, c. 45, § 2; L.1983, c. 90, § 1, eff. March 11, 1983; L.1986, c. 38, § 1, eff. June 25, 1986; L.1992, c. 203, § 1, eff. Dec. 24, 1992; L.1994, c. 64, § 2, eff. June 30, 1994; L.1995, c. 286, § 1, eff. June 1, 1996; L.1999, c. 185, § 3; L.1999, c. 423, § 3, eff. Jan. 18, 2000; L.2001, c. 213, § 1, eff. Aug. 20, 2001; L.2002, c. 28, § 1, eff. June 24, 2002; L.2007, c. 187, § 1, eff. Jan. 1, 2008; L.2009, c. 224, § 1, eff. Jan. 16, 2010; L.2009, c. 332, § 1, eff. Aug. 1, 2011.

39:3–40.1. Revocation of registration certificate and plates

a. Any motor vehicle registration certificate and registration plates shall be revoked if a person is convicted of violating the provisions of:

(1) subsection a. of R.S.39:3–40 for operating a motor vehicle during a period when that violator's driver's license has been suspended for a violation of R.S.39:4–50; or

(2) subsection b. or c. of R.S.39:3–40 for operating a motor vehicle during a period when that violator's driver's license has been suspended within a five-year period.

This revocation of registration certificate and registration plates shall apply to all passenger automobiles and motorcycles owned or leased by the violator and registered under the provisions of R.S.39:3–4 and all noncommercial trucks owned or leased by the violator and registered under the provisions of section 2 of P.L.1968, c. 439 (C.39:3–8.1), including those passenger automobiles, motorcycles and noncommercial trucks registered or leased jointly in the name of the violator and the other owner of record.

b. At the time of conviction, the court shall notify each violator that the person's passenger automobile, motorcycle, and noncommercial truck registrations are revoked. Notwithstanding the provisions of R.S.39:5–35, the violator shall surrender the registration certificate and registration plates of all passenger automobiles, motorcycles, and noncommercial truck registrations subject to revocation under the provisions of this section within 48 hours of the court's notice. The surrender shall be at a place and in a manner prescribed by the Chief Administrator of the New Jersey Motor Vehicle Commission pursuant to rule and regulation. The court also shall notify the violator that a failure to surrender that vehicle registration certificate and registration plates shall result in the impoundment of the vehicle in accordance with the provisions of section 4 of P.L.1995, c. 286 (C.39:3–40.3) and the seizure of said registration certificate and registration plates. The revocation authorized under the provisions of this subsection shall remain in effect for the period during which the violator's license to operate a motor vehicle is suspended and shall be enforced so as to prohibit the violator from registering or leasing any other vehicle, however acquired, during that period.

c. If the violator subject to the penalties set forth in subsections a. and b. of this section for conviction of violating the provisions of R.S.39:3–40 was operating a motor vehicle owned or leased by another person and that other owner or lessee permitted that operation with knowledge that the violator's driver's license was suspended, the court shall suspend the person's license to operate a motor vehicle and revoke the registration certificate and registration plates for that vehicle for a period of not more than six months. Notwithstanding the provisions of R.S.39:3–35, the owner or lessee shall surrender the registration certificate and registration plates of that vehicle within 48 hours of the court's notice of revocation. The surrender shall be at a place and in a manner prescribed by the Chief Administrator of the New Jersey Motor Vehicle Commission pursuant to rule and regulation. The court also shall notify the owner or lessee that a failure to surrender the revoked registration certificate and registration plates shall result in the impoundment of the vehicle in accordance with the provisions of section 4 of P.L.1995, c. 286 (C.39:3–40.3) and the seizure of said registration certificate and registration plates. Nothing in this subsection shall be construed to limit the court from finding that owner or lessee guilty of violating R.S.39:3–39 or any other such statute concerning the operation of a motor vehicle by an unlicensed driver.

L.1995, c. 286, § 2, eff. June 1, 1996. Amended by L.2000, c. 83, § 2, eff. Sept. 30, 2000; L.2009, c. 201, § 4, eff. Jan. 14, 2010.

39:3–40.2. Issuance of temporary registration certificate and plates to spouse, child, dependent or legal guardian of violator or to owner or lessee of vehicle

a. The director may issue a temporary registration certificate and temporary registration plates for a motor vehicle for which the registration certificate and registration plates have been revoked under the provisions of section 2 of P.L.1995, c. 286 (C.39:3–40.1) if:

(1) the name of the applicant for the temporary registration appeared upon the revoked registration certificate as a joint owner or joint lessee of the motor vehicle; or

(2) the applicant for the temporary registration is the spouse, child, dependent, parent or legal guardian of the violator or owner and certifies, in a manner prescribed by the director, that the operation of the motor vehicle is necessary for specified employment, educational, health or medical purposes.

The application shall be in a manner and form prescribed by the director. The application also shall include a signed certification that the applicant shall not knowingly permit the violator to operate the motor vehicle until the violator's license and driving privileges have been restored by the director and that any violation of this provision shall result in the revocation of the temporary registration issued for the motor vehicle under the provisions of this section, that the motor vehicle shall be ineligible for the temporary registration authorized under this act, and that the motor vehicle may be impounded in accordance with the provisions of section 4 of P.L.1995, c. 286 (C.39:3–40.3) and the temporary registration certificate and temporary registration plates seized.

b. The director shall issue a temporary registration certificate and temporary registration plates for a motor vehicle registered under the provisions of this section. As prescribed by the director, the temporary registration plates shall bear a special series of numbers or letters so as to be readily identifiable by law enforcement officers.

c. The director may issue a new registration to a lessor of a vehicle for which the registration has been revoked pursuant to section 2 of P.L.1995, c. 286 (C.39:3–40.1) provided that the vehicle is not leased to the same lessee.

d. The temporary registration authorized under this section shall expire and become void on the last day of the sixth month following the calendar month in which it was issued. All such temporary registrations may be renewed, upon application, by the director.

The fee schedule for the temporary registration authorized under this section shall be prescribed by the director. The schedule may provide for differing fees based upon the manufacturer's shipping weight and the model year of the motor vehicle; provided, however, that no such temporary registration fee shall exceed $75. The registrant also shall pay a non-recurring $25 fee for the temporary registration plates issued by the director.
L.1995, c. 286, § 3, eff. June 1, 1996. Amended by L.2000, c. 83, § 3, eff. Sept. 30, 2000.

39:3–40.3. Impoundment of motor vehicle subject to registration restriction

a. A motor vehicle subject to the provisions of this act may be impounded by any law enforcement officer if the registrant:

(1) knowingly permits an unlicensed driver to operate that motor vehicle;

(2) operates or permits the operation of that motor vehicle without a valid temporary registration or valid temporary registration plates as authorized under section 3 of P.L.1995, c. 286 (C. 39:3–40.2); or

(3) fails to surrender a registration certificate and registration plates in accordance with the provisions of subsection b. or c. of section 2 of P.L.1995, c. 286 (C.39:3–40.1).

A motor vehicle impounded under the provisions of this subsection shall be removed to storage space or garage and its registration certificate and registration plates seized. The registrant shall be responsible for the cost of the removal and storage of the impounded motor vehicle.

b. (1) If the registrant fails to claim the motor vehicle and pay the reasonable costs of removal and storage by midnight of the 30th day following impoundment, along with a fine of $50 to cover the administrative costs of the municipality wherein the violation occurred, the municipality may sell the motor vehicle at public auction. The municipality shall give notice of the sale by certified mail to the registrant of the motor vehicle and to the holder of any security interest filed with the director, and by publication in a form to be prescribed by the director by one insertion, at least five days before the date of the sale, in one or more newspapers published in this State and circulating in the

municipality in which the motor vehicle has been impounded.

(2) At any time prior to the sale, the registrant or other person entitled to the motor vehicle may reclaim possession of it upon payment of the reasonable costs of removal and storage of the motor vehicle and any outstanding fines or penalties; provided, however, if the other person entitled to the motor vehicle is a lessor or the holder of a lien on the motor vehicle, he may reclaim the motor vehicle without payment. In such cases, the violator shall be liable for all outstanding costs, fines and penalties, and the municipality shall have a lien against the property and income of that violator for the total amount of those outstanding costs, fines and penalties.

(3) Any proceeds obtained from the sale of a motor vehicle at public auction pursuant to paragraph (1) of this subsection in excess of the amount owed to the municipality for the reasonable costs of removal and storage of the motor vehicle and any outstanding fines or penalties shall be returned to the registrant of the vehicle.
L.1995, c. 286, § 4, eff. June 1, 1996.

39:3–40.4. Sale or transfer of vehicle subject to registration restrictions

A motor vehicle subject to the registration restrictions set forth in sections 2 and 3 of P.L.1995, c. 286 (C.39:3–40.1 and C.39:3–40.2) may not be sold or its ownership transferred; and the Division of Motor Vehicles shall not issue a certificate of registration for that vehicle; during the period in which those restrictions remain in effect unless that motor vehicle is sold or transferred for a fair market value.
L.1995, c. 286, § 5, eff. June 1, 1996.

39:3–40.5. Rules and regulations

The director, in accordance with the provisions of the "Administrative Procedure Act," P.L.1968, c. 410 (C. 52:14B–1 et seq.), shall promulgate rules and regulations to effectuate the purposes of this act. Those rules and regulations shall include, but not be limited to, provisions providing for a notice:

a. to the lessor or lienholder of any motor vehicle subject to a revocation of registration under the provisions of this act; and

b. to each person whose driver's license has been suspended of the penalties which may be imposed under the provisions of this act.
L.1995, c. 286, § 6, eff. June 1, 1996.

39:3–40.6. Release of impounded vehicle; proof of insurance

No motor vehicle which has been impounded pursuant to the laws of this State shall be released by the State or local law enforcement authority which impounded the vehicle unless proof of valid motor vehicle insurance for that vehicle is presented to the law enforcement authority. The recovery or salvage of the impounded motor vehicle by, or on behalf of, an insurer, financial institution or other lending entity, shall not require proof of valid motor vehicle insurance for that vehicle.

L.2000, c. 61, § 1.

39:3–41. Driver's manual; distribution

a. At the time of the issuance of an examination permit or a special learner's permit to operate a motor vehicle, the director shall make available to each applicant for the examination permit or special learner's permit a driver's manual containing information required to be known and followed by licensed drivers relating to licensing requirements.

b. At the time of any required examination for renewal of a driver's license, the director shall upon request make available to each applicant for renewal a copy of the manual and any supplements thereto.

c. The driver's manual and any supplements thereto or any other booklet or writing prepared in connection with examinations for drivers' licenses or for renewals of drivers' licenses shall contain all information necessary to answer any question on an examination for a driver's license or for a renewal of a driver's license.

d. The director, following consultation with the organ procurement organizations designated pursuant to 42 U.S.C. s.1320b–8 to serve in the State of New Jersey, shall include in the driver's manual information explaining the provisions of the "Revised Uniform Anatomical Gift Act," P.L.2008, c. 50 (C.26:6–77 et al.), the beneficial uses of donated organs and tissues, and the procedure for indicating on the driver's license the intention to make such a donation pursuant to P.L.1978, c. 181 (C.39:3–12.2). The director may distribute all remaining copies of the existing driver's manual before reprinting the manual with the information required pursuant to this subsection.

Amended by L.1941, c. 341, p. 900, § 1; L.1977, c. 24, § 1, eff. Feb. 24, 1977; L.1992, c. 110, § 2, eff. Sept. 25, 1992; L.2008, c. 50, § 26, eff. July 22, 2008.

39:3–41.1. Driver's manual; distribution of remaining copies before reprinting

The administrator may distribute all remaining copies of the existing manual before reprinting it with the information required pursuant to subsection b. of R.S.39:4–72.

L.2004, c. 163, § 2, eff. Dec. 7, 2004.

39:3–42. Compliance with chapter sufficient

No owner, purchaser or driver of a motor vehicle who has complied with this chapter shall be required to obtain any other license or permit to use or operate the vehicle, be excluded or prohibited from or limited in the free use thereof or be required to comply with other provisions or conditions as to the use of the motor vehicle, except as provided in this subtitle and as otherwise provided by law.

ARTICLE 3. EQUIPMENT

39:3–43. Powers of commissioner

The commission is hereby given authority to pass upon the construction and equipment of any vehicle, motor vehicle or motor-drawn vehicle with a view to its safety for use on a street or highway and it shall be lawful for the commission to refuse registration to any vehicle that in its estimation is not a proper vehicle to be used upon a highway. The commission is hereby authorized to promulgate regulations, not inconsistent with this chapter, concerning the construction and equipment of any vehicle, motor vehicle or motor-drawn vehicle. The commission may require the approval of any equipment or device and may set up the procedure which shall be followed when any equipment or device is submitted for approval. The commission may revoke or suspend for cause and after hearing any certificate of approval that may be issued under this article. The commission at its discretion is hereby authorized to disapprove any equipment or device.

Amended by L.2003, c. 13, § 103.

39:3–44. Scope and effect

No person shall hereafter drive, move, park or be in custody of nor shall any owner or lessee hereafter cause or knowingly permit to be driven, moved or parked on any highway any vehicle, motor vehicle or motor-drawn vehicle or combination of vehicles which is in such unsafe condition as to endanger or be likely to endanger any person or property, or which does not contain those parts or is not at all times, equipped with such equipment in proper condition and adjustment as required in this article, or which is equipped in any manner in violation of this article. No person shall do any act forbidden or fail to perform any act required under this article.

39:3–45. Certain vehicles excepted

The subsequent provisions of this article with respect to equipment and lights on vehicles shall not apply to agricultural machinery and implements, road machinery, road rollers, traction engines or farm tractors except as hereinafter in this article made applicable.

39:3–46. Words and phrases defined

As used in this article, unless the context requires another or different construction:

"Approved" means approved by the commission and when applied to lamps and other illuminating devices means that such lamps and devices must be in good working order and capable of operating at least 50% of their designed efficiency.

"Vehicle" means every device in, upon or by which a person or property is or may be transported upon a highway, excepting devices moved by human power or used exclusively upon stationary rails or tracks.

"When lighted lamps are required" means at any time from a half-hour after sunset to a half-hour before sunrise; whenever rain, mist, snow or other precipitation or atmospheric moisture requires the use of windshield wipers by motorists; and during any time when, due to smoke, fog, unfavorable atmospheric conditions or for any other cause there is not sufficient light to render clearly discernible persons and vehicles on the highway at a distance of 500 feet ahead.

"Headlamp" means a major lighting device capable of providing general illumination ahead of a vehicle.

"Auxiliary driving lamp" means an additional lighting device on a motor vehicle used primarily to supplement the headlamps in providing general illumination ahead of a vehicle.

"Single beam headlamps" means headlamps or similar devices arranged so as to permit the driver of the vehicle to use but one distribution of light on the road.

"Multiple-beam headlamps" means headlamps or similar devices arranged so as to permit the driver of the vehicle to use one of two or more distributions of light on the road.

"Asymmetric headlamps" means headlamps or similar devices arranged so as to permit the driver of the vehicle to use one of several distributions of light on the road, at least one of which is asymmetric about the median vertical axis.

"Clear road beam" means the beam from multiple-beam headlamps designed to be used when not approaching other vehicles and designed to provide sufficient candlepower ahead to reveal obstacles at a safe distance ahead under ordinary conditions of road contour and of vehicle loading.

"Meeting beam" means the beam from multiple beam or asymmetric headlamps designed to be used when other vehicles are approaching within 500 feet or when signaled and designed so that the illumination on the left side of the road is reduced sufficiently to avoid dangerous glare for the approaching driver.

"Lower beam" means the beam from multiple beam or asymmetric headlamps designed to be directed low enough to avoid dangerous glare on both sides of the roadway.

"Reflector" means an approved device designed and used to give an indication by reflected light.

Amended by L.1983, c. 285, § 1, eff. July 29, 1983; L.1995, c. 305, § 1, eff. Jan. 5, 1996; L.2003, c. 13, § 104 (contingent effective date).

39:3–47. Certain acts forbidden

No person shall drive, move, park or be in custody of any vehicle or combination of vehicles on any street or highway unless such vehicle or combination of vehicles is equipped with lamps and illuminating devices as hereinafter in this article respectively required for different classes of vehicles.

a. No person shall drive, move, park or be in custody of any vehicle or combination of vehicles on any street or highway during the times when lighted lamps are required unless such vehicle or combination of vehicles displays lighted lamps and illuminating devices as hereinafter in this article required. Failure to use lighted lamps when lighted lamps are required may result in a fine not to exceed $50.00. In no case shall motor vehicle points or automobile insurance eligibility points pursuant to section 26 of P.L.1990, c. 8 (C:17:33B–14) be assessed against any person for a violation of this subsection. A person who is fined under this subsection for a violation of this subsection shall not be subject to a surcharge under the New Jersey Merit Rating Plan as provided in section 6 of P.L.1983, c. 65 (C:17:29A–35).

b. No person shall use on any vehicle any approved electric lamp or similar device unless the light source of such lamp or device complies with the conditions of approval as to focus and rated candlepower.

c. No person shall alter the equipment or performance of equipment of any vehicle which has been approved at an official inspection station designated by the commission with intent to defeat the purpose of such inspection, and no person shall drive or use any vehicle with equipment so altered.

Amended by L.1995, c. 305, § 2, eff. Jan. 5, 1996; L.2003, c. 13, § 44 (contingent effective date).

39:3–48. Visibility

(a) Whenever there shall be in this article a requirement declared as to the distance from which certain lamps and devices shall render objects visible or within which such lamps or devices shall be visible, said provisions shall apply during the times when lighted lamps are required upon a straight level unlighted highway under normal atmospheric conditions unless a different time or condition is expressly stated.

(b) The light from every required exterior lamp on a vehicle shall be visible from a distance of 500 feet in the directions set forth therefor in paragraph (d) of this section except that the light illuminating a license plate shall cause the license plate to be clearly legible from a distance of 50 feet to the rear. Such visibility is not required when the light is obscured by another vehicle in a combination of vehicles.

(c) Every required Class A reflector shall be visible from all distances between 100 and 600 feet, and every required Class B reflector shall be visible from all distances between 100 and 350 feet, when illuminated by the upper beam of headlamps.

(d) Light from every headlamp, other driving lamp, clearance lamp, identification lamp and single-faced turn signal mounted on or at the front of a vehicle, and front parking light, shall be visible to the front; that from every side-marker lamp and side reflector shall be visible to the side; that from every stop lamp, tail lamp, clearance lamp, identification lamp, back-up lamp and reflector mounted on the rear, from every turn signal mounted on the rear of a vehicle or the cab of a truck tractor, and from any rear parking lamp, shall be visible to the rear; that from any double-faced turn signal shall be visible to the front and to the rear at the side on which such lamp is mounted; and that from any projecting load marker lamp or combination marker lamp shall be visible from the direction stated in the provision requiring it.

Amended by L.1964, c. 136, § 1.

39:3–49. Headlamps

Except as hereinafter in this article provided, every motor vehicle other than a motor-drawn vehicle and other than a motor cycle shall be equipped with at least 2 approved headlamps mounted at the same level with an equal number on each side of the front of the vehicle. Every motor cycle shall be equipped with at least 1 and not more than 2 approved headlamps. Every motor cycle equipped with a side car or other attachment shall be equipped with a lamp on the outside limit of such attachment capable of displaying a white light to the front.

Amended by L.1964, c. 136, § 2.

39:3–50. Color of lights, permits; cancellation or revocation of permits

All lamps and reflectors, which display a light visible from directly in front of a vehicle as authorized by this subtitle, shall exhibit lights substantially white, yellow or amber in color.

(a) The color of light emitted or reflected by exterior lamps or reflectors on a vehicle shall be as follows, except as otherwise provided in paragraphs (b), (c) and (d) of this section:

White when the lamp is a headlamp, or spot lamp, or illuminates a license plate or a destination sign; or is located on the outside limit of a side car or other attachment on a motor cycle;

Substantially white or amber when the lamp is a side-cowl or fender lamp, running-board or other courtesy lamp, front parking lamp, back-up lamp, auxiliary driving lamp; or a turn signal on or facing the front;

Substantially red or amber when the lamp is a turn signal or a stop lamp on or facing the rear;

Red when any other lamp or any reflector is on the rear or on either side at or near the rear, except as otherwise provided in paragraph (f) of section 39:3–61 for a combination marker lamp;

Amber when any other lamp or reflector is on the front or on either side other than at or near the rear.

(b) Lamps and reflectors on projecting loads shall emit or reflect light with color as provided in section 10 of this act.

(c) No person shall drive or move any vehicle or equipment upon any street or highway equipped with any device or lamp thereon capable of or displaying a light of any other color than permitted by this section, except: an authorized emergency vehicle, an authorized school bus, or a vehicle authorized by a permit issued by the chief administrator.

(d) A permit authorizing a vehicle to be equipped with a lamp capable of or displaying a flashing light, except as provided in 39:3–54 or a light of a color other than permitted by this section, visible from directly in front of said vehicle, may be issued by the director when necessary, in his discretion, for the reasonable and safe movement of traffic. The permit shall specify the type and color of such lamp and the conditions under which a person may drive or move the vehicle with said lamp displaying a light. The permit shall be valid only when the specifications and conditions contained therein are complied with. The chief administrator shall collect a $25 fee for the initial issuance and for each subsequent renewal of the permit for each vehicle for which the applicant seeks to use such a light, provided, however, that no fee shall be charged for a permit authorizing the use of a light that is red or blue. The fee set forth in this section shall not apply to a motor vehicle registered at no fee pursuant to R.S.39:3–27. The fees collected pursuant to this section shall be considered revenue of the commission and shall not be subject to the calculation of proportional revenue remitted to the commission pursuant to section 105 of P.L.2003, c. 13 (C.39:2A–36).

The chief administrator may cancel or revoke a permit issued under authority of this section whenever the conditions for its issuance no longer exist or on any other reasonable grounds.

Amended by L.1951, c. 24, p. 121, § 1; L.1964, c. 136, § 3; L.2007, c. 242, § 5, eff. Feb. 1, 2009.

39:3–51. Auxiliary driving lamps

Any motor vehicle may be equipped with not to exceed two auxiliary driving lamps mounted on the front at a height not less than twelve inches nor more than forty-two inches above the level surface upon which the vehicle stands, and every such auxiliary driving lamp or lamps shall be so aimed and used that no part of the high-intensity portion of the beam will be directed to the left of the prolongation of the extreme left side of the vehicle nor more than one hundred feet ahead of the vehicle.

39:3–52. Additional lighting equipment

Any motor vehicle may be equipped with not more than two side cowl or fender lamps which shall emit a white or yellow light without glare. Any motor vehicle may be equipped with not more than one running board courtesy lamp on each side thereof which shall emit a white or yellow light without glare. Any motor vehicle may be equipped with a back-up lamp either separately or in combination with another lamp; except that no such back-up lamp shall be continuously lighted when the motor vehicle is in forward motion.

39:3–53. Spot lamps

Any motor vehicle may be equipped with not to exceed one spot lamp but the use of any such spot lamp for driving purposes is prohibited and every lighted spot lamp shall be so aimed and used so as not to be dazzling or glaring to any person.

39:3–54. Special restrictions on lamps, emergency warning lighting

a. Any lighted lamp or illuminating device upon a motor vehicle other than a headlamp, spot lamp or auxiliary driving lamp which projects a beam of light of an intensity greater than 300 candlepower shall be so directed that no part of the beam will strike the level of the roadway on which the vehicle stands at a distance of more than 75 feet from the vehicle. Flashing lights are prohibited on motor vehicles, motorcycles and motor-drawn vehicles except as a means for indicating a right or left turn; provided, however, any vehicle may be equipped, and when required under this article shall be equipped, with lamps for the purpose of warning the operators of other vehicles of the presence of a vehicular traffic hazard requiring the exercise of unusual care in approaching, overtaking or passing, and when so equipped, shall display such warning in addition to any other warning signals required by law. The lamps used to display such warning shall be of a type approved by the Director of the Division of Motor Vehicles; those used to display warning to the front shall be mounted at the same level and as widely spaced laterally as practicable, and shall display simultaneously flashing white or amber lights, or any shade of color between white and amber. The lamps used to display such warning to the rear shall be mounted at the same level and as widely spaced laterally as practicable, and shall show simultaneously flashing amber or red lights, or any shade of color between amber and red. These warning lights shall be visible from a distance of not less than 500 feet at any time when lighted lamps are required. The two front and two rear turn signals shall be flashed simultaneously to display such warning on vehicles of the types mentioned in section 39:3–64.

b. In addition to the flashing devices permitted in subsection a. of this section, an omnibus may be equipped with two flashing devices for the purpose of warning the operators of other vehicles and law enforcement officials that an emergency situation exists within the omnibus.

These devices shall be capable of activation by the operator of the omnibus and shall be of a type approved by the Director of the Division of Motor Vehicles.

They shall be mounted one at the front and one at the rear of the omnibus and shall display flashing red lights which shine on the roadway under the vehicle.

Amended by L.1956, c. 27, p. 70, § 1; L.1964, c. 136, § 4; L.1985, c. 536, § 1.

39:3–54.1 to 39:3–54.6. Repealed by L.1977, c. 223, § 8

39:3–54.7. Members of certain organizations; display of emergency warning lights

a. An active member in good standing of any of the following organizations may mount and operate, on a motor vehicle operated by that member, an emergency warning light or lights as provided in P.L.1977, c. 223 (C.39:3–54.7 et seq.):

(1) a volunteer fire company or a volunteer first aid or rescue squad recognized by and rendering service in any municipality; or

(2) any county or municipal volunteer Office of Emergency Management recognized by and rendering service in any county or municipality, provided the member's official duties include responding to a fire or emergency call.

b. The Chief Administrator of the New Jersey Motor Vehicle Commission shall not require the member to specify on which motor vehicles the emergency warning light or lights may be mounted.

L.1977, c. 223, § 1, eff. Sept. 16, 1977. Amended by L.1979, c. 71, § 1, eff. April 10, 1979; L.1995, c. 37, § 1, eff. March 7, 1995; L.2005, c. 34, § 2, eff. May 1, 2005; L.2005, c. 218, § 1, eff. April 1, 2006.

39:3–54.8. Time of operation

Emergency warning lights may be operated only while the vehicle is being used in answering a fire or emergency call.

L.1977, c. 223, § 2, eff. Sept. 16, 1977.

39:3–54.9. Specifications

Emergency warning lights shall be removable or permanently attached, of the flashing or revolving type, equipped with a blue lens and controlled by a switch installed inside the vehicle or shall be blue of the light bar type, in accordance with the specifications prescribed by the chief administrator.

L.1977, c. 223, § 3, eff. Sept. 16, 1977. Amended by L.1979, c. 71, § 2, eff. April 10, 1979; L.2005, c. 218, § 2, eff. April 1, 2006.

39:3–54.10. Placement on motor vehicle

No more than two emergency warning lights shall be installed on a vehicle. If one light is used it shall be installed in the center of the roof of the car, or on the front of the vehicle so that the top of the emergency warning light is no higher than the top of the vehicle's headlights, or in the center of the dashboard. It may be a low profile light bar of the strobe, halogen or incandescent type, or a combination thereof. If two lights are used they may be placed on the windshield columns on each side of the vehicle where spotlights are normally mounted, or on either side of the roof at the front of the vehicle directly back of the top of the windshield. Under no circumstances may one light be placed on the roof and one on the windshield column in the spotlight position. Light elements shall be shielded from direct sight or view of the driver.

L.1977, c. 223, § 4, eff. Sept. 16, 1977. Amended by L.1979, c. 71, § 3, eff. April 10, 1979; L.2005, c. 218, § 3, eff. April 1, 2006.

39:3–54.11. Display of emergency warning lights; identification cards

a. The Chief Administrator of the New Jersey Motor Vehicle Commission shall prepare suitable identification cards bearing the signature of the chief administrator which, upon the request of the mayor or chief executive officer of any municipality recognizing and being served by a volunteer fire company or a volunteer first aid or rescue squad on a form and in a manner prescribed by the chief administrator, shall be forwarded to the mayor or chief executive officer, to be countersigned and issued by the mayor or chief executive officer to the members in good standing of the volunteer fire company or first aid or rescue squad.

b. Identification cards issued pursuant to this section and sections 5 and 6 of P.L.2005, c. 34 (C.39:3–54.22 and C.39:3–54.23) shall be considered permits to mount and operate emergency warning lights as provided for in P.L.1977, c. 223 (C.39:3–54.7 et seq.) and shall apply to any motor vehicle driven by the member of a volunteer fire company, a volunteer first aid or rescue squad or a volunteer Office of Emergency Management. Emergency warning lights shall not be mounted prior to the issuance of the identification cards. Each member of a volunteer fire company, a volunteer first aid or rescue squad or a volunteer Office of Emergency Management must carry the identification card while an emergency warning light or lights are operated on the vehicle.

L.1977, c. 223, § 5, eff. Sept. 16, 1977. Amended by L.1995, c. 37, § 2, eff. March 7, 1995; L.2005, c. 34, § 3, eff. May 1, 2005; L.2005, c. 218, § 4, eff. April 1, 2006.

39:3–54.12. Rights of motor vehicle with emergency warning lights in operation

Nothing contained herein is intended to grant to any member of a volunteer fire company, a volunteer first aid or rescue squad or a volunteer Office of Emergency Management any privileges or exemptions denied to the drivers of other vehicles, and such members operating emergency warning lights shall drive with due regard for the safety of all persons and shall obey all the traffic laws of this State including R.S.39:4–81, provided, however, that the drivers of non-emergency vehicles upon any highway shall yield the right of way to the vehicle of any member of a volunteer fire company, a volunteer first aid or rescue squad or a volunteer Office of Emergency Management operating emergency warning lights in the same manner as is provided for

authorized emergency vehicles pursuant to R.S. 39:4–92.

L.1977, c. 223, § 6, eff. Sept. 16, 1977. Amended by L.2005, c. 34, § 4, eff. May 1, 2005; L.2005, c. 218, § 5, eff. April 1, 2006.

39:3–54.13. Violations; penalty

Any person authorized to operate emergency warning lights pursuant to P.L.1977, c. 223 (C.39:3–54.7 et seq.) who willfully operates such emergency warning lights in violation of the provisions of P.L.1977, c. 223 (C.39:3–54. 7 et seq.) shall be liable to a penalty of not more than $ 100 and the person's privilege to operate such emergency warning lights may be suspended or revoked by the Chief Administrator of the New Jersey Motor Vehicle Commission. A person who is not authorized to operate emergency warning lights who willfully operates such emergency warning lights shall be liable to a penalty of not more than $ 200.

L.1977, c. 223, § 7, eff. Sept. 16, 1977. Amended by L.1995, c. 37, § 3, eff. March 7, 1995; L.2005, c. 218, § 6, eff. April 1, 2006.

39:3–54.14. Special identification lights; vehicles of licensed private detective businesses; permits; penalty for violation

a. The director may issue permits authorizing vehicles of licensed private detective businesses under contractual agreement to provide community security services in planned developments as defined in the "Municipal Land Use Law" P.L.1975, c. 291 (C. 40:55D–1 et seq.), to be equipped with and display a special identification light. Issuance of such permits shall, in addition, be approved and signed by the chief law enforcement official in the municipality in which such permit shall be used. The permit shall specify the type of light, the manner in which it shall be displayed and the conditions under which the operator of the vehicle may drive or move the vehicle when the light is in use. The permit shall also specify the color of the light, which shall be other than red. The permit for the use of the special identification light shall be carried by the operator while the light is displayed on the vehicle.

b. The permit shall be valid only when the specifications and conditions contained therein are complied with, and the director may cancel or revoke a permit issued pursuant to this act whenever the conditions for its issuance no longer exist or on any other reasonable grounds. The director shall charge a $25.00 fee for the issuance of each such permit.

c. Any person authorized to display a special identification light pursuant to this act who displays or uses said light in violation of the provisions of this act shall be liable to a penalty of $50.00 for the first offense, and $100.00 for the second and each subsequent offense.

L.1979, c. 314, § 1, eff. Jan. 18, 1980.

39:3–54.15. Red emergency warning lights and/or siren on motor vehicles owned by current volunteer fire chief or first assistant chief or chief officer of first aid or rescue squad

A current chief or first assistant chief of a volunteer fire company, or chief officer of a first aid or rescue squad, recognized by and rendering service in any municipality may mount and operate on a motor vehicle owned by him and registered in his name a red emergency warning light or lights, a siren, or both, as prescribed in P.L.1985, c. 171 (C.39:3–54.15 et seq.). The size and type of lights and siren, and the location of their controls, shall be determined by the Chief Administrator of the New Jersey Motor Vehicle Commission.

L.1985, c. 171, § 1, eff. May 31, 1985. Amended by L.2005, c. 218, § 7, eff. April 1, 2006.

39:3–54.16. Placement of red emergency warning lights

All red emergency lights shall be mounted on the exterior of the motor vehicle. No more than two red emergency warning lights shall be installed on a vehicle. If one light is used it shall be installed in the center of the roof of the vehicle, or on the left windshield column in a position where a spotlight is normally located. If two lights are used they may be placed on the windshield columns on each side of the vehicle where spotlights are normally mounted, or on either side of the roof at the front of the vehicle directly back of the top of the windshield. Under no circumstances may one light be placed on the roof and one on a windshield column in the spotlight position. They shall be operated only while the vehicle is being used by the registered owner chief or first assistant chief in answering a fire or emergency call.

L.1985, c. 171, § 2, eff. May 31, 1985.

39:3–54.17. Placement of sirens

All sirens shall be mounted under the hood of the motor vehicle and shall be operated only while the vehicle is being used by the registered owner chief or first assistant chief in answering a fire or emergency call.

L.1985, c. 171, § 3, eff. May 31, 1985.

39:3–54.18. Identification cards for chief or first assistant chief; issuance; purpose

The Director of the Division of Motor Vehicles shall prepare suitable identification cards bearing the signature of the director, which, upon the request of the mayor or chief executive officer of any municipality recognizing and being served by a volunteer fire company, on a form and in a manner prescribed by the director, shall be forwarded to the mayor or chief executive officer, to be countersigned and issued by the mayor or chief executive officer to the chief or first assistant chief of the volunteer fire company. Identification cards issued pursuant to this section shall be considered permits to display and operate red emergen-

cy warning lights, sirens, or both, as provided for in this act, and no lights or sirens shall be mounted prior to the issuance of the identification cards. Each chief or first assistant chief of a volunteer fire company shall carry the identification card while red emergency warning lights, sirens, or both, are displayed on his vehicle.

L.1985, c. 171, § 4, eff. May 31, 1985.

39:3–54.19. Operation of motor vehicles with red emergency warning lights or sirens; yielding right of way

This act shall not grant to any chief or first assistant chief of a volunteer fire company any privileges or exemptions denied to the drivers of other vehicles, and persons displaying red emergency warning lights, sirens, or both, shall drive with due regard for the safety of all persons and shall obey the traffic laws of this State; but drivers of nonemergency vehicles upon any highway shall yield the right of way to the vehicle of any chief or first assistant chief of a volunteer fire company displaying red emergency warning lights, sirens, or both, in the same manner as is provided for authorized emergency vehicles pursuant to R.S. 39:4–92.

L.1985, c. 171, § 5, eff. May 31, 1985.

39:3–54.20. Unlawful use of red emergency warning lights or sirens; penalty

Any person authorized to display red emergency warning lights, sirens, or both, pursuant to this act, who willfully displays or uses the lights or sirens in violation of the provisions of this act, shall be liable to a penalty of not more than $50.00 and his privilege to display the lights or sirens may be suspended or revoked by the Director of the Division of Motor Vehicles.

L.1985, c. 171, § 6, eff. May 31, 1985.

39:3–54.21. Use of amber warning lights by United States Postal Service employees

a. Any employee of the United States Postal Service who, as part of his assigned duties as a rural route letter carrier, is required to use a motor vehicle owned or leased by him or a member of his family in the performance of his duties may display on that motor vehicle an amber warning light.

The amber warning light may be operated only while the motor vehicle is being used by the United States Postal Service employee in the performance of his duties as a rural letter carrier.

The amber warning light authorized under the provisions of this act shall be temporarily attached, removable lights of the flashing or revolving type, not more than 7½ inches in diameter, not more than 51 candlepower, and shall be controlled by a switch installed inside the vehicle.

While in operation, the amber warning light shall be conspicuously displayed on the roof of the motor vehicle.

Nothing herein shall be construed to grant any person displaying and operating an amber warning light pursuant to the provisions of this act any privileges or exemptions denied to the drivers of other motor vehicles and all such persons shall drive with due regard for the safety of all persons and shall obey the traffic laws of this State.

b. The Director of the Division of Motor Vehicles, in accordance with the provisions of the "Administrative Procedure Act," P.L.1968, c. 410 (C.52:14B–1 et seq.), shall promulgate rules and regulations to effectuate the purposes of this act.

L.1991, c. 4, § 1, eff. April 1, 1991.

39:3–54.22. Permit to display emergency warning lights; application to County Emergency Management Coordinator

An active member of a county volunteer Office of Emergency Management shall submit an application for a permit to the County Emergency Management Coordinator prior to displaying an emergency warning light or lights pursuant to the provisions of this act. The coordinator shall approve the application if the volunteer's official duties require him to respond to fire or emergency calls. The completed application shall be forwarded to the Director of the Board of Chosen Freeholders or other appropriate authority of the county that recognizes and serves the applicant's Office of Emergency Management. Upon approval, the mayor or chief executive officer shall forward the application to the Chief Administrator of the New Jersey Motor Vehicle Commission for issuance of the permit.

L.2005, c. 34, § 5, eff. May 1, 2005.

39:3–54.23. Permit to display emergency warning lights; application to Municipal Emergency Management Coordinator

An active member of a municipal volunteer Office of Emergency Management shall submit an application to the Municipal Emergency Management Coordinator to display an emergency warning light or lights pursuant to the provisions of this act. The coordinator shall approve the application if the volunteer's official duties require him to respond to fire or emergency calls. The completed application shall be forwarded to the mayor or chief executive officer of the municipality that recognizes and serves the applicant's Office of Emergency Management. Upon approval, the mayor or chief executive officer shall forward the application to the Chief Administrator of the New Jersey Motor Vehicle Commission for issuance of the permit.

L.2005, c. 34, § 6, eff. May 1, 2005.

39:3–54.24. Amber warning lights for use by an authorized public utility company employee; permit authorizing display; fees; approved operation

An authorized employee of a public utility company who, as part of the official duties of a public utility employee, is required to use a motor vehicle owned or leased by him or a member of his family in the performance of his duties may apply for and be issued a permit by the chief administrator authorizing the display on that motor vehicle of an amber warning light that is provided by the public utility company. The permit for the amber warning light shall be in the possession of the public utility employee while the light is displayed on the motor vehicle. The chief administrator may cancel, suspend, or revoke a permit issued pursuant to this act [1] whenever the conditions for its issuance no longer exist or for any other reasonable grounds. The chief administrator shall collect a $25 fee for the initial issuance and for each subsequent renewal of the permit for each vehicle for which the applicant seeks authorization to use an amber warning light. The fees collected pursuant to this section shall be considered revenue of the commission and shall not be subject to the calculation of proportional revenue remitted to the commission pursuant to section 105 of P.L.2003, c. 13 (C.39:2A–36).

The amber warning light may be operated for the protection of the public and the public utility employee only while the motor vehicle is being used on a public highway by the authorized public utility employee in the performance of his official duties as a public utility employee.

The amber warning lights authorized under the provisions of this act shall be temporarily attached, removable lights of the flashing or revolving type, not more than 7 ½ inches in diameter, and shall be controlled by a switch installed inside the vehicle.

While in operation, the amber warning light shall be conspicuously displayed on the roof of the motor vehicle.

Nothing herein shall be construed to grant any person displaying and operating an amber warning light pursuant to the provisions of this act any privileges or exemptions denied to the drivers of other motor vehicles and all such persons shall drive with due regard for the safety of all persons and shall obey the traffic laws of this State.

L.2007, c. 242, § 1, eff. Feb. 1, 2009.

[1] L.2007, c. 242 (N.J.S.A. § 39:3–54.24 et al.).

39:3–54.25. Magnetic sign with utility logo affixed on to vehicle; authorized display

Notwithstanding the provisions of section 2 of P.L. 1968, c. 439 (C.39:3–8.1), an authorized employee of a public utility company who, as part of the official duties of a public utility employee, is required to use a motor vehicle owned or leased by him or a member of his family in the performance of his duties may affix on that motor vehicle a magnetic sign, provided by the public utility company, that displays the corporate logo of the public utility company. The sign shall be placed on the exterior of the front driver's side door of the motor vehicle.

The sign may only be displayed while the motor vehicle is being used on a public highway by the authorized public utility employee in the performance of his official duties as a public employee, and shall be removed from the motor vehicle when the vehicle is not being used in the performance of these duties.

L.2007, c. 242, § 2, eff. Feb. 1, 2009.

39:3–54.26. Violation of authorized use of amber warning lights or magnetic sign; penalties

Any person authorized to display an amber warning light or a magnetic sign pursuant to this act,[1] who willfully uses the light or displays the sign in violation of the provisions of this act, shall be liable to a penalty of not more than $100 and his permit to display the light may be cancelled, suspended, or revoked by the chief administrator.

L.2007, c. 242, § 3, eff. Feb. 1, 2009.

[1] L.2007, c. 242 (N.J.S.A. § 39:3–54.24 et al.).

39:3–55. Alternate road lighting equipment

Any motor vehicle need not be equipped with approved headlamps provided that every such vehicle during the times when lighted lamps are required is equipped with two lighted lamps on the front thereof displaying white or yellow lights without glare capable of revealing persons and objects seventy-five feet ahead; provided, however, that no such motor vehicle shall be operated at a speed in excess of twenty miles per hour during the times when lighted lamps are required.

39:3–56. Number of driving lamps required or permitted

At the times when lighted lamps are required, at least 2 lighted driving lamps shall be displayed, an equal number on each side of the front of every motor vehicle other than a motorcycle and other than a motor-drawn vehicle except when such vehicle is parked subject to the provisions governing lights on parked vehicles or is flashing vehicular traffic hazard warning signals as provided for in sections 39:3–54 and 39:3–64. Whenever a motor vehicle equipped with headlamps as in this article required is also equipped with auxiliary lamps or a spot lamp or any other lamp on the front thereof projecting a beam of an intensity greater than 300 candlepower, not more than a total of 4 of any such lamps on the front of a vehicle shall be lighted at any one time when upon a highway.

Amended by L.1964, c. 136, § 5.

39:3–57. Single-beam road lighting

Approved single-beam headlamps shall be so aimed that when the vehicle is not loaded none of the high-intensity portion of the light shall at a distance of twenty-five feet ahead project higher than a level of five inches below the level of the center of the lamp from which it comes, and in no case higher than forty-two inches above the level on which the vehicle stands at a distance of seventy-five feet ahead. The intensity shall be sufficient to reveal persons and vehicles at a distance of at least two hundred feet.

39:3–58. Multiple-beam road lighting

Approved multiple beam headlamps shall be so arranged that the driver may control the selection between different distributions of light subject to the following requirements and limitations:

There shall be an uppermost distribution of light, or composite beam, so aimed and of such intensity as to reveal persons and vehicles at a distance of at least 350 feet ahead for all conditions of loading.

There shall be a lowermost distribution of light, or composite beam, so aimed and of sufficient intensity to reveal persons and vehicles at a distance of at least 100 feet ahead; and on a straight level road under any condition of loading none of the high-intensity portion of the beam shall be directed to strike the eyes of an approaching driver.

Amended by L.1954, c. 124, p. 600, § 1.

39:3–59. Beam indicator lights

Every New Jersey registered motor vehicle hereafter equipped with multiple-beam road lighting equipment shall be equipped with a beam indicator, which shall be lighted whenever the uppermost distribution of light from the head lamps is in use, and shall not otherwise be lighted. Said indicator shall be so designed and located that when lighted it will be readily visible without glare to the driver of the vehicle so equipped.

Amended by L.1941, c. 342, p. 901, § 1.

39:3–60. Use of multiple-beam road lighting equipment

Every person driving a motor vehicle equipped with multiple-beam road lighting equipment, during the times when lighted lamps are required, shall use a distribution of light, or composite beam, directed high enough and of sufficient intensity to reveal persons and vehicles at a safe distance in advance of the vehicle, subject to the following requirements and limitations: whenever the driver of a vehicle approaches an oncoming vehicle within five hundred feet, such driver shall use a distribution of light or composite beam so aimed that the glaring rays are not projected into the eyes of the oncoming driver, and in no case shall the high-intensity portion which is projected to the left of the prolongation of the extreme left side of the vehicle be aimed higher than the center of the lamp from which it comes at a distance of twenty-five feet ahead, and in no case higher than a level of forty-two inches above the level upon which the vehicle stands at a distance of seventy-five feet ahead.

39:3–61. Lamps and reflectors required on particular vehicles

(a) Every motor vehicle other than a motorcycle and other than a motor-drawn vehicle shall be equipped on the front with at least 2 headlamps, an equal number at each side, and with 2 turn signals, one on each side; and on the rear with 2 tail lamps, 2 stop lamps, 2 turn signals and 2 reflectors, one of each at each side; except that a passenger vehicle manufactured before July 2, 1954, and registered in this State may be equipped with one stop lamp, one reflector and one tail lamp and is not required to be equipped with turn signals. In addition, every such vehicle shall be equipped with adequate license plate illumination, and with one or more lamps capable of providing parking light as required in section 39:3–62. Turn signals are not required on the rear of a truck tractor equipped with double-faced turn signals on or near the front and so constructed and located as to be visible to passing drivers.

(b) Every truck tractor manufactured after January 1, 1965, shall be equipped on the front with 2 clearance lamps, one at each side, and 3 identification lamps, which shall be in addition to the lamps provided for in paragraph (a) of this section. Where the cab is not more than 42 inches wide at the front roof line, a single lamp at the center of the cab shall be deemed to comply with the requirement for front identification lamps. Reflectors required on the rear of a truck tractor may be located on the rear of the cab, one at each side.

(c) Every truck 80 inches or more in over-all width except a dump truck and except a truck 80 inches or more in over-all width which is not in excess of 25 feet in over-all length and manufactured prior to January 1, 1965, shall be equipped with the following lamps and reflectors in addition to those provided for in paragraph (a) of this section;

On the front, 2 clearance lamps, one at each side, and 3 identification lamps except that where the cab is not more than 42 inches wide at the front roof line, a single lamp at the center of the cab shall be deemed to comply with the requirement for front identification lamps;

On the rear, 2 clearance lamps, one at each side, and 3 identification lamps;

On each side, one side-marker lamp and one reflector at or near the front, and one side-marker lamp and one reflector at or near the rear.

(d) Every trailer or semitrailer shall be equipped on the rear with 2 tail lamps, 2 stop lamps, 2 turn signals and 2 reflectors, one of each at each side, and with adequate license plate illumination.

(e) Every trailer or semitrailer 80 inches or more in over-all width, except a dump truck trailer, a dump truck semitrailer or a converter dolly, shall be equipped with the following lamps and reflectors in addition to those provided for in paragraph (d) of this section:

On the front, 2 clearance lamps, one at each side;

On the rear, 2 clearance lamps, one at each side, and except with respect to cable reel trailers, 3 identification lamps;

On each side, one side-marker lamp and one reflector at or near the front, and one side-marker lamp and one reflector at or near the rear; and on any such vehicle 30 feet or more in length, at least one additional side-marker lamp at optional height and at least one additional reflector, the additional lamp (or lamps) and reflector (or reflectors) to be at or near the center or at approximately uniform spacing in the length of the vehicle.

(f) Every pole trailer shall be equipped as follows:

On the rear, 2 tail lamps, one at each side; 2 stop lamps, one at each side; 2 turn signals, one at each side; 2 reflectors, one at each side, placed to indicate extreme width of the pole trailer; 3 identification lamps mounted on the vertical center line of the pole trailer or in lieu thereof mounted on the vertical center line of the rear of the cab of the truck tractor drawing the pole trailer and higher than the load being transported.

On each side, one amber side-marker lamp at or near the front of the load; one amber reflector at or near the front of the load; on the rearmost support for the load, one combination marker lamp showing amber to the front and red to the rear and side, mounted to indicate maximum width of the pole trailer; on the rearmost support for the load, one red reflector.

Nothing in this subsection (f) shall apply to a single axle, skeleton frame trailer, not exceeding 2,500 pounds net weight and not exceeding 80 inches in over-all width which is designed to transport poles and is owned by a public utility as defined in section 48:2–13 of the Revised Statutes except that such vehicles shall be required to have on the rear, 2 tail lamps, one at each side; 2 stop lamps, one at each side; 2 turn signals, one at each side; 2 reflectors, one at each side on each side; and one amber side-marker lamp at or near the front of the load.

(g) Every converter dolly not permanently attached to a semitrailer shall be equipped on the rear with one stop lamp, one tail lamp, 2 reflectors, one at each side, and adequate license plate illumination. These lamps need be lighted only when the converter dolly is being towed singly by another vehicle. A "converter dolly" is a vehicle with a fifth wheel lower half or equivalent mechanism, the attachment of which converts a semitrailer to a trailer.

(h) Every motorcycle shall be equipped with at least one and not more than 2 headlamps, one tail lamp, one stop lamp, at least one reflector on the rear, adequate license plate illumination and, if a side car or any other extension is attached to the side thereof, one lamp located on the outside limit of the attachment capable of displaying white light to the front.

(i) Required lamps and reflectors shall be of a type approved by the director. Turn signals shall be Class A Type 1 lamps except that on passenger cars, and on commercial vehicles less than 80 inches in over-all width they may be Class B lamps. Reflectors shall be Class A reflex reflectors except that on passenger cars they may be Class B reflex reflectors.

(j) Required headlamps, tail lamps, clearance lamps, identification lamps and side-marker lamps shall be lighted and adequate license plate illumination displayed whenever the vehicle other than a converter dolly is upon a highway when lighted lamps are required except when parked and exhibiting lights as provided for in section 39:3–62 or when stopped and displaying emergency warning lights or devices as provided for in section 39:3–64 or section 39:3–54. Lamps on a converter dolly shall be lighted as provided for in paragraph (g) of this section. Turn signals on the side toward which a vehicle turn is made shall be flashed to indicate the turning movement. Stop lamps shall be lighted as provided in section 9 of this act.[1]

(k) License plate illumination will be deemed to be adequate when either a tail lamp or a separate lamp is so constructed and placed as to illuminate with a white light the rear registration plate on a vehicle and render it clearly legible from a distance of 50 feet to the rear. Any lamp or lamps providing such illumination shall be lighted whenever the headlamps or other driving lamps are lighted.

(*l*) Whenever a law enforcement officer detects a motor vehicle with a lamp not in working order, the driver may be permitted to park the vehicle temporarily at some safe place nearby and make the necessary repairs or replacement to restore the lamp to working order before moving the vehicle, in which event, there is no violation of this Title.

(m) Every motorbus manufactured before January 1, 1960, that has been inspected and approved as to construction and safety devices by the Board of Public Utility Commissioners shall be deemed in compliance with the requirements of this section.

Amended by L.1953, c. 237, p. 1755, § 1; L.1958, c. 112, p. 584, § 1; L.1959, c. 187, p. 757, § 1; L.1962, c. 247, § 1; L.1964, c. 136, § 6; L.1964, c. 281, § 1.

[1] N.J.S.A. § 39:3–61.3.

39:3–61.1. Mounting of lamps and reflectors

Lamps and reflectors required by section 39:3–61 shall be mounted on a vehicle as follows:

(a) Every lamp and every reflector shall be permanently and securely mounted in a workmanlike manner on a permanent part of the vehicle.

(b) When two lamps or two reflectors of the same type are required on the front or on the rear of a vehicle, they shall be mounted at the same level and spaced as widely laterally [1] as practicable.

(c) The mounted height of a lamp or reflector shall be measured from the center thereof to the level surface upon which the vehicle stands.

(d) Headlamps shall be so mounted that their beams are readily adjustable, both vertically and horizontally, and their aim is not readily disturbed by ordinary

conditions of service. The mounted height of headlamps shall be not more than 54 inches nor less than 24 inches, but these height requirements shall not apply to trucks prepared for snowplowing.

(e) The mounted height of tail lamps shall be not more than 72 inches nor less than 15 inches; eye-level tail lamps may be mounted outside the passenger vehicle; provided their height does not exceed 72 inches. Rear lamps may be mounted higher than 72 inches on any vehicle designed for carrying flammable liquids as a cargo.

(f) Clearance lamps shall be mounted to indicate the extreme width and height of the vehicle so far as is practicable, except that on a truck tractor, they shall be mounted to indicate the extreme width of the cab. On flatbed vehicles and vehicles designed for carrying flammable liquids, rear clearance lamps may be located on the chassis, and front clearance lamps may be located on the cab of trucks or truck tractors or the vehicle's chassis, provided the lamps are clearly visible from a distance of 500 feet in the direction set forth therefor.

(g) Side-marker lamps may be mounted at optional height on the side of a vehicle.

(h) Turn signals required on the rear of a truck tractor not equipped with double-faced turn signals on or near the front shall be mounted on the rear in a manner to be visible to passing drivers.

(i) Identification lamps shall be mounted on the front and rear of the vehicle as close as practicable to the vertical center line of the vehicle, and shall be grouped in a horizontal row, with lamp centers spaced not less than six nor more than 12 inches apart; provided, however, that where the cab is not more than 42 inches wide at the front roof line, a single identification lamp at the center line of the cab shall be deemed to comply with the requirements for front identification lamps. No part of front identification lamps or their mountings may extend below the top of the vehicle windshield. Rear identification lamps on a truck, trailer, or semi-trailer need not be lighted if they are obscured by another vehicle towed by the truck or in the same combination of vehicles.

(j) The mounted height of reflectors shall be not less than 20 inches nor more than 60 inches. Every reflector shall be so installed in a workmanlike manner as to perform its function adequately, and to provide maximum stability and minimum likelihood of damage. Any reflector otherwise properly mounted may be securely installed on flexible strapping or belting; provided that under conditions of normal operation it reflects light in the required direction.

(k) The director in his discretion may prescribe additional requirements for mounting lamps or reflectors on vehicles, provided they are not inconsistent with the provisions of this article.

L.1964, c. 136, § 7. Amended by L.1983, c. 59, § 1, eff. Feb. 7, 1983; L.1984, c. 145, § 1, eff. Sept. 8, 1984.

¹ So in enrolled bill.

39:3–61.2. Combination of lighting devices and reflectors; prohibited combinations

(a) Any 2 or more lighting devices and reflectors may be combined into one shell or housing except as stated below, provided that the requirements for each required lighting device or reflector are met and that neither the mounting nor the use of any nonrequired lighting device is inconsistent with this article in any respect:

(1) No turn signal may be combined with a headlamp or other lighting device or combination of lighting devices capable of producing a greater intensity of light than the turn signal when the turn signal is operating.

(2) No turn signal may be combined with a stop lamp unless the arrangement of switches or other parts is such that the stop light is extinguished whenever the turn signal is in use.

(3) No clearance lamp may be combined with a tail lamp or an identification lamp.

(b) Any lamp or lamps combined in the same shell or housing with a turn signal may be turned off by the same switch that turns the signal on for flashing, and turned on again when the turn signal as such is turned off.

L.1964, c. 136, § 8.

39:3–61.3. Stop lamps; construction, placement and use

Every stop lamp shall be so constructed, placed and used as to indicate by a substantial increase in illumination that the service brakes of the vehicle have been applied, except as otherwise provided in this section. Stop lamps are not required to be lighted when the emergency feature of trailer brakes is activated by means of either manual or automatic control on the towing vehicle. Stop lamps on a towing vehicle need not be lighted when service brakes are applied to the towed vehicle or vehicles only. No stop lamp need be lighted as such when it is in use as a turn signal or when it is turned off by the turn signal switch as provided in paragraph (b) of section 8 of this act.¹

L.1964, c. 136, § 9.

¹ N.J.S.A. § 39:3–61.2.

39:3–61.4. Overhang loads; placement and use of red lamps and flags

(a) Whenever the load upon any vehicle extends to the rear 4 feet or more beyond the bed or body of such vehicle there shall be displayed at the extreme rear end of the load, at the times when lighted lamps are required 2 red lamps, visible from a distance of at least 500 feet to the rear, 2 red reflectors visible from the rear

and located so as to indicate maximum width, when the width of the overhang load is in excess of 50% of the width of the vehicle, otherwise one red lamp is required, and on each side one red lamp, visible from a distance of at least 500 feet to the side, located so as to indicate maximum overhang. There shall be displayed at all other times on any vehicle having a load which extends beyond its sides or more than 4 feet beyond its rear, red flags, not less than 18 inches square, marking the extremities of such loads, at each point where a lamp would otherwise be required by this section.

(b) During the times when lighted lamps are required, any vehicle transporting a load which projects beyond the sides thereof shall be equipped with additional lamps as follows:

(1) The foremost edge of the projecting load at its outermost extremity shall be marked with an amber lamp visible from the front and side;

(2) The rearmost edge of the projecting load at its outermost extremity shall be marked with a red lamp visible from the rear and side.

(c) Projecting load marker lamps shall conform to the requirements for clearance, side-marker and identification lamps.

L.1964, c. 136, § 10.

39:3–62. Lamps on parked vehicles

Whenever a vehicle is parked or stopped in areas other than business or residential districts, upon a highway or shoulder adjacent thereto, whether attended or unattended, during the times when lighted lamps are required, except when it is displaying vehicular traffic hazard warning signals as permitted by section 39:3–54 or as required by section 39:3–64, such vehicle shall be equipped with 2 or more lamps which shall exhibit a light substantially white, yellow or amber in color visible from a distance of 500 feet to the front of such vehicle and 2 or more lamps which shall exhibit a red light visible from a distance of 500 feet to the rear. Any lighted headlamps upon a parked vehicle shall be depressed or dimmed.

Amended by L.1959, c. 186, p. 757, § 1; L.1964, c. 136, § 11.

39:3–63. Regulations governing lamps, turn signals and reflectors; promulgation by commissioner

The director is hereby authorized to promulgate regulations in his discretion not inconsistent with this article, governing the size, type, construction, location and use of lamps, turn signals, and reflectors, and to exclude from compliance with the requirements of this article any vehicle when in his discretion the construction or use of the vehicle makes compliance impracticable. The authority granted herein to regulate reflectors includes the power to regulate any retroreflective surface on a vehicle. In promulgating such regulations, the director shall take into account and so far as he deems appropriate be guided by established applicable standards or recommended practices.

Amended by L.1964, c. 136, § 12.

39:3–64. Vehicular traffic hazard warning signals

(a) Every truck, truck tractor, trailer, semitrailer, or pole trailer, 80 inches or more in width shall be equipped with a signaling system that in addition to signaling turning movements as provided for in section 39:4–126 shall have a switching arrangement that will cause the 2 front turn signals and the 2 rear turn signals on the vehicle or combination of vehicles to flash simultaneously as a vehicular traffic hazard warning signal as required in paragraph (c) of this section. The system shall be capable of flashing simultaneously with the engine operating or stopped.

(b) During the times when lighted lamps are required, no person shall drive on any highway any commercial motor vehicle 80 inches or more in width or any omnibus having a carrying capacity of over 10 passengers except an omnibus operated within business or residential districts on a route under the jurisdiction of the Board of Public Utility Commissioners unless it carries ready for immediate use portable emergency warning devices as follows: at least 3 liquid burning flares (pot torches), or 3 red electric lanterns, or 3 portable red emergency reflectors, and at least 3 red-burning fusees unless red electric lanterns or portable red emergency reflectors are carried. Each such device other than a fusee shall be capable of displaying light visible from a distance of at least 600 feet for a period of at least 12 hours, except that a commercial motor vehicle transporting inflammable liquids in bulk or compressed inflammable gases or explosives as a cargo or part of a cargo shall carry red electric lanterns or portable red emergency reflectors. Every such flare, lantern, reflector or fusee shall be of a type approved by the director.

(c) At the times when lighted lamps are required, whenever any motor-drawn vehicle or any motor vehicle of a type mentioned in paragraph (b) of this section other than motorbuses manufactured before January 1, 1960, that have been inspected and approved as to construction and safety devices by the Board of Public Utility Commissioners, or any combination of such vehicles, shall become disabled on any roadway or the shoulder thereof, except where there is sufficient all-night street or highway lighting provided as such to make it clearly discernible to persons on the highway at a distance of 500 feet, the driver of such vehicle or combination of vehicles shall immediately, upon learning of the disability, flash the 2 front and 2 rear turn signals simultaneously as a vehicular traffic hazard warning signal and continue such flashing until he shall have placed the portable emergency warning devices required in paragraph (b) of this section in use on the roadway, and during the time such portable emergency warning devices are being picked up for storage prior to movement of the vehicle or combination of vehicles.

These warning signals may be given at other times during vehicle disablement in addition to but not in lieu of placement of portable emergency warning devices on the highway as required herein. The driver also shall immediately place on the traveled portion of the highway at the traffic side of the disabled vehicle or combination of vehicles, a lighted fusee, a lighted red electric lantern, or a portable red emergency reflector. As soon thereafter as possible, but in any event within the burning period of the fusee, the driver shall place 3 lighted liquid burning flares (pot torches), or 3 lighted red electric lanterns, or 3 portable red emergency reflectors on the traveled portion of the highway in the following order: one at a distance of approximately 100 feet from the disabled vehicle or combination of vehicles in the center of the traffic lane occupied thereby and toward traffic approaching in that lane; one at a distance of approximately 100 feet in the opposite direction from the disabled vehicle or combination of vehicles in the center of the traffic lane occupied thereby; and one at the traffic side of the disabled vehicle or combination of vehicles, not less than 10 feet to the front or rear thereof. If a lighted red electric lantern or a portable red emergency reflector has been placed at the traffic side of the disabled vehicle or combination of vehicles, it may be used for this purpose. If the vehicle disablement occurs within 500 feet of a curve, crest of a hill or other obstruction to view, the driver shall so place the warning device in that direction as to afford ample warning to other users of the highway, but in no case less than 100 feet nor more than 500 feet from the disabled vehicle or combination of vehicles. If the vehicle disablement occurs upon any roadway of a divided or one-way highway, the driver shall place one required emergency warning device at a distance of 200 feet and one such device at a distance of 100 feet to the rear of the disabled vehicle or combination of vehicles in the center of the lane occupied thereby; and one such device at the traffic side not less than 10 feet to the rear thereof.

(d) If gasoline or any other inflammable liquid, or combustible liquid or gas seeps or leaks from a fuel container of a motor vehicle disabled or otherwise stopped upon a highway, no portable emergency warning device producing a flame shall be lighted or placed except at such distance from any such liquid or gas as will assure the prevention of a fire or explosion.

(e) Whenever a vehicle or combination of vehicles 80 inches or more in width is stopped or parked on a roadway or shoulder thereof at a time and under conditions where the immediate activating of vehicular traffic hazard warning signal is required in paragraph (c) of this section, the driver shall immediately flash the 2 front and 2 rear turn signals simultaneously and continue the flashing while the vehicle is so stopped or parked.

Amended by L.1947, c. 82, p. 461, § 1; L.1964, c. 136, § 13; L.1964, c. 281, § 2.

39:3–64.1. Itinerant vendors' vehicle

"Itinerant vendors' vehicle" as used in this act means a motor vehicle used in the operation of the business of an itinerant vendor to carry the goods, wares or other merchandise offered for sale to the general public and from which sales are made to customers invited to the vehicle and solicited for such purpose through the ringing of a bell or the use of any other device or means designed to attract attention to the vehicle.

L.1968, c. 90, § 1, eff. June 21, 1968.

39:3–64.2. Signaling system; flashing simultaneously

Every itinerant vendor's vehicle shall be equipped with a signaling system that in addition to signaling turning movements as provided for in section 39:4–126 of the Revised Statutes shall have a switching arrangement that will cause the 2 front turn signals and the 2 rear turn signals on the vehicle to flash simultaneously as a vehicular traffic hazard warning signal. The system shall be capable of flashing simultaneously with the engine operating or stopped.

L.1968, c. 90, § 2, eff. June 21, 1968.

39:3–64.3. Signals to flash simultaneously when stopped for purpose of transacting business

At all times during the daylight or at night, whenever the driver of an itinerant vendor's vehicle shall stop or park the vehicle on any roadway or the shoulder thereof for the purpose of transacting business, he shall immediately flash the 2 front and 2 rear turn signals of the vehicle simultaneously as a vehicular traffic hazard warning signal and continue such flashing so long as the vehicle remains stopped or parked for such purpose.

L.1968, c. 90, § 3, eff. June 21, 1968.

39:3–64.4. Rules and regulations

The director shall adopt such rules and regulations as shall be necessary to effectuate the provisions of this act.

L.1968, c. 90, § 4, eff. June 21, 1968.

39:3–65. Lamps on other vehicles and equipment

All vehicles, including agricultural machinery or implements, road machinery, road rollers, traction engines and farm tractors not hereinbefore in this article specifically required to be equipped with lamps, shall be equipped during the times when lighted lamps are required with at least one lighted lamp or lantern exhibiting a white light visible from a distance of five hundred feet to the front of such vehicle and with a lamp or lantern exhibiting a red light visible from a distance of five hundred feet to the rear, and such lamps and lanterns shall exhibit lights to the sides of such vehicle.

39:3–66. Maintenance of lamps, reflectors, etc.

All lamps, reflectors and other illuminating devices required by this article shall be kept clean and in good working order and, as far as practicable, shall be mounted in such a manner as to reduce the likelihood of their being obscured by mud or dust thrown up by the wheels.

39:3–66.1. Repealed by Laws 1964, c. 136, § 14

39:3–66.2. Punishment for violation

Any person violating the provisions of this act[1] shall be subject to a fine of not more than twenty-five dollars ($25.00) or imprisonment for a term not exceeding ten days, or both.

L.1953, c. 188, p. 1484, § 2.

  1 N.J.S.A. §§ 39:3–66.1, 39:3–66.2.

39:3–67. Brake equipment required

Every motorcycle when operated upon a highway shall be equipped with at least one brake adequate to control the movement of and to stop such vehicle.

Every motor vehicle, except a motorcycle and except a motor-drawn vehicle, shall be equipped with brakes adequate to control the movement of and to stop and to hold such vehicle, including 2 separate means of applying the brakes. If these 2 separate means of applying the brakes are connected in any way, they shall be so constructed that failure of any one part of the operating mechanism shall not leave the vehicle without brakes adequate to stop and to hold such vehicle. One of these means of applying the brakes shall be so constructed that it can be set to hold the vehicle, or any combination of which it forms a part, stationary on any up or down grade upon which it is operated, whether the vehicle or combination is empty or loaded.

Every combination of motor vehicles shall be equipped with brakes upon one or more of such motor vehicles, adequate to stop and to hold such combination of motor vehicles. Every motor vehicle, except a motorcycle, manufactured on or after July 1, 1938 when used on a highway shall be equipped with brakes on all wheels, except the front wheels of a 3-axle truck tractor and except any trailer or semitrailer of a gross weight not exceeding 3,000 pounds; provided, however, that the gross weight of any such trailer without brakes shall not exceed 40% of the gross weight of the towing vehicle, and that the gross weight of any such semitrailer without brakes shall not exceed 40% of the gross weight of the towing vehicle when the vehicles are connected. All brakes on a combination of vehicles shall be controlled by the driver thereof.

Every trailer and semitrailer, required to be equipped with brakes, shall be equipped with brakes of such a character as to be automatically applied upon breakaway from the towing vehicle, and means shall be provided to stop and hold such vehicle for an adequate period of time.

In any combination of motor vehicles, means shall be provided for applying the trailer or semitrailer brakes, of any trailer or semitrailer equipped with brakes, in approximate synchronism with the brakes on the towing vehicle and developing the required braking effort on the wheels of the rearmost vehicle at the fastest rate; or means shall be provided for applying braking effort first on the rearmost vehicle equipped with brakes; or both of the above means capable of being used alternatively may be employed.

No person shall drive, move, park or be in custody of on any highway any motor vehicle not equipped as herein required.

Amended by L.1962, c. 153, § 1, eff. Aug. 7, 1962.

39:3–68.   Brake performance

Every motor vehicle or combination of motor vehicles, according to its type, shall be capable at all times and under all conditions of loading, of stopping on a dry, smooth, level pavement of approximately .6 coefficient of friction and free from loose material, upon application of the service (foot) brake, within the distances specified below, or shall be capable of decelerating at a sustained rate corresponding to these distances:

	Feet to stop from twenty miles per hour	Approximate deceleration in feet per second per second
Vehicles or combination of vehicles having brakes on all wheels	30	14
Vehicles or combination of vehicles not having brakes on all wheels	45	9.5

The stopping ability, or decelerating capacity, of a motor vehicle or combination of motor vehicles shall be determined by an approved instrument or an approved machine capable of being read in feet to stop from a speed of twenty miles per hour, deceleration in feet per second per second or other equivalent units.

Agricultural machinery and implements, road machinery, road rollers, traction engines and farm tractors when used upon any highway shall have means adequate to control the movement of and to stop and to hold such machines on any up or down grade upon which they may be operated.

No person shall hereafter drive, move or be in custody of any motor vehicle or combination of motor vehicles unless such vehicle or combination is capable of being controlled, stopped and held as provided for herein.

39:3–68.1.   Towing vehicle and towed vehicle defined

As used in this act:

a. "Towing vehicle" means a road tractor or truck tractor.

b. "Towed vehicle" means a motor-drawn vehicle, pole trailer, semitrailer or trailer.

L.1987, c. 402, § 1, eff. Jan. 14, 1988.

39:3–68.2.   Emergency stopping system for vehicles using compressed air at wheels for application of service brakes; requirement

Every vehicle or combination of vehicles using compressed air at the wheels for applying the service brakes shall be equipped with an emergency stopping system meeting the requirements of this section and capable of stopping the vehicle or combination of vehicles in the event of failure in the service brake air system as follows:

a. Towing vehicles which use compressed air at the wheels for applying the service brakes shall be equipped with a device with an automatic means of actuating an emergency stopping system on the towed vehicle. The device shall operate automatically in the event of a reduction of the service air brake supply of the towing vehicle to a fixed pressure which shall not be lower than 20 pounds per square inch nor higher than 45 pounds per square inch.

b. Towed vehicles shall be deemed to be in compliance with this section when:

(1) The towed vehicle is equipped with a no-bleed-back relay-emergency valve or equivalent device, so designed that the supply reservoir used to provide air for the brakes is safeguarded against backflow of air from the reservoir through the supply line; and

(2) The combination of vehicles is capable of stopping within the distance and under the conditions specified in subsections g. and h. of this section.

c. If the service brake system and the emergency stopping system are connected in any way, they shall be so constructed that a failure or malfunction in any one part of either system, including brake chamber diaphragm failure but not including failure in the drums, brakeshoes, or other mechanical parts of the wheel brake assemblies, shall not leave the vehicle without one operative stopping system capable of complying with the performance requirements in subsection g. of this section.

d. No vehicle or combination of vehicles upon failure of the service brake air system shall be driven on a highway under its own power except to the extent necessary to move the vehicles off the roadway to the nearest place of safety.

e. No vehicle or combination of vehicles shall be equipped with an emergency stopping system that creates a hazard on the highway, or increases the service brake stopping distance of a vehicle or combination of vehicles, or interferes in any way with the application of the service brakes on any vehicle or combination of vehicles.

f. Any energy-storing device which is a part of the emergency stopping system shall be designed so that it is recharged or reset from the source of compressed air or other energy produced by the vehicle, except that energy to release the emergency stopping system may be produced by the driver's muscular effort from the driver's seat. No device shall be used which can be set to prevent automatic delivery of air to protected air supply reservoirs of motor vehicle emergency stopping systems when air is available in the service brake air supply system.

g. Every motor vehicle or combination of vehicles, at all times and under all conditions of loading, upon application of the emergency stopping system, shall be capable of stopping from a speed of 20 miles per hour in not more than the distance tabulated herein for its classification, this distance to be measured from the point at which movement of the emergency stopping system control begins.

EMERGENCY STOPPING SYSTEM REQUIRE-
MENTS

Classification of vehicle and combination of vehicles	Stopping Distance In Feet
A. Passenger-carrying vehicles.	
(1) Vehicles with a seating capacity of 10 persons or less, including driver, and built on a passenger car chassis	54
(2) Vehicles with a seating capacity of more than 10 persons, including driver, and built on a passenger car chassis; vehicles built on a truck or bus chassis and having a manufacturer's Gross Vehicle Weight Rating of 10,000 pounds or less	66
(3) All other passenger-carrying vehicles	85
B. Property-carrying vehicles.	
(1) Single unit vehicles having a manufacturer's Gross Vehicle Weight Rating of 10,000 pounds or less	66
(2) Single unit vehicles having a manufacturer's Gross Vehicle Weight Rating of more than 10,000 pounds, except truck tractors. Combinations of a 2-axle towing vehicle and trailer having a Gross Vehicle Weight Rating of 3,000 pounds or less. All combinations of 2 or less vehicles in driveaway or towaway operation	85
(3) All other property-carrying vehicles and combination of property-carrying vehicles	90

h. Tests of deceleration and stopping distance shall be made on a substantially level dry, smooth, hard surface that is free from loose material and where the grade does not exceed plus or minus 1%. No test of emergency stopping system performance shall be made upon a highway at a speed in excess of 25 miles per hour.

i. The provisions of this section shall not apply to:

(1) Auxiliary dollies, special mobile equipment, or special construction equipment; or

(2) Disabled vehicles when being towed.

j. Every owner or lessee shall instruct and require that the driver be thoroughly familiar with the requirements of this section.

The driver of a vehicle or combination of vehicles required to comply with the requirements of this section shall be able to demonstrate the application and release of the emergency system on the vehicle and each vehicle in combination.

L.1987, c. 402, § 2, eff. Jan. 14, 1988.

39:3–69. Horns and audible warning devices

Every motor vehicle except a motor-drawn vehicle when operated upon a highway shall be equipped with a horn in good working order and capable of emitting sound audible under normal conditions from a distance of not less than 200 feet, but no horn or other warning device shall emit an unreasonably loud or harsh sound or a whistle. The driver of a motor vehicle shall, when reasonably necessary to insure safe operation, give audible warning with his horn but shall not otherwise use such horn when upon a highway.

No vehicle shall be equipped with nor shall any person use upon a vehicle any siren, whistle or bell except as otherwise permitted in this section. It is permissible but not required that any vehicle be equipped with a theft alarm signal device which is so arranged that it cannot be used by the driver as an ordinary warning signal. Any emergency vehicle authorized by the commission may be equipped with a siren, whistle, or bell capable of emitting sound audible under normal conditions from a distance of not less than 500 feet and of a type approved by the commission, but such siren, whistle or bell shall not be used except when such vehicle is operated in response to an emergency call or in the immediate pursuit of an actual or suspected violator of the law, in which said latter events the driver of such vehicle shall sound said siren, whistle or bell when necessary to warn pedestrians and other drivers of the approach thereof.

No person shall install or use on the exhaust system of any motor vehicle any device which emits an audible sound unless authorized to do so by the commission.

No bicycle shall be equipped with nor shall any person use upon a bicycle any siren or whistle.

The commission is hereby authorized in its discretion to promulgate standards concerning the audibility of audible warning devices.

Amended by L.1968, c. 97, § 1, eff. June 21, 1968; L.2003, c. 13, § 45 (contingent effective date).

Historical and Statutory Notes

L.2003, c. 13, § 127, approved Jan. 28, 2003, provides:

"Sections 1, 2, 3, 12, 38, 109, 110 and 121 shall take effect immediately, sections 105, 106, 107, 108, and 120 shall take effect on July 1, 2003 and the remainder of this act shall take effect on the date the Commissioner of Transportation certifies to the Governor (hereinafter the "date of certification") that a majority of the members of the commission have been appointed or are in office and that all necessary anticipatory actions have been accomplished, provided, that the amount of revenues received pursuant to sections 109 and 110 prior to the date of certification are hereby appropriated to the division. Upon the date of certification, all such collected revenue shall be revenue of the commission. The Commissioner of Transportation, the Director of the Division of Motor Vehicles and the commission may take such anticipatory administrative action in advance as shall be necessary for the implementation of the act."

39:3–70. Mufflers

Text of section effective until May 18, 2010.

Every motor vehicle having a combustion motor shall at all times be equipped with a muffler in good working order and in constant operation to prevent excessive or unusual noise and annoying smoke, and no person shall use a muffler cut-out, bypass or similar device upon a motor vehicle on a highway.

39:3–70. Mufflers

Text of section effective on May 18, 2010.

Every motor vehicle having a combustion motor shall at all times be equipped with a muffler in good working order and in constant operation to prevent excessive or unusual noise and no person shall use a muffler cut-out, bypass, or similar device upon a motor vehicle on a highway.

Amended by L.2009, c. 331, § 1, eff. May 18, 2010.

39:3–70.1. Air pollution control; tests

Any motor vehicle which is subject to inspection by the Division of Motor Vehicles or any other duly authorized body shall, as a condition of compliance with said inspection, pass such tests as may be required to demonstrate that the motor vehicle complies with any standards and requirements for the control of air contaminants established by the Air Pollution Control Commission which are applicable to such motor vehicle.

L.1966, c. 15, § 1, eff. April 7, 1966.

39:3–70.2. Idling and operation of motor vehicles and school buses; emission of smoke and other air contaminants; penalties; exceptions

Text of section effective until May 18, 2010.

Any person who operates a motor vehicle or owns a motor vehicle, other than a school bus, which the person permits to idle in violation of rules and regulations, or to be operated upon the public highways of the State when the motor vehicle is emitting smoke and other air contaminants in excess of standards adopted by the Department of Environmental Protection pursuant to the "Air Pollution Control Act (1954)," P.L.1954, c. 212 (C.26:2C–1 et seq.) shall be liable to a penalty of not less than $250 nor more than $1,000 per day, per vehicle, which shall be enforced in accordance with the provisions of chapter 5 of Title 39 of the Revised Statutes [1] and P.L.2005, c. 219 (C.26:2C–8.26 et al.).

The owner of any school bus that is operated or is permitted to idle in violation of rules and regulations adopted pursuant to the Department of Environmental Protection pursuant to the "Air Pollution Control Act (1954)," P.L.1954, c. 212 (C.26:2C–1 et seq.) or any applicable rules and regulations adopted pursuant to P.L.2005, c. 219 (C.26:2C–8.26 et al.) shall be liable for a penalty of not less than $250 nor more than $1,000 per day, per vehicle, which shall be enforced in accordance with the provisions of chapter 5 of Title 39 of the Revised Statutes, except that no penalty may be assessed against any driver of a school bus who is not the owner of the school bus.

The provisions of this section shall not apply to a motor vehicle idling in traffic, or a motor vehicle other than a school bus idling in a queue of motor vehicles, that are intermittently motionless and moving because the progress of the motor vehicles in the traffic or the queue has been stopped or slowed by the congestion of traffic on the roadway or other conditions over which the driver of the idling motor vehicle has no control.

L.1966, c. 15, § 2.   Amended by L.2005, c. 219, § 33, eff. Sept. 7, 2005.

[1] N.J.S.A. §§ 39:5–1 et seq.

39:3–70.2. Idling and operation of motor vehicles and school buses; emission of smoke and other air contaminants; penalties; exceptions

Text of section effective on May 18, 2010.

Any person who operates a motor vehicle or owns a motor vehicle, other than a school bus, which the person permits to idle in violation of rules and regulations, or to be operated upon the public highways of the State when the motor vehicle is emitting smoke or other air contaminants in excess of standards adopted by the Department of Environmental Protection pursuant to the "Air Pollution Control Act (1954)," P.L.1954, c. 212 (C.26:2C–1 et seq.) shall be liable to a penalty of not less than $250 nor more than $1,000 per day, per vehicle, which shall be enforced in accordance with the provisions of chapter 5 of Title 39 of the Revised Statutes [1] and P.L.2005, c. 219 (C.26:2C–8.26 et al.).

The owner of any school bus that is operated or is permitted to idle in violation of rules and regulations adopted pursuant to the Department of Environmental Protection pursuant to the "Air Pollution Control Act (1954)," P.L.1954, c. 212 (C.26:2C–1 et seq.) or any applicable rules and regulations adopted pursuant to P.L.2005, c. 219 (C.26:2C–8.26 et al.) shall be liable for a penalty of not less than $250 nor more than $1,000 per day, per vehicle, which shall be enforced in accordance with the provisions of chapter 5 of Title 39 of the Revised Statutes, except that no penalty may be assessed against any driver of a school bus who is not the owner of the school bus.

The provisions of this section shall not apply to a motor vehicle idling in traffic, or a motor vehicle other than a school bus idling in a queue of motor vehicles, that are intermittently motionless and moving because the progress of the motor vehicles in the traffic or the queue has been stopped or slowed by the congestion of traffic on the roadway or other conditions over which the driver of the idling motor vehicle has no control.

L.1966, c. 15, § 2. Amended by L.2005, c. 219, § 33, eff. Sept. 7, 2005; L.2009, c. 331, § 2, eff. May 18, 2010.

1 N.J.S.A. §§ 39:5–1 et seq.

39:3–71. Mirrors

Every motor vehicle shall have rear view mirrors so located and angled as to give the driver adequate rear view vision. Every passenger automobile manufactured after January 1, 1965 and registered in this State, shall be equipped with an interior mirror and an exterior mirror on the driver's side. On and after January 1, 1965, every commercial motor vehicle registered in this State, other than a trailer or semitrailer, shall be equipped with an interior mirror and an exterior mirror on the driver's side, except that every such vehicle so constructed or loaded as to obstruct or obscure a rear view from an interior mirror shall, in lieu of an interior mirror, be equipped with an exterior mirror on the side of the vehicle opposite the driver's side. The director may by regulation establish other mirror requirements for special or unusual types of vehicles. Any person operating a motor vehicle without the equipment prescribed by this section shall, on conviction, be fined as provided in Revised Statutes 39:3–79.

Amended by L.1964, c. 119, § 1.

39:3–71.1. Backup monitoring device or rear crossview mirrors

a. Every delivery van or truck registered in this State with a cube-style, walk-in cargo box up to 18–feet long that is used in the commercial delivery of goods and services shall be equipped with either an electronic rear backup monitoring device or a rear crossview mirror located at the top left rear corner of the cargo box. The mirror shall be convex and located to reflect to the vehicle operator an unobstructed, overall view of the lower six feet of the entire rear width of the van or truck body.

b. The director may adopt regulations pursuant to the "Administrative Procedure Act," P.L.1968, c. 410 (C.52:14B–1 et seq.) necessary to implement the provisions of this act.

L.2002, c. 131, § 1, eff. April 1, 2003.

39:3–72. Tire equipment

No person shall drive or move any motor vehicle equipped with solid rubber tires unless every such tire shall have rubber on its entire traction surface at least one inch thick above the edge of the flange of the entire periphery. No person shall drive or move any motor vehicle or trailer upon the public highways, unless such motor vehicle or trailer is equipped with tires in safe operating condition in accordance with requirements approved by the director.

The director shall promulgate rules of safe operating condition capable of being employed by a law enforcement officer for visual inspection of tires mounted on vehicles including visual comparison with simple measuring gauges. Said requirements shall encompass effects of tread wear and depth of tread. A tire shall be considered unsafe if it has: (1) any ply or cord exposed; or (2) any bump, bulge or knot affecting tire structure; or (3) any break repaired with boot or patch; or (4) worn so that the tread wear indicators contact the road in any two adjacent major grooves at three locations spaced approximately equally around the outside of the tire. Nothing herein shall apply to farm vehicles registered under section 39:3–24 of this Title.

Any law enforcement officer, at any time, upon reasonable cause to believe that a vehicle is unsafe or equipped with tires in violation of the provisions of this section or of the rules promulgated hereunder, may require the operator of such vehicle to stop and submit such vehicle to an inspection. If the inspection discloses the vehicle to be in violation, the officer may issue a summons for such violation.

Amended by L.1970, c. 129, § 1, eff. July 8, 1970.

39:3–73. Tire-chains

Motor vehicle tires may be fitted with tire-chains of reasonable proportions when roads, streets and highways are slippery, because of rain, snow, ice, oil, manner of construction or other reason; provided, however, that no tire-chains shall be used at any time on improved highways when highway conditions do not make such use necessary for the safety of life or property. No person shall use any tire-chains so constructed or installed as to be likely to be thrown so as to endanger any person or property.

39:3–74. Windshields must be unobstructed and equipped with cleaners

Every motor vehicle having a windshield shall be equipped with at least one device in good working order for cleaning rain, snow or other moisture from the windshield so as to provide clear vision for the driver, and all such devices shall be so constructed and installed as to be operated or controlled by the driver.

No person shall drive any motor vehicle with any sign, poster, sticker or other non-transparent material upon the front windshield, wings, deflectors, side shields, corner lights adjoining windshield or front side windows of such vehicle other than a certificate or other article required to be so displayed by statute or by regulations of the commissioner.

No person shall drive any vehicle so constructed, equipped or loaded as to unduly interfere with the driver's vision to the front and to the sides.

39:3–75. Safety glass

The term "safety glass" shall be construed as meaning glass so treated or combined with other materials as to reduce, in comparison with ordinary sheet glass or plate glass, the likelihood of injury to persons by objects from exterior sources or by glass when the glass is cracked or broken. The term "safety glazing material" shall be construed as meaning "safety glass"; or other glazing materials, such as plastics, produced for the purpose of safety in glazing; or a combination of safety glass and other safety glazing material. The term "approved safety glazing material" shall be construed as meaning safety glazing material of a type approved by the director. In the approving of safety glazing materials, the director is hereby given authority to make use of recognized standards to confine the use of certain types of safety glazing materials to a specific location in or on the vehicle, or to a certain purpose.

No person shall drive any motor vehicle manufactured on or after July first, nineteen hundred and thirty-five and registered in this State unless such vehicle is equipped with approved safety glazing material wherever glazing is used in doors, windows and windshields. The term "windshield" shall be construed to include wings, deflectors and side shields; also front corner lights adjoining windshields.

Every section of safety glazing material shall be legibly and permanently marked with the manufacturers' distinctive designations, under which the safety glazing material was approved, so as to be visible when installed.

No person shall drive any motor vehicle equipped with safety glazing material which causes undue or unsafe distortion of visibility or equipped with unduly fractured, discolored or deteriorated safety glazing material, and the director may revoke the registration of any such vehicle.

Amended by L.1949, c. 258, p. 823, § 1.

39:3–75.1. Regular transport of persons with medical conditions; application for windshield treatment

Notwithstanding the provisions of any other law to the contrary, the owner or lessee of a motor vehicle that is driven by or is used to regularly transport a person who has a medical condition involving ophthalmic or dermatologic photosensitivity may apply to the director for permission to have the windshield and windows of that vehicle covered by or treated with a product or material that increases its light reflectance or reduces its light transmittance.

The application shall be in a form and manner prescribed by the director and shall include, but not be limited to, a written certification by a certified ophthalmologist or a physician with a plenary license to practice medicine and surgery in this State or a bordering state that the person for whom the application is submitted has a medical condition involving ophthalmic or dermatologic photosensitivity. For the purposes of this act,

medical conditions involving ophthalmic or dermatologic photosensitivity shall include:

   a.   polymorphous light eruption;

   b.   persistent light reactivity;

   c.   actinic reticuloid;

   d.   porphyrins;

   e.   solar urticaria;

   f.   lupus erythematosus; and

   g.   such other photosensitive disorders or conditions as the director shall determine.

L.1999, c. 308, § 1.

39:3–75.2. Rules and regulations

The director, pursuant to the "Administrative Procedure Act," P.L.1968, c. 410 (C.52:14B–1 et seq.), shall promulgate rules and regulations to effectuate the purposes of this act. The rules and regulations shall include, but shall not be limited to:

   a.   Standards and specifications governing the types of materials and products that may be applied to a motor vehicle windshield and windows under this act. These standards and specifications shall include the color of the materials or products, the maximum allowable percentage of total light reflectance of the materials or products, the maximum allowable percentage of the light transmittance and ultraviolet transmittance of the materials or products, and such other matters as the director shall deem appropriate and necessary. In establishing the standards and specifications, the director shall consider, to the greatest extent possible, the safety of law enforcement officers, who during the performance of their duties may find it necessary to inspect or otherwise observe the interior of a motor vehicle having a windshield and windows to which an approved material or product is applied.

   b.   The issuance of a certificate or card to each approved applicant authorizing the approved covering or treatment. The certificate or card shall be valid for a period of not more than 48 months and shall be exhibited to any law enforcement officer, when so requested, and to a designated motor vehicle examiner whenever the motor vehicle is inspected.

   c.   Standards and specifications governing the installation and application of approved materials and products, including the affixation of an appropriate label, in a manner and form prescribed by the director, on each windshield and window to which an approved material or product is applied. The label may identify the name and the location of the installer and the name of the manufacturer of the material or product applied.

   d.   The registration of persons in the business of installing or applying approved materials and products, including the establishment of a fee to cover the costs of that registration.

L.1999, c. 308, § 2, eff. Jan. 4, 2000.

39:3–75.3. Violations and penalties

a. A person who violates the provisions of subsection b. of section 2 of P.L.1999, c. 308 (C.39:3–75.2) shall be subject to a fine not exceeding $ 100; provided, however, if a person charged with such a violation can exhibit a certificate or card which was valid on the day he was charged to the judge of the municipal court before whom he is summoned to answer the charge, the judge may dismiss the charge. The judge, however, may impose court costs.

b. A person who violates the provisions of the regulations adopted pursuant to subsection c. or d. of section 2 of P.L.1999, c. 308 (C.39: 3–75.2) shall be subject to a fine not to exceed $1,000 for a first offense and not to exceed $5,000 for a second or subsequent offense.

L.1999, c. 308, § 3.

39:3–76. Dangerous exhaust gases

Every motor vehicle shall be equipped and maintained so that exhaust gases cannot injure any person or animal, and no person shall use any motor vehicle so as to cause or be likely to cause any such injury.

39:3–76.1. Use of sign "Press" on motor vehicle

No person shall operate a motor vehicle on which is affixed any sign, poster or sticker with the word "Press" or any other word or words indicating that the motor vehicle is in use by a reporter for a newspaper or other periodical except during such time as such motor vehicle is in actual use by a reporter for a newspaper or other periodical while engaged in his duties as such reporter.

L.1943, c. 101, p. 332, § 1.

39:3–76.2. Safety belts or restraining devices

No person shall sell or operate any passenger automobile manufactured after July 1, 1966, and registered in this State unless such passenger automobile is equipped with at least two sets of seat safety belts for the front seat of the passenger automobile and the anchorage units necessary for their attachment or other suitable restraining device. Such seat safety belts and anchorage units or such restraining device shall be of a type approved by the Director of the Division of Motor Vehicles in the Department of Law and Public Safety, and in making any such approval the director shall be guided by the specifications of the Society of Automotive Engineers and the standards of the Federal Department of Transportation.

L.1965, c. 107, § 1. Amended by L.1973, c. 194, § 1, eff. June 28, 1973.

39:3–76.2a. Child passenger restraint system; use; failure to use not contributory negligence; inadmissibility in evidence

Every person operating a motor vehicle, other than a school bus, equipped with safety belts who is transporting a child under the age of eight years and weighing less than 80 pounds on roadways, streets or highways of this State, shall secure the child in a child passenger restraint system or booster seat, as described in Federal Motor Vehicle Safety Standard Number 213, in a rear seat. If there are no rear seats, the child shall be secured in a child passenger restraint system or booster seat, as described in Federal Motor Vehicle Safety Standard Number 213. In no event shall failure to wear a child passenger restraint system or to use a booster seat be considered as contributory negligence, nor shall the failure to wear the child passenger restraint system be admissible as evidence in the trial of any civil action.

L.1983, c. 128, § 1, eff. April 7, 1983. Amended by L.2001, c. 244, § 1, eff. Dec. 1, 2001.

39:3–76.2b. Repealed by L.2001, c. 244, § 3

39:3–76.2c. Informational material

The Division of Motor Vehicles shall print such materials as to adequately inform the public about the types of child passenger restraint systems meeting federal motor vehicle safety standards. These materials may be made available to car dealers, parent groups, hospitals and the general public.

L.1983, c. 128, § 3, eff. April 7, 1983.

39:3–76.2d. Fines; suspension of fine

Any person guilty of violating any of the provisions of this act shall be fined not less than $10.00 and not more than $25.00. The court shall suspend any fine imposed for failure to use a child restraint system if the defendant demonstrates that he possesses a child restraint system that complies with the federal standard applicable when it was manufactured and is using it according to the manufacturer's instructions.

L.1983, c. 128, § 4, eff. April 7, 1983.

39:3–76.2e. Short title

This act shall be known and may be cited as the "Passenger Automobile Seat Belt Usage Act."

L.1984, c. 179, § 1, eff. March 1, 1985.

39:3–76.2f. Seat belt usage by drivers and passengers required

a. Except as provided in P.L.1983, c. 128 (C.39:3–76.2a et al.) for children under eight years of age and weighing less than 80 pounds, all passengers under eight years of age and weighing more than 80 pounds, and all passengers who are at least eight years of age but less than 18 years of age, and each driver and front seat passenger of a passenger automobile operated on a street or highway in this State shall wear a properly adjusted and fastened safety seat belt system as defined by Federal Motor Vehicle Safety Standard Number 209.

b. The driver of a passenger automobile shall secure or cause to be secured in a properly adjusted and fastened safety seat belt system, as defined by Federal

Motor Vehicle Safety Standard Number 209, any passenger who is at least eight years of age but less than 18 years of age.

c. All rear seat passengers 18 years of age or older of a passenger automobile operated on a street or highway in this State shall wear a properly adjusted and fastened safety seat belt system as defined by Federal Motor Vehicle Safety Standard Number 209.

For the purposes of the "Passenger Automobile Seat Belt Usage Act," the term "passenger automobile" shall include vans, pick-up trucks, and utility vehicles.

L.1984, c. 179, § 2, eff. March 1, 1985. Amended by L.1999, c. 422, § 1; L.2001, c. 244, § 2, eff. Dec. 1, 2001; L.2009, c. 318, § 1, eff. Jan. 18, 2010.

39:3–76.2g. Exceptions to seat belt usage requirements

This act shall not apply to a driver or passenger of:

a. A passenger automobile manufactured before July 1, 1966;

b. A passenger automobile in which the driver or passenger possesses a written verification from a licensed physician that the driver or passenger is unable to wear a safety seat belt system for physical or medical reasons;

c. A passenger automobile which is not required to be equipped with a safety seat belt system under federal law;

d. A passenger automobile operated by a rural letter carrier of the United States Postal Service while performing the duties of a rural letter carrier; or

e. A passenger automobile which was originally constructed with fewer safety seat belt systems than are necessary to allow the passenger to be buckled.

L.1984, c. 179, § 3, eff. March 1, 1985. Amended by L.1999, c. 422, § 2; L.2009, c. 318, § 2, eff. Jan. 18, 2010.

39:3–76.2h. Personal injury or death actions; effect of act

This act shall not be deemed to change existing laws, rules, or procedures pertaining to a trial of a civil action for damages for personal injuries or death sustained in a motor vehicle accident.

L.1984, c. 179, § 4, eff. March 1, 1985.

39:3–76.2i. Repealed by L.1999, c. 422, § 4

39:3–76.2j. Violations; fines

A person who violates section 2 of this act [1] shall be fined $20.00. In no case shall motor vehicle points or automobile insurance eligibility points pursuant to section 26 of P.L.1990, c. 8 (C.17:33B–14) be assessed against any person for a violation of this act. A person who is fined under this section for a violation of this act shall not be subject to a surcharge under the New Jersey

Merit Rating Plan as provided in section 6 of P.L.1983, c. 65 (C.17:29A–35).

L.1984, c. 179, § 6, eff. March 1, 1985. Amended by L.1999, c. 422, § 3.

[1] N.J.S.A. § 39:3–76.2f.

39:3–76.2k. Informational booklet; availability to public

The Director of the Division of Motor Vehicles shall develop a booklet containing information on the benefits of wearing safety seat belt systems. The booklet shall be made available upon request to the general public.

L.1984, c. 179, § 7, eff. March 1, 1985.

39:3–76.2l. Wheelchair passengers; restraint and securement systems in passenger vehicles

The driver of a passenger automobile shall secure or cause to be secured any wheelchaired passenger in a properly adjusted and fastened wheelchair securement and occupant securement device. The securement devices shall be in compliance with Federal Motor Vehicle Safety Standards.

For the purposes of this act, [1] the term "passenger automobile" shall include vans, pick-up trucks, and utility vehicles.

L.2008, c. 79, § 1, eff. Sept. 9, 2008.

[1] L.2008, c. 79, eff. Sept. 9, 2008.

39:3–76.2m. Violations; fines

A person who violates this act [1] shall be fined $100. In no case shall motor vehicle points or automobile insurance eligibility points pursuant to section 26 of P.L.1990, c. 8 (C.17:33B–14) be assessed against any person for a violation of this act. A person who is fined under this section for a violation of this act shall not be subject to a surcharge under the Motor Vehicle Violations Surcharge System as provided in section 6 of P.L.1983, c. 65 (C.17:29A–35).

L.2008, c. 79, § 2, eff. Sept. 9, 2008.

[1] L.2008, c. 79, eff. Sept. 9, 2008.

39:3–76.2n. Offense level for violation of seat belt laws; fines for back seat violations

Enforcement of the provisions of subsection c. of section 2 of P.L.1984, c. 179 (C.39:3–76.2f) by State or local law enforcement officials shall be accomplished by treating a violation thereof only as a secondary offense when a driver of a passenger automobile has been detained for some other suspected violation of Title 39 of the Revised Statutes or other law. Each rear seat passenger 18 years of age or older of a passenger automobile shall be responsible for any fine imposed pursuant to section 6 of P.L.1984, c. 179 (C.39:3–76.2j) for failure to wear a seat belt pursuant to subsection c. of section 2 of P.L.1984, c. 179 (C.39:3–76.2f).

L.2009, c. 318, § 3, eff. Jan. 18, 2010.

39:3–76.3. Motorcycles; height of handle bar grips

No person shall operate on a public highway a motorcycle on which the handle bar grips are higher than the shoulder height of the operator when seated.

L.1967, c. 237, § 2, eff. Jan. 1, 1968. Amended by L.1979, c. 434, § 1, eff. Feb. 14, 1980.

39:3–76.3a. Motorcycle operation; conformance to federal standards; NHTSA certification

No motorcycle shall be operated on the public highways or roadways of this State unless the motorcycle was manufactured in compliance with applicable Federal Motor Safety Standards that were in effect on the day the motorcycle was manufactured and the motorcycle has a certification label, in the format prescribed by the National Highway Traffic Safety Administration, attesting to that compliance, permanently affixed by the original manufacturer.

L.2005, c. 159, § 5, eff. July 19, 2005.

39:3–76.4. Muffler systems for motorcycles

In addition to the muffler requirements contained in section 39:3–70 of the Revised Statutes, motorcycles shall be equipped with muffler systems designed especially for motorcycles and of a type approved by the director.

L.1967, c. 237, § 3, eff. Jan. 1, 1968.

39:3–76.5. Permanent seat; passengers; seat, handholds and footrests; helmets; method of riding; violations; penalties

a. A person operating a motorcycle shall ride only upon the permanent and regular seat attached thereto, and such operator shall not carry any other person nor shall any other person ride on a motorcycle unless such motorcycle is designed to carry more than one person, in which event a passenger may ride upon the permanent and regular seat if designed for two persons, or upon another seat firmly attached to the rear or side of the operator. A passenger shall ride astride on a motorcycle only if the feet of that passenger rest firmly upon the footrests attached to the motorcycle as required by subsection b. of this section. A passenger on a motorcycle, whether riding astride or in a sidecar attached to the motorcycle, shall wear a securely fitted helmet of a size proper for that passenger as required under section 6 of P.L.1967, c. 237 (C. 39:3–76.7).

A motorcycle operator who carries a passenger in violation of this subsection shall be fined not less than $50.00 nor more than $100.00.

b. Motorcycles designed to carry more than one person shall be equipped with adequate footrests for each passenger. Seats and footrests shall be of a type approved by the director. Handholds shall be required

only insofar as they are necessary to comply with federal regulations.

L.1967, c. 237, § 4, eff. Jan. 1, 1968. Amended by L.1979, c. 57, § 1, eff. March 27, 1979; L.1985, c. 15, § 1, eff. Jan. 23, 1985.

39:3–76.6. Rules and regulations; motorcycle equipment

The director is authorized to adopt rules and regulations covering the types and specifications of the equipment for motorcycles required by this act.

L.1967, c. 237, § 5, eff. Jan. 1, 1968.

39:3–76.7. Protective helmet of proper size to be worn by operator and passenger; points not assessed for violations

a. No person shall operate or ride upon a motorcycle unless he wears a securely fitted protective helmet of a size proper for that person and of a type approved by the director. Such a helmet must be equipped with either a neck or chin strap and be reflectorized on both sides thereof. The director is authorized and empowered to adopt rules and regulations covering the types of helmets and the specifications therefor and to establish and maintain a list of approved helmets which meet the specifications as established hereunder. For the purposes of this section, motorcycle shall not include any three-wheeled motor vehicle equipped with a single cab with glazing enclosing the occupant, seats similar to those of a passenger vehicle or truck, seat belts and automotive steering.

b. The director shall not assess motor vehicle points for the failure of a motorcycle operator or rider to wear a protective helmet.

L.1967, c. 237, § 6, eff. Jan. 1, 1968. Amended by L.1984, c. 33, § 3; L.1985, c. 15, § 2, eff. Jan. 23, 1985; L.1992, c. 153, § 1, eff. Nov. 25, 1992.

39:3–76.8. Goggles or face shield to be worn by motorcycle operator

No person shall operate a motorcycle unless he wears goggles or a face shield of a type approved by the director. The director is authorized and empowered to adopt rules and regulations covering types of goggles and face shields and the specifications therefor and to establish and maintain a list of approved goggles and face shields which meet the specifications as established hereunder. For the purposes of this section, motorcycle shall not include any three-wheeled motor vehicle equipped with a single cab with glazing enclosing the occupant, seats similar to those of a passenger vehicle or truck, seat belts and automotive steering.

L.1967, c. 237, § 7, eff. Jan. 1, 1968. Amended by L.1984, c. 33, § 4.

39:3–76.9. Wind screen; goggles or face shield not necessary

The provisions of section 7 of this act [1] with respect to goggles and face shields shall not apply to the operator of a motorcycle equipped with a wind screen meeting specifications established by the director.

L.1967, c. 237, § 8, eff. Jan. 1, 1968.

[1] N.J.S.A. § 39:3–76.8.

39:3–76.10. Sale of helmets, goggles or face shields; type and specifications approved by director

No person shall sell, offer for sale or distribute any protective helmets, goggles or face shields for use by the operators of motorcycles, or protective helmets for the use of passengers thereon, unless they are of a type and specifications approved by the director and appear on the list of approved devices maintained by the director.

L.1967, c. 237, § 9, eff. Jan. 1, 1968.

39:3–77. Selling or using unapproved devices or equipment

No person shall have for sale, sell or offer for sale for use upon or as a part of the equipment of a motor vehicle any unapproved device or equipment of a type which is required to be approved by the commissioner.

No person shall have for sale, sell, offer for sale or use any device, part or accessory which changes or is intended to change the design or designed performance of any device or equipment required to be approved.

No person shall have for sale, sell or offer for sale for use upon or as part of the equipment of any motor vehicle or motor-drawn vehicle any device or equipment of a type required to be approved unless such device or equipment bears thereon the trade-mark or name under which it is approved so as to be plainly visible when installed.

39:3–77.1. Use of national school bus chrome paint on motor vehicles

No motor vehicle with a capacity of more than 16 passengers shall be painted National School Bus Chrome, unless that vehicle is used to transport children to or from school, or a summer day camp, or any school connected activity.

Whenever any motor vehicle with a capacity of more than 16 passengers, which has been used for the transportation of children to or from school, or a summer day camp, or any school connected activity, is no longer used for these purposes, it shall be repainted a color distinctively different from National School Bus Chrome.

L.1971, c. 86, § 1, eff. April 8, 1971.

39:3–77.2. Motor vehicles to which persons admitted to purchase merchandise or view exhibit; exit door

Every motor vehicle, including any van or trailer, to which persons are admitted for the purpose of purchasing merchandise, including books, or for the purpose of viewing any exhibit, shall in addition to an entrance door be equipped with a separate exit door. Such exit shall be plainly identified as an exit and shall be kept unobstructed at all times.

L.1971, c. 457, § 1, eff. Feb. 29, 1972.

39:3–78. Construction of article

Nothing in this article contained shall be construed to amend, repeal or in any manner impair the operation or effect of section 39:3–4.1 of this title.

39:3–79. Fine for violating article

Any person violating any of the provisions of this article shall be subject to a fine not exceeding twenty-five dollars.

39:3–79.1. Devices to prevent throwing of dirt on windshields of following vehicles

No person shall operate or cause to be operated any bus, truck, full trailer or semitrailer of registered gross weight exceeding three tons on any public highway unless the same is equipped with suitable metal protectors or substantial flexible flaps on the rearmost wheels, and, in case the rear wheels are not covered at the top by fender, body or other parts of the vehicle, the rear wheels shall be covered at the top by protective means, of such standard type or design and installed in such manner as shall be approved by the Director of the Division of Motor Vehicles in the Department of Law and Public Safety and as shall conform substantially to any requirements of the Interstate Commerce Commission governing similar subject matter, in order to prevent, as far as practical, such wheels from throwing dirt, water or other materials on the windshields of the following vehicles, except in cases in which the motor vehicle is so designed and constructed that the above requirements are accomplished by reason of fender or body construction or other means of enclosure; provided, however, this act shall not apply to pole trailers, dump trucks, tanks, or other vehicles where the construction thereof is such that complete freedom around the wheel area is necessary to secure the designed use of the vehicle.

L.1952, c. 343, p. 1122, § 1.

39:3–79.2. Violations

Any person who shall violate any of the provisions of this act shall, upon conviction, suffer and pay a penalty not exceeding fifty dollars ($50.00), or suffer imprisonment for a term not exceeding thirty days, or by both such fine and imprisonment, in the discretion of the magistrate before whom such conviction is had.

L.1952, c. 343, p. 1123, § 2.

39:3–79.3. Effective date

This act shall take effect January first, one thousand nine hundred and fifty-three.

L.1952, c. 343, p. 1123, § 3.

39:3–79.4. Motor vehicle powered by compressed or liquified gaseous fuel; identification with diamond shaped label; fee

a. No person shall drive upon a public highway, road or street a motor vehicle registered or principally garaged in this State and powered primarily or secondarily by a compressed or liquified gaseous fuel unless the vehicle is identified with a weather resistant, diamond shaped label which may be obtained from the Division of Motor Vehicles in the Department of Law and Public Safety or from a gas industry source.

b. A fee may be charged for the label. The amount of the fee shall be established by rule and regulation of the Director of the Division of Motor Vehicles and shall not exceed the reasonable cost of preparation and distribution.

L.1984, c. 55, § 1, eff. Sept. 1, 1984.

39:3–79.5. Diamond shaped label; requirements; rules and regulations on placement and appearance

The Director of the Division of Motor Vehicles may promulgate rules and regulations governing the placement and appearance of the label in addition to the following requirements:

a. The label shall be located on an exterior vertical or near vertical surface on the lower right rear of the vehicle, but not on the bumper, and toward the center and away from any other markings.

b. The label shall contain a border and one inch minimum height letters centered in the diamond.

c. The markings shall be of a silver or white reflective luminous material on a black background and the letters shall indicate the type of compressed or liquified gas used as fuel for the vehicle.

L.1984, c. 55, § 2, eff. Sept. 1, 1984.

39:3–79.6. Inspection for compliance with provisions of act

The vehicle identification required in this act shall, at the time of an inspection pursuant to this Title, be inspected for compliance with the provisions of this act.

L.1984, c. 55, § 3, eff. Sept. 1, 1984.

39:3–79.7. Failure to comply; penalties

Any person who fails to comply with sections 1 and 2 of this act [1] following an inspection shall be subject to the penalties of R.S. 39:8–9.

L.1984, c. 55, § 4, eff. Sept. 1, 1984.

[1] N.J.S.A. §§ 39:3–79.4 and 39:3–79.5.

39:3–79.8. Prohibition of supplying fuel to vehicle without label; violations; penalty

a. Any person requested to supply the compressed or liquified gaseous fuel for any vehicle covered under this act shall refuse to provide the fuel unless the vehicle for which the fuel is intended displays the label required herein.

b. Any person who violates subsection a. of this section shall be liable for a penalty of $25.00 for the first offense and $50.00 for each subsequent offense which may be collected in accordance with "the penalty enforcement law" (N.J.S. 2A:58–1 et seq.) by the Attorney General.

L.1984, c. 55, § 5, eff. Sept. 1, 1984.

39:3–79.9. Publicity of provisions of act

The Director of the Division of Motor Vehicles in the Department of Law and Public Safety shall periodically publicize the provisions of this act following its enactment.

L.1984, c. 55, § 6, eff. Sept. 1, 1984.

39:3–79.10. Intermodal chassis; definitions

As used in this act:

"Department" means the New Jersey Department of Transportation.

"Equipment interchange receipt" or "interchange receipt" means the receipt exchanged between an intermodal equipment provider or its agent and a motor carrier or its driver confirming acceptance of an intermodal chassis by a motor carrier and indicating the name of the intermodal equipment provider for such equipment.

"Intermodal chassis" or "chassis" means a trailer designed to carry intermodal freight containers.

"Intermodal equipment facility" means any facility in New Jersey at which intermodal chassis are maintained and interchanged to motor carriers by or on behalf of an intermodal equipment provider.

"Intermodal equipment provider" or "equipment provider" means the person or entity that provides an intermodal chassis to a motor carrier pursuant to a written interchange agreement or has responsibility for maintenance of the intermodal chassis.

"Systematic maintenance check program" or "SMC" means the eight-point intermodal chassis inspection program established by this act.

L.2005, c. 234, § 1, eff. Sept. 1, 2006.

Expiration

L.2005, c. 234, § 13, shall expire upon: a. the effective date of a federal statute to regulate the inspection and maintenance of intermodal chassis; or b. when final rules by the Federal Motor Carrier Safety Administration regulating the inspection and maintenance of intermodal chassis take effect.

39:3–79.11. Intermodal equipment provider; violations

a. An intermodal equipment provider shall not tender for interchange in New Jersey with a motor carrier an intermodal chassis that has not passed the systematic maintenance check program required by this act or that fails to meet the requirements set forth in the Federal Motor Carrier Safety Regulations, 49 C.F.R. sections 393 and 396. Any intermodal equipment provider tendering to, or interchanging with, a motor carrier such equipment shall provide certification that the chassis is currently in compliance with the SMC program set forth in this act.

b. An intermodal equipment provider that violates this section shall be assessed a civil administrative penalty by the department up to $5,000, per occurrence, commensurate with the gravity of the offense. A civil administrative penalty imposed pursuant to this subsection may be recovered by a summary proceeding pursuant to the "Penalty Enforcement Law of 1999," P.L.1999, c. 274 (C.2A:58–10 et seq.).

c. Nothing in this act is intended to supersede or interfere with the commercial motor vehicle inspection requirements and standards set forth in 49 C.F.R. sections 393 and 396. Rather, this act imposes an additional requirement that an intermodal equipment provider inspect chassis on a routine basis and as otherwise required by this act.

L.2005, c. 234, § 2, eff. Sept. 1, 2006.

Expiration

L.2005, c. 234, § 13, shall expire upon a. the effective date of a federal statute to regulate the inspection and maintenance of intermodal chassis; or: b. when final rules by the Federal Motor Carrier Safety Administration regulating the inspection and maintenance of intermodal chassis take effect.

39:3–79.12. Systematic maintenance check program for intermodal chassis; requirements; reports

a. An intermodal equipment provider shall establish and implement a systematic maintenance check program for the intermodal chassis that it tenders for interchange to motor carriers. The SMC program shall be consistent with Federal Motor Carrier Safety Regulations set forth in 49 C.F.R. sections 393 and 396 and shall include, but not be limited to, the following components or actions:

(1) tires;

(2) brakes;

(3) lights;

(4) a twist lock and safety lock inspection which includes ensuring that twist locks are operational and safety locks are working;

(5) wheel lubrication;

(6) frame;

(7) registration and federal and State inspection stickers; and

(8) upon the satisfactory completion of the inspection and any required actions necessary to bring the chassis into compliance with the inspection standards, the application of an SMC inspection sticker with the equipment provider's name, the inspector's name, and an expiration date set at six months following the inspection. Chassis which fail a SMC inspection shall be processed in accordance with section 4 of this act. [1]

b. Each SMC inspection shall be recorded on a SMC inspection report that shall include, but not be limited to, all of the following:

(1) Positive identification of the intermodal chassis, including company identification number and vehicle license plate number;

(2) Date of and reason for each SMC inspection; and

(3) Signature, under penalty of perjury, of the inspector that the SMC inspection has been performed and that the chassis is roadworthy or, if the chassis failed the inspection, the specific reason for the failure.

L.2005, c. 234, § 3, eff. Sept. 1, 2006.

[1] N.J.S.A. § 39:3–79.13.

Expiration

L.2005, c. 234, § 13, shall expire upon a. the effective date of a federal statute to regulate the inspection and maintenance of intermodal chassis; or b. when final rules by the Federal Motor Carrier Safety Administration regulating the inspection and maintenance of intermodal chassis take effect.

39:3–79.13. Identification of out–of–service intermodal chassis; tags; repair of defects

a. Intermodal equipment providers shall implement a process to positively identify by means of a tag those intermodal chassis that are out-of-service as a result of having failed an inspection required by this act. The tag shall contain the name of the intermodal equipment provider, the inspector and the date that the chassis failed inspection. The tag shall be supplied by the intermodal equipment provider and shall meet the specifications determined by the department.

b. A chassis which is out-of-service as a result of having failed an inspection required by this act shall be transported, without a container, to a facility where repairs and maintenance may be performed. Defects identified during an SMC inspection of a chassis shall be repaired, and the repairs shall be recorded on the chassis maintenance file and on the SMC inspection report.

A chassis subject to this section shall not be interchanged with a motor carrier or operated on a public road in New Jersey until all defects listed during the inspection have been corrected, the chassis passes an SMC inspection, and an authorized inspector attests to that fact and affixes an SMC inspection sticker to the chassis.

L.2005, c. 234, § 4, eff. Sept. 1, 2006.

39:3–79.14. Events triggering full SMC eight–point inspection

In addition to the routine SMC inspection which must take place at least once every six months in accordance with section 3 of this act,[1] the following events shall cause a full SMC eight-point inspection to be done immediately:

a. a repair is done to remedy a defect that would be the basis for failure of an SMC inspection other than a minor repair or minor equipment defect,

b. a defect is noted on an in-gate interchange receipt that would be the basis for failure of an SMC inspection other than a minor repair or minor equip- ment defect, or

c. an SMC inspection sticker has expired.

For purposes of this section, "minor repair or minor equipment defect" means any one of the following: the need to inflate tires; the need to replace lights, a lens or a reflector; a twistlock or safety lock inspection or a safety latch replacement; a simple confirmation of federal or State inspection stickers; or the reapplication of an SMC inspection sticker that has not expired.

L.2005, c. 234, § 5, eff. Sept. 1, 2006.

[1] N.J.S.A. § 39:3–79.12.

39:3–79.15. Qualifications of SMC inspectors

Individuals performing SMC inspections pursuant to this act shall be qualified, at a minimum, as set forth in 49 C.F.R. sections 396.19 and 396.25. Evidence of each inspector's qualification shall be retained by the inter- modal equipment provider at the intermodal equipment facility for the period of time during which the inspector is performing SMC inspections at that facility.

L.2005, c. 234, § 6, eff. Sept. 1, 2006.

39:3–79.16. Driver request for repair or replacement of intermodal chassis; driver compensation; com- plaint; penalty

a. Any motor carrier or driver who, as a result of the pre-trip inspection of the intermodal chassis, determines the intermodal chassis to be in an unsafe operating condition shall request that the intermodal equipment provider repair or replace the intermodal chassis prior to completion of the interchange. It shall be at the discretion of the intermodal equipment provider wheth- er to repair or to replace the chassis.

In the event a driver is forced to wait for more than one hour while the chassis is repaired or replaced, the intermodal equipment provider shall compensate the driver at an hourly rate to be set by the department based upon the average rate in comparable situations.

b. If a driver's request for repair or replacement is refused by the equipment provider, which shall be a violation of this section, the driver may file a complaint with the department. If, after an equipment provider has been afforded an opportunity for a hearing pursuant to the "Administrative Procedure Act," P.L.1968, c. 410 (C.52:14B–1 et seq.), the department determines that the equipment provider has violated this section, that person shall be subject to a civil administrative penalty to be imposed by the department not to exceed $1,000 for the first violation and not more than $5,000 for each subsequent violation. A civil administrative penalty imposed pursuant to this subsection may be recovered by a summary proceeding pursuant to the "Penalty Enforcement Law of 1999," P.L.1999, c. 274 (C.2A:58–10 et seq.).

L.2005, c. 234, § 7, eff. Sept. 1, 2006.

39:3–79.17. Maintenance of records

Records of inspections, maintenance or repairs of chassis performed pursuant to this act shall be main- tained for three years and made available upon request of the department or a motor carrier which has transported the chassis.

All records required by this act may be kept in a digital format or other media allowing for the storage and retrieval of data if printouts of those records can be provided upon request at the intermodal equipment facility.

L.2005, c. 234, § 8, eff. Sept. 1, 2006.

Expiration

L.2005, c. 234, § 13, shall expire upon: a. the effective date of a federal statute to regulate the inspection and maintenance of intermodal chassis; or b. when final rules by the Federal Motor Carrier Safety Administration regulating the inspection and maintenance of intermodal chassis take effect.

39:3–79.18. Intermodal equipment providers; registration; annual certification; audits; compliance and penalty

a. Any intermodal equipment provider that tenders intermodal chassis for interchange in New Jersey with a motor carrier shall register with the New Jersey Department of Transportation in accordance with regulations promulgated pursuant to this act.

b. Every registered intermodal equipment provider shall certify to the department on an annual basis that the equipment provider is conducting a systematic maintenance check program for intermodal chassis that is in compliance with this act.

c. The department may conduct audits at an intermodal equipment facility as it deems necessary to effectuate the purposes of this act, including, but not limited to, when an intermodal equipment provider has demonstrated a history of non-compliance with any requirements of this act. The audit shall include, but not be limited to, SMC inspection, tagging and processing of failed chassis, repair, and record-keeping requirements. The department is authorized to enter any intermodal equipment facility for the purposes of conducting the audits.

As part of the audits, the department may request the New Jersey State Police or, if the chassis is tendered at a port, the police of the authority operating that port, to accompany the department and to conduct a limited number of chassis inspections in order to determine that SMC inspection and identification requirements are being met. Any New Jersey State Police officer trained to inspect intermodal chassis is authorized to enter any intermodal equipment facility for the purposes of conducting inspections as part of an audit by the department. Nothing herein shall limit the authority of an authorized member of the State Police or the police of the authority operating the port to enter upon and perform inspections of vehicles in operation upon the highways of this State or at the premises or places of business of the owner or lessee of such vehicles.

d. If, during an audit, the department determines that an intermodal equipment provider has failed to comply with any of the requirements of this act, the department shall:

(1) direct the intermodal equipment provider to comply immediately with the requirements of this act; and

(2) impose a civil administrative penalty on the intermodal equipment provider of up to $5,000, commensurate with the gravity of the offense, for every day

that the intermodal equipment provider fails to comply with the requirements of this act. A civil administrative penalty imposed pursuant to this subsection may be recovered by a summary proceeding pursuant to the "Penalty Enforcement Law of 1999," P.L.1999, c. 274 (C.2A:58–10 et seq.).

L.2005, c. 234, § 9, eff. Sept. 1, 2006.

Expiration

L.2005, c. 234, § 13, shall expire upon: a. the effective date of a federal statute to regulate the inspection and maintenance of intermodal chassis; or b. when final rules by the Federal Motor Carrier Safety Administration regulating the inspection and maintenance of intermodal chassis take effect.

39:3–79.19. Roadside inspection; summons, complaint or violation report

a. When, upon roadside inspection of an intermodal chassis, there is found a violation of State law or regulations or Federal Motor Carrier Safety Administration Regulations, 49 C.F.R. sections 393 and 396, relating to the chassis, any summons, complaint, or violation report shall cite the motor carrier, the intermodal equipment provider, or the registered owner as follows:

(1) for latent equipment defects on the chassis, the summons, complaint, or violation report shall cite the intermodal equipment provider identified on the equipment interchange receipt; in the event there is no equipment interchange receipt, the summons, complaint or violation report shall cite the equipment provider shown on the SMC inspection sticker. If there is neither an interchange receipt or a SMC inspection sticker, the summons, complaint or violation report shall cite the registered owner of the chassis as determined by a registration document, a company identification number or the chassis license plate number. When the summons, complaint or violation report cites the registered owner because it is not possible to identify an equipment provider, the registered owner may seek reimbursement for any fine from the equipment provider; and

(2) for equipment defects when the equipment is one of the specific equipment components required to be inspected by the driver during the pre-trip inspection, the summons, complaint or violation report shall cite the motor carrier. The pre-trip inspection shall be conducted as part of the walk-around inspection required by federal law prior to use of the chassis.

The department, in conjunction with representatives of intermodal equipment providers, motor carriers and the New Jersey State Police, shall establish a list of the specific chassis equipment components to be inspected during the pre-trip inspection and for which the driver shall be cited on the summons, complaint or violation report.

b. (1) An intermodal equipment provider, registered chassis owner, or any other entity shall not seek reimbursement of a fine or penalty imposed by a municipal court for a violation of State law or regulations or Federal Motor Carrier Safety Administration Regulations, 49 C.F.R. sections 393 and 396, relating to the chassis from the motor carrier or its driver, or otherwise hold the motor carrier or its driver responsible for summons or complaint related to the chassis, unless the violation was caused by the negligence or willful misconduct of the motor carrier, its driver, agent, subcontractor or assigns.

(2) A motor carrier or its driver shall not seek reimbursement of a fine or penalty imposed by a municipal court for a violation of State law or regulations or Federal Motor Carrier Safety Administration Regulations, 49 C. F.R. sections 393 and 396, relating to the chassis from the intermodal equipment provider, registered chassis owner, or any other entity, or otherwise hold the intermodal equipment provider, registered chassis owner, or any other entity responsible for summons or complaint related to the chassis, unless the violation was caused by the negligence or willful misconduct of the intermodal equipment provider, registered chassis owner, or other entity.

c. (1) Whenever the act or omission of an intermodal equipment provider is deemed the cause for a violation report citing a motor carrier, the motor carrier may petition the appropriate authorities to request that the violation not be used or applied against the motor carrier's overall compliance record maintained in accordance with Federal Motor Carrier Safety Administration Regulations.

(2) Whenever the act or omission of a motor carrier or its driver is deemed the cause for a violation report citing an intermodal equipment provider, the intermodal equipment provider may petition the appropriate authorities to request that the violation not be used or applied against the intermodal equipment provider's overall compliance record maintained in accordance with Federal Motor Carrier Safety Administration Regulations.

(3) The State Police and the department shall establish a process whereby, upon application of a motor carrier, a violation report improperly citing a motor carrier may be administratively removed from its compliance record.

The State Police and the department shall establish a process whereby, upon application of an intermodal equipment provider, a violation report improperly citing an intermodal equipment provider may be administratively removed from its compliance record.

d. The provisions of this section shall apply only to a summons, complaint, or violation report issued on or after the effective date of this act. [1]

e. This section is intended solely to determine which party shall be cited on a summons, complaint or violation report for a violation of State law or regulations or Federal Motor Carrier Safety Administration Regulations, 49 C.F.R. sections 393 and 396, relating to

an intermodal chassis. Nothing in this section is intended to affect any indemnification agreement among an intermodal equipment provider, a motor carrier or any other entity concerning intermodal chassis.

L.2005, c. 234, § 10, eff. Sept. 1, 2006.

[1] Sept. 1, 2006.

Expiration

L.2005, c. 234, § 13, shall expire upon: a. the effective date of a federal statute to regulate the inspection and maintenance of intermodal chassis; or b. when final rules by the Federal Motor Carrier Safety Administration regulating the inspection and maintenance of intermodal chassis take effect.

39:3–79.20. Interference with motor carrier or driver, intermodal equipment provider or SMC inspector; penalty

It shall be a violation of this act to interfere with or attempt to interfere with the duties, obligations, rights or remedies of a motor carrier or its driver, an intermodal equipment provider, or an SMC inspector as provided in this act. If, after a person has been afforded an opportunity for a hearing pursuant to the "Administrative Procedure Act," P.L.1968, c. 410 (C.52:14B–1 et seq.), the department determines that the person has violated this section, that person shall be subject to a civil administrative penalty to be imposed by the department not to exceed $1,000 for the first violation and not more than $5,000 for each subsequent violation. A civil administrative penalty imposed pursuant to this subsection may be recovered by a summary proceeding pursuant to the "Penalty Enforcement Law of 1999," P.L.1999, c. 274 (C.2A:58–10 et seq.).

L.2005, c. 234, § 11, eff. Sept. 1, 2006.

Expiration

L.2005, c. 234, § 13, shall expire upon: a. the effective date of a federal statute to regulate the inspection and maintenance of intermodal chassis; or b. when final rules by the Federal Motor Carrier Safety Administration regulating the inspection and maintenance of intermodal chassis take effect.

39:3–79.21. Intermodal chassis; rules and regulations

The department shall adopt such rules and regulations pursuant to the provisions of the "Administrative Procedure Act," P.L.1968, c. 410 (C.52:14B–1 et seq.) necessary to effectuate the purposes of this act.

L.2005, c. 234, § 12, eff. Sept. 1, 2006.

Expiration

L.2005, c. 234, § 13, shall expire upon: a. the effective date of a federal statute to regulate the inspection and maintenance of intermodal chassis; or b. when final rules by the Federal Motor Carrier Safety Administration regulating the inspection and maintenance of intermodal chassis take effect.

39:3–79.22. Omnibus owner or operators without a certificate of public convenience and necessity; additional fine

Whenever an owner or operator of an omnibus, as defined pursuant to R.S.39:1–1, does not have a certificate of public convenience and necessity as required pursuant to R.S.48:4–3 and that owner or operator is convicted of an equipment violation pursuant to any provision in chapter 3 of Title 39 of the Revised Statutes, or any regulation promulgated pursuant thereto, in addition to and independent of any fine or other penalty provided for under law, the court shall impose an additional fine of $150 on that owner or operator. The State Treasurer shall annually deposit the monies collected from the fines imposed pursuant to this section to the "Omnibus Safety Enforcement Fund" established pursuant to section 4 of P.L.2007, c. 40 (C.39:3–79.23). The fine described herein shall not be deemed a fine, penalty, or forfeiture pursuant to R.S.39:5–41.

L.2007, c. 40, § 3, eff. July 1, 2007.

39:3–79.23. Omnibus Safety Enforcement Fund within the Department of Treasury; deposit and utilization of funds

There is created in the Department of the Treasury a separate, non-lapsing revolving fund to be known as the "Omnibus Safety Enforcement Fund." This fund is to be the depository for monies collected from certain fines imposed pursuant to R.S.39:3–19.1, R.S.39:3–29, and section 3 of P.L.2007, c. 40 (C.39:3–79.22). The money in the fund shall be administered by the State Treasurer and all interest on monies deposited in the fund shall be credited to the fund. Unless otherwise specifically provided by law, monies in the fund shall be utilized exclusively by the New Jersey Motor Vehicle Commission to administer and enforce the provisions of this act, or any rule or regulation adopted pursuant thereto. Beginning in the fiscal year next following the effective date of this act, the State Treasurer shall annually allocate the money pursuant to this section to the commission.

L.2007, c. 40, § 4, eff. July 1, 2007.

39:3–79.24. Omnibus Safety Enforcement Fund within the Motor Vehicle Commission; deposit and utilization of funds

There is created within the New Jersey Motor Vehicle Commission, a separate, non-lapsing account to be known as the " Omnibus Safety Enforcement Fund." All monies paid to the commission pursuant to section 4 of P.L.2007, c. 40 (C.39:3–79.23)shall be deposited in the fund. Unless otherwise specifically provided by law, monies in the fund shall be utilized exclusively by the commission to administer and enforce the provisions of this act, or any rule or regulation adopted pursuant thereto.

L.2007, c. 40, § 5, eff. July 1, 2007.

ARTICLE 4. TIRES AND LOADS

39:3–80. Rubber tires or tires of approved material required; penalties

Any person who shall operate an automobile, commercial vehicle, trailer or semitrailer or tractor not equipped on all wheels with rubber tires or tires, of a material other than rubber which have been approved by the commissioner, or who shall operate a commercial vehicle, trailer, semitrailer or tractor equipped with solid rubber tires impaired to such an extent as to be likely to cause damage to the public highways, shall be fined, in either case, not less than fifty dollars ($50.00) nor more than one hundred dollars ($100.00) for the first offense, and for any subsequent offense not less than one hundred dollars ($100.00) nor more than two hundred dollars ($200.00).

Tractors used for agricultural purposes may be operated over the highways of this State without being equipped with rubber tires, under such regulations as shall, from time to time, be adopted by the commissioner.

Traction or tractor well-drill machines or well-drilling equipment may be operated on the highways as provided by section 39:3–26 of this Title.

Amended by L.1942, c. 227, p. 608, § 2.

39:3–81. Sale, possession or use of tires of type approved by director; regulations; penalties

No person shall sell, offer for sale or possess with intent to sell or use on a highway any motor vehicle tire fitted with blocks, hobs, studs or other projections unless such tire is in safe operating condition and provided that such tire is of a type approved by the director. The director shall promulgate regulations concerning the design, construction and use of such tires and the procedure which shall be followed when such tires are submitted for approval.

Any person violating this section shall be subject to a fine of not less than $25.00 nor more than $50.00 to be recovered in a summary proceeding pursuant to the Penalty Enforcement Law (N.J.S. 2A:58–1 et seq.).

Amended by L.1964, c. 266, § 1.

39:3–82. Tires on commercial vehicles, tractors and motordrawn vehicles; distribution of load; fine for violation of section

No commercial motor vehicle or tractor not equipped on all wheels with pneumatic tires shall be used on the public highways, unless there is attached to the chassis, in plain view, a metal plate giving information as follows: Maker's name, number, motor number, weight of vehicle in pounds, allowable load in pounds, gross weight in pounds and maximum speed in miles per hour.

The size of tires on all commercial motor vehicles or motor-drawn vehicles shall be determined on the maximum width of rubber, and the load shall be so distributed that there shall not be more than eight hundred pounds per inch in width of tire on any one wheel.

A person who violates this section shall be subject to a fine not exceeding one hundred dollars. In default of the payment thereof, imprisonment in the county jail for a period not exceeding ten days shall be imposed.

39:3–83. Repealed by L.1950, c. 142, p. 283, § 4

ARTICLE 5. DIMENSIONS AND WEIGHT

39:3–84. Dimensional restrictions; outside width; height; overall length; weight; special written permit for exceptions

a. The following constitute the maximum dimensional limits for width, height and length for any vehicle or combination of vehicles, including load or contents or any part or portion thereof, found or operated on any public road, street or highway or any public or quasi-public property in this State. Violations shall be enforced pursuant to subsection i. of section 5 of P.L.1950, c. 142 (C.39:3–84.3).

The dimensional limitations set forth in this subsection are exclusive of safety and energy conservation devices necessary for safe and efficient operation of a vehicle or combination of vehicles, including load or contents, except that no device excluded herein shall have by its design or use the capability to carry, transport or otherwise be utilized for cargo.

Any rules and regulations authorized to be promulgated pursuant to this subsection shall be consistent with any rules and regulations promulgated by the Secretary of Transportation of the United States of America, and shall be in accordance with the provisions of the "Administrative Procedure Act," P.L.1968, c. 410 (C.52:14B–1 et seq.). In addition to the other requirements of this subsection and notwithstanding any other provision of this Title, no vehicle or combination of vehicles, including load or contents or any part or portion thereof, except as otherwise provided by this subsection shall be operated in this State, unless by special permit authorized by subsection d. of this section with a dimension, the allowance of which would disqualify the State of New Jersey or any department, agency or governmental subdivision thereof for the purpose of receiving federal highway funds.

As used herein and pursuant to R.S.39:1–1, the term "vehicle" includes, but is not limited to, commercial motor vehicles, trucks, truck tractors, tractors, road tractors, recreation vehicles, or omnibuses. As used herein and pursuant to R.S.39:1–1, the term "combination of vehicles" includes, but is not limited to, vehicles as heretofore designated, when those vehicles are the drawing or power unit of a combination of vehicles and motor-drawn vehicles, such as, but not limited to, trailers, semi-trailers, or other vehicles. As used herein, the term "recycling vehicle" means a commercial motor vehicle used for the collection or transportation of recyclable material; or any truck, trailer or other vehicle approved by the New Jersey Office of Recycling for use by persons engaging in the business of recycling or otherwise providing recycling services in this State; and "recyclable material" means those materials which would otherwise become solid waste, and which may be collected, separated or processed and returned to the economic mainstream in the form of raw materials or products.

(1) The maximum outside width of any vehicle or combination of vehicles, including load or contents of any part or portion thereof, except as otherwise provided by this subsection, shall be no more than 102 inches; except that the Commissioner of Transportation, after consultation with the Chief Administrator of the New Jersey Motor Vehicle Commission and the Superintendent of State Police, may promulgate rules and regulations for those public roads, streets or highways or public or quasi-public property in this State, where it is determined that the interests of public safety and welfare require the maximum outside width be no more than 96 inches.

(2) The maximum height of any vehicle or combination of vehicles, including load or contents of any part or portion thereof, except as otherwise provided by this subsection, shall not exceed 13 feet, 6 inches.

(3) The maximum overall length of any vehicle, as set forth in this subsection, including load or contents or any part or portion thereof, except as otherwise provided by this subsection, shall not exceed 40 feet, except that the overall length of a vehicle, including load or contents or any part or portion thereof, otherwise subject to the provisions of this paragraph shall not exceed 50 feet when transporting poles, pilings, structural units or other articles which cannot be dismembered, dismantled or divided. When a vehicle, subject to this paragraph, is the drawing or power unit of a combination of vehicles, as set forth in this subsection, the overall length of the combination of vehicles, including load or contents or any part or portion thereof, shall not exceed 62 feet. The provisions of this paragraph shall not apply to omnibuses, recreation vehicles, or to vehicles which are not designed, built or otherwise capable of carrying cargo or loads.

(4) The maximum overall length of a motor-drawn vehicle, as set forth in this subsection, including load or contents or any part or portion thereof, except as otherwise provided by this subsection, shall not exceed 53 feet when operated as part of a combination of vehicles consisting of one motor-drawn vehicle and a drawing or power unit vehicle not designed, built or otherwise capable of carrying cargo or loads, except that a motor-drawn vehicle, the overall length of which is greater than 48 feet and not more than 53 feet, shall be constructed so that the distance between the kingpin of the motor-drawn vehicle and the centerline of its rear axle or rear axle group does not exceed 41 feet; the motor-drawn vehicle shall be equipped with a rear-end protection device of substantial construction consisting

of a continuous lateral beam extending to within four inches of the lateral extremities of the motor-drawn vehicle and located not more than 22 inches from the surface as measured with the vehicle empty and on a level surface; the kingpin of the trailer shall not be set back further than 3.5 feet from the front of the semitrailer; the rear overhang, measured from the center of the rear tandem axles to the rear of the semitrailer shall not exceed 35% of the semitrailer's wheelbase; the width of the semitrailer and the distance between the outside edges of the trailer tires shall be 102 inches; and the vehicle shall be equipped with such reflectorization, including but not limited to side-marker reflectorization strips located between the rear axle and the rear of the motor-drawn vehicle, as shall be prescribed by the Motor Vehicle Commission, and as is consistent with any applicable federal standards concerning reflectorization. The overall length of a motor-drawn vehicle otherwise subject to the provisions of this paragraph shall not exceed 63 feet when transporting poles, pilings, structural units or other articles that cannot be dismembered, dismantled or divided. The provisions of this paragraph shall not apply to any vehicle or combination of vehicles designed, built and utilized solely to transport other motor vehicles. The Commissioner of Transportation, after consultation with the Chief Administrator of the New Jersey Motor Vehicle Commission and the Superintendent of State Police, shall promulgate rules and regulations specifying those portions or parts of the National System of Interstate and Defense Highways, Federal-aid Primary System Highways and public roads, streets, highways, toll roads, freeways or parkways in this State where the combination of vehicles as described in this paragraph may lawfully operate. The commissioner shall promulgate rules and regulations within 120 days after the effective date of this amendatory act to identify a network of roads with reasonable access for motor-drawn vehicles greater than 48 feet in length but not more than 53 feet in length. The commissioner shall, in establishing this network, consider all portions of the network for 48 foot long and 102 inch wide motor-drawn vehicles and specify those routes or portions thereof where motor-drawn vehicles greater than 48 feet in length but not more than 53 feet in length shall be excluded from lawful operation for reasons of safety.

(5) No combination of vehicles, including load or contents, consisting of more than two motor-drawn vehicles, as set forth in this subsection, and any other vehicle, shall be found or operated on any public road, street or highway or any public or quasi-public property in this State.

(6) The maximum overall length of a motor-drawn vehicle, as set forth in this section, including load or contents or any part or portion thereof, except as otherwise provided by this subsection, when operated as part of a combination of vehicles consisting of two motor-drawn vehicles and a drawing or power unit vehicle which is not designed, built or otherwise capable of carrying cargo or loads, shall not exceed 28 feet for each motor-drawn vehicle in the combination of vehicles. The provision of this paragraph shall not apply to any vehicle or combination of vehicles designed, built and utilized solely to transport other motor vehicles. The Commissioner of Transportation, after consultation with the Chief Administrator of the New Jersey Motor Vehicle Commission and the Superintendent of State Police, shall promulgate rules and regulations specifying those portions or parts of the National System of Interstate and Defense Highways, Federal-aid Primary System Highways and public roads, streets, highways, toll roads, freeways or parkways in this State where combinations of vehicles as described in this paragraph may lawfully operate.

(7) The maximum length and outside width of an omnibus found or operated in this State shall be established by rules and regulations promulgated by the Commissioner of Transportation, after consultation with the Chief Administrator of the New Jersey Motor Vehicle Commission and the Superintendent of State Police. Unless otherwise specified in the aforesaid rules and regulations, the maximum outside width shall be 102 inches; any other dimension established for width in the aforesaid rules and regulations shall be based upon a determination that operation of an omnibus with a width of less than 102 inches, but no less than 96 inches is required in the interest of public safety on those public roads, streets, highways, toll roads, freeways, parkways or the National System of Interstate and Defense Highways in this State specified in the aforesaid rules and regulations, or that operation of an omnibus with a width greater than 102 inches is not unsafe on those public roads, streets, highways, toll roads, freeways, parkways or the National System of Interstate and Defense Highways in this State specified in the aforesaid rules and regulations.

(8) The maximum width and length of farm tractors and traction equipment and farm machinery and implements shall be established by rules and regulations promulgated by the Chief Administrator of the New Jersey Motor Vehicle Commission. The operation of the aforesaid vehicles shall be subject to the provisions of R.S.39:3–24 and they shall not be operated on any highway which is part of the National System of Interstate and Defense Highways or on any highway which has been designated a freeway or parkway as provided by law.

(9) The maximum outside width of the cargo or load of a vehicle or combination of vehicles, including farm trucks, loaded with hay or straw shall not exceed 105 1/2 inches, but the maximum outside width of the vehicle or combination of vehicles, including farm trucks, shall otherwise comply with the provisions of paragraph (1) of this subsection. The Commissioner of Transportation, after consultation with the Chief Administrator of the New Jersey Motor Vehicle Commission and the Superintendent of State Police, may promulgate rules and regulations establishing a maximum outside width of 102 inches for the aforesaid cargo or load when

operating on those highways where a greater width is prohibited by operation of law.

(10) Notwithstanding the provisions of paragraphs (4) and (6) of this subsection pertaining to length, the Chief Administrator of the New Jersey Motor Vehicle Commission may adopt rules and regulations specifying maximum length dimensions for any vehicle or combination of vehicles designed, built and utilized solely to transport other motor vehicles.

(11) The provisions of this subsection pertaining to length shall not apply to a vehicle or combination of vehicles or special mobile equipment operated by a public utility, as defined in R.S.48:2–13, when that vehicle or combination of vehicles or special mobile equipment is used by the public utility in the construction, reconstruction, repair or maintenance of its property or facilities.

(12) The provisions of this subsection pertaining to width shall not apply to a recycling vehicle when that vehicle is used for the collection of recyclable material on a street or highway other than a highway which is designated part of the National System of Interstate and Defense Highways in this State or as a freeway or parkway as provided by law. The maximum outside width of any recycling vehicle so used, including load or contents of any part or portion thereof, shall be no more than 96 inches, except that the width may be up to 105 inches whenever that vehicle is operating at 15 miles per hour or less, and access steps are deployed and recyclable materials are actually being collected.

(13) The maximum overall length of a recreation vehicle including any load or truck camper thereon found or operated in this State shall not exceed 45 feet and no combination of a recreation vehicle with any vehicle, including the load thereon, nor any combination of any motor vehicle with any camping trailer, fifth wheel trailer or park trailer attached thereto, as these terms are defined in section 1 of P.L.1991, c. 483 (C.46:8C–10), shall exceed 65 feet in length. Further, the outside width of a recreation vehicle found or operated in this State shall not exceed 102 inches, excluding safety appurtenances such as awnings and lights which are integral to the construction of the vehicle, installed by the vehicle's manufacturer or dealer, and do not extend more than three inches wide on each side of the vehicle, provided however, that such vehicles permissibly exceeding the 102 inch width with their attached equipment or appurtenances shall only be operated:

(a) On roadways having travel lanes at least 11 feet in width, unless prohibited by the Department of Transportation or by a municipality based on safety reasons and marked with signs prohibiting such vehicles; or

(b) On any roadway of the State when such a vehicle is being operated between roadways permitted under subparagraph (a) of this paragraph; and

(i) The location where the recreation vehicle, fifth wheel trailer, park trailer, camping trailer or truck camper is garaged; or

(ii) The destination of the recreation vehicle, fifth wheel trailer, park trailer, camping trailer or truck camper; or

(iii) A facility for food, fuel, repair, services or rest.

b. No vehicle or combination of vehicles, including load or contents, found or operated on any public road, street or highway or any public or quasi-public property in this State shall exceed the weight limitations set forth in this Title. Violations shall be enforced pursuant to subsection j. of section 5 of P.L.1950, c. 142 (C.39:3–84.3).

Where enforcement of a weight limit provision of this Title requires a measurement of length between axle centers, the distance between axle centers shall be measured to the nearest whole foot or whole inch, whichever is applicable, and when the measurement includes a fractional part of a foot equaling six inches or more or a fractional part of an inch equaling one-half inch or more, the next larger whole foot or whole inch, whichever is applicable, shall be utilized. The term "tandem axle" as used in this act is defined as a combination of consecutive axles, consisting of only two axles, where the distance between axle centers is 40 inches or more but no more than 96 inches.

In addition to the other requirements of this section and notwithstanding any other provision of this Title, no vehicle or combination of vehicles, including load or contents, shall be operated in this State, unless by special permit authorized by this Title, with a gross weight, single or multiple axle weight, or gross weight of two or more consecutive axles, the allowance of which would disqualify the State of New Jersey or any department, agency or governmental subdivision thereof for the purpose of receiving federal highway funds.

(1) The gross weight imposed on the highway or other surface by the wheels of any one axle of a vehicle or combination of vehicles, including load or contents, shall not exceed 22,400 pounds; provided, however, that notwithstanding any provision of this section or any other law, rule, or regulation to the contrary, any vehicle, registered as an omnibus pursuant to R.S.39:3–19 having an axle weight greater than that provided for in this paragraph, may operate with the approval of the Commissioner of Transportation consistent with federal law and regulation.

For the purpose of this Title the combined gross weight imposed on the highway or other surface by all the wheels of any one axle of a vehicle or combination of vehicles, including load or contents, shall be deemed to mean the total gross weight of all wheels whose axle centers are spaced less than 40 inches apart.

(2) The gross weight imposed on the highway or other surface by all the wheels of all consecutive axles of a vehicle or combination of vehicles, including load or

contents, shall not exceed 34,000 pounds where the distance between consecutive axle centers is 40 inches or more, but no more than 96 inches apart.

(3) The combined gross weight imposed on the highway or other surface by all the wheels of consecutive axles of a vehicle or combination of vehicles, including load or contents, shall not exceed 22,400 pounds for each single axle where the distance between consecutive axle centers is more than 96 inches; except that on any highway in this State which is part of, or designated as part of, the National Interstate System, as provided at 23 U.S.C. s.103(c), this single axle limitation shall not apply and in those instances the provisions of this Title as set forth at R.S.39:3–84b.(5) shall apply.

(4) The maximum total gross weight imposed on the highway or other surface by a vehicle or combination of vehicles, including load or contents, shall not exceed 80,000 pounds.

(5) On any highway in this State which is part of, or designated as part of, the National Interstate System, as provided at 23 U.S.C. s.103(c), the total gross weight, in pounds, imposed on the highway or other surface by any group of two or more consecutive axles of a vehicle or combination of vehicles, including load or contents, shall not exceed that listed in the following Table of Maximum Gross Weights, for the respective distance, in feet, between the axle centers of the first and last axles of the group of two or more consecutive axles under consideration; except that in addition to the weights specified in that Table, two consecutive sets of tandem axles may carry a gross weight of 34,000 pounds each if the overall distance between the first and last axles of the consecutive sets of tandem axles is 36 feet or more. The gross weight of each set of tandem axles shall not exceed 34,000 pounds and the combined gross weight of the two consecutive sets of tandem axles shall not exceed 68,000 pounds.

In all cases the combined gross weight for a vehicle or combination of vehicles, including load or contents, or the maximum gross weight for any axle or combination of axles of the vehicle or combination of vehicles, including load or contents, shall not exceed that which is permitted pursuant to this paragraph or R.S.39:3–84b.(2); R.S.39:3–84b.(3); or R.S.39:3–84b.(4) of this act, whichever is the lesser allowable gross weight.

TABLE OF MAXIMUM GROSS WEIGHTS

Distance in feet between axle centers of first and last axles of any group of two or more consecutive axles

	2 axles	3 axles	4 axles	5 axles	6 axles	7 axles
3	22400	22400	22400	22400	22400	22400
4	34000	34000	34000	34000	34000	34000
5	34000	34000	34000	34000	34000	34000
6	34000	34000	34000	34000	34000	34000
7	34000	34000	34000	34000	34000	34000
8	34000	34000	34000	34000	34000	34000
9	39000	42500	42500	42500	42500	42500
10	40000	43500	43500	43500	43500	43500
11	41000	44000	44000	44000	44000	44000
12	42000	45000	50000	50000	50000	50000
13	43000	45500	50500	50500	50500	50500
14	44000	46500	51500	51500	51500	51500
15	44800	47000	52000	52000	52000	52000
16	44800	48000	52500	58000	58000	58000
17	44800	48500	53500	58500	58500	58500
18	44800	49500	54000	59000	59000	59000
19	44800	50000	54500	60000	60000	60000
20	44800	51000	55500	60500	66000	66000
21	44800	51500	56000	61000	66500	66500
22	44800	52500	56500	61500	67000	67000
23	44800	53000	57500	62500	68000	68000
24	44800	54000	58000	63000	68500	74000
25	44800	54500	58500	63500	69000	74500
26	44800	55500	59500	64000	69500	75000
27	44800	56000	60000	65000	70000	75500
28	44800	57000	60500	65500	71000	76500
29	44800	57500	61500	66000	71500	77000
30	44800	58500	62000	66500	72000	77500
31	44800	59000	62500	67500	72500	78000
32	44800	60000	63500	68000	73000	78500
33	44800	60500	64000	68500	74000	79000

	2 axles	3 axles	4 axles	5 axles	6 axles	7 axles
34	44800	61500	64500	69000	74500	80000
35	44800	62000	65500	70000	75000	80000
36	44800	63000	66000	70500	75500	80000
37	44800	63500	66500	71000	76000	80000
38	44800	64500	67500	71500	77000	80000
39	44800	65000	68000	72500	77500	80000
40	44800	66000	68500	73000	78000	80000
41	44800	66500	69500	73500	78500	80000
42	44800	67200	70000	74000	79000	80000
43	44800	67200	70500	75000	80000	80000
44	44800	67200	71500	75500	80000	80000
45	44800	67200	72000	76000	80000	80000
46	44800	67200	72500	76500	80000	80000
47	44800	67200	73500	77500	80000	80000
48	44800	67200	74000	78000	80000	80000
49	44800	67200	74500	78500	80000	80000
50	44800	67200	75500	79000	80000	80000
51	44800	67200	76000	80000	80000	80000
52	44800	67200	76500	80000	80000	80000
53	44800	67200	77500	80000	80000	80000
54	44800	67200	78000	80000	80000	80000
55	44800	67200	78500	80000	80000	80000
56	44800	67200	79500	80000	80000	80000
57	44800	67200	80000	80000	80000	80000
58	44800	67200	80000	80000	80000	80000
59	44800	67200	80000	80000	80000	80000
60	44800	67200	80000	80000	80000	80000
61	44800	67200	80000	80000	80000	80000
62	44800	67200	80000	80000	80000	80000
63	44800	67200	80000	80000	80000	80000
64	44800	67200	80000	80000	80000	80000
65	44800	67200	80000	80000	80000	80000
66	44800	67200	80000	80000	80000	80000
67	44800	67200	80000	80000	80000	80000
68	44800	67200	80000	80000	80000	80000
69	44800	67200	80000	80000	80000	80000
70	44800	67200	80000	80000	80000	80000

c. The dimensional and weight restrictions set forth herein shall not apply to a combination of vehicles which includes a disabled vehicle or a combination of vehicles being removed from a highway in this State, provided that such oversize or overweight vehicle combination may not travel on the public highways more than 75 miles from the point where such disablement occurred. If the disablement occurred on a limited access highway, the distance to the nearest exit of such highway shall be added to the 75–mile limitation. A heavy-duty tow truck, as defined in section 1 of P.L. 1999, c. 396 (C.39:3–84.6), shall be permitted, in combination with the towed unit or units, to exceed the axle, dimensional and maximum gross weight limits for tow trucks and towed unit combinations; except that the limit shall not exceed 150,000 pounds gross combined weight. This provision shall not affect the application of section 6 of P.L.1950, c. 142 (C.39:3–84.4) concerning driver liability for damages and does not provide an exemption to exceed the height and weight restrictions marked or posted on a bridge or overpass in the State. A heavy-duty tow truck in combination with the towed unit or units shall not be operated at a speed greater than 45 miles per hour when the heavy-duty tow truck in combination with the towed unit or units weighs more than 80,000 pounds, or one or more of its axles exceeds the limitations prescribed herein in the Table of Maximum Gross Weights, or the tow truck in combination with the towed unit exceeds maximum length and width standards as prescribed by law.

d. The Chief Administrator of the New Jersey Motor Vehicle Commission may promulgate rules and regulations, including the establishment of fees, for the issuance, at his discretion and if good cause appears, of a special written permit authorizing the applicant:

(1) To operate or move a vehicle or combination of vehicles or special mobile equipment, transporting one piece loads that cannot be dismembered, dismantled or divided in order to comply with the weight limitations set forth in this act. The special written permit issued by the director shall be in the possession of the driver or operator of the vehicle or combination of vehicles or special mobile equipment for which said permit was issued; and

(2) To operate or move a vehicle or combination of vehicles or specialized mobile equipment, transporting a load or cargo that cannot be dismembered, dismantled

or divided in order to comply with the dimensional limitations set forth in this act. The special written permit shall be in the possession of the driver or operator of the vehicle or combination of vehicles or special mobile equipment for which the permit was issued; and

(3) Under emergency conditions, to operate or move a type of vehicle or combination of vehicles or special mobile equipment of a size or weight, including load or contents, which exceeds the maximum size or weight limitations specified in this act.

e. If the Commissioner of Transportation has, by regulations adopted pursuant to the "Administrative Procedure Act," P.L.1968, c. 410 (C.52:14B–1 et seq.), designated certain routes within the State for use by a combination of vehicles with a prescribed maximum width or length or consisting of a drawing vehicle and two motor drawn vehicles with a prescribed maximum length, no such combination of vehicles shall be found or operated on any other public road, street or highway or any other public or quasi-public property in this State, unless otherwise permitted by such regulations.
Amended by L.1942, c. 268, p. 711, § 1; L.1950, c. 142, p. 281, § 2; L.1955, c. 198, p. 775, § 1; L.1957, c. 161, p. 577, § 2; L.1959, c. 171, p. 703, § 1; L.1961, c. 71, p. 594, § 1; L.1961, c. 113, p. 703, § 2; L.1963, c. 49, § 2; L.1964, c. 136, § 15; L.1967, c. 137, § 1; L.1971, c. 383, § 1, eff. Dec. 30, 1971; L.1973, c. 11, § 11, eff. Jan. 25, 1973; L.1975, c. 91, § 1; L.1977, c. 51, § 3; L.1983, c. 126, § 1, eff. April 6, 1983; L.1983, c. 349, § 2; L.1989, c. 47, § 1, eff. March 14, 1989; L.1991, c. 115, § 1, eff. April 19, 1991; L.1991, c. 449, § 1, eff. Jan. 18, 1992; L.1995, c. 397, § 3, eff. Jan. 10, 1996; L.1999, c. 29, § 1, eff. Feb. 26, 1999; L.1999, c. 348, § 2, eff. Jan. 13, 2000; L.1999, c. 396, § 9, eff. Jan. 18, 2000; L.2007, c. 249, § 1, eff. Jan. 4, 2008; L.2009, c. 3, § 1, eff. Jan. 15, 2009.

39:3–84a. Repealed by L.1983, c. 349, § 5, eff. April 6, 1983

39:3–84.1. Application of weight limitations

a. The axle weight limitations as provided at R.S. 39:3–84b. shall apply to all vehicles registered in New Jersey subsequent to March 1, 1950, which have not been registered therein or contracted for purchase by New Jersey residents prior to that date. The weight limitations provided at R.S. 39:3–84 b.(1); R.S. 39:3–84 b.(2); and R.S. 39:3–84 b.(3) relative to maximum gross axle weights shall not apply to vehicles registered as "constructor" or "solid waste" vehicles or to a combination of vehicles of which the "constructor" or "solid waste" vehicle is the drawing vehicle as provided at R.S. 39:3–20, except that said limitations shall apply to vehicles registered as "solid waste" when operated on any highway which is part of the National System of Interstate and Defense Highways, as provided at 23 U.S.C. § 103(e). Except as otherwise provided in this section, the provisions of R.S. 39:3–84 b.(5) shall apply to vehicles registered as "constructor" or "solid waste" or to a combination of vehicles of which the "construc-

tor" or "solid waste" vehicle is the drawing vehicle as provided in R.S. 39:3–20, except that for any vehicle registered as a "constructor" or any combination of vehicles of which the drawing vehicle is registered as a "constructor," the provisions of R.S. 39:3–84 b.(5) shall not apply; provided the vehicle or combination of vehicles is operated within an area that is 30 miles or less from the point established as a headquarters for the particular construction operation. Vehicles registered as "constructor" or "solid waste" or a combination of vehicles of which the "constructor" or "solid waste" vehicle is the drawing vehicle shall be limited to a maximum gross vehicle weight, including load or contents, as shown on the registration certificate of that vehicle.

b. The Commissioner of Transportation is authorized to adopt rules and regulations providing for exemptions from the provisions of R.S. 39:3–84 b.(5) for the following:

(1) Vehicles registered as "solid waste" or combinations of vehicles of which the "solid waste" vehicle is the drawing vehicle as provided in R.S. 39:3–20.

(2) Vehicles not in excess of 73,280 pounds.

The commissioner is also authorized to adopt rules and regulations providing for any time limits, distinctions among classes of vehicles, or other conditions with respect to these exemptions.

c. In addition to any exemptions provided for by regulations adopted pursuant to subsection b. of this section, the commissioner is authorized to adopt rules and regulations providing for exemptions for a transitional period from the provisions of R.S. 39:3–84 b.(5) for the following:

(1) Tandem-axle dump trucks;

(2) Five-axle dump trailers;

(3) Two-axle dump trucks;

(4) Three-axle dump trucks;

(5) Four-axle dump trucks;

(6) Three-axle and four-axle ready-mix transit trucks;

(7) Four-axle and five-axle flatbed tractor trailers;

(8) Five-axle bulk carriers;

(9) Two-axle, three-axle, four-axle and five-axle liquid bulk carriers;

(10) Two-axle and three-axle emergency equipment wreckers;

(11) Solid waste rear-end loaders;

(12) Solid waste front-end loaders;

(13) Solid waste four-axle roll-offs;

(14) Four-axle and five-axle waste transfer tractor trailers;

(15) Two-axle, three-axle, four-axle and five-axle general freight carriers; and

(16) Intermodal ocean containers.

L.1950, c. 142, p. 282, § 3.   Amended by L.1954, c. 166, p. 673, § 1; L.1958, c. 2, p. 19, § 1; L.1973, c. 373, § 2, eff. Jan. 7, 1974; L.1977, c. 51, § 4, eff. July 1, 1976; L.1983, c. 349, § 3; L.1983, c. 374, § 1.

39:3–84.2. Repeal

Sections 39:3–83, 39:3–85 and 39:4–73 of the Revised Statutes are hereby repealed.

L.1950, c. 142, p. 283, § 4.

39:3–84.3. Violations as to weights and measurements of vehicles

a. Officers shall have authority as set forth in paragraphs (1) through (3) of this subsection to require the driver, operator, owner, lessee or bailee of any vehicle or combination of vehicles found on any public road, street, or highway or any public or quasi-public property in this State to facilitate and permit the measurement or weighing of the vehicle or combination of vehicles, including load or contents, for the purpose of determining whether the size or weight of the vehicle or combination of vehicles, including load or contents, is in excess of that permitted in this Title:

(1) Officers of the Division of State Police shall have the exclusive authority to conduct random roadside examinations for the purpose of determining whether size or weight is in excess of that permitted in this Title, and officers of the Division of State Police shall have the authority, with or without probable cause to believe that the size or weight is in excess of that permitted, to require the driver, operator, owner, lessee or bailee, to stop, drive or otherwise move to a location for measurement or weighing and submit the vehicle or combination of vehicles, including load or contents, to measurement or weighing;

(2) Police or peace officers or inspectors appointed by any municipality or county shall have the authority to require the driver, operator, owner, lessee or bailee to stop, drive or otherwise move to a location for measurement or weighing and submit the vehicle or combination of vehicles, including load or contents, to measurement or weighing, only if the officer has probable cause to believe that the size or weight of the vehicle or combination of vehicles, including load or contents, is in excess of that permitted by this Title; and

(3) The Division of State Police and the director shall have the exclusive authority to establish and operate locations for the measurement and weighing of vehicles, including load and contents, and all measuring and weighing devices or scales employed at such locations shall be approved and certified by the State Superintendent of Weights and Measures or the State Superintendent's agent.   Copies of documents displaying the State Superintendent's seal or certification shall be prima facie evidence of the reliability and accuracy of the measuring or weighing devices or scales utilized.

b.   Whenever the officer, upon measuring or weighing a vehicle or combination of vehicles, including load or contents, determines that the size or weight is in excess of the limits permitted in this Title, the officer or inspector shall require the driver, operator, owner, lessee or bailee to stop the vehicle or combination of vehicles in a suitable place and remain in that place until a portion of the load or contents of the vehicle or combination of vehicles is removed by the driver, operator, owner, lessee, bailee or duly appointed agent thereof, as may be necessary to conform or reduce the size or weight of the vehicle or combination of vehicles, including load or contents, to those limits as permitted under this act, or permitted by the certificate of registration for the vehicle or combination of vehicles, whichever may be lower.   All materials so unloaded or removed shall be cared for by the driver, owner, operator, lessee or bailee of the vehicle or combination of vehicles, or duly appointed agent thereof, at the risk, responsibility and liability of the driver, owner, operator, lessee, bailee or duly appointed agent thereof.

c.   No vehicle or combination of vehicles shall be deemed to be in violation of the weight limitation provision of this act, when, upon examination by the officer, the dispatch papers for the vehicle or combination of vehicles, including load or contents, show it is proceeding from its last preceding freight pickup point within the State of New Jersey by a reasonably expeditious route to the nearest available scales or to the first available scales in the general direction towards which the vehicle or combination of vehicles has been dispatched, or is returning from such scales after weighing-in to the last preceding pickup point.

d.   When the officer determines that a vehicle or combination of vehicles, including load or contents, is in violation of the weight limitations of this Title as provided at paragraph (1) of subsection b. of R.S.39:3–84;   paragraph (2) of subsection b. of R.S.39:3–84;   paragraph (3) of subsection b. of R.S.39:3–84;   or paragraph (5) of subsection b. of R.S.39:3–84 relative to maximum gross axle weights, but is within the permissible maximum gross vehicle weight of this Title as provided at paragraph (4) of subsection b. of R.S.39:3–84 or paragraph (5) of subsection b. of R.S.39:3–84, whichever is applicable, the driver, operator, owner, lessee, bailee or duly appointed agent thereof shall be permitted, before proceeding, to redistribute the weight of the vehicle or combination of vehicles or the load or contents of the vehicle or combination of vehicles so that no axle or combination of consecutive axles are in excess of the limits set by this act, in which event there is no violation.

e.   When the officer determines that a vehicle or combination of vehicles, including load or contents, is in violation of the height, width or length limits of this Title as provided at subsection a. of R.S.39:3–84, the driver, operator, owner, lessee or bailee of the vehicle or combination of vehicles or duly appointed agent thereof shall be permitted, before proceeding, to adjust, reduce or conform the vehicle or combination of vehicles, including load or contents, so that the vehicle or combination of vehicles, including load or contents, are not in excess of the height, width, or length limits set by this act, in which event there is no violation.

f. The provisions of this subsection shall not apply to a vehicle or combination of vehicles, including load or contents, found or operated on any highway in this State which is part of or designated as part of the National Interstate System, as provided at 23 U.S.C. s. 103(e). No arrest shall be made or summons issued for a violation of the weight limitations provided in this act at subsection b. of R.S.39:3–84 where the excess weight is no more than 5% of the weight permitted, provided the gross weight of the vehicle or combination of vehicles, including load or contents, does not exceed the maximum gross weight of 80,000 pounds as set forth at paragraph (4) of subsection b. of R.S.39:3–84.

g. Any person who presents to the officer, or has in his possession, or who prepares false dispatch papers, that is to say, dispatch papers which do not correspond to the cargo carried, shall be subject to a fine not to exceed $300.

h. Any driver of a vehicle or combination of vehicles who fails or refuses to stop and submit the vehicle or combination of vehicles, including load or contents, to measurement or weighing, as provided in this Title, or otherwise fails to comply with the provisions of this section, shall be subject to a fine not exceeding $200.00.

i. The owner, lessee, bailee or any one of the aforesaid of any vehicle or combination of vehicles found or operated on any public road, street or highway or on any public or quasi-public property in this State in violation of the height, width or length limits as set forth in subsection a. of R.S.39: 3–84 shall be fined not less than $150.00 nor more than $500.00.

j. The owner, lessee, bailee or any one of the aforesaid of any vehicle or combination of vehicles found or operated on any public road, street or highway or on any public or quasi-public property in this State, with a gross weight of the vehicle or combination of vehicles, including load or contents, in excess of the weight limitations as provided at subsection b. of R.S.39: 3–84 or section 3 of P.L.1950, c. 142 (C.39:3–84.1) shall be fined an amount equal to $0.02 per pound for each pound of the total excess weight; provided the total excess weight is 10,000 pounds or less, or shall be fined an amount equal to $0.03 per pound for each pound of the total excess weight; provided the total excess weight is more than 10,000 pounds, but in no event shall the fine be less than $50.00. However, in the case of any vehicle or combination of vehicles carrying a sealed ocean container, either the shipper, the consignee or both, shall be liable for a violation of the weight limitations as provided at subsection b. of R.S.39:3–84 relative to maximum gross axle weights.

k. Whenever a vehicle or combination of vehicles, including load or contents, is found to be in violation of any two or more of the weight limitations as provided at subsection b. of R.S.39:3–84 or section 3 of P.L.1950, c. 142 (C.39:3–84.1), the fine levied shall be only for the violation involving the greater or greatest excess weight.

l. The driver, owner, lessee, bailee or any one of the foregoing of any combination of vehicles found or operated on any public road, street or highway or on any public or quasi-public property in the State in violation of the regulations of the Commissioner of Transportation regarding designated routes for such combinations as provided in subsection e. of R.S. 39:3–84 shall be fined not more than $400 for the first offense, and shall be subject to a fine of $700 for the second offense and a fine of $1,000 for each subsequent offense. The officer may direct that a combination of vehicles so found or operated proceed by the most direct route to a permitted route or return to a permitted route by making use of the route already traversed.

L.1950, c. 142, p. 283, § 5. Amended by L.1951, First Sp.Sess., c. 356, p. 1472, § 1; L.1955, c. 86, p. 258, § 1; L.1956, c. 165, p. 657, § 1; L.1957, c. 161, p. 575, § 1; L.1961, c. 113, p. 705, § 3; L.1963, c. 166, § 2; L.1966, c. 209, § 3, eff. April 1, 1967; L.1975, c. 92, § 1, eff. May 8, 1975; L.1983, c. 349, § 4; L.1983, c. 403, § 12, eff. Dec. 23, 1983; L.1993, c. 12, § 2, eff. Jan. 15, 1993; L.1994, c. 60, § 33, eff. July 1, 1994; L.1999, c. 348, § 3, eff. Jan. 13, 2000.

39:3–84.4. Damage to highways or structures by over-weight vehicles; liability

Any person driving any vehicle, object or contrivance referred to in section 39:3–84 of the Revised Statutes, in excess of the gross weight limits set forth therein upon any highway or highway structure, whether temporary or permanent, shall be liable for all damage which said highway or highway structure may sustain as a result of any such operation, driving or moving of such vehicle, object or contrivance.

Such damage may be recovered in a civil action brought by the authorities in control of such highway or highway structure.

The fact that the vehicle, object, or contrivance causing the damage was being operated, driven or moved within the size and weight limitations authorized in this Title or permitted by a special permit as provided by law, shall not be accepted as a defense to any action brought as provided herein if damage is caused to highways or bridges posted for less weight limits than those set forth in this act.[1]

Whenever the driver is not the owner of such vehicle, object or contrivance, but is so operating, driving or moving the same with the express or implied permission of said owner, then the owner and the driver shall be jointly and severally liable for any damage.

L.1950, c. 142, p. 284, § 6.

1 N.J.S.A. §§ 39:3–20, 39:3–84 and 39:3–84.1 to 39:3–84.5.

39:3–84.5. Partial invalidity

If any section, subsection, clause or provision of this act [1] shall be adjudged unconstitutional or to be ineffective in whole or in part, to the extent that it is not adjudged unconstitutional or is not ineffective it shall be valid and effective and no other section, subsection, clause or provision of this act shall on account thereof be deemed invalid or ineffective, and the inapplicability or invalidity of any section, subsection, clause or provision of this act in any one or more instances or under any one or more circumstances shall not be taken to affect or prejudice in any way its applicability or validity in any other instance or under any other circumstance.

L.1950, c. 142, p. 284, § 7.

1 N.J.S.A. §§ 39:3–20, 39:3–84 and 39:3–84.1 to 39:3–84.5.

39:3–84.6. Definitions

As used in this act:

"Director" means the Director of the Division of Motor Vehicles in the Department of Transportation.

"Division" means the Division of Motor Vehicles in the Department of Transportation.

"Garage keeper's legal liability" means the protection of customer vehicles under various conditions pertaining to specific garage functions.

"Heavy-duty" means a gross weight of at least 32,000 pounds.

"Light-medium duty" means a gross weight of less than 32,000 pounds.

"Marker" means a type of vehicle identification issued by the director to be displayed on a tow truck.

"Towing company" means any person or entity owning or operating a tow truck service for compensation.

"Tow truck" means a motor vehicle equipped with a boom or booms, winches, slings, tilt beds or similar equipment designed for the towing or recovery of vehicles and other objects.

"Transporter" means equipment designed to transport more than one vehicle on a non-emergency basis.

L.1999, c. 396, § 1, eff. Jan. 18, 2000.

39:3–84.7. Issuance of distinctive markers

a. Unless determined otherwise by the director pursuant to subsection b. of this section, the director shall issue distinctive markers for tow trucks operating under the provisions of this act. A fee of $25 annually shall be charged for such markers. The fee for such markers is in addition to the fees otherwise prescribed by law for the registration of motor vehicles and the amount received from the fees shall be annually appropriated to the department to defray costs incurred by the division in issuing the markers and implementing the provisions of P.L.1999, c. 396 (C.39:3–84.6 et al.). The markers shall be available for tow trucks in two gross weight categories: light-medium duty and heavy-duty. The markers for each weight category shall have distinctive features.

b. The director may issue, in lieu of markers issued pursuant to subsection a. of this section, license plates for tow trucks operating under the provisions of this act. The license plates shall be issued for 12 months upon the filing of an application pursuant to section 3 of P.L.1999, c. 396 (C.39:3–84.8) and upon payment of the registration fee. A surcharge on the registration fee shall be imposed by the director in the amount of $25 and the amount received from the surcharge shall be annually appropriated to the department to defray costs incurred by the division in issuing the plates and implementing the provisions of P.L.1999, c. 396 (C.39:3–84.6 et al.). The plates shall be available for tow trucks in two gross weight categories: light-medium duty and heavy-duty. The plates for each weight category shall have distinctive features conspicuous to passing motorists.

c. A person shall not operate or offer to operate a tow truck to tow, winch, or otherwise move a motor vehicle for any direct or indirect compensation unless the tow truck displays the proper marker or valid tow truck license plate issued by the Division of Motor Vehicles pursuant to this act. The director may exempt tow trucks that meet the definition of an apportioned vehicle pursuant to section 21 of P.L.1995, c. 157 (C.39:3–6.11) from the requirement to display a tow truck license plate.

L.1999, c. 396, § 2, eff. July 1, 2001.

39:3–84.8. Tow truck registration; application contents

a. An application for tow truck registration shall contain the following information:

(1) The name and address of the towing company's principal owner or owners;

(2) The address of the principal business office of the towing company;

(3) The location of any garage, parking lot, or other storage area, where motor vehicles or other objects moved by the towing company may be stored or placed;

(4) A valid certificate of insurance and a schedule of insured vehicles that are to be utilized by the towing company from an insurer authorized to do business in the State, including the amounts of the garage keeper's legal liability coverage and any "on hook" coverage as an endorsement or contained in a separate schedule, and liability insurance coverage, including in the case of each light-medium duty tow truck, motor vehicle liability insurance coverage for the death of, or injury to persons and damage to property for each accident or occurrence in the amount of at least $750,000 single

limit, and in the case of each heavy-duty tow truck, motor vehicle liability insurance coverage for the death of, or injury to, persons and damage to property for each accident or occurrence in the amount of at least $1,000,000 single limit; and

(5) Documentation of the manufacturer's gross vehicle weight rating for each tow truck.

Except as otherwise provided in this act, the registration for these vehicles shall be issued and renewed pursuant to the provisions of this Title.

L.1999, c. 396, § 3, eff. July 1, 2001.   Amended by L.2007, c. 193, § 18, eff. Oct. 18, 2008; L.2009, c. 39, § 13, eff. April 15, 2009.

39:3–84.9.   Repealed by L.2007, c. 193, § 24, operative Oct. 18, 2008

39:3–84.10.   Suspension, revocation or refusal of registration

The director may suspend, revoke or refuse to issue or renew any registrations issued pursuant to this act upon proof that the applicant:

a.   Used fraud or deception in securing such registration;

b.   Violated any provision of this act; or

c.   Has been convicted of theft of a motor vehicle.

L.1999, c. 396, § 5, eff. July 1, 2001.

39:3–84.11.   Proper display of license plates or markers

A towing company shall display valid tow truck license plates or markers as required by law on each of its tow trucks. The name of the towing company and the municipality and state where the business is located shall be conspicuously displayed on all tow trucks used by the company as provided by law and regulation. Transporters shall be exempt from the provisions of this act.

L.1999, c. 396, § 6, eff. July 1, 2001.

39:3–84.12.   Preemption of certain political subdivision actions

The provisions of this act shall preempt a political subdivision from regulating, requiring or issuing any registration, license plate or marker or surety registration of any towing company. This section shall not limit the existing authority of a political subdivision to:

a.   License and collect a general and nondiscriminatory tax upon all businesses;

b.   License and collect a tax upon towing operations domiciled within its jurisdiction; or

c.   Impose any additional requirements or conditions as part of any contract to perform towing and recovery services for that jurisdiction.

L.1999, c. 396, § 7, eff. July 1, 2001.

39:3–84.13.   Violations; fines

A towing company operating a light-medium duty tow truck without displaying a proper marker or valid tow truck license plate as required by this act or violating section 6 of this act shall be subject to a fine of $600 for the first offense and a fine of $900 for each subsequent offense and a towing company operating a heavy-duty tow truck without displaying a proper marker or valid tow truck license plate as required by this act or violating section 6 of this act shall be subject to a fine of $1,200 for the first offense and a fine of $1,800 for each subsequent offense.   A person or towing company knowingly displaying a false tow truck marker or license plate or using fraud or deception in securing tow truck registration under this act shall be subject to a fine of not less than $1,000 nor more than $7,500.

L.1999, c. 396, § 8, eff. July 1, 2001.

39:3–84.14.   Rules and regulations

The director shall adopt, pursuant to the " Administrative Procedure Act," P.L.1968, c. 410 (C.52:14B–1 et seq.), rules and regulations necessary to implement the provisions of this act.

L.1999, c. 396, § 10, eff. Jan. 18, 2000.

39:3–85.   Repealed by L.1950, c. 142, p. 283, § 4

ARTICLE 6.   REPORTS OF THEFT, ETC.

39:3–85.1.   Stolen motor vehicles or registration plates; notification of police

Any person or persons whose motor vehicle has been stolen, and any person or persons whose registration plates have been lost or stolen, shall immediately notify the chief of police or other peace officer within whose jurisdiction the theft or loss occurred.

Any person or persons who have given any such report shall immediately, upon the recovery of same, notify the chief of police or other peace officer to whom the original report had been made, of the recovery of the motor vehicle or registration plates.

L.1938, c. 352, p. 880, § 1.

39:3–85.2.   Report to Superintendent of State Police and Commissioner of Motor Vehicles

Every chief of police or other peace officer in the State of New Jersey, upon receiving reliable information that any motor vehicle has been stolen or any registration plates have been lost or stolen, shall within twenty-four hours report this information to the Superintendent of State Police and the commission.

Any chief of police or other peace officer, upon receiving reliable information that any motor vehicle or registration plates, which he previously reported as stolen or lost has been recovered, shall within twenty-four hours report the fact of such recovery to the Superintendent of State Police and the commission.

L.1938, c. 352, p. 880, § 2.   Amended by L.2003, c. 13, § 46 (contingent effective date).

Historical and Statutory Notes

L.2003, c. 13, § 127, approved Jan. 28, 2003, provides:

"Sections 1, 2, 3, 12, 38, 109, 110 and 121 shall take effect immediately, sections 105, 106, 107, 108, and 120 shall take effect on July 1, 2003 and the remainder of this act shall take effect on the date the Commissioner of Transportation certifies to the Governor (hereinafter the "date of certification") that a majority of the members of the commission have been appointed or are in office and that all necessary anticipatory actions have been accomplished, provided, that the amount of revenues received pursuant to sections 109 and 110 prior to the date of certification are hereby appropriated to the division. Upon the date of certification, all such collected revenue shall be revenue of the commission. The Commissioner of Transportation, the Director of the Division of Motor Vehicles and the commission may take such anticipatory administrative action in advance as shall be necessary for the implementation of the act."

39:3–85.3. Record of stolen motor vehicles and registration plates

The Superintendent of State Police and the commission having been notified of the theft of a motor vehicle or the loss or theft of registration plates by a chief of police or other peace officer, shall index and file this information in such a manner that a motor vehicle or registration plates can be properly identified. These records shall be available to all police officers and other interested agencies. The Superintendent of State Police and the commission shall co-operate with and assist all peace officers and other agencies in tracing or examining any questionable automobiles to determine the ownership thereof.

L.1938, c. 352, p. 880, § 3.   Amended by L.2003, c. 13, § 47 (contingent effective date).

Historical and Statutory Notes

L.2003, c. 13, § 127, approved Jan. 28, 2003, provides:

"Sections 1, 2, 3, 12, 38, 109, 110 and 121 shall take effect immediately, sections 105, 106, 107, 108, and 120 shall take effect on July 1, 2003 and the remainder of this act shall take effect on the date the Commissioner of Transportation certifies to the Governor (hereinafter the "date of certification") that a majority of the members of the commission have been appointed or are in office and that all necessary anticipatory actions have been accomplished, provided, that the amount of revenues received pursuant to sections 109 and 110 prior to the date of certification are hereby appropriated to the division. Upon the date of certification, all such collected revenue shall be revenue of the commission. The Commissioner of Transportation, the Director of the Division of Motor Vehicles and the commission may take such anticipatory administrative action in advance as shall be necessary for the implementation of the act."

39:3–85.4. Partial invalidity

Should any section or provision of this act be held to be invalid by any court of competent jurisdiction, same shall not affect the validity of the act as a whole or any part thereof other than the portion so held to be invalid.

L.1938, c. 352, p. 881, § 4.

39:3–85.5. Program to combat theft of motor vehicles; establishment; consent agreement; decal

The Superintendent of the Division of State Police shall establish a program, as hereinafter provided, to combat the theft of motor vehicles in this State. Participation in the program shall be voluntary in nature and shall involve the following:

a. The registered owner of a motor vehicle shall, in the presence of the chief law enforcement officer of the municipality, or his designee, sign an informed consent agreement, designed by the superintendent pursuant to the provisions of section 3 of this act, indicating that the motor vehicle registered to him is not normally operated between the hours of 1:00 a.m. and 5:00 a.m.

b. Upon signing the informed consent agreement, the registered owner shall be issued a decal, designed by the superintendent and provided by the local police department and force. The registered owner shall affix the decal, in a conspicuous place prescribed by the superintendent, to his motor vehicle.

L.1990, c. 98, § 1, eff. Jan. 28, 1991.

39:3–85.6. Authority of law enforcement officer to stop vehicle displaying decal

Whenever any law enforcement officer shall see a motor vehicle displaying a decal issued pursuant to the provisions of section 1 of this act being operated upon the public highways of this State between the hours of 1:00 a.m. and 5:00 a.m., the officer is hereby authorized to stop that motor vehicle and to request the driver thereof to produce a valid driver's license, motor vehicle registration card, and insurance identification card.

Whenever the operator of a motor vehicle displaying such a decal is unable to produce the documentation set forth in this section, the police officer shall investigate further to determine if the person operating the motor vehicle is the registered owner or has the authorization of the owner to operate the vehicle.

L.1990, c. 98, § 2, eff. Jan. 28, 1991.

39:3–85.7. Form of consent agreement

The superintendent shall design the manner and form of the informed consent agreement required under the provisions of section 1 of this act. The chief law enforcement officer of any municipality shall make copies of the document available upon request.

L.1990, c. 98, § 3, eff. Jan. 28, 1991.

39:3–85.8. Recording of participants in program

The superintendent shall provide for the recording of the registered owners of motor vehicles who participate in this program. The records shall be available to all law enforcement departments, agencies and forces. The superintendent shall cooperate with and assist all law enforcement officers and other agencies in tracing or examining any questionable motor vehicles in order to determine the ownership thereof.

L.1990, c. 98, § 4, eff. Jan. 28, 1991.

39:3–85.9. Fees for consent forms and decals

The chief law enforcement officer of the municipality may charge a fee for the informed consent forms and the decals provided under this act. The fee charged shall not exceed the actual costs incurred by the municipality in providing the informed consent forms and decals and in administering the program authorized under this act.

L.1990, c. 98, § 5, eff. Jan. 28, 1991.

39:3–85.10. Rules and regulations

The Superintendent of the Division of State Police shall promulgate pursuant to the provisions of the "Administrative Procedure Act," P.L.1968, c. 410 (C. 52:14B–1 et seq.), rules and regulations to effectuate the purposes of this act.

L.1990, c. 98, § 6, eff. Jan. 28, 1991.

ARTICLE 7. GENERAL PENALTIES

39:3–86. Penalty where no specific penalty provided

For a violation of a provision of chapter three of Title 39 of the Revised Statutes for which no specific penalty is provided, the offender shall be liable to a penalty of not less than $25 or more than $500 or imprisonment for a term of not exceeding fifteen days or both.

L.1941, c. 343, p. 901, § 1. Amended by L.1999, c. 28, § 12, eff. Jan. 1, 2000.

Historical and Statutory Notes

L.2001, c. 391, § 17, approved Jan. 8, 2002, provides:

"Notwithstanding the provisions of P.L.1999, c. 28 (C.39:3–10f1 et al.) to the contrary, the Director of the Division of Motor Vehicles may delay the implementation of the provisions of that act, other than those set forth in section 14 thereof, until the 60th day after the director certifies to the Commissioner of Transportation that the division is prepared to issue drivers' licenses with digitized pictures of licensees, but such implementing date shall be not later than January 1, 2003. The director shall make every effort to provide the certification required for P. L.1999, c. 28 to be implemented as soon as practicable."

ARTICLE 8. APPROPRIATIONS

39:3–87. Expenditure of receipts, apportionment

The receipts for licenses covering a 3-year period shall not be expended during any 1 year, but shall be apportioned for the purpose of expenditure upon an annual basis throughout the entire period so covered.
L.1955, c. 8, p. 49, § 13.

CHAPTER 3A

ADDITIONAL EQUIPMENT REGULATIONS

Section
39:3A–1.   Television set with screen visible to driver of vehicle prohibited.
39:3A–2.   Punishment for violations.

39:3A–1. Television set with screen visible to driver of vehicle prohibited

It shall be unlawful to operate upon any public highway in this State a motor vehicle which is equipped with or in which is located a television set so placed that the viewing screen thereof is visible to the driver while operating such vehicle.

L.1951, c. 134, p. 569, § 1.

39:3A–2. Punishment for violations

A person violating the provisions of this act shall, for each violation, be subject to a fine of not more than fifty dollars ($50.00), or imprisonment for a period not exceeding ten days or both.

L.1951, c. 134, p. 569, § 2.

CHAPTER 3B

SCHOOL BUSES, EQUIPMENT AND REGULATIONS

Section
39:3B–1.   Electric identification and warning lamps.
39:3B–1.1.   Installation of crossing control arms on school buses.
39:3B–1.2.   School districts to be reimbursed for installation costs; amount of reimbursements.
39:3B–1.3.   List of vehicles used to transport students to be submitted to commissioner; application for reimbursement.
39:3B–1.4.   Repealed.
39:3B–2.   Signs or legends displayed on bus.
39:3B–3.   Information on back of certificates of approval.
39:3B–4.   Convex mirror or other device for observing road condition in front of bus.
39:3B–5.   Rules and regulations.
39:3B–5.1.   Duration of use of school buses.
39:3B–5.2.   Duration of use of school buses with gross vehicle weight over 25,000 pounds.
39:3B–5.3.   Inspection of school buses.
39:3B–5.4.   Retired school buses; use to transport children or senior citizens to certain programs and events; safety regulations.

Section
39:3B–6.   Violations.
39:3B–7.   Repeal.
39:3B–8.   Van type II school vehicle.
39:3B–9.   Identification lettering, color and warning lights.
39:3B–10.   Seats, seat belts and child restraint systems; regulations.
39:3B–11.   Use of seat belts or child restraint systems during operation of bus; liability of owner or operator.
39:3B–12.   Emergency exits on type I school bus.
39:3B–13.   Definitions relating to liquified petroleum gas.
39:3B–14.   Liquified petroleum gas; alternative fuel for school buses.
39:3B–15.   School bus conversion or modification; use of liquified petroleum gas.
39:3B–16.   Limited immunity from civil liability for use of liquified petroleum gas.
39:3B–17.   Adoption of rules and regulations; use of liquified petroleum gas in school buses.
39:3B–18.   Short title.
39:3B–19.   Legislative findings.
39:3B–20.   Definitions.
39:3B–21.   Inspection program; elements.
39:3B–21.   Inspection program; elements.
39:3B–22.   Violations; enforcement of penalties.
39:3B–23.   Removal from service.
39:3B–24.   Rules and regulations.
39:3B–25.   Wireless telephones.

39:3B–1.   Electric identification and warning lamps

Every bus when being used to transport children to and from school pursuant to sections 18:14–8 to 18:14–12,[1] inclusive, of the Revised Statutes shall be equipped with electric identification and warning lamps which, when such bus has stopped for the purpose of receiving or discharging any school child, will exhibit a flashing red light plainly visible at such a distance as will enable the driver of a vehicle approaching or overtaking the bus to see the red light in sufficient time to bring the same to a stop within 10 feet of the bus. Such lamps shall meet the requirements prescribed by the State Board of Education,[2] which requirements shall not be inconsistent with the provisions of this Title or any rule or regulation made pursuant thereto.

Nothing contained herein shall be construed to apply to any motorbus when carrying passengers for hire over any street or road and accepting and discharging indiscriminately such persons as may offer themselves for transportation either at the termini or points along the route on which it is being operated.

L.1965, c. 119, § 1.

[1] Repealed. See, now, §§ 18A:39–1 to 18A:39–21.
[2] Continuation and transfer of powers, functions and duties relating to construction, design, equipment and maintenance of school buses to the Division of Motor Vehicles in the Department of Transportation; see Reorganization Plan No. 005–1998, set out below.

39:3B–1.1.   Installation of crossing control arms on school buses

Every school bus as defined under R.S.39:1–1, which was originally designed to carry 10 or more passengers and which is in operation on August 6, 1996, transporting public and nonpublic school pupils and every new or used such school bus purchased on or after that date to transport public and nonpublic school pupils shall be equipped with a crossing control arm at the right front corner of the bus. In each year subsequent to August 6, 1996, 50 percent of all school bus fleets in operation on that date owned by any agency, a board of education, a nonpublic school or a school bus contractor not already equipped with a crossing control arm shall be so equipped, provided that each vehicle used to transport elementary school students shall be given priority to be equipped with a crossing control arm in the first year following August 6, 1996. The arm shall open and extend out from the front of the bus at least 5 ½ feet each time the bus door is opened.

L.1996, c. 96, § 1, eff. Aug. 6, 1996. Amended by L.1998, c. 80, § 1, eff. Aug. 14, 1998.

39:3B–1.2.   School districts to be reimbursed for installation costs; amount of reimbursements

Each agency, school district and nonpublic school that owns and operates its own school buses and each school bus contractor that operates school buses, as defined in section 1 of P.L.1996, c. 96 (C.39:3B–1.1), shall receive reimbursement from the Department of Education in an amount up to, but not to exceed, $300 per bus for retrofitting those school buses in operation on August 6, 1996, and an amount up to, but not to exceed, $200 per bus for buses put into operation after that date for the cost of including the crossing control arm on those buses. If any agency, school district, nonpublic school or school bus contractor chooses to equip more than 50 percent of its school buses in any one year, it shall receive a maximum reimbursement for 50 percent of its school buses for that year. Reimbursement for retrofitting more than 50 percent of its school buses will be paid in the subsequent year based on a schedule to be determined by the commissioner, not to exceed two years.

L.1996, c. 96, § 2, eff. Aug. 6, 1996. Amended by L.1998, c. 80, § 2, eff. Aug. 14, 1998.

39:3B–1.3.   List of vehicles used to transport students to be submitted to commissioner; application for reimbursement

No later than 60 days after the effective date of P.L.1998, c. 80 (C.39:3B–1.1 et seq.), each agency, board of education, nonpublic school and school bus contractor shall submit to the Commissioner of Education a list of all vehicles, as defined in section 1 of P.L.1996, c. 96 (C.39:3B–1.1), that are used to transport students on August 6, 1996, including: the vehicle serial number; the year, make and license plate number as noted on the vehicle registration; and an indication as to whether the vehicle is currently equipped with a crossing control arm.

The owners of such vehicles may apply for reimbursement through the Department of Education in accordance with section 2 of P.L.1996, c. 96 (C.39:3B–1.2) on an application form as the Commissioner of Education shall prescribe. The application shall be accompanied by a receipt for the purchase of the crossing control arm through an authorized dealer.

L.1996, c. 96, § 3, eff. Aug. 6, 1996. Amended by L.1998, c. 80, § 3, eff. Aug. 14, 1998.

39:3B–1.4. Repealed by Laws 1998, c. 80, § 4, eff. Aug. 14, 1998

39:3B–2. Signs or legends displayed on bus

There shall be displayed on every bus subject to the provisions of section 1 of this act [1] signs or legends which will, insofar as practicable, inform the driver of any vehicle concerning the duty imposed upon him by law with respect to passing such bus, while it is loading or unloading. Such signs or legends shall be in such color, form and design as will meet the requirements prescribed by the State Board of Education,[2] which requirements shall not be inconsistent with the provisions of this Title or any rule or regulation made pursuant thereto.

L.1965, c. 119, § 2.

[1] N.J.S.A. § 39:3B–1.

[2] Continuation and transfer of powers, functions and duties relating to construction, design, equipment and maintenance of school buses to the Division of Motor Vehicles in the Department of Transportation; see Reorganization Plan No. 005–1998.

39:3B–3. Information on back of certificates of approval

The Director of the Division of Motor Vehicles shall, at such times as in his discretion he shall determine, cause to be displayed upon the back of each certificate of approval designed for pasting upon the windshield of any motor vehicle, pursuant to chapter 8 of this Title, such information, as he may deem practicable and advisable, concerning the duty imposed by law upon the driver of any vehicle with respect to passing any bus referred to in section 1 of this act while it is loading or unloading.

L.1965, c. 119, § 3.

39:3B–4. Convex mirror or other device for observing road condition in front of bus

Every bus subject to the provisions of section 1 of this act shall be equipped with a mirror of the convex type, or such other comparable device as the State Board of Education [1] may authorize or prescribe, which is affixed to the bus in such a manner that the seated driver may observe or otherwise ascertain through its use the condition of the road from the front bumper forward to the point where direct observation is possible. Such mirror or other comparable device, and its location on the bus, shall meet the requirements specified by the State Board of Education, which requirements shall not

be inconsistent with the provisions of this Title or any rule or regulation made pursuant thereto.

L.1965, c. 119, § 4.

[1] Continuation and transfer of powers, functions and duties relating to construction, design, equipment and maintenance of school buses to the Division of Motor Vehicles in the Department of Transportation; see Reorganization Plan No. 005–1998.

39:3B–5. Rules and regulations

The State Board of Education [1] is hereby authorized to make rules and regulations not inconsistent with the provisions of this Title or any rule or regulation made pursuant thereto, concerning the construction, design, equipment, maintenance, operation and inspection of any bus subject to the provisions of section 1 of this act.[2] Such rules and regulations shall be filed with the Director of the Division of Motor Vehicles and, upon such filing, shall be enforced by the director in the same manner as all other rules and regulations made pursuant to this Title.

Nothing contained in this section shall be deemed to limit the existing authority of the State Board of Education to make rules and regulations governing the transportation of school pupils, pursuant to Title 18 of the Revised Statutes.

L.1965, c. 119, § 6.

[1] Continuation and transfer of powers, functions and duties relating to construction, design, equipment and maintenance of school buses to the Division of Motor Vehicles in the Department of Transportation; see Reorganization Plan No. 005–1998.

[2] N.J.S.A. § 39:3B–1.

39:3B–5.1. Duration of use of school buses

School buses, under the jurisdiction of the public schools and manufactured prior to April 1, 1977, other than those of the transit type whose gross vehicle weight (G.V.W.) exceeds 25,000 pounds, shall not be used for pupil transportation purposes beyond the end of the tenth year from the date of manufacture, as noted on the vehicle registration, or at the end of the school year in which that date falls, whichever is later. School buses manufactured on or after April 1, 1977, other than those of the transit type whose gross vehicle weight (G.V.W.) exceeds 25,000 pounds, shall not be used for pupil transportation purposes beyond the end of the twelfth year from the date of manufacture, as noted on the vehicle registration, or at the end of the school year in which that date falls, whichever is later.

L.1983, c. 206, § 1, eff. July 1, 1983.

39:3B–5.2. Duration of use of school buses with gross vehicle weight over 25,000 pounds

School buses of the transit type whose gross vehicle weight (G.V.W.) exceeds 25,000 pounds shall not be used for pupil transportation purposes beyond the end of the twentieth year from the date of manufacture, as noted on the vehicle registration, or at the end of the school year in which that date falls, whichever is later.

L.1983, c. 206, § 2, eff. July 1, 1983.

39:3B-5.3. Inspection of school buses

School buses manufactured on or after April 1, 1977, when used beyond the tenth year, other than the transit type whose gross vehicle weight (G.V.W.) exceeds 25,000 pounds, shall have an annual in-depth inspection by the Division of Motor Vehicles prior to the beginning of the school year.

L.1983, c. 206, § 3, eff. July 1, 1983.

39:3B-5.4. Retired school buses; use to transport children or senior citizens to certain programs and events; safety regulations

A motor vehicle retired from use as a school bus as defined in R.S. 39:1-1 which is used to transport children or senior citizens to entertainment programs, recreational areas, sporting events, or camping activities shall not be used for those purposes unless the motor vehicle has met the safety regulations for school buses dealing with mechanical condition and body integrity adopted in accordance with the "Administrative Procedure Act," P.L.1968, c. 410 (C. 52:14B-1 et seq.) by the Department of Education,[1] with the exception of school bus chrome yellow color and amber and red warning lamp system regulations. No motor vehicle retired from use as a school bus shall be required to meet the safety regulations for school buses adopted by the Department of Education other than those in effect for the class of vehicle of which the bus was a member on the date upon which the vehicle was last inspected prior to its retirement as a school bus.

L.1986, c. 92, § 1, eff. Aug. 27, 1986.

[1] Continuation and transfer of powers, functions and duties relating to construction, design, equipment and maintenance of school buses to the Division of Motor Vehicles in the Department of Transportation; see Reorganization Plan No. 005-1998.

39:3B-6. Violations

Any person who willfully violates any provision of this act, or any rule or regulation promulgated pursuant thereto, shall be subject to a fine of not more than $50.00 or imprisonment for a term not exceeding 30 days, or both.

L.1965, c. 119, § 7.

39:3B-7. Repeal

"An act concerning public school buses, and supplementing chapter 14 of Title 18 of the Revised Statutes," approved June 12, 1948 (P.L.1948, c. 133),[1] is hereby repealed.

L.1965, c. 119, § 8.

[1] N.J.S.A. §§ 18:14-12.1 to 18:14-12.4.

39:3B-8. Van type II school vehicle

As used herein "van type II school vehicle" is a vehicle transporting pupils, under the jurisdiction of a local board of education, manufactured after April 1, 1977, and having a pupil capacity of not less than 10 nor more than 16.

L.1980, c. 148, § 1, eff. Nov. 22, 1980.

39:3B-9. Identification lettering, color and warning lights

In addition to owner identification, lettering shall be permitted on van type II school vehicles to identify the vehicles as school vehicles and all such vehicles shall be painted school bus yellow and equipped with warning lights.

With respect to any such vehicle transporting handicapped pupils, the national symbol for the handicapped may also be imprinted on the lower right side of the rear door.

L.1980, c. 148, § 2, eff. Nov. 22, 1980.

39:3B-10. Seats, seat belts and child restraint systems; regulations

In addition to the requirements in Federal Motor Vehicle Safety Standard No. 222 (49 CFR § 571.222) concerning school bus passenger seating and crash protection, each school bus as defined in R.S. 39:1-1 shall be equipped with seats of a minimum seat back height of 28 inches, or 24 inches as measured from the seating reference point, and seat belts of the lap belt type for each seating position on the bus or other child restraint systems that are in conformity with applicable federal standards. The design and installation of seat belts or other child restraint systems that are in conformity with applicable federal standards shall conform to the regulations promulgated by the State Board of Education,[1] in consultation with the Director of the Division of Motor Vehicles in the Department of Law and Public Safety. The State board shall promulgate regulations, pursuant to the "Administrative Procedure Act," P.L.1968, c. 410 (C.52:14B-1 et seq.), for the design and installation of seat belts or other child restraint systems that are in conformity with applicable federal standards.

As used in this section, "seating reference point" shall be defined as the term is defined in 49 CFR § 571.3.

L.1992, c. 92, § 1.

[1] Continuation and transfer of powers, functions and duties relating to construction, design, equipment and maintenance of school buses to the Division of Motor Vehicles in the Department of Transportation; see Reorganization Plan No. 005-1998.

39:3B-11. Use of seat belts or child restraint systems during operation of bus; liability of owner or operator

Beginning on September 1 of the second year next following the year of enactment of P.L.1992, c. 92 (C. 39:3B-10 et al.), each passenger on a school bus which is equipped with seat belts shall wear a properly adjusted and fastened seat belt or other child restraint system that is in conformity with applicable federal standards at all times while the bus is in operation. Nothing in this section shall make the owner or operator of a school bus liable for failure to properly adjust and fasten a seat belt or other child restraint system that is in conformity with applicable federal standards for a passenger who sustains injury as a direct result of the passenger's failure to comply with the requirement established by this section.

L.1992, c. 92, § 2, eff. Sept. 8, 1992.

39:3B–12. Emergency exits on type I school bus

A type I school bus when used to transport children to and from school, or to and from school-related activities, shall be equipped with emergency exits to conform with emergency evacuation standards to be prescribed by rule or regulation of the State Board of Education.[1] The emergency exits shall at a minimum consist of a rear emergency door and two roof hatches.

L.1992, c. 93, § 1.

[1] Continuation and transfer of powers, functions and duties relating to construction, design, equipment and maintenance of school buses to the Division of Motor Vehicles in the Department of Transportation; see Reorganization Plan No. 005–1998.

39:3B–13. Definitions relating to liquified petroleum gas

As used in this act:

"Conventional fuel" means gasoline or diesel fuel;

"Governmental entity" means the State, any agency, authority, or employee thereof, or any political subdivision of the State, including but not limited to any county, municipality, or school district, or any agency, authority, or employee thereof;

"Liquefied petroleum gas" means LPG, butane, butylene, propane, or propylene, or other related or similar compounds commonly regarded to be liquefied petroleum gases as prescribed by rule or regulation adopted by the Department of Environmental Protection pursuant to the "Administrative Procedure Act," P.L.1968, c. 410 (C.52:14B–1 et seq.); and

"School bus" means a school bus as defined pursuant to R.S.39:1–1.

L.1997, c. 367, § 1, eff. Jan. 19, 1998.

39:3B–14. Liquified petroleum gas; alternative fuel for school buses

a. Liquefied petroleum gas may be used as an alternative fuel for a school bus instead of, in addition to, or in combination with a conventional fuel.

b. A school bus may be equipped or converted to operate with liquefied petroleum gas as the sole fuel or in addition to or in combination with a conventional fuel.

L.1997, c. 367, § 2, eff. Jan. 19, 1998.

39:3B–15. School bus conversion or modification; use of liquified petroleum gas

No school bus may be operated using liquefied petroleum gas as the sole fuel, or in addition to or in combination with a conventional fuel, unless the school bus has been equipped or converted for such use and is operated in accordance with (1) all applicable federal and State laws, rules, regulations, codes, standards, and guidelines pertaining thereto, including but not limited to any such rules, regulations, codes, standards, and guidelines that may be adopted by the National Highway Traffic Safety Administration, and (2) all applicable codes, standards, and guidelines established by the National Fire Protection Association for the storage, handling, and use of liquefied petroleum gas.

L.1997, c. 367, § 3, eff. Jan. 19, 1998.

39:3B–16. Limited immunity from civil liability for use of liquified petroleum gas

a. In any action brought for any injury or damages caused either directly or indirectly by the use of liquefied petroleum gas as the sole fuel, or in addition to or in combination with a conventional fuel, to operate a school bus, or the equipping or converting of a school bus to operate using liquefied petroleum gas as the sole fuel or in addition to or in combination with a conventional fuel, neither the owner or operator of the school bus nor any governmental entity may be found negligent in connection therewith if the school bus was equipped or converted, and operated, as required by section 3 of this act.

b. The immunity provided by subsection a. of this section: (1) shall be in addition to any other immunity that may apply under the "New Jersey Tort Claims Act," N.J.S.59:1–1 et seq., or any other law, rule, or regulation; and (2) shall not apply if it is established that the act or omission causing the injury or damages constitutes gross negligence, recklessness, actual fraud, actual malice, willful misconduct, or criminal conduct.

L.1997, c. 367, § 4, eff. Jan. 19, 1998.

39:3B–17. Adoption of rules and regulations; use of liquified petroleum gas in school buses

The Department of Environmental Protection, in consultation with the Department of Transportation, the Division of Motor Vehicles in the Department of Transportation, and the Department of Education, may adopt, pursuant to the "Administrative Procedure Act," P.L.1968, c. 410 (C.52:14B–1 et seq.), any rules or regulations necessary to implement this act.

L.1997, c. 367, § 5, eff. Jan. 19, 1998.

39:3B–18. Short title

This act shall be known and may be cited as the "School Bus Enhanced Safety Inspection Act."

L.1999, c. 5, § 1, eff. Jan. 1, 1999.

39:3B–19. Legislative findings

The Legislature finds and declares that school bus safety is of paramount importance to the health and welfare of the school children of this State. The Legislature further finds that school buses are cited for safety violations during scheduled and random inspections at an unacceptably high level and that recent random school bus inspections conducted by the Division of State Police and the Division of Motor Vehicles found a high percentage of school buses operating with significant violations that warranted the removal of these vehicles from service.

The Legislature concurs with the findings of the Governor's School Bus Safety Task Force that it is appropriate and necessary to revise the existing system of in-lane inspections to a system of in-terminal inspections conducted by motor vehicle inspectors at the facility of the school bus operator. Such a system would provide insight into the carrier's overall operation and commitment to maintenance; allow interaction with the carrier's mechanics and operational personnel to facilitate the immediate repair of vehicles; provide a mechanism for the audit of a carrier's maintenance records, including daily defect slips, vehicle history records, and driver history and credential records; and, insure the timely inspection of all school buses.

L.1999, c. 5, § 2, eff. Jan. 1, 1999.

39:3B–20. Definitions

As used in this act:

"Director" means the Director of the Division of Motor Vehicles in the Department of Transportation;

"Division" means the Division of Motor Vehicles in the Department of Transportation;

"In-terminal inspection" means an inspection conducted by the Division of Motor Vehicles at the operator's terminal of any motor vehicle required to meet the safety regulations for school buses adopted by the Department of Transportation pursuant to R.S.39:3B–5 and P.L.1986, c. 92 (C.18A:3B–5.4) and vehicle emissions standards established for engine type pursuant to R.S.39:8–2 and section 3 of P.L.1995, c. 157 (C.39:8–61);

"Operator" means the owner or person responsible for the day to day operation and maintenance of school buses;

"School bus" means all Type I and Type II school buses as defined in R.S.39:1–1 and school buses retired pursuant to P.L.1986, c. 99:3B2 (C.39:3B–5.4), under the jurisdiction of the division.

L.1999, c. 5, § 3, eff. Jan. 1, 1999.

39:3B–21. Inspection program; elements

Text of section effective until May 18, 2010.

a. The director shall establish a school bus enhanced safety inspection program which shall include, but not be limited to, the following elements:

(1) an in-terminal school bus inspection program which provides for the semi-annual or annual inspection of school buses by division inspection teams;

(2) standards and requirements pertaining to the equipment, maintenance, and repair of school buses subject to inspection pursuant to this act; all in-terminal inspections, including those involving diesel vehicles, shall include an emission inspection to determine whether that vehicle meets the State's emission specifications and standards;

(3) standards and requirements pertaining to the establishment and maintenance of school bus maintenance, repair, and inspection records for all school buses in the operator's fleet; and

(4) standards and requirements pertaining to the establishment and maintenance of driver employment records, including records which demonstrate a driver's compliance with all statutory and regulatory requirements for authorization to operate a school bus, and any other records and credentials deemed necessary by the director for school bus drivers employed by the operator. The records shall be made available to division inspectors during each in-terminal inspection.

b. If an operator does not have adequate terminal facilities to allow for a proper and thorough in-terminal inspection, the director shall designate an in-lieu-of terminal site and direct the operator to present his buses and records to that site for inspection on such terms and conditions as determined by the director.

c. The time and location of any inspection or reinspection conducted pursuant to this section shall be determined by the director. Unless an owner agrees to a different time schedule, the director shall schedule a reinspection within three days of the date of the inspection that necessitated the reinspection.

L.1999, c. 5, § 4, eff. Jan. 1, 1999.

39:3B–21. Inspection program; elements

Text of section effective on May 18, 2010.

a. The chief administrator shall establish a school bus enhanced safety inspection program which shall include, but not be limited to, the following elements:

(1) an in-terminal school bus inspection program which provides for the semi-annual or annual inspection of school buses by commission inspectors;

(2) standards and requirements pertaining to the equipment, maintenance, and repair of school buses subject to inspection pursuant to this act; all in-terminal inspections, including those involving diesel vehicles, shall include an emission inspection to determine whether that vehicle meets the State's emission specifications and standards;

(3) standards and requirements pertaining to the establishment and maintenance of school bus maintenance, repair, and inspection records for all school buses in the operator's fleet; and

(4) standards and requirements pertaining to the establishment and maintenance of driver employment records, including records which demonstrate a driver's

compliance with all statutory and regulatory requirements for authorization to operate a school bus, and any other records and credentials deemed necessary by the chief administrator for school bus drivers employed by the operator. The records shall be made available to commission inspectors during each in-terminal inspection.

b. If an operator does not have adequate terminal facilities to allow for a proper and thorough in-terminal inspection, the chief administrator shall designate an in-lieu-of terminal site and direct the operator to present his buses and records to that site for inspection on such terms and conditions as determined by the chief administrator.

c. The time and location of any inspection or reinspection conducted pursuant to this section shall be determined by the chief administrator. Unless an owner agrees to a different time schedule, the chief administrator shall schedule a reinspection within three days of the date of the inspection that necessitated the reinspection.

L.1999, c. 5, § 4, eff. Jan. 1, 1999. Amended by L.2009, c. 331, § 3, eff. May 18, 2010.

39:3B–22. Violations; enforcement of penalties

a. Any operator who violates the standards for driver employment records established pursuant to subsection a. of section 4 of this act, or who fails to retain proper records for inspection as required, or who fails to make available any record or document required at the time of inspection, or who falsifies any record, or who fails to present or otherwise make available any school bus or buses due for inspection, as requested by an examiner, unless notification of the intent to withhold a bus or buses from an examiner is made in writing at least 24 hours prior to the scheduled inspection, shall be fined not less than $50 and not more than $500 per violation, in accordance with a schedule of fines to be established by the director. The director shall waive the requirement of notice upon a showing of good cause by an operator. A bus withheld from an examiner pursuant to this section shall be inspected within 30 days of the date of the originally scheduled inspection, unless otherwise agreed by the operator and the director. The operator shall be responsible for all fines.

Nothing in this subsection shall be deemed to preclude any other enforcement actions provided by law.

b. Any fine imposed pursuant to the provisions of this section may be collected, with costs, in a summary proceeding pursuant to "the penalty enforcement law," N.J.S.2A:58–1 et seq. The Superior Court or municipal court of the county or municipality in which the violation occurs or in which the operator resides or has a place of business or principal office in this State, shall have jurisdiction to enforce the provisions of "the penalty enforcement law" in connection with any violation of this act.

The director or any duly authorized representative of the director may issue a summons and complaint returnable in any court of competent jurisdiction for a violation of this act or any rule or regulation adopted pursuant to this act. A municipal, county, or State prosecutor is authorized to assist the director in the enforcement of this act. The director may institute an action in the Superior Court for injunctive relief to prevent or restrain any violation of this act, or any rule or regulation adopted, or any administrative or judicial order issued, pursuant to this act.

c. Any officer charged with the enforcement of State and municipal laws is authorized to assist the director or any duly authorized representative of the director in the enforcement of the provisions of this act, or any rule or regulation adopted, or any administrative or judicial order issued, pursuant to this act.

L.1999, c. 5, § 5, eff. Jan. 1, 1999.

39:3B–23. Removal from service

Any school bus that fails an inspection based on out-of-service criteria as established by the director shall be immediately removed from service.

L.1999, c. 5, § 6, eff. Jan. 1, 1999.

39:3B–24. Rules and regulations

The director shall adopt, pursuant to the "Administrative Procedure Act," P.L.1968, c. 410 (C.52:14B–1 et seq.), rules and regulations to implement the provisions of this act, including the schedule of fines required pursuant to section 5 of this act and the out of service criteria required pursuant to section 6 of this act.

L.1999, c. 5, § 7, eff. Jan. 1, 1999.

39:3B–25. Wireless telephones

a. It shall be unlawful for the driver of a school bus, as defined in R.S.39:1–1, to use a cellular or other wireless telephone while operating the school bus.

b. The prohibition contained in subsection a. of this section shall not apply:

(1) when the school bus is parked in a safe area off of a highway; or

(2) in an emergency situation.

c. A person who violates this section shall be fined not less than $250 or more than $500.

d. No motor vehicle points or automobile insurance eligibility points pursuant to section 26 of P.L.1990, c. 8 (C.17:33B–14) shall be assessed for this offense.

L.2002, c. 120, § 1, eff. Dec. 12, 2002.

CHAPTER 3C

SNOWMOBILES, ALL-TERRAIN VEHICLES AND DIRT BIKES

Section
39:3C–1.   Definitions.

Section
39:3C–1. Definitions.
39:3C–2. Director and commissioner; powers, duties and authority.
39:3C–2. Chief administrator and commissioner; powers, duties and authority.
39:3C–3. Registration; necessity; fee; expiration.
39:3C–3. Registration; necessity; fee; expiration.
39:3C–3.1. Off-Road Vehicle Recreational Fund; establishment; deposit of revenue and allocation of funds.
39:3C–4. Duration of registration number.
39:3C–4. Duration of registration number.
39:3C–5. Registration; issuance; inspection of certificate; display of number; transfer of ownership.
39:3C–5. Time to register with the Commissioner; verification upon resale; change of ownership.
39:3C–6. Exemptions; operation on private property; payment of fee by governments.
39:3C–6. Exemption; operation for use on a farm; payment of fee by government.
39:3C–7. Exemptions; nonresidents.
39:3C–7. Exemptions; nonresidents.
39:3C–8. Display of registration number.
39:3C–8. Display of assigned number.
39:3C–9. Production of registration certificate for inspection; persons under 18 to produce certificate of completion of safety course.
39:3C–9. Production of registration certificate for inspection; persons under 18 to produce certificate of completion of safety course.
39:3C–10. Notice of change of address.
39:3C–10. Notice of change of address.
39:3C–11. Transfer of ownership or discontinuance of use.
39:3C–11. Transfer of ownership; application and proof of ownership.
39:3C–12. Destruction, theft or removal from state; notice to division.
39:3C–12. Destruction, theft or removal from state; notice to commission.
39:3C–13. Licensing or registration by political subdivision; prohibition.
39:3C–13. Licensing or registration by political subdivision; prohibition.
39:3C–14. Rules and regulations; scope of commissioner action with respect to use of vehicles; designated locations for safety education and training programs.
39:3C–15. Rules and regulations of director; establishment of all-terrain vehicle safety education and training program.
39:3C–15. Rules and regulations; scope and content of safety education and training program; permits for special events.
39:3C–16. Minimum age to be operator.
39:3C–16. Minimum age to be operator.
39:3C–17. Prohibition of operation on highways, streets and right-of-way limits; exceptions.
39:3C–17. Prohibition of operation on highways, streets and right-of-way limits; exceptions.
39:3C–18. Prohibition of operation on private property without consent.
39:3C–18. Prohibition of operation on private property without consent.
39:3C–19. Unlawful acts.
39:3C–19. Unlawful acts.
39:3C–20. Liability insurance.
39:3C–20. Liability insurance.
39:3C–21. Report of accidents.
39:3C–21. Report of accidents.
39:3C–22. Special events.
39:3C–22. Special events.
39:3C–23. Special events; exemption from registration and light requirements.
39:3C–23. Special events; exemption from registration and light requirements.
39:3C–24. Equipment.
39:3C–24. Equipment.
39:3C–25. Inspection and testing.
39:3C–25. Inspection and testing.
39:3C–26. Sale of vehicle not in compliance with provisions of law; prohibition.
39:3C–26. Sale of vehicle not in compliance with provisions of law; prohibition.
39:3C–27. Law enforcement officers; duties.
39:3C–27. Law enforcement officers; duties.
39:3C–28. Violations; penalty.
39:3C–28. Violations; penalty.
39:3C–29. Deposit of moneys to credit of general treasury; allocation to defray cost of all-terrain vehicle education and training manuals or programs.
39:3C–29. Deposit of moneys into fund.
39:3C–30. Other laws applicable to operation on public highways and lands; violations; penalties.
39:3C–30. Other laws applicable to operation on public highways, lands or waters.
39:3C–30.1. All-terrain vehicles; operation and use on golf courses; operation on public lands, waters or highways as incident to adjacent farm operations.
39:3C–31. Severability.
39:3C–32. Definitions.
39:3C–33. Penalties for operating any vehicle or off-road vehicle on public lands contrary to law.
39:3C–34. Additional penalties; impoundment; disposition of impounded vehicles; use of proceeds.

39:3C–1. Definitions

Text of section effective until the third month after the date the commissioner has designated the first of the three sites pursuant to paragraph (1) of subsection a. of section 38 of P.L.2009, c. 275 (C.13:1L–5.1).

As used in this act:

a. "Commissioner" means the Commissioner of the Department of Environmental Protection.

b. "Director" means the Director of the Division of Motor Vehicles in the Department of Law and Public Safety.

c. "Snowmobile" means any motor vehicle, designed primarily to travel over ice or snow, of a type which uses sled type runners, skis, an endless belt tread, cleats or any combination of these or other similar means of contact with the surface upon which it is operated, but does not include any farm tractor, highway or other construction equipment, or any military vehicle.

d. "Special event" means an organized race, exhibition or demonstration of limited duration which is conducted according to a prearranged schedule and in which general public interest is manifested.

e. "All-terrain vehicle" means a motor vehicle, designed to travel over any terrain, of a type possessing between three and six rubber tires and powered by a gasoline engine not exceeding 600 cubic centimeters, but shall not include golf carts.

L.1973, c. 307, § 1, eff. Dec. 14, 1973. Amended by L.1985, c. 375, § 2; L.1991, c. 496, § 7, eff. Jan. 18, 1992.

39:3C–1. Definitions

Text of section effective on the third month after the date the commissioner has designated the first of the three sites pursuant to paragraph (1) of subsection a. of section 38 of P.L.2009, c. 275 (C.13:1L–5.1).

As used in this act:[1]

"All-terrain vehicle" means a motor vehicle, designed and manufactured for off-road use only, of a type possessing between three and six rubber tires and powered by a gasoline engine not exceeding 600 cubic centimeters, but shall not include golf carts or any all-terrain vehicle operated by an employee or agent of the State of New Jersey and used while in the performance of the employee's or agent's official duties.

"Chief administrator" means the Chief Administrator of the New Jersey Motor Vehicle Commission.

"Commission" means the New Jersey Motor Vehicle Commission established by section 4 of P.L.2003, c. 13 (C.39:2A–4).

"Commissioner" means the Commissioner of Environmental Protection.

"Department" means the Department of Environmental Protection.

"Dirt bike" means any two-wheeled motorcycle that is designed and manufactured for off-road use only and that does not comply with Federal Motor Vehicle Safety Standards or United States Environmental Protection Agency on-road emissions standards.

"Natural resource" means all land, fish, shellfish, wildlife, biota, air, waters, and other such resources owned, managed, held in trust, or otherwise controlled by the State.

"Public land" means all land owned, operated, managed, maintained, or under the jurisdiction of the Department of Environmental Protection, including any and all land owned, operated, managed, maintained, or purchased jointly by the Department of Environmental Protection with any other party and any land so designated by municipal or county ordinance. Public land shall also mean any land used for conservation purposes, including, but not limited to, beaches, forests, greenways, natural areas, water resources, wildlife preserves, land used for watershed protection, or biological or ecological studies, and land exempted from taxation pursuant to section 2 of P.L.1974, c. 167 (C.54:4–3.64).

"Snowmobile" means any motor vehicle, designed primarily to travel over ice or snow, of a type which uses sled type runners, skis, an endless belt tread, cleats or any combination of these or other similar means of contact with the surface upon which it is operated, but does not include any farm tractor, highway or other construction equipment, or any military vehicle.

"Special event" means an organized race, exhibition, or demonstration of limited duration which is conducted according to a prearranged schedule and in which general public interest is manifested.

L.1973, c. 307, § 1, eff. Dec. 14, 1973. Amended by L.1985, c. 375, § 2; L.1991, c. 496, § 7, eff. Jan. 18, 1992; L.2009, c. 275, § 1, (contingent effective date).

[1] P.L.1973, c. 307 (C.39:3C–1 et seq.)

39:3C–2. Director and commissioner; powers, duties and authority

Text of section effective until the third month after the date the commissioner has designated the first of the three sites pursuant to paragraph (1) of subsection a. of section 38 of P.L.2009, c. 275 (C.13:1L–5.1).

For the purpose of carrying out the provisions of this act:

a. The director shall have the power, duty and authority to administer and enforce all statutes, rules and regulations, except as otherwise provided by statute, relating to the operation and use of snowmobiles and all-terrain vehicles on or across a public highway or on public lands or waters, including but not limited to the following:

(1) Registration, identification, numbering and classification

(2) Equipment

(3) Standards of safety

(4) Educational programs

(5) Promulgate rules and regulations to effectuate the purposes of this act.

b. The Commissioner of Environmental Protection shall have the power, duty and authority to administer and enforce all statutes, rules and regulations, except as otherwise provided by statute, relating to snowmobiles and all-terrain vehicles on the public lands and waters under the jurisdiction of the Department of Environmental Protection.

L.1973, c. 307, § 2, eff. Dec. 14, 1973. Amended by L.1985, c. 375, § 3.

39:3C–2. Chief administrator and commissioner; powers, duties and authority

Text of section effective on the third month after the date the commissioner has designated the first of the three sites pursuant to paragraph (1) of subsection a. of section 38 of P.L.2009, c. 275 (C.13:1L–5.1).

For the purpose of carrying out the provisions of P.L.1973, c. 307 (C.39:3C–1 et seq.):

a. The chief administrator shall have the power, duty, and authority to administer and enforce all statutes, rules, and regulations, except as otherwise provided by statute, relating to the operation and use of snowmobiles, all-terrain vehicles, and dirt bikes on or across a public highway or on public lands or waters, including but not limited to the following:

(1) Registration, identification, numbering, and classification;

(2) Equipment;

(3) Standards of safety;

(4) (Deleted by amendment, P.L.2009, c. 275); and

(5) Promulgation of rules and regulations to effectuate the purposes of P.L.1973, c. 307 (C.39:3C–1 et seq.).

b. The Commissioner of Environmental Protection shall have the power, duty, and authority to administer and enforce all other statutes, permits, rules, and regulations relating to snowmobiles, all-terrain vehicles, and dirt bikes on the public lands and waters under the jurisdiction of the Department of Environmental Protection such that:

(1) snowmobiles, all-terrain vehicles, and dirt bikes shall be operated only on highways and roads designated and marked for such operation, unless specifically authorized by the commissioner; and

(2) snowmobiles, all-terrain vehicles, and dirt bikes shall be operated only in areas designated and marked for such operation and only with a special use permit issued by the Department of Environmental Protection.

L.1973, c. 307, § 2, eff. Dec. 14, 1973. Amended by L.1985, c. 375, § 3; L.2009, c. 275, § 2, (contingent effective date).

39:3C–3. Registration; necessity; fee; expiration

Text of section effective until the third month after the date the commissioner has designated the first of the three sites pursuant to paragraph (1) of subsection a. of section 38 of P.L.2009, c. 275 (C.13:1L–5.1).

Except as otherwise provided, no snowmobile or all-terrain vehicle shall be operated or permitted to be operated on or across a public highway or on public lands or waters of this State unless registered by the owner thereof as provided by this act. The Director of the Division of Motor Vehicles in the Department of Law and Public Safety is authorized to register and assign a registration number to snowmobiles and all-terrain vehicles, upon application and payment of the appropriate fee in accordance with the following schedule:

a. For each individual resident snowmobile registration, $5.00, and for each individual resident all-terrain vehicle registration, $10.00, annually;

b. For each individual nonresident snowmobile registration, $7.00, and for each individual nonresident all-terrain vehicle registration, $12.00, annually;

c. For replacement of a lost, mutilated or destroyed certificate, $5;

d. For a duplicate registration, $5 at the time of issuance;

e. For an amended registration, $5.

All such registrations shall be issued on or after September 1 in any year and shall be valid through September 30 of the following year, except that the director may suspend or revoke such registration for any violations of this act or of the rules promulgated hereunder.

L.1973, c. 307, § 3, eff. Dec. 14, 1973. Amended by L.1975, c. 28, § 1, eff. March 5, 1975; L.1985, c. 375, § 4; L.1991, c. 322, § 1, eff. May 30, 1992; L.1994, c. 60, § 22, eff. July 1, 1994.

39:3C–3. Registration; necessity; fee; expiration

Text of section effective on the third month after the date the commissioner has designated the first of the three sites pursuant to paragraph (1) of subsection a. of section 38 of P.L.2009, c. 275 (C.13:1L–5.1).

Except as otherwise provided, no snowmobile, all-terrain vehicle, or dirt bike shall be operated or permitted to be operated on or across a public highway or on public lands or waters of this State unless registered and numbered by the owner thereof as provided by P.L.1973, c. 307 (C.39:3C–1 et seq.). The chief administrator is authorized to register and assign a number to snowmobiles, all-terrain vehicles, and dirt bikes upon application and payment of the appropriate fee in accordance with the following schedule:

a. For each individual resident snowmobile registration, all-terrain vehicle registration, and dirt bike registration, $50, for a period not to exceed 24 months, in accordance with the provisions of section 29 of P.L. 1973, c. 307 (C.39:3C–29).

b. For each individual nonresident snowmobile registration, all-terrain vehicle registration, and dirt bike registration, $50, for a period not to exceed 24 months, in accordance with the provisions of section 29 of P.L.1973, c. 307 (C.39:3C–29).

c. For replacement of a lost, mutilated, or destroyed certificate, $5.

d. For a duplicate registration, $5 at the time of issuance.

e. For an amended registration, $5.

f. In addition to the registration fees imposed pursuant to this section, the chief administrator shall impose and collect an additional fee of $10 to be deposited in the "Off–Road Vehicle Recreational Fund" created by section 31 of P.L.2009, c. 275 (C.39:3C–3.1).

All registrations shall be valid for a period not to exceed 24 months from the date on which the registration was issued, except that the chief administrator may suspend or revoke such registration for any violations of P.L.1973, c. 307 (C.39:3C–1 et seq.) or of the rules promulgated hereunder.

L.1973, c. 307, § 3, eff. Dec. 14, 1973. Amended by L.1975, c. 28, § 1, eff. March 5, 1975; L.1985, c. 375, § 4; L.1991, c. 322, § 1, eff. May 30, 1992; L.1994, c. 60, § 22, eff. July 1, 1994; L.2009, c. 275, § 3, (contingent effective date).

39:3C–3.1. Off-Road Vehicle Recreational Fund; establishment; deposit of revenue and allocation of funds

Section effective on the third month after the date the commissioner has designated the first of the three sites pursuant to paragraph (1) of subsection a. of section 38 of P.L.2009, c. 275 (C.13:1L–5.1).

a. There is established in the General Fund a separate, non-lapsing, dedicated account to be known as the "Off–Road Vehicle Recreational Fund," hereinafter referred to as "the fund." Notwithstanding any provision of law to the contrary, each fiscal year the State Treasurer shall credit the revenue collected pursuant to subsection f. of section 3 of P.L.1973, c. 307 (C.39:3C–3) into the fund. Each fiscal year, the State Treasurer shall allocate the monies contained in the fund to the Department of Environmental Protection. Each fiscal year, the State Treasurer shall credit all earnings received from the investment or deposit of revenue in the fund, to the fund. All revenues and earnings deposited in the fund shall be appropriated in the same fiscal year to the department.

b. The monies credited to the fund shall be used by the Department of Environmental Protection for designating and maintaining sites in the State for the use of snowmobiles, all-terrain vehicles, and dirt bikes; sites shall be designated and shall be maintained in a manner that, to the greatest possible extent, mitigates any detrimental effects on the environment and protects public safety.

L.2009, c. 275, § 31, (contingent effective date).

39:3C–4. Duration of registration number

Text of section effective until the third month after the date the commissioner has designated the first of the three sites pursuant to paragraph (1) of subsection a. of section 38 of P.L.2009, c. 275 (C.13:1L–5.1).

Once a registration number is assigned, it shall remain with the registered snowmobile or all-terrain vehicle until the snowmobile or all-terrain vehicle is destroyed, abandoned or permanently removed from the State, or until changed or terminated by the director.

L.1973, c. 307, § 4, eff. Dec. 14, 1973. Amended by L.1985, c. 375, § 5.

39:3C–4. Duration of registration number

Text of section effective on the third month after the date the commissioner has designated the first of the three sites pursuant to paragraph (1) of subsection a. of section 38 of P.L.2009, c. 275 (C.13:1L–5.1).

Once a registration number is assigned, it shall remain with the registered snowmobile, all-terrain vehicle, or dirt bike until the snowmobile, all-terrain vehicle, or dirt bike is destroyed, abandoned or permanently removed from the State, or until changed or terminated by the chief administrator.

L.1973, c. 307, § 4, eff. Dec. 14, 1973. Amended by L.1985, c. 375, § 5; L.2009, c. 275, § 4, (contingent effective date).

39:3C–5. Registration; issuance; inspection of certificate; display of number; transfer of ownership

Text of section effective until the third month after the date the commissioner has designated the first of the three sites pursuant to paragraph (1) of subsection a. of section 38 of P.L.2009, c. 275 (C.13:1L–5.1).

Such registration shall be issued by the director or by agents as designated by him when a snowmobile or all-terrain vehicle is operated across a public highway or on public lands or waters and shall be in such form as the director shall prescribe. The registration certificate shall be subject to inspection by any law enforcement officer on demand and shall be on the vehicle at all times when in operation.

The registration number assigned shall be displayed on each side of the vehicle in such form, location and manner as prescribed by the director.

Whenever ownership is transferred or the use of a snowmobile or all-terrain vehicle for which a registration certificate has already been issued is discontinued, the old registration shall be properly signed and executed by the owner, showing that the ownership has been transferred or its use discontinued, and returned to the director within 10 days of said event. If there is a change of ownership for which a registration certificate has been previously issued, the new owner shall apply for a new registration certificate and set forth the original number in the application. He shall pay the regular fee for the particular snowmobile or all-terrain vehicle involved. The owner of any registration certificate issued under this section may obtain a duplicate from the division upon application and payment of the fee prescribed.

L.1973, c. 307, § 5, eff. Dec. 14, 1973. Amended by L.1985, c. 375, § 6.

39:3C–5. Time to register with the Commissioner; verification upon resale; change of ownership

Text of section effective on the third month after the date the commissioner has designated the first of the three sites pursuant to paragraph (1) of subsection a. of section 38 of P.L.2009, c. 275 (C.13:1L–5.1).

The owner of a snowmobile, all-terrain vehicle, or dirt bike required to be registered and numbered in this State shall do so with the commission no later than six months after the effective date of P.L.2009, c. 275 (C.39:3C–3.1 et al.).

Every person in the business of selling a snowmobile, all-terrain vehicle, or dirt bike shall require proof that the vehicle is properly registered with the New Jersey Motor Vehicle Commission, pursuant to section 3 of P.L.1973, c. 307 (C.39:3C–3), before transferring actual physical possession of the snowmobile, all-terrain vehicle, or dirt bike to a purchaser of the vehicle.

If there is a change of ownership for which a registration certificate has been previously issued, the new owner shall apply for a new registration certificate and set forth the original number in the application. The owner shall demonstrate to the commission a notarized bill of sale, assignable certificate of origin, or other formal proof of ownership deemed acceptable by the commission when transferring ownership or selling a snowmobile, all-terrain vehicle, or dirt bike. The owner shall pay the regular fee for the particular snowmobile, all-terrain vehicle, or dirt bike involved. The owner of any registration certificate issued under this section may obtain a duplicate from the commission upon application and payment of the fee prescribed.

L.1973, c. 307, § 5, eff. Dec. 14, 1973. Amended by L.1985, c. 375, § 6; L.2009, c. 275, § 5, (contingent effective date).

39:3C–6. Exemptions; operation on private property; payment of fee by governments

Text of section effective until the third month after the date the commissioner has designated the first of the three sites pursuant to paragraph (1) of subsection a. of section 38 of P.L.2009, c. 275 (C.13:1L–5.1).

a. No registration shall be required for a snowmobile or all-terrain vehicle operated on private property.

b. No registration fee shall be charged for a snowmobile or all-terrain vehicle owned by the federal government, the State, county or municipal government or subdivision thereof.

L.1973, c. 307, § 6, eff. Dec. 14, 1973. Amended by L.1985, c. 375, § 7.

39:3C–6. Exemption; operation for use on a farm; payment of fee by government

Text of section effective on the third month after the date the commissioner has designated the first of the three sites pursuant to paragraph (1) of subsection a. of section 38 of P.L.2009, c. 275 (C.13:1L–5.1).

a. Any snowmobile, all-terrain vehicle, or dirt bike solely operated for use on a farm shall be exempt from the registration and numbering requirements of P.L. 1973, c. 307 (C.39:3C–1 et seq.).

b. No registration fee shall be charged for a snowmobile, all-terrain vehicle, or dirt bike owned by the federal government, the State, county or municipal government or subdivision thereof.

L.1973, c. 307, § 6, eff. Dec. 14, 1973. Amended by L.1985, c. 375, § 7; L.2009, c. 275, § 6, (contingent effective date).

39:3C–7. Exemptions; nonresidents

Text of section effective until the third month after the date the commissioner has designated the first of the three sites pursuant to paragraph (1) of subsection a. of section 38 of P.L.2009, c. 275 (C.13:1L–5.1).

The registration provisions of this act shall not apply to nonresident owners who have complied with the registration and licensing laws of the state or country of residence, provided that the snowmobile or all-terrain vehicle is appropriately identified in accordance with the laws of the state of residence and conspicuously displays the registration number issued by the state or country of residence. Nothing in this section shall be construed to authorize the operation of any snowmobile or all-terrain vehicle contrary to the provisions of this act.

L.1973, c. 307, § 7, eff. Dec. 14, 1973. Amended by L.1985, c. 375, § 8.

39:3C–7. Exemptions; nonresidents

Text of section effective on the third month after the date the commissioner has designated the first of the three sites pursuant to paragraph (1) of subsection a. of section 38 of P.L.2009, c. 275 (C.13:1L–5.1).

The registration provisions of P.L.1973, c. 307 (C.39:3C–1 et seq.) shall not apply to nonresident owners who have complied with the registration and licensing laws of the state or country of residence, provided that the snowmobile, all-terrain vehicle, or dirt bike is appropriately identified in accordance with the laws of the state or country of residence and conspicuously displays the number issued by the state or country of residence. Nothing in this section shall be construed to authorize the operation of any snowmobile, all-terrain vehicle, or dirt bike contrary to the provisions of P.L.1973, c. 307 (C.39:3C–1 et seq.).

L.1973, c. 307, § 7, eff. Dec. 14, 1973. Amended by L.1985, c. 375, § 8; L.2009, c. 275, § 7, (contingent effective date).

39:3C–8. Display of registration number

Text of section effective until the third month after the date the commissioner has designated the first of the three sites pursuant to paragraph (1) of subsection a. of section 38 of P.L.2009, c. 275 (C.13:1L–5.1).

The registration number assigned to a snowmobile or all-terrain vehicle shall be displayed on the vehicle at all times in such manner as the director may, by regulation, prescribe. No number other than the number assigned by the director, or the identification number of the registration in another state, shall be painted, attached or otherwise displayed on either side of the cowling, except that racing numbers on a snowmobile or all-terrain vehicle being operated in prearranged organized special events may be temporarily displayed for the duration of the race.

L.1973, c. 307, § 8, eff. Dec. 14, 1973. Amended by L.1985, c. 375, § 9.

39:3C–8.　Display of assigned number

Text of section effective on the third month after the date the commissioner has designated the first of the three sites pursuant to paragraph (1) of subsection a. of section 38 of P.L.2009, c. 275 (C.13:1L–5.1).

The number assigned to a snowmobile, all-terrain vehicle, or dirt bike and required to be displayed pursuant to section 3 of P.L.1973, c. 307 (C.39:3C–3) shall be displayed on the snowmobile, all-terrain vehicle, or dirt bike at all times in such manner as the chief administrator may, by regulation, prescribe. No number other than the number assigned by the chief administrator, or a comparable identification number of the snowmobile, all-terrain vehicle, or dirt bike properly registered in another state, shall be painted, attached, or otherwise displayed on either side of the cowling, except that racing numbers on a snowmobile, all-terrain vehicle, or dirt bike being operated in prearranged organized special events may be temporarily displayed for the duration of the race.

L.1973, c. 307, § 8, eff. Dec. 14, 1973. Amended by L.1985, c. 375, § 9; L.2009, c. 275, § 8, (contingent effective date).

39:3C–9.　Production of registration certificate for inspection; persons under 18 to produce certificate of completion of safety course

Text of section effective until the third month after the date the commissioner has designated the first of the three sites pursuant to paragraph (1) of subsection a. of section 38 of P.L.2009, c. 275 (C.13:1L–5.1).

a.　Every person operating a snowmobile or all-terrain vehicle registered or transferred in accordance with any of the provisions of this act shall, upon demand of any peace officer, law enforcement officer, duly authorized official of the Department of Environmental Protection, or a police officer, produce for inspection the certificate of registration and shall furnish to such officer any information necessary for the identification of such snowmobile or all-terrain vehicle and its owner. The failure to produce the certificate of registration when operating a snowmobile or all-terrain vehicle on public lands and waters or when crossing a public highway shall be presumptive evidence in any court of competent jurisdiction of operating a snowmobile or all-terrain vehicle which is not registered as required by this act.

b.　A person less than 18 years of age who operates an all-terrain vehicle which is registered in this State shall produce upon demand a certificate indicating that person's successful completion of an all-terrain vehicle safety education and training course established or

certified by the director in accordance with section 15 of P.L.1973, c. 307 (C. 39:3C–15). The failure to produce the certificate when operating an all-terrain vehicle on public lands or waters, or when crossing a public highway, shall be presumptive evidence in any court of competent jurisdiction of the operation of the all-terrain vehicle in violation of the requirement in subsection c. of section 16 of P.L.1973, c. 307 (C. 39:3C–16).

L.1973, c. 307, § 9, eff. Dec. 14, 1973. Amended L.1983, c. 403, § 13, eff. Dec. 23, 1983; L.1985, c. 375, § 10; L.1991, c. 322, § 2, eff. May 30, 1992.

39:3C–9.　Production of registration certificate for inspection; persons under 18 to produce certificate of completion of safety course

Text of section effective on the third month after the date the commissioner has designated the first of the three sites pursuant to paragraph (1) of subsection a. of section 38 of P.L.2009, c. 275 (C.13:1L–5.1).

a.　Every person operating a snowmobile, all-terrain vehicle, or dirt bike registered or transferred in accordance with any of the provisions of P.L.1973, c. 307 (C.39:3C–1 et seq.) shall, upon demand of any law enforcement officer, duly authorized conservation officer of the Division of Fish and Wildlife or park police officer or law enforcement operation officer of the Division of Parks and Forestry within the Department of Environmental Protection, or any other police officer, produce for inspection the certificate of registration and shall furnish to the officer any information necessary for the identification of the snowmobile, all-terrain vehicle, or dirt bike and its owner. The failure to produce the certificate of registration when operating a snowmobile, all-terrain vehicle, or dirt bike on public lands and waters, or when crossing a public highway, shall be presumptive evidence in any court of competent jurisdiction of operating a snowmobile, all-terrain vehicle, or dirt bike which is not registered as required by P.L.1973, c. 307 (C.39:3C–1 et seq.).

b.　A person less than 18 years of age who operates a snowmobile, all-terrain vehicle, or a dirt bike which is registered in this State shall produce upon demand a certificate indicating that person's successful completion of a safety education and training course established or certified by the commissioner in accordance with section 15 of P.L.1973, c. 307 (C.39:3C–15). The failure to produce the certificate when operating a snowmobile, all-terrain vehicle, or dirt bike on public lands or waters, or when crossing a public highway, shall be presumptive evidence in any court of competent jurisdiction of the operation of the snowmobile, all-terrain vehicle, or dirt bike in violation of the requirement in subsection c. of section 16 of P.L.1973, c. 307 (C.39:3C–16).

L.1973, c. 307, § 9, eff. Dec. 14, 1973. Amended L.1983, c. 403, § 13, eff. Dec. 23, 1983; L.1985, c. 375, § 10; L.1991, c. 322, § 2, eff. May 30, 1992; L.2009, c. 275, § 9, (contingent effective date).

39:3C–10. Notice of change of address

Text of section effective until the third month after the date the commissioner has designated the first of the three sites pursuant to paragraph (1) of subsection a. of section 38 of P.L.2009, c. 275 (C.13:1L–5.1).

a. It shall be the duty of every owner holding a certificate of registration to notify the commission, in writing, of any change of residence of such person within seven days after the change occurs.

b. The chief administrator shall establish a public awareness campaign to inform the general public about the importance of maintaining a current address with the commission.

L.1973, c. 307, § 10, eff. Dec. 14, 1973. Amended by L.2007, c. 281, § 1, eff. July 1, 2008.

39:3C–10. Notice of change of address

Text of section effective on the third month after the date the commissioner has designated the first of the three sites pursuant to paragraph (1) of subsection a. of section 38 of P.L.2009, c. 275 (C.13:1L–5.1).

a. It shall be the duty of every owner holding a certificate of registration to notify the commission, in writing, of any change of residence of such person within one week after the change occurs.

b. The chief administrator shall establish a public awareness campaign to inform the general public about the importance of maintaining a current address with the commission.

L.1973, c. 307, § 10, eff. Dec. 14, 1973. Amended by L.2007, c. 281, § 1, eff. July 1, 2008; L.2009, c. 275, § 10, (contingent effective date).

39:3C–11. Transfer of ownership or discontinuance of use

Text of section effective until the third month after the date the commissioner has designated the first of the three sites pursuant to paragraph (1) of subsection a. of section 38 of P.L.2009, c. 275 (C.13:1L–5.1).

Whenever the ownership of a snowmobile or all-terrain vehicle is transferred or the use for which a registration certificate has already been issued is discontinued, the old registration certificate shall be properly signed and executed by the owner, showing that the ownership of the snowmobile or all-terrain vehicle has been transferred or its use discontinued, and returned to the division within 10 days after transfer or discontinuance. If there is a change of ownership for which a registration certificate has previously been issued, the new owner shall apply for a new certificate. He shall set forth the original number issued in the application accompanied by the old registration properly signed by the previous owner and with the required fee submitted to the division, for registration.

L.1973, c. 307, § 11, eff. Dec. 14, 1973. Amended by L.1985, c. 375, § 11.

39:3C–11. Transfer of ownership; application and proof of ownership

Text of section effective on the third month after the date the commissioner has designated the first of the three sites pursuant to paragraph (1) of subsection a. of section 38 of P.L.2009, c. 275 (C.13:1L–5.1).

In accordance with the provisions of P.L.1973, c. 307 (C.39:3C–1 et seq.), whenever there is a change of ownership for which a registration certificate has previously been issued, the new owner shall apply for a new certificate. The new owner shall set forth the original number issued in the application accompanied by the old registration, if available, and with the required fee submitted to the commission, for registration. The new owner shall demonstrate to the commission a notarized bill of sale, assignable certificate of origin, or other formal proof of ownership deemed acceptable by the commission when transferring ownership or selling a snowmobile, all-terrain vehicle, or dirt bike.

L.1973, c. 307, § 11, eff. Dec. 14, 1973. Amended by L.1985, c. 375, § 11; L.2009, c. 275, § 11, (contingent effective date).

39:3C–12. Destruction, theft or removal from state; notice to division

Text of section effective until the third month after the date the commissioner has designated the first of the three sites pursuant to paragraph (1) of subsection a. of section 38 of P.L.2009, c. 275 (C.13:1L–5.1).

It shall be the duty of every owner of a snowmobile or all-terrain vehicle registered pursuant to this act to notify the division, in writing, of the destruction, theft or permanent removal of such from the State, within 10 days thereafter; and in the event of the destruction or theft of such, shall surrender the certificate of registration with such notice.

L.1973, c. 307, § 12, eff. Dec. 14, 1973. Amended by L.1985, c. 375, § 12.

39:3C–12. Destruction, theft or removal from state; notice to commission

Text of section effective on the third month after the date the commissioner has designated the first of the three sites pursuant to paragraph (1) of subsection a. of section 38 of P.L.2009, c. 275 (C.13:1L–5.1).

It shall be the duty of every owner of a snowmobile, all-terrain vehicle, or dirt bike registered pursuant to P.L.1973, c. 307 (C.39:3C–1 et seq.) to notify the commission, in writing, of the destruction, theft, or permanent removal of the snowmobile, all-terrain vehicle, or dirt bike from the State, to surrender the certificate of registration within 10 days in the event of the destruction, theft, or permanent removal of the snowmobile, all-terrain vehicle, or dirt bike from the State.

L.1973, c. 307, § 12, eff. Dec. 14, 1973. Amended by L.1985, c. 375, § 12; L.2009, c. 275, § 12, (contingent effective date).

39:3C–13. Licensing or registration by political subdivision; prohibition

Text of section effective until the third month after the date the commissioner has designated the first of the three sites pursuant to paragraph (1) of subsection a. of section 38 of P.L.2009, c. 275 (C.13:1L–5.1).

No political subdivision of the State shall require additional licensing or registration of snowmobiles or all-terrain vehicles which are covered by the provisions of this act.

Nothing herein shall however prohibit the requirement of a permit by State or local parks for use of snowmobiles on park lands or in any way affect the authority of the Department of Environmental Protection, the commissioner thereof, or those responsible for the operation of a park from adopting rules and regulations concerning the use of snowmobiles and all-terrain vehicles.

L.1973, c. 307, § 13, eff. Dec. 14, 1973. Amended by L.1985, c. 375, § 13.

39:3C–13. Licensing or registration by political subdivision; prohibition

Text of section effective on the third month after the date the commissioner has designated the first of the three sites pursuant to paragraph (1) of subsection a. of section 38 of P.L.2009, c. 275 (C.13:1L–5.1).

No political subdivision of the State shall require additional licensing or registration of snowmobiles, all-terrain vehicles, or dirt bikes which are covered by the provisions of P.L.1973, c. 307 (C.39:3C–1 et seq.).

Nothing herein shall prohibit the requirement of a permit by State or local parks for use of snowmobiles, all-terrain vehicles, or dirt bikes on park lands or in any way affect the authority of the Department of Environmental Protection, the commissioner thereof, or those responsible for the operation of a park from adopting rules and regulations concerning the use of snowmobiles, all-terrain vehicles, and dirt bikes.

L.1973, c. 307, § 13, eff. Dec. 14, 1973. Amended by L.1985, c. 375, § 13; L.2009, c. 275, § 13, (contingent effective date).

39:3C–14. Rules and regulations; scope of commissioner action with respect to use of vehicles; designated locations for safety education and training programs

The commissioner, with a view towards minimizing detrimental effects on the environment and protecting public safety, shall adopt rules and regulations relating to and including, but not limited to, the following:

a. Use of snowmobiles, all-terrain vehicles, and dirt bikes, insofar as fish, wildlife, and plantlife resources, and public safety are affected;

b. Use of snowmobiles, all-terrain vehicles, and dirt bikes on public lands and waters under the jurisdiction of the Department of Environmental Protection; and

c. Use of snowmobiles, all-terrain vehicles, and dirt bikes at three sites on State-owned land pursuant to section 38 of P.L.2009, c. 275 (C.13:1L–5.1).

The commissioner may locate, designate, and make available by the effective date of P.L.1991, c. 322 appropriate areas of public lands upon which snowmobile, all-terrain vehicle, and dirt bike safety education and training programs established or certified by the commissioner in accordance with section 15 of P.L.1973, c. 307 (C.39:3C–15) may be conducted. The commissioner shall report to the Legislature and the Governor within one year after the effective date of P.L.1991, c. 322 on the size and location of the public lands located, designated, and made available; on the frequency of the use, or the estimated frequency of use, of these public lands for safety education and training programs; and the environmental impact of this use on the lands.

L.1973, c. 307, § 14, eff. Dec. 14, 1973. Amended by L.1985, c. 375, § 14; L.1991, c. 322, § 3, eff. Nov. 22, 1991; L.2009, c. 275, § 14, eff. Jan. 17, 2010.

39:3C–15. Rules and regulations of director; establishment of all-terrain vehicle safety education and training program

Text of section effective until the third month after the date the commissioner has designated the first of the three sites pursuant to paragraph (1) of subsection a. of section 38 of P.L.2009, c. 275 (C.13:1L).

The Director of the Division of Motor Vehicles shall adopt rules and regulations relating to and including, but not limited to:

a. Specifications relating to equipment required for safety as provided herein.

b. Establishment of a comprehensive snowmobile and all-terrain vehicle information and safety education and training program.

c. The regulations pertaining to and the granting of permits for the conduct of all prearranged special events as provided in this act, except that in the case of those special events conducted on public lands and waters under the jurisdiction of the Department of Environmental Protection any regulations must be approved jointly by the director and the commissioner.

In accordance with the requirement in paragraph b. of this section, the director shall establish an all-terrain vehicle safety education and training program to be offered by the division, or shall certify other all-terrain vehicle safety education and training programs to be offered by public or private agencies or organizations, the successful completion of which shall satisfy the training requirements in subsection c. of section 16 of P.L.1973, c. 307 (C. 39:3C–16). A person less than 16 years of age participating in an all-terrain vehicle safety education and training course established or certified by the director shall operate during the training only an all-terrain vehicle with an engine capacity of 90 cubic centimeters or less.

L.1973, c. 307, § 15, eff. Dec. 14, 1973. Amended by L.1985, c. 375, § 15; L.1991, c. 322, § 4, eff. Nov. 22, 1991.

39:3C–15. Rules and regulations; scope and content of safety education and training program; permits for special events

Text of section effective on the third month after the date the commissioner has designated the first of the three sites pursuant to paragraph (1) of subsection a. of section 38 of P.L.2009, c. 275 (C.13:1L–5.1).

The commissioner may adopt rules and regulations relating to and including, but not limited to:

a.   (Deleted by amendment, P.L.2009, c. 275).

b.   Establishment of a comprehensive snowmobile, all-terrain vehicle, and dirt bike information and safety education and training program.

c.   Granting of permits for the conduct of all prearranged special events as provided in P.L.1973, c. 307 (C.39:3C–1 et seq.), including those permits necessary for special events conducted on public lands and waters under the jurisdiction of the Department of Environmental Protection.

In accordance with the requirement in subsection b. of this section, the commissioner shall certify snowmobile, all-terrain vehicle, and dirt bike safety education and training programs to be offered by public or private agencies or organizations, the successful completion of which shall satisfy the training requirements in subsection c. of section 16 of P.L.1973, c. 307 (C.39:3C–16). A person less than 16 years of age participating in an all-terrain vehicle safety education and training course established or certified by the commissioner shall operate during the training only an all-terrain vehicle with an engine capacity of 90 cubic centimeters or less.

L.1973, c. 307, § 15, eff. Dec. 14, 1973. Amended by L.1985, c. 375, § 15; L.1991, c. 322, § 4, eff. Nov. 22, 1991; L.2009, c. 275, § 15, (contingent effective date).

39:3C–16. Minimum age to be operator

Text of section effective until the third month after the date the commissioner has designated the first of the three sites pursuant to paragraph (1) of subsection a. of section 38 of P.L.2009, c. 275 (C.13:1L–5.1).

a.   A person under the age of 14 years shall not operate or be permitted to operate any snowmobile or all-terrain vehicle on public lands or waters or across a public highway.

b.   A person less than 16 years of age shall not operate on public lands or waters or across a public highway of this State an all-terrain vehicle with an engine capacity greater than 90 cubic centimeters.

c.   A person less than 18 years of age shall not operate an all-terrain vehicle registered in this State on public lands or waters or across a public highway of this State unless the person has completed an all-terrain vehicle safety education and training course established or certified by the director pursuant to section 15 of P.L.1973, c. 307 (C. 39:3C–15). At all times during the operation of the all-terrain vehicle, the person shall have in his possession a certificate indicating successful completion of the course.

L.1973, c. 307, § 16, eff. Dec. 14, 1973. Amended by L.1985, c. 375, § 16; L.1991, c. 322, § 5, eff. May 30, 1992.

39:3C–16. Minimum age to be operator

Text of section effective on the third month after the date the commissioner has designated the first of the three sites pursuant to paragraph (1) of subsection a. of section 38 of P.L.2009, c. 275 (C.13:1L–5.1).

a.   A person under the age of 14 years shall not operate or be permitted to operate any snowmobile, all-terrain vehicle, or dirt bike on public lands or waters or across a public highway.

b.   A person less than 16 years of age shall not operate on public lands or waters or across a public highway of this State an all-terrain vehicle with an engine capacity greater than 90 cubic centimeters.

c.   A person less than 18 years of age shall not operate a snowmobile, all-terrain vehicle, or dirt bike registered in this State on public lands or waters or across a public highway of this State unless the person has completed a safety education and training course established or certified by the commissioner pursuant to section 15 of P.L.1973, c. 307 (C.39:3C–15). At all times during the operation of the snowmobile, all-terrain vehicle, or dirt bike the person shall possess a certificate indicating successful completion of the course.

L.1973, c. 307, § 16, eff. Dec. 14, 1973. Amended by L.1985, c. 375, § 16; L.1991, c. 322, § 5, eff. May 30, 1992; L.2009, c. 275, § 16, (contingent effective date).

39:3C–17. Prohibition of operation on highways, streets and right-of-way limits; exceptions

Text of section effective until the third month after the date the commissioner has designated the first of the three sites pursuant to paragraph (1) of subsection a. of section 38 of P.L.2009, c. 275 (C.13:1L–5.1).

a.   No person shall operate a snowmobile or all-terrain vehicle upon limited access highways or within the right-of-way limits thereof.

b.   No person shall operate a snowmobile or all-terrain vehicle upon the main traveled portion or the plowed snowbanks of any public street or highway or within the right-of-way limits thereof except as follows:

(1) Properly registered snowmobiles or all-terrain vehicles may cross, as directly as possible, public streets or highways, except limited access highways, provided that such crossing can be made in safety and that it does not interfere with the free movement of vehicular traffic

approaching from either direction on such public street or highway. Prior to making any such crossing, the operator shall bring the snowmobile or all-terrain vehicle to a complete stop. It shall be the responsibility of the operator of a snowmobile or all-terrain vehicle to yield the right-of-way to all vehicular traffic upon any public street or highway before crossing same.

(2) Whenever it is impracticable to gain immediate access to an area adjacent to a public highway where a snowmobile or all-terrain vehicle is to be operated, it may be operated adjacent and parallel to such public highway for the purpose of gaining access to the area of operation. This subsection shall apply to the operation of a snowmobile or all-terrain vehicle from the point where it is unloaded from a motorized conveyance to the area where it is to be operated, or from the area where operated to a motorized conveyance, when such loading or unloading cannot be effected in the immediate vicinity of the area of operation without causing a hazard to vehicular traffic approaching from either direction on said public highway. Such loading or unloading must be accomplished with due regard to safety, at the nearest possible point to the area of operation.

L.1973, c. 307, § 17, eff. Dec. 14, 1973. Amended by L.1985, c. 375, § 17.

39:3C–17. Prohibition of operation on highways, streets and right-of-way limits; exceptions

Text of section effective on the third month after the date the commissioner has designated the first of the three sites pursuant to paragraph (1) of subsection a. of section 38 of P.L.2009, c. 275 (C.13:1L–5.1).

a. No person shall operate a snowmobile, all-terrain vehicle, or dirt bike upon limited access highways or within the right-of-way limits thereof.

b. No person shall operate a snowmobile, all-terrain vehicle, or dirt bike upon the main traveled portion or the plowed snowbanks of any public street or highway or within the right-of-way limits thereof except as follows:

(1) Properly registered snowmobiles, all-terrain vehicles, and dirt bikes may cross, as directly as possible, public streets or highways, except limited access highways, provided that such crossing can be made in safety and that it does not interfere with the free movement of vehicular traffic approaching from either direction on the public street or highway. Prior to making any such crossing, the operator shall bring the snowmobile, all-terrain vehicle, or dirt bike to a complete stop. It shall be the responsibility of the operator of a snowmobile, all-terrain vehicle, or dirt bike to yield the right-of-way to all vehicular traffic upon any public street or highway before crossing the public street or highway.

(2) Whenever it is impracticable to gain immediate access to an area adjacent to a public highway where a snowmobile, all-terrain vehicle, or dirt bike is to be operated, the snowmobile, all-terrain vehicle, or dirt bike may be operated adjacent and parallel to the public highway for the purpose of gaining access to the area of operation. This subsection shall apply to the operation of a snowmobile, all-terrain vehicle, or dirt bike from the point where the snowmobile, all-terrain vehicle, or dirt bike is unloaded from a motorized conveyance to the area where it is to be operated, or from the area where operated to a motorized conveyance, when the loading or unloading cannot be effected in the immediate vicinity of the area of operation without causing a hazard to vehicular traffic approaching from either direction on the public highway. The loading or unloading must be accomplished with due regard to safety, at the nearest possible point to the area of operation.

L.1973, c. 307, § 17, eff. Dec. 14, 1973. Amended by L.1985, c. 375, § 17; L.2009, c. 275, § 17, (contingent effective date).

39:3C–18. Prohibition of operation on private property without consent

Text of section effective until the third month after the date the commissioner has designated the first of the three sites pursuant to paragraph (1) of subsection a. of section 38 of P.L.2009, c. 275 (C.13:1L–5.1).

a. No person shall operate a snowmobile or all-terrain vehicle on the property of another without receiving the consent of the owner of the property and the person who has a contractual right to the use of such property;

b. No person shall continue to operate a snowmobile or all-terrain vehicle on the property of another after consent, as provided in subsection a. above, has been withdrawn.

c. No owner of real property and no person or entity having a contractual right to the use of real property, no matter where such property is situate in this State, shall assume responsibility or incur liability for any injury or damage to an owner, operator or occupant of a snowmobile or all terrain vehicle where such injury or damage occurs during, or arises out of the operation or use of such vehicle, unless: (1) the operation or use is with the express consent of the owner and contractual user of the property and (2) the provisions of P.L.1968, c. 73 (C.2A:42A–2 et seq.) or P.L.1985, c. 431 (C. 2A:42A–6 et seq.) do not limit liability. This subsection shall not limit the liability which would otherwise exist for the willful or malicious creation of a hazardous condition.

L.1973, c. 307, § 18, eff. Dec. 14, 1973. Amended by L.1985, c. 375, § 18; L.1991, c. 496, § 8, eff. Jan. 18, 1992.

39:3C–18. Prohibition of operation on private property without consent

Text of section effective on the third month after the date the commissioner has designated the first of the three sites pursuant to paragraph (1) of subsection a. of section 38 of P.L.2009, c. 275 (C.13:1L–5.1).

a. No person shall operate a snowmobile, all-terrain vehicle, or dirt bike on the property of another without receiving the consent of the owner of the property and the person who has a contractual right to the use of the property.

b. No person shall continue to operate a snowmobile, all-terrain vehicle, or dirt bike on the property of another after consent, as provided in subsection a. above, has been withdrawn.

c. No owner of real property and no person or entity having a contractual right to the use of real property, no matter where the property is situate in this State, shall assume responsibility or incur liability for any injury or damage to an owner, operator, or occupant of a snowmobile, all terrain vehicle, or dirt bike if the injury or damage occurs during, or arises out of the operation or use of, the snowmobile, all-terrain vehicle, or dirt bike unless: (1) the operation or use is with the express consent of the owner and contractual user of the property, and (2) the provisions of P.L.1968, c. 73 (C.2A:42A–2 et seq.) or P.L.1985, c. 431 (C.2A:42A–6 et seq.) do not limit liability. This subsection shall not limit the liability which would otherwise exist for the willful or malicious creation of a hazardous condition.
L.1973, c. 307, § 18, eff. Dec. 14, 1973. Amended by L.1985, c. 375, § 18; L.1991, c. 496, § 8, eff. Jan. 18, 1992; L.2009, c. 275, § 18, (contingent effective date).

39:3C–19. Unlawful acts

Text of section effective until the third month after the date the commissioner has designated the first of the three sites pursuant to paragraph (1) of subsection a. of section 38 of P.L.2009, c. 275 (C.13:1L–5.1).

It shall be unlawful for:

a. Any person to operate or ride as a passenger on any snowmobile or all-terrain vehicle without wearing a protective helmet approved by the director. Any such helmet shall be of a type acceptable for use in conjunction with motorcycles as provided in sections 6 to 9 of P.L.1967, c. 237 (C. 39:3–76.7 through 39:3–76.10).

b. Any person to operate a snowmobile or all-terrain vehicle that is not equipped with working headlights, taillights, brakes and proper mufflers as supplied by the motor manufacturer for the particular model, without modifications, nor shall any person operate any snowmobile or all-terrain vehicle in such a manner as to cause a harsh, objectionable or unreasonable noise.

c. Any person to operate a snowmobile or all-terrain vehicle at any time and in any manner intended or reasonably to be expected to harass, drive or pursue any wildlife.

d. Any person to operate any snowmobile or all-terrain vehicle during the hours from ½ hour before sunset to ½ hour after sunrise without having lighted headlights and lighted taillights.

e. Any person to operate any snowmobile or all-terrain vehicle on the land of another without first securing the permission of the landowner or his duly authorized representative.

f. Any person to operate a snowmobile or all-terrain vehicle upon railroad or right-of-way of an operating railroad, except railroad personnel in the performance of their duties.

g. Any person to violate any provision of this act or any rule or regulation adopted pursuant to this act.
L.1973, c. 307, § 19, eff. Dec. 14, 1973. Amended by L.1985, c. 375, § 19.

39:3C–19. Unlawful acts

Text of section effective on the third month after the date the commissioner has designated the first of the three sites pursuant to paragraph (1) of subsection a. of section 38 of P.L.2009, c. 275 (C.13:1L–5.1).

It shall be unlawful for:

a. Any person to operate or ride as a passenger on any snowmobile, all-terrain vehicle, or dirt bike without wearing a protective helmet approved by the chief administrator. Any helmet shall be of a type acceptable for use in conjunction with motorcycles as provided in sections 6 to 9 of P.L.1967, c. 237 (C.39:3–76.7 through 39:3–76.10).

b. Any person to operate a snowmobile, all-terrain vehicle, or dirt bike that is not equipped with working headlights, taillights, brakes, and proper mufflers as supplied by the motor manufacturer for the particular model, without modifications, nor shall any person operate any snowmobile, all-terrain vehicle, or dirt bike in any manner as to cause a harsh, objectionable, or unreasonable noise.

c. Any person to operate a snowmobile, all-terrain vehicle, or dirt bike at any time and in any manner intended or reasonably to be expected to harass, drive, or pursue any wildlife.

d. Any person to operate any snowmobile, all-terrain vehicle, or dirt bike during the hours from 1/2 hour before sunset to 1/2 hour after sunrise without having lighted headlights and lighted taillights.

e. Any person to operate any snowmobile, all-terrain vehicle, or dirt bike on the land of another without first securing the permission of the landowner or the landowner's duly authorized representative.

f. Any person to operate a snowmobile, all-terrain vehicle, or dirt bike upon railroad or right-of-way of an operating railroad, except railroad personnel in the performance of their duties.

g. Any person to violate any provision of P.L.1973, c. 307 (C.39:3C–1 et seq.) or any rule or regulation adopted pursuant to P.L.1973, c. 307 (C.39:3C–1 et seq.).

L.1973, c. 307, § 19, eff. Dec. 14, 1973. Amended by L.1985, c. 375, § 19; L.2009, c. 275, § 19, (contingent effective date).

39:3C–20. Liability insurance

Text of section effective until the third month after the date the commissioner has designated the first of the three sites pursuant to paragraph (1) of subsection a. of section 38 of P.L.2009, c. 275 (C.13:1L–5.1).

a. No snowmobile or all-terrain vehicle shall be operated or permitted to be operated unless the owner thereof has obtained a policy of insurance, in such language and form as shall be determined by the Commissioner of the Department of Insurance, from an insurance carrier authorized to do business in this State, the terms of which policy shall indemnify an amount or limit of $15,000.00, exclusive of interest and costs, on account of injury to, or death of, one person, in any one accident; and an amount or limit, subject to such limit for any one person so injured, or killed, of $30,000.00, exclusive of interest and costs, on account of injury to or death of, more than one person, in any one accident; and an amount or limit of $5,000.00, exclusive of interest and costs, for damage to property in any one accident, for damages arising out of the negligent operation of said snowmobile or all-terrain vehicle. In lieu of such insurance coverage as hereinabove provided, the director, in his discretion and upon application of the State or a municipality having registered in its name one or more snowmobiles or all-terrain vehicles, may waive the requirement of insurance by a private insurance carrier and issue a certificate of self-insurance, when he is satisfied of financial ability to respond to judgments obtained against it or them, arising out of the ownership, use or operation of the snowmobiles or all-terrain vehicles.

b. Proof of insurance as hereinabove required shall be produced and displayed by the owner or operator of such snowmobile or all-terrain vehicle upon request to any law enforcement officer or to any person who has suffered or claims to have suffered either personal injury or property damage as a result of the operation of it by the owner or operator.

c. An owner of a snowmobile or all-terrain vehicle who shall operate or permit the same to be operated without having in effect the required liability insurance coverage, and any other person who shall operate any snowmobile or all-terrain vehicle with the knowledge that the owner thereof does not have in effect such insurance coverage shall be guilty of a violation of this act and be subject to a fine of not less than $25.00 nor more than $100.00.

d. The director is hereby authorized to promulgate reasonable regulations to provide effective administra-

tion and enforcement of the provisions of this section in accordance with the purposes thereof.

L.1973, c. 307, § 20, eff. Dec. 14, 1973. Amended by L.1985, c. 375, § 20.

39:3C–20. Liability insurance

Text of section effective on the third month after the date the commissioner has designated the first of the three sites pursuant to paragraph (1) of subsection a. of section 38 of P.L.2009, c. 275 (C.13:1L–5.1).

a. No snowmobile, all-terrain vehicle, or dirt bike shall be operated or permitted to be operated unless the owner thereof has obtained a policy of insurance, in such language and form as shall be determined by the Commissioner of Banking and Insurance, from an insurance carrier authorized to do business in this State, the terms of which policy shall indemnify an amount or limit of $15,000, exclusive of interest and costs, on account of injury to, or death of, one person, in any one accident; and an amount or limit, subject to such limit for any one person so injured, or killed, of $30,000, exclusive of interest and costs, on account of injury to or death of, more than one person, in any one accident; and an amount or limit of $5,000, exclusive of interest and costs, for damage to property in any one accident, for damages arising out of the negligent operation of the snowmobile, all-terrain vehicle, or dirt bike. In lieu of the insurance coverage as hereinabove provided, the chief administrator, in the chief administrator's discretion and upon application of the State or a municipality having registered in its name one or more snowmobiles, all-terrain vehicles, or dirt bikes, may waive the requirement of insurance by a private insurance carrier and issue a certificate of self-insurance, when the chief administrator is satisfied of financial ability to respond to judgments obtained against it or them, arising out of the ownership, use or operation of the snowmobiles, all-terrain vehicles, or dirt bikes.

b. Proof of insurance as hereinabove required shall be produced and displayed by the owner or operator of the snowmobile, all-terrain vehicle, or dirt bike upon request to any law enforcement officer or to any person who has suffered or claims to have suffered either personal injury or property damage as a result of the operation of the snowmobile, all-terrain vehicle, or dirt bike by the owner or operator.

c. An owner of a snowmobile, all-terrain vehicle, or dirt bike who shall operate or permit the snowmobile, all-terrain vehicle, or dirt bike to be operated without having in effect the required liability insurance coverage, and any other person who shall operate any snowmobile, all-terrain vehicle, or dirt bike with the knowledge that the owner thereof does not have in effect the insurance coverage shall be guilty of a violation of P.L.1973, c. 307 (C.39:3C–1 et seq.) and be subject to a fine of not less than $25 nor more than $100.

d. The chief administrator is hereby authorized to promulgate reasonable regulations to provide effective administration and enforcement of the provisions of this section in accordance with the purposes thereof.

L.1973, c. 307, § 20, eff. Dec. 14, 1973. Amended by L.1985, c. 375, § 20; L.2009, c. 275, § 20, (contingent effective date).

39:3C–21.   Report of accidents

Text of section effective until the third month after the date the commissioner has designated the first of the three sites pursuant to paragraph (1) of subsection a. of section 38 of P.L.2009, c. 275 (C.13:1L–5.1).

The operator of any snowmobile or all-terrain vehicle involved in an accident resulting in injuries or death of any person or property damage shall comply with the procedures in R.S. 39:4–129 and R.S. 39:4–130.

L.1973, c. 307, § 21, eff. Dec. 14, 1973. Amended by L.1985, c. 375, § 21.

39:3C–21.   Report of accidents

Text of section effective on the third month after the date the commissioner has designated the first of the three sites pursuant to paragraph (1) of subsection a. of section 38 of P.L.2009, c. 275 (C.13:1L–5.1).

The operator of any snowmobile, all-terrain vehicle, or dirt bike involved in an accident resulting in injuries or death of any person or property damage shall comply with the procedures in R.S. 39:4–129 and R.S. 39:4–130.

L.1973, c. 307, § 21, eff. Dec. 14, 1973. Amended by L.1985, c. 375, § 21; L.2009, c. 275, § 21, (contingent effective date).

39:3C–22.   Special events

Text of section effective until the third month after the date the commissioner has designated the first of the three sites pursuant to paragraph (1) of subsection a. of section 38 of P.L.2009, c. 275 (C.13:1L–5.1).

The director may authorize the holding of organized special events. He shall adopt and may, from time to time, amend rules and regulations determining the special events which shall be subject to division permit and designating the equipment and facilities necessary for safe operation of snowmobiles and all-terrain vehicles and for the safety of operators, participants, and observers in such special events. Whenever such special event requiring permit of the division is proposed to be held in the State of New Jersey, the person in charge thereof shall, at least 20 days prior thereto, file an application with the director to hold such special event. The application shall set forth the date of and location where it is proposed to hold such rally, race, exhibition, or organized event, and such other information as the director may require, and it shall not be conducted without written authorization of the director and, if the event is desired to be held upon public lands or waters, a written authorization of the commissioner. Copies of such regulations shall be furnished by the division to any person making an application therefor.

Any person sponsoring the event who shall violate any regulation adopted pursuant to this section shall for every such violation be subject to a fine not to exceed $250.00.

L.1973, c. 307, § 22, eff. Dec. 14, 1973. Amended by L.1985, c. 375, § 22.

39:3C–22.   Special events

Text of section effective on the third month after the date the commissioner has designated the first of the three sites pursuant to paragraph (1) of subsection a. of section 38 of P.L.2009, c. 275 (C.13:1L–5.1).

The commissioner may authorize the holding of organized special events. The commissioner shall adopt and may, from time to time, amend rules and regulations determining the special events which shall be subject to a permit and designating the equipment and facilities necessary for safe operation of snowmobiles, all-terrain vehicles, and dirt bikes and for the safety of operators, participants, and observers in such special events. Whenever a special event requiring authorization of the department is proposed to be held in the State of New Jersey, the person in charge thereof shall, at least 90 days prior thereto, file an application with the commissioner to hold the special event. The application shall set forth the date of and location where it is proposed to hold the rally, race, exhibition, or organized event, and any other information as the commissioner may require, and it shall not be conducted without written authorization of the commissioner. Copies of such regulations shall be furnished by the commissioner to any person making an application therefor.

Any person sponsoring the event who shall violate any regulation adopted pursuant to this section shall for every violation be subject to a fine not to exceed $250.

L.1973, c. 307, § 22, eff. Dec. 14, 1973. Amended by L.1985, c. 375, § 22; L.2009, c. 275, § 22, (contingent effective date).

39:3C–23.   Special events; exemption from registration and light requirements

Text of section effective until the third month after the date the commissioner has designated the first of the three sites pursuant to paragraph (1) of subsection a. of section 38 of P.L.2009, c. 275 (C.13:1L–5.1).

Snowmobiles and all-terrain vehicles operated at special events shall be exempt from the provisions of this chapter concerning registration and lights during the time of such operation, including all prerace practice at the location of the meet. In addition, all-terrain vehicles operated at special events shall be exempt from the provisions of subsection c. of section 16 of P.L.1973, c. 307 (C. 39:3C–16) and subsection b. of section 9 of P.L.1973, c. 307 (C. 39:3C–9); however, subsection b. of section 16 of P.L.1973, c. 307 (C. 39:3C–16) shall apply to persons operating all terrain vehicles at special events and prerace practice.

L.1973, c. 307, § 23, eff. Dec. 14, 1973. Amended by L.1985, c. 375, § 23; L.1991, c. 322, § 6, eff. May 30, 1992.

39:3C–23. Special events; exemption from registration and light requirements

Text of section effective on the third month after the date the commissioner has designated the first of the three sites pursuant to paragraph (1) of subsection a. of section 38 of P.L.2009, c. 275 (C.13:1L–5.1).

Snowmobiles, all-terrain vehicles, and dirt bikes operated at special events shall be exempt from the provisions of this chapter concerning registration and lights during the time of operation of the special event, including all prerace practice at the location of the meet. In addition, snowmobiles, all-terrain vehicles, and dirt bikes operated at special events shall be exempt from the provisions of subsection c. of section 16 of P.L.1973, c. 307 (C.39:3C–16) and subsection b. of section 9 of P.L.1973, c. 307 (C.39:3C–9); however, subsection b. of section 16 of P.L.1973, c. 307 (C.39:3C–16) shall apply to persons operating snowmobiles, all-terrain vehicles, and dirt bikes at special events and prerace practice.

L.1973, c. 307, § 23, eff. Dec. 14, 1973. Amended by L.1985, c. 375, § 23; L.1991, c. 322, § 6, eff. May 30, 1992; L.2009, c. 275, § 23, (contingent effective date).

39:3C–24. Equipment

Text of section effective until the third month after the date the commissioner has designated the first of the three sites pursuant to paragraph (1) of subsection a. of section 38 of P.L.2009, c. 275 (C.13:1L–5.1).

All snowmobiles and all-terrain vehicles operating within the State of New Jersey shall be equipped with:

a. Headlights. At least one white or amber headlamp having a minimum candlepower of sufficient intensity to reveal persons and vehicles at a distance of at least 100 feet ahead during hours of darkness under normal atmospheric conditions.

b. Taillights. At least one red taillamp having a minimum candlepower of sufficient intensity to exhibit a red light plainly visible from a distance of 500 feet to the rear during hours of darkness under normal atmospheric conditions.

c. Brakes. A brake system in good mechanical condition.

d. Reflector material. Reflector material of a minimum area of 16 square inches mounted on each side of the cowling. Registration numbers or other decorative material may be included in computing the required 16-square-inch area.

e. Mufflers. An adequate muffler system in good working condition.

L.1973, c. 307, § 24, eff. Dec. 14, 1973. Amended by L.1985, c. 375, § 24.

39:3C–24. Equipment

Text of section effective on the third month after the date the commissioner has designated the first of the three sites pursuant to paragraph (1) of subsection a. of section 38 of P.L.2009, c. 275 (C.13:1L–5.1).

All snowmobiles, all-terrain vehicles, and dirt bikes operating within the State of New Jersey shall be equipped with:

a. Headlights. At least one white or amber headlamp having a minimum candlepower of sufficient intensity to reveal persons and vehicles at a distance of at least 100 feet ahead during hours of darkness under normal atmospheric conditions.

b. Taillights. At least one red taillamp having a minimum candlepower of sufficient intensity to exhibit a red light plainly visible from a distance of 500 feet to the rear during hours of darkness under normal atmospheric conditions.

c. Brakes. A brake system in good mechanical condition.

d. Reflector material. Reflector material of a minimum area of 16 square inches mounted on each side of the cowling. Registration numbers or other decorative material may be included in computing the required 16–square–inch area.

e. Mufflers. An adequate muffler system in good working condition.

L.1973, c. 307, § 24, eff. Dec. 14, 1973. Amended by L.1985, c. 375, § 24; L.2009, c. 275, § 24, (contingent effective date).

39:3C–25. Inspection and testing

Text of section effective until the third month after the date the commissioner has designated the first of the three sites pursuant to paragraph (1) of subsection a. of section 38 of P.L.2009, c. 275 (C.13:1L–5.1).

The director may adopt rules and regulations with respect to the inspection of snowmobiles and all-terrain vehicles and the testing of mufflers for those vehicles.

L.1973, c. 307, § 25, eff. Dec. 14, 1973. Amended by L.1985, c. 375, § 25.

39:3C–25. Inspection and testing

Text of section effective on the third month after the date the commissioner has designated the first of the three sites pursuant to paragraph (1) of subsection a. of section 38 of P.L.2009, c. 275 (C.13:1L–5.1).

The chief administrator may adopt rules and regulations with respect to the inspection of snowmobiles, all-terrain vehicles, and dirt bikes and the testing of mufflers for those vehicles.

L.1973, c. 307, § 25, eff. Dec. 14, 1973. Amended by L.1985, c. 375, § 25; L.2009, c. 275, § 25, (contingent effective date).

39:3C–26. Sale of vehicle not in compliance with provisions of law; prohibition

Text of section effective until the third month after the date the commissioner has designated the first of the three sites pursuant to paragraph (1) of subsection a. of section 38 of P.L.2009, c. 275 (C.13:1L–5.1).

a.   No person shall have for sale, sell, or offer for sale in this State any snowmobile or all-terrain vehicle which fails to comply with the provisions of this act or which does not comply with the specifications for such equipment required by the rules and regulations of the director, after the effective date of such rules and regulations.

b.   A person shall not knowingly sell or offer to sell an all-terrain vehicle with an engine capacity of greater than 90 cubic centimeters for use by a person less than 16 years of age.

c.   Retail dealers and distributors of all-terrain vehicles shall comply with those requirements of the consent decree entered into by all-terrain vehicle distributors and the United States Consumer Product Safety Commission on April 28, 1988 which require the providing of safety information on all-terrain vehicles to either the purchasers or retail dealers of such vehicles, as appropriate.

L.1973, c. 307, § 26, eff. Dec. 14, 1973. Amended by L.1985, c. 375, § 26; L.1991, c. 322, § 7, eff. Nov. 22, 1991.

39:3C–26. Sale of vehicle not in compliance with provisions of law; prohibition

Text of section effective on the third month after the date the commissioner has designated the first of the three sites pursuant to paragraph (1) of subsection a. of section 38 of P.L.2009, c. 275 (C.13:1L–5.1).

a.   No person shall have for sale, sell, or offer for sale in this State any snowmobile, all-terrain vehicle, or dirt bike which fails to comply with the provisions of P.L.1973, c. 307 (C.39:3C–1 et seq.) or which does not comply with the specifications for the equipment required by the rules and regulations of the commission, after the effective date of such rules and regulations.

b.   A person shall not knowingly sell or offer to sell an all-terrain vehicle with an engine capacity of greater than 90 cubic centimeters for use by a person less than 16 years of age.

c.   Retail dealers and distributors of all-terrain vehicles shall comply with those requirements of the consent decree entered into by all-terrain vehicle distributors and the United States Consumer Product Safety Commission on April 28, 1988 which require the providing of

safety information on all-terrain vehicles to either the purchasers or retail dealers of all-terrain vehicles, as appropriate.

L.1973, c. 307, § 26, eff. Dec. 14, 1973. Amended by L.1985, c. 375, § 26; L.1991, c. 322, § 7, eff. Nov. 22, 1991; L.2009, c. 275, § 26, (contingent effective date).

39:3C–27. Law enforcement officers; duties

Text of section effective until the third month after the date the commissioner has designated the first of the three sites pursuant to paragraph (1) of subsection a. of section 38 of P.L.2009, c. 275 (C.13:1L–5.1).

Every law enforcement officer in the State, including authorized officers of the Division of Motor Vehicles, Department of Environmental Protection, forest rangers and State park police and other designated officers and employees of the department shall enforce this act within their respective jurisdictions.

L.1973, c. 307, § 27, eff. Dec. 14, 1973.

39:3C–27. Law enforcement officers; duties

Text of section effective on the third month after the date the commissioner has designated the first of the three sites pursuant to paragraph (1) of subsection a. of section 38 of P.L.2009, c. 275 (C.13:1L–5.1).

Every law enforcement officer in the State, including any authorized officer of the commission, conservation officers of the Division of Fish and Wildlife, and park police officers and law enforcement operation officers of the Division of Parks and Forestry within the Department of Environmental Protection, and other designated officers and employees of the department shall enforce P.L.1973, c. 307 (C.39:3C–1 et seq.) within their respective jurisdictions.

L.1973, c. 307, § 27, eff. Dec. 14, 1973. Amended by L.2009, c. 275, § 27, (contingent effective date).

39:3C–28. Violations; penalty

Text of section effective until the third month after the date the commissioner has designated the first of the three sites pursuant to paragraph (1) of subsection a. of section 38 of P.L.2009, c. 275 (C.13:1L–5.1).

Any person who shall violate any provisions of this act, if no other penalty is specifically provided, or any rule or regulation promulgated pursuant to this act shall be punished by a fine of not less than $100 or more than $200. For a second or subsequent violation of section 26 of P.L.1973, c. 307 (C. 39:3C–26), a fine of not less than $200 or more than $500 shall be imposed.

L.1973, c. 307, § 28, eff. Dec. 14, 1973. Amended by L.1991, c. 322, § 8, eff. Nov. 22, 1991.

39:3C–28. Violations; penalty

Text of section effective on the third month after the date the commissioner has designated the first of the three sites pursuant to paragraph (1) of subsection a. of section 38 of P.L.2009, c. 275 (C.13:1L–5.1).

Any person who shall violate any provision of P.L. 1973, c. 307 (C.39:3C–1 et seq.), if no other penalty is specifically provided, or any rule or regulation promulgated pursuant to P.L.1973, c. 307 (C.39:3C–1 et seq.) shall be punished by a fine of not less than $250 nor more than $500. For a second or subsequent violation of section 26 of P.L.1973, c. 307 (C.39:3C–26), a fine of not less than $500 nor more than $1,000 shall be imposed.

L.1973, c. 307, § 28, eff. Dec. 14, 1973. Amended by L.1991, c. 322, § 8, eff. Nov. 22, 1991; L.2009, c. 275, § 28, (contingent effective date).

39:3C–29. Deposit of moneys to credit of general treasury; allocation to defray cost of all-terrain vehicle education and training manuals or programs

Text of section effective until the third month after the date the commissioner has designated the first of the three sites pursuant to paragraph (1) of subsection a. of section 38 of P.L.2009, c. 275 (C.13:1L–5.1).

The director shall deposit all moneys received by him from the registration of snowmobiles and all-terrain vehicles, the sale of registration information, publications and other services provided by the department and all fees collected by him under this act to the credit of the General Treasury, except that $5 of a registration fee paid by a resident or nonresident of this State shall be allocated to the division to defray the cost of providing all-terrain vehicle safety education and training manuals or all-terrain vehicle safety education and training programs in accordance with section 15 of P.L.1973, c. 307 (C. 39:3C–15), or both.

L.1973, c. 307, § 29, eff. Dec. 14, 1973. Amended by L.1985, c. 375, § 27; L.1991, c. 322, § 10, eff. Nov. 22, 1991.

39:3C–29. Deposit of moneys into fund

Text of section effective on the third month after the date the commissioner has designated the first of the three sites pursuant to paragraph (1) of subsection a. of section 38 of P.L.2009, c. 275 (C.13:1L–5.1).

The chief administrator shall deposit in the "Off–Road Vehicle Recreational Fund," established pursuant to section 31 of P.L.2009, c. 275 (C.39:3C–3.1) all moneys received by the chief administrator from the additional $10 payment required to be made at the time of registration of snowmobiles, all-terrain vehicles, and dirt bikes in accordance with subsection f. of section 3 of P.L.1973, c. 307 (C.39:3C–3).

L.1973, c. 307, § 29, eff. Dec. 14, 1973. Amended by L.1985, c. 375, § 27; L.1991, c. 322, § 10, eff. Nov. 22, 1991; L.2009, c. 275, § 29, (contingent effective date).

39:3C–30. Other laws applicable to operation on public highways and lands; violations; penalties

Text of section effective until the third month after the date the commissioner has designated the first of the three sites pursuant to paragraph (1) of subsection a. of section 38 of P.L.2009, c. 275 (C.13:1L–5.1).

Owners and operators of snowmobiles and all-terrain vehicles shall, when operating such across a public highway or on public lands or waters, comply with the following provisions of chapter 4 of Title 39 of the Revised Statutes: R.S. 39:4–48 through R.S. 39:4–51; R.S. 39:4–64; R.S. 39:4–72; R.S. 39:4–80; R.S. 39:4–81; R.S. 39:4–92; R.S. 39:4–96 through R.S. 39:4–98; R.S. 39:4–99; R.S. 39:4–100; R.S. 39:4–104; R.S. 39:4–129 through R.S. 39:4–134; R.S. 39:4–203. The failure to comply with any of these provisions shall be a violation of this act and the penalty for such a violation shall be as provided in section 28 of P.L.1973, c. 307 (C. 39:3C–28) rather than the penalty provided in the sections cited above.

L.1973, c. 307, § 30, eff. Dec. 14, 1973. Amended by L.1985, c. 375, § 28.

39:3C–30. Other laws applicable to operation on public highways, lands or waters

Text of section effective on the third month after the date the commissioner has designated the first of the three sites pursuant to paragraph (1) of subsection a. of section 38 of P.L.2009, c. 275 (C.13:1L–5.1).

Owners and operators of snowmobiles, all-terrain vehicles, and dirt bikes shall, when operating such across a public highway or on public land or waters, comply with the following provisions of chapter 4 of Title 39 of the Revised Statutes: R.S.39:4–48 through R.S.39:4–51; R.S.39:4–64; R.S.39:4–72; R.S.39:4–80; R.S.39:4–81; R.S.39:4–92; R.S.39:4–96 through R.S.39:4–98; R.S.39:4–99; R.S.39:4–100; R.S.39:4–104; R.S.39:4–129 through R.S.39:4–134; R.S.39:4–203.

L.1973, c. 307, § 30, eff. Dec. 14, 1973. Amended by L.1985, c. 375, § 28; L.2009, c. 275, § 30, (contingent effective date).

39:3C–30.1. All-terrain vehicles; operation and use on golf courses; operation on public lands, waters or highways as incident to adjacent farm operations

a. The provisions of this 1985 amendatory and supplementary act and this 1991 amendatory act insofar as they pertain to all-terrain vehicles shall not be applicable to their operation and use on golf courses in this State, except that, subsection b. of section 16 of P.L.1973, c. 307 (C. 39:3C–16) and subsection b. of section 26 of P.L.1973, c. 307 (C. 39:3C–26) shall be applicable to the operation and use of all-terrain vehicles on the golf courses of this State.

b. The requirements of subsection b. of section 9 of P.L.1973, c. 307 (C. 39:3C–9) and subsection c. of section 16 of P.L.1973, c. 307 (C. 39:3C–16) shall not apply to a person less than 18 years of age when the person operates an all-terrain vehicle on public lands or waters or across a public highway as an incident to or in the actual performance of the operations of a farm adjacent to the public land or water or the public highway upon which the vehicle is being operated. As used in this section, "farm" means land used for commercial raising, growing and producing of any crop, livestock, or fur products on land not less than five acres in area and which is not used in the business of buying farm products for resale.

L.1985, c. 375, § 29. Amended by L.1991, c. 322, § 9, eff. May 30, 1992.

39:3C–31. Severability

If any clause, sentence, paragraph or part of this act shall, for any reason be adjudged by any court of competent jurisdiction to be invalid, such judgment shall not affect, impair or invalidate the remainder thereof but shall be confined in its operation to the clause, sentence, paragraph or part thereof, directly involved in the controversy in which such judgment shall have been rendered.

L.1973, c. 307, § 31, eff. Dec. 14, 1973.

39:3C–32. Definitions

Section effective on the third month after the date the commissioner has designated the first of the three sites pursuant to paragraph (1) of subsection a. of section 38 of P.L.2009, c. 275 (C.13:1L–5.1).

As used in sections 33 and 34 of P.L.2009, c. 275 (C.39:3C–33 and C.39:3C–34):

"Off-road vehicle" means any motorized vehicle with two or more wheels or tracks that is capable of being operated off of regularly improved and maintained roads including, but not limited to, motorcycles as defined in R.S.39:1–1, snowmobiles and all-terrain vehicles, and dirt bikes as defined in section 5 of P.L.1991, c. 496 (C.2A:42A–6.1).

"Public land" means all land owned, operated, managed, or maintained, or under the jurisdiction of the Department of Environmental Protection, including any and all land owned, operated, managed, maintained, or purchased jointly by the Department of Environmental Protection with any other party and any land so designated by municipal or county ordinance. Public land shall also mean any land used for conservation purposes, including, but not limited to, beaches, forests, greenways, natural areas, water resources, wildlife preserves, land used for watershed protection, or biological or ecological studies, and land exempted from taxation pursuant to section 2 of P.L.1974, c. 167 (C.54:4–3.64).

"Vehicle" means every device in, upon or by which a person or property is or may be transported upon a highway, excepting devices moved by human power or used exclusively upon stationary rails or tracks or motorized bicycles.

L.2009, c. 275, § 32, (contingent effective date).

39:3C–33. Penalties for operating any vehicle or off-road vehicle on public lands contrary to law

Section effective on the third month after the date the commissioner has designated the first of the three sites pursuant to paragraph (1) of subsection a. of section 38 of P.L.2009, c. 275 (C.13:1L–5.1).

Any person who operates any vehicle or off-road vehicle on public lands in violation of P.L.1973, c. 307 (C:39:3C–1 et seq.) or in violation of any law, rule, or regulation adopted pursuant thereto shall be subject to:

a. For a first offense, a fine of not less than $250 nor more than $500.

b. For a second offense, a fine of not less than $500 nor more than $1,000.

c. For a third or subsequent offense, a fine of not less than $1,000.

d. For any offense on public lands in which the use of a vehicle is found responsible for damage to or destruction of natural resources valued in excess of $100, a fine of five times the amount, as determined by the Department of Environmental Protection, of restoration and replacement, where possible, of any natural resource damaged or destroyed by the use of the vehicle. If a person at the time of the imposition of the sentence is less than 17 years of age, the owner of the vehicle shall be liable for the fine of five times the amount, as determined by the Department of Environmental Protection, of restoration and replacement, where possible, of any natural resource damaged or destroyed by the use of the vehicle.

L.2009, c. 275, § 33, (contingent effective date).

39:3C–34. Additional penalties; impoundment; disposition of impounded vehicles; use of proceeds

Section effective on the third month after the date the commissioner has designated the first of the three sites pursuant to paragraph (1) of subsection a. of section 38 of P.L.2009, c. 275 (C.13:1L–5.1).

a. In addition to the fines set forth in section 33 of P.L.2009, c. 275 (C.39:3C–33), any vehicle or off-road vehicle operated on public lands in violation of P.L. 1973, c. 307 (C.39:3C–1 et seq.), may be impounded by the law enforcing agency and held until the payment of the fee required pursuant to subsection b. or c. of this section, as appropriate.

The prosecutor may waive the requirements of subsections b. and c. of this section for the owner of the vehicle or off-road vehicle if the owner is not a defendant in the case and did not know, or reasonably could not have known, that the vehicle or off-road vehicle would be used in violation of P.L.1973, c. 307 (C.39:3C–1 et seq.), or any law, or rule or regulation adopted pursuant thereto, concerning the operation of vehicles or off-road vehicles on public lands.

b. (1) For a first offense, the vehicle or off-road vehicle may be impounded for not less than 48 hours and shall be released to the registered owner upon proof of registration and insurance as applicable to the type of vehicle or off-road vehicle and payment of a fee of $500 to the Department of Environmental Protection, plus reasonable towing and storage costs.

(2) For a second offense, the vehicle or off-road vehicle may be impounded for not less than 96 hours

and shall be released to the registered owner upon proof of registration and insurance as applicable to the type of vehicle or off-road vehicle and payment of a fee of $750 to the Department of Environmental Protection, plus reasonable towing and storage costs.

(3) For a third or subsequent offense, the vehicle or off-road vehicle impounded may be forfeited and sold at auction and the registered owner shall be responsible for payment of a fee of $1,000 to the Department of Environmental Protection, plus reasonable towing and storage costs.

c. (1) If the owner fails to claim the impounded vehicle or off-road vehicle, and the fee required pursuant to subsection b. of this section has not been paid, by noon of the 30th day following the date of conviction, the vehicle or off-road vehicle may be sold at auction. Notice of the sale shall be given by the impounding entity by certified mail to the owner of the vehicle or off-road vehicle, if the owner's name and address are known, and to the holder of any security interest filed with the chief administrator of the New Jersey Motor Vehicle Commission, and by publication in a form prescribed by the chief administrator by one insertion, at least five days before the date of the sale, in one or more newspapers published in the State and circulating in the municipality in which the vehicle or off-road vehicle is impounded.

(2) At any time prior to the sale, the owner or other person entitled to the vehicle or off-road vehicle may reclaim possession upon (a) showing proof of registration and insurance as applicable to the vehicle or off-road vehicle, (b) payment of the required fee, (c) payment of reasonable towing and storage costs, and (d) payment of all outstanding fees and costs associated with the impoundment.

The owner-lessor of an impounded vehicle or off-road vehicle shall be entitled to reclaim possession and the lessee shall be liable for all outstanding fines and restitution and fees and costs associated with the impoundment, towing and storage of the vehicle or off-road vehicle.

d. Any proceeds obtained from the sale of a vehicle or off-road vehicle at public auction pursuant to subsection c. of this section in excess of the amount owed to the impounding entity for the reasonable costs of towing and storage and any fees or other costs associated with the impoundment of the vehicle or off-road vehicle shall be returned to the owner of that vehicle or off-road vehicle, if the owner's name and address are known. If the owner's name and address are unknown or such person or entity cannot be located, the net proceeds shall be administered in accordance with the "Uniform Unclaimed Property Act," R.S.46:30B–1 et seq.

e. (1) Whenever a vehicle or off-road vehicle is subject to forfeiture pursuant to paragraph (3) of subsection b. of this section, the forfeiture may be enforced by a civil action, instituted within 90 days of the impoundment and commenced by the State against the property sought to be forfeited. The complaint for forfeiture shall be verified on oath or affirmation. It shall describe with reasonable accuracy the vehicle or off-road vehicle that is subject to the forfeiture action. The complaint shall contain all allegations setting forth the reason for forfeiture.

(2) Notice of the action shall be given to any person known to have property interest in the vehicle or off-road vehicle and the notice requirements of the Rules of Court for an in rem action shall be followed. The claimant of the vehicle or off-road vehicle that is subject to action under this subsection shall file and serve the claim in the form of an answer in accordance with the Rules of Court. The answer shall be verified on oath or affirmation and state the interest in the property by virtue of which the claimant demands its restitution and the right to defend the action. If the claim is made on behalf of the person entitled to possession by an agent or attorney, it shall state that the agent or attorney is duly authorized to make the claim. If no answer is filed and served within the applicable time, the property seized shall be disposed of pursuant to N.J.S.2C:64–6 and N.J.S.2C:64–7.

L.2009, c. 275, § 34, (contingent effective date).

CHAPTER 4

TRAFFIC REGULATION

ARTICLE 1. CONSTRUCTION OF CHAPTER

Section
39:4–1.   Application of chapter.

ARTICLE 2. GENERAL POWERS AND DUTIES OF COMMISSIONER

39:4–2.   Transfer of powers and duties of commissioner to director of Division of Motor Vehicles.
39:4–3 to 39:4–5.   Repealed.
39:4–6.   Director's duties.
39:4–7.   Director's hearings; subpoenas.
39:4–8.   Municipal or county regulatory actions governing traffic or traffic conditions; commission approval; certain authorized action permitted without commissioner approval.
39:4–8.1.   Handicapped parking spaces and signs; inspection by municipal engineer.
39:4–8.2.   Definitions relating to traffic and parking on public highways or transportation systems.
39:4–8.3.   Regulation of traffic and parking on public highways and transportation systems.
39:4–8.4.   Contents of order, mailing and publication requirements.
39:4–8.5.   Maintenance of official and informational records of orders.
39:4–8.6.   Continued effectiveness of orders issued prior to the effective date of this act.
39:4–8.7.   Regulation provisions of Title 39 under the jurisdiction of the commissioner.
39:4–8.8.   Authority of the commissioner.
39:4–8.9.   Definitions.

Section

39:4–8.10.   Construction of speed hump on residential streets; construction of traffic calming measures.

39:4–8.11.   Design and construction of speed humps.

39:4–8.12.   Legislative findings and declarations; traffic control signal monitoring systems; pilot program.

39:4–8.13.   Definitions.

39:4–8.14.   Five-year pilot program; municipal participation in program; authorization to install and utilize traffic control signal monitoring systems; public awareness.

39:4–8.15.   Recorded data to be reviewed by designated law enforcement official; issuance of a summons; public access to data; owner liability for violations.

39:4–8.16.   Rules and regulations.

39:4–8.17.   Annual reports by municipalities; reports to the legislature and governor.

39:4–8.18.   Expiration of pilot program.

39:4–8.19.   Consultation with commissioner at request of municipality or county; authority to give advisory review; fees.

39:4–8.20.   Fines paid to the municipal court; distribution of funds.

39:4–8.21.   Construction of a curb extension or bulbout; municipal authority.

39:4–9.   Repealed.

39:4–9.1.   Exchange of information between states concerning certain violations.

ARTICLE 3. BICYCLES AND ROLLER SKATES

39:4–10.   Lights and reflectors on bicycles.

39:4–10.1.   Bicycle operators and passengers under age 17 required to wear helmets.

39:4–10.2.   Violation of bicycle helmet requirement; fines.

39:4–10.3.   Posting of sign regarding bicycle helmet requirement; penalties.

39:4–10.4.   Rules and regulations.

39:4–10.5.   Definitions relating to roller skating and skateboarding.

39:4–10.6.   Violations by roller skaters or skateboarders; fines.

39:4–10.7.   Personal injury or wrongful death actions.

39:4–10.8.   Sale of roller skates or skateboards; protective gear warning.

39:4–10.9.   Sale or rental of roller skates or skateboards; notice of helmet requirement.

39:4–10.10.   Rights and duties of roller skaters and skateboarders.

39:4–10.10a.   Municipal ordinances; skateboards and roller skates.

39:4–10.10b.   Maintenance or construction of roadways; accommodation of roller skates or skateboards.

39:4–10.11.   Rules of operation of roller skates and skateboards on roadways.

39:4–10.12.   Nonapplicability of act; roller skating rinks.

39:4–10.13.   Adoption of rules and regulations; roller skates and skateboards.

39:4–11.   Audible signal.

39:4–11.1.   Brake required.

39:4–12.   Position of hands and feet; carrying another person.

39:4–13.   Repealed.

39:4–14.   Hitching on vehicles prohibited.

39:4–14.1.   Rights and duties of persons on bicycles.

Section

39:4–14.2.   Keeping to right; exceptions; single file.

39:4–14.3.   Motorized bicycles; limitations on use; age of operator; license to operate; issuance; examination; learner's permit; fee; possession; exhibit on request; violations; fine; applicable traffic regulations.

39:4–14.3a.   Retail sales; conformance of bicycles to act and regulations.

39:4–14.3b.   Violations; penalties.

39:4–14.3c.   Rules and regulations.

39:4–14.3d.   Operator only on bicycle.

39:4–14.3e.   Compulsory liability insurance coverage.

39:4–14.3f.   Accident reports.

39:4–14.3g.   Operation by person under influence of liquor or drugs; penalty.

39:4–14.3h.   Suspension of privilege; second violation.

39:4–14.3i.   Registration; requirements; form and content of certificate; expiration; renewal.

39:4–14.3j.   Form completed by dealer at original sale; content; temporary registration; temporary license plates; registration; fee.

39:4–14.3k.   License plate.

39:4–14.3l.   Removal from state, destruction, theft or discontinued usage; notice; transfer of ownership.

39:4–14.3m.   Display of license.

39:4–14.3n.   Make and model numbers; certification; list of approved bicycles.

39:4–14.3o.   Nonresident motorized bicycle owner; registration.

39:4–14.3p.   Proof of ownership; bicycle purchased prior to effective date of act.

39:4–14.3q.   Helmet.

39:4–14.3r.   Dealer licensed as motor vehicle dealer; inapplicability of restrictions contained in Municipal Land Use Law.

39:4–14.3s.   Rules and regulations.

39:4–14.3t.   Violations; fine.

39:4–14.3u.   Ownership acquired prior to effective date of act; compliance with act.

39:4–14.3v.   Education program for safe operation; fund.

39:4–14.3v1.   Educational program for safe operation of bicycles; fund.

39:4–14.3w.   Disposition of fees.

39:4–14.3x.   Emerging from or entering alley, driveway, garage, or private road or driveway; violation; penalties.

39:4–14.4.   Sale or rent of bicycle; equipment with reflectors.

39:4–14.4a.   Rules and regulations for promotion of bicycle helmets.

39:4–14.5.   Bicycle defined.

39:4–14.6.   Inapplicability of act to person not regularly engaged in selling or renting bicycles.

39:4–14.7.   Equipment; rules and regulations.

39:4–14.7a.   Statement promoting use of helmet to be affixed to bicycle or to carton of unassembled bicycle.

39:4–14.8.   Violations; penalties.

39:4–14.9.   Enforcement; collection of penalties; jurisdiction; process.

39:4–14.10.   Definitions.

39:4–14.11.   Failure to comply with act; fines.

39:4–14.12.   Restriction on operation of motorized scooter.

39:4–14.13.   Violations; penalties.

Section

39:4–14.14. Operation of motorized scooters in designated locations permitted by municipal ordinance or county resolution; requirements.

39:4–14.15. Conditions for operation of motor scooter on public streets.

ARTICLE 4. HORSES AND HORSE–DRAWN VEHICLES

39:4–15. Sleigh bells on horses attached to a sleigh.

39:4–16. Unattended horses; precautions used.

39:4–17. Unbitted horses.

39:4–18. Removing part of vehicle or harness.

39:4–19. Obstructing sidewalk with tie rope, etc., prohibited.

39:4–20. Hitching horses to pole, post, tree or hydrant prohibited.

39:4–21. Racing on highway prohibited; exception.

39:4–22. Reins held in hands.

39:4–23. Ill-treatment of horses.

39:4–24. Use of whip.

39:4–25. Lights on animal-drawn vehicles.

39:4–25.1. Rights and duties of persons riding or driving animals.

ARTICLE 5. MACHINERY, VEHICLES OR APPARATUS OF UNUSUAL SIZE OR WEIGHT

39:4–26. Moving heavy machinery, apparatus, etc.; registration fee; permits; reciprocity.

39:4–27. Loading and operation of trailer; permittee's responsibility in damages.

39:4–28. Height; overhead wires.

39:4–29. Time for moving along street railway tracks.

39:4–30. Exceptions to application of article; "temporary" or "in-transit" registration plates.

39:4–31. Violations of article; fine.

ARTICLE 5A. LOW SPEED VEHICLES

39:4–31.1. Operation of low-speed vehicles on public roads; conditions.

39:4–31.2. Maintenance and equipment requirements for low-speed vehicles operated on public roads; violation.

39:4–31.3. Valid driver's license required for operation of low-speed vehicle; registration; insurance; license plates; safety information decal; violation.

39:4–31.4. Certificate of origin of low-speed vehicle; waiver and certification by purchaser.

39:4–31.5. Low-speed vehicle exempt from inspection.

ARTICLE 6. PEDESTRIANS

39:4–32. Pedestrian crossing at controlled intersection; pedestrian duties; driver duties; inference of no due care exercised.

39:4–33. Use of designated crosswalk; keeping to right.

39:4–34. Pedestrians to cross within crosswalk or at right angles; facing traffic; sidewalks.

39:4–35. Repealed.

39:4–36. Driver to yield to pedestrian at crosswalk; exceptions; vehicles approaching stopped vehicle from rear; yield of right-of-way by pedestrian;

Section

penalties; portion of fine deposited in Pedestrian Safety Enforcement and Education Fund.

39:4–36.1. Crossing having pedestrian tunnel or overhead crossing; right of way.

39:4–36.2. Pedestrian Safety Enforcement and Education Fund.

39:4–36.3. Legislative findings.

39:4–36.4. Identification of intersections controlled by traffic control signals presenting demonstrated pedestrian safety problems.

39:4–37. Regulating crossing at intersections by local authorities.

39:4–37.1. Blind persons; right of way.

ARTICLE 7. STREET CARS

39:4–38. Vehicles travelling upon street car route to give way to street car; intersections; overtaking and passing street cars.

39:4–39. Distance to be kept behind street car.

39:4–40. Passing street car.

39:4–41. Driving through safety zones prohibited.

39:4–42. Action of motorman on collision.

39:4–43. Crossing signals.

39:4–44. Car stops.

39:4–45. Obstruction of crosswalks by street cars.

ARTICLE 8. DISPLAY OF NAME AND PLACE OF OWNER OF COMMERCIAL VEHICLE

39:4–46. Commercial vehicles to display name and municipality of owner and gross vehicle weight rating; exception; exemption from municipality requirement.

39:4–47. Violations of article; fine.

ARTICLE 9. OPERATION OF OR ACTS AFFECTING OPERATION OF VEHICLES AND STREET CARS

39:4–48. Operating or using motor vehicle without consent of owner; fine.

39:4–49. Tampering with vehicle; fine.

39:4–49.1. Operating motor vehicle with controlled dangerous substance or prescription legend drug in possession or in motor vehicle.

39:4–49.2. Exemption; physicians, dentists, etc.

39:4–49.3. Exemption; common carriers, warehousemen, etc.

39:4–50. Driving while intoxicated.

39:4–50.1. Repealed.

39:4–50.2. Consent to taking samples of breath; record of test; independent test; prohibition of use of force; informing accused.

39:4–50.2a. Guidelines to promote uniform enforcement.

39:4–50.3. Method of analyses; approval of techniques; certification of analysts; reports; forms.

39:4–50.4. Repealed.

39:4–50.4a. Refusal to submit to chemical test; penalties.

39:4–50.5. Severability.

39:4–50.6, 39:4–50.7. Repealed.

39:4–50.8. Conviction for violation of § 39:4–50; surcharge; distribution.

39:4–50.9. Short title.

39:4–50.10. Victim defined.

39:4–50.11. Victims' rights.

39:4–50.12. Consultation with prosecutor prior to dismissal or plea negotiation.

Section

39:4–50.13.	Effect on New Jersey Tort Claims Act.
39:4–50.14.	Operation of motor vehicle by person who has consumed alcohol but is under the legal age to purchase alcoholic beverages; penalties.
39:4–50.15.	Additional definitions.
39:4–50.16.	Legislative findings.
39:4–50.17.	Ignition interlock device as an additional penalty.
39:4–50.17a.	Fees for ignition interlock device installation.
39:4–50.18.	Notification of the Director of the Division of Motor Vehicles.
39:4–50.19.	Failure to install interlock device; penalties.
39:4–50.20.	Certification of ignition interlock devices.
39:4–50.21.	Rules and regulations; consistency with federal model.
39:4–50.22.	Criminal and civil liability for permitting or facilitating the arrestee's operation of a motor vehicle; content and form of the written statement and acknowledgment.
39:4–50.23.	Vehicle impoundment; detainment, and release; fees.
39:4–51.	Sentence for violation of section 39:4–50 must be served; release on work release program.
39:4–51a.	Consumption of alcoholic beverage by operator or passenger; prohibition; presumption; violations; penalty.
39:4–51b.	Open container; occupants of motor vehicle.
39:4–52.	Racing on highway prohibited; fine.
39:4–53.	Leaving vehicle with engine running prohibited; fine.
39:4–54.	Trailers; number permitted; towing methods; auxiliary axles; converter dolly.
39:4–55.	Action on steep grades and curves.
39:4–56.	Delaying traffic prohibited.
39:4–56.1.	Willfully causing vehicle to become disabled; abandonment of vehicle upon public highway.
39:4–56.2.	Violations; penalties.
39:4–56.3.	Suspension of registration.
39:4–56.4.	Legislative findings and declarations.
39:4–56.5.	Abandonment of motor vehicles; penalty.
39:4–56.6.	Abandonment of vehicle on private property; removal by owner of property; costs; sale of vehicle.
39:4–56.7.	Issuance of summons for violation by law enforcement officer.
39:4–56.8.	Definitions; removal of disabled motor vehicles by towing service under contract; failure to remove debris surrounding vehicle; penalty.
39:4–57.	Observance of directions of officers.
39:4–57.1.	Vehicle stopped by law enforcement officer; activation of interior light.
39:4–58.	Driving vehicle with view to rear and sides obstructed.
39:4–59.	Begging rides prohibited.
39:4–60.	Soliciting trade or contributions prohibited; designation of particular highway as hazardous for such purposes; signs.
39:4–60.1.	Certain rotating or flashing lights prohibited.
39:4–60.2.	Removal without notice.
39:4–60.3.	Emergency use.
39:4–61.	Tailboard riding.
39:4–62.	Leaving curb.
39:4–63.	Placing, throwing or depositing from motor vehicle, injurious substance on highway; fine; forfeiture of right to operate motor vehicle.

Section

39:4–64.	Throwing or dropping bundles, objects or debris from vehicles; fine; rebuttable presumption.
39:4–64.1.	Signs informing of consequences of violation.
39:4–65.	Letting off or taking on persons.
39:4–66.	Emerging from alley, driveway, garage, or private road or driveway.
39:4–66.1.	Entering alley, driveway, garage, or private road or driveway from highway over sidewalk.
39:4–66.2.	Operation of motor vehicles on public or private property to avoid traffic signals or signs prohibited; exceptions; penalties for violations.
39:4–67.	Obstructing passage of other vehicles or street cars prohibited; clearance of intersections.
39:4–68.	Doors of street car or autobus closed.
39:4–69.	Riding on part not intended for passengers prohibited.
39:4–70.	Repealed.
39:4–71.	Driving on sidewalk.
39:4–72.	Operating motor vehicle near horses; violation and penalties.

ARTICLE 10. LOAD AND LOADING OF VEHICLES

39:4–73.	Repealed.
39:4–74.	Blank.
39:4–75.	Driving overweight vehicles on intrastate bridges; approaching signs; fines; liability for damage to bridges.
39:4–76.	Driving overweight vehicles on interstate bridges; penalty; liability for damages; disposition of penalties.
39:4–77.	Loading so as to spill prohibited; minimum safety standards; penalty.
39:4–77.1.	Snow or ice falling off moving vehicle; damage to vehicles or property; penalties.
39:4–77.1.	Snow or ice accumulated on motor vehicles; duty to remove; penalties; commercial vehicles; damage to other vehicles; public awareness campaign.
39:4–77.2.	Motor Vehicle Snow and Ice Removal Safety Fund.
39:4–78.	Carrying metals.
39:4–79.	Backing to curb.

ARTICLE 11. LAW OF ROAD AND RIGHT OF WAY

39:4–80.	Traffic control by officers.
39:4–80.1.	School crossing guards; duty to obey; penalty.
39:4–81.	Observing traffic signals.
39:4–82.	Keeping to right.
39:4–82.1.	Two roadway highways; driving upon.
39:4–83.	Keeping to right at intersections; exception on one-way roadway.
39:4–84.	Passing to right when proceeding in opposite directions.
39:4–85.	Passing to left when overtaking; passing when in lines; signalling to pass; passing upon right.
39:4–85.1.	One-way traffic, designation of highways for; signs.
39:4–86.	Overtaking and passing vehicles; crossing "No Passing" lines.
39:4–86.1 to 39:4–86.3.	Repealed.
39:4–87.	Overtaken vehicle to give way.
39:4–87.1.	Right of way for busses.
39:4–88.	Traffic on marked lanes.
39:4–89.	Following; space between trucks.

Section

39:4–90. Right of way at intersections.
39:4–90.1. Limited access highways, driving onto or from.
39:4–91. Right of way of emergency vehicles; liability of drivers.
39:4–92. Authorized emergency vehicles; clearance for; following or parking near.
39:4–92.1. Fire department vehicle returning to fire station; flashing red light.
39:4–92.2. Authorized emergency vehicles displaying flashing, blinking or alternating lights; driver duty when approaching stationary emergency vehicles; penalties.
39:4–93. Processions.
39:4–94. Railroad blocking highway.
39:4–94.1. Repealed.
39:4–94.2. State, county or municipal highway, road or street closed with posted notice and barricade; violations; penalty.

ARTICLE 12. SPEED

39:4–95. "Vehicle" defined.
39:4–96. Reckless driving; punishment.
39:4–97. Careless driving.
39:4–97a. Motor vehicle operation causing property destruction; prohibition; exception; recreational property defined.
39:4–97.1. Slow speeds as blocking traffic.
39:4–97.2. Driving or operating a motor vehicle in an unsafe manner; endangering persons or property; fines; surcharges.
39:4–97.3. Use of hands-free and hand-held wireless communication devices while driving; when permitted; penalty.
39:4–97.4. Application to law enforcement, fire department and emergency personnel.
39:4–97.5. Construction with other laws.
39:4–98. Rates of speed.
39:4–98.1. Designation of lower maximum speed limits for trucks of registered gross weight of 10,000 pounds and over.
39:4–98.2. Counties or municipalities; reduction of regular speed limit for 72 hours for maintenance or repairs; notice to commissioner.
39:4–98.3. Short title.
39:4–98.4. Definitions relative to 65mph speed limit.
39:4–98.5. Speed limit of 65mph established, certain highways.
39:4–98.6. Certain fines doubled where speed limit is 65mph.
39:4–98.7. Speeding 20mph or more over limit; fines; certain; doubled.
39:4–98.8. Study to determine effect of 65mph speed limit; report; implementation.
39:4–98.9. Temporary changes to speed limit; emergency orders.
39:4–99. Exceeding speed limitations; speed specified in charge.
39:4–100. Rate of speed across sidewalk.
39:4–101. Speedways.
39:4–102. Speeding by physicians in emergencies.
39:4–103. Exemptions from speed regulations.
39:4–103.1. Use of photo radar to enforce speeding laws prohibited.
39:4–104. Violations of article; penalty.

Section

ARTICLE 13. TRAFFIC SIGNALS

39:4–105. Color system.
39:4–106. Sequence of lights.
39:4–107. Period or cycle.
39:4–108. Semaphores.
39:4–109. Position of lenses.
39:4–110. Height of signals.
39:4–111. Power of lights.
39:4–112. Visibility of signals to traffic at intersections.
39:4–113. Continuously controlled highway.
39:4–114. Traffic signal in paved roadway or poles in crosswalk lanes prohibited.
39:4–115. Making right or left turn.
39:4–116. Special right or left turn.
39:4–117. Special pedestrian interval.
39:4–118. Beacon or flashing signal.
39:4–119. Traffic control signals operating as flashing mechanisms; red; amber.
39:4–120. Director to determine signals; uniform system.
39:4–120.1. Official traffic control signals.
39:4–120.2. Flashing mechanism; use by municipalities.
39:4–120.3. Submission of written information to commissioner.
39:4–120.4. Ordinance, regulation or resolution; effective date.
39:4–120.5. Definitions.
39:4–120.6. Official traffic control device erected at public-private intersection.
39:4–120.7. Public-private intersection containing state or local highway; approval by commissioner or local authority.
39:4–120.8. Traffic device to be installed and maintained by owner of private road.
39:4–120.9. Motorists required to obey traffic control device at public-private intersection.
39:4–120.10. Violations; penalties.
39:4–120.11. Rules and regulations.
39:4–121. Traffic lights on state roads in suburban districts at location of fire engine houses; installation by state highway commission.
39:4–121.1. Dangerous intersections in counties or municipalities; traffic lights.
39:4–121.2. Expenses paid from state highway fund.
39:4–121.3. Counties or municipalities; agreements with department of transportation for installation, alteration or maintenance of traffic control device.
39:4–122. Signal by police whistle.

ARTICLE 14. TURNS, HAND SIGNALS, STARTING AND STOPPING

39:4–123. Right and left hand turns.
39:4–124. Method of turning at intersection; local authorities may determine.
39:4–125. Turning on curve, grade or place where view obstructed or highway marked with "no U turn" sign.
39:4–126. Signaling before starting, turning or stopping.
39:4–127. Backing or turning in street.
39:4–127.1. Railroad crossings; stopping.
39:4–127.2. Movable span bridges.
39:4–128. Vehicles required to stop at grade crossings; method of crossing; exceptions; notice to railroad of intention to cross with certain vehicles or machinery; violations; penalties.

Section

39:4–128.1. Buses used for transportation of children stopped to receive or discharge passengers; duty of motorists and of bus driver; violations; penalties.
39:4–128.2. Repealed.
39:4–128.3. Definitions.
39:4–128.4. Approaching or overtaking stopped frozen dessert truck; stopping.
39:4–128.5. Frozen dessert truck; equipment.
39:4–128.6. Stopped frozen dessert truck; duty of driver.
39:4–128.7. Conditions for vending.
39:4–128.8. Backing up truck to make sale; prohibition.
39:4–128.9. Riding in or on frozen dessert truck; authorized persons only.
39:4–128.10. Violations; penalty.
39:4–128.11. Railroad crossings; requirements for certain commercial motor vehicles; employer liability for violations.

ARTICLE 15. ACCIDENTS AND REPORTS

39:4–129. Action in case of accident.
39:4–130. Report of accidents; notice when person is injured or killed.
39:4–131. Reports; forms; use as evidence; inspection; confidentiality.
39:4–131.1. Inconsistent rule, regulation, resolution or ordinance inconsistent with act or establishing fee in excess of fee under Right to Know Law; supersedure.
39:4–132. Certain damages reported by repairman.
39:4–133. Repealed.
39:4–134. Report of death to director.
39:4–134.1. Application of article.

ARTICLE 16. PARKING

39:4–135. Parking; direction and side of street; angle parking; one-way street.
39:4–136. Parking on highway; removing vehicle; disabled vehicle.
39:4–137. Vehicle without driver; brakes set; motor stopped; wheels turned to curb.
39:4–138. Places where parking prohibited; exceptions; moving vehicle not under one's control into prohibited area.
39:4–138.1. "No parking" zones on highways.
39:4–138.2. Repealed.
39:4–138.3. Ordinance permitting parking in front of private driveway.
39:4–138.4. Issuance of permit for parking in front of driveway; application; number of permits.
39:4–138.5. Display of permit required; fees.
39:4–138.6. Ordinance setting forth permissible parking distances; exception.
39:4–139. Loading or unloading passengers or materials; period at certain places.
39:4–139.1. Repealed.
39:4–139.2. Short title.
39:4–139.3. Definitions.
39:4–139.4. Uniform traffic ticket; complaint and summons; contents; personal service.
39:4–139.5. Joint liability of owner and operator; recovery by owner against operator; leased vehicles.
39:4–139.6. Failure to answer or appear; rule applicable; procedures; notice.

Section

39:4–139.7. Answer to parking ticket or failure to appear notice.
39:4–139.8. Evidence; submission to court; presence of officer; default judgment after failure to answer or pay fine and penalties; effect; assessment of costs; appeals; limitation of actions.
39:4–139.9. Distribution of $2.00 of parking penalty to municipal court; civil contempt for failure to pay fine, penalty or costs.
39:4–139.10. Failure to respond to a failure to appear notice or to pay parking judgment; notice to division; suspension of driver's license or motor vehicle registration; record.
39:4–139.10a. Parking cases; dismissal.
39:4–139.11. Restoration of driver's license or motor vehicle registration after satisfaction of fines and penalties; recordation.
39:4–139.12. Suspension of license; fee; deposit.
39:4–139.13. Impoundment or immobilization of vehicle with outstanding warrants; authorization by municipalities by ordinance; sale at auction; reclamation of possession prior to sale; disposition of proceeds.
39:4–139.14. Contracts by municipalities with public agency or private organization for services to process parking offenses; plan by municipality; approval by Supreme Court.

ARTICLE 17. THROUGH STREETS

39:4–140. Designation of through highways, stop intersections and yield intersections; erection of stop or yield signs.
39:4–141. Placing of signs.
39:4–142. Repealed.
39:4–143. Intersecting through streets.
39:4–144. Stopping or yielding right of way before entering stop or yield intersections.
39:4–145. Repealed.

ARTICLE 18. SIGNS [REPEALED]

39:4–146 to 39:4–183. Repealed.

ARTICLE 18A. HIGHWAY AND TRAFFIC SIGNS

A. GENERAL PROVISIONS

39:4–183.1. Legal authority.
39:4–183.1a. Municipalities; installations at school crossing intersections; ordinance; approval by commissioner.
39:4–183.1b. Designation of older and walking impaired persons crossing areas; appropriate signs.
39:4–183.2. Signs hereafter erected.
39:4–183.3. Display of unauthorized traffic signs.
39:4–183.4. Prohibited signs deemed a nuisance; action for removal.
39:4–183.5. Repealed.
39:4–183.6. Director to determine signs.

B. SPECIFICATIONS

39:4–183.7. Repealed.
39:4–183.8. Materials.
39:4–183.9. Dimensions.
39:4–183.10. Message; wording and symbols.

Section

39:4–183.11.   Illumination; reflectorization.

C. LOCATION

39:4–183.12.   Location.
39:4–183.13, 39:4–183.14.   Repealed.

D. MAINTENANCE

39:4–183.15.   Continuous maintenance.

E. DETAILED DESIGN AND INSTALLATION

39:4–183.16 to 39:4–183.21.   Repealed.
39:4–183.21a.   Abandonment of line and grade crossings; notice; removal of railroad advance warning signs.
39:4–183.22.   Repealed.
39:4–183.22a.   Construction warning signs.
39:4–183.23.   Repealed.
39:4–183.24.   Location and information signs.
39:4–183.25.   Repeal.
39:4–183.26.   Repealed.
39:4–183.27.   Rules and regulations; placement, specifications, location and maintenance of traffic signs and markings.
39:4–183.28.   Repeals.
39:4–183.29.   Continuance of rules and regulations promulgated by department of transportation prior to act.
39:4–183.30.   Effect of act on offenses, liabilities, penalties or forfeitures prior to date of act.
39:4–183.31.   Uncontrolled intersections having demonstrated pedestrian safety problems; posting pedestrian crossing yield signs.

ARTICLE 19.   CURB AND PAVEMENT MARKINGS [REPEALED]

39:4–184 to 39:4–191.   Repealed.

ARTICLE 19A.   MARKINGS

39:4–191.1.   Legal authority; uniformity.
39:4–191.2.   Types of markings.
39:4–191.3 to 39:4–191.5.   Repealed.
39:4–191.6.   Illumination and reflectorization.
39:4–191.7.   Word markings limited.

ARTICLE 20.   SAFETY ZONES [REPEALED]

39:4–192 to 39:4–196.   Repealed.

ARTICLE 20A.   SAFETY ZONES AND TRAFFIC ISLANDS

39:4–196.1.   Local authority.
39:4–196.2.   Types of safety zones and traffic islands.
39:4–196.3.   Location, design and protection.

ARTICLE 21.   POWERS OF MUNICIPALITIES, COUNTIES AND HIGHWAY COMMISSIONER

39:4–197.   Ordinance or resolution on matters covered by chapter.

Section

39:4–197.1.   Prohibiting normal traffic on county or state highway; consent of board of chosen freeholders or highway commission necessary.
39:4–197.2.   County road lying within municipality; regulation of traffic and parking.
39:4–197.3.   Special traffic regulations.
39:4–197.4.   Angle parking ordinances; exemption from approval by state; conditions.
39:4–197.5.   Restricted parking for use by handicapped persons; ordinances, resolutions or regulations.
39:4–197.6.   Restricted parking zones in front of residences occupied by handicapped persons; ordinance; conditions.
39:4–197.7.   Permits for motor vehicle; fee.
39:4–197.8.   State Highway Route No. 94 in Sussex and Warren Counties; regulations limiting use.
39:4–197.9.   Municipal handicapped parking enforcement unit; creation; purpose.
39:4–197.10.   Eligibility for participation.
39:4–197.11.   Preference for participation by handicapped persons.
39:4–197.12.   Reimbursement for actual expenses.
39:4–197.13.   Course of instruction required; curriculum.
39:4–197.14.   Appropriations.
39:4–197.15.   Uniform and patch.
39:4–197.16.   State Highway Route 29; Legislative findings.
39:4–197.17.   Truck traffic exceeding 26,000 pounds prohibited.
39:4–197.18.   Exceptions.
39:4–197.19.   Use of prohibited portions.
39:4–197.20.   Enforceability.
39:4–197.21.   Violation; fines.
39:4–198.   Notice of ordinance, resolution or regulation by signs; handicapped parking signs.
39:4–199.   Safety zones, signals, guideposts and other structures on state highway; approval by highway commission.
39:4–199.1.   Official traffic signs at traffic islands, safety zones and grade separations, etc.
39:4–200.   Repealed.
39:4–201.   Resolutions or ordinances regulating traffic on county roads; notice; penalties.
39:4–201.1.   "No passing" zones; notice.
39:4–201.2.   Repealed.
39:4–202.   Approval of resolutions, ordinances or regulation by commissioner.

ARTICLE 22.   GENERAL PENALTY

39:4–203.   General penalty for violations of chapter.
39:4–203.1.   Indigents; fine for traffic offense; payment in installments.
39:4–203.2.   Failure to comply with installment order; additional penalties.
39:4–203.3.   Violations pertaining to pedestrians and bicycles by juvenile under 17; warning; penalties.
39:4–203.4.   Conviction for violation after Jan. 1, 1983; petition for reduction in sentence.
39:4–203.5.   Traffic offenses committed in areas of highway construction or repair; fines doubled.

ARTICLE 23.   SPECIAL PRIVILEGES

39:4–204.   "Handicapped person" defined.
39:4–205.   Handicapped person identification cards; application; issuance; forfeiture or revocation; indefinite validity.

Section

39:4–206.   Placard; issuance; display on motor vehicle; temporary placards; grant upon certification by physician; renewal; fees; license plates with wheelchair symbol.

39:4–207.   Parking overtime; motor vehicle with display of placard or wheelchair symbol license plates.

39:4–207.1.   Rules and regulations.

39:4–207.2.   Mentally retarded person defined.

39:4–207.3.   Motor vehicles used to transport mentally retarded persons; special insignia; issuance; fee; annual renewal; special vehicle identification cards; placard for display.

39:4–207.4.   Authorization to park in space marked for physically handicapped.

39:4–207.5.   Handicapped parking privileges; vehicles with permit from another state, district or territory of United States or Canada.

39:4–207.6.   Definitions.

39:4–207.7.   Request by eligible handicapped person to law enforcement officer for removal and storage of motor vehicle unlawfully parked in handicapped parking space or zone.

39:4–207.8.   Handicapped nursing home resident identification card and windshield placard.

39:4–207.9.   Parking spaces for handicapped motorists; maintenance.

ARTICLE 24.   REGULATION OF TRAFFIC AND PARKING ON STATE PROPERTY

39:4–208.   Trenton, State's property at; regulations authorized.

39:4–209.   Violations; penalties.

39:4–210.   Jurisdiction of offenses; disposition of fines.

39:4–211.   Enforcement of regulations.

39:4–212.   Cooperation in making and enforcing regulations.

ARTICLE 25.   EMERGENCY TRAFFIC CONTROL

39:4–213.   Control of traffic during emergency conditions; Attorney-General's powers.

39:4–214.   Signals; signs; police personnel.

39:4–215.   Failure to obey signals, signs or directions.

ARTICLE 26.   REGULATION OF USE BY STATE AND INTERSTATE HIGHWAY SYSTEM. RIGHTS OF WAY AND REST AREAS

39:4–216.   Commercial activity or solicitation of contributions; prohibition.

ARTICLE 1.   CONSTRUCTION OF CHAPTER

39:4–1.   Application of chapter

The provisions of this chapter applicable to the drivers of vehicles on the highways shall also apply to the drivers of all vehicles owned or operated by this State, the United States, any territorial or Federal district, any other State or any county, municipality or any other political subdivision thereof, subject to such specific exceptions as are set forth in this chapter.

The provisions of this chapter shall apply to the owners and drivers of vehicles on highways, roadways, driveways, parking areas or upon any grounds owned and maintained by the State of New Jersey, or any State department or agency, the counties, the municipalities and the school district boards of education of this State.

This chapter shall not apply to persons, teams, motor vehicles and other equipment while actually engaged in work on the surface of a highway, but shall apply to such persons and vehicles when traveling to or from the work.

Amended by L.1950, c. 15, p. 42, § 1; L.1951, c. 23, p. 66, § 1; L.1995, c. 70, § 1, eff. April 10, 1995.

ARTICLE 2.   GENERAL POWERS AND DUTIES OF COMMISSIONER

39:4–2.   Transfer of powers and duties of commissioner to director of Division of Motor Vehicles

All the powers and duties heretofore exercised and performed by the commission created by an act entitled "An act to establish a traffic commission and to define its powers and duties," approved April fifteenth, one thousand nine hundred and thirty (L.1930, c. 148, p. 564), and its amendments and supplements,[1] which powers and duties were transferred to and vested in the commissioner by an act entitled "An act vesting in the Commissioner of Motor Vehicles of this State all the powers and duties heretofore exercised and performed by the commission created by an act entitled 'An act to establish a traffic commission and to define its powers and duties,' approved April fifteenth, one thousand nine hundred and thirty, and the acts amendatory thereof and supplemental thereto," approved June twelfth, one thousand nine hundred and thirty-two (L.1932, c. 179, § 1, p. 306),[2] and which powers and duties were transferred to and vested in the director by an act entitled "An act relating to the reorganization of the executive and administrative offices, departments, and instrumentalities of the State Government; and establishing and concerning a Department of Law and Public Safety as a principal department in the executive branch of the State Government," approved October fifteenth, one thousand nine hundred and forty-eight (P.L.1948, c. 439),[3] shall continue to be so vested in the director.

Amended by L.1951, c. 23, p. 66, § 2.

[1] N.J.S.A. § 39:4–4 et seq.

[2] This section.

[3] N.J.S.A. § 52:17B–1 et seq.

39:4–3 to 39:4–5.   Repealed by L.2003, c. 13, § 126

39:4–6.   Director's duties

The commissioner shall investigate traffic conditions, means for their improvement and the enforcement of laws and regulations relating to traffic, including pedestrian travel on the public streets and highways. He may determine, regulate and control the character, type, location, placing of and operation of all official traffic control devices on the streets, highways and public places in the State, or cause the removal of such devices determined to be unnecessary. He shall see that the laws relating to such devices are enforced, investigate the manner of enforcing the laws regarding the parking of vehicles on public highways, the use of streets by pedestrians, investigate the location of "stop" signs and cause the removal of those which in his opinion are installed in violation of this chapter, and cause the removal of all colored lights so located as to be confused with traffic signals. He shall also enforce the provisions of this chapter and promulgate rules and regulations for the enforcement of his duties hereunder.

This section shall not be construed to in any way curtail the powers of actual enforcement vested by law in the local authorities.

Amended by L.1951, c. 23, p. 68, § 6; L.2003, c. 13, § 48 (contingent effective date).

39:4–7. Director's hearings; subpoenas

The director shall hold hearings when in his judgment they are necessary. He may issue subpoenas to compel the attendance of witnesses and the production of books, papers and records applicable to the provisions of this chapter.

Amended by L.1951, c. 23, p. 69, § 7.

39:4–8. Municipal or county regulatory actions governing traffic or traffic conditions; commission approval; certain authorized action permitted without commissioner approval

a. Except as otherwise provided in this section, no ordinance, resolution, or regulation concerning, regulating, or governing traffic or traffic conditions, adopted or enacted by any board or body having jurisdiction over highways, shall be of any force or effect unless the same is approved by the commissioner, according to law. The commissioner shall not be required to approve any such ordinance, resolution, or regulation, unless, after investigation by the commissioner, the same shall appear to be in the interest of safety and the expedition of traffic on the public highways. The commissioner's investigation need not include more than a review of the ordinance, resolution, or regulation, and the supporting documentation submitted by a board or body having jurisdiction over highways, unless the commissioner determines that additional investigation is warranted.

Prior to the adoption of any municipal or county ordinance, resolution, or regulation, which places any impact on roadways in an adjoining municipality or county, the governing board or body of the municipality or county shall provide appropriate notice to the adjoining municipality or county.

Notwithstanding any other provision of this section to the contrary, any municipal or county ordinance, resolution, or regulation which places any impact on a State roadway shall require the approval of the commissioner.

Where the commissioner's approval is required, a certified copy of the adopted ordinance, resolution, or regulation shall be transmitted by the clerk of the municipality or county, as applicable, to the commissioner within 30 days of adoption, together with: a copy of the municipal or county engineer's certification, a statement of the reasons for the municipal or county engineer's decision, detailed information as to the location of streets, intersections, and signs affected by the ordinance, resolution, or regulation, and traffic count, crash, and speed sampling data, when appropriate. The commissioner may invalidate the provisions of the ordinance, resolution, or regulation if the commissioner finds that the provisions of the ordinance, resolution, or regulation are inconsistent with the Manual on Uniform Traffic Control Devices for Streets and Highways, inconsistent with accepted engineering standards, are not based on the results of an accurate traffic and engineering survey, or place an undue traffic burden or impact on the State highway system, or affect the flow of traffic on the State highway system.

b. (1) A municipality may, without the approval of the commissioner, and consistent with the current standards prescribed by the Manual on Uniform Traffic Control Devices for Streets and Highways, establish by ordinance, resolution, or regulation, any of the provisions contained in R.S.39:4–197.

(a) (Deleted by amendment, P.L.2008, c. 110)

(b) (Deleted by amendment, P.L.2008, c. 110)

(c) (Deleted by amendment, P.L.2008, c. 110)

(d) (Deleted by amendment, P.L.2008, c. 110)

(2) A county may, without the approval of the commissioner, and consistent with the current standards prescribed by the Manual on Uniform Traffic Control Devices for Streets and Highways, establish by ordinance, resolution, or regulation, any of the provisions contained in R.S.39:4–197.

(a) (Deleted by amendment, P.L.2008, c. 110)

(b) (Deleted by amendment, P.L.2008, c. 110)

(c) (Deleted by amendment, P.L.2008, c. 110)

(d) (Deleted by amendment, P.L.2008, c. 110)

(3) The municipal or county engineer shall, under his seal as a licensed professional engineer, certify to the governing body of the municipality or county, as appropriate, that any designation or erections of signs or placement of pavement markings has been approved by the engineer after investigation of the circumstances, appears to the engineer to be in the interest of safety and the expedition of traffic on the public highways, and conforms to the current standards prescribed by the Manual on Uniform Traffic Control Devices for Streets and Highways, as adopted by the commissioner.

The provisions of the ordinance, resolution, or regulation shall be consistent with the Manual on Uniform Traffic Control Devices for Streets and Highways, consistent with accepted engineering standards, based on the results of an accurate traffic and engineering survey, and not place an undue traffic burden or impact on streets in an adjoining municipality or negatively affect the flow of traffic on the State highway system.

Nothing in this subsection shall allow municipalities to designate any intersection with any highway under State or county jurisdiction as a stop or yield intersection or counties to designate any intersection with any highway under State or municipal jurisdiction as a stop or yield intersection.

c. Subject to the provisions of R.S.39:4–138, in the case of any street under municipal or county jurisdiction, a municipality or county may, without the approval of the commissioner, and consistent with the current standards prescribed by the Manual on Uniform Traffic Control Devices for Streets and Highways, by ordinance, resolution, or regulation:

(1) prohibit or restrict general parking;

(2) designate restricted parking under section 1 of P.L.1977, c. 309 (C.39:4–197.6);

(3) designate time limit parking;

(4) install parking meters;

(5) designate loading and unloading zones and taxi stands;

(6) approve street closings for periods up to 48 continuous hours;

(7) designate restricted parking under section 1 of P.L.1977, c. 202 (C.39:4–197.5);

(8) establish angle parking; and

(9) reinstate or add parking on any street.

d. A municipality or county may, without the approval of the commissioner, and consistent with the current standards prescribed by the Manual on Uniform Traffic Control Devices for Streets and Highways, by ordinance, resolution, or regulation, regarding any street under its jurisdiction, install or place an in-street pedestrian crossing right-of-way sign at a marked crosswalk or unmarked crosswalk at an intersection. The installation shall be subject to guidelines issued by the commissioner after consultation with the Director of the Division of Highway Traffic Safety in the Department of Law and Public Safety. The guidelines shall be aimed at ensuring safety to both pedestrians and motorists including, but not limited to, the proper method of sign installation, dimensions, composition of material, proper placement points and maintenance. A claim against the State or a municipality or county for damage or injury under this subsection for a wrongful act or omission shall be dismissed if the municipality or county is deemed to have conformed to the guidelines required hereunder.

e. A municipality or county may, without the approval of the commissioner, and consistent with the current standards prescribed by the Manual on Uniform Traffic Control Devices for Streets and Highways, by ordinance, resolution, or regulation in any street under its jurisdiction, designate stops, stations, or stands for omnibuses. The designation shall be subject to guidelines issued by the commissioner. The guidelines shall be aimed at ensuring safety to both pedestrians and motorists including, but not limited to, the proper method of sign installation, dimensions, composition of material, proper placement points, and maintenance. A claim against the State or a municipality or county for damage or injury under this subsection for a wrongful act or omission shall be dismissed if the municipality or county is deemed to have conformed to the guidelines required hereunder.

Amended by L.1951, c. 23, p. 69, § 8; L.1983, c. 227, § 1, eff. June 27, 1983; L.1993, c. 122, § 1, eff. May 28, 1993; L.1995, c. 412, § 1, eff. Jan. 10, 1996; L.1996, c. 113, § 6, eff. Sept. 5, 1996; L.1999, c. 191, § 1, eff. Aug. 31, 1999; L.2001, c. 119, § 1; L.2001, c. 342, § 2, eff. Jan. 5, 2002; L.2004, c. 169, § 1, eff. Dec. 7, 2004; L.2008, c. 110, § 1, eff. Dec. 4, 2008.

39:4–8.1. Handicapped parking spaces and signs; inspection by municipal engineer

Any municipality, which pursuant to the provisions of R.S. 39:4–8, R.S. 39:4–197, section 1 of P.L.1977, c. 202 (C. 39:4–197.5) or section 1 of P.L.1977, c. 309 (C. 39:4–197.6) designates restricted parking spaces for use by handicapped persons, may, in lieu of having the Department of Transportation inspect those parking spaces and any signs erected in association therewith, designate the municipal engineer to determine whether or not those parking spaces and signs conform to the current standards prescribed by the Manual of Uniform Traffic Control Devices for Streets and Highways, adopted by the Commissioner of Transportation, and any other Department of Transportation rules and regulations governing such parking spaces and signs.

Any such parking spaces and signs shall be deemed approved and operational, and in need of no additional inspection by the Department of Transportation, when the municipal engineer, under his seal as a licensed professional engineer, shall certify to the commissioner that the parking spaces and signs:

a. have been approved by him after investigation; and

b. conform to the current standards prescribed by the Manual of Uniform Traffic Control Devices for Streets and Highways, as adopted by the commissioner, and any other Department of Transportation rules and regulations governing such parking spaces and signs.

The municipal engineer shall submit to the commissioner, together with his certification, detailed information as to the location and number of parking spaces, a certified copy of the ordinance, resolution or regulation designating the restricted parking spaces, and such other information as the commissioner shall deem necessary.

L.1991, c. 285, § 1, eff. Sept. 18, 1991.

39:4–8.2. Definitions relating to traffic and parking on public highways or transportation systems

As used in this act:

"Public highways" means public highways as defined in section 3 of P.L.1984, c. 73 (C.27:1B–3).

"Transportation system" means transportation system as defined in section 3 of P.L.1984, c. 73 (C.27:1B–3).

"Under the jurisdiction of the commissioner" means that which has been taken over, or is owned, controlled, or maintained by the Department of Transportation.
L.1998, c. 28, § 1.

39:4–8.3. Regulation of traffic and parking on public highways and transportation systems

a. Notwithstanding the provisions of any other law to the contrary, the Commissioner of Transportation, in accordance with the provisions of this act, may by written order provide for the regulation of traffic and parking on public highways or transportation systems under the jurisdiction of the commissioner and for the establishment, operation, control and maintenance of official traffic control devices thereon where the provisions of chapter 4 of this Title authorize the commissioner to regulate such traffic and parking by rule or regulation. An order issued pursuant to this act shall conform to the same requirements of this Title concerning examination, investigation or study as apply in the case of the rule or regulation in place of which the order is being issued.

b. An order issued pursuant to subsection a. of this section shall be binding and enforceable in accordance with the provisions of this act and any official traffic control device established thereby shall conform to the "Manual on Uniform Traffic Control Devices."

c. The provisions of this act shall not apply to public highways or transportation systems under the jurisdiction of a county or municipality.
L.1998, c. 28, § 2.

39:4–8.4. Contents of order, mailing and publication requirements

a. An order to be issued pursuant to this act shall cite the public highway or transportation system under the jurisdiction of the commissioner to which it is to be applicable; provide an explanation in plain language as to why the order is needed at the location in question; provide a description in plain language of what the order requires; identify the individual or public body who or which requested the order or initiated a request leading to the order; name the date on which the order became final and the effective date of the order; and contain any other information the commissioner deems necessary.

b. A copy of a proposed order shall be mailed to the governing body and chief uniformed law enforcement official of each county and municipality in which that portion of the public highway or transportation system

under the jurisdiction of the commissioner affected by the order is located. On or after the date of mailing, the commissioner shall cause an informational notice of the proposed order, including therein a summary of the provisions of the proposed order, to be published in a newspaper or newspapers having general circulation in the municipality or municipalities affected by the order. The notice shall provide for a telephone number or address which a member of the public may use to receive a copy of the complete text of the proposed order and shall provide for a 30–day period from the date of publication for public comment. The order shall be final on the 31st day after publication of the informational notice or on a later date if the commissioner so determines, except that if comments are received during the 30–day period the order shall be final after the commissioner reviews and responds in writing to the comments received but in no event shall the order be final earlier than the 31st day after publication. Nothing in this section shall be construed as prohibiting the commissioner from extending the comment period or from modifying or withdrawing the proposed order as a result of the review of public comment.

c. Notwithstanding the provisions of subsection b. of this section to the contrary, an order may be made final immediately or at a later date and without the requirement of mailing or publication by the commissioner if it is issued in response to a resolution from the governing body of a municipality and if the order pertains exclusively to a public highway or transportation system located within the boundaries of that municipality. Such a resolution shall be adopted by the governing body and shall memorialize the commissioner to issue an order regulating traffic or parking on a public highway or transportation system located within the boundaries of the municipality. The governing body shall cause an informational notice of the proposed resolution to be published in the official newspaper if there be one or, if that is not the case, in a newspaper of general circulation in the municipality in question, in advance of a meeting at which the resolution is to be considered. A copy of the final order shall be mailed to the governing body and the chief uniformed law enforcement official of the county and municipality in which that portion of the public highway or transportation system under the jurisdiction of the commissioner affected by the order is located.

d. Notwithstanding the provisions of this section to the contrary, upon a finding by the commissioner that an emergent condition exists with respect to a public highway or transportation system under the jurisdiction of the commissioner, an order may be made final immediately. In such an event, a copy of the final order issued pursuant to this subsection shall be provided within 24 hours of issuance to the governing body and the chief uniformed law enforcement official of the county and municipality in which that portion of the public highway or transportation system under the jurisdiction of the commissioner affected by the order is located. Nothing in this section shall be construed to supersede, limit or alter the authority and powers of the Attorney General pursuant to P.L.1950, c. 70 (C.39:4–213 et seq.) to control traffic during emergency conditions. The exercise of the Attorney General's authority and powers pursuant to P.L.1950, c. 70 (C.39:4–213 et seq.) shall supersede an order issued by the commissioner pursuant to this act.

e. A final order shall be effective upon compliance with the notice and briefing provisions of R.S.39:4–198 and shall be binding and enforceable on that date.

L.1998, c. 28, § 3.

39:4–8.5. Maintenance of official and informational records of orders

The commissioner shall maintain an official permanent record of orders issued pursuant to this act providing for the regulation of traffic and parking on public highways or transportation systems under the jurisdiction of the commissioner and of any rule or regulation removed from the New Jersey Administrative Code pursuant to subsection b. of section 5 of this act, which shall be made available upon request, pursuant to P.L.1963, c. 73 (C.47:1A–1 et seq.). In addition, an informational record concerning those public highways, or portions thereof, and transportation systems affected by the orders issued pursuant to this act shall be accessible in electronic form by members of the public without fee or charge.

L.1998, c. 28, § 4.

39:4–8.6. Continued effectiveness of orders issued prior to the effective date of this act

a. Rules or regulations adopted pursuant to chapter 4 of this Title before the effective date of this act and in effect on the effective date thereof and dealing with the regulation of traffic or parking on public highways or transportation systems under the jurisdiction of the commissioner shall continue in effect and shall be enforceable under the provisions of Title 39 of the Revised Statutes and all other applicable Statutes, in any court of competent jurisdiction, until superseded by order of the commissioner pursuant to this act.

b. The Commissioner of Transportation shall, within 60 days of the effective date of this act, issue an order which shall in substance include all rules and regulations adopted pursuant to chapter 4 of this Title before the effective date of this act and in effect on the effective date thereof and dealing exclusively with the regulation of traffic or parking on public highways or transportation systems under the jurisdiction of the commissioner, which order shall be final and effective on the date of issuance, without the requirement of any other action or proceeding, notwithstanding the provisions of this act to the contrary. Upon the issuance of the order the rules and regulations included in substance therein shall be superseded. The commissioner shall forbear from adopting any rule or regulation dealing with the regulation of traffic or parking on public highways or transpor-

tation systems under the jurisdiction of the commissioner from the effective date of this act until the issuance of the order required by this subsection.

c. Sixty days after the effective date of this act, the Office of Administrative Law may remove from the New Jersey Administrative Code any rule or regulation which deals exclusively with the regulation of traffic and parking on public highways or transportation systems under the jurisdiction of the commissioner and which has been superseded by order of the commissioner.

L.1998, c. 28, § 5.

39:4–8.7. Regulation provisions of Title 39 under the jurisdiction of the commissioner

Any provision of chapter 4 of this Title authorizing or requiring the commissioner to provide for the regulation of traffic or parking on public highways or transportation systems under the jurisdiction of the commissioner by means of rule or regulation shall on and after the effective date of this act be construed as authorizing or requiring the commissioner to proceed by order, as the case may be, pursuant to the provisions of this act. Such an order, however, shall not be considered a rule or regulation pursuant to the provisions of the "Administrative Procedure Act," P.L.1968, c. 410 (C.52:14B–1 et seq.).

L.1998, c. 28, § 6.

39:4–8.8. Authority of the commissioner

a. Nothing in this act shall be construed as expanding or diminishing the authority of the commissioner to regulate traffic and parking on public highways or transportation systems under the jurisdiction of the commissioner and to establish, operate, control and maintain official traffic control devices thereon.

b. Nothing in this act shall be construed as superseding any provision or expending or diminishing the authority of the commissioner in regard to the "State Highway Access Management Act," P.L.1989, c. 32 (C.27:7–89 et al.).

L.1998, c. 28, § 7.

39:4–8.9. Definitions

As used in this act: [1]

"Department" means the Department of Transportation.

"Private roads" means semipublic or private roads, streets, driveways, parkways, parking areas, or other roadways owned by a private person, corporation or institution open to or used by the public for the purposes of vehicular travel by permission of such persons, corporations or institutions and not as a matter of public right.

"Speed hump" means one of several traffic calming measures which use forces of vertical acceleration to discourage speeding. For purposes of this chapter, speed humps means all vertical speed deflectors, including but not limited to, speed tables, raised crosswalks, raised intersections, and modified speed humps.

"Vertical speed deflector" means a raised area in the roadway pavement surface extending transversely across the travel way.

L.2004, c. 107, § 1, eff. Nov. 11, 2004. Amended by L.2008, c. 110, § 4, eff. Dec. 4, 2008.

[1]N.J.S.A. §§ 39:4–8.9 to 39:4–8.11.

39:4–8.10. Construction of speed hump on residential streets; construction of traffic calming measures

a. Pursuant to the provisions of section 3 of P.L. 2004, c. 107 (C.39:4–8.11), a municipality or county may, without the approval of the commissioner, construct a speed hump on two-lane residential streets and on one-way residential streets under municipal or county jurisdiction with a posted speed of 30 mph or less and which have fewer than 3,000 vehicles per day. The board of directors of any corporation, or the board of trustees of any corporation or other institution of a public or semipublic nature not for pecuniary profit, having control over private roads, may construct or provide for the construction of a speed hump on any private road subject to the provisions of Title 39 of the Revised Statutes, pursuant to P.L.1945, c. 284 (C.39:5A–1 et seq.).

b. Pursuant to the provisions of section 3 of P.L. 2004, c. 107 (C.39:4–8.11), a municipality or county may, without the approval of the commissioner, construct traffic calming measures where appropriate, which may include, but are not limited to, speed humps on streets under municipal or county jurisdiction with a posted speed of 30 mph or less and which have fewer than 3,000 vehicles per day when any road construction project or repair of a street set forth in this subsection is undertaken and located within 500 feet of that street is a school or any property used for school purposes.

c. Prior to a municipality or county constructing a speed hump which places any impact on roadways in an adjoining municipality or county, the governing board or body of the municipality or county shall provide appropriate notice to the adjoining municipality or county.

d. Prior to a municipality or county constructing a speed hump which places any impact on a State roadway, the county or municipality shall obtain the approval of the commissioner.

L.2004, c. 107, § 2, eff. Nov. 11, 2004. Amended by L.2005, c. 221, § 1, eff. Dec. 12, 2005; L.2008, c. 110, § 5, eff. Dec. 4, 2008.

39:4–8.11. Design and construction of speed humps

Any speed hump constructed by a municipality or a board of directors or trustees shall conform in design and construction to the technical standards established by the Department of Transportation.

A municipality or board shall provide advance warning, including but not limited to, the erection of appropriate signs giving notice of the presence of speed humps before the first speed hump in a series of speed humps and provide for a pavement marker to be placed at the location of the first speed hump. The signing and pavement markings for a speed hump shall conform to the current standards prescribed in the Manual of Uniform Traffic Control Devices for Streets and Highways as adopted by the Commissioner of Transportation.

L.2004, c. 107, § 3, eff. Nov. 11, 2004.

39:4–8.12. Legislative findings and declarations; traffic control signal monitoring systems; pilot program

The Legislature finds:

The disregard of traffic control devices at intersections impedes the efficient flow of traffic, and more importantly, dramatically increases the likelihood of accidents that endanger the safety and well being of motor vehicle occupants and pedestrians.

The installation and use of a traffic control signal monitoring system, which complements the efforts of local law enforcement, could serve as an effective tool in encouraging drivers to strictly obey traffic control devices at intersections, facilitating the flow of traffic and protecting the safety and well being of motor vehicle occupants and pedestrians.

The Legislature, therefore, declares:

It is altogether fitting and proper, and within the public interest, to require the Commissioner of Transportation to establish a pilot program to determine the effectiveness of the installation and utilization of traffic control signal monitoring systems in this State and to approve applications from municipalities where such systems may be installed.

L.2007, c. 348, § 1, eff. April 12, 2008.

39:4–8.13. Definitions

As used in this act: [1]

"Recorded image" means a digital image recorded by a traffic control signal monitoring system.

"Summons" means a citation alleging a violation of a traffic control signal.

"Traffic control signal" means a device, whether manually, electrically, mechanically, or otherwise controlled, by which traffic is alternatively directed to stop and to proceed, and which has been approved by the Commissioner of Transportation in accordance with the "Manual on Uniform Traffic Control Devices for Streets and Highways."

"Traffic control signal monitoring system" means an integrated system or device utilizing a camera, or a multiple camera system, and vehicle sensors which work in conjunction with a traffic control signal and is capable of producing:

a.   high resolution color digital recorded images that show: (1) the traffic control signal while it is displaying a red light; (2) a motor vehicle unlawfully entering and continuing through the intersection while the traffic control signal is displaying a red light; and (3) a portion of the rear of the motor vehicle unlawfully in the intersection sufficient to clearly reveal the vehicle's license plate and the make and model of the vehicle a unique close-up image obtained from an independent camera, integrated as part of the traffic control signal monitoring system that has been installed, resulting in a series of synchronized images; and

b.   a video recording of the violation that shows the violation occurring.

A digital camera may be used as part of a traffic control signal monitoring system provided the violation images are captured by a digital camera, or a multiple camera system, which produces a set of at least two images for each violation. At least one of the digital color images shall contain the following: (1) the scene of the location where the violation occurred; (2) the violating motor vehicle; (3) the license plate numbers, letters, and issuing jurisdiction; (4) the day, month, and year of the violation; (5) the time of the violation in hours, minutes, and seconds; (6) the amount of time that had passed between the time the light turned red and the violation occurred; and (7) the frame sequence code. This information shall be imprinted along the bottom or top edge of the image frame so as not to obstruct the violation image.

L.2007, c. 348, § 2, eff. April 12, 2008.

1 L.2007, c. 348, (N.J.S.A. § 39:4–8.12 to 39:4–8.18).

39:4–8.14.   Five-year pilot program; municipal participation in program; authorization to install and utilize traffic control signal monitoring systems; public awareness

a.   The Commissioner of Transportation shall establish a five-year pilot program to determine the effectiveness of the installation and utilization of traffic control signal monitoring systems in this State. A municipality desiring to participate in the program shall submit an application to the Commissioner of Transportation. The application shall include:

(1) The intersection or intersections in the municipality at which it is desired to install and utilize a traffic control signal monitoring system;

(2) Data which indicate that the intersection or intersections in question have a high number of violations of the traffic control signals, and any additional safety data the municipality deems appropriate;

(3) A certification by the municipal engineer that (a) the intersection or intersections in question have a minimum duration of the amber light at the traffic control signal of three seconds if at least 85 percent of the vehicular traffic approaching the signal is traveling at a speed of 25 miles per hour or less; and (b) for each five mile increase in the speed of vehicular traffic

referred to in subparagraph (a) of this paragraph above 30 miles per hour this minimum duration of the amber light shall be increased by one-half second;

(4) Such other information as the Commissioner of Transportation may require.

The commissioner may approve as many municipalities making application as he deems appropriate, and shall indicate which of the intersections in those applications are approved for the installation and utilization of traffic control signal monitoring systems.

b.   Notwithstanding the provisions of P.L.1992, c. 91 (C.39:4–103.1), the governing body of a municipality, by ordinance, may determine to install and utilize a traffic control signal monitoring system to facilitate the lawful observance of and compliance with traffic control signals governing the flow of traffic at intersections under its jurisdiction approved by the Commissioner of Transportation pursuant to subsection a. of this section.

c.   A traffic control signal monitoring system installed and utilized pursuant to this section shall be of a type approved by the governing body of the municipality.

d.   In any municipality where the governing body has authorized the installation and use of a traffic control signal monitoring system pursuant to subsection b. of this section, a sign notifying drivers that such a monitoring system is being utilized shall be placed on each street converging into the affected intersection. The sign shall be of a design and placed in accordance with specifications approved by the municipal engineer. The specifications so approved shall conform with the uniform system set forth in the "Manual on Uniform Traffic Control Devices for Streets and Highways."

e.   A traffic control signal monitoring system shall be inspected and certified at least once every six months by the municipal engineer from the date of its installation for the duration of the five-year pilot program prescribed by P.L.2007, c. 348 (C.39:4–8.12 et seq.).

f.   In any municipality in which the governing body has authorized the installation and use of a traffic control signal monitoring system pursuant to subsection b. of this section, a vendor contracting with that municipality concerning the installation and use of such system shall establish a public awareness campaign to notify the public of the intersection at which the system will be installed and of the date on which the system will be activated. The public awareness campaign shall, at a minimum, utilize electronic and print media and shall make available electronically on an Internet website the information required under this subsection.

L.2007, c. 348, § 3, eff. April 12, 2008. Amended by L.2009, c. 52, § 2, eff. July 3, 2009.

39:4–8.15.   Recorded data to be reviewed by designated law enforcement official; issuance of a summons; public access to data; owner liability for violations

a.   In any municipality where the governing body has authorized the installation and use of a traffic control signal monitoring system, a law enforcement official of such municipality shall review the recorded images produced by the traffic control signal monitoring system. In conducting such review, the law enforcement official shall determine whether there is sufficient evidence to conclude that a traffic control signal violation has occurred and shall issue, within 90 days from the date on which the violation occurred, a summons where it is deemed appropriate. A traffic control signal violation summons issued pursuant to a traffic control signal monitoring system established in accordance with this act [1] shall be served by a law enforcement official in accordance with the Rules of Court. Except as otherwise provided in this subsection, the recorded images produced by the traffic control signal monitoring system shall be available for the exclusive use of any law enforcement official for the purposes of discharging the official's duties pursuant to P.L.2007, c. 348 (C.39:4–8.12 et seq.). Any recorded image or information produced in connection with the traffic control signal monitoring system shall not be deemed a public record under P.L.1963, c. 73 (C.47:1A–1 et seq.) or the common law concerning access to public records. The recorded images shall not be discoverable as a public record by any person, entity, or governmental agency, except upon a subpoena issued by a grand jury or a court order in a criminal matter, nor shall they be offered in evidence in any civil or administrative proceeding not directly related to a traffic control signal violation.

Any recorded image or information produced in connection with the traffic control signal monitoring system pertaining to a specific violation shall be purged and not retained later than 60 days after the collection of any fine or penalty. If a law enforcement official does not issue a summons for a traffic control signal violation within 90 days, all recorded images and information collected pertaining to that alleged violation shall be purged within three days. Any municipality operating a traffic control signal monitoring system shall certify compliance with this subsection in the report required to be filed with the Commissioner of Transportation pursuant to section 6 of P.L.2007, c. 348 (C.39:4–8.17).

b. Except as provided in subsection c. of this section, the owner and operator shall be jointly liable for a traffic control signal violation summons issued pursuant to a traffic control signal monitoring system established in accordance with this act, unless the owner can show that the vehicle was used without his consent, express or implied. An owner who pays any fine, penalty, civil judgment, costs or administrative fees in connection with a traffic control signal violation issued pursuant to a traffic control signal monitoring system shall have the right to recover that sum from the operator in a court of competent jurisdiction.

c. The owner of a motor vehicle who is a lessor shall not be liable for a traffic control signal violation summons issued pursuant to this act when the motor vehicle is under the control or in the possession of the lessee, if upon notice of a traffic control signal violation, the owner of the motor vehicle which was leased at the time of the offense notifies the clerk of the court where the case is pending, by an affidavit of the name and address of the lessee. The affidavit shall be in a form prescribed by the Administrative Director of the Courts.

After providing the name and address of the lessee, the owner shall not be required to attend a hearing of the offense, unless otherwise notified by the court.

d. In no case shall motor vehicle points or automobile insurance eligibility points pursuant to section 26 of P.L.1990, c. 8 (C.17:33B–14) be assessed against any person for a violation occurring under the provisions of this act.

(Deleted by amendment, P.L.2009, c. 52)

L.2007, c. 348, § 4, eff. April 12, 2008. Amended by L.2009, c. 52, § 3, eff. July 3, 2009.

[1] L.2007, c. 348 (N.J.S.A. § 39:4–8.12 et seq.)

39:4–8.16. Rules and regulations

The Commissioner of Transportation, the Chief Administrator of the Motor Vehicle Commission, and the Superintendent of the State Police may, in accordance with the "Administrative Procedure Act," P.L.1968, c. 410 (C.52:14B–1 et seq.), promulgate rules and regulations to effectuate the purposes of this act.[1] The Supreme Court of New Jersey may adopt Rules of Court appropriate or necessary to effectuate the purposes of this act.

L.2007, c. 348, § 5, eff. April 12, 2008.

[1] L.2007, c. 348, (N.J.S.A. § 39:4–8.12 to 39:4–8.18).

39:4–8.17. Annual reports by municipalities; reports to the legislature and governor

The municipalities whose applications have been approved for the pilot program established pursuant to this act [1] shall submit reports every 12 months after a traffic control signal monitoring system has been installed to the Commissioner of Transportation detailing increases or decreases in violations and accidents at intersections where traffic control signal monitoring systems have been installed. The Commissioner of Transportation shall prepare and submit an annual report to the Governor, the President of the Senate, the Speaker of the General Assembly, and the Senate Transportation Committee and the Assembly Transportation and Public Works Committee or their successor committees describing the pilot program developed pursuant to this act, including accident and violation information reported by the affected municipalities. The first such report shall be submitted no later than one year after the installation of the first traffic control signal monitoring system authorized pursuant to this act. Thereafter, subsequent reports shall be submitted annually for the duration of the five-year pilot program prescribed by P.L.2007, c. 348 (C.39:4–8.12 et seq.), with the fifth and final report providing a comprehensive review of the pilot program, including but not limited to, an evaluation of the program's effectiveness, a discussion of extending the program to other intersections in the State, and any other information relevant to the report.

L.2007, c. 348, § 6, eff. April 12, 2008.

1 L.2007, c. 348 (N.J.S.A. § 39:4–8.12 et seq.).

39:4–8.18.   Expiration of pilot program

This act [1] shall take effect ninety days following enactment and shall expire upon the submission of the Commissioner of Transportation's fifth and final report to the appropriate parties pursuant to section 6 of this act. [2]

L.2007, c. 348, § 7, eff. April 12, 2008.

1 L.2007, c. 348 (N.J.S.A. § 39:4–8.12 et seq.).
2 N.J.S.A. § 39:4–8.17.

39:4–8.19.   Consultation with commissioner at request of municipality or county; authority to give advisory review; fees

a.   Notwithstanding the provisions of R.S.39:4–8, a municipality or county may request the commissioner's review and non-binding recommendation regarding any proposed municipal or county ordinance, resolution, or regulation that would concern, regulate, or otherwise govern traffic or traffic conditions, and for which the approval of the commissioner is not required pursuant to R.S.39:4–8, prior to the adoption or enactment of that proposed ordinance, resolution, or regulation. Any ordinance, resolution, or regulation submitted for the commissioner's review shall include a municipal or county traffic engineer's recommendation regarding the proposed traffic regulation. The commissioner shall assess a municipality or a county a non-refundable fee for the commissioner's review. All fees collected by the commissioner for the review shall be utilized by the department to offset costs incurred by the department in processing the request.

b.   The commissioner shall adopt, pursuant to the "Administrative Procedure Act," P.L.1968, c. 410 (C.52:14B–1 et seq.), any rules and regulations necessary to effectuate the purposes of this section, including but not limited to, establishing guidelines for the review process and applicable fees.

L.2008, c. 110, § 7, eff. Dec. 4, 2008.

39:4–8.20.   Fines paid to the municipal court; distribution of funds

a.   Notwithstanding the provisions of R.S.39:5–41, in the case of a violation of R.S.39:4–81, the evidence of which was captured by a traffic control signal monitoring system installed pursuant to section 3 of P.L.2007, c. 348, (C.39:4–8.14) the full amount of a fine assessed by a municipal court shall be paid to the financial officer of the municipality in which the offense occurred, unless the governing body of the county has elected to pay one-half of the cost of the installation, maintenance, and

administration of the traffic control signal monitoring system, in which case, one-half of the fine amount shall be distributed to the financial officer of the county where the offense occurred. Any change in this distribution of revenue shall be applicable only to fines attributable to complaints filed with the municipal court after the date on which applicable notice under subsection b. of this section shall have been received by the Administrative Office of the Courts.

b.   A municipality that has installed a traffic control signal monitoring system shall notify the Administrative Office of the Courts when the governing body of a county has agreed to participate in a traffic control signal monitoring system program within its jurisdiction. Such notice shall be applicable to any violation of R.S.39:4–81, evidence of which shall have been captured by a traffic control signal monitoring system within the municipality's jurisdiction.

L.2009, c. 52, § 4, eff. July 3, 2009.

39:4–8.21.   Construction of a curb extension or bulb-out; municipal authority

A county, municipality, or the board of directors or the board of trustees of any corporation or other institution of a public or semipublic nature, not for pecuniary profit, having control over private roads subject to the provisions of Title 39, may construct, without the approval of the Commissioner, a curb extension or a bulbout on any street under its jurisdiction.

L.2009, c. 107, § 3, eff. Aug. 6, 2009.

39:4–9.   Repealed by L.1967, c. 189, § 6, eff. July 27, 1967

39:4–9.1.   Exchange of information between states concerning certain violations

Whenever another State shall have enacted a law providing for reciprocal exchange thereof, the director, upon receiving a certificate of conviction of a nonresident operator or chauffeur of a violation of the provisions of sections 39:4–50, 39:4–96, 39:4–98 and 39:4–129 of the Revised Statutes, or of notice of the forfeiture of any bond or collateral given for such violation, shall transmit forthwith, a certified copy of such record to the motor vehicle administrator of the State wherein the person named in such record shall reside.

L.1938, c. 360, p. 900, § 1.   Amended by L.1951, c. 23, p. 70, § 10.

ARTICLE 3.   BICYCLES AND ROLLER SKATES

39:4–10.   Lights and reflectors on bicycles

Every bicycle when in use at nighttime shall be equipped with a lamp on the front which shall emit a white light visible from a distance of at least five hundred feet to the front, and with a lamp on the rear which shall emit a red light visible from a distance of at least five hundred feet to the rear. In addition to the red lamp, a red reflector may be mounted on the rear, of a type approved by the division which shall be visible from all distances from fifty feet to three hundred feet to the rear when directly in front of lawful upper beams of head lamps on a motor vehicle.

Amended by L.1951, c. 23, p. 70, § 11.

39:4–10.1. Bicycle operators and passengers under age 17 required to wear helmets

a. A person under 17 years of age shall not operate, or ride upon a bicycle as a passenger, unless that person is wearing a properly fitted and fastened bicycle helmet which meets the standards of the American National Standards Institute (ANSI Z90.4 bicycle helmet standard) or the Snell Memorial Foundation's 1990 Standard for Protective Headgear for Use in Bicycling. This requirement shall apply to a person who rides upon a bicycle while in a restraining seat which is attached to the bicycle or in a trailer towed by the bicycle.

As used in this act, "bicycle" means a vehicle with two wheels propelled solely by human power and having pedals, handle bars and a saddle-like seat. The term shall include a bicycle for two or more persons having seats and corresponding sets of pedals arranged in tandem.

b. The director shall publish a list of bicycle helmets which meet the standards described in subsection a. of this section and shall provide for its distribution in as many locations frequented by the public as the director deems appropriate and practicable.

c. The requirement in subsection a. of this section shall apply at all times while a bicycle is being operated on any property open to the public or used by the public for pedestrian and vehicular purposes; however, a municipality may by ordinance exempt from this requirement a person operating or riding on a bicycle as a passenger when the bicycle is operated:

(1) on a road or highway closed to motor vehicle traffic and limited to pedestrian or bicycle use at all times or only during specified periods of time during which bicycles may be operated; or

(2) exclusively on a trail, route, course, boardwalk, path or other area which is set aside for the use of bicycles or for the use of pedestrians and bicycle operation is not otherwise prohibited. However, an exemption may not be granted under this paragraph for any portion of a trail, route, course, boardwalk, path or other area which is immediately adjacent to a road or highway used by motor vehicle traffic and which does not contain a barrier of sufficient height and rigidity to prevent the inadvertent or deliberate entry of a bicycle operator onto the road or highway.

d. An ordinance enacted pursuant to subsection c. of this section shall specify those roads, highways, trails, routes, courses, boardwalks, paths or areas within the municipality where helmets are not required during the operation of a bicycle.

e. When a bicycle is being operated in an area where bicycle helmets are not required, the operator or a passenger, except a passenger in a restraining seat or trailer, shall dismount from the bicycle and walk whenever it is necessary to enter a crosswalk or to cross a road or highway upon which motor vehicle traffic is permitted.

L.1991, c. 465, § 1, eff. July 1, 1992. Amended by L.1997, c. 411, § 10; L.2005, c. 208, § 1, eff. March 1, 2006.

39:4–10.2. Violation of bicycle helmet requirement; fines

a. A person who violates a requirement of this act shall be warned of the violation by the enforcing official. The parent or legal guardian of that person also may be fined a maximum of $25 for the person's first offense and a maximum of $100 for a subsequent offense if it can be shown that the parent or guardian failed to exercise reasonable supervision or control over the person's conduct. Penalties provided in this section for a failure to wear a helmet may be waived if an offender or his parent or legal guardian presents suitable proof that an approved helmet was owned at the time of the violation or has been purchased since the violation occurred.

b. All money collected as fines under subsection a. of this section and subsection a. of section 2 of P.L.1997, c. 411 (C. 39:4–10.6) shall be deposited in a nonlapsing revolving fund to be known as the "Bicycle and Skating Safety Fund." Interest earned on money deposited in the fund shall accrue to the fund. Money in the fund shall be utilized by the director to provide educational programs devoted to bicycle, roller skating and skateboarding safety. If the director determines that sufficient money is available in the fund, he also may use, in a manner prescribed by rule and regulation, the money to assist low income families in purchasing approved bicycle helmets. For the purposes of this subsection, "low income family" means a family which qualifies for low income housing under the standards promulgated by the Council on Affordable Housing pursuant to the provisions of P.L.1985, c. 222 (C.52:27D–301 et seq.).

L.1991, c. 465, § 2, eff. July 1, 1992. Amended by L.1997, c. 411, § 11.

39:4–10.3. Posting of sign regarding bicycle helmet requirement; penalties

a. A person regularly engaged in the business of selling or renting bicycles shall post a sign at the point where the sale or rental transaction is completed stating: "STATE LAW REQUIRES A BICYCLE RIDER UNDER 17 YEARS OF AGE TO WEAR A HELMET." The size of the sign shall be at a minimum 15 inches in length and 8 inches in width. This notification requirement shall not apply to a seller when a bicycle is sold through the use of a catalog or brochure and the purchase and payment are made by mail, telephone or another telecommunications or electronic method.

A person who fails to post a sign required by this subsection within 60 days after the effective date of this amendatory act (P.L.1995, c. 177) shall be subject to a penalty not to exceed $25 a day for each day the business is open to the public and the sign is not posted. The enforcement of this subsection shall be vested in the Director of the Division of Consumer Affairs of the Department of Law and Public Safety, the inspectors appointed under his authority, and the police or peace officers of, or inspectors duly appointed for this purpose, by any municipality or county or by the State. Jurisdiction of proceedings to collect the penalties prescribed by this act is vested in the Superior Court and the municipal court in any municipality where the defendant may be apprehended or where he may reside. Process shall be either a summons or warrant and shall be executed in a summary manner pursuant to "the Penalty Enforcement Law of 1999," P.L. 1999, c.274 (C.2A:58–10 et seq.).

b.　A person regularly engaged in the business of renting bicycles shall provide a helmet to a person under 17 years of age who will operate the bicycle in an area where a helmet is required, if the person does not already have a helmet in his possession. A fee may be charged for the helmet rental.

c.　A person regularly engaged in the business of selling or renting bicycles who complies with the applicable requirements of this section shall not be liable in a civil action for damages for any physical injury sustained by a bicycle operator or passenger who is under the age of 17 years as a result of the operator's or passenger's failure to wear a helmet or to wear a properly fitted or fastened helmet in violation of the requirements of this act.

d.　Within 60 days after the effective date of this amendatory act (P.L.1995, c. 177)[1], the Division of Consumer Affairs in the Department of Law and Public Safety shall make a reasonable effort to notify any person who is regularly engaged in the business of selling or renting bicycles of the requirements of this section. The responsibility of a person under this section shall not be abrogated or diminished in any manner if the person fails to receive or become aware of a notice from the division.

L.1991, c. 465, § 3, eff. July 1, 1992. Amended by L.1995, c. 177, § 1, eff. July 11, 1995; L.2005, c. 208, § 2, eff. March 1, 2006.

[1] L.1995, c. 177, eff. July 11, 1995.

39:4–10.4.　Rules and regulations

The director, in accordance with the provisions of the "Administrative Procedure Act," P.L.1968, c. 410 (C.52:14B–1 et seq.), shall promulgate rules and regulations which may be necessary to effectuate the purposes of this act.

L.1991, c. 465, § 4, eff. July 1, 1992.

39:4–10.5.　Definitions relating to roller skating and skateboarding

a.　As used in this act:

"Director" means the Director of Consumer Affairs in the Department of Law and Public Safety.

"Roller skates" means a pair of devices worn on the feet with a set of wheels attached, regardless of the number or placement of those wheels, and used to glide or propel the user over the ground.

b.　A person under 17 years of age shall not operate any roller skates or skateboard unless that person is wearing a properly fitted and fastened helmet which meets the standards of the American National Standards Institute (ANSI Z90.4 bicycle helmet standard), the Snell Memorial Foundation's 1990 Standard for Protective Headgear for Use in Bicycling, the American Society for Testing and Materials (ASTM) standard or other such standard, as appropriate.

c.　The requirement in subsection b. of this section shall apply at all times while a person subject to the provisions of this act is operating roller skates or skateboarding on any property open to the public or used by the public for roller skating or skateboarding.

L.1997, c. 411, § 1.　Amended by L.2005, c. 208, § 3, eff. March 1, 2006.

39:4–10.6.　Violations by roller skaters or skateboarders; fines

a.　A person who violates the provisions of section 1 of this act[1] by failing to wear an approved helmet shall be warned of the violation by the enforcing official. The parent or legal guardian of the violator may be fined a maximum of $25 for a first offense and a maximum of $100 for a subsequent offense. The penalties provided under the provisions of this subsection for failing to wear an approved helmet may be waived if the parent or legal guardian of the violator presents suitable proof that an approved helmet or appropriate personal protection equipment has been purchased since the violation occurred.

b.　All moneys collected as fines under subsection a. of this section shall be deposited in the "Bicycle and Skating Safety Fund" pursuant to section 2 of P.L.1991, c. 465 (C.39:4–10.2).

L.1997, c. 411, § 2.

[1] N.J.S.A. § 39:4–10.5.

39:4–10.7.　Personal injury or wrongful death actions

The failure of any person to comply with the provisions of section 1 of this act[1] shall not constitute negligence per se, contributory negligence or assumption of risk, and shall not in any way bar, preclude or foreclose an action for personal injury or wrongful death by or on behalf of such person.

L.1997, c. 411, § 3.

[1] N.J.S.A. § 39:4–10.5.

39:4–10.8. Sale of roller skates or skateboards; protective gear warning

a. It shall be unlawful to manufacture, assemble, sell, offer to sell or distribute roller skates, skateboards or electric personal assistive mobility devices unless such roller skates, skateboards or electric personal assistive mobility devices contain a warning notice consistent with the requirements of this section.

b. The warning notice required by subsection a. of this section shall be placed in at least one of the following locations and shall be clearly visible to the consumer: (1) on one roller skate in each pair of roller skates or on the skateboard; (2) on the outside of the box or other container in which the roller skates, skateboard or electric personal assistive mobility device are offered for sale at retail; or (3) on any user's guide or instruction manual provided with the roller skates, skateboard or electric personal assistive mobility device.

c. The warning notice required by subsection a. of this section must be printed in clear and conspicuous type and be substantially similar to the following notice: "WARNING! REDUCE THE RISK OF SERIOUS INJURY AND ONLY USE WHILE WEARING FULL PROTECTIVE GEAR—HELMET, WRIST GUARDS, ELBOW PADS AND KNEE PADS."

d. A person, firm, corporation or other legal entity regularly engaged in the business of manufacturing or assembling roller skates, skateboards or electric personal assistive mobility devices who complies with the requirements of this section shall not be liable in a civil action for damages for any physical injury sustained by a user of roller skates, a skateboard or an electric personal assistive mobility device as a result of that user's failure to wear a helmet in accordance with the provisions of this act.

L.1997, c. 411, § 4. Amended by L.2001, c. 430, § 2, eff. Jan. 8, 2002.

39:4–10.9. Sale or rental of roller skates or skateboards; notice of helmet requirement

a. A person, firm, corporation or other legal entity regularly engaged in the business of selling or renting roller skates or skateboards shall post a sign at the point where the sale or rental transaction is completed stating: "STATE LAW REQUIRES A PERSON UNDER 17 YEARS OF AGE TO WEAR A HELMET WHEN ROLLER SKATING OR SKATEBOARDING." The size of the sign shall be at a minimum 15 inches in length and 8 inches in width. This notification requirement shall not apply to a seller when roller skates are sold through the use of a mail order catalog or brochure where the purchase and payment are made by mail, telephone or another telecommunications or electronic method.

b. A person, firm, corporation or other legal entity who fails to post the sign required by subsection a. of this section shall be subject to a penalty not to exceed $25 a day for each day the business is open to the public

and the sign is not posted. The enforcement of this subsection shall be vested in the director, the inspectors appointed under his authority and the police or peace officers of, or inspectors duly appointed for this purpose by, any municipality or county or the State. Jurisdiction of proceedings to collect the penalties prescribed by this act is vested in the Superior Court and the municipal court in any municipality where the defendant resides. Process shall be either a summons or warrant and shall be executed in a summary manner pursuant to "the Penalty Enforcement Law of 1999," P.L.1999, c.274 (C.2A:58–10 et seq.).

c. A person, firm, corporation or other legal entity regularly engaged in the business of renting roller skates or skateboards shall make available an approved helmet to a person under 17 years of age who rents the roller skates or skateboards for use in an area where a helmet is required, if the person does not already have a helmet in his possession. A fee may be charged for the helmet rental.

d. A person, firm, corporation or other legal entity regularly engaged in the business of selling or renting roller skates or skateboards who complies with the applicable requirements of this section shall not be liable in a civil action for damages for any physical injury sustained by a user of roller skates or a skateboard who is under the age of 17 years as a result of that person's failure to wear a helmet in accordance with the provisions of this act.

e. Sixty days before the effective date of this act,[1] the Division of Consumer Affairs in the Department of Law and Public Safety shall make a reasonable effort to notify any person, firm, corporation or other legal entity who is regularly engaged in the business of selling or renting roller skates or skateboards of the requirements of this section. The responsibility of a person, firm, corporation or other legal entity under this section shall not be abrogated or diminished in any manner if the person fails to receive or become aware of a notice from the division.

L.1997, c. 411, § 5. Amended by L.2005, c. 208, § 4, eff. March 1, 2006.

[1] L.1997, c. 411, eff. July 1, 1998.

39:4–10.10. Rights and duties of roller skaters and skateboarders

Every person operating any roller skates or skateboard upon a roadway shall be granted all of the rights and shall be subject to all of the duties applicable to the driver of a vehicle by chapter four of Title 39 of the Revised Statutes and all supplements thereto, except as to those provisions thereof which by their nature can have no application.

Regulations applicable to roller skates and skateboards shall apply whenever any person operates any roller skates or skateboard upon any highway or upon any path set aside for the exclusive use of roller skates or skateboards subject to those exceptions stated herein.

L.1997, c. 411, § 6.

39:4–10.10a. Municipal ordinances; skateboards and roller skates

The governing body of any municipality may, by ordinance, regulate the operation of skateboards and roller skates upon the roadways and public properties under municipal jurisdiction; provided, however, that no such ordinance shall:

a. absolve any person operating roller skates or a skateboard upon a permitted roadway of any of the duties applicable to the operator of a bicycle pursuant to Article 3 of chapter 4 of Title 39 of the Revised Statutes and all supplements thereto, except as to those provisions thereof which by their nature can have no application;

b. prohibit any person from operating a skateboard upon any public roadway, except those specifically designated by ordinance.

For the purpose of this section, "roller skates" means a pair of devices worn on the feet with a set of wheels attached, regardless of the number or placement of those wheels, and used to glide or propel the user over the ground.

L.1998, c. 36, § 1, eff. June 30, 1998.

39:4–10.10b. Maintenance or construction of roadways; accommodation of roller skates or skateboards

Nothing in P.L.1998, c.36 (C.39:4–10.10a et seq.) or in P.L.1997, c. 411 (C.39:4–10.5 et al.) shall obligate the Commissioner of Transportation to in any way maintain, plan, design or construct roadways to accommodate the operation of roller skates or skateboards.

L.1998, c. 36, § 2, eff. June 30, 1998.

39:4–10.11. Rules of operation of roller skates and skateboards on roadways

Every person operating any roller skates or skateboard upon a roadway shall ride as near to the right side of the roadway as practicable, exercising due care when passing a standing vehicle or one proceeding in the same direction; provided, however, that any person may move to the left under any of the following situations:

(a) to make a left turn from a left-turn lane or pocket;

(b) to avoid debris, drains or other hazardous conditions that make it impracticable to ride at the right side of the roadway;

(c) to pass a slower moving vehicle;

(d) to occupy any available lane when traveling at the same speed as other traffic;

(e) to travel no more than two abreast when traffic is not impeded.

Persons operating any roller skates or skateboards upon a roadway may travel no more than two abreast when traffic is not impeded, but otherwise shall ride in single file, except on paths or parts of roadways set aside for the exclusive use of bicycles, roller skates or skateboards.

L.1997, c. 411, § 7.

39:4–10.12. Nonapplicability of act; roller skating rinks

The provisions of this act shall not apply to the operators and patrons of roller skating rinks governed by the provisions of the "New Jersey Roller Skating Rink Safety and Fair Liability Act," P.L.1991, c. 28 (C.5:14–1 et seq.).

L.1997, c. 411, § 8.

39:4–10.13. Adoption of rules and regulations; roller skates and skateboards

The director, in accordance with the provisions of the "Administrative Procedure Act," P.L.1968, c. 410 (C.52:14B–1 et seq.), may promulgate rules and regulations to effectuate the purposes of this act.

L.1997, c. 411, § 9, eff. Jan. 19, 1998.

39:4–11. Audible signal

No person shall operate a bicycle unless it is equipped with a bell or other device capable of giving a signal audible for a distance of at least one hundred feet, except that a bicycle shall not be equipped with nor shall any person use upon a bicycle any siren or whistle.

Amended by L.1951, c. 23, p. 70, § 12.

39:4–11.1. Brake required

Every bicycle shall be equipped with a brake which will enable the operator to make the braked wheels skid on dry, level, clean pavement.

L.1951, c. 23, p. 71, § 15.

39:4–12. Position of hands and feet; carrying another person

A person propelling or riding on a bicycle shall not ride other than upon or astride a permanent and regular seat attached thereto, nor shall he ride with his feet removed from the pedals, or with both hands removed from the handlebars, nor shall he practice any trick or fancy riding in a street. No bicycle shall be used to carry more persons at one time than the number for which it is designed and equipped.

Amended by L.1951, c. 23, p. 70, § 13.

39:4–13. Repealed by L.1951, c. 23, p. 120, § 119

39:4–14. Hitching on vehicles prohibited

No person riding upon any bicycle, coaster, skates, sled, or toy vehicle shall attach the same or himself to any streetcar or vehicle upon a roadway and no operator of any streetcar or vehicle shall knowingly allow any person riding upon any bicycle, coaster, skates, sled or toy vehicle to attach the same or himself to the streetcar or vehicle.

Amended by L.1951, c. 23, p. 71, § 14.

39:4–14.1. Rights and duties of persons on bicycles

a. Every person riding a bicycle upon a roadway shall be granted all of the rights and shall be subject to all of the duties applicable to the driver of a vehicle by chapter four of Title 39 of the Revised Statutes and all supplements thereto except as to those provisions thereof which by their nature can have no application.

Regulations applicable to bicycles shall apply whenever a bicycle is operated upon any highway or upon any path set aside for the exclusive use of bicycles subject to those exceptions stated herein.

b. A law enforcement officer operating a bicycle while in the performance of his duty, and who is engaged in the apprehension of violators of the law or of persons charged with, or suspected of, a violation shall not be subject to the provisions of this section.

L.1951, c. 23, p. 71, § 16. Amended by L.1999, c. 283, § 1, eff. Dec. 20, 1999.

39:4–14.2. Keeping to right; exceptions; single file

Every person operating a bicycle upon a roadway shall ride as near to the right side of the roadway as practicable, exercising due care when passing a standing vehicle or one proceeding in the same direction; provided, however, that any person may move to the left under any of the following situations:

(a) to make a left turn from a left-turn lane or pocket;

(b) to avoid debris, drains or other hazardous conditions that make it impracticable to ride at the right side of the roadway;

(c) to pass a slower moving vehicle;

(d) to occupy any available lane when traveling at the same speed as other traffic;

(e) to travel no more than two abreast when traffic is not impeded.

Persons riding bicycles upon a roadway may travel no more than two abreast when traffic is not impeded, but otherwise shall ride in single file except on paths or parts of roadways set aside for the exclusive use of bicycles.

L.1951, c. 23, p. 71, § 17. Amended by L.1977, c. 388, § 1, eff. Feb. 23, 1978; L.1983, c. 257, § 1, eff. July 7, 1983.

39:4–14.3. Motorized bicycles; limitations on use; age of operator; license to operate; issuance; examination; learner's permit; fee; possession; exhibit on request; violations; fine; applicable traffic regulations

a. Motorized bicycles shall not be operated upon interstate highways or upon public highways divided by

a grass or concrete median or highways with posted speed limits in excess of 50 miles per hour or upon the railroad or right-of-way of an operating railroad within the State of New Jersey or upon any public land where expressly prohibited by the governing body, department or agency having jurisdiction thereof.

The commissioner is authorized to adopt regulations either prohibiting the operation of motorized bicycles on any public road or highway with a speed limit in excess of 40 miles per hour, which in his discretion are hazardous for the operation of motorized bicycles or permitting the operation of motorized bicycles on any public road or highway, upon which the operation of motorized bicycles is otherwise prohibited by the provisions of this section, which in his discretion are safe for the operation of motorized bicycles. In no case, however, shall the commissioner adopt a regulation permitting motorized bicycles to be operated on any highway with a posted speed in excess of 50 miles per hour.

b. No municipality shall limit or otherwise restrict the operation of motorized bicycles on any public roads or highways under its jurisdiction in contravention of the provisions of this act or any regulations adopted by the director pursuant thereto.

c. Motorized bicycles shall not be operated by a person under 15 years of age.

d. No person shall operate a motorized bicycle unless he is in possession of a valid driver's license of any class or a motorized bicycle license, which shall be issued by the commission to any person 15 years of age or older, upon proof of identity and date of birth, and after he has passed a satisfactory examination as to his ability as an operator. Such examination shall include a test of the applicant's knowledge of such portions of the mechanism of motorized bicycles as is necessary to insure their safe operation and of the laws and ordinary usages of the road and a demonstration of his ability to operate a motorized bicycle.

The demonstration of an applicant's ability to operate a motorized bicycle shall be administered at such municipalities that the commission shall designate, under the supervision of the commission, or an officer, employee, or authorized agent of the commission, in accordance with rules and regulations promulgated by the commission.

The administrator may, in his discretion, issue a learner's permit to a person 15 years of age or older, upon proof of identity and date of birth, allowing such person, for the purpose of fitting himself to become a motorized bicycle driver, to operate a motorized bicycle during daylight hours without supervision for a period not to exceed 45 days. The permit shall be sufficient license for the person to operate a motorized bicycle. No permit shall be issued unless the person applying therefor shall pay the sum of $5.00 to the commission, or an officer, employee or agent of the commission.

e. The valid driver's license, the insurance identification card, and the registration certificate shall be in the possession of the operator at all times when he is operating a motorized bicycle with motor engaged on the highways of this State. The operator shall exhibit his driver's license when requested to do so by any police officer or magistrate, while in the performance of the duties of his office and shall write his name in the presence of the officer, so that the officer may thereby determine the identity of the licensee and at the same time determine the correctness of the registration certificate, as it relates to the registration number and number plates of the motorized bicycle for which it was issued and the correctness of the evidence of a policy of insurance, as it relates to the coverage of the motorized bicycle for which it was issued. Any person violating this subsection shall be subject to a fine not exceeding $50.00.

If a person charged with a violation of this subsection can exhibit his valid driver's license, insurance identification card, and registration certificate, which were valid on the day he was charged, to the judge of the municipal court before whom he is summoned to answer to the charge, the judge may dismiss the charge; however, the judge may impose court costs.

f. Unless otherwise determined by the commissioner, statutes, rules and regulations applicable to bicycles shall apply whenever a motorized bicycle is operated upon any highway or upon any public land.

Every person operating a motorized bicycle upon a public road or highway shall be subject to all of the duties applicable to the driver of a vehicle by chapter 4 of Title 39 and N.J.S.2C:11–5 and all amendments and supplements thereto.

L.1975, c. 250, § 2. Amended by L.1977, c. 267, § 2; L.1983, c. 16, § 1; L.1983, c. 105, § 7; L.2003, c. 13, § 49 (contingent effective date).

39:4–14.3a. Retail sales; conformance of bicycles to act and regulations

No person engaged in the business of selling motorized bicycles at retail shall sell or offer to sell any motorized bicycle unless such motorized bicycle is in conformity with this act and regulations promulgated hereunder by the director.

L.1977, c. 267, § 3.

39:4–14.3b. Violations; penalties

Except as otherwise provided by this act, any person who violates any of the provisions of this act shall be subject to a fine not exceeding $200.00 or imprisonment for a term not exceeding 15 days or both.

L.1977, c. 267, § 4.

39:4–14.3c. Rules and regulations

The director may promulgate such rules and regulations as may be necessary to effectuate the purposes of this act.

L.1977, c. 267, § 5.

39:4–14.3d. Operator only on bicycle

A motorized bicycle shall carry only the operator.

L.1977, c. 267, § 6.

39:4–14.3e. Compulsory liability insurance coverage

Every owner of a motorized bicycle principally garaged or operated in this State and every person in the business of renting motorized bicycles shall maintain liability insurance coverage, under provisions approved by the Commissioner of Insurance, insuring against loss resulting from liability imposed by law for bodily injury, death and property damage sustained by any person arising out of the ownership, operation or use of a motorized bicycle.

The Commissioner of Insurance, in consultation with the Director of the Division of Motor Vehicles, shall by regulation fix the amounts and limits of coverage of, and requirements for, such insurance.

L.1977, c. 267, § 7.

39:4–14.3f. Accident reports

Article 15 of chapter 4 of Title 39 of the Revised Statutes pertaining to accidents and reports shall be applicable to all accidents involving motorized bicycles. Any law enforcement officer investigating an accident in which a motorized bicycle is involved shall report the accident to the Division of Motor Vehicles. Said report shall include information relating to the cause of the accident and extent of injury, if any, to the operator and such other information as may be required.

L.1977, c. 267, § 8.

39:4–14.3g. Operation by person under influence of liquor or drugs; penalty

It is unlawful for any person to operate a motorized bicycle while under the influence of intoxicating liquor, or a narcotic, hallucinogenic or habit-producing drug. Any person who violates the provisions of this act shall be subject to the same penalties as provided in R.S. 39:4–50 for conviction of operating a motor vehicle while under the influence of any such substance. In any prosecution for a violation of this act, the presumptions, consent and procedures set forth in P.L.1951, c. 23, s. 30 (C. 39:4–50.1) and P.L.1966, c. 142, ss. 2–5 (C. 39:4–50.2 to 39:4–50.5) [1] shall be applicable.

L.1981, c. 97, § 1, eff. March 31, 1981.

[1] N.J.S.A. § 39:4–50.4 was repealed. See, now, § 39:4–50.4a.

39:4–14.3h. Suspension of privilege; second violation

Any person under the age of 17 who commits a second violation of the provisions of P.L.1975, c. 250 (C.

39:4–14.3) or P.L.1977, c. 267 (C. 39:4–14.3a et seq.) or any other provision of chapter 4 of Title 39 of the Revised Statutes shall have his privilege to operate a motorized bicycle suspended for a period of 30 days from the date of conviction. For a subsequent violation a person shall have his privilege to operate a motorized bicycle suspended until he reaches the age of 17.

L.1982, c. 28, § 1, eff. April 29, 1982.

39:4–14.3i. Registration; requirements; form and content of certificate; expiration; renewal

In addition to the requirements of section 2 of P.L.1975, c. 250 (C. 39:4–14.3) and P.L.1977, c. 267 (C. 39:4–14.3a et seq.), no motorized bicycle as defined by R.S. 39:1–1 shall be operated on the public highways or on public lands of this State unless registered by the owner thereof as provided by this act. The Director of the Division of Motor Vehicles in the Department of Law and Public Safety is authorized to grant a registration to the owner of a motorized bicycle who is at least 15 years of age, provided that the application for registration has been properly made, the registration fee has been paid, and the motorized bicycle is of a type approved by the director.

The form and contents of the registration certificate shall be prescribed by the director. The director shall maintain a record of all registration certificates issued and their contents.

The registration shall expire and the registration certificate shall become void on the last day of the 11th calendar month following the calendar month in which the certificate was issued, except that the director may suspend or revoke a registration for any violation of this act or of any of the rules promulgated hereunder.

The director shall issue registration certificates for the following registration period, on and after the first day of the calendar month immediately preceding the commencement of the registration period, the registration certificates to be effective immediately.

Application forms for all renewals of registrations for motorized bicycles shall be mailed by the director from the division to the last address of the owner of a motorized bicycle as it appears on the records of the division.

L.1983, c. 105, § 9.

39:4–14.3j. Form completed by dealer at original sale; content; temporary registration; temporary license plates; registration; fee

At the time of original sale of a motorized bicycle in this State, a motorized bicycle dealer shall complete a form, of a kind to be approved by the director, which shall contain the following information:

a. The year of manufacture, make, model, color, and unladen weight of the motorized bicycle;

b. The United States Department of Transportation head tag serial number of the motorized bicycle;

c. The name, street address, and age of the purchaser of the motorized bicycle;

d. The business name and address of the motorized bicycle dealer from whom the bicycle was purchased;

e. The amount of New Jersey sales tax collected by the dealer;

f. The motorized bicycle dealer's New Jersey sales tax authorization number;

g. Signatures of both the motorized bicycle dealer and the purchaser;

h. The month, day and year of sale;

i. The name of the insurer of the motorized bicycle and the policy number;

j. Any other information required by the director.

The dealer shall retain one copy of the form and present the other two to the purchaser. The form shall constitute temporary registration for the vehicle for a period of 20 days from the date of purchase; provided, however, that the purchaser shall comply with all other laws, rules and regulations regarding operation of motorized bicycles.

The dealer shall issue the purchaser temporary license plates to be displayed on the motorized bicycle until permanent registration is completed and a motorized bicycle license plate is issued.

Within 20 days the purchaser shall present one copy of the form to the Division of Motor Vehicles, together with any additional information which the director may require, pay the requisite fee and register the motorized bicycle in the manner provided in this act.

The fee for the initial registration of a motorized bicycle by a given owner shall be $8.00. The yearly fee for each renewal of registration shall be $8.

L.1983, c. 105, § 10. Amended by L.1994, c. 60, § 23, eff. July 1, 1994.

39:4–14.3k. License plate

At the time of issuance of the registration of the motorized bicycle, the director shall also issue to the registrant, at no additional cost, a motorized bicycle license plate to be attached to the bicycle by the registrant. Each plate shall contain a clearly visible license number to be assigned by the director and shall bear the insignia "MOPED" in clear lettering. The license plate number shall be contained on the certificate of registration.

L.1983, c. 105, § 11.

39:4–14.3l. Removal from state, destruction, theft or discontinued usage; notice; transfer of ownership

Whenever a motorized bicycle for which a registration certificate has been issued has been permanently removed from the State, the owner shall notify the director in writing within 10 days.

Whenever a motorized bicycle for which a registration certificate has been issued has been destroyed, stolen, or whenever its use has been discontinued, the owner shall notify the director in writing, sign and execute the registration certificate, and return it to the director within 10 days.

Whenever there is a transfer of ownership of a motorized bicycle for which a registration certificate has been issued, the owner shall sign over the registration to the purchaser.

The new owner shall apply to the director for a new registration certificate and license plate and submit the original registration certificate and license plate with the application. The new owner shall not operate the motorized bicycle until the new registration is completed.

The application form for registering a motorized bicycle whose ownership has been transferred shall contain the same information contained in the application completed by a motorized bicycle dealer at the time of original sale, with modifications made by the director.

The new owner shall pay the fees for registering the motorized bicycle established pursuant to section 10 of this act.

L.1983, c. 105, § 12.

39:4–14.3m.   Display of license

No person shall operate a motorized bicycle in this State unless a license plate is displayed in accordance with the provisions of R.S. 39:3–33 applicable to motorcycles.

L.1983, c. 105, § 13.

39:4–14.3n.   Make and model numbers; certification; list of approved bicycles

a.   The director shall promulgate rules and regulations pursuant to the "Administrative Procedure Act," P.L.1968, c. 410 (C. 52:14B–1 et seq.), requiring manufacturers or distributors to certify in writing to the division the make and model numbers of motorized bicycles which they sell or distribute in this State.

b.   The director shall compile and maintain a list of approved motorized bicycles and shall only permit approved makes and models of motorized bicycles which are sold or distributed in this State after the effective date of this act to be registered pursuant thereto.

c.   Nothing contained herein, however, shall preclude registration of a motorized bicycle pursuant to this act where the registrant of the motorized bicycle establishes with reasonable specificity that the motorized bicycle conforms to the definition in R.S. 39:1–1 and the requirements of section 2 of P.L.1975, c. 250 (C. 39:4–14.3) and P.L.1977, c. 267 (C. 39:4–14.3a et seq.).

L.1983, c. 105, § 14.

39:4–14.3o.   Nonresident motorized bicycle owner; registration

The registration provisions governing motorized bicycles shall not apply to a nonresident motorized bicycle owner who has complied with the registration and licensing laws of his state of residence, if the motorized bicycle is appropriately identified in accordance with the laws of his state of residence. Nothing in this section shall authorize the operation of a motorized bicycle contrary to the provisions of this act, section 2 of P.L.1975, c. 250 (C. 39:4–14.3) and P.L.1977, c. 267 (C. 39:4–14.3a et seq.).

L.1983, c. 105, § 15.

39:4–14.3p.   Proof of ownership; bicycle purchased prior to effective date of act

With respect to motorized bicycles purchased prior to the effective date of this act, and for which no bill of sale or other formal proof of ownership is available, the director may accept as proof of ownership a sworn affidavit from the owner, setting forth with reasonable specificity facts regarding the acquisition of ownership of the motorized bicycle, together with any supporting documents, as proof of ownership of the motorized bicycle.

A person who knowingly submits a false bill of sale, false receipt for purchase, or any other false proof of ownership, or who knowingly submits any false affidavit or false supporting document regarding proof of ownership of a motorized bicycle, commits a crime of the fourth degree.

L.1983, c. 105, § 16.

39:4–14.3q.   Helmet

No person shall operate a motorized bicycle unless he wears a protective helmet of a type approved by the director.

L.1983, c. 105, § 17.

39:4–14.3r.   Dealer licensed as motor vehicle dealer; inapplicability of restrictions contained in Municipal Land Use Law

Requiring a motorized bicycle dealer to be licensed as a motor vehicle dealer under R.S. 39:10–19 for the purposes of this act shall not mean that he is a motor vehicle dealer for the purpose of meeting any restrictions or regulations contained in a planning or zoning ordinance under the "Municipal Land Use Law," P.L. 1975, c. 291 (C. 40:55D–1 et seq.).

L.1983, c. 105, § 18.

39:4–14.3s.   Rules and regulations

The director shall have the authority to promulgate rules and regulations pursuant to the "Administrative Procedure Act," P.L.1968, c. 410 (C. 52:14B–1 et seq.) to effectuate the purposes of this act.

L.1983, c. 105, § 19.

39:4–14.3t. Violations; fine

Except as otherwise provided by this act, a person who violates any of the provisions of this act or any rule or regulation promulgated pursuant to this act shall be subject to a fine of not more than $100.00 for each offense.

L.1983, c. 105, § 20.

39:4–14.3u. Ownership acquired prior to effective date of act; compliance with act

The owner of a motorized bicycle who acquired ownership prior to the effective date of this act shall have 90 days from the effective date to comply with the registration, titling, and license plate requirements contained herein.

L.1983, c. 105, § 21.

39:4–14.3v. Education program for safe operation; fund

The director shall establish a fund not to exceed $50,000.00 per year for the purpose of providing an educational program for the safe operation of motorized bicycles.

L.1983, c. 105, § 22.

39:4–14.3v1. Educational program for safe operation of bicycles; fund

The Director of the Division of Motor Vehicles shall use a portion of the fund established pursuant to section 22 of P.L.1983, c. 105 (C. 39:4–14.3v) for the purpose of providing an educational program for the safe operation of bicycles.

L.1983, c. 459, § 1, eff. Jan. 12, 1984.

39:4–14.3w. Disposition of fees

The fees collected pursuant to this act shall be appropriated to the Division of Motor Vehicles.

L.1983, c. 105, § 23.

39:4–14.3x. Emerging from or entering alley, driveway, garage, or private road or driveway; violation; penalties

An operator of a motorized bicycle who is convicted of a violation of R.S. 39:4–66 concerning the operation of a vehicle when emerging from an alley, driveway, garage, or private road or driveway or section 48 of P.L.1951, c. 23 (C. 39:4–66.1) concerning the operation of a vehicle when entering an alley, driveway, garage, or private road or driveway from a highway shall be subject to the penalties set forth in R.S. 39:4–203.

L.1989, c. 147, § 3.

39:4–14.4. Sale or rent of bicycle; equipment with reflectors

No person shall sell or offer to sell, or rent or offer to rent, whether it be by retail, wholesale or by auction, any bicycle manufactured on or after the effective date of this act unless such bicycle is equipped with front, rear and pedal reflectors and either (a) side reflectors; or (b) retroreflective tire sidewalls which shall form a continuous circle on each sidewall, in order to permit recognition and identification under illumination from motor vehicle headlamps. Such front, rear, pedal and side reflectors shall be colored and mounted in conformity with regulations promulgated by the Director of the Division of Consumer Affairs.

L.1975, c. 328, § 1.

39:4–14.4a. Rules and regulations for promotion of bicycle helmets

No person shall sell or offer to sell at retail any bicycle unless there is affixed to that bicycle a statement promoting the use of helmets by bicycle riders. If a bicycle is sold unassembled, the statement shall be displayed in a prominent manner on the carton or package containing the unassembled bicycle.

L.1991, c. 323, § 1, eff. Feb. 1, 1992.

39:4–14.5. Bicycle defined

As used in this act "bicycle" means any two-wheeled vehicle having a rear drive wheel which is solely human-powered and having a seat height of 25 inches or greater when the seat is in the lowest adjustable position.

L.1975, c. 328, § 2.

39:4–14.6. Inapplicability of act to person not regularly engaged in selling or renting bicycles

This act shall not apply to the sale or rental of a bicycle by any person who is not regularly engaged in the business of selling or renting bicycles and where such bicycle was obtained by the person making the sale or rental for his own use.

L.1975, c. 328, § 3.

39:4–14.7. Equipment; rules and regulations

The Director of the Division of Consumer Affairs in the Department of Law and Public Safety is authorized and empowered to adopt rules and regulations covering the types of equipment and the specifications therefor, including the color and mounting thereof, which shall be in accordance with Federal standards regulating bicycles promulgated by the Consumer Product Safety Commission entitled "Requirements For Bicycles" (16 CFR Part 1512) and pursuant to the Federal Hazardous Substances Act (15 U.S.C. 1261, et seq.) and any amendatory or supplemental acts or regulations promulgated thereto.

L.1975, c. 328, § 4.

39:4–14.7a. Statement promoting use of helmet to be affixed to bicycle or to carton of unassembled bicycle

The Director of the Division of Consumer Affairs in the Department of Law and Public Safety shall, pursuant to the provisions of the "Administrative Procedure Act," P.L.1968, c. 410 (C. 52:14B–1 et seq.), promulgate rules and regulations to effectuate the purposes of this act. In addition to such other matters as the director shall deem appropriate and necessary, those rules and regulations so promulgated shall provide that the affixing of the warning cards "This Bike Is Missing One Part," designed by the New Jersey Coalition for Prevention of Developmental Disabilities and funded by the Office for the Prevention of Mental Retardation and Developmental Disabilities in the Department of Human Services, to a bicycle offered for sale at retail shall fulfill the requirements of section 1 of this act [1] and that those warning cards shall be readily available to the retail sellers of bicycles at cost.

L.1991, c. 323, § 2, eff. Feb. 1, 1992.

[1] N.J.S.A. § 39:4–14.4a.

39:4–14.8. Violations; penalties

Any person who shall violate any of the provisions of this act shall be subject to a fine of not more than $50.00 for a first offense and a fine of $100.00 for each subsequent offense.

L.1975, c. 328, § 5.

39:4–14.9. Enforcement; collection of penalties; jurisdiction; process

The enforcement of this act shall be vested in the Director of the Division of Consumer Affairs of the Department of Law and Public Safety, the inspectors appointed under his authority, and the police or peace officers of, or inspectors duly appointed for that purpose by, any municipality or county or by the State. Jurisdiction of proceedings to collect the penalties prescribed by this act is vested in the Superior Court and the municipal court in any municipality where the defendant may be apprehended or where he may reside. Process shall be either a summons or warrant and shall be prosecuted in a summary manner pursuant to "the penalty enforcement law" (N.J.S.2A:58–1 et seq.).

L.1975, c. 328, § 6. Amended by L.1991, c. 91, § 370, eff. April 9, 1991.

39:4–14.10. Definitions

a. As used in this act, "electric personal assistive mobility device" means a self-balancing non-tandem two wheeled device designed to transport one person which uses an electric propulsion system with average power of 750 watts (one horsepower), whose maximum speed on a paved level surface, when operated solely by such a propulsion system while operated by a person weighing 170 pounds is less than 20 miles per hour. The device shall not be considered a motorized wheelchair, motorized bicycle, motorcycle, motorized scooter, motorized skateboard, vehicle or motor vehicle.

b. An electric personal assistive mobility device may be operated on the public highways, sidewalks and bicycle paths of the State. Every person operating such a device shall be granted all of the rights and be subject to all of the duties applicable to the driver of a bicycle by chapter four of Title 39 of the Revised Statutes except as to those provisions thereof which by their nature can have no application. An electric personal assistive mobility device shall be subject to the safety and equipment requirements applicable to the bicycle provisions of chapter 4 of Title 39 of the Revised Statutes, except as to those provisions thereof which by their nature can have no application.

c. The operator of an electric personal assistive mobility device shall not be required to obtain a driver's license therefor or to register the device. The operator shall not be required to furnish proof of having liability insurance for the device or other proof of financial responsibility.

d. The governing body of any municipality may, by ordinance, regulate the operation of electric personal assistive mobility devices upon the roadways and public properties under municipal jurisdiction. The State or the governing body of any county or municipality may prohibit or regulate their operation on any public highway under its jurisdiction.

e. Notwithstanding the other provisions of this section, an operator of an electric personal assistive mobility device shall:

(1) wear a helmet while operating that device; and

(2) be 16 years of age or older, except for an operator with a mobility-related disability.

L.2001, c. 430, § 1, eff. Jan. 8, 2002. Amended by L.2003, c. 88, § 1, eff. June 8, 2003.

39:4–14.11. Failure to comply with act; fines

An operator who fails to comply with the requirements of this act shall receive a warning for the first offense. For a second offense, the operator shall be fined $10. For a subsequent offense, the device shall be impounded for not more than 30 days. A person who fails to comply with the requirements governing warning notices shall be fined not more than $100 for each violation.

L.2001, c. 430, § 3, eff. Jan. 8, 2002.

39:4–14.12. Restriction on operation of motorized scooter

a. No person, except for an operator with a mobility-related disability, as authorized by section 2 of P.L.2007, c. 21 (C.39:4–14.15), shall operate a motorized scooter upon any public street, highway or sidewalk.

b. Except as otherwise provided in section 4 of P.L.2005, c. 159 (C.39:4–14.14), no person, except for an operator with a mobility-related disability, as authorized by section 2 of P.L.2007, c. 21 (C.39:4–14.15), shall operate a motorized scooter upon any public property or lands.

c. No person shall operate a motorized scooter on the property of another without the consent of the owner of that property or the person who has a contractual right to the use of that property.

L.2005, c. 159, § 2, eff. July 19, 2005. Amended by L.2007, c. 21, § 1, eff. May 1, 2007.

39:4–14.13. Violations; penalties

A person violating the provisions of section 2[1] of this act shall be subject:

a. For the first offense, to a fine of not less than $100 nor more than $200, and seizure of the motorized scooter. The seized scooter may only be retrieved from the police by the operator of the scooter or if the operator is under 18 years of age by the operator accompanied by the operator's parent or guardian.

b. For the second offense, to a fine of not less than $200 nor more than $500, and seizure of the motorized scooter. The seized scooter may only be retrieved from the police by the operator of the scooter or if the operator is under 18 years of age by the operator accompanied by the operator's parent or guardian, provided that the court adjudicating the matter approves the return of the scooter. In addition to the fine and seizure provided for in this subsection, the court shall order the violator to perform community service for a period of not greater than 25 hours.

c. For the third or subsequent offense, to a fine of not less than $500 nor more than $750, and seizure and forfeiture of the motorized scooter. In addition to the fine, and seizure and forfeiture provided in this subsection, the court shall order the violator to perform community service for a period of not greater than 50 hours.

L.2005, c. 159, § 3, eff. July 19, 2005.

[1] N.J.S.A. § 39:4–14.12.

39:4–14.14. Operation of motorized scooters in designated locations permitted by municipal ordinance or county resolution; requirements

The governing body of any municipality may, by ordinance, permit the operation of motorized scooters upon designated municipal property, other than the streets, highways and sidewalks under municipal jurisdiction. The governing body of any county may, by resolution, permit the operation of motorized scooters upon designated county property, other than the streets, highways and sidewalks under county jurisdiction.

Such an ordinance or resolution permitting the operation of motorized scooters upon designated municipal or county property shall include, but not be limited to, the following provisions:

a. A designation of the municipal or county property upon which motorized scooters may be operated;

b. The days and hours of the day during which motorized scooters may be operated upon that municipal or county property;

c. A requirement that each motorized scooter operated upon the designated municipal or county property be registered with the municipality or county and receive a certificate of registration from the municipality or county. As a condition for such registration, the owner or operator shall produce or display appropriate proof that a policy of liability insurance is in effect for that motorized scooter. The municipality or county may impose a reasonable fee to cover the costs of registration;

d. A requirement that no person under the age of 12 years or older if so determined by the municipality or county be permitted to operate a motorized scooter upon the designated municipal or county property;

e. A requirement that every operator of a motorized scooter wear a properly fitted and fastened helmet which meets the standards of the American National Standards Institute (ANSI Z90.4 bicycle helmet), the Snell Memorial Foundation's 1990 Standard for Protective Headgear for Use in Bicycling, the American Society for Testing and Materials (ASTM) standard or such other standard, as appropriate;

f. A requirement that each motorized scooter operated upon the designated municipal or county property be equipped with a brake that will enable the operator to stop the scooter in a safe and effective manner;

g. A requirement that prior to operating a motorized scooter upon the designated municipal or county property, the prospective operator demonstrate, in a manner prescribed by a designated local authority, a capability to safely operate the scooter; and

h. A schedule setting forth the penalties for violating the provisions of the ordinance. The schedule shall be prominently posted upon the designated municipal or county property, along with a warning that operators may also be subject to applicable provisions and penalties set forth in chapter 4 of Title 39 of the Revised Statutes [1].

L.2005, c. 159, § 4, eff. July 19, 2005.

[1] N.J.S.A. § 39:4–1 et seq.

39:4–14.15 Conditions for operation of motor scooter on public streets

a. Upon request, the Chief Administrator of the New Jersey Motor Vehicle Commission shall issue to any holder of a handicapped person identification card, a placard or sticker of such size and design as shall be determined by the chief administrator in consultation with the Division of Vocational Rehabilitation Services in the Department of Labor and Workforce Development and the Division of Disability Services in the Department of Human Services, indicating that a handicapped person identification card has been issued to the person designated therein and that the person so designated may operate the motorized scooter on public streets as provided in subsection e. of this section. The placard or sticker shall be displayed in such manner as the chief administrator shall determine on the motorized scooter used by the named individual with a mobility-related disability.

b. Any motorized scooter operated by a person with a mobility-related disability shall be registered with the municipality in which the operator resides. As a condition for such registration, the owner or operator shall produce or display appropriate proof that a policy of liability insurance is in effect for that motorized scooter. The municipality or county may impose a reasonable fee to cover the costs of registration.

c. Any person with a mobility-related disability who operates a motorized scooter shall wear a properly fitted and fastened helmet which meets the Consumer Product Safety Commission standard or such other standard, as appropriate.

d. Any motorized scooter operated by a person with a mobility-related disability shall be equipped with a brake that will enable the operator to stop the scooter in a safe and effective manner.

e. A properly registered motorized scooter may be operated by a properly designated person with a mobility-related disability on any public street with a posted speed limit not exceeding 25 miles per hour. If the authority having jurisdiction over the public street determines that a properly registered motorized scooter operated by a properly designated person with a mobility-related disability may be operated on a public street with a posted speed limit in excess of 25 miles per hour, but not exceeding 35 miles per hour, or any portion thereof, without posing a danger to the safety and well-being of the operator of the motorized scooter or impeding the safe flow and operation of traffic, a properly registered motorized scooter may be operated on that designated public street, or designated portion thereof, by a properly designated person. A municipality or county may make such a determination by ordinance or resolution, as appropriate, but such ordinance or resolution shall not require the approval of the Commissioner of Transportation.

f. No motorized scooter that is capable of a maximum speed of more than 15 miles per hour shall be registered or operated on a public street under the provisions of this section.

g. Neither the State nor any municipality or county, nor any agency, official or employee thereof, shall assume responsibility for or incur liability for any injury to person or property caused by any act of a person with a mobility-related disability who operates a motorized scooter upon its designated municipal, county or State property.

h. For the purposes of this section, "motorized scooter" shall mean a gas or electric powered scooter or mini scooter which is capable of a maximum speed of not more than 15 miles per hour on a flat surface. Nothing in this section shall be construed to authorize or permit the registration or operation of any pocket bike, super pocket bike, sport scooter, mini chopper, mini motorcycle, or motorized skateboard on any public street by a person with a mobility-related disability. *L.2007, c. 21, § 2, eff. May 1, 2007.*

ARTICLE 4. HORSES AND HORSE–DRAWN VEHICLES

39:4–15. Sleigh bells on horses attached to a sleigh

No person shall drive a horse attached to a sleigh or sled on a highway unless there are a sufficient number of bells attached to the horse's harness to give warning of its approach.

39:4–16. Unattended horses; precautions used

No horse shall be left unattended in a highway unless securely fastened or unless the wheels of the vehicle to which he is harnessed are securely tied, fastened or chained, and the vehicle is of sufficient weight to prevent its being dragged at a dangerous speed with the wheels so secured.

39:4–17. Unbitted horses

No horse shall be unbitted in a highway unless secured by a halter.

39:4–18. Removing part of vehicle or harness

No person shall remove a wheel, pole shaft, whiffle-tree, swinglebar or a part of a vehicle or harness likely to cause accident if the horse starts, without first unhitching the horse attached to the vehicle.

39:4–19. Obstructing sidewalk with tie rope, etc., prohibited

No person shall fasten a horse in such a manner that the tie rope, reins, or lines are an obstruction to the free use of a sidewalk or crosswalk.

39:4–20. Hitching horses to pole, post, tree or hydrant prohibited

No horse shall be hitched or fastened to a pole carrying any wires, a public lamp-post, or pole, a shade tree or its protecting box or casing, or to a water hydrant in a street.

39:4–21. Racing on highway prohibited; exception

No person shall run or race a horse on a highway, whether the running, racing or trotting is for trial of speed or for the purpose of passing another horse or vehicle. This section shall not apply where permission for racing is given by the proper municipal authorities and the portion of the highway which is devoted to the racing is properly closed to other traffic.

39:4–22. Reins held in hands

No person shall cease to hold the reins in his hands while riding, driving, or conducting a horse.

39:4–23. Ill-treatment of horses

No person shall either ill-treat, overdrive, override or unnecessarily or cruelly beat a horse. A person who violates this section shall be guilty of a disorderly persons offense, except that a person who unnecessarily or cruelly beats a horse shall be guilty of a crime of the fourth degree, and shall be subject to the provisions of R.S.4:22–17, R.S.4:22–21, and R.S.4:22–26, as appropriate.

Amended by L.1998, c. 105, § 1, eff. Sept. 14, 1998; L.2001, c. 229, § 5, eff. Aug. 27, 2001.

39:4–24. Use of whip

No person shall crack or so use a whip as to annoy, interfere with or endanger a person or excite a horse other than a horse which he is using.

39:4–25. Lights on animal-drawn vehicles

Every vehicle drawn by a horse or other beast shall carry, during the period from thirty minutes after sunset and thirty minutes before sunrise, and when fog renders it impossible to see a long distance, at least one lighted lamp on the front of the vehicle. The lamp shall show a white light and shall be of such a nature and so displayed that it may be seen from a point at least five hundred feet distant in the direction toward which the vehicle is proceeding. There shall be attached to the rear of the vehicle two lighted lamps showing a red light visible for a distance of at least five hundred feet in the direction from which the vehicle is proceeding.

Amended by L.1951, c. 23, p. 72, § 18.

39:4–25.1. Rights and duties of persons riding or driving animals

Every person riding an animal or driving any animal-drawn vehicle upon a roadway shall be granted all of the rights and shall be subject to all of the duties applicable to the driver of a vehicle by chapter four of Title 39 of the Revised Statutes and all supplements thereto, except those provisions thereof which by their very nature can have no application.

L.1951, c. 23, p. 72, § 19.

ARTICLE 5. MACHINERY, VEHICLES OR APPARATUS OF UNUSUAL SIZE OR WEIGHT

39:4–26. Moving heavy machinery, apparatus, etc.; registration fee; permits; reciprocity

A person may move along or across a public road or highway, road building machinery, vehicles, traction engines, rollers, structural units incapable of dismemberment or other apparatus or machinery of unusual size or weight, on trailers or semitrailers, after registering the trailers or semitrailers with the Director of Motor Vehicles and paying him a registration fee of $200.00 and obtaining a permit therefor from the director for the State highways traversed by them, or from the county supervisor or supervisors of roads of the county or counties for the county roads traversed by them or from the duly authorized official or officials of the municipality or municipalities for the municipal roads traversed by them, subject to the provisions of this article, provided, however, that the provisions for registration and registration fee shall not apply to such vehicles duly registered in any other State or Federal district which grants exemption from registration and registration fee to vehicles properly registered in New Jersey under provisions of this article, traversing the roads of said other State or Federal district.

A trailer or semitrailer, having a width in excess of 96 but not more than 144 inches, used to transport divisible loads for industrial processing or storage may be registered with the director at a fee of $200.00. A trailer or semitrailer so registered may be operated on any public highway, except limited access highways, provided the distance operated on the highway is not more than 1,000 feet from the point of entrance to the point of exit and further provided that a permit valid for the duration of the registration year is obtained from the director. Such movements may be made at any hour of any day of the year and no escort vehicles shall be required. The limitation as to distance operated shall not apply when the vehicle is empty and proceeding to or from an inspection, service, maintenance, or repair facility.

The director, board of chosen freeholders and a municipality, may be[1] regulation in the case of the director and by resolution in the case of the board of freeholders or municipality, adopt general rules and regulations with respect to the issuance and use of permits, but not contrary to those stated above, and may impose reasonable fees therefor provided that no permit shall be issued unless the said director, county supervisor or authorized municipal official is reasonably satisfied as to the financial responsibility of the applicant for permit to meet any claims for damages which may arise and reasonable evidence of such financial responsibility is filed with the said director, supervisor or municipal official.

Amended by L.1941, c. 260, p. 690, § 1; L.1951, c. 23, p. 72, § 20; L.1952, c. 149, p. 508, § 1; L.1960, c. 13, p. 33, § 1; L.1961, c. 113, p. 707, § 4; L.1971, c. 310, § 1, eff. Sept. 2, 1971; L.1975, c. 180, § 10, eff. Jan. 1, 1976.

1 Probably should read "by".

39:4–27. Loading and operation of trailer; permittee's responsibility in damages

In the transportation of any such road building machinery, vehicle, traction engine, roller, structural unit incapable of dismemberment or other apparatus or machinery in accordance with the provisions of section 39:4–26 of this Title, such trailer or semitrailer shall be so loaded and operated as not to cause damage to the surface of any public road, street, highway, bridge or railroad crossing. When operated the gross weight of the combination of vehicle and load shall be limited to eight hundred pounds for each inch of width of the tires on all wheels.

Every permittee shall be responsible in money damages to the municipality, county, State Highway Commissioner or railroad company maintaining a highway, bridge or railroad crossing by reason of the failure of the permittee to comply with the statutes or posted regulations governing the use of the said highway, bridge or crossing or the rules and regulations governing the movement authorized under said permit.

Amended by L.1941, c. 260, p. 690, § 2; L.1952, c. 149, p. 509, § 2.

39:4–28. Height; overhead wires

No such road building machinery, vehicle, traction engine, steam roller or other apparatus or machinery having a height, including load or equipment or apparatus connected therewith, in excess of fourteen feet shall be operated, driven, propelled or conveyed along or across a public road or highway in which is located overhead wires of a street railway, traction company or electric light or power company at any time, unless employees of the street railway, traction company or electric light or power company are present prepared to superintend the necessary movement or change in the wires, or to make immediate repairs thereof in case of injury thereto.

39:4–29. Time for moving along street railway tracks

No such road building machinery, vehicle, traction engine, steam roller or other apparatus or machinery shall be operated, driven, propelled or conveyed along the tracks of a street railway excepting between the hours of nine o'clock P.M. and six o'clock A.M.

39:4–30. Exceptions to application of article; "temporary" or "in-transit" registration plates

Nothing in this article shall apply to any road building machinery, vehicle, traction engine, steam roller or other apparatus or machinery running upon railroad or street railway tracks, or a private railroad or railway, spur track or switch, nor shall a license hereunder be required for any road building machinery, vehicle, traction engine, steam roller or other apparatus or machinery while actually used in any type of construction; provided, further, however, that any such road building machinery, vehicle, traction engine, roller or other apparatus or machinery of the kind may be operated or drawn, subject to the following conditions:

Any person, partnership or corporation may, with regard to such road building machinery, vehicle, traction engine, roller or other apparatus or machinery of the kind owned or controlled by it, obtain general registration and registration plates therefor of the style and kind provided for in this article, with the word "temporary" or "in-transit" stated thereon, but only if the director is satisfied as to the financial responsibility of such person, partnership or corporation to meet any claim for damages arising out of an accident and satisfactory evidence of such responsibility has been filed with him.

The annual fee for the issuance of a certificate of registration, or duplicates thereof and five sets of "temporary" or "in-transit" plates bearing a number, corresponding to the number on the certificate of registration shall be $100.00.

Such plates can be placed on any such road building machinery, vehicle, traction engine, roller or other apparatus or machinery, owned or operated by the person, partnership or corporation to whom the registration is issued, only in moving to and from the location of any type of construction.

Amended by L.1941, c. 257, p. 686, § 1; L.1949, c. 250, p. 804, § 1; L.1951, c. 23, p. 73, § 21; L.1968, c. 130, § 11, eff. Aug. 1, 1968; L.1975, c. 180, § 11, eff. Jan. 1, 1976.

39:4–31. Violations of article; fine

A person violating a provision of this article shall, upon conviction thereof, pay such fine as may be imposed by the court, not exceeding one hundred dollars ($100.00) for each violation. In default of the payment thereof, the court imposing the fine may cause him to be imprisoned in the county jail of the county for a term not exceeding ninety days.

The fine shall be paid over to the board or body charged with the maintenance of the road or highway upon which the violation occurs.

Amended by L.1953, c. 36, p. 618, § 4.

ARTICLE 5A.   LOW SPEED VEHICLES

39:4–31.1. Operation of low-speed vehicles on public roads; conditions

a.   A low-speed vehicle may be operated upon any public road or highway under the jurisdiction of the Department of Transportation with a posted speed of 25 miles per hour or less. The commissioner may in the commissioner's discretion, by order, pursuant to the provisions of P.L.1998, c. 28 (C.39:4–8.2 et seq.), permit the use of low-speed vehicles upon any road and highway under the jurisdiction of the Department of Transportation where the posted speed limit is greater than 25 miles per hour but not greater than 35 miles per hour. Notwithstanding the foregoing, the commissioner may by order prohibit the use of low-speed vehicles on any street under the jurisdiction of the Department of Transportation where the commissioner determines that the operation of low- speed vehicles would constitute a hazard.

b.   A low-speed vehicle may be operated upon any public road or highway under the jurisdiction of a county or municipality with a posted speed of 25 miles per hour or less. A municipality or county may, by ordinance, or a county may, by ordinance or resolution, as appropriate, in the case of any street under municipal or county jurisdiction, permit the use of low- speed vehicles where the posted speed limit is greater than 25 miles per hour but not greater than 35 miles per hour. Notwithstanding the foregoing, a municipality or county may, by ordinance, or a county may, by ordinance or resolution, as appropriate, prohibit the use of low-speed vehicles on any street where the municipality or county determines that the operation of low- speed vehicles would constitute a hazard.

c. A low-speed vehicle may enter an intersection and cross any public road or highway under the jurisdiction of the Department of Transportation where the posted speed is 35 miles per hour or less, provided that if the road or highway is more than two lanes or is divided, such crossings shall only occur at signalized intersections or at such non-signalized intersections as the commissioner in the commissioner's discretion determines are appropriate for such crossings either on the commissioner's own motion or at the request of a county or municipality. A low-speed vehicle may enter an intersection and cross any public road or highway under the jurisdiction of the Department of Transportation where the posted speed is in excess of 35 miles per hour only at signalized intersections or at such non-signalized intersections as the commissioner in the commissioner's discretion determines are appropriate for such crossings either upon the commissioner's own motion or at the request of a county or municipality.

d. A low-speed vehicle may enter an intersection and cross any public road or highway under the jurisdiction of a county or municipality where the posted speed is 35 miles per hour or less, provided that if the road or highway is more than two lanes or is divided, such crossings shall only occur at signalized intersections or at such non-signalized intersections as the municipality by ordinance or the county, by ordinance or resolution, as appropriate, determines are appropriate for such crossing. A low-speed vehicle may enter an intersection and cross any public road or highway under the jurisdiction of a county or municipality where the posted speed is in excess of 35 miles per hour only at signalized intersections or at such non-signalized intersections as the municipality by ordinance or the county by ordinance or resolution, as appropriate, determines are appropriate for such crossing.

e. Persons operating a low-speed vehicle upon a public road, street or highway or crossing a public road, street or highway in violation of this section shall be subject to the general penalties of this chapter.

L.2005, c. 273, § 2, eff. April 6, 2006.

39:4–31.2. Maintenance and equipment requirements for low-speed vehicles operated on public roads; violation

a. Low-speed vehicles operated upon any public road or highway in this State shall be maintained in proper condition and comply with the equipment requirements and standards as set forth in 49 CFR s. 571.500, as amended and supplemented.

Low-speed vehicles operated upon any public road or highway in this State shall be equipped with the following additional equipment:

(1) Brakes adequate to control the movement of and to stop such vehicle;

(2) An odometer;

(3) A speedometer; and

(4) The original manufacturer's vehicle identification number die stamped upon the body, or frame, or either or both of them, of the vehicle or the original manufacturer's vehicle identification number die stamped upon the engine or motor of the vehicle.

b. All low-speed vehicles shall have a safety information decal as provided by the manufacturer affixed in a conspicuous place on the rear of the vehicle which shall display in prominent lettering "25 MPH Vehicle."

c. Any person operating a low-speed vehicle without the equipment prescribed in this section shall, on conviction, be fined for each violation as provided in R.S.39:3–79.

L.2005, c. 273, § 3, eff. April 6, 2006.

39:4–31.3. Valid driver's license required for operation of low-speed vehicle; registration; insurance; license plates; safety information decal; violation

a. Any person operating a low-speed vehicle in this State authorized pursuant to section 2 of P.L.2005, c. 273 (C.39:4–31.1) shall be in possession of a valid driver's license pursuant to the applicable provisions of R.S.39:3–10.

b. Low-speed vehicles operated on the roads and highways of this State shall be properly registered and insured in accordance with the provisions of R.S.39:3–4. All low-speed vehicles operated on the roads and highways of this State shall properly display a license plate issued by the New Jersey Motor Vehicle Commission or issued pursuant to the laws of another state.

The driver's license, the registration certificate of a motor vehicle and an insurance identification card shall be in the possession of the driver or operator at all times when he is in charge of a low-speed vehicle on the highways of this State.

c. Every person operating a low-speed vehicle upon a public road, street or highway shall be subject to the provisions of chapter 4 of Title 39 of the Revised Statutes, and chapter 11 and chapter 12 of Title 2C of the New Jersey Statutes applicable to the drivers of motor vehicles.

L.2005, c. 273, § 4, eff. April 6, 2006.

39:4–31.4. Certificate of origin of low-speed vehicle; waiver and certification by purchaser

a. When a new low-speed vehicle is delivered in this State by the manufacturer to his agent or a dealer, or a person purchasing directly from the manufacturer, the manufacturer shall execute and deliver to his agent or a dealer, or a person purchasing directly from the manufacturer, a certificate of origin, and no person shall bring into this State any new low-speed vehicle unless he has in his possession the certificate of origin. The certificate of origin shall contain the manufacturer's vehicle identification number and the motor number, if available, when the vehicle is sold, the name of the manufacturer, the manufacturer's shipping weight, and identify the vehicle as a low-speed vehicle, and provide a general description of the body, if any, the type and model and the gross vehicle weight rating.

When a new low-speed vehicle is sold in this State, the manufacturer, his agent or a dealer shall execute and deliver to the purchaser an assignment of the certificate of origin, with the genuine names and business or residence addresses of both stated thereon, and certified to have been executed with full knowledge of the contents and with the consent of both purchaser and seller. If, in connection with such sale, a security interest is taken or retained by the seller to secure all or a part of the purchase price of the vehicle, or is taken by a person who by making an advance or incurring an obligation gives value to enable the purchaser to acquire rights in the motor vehicle, the name and the business or residence address of the secured party or his assignee shall be noted on the manufacturer's certificate of origin. Nothing in this section shall apply to security interests in motor vehicles which constitute inventory held for sale, but such interests shall be subject to chapter 9 of Title 12A of the New Jersey Statutes.

b. Each purchaser of a new low-speed vehicle in this State shall execute a waiver and certify to have purchased a low-speed vehicle with full knowledge of the potentially hazardous characteristics of such vehicles as detailed by the manufacturer or his agent or dealer. The waiver shall be prepared by the manufacturer and kept in the possession of the manufacturer and his agent or dealer of low-speed vehicles. An executed copy shall be provided to the purchaser. The signing of this waiver by the purchaser shall serve to eliminate any liability of the manufacturer and his agent or dealer of low- speed vehicles.

L.2005, c. 273, § 5, eff. April 6, 2006.

39:4–31.5. Low-speed vehicle exempt from inspection

No low-speed vehicle shall be subject to a motor vehicle inspection by the New Jersey Motor Vehicle Commission. The registered owner of a low-speed vehicle shall be required to maintain the vehicle in proper condition as required by section 3 of this act. [1]

L.2005, c. 273, § 6, eff. April 6, 2006.

[1] N.J.S.A. § 39:4–31.2.

ARTICLE 6. PEDESTRIANS

39:4–32. Pedestrian crossing at controlled intersection; pedestrian duties; driver duties; inference of no due care exercised

On highways where traffic is controlled by a traffic control signal or by traffic or police officers:

a. Pedestrians shall not cross a roadway against the "stop" or red signal at a crosswalk, whether marked or unmarked, unless otherwise specifically directed to go by a traffic or police officer, or official traffic control device.

b. No driver of a vehicle shall fail to stop and remain stopped for a pedestrian crossing a roadway at a crosswalk when the pedestrian is upon, or within one lane of, the half of the roadway upon which the vehicle is traveling or onto which it is turning during the "go" or green signal. As used in this subsection, "half of the roadway" means all traffic lanes conveying traffic in one direction of travel, and includes the entire width of a one-way roadway.

c. A pedestrian crossing or starting across the intersection on a "go" or green signal, but who is still within the crosswalk when the signal changes, shall have the right of way until the pedestrian has reached the opposite curb or place of safety.

d. No pedestrian shall leave a curb or other place of safety and walk or run into the path of a vehicle which is so close that it is impossible for the driver to yield or stop.

e. Whenever any vehicle is stopped to permit a pedestrian to cross the roadway, the driver of any other vehicle approaching from the rear shall not overtake and pass such stopped vehicle.

f. Every pedestrian upon a roadway at any point other than within a marked crosswalk or within an unmarked crosswalk at an intersection shall yield the right-of-way to all vehicles upon the roadway.

g. Nothing contained herein shall relieve a driver from the duty to exercise due care for the safety of any pedestrian upon a roadway. Nothing herein shall relieve a pedestrian from using due care for his safety.

h. In the event of a collision between a vehicle and a pedestrian within a marked crosswalk, or at an unmarked crosswalk at an intersection, there shall be a permissive inference that the driver did not exercise due care for the safety of the pedestrian.

Amended by L.1951, c. 23, p. 74, § 22; L.2009, c. 319, § 1, eff. April 1, 2010.

39:4–33. Use of designated crosswalk; keeping to right

At intersections where traffic is directed by a police officer or traffic signal, no pedestrian shall enter upon or cross the highway at a point other than a crosswalk. Pedestrians shall move, whenever practicable, upon the right half of crosswalks.

Amended by L.1951, c. 23, p. 74, § 23.

39:4–34. Pedestrians to cross within crosswalk or at right angles; facing traffic; sidewalks

Where traffic is not controlled and directed either by a police officer or a traffic control signal, pedestrians shall cross the roadway within a crosswalk or, in the absence of a crosswalk, and where not otherwise prohibited, at right angles to the roadway. It shall be unlawful for a pedestrian to cross any highway having roadways separated by a medial barrier, except where provision is made for pedestrian crossing. On all highways where there are no sidewalks or paths provided for pedestrian use, pedestrians shall, when practicable, walk only on the extreme left side of the roadway or its shoulder facing approaching traffic.

Where sidewalks are provided it shall be unlawful for any pedestrian to walk along and upon an adjacent roadway.

Amended by L.1951, c. 23, p. 74, § 25; L.1970, c. 156, § 1, eff. July 24, 1970; L.1981, c. 220, § 1, eff. July 20, 1981.

39:4–35. Repealed by L.2009, c. 319, § 5, eff. April 1, 2010

39:4–36. Driver to yield to pedestrian at crosswalk; exceptions; vehicles approaching stopped vehicle from rear; yield of right-of-way by pedestrian; penalties; portion of fine deposited in Pedestrian Safety Enforcement and Education Fund

a. The driver of a vehicle shall yield the right-of-way to a pedestrian crossing the roadway within any unmarked crosswalk at an intersection, except at crosswalks when the movement of traffic is being regulated by police officers or traffic control signals, or where otherwise regulated by municipal, county, or State regulation, and except where a pedestrian tunnel or overhead pedestrian crossing has been provided:

(1) The driver of a vehicle shall stop and remain stopped to allow a pedestrian to cross the roadway within a marked crosswalk, when the pedestrian is upon, or within one lane of, the half of the roadway, upon which the vehicle is traveling or onto which it is turning. As used in this paragraph, "half of the roadway" means all traffic lanes conveying traffic in one direction of travel, and includes the entire width of a one-way roadway.

(2) No pedestrian shall leave a curb or other place of safety and walk or run into the path of a vehicle which is so close that it is impossible for the driver to yield or stop.

(3) Whenever any vehicle is stopped to permit a pedestrian to cross the roadway, the driver of any other vehicle approaching from the rear shall not overtake and pass such stopped vehicle.

(4) Every pedestrian upon a roadway at any point other than within a marked crosswalk or within an unmarked crosswalk at an intersection shall yield the right-of-way to all vehicles upon the roadway.

(5) Nothing contained herein shall relieve a driver from the duty to exercise due care for the safety of any pedestrian upon a roadway. Nothing contained herein shall relieve a pedestrian from using due care for his safety.

b. A person violating any paragraph of subsection a. of this section shall, upon conviction thereof, pay a fine to be imposed by the court in the amount of $200. The court may also impose upon a person violating any paragraph of subsection a. of this section, a penalty of community service not to exceed 15 days in such form and on such terms as the court shall deem appropriate. If the violation results in serious bodily injury to a pedestrian, the person convicted of the violation shall be subject to a fine of not less than $100 or more than $500, and may additionally be subject to a sentence of imprisonment not to exceed 25 days, or a license suspension not to exceed six months, or both, in the discretion of the court. As used in this section, "serious bodily injury" means serious bodily injury as defined in subsection b. of N.J.S.2C:11–1.

c. Of each fine imposed and collected pursuant to subsection b. of this section, $100 shall be forwarded to the State Treasurer who shall annually deposit the moneys into the "Pedestrian Safety Enforcement and Education Fund" created by section 1 of P.L.2005, c. 86 (C.39:4–36.2).

d. In the event of a collision between a vehicle and a pedestrian within a marked crosswalk, or at an unmarked crosswalk at an intersection, there shall be a permissive inference that the driver did not exercise due care for the safety of the pedestrian.

Amended by L.1951, c. 23, p. 75, § 26; L.1981, c. 220, § 3, eff. July 20, 1981; L.2005, c. 86, § 2, eff. Nov. 1, 2005; L.2009, c. 312, § 1, eff. Jan. 18, 2010; L.2009, c. 319, § 2, eff. April 1, 2010.

39:4–36.1. Crossing having pedestrian tunnel or overhead crossing; right of way

Any pedestrian crossing a roadway at a point where a pedestrian tunnel or overhead pedestrian crossing has been provided shall yield the right of way to all vehicles upon the roadway.

L.1951, c. 23, p. 74, § 24.

39:4–36.2. Pedestrian Safety Enforcement and Education Fund

There is created in the Division of Highway and Traffic Safety in the Department of Law and Public Safety a nonlapsing revolving fund to be known as the "Pedestrian Safety Enforcement and Education Fund." This fund shall be a repository for moneys provided pursuant to subsection c. of R.S.39:4–36 and shall be administered by the Division of Highway and Traffic Safety. Moneys deposited in the fund, and any interest earned thereon, shall be used for the purpose of making grants to municipalities and counties with pedestrian safety problems. Priority in awarding grants shall be given to municipalities and counties requesting funds in order to take remedial steps for intersections that have been identified as demonstrating pedestrian safety problems in accordance with P.L.2005, c.158 (C.39:4-36.3 et al.).

L.2005, c. 86, § 1, eff. Nov. 1, 2005.

39:4–36.3.   Legislative findings

The Legislature finds and declares:

a.   every year almost 5,000 pedestrians are killed in automobile accidents in the United States, accounting for roughly 12 percent of all persons killed in motor vehicle crashes;

b.   in New Jersey, from 1996 to 2001, the number of pedestrian fatalities declined by an average of seven percent per year; but this promising trend ended in 2002 when the number of pedestrian deaths in the State increased 26 percent from 2001;

c.   the 183 pedestrian fatalities in 2002 constitute 23 percent of all traffic-related deaths in the State, the highest rate since 1993; and

d.   therefore, it is fitting and appropriate that this State assess the safety of its intersections and take steps to increase the safety of its pedestrians.

L.2005, c. 158, § 1, eff. July 19, 2005.

39:4–36.4.   Identification of intersections controlled by traffic control signals presenting demonstrated pedestrian safety problems

The Commissioner of Transportation shall identify intersections controlled by a traffic control signal where making a right turn upon "Stop" or "Caution" signals presents demonstrated pedestrian safety problems. If an intersection identified by the commissioner is under State jurisdiction, the commissioner shall prohibit drivers from making right turns upon "Stop" or "Caution" signals at the intersection. If an intersection identified by the commissioner is under municipal or county authority, the commissioner shall request that the relevant authority prohibit drivers from making right turns upon "Stop" or "Caution" signals at the intersection.

L.2005, c. 158, § 2, eff. July 19, 2005.

39:4–37.   Regulating crossing at intersections by local authorities

Local authorities in their respective jurisdictions may regulate by ordinance, which shall first be approved by the director, the crossing of pedestrians at intersections of roadways where traffic on the roadways is controlled by traffic control signals.

Amended by L.1951, c. 23, p. 75, § 27.

39:4–37.1.   Blind persons; right of way

Any blind person using as a guide a walking cane, predominantly white or metallic in color or any blind person using as a guide a seeing-eye dog or other dog trained as a guide for the blind, equipped with a rigid "U"-shaped harness such as customarily used on dog guides or any guide dog instructor engaged in instruct-

ing a guide dog shall have the right-of-way in crossing any highway or any intersection thereof, and all drivers of vehicles shall yield the right-of-way to such blind person or guide dog instructor engaged in instructing a guide dog although traffic on said highway or intersection thereof is controlled by traffic signals, anything in the motor vehicle and traffic laws of this State to the contrary notwithstanding. The failure of a blind person or guide dog instructor to comply with the provisions of this act shall not give rise to a conclusive presumption of contributory negligence by such person. The provisions of this section shall not apply where traffic is specially directed by a traffic or police officer.

L.1939, c. 274, p. 696, § 1.   Amended by L.1946, c. 208, p. 805, § 1;   L.1971, c. 81, § 1, eff. April 8, 1971;   L.1999, c. 264, § 2, eff. Oct. 26, 1999.

ARTICLE 7.   STREET CARS

39:4–38.   Vehicles travelling upon street car route to give way to street car; intersections; overtaking and passing street cars

The driver or person in control of a vehicle traveling upon a regular street car route, and proceeding so as to obstruct the passage of the street car, shall immediately upon signal from the person in control thereof, give way thereto.

When a street car has lawfully entered and is crossing an intersection, no driver of a vehicle shall drive upon or across the car tracks within the intersection in front of the street car when there is hazard of a collision.

The driver of a vehicle upon overtaking and passing a street car shall not turn in front of such street car so as to interfere with or impede its movement.

Amended by L.1951, c. 23, p. 75, § 28.

39:4–39.   Distance to be kept behind street car

A driver of a vehicle when following a street car, upon the street car tracks, shall keep at least ten feet behind the car.

39:4–40.   Passing street car

The driver of a vehicle shall not overtake and pass upon the left, a street car proceeding in the same direction, whether actually in motion or temporarily at rest, when a travelable portion of the highway exists to the right of the street car, even though that portion of the highway is occupied by traffic, but this provision shall not apply to one-way streets.

The driver of a vehicle overtaking a street car, stopped for the purpose of receiving or discharging a passenger, shall bring the vehicle to a full stop, at least ten feet in the rear of the nearest entrance or exit of the street car then in use, and shall remain stationary until the passenger has boarded the car or reached the adjacent sidewalk. Where a safety zone has been established, a vehicle if otherwise permitted to proceed need not be brought to a full stop before passing the street car but may proceed past the car at a speed not greater than is reasonable and proper and with due caution for the safety of pedestrians.

39:4–41. Driving through safety zones prohibited

No driver of a vehicle shall drive through a safety zone, unless directed to do so by a police or traffic officer or official sign.

39:4–42. Action of motorman on collision

The motorman or driver of a street car which collides with a person or vehicle shall stop immediately, give his name and address and render any assistance that may be required to an injured person.

39:4–43. Crossing signals

The motorman or driver of a street car, on approaching road intersections or street crossings, shall sound his signal in quick succession at a reasonable distance from the intersection. No person shall knowingly delay or hinder the passage of the car.

39:4–44. Car stops

Every street railway company may establish certain road intersections, street crossings or other points along its railway as regular stops, and unless otherwise ordered by the board of public utility commissioners, or by the board or body having charge of streets in a municipality it shall not be necessary for the railway company to stop its cars for the purpose of taking on or letting off passengers at any place other than at the established stops.

When the established stops are at road intersections or street crossings, the near side of the intersection or crossing shall be designated as the established stop, except that, at special intersections or crossings or under special conditions where in the judgment of the street railway company, the board of public utility commissioners or the local authorities, the convenience or safety of the public will be better served, the far side may be designated as the established stop.

39:4–45. Obstruction of crosswalks by street cars

The cars of a street railway company shall not be allowed to obstruct the crosswalks of a street.

ARTICLE 8. DISPLAY OF NAME AND PLACE OF OWNER OF COMMERCIAL VEHICLE

39:4–46. Commercial vehicles to display name and municipality of owner and gross vehicle weight rating; exception; exemption from municipality requirement

a. Every vehicle used for commercial purposes on a street or highway, except for passenger automobiles and vehicles owned or leased by a pharmacy and utilized for the transportation or delivery of drugs, shall have conspicuously displayed thereon, or on a name plate

affixed thereto, the name of the owner, lessee or lessor of the vehicle and the name of the municipality in which the owner, lessee or lessor has his principal place of business. Franchised public utilities and operators of fleets of 50 or more commercial vehicles, shall be exempted from displaying the name of the municipality, provided that their vehicles display a corporate identification number. The sign or name plate shall be in plain view and not less than three inches high. Where available space for lettering is limited, either by the design of the vehicle or by the presence of other legally specified identification markings, making a strict compliance herewith impractical, the size of the lettering required by this section shall be as close to three inches high as is possible, within the limited space area, provided the name is clearly visible and readily identifiable. In the case of a combination of two vehicles the requirements of this section will be served when either unit of the combination conforms with the above identification specifications. No person shall operate or drive or cause or permit to be operated or driven on a road or highway a commercial vehicle, except for passenger automobiles and vehicles owned or leased by a pharmacy and utilized for the transportation or delivery of drugs, which does not conform hereto.

For purposes of this section, a franchised public utility means a public utility, as defined in R.S.48:2–13, that has a defined geographical service territory approved by the Board of Public Utilities.

b. Every owner of a commercial motor vehicle as defined in section 3 of P.L.1990, c. 103 (C.39:3–10.11) which has a gross vehicle weight rating or a combined gross vehicle weight rating of 26,001 pounds or more and is registered or principally garaged in this State shall display the gross vehicle weight rating (GVWR) for the vehicle in the manner set forth in subsection a. of this section. For purposes of this subsection, GVWR means the value specified by the manufacturer as the maximum loaded weight of a single or combination (articulated) vehicle, or registered gross weight, whichever is greater. Any person who knowingly displays or causes to be displayed on a commercial motor vehicle a GVWR less than the actual GVWR, or an owner who knowingly permits a commercial motor vehicle owned by him to be operated in this State with a displayed GVWR less than the actual GVWR shall, for each offense, be fined not more than $5,000, or imprisoned for a term of not more than 90 days, or both.

Amended by L.1959, c. 76, p. 194, § 1; L.1964, c. 66, § 1; L.1986, c. 77, § 1, eff. Aug. 5, 1986; L.1990, c. 103, § 32, eff. Nov. 9, 1990; L.1997, c. 158, § 1, eff. July 3, 1997.

39:4–47. Violations of article; fine

A person violating this article shall be fined not more than ten dollars ($10.00). In default of the payment thereof he shall be imprisoned in the county jail for a period not exceeding ten days.

Moneys received from fines under this article shall be accounted for and forwarded to the director and by him paid over to the State Treasurer, to be used as a fund for the repair of the improved roads throughout the State, regard being had to the repair of the most improved roads and the distribution of the benefits of this article throughout the several counties of the State.

Amended by L.1951, c. 23, p. 76, § 29.

ARTICLE 9. OPERATION OF OR ACTS AFFECTING OPERATION OF VEHICLES AND STREET CARS

39:4–48. Operating or using motor vehicle without consent of owner; fine

No person shall operate or use any motor vehicle without the permission of the owner. Any person violating this section shall be fined not less than one hundred dollars.

39:4–49. Tampering with vehicle; fine

No person shall interfere or tamper with a motor vehicle or put its engine in motion while it is standing, without its owner's permission.

A person who violates this section shall be fined, for a first offense, not less than ten nor more than fifty dollars, and for a subsequent offense, not less than fifty nor more than one hundred dollars or be imprisoned for not more than thirty days or both.

39:4–49.1. Operating motor vehicle with controlled dangerous substance or prescription legend drug in possession or in motor vehicle

No person shall operate a motor vehicle on any highway while knowingly having in his possession or in the motor vehicle any controlled dangerous substance as classified in Schedules I, II, III, IV and V of the "New Jersey Controlled Dangerous Substances Act," P.L. 1970, c. 226 (C. 24:21–1 et seq.) or any prescription legend drug, unless the person has obtained the substance or drug from, or on a valid written prescription of, a duly licensed physician, veterinarian, dentist or other medical practitioner licensed to write prescriptions intended for the treatment or prevention of disease in man or animals or unless the person possesses a controlled dangerous substance pursuant to a lawful order of a practitioner or lawfully possesses a Schedule V substance.

A person who violates this section shall be fined not less than $50.00 and shall forthwith forfeit his right to operate a motor vehicle for a period of two years from the date of his conviction.

L.1964, c. 289, § 1. Amended by L.1985, c. 239, § 1, eff. July 17, 1985.

39:4–49.2. Exemption; physicians, dentists, etc.

The provisions of section 1 of this act[1] shall not apply to a duly licensed physician, dentist, registered pharma-cist, veterinarian, nurse, podiatrist, interne or resident physician of a hospital, sanitarium or other medical institution; or to a hospital, sanitarium, clinical laboratory or any other medical institution; or to a State or governmental agency; or to any manufacturer, wholesaler, retailer or regular dealer in drugs.

L.1964, c. 289, § 2.

[1] N.J.S.A. § 39:4–49.1.

39:4–49.3. Exemption; common carriers, warehousemen, etc.

The provisions of section 1 of this act[1] shall not apply to common carriers or to warehousemen while engaged in lawfully transporting or storing such drugs or to any employee of the same acting within the scope of his employment; or to public officers or employees in the performance of their official duties requiring possession or control of these drugs; or to temporary incidental possession by employees or agents of persons lawfully entitled to possession; or to persons whose possession is for the purpose of aiding public officers in performing their official duties.

L.1964, c. 289, § 3.

[1] N.J.S.A. § 39:4–49.1.

39:4–50 Driving while intoxicated

(a) Except as provided in subsection (g) of this section, a person who operates a motor vehicle while under the influence of intoxicating liquor, narcotic, hallucinogenic or habit-producing drug, or operates a motor vehicle with a blood alcohol concentration of 0.08% or more by weight of alcohol in the defendant's blood or permits another person who is under the influence of intoxicating liquor, narcotic, hallucinogenic or habit-producing drug to operate a motor vehicle owned by him or in his custody or control or permits another to operate a motor vehicle with a blood alcohol concentration of 0.08% or more by weight of alcohol in the defendant's blood shall be subject:

(1) For the first offense:

(i) if the person's blood alcohol concentration is 0.08% or higher but less than 0.10%, or the person operates a motor vehicle while under the influence of intoxicating liquor, or the person permits another person who is under the influence of intoxicating liquor to operate a motor vehicle owned by him or in his custody or control or permits another person with a blood alcohol concentration of 0.08% or higher but less than 0.10% to operate a motor vehicle, to a fine of not less than $250 nor more than $400 and a period of detainment of not less than 12 hours nor more than 48 hours spent during two consecutive days of not less than six hours each day and served as prescribed by the program requirements of the Intoxicated Driver Resource Centers established under subsection (f) of this section and, in the discretion of the court, a term of imprisonment of not more than 30 days and shall forthwith forfeit his right to operate a motor vehicle over the highways of this State for a period of three months;

(ii) if the person's blood alcohol concentration is 0.10% or higher, or the person operates a motor vehicle while under the influence of narcotic, hallucinogenic or habit-producing drug, or the person permits another person who is under the influence of narcotic, hallucinogenic or habit-producing drug to operate a motor vehicle owned by him or in his custody or control, or permits another person with a blood alcohol concentration of 0.10% or more to operate a motor vehicle, to a fine of not less than $300 nor more than $500 and a period of detainment of not less than 12 hours nor more than 48 hours spent during two consecutive days of not less than six hours each day and served as prescribed by the program requirements of the Intoxicated Driver Resource Centers established under subsection (f) of this section and, in the discretion of the court, a term of imprisonment of not more than 30 days and shall forthwith forfeit his right to operate a motor vehicle over the highways of this State for a period of not less than seven months nor more than one year;

(iii) For a first offense, a person also shall be subject to the provisions of P.L.1999, c. 417 (C.39:4–50.16 et al.).

(2) For a second violation, a person shall be subject to a fine of not less than $500.00 nor more than $1,000.00, and shall be ordered by the court to perform community service for a period of 30 days, which shall be of such form and on such terms as the court shall deem appropriate under the circumstances, and shall be sentenced to imprisonment for a term of not less than 48 consecutive hours, which shall not be suspended or served on probation, nor more than 90 days, and shall forfeit his right to operate a motor vehicle over the highways of this State for a period of two years upon conviction, and, after the expiration of said period, he may make application to the Chief Administrator of the New Jersey Motor Vehicle Commission for a license to operate a motor vehicle, which application may be granted at the discretion of the chief administrator, consistent with subsection (b) of this section. For a second violation, a person also shall be required to install an ignition interlock device under the provisions of P.L.1999, c. 417 (C.39:4–50.16 et al.).

(3) For a third or subsequent violation, a person shall be subject to a fine of $1,000.00, and shall be sentenced to imprisonment for a term of not less than 180 days in a county jail or workhouse, except that the court may lower such term for each day, not exceeding 90 days, served participating in a drug or alcohol inpatient rehabilitation program approved by the Intoxicated Driver Resource Center and shall thereafter forfeit his right to operate a motor vehicle over the highways of this State for 10 years. For a third or subsequent violation, a person also shall be required to install an ignition interlock device under the provisions of P.L. 1999, c. 417 (C.39:4–50.16 et al.).

As used in this section, the phrase "narcotic, hallucinogenic or habit-producing drug" includes an inhalant or other substance containing a chemical capable of releasing any toxic vapors or fumes for the purpose of inducing a condition of intoxication, such as any glue, cement or any other substance containing one or more of the following chemical compounds: acetone and acetate, amyl nitrite or amyl nitrate or their isomers, benzene, butyl alcohol, butyl nitrite, butyl nitrate or their isomers, ethyl acetate, ethyl alcohol, ethyl nitrite or ethyl nitrate, ethylene dichloride, isobutyl alcohol or isopropyl alcohol, methyl alcohol, methyl ethyl ketone, nitrous oxide, n-propyl alcohol, pentachlorophenol, petroleum ether, propyl nitrite or propyl nitrate or their isomers, toluene, toluol or xylene or any other chemical substance capable of causing a condition of intoxication, inebriation, excitement, stupefaction or the dulling of the brain or nervous system as a result of the inhalation of the fumes or vapors of such chemical substance.

Whenever an operator of a motor vehicle has been involved in an accident resulting in death, bodily injury or property damage, a police officer shall consider that fact along with all other facts and circumstances in determining whether there are reasonable grounds to believe that person was operating a motor vehicle in violation of this section.

A conviction of a violation of a law of a substantially similar nature in another jurisdiction, regardless of whether that jurisdiction is a signatory to the Interstate Driver License Compact pursuant to P.L.1966, c. 73 (C.39:5D–1 et seq.), shall constitute a prior conviction under this subsection unless the defendant can demonstrate by clear and convincing evidence that the conviction in the other jurisdiction was based exclusively upon a violation of a proscribed blood alcohol concentration of less than 0.08%.

If the driving privilege of any person is under revocation or suspension for a violation of any provision of this Title or Title 2C of the New Jersey Statutes at the time of any conviction for a violation of this section, the revocation or suspension period imposed shall commence as of the date of termination of the existing revocation or suspension period. In the case of any person who at the time of the imposition of sentence is less than 17 years of age, the forfeiture, suspension or revocation of the driving privilege imposed by the court under this section shall commence immediately, run through the offender's seventeenth birthday and continue from that date for the period set by the court pursuant to paragraphs (1) through (3) of this subsection. A court that imposes a term of imprisonment for a first or second offense under this section may sentence the person so convicted to the county jail, to the workhouse of the county wherein the offense was committed, to an inpatient rehabilitation program or to an Intoxicated Driver Resource Center or other facility approved by the chief of the Intoxicated Driving Program Unit in the Department of Health and Senior Services. For a third or subsequent offense a person shall not serve a term of imprisonment at an Intoxicated Driver Resource Center as provided in subsection (f).

A person who has been convicted of a previous violation of this section need not be charged as a second or subsequent offender in the complaint made against him in order to render him liable to the punishment imposed by this section on a second or subsequent offender, but if the second offense occurs more than 10 years after the first offense, the court shall treat the second conviction as a first offense for sentencing purposes and if a third offense occurs more than 10 years after the second offense, the court shall treat the third conviction as a second offense for sentencing purposes.

(b) A person convicted under this section must satisfy the screening, evaluation, referral, program and fee requirements of the Division of Alcoholism and Drug Abuse's Intoxicated Driving Program Unit, and of the Intoxicated Driver Resource Centers and a program of alcohol and drug education and highway safety, as prescribed by the chief administrator. The sentencing court shall inform the person convicted that failure to satisfy such requirements shall result in a mandatory two-day term of imprisonment in a county jail and a driver license revocation or suspension and continuation of revocation or suspension until such requirements are satisfied, unless stayed by court order in accordance with the Rules Governing the Courts of the State of New Jersey, or R.S.39:5–22. Upon sentencing, the court shall forward to the Division of Alcoholism and Drug Abuse's Intoxicated Driving Program Unit a copy of a person's conviction record. A fee of $100.00 shall be payable to the Alcohol Education, Rehabilitation and Enforcement Fund established pursuant to section 3 of P.L. 1983, c. 531 (C.26:2B–32) to support the Intoxicated Driving Program Unit.

(c) Upon conviction of a violation of this section, the court shall collect forthwith the New Jersey driver's license or licenses of the person so convicted and forward such license or licenses to the chief administrator. The court shall inform the person convicted that if he is convicted of personally operating a motor vehicle during the period of license suspension imposed pursuant to subsection (a) of this section, he shall, upon conviction, be subject to the penalties established in R.S.39:3–40. The person convicted shall be informed orally and in writing. A person shall be required to acknowledge receipt of that written notice in writing. Failure to receive a written notice or failure to acknowledge in writing the receipt of a written notice shall not be a defense to a subsequent charge of a violation of R.S.39:3–40. In the event that a person convicted under this section is the holder of any out-of-State driver's license, the court shall not collect the license but shall notify forthwith the chief administrator, who shall, in turn, notify appropriate officials in the licensing jurisdiction. The court shall, however, revoke the nonresident's driving privilege to operate a motor vehicle in this State, in accordance with this section.

Upon conviction of a violation of this section, the court shall notify the person convicted, orally and in writing, of the penalties for a second, third or subsequent violation of this section. A person shall be required to acknowledge receipt of that written notice in writing. Failure to receive a written notice or failure to acknowledge in writing the receipt of a written notice shall not be a defense to a subsequent charge of a violation of this section.

(d) The chief administrator shall promulgate rules and regulations pursuant to the "Administrative Procedure Act," P.L.1968, c. 410 (C.52:14B–1 et seq.) in order to establish a program of alcohol education and highway safety, as prescribed by this act.

(e) Any person accused of a violation of this section who is liable to punishment imposed by this section as a second or subsequent offender shall be entitled to the same rights of discovery as allowed defendants pursuant to the Rules Governing the Courts of the State of New Jersey.

(f) The counties, in cooperation with the Division of Alcoholism and Drug Abuse and the commission, but subject to the approval of the Division of Alcoholism and Drug Abuse, shall designate and establish on a county or regional basis Intoxicated Driver Resource Centers. These centers shall have the capability of serving as community treatment referral centers and as court monitors of a person's compliance with the ordered treatment, service alternative or community service. All centers established pursuant to this subsection shall be administered by a counselor certified by the Alcohol and Drug Counselor Certification Board of New Jersey or other professional with a minimum of five years' experience in the treatment of alcoholism. All centers shall be required to develop individualized treatment plans for all persons attending the centers; provided that the duration of any ordered treatment or referral shall not exceed one year. It shall be the center's responsibility to establish networks with the community alcohol and drug education, treatment and rehabilitation resources and to receive monthly reports from the referral agencies regarding a person's participation and compliance with the program. Nothing in this subsection shall bar these centers from developing their own education and treatment programs; provided that they are approved by the Division of Alcoholism and Drug Abuse.

Upon a person's failure to report to the initial screening or any subsequent ordered referral, the Intoxicated Driver Resource Center shall promptly notify the sentencing court of the person's failure to comply.

Required detention periods at the Intoxicated Driver Resource Centers shall be determined according to the individual treatment classification assigned by the Intoxicated Driving Program Unit. Upon attendance at an Intoxicated Driver Resource Center, a person shall be required to pay a per diem fee of $75.00 for the first offender program or a per diem fee of $100.00 for the second offender program, as appropriate. Any increases in the per diem fees after the first full year shall be determined pursuant to rules and regulations adopted by the Commissioner of Health and Senior Services in consultation with the Governor's Council on Alcoholism and Drug Abuse pursuant to the "Administrative Procedure Act," P.L.1968, c. 410 (C.52:14B–1 et seq.).

The centers shall conduct a program of alcohol and drug education and highway safety, as prescribed by the chief administrator.

The Commissioner of Health and Senior Services shall adopt rules and regulations pursuant to the "Administrative Procedure Act," P.L.1968, c. 410 (C.52:14B–1 et seq.), in order to effectuate the purposes of this subsection.

(g) When a violation of this section occurs while:

(1) on any school property used for school purposes which is owned by or leased to any elementary or secondary school or school board, or within 1,000 feet of such school property;

(2) driving through a school crossing as defined in R.S.39:1–1 if the municipality, by ordinance or resolution, has designated the school crossing as such; or

(3) driving through a school crossing as defined in R.S.39:1–1 knowing that juveniles are present if the municipality has not designated the school crossing as such by ordinance or resolution, the convicted person shall: for a first offense, be fined not less than $500 or more than $800, be imprisoned for not more than 60 days and have his license to operate a motor vehicle suspended for a period of not less than one year or more than two years; for a second offense, be fined not less than $1,000 or more than $2,000, perform community service for a period of 60 days, be imprisoned for not less than 96 consecutive hours, which shall not be suspended or served on probation, nor more than 180 days, except that the court may lower such term for each day, not exceeding 90 days, served performing community service in such form and on such terms as the court shall deem appropriate under the circumstances and have his license to operate a motor vehicle suspended for a period of four years; and, for a third offense, be fined $2,000, imprisoned for 180 days in a county jail or workhouse, except that the court may lower such term for each day, not exceeding 90 days, served participating in a drug or alcohol inpatient rehabilitation program approved by the Intoxicated Driver Resource Center, and have his license to operate a motor vehicle suspended for a period of 20 years; the period of license suspension shall commence upon the completion of any prison sentence imposed upon that person.

A map or true copy of a map depicting the location and boundaries of the area on or within 1,000 feet of any property used for school purposes which is owned by or leased to any elementary or secondary school or school board produced pursuant to section 1 of P.L. 1987, c. 101 (C.2C:35–7) may be used in a prosecution under paragraph (1) of this subsection.

It shall not be relevant to the imposition of sentence pursuant to paragraph (1) or (2) of this subsection that the defendant was unaware that the prohibited conduct took place while on or within 1,000 feet of any school property or while driving through a school crossing. Nor shall it be relevant to the imposition of sentence that no juveniles were present on the school property or crossing zone at the time of the offense or that the school was not in session.

(h) A court also may order a person convicted pursuant to subsection a. of this section, to participate in a supervised visitation program as either a condition of probation or a form of community service, giving preference to those who were under the age of 21 at the time of the offense. Prior to ordering a person to participate in such a program, the court may consult with any person who may provide useful information on the defendant's physical, emotional and mental suitability for the visit to ensure that it will not cause any injury to the defendant. The court also may order that the defendant participate in a counseling session under the supervision of the Intoxicated Driving Program Unit prior to participating in the supervised visitation program. The supervised visitation program shall be at one or more of the following facilities which have agreed to participate in the program under the supervision of the facility's personnel and the probation department:

(1) a trauma center, critical care center or acute care hospital having basic emergency services, which receives victims of motor vehicle accidents for the purpose of observing appropriate victims of drunk drivers and victims who are, themselves, drunk drivers;

(2) a facility which cares for advanced alcoholics or drug abusers, to observe persons in the advanced stages of alcoholism or drug abuse; or

(3) if approved by a county medical examiner, the office of the county medical examiner or a public morgue to observe appropriate victims of vehicle accidents involving drunk drivers.

As used in this section, "appropriate victim" means a victim whose condition is determined by the facility's supervisory personnel and the probation officer to be appropriate for demonstrating the results of accidents involving drunk drivers without being unnecessarily gruesome or traumatic to the defendant.

If at any time before or during a visitation the facility's supervisory personnel and the probation officer determine that the visitation may be or is traumatic or otherwise inappropriate for that defendant, the visitation shall be terminated without prejudice to the defendant. The program may include a personal conference after the visitation, which may include the sentencing judge or the judge who coordinates the program for the court, the defendant, defendant's counsel, and, if available, the defendant's parents to discuss the visitation and its effect on the defendant's future conduct. If a personal conference is not practicable because of the defendant's absence from the jurisdiction, conflicting time schedules, or any other reason, the court shall require the defendant to submit a written report concerning the visitation experience and its impact on the defendant. The county, a court, any facility visited pursuant to the program, any agents, employees, or independent contractors of the court, county, or facility visited pursuant to the program, and any person supervising a defendant during the visitation, are not liable for any civil damages resulting from injury to the defendant, or for civil damages associated with the visitation which are caused by the defendant, except for willful or grossly negligent acts intended to, or reasonably expected to result in, that injury or damage.

The Supreme Court may adopt court rules or directives to effectuate the purposes of this subsection.

(i) In addition to any other fine, fee, or other charge imposed pursuant to law, the court shall assess a person convicted of a violation of the provisions of this section a surcharge of $100, of which amount $50 shall be payable to the municipality in which the conviction was obtained and $50 shall be payable to the Treasurer of the State of New Jersey for deposit into the General Fund.

Amended by L.1952, c. 286, p. 972, § 1; L.1964, c. 137, § 1; L.1965, c. 134, § 1; L.1966, c. 141, § 1; L.1971, c. 103, § 1, eff. April 16, 1971; L.1977, c. 29, § 1; L.1981, c. 47, § 1, eff. Feb. 25, 1981; L.1981, c. 537, § 1; L.1982, c. 53, § 2, eff. July 1, 1982; L.1982, c. 58, § 1, eff. July 6, 1982; L.1983, c. 90, § 2, eff. March 11, 1983; L.1983, c. 129, § 1, eff. April 7, 1983; L.1983, c. 444, § 1; L.1984, c. 243, § 1, eff. Jan. 2, 1985; L.1986, c. 126, § 1, eff. Oct. 9, 1986; L.1993, c. 296, § 6; L.1994, c. 184, § 1, eff. Dec. 23, 1994; L.1995, c. 243, § 1, eff. April 1, 1996; L.1997, c. 277, § 1, eff. Dec. 30, 1997; L.1999, c. 185, § 4; L.1999, c. 417, § 7; L.2000, c. 83, § 1, eff. Sept. 30, 2000; L.2000, c. 117, § 1, eff. Sept. 13, 2000; L.2001, c. 12, § 1; L.2002, c. 34, § 17, eff. July 1, 2002; L.2003, c. 314, § 2, eff. Jan. 20, 2004; L.2003, c. 315, § 2, eff. Jan. 20, 2004; L.2004, c. 8, § 2, eff. April 26, 2004; L.2009, c. 201, § 1, eff. Jan. 14, 2010.

39:4–50.1. Repealed by L.1990, c. 103, § 38, eff. Nov. 9, 1990

39:4–50.2. Consent to taking samples of breath; record of test; independent test; prohibition of use of force; informing accused

(a) Any person who operates a motor vehicle on any public road, street or highway or quasi-public area in this State shall be deemed to have given his consent to the taking of samples of his breath for the purpose of making chemical tests to determine the content of alcohol in his blood; provided, however, that the taking of samples is made in accordance with the provisions of this act and at the request of a police officer who has reasonable grounds to believe that such person has been operating a motor vehicle in violation of the provisions

of R.S.39:4–50 or section 1 of P.L.1992, c. 189 (C.39:4–50.14).

(b) A record of the taking of any such sample, disclosing the date and time thereof, as well as the result of any chemical test, shall be made and a copy thereof, upon his request, shall be furnished or made available to the person so tested.

(c) In addition to the samples taken and tests made at the direction of a police officer hereunder, the person tested shall be permitted to have such samples taken and chemical tests of his breath, urine or blood made by a person or physician of his own selection.

(d) The police officer shall inform the person tested of his rights under subsections (b) and (c) of this section.

(e) No chemical test, as provided in this section, or specimen necessary thereto, may be made or taken forcibly and against physical resistance thereto by the defendant. The police officer shall, however, inform the person arrested of the consequences of refusing to submit to such test in accordance with section 2 of this amendatory and supplementary act.[1] A standard statement, prepared by the chief administrator, shall be read by the police officer to the person under arrest.

L.1966, c. 142, § 2. Amended by L.1977, c. 29, § 3; L.1981, c. 512, § 1, eff. Jan. 12, 1982; L.2007, c. 267, § 1, eff. March 1, 2008.

[1] N.J.S.A. § 39:4–50.4a.

39:4–50.2a. Guidelines to promote uniform enforcement

In order to promote the uniform enforcement of R.S.39:4–50 and section 2 of P.L.1966, c. 142 (C.39:4–50.2), the Attorney General shall promulgate guidelines concerning the prosecution of such violations. The guidelines shall be disseminated to county and municipal prosecutors within 120 days of the effective date of this act.

L.2004, c. 8, § 3, eff. April 26, 2004.

39:4–50.3. Method of analyses; approval of techniques; certification of analysts; reports; forms

Chemical analyses of the arrested person's breath, to be considered valid under the provisions of this act, shall have been performed according to methods approved by the Attorney General, and by a person certified for this purpose by the Attorney General. The Attorney General is authorized to approve satisfactory techniques or methods, to ascertain the qualifications and competence of individuals to conduct such analyses, and to make certifications of such individuals, which certifications shall be subject to termination or revocation at the discretion of the Attorney General. The Attorney General shall prescribe a uniform form for reports of such chemical analysis of breath to be used by law enforcement officers and others acting in accordance with the provisions of this act. Such forms shall be sequentially numbered. Each chief of police, in the case of forms distributed to law enforcement officers and others in his municipality, or the other officer, board, or official having charge or control of the police department where there is no chief, and the Director of the Division of Motor Vehicles and the Superintendent of State Police, in the case of such forms distributed to law enforcement officers and other personnel in their divisions, shall be responsible for the furnishing and proper disposition of such uniform forms. Each such responsible party shall prepare or cause to be prepared such records and reports relating to such uniform forms and their disposition in such manner and at such times as the Attorney General shall prescribe.

L.1966, c. 142, § 3. Amended by L.1971, c. 273, § 1.

39:4–50.4. Repealed by L.1981, c. 512, § 3, eff. Jan. 12, 1982

39:4–50.4a. Refusal to submit to chemical test; penalties

a. Except as provided in subsection b. of this section, the municipal court shall revoke the right to operate a motor vehicle of any operator who, after being arrested for a violation of R.S.39:4–50 or section 1 of P.L.1992, c. 189 (C.39:4–50.14), shall refuse to submit to a test provided for in section 2 of P.L.1966, c. 142 (C.39:4–50.2) when requested to do so, for not less than seven months or more than one year unless the refusal was in connection with a second offense under this section, in which case the revocation period shall be for two years or unless the refusal was in connection with a third or subsequent offense under this section in which case the revocation shall be for ten years. A conviction or administrative determination of a violation of a law of a substantially similar nature in another jurisdiction, regardless of whether that jurisdiction is a signatory to the Interstate Driver License Compact pursuant to P.L.1966, c. 73 (C.39:5D–1 et seq.), shall constitute a prior conviction under this section.

The municipal court shall determine by a preponderance of the evidence whether the arresting officer had probable cause to believe that the person had been driving or was in actual physical control of a motor vehicle on the public highways or quasi-public areas of this State while the person was under the influence of intoxicating liquor or a narcotic, hallucinogenic, or habit-producing drug or marijuana; whether the person was placed under arrest, if appropriate, and whether he refused to submit to the test upon request of the officer; and if these elements of the violation are not established, no conviction shall issue. In addition to any other requirements provided by law, a person whose operator's license is revoked for refusing to submit to a test shall be referred to an Intoxicated Driver Resource Center established by subsection (f) of R.S.39:4–50 and shall satisfy the same requirements of the center for refusal to submit to a test as provided for in section 2 of P.L.1966, c. 142 (C.39:4–50.2) in connection with a first, second, third or subsequent offense under this section that must be satisfied by a person convicted of a

commensurate violation of this section, or be subject to the same penalties as such a person for failure to do so. For a first offense, the revocation may be concurrent with or consecutive to any revocation imposed for a conviction under the provisions of R.S.39:4–50 arising out of the same incident. For a second or subsequent offense, the revocation shall be consecutive to any revocation imposed for a conviction under the provisions of R.S.39:4–50. In addition to issuing a revocation, except as provided in subsection b. of this section, the municipal court shall fine a person convicted under this section, a fine of not less than $300 or more than $500 for a first offense; a fine of not less than $500 or more than $1,000 for a second offense; and a fine of $1,000 for a third or subsequent offense. The person also shall be required to install an ignition interlock device pursuant to the provisions of P.L.1999, c. 417 (C.39:4–50.16 et al.).

b. For a first offense, the fine imposed upon the convicted person shall be not less than $600 or more than $1,000 and the period of license suspension shall be not less than one year or more than two years; for a second offense, a fine of not less than $1,000 or more than $2,000 and a license suspension for a period of four years; and for a third or subsequent offense, a fine of $2,000 and a license suspension for a period of 20 years when a violation of this section occurs while:

(1) on any school property used for school purposes which is owned by or leased to any elementary or secondary school or school board, or within 1,000 feet of such school property;

(2) driving through a school crossing as defined in R.S.39:1–1 if the municipality, by ordinance or resolution, has designated the school crossing as such; or

(3) driving through a school crossing as defined in R.S.39:1–1 knowing that juveniles are present if the municipality has not designated the school crossing as such by ordinance or resolution.

A map or true copy of a map depicting the location and boundaries of the area on or within 1,000 feet of any property used for school purposes which is owned by or leased to any elementary or secondary school or school board produced pursuant to section 1 of P.L. 1987, c. 101 (C.2C:35–7) may be used in a prosecution under paragraph (1) of this subsection.

It shall not be relevant to the imposition of sentence pursuant to paragraph (1) or (2) of this subsection that the defendant was unaware that the prohibited conduct took place while on or within 1,000 feet of any school property or while driving through a school crossing. Nor shall it be relevant to the imposition of sentence that no juveniles were present on the school property or crossing zone at the time of the offense or that the school was not in session.

L.1981, c. 512, § 2, eff. Jan. 12, 1982. Amended by L.1981, c. 537, § 2, eff. Jan. 12, 1982; L.1994, c. 184, § 2, eff. Dec. 23, 1994; L.1997, c. 277, § 2, eff. Dec. 30, 1997; L.1999, c. 185, § 5; L.2004, c. 8, § 1, eff. April 26, 2004; L.2007, c. 267, § 2, eff. March 1, 2008; L.2009, c. 201, § 5, eff. Jan. 14, 2010.

39:4–50.5. Severability

If any provision of this act, or any particular application thereof, be found invalid, the same shall be deemed severable to the end that such invalidity shall not affect other provisions or applications hereof.

L.1966, c. 142, § 5.

39:4–50.6, 39:4–50.7. Repealed by L.1977, c. 29, § 8

39:4–50.8. Conviction for violation of § 39:4–50; surcharge; distribution

Upon a conviction of a violation of R.S. 39:4–50 or section 2 of P.L.1981, c. 512 (C. 39:4–50.4a), the court shall collect from the defendant a surcharge of $100.00 in addition to and independently of any fine imposed on that defendant. The court shall forward the surcharge to the Director of the Division of Motor Vehicles who shall deposit $95.00 of the surcharge into a "Drunk Driving Enforcement Fund" (hereinafter referred to as the "fund"). This fund shall be used to establish a Statewide drunk driving enforcement program to be supervised by the director. The remaining $5.00 of each surcharge shall be deposited by the director into a separate fund for administrative expenses.

A municipality shall be entitled to periodic grants from the "Drunk Driving Enforcement Fund" in amounts representing its proportionate contribution to the fund. A municipality shall be deemed to have contributed to the fund the portion of the surcharge allocated to the fund, collected pursuant to this section if the violation of R.S. 39:4–50 or section 2 of P.L.1981, c. 512 (C. 39:4–50.4a) occurred within the municipality and the arrest resulting in conviction was made by the member of a municipal police force. The grants from the fund shall be used by the municipality to increase enforcement of R.S. 39:4–50 by subsidizing additional law enforcement patrols and through other measures approved by the director. The Division of State Police, interstate law enforcement agencies and county law enforcement agencies shall be entitled to periodic grants from the fund in amounts representing their proportionate contribution to the fund. The Division of State Police or county or interstate law enforcement agency shall be deemed to have contributed to the fund the portion of the surcharge allocated to the fund collected pursuant to this section if the arrest resulting in a conviction was made by a member of the Division of State Police or county or interstate law enforcement agency. The grants from the fund shall be used by the Division of State Police or county or interstate law enforcement agency to increase enforcement of R.S. 39:4–50 by subsidizing additional law enforcement patrols and through other measures approved by the director.

The surcharge described herein shall not be considered a fine, penalty or forfeiture to be distributed pursuant to R.S. 39:5–41.

The director shall promulgate rules and regulations in order to effectuate the purposes of this section.

L.1984, c. 4, § 1, eff. Feb. 9, 1984. Amended by L.1994, c. 184, § 3, eff. Dec. 23, 1994.

39:4–50.9. Short title

This act shall be known and may be cited as the "Drunk Driving Victim's Bill of Rights."

L.1985, c. 442, § 1.

39:4–50.10. Victim defined

As used in this act, "victim" means, unless otherwise indicated, a person who suffers personal physical or psychological injury or death or incurs loss of or injury to personal or real property as a result of a motor vehicle accident involving another person's driving while under the influence of drugs or alcohol. In the event of a death, "victim" means the surviving spouse, a child or the next of kin.

L.1985, c. 442, § 2.

39:4–50.11. Victims' rights

Victims shall have the right to:

a. Make statements to law enforcement officers regarding the facts of the motor vehicle accident and to reasonable use of a telephone;

b. Receive medical assistance for injuries resulting from the accident;

c. Contact the investigating officer and see copies of the accident reports and, in the case of a surviving spouse, child or next of kin, the autopsy reports;

d. Be provided by the court adjudicating the offense, upon the request of the victim in writing, with:

(1) Information about their role in the court process;

(2) Timely advance notice of the date, time and place of the defendant's initial appearance before a judicial officer, submission to the court of any plea agreement, the trial and sentencing;

(3) Timely notification of the case disposition, including the trial and sentencing;

(4) Prompt notification of any decision or action in the case which results in the defendant's provisional or final release from custody; and

(5) Information about the status of the case at any time from the commission of the offense to final disposition or release of the defendant;

e. Receive, when requested from any law enforcement agency involved with the offense, assistance in obtaining employer cooperation in minimizing loss of pay and other benefits resulting from their participation in the court process;

f. A secure waiting area, after the motor vehicle accident, during investigations, and prior to a court appearance;

g. Submit to the court adjudicating the offense a written or oral statement to be considered in deciding upon sentencing and probation terms. This statement may include the nature and extent of any physical harm or psychological or emotional harm or trauma suffered by the victim, the extent of any loss of earnings or ability to work suffered by the victim and the effect of the offense upon the victim's family.

When a need is demonstrated, the information in this section shall be provided in the Spanish as well as the English language.

L.1985, c. 442, § 3.

39:4–50.12. Consultation with prosecutor prior to dismissal or plea negotiation

A victim shall be provided with an opportunity to consult with the prosecutor prior to dismissal of the case or the filing of a proposed plea negotiation with the court, if the victim sustained bodily injury or serious bodily injury as defined in N.J.S. 2C:11–1.

Nothing contained herein shall be construed to alter or limit the authority or discretion of the prosecutor to enter into any plea agreement which the prosecutor deems appropriate.

L.1985, c. 442, § 4.

39:4–50.13. Effect on New Jersey Tort Claims Act

Nothing contained in the act shall mitigate any right which the victim may have pursuant to the "New Jersey Tort Claims Act" (N.J.S. 59:1–1 et seq.).

L.1985, c. 442, § 5.

39:4–50.14. Operation of motor vehicle by person who has consumed alcohol but is under the legal age to purchase alcoholic beverages; penalties

Any person under the legal age to purchase alcoholic beverages who operates a motor vehicle with a blood alcohol concentration of 0.01% or more, but less than 0.08%, by weight of alcohol in his blood, shall forfeit his right to operate a motor vehicle over the highways of this State or shall be prohibited from obtaining a license to operate a motor vehicle in this State for a period of not less than 30 or more than 90 days beginning on the date he becomes eligible to obtain a license or on the day of conviction, whichever is later, and shall perform community service for a period of not less than 15 or more than 30 days.

In addition, the person shall satisfy the program and fee requirements of an Intoxicated Driver Resource Center or participate in a program of alcohol education and highway safety as prescribed by the chief administrator.

The penalties provided under the provisions of this section shall be in addition to the penalties which the

court may impose under N.J.S.2C:33–15, R. S.33:1–81, R.S.39:4–50 or any other law.

L.1992, c. 189, § 1, eff. Dec. 17, 1992. Amended by L.2003, c. 314, § 3, eff. Jan. 20, 2004.

39:4–50.15. Additional definitions

a. As used in this act:

"Minor" means a person who is 17 years of age or younger.

"Parent or guardian" means any natural parent, adoptive parent, resource family parent, stepparent, or any person temporarily responsible for the care, custody or control of a minor or upon whom there is a legal duty for such care, custody or control.

b. A parent or guardian who is convicted of a violation of R.S.39:4–50 and who, at the time of the violation, has a minor as a passenger in the motor vehicle is guilty of a disorderly persons offense.

c. In addition to the penalties otherwise prescribed by law, a person who is convicted under subsection b. of this section shall forfeit the right to operate a motor vehicle over the highways of this State for a period of not more than six months and shall be ordered to perform community service for a period of not more than five days.

L.1999, c. 410, § 1, eff. Jan. 18, 2000. Amended by L.2004, c. 130, § 112, eff. Aug. 27, 2004.

39:4–50.16. Legislative findings

The Legislature finds and declares:

a. This State's penalties for drunk driving, including the mandatory suspension of driver's licenses and counseling for offenders, are among the strongest in the nation. However, despite the severity of existing penalties, far too many persons who have been convicted under the drunk driving law continue to imperil the lives of their fellow citizens by driving while intoxicated.

b. Ignition interlock devices, which permit a motor vehicle to be started only when the driver is sober, offer a technically feasible and effective means of further reducing the incidence of drunk driving. The use of these devices was initiated in California in 1986 and, according to the National Highway Traffic Safety Administration, they are presently being used or tested in at least 37 states.

c. The judicious deployment of ignition interlock devices, as provided under this act, will enhance and strengthen this State's existing efforts to keep drunk drivers off the highways.

L.1999, c. 417, § 1.

L.2000, c. 83, § 4, approved Aug. 14, 2000, provides:

39:4–50.17. Ignition interlock device as an additional penalty

a. (1) Except as provided in paragraph (2) of this subsection, in sentencing a first offender under

R.S.39:4–50, the court may order, in addition to any other penalty imposed by that section, the installation of an ignition interlock device in the motor vehicle principally operated by the offender following the expiration of the period of license suspension imposed under that section. In sentencing a first offender under section 2 of P.L.1981, c. 512 (C.39:4–50.4a), the court shall order, in addition to any other penalty imposed by that section, the installation of an ignition interlock device in the motor vehicle principally operated by the offender during and following the expiration of the period of license suspension imposed under that section. The device shall remain installed for not less than six months or more than one year, commencing immediately upon the return of the offender's driver's license after the required period of suspension has been served.

(2) If the first offender's blood alcohol concentration is 0.15 % or higher, the court shall order, in addition to any other penalty imposed under R.S.39:4–50, the installation of an ignition interlock device in the motor vehicle principally operated by the offender during and following the expiration of the period of license suspension imposed under that section. In addition to installation during the period of license suspension, the device shall remain installed for not less than six months or more than one year, commencing immediately upon the return of the offender's driver's license after the required period of suspension has been served.

b. In sentencing a second or subsequent offender under R.S.39:4–50 or section 2 of P.L.1981, c. 512 (C.39:4–50.4a), the court shall order, in addition to any other penalty imposed by that section, the installation of an ignition interlock device in the motor vehicle principally operated by the offender during and following the expiration of the period of license suspension imposed under R.S.39:4–50 or section 2 of P.L.1981, c. 512 (C.39:4–50.4a). In addition to installation during the period of license suspension, the device shall remain installed for not less than one year or more than three years, commencing immediately upon the return of the offender's driver's license after the required period of suspension has been served.

c. The court shall require that, for the duration of its order, an offender shall drive no vehicle other than one in which an interlock device has been installed pursuant to the order.

d. As used in this act, "ignition interlock device" or "device" means a blood alcohol equivalence measuring device which will prevent a motor vehicle from starting if the operator's blood alcohol content exceeds a predetermined level when the operator blows into the device.

e. The provisions of P.L.1999, c. 417 (C.39:4–50.16 et al.) and any amendments and supplements thereto shall be applicable only to violations of R.S.39:4–50 and section 2 of P.L.1981, c. 512 (C.39:4–50.4a).

L.1999, c. 417, § 2. Amended by L.2009, c. 201, § 2, eff. Jan. 14, 2010.

39:4–50.17a. Fees for ignition interlock device installation

a. If a person is required to install an ignition interlock device and that person's family income does not exceed 100% of the federal poverty level, the monthly leasing fee shall be 50% of the fee established by regulation for persons who do not qualify for the reduced fee.

b. If a person is required to install an ignition interlock device and that person's family income does not exceed 149% of the federal poverty level, the monthly leasing fee shall be 75% of the fee established by regulation for persons who do not qualify for the reduced fee.

c. Persons who qualify for a reduced fee pursuant to the provisions of this section shall not be required to pay the installation fee, the cost for monitoring of the device, or any fees for calibration or removal of the device.

L.2009, c. 201, § 6, eff. Jan. 14, 2010.

39:4–50.18. Notification of the Director of the Division of Motor Vehicles

The court shall notify the Director of the Division of Motor Vehicles when a person has been ordered to install an interlock device in a vehicle owned, leased or regularly operated by the person. The division shall require that the device be installed before reinstatement of the person' s driver's license that has been suspended pursuant to R.S.39:4–50. The division shall imprint a notation on the driver's license stating that the person shall not operate a motor vehicle unless it is equipped with an interlock device and shall enter this requirement in the person's driving record.

L.1999, c. 417, § 3.

39:4–50.19. Failure to install interlock device; penalties

a. A person who fails to install an interlock device ordered by the court in a motor vehicle owned, leased or regularly operated by him shall have his driver's license suspended for one year, in addition to any other suspension or revocation imposed under R.S.39:4–50, unless the court determines a valid reason exists for the failure to comply. A person in whose vehicle an interlock device is installed pursuant to a court order who drives that vehicle after it has been started by any means other than his own blowing into the device or who drives a vehicle that is not equipped with such a device shall have his driver's license suspended for one year, in addition to any other penalty applicable by law.

b. A person is a disorderly person who:

(1) blows into an interlock device or otherwise starts a motor vehicle equipped with such a device for the purpose of providing an operable motor vehicle to a person who has been ordered by the court to install the device in the vehicle;

(2) tampers or in any way circumvents the operation of an interlock device; or

(3) knowingly rents, leases or lends a motor vehicle not equipped with an interlock device to a person who has been ordered by the court to install an interlock device in a vehicle he owns, leases or regularly operates.

c. The provisions of subsection b. of this section shall not apply if a motor vehicle required to be equipped with an ignition interlock device is started by a person for the purpose of safety or mechanical repair of the device or the vehicle, provided the person subject to the court order does not operate the vehicle.

L.1999, c. 417, § 4. Amended by L.2009, c. 201, § 3, eff. Jan. 14, 2010.

39:4–50.20. Certification of ignition interlock devices

The director shall certify or cause to be certified ignition interlock devices required by this act and shall publish a list of approved devices. A device shall not be certified unless the manufacturer enters into an agreement with the division for the provision of devices to indigent offenders, as determined by the director, at a reduced cost. The director shall provide a copy of this list along with information on the purpose and proper use of interlock devices to persons who have been ordered by the court to install such a device in their vehicles.

L.1999, c. 417, § 5.

39:4–50.21. Rules and regulations; consistency with federal model

Pursuant to the "Administrative Procedure Act," P.L.1968, c. 410 (C.52:14B–1 et seq.), the division shall promulgate rules and regulations for the installation and use of ignition interlock devices. These regulations shall be consistent with the federal model specifications for ignition interlock devices issued by the National Highway Traffic Safety Administration. They shall include, but not be limited to, the following:

a. requiring that the ignition interlock system selected shall:

(1) not impede the safe operation of the vehicle;

(2) incorporate features that make circumvention difficult and that do not interfere with the normal use of the vehicle;

(3) correlate closely with established measures of alcohol impairment;

(4) operate accurately and reliably in an unsupervised environment;

(5) resist tampering and give evidence when tampering is attempted;

(6) be difficult to circumvent and require premeditation to do so;

(7) require a deep lung breath sample as a measure of blood alcohol concentration equivalence;

(8) operate reliably over the range of automobile environments; and

(9) be manufactured by a party who will provide liability insurance.

b. designating the facilities where ignition interlock devices may be installed;

c. establishing guidelines for the proper use of ignition interlock devices; and

d. establishing guidelines for the provision of ignition interlock devices at reduced rates to persons who, according to standards specified by the division, qualify as indigent.

The director may adopt at his discretion, in whole or in part, the guidelines, rules, regulations, studies, or independent laboratory tests performed on and relied upon in the certification of ignition interlock devices by other states, their agencies or commissions.

L.1999, c. 417, § 6.

39:4–50.22. Criminal and civil liability for permitting or facilitating the arrestee's operation of a motor vehicle; content and form of the written statement and acknowledgment

Whenever a person is summoned by or on behalf of a person who has been arrested for a violation of R.S.39:4–50 or section 2 of P.L.1981, c. 512 (C.39:4–50.4a) in order to transport or accompany the arrestee from the premises of a law enforcement agency, the law enforcement agency shall provide that person with a written statement advising him of his potential criminal and civil liability for permitting or facilitating the arrestee's operation of a motor vehicle while the arrestee remains intoxicated. The person to whom the statement is issued shall acknowledge, in writing, receipt of the statement, or the law enforcement agency shall record the fact that the written statement was provided, but the person refused to sign an acknowledgment.

Nothing in this section shall impose any obligation on a physician or other health care provider involved in the treatment or evaluation of the arrestee.

The Attorney General shall establish the content and form of the written statement and acknowledgment to be used by law enforcement agencies throughout the State and may issue directives to ensure the uniform implementation of this act.

L.2001, c. 69, § 1, eff. Aug. 1, 2001.

39:4–50.23. Vehicle impoundment; detainment, and release; fees

a. Whenever a person has been arrested for a violation of R.S.39:4–50 or section 2 of P.L.1981, c. 512 (C.39:4–50.4a), the arresting law enforcement agency shall impound the vehicle that the person was operating at the time of arrest.

b. A vehicle impounded pursuant to this section shall be impounded for a period of 12 hours after the time of arrest or until such later time as the arrestee claiming the vehicle meets the conditions for release in subsection d. of this section.

c. A vehicle impounded pursuant to this section may be released to a person other than the arrestee prior to the end of the impoundment period only if:

(1) The vehicle is not owned or leased by the person under arrest and the person who owns or leases the vehicle claims the vehicle and meets the conditions for release in subsection d. of this section; or

(2) The vehicle is owned or leased by the arrestee, the arrestee gives permission to another person, who has acknowledged in writing receipt of the statement required in section 1 of P.L.2001, c. 69 (C.39:4–50.22), to operate the vehicle and the conditions for release in subsection d. of this section are met.

d. A vehicle impounded pursuant to this section shall not be released unless the person claiming the vehicle:

(1) presents a valid operator's license, proof of ownership or lawful authority to operate the motor vehicle, and proof of valid motor vehicle insurance for that vehicle;

(2) is able to operate the vehicle in a safe manner and would not be in violation of Title 39 of the Revised Statutes; and

(3) meets any other conditions for release established by the law enforcement agency.

e. A law enforcement agency impounding a vehicle pursuant to this section is authorized to charge a reasonable fee for towing and storage of the vehicle. The law enforcement agency is further authorized to retain custody of the vehicle until that fee is paid.
L.2001, c. 69, § 2, eff. Aug. 1, 2001.

39:4–51. Sentence for violation of section 39:4–50 must be served; release on work release program

A person who has been convicted of a first or second violation of section 39:4–50 of this Title, and in pursuance thereof has been imprisoned in a county jail or workhouse in the county in which the offense was committed, shall not, after commitment, be released therefrom until the term of imprisonment imposed has been served. A person imprisoned in the county jail or workhouse may in the discretion of the court, be released on a work release program.

No warden or other officer having custody of the county jail or workhouse shall release therefrom a person so committed, unless the person has been released by the court on a work release program, until the sentence has been served. A person sentenced to an inpatient rehabilitation program may upon petition by the treating agency be released, by the court, to an

outpatient rehabilitation program for the duration of the original sentence.

Nothing in this section shall be construed to interfere in any way with the operation of a writ of habeas corpus, a proceeding in lieu of the prerogative writs, or an appeal.

The chief administrator shall adopt such rules and regulations to effectuate the provisions of this section as he shall deem necessary.
Amended by L.1951, c. 23, p. 77, § 31; L.1977, c. 29, § 5; L.2003, c. 315, § 3, eff. Jan. 20, 2004.

39:4–51a. Consumption of alcoholic beverage by operator or passenger; prohibition; presumption; violations; penalty

a. A person shall not consume an alcoholic beverage while operating a motor vehicle. A passenger in a motor vehicle shall not consume an alcoholic beverage while the motor vehicle is being operated. This subsection shall not apply to a passenger of a charter or special bus operated as defined under R.S.48:4–1 or a limousine service.

b. A person shall be presumed to have consumed an alcoholic beverage in violation of this section if an unsealed container of an alcoholic beverage is located in the passenger compartment of the motor vehicle, the contents of the alcoholic beverage have been partially consumed and the physical appearance or conduct of the operator of the motor vehicle or a passenger may be associated with the consumption of an alcoholic beverage. For the purposes of this section, the term "unsealed" shall mean a container with its original seal broken or a container such as a glass or cup.

c. For the first offense, a person convicted of violating this section shall be fined $200.00 and shall be informed by the court of the penalties for a second or subsequent violation of this section. For a second or subsequent offense, a person convicted of violating this section shall be fined $250.00 or shall be ordered by the court to perform community service for a period of 10 days in such form and on such terms as the court shall deem appropriate under the circumstances.
L.1983, c. 307, § 1, eff. Aug. 26, 1983. Amended by L.1999, c. 356, § 20.

39:4–51b. Open container; occupants of motor vehicle

a. All occupants of a motor vehicle located on a public highway, or the right-of-way of a public highway, shall be prohibited from possessing any open or unsealed alcoholic beverage container. This subsection shall not apply to a passenger of a charter or special bus operated as defined under R.S.48:4–1 or a limousine service.

b. A person shall not be deemed to be in possession of an opened or unsealed alcoholic beverage container pursuant to this section if such container is located in the trunk of a motor vehicle, behind the last upright seat in a trunkless vehicle, or in the living quarters of a motor home or house trailer. For the purposes of this section, the term "open or unsealed" shall mean a container with its original seal broken or a container such as a glass or cup.

c. For a first offense, a person convicted of violating this section shall be fined $200 and shall be informed by the court of the penalties for a second or subsequent violation of this section. For a second or subsequent offense, a person convicted of violating this section shall be fined $250 or shall be ordered by the court to perform community service for a period of 10 days in such form and on such terms as the court shall deem appropriate under the circumstances.

L.2000, c. 83, § 6, eff. Aug. 14, 2000.

39:4–52. Racing on highway prohibited; fine

No person shall operate a motor vehicle upon a public highway for a wager or in a race or for the purpose of making a speed record.

A person who violates this section shall be fined not less than twenty-five nor more than one hundred dollars for the first offense, and, for a subsequent offense, not less than one hundred nor more than two hundred dollars.

39:4–53. Leaving vehicle with engine running prohibited; fine

A person who leaves a motor vehicle, with its engine running, stationary on the highway and unoccupied by a person able to control it, and without setting the hand brake in such manner as to prevent the vehicle from moving, shall be fined not less than ten nor more than twenty-five dollars for each offense.

39:4–54. Trailers; number permitted; towing methods; auxiliary axles; converter dolly

No motor vehicle shall be used on the public highways while drawing more than 2 motor-drawn vehicles. A "double saddle-mount," herein defined, means mounting the front of a motor vehicle by use of a coupling device, known as a "saddle-mount," on the rear of a towing vehicle and mounting the front of another motor vehicle by use of another "saddle-mount" on the rear of the towed vehicle. The director by regulation may prescribe standards to insure the sufficiency of the coupling, or "saddle-mount," devices, the lighting, braking and towing methods in double saddle-mount operations or in any other combination of 2 motor-drawn vehicles. In no event shall the over-all length of a double saddle-mount operation or any other combination of vehicles exceed the over-all length limitation prescribed in Revised Statutes 39:3–84 for combinations of vehicles, and any violation thereof shall be subject to the penalty provided in this Title for violations of the over-all length limitation in said section.

Trailers shall, when operated on the highways of this State, be connected to the towing vehicle by at least one chain or cable, in addition to the hitch bar, of sufficient strength to hold the motor-drawn vehicle on a hill if the hitching bar becomes disconnected, or shall be provided with an adequate device to prevent its rolling backward.

An attachable auxiliary motor vehicle axle, herein defined, means a single axle mounted on 2 or more wheels, an equal number of wheels on each side, which may be attached, and at times dismounted, to a truck or truck tractor to form a tandem axle.

When a tandem axle is thus formed, the allowable gross weight thereon shall be the same as set forth in Revised Statutes 39:3–84 for tandem axles, if the centers of the axles are on or between 2 parallel transverse vertical planes spaced 40 inches, but less than 96 inches apart. Violations of the allowable gross weight shall be treated in the same manner and be subject to the same penalty as provided in Revised Statutes 39:3–84.3.

An attachable auxiliary axle, upon proof of ownership satisfactory to the director, may be registered on a gross weight basis in the same manner as commercial vehicles under Revised Statutes 39:3–20 and shall display one registration plate or tab of a classification to be determined by the director and located on the auxiliary axle in a manner as may be prescribed by the director. Unless so registered and displaying a registration plate or tab no such attachable auxiliary axle owned by a resident of this State shall be operated on the highways of this State, and no such attachable auxiliary axle owned by a non-resident shall be operated on the highways of this State unless registered in accordance with the laws respecting the registration of motor vehicles of the State, Territory, Federal district of the United States or province of the Dominion of Canada, or foreign country, in which the non-resident resides, if such registration is required therein, and which has conspicuously displayed thereon an identification marker if furnished by said jurisdiction.

When an attachable auxiliary axle registered under this Title is operated on a highway in conjunction with a tractor-semitrailer combination, and one unit of the combination is registered in this State and the other in a foreign jurisdiction, known as a "mixed combination," the registered weight of the auxiliary axle may be added to the registered weight of the New Jersey registered unit in determining if the over-all registered weight conforms with the "mixed combination" registration requirements of Revised Statutes 39:3–20. If the over-all registered weight of the auxiliary axle and the New Jersey registered unit is less than ½ the combined gross weight of the entire combination, then the owner, lessee and bailee shall be subject to the penalty formula set forth in Revised Statutes 39:3–20.

When an auxiliary axle or a converter dolly registered under this Title appears on a highway as part of a tractor-semitrailer combination or a combination of 2 motor-drawn vehicles registered in a foreign jurisdiction or jurisdictions, the entire combination shall be deemed to be of foreign origin and the registration requirements as to "mixed combinations" shall not apply, provided the auxiliary axle or converter dolly is registered with the director for a gross weight of 10,000 pounds.

A converter dolly, herein defined, means an attachable auxiliary frame with hitch bar and fifth wheel with the axle or axles mounted on 2 or more wheels, an equal number of wheels on each side, which may be attached, and at times dismounted, to a semitrailer to form a trailer.

A converter dolly, upon proof of ownership satisfactory to the director, may be registered on a gross weight basis in the same manner as commercial vehicles under Revised Statutes 39:3–20 and shall display one registration plate or tab of a classification to be determined by the director and located on the dolly in a manner as may be prescribed by the director. Unless so registered and displaying a registration plate or tab no such converter dolly owned by a resident of this State shall be operated on the highways of this State, and no such converter dolly owned by a non-resident shall be operated on the highways of this State unless registered in accordance with the laws respecting the registration of motor vehicles of the State, Territory, Federal district of the United States or province of the Dominion of Canada, or foreign country, in which the non-resident resides if such registration is required therein, and which has conspicuously displayed thereon an identification marker if furnished by said jurisdiction.

It shall be unlawful for any combination of 2 motor-drawn vehicles registered under this Title having gross weight of load and vehicles in excess of the gross weight provided on the registration certificates to be operated on the highways of this State. In any violation thereof, the owner, lessee and bailee shall be subject to the penalty formula provided in Revised Statutes 39:3–20.

In any combination of 2 motor-drawn vehicles, with or without use of a converter dolly, and part or parts of the combination is registered in New Jersey and part or parts in a foreign jurisdiction or jurisdictions, the registration requirements as to "mixed combinations" and the penalty formula for violations thereof as provided in Revised Statutes 39:3–20 shall apply.

An auxiliary axle or converter dolly, for the purposes of this section shall not be considered a "vehicle" or "motor vehicle" as defined in Revised Statutes 39:1–1.

A person violating this section, except as specifically provided herein, shall be subject to a fine not exceeding $100.00. In default of the payment thereof, there shall be imposed imprisonment in the county jail for a period not exceeding 10 days.

Amended by L.1951, c. 23, p. 77, § 32; L.1964, c. 180, § 1; L.1965, c. 158, § 1.

39:4–55. Action on steep grades and curves

The driver of a motor vehicle traversing a steep grade or mountain highway shall hold the vehicle under control and as near the right-hand side of the highway as reasonably possible, and when traveling upon a down grade upon a highway, shall not coast with the gears of the vehicle in neutral. When approaching a curve where the view is obstructed within a distance of two hundred feet along the highway, he shall give audible warning with a horn or other warning device.

39:4–56. Delaying traffic prohibited

No person shall drive or conduct a vehicle in such condition, so constructed or so loaded, as to be likely to cause delay in traffic or accident to man, beast or property.

39:4–56.1. Willfully causing vehicle to become disabled; abandonment of vehicle upon public highway

(a) No person shall operate a vehicle upon the public highways, bridges or tunnels of this State or upon any highways, bridges or tunnels in this State operated by any authority of this State or by any authority created jointly by this State and any other State in such a manner as to willfully cause such vehicle to become disabled, by reason of lack of fuel or otherwise, for the purpose of interfering with or obstructing the passage of other vehicles.

(b) No person shall willfully abandon a vehicle upon the public highways, bridges or tunnels of this State, or upon any highways, bridges or tunnels in this State operated by any authority of this State or by any authority created jointly by this State and any other State for the purpose of interfering with or obstructing the passage of other vehicles.

L.1964, c. 18, § 1.

39:4–56.2. Violations; penalties

Any person who has been convicted of a violation of this act shall be subject, for a first offense, to a fine of not less than $200.00 nor more than $500.00 and shall have his license to operate a motor vehicle suspended for a period of not less than 1 year nor more than 5 years. For a subsequent violation, he shall be fined not less than $500.00 nor more than $1,000.00 and shall have his license to operate a motor vehicle suspended for 5 years from the date of his conviction. In fixing the penalty to be imposed, the magistrate shall give consideration to the hazard to the public safety and the public inconvenience created by the conduct of such person.

L.1964, c. 18, § 2.

39:4–56.3. Suspension of registration

The registration of any motor vehicle which is used by any person in violation of section 1 of this act shall[1] be suspended for not less than 90 days nor more than 1 year unless the owner thereof can demonstrate to the satisfaction of the Director of Motor Vehicles that said vehicle was used in such a manner without his knowledge and consent. In fixing the period of suspension, the director shall give consideration to the threat to public safety and the public inconvenience caused by the use of said vehicle.

L.1964, c. 18, § 3.

¹ N.J.S.A. § 39:4–56.1.

39:4–56.4. Legislative findings and declarations

The Legislature finds and declares that a serious threat to the health, safety and welfare of the people of this State may be presented by any concerted effort, plan or demonstration involving the use and operation of vehicles in such a way as to impede, hamper, stall and interfere with the ordinary progress of vehicular traffic on, in and through the roads, highways and bridges of the State. Because of the special road hazards, with consequent danger to the lives and property of the people of this State, and economic loss which would inevitably flow from any such course of conduct, the Legislature determines that the penalties and sanctions provided by this act shall be applicable under such circumstances.

L.1964, c. 18, § 4.

39:4–56.5. Abandonment of motor vehicles; penalty

a. It shall be unlawful for any person to abandon a motor vehicle on or along any highway, other than a limited access highway, or other public property or on any private property without the consent of the owner or other person in charge of the private property. A vehicle which has remained on or along any highway or other public property or on private property without such consent for a period of more than 48 hours or for any period without current license plates shall be presumed to be an abandoned motor vehicle. Vehicles used or to be used in the construction, operation or maintenance of public utility facilities and which are left in a manner which does not interfere with the normal movement of traffic shall not be considered abandoned vehicles for the purposes of this section.

b. It shall be unlawful for any person to abandon a motor vehicle on or along any limited access highway without the consent of the State Department of Transportation or other entity having jurisdiction over the limited access highway, as the case may be. A vehicle which remains on or along such a highway for a period of more than four hours or for any period without current license plates shall be presumed to be an abandoned motor vehicle. Legally parked vehicles, such as vehicles parked in a designated rest area for not more than 12 hours, or vehicles used or to be used in the construction, operation or maintenance of public utility facilities and which are left in a manner which does not interfere with the normal movement of traffic shall not be considered abandoned vehicles for the purposes of this section.

c. Any person who violates this section shall be subject for the first offense to a fine of not less than $100 nor more than $500 and his license or driving privilege may be suspended or revoked by the director for not more than two years. For any subsequent violation he shall be subject to a fine of not less than $500 nor more than $1,000, and his license or driving privilege be suspended or revoked for a period of not more than five years.

L.1967, c. 305, § 1. Amended by L.1971, c. 330, § 1, eff. Nov. 12, 1971; L.1999, c. 411, § 1, eff. Jan. 18, 2000.

39:4–56.6. Abandonment of vehicle on private property; removal by owner of property; costs; sale of vehicle

No person shall park or leave unattended a vehicle on private property without the consent of the owner or other person in control or possession of the property or for a period in excess of that for which consent was given, except in the case of emergency or disablement of the vehicle in which case the owner or operator thereof shall arrange for the expeditious removal of the vehicle. This section shall not apply to manufactured or mobile homes left unattended and for which there exists or existed a rental agreement to occupy a space on the property.

Subject to the requirements of section 7 of P.L.2007, c. 193 (C.56:13–13),¹ the owner or other person in control or possession of the property on which a vehicle is parked or left unattended in violation of this section may remove or hire another person to remove and store the vehicle. It shall be the obligation of the owner of the vehicle to pay the reasonable costs for the removal and for any storage which may result from such removal before he shall be entitled to recover the possession of the vehicle. If the owner of the vehicle refuses to pay such costs or fails to make any claim for the return of the vehicle within 90 days after such removal, the vehicle may be sold at public auction in accordance with the provisions of N.J.S.2A:44–20 through N.J.S.2A:44–31.

L.1973, c. 137, § 1, eff. May 17, 1973. Amended by L.1999, c. 340, § 10, eff. Jan. 10, 2000; L.2007, c. 193, § 22, eff. Oct. 18, 2008.

¹ The Predatory Towing Prevention Act.

39:4–56.7. Issuance of summons for violation by law enforcement officer

Any law enforcement officer may in the performance of his duty enter upon the property upon request of the property owner wherein a vehicle is parked in violation of section 1 of this act for the purpose of issuing a summons for such violation.

L.1973, c. 137, § 2, eff. May 17, 1973.

39:4–56.8. Definitions; removal of disabled motor vehicles by towing service under contract; failure to remove debris surrounding vehicle; penalty

a. As used in this act:

(1) "Public entity" means the State, and any county, municipality, district, or political subdivision and any authority, agency, board or body thereof.

(2) "Public road or highway" means every street, road or highway open to the use of the public for the purpose of vehicular travel.

(3) "Private entity" means any entity other than a public entity with jurisdiction over a road or highway in the State open to the use of the public.

b. Any towing service under contract to a public or private entity to tow disabled motor vehicles which, after being called upon to remove a disabled motor vehicle, fails to remove from public roads or highways any motor vehicle debris or material in the area surrounding that vehicle shall be subject to a fine of not less than $25.00 nor more than $50.00 if the debris or material is likely to cause injury to a person operating a motor vehicle or substantial damage to another motor vehicle. A towing service shall not be required to remove any debris or material which may be hazardous such as oil, gasoline, kerosene or other petroleum or chemical products, or debris or material which the service is not equipped to remove.

L.1983, c. 271, § 1, eff. July 18, 1983.

39:4–57. Observance of directions of officers

Drivers of vehicles, street cars or horses shall at all times comply with any direction, by voice or hand, of a member of a police department, a peace officer, or the director, when enforcing a provision of this chapter.

Amended by L.1951, c. 23, p. 78, § 33; L.1983, c. 403, § 15, eff. Dec. 23, 1983.

39:4–57.1. Vehicle stopped by law enforcement officer; activation of interior light

The driver of a motor vehicle equipped with an interior light, when stopped by a law enforcement officer during the period when lighted lamps are required, shall, upon request of the officer, activate an interior light of the vehicle in order to illuminate the driver's compartment of the vehicle. A fine of $50 shall be imposed upon any person who purposely refuses to comply with this section.

L.1997, c. 374, § 1, eff. March 1, 1998.

39:4–58. Driving vehicle with view to rear and sides obstructed

No person shall drive a vehicle that is so constructed, loaded or covered in as to prevent its driver from having a clear view of the traffic following and at its sides, unless it is equipped with a device that will show the driver the road to the rear and side.

39:4–59. Begging rides prohibited

No person shall stand in a highway for the purpose of or while soliciting a ride from the operator of any vehicle other than an omnibus or a street car.

Amended by L.1951, c. 23, p. 78, § 34.

39:4–60. Soliciting trade or contributions prohibited; designation of particular highway as hazardous for such purposes; signs

Except as provided herein, no person shall stand in the roadway of a highway to stop, impede, hinder or delay the progress of a vehicle for the purpose of soliciting the purchase of goods, merchandise or tickets, or for the purpose of soliciting contributions for any cause, and the only question of law and fact in determining guilt under this section shall be whether goods, merchandise or tickets were tendered or offered for sale, or whether a contribution was solicited.

A municipal governing body by ordinance may authorize charitable organizations as defined in section 3 of P.L.1994, c. 16 (C. 45:17A–20) to solicit contributions in the roadway of a highway, other than interstate highways or toll roads maintained pursuant to P.L.1962, c. 10 (C. 27:12C–1 et seq.) or P.L.1991, c. 252 (C. 27:25A–1 et seq.), P.L.1952, c. 16 (C. 27:12B–1 et seq.), or P.L.1948, c. 454 (C. 27:23–1 et seq.), subject to regulations promulgated pursuant to the "Administrative Procedure Act," P.L.1968, c. 410 (C. 52:14B–1 et seq.), by the Department of Transportation in consultation with the Division of Highway Traffic Safety.

A municipality shall not authorize charitable organizations to solicit on any county highway or intersection of a county highway without the approval of the board of chosen freeholders. A municipality shall not authorize charitable organizations to solicit on any State highway or intersection of a State highway without the approval of the Commissioner of Transportation. The board of chosen freeholders and the Commissioner of Transportation shall not unreasonably withhold approval.

In addition to the prohibition contained in the first paragraph of this section, whenever in his judgment the public safety so requires, the Commissioner of Transportation may, by regulation, designate any highway or sections of any highway as a location wherein the standing of any person or the parking of any vehicle for the purpose of soliciting the purchase of goods, merchandise or tickets, or for the purpose of soliciting contributions for any cause, is deemed hazardous or inimical to the proper flow of traffic, and shall be prohibited. Each highway or section thereof so designated shall be clearly marked by appropriate signs which shall be erected and maintained by the authority having the responsibility for the maintenance of such highway, upon receipt by such authority of written notice from the director of the adoption of such regulation. No person shall stand in, and no operator shall allow a vehicle to stand in, any section of a highway so designated and marked to stop, impede, hinder or delay the progress of a vehicle for the purpose of soliciting the purchase of goods, merchandise or tickets, or for the purpose of soliciting contributions for any cause, and the only question of law and fact in determining guilt under this section shall be whether goods, merchandise or tickets were tendered or offered for sale, or whether a contribution was solicited. Whenever in his judgment the public safety so requires the Commissioner of Transportation may, by regulation, amend or alter any designation made by him pursuant to the provisions of this paragraph. Nothing contained in this paragraph shall be construed to authorize or permit any person to stand in or to allow a vehicle to stand in any highway where the same is or shall be prohibited by any other provision of this Title or by any amendment thereof or supplement thereto, or by any ordinance, resolution, regulation or order duly adopted pursuant to authority thereunder.

Any person who shall violate any of the provisions of this section shall pay, upon conviction, a penalty not to exceed $100.

Amended by L.1951, c. 23, p. 78, § 35; L.1997, c. 82, § 1, eff. Aug. 1, 1997.

39:4–60.1. Certain rotating or flashing lights prohibited

On and after the effective date of this act no rotating or flashing light which imitates or resembles rotating or flashing lights such as are used by public and governmental agencies or any public utility to indicate emergency or hazardous conditions shall be erected or used within 100 feet of the roadway of a highway within the State.

L.1970, c. 134, § 1, eff. July 9, 1970.

39:4–60.2. Removal without notice

Every such prohibited light or signal is hereby declared to be a public nuisance and the authority having jurisdiction over the highway or the municipality in which the prohibited act takes place is empowered to remove the same or cause it to be removed without notice.

L.1970, c. 134, § 2, eff. July 9, 1970.

39:4–60.3. Emergency use

This act shall not apply to any rotating or flashing light used to indicate an emergency or hazardous condition.

L.1970, c. 134, § 3, eff. July 9, 1970.

39:4–61. Tailboard riding

No person shall ride upon the rear end of a vehicle, without the consent of the driver, and when so riding, no part of the person's body shall protrude beyond the limits of the vehicle.

39:4–62. Leaving curb

A vehicle waiting at the curb shall promptly give place to a vehicle about to take on or let off passengers.

39:4–63. Placing, throwing or depositing from motor vehicle, injurious substance on highway; fine; forfeiture of right to operate motor vehicle

A person who throws, places or deposits, or who permits to be thrown, placed, or deposited from a motor vehicle, any glass or other sharp, injurious or cutting substance in or upon a public highway of this State shall, except when acting under the authority of the governing body of a municipality, be punished by a fine of not less than $100.00 nor more than $500.00 and may forfeit his right to operate a motor vehicle over the highways of this State for a period of 30 days.

Amended by L.1980, c. 100, § 1, eff. Sept. 11, 1980.

39:4–64. Throwing or dropping bundles, objects or debris from vehicles; fine; rebuttable presumption

a. No person shall throw or drop any bundle, object, article or debris of any nature from a vehicle whether in motion or not when such vehicle is on a highway. The words "object, article or debris of any nature" as used in this section shall be deemed to include a cigarette, cigar, match, or ashes, or any substance or thing in and of itself likely to cause or fuel a fire, but such inclusion shall not be deemed to in any way limit the generality of the words "object, article or debris of any nature." Any person who violates this section shall be subject to a fine of not less than $200 or more than $1,000 for each offense.

b. There shall be a rebuttable presumption that the registered owner of the vehicle, if present in the vehicle, or, in his absence, the driver of the vehicle, is presumed to be responsible for any violation of this section, if:

(1) A bundle, object, article or debris of any nature is thrown or dropped from the vehicle by an occupant of the vehicle;

(2) There are two or more occupants in the vehicle; and

(3) It cannot be determined which occupant of the vehicle is the violator.

Amended by L.1954, c. 37, p. 107, § 1; L.1975, c. 154, § 1, eff. July 15, 1975; L.1981, c. 143, § 1, eff. May 14, 1981; L.1983, c. 346, § 1, eff. Sept. 22, 1983; L.1992, c. 171, § 1, eff. June 1, 1993.

39:4–64.1. Signs informing of consequences of violation

The Director of the Division of Motor Vehicles shall cause to be erected on the highways such signs as he deems necessary to inform those people using the highways of the consequences of violating the provisions of R.S. 39:4–64.

L.1975, c. 154, § 2, eff. July 15, 1975.

39:4–65. Letting off or taking on persons

No operator of a vehicle shall stop the vehicle on the highway for the purpose of letting off or taking on a person, other than at the curb or side of the road or highway, or knowingly permit a person to alight from or enter upon the vehicle while it is in motion.

39:4–66. Emerging from alley, driveway, garage, or private road or driveway

a. The operator of a vehicle emerging from an alley, driveway, garage, or private road or driveway, shall stop the vehicle immediately prior to driving upon the sidewalk, and shall proceed to enter the sidewalk only after yielding the right of way to a pedestrian on the sidewalk, if the pedestrian is so close as to constitute an immediate hazard.

b. In addition to any duty imposed under subsection a. of this section, the operator of a vehicle emerging from an alley, driveway, garage, or private road or driveway, shall stop the vehicle immediately prior to entering or crossing a highway, and shall proceed to enter or cross the highway only after yielding the right of way to the traffic on the highway, if the traffic is so close as to constitute an immediate hazard.

Amended by L.1989, c. 147, § 1.

39:4–66.1. Entering alley, driveway, garage, or private road or driveway from highway over sidewalk

When the driver of a vehicle, about to enter an alley, driveway, garage, or private road or driveway from a highway, shall find it necessary to drive upon the sidewalk, he first shall yield the right of way to all pedestrians on the sidewalk, if the pedestrians are so close as to constitute an immediate hazard.

L.1951, c. 23, p. 84, § 48. Amended by L.1989, c. 147, § 2.

39:4–66.2. Operation of motor vehicles on public or private property to avoid traffic signals or signs prohibited; exceptions; penalties for violations

Except for emergency vehicles and motor vehicles being operated at the direction of a law enforcement officer, no person shall drive a motor vehicle on public property, except public roads or highways, or private property, with or without the permission of the owner, for the purpose of avoiding a traffic control signal or sign.

Any person found guilty of violating the provisions of this act shall be liable for a penalty of not less than $50.00 or more than $200.00 or imprisonment for a term not exceeding 15 days, or both.

L.1993, c. 326, § 1, eff. Dec. 23, 1993.

39:4–67. Obstructing passage of other vehicles or street cars prohibited; clearance of intersections

No vehicle or street car shall be permitted by the owner or driver thereof to so occupy a street as to interfere with or interrupt the passage of other street cars or vehicles, nor shall the driver of a vehicle or street car drive such vehicle or street car into an intersection if preceding traffic prevents immediate clearance of the intersection.

Amended by L.1956, c. 107, p. 484, § 1.

39:4–68. Doors of street car or autobus closed

No operator of a street car or autobus shall knowingly operate the same while any door thereof is open.

39:4–69. Riding on part not intended for passengers prohibited

No person shall ride on, and no operator shall knowingly allow a person to ride on a street car or vehicle, or on a portion thereof not designed or intended for the conveyance of passengers. This section shall not apply to an employee engaged in the necessary discharge of a duty.

Amended by L.1951, c. 23, p. 79, § 36.

39:4–70. Repealed by L.1964, c. 136, § 14

39:4–71. Driving on sidewalk

No person shall drive or back a horse or vehicle across, or allow the same to stand on a sidewalk unless it be in crossing the sidewalk to go into a yard or lot, and then not without the consent of the owner of the premises. This section shall not prohibit the passing of a horse or vehicle over a sidewalk in front of an alley or passageway with the owner's consent, or any municipality from driving or operating or causing to be driven or operated along or over the sidewalks within the municipality any vehicle for the purpose of maintaining or cleaning said sidewalks.

Amended by L.1963, c. 24, § 1, eff. May 8, 1963.

39:4–72. Operating motor vehicle near horses; violation and penalties

a. When approaching or passing a person riding or driving a horse, a person driving a motor vehicle shall reduce the vehicle's speed to a rate not exceeding 25 miles an hour and proceed with caution. At the request of or upon a signal by putting up the hand or otherwise, from a person riding or driving a horse in the opposite direction, the motor vehicle driver shall cause the motor vehicle to stop and remain stationary so long as may be necessary to allow the horse to pass.

b. The administrator shall include in the New Jersey Driver Manual information explaining the requirements of subsection a. of this section and cautioning licensees on the need to exercise caution when operating a motor vehicle near horses.

c. A person who violates subsection a. of this section shall be subject to a fine of $150.

Amended by L.2004, c. 163, § 1, eff. Dec. 7, 2004.

ARTICLE 10. LOAD AND LOADING OF VEHICLES

39:4–73. Repealed by L.1950, c. 142, p. 283, § 4

39:4–74. Blank

39:4–75. Driving overweight vehicles on intrastate bridges; approaching signs; fines; liability for damage to bridges

a. No motor vehicle shall be driven over a bridge in this State if the gross weight of the vehicle and load is greater than the gross posted weight limit of the bridge.

b. Signs warning persons driving motor vehicles that they are approaching a bridge with a maximum gross weight limit shall be posted in a conspicuous place upon the bridge or immediately adjacent thereto and at the last safe exit or detour preceding the bridge. These signs shall indicate the maximum gross weight permitted on the bridge and shall be in accordance with the current standards prescribed by the Manual on Uniform Traffic Control Devices for Streets and Highways. The signs required by this section shall be posted and maintained by the entity which has jurisdiction over the bridge.

c. A person violating this section shall be subject to a fine not exceeding $1,000.00. In default of the payment thereof imprisonment in the county jail for a period not exceeding 10 days shall be imposed.

The owner and operator of any vehicle used in violation of this section shall be responsible to the municipal or other corporation owning or maintaining such bridge, or to the State if such bridge is maintained by the State, for any damage done to the bridge by reason of the violation.

Amended by L.1971, c. 40, § 1, eff. March 4, 1971; L.1987, c. 315, § 1, eff. Dec. 15, 1987.

39:4–76. Driving overweight vehicles on interstate bridges; penalty; liability for damages; disposition of penalties

No vehicle shall be driven over any interstate bridge owned or maintained in whole or in part by this State, upon which is posted in a conspicuous place a sign stating the gross weight that the bridge will carry, if the gross weight of any such vehicle and the load is greater than the gross weight stated on the sign.

Any person violating any of the provisions of this section, and the owner of any vehicle driven upon any bridge in violation of this section, with a gross weight or with weight on any axle or wheel exceeding by more than 3% the maximum weight allowed in that particular case, shall be fined an amount equal to $0.02 per pound for each pound of excess weight if the excess does not exceed 10,000 pounds, and $0.03 per pound for each pound of excess weight if the excess weight exceeds 10,000 pounds, but in no event less than $50.00.

The owner of any vehicle driven in violation of this section shall, in addition to the penalty herein prescribed, be responsible to the commission, body or authority having control of said bridge, for damages which may be done to any such bridge by reason of any violation of this section.

Moneys received from penalties imposed for violations of this section shall be accounted for and forwarded to the director, who shall pay the same to the State Treasurer.

Amended by L.1951, c. 23, p. 80, § 37; L.1970, c. 280, § 1, eff. Dec. 3, 1970.

39:4–77. Loading so as to spill prohibited; minimum safety standards; penalty

No person shall cause or permit a vehicle to be so loaded or operate a vehicle so loaded that the contents or any part thereof may be scattered in any street. Whenever the load of any vehicle is of material other than farm products susceptible to scattering on a street and such load extends above the height of the sides or tail gate or rear of the body of the vehicle, such load shall be securely covered by a tarpaulin or other cover. The director, where public safety so warrants, shall, after a public hearing, prescribe by rule or regulation minimum safety standards for fastening loads on and fix loading procedures for any commercial type flat bed motor vehicle or motor-drawn vehicle. Any rule or regulation so promulgated by the director shall be filed in the Secretary of State's office and copies thereof shall be available, upon request, in the director's office.

The owner, lessee, bailee, or operator of any vehicle described above found on a highway in violation of any such safety standard or procedure that may be prescribed by the director shall be fined not more than $500.00 for each violation.

Amended by L.1951, c. 23, p. 80, § 38; L.1966, c. 251, § 1; L.1968, c. 272, § 1, eff. Sept. 4, 1968.

39:4–77.1. Snow or ice falling off moving vehicle; damage to vehicles or property; penalties

Text of section effective until October 19, 2010.

When snow or ice is dislodged from a moving vehicle and strikes another vehicle or pedestrian causing injury or property damage, the following penalties shall apply:

The operator of a non-commercial motor vehicle shall be subject to a fine of not less than $200 or more than $1,000 for each offense.

The operator, owner, lessee, bailee or any one of the aforesaid of a commercial motor vehicle shall be subject to a fine of not less than $500 or more than $1,500 for each offense.

No motor vehicle points or automobile insurance eligibility points pursuant to section 26 of P.L.1990, c. 8 (C.17:33B–14) shall be assessed for this offense.

L.1997, c. 124, § 1, eff. June 20, 1997.

39:4–77.1. Snow or ice accumulated on motor vehicles; duty to remove; penalties; commercial vehicles; damage to other vehicles; public awareness campaign

Text of section effective on October 19, 2010.

a. (1) Each driver of a motor vehicle operated on a street or highway in this State shall have an affirmative duty to make all reasonable efforts to remove accumulated ice or snow from exposed surfaces of the motor vehicle prior to operation, which surfaces shall include, but not be limited to, the hood, trunk, windshield, windows, and roof of the motor vehicle, the cab of a truck, the top of a trailer or semitrailer being drawn by a motor vehicle, and the top of an intermodal freight container being carried by an intermodal chassis. A person who violates the provisions of this subsection may be stopped on a street or highway by a law enforcement officer who believes the accumulated ice or snow may pose a threat to persons or property and shall be subject to a fine of not less than $25 or more than $75 for each offense regardless of whether any snow or ice is dislodged from the motor vehicle. No motor vehicle points or automobile insurance eligibility points pursuant to section 26 of P.L.1990, c. 8 (C.17:33B–14) shall be assessed for a violation of this paragraph. Every day upon which a violation occurs shall be considered a separate violation, but no person shall be subject to more than one fine for a violation of this paragraph in a period of 24 consecutive hours.

(2) This subsection shall not apply to any driver of a motor vehicle operated during a snow or ice storm that began and continued for the duration of the motor vehicle's operation or to any operator of a motor vehicle while it is parked.

(3) No fine shall be imposed pursuant to paragraph (1) of this subsection on the driver of a commercial motor vehicle, as the term is defined in R.S.39:1–1, that is traveling to a location where equipment or technology that is used to remove snow and ice from commercial motor vehicles is available, provided that the driver has not already passed a location with snow and ice removal equipment or technology after snow or ice shall have accumulated on the exposed surfaces of the commercial motor vehicle. In determining whether the vehicle has already passed a location with equipment or technology that is used to remove snow and ice from commercial motor vehicles, a law enforcement officer shall have the authority to inspect any documentation relating to the route traveled by the driver of the commercial motor vehicle prior to being stopped, including, but not limited to, a log book or map depicting the route traveled by the vehicle.

(4) Notwithstanding the provisions of paragraph (1) of this subsection:

(a) the person who is in physical possession of a motor vehicle at the time snow or ice accumulates on the exposed surfaces of the motor vehicle shall be responsible for removing the accumulated snow or ice

from the exposed surfaces of the motor vehicle and shall be liable for a violation of the duty to remove accumulated snow or ice prior to operation of the motor vehicle pursuant to paragraph (1) of this subsection. If the driver of the motor vehicle was not in physical possession of the motor vehicle at the time the snow or ice accumulated, then such driver shall not be liable for a violation of paragraph (1) of this subsection.

(b) in the case of any trailer or semitrailer being drawn by a motor vehicle or of any vehicle or combination of vehicles carrying an intermodal freight container, the person, including, but not limited to a shipper or consignee, who is in physical possession of the trailer, semitrailer, or container at the time snow or ice accumulates on such trailer, semitrailer, or container shall be responsible for removing the accumulated snow or ice from the trailer, semitrailer, or container and shall be liable for a violation of the duty to remove accumulated snow or ice prior to operation of a motor vehicle pursuant to paragraph (1) of this subsection. If the driver of the motor vehicle was not in physical possession of the trailer, semitrailer, or container at the time the snow or ice accumulated, then such driver shall not be liable for a violation of paragraph (1) of this subsection.

b. When snow or ice is dislodged from a moving vehicle and strikes another vehicle or pedestrian causing injury or property damage, the following penalties shall apply:

The operator of a non-commercial motor vehicle shall be subject to a fine of not less than $200 or more than $1,000 for each offense.

The operator, owner, lessee, bailee or any one of the aforesaid of a commercial motor vehicle shall be subject to a fine of not less than $500 or more than $1,500 for each offense.

No motor vehicle points or automobile insurance eligibility points pursuant to section 26 of P.L.1990, c. 8 (C.17:33B–14) shall be assessed for a violation of this subsection.

c. The Director of the Division of Highway Traffic Safety in the Department of Law and Public Safety shall establish a public awareness campaign that educates the public on the importance of removing snow and ice from the exposed surfaces of motor vehicles prior to the operation of such vehicles. This campaign shall educate the public on the potential dangers associated with failing to remove snow or ice from motor vehicles as well as on the penalties that may be imposed as a result of failing to remove snow or ice from a motor vehicle prior to operation.

d. The Director of the Division of Highway Traffic Safety in the Department of Law and Public Safety, in conjunction with the Division of State Police and other law enforcement agencies, shall establish and maintain a data collection system to be used to determine the number and seriousness of motor vehicle accidents caused by snow or ice becoming dislodged from motor vehicles. In its annual report to the Legislature pursuant to section 16 of P.L.1987, c. 284 (C.27:5F–33), the Division of Highway Traffic Safety shall provide an analysis of the information gathered through the data collection system and any recommendations, including any proposed legislation, for reducing the number and seriousness of accidents caused by snow or ice becoming dislodged from motor vehicles.

e. All fines imposed and collected in the enforcement of this section shall be forwarded by the person to whom they are paid to the State Treasurer, who shall annually deposit those moneys in the "Motor Vehicle Snow and Ice Removal Safety Fund" established pursuant to section 2 of P.L.2009, c. 138 (C.39:4–77.2).

L.1997, c. 124, § 1, eff. June 20, 1997. Amended by L.2009, c. 138, § 1, eff. Oct. 19, 2010.

39:4–77.2. Motor Vehicle Snow and Ice Removal Safety Fund

Section effective on October 19, 2010.

a. There is established in the General Fund a separate, nonlapsing, dedicated account to be known as the "Motor Vehicle Snow and Ice Removal Safety Fund." All fines imposed and collected as a result of enforcement of section 1 of P.L.1997, c. 124 (C.39:4–77.1) shall be forwarded to the State Treasurer for deposit in the Motor Vehicle Snow and Ice Removal Safety Fund account. The fund shall be administered by the Division of Highway Traffic Safety in the Department of Law and Public Safety.

b. Moneys in the account shall be used exclusively for the following purposes:

(1) To offset the costs associated with the public awareness campaign established by the Director of the Division of Highway Traffic Safety in the Department of Law and Public Safety pursuant to subsection c. of section 1 of P.L.1997, c. 124 (C.39:4–77.1);

(2) To offset the costs associated with the data collection system established and maintained by the Division of Highway Traffic Safety in the Department of Law and Public Safety pursuant to subsection d. of section 1 of P.L.1997, c. 124 (C.39:4–77.1); and

(3) To establish a grant program to provide incentives to encourage private companies to purchase, install, and maintain equipment and technology to be used to remove snow and ice from commercial motor vehicles, as the term is defined in R.S.39:1–1. Recipients of grants provided pursuant to this subsection shall place snow and ice removal equipment and technology at locations around the State that are convenient and easily accessible to commercial motor vehicles, including, but not limited to, service areas, weigh stations, inspection facilities, ports, terminals, and other intermodal transportation facilities.

L.2009, c. 138, § 2, eff. Oct. 19, 2010.

39:4–78. Carrying metals

No person shall load a vehicle or drive a vehicle so loaded with iron or other material that may strike together, unless it is properly deafened so as to cause no unnecessary noise.

39:4–79. Backing to curb

No operator shall allow a vehicle to stand backed to the curb when loading or unloading, except when it is impracticable to load or unload it while standing parallel to the curb, but no vehicle may completely block the passage of another vehicle or street car by remaining backed up to the curb. When necessary to back up to the curb, the towing vehicle in any combination of vehicles and the horse, if the vehicle is horse drawn, shall stand as nearly parallel as practicable to the curb and facing the direction of traffic.

Amended by L.1951, c. 23, p. 80, § 39.

ARTICLE 11. LAW OF ROAD AND RIGHT OF WAY

39:4–80. Traffic control by officers

When a traffic or police officer is stationed in a highway for the purpose of directing traffic, he may regulate and control traffic at that point, and all drivers of vehicles shall obey his orders and directions, notwithstanding anything contained in this article.

39:4–80.1. School crossing guards; duty to obey; penalty

A motor vehicle operator who fails to comply with a school crossing guard's signal to stop during those time periods when that guard is duly authorized to control or direct vehicular or pedestrian traffic pursuant to section 4 of P.L.1979, c. 82 (C.40A:9–154.4) shall be fined not less than $150 for a first offense. For a subsequent offense, the operator shall be fined not less than $300.

L.2007, c. 78, § 1, eff. Aug. 1, 2007.

39:4–81. Observing traffic signals

a. The driver of every vehicle, the motorman of every street car and every pedestrian shall obey the instructions of any official traffic control device applicable thereto, placed in accordance with the provisions of this chapter, unless otherwise directed by a traffic or police officer.

b. When, by reason of a power failure or other malfunction, a traffic control signal at an intersection is not illuminated, the driver of a vehicle or street car shall, with respect to that intersection, observe the requirement for a stop intersection, as provided in R.S.39:4–144.

Amended by L.1951, c. 23, p. 81, § 40; L.2004, c. 92, § 1, eff. July 9, 2004.

39:4–82. Keeping to right

Upon all highways of sufficient width, except upon one-way streets, the driver of a vehicle shall drive it on the right half of the roadway. He shall drive a vehicle as closely as possible to the right-hand edge or curb of the roadway, unless it is impracticable to travel on that side of the roadway, and except when overtaking and passing another vehicle subject to the provisions of sections 39:4–84 and 39:4–85 of this Title.

Amended by L.1951, c. 23, p. 81, § 43.

39:4–82.1. Two roadway highways; driving upon

Whenever any highway has been divided into two roadways by leaving an intervening space or by a physical barrier or clearly indicated dividing section so constructed so as to impede vehicular traffic, every vehicle shall be driven only upon the right-hand roadway and no vehicle shall be driven over, across or within any such dividing space, barrier or section, except through an appropriate opening in such physical barrier or dividing section or space or at a cross over or intersection established by public authority.

L.1951, c. 23, p. 81, § 41.

39:4–83. Keeping to right at intersections; exception on one-way roadway

In crossing an intersection of highways or the intersection of a highway and a railroad right of way, the driver of a vehicle shall at all times cause the vehicle to travel on the right half of the roadway unless the right half is obstructed or impassable. The foregoing limitations shall not apply upon a one-way roadway.

Amended by L.1951, c. 23, p. 82, § 44.

39:4–84. Passing to right when proceeding in opposite directions

Drivers of vehicles proceeding in opposite directions shall pass each other to the right, each giving to the other at least one-half of the available traveled portion of the highway as nearly as possible.

39:4–85. Passing to left when overtaking; passing when in lines; signalling to pass; passing upon right

The driver of a vehicle overtaking another vehicle proceeding in the same direction shall pass at a safe distance to the left thereof and shall not again drive to the right side of the roadway until safely clear of the overtaken vehicle. If vehicles on the roadway are moving in two or more substantially continuous lines, the provisions of this paragraph and section 39:4–87 of this Title shall not be considered as prohibiting the vehicles in one line overtaking and passing the vehicles in another line either upon the right or left, nor shall those provisions be construed to prohibit drivers overtaking and passing upon the right another vehicle which is making or about to make a left turn.

The driver of an overtaking motor vehicle not within a business or residence district shall give audible warning with his horn or other warning device before passing or attempting to pass a vehicle proceeding in the same direction.

The driver of a vehicle may overtake and pass another vehicle upon the right as provided in this section only under conditions permitting such movement in safety. In no event shall such movement be made by driving off the pavement or main-traveled portion of the roadway.

Amended by L.1951, c. 23, p. 82, § 45.

39:4–85.1. One-way traffic, designation of highways for; signs

The commissioner with respect to highways under his jurisdiction may by regulation, and local and county authorities with respect to highways under their jurisdiction may by ordinance or resolution designate any such highway or any separate roadway of such highway for one-way traffic and shall erect appropriate signs giving notice thereon.

Upon a highway or roadway properly designated and signed for one-way traffic, a vehicle shall be driven only in the direction designated.

L.1951, c. 23, p. 81, § 42. Amended by L.2003, c. 13, § 50 (contingent effective date).

39:4–86. Overtaking and passing vehicles; crossing "No Passing" lines

The driver of a vehicle shall not drive to the left side of the center line of a highway in overtaking and passing another vehicle proceeding in the same direction unless the left side is clearly visible and free of oncoming traffic for a sufficient distance ahead to permit the overtaking and passing to be made in safety.

The driver of a vehicle shall not drive to the left of the center of a highway in order to overtake and pass another vehicle proceeding in the same direction upon the crest of a grade or upon a curve in the highway where the driver's view along the highway is obstructed within a distance of five hundred feet.

Except when otherwise directed by a duly constituted traffic or police officer or when the lane in which he is operating is obstructed and impassable, the driver of a vehicle shall not cross an appropriately marked "No Passing" line in a "No Passing" zone duly established pursuant to a duly promulgated regulation of the State Highway Commissioner or an ordinance or resolution duly adopted by a municipal governing body or a board of chosen freeholders, whichever has jurisdiction over the highway.

Amended by L.1948, c. 170, p. 912, § 3; L.1951, c. 23, p. 82, § 46.

39:4–86.1 to 39:4–86.3. Repealed by L.1951, c. 23, p. 120, § 122

39:4–87. Overtaken vehicle to give way

The driver of a vehicle on a highway, about to be overtaken and passed by another vehicle, approaching from the rear, shall give way to the right in favor of the overtaking vehicle on suitable and audible signal being given by the driver of the overtaking vehicle, and shall not increase the speed of his vehicle until completely passed by the overtaking vehicle.

39:4–87.1. Right of way for busses

a. The driver of a non-emergency vehicle upon a highway shall yield the right of way to any bus, provided that:

(1) The driver is operating a vehicle that is in a position to overtake the bus from its rear; and

(2) The bus, after exiting an active traffic lane for the purpose of stopping to receive or discharge passengers is attempting to reenter the lane from which it exited and to enter the traffic lane occupied by the driver by signaling its intention to do so. No other lane changes shall be applicable.

As used in this act, "bus" means a bus as defined in section 3 of P.L. 1995, c. 225 (C. 48:4–2.1e), in regular scheduled service, and a motorbus operated in regular route service pursuant to P.L. 1979, c. 150 (C. 27:25–1 et seq.).

b. The New Jersey Transit Corporation shall conduct a public education program to inform motorists of the requirements imposed by this section relating to bus rights-of-way.

c. The Commissioner of Transportation shall study the need for further action to effectuate the purposes of this 2003 act and shall, no later than 18 months after the effective date of this 2003 act, report to the Governor and the Legislature.

d. This section shall not relieve the driver of any bus from the duty to drive with due regard for the safety of all persons, nor shall it protect the driver from the consequences of his reckless disregard for the safety of others. Nothing in this section shall be construed to limit any immunity or defense otherwise provided by law.

L.2003, c. 226, § 1, eff. Aug. 1, 2004.

39:4–88. Traffic on marked lanes

When a roadway has been divided into clearly marked lanes for traffic, drivers of vehicles shall obey the following regulations:

a. A vehicle shall normally be driven in the lane nearest the right-hand edge or curb of the roadway when that lane is available for travel, except when overtaking another vehicle or in preparation for a left turn.

b. A vehicle shall be driven as nearly as practicable entirely within a single lane and shall not be moved from that lane until the driver has first ascertained that the movement can be made with safety.

c. Upon a highway which is divided into 3 lanes, a vehicle shall not be driven in the center lane except when overtaking or passing another vehicle or in preparation for a left turn or unless the center lane is at the time allocated for traffic moving in the direction the vehicle is proceeding and is signposted to give notice of that allocation.

d. The State Highway Commissioner may by regulation or local authorities may by resolution or ordinance with respect to highways under their jurisdiction designate right-hand lanes for slow moving traffic and inside lanes for traffic moving at the speed designated for the district as provided under this chapter, and when the lanes are signposted or marked to give notice of the designation a vehicle may be driven in any lane allocated to traffic moving in the direction in which it is proceeding, but when traveling within the inside lanes the vehicle shall be driven at approximately the speed authorized in such lanes and speed shall not be decreased unnecessarily so as to block, hinder or retard traffic.

e. When such roadway has been divided in such a manner that there are 3 or more lanes for traffic in any one direction, no truck of 10,000 pounds registered gross weight or over shall be driven in the farthest left-hand lane, except when and to the extent necessary to prepare for a left turn, or when necessary to enter or leave such roadway by entrance or exit to or from the left lane or when reasonably necessary in response to emergency conditions.

Amended by L.1951, c. 23, p. 83, § 47; L.1968, c. 432, § 1, eff. Feb. 11, 1969.

39:4–89. Following; space between trucks

The driver of a vehicle shall not follow another vehicle more closely than is reasonable and prudent, having due regard to the speed of the preceding vehicle and the traffic upon, and condition of, the highway.

The driver of a motor truck when traveling upon a highway, outside of a business or residence district, shall not follow another motor truck within one hundred feet, but this shall not be construed to prevent one motor truck overtaking and passing another.

39:4–90. Right of way at intersections

The driver of a vehicle approaching an intersection shall yield the right of way to a vehicle which has entered the intersection. When 2 vehicles enter an intersection at the same time the driver of the vehicle on the left shall yield the right of way to the driver of the vehicle on the right.

The driver of a vehicle within an intersection intending to turn to the left shall yield to a vehicle approaching from the opposite direction which is within the intersection or so close thereto as to constitute an immediate hazard, but the driver having so yielded, and having given a signal when and as required by law, may make the left turn; and other vehicles approaching the intersection from the opposite direction shall yield to the driver making the left turn.

Amended by L.1958, c. 114, p. 587, § 1.

39:4–90.1. Limited access highways, driving onto or from

No person shall drive a vehicle onto or from any limited-access highway except at such entrances and exits as are established by public authority.

L.1951, c. 23, p. 85, § 51.

39:4–91. Right of way of emergency vehicles; liability of drivers

a. The driver of a vehicle upon a highway shall yield the right of way to any authorized emergency vehicle when it is operated on official business, or in the exercise of the driver's profession or calling, in response to an emergency call or in the pursuit of an actual or suspected violator of the law and when an audible signal by bell, siren, exhaust whistle or other means is sounded from the authorized emergency vehicle and when the authorized emergency vehicle, except a police vehicle, is equipped with at least one lighted lamp displaying a red light visible under normal atmospheric conditions from a distance of at least five hundred feet to the front of the vehicle.

b. This section shall not relieve the driver of any authorized emergency vehicle from the duty to drive with due regard for the safety of all persons, nor shall it protect the driver from the consequences of his reckless disregard for the safety of others. Nothing in this section shall be construed to limit any immunity or defense otherwise provided by law.

Amended by L.1951, c. 23, p. 84, § 49; L.1997, c. 423, § 1, eff. Jan. 19, 1998.

39:4–92. Authorized emergency vehicles; clearance for; following or parking near

Upon the immediate approach of an authorized emergency vehicle giving audible signal, and equipped, as required by section 39:4–91 of this Title, and unless otherwise directed by a police or traffic officer,

(a) The driver of every vehicle shall immediately drive to a position as near as possible and parallel to the right-hand edge or curb of the highway, clear of an intersection of highways, and shall stop and remain in that position until the authorized emergency vehicle has passed and

(b) The driver or person in control of a street car shall immediately stop the car clear of an intersection of highways and keep it stationary until the authorized emergency vehicle has passed.

No driver of any vehicle other than one on official business shall follow any authorized emergency vehicle, traveling in response to an emergency call, closer than 300 feet, or drive nearer to, or park the vehicle within

200 feet of, where any fire apparatus has stopped in answer to a fire alarm.

Amended by L.1951, c. 23, p. 85, § 50; L.1962, c. 148, § 1.

39:4–92.1. Fire department vehicle returning to fire station; flashing red light

It shall be lawful for any fire department vehicle when returning to its fire station from an emergency call to display a flashing red light visible under normal atmospheric conditions from a distance of at least 500 feet to the rear of the vehicle and no driver of any vehicle other than one on official business shall follow any such vehicle displaying said light closer than 300 feet.

L.1966, c. 289, § 1, eff. Oct. 6, 1966.

39:4–92.2. Authorized emergency vehicles displaying flashing, blinking or alternating lights; driver duty when approaching stationary emergency vehicles; penalties

a. The operator of a motor vehicle approaching a stationary authorized emergency vehicle as defined in R.S.39:1–1 that is displaying a flashing, blinking or alternating red or blue light or, any configuration of lights containing one of these colors, shall approach the authorized emergency vehicle with due caution and shall, absent any other direction by a law enforcement officer, proceed as follows:

(1) Make a lane change into a lane not adjacent to the authorized emergency vehicle if possible in the existing safety and traffic conditions; or

(2) If a lane change pursuant to paragraph (1) of subsection a. of this section would be impossible, prohibited by law or unsafe, reduce the speed of the motor vehicle to a reasonable and proper speed for the existing road and traffic conditions, which speed shall be less than the posted speed limit, and be prepared to stop.

b. The operator of a motor vehicle approaching a stationary tow truck as defined in section 1 of P.L.1999, c. 396 (C.39:3–84.6) that is displaying a flashing amber light or a stationary highway maintenance or emergency service vehicle that is operated by the State, an authority or a county or municipality and displaying flashing yellow, amber, or red lights shall approach the vehicle with due caution and shall, absent any other direction by a law enforcement officer, proceed as follows:

(1) Make a lane change into a lane not adjacent to the tow truck or highway maintenance or emergency service vehicle if possible in the existing safety and traffic conditions; or

(2) If a lane change under paragraph (1) of subsection b. of this section would be impossible, prohibited by law or unsafe, reduce the speed of the motor vehicle to a reasonable and proper speed for the existing road and traffic conditions, which speed shall be less than the posted speed limit, and be prepared to stop.

c. A violation of this section shall be punished by a fine of not less than $100 and not more than $500. *L.2009, c. 5, § 1, eff. Jan. 27, 2009.*

39:4–93. Processions

If a procession takes longer than five minutes to pass a given point, it shall be interrupted every five minutes for the passage of traffic which may be waiting.

Authorized emergency vehicles, United States mail vehicles and physicians vehicles shall have the right of way through a procession.
Amended by L.1951, c. 23, p. 86, § 53.

39:4–94. Railroad blocking highway

No employee of a steam or electric railroad company shall operate a locomotive, train or crossing gate in such a manner as to unnecessarily prevent or interfere with the use of a highway for the purpose of travel.

39:4–94.1. Repealed by L.1989, c. 32, § 30

39:4–94.2. State, county or municipal highway, road or street closed with posted notice and barricade; violations; penalty

Whenever by order of the Commissioner of the Department of Transportation, a State highway, or by resolution of a county governing body, a county public road, or by appropriate action of the governing body of a municipality, a municipal street or road is declared closed to traffic for any lawful purpose, and a notice of the closing has been posted at the beginning and ending points of the closed section of the highway, road, or street, and a barricade erected at those points, any person who without the permission of the commissioner or governing body of the county, or municipality, as the case may be:

a. Mutilates or removes the notice, or damages, destroys or removes any warning sign or signal, or removes the barricade placed or posted by the commissioner or county or municipal governing body, at any point along the highway, road or street in connection with or relating to the closed portion thereof; or

b. Drives a vehicle over or upon the closed section of the highway, road or street which he knows or should have reason to know has been closed to traffic; or

c. Violates any rule or regulation for the use of the highway, road or street duly made by the commissioner or county or municipal governing body, as authorized by law, he shall be subject to a fine of not more than $100.00.
L.1981, c. 229, § 1, eff. July 27, 1981.

ARTICLE 12. SPEED

39:4–95. "Vehicle" defined

As used in this article, the word "vehicle" includes street cars.

39:4–96. Reckless driving; punishment

A person who drives a vehicle heedlessly, in willful or wanton disregard of the rights or safety of others, in a manner so as to endanger, or be likely to endanger, a person or property, shall be guilty of reckless driving and be punished by imprisonment in the county or municipal jail for a period of not more than 60 days, or by a fine of not less than $50.00 or more than $200.00, or both.

On a second or subsequent conviction he shall be punished by imprisonment for not more than three months, or by a fine of not less than $100 or more than $500, or both.
Amended by L.1955, c. 220, p. 868, § 1; L.1982, c. 45, § 3, eff. Sept. 1, 1982; L.1995, c. 70, § 2, eff. April 10, 1995.

39:4–97. Careless driving

A person who drives a vehicle carelessly, or without due caution and circumspection, in a manner so as to endanger, or be likely to endanger, a person or property, shall be guilty of careless driving.
Amended by L.1951, c. 23, p. 87, § 54; L.1955, c. 220, p. 869, § 2; L.1995, c. 70, § 3, eff. April 10, 1995.

39:4–97a. Motor vehicle operation causing property destruction; prohibition; exception; recreational property defined

No person shall operate a motor vehicle, except a motor vehicle operated for emergency purposes by a fire department or ambulance or rescue squad, in a manner which causes the destruction of agricultural crops, fences, fields or other agricultural or recreational property. "Recreational property" means any public or private property used as a golf course, park, or other similar purpose.
L.1985, c. 154, § 1, eff. April 25, 1985.

39:4–97.1. Slow speeds as blocking traffic

No person shall drive a motor vehicle at such a slow speed as to impede or block the normal and reasonable movement of traffic except when reduced speed is necessary for safe operation or in compliance with law.
L.1955, c. 220, p. 869, § 3.

39:4–97.2. Driving or operating a motor vehicle in an unsafe manner; endangering persons or property; fines; surcharges

a. Notwithstanding any other provision of law to the contrary, it shall be unlawful for any person to drive or operate a motor vehicle in an unsafe manner likely to endanger a person or property.

b. A person convicted of a first offense under subsection a. shall be subject to a fine of not less than $50.00 or more than $150.00 and shall not be assessed any motor vehicle penalty points pursuant to section 1 of P.L.1982, c. 43 (C.39:5–30.5).

c. A person convicted of a second offense under subsection a. shall be subject to a fine of not less than $100.00 or more than $250.00 and shall not be assessed any motor vehicle penalty points pursuant to section 1 of P.L.1982, c. 43 (C.39:5–30.5).

d. A person convicted of a third or subsequent offense under subsection a. shall be subject to a fine of not less than $200.00 or more than $500.00 and shall be assessed motor vehicle penalty points pursuant to section 1 of P.L.1982, c. 43 (C.39:5–30.5).

e. An offense committed under this section that occurs more than five years after the prior offense shall not be considered a subsequent offense for the purpose of assessing motor vehicle penalty points under subsection d. of this section.

f. In addition to any fine, fee or other charge imposed pursuant to law, the court shall assess a person convicted of an offense under subsection a. of this section a surcharge of $250 which shall be collected by the court and distributed to the Division of Revenue in the Department of the Treasury as a New Jersey Merit Rating Plan surcharge pursuant to subparagraph (a) of paragraph (2) of subsection b. of section 6 of P.L.1983, c. 65 (C.17:29A–35).

L.2000, c. 75, § 1, eff. July 24, 2000. Amended by L.2004, c. 69, § 1, eff. July 1, 2004.

39:4–97.3. Use of hands-free and hand-held wireless communication devices while driving; when permitted; penalty

a. The use of a wireless telephone or electronic communication device by an operator of a moving motor vehicle on a public road or highway is unlawful except when the telephone is a hands-free wireless telephone or the electronic communication device is used hands-free, provided that its placement does not interfere with the operation of federally required safety equipment and the operator exercises a high degree of caution in the operation of the motor vehicle. For the purposes of this section, an "electronic communication device" shall not include an amateur radio.

b. The operator of a motor vehicle may use a hand-held wireless telephone while driving with one hand on the steering wheel only if:

(1) The operator has reason to fear for his life or safety, or believes that a criminal act may be perpetrated against himself or another person; or

(2) The operator is using the telephone to report to appropriate authorities a fire, a traffic accident, a serious road hazard or medical or hazardous materials emergency, or to report the operator of another motor vehicle who is driving in a reckless, careless or otherwise unsafe manner or who appears to be driving under the influence of alcohol or drugs. A hand-held wireless telephone user's telephone records or the testimony or written statements from appropriate authorities receiv-

ing such calls shall be deemed sufficient evidence of the existence of all lawful calls made under this paragraph.

As used in this act, "hands-free wireless telephone" means a mobile telephone that has an internal feature or function, or that is equipped with an attachment or addition, whether or not permanently part of such mobile telephone, by which a user engages in a conversation without the use of either hand; provided, however, this definition shall not preclude the use of either hand to activate, deactivate, or initiate a function of the telephone.

"Use" of a wireless telephone or electronic communication device shall include, but not be limited to, talking or listening to another person on the telephone, text messaging, or sending an electronic message via the wireless telephone or electronic communication device.

c. (Deleted by amendment, P.L.2007, c. 198).

d. A person who violates this section shall be fined $100.

e. No motor vehicle points or automobile insurance eligibility points pursuant to section 26 of P.L.1990, c. 8 (C.17:33B–14) shall be assessed for this offense.

f. The Chief Administrator of the New Jersey Motor Vehicle Commission shall develop and undertake a program to notify and inform the public as to the provisions of this act.

g. Whenever this section is used as an alternative offense in a plea agreement to any other offense in Title 39 of the Revised Statutes that would result in the assessment of motor vehicle points, the penalty shall be the same as the penalty for a violation of section 1 of P.L.2000, c. 75 (C.39:4–97.2), including the surcharge imposed pursuant to subsection f. of that section, and a conviction under this section shall be considered a conviction under section 1 of P.L.2000, c. 75 (C.39:4–97.2) for the purpose of determining subsequent enhanced penalties under that section.

L.2003, c. 310, § 1, eff. July 1, 2004. Amended by L.2007, c. 198, § 1, eff. March 1, 2008.

39:4–97.4. Application to law enforcement, fire department and emergency personnel

The prohibitions set forth in this act shall not be applicable to any of the following persons while in the actual performance of their official duties: a law enforcement officer; a member of a paid, part-paid, or volunteer fire department or company; or an operator of an authorized emergency vehicle.

L.2003, c. 310, § 2, eff. July 1, 2004.

39:4–97.5. Construction with other laws

This act supersedes and preempts all ordinances of any county or municipality with regard to the use of a wireless telephone or electronic communication device by an operator of a motor vehicle.

L.2003, c. 310, § 3, eff. July 1, 2004. Amended by L.2007, c. 198, § 2, eff. March 1, 2008.

39:4–98. Rates of speed.

Subject to the provisions of R.S.39:4–96 and R.S.39:4–97 and except in those instances where a lower speed is specified in this chapter, it shall be prima facie lawful for the driver of a vehicle to drive it at a speed not exceeding the following:

a. Twenty-five miles per hour, when passing through a school zone during recess, when the presence of children is clearly visible from the roadway, or while children are going to or leaving school, during opening or closing hours;

b. (1) Twenty-five miles per hour in any business or residential district;

(2) Thirty-five miles per hour in any suburban business or residential district;

c. Fifty miles per hour in all other locations, except as otherwise provided in the "Sixty–Five MPH Speed Limit Implementation Act," pursuant to section 2 of P.L.1997, c. 415 (C.39:4–98.3 et al.).

Whenever it shall be determined upon the basis of an engineering and traffic investigation that any speed hereinbefore set forth is greater or less than is reasonable or safe under the conditions found to exist at any intersection or other place or upon any part of a highway, the Commissioner of Transportation, with reference to State highways, may by regulation and municipal or county authorities, with reference to highways under their jurisdiction, may by ordinance, in the case of municipal authorities, or by ordinance or resolution, in the case of county authorities, subject to the approval of the Commissioner of Transportation, except as otherwise provided in R.S.39:4–8, designate a reasonable and safe speed limit thereat which, subject to the provisions of R.S.39:4–96 and R.S.39:4–97, shall be prima facie lawful at all times or at such times as may be determined, when appropriate signs giving notice thereof are erected at such intersection, or other place or part of the highway. Appropriate signs giving notice of the speed limits authorized under the provisions of paragraph (1) of subsection b. and subsection c. of this section may be erected if the commissioner or the municipal or county authorities, as the case may be, so determine they are necessary. Appropriate signs giving notice of the speed limits authorized under the provisions of subsection a. and paragraph (2) of subsection b. of this section shall be erected by the commissioner or the municipal or county authorities, as appropriate.

When designating reasonable and safe speed limits for a street under its jurisdiction pursuant to this subsection, as part of an engineering and traffic investigation, a municipality or county shall consider, but not be limited to, the following criteria: residential density; the presence, or lack, of sidewalks; the prevalence of entry and exit ways for business and commercial establishments; whether school children walk adjacent to the street on their way to and from school; and the proximity of recreational or park areas, schools, community residences, family day care homes, child care centers, assisted living facilities or senior communities. Nothing in this paragraph shall substitute for traffic count, accident, and speed sampling data as appropriate.

The driver of every vehicle shall, consistent with the requirements of this section, drive at an appropriate reduced speed when approaching and crossing an intersection or railway grade crossing, when approaching and going around a curve, when approaching a hill crest, when traveling upon any narrow or winding roadway, and when special hazard exists with respect to pedestrians or other traffic or by reason of weather or highway conditions.

The Commissioner of Transportation shall cause the erection and maintenance of signs at such points of entrance to the State as are deemed advisable, setting forth the lawful rates of speed, the wording of which shall be within his discretion.

Amended by L.1939, c. 211, p. 607, § 1; L.1951, c. 23, p. 87, § 55; L.1983, c. 227, § 2, eff. June 27, 1983; L.1993, c. 315, § 2, eff. Dec. 23, 1993; L.1997, c. 415, § 1, eff. Jan. 19, 1998; L.2009, c. 258, § 1, eff. Jan. 17, 2010.

39:4–98.1. Designation of lower maximum speed limits for trucks of registered gross weight of 10,000 pounds and over

In accordance with the provisions of section 39:4–98 of the Revised Statutes, the State Highway Commissioner may, by regulation and identification by appropriate signs, designate lower maximum speed limits for trucks of a registered gross weight of 10,000 pounds and over, at a differential of 5 miles per hour, on State highways, or appropriate portions thereof, having 4 or more traffic lanes, where the legal speed limit is 50 miles per hour or greater.

L.1960, c. 100, p. 588, § 1.

39:4–98.2. Counties or municipalities; reduction of regular speed limit for 72 hours for maintenance or repairs; notice to commissioner

Any county or municipal governing body may adopt an ordinance or resolution, as appropriate, designating a county or municipal official who may order a reduction of a regular speed limit for periods not to exceed 72 hours on segments of highways under its jurisdiction for the purpose of maintenance or repairs. Any resolution or ordinance adopted pursuant to this act shall specify the circumstance under which a speed limit may be reduced.

An order reducing the speed limit pursuant to this act shall not require the approval of the Commissioner of Transportation; provided, however, that it shall be the duty of the designated county or municipal official to notify the commissioner of the affected segment of highway no less than 7 days before any reduced speed limit takes effect; except that in cases of emergency situations the notification period may be waived by the commissioner. It shall be the duty of the designated county or municipal official to place one or more signs indicating the reduced speed limit along the affected highway.

Any speed limit established pursuant to this act shall be prima facie lawful and subject to the provisions of R.S. 39:4–96 and 39:4–97 when appropriate signs giving notice thereof are erected.

L.1981, c. 237, § 1, eff. July 27, 1981.

39:4–98.3. Short title

This act may be known and shall be cited as the "Sixty–Five MPH Speed Limit Implementation Act."
L.1997, c. 415, § 2, eff. Jan. 19, 1998.

39:4–98.4. Definitions relative to 65mph speed limit

As used in this act:

"Authorities" means the New Jersey Highway Authority, the New Jersey Turnpike Authority and the South Jersey Transportation Authority.

"Commissioner" means the Commissioner of Transportation.

"Eligible public highways" means public highways as defined in section 3 of P.L. 1984, c. 73 (C.27:1B–3) of which portions have been determined by the commissioner to be appropriate for a 65 miles per hour speed limit based on such criteria as determined by the commissioner. Public highways under the jurisdiction of counties and municipalities shall not be eligible public highways.

L.1997, c. 415, § 3, eff. Jan. 19, 1998.

39:4–98.5. Speed limit of 65mph established, certain highways

a. Within four months following the effective date of this act, the commissioner, in consultation with the Attorney General and the authorities, shall establish by written order speed limits of 65 miles per hour on approximately 400 miles of eligible public highways. The commissioner, pursuant to section 7 of this act, may increase or decrease the number of miles of eligible public highways on which a 65 miles per hour speed limit has been established.

b. An order to be issued pursuant to subsection a. of this section shall cite the eligible public highways to which it is to be applicable and contain a description in plain language of the order's contents, the effective date of the order and any other information the commissioner deems necessary.

c. The commissioner shall cause a general public notice of the proposed order, including a summary of the provisions of the proposed order, to be published in a newspaper or newspapers having general circulation in the municipality or municipalities affected by the order. The notice shall include a telephone number or address which a member of the public may use to receive a copy of the complete text of the proposed order and shall provide for a 30–day period from the date of publication for public comment. The order shall be final on the 31st day after publication of the notice or on a later date if the commissioner so determines. Nothing in this subsection shall be construed as prohibiting the commissioner from extending the comment period or from modifying or withdrawing the proposed order as a result of the review of public comment.

d. A final order shall be effective and enforceable upon compliance with the requirement for the posting of signs providing notice of the speed limit, as provided under the applicable provisions of R.S.39:4–98 and R.S.39:4–198.

e. Any official traffic control device established pursuant to this section shall conform to the "Manual on Uniform Traffic Control Devices."

f. Any order issued pursuant to this section shall be binding and enforceable under the provisions of Title 39 of the Revised Statutes and all other applicable laws, in any court of competent jurisdiction, until superseded by order of the commissioner pursuant to this act.

L.1997, c. 415, § 4, eff. Jan. 19, 1998.

39:4–98.6. Certain fines doubled where speed limit is 65mph

a. The fine for a motor vehicle offense embodied in the following sections of statutory law, when committed in an area which has been designated as having a speed limit of 65 miles per hour, shall be double the amount specified by law:

R.S. 39:4–52;

R.S. 39:4–57;

R.S. 39:4–80;

R.S. 39:4–81;

R.S. 39:4–84;

R.S. 39:4–85;

R.S. 39:4–86;

R.S. 39:4–88;

R.S. 39:4–89;

R.S. 39:4–90;

R.S. 39:4–96;

R.S. 39:4–97;

R.S. 39:4–98, when guilty of driving at a speed that is 10 miles per hour or more over the established speed limit;

R.S. 39:4–126;

R.S. 39:4–127;

R.S. 39:4–129;

R.S. 39:4–144;

P.L. 1955, c. 217 (C.39:5C–1);

Section 41 of P.L. 1951, c. 23 (C.39:4–82.1);

Section 51 of P.L. 1951, c. 23 (C.39:4–90.1);

Section 5 of P.L. 1951, c. 264 (C.27:23–29);

Section 18 of P.L. 1952, c. 16 (C.27:12B–18); and

Section 21 of P.L. 1991, c. 252 (C.27:25A–21).

b. (1) Signs designed in compliance with the specifications of the Department of Transportation or, if appropriate, the authority having jurisdiction over the appropriate highway, shall be appropriately placed, by order of the commissioner or the affected authority, as the case may be, to notify drivers approaching areas designated as having a speed limit of 65 miles per hour that the fines are doubled for motor vehicle offenses in those areas.

(2) In addition, all traffic control signs and devices erected or displayed by the State Department of Transportation or an authority within an area designated as having a speed limit of 65 miles per hour shall conform to the uniform system specified in the most current "Manual on Uniform Traffic Control Devices for Streets and Highways, "prepared by the Federal Highway Administration in the United States Department of Transportation.

c. It shall not be a defense to the imposition of the fines authorized under the provisions of this act that a sign notifying drivers that fines are doubled was not posted, improperly posted, wrongfully removed or stolen, or that signs or devices were not placed in compliance with the most current "Manual on Uniform Traffic Control Devices for Streets and Highways."

d. The Director of Motor Vehicles in the Department of Transportation shall include information concerning the penalties imposed pursuant to this section in any subsequent revision of the New Jersey Driver Manual and the New Jersey Motorist Guide.

L.1997, c. 415, § 5, eff. Jan. 19, 1998.

39:4–98.7. Speeding 20mph or more over limit; fines; certain; doubled

The fine for a motor vehicle offense shall be double the amount specified by law when traveling 20 miles per hour or more over the designated speed limit as set forth in R.S.39:4–98, except as provided in subsection b. of section 1 of P.L.1993, c.332 (C.39:4–203.5) and subsection a. of section 5 of P.L.1997, c.415 (C.39:4–98.6).

L.1997, c. 415, § 6, eff. Jan. 19, 1998.

39:4–98.8. Study to determine effect of 65mph speed limit; report; implementation

a. During the first 18 months following the establishment of 65 miles per hour speed limits on eligible public highways pursuant to section 4 of this act, the commissioner, in consultation with the Attorney General and the authorities, shall conduct a study to determine the overall impact of this act. The study shall consider public safety, environmental and cost issues, including, but not limited to speed, accident rates, fatalities, enforcement, air quality and such other issues as the commissioner deems appropriate to evaluate fully the effect of the 65 miles per hour speed limit on the State.

b. A report of the study's findings and recommendations, including a recommendation as to whether the number of miles of eligible public highways should increase, decrease or remain the same, shall be submitted to the Governor, President of the Senate and Speaker of the General Assembly no later than 21 months after the establishment of 65 miles per hour speed limits on eligible public highways pursuant to section 4 of this act.

c. The commissioner shall implement the recommendations contained in the report 60 days following the report's submission to the Governor and Legislature unless the recommendations, either all or in part, are disapproved each by the Senate and the General Assembly by passage of a concurrent resolution stating, in substance, that the Legislature does not favor the recommendations. If the recommendations are disapproved in part by concurrent resolution, the commissioner shall implement those recommendations that are not disapproved.

L.1997, c. 415, § 7, eff. Jan. 19, 1998.

39:4–98.9. Temporary changes to speed limit; emergency orders

a. Notwithstanding any other provision of law to the contrary, the commissioner is authorized to set or change by emergency order, for periods of up to 60 days, the speed limit on any public highway based on emergent conditions, such as construction work, dangerous conditions, extreme congestion or traffic problems, imminent peril, or imminent risk to motorists or to the public safety.

b. An emergency order issued pursuant to this section shall cite the portions of public highway to which it is to be applicable, a description in plain language of what the order requires, the effective date of the order, and any other information the commissioner deems necessary.

c. An emergency order issued pursuant to this section shall be final upon the signature of the commissioner, or on a later date if the commissioner so determines, and shall be effective and enforceable upon compliance with the requirement for the posting of signs providing notice of the speed limit, as provided under the applicable provisions of R.S.39:4–98 and R.S.39:4–198.

d. An emergency order issued pursuant to this section may, upon its expiration date, be renewed by the commissioner for additional 60-day periods, until the emergent condition necessitating the emergency order is mitigated.

e. Any official traffic control device established pursuant to this section shall conform to the "Manual on Uniform Traffic Control Devices."

L.1997, c. 415, § 8, eff. Jan. 19, 1998.

39:4–99. Exceeding speed limitations; speed specified in charge

It shall be prima facie unlawful for a person to exceed any of the foregoing speed limitations or any speed limitation in effect as established by authority of section 39:4–98 of this Title.

In every charge of violation of section 39:4–98 of this Title, the complaint and the summons or notice to appear, shall specify the speed at which the defendant is alleged to have driven and the speed which this article declares shall be prima facie lawful at the time and place of the alleged violation.

Amended by L.1951, c. 23, p. 88, § 56.

39:4–100. Rate of speed across sidewalk

No vehicle or horse shall be driven or ridden across a sidewalk at a rate of speed greater than four miles per hour.

39:4–101. Speedways

Nothing in this article shall apply to a speedway, constructed with the permission of the local authorities or the board of freeholders, as the case may be, of the county or counties in which the speedway is located, and built or intended for the exclusive use of motor vehicles, if the speedway at no point crosses a highway, railroad or railway at grade.

39:4–102. Speeding by physicians in emergencies

If a physician's motor vehicle is stopped for exceeding the speed limit while in the act of responding to an emergency call, the registration number of the vehicle and the driver's license number may be inspected and noted and the physician shall then be allowed to proceed in the vehicle to his destination. Such proceedings may be taken subsequently as would have been proper had the person not been a physician.

39:4–103. Exemptions from speed regulations

Motor vehicles belonging to the military establishment, while in use for official purposes in time of riot, insurrection or invasion; all police officers, while the officers are engaged in the apprehension of violators of the law, or of persons charged with, or suspected of, a violation, are exempt from the provisions of this chapter relating to speed.

Amended by L.1951, c. 23, p. 89, § 57; L.1983, c. 403, § 16, eff. Dec. 23, 1983.

39:4–103.1. Use of photo radar to enforce speeding laws prohibited

a. Notwithstanding any law, rule or regulation to the contrary, a law enforcement officer or agency shall not use photo radar to enforce the provisions of chapter 4 of Title 39 of the Revised Statutes.

b. As used in this act, "photo radar" means a device used primarily for highway speed limit enforcement substantially consisting of a radar unit linked to a camera, which automatically produces a photograph of a vehicle traveling at a speed in excess of the legal limit.

L.1992, c. 91, § 1, eff. Sept. 4, 1992.

39:4–104. Violations of article; penalty

A person violating a section of this article shall, for each violation, be subject to a fine of not less than $50.00 or more than $200.00, or imprisonment for a period not exceeding 15 days, or both, except as herein otherwise provided.

Amended by L.1955, c. 221, p. 869, § 1; L.1982, c. 45, § 4, eff. Sept. 1, 1982.

ARTICLE 13. TRAFFIC SIGNALS

39:4–105. Color system

Traffic signals or signal devices shall conform strictly with the provisions of this article.

A three-color system shall be used; red, amber and green. Green means permission for traffic to go, subject to the safety of others or the specific directions of an officer, official sign or special signal. Red means traffic to stop before entering the intersection or crosswalk and remain standing until green is shown alone, unless otherwise specifically directed to go by an officer, official sign or special signal. Amber, or yellow, when shown alone following green means traffic to stop before entering the intersection or nearest crosswalk, unless when the amber appears the vehicle or street car is so close to the intersection that with suitable brakes it cannot be stopped in safety. A distance of fifty feet from the intersection is considered a safe stopping distance for a speed of twenty miles per hour, and vehicles and street cars if within that distance when the amber appears alone, and which cannot be stopped with safety, may proceed across the intersection or make a right or left turn unless the turning movement is specifically limited.

All other uses of green, red, amber or yellow lights so located as to be confused with traffic signals shall be discontinued.

39:4–106. Sequence of lights

The colors shall be shown in the following sequence: A green light displayed for a predetermined number of seconds followed by an amber light for a reasonable time necessary for the clearance of traffic, followed by a red light, followed by a green light. The timing of all lights shall be determined by the volume of traffic.

39:4–107. Period or cycle

The period or cycle shall be based on counts of turning and through traffic and study of turns, special intersections, distance between intersections and speeds permitted.

39:4–108. Semaphores

Semaphores shall have four vanes or sides, the stop vanes having a red field with the word "stop" plainly visible thereon, and the go vanes a green field with the word "go" plainly visible thereon.

When used at night, semaphores shall be equipped with red and green lights, corresponding with the vanes or sides, and with the same meaning and visibility as electrically equipped signals.

39:4–109. Position of lenses

When a vertical arrangement of lenses is used, red shall be placed at the top, amber in the middle and green at the bottom. When it is necessary to place the lights horizontally, the order of the lights shall be red at the left, amber in the middle and green at the right.

39:4–110. Height of signals

Traffic signals shall be placed at such height as to be plainly visible to approaching traffic at a distance of at least one hundred and fifty feet from the intersection, and shall, if within the curb line and operated by electricity, be placed at a height of from eight to ten feet above the pavement. If on bracket, mast arm or cable, the signal shall clear the pavement by fourteen feet and six inches.

Amended by L.1948, c. 422, p. 1660, § 1.

39:4–111. Power of lights

The light shall be of such power as to cause the signal to be visible for at least three hundred feet.

39:4–112. Visibility of signals to traffic at intersections

Traffic control signals shall be so located as to be plainly visible to all traffic to be regulated and shall provide at least two indications for each approach at the intersection. At least one signal face shall give an unmistakable indication to traffic approaching, as well as passing through the intersection area. This shall be accomplished by means of posts, brackets, mast arms or cables so located that at least one signal face shall be to the right of, or over the traffic it is intended to control.

Amended by L.1948, c. 422, p. 1660, § 2.

39:4–113. Continuously controlled highway

Each intersection on a continuously controlled highway shall be controlled by signals or suitable signs. If traffic signals are not erected at every intersection it shall not be construed as a continuously controlled highway.

39:4–114. Traffic signal in paved roadway or poles in crosswalk lanes prohibited

No traffic signal shall be so located as to obstruct the paved width of the highway, nor shall poles carrying signal supports be so placed as to be in pedestrian crosswalk lanes. Where there is, or may hereafter be erected a fixed raised safety zone, the highway area covered by the raised safety zone shall not be construed to mean the paved width of the highway.

39:4–115. Making right or left turn

The driver of a vehicle or the motorman of a streetcar: a. intending to turn to the right or left at an intersection where traffic is controlled by traffic control signals or by a traffic or police officer, shall proceed to make either turn with proper care to avoid accidents and, except as provided in b. below, only upon the "go" signal unless otherwise directed by a traffic or police officer, an official sign or special signal; or b. intending to turn right at an intersection where traffic is controlled by a traffic control signal shall, unless an official sign of the State, municipality, or county authority having jurisdiction over the intersection prohibits the same, proceed to make the turn upon a "stop" or "caution" signal with proper care to avoid accidents after coming to a full stop, observing traffic in all directions, yielding to other vehicular traffic traveling in a direction in which the turn will be made, and stopping and remaining stopped for pedestrians crossing the roadway within a marked crosswalk, or at an unmarked crosswalk, into which the driver is turning. Both the approach for and the turn shall be made as close as practicable to the right-hand curb or edge of the roadway, unless such intersection is otherwise posted.

Amended by L.1976, c. 46, § 1; L.2009, c. 319, § 3, eff. April 1, 2010.

39:4–116. Special right or left turn

Special right or left turn movements may be provided when approved by the director at intersections where traffic is controlled by traffic control signals, by incorporating an additional lens in the signal. This additional lens shall be a green arrow lens and shall designate the special right or left turn movement by the direction of the arrow.

When a green arrow lens is incorporated in a traffic control signal and the signal is operating to control traffic at an intersection, vehicles shall make turning movements in the direction of the arrow only when the lens is illuminated.

Amended by L.1951, c. 23, p. 89, § 58.

39:4–117. Special pedestrian interval

A special pedestrian interval may be provided when approved by the director at intersections where traffic is controlled by traffic control signals.

When a special pedestrian interval is incorporated in the operation of a traffic control signal and signified by means of an approved indication, pedestrians shall cross the roadway only when the indication is illuminated, and vehicles and street cars shall stop and remain standing until the green is shown alone.

Amended by L.1951, c. 23, p. 89, § 59.

39:4–118. Beacon or flashing signal

Beacon or flashing signals may be erected on pedestals or posts or suspended by means of mast arms or cables over the intersection, but the signal shall not be erected within the travelable portion of a highway, except as provided in section 39:4–114 of this Title.

Amended by L.1951, c. 23, p. 89, § 60.

39:4–119. Traffic control signals operating as flashing mechanisms; red; amber

Traffic control signals and beacon or flashing signals when operating as flashing mechanisms shall conform to the following:

a.   Flashing red: The red lens when illuminated with rapid intermittent flashes shall require drivers to come to a complete stop before entering or crossing the intersection. The driver shall proceed only after yielding the right of way to all traffic on the intersecting street, which traffic is so close as to constitute an immediate hazard.

b.   Flashing amber: The amber lens when illuminated with rapid intermittent flashes shall indicate the presence of danger and require drivers to proceed only with caution.

Amended by L.1985, c. 59, § 1, eff. Feb. 27, 1985.

39:4–120. Director to determine signals; uniform system

The commissioner may determine the character, type, location, placing and operation of all traffic control signal devices on the highways of this State. The commissioner may adopt a manual and specifications for a uniform system of traffic control signals consistent with the provisions of this act for use upon public highways within the State. Such uniform system shall correlate with and so far as possible conform to the system then current as specified in the "Manual on Uniform Traffic Control Devices for Streets and Highways."

Amended by L.1951, c. 23, p. 90, § 61; L.2003, c. 13, § 51 (contingent effective date).

39:4–120.1. Official traffic control signals

Official traffic control signals shall be placed only by the authority of a public body or official having jurisdiction as authorized by law and only for the purpose of regulating traffic.

L.1951, c. 23, p. 90, § 62.

39:4–120.2. Flashing mechanism; use by municipalities

Subject to the provisions of R.S. 39:4–8 and P.L.1969, c. 65 (C. 27:1A–43 et seq.), a municipality may determine the operation of any approved traffic control device as a flashing mechanism on municipally-owned and maintained streets and roads during the offpeak hours between 10 p.m. to 6 a.m. of any day of the week.

L.1981, c. 437, § 1, eff. Jan. 9, 1982.

39:4–120.3. Submission of written information to commissioner

Any municipality seeking to enact an ordinance, regulation or resolution under this act shall first submit written information to the Commissioner of the Department of Transportation indicating the location of the traffic control device where the use of flashing signals is requested, the intended hours of operation of such signal, data as to the traffic volume at, and the site distances from, each intersection of, each location, and any other information requested by the commissioner.

L.1981, c. 437, § 2, eff. Jan. 9, 1982.

39:4–120.4. Ordinance, regulation or resolution; effective date

Any ordinance, regulation or resolution adopted hereunder shall become effective on the ninetieth day following enactment unless it shall have been disapproved before that time by the commissioner; provided that the commissioner shall have received a certified copy of the ordinance, regulation or resolution, as the case may be, within 5 days of its enactment.

L.1981, c. 437, § 3, eff. Jan. 9, 1982.

39:4–120.5. Definitions

As used in this act:

a.   "Private road open to the public" means a private road leading from an establishment open to the public including but not limited to a shopping center, restaurant, movie theater or arena.

b.   "Public-private intersection" means the intersection of a private road open to the public with a highway.

L.1991, c. 298, § 1, eff. Feb. 1, 1992.

39:4–120.6. Official traffic control device erected at public-private intersection

The owner of a private road open to the public which forms a public-private intersection may erect an official traffic control device at the public-private intersection after obtaining the necessary approval in accordance with section 3 of this act.[1] All official traffic control devices shall conform to the same specifications as those regulating intersections.

L.1991, c. 298, § 2, eff. Feb. 1, 1992.

1 N.J.S.A. § 39:4–120.7.

39:4–120.7. Public-private intersection containing state or local highway; approval by commissioner or local authority

a. Where the public-private intersection contains a State highway, the Commissioner of Transportation by regulation shall approve the erection of an official traffic control device.

b. Where the public-private intersection contains a highway under the jurisdiction of local authorities, the local authorities by ordinance or resolution shall approve the erection of an official traffic control device, subject to the approval of the commissioner.

c. The commissioner by appropriate order may withdraw an official traffic control device from a public-private intersection.

L.1991, c. 298, § 3, eff. Feb. 1, 1992.

39:4–120.8. Traffic device to be installed and maintained by owner of private road

The owner of the private road open to the public shall obtain, install and maintain any official traffic control device at a public-private intersection.

L.1991, c. 298, § 4, eff. Feb. 1, 1992.

39:4–120.9. Motorists required to obey traffic control device at public-private intersection

The driver of a motor vehicle shall observe and obey an official traffic control device erected at a public-private intersection in the same manner as those erected at any other intersection.

L.1991, c. 298, § 5, eff. Feb. 1, 1992.

39:4–120.10. Violations; penalties

For a violation of this act, the offender shall be subject to the same penalties as exist in connection with violations at public intersections.

L.1991, c. 298, § 6, eff. Feb. 1, 1992.

39:4–120.11. Rules and regulations

The Commissioner of Transportation may promulgate rules and regulations pursuant to the "Administrative Procedure Act," P.L.1968, c. 410 (C. 52:14B–1 et seq.) to effectuate the purposes of this act.

L.1991, c. 298, § 7, eff. Oct. 4, 1991.

39:4–121. Traffic lights on state roads in suburban districts at location of fire engine houses; installation by state highway commission

The State Highway Commissioner, after proper investigation and survey, subject to the approval of the director, may install and maintain traffic lights upon State roads in suburban districts wherever a fire engine house is located within one thousand feet of such road or is located upon such road. The investigation and survey must clearly indicate a special hazard existing because of heavy traffic congestion or of traffic speed upon such road at the locality in question.

Amended by L.1951, c. 23, p. 90, § 63.

39:4–121.1. Dangerous intersections in counties or municipalities; traffic lights

Any county or municipality, wherein a dangerous intersection has been established by reason of the construction of a State highway within the territorial limits thereof, may apply to the State Highway Commissioner for the installation and maintenance of traffic lights at such intersection, and after an application is so made the commissioner shall cause to be made a proper investigation and survey concerning the traffic hazards which exist at such intersection. The State Highway Commissioner, after an investigation and survey, may install and maintain traffic lights at any intersection where an application, as hereinbefore provided for, has been made, but the installation of any traffic lights pursuant to this section shall receive the approval of the director.

Amended by L.1951, c. 23, p. 90, § 64.

39:4–121.2. Expenses paid from state highway fund

The state highway commissioner may expend such moneys as may be necessary to install and maintain traffic lights at the places mentioned in section 39:4–121.1 of this title, said moneys to be withdrawn from those appropriated to the state highway commissioner from the state highway fund.

39:4–121.3. Counties or municipalities; agreements with department of transportation for installation, alteration or maintenance of traffic control device

Upon approval by the Department of Transportation of a request by a county or municipality for the installation, alteration or maintenance of a traffic control device on a county or municipal street or highway, the county or municipality may, and is authorized to, enter into an agreement with the Commissioner of Transportation for the Department to perform the work or contract for the installation, alteration or maintenance at the expense of the county or municipality.

L.1972, c. 97, § 1, eff. July 18, 1972. Amended by L.1989, c. 72, § 1, eff. April 14, 1989.

39:4–122. Signal by police whistle

A driver shall, upon one blast of a police whistle given by a police officer with hand raised, bring the vehicle to a full stop, and shall not proceed again until he receives a signal so to do from the officer. Three or more blasts of the police whistle is the signal for alarm and indicates the approach of a fire engine or other danger.

ARTICLE 14. TURNS, HAND SIGNALS, STARTING AND STOPPING

39:4–123. Right and left hand turns

Except as otherwise provided in this article, the driver of a vehicle intending to turn at an intersection shall do so as follows:

(a) Right turns. Both the approach for a right turn and a right turn shall be made as close as practicable to the right-hand curb or edge of the roadway.

(b) Left turns on two-way roadways. At any intersection where traffic is permitted to move in both directions on each roadway entering the intersection, an approach for a left turn shall be made in that portion of the right half of the roadway nearest the center line thereof and by passing to the right of such center line where it enters the intersection and after entering the intersection the left turn shall be made so as to leave the intersection to the right of the center line of the roadway being entered. Whenever practicable the left turn shall be made in that portion of the intersection to the left of the center of the intersection.

(c) Left turns on other than two-way roadways. At any intersection where traffic is restricted to one direction on one or more of the roadways, the driver of a vehicle intending to turn left at any such intersection shall approach the intersection in the extreme left-hand lane lawfully available to traffic moving in the direction of travel of such vehicle and after entering the intersection the left turn shall be made so as to leave the intersection, as nearly as practicable, in the left-hand lane lawfully available to traffic moving in such direction upon the roadway being entered.

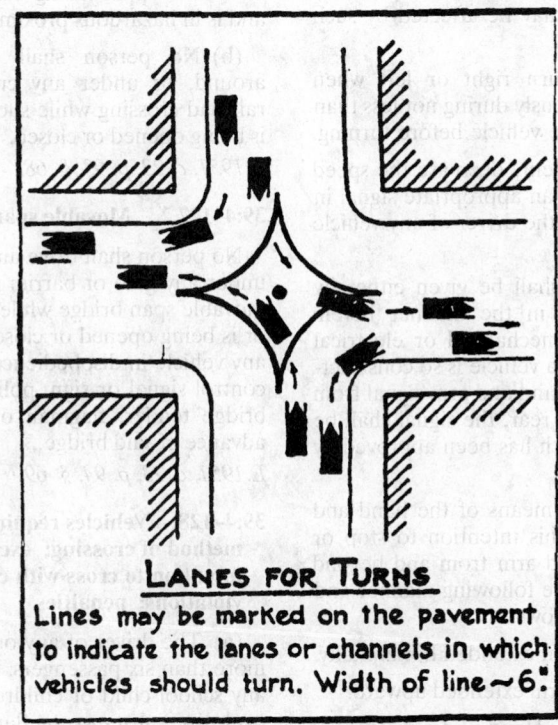

LANES FOR TURNS

Lines may be marked on the pavement to indicate the lanes or channels in which vehicles should turn. Width of line ~6"

Amended by L.1951, c. 23, p. 91, § 65.

39:4–124. Method of turning at intersection; local authorities may determine

The State Highway Commissioner and local authorities, with reference to highways under their respective jurisdictions, may modify the method provided in section 39:4–123 of this Title, of turning at intersections by clearly indicating by buttons, markers or other direction signs, within an intersection, the course to be followed by vehicles turning therein. No driver shall fail to turn in the manner so directed when such direction signs are installed by said authorities.

Amended by L.1951, c. 23, p. 92, § 66.

39:4–125. Turning on curve, grade or place where view obstructed or highway marked with "no U turn" sign

The driver of a vehicle shall not turn such vehicle around so as to proceed in the opposite direction upon any curve or upon the approach to or near the crest of a grade or at any place upon a highway as defined in R.S. 39:1–1 where the view of such vehicle is obstructed within a distance of five hundred feet along the highway in either direction; and no such vehicle shall be turned around so as to proceed in the opposite direction on a highway[1] which shall be conspicuously marked with signs stating "no U turn".

Amended by L.1987, c. 81, § 1, eff. March 11, 1987.

[1] Correction to main volume: "state" does not precede "highway" in the pamphlet copy of the law.

39:4–126. Signaling before starting, turning or stopping

No person shall turn a vehicle at an intersection unless the vehicle is in proper position upon the roadway as required in section 39:4–123, or turn a vehicle to enter a private road or driveway or otherwise turn a vehicle from a direct course or move right or left upon a roadway, or start or back a vehicle unless and until such movement can be made with safety. No person shall so turn any vehicle without giving an appropriate signal in the manner hereinafter provided in the event any other traffic may be affected by such movement.

A signal of intention to turn right or left when required shall be given continuously during not less than the last 100 feet traveled by the vehicle before turning.

No person shall stop or suddenly decrease the speed of a vehicle without first giving an appropriate signal in the manner provided herein to the driver of any vehicle immediately to the rear.

The signal herein required shall be given either by means of the hand and arm in the manner herein specified, or by an approved mechanical or electrical signal device, except that when a vehicle is so constructed or loaded as to prevent the hand and arm signal from being visible, both to front and rear, the signal shall be given by a device of a type which has been approved by the division.

When the signal is given by means of the hand and arm, the driver shall indicate his intention to stop or turn by extending the hand and arm from and beyond the left side of the vehicle in the following manner and such signals shall indicate as follows:

(a) Left turn.—Hand and arm extended horizontally.

(b) Right turn.—Hand and arm extended upward.

(c) Stop or decrease speed.—Hand and arm extended downward.

Amended by L.1951, c. 23, p. 92, § 67; L.1956, c. 107, p. 485, § 2.

39:4–127. Backing or turning in street

No vehicle shall back or make a turn in a street, if by so doing it interferes with other vehicles, but shall go around a block or to a street sufficiently wide to turn in without backing.

39:4–127.1. Railroad crossings; stopping

(a) Whenever any person driving a vehicle approaches a railroad grade crossing under any of the circumstances stated in this section, the driver of such vehicle shall stop within fifty feet but not less than fifteen feet from the nearest rail of such railroad, and shall not proceed until he can do so safely. The foregoing requirements shall apply when:

1. A clearly visible electric or mechanical signal device gives warning of the immediate approach of a railroad train;

2. A crossing gate is lowered or when a human flagman gives or continues to give a signal of the approach or passage of a railroad train;

3. A railroad train approaching within approximately one thousand five hundred feet of the highway crossing emits a signal audible from such distance and such railroad train, by reason of its speed or nearness to such crossing, is an immediate hazard;

4. An approaching railroad train is plainly visible and is in hazardous proximity to such crossing.

(b) No person shall drive any vehicle through, around, or under any crossing gate or barrier at a railroad crossing while such gate or barrier is closed or is being opened or closed.

L.1951, c. 23, p. 93, § 68.

39:4–127.2. Movable span bridges

No person shall drive any vehicle through, around, or under any gate or barrier at or on the approaches to a movable span bridge while such gate or barrier is closed or is being opened or closed, nor shall any person drive any vehicle in disobedience to the directions of a traffic control signal or sign, police officer or duly authorized bridge tender, flagman or gateman, located at or in advance of said bridge.

L.1951, c. 23, p. 94, § 69.

39:4–128. Vehicles required to stop at grade crossings; method of crossing; exceptions; notice to railroad of intention to cross with certain vehicles or machinery; violations; penalties

(a) The driver of any omnibus, designed for carrying more than six passengers, or of any school bus carrying any school child or children, or of any vehicle carrying explosive substance or flammable liquids as a cargo or part of a cargo, or of any commercial motor vehicle specified in 49 C.F.R. s.392.10(a) (1) through (6), before crossing at grade any track or tracks of a railroad shall stop such vehicle within 50 feet but not less than 15 feet from the nearest rail of such railroad and while so stopped listen and look in both directions along such track or tracks, for any approaching train, and for signals indicating the approach of a train. After stopping as required herein and upon proceeding when it is safe to do so, the driver of any said vehicle shall cross only in such gear of the vehicle that there will be no necessity for changing gears while traversing such crossing and the driver shall not shift gears while crossing the track or tracks. This section shall not apply to grade crossings which are no longer used for railroad traffic and which have been abandoned by the railroad company provided that appropriate signs have been posted to indicate that such grade crossing has been abandoned or is no longer used for any railroad traffic. This section shall not apply to grade crossings where the railroad track has been removed or paved over and the warning signs erected by the railroad in accordance with R.S.48:12–58 have been removed, provided that in such case written notice is given to the Commissioner of Transportation and to the appropriate State or local authority having jurisdiction over the highway, road, or street prior to the undertaking of such removal or paving of railroad track. This section shall also not apply to grade crossings marked with a sign reading "Exempt Crossing."

The Commissioner of Transportation is hereby vested with the exclusive authority to designate and mark any railroad grade crossings across any street or highway in this State with a sign "Exempt Crossing." The commissioner shall hold a public hearing before designating any crossing as exempt with notice of such hearing to be served in accordance with regulations promulgated by the commissioner.

The commissioner shall designate a grade crossing an exempt crossing when the potential for damage and injury from accidents between motor vehicles required to stop at grade crossings and other motor vehicles traveling in the same direction exceeds that between a train and the vehicles required to stop by law. Crossings designated as exempt crossings may include, but shall not be limited to, industrial, spurline and secondary crossings. The commissioner shall promulgate such regulations as are necessary to effectuate the purpose of the establishment of exempt crossings.

(b) No person shall operate or move any crawler-type tractor, wheel tractor, tractor engine with or without trailer or trailers attached, steam shovel, derrick, roller, self-propelled concrete mixer, or any self-propelled vehicle, commercial motor vehicle, equipment, machinery, apparatus or structure having a normal operating speed of 10 or less miles per hour or a vertical body or load clearance of less than ½ inch per foot of the distance between any two adjacent axles or in any event of less than 9 inches, measured above the level surface of a roadway, upon or across any track or tracks at a railroad grade crossing without first complying with the following requirements.

Notice of any such intended crossing shall be given to the nearest superintendent or trainmaster of such railroad. Such notice shall specify the approximate time of crossing and a reasonable time shall be given to such railroad to provide proper protection at such crossing.

After concluding satisfactory arrangements with the proper officer of the railroad and before making any such crossing, the person operating or moving any such vehicle or equipment shall first stop the same not less than 15 feet nor more than 50 feet from the nearest rail of such railroad, and while so stopped shall listen and look in both directions along such track or tracks for any approaching train and for signals indicating the approach of a train, and shall not proceed until the crossing can be made safely.

No such crossing shall be made when warning is given by automatic signal or crossing gates or a flagman or otherwise of the immediate approach of a railroad train or car. If the flagman is provided by the railroad, movement over the crossing shall be made under his jurisdiction.

(c) Any person violating the provisions of this section shall be punished by a fine of not more than $50.00 for the first offense and for the second offense a fine of not more than $100.00, or by imprisonment for not more than 30 days, or by both such fine and imprisonment.

(d) This section shall not be construed as limiting the authority of any municipality to adopt police regulations governing the operation of omnibuses and to provide penalties for their violation, or to relieve the owner or operator of such omnibus subject to the jurisdiction of the Board of Public Utilities from any penalty prescribed by the laws of this State for violation of orders of such board.

Amended by L.1938, c. 164, p. 373, § 1, eff. May 12, 1938; L.1941, c. 260, p. 691, § 3; L.1953, c. 294, p. 1832, § 1; L.1971, c. 393, § 1, eff. Jan. 7, 1972; L.1973, c. 177, § 1, eff. June 8, 1973; L.1979, c. 48, § 1, eff. March 21, 1979; L.2005, c. 147, § 9, eff. Sept. 30, 2005.

39:4–128.1. Buses used for transportation of children stopped to receive or discharge passengers; duty of motorists and of bus driver; violations; penalties

On highways having roadways not divided by safety islands or physical traffic separation installations, the driver of a vehicle approaching or overtaking a bus, which is being used solely for the transportation of children to or from school or a summer day camp or any school connected activity and which has stopped for the purpose of receiving or discharging any child, shall stop such vehicle not less than 25 feet from such school bus and keep such vehicle stationary until such child has entered said bus or has alighted and reached the side of such highway and until a flashing red light is no longer exhibited by the bus; provided, such bus is designated as a school bus by one sign on the front and one sign on the rear, with each letter on such signs at least four inches in height.

On highways having dual or multiple roadways separated by safety islands or physical traffic separation installations, the driver of a vehicle overtaking a school bus, which has stopped for the purpose of receiving or discharging any child, shall stop such vehicle not less than 25 feet from such school bus and keep such vehicle stationary until such child has entered said bus or has alighted and reached the side of the highway and until a flashing red light is no longer exhibited by the bus.

On highways having dual or multiple roadways separated by safety islands or physical traffic separation installations, the driver of a vehicle on another roadway approaching a school bus, which has stopped for the purpose of receiving or discharging any child, shall reduce the speed of his vehicle to not more than 10 miles per hour and shall not resume normal speed until the vehicle has passed the bus and has passed any child who may have alighted therefrom or be about to enter said bus.

For purposes of this section, "highway" means the entire width between the boundary lines of every way whether publicly or privately maintained when any part thereof is open to the public for purposes of vehicular travel.

Whenever a school bus is parked at the curb for the purpose of receiving children directly from a school or a summer day camp or any school connected activity or discharging children to enter a school, or a summer day camp or any school connected activity, which is located on the same side of the street as that on which the bus is parked, drivers of vehicles shall be permitted to pass said bus without stopping, but at a speed not in excess of 10 miles per hour.

The driver of a bus which is being used solely for the transportation of children to or from school or a summer day camp or any school connected activity shall continue to exhibit a flashing red light and shall not start his bus until every child who may have alighted therefrom shall have reached a place of safety.

Any person who shall violate any provision of this act shall be subject to (1) a fine of not less than $100.00, (2) imprisonment for not more than 15 days or community service for 15 days in such form and on such terms as the court shall deem appropriate, (3) or both for the first offense, and a fine not less than $250.00, imprisonment for not more than 15 days, or both for each subsequent offense. The penalties shall be enforced and recovered pursuant to the provisions of chapter 5 of Title 39 of the Revised Statutes. There shall be a rebuttable presumption that the registered owner of the vehicle which was involved in the violation of this section was the person who committed the act. Any person who suppresses, by way of concealment or destruction, any evidence of a violation of this section or who suppresses the identity of the violator shall be subject to a fine of $100.

The Director of the Division of Motor Vehicles may also revoke the license to drive a motor vehicle of any person who shall have been guilty of such willful violation of any of the provisions of this act as shall, in the discretion of the director, justify such revocation, but the director shall, at all times, have power to validate such a license which has been revoked, or to grant a new license to any person whose license to drive

a motor vehicle shall have been revoked pursuant to this act.

L.1942, c. 192, p. 564, § 1. Amended by L.1948, c. 132, p. 854, § 1; L.1949, c. 102, p. 425, § 1; L.1951, c. 23, p. 96, § 71; L.1966, c. 234, § 1; L.1968, c. 171, § 1, eff. July 16, 1968; L.1983, c. 27, § 1, eff. Jan. 25, 1983; L.1989, c. 319, § 1, eff. Jan. 12, 1990; L.1992, c. 72, § 1, eff. July 30, 1992; L.2000, c. 85, § 2, eff. Aug. 14, 2000.

39:4–128.2.   Repealed by L.1989, c. 36, § 1, eff. March 9, 1989

39:4–128.3.   Definitions

For the purposes of this act:

a.   "Division" means the Division of Motor Vehicles.

b.   "Frozen dessert truck" means every motor vehicle in which frozen desserts are carried for purposes of retail sale on the streets of the State.

c.   "Vend" or "vending" means offering frozen desserts for sale from a motor vehicle on the streets of the State.

d.   "Frozen desserts" means ice cream, frozen custard, French ice cream, French custard ice cream, sherbet, fruit sherbet, ice milk, ice, water ice, nonfruit sherbets, nonfruit water ices, freezer made milk shakes, quiescently frozen confection, quiescently frozen dairy confection, whipped cream confection, bisque tortoni, artificially sweetened ice cream, or artificially sweetened ice milk, special frozen dietary foods, frozen yogurt, mellorine frozen desserts, as all such products are commonly known, together with any such mix used in frozen desserts and any products which are similar in appearance, odor or taste to such products or are prepared or frozen as such products are customarily prepared or frozen whether made with dairy or non-dairy products and ice flavored with syrup.

L.1979, c. 438, § 1.

39:4–128.4.   Approaching or overtaking stopped frozen dessert truck; stopping

a.   The driver of a vehicle approaching or overtaking from either direction a frozen dessert truck stopped on the highway shall stop before reaching the truck when the flashing red lights and stop signal arm described in section 3 are in use. After stopping, a driver may proceed past such truck at a reasonable and prudent speed, not exceeding 15 miles per hour, and shall yield the right of way to any pedestrian who crosses the roadway to or from the frozen dessert truck.

b.   The driver of a vehicle on a highway having dual or multiple roadways separated by safety islands or physical traffic separation installations need not stop upon meeting or passing a frozen dessert truck on another roadway.

L.1979, c. 438, § 2.

39:4–128.5.   Frozen dessert truck; equipment

In addition to other equipment required by law, every frozen dessert truck shall be equipped with:

a.   Signal lamps mounted at the same level and as high and as widely spaced laterally as practicable. These lamps shall be 5 to 7 inches in diameter and shall display two alternately flashing red lights visible at 500 feet to the front and rear in normal sunlight upon a straight level highway.

b.   A stop signal arm that can be extended horizontally from the left side of the truck. When such arm is extended, the side of the stop signal arm nearest the truck shall be 7¼ inches long and parallel to the side of the truck. The side furthest from the truck shall be 18 inches long and parallel to the side nearest the truck. The two sides shall be 18 inches apart creating a symmetrical, trapezoidal shape. Two alternately flashing red lights shall be located in the outside corners of the extended signal arm and such corners shall be rounded to conform with the shape of the lights. Each red light shall be 3 to 5 inches in diameter and visible at 300 feet to the front and rear in normal sunlight upon a straight and level street. Both sides of the signal arm shall have a red reflectorized background and the following legend: The word "STOP" shall appear in 6-inch high, 1 inch wide white letters in the middle of the signal arm; above the word "STOP," the phrase "IF SAFE" shall appear in 2 inch high, one-quarter inch wide white letters; below the word "STOP," the phrase "THEN GO" shall appear in 2 inch high, one-quarter inch wide white letters. All colors shall meet specifications in the most recently published Federal Highway Administration Standard Color Charts. The bottom of the extended signal arm shall be 42 inches above the street.

c.   A convex mirror mounted on the front so the driver in his normal seating position can see the area in front of the truck obscured by the hood.

L.1979, c. 438, § 3.

39:4–128.6.   Stopped frozen dessert truck; duty of driver

a.   The driver of a frozen dessert truck stopped on the highway for the purpose of vending shall actuate the special red flashing lights and extend the stop signal arm required by section 3 [1].

b.   These lights and the stop signal arm shall not be used when the truck is in motion nor at any time the truck is stopped for a purpose other than vending.

L.1979, c. 438, § 4.

[1] N.J.S.A. § 39:4–128.5.

39:4–128.7.   Conditions for vending

a.   A person shall not vend on streets where the speed limit exceeds 30 miles per hour.

b.   A person shall not vend within 500 feet of any property used as a grade or junior high or middle school

from 1 hour before the regular school day to 1 hour after the regular school day; provided, this subsection shall not apply on days when school is not attended by children nor on school property when vending has been approved in writing by the board of education.

c.   A person shall vend only when the frozen dessert truck is lawfully parked or stopped.

d.   A person shall vend only from the side of the truck away from moving traffic and as near as possible to the curb or edge of the highway.

e.   A person shall not vend to a person standing in the roadway.

f.   A person shall not stop on the left side of a one-way highway to vend.

L.1979, c. 438, § 5.

39:4–128.8.   Backing up truck to make sale; prohibition

The driver of a frozen dessert truck shall not back up the same to make or attempt a sale.

L.1979, c. 438, § 6.

39:4–128.9.   Riding in or on frozen dessert truck; authorized persons only

a.   The driver of a frozen dessert truck shall not permit any unauthorized person to ride in or on the vehicle.

b.   A person shall not ride in or on a frozen dessert truck unless employed by its owner or unless authorized in writing to do so by the owner or police department.

L.1979, c. 438, § 7.

39:4–128.10.   Violations; penalty

Any person violating any provision of this act shall be liable for a penalty of not more than $100.00 for each offense, which may be enforced by summary proceedings.

L.1979, c. 438, § 8.

39:4–128.11.   Railroad crossings; requirements for certain commercial motor vehicles; employer liability for violations

a.   A driver of a commercial motor vehicle, other than a commercial motor vehicle that is required to stop at a railroad crossing in accordance with R.S.39:4–128, shall, upon approaching a railroad grade crossing, drive at a rate of speed that will permit the commercial motor vehicle to be stopped before reaching the nearest rail of the crossing. A driver shall not drive a commercial motor vehicle upon or over a railroad crossing until he has exercised due caution to ascertain that a train is not approaching the crossing.

b.   A driver of a commercial motor vehicle, other than a commercial motor vehicle that is required to stop at a railroad crossing in accordance with R. S.39:4–128, shall stop that commercial motor vehicle before reaching the nearest rail of the crossing, if the tracks of the crossing are not clear of other vehicles or if there is insufficient space to drive the commercial motor vehicle completely through the crossing without stopping the commercial motor vehicle.

c. An employer shall not knowingly allow, require, permit or authorize a driver to operate a commercial motor vehicle in violation of R.S.39:4–128, section 68 of P.L.1951, c. 23 (C.39:4–127.1) or this section. An employer who is convicted of any such violation shall be fined not more than $10,000.

L.2005, c. 147, § 10, eff. Sept. 30, 2005.

ARTICLE 15. ACCIDENTS AND REPORTS

39:4–129. Action in case of accident

(a) The driver of any vehicle, knowingly involved in an accident resulting in injury or death to any person shall immediately stop the vehicle at the scene of the accident or as close thereto as possible but shall then forthwith return to and in every event shall remain at the scene until he has fulfilled the requirements of subsection (c) of this section. Every such stop shall be made without obstructing traffic more than is necessary. Any person who shall violate this subsection shall be fined not less than $2,500 nor more than $5,000, or be imprisoned for a period of 180 days, or both. The term of imprisonment required by this subsection shall be imposed only if the accident resulted in death or injury to a person other than the driver convicted of violating this section.

In addition, any person convicted under this subsection shall forfeit his right to operate a motor vehicle over the highways of this State for a period of one year from the date of his conviction for the first offense and for a subsequent offense shall thereafter permanently forfeit his right to operate a motor vehicle over the highways of this State.

(b) The driver of any vehicle knowingly involved in an accident resulting only in damage to a vehicle, including his own vehicle, or other property which is attended by any person shall immediately stop his vehicle at the scene of such accident or as close thereto as possible, but shall then forthwith return to and in every event shall remain at the scene of such accident until he has fulfilled the requirements of subsection (c) of this section. Every such stop shall be made without obstructing traffic more than is necessary. Any person who shall violate this subsection shall be fined not less than $200 nor more than $400, or be imprisoned for a period of not more than 30 days, or both, for the first offense, and for a subsequent offense, shall be fined not less than $400 nor more than $600, or be imprisoned for a period of not less than 30 days nor more than 90 days or both.

In addition, a person who violates this subsection shall, for a first offense, forfeit the right to operate a motor vehicle in this State for a period of six months

from the date of conviction, and for a period of one year from the date of conviction for any subsequent offense.

(c) The driver of any vehicle knowingly involved in an accident resulting in injury or death to any person or damage to any vehicle or property shall give his name and address and exhibit his operator's license and registration certificate of his vehicle to the person injured or whose vehicle or property was damaged and to any police officer or witness of the accident, and to the driver or occupants of the vehicle collided with and render to a person injured in the accident reasonable assistance, including the carrying of that person to a hospital or a physician for medical or surgical treatment, if it is apparent that the treatment is necessary or is requested by the injured person.

In the event that none of the persons specified are in condition to receive the information to which they otherwise would be entitled under this subsection, and no police officer is present, the driver of any vehicle involved in such accident after fulfilling all other requirements of subsections (a) and (b) of this section, insofar as possible on his part to be performed, shall forthwith report such accident to the nearest office of the local police department or of the county police of the county or of the State Police and submit thereto the information specified in this subsection.

(d) The driver of any vehicle which knowingly collides with or is knowingly involved in an accident with any vehicle or other property which is unattended resulting in any damage to such vehicle or other property shall immediately stop and shall then and there locate and notify the operator or owner of such vehicle or other property of the name and address of the driver and owner of the vehicle striking the unattended vehicle or other property or, in the event an unattended vehicle is struck and the driver or owner thereof cannot be immediately located, shall attach securely in a conspicuous place in or on such vehicle a written notice giving the name and address of the driver and owner of the vehicle doing the striking or, in the event other property is struck and the owner thereof cannot be immediately located, shall notify the nearest office of the local police department or of the county police of the county or of the State Police and in addition shall notify the owner of the property as soon as the owner can be identified and located. Any person who violates this subsection shall be punished as provided in subsection (b) of this section.

(e) There shall be a permissive inference that the driver of any motor vehicle involved in an accident resulting in injury or death to any person or damage in the amount of $250.00 or more to any vehicle or property has knowledge that he was involved in such accident.

For purposes of this section, it shall not be a defense that the operator of the motor vehicle was unaware of the existence or extent of personal injury or property damage caused by the accident as long as the operator was aware that he was involved in an accident.

There shall be a permissive inference that the registered owner of the vehicle which was involved in an accident subject to the provisions of this section was the person involved in the accident; provided, however, if that vehicle is owned by a rental car company or is a leased vehicle, there shall be a permissive inference that the renter or authorized driver pursuant to a rental car contract or the lessee, and not the owner of the vehicle, was involved in the accident, and the requirements and penalties imposed pursuant to this section shall be applicable to that renter or authorized driver or lessee and not the owner of the vehicle.

Any person who suppresses, by way of concealment or destruction, any evidence of a violation of this section or who suppresses the identity of the violator shall be subject to a fine of not less than $250 or more than $1,000.

Amended by L.1940, c. 147, p. 313, § 1; L.1967, c. 189, § 1, eff. July 27, 1967; L.1977, c. 407, § 1, eff. Feb. 23, 1978; L.1978, c. 180, § 1, eff. Jan. 3, 1979; L.1979, c. 463, § 1, eff. Feb. 27, 1980; L.1994, c. 183, § 1, eff. Dec. 23, 1994; L.2003, c. 55, § 1, eff. June 1, 2003; L.2007, c. 266, § 1, eff. Jan. 13, 2008.

39:4–130. Report of accidents; notice when person is injured or killed

The driver of a vehicle or street car involved in an accident resulting in injury to or death of any person, or damage to property of any one person in excess of $500.00 shall by the quickest means of communication give notice of such accident to the local police department or to the nearest office of the county police of the county or of the State Police, and in addition shall within 10 days after such accident forward a written report of such accident to the commission on forms furnished by it. Such written reports shall contain sufficiently detailed information with reference to a motor vehicle accident, including the cause, the conditions then existing, the persons and vehicles involved and such information as may be necessary to enable the chief administrator to determine whether the requirements for the deposit of security required by law are inapplicable by reason of the existence of insurance or other circumstances. The chief administrator may rely upon the accuracy of the information contained in any such report, unless he has reason to believe that the report is erroneous. The commission may require operators involved in accidents to file supplemental reports of accidents upon forms furnished by it when in the opinion of the commission, the original report is insufficient. The reports shall be without prejudice, shall be for the information of the commission, and shall not be open to public inspection. The fact that the reports have been so made shall be admissible in evidence solely to prove a compliance with this section, but no report or any part thereof or statement contained therein shall be admissible in evidence for any other purpose in any proceeding or action arising out of the accident.

Whenever the driver of a vehicle is physically incapable of giving immediate notice or making a written report of an accident as required in this section and there was another occupant in the vehicle at the time of the accident capable of giving notice or making a report, such occupant shall make or cause to be made said notice or report not made by the driver.

Whenever the driver is physically incapable of making a written report of an accident as required by this section and such driver is not the owner of the vehicle, then the owner of the vehicle involved in such accident shall make such report not made by the driver.

In those cases where a driver knowingly violates the provisions of this section by failing to make a written report of an accident, there shall be a permissive inference that the registered owner of the vehicle which was involved in that accident was the person involved in the accident; provided, however, if that vehicle is owned by a rental car company or is a leased vehicle, there shall be a permissive inference that the renter or authorized driver pursuant to a rental car contract or the lessee, and not the owner of the vehicle, was the person involved in the accident, and the requirements and penalties imposed pursuant to this section shall be applicable to that renter or authorized driver or lessee and not the owner of the vehicle.

Any person who suppresses, by way of concealment or destruction, any evidence of a violation of this section or who suppresses the identity of the violator shall be subject to a fine of not less than $250 or more than $1,000.

A written report of an accident shall not be required by this section if a law enforcement officer submits a written report of the accident to the commission pursuant to R.S.39:4–131.

Except as otherwise provided in this section, a person who knowingly violates this section shall be fined not less than $30 or more than $100.

The chief administrator may revoke or suspend the operator's license privilege and registration privilege of a person who violates this section.

For purposes of this section, it shall not be a defense that the operator of the motor vehicle was unaware of the existence or extent of personal injury or property damage caused by the accident as long as the operator was aware that he was involved in an accident.

Amended by L.1951, c. 23, p. 97, § 72; L.1953, c. 187, p. 1483, § 1; L.1967, c. 189, § 2, eff. July 29, 1967; L.1983, c. 193, § 1, eff. May 24, 1983; L.1994, c. 183, § 2, eff. Dec. 23, 1994; L.2007, c. 266, § 2, eff. Jan. 13, 2008.

39:4–131. Reports; forms; use as evidence; inspection; confidentiality

The commission shall prepare and supply to police departments and other suitable agencies, forms for accident reports calling for sufficiently detailed information with reference to a motor vehicle accident, including the cause, the conditions then existing, the persons and vehicles involved, the compliance with P.L.1984, c. 179 (C.39:3–76.2e et seq.) by the operators and passengers of the vehicles involved in the accident, whether the operator of the vehicle was using a cellular telephone when the accident occurred, and such other information as the chief administrator may require.

Every law enforcement officer who investigates a vehicle accident of which report must be made as required in this Title, or who otherwise prepares a written report as a result of an accident or thereafter by interviewing the participants or witnesses, shall forward a written report of such accident to the commission, on forms furnished by it, within five days after his investigation of the accident.

Such written reports required to be forwarded by law enforcement officers and the information contained therein shall not be privileged or held confidential. Every citizen of this State shall have the right, during regular business hours and under supervision, to inspect and copy such reports and shall also have the right in person to purchase copies of the reports at the same fee established by section 6 of P.L.2001, c. 404 (C.47:1A–5). If copies of reports are requested other than in person, an additional fee of up to $5.00 for the first three pages and $1.00 per page thereafter may be added to cover the administrative costs of the report. Upon request, a police department shall send an accident report to a person through the mail or via fax as defined in section 2 of P.L.1976, c. 23 (C.19:59–2). The police department may require the person requesting the report to provide a completed request form and the appropriate fee prior to faxing or mailing the report. The police department shall provide the person requesting the report with the option of submitting the form and providing the appropriate fee either in person, through the mail, or via fax as defined in section 2 of P.L.1976, c. 23 (C.19:59–2).

The provisions of any other law or regulation to the contrary notwithstanding, reports obtained pursuant to this act shall not be subject to confidentiality requirements except as provided by section 28 of P.L.1960, c. 52 (C.2A:84A–28).

When a motor vehicle accident results in the death or incapacitation of the driver or any passenger, the law enforcement officer responsible for notifying the next of kin that their relative is deceased or incapacitated, also shall inform the relative, in writing, how to obtain a copy of the accident report required by this section and the name, address, and telephone number of the person storing the motor vehicle pursuant to section 1 of P.L.1964, c. 81 (C.39:10A–1).

Amended by L.1951, c. 23, p. 98, § 73; L.1952, c. 177, p. 599, § 1; L.1967, c. 189, § 3, eff. July 27, 1967; L.1979, c. 412, § 1, eff. Feb. 8, 1980; L.1981, c. 105, § 1, eff. April 2, 1981; L.1987, c. 26, § 1; L.2001, c. 161, § 2, eff. Jan. 1, 2002; L.2007, c. 20, § 1, eff. Jan. 26, 2007; L.2008, c. 107, § 1, eff. April 1, 2009.

39:4–131.1. Inconsistent rule, regulation, resolution or ordinance inconsistent with act or establishing fee in excess of fee under Right to Know Law; supersedure

Any rule, regulation, resolution or ordinance inconsistent with this act or establishing a fee in excess of the fee permitted by section 2 of P.L.1963, c. 73 (C. 47:1A–2) is superseded insofar as it is inconsistent or to the extent that it exceeds the fee so established.
L.1979, c. 412, § 2, eff. Feb. 8, 1980.

39:4–132. Certain damages reported by repairman

The person in charge of a garage or repair shop to which is brought a motor vehicle which shows evidence of having been involved in an accident of which report must be made by the driver thereof as provided in section 39:4–130 of the Revised Statutes or of having been struck by a bullet shall report to the nearest office of the local police department or of the county police of the county or of the State Police within 24 hours after the motor vehicle is received, giving the serial number, registration number and, if known, the name and address of the owner or operator of the vehicle.

Any person who shall violate this section shall be fined not less than $100.00 nor more than $500.00 or be imprisoned for a period of not less than 30 days nor more than 90 days, or both.
Amended by L.1967, c. 189, § 4, eff. July 27, 1967.

39:4–133. Repealed by L.1967, c. 189, § 6, eff. July 27, 1967

39:4–134. Report of death to director

Every county prosecutor, county medical examiner, or other official performing like functions shall make a report to the director with respect to a death found to have been the result of a motor vehicle accident.
Amended by L.1951, c. 23, p. 99, § 74; L.1971, c. 2, § 17, eff. Jan. 15, 1971.

39:4–134.1. Application of article

The duties and responsibilities imposed by the provisions of this article upon all persons designated therein shall apply to accidents occurring upon highways and elsewhere throughout the State.
L.1967, c. 189, § 5.

ARTICLE 16. PARKING

39:4–135. Parking; direction and side of street; angle parking; one-way street

The operator of a vehicle shall not stop, stand or park the vehicle in a roadway other than parallel with the edge of the roadway headed in the direction of traffic, on the right-hand side of the road and with the curb side of the vehicle within six inches of the edge of the roadway, except as follows:

a.   Upon those streets which have been designated by ordinance and have been marked or signed for angle parking, vehicles shall be parked at the angle to the curb designated and indicated by the ordinance and marks or signs.

b.   Upon one-way streets, local authorities may permit parking of vehicles parallel with the left-hand edge of the roadway headed in the direction of traffic, on the left-hand side of the road and with the curb side of the vehicle within six inches of the edge of the roadway.
Amended by L.1951, c. 23, p. 99, § 75.

39:4–136.   Parking on highway; removing vehicle; disabled vehicle

No person shall park or leave standing a vehicle, whether attended or unattended, upon the roadway, outside of a business or residence district, when it is practicable to park or leave it standing off the roadway. In no event shall a person park or leave standing a vehicle whether attended or unattended, upon a roadway, unless a clear and unobstructed width of not less than fifteen feet upon the roadway opposite the standing vehicle is left for free passage of other vehicles thereon, nor unless a clear view of the vehicle may be obtained from a distance of two hundred feet in each direction upon the roadway.

In the event that a vehicle is disabled or otherwise unable to proceed while on the roadway of a highway, the driver or person in charge of such vehicle shall immediately, by the quickest means of communication, notify the nearest police authority.

Any vehicle, upon a roadway, which is disabled to the extent that the operator cannot move it, or any unoccupied vehicle parked or standing in violation of this chapter shall be deemed a nuisance and a menace to the safe and proper regulation of traffic and any peace officer may provide for the removal of such vehicle. The owner shall pay the reasonable costs of the removal and storage which may result from such removal, before regaining possession of the vehicle.
Amended by L.1951, c. 23, p. 99, § 76.

39:4–137.   Vehicle without driver; brakes set; motor stopped; wheels turned to curb

No person having control or charge of a motor vehicle shall allow it to stand on a highway unattended without first effectively setting the brakes thereon and stopping the motor thereof, and, when standing on a grade, without turning the wheels thereof to the curb or side of the highway.

39:4–138.   Places where parking prohibited; exceptions; moving vehicle not under one's control into prohibited area

Except when necessary to avoid conflict with other traffic or in compliance with the directions of a traffic or police officer or traffic sign or signal, no operator of a vehicle shall stand or park the vehicle in any of the following places:

a.   Within an intersection;

b.   On a crosswalk;

c.   Between a safety zone and the adjacent curb or within at least 20 feet of a point on the curb immediately opposite the end of a safety zone;

d.   In front of a public or private driveway;

e.   (1) Within 25 feet of the nearest crosswalk or side line of a street or intersecting highway, except at alleys and as provided in section 2 of P.L. 2009, c. 257 (C.39:4–138.6); or

(2) Within 10 feet of the nearest crosswalk or side line of a street or intersecting highway, if a curb extension or bulbout has been constructed at that crosswalk;

f.   On a sidewalk;

g.   In any appropriately marked "No Parking" space established pursuant to the duly promulgated regulations of the Commissioner of Transportation;

h.   Within 50 feet of a "stop" sign except as provided in section 2 of P.L.2009, c. 257 (C.39:4–138.6);

i.   Within 10 feet of a fire hydrant;

j.   Within 50 feet of the nearest rail of a railroad crossing;

k.   Within 20 feet of the driveway entrance to any fire station and on the side of a street opposite the entrance to any fire station within 75 feet of said entrance, when properly signposted;

l.   Alongside or opposite any street excavation or obstruction when stopping, standing, or parking would obstruct traffic, when properly signposted;

m.   On the roadway side of any vehicle stopped or parked at the edge or curb of a street;

n.   Upon any bridge or other elevated structure upon a highway, or within a highway tunnel or underpass, or on the immediate approaches thereto except where space for parking is provided;

o.   In any space on public or private property appropriately marked for vehicles for the physically handicapped pursuant to P.L.1977, c. 202 (C.39:4–197.5), P.L.1975, c. 217 (C.52:27D–119 et seq.) or any other applicable law unless the vehicle is authorized by law to be parked therein and a handicapped person is either the driver or a passenger in that vehicle. State, county or municipal law enforcement officers or parking enforcement authority officers shall enforce the parking restrictions on spaces appropriately marked for vehicles for the physically handicapped on both public and private property.

No person shall move a vehicle not lawfully under his control into any such prohibited area or away from a curb such distance as is unlawful.

Amended by L.1948, c. 342, p. 1346, § 2; L.1951, c. 23, p. 100, § 77; L.1981, c. 20, § 1, eff. Feb. 6, 1981; L.1989, c. 201, § 1, eff. June 1, 1990; L.2009, c. 107, § 2, eff. Aug. 6, 2009; L.2009, c. 257, § 1, eff. April 1, 2010.

39:4–138.1. "No parking" zones on highways

The commissioner, by regulations, shall have authority to establish and maintain "no parking" zones on portions of State highways where parking is deemed hazardous or inimical to the proper flow of traffic.

"No parking" zones so established shall be clearly marked by appropriate signs of a type and design according to specifications adopted by the commissioner.

L.1948, c. 342, p. 1346, § 1. Amended by L.1951, c. 23, p. 101, § 78; L.2003, c. 13, § 52 (contingent effective date).

39:4–138.2. Repealed by L.1999, c. 319, § 2, eff. Jan. 6, 2000

39:4–138.3. Ordinance permitting parking in front of private driveway

Notwithstanding the provisions of R.S. 39:4–138 to the contrary, any municipality may by ordinance, permit the parking of motor vehicles in front of private driveways whenever both the motor vehicle and driveway involved are owned by the same person, whenever the motor vehicle is owned by a member of the same household as the owner of the private driveway, or whenever the owner of the private driveway authorizes the parking of a motor vehicle in front of the private driveway; and where such parking is not otherwise prohibited and the permitting thereof would not interfere with the normal flow of traffic.

L.1991, c. 297, § 1, eff. Oct. 4, 1991.

39:4–138.4. Issuance of permit for parking in front of driveway; application; number of permits

Any municipality enacting an ordinance pursuant to section 1 of this act [1] shall provide for the issuance of permits which authorize the parking of motor vehicles in front of private driveways and identify the location of the driveway in front of which the parking of a motor vehicle is permitted. The permits shall be issued to owners of private driveways and to members of the same household as the owner of a private driveway provided that a completed application for a permit has been filed as required by the municipality.

An owner of a private driveway shall be eligible to apply for up to three permits for his own motor vehicles or for use by other parties authorized by the owner to park in front of the private driveway. Each member of the owner's household who owns a motor vehicle shall also be eligible to apply for a permit issued under this section. The permit shall be 5½ inches by 8½ inches in size, shall bear an appropriate certification of authenticity and shall be displayed prominently within the vehicle when it is parked so as to be seen from the middle of the street.

L.1991, c. 297, § 2, eff. Oct. 4, 1991.

[1] N.J.S.A. § 39:4–138.3.

39:4–138.5. Display of permit required; fees

A motor vehicle shall not be permitted to be parked in front of a private driveway unless the owner of the private driveway or a member of the owner's household has been issued a valid permit and the permit is properly displayed, or unless the owner has authorized another party to use and display the owner's permit for parking in front of the private driveway, and the permit is valid and properly displayed. A municipality may, by ordinance, establish a fee for these permits.

L.1991, c. 297, § 3, eff. Oct. 4, 1991.

39:4–138.6. Ordinance setting forth permissible parking distances; exception

A municipality may mandate by ordinance the permissible distance a person may park a motor vehicle from a crosswalk, side line of a street or intersecting highway, or "stop" sign. A municipality may not, however, permit parking within 25 feet of a crosswalk or side line of a street or intersecting highway or within 50 feet of a "stop" sign in a school zone during hours when school is in session.

L.2009, c. 257, § 2, eff. April 1, 2010.

39:4–139. Loading or unloading passengers or materials; period at certain places

No operator of a vehicle shall stand or park the vehicle for a period of time longer than is necessary for the loading or unloading of passengers or materials or longer than is hereinafter provided. The loading or unloading of passengers shall not consume more than three minutes in an alley or at a curb adjacent to the entrance of a school, church, theatre, hotel, hospital or any other place of public assemblage during hours designated by official signs.

39:4–139.1. Repealed by L.1985, c. 14, § 14

39:4–139.2. Short title

This act shall be known and may be cited as "The Parking Offenses Adjudication Act."

L.1985, c. 14, § 1.

39:4–139.3. Definitions

As used in this act:

a. "Director" means the Director of the Division of Motor Vehicles.

b. "Division" means the Division of Motor Vehicles in the Department of Law and Public Safety.

c. "Parking offense" means a violation of a State statute, an ordinance or resolution adopted by a county, municipality or authority or a regulation issued by a State authority which regulates the parking of vehicles. For purposes of this act, violations of ordinances or regulations will be within the civil jurisdiction of the court.

d. "Parking ticket" means the summons issued alleging that a parking offense has occurred.

L.1985, c. 14, § 2.

39:4–139.4. Uniform traffic ticket; complaint and summons; contents; personal service

a. The complaint and summons shall be a uniform traffic ticket in the form prescribed by the Administrative Director of the Courts and shall contain information advising the person to whom it is issued of the manner in which and the time within which an answer to the offense alleged is required. The parking ticket shall also advise that penalties may result from a failure to answer, that the failure to answer or appear shall be considered an admission of liability, and that a default judgment may be entered against the owner of the vehicle.

b. A parking ticket shall be served personally upon the operator of a vehicle who is present at the time of service, and his name shall be recorded on the parking ticket, together with the plate number and type as shown by the registration plates of the vehicle and the make or model of the vehicle. If the operator is not present, the parking ticket shall be served upon the owner of the vehicle by affixing the parking ticket to the vehicle in a conspicuous place, or by any other method appropriate under R. 4:4–4 of the Rules Governing the Courts of the State of New Jersey.

c. A parking ticket shall also contain sufficient information to inform the person of the nature, date, time and location of the offense alleged. Service of a parking ticket by affixation as provided in subsection b. of this section shall have the same effect as if the parking ticket was personally served on the owner or operator of the vehicle.

d. The original parking ticket shall be signed by the complainant, who shall certify to the truth of the facts set forth therein. The original parking ticket or a true copy of the parking ticket shall be considered a record kept in the ordinary business of the enforcement agency and shall be prima facie evidence of the facts contained therein.

e. An operator of a vehicle who is not the owner, but who uses or operates the vehicle with the permission of the owner, express or implied, shall be considered the agent of the owner to receive parking tickets served in accordance with subsection b. of this section.

L.1985, c. 14, § 3.

39:4–139.5. Joint liability of owner and operator; recovery by owner against operator; leased vehicles

a. Except as provided in subsection b. of this section, the owner and operator shall be jointly liable for parking offenses, unless the owner can show that the vehicle was used without his consent, express or implied. An owner who pays any fine, penalty, civil judgment, costs or administrative fees in connection with a parking offense shall have the right to recover that sum from the operator in a court of competent jurisdiction.

b. (1) The owner of a motor vehicle who has leased the motor vehicle shall not be liable for a parking offense when the motor vehicle is under the control or in the possession of the lessee if, upon notice of a parking offense, the owner of a motor vehicle which was leased at the time of the offense notifies the clerk of the court where the case is pending, by a notarized statement of the name and address of the lessee. The notarized statement shall be in a form prescribed by the Administrative Director of the Courts.

(2) After providing the name and address of the lessee, the owner shall not be required to attend a hearing on the offense, unless notified that the offense may have been caused by mechanical failure of the vehicle which resulted from the owner's failure to maintain the vehicle.

(3) Paragraph (1) of this subsection shall not apply to a parking offense which was caused by mechanical failure of the vehicle which resulted from the owner's failure to maintain the vehicle.

The lessee of the motor vehicle who intends to claim the offense resulted from the owner's failure to maintain the vehicle shall notify the clerk of the court where the case is pending and the owner of the vehicle of this claim within five days after receiving notice of the offense or at least seven days prior to the date the case will be heard by the court, whichever is later.

(4) If the owner of the vehicle fails to comply with the provisions of paragraph (1) of this subsection, the court hearing the violation may take any action which the interests of justice require, including finding the owner of the motor vehicle liable for the parking offense.

L.1985, c. 14, § 4.

39:4–139.6. Failure to answer or appear; rule applicable; procedures; notice

The municipal court shall immediately upon expiration of time to answer or appear, with respect to residents of New Jersey, follow the procedures set forth in R. 7:6–3(a) [1] of the Rules Governing the Courts of the State of New Jersey. These procedures include the mailing of a notice of offense or a failure to appear notice to defendant. That notice shall be on a form approved by the Administrative Director of the Courts and shall inform the defendant of the parking offense charged; the time and date of the parking offense; the amount of fines, penalties and costs due; of his right to have a hearing; that a civil judgment may be entered against him for failure to appear or pay the amount due; and that his driver's license may be suspended; that his driving privileges may be revoked; and that a warrant may be issued for his arrest.

The procedures set forth in R. 7:6–3(c) [1] of the Rules Governing the Courts of the State of New Jersey shall be followed in the case of a nonresident.

L.1985, c. 14, § 5.

[1] Deleted by amendment; see, now, R. 7:8–9.

39:4–139.7. Answer to parking ticket or failure to appear notice

a. In answer to a parking ticket or failure to appear notice, a person to whom a parking ticket or failure to appear notice was issued may:

(1) Admit the commission of the parking offense by payment of the fine and penalty due; or

(2) Deny liability and appear in court in accordance with the instructions on the summons or otherwise as provided by court rule.

b. A person to whom a parking ticket or failure to appear notice has been issued may answer by personal appearance or by mail in accordance with instructions on the summons.

c. A person who admits the commission of a parking offense shall, at the same time he submits his answer, pay the civil fine and any additional penalties established pursuant to local ordinance or regulation, which may be due for failure to answer within the time required.

L.1985, c. 14, § 6.

39:4–139.8. Evidence; submission to court; presence of officer; default judgment after failure to answer or pay fine and penalties; effect; assessment of costs; appeals; limitation of actions

a. The officer issuing the ticket shall not be required to appear at the hearing of a case unless the respondent has denied that the parking offense occurred by his commission and the court determines that the officer's presence is required. The court may grant a reasonable adjournment if the officer is not available at the time of hearing. It shall not be required that evidence other than the parking ticket and information from the division identifying the owner of the vehicle be submitted to the court, and that documentation in proper form shall be considered prima facie evidence that the registered owner of the vehicle was the person who committed the parking offense.

b. If a person to whom a failure to appear notice has been issued fails to answer or fails to appear at a hearing when he is required to do so, or, having admitted commission of the parking offense, fails to pay the fine and penalties assessed by the court, the court may, in addition to all other remedies and penalties

currently available to the court for failure to appear, enter a judgment by default sustaining the charges, fix the appropriate fine and assess appropriate penalties and costs, if any.

c. A judgment by default may be vacated by the court within one year after its entry only upon written application setting forth both a sufficient defense to the charge and an excusable neglect as to the respondent's failure to attend the hearing. If a failure to appear notice was mailed to the registered owner at the address appearing on the records of the division, the failure to receive the notice shall not be considered a defense unless the owner can prove that the division was advised of the owner's correct address prior to the date of the parking offense.

d. If payment is not made within 10 days after entry of a default judgment for a parking offense, the order of the court may be filed in the office of the clerk of the Superior Court and, when filed, shall have the effect of a civil money judgment. Judgments for parking offenses shall be maintained in a separate judgment roll from other civil judgments. Execution may be levied and other measures may be taken for the collection of the judgment which are authorized for the collection of an unpaid civil judgment. The court may assess costs against a judgment debtor, not to exceed $25.00 for each violation, to be paid upon satisfaction of the judgment.

e. If a notice of appeal is filed by the person against whom judgment is entered within 10 days after entry of the judgment and the payment of costs which the court shall require, a hearing de novo shall be held in accordance with the rules of the court. Service of a notice of appeal shall not stay the enforcement of a judgment appealed from unless the appellant shall have posted a bond in the amount of the judgment plus court costs at or before service of the notice of appeal.

f. A default judgment under this act may be filed by the court at any time within three years after the parking ticket was issued.

L.1985, c. 14, § 7.

39:4–139.9. Distribution of $2.00 of parking penalty to municipal court; civil contempt for failure to pay fine, penalty or costs

a. Out of each parking penalty assessed and disbursed to the municipality where a failure to appear notice was issued under these provisions, $2.00 shall be designated and distributed to the municipal court by the municipality to provide for the operating costs to administer this act. These funds shall be in addition to the municipal court's normal budget allocation but in no event shall exceed those additional costs to the court incurred as a result of this act.

b. If a respondent defaults in the payment of a fine, penalty or costs, or of an installment, the court may require the respondent to show cause why the default should not be treated as a civil contempt and may issue a summons or order to show cause or a bench warrant of arrest for the respondent's appearance. The officers of a corporation or the partners, directors or officers of an association may be held in contempt upon a default by the corporation or association.

L.1985, c. 14, § 8. Amended by L.1989, c. 137, § 1, eff. Aug. 2, 1989.

39:4–139.10. Failure to respond to a failure to appear notice or to pay parking judgment; notice to division; suspension of driver's license or motor vehicle registration; record

a. If a person has failed to respond to a failure to appear notice or has failed to pay a parking judgment, the municipal court may give notice of that fact to the commission in a manner prescribed by the chief administrator. If notice has been given under this section of a person's failure to respond to a failure to appear notice or to pay a parking judgment and if the fines and penalties are paid or if the case is dismissed or otherwise disposed of, the municipal court shall promptly give notice to that effect to the commission.

b. The judge or the commission may suspend the driver's license, or the registration of the motor vehicle of an owner, lessee, or operator who has not answered or appeared in response to a failure to appear notice or has not paid or otherwise satisfied outstanding parking fines or penalties. If an owner, lessee or operator has been found guilty of a parking offense, the court shall provide notice and an opportunity to appear before a judge prior to suspending that person's driver's license or motor vehicle registration. In determining whether to suspend the person's driver's license or the motor vehicle registration, the judge and the commission shall take into consideration the area where the person resides and whether or not the person has access to off-street parking. If the owner, lessee or operator is found by the court to be indigent or is participating in a government-based income maintenance program, that person shall be permitted to pay the parking fine and other penalties in installments in accordance with section 1 of P.L.1981, c. 365 (C.39:4–203.1).

c. The commission shall keep a record of a suspension ordered by the court pursuant to subsection b. of this section.

L.1985, c. 14, § 9. Amended by L.1999, c. 397, § 1; L.2007, c. 280, § 1, eff. July 1, 2008.

39:4–139.10a. Parking cases; dismissal

In any parking case, if the municipal court fails, within three years of the date of the violation, to either issue a warrant for the defendant's arrest, or to order a suspension of the defendant's driving privileges or the defendant's non-resident reciprocity privileges or prohibit the person from receiving or obtaining driving privileges, the matter shall be dismissed and shall not be reopened.

L.1999, c. 423, § 1, eff. Jan. 18, 2000.

39:4–139.11. Restoration of driver's license or motor vehicle registration after satisfaction of fines and penalties; recordation

a. When a person whose license or motor vehicle registration has been suspended pursuant to subsection b. of section 9 of P.L.1985, c. 14 (C.39:4–139.10) satisfies the fines and any penalties imposed by the court, the court shall forward to the commission a notice to restore the person's driver's license or motor vehicle registration.

b. Upon receiving a notice to restore pursuant to subsection a. of this section, the commission shall record the restoration and notify the person of the restoration.

L.1985, c. 14, § 10. Amended by L.2007, c. 280, § 2, eff. July 1, 2008.

39:4–139.12. Suspension of license; fee; deposit

There shall be included in the fines and penalties imposed by the court on a person whose license has been suspended pursuant to subsection b. of section 9 of this act [1] a fee of $3.00 which shall be transferred by the court to the division. All fees so transferred shall be deposited in a fund established to effectuate the purposes of this act.

L.1985, c. 14, § 11.
[1] N.J.S.A. § 39:4–139.10.

39:4–139.13. Impoundment or immobilization of vehicle with outstanding warrants; authorization by municipalities by ordinance; sale at auction; reclamation of possession prior to sale; disposition of proceeds

a. The governing body of every municipality may make, amend, repeal and enforce an ordinance authorizing the impoundment or immobilization of a vehicle found within the jurisdiction of that municipality if there are any outstanding warrants against the vehicle.

b. Except for vehicles owned by lessors who have complied with paragraphs (1) and (2) of subsection b. of section 4 of this act,[1] if the outstanding warrants are not paid by midnight on the 30th day following the day on which the vehicle was impounded or immobilized, the vehicle may be sold at a public auction. The municipality shall give notice of the sale by certified mail to the owner, if his name and address are known, and to the holder of any security interest filed with the director, and by publication in a form to be prescribed by the director by one insertion, at least five days before the date of the sale, in one or more newspapers published in this State and circulating in the municipality in which the motor vehicle has been impounded or immobilized.

c. At any time prior to the sale, the owner of the motor vehicle or other person entitled to the motor vehicle may reclaim possession of the motor vehicle upon payment of the reasonable costs of removal and storage of the motor vehicle, any fine or penalty and court costs assessed against him for a violation that gave rise to the impoundment or immobilization of the motor vehicle, and any outstanding warrants against the vehicle; however, the owner-lessor of a motor vehicle who has complied with paragraphs (1) and (2) of subsection b. of section 4 of this act shall be entitled to reclaim possession without payment and the lessee shall be liable for any fine, penalty, court costs and outstanding warrants against the vehicle.

d. Any proceeds obtained from the sale of a vehicle at public auction pursuant to subsection b. of this section in excess of the amount owed to the municipality for the reasonable costs of removal and storage of the motor vehicle, any fine or penalty and court costs assessed against him for a violation that gave rise to the impoundment or immobilization of the motor vehicle, and any outstanding warrants against the vehicle, shall be returned to the owner of the vehicle, if his name and address are known.

L.1985, c. 14, § 12.

1 N.J.S.A. § 39:4–139.5.

39:4–139.14. Contracts by municipalities with public agency or private organization for services to process parking offenses; plan by municipality; approval by Supreme Court

A municipality may enter into a contract with a public agency or private organization for services to be rendered in the processing of parking offenses under this act. A municipality which contracts for processing services shall submit a plan to the Supreme Court describing the services to be provided and the procedures to be used. The Supreme Court shall approve a plan submitted by a municipality prior to the implementation of that plan.

L.1985, c. 14, § 13.

ARTICLE 17. THROUGH STREETS

39:4–140. Designation of through highways, stop intersections and yield intersections; erection of stop or yield signs

The Commissioner of Transportation, with reference to State highways, may by regulation and the local authorities, with reference to any highway under their jurisdiction, may by ordinance or resolution, subject to the approval of the commissioner, except as otherwise provided in R.S. 39:4–8, designate through highways and erect "stop" signs or "yield" signs at specified entrances thereto, or may designate any intersection as a stop intersection or as a yield intersection and may erect "stop" signs or "yield" signs at one or more entrances to such intersections.

The commissioner on his own motion may designate through streets, stop intersections and yield intersections, and upon the designation shall give notice thereof to the board or body charged with the maintenance of such streets or intersections. The board or body shall thereupon comply with section 39:4–141 of this Title.

The commissioner may by appropriate order withdraw the designation of through streets, stop intersections or yield intersections and thereafter cause the removal of "stop" signs or "yield" signs indicating such streets or intersections.

Amended by L.1951, c. 23, p. 101, § 79; L.1956, c. 107, p. 486, § 3; L.1958, c. 114, p. 587, § 2; L.1971, c. 428, § 1, eff. Feb. 1, 1972; L.1983, c. 227, § 3, eff. June 27, 1983.

39:4–141. Placing of signs

The official, board or body charged with the maintenance of a highway or section thereof designated as a through street, or of an intersection designated as a stop intersection or a yield intersection, as provided in section 39:4–140 of this Title shall place "stop" signs or "yield right of way" signs, as in the designation provided, on the near right side of each highway intersecting the through street or of each entrance to the intersection where such sign is deemed necessary; except that on one-way streets, such signs may be placed on either or both near sides of the intersecting street or entrance, if approved by the director.

Amended by L.1951, c. 23, p. 102, § 80; L.1956, c. 107, p. 486, § 4; L.1958, c. 114, p. 588, § 3.

39:4–142. Repealed by L.1951, c. 23, p. 120, § 119

39:4–143. Intersecting through streets

When through streets intersect each other the director shall determine the highway to be known as the through street and cause the board or body having control of the highways to post only one of the highways.

Amended by L.1951, c. 23, p. 102, § 81.

39:4–144. Stopping or yielding right of way before entering stop or yield intersections

No driver of a vehicle or street car shall enter upon or cross an intersecting street marked with a "stop" sign unless:

a. The driver has first brought the vehicle or street car to a complete stop at a point within five feet of the nearest crosswalk or stop line marked upon the pavement at the near side of the intersecting street and shall proceed only after yielding the right of way to all vehicular traffic on the intersecting street which is so close as to constitute an immediate hazard.

b. No driver of a vehicle or street car shall enter upon or cross an intersecting street marked with a "yield right of way" sign without first slowing to a reasonable speed for existing conditions and visibility, stopping if necessary, and the driver shall yield the right of way to all vehicular traffic on the intersecting street which is so close as to constitute an immediate hazard; unless, in either case, the driver is otherwise directed to proceed by a traffic or police officer or traffic control signal.

c. No driver of a vehicle or street car shall turn right at an intersecting street marked with a "stop" sign or "yield right of way" sign unless the driver stops and remains stopped for pedestrians crossing the roadway within a marked crosswalk, or at an unmarked crosswalk, into which the driver is turning.

Amended by L.1956, c. 107, p. 486, § 5; L.1958, c. 114, p. 588, § 4; L.2008, c. 9, § 1, eff. June 6, 2008; L.2009, c. 319, § 4, eff. April 1, 2010.

39:4–145. Repealed by L.2008, c. 9, § 2, eff. June 6, 2008

ARTICLE 18.   SIGNS [REPEALED]

39:4–146 to 39:4–183.   Repealed by L.1941, c. 345, p. 915, § 26

ARTICLE 18A.   HIGHWAY AND TRAFFIC SIGNS

A.   GENERAL PROVISIONS

39:4–183.1.   Legal authority

Traffic signs shall be placed only by the authority of a public body or official having jurisdiction as authorized by law and only for the purpose of regulating, warning or guiding traffic.

This section, however, shall not prohibit public utility companies or other authorized persons or companies from erecting temporary MEN WORKING signs to protect construction, maintenance or repair work on or within a public highway; provided, such signs conform reasonably to the specifications included in this act.

L.1941, c. 345, p. 903, § 2.

39:4–183.1a.   Municipalities; installations at school crossing intersections; ordinance; approval by commissioner

Notwithstanding any law to the contrary, a municipality may, upon the request of the appropriate board of education or, in the case of a private school, by the school's governing body, provide by resolution for the installation of a traffic control device or sign consistent with the current standards prescribed by the Manual of Uniform Traffic Control Devices for Streets and Highways as adopted by the Commissioner of Transportation, to regulate motor vehicle traffic at an intersection located within 300 feet of any public or private school; provided that the municipal or county engineer shall, under the engineer's seal as a licensed professional engineer, certify to the municipal or county governing body, as appropriate, that the traffic control or device has been approved by the engineer after the engineer's investigation of the circumstances. Before a resolution shall take effect, however, the governing body shall submit a copy of the resolution to the Commissioner of Transportation for his review and approval together with detailed information as to the location of streets,

intersections and signs affected by any installation, traffic court, accident and speed sampling data when appropriate, the municipal or county engineer's certification, under the engineer's seal as a licensed professional engineer, to the municipal or county governing body, and any other information as the commissioner may require. If the commissioner disapproves the resolution, he shall file his disapproval, in writing, with a statement of the reasons for his disapproval, with the governing body within 90 days following the receipt of the resolution. If the commissioner approves the resolution or fails to file his disapproval within the 90–day review period, the resolution shall take effect immediately.

For the purposes of this section, the term "public or private school" has the meaning that term is given in N.J.S.18A:1–1.

L.1984, c. 219, § 1, eff. Dec. 20, 1984. Amended by L.2001, c. 342, § 3, eff. Jan. 5, 2002.

39:4–183.1b.   Designation of older and walking impaired persons crossing areas; appropriate signs

The Commissioner of Transportation, with reference to State highways, may by regulation and the local authorities, with reference to any highway under their jurisdiction, may by ordinance or resolution, subject to the approval of the commissioner, designate "Older and Walking Impaired Persons Crossing" areas and erect appropriate signs.

L.1991, c. 120, § 1, eff. April 25, 1991.

39:4–183.2.   Signs hereafter erected

All traffic signs hereafter erected, whether initial installations or replacements, must conform in all respects to the provisions of this act.

L.1941, c. 345, p. 903, § 3.

39:4–183.3.   Display of unauthorized traffic signs

No person shall place, maintain or display upon or in view of any highway, any unauthorized traffic sign, device or other contrivance which purports to be or is an imitation of or of such a nature as to be mistaken for an official traffic sign or which attempts to direct the movement of traffic or which hides from view or interferes with the effectiveness of any official traffic sign and no person shall place or maintain, nor shall any public authority permit upon any highway, any traffic sign or signal bearing thereon or its support, any commercial advertising.

This shall not be deemed to prohibit the erection upon private property adjacent to highways of signs giving useful directional information and of a type that cannot be mistaken for official signs.

L.1941, c. 345, p. 903, § 4.

39:4–183.4. Prohibited signs deemed a nuisance; action for removal

A sign, device or other contrivance prohibited by section four of this act[1] shall be deemed a public and private nuisance and any citizen may maintain an action at law or in equity for its removal. The sole question of law and fact shall be whether it is in imitation of or of a nature as to be mistaken for an official traffic sign.

L.1941, c. 345, p. 904, § 5.

[1] N.J.S.A. § 39:4–183.3.

39:4–183.5. Repealed by L.1998, c. 54, § 4, eff. July 10, 1998

39:4–183.6. Director to determine signs

The commissioner may determine the character, type, location, wording or symbol, and use of all traffic signs on the highways of this State; may adopt a manual and specifications for a uniform system of traffic signs consistent with the provisions of this act for use upon public highways within the State. Such uniform system shall correlate with and so far as possible conform to the system then current as specified in the "Manual on Uniform Traffic Control Devices for Streets and Highways."

L.1941, c. 345, p. 904, § 7. Amended by L.1951, c. 23, p. 102, § 82; L.2003, c. 13, § 53 (contingent effective date).

Historical and Statutory Notes

L.2003, c. 13, § 127, approved Jan. 28, 2003, provides:

"Sections 1, 2, 3, 12, 38, 109, 110 and 121 shall take effect immediately, sections 105, 106, 107, 108, and 120 shall take effect on July 1, 2003 and the remainder of this act shall take effect on the date the Commissioner of Transportation certifies to the Governor (hereinafter the "date of certification") that a majority of the members of the commission have been appointed or are in office and that all necessary anticipatory actions have been accomplished, provided, that the amount of revenues received pursuant to sections 109 and 110 prior to the date of certification are hereby appropriated to the division. Upon the date of certification, all such collected revenue shall be revenue of the commission. The Commissioner of Transportation, the Director of the Division of Motor Vehicles and the commission may take such anticipatory administrative action in advance as shall be necessary for the implementation of the act."

B. SPECIFICATIONS

39:4–183.7. Repealed by L.1972, c. 43, § 2

39:4–183.8. Materials

Permanent traffic signs should be made of metal or comparable durable material; wood may be used for large signs and also for temporary and seasonal signs; heavy cardboard may be used for special occasions or emergencies.

L.1941, c. 345, p. 906, § 9. Amended by L.1951, c. 23, p. 104, § 84.

39:4–183.9. Dimensions

The design of all traffic signs shall conform to and have the minimum dimensions of the specifications adopted by the commissioner, except as otherwise approved by the commissioner. Where conditions require greater visibility necessitating a larger sign, standard shapes and colors shall be used, and standard proportions shall be retained, so far as practicable.

This is not to be deemed to prohibit the erection of enlarged bridge type signs or narrow longitudinal type signs suspended from mast arms, over the roadway.

L.1941, c. 345, p. 906, § 10. Amended by L.1951, c. 23, p. 104, § 85; L.1956, c. 107, p. 488, § 7; L.2003, c. 13, § 54 (contingent effective date).

"Sections 1, 2, 3, 12, 38, 109, 110 and 121 shall take effect immediately, sections 105, 106, 107, 108, and 120 shall take effect on July 1, 2003 and the remainder of this act shall take effect on the date the Commissioner of Transportation certifies to the Governor (hereinafter the "date of certification") that a majority of the members of the commission have been appointed or are in office and that all necessary anticipatory actions have been accomplished, provided, that the amount of revenues received pursuant to sections 109 and 110 prior to the date of certification are hereby appropriated to the division. Upon the date of certification, all such collected revenue shall be revenue of the commission. The Commissioner of Transportation, the Director of the Division of Motor Vehicles and the commission may take such anticipatory administrative action in advance as shall be necessary for the implementation of the act."

39:4–183.10. Message; wording and symbols

Wording and arrangement for each type of traffic sign shall be as specified in subsequent sections of this act; symbols on the sign shall take the place of a word message wherever indicated in subsequent sections of this act. In situations where messages or symbols are required other than those herein provided for, the signs shall be of the same shape and color as standard signs of the same functional type.

L.1941, c. 345, p. 907, § 11. Amended by L.1951, c. 23, p. 104, § 86.

39:4–183.11. Illumination; reflectorization

All warning signs, and all regulatory signs, with the exception of pedestrian signs, urban parking signs and signs having a significance only during daylight hours, shall be illuminated or reflectorized so as to be visible during hours of darkness from all distances up to five hundred feet. All other traffic signs may be illuminated or reflectorized if desirable.

All illumination shall normally be by white light, except that a flashing light incorporated in a sign installation shall be yellow when displayed with a warning sign or red when displayed with a stop sign, and shall be provided by means of:

(a) A light, within or behind the sign, illuminating the main message or symbol, or luminous tubing shaped to the lettering or symbol;

(b) An attached or independently mounted flood light or flood lights, directed on the face of the sign.

Reflectorization of traffic signs shall reflect white light, except that if a reflecting coating is used as a background of a yellow sign it shall reflect yellow light, and shall be provided by means of:

(a) Reflector buttons or units set into the symbol or message;

(b) Reflecting coatings, either on the sign background or, where a black background or panel is used, in the symbol or message.

L.1941, c. 345, p. 907, § 12. Amended by L.1951, c. 23, p. 105, § 87.

C. LOCATION

39:4–183.12. Location

All traffic signs shall be located as provided in subsequent sections of this act covering details of design and installation. Signs other than temporary signs in the roadway shall be placed on the right side of the roadway, except traffic signs erected on or within traffic circles, islands and safety zones. All signs shall be mounted approximately at right angles to the direction of, and facing the traffic that they are intended to serve. This section shall not prohibit location of traffic signs over the roadway.

L.1941, c. 345, p. 907, § 13. Amended by L.1951, c. 23, p. 106, § 88.

39:4–183.13, 39:4–183.14. Repealed by L.1972, c. 43, § 2

D. MAINTENANCE

39:4–183.15. Continuous maintenance

All traffic signs shall be kept in good order and clearly legible at all times. Signs damaged or destroyed shall be replaced promptly.

Signs no longer applicable shall be removed immediately.

L.1941, c. 345, p. 908, § 16.

E. DETAILED DESIGN AND INSTALLATION

39:4–183.16 to 39:4–183.21. Repealed by L.1951, c. 23, p. 120, § 123; L.1972, c. 43, § 2

39:4–183.21a. Abandonment of line and grade crossings; notice; removal of railroad advance warning signs

The commissioner shall, upon receiving notice from a railroad company that it has abandoned a particular line and the grade crossings thereon, order the removal of any advance warning signs erected pursuant to section 22 of P.L.1941, c. 345 (C.39:4–183.21).

L.1971, c. 393, § 3, eff. Jan. 7, 1972. Amended by L.2003, c. 13, § 55 (contingent effective date).

39:4–183.22. Repealed by L.1972, c. 43, § 2

39:4–183.22a. Construction warning signs

The design and location of standard construction warning signs should be as follows:

(a) Shape—Rectangle with longer dimension horizontal;

(b) Color—White background with black letters;

(c) Dimensions—Four feet by six feet, or larger for higher approach speeds;

(d) Message—CONSTRUCTION AHEAD or other appropriate wording, the distance over which the warning applies, and the approved speed limit.

(e) Location—Where construction work is in progress within the roadway area, a construction warning sign shall be located on each side of the roadway, facing approaching traffic, five hundred feet to one thousand feet in advance of the beginning of the construction area, the distance depending on the approach speeds on that roadway.

L.1951, c. 23, p. 112, § 96.

39:4–183.23. Repealed by L.1972, c. 43, § 2

39:4–183.24. Location and information signs

Standard location and information signs shall conform to the design and specifications adopted by the commissioner.

L.1941, c. 345, p. 915, § 25. Amended by L.1951, c. 23, p. 113, § 98; L.2003, c. 13, § 56 (contingent effective date).

Historical and Statutory Notes

L.2003, c. 13, § 127, approved Jan. 28, 2003, provides:

"Sections 1, 2, 3, 12, 38, 109, 110 and 121 shall take effect immediately, sections 105, 106, 107, 108, and 120 shall take effect on July 1, 2003 and the remainder of this act shall take effect on the date the Commissioner of Transportation certifies to the Governor (hereinafter the "date of certification") that a majority of the members of the commission have been appointed or are in office and that all necessary anticipatory actions have been accomplished, provided, that the amount of revenues received pursuant to sections 109 and 110 prior to the date of certification are hereby appropriated to the division. Upon the date of certification, all such collected revenue shall be revenue of the commission. The Commissioner of Transportation, the Director of the Division of Motor Vehicles and the commission may take such anticipatory administrative action in advance as shall be necessary for the implementation of the act."

39:4–183.25. Repeal

Article eighteen of chapter four of Title 39 of the Revised Statutes (R.S. 39:4–146 to and including R.S. 39:4–183) is repealed.

L.1941, c. 345, p. 915, § 26.

39:4–183.26. Repealed by L.1972, c. 43, § 2

39:4–183.27. Rules and regulations; placement, specifications, location and maintenance of traffic signs and markings

The Commissioner of Transportation shall, from time to time, promulgate rules and regulations concerning the placing, specifications, location and maintenance of highway and traffic signs and markings. In promulgating such rules and regulations, the commissioner shall be guided by the Manual on Uniform Traffic Control Devices for streets and highways which has been adopted by the Federal Highway Administrator as a national standard for application on all classes of highways.

L.1972, c. 43, § 1.

39:4–183.28. Repeals

Sections 8, 14 and 15 of P.L.1941, c. 345 (C. 39:4–183.7, 39:4–183.13 and 39:4–183.14), sections 17 to 20 of P.L.1941, c. 345 (C. 39:4–183.16 to 39:4–183.19), sections 22 to 24 of P.L.1941, c. 345 (C. 39:4–183.21, 39:4–183.22, 39:4–183.23), section 99 of P.L.1951, c. 23 (C. 39:4–183.26) and sections 102 to 104 of P.L.1951, c. 23 (C. 39:4–191.3 to 39:4–191.5) are repealed.

L.1972, c. 43, § 2.

39:4–183.29. Continuance of rules and regulations promulgated by department of transportation prior to act

This act shall not affect the orders, rules and regulations heretofore made or promulgated by the Department of Transportation relating to the placing, specifications, location and maintenance of highway and traffic signs and markings, but such orders, rules and regulations shall continue with full force and effect until amended or repealed pursuant to law.

L.1972, c. 43, § 3.

39:4–183.30. Effect of act on offenses, liabilities, penalties or forfeitures prior to date of act

No offense committed, and no liability, penalty, or forfeiture, either civil or criminal, incurred, prior to the repeal or revision of any act or any part thereof by the enactment of this act, shall be discharged, released or affected by the repeal or revision of the act or part thereof under which such offense, liability, penalty or forfeiture was incurred, and prosecutions and actions for such offenses, liabilities, penalties or forfeitures committed or incurred prior to the effective date of this act shall be commenced or continued and be proceeded with in all respects as if the act or part thereof had not been repealed or revised.

L.1972, c. 43, § 4.

39:4–183.31. Uncontrolled intersections having demonstrated pedestrian safety problems; posting pedestrian crossing yield signs

The Commissioner of Transportation shall post, and shall request county and municipal authorities to post, pedestrian crossing yield signs that make reference to State law at all crosswalks at intersections that have demonstrated pedestrian safety problems and are not controlled by a traffic control signal. The signs shall conform to the "Manual on Uniform Traffic Control Devices".

L.2005, c. 158, § 3, eff. Dec. 1, 2005.

ARTICLE 19. CURB AND PAVEMENT MARKINGS [REPEALED]

39:4–184 to 39:4–191. Repealed by L.1951, c. 23, p. 120, § 120

ARTICLE 19A. MARKINGS

39:4–191.1. Legal authority; uniformity

Markings shall be placed only by the authority of a public body or official having jurisdiction as authorized by law, and only for the purpose of regulating, warning or guiding traffic. Where used, these markings shall be uniform in design, position and application. The director may adopt a uniform system of markings consistent with the provisions of this act for use upon public highways within the State. Such a uniform system of markings shall correlate with and so far as possible conform to the current "Manual on Uniform Traffic Control Devices for Streets and Highways."

L.1951, c. 23, p. 114, § 100.

39:4–191.2. Types of markings

Markings shall be of the following types:

a. Pavement markings, including lines and word markings on the pavement.

b. Curb markings for parking prohibitions.

c. Object markings, including objects within and adjacent to the roadway.

d. Reflector markers, including reflector buttons, panels, delineators or similar devices, within or adjacent to the roadway.

L.1951, c. 23, p. 115, § 101.

39:4–191.3 to 39:4–191.5. Repealed by L.1972, c. 43, § 2

39:4–191.6. Illumination and reflectorization

All markings may be reflectorized, and all obstructions, within the roadway, shall be properly illuminated or reflectorized. The following markings shall normally be reflectorized:

a. Center lines on pavement.

b. "No Passing" lines.

c. Striping or checkerboard squares on vertical surfaces of obstructions in or adjacent to the roadway.

d. Reflector markers.

L.1951, c. 23, p. 116, § 105.

39:4–191.7. Word markings limited

The use of words painted on the pavement shall be limited to very brief warning messages expressed in the shortest possible words. Regulatory messages may be used, but only in support of standard signs. All letters should be greatly elongated in the direction of traffic movement.

L.1951, c. 23, p. 116, § 106.

ARTICLE 20.   SAFETY ZONES [REPEALED]

39:4–192 to 39:4–196.   Repealed by L.1951, c. 23, p. 120, § 121

ARTICLE 20A.   SAFETY ZONES AND TRAFFIC ISLANDS

39:4–196.1.   Local authority

Safety zones and traffic islands shall be established and installed only by authority of a public body or official having jurisdiction as authorized by law, and for the purpose of regulating, segregating or guiding traffic.

L.1951, c. 23, p. 116, § 107.

39:4–196.2.   Types of safety zones and traffic islands

Safety zones and traffic islands shall be of the following types:

1. Safety zones

   a. Loading islands

   b. Refuge islands

2. Traffic islands

   a. Divisional islands

   b. Channelization islands.

L.1951, c. 23, p. 116, § 108.

39:4–196.3.   Location, design and protection

The location, design and protection of safety zones and traffic islands shall conform to the specifications adopted by the director.

L.1951, c. 23, p. 117, § 109.

ARTICLE 21.   POWERS OF MUNICIPALITIES, COUNTIES AND HIGHWAY COMMISSIONER

39:4–197.   Ordinance or resolution on matters covered by chapter

Except as otherwise provided in R.S.39:4–8, no municipality shall pass an ordinance or resolution on a matter covered by or which alters or in any way nullifies the provisions of this chapter or any supplement to this chapter; except that a municipality may pass, without the approval of the commissioner, and consistent with the current standards prescribed by the Manual on Uniform Traffic Control Devices for Streets and Highways, ordinances or resolutions, or by ordinances or resolutions may authorize the adoption of regulations by the board, body, or official having control of traffic in the public streets, regulating special conditions existent in the municipality on the subjects and within the limitations following:

(1) Ordinance:

a. Altering speed limitations as provided in R.S.39:4–98;

b. Limiting use of streets to certain class of vehicles, except that nothing in this paragraph shall permit a municipality to pass an ordinance or resolution limiting use of streets by commercial motor vehicles without the approval of the commissioner;

c. Designating one-way streets;

d. Regulating the stopping or starting of street cars at special places, such as railroad stations, public squares or in front of certain public buildings;

e. Regulating the passage or stopping of traffic at certain congested street corners or other designated points, including the establishment of multi-way stop controls;

f. Regulating the parking of vehicles on streets and portions thereof, including angle parking as provided in R.S.39:4–135;

g. Regulating the parking of vehicles upon land owned or leased and maintained by the municipality, a parking authority or the board of education of a school district, including any lands devoted to the public parking of vehicles, the entrances thereto and exits therefrom;

h. Regulating the entrances to and exits from parking yards and parking places which are open to the public or to which the public is invited, except that this shall not apply to entrances or exits to and from State highways;

i. Designating streets or roads upon which buses and trucks over four tons gross weight may be required not to exceed specially fixed limits based on engineering and traffic investigation and to use a lower gear in descending steep declivities having a grade in excess of

5% fixing such special speed limits and providing for the use of such a gear thereon; and

j. Designating any intersection as a stop intersection and erecting appropriate signs, on streets under municipal jurisdiction if that intersection is located within 500 feet of a school, or of a playground or youth recreational facility and the street on which the stop sign will be erected is contiguous to that school, playground, or youth recreational facility. The municipal engineer shall certify to the following in regard to the designated site in which a stop intersection is being designated: (i) that both intersecting streets are under municipal jurisdiction; (ii) that the intersection is within 500 feet of a school, playground, or youth recreational facility as defined herein; and (iii) that the intersection is on a street contiguous to a school, playground, or youth recreational facility. A claim against a municipality for damage or injury under this subparagraph for a wrongful act or omission shall be dismissed if the municipality is deemed to have conformed to the provisions contained in this subparagraph.

(2) Ordinance or resolution:

a. Designating through streets, as provided in article 17 of this chapter (R.S.39:4–140 et seq.); and

b. Designating and providing for the maintenance as "no passing" zones of portions of highway where overtaking and passing or driving to the left of the roadway is deemed especially hazardous.

(3) Ordinance, resolution, or regulation:

a. Designating stops, stations, or stands for omnibuses and taxis;

b. Designating curb loading zones; and

c. Designating restricted parking spaces for use by persons who have been issued special vehicle identification cards by the New Jersey Motor Vehicle Commission pursuant to the provisions of P.L.1949, c. 280 (C.39:4–204 et seq.) and section 1 of P.L.1977, c. 202 (C.39:4–197.5). Any person parking a motor vehicle in a restricted parking space without a special vehicle identification card shall be liable to a fine of $250 for the first offense and, for subsequent offenses, a fine of at least $250 and up to 90 days' community service on such terms and in such form as the court shall deem appropriate, or any combination thereof.

Amended by L.1951, c. 23, p. 117, § 110; L.1954, c. 27, p. 96, § 1; L.1955, c. 74, p. 239, § 1; L.1956, c. 46, p. 94, § 1; L.1956, c. 186, p. 697, § 1; L.1965, c. 226, § 2, eff. Jan. 10, 1966; L.1967, c. 279, § 1, eff. Jan. 12, 1968; L.1968, c. 32, § 1, eff. May 6, 1968; L.1980, c. 178, § 3, eff. Dec. 31, 1980; L.1983, c. 227, § 4, eff. June 27, 1983; L.1989, c. 201, § 2, eff. June 1, 1990; L.2003, c. 161, § 1, eff. Oct. 1, 2003; L.2008, c. 110, § 2, eff. Dec. 4, 2008.

39:4–197.1. Prohibiting normal traffic on county or state highway; consent of board of chosen freeholders or highway commission necessary

No municipality in the exercise of its power to regulate parades, processions or assemblages, shall prohibit normal traffic on any county or State highway without the consent of the Board of Chosen Freeholders in the case of a county highway or the consent of the State Highway Commissioner in the case of a State highway.

L.1951, c. 23, p. 118, § 111.

39:4–197.2. County road lying within municipality; regulation of traffic and parking

Any municipality, which maintains a paid police force, may, by ordinance, resolution, or regulation, pursuant to R.S. 39:4–197 and with the consent of the governing body of the county, regulate traffic and parking along and upon any county road or part thereof, lying within its corporate limits, in the same manner and to the same extent that it is authorized by law to regulate the same upon municipal roads and streets.

L.1957, c. 69, p. 133, § 1. Amended by L.1980, c. 143, § 1, eff. Nov. 12, 1980.

39:4–197.3. Special traffic regulations

The governing body of any municipality may, upon the adoption of a resolution declaring that an emergent or temporary condition dictates adoption of special traffic regulations within the scope of any of the items listed in subparagraphs (1) b. through h., (2) and (3) of Revised Statutes 39:4–197, provide by said resolution for such special traffic regulation and for a period of effectiveness thereof not in excess of 3 months from the effective date thereof. Notice of special regulations adopted pursuant to this act shall be given as provided in Revised Statutes 39:4–198.

L.1964, c. 131, § 1.

39:4–197.4. Angle parking ordinances; exemption from approval by state; conditions

Notwithstanding the provisions of the chapter to which this act is a supplement, or any supplement to said chapter, no ordinance adopted by any municipality designating any street or streets under the jurisdiction of any such municipality for angle parking shall require the approval of the Commissioner of the State Department of Transportation or of any other State officer or employee, and any such ordinance shall be of full force and effect from the date of its adoption or from any effective date prescribed therein if the street or streets designated in said ordinance have been marked or signed for angle parking by the municipality for a period of not less than 10 consecutive years prior to the adoption of the said ordinance or for a period not less than any 20 years during which such street or streets have been under the jurisdiction of the municipality.

L.1975, c. 152, § 1, eff. July 9, 1975.

39:4–197.5. Restricted parking for use by handicapped persons; ordinances, resolutions or regulations

Any municipality may, by ordinance, resolution or regulation, establish restricted parking spaces in front of residences, schools, hospitals and other public buildings and in shopping and business districts for use by persons who have been issued special vehicle identification cards by the Division of Motor Vehicles pursuant to the provisions of section 2 of P.L.1949, c. 280 (C. 39:4–205), when using a motor vehicle on which is displayed a certificate, for which a special vehicle identification card has been issued, pursuant to section 3 of said law (C. 39:4–206).

L.1977, c. 202, § 1, eff. Aug. 30, 1977. Amended by L.1980, c. 178, § 2, eff. Dec. 31, 1980.

39:4–197.6. Restricted parking zones in front of residences occupied by handicapped persons; ordinance; conditions

Any municipality may, by ordinance, establish a restricted parking zone in front of a residence occupied by a handicapped person if a windshield placard or wheelchair symbol license plates have been issued for a vehicle owned by the handicapped person, or by another occupant of the residence who is a member of the immediate family of the handicapped person, by the Division of Motor Vehicles pursuant to the provisions of P.L.1949, c. 280 (C. 39:4–204 et seq.), provided such parking is not otherwise prohibited and the permitting thereof would not interfere with the normal flow of traffic.

L.1977, c. 309, § 1, eff. Jan. 5, 1978. Amended by L.1991, c. 406, § 1, eff. Jan. 17, 1992.

39:4–197.7. Permits for motor vehicle; fee

Any municipality enacting an ordinance pursuant to section 1 of this act [1] shall provide for the issuance of permits which identify a specific motor vehicle and the location wherein it is to be parked. Such permits shall only be issued to persons who can prove ownership and operation of the motor vehicle and residency at the location specified thereon. The permit shall be 5½ inches by 8½ inches in size, shall bear an appropriate certification of authenticity and shall be displayed prominently within the vehicle when it is parked so as to be seen from the middle of the street. Only a motor vehicle for which a valid permit has been issued and which has such permit properly displayed shall be permitted to be parked in the restricted parking zone indicated on such permit. A municipality may, by ordinance, establish a fee for such permits.

L.1977, c. 309, § 2, eff. Jan. 5, 1978.

[1] N.J.S.A. § 39:4–197.6.

39:4–197.8. State Highway Route No. 94 in Sussex and Warren Counties; regulations limiting use

Notwithstanding any other law, the Commissioner of Transportation may adopt regulations limiting the operation of commercial motor vehicles, tractors, trailers or semi-trailers upon that portion of State Highway Route No. 94 located in Sussex county and Warren county. In adopting regulations the commissioner shall give consideration to normal traffic volume in the municipalities of the respective counties so that the residents and the business establishments of these counties shall not be penalized.

L.1983, c. 416, § 1, eff. Jan. 4, 1984.

39:4–197.9. Municipal handicapped parking enforcement unit; creation; purpose

In order to implement the enforcement of P.L.1977, c. 202 (C. 39:4–197.5) subject to R.S. 39:4–138, and of P.L.1975, c. 221 (C. 52:32–11 et seq.) and spaces established pursuant to P.L.1975, c. 217 (C. 52:27D–119 et seq.) within its jurisdiction, a municipality may establish a handicapped parking enforcement unit under the supervision of the chief law enforcement officer of the municipality. The municipality may, by ordinance or resolution, provide procedures and other guidelines for the program consistent with this act which may give persons selected and trained for the unit the full power and authority to issue warnings or summonses for violations of any provision of any law, regulation, ordinance or resolution pertaining to illegal parking in restricted parking spaces for the handicapped. The unit shall concentrate its enforcement activity at any shopping centers or malls in the municipality.

L.1991, c. 442, § 1, eff. Jan. 18, 1992.

39:4–197.10. Eligibility for participation

No person shall be appointed to or continue to be eligible for participation in the handicapped parking enforcement unit unless he:

a. Evidences no criminal record as a result of a State criminal history record background check through the State Bureau of Identification in the Division of State Police in the Department of Law and Public Safety;

b. Is a resident of the municipality in which the unit is established; and

c. Is at least 18 years of age.

L.1991, c. 442, § 2, eff. Jan. 18, 1992.

39:4–197.11. Preference for participation by handicapped persons

Preference for participation in this program may be given to persons who are handicapped as defined in P.L.1949, c. 280 (C. 39:4–204 et seq.).

L.1991, c. 442, § 3, eff. Jan. 18, 1992.

39:4–197.12. Reimbursement for actual expenses

Any person appointed to the municipality's handicapped parking enforcement unit shall be reimbursed for actual expenses of transportation incurred in the course of his work at a rate at least equal to the rate established by the State and adjusted pursuant to section 2 of P.L.1980, c. 19 (C. 52:14–17.1a).

L.1991, c. 442, § 4, eff. Jan. 18, 1992.

39:4–197.13. Course of instruction required; curriculum

The municipality shall require any person who fulfills the requirements for appointment in section 2 of P.L.1991, c. 442 (C. 39:4–197.10) to take a course of instruction designed to prepare the person to properly fulfill his responsibilities under the law. The curriculum for the course shall include, but may not be limited to, appropriate information concerning public relations, the laws, regulations, resolutions, ordinances and other guidelines concerning restricted parking enforcement and court proceedings. Before the person may commence enforcement activity with the unit, he shall satisfactorily complete the prescribed course of instruction.

L.1991, c. 442, § 5, eff. Jan. 18, 1992.

39:4–197.14. Appropriations

The governing body of a municipality, by ordinance, may appropriate annually sums of money as it shall deem necessary for the purpose of compensating any such person for his services. The governing body of a municipality may provide the members of the handicapped parking enforcement unit with coverage under chapter 15 of Title 34 of the Revised Statutes (Workers' Compensation) or if the governing body chooses not to provide such coverage, it may appropriate annually sums of money as it shall deem necessary for the purpose of compensating such persons for any losses which would otherwise be compensable under chapter 15 of Title 34 of the Revised Statutes (Workers' Compensation). However, neither the municipality nor the State shall be required to provide any benefits thereto whatsoever.

L.1991, c. 442, § 6, eff. Jan. 18, 1992.

39:4–197.15. Uniform and patch

Any person who is selected for the handicapped parking enforcement unit shall be provided, at the expense of the municipality, with a distinctive uniform on which is affixed a special patch designating his function and shall be provided with reasonable maintenance thereof.

L.1991, c. 442, § 7, eff. Jan. 18, 1992.

39:4–197.16. State Highway Route 29; Legislative findings

The Legislature finds that sections of State Highway Route 29, from its intersection with Interstate Route 95 to its northern terminus at State Highway Route 12, have sharp curves, minimal shoulders and limited sight distances. The Legislature further finds that the use of Route 29 between the stated points by heavy vehicles constitutes a hazard to the traveling public, as evidenced by serious accidents on that roadway, some including fatalities, and confirmed by extensive formal public comments, in recognition of which the Department of Transportation issued a traffic regulation order on November 15, 2000 temporarily prohibiting heavy trucks and truck-trailer combinations from using Route 29 between the stated points for through travel. The Legislature further finds that there are nearby alternative through routings which have significantly better overall roadway conditions and geometric designs.

The Legislature finds and declares that State Highway Route 29, from its intersection with Interstate 95 to its northern terminus at State Highway Route 12, is inappropriate for through travel by truck and truck-trailer combinations which exceed 26,000 pounds in weight, and that these vehicles should be permanently prohibited from using that roadway.

L.2001, c. 45, § 1, eff. March 30, 2001.

39:4–197.17. Truck traffic exceeding 26,000 pounds prohibited

Except as otherwise provided in section 3 of this act, truck and truck-trailer combinations which exceed 26,000 pounds in gross registered vehicle weight, gross vehicle weight rating, or gross combination weight rating regardless of their dimensions, are prohibited from using State Highway Route 29, in either the northbound or southbound travel lanes, from its intersection with Interstate Route 95 to its northern terminus at State Highway Route 12.

L.2001, c. 45, § 2, eff. March 30, 2001.

39:4–197.18. Exceptions

The prohibitions contained in section 2 of this act shall not apply to emergency vehicles, government owned or leased vehicles, vehicles which have an origin or final destination on or within three miles of the prohibited sections of State Highway Route 29, or vehicles making an actual pickup, delivery or providing services at a location on or within three miles of the prohibited sections.

L.2001, c. 45, § 3, eff. March 30, 2001.

39:4–197.19. Use of prohibited portions

Notwithstanding the provisions of section 2 of this act, the Commissioner of Transportation in accordance with the provisions of section 2 of P.L.1998, c. 28 (C.39:4–8.3) may after the holding of a public meeting by written order provide for the use of the prohibited portions of State Route 29 by vehicles engaged in the commercial transportation of certain rapidly setting concrete mixtures under circumstances in which adherence to the prohibitions set forth in this act makes delivery impossible or economically impracticable.

L.2001, c. 45, § 4, eff. March 30, 2001.

39:4–197.20. Enforceability

The provisions of this act shall not be enforceable until the Commissioner of Transportation has caused to be erected such signage as may be necessary to effectuate the purposes of this act, which shall be done no later than 90 days following enactment.

L.2001, c. 45, § 5, eff. March 30, 2001.

39:4–197.21. Violation; fines

The driver, owner, lessee, bailee or any one of the foregoing of any truck or truck-trailer combination found or operated in violation of the provisions of this act shall be fined not more than $400 for the first offense, and shall be subject to a fine of $700 for the second offense and a fine of $1,000 for each subsequent offense.

L.2001, c. 45, § 6, eff. March 30, 2001.

39:4–198. Notice of ordinance, resolution or regulation by signs; handicapped parking signs

No ordinance, resolution or regulation enacted, passed, or adopted by local authorities nor any regulation adopted by the Commissioner of Transportation under any power given by this chapter or any supplement thereto shall be effective unless due notice thereof is given to the public by placing a sign at the places where the ordinance, resolution or regulation is effective, and by briefing its provisions on signs according to specifications contained in this chapter or as specified by the current Manual on Uniform Traffic Control Devices for streets and highways. These signs shall be so placed as to be easily read by pedestrians or operators of vehicles. Except, in the case of "No Passing" zones, in lieu of or in addition to signs, notice shall be given to the public by highway pavement markings which conform to the current Manual on Uniform Traffic Control Devices for streets and highways.

In addition to the specifications in the Manual on Uniform Traffic Control Devices, any sign erected after the effective date of this amendatory and supplementary act to notify the public that parking in a space is reserved for the handicapped shall also state the penalties set forth in paragraph c. of subsection (3) of R.S.39:4–197 which may be imposed for a violation. Signs which were erected prior to the effective date shall be modified within 12 months after the effective date to include the penalty information.

It shall not be a defense to the unauthorized use of a parking space reserved for the handicapped pursuant to R.S.39:4–138 that the penalties set forth in paragraph c.

of subsection (3) of R.S.39:4–197 were not posted or were improperly posted.

Amended by L.1951, c. 23, p. 118, § 112; L.1956, c. 186, p. 698, § 2; L.1987, c. 209, § 1, eff. July 23, 1987; L.1989, c. 201, § 5, eff. June 1, 1990; L.2007, c. 164, § 1, eff. Sept. 10, 2007.

39:4–199. Safety zones, signals, guideposts and other structures on state highway; approval by highway commission

No safety zones or platforms, commonly called "safety isles", traffic signal devices, guideposts or any other structures shall be erected, constructed, operated or maintained in, over or upon a state highway, without the permission of the state highway commission first having been obtained.

39:4–199.1. Official traffic signs at traffic islands, safety zones and grade separations, etc.

Local, county and State authorities, with respect to highways under their jurisdiction, may erect and maintain appropriate official traffic signs not inconsistent with the provisions of chapter 4 of Title 39 of the Revised Statutes,[1] on a highway or at an intersection where the movements of traffic are regulated and controlled by traffic islands, traffic circles, channelizing islands, divisional islands, safety zones, grade separations or other physical structures which have been erected by such authority; and such authorities may erect and maintain railroad advance warning signs and other appropriate official traffic signs where any such highway crosses a railroad at grade.

L.1951, c. 23, p. 120, § 118. Amended by L.1963, c. 167, § 1.

[1] N.J.S.A. § 39:4–1 et seq.

39:4–200. Repealed by L.1951, c. 23, p. 120, § 119

39:4–201. Resolutions or ordinances regulating traffic on county roads; notice; penalties

Except as otherwise provided in R.S.39:4–8, no governing body of any county in this State may adopt resolutions, ordinances, or regulations on a matter covered by or which alters or in any way nullifies the provisions of this chapter or of any supplement thereto, except that, without the approval of the commissioner, and consistent with the current standards prescribed by the Manual on Uniform Traffic Control Devices for Streets and Highways, ordinances , resolutions, or regulations may be passed by a governing body for the supervision and regulation of traffic on any county roads of the county upon the subject matter and within the limitations prescribed in R.S.39:4–197, and the governing body may prescribe penalties for violations of the resolutions , ordinances, or regulations; provided, however, that a fine of not less than $50.00 be imposed upon the violator of an ordinance, resolution, or regulation, as the case may be, establishing parking spaces for the handicapped.

Matters pertaining to the supervision and regulation of traffic, to be established by ordinance, resolution, or regulation pursuant to R.S.39:4–197, shall in counties operating under the "Optional County Charter Law," P.L.1972, c. 154 (C.40:41A–1 et seq.) be established by ordinance.

No ordinance, resolution, or regulation adopted pursuant to this section shall be effective unless due notice to the public is given as provided in R.S.39:4–198.

The penalties may be enforced by the proper method of procedure before a magistrate. In default of the payment of the penalty, the magistrate may commit the offender to the county jail for a period not exceeding 5 days.

Amended by L.1951, c. 23, p. 118, § 113; L.1980, c. 143, § 2, eff. Nov. 12, 1980; L.1983, c. 227, § 5, eff. June 27, 1983; L.2008, c. 110, § 3, eff. Dec. 4, 2008.

39:4–201.1. "No passing" zones; notice

With respect to highways under his jurisdiction the commissioner, by regulations, shall have authority to establish and maintain as "no passing" zones portions of such highways where overtaking and passing, or driving to the left of the roadway is deemed especially hazardous. Notice to the public of the establishment of said "no-passing" zones, shall be given in the manner provided in section 39:4–198 of the Revised Statutes.

L.1951, c. 23, p. 119, § 114. Amended by L.2003, c. 13, § 57 (contingent effective date).

Historical and Statutory Notes

L.2003, c. 13, § 127, approved Jan. 28, 2003, provides:

"Sections 1, 2, 3, 12, 38, 109, 110 and 121 shall take effect immediately, sections 105, 106, 107, 108, and 120 shall take effect on July 1, 2003 and the remainder of this act shall take effect on the date the Commissioner of Transportation certifies to the Governor (hereinafter the "date of certification") that a majority of the members of the commission have been appointed or are in office and that all necessary anticipatory actions have been accomplished, provided, that the amount of revenues received pursuant to sections 109 and 110 prior to the date of certification are hereby appropriated to the division. Upon the date of certification, all such collected revenue shall be revenue of the commission. The Commissioner of Transportation, the Director of the Division of Motor Vehicles and the commission may take such anticipatory administrative action in advance as shall be necessary for the implementation of the act."

39:4–201.2. Repealed by L.1999, c. 319, § 2, eff. Jan. 6, 2000

39:4–202. Approval of resolutions, ordinances or regulation by commissioner

No resolution, ordinance or regulation passed, enacted or established under authority of this article shall be effective until submitted to and approved by the Com-

missioner of Transportation, as provided in R.S. 39:4–8, except as otherwise provided therein.

Amended by L.1951, c. 23, p. 119, § 116; L.1983, c. 227, § 6, eff. June 27, 1983.

ARTICLE 22. GENERAL PENALTY

39:4–203. General penalty for violations of chapter

For a violation of a provision of this chapter or any supplement thereto for which no specific penalty is provided, the offender shall be liable to a penalty of not more than $50.00 or imprisonment for a term not exceeding 15 days, or both; except that for a violation of a section of article 11, 13, 14 or 17 of this chapter[1] or any supplement thereto for which no specific penalty is provided, the offender shall be liable to a penalty of not less than $50.00 or more than $200.00 or imprisonment for a term not exceeding 15 days, or both.

Amended by L.1951, c. 23, p. 119, § 117; L.1982, c. 45, § 5, eff. Sept. 1, 1983.

[1] N.J.S.A. § 39:4–80 et seq., § 39:4–105 et seq., § 39:4–123 et seq., or § 39:4–140 et seq.

39:4–203.1. Indigents; fine for traffic offense; payment in installments

Any defendant convicted of a traffic offense pursuant to Title 39 of the Revised Statutes or a parking offense, shall, upon a satisfactory showing of a condition of indigency or participation in a government-based income maintenance program, be permitted by the court to pay the fine in installments. The court shall set the amount and frequency of each installment. In addition, the court may waive an unpaid portion, up to $200, of any court-imposed time-payment order, as a result of a conviction for a motor vehicle traffic violation or a parking offense, except for a violation of R.S.39:4–50 or section 2 of P.L.1981, c. 512 (C.39:4–50.4a), for a defendant who is indigent or is participating in a government-based income maintenance program and who has demonstrated an inability to comply with the time-payment order, and in lieu of the remaining unpaid amount, require the defendant to perform community service for a period of time to be determined by the court, or participate in any program authorized by law, or satisfy any other aspect of a sentence imposed. For the purposes of this section, the guideline for the court to determine indigency is an income up to 250 percent of the poverty level, as defined in section 4 of P.L.2005, c. 156 (C.30:4J–11).

L.1981, c. 365, § 1. Amended by L.1999, c. 397, § 2; L.2007, c. 283, § 1, eff. July 1, 2008.

39:4–203.2. Failure to comply with installment order; additional penalties

If the defendant fails to comply with any of the terms of the installment order, the court may, in addition to any other penalties it may impose, order the suspension

of the defendant's driver's license and notify the Director of the Division of Motor Vehicles of the action.
L.1981, c. 365, § 2.

39:4–203.3. Violations pertaining to pedestrians and bicycles by juvenile under 17; warning; penalties

Notwithstanding the provisions of Title 39 of the Revised Statutes to the contrary, a juvenile under the age of 17 who commits an act which constitutes a violation of that Title pertaining to pedestrians and bicycles may be warned of the violation by a police officer or may be subject to a fine not to exceed $10.00. No points shall be assessed pursuant to section 1 of P.L.1982, c. 43 (C. 39:5–30.5) for these violations.
L.1984, c. 90, § 1.

39:4–203.4. Conviction for violation after Jan. 1, 1983; petition for reduction in sentence

A juvenile convicted of a violation of Title 39 of the Revised Statutes pertaining to pedestrians or bicycles, which violation occurred on or after January 1, 1983, may petition the sentencing court for reduction of the sentence in accordance with the provisions of this act. The court shall sentence pursuant to the provisions of this act unless, for good cause shown, it determines that the original sentence was proper under the circumstances.
L.1984, c. 90, § 2.

39:4–203.5. Traffic offenses committed in areas of highway construction or repair; fines doubled

a. For the purposes of this act:

"Area of highway construction or repair" means that segment of any highway which is identified by properly posted traffic control devices or signs as undergoing construction, reconstruction, repair, or maintenance operation. An area of highway construction or repair shall consist of that area between the first traffic control device or sign informing motor vehicle operators of their approaching highway construction or repair and the last traffic control device or sign indicating all restrictions are removed and normal motor vehicle operations may resume.

"Highway" means any highway under the jurisdiction of the State Department of Transportation, a county, a municipality or a toll road authority.

"Safe corridor" or "safe corridor area" means a segment of highway under the jurisdiction of the Department of Transportation which, based upon accident rates, fatalities, traffic volume and other highway traffic safety criteria, is identified by the Commissioner of Transportation as a segment warranting designation as a "safe corridor."

"Toll road authority" means the New Jersey Turnpike Authority, the New Jersey Highway Authority, or the South Jersey Transportation Authority.

b. The fine for a motor vehicle offense embodied in the following sections of statutory law, when committed in an area of highway construction or repair, or when committed in a designated safe corridor, shall be double the amount specified by law:

Subsection b. of R.S. 39:3–20;

R.S. 39:4–52;

R.S. 39:4–57;

R.S. 39:4–71;

R.S. 39:4–80;

R.S. 39:4–81;

R.S. 39:4–82;

R.S. 39:4–83;

R.S. 39:4–84;

R.S. 39:4–85;

R.S. 39:4–86;

R.S. 39:4–88;

R.S. 39:4–89;

R.S. 39:4–90;

R.S. 39:4–96;

R.S. 39:4–97;

R.S. 39:4–98;

R.S. 39:4–99;

R.S. 39:4–105;

R.S. 39:4–115;

R.S. 39:4–119;

R.S. 39:4–122;

R.S. 39:4–123;

R.S. 39:4–124;

R.S. 39:4–125;

R.S. 39:4–127;

R.S. 39:4–129;

R.S. 39:4–144;

P.L.1955, c. 217 (C. 39:5C–1);

Section 48 of P.L.1951, c. 23 (C. 39:4–66.1);

Section 41 of P.L.1951, c. 23 (C. 39:4–82.1);

Section 51 of P.L.1951, c. 23 (C. 39:4–90.1);

Section 1 of P.L.2000, c. 75 (C. 39:4–97.2);

Section 6 of P.L.1997, c. 415 (C. 39:4–98.7);

Section 5 of P.L.1951, c. 264 (C. 27:23–29);

Section 18 of P.L.1952, c. 16 (C. 27:12B–18); and

Section 21 of P.L.1991, c. 252 (C. 27:25A–21).

When an area of highway construction or repair is within a safe corridor, the fine for a motor vehicle offense embodied in the preceding sections of statutory law shall be doubled only once. When a safe corridor is within an area of highway construction or repair, the fine for a motor vehicle offense embodied in the preceding sections of statutory law shall be doubled only once. Fines for violation of section 6 of P.L.1997, c. 415 (C.39:4–98.7) in a safe corridor or an area of highway construction or repair shall be doubled only once. Notwithstanding any other provision of law, the increase from the doubled fines imposed and collected in designated safe corridor areas shall be forwarded by the person to whom they are paid to the State Treasurer, who shall annually deposit those moneys in the "Highway Safety Fund" established pursuant to section 5 of P.L.2003, c. 131 (C.39:3–20.4).

c. (1) Signs designed in compliance with the specifications of the Department of Transportation or, if appropriate, the toll road authority having jurisdiction over the appropriate highway, shall be appropriately placed, by order of the Commissioner of Transportation, the appropriate local official, or the affected toll road authority, as the case may be, to notify drivers approaching areas of highway construction or repair, or designated safe corridor areas, that the fines are doubled for motor vehicle offenses in those areas.

(2) In addition, all traffic control signs and devices erected or displayed by the State Department of Transportation, a county, a municipality or a toll road authority within an area of highway construction or repair or safe corridor area shall conform to the uniform system specified in the most current "Manual on Uniform Traffic Control Devices for Streets and Highways," prepared by the Federal Highway Administration in the United States Department of Transportation.

d. It shall not be a defense to the imposition of the fines authorized under the provisions of this act that a sign notifying drivers who are approaching highway construction or repair areas, or designated safe corridor areas, that fines are doubled for motor vehicle offenses in those areas was not posted, improperly posted, wrongfully removed or stolen, or that signs or devices were not placed in compliance with the most current "Manual on Uniform Traffic Control Devices for Streets and Highways" as required pursuant to paragraph (2) of subsection c. of this section.

e. The director shall include information concerning the penalties imposed pursuant to this act in any subsequent revision of the New Jersey Driver Manual and the New Jersey Motorist Guide.

f. Safe corridor areas shall be designated by traffic order issued pursuant to P.L.1998, c. 28 (C.39:4–8.2 et seq.).

L.1993, c. 332, § 1, eff. Feb. 21, 1994. Amended by L.2003, c. 131, § 1, eff. Feb. 15, 2004.

ARTICLE 23. SPECIAL PRIVILEGES

39:4–204. "Handicapped person" defined

The term "handicapped person" as employed herein shall include any person who has lost the use of one or more limbs as a consequence of paralysis, amputation, or other permanent disability or who is permanently disabled as to be unable to ambulate without the aid of an assisting device or whose mobility is otherwise limited as certified by a physician with a plenary license to practice medicine and surgery; a podiatrist licensed to practice in this State or a bordering state; a physician stationed at a military or naval installation located in this State who is licensed to practice in any state; or, a chiropractic physician licensed to practice in this State or a bordering state.

L.1949, c. 280, p. 871, § 1. Amended by L.1950, c. 191, p. 428, § 1; L.1981, c. 36, § 1; L.1991, c. 49, § 1, eff. March 6, 1991; L.1997, c. 267, § 1, eff. March 1, 1998; L.1999, c. 326, § 1, eff. Jan. 6, 2000.

39:4–205. Handicapped person identification cards; application; issuance; forfeiture or revocation; indefinite validity

The Director of the Division of Motor Vehicles in the Department of Law and Public Safety shall issue, at the expense of the State of New Jersey, handicapped person identification cards upon the application of qualifying handicapped persons, as heretofore defined, and after due investigation of the qualifying status of each applicant. Said card shall, amongst other things, identify the handicapped persons and the registration number of the vehicle for which any wheelchair symbol license plates have been issued under the provisions of section 3 of this act and shall state that he is a handicapped person validly qualified hereunder to receive such card, that said card is for the exclusive use of the person to whom it has been duly issued, is nontransferable and will be forfeited if presented by any other person, and that any abuse of any privilege, benefit, precedence or consideration granted to any person to whom such card may be issued will be sufficient cause for revocation of said card, corresponding windshield placard and wheelchair symbol license plates, and the same may be forfeited or revoked accordingly, and in the absence of any such forfeiture or revocation said card shall be valid indefinitely.

L.1949, c. 280, p. 871, § 2. Amended by L.1981, c. 36, § 2.

39:4–206. Placard; issuance; display on motor vehicle; temporary placards; grant upon certification by physician; renewal; fees; license plates with wheelchair symbol

The director shall issue to such applicant, also, a placard of such size and design as shall be determined by the director in consultation with the Division of Vocational Rehabilitation Services in the Department of Labor and the Office of Disability Services in the

Department of Human Services, indicating that a handicapped person identification card has been issued to the person designated therein, which shall be displayed in such manner as the director shall determine on the motor vehicle used to transport the handicapped person, when the vehicle is parked overtime or in special parking places established for use by handicapped persons.

Notwithstanding any provision of P.L.1949, c. 280 (C. 39:4–204 et seq.) to the contrary, the chief of police of each municipality in this State shall issue a temporary placard of not more than six months' duration to any person who has temporarily lost the use of one or more limbs or is temporarily disabled as to be unable to ambulate without the aid of an assisting device or whose mobility is otherwise temporarily limited, as certified by a physician with a plenary license to practice medicine and surgery; a podiatrist licensed to practice in this State or a bordering state; a physician stationed at a military or naval installation located in this State who is licensed to practice in any state; or a chiropractic physician licensed to practice in this State or a bordering state. Each temporary handicapped placard issued under the provisions of this section shall set forth the date on which it shall become invalid.

The temporary placard shall be granted upon written certification by a physician with a plenary license to practice medicine and surgery or a podiatrist licensed to practice in this State or a bordering state or a physician stationed at a military or naval installation located in this State who is licensed to practice in any state that the person meets the conditions constituting temporary disability as provided in this section. This certification shall be provided on a standard form to be developed by the director in consultation with local chiefs of police and representatives of the handicapped. The form shall contain only those conditions constituting temporary disability as are provided in this section. The physical presence of the handicapped person shall not be required for the issuance of a temporary handicapped placard.

The placard may be renewed one time at the discretion of the issuing authority for a period of not more than six months' duration. The placard shall be displayed on the motor vehicle used by the temporarily handicapped person and shall give the person the right to park overtime or to use special parking places established for use by handicapped persons in any municipality of this State.

The fee for the issuance of such temporary or permanent placard issued pursuant to this section shall be $4.00 and payable to the Director of the Division of Motor Vehicles.

The director may, in addition, issue license plates bearing the national wheelchair symbol for:

a. Not more than two motor vehicles owned, operated or leased by a handicapped person or by any person furnishing transportation on his behalf; or

b. Any two motorcycles owned, operated or leased by a handicapped person.

The fee for the issuance of such plates shall be $10.00 for each vehicle.

L.1949, c. 280, p. 872, § 3. Amended by L.1954, c. 133, p. 610, § 1; L.1966, c. 204, § 1, eff. July 21, 1966; L.1975, c. 330, § 1; L.1981, c. 36, § 3; L.1983, c. 96, § 1, eff. March 11, 1983; L.1989, c. 201, § 3, eff. June 1, 1990; L.1991, c. 49, § 2, eff. March 6, 1991; L.1993, c. 277, § 1, eff. March 1, 1994; L.1997, c. 267, § 2, eff. March 1, 1998; L.1999, c. 91, § 13, eff. May 3, 1999; L.1999, c. 326, § 2, eff. Jan. 6, 2000.

39:4–207. Parking overtime; motor vehicle with display of placard or wheelchair symbol license plates

No penalty shall be imposed for the parking overtime of any motor vehicle which has displayed thereon a placard or wheelchair symbol license plates issued pursuant to the provisions of this act under any law or municipal ordinance now in effect or hereafter enacted unless such vehicle shall have been parked in one location for more than 24 hours. This provision shall apply only when the person to whom the placard or special license plate has been issued is either the driver or a passenger of the vehicle.

L.1949, c. 280, p. 872, § 4. Amended by L.1981, c. 36, § 4; L.1989, c. 201, § 4, eff. June 1, 1990.

39:4–207.1. Rules and regulations

The Director of the Division of Motor Vehicles shall promulgate rules and regulations necessary to effectuate the purposes of this act.

L.1981, c. 36, § 5.

39:4–207.2. Mentally retarded person defined

For purposes of this act "mentally retarded person" means a person in a state of significant subnormal intellectual development with reduction of social competence which state shall have existed prior to adolescence and is expected to be of lifelong duration.

L.1984, c. 50, § 1.

39:4–207.3. Motor vehicles used to transport mentally retarded persons; special insignia; issuance; fee; annual renewal; special vehicle identification cards; placard for display

a. The Director of the Division of Motor Vehicles shall issue a special insignia upon the application of a federal, State, county or municipal entity or a public or private nonprofit organization incorporated under the laws of this State for motor vehicles owned or operated by the applicant and used to transport mentally retarded persons. The insignia shall be of a design and shall be posted or attached to the motor vehicle in a place and manner to be determined by the director. The fee for the issuance of an insignia shall be determined by the director and the insignia shall be renewable annually by the director at the time fixed for the annual registration of the vehicle.

b. The director may also issue to an applicant, at the expense of the State, special vehicle identification cards to be carried by the operators of motor vehicles used to transport mentally retarded persons. The cards shall be renewable annually by the director at the time fixed for the annual registration of the vehicles.

c. The director may also issue to an applicant a placard to be displayed on the motor vehicle.

L.1984, c. 50, § 2.

39:4–207.4. Authorization to park in space marked for physically handicapped

A motor vehicle owned or operated by a federal, State, county or municipal entity or a public or private nonprofit organization incorporated under the laws of this State and used to transport mentally retarded persons, and which is properly identified in accordance with the provisions of section 1 of this act,[1] is authorized to park in a space appropriately marked for vehicles for the physically handicapped pursuant to law whenever the vehicle is being used to transport mentally retarded persons.

L.1984, c. 50, § 3.

[1] N.J.S.A. § 39:4–207.2.

39:4–207.5. Handicapped parking privileges; vehicles with permit from another state, district or territory of United States or Canada

A motor vehicle with a special license plate, placard or parking permit issued to a handicapped person by another state, district or territory of the United States, or by Canada shall be entitled to special parking privileges for the handicapped established by any law or by any ordinance, resolution or regulation.

L.1986, c. 25, § 1, eff. June 6, 1986.

39:4–207.6. Definitions

As used in this act:

a. "Appropriate identification" means, in the case of a restricted parking zone, a permit issued by a municipality under the authority granted by section 2 of P.L.1977, c. 309 (C.39:4–197.7) and, in the case of a restricted parking space, a placard or wheelchair symbol license plates issued by the Division of Motor Vehicles under section 3 of P.L.1949, c. 280 (C.39:4–206).

b. "Eligible handicapped person" means a handicapped person who is the holder of (1) an identification card issued by the Division of Motor Vehicles under section 2 of P.L.1949, c. 280 (C.39:4–205), or (2) a permit issued by a municipality under the authority granted by section 2 of P.L.1977, c. 309 (C.39:4–197.7).

c. "Park unlawfully" means to park a motor vehicle in a restricted parking space or a restricted parking zone if the motor vehicle does not display appropriate identification.

d. "Restricted parking space" means a parking space which the State or a local government has established for the exclusive use of a handicapped person but shall not include a restricted parking zone established under section 1 of P.L.1977, c. 309 (C.39:4–197.6).

e. "Restricted parking zone" means a parking zone in front of the residence of a handicapped person which a municipality has established for the use of that handicapped person under the authority granted by section 1 of P.L.1977, c. 309 (C.39:4–197.6).

L.1989, c. 200, § 1, eff. Nov. 29, 1989.

39:4–207.7. Request by eligible handicapped person to law enforcement officer for removal and storage of motor vehicle unlawfully parked in handicapped parking space or zone

a. An eligible handicapped person may request a law enforcement officer to arrange for the removal and storage of a motor vehicle which is parked unlawfully in a parking space or zone which is restricted for use by a handicapped person. It shall be the obligation of the owner of the motor vehicle to pay the reasonable costs for the removal and for any storage which may result from the removal.

b. The removal of a motor vehicle under this section is subject to local ordinances concerning the regulation of that practice, including, but not limited to, the fees charged for the removal, notice requirements therefor, and the licensing of persons engaged in that practice.

c. The assessment of removal and storage costs against a person under this section shall be in addition to any other penalty assessed against the person.

L.1989, c. 200, § 2, eff. Nov. 29, 1989.

39:4–207.8. Handicapped nursing home resident identification card and windshield placard

The Director of the Division of Motor Vehicles in the Department of Law and Public Safety shall issue a handicapped nursing home resident identification card and corresponding windshield placard upon the application of a nursing home owner or operator for use in a vehicle owned or operated by the nursing home when that vehicle is used to transport handicapped nursing home residents. The identification card and corresponding windshield placard shall identify the nursing home owner or operator and the registration number of the nursing home's vehicle for which the card is issued, and shall state that: the nursing home owner or operator is validly qualified to receive the identification card and corresponding windshield placard; the identification card and corresponding windshield placard are for the exclusive use of the nursing home's vehicle when transporting a handicapped nursing home resident; the identification card and corresponding windshield placard are not transferable and will be forfeited if used for purposes not authorized under this act; and an abuse of any privilege, benefit, precedence or consideration granted to a person to whom the identification card and corresponding windshield placard are issued will be sufficient cause for revocation of the identification card and corresponding windshield placard and the same may be forfeited or revoked accordingly, and in the absence of a forfeiture or revocation, the identification card and corresponding windshield placard are valid indefinitely.

The windshield placard shall be displayed on the vehicle when the vehicle is used to transport handicapped nursing home residents. A vehicle displaying this windshield placard is authorized to park in a space appropriately marked for vehicles for the physically handicapped only when delivering or receiving handicapped nursing home residents from one location to another. The vehicle is not permitted to park in designated handicapped parking spaces when it is not transporting handicapped nursing home residents.

The fee for the issuance of the identification card and corresponding windshield placard issued pursuant to this section is $4.00 and is payable to the Director of the Division of Motor Vehicles.

L.1989, c. 201, § 6, eff. June 1, 1990.

39:4–207.9. Parking spaces for handicapped motorists; maintenance

a. A person who owns or controls a parking area which is open to the public or to which the public is invited and which contains special parking spaces for the use of persons who have been issued a placard or wheelchair symbol license plates pursuant to P.L.1949, c. 280 (C.39:4–204 et seq.) shall be responsible for assuring that access to these special parking spaces and to curb cuts or other improvements designed to provide accessibility for handicapped persons is not obstructed.

b. If snow or ice is obstructing the special parking space, curb cut or other improvement designed to provide accessibility for the handicapped, it shall be removed within 24 hours after the weather condition causing the snow or ice ceases.

c. A person who violates this act shall be liable for a penalty of not less than $500 or more than $1,000 for each space that is obstructed.

L.1999, c. 182, § 1, eff. Aug. 16, 1999. Amended by L.2007, c. 287, § 1, eff. Jan. 13, 2008.

ARTICLE 24. REGULATION OF TRAFFIC AND PARKING ON STATE PROPERTY

39:4–208. Trenton, State's property at; regulations authorized

The Division of State Police in the Department of Law and Public Safety is authorized and empowered to regulate traffic and the parking of motor vehicles on the grounds, and roadways or highways therein, owned by the State of New Jersey at Trenton, and the board, body or officer in charge and control of any State institution

may likewise regulate traffic and the parking of motor vehicles on the grounds of such institution and roadways or highways on such grounds, and for such purpose may adopt, promulgate and enforce rules and regulations to prevent traffic congestion and insure a proper, reasonable, orderly and safe use of said grounds, roadways and highways by motorists.

L.1950, c. 16, p. 43, § 1. Amended by L.1956, c. 47, p. 96, § 1.

39:4–209. Violations; penalties

Any person who shall violate any of the said regulations shall be subject to a fine of not less than $1.00 nor more than $15.00; provided, however, that any person who shall violate any of said regulations concerning the altering, counterfeiting or misuse of parking permits shall be subject to a fine of not more than $50.00.

L.1950, c. 16, p. 43, § 2. Amended by L.1973, c. 116, § 1, eff. May 7, 1973.

39:4–210. Jurisdiction of offenses; disposition of fines

Every magistrate and every court having jurisdiction of criminal offenses and the violations of public laws committed in the municipality in which such grounds are located shall have jurisdiction to hear and determine violations of the said regulations to be made by the said division under the provisions of this act and to fix, impose and enforce payment of fines therefor. All such fines shall be for the use and benefit of the State of New Jersey.

L.1950, c. 16, p. 43, § 3. Amended by L.1956, c. 47, p. 96, § 2.

39:4–211. Enforcement of regulations

The State Police, the State Capitol Police, the city police of the city of Trenton, and other police officers of this State, including those specially appointed or designated to police the grounds of any such State institution, shall have the power and authority to enforce the provisions of this act and said regulations upon the public highways located on the said grounds of the State of New Jersey within their respective jurisdictions.

L.1950, c. 16, p. 43, § 4. Amended by L.1956, c. 47, p. 97, § 3; L.1983, c. 403, § 17, eff. Dec. 23, 1983.

39:4–212. Cooperation in making and enforcing regulations

The said division and any such board, body or officer is authorized to consult and co-operate with the commissioner, and the county and municipal officials having jurisdiction over the highways and traffic regulations and enforcement in the city of Trenton, or in the municipality in which the State institution may be located, as the case may be, in making and enforcing the said regulations.

L.1950, c. 16, p. 44, § 5. Amended by L.1956, c. 47, p. 97, § 4; L.2003, c. 13, § 58 (contingent effective date).

ARTICLE 25. EMERGENCY TRAFFIC CONTROL

39:4–213. Control of traffic during emergency conditions; Attorney-General's powers

Whenever the Attorney-General shall determine that an emergency condition exists with regard to the flow of vehicular traffic in this State, he may, through police agencies under his control, determine and control the direction of the flow of such traffic on any State highway, municipal or county road, including the right to detour, reroute or divert any or all traffic necessary to remove the emergency then existing. Said traffic may be detoured, rerouted or diverted to other State highways, or municipal or county roads. The Attorney-General further shall determine the type of vehicle or vehicles permitted to be operated on such State highway, or municipal or county road.

L.1950, c. 70, p. 128, § 1.

39:4–214. Signals; signs; police personnel

For the purpose of carrying into effect the provisions of this act, the Attorney-General is authorized to erect directional signals or signs, and assign such police personnel as may be necessary for the manual direction of traffic during said emergency.

L.1950, c. 70, p. 129, § 2.

39:4–215. Failure to obey signals, signs or directions

Any person who fails to obey the directions of a police officer or fails to obey the directional signals or signs provided hereunder shall be subject to a fine of not more than one hundred dollars ($100.00) or imprisonment for ten days in jail, or both.

L.1950, c. 70, p. 129, § 3.

ARTICLE 26. REGULATION OF USE BY STATE AND INTERSTATE HIGHWAY SYSTEM. RIGHTS OF WAY AND REST AREAS

39:4–216. Commercial activity or solicitation of contributions; prohibition

No person shall tender or offer for sale goods or merchandise of any kind, engage in any other commercial activity, or solicit contributions for any cause, on any portion of the right of way of a State or interstate highway system, including any rest areas located on such right of way.

Nothing in this section shall be construed to inhibit the operation of commercial traffic, the rendering of emergency services to vehicles or travelers on the State or interstate highway system nor the installation and use of public telephones at locations on the rights of way approved by the State Department of Transportation.

L.1979, c. 66, § 1, eff. April 4, 1979.

CHAPTER 5

ENFORCEMENT AND PROCEDURE

Section

39:5–1.   Enforcement.

39:5–2.   Judicial powers of director; holding court; notice to defendants; fees and costs; appeal.

39:5–3.   Process for appearance or arrest; complaint; venue.

39:5–4.   Repealed.

39:5–5.   Entitling proceedings; bond to secure costs.

39:5–6.   Performance of ministerial acts.

39:5–7.   Suspension of sentence; probation.

39:5–8.   Repealed.

39:5–9.   Forfeiture of bond or cash deposit; disposition of moneys.

39:5–10.   Repealed.

39:5–11.   Appeal to Superior Court; effect.

39:5–12 to 39:5–19.   Repealed.

39:5–20.   Complainant represented on trial on appeal by county prosecutor, attorney general or municipal attorney; aid in prosecution.

39:5–21.   Repealed.

39:5–22.   Revoked license not restored by appeal.

39:5–23.   Repealed.

39:5–24.   Proceedings on Sunday.

39:5–25.   Arrest without warrant; detention of offender; summons instead of arrest.

39:5–25.1.   Summons or complaint; identification of motorist as commercial driver license holder.

39:5–26.   Repealed.

39:5–27.   License exhibited to magistrate upon arrest.

39:5–28.   Validity, service and effect of summons or warrant and arrest thereon in county other than where issued.

39:5–29.   Repealed.

39:5–30.   Suspension or revocation of drivers's license, registration certificate or nonresident reciprocity privileges; plenary hearing; preliminary suspension without hearing.

39:5–30a.   Habitual offender defined.

39:5–30b.   Suspension of license; period of time; notice; hearing.

39:5–30c.   Maximum suspension period; circumstances determining.

39:5–30d.   Concurrent suspension; application for reinstatement.

39:5–30e.   Operation of motor vehicle during suspension; fine and imprisonment.

39:5–30.1.   Suspension or revocation of driver's license where reciprocity driving privilege is suspended or revoked in another state.

39:5–30.2.   Review of suspension or revocation; attendance of driver improvement program in lieu of suspension; administration authority relating to driver improvement program.

39:5–30.3.   Repealed.

39:5–30.4.   Driver improvement program; fees.

39:5–30.5.   Penalty points; rules and regulations; authority to adopt.

39:5–30.5a.   Penalty points; motor vehicle operation causing property destruction.

39:5–30.6.   Penalty points; assessment; record.

39:5–30.7.   Accumulated points; notification.

Section

39:5–30.8.   Suspension of License; accumulated points; notice; effective date; hearing; failure to appear.

39:5–30.9.   Reduction of points.

39:5–30.10.   Subsequent violations; suspension; notice; hearing; failure to appear.

39:5–30.11.   Initial notification; defense; accumulated points.

39:5–30.12.   Definitions.

39:5–30.13.   Suspension of license for drug convictions; period of suspension for persons under 17 years of age.

39:5–30.14.   Notification: effective date of suspension; hearing.

39:5–30.15.   Responsibility of director for drug conviction reports.

39:5–30.16.   Rules and regulations.

39:5–31.   Revocation of driver's license by director or magistrate.

39:5–32.   Validation of or grant of new driver's license when same revoked.

39:5–33.   New license to driver whose license suspended or revoked to be granted by commissioner personally.

39:5–34.   New registration or registration certificate when old suspended or revoked to be issued under personal direction of commissioner.

39:5–35.   Return or surrender of suspended or revoked driver's license or registration certificate and registration plates.

39:5–36.   Imprisonment on default of payment of fine.

39:5–36.1.   Fee for dishonored check or similar sight order.

39:5–37, 39:5–38.   Repealed.

39:5–39.   Physician's fee in certain cases.

39:5–40.   Disposition of moneys received under motor vehicle law.

39:5–41.   Fines, penalties and forfeitures; disposition; exceptions.

39:5–42.   Reports by magistrate to commissioner; motor vehicle violations; crimes in which a motor vehicle was used.

39:5–43.   Failure to pay over fines collected; penalty.

39:5–44.   Record of fines payable to county; inspection.

39:5–45.   Receipt for offender.

39:5–46.   Conviction of stealing produce reported to commissioner.

39:5–47.   Seizure and sale of stolen motor vehicles.

39:5–48 to 39:5–50.   Transferred.

39:5–51.   Case involving violation of law on motor vehicles and traffic regulation or motor vehicle accident; prosecutor's responsibility to inform court of death of or injury to victim.

39:5–52.   Information available to victim; request; "victim" defined; consultation with prosecutor.

39:5–53.   Definitions.

39:5–54.   Law enforcement procedures.

39:5–55.   Duties of Division of Motor Vehicles.

39:5–56.   Construction with other laws.

39:5–1.   Enforcement

Except as otherwise provided, the enforcement of this subtitle shall be vested in the director and the police or peace officers of, or inspectors duly appointed for that purpose by, any municipality or county or by the State. Nothing in this section shall be construed to authorize police or peace officers or inspectors appointed by any municipality or county to conduct random roadside examinations of any vehicle.

Amended by L.1938, c. 164, p. 374, § 2, eff. May 12, 1938; L.1972, c. 169, § 3, eff. Nov. 3, 1972; L.1983, c. 403, § 18, eff. Dec. 23, 1983; L.1994, c. 60, § 34, eff. July 1, 1994.

39:5–2.   Judicial powers of director; holding court; notice to defendants; fees and costs; appeal

The director shall have the same powers as are conferred by this subtitle on a magistrate.

In considering violations of this subtitle, the director may hold court in any municipality in the State, upon five days' notice given to the defendants summoned to appear before him and shall conduct the proceedings in compliance with, insofar as they are applicable, the rules of the Supreme Court governing municipal courts. The fees and costs shall be the same as in a municipal court. Appeals from a court held by the director shall, in the manner provided for an appeal from a municipal court, be taken to the Superior Court .

Amended by L.1939, c. 216, p. 614, § 1, eff. July 12, 1939; L.1953, c. 36, p. 619, § 5; L.1991, c. 91, § 371, eff. April 9, 1991.

39:5–3.   Process for appearance or arrest; complaint; venue

a. When a person has violated a provision of this subtitle, the judge may, within 30 days after the commission of the offense, issue process directed to a constable, police officer, or the chief administrator for the appearance or arrest of the person so charged and for a violation of R.S.39:4–81, issue process within 90 days after the commission of the offense. In the case of a violation enumerated in subsection b. of this section, this period shall commence upon the filing of a complaint.

b. A complaint may be made to a judge for a violation of R.S.39:3–12, R.S. 39:3–34, R.S.39:3–37, R.S.39:4–129 or R.S.39:10–24 at any time within one year after the commission of the offense; for a violation of R.S.39:4–50, section 2 of P.L.1981, c. 512 (C.39:4–50.4a), section 5 of P.L.1990, c. 103 (C.39:3–10.13), section 16 of P.L.1990, c. 103 (C.39:3–10.24), section 3 of P.L.1952, c. 157 (C.12:7–46), section 9 of P.L.1986, c. 39 (C.12:7–57), R.S.39:3–40, or section 1 of P.L.1942, c. 192 (C.39:4–128.1), at any time within 90 days after the commission of the offense.

c. All proceedings shall be brought before a judge having jurisdiction in the municipality in which it is alleged that the violation occurred, but when a violation occurs on a street through which the boundary line of two or more municipalities runs or crosses, then the proceeding may be brought before the judge having jurisdiction in any one of the municipalities divided by said boundary line, and in the event there shall be no judge or should no judge having such jurisdiction be available for the acceptance of bail and disposition of the case, or should the judges having such jurisdiction be disqualified because of personal interest in the proceedings, or for any other legal cause, said proceeding shall be brought before a judge having jurisdiction in the nearest municipality to the one in which it is alleged such a violation occurred.

Amended by L.1940, c. 212, p. 874, § 1; L.1942, c. 334, p. 1178, § 1; L.1951, c. 251, p. 887, § 1; L.1953, c. 36, p. 619, § 6; L.1959, c. 58, p. 167, § 1; L.1983, c. 403, § 19, eff. Dec. 23, 1983; L.2000, c. 85, § 1, eff. Aug. 14, 2000; L.2002, c. 56, § 1, eff. Aug. 3, 2002; L.2009, c. 52, § 1, eff. July 3, 2009.

39:5–4. Repealed by L.1953, c. 36, p. 620, § 7

39:5–5. Entitling proceedings; bond to secure costs

All proceedings for the violation of this subtitle shall be brought in the name of the State, with the director, police officer, peace officer, constable or any other person who institutes the proceedings as prosecutor. A judge may, at his discretion, refuse to issue a warrant on the complaint of a person other than the director or a police officer, until a sufficient bond to secure costs has been executed and delivered to the judge.

Amended by L.1953, c. 36, p. 620, § 8; L.1983, c. 403, § 20, eff. Dec. 20, 1983.

39:5–6. Performance of ministerial acts

All acts, whether in connection with the taking of complaints, issuing of process, return thereof, taking of bail for appearance or committing to custody for failure to deposit such bail and all proceedings preliminary to trial, including the arraignment, taking of plea and postponement of trial and all ministerial acts and proceedings subsequent to trial, may be performed by the clerk or deputy clerk of a magistrate, and the jurisdiction so to do with respect to a violation of this subtitle is hereby conferred.

Amended by L.1952, c. 288, p. 975, § 1.

39:5–7. Suspension of sentence; probation

In any proceeding instituted pursuant to the provisions of this subtitle, except where a mandatory penalty is fixed herein, the magistrate may suspend the imposition or execution of sentence, and may also place the defendant on probation under the supervision of the chief probation officer of the county for a period of not less than six months nor more than one year. The probation shall be effected and administered pursuant to the provisions of sections 2A:168–1 to 2A:168–13 of the New Jersey Statutes.[1]

Amended by L.1953, c. 36, p. 620, § 9.

[1] N.J.S.A. §§ 2A:168–1 to 2A:168–4 repealed. See, now, §§ 2C:44–1, 2C:44–6, 2C:45–1 to 2C:45–4, 2C:46–1.

39:5–8. Repealed by L.1953, c. 36, p. 620, § 10

39:5–9. Forfeiture of bond or cash deposit; disposition of moneys

A bail bond, if forfeited, may be enforced by the director, and any cash deposit in lieu of bond, if forfeited, shall be paid to the director by the magistrate with whom it was deposited; provided, that such forfeiture is in a proceeding instituted by the director, or a member of his staff, or by the State Police, or an inspector of the Public Utility Commission, or a law enforcement officer of any other State agency. The director shall dispose of the proceeds of said forfeiture in the manner provided by section 39:5–40 of this Title and the proceeds of forfeitures in a proceeding instituted by a local officer shall be forwarded by the magistrate to the proper financial officer of the county, wherein they were collected, to be used by the county as a fund for road repairs therein; provided, however, that the magistrate may first deduct costs and fees from forfeited bail in an amount not to exceed the amount of the costs and fees authorized by section 22A:3–4 of the New Jersey Statutes, and pay the same to the municipal treasurer.

Amended by L.1942, c. 334, p. 1179, § 2; L.1953, c. 36, p. 621, § 11; L.1965, c. 230, § 1, eff. Jan. 10, 1966.

39:5–10. Repealed by L.1953, c. 36, p. 621, § 12

39:5–11. Appeal to Superior Court; effect

If the defendant appeals to the Superior Court, the appeal shall operate as a consent to an amendment of the complaint in that court so as to substitute a new or different charge growing out of the act or acts complained of or the circumstances surrounding such acts; and any provision of law limiting the time within which any such charge may be brought or proceedings taken in the prosecution thereof shall not operate and shall be deemed to have been waived by the appeal.

Amended by L.1953, c. 36, p. 621, § 13; L.1991, c. 91, § 372, eff. April 9, 1991.

39:5–12 to 39:5–19. Repealed by L.1953, c. 36, pp. 621, 622, §§ 14 to 21

39:5–20. Complainant represented on trial on appeal by county prosecutor, attorney general or municipal attorney; aid in prosecution

On an appeal by the defendant in any proceeding instituted under this subtitle, the county prosecutor of the county wherein the alleged violation was committed shall represent the complainant; but where a complaint is made by a member of the State Police charging a violation of either section 39:3–40, 39:4–50 or 39:4–96 of this Title, the Attorney General, and not the prosecutor, shall represent the complainant, and where there is violation of a municipal ordinance relating to traffic regulations and the proceeding was instituted by a municipal officer, the municipal attorney shall represent the complainant. The county prosecutor, charged with the enforcement of this subtitle, may request the Attorney General to attend personally, or by such assistant or assistants as he shall designate, to aid in the prosecution of the appeal.

Amended by L.1953, c. 36, p. 622, § 22; L.1967, c. 41, § 1, eff. April 28, 1967; L.1983, c. 403, § 21, eff. Dec. 23, 1983.

39:5–21. Repealed by L.1953, c. 36, p. 622, § 23

39:5–22. Revoked license not restored by appeal

Where a license has been revoked for a violation of section 39:4–50 of this Title, and an appeal has been taken from the judgment, the appeal shall not operate to restore the license during the pendency of the appeal, however, the license may be restored either by the trial court or the appellate court pending disposition of the appeal.

Amended by L.1953, c. 36, p. 622, § 24; L.1965, c. 237, § 1, eff. Feb. 16, 1966.

39:5–23. Repealed by L.1953, c. 36, p. 622, § 25

39:5–24. Proceedings on Sunday

Proceedings under this subtitle may be instituted on any day of the week, and the institution of the proceedings on Sunday shall be no bar to the successful prosecution thereof. Any process served on Sunday shall be as valid as if served on any other day of the week.

39:5–25. Arrest without warrant; detention of offender; summons instead of arrest

Any law enforcement officer may, without a warrant, arrest any person violating in his presence any provision of chapter 3 of this Title,[1] or any person, other than a motorman or person having control of a street car or auto bus, running upon a route approved by the Board of Public Utilities, violating in his presence any provision of chapter 4 of this Title.[2] A law enforcement officer may arrest without a warrant any person who the officer has probable cause to believe has operated a motor vehicle in violation of R.S. 39:4–50 or section 5 of P.L. 1990, c. 103 (C. 39:3–10.13), regardless of whether the suspected violation occurs in the officer's presence. The exemption from arrest of a motorman or person having control of a street car or auto bus, as conferred herein, shall not operate to prevent his arrest, however, for a violation of R.S. 39:4–50. The arresting officer shall bring any person so arrested before any judge of the municipal court of the municipality wherein the offense is committed, or before the director at any place designated as his office. If the arrest is for a violation of R.S. 39:4–50, the arresting officer may, if no judge, clerk or deputy clerk is available, detain the person arrested, either in any police station, lockup or other place maintained by any municipality for the detention of offenders or in the common jail of the county, for such reasonable time as will permit the arresting officer to obtain a warrant for the offender's further detention, which temporary detention shall not exceed 24 hours from the time of the arrest. If the arrest is for a

violation of any other provision of this subtitle, the person arrested shall be detained in the police station or municipal court until the arresting officer makes a complaint and a warrant issues.

Any law enforcement officer may, instead of arresting an offender as herein provided, serve upon him a summons.

Amended by L.1940, c. 139, p. 303, § 1; L.1953, c. 36, p. 622, § 26; L.1983, c. 403, § 22, eff. Dec. 23, 1983; L.1983, c. 563, § 1, eff. Jan. 17, 1984; L.1994, c. 184, § 4, eff. Dec. 23, 1994.

    1 N.J.S.A. § 39:3–1 et seq.
    2 N.J.S.A. § 39:4–1 et seq.

39:5–25.1. Summons or complaint; identification of motorist as commercial driver license holder

Upon issuance of a summons or complaint charging a motorist with any violation, other than a parking violation, under Title 39 of the Revised Statutes, a law enforcement officer shall identify on the face of the summons or complaint, whether the motorist is a holder of a commercial driver license.

L.2005, c. 147, § 11, eff. Sept. 30, 2005.

39:5–26. Repealed by L.1953, c. 36, p. 623, § 27

39:5–27. License exhibited to magistrate upon arrest

Any driver arrested for a violation of any provision of this subtitle shall, on demand of the magistrate hearing the complaint against him, produce his license for inspection. If he fails to produce his license or to give satisfactory excuse for its nonproduction, he shall, in addition to any other penalties imposed by the magistrate, be subject to a fine of not more than twenty-five dollars.

39:5–28. Validity, service and effect of summons or warrant and arrest thereon in county other than where issued

A summons or warrant issued by a magistrate under this chapter shall be valid throughout the State. An officer who may serve the summons or warrant and make arrest on the warrant in the county in which it was issued may also serve the summons or warrant and make arrest on the warrant in any county of the State.

Amended by L.1953, c. 36, p. 623, § 28.

39:5–29. Repealed by L.1953, c. 36, p. 624, § 29

39:5–30. Suspension or revocation of drivers's license, registration certificate or nonresident reciprocity privileges; plenary hearing; preliminary suspension without hearing

a. Every registration certificate, every license certificate, every privilege to drive motor vehicles, including commercial motor vehicles as defined in P.L.1990, c. 103 (C.39:3–10.9 et al.), every endorsement, class of license, and commercial driver's license, may be suspended or revoked, and any person may be prohibited from obtaining a driver's license or a registration certificate, or disqualified from obtaining any class of or endorsement on a commercial driver's license, and the reciprocity privilege of any nonresident may be suspended or revoked by the director for a violation of any of the provisions of this Title or on any other reasonable grounds, after due notice in writing of such proposed suspension, revocation, disqualification or prohibition and the ground thereof.

He may also summon witnesses to appear before him at his office or at any other place he designates, to give testimony in a hearing which he holds looking toward a revocation of a license or registration certificate issued by or under his authority. The summons shall be served at least five days before the return date, either by registered mail or personal service. A person who fails to obey the summons shall be subject to a penalty not exceeding $100.00, to be recovered with costs in an action at law, prosecuted by the Attorney General, and in addition the vehicle registration or driver's license, or both, as the case may be, shall forthwith be revoked. The fee for witnesses required to attend before the director shall be $1.00 for each day's attendance and $0.03 for every mile of travel by the nearest generally traveled route in going to and from the place where the attendance of the witness is required. These fees shall be paid when the witness is excused from further attendance, and the disbursements made from payment of the fees shall be audited and paid in the manner provided for expenses of the department. The actual conduct of said hearing may be delegated by the director to such departmental employees as he may designate, in which case the said employees shall recommend to the director in writing whether the said licenses or certificates shall or shall not be suspended or revoked.

b. Whenever a matter is presented to the director involving an alleged violation of

(1) R.S.39:4–98, where an excess of 20 miles per hour over the authorized speed limit is alleged, and which has resulted in the death of another;

(2) R.S.39:4–50, and which has resulted in the death of another;

(3) R.S.39:4–96, and which has resulted in the death of another; or

(4) R.S.39:4–129, wherein the death of another has occurred, and the director has not determined to immediately issue a preliminary suspension pursuant to subsection e. of this section, the director shall issue a notice of proposed final suspension or revocation of any license certificate or any nonresident reciprocity privilege to operate any motor vehicle or motorized bicycle held by the individual charged or temporary order prohibiting the individual from obtaining any license to operate any motor vehicle or motorized bicycle in this State.

In the notice, the director shall provide the individual charged with an opportunity for a plenary hearing to contest the proposed final suspension, revocation or other final agency action. Unless the division receives, no later than the 10th day from the date the notice was mailed, a written request for hearing, the proposed final agency action shall take effect on the date specified in the notice.

Upon receipt of a timely request for a plenary hearing, a preliminary hearing shall be held by an administrative law judge within 15 days of the receipt of the request. The preliminary hearing shall be for the purpose of determining whether, pending a plenary hearing on the proposed final agency action, a preliminary suspension shall be immediately issued by the judge. Adjournment of such hearing upon motion by the individual charged shall be given only for good cause shown.

At the preliminary hearing, the parties shall proceed on the papers submitted to the judge, including the summons, the police reports and the charged individual's prior driving record submitted by the division, and any brief affidavits permitted by the judge from persons who shall be witnesses at the plenary hearing, and the parties may present oral argument. Based on the papers, on any oral argument, on the individual's prior driving record, and on the circumstances of the alleged violation presented in the papers, the judge shall determine whether the individual was properly charged with a violation of the law and a death occurred; and, if so, whether in the interest of public safety, a preliminary suspension shall be immediately ordered pending the plenary hearing on the proposed suspension or revocation. The administrative law judge shall transmit his findings to the director.

A plenary hearing shall be held no later than the 45th day following the preliminary hearing. Adjournment of the hearing shall be given only for good cause shown. If the hearing is otherwise postponed or delayed solely at the instance of the individual charged, the administrative law judge shall immediately issue a preliminary suspension of any license certificate or any nonresident reciprocity privilege held by the individual charged, or if any such preliminary suspension or order is in effect, he shall continue such suspension or order. Such preliminary suspension or temporary order shall remain in effect pending a final agency decision on the matter. If the hearing is otherwise postponed or delayed at the instance of anyone other than the individual charged, the judge shall immediately issue an order restoring the individual's license certificate or any nonresident reciprocity privilege pending final agency decision in the matter. The period of any preliminary suspension imposed under this section shall be deducted from any suspension imposed by the final agency decision in the matter.

c. Whenever any other matter is presented to the director involving an alleged violation of this title, wherein the death of another occurred and for which he determines immediate action is warranted, he may proceed in the manner prescribed in subsection b. above.

d. Whenever a fatal accident occurs in this State, an investigation of the incident, whether performed by the State Police or by local police, shall be completed and forwarded to the director within 72 hours of the time of the accident.

e. Whenever a matter is presented to the director involving an alleged violation of

(1) R.S.39:4–98, where an excess of 20 miles per hour over the authorized speed limit is alleged, and which has resulted in the death or serious bodily injury of another;

(2) R.S.39:4–50, which has resulted in the death or serious bodily injury of another;

(3) R.S.39:4–96 or R.S.39:4–97, which has resulted in the death or serious bodily injury of another; or

(4) R.S.39:4–129, wherein the death or serious bodily injury of another has occurred, the director for good cause may, without hearing, immediately issue a preliminary suspension of any license certificate or any nonresident reciprocity privilege to operate any motor vehicle or motorized bicycle held by an individual charged or temporary order prohibiting the individual from obtaining any license to operate any motor vehicle or motorized bicycle in this State. For purposes of this subsection, "serious bodily injury" means bodily injury which creates a substantial risk of death or which causes serious, permanent disfigurement, or protracted loss or impairment of the function of any bodily member or organ. Along with the notice of preliminary suspension, the director shall issue a notice of proposed final suspension, revocation or other final agency action, and shall afford the individual the right to a preliminary hearing to contest the preliminary suspension and a plenary hearing to contest the proposed final agency action.

The preliminary suspension shall remain in effect pending a final agency decision on the proposed final agency action, unless a request for a preliminary hearing is received by the division no later than the 10th day from the date on which the notice was mailed. The proposed final agency action shall take effect on the date specified in the notice unless a request for a plenary hearing is received by the division no later than the 10th day from the date on which the notice was mailed.

Upon timely request by the individual, a preliminary hearing shall be held by an administrative law judge, no later than the 15th day from the date on which the division receives the request. The preliminary hearing shall be for the purpose of determining whether, pending a final agency decision on the matter, the preliminary suspension issued by the director shall remain in effect. Adjournment of the hearing shall be given only for good cause shown. If the preliminary hearing is otherwise postponed or delayed solely at the instance of someone other than the individual charged,

the judge shall immediately order that the individual's license certificate or any nonresident reciprocity privilege be restored pending the rescheduled preliminary hearing.

At the preliminary hearing, the parties shall proceed on the papers submitted to the judge, including the summons, the police reports and the charged individual's prior driving record submitted by the division, and any brief affidavits permitted by the judge from persons who shall be witnesses at the final hearing, and the parties may present oral arguments. Based on the papers, on any oral argument, on the individual's prior driving record, and on the circumstances of the alleged violation presented in the papers, the judge shall immediately determine whether the individual was properly charged with a violation of the law and a death occurred; and, if so, whether in the interest of public safety, the preliminary suspension shall be continued pending the final agency decision on the matter. The administrative law judge shall transmit his findings to the director.

Any plenary hearing to contest the proposed final agency action shall conform to the requirements for a plenary hearing contained in subsection b. of this section.

f. In addition to any other final agency action, the director shall require any person whose privileges to operate a motor vehicle or motorized bicycle are suspended or who has been prohibited from obtaining a license, pursuant to this section, to be reexamined to determine the person's ability to operate a motor vehicle or motorized bicycle, prior to regaining or obtaining any driving privileges in this State.

Any determination resulting from any preliminary or plenary hearing held pursuant to subsection b., c., or e. of this section shall not be admissible at any criminal or quasi-criminal proceedings on the alleged violation or violations.

g. In addition to any other requirements imposed by statute or regulation, as a condition for the restoration of a revoked or suspended license issued under the provisions of the "New Jersey Commercial Driver License Act," P.L.1990, c. 103 (C.39:3–10.9 et seq.), the person whose commercial driving privileges are revoked or suspended shall successfully complete a commercial driver improvement program. The director, in accordance with the provisions of the "Administrative Procedure Act," P.L.1968, c. 410 (C.52:14B–1 et seq.), shall promulgate rules and regulations prescribing the scope and content of the program, the qualifications of third parties that may offer a commercial driver improvement program, a fee schedule for persons attending a commercial driver improvement program and such other matters as the director may deem appropriate and necessary. The successful completion of a commercial driver improvement program pursuant to this subsection shall not entitle a person to any reduction in the points assessed and recorded under P.L.1982, c. 43

(C.39:5–30.5 et seq.). In addition, the director may also require a person holding a commercial driver's license pursuant to P.L.1990, c. 103 (C.39:3–10.9 et seq.) who receives 12 or more points during a 24–month period to complete a commercial driver improvement program successfully or face full suspension of the commercial driver's license driving privilege.

Amended by L.1939, c. 216, p. 614, § 2, eff. July 12, 1939; L.1945, c. 256, p. 782, § 1; L.1979, c. 463, § 2, eff. Feb. 27, 1980; L.1982, c. 43, § 8; L.1990, c. 103, § 33, eff. Nov. 9, 1990; L.2003, c. 131, § 3, eff. May 15, 2004.

39:5–30a. Habitual offender defined

As used in this act:

"Habitual offender" means a person who has his license to operate a motor vehicle suspended three times for violations occurring within a 3-year period.

L.1982, c. 85, § 1, eff. Oct. 1, 1982.

39:5–30b. Suspension of license; period of time; notice; hearing

The director may suspend for a period of no more than 3 years, the license to operate a motor vehicle of any person who, within a period of 3 years, commits motor vehicle violations, other than a violation of section 2 of P.L.1972, c. 197 (C. 39:6B–2), which ultimately result in the licensee having his license suspended three times. Where any given suspension is based on an accumulation of points involving more than one conviction for violations, the period of suspension shall be calculated from the date of commission of the latest violation.

The proposed notice of suspension shall be mailed to the licensee at his last address of record with the Division of Motor Vehicles and shall clearly state the reason for the suspension. The suspension shall become effective 15 days from the date of the mailing of the notice unless the director for cause establishes another date for commencement of the suspension, or the licensee notifies the director in writing within 10 days of the mailing of the notice of his intention to personally appear at a hearing to challenge the suspension.

The administrative law judge presiding at a hearing held pursuant to this section shall only consider evidence of the actual number of suspensions and the time period during which the violations leading to the suspensions were committed in issuing a suspension for the period provided for by this act. He may admit evidence relevant to the circumstances set out in section 3 of this act [1] in considering the appropriateness of any portion of in excess of the 3 year period suspension issued.

Any person who fails without reasonable cause to appear at a hearing provided for by this section shall have his license to operate a motor vehicle suspended

forthwith by the director for a fixed minimum period of 3 years.

L.1982, c. 85, § 2, eff. Oct. 1, 1982.

[1] N.J.S.A. § 39:5–30c.

39:5–30c. Maximum suspension period; circumstances determining

In determining the appropriateness of issuing a suspension for the maximum period of 3 years established by this act, the director may consider the following circumstances:

a. The latest offense was of such a nature that it evinced an unreasonable disregard by the licensee for the safety and welfare of himself or others;

b. The number and seriousness of the offenses contained in the prior driving record of the licensee evince a pattern or patterns of unreasonable disregard by the licensee for the safety and welfare of himself or others;

c. The nature and extent of the driving record of the licensee establish a substantial risk that licensee will commit another offense.

L.1982, c. 85, § 3, eff. Oct. 1, 1982.

39:5–30d. Concurrent suspension; application for reinstatement

A suspension issued pursuant to this act shall not run concurrently with any other suspension issued pursuant to law. A licensee may apply to the director for reinstatement of his license following the period of suspension issued.

L.1982, c. 85, § 4, eff. Oct. 1, 1982.

39:5–30e. Operation of motor vehicle during suspension; fine and imprisonment

Unless otherwise provided, an habitual offender convicted of operating a motor vehicle or motorized bicycle, while suspended pursuant to this act, shall pay a fine of $1,000.00 and may be sentenced to a term of imprisonment in a county jail, penitentiary, or workhouse, as the case may be, for a period of 30 days, provided, however, that if the habitual offender is involved in an accident resulting in bodily injury to another, he shall, in addition to the fine, be sentenced to a term of imprisonment for not less than 45 days.

L.1982, c. 85, § 5, eff. Oct. 1, 1982.

39:5–30.1. Suspension or revocation of driver's license where reciprocity driving privilege is suspended or revoked in another state

Whenever the reciprocity driving privilege of any New Jersey resident is suspended or revoked by lawful authority in another State upon a conviction of a violation of the Motor Vehicle Act of such State and the report of such conviction is transmitted by the motor vehicle administrator of such State to the Director of the Division of Motor Vehicles of this State pursuant to any law providing for reciprocal exchange thereof, the director may suspend or revoke the driving privilege of such resident in this State, in the manner prescribed by section 39:5–30 of the Revised Statutes, for a period not less than that for which the reciprocity driving privilege was suspended or revoked in such other State nor more than the period for which the driving privilege would have been suspended or revoked had a conviction of a like offense occurred in this State.

L.1953, c. 429, p. 2164, § 1. Amended by L.1957, c. 71, p. 138, § 1.

39:5–30.2. Review of suspension or revocation; attendance of driver improvement program in lieu of suspension; administration authority relating to driver improvement program

Any moving violation of the motor vehicle law which carries with it a penalty of suspension or revocation of a driver's license may be subject to review by the chief administrator. The chief administrator, in his or his designee's discretion, may permit a driver subject to suspension or revocation to elect to attend a New Jersey Motor Vehicle Commission Driver Improvement Program in lieu of all or part of a period of suspension. This discretionary authority shall not apply to those sections of the motor vehicle law which require the imposition of a mandatory suspension term. In addition to, or in lieu of, the Driver Improvement Program offered by the commission, the chief administrator may authorize a drivers' school licensed pursuant to section 2 of P.L.1951, c. 216 (C.39:12–2) or any statewide safety organization to provide a Driver Improvement Program, the course of which shall be subject to the oversight of, and any guidelines established by, the commission. The authority of the chief administrator to suspend, revoke, or deny issuance of an initial or renewal license to operate a driving school, or an instructor's license, and to assess fines, pursuant to P.L.1951, c. 216 (C.39:12–1 et seq.) shall apply to any violations related to the administration of a Driver Improvement Program.

L.1969, c. 261, § 1, eff. Jan. 8, 1970. Amended by L.1977, c. 27, § 1, eff. Feb. 24, 1977; L.2009, c. 298, § 6, eff. Jan. 17, 2010.

39:5–30.3. Repealed by L.1982, c. 43, § 9

39:5–30.4. Driver improvement program; fees

Persons attending a Driver Improvement Program offered by the New Jersey Motor Vehicle Commission, an approved drivers' school, or a Statewide safety organization, as approved by the commission, shall pay such fee therefor not to exceed $100, as prescribed in regulations promulgated by the chief administrator. The driver's license of any person failing to pay the prescribed fee shall be subject to suspension or revocation.

L.1972, c. 38, § 1, eff. May 25, 1972. Amended by L.1977, c. 27, § 3, eff. Feb. 24, 1977; L.1982, c. 53, § 9, eff. July 1, 1982; L.1994, c. 60, § 24, eff. July 1, 1994; L.2009, c. 298, § 7, eff. Jan. 17, 2010.

39:5–30.5. Penalty points; rules and regulations; authority to adopt

The Director of the Division of Motor Vehicles shall have the authority, pursuant to the "Administrative Procedure Act," P.L.1968, c. 410 (C. 52:14B–1 et seq.), to continue to adopt rules and regulations to determine the motor vehicle offenses for which penalty points may be assessed under this act, and the amount of points to be assessed for each offense and to adopt rules and regulations to determine the motorized bicycle offenses for which penalty points may be assessed and the number of points to be assessed for each offense.

L.1982, c. 43, § 1, eff. Oct. 26, 1982. Amended by L.1983, c. 105, § 8, eff. June 12, 1984.

39:5–30.5a. Penalty points; motor vehicle operation causing property destruction

a. The director shall, in establishing a motor vehicle point system, pursuant to section 1 of P.L.1982, c. 43 (C. 39:5–30.5), include in that system a schedule of points to be assessed against a person operating a motor vehicle, except a motor vehicle operated for emergency purposes by a fire department or ambulance or rescue squad, in a manner which causes the destruction of agricultural crops, fences, fields or other agricultural or recreational property. "Recreational property" means any public or private property used as a golf course, park, or other similar purpose.

b. A person who operates a motor vehicle in the manner described in subsection a. of this section, who is not a licensed driver of this State at the time of the violation, shall have the points established pursuant to this section assessed against his record upon being issued a license to operate a motor vehicle in this State.

L.1985, c. 154, § 2, eff. April 25, 1985.

39:5–30.6. Penalty points; assessment; record

The court shall assess points at the time of conviction for any offense committed in this State, and the Director of the Division of Motor Vehicles in the Department of Law and Public Safety shall, upon receiving notice, assess points for any conviction occurring in another jurisdiction. The court shall transmit a record of all points assessed, along with the record of conviction to the director. The director shall maintain records of all points assessed in a manner which he shall prescribe. In addition to any requirements the director may prescribe, the record shall include the respective dates of commission and conviction of the offense or offenses.

L.1982, c. 43, § 2, eff. Oct. 26, 1982.

39:5–30.7. Accumulated points; notification

Whenever a licensee has accumulated six or more points, the director shall notify him at his last address of record with the Division of Motor Vehicles of the number of points he has been assessed and the general nature and effect of the point system.

L.1982, c. 43, § 3, eff. Oct. 26, 1982.

39:5–30.8. Suspension of License; accumulated points; notice; effective date; hearing; failure to appear

Except for good cause, the director shall suspend for a period of no less than 30 days and no more than 180 days, except as provided in section 6 of this act,[1] the license to operate a motor vehicle of any person who accumulates

    a.   12 or more points in a period of 2 years or less, or

    b.   15 or more points in a period greater than 2 years, or

    c.   at least 12 points but fewer than 15 points in a period greater than 2 years, unless the licensee notifies the division in writing within 10 days of the date of mailing of the proposed notice of suspension of his intention to attend a driver improvement course that is approved by the director, and satisfactorily completes such course.

The proposed notice of suspension shall be mailed to the licensee at his last address of record with the Division of Motor Vehicles and shall clearly state the length of the suspension, the reason for the suspension and that the licensee has a right to be heard on the suspension.

The suspension shall become effective 15 days from the date of the mailing of the notice unless the director for cause establishes another date for commencement of the suspension, or the licensee notifies the director in writing within 10 days of the mailing of the notice of his intention to personally appear at a hearing to challenge the suspension.

The administrative law judge presiding at a hearing held pursuant to this section shall only consider evidence of the actual number of points assessed and the period of time during which such points were accumulated, taking into consideration any point reduction credits earned by the licensee, in issuing a suspension. He may consider other relevant evidence in considering the appropriateness of any portion of a suspension issued in excess of 30 days.

Any person who fails without reasonable cause to appear at a hearing provided for by this section, or who fails to satisfactorily complete the approved driver improvement course, as the case may be, shall have his license to operate a motor vehicle suspended forthwith by the director for the period contained in the proposed notice of suspension.

L.1982, c. 43, § 4, eff. Oct. 26, 1982.

[1] N.J.S.A. § 39:5–30.10.

39:5–30.9. Reduction of points

Points recorded against a licensee shall be reduced at the rate of three points for each 12 consecutive months in which the licensee has not committed any violation either resulting in the assessment of points or in the suspension of driving privileges. Points recorded against a licensee shall also be reduced by three points, where the licensee attends and satisfactorily completes an approved license improvement course; provided, however, that no licensee may receive point reduction credits for completion of the same or a similar course within two years of having completed the original course. Points recorded against a licensee shall also be reduced by two points if the licensee attends and satisfactorily completes an approved motor vehicle defensive driving course pursuant to section 55 of P.L.1990, c. 8 (C.17:33B–45), except that no licensee may receive point reduction credits for completion of an approved motor vehicle defensive driving course within five years of having completed a previously approved motor vehicle defensive driving course. No point totals shall be reduced below zero. Computation of the time periods used in granting point reduction credits shall in all cases be based upon the respective dates of commission of the offenses for which the licensee was convicted and assessed points.

L.1982, c. 43, § 5, eff. Oct. 26, 1982. Amended by L.1990, c. 8, § 54, eff. March 12, 1990.

39:5–30.10. Subsequent violations; suspension; notice; hearing; failure to appear

Except for good cause, the director shall suspend for a period as provided herein the license to operate a motor vehicle of any person who, having had his license suspended pursuant to subsection a., b., or c. of section 4 of this act,[1] or having satisfactorily completed an approved driver improvement course pursuant to subsection c. of section 4 of this act, is convicted of a violation committed within 1 year of the date of restoration of the driving privilege or the date of completion of the approved driver improvement course, as the case may be. For commission of one violation within 1 year, the period of suspension shall be no less than 45 days and no more than 90 days. For a second violation the period of suspension shall be no less than 90 days and no more than 180 days.

The proposed notice of suspension shall be mailed to the licensee at his last address of record with the Division of Motor Vehicles. The notice shall clearly state the length of the suspension, the reason for the suspension and that the licensee has a right to be heard on the suspension, which shall become effective 15 days from the date of the mailing of the notice, unless the director for cause establishes another date for commencement of the suspension, or unless the licensee notifies the director in writing within 10 days of the notice of his intention to personally appear at a hearing to challenge the suspension.

The administrative law judge presiding at a hearing held pursuant to this section shall only consider evidence of the actual number of points assessed and the period of time during which such points were accumulated, taking into consideration any point reduction credits earned by the licensee. He may consider other relevant evidence in considering the appropriate length of a suspension for each case.

Any person who fails without reasonable cause to appear at a hearing provided for by this section shall have his license to operate a motor vehicle suspended forthwith for the term contained in the proposed notice of suspension.

L.1982, c. 43, § 6, eff. Oct. 26, 1982.

1 N.J.S.A. § 39:5–30.8.

39:5–30.11. Initial notification; defense; accumulated points

It shall not be a defense to nor a reason for an adjournment of any suspension proceeding instituted pursuant to this act that a. the director initially notified the licensee of any less stringent administrative alternatives then available to the licensee, prior to the division receiving notification of more recent points accumulated by the licensee, or b. the director failed to notify the licensee, pursuant to the provisions of section 3 of this act,[1] of the number of points he had accumulated. At any hearing held pursuant to this act, the administrative law judge shall consider as reason for the suspension and the length of the suspension the actual number of points accumulated by the licensee prior to the date of the hearing.

L.1982, c. 43, § 7, eff. Oct. 26, 1982.

1 N.J.S.A. § 39:5–30.7.

39:5–30.12. Definitions

As used in sections 1 through 5 of this act:[1]

"Conviction" means a final adjudication that a violation has occurred, a final judgment on a verdict, a finding of guilt in a tribunal of original jurisdiction, or a conviction following a plea of guilty, non vult or nolo contendere accepted by a court. It also includes an unvacated forfeiture of bail, bond or collateral deposited to secure the person's appearance in court, or the payment of a fine or court costs, or violation of a condition of release without bail, regardless of whether the penalty is rebated, suspended or probated.

"Drug offense" means a conviction or an adjudication under juvenile proceedings for the possession, distribution, manufacture, cultivation, sale, transfer, or the attempt or conspiracy to possess, distribute, manufacture, cultivate, sell, or transfer any substance, the possession of which is prohibited under the federal Controlled Substances Act or a conviction or adjudication of delinquency for any violation of a law substantially similar in nature to the "Comprehensive Drug Reform Act of 1987," N.J.S. 2C:35–1 et al.

"Person" means a natural person who is a resident of New Jersey at the time of the violation resulting in the conviction or adjudication of delinquency or who holds a New Jersey driver's license or permit at the time of the violation resulting in the conviction or adjudication of delinquency.

L.1993, c. 296, § 1, eff. Dec. 22, 1993.

1 N.J.S.A. §§ 39:5–30.12 to 39:5–30.16.

39:5–30.13. Suspension of license for drug convictions; period of suspension for persons under 17 years of age

The Director of the Division of Motor Vehicles shall suspend, revoke, or postpone the driving privilege in this State for a period of not less than six months or more than two years of every person convicted of or adjudicated delinquent for a drug offense in any federal court or in the court of any other state, or the District of Columbia. When a person whose license is subject to suspension, revocation, or postponement under this act is less than 17 years of age, the period of suspension, revocation or postponement imposed by the director shall commence immediately and shall run for a period of not less than six months or more than two years after the date the person reaches the age of 17. If the driving privilege of any person is under revocation, suspension, or postponement for a violation of Title 2C or Title 39 of the Revised Statutes at the time of the imposition of suspension, revocation, or postponement under this act, the revocation, suspension, or postponement imposed herein shall commence as of the date of termination of the existing suspension, revocation, or postponement.

L.1993, c. 296, § 2, eff. Dec. 22, 1993.

39:5–30.14. Notification: effective date of suspension; hearing

The proposed notice of suspension, revocation, or postponement shall be mailed to the person at his last address of record with the Division of Motor Vehicles. The suspension, revocation, or postponement shall become effective 20 days from the date of mailing of the notice, unless the director establishes another date for the commencement, or the person notifies the director in writing within 15 days of the mailing of the notice of his intention to challenge the suspension, revocation, or postponement. A hearing request shall contain a detailed statement of the factual and legal basis upon which the person challenges the suspension.

L.1993, c. 296, § 3, eff. Dec. 22, 1993.

39:5–30.15. Responsibility of director for drug conviction reports

The Director of the Division of Motor Vehicles shall be responsible for the receipt of all reports of drug offense convictions submitted to this State by federal courts, courts of any other state, or courts of the District of Columbia.

L.1993, c. 296, § 4, eff. Dec. 22, 1993.

39:5–30.16. Rules and regulations

The Director of the Division of Motor Vehicles may promulgate rules and regulations pursuant to the Administrative Procedure Act, P.L.1968, c. 410 (C. 52:14B–1 et seq.) to implement sections 1 through 5 of this act.[1]

L.1993, c. 296, § 5, eff. Dec. 22, 1993.

[1] N.J.S.A. §§ 39:5–30.12 to 39:5–30.16.

39:5–31. Revocation of driver's license by director or magistrate

The director or any magistrate before whom any hearing under this subtitle is had may revoke the license of any person to drive a motor vehicle, when such person shall have been guilty of such willful violation of any of the provisions of this subtitle as shall, in the discretion of the magistrate, justify such revocation.

Amended by L.1953, c. 36, p. 624, § 30, eff. March 19, 1953.

39:5–32. Validation of or grant of new driver's license when same revoked

The commission shall, at all times, have the power to validate a driver's license that has been revoked, or to grant a new license to any person whose license to drive motor vehicles shall have been revoked.

Amended by L.2003, c. 13, § 59.

Historical and Statutory Notes

L.2003, c. 13, § 127, approved Jan. 28, 2003, provides:

"Sections 1, 2, 3, 12, 38, 109, 110 and 121 shall take effect immediately, sections 105, 106, 107, 108, and 120 shall take effect on July 1, 2003 and the remainder of this act shall take effect on the date the Commissioner of Transportation certifies to the Governor (hereinafter the "date of certification") that a majority of the members of the commission have been appointed or are in office and that all necessary anticipatory actions have been accomplished, provided, that the amount of revenues received pursuant to sections 109 and 110 prior to the date of certification are hereby appropriated to the division. Upon the date of certification, all such collected revenue shall be revenue of the commission. The Commissioner of Transportation, the Director of the Division of Motor Vehicles and the commission may take such anticipatory administrative action in advance as shall be necessary for the implementation of the act."

39:5–33. New license to driver whose license suspended or revoked to be granted by commissioner personally

If a driver of motor vehicles shall have had his license suspended or revoked, a new license granted to him shall be void and of no effect, unless it shall be granted by the commission.

Amended by L.2003, c. 13, § 60.

Historical and Statutory Notes

L.2003, c. 13, § 127, approved Jan. 28, 2003, provides:

"Sections 1, 2, 3, 12, 38, 109, 110 and 121 shall take effect immediately, sections 105, 106, 107, 108, and 120 shall take effect on July 1, 2003 and the remainder of this act shall take effect on the date the Commissioner of Transportation certifies to the Governor (hereinafter the "date of certification") that a majority of the members of the commission have been appointed or are in office and that all necessary anticipatory actions have been accomplished, provided, that the amount of revenues received pursuant to sections 109 and 110 prior to the date of certification are hereby appropriated to the division. Upon the date of certification, all such collected revenue shall be revenue of the commission. The Commissioner of Transportation, the Director of the Division of Motor Vehicles and the commission may take such anticipatory administrative action in advance as shall be necessary for the implementation of the act."

39:5–34. New registration or registration certificate when old suspended or revoked to be issued under personal direction of commissioner

If a registration or registration certificate shall have been suspended or revoked, a new registration or registration certificate issued shall be void and of no effect, unless the new registration shall be made and the new certificate issued under the direction of the commission.

Amended by L.2003, c. 13, § 61.

Historical and Statutory Notes

L.2003, c. 13, § 127, approved Jan. 28, 2003, provides:

"Sections 1, 2, 3, 12, 38, 109, 110 and 121 shall take effect immediately, sections 105, 106, 107, 108, and 120 shall take effect on July 1, 2003 and the remainder of this act shall take effect on the date the Commissioner of Transportation certifies to the Governor (hereinafter the "date of certification") that a majority of the members of the commission have been appointed or are in office and that all necessary anticipatory actions have been accomplished, provided, that the amount of revenues received pursuant to sections 109 and 110 prior to the date of certification are hereby appropriated to the division. Upon the date of certification, all such collected revenue shall be revenue of the commission. The Commissioner of Transportation, the Director of the Division of Motor Vehicles and the commission may take such anticipatory administrative action in advance as shall be necessary for the implementation of the act."

39:5–35. Return or surrender of suspended or revoked driver's license or registration certificate and registration plates

Any person, whose driver's license or registration certificate has been suspended or revoked, who fails to return it or them to the director, together with any registration plates issued under such certificate, within five days of the date of suspension or revocation of such license or certificate, or both, or who fails to surrender it or them upon demand of an authorized representative of the Division of Motor Vehicles, member of the State Police or other police officer who has been directed to secure possession thereof, shall be fined not more than $25.00.

Amended by L.1983, c. 403, § 23, eff. Dec. 23, 1983.

39:5–36. Imprisonment on default of payment of fine

Unless otherwise expressly provided in this subtitle, any person who shall be convicted of a violation of any of the provisions of this subtitle, and upon whom a fine shall be imposed, shall, in default of payment thereof, be imprisoned in the county jail or workhouse of the county where the offense was committed, but in no case shall such imprisonment exceed 1 day for each $20.00 of the fine so imposed, nor shall such imprisonment exceed, in any case, a period of 3 months.

Whenever a person is imprisoned by reason of default in the payment of a fine or fines and costs imposed and assessed upon conviction of any violation of this subtitle wherein the committing court, as a part of the sentence, ordered that such person stand committed to the county jail or workhouse until such fine and costs are paid, he shall be given credit against the amount of such fines and costs at the rate of $20.00 for each day of such confinement. When such person shall have been confined for a sufficient number of days to establish credits equal to the aggregate amount of such fines and costs, and is not held by reason of any other sentence or commitment, he shall be discharged from such imprisonment by the officer in charge of the county jail or workhouse.

Amended by L.1942, c. 334, p. 1183, § 7, eff. Dec. 21, 1942; L.1963, c. 142, § 4, eff. Aug. 26, 1963; L.1975, c. 144, § 4, eff. July 7, 1975.

39:5–36.1. Fee for dishonored check or similar sight order

The Director of the Division of Motor Vehicles shall collect a $25 fee from a person who issues or passes to the division a check, or similar sight order for the payment of money, which is not honored by the drawee. This fee shall be in addition to all other fees owed by the person to the division. The amount sought to be satisfied by such dishonored check, or similar sight order for the payment of money, shall not be deemed paid until such amount and the fee required under this section are paid. This section shall be applicable to any check or similar sight order for the payment of money, made to the division.

L.1994, c. 60, § 31, eff. July 1, 1994.

39:5–37, 39:5–38. Repealed by L.1953, c. 36, p. 624, §§ 31, 32

39:5–39. Physician's fee in certain cases

The judge, either in an original proceeding or on appeal for a violation of R.S. 39:4–50, may tax in the costs a sum not exceeding $20.00, which shall be paid to any physician testifying in the proceeding. This amount, when included in the taxed costs authorized by this chapter, shall be paid as costs are now paid. If the defendant is found not guilty of the charges laid against him for a violation of R.S. 39:4–50, the costs shall be paid by the prosecutor, except in those instances in which the director, a member of the Division of State Police or a police officer has been the prosecutor.

Amended by L.1983, c. 403, § 24, eff. Dec. 23, 1983.

39:5–40. Disposition of moneys received under motor vehicle law

Except as otherwise provided by this subtitle all moneys received in accordance with the provisions of this Title, whether from fines, penalties, forfeitures, registration fees, license fees, or otherwise, shall be accounted for and forwarded to the commissioner, who shall pay the same over to the State Treasurer, to be credited to the State Highway Fund and used for the purposes of such fund as provided by section 52:22–20 of the Title,[1] State Government, Departments and Officers.

Amended by L.1938, c. 75, p. 189, § 1, eff. April 4, 1938; L.1942, c. 334, p. 1184, § 8, eff. Dec. 21, 1942.

1 Repealed 1944. See, now, § 52:27B–10 et seq.

39:5–41. Fines, penalties and forfeitures; disposition; exceptions

a. All fines, penalties and forfeitures imposed and collected under authority of law for any violations of R.S.39:4–63 and R.S.39:4–64 shall be forwarded by the judge to whom the same have been paid to the proper financial officer of a county, if the violation occurred within the jurisdiction of that county's central municipal court, established pursuant to N.J.S.2B:12–1 et seq. or the municipality wherein the violation occurred, to be used by the county or municipality to help finance litter control activities in addition to or supplementing existing litter pickup and removal activities in the municipality.

b. Except as otherwise provided by subsection a. of this section, all fines, penalties and forfeitures imposed and collected under authority of law for any violations of the provisions of this Title, other than those violations in which the complaining witness is the chief administrator, a member of his staff, a member of the State Police, a member of a county police department and force or a county park police system in a county that has established a central municipal court, an inspector of the Board of Public Utilities, or a law enforcement officer of any other State agency, shall be forwarded by the judge to whom the same have been paid as follows: one-half of the total amount collected to the financial officer, as designated by the local governing body, of the respective municipalities wherein the violations occurred, to be used by the municipality for general municipal use and to defray the cost of operating the municipal court; and one-half of the total amount collected to the proper financial officer of the county wherein they were collected, to be used by the county as a fund for the construction, reconstruction, maintenance and repair of roads and bridges, snow removal, the acquisition and purchase of rights-of-way, and the purchase, replacement and repair of equipment for use on said roads and bridges therein. Up to 25%

of the money received by a municipality pursuant to this subsection, but not more than the actual amount budgeted for the municipal court, whichever is less, may be used to upgrade case processing.

All fines, penalties and forfeitures imposed and collected under authority of law for any violations of the provisions of this Title, in which the complaining witness is a member of a county police department and force or a county park police system in a county that has established a central municipal court, shall be forwarded by the judge to whom the same have been paid to the financial officer, designated by the governing body of the county, for all violations occurring within the jurisdiction of that court, to be used for general county use and to defray the cost of operating the central municipal court.

Whenever any county has deposited moneys collected pursuant to this section in a special trust fund in lieu of expending the same for the purposes authorized by this section, it may withdraw from said special trust fund in any year an amount which is not in excess of the amount expended by the county over the immediately preceding three-year period from general county revenues for said purposes. Such moneys withdrawn from the trust fund shall be accounted for and used as are other general county revenues.

c. (Deleted by amendment, P.L.1993, c. 293.)

d. Notwithstanding the provisions of subsections a. and b. of this section, $1 shall be added to the amount of each fine and penalty imposed and collected through a court under authority of any law for any violation of the provisions of Title 39 of the Revised Statutes or any other motor vehicle or traffic violation in this State and shall be forwarded by the person to whom the same are paid to the State Treasurer. In addition, upon the forfeiture of bail, $1 of that forfeiture shall be forwarded to the State Treasurer. The State Treasurer shall annually deposit those moneys so forwarded in the "Body Armor Replacement" fund established pursuant to section 1 of P.L.1997, c. 177 (C.52:17B–4.4). Beginning in the fiscal year next following the effective date of this act, the State Treasurer annually shall allocate from those moneys so forwarded an amount not to exceed $400,000 to the Department of the Treasury to be expended exclusively for the purposes of funding the operation of the "Law Enforcement Officer Crisis Intervention Services" telephone hotline established and maintained under the provisions of sections 115 and 116 of P.L.2008, c. 29 (C.26:2NN–1 and C.26:2NN–2).

e. Notwithstanding the provisions of subsections a. and b. of this section, $1 shall be added to the amount of each fine and penalty imposed and collected through a court under authority of any law for any violation of the provisions of Title 39 of the Revised Statutes or any other motor vehicle or traffic violation in this State and shall be forwarded by the person to whom the same are paid to the State Treasurer. The State Treasurer shall annually deposit those moneys so forwarded in the "New Jersey Spinal Cord Research Fund" established pursuant to section 9 of P.L.1999, c. 201 (C.52:9E–9). In order to comply with the provisions of Article VIII, Section II, paragraph 5 of the State Constitution, a municipal or county agency which forwards moneys to the State Treasurer pursuant to this subsection may retain an amount equal to 2% of the moneys which it collects pursuant to this subsection as compensation for its administrative costs associated with implementing the provisions of this subsection.

f. Notwithstanding the provisions of subsections a. and b. of this section, $1 shall be added to the amount of each fine and penalty imposed and collected through a court under authority of any law for any violation of the provisions of Title 39 of the Revised Statutes or any other motor vehicle or traffic violation in this State and shall be forwarded by the person to whom the same are paid to the State Treasurer. The State Treasurer shall annually deposit those moneys so forwarded in the "Autism Medical Research and Treatment Fund" established pursuant to section 1 of P. L.2003, c. 144 (C.30:6D–62.2).

g. Notwithstanding the provisions of subsections a. and b. of this section, $2 shall be added to the amount of each fine and penalty imposed and collected by a court under authority of any law for any violation of the provisions of Title 39 of the Revised Statutes or any other motor vehicle or traffic violation in this State and shall be forwarded by the person to whom the same are paid to the State Treasurer. The State Treasurer shall annually deposit those moneys so forwarded in the "New Jersey Forensic DNA Laboratory Fund" established pursuant to P.L.2003, c. 183. Prior to depositing the moneys into the fund, the State Treasurer shall forward to the Administrative Office of the Courts an amount not to exceed $475,000 from moneys initially collected pursuant to this subsection to be used exclusively to establish a collection mechanism and to provide funding to update the Automated Traffic System Fund created pursuant to N.J.S.2B:12–30 to implement the provisions of this subsection.

h. Notwithstanding the provisions of subsections a. and b. of this section, $1 shall be added to the amount of each fine and penalty imposed and collected under authority of any law for any violation of the provisions of Title 39 of the Revised Statutes or any other motor vehicle or traffic violation in this State and shall be forwarded by the person to whom the same are paid to the State Treasurer. The State Treasurer shall annually deposit those moneys so forwarded in the "New Jersey Brain Injury Research Fund" established pursuant to section 9 of P.L.2003, c.200 (C.52:9EE–9). The Administrative Office of the Courts may retain an amount equal to $475,000 from the moneys which it initially collects pursuant to this subsection, prior to depositing any moneys in the "New Jersey Brain Injury Research Fund," in order to meet the expenses associated with utilizing the Automated Traffic System Fund created pursuant to N.J.S.2B:12–30 to implement the provisions of this subsection and serve other statutory purposes.

i. Notwithstanding the provisions of subsections a. and b. of this section, all fines and penalties imposed and collected under authority of law for any violation related to the unlawful operation or the sale of a vehicle under section 1 of P.L.1955, c.53 (C.39:3–17.1) shall be forwarded by the judge to whom the same have been paid to the State Treasurer, if the complaining witness is the chief administrator, a member of his staff, a member of the State Police, an inspector of the Board of Public Utilities, or a law enforcement officer or other official of any other State agency; or, if the complaining witness is not one of the foregoing, one-half to the chief financial officer of the county and one-half to the chief financial officer of the municipality wherein the violation occurred.

Amended by L.1938, c. 75, p. 190, § 2, eff. April 4, 1938; L.1942, c. 334, p. 1184, § 9, eff. Dec. 21, 1942; L.1975, c. 309, § 1, eff. Feb. 17, 1976; L.1982, c. 31, § 1, eff. Jan. 1, 1983; L.1985, c. 533, § 13, eff. April 21, 1986; L.1986, c. 197, § 1, eff. Jan. 1, 1987; L.1990, c. 95, § 2; L.1992, c. 143, § 7, eff. Nov. 19, 1992; L.1993, c. 293, § 5, eff. Feb. 15, 1994; L.1996, c. 95, § 16, eff. Oct. 24, 1996; L.1997, c. 177, § 2, eff. Sept. 1, 1997; L.1998, c. 149, § 4, eff. May 1, 1999; L.1999, c. 201, § 10; L.2003, c. 144, § 2; L.2003, c. 183, § 6, eff. Sept. 22, 2003; L.2003, c. 200, § 10, eff. June 30, 2004; L.2007, c. 174, § 1, eff. Sept. 12, 2007; L.2007, c. 178, § 2, eff. Sept. 27, 2007; L.2008, c. 29, § 95, eff. June 30, 2008; L.2008, c. 116, § 1, eff. Dec. 15, 2008.

39:5–42. Reports by magistrate to commissioner; motor vehicle violations; crimes in which a motor vehicle was used

Every judge or magistrate shall make a report, in such form as the director may require, to the director (1) of all cases heard before him for violation of this title, or for any other violation in which a motor vehicle was used in any way, and (2) of the conviction of any person of having committed a penal offense or crime in the commission of which a motor vehicle was used, within three days after the disposition of the case before him as a judge or magistrate. The report shall state the nature of the violation, the full facts concerning the use of the motor vehicle in the commission of the penal offense or crime, the disposition of the case by the judge or magistrate and any recommendations which the judge or magistrate may deem of value to the director in determining whether action should be taken against the driving, registration, or other privilege of the driver or owner of the motor vehicle.

Amended by L.1941, c. 60, p. 145, § 1, eff. April 28, 1941; L.1942, c. 334, p. 1184, § 10, eff. Dec. 21, 1942; L.1990, c. 103, § 34, eff. Nov. 9, 1990.

39:5–43. Failure to pay over fines collected; penalty

Any person who, having collected any fine for any violation of this subtitle, fails, within 30 days, to return the same to the director or the proper financial officer of the county or municipality, as the case may be, shall be subject to a penalty not exceeding $500.00 for the first offense, and a penalty of $1,000.00 or imprisonment not exceeding 1 year, or both, at the discretion of the court, upon any subsequent conviction.

Amended by L.1982, c. 31, § 2, eff. Jan. 1, 1983.

39:5–44. Record of fines payable to county; inspection

Every court having jurisdiction to hear complaints for violations of the provisions of this Title shall keep a record of the disposition of all complaints under this subtitle, for which a fine may be imposed which record shall be open to inspection by the treasurer or auditor of a county or his duly authorized representative, or by the director or his duly authorized representative, or by the financial officers of the respective municipalities which are entitled to fines imposed by the court.

Amended by L.1942, c. 334, p. 1185, § 11, eff. Dec. 21, 1942; L.1953, c. 36, p. 624, § 33, eff. March 19, 1953; L.1982, c. 31, § 3, eff. Jan. 1, 1983.

39:5–45. Receipt for offender

Any person who collects fines, costs or cash bail, for a violation of this subtitle, shall deliver to the defendant a proper itemized receipt, which may be either a "proper itemized manual receipt" or a "proper itemized computer generated receipt." Such receipt shall be created either manually or by computer. In the event that the payment was made by mail, the defendant shall only be entitled to a copy of the receipt if the defendant provides the court with a stamped self-addressed envelope. If a manual receipt is issued, a copy of that receipt shall be filed with the case. For the purposes of this section, a "proper itemized manual receipt" is one that is pre-numbered and which includes: the name and signature of the person who received the payment, the date the payment was received, the name of the defendant, the amount paid and the complaint or docket number. A "proper itemized computer generated receipt" is one that is pre-numbered and which includes: the identifying code of the person who received the payment, the date and time the payment was received, the name of the defendant, the amount paid and the complaint or docket number. Any outstanding charges against an offender may be immediately dismissed upon the offender's presentation of a proper itemized receipt issued pursuant to this section evidencing the payment of the required fines and costs. Properly itemized receipts, for use by municipal courts, may contain supplemental information as appropriate, but shall be on a form approved by the Administrative Director of the Courts.

Amended by L.1942, c. 334, p. 1185, § 12, eff. Dec. 21, 1942; L.1999, c. 423, § 2, eff. Jan. 18, 2000.

39:5–46. Conviction of stealing produce reported to commissioner

The clerk of every court wherein a person licensed to operate a motor vehicle in this or another state is convicted of stealing produce from a farm in this state, shall, within three days after the conviction, make a report in writing to the commission of all such cases heard before the court, upon blanks provided by the commission for the purpose. The report shall state the name and address of the person convicted, the date thereof, the sentence imposed by the court and any recommendations the court may deem of value to the commission in determining whether action should be taken against the convicted person's license.

Amended by L.2003, c. 13, § 62.

Historical and Statutory Notes

L.2003, c. 13, § 127, approved Jan. 28, 2003, provides:

"Sections 1, 2, 3, 12, 38, 109, 110 and 121 shall take effect immediately, sections 105, 106, 107, 108, and 120 shall take effect on July 1, 2003 and the remainder of this act shall take effect on the date the Commissioner of Transportation certifies to the Governor (hereinafter the "date of certification") that a majority of the members of the commission have been appointed or are in office and that all necessary anticipatory actions have been accomplished, provided, that the amount of revenues received pursuant to sections 109 and 110 prior to the date of certification are hereby appropriated to the division. Upon the date of certification, all such collected revenue shall be revenue of the commission. The Commissioner of Transportation, the Director of the Division of Motor Vehicles and the commission may take such anticipatory administrative action in advance as shall be necessary for the implementation of the act."

39:5–47. Seizure and sale of stolen motor vehicles

The commission may authorize the seizure of a motor vehicle operated over the highways of this state when it has reason to believe that the motor vehicle has been stolen or is otherwise being operated under suspicious circumstances and may retain it in the name of the commission until such time as the identity of ownership is established, whereupon it shall order the release of the motor vehicle to its owner.

After the expiration of ninety days from the date the motor vehicle came into the possession of the commission by seizure or otherwise, it shall sell it at public sale, upon notice of the sale being first published for the space of two weeks in one or more newspapers published and circulating in this state, and also by posting the notice in five public places in this state. The newspapers and places of posting shall be designated by the commission. Upon the sale of the motor vehicle all claims for interest therein shall be forever barred and the proceeds realized therefrom shall become the sole property of the state, to be used as other moneys received under chapter 3 of this title (R.S.39:3–1 et seq.).

Amended by L.2003, c. 13, § 63.

Historical and Statutory Notes

L.2003, c. 13, § 127, approved Jan. 28, 2003, provides:

"Sections 1, 2, 3, 12, 38, 109, 110 and 121 shall take effect immediately, sections 105, 106, 107, 108, and 120 shall take effect on July 1, 2003 and the remainder of this act shall take effect on the date the Commissioner of Transportation certifies to the Governor (hereinafter the "date of certification") that a majority of the members of the commission have been appointed or are in office and that all necessary anticipatory actions have been accomplished, provided, that the amount of revenues received pursuant to sections 109 and 110 prior to the date of certification are hereby appropriated to the division. Upon the date of certification, all such collected revenue shall be revenue of the commission. The Commissioner of Transportation, the Director of the Division of Motor Vehicles and the commission may take such anticipatory administrative action in advance as shall be necessary for the implementation of the act."

39:5–48 to 39:5–50. Transferred. See §§ 39:3–85.1 to 39:3–85.4

39:5–51. Case involving violation of law on motor vehicles and traffic regulation or motor vehicle accident; prosecutor's responsibility to inform court of death of or injury to victim

In a municipal court case which involves a violation of the motor vehicle and traffic laws as set forth in Title 39 of the Revised Statutes or in any other case which involves directly or indirectly a motor vehicle accident, the municipal prosecutor shall inform the municipal court judge in writing during the initial appearance of a defendant before the court of the death of any person or the extent of any personal injury sustained by a person as a result of the violation of the motor vehicle or traffic laws by the defendant or as a result of a motor vehicle accident which occurred during the violation of any other law by the defendant.

L.1987, c. 307, § 1, eff. Dec. 2, 1987.

39:5–52. Information available to victim; request; "victim" defined; consultation with prosecutor

a. A victim of a motor vehicle accident as defined in this section shall, upon his request, be provided in writing by the court adjudicating any offense committed during that motor vehicle accident with the following information:

(1) Information about the victim's role in the court process;

(2) Timely advance notice of the date, time, and place of the defendant's initial appearance before a judicial officer, submission to the court of any plea agreement, the trial and sentencing;

(3) Timely notification of the case disposition, including the trial and sentencing;

(4) Prompt notification of any decision or action in the case which results in the defendant's provisional or final release from custody; and

(5) Information about the status of the case at any time from the commission of the offense to final disposition or release of the defendant.

As used in this section, "victim" means, unless otherwise indicated, a person who suffers death, or any personal, physical, or psychological injury as a result of a motor vehicle accident. In the case of death, "victim" means a surviving spouse, child, or the next of kin.

When a need is demonstrated, the information in this section shall be provided in the Spanish as well as the English language.

b.   A victim shall be provided with an opportunity to consult with the prosecutor prior to a dismissal of a case or the filing of a proposed plea negotiation with the court if a victim suffered death or sustained bodily injury or serious bodily injury as defined in N.J.S. 2C:11-1.

c.   This section shall not be construed to alter or limit the authority or discretion of the Supreme Court to regulate the practice of plea agreements in municipal court, or alter or limit the authority or discretion of a prosecutor.

L.1987, c. 307, § 2, eff. Dec. 2, 1987.

39:5-53. Definitions

As used in this act:

"Motor vehicle moving violation" means any violation of the motor vehicle laws of this State for which motor vehicle points are assessed by the Director of the Division of Motor Vehicles pursuant to P.L.1982, c. 43 (C.39:5-30.5).

"Person with diplomatic immunity" means a person who displays to a law enforcement officer a driver's license issued by the United States Department of State or who otherwise claims immunities or privileges under Title 22, chapter 6 of the United States Code.

L.2003, c. 23, § 1, eff. May 1, 2003.

39:5-54. Law enforcement procedures

Whenever a person with diplomatic immunity is stopped by a State, county or municipal law enforcement officer who has probable cause to believe that the person has violated N.J.S.2C:11-5, subsection c. of N.J.S.2C:12-1, R.S.39:4-50, section 2 of P.L.1981, c. 512 (C.39:4-50.4a) or section 2 of P.L.1972, c. 197 (C.39:6B-2), or has committed a motor vehicle moving violation, the law enforcement officer shall:

a.   As soon as practicable, contact the United States Department of State office to verify the driver's status and immunity;

b.   Record all relevant information from the person's driver's license or identification card, including a driver's license or identification card issued by the United States Department of State;

c.   Within five working days after the date of the stop, forward to the Division of Motor Vehicles the following information:

(1) A vehicle accident report if the person was involved in an accident;

(2) A copy of any citation or other charging document that was issued, if any; and

(3) A written report describing the incident if no citation or charging document was issued.

L.2003, c. 23, § 2, eff. May 1, 2003.

39:5-55. Duties of Division of Motor Vehicles

The Division of Motor Vehicles shall:

a.   Keep records of each accident report, citation or other charging document, and incident report received by law enforcement officers pursuant to subsection c. of section 2 of this act;

b.   Send copies of the reports and documents specified in subsection a. of this section to the Bureau of Diplomatic Security, Office of Foreign Missions in the United States Department of State.

L.2003, c. 23, § 3, eff. May 1, 2003.

39:5-56. Construction with other laws

The provisions of this act do not prohibit or limit the application of any law to a criminal or motor vehicle violation by a person who claims immunities or privileges under Title 22 of the United States Code.

L.2003, c. 23, § 4, eff. May 1, 2003.

CHAPTER 5A

APPLICATION OF SUBTITLE TO HIGHWAYS OWNED BY PUBLIC OR SEMIPUBLIC CORPORATIONS

Section
39:5A-1.   Written request; provisions made applicable.
39:5A-2.   Rescission of request.
39:5A-3.   Request not dedication; prohibition of use; different or additional conditions.
39:5A-4.   Application of motor vehicle and traffic laws.

39:5A-1. Written request; provisions made applicable

Upon the filing of a written request by a person, or by the board of directors of any corporation, or by the board of trustees of any corporation or other institution of a public or semipublic character not for pecuniary profit, incorporated under Title 15 of the Revised Statutes, with the clerk of any municipality of this State within which the property of such person, corporation or institution is situate, that the provisions of subtitle 1, Title 39, of the Revised Statutes shall be made applicable to the semipublic or private roads, streets, driveways, trails, terraces, bridle paths, parkways, parking areas, or other roadways open to or used by the public, tenants, employees, and the members of such institutions for purposes of vehicular travel by permission of such persons, corporations, or institutions and not as matter of public right, the provisions of subtitle 1, Title 39, of the Revised Statutes, shall, in the discretion of the municipal authorities vested with the police powers in the locality within which the property of such persons, corporations, or institutions is situate, be made applicable thereto. Such written request shall contain the name and post office address of the person, corporation or institution and shall designate with reasonable accuracy the semipublic or private roads, streets, driveways, trails, terraces, bridle paths, parkways, parking areas, or other roadway open to or used by vehicular traffic, to be affected thereby.

L.1945, c. 284, p. 834, § 1, eff. May 2, 1945. Amended by L.1954, c. 139, p. 639, § 2, eff. July 12, 1954; L.1964, c. 204, § 1, eff. Oct. 13, 1964; L.1970, c. 315, § 1, eff. Dec. 21, 1970; L.2008, c. 110, § 6, eff. Dec. 4, 2008.

39:5A–2. Rescission of request

Any such institution may rescind any request filed by it in conformity with the provisions of the foregoing section, by filing with the clerk of the municipality in which the original request was filed, a written rescission of such request, and thereupon the provisions of subtitle one, Title 39, of the Revised Statutes shall cease to be applicable to the road, street, driveway, trail, terrace, bridle-path, parkway or other roadway, used by vehicular traffic, set forth in such written rescission, effective as of the first day of January in the year next ensuing the filing of the said rescission; provided, however, that no rescission may be filed in the same year in which a request has been filed pursuant to section one of this act.

L.1945, c. 284, p. 835, § 2, eff. May 2, 1945.

39:5A–3. Request not dedication; prohibition of use; different or additional conditions

The filing of a written request, in pursuance of section 1 of this act,[1] shall not be deemed to constitute a dedication to public use, of any such roads, streets, driveways, trails, terraces, bridle paths, parkways, parking areas, or other roadways open to or used by vehicular traffic, nor shall it be construed to prevent such persons, corporations or institutions, as owners of such property open to or used by the public for purposes of vehicular travel by permission of such persons, corporations or institutions and not as a matter of public right, from prohibiting such use or from requiring other or different or additional conditions than those specified in subtitle 1, Title 39, of the Revised Statutes, or otherwise regulating such use as may seem best to such persons, corporations or institutions.

L.1945, c. 284, p. 835, § 3, eff. May 2, 1945. Amended by L.1954, c. 139, p. 640, § 3, eff. July 12, 1954.

[1] N.J.S.A. § 39:5A–1.

39:5A–4. Application of motor vehicle and traffic laws

The provisions of subtitle one of Title 39 of the Revised Statutes [1] shall be applicable to the semipublic or private roads, streets, driveways, trails, terraces, bridle paths, parkways or other roadways open to or used by the public for purposes of vehicular traffic, either as a matter of right or otherwise, within any park maintained in whole or in part by any municipality.

L.1953, c. 400, p. 2038, § 1, eff. Sept. 16, 1953.

[1] N.J.S.A. § 39:1–1 et seq.

CHAPTER 5B

TRANSPORTATION OF DANGEROUS ARTICLES ON HIGHWAY

Section
39:5B–1 to 39:5B–17. Repealed.
39:5B–18. Definitions.
39:5B–19. Radioactive material; production of certificate of handling, certificate number or other documents upon request.
39:5B–20. Placard on vehicle.
39:5B–21. Possession of certificate of handling or certification number by driver or operator.
39:5B–22. Conditions of certificate of handling; deviations; prohibition.
39:5B–23. Inspection.
39:5B–24. Violations; penalties.
39:5B–25. Definitions.
39:5B–26. Rules and regulations.
39:5B–27. Office of hazardous materials transportation compliance and enforcement; responsibilities.
39:5B–28. Annual report; recommendations.
39:5B–29. Penalties and injunctive relief.
39:5B–30. Transportation of hazardous materials; applicable law; reporting requirements of hazardous wastes.
39:5B–31. Inspection of hazardous materials being transported; authorized personnel; rules and regulations.
39:5B–31.1. Annual report of number of placarded rail freight cars transporting hazardous materials; fees; rules and regulations.
39:5B–32. Qualifications of interstate motor carrier operators and vehicles; rules and regulations; registration; financial responsibility; alcohol and controlled substances programs.

39:5B–1 to 39:5B–17. Repealed by L.1985, c. 415, § 6, eff. Jan. 13, 1986

39:5B–18. Definitions

As used in this act:

a. "Certificate of handling" means a written document issued by the Department of Environmental Protection pursuant to the terms of P.L.1977, c. 233 (C. 26:2D–18 et seq.), approving the use of certain specified New Jersey highways for the transport of specified quantities of radioactive materials.

b. "Certificate number" means the number associated with the certificate of handling issued by the Department of Environmental Protection.

L.1983, c. 102, § 1, eff. March 14, 1983.

39:5B–19. Radioactive material; production of certificate of handling, certificate number or other documents upon request

For the transport of certain types and quantities of radioactive material as specified by P.L.1977, c. 233 (C. 26:2D–18 et seq.), the driver or operator of the motor vehicle shall produce the certificate of handling or certificate number when requested to do so by any State Police officer or any representative of the State Department of Environmental Protection, while in the performance of his office, and shall also produce any other documents in such manner as may be required by law so that the officer or representative may thereby determine the identity of the certificate holder.

L.1983, c. 102, § 2, eff. March 14, 1983.

39:5B–20. Placard on vehicle

Where a radioactive material shipment has been certified pursuant to the provisions of P.L.1977, c. 233 (C. 26:2D–18 et seq.), and the rules and regulations promulgated pursuant thereto, and it does not require placarding on the outside of the shipping vehicle pursuant to federal law or regulations, the driver or operator of the vehicle shall conspicuously post a placard in the cab to be readily visible from outside the cab of the vehicle bearing the conventional radiation symbol and the words:

"CAUTION: THIS VEHICLE CONTAINS
RADIOACTIVE MATERIAL".

Compliance with this section shall be deemed compliance with section 11 of P.L.1950, c. 128 (C. 39:5B–11).[1]

L.1983, c. 102, § 3, eff. March 14, 1983.

1 Repealed 1985.

39:5B–21. Possession of certificate of handling or certification number by driver or operator

In addition to any other conditions or liability imposed by law, it shall be unlawful to ship or transport, or cause to be shipped or transported, by motor vehicle over the highways of this State those types and quantities of radioactive material for which a certificate of handling is required pursuant to the terms of P.L.1977, c. 233 (C. 26:2D–18 et seq.), unless the certificate of handling or certification number is obtained from the State Department of Environmental Protection and is in the possession of the driver or operator of any motor vehicle used for the transport of the material on the highways of this State.

L.1983, c. 102, § 4, eff. March 14, 1983.

39:5B–22. Conditions of certificate of handling; deviations; prohibition

Where a certificate of handling is required by law and has been issued by the State Department of Environmental Protection, it shall be unlawful to ship or transport, or cause to be shipped or transported, by motor vehicle over the highways of this State the radioactive material in any manner or condition that constitutes a deviation from the conditions of the certificate of handling.

L.1983, c. 102, § 5, eff. March 14, 1983.

39:5B–23. Inspection

Any State Police officer or representative of the State Department of Environmental Protection, while in the performance of the duties of his office, is authorized to inspect any motor vehicle to investigate any actual or suspected source of radiation for the purpose of determining compliance with the provisions of, or the need for, a certificate of handling.

L.1983, c. 102, § 6, eff. March 14, 1983.

39:5B–24. Violations; penalties

The civil penalty for violation of this act for a first offense is not more than $250.00 and for each subsequent offense is not more than $500.00, which penalty shall be recovered in accordance with "the penalty enforcement law" (N.J.S. 2A:58–1 et seq.).

L.1983, c. 102, § 7, eff. March 14, 1983.

39:5B–25. Definitions

As used in this act:

a. "Department" means the Department of Transportation;

b. "Hazardous material" means a substance or material determined by the Secretary of the United States Department of Transportation to be capable of posing an unreasonable risk to health, safety, and property when transported in commerce and so designated pursuant to the provisions of the "Hazardous Materials Transportation Act," Pub.L. 93–633 (49 U.S.C. § 1801 et seq.).

L.1983, c. 401, § 1, eff. Dec. 23, 1983.

39:5B–26. Rules and regulations

The department, in consultation with the Department of Environmental Protection, the Department of Labor, the Department of Commerce and Economic Development, the Divisions of Motor Vehicles and State Police of the Department of Law and Public Safety, and other appropriate State departments and agencies shall adopt, within 12 months of the effective date of this act and pursuant to the provisions of the "Administrative Procedure Act," P.L.1968, c. 410 (C. 52:14B–1 et seq.), rules and regulations concerning the transportation of hazardous materials, which shall, to the maximum extent practicable, conform to the requirements established by

49 CFR Parts 100–199, adopted by the United States Department of Transportation pursuant to the provisions of the "Hazardous Materials Transportation Act," Pub.L. 93–633 (49 U.S.C. § 1801 et seq.).

L.1983, c. 401, § 2, eff. Dec. 23, 1983.

39:5B–27. Office of hazardous materials transportation compliance and enforcement; responsibilities

There is created in the Division of State Police of the Department of Law and Public Safety, an Office of Hazardous Materials Transportation Compliance and Enforcement. It shall be the responsibility of this office to coordinate the implementation and enforcement of the provisions of this act and the rules and regulations adopted pursuant thereto.

L.1983, c. 401, § 3, eff. Dec. 23, 1983.

39:5B–28. Annual report; recommendations

The department, in consultation with the Department of Environmental Protection, the Department of Labor, the Department of Commerce and Economic Development, the Divisions of Motor Vehicles and State Police of the Department of Law and Public Safety, and other appropriate State departments and agencies, shall, within one year of the effective date of this act and annually thereafter, prepare and submit to the Governor and the Legislature a report detailing the incidence and means of the transportation of hazardous materials in this State, evaluating the protection afforded New Jersey citizens therefrom by all relevant federal and State statutes and regulations, and recommending executive or legislative actions necessary to insure the safe and proper transportation of hazardous materials.

L.1983, c. 401, § 4, eff. Dec. 23, 1983. Amended by L.1985, c. 415, § 4, eff. Jan. 13, 1986.

39:5B–29. Penalties and injunctive relief

a. Any person who violates the provisions of this act or any rule or regulation adopted pursuant thereto shall be subject to a penalty of not less than $100 nor more than $5,000.00 for the first offense, nor less than $200 nor more than $10,000.00 for the second offense, nor less than $500 nor more than $25,000.00 for the third or any subsequent offense. Notwithstanding any other provision of law, 50 percent of the penalty moneys collected pursuant to this paragraph shall be deposited into the "Highway Safety Fund" created pursuant to section 5 of P.L.2003, c. 131 (C.39:3–20.4).

The complaint and summons shall state whether the charges pertain to a first offense, or to a second or subsequent offense, but if the complaint or summons fails to allege a second or subsequent offense, the penalty imposed shall be for a first offense. The penalty may be reduced to $25 for a first offense, $50 for a second offense, and $125 for a third and subsequent offense for a non-out-of-service equipment violation if the defendant provides proof of repair to the vehicle that is satisfactory to the court. Proof that the violation has been corrected shall be by a document certifying that the non-out-of-service equipment violation has been corrected. The Division of State Police, a diesel emissions inspection center licensed by the New Jersey Motor Vehicle Commission, a certified fleet mechanic approved by the New Jersey Motor Vehicle Commission, or any other entity approved by the New Jersey Motor Vehicle Commission shall be authorized to issue the requisite certifying documentation. The Division of State Police may, in its discretion, designate times and locations where a defendant may bring a vehicle for an inspection pursuant to which a requisite certifying document may be issued. Nothing in this act shall be construed as requiring the Division of State Police to conduct a vehicle inspection pursuant to which a requisite certifying document may be issued other than at the time and locations as the Division of State Police may provide.

Repairs to effect a reduction of penalty under the provisions of this section shall be made before the hearing date. A defendant may be permitted to submit the certification of repairs by mail; provided that if the court deems the certification to be inadequate, it shall afford the defendant the option to withdraw the defendant's guilty plea.

The Department of Transportation is authorized to adopt a schedule of penalties for any specific violation of P.L.1983, c. 401 (C.39:5B–25 et seq.) or any rule or regulation adopted pursuant thereto. A penalty imposed pursuant to this act may be collected in a civil action by a summary proceeding under the "Penalty Enforcement Law of 1999," P.L.1999, c. 274 (C.2A:58–10 et seq.), or in a summary proceeding before a court of competent jurisdiction wherein injunctive relief has been sought. The State Police and police officers of the Port Authority of New York and New Jersey may issue a summons and complaint returnable in a municipal court or other court of competent jurisdiction for violations of P.L. 1983, c. 401 (C. 39:5B–25 et seq.) and this amendatory and supplementary act or any rule or regulation adopted pursuant thereto. In addition to the jurisdiction conferred by the "Penalty Enforcement Law of 1999," the Law and Chancery Divisions of the Superior Court shall have jurisdiction of proceedings for the enforcement of the penalties provided in this act. The various municipal courts shall have jurisdiction of proceedings for the enforcement of penalties under $5,000.00 provided in P.L. 1983, c. 401 (C. 39:5B–25 et seq.).

b. Penalties imposed pursuant to this act shall in no way reduce or otherwise limit the liability of any person, pursuant to the laws of this State, for cleanup costs or other damages arising from a discharge of hazardous materials.

c. The Superintendent of the State Police, police officers of the Port Authority of New York and New Jersey and personnel of the Department of Transportation and of the Department of Environmental Protection duly authorized by the superintendent may, in addition to seeking a civil penalty, seek injunctive relief in the Chancery Division, General Equity Part of the Superior Court as to any person found to have violated any provision of P.L.1983, c. 401 (C. 39:5B–25 et seq.) or this amendatory and supplementary act or any rule or regulation adopted pursuant to either.

d.   (Deleted by amendment, P.L.2003, c. 131).

L.1983, c. 401, § 5, eff. Dec. 23, 1983. Amended by L.1985, c. 415, § 5, eff. Jan. 13, 1986; L.2003, c. 131, § 2, eff. Feb. 15, 2004.

39:5B–30. Transportation of hazardous materials; applicable law; reporting requirements of hazardous wastes

The transportation of hazardous materials in this State shall be carried out in accordance with the provisions of P.L.1983, c. 401 (C. 39:5B–25 et seq.) and this amendatory and supplementary act, except that this section shall not be construed to limit the application or enforcement of the system of reporting the generation, transportation, storage and disposal of hazardous wastes required to be reported to the Department of Environmental Protection on the special waste manifest pursuant to N.J.A.C. 7:26–7.1 et seq., or as otherwise provided by law.

L.1985, c. 415, § 1, eff. Jan. 13, 1986.

39:5B–31. Inspection of hazardous materials being transported; authorized personnel; rules and regulations

a.   The Superintendent of the State Police may inspect such vehicles, railroad cars, and places of origin or destination in the State of the hazardous materials being transported, as may be necessary to carry out the provisions of P.L.1983, c. 401 and this amendatory and supplementary act.[1] The superintendent may also break such cargo seals on vehicles and railroad cars as may be necessary to inspect vehicles and railroad cars transporting hazardous materials to ascertain that packages as defined in 49 C.F.R. § 171.8 have been properly classified, described, packaged, marked, labeled, blocked and braced and are in proper condition for shipment.

b.   The powers exercised by the superintendent pursuant to this section may also be exercised by police officers of the Port Authority of New York and New Jersey, and by personnel of the Department of Transportation duly authorized by the superintendent. Appropriate personnel of the Department of Environmental Protection duly authorized by the superintendent may, consistent with federal regulations, inspect the contents of packages referred to in subsection a. of this section at places of origin prior to acceptance by the transporter or at places of destination after acceptance by the consignee. In addition, personnel of the Department of Environmental Protection so authorized may conduct, in conjunction with and under the direction of State Police personnel, inspections and break cargo seals as described in subsection a. of this section when at off-highway facilities, including, but not limited to,

public truck stops, public rest areas, State weigh stations, and commercial motor vehicle inspection stations.

c.   The Commissioner of Transportation is authorized to adopt, in consultation with the Superintendent of the State Police and pursuant to the "Administrative Procedure Act," P.L.1968, c. 410 (C. 52:14B–1 et seq.), rules and regulations governing inspection and breaking of cargo seals by those authorized to do so under this section. No person not given specific authority in this section to do so shall break cargo seals under this section or otherwise implement the provisions of this section.

L.1985, c. 415, § 2, eff. Jan. 13, 1986.

1 N.J.S.A. § 39:5B–30 et seq.

39:5B–31.1. Annual report of number of placarded rail freight cars transporting hazardous materials; fees; rules and regulations

a.   Notwithstanding any provision of Title 39 or Title 48 of the Revised Statutes to the contrary, the Commissioner of Transportation shall require all railroads operating in the State of New Jersey to annually report to the department the number of placarded rail freight cars transporting hazardous materials, as defined pursuant to P.L.1983, c. 401 (C.39:5B–25 et seq.), originating or terminating in the State, and shall annually pay the department a $3 fee per placarded rail freight car transporting hazardous materials which originates or terminates in this State during the reporting year.

b.   After a 24–month period following the effective date of this amendatory and supplementary act, the Commissioner of Transportation may, annually or less frequently, adopt regulations in accordance with the "Administrative Procedure Act," P.L.1968, c. 410 (C.52:14B–1 et seq.) providing for the revision of the fee set forth in subsection a. of this section, provided, however that such fee shall not be increased by more than the increase in the consumer price index for all urban wage earners and clerical workers (CPI–W) in the Philadelphia–New Jersey Area, as reported by the United States Department of Labor for the period since the fee was last determined.

c.   Moneys received from fees collected pursuant to this section shall be deposited in the General Fund and shall be disbursed to the department, subject to appropriation, to defray the expenses of the placarded rail freight car transporting hazardous materials program.

L.1993, c. 124, § 3, eff. June 7, 1993.

39:5B–32. Qualifications of interstate motor carrier operators and vehicles; rules and regulations; registration; financial responsibility; alcohol and controlled substances programs

a.   The Superintendent of the State Police shall adopt, within six months of the effective date of this amendatory and supplementary act and pursuant to the "Administrative Procedure Act," P.L.1968, c. 410 (C.52:14B–1 et seq.), rules and regulations concerning the qualifications of interstate motor carrier operators and vehicles, which shall substantially conform to the requirements established pursuant to sections 401 to 404 of the "Surface Transportation Assistance Act of 1982," Pub.L.97–424 (49 U.S.C. App. s. 2301–2304).

b. The superintendent, in consultation with the New Jersey Motor Vehicle Commission and with the Department of Transportation, shall revise and readopt, within six months of the effective date of P.L.1991, c. 491, the rules and regulations adopted pursuant to subsection a. of this section to provide that the regulations:

(1) Substantially conform to the requirements concerning the qualifications of interstate motor carrier operators and vehicles established pursuant to sections 401 to 404 of the "Surface Transportation Assistance Act of 1982," Pub.L.97–424 (49 U.S.C. App. s.2301–2304) and the federal "Motor Carrier Safety Act of 1984," Pub.L.98–554 (49 U.S.C. App. s. 2501 et seq.); and

(2) Include provisions with regard to motor carrier operators and vehicles engaged in intrastate commerce or used wholly within a municipality or a municipality's commercial zone, except for farm vehicles weighing 26,000 pounds or less that are operated exclusively in intrastate commerce and are registered pursuant to R.S.39:3–24 and R.S.39:3–25, that are compatible with federal rules and regulations.

Notwithstanding subsection c. of this section, the hours of service variances as adopted in 49 CFR s.350.341(e), as amended and supplemented, are hereby adopted effective immediately for commercial motor vehicles weighing 26,001 pounds or more operating in intrastate commerce provided that these vehicles are not designed to transport 16 or more passengers, including the driver, or used in the transportation of hazardous materials and required to be placarded in accordance with 49 CFR s.172.500 et seq., or display a hazardous materials placard. The superintendent shall adopt rules and regulations that conform to the requirements established in 49 CFR s. 350.341(e) as amended and supplemented.

c. Notwithstanding any provision of law or regulation to the contrary, no person shall operate a commercial motor vehicle, as defined in rules adopted pursuant to this section, in this State unless the operation of the commercial motor vehicle is in accordance with the rules adopted by the Superintendent of State Police pursuant to this section.

The rules adopted pursuant to this section shall include rules concerning protection against shifting or falling cargo contained in 49 C.F.R. s. 393.100 to 393.106.

d. The superintendent shall enforce registration requirements under 49 U.S.C. 13902, 49 CFR Parts 356 and 365 and 49 CFR s.392.9a by placing out of service a commercial motor vehicle in interstate commerce discovered to be operating without its Federal Motor Carrier Safety Administration registration as required

by 49 U.S.C. 13902, 49 CFR Parts 356 and 365 and 49 CFR s.392.9a, or beyond the scope of its Federal Motor Carrier Safety Administration registration.

e. The superintendent shall enforce financial responsibility requirements under 49 U.S.C. 13906 and 31139, and 49 CFR Part 387.

f. The superintendent shall enforce the implementation of programs designed to help prevent accidents and injuries resulting from the misuse of alcohol or use of controlled substances by drivers of commercial motor vehicles, pursuant to 49 CFR Part 382, and the implementation of federal procedures for transportation workplace drug and alcohol testing programs, pursuant to 49 CFR Part 40.

L.1985, c. 415, § 3, eff. Jan. 13, 1986. Amended by L.1991, c. 491, § 1, eff. Jan. 18, 1992; L.2004, c. 97, § 1, eff. July 12, 2004; L.2005, c. 109, § 1, eff. April 15, 2006.

CHAPTER 5C

MOTOR VEHICLE RACING ON HIGHWAYS

Section
39:5C–1.   Racing or making of speed records; penalty.

39:5C–1.   Racing or making of speed records; penalty

A person who shall operate or attempt or agree to operate a motor vehicle on a public highway in a race with any other motor vehicle or for the purpose of making a speed record or who shall arrange for, manage, encourage, or assist in, the holding of, or the attempting to hold, any such race or speed race event, is a disorderly person, and, upon conviction, shall be punished by a fine of not less than $25.00 nor more than $100.00 for the first offense and for each subsequent offense a fine of not less than $100.00 nor more than $200.00 or by imprisonment for not more than 90 days or both.

L.1955, c. 217, p. 840, § 1.

CHAPTER 5D

INTERSTATE COMPACT; DRIVERS LICENSES

DRIVER LICENSE COMPACT

Section
39:5D–1.   Findings and declaration of policy.
39:5D–2.   Definitions.
39:5D–3.   Reports of conviction.
39:5D–4.   Effect of conviction.
39:5D–5.   Applications for new licenses.
39:5D–6.   Applicability of other laws.
39:5D–7.   Compact administrator and interchange of information.
39:5D–8.   Entry into force and withdrawal.
39:5D–9.   Construction and severability.
39:5D–10. Licensing authority defined; duty of furnishing information.

Section

39:5D–11.   Compact administrator; expenses.

39:5D–12.   Executive head defined.

39:5D–13.   Report of action suspending, revoking or otherwise limiting license.

39:5D–14.   Suspension of enforcement against party State.

DRIVER LICENSE COMPACT

39:5D–1. Findings and declaration of policy

ARTICLE I

(a) The party States find that:

(1) The safety of their streets and highways is materially affected by the degree of compliance with State laws and local ordinances relating to the operation of motor vehicles.

(2) Violation of such a law or ordinance is evidence that the violator engages in conduct which is likely to endanger the safety of persons and property.

(3) The continuance in force of a license to drive is predicated upon compliance with laws and ordinances relating to the operation of motor vehicles, in whichever jurisdiction the vehicle is operated.

(b) It is the policy of each of the party States to:

(1) Promote compliance with the laws, ordinances, and administrative rules and regulations relating to the operation of motor vehicles by their operators in each of the jurisdictions where such operators drive motor vehicles.

(2) Make the reciprocal recognition of licenses to drive and eligibility therefor more just and equitable by considering the over-all compliance with motor vehicle laws, ordinances and administrative rules and regulations as a condition precedent to the continuance or issuance of any license by reason of which the licensee is authorized or permitted to operate a motor vehicle in any of the party States.

L.1966, c. 73, § 1, eff. Jan. 1, 1967.

39:5D–2. Definitions

ARTICLE II

As used in this compact:

(a) "State" means a State, territory or possession of the United States, the District of Columbia, or the Commonwealth of Puerto Rico.

(b) "Home State" means the State which has issued and has the power to suspend or revoke the use of the license or permit to operate a motor vehicle.

(c) "Conviction" means a conviction of any offense related to the use or operation of a motor vehicle which is prohibited by State law, municipal ordinance or administrative rule or regulation, or a forfeiture of bail, bond or other security deposited to secure appearance by a person charged with having committed any such

offense, and which conviction or forfeiture is required to be reported to the licensing authority.

L.1966, c. 73, § 1, eff. Jan. 1, 1967.

39:5D–3. Reports of conviction

ARTICLE III

The licensing authority of a party State shall report each conviction of a person from another party State occurring within its jurisdiction to the licensing authority of the home State of the licensee. Such report shall clearly identify the person convicted; describe the violation specifying the section of the statute, code or ordinance violated; identify the court in which action was taken; indicate whether a plea of guilty or not guilty was entered, or the conviction was a result of the forfeiture of bail, bond or other security; and shall include any special findings made in connection therewith.

L.1966, c. 73, § 1, eff. Jan. 1, 1967.

39:5D–4. Effect of conviction

ARTICLE IV

(a) The licensing authority in the home State, for the purposes of suspension, revocation or limitation of the license to operate a motor vehicle, shall give the same effect to the conduct reported, pursuant to Article III of this compact, [1] as it would if such conduct had occurred in the home State, shall apply the penalties of the home State or of the State in which the violation occurred, in the case of convictions for:

(1) Manslaughter or negligent homicide resulting from the operation of a motor vehicle;

(2) Driving a motor vehicle while under the influence of intoxicating liquor or a narcotic drug, or under the influence of any other drug to a degree which renders the driver incapable of safely driving a motor vehicle;

(3) Any felony in the commission of which a motor vehicle is used;

(4) Failure to stop and render aid in the event of a motor vehicle accident resulting in the death or personal injury of another.

(b) As to other convictions, reported pursuant to Article III, the licensing authority in the home State shall give such effect to the conduct as is provided by the laws of the home State.

(c) If the laws of a party State do not provide for offenses or violations denominated or described in precisely the words employed in subdivision (a) of this article, such party State shall construe the denominations and descriptions appearing in subdivision (a) hereof as being applicable to and identifying those offenses or violations of a substantially similar nature and the laws of such party State shall contain such provisions as may be necessary to ensure that full force and effect is given to this article.

L.1966, c. 73, § 1, eff. Jan. 1, 1967.

1 N.J.S.A. § 39:5D–3.

39:5D–5. Applications for new licenses

ARTICLE V

Upon application for a license to drive, the licensing authority in a party State shall ascertain whether the applicant has ever held, or is the holder of a license to drive issued by any other party State. The licensing authority in the State where application is made shall not issue a license to drive to the applicant if:

(1) The applicant has held such a license, but the same has been suspended by reason, in whole or in part, of a violation and if such suspension period has not terminated.

(2) The applicant has held such a license, but the same has been revoked by reason, in whole or in part, of a violation and if such revocation has not terminated, except that after the expiration of 1 year from the date the license was revoked, such person may make application for a new license if permitted by law. The licensing authority may refuse to issue a license to any such applicant if, after investigation, the licensing authority determines that it will not be safe to grant to such person the privilege of driving a motor vehicle on the public highways.

(3) The applicant is the holder of a license to drive issued by another party State and currently in force unless the applicant surrenders such license.

L.1966, c. 73, § 1, eff. Jan. 1, 1967.

39:5D–6. Applicability of other laws

ARTICLE VI

Except as expressly required by provisions of this compact, nothing contained herein shall be construed to affect the right of any party State to apply any of its other laws relating to licenses to drive to any person or circumstance, nor to invalidate or prevent any driver license agreement or other co-operative arrangement between a party State and a nonparty State.

L.1966, c. 73, § 1, eff. Jan. 1, 1967.

39:5D–7. Compact administrator and interchange of information

ARTICLE VII

(a) The head of the licensing authority of each party State shall be the administrator of this compact for his State. The administrators, acting jointly, shall have the power to formulate all necessary and proper procedures for the exchange of information under this compact.

(b) The administrator of each party State shall furnish to the administrator of each other party State any information or documents reasonably necessary to facilitate the administration of this compact.

L.1966, c. 73, § 1, eff. Jan. 1, 1967.

39:5D–8. Entry into force and withdrawal

ARTICLE VIII

(a) This compact shall enter into force and become effective as to any State when it has enacted the same into law.

(b) Any party State may withdraw from this compact by enacting a statute repealing the same, but no such withdrawal shall take effect until 6 months after the executive head of the withdrawing State has given notice of the withdrawal to the executive heads of all other party States. No withdrawal shall affect the validity or applicability by the licensing authorities of States remaining party to the compact of any report of conviction occurring prior to the withdrawal.

L.1966, c. 73, § 1, eff. Jan. 1, 1967.

39:5D–9. Construction and severability

ARTICLE IX

This compact shall be liberally construed so as to effectuate the purposes thereof. The provisions of this compact shall be severable and if any phrase, clause, sentence or provision of this compact is declared to be contrary to the constitution of any party State or of the United States or the applicability thereof to any government, agency, person or circumstance is held invalid, the validity of the remainder of this compact and the applicability thereof to any government, agency, person or circumstance shall not be affected thereby. If this compact shall be held contrary to the constitution of any State party thereto, the compact shall remain in full force and effect as to the remaining States and in full force and effect as to the State affected as to all severable matters.

L.1966, c. 73, § 1, eff. Jan. 1, 1967.

39:5D–10. Licensing authority defined; duty of furnishing information

As used in the compact, the term "licensing authority" with reference to this State, shall mean the Division of Motor Vehicles, Department of Law and Public Safety. Said division shall furnish to the appropriate authorities of any other party State any information or documents reasonably necessary to facilitate the administration of Articles III, IV and V of the compact.[1]

L.1966, c. 73, § 2, eff. Jan. 1, 1967.

1 N.J.S.A. §§ 39:5D–3 to 39:5D–5.

39:5D–11. Compact administrator; expenses

The compact administrator provided for in Article VII[1] of the compact shall not be entitled to any additional compensation on account of his service as such administrator, but shall be entitled to expenses incurred in connection with his duties and responsibilities as such administrator, in the same manner as for expenses incurred in connection with any other duties or responsibilities of his office or employment.

L.1966, c. 73, § 3, eff. Jan. 1, 1967.

1 N.J.S.A. § 39:5D–7.

39:5D–12. Executive head defined

As used in the compact, with reference to this State, the term "executive head" shall mean the Governor.

L.1966, c. 73, § 4, eff. Jan. 1, 1967.

39:5D–13. Report of action suspending, revoking or otherwise limiting license

Any court or other agency of this State, or a subdivision thereof, which has jurisdiction to take any action suspending, revoking or otherwise limiting a license to drive, shall report any such action and the adjudication upon which it is based to the Division of Motor Vehicles within 3 days on forms furnished by the division.

L.1966, c. 73, § 5, eff. Jan. 1, 1967.

39:5D–14. Suspension of enforcement against party State

If it is determined by the Director of Motor Vehicles of the State of New Jersey that the provisions of the compact, in full or in part, are not being implemented with respect to violations reported from the State of New Jersey by any other party State, the director with the approval of the Governor of New Jersey, may suspend the enforcement of the provisions of this agreement as against such party State until such time as he shall determine that such implementation by the other party State is being had.

L.1966, c. 73, § 6, eff. Jan. 1, 1967.

CHAPTER 5E

TRANSPORTATION OF BULK COMMODITIES
[REPEALED]

39:5E–1 to 39:5E–26. Repealed by L.1995, c. 157, § 38

CHAPTER 5F

NONRESIDENT VIOLATOR COMPACT

ARTICLE I

Section
39:5F–1.   Findings of party jurisdictions.
39:5F–2.   Policy of party jurisdictions.
39:5F–3.   Purpose.

ARTICLE II

39:5F–4.   Definitions.

Section

ARTICLE III

39:5F–5.   Collateral to secure appearance; personal recognizance.
39:5F–6.   Personal recognizance.
39:5F–7.   Report of motorists failure to comply with terms of citation.
39:5F–8.   Transmission of report to home jurisdiction of motorist.
39:5F–9.   Suspension of driving privilege by issuing jurisdiction.
39:5F–10.   Limitation on transmission of report; date of transmission.
39:5F–11.   Limitation on transmission of report; date of issuance of citation.

ARTICLE IV

39:5F–12.   Suspension of drivers license by home jurisdiction.
39:5F–13.   Record of actions; reports to issuing jurisdiction.

ARTICLE V

39:5F–14.   Effect on other laws or agreements.

ARTICLE VI

39:5F–15.   Board of compact administrators.
39:5F–16.   Voting; action of board.
39:5F–17.   Chairman and vice-chairman.
39:5F–18.   Bylaws.
39:5F–19.   Donations and grants.
39:5F–20.   Contracts for or acceptance of services or personnel.
39:5F–21.   Procedures and forms.

ARTICLE VII

39:5F–22.   Effective upon adoption by at least two jurisdictions.
39:5F–23.   Entry into compact; resolution of ratification; effective date.
39:5F–24.   Withdrawal.

ARTICLE VIII

39:5F–25.   Violations not covered by compact.

ARTICLE IX

39:5F–26.   Amendment.
39:5F–27.   Endorsement of amendment.
39:5F–28.   Failure to respond as endorsement.

ARTICLE X

39:5F–29.   Construction; severability.

ARTICLE XI

39:5F–30.   Title of compact.

ARTICLE I

39:5F–1. Findings of party jurisdictions

The party jurisdictions find that:

a. In most instances, a motorist who is cited for a traffic violation in a jurisdiction other than his home jurisdiction:

(1) Must post collateral or bond to secure appearance for trial at a later date; or

(2) If unable to post collateral or bond, is taken into custody until the collateral or bond is posted; or

(3) Is taken directly to court for his trial to be held.

b. In some instances, the motorist's driver's license may be deposited as collateral to be returned after he has complied with the terms of the citation.

c. The purpose of the practices described in subsections 1a. and b. above is to ensure compliance with the terms of a traffic citation by the motorist who, if permitted to continue on his way after receiving the traffic citation, could return to his home jurisdiction and disregard his duty under the terms of the traffic citation.

d. A motorist receiving a traffic citation in his home jurisdiction is permitted, except for certain violations, to accept the citation from the officer at the scene of the violation and to immediately continue on his way after promising or being instructed to comply with the terms of the citation.

e. The practice described in subsection a. above causes unnecessary inconvenience and, at times, a hardship for the motorist who is unable at the time to post collateral, furnish a bond, stand trial, or pay the fine, and thus is compelled to remain in custody until some arrangement can be made.

f. The deposit of a driver's license as a bail bond, as described in subsection 1b. above, is viewed with disfavor.

g. The practices described herein consume an undue amount of law enforcement time.

L.1983, c. 46, § 1, eff. Jan. 28, 1983.

39:5F–2. Policy of party jurisdictions

It is the policy of the party jurisdictions to:

a. Seek compliance with the laws, ordinances, and administrative rules and regulations relating to the operation of motor vehicles in each of the jurisdictions.

b. Allow motorists to accept a traffic citation for certain violations and proceed on their way without delay, whether or not the motorist is a resident of the jurisdiction in which the citation was issued.

c. Extend cooperation to its fullest extent among the jurisdictions for obtaining compliance with the terms of a traffic citation issued in one jurisdiction to a resident of another jurisdiction.

d. Maximize effective utilization of law enforcement personnel and assist court systems in the efficient disposition of traffic violations.

L.1983, c. 46, § 2, eff. Jan. 28, 1983.

39:5F–3. Purpose

The purpose of this compact is to:

a. Provide a means through which the party jurisdictions may participate in a reciprocal program to effectuate the policies enumerated in section 2 [1] above in a uniform and orderly manner.

b. Provide for the fair and impartial treatment of traffic violators operating within party jurisdictions in recognition of the motorist's right of due process and the sovereign status of a party jurisdiction.

L.1983, c. 46, § 3, eff. Jan. 28, 1983.

[1] N.J.S.A. § 39:5F–2.

ARTICLE II

39:5F–4. Definitions

As used in this compact:

a. "Citation" means any summons, ticket, or other official document issued by a police officer for a traffic violation, containing an order which requires the motorist to respond;

b. "Collateral" means any cash or other security deposited to secure an appearance for trial, following the issuance by a police officer of a citation for a traffic violation;

c. "Compliance" means the act of answering a citation, summons or subpena through appearance at court, or payment of fines and costs, or both;

d. "Court" means a court of law or traffic tribunal;

e. "Driver's license" means any license or privilege to operate a motor vehicle issued under the laws of the home jurisdiction;

f. "Home jurisdiction" means the jurisdiction that issued the driver's license of the traffic violator;

g. "Issuing jurisdiction" means the jurisdiction in which the traffic citation was issued to the motorist;

h. "Jurisdiction" means a state, territory, or possession of the United States, the District of Columbia, Commonwealth of Puerto Rico, Provinces of Canada, or other countries;

i. "Motorist" means a driver of a motor vehicle operating in a party jurisdiction other than the home jurisdiction;

j. "Personal recognizance" means an agreement by a motorist made at the time of issuance of the traffic citation that he will comply with the terms of that traffic citation;

k. "Police officer" means any individual authorized by the party jurisdiction to issue a citation for a traffic violation;

l. "Terms of the citation" means those options expressly stated upon the citation.

L.1983, c. 46, § 4, eff. Jan. 28, 1983.

ARTICLE III

39:5F–5. Collateral to secure appearance; personal recognizance

When issuing a citation for a traffic violation, a police officer shall issue the citation to a motorist who possesses a driver's license issued by a party jurisdiction and shall not, subject to the exceptions noted in section 6 of this act,[1] require the motorist to post collateral to secure appearance, if the officer receives the motorist's personal recognizance that he will comply with the terms of the citation.

L.1983, c. 46, § 5, eff. Jan. 28, 1983.

[1] N.J.S.A. § 39:5F–6.

39:5F–6. Personal recognizance

Personal recognizance is acceptable only if not prohibited by law. If mandatory appearance is required, it shall take place immediately following issuance of the citation.

L.1983, c. 46, § 6, eff. Jan. 28, 1983.

39:5F–7. Report of motorists failure to comply with terms of citation

Upon failure of a motorist to comply with the terms of a traffic citation, the appropriate official shall report the failure to comply to the licensing authority of the jurisdiction in which the traffic citation was issued. The report shall be made in accordance with procedures specified by the issuing jurisdiction and shall contain information as specified in the Compact Manual as minimum requirements for effective processing by the home jurisdiction.

L.1983, c. 46, § 7, eff. Jan. 28, 1983.

39:5F–8. Transmission of report to home jurisdiction of motorist

Upon receipt of the report, the licensing authority of the issuing jurisdiction shall transmit to the licensing authority in the home jurisdiction of the motorist the information in a form and content as contained in the Compact Manual.

L.1983, c. 46, § 8, eff. Jan. 28, 1983.

39:5F–9. Suspension of driving privilege by issuing jurisdiction

The licensing authority of the issuing jurisdiction need not suspend the driving privilege of a motorist for whom a report has been transmitted.

L.1983, c. 46, § 9, eff. Jan. 28, 1983.

39:5F–10. Limitation on transmission of report; date of transmission

The licensing authority of the issuing jurisdiction shall not transmit a report on any violation if the date of transmission is more than 6 months after the date on which the traffic citation was issued.

L.1983, c. 46, § 10, eff. Jan. 28, 1983.

39:5F–11. Limitation on transmission of report; date of issuance of citation

The licensing authority of the issuing jurisdiction shall not transmit a report on any violation where the date of issuance of the citation predates the most recent of the effective dates of entry for the two jurisdictions affected.

L.1983, c. 46, § 11, eff. Jan. 28, 1983.

ARTICLE IV

39:5F–12. Suspension of drivers license by home jurisdiction

Upon receipt of a report of a failure to comply from the licensing authority of the issuing jurisdiction, the licensing authority of the home jurisdiction shall notify the motorist and initiate a suspension action, in accordance with the home jurisdiction's procedures, to suspend the motorist's driver's license until satisfactory evidence of compliance with the terms of the traffic citation has been furnished to the home jurisdiction licensing authority. Due process safeguards will be accorded.

L.1983, c. 46, § 12, eff. Jan. 28, 1983.

39:5F–13. Record of actions; reports to issuing jurisdiction

The licensing authority of the home jurisdiction shall maintain a record of actions taken and make reports to issuing jurisdictions as provided in the Compact Manual.

L.1983, c. 46, § 13, eff. Jan. 28, 1983.

ARTICLE V

39:5F–14. Effect on other laws or agreements

Except as expressly required by provisions of this compact, nothing contained herein shall be construed to affect the right of any party jurisdiction to apply any of its other laws relating to license to drive to any person or circumstance, or to invalidate or prevent any driver license agreement or other cooperative arrangements between a party jurisdiction and a nonparty jurisdiction.

L.1983, c. 46, § 14, eff. Jan. 28, 1983.

ARTICLE VI

39:5F–15. Board of compact administrators

For the purpose of administering the provisions of this compact and to serve as a governing body for the resolution of all matters relating to the operation of this compact, a Board of Compact Administrators is established. The board shall be composed of one representative from each party jurisdiction, to be known as the compact administrator. The compact administrator shall be appointed by the chief executive of the jurisdiction and shall serve and be subject to removal in accordance with the laws of his jurisdiction. A compact administrator may provide for the discharge of his duties and the performance of his functions as a board member by an alternate. An alternate may not serve on the board unless written notification of his identity has been given to the board.

L.1983, c. 46, § 15, eff. Jan. 28, 1983.

39:5F–16. Voting; action of board

Each member of the Board of Compact Administrators shall be entitled to one vote. No action of the board shall be binding unless taken at a meeting at which a majority of the total number of votes on the board are cast in favor. Action by the board shall be only at a meeting at which a majority of the party jurisdictions are represented.

L.1983, c. 46, § 16, eff. Jan. 28, 1983.

39:5F–17. Chairman and vice-chairman

The board shall elect annually, from its membership, a chairman and vice-chairman.

L.1983, c. 46, § 17, eff. Jan. 28, 1983.

39:5F–18. Bylaws

The board shall adopt bylaws, not inconsistent with the provisions of this compact or the laws of a party jurisdiction, for the conduct of its business and shall have the power to amend and rescind its bylaws.

L.1983, c. 46, § 18, eff. Jan. 28, 1983.

39:5F–19. Donations and grants

The board may accept for any of its purposes and functions under this compact any and all donations, and grants of money, equipment, supplies, materials, and services, conditional or otherwise, from any jurisdiction, the United States, or any other governmental agency, and may receive, utilize and dispose of the same.

L.1983, c. 46, § 19, eff. Jan. 28, 1983.

39:5F–20. Contracts for or acceptance of services or personnel

The board may contract with, or accept services or personnel from any governmental or intergovernmental agency, persons, firm or corporation, or any private, nonprofit organization or institution.

L.1983, c. 46, § 20, eff. Jan. 28, 1983.

39:5F–21. Procedures and forms

The board shall formulate all necessary procedures and develop uniform forms and documents for administering the provisions of this compact. All procedures and forms adopted pursuant to board action shall be contained in the Compact Manual.

L.1983, c. 46, § 21, eff. Jan. 28, 1983.

ARTICLE VII

39:5F–22. Effective upon adoption by at least two jurisdictions

This compact shall become effective when it has been adopted by at least two jurisdictions.

L.1983, c. 46, § 22, eff. Jan. 28, 1983.

39:5F–23. Entry into compact; resolution of ratification; effective date

a. Entry into the compact shall be made by a Resolution of Ratification executed by the authorized officials of the applying jurisdiction and submitted to the chairman of the board.

b. The resolution shall be in a form and content as provided in the Compact Manual and shall include statements that in substance are as follows:

(1) A citation of the authority by which the jurisdiction is empowered to become a party to this compact.

(2) Agreement to comply with the terms and provisions of the compact.

(3) That compact entry is with all jurisdictions then party to the compact and with any jurisdiction that legally becomes a party to the compact.

c. The effective date of entry shall be specified by the applying jurisdiction, but it shall not be less than 60 days after notice has been given by the chairman of the Board of Compact Administrators or by the secretariat of the board to each party jurisdiction that the resolution from the applying jurisdiction has been received.

L.1983, c. 46, § 23, eff. Jan. 28, 1983.

39:5F–24. Withdrawal

A party jurisdiction may withdraw from this compact by official written notice to the other party jurisdictions, but a withdrawal shall not take effect until 90 days after notice of withdrawal is given. The notice shall be directed to the compact administrator of each member jurisdiction. No withdrawal shall affect the validity of this compact as to the remaining party jurisdictions.

L.1983, c. 46, § 24, eff. Jan. 28, 1983.

ARTICLE VIII

39:5F–25. Violations not covered by compact

The provisions of this compact shall not apply to parking or standing violations, highway weight limit violations, and violations of law governing the transportation of hazardous materials.

L.1983, c. 46, § 25, eff. Jan. 28, 1983.

ARTICLE IX

39:5F–26. Amendment

This compact may be amended from time to time. Amendments shall be presented in resolution form to the chairman of the Board of Compact Administrators and may be initiated by one or more party jurisdictions.

L.1983, c. 46, § 26, eff. Jan. 28, 1983.

39:5F–27. Endorsement of amendment

Adoption of an amendment shall require endorsement of all party jurisdictions and shall become effective 30 days after the date of the last endorsement.

L.1983, c. 46, § 27, eff. Jan. 28, 1983.

39:5F–28. Failure to respond as endorsement

Failure of a party jurisdiction to respond to the compact chairman within 120 days after receipt of the proposed amendment shall constitute endorsement.

L.1983, c. 46, § 28, eff. Jan. 28, 1983.

ARTICLE X

39:5F–29. Construction; severability

This compact shall be liberally construed so as to effectuate the purposes stated herein. The provisions of this compact shall be severable and if any phrase, clause, sentence, or provision of this compact is declared to be contrary to the constitution of any party jurisdiction or of the United States or the applicability thereof to any government agency, person, or circumstance, the compact shall not be affected thereby. If this compact shall be held contrary to the constitution of any jurisdiction party thereto, the compact shall remain in full force and effect as to the remaining jurisdictions and in full force and effect as to the jurisdiction affected as to all severable matters.

L.1983, c. 46, § 29, eff. Jan. 28, 1983.

ARTICLE XI

39:5F–30. Title of compact

This compact shall be known and may be cited as the "Nonresident Violator Compact".

L.1983, c. 46, § 30, eff. Jan. 28, 1983.

CHAPTER 5G

LIMOUSINE OPERATION AND ENFORCEMENT

Section
39:5G–1.   Ownership and operation of a limousine; certain violations and penalties; law enforcement investigations.
39:5G–2.   Chauffeur driver endorsement required for prearranged passenger transportation; penalty for violation; application requirements; "certification date" defined.

39:5G–1. Ownership and operation of a limousine; certain violations and penalties; law enforcement investigations

A person who shall own and operate a limousine in any street in this State in violation of the provisions of article 2 of chapter 16 of Title 48 of the Revised Statutes or of Title 39 of the Revised Statutes shall be subject to the following penalties:

a. (1) For operating a limousine without a license issued by a municipality pursuant to R.S.48:16–17, knowingly permitting a driver to operate a limousine without a validly issued driver's license or a validly issued commercial driver license if required pursuant to N.J.A.C.13:21–23.1, failure to have filed an insurance policy in the amount of $1,500,000 which is currently in force as provided in R.S.48:16–14 or in the amounts required pursuant to section 14 of P.L.1999, c. 356 (C.48:16–22.4), operating a limousine in which the number of passengers exceeds the maximum seating capacity as provided in R.S.48:16–13 or section 2 of P.L.1997, c. 356 (C.48:16–13.1): a fine of $2,500 for the first offense and a fine of $5000 for the second or subsequent offense;

(2) For operating a limousine without the special registration plates required pursuant to section 12 of P.L.1979, c. 224 (C.39:3–19.5), or operating a limousine without the limousine being properly inspected as provided in R.S.39:8–1: a fine of $1,250 for the first offense and a fine of $2,500 for the second or subsequent offense;

(3) For operating a limousine without the attached sideboards required by section 11 of P.L.1999, c. 356 (C.48:16–22.1), failure to retain within the limousine appropriate proof of insurance pursuant to R.S.48:16–17 or failure to execute and deliver to the chief administrator the power of attorney required pursuant to R.S.48:16–16: a fine of $250 for the first offense and $500 for the second and subsequent offense;

(4) For failure to be equipped with a two-way communications system, a removable first-aid kit, and an operable fire extinguisher as required by section 11 of P.L.1999, c. 356 (C.48:16–22.1), or any other violation of the provisions of article 2 of chapter 16 of Title 48 of the Revised Statutes other than those enumerated in this subsection: a fine of $50 for the first offense and $100 for the second and subsequent offense.

b. Violations of this section shall be enforced and penalties collected in a summary proceeding pursuant to "The Penalty Enforcement Law of 1999," P.L.1999, c. 274 (C.2A:58–10 et seq.). The Superior Court or any municipal court where the violation was detected, or where the defendant was apprehended, shall have jurisdiction to enforce this section. Penalties imposed pursuant to this section shall be in addition to those otherwise imposed according to law. All penalties collected pursuant to the provisions of this section shall be forwarded as provided in R.S.39:5–40 and subsection b. of R.S.39:5–41.

c. State Police officers may enter the property of the operator of a limousine service to conduct an inspection of documents and vehicles upon probable cause that the operator is violating R.S.48:16–14, R.S.48:16–17, R.S.48:16–22, section 11 of P.L.1999, c. 356 (C.48:16–22.1), section 14 of P. L.1999, c. 356 (C.48:16–22.4), or section 12 of P.L.1979, c. 224 (C.39:3–19.5).

L.1999, c. 356, § 18. Amended by L.2001, c. 416, § 11, eff. Jan. 8, 2002; L.2009, c. 325, § 1, eff. Jan. 18, 2010.

39:5G–2. Chauffeur driver endorsement required for prearranged passenger transportation; penalty for violation; application requirements; "certification date" defined

Section effective on the date the chief administrator certifies to the Governor that the Motor Vehicle Automated Transaction System (MATRX) is capable of accommodating the new chauffeur endorsement.

a. No person shall operate a limousine, or any other passenger automobile, as defined in R.S.39:1–1, provided through a company or service which pairs a passenger automobile and a driver with a private customer to provide prearranged passenger transportation at a premium fare on a dedicated, nonscheduled, charter basis that is not conducted on a regular route, including, but not limited to, the use of authorized drivers of rental vehicles to provide such passenger transportation, in this State unless the person has a chauffeur endorsement. An owner of a limousine service, or any other company or service which pairs a passenger automobile, as defined in R.S.39:1–1, and a driver with a private customer to provide prearranged passenger transportation at a premium fare on a dedicated, nonscheduled, charter basis that is not conducted on a regular route, who permits the operation of a limousine, or any other passenger automobile provided through a company or service which pairs a passenger automobile and a driver with a private customer to provide prearranged passenger transportation at a premium fare on a dedicated, nonscheduled, charter basis that is not conducted on a regular route, by any person who does not hold a chauffeur endorsement shall be subject to a penalty of $500.

Actions to impose a penalty under this subsection shall be brought, and any such penalty shall be collected, in a summary proceeding pursuant to the "Penalty Enforcement Law of 1999," P.L.1999, c. 274 (C.2A:58–10 et seq.). The Superior Court or any municipal court where the violation was detected, or where the defendant was apprehended, shall have jurisdiction to hear any action brought for violation of this subsection. Penalties imposed pursuant to this subsection shall be in addition to those otherwise imposed according to law. All penalties collected pursuant to the provisions of this subsection shall be forwarded as provided in R.S.39:5–40 and subsection b.

of R.S.39:5–41. If the violation is of a continuing nature, each day during which it continues shall constitute an additional, separate, and distinct offense.

b. To qualify for a chauffeur endorsement, an applicant shall provide the New Jersey Motor Vehicle Commission (hereinafter "the commission") with the applicant's name, home address, citizenship status, photographic identification, birth certificate, and such other information as the Chief Administrator of the New Jersey Motor Vehicle Commission (hereinafter the "chief administrator") may require.

c. The fee for the chauffeur endorsement shall be set by the chief administrator.

d. An applicant shall be required to submit proof that the applicant meets the medical standards for commercial drivers which are contained in 49 CFR 391.41.

e. An applicant shall submit to being fingerprinted by the Division of State Police in the Department of Law and Public Safety or by agents appointed by, or under contract to, the division and shall also provide written consent to the performance of a criminal history record background check unless the applicant was previously fingerprinted and had a criminal history background check conducted as part of an application for a Commercial Driver License or a passenger endorsement under a Commercial Driver License or both. The chief administrator is authorized to exchange fingerprint data and photographic identification with and receive criminal history record background information results from the Division of State Police. The division shall inform the chief administrator if an applicant's criminal history record background check reveals a conviction of a disqualifying crime as specified in subsection g. of this section. The applicant shall bear the cost of fingerprinting and the cost for the background checks, including all costs of administering and processing the checks. As used in this section, "criminal history record background check" means a determination of whether a person has a criminal record by cross-referencing that person's name and fingerprint data with those on file with the State Bureau of Identification in the Division of State Police.

f. No applicant shall be issued a chauffeur endorsement unless the applicant is 21 years of age or older.

g. An applicant shall be disqualified from obtaining a chauffeur endorsement if the applicant's criminal history record background check reveals a record of conviction of any of the following crimes:

(1) In New Jersey or elsewhere any crime as follows: aggravated assault, arson, burglary, escape, extortion, homicide, kidnapping, robbery, aggravated sexual assault, sexual assault or endangering the welfare of a child pursuant to N.J.S.2C:24–4, whether or not armed with or having in his possession any weapon enumerated in subsection r. of N.J.S.2C:39–1, a crime pursuant to the provisions of N.J.S.2C:39–3, N.J.S.2C:39–4, or N.J.S.2C:39–9, or other than a disorderly persons or

petty disorderly persons offense for the unlawful use, possession or sale of a controlled dangerous substance as defined in N.J.S.2C:35–2.

(2) In any other state, territory, commonwealth, or other jurisdiction of the United States, or any country in the world, as a result of a conviction in a court of competent jurisdiction, a crime which in that other jurisdiction or country is comparable to one of the crimes enumerated in paragraph (1) of this subsection.

h. If an applicant who has been convicted of one of the crimes enumerated in paragraph (1) of subsection g. of this section can produce a certificate of rehabilitation issued pursuant to N.J.S.2A:168A–8 or, if the criminal offense occurred outside New Jersey, an equivalent certificate from the jurisdiction where the criminal offense occurred, the criminal offense will not disqualify the applicant from obtaining a chauffeur endorsement.

i. Nothing in this section shall be construed to require operators of taxicabs, hotel buses, buses employed solely in transporting school children or teachers, vehicles owned and operated directly or indirectly by businesses engaged in the practice of mortuary science when those vehicles are used exclusively for providing transportation related to the provision of funeral services, autobuses which are subject to the jurisdiction of the Department of Transportation or interstate autobuses required by federal or State law or regulations of the Department of Transportation to carry insurance against loss from liability imposed by law on account of bodily injury or death to obtain a chauffeur endorsement pursuant to subsection a. of this section.

j. The chief administrator is authorized to adopt regulations, pursuant to the "Administrative Procedure Act," P.L.1968, c. 410 (C.52:14B–1 et seq.), to effectuate the purposes of this section.

k. "Certification date" means the date on which the chief administrator certifies to the Governor that the Motor Vehicle Automated Transaction System (MATRX) is capable of accommodating the new chauffeur endorsement. The chief administrator shall make such certification when the MATRX system can denote the existence of the endorsement and can monitor and track the status of the endorsement on a person's driving record.

L.2009, c. 325, § 5 (contingent effective date).

SUBTITLE 2

OTHER LAWS REGULATING MOTOR VEHICLES

Chapter
6. Financial Responsibility.
6A. Compulsory Automobile Liability Insurance—No Fault Provisions.
6B. Compulsory Motor Vehicle Insurance.
7. Service of Process Upon Nonresidents.
8. Inspection of Motor Vehicles.
9. Hours of Duty of Operators of Certain Motor Vehicles.
10. Purchase, Sale and Transfer of Motor Vehicles.
10A. Abandoned and Unclaimed Motor Vehicles.
10B. Motor Vehicle Component Parts.
11. Junk Yards.
12. Driving Schools.
13. Auto Body Repair Facilities.

CHAPTER 6

FINANCIAL RESPONSIBILITY

Section
39:6–1 to 39:6–22. Repealed.
39:6–23. Short title.
39:6–24. Definitions.
39:6–25. Security to satisfy judgments, damages or claims; suspension of license; inapplicability; requirements for insurance or surety company.
39:6–26. Inapplicability of requirements as to security and suspension.
39:6–27. Duration of suspension; default in payment of installment.
39:6–28. Operator or owner involved in accident without license or a nonresident.
39:6–29. Security, requirements as to.
39:6–30. Application of security; return of deposit or balance.
39:6–30.1. Remission of funds to state treasurer; investments.
39:6–31 to 39:6–34. Repealed.
39:6–35. Failure to satisfy judgment; discharge in bankruptcy.
39:6–36. Nonresident; judgment unsatisfied.
39:6–37. Insolvency or bankruptcy of liability insurer.
39:6–38. Partial payments which are deemed satisfaction of judgment.
39:6–39. Payment of judgment in installments.
39:6–40, 39:6–41. Repealed.
39:6–42. Certified abstract of operating record.
39:6–43 to 39:6–47. Repealed.
39:6–48. Form of liability policy; provisions to which it is subject; binders; indorsements.
39:6–49. Transfer of registration while owner's registration suspended.
39:6–50. Enforcement of act; rules and regulations; review.
39:6–50.1. Self-insurance; rules and regulations.
39:6–51. Informing persons as to contents of act.
39:6–52. Self insurance; cancellation.
39:6–53. Commissioner's action and findings and security filed not evidence as to negligence.

Section
39:6–54. Exemptions; self-insurance by public entity or group of public entities.
39:6–55. Prohibited acts; violations; enforcement; remedies; procedure; revocation of license.
39:6–56. Repeal.
39:6–57. Effective date.
39:6–58. Expense of administering Motor Vehicle Security-Responsibility Law; ascertainment; certifying annually.
39:6–59. Apportionment of amount certified among liability insurers.
39:6–60. Effective date.
39:6–61. Title.
39:6–62. Definitions.
39:6–63. Creation and maintenance of fund.
39:6–63.1. Assessment rescinded; registration of uninsured vehicles; fee.
39:6–63.2. Repealed.
39:6–64 to 39:6–64b. Repealed.
39:6–64c. Abolition of the Unsatisfied Claim and Judgment Fund Board in the Department of Banking and Insurance; transfer to the New Jersey Property-Liability Insurance Guaranty Association.
39:6–64.1. Rules and regulations; liability.
39:6–65. Notice of accident and intention to file claim.
39:6–66. Repealed.
39:6–67. Defense of actions against motorists.
39:6–68. Co-operation of defendant.
39:6–69. Application for payment of judgment.
39:6–70. Hearing on application for payment of judgment.
39:6–71. Order for payment of judgment.
39:6–72. Settlement of actions against motorist.
39:6–73. Limitation on amounts payable from fund.
39:6–73.1. Assumption of excess payment by fund; exceptions.
39:6–74. Default and consent judgments.
39:6–75. Repealed.
39:6–76. Collusive judgments.
39:6–77. Assignment of judgments to association.
39:6–78. "Hit-and-run" cases.
39:6–79. Other "hit-and-run" cases.
39:6–80. Impleading association in "hit-and-run" cases.
39:6–81. Defense of such actions by association.
39:6–82. Settlement of actions against the association.
39:6–83. Credits against judgment.
39:6–84. Judgment against commissioner.
39:6–84.1. Increase in payment of maximum amounts from fund; application to accidents on or after January 1, 1973.
39:6–85. Subrogation.
39:6–86. Repealed.
39:6–86.1. Unsatisfied Claim and Judgment Fund claims; benefits.
39:6–86.2. Payments of benefits.
39:6–86.3. Denial of benefits; grounds.
39:6–86.4. Death or injury due to unidentifiable operator or owner, or to operator using automobile without consent of owner; benefits payable; conditions.

Section
39:6–86.5.   Application for benefits; payment.
39:6–86.6.   Recovery of benefits paid by fund.
39:6–86.7.   Personal injury protection benefits to pedestrians.
39:6–87.   Registration, etc. not restored until fund is reimbursed.
39:6–88.   Fund to be held in trust.
39:6–89.   Repealed.
39:6–90.   Penalty for false statements.
39:6–90.1.   Partial invalidity.
39:6–91.   Repealed.
39:6–92 to 39:6–104.   Repealed.

39:6–1 to 39:6–22.   Repealed by L.1952, c. 173, p. 570, § 34

39:6–23.   Short title

This act shall be known and may be cited as the "Motor Vehicle Security-Responsibility Law."

L.1952, c. 173, p. 548, § 1, eff. April 1, 1953.

39:6–24.   Definitions

The following words and phrases, when used in this act, shall, for the purposes of this act, have the meanings respectively ascribed to them in this section, except in those instances where the context clearly indicates a different meaning:

"Director"—The Director of the Division of Motor Vehicles in the Department of Law and Public Safety.

"License"—Any license, temporary instruction permit or temporary license issued under the laws of this State pertaining to the licensing of persons to operate motor vehicles.

"Nonresident's operating privilege"—The privilege conferred upon a nonresident by the laws of this State pertaining to the operation by him of a motor vehicle, or the use of a motor vehicle owned by him, in this State.

"State"—Any State, territory or possession of the United States, the District of Columbia, or any province of the Dominion of Canada.

L.1952, c. 173, p. 548, § 2, eff. April 1, 1953.

39:6–25.   Security to satisfy judgments, damages or claims; suspension of license; inapplicability; requirements for insurance or surety company

(a) If 20 days after the receipt of a report of a motor vehicle accident within this State which has resulted in bodily injury or death, or damage to the property of any one person in excess of $500.00, the director does not have on file evidence satisfactory to him that the person who would otherwise be required to file security under subsection (b) of this section has been released from liability, or has been finally adjudicated not to be liable, or has executed a duly acknowledged written agreement providing for the payment of an agreed amount in installments with respect to all claims for injuries or damages resulting from the accident, and in the event of an accident involving an automobile, required to have coverage for personal injury protection benefits pursuant to P.L.1972, c. 70 (C. 39:6A–1 et seq.), has also reimbursed or has executed a duly acknowledged written agreement to pay an agreed amount in installments to reimburse the Unsatisfied Claim and Judgment Fund for the payment of all personal injury protection benefits the fund has made or shall make pursuant to section 7 or section 10 of P.L.1972, c. 198 (C. 39:6–86.1 and C. 39:6–86.4) by reason of the failure of such person to have the requisite insurance coverage in effect, the director shall determine the amount of security which may be necessary in his judgment to satisfy any reimbursement, judgment or judgments for damages resulting from such accident as may be recovered against each operator or owner in view of the total insurance protection available to the injured party.   The Director of the Division of Motor Vehicles shall promulgate such rules as may be necessary to set forth those instances where deposit of security is necessary.

(b) The director may, within 90 days after the receipt of such report of a motor vehicle accident, suspend the license of each operator and all registrations of each owner of a motor vehicle in any manner involved in such accident, and if such operator is a nonresident the privilege of operating a motor vehicle within this State, and if such owner is a nonresident the privilege of the use within this State of any motor vehicle owned by him, unless such operator or owner or both shall deposit security in the sum so determined by the director; provided, notice of such suspension shall be sent by the director to such operator and owner not less than 10 days prior to the effective date of such suspension and shall state the amount required as security.   Where erroneous information is given the director with respect to the matters set forth in paragraph (1), (2) or (3) of subsection (c) of this section, he may take appropriate action as hereinbefore provided, within 90 days after receipt by him of correct information with respect to said matters.

(c) This section shall not apply under the conditions stated in section 4 of this act[1] nor:

(1) To such operator or owner, if such owner had in effect, at the time of such accident, a motor vehicle liability policy with respect to the motor vehicle involved in such accident;

(2) To such operator, if not the owner of such motor vehicle, if there was in effect at the time of such accident a motor vehicle liability policy or bond with respect to his operation of motor vehicles not owned by him;

(3) To such operator or owner if the liability of such operator or owner for damages resulting from such accident is, in the judgment of the director, covered by any other form of liability insurance policy or bond;   nor

(4) To any person qualifying as a self-insurer under section 30 of this act,[2] or to any person operating a motor vehicle for such self-insurer.

No such policy or bond shall be effective under this section unless issued by an insurance company or surety company authorized to do business in this State, except that if such motor vehicle was not registered in this State, or was a motor vehicle which was registered elsewhere than in this State at the effective date of the policy or bond, or the most recent renewal thereof, such policy or bond shall not be effective under this section unless the insurance company or surety company if not authorized to do business in this State shall execute a power of attorney authorizing the director to accept service on its behalf of notice or process in any action upon such policy or bond arising out of such accident; provided, however, every such policy or bond is subject, if the accident has resulted in bodily injury or death, to a limit, exclusive of interest and costs, of not less than $15,000.00 because of bodily injury to or death of one person in any one accident and, subject to said limit for one person, to a limit of not less than $30,000.00 because of bodily injury to or death of two or more persons in any one accident, and, if the accident has resulted in injury to or destruction of property, to a limit of not less than $5,000.00 because of injury to or destruction of property of others in any one accident and if policy or bond is applicable to an automobile required to have coverage for personal injury protection benefits pursuant to P.L.1972, c. 70 (C. 39:6A–1 et seq.), it shall include an amount to cover personal injury protection benefits as required by that act.

L.1952, c. 173, p. 549, § 3, eff. April 1, 1953. Amended by L.1958, c. 95, p. 541, § 1, eff. Jan. 1, 1959; L.1959, c. 78, p. 196, § 1, eff. June 8, 1959; L.1967, c. 188, § 1, eff. July 27, 1967; L.1971, c. 217, § 2, eff. June 17, 1971; L.1972, c. 199, § 1, eff. Jan. 1, 1973; L.1975, c. 252, § 1, eff. Nov. 13, 1975; L.1988, c. 119, § 12, eff. Jan. 1, 1989.

[1] N.J.S.A. § 39:6–26.
[2] N.J.S.A. § 39:6–52.

39:6–26. Inapplicability of requirements as to security and suspension

The requirements as to security and suspension in section 3 of this act [1] shall not apply:

(a) to the operator or the owner of a motor vehicle involved in an accident wherein no injury or damage was caused to the person or property of any one other than such operator or owner;

(b) to the operator or the owner of a motor vehicle legally parked at the time of the accident;

(c) to the owner of a motor vehicle if at the time of the accident the vehicle was being operated without his permission, express or implied, or was parked by a person who had been operating such motor vehicle without such permission; or to the operator if he was a chauffeur or operator employed by the owner of the motor vehicle and was operating with the permission of the owner.

(d) if, prior to the date that the director would otherwise suspend license and registration or nonresi-

dent's operating privilege under section 3 of this act, there shall be filed with the director evidence satisfactory to him that the person who would otherwise have to file security has been released from liability or been finally adjudicated not to be liable or has executed a duly acknowledged written agreement providing for the payment of an agreed amount in installments, with respect to all claims for injuries or damages resulting from the accident and with respect to an accident involving an automobile, required to have coverage for personal injury protection benefits pursuant to P.L. 1972, c. 70,[2] has also reimbursed or executed a duly acknowledged written agreement to pay an agreed amount in installments to reimburse the Unsatisfied Claim and Judgment Fund for the payments it has made or shall make pursuant to section 7 or section 10 of P.L.1972, c. 198 (Assembly Bill No. 803 presently pending in the Legislature) [3] by reason of the failure of such person to have the requisite insurance coverage in effect.

L.1952, c. 173, p. 551, § 4, eff. April 1, 1953. Amended by L.1972, c. 199, § 2, eff. Jan. 1, 1973.

[1] N.J.S.A. § 39:6–25.
[2] N.J.S.A. §§ 39:6A–1 to 39:6A–18.
[3] N.J.S.A. §§ 39:6–86.1, 39:6–86.4.

39:6–27. Duration of suspension; default in payment of installment

The license and registration and nonresident's operating privilege suspended as provided in section three of this act [1] shall remain so suspended and shall not be renewed nor shall any such license or registration be issued to such person until:

(a) such person shall deposit or there shall be deposited on his behalf the security required under said section 3 of this act; or

(b) one year shall have elapsed following the date of such suspension and evidence satisfactory to the director has been filed with him that during such period no action for damages arising out of the accident has been instituted; or

(c) evidence satisfactory to the director has been filed with him of a release from liability, or a final adjudication of nonliability, or a duly acknowledged written agreement, in accordance with section 4(d) of P.L.1952, c. 173 (C. 39:6–26) and with respect to an automobile required to have coverage for personal injury protection benefits pursuant to P.L.1972, c. 70 [2] has filed evidence satisfactory to the director that he has also met the additional requirements of section 4(d) of P.L.1952, c. 173 (C. 39:6–26) pertaining to such automobile; provided, however, in the event there shall be any default in the payment of any installment under any duly acknowledged written agreement, then, upon notice of such default, the director shall forthwith suspend the license and registration or nonresident's operating privilege of such person defaulting which shall not be restored unless and until

(1) such person deposits and thereafter maintains security as required under said section 3 of this act in such amount as the director may then determine; or

(2) one year shall have elapsed following the date when such security was required and during such period no action upon such agreement has been instituted in a court in this State.

Subsections 5(b) and 5(c)(1) of this section shall not apply to amounts in reimbursement of the Unsatisfied Claim and Judgment Fund which remain unpaid after 1 year.

L.1952, c. 173, p. 552, § 5, eff. April 1, 1953. Amended by L.1972, c. 199, § 3, eff. Jan. 1, 1973.

1 N.J.S.A. § 39:6–25.
2 N.J.S.A. §§ 36:6A–1 to 36:6A–18.

39:6–28. Operator or owner involved in accident without license or a nonresident

(a) In case the operator or the owner of a motor vehicle involved in an accident within this State has no license or registration, or is a nonresident, he shall not be allowed a license or registration until he has complied with the requirements of this act to the same extent that would be necessary if, at the time of the accident, he had held a license and registration.

(b) When a nonresident's operating privilege is suspended pursuant to section three or section five of this act,[1] the director shall transmit a certified copy of the record of such action to the official in charge of the issuance of licenses and registration certificates in the State in which such nonresident resides, if the law of such other State provides for action in relation thereto similar to that provided for in subsection (c) of this section.

(c) Upon receipt of such certification that the operating privilege of a resident of this State has been suspended or revoked in any such other State pursuant to a law providing for its suspension or revocation for failure to deposit security for the payment of judgments arising out of a motor vehicle accident, under circumstances which would require the director to suspend a nonresident's operating privilege had the accident occurred in this State, the director shall suspend the license of such resident if he was the operator, and all of his registrations if he was the owner of a motor vehicle involved in such accident. Such suspension shall continue until such resident furnishes evidence of his compliance with the law of such other State relating to the deposit of such security.

L.1952, c. 173, p. 552, § 6, eff. April 1, 1953.

1 N.J.S.A. § 39:6–25 or 39:6–27.

39:6–29. Security, requirements as to

The security under this act shall be in such form and in such amount as the director may require but in no case in excess of the limits specified in section three of this act[1] in reference to the acceptable limits of a policy or bond. The person depositing security shall specify in

writing the person or persons on whose behalf the deposit is made and, at any time while such deposit is in the custody of the director or State Treasurer, the person depositing it may, in writing, amend the specification of the person or persons on whose behalf the deposit is made to include an additional person or persons; provided, however, that a single deposit of security shall be applicable only on behalf of persons required to furnish security because of the same accident.

The director may reduce the amount of security ordered in any case within six months after the date of the accident if, in his judgment, the amount ordered is excessive. In case the security originally ordered has been deposited the excess deposited over the reduced amount ordered shall be returned to the depositor or his personal representative forthwith, notwithstanding the provisions of section eight of this act.[2]

L.1952, c. 173, p. 553, § 7, eff. April 1, 1953.

1 N.J.S.A. § 39:6–25.
2 N.J.S.A. § 39:6–30.

39:6–30. Application of security; return of deposit or balance

Security deposited in compliance with the requirements of this act shall be applicable only to the payment of a judgment or judgments rendered against the person or persons on whose behalf the deposit was made, for damages arising out of the accident in question in a civil action, begun not later than 1 year after the date of such accident, or within 1 year after the date of deposit of any security under subparagraph (c) of section 5 of this act,[1] or to the payment in settlement, agreed to by the depositor, of a claim or claims arising out of such accident or to the reimbursement of the Unsatisfied Claim and Judgment Fund for the payment of personal injury protection benefits pursuant to section 7 or section 10 of P.L. 1972, c. 198 (Assembly Bill No. 803 presently pending in the Legislature).[2] Such deposit or any balance thereof shall be returned to the depositor or his personal representative when evidence satisfactory to the director has been filed with him that there has been a release from liability, or a final adjudication of nonliability, or a duly acknowledged agreement in accordance with subparagraph (d) of section 4 of this act,[3] and in the event of an accident involving an automobile required to have coverage for personal injury protection benefits pursuant to P.L.1972, c. 70, if the depositor has also met the additional requirements of section 4(d) of P.L.1952, c. 173 (C. 39:6–26) pertaining to such automobile or whenever, after the expiration of 1 year (1) from the date of the accident, or (2) from the date of any security under subparagraph (c) of section 5 of this act, the director shall be given reasonable evidence that there is no such action pending and no judgment rendered in such action left unpaid and no amount in reimbursement, to the Unsatisfied Claim and Judgment Fund for payment of personal injury protection benefits, remains unpaid by such person.

L.1952, c. 173, p. 554, § 8, eff. April 1, 1953. Amended by L.1959, c. 146, p. 588, § 1, eff. July 1, 1959; L.1972, c. 199, § 4, eff. Jan. 1, 1973.

  [1] N.J.S.A. § 39:6–27.

  [2] N.J.S.A. §§ 39:6–86.1, 39:6–86.4.

  [3] N.J.S.A. § 39:6–26.

39:6–30.1. Remission of funds to state treasurer; investments

All sums deposited with the director in compliance with the requirements of the "Motor Vehicle Security-Responsibility Law"[1] shall be remitted forthwith to the State Treasurer and shall be kept separate and apart from all other State funds. The State Treasurer shall be the custodian of said funds and shall make all disbursements from said funds in the same manner as other State disbursements are made. Said funds may be invested and reinvested by the Director of the Division of Investment, Department of the Treasury, in the same manner as other State funds. All earnings received from the investment of such funds shall be paid into the General Treasury and become a part of the General State Fund.

L.1959, c. 146, p. 589, § 2, eff. July 1, 1959.

  [1] N.J.S.A. § 39:6–23 et seq.

39:6–31 to 39:6–34. Repealed by L.1979, c. 169, § 5, eff. Aug. 9, 1979

39:6–35. Failure to satisfy judgment; discharge in bankruptcy

If a person fails to pay and satisfy every judgment rendered against him for damages because of personal injury or death, or damage to property in excess of $500.00, resulting from the ownership, maintenance, use or operation of a motor vehicle and every judgment based on an agreement or contract made in settlement of damages arising out of a motor vehicle accident, within 60 days after its entry, or if an appeal is taken therefrom within that time, within 60 days after the judgment as entered or modified becomes final, the operator's license and all registration certificates of any such person, other than a chauffeur or operator employed by the owner of a motor vehicle and so acting at the time of the damage, injuries or death resulting in the judgment, shall, upon receiving a certified copy of a transcript of the final judgment from the court in which it was rendered showing it to have been still unsatisfied more than 60 days after it became final, be forthwith suspended by the director.

If the director is satisfied that a judgment debtor or his insurance carrier was, within the said 60–day period, ready, willing and able to pay the said judgment but was prevented from so doing by reason of the refusal or legal inability of the judgment creditor to accept payment, or that the failure to pay said judgment within the said 60–day period was due to the act or neglect of the judgment debtor's insurance carrier and not to any fault of the judgment debtor then the director may, in his discretion, extend the 60–day limitation herein prescribed for any reasonable time necessary to complete the formality of payment of the judgment and shall not suspend the judgment debtor's driver's license, operating privilege or certificate of registration.

The judgment herein mentioned shall be a judgment of a court of competent jurisdiction of this State or any other state or of a District Court of the United States.

The license and registration certificates shall remain so suspended and shall not be renewed, nor shall a motor vehicle be thereafter registered in the name of that person while the judgment remains unstayed, unsatisfied, subsisting and until every such judgment is satisfied or discharged, except that in the event that the judgment debtor shall be relieved of liability for payment of said judgment by an adjudication of the court in which the same was entered, or if the right to enforce said judgment by docketing and revival, or by revival, or by bringing an action thereon, shall have expired without such revival or the bringing of any such action thereon, the judgment debtor's license shall be restored to him, and one or more motor vehicles may be registered in his name, upon application to the Division of Motor Vehicles.

A discharge in bankruptcy shall relieve the judgment debtor from any of the requirements of this act, provided that the underlying judgment was not based on a willful or malicious tort.

The clerk of the court in which the judgment is rendered, or the court where it has no clerk, shall forward to the director, at the request of the judgment creditor or his attorney, after the expiration of the 60 days a certified copy of the judgment or a transcript thereof, as aforesaid.

Upon the filing with the court of proof of satisfaction or discharge of a judgment, the nonpayment of which has been previously certified to the director, the clerk of the court, or the court where it has no clerk shall immediately forward notice of such satisfaction or discharge to the director.

If the defendant is a nonresident the director shall transmit to the officer in charge of the issuance of driver licenses and registration certificates of the state of which the defendant is a resident a certified copy of the judgment.

If after proof is given, another such judgment is recovered against that person for an accident occurring before the proof was given, the license and certificate shall again be and remain suspended, and no other license or certificate shall be issued to him while the judgment so remains unsatisfied and subsisting.

L.1952, c. 173, p. 557, § 13, eff. April 1, 1953. Amended by L.1956, c. 175, p. 673, § 1, eff. Dec. 20, 1956; L.1957, c. 106, p. 207, § 1, eff. June 27, 1957; L.1964, c. 113, § 1, eff. June 16, 1964; L.1973, c. 5, § 1, eff. Jan. 16, 1973; L.1979, c. 169, § 1, eff. Aug. 9, 1979; L.1988, c. 119, § 13, eff. Jan. 1, 1989.

39:6–36. Nonresident; judgment unsatisfied

While a final judgment against a nonresident motor vehicle owner or operator is so unstayed, unsatisfied and subsisting for more than 60 days, his privilege of operating a motor vehicle, whether owned by him or not, in this State, shall be withdrawn and shall not be renewed. No operator's or chauffeur's license shall be issued to him nor shall a motor vehicle be registered in his name until every such judgment is stayed, satisfied or discharged as herein provided.

L.1952, c. 173, p. 559, § 14, eff. April 1, 1953. Amended by L.1979, c. 169, § 2, eff. Aug. 9, 1979.

39:6–37. Insolvency or bankruptcy of liability insurer

Whenever it appears to the satisfaction of the director that: at the time of a motor vehicle accident resulting in the death of or injury to any person, or damage to property to the extent of $500.00, the judgment debtor, against whom a judgment has been obtained as a result of such accident, was insured in an insurance company, authorized to do business in this State, against public liability for injuries or death to one person to the extent of $15,000.00 and for injuries or death to more than one person to the extent of $30,000.00 and for damage to property to the extent of $5,000.00 arising out of a single motor vehicle accident and with respect to an automobile, as defined in section 2 of P.L.1972, c. 70 (C. 39:6A–2), registered or principally garaged in New Jersey; personal injury protection coverage as provided in the "New Jersey Automobile Reparation Reform Act," P.L.1972, c. 70 (C. 39:6A–1 et seq.), and that the judgment has not been paid or the personal injury protection benefits have not been paid because, subsequent to the date of such accident, such insurance company has become insolvent or bankrupt, or the Commissioner of Insurance has undertaken control thereof for the purpose of liquidation, he shall not suspend the operator's license and the registration certificates of such judgment debtor.

L.1952, c. 173, p. 559, § 15, eff. April 1, 1953. Amended by L.1958, c. 95, p. 544, § 3, eff. Jan. 1, 1959; L.1972, c. 199, § 7, eff. Jan. 1, 1973; L.1979, c. 169, § 3, eff. Aug. 9, 1979; L.1988, c. 119, § 14, eff. Jan. 1, 1989.

39:6–38. Partial payments which are deemed satisfaction of judgment

For the purposes of sections 9 to 14 of this act [1] when:

(a) $10,000.00 has been credited upon any judgment or judgments rendered in excess of that amount for bodily injury to or the death of 1 person as the result of 1 accident;

(b) Subject to the limit of $10,000.00 for 1 person so injured or killed, the sum of $20,000.00 has been credited upon any judgment or judgments rendered in excess of that amount for bodily injury to or the death of more than 1 person as the result of 1 accident; or

(c) $5,000.00 has been credited upon any judgment or judgments rendered in excess of that amount for damage to property as the result of 1 accident—

Such payment or payments shall be deemed a satisfaction of the judgment or judgments.

L.1952, c. 173, p. 559, § 16, eff. April 1, 1953. Amended by L.1958, c. 95, p. 545, § 4, eff. Jan. 1, 1959.

    1 N.J.S.A. §§ 39:6–31 to 39:6–36.

39:6–39. Payment of judgment in installments

A judgment debtor to whom this chapter applies may, for the sole purpose of giving authority to the director to authorize the judgment debtor to operate a motor vehicle thereafter, on due notice to the judgment creditor, apply to the court in which the trial judgment was obtained for the privilege of paying the judgment in installments. The court, in its discretion and without prejudice to any other legal remedies which the judgment creditor may have, may so order, fixing the amounts and times of payment of the installments. The director may, in his discretion, while the judgment debtor is not in default in paying the installments, restore, or refrain from suspending his license or registration certificate or certificates, or either or both of them. The license or certificate or certificates, or either or both or all of them, shall be suspended as hereinbefore provided when the director is satisfied that the judgment debtor has failed to comply with the terms of the court order.

L.1952, c. 173, p. 560, § 17, eff. April 1, 1953. Amended by L.1979, c. 169, § 4, eff. Aug. 9, 1979.

39:6–40, 39:6–41. Repealed by L.1979, c. 169, § 5, eff. Aug. 9, 1979

39:6–42. Certified abstract of operating record

Upon the request of any insurance company, any person furnishing any financial responsibility or any surety on a bond herein provided for, the director shall furnish such company person or surety a certified abstract of the operating record of any person subject to the provisions of this act. If there is no record of his conviction of a violation of a provision of law relating to the operation of motor vehicles or of an injury or damage caused by him as herein provided, the director shall so certify. The director shall collect a fee of $10 for each certified or uncertified abstract so issued. The director shall use the same schedule of fees established above for abstracts requested by persons authorized by law to receive them.

L.1952, c. 173, p. 562, § 20, eff. April 1, 1953. Amended by L.1975, c. 180, § 12, eff. Jan. 1, 1976; L.1994, c. 60, § 25, eff. July 1, 1994; L.2002, c. 34, § 16, eff. July 1, 2002.

39:6–43 to 39:6–47. Repealed by L.1979, c. 169, § 5, eff. Aug. 9, 1979

39:6–48. Form of liability policy; provisions to which it is subject; binders; indorsements

No motor vehicle liability policy shall be issued or delivered in this State, as proof of financial responsibility, unless such policy discloses the name, address and business of the insured, the coverage afforded by the policy, the premium charged therefor, the policy period, the limit of liability and the agreement that the insurance thereunder is provided in accordance with the coverage defined in sections twenty-four and twenty-five of this act [1] and in this section and is subject to all of the provisions of this act.

The motor vehicle liability policy shall be subject to the following provisions which need not be contained therein:

(a) The liability of a company under a motor vehicle liability policy shall become absolute when loss or damage covered by the policy occurs and the satisfaction by the insured of a final judgment of the loss or damage shall not be a condition precedent to the right or duty of the carrier to make payment on account of the loss or damage. No such policy shall be canceled or annulled as respects any loss or damage by any agreement between the carrier and the insured after the insured has become responsible for the loss or damage and any such cancellation or annulment shall be void. Upon the recovery of a final judgment against a person for the loss or damage if the judgment debtor was at the accrual of the cause of action insured against liability therefor under a motor vehicle liability policy, the judgment creditor shall be entitled to have the insurance money applied to the satisfaction of the judgment. The policy may provide that the insured or a person covered by the policy shall reimburse the company for payments made on account of an accident, claim or suit involving a breach of the terms, provisions or conditions of the policy; and, if the policy provides for limits in excess of the limits designated in this section the insurance carrier may plead against the judgment creditor, with respect to the amount of the excess limits of liability any defenses which it may be entitled to plead against the insured. The policy may further provide for the prorating of the insurance thereunder with other applicable valid and collectible insurance.

(b) The policy, any written application therefor and any rider or indorsement which shall not conflict with the provisions of this act shall constitute the entire contract between the parties.

Effective as of the date such proof is furnished and to the extent of the coverage required by this act and to the extent of the limits of liability specified in section twenty-four of this act, any policy of motor vehicle liability insurance furnished as proof of financial responsibility pursuant to section eighteen of this act,[2] either by the filing of a certificate signed by a duly licensed agent of the company issuing the policy as provided in the said section, or otherwise, shall be deemed amended to conform with and to contain all the provisions required by this act, any provision of the policy or certificate to the contrary notwithstanding.

An insurance carrier authorized to issue motor vehicle liability policies as provided for in this act may, pending the issuance of the policy, execute an agreement, to be known as a binder; or may, in lieu of the policy, issue an indorsement to an existing policy, each of which shall be construed to provide indemnity or protection in like manner and to the same extent as the policy. The provisions of said sections twenty-four and twenty-five and this section shall apply to the binders and indorsements.

L.1952, c. 173, p. 566, § 26, eff. April 1, 1953.

  [1] N.J.S.A. §§ 39:6–46, 39:6–47 (repealed).

  [2] N.J.S.A. § 39:6–40 (repealed).

39:6–49. Transfer of registration while owner's registration suspended

(a) The owner's registration of a vehicle involved in an accident to which this act applies shall not be transferred nor the vehicle, in respect to which such registration was issued, registered in any other name until the provisions of this act relating to the deposit of security are complied with, unless such provisions are inapplicable because of the exceptions stated in section three[1] or because of other exceptions specified in this act, or until the director is satisfied that such transfer is proposed in good faith and not for the purpose or with the effect of defeating the purposes of this act.

(b) If an owner's registration has been suspended hereunder, such registration shall not be transferred nor the vehicle, in respect to which such registration was issued, registered in any other name until the director is satisfied that such transfer of registration is proposed in good faith and not for the purpose or with the effect of defeating the purposes of this act.

(c) Nothing in this section shall in anywise affect the rights of any conditional vendor, chattel mortgagee or lessor of such a vehicle registered in the name of another as owner who becomes subject to the provisions of this act.

(d) The director shall suspend the registration of any vehicle transferred in violation of the provisions of this section.

L.1952, c. 173, p. 568, § 27, eff. April 1, 1953.

  [1] N.J.S.A. § 39:6–25.

39:6–50. Enforcement of act; rules and regulations; review

(a) The director shall administer and enforce the provisions of this act and may make rules and regulations necessary for the administration thereof and shall provide for hearings upon request of persons aggrieved by orders or acts of the director under the provisions of this act.

(b) Any order or act of the director, under the provisions of this act, shall be subject to review by a proceeding in lieu of the prerogative writs.

L.1952, c. 173, p. 568, § 28, eff. April 1, 1953.

39:6–50.1. Self-insurance; rules and regulations

The commissioner shall have the authority to issue any rules and regulations or exercise any power granted to him by Title 17 of the Revised Statutes with respect to vehicles which are self-insured pursuant to the provisions of sections 30, 31, and 32 of P.L.1952, c. 173 (C. 39:6A–52, 39:6A–53, and 39:6A–54).[1]

L.1987, c. 428, § 4, eff. Jan. 14, 1988.

  [1] Probably should read: "(C. 39:6–52, 39:6–53, and 39:6–54)".

39:6–51. Informing persons as to contents of act

The director shall, by means of any printed form he provides, inform every person to whom a driver's license or registration certificate is issued of the contents of this act.

L.1952, c. 173, p. 568, § 29, eff. April 1, 1953.

39:6–52. Self insurance; cancellation

(a) Any person in whose name more than 25 motor vehicles are registered or in whose name more than 25 motor vehicles are leased may qualify as a self-insurer by obtaining a certificate of self-insurance issued by the Commissioner of Insurance as provided in subsection (b) of this section.

(b) The commissioner may, in his discretion, upon the application of such a person, issue a certificate of self-insurance when he is satisfied that such person is possessed and will continue to be possessed of ability to pay judgments obtained against such person.

(c) The application shall be on a form prescribed by the commissioner, and shall include any information which the commissioner deems to be necessary to determine the applicant's eligibility for self-insurance, including, but not limited to, information on the number and types of the motor vehicles which are to be self-insured, the proposed use of the vehicles, and financial information regarding the applicant. The certificate shall be issued for a one-year period and each holder of a certificate shall make application for renewal.

(d) If the applicant for a certificate of self-insurance is a corporation, the commissioner may also include in the certificate of self-insurance any subsidiary corporation under the control of that corporation if the parent corporation guarantees that it will discharge the subsidiary corporation's liability pursuant to the provisions of this act. In the event that the ownership of the parent or a subsidiary corporation changes, the parent or subsidiary shall reapply for a certificate of self-insurance within 30 days of the ownership change. If the parent corporation does not provide a guarantee that it will discharge the subsidiary corporation's liability, the subsidiary shall make separate application and receive independent qualification as a self-insurer.

(e) The commissioner may make or cause to be made audits or examinations as he may deem necessary to determine the financial ability of the applicant or certificate holder to discharge his obligations as a self-insurer. The reasonable expenses of the audit or examination shall be fixed and determined by the commissioner, and shall be payable by the applicant or certificate holder upon presentation of a detailed account of expenses.

(f) The commissioner may require the furnishing of a surety bond or evidence of excess insurance.

(g) A filing fee of $1,000.00 shall accompany every application for a certificate of self-insurance or a renewal thereof, except that no filing fee shall be required of any public entity which applies for a certificate of self-insurance pursuant to this section or a renewal thereof.

(h) Upon not less than five days' notice and a hearing pursuant to such notice, the commissioner may upon reasonable grounds cancel a certificate of self-insurance. Failure to pay any judgment within 30 days after such judgment shall have become final shall constitute a reasonable ground for the cancellation of a certificate of self-insurance.

L.1952, c. 173, p. 569, § 30, eff. April 1, 1953. Amended by L.1987, c. 428, § 1, eff. Jan. 14, 1988.

39:6–53. Commissioner's action and findings and security filed not evidence as to negligence

No action taken by the commissioner pursuant to this act, the findings, if any, of the commissioner upon which such action is based, nor the security filed, as provided by this act, shall be referred to in any way, nor be any evidence of the negligence or due care of either party, at the trial of any civil action to recover damages.

L.1952, c. 173, p. 569, § 31, eff. April 1, 1953. Amended by L.1987, c. 428, § 2, eff. Jan. 14, 1988.

39:6–54. Exemptions; self-insurance by public entity or group of public entities

a. This act shall not apply with respect to any motor vehicle owned by the United States, this State or any political subdivision of this State or any municipality therein; nor with respect to any motor vehicle which is subject to the requirements of law requiring insurance or other security on certain types of vehicles, other than the requirements of P.L.1972, c. 70 (C. 39:6A–1 et seq.) or P.L.1972, c. 197 (C. 39:6B–1 et seq.).

b. Notwithstanding the provisions of subsection a. to the contrary, the commissioner may issue a certificate of self-insurance to any public entity or group of public entities upon receipt of a resolution from the public entity or group of public entities that they have established a self-insurance program or a group self-insurance program, as the case may be.

L.1952, c. 173, p. 569, § 32, eff. April 1, 1953. Amended by L.1987, c. 428, § 3, eff. Jan. 14, 1988.

39:6–55. Prohibited acts; violations; enforcement; remedies; procedure; revocation of license

(a) Any person who shall forge, or, without authority, sign any evidence of proof of financial responsibility, or who files or offers for filing any such evidence of proof, knowing or having reason to believe that it is forged or signed without authority, shall be fined not more than $1,000.00 or imprisoned for not more than one year, or both.

(b) Any person willfully failing to return license or registration as required in section 22 of this act [1] shall be fined not more than $500.00 or imprisoned not to exceed 30 days, or both.

(c) Any person who shall violate any provision of this act for which no penalty is otherwise provided shall be fined not more than $500.00 or imprisoned not more than 90 days, or both.

The provisions of this act shall be enforced and all penalties for the violation thereof shall be recovered in accordance with the provisions of "the penalty enforcement law" (N.J.S. 2A:58–1 et seq.), and in addition to the provisions and remedies therein contained, the following provisions and remedies shall be applicable in any proceeding brought for a violation of any of the provisions of this act:

a. The several municipal courts shall have jurisdiction of any such proceeding, in addition to the courts prescribed in "the penalty enforcement law";

b. The complaint in any such proceeding may be made on information and belief by the director, or the police or peace officer of any municipality, any county or the State;

c. A warrant may issue in lieu of summons;

d. Any police or peace officer shall be empowered to serve and execute process in any such proceeding;

e. The hearing in any such proceeding shall be without a jury;

f. Any such proceeding may be brought in the name of the Director of the Division of Motor Vehicles in the Department of Law and Public Safety or in the name of the State of New Jersey;

g. Any sums received in payment of any fines imposed in any such proceeding shall be paid to the Director of the Division of Motor Vehicles and shall be paid by him into the State treasury;

h. The director or judge before whom any hearing under this act is had may revoke the license of any person to drive a motor vehicle or the registration certificate of any motor vehicle owned by any person, when such person shall have been guilty of such willful violation of any of the provisions of this act as shall in the discretion of the director or judge justify such revocation.

L.1952, c. 173, p. 569, § 33, eff. April 1, 1953. Amended by L.1954, c. 77, p. 448, § 1, eff. July 1, 1954; L.1983, c. 403, § 25, eff. Dec. 23, 1983.

[1] N.J.S.A. § 39:6–44.

39:6–56. Repeal

Chapter six of Title 39 of the Revised Statutes is repealed so far as it relates to any motor vehicle accident within this State, or to any conviction or forfeiture of bail, occurring on or after the effective date of this act.

L.1952, c. 173, p. 570, § 34, eff. April 1, 1953.

39:6–57. Effective date

This act shall take effect April first, one thousand nine hundred and fifty-three.

L.1952, c. 173, p. 570, § 35, eff. April 1, 1953.

39:6–58. Expense of administering Motor Vehicle Security-Responsibility Law; ascertainment; certifying annually

The Director of the Division of Budget and Accounting in the Department of the Treasury shall, on or before September first in each year, ascertain and certify to the Commissioner of Banking and Insurance the total amount of expense incurred by the State in connection with the administration of the Motor Vehicle Security-Responsibility Law during the preceding fiscal year, which expenses shall include, in addition to the direct cost of personal service, the cost of maintenance and operation, the cost of retirement contributions made and workmen's compensation paid for and on account of personnel, rentals for space occupied in State owned or State leased buildings and all other direct and indirect costs of the administration thereof.

L.1952, c. 176, p. 598, § 1, eff. April 1, 1953.

39:6–59. Apportionment of amount certified among liability insurers

The commissioner shall, on or before the fifteenth day of October in each year, apportion the amount so certified to him among the mutual associations and stock companies writing motor vehicle liability insurance within this State or motor vehicle liability bonds, or both, in the proportion that the net premiums received by each of them for such insurance and bonds written or renewed on risks within this State during the calendar year immediately preceding, as reported to him, bears to the sum total of all such net premiums received by all mutual associations and stock companies writing such insurance or bonds, or both, within the State during such year, as so reported, and shall certify the sum so apportioned to each such mutual association and stock company on or before November fifteenth next ensuing, to the Division of Taxation in the Department of the Treasury and each such mutual association and stock company shall pay the amount so certified as apportioned to it to the said Division of Taxation on or before the thirty-first day of December next ensuing, and the sum so paid shall be paid into the State Treasury in reimbursement to the State for the expenses so paid.

L.1952, c. 176, p. 598, § 2, eff. April 1, 1953.

39:6–60. Effective date

This act shall take effect April first, one thousand nine hundred and fifty-three.

L.1952, c. 176, p. 599, § 3, eff. April 1, 1953.

39:6–61. Title

This act shall be known and may be cited as the "Unsatisfied Claim and Judgment Fund Law."

L.1952, c. 174, p. 570, § 1, eff. April 1, 1955.

39:6–62. Definitions

As used in this act:

"Association" means the New Jersey Property–Liability Insurance Guaranty Association created pursuant to P.L.1974, c. 17 (C.17:30A–1 et seq.).

"Commissioner" means the Commissioner of Banking and Insurance.

"Unsatisfied Claim and Judgment Fund" or "Fund" means the fund derived from the sources specified in this act.

"Qualified person" means a resident of this State or the owner of a motor vehicle registered in this State or a resident of another state, territory, or federal district of the United States or province of Canada or of a foreign country, in which recourse is afforded, to residents of this State, of substantially similar character to that provided for by this act; provided, however, that no person shall be a qualified person where such person is an insured under a policy provision providing coverage for damages sustained by the insured as a result of the operation of an uninsured motor vehicle in a form authorized to be included in automobile liability policies of insurance delivered or issued for delivery in this State, pursuant to the provisions of, or any supplement to, chapter 28 of Title 17 of the Revised Statutes or in a form substantially similar thereto.

"Uninsured motor vehicle" means a motor vehicle as to which there is not in force a liability policy meeting the requirements of section 3 or 26 of the "Motor Vehicle Security–Responsibility Law," P.L.1952, c. 173 (C.39:6–25 or C.39:6–48), and which is not owned by a holder of a certificate of self-insurance under said law, but shall not include a motor vehicle with a policy in force which is insured pursuant to section 4 of P.L.1998, c. 21 (C.39:6A–3.1).

"Person" includes natural persons, firms, copartnerships, associations and corporations.

"Insurer" means any insurer authorized in this State to write the kinds of insurance specified in paragraphs d. and e. of R.S.17:17–1.

"Net direct written premiums" means direct gross premiums written on policies, insuring against legal liability for bodily injury or death and for damage to property arising out of the ownership, operation or maintenance of motor vehicles, which are principally garaged in this State, less return premiums thereon and dividends paid to policyholders on such direct business.

L.1952, c. 174, p. 570, § 2, eff. April 1, 1955. Amended by L.1955, c. 1, p. 11, § 1, eff. March 30, 1955; L.1956, c. 22, p. 63, § 1, eff. May 7, 1956; L.1968, c. 323, § 1, eff. Nov. 8, 1968; L.1968, c. 385, § 4, eff. April 2, 1969; L.1985, c. 148, § 3, eff. April 24, 1985; L.1998, c. 21, § 21; L.2003, c. 89, § 8, eff. June 9, 2003.

39:6–63. Creation and maintenance of fund

For the purpose of creating and maintaining the fund:

(a) (Deleted by amendment, P.L.1968, c. 323, s.3.)

(b) (Deleted by amendment, P.L.1968, c. 323, s.3.)

(c) (Deleted by amendment, P.L.1968, c. 323, s.3.)

(d) Commencing on or before December 30, 2003, and on or before December 30 in each year thereafter, the association shall calculate the probable amount which will be needed to carry out its responsibilities under section 35 of P.L.2003, c.89 (C.39:6–86.7), section 9 of P.L.1952, c. 174 (C.39:6–69) and section 7 of P.L.1972, c. 198 (C.39:6–86.1) during the ensuing year. In that calculation, the association shall take into consideration the amount presently reserved for pending claims, anticipated payments from the fund during that year and during the two years after that year, anticipated amounts to be reserved for claims pending during that year, and the desirability of maintaining a surplus over and above those anticipated payments and present and anticipated reserves, which surplus shall not exceed the amount actually paid from the fund during the 12 full calendar months immediately preceding the date of calculation. The probable amount needed to carry out the provisions of this section shall be assessed against insurers for that year's contribution to the fund.

(e) Whenever any of the provisions concerning the method and sources of assessments on insurers, the maximum amounts payable from the fund, eligibility or qualifications of claimants, or amounts to be deducted from payments made from the fund are amended by law, the association may, if the association deems it necessary, rescind any assessment on insurers. The association shall then, within 30 days of the adoption of such amendment, recalculate the probable amount which will be needed to carry out the provisions of P.L.2003, c.89 (C.17: 30A–2.1 et al.) during the ensuing fiscal year, in accordance with the provisions of subsection (d) of this section. If, in the judgment of the association, the estimated balance of the fund at the beginning of the next year will be sufficient to meet those needs, the association shall determine the contributions of insurers, if any, in accordance with the provisions of subsection (d) of this section.

L.1952, c. 174, p. 572, § 3, eff. May 10, 1952. Amended by L.1955, c. 1, p. 12, § 2, eff. March 30, 1955; L.1956, c. 22, p. 64, § 2, eff. May 7, 1956; L.1958, c. 99, p. 554, § 1, eff. July 1, 1958; L.1965, c. 72, § 1, eff. May 28, 1965; L.1968, c. 323, § 2, eff. Nov. 8, 1968; L.1972, c. 198, § 1, eff. Dec. 26, 1972; L.1977, c. 310, § 3, eff. Jan. 5, 1978; L.1983, c. 125, § 1, eff. April 5, 1983; L.1985, c. 148, § 4, eff. April 24, 1985; L.1988, c. 119, § 2, eff. Jan. 1, 1989; L.1990, c. 8, § 85, eff. March 12, 1990; L.2003, c. 89, § 9, eff. June 9, 2003.

39:6–63.1. Assessment rescinded; registration of uninsured vehicles; fee

Any assessment made under the provisions of subparagraph (2), of paragraph (d) of section 3 of the act [1] of which this act is amendatory which has not been collected prior to the effective date of this act, is hereby rescinded and shall not be collected. Every person registering an uninsured motor vehicle in this State, during the period commencing June 1, 1956 and ending May 31, 1957, shall pay at the time of registering the same, in addition to any other fee prescribed by any other law, a fee of $8.00.

L.1956, c. 22, p. 66, § 3, eff. May 7, 1956.

[1] N.J.S.A. § 39:6–63.

39:6–63.2. Repealed by L.1969, c. 113, § 1, eff. June 26, 1969

39:6–64 to 39:6–64b. Repealed by L.2003, c. 89, § 85, eff. June 9, 2003

39:6–64c. Abolition of the Unsatisfied Claim and Judgment Fund Board in the Department of Banking and Insurance; transfer to the New Jersey Property-Liability Insurance Guaranty Association

The Unsatisfied Claim and Judgment Fund Board in the Department of Banking and Insurance, established pursuant to P.L.1952, c. 174 (C.39:6–61 et seq.), is hereby abolished and all its functions, powers and duties, along with the Unsatisfied Claim and Judgment Fund, including all its assets, liabilities and balances, are transferred from the Department of Banking and Insurance to the New Jersey Property–Liability Insurance Guaranty Association, established pursuant to P.L.1974, c. 17 (C.17:30A–1 et seq.). Wherever in any law, rule or regulation, reference is made to the Unsatisfied Claim and Judgment Fund Board, the same shall mean and refer to the New Jersey Property–Liability Insurance Guaranty Association.

L.2003, c. 89, § 7, eff. June 9, 2003.

39:6–64.1. Rules and regulations; liability

a. The association may from time to time, adopt and amend a plan of operation, subject to the approval of the commissioner, necessary or desirable in connection with its functions, duties and responsibilities in administering this act.

The plan of operation shall provide that the Unsatisfied Claim and Judgment Fund may (1) borrow and separately account for moneys from any source, including, but not limited to, the New Jersey Property–Liability Insurance Guaranty Association and the New Jersey Surplus Lines Insurance Guaranty Fund, in such amounts and on such terms as the board of directors may determine, are necessary or appropriate and (2) make loans, in such amounts and on such terms as the board of directors may determine are necessary or appropriate, to the New Jersey Property–Liability Insurance Guaranty Association and the New Jersey Surplus Lines Insurance Guaranty Fund.

b. There shall be no liability on the part of and no cause of action of any nature shall arise against the association, its agents, employees, or the commissioner or his designees for any action taken by them in the performance of their powers and duties under P.L.2003, c.89 (C.17:30A–2.1 et al.).

L.1955, c. 1, p. 24, § 18, eff. March 30, 1955. Amended by L.1961, c. 69, p. 588, § 1, eff. June 3, 1961; L.1985, c. 148, § 6, eff. April 24, 1985; L.2003, c. 89, § 10, eff. June 9, 2003.

39:6–64.2. Transferred. See § 39:6–90.1

39:6–65. Notice of accident and intention to file claim

Any qualified person, or the personal representative of such person, who suffers damages resulting from bodily injury or death or damage to property arising out of the ownership, maintenance or use of a motor vehicle in this State on or after April 1, 1955, and whose damages may be satisfied in whole or in part from the fund, shall, except in cases in which the claim is asserted by actions brought under section 18 [1] of this act pursuant to section 19 [2] of this act, within 180 days after the accident, as a condition precedent to the right thereafter to apply for payment from the fund, give notice to the association, the form and contents of which shall be prescribed by the association, of his intention to make a claim thereon for such damages if otherwise uncollectible; provided, any such qualified person may, in lieu of giving said notice within said time, make proof to the court on the hearing of the application for the payment of a judgment (a) that he was physically incapable of giving said notice within said period and that he gave said notice within 180 days after he became physically capable to do so or in the event he did not become so capable, that a notice was given on his behalf within a reasonable period, or (b) that he gave notice to the association within 15 days of receiving notice that an insurer had disclaimed on a policy of insurance so as to remove or withdraw liability insurance coverage for his claim against a person or persons who allegedly caused him to suffer damages. A copy of the complaint shall be furnished to the association if an action has theretofore been brought for the enforcement of such claim. Such person shall also notify the association of any action thereafter instituted for the enforcement of such claim within 15 days after the institution thereof and such notice shall be accompanied by a copy of the complaint.

The New Jersey Motor Vehicle Commission is hereby authorized and empowered, the provisions of any other law relating to the confidential nature of any reports or information furnished to or filed with the division notwithstanding, to furnish to the association upon its request, for such use, utilization and purposes as the association may deem reasonably appropriate to administer this act and discharge its functions hereunder, any reports or information filed by any person or persons claiming benefits under the provisions of this act, that the director has with regard to any accident, and any operator or owner of a motor vehicle involved in any accident, and as to any automobile or motor vehicle liability insurance or bond carried by an operator or owner of any motor vehicle.

L.1952, c. 174, p. 574, § 5, eff. April 1, 1955. Amended by L.1955, c. 1, p. 15, § 4, eff. March 30, 1955; L.1956, c. 200, p. 737, § 1, Feb. 2, 1957, retroactive to July 1, 1956; L.1958, c. 99, p. 556, § 2, eff. July 1, 1958; L.1963, c. 81, § 10, eff. June 4, 1963; L.1985, c. 148, § 7, eff. April 24, 1985; L.2003, c. 89, § 11, eff. June 9, 2003.

1 N.J.S.A. § 39:6–78.
2 N.J.S.A. § 39:6–79.

39:6–66. Repealed by L.2003, c. 89, § 85, eff. June 9, 2003

39:6–67. Defense of actions against motorists

The association may through counsel enter an appearance on behalf of the defendant, file a defense, appear at the trial or take such other steps as it may deem appropriate on the behalf and in the name of the defendant, and may thereupon, on the behalf and in the name of the defendant, conduct his defense, take recourse to any appropriate method of review on behalf of, and in the name of, the defendant, and all such acts shall be deemed to be the acts of such defendant; provided, however, that nothing contained herein shall deprive the defendant of the right to also employ his own counsel and defend the action. All expense incurred by the association in connection with any review prosecuted or defended by it from a judgment rendered in such action, including its attorneys' fees in connection therewith, shall be borne by the fund.

L.1952, c. 174, p. 576, § 7, eff. April 1, 1955. Amended by L.1968, c. 323, § 4, eff. Nov. 8, 1968; L.2003, c. 89, § 12, eff. June 9, 2003.

39:6–68. Co-operation of defendant

In any case in which the association has assumed under this act, the defense of any action, the defendant shall co-operate with the association in the defense of such action. In the event of his failure to do so, the association may apply to the court for an order directing such co-operation.

L.1952, c. 174, p. 576, § 8, eff. April 1, 1955. Amended by L.2003, c. 89, § 13, eff. June 9, 2003.

39:6–69. Application for payment of judgment

When any qualified person recovers a valid judgment in any court of competent jurisdiction in this State against any other person, who was the operator or owner of a motor vehicle, for injury to, death of, any person or persons, or a similar valid judgment in such court against such a defendant for an amount in excess of $500.00, exclusive of interest and costs, for damage to property, except property of others in charge of such operator or owner or such operator's or owner's employees, arising out of the ownership, maintenance or use of the motor vehicle in this State on or after April 1, 1955, and any amount remains unpaid thereon in the case of a judgment for bodily injury or death, or any amount in excess of $500.00 remains unpaid thereon in case of a judgment for damage to property, such judgment creditor may, upon the termination of all proceedings, including reviews and appeals in connection with such judgment, file a verified claim in the court in which the judgment was entered, and upon 10 days' written notice to the association may apply to the court for an order directing payment out of the fund, of the amount unpaid upon such judgment for bodily injury or death, which does not exceed, or upon such judgment for damage to property, which exceeds the sum of $500.00 and does not exceed—

(a) The maximum amount or limit of $15,000.00, exclusive of interest and costs, on account of injury to, or death of, one person, in any one accident, and

(b) The maximum amount or limit, subject to such limit for any one person so injured or killed, of $30,000.00, exclusive of interest and costs, on account of injury to, or death of, more than one person, in any one accident, and

(c) The maximum amount or limit of $5,000.00, exclusive of interest and costs, for damage to property in any one accident.

L.1952, c. 174, p. 576, § 9, eff. April 1, 1955. Amended by L.1958, c. 99, p. 557, § 3, eff. July 1, 1958; L.1972, c. 198, § 3, eff. Jan. 1, 1973; L.1983, c. 362, § 21, eff. Oct. 4, 1983; L.1988, c. 119, § 15, eff. Jan. 1, 1989; L.2003, c. 89, § 14, eff. June 9, 2003.

39:6–70. Hearing on application for payment of judgment

The court shall proceed upon such application, in a summary manner, and, upon the hearing thereof, the applicant shall be required to show:

(a) He is not a person covered with respect to such injury or death by any workers' compensation law, or the personal representative of such a person,

(b) He is not a spouse, parent or child of the judgment debtor, or the personal representative of such spouse, parent or child,

(c) He was not at the time of the accident a person (1) operating or riding in a motor vehicle which he had stolen or participated in stealing or (2) operating or riding in a motor vehicle without the permission of the owner, and is not the personal representative of such a person,

(d) He was not at the time of the accident, the owner or registrant of an uninsured motor vehicle, or was not operating a motor vehicle in violation of an order of suspension or revocation,

(e) He has complied with all of the requirements of section 5,[1]

(f) The judgment debtor at the time of the accident was not insured under a policy of automobile liability insurance under the terms of which the insurer is liable to pay in whole or in part the amount of the judgment,

(g) He has obtained a judgment as set out in section 9 of this act,[2] stating the amount thereof and the amount owing thereon at the date of the application,

(h) He has caused to be issued a writ of execution upon said judgment and the sheriff or officer executing the same has made a return showing that no personal or real property of the judgment debtor, liable to be levied upon in satisfaction of the judgment, could be found or that the amount realized on the sale of them or of such of them as were found, under said execution, was insufficient to satisfy the judgment, stating the amount so realized and the balance remaining due on the judgment after application thereon of the amount realized,

(i) He has caused the judgment debtor to make discovery under oath, pursuant to law, concerning his personal property and as to whether such judgment debtor was at the time of the accident insured under any policy or policies of insurance described in subsection (f) of this section,

(j) He has made all reasonable searches and inquiries to ascertain whether the judgment debtor is possessed of personal or real property or other assets, liable to be sold or applied in satisfaction of the judgment,

(k) By such search he has discovered no personal or real property or other assets, liable to be sold or applied or that he has discovered certain of them, describing them, owned by the judgment debtor and liable to be so sold and applied and that he has taken all necessary action and proceedings for the realization thereof and that the amount thereby realized was insufficient to satisfy the judgment, stating the amount so realized and the balance remaining due on the judgment after application of the amount realized,

(*l*) The application is not made by or on behalf of any insurer by reason of the existence of a policy of insurance, whereby the insurer is liable to pay, in whole or in part, the amount of the judgment and that no part of the amount to be paid out of the fund is sought in lieu of making a claim or receiving a payment which is payable by reason of the existence of such a policy of insurance and that no part of the amount so sought will be paid to an insurer to reimburse or otherwise indemnify the insurer in respect of any amount paid or payable by the insurer by reason of the existence of such a policy of insurance,

(m) Whether or not he has recovered a judgment in an action against any other person against whom he has a cause of action in respect of his damages for bodily injury or death or damage to property arising out of the accident and what amounts, if any, he has received by way of payments upon the judgment, or by way of settlement of such cause of action, in whole or in part, from or on behalf of such other person,

(n) In order to recover for noneconomic loss, as defined in section 2 of P.L.1972, c. 70 (C.39:6A–2) for accidents to which the benefits of sections 7 and 10 of P.L.1972, c. 198 (C.39:6–86.1 and C.39:6–86.4) apply, the injured person shall have sustained an injury described in subsection a. of section 8 of P.L.1972, c. 70 (C.39:6A–8).

Whenever the applicant satisfies the court that it is not possible to comply with one or more of the requirements enumerated in subsections (h) and (i) of this section and that the applicant has taken all reasonable steps to collect the amount of the judgment or the unsatisfied part thereof and has been unable to collect the same, the court may dispense with the necessity for complying with such requirements.

The association may appear and be heard on application and show cause why the order should not be made.
L.1952, c. 174, p. 577, § 10, eff. April 1, 1955. Amended by L.1958, c. 98, p. 550, § 1, eff. July 1, 1958; L.1961, c. 19, p. 95, § 1; L.1983, c. 362, § 2, eff. Oct. 4, 1983; L.1988, c. 119, § 19, eff. Jan. 1, 1989; L.2003, c. 89, § 15, eff. June 9, 2003.

[1] N.J.S.A. § 39:6–65.
[2] N.J.S.A. § 39:6–69.

39:6–71. Order for payment of judgment

The court shall make an order directed to the association requiring the association to make payment from the fund of such sum, if any, as it shall find to be payable upon said claim, pursuant to the provisions of and in accordance with the limitations contained in this act, if the court is satisfied, upon the hearing:

(a) Of the truth of all matters required to be shown by the applicant by section 10,[1]

(b) That the applicant has fully pursued and exhausted all remedies available to him for recovering damages against all persons mentioned in subparagraph (m) of section 10 by

(1) Commencing action against all such persons against whom the applicant might reasonably be considered as having a cause of action in respect of such damages and prosecuting every such action in good faith to judgment and

(2) Taking all reasonable steps available to him to collect on every judgment so obtained and by applying the proceeds of any judgment or recovery so obtained

towards satisfaction of the amount due upon the judgment for payment of which the claim is made.

Any amount which the plaintiff has received or can collect by way of payments upon the judgment or by way of settlement of the cause of action, in whole or in part, from or on behalf of any person other than the judgment debtor, described in subparagraph (m) of section 10, shall be deducted from the amount due upon the judgment for payment of which claim is made.

L.1952, c. 174, p. 580, § 11, eff. April 1, 1955. Amended by L.1955, c. 1, p. 16, § 5, eff. March 30, 1955; L.1958, c. 98, p. 552, § 2, eff. July 1, 1958; L.2003, c. 89, § 16, eff. June 9, 2003.

   1 N.J.S.A. § 39:6–70.

39:6–72. Settlement of actions against motorist

(a) In any action against an operator or owner of a motor vehicle for injury to or death of any person or for damage to property arising out of the ownership, maintenance or use of said vehicle in this State on or after April 1, 1955, pending in any court of competent jurisdiction in this State, the plaintiff may upon notice to the association file a verified petition with the court alleging:

(1) the matters set forth in subparagraphs (a), (b), (c), (d), (e) and (f) of section 10;[1]

(2) that the petition is not presented on behalf of an insurer under circumstances set forth in subparagraph (1) of section 10;

(3) that he has entered into an agreement with the defendant to settle all claims set forth in the complaint in said action and the amount proposed to be paid to him pursuant thereto;

(4) that the said proposed settlement has been entered into with and by the consent of the Superior Court and approved by the association;

(5) that the defendant has executed and delivered to the association a verified statement of his financial condition;

(6) that a judgment against the defendant would be uncollectible;

(7) that the defendant has undertaken in writing to repay to the association the sum that he would be required to pay under such settlement, and has executed a confession of judgment in connection therewith.

If the court be satisfied of the truth of the allegations in said petition and of the fairness of such proposed settlement, it may enter an order approving the same and directing the association, upon receipt of the undertaking and confession of judgment mentioned in subparagraph (7) of this section, to make payment to the plaintiff of the amount agreed to be accepted.

(b) The association may settle any claim, without court approval, if satisfied:

(1) that the claimant is not a person of the character described in subparagraphs (a), (b), (c), (d), (e) and (f) of section 10;

(2) that the settlement is not made on behalf of an insurer under circumstances set forth in subparagraph (e) of section 10; and

(3) that a judgment against the owner or operator of the motor vehicle involved in the accident would be uncollectible, and that such owner or operator has consented to such settlement, executed and delivered to the association a verified statement of his financial condition and undertaken in writing to repay to the association the sum to be paid under the settlement, and executed a confession of judgment in connection therewith.

L.1952, c. 174, p. 581, § 12, eff. April 1, 1955. Amended by L.1955, c. 1, p. 17, § 6, eff. March 30, 1955; L.1958, c. 99, p. 558, § 4, eff. July 1, 1958; L.1968, c. 323, § 5, eff. Nov. 8, 1968; L.1985, c. 148, § 8, eff. April 24, 1985; L.2003, c. 89, § 17, eff. June 9, 2003.

   1 N.J.S.A. § 39:6–70.

39:6–73. Limitation on amounts payable from fund

Except with respect to medical expense benefits paid pursuant to section 2 of P.L.1977, c. 310 (C.39:6–73.1), no order shall be made for the payment and the association shall make no payment, out of the fund, of

(a) Any claim for damage to property for less than $500.00,

(b) The first $500.00 of any judgment for damage to property or of the unsatisfied portion thereof, or

(c) The unsatisfied portion of any judgment which, after deducting $500.00 therefrom if the judgment is for damage to property, exceeds

(1) the maximum or limit of $15,000.00, exclusive of interest and costs, on account of injury to, or death of, one person in any one accident, and

(2) the maximum amount or limit, subject to such limit for any one person so injured or killed, of $30,000.00, exclusive of interest and costs, on account of injury to, or death of, more than one person, in any one accident, and

(3) the maximum amount or limit of $5,000.00, exclusive of interest and costs, for damage to property in any one accident; provided, that such maximum amounts shall be reduced by any amount received or recovered as specified in subsection (m) of section 10.[1]

(d) Any claim for damage to property which includes any sum greater than the difference between said maximum amounts and the sum of $500.00, and any amount paid out of the fund in excess of the amount so authorized may be recovered by the association in an action brought to it against the person receiving the same.

L.1952, c. 174, p. 582, § 13, eff. April 1, 1955. Amended by L.1958, c. 99, p. 560, § 5, eff. July 1, 1958; L.1972, c. 198, § 4, eff. Jan. 1, 1973; L.1977, c. 310, § 4, eff. Jan. 5, 1978; L.1983, c. 362, § 22, eff. Oct. 4, 1983; L.1988, c. 119, § 16, eff. Jan. 1, 1989; L.2003, c. 89, § 18, eff. June 9, 2003.

1 N.J.S.A. § 39:6–70.

39:6–73.1. Assumption of excess payment by fund; exceptions

In the event medical expense benefits paid by an insurer, in accordance with subsection a. of section 4 of P.L.1972, c. 70 (C.39:6A–4) or section 4 of P.L.1998, c. 21 (C.39:6A–3.1), are in excess of $75,000.00 on account of personal injury to any one person in any one accident covered under a policy issued prior to January 1, 2004, the Unsatisfied Claim and Judgment Fund shall assume the following: a. the entire excess for a medical expense benefits claim covered under a policy issued before January 1, 1991; and b. such excess up to $250,000 for a medical expense benefits claim covered under a policy issued on or after January 1, 1991 and the Unsatisfied Claim and Judgment Fund shall reimburse the insurer therefor in accordance with rules and regulations promulgated by the commissioner; provided, however, that this provision is not intended to broaden the coverage available to accidents involving uninsured or hit-and-run automobiles, to provide extraterritorial coverage, or to pay excess medical expenses.

The Unsatisfied Claim and Judgment Fund shall cease to reimburse an insurer for medical expense benefits under this section for injuries covered under a policy issued on or after January 1, 2004.

L.1977, c. 310, § 2, eff. Jan. 5, 1978. Amended by L.1985, c. 148, § 9, eff. April 24, 1985; L.1990, c. 8, § 14, eff. March 12, 1990; L.1998, c. 21, § 69; L.2003, c. 89, § 19, eff. June 9, 2003.

39:6–74. Default and consent judgments

No claim shall be allowed and ordered to be paid out of the fund if the court shall find, upon the hearing for the allowance of the claim, that it is founded upon a judgment which was entered by default unless (1) the claimant shall have complied with the requirements of section 5,[1] and (2) prior to the entry of such judgment the association shall have been given notice of intention to enter the judgment and file a claim thereon against the fund and shall have been afforded an opportunity to take such action as it shall deem advisable.

If the court, upon a hearing for the allowance of any claim against the fund, finds that it was a claim which was not assigned by the association for defense, or that the action upon such claim was not fully and fairly defended, or that the judgment thereon was entered upon the consent or with the agreement of the defendant, the court shall allow such claim but shall order it to be paid only in such sum as the court shall determine to be justly due and payable out of the fund, on the basis of the actual amount of damages for which the defendant was liable to the plaintiff under the cause of action, upon which the judgment was rendered and reduced by any amount received from any person mentioned in subparagraph (m) of section 10,[2] notwithstanding that the judgment is for a greater amount.

L.1952, c. 174, p. 583, § 14, eff. April 1, 1955. Amended by L.1955, c. 1, p. 19, § 7, eff. March 30, 1955; L.2003, c. 89, § 20, eff. June 9, 2003.

1 N.J.S.A. § 39:6–65.
2 N.J.S.A. § 39:6–70.

39:6–75. Repealed by L.2003, c. 89, § 85, eff. June 9, 2003

39:6–76. Collusive judgments

No claim against the fund shall be allowed in any case in which the court shall find, upon the hearing for the allowance of the claim, that the judgment upon which the claim is founded was obtained by fraud, or by collusion of the plaintiff and of any defendant in the action, relating to any matter affecting the cause of action upon which such judgment is founded or the amount of damages assessed therein.

L.1952, c. 174, p. 583, § 16, eff. April 1, 1955.

39:6–77. Assignment of judgments to association

Assignment of judgments to commissioner. The association shall not pay any sum from the fund, in compliance with an order made for that purpose, in any case in which the claim is founded upon a judgment, except a judgment obtained against the association under this act, until the applicant assigns the judgment to the association and, thereupon, the association shall be deemed to have all the rights of the judgment creditor under the judgment and shall enforce and collect the same for the full amount thereof with interest and costs and if more money is collected upon any such judgment than the amount paid out of the fund, the association shall pay the balance, after reimbursing the fund, to the judgment creditor. Upon assignment of a judgment to the association the association may enter into agreement with the defendant for reimbursement of the fund by lump sum or installment payments, including waiver of interest and subordination of the lien of the judgment where the same is determined to be advantageous in obtaining reimbursement of payments made by the fund. Any such agreement may be annexed to an application for a court order made pursuant to section 27(b).[1]

L.1952, c. 174, p. 583, § 17, eff. April 1, 1955. Amended by L.1955, c. 1, p. 20, § 8, eff. March 30, 1955; L.1968, c. 323, § 6, eff. Nov. 8, 1968; L.1985, c. 148, § 10, eff. April 24, 1985; L.2003, c. 89, § 21, eff. June 9, 2003.

1 N.J.S.A. § 39:6–87.

39:6–78. "Hit-and-run" cases

When the death of, or personal injury to, any person arises out of ownership, maintenance or use of a motor vehicle in this State on or after April 1, 1955, but the identity of the motor vehicle and of the operator and owner thereof cannot be ascertained or it is established that the motor vehicle was, at the time said accident occurred, in the possession of some person other than the owner without the owner's consent and that the identity of such person cannot be ascertained, any qualified person who would have a cause of action against the operator or owner or both in respect to such death or personal injury may bring an action therefor against the association in any court of competent jurisdiction, but no judgment against the association shall be entered in such an action unless the court is satisfied, upon the hearing of the action, that—

(a) The claimant has complied with the requirements of section 5,[1]

(b) The claimant is not a person covered with respect to such injury or death by any workers' compensation law, or the personal representative of such a person,

(c) The claimant was not at the time of the accident the owner or registrant of an uninsured motor vehicle, or was not operating a motor vehicle in violation of an order of suspension or revocation,

(d) The claimant has a cause of action against the operator or owner of such motor vehicle or against the operator who was operating the motor vehicle without the consent of the owner of the motor vehicle,

(e) All reasonable efforts have been made to ascertain the identity of the motor vehicle and of the owner and operator thereof and either that the identity of the motor vehicle and the owner and operator thereof cannot be established, or that the identity of the operator, who was operating the motor vehicle without the owner's consent, cannot be established,

(f) The action is not brought by or on behalf of an insurer under circumstances set forth in paragraph (1) of section 10.[2]

L.1952, c. 174, p. 585, § 18, eff. April 1, 1955. Amended by L.1955, c. 1, p. 20, § 9, eff. March 30, 1955; L.1956, c. 150, p. 618, § 1, eff. Sept. 10, 1956; L.1958, c. 99, p. 561, § 6, eff. July 1, 1958; L.1983, c. 362, § 2.1, eff. Oct. 4, 1983; L.1985, c. 148, § 11, eff. April 24, 1985; L.2003, c. 89, § 22, eff. June 9, 2003.

[1] N.J.S.A. § 39:6–65.
[2] N.J.S.A. § 39:6–70.

39:6–79. Other "hit-and-run" cases

When in an action in respect to the death of, or personal injury to, any person, arising out of the ownership, maintenance or use of a motor vehicle in this State on or after April 1, 1955, judgment is rendered for the defendant on the sole ground that such death or personal injury was occasioned by a motor vehicle—

(a) The identity of which, and of the owner and operator of which, has not been established, or

(b) Which was in the possession of some person other than the owner or his agent without the consent of the owner and the identity of the operator has not been established, such cause shall be stated in the judgment and the plaintiff in such action may within 180 days from the date of the entry of such judgment bring an action upon said cause of action against the association in the manner provided in section 18.[1]

L.1952, c. 174, p. 586, § 19, eff. April 1, 1955. Amended by L.1955, c. 1, p. 21, § 10, eff. March 30, 1955; L.1958, c. 99, p. 562, § 7, eff. July 1, 1958; L.1963, c. 81, § 11, eff. June 4, 1963; L.1985, c. 148, § 12, eff. April 24, 1985; L.2003, c. 89, § 23, eff. June 9, 2003.

[1] N.J.S.A. § 39:6–78.

39:6–80 Impleading association in "hit-and-run" cases

When an action has been commenced in respect of the death or injury of any person arising out of the ownership, maintenance or use of a motor vehicle in this State on or after April 1, 1955, the plaintiff shall be entitled to make the association a party thereto if the provisions of section 18 or 19[1] shall apply in any such case, and the plaintiff has made the application and the court has entered the order provided for in section 18.

L.1952, c. 174, p. 586, § 20, eff. April 1, 1955. Amended by L.1955, c. 1, p. 22, § 11, eff. March 30, 1955; L.1985, c. 148, § 13, eff. April 24, 1985; L.2003, c. 89, § 24, eff. June 9, 2003.

[1] N.J.S.A. § 39:6–78 or 39:6–79.

39:6–81 Defense of such actions by association

In any action brought under sections 18 and 19 of this act,[1] the association may appear. The association shall for all purposes of the action be deemed to be the defendant. The association shall have available to it any and all defenses which would have been available to said operator or owner or both if the action had been brought against them or either of them and process upon them or either of them had been duly served within this State, but the association shall be entitled to defend in all cases without asserting any specific facts.

L.1952, c. 174, p. 587, § 21, eff. April 1, 1955. Amended by L.1955, c. 1, p. 22, § 12, eff. March 30, 1955; L.1985, c. 148, § 14, eff. April 24, 1985; L.2003, c. 89, § 25, eff. June 9, 2003.

[1] N.J.S.A. §§ 39:6–78 and 39:6–79.

39:6–82 Settlement of actions against the association

In any action brought against the association pursuant to an order by the court entered in accordance with the provisions of section 18,[1] the plaintiff may file a verified petition alleging that he has entered into an agreement with the association to settle all claims set forth in the complaint in said action and the amount proposed to be paid to him pursuant thereto. If the court be satisfied of the fairness of such proposed settlement, it may enter an order approving such settlement and enter a judgment against the association for the amount so agreed to be paid thereunder.

L.1952, c. 174, p. 587, § 22, eff. April 1, 1955. Amended by L.1955, c. 1, p. 22, § 13, eff. March 30, 1955; L.1985, c. 148, § 15, eff. April 24, 1985; L.2003, c. 89, § 26, eff. June 9, 2003.

1 N.J.S.A. § 39:6–78.

39:6–83. Credits against judgment

A judgment against the association shall be reduced by any amounts which such plaintiff has received from any person mentioned in subparagraph (m) of section 10.[1]

L.1952, c. 174, p. 587, § 23, eff. April 1, 1955. Amended by L.1955, c. 1, p. 23, § 14, eff. March 30, 1955; L.1985, c. 148, § 16, eff. April 24, 1985; L.2003, c. 89, § 27, eff. June 9, 2003.

1 N.J.S.A. § 39:6–70.

39:6–84. Judgment against commissioner

When a judgment is obtained against the association, in an action brought under this act, upon the determination of all proceedings including appeals and reviews, the court shall make an order directed to the association directing it to pay out of the fund to the plaintiff in the action the amount thereof which does not exceed $15,000.00, exclusive of interest and costs, on account of injury to, or death of, one person and, subject to such limits for the death of, or injury to, any one person, does not exceed $30,000.00, exclusive of interest and costs, on account of the injury to, or death of, more than one person, in any one accident, provided that such maximum amount shall be reduced by any amount received or recovered by the plaintiff as specified in subparagraph (m) of section 10.[1]

L.1952, c. 174, p. 588, § 24, eff. April 1, 1955. Amended by L.1955, c. 1, p. 23, § 15, eff. March 30, 1955; L.1958, c. 99, p. 562, § 8, eff. July 1, 1958; L.1972, c. 198, § 5, eff. Jan. 1, 1973; L.1985, c. 148, § 17, eff. April 24, 1985; L.2003, c. 89, § 28, eff. June 9, 2003.

1 N.J.S.A. § 39:6–70.

39:6–84.1. Increase in payment of maximum amounts from fund; application to accidents on or after January 1, 1973

The provisions of sections 9, 13 and 24 of the act of which this act is supplementary (C. 39:6–69, 39:6–73 and 39:6–84) as amended by sections 3, 4 and 5 of P.L.1972, c. 198 which increase the maximum amounts payable from the fund shall be applicable only to claims made by qualified persons, or the personal representatives of such persons, who suffered damages resulting from bodily injury or death or damage to property arising out of the ownership, maintenance or use of a motor vehicle in this State on or after January 1, 1973, and whose

damages may be satisfied in whole or in part from the fund.

L.1975, c. 6, § 1, eff. Feb. 4, 1975, retroactive to Jan. 1, 1973.

39:6–85. Subrogation

When judgment has been obtained against the association in an action brought under this act, the association shall, upon payment from the fund of the amount of the judgment to the extent provided in this act, be subrogated to the cause of action of the judgment creditor against the operator and owner of the motor vehicle by which the accident was occasioned and shall bring an action against either or both of such persons for the amount of the damage sustained by the judgment creditor when and in the event that the identity of either or both of such persons shall be established, and shall recover the same out of any funds which would be payable in respect to the death or injury under any policy of insurance, which was in force at the time of the accident and in event that more is recovered and collected in any such action than the amount paid out of the fund by reason of the judgment, the association shall pay the balance, after reimbursing the fund, to the judgment creditor.

L.1952, c. 174, p. 588, § 25, eff. April 1, 1955. Amended by L.1955, c. 1, p. 23, § 16, eff. March 30, 1955; L.1968, c. 323, § 7, eff. Nov. 8, 1968; L.1985, c. 148, § 18, eff. April 24, 1985; L.2003, c. 89, § 29, eff. June 9, 2003.

39:6–86. Repealed by L.1955, c. 1, p. 24, § 17

39:6–86.1. Unsatisfied Claim and Judgment Fund claims; benefits

When any person qualified to receive payments under the provisions of the "Unsatisfied Claim and Judgment Fund Law"[1] suffers bodily injury or death as a pedestrian, as defined in section 2 of P.L.1972, c. 70 (C.39:6A–2), caused by a motor vehicle, including an automobile as defined in section 2 of P.L.1972, c. 70 (C.39:6A–2), and a motorcycle, or by an object propelled therefrom, or arising out of an accident while occupying, entering into, alighting from, or using an automobile, registered or principally garaged in this State for which personal injury protection benefits under the "New Jersey Automobile Reparation Reform Act," P.L.1972, c. 70 (C.39:6A–1 et seq.), or section 19 of P.L.1983, c. 362 (C.17:28–1.3), would be payable to such person if personal injury protection coverage were in force and the damages resulting from such accident or death are not satisfied due to the personal injury protection coverage not being in effect with respect to such accident, or when a pedestrian suffers bodily injury as provided by section 35 of P.L.2003,c.89 (C.39:6–86.7) then in such event the Unsatisfied Claim and Judgment Fund shall provide, under the following conditions, the following benefits:

a. Medical expenses benefits. Payment of all medical expense benefits in accordance with a benefits plan, subject to the approval of the commissioner, for reasonable, necessary and appropriate treatment and provision of services in an amount not exceeding $250,000 per person per accident. In the event of death, payment shall be made to the estate of the decedent. The benefits plan shall set forth the benefits provided by the Unsatisfied Claim and Judgment Fund, including eligible medical treatments, diagnostic tests and services as well as such other benefits as the Unsatisfied Claim and Judgment Fund may provide.

Medical expense benefit payments shall be subject to a deductible of $250.00 on account of injury in any one accident and a copayment of 20% of any benefits payable between $250.00 and $5,000.00.

b. Income continuation benefits. The payment of the loss of income of an income producer as a result of bodily injury disability, subject to a maximum weekly payment of $100.00. Such sums shall be payable during the life of the injured person and shall be subject to an amount or limit of $5,200.00, on account of injury to any one person in any one accident, except that in no case shall income continuation benefits exceed the net income normally earned during the period in which the benefits are payable.

c. Essential services benefits. Payment of essential services benefits to an injured person shall be made in reimbursement of necessary and reasonable expenses incurred for such substitute essential services ordinarily performed by the injured person for himself, his family and members of the family residing in the household, subject to an amount or limit of $12.00 per day. Such benefits shall be payable during the life of the injured person and shall be subject to an amount or limit of $4,380.00, on account of injury to any one person in any one accident.

d. Death benefits. In the event of the death of an income producer as a result of injuries sustained in an accident entitling such person to benefits under this section, the maximum amount of benefits which could have been paid to the income producer, but for his death, under subsection b. of this section shall be paid to the surviving spouse, or in the event there is no surviving spouse, then to the surviving children, and in the event there are no surviving spouse or surviving children, then to the estate of the income producer.

In the event of the death of one performing essential services as a result of injuries sustained in an accident entitling such person to benefits under subsection c. of this section, the maximum amount of benefits which could have been paid such person, under subsection c., shall be paid to the person incurring the expense of providing such essential services.

e. Funeral expenses benefits. All reasonable funeral, burial and cremation expenses, subject to a maximum benefit of $1,000.00, on account of the death to any one person in any one accident shall be payable to decedent's estate.

Provided, however, that no benefits shall be paid under this section unless the person applying for benefits has demonstrated that he is not disqualified by reason of the provisions of subsection (a), (c), (d) or (*l*) of section 10 of P.L.1952, c. 174 (C.39:6–70), or any other provision of law.

L.1972, c. 198, § 7, eff. Jan. 1, 1973. Amended by L.1983, c. 362, § 3, eff. Oct. 4, 1983; L.1988, c. 119, § 5, eff. Jan. 1, 1989; L.1990, c. 8, § 101, eff. March 12, 1990; L.2003, c. 89, § 30, eff. June 9, 2003.

 1 N.J.S.A. § 39:6–61 et seq.

39:6–86.2. Payments of benefits

The benefits provided in sections 7 and 10 [1] shall be payable as loss accrues, upon written notice of such loss, including reasonable proof of such loss, except that benefits collectible under:

a. Employees' temporary disability benefit statutes and medicare provided under federal law shall be deducted from the benefits collectible under sections 7 and 10; and

b. Any hospital, medical or dental benefit plan or policy coverage with benefits similar to those provided under section 7, in an amount not to exceed in the aggregate $2,500.00 for any one accident, shall be deducted from the benefits collectible under sections 7 and 10.

Evidence of benefit payments collectible under subsections a. and b. of this section shall not be admissible in a civil action by the claimant for recovery of damages for bodily injury from the fund.

The amount of $2,500.00 shall be deemed to have been exceeded, whether the amount is paid or benefits in that amount are provided to one or more persons eligible for benefits under the hospital, medical or dental plan or policy, for injuries sustained in any one accident.

L.1972, c. 198, § 8, eff. Jan. 1, 1973. Amended by L.1983, c. 362, § 4, eff. Oct. 4, 1983; L.1984, c. 40, § 2, eff. May 15, 1984.

 1 N.J.S.A. §§ 39:6–86.1 and 39:6–86.4.

39:6–86.3. Denial of benefits; grounds

Any qualified person entitled to receive benefits as provided in section 7 of this act [1] shall be precluded from receiving such benefits where such person's conduct contributed to his personal injuries or death in any of the following ways:

a. While committing a high misdemeanor or felony or seeking to avoid lawful apprehension or arrest by a police officer; or

b. While acting with specific intent of causing injury or damage to himself or others.

L.1972, c. 198, § 9, eff. Jan. 1, 1973.

 1 N.J.S.A. § 39:6–86.1.

39:6–86.4. Death or injury due to unidentifiable operator or owner, or to operator using automobile without consent of owner; benefits payable; conditions

When the death of or personal injury to any person arises out of the ownership, maintenance or use of an automobile in this State on or after the effective date of this act, but the identity of the automobile and of the operator and owner thereof cannot be ascertained or it is established that the automobile was, at the time said accident occurred, in the possession of some person other than the owner without the owner's consent and that the identity of such person cannot be ascertained, any person qualified to receive payments under the provisions of the "Unsatisfied Claim and Judgment Fund Law" [1] shall be entitled to receive payment under sections 7 and 10 of this act,[2] provided that:

a. The claimant is not a person covered with respect to such injury or death by any workers' compensation law, or the personal representative of such a person,

b. The claimant was not at the time of the accident the owner or registrant of an uninsured motor vehicle, or was not operating a motor vehicle in violation of an order of suspension or revocation,

c. The claimant was not at the time of the accident:

(1) A person operating or riding in a motor vehicle which he had stolen or participated in stealing, or

(2) Operating a motor vehicle without the permission of the owner, and is not the personal representative of such a person,

d. All reasonable efforts have been made to ascertain the identity of the motor vehicle and of the owner and operator thereof and either that the identity of the motor vehicle and the owner and operator thereof cannot be established, or that the identity of the operator, who was operating the motor vehicle without the owner's consent, cannot be established, or

e. (Deleted by amendment, P.L. 1983, c. 362.)

f. The action or claim is not brought by or on behalf of an insurer.

L.1972, c. 198, § 10, eff. Jan. 1, 1973. Amended by L.1983, c. 362, § 5, eff. Oct. 4, 1983.

  [1] N.J.S.A. § 39:6–61 et seq.
  [2] N.J.S.A. §§ 39:6–86.1, 39:6–86.4.

39:6–86.5. Application for benefits; payment

Any qualified person seeking to receive benefits as provided in sections 7 and 10 of this act [1] shall comply with the provisions of section 5 of P.L.1952, c. 174 (C. 39:6–65) and payment under these sections shall be payable to the qualified person entitled to receive such benefits, as the loss accrues, upon receipt of reasonable proof of such loss and without the need of a judgment as to damages, or a hearing as provided in section 10 of

P.L.1954, c. 174 (C. 39:6–70) or an order for payment as provided in section 11 of P.L.1954, c. 174 (C. 39:6–71).

L.1972, c. 198, § 11, eff. Jan. 1, 1973.

  [1] N.J.S.A. §§ 39:6–86.1, 39:6–86.4.

39:6–86.6. Recovery of benefits paid by fund

The association shall be entitled to recover on behalf of the Unsatisfied Claim and Judgment Fund for all payments made by it pursuant to sections 7 and 10 of this act,[1] regardless of fault, from any person who owned or operated the automobile involved in the accident and whose failure to have the required insurance coverage in effect at the time of the accident resulted in the payment of personal injury protection benefits. If the identity of the owner and operator is not ascertained until after personal injury protection benefits have been paid then the association shall be entitled to recover for such payments, regardless of fault, from the operator if he was driving without the owner's permission or from the operator and the owner if he was driving with the owner's permission or, in either case, from the insurer if there is an insurance policy providing personal injury protection benefits that was in effect at the time of the accident with respect to such automobile.

The association is authorized to bring an action, which shall be a summary proceeding, in the Superior Court to reduce the right provided by this section to judgment.

L.1972, c. 198, § 12, eff. Jan. 1, 1973. Amended by L.1985, c. 148, § 19, eff. April 24, 1985; L.2003, c. 89, § 31, eff. June 9, 2003.

  [1] N.J.S.A. §§ 39:6–86.1 and 39:6–86.4.

39:6–86.7. Personal injury protection benefits to pedestrians

The Unsatisfied Claim and Judgment Fund created pursuant to P.L.1952, c. 174 (C.39:6–61 et seq.) shall provide personal injury protection benefits pursuant to section 7 of P.L.1972, c. 198 (C.39:6–86.1) to a pedestrian sustaining bodily injury in this State caused by an automobile, other than to a named insured or a member of the named insured's family residing in his household, if that pedestrian is entitled to personal injury protection coverage under an automobile insurance policy.

L.2003, c. 89, § 35, eff. June 9, 2003.

39:6–87. Registration, etc. not restored until fund is reimbursed

Where the license or privileges of any person, or the registration of a motor vehicle registered in his name, has been suspended or cancelled under the Motor Vehicle Security–Responsibility Law of this State,[1] and the association has paid from the fund any amount in settlement of a claim or towards satisfaction of a judgment against that person, or for the payment of personal injury protection benefits as provided in section 7 and section 10 of this act,[2] the cancellation or suspension shall not be removed, nor the license, privileges, or registration restored, nor shall any new license or privilege be issued or granted to, or registration be permitted to be made by, that person until he has

(a) Repaid in full to the association the amount so paid by him together with interest thereon at 8% per annum from the date of such payment; and

(b) Satisfied all requirements of said Motor Vehicle Security–Responsibility Law in respect of giving proof of ability to respond in damages for future accidents, provided, that the court in which such judgment was rendered may, upon 10 days' notice to the association, make an order permitting payment of the amount of such person's indebtedness to the fund, to be made in installments, or in the event the fund makes personal injury protection benefit payments, such person and the fund by agreement may provide for repayment to the fund to be made in installments, and in such case, such person's driver's license, or his driving privileges, or registration certificate, if the same have been suspended or revoked, or have expired, may be restored or renewed and shall remain in effect unless and until such person defaults in making any installment payment specified in such order. In the event of any such default, the New Jersey Motor Vehicle Commission shall upon notice of such default suspend such person's driver's license, or driving privileges or registration certificate until the amount of his indebtedness to the fund has been paid in full.

L.1952, c. 174, p. 589, § 27, eff. April 1, 1955. Amended by L.1968, c. 323, § 8, eff. Nov. 8, 1968; L.1972, c. 198, § 6, eff. Jan. 1, 1973; L.1981, c. 175, § 1, eff. June 19, 1981; L.1985, c. 148, § 20, eff. April 24, 1985; L.2003, c. 89, § 32, eff. June 9, 2003.

1 N.J.S.A. § 39:6–23 et seq.
2 N.J.S.A. §§ 39:6–67, 39:6–70.

39:6–88. Fund to be held in trust

All sums received by the association pursuant to any of the provisions of this act shall become part of the fund, and shall be held by the association in trust for the carrying out of the purposes of this act and for the payment of the cost of administering this act.

L.1952, c. 174, p. 590, § 28, eff. April 1, 1955. Amended by L.1975, c. 174, § 1, eff. Aug. 4, 1975; L.1977, c. 310, § 5, eff. Jan. 5, 1978; L.1983, c. 125, § 2, eff. April 5, 1983; L.1985, c. 148, § 21, eff. April 24, 1985; L.2003, c. 89, § 33, eff. June 9, 2003.

39:6–89. Repealed by L.2003, c. 89, § 85, eff. June 9, 2003

39:6–90. Penalty for false statements

Any person and any agent or servant of such person, who knowingly files with the fund or the association or either of them, any notice, statement or other document required under this act, which is false or untrue or contains any material misstatement of fact shall be subject to a penalty as provided in section 5 of P.L.1983, c. 320 (C.17:33A–5) and damages as provided in section 7 of P.L.1983, c. 320 (C.17:33A–7).

L.1952, c. 174, p. 590, § 30, eff. April 1, 1955. Amended by L.2003, c. 89, § 34, eff. June 9, 2003.

39:6–90.1. Partial invalidity

In the event any section, term or provision of this act or of the act to which this act is amendatory and supplementary[1] shall be adjudged invalid for any reason, such judgment shall not affect, impair or invalidate any other section, term or provision of said acts, but the remaining sections, terms and provisions shall be and remain in full force and effect.

L.1955, c. 1, p. 24, § 19, eff. March 30, 1955.

1 N.J.S.A. §§ 39:6–61 to 39:6–91.

39:6–91. Repealed by L.2003, c. 89, § 85, eff. June 9, 2003

39:6–92 to 39:6–104. Repealed by L.1975, c. 175, § 1, eff. Aug. 4, 1975

CHAPTER 6A

COMPULSORY AUTOMOBILE LIABILITY INSURANCE—NO FAULT PROVISIONS

Section
39:6A–1. Short title.
39:6A–1.1. Short title; legislative findings and declarations.
39:6A–1.2. Adoption of rules and regulations.
39:6A–2. Definitions.
39:6A–3. Compulsory automobile insurance coverage; limits.
39:6A–3.1. Alternate coverage; minimum required coverages.
39:6A–3.2. Automobile policies; minimum required coverages.
39:6A–3.3. Automobile insurance policy for low income individuals.
39:6A–4. Personal injury protection coverage, regardless of fault.
39:6A–4.1. Additional automobiles; reduced personal injury protection premium.
39:6A–4.2. Primacy of coverages.
39:6A–4.3. Personal injury protection coverage options.
39:6A–4.4. Application of amendment of § 39:6A–4.3 by L.1984, c. 40.
39:6A–4.5. Failure to maintain required medical expense coverage; effect on recovery for noneconomic loss.
39:6A–4.6. Medical fee schedules for reimbursement of health care providers; biannual review.
39:6A–4.7. Promulgation of rules and regulations; valid diagnostic tests for persons sustaining bodily injury.
39:6A–5. Payment of personal injury protection coverage benefits.
39:6A–5.1. Personal injury protection benefits; dispute resolution.
39:6A–5.2. Medical review organizations; certification standards.

Section

39:6A–6.   Collateral source.

39:6A–7.   Exclusions.

39:6A–8.   Tort exemption; limitation on the right to noneconomic loss.

39:6A–8.1. Election of tort option.

39:6A–9.   Inoperative.

39:6A–9.1. Recovery of personal injury protection benefits from tortfeasor.

39:6A–10. Additional personal injury protection coverage.

39:6A–11. Contribution among insurers.

39:6A–12. Inadmissibility of evidence of losses collectible under personal injury protection coverage.

39:6A–13. Discovery of facts as to personal injury protection coverage.

39:6A–13.1. Limitation of actions.

39:6A–14. Compulsory uninsured motorist protection.

39:6A–15. Penalties for false and fraudulent representation.

39:6A–16. Construction and severability.

39:6A–17. General repeal of inconsistent statutory provisions.

39:6A–18. Mandatory reduction of bodily injury insurance rates.

39:6A–19. Rules and regulations.

39:6A–20. Powers of commissioner of insurance.

39:6A–21. The New Jersey Automobile Insurance Risk Exchange: membership, board of directors.

39:6A–22. Powers of exchange.

39:6A–22.1. Investment of moneys; annual report.

39:6A–23. Written notice—buyer's guide and coverage selection form.

39:6A–23.1. Comparative premium data; publication and distribution.

39:6A–24. Purpose and intent of act.

39:6A–25. Actions to be submitted to arbitration.

39:6A–26. Tolling statute of limitations.

39:6A–27. Selection of arbitrators.

39:6A–28. Compensation and fees; rules governing offers of judgment.

39:6A–29. Subpoenas.

39:6A–30. Award; decision of arbitrator.

39:6A–31. Confirming arbitration decision.

39:6A–32. Arbitrators fee; payment.

39:6A–33. Admissibility of evidence at trial de novo.

39:6A–34. Assessment of costs for trial de novo.

39:6A–35. Rules; report.

39:6A–1. Short title

This act may be cited and known as the "New Jersey Automobile Reparation Reform Act."

L.1972, c. 70, § 1.

39:6A–1.1. Short title; legislative findings and declarations

a. This act shall be known and may be cited as the "Automobile Insurance Cost Reduction Act."

b. The Legislature finds and declares:

Whereas, While New Jersey's automobile insurance no-fault law, enacted twenty-six years ago, has provided valuable benefits in the form of medical benefits and wage replacement benefits, without regard to fault, to New Jersey residents who have been injured in an automobile accident; and

Whereas, Medical benefits paid by no-fault policies over those years amount to billions of dollars, which would otherwise have been paid by health insurance, thus raising the cost of health insurance for everyone; and

Whereas, While medical benefits under no-fault insurance were unlimited under the law enacted in 1972, the rapidly escalating cost of those benefits made it necessary for the Legislature to reduce those benefits to a limit of $250,000 in 1990; and

Whereas, Since the enactment of the verbal threshold in 1988, the substantial increase in the cost of medical expense benefits indicates that the benefits are being overutilized for the purpose of gaining standing to sue for pain and suffering, thus undermining the limitations imposed by the threshold and necessitating the imposition of further controls on the use of those benefits, including the establishment of a basis for determining whether treatments or diagnostic tests are medically necessary; and

Whereas, The present arbitration system has not sufficiently addressed the Legislature's goal of eliminating payment for treatments and diagnostic tests which are not medically necessary, leading to the belief that a revised dispute resolution mechanism needs to be established which will accomplish this goal; and

Whereas, The principle underlying the philosophical basis of the no-fault system is that of a trade-off of one benefit for another; in this case, providing medical benefits in return for a limitation on the right to sue for non-serious injuries; and

Whereas, While the Legislature believes that it is good public policy to provide medical benefits on a first party basis, without regard to fault, to persons injured in automobile accidents, it recognizes that in order to keep premium costs down, the cost of the benefit must be offset by a reduction in the cost of other coverages, most notably a restriction on the right of persons who have non-permanent or non-serious injuries to sue for pain and suffering; and

Whereas, The high cost of automobile insurance in New Jersey has presented a significant problem for many-lower income residents of the state, many of whom have been forced to drop or lapse their coverage in violation of the State's mandatory motor vehicle insurance laws, making it necessary to provide a lower-cost option to protect people by providing coverage to pay their medical expenses if they are injured; and

Whereas, To meet these goals, this legislation provides for the creation of two insurance coverage options, a basic policy and a standard policy, provides for cost containment of medical expense benefits through a revised dispute resolution proceeding, provides for a revised lawsuit threshold for suits for pain and suffering which will eliminate suits for injuries which are not serious or permanent, including those for soft tissue injuries, would more precisely define the benefits available under the medical expense benefits coverage, and establishes standard treatment and diagnostic procedures against which the medical necessity of treatments reimbursable under medical expense benefits coverage would be judged; and

Whereas, It is generally recognized that fraud, whether in the form of inappropriate medical treatments, inflated claims, staged accidents, falsification of records, or in any other form, has increased premiums, and must be uncovered and vigorously prosecuted, and while the pursuit of those who defraud the automobile insurance system has heretofore been addressed by the State through various agencies, it has been without sufficient coordination to aggressively combat fraud, leading to the conclusion that greater consolidation of agencies which were created to combat fraud is necessary to accomplish this purpose; and

Whereas, With these many objectives, the Legislature nevertheless recognizes that to provide a healthy and competitive automobile insurance market, insurers are entitled to earn an adequate rate of return through the ratemaking process, which shall reflect the impact of the cost-saving provisions of this act and other recent legislative insurance reforms; and

Whereas, The Legislature has thus addressed these and other issues in this comprehensive legislation designed to preserve the no-fault system, while at the same time reducing unnecessary costs which drive premiums higher.

L.1998, c. 21, § 1, eff. May 19, 1998.

39:6A–1.2. Adoption of rules and regulations

The commissioner may promulgate any rules and regulations pursuant to P.L.1968, c. 410 (C.52:14B–1 et seq.) deemed necessary in order to effectuate the provisions of this amendatory and supplementary act. *L.1998, c. 21, § 73.*

39:6A–2. Definitions

As used in this act:

a. "Automobile" means a private passenger automobile of a private passenger or station wagon type that is owned or hired and is neither used as a public or livery conveyance for passengers nor rented to others with a driver; and a motor vehicle with a pickup body, a delivery sedan, a van, or a panel truck or a camper type vehicle used for recreational purposes owned by an individual or by husband and wife who are residents of the same household, not customarily used in the occupation, profession or business of the insured other than farming or ranching. An automobile owned by a farm family copartnership or corporation, which is principally garaged on a farm or ranch and otherwise meets the definitions contained in this section, shall be considered a private passenger automobile owned by two or more relatives resident in the same household.

b. "Essential services" means those services performed not for income which are ordinarily performed by an individual for the care and maintenance of such individual's family or family household.

c. "Income" means salary, wages, tips, commissions, fees and other earnings derived from work or employment.

d. "Income producer" means a person who, at the time of the accident causing personal injury or death, was in an occupational status, earning or producing income.

e. "Medical expenses" means reasonable and necessary expenses for treatment or services as provided by the policy, including medical, surgical, rehabilitative and diagnostic services and hospital expenses, provided by a health care provider licensed or certified by the State or by another state or nation, and reasonable and necessary expenses for ambulance services or other transportation, medication and other services as may be provided for, and subject to such limitations as provided for, in the policy, as approved by the commissioner. "Medical expenses" shall also include any nonmedical remedial treatment rendered in accordance with a recognized religious method of healing.

f. "Hospital expenses" means the cost of treatment and services, as provided in the policy approved by the commissioner, by a licensed and accredited acute care facility which engages primarily in providing diagnosis, treatment and care of sick and injured persons on an inpatient or outpatient basis; the cost of covered treatment and services provided by an extended care facility which provides room and board and skilled nursing care 24 hours a day and which is recognized by the administrators of the federal Medicare program as an extended care facility; and the cost of covered services at an ambulatory surgical facility supervised by a physician licensed in this State or in another jurisdiction and recognized by the Commissioner of Health and Senior Services, or any other facility licensed, certified or recognized by the Commissioner of Health and Senior Services or the Commissioner of Human Services or a nationally recognized system such as the Commission on Accreditation of Rehabilitation Facilities, or by another jurisdiction in which it is located.

g. "Named insured" means the person or persons identified as the insured in the policy and, if an individual, his or her spouse, if the spouse is named as a resident of the same household, except that if the spouse ceases to be a resident of the household of the named insured, coverage shall be extended to the spouse for the full term of any policy period in effect at the time of the cessation of residency.

h. "Pedestrian" means any person who is not occupying, entering into, or alighting from a vehicle propelled by other than muscular power and designed primarily for use on highways, rails and tracks.

i. "Noneconomic loss" means pain, suffering and inconvenience.

j. "Motor vehicle" means a motor vehicle as defined in R.S.39:1–1, exclusive of an automobile as defined in subsection a. of this section.

k. "Economic loss" means uncompensated loss of income or property, or other uncompensated expenses, including, but not limited to, medical expenses.

l. "Health care provider" or "provider" means those persons licensed or certified to perform health care treatment or services compensable as medical expenses and shall include, but not be limited to, (1) a hospital or health care facility which is maintained by a state or any of its political subdivisions, (2) a hospital or health care facility licensed by the Department of Health and Senior Services, (3) other hospitals or health care facilities designated by the Department of Health and Senior Services to provide health care services, or other facilities, including facilities for radiology and diagnostic testing, freestanding emergency clinics or offices, and private treatment centers, (4) a nonprofit voluntary visiting nurse organization providing health care services other than in a hospital, (5) hospitals or other health care facilities or treatment centers located in other states or nations, (6) physicians licensed to practice medicine and surgery, (7) licensed chiropractors, (8) licensed dentists, (9) licensed optometrists, (10) licensed pharmacists, (11) licensed podiatrists, (12) registered bio-analytical laboratories, (13) licensed psychologists, (14) licensed physical therapists, (16) certified nurse-midwives, (17) certified nurse–practitioners/clinical nurse-specialists, (18) licensed health maintenance organizations, (19) licensed orthotists and prosthetists, (20) licensed professional nurses, and (21) providers of other health care services or supplies, including durable medical goods.

m. "Medically necessary" means that the treatment is consistent with the symptoms or diagnosis, and treatment of the injury (1) is not primarily for the convenience of the injured person or provider, (2) is the most appropriate standard or level of service which is in accordance with standards of good practice and standard professional treatment protocols, as such protocols may be recognized or designated by the Commissioner of Banking and Insurance, in consultation with the Commissioner of Health and Senior Services or with a professional licensing or certifying board in the Division of Consumer Affairs in the Department of Law and Public Safety, or by a nationally recognized professional organization, and (3) does not involve unnecessary diagnostic testing.

n. "Standard automobile insurance policy" means an automobile insurance policy with at least the coverage required pursuant to sections 3 and 4 of P.L.1972, c. 70 (C.39:6A–3 and 39:6A–4).

o. "Basic automobile insurance policy" means an automobile insurance policy pursuant to section 4 of P.L.1998, c. 21 (C.39:6A–3.1).

L.1972, c. 70, § 2. Amended by L.1972, c. 203, § 1, eff. Dec. 26, 1972; L.1983, c. 362, § 6, eff. Oct. 4, 1983; L.1998, c. 21, § 2; L.2005, c. 259, § 35, eff. Jan. 4, 2006.

39:6A–3. Compulsory automobile insurance coverage; limits

Except as provided by section 4 of P.L.1998, c. 21 (C.39:6A–3.1), every owner or registered owner of an automobile registered or principally garaged in this State shall maintain automobile liability insurance coverage, under provisions approved by the Commissioner of Banking and Insurance, insuring against loss resulting from liability imposed by law for bodily injury, death and property damage sustained by any person arising out of the ownership, maintenance, operation or use of an automobile wherein such coverage shall be at least in:

a. an amount or limit of $15,000.00, exclusive of interest and costs, on account of injury to, or death of, one person, in any one accident; and

b. an amount or limit, subject to such limit for any one person so injured or killed, of $30,000.00, exclusive of interest and costs, on account of injury to or death of, more than one person, in any one accident; and

c. an amount or limit of $5,000.00, exclusive of interest and costs, for damage to property in any one accident.

No licensed insurance carrier shall refuse to renew the required coverage stipulated by this act of an eligible person as defined in section 25 of P.L.1990, c. 8 (C.17:33B–13) except in accordance with the provisions of section 26 of P.L.1988, c. 119 (C.17:29C–7.1) or with the consent of the Commissioner of Banking and Insurance.

L.1972, c. 70, § 3. Amended by L.1972, c. 203, § 2, eff. Dec. 26, 1972; L.1988, c. 119, § 9, eff. Jan. 1, 1989; L.1990, c. 8, § 3, eff. March 12, 1990; L.1998, c. 21, § 3.

39:6A–3.1. Alternate coverage; minimum required coverages

As an alternative to the mandatory coverages provided in sections 3 and 4 of P.L.1972, c. 70 (C.39:6A–3 and 39:6A–4), any owner or registered owner of an automobile registered or principally garaged in this State may elect a basic automobile insurance policy providing the following coverage:

a. Personal injury protection coverage, for the payment of benefits without regard to negligence, liability or fault of any kind, to the named insured and members of his family residing in his household, who sustained bodily injury as a result of an accident while occupying, entering into, alighting from or using an automobile, or as a pedestrian, caused by an automobile or by an object propelled by or from an automobile, and to other persons sustaining bodily injury while occupying, entering into, alighting from or using the automobile of the named insured, with the permission of the named insured. "Personal injury protection coverage" issued pursuant to this section means and includes payment of medical expense benefits, as provided in the policy and approved by the commissioner, for the reasonable and necessary treatment of bodily injury in an amount not to exceed $15,000 per person per accident; except that, medical expense benefits shall be paid in an amount not to exceed $250,000: (1) for all medically necessary treatment of permanent or significant brain injury, spinal cord injury or disfigurement or (2) for medically necessary treatment of other permanent or significant injuries rendered at a trauma center or acute care hospital immediately following the accident and until the patient is stable, no longer requires critical care and can be safely discharged or transferred to another facility in the judgment of the attending physician. In the event benefits paid by an insurer pursuant to this subsection are in excess of $75,000 on account of personal injury to any one person in any one accident covered by a policy issued or renewed prior to January 1, 2004, such excess shall be paid by the insurer and shall be reimbursable to the insurer from the Unsatisfied Claim and Judgment Fund pursuant to section 2 of P.L.1977, c. 310 (C.39:6–73.1). Benefits provided under basic coverage shall be in accordance with a benefit plan provided in the policy and approved by the commissioner. The policy form, which shall be subject to the approval of the commissioner, shall set forth the benefits provided under the policy, including eligible medical treatments, diagnostic tests and services as well as such other benefits as the policy may provide. The commissioner shall set forth by regulation a statement of the basic benefits which shall be included in the policy. Medical treatments, diagnostic tests, and services provided by the policy shall be rendered in accordance with commonly accepted protocols and professional standards and practices which are commonly accepted as being beneficial for the treatment of the covered injury. Protocols and professional standards and practices which are deemed to be commonly accepted pursuant to this section shall be those recognized by national standard setting organizations, national or state professional organizations of the same discipline as the treating provider, or those designated or approved by the commissioner in consultation with the professional licensing boards in the Division of Consumer Affairs in the Department of Law and Public Safety. The commissioner, in consultation with the Commissioner of the Department of Health and Senior Services and the applicable licensing boards, may reject the use of protocols, standards and practices or lists of diagnostic tests set by any organization deemed not to have standing or general recognition by the provider community or the applicable licensing boards. Protocols shall be deemed to establish guidelines as to standard appropriate treatment and diagnostic tests for injuries sustained in automobile accidents, but the establishment of standard treatment protocols or protocols for the administration of diagnostic tests shall not be interpreted in such a manner as to preclude variance from the standard when warranted by reason of medical necessity. The policy form may provide for the precertification of certain procedures, treatments, diagnostic tests, or other services or for the purchase of durable

medical goods, as approved by the commissioner, provided that the requirement for precertification shall not be unreasonable, and no precertification requirement shall apply within ten days of the insured event. The policy may provide that certain benefits provided by the policy which are in excess of the basic benefits required by the commissioner to be included in the policy may be subject to reasonable copayments in addition to the copayments provided for herein, provided that the copayments shall not be unreasonable and shall be established in such a manner as not to serve to encourage underutilization of benefits subject to the copayments, nor encourage overutilization of benefits. The policy form shall clearly set forth any limitations on benefits or exclusions, which may include, but need not be limited to, benefits which are otherwise compensable under workers' compensation, or benefits for treatments deemed to be experimental or investigational, or benefits deducted pursuant to section 6 of P.L.1972, c. 70 (C.39:6A–6). The commissioner may enlist the services of a benefit consultant in establishing the basic benefits level provided in this subsection, which shall be set forth by regulation no later than 120 days following the enactment date of this amendatory and supplementary act. The commissioner shall not advertise for the consultant as provided in sections 3 and 4 of P.L.1954, c. 48 (C.52:34–8 and 52:34–9).

Medical expense benefits payable under this subsection shall not be assignable, except to a provider of service benefits, in accordance with policy terms approved by the commissioner, nor shall they be subject to levy, execution, attachment or other process for satisfaction of debts. Medical expense benefits payable in accordance with this subsection may be subject to a deductible and copayments as provided for in the policy, if any. No insurer or provider providing service benefits to an insured shall have a right of subrogation for the amount of benefits paid pursuant to any deductible or copayment under this section.

Notwithstanding the provisions of P.L.2003, c. 18, physical therapy treatment shall not be reimbursable as medical expense benefits pursuant to this subsection unless rendered by a licensed physical therapist pursuant to a referral from a licensed physician, dentist, podiatrist or chiropractor within the scope of their respective practices. Notwithstanding the provisions of P.L.2009, c. 56 (C.45:2C–19 et al.), acupuncture treatment shall not be reimbursable as medical expense benefits pursuant to this subsection unless rendered by a licensed acupuncturist pursuant to a referral from a licensed physician within the scope of the physician's practice.

b. Liability insurance coverage insuring against loss resulting from liability imposed by law for property damage sustained by any person arising out of the ownership, maintenance, operation or use of an automobile in an amount or limit of $5,000, exclusive of interest and costs, for damage to property in any one accident.

c. In addition to the aforesaid coverages required to be provided in a basic automobile insurance policy, optional liability insurance coverage insuring against loss resulting from liability imposed by law for bodily injury or death in an amount or limit of $10,000, exclusive of interests and costs, on account of injury to, or death of, one or more persons in any one accident.

If a named insured has elected the basic automobile insurance policy option and an immediate family member or members or relatives resident in his household have one or more policies with the coverages provided for in sections 3 and 4 of P.L.1972, c. 70 (C.39:6A–3 and 39:6A–4), the provisions of section 12 of P.L.1983, c. 362 (C.39:6A–4.2) shall apply.

Every named insured and any other person to whom the basic automobile insurance policy, with or without the optional $10,000 liability coverage insuring against loss resulting from liability imposed by law for bodily injury or death provided for in subsection c. of this section, applies shall be subject to the tort option provided in subsection a. of section 8 of P.L.1972, c. 70 (C.39:6A–8).

No licensed insurance carrier shall refuse to renew the coverage stipulated by this section of an eligible person as defined in section 25 of P.L.1990, c. 8 (C.17:33B–13) except in accordance with the provisions of section 26 of P.L.1988, c. 119 (C.17:29C–7.1) or with the consent of the Commissioner of Banking and Insurance.

L.1998, c. 21, § 4. Amended by L.1998, c. 22, § 1, eff. May 19, 1998; L.2003, c. 18, § 26, eff. Feb. 13, 2003; L.2003, c. 89, § 36, eff. June 9, 2003; L.2009, c. 56, § 17, eff. Nov. 2, 2009.

39:6A–3.2. Automobile policies; minimum required coverages

a. All automobile insurance policies issued or renewed on or after the effective date of P.L.1998, c. 21 (C.39:6A–1.1 et al.) shall be issued or renewed including at least the coverages required pursuant to sections 3 and 4 of P.L.1972, c. 70 (C.39:6A–3 and 39:6A–4), unless the named insured elects a basic automobile insurance policy pursuant to section 4 of P.L.1998, c. 21 (C.39:6A–3.1) or, after the effective date of P.L.2003, c.89 (C.17:30A–2.1 et al.), a special automobile insurance policy pursuant to section 45 of P.L.2003, c.89 (C.39:6A–3.3). Election of a basic automobile insurance policy or a special automobile insurance policy shall be in writing and signed by the named insured on the coverage selection form required by section 17 of P.L.1983, c. 362 (C.39:6A–23). The coverage selection form shall contain a statement, clearly readable and in 12–point bold type, in a form approved by the commissioner, that: (1) election of a basic automobile insurance policy will result in less coverage than the $250,000 medical expense benefits coverage mandated prior to the effective date of P.L.1998, c. 21 (C.39:6A–1.1 et al.); or (2) election of a special automobile insurance policy will result in coverage only

for emergency care. Furthermore, the coverage election form shall contain a statement, clearly readable and in 12–point bold type, in a form approved by the commissioner, that election of a special automobile insurance policy, or a basic automobile insurance policy without the optional $10,000 liability coverage provided for in section 4 of P.L.1998, c. 21 (C.39:6A–3.1) may subject the named insured to a claim or judgment for noneconomic loss which is not covered by the basic or special automobile insurance policy, and which may place his assets at risk, and in the event the named insured is sued, the insurer shall not provide legal counsel.

b. The insurance coverages provided for in section 4 of P.L.1998, c. 21 (C.39:6A–3.1) shall be offered by every insurer which writes insurance coverages pursuant to sections 3 and 4 of P.L.1972, c. 70 (C.39:6A–3 and 39:6A–4) for a period of five years after the effective date of P.L.1998, c. 21 (C.39:6A–1.1 et al.). The commissioner shall require every company writing such insurance coverage to report to him annually during that five-year period as to the number of policies written pursuant to this subsection in the previous year, the number of policies with the coverage offered pursuant to section 4 of P.L.1972, c. 70 (C.39:6A–4) which have been converted to policies with the coverage offered pursuant to section 4 of P.L. 1998, c. 21 (C.39:6A–3.1) and any other information the commissioner may require such as, but not limited to, the age of the policyholders and the territories in which the policyholders reside. The commissioner shall then report to the Governor and the Legislature regarding the acceptance of the basic automobile insurance policy by the automobile insurance consumers of this State annually for the first four years the basic policy is sold. On or before January 1, 2003, the commissioner shall make a final, cumulative report which shall include recommendations as to the continuation of the basic policy to the Governor and the Legislature.

c. The insurance coverages provided for in section 45 of P.L.2003, c.89 (C.39:6A–3.3) shall be offered or provided pursuant to subsection f. of that section for a period of five years after the effective date of P.L.2003, c.89 (C.17:30A–2.1 et al.). On or before January 1, 2008, the commissioner shall make a final report which shall include recommendations as to the continuation of the special policy to the Governor and the Legislature.

L.1998, c. 21, § 5. Amended by L.2003, c. 89, § 46, eff. June 9, 2003.

39:6A–3.3. Automobile insurance policy for low income individuals

a. In order to assist certain low income individuals in this State and encourage their greater compliance in satisfying the mandatory private passenger automobile insurance requirements, the Legislature intends to establish a special automobile insurance policy. The special automobile insurance policy shall be offered only to individuals who qualify for and are actively covered by designated government subsidized programs in the State. For the purpose of this section, "eligible low income individual" means an individual who meets the income criteria established by the commissioner by regulation. In setting the low income criteria, the commissioner shall limit availability to those persons eligible and enrolled in the federal Medicaid program.

b. As an additional option to the mandatory coverage provided in sections 3 and 4 of P.L.1972, c. 70 (C.39:6A–3 and 39:6A–4) or the alternative covered provided in section 4 of P.L.1998, c. 21 (C.39:6A–3.1), an owner or registered owner of an automobile registered or principally garaged in this State, who is an eligible low income individual, may elect a special automobile insurance policy providing the following coverage:

(1) Emergency personal injury protection coverage, for the payment of benefits without regard to negligence, liability or fault of any kind, only to the named insured and dependent members of his family, as defined by the federal Medicaid program, residing in his household, who sustain bodily injury as a result of an accident while occupying, entering into, alighting from or using an automobile, or as a pedestrian, caused by an automobile or by an object propelled by or from an automobile, and to other persons sustaining bodily injury while occupying, entering into, alighting from or using the automobile of the named insured, with the permission of the named insured. "Emergency personal injury protection coverage" issued pursuant to this section means and includes only payment of treatment for emergency care in an amount not to exceed $250,000 per person per accident. "Emergency care" means all medically necessary treatment of a traumatic injury or a medical condition manifesting itself by acute symptoms of sufficient severity such that absence of immediate attention could reasonably be expected to result in: death; serious impairment to bodily functions; or serious dysfunction of a bodily organ or part. Such emergency care shall include all medically necessary care immediately following an automobile accident, including, but not limited to, immediate pre-hospitalization care, transportation to a hospital or trauma center, emergency room care, surgery, critical and acute care. Emergency care extends during the period of initial hospitalization until the patient is discharged from acute care by the attending physician. Emergency care shall be presumed when medical care is initiated at a hospital within 120 hours of the accident. "Emergency personal injury protection coverage" shall also include all medically necessary treatment of permanent or significant brain injury, spinal cord injury or disfigurement after the patient is discharged from acute care. In the event benefits paid by an insurer pursuant to this subsection are in excess of $75,000 on account of bodily injury to any one person in any one accident covered by a policy issued or renewed prior to January 1, 2004, that excess shall be paid by the insurer and shall be reimbursable to the insurer from the Unsatisfied Claim and Judgment

Fund pursuant to section 2 of P.L.1977, c. 310 (C.39:6–73.1);

(2) Death benefit in the amount of $10,000;

(3) The tort option provided in subsection a. of section 8 of P.L.1972, c. 70 (C.39:6A–8) shall apply to every named insured and any other person to whom the special automobile insurance policy applies.

c. A special automobile insurance policy shall not provide liability, collision, comprehensive, uninsured or underinsured motorist coverage.

d. The policy form for special automobile insurance policies shall be subject to the approval of the Commissioner of Banking and Insurance and shall clearly and conspicuously set forth the limitations on benefits provided under the policy.

e. The commissioner shall approve the rating system to be used for a special automobile insurance policy, which shall be administered by the plan created pursuant to section 1 of P.L.1970, c. 215 (C.17:29D–1), to provide a uniform Statewide rate to be utilized by all insurers providing coverage through a special automobile insurance policy. The rate established by the commissioner shall be sufficient to reimburse the insurer for the cost of writing the policy and an amount set by the commissioner to be forwarded to the Unsatisfied Claim and Judgment Fund to offset claims paid by the Unsatisfied Claim and Judgment Fund. The commissioner may adjust the rate annually.

f. Special automobile insurance policies shall be assigned to insurers pursuant to the apportionment methodology of the plan created pursuant to section 1 of P.L.1970, c. 215 (C.17:29D–1). The number of policies assigned pursuant to this subsection shall not be included in the determination of a competitive market pursuant to subsection d. of section 27 of P.L.1990, c. 8 (C.17:33B–15).

L.2003, c. 89, § 45.

39:6A–4. Personal injury protection coverage, regardless of fault

Except as provided by section 45 of P.L.2003, c. 89 (C.39:6A–3.3) and section 4 of P.L.1998, c. 21 (C.39:6A–3.1), every standard automobile liability insurance policy issued or renewed on or after the effective date of P.L.1998, c. 21 (C.39:6A–1.1 et al.) shall contain personal injury protection benefits for the payment of benefits without regard to negligence, liability or fault of any kind, to the named insured and members of his family residing in his household who sustain bodily injury as a result of an accident while occupying, entering into, alighting from or using an automobile, or as a pedestrian, caused by an automobile or by an object propelled by or from an automobile, and to other persons sustaining bodily injury while occupying, entering into, alighting from or using the automobile of the named insured, with permission of the named insured.

"Personal injury protection coverage" means and includes:

a. Payment of medical expense benefits in accordance with a benefit plan provided in the policy and approved by the commissioner, for reasonable, necessary, and appropriate treatment and provision of services to persons sustaining bodily injury, in an amount not to exceed $250,000 per person per accident. In the event benefits paid by an insurer pursuant to this subsection are in excess of $75,000 on account of bodily injury to any one person in any one accident, that excess shall be paid by the insurer and shall be reimbursable to the insurer from the Unsatisfied Claim and Judgment Fund pursuant to section 2 of P.L.1977, c. 310 (C.39:6–73.1). The policy form, which shall be subject to the approval of the commissioner, shall set forth the benefits provided under the policy, including eligible medical treatments, diagnostic tests and services as well as such other benefits as the policy may provide. The commissioner shall set forth by regulation a statement of the basic benefits which shall be included in the policy. Medical treatments, diagnostic tests, and services provided by the policy shall be rendered in accordance with commonly accepted protocols and professional standards and practices which are commonly accepted as being beneficial for the treatment of the covered injury. Protocols and professional standards and practices and lists of valid diagnostic tests which are deemed to be commonly accepted pursuant to this section shall be those recognized by national standard setting organizations, national or state professional organizations of the same discipline as the treating provider, or those designated or approved by the commissioner in consultation with the professional licensing boards in the Division of Consumer Affairs in the Department of Law and Public Safety. The commissioner, in consultation with the Commissioner of the Department of Health and Senior Services and the applicable licensing boards, may reject the use of protocols, standards and practices or lists of diagnostic tests set by any organization deemed not to have standing or general recognition by the provider community or the applicable licensing boards. Protocols shall be deemed to establish guidelines as to standard appropriate treatment and diagnostic tests for injuries sustained in automobile accidents, but the establishment of standard treatment protocols or protocols for the administration of diagnostic tests shall not be interpreted in such a manner as to preclude variance from the standard when warranted by reason of medical necessity. The policy form may provide for the precertification of certain procedures, treatments, diagnostic tests, or other services or for the purchase of durable medical goods, as approved by the commissioner, provided that the requirement for precertification shall not be unreasonable, and no precertification requirement shall apply within ten days of the insured event. The policy may provide that certain benefits provided by the policy which are in excess of the basic benefits required by the commissioner to be included in the policy may be

subject to reasonable copayments in addition to the copayments provided for pursuant to subsection e. of this section, provided that the copayments shall not be unreasonable and shall be established in such a manner as not to serve to encourage underutilization of benefits subject to the copayments, nor encourage overutilization of benefits. The policy form shall clearly set forth any limitations on benefits or exclusions, which may include, but need not be limited to, benefits which are otherwise compensable under workers' compensation, or benefits for treatments deemed to be experimental or investigational, or benefits deducted pursuant to section 6 of P.L.1972, c. 70 (C.39:6A–6). The commissioner may enlist the services of a benefit consultant in establishing the basic benefits level provided in this subsection, which shall be set forth by regulation no later than 120 days following the enactment date of P.L.1998, c. 21 (C.39:6A–1.1 et al.). The commissioner shall not advertise for bids for the consultant as provided in sections 3 and 4 of P.L.1954, c. 48 (C.52:34–8 and 52:34–9).

Notwithstanding the provisions of P.L.2003, c. 18, physical therapy treatment shall not be reimbursable as medical expense benefits pursuant to this subsection unless rendered by a licensed physical therapist pursuant to a referral from a licensed physician, dentist, podiatrist or chiropractor within the scope of their respective practices. Notwithstanding the provisions of P.L.2009, c. 56 (C.45:2C–19 et al.), acupuncture treatment shall not be reimbursable as medical expense benefits pursuant to this subsection unless rendered by a licensed acupuncturist pursuant to a referral from a licensed physician within the scope of the physician's practice.

b. Income continuation benefits. The payment of the loss of income of an income producer as a result of bodily injury disability, subject to a maximum weekly payment of $100. Such sum shall be payable during the life of the injured person and shall be subject to an amount or limit of $5,200, on account of injury to any one person in any one accident, except that in no case shall income continuation benefits exceed the net income normally earned during the period in which the benefits are payable.

c. Essential services benefits. Payment of essential services benefits to an injured person shall be made in reimbursement of necessary and reasonable expenses incurred for such substitute essential services ordinarily performed by the injured person for himself, his family and members of the family residing in the household, subject to an amount or limit of $12 per day. Such benefits shall be payable during the life of the injured person and shall be subject to an amount or limit of $4,380, on account of injury to any one person in any one accident.

d. Death benefits. In the event of the death of an income producer as a result of injuries sustained in an accident entitling such person to benefits under this section, the maximum amount of benefits which could have been paid to the income producer, but for his death, under subsection b. of this section shall be paid to the surviving spouse, or in the event there is no surviving spouse, then to the surviving children, and in the event there are no surviving spouse or surviving children, then to the estate of the income producer.

In the event of the death of one performing essential services as a result of injuries sustained in an accident entitling such person to benefits under subsection c. of this section, the maximum amount of benefits which could have been paid to such person, under subsection c., shall be paid to the person incurring the expense of providing such essential services.

e. Funeral expenses benefits. All reasonable funeral, burial and cremation expenses, subject to a maximum benefit of $1,000, on account of the death of any one person in any one accident shall be payable to the decedent's estate.

Benefits payable under this section shall:

(1) Be subject to any option elected by the policyholder pursuant to section 13 of P.L.1983, c. 362 (C.39:6A–4.3);

(2) Not be assignable, except to a provider of service benefits under this section in accordance with policy terms approved by the commissioner, nor subject to levy, execution, attachment or other process for satisfaction of debts.

Medical expense benefit payments shall be subject to any deductible and any copayment which may be established as provided in the policy. Upon the request of the commissioner or any party to a claim for benefits or payment for services rendered, a provider shall present adequate proof that any deductible or copayment related to that claim has not been waived or discharged by the provider.

No insurer or health provider providing benefits to an insured shall have a right of subrogation for the amount of benefits paid pursuant to any deductible or copayment under this section.

L.1972, c. 70, § 4. Amended by L.1972, c. 203, § 3, eff. Dec. 26, 1972; L.1977, c. 310, § 1, eff. Jan. 5, 1978; L.1981, c. 562, § 1, eff. Jan. 18, 1982; L.1983, c. 362, § 7, eff. Oct. 4, 1983; L.1984, c. 40, § 3, eff. May 15, 1984; L.1988, c. 119, § 3, eff. Jan. 1, 1989; L.1990, c. 8, § 4, eff. March 12, 1990; L.1998, c. 21, § 6; L.1998, c. 22, § 2, eff. May 19, 1998; L.2003, c. 18, § 27, eff. Feb. 13, 2003; L.2003, c. 89, § 37, eff. June 9, 2003; L.2009, c. 56, § 18, eff. Nov. 2, 2009.

39:6A–4.1. Additional automobiles; reduced personal injury protection premium

When a named insured is the owner and only designated operator of two or more automobiles and the only licensed driver residing in the household, he shall be charged a reduced personal injury protection premium for each automobile listed in addition to the principal automobile on the policy in an amount deter-mined by the commissioner for the benefits provided in section 4 of P.L.1972, c. 70 (C. 39:6A–4). Three years after the initial reduction in such premiums the personal injury protection premium for such additional automobiles shall be determined by the loss experience of the rate filer with respect to the payment of personal injury protection benefits which are attributable to such additional automobiles.

L.1983, c. 212, § 1, eff. June 15, 1983.

39:6A–4.2. Primacy of coverages

Except as provided in subsection d. of section 13 of P.L.1983, c. 362 (C. 39:6A–4.3), the personal injury protection coverage of the named insured shall be the primary coverage for the named insured and any resident relative in the named insured's household who is not a named insured under an automobile insurance policy of his own. No person shall recover personal injury protection benefits under more than one automobile insurance policy for injuries sustained in any one accident.

L.1983, c. 362, § 12, eff. Oct. 4, 1983. Amended by L.1990, c. 8, § 5, eff. March 12, 1990.

39:6A–4.3. Personal injury protection coverage options

Personal injury protection coverage options. With respect to personal injury protection coverage provided on an automobile in accordance with section 4 of P.L.1972, c. 70 (C.39:6A–4), the automobile insurer shall provide the following coverage options:

a. Medical expense benefit deductibles in amounts of $500.00, $1,000.00, $2,000.00 and $2,500.00 for any one accident;

b. The option to exclude all benefits offered under subsections b., c., d., and e. of section 4;

c. (Deleted by amendment, P.L.1988, c. 119.)

d. For policies issued or renewed on or after January 1, 1991, the option that other health insurance coverage or benefits of the insured, including health care services provided by a health maintenance organization and any coverage or benefits provided under any federal or State program, are the primary coverage in regard to medical expense benefits pursuant to section 4 of P.L.1972, c. 70 (C.39:6A–4). If health insurance coverage or benefits are primary, an automobile insurer providing medical expense benefits under personal injury protection coverage shall be liable for reasonable medical expenses not covered by the health insurance coverage or benefits up to the limit of the medical expense benefits coverage. The principles of coordination of benefits shall apply to personal injury protection medical expense benefits coverage pursuant to this subsection;

e. Medical expense benefits in amounts of $150,000, $75,000, $50,000 or $15,000 per person per accident; except that, medical expense benefits shall be paid in an amount not to exceed $250,000 for all medically necessary treatment of permanent or significant brain injury, spinal cord injury or disfigurement or for medically necessary treatment of other permanent or significant injuries rendered at a trauma center or acute care hospital immediately following the accident and until the patient is stable, no longer requires critical care and can be safely discharged or transferred to another facility in the judgment of the attending physician. The coverage election form shall contain a statement, clearly readable and in 12–point bold type, in a form approved by the commissioner, that election of any of the aforesaid medical expense benefits options results in less coverage than the $250,000 medical expense benefits coverage mandated prior to the effective date of P.L.1998, c. 21.

If none of the aforesaid medical expense benefits options is affirmatively chosen in writing, the policy shall provide $250,000 medical expense benefits coverage;

f. The insurer shall provide an appropriate reduction from the territorial base rate for personal injury protection coverage for those electing any of the options in subsections a., b., d. and e. of this section.

Any named insured who chooses the option provided by subsection d. of this section shall provide proof that he and members of his family residing in his household are covered by health insurance coverage or benefits in a manner and to an extent approved by the commissioner. Nothing in this section shall be construed to require a health insurer, health maintenance organization or governmental agency to cover individuals or treatment which is not normally covered under the applicable benefit contract or plan. If it is determined that an insured who selected or is otherwise covered by the option provided in subsection d. of this section did not have such health coverage in effect at the time of an accident, medical expense benefits shall be payable by the person's automobile insurer and shall be subject to any deductible required by law or otherwise selected as an option pursuant to subsection a. of this section, any copayment required by law and an additional deductible in the amount of $750.

An option elected by the named insured in accordance with this section shall apply only to the named insured and any resident relative in the named insured's household who is not a named insured under another automobile insurance policy, and not to any other person eligible for personal injury protection benefits required to be provided in accordance with section 4 of P.L.1972, c. 70 (C.39:6A–4).

Medical expense benefits payable in any amount between the deductible selected pursuant to subsection a. of this section and $5,000.00 shall be subject to the copayment provided in the policy, if any.

No insurer or health provider providing benefits to an insured who has elected a deductible pursuant to subsection a. of this section shall have a right of subrogation for the amount of benefits paid pursuant to a deductible elected thereunder or any applicable copayment.

The Commissioner of Banking and Insurance shall adopt rules and regulations to effectuate the purposes of this section and may

promulgate standards applicable to the coordination of personal injury protection medical expense benefits coverage.

L.1983, c. 362, § 13, eff. Oct. 4, 1983. Amended by L.1984, c. 40, § 1, eff. May 15, 1984; L.1988, c. 119, § 38, eff. Jan. 1, 1989; L.1990, c. 8, § 6, eff. March 12, 1990; L.1997, c. 151, § 32, eff. Jan. 1, 1998; L.1998, c. 21, § 7; L.1998, c. 22, § 3, eff. May 19, 1998.

39:6A–4.4. Application of amendment of § 39:6A–4.3 by L.1984, c. 40

The amendments to section 13 of P.L.1983, c. 362 (C. 39:6A–4.3) contained in section 1 of this amendatory and supplementary act shall apply to any accident occurring on or after the effective date of this amendatory and supplementary act involving an automobile insurance policy in force on, or issued on or after that date, under which the named insured has elected a medical expense deductible in accordance with subsection a. of section 13 of P.L.1983, c. 362 (C. 39:6A–4.3). Any additional premium that may be owing on an existing policy by reason of the application of those amendments shall be debited to the account of the named insured and shall be payable at the time of payment of the next policy premium.

L.1984, c. 40, § 4, eff. May 15, 1984.

39:6A–4.5. Failure to maintain required medical expense coverage; effect on recovery for noneconomic loss

a. Any person who, at the time of an automobile accident resulting in injuries to that person, is required but fails to maintain medical expense benefits coverage mandated by section 4 of P.L.1972, c. 70 (C.39:6A–4), section 4 of P.L.1998, c. 21 (C.39:6A–3.1) or section 45 of P.L.2003, c.89 (C.39:6A–3.3) shall have no cause of action for recovery of economic or noneconomic loss sustained as a result of an accident while operating an uninsured automobile.

b. Any person who is convicted of, or pleads guilty to, operating a motor vehicle in violation of R.S.39:4–50, section 2 of P.L.1981, c. 512 (C.39:4–50.4a), or a similar statute from any other jurisdiction, in connection with an accident, shall have no cause of action for recovery of economic or noneconomic loss sustained as a result of the accident.

c. Any person acting with specific intent of causing injury to himself or others in the operation or use of an automobile shall have no cause of action for recovery of economic or noneconomic loss sustained as a result of an accident arising from such conduct.

L.1985, c. 520, § 14, eff. Jan. 21, 1986. Amended by L.1988, c. 119, § 4, eff. Jan. 1, 1989; L.1997, c. 151, § 13, eff. June 30, 1997; L.1998, c. 21, § 8; L.2003, c. 89, § 47, eff. June 9, 2003.

39:6A–4.6. Medical fee schedules for reimbursement of health care providers; biannual review

a. The Commissioner of Banking and Insurance shall, within 90 days after the effective date of P.L.1990, c. 8 (C.17:33B–1 et al.), promulgate medical fee schedules on a regional basis for the reimbursement of health care providers providing services or equipment for medical expense benefits for which payment is to be made by an automobile insurer under personal injury protection coverage pursuant to P.L.1972, c. 70 (C.39:6A–1 et seq.), or by an insurer under medical expense benefits coverage pursuant to section 2 of P.L.1991, c. 154 (C.17:28–1.6). These fee schedules shall be promulgated on the basis of the type of service provided, and shall incorporate the reasonable and prevailing fees of 75% of the practitioners within the region. If, in the case of a specialist provider, there are fewer than 50 specialists within a region, the fee schedule shall incorporate the reasonable and prevailing fees of the specialist providers on a Statewide basis. The commissioner may contract with a proprietary purveyor of fee schedules for the maintenance of the fee schedule, which shall be adjusted biennially for inflation and for the addition of new medical procedures.

b. The fee schedule may provide for reimbursement for appropriate services on the basis of a diagnostic-related (DRG) payment by diagnostic code where appropriate, and may establish the use of a single fee, rather than an unbundled fee, for a group of services if those services are commonly provided together. In the case of multiple procedures performed simultaneously, the fee schedule and regulations promulgated pursuant thereto may also provide for a standard fee for a primary procedure, and proportional reductions in the cost of the additional procedures.

c. No health care provider may demand or request any payment from any person in excess of those permitted by the medical fee schedules established pursuant to this section, nor shall any person be liable to any health care provider for any amount of money which results from the charging of fees in excess of those permitted by the medical fee schedules established pursuant to this section.

Amended by L.1991, c. 154, § 6, eff. Oct. 5, 1991; L.1997, c. 151, § 33, eff. June 30, 1997.

39:6A–4.7. Promulgation of rules and regulations; valid diagnostic tests for persons sustaining bodily injury

The professional licensing boards governing health care providers in the Division of Consumer Affairs shall promulgate, pursuant to the "Administrative Procedure Act," P.L.1968, c. 410 (C.52:14B–1 et seq.), a list of valid diagnostic tests to be used in conjunction with the appropriate health care protocols in the treatment of persons sustaining bodily injury and subject to subsection a. of section 8 of P.L.1972, c. 70 (C.39:6A–8). Inclusion of a test on the list of valid diagnostic tests shall be based on demonstrated medical value, and a level of general acceptance by the relevant provider community and shall not be dependent for results entirely upon subjective patient response. The initial lists shall be promulgated within 180 days of the effective date of this section and shall be revised from time to time as determined by the respective boards to reflect new testing procedures and emerging technologies enjoying a level of general acceptance within the appropriate provider community. In updating its list, a board may take action at a regularly scheduled meeting, notwithstanding the provisions of P.L.1968, c. 410 (C.52:14B–1 et seq.) to the contrary, after notice as provided herein. The professional boards, individually or collectively, may enlist the services of a consulting firm to assist in compiling and updating the list. The Commissioner of Banking and Insurance may reimburse the boards for the cost of the services of the consultant. The list of valid diagnostic tests, once approved by the commissioner shall apply only to benefits under section 4 of P.L.1972, c. 70 (C.39:6A–4) and section 4 of P.L.1998, c.21 (C.39:6A–3.1). The board or boards hiring a consultant shall not advertise for bids, as provided in sections 3 and 4 of P.L.1954, c. 48 (C.52:34–8 and 52:34–9). Notwithstanding any of the provisions of this section to the contrary, a diagnostic test performed in an acute care facility, or extended care facility recognized by Medicare, shall not be excluded from a list of valid diagnostic tests promulgated pursuant to this section.

a. For the purposes of this section, "action" includes, but is not limited to:

(1) the addition or deletion of a test to the list; or

(2) procedures and standards for the performance of a test.

"Action" shall not include the hearing and resolution of contested cases, licensing matters, personnel matters or any other duties of a professional licensing board.

b. Prior to the adoption of an action by the board, the board shall forward the notice of intended action and a detailed description of the intended action to the Office of Administrative Law for publication in the New Jersey Register.

A copy of the text of the intended action shall be available in the Division of Consumer Affairs in accordance with the provisions of P.L.1963, c. 73 (C.47:1A–1 et seq.).

c. The board may hold a public hearing on any intended action.

d. Whether or not a public hearing is held, the board shall afford all interested persons an opportunity to comment in writing on the intended action. Written comments shall be submitted to the board within the time established by the board in the notice of intended action, which time shall not be less than 10 calendar days from the date of notice. The board shall give due consideration to all comments received. A copy of the submissions shall be filed with the Office of Administrative Law for publication in the New Jersey Register.

e. The board may adopt the intended action immediately following the expiration of the public comment period provided in subsection d. of this section, or the hearing provided for in subsection c. of this section, whichever date is later. The final action adopted by the board shall be submitted for publication in the New Jersey Register to the Office of Administrative Law, and shall be effective on the date of the submission or such later date as the board may establish.

f. Actions filed with the Office of Administrative Law pursuant to this section shall be filed subject to the provisions of subsections (a), (c), (d) and (e) of section 5 of P.L.1968, c. 410 (C.52:14B–5).

g. Nothing in this section shall be construed to prohibit the board from adopting any action pursuant to the provisions of the "Administrative Procedure Act," P.L.1968, c. 410 (C.52:14B–1 et seq.).

h. Nothing in this section shall be construed to prohibit the Director of the Division of Consumer Affairs from adopting any rule or regulation pursuant to the provisions of the "Administrative Procedure Act," P.L.1968, c. 410 (C.52:14B–1 et seq.).

L.1998, c. 21, § 12, eff. May 19, 1998.

39:6A–5. Payment of personal injury protection coverage benefits

a. An insurer may require written notice to be given as soon as practicable after an accident involving an automobile with respect to which the policy affords personal injury protection coverage benefits payable under a standard automobile insurance policy pursuant to section 4 of P.L.1972, c. 70 (C.34:6A–4), medical expense benefits payable under a basic automobile insurance policy pursuant to section 4 of P.L.1998, c. 21 (C.39:6A–3.1) or emergency care medical expense benefits payable under a special automobile insurance policy pursuant to section 45 of P.L.2003, c.89 (C.39:6A–3.3). In the case of claims for medical expense benefits under any of those policies, written notice shall be provided to the insurer by the treating health care provider no later than 21 days following the commencement of treatment. Notification required under this section shall be made in accordance with regulations adopted by the Commissioner of Banking and Insurance and on a form prescribed by the Commissioner of Banking and Insurance. Within a reasonable time after receiving notification required pursuant to this act, the insurer shall confirm to the treating health care provider that its policy affords the claimant personal injury protection coverage benefits as required by section 4 of P.L.1972, c.

70 (C.39:6A–4), medical expense benefits pursuant to section 4 of P.L.1998, c. 21 (C.39:6A–3.1) or emergency care medical expense benefits payable under a special automobile insurance policy pursuant to section 45 of P.L.2003, c. 89 (C.39:6A–3.3).

b. For the purposes of this section, notification shall be deemed to be met if a treating health care provider submits a bill or invoice to the insurer for reimbursement of services within 21 days of the commencement of treatment.

c. In the event that notification is not made by the treating health care provider within 21 days following the commencement of treatment, the insurer shall reserve the right to deny, in accordance with regulations established by the Commissioner of Banking and Insurance, payment of the claim and the treating health care provider shall be prohibited from seeking any payment directly from the insured. In establishing the standards for denial of payment, the Commissioner of Banking and Insurance shall consider the length of delay in notification, the severity of the treating health care provider's failure to comply with the notification provisions of this act based upon the potential adverse impact to the public and whether or not the provider has engaged in a pattern of noncompliance with the notification provisions of this act. In establishing the regulations necessary to effectuate the purposes of this subsection, the Commissioner of Banking and Insurance shall define specific instances where the sanctions permitted pursuant to this subsection shall not apply. Such instances may include, but not be limited to, a treating medical provider's failure to provide notification to the insurer as required by this act due to the insured's medical condition during the time period within which notification is required.

d. A health care provider who fails to notify the insurer within 21 days and whose claim for payment has been denied by the insurer pursuant to the standards established by the Commissioner of Banking and Insurance may, in the discretion of a judge of the Superior Court, be permitted to refile such claim provided that the insurer has not been substantially prejudiced thereby. Application to the court for permission to refile a claim shall be made within 14 days of notification of denial of payment and shall be made upon motion based upon affidavits showing sufficient reasons for the failure to notify the insurer within the period of time prescribed by this act.

e. (Deleted by amendment, P.L.1998, c. 21.)

f. In instances when multiple treating health care providers render services in connection with emergency care, the Commissioner of Banking and Insurance shall designate, through regulation, a process whereby notification by one treating health care provider to the insurer shall be deemed to meet the notification requirements of all the treating health care providers who render services in connection with emergency care.

g. Personal injury protection coverage benefits pursuant to section 4 of P.L.1972, c. 70 (C.39:6A–4) and medical expense benefits pursuant to section 4 of P.L.1998, c. 21 (C.39:6A–3.1) or emergency care medical expense benefits payable under a special automobile insurance policy pursuant to section 45 of P.L.2003, c. 89 (C.39:6A–3.3) shall be overdue if not paid within 60 days after the insurer is furnished written notice of the fact of a covered loss and of the amount of same. If such written notice is not furnished to the insurer as to the entire claim, any partial amount supported by written notice is overdue if not paid within 60 days after such written notice is furnished to the insurer. Any part or all of the remainder of the claim that is subsequently supported by written notice is overdue if not paid within 60 days after such written notice is furnished to the insurer; provided, however, that any payment shall not be deemed overdue where, within 60 days of receipt of notice of the claim, the insurer notifies the claimant or his representative in writing of the denial of the claim or the need for additional time, not to exceed 45 days, to investigate the claim, and states the reasons therefor. The written notice stating the need for additional time to investigate the claim shall set forth the number of the insurance policy against which the claim is made, the claim number, the address of the office handling the claim and a telephone number, which is toll free or can be called collect, or is within the claimant's area code. Written notice to the organization administering dispute resolution pursuant to sections 24 and 25 of P.L.1998, c. 21 (C.39:6A–5.1 and C.39:6A–5.2) shall satisfy the notice request for additional time to investigate a claim pursuant to this subsection. For the purpose of determining interest charges in the event the injured party prevails in a subsequent proceeding where an insurer has elected a 45–day extension pursuant to this subsection, payment shall be considered overdue at the expiration of the 45–day period or, if the injured person was required to provide additional information to the insurer, within 10 business days following receipt by the insurer of all the information requested by it, whichever is later.

For the purpose of calculating the extent to which any benefits are overdue, payment shall be treated as being made on the date a draft or other valid instrument which is equivalent to payment was placed in the United States mail in a properly addressed, postpaid envelope, or, if not so posted, on the date of delivery.

h. All overdue payments shall bear interest at the percentage of interest prescribed in the Rules Governing the Courts of the State of New Jersey for judgments, awards and orders for the payment of money.

i. All automobile insurers and the Unsatisfied Claim and Judgment Fund shall provide any claimant with the option of submitting a dispute under this section to dispute resolution pursuant to sections 24 and 25 of P.L.1998, c. 21 (C.39:6A–5.1 and C.39:6A–5.2).

L.1972, c. 70, § 5. Amended by L.1983, c. 362, § 8, eff. Oct. 4, 1983; L.1990, c. 8, § 8, eff. March 12, 1990; L.1995, c. 407, § 1; L.1998, c. 21, § 23; L.2003, c. 89, § 48, eff. June 9, 2003.

39:6A–5.1. Personal injury protection benefits; dispute resolution

a. Any dispute regarding the recovery of medical expense benefits or other benefits provided under personal injury protection coverage pursuant to section 4 of P.L.1972, c. 70 (C.39:6A–4), section 4 of P.L.1998, c. 21 (C.39:6A–3.1) or section 45 of P.L.2003, c.89 (C.39:6A–3.3) arising out of the operation, ownership, maintenance or use of an automobile may be submitted to dispute resolution on the initiative of any party to the dispute, as hereinafter provided.

b. The Commissioner of Banking and Insurance shall designate an organization, and for that purpose may, at his discretion, advertise for proposals, for the purpose of administering dispute resolution proceedings regarding medical expense benefits and other benefits provided under personal injury protection pursuant to section 4 of P.L.1972, c. 70 (C.39:6A–4), medical expense benefits coverage pursuant to section 4 of P.L.1998, c. 21 (C.39:6A–3.1) or emergency care medical expense benefits pursuant to section 45 of P.L.2003, c. 89 (C.39:6A–3.3). The commissioner shall promulgate rules and regulations with respect to the conduct of the dispute resolution proceedings. The organization administering dispute resolution shall utilize qualified professionals who serve on a full-time basis and who meet standards of competency established by the commissioner. The commissioner shall establish standards of performance for the organization to ensure the independence and fairness of the review process, including, but not limited to, standards relative to the professional qualifications of the professionals presiding over the dispute resolution process, and standards to ensure that no conflict of interest exists which would prevent the professional from performing his duties in an impartial manner. The standards of performance shall include a requirement that the organization establish an advisory council composed of parties who are users of the dispute resolution mechanism established herein. The commissioner may contract with a consulting firm for the formulation of the standards of performance of the organization and establishment of qualifications for the persons who are to conduct the dispute resolution proceedings. The commissioner shall not advertise for bids for the consulting firm, as provided in sections 3 and 4 of P.L.1954, c. 48 (C.52: 34–8 and 52:34–9). Compensation to the dispute resolution professionals shall be established by the commissioner and adjusted from time to time as appropriate, with the approval of the commissioner. In no case shall compensation be paid on a contingency basis. The organization shall establish a dispute resolution plan, which shall include procedures and rules governing the dispute resolution process and provisions for monitoring the dispute resolution process to ensure adherence to the standards of performance established by the commissioner. The plan, and any amendments thereto, shall be subject to the approval of the commissioner.

c. Dispute resolution proceedings under this section 24 and section 25 of this amendatory and supplementary act shall include disputes arising regarding medical expense benefits provided under subsection a. of section 4 of P.L.1972, c. 70 (C.39:6A–4), section 4 of P.L.1998, c. 21 (C.39:6A–3.1) or section 45 of P.L.2003, c. 89 (C.39:6A–3.3), benefits provided pursuant to subsection b., c., d. or e. of section 4 of P.L.1972, c. 70 (C.39:6A–4), subsection b., c., d. or e. of section 7 of P.L.1972, c. 198 (C.39:6–86.1), and disputes as to additional first party coverage benefits required to be offered pursuant to section 10 of P.L.1972, c. 70 (C.39:6A–10). Disputes involving medical expense benefits may include, but not necessarily be limited to, matters concerning: (1) interpretation of the insurance contract; (2) whether the treatment or health care service which is the subject of the dispute resolution proceeding is in accordance with the provisions of section 4 of P.L.1972, c. 70 (C.39:6A–4), section 4 of P.L.1998, c. 21 (C.39:6A–3.1) or section 45 of P.L.2003, c. 89 (C.39: 6A–3.3) or the terms of the policy; (3) the eligibility of the treatment or service for compensation; (4) the eligibility of the provider performing the treatment or service to be compensated under the terms of the policy or under regulations promulgated by the commissioner, including whether the person is licensed or certified to perform such treatment; (5) whether the disputed medical treatment was actually performed; (6) whether diagnostic tests performed in connection with the treatment are those recognized by the commissioner; (7) the necessity or appropriateness of consultations by other health care providers; (8) disputes involving application of and adherence to fee schedules promulgated by the commissioner; and (9) whether the treatment performed is reasonable, necessary, and compatible with the protocols provided for pursuant to P.L.1998, c. 21 (C.39:6A–1.1 et al.). The dispute resolution professionals may review the entire claims file of the insurer, subject to any confidentiality requirement established pursuant to State or federal law. All decisions of the dispute resolution professional shall be in writing, in a form prescribed by the commissioner, shall state the issues in dispute, the findings and conclusions on which the decision is based, and shall be signed by the dispute resolution professional. All decisions of a dispute resolution professional shall be binding. The dispute resolution organization shall provide for the retention of all documents used in dispute resolution proceedings under this section and section 25 of this amendatory and supplementary act, including the written decision, for a period of at least five years, in a form approved by the commissioner, or for such additional time as may be established by the commissioner. The written decisions of the dispute resolution professional shall be forwarded to the commissioner, who shall establish a record of the proceedings conducted under the dispute resolution procedure, which shall be accessible to the public and may be used as guidance in subsequent dispute resolution proceedings.

d. With respect to disputes as to the diagnosis, the medical necessity of the treatment or diagnostic test administered to the injured person, whether the injury is causally related to the insured event or is the product of a preexisting condition, or disputes as to the appropriateness of the protocols utilized by the provider, the dispute resolution professional shall, either at his option or at the request of any party to the dispute, refer the matter to a medical review organization for a determination. The determination of the medical review organization on the dispute referred shall be presumed to be correct by the dispute resolution professional, which presumption may be rebutted by a preponderance of the evidence. Should the dispute resolution professional find that the decision of the medical review organization is not correct, the reasons supporting that finding shall be set forth in the dispute resolution professional's written decision.

e. Any person submitting a matter to the dispute resolution process established herein may submit for review all or a portion of a disputed treatment or treatments or a dispute regarding a diagnostic test or tests or a dispute regarding the providing of services or durable medical goods. Any portion of a treatment or diagnostic test or service which is not under review shall be reimbursed in accordance with the provisions of section 5 of P.L.1972, c. 70 (C.39:6A–5). If the dispute resolution proceeding results in a determination that all or part of a treatment or treatments, diagnostic test or tests or service performed, or durable medical goods provided are medically necessary and appropriate, reimbursement shall be made with interest payable in accordance with the provisions of section 5 of P.L.1972, c. 70 (C.39:6A–5).

L.1998, c. 21, § 24. Amended by L.1998, c. 22, § 4, eff. May 19, 1998; L.2003, c. 89, § 49, eff. June 9, 2003.

39:6A–5.2. Medical review organizations; certification standards

a. The commissioner shall establish standards for the certification of medical review organizations, which shall include standards of performance formulated by the commissioner in consultation with the Commissioner of Health and Senior Services. The standards of performance shall set forth procedures to ensure a timely and impartial review of the medical records of the injured person by a medical review organization, including, but not limited to, a review of the necessity or appropriateness of treatments for injuries, including diagnostic tests, sustained in an automobile accident. The commissioner shall establish standards for persons conducting the medical review, including standards with respect to credentials, experience, licensure, fees, and confidentiality. The standards shall include a requirement that all persons performing reviews are New Jersey licensed or certified health care providers, and a requirement that any medical review panel contain a health care provider licensed or certified in the same profession as the treating health care provider and that it contain a sufficient representation of reviewers to judge the appropriateness of treatment or treatments in dispute, including, but not limited to, the medical necessity of such treatments, appropriateness of the protocols used by the treating provider, issues regarding causality and preexisting conditions, the appropriateness and efficacy of diagnostic tests performed in connection with the diagnosis, and whether the diagnostic tests meet the requirements established by the commissioner. The commissioner may contract with a consultant for the formulation of the standards governing the certification of the persons conducting the medical reviews. The commissioner shall not advertise for bids for the consultant, as provided in sections 3 and 4 of P.L.1954, c. 48 (C.52:34–8 and 52:34–9).

b. Before certifying a medical review organization to receive referrals from dispute resolution proceedings, the commissioner shall determine that the organization has a sufficient number of qualified health care providers, by specialty, to perform the reviews, has a satisfactory procedure for maintaining the confidentiality of medical records, is not owned or controlled by an insurer, and has met any other requirements established by the commissioner.

c. The medical review organization shall establish and utilize written review procedures, which shall be filed with the commissioner. Every determination made by a medical review organization shall be in writing and shall be retained by the organization for a period of no less than five years.

d. The medical review organization may review the medical treatment or treatments in dispute to determine whether: (1) the treatment or diagnostic test being given for the injury or the services provided in connection with the injury is medically necessary; (2) the treatment is in accordance with or compatible with medically recognized standard protocols, professional standards, and commonly accepted medical practice in the same health care discipline as the treating provider; (3) the treatment is consistent with the symptoms or diagnosis of the injury; (4) the treatment or health care service is related to the injury sustained in the insured event, or is required for the diagnosis, evaluation or confirmation of the injury; (5) the treatment is of a palliative, rather than restorative, nature; and (6) medical procedures, treatment, or testing which have been repeated are medically necessary and consistent with standard practice.

e. Cases referred by a dispute resolution professional for medical review shall be referred to appropriate certified medical reviewers affiliated with the certified medical review organization by a dispute resolution organization. The dispute resolution organization shall forward the referrals to certified medical reviewers on a random basis, so that there is a relatively equal apportionment among all medical reviewers. Referrals shall be made in such a manner so as not to disclose to the medical reviewers the identity of the insurer, nor shall the identity of the reviewer be disclosed to the insurer.

f. When appropriate in the context of its review of services or treatments under dispute, a medical reviewer may request and shall receive a written report or copy of the provider's records regarding the case history, treatment dates, or the dates diagnostic tests or other services were performed, and the provider's projected treatment plan. The injured person or provider, as applicable, shall provide or make available to the medical reviewer any pertinent medical records or medical history which the medical reviewer may request. The medical reviewer shall complete its review and make a determination within 20 business days of receipt of all of the requested information from the dispute resolution professional or provider, as the case may be. The medical reviewer shall submit its determination in writing to the referring dispute resolution organization, which shall forward it to the dispute resolution professional.

g. The cost of the proceedings shall be apportioned by the dispute resolution professional. Fees shall be determined to be reasonable if they are consonant with the amount of the award, in accordance with a schedule established by the New Jersey Supreme Court. If the treatment, diagnostic test, or service performed is not determined to be medically necessary or appropriate, the injured person shall not be liable to pay the provider the disputed amount.

L.1998, c. 21, § 25.

Historical and Statutory Notes

L.1998, c. 21, § 74, approved May 19, 1998, provides:

"a. This act shall take effect 90 days following the establishment by the Commissioner of Banking and Insurance of basic benefits required to be provided pursuant to section 4 of P.L.1972, c. 70 (C.39:6A–4) or the adoption by rule of the professional boards of the designation of valid diagnostic tests pursuant to the provisions of section 12 of this act, whichever is later, except that 1: (1) sections 47 through 61 shall take effect on the 90th day after the date of enactment; (2) sections 1, 12, 26 through 46, 62 through 65 and 67 shall take effect immediately.

"b. Prior to the effective date of any section of this act, the Commissioner of Banking and Insurance may take those actions and promulgate those regulations necessary to implement the provisions of this act."

39:6A–6. Collateral source

The benefits provided in sections 4 and 10 of P.L.1972, c. 70 (C.39:6A–4 and 39:6A–10), the medical expense benefits provided in section 4 of P.L.1998, c. 21 (C.39:6A–3.1) and the benefits provided in section 45 of P.L.2003, c. 89 (C.39:6A–3.3) shall be payable as loss accrues, upon written notice of such loss and without regard to collateral sources, except that benefits, collectible under workers' compensation insurance, employees' temporary disability benefit statutes, Medicare provided under federal law, and benefits, in fact collected, that are provided under federal law to active and retired military personnel shall be deducted from the benefits collectible under sections 4 and 10 of P.L.1972,

c. 70 (C.39:6A–4 and 39:6A–10), the medical expense benefits provided in section 4 of P.L.1998, c. 21 (C.39:6A–3.1) and the benefits provided in section 45 of P.L.2003, c. 89 (C.39:6A–3.3).

If an insurer has paid those benefits and the insured is entitled to, but has failed to apply for, workers' compensation benefits or employees' temporary disability benefits, the insurer may immediately apply to the provider of workers' compensation benefits or of employees' temporary disability benefits for a reimbursement of any benefits pursuant to sections 4 and 10 of P.L.1972, c. 70 (C.39:6A–4 and 39:6A–10), medical expense benefits pursuant to section 4 of P.L.1998, c. 21 (C.39:6A–3.1) or benefits pursuant to section 45 of P.L.2003, c. 89 (C.39:6A–3.3) it has paid.

L.1972, c. 70, § 6. Amended by L.1972, c. 203, § 4, eff. Dec. 26, 1972; L.1981, c. 95, § 1, eff. March 31, 1981; L.1983, c. 362, § 9, eff. Oct. 4, 1983; L.1998, c. 21, § 9; L.2003, c. 89, § 50, eff. June 9, 2003.

39:6A–7. Exclusions

a. Insurers may exclude a person from benefits under sections 4 and 10 of P.L.1972, c. 70 (C.39:6A–4 and 39:6A–10), medical expense benefits provided in section 4 of P.L.1998, c. 21 (C.39:6A–3. 1) and benefits provided in section 45 of P.L.2003, c. 89 (C.39:6A–3.3) if that person's conduct contributed to his personal injuries or death occurred in any of the following ways:

(1) while committing a high misdemeanor or felony or seeking to avoid lawful apprehension or arrest by a police officer; or

(2) while acting with specific intent of causing injury or damage to himself or others.

b. An insurer may also exclude from the benefits provided in sections 4 and 10 of P.L.1972, c. 70 (C.39:6A–4 and 39:6A–10), the medical expense benefits provided in section 4 of P.L.1998, c. 21 (C.39:6A–3.1) and benefits provided in section 45 of P.L.2003, c. 89 (C.39:6A–3.3) any person having incurred injuries or death, who, at the time of the accident:

(1) was the owner or registrant of an automobile registered or principally garaged in this State that was being operated without personal injury protection coverage;

(2) was occupying or operating an automobile without the permission of the owner or other named insured;

(3) was a person other than the named insured or a member of the named insured's family residing in his household, if that person is entitled to coverage under section 4 or section 10 of P.L.1972, c. 70 (C.39:6A–4 or 39:6A–10), or both, section 4 of P.L.1998, c. 21 (C.39:6A–3.1) or section 45 of P.L.2003, c. 89 (C.39:6A–3.3), as a named insured or member of the named insured's family residing in his household under the terms of another policy; or

(4) was a member of the named insured's family residing in the named insured's household, if that person is entitled to coverage under section 4 or section 10 of P.L.1972, c. 70 (C.39:6A–4 or 39:6A–10), or both, section 4 of P.L.1998, c. 21 (C.39:6A–3.1) or section 45 of P.L.2003, c. 89 (C.39:6A–3.3) as a named insured under the terms of another policy.

L.1972, c. 70, § 7. Amended by L.1972, c. 203, § 5, eff. Dec. 26, 1972; L.1983, c. 362, § 10, eff. Oct. 4, 1983; L.1997, c. 270, § 1, eff. Dec. 22, 1997; L.1998, c. 21, § 10; L.2003, c. 89, § 51, eff. June 9, 2003.

39:6A–8. Tort exemption; limitation on the right to noneconomic loss

One of the following two tort options shall be elected, in accordance with section 14.1 of P.L.1983, c. 362 (C.39:6A–8.1), by any named insured required to maintain personal injury protection coverage pursuant to section 4 of P.L.1972, c. 70 (C.39:6A–4):

a. Limitation on lawsuit option. Every owner, registrant, operator or occupant of an automobile to which section 4 of P.L.1972, c. 70 (C.39:6A–4), personal injury protection coverage, section 4 of P.L.1998, c. 21 (C.39:6A–3.1), medical expense benefits coverage, or section 45 of P.L.2003, c.89 (C.39:6A–3.3) regardless of fault, applies, and every person or organization legally responsible for his acts or omissions, is hereby exempted from tort liability for noneconomic loss to a person who is subject to this subsection and who is either a person who is required to maintain personal injury protection coverage pursuant to section 4 of P.L.1972, c. 70 (C.39:6A–4), medical expense benefits pursuant to section 4 of P.L.1998, c. 21 (C.39:6A–3.1) or benefits pursuant to section 45 of P.L.2003, c.89 (C.39:6A–3.3), or is a person who has a right to receive benefits under section 4 of P.L.1972, c. 70 (C.39:6A–4), section 4 of P.L.1998, c. 21 (C.39:6A–3.1) or section 45 of P.L.2003, c.89 (C.39:6A–3.3), as a result of bodily injury, arising out of the ownership, operation, maintenance or use of such automobile in this State, unless that person has sustained a bodily injury which results in death; dismemberment; significant disfigurement or significant scarring; displaced fractures; loss of a fetus; or a permanent injury within a reasonable degree of medical probability, other than scarring or disfigurement. An injury shall be considered permanent when the body part or organ, or both, has not healed to function normally and will not heal to function normally with further medical treatment. For the purposes of this subsection, " physician" means a physician as defined in section 5 of P. L.1939, c. 115 (C.45:9–5.1).

In order to satisfy the tort option provisions of this subsection, the plaintiff shall, within 60 days following the date of the answer to the complaint by the defendant, provide the defendant with a certification from the licensed treating physician or a board-certified licensed physician to whom the plaintiff was referred by the treating physician. The certification shall state, under penalty of perjury, that the plaintiff has sustained an injury described above. The certification shall be based on and refer to objective clinical evidence, which may include medical testing, except that any such testing shall be performed in accordance with medical protocols pursuant to subsection a. of section 4 of P.L.1972, c. 70 (C.39:6A–4) and the use of valid diagnostic tests administered in accordance with section 12 of P.L.1998, c. 21 (C.39:6A–4.7). Such testing may not be experimental in nature or dependent entirely upon subjective patient response. The court may grant no more than one additional period not to exceed 60 days to file the certification pursuant to this subsection upon a finding of good cause.

A person is guilty of a crime of the fourth degree if that person purposefully or knowingly makes, or causes to be made, a false, fictitious, fraudulent, or misleading statement of material fact in, or omits a material fact from, or causes a material fact to be omitted from, any certification filed pursuant to this subsection. Notwithstanding the provisions of subsection e. of N.J.S.2C:44–1, the court shall deal with a person who has been convicted of a violation of this subsection by imposing a sentence of imprisonment unless, having regard to the character and condition of the person, the court is of the opinion that imprisonment would be a serious injustice which overrides the need to deter such conduct by others. If the court imposes a noncustodial or probationary sentence, such sentence shall not become final for 10 days in order to permit the appeal of such sentence by the prosecution. Nothing in this subsection a. shall preclude an indictment and conviction for any other offense defined by the laws of this State. In addition, any professional license held by the person shall be forfeited according to the procedures established by section 4 of P.L.1997, c. 353 (C.2C:51–5); or

b. No limitation on lawsuit option. As an alternative to the basic tort option specified in subsection a. of this section, every owner, registrant, operator, or occupant of an automobile to which section 4 of P.L.1972, c. 70 (C.39:6A–4), personal injury protection coverage, section 4 of P.L.1998, c. 21 (C.39:6A–3.1), medical expense benefits coverage, or section 45 of P.L.2003, c.89 (C.39:6A–3.3), regardless of fault, applies, and every person or organization legally responsible for his acts or omissions, shall be liable for noneconomic loss to a person who is subject to this subsection and who is either a person who is required to maintain the coverage mandated by P.L.1972, c. 70 (C.39:6A–1 et seq.) or is a person who has a right to receive benefits under section 4 of that act (C.39:6A–4), as a result of bodily injury, arising out of the ownership, operation, maintenance or use of such automobile in this State.

The tort option provisions of subsection b. of this section shall also apply to the right to recover for noneconomic loss of any person eligible for benefits pursuant to section 4 of P.L.1972, c. 70 (C.39:6A–4), section 4 of P.L.1998, c. 21 (C.39:6A–3.1) or section 45 of P.L.2003, c.89 (C.39:6A–3.3) but who is not required

to maintain personal injury protection coverage pursuant to section 4 of P.L.1972, c. 70 (C.39: 6A–4), medical expense benefits coverage pursuant to section 4 of P.L.1998, c. 21 (C.39:6A–3.1) or benefits pursuant to section 45 of P.L.2003, c.89 (C.39:6A–3.3) and is not an immediate family member, as defined in section 14.1 of P.L.1983, c. 362 (C.39:6A–8.1), under a standard automobile insurance policy or basic automobile insurance policy.

The tort option provisions of subsection a. of this section shall also apply to any person subject to section 14 of P.L.1985, c. 520 (C.39:6A–4.5) and to every named insured and any other person to whom the benefits of the special automobile insurance policy provided in section 45 of P.L.2003, c.89 (C.39:6A–3.3) or the medical expense benefits of the basic automobile insurance policy pursuant to section 4 of P. L.1998, c. 21 (C.39:6A–3.1) apply whether or not the person has elected the optional $10,000 liability coverage insuring against loss resulting from liability imposed by law for bodily injury or death provided for in subsection c. of section 4 of P.L.1998, c. 21 (C.39:6A–3.1).

The tort option provisions of subsections a. and b. of this section as provided in this 1998 amendatory and supplementary act shall apply to automobile insurance policies issued or renewed on or after the effective date of P.L.1998, c. 21 (C.39:6A–1.1 et al.) and as otherwise provided by law.

L.1972, c. 70, § 8. Amended by L.1972, c. 203, § 6, eff. Dec. 26, 1972; L.1983, c. 362, § 14, eff. Oct. 4, 1983; L.1985, c. 520, § 15, eff. Jan. 21, 1986; L.1988, c. 119, § 6, eff. Jan. 1, 1989; L.1990, c. 8, § 9, eff. March 12, 1990; L.1998, c. 21, § 11; L.2003, c. 89, § 52, eff. June 9, 2003.

39:6A–8.1. Election of tort option

a. Election of a tort option pursuant to section 8 of P.L.1972, c. 70 (C. 39:6A–8) shall be in writing and signed by the named insured on the coverage selection form required by section 17 of P.L.1983, c. 362 (C. 39:6A–23). The form shall state the percentage difference in the premium rates or the dollar savings between the two tort options. The tort option elected shall apply to the named insured and any immediate family member residing in the named insured's household. "Immediate family member" means the spouse of the named insured and any child of the named insured or spouse residing in the named insured's household, who is not a named insured under another automobile insurance policy.

b. If the named insured fails to elect, in writing, any of the tort options offered pursuant to section 8 of P.L.1972, c. 70 (C. 39:6A–8), the named insured shall be deemed to elect the tort option of subsection a. of that section 8.

c. The tort option elected by a named insured for an automobile policy issued or renewed on or after January 1, 1989 shall continue in force as to subsequent renewal or replacement policies until the insurer or its authorized representative receives a properly executed form electing the other tort option.

d. The tort option elected by the named insured shall apply to all automobiles owned by the named insured and to any immediate family member who is not a named insured under another automobile insurance policy, except that in the case where more than one policy is applicable to the named insured or immediate family member, and the policies have different tort options, the tort option elected by the injured named insured shall apply or, in the case of an immediate family member who is not a named insured and is injured in an accident involving an automobile to which a policy issued to a named insured in the household of the injured immediate family member applies, the tort option elected by that named insured shall apply.

e. Notwithstanding any other provision of law to the contrary, no person, including, but not limited to, an insurer, an insurance producer as defined in section 2 of P.L.1987, c. 293 (C. 17:22A–2), a servicing carrier or non-insurer servicing carrier acting in that capacity pursuant to P.L.1983, c. 65 (C. 17:30E–1 et seq.), and the New Jersey Automobile Full Insurance Underwriting Association created pursuant to P.L.1983, c. 65 (C. 17:30E–1 et seq.), shall be liable in an action for damages on account of the election of a tort option by a named insured or on account of the tort option imposed pursuant to subsection b. of this section or otherwise imposed by law. Nothing in this subsection shall be deemed to grant immunity to any person causing damage as the result of his willful, wanton or grossly negligent act of commission or omission.

In the case of automobile insurance policies in force on January 1, 1989, notice of the tort options available pursuant to the aforesaid section 8 shall be given in accordance with section 17 of P.L.1983, c. 362 (C. 39:6A–23).

L.1983, c. 362, § 14.1, eff. Oct. 4, 1983. Amended by L.1988, c. 119, § 7, eff. Jan. 1, 1989.

39:6A–9. Inoperative

39:6A–9.1. Recovery of personal injury protection benefits from tortfeasor

An insurer, health maintenance organization or governmental agency paying benefits pursuant to subsection a., b. or d. of section 13 of P.L.1983, c. 362 (C.39:6A–4.3), personal injury protection benefits in accordance with section 4 or section 10 of P.L.1972, c. 70 (C.39:6A–4 or 39:6A–10), medical expense benefits pursuant to section 4 of P.L.1998, c. 21 (C.39:6A–3.1) or benefits pursuant to section 45 of P.L.2003, c.89 (C.39:6A–3.3), as a result of an accident occurring within this State, shall, within two years of the filing of the claim, have right to recover the amount of payments from any tortfeasor who was not, at the time of the accident, required to maintain personal injury protection or medical expense benefits coverage, other

than for pedestrians, under the laws of this State, including personal injury protection coverage required to be provided in accordance with section 18 of P.L.1985, c. 520 (C.17:28–1.4), or although required did not maintain personal injury protection or medical expense benefits coverage at the time of the accident. In the case of an accident occurring in this State involving an insured tortfeasor, the determination as to whether an insurer, health maintenance organization or governmental agency is legally entitled to recover the amount of payments and the amount of recovery, including the costs of processing benefit claims and enforcing rights granted under this section, shall be made against the insurer of the tortfeasor, and shall be by agreement of the involved parties or, upon failing to agree, by arbitration.

L.1983, c. 362, § 20, eff. Oct. 4, 1983. Amended by L.1985, c. 520, § 17, eff. Jan. 21, 1986; L.1990, c. 8, § 10, eff. March 12, 1990; L.1998, c. 21, § 13; L.2003, c. 89, § 53, eff. June 9, 2003.

39:6A–10. Additional personal injury protection coverage

Insurers shall make available to the named insured electing the standard automobile insurance policy and covered under section 4 of P.L.1972, c. 70 (C.39:6A–4), and, at his option, to resident relatives in the household of the named insured, suitable additional first party coverage for income continuation benefits, essential services benefits, death benefits and funeral expense benefits, but the income continuation and essential services benefits shall cease upon the death of the claimant, and shall not operate to increase the amount of any death benefits payable under section 4 of P.L.1972, c. 70 (C.39:6A–4) and such additional first party coverage shall be payable only to the extent that the claimant establishes that the amount of loss sustained exceeds the coverage specified in section 4 of P.L.1972, c. 70 (C.39:6A–4). Insurers may also make available to named insureds electing a standard automobile insurance policy and covered under section 4 of P.L.1972, c. 70 (C.39:6A–4), and, at their option, to resident relatives in the household of the named insured or to other persons provided medical expense benefits coverage pursuant to section 4 of P.L.1972, c. 70 (C.39:6A–4), or both, additional first party medical expense benefits coverage. The additional coverage shall be offered by the insurer at least annually as part of the coverage selection form applicable to the standard automobile insurance policy and required by section 17 of P.L.1983, c. 362 (C.39:6A–23). Income continuation in excess of that provided for in section 4 of P.L.1972, c. 70 (C.39:6A–4) shall be provided as an option by insurers for disabilities, as long as the disability persists, up to an income level of $35,000.00 per year, provided that a. the excess between $5,200.00 and the amount of coverage contracted for shall be written on the basis of 75% of said difference, and b. regardless of the duration of the disability, the benefits payable shall not exceed the total maximum amount of income continuation benefits contracted for. Death benefits provided pursuant to this section shall be payable without regard to the period of time elapsing between the date of the accident and the date of death, if death occurs within two years of the accident and results from bodily injury from that accident to which coverage under this section applies. The Commissioner of Banking and Insurance is hereby authorized and empowered to establish, by rule or regulation, the amounts and terms of income continuation insurance to be provided pursuant to this section.

L.1972, c. 70, § 10.   Amended by L.1972, c. 203, § 8, eff. Dec. 26, 1972; L.1981, c. 533, § 1; L.1985, c. 520, § 16; L.1990, c. 8, § 11, eff. March 12, 1990; L.1998, c. 21, § 14.

Historical and Statutory Notes

L.1998, c. 21, § 74, approved May 19, 1998, provides:

"a. This act shall take effect 90 days following the establishment by the Commissioner of Banking and Insurance of basic benefits required to be provided pursuant to section 4 of P.L.1972, c. 70 (C.39:6A-4) or the adoption by rule of the professional boards of the designation of valid diagnostic tests pursuant to the provisions of section 12 of this act, whichever is later, except that 1: (1) sections 47 through 61 shall take effect on the 90th day after the date of enactment; (2) sections 1, 12, 26 through 46, 62 through 65 and 67 shall take effect immediately.

"b.   Prior to the effective date of any section of this act, the Commissioner of Banking and Insurance may take those actions and promulgate those regulations necessary to implement the provisions of this act."

39:6A-11.   Contribution among insurers

If two or more insurers are liable to pay benefits under sections 4 and 10 of P.L.1972, c. 70 (C.39:6A-4 and 39:6A-10) under a standard automobile insurance policy for the same bodily injury, or death, of any one person, the maximum amount payable shall be as specified in those sections 4 and 10 of P.L.1972, c. 70 (C.39:6A-4 and 39:6A-10), section 4 of P.L.1998, c. 21 (C.39:6A-3.1) and section 45 of P.L.2003, c. 89 (C.39:6A-3.3), respectively, if additional first party coverage applies and any insurer paying the benefits shall be entitled to recover from each of the other insurers, only by inter-company arbitration or inter-company agreement, an equitable pro-rata share of the benefits paid.

L.1972, c. 70, § 11.   Amended by L.1998, c. 21, § 15; L.2003, c. 89, § 54, eff. June 9, 2003.

39:6A-12.   Inadmissibility of evidence of losses collectible under personal injury protection coverage

Except as may be required in an action brought pursuant to section 20 of P.L.1983, c. 362 (C.39:6A-9.1), evidence of the amounts collectible or paid under a standard automobile insurance policy pursuant to sections 4 and 10 of P.L.1972, c. 70 (C.39:6A-4 and 39:6A-10), amounts collectible or paid for medical expense benefits under a basic automobile insurance

policy pursuant to section 4 of P.L.1998, c. 21 (C.39:6A-3.1) and amounts collectible or paid for benefits under a special automobile insurance policy pursuant to section 45 of P.L.2003, c.89 (C.39:6A-3.3), to an injured person, including the amounts of any deductibles, copayments or exclusions, including exclusions pursuant to subsection d. of section 13 of P.L. 1983, c. 362 (C.39:6A-4.3), otherwise compensated is inadmissible in a civil action for recovery of damages for bodily injury by such injured person.

The court shall instruct the jury that, in arriving at a verdict as to the amount of the damages for noneconomic loss to be recovered by the injured person, the jury shall not speculate as to the amount of the medical expense benefits paid or payable by an automobile insurer under personal injury protection coverage payable under a standard automobile insurance policy pursuant to sections 4 and 10 of P.L.1972, c. 70 (C.39:6A-4 and 39:6A-10), medical expense benefits under a basic automobile insurance policy pursuant to section 4 of P.L.1998, c. 21 (C.39:6A-3.1) or benefits under a special automobile insurance policy pursuant to section 45 of P.L.2003, c. 89 (C.39:6A-3.3)) to the injured person, nor shall they speculate as to the amount of benefits paid or payable by a health insurer, health maintenance organization or governmental agency under subsection d. of section 13 of P.L.1983, c. 362 (C.39:6A-4.3).

Nothing in this section shall be construed to limit the right of recovery, against the tortfeasor, of uncompensated economic loss sustained by the injured party.

L.1972, c. 70, § 12.   Amended by L.1983, c. 362, § 11, eff. Oct. 4, 1983; L.1988, c. 119, § 44, eff. Jan. 1, 1989; L.1990, c. 8, § 12, eff. March 12, 1990; L.1998, c. 21, § 16; L.2003, c. 89, § 55, eff. June 9, 2003.

39:6A-13.   Discovery of facts as to personal injury protection coverage

Discovery of facts as to personal injury protection coverage. The following apply to personal injury protection coverage benefits payable under a standard automobile insurance policy pursuant to sections 4 and 10 of P.L.1972, c. 70 (C.39:6A-4 and 39:6A-10), medical expense benefits payable under a basic automobile insurance policy pursuant to section 4 of P.L.1998, c. 21 (C.39:6A-3.1) and benefits payable under a special automobile insurance policy pursuant to section 45 of P.L.2003, c. 89 (C.39:6A-3.3):

a. Every employer shall, if a request is made by an insurer or the Unsatisfied Claim and Judgment Fund providing personal injury protection benefits under a standard automobile insurance policy or medical expense benefits payable under a basic automobile insurance policy against whom a claim has been made, furnish forthwith, in a form approved by the Commissioner of Banking and Insurance, a signed statement of the lost earnings since the date of the bodily injury and for a reasonable period before the injury, of the person upon whose injury the claim is based.

b. Every physician, hospital, or other health care provider providing, before and after the bodily injury upon which a claim for personal injury protection benefits or medical expense benefits is based, any products, services or accommodations in relation to such bodily injury or any other injury, or in relation to a condition claimed to be connected with such bodily injury or any other injury, shall, if requested to do so by the insurer or the Unsatisfied Claim and Judgment Fund against whom the claim has been made, furnish forthwith a written report of the history, condition, treatment, dates and costs of such treatment of the injured person, and produce forthwith and permit the inspection and copying of his or its records regarding such history, condition, treatment dates and costs of treatment. The person requesting such records shall pay all reasonable costs connected therewith.

c. The injured person shall be furnished upon demand a copy of all information obtained by the insurer or the Unsatisfied Claim and Judgment Fund under the provisions of this section, and shall pay a reasonable charge, if required by the insurer and the Unsatisfied Claim and Judgment Fund.

d. Whenever the mental or physical condition of an injured person covered by personal injury protection under a standard automobile insurance policy or medical expense benefits under a basic automobile insurance policy is material to any claim that has been or may be made for such past or future personal injury protection benefits or medical expense benefits, such person shall, upon request of an insurer or the Unsatisfied Claim and Judgment Fund submit to mental or physical examination conducted by a health care provider licensed in this State in the same profession or specialty as the health care provider whose services are subject to review under this section and who is located within a reasonable proximity to the injured person's residence. The injured person shall provide or make available to the provider any pertinent medical records or medical history that the provider deems necessary to the examination. The costs of any examinations requested by an insurer or the Unsatisfied Claim and Judgment Fund shall be borne entirely by whomever makes such request. Such examination shall be conducted within the municipality of residence of the injured person. If there is no qualified health care provider to conduct the examination within the municipality of residence of the injured person, then such examination shall be conducted in an area of the closest proximity to the injured person's residence. Insurers providing personal injury protection coverage under a standard automobile insurance policy or medical expense benefits under a basic automobile insurance policy are authorized to include reasonable provisions requiring those claiming personal injury protection coverage benefits or medical expense benefits to submit to mental or physical examination as requested by an insurer or the Unsatisfied Claim and Judgment Fund pursuant to the provisions of this section. Failure to submit to a mental or physical examination requested by an insurer or the Unsatisfied

Claim and Judgment Fund pursuant to the provisions of this section shall subject the injured person to certain limitations in coverage as specified in regulations promulgated by the commissioner.

e. If requested by the person examined, a party causing an examination to be made, shall deliver to him a copy of every written report concerning the examination rendered by an examining health care provider, at least one of which reports must set out his findings and conclusions in detail. After such request and delivery, the party causing the examination to be made is entitled upon request to receive from the person examined every written report available to him, or his representative, concerning any examination, previously or thereafter made of the same mental or physical condition.

f. The injured person, upon reasonable request by the insurer or the Unsatisfied Claim and Judgment Fund, shall sign all forms, authorizations or releases for information, approved by the Commissioner of Banking and Insurance, which may be necessary to the discovery of the above facts, in order to reasonably prove the injured person's losses.

g. In the event of any dispute regarding an insurer's or the Unsatisfied Claim and Judgment Fund's or an injured person's right as to the discovery of facts about the injured person's earnings or about his history, condition, treatment, dates and costs of such treatment, or the submission of such injured person to a mental or physical examination subject to the provisions of this section, the insurer, Unsatisfied Claim and Judgment Fund or the injured person may petition a court of competent jurisdiction for an order resolving the dispute and protecting the rights of all parties. The order may be entered on motion for good cause shown giving notice to all persons having an interest therein. Such court may protect against annoyance, embarrassment or oppression and may as justice requires, enter an order compelling or refusing discovery, or specifying conditions of such discovery; the court may further order the payment of costs and expenses of the proceeding, as justice requires.

L.1972, c. 70, § 13. Amended by L.1993, c. 186, § 1, eff. July 16, 1993; L.1998, c. 21, § 17; L.2003, c. 89, § 56, eff. June 9, 2003.

39:6A–13.1. Limitation of actions

a. Every action for the payment of benefits payable under a standard automobile insurance policy pursuant to sections 4 and 10 of P.L.1972, c. 70 (C.39:6A–4 and 39:6A–10), medical expense benefits payable under a basic automobile insurance policy pursuant to section 4 of P.L.1998, c. 21 (C.39:6A–3.1) or benefits payable under a special automobile insurance policy pursuant to section 45 of P.L.2003, c.89 (C.39:6A–3.3), except an action by a decedent's estate, shall be commenced not later than two years after the injured person or survivor suffers a loss or incurs an expense and either knows or in the exercise of reasonable diligence should know that the loss or expense was caused by the accident, or not later than four years after the accident whichever is earlier, provided, however, that if benefits have been paid before then an action for further benefits may be commenced not later than two years after the last payment of benefits.

b. Every action by a decedent's estate for the payment of benefits provided under a standard automobile insurance policy pursuant to sections 4 and 10 of P.L.1972, c. 70 (C.39:6A–4 and 39:6A–10), medical expense benefits provided under a basic automobile insurance policy pursuant to section 4 of P.L.1998, c. 21 (C.39:6A–3.1) or benefits payable under a special automobile insurance policy pursuant to section 45 of P.L.2003, c. 89 (C.39:6A–3.3), shall be commenced not later than two years after death or four years after the accident from which death results, whichever is earlier, provided, however, that if benefits had been paid to the decedent prior to his death then an action may be commenced not later than two years after his death or four years after the last payment of benefits, whichever is earlier, provided, further, that if the decedent's estate has received benefits before then an action for further benefits shall be commenced not later than two years from the last payment of benefits.

L.1972, c. 203, § 11, eff. Dec. 26, 1972. Amended by L.1998, c. 21, § 18; L.2003, c. 89, § 57, eff. June 9, 2003.

39:6A–14.   Compulsory uninsured motorist protection

Every owner or registrant of an automobile registered or principally garaged in this State shall maintain uninsured motorist coverage as provided in P.L.1968, c. 385 (C. 17:28–1.1).

L.1972, c. 70, § 14.

39:6A–15.   Penalties for false and fraudulent representation

In any claim or action arising for benefits payable under a standard automobile insurance policy under section 4 of P.L.1972, c. 70 (C.39:6A–4), any claim or action arising for medical expense benefits payable under a basic automobile insurance policy under section 4 of P.L.1998, c. 21 (C.39:6A–3.1) or any claim or action arising for benefits payable under a special automobile insurance policy pursuant to section 45 of P.L.2003, c. 89 (C.39:6A–3.3) wherein any person obtains or attempts to obtain from any other person, insurance company or Unsatisfied Claim and Judgment Fund any money or other thing of value by (1) falsely or fraudulently representing that such person is entitled to such benefits; (2) falsely and fraudulently making statements or presenting documentation in order to obtain or attempt to obtain such benefits; or (3) cooperates, conspires or otherwise acts in concert with any person seeking to falsely or fraudulently obtain, or attempt to obtain, such benefits may upon conviction be fined not more than $5, 000.00, or imprisoned for not more than three years or both, or in the event the sum so obtained or attempted to be obtained is not more than $500.00, may upon conviction, be fined not more than $500.00,

or imprisoned for not more than six months or both, as a disorderly person.

In addition to any penalties imposed by law, any person who is either found by a court of competent jurisdiction to have violated any provision of P.L.1983 c.320 (C.17:33A–1 et seq.) pertaining to automobile insurance or been convicted of any violation of Title 2C of the New Jersey Statutes arising out of automobile insurance fraud shall not operate a motor vehicle over the highways of this State for a period of one year from the date of judgment or conviction.

L.1972, c. 70, § 15. Amended by L.1973, c. 298, § 1, eff. Dec. 7, 1973; L.1997, c. 151, § 9, eff. June 30, 1997; L.1998, c. 21, § 19; L.2003, c. 89, § 58, eff. June 9, 2003.

39:6A–16.   Construction and severability

This act shall be liberally construed so as to effect the purpose thereof. The provisions of this act shall be severable and if any phrase, clause, sentence or provision of this act is declared to be contrary to the Constitution of this State or of the United States or the applicability thereof to any person, government, agency or circumstance is held invalid, the validity of the remainder of this act and the applicability thereof to any person, government, agency or circumstance shall not be affected thereby.

L.1972, c. 70, § 16.

39:6A–17.   General repeal of inconsistent statutory provisions

All laws or parts of laws which are inconsistent with the provisions of this act are repealed and superseded to the extent of such inconsistency.

L.1972, c. 70, § 17.

39:6A–18.   Mandatory reduction of bodily injury insurance rates

Bodily injury insurance rates in effect on July 1, 1972 shall be reduced by at least 15% and shall become effective upon the effective date of this act.

L.1972, c. 70, § 18.

39:6A–19.   Rules and regulations

The Commissioner of Insurance is hereby authorized and empowered to prescribe, adopt, promulgate, rescind and enforce such reasonable rules and regulations as may be required to effectuate the purposes of this act.

L.1972, c. 203, § 9, eff. Dec. 26, 1972.

39:6A–20.   Powers of commissioner of insurance

For the purpose of implementing and enforcing this act, the Commissioner of Insurance shall possess all of those general powers as enumerated in Title 17 of the Revised Statutes.

L.1972, c. 203, § 10, eff. Dec. 26, 1972.

39:6A–21. The New Jersey Automobile Insurance Risk Exchange: membership, board of directors

There shall be created, within 45 days of the operative date of this act, an unincorporated association, to operate on a nonprofit-nonloss basis, to be known as the New Jersey Automobile Insurance Risk Exchange, with its headquarters to be located within the State of New Jersey. Every insurer licensed to transact private-passenger automobile insurance in this State shall be a member of the exchange and shall be bound by the rules of the exchange as a condition of the authority to transact insurance business in this State. Any insurer which ceases to transact automobile insurance business in this State shall remain liable for any amounts due to the exchange for business transacted prior to the effective date of its cessation of business in the State.

The exchange shall adopt a plan of operation which shall become effective upon approval by the Commissioner of Banking and Insurance. The business affairs of the exchange shall be governed by a board of directors to be comprised of 12 members. Nine members shall be appointed, from a list of names submitted by the Commissioner of Banking and Insurance, by the Governor, with the advice and consent of the Senate, of whom two shall represent the Property Casualty Insurers Association of America, or its successor organization; two shall represent the American Insurance Association, or its successor organization; two shall represent the independent companies; two shall represent New Jersey domiciled insurance companies as nominated to the commissioner by the exchange; and one shall be a public member. If no name is submitted by an aforementioned association or company to serve as its representative on the board of the exchange, the exchange shall submit to the commissioner the name of an individual employed by an insurer transacting automobile insurance in this State. Additionally, the Governor, the Speaker of the General Assembly and the President of the Senate shall each appoint one public member. The board shall elect a chairman who shall be a representative of an insurer domiciled in New Jersey. No insurer shall represent more than one organization on the board of directors of the exchange.

All appointments made on or after the effective date of this amendatory act shall be for five-year terms. A director shall serve until his successor is appointed. Vacancies on the board of directors of the exchange shall be filled for the remainders of the terms in the same manner as the original appointments. Public members shall be compensated in an amount to be determined by the commissioner, and shall be reimbursed for necessary expenses actually incurred in the performance of their duties. All expenses incurred by the board shall be payable from moneys collected by the exchange.

L.1983, c. 362, § 15, eff. Oct. 4, 1983. Amended by L.1985, c. 520, § 10, eff. Jan. 21, 1986; L.2000, c. 66, § 1, eff. July 13, 2000; L.2007, c. 72, § 1, eff. April 30, 2007.

39:6A–22. Powers of exchange

a. The exchange shall be empowered to raise sufficient moneys (1) to pay its operating expenses, and (2) to compensate members of the exchange for claims paid for noneconomic loss, and associated claim adjustment expenses, which would not have been incurred had the tort limitation option provided in subsection b. of section 8 of P.L.1972, c. 70 (C. 39:6A–8) or, in the case of policies issued or renewed on or after January 1, 1989, subsection a. of section 8 of P.L.1972, c. 70 (C. 39:6A–8), been elected by the injured party filing the claim for noneconomic loss.

b. In order to enable the exchange to meet its obligations under subsection a. of this section, every member insurer or servicing carrier of the New Jersey Automobile Full Insurance Underwriting Association shall forward on a monthly basis, within 15 days of the close of the member's accounting month, a charge, to be known as the AIRE charge, in an amount and manner to be prescribed by the board of directors.

AIRE charge amounts required to be paid to the exchange in accordance with this subsection shall, in the case of those amounts determined by the board of directors to be applicable during the period from July 1, 1984 to the effective date of P.L.1985, c. 520, be paid to the exchange within 60 days of that date.

A 10% per annum penalty charge shall be assessed by the exchange on any overdue AIRE charges.

c. The board of directors shall establish guidelines by which members or servicing carriers and the exchange may verify the tort limitation options elected by claimants.

d. Moneys collected by or otherwise available to the exchange shall be invested as hereinafter provided in section 12 of P.L.1985, c. 520 (C. 39:6A–22.1).

e. The exchange shall have such powers as may be necessary or appropriate to effectuate the purposes of the exchange.

L.1983, c. 362, § 16, eff. Oct. 4, 1983. Amended by L.1985, c. 520, § 11, eff. Jan. 21, 1986; L.1988, c. 119, § 31, eff. Jan. 1, 1989.

39:6A–22.1. Investment of moneys; annual report

Moneys collected by or available to the exchange shall be invested by the board of directors in accordance with the liabilities of the fund and the statutory limitations on insurer investments in Title 17 of the Revised Statutes; except that the board shall invest moneys of the exchange in New Jersey or in equity securities or debt obligations of businesses incorporated in New Jersey for operations in the State, if at least equivalent to any alternative investment opportunities outside New Jersey, with respect to risk exposure, rates of return and other investment objectives established by the board.

The exchange shall at least annually file a report with the Commissioner of Insurance and the chairmen of the Assembly Banking and Insurance Committee and the

Senate Labor, Industry and Professions Committee, or the successors of those committees, setting forth, among other things, the income, claims and investment experience of the exchange. The commissioner shall prescribe, by regulation, the contents and form of the report.

L.1985, c. 520, § 12, eff. Jan. 21, 1986.

39:6A–23. Written notice—buyer's guide and coverage selection form

a. No new automobile insurance policy shall be issued on or after the 180th day following the effective date of P.L.1985, c. 520, unless the application for the policy is accompanied by a written notice identifying and containing a buyer's guide and coverage selection form. The buyer's guide shall contain a brief description of all available policy coverages and benefit limits, and shall identify which coverages are mandatory and which are optional under State law, as well as all options offered by the insurer.

The buyer's guide shall also contain a statement on the possible coordination of other health benefits coverages with the personal injury protection coverage options, the form and contents of which shall be prescribed by the Commissioner of Insurance.

The coverage selection form shall identify the range of premium rate credit or dollar savings, or both, and shall provide any other information required by the commissioner by regulation.

The applicant shall indicate the options elected on the coverage selection form which shall be signed and returned to the insurer.

b. (Deleted by amendment, P.L.1985, c. 520.)

c. Any notice of renewal of an automobile insurance policy with an effective date subsequent to July 1, 1984, shall be accompanied by a written notice of all policy coverage information required to be provided under subsection a. of this section.

The Commissioner of Insurance shall, within 45 days following the effective date of this act, promulgate standards for the written notice and buyer's guide required to be provided under this section.

d. Written notices provided by any insurer writing at least 2% of the New Jersey private passenger automobile market, including the New Jersey Automobile Full Insurance Underwriting Association established pursuant to section 16 of P.L.1983, c. 65 (C. 17:30E–4), shall also contain a statement advising that if the insured or applicant has any questions concerning his automobile insurance policy, including questions as to coverage or premiums, he may contact his producer, or the company directly, by using a toll free number which shall be set forth in the notice. Written notice shall be given to all insureds of any change in the toll free number.

e. A properly completed and executed coverage selection form shall be prima facie evidence of the named insured's knowing election or rejection of any option.

f. Each named insured of an automobile insurance policy shall, at least annually or as otherwise ordered by the commissioner, receive a buyer's guide and coverage selection form.

g. On and after January 1, 1991, each buyer's guide and coverage selection form shall be written in plain language.

L.1983, c. 362, § 17, eff. Oct. 4, 1983. Amended by L.1985, c. 520, § 5; L.1988, c. 119, § 35, eff. Jan. 1, 1989; L.1990, c. 8, § 13, eff. March 12, 1990.

39:6A–23.1. Comparative premium data; publication and distribution

Within nine months of the effective date of this 1988 amendatory and supplementary act, the Commissioner of Insurance shall cause to have published a representative sample of the premiums being charged by insurers in each territory to facilitate price comparison by insureds or prospective insureds who are seeking new coverage. The commissioner may act to make comparative premium data available to all insureds and prospective insureds.

L.1988, c. 119, § 36, eff. Jan. 1, 1989.

39:6A–24. Purpose and intent of act

The purpose and intent of this act is to establish an informal system of settling tort claims arising out of automobile accidents in an expeditious and least costly manner, and to ease the burden and congestion of the State's courts.

L.1983, c. 358, § 1.

39:6A–25. Actions to be submitted to arbitration

a. Any cause of action filed in the Superior Court after the operative date of this act, for the recovery of noneconomic loss, as defined in section 2 of P.L.1972, c. 70 (C. 39:6A–2), or the recovery of uncompensated economic loss, other than for damages to property, arising out of the operation, ownership, maintenance or use of an automobile, as defined in that section 2, shall be submitted, except as hereinafter provided, to arbitration by the assignment judge of the court in which the action is filed, if the court determines that the amount in controversy is $15,000.00 or less, exclusive of interest and costs; provided that if the action is for recovery for both noneconomic and economic loss, the controversy shall be submitted to arbitration if the court determines that the amount in controversy for noneconomic loss is $15,000.00 or less, exclusive of interest and costs.

b. Notwithstanding that the amount in controversy of an action for noneconomic loss is in excess of $15,000.00, the court may refer the matter to arbitration, if all of the parties to the action consent in writing to arbitration and the court determines that the controversy does not involve novel legal or unduly complex factual issues.

No cause of action determined by the court to be, upon proper motion of any party to the controversy, frivolous, insubstantial or without actionable cause shall be submitted to arbitration.

The provisions of this section shall not apply to any controversy on which an arbitration decision was rendered prior to the filing of the action.

The provisions of this section shall apply to any cause of action, subject to this section, filed prior to the operative date of this act, if a pretrial conference has not been concluded thereon.

L.1983, c. 358, § 2.

39:6A-26. Tolling statute of limitations

Submission of a controversy to arbitration shall toll the statute of limitations for filing an action until the filing of the arbitration decision in accordance with section 7 of this act.[1]

L.1983, c. 358, § 3.

[1] N.J.S.A. § 39:6A-30.

39:6A-27. Selection of arbitrators

a. The number or selection of arbitrators may be stipulated by mutual consent of all of the parties to the action, which stipulation shall be made in writing prior to or at the time notice is given that the controversy is to be submitted to arbitration. The assignment judge shall approve the arbitrators agreed to by the parties, whether or not the designated arbitrators satisfy the requirements of subsection b. of this section, upon a finding that the designees are qualified and their serving would not prejudice the interest of any of the parties.

b. If the parties fail to stipulate the number or names of the arbitrators, the arbitrators shall be selected, in accordance with the Rules of Court adopted by the Supreme Court of New Jersey, from a list of arbitrators compiled by the assignment judge, to be comprised of retired judges and qualified attorneys in this State with at least seven years' negligence experience and recommended by the county or State bar association.

L.1983, c. 358, § 4.

39:6A-28. Compensation and fees; rules governing offers of judgment

Compensation for arbitrators shall be set by the Rules of the Supreme Court of New Jersey. The Supreme Court may also establish a schedule of fees for attorneys representing the parties to the dispute and for witnesses in arbitration proceedings. Attorney's fees may exceed these limits upon application made to the assignment judge in accordance with the Rules of the Court for the purpose of determining a reasonable fee in the light of all the circumstances.

The Supreme Court may adopt rules governing offers of judgment by the claimant or defendant prior to the start of arbitration, including the assessment of the costs of arbitration proceedings and attorney's fees, where an offer is made but refused by the other party to the controversy.

L.1983, c. 358, § 5.

39:6A-29. Subpoenas

The arbitrators may, at their initiative or at the request of any party to the arbitration, issue subpenas for the attendance of witnesses and the production of books, records, documents and other evidence. Subpenas shall be served and shall be enforceable in the manner provided by law.

L.1983, c. 358, § 6.

39:6A-30. Award; decision of arbitrator

Notwithstanding that a controversy was submitted pursuant to subsection a. of section 2 of this act,[1] the arbitration award for noneconomic loss may exceed $15,000.00. The arbitration decision shall be in writing, and shall set forth the issues in controversy, and the arbitrators' findings and conclusions of law and fact.

L.1983, c. 358, § 7.

[1] N.J.S.A. § 39:6A-25.

39:6A-31. Confirming arbitration decision

Unless one of the parties to the arbitration petitions the court, within 30 days of the filing of the arbitration decision with the court: a. for a trial de novo, or b. for the modification or vacation of the arbitration decision for any of the reasons set forth in chapter 24 of Title 2A of the New Jersey Statutes, or an error of law or factual inconsistencies in the arbitration findings, the court shall, upon motion of any of the parties, confirm the arbitration decision, and the action of the court shall have the same effect and be enforceable as a judgment in any other action.

L.1983, c. 358, § 8.

39:6A-32. Arbitrators fee; payment

Except in the case of an arbitration decision vacated by the court or offers of judgment made pursuant to court rules, the party petitioning the court for a trial de novo shall pay to the court a trial de novo fee in an amount established pursuant to the Rules of Court, which shall be utilized by the judiciary to pay the costs of arbitration including the fees of the arbitrators.

L.1983, c. 358, § 9. Amended by L.1993, c. 88, § 1, eff. March 19, 1993.

39:6A-33. Admissibility of evidence at trial de novo

No statements, admissions or testimony made at the arbitration proceedings, nor the arbitration decision, as confirmed or modified by the court, shall be used or referred to at the trial de novo by any of the parties, except that the court may consider any of those matters in determining the amount of any reduction in assessments made pursuant to section 11 of this act.[1]

L.1983, c. 358, § 10.

¹ N.J.S.A. § 39:6A–34.

39:6A–34. Assessment of costs for trial de novo

The party having filed for a trial de novo shall be assessed court costs and other reasonable costs of the other party to the judicial proceeding, including attorney's fees, investigation expenses and expenses for expert or other testimony or evidence, which amount shall be, if the party assessed the costs is the one to whom the award is made, offset against any damages awarded to that party by the court, and only to that extent; except that if the judgment is more favorable to the party having filed for a trial de novo, the court may reduce or eliminate the amount of the assessment in accordance with the extent to which the decision of the court is more favorable to that party than the arbitration decision, and as best serves the interest of justice. The court may waive an assessment of costs required by this section upon a finding that the imposition of costs would create a substantial economic hardship as not to be in the interest of justice.

L.1983, c. 358, § 11.

39:6A–35. Rules; report

The Supreme Court of New Jersey shall adopt Rules of Court appropriate or necessary to effectuate the purpose of this act. The Administrative Office of the Courts shall not later than March 1 of each year file with the Governor and Legislature a report on the impact of the implementation of this act on automobile insurance settlement practices and costs, and on court calendars and workload.

L.1983, c. 358, § 12.

CHAPTER 6B

COMPULSORY MOTOR VEHICLE INSURANCE

Section
39:6B–1.   Liability insurance; amount of coverage.
39:6B–2.   Penalties for failure to carry motor vehicle insurance coverage.
39:6B–3.   Uninsured motorist prevention fund.

39:6B–1. Liability insurance; amount of coverage

a. Every owner or registered owner of a motor vehicle registered or principally garaged in this State shall maintain motor vehicle liability insurance coverage, under provisions approved by the Commissioner of Banking and Insurance, insuring against loss resulting from liability imposed by law for bodily injury, death and property damage sustained by any person arising out of the ownership, maintenance, operation or use of a motor vehicle wherein such coverage shall be at least in: (1) an amount or limit of $15,000.00, exclusive of interest and costs, on account of injury to, or death of, one person, in any one accident; and (2) an amount or limit, subject to such limit for any one person so injured or killed, of $30,000.00, exclusive of interest and costs, on account of injury to or death of, more than one person, in any one accident; and (3) an amount or limit of $5,000.00, exclusive of interest and costs, for damage to property in any one accident.

b. Notwithstanding the provisions of subsection a. of this section, an owner or registered owner of an automobile, as defined in section 2 of P.L.1972, c. 70 (C.39:6A–2), registered or primarily garaged in the State may satisfy the requirements of subsection a. of this section by maintaining a basic automobile insurance policy containing coverages provided pursuant to subsections a. and b. of section 4 of P.L.1998, c. 21 (C.39:6A–3.1).

c. Notwithstanding the provisions of subsection a. of this section, an owner or registered owner of an automobile, as defined in section 2 of P.L.1972, c. 70 (C.39:6A–2), registered or primarily garaged in the State may satisfy the requirements of subsection a. of this section by maintaining a special automobile insurance policy containing coverages provided pursuant to subsection b. of section 45 of P.L.2003, c. 89 (C.39:6A–3.3).

L.1972, c. 197, § 1, eff. Jan. 1, 1973. Amended by L.1998, c. 21, § 20; L.2003, c. 89, § 60, eff. June 9, 2003.

39:6B–2. Penalties for failure to carry motor vehicle insurance coverage

Any owner or registrant of a motor vehicle registered or principally garaged in this State who operates or causes to be operated a motor vehicle upon any public road or highway in this State without motor vehicle liability insurance coverage required by this act, and any operator who operates or causes a motor vehicle to be operated and who knows or should know from the attendant circumstances that the motor vehicle is without motor vehicle liability insurance coverage required by this act shall be subject, for the first offense, to a fine of not less than $300 nor more than $1,000 and a period of community service to be determined by the court, and shall forthwith forfeit his right to operate a motor vehicle over the highways of this State for a period of one year from the date of conviction. Upon subsequent conviction, he shall be subject to a fine of up to $5,000 and shall be subject to imprisonment for a term of 14 days and shall be ordered by the court to perform community service for a period of 30 days, which shall be of such form and on such terms as the court shall deem appropriate under the circumstances, and shall forfeit his right to operate a motor vehicle for a period of two years from the date of his conviction, and, after the expiration of said period, he may make application to the Director of the Division of Motor Vehicles for a license to operate a motor vehicle, which application may be granted at the discretion of the director. The director's discretion shall be based upon an assessment of the likelihood that the individual will operate or cause a motor vehicle to be operated in the future without the insurance coverage required by this act. A complaint for violation of this act may be made to a municipal court at any time within six months after the date of the alleged offense.

Failure to produce at the time of trial an insurance identification card or an insurance policy which was in force for the time of operation for which the offense is charged creates a rebuttable presumption that the person was uninsured when charged with a violation of this section.

L.1972, c. 197, § 2, eff. Jan. 1, 1973. Amended by L.1983, c. 141, § 1, eff. April 20, 1983; L.1987, c. 46, § 1, eff. Feb. 19, 1987; L.1988, c. 156, § 15, eff. Nov. 14, 1988; L.1990, c. 8, § 49, eff. March 12, 1990; L.1997, c. 151, § 12, eff. June 30, 1997.

39:6B–3. Uninsured motorist prevention fund

The Uninsured Motorist Prevention Fund (hereinafter referred to as the "fund") is established as a nonlapsing, revolving fund into which shall be deposited all revenues from the fines imposed pursuant to section 2 of P.L.1972, c. 197 (C.39:6B–2) and $25 from each fine imposed pursuant to R.S.39:3–29. Interest received on moneys in the fund shall be credited to the fund. The fund shall be administered by the New Jersey Motor Vehicle Commission. Moneys in the fund shall be allocated and used for the purpose of the administrative expenses of the fund and enforcement of the compulsory motor vehicle insurance law, P.L.1972, c. 197 (C.39:6B–1 et seq.) by the New Jersey Motor Vehicle Commission.

L.1983, c. 141, § 2, eff. April 20, 1983. Amended by L.2003, c. 89, § 80, eff. June 9, 2003.

CHAPTER 7

SERVICE OF PROCESS UPON NONRESIDENTS

Section
39:7–1.   Construction of chapter.
39:7–2.   Director of Division of Motor Vehicles as agent for service of process; effect of service.
39:7–2.1.   Director of Division of Motor Vehicles as agent for service of process of residents who become nonresidents.
39:7–2.2.   Manner of service; notice; fees.
39:7–3.   Methods of service; notice; fees and expenses of service.
39:7–4.   Continuances to permit defendant to defend.
39:7–5.   Fees and expenses as taxable costs.
39:7–6.   Record kept by commissioner.
39:7–7.   Power of attorney constituting director agent for service condition precedent to release on bail.
39:7–8.   Other methods of service of process.

39:7–1. Construction of chapter

This chapter shall be construed as extending the right and manner of service of process upon nonresidents, and not as limiting any other lawful manner for such service.

39:7–2. Director of Division of Motor Vehicles as agent for service of process; effect of service

(a) Any person, not being a resident of this State, who shall drive a motor vehicle in this State, whether or not such person shall be licensed to do so in accordance with the laws of this State or of any other State or otherwise; and

(b) Any person or persons, not being a resident or residents of this State or any corporation or association, not incorporated under the laws of this State and not duly authorized to transact business in this State, who by his, their or its agent or servant, shall cause to be driven in this State, any motor vehicle which is not registered in this State to be driven upon the public highways thereof, pursuant to the laws thereof, whether or not the driver thereof shall be licensed to drive a motor vehicle upon the public highways of this State; shall, by the operation of such motor vehicle, or by causing the same to be operated, within this State, make and constitute the Director of the Division of Motor Vehicles in the Department of Law and Public Safety, his or their agent for the acceptance of process in any civil action or proceeding, issuing out of the Superior Court, or other court of civil jurisdiction, against any such person or persons, corporation or association arising out of or by reason of any accident or collision occurring within this State in which any such motor vehicle, so driven or caused to be driven within this State is involved.

The agreement that the Director of the Division of Motor Vehicles in the Department of Law and Public Safety shall be constituted the agent, of a nonresident operator or owner of a motor vehicle, which is involved in any accident in this State, for the acceptance of process in any such action or proceeding, shall be irrevocable and binding upon the executor or administrator of such operator or owner, and service of process shall be made upon the executor or administrator of any such operator or owner dying prior to the commencement of such action or proceeding in the same manner and on the same notice as herein provided for service of process upon such operator or owner, and any such action or proceeding, duly commenced by service upon such an operator or owner under the provisions of this chapter, who shall die thereafter during the pendency of such action or proceeding, shall be continued against his executor or administrator by the court in which the same is pending, upon such application and notice as the court shall prescribe. The operating or causing to be operated of any such motor vehicle within this State shall be the signification of the agreement of such nonresident person operating the same, or of such person or persons or corporation or association for whom such motor vehicle is operated, of his, their or its agreement that any such process against him, or them, or it, or against his or their executors or administrators, which is so served shall be of the same legal force and validity as if served upon him or them personally or upon it in accordance with law within this State.

Amended by L.1941, c. 262, p. 695, § 1; L.1949, c. 190, p. 635, § 1; L.1950, c. 251, p. 866, § 1; L.1958, c. 59, p. 179, § 1; L.1971, c. 104, § 1, eff. April 16, 1971; L.1991, c. 91, § 373, eff. April 9, 1991.

39:7–2.1. Director of Division of Motor Vehicles as agent for service of process of residents who become nonresidents

Any resident of this State who shall drive a motor vehicle, or cause a motor vehicle to be driven in this State, whether or not such motor vehicle is registered under the laws of this State and whether or not such person or the driver of such motor vehicle is licensed to drive a motor vehicle upon the highways of this State, shall by the operation of such motor vehicle, or by causing the same to be operated, within this State, make and constitute the Director of the Division of Motor Vehicles in the Department of Law and Public Safety his agent for the acceptance of process, in any civil action or proceeding, issuing out of the Superior Court or other court of civil jurisdiction of this State against him by reason of an accident or collision in this State in which such motor vehicle, while so driven or caused to be driven, shall be involved if, and in case, such person shall cease to be a resident of this State and service of such process upon him within this State cannot be made by reason of his nonresidence. The operating or causing to be operated of any such motor vehicle within this State shall be his signification of the agreement of such person operating the same or the person for whom such motor vehicle is operated of his agreement that any such process against him which is so served after he becomes a nonresident of this State shall be of the same legal force and validity as if served upon him personally in accordance with law within this State. The agreement that the Director of the Division of Motor Vehicles in the Department of Law and Public Safety shall be constituted the agent, of a resident operator or owner of a motor vehicle who becomes a nonresident, which is involved in any accident in this State, for the acceptance of process in any such action or proceeding, shall be irrevocable and binding upon the executor or administrator of such operator or owner, whether appointed within or without the State, and service of process shall be made upon the said executor or administrator of any such operator or owner dying prior to the commencement of such action or proceeding in the same manner and on the same notice as herein provided for service of process upon such operator or owner, and any such action or proceeding, duly commenced by service upon such an operator or owner under the provisions of this act, who shall die thereafter during the pendency of such action or proceeding, shall be continued against his said executor or administrator

by the court in which the same is pending, upon such application and notice as the court shall prescribe.

L.1954, c. 61, p. 412, § 1. Amended by L.1963, c. 163, § 1; L.1971, c. 104, § 3, eff. April 16, 1971; L.1991, c. 91, § 374, eff. April 9, 1991.

39:7–2.2. Manner of service; notice; fees

Service of process shall be made, and notice thereof shall be given, under this act in the same manner and with the same effect, the same fees shall be chargeable and payable, continuance may be ordered and the same records shall be kept, as is provided in the act to which this act is a supplement.[1]

L.1954, c. 61, p. 413, § 2.

   [1] N.J.S.A. § 39:7–1 et seq.

39:7–3. Methods of service; notice; fees and expenses of service

Service of process upon the director shall be made by leaving the original and a copy of the summons and two copies of the complaint, with a fee of $10.00, in the hands of the director, or someone designated by him in his office, or, in an action commenced in any county other than Mercer county, then the sheriff or other authorized person may serve the director by mailing such papers to him by registered mail, with the said fee. Such service shall be sufficient service upon the nonresident chauffeur, operator or owner, if

a. Notice of such service and a copy of the summons with a copy of the complaint are forthwith sent by registered mail to the defendant by the director, or someone designated by him in his office; and

b. Defendant's return receipt and the affidavit of the director, or such person in his office acting for him, of the compliance herewith, including a statement of the date of such mailing and of the receipt of the return card, are appended to the original of the summons and the other copy of the complaint and filed in the office of the clerk of the court wherein the action may be pending; or

c. Notice of such service with a copy thereof and the original and a copy of the summons and two copies of the complaint are forthwith sent by registered mail by the director, or the person in his office acting for him, to the sheriff or other process server in the jurisdiction in which the defendant resides, with directions that such sheriff or process server, or someone acting for such sheriff or process server, shall serve the same upon the defendant in the same manner that service is legally effected in that jurisdiction, and the return of such sheriff or process server, or the person acting for such sheriff or process server in such jurisdiction, shall be appended to or endorsed upon the original summons and a copy of the complaint and returned to the director, and thereafter filed in the office of the clerk of the court wherein the action may be pending in this State; or

d. Notice of such service and a copy of the summons and complaint may be served on the defendant personally by any official or private individual, wherever such service may be made, and, upon service being so made, an affidavit shall be made by the person effecting such service, showing the person served and the time and place of such service, which affidavit shall be appended to the original summons and one copy of the complaint and returned to the director, and be thereafter filed in the office of the clerk of the court wherein the action may be pending in this State; or

e. Notice of such service and a copy of the summons and complaint may be served on the defendant in any other manner that the court in which the cause is pending shall deem sufficient and expedient.

If, by direction of plaintiff, notice of service is given as provided by paragraph c. of this section, plaintiff shall, in addition to the fee of $10.00 required by the first paragraph of this section, deposit with the director sufficient money to effectuate the same.

Upon giving notice to the defendant of the service of process as required by this chapter, where service of process is made upon the director, he shall file with the clerk of the court his certificate of the notice given.

If notice of service is given as provided by paragraph d. of this section, plaintiff shall pay the cost thereof.
Amended by L.1949, c. 190, p. 636, § 2; L.1953, c. 36, p. 624, § 34; L.1975, c. 180, § 13, eff. Jan. 1, 1976; L.1982, c. 53, § 3, eff. July 1, 1982; L.1991, c. 91, § 375, eff. April 9, 1991.

39:7–4. Continuances to permit defendant to defend

The court in which an action against a chauffeur, operator or owner mentioned in section 39:7–2 of this title is pending may order such continuances as may be necessary to afford the defendant reasonable opportunity to defend the action.

39:7–5. Fees and expenses as taxable costs

The fee of $5.00 paid by the plaintiff to the director at the time of service and the cost of giving notice as provided in this chapter shall be taxed in plaintiff's costs if he prevails in the action.
Amended by L.1949, c. 190, p. 637, § 3; L.1975, c. 180, § 14, eff. Jan. 1, 1976.

39:7–6. Record kept by commissioner

The director shall keep a record of processes served pursuant to the provisions of this chapter, which shall show the day and hour of such service.
Amended by L.1949, c. 190, p. 638, § 4.

39:7–7. Power of attorney constituting director agent for service condition precedent to release on bail

Whenever any collision or accident shall occur in this State and the driver of any motor vehicle involved therein shall be a nonresident and not licensed under the laws of this State to operate a motor vehicle, or a motor vehicle involved in any such collision or accident shall not be registered or licensed under the laws of this State, the magistrate before whom the nonresident owner or operator of such motor vehicle shall be brought shall require such nonresident owner or operator, as a condition to his release on bail or otherwise, to execute a written power of attorney to the director, appointing such director his lawful agent for the acceptance of service of process in any civil action instituted or to be instituted by any resident of this State against such nonresident for or on account of any claim, demand or cause of action arising out of such collision or accident. The power of attorney herein required shall be upon a form prepared and furnished to recorders and other committing magistrates by the director and shall, after the execution thereof, be filed with the director.

The requirements of this section shall be in addition to, and not in limitation of any other law concerning the giving of bail or other security.
Amended by L.1949, c. 190, p. 638, § 5.

39:7–8. Other methods of service of process

From and after April seventh, one thousand nine hundred and thirty, civil process in any action or proceeding arising out of a collision or accident in which any motor vehicle of a nonresident owner, not registered or licensed under the laws of this state, may be served upon such nonresident owner, by service upon any chauffeur or operator of such or any other motor vehicle of such nonresident owner, while such motor vehicle is being operated in this state by such chauffeur or operator. Process in any such action may be also lawfully served upon any such nonresident owner by service thereof upon any person over the age of fourteen years who has the custody of such motor vehicle, whether held by him as security or driven, if a copy of such process is also posted in a conspicuous place upon such motor vehicle.

CHAPTER 8

INSPECTION OF MOTOR VEHICLES

Section

39:8–1.   Inspection of registered motor vehicles; exceptions.
39:8–1.   Inspection of registered motor vehicles; exceptions.
39:8–2.   Examiners of motor vehicles; appointment; rules and regulations; annual inspections; certificates of approval; acquisition of property; random roadside inspections; inspections and audits of licensed private inspection centers; fees.
39:8–2.   Inspectors of motor vehicles; appointment; rules and regulations; annual inspections; certificates of approval; acquisition of property; random roadside inspections; inspections and audits of licensed private inspection centers; fees.
39:8–2.1.   Uniforms for motor vehicle inspectors.
39:8–2.2.   Inspection stations; hours open; rules and regulations.

Section
39:8–2.3.   Possession of property in advance of compensation.
39:8–3.   Issuance of certificates of approval; prerequisites.
39:8–4.   Adjustments, corrections or repairs to be made; issuance of rejection sticker; certificate of approval; issuance; notice to correct deficiency.
39:8–4.1.   Rules and regulations.
39:8–5.   Reports concerning inspections.
39:8–5.   Reports concerning inspections.
39:8–6.   Display of approval certificate on request.
39:8–7.   Revocation, suspension or denial of registration for failure to display appropriate certificate; vehicles incapable of being made safe or of being brought within emission standards.
39:8–8.   Certificate of approval as prerequisite for registration.
39:8–9.   Enforcement of chapter; violations; punishment; remedies; procedure; revocation of certificate.
39:8–10.   Authority of director; adoption of rules and regulations for enforcement; hiring and compensation of employees.
39:8–11.   Private inspection centers; license; initial motor vehicle inspections and certification of corrections, adjustments or repairs; approval sticker.
39:8–12.   Certification or rejection of motor vehicle on initial inspection or adjustment, correction or repair of previously rejected vehicle.
39:8–13.   Charges for certification, reinspection and initial inspection; posting schedule; repairs or adjustments at licensed private center; conditions.
39:8–14.   Owner or lessee of 10 or more vehicles; license; certification of initial inspections and reinspections; approval sticker.
39:8–15.   Annual expiration of license.
39:8–16.   Application or renewal of license; form and contents; fee; proof of financial responsibility.
39:8–17.   Private inspection approval stickers; provision to licensee; fee; records; safeguards; accounting.
39:8–18.   Affixation of sticker without reinspection or determination of conformity to standards or after charge of fee for repair work not performed or performed unnecessarily; penalty.
39:8–19.   Denial, suspension, revocation or refusal of renewal of license; grounds.
39:8–20.   Discontinuance of operation or suspension or revocation of license; delivery of items to director; failure to deliver; disorderly person.
39:8–21.   Unauthorized display or advertisement as private inspection center or transfer of license; disorderly persons offense.
39:8–22.   Employees and expenditures for supervision of private inspection centers.
39:8–23.   Rules and regulations.
39:8–24.   Effective date.
39:8–25 to 39:8–36.   Repealed.
39:8–37.   Reinspection centers; redesignation as private inspection centers; authority; renewal of license.
39:8–38.   Licensed private inspection centers; emissions test equipment.
39:8–39.   Qualifications of licensee or employee.
39:8–40.   Rules and regulations; encouragement of participation in inspection program.
39:8–41.   Federal clean air mandate compliance act; short title.
39:8–42.   Legislative findings and declaration.
39:8–43.   Definitions.

Section
39:8–44.   Design, construction and operation of inspection facilities; training grants.
39:8–45.   Licensure of private inspection facilities.
39:8–45.   Licensure of private inspection facilities.
39:8–46.   Inspection procedures and fees.
39:8–47.   Certificates and stickers.
39:8–48.   Civil penalties for improper inspections.
39:8–49.   Denial, suspension and revocation of licenses.
39:8–50.   Approved testing equipment.
39:8–51.   Expiration of licenses under prior law.
39:8–52.   Licensure of emission inspectors.
39:8–52.   Licensure of inspectors; standards for licensure; denial, suspension or revocation of license.
39:8–53.   Emission-related repairs.
39:8–54.   False claim of licensure; transfer of license.
39:8–55.   Waivers.
39:8–56.   Voluntary emissions recalls; remedial plans.
39:8–57.   Rules and regulations.
39:8–58.   Continuing applicability of prior law.
39:8–59.   Legislative findings and declarations.
39:8–60.   Definitions.
39:8–61.   Exhaust emission standards and test methods; rules and regulations.
39:8–62.   Operation of diesel-powered motor vehicles.
39:8–63.   Violations; civil penalties.
39:8–64.   Periodic inspection and roadside enforcement programs.
39:8–65.   Pilot roadside enforcement program.
39:8–66.   Test methods; procedures for periodic inspection and roadside enforcement programs.
39:8–67.   State police officers to assist roadside enforcement programs; records of inspections.
39:8–68.   Additional civil penalties.
39:8–69.   Licensing of diesel emission inspection centers; grounds for revocation or suspension of license.
39:8–69.   Licensing of private inspection facilities for diesel-powered vehicles; grounds for revocation or suspension of license.
39:8–70.   Amount of civil penalty; suspension of registration.
39:8–71.   Tickets; process; proceedings on violations.
39:8–72.   Action to recover civil penalty.
39:8–73.   Municipal court proceedings for collection of unpaid penalties; suspension of registration; placement of administrative out-of-service order against vehicle.
39:8–74.   Disbursement of fees, charges and expenses collected.
39:8–75.   Commercial vehicle enforcement fund.
39:8–76.   Receivable account established for expenses of program implementation and administration.
39:8–77.   Rules and regulations.
39:8–78.   Report to governor and legislature.
39:8–79 to 39:8–89.   [Reallocated.
39:8–90.   Diesel emission inspection centers redesignation as private inspection facilities.

39:8–1. Inspection of registered motor vehicles; exceptions

Text of section effective until May 18, 2010.

a. Every motor vehicle registered in this State which is used over any public road, street, or highway or any public or quasi-public property in this State, and every vehicle subject to enhanced inspection and maintenance programs pursuant to 40 C.F.R. § 51.356, except historic motor vehicles registered as such, collector motor vehicles designated as such pursuant to this subsection, and those vehicles over 8,500 pounds gross weight that are under the inspection jurisdiction of the commission pursuant to Titles 27 and 48 (as amended by this legislation) of the Revised Statutes, shall be inspected by designated examiners or at official inspection facilities to be designated by the commission or at licensed private inspection facilities. The commission shall adopt rules and regulations establishing a procedure for the designation of motor vehicles as collector motor vehicles, which designation shall include consideration by the commission of one or more of the following factors: the age of the vehicle, the number of such vehicles originally manufactured, the number of such vehicles that are currently in use, the total number of miles the vehicle has been driven, the number of miles the vehicle has been driven during the previous year or other period of time determined by the commission, and whether the vehicle has a collector classification for insurance purposes.

b. The commission shall determine the official inspection facility or private inspection facility at which a motor vehicle, depending upon its characteristics, shall be inspected. The commission, with the concurrence of the Department of Environmental Protection, may exclude by regulation from this inspection requirement any category of motor vehicle if good cause for such exclusion exists, unless the exclusion is likely to prevent this State from meeting the applicable performance standard established by the United States Environmental Protection Agency. The commission may determine that a vehicle is in compliance with the inspection requirements of this section if the vehicle has been inspected and passed under a similar inspection program of another state, district, or territory of the United States.

Amended by L.1963, c. 128, § 2, eff. July 8, 1963; L.1964, c. 195, § 3; L.1967, c. 237, § 1, eff. Jan. 1, 1968; L.1976, c. 43, § 3; L.1983, c. 236, § 2, eff. June 30, 1983; L.1983, c. 403, § 26, eff. Dec. 23, 1983; L.1986, c. 22, § 1, eff. June 2, 1986; L.1995, c. 112, § 19, eff. June 2, 1995; L.2003, c. 13, § 75.

39:8–1. Inspection of registered motor vehicles; exceptions

Text of section effective on May 18, 2010.

a. Every motor vehicle registered in this State which is used over any public road, street, or highway or any public or quasi-public property in this State, and every vehicle subject to enhanced inspection and maintenance programs pursuant to 40 C.F.R. s.51.356, except historic motor vehicles registered as such, collector motor vehicles designated as such pursuant to this subsection, and those vehicles over 8,500 pounds gross weight that are under the inspection jurisdiction of the commission pursuant to Titles 27 and 48 (as amended by this legislation) of the Revised Statutes, shall be inspected by designated inspectors or at official inspection facili-

ties to be designated by the commission or at licensed private inspection facilities. The commission shall adopt rules and regulations establishing a procedure for the designation of motor vehicles as collector motor vehicles, which designation shall include consideration by the commission of one or more of the following factors: the age of the vehicle, the number of such vehicles originally manufactured, the number of such vehicles that are currently in use, the total number of miles the vehicle has been driven, the number of miles the vehicle has been driven during the previous year or other period of time determined by the commission, and whether the vehicle has a collector classification for insurance purposes.

b. The commission shall determine the official inspection facility or private inspection facility at which a motor vehicle, depending upon its characteristics, shall be inspected. The commission, with the concurrence of the Department of Environmental Protection, may exclude by regulation from this inspection requirement any category of motor vehicle if good cause for such exclusion exists, unless the exclusion is likely to prevent this State from meeting the applicable performance standard established by the United States Environmental Protection Agency. The commission may determine that a vehicle is in compliance with the inspection requirements of this section if the vehicle has been inspected and passed under a similar inspection program of another state, district, or territory of the United States.

Amended by L.1963, c. 128, § 2, eff. July 8, 1963; L.1964, c. 195, § 3; L.1967, c. 237, § 1, eff. Jan. 1, 1968; L.1976, c. 43, § 3; L.1983, c. 236, § 2, eff. June 30, 1983; L.1983, c. 403, § 26, eff. Dec. 23, 1983; L.1986, c. 22, § 1, eff. June 2, 1986; L.1995, c. 112, § 19, eff. June 2, 1995; L.2003, c. 13, § 75; L.2009, c. 331, § 4, eff. May 18, 2010.

39:8–2. Examiners of motor vehicles; appointment; rules and regulations; annual inspections; certificates of approval; acquisition of property; random roadside inspections; inspections and audits of licensed private inspection centers; fees

Text of section effective until May 18, 2010.

a. The commission may designate and appoint, subject to existing laws, competent examiners of motor vehicles to conduct examinations, other than the periodic inspections required pursuant to subsection b. of this section, of motor vehicles required to be inspected in accordance with the provisions of this chapter. The examiners may be delegated to enforce the provisions of the motor vehicle and traffic law.

b. (1) The commission shall adopt, pursuant to the "Administrative Procedure Act," P.L.1968, c. 410 (C.52:14B–1 et seq.), rules and regulations consistent with P.L.1966, c. 16 (C.26:2C–8.1 et seq.) and with the requirements of the federal Clean Air Act[1] with respect to the type and character of the inspections to be made, the facility at which the vehicle shall be inspected, the frequency of inspections of motor vehicles and the approval or rejection of motor vehicles as a result of these inspections. These rules and regulations shall require the use of inspection tests that are designed to meet the enhanced inspection and maintenance requirements of the federal Clean Air Act and that have been proven to be feasible and effective for the inspection of large numbers of motor vehicles, except that these tests shall not include the "I/M 240" test. Nothing in this subsection shall preclude the use of the "I/M 240" test in sampling for performance evaluations only or the use of the test at the option of a private inspection facility. The rules and regulations may distinguish between vehicles based on model year, type, or other vehicle characteristics in order to facilitate inspections or to comply with the federal Clean Air Act. A low mileage vehicle shall not be subject to a tailpipe inspection test utilizing a dynamometer but may be subject to an idle test and a purge and pressure test. For the purpose of this paragraph, "low mileage vehicle" means a motor vehicle that is driven less than 10,000 miles during the biennial inspection period, except that the commission may set the qualifying number of miles for this exemption at a lower number in order to meet the federal enhanced inspection and maintenance performance standard.

(2) The Department of Environmental Protection and the commission shall investigate advanced testing technologies, including but not limited to remote sensing and onboard diagnostics, and shall, to the extent permitted by law, pursue the use of such technologies, other than the "I/M 240" test, in motor vehicle emission inspections required by the United States Environmental Protection Agency pursuant to the federal Clean Air Act. The commission shall adopt, to the extent practicable, advanced technologies to facilitate the retrieval of testing and other information concerning motor vehicles, which technologies shall include but not be limited to the use of computer bar codes and personal cards containing encoded information, such as a person's operating license, motor vehicle registration, and motor vehicle insurance, the inspection status of a motor vehicle, and mass transit fares, that can be accessed quickly by a computer.

c. Except as modified by the commission to distribute evenly the volume of inspections, all motor vehicles required by the commission, in accordance with the provisions of R.S.39:8–1, to be inspected under this chapter shall be inspected biennially, except that (i) after certification by the commission of the federal approval by the Environmental Protection Agency of the State waiver request, model year 2000 and newer motor vehicles shall be inspected no later than four years from the last day of the month in which they were initially registered and thereafter biennially; and (ii) classes of vehicles that require more frequent inspections, such as school buses, shall be inspected at such shorter intervals as may be established by the commission after consultation with the Department of Environmental Protection. At any time, the commission may

require the owner, lessee, or operator of a motor vehicle to submit the vehicle for inspection.

d. The commission shall furnish to designated examiners or to other persons authorized to conduct inspections or to grant waivers official certificates of approval, rejection stickers or waiver certificates, the form, content and use of which it shall establish. The certificates of approval, rejection stickers and waiver certificates shall be of a type, such as a windshield sticker or license plate decal, that can be attached to the vehicle or license plate in a location that is readily visible to anyone viewing the vehicle. If a certificate of approval cannot be issued, the driver shall be provided with a written inspection report describing the reasons for rejection and, if appropriate, the repairs needed or likely to be needed to bring the vehicle into compliance with applicable standards.

e. The commission may, with the approval of the State House Commission, purchase, lease or acquire by the exercise of the power of eminent domain any property for the purpose of assisting it in carrying out the provisions of this chapter. This property may also be used by the commission for the exercise of the duties and powers conferred upon it by the other chapters of this Title.

f. For the purpose of implementing the motor vehicle inspection requirements of the federal Clean Air Act and subject to the approval of the Attorney General, the State Treasurer, prior to January 1, 1997, may:

(1) Purchase, lease or acquire by eminent domain any property for vehicle inspection purposes. Any other provision of law to the contrary notwithstanding, no further approval shall be required for transactions authorized by this paragraph, except that a proposed purchase, lease or acquisition by eminent domain shall require the approval of the Joint Budget Oversight Committee, and shall be submitted to the Joint Budget Oversight Committee, which shall review the proposed purchase, lease or acquisition by eminent domain within 15 business days; and

(2) Sell or lease, or grant an easement in, any property acquired, held or used for vehicle inspection purposes or any other suitable property held by the State that is not currently in use or dedicated to another purpose. For the purpose of this paragraph and notwithstanding any provision of R.S.52:20–1 et seq. to the contrary, the sale or lease of, or the granting of an easement in, real property owned by the State shall be subject to the approval of the State House Commission, which shall meet at the call of the Governor to act on a proposed sale or lease or grant of an easement pursuant to this paragraph. A member of the State House Commission may permit a representative to act on that member's behalf in considering and voting on a sale or lease or grant of an easement pursuant to this paragraph. Any other provision of law to the contrary notwithstanding, any moneys derived from a sale, lease

or granting of an easement by the State pursuant to this paragraph shall not be expended unless approved by the Joint Budget Oversight Committee for the purpose of purchasing, leasing or acquiring property pursuant to paragraph (1) of this subsection, except that any moneys derived therefrom and not approved for that purpose shall be appropriated to the Department of Transportation to provide for mass transit improvements.

g. The commission shall conduct roadside examinations of motor vehicles required to be inspected, using such inspection equipment and procedures, and standards established pursuant to section 1 of P.L.1966, c. 16 (C.26:2C–8.1), including, but not limited to, remote sensing technology, as the commission shall deem appropriate to provide for the monitoring of motor vehicles pursuant to this subsection. At least 20,000 vehicles or 0.5 percent of the total number of motor vehicles required to be inspected under this chapter, whichever is less, shall be inspected during each inspection cycle by roadside examination teams under the supervision of the commission. The commission may require any vehicle failing a roadside examination to be inspected at an official inspection facility or a private inspection facility within a time period fixed by the commission. Failure to appear and pass inspection within the time period fixed by the commission shall result in registration suspension in addition to any other penalties provided in this Title. The commission shall conduct an aggressive roadside inspection program to ensure that all motor vehicles that are required to be inspected in this State are in compliance with State law.

h. The commission, and, when appropriate, the Department of Environmental Protection, shall conduct inspections and audits of licensed private inspection facilities, official inspection facilities and designated examiners to ensure accurate test equipment calibration and use, and compliance with proper inspection procedures and with the provisions of P.L.1995, c. 112 (C.39:8–41 et al.) and any regulations adopted pursuant thereto by the commission or by the Department of Environmental Protection. These inspections and audits shall be conducted at such times and in such manner as the commission, upon consultation with the Department of Environmental Protection, shall determine in order to provide quality assurance in the performance of the inspection and maintenance program.

i. (1) The commission shall make a charge of $2.50 for the initial inspection for each vehicle subject to inspection, which amount shall be paid to the commission or its representative when payment of the registration fees fixed in chapter 3 of this Title is made which inspection charge shall be considered a service charge and shall be subject to the calculation of proportional revenue remitted to the commission pursuant to section 105 of P.L.2003, c. 13 (C.39:2A–36); provided however, that on and after January 1, 1999, a school bus as defined pursuant to section 3 of P.L.1999, c. 5 (C.39:3B–20) and having a registration period commencing on or after January 1, 1999, shall be subject to an inspection fee for each in-terminal or in-lieu-of terminal inspection in accordance with the following schedule:

School Bus Specification Inspection	$50 per bus
School Bus Inspection	$25 per bus
School Bus Reinspection	$25 per bus subject to the conditions set forth below

The specification inspection is required when a school bus is put into service in New Jersey, whether a new bus or a bus from another state. The specification inspection is conducted to ensure that the school bus meets New Jersey specification standards. The school bus inspection fee shall be charged to the operator for each in-terminal or in-lieu-of terminal inspection. School Vehicle Type I and School Vehicle Type II buses shall be inspected semiannually. Retired school buses shall be inspected annually. No school bus inspection fee shall be charged for any reinspection conducted by the commission if the reinspection is conducted on the same day as the inspection that necessitated the reinspection. If an additional trip is required by the commission's inspectors, a fee of $25 per bus shall be charged. School bus inspection fees shall be paid to the commission or the commission's designee subject to the terms and conditions prescribed by the commission and shall be considered service charges of the commission and not subject to the calculation of proportional revenue remitted to the commission pursuant to section 105 of P.L.2003, c. 13 (C.39:2A–36). Any law or rule or regulation adopted pursuant thereto to the contrary notwithstanding, a registration fee authorized pursuant to chapter 3 of Title 39 of the Revised Statutes shall not be increased for the purpose of paying any costs associated in any manner with the establishment, implementation or operation of the motor vehicle inspection and maintenance program established pursuant to P.L. 1995, c. 112 (C.39:8–41 et al.).

(2) The commission shall establish by regulation a fee to cover the costs of inspecting any vehicle that is required, or has the option, under federal law to be inspected in this State but is registered in another state or is owned or leased by the federal government. In determining these costs, the commission shall include all capital and direct and indirect operating costs associated with the inspection of these vehicles including, but not limited to, the costs of the actual inspection, the creation and maintenance of the vehicle inspection record, administrative, oversight and quality assurance costs and the costs associated with reporting inspection information to the owner, the federal government and agencies of other states. All fees collected pursuant to this subsection shall be paid to the State Treasurer and deposited in the "Motor Vehicle Inspection Fund" established pursuant to subsection j. of this section.

j. There is established in the General Fund a special dedicated, non-lapsing fund to be known as the "Motor Vehicle Inspection Fund," which shall be administered by the State Treasurer. The State Treasurer shall deposit into the "Motor Vehicle Inspection Fund" $11.50 from each motor vehicle registration fee received by the State after June 30, 1995. This fee shall be considered a service charge of the commission and shall be subject to the calculation of proportional revenue remitted to the commission pursuant to section 105 of P.L.2003, c. 13 (C.39:2A–36). The Legislature shall annually appropriate from the fund an amount necessary to pay the reasonable and necessary expenses of the implementation and operation of the motor vehicle inspection program. The State Treasurer shall:

(1) Pay to a private contractor or contractors contracted to design, construct, renovate, equip, establish, maintain and operate official inspection facilities under a contract or contracts entered into with the State Treasurer pursuant to subsection a. of section 4 of P.L.1995, c. 112 (C.39:8–44) from the fund the amount necessary to meet the costs agreed to under the contract or contracts; and

(2) Transfer from the fund to the commission as provided pursuant to section 105 of P.L.2003, c. 13 (C.39:2A–36) and the Department of Environmental Protection the amounts necessary to finance the costs of administering and implementing all aspects of the inspection and maintenance program, and to the Office of Telecommunications and Information Systems in the Department of the Treasury the amount necessary for computer support upgrades;

Moneys remaining in the fund and any unexpended balance of appropriations from the fund at the end of each fiscal year shall be reappropriated for the purposes of the fund. Any interest earned on moneys in the fund shall be credited to the fund.

Amended by L.1955, c. 9, p. 50, 1; L.1975, c. 156, 1, eff. July 16, 1975; L.1976, c. 43, 4; L.1983, c. 236, 3, eff. June 30, 1983; L.1986, c. 22, 2, eff. June 2, 1986; L.1989, c. 167, 1; L.1995, c. 112, 20, eff. June 2, 1995; L.1999, c. 5, 8, eff. Jan. 1, 1999; L.2002, c. 34, 15, eff. July 1, 2002; L .2003, c. 13, § 107, eff. July 1, 2003.

1 42 U.S.C.A. § 7401 et seq.

39:8–2. Inspectors of motor vehicles; appointment; rules and regulations; annual inspections; certificates of approval; acquisition of property; random roadside inspections; inspections and audits of licensed private inspection centers; fees

Text of section effective on May 18, 2010.

a. The commission may designate and appoint, subject to existing laws, competent inspectors of motor vehicles to conduct examinations, other than the periodic inspections required pursuant to subsection b. of this section, of motor vehicles required to be inspected in accordance with the provisions of this chapter. The

inspectors may be delegated to enforce the provisions of the motor vehicle and traffic law.

b. (1) The commission shall adopt, pursuant to the "Administrative Procedure Act," P.L.1968, c. 410 (C.52:14B–1 et seq.), rules and regulations consistent with P.L.1966, c. 16 (C.26:2C–8.1 et seq.) and with the requirements of the federal Clean Air Act[1] with respect to the type and character of the inspections to be made, the facility at which the vehicle shall be inspected, the frequency of inspections of motor vehicles and the approval or rejection of motor vehicles as a result of these inspections. These rules and regulations shall require the use of inspection tests that are designed to meet the enhanced inspection and maintenance requirements of the federal Clean Air Act and that have been proven to be feasible and effective for the inspection of large numbers of motor vehicles, except that these tests shall not include the "I/M 240" test. Nothing in this subsection shall preclude the use of the "I/M 240" test in sampling for performance evaluations only or the use of the test at the option of a private inspection facility. The rules and regulations may distinguish between vehicles based on model year, type, or other vehicle characteristics in order to facilitate inspections or to comply with the federal Clean Air Act.

(2) The Department of Environmental Protection and the commission shall investigate advanced testing technologies, including but not limited to remote sensing and onboard diagnostics, and shall, to the extent permitted by law, pursue the use of such technologies, other than the "I/M 240" test, in motor vehicle emission inspections required by the United States Environmental Protection Agency pursuant to the federal Clean Air Act. The commission shall adopt, to the extent practicable, advanced technologies to facilitate the retrieval of testing and other information concerning motor vehicles, which technologies shall include but not be limited to the use of computer bar codes and personal cards containing encoded information, such as a person's operating license, motor vehicle registration, and motor vehicle insurance, the inspection status of a motor vehicle, and mass transit fares, that can be accessed quickly by a computer.

c. Except as modified by the commission to distribute evenly the volume of inspections, all motor vehicles required by the commission, in accordance with the provisions of R.S.39:8–1, to be inspected under this chapter shall be inspected biennially, except that:

(i) after certification by the commission of the federal approval by the Environmental Protection Agency of the State waiver request, model year 2004 and newer motor vehicles shall be inspected no later than four years from the last day of the month in which they were initially registered and thereafter biennially. Motor vehicles four model years old or newer, purchased in a foreign jurisdiction, and to be registered in this State, shall receive a temporary inspection certificate of approval. Motor vehicles four model years old or newer, purchased in a foreign jurisdiction, shall be subject to inspection not later than four years from the last day of the last calendar month of the model year of the vehicle, and thereafter, inspected biennially. Whenever a used motor vehicle four model years old or newer is purchased in this or any other state which has an unexpired New Jersey inspection certificate of approval and is initially registered by the purchaser in this State, the New Jersey inspection certificate of approval displayed on the windshield shall be valid for the remaining time indicated on the inspection certificate of approval. Upon expiration of the inspection certificate of approval, such vehicle shall be subject to inspection and inspected biennially thereafter; and

(ii) classes of vehicles that require more frequent inspections, such as school buses, shall be inspected at such shorter intervals as may be established by the commission after consultation with the Department of Environmental Protection. At any time, the commission may require the owner, lessee, or operator of a motor vehicle to submit the vehicle for inspection.

d. The commission shall furnish to designated inspectors or to other persons authorized to conduct inspections or to grant waivers official certificates of approval, rejection stickers or waiver certificates, the form, content and use of which it shall establish. The certificates of approval, rejection stickers and waiver certificates shall be of a type, such as a windshield sticker or license plate decal, that can be attached to the vehicle or license plate in a location that is readily visible to anyone viewing the vehicle. If a certificate of approval cannot be issued, the driver shall be provided with a written inspection report describing the reasons for rejection and, if appropriate, the repairs needed or likely to be needed to bring the vehicle into compliance with applicable standards.

e. The commission may, with the approval of the State House Commission, purchase, lease or acquire by the exercise of the power of eminent domain any property for the purpose of assisting it in carrying out the provisions of this chapter. This property may also be used by the commission for the exercise of the duties and powers conferred upon it by the other chapters of this Title.

f. For the purpose of implementing the motor vehicle inspection requirements of the federal Clean Air Act and subject to the approval of the Attorney General, the State Treasurer, prior to January 1, 1997, may:

(1) Purchase, lease or acquire by eminent domain any property for vehicle inspection purposes. Any other provision of law to the contrary notwithstanding, no further approval shall be required for transactions authorized by this paragraph, except that a proposed purchase, lease or acquisition by eminent domain shall require the approval of the Joint Budget Oversight Committee, and shall be submitted to the Joint Budget Oversight Committee, which shall review the proposed

purchase, lease or acquisition by eminent domain within 15 business days; and

(2) Sell or lease, or grant an easement in, any property acquired, held or used for vehicle inspection purposes or any other suitable property held by the State that is not currently in use or dedicated to another purpose. For the purpose of this paragraph and notwithstanding any provision of R.S.52:20–1 et seq. to the contrary, the sale or lease of, or the granting of an easement in, real property owned by the State shall be subject to the approval of the State House Commission, which shall meet at the call of the Governor to act on a proposed sale or lease or grant of an easement pursuant to this paragraph. A member of the State House Commission may permit a representative to act on that member's behalf in considering and voting on a sale or lease or grant of an easement pursuant to this paragraph. Any other provision of law to the contrary notwithstanding, any moneys derived from a sale, lease or granting of an easement by the State pursuant to this paragraph shall not be expended unless approved by the Joint Budget Oversight Committee for the purpose of purchasing, leasing or acquiring property pursuant to paragraph (1) of this subsection, except that any moneys derived therefrom and not approved for that purpose shall be appropriated to the Department of Transportation to provide for mass transit improvements.

g. The commission shall conduct roadside examinations of motor vehicles required to be inspected, using such inspection equipment and procedures, and standards established pursuant to section 1 of P.L.1966, c. 16 (C.26:2C–8.1), including, but not limited to, remote sensing technology, as the commission shall deem appropriate to provide for the monitoring of motor vehicles pursuant to this subsection. At least 20,000 vehicles or 0.5 percent of the total number of motor vehicles required to be inspected under this chapter, whichever is less, shall be inspected during each inspection cycle by roadside examination teams under the supervision of the commission. The commission may require any vehicle failing a roadside examination to be inspected at an official inspection facility or a private inspection facility within a time period fixed by the commission. Failure to appear and pass inspection within the time period fixed by the commission shall result in registration suspension in addition to any other penalties provided in this Title. The commission shall conduct an aggressive roadside inspection program to ensure that all motor vehicles that are required to be inspected in this State are in compliance with State law.

h. The commission, and, when appropriate, the Department of Environmental Protection, shall conduct inspections and audits of licensed private inspection facilities, official inspection facilities and designated inspectors to ensure accurate test equipment calibration and use, and compliance with proper inspection procedures and with the provisions of P.L.1995, c. 112 (C.39:8–41 et al.) and any regulations adopted pursuant thereto by the commission or by the Department of

Environmental Protection. These inspections and audits shall be conducted at such times and in such manner as the commission, upon consultation with the Department of Environmental Protection, shall determine in order to provide quality assurance in the performance of the inspection and maintenance program.

i. (1) The commission shall make a charge of $2.50 for the initial inspection for each vehicle subject to inspection, which amount shall be paid to the commission or its representative when payment of the registration fees fixed in chapter 3 of this Title is made which inspection charge shall be considered a service charge and shall be subject to the calculation of proportional revenue remitted to the commission pursuant to section 105 of P.L.2003, c. 13 (C.39:2A–36); provided however, that on and after January 1, 1999, a school bus as defined pursuant to section 3 of P.L.1999, c. 5 (C.39:3B–20) and having a registration period commencing on or after January 1, 1999, shall be subject to an inspection fee for each in-terminal or in-lieu-of terminal inspection in accordance with the following schedule:

School Bus Specification Inspection	$50 per bus
School Bus Inspection	$25 per bus
School Bus Reinspection	$25 per bus subject to the conditions set forth below

The specification inspection is required when a school bus is put into service in New Jersey, whether a new bus or a bus from another state. The specification inspection is conducted to ensure that the school bus meets New Jersey specification standards. The school bus inspection fees shall be charged to the operator for each in-terminal or in-lieu-of terminal inspection. School Vehicle Type I and School Vehicle Type II buses shall be inspected semiannually. Retired school buses shall be inspected annually. No school bus inspection fee shall be charged for any reinspection conducted by the commission if the reinspection is conducted on the same day as the inspection that necessitated the reinspection. If an additional trip is required by the commission's inspectors, a fee of $25 per bus shall be charged. School bus inspection fees shall be paid to the commission or the commission's designee subject to the terms and conditions prescribed by the commission and shall be considered service charges of the commission and not subject to the calculation of proportional revenue remitted to the commission pursuant to section 105 of P.L.2003, c. 13 (C.39:2A–36). Any law or rule or regulation adopted pursuant thereto to the contrary notwithstanding, a registration fee authorized pursuant to chapter 3 of Title 39 of the Revised Statutes shall not be increased for the purpose of paying any costs associated in any manner with the establishment, implementation or operation of the motor vehicle inspection

and maintenance program established pursuant to P.L. 1995, c. 112 (C.39:8–41 et al.).

(2) The commission shall establish by regulation a fee to cover the costs of inspecting any vehicle that is required, or has the option, under federal law to be inspected in this State but is registered in another state or is owned or leased by the federal government. In determining these costs, the commission shall include all capital and direct and indirect operating costs associated with the inspection of these vehicles including, but not limited to, the costs of the actual inspection, the creation and maintenance of the vehicle inspection record, administrative, oversight and quality assurance costs and the costs associated with reporting inspection information to the owner, the federal government and agencies of other states. All fees collected pursuant to this subsection shall be paid to the State Treasurer and deposited in the "Motor Vehicle Inspection Fund" established pursuant to subsection j. of this section.

j. There is established in the General Fund a special dedicated, non-lapsing fund to be known as the "Motor Vehicle Inspection Fund," which shall be administered by the State Treasurer. The State Treasurer shall deposit into the "Motor Vehicle Inspection Fund" $11.50 from each motor vehicle registration fee received by the State after June 30, 1995. This fee shall be considered a service charge of the commission and shall be subject to the calculation of proportional revenue remitted to the commission pursuant to section 105 of P.L.2003, c. 13 (C.39:2A–36). The Legislature shall annually appropriate from the fund an amount necessary to pay the reasonable and necessary expenses of the implementation and operation of the motor vehicle inspection program. The State Treasurer shall:

(1) Pay to a private contractor or contractors contracted to design, construct, renovate, equip, establish, maintain and operate official inspection facilities under a contract or contracts entered into with the State Treasurer pursuant to subsection a. of section 4 of P.L.1995, c. 112 (C.39:8–44) from the fund the amount necessary to meet the costs agreed to under the contract or contracts; and

(2) Transfer from the fund to the commission as provided pursuant to section 105 of P.L.2003, c. 13 (C.39:2A–36) and the Department of Environmental Protection the amounts necessary to finance the costs of administering and implementing all aspects of the inspection and maintenance program, and to the Office of Telecommunications and Information Systems in the Department of the Treasury the amount necessary for computer support upgrades;

Moneys remaining in the fund and any unexpended balance of appropriations from the fund at the end of each fiscal year shall be reappropriated for the purposes of the fund. Any interest earned on moneys in the fund shall be credited to the fund.

Amended by L.1955, c. 9, p. 50, 1; L.1975, c. 156, 1, eff. July 16, 1975; L.1976, c. 43, 4; L.1983, c. 236, 3, eff. June 30, 1983; L.1986, c. 22, 2, eff. June 2, 1986; L.1989, c. 167, 1; L.1995, c. 112, 20, eff. June 2, 1995; L.1999, c. 5, 8, eff. Jan. 1, 1999; L.2002, c. 34, 15, eff. July 1, 2002; L .2003, c. 13, § 107, eff. July 1, 2003; L.2009, c. 331, § 5, eff. May 18, 2010.

1 42 U.S.C.A. § 7401 et seq.

39:8–2.1. Uniforms for motor vehicle inspectors

The Division of Motor Vehicles in the Department of Law and Public Safety shall provide uniforms for its employees engaged in examining and inspecting motor vehicles at official inspection stations, and shall pay for such uniforms out of any available appropriations.

L.1949, c. 221, p. 703, § 1.

39:8–2.2. Inspection stations; hours open; rules and regulations

During the 12 calendar months following the effective date of this act the Director of the Division of Motor Vehicles in the State Department of Law and Public Safety shall provide for the keeping open of such of the motor vehicle inspection stations as he shall designate from 8:00 A.M. to 8:00 P.M. on all the days of the week except Sundays. The said director shall make and enforce such rules, regulations and directions as may be necessary to effectuate the purposes of this act.

L.1956, c. 25, p. 68, § 1.

39:8–2.3. Possession of property in advance of compensation

In addition to the powers now vested in the Director of the Division of Motor Vehicles under section 39:8–2 of the Revised Statutes for the acquisition of property by the power of eminent domain, the Director, upon or after exercising the right of condemnation by instituting an action in the Superior Court in the manner provided by chapter 1 of Title 20 of the Revised Statutes,[1] may in advance of making compensation therefor take immediate possession of and occupy, use and improve the property, notwithstanding any other law.

L.1956, c. 120, p. 514, § 1.

1 N.J.S.A. § 20:1–1 et seq. (Repealed. See, now, § 20:3–1 et seq.)

39:8–3. Issuance of certificates of approval; prerequisites

a. No certificate of approval shall be issued by an examiner, official inspection facility or private inspection facility until the motor vehicle inspected successfully passes all emission tests required by the director and the mechanism, brakes and equipment of the motor vehicle inspected have been found to be in a proper and safe condition and complying with the laws of this State.

b. Notwithstanding the issuance or non-issuance of a certificate of approval, the obligation to ensure that a

vehicle is in a proper and safe condition rests with the owner, operator or lessee, as appropriate, of the vehicle.

Amended by L.1995, c. 112, § 21, eff. June 2, 1995.

39:8–4. Adjustments, corrections or repairs to be made; issuance of rejection sticker; certificate of approval; issuance; notice to correct deficiency

a. If inspections as required by R.S. 39:8–1 disclose the necessity for adjustments, corrections or repairs, the director shall cause a rejection sticker to be issued.

b. The director may require the owner of a motor vehicle requiring an adjustment, correction or repair that is not emission-related to have that adjustment, correction or repair made and thereafter have the vehicle reinspected at an official inspection facility or at a licensed private inspection facility within the period designated by the director.

The director may cause a certificate of approval to be issued for a motor vehicle needing an adjustment, correction or repair that is not emission-related in order to conform to the requirements of chapter 3 and chapter 8 of this Title, but which, in the director's determination, is nevertheless safe. In such cases the director shall issue notice to the vehicle owner to have the adjustment, correction or repair made within a specified period of time, subject to the penalties of R.S. 39:8–9.

c. The director shall require the owner of a motor vehicle requiring an adjustment, correction or repair that is emission-related to have that adjustment, correction or repair made and thereafter have the vehicle reinspected at an official inspection facility or at a private inspection facility, as determined by the director, within the period designated by the director.

Amended by L.1975, c. 156, § 2, eff. July 16, 1975; L.1975, c. 157, § 1, eff. July 16, 1975; L.1986, c. 22, § 3, eff. June 2, 1986; L.1995, c. 112, § 22, eff. June 2, 1995.

39:8–4.1. Rules and regulations

The director may promulgate such rules and regulations as may be necessary to effectuate the purposes of this act.

L.1975, c. 157, § 2, eff. July 16, 1975.

39:8–5. Reports concerning inspections

Text of section effective until May 18, 2010.

a. Every designated examiner, official inspection facility or private inspection facility shall make such reports to the director concerning inspections made and the results thereof, and in such form and at such time, as the director may require. The director may furnish to the examiners and inspection facilities forms for such reports. The director may require the use of electronic media for the gathering and transmission of inspection data and reports when the director deems it appropriate or when electronic media are required by federal law.

b. Every motor vehicle repair facility that is registered pursuant to section 13 of P.L.1995, c. 112 (C. 39:8–53) shall make such reports to the director concerning emission repairs made and the results thereof, as the director may require. The director may furnish to registered motor vehicle repair facilities forms to be completed by them in documenting emission repairs to motor vehicles, which forms shall be presented by the operator of the vehicle to an emission inspector at the time of vehicle reinspection.

Amended by L.1955, c. 9, p. 51, § 2; L.1995, c. 112, § 23, eff. June 2, 1995.

39:8–5. Reports concerning inspections

Text of section effective on May 18, 2010.

a. Every designated inspector, official inspection facility or private inspection facility shall make such reports to the chief administrator concerning inspections made and the results thereof, and in such form and at such time, as the chief administrator may require. The chief administrator may furnish to the inspectors and inspection facilities forms for such reports. The chief administrator may require the use of electronic media for the gathering and transmission of inspection data and reports when the chief administrator deems it appropriate or when electronic media are required by federal law.

b. Every motor vehicle repair facility that is registered pursuant to section 13 of P.L.1995, c. 112 (C.39:8–53) shall make such reports to the chief administrator concerning emission repairs made and the results thereof, as the chief administrator may require. The chief administrator may furnish to registered motor vehicle repair facilities forms to be completed by them in documenting emission repairs to motor vehicles, which forms shall be presented by the operator of the vehicle to an emission inspector at the time of vehicle reinspection.

Amended by L.1955, c. 9, p. 51, § 2; L.1995, c. 112, § 23, eff. June 2, 1995; L.2009, c. 331, § 6, eff. May 18, 2010.

39:8–6. Display of approval certificate on request

During the period designated by the director, any police officer who shall exhibit his badge or other sign of authority may stop any motor vehicle and require the owner or operator to display an official certificate of approval for the motor vehicle being operated.

Amended by L.1983, c. 403, § 27, eff. Dec. 23, 1983.

39:8–7. Revocation, suspension or denial of registration for failure to display appropriate certificate; vehicles incapable of being made safe or of being brought within emission standards

Except as otherwise provided pursuant to R.S. 39:3–5, the director may suspend, revoke or deny the registration of a motor vehicle registered or required to be registered in this State, or the reciprocity privilege of a motor vehicle registered in another state, if the motor vehicle is subject to the inspection requirement of this State and operated or parked on any public road, street or highway or any public or quasi-public property in this State, and:

a. Does not have displayed upon it a current certificate of approval, current rejection sticker or current waiver certificate issued in accordance with this chapter; or

b. Has not successfully passed inspection or been granted a waiver within the time period prescribed by the director; or

c. Is shown by the inspection to be incapable of being placed in a proper condition to make its use safe on the highway or incapable of being brought within the emission standards or requirements established by law or regulation, and for which a certificate of approval or waiver certificate cannot be issued.

Amended by L.1995, c. 112, § 24, eff. June 2, 1995.

39:8–8. Certificate of approval as prerequisite for registration

The director may rule that a certificate of approval shall serve as a prerequisite for obtaining a registration for the following registration period.

Amended by L.1955, c. 9, p. 51, § 3.

39:8–9. Enforcement of chapter; violations; punishment; remedies; procedure; revocation of certificate

a. The enforcement of this chapter shall be vested in the director and the police or peace officers of any municipality, any county or the State.

b. An owner or lessee who:

(1) Fails or refuses to have a motor vehicle examined within the time period prescribed by the director; or

(2) After having had it examined, fails or refuses to place or display a certificate of approval, rejection sticker or waiver certificate upon the windshield or other location on the vehicle as may be prescribed by the director; or

(3) Fails or refuses to place the motor vehicle in proper condition after having had the same examined; or

(4) In any manner, fails to conform to the provisions of this chapter or the regulations adopted by the director pursuant thereto, shall be guilty of violating the provisions of this chapter, and shall be subject to a fine of not less than $100 or more than $200 or to imprisonment for not more than 30 days, or to both such fine and imprisonment.

c. A person who fraudulently obtains a certificate of approval, rejection sticker or waiver certificate, or displays or has in his possession a fictitious, altered, or stolen certificate of approval, rejection sticker or waiver certificate shall be subject to a fine of $500 for each such certificate or sticker.

d. The provisions of this chapter shall be enforced and all penalties for the violation thereof shall be recovered in accordance with the provisions of "the penalty enforcement law" (N.J.S. 2A:58–1 et seq.), and in addition to the provisions and remedies therein contained, the following provisions and remedies shall be applicable in any proceeding brought for a violation of any of the provisions of this chapter:

(1) The several municipal courts shall have jurisdiction of such proceeding, in addition to the courts prescribed in "the penalty enforcement law";

(2) The complaint in any such proceeding may be made on information and belief by the director, or any police or peace officer of any municipality, any county or the State;

(3) A warrant may issue in lieu of summons;

(4) Any police or peace officer shall be empowered to serve and execute process in any such proceeding;

(5) The hearing in any such proceeding shall be without a jury;

(6) Any such proceeding may be brought in the name of the Director of the Division of Motor Vehicles in the Department of Law and Public Safety or in the name of the State of New Jersey;

(7) Any sums received in payment of any fines imposed in any such proceeding shall be paid to the Director of the Division of Motor Vehicles and shall be paid by him to the State Treasurer, who shall deposit one-half of such sums in the "Motor Vehicle Inspection Fund" established pursuant to subsection j. of R.S. 39:8–2, and who shall pay the remaining one-half of such sums to the county or municipality initiating the complaint or summons or, if initiated by State law enforcement personnel, to the State Treasury;

(8) The director or judge before whom any hearing under this chapter is had may revoke the registration certificate of any motor vehicle owned or leased by any person, when such person shall have been found to be in violation of any of the provisions of this chapter as shall in the discretion of the director or judge justify such revocation.

e. The director may order the suspension of the registration or reciprocity privilege of any motor vehicle found to be in violation of any of the provisions of this chapter. If the owner or lessee fails to surrender the license plates for that vehicle to the division within 45 days of the mailing of an order requiring their surrender, the director may order the confiscation of the license plates of the vehicle that is in violation. An order of license plate confiscation issued by the director shall include an order imposing a civil penalty of $200 on the owner or lessee of the vehicle. This civil penalty shall be paid to the State Treasurer, who shall deposit one-half of the amount in the "Motor Vehicle Inspection Fund" established pursuant to subsection j. of R.S. 39:8–2 and pay the remaining one-half to any municipality or county whose law enforcement, police or peace

officers confiscated the plates in accordance with the order of the director, or if the plates were confiscated by State law enforcement personnel, to the State Treasury. A civil penalty imposed pursuant to this subsection shall be in addition to any other penalty provided by this chapter.

Amended by L.1954, c. 75, p. 444, § 1; L.1983, c. 403, § 28, eff. Dec. 23, 1983; L.1995, c. 112, § 25, eff. June 2, 1995.

39:8–10. Authority of director; adoption of rules and regulations for enforcement; hiring and compensation of employees

The director shall have authority to make rules and regulations necessary for the administration and enforcement of this chapter. The director may employ, subject to existing laws, such persons as the director requires for the administration and enforcement of this chapter and the director may fix their compensation.

Amended by L.1955, c. 9, p. 51, § 4; L.1995, c. 112, § 26, eff. June 2, 1995.

39:8–11. Private inspection centers; license; initial motor vehicle inspections and certification of corrections, adjustments or repairs; approval sticker

The director may, after appropriate inquiry and investigation, license to operate private inspection centers as many qualified and properly equipped persons engaged in the business of motor vehicle repairs and service as are necessary, to conduct initial motor vehicle inspections, and to certify that the specific items for which a vehicle was initially rejected have been adjusted, corrected or repaired by him or under his direction, and that the condition of the items conforms to the standards established by law or regulation. The certification shall be evidenced by a private inspection approval sticker placed on the vehicle as prescribed by the director.

L.1975, c. 156, § 3, eff. July 16, 1975. Amended by L.1986, c. 22, § 4, eff. June 2, 1986.

39:8–12. Certification or rejection of motor vehicle on initial inspection or adjustment, correction or repair of previously rejected vehicle

A licensee shall inspect and certify or reject a motor vehicle presented to him for an initial inspection. Certification shall indicate that the licensee or his employee has inspected the motor vehicle as prescribed by the director and has found that the motor vehicle conforms to the standards established by law or regulation.

A licensee shall reinspect and certify or reject any previously rejected vehicle presented to him for adjustment, correction or repair, and any vehicle presented by an owner who himself has made the necessary adjustment, correction or repair. Such certification shall indicate that the licensee or his employee has reinspected the items for which a vehicle has been rejected, as prescribed by the director, and has found that the condition of the items conforms to the standards established by law or regulation.

L.1975, c. 156, § 4, eff. July 16, 1975. Amended by L.1986, c. 22, § 5, eff. June 2, 1986.

39:8–13. Charges for certification, reinspection and initial inspection; posting schedule; repairs or adjustments at licensed private center; conditions

a. A licensee may charge any owner whose vehicle was adjusted, corrected or repaired by or under the direction of the licensee an amount for certification to be determined by the director.

b. A licensee may charge any owner who himself has made the necessary adjustments, corrections or repairs an amount for reinspection computed at the hourly rate charged by the licensee for normal on premises repairs, and an amount for certification. The director shall determine the average length of time required to reinspect a specific rejected item, which shall be the maximum time for which a licensee may charge, and shall determine the charge for certification.

c. Licensees shall post a schedule of charges for initial inspection, reinspection and for certification in a prominent place on the premises, and shall file a copy thereof with the director.

d. A licensee may charge an owner whose motor vehicle has been initially inspected by or under the direction of the licensee an amount to be determined by the director.

e. No licensed private inspection center shall require, as a condition of performing the inspection, that any needed repairs or adjustments be done by the person or at the facility of the person performing the inspection.

f. No service or adjustment shall be performed on the vehicle at the licensed private inspection center where the vehicle was initially inspected unless the customer signs a written acknowledgment and waiver indicating that he understands his right to have service and adjustment done elsewhere and expressly waives his right.

L.1975, c. 156, § 5, eff. July 16, 1975. Amended by L.1986, c. 22, § 6, eff. June 2, 1986.

39:8–14. Owner or lessee of 10 or more vehicles; license; certification of initial inspections and reinspections; approval sticker

a. The director may license any person who is the owner or lessee of 10 or more motor vehicles to initially inspect, reinspect and certify those vehicles if such person has available to him the equipment, facilities and qualified employees, or other qualified person under his control by contract, necessary to make the required initial inspection, adjustments, corrections or repairs. When the licensee, or his employee, or other qualified person under his control conducts an initial inspection, he shall certify that he or his employee or other

qualified person under his control by contract has inspected the motor vehicle as prescribed by the director and has found that the motor vehicle conforms to the standards established by law or regulation. When a motor vehicle is reinspected, the licensee shall certify that the items for which a vehicle was initially rejected have been adjusted, corrected or repaired by him or under his direction and that the condition of the items conforms to the standards established by law or regulation. The certification shall be evidenced by a private inspection approval sticker placed on the vehicle as prescribed by the director.

b. Any inspection or reinspection conducted pursuant to this section relating to emissions from a motor vehicle powered with diesel fuel that is also subject to the provisions of P.L.1995, c. 157 (C. 39:8–59 et al.) shall be conducted in accordance with the provisions of that act.

L.1975, c. 156, § 6, eff. July 16, 1975. Amended by L.1983, c. 236, § 4, eff. June 30, 1983; L.1986, c. 22, § 7, eff. June 2, 1986; L.1995, c. 157, § 35.

39:8–15. Annual expiration of license

Every private inspection center license issued on or after May 1 in any year shall be valid through June 30 of the following year.

L.1975, c. 156, § 7, eff. July 16, 1975. Amended by L.1986, c. 22, § 8, eff. June 2, 1986.

39:8–16. Application or renewal of license; form and contents; fee; proof of financial responsibility

An application or renewal for a private inspection center license shall be in such form and shall contain such information as the director may prescribe, and shall be accompanied annually by a nonrefundable $25.00 fee, which shall be remitted to the General Treasury. The director shall require a licensee to have in effect at all times liability insurance or such other proof of financial responsibility as he may prescribe, and may require such other qualifications of a licensee and his premises as are necessary.

L.1975, c. 156, § 8, eff. July 16, 1975. Amended by L.1982, c. 53, § 4, eff. July 1, 1982; L.1986, c. 22, § 9, eff. June 2, 1986.

39:8–17. Private inspection approval stickers; provision to licensee; fee; records; safeguards; accounting

The director shall provide each licensee as many numbered private inspection approval stickers as may be required, and may charge the licensee $1.00 for each sticker. There shall be no refund or credit for expired or unused private inspection approval stickers. Every licensee shall keep such records of inspections, reinspections and approval stickers issued as the director may prescribe, shall make such records available to the director upon demand, shall institute such safeguards to secure the stickers from theft, loss or fraudulent use as the director may prescribe, shall return any unused expired stickers to the director, and shall upon request account to the director for all stickers.

L.1975, c. 156, § 9, eff. July 16, 1975. Amended by L.1982, c. 53, § 5, eff. July 1, 1982; L.1986, c. 22, § 10, eff. June 2, 1986.

39:8–18. Affixation of sticker without reinspection or determination of conformity to standards or after charge of fee for repair work not performed or performed unnecessarily; penalty

A person who affixes a private inspection approval sticker to a motor vehicle without having reinspected the specific item for which the vehicle was initially rejected, or without having determined that the condition of the item conforms to standards established by law or regulation, shall be guilty of violating the provisions of this chapter, and shall be fined not less than $1,000.00 or more than $1,500.00 and shall have the license suspended for a period of at least one year but not more than three years for a first offense or not less than $2,000.00 or more than $3,500.00 and shall have the license permanently revoked for a subsequent offense. This section shall be enforced pursuant to R.S. 39:8–9.

A person who charges a fee for repair work not performed or performed unnecessarily and affixes a private inspection approval sticker shall be punished under the terms of P.L.1960, c. 39 (C. 56:8–1 et seq.), and any regulation adopted thereunder.

L.1975, c. 156, § 10, eff. July 16, 1975. Amended by L.1986, c. 22, § 11, eff. June 2, 1986.

39:8–19. Denial, suspension, revocation or refusal of renewal of license; grounds

a. The director may deny, suspend or revoke a private inspection center license or refuse renewal thereof for cause, including but not limited to one or more of the following:

(1) Violation of any provision of this act or of any regulation adopted thereunder, including a finding of guilt made pursuant to section 10 of this act; [1]

(2) Fraud or misrepresentation in securing the license or in the conduct of the licensed activity;

(3) Making initial inspection or reinspection service charges in excess of those posted on the licensed premises and filed with the director;

(4) Conviction of a crime involving moral turpitude;

(5) Violation of P.L.1960, c. 39 (C. 56:8–1 et seq.) or of any regulation adopted thereunder;

(6) Other good cause.

b. The director may suspend a license for such period as he deems fit, pursuant to the "Administrative Procedure Act," P.L.1968, c. 410 (C. 52:14B–1 et seq.). If the director determines that the public interest requires suspension of a license pursuant to this act prior to hearing, the director may do so, provided that the licensee is afforded the opportunity to request in writing a hearing within 10 days of the effective date of the suspension, and an administrative adjudication shall be held as soon thereafter as possible.

c. The suspension or revocation of a private inspection center license shall not of itself be cause for the denial, suspension or revocation of any other business license held by the private inspection center licensee, issued by the State or any of its political subdivisions.

L.1975, c. 156, § 11, eff. July 16, 1975. Amended by L.1986, c. 22, § 12, eff. June 2, 1986.

[1] N.J.S.A. § 39:8–18.

39:8–20. Discontinuance of operation or suspension or revocation of license; delivery of items to director; failure to deliver; disorderly person

Any licensee who discontinues operation of a private inspection center, or whose license has been suspended or revoked, or whose renewal thereof has been denied, shall forthwith deliver to the director the license, all unused private inspection approval stickers, all reinspection records and other items issued to the licensee or required by the director to be kept in connection with the operation of the private inspection center. Any person who fails to deliver these items to the director is a disorderly person.

L.1975, c. 156, § 12, eff. July 16, 1975. Amended by L.1986, c. 22, § 13, eff. June 2, 1986.

39:8–21. Unauthorized display or advertisement as private inspection center or transfer of license; disorderly persons offense

Any person who shall display or cause or permit to be displayed any sign, mark, or advertisement as a private inspection center when a license has not been issued by the director or is not then in effect, or who shall transfer or attempt to transfer a private inspection center license is a disorderly person.

L.1975, c. 156, § 13, eff. July 16, 1975. Amended by L.1986, c. 22, § 14, eff. June 2, 1986.

39:8–22. Employees and expenditures for supervision of private inspection centers

The director may, subject to existing law, employ such persons and make such expenditures as are necessary to supervise the operation of licensed private inspection centers to insure compliance with the provisions of this act and the regulations adopted pursuant thereto.

L.1975, c. 156, § 14, eff. July 16, 1975. Amended by L.1986, c. 22, § 15, eff. June 2, 1986.

39:8–23. Rules and regulations

The director may adopt such rules and regulations as may be required or appropriate to effectuate the purposes of this act.

L.1975, c. 156, § 15, eff. July 16, 1975.

39:8–24. Effective date

This act shall take effect immediately.

L.1975, c. 156, § 16, eff. July 16, 1975. Amended by L.1977, c. 270, § 1, eff. Oct. 20, 1977.

39:8–25 to 39:8–36. Repealed by L.1986, c. 22, § 21, eff. June 2, 1986

39:8–37. Reinspection centers; redesignation as private inspection centers; authority; renewal of license

All reinspection centers licensed pursuant to P.L. 1975, c. 156 (C. 39:8–11 et seq.) shall be redesignated by virtue of this 1986 amendatory and supplementary act as private inspection centers with the authority to make initial motor vehicle inspections, reinspections and repairs to the extent and under the conditions permitted herein. All reinspection center licenses shall be renewed as if they were private inspection center licenses upon their expiration.

L.1986, c. 22, § 17, eff. June 2, 1986.

39:8–38. Licensed private inspection centers; emissions test equipment

All licensed private inspection centers shall use emissions test equipment which has been certified by the Department of Environmental Protection. The department shall adopt standards for the certification of the equipment, which shall include but not be limited to all of the following:

a. An automated system to control test sequencing, the automatic pass or fail decision, and the format for the test report and recorded magnetic tape file;

b. An exhaust gas analysis portion;

c. A device to accept and record vehicle identification information; and

d. A device to provide a printed record of the test results to the consumer.

L.1986, c. 22, § 18, eff. June 2, 1986.

39:8–39. Qualifications of licensee or employee

A licensee or his employee shall not perform initial inspections or reinspections and make repairs for compensation pursuant to this act unless qualified by the completion of training courses prescribed by the division, in cooperation with the Department of Environmental Protection, through regulations which establish standards for the training and certification of mechanics employed at private inspection centers.

L.1986, c. 22, § 19, eff. June 2, 1986.

39:8–40. Rules and regulations; encouragement of participation in inspection program

The director may promulgate rules and regulations pursuant to the "Administrative Procedure Act," P.L. 1968, c. 410 (C. 52:14B–1 et seq.), to effectuate the purposes of this act. The director shall also take the appropriate steps necessary to ensure the widespread participation in the public and private motor vehicle inspection program by the private commercial sector and by the public at large.

L.1986, c. 22, § 20, eff. June 2, 1986.

39:8–41. Federal clean air mandate compliance act; short title

Sections 1 through 18 of this act shall be known and may be cited as the "Federal Clean Air Mandate Compliance Act."

L.1995, c. 112, § 1, eff. June 2, 1995.

39:8–42. Legislative findings and declaration

The Legislature finds and declares that the federal Clean Air Act requires states that have been determined to be in nonattainment for certain ambient air quality standards to take extraordinary measures to reduce air emissions; and that among these measures is an enhanced motor vehicle inspection and maintenance program.

The Legislature further finds and declares that the standards established by the United States Environmental Protection Agency are based on computer modeling and not on scientific testing; that the requirements of the Environmental Protection Agency regulations therefore may not achieve the federal emission reduction goals for New Jersey; and that officials of the Environmental Protection Agency are no longer mandating that the State program require the use of the "I/M 240" test and have recently expressed a greater flexibility in allowing states to make certain decisions in the implementation of this enhanced inspection and maintenance program.

The Legislature further finds and declares that the inspection and maintenance program being imposed by the Environmental Protection Agency pursuant to the federal law will be expensive and burdensome on the citizens of this State, but that the alternative to adopting this program is a series of federal sanctions that would result in the loss of federal highway monies, more stringent permitting criteria for industry and the imposition of an air pollution control program by the Environmental Protection Agency.

The Legislature further finds and declares that it would not adopt this enhanced motor vehicle inspection and maintenance program if the federal government were not forcing such action by the threat of the above-mentioned sanctions.

The Legislature further finds and declares that it shall take this opportunity to improve the existing motor vehicle inspection system by authorizing competitive contracting for or privatization of motor vehicle inspections and making other necessary legislative reforms to the provisions of Title 39 of the Revised Statutes.

The Legislature therefore determines that an enhanced inspection and maintenance program shall be adopted, that this inspection and maintenance program shall be as consumer-friendly as possible and shall not use the "I/M 240" test, except as hereinafter specified, and that advanced testing technologies, including but not limited to remote sensing, shall be investigated and used for emission testing to the extent permitted by the Environmental Protection Agency.

L.1995, c. 112, § 2, eff. June 2, 1995.

39:8–43. Definitions

As used in chapter 8 of Title 39 of the Revised Statutes:

"Certificate of Approval" means a document, in a form determined by the director, issued in accordance with guidelines set by the division certifying that a motor vehicle complies with the requirements of Title 39 and Title 26 of the Revised Statutes and the regulations regarding the inspection of motor vehicles adopted pursuant thereto;

"Director" means the Director of the Division of Motor Vehicles in the Department of Law and Public Safety;

"Division" means the Division of Motor Vehicles in the Department of Law and Public Safety;

"Federal Clean Air Act" means the federal "Clean Air Act," 42 U.S.C. § 7401 et seq., and any subsequent amendments or supplements to that act;

"Gross weight" means gross vehicle weight rating, as that term is defined in section 3 of P.L.1990, c. 103 (C. 39:3–10.11);

"Official inspection facility" means a test-only inspection facility that is operated by the division or that the State Treasurer has contracted for pursuant to section 4 of P.L.1995, c. 112 (C. 39:8–44); and

"Private inspection facility" means an inspection facility licensed by the director pursuant to section 5 of P.L.1995, c. 112 (C. 39:8–45).

L.1995, c. 112, § 3, eff. June 2, 1995.

39:8–44. Design, construction and operation of inspection facilities; training grants

a. The State Treasurer shall either:

(1) Assign to the State the full responsibility for the design, construction, renovation, equipment, establishment, maintenance, and operation of official inspection facilities and other aspects of the inspection and maintenance program, including safety inspections;

(2) Enter into a contract or contracts with a private contractor or contractors for the design, construction, renovation, equipment, establishment, maintenance, and operation of official inspection facilities and other aspects of the inspection and maintenance program, including safety inspections; or

(3) Assign to the State partial responsibility and enter into a contract or contracts with a private contractor or contractors for the remaining responsibili-

ty for the design, construction, renovation, equipment, establishment, maintenance, and operation of official inspection facilities and other aspects of the inspection and maintenance program, including safety inspections.

The State Treasurer shall choose one of the options pursuant to this subsection based on a determination of the best interests of the citizens of New Jersey. At least seven business days prior to the award of a contract that includes the operation or maintenance of an official inspection facility pursuant to this section, the State Treasurer shall issue a notice of intent to award the contract and shall submit to the Legislature the notice of intent and a report describing the option chosen, which shall include an economic analysis of the three options listed in this subsection with respect to the operation or maintenance portion of the contract.

b. (1) A contract authorized by this section may, subject to the provisions of subsection f. of R.S. 39:8–2, include the purchase, lease or sale of an interest in real or personal property. The State Treasurer is authorized to exercise all authority of the Directors of the Division of Purchase and Property and of the Division of Building and Construction[1] to award the contract or contracts authorized by this section as a single contract, multiple branch contracts or multiple single contracts. Any contract awarded pursuant to this section shall be awarded in accordance with the provisions of P.L.1954, c. 48 (C. 52:34–6 et seq.) and any rules and regulations promulgated pursuant to that act. The provisions of R.S. 52:32–2 shall not apply to any contract authorized by this section.

(2) Notwithstanding the provisions of chapter 35 of Title 52 of the Revised Statutes, the State Treasurer is not required to limit bids to persons who are prequalified. The State Treasurer is authorized to require each person who submits a bid for a contract pursuant to this section to submit statements under oath in response to a questionnaire that develops fully that person's financial ability, adequacy of plant and equipment, organization, prior experience and any other facts pertinent and material to qualification, including qualification of any subcontractors, for the contract sought. Any such questionnaire required shall be standardized with respect to, and shall be set forth in, each invitation to bid.

(3) Any other provision of law to the contrary notwithstanding, and subject to guidelines for conflict of interest established by the Attorney General, for the purposes of this section a State officer or employee or a group of State officers or employees may enter into a contract or contracts as a private contractor. A State officer or employee having any duties or responsibilities in connection with the evaluation or awarding of a contract pursuant to this section shall not individually or through any person or entity acting on behalf of that officer or employee bid on or enter into a contract as a private contractor.

(4) A contractor for the operation of an official inspection facility, or any of its officers or employees,

may not be engaged in the business of selling, maintaining, or repairing motor vehicles or selling motor vehicle replacement or repair parts. A contractor's employees shall not be deemed employees of the State for any purpose.

c. A contract for the operation of an official inspection facility shall provide for motor vehicle inspection services that are consumer-friendly to the maximum extent feasible. A contract shall at a minimum specify that:

(1) New or relocated inspection facilities shall be sited close to population centers, but in locations that remain convenient for suburban and rural residents;

(2) An inspection facility shall be open for inspections, exclusive of holidays, at least 55 hours each week, including hours prior to 9:00 am or after 5:00 pm on weekdays and hours on the weekend, except that the facility may lessen or expand these hours based on the results of a survey of persons who use the facility for motor vehicle inspections;

(3) An inspection facility shall maintain a climate-controlled waiting area for persons whose motor vehicles are being inspected;

(4) At least one lane at each inspection facility shall be reserved to the extent practicable for reinspections, although this lane may be opened to initial inspections whenever there are no reinspections being performed;

(5) The number of inspection lanes provided for in the contract to be constructed may be increased to meet the standards set by the director pursuant to subsection d. of this section only if the contractor can show that this increase is more cost-effective than extending the hours of operation;

(6) A toll-free telephone number and a network of computerized signs shall be established, and public service announcements shall be aired to advise motorists of the length of lines at inspection facilities. Periodic surveys concerning hours and methods of operation shall be conducted. Each motor vehicle operator who arrives at a facility for an inspection shall be provided with a written document containing the following statement:

"The motor vehicle emission test being conducted at this facility has been imposed on the residents of this State by an act of the Congress of the United States and the regulations of the United States Environmental Protection Agency."

In addition, the written document shall include the name and address of the Administrator of the federal Environmental Protection Agency and of each member of Congress elected from this State.

A contractor shall spend not less than one percent of its operating budget to provide an ongoing public information program; and

(7) All qualified full-time employees whose employment with the division is terminated as a result of

P.L.1995, c. 112 (C. 39:8–41 et al.) shall be offered full-time employment. If more than one contract for the operation of official inspection facilities is awarded, each contractor shall offer full-time employment to a percentage of the number of such employees that is equal to the percentage of the total number of inspection lanes that will be operated by that contractor.

d. The director shall adopt, pursuant to the "Administrative Procedure Act," P.L.1968, c. 410 (C. 52:14B–1 et seq.), regulations to establish the conduct of inspections by any person who has entered into a contract with the State pursuant to subsection a. of this section, and may issue directives or guidelines or enter into contracts or agreements for the oversight and regulation of any person who has entered into a contract with the State pursuant to subsection a. of this section. The director shall establish standards that are designed to achieve average wait times of 30 minutes or less and to keep the overall operating cost of the facilities to a minimum. The director shall develop a system of incentives that are designed to achieve average wait times of 15 minutes or less. Data generated at any official inspection facility shall be the property of the State and shall be fully accessible to the division at any time.

e. If a dispute over contract compliance, performance or termination cannot be resolved by the State Treasurer and the private contractor pursuant to the procedures set forth in a contract entered into pursuant to the provisions of this section, either party to the contract may file with the Superior Court a request either for an order either to terminate the contract or for an order for other appropriate relief to the dispute. Any provision of N.J.S. 59:13–5 to the contrary notwithstanding, the State Treasurer may consent to the filing of such a request prior to the expiration of 90 days from the date that the notice of claim is received. The court may take such action as it may deem necessary to facilitate the expeditious resolution of the dispute and an expeditious response to the request, including ordering the parties to undertake dispute resolution, mediation, or arbitration as provided in N.J.S. 59:13–7. Within 90 days after the filing of a request, the court shall either grant the request or deny the request. If the request is granted, the court shall order such appropriate relief measures or remedies as it deems appropriate and necessary.

f. (1) A person whose employment with the Division of Motor Vehicles is terminated as a result of a contract entered into pursuant to subsection a. of this section, who does not accept an offer of employment with a contractor pursuant to paragraph (7) of subsection c. of this section, and who undergoes counseling pursuant to section 7 of P.L.1992, c. 43 (C. 34:15D–7), may apply for a training grant pursuant to section 6 of P.L.1992, c. 43 (C. 34:15D–6).

(2) Any provision of P.L.1992, c. 43 (C. 34:15D–1 et al.) to the contrary notwithstanding, the Workforce Development Program in the Department of Labor may

provide a training grant to each person who applies pursuant to paragraph (1) of this subsection for a training grant to pay for employment and training services as provided pursuant to section 6 of P.L.1992, c. 43 (C. 34:15D–6).

L.1995, c. 112, § 4, eff. June 2, 1995.

[1]Title of the Director of Building and Construction changed to the Director of Property Management and Construction by Reorganization Plan 003–1997.

39:8–45. Licensure of private inspection facilities

Text of section effective until May 1, 2010.

a. (1) The chief administrator, after appropriate inquiry and investigation, may license persons to operate private inspection facilities to inspect initially, reinspect and certify all motor vehicles that are subject to inspection pursuant to R.S.39:8–1. A person shall not be licensed unless qualified to conduct the inspections and reinspections, and in possession of the necessary equipment.

(2) The chief administrator, by regulation with the concurrence of the Department of Environmental Protection, may establish a limited number of distinct classes of licenses, may restrict the activities authorized by each distinct class of license, including restrictions as to the vehicles that may be inspected or reinspected, and may restrict the services that holders of each class may perform in addition to the activities authorized by the license. These regulations shall permit private inspection facilities to perform initial inspections on motor vehicles four years old or newer and, to the maximum extent feasible, permit private inspection facilities to perform initial inspections on motor vehicles that are more than four years old and to repair and reinspect all motor vehicles.

b. (1) The chief administrator may license as a private inspection facility any person that is the owner or lessee of 10 or more motor vehicles to initially inspect, reinspect and certify vehicles that the person owns or leases.

(2) The chief administrator, by regulation with the concurrence of the Department of Environmental Protection, may restrict the activities authorized by a license issued pursuant to this subsection, including restrictions as to the vehicles that may be inspected or reinspected, and may restrict the services that holders of this license may perform in addition to the activities authorized by the license.

c. The chief administrator shall require a private inspection facility licensee to have in effect at all times liability insurance or such other proof of financial responsibility as the chief administrator may prescribe; and may require a performance bond.

d. The chief administrator shall prescribe the form and content of the application for a private inspection facility license, and may charge a nonrefundable application fee not to exceed $20. The chief administrator may charge a license fee, not to exceed $250, to be paid

by a person for each year or part of a year in which that person holds a private inspection facility license. All fees collected pursuant to this subsection shall be paid to the State Treasurer and deposited in the "Motor Vehicle Inspection Fund" established pursuant to subsection j. of R.S.39:8–2.

e. For the purposes of this section, each applicant for a license shall submit to the chief administrator the applicant's name, address, fingerprints and written consent for a criminal history record background check to be performed. The chief administrator is hereby authorized to exchange fingerprint data with and receive criminal history record information from the State Bureau of Identification in the Division of State Police and the Federal Bureau of Investigation consistent with applicable State and federal laws, rules and regulations, for purposes of facilitating determinations concerning licensure eligibility. The applicant shall bear the cost for the criminal history record background check, including all costs of administering and processing the check. The Division of State Police shall promptly notify the chief administrator in the event a current holder of a license or prospective applicant, who was the subject of a criminal history record background check pursuant to this section, is arrested for a crime or offense in this State after the date the background check was performed.

L.1995, c. 112, § 5, eff. June 2, 1995. Amended by L.2003, c. 199, § 21, eff. Dec. 24, 2003.

39:8–45. Licensure of private inspection facilities

Text of section effective on May 18, 2010.

a. (1) The chief administrator, after appropriate inquiry and investigation, may license persons to operate private inspection facilities to inspect initially, reinspect and certify all motor vehicles that are subject to inspection pursuant to R.S.39:8–1. A person shall not be licensed unless qualified to conduct the inspections and reinspections, and in possession of the necessary equipment.

(2) The chief administrator, by regulation with the concurrence of the Department of Environmental Protection, may establish a limited number of distinct classes of licenses, may restrict the activities authorized by each distinct class of license, including restrictions as to the vehicles that may be inspected or reinspected, and may restrict the services that holders of each class may perform in addition to the activities authorized by the license. These regulations shall permit private inspection facilities to perform initial inspections on motor vehicles four years old or newer and, to the maximum extent feasible, permit private inspection facilities to perform initial inspections on motor vehicles that are more than four years old and to repair and reinspect all motor vehicles.

b. (1) The chief administrator may license as a private inspection facility any person who is the owner or lessee of 10 or more motor vehicles or any owner or lessee of diesel buses, heavy-duty diesel trucks, or other diesel-powered motor vehiclesto initially inspect, reinspect and certify vehicles that the person owns or leases.

(2) The chief administrator, by regulation with the concurrence of the Department of Environmental Protection, may restrict the activities authorized by a license issued pursuant to this subsection, including restrictions as to the vehicles that may be inspected or reinspected, and may restrict the services that holders of this license may perform in addition to the activities authorized by the license.

c. The chief administrator shall require a private inspection facility licensee to have in effect at all times liability insurance or such other proof of financial responsibility as the chief administrator may prescribe; and may require a performance bond.

d. The chief administrator shall prescribe the form and content of the application for a private inspection facility license, and may charge a nonrefundable application fee not to exceed $20. The chief administrator may charge a license fee, not to exceed $250, to be paid by a person for each year in which that person holds a private inspection facility license. The chief administrator may require licenses that shall expire on a date fixed by the chief administrator. All fees collected pursuant to this subsection shall be paid to the State Treasurer and deposited in the "Motor Vehicle Inspection Fund" established pursuant to subsection j. of R.S.39:8–2.

e. For the purposes of this section, each applicant for a license shall submit to the chief administrator the applicant's name, address, fingerprints and written consent for a criminal history record background check to be performed. The chief administrator is hereby authorized to exchange fingerprint data with and receive criminal history record information from the State Bureau of Identification in the Division of State Police and the Federal Bureau of Investigation consistent with applicable State and federal laws, rules and regulations, for purposes of facilitating determinations concerning licensure eligibility. The applicant shall bear the cost for the criminal history record background check, including all costs of administering and processing the check. The Division of State Police shall promptly notify the chief administrator in the event a current holder of a license or prospective applicant, who was the subject of a criminal history record background check pursuant to this section, is arrested for a crime or offense in this State after the date the background check was performed.

L.1995, c. 112, § 5, eff. June 2, 1995. Amended by L.2003, c. 199, § 21, eff. Dec. 24, 2003; L.2009, c. 331, § 7, eff. May 18, 2010.

39:8–46. Inspection procedures and fees

a. Whenever a private inspection facility licensee conducts an initial inspection, the private inspection facility shall either reject the vehicle or certify that the vehicle was inspected pursuant to chapter 8 of Title 39

of the Revised Statutes and was found to conform to the standards established by law and regulation. When a vehicle is reinspected, the private inspection facility licensee shall either reject the vehicle or certify that the items for which a vehicle was initially rejected conform to the standards established by law and regulation. The certification shall be evidenced by a private inspection certificate of approval placed on the vehicle as prescribed by the director.

b. A private inspection facility licensee may charge an amount approved by and on file with the director for initial inspection, reinspection, and certification of a vehicle, which amount shall be subject to any maximum limits that may be established by the director by regulation. The director may establish maximum amounts that may be charged for initial inspection or reinspection based on the average length of time required to inspect a vehicle or reinspect a specific rejected item.

c. A private inspection facility licensee shall post a schedule of charges for initial inspection, reinspection and certification in a prominent place on the premises, and shall file a copy thereof with the director.

d. A private inspection facility licensee shall not require, as a condition of performing an inspection, that any needed repairs or adjustments be done by the licensee or at a specific facility identified by the licensee or by an agent thereof.

L.1995, c. 112, § 6, eff. June 2, 1995.

39:8–47. Certificates and stickers

a. The director shall provide each private inspection facility with as many certificates of approval and rejection stickers as may be required and may charge the private inspection facility licensee a fee of $1 for each certificate or sticker, which fee shall be refunded for any expired or unused certificates or stickers. All fees collected pursuant to this subsection shall be paid to the State Treasurer and deposited in the "Motor Vehicle Inspection Fund" established pursuant to subsection j. of R.S. 39:8–2. Every private inspection facility licensee shall:

(1) Keep such records of inspections and reinspections and of certificates and stickers issued in such form as the director may determine;

(2) Make such records available to the director upon demand;

(3) Institute such safeguards to secure the certificates and stickers from theft, loss or fraudulent use as the director may prescribe;

(4) Return any unused expired certificates or stickers to the director; and

(5) Upon request account to the director for all certificates and stickers.

b. An owner or operator of a private inspection facility that for any reason, including but not limited to theft, destruction, loss, or damage, does not upon request either promptly return or properly account for a certificate or sticker shall be liable to a civil penalty of not less than $100 for each such certificate or sticker, to be collected in a civil action commenced by the director. Any penalty imposed pursuant to this subsection may be collected with costs in a summary proceeding pursuant to "the penalty enforcement law," N.J.S. 2A:58–1 et seq. The Superior Court and the municipal court shall have jurisdiction to enforce the provisions of "the penalty enforcement law" in connection with this subsection. Any fine collected pursuant to this subsection shall be paid to the State Treasurer and deposited in the "Motor Vehicle Inspection Fund" established pursuant to subsection j. of R.S. 39:8–2.

L.1995, c. 112, § 7, eff. June 2, 1995.

39:8–48. Civil penalties for improper inspections

A person who is employed by or under contract with a private inspection facility and who affixes a certificate of approval or a waiver certificate to a motor vehicle without having properly inspected the vehicle or without having determined that the condition of the vehicle conforms to standards established by law or regulation shall be liable to a civil penalty of not less than $500, to be collected in a civil action commenced by the director. Any penalty imposed pursuant to this section may be collected with costs in a summary proceeding pursuant to "the penalty enforcement law," N.J.S. 2A:58–1 et seq. The Superior Court and the municipal court shall have jurisdiction to enforce the provisions of "the penalty enforcement law" in connection with this section. A private inspection facility licensee shall be severally liable for any violation of this section by any person employed by or under contract with the private inspection facility licensee. Any fine collected pursuant to this section shall be paid to the State Treasurer and deposited in the "Motor Vehicle Inspection Fund" established pursuant to subsection j. of R.S. 39:8–2.

In addition to any civil penalty imposed, the director may suspend the license of a private inspection facility that violates this section for a period of not less than six months. The director may also file an action in Superior Court to enjoin any violation of this section.

L.1995, c. 112, § 8, eff. June 2, 1995.

39:8–49. Denial, suspension and revocation of licenses

a. The director may, pursuant to the "Administrative Procedure Act," P.L.1968, c. 410 (C. 52:14B–1 et seq.), deny, suspend or revoke a private inspection facility license or refuse renewal thereof for cause, including but not limited to one or more of the following:

(1) Violation of any provision of P.L.1995, c. 112 (C. 39:8–41 et al.) or of any rule or regulation adopted pursuant thereto;

(2) Fraud or misrepresentation in securing the license or in the conduct of the licensed activity;

(3) Making initial inspection or reinspection service charges in excess of those posted on the licensed premises and filed with the director;

(4) Conviction of a crime involving fraud or moral turpitude;

(5) Violation of P.L.1960, c. 39 (C. 56:8–1 et seq.) or of any regulation adopted thereunder;

(6) Failure to successfully complete any training or testing requirements that are a prerequisite to licensure;

(7) Fraudulently, willfully or negligently performing an improper inspection on a motor vehicle;

(8) Failure to pay a fee required by law; or

(9) Other good cause.

b. If the director determines that the public interest requires immediate suspension of a private inspection facility license prior to hearing, the director may do so, provided that the private inspection facility licensee is afforded the opportunity to request in writing a hearing within 10 days of the effective date of the suspension, and an administrative adjudication shall be held as soon thereafter as possible. The ordered suspension shall become final if a written request is not received by the director within 10 days of service of the notice or the scheduled suspension or order of suspension as the case may be. If the director determines it necessary to suspend a license prior to hearing and the private inspection facility licensee files a request for a hearing within the time prescribed by this section, the director may hold a preliminary hearing to determine whether sufficient cause exists to continue such suspension until a plenary hearing can be conducted.

L.1995, c. 112, § 9, eff. June 2, 1995.

39:8–50. Approved testing equipment

A private inspection facility or an official inspection facility shall use emission testing equipment that has been certified by the Department of Environmental Protection. The Department of Environmental Protection shall adopt standards for the certification of the equipment, which may include but shall not be limited to any of the following:

a. An automated system to control test sequencing, the automatic pass or fail decision, and the format for the test report and electronic medium for storage and transmission of test results;

b. An exhaust gas analysis portion;

c. A device to accept and record vehicle identification information;

d. A device to provide a printed record of the test results to the owner or lessee; and

e. A chassis dynamometer.

L.1995, c. 112, § 10, eff. June 2, 1995.

39:8–51. Expiration of licenses under prior law

All licenses issued pursuant to section 3 of P.L.1975, c. 156 (C. 39:8–11) shall expire and be of no force and effect on or after January 1, 1996, unless extended by the director. All licensed private inspection centers shall deliver to the director the license, all unused private inspection approval stickers, all inspection records and other items issued to the licensee or required by the director to be kept in connection with the operation of the private inspection center.

L.1995, c. 112, § 11, eff. June 2, 1995.

39:8–52. Licensure of emission inspectors

Text of section effective until May 18, 2010.

a. A person shall not conduct any emission inspection required by the director on a motor vehicle unless that person is licensed as an emission inspector by the director. The director may establish a fee not to exceed $50 for the licensure and relicensure of emission inspectors and shall establish standards and requirements for the licensure and relicensure of emission inspectors including, at a minimum, the successful completion of emission training and testing requirements determined by the director in consultation with the Department of Environmental Protection as a prerequisite to licensing. Any license issued pursuant to this section shall be valid for the period set by the director, which shall not be longer than two years. The successful completion of refresher training and testing, at a minimum, shall be required prior to license renewal. All fees collected pursuant to this subsection shall be turned over to the State Treasurer and deposited in the "Motor Vehicle Inspection Fund" established pursuant to subsection j. of R.S. 39:8–2.

b. The director may deny, suspend or revoke any license authorized to be issued by this section or refuse renewal thereof for cause, including but not limited to one or more of the following:

(1) Violation of any provision of P.L.1995, c. 112 (C. 39:8–41 et al.) or of any regulation adopted pursuant thereto;

(2) Fraud, misrepresentation or misstatement in securing the license or in the conduct of the licensed activity;

(3) Conviction of a crime involving fraud or moral turpitude;

(4) Violation of P.L.1960, c. 39 (C. 56:8–1 et seq.) or of any regulation adopted pursuant thereto;

(5) Failure to successfully complete any training or testing requirements that are a prerequisite to licensure;

(6) Failure to pay any fee required by law; or

(7) Other good cause.

L.1995, c. 112, § 12, eff. June 2, 1995.

39:8–52. Licensure of inspectors; standards for licensure; denial, suspension or revocation of license

Text of section effective on May 18, 2010.

a. A person shall not conduct any inspection required by the chief administrator on a motor vehicle or diesel bus, heavy-duty diesel truck, or any diesel-powered vehicle unless that person is licensed as an inspector by the chief administrator. The chief administrator may establish a fee not to exceed $50 for the licensure and relicensure of inspectors and shall establish standards and requirements for the licensure and relicensure of inspectors including, at a minimum, the successful completion of emission training and testing requirements determined by the chief administrator in consultation with the Department of Environmental Protection as a prerequisite to licensing. Any license issued pursuant to this section shall be valid for the period set by the chief administrator, which shall not be longer than two years. The successful completion of refresher training and testing, at a minimum, shall be required prior to license renewal. All fees collected pursuant to this subsection shall be turned over to the State Treasurer and deposited in the "Motor Vehicle Inspection Fund" established pursuant to subsection j. of R.S.39:8–2.

b. The chief administrator may deny, suspend or revoke any license authorized to be issued by this section or refuse renewal thereof for cause, including, but not limited to, one or more of the following:

(1) Violation of any provision of P.L.1995, c. 112 (C.39:8–41 et al.) or of any regulation adopted pursuant thereto;

(2) Fraud, misrepresentation or misstatement in securing the license or in the conduct of the licensed activity;

(3) Conviction of a crime involving fraud or moral turpitude;

(4) Violation of P.L.1960, c. 39 (C.56:8–1 et seq.) or of any regulation adopted pursuant thereto;

(5) Failure to successfully complete any training or testing requirements that are a prerequisite to licensure;

(6) Failure to pay any fee required by law;

(7) Other good cause; or

(8) Violation of P.L.1995, c. 157 (C.39:8–59 et seq.), or of any regulation adopted pursuant thereto.

L.1995, c. 112, § 12, eff. June 2, 1995. Amended by L.2009, c. 331, § 8, eff. May 18, 2010.

39:8–53. Emission-related repairs

a. The director shall adopt, after consultation with the Division of Consumer Affairs in the Department of Law and Public Safety, rules and regulations for the registration of facilities authorized to perform emission-related repairs on vehicles that fail a required emission test. A facility or business shall not correct, adjust or repair, for compensation, any motor vehicle that has failed an emission test required by the director unless it has first obtained from the director a motor vehicle repair facility registration authorizing the facility or business to repair vehicles that have failed an emission test required by the director. The director may establish an annual registration fee, which shall not exceed $50, to defray the cost of registering these businesses and facilities. All fees collected pursuant to this section shall be paid to the State Treasurer and deposited in the "Motor Vehicle Inspection Fund" established pursuant to subsection j. of R.S. 39:8–2.

b. The director may deny, suspend or revoke any registration issued pursuant to this section, or refuse renewal thereof, for performance by a registered business or facility of an improper repair on a motor vehicle or for other good cause.

c. The director may establish or approve a repair technician certification program for persons who perform, for compensation, emission-related repairs on vehicles that fail a required emission test.

d. The Department of Education, in consultation with the Department of Environmental Protection, shall develop and make available a course of instruction, to be offered at State community colleges and other appropriate educational institutions, for the purpose of training repair technicians in the diagnosis and repair of motor vehicle emission control systems.

L.1995, c. 112, § 13, eff. June 2, 1995.

39:8–54. False claim of licensure; transfer of license

A person who displays or causes or permits to be displayed any sign, mark, or advertisement, or otherwise identifies that person as a private inspection facility, a registered motor vehicle repair facility or an emission inspector when not holding a valid license or registration issued by the director, or who inspects a motor vehicle without being licensed as a private inspection facility, or who conducts an emission inspection without being licensed as an emission inspector, or who performs for compensation an emission-related repair on a motor vehicle that has failed an emission test without being registered as a motor vehicle emission repair facility, or who transfers or attempts to transfer a valid license or registration, shall be subject to a fine of not less than $1,000 or imprisonment for not more than 30 days, or both. Any fine collected under the provisions of this section shall be paid to the State Treasurer and deposited in the "Motor Vehicle Inspection Fund" established pursuant to subsection j. of R.S.39:8–2.

L.1995, c. 112, § 14, eff. June 2, 1995. Amended by L.2003, c. 13, § 39.

39:8–55. Waivers

The director, either directly or through an agent, may grant a waiver from the requirement that a vehicle satisfy emission standards. A waiver shall be valid for one inspection cycle. The waiver may be issued to any

vehicle that cannot successfully pass the emission tests upon reinspection, provided the vehicle owner or lessee demonstrates compliance with the following to the satisfaction of the director or agent:

a. All available warranty coverage for vehicle emission systems has been used to obtain needed repairs on the vehicle or written denial of warranty coverage in a form and manner prescribed by the director has been provided; and

b. The owner has expended, within 30 days prior to an emission test that is failed on or after January 1, 1998 or following the failed emission test, the amount for emission related repairs specified in rules and regulations adopted by the United States Environmental Protection Agency pursuant to the federal Clean Air Act;[1] and

c. The repairs made on the vehicle were appropriate to the cause of the emission test failure; and

d. The repairs were made by a registered motor vehicle repair facility or by the owner of the vehicle provided he possesses a nationally recognized certification for emission-related diagnosis and repair; and

e. The vehicle complies with the safety inspection requirements of this chapter and the rules adopted by the director; and

f. Any other requirements established by the director by regulation; and

g. Any other requirements established by the Department of Environmental Protection with the concurrence of the director.

L.1995, c. 112, § 15, eff. June 2, 1995.

[1] 42 U.S.C.A. § 7401 et seq.

Repeal

L.2009, c. 331, § 11, approved Jan. 18, 2010, provides for repeal of this section, effective May 18, 2010.

39:8–56. Voluntary emissions recalls; remedial plans

The owner or lessee of a motor vehicle that is subject to inspection pursuant to R.S. 39:8–1 and that is included in either a "Voluntary Emissions Recall" as defined at 40 C.F.R. § 85.1902(d) or any amendment thereto or in a remedial plan determination made pursuant to section 207(c) of the federal Clean Air Act [1] or any amendment thereto, for which owner notification occurs after the effective date of P.L.1995, c. 112 (C. 39:8–41 et al.), shall obtain the required repairs within the time period established by the director, in consultation with the Department of Environmental Protection, in order to obtain a certificate of approval. The director shall allow the owner or lessee of a motor vehicle which is subject to recall a minimum of 60 days in which to comply with such recall notice. It shall be the responsibility of the owner and lessee of a vehicle to submit proof of required repairs in response to such recall notice in a form and manner determined by the director. The director shall suspend the registration privileges or deny an application for registration for any vehicle that has failed to receive necessary repairs in response to a "Voluntary Emissions Recall" or to a remedial plan determination within the time period established by the director in consultation with the Department of Environmental Protection.

L.1995, c. 112, § 16, eff. June 2, 1995.

1 42 U.S.C.A. § 7541.

39:8–57. Rules and regulations

The director shall adopt, after consultation with the Department of Environmental Protection and pursuant to the "Administrative Procedure Act," P.L.1968, c. 410 (C. 52:14B–1 et seq.), any rules and regulations necessary to implement the provisions of P.L.1995, c. 112 (C. 39:8–41 et al.) or to place this State in substantial compliance with the motor vehicle emission inspection and maintenance requirements established by federal law, except that these rules and regulations shall not require the use of the "I/M 240" test.

L.1995, c. 112, § 17, eff. June 2, 1995.

39:8–58. Continuing applicability of prior law

The provisions of P.L.1995, c. 112 (C. 39:8–41 et al.) shall not apply to violations committed prior to its effective date, and prosecutions and dispositions for such violations shall be governed by the prior law, which is continued in effect for that purpose, as if P.L.1995, c. 112 (C. 39:8–41 et al.) were not in force.

L.1995, c. 112, § 18, eff. June 2, 1995.

39:8–59. Legislative findings and declarations

The Legislature finds and declares that exhaust emissions from diesel buses, heavy-duty diesel trucks, and other diesel-powered motor vehicles contribute significantly to air pollution problems within the State; that such emissions diminish the quality of life and health of our citizens; and that the technology and state of the art in determining and controlling the level of unacceptable exhaust emissions from diesel buses, heavy-duty diesel trucks, and other diesel-powered motor vehicles are continually being advanced and that the procedures, test methods and standards for determination of such unacceptable levels must be reflective of those advances.

The Legislature therefore determines that it is in the public interest to establish a program regulating exhaust emissions from diesel buses, heavy-duty diesel trucks, and certain other diesel-powered motor vehicles.

L.1995, c. 157, § 1, eff. June 30, 1995.

39:8–60. Definitions

As used in this act:

"Diesel bus" means any diesel-powered autobus or motorbus of any size or configuration, whether registered in this State or elsewhere, that is designed or used for intrastate or interstate transportation of passengers for hire or otherwise on a public road, street or highway or any public or quasi-public property in this State, and shall include, but need not be limited to: autobuses under the jurisdiction of the commission pursuant to Titles 27 or 48 of the Revised Statutes; autobuses of the New Jersey Transit Corporation and its contract carriers that are under the inspection jurisdiction of the commission; autobuses that are subject to federal motor carrier safety regulations; autobuses under the authority of the Interstate Commerce Commission or its successor agency; school buses, as defined pursuant to R.S.39:1–1; hotel, casino, charter, and special buses; and any other diesel-powered autobus or motorbus as determined by rule or regulation adopted by the commission in consultation with the Department of Transportation;

"Diesel-powered motor vehicle" means a vehicle, whether registered in this State or elsewhere, that is self-propelled by a compression ignition type of internal combustion engine using diesel fuel and that (1) is designed or used for transporting persons or property on any public road, street or highway or any public or quasi-public property in this State, (2) is greater than 8,500 pounds gross vehicle weight, (3) is not a diesel bus or heavy-duty diesel truck, and (4) is not a heavy-duty diesel truck or other diesel-powered motor vehicle owned and operated by a county, municipality, fire district, or duly incorporated nonprofit organization for first aid, emergency, ambulance, rescue, or fire-fighting purposes. Diesel–powered motor vehicle shall also mean a vehicle that is designed or used for construction or farming purposes and is greater than 8,500 pounds gross vehicle weight, except that the commission, in consultation with the Department of Environmental Protection, may exempt from the requirements of this act diesel-powered motor vehicles that are registered as construction vehicles under Titles 39 and 41 of the Revised Statutes or that are greater than 8,500 pounds gross vehicle weight and are designed or used for construction or farming purposes;

"EPA" means the United States Environmental Protection Agency;

"Gross vehicle weight rating" or "GVWR" means the value specified by the manufacturer as the loaded weight of a single or combination (articulated) vehicle. The GVWR of a combination (articulated) vehicle, commonly referred to as the "gross combination weight rating" or "GCWR," is the GVWR of the power unit plus the GVWR of the towed unit or units;

"Heavy-duty diesel truck" means any diesel-powered motor vehicle, whether registered in this State or elsewhere, with a GVWR of 18,000 or more pounds that is designed or used for the transporting of property on any public road, street or highway or any public or quasi-public property in this State. Heavy–duty diesel truck shall not mean a heavy-duty diesel truck owned and operated by a county, municipality, fire district, or duly incorporated nonprofit organization for first aid, emergency, ambulance, rescue, or fire-fighting purposes;

"Periodic inspection program" or "periodic inspection" means a program in which diesel buses, heavy-duty diesel trucks, and other diesel-powered motor vehicles registered in this State are periodically inspected in accordance with the provisions of this act;

"Person" means a corporation, company, association, society, firm, partnership, or joint stock company, or an individual, and shall also include the State and all of its political subdivisions and any agencies, authorities, corporations, or instrumentalities of the State or any political subdivision thereof; and

"Roadside enforcement program" or "roadside inspection" means a roadside examination program conducted pursuant to this act for the inspection of exhaust emissions, emission control apparatus and such other items as the Department of Environmental Protection, in consultation with the commission and the Commissioner of Transportation, prescribes, of diesel buses, heavy-duty diesel trucks, and other diesel-powered motor vehicles along any public road, street or highway or any public or quasi-public property in this State or at such other locations as may be designated by the commission in consultation with the Commissioner of Transportation.

L.1995, c. 157, § 2. Amended by L.2003, c. 13, § 76.

Historical and Statutory Notes

L.2003, c. 13, § 127, approved Jan. 28, 2003, provides:

"Sections 1, 2, 3, 12, 38, 109, 110 and 121 shall take effect immediately, sections 105, 106, 107, 108, and 120 shall take effect on July 1, 2003 and the remainder of this act shall take effect on the date the Commissioner of Transportation certifies to the Governor (hereinafter the "date of certification") that a majority of the members of the commission have been appointed or are in office and that all necessary anticipatory actions have been accomplished, provided, that the amount of revenues received pursuant to sections 109 and 110 prior to the date of certification are hereby appropriated to the division. Upon the date of certification, all such collected revenue shall be revenue of the commission. The Commissioner of Transportation, the Director of the Division of Motor Vehicles and the commission may take such anticipatory administrative action in advance as shall be necessary for the implementation of the act."

39:8–61. Exhaust emission standards and test methods; rules and regulations

The Department of Environmental Protection, in consultation with the commission and the Department of Transportation, shall adopt rules and regulations pursuant to the "Administrative Procedure Act," P.L. 1968, c. 410 (C.52:14B–1 et seq.) establishing exhaust emissions standards and test methods, and standards for emission control apparatus and related items, in accordance with P.L.1966, c. 16 (C.26:2C–8.1 et seq.) or as may be authorized or provided otherwise by federal law, rule or regulation, for diesel buses, heavy-duty diesel trucks, and other diesel-powered motor vehicles. The

test methods shall be accurate, objective, and capable of being performed routinely in the periodic inspection program and the roadside enforcement program. In adopting such standards and test methods, the Department of Environmental Protection may consider, but need not necessarily adopt, exhaust control technology current at the time of adoption of the rules and regulations, as well as guidance, standards, directives, and other information issued by the EPA, any other state, or any governmental agency, scientific research entity, or industry. The Department of Environmental Protection may provide that the standards and test methods vary according to the age of the vehicle or according to other relevant factors, and the department may provide exemptions based upon good cause, including, but not limited to, whether the vehicle has been tested within the previous six months or other reasonable period of time in accordance with the law of another state or jurisdiction and has been found to be in compliance with the exhaust emissions standards of the state or jurisdiction in which the vehicle was tested. The provisions of this act shall not apply to any heavy-duty diesel truck or other diesel-powered motor vehicle owned and operated by a county, municipality, fire district, or duly incorporated nonprofit organization for first aid, emergency, ambulance, rescue, or fire-fighting purposes.

L.1995, c. 157, § 3. Amended by L.2003, c. 13, § 77.

Historical and Statutory Notes

L.2003, c. 13, § 127, approved Jan. 28, 2003, provides:

"Sections 1, 2, 3, 12, 38, 109, 110 and 121 shall take effect immediately, sections 105, 106, 107, 108, and 120 shall take effect on July 1, 2003 and the remainder of this act shall take effect on the date the Commissioner of Transportation certifies to the Governor (hereinafter the "date of certification") that a majority of the members of the commission have been appointed or are in office and that all necessary anticipatory actions have been accomplished, provided, that the amount of revenues received pursuant to sections 109 and 110 prior to the date of certification are hereby appropriated to the division. Upon the date of certification, all such collected revenue shall be revenue of the commission. The Commissioner of Transportation, the Director of the Division of Motor Vehicles and the commission may take such anticipatory administrative action in advance as shall be necessary for the implementation of the act."

39:8–62. Operation of diesel-powered motor vehicles

No owner or lessee of a diesel bus, heavy-duty diesel truck, or other diesel-powered motor vehicle shall operate, or cause or allow the operation of, that diesel bus, heavy-duty diesel truck, or other diesel-powered motor vehicle in this State in violation of the standards established by the Department of Environmental Protection and determined in accordance with test methods and procedures established pursuant to this act.

L.1995, c. 157, § 4.

39:8–63. Violations; civil penalties

a. The owner and the lessee, if any, of a heavy-duty diesel truck operated in violation of section 4 of this act[1] shall be jointly and severally liable for a civil penalty of: $700 for the first violation, except as otherwise provided in this subsection; and $1,300 for the second or subsequent violation, except as otherwise provided in this subsection. A second or subsequent violation is one that occurs within one year of the occurrence of a previous violation committed with respect to the same heavy-duty diesel truck, without regard to the date of the hearing that adjudicated the violation and without regard to the identity of the defendant against whom it was adjudicated. The complaint and summons shall state whether the charges pertain to a first violation or to a second or subsequent violation, but if the complaint and summons fail to allege a second or subsequent violation, the civil penalty imposed shall be that for a first violation. The penalty for a first violation may be reduced to $150 and the penalty for a second or subsequent violation may be reduced to $500 if the defendant provides a certification of the repairs to the vehicle that is satisfactory to the court and in compliance with emissions standards. The commission may specify by rule or regulation the manner of the repairs and the certification necessary to effect a reduction of penalty. The commission may, by rule or regulation, provide that information pertaining to penalties, the repairs that may effect a reduction of penalty, and the certification necessary to substantiate those repairs and compliance with emissions standards be served with the complaint and summons. The commission may, by rule or regulation, prescribe a form for certifying repairs and compliance with emissions standards, with instructions as to how the form should be completed and certified. The commission may provide that the form be served with the complaint and summons.

Notwithstanding any other provision of law or any rule or regulation adopted pursuant thereto to the contrary, repairs to effect a reduction of penalty under the provisions of this subsection shall be made before the hearing date or within 45 days of the occurrence of the violation, whichever is sooner. A defendant who is permitted to waive appearance and plead guilty by mail shall also be permitted to submit the certification of repairs by mail; provided that if the court deems the certification to be inadequate, it shall afford the defendant the option to withdraw the defendant's guilty plea.

b. The owner and the lessee, if any, of a diesel bus operated in violation of section 4 of this act shall be jointly and severally liable for a civil penalty determined by a penalty schedule that the commission, in consultation with the Commissioner of Transportation, shall adopt by rule or regulation pursuant to the "Administrative Procedure Act," P.L.1968, c. 410 (C.52:14B–1 et seq.), but in no event shall the penalties established thereby exceed the penalties established by subsection a. of this section for heavy-duty diesel trucks. The penalty schedule may provide for a reduction of penalty if the

defendant provides a certification of the repairs to the vehicle that is satisfactory to the court and in compliance with emissions standards. The commission, in consultation with the Commissioner of Transportation, may, by rule or regulation, specify the timing and manner of the repairs and compliance with emissions standards, and the certification necessary to effect a reduction of penalty. The commission, in consultation with the Commissioner of Transportation, may, by rule or regulation, provide whether information pertaining to repairs and compliance with emissions standards, and whether a form to certify those repairs and that compliance, should be served with the complaint and summons.

Notwithstanding the provisions of this subsection to the contrary, the New Jersey Transit Corporation shall not be liable for any civil penalty assessed for a violation of section 4 or a violation of any other provision of this act if the diesel bus that is the subject of the violation is operated by a lessee or contractor, or an employee or agent of a lessee or contractor, of the New Jersey Transit Corporation. However, if a diesel bus that is the subject of a violation is leased by the New Jersey Transit Corporation from another person, and the diesel bus is operated by the New Jersey Transit Corporation or an employee thereof, the New Jersey Transit Corporation as lessee, and not the owner of the diesel bus, shall be liable for any civil penalty assessed for the violation.

c. The owner and the lessee, if any, of a diesel-powered motor vehicle operated in violation of section 4 of this act shall be jointly and severally liable for a civil penalty determined by a penalty schedule that the commission shall adopt by rule or regulation pursuant to the "Administrative Procedure Act," P.L.1968, c. 410 (C.52:14B–1 et seq.), but in no event shall the penalties established thereby exceed the penalties established by subsection a. of this section for heavy-duty diesel trucks. The penalty schedule may provide for a reduction of penalty if the defendant provides a certification of the repairs to the vehicle that is satisfactory to the court and in compliance with emissions standards. The commission may, by rule or regulation, specify the timing and manner of the repairs and compliance with emissions standards, and the certification necessary to effect a reduction of penalty. The commission may, by rule or regulation, provide whether information pertaining to repairs and compliance with emissions standards, and whether a form to certify those repairs and that compliance, should be served with the complaint and summons.

L.1995, c. 157, § 5. Amended by L.2003, c. 13, § 78.

1 N.J.S.A. § 39:8–62.

Historical and Statutory Notes

L.2003, c. 13, § 127, approved Jan. 28, 2003, provides:

"Sections 1, 2, 3, 12, 38, 109, 110 and 121 shall take effect immediately, sections 105, 106, 107, 108, and 120 shall take effect on July 1, 2003 and the remainder of this act shall take effect on the date the Commissioner of Transportation certifies to the Governor (hereinafter the "date of certification") that a majority of the members of the commission have been appointed or are in office and that all necessary anticipatory actions have been accomplished, provided, that the amount of revenues received pursuant to sections 109 and 110 prior to the date of certification are hereby appropriated to the division. Upon the date of certification, all such collected revenue shall be revenue of the commission. The Commissioner of Transportation, the Director of the Division of Motor Vehicles and the commission may take such anticipatory administrative action in advance as shall be necessary for the implementation of the act."

39:8–64. Periodic inspection and roadside enforcement programs

a. The commission, in consultation with the Department of Environmental Protection and the Department of Transportation and with the approval of the Attorney General, shall establish and implement a periodic inspection program and a roadside enforcement program to implement the standards and test methods adopted pursuant to section 3[1] of this act. These programs shall be designed to measure exhaust emissions and to inspect emission control apparatus and related items on diesel buses, heavy-duty diesel trucks, and other diesel-powered motor vehicles. The programs shall include, at a minimum, diesel buses and heavy-duty diesel trucks subject to the rules and regulations adopted pursuant to section 3 of this act; provided that the commission, in consultation with the Department of Transportation, may exempt vehicles from either program for good cause, which may include that vehicles belonging to an exempted class are, by law, subject to emissions testing in another program. The commission, in consultation with the Department of Environmental Protection and with the approval of the Attorney General, may, by rule or regulation, expand the periodic inspection program and the roadside enforcement program to include other diesel-powered motor vehicles that are subject to the rules and regulations adopted pursuant to section 3 of this act. The commission, in consultation with the Commissioner of Transportation, may, by rule or regulation, impose upon every owner and lessee of a diesel bus, heavy-duty diesel truck, or other diesel-powered motor vehicle subject to periodic inspection the obligation to have the vehicle periodically inspected in a manner determined by the commission in consultation with the Commissioner of Transportation, to effect repairs or to abstain from operating or to limit the operation of a rejected vehicle or a vehicle overdue for inspection, and may take other action necessary or appropriate for implementation of the periodic inspection program. The commission, in consultation with the Commissioner of Transportation, may, by rule or regulation, impose upon every owner and lessee of a diesel bus, heavy-duty diesel truck, or other diesel-powered motor vehicle subject to roadside inspection the obligation to abstain from operating or to limit the operation of a vehicle that has been tested and found to be in violation of the rules and regulations adopted pursuant to section 3 of this act, or to effect

repairs, and may take other action necessary or appropriate for implementation of the roadside enforcement program. A school bus, as defined pursuant to R.S.39:1–1, shall be exempt from the roadside enforcement program. However, nothing in this subsection allowing or mandating exemptions from the periodic inspection program or the roadside enforcement program shall be construed to limit any other enforcement actions permitted by law.

b. The commission shall exercise all authority, including but not limited to administrative, implementation, enforcement, and penalty authority, in connection with the periodic inspection program for diesel buses and the roadside enforcement program for diesel buses that are under the jurisdiction of the commission pursuant to Titles 27 and 48 of the Revised Statutes or any other law, rule, or regulation. The commission shall consult with the Department of Environmental Protection and the Department of Transportation in conducting the periodic inspection program for diesel buses and the roadside enforcement program for diesel buses that are under the jurisdiction of the commission. Any periodic inspection that may be required pursuant to this act for a diesel bus under the jurisdiction of the commission shall be conducted only in conjunction with any periodic safety inspection required for that diesel bus pursuant to law, rule, or regulation. Any suspension of registration privileges with respect to diesel buses for a violation of this act or any rule or regulation adopted pursuant thereto shall be implemented by the commission.

L.1995, c. 157, § 6. Amended by L.2003, c. 13, § 79.
[1] N.J.S.A. § 39:8–61.

Historical and Statutory Notes

L.2003, c. 13, § 127, approved Jan. 28, 2003, provides:

"Sections 1, 2, 3, 12, 38, 109, 110 and 121 shall take effect immediately, sections 105, 106, 107, 108, and 120 shall take effect on July 1, 2003 and the remainder of this act shall take effect on the date the Commissioner of Transportation certifies to the Governor (hereinafter the "date of certification") that a majority of the members of the commission have been appointed or are in office and that all necessary anticipatory actions have been accomplished, provided, that the amount of revenues received pursuant to sections 109 and 110 prior to the date of certification are hereby appropriated to the division. Upon the date of certification, all such collected revenue shall be revenue of the commission. The Commissioner of Transportation, the Director of the Division of Motor Vehicles and the commission may take such anticipatory administrative action in advance as shall be necessary for the implementation of the act."

39:8–65. Pilot roadside enforcement program

In implementing the roadside enforcement program, the commission, in consultation with the Commissioner of Transportation, shall phase in roadside inspections by establishing a pilot roadside enforcement program providing a six-month grace period in which warnings shall be issued in lieu of the civil penalties established by this act or any rule or regulation adopted pursuant thereto.

Notwithstanding the provisions of the "Administrative Procedure Act," P.L.1968, c. 410 (C.52:14B–1 et seq.), procedures for the pilot program may be adopted immediately.

L.1995, c. 157, § 7. Amended by L.2003, c. 13, § 80.

Historical and Statutory Notes

L.2003, c. 13, § 127, approved Jan. 28, 2003, provides:

"Sections 1, 2, 3, 12, 38, 109, 110 and 121 shall take effect immediately, sections 105, 106, 107, 108, and 120 shall take effect on July 1, 2003 and the remainder of this act shall take effect on the date the Commissioner of Transportation certifies to the Governor (hereinafter the "date of certification") that a majority of the members of the commission have been appointed or are in office and that all necessary anticipatory actions have been accomplished, provided, that the amount of revenues received pursuant to sections 109 and 110 prior to the date of certification are hereby appropriated to the division. Upon the date of certification, all such collected revenue shall be revenue of the commission. The Commissioner of Transportation, the Director of the Division of Motor Vehicles and the commission may take such anticipatory administrative action in advance as shall be necessary for the implementation of the act."

39:8–66. Test methods; procedures for periodic inspection and roadside enforcement programs

a. The commission, in consultation with the Department of Environmental Protection and the Department of Transportation, shall establish procedures by which test methods established pursuant to section 3 of this act[1] shall be conducted in the periodic inspection program and in the roadside enforcement program.

b. The commission, in consultation with the Department of Transportation and with the approval of the Attorney General, may, by rule or regulation, require that personnel from, and agents of, the commission and the Department of Transportation, and personnel from the Division of State Police, who perform the test methods utilized in the roadside enforcement program, and licensees and persons employed by licensees who perform the tests and test methods utilized in the periodic inspection program in accordance with the provisions of section 11 of this act,[2] be trained to do so and be examined, periodically if the rule or regulation so provides, to ensure that their training and competence are adequate. Testing in the roadside enforcement program may be conducted by personnel from the commission, or the Division of State Police, or by agents appointed by or under contract with the commission.

c. The commission, in consultation with the Department of Environmental Protection and the Department of Transportation and with the approval of the Attorney General, shall designate one or more test methods among those established pursuant to section 3 of this act that shall be utilized in the roadside enforcement program established pursuant to section 6 of this act.[3] The commission, in consultation with the Department of Transportation and with the approval of the Attorney General, shall establish a form or forms upon which the results of these designated tests or test methods shall be

reported in the ordinary course. The form shall contain a statement or statements establishing the following: the type of test performed; the result achieved; that the person completing the form is the person who performed the test; that the tester has been certified by the commission as having adequate training and competence to perform the test; that the tester is an employee or agent of the State and was acting in an official capacity when the tester performed the test; and any other information that the commission may prescribe. The form shall contain a certification subscribed by the person performing the test and certifying that that person did perform the test in a proper manner and believes the test results to be valid and accurate. The presentation of a form prepared in accordance with the provisions of this subsection to a court by any party to a proceeding shall be evidence that all of the requirements and provisions of this subsection have been met and that the form has been prepared in accordance with the provisions of this subsection. The form shall be admissible evidence as proof of the statements contained therein in any civil penalty proceeding brought pursuant to the provisions of this act or any rule or regulation adopted pursuant thereto. A copy of the form shall be served, if practicable, with the complaint and summons upon the defendant or the defendant's agent for service of process; and, in any event, shall be served upon such person at least 20 days before the hearing. Whenever the form is served upon a defendant or a defendant's agent, together with the complaint and summons, the law enforcement officer serving the form shall execute and file with the court a proof of service on a form prescribed by the Administrative Director of the Courts and in a manner consistent with the Rules Governing the Courts of the State of New Jersey. The form shall not be admissible if it is not served at least 20 days before the hearing, provided that the court, upon a showing of good cause and that the defendant is not prejudiced, may postpone the hearing, subject to the Rules Governing the Courts of the State of New Jersey.

d. A roadside inspection of a diesel bus to enforce standards adopted pursuant to section 3 of this act shall be conducted only in conjunction with a roadside safety inspection that is conducted pursuant to law, rule or regulation.

L.1995, c. 157, § 8. Amended by L.2003, c. 13, § 81.

[1] N.J.S.A. § 39:8–61.
[2] N.J.S.A. § 39:8–69.
[3] N.J.S.A. § 39:8–64.

Historical and Statutory Notes

L.2003, c. 13, § 127, approved Jan. 28, 2003, provides:

"Sections 1, 2, 3, 12, 38, 109, 110 and 121 shall take effect immediately, sections 105, 106, 107, 108, and 120 shall take effect on July 1, 2003 and the remainder of this act shall take effect on the date the Commissioner of Transportation certifies to the Governor (hereinafter the "date of certification") that a majority of the members of the commission have been appointed or are in office and that all necessary anticipatory actions have been accomplished, provided, that the amount of revenues received pursuant to sections 109 and 110 prior to the date of certification are hereby appropriated to the division. Upon the date of certification, all such collected revenue shall be revenue of the commission. The Commissioner of Transportation, the Director of the Division of Motor Vehicles and the commission may take such anticipatory administrative action in advance as shall be necessary for the implementation of the act."

39:8–67. State police officers to assist roadside enforcement programs; records of inspections

The Superintendent of the State Police, in consultation with and subject to the approval of the Attorney General, shall provide State Police officers to assist the commission in conducting the roadside enforcement program and the pilot roadside enforcement program. The State Police officers shall have authority to direct diesel buses, heavy-duty diesel trucks, or other diesel-powered motor vehicles from the roadway for the purpose of inspection, and shall perform other police duties necessary for or helpful to the implementation of the programs. The State Police officers shall maintain records of these inspections and shall forward the information concerning the number of inspections, and the type of violations and the number of each type of violation to the Department of Environmental Protection.

L.1995, c. 157, § 9. Amended by L.2003, c. 13, § 82; L.2005, c. 219, § 34, eff. Sept. 7, 2005.

Historical and Statutory Notes

L.2003, c. 13, § 127, approved Jan. 28, 2003, provides:

"Sections 1, 2, 3, 12, 38, 109, 110 and 121 shall take effect immediately, sections 105, 106, 107, 108, and 120 shall take effect on July 1, 2003 and the remainder of this act shall take effect on the date the Commissioner of Transportation certifies to the Governor (hereinafter the "date of certification") that a majority of the members of the commission have been appointed or are in office and that all necessary anticipatory actions have been accomplished, provided, that the amount of revenues received pursuant to sections 109 and 110 prior to the date of certification are hereby appropriated to the division. Upon the date of certification, all such collected revenue shall be revenue of the commission. The Commissioner of Transportation, the Director of the Division of Motor Vehicles and the commission may take such anticipatory administrative action in advance as shall be necessary for the implementation of the act."

39:8–68. Additional civil penalties

In addition to any other penalties that may be applicable, the operator of a diesel bus, heavy-duty diesel truck, or other diesel-powered motor vehicle who fails to comply with any direction given pursuant to section 9 of this act,[1] or who refuses to submit or resists submitting a vehicle under the operator's control for roadside inspection, or who fails to comply with any other obligation imposed upon that person as part of the roadside enforcement program shall be jointly and severally liable with the owner and the lessee, if any, of the vehicle for a civil penalty of $500. The owner and the lessee, if any, of a diesel bus, heavy-duty diesel

truck, or other diesel-powered motor vehicle subject to periodic inspections who violates any rule or regulation adopted pursuant to section 6 of this act[2] pertaining to periodic inspections shall be liable for a civil penalty determined by a penalty schedule that the commission, in consultation with the Commissioner of Transportation, shall adopt by rule or regulation pursuant to the "Administrative Procedure Act," P.L.1968, c. 410 (C.52:14B–1 et seq.), but in no event shall a penalty established thereby exceed $500.

Notwithstanding the provisions of this section to the contrary, the New Jersey Transit Corporation shall not be liable for any civil penalty assessed for a violation of this section if the diesel bus that is the subject of the violation is operated by a lessee or contractor, or an employee or agent of a lessee or contractor, of the New Jersey Transit Corporation. However, if a diesel bus that is the subject of a violation of this section is leased by the New Jersey Transit Corporation from another person, and the diesel bus is operated by the New Jersey Transit Corporation or an employee thereof, the New Jersey Transit Corporation as lessee, and not the owner of the diesel bus, shall be liable for any civil penalty assessed for the violation.

L.1995, c. 157, § 10. Amended by L.2003, c. 13, § 83.

[1] N.J.S.A. § 39:8–67.
[2] N.J.S.A. § 39:8–64.

Historical and Statutory Notes

L.2003, c. 13, § 127, approved Jan. 28, 2003, provides:

"Sections 1, 2, 3, 12, 38, 109, 110 and 121 shall take effect immediately, sections 105, 106, 107, 108, and 120 shall take effect on July 1, 2003 and the remainder of this act shall take effect on the date the Commissioner of Transportation certifies to the Governor (hereinafter the "date of certification") that a majority of the members of the commission have been appointed or are in office and that all necessary anticipatory actions have been accomplished, provided, that the amount of revenues received pursuant to sections 109 and 110 prior to the date of certification are hereby appropriated to the division. Upon the date of certification, all such collected revenue shall be revenue of the commission. The Commissioner of Transportation, the Director of the Division of Motor Vehicles and the commission may take such anticipatory administrative action in advance as shall be necessary for the implementation of the act."

39:8–69. Licensing of diesel emission inspection centers; grounds for revocation or suspension of license

Text of section effective until May 18, 2010.

a. The commission, in consultation with the Department of Transportation and after appropriate inquiry and investigation, shall issue licenses to operate diesel emission inspection centers to as many qualified and properly equipped persons, including owners or lessees of diesel buses, heavy-duty diesel trucks, or other diesel-powered motor vehicles, as the commission determines shall be necessary to conduct periodic inspections. A licensee shall inspect and pass or reject a diesel bus, heavy-duty diesel truck, or other diesel-powered motor vehicle presented to the licensee for inspection. Passing shall indicate that the licensee or the licensee's employee has inspected the diesel bus, heavy-duty diesel truck, or other diesel-powered motor vehicle as prescribed by the commission and has found that the vehicle conforms to the standards established by law and rule or regulation. The commission, in consultation with the Department of Transportation and with the approval of the Attorney General, may establish by rule or regulation adopted pursuant to the "Administrative Procedure Act," P.L.1968, c. 410 (C.52:14B–1 et seq.) an application fee for the licensing of diesel emission inspection centers, which fee shall not exceed $250 per year.

b.   For the purpose of documenting compliance with periodic inspection requirements, the commission shall furnish official inspection forms to licensed diesel emission inspection centers. The commission shall require each diesel emission inspection center and each owner or lessee of a diesel bus, heavy-duty diesel truck, or other diesel-powered motor vehicle subject to periodic inspection to keep such records and file such reports regarding these inspections as the commission shall deem necessary. The commission may conduct such audits or inspections of these centers as the commission deems appropriate.

c.   The commission may deny, suspend or revoke a diesel emission inspection center license or refuse renewal thereof for cause, including, but not limited to, one or more of the following:

(1) Violation of any provision of this act or of any rule or regulation adopted pursuant thereto; or

(2) Fraud or misrepresentation in securing a license or in the conduct of the licensed activity; or

(3) Conviction of a crime demonstrating that the applicant or licensee is unfit; or

(4) Improper, negligent, or fraudulent inspection of a diesel bus, heavy-duty diesel truck, or other diesel-powered motor vehicle; or

(5) Other good cause.

d.   In addition to any other civil or criminal penalties that may be applicable, a person licensed by the commission to operate a diesel emission inspection center who commits fraud or misrepresentation in securing a license or in the conduct of the licensed activity or who improperly or negligently or fraudulently conducts an inspection of a diesel bus, heavy-duty diesel truck, or other diesel-powered motor vehicle shall be liable for a civil penalty of $1,500. In addition to any other civil or criminal penalties that may be applicable, a person licensed by the commission to operate a diesel emission inspection center who otherwise violates any provision of this act or of any rule or regulation adopted pursuant thereto shall be liable for a civil penalty of $500.

L.1995, c. 157, § 11.   Amended by L.2003, c. 13, § 84.

39:8–69.   Licensing of private inspection facilities for diesel-powered vehicles; grounds for revocation or suspension of license

Text of section effective on May 18, 2010.

a.   The commission shall designate as many qualified and properly equipped duly licensed private inspection facilities as the commission determines shall be necessary to conduct periodic inspections. A licensee shall inspect and pass or reject a diesel bus, heavy-duty diesel truck, or other diesel-powered motor vehicle presented to the licensee for inspection. Passing shall indicate that the licensee or the licensed inspector has inspected the diesel bus, heavy-duty diesel truck, or other diesel-powered motor vehicle as prescribed by the commission and has found that the vehicle conforms to the standards established by law and rule or regulation. The commission may establish by rule or regulation adopted pursuant to the "Administrative Procedure Act," P.L. 1968, c. 410 (C.52:14B–1 et seq.) an application fee for the authority to conduct diesel emission inspections, which fee shall not exceed $250 per year.

b.   For the purpose of documenting compliance with periodic inspection requirements, the commission shall furnish official inspection forms to licensed private inspection facilities authorized to conduct diesel emission inspections. The commission shall require each licensee and each owner or lessee of a diesel bus, heavy-duty diesel truck, or other diesel-powered motor vehicle subject to periodic inspection to keep such records and file such reports regarding these inspections as the commission shall deem necessary. The commission may conduct such audits or inspections of licensee facilities as the commission deems appropriate.

c.   The commission may deny, suspend or revoke the authority to conduct diesel emission inspections or refuse renewal thereof for cause, including, but not limited to, one or more of the following:

(1) Violation of any provision of this act or of any rule or regulation adopted pursuant thereto; or

(2) Fraud or misrepresentation in securing a license or in the conduct of the licensed activity; or

(3) Conviction of a crime demonstrating that the applicant or licensee is unfit; or

(4) Improper, negligent, or fraudulent inspection of a diesel bus, heavy-duty diesel truck, or other diesel-powered motor vehicle; or

(5) Other good cause.

d.   In addition to any other civil or criminal penalties that may be applicable, a person licensed by the commission to conduct diesel emission inspections who commits fraud or misrepresentation in securing a license or in the conduct of the licensed activity or who improperly or negligently or fraudulently conducts an inspection of a diesel bus, heavy-duty diesel truck, or other diesel-powered motor vehicle shall be liable for a civil penalty of $1,500. In addition to any other civil or criminal penalties that may be applicable, a person licensed by the commission to conduct diesel emission inspections, who otherwise violates any provision of this act or of any rule or regulation adopted pursuant thereto, shall be liable for a civil penalty of $500.

L.1995, c. 157, § 11. Amended by L.2003, c. 13, § 84; L.2009, c. 331, § 9, eff. May 18, 2010.

Historical and Statutory Notes

L.2003, c. 13, § 127, approved Jan. 28, 2003, provides:

"Sections 1, 2, 3, 12, 38, 109, 110 and 121 shall take effect immediately, sections 105, 106, 107, 108, and 120 shall take effect on July 1, 2003 and the remainder of this act shall take effect on the date the Commissioner of Transportation certifies to the Governor (hereinafter the "date of certification") that a majority of the members of the commission have been appointed or are in office and that all necessary anticipatory actions have been accomplished, provided, that the amount of revenues received pursuant to sections 109 and 110 prior to the date of certification are hereby appropriated to the division. Upon the date of certification, all such collected revenue shall be revenue of the commission. The Commissioner of Transportation, the Director of the Division of Motor Vehicles and the commission may take such anticipatory administrative action in advance as shall be necessary for the implementation of the act."

39:8–70. Amount of civil penalty; suspension of registration

Any person who violates any provision of sections 2 through 20 of this act[1] or any rule or regulation adopted pursuant thereto shall be liable for a civil penalty. The amount of the penalty shall be that specified in the other sections of this act or in the rules or regulations adopted pursuant to this act; but if no amount is otherwise specified, then the amount shall be $200. Additionally, the commission may suspend the registration privileges of a vehicle registered in this State that is operated in violation of this act or any rule or regulation adopted pursuant thereto.

L.1995, c. 157, § 12. Amended by L.2003, c. 13, § 85.

[1] N.J.S.A. §§ 39:8–60 to 39:8–80.

Historical and Statutory Notes

L.2003, c. 13, § 127, approved Jan. 28, 2003, provides:

"Sections 1, 2, 3, 12, 38, 109, 110 and 121 shall take effect immediately, sections 105, 106, 107, 108, and 120 shall take effect on July 1, 2003 and the remainder of this act shall take effect on the date the Commissioner of Transportation certifies to the Governor (hereinafter the "date of certification") that a majority of the members of the commission have been appointed or are in office and that all necessary anticipatory actions have been accomplished, provided, that the amount of revenues received pursuant to sections 109 and 110 prior to the date of certification are hereby appropriated to the division. Upon the date of certification, all such collected revenue shall be revenue of the commission. The Commissioner of Transportation, the Director of the Division of Motor Vehicles and the commission may take such anticipatory administrative action in advance as shall be necessary for the implementation of the act."

39:8–71. Tickets; process; proceedings on violations

a. A complaint and summons charging a violation of this act or any rule or regulation adopted pursuant thereto and seeking the imposition of a civil penalty in accordance with the provisions of this act or any rule or regulation adopted pursuant to this act shall be a ticket in the form prescribed by the Administrative Director of the Courts pursuant to the Rules Governing the Courts of the State of New Jersey and may contain information advising the persons to whom it is issued of the manner in which and time within which an answer to the alleged violation is required. The ticket may also advise that penalties may result from a failure to answer, that the failure to answer or appear shall be considered an admission of liability, and that a default judgment may be entered. Service of the ticket shall be subject to the Rules Governing the Courts of the State of New Jersey. The ticket may be served personally upon the operator of a vehicle, and the owner's or the lessee's name may be recorded on the ticket, together with the plate number and state or jurisdiction as shown by the registration plates of the vehicle and the make or model of the vehicle. A ticket may be served upon the owner or the lessee of the vehicle by affixing the ticket to the vehicle in a conspicuous place. A ticket may be served by mail upon the owner or the lessee of the vehicle on file with the commission, or the licensing authority of another jurisdiction by mailing the ticket to the vehicle owner or lessee by regular or certified mail to the address on file with the commission, or the licensing authority of another jurisdiction. Service of a ticket by regular or certified mail shall have the same effect as if the ticket were served personally, subject to the Rules Governing the Courts of the State of New Jersey.

b. Subject to the Rules Governing the Courts of the State of New Jersey, the ticket shall contain sufficient information to identify the person or persons charged and to inform them of the nature, date, time and location of the alleged violation. Subject to the Rules Governing the Courts of the State of New Jersey, the original of the ticket shall be signed by the complaining witness, who shall certify to the truth of the facts set forth therein. Any person may serve as the complaining witness. For the purposes of the certification, the complaining witness may rely upon information from the commission, or the Division of State Police, upon official reports, and upon any form prepared in accordance with subsection c. of section 8 of this act.[1] The original ticket or a true copy of the ticket shall be considered a record kept in the ordinary business of the commission and shall be prima facie evidence of the facts contained therein.

c. Any operator who drives a vehicle in this State when the owner or lessee of that vehicle causes, authorizes, or otherwise permits such operation shall be the owner's or lessee's agent for service of any ticket, process, or penalty or other notice against the owner or lessee arising out of any alleged violation of this act or any rule or regulation adopted pursuant thereto. The owner and the lessee, if any, of a vehicle driven by any operator in this State shall be the operator's agent or agents for service of any ticket, process, or penalty or other notice arising out of any alleged violation of section 10 of this act[2] pertaining to a roadside inspection. Subject to the Rules Governing the Courts of the State of New Jersey, any service of ticket, process, or penalty or other notice served on an operator who operates in this State, or on an owner or lessee of the vehicle, shall also constitute service upon the remaining persons, so long as the ticket, process, or penalty or other notice advises the person actually served of that person's responsibility to notify the remaining persons.

d. Subject to the Rules Governing the Courts of the State of New Jersey, judicial proceedings under this act may be instituted on any day of the week, and the institution of the proceedings on a Sunday or a holiday shall not be a bar to the successful prosecution thereof. Subject to the Rules Governing the Courts of the State of New Jersey, any process served on a Sunday or holiday shall be as valid as if served on any other day of the week.

e. A municipal court before which proceedings pursuant to this act are instituted shall, subject to the Rules Governing the Courts of the State of New Jersey, immediately, upon expiration of the time for a defendant to answer or appear: (1) with respect to a resident of New Jersey, mail notice as provided in the Rules Governing the Courts of the State of New Jersey; or (2) with respect to a non-resident of New Jersey, mail notice as provided in the Rules Governing the Courts of the State of New Jersey. The notice shall be upon a form approved by the Administrative Director of the Courts that informs the defendant of the following: the infraction charged; the time and date of the infraction; the amount of penalties due; the defendant's right to have a hearing; and that a civil judgment may be entered against the defendant for failure to answer or appear or pay the amount of penalties due. Upon failure to answer or appear in response to the notice, the court shall give notice of that fact to the commission in a manner prescribed by the commission, and money judgment shall be entered and execution shall issue in accordance with the Rules Governing the Courts of the State of New Jersey. If the judgment has been docketed in the Superior Court pursuant to section 15 of this act,[3] execution shall be under the jurisdiction of that court. In no case of an unsatisfied judgment shall an arrest warrant or execution against the body of the defendant issue unless otherwise provided by the Rules Governing the Courts of the State of New Jersey. If notice has been given under this subsection of a person's failure to respond to a failure to appear notice and if the person appears or if the case is dismissed or otherwise disposed of, the court shall promptly give notice to that effect to the commission.

f. If the defendant is the owner or lessee of a vehicle that is the subject of the violation and if the defendant fails to respond to a failure to appear notice, the judge

or the commission may suspend the registration privileges of the defendant in this State. The commission shall keep a record of a suspension ordered by the court pursuant to this subsection. If the registration privileges of the defendant have been suspended pursuant to this subsection and if the defendant appears or the case is disposed of and if the defendant satisfies all penalties and costs that are owing, the court shall forward to the commission a notice to restore the defendant's registration privileges. Upon receiving a notice to restore and upon the defendant's payment of the restoration fee in accordance with section 23 of P.L.1975, c. 180 (C.39:3–10a), the commission shall record the restoration and notify the defendant of the restoration.

L.1995, c. 157, § 13. Amended by L.2003, c. 13, § 86.

[1] N.J.S.A. § 39:8–66.
[2] N.J.S.A. § 39:8–68.
[3] N.J.S.A. § 39:8–73.

Historical and Statutory Notes

L.2003, c. 13, § 127, approved Jan. 28, 2003, provides:

"Sections 1, 2, 3, 12, 38, 109, 110 and 121 shall take effect immediately, sections 105, 106, 107, 108, and 120 shall take effect on July 1, 2003 and the remainder of this act shall take effect on the date the Commissioner of Transportation certifies to the Governor (hereinafter the "date of certification") that a majority of the members of the commission have been appointed or are in office and that all necessary anticipatory actions have been accomplished, provided, that the amount of revenues received pursuant to sections 109 and 110 prior to the date of certification are hereby appropriated to the division. Upon the date of certification, all such collected revenue shall be revenue of the commission. The Commissioner of Transportation, the Director of the Division of Motor Vehicles and the commission may take such anticipatory administrative action in advance as shall be necessary for the implementation of the act."

39:8–72. Action to recover civil penalty

An action for the recovery of a civil penalty for violation of this act or any rule or regulation adopted pursuant to this act shall be within the jurisdiction of and may be brought before the municipal court in the municipality where the offense was committed or where the defendant may be found, or where the measurement of emissions was physically made. The municipal prosecutor shall proceed in the matter on behalf of the State, unless the county prosecutor or the Attorney General assumes responsibility for the prosecution. The civil penalties provided by this act or any rule or regulation adopted pursuant thereto shall be recovered in the name of the commission, as appropriate, and any money collected by the court in payment of a civil penalty shall be conveyed to the State Treasurer for deposit into the State General Fund. The civil penalties provided by this act or any rule or regulation adopted pursuant thereto shall be collected and enforced by summary proceedings pursuant to "The Penalty Enforcement Law of 1999," P.L.1999, c. 274 (C.2A:58–10 et seq.). If the ticket has not been marked to indicate that a court appearance is required, the defendant shall have the option to waive trial, enter a plea of guilty, and pay the penalty, either by mail or in person, to the violations clerk, subject to the Rules Governing the Courts of the State of New Jersey. *L.1995, c. 157, § 14. Amended by L.2003, c. 13, § 87.*

Historical and Statutory Notes

L.2003, c. 13, § 127, approved Jan. 28, 2003, provides:

"Sections 1, 2, 3, 12, 38, 109, 110 and 121 shall take effect immediately, sections 105, 106, 107, 108, and 120 shall take effect on July 1, 2003 and the remainder of this act shall take effect on the date the Commissioner of Transportation certifies to the Governor (hereinafter the "date of certification") that a majority of the members of the commission have been appointed or are in office and that all necessary anticipatory actions have been accomplished, provided, that the amount of revenues received pursuant to sections 109 and 110 prior to the date of certification are hereby appropriated to the division. Upon the date of certification, all such collected revenue shall be revenue of the commission. The Commissioner of Transportation, the Director of the Division of Motor Vehicles and the commission may take such anticipatory administrative action in advance as shall be necessary for the implementation of the act."

39:8–73. Municipal court proceedings for collection of unpaid penalties; suspension of registration; placement of administrative out-of-service order against vehicle

a. The court administrator of the municipal court shall docket in the Superior Court a municipal court judgment imposing a civil penalty pursuant to this act, or any rule or regulation adopted pursuant thereto, that remains unpaid at the time of the judgment's entry in the municipal court. The court administrator shall give notice of the docketing to the commission in a manner prescribed by the commission. The provisions and procedures of N.J.S.2B:12–26 shall apply to the docketing, except that the court administrator of the municipal court, rather than the commission, shall effect the docketing; provided that nothing in this act shall be construed to prohibit the commission or its designee from docketing the judgment on behalf of the commission and in accordance with N.J.S.2B:12–26 if the court administrator of the municipal court fails to do so or if the commission or its designee chooses to do so for any other reason. No fee shall be charged to docket the judgment. The docketing shall have the same force and effect as a civil judgment docketed in the Superior Court, and the commission and its designee shall have all of the remedies and may take all of the proceedings for the collection thereof that may be had or taken upon recovery of a judgment in an action, but without prejudice to any right of appeal.

b. If the defendant is the owner or lessee of a vehicle that is the subject of the violation, and if the defendant fails to pay a civil penalty imposed pursuant to this act or any rule or regulation adopted pursuant thereto, the commission may suspend the registration privileges of the defendant in this State.

c. Any vehicle that is registered or present in this State and for which a civil penalty has been assessed pursuant to this act or any rule or regulation adopted pursuant thereto may be placed out of service by the commission or the Division of State Police if the civil penalty remains unpaid after the date on which it became due and owing. A vehicle placed out of service pursuant to this act by either the commission or the Division of State Police shall not be operated until all civil penalties that are due and owing are paid to the commission. When a vehicle is placed out of service pursuant to this act, an administrative out-of-service order shall be prepared on a form or forms specified by the commission and a copy served upon the operator of the vehicle or upon the owner or lessee of the vehicle. The operator of a vehicle served with an out-of-service order pursuant to this act shall report the issuance of the out-of-service order to the owner and the lessee, if any, of the vehicle within 24 hours. When a vehicle is placed out of service pursuant to this act it shall be the responsibility of the owner or lessee of that vehicle to arrange for the prompt removal of that vehicle, by means other than operating the vehicle, and to pay all costs associated therewith. The vehicle shall be removed to a secure storage place where the commission and the Division of State Police can readily confirm its non-operation. If the owner or lessee fails to comply, or is otherwise incapable of complying with this subsection, the commission or the Division of State Police may make such arrangements for the removal of the vehicle to a secure storage place where the commission and the Division of State Police can readily confirm its non-operation, with all attendant charges and expenses to be paid by the owner, lessee, or bailee. No entity of government of this State or any political subdivision thereof shall be held liable for costs associated with or incurred in the enforcement of this subsection. Upon payment by cashier's check or money order, or in such other form as may be determined by the commission, subject to law or the Rules Governing the Courts of the State of New Jersey, of all unpaid civil penalties and attendant storage charges and expenses for a vehicle that has been placed out of service, the commission shall remove the out-of-service order. Any person who operates, and any owner or lessee who causes or allows to be operated, a vehicle in violation of an out-of-service order prepared and served in accordance with the provisions of this subsection shall be liable for a civil penalty of $1,500, and, if the person has the vehicle registered in this State, the commission may suspend the registration privileges of the vehicle.

d. The commission shall exercise all duties, powers and responsibilities set forth in this section with respect to the periodic inspection program for diesel buses and the roadside enforcement program for diesel buses under the jurisdiction of the commission as set forth in subsection b. of section 6 of this act.[1]

L.1995, c. 157, § 15. Amended by L.2003, c. 13, § 88.

[1] N.J.S.A. § 39:8–64.

Historical and Statutory Notes

L.2003, c. 13, § 127, approved Jan. 28, 2003, provides:

"Sections 1, 2, 3, 12, 38, 109, 110 and 121 shall take effect immediately, sections 105, 106, 107, 108, and 120 shall take effect on July 1, 2003 and the remainder of this act shall take effect on the date the Commissioner of Transportation certifies to the Governor (hereinafter the "date of certification") that a majority of the members of the commission have been appointed or are in office and that all necessary anticipatory actions have been accomplished, provided, that the amount of revenues received pursuant to sections 109 and 110 prior to the date of certification are hereby appropriated to the division. Upon the date of certification, all such collected revenue shall be revenue of the commission. The Commissioner of Transportation, the Director of the Division of Motor Vehicles and the commission may take such anticipatory administrative action in advance as shall be necessary for the implementation of the act."

39:8–74. Disbursement of fees, charges and expenses collected

Notwithstanding any other provisions of this title to the contrary, all fees and other monies that the commission, or the State Treasurer receives pursuant to the provisions of this act or any rule or regulation adopted pursuant thereto shall be paid to the Commercial Vehicle Enforcement Fund established pursuant to section 17 of this act;[1] except that monies received for attendant storage charges and expenses as provided in subsection c. of section 15 of this act[2] shall be paid to the entity that incurred those charges and expenses.

L.1995, c. 157, § 16. Amended by L.2003, c. 13, § 89.

1 N.J.S.A. § 39:8–75.
2 N.J.S.A. § 39:8–73.

Historical and Statutory Notes

L.2003, c. 13, § 127, approved Jan. 28, 2003, provides:

"Sections 1, 2, 3, 12, 38, 109, 110 and 121 shall take effect immediately, sections 105, 106, 107, 108, and 120 shall take effect on July 1, 2003 and the remainder of this act shall take effect on the date the Commissioner of Transportation certifies to the Governor (hereinafter the "date of certification") that a majority of the members of the commission have been appointed or are in office and that all necessary anticipatory actions have been accomplished, provided, that the amount of revenues received pursuant to sections 109 and 110 prior to the date of certification are hereby appropriated to the division. Upon the date of certification, all such collected revenue shall be revenue of the commission. The Commissioner of Transportation, the Director of the Division of Motor Vehicles and the commission may take such anticipatory administrative action in advance as shall be necessary for the implementation of the act."

39:8–75. Commercial vehicle enforcement fund

a. There is established in the General Fund a separate, nonlapsing, dedicated account to be known as the "Commercial Vehicle Enforcement Fund." The Commercial Vehicle Enforcement Fund shall be administered by the commission. All fees and other monies collected pursuant to this act or any rule or regulation adopted pursuant thereto shall be forwarded to the State Treasury for deposit into the Commercial Vehicle Enforcement Fund account. The commission shall receive 40 percent of this fund annually, which monies shall be considered revenue of the commission. All remaining fees and other monies deposited in the Commercial Vehicle Enforcement Fund account shall be used to fund the costs of administering the programs and activities of the Department of Law and Public Safety, the Department of Transportation, the commission and the Department of Environmental Protection established or specified in this act and in subsection f. of R.S.39:3–20, subject to the approval of the Director of the Division of Budget and Accounting in the Department of the Treasury.

b. A municipality may be eligible for periodic grants from the fund in such amounts as the commission, in consultation with the Commissioner of Transportation, may determine pursuant to rule or regulation to subsidize costs of prosecuting and trying actions pursuant to this act.

L.1995, c. 157, § 17. Amended by L.2003, c. 13, § 106, eff. July 1, 2003.

39:8–76. Receivable account established for expenses of program implementation and administration

The State Treasurer shall establish a receivable account for the sole purpose of defraying the expenses incurred for program implementation and administration of this act. The receivable account shall be relieved by monies deposited into the Commercial Vehicle Enforcement Fund established pursuant to section 17 of this act.[1]

L.1995, c. 157, § 18.

1 N.J.S.A. § 39:8–75.

39:8–77. Rules and regulations

Except as otherwise provided in this act, the commission, the Department of Environmental Protection, and the Department of Transportation may adopt rules and regulations pursuant to the "Administrative Procedure Act," P.L.1968, c. 410 (C.52:14B–1 et seq.) to effectuate the purposes of this act.

L.1995, c. 157, § 19. Amended by L.2003, c. 13, § 90.

Historical and Statutory Notes

L.2003, c. 13, § 127, approved Jan. 28, 2003, provides:

"Sections 1, 2, 3, 12, 38, 109, 110 and 121 shall take effect immediately, sections 105, 106, 107, 108, and 120 shall take effect on July 1, 2003 and the remainder of this act shall take effect on the date the Commissioner of Transportation certifies to the Governor (hereinafter the "date of certification") that a majority of the members of the commission have been appointed or are in office and that all necessary anticipatory actions have been accomplished, provided, that the amount of revenues received pursuant to sections 109 and 110 prior to the date of certification are hereby appropriated to the division. Upon the date of certification, all such collected revenue shall be revenue of the commission. The Commissioner of Transportation, the Director of the Division of Motor Vehicles and the commission may take such anticipatory administrative action in advance as shall be necessary for the implementation of the act."

39:8–78. Report to governor and legislature

On the first day of the forty-eighth month after this act takes effect, the Attorney General, in consultation with the Commissioner of Environmental Protection, the commission, and the Commissioner of Transportation, shall submit to the Governor and to the members of the Legislature a report assessing the effectiveness of the programs required by this act and the necessity and feasibility of providing for periodic centralized emissions inspections of diesel buses, heavy-duty diesel trucks, and other diesel-powered motor vehicles.

L.1995, c. 157, § 20. Amended by L.2003, c. 13, § 91.

Historical and Statutory Notes

L.2003, c. 13, § 127, approved Jan. 28, 2003, provides:

"Sections 1, 2, 3, 12, 38, 109, 110 and 121 shall take effect immediately, sections 105, 106, 107, 108, and 120 shall take effect on July 1, 2003 and the remainder of this act shall take effect on the date the Commissioner of Transportation certifies to the Governor (hereinafter the "date of certification") that a majority of the members of the commission have been appointed or are in office and that all necessary anticipatory actions have been accomplished, provided, that the amount of revenues received pursuant to sections 109 and 110 prior to the date of certification are hereby appropriated to the division. Upon the date of certification, all such collected revenue shall be revenue of the commission. The Commissioner of Transportation, the Director of the Division of Motor Vehicles and the commission may take such anticipatory administrative action in advance as shall be necessary for the implementation of the act."

39:8–79 to 39:8–89. [Reallocated to §§ 39:3–6.11 to 39:3–6.21]

39:8–90. Diesel emission inspection centers redesignation as private inspection facilities

Section effective on May 18, 2010.

All diesel emission inspection centers licensed pursuant to section 11 of P.L.1995, c. 157 (C.39:8–69) shall be redesignated by virtue of this act as private inspection facilities with the authority to make diesel emission inspections to the extent and under the conditions permitted herein. All diesel emission inspection center licenses shall be renewed as private inspection facility licenses upon their current expiration.

L.2009, c. 331, § 10, eff. May 18, 2010.

CHAPTER 9

HOURS OF DUTY OF OPERATORS OF CERTAIN MOTOR VEHICLES

Section
39:9–1.   Citation of chapter.
39:9–2.   Hours of duty limited; hours off duty; emergencies.
39:9–3.   Repealed.
39:9–4.   Violations of chapter; punishment; enforcement; remedies; procedure; revocation of certificate.

39:9–1. Citation of chapter

This chapter shall be known, and may be cited, as the "hours of service law of 1936."

39:9–2. Hours of duty limited; hours off duty; emergencies

It shall be unlawful for any person to operate, or to require or permit any person to operate, any commercial motor vehicle weighing 26,000 pounds or less that is operated exclusively in intrastate commerce after the operator has been continuously on duty for a longer period than 12 hours, or after the operator has been on duty for more than 12 hours in the aggregate during any 16 consecutive hours. When the operator has been continuously on duty for 12 hours or has been on duty for 12 hours in the aggregate during any 16 consecutive hours, that person shall have at least 10 consecutive hours off duty.   The periods of release from duty provided for in this section shall be spent at a place and under circumstances where rest and relaxation from the strain of the duties of driving may be obtained; provided, however, that in case of accident or emergency, the operator of a commercial motor vehicle may complete his run or tour of duty, and neither the operator nor the person who requires or permits that person to drive for a longer period shall be deemed to have violated the provisions of this chapter.

Nothing in this section shall apply to a vehicle designed to transport 16 or more passengers, including the driver, or a vehicle used in the transportation of hazardous materials and required to be placarded in accordance with 49 CFR s. 172.500 et seq., or a vehicle that displays a hazardous materials placard.

Amended by L.2004, c. 97, § 2, eff. July 12, 2004.

39:9–3. Repealed by L.1956, c. 51, p. 102, § 1

39:9–4. Violations of chapter; punishment; enforcement; remedies; procedure; revocation of certificate

Any person violating any provision of this chapter shall, upon summary conviction by a court of competent jurisdiction, be sentenced to pay a fine of $25.00 for the first offense and, in default of payment thereof, shall undergo imprisonment for not more than five days; and for each subsequent violation shall be sentenced to pay a fine of $50.00 and, in default of such payment, shall undergo imprisonment for not more than 10 days.

The provisions of this chapter shall be enforced and all penalties for the violation thereof shall be recovered in accordance with the provisions of "the penalty enforcement law" (N.J.S. 2A:58–1 et seq.), and in addition to the provisions and remedies therein contained, the following provisions and remedies shall be applicable in any proceeding brought for a violation of any of the provisions of this chapter:

a.   The several municipal courts shall have jurisdiction of such proceeding, in addition to the courts prescribed in "the penalty enforcement law";

b. The complaint in any such proceeding may be made on information and belief by the director or any police or peace officer of any municipality, any county or the State;

c. A warrant may issue in lieu of summons;

d. Any police or peace officer shall be empowered to serve and execute process in any such proceeding;

e. The hearing in any such proceeding shall be without a jury;

f. Any such proceeding may be brought in the name of the Director of the Division of Motor Vehicles in the Department of Law and Public Safety or in the name of the State of New Jersey;

g. Any sums received in payment of any fines imposed in any such proceeding shall be paid to the Director of the Division of Motor Vehicles and shall be paid by him into the State treasury;

h. The director or judge before whom any hearing under this chapter is had may revoke the license of any person to drive a motor vehicle or the registration certificate of any motor vehicle owned by any person, when such person shall have been guilty of such willful violation of any of the provisions of this chapter as shall in the discretion of the director or judge justify such revocation.

Amended by L.1954, c. 76, p. 446, § 1; L.1956, c. 51, p. 102, § 2; L.1983, c. 403, § 29, eff. Dec. 23, 1983.

CHAPTER 10

PURCHASE, SALE AND TRANSFER OF MOTOR VEHICLES

I.   GENERAL PROVISIONS

Section
39:10–1.   Short title.
39:10–2.   Definitions.
39:10–3.   Interpretation of chapter.
39:10–4.   Chapter enforced by commissioner; rules and regulations.
39:10–5.   Sale contrary to chapter unlawful.
39:10–5.1.   Lease containing terminal rental adjustment clause not to constitute conditional sale of or security interest in vehicle; definitions.
39:10–6.   Necessary certificates.
39:10–7.   Manufacturer's numbers required on motor vehicles.
39:10–8.   Certificate of origin of new motor vehicle; security interests.
39:10–9.   Subsequent sales; security interests.
39:10–9.1.   Used police patrol car; designation on certificate of ownership.
39:10–9.2.   Failure to designate; penalty.
39:10–9.3.   Certificate of ownership to contain notice if vehicle returned due to nonconformity with manufacturer's warranty; penalty for violation.
39:10–9.4.   Identifying markings of ambulances to be removed prior to certain sales or transfers; enforcement; violation.

Section
39:10–10.   Delivery of certificate of ownership; filing of evidence of satisfaction of contract or termination of security interest; penalty for noncompliance.
39:10–11.   Submitting evidence of purchase; recording; certificate of ownership; fee; creation of security interest; penalty.
39:10–11.1.   Certificate of ownership for mobile or manufactured home in mobile home park; cancellation on relocation on land with interest or title in owner.
39:10–12.   Lost papers; duplicate certificate; false statements in application.
39:10–13.   File of certificates kept; destruction of other certificates.
39:10–14.   Notations; index; certificates; security interests; fees; furnishing information from records.
39:10–15.   Procedure and delivery of title papers upon seizure of motor vehicle.
39:10–15.1.   Sale or disposal of manufactured homes.
39:10–16.   Defective or improper title papers or sale in other state or country; procedure to correct or to permit receipt of title papers.
39:10–17.   Repealed.
39:10–18.   Title papers necessary to registration.
39:10–19.   Motor vehicle dealer's license; eligibility; duration; renewal; fee.
39:10–19.1.   Definitions applicable to off–site sales of new or used recreational vehicles or used motor vehicles.
39:10–19.2.   Off–site vehicle sales permitted to certain dealers.
39:10–19.3.   Provisional and final permits for off–site vehicle sales.
39:10–19.4.   Off–site vehicle sales; booth or desk at sale premises; information required for agreements of sale, offerings or contracts.
39:10–20.   Fines; suspension or revocation of license; notice; subpoenas; depositions; review.
39:10–21.   Possession of title papers by dealer; seizure and sale for nonconformity.
39:10–22.   Forms; seizure of papers to which chief administrator entitled.
39:10–23.   Certificate surrendered when vehicle junked, etc.
39:10–24.   Violations of chapter; misdemeanor; punishment.
39:10–25.   Agency to issue certificates; fees.

II.   STANDARDS FOR USED MOTOR VEHICLES

39:10–26.   Standards for used motor vehicles for sale.
39:10–27.   Failure to meet standards; liability of seller.
39:10–28.   Specification of intended registration in written agreement; informing purchaser of dealer's responsibilities.
39:10–29.   Waiver of dealer's obligation; effect.
39:10–30.   Violations; penalty.

III.   SALVAGE CERTIFICATES OF TITLE

39:10–31.   "Salvage certificate of title" defined.
39:10–32.   Vehicle reported stolen or damaged; surrender of certificate of ownership; issuance of salvage certificate of title.
39:10–33.   Recovery of stolen vehicle; conditions for issuance of certificate of ownership.

Section

39:10–34. Repair of damaged vehicle; conditions for issuance of certificate of ownership.
39:10–35. Fee for inspection.
39:10–36. Vehicle issued salvage certificate of title by another state.
39:10–37. Rules and regulations.

I. GENERAL PROVISIONS

39:10–1. Short title

This chapter may be known and cited as the "motor vehicle certificate of ownership law."
Amended by L.1946, c. 136, p. 622, § 1.

39:10–2. Definitions

As used in this chapter unless other meaning is clearly apparent from the language or context, or unless inconsistent with the manifest intention of the Legislature:

"New motor vehicle" means only a newly manufactured motor vehicle, except a nonconventional type motor vehicle, and includes all such vehicles propelled otherwise than by muscular power, and motorcycles, motorized bicycles, trailers and tractors, and manufactured homes not subject to real property taxation pursuant to P.L.1983, c. 400 (C. 54:4–1.2 et seq.), excepting such vehicles as run only upon rails or tracks and manufactured homes subject to real property taxation.

"Used motor vehicle" means every motor vehicle and motorized bicycle, except a nonconventional type motor vehicle, title to, or possession of, which has been transferred from the person who first acquired it from the manufacturer or dealer, and so used as to become what is commonly known as "secondhand" within the ordinary meaning thereof, and includes every motor vehicle and motorized bicycle other than a "new motor vehicle," a "nonconventional type motor vehicle" or a manufactured home subject to real property taxation.

"Any motor vehicle," "every motor vehicle," or similar term, means both new and used motor vehicles, except a "nonconventional type motor vehicle."

"Nonconventional type motor vehicle" means every vehicle not designed or used primarily for the transportation of persons or property and only incidentally operated or moved over a highway, including, but not limited to, ditch-digging apparatus, well-boring apparatus, road and general purpose construction and maintenance machinery, asphalt spreaders, bituminous mixers, bucket loaders, ditchers, leveling graders, finishing machines, motor graders, road rollers, scarifiers, earth-moving carryalls, scrapers, power shovels, drag lines, self-propelled cranes, earth-moving equipment, trailers and semitrailers which weigh less than 2,500 pounds, except that no mobile or manufactured home or travel trailer shall be classified as a nonconventional type motor vehicle, motorized wheelchairs, motorized lawn mowers, bogies, farm equipment having a factory shipping weight of less than 1,500 pounds, whether or not motorized, including farm tractors within said weight limitation, industrial tractors, scooters, go-carts, gas buggies and golf carts. The Director of Motor Vehicles shall have power to make, amend and repeal regulations, not inconsistent with the provisions of this paragraph, prescribing what further vehicles or types of vehicles, not specified in this paragraph, shall be included in the category of nonconventional type motor vehicles.

"Motor vehicles which constitute inventory held for sale" means new motor vehicles and used motor vehicles held for the purpose of sale by dealers and used motor vehicles held for the purpose of sale by used motor vehicle dealers, and excludes motor vehicles held for the purpose of lease or rental by a person engaged in the motor vehicle leasing or rental business.

"Manufacturer's or importer's certificate of origin" means the original written instrument or document required to be executed and delivered by the manufacturer to his agent or a dealer, or a person purchasing direct from the manufacturer, certifying the origin of the vehicle.

"Certificate of ownership" means the document issued in conformance with this chapter, certifying ownership of a motor vehicle, other than manufacturer's or importer's certificate of origin.

"Assignment" means the execution of a prescribed form transferring ownership of a motor vehicle from the person named therein to the purchaser.

"Contract" means conditional sale agreement, bailment, lease, chattel mortgage, trust receipt or any other form of security or possession agreement executed prior to January 1, 1963, wherein and whereby possession of a motor vehicle is delivered to the buyer and title therein is to vest in the buyer at a subsequent time upon the payment of part or all of the price, or upon the performance of any other condition or happening of any contingency, or upon the payment of a sum substantially equivalent to the value of the motor vehicle, by which contract it is agreed that the buyer is bound to become, or has the option of becoming, the owner of the motor vehicle upon full compliance with the terms of the contract.

"Abstract" means the duplicate copy of the original certificate of ownership recording any encumbrance or upon which the existence of a security interest is noted.

"Title papers" means any instrument or document that is evidence of ownership of a vehicle.

"Director" means the Director of Motor Vehicles, his deputy or duly authorized agent.

"Manufacturer" means the person who originally manufactured the motor vehicle.

"Dealer" means the agent, distributor or authorized dealer of the manufacturer of the new motor vehicle, and who has an established place of business.

"Used motor vehicle dealer" means a person engaged in the business of selling, buying or dealing in used motor vehicles, and who has an established place of business.

"Person" includes natural persons, firms or copartnerships, corporations, associations, or other artificial bodies, receivers, trustees, common law or statutory assignees, executors, administrators, sheriffs, constables, marshals, or other persons in representative or official capacity, and members, officers, agents, employees, or other representatives of those hereinbefore enumerated.

"Buyer" includes purchaser, debtor, lessee, bailee, transferee, and any person buying, attempting to buy, or receiving a motor vehicle subject to a security interest, lease, bailment or transfer agreement, and their legal successors in interest.

"Seller" means manufacturer, dealer, lessor, bailor, transferor with or without a security interest, and any other person selling, attempting to sell, or delivering a motor vehicle, and their legal successors in interest.

The terms "sell" or "sale" or "purchase" and any form thereof include absolute or voluntary sales and purchases, agreements to sell and purchase, bailments, leases, security agreements whereby any motor vehicles are sold and purchased, or agreed to be sold and purchased, involuntary, statutory and judicial sales, inheritance, devise, or bequest, gift or any other form or manner of sale or agreement of sale thereof, or the giving or transferring possession of a motor vehicle to a person for a permanent use; continued possession for 60 days or more is to be construed as permanent use.

"Manufacturer's number" means the original manufacturer's vehicle identification number die stamped upon the body, or frame, or either or both of them, of a motor vehicle or the original manufacturer's number die stamped upon the engine or motor of a motor vehicle.

"Purchaser" means a person who takes possession of a motor vehicle by transfer of ownership, either for use or resale, except a dealer when he takes possession through a certificate of origin.

"Debtor" means the person who owes payment or other performance of the obligation secured by a security interest in a motor vehicle.

"Security interest" means an interest in a motor vehicle which secures payment or other performance of an obligation.

"Security agreement" means an agreement which creates or provides for a security interest in a motor vehicle.

"Secured party" means a lender, seller or other person in whose favor there is a security interest.

"Gross vehicle weight rating" means the value specified by the manufacturer as the loaded weight of the single or combination vehicle and, if the manufacturer has not specified a value for a towed vehicle, means the value specified for the towing vehicle plus the loaded weight of the towed unit.

Amended by L.1946, c. 136, p. 622, § 2; L.1949, c. 235, p. 734, § 1; L.1961, c. 122, p. 732, § 1; L.1964, c. 238, § 1; L.1965, c. 10, § 1; L.1983, c. 105, § 4; L.1983, c. 387, § 1, eff. Jan. 1, 1984; L.1990, c. 115, § 4, eff. Nov. 19, 1990.

39:10–3. Interpretation of chapter

This chapter shall be so interpreted and construed as to effectuate its general purpose to regulate and control titles to, and possession of, all motor vehicles in this state, so as to prevent the sale, purchase, disposal, possession, use or operation of stolen motor vehicles, or motor vehicles with fraudulent titles, within this state.

39:10–4. Chapter enforced by commissioner; rules and regulations

The enforcement of this chapter shall be intrusted to the commission and it may make rules and regulations necessary in its judgment for the administration and enforcement thereof in addition thereto but not inconsistent therewith. The commission may employ and discharge any person it requires for the administration and enforcement of this chapter and fix their compensation.

Amended by L.2003, c. 13, § 64.

Historical and Statutory Notes

L.2003, c. 13, § 127, approved Jan. 28, 2003, provides:

"Sections 1, 2, 3, 12, 38, 109, 110 and 121 shall take effect immediately, sections 105, 106, 107, 108, and 120 shall take effect on July 1, 2003 and the remainder of this act shall take effect on the date the Commissioner of Transportation certifies to the Governor (hereinafter the "date of certification") that a majority of the members of the commission have been appointed or are in office and that all necessary anticipatory actions have been accomplished, provided, that the amount of revenues received pursuant to sections 109 and 110 prior to the date of certification are hereby appropriated to the division. Upon the date of certification, all such collected revenue shall be revenue of the commission. The Commissioner of Transportation, the Director of the Division of Motor Vehicles and the commission may take such anticipatory administrative action in advance as shall be necessary for the implementation of the act."

39:10–5. Sale contrary to chapter unlawful

No person shall sell or purchase any motor vehicle in this state, except in the manner and subject to the conditions provided in this chapter.

39:10–5.1. Lease containing terminal rental adjustment clause not to constitute conditional sale of or security interest in vehicle; definitions

a. Notwithstanding any other provision of law to the contrary, no agreement stating that it is for the lease of a vehicle shall be deemed to create a conditional sale of, or security interest in, the property which is the subject of the agreement merely because the agreement contains a terminal rental adjustment clause.

b. For purposes of this section:

(1) "terminal rental adjustment clause" means a provision of an agreement which permits or requires the rental price to be adjusted upward or downward by reference to the amount realized by the lessor upon sale or other disposition of the vehicle.

(2) "vehicle" means every device in, upon or by which a person or property is or may be transported upon a highway, excepting devices moved by human power or used exclusively upon stationary rails or tracks or motorized bicycles.

L.1992, c. 28, § 1, eff. June 29, 1992.

39:10–6. Necessary certificates

Every person shall have for each motor vehicle in his possession in this State: (a) certificate of ownership therefor in conformity with this chapter, and (b) the registration certificate for the motor vehicle, if it is registered by the chief administrator and a registration certificate has been issued therefor. He shall produce either the certificate of ownership or registration certificate, at the discretion of the chief administrator¢, upon demand for production thereof by the chief administrator¢. If he fails to do so, the director may seize and take possession of the motor vehicle and hold and dispose of it in accordance with R.S.39:10–21.

If a motor vehicle is registered in or bears the registration plates of another state or country and is being used or operated in this State, the person in possession of it or using or operating it in this State must be entitled to ownership or possession in accordance with the laws of the state or country where it is registered or the registration plates of which it bears, and shall produce to the chief administrator¢ documents showing title to, or right of possession in, the motor vehicle in that person or in the person who has authorized him to use and operate it, or registration certificate or other evidence of registration, besides plates, issued by the state or country or department thereof to that person, or to the person who has authorized him to use and operate the motor vehicle, evidencing the registration of the motor vehicle in that state or country.

When a motor vehicle is in the possession of a garage keeper, motor vehicle dealer, both new and used, or motor vehicle service station in this State, the production of a writing signed by the person delivering possession of the motor vehicle to the garage keeper, dealer or service station, stating that the person is the owner or entitled to the possession of the motor vehicle and has title papers or the registration certificate therefor, shall be deemed a compliance with this section insofar as the garage keeper, dealer and service station are concerned. In the case of a licensed motor vehicle dealer, the production of a writing signed by the person or persons delivering possession of the motor vehicle to the dealer, assigning to that dealer the right to title or possession or both of and to the vehicle, or in the case of a new vehicle, a copy of the manufacturer's certificate of origin, shall constitute compliance with this section.

Amended by L.1946, c. 136, p. 625, § 3; L.1983, c. 403, § 30, eff. Dec. 23, 1983; L.1990, c. 115, § 5, eff. Nov. 19, 1990; L.2007, c. 335, § 21, eff. Feb. 12, 2008.

39:10–7. Manufacturer's numbers required on motor vehicles

Every motor vehicle and nonconventional type motor vehicle shall have and contain a manufacturer's vehicle identification number, which number shall not be obliterated, erased, mutilated, removed or missing. This section shall not affect those persons authorized by law to have in their possession a motor vehicle on which the manufacturer's number or numbers have been obliterated, erased, mutilated, removed or missing.

Amended by L.1949, c. 235, p. 737, § 2; L.1964, c. 238, § 1.

39:10–8. Certificate of origin of new motor vehicle; security interests

When a new motor vehicle is delivered in this State by the manufacturer to his agent or a dealer, or a person purchasing directly from the manufacturer, the manufacturer shall execute and deliver to his agent or a dealer, or a person purchasing directly from the manufacturer, a certificate of origin in the form prescribed by the chief administrator of the New Jersey Motor Vehicle Commission, and no person shall bring into this State any new motor vehicle unless he has in his possession the certificate of origin as prescribed by the chief administrator. The certificate of origin shall contain the manufacturer's vehicle identification number and the motor number when used of the motor vehicle sold, name of the manufacturer, the manufacturer's shipping weight, a general description of the body, if any, the type and model and the gross vehicle weight rating.

When a new motor vehicle is sold in this State, the manufacturer, his agent or a dealer shall execute and deliver to the purchaser an assignment of the certificate of origin, with the genuine names and business or residence addresses of both stated thereon, and certified to have been executed with full knowledge of the contents and with the consent of both purchaser and seller. If, in connection with such sale, a security interest is taken or retained by the seller to secure all or a part of the purchase price of the motor vehicle, or is taken by a person who by making an advance or incurring an obligation gives value to enable the purchaser to acquire rights in the motor vehicle, the original certificate of origin need not be delivered to the buyer at time of sale, and the original certificate of origin, with the name and business address of the secured party noted, may be delivered directly to the Motor Vehicle Commission for issuance of a certificate of title in the name of the purchaser. The name and the business or residence address of the secured party or his assignee shall be noted on the manufacturer's certificate of origin. Nothing in this section shall apply to security interests in motor vehicles which constitute inventory held for sale, but such interests shall be subject to chapter 9 of Title 12A of the New Jersey Statutes.

Amended by L.1946, c. 136, p. 626, § 4; L.1949, c. 235, p. 737, § 3; L.1955, c. 8, p. 48, § 11; L.1961, c. 122, p. 735, § 2; L.1962, c. 193, § 1, eff. Jan. 1, 1963; L.1990, c. 115, § 6, eff. Nov. 19, 1990; L.2007, c. 335, § 22, eff. Feb. 12, 2008.

39:10–9. Subsequent sales; security interests

When a used motor vehicle is sold in this State, the seller shall, except as provided in section 39:10–15 of this Title, execute and deliver to the purchaser, an assignment of the certificate of ownership or an assignment of the bill of sale issued prior to October 1, 1946, or, in the event the vehicle is subject to a security interest, or for some other reason the original certificate of ownership is not in the possession of the seller, and where the purchaser is a licensed New Jersey motor vehicle dealer, the seller may execute a secure power of attorney as required under the federal Truth in Mileage Act of 1986, Pub.L. 99–579 (49 U.S.C. s.32705) or such other documents as the chief administrator may require, authorizing the licensed dealer to execute the original title upon obtaining possession of same. If a security interest exists at the time of such sale and will continue in effect afterwards or if, in connection with such sale, a security interest is taken or retained by the seller to secure all or a part of the purchase price of the motor vehicle, or is taken by a person who by making an advance or incurring an obligation gives value to enable the purchaser to acquire rights in the motor vehicle, the name and the business or residence address of the secured party or his assignee shall be noted on the certificate of ownership. If the seller is a licensed New Jersey motor vehicle dealer, the seller shall not be required to deliver an assignment or certificate of ownership at the time of sale, provided that the dealer has satisfied all liens noted on the certificate of title and has the right to title as of the time of sale, and provided that the dealer represents and attests to the same in a writing to be delivered to the purchaser at the time of sale. Nothing in this section shall apply to security interests in motor vehicles which constitute inventory held for sale, but such interests shall be subject to chapter 9 of Title 12A of the New Jersey Statutes.

Amended by L.1946, c. 136, p. 627, § 5, eff. Oct. 1, 1946; L.1961, c. 122, p. 736, § 3; L.1962, c. 193, § 2; L.2007, c. 335, § 23, eff. Feb. 12, 2008.

39:10–9.1. Used police patrol car; designation on certificate of ownership

In every sale or transfer of a used motor vehicle which has been used as a police patrol car, whether said patrol car bore markings identifying it as such or not, the certificate of ownership shall state that said motor vehicle was used as a police patrol car, and shall continue to so state on each subsequent sale or transfer.

L.1971, c. 311, § 1, eff. Sept. 2, 1971.

39:10–9.2. Failure to designate; penalty

Any person who transfers or attempts to transfer a motor vehicle in violation of this act shall be subject to a fine of $150.00 for a first offense and $250.00 for each subsequent offense. Such offense shall be prosecuted in the Superior Court or in the municipal court.

L.1971, c. 311, § 2, eff. Sept. 2, 1971. Amended by L.1991, c. 91, § 376, eff. April 9, 1991.

39:10–9.3. Certificate of ownership to contain notice if vehicle returned due to nonconformity with manufacturer's warranty; penalty for violation

a. In every sale or transfer of a motor vehicle returned to the manufacturer under the provisions of P.L.1988, c. 123 (C.56:12–29 et seq.), a similar statute of another state, or as the result of a legal action or an informal dispute settlement procedure, the certificate of ownership shall indicate, in a conspicuous and understandable manner, that the motor vehicle was returned to the manufacturer because it did not conform to the manufacturer's warranty and the nonconformity was not corrected within a reasonable time as provided by law. The notice required under the provisions of this subsection shall continue to appear on each certificate of ownership issued as a result of any subsequent sale or transfer of that motor vehicle.

b. Any person who transfers or attempts to transfer a motor vehicle in violation of this section shall be subject to a fine of not more than $7,500.

c. The Director of the Division of Motor Vehicles in the Department of Law and Public Safety, in accordance with the provisions of the "Administrative Procedure Act" P.L.1968, c. 410 (C. 52:14B–1 et seq.), shall promulgate rules and regulations to effectuate the purposes of this section.

L.1993, c. 21, § 1, eff. April 1, 1993.

39:10–9.4. Identifying markings of ambulances to be removed prior to certain sales or transfers; enforcement; violation

a. Any ambulance sold, transferred, gifted, discarded or abandoned to an entity other than a hospital, licensed ambulance dealership, an emergency service organization as defined in section 2 of P.L.1997, c. 388 (C.40A:14–184) or any entity licensed by the Department of Health and Senior Services as an ambulance operator shall, prior to sale or transfer, be stripped of all markings that would identify the vehicle as an ambulance.

b. The Commissioner of the Department of Health and Senior Services shall be responsible for the enforcement of this act.

c. An action for a violation of this act may be brought in any court of competent jurisdiction, and shall be punishable as a crime of the fourth degree.

L.2005, c. 295, § 1, eff. Jan. 9, 2006.

39:10–10. Delivery of certificate of ownership; filing of evidence of satisfaction of contract or termination of security interest; penalty for noncompliance

When the contract or terms of the security agreement noted on the certificate of origin, or certificate of ownership have been performed the seller or secured party shall deliver to the buyer the certificate of ownership thereto, executed as provided in this chapter, with proper evidence of satisfaction of the contract or termination of the security interest. Within 15 days after the performance of the contract or termination of the security interest, the seller or secured party shall file with the director a notice, in such form as the director shall prescribe, containing evidence of such performance or termination. The director shall thereupon cause a notation to be made on his records of certificate of ownership of the motor vehicle that the contract has been satisfied or the security interest terminated.

Any person violating the provisions of this section shall pay a fine of $25.00.

Amended by L.1939, c. 270, p. 692, § 1; L.1946, c. 136, p. 627, § 6; L.1951, c. 295, p. 1075, § 1; L.1961, c. 122, p. 736, § 4.

39:10–11. Submitting evidence of purchase; recording; certificate of ownership; fee; creation of security interest; penalty

A. The purchaser of a motor vehicle in this State, other than a dealer licensed pursuant to the provisions of R.S. 39:10–19, shall, within 10 working days after its purchase, submit to the director evidence of the purchase. Upon presentation to the director of the certificate of origin, or certificate of ownership, or bill of sale issued prior to October 1, 1946, with proper assignment and certification of the seller, a record of the transaction shall be made and filed. A certificate of ownership shall be issued by the director and delivered to the buyer, in case of a sale not subject to a security interest, and the director shall collect a fee of $20 for the issuance and filing thereof.

B. In the case of a sale subject to a security interest, a certificate of ownership, with the name and address of the holder of the encumbrance or secured party or his assignee recorded thereon, shall be delivered to the holder of the encumbrance or secured party or his assignee and a copy thereof shall be delivered to the buyer. The director shall collect a fee of $30 for his services in issuing a certificate and copy thereof, and for

making a record of and filing the record of the transaction, pursuant to this subsection.

C. Except as hereinafter in this section otherwise expressly provided, whenever a security interest is created in a motor vehicle, other than a security interest which is required to be noted on the certificate of origin or the certificate of ownership, as provided in R.S. 39:10–8 and R.S. 39:10–9, there shall be filed with the director the certificate of ownership of the motor vehicle, together with a financing statement on a form prescribed by the director. The director shall make and file a record of the transaction and shall issue a certificate of ownership, recording the name and address of the secured party or his assignee thereon, and shall deliver it to the secured party or his assignee. A copy of the certificate of ownership so issued shall be delivered to the buyer. The director shall collect a fee of $20 for his services in issuing a certificate and copy thereof and for making a record of and filing the record of the transaction, pursuant to this subsection.

D. The financing statement required to be filed pursuant to subsection C. hereof shall be signed only by the buyer, shall not be required to be acknowledged or proved, and shall show, in addition to such matters as the director may require for the proper identification of the motor vehicle affected, the date of the security agreement, and the names and addresses of the parties thereto. Nothing in this section 39:10–11 contained shall be construed as requiring that the security agreement or a copy thereof, or any proof of execution thereof other than that contained in the financing statement, shall be presented to the director. When the buyer is a corporation, it shall be sufficient if the financing statement is signed by any officer thereof, or by any agent designated by the corporation for that purpose, and it shall not be necessary that the financing statement recite the authorization of the agent. When there is more than one buyer, it shall be sufficient if the financing statement is signed by any one of them.

E. Nothing in subsections C. and D. of this section shall apply to security interests in motor vehicles which constitute inventory held for sale, but such interests shall be subject to chapter 9 of Title 12A of the New Jersey Statutes, nor shall anything in the said subsections apply to interests in personal property subject to chapter 28 of Title 46 of the Revised Statutes.

F. In addition to the fees elsewhere in this section provided for, there shall be paid to the director at the time a certificate of ownership is issued a fee of $10 for notice of satisfaction of the lien or encumbrance of the record or abstract, or of the termination of the security interest, where the motor vehicle is subject to a lien or encumbrance or a security interest as provided in R.S. 39:10–14.

G. Notwithstanding any other provision of this chapter, when any dealer licensed under the provisions of R.S. 39:10–19 is the purchaser of a motor vehicle in this State, he may, within 10 working days after its purchase, submit to the director the evidence of purchase. Upon presentation of the certificate of ownership with proper assignment and certification of the seller to the director, a record of the transaction shall be made and filed. A certificate of ownership shall be issued by the director and delivered to such purchaser, and the director shall collect a fee of $10 for the issuing and filing thereof.

If a dealer does not submit the evidence of purchase, upon resale of the motor vehicle he shall execute and attach to the certificate of ownership a dealer reassignment certificate. The director shall issue dealer reassignment certificates in lots upon payment of a fee of $10 for each certificate.

H. Any purchaser of a motor vehicle who fails to comply with the provisions of this section shall pay to the director a penalty of $25 plus the issuing and filing fee.

I. The failure of any person to comply with the requirements of this section shall not constitute a misdemeanor within the provisions of R.S. 39:10–24, nor shall such failure affect the validity of any instrument creating or reserving a security interest in a motor vehicle, as between the parties to such instrument.

J. The notation of the name and business or residence address of a secured party or his assignee, on the certificate of origin or on the certificate of ownership, as provided in R.S. 39:10–8 and R.S. 39:10–9, and the presentation to the director, in accordance with R.S. 39:10–11, of the certificate of origin or certificate of ownership so noted, and the compliance with the requirements of subsections C. and D. of R.S. 39:10–11 shall be in lieu of all filing requirements imposed by chapter 9 of Title 12A of the New Jersey Statutes and shall constitute the perfection of a security interest in the motor vehicle, and the rights and remedies of the debtors and the secured parties in respect to such security interest shall, except as otherwise expressly provided in this chapter, be subject to and governed by chapter 9 of Title 12A of the New Jersey Statutes.

Amended by L.1939, c. 270, p. 693, § 2; L.1946, c. 136, p. 628, § 7; L.1951, c. 334, p. 1173, § 1; L.1954, c. 207, p. 767, § 1; L.1955, c. 209, p. 820, § 1; L.1956, c. 92, p. 185, § 1; L.1961, c. 122, p. 737, § 5; L.1962, c. 193, § 3; L.1963, c. 34, § 3; L.1968, c. 130, § 12, eff. Aug. 1, 1968; L.1975, c. 180, § 15, eff. Jan. 1, 1976; L.1982, c. 27, § 1, eff. April 29, 1982; L.1982, c. 53, § 6, eff. July 1, 1982; L.1994, c. 60, § 26, eff. July 1, 1994.

39:10–11.1. Certificate of ownership for mobile or manufactured home in mobile home park; cancellation on relocation on land with interest or title in owner

A person who has a certificate of ownership issued by the director for a mobile or manufactured home located in a mobile home park that shall be relocated on land which the owner of the home has an interest in or the title to, shall, at least 10 days prior to that relocation,

file with the director a notice of relocation in a form and with evidence as the director shall prescribe. If the director shall accept the notice as complete, the director shall cancel the certificate of ownership on the date of relocation.

L.1983, c. 387, § 2, eff. Jan. 1, 1984.

39:10–12. Lost papers; duplicate certificate; false statements in application

If certificate of ownership, or title papers, are lost, the director may, upon proof of certification or otherwise in the manner required by him and if satisfied of the bona fides of the application, prepare a certificate of ownership, certify it and authorize its use in place of the original, with the same effect as the original. The director shall collect a fee of $25 for this duplicate certificate.

A person who falsely states, in any application to the director for a duplicate certificate of ownership, that a certificate of ownership, or title papers, are lost, shall be subject to a fine of not less than $200.00 nor more than $500.00 or imprisonment for a term not exceeding 30 days or both.

Amended by L.1946, c. 136, p. 629, § 8; L.1951, c. 295, p. 1076, § 2; L.1963, c. 34, § 4; L.1968, c. 130, § 13, eff. Aug. 1, 1968; L.1975, c. 180, § 16, eff. Jan. 1, 1976; L.1994, c. 60, § 27, eff. July 1, 1994.

39:10–13. File of certificates kept; destruction of other certificates

The commissioner shall retain a file of all certificates of ownership until the vehicles described therein shall be eight years old according to the year of manufacture stated in such certificate of ownership. Authority is hereby granted to the commissioner to destroy all other certificates of ownership.

Amended by L.1946, c. 136, p. 629, § 9.

39:10–14. Notations; index; certificates; security interests; fees; furnishing information from records

A. The director shall, on the record or abstract of every motor vehicle registered with him, which is subject to a security interest of which notice is required to be filed with him, make a notation of the existence of such security interest and shall index the same under the name of the owner of record of the vehicle, so long as the security interest remains unterminated of record.

B. Upon request from any person, the director shall issue a certificate showing names and addresses of the parties to any contract of conditional sale or chattel mortgage or other instrument, or to any financing statement, the name and address of the holder of the lien or liens under such contract, chattel mortgage or other instrument or of the secured party, the date thereof or of the financing statement, the date of filing, the make, model, identification number or numbers of the motor vehicle, and, if the condition in the contract of conditional sale or chattel mortgage has been performed or the security interest has been terminated, a statement to that effect, for which he shall be entitled to a fee of $5.00.

C. For a full certified copy of any instrument showing a lien on or a security interest in a motor vehicle the director shall be entitled to a fee of $10.00 for the certificate plus $0.50 for each copy of any paper certified.

D. When evidence of satisfaction of any contract of conditional sale or chattel mortgage or other instrument, or evidence of the termination of a security interest, as aforesaid, shall be presented to the director, he shall make a notation thereof on the record of the sale of such motor vehicle, showing that the condition in the contract of conditional sale or chattel mortgage has been performed or the security interest has been terminated; provided, however, that the evidence of satisfaction of a chattel mortgage on a motor vehicle executed after September 1, 1951 shall be submitted by the county recording officer on a form prescribed by the director, unless the chattel mortgage is one that is not required, under the provisions of this section R.S. 39:10–11, to be presented to and recorded by the director.

E. The director, his agents, and employees of the Division of Motor Vehicles shall not incur any personal liability in carrying out the provisions of this section or in furnishing any information provided herein from the records of the Division of Motor Vehicles.

Amended by L.1946, c. 136, p. 629, § 10; L.1951, c. 334, p. 1174, § 2; L.1961, c. 122, p. 739, § 6; L.1968, c. 130, § 14, eff. Aug. 1, 1968; L.1975, c. 180, § 17, eff. Jan. 1, 1976; L.1982, c. 53, § 7, eff. July 1, 1982.

39:10–15. Procedure and delivery of title papers upon seizure of motor vehicle

If a motor vehicle is seized, levied upon, or attached and taken into possession, actually or constructively, by virtue of judicial process issued by a court of competent jurisdiction in this State, or by virtue of a statute, State, Federal or otherwise, the person from whose possession the motor vehicle was taken, and without prejudice to his rights in the premises, shall surrender the title papers to the commissioner upon written notice or demand from the commissioner. The officer or person so seizing and taking possession of the motor vehicle shall immediately file with the commissioner a notice in writing giving a full description of the motor vehicle, as provided in section 39:10–8 of this Title, and the name and address of the person from whom taken, and shall attach a copy of process or statutory or other authority to the notice. If the motor vehicle is sold in pursuance thereof, the officer so selling it shall execute and deliver to the purchaser at the sale an application for certificate of ownership, in the same form and manner as provided in said section 39:10–8, which shall also contain the name and address of the person from whom the motor vehicle was taken. A copy of the writ, order, decree, execution or other process under which the motor

vehicle is sold and a copy of the notice of sale, which notice of sale shall contain a description of the motor vehicle as required by this chapter, shall be attached thereto. If the sale is held by a bailiff or attorney in fact for a lienor, the lienor shall also execute the application for certificate of ownership. The commissioner, upon due application to him by the purchaser at the sale, shall file and record purchase of the vehicle as provided in section 39:10–8.

Amended by L.1946, c. 136, p. 630, § 11.

39:10–15.1. Sale or disposal of manufactured homes

If a manufactured home is sold or otherwise disposed of pursuant to P.L.1999, c. 340 (C.2A:18–72 et al.), the Director of the Division of Motor Vehicles shall issue, upon proof of purchase, a certificate of ownership to the purchaser, with no encumbrances listed thereon.

L.1999, c. 340, § 8, eff. Jan. 10, 2000.

39:10–16. Defective or improper title papers or sale in other state or country; procedure to correct or to permit receipt of title papers

If the title papers or certificate of ownership are defective or improper, or if the motor vehicle was purchased and its sale consummated in another state or country, in accordance with the laws of such state or country regulating the sale of motor vehicles, and not made for the purpose of evading the provisions of this chapter, the bona fide owner of the motor vehicle may apply to the director to correct the defects, or permit the title papers to be received.

The director shall, upon such proof as he requires showing that it is just and equitable that the defects be corrected or that the title papers or certificate of ownership be received, with or without hearing, determine the truth and merits of the application and whether the holder appears to be the bona fide owner of the motor vehicle, and may issue his certificate correcting the defects or permitting the title papers or certificate of ownership to be so recorded and filed. The person submitting the papers shall pay to the director a fee of $20 for the issuing and filing of the certificate.

Before issuing the certificate the director may, in his discretion, require the person to advertise in a newspaper having a general circulation in the county where he resides, for the space of two weeks, at least once a week, making three insertions in all, a notice briefly stating that the person has applied to the director to correct defects in the motor vehicle title papers or to receive the title papers out of time, or, as the case may be, giving a description of the motor vehicle as provided in R.S. 39:10–8, and that if anyone desires to be heard in opposition thereto, he may do so by appearing before the director on a date and at a place named, or communicating with him prior thereto. He shall also serve like notice on local police, State Police and any other person or agency, as prescribed by the director, personally or by registered mail. Proofs of the publication and service shall be submitted to the director. The director or his agent may have the notice advertised or served at the cost and expense of that person.

Amended by L.1946, c. 136, p. 631, § 12; L.1949, c. 235, p. 738, § 4; L.1968, c. 130, § 15, eff. Aug. 1, 1968; L.1975, c. 180, § 18, eff. Jan. 1, 1976; L.1982, c. 53, § 8, eff. July 1, 1982; L.1983, c. 403, § 31, eff. Dec. 23, 1983; L.1994, c. 60, § 28, eff. July 1, 1994.

39:10–17. Repealed by L.1946, c. 136, p. 632, § 13

39:10–18. Title papers necessary to registration

The commissioner may refuse to grant a registration certificate and plates for a motor vehicle, unless there is furnished to him or his agent title papers or certificate of ownership in conformity with this chapter, in addition to the requirements of subtitle one, this Title (39:1–1 et seq.).

Amended by L.1946, c. 136, p. 632, § 14.

39:10–19. Motor vehicle dealer's license; eligibility; duration; renewal; fee

No person shall engage in the business of buying, selling or dealing in motor vehicles in this State, nor shall a person engage in activity that would qualify the person as a leasing dealer, as defined in section 2 of P.L.1994, c. 190 (C.56:12–61), unless: a. the person is a licensed real estate broker acting as an agent or broker in the sale of mobile homes without their own motor power other than recreation vehicles as defined in section 3 of P.L.1990, c. 103 (C.39:3–10.11), or manufactured homes as defined in section 3 of P.L.1983, c. 400 (C.54:4–1.4); or b. the person is authorized to do so under the provisions of this chapter. The chief administrator may, upon application in such form as the chief administrator prescribes, license any proper person as such dealer or leasing dealer. A licensed real estate broker shall be entitled to act as an agent or broker in the sale of a mobile or manufactured home as defined in subsection a. of this section without obtaining a license from the chief administrator. For the purposes of this chapter, a "licensed real estate broker" means a real estate broker licensed by the New Jersey Real Estate Commission pursuant to the provisions of chapter 15 of Title 45 of the Revised Statutes. Any sale or transfer of a mobile or manufactured home, in which a licensed real estate broker acts as a broker or agent pursuant to this section, which sale or transfer is subject to any other requirements of R.S.39:10–1 et seq., shall comply with all of those requirements. No person who has been convicted of a crime, arising out of fraud or misrepresentation in the sale, leasing or financing of a motor vehicle, shall be eligible to receive a license. For the purposes of this section, each applicant for a license shall submit to the chief administrator the applicant's name, address, fingerprints, and written consent for a criminal history record background check to be performed. The chief administrator is hereby authorized to exchange fingerprint data with and receive criminal history record information from the State Bureau of Identification in the Division of State Police and the

Federal Bureau of Investigation consistent with applicable State and federal laws, rules, and regulations, for purposes of facilitating determinations concerning licensure eligibility. The applicant shall bear the cost for the criminal history record background check, including all costs of administering and processing the check. The Division of State Police shall promptly notify the chief administrator in the event a current holder of a license or prospective applicant, who was the subject of a criminal history record background check pursuant to this section, is arrested for a crime or offense in this State after the date the background check was performed. Each applicant for a license shall at the time such license is issued have established and maintained, or by that application shall agree to establish and maintain, within 90 days after the issuance thereof, a place of business consisting of a permanent building not less than 1,000 square feet in floor space located in the State of New Jersey to be used principally for the servicing and display of motor vehicles with such equipment installed therein as shall be requisite for the servicing of motor vehicles in such manner as to make them comply with the laws of this State and with any rules and regulations made by the board governing the equipment, use, and operation of motor vehicles within the State. However, a leasing dealer, who is not engaged in the business of buying, selling, or dealing in motor vehicles in the State, shall not be required to maintain a place of business with floor space available for the servicing or display of motor vehicles or to have an exterior sign at the lessor's place of business. A license fee of $200 shall be paid by an applicant upon the applicant's initial application for a license. The chief administrator may renew an applicant's license upon application for renewal on a form prescribed by the chief administrator and accompanied by a renewal fee of $200. Every license shall expire 24 months from the date on which it is issued. The chief administrator may, at the chief administrator's discretion and for good cause shown, extend an applicant's license for an additional period not to exceed 12 months from the date on which it is scheduled to expire. The chief administrator may, at the chief administrator's discretion and for good cause shown, issue a license which shall expire on a date fixed by the chief administrator. The fee for licenses with an expiration date fixed by the chief administrator shall be fixed by the chief administrator in an amount proportionately less or greater than the fee established herein.

For the purposes of this section, a leasing dealer or an assignee of a leasing dealer whose leasing activities are limited to buying motor vehicles for the purpose of leasing them and selling motor vehicles at the termination of a lease shall not be deemed to be engaged in the business of buying, selling, or dealing in motor vehicles in this State.

Amended by L.1940, c. 75, p. 199, § 1, eff. May 29, 1940; L.1946, c. 136, p. 632, § 15; L.1963, c. 34, § 5; L.1994, c. 150, § 1, eff. Dec. 2, 1994; L.1994, c. 190, § 9, eff. June 21, 1995; L.2003, c. 199, § 22, eff. Dec. 24, 2003; L.2007, c. 335, § 24, eff. July 11, 2008.

39:10–19.1. Definitions applicable to off–site sales of new or used recreational vehicles or used motor vehicles

As used in this act:

"Off-site sale" means the display and sale of new or used recreational vehicles by a recreational vehicle dealer, or used motor vehicles registered in New Jersey by a used motor vehicle dealer, licensed under the provisions of R.S.39:10–19, at a location other than the dealer's established place of business. An "off-site sale" includes any off-site display of vehicles at which a recreational vehicle or used motor vehicle dealer has a sales person or employee present. For the purposes of this act, "off-site sale" does not include:

a. An off-site display of vehicles at which a recreational vehicle or used motor vehicle dealer has no sales personnel present;

b. The sale of a vehicle at an auction at which only wholesale purchases are permitted; or

c. The use of telephones, telephone call-forwarding, email, internet websites or other internet communications which allow a licensed dealer or dealership employee to communicate with customers while either the customer or the dealer or employee thereof is not present at the licensed physical location of the dealership, provided the contract for the sale of a vehicle is finalized and the sale transaction completed at the licensed location.

"Sponsoring organization" means:

a. a credit union, automobile club, or other such not for profit organization or entity that makes the opportunity to attend and purchase a motor vehicle at an off-site sale available to its members; or

b. a trade show coordinator, or other such organization, entity, or individual that makes the opportunity to attend and purchase a recreational vehicle at an off-site sale available to ticketed individuals.

L.2005, c. 351, § 1, eff. Aug. 1, 2006. Amended by L.2007, c. 335, § 25, eff. Feb. 12, 2008.

39:10–19.2. Off–site vehicle sales permitted to certain dealers

Notwithstanding any other provision of law to the contrary, a recreational vehicle or used motor vehicle dealer, licensed under the provisions of R.S.39:10–19, may hold an off-site sale provided he is granted a final permit to do so pursuant to section 3 of this act.[1]

L.2005, c. 351, § 2, eff. Aug. 1, 2006.

[1] N.J.S.A. § 39:10–19.3

39:10–19.3. Provisional and final permits for off–site vehicle sales

a. The Chief Administrator of the Motor Vehicle Commission may issue a provisional permit, subject to a fee, for an off-site sale to a licensed recreational vehicle or used motor vehicle dealer, provided:

(1) No more than one permit for a particular location is issued during any calendar quarter;

(2) A completed application and fee, in an amount determined by the chief administrator, is received by the commission at least 15 days prior to the first day of the sale;

(3) The applicant is a recreational vehicle or used motor vehicle dealer, licensed under the provisions of R.S.39:10–19, in good standing;

(4) The sale is not conducted within 1,000 feet of the established place of business of any motor vehicle dealer licensed under the provisions of R.S. 39:10–19;

(5) The display and sale of vehicles is conducted for no more than five consecutive days; and

(6) The sale is not open to the general public, but limited to members of the sponsoring organization or in the case of the off-site sales of recreational vehicles, only to ticketed individuals.

b. Following the issuance of a provisional permit for an off-site sale, and in the event that the chief administrator determines that neither the dealer, the sponsoring organization, nor the off-site sale location has an unsatisfactory history of violations of Title 39, the chief administrator shall issue a final permit for an off-site sale to the applicant, provided the dealer applicant delivers to the commission, no later than five days prior to the sale

, a surety bond in the amount of

$500,000 in the case of a permit for an off-site sale to a licensed used motor vehicle dealer; or $10,000 in the case of a permit for an off-site sale to a licensed recreational vehicle dealer issued by a company authorized to transact surety business in this State and payable to the New Jersey Motor Vehicle Commission. If a surety bond is cancelled or terminated for any reason prior to the end date of the sale, the company that issued the surety bond shall immediately notify the chief administrator of the cancellation or termination. The dealer applicant shall immediately obtain and file with the chief administrator a replacement surety bond prior to the end date of the sale that shall cover the uninsured term of the sale. In lieu of a surety bond, a dealer applicant may submit a notarized copy of a certificate of self-insurance issued pursuant to section 30 of P.L.1952, c. 173 (C.39:6–52).

L.2005, c. 351, § 3, eff. Aug. 1, 2006. Amended by L.2008, c. 73, § 1, eff. Sept. 6, 2008.

39:10–19.4. Off–site vehicle sales; booth or desk at sale premises; information required for agreements of sale, offerings or contracts

a. A dealer conducting an off-site sale shall maintain a booth or desk at the off-site sale premises location for the duration of the sale. The final permit for the sale and the name of the recreational vehicle or used motor vehicle dealer to whom the permit was issued shall be prominently displayed at the booth or desk at all times during the off-site sale.

b. Any agreements of sale, offerings, or contracts entered into during the off-site sale shall include, or have attached, the following information, in a clearly identifiable manner:

(1) The address and telephone number of the established place of business of the recreational vehicle or used motor vehicle dealer conducting the off- site sale; and

(2) The recreational vehicle or used motor vehicle dealer's license number; and

(3) A copy of the final permit issued to the recreational vehicle or used motor vehicle dealer authorizing him to conduct the off-site sale.

L.2005, c. 351, § 4, eff. Aug. 1, 2006.

39:10–20. Fines; suspension or revocation of license; notice; subpoenas; depositions; review

The chief administrator may impose a fine not to exceed $500 for a first offense and $1,000 for any subsequent offense upon the holder of a license for a violation of any provision of this chapter. The board is authorized to adopt rules and regulations, in accordance with the "Administrative Procedure Act," P.L.1968, c. 410 (C.52:14B–1 et seq.), implementing the provisions of this chapter and authorizing the chief administrator to impose fines for the violation of these rules and regulations. The chief administrator may suspend for a period less than the unexpired term of a license or revoke a license, after hearing, for a violation of any provision of this chapter, or for a violation of the rules and regulations promulgated pursuant thereto, or upon the final conviction of the licensee of a crime, arising out of fraud or misrepresentation in the sale, leasing or financing of a motor vehicle, or upon proof of the failure of a licensee to make payment of the amount of any final judgment, rendered by a court of competent jurisdiction against such licensee and founded upon a claim arising out of fraud or misrepresentation in the sale or leasing of a motor vehicle, within 90 days after the same is finally entered, or for final conviction of the licensee for violating any provision of chapter 171 of Title 2A or of any supplement thereof (Observance of Sabbath Days). The clerk of the court in which any conviction is rendered, or the court where it has no clerk, shall forward to the chief administrator, immediately upon the entry thereof, a certified copy of the conviction or a transcript thereof. The clerk of the court in which any judgment founded upon fraud or misrepresentation is rendered, or the court where it has no clerk, shall forward to the chief administrator, immediately after the expiration of the 90 days, a certified copy of the judgment, or a transcript thereof, showing it to have been unsatisfied more than 90 days after it became final. The chief administrator shall, before suspending or revoking the license, and at least 10 days prior to the date set for the hearing, notify the holder of the license, in writing, of any charges made, and shall afford him an opportunity to be heard in person or by counsel. The written notice may be served either personally or by registered mail addressed to the last-known address of the licensee. The chief administrator may subpoena and bring before the chief administrator any person in this State, or take testimony by deposition, in the same manner as prescribed by law in judicial proceedings in the courts of this State, and shall also issue and deliver to the dealer such subpoenas as are requested by the chief administrator. The Appellate Division of the Superior Court shall have power to review, by an appeal in lieu of prerogative writ taken by an aggrieved person, a final determination of the chief administrator.

Any fine imposed and collected pursuant to this section shall be remitted to the commission and used to defray the costs of the commission.

Amended by L.1946, c. 136, p. 633, § 16; L.1953, c. 36, p. 626, § 35; L.1955, c. 253, p. 935, § 1; L.1994, c. 190, § 10, eff. June 21, 1995; L.2007, c. 335, § 26, eff. Feb. 12, 2008.

39:10–21. Possession of title papers by dealer; seizure and sale for nonconformity

All dealers for both new and used motor vehicles in this State shall have a certificate of origin, certificate of ownership, or writing provided in R.S. 39:10–6 for all motor vehicles in their possession. The director, either personally or by his agent, may demand production of, and examine, the certificate of origin, certificate of ownership, or writing provided in R.S. 39:10–6 for any motor vehicle in a dealer's possession, and examine and inspect any motor vehicle in his possession.

If the demand is not complied with, or there is no certificate of origin, certificate of ownership or writing provided in R.S. 39:10–6 for a motor vehicle in the possession of a dealer, or if it is not in conformity with this chapter, the director or his agent may seize and take possession of the motor vehicle, and hold it until the certificate of origin, certificate of ownership or writing provided in R.S. 39:10–6 is produced or is corrected, if defective, or ownership of the motor vehicle is established according to law. After the expiration of 90 days from the date the motor vehicle came into his possession, the director may sell it at public sale, upon at least 10 days' written notice of sale to the dealer, served personally or by registered mail, addressed to the dealer at his last known place of business, and notice of the sale being published for a space of two weeks, once a week, making three insertions in all, in one or more newspapers published and circulating in the county where the dealer has his established place of business and also by posting the notice in five public places in the county. The newspapers and places of posting shall be designated by the director. Upon the sale of the motor vehicle, all valid liens and claims for interest therein, if any, shall be transferred from the vehicle to the proceeds of sale, which, subject thereto, shall become the sole property of the State, to be used as other moneys received by the director.

Amended by L.1946, c. 136, p. 635, § 17; L. 1983, c. 403, § 32, eff. Dec. 23, 1983.

39:10–22. Forms; seizure of papers to which chief administrator entitled

The chief administrator may prepare and prescribe any or all forms necessary for the proper administration of this chapter. The chief administrator or his agent may seize and take possession of any certificate of ownership or other title papers to which the chief administrator may be entitled, for which a person is under duty to return to the chief administrator, from any person or place in this State, with all the rights, privileges and immunities conferred by law on an officer executing a writ of replevin.

A licensed dealer shall keep and store all required forms, papers, and records as the Motor Vehicle Commission may by regulation require at the licensed premises. In the event a licensee operates multiple licensed dealerships under common ownership or control, such forms, papers, and records may be stored at a centralized record-keeping facility.

Amended by L.1946, c. 136, p. 636, § 18; L.1983, c. 403, § 33, eff. Dec. 23, 1983; L.2007, c. 335, § 27, eff. Feb. 12, 2008.

39:10–23. Certificate surrendered when vehicle junked, etc.

When a motor vehicle is scrapped, junked or destroyed, or a person permanently parts with its possession other than by sale, he shall immediately surrender and deliver the certificate of ownership to the commissioner, who shall issue a receipt therefor to the person surrendering it. When a motor vehicle is sold to be scrapped, junked or destroyed, assignment shall be made to the purchaser in accordance with the provisions of section 39:10–8 of this Title. The purchaser shall within five days deliver the certificate of ownership to the commissioner, who shall issue a receipt therefor to the person surrendering it.

Amended by L.1946, c. 136, p. 636, § 19.

39:10–24. Violations of chapter; misdemeanor; punishment

A person who

purposely or knowingly violates a provision of this chapter for which a specific penalty

is not provided herein shall be subject to the penalty provided in section 2 of P.L.2003, c. 217 (C.2C:21–4.8).

Amended by L.1946, c. 136, p. 636, § 20; L.2003, c. 217, § 1, eff. Jan. 9, 2004.

39:10–25. Agency to issue certificates; fees

The commission may designate any person to be its agent for the issuing and filing of certificates of origin, certificates of registration and certificates of ownership in accordance with the provisions of section 39:10–11 of this Title, subject to the requirements of chapter 10, and to any rules and regulations the commission shall impose. The agent shall so act until the agent's authority is revoked by the commission. All moneys received by such agents for the issuing and filing of certificates of origin and certificates of ownership under the provisions of this section shall forthwith be deposited as received with the State Treasurer. The fee allowed the agent for issuing and filing each certificate of ownership shall be fixed by the commission on the basis of the fees collected by the agent for the issuing and filing of such certificates. The commission may limit the fee so paid to a maximum. Such fee shall be paid to the agent by the State Treasurer upon the voucher of the commission in the same manner as other State expenses are paid.

Amended by L.1946, c. 136, p. 637, § 21; L.1959, c. 145, p. 588, § 2; L.2003, c. 13, § 125.

Historical and Statutory Notes

L.2003, c. 13, § 127, approved Jan. 28, 2003, provides:

"Sections 1, 2, 3, 12, 38, 109, 110 and 121 shall take effect immediately, sections 105, 106, 107, 108, and 120 shall take effect on July 1, 2003 and the remainder of this act shall take effect on the date the Commissioner of Transportation certifies to the Governor (hereinafter the "date of certification") that a majority of the members of the commission have been appointed or are in office and that all necessary anticipatory actions have been accomplished, provided, that the amount of revenues received pursuant to sections 109 and 110 prior to the date of certification are hereby appropriated to the division. Upon the date of certification, all such collected revenue shall be revenue of the commission. The Commissioner of Transportation, the Director of the Division of Motor Vehicles and the commission may take such anticipatory administrative action in advance as shall be necessary for the implementation of the act."

II. STANDARDS FOR USED MOTOR VEHICLES

39:10–26. Standards for used motor vehicles for sale

Unless otherwise provided in this act, no motor vehicle dealer shall sell at retail any used passenger motor vehicle to be registered in this State, unless such vehicle, meets the standards for the issuance of a certificate of approval as provided in chapter 8 of Title 39 of the Revised Statutes.

L.1971, c. 76, § 1.

39:10–27. Failure to meet standards; liability of seller

In the event that any such used passenger motor vehicle is sold at retail and has any defect, which results in its rejection for failure to meet the standards for issuance of such a certificate of approval, in the absence of a waiver as provided in this act, the seller shall make, or cause to be made, all the necessary repairs, without charge, or return the full purchase price to the purchaser; provided that such defect or defects are not the result of the purchaser's own act.

L.1971, c. 76, § 2.

39:10–28. Specification of intended registration in written agreement; informing purchaser of dealer's responsibilities

Prior to entering into any agreement for the retail sale of a used passenger motor vehicle, the dealer shall inquire as to whether the vehicle to be purchased is intended for registration in this State in the condition sold and, if so, such fact shall be specified in the written agreement between the dealer and the purchaser, and the dealer, prior to execution of the agreement of sale, shall inform the purchaser of the dealer's responsibilities under this act.

L.1971, c. 76, § 3.

39:10–29. Waiver of dealer's obligation; effect

Any agreement of retail sale may contain a provision whereby the purchaser waives the dealer's obligation under section 2 of this act;[1] provided, however, any such waiver must be separately stated in the agreement of retail sale and separately signed by the purchaser.

The signing of such a waiver by the purchaser shall also serve to eliminate any criminal responsibility placed upon any motor vehicle dealer by this act.

L.1971, c. 76, § 4.

[1] N.J.S.A. § 39:10–27.

39:10–30. Violations; penalty

Any dealer who fails to comply with the provisions of this act is a disorderly person.

L.1971, c. 76, § 5.

III. SALVAGE CERTIFICATES OF TITLE

39:10–31. "Salvage certificate of title" defined

As used in this act "salvage certificate of title" means a document issued by the Director of the Division of Motor Vehicles which serves as proof of ownership of a motor vehicle and provides a method of transfer of the vehicle only as a salvage motor vehicle.

L.1983, c. 323, § 1.

39:10–32. Vehicle reported stolen or damaged; surrender of certificate of ownership; issuance of salvage certificate of title

a. If a motor vehicle has either been reported as being stolen or suffered sufficient damage to render it economically impractical to repair, the person in possession of the certificate of ownership for the vehicle shall surrender the certificate of ownership to the director along with a statement setting forth how the person acquired the certificate of ownership.

b. The director, after determining ownership, shall issue a salvage certificate of title to a person who

surrenders a certificate of ownership pursuant to subsection a. of this section.

L.1983, c. 323, § 2.

39:10–33. Recovery of stolen vehicle; conditions for issuance of certificate of ownership

If a motor vehicle reported as being stolen is subsequently recovered, a certificate of ownership for the vehicle which had been surrendered to the director by a person pursuant to subsection a. of section 2 of this act[1] may be issued by the director to that person only if:

a. The person presents to the director a salvage certificate of title for the motor vehicle;

b. The person presents to the director a report from the law enforcement agency which recovered the vehicle; and

c. The vehicle passes an inspection at a State inspection facility to determine the accuracy of its vehicle identification number.

L.1983, c. 323, § 3.

[1] N.J.S.A. § 39:10–32.

39:10–34. Repair of damaged vehicle; conditions for issuance of certificate of ownership

If a motor vehicle which has suffered sufficient damage to render it economically impractical to repair is subsequently repaired, a certificate of ownership for the vehicle may be issued to a person only if:

a. The person presents to the director a salvage certificate of title;

b. The repaired vehicle is inspected by an official specially designated by the director to determine the accuracy of its vehicle identification number;

c. The person submits proof of ownership of repair parts used to the director; and

d. The person complies with any other requirement the director deems appropriate.

L.1983, c. 323, § 4.

39:10–35. Fee for inspection

The director shall establish a fee for the inspections required under sections 3 and 4 of this act.[1] The fees shall be deposited in a non-lapsing fund which is dedicated to the administration of this act.

L.1983, c. 323, § 5.

[1] N.J.S.A. §§ 39:10–33 and 39:10–34.

39:10–36. Vehicle issued salvage certificate of title by another state

If a motor vehicle has been issued a salvage certificate of title, or similar document, by another state, that vehicle may be issued a certificate of ownership pursuant to section 3 or 4 of this act.[1]

L.1983, c. 323, § 6.

[1] N.J.S.A. §§ 39:10–33 or 39:10–34.

39:10–37. Rules and regulations

The director shall promulgate rules and regulations pursuant to the "Administrative Procedure Act," P.L. 1968, c. 410 (C. 52:14B–1 et seq.) he deems advisable to effectuate the purposes of this act.

L.1983, c. 323, § 7.

CHAPTER 10A

ABANDONED AND UNCLAIMED MOTOR VEHICLES

Section
39:10A–1.   Report of taking of possession; sale at auction; conditions; notice.
39:10A–2.   Reclaiming possession; payment of costs and penalties.
39:10A–3.   Issuance of junk title certificate; grounds.
39:10A–4.   Execution and delivery of application for certificate of ownership; issuance of certificate; fee.
39:10A–5.   Sale as barring claims of interest; remission of proceeds of sale.
39:10A–6.   Rules and regulations.
39:10A–7.   Additional remedy.
39:10A–8.   Motor vehicle abandoned at repair facility.
39:10A–9.   Removal and storage, sale or obtaining junk title certificate; inapplicability if dispute between repair facility and owner on amount due.
39:10A–10.   Notice to owner of intent to remove and store.
39:10A–11.   Notice of intent to and of date, time, place and manner of sale.
39:10A–12.   Junk title certificate; issuance; notice.
39:10A–13.   Notices; writing; method of delivery; publication.
39:10A–14.   Reclamation of possession by owner prior to sale or issuance of junk title certificate.
39:10A–15.   Sale of motor vehicle; certificate of ownership; application; issuance; fee.
39:10A–16.   Bar of claims of former owner, other person formerly having legal right and holder of security interest.
39:10A–17.   Claims allowable against repair facility in compliance with act only for balance of proceeds of sale.
39:10A–18.   Pattern or practice of knowingly violating act or aids or advises such pattern or practice; penalty.
39:10A–19.   Rules and regulations.
39:10A–20.   Act as additional remedy; priority of perfected lien or security interest.

39:10A–1. Report of taking of possession; sale at auction; conditions; notice

a. When the State or any county, county park commission, municipality or any authority created by any thereof, hereinafter referred to as a "public agency," shall have taken possession of a motor vehicle found abandoned, such taking of possession shall be reported immediately to

(1) the Chief Administrator of the Motor Vehicle Commission on a form prescribed by the administrator, for verification of ownership and

(2) the National Insurance Crime Bureau.

(3) Upon receipt of verification of ownership of the vehicle from the administrator, the public agency shall within three business days provide notice of possession of the vehicle to the owner of record and the holder of any security interest filed with the administrator by telephone, mail, facsimile or electronically. The public agency may assess the person claiming the vehicle, be it the owner of record or the holder of any security interest, for the actual costs of providing the notice required under this paragraph.

(4) The public agency shall also within three business days notify the person storing the abandoned motor vehicle. The notice shall be given in the same manner as in the case of notification of the owner of record and the security interest holder and shall include the name and address of the owner of record and the holder of any security interest in the stored motor vehicle.

(5) Upon receipt of the notice required by paragraph (4) of this subsection, the person storing the abandoned motor vehicle shall provide notice to the owner of record and to any security interest holder.

(a) The notice shall be by first class mail, with a certificate of mailing, and shall include a schedule of the costs imposed for storing the motor vehicle and instructions explaining how the owner of record or the security interest holder may claim the stored motor vehicle.

(b) Except as provided in subparagraph (c) of this paragraph, if the person storing the motor vehicle fails to provide this notice to the owner of record and to the security interest holder within 30 days of the date on which the storer of the vehicle received the notice required under paragraph (4) from the public agency, the maximum amount that person may charge the owner of record or the security interest holder for storing that motor vehicle shall be $750, provided that the owner of record or security interest holder submits a proper claim for the vehicle not later than the 30th day following the date the notice is delivered from the public agency to the person storing the motor vehicle.

(c) When a vehicle is abandoned due to the death or incapacitation of the driver or any passenger, the person storing the vehicle shall charge the owner of record or the security interest holder no more than $100 for the first 72 hours after the vehicle is placed on the premises.

(d) If the owner of record or security interest holder fails to submit a proper claim for the vehicle on or before that 30th day, the person storing the motor vehicle may charge the security interest holder reasonable costs for the removal and storage of the motor vehicle. If the notice is properly provided by the person storing the motor vehicle, that person may charge the owner of record or the security interest holder reasonable costs for the removal and storage of the motor vehicle from the date the person removed and stored the motor vehicle.

(e) The public agency may assess the person storing the abandoned motor vehicle, and the person storing the abandoned motor vehicle may assess the security interest holder, for the actual costs of providing the notices required under paragraphs (4) and (5) of this subsection.

b. When such motor vehicle which has been ascertained not to be stolen and to be one which can be certified for a junk title certificate under section 3 of P.L.1964, c. 81 (C.39:10A-3) shall have remained unclaimed by the owner or other person having a legal right thereto for a period of 15 business days, even if at that time the owner has not been identified as a result of efforts to make identification by the public agency or the Motor Vehicle Commission, the same may be sold at auction in a public place. If the certified motor vehicle is sold at auction prior to identification of the owner, the public agency shall document the condition of the motor vehicle in writing and with photographs prior to the sale; document the amount obtained from the sale of the motor vehicle; and notify the owner, if his name and address are identified after the sale, of the actions taken by the public agency to dispose of the motor vehicle.

c. When a motor vehicle which cannot be certified for a junk title certificate under section 3 of P.L.1964, c. 81 (C.39:10A-3) remains unclaimed by the owner or other person having a legal right thereto for a period of 20 business days, the motor vehicle may be sold at auction in a public place, but shall be sold no later than 90 business days after the public agency takes possession of the vehicle, except that a waiver of the 90-day limit may be obtained for good cause from the Division of Local Government Services in the Department of Community Affairs.

d. The public agency shall give notice of a sale conducted pursuant to subsection b. or c. of this section, by certified mail, to the owner, if his name and address be known and to the holder of any security interest filed with the administrator, and by publication in a form to be prescribed by the administrator by one insertion, at least five days before the date of the sale, in one or more newspapers published in this State and circulating in the municipality in which such motor vehicle is held.

L.1964, c. 81, § 1. Amended by L.1986, c. 173, § 1, eff. Dec. 8, 1986; L.1987, c. 127, § 5, eff. May 26, 1987; L.1989, c. 66, § 1, eff. April 14, 1989; L.2006, c. 91, § 1, eff. Nov. 1, 2006; L.2008, c. 107, § 2, eff. April 1, 2009.

39:10A-2. Reclaiming possession; payment of costs and penalties

At any time prior to sale the owner or other person entitled thereto may reclaim possession of the motor vehicle upon payment of the reasonable costs of removal and storage of the vehicle and any fine or penalty and court costs assessed against him for a violation which gave rise to the seizure or taking possession of such vehicle.

L.1964, c. 81, § 2.

39:10A-3. Issuance of junk title certificate; grounds

If the public agency taking possession of a motor vehicle pursuant to this act shall, in its report thereof to the director, certify on an application prescribed by him that such motor vehicle is incapable of being operated safely or of being put in safe operational condition except at a cost in excess of the value thereof, the division shall, without further certification or verification, issue to the public agency for a fee of $2.00 a junk title certificate thereto, with proper assignment thereon, which shall be assigned and delivered to the purchaser of the vehicle at public sale.

L.1964, c. 81, § 3. Amended by L.1975, c. 180, § 19, eff. Jan. 1, 1976.

39:10A-4. Execution and delivery of application for certificate of ownership; issuance of certificate; fee

Upon the sale of any motor vehicle for which no junk title certificate shall have been issued, the public agency shall execute and deliver to the purchaser an application for certificate of ownership prescribed by the director in the same form and manner as provided in Revised Statutes 39:10-15, which shall also contain the name and address, if known, of the former owner. Such application shall be accepted by the director for issuance of a certificate of ownership for a fee of $3.00.

L.1964, c. 81, § 4. Amended by L.1968, c. 130, § 16, eff. Aug. 1, 1968.

39:10A-5. Sale as barring claims of interest; remission of proceeds of sale

Upon the sale of a motor vehicle pursuant to the provisions of this act all claims of interest therein shall be forever barred and the proceeds realized therefrom after payment of the expenses of possession and sale, shall be remitted to the treasury of the public agency as its sole property.

L.1964, c. 81, § 5.

39:10A-6. Rules and regulations

The Director of the Division of Motor Vehicles may make and promulgate rules and regulations to implement the provisions of this act.

L.1964, c. 81, § 6.

39:10A-7. Additional remedy

This act is intended to provide an additional remedy and shall not be construed to supersede procedures provided under any other act.

L.1964, c. 81, § 7.

39:10A-8. Motor vehicle abandoned at repair facility

For purposes of this act a motor vehicle shall be deemed to be abandoned if it is left at a motor vehicle repair facility without an attempt by the owner, a person on the owner's behalf or any other person having a legal right thereto to regain possession thereof:

a. For a period in excess of 60 days without the consent of an authorized representative of the motor vehicle repair facility;

b. For a period of 60 days in excess of the period for which consent has been given by an authorized representative of the motor vehicle repair facility; or

c. For a period in excess of 60 days after being notified by an authorized representative of the motor vehicle repair facility that service or repairs to the motor vehicle have been completed.

L.1983, c. 455, § 1.

39:10A–9. Removal and storage, sale or obtaining junk title certificate; inapplicability if dispute between repair facility and owner on amount due

a. An authorized representative of a motor vehicle repair facility may take one or more of the following actions with respect to an abandoned motor vehicle:

(1) Remove and store, or hire another person to remove and store the motor vehicle pursuant to section 3 of this act;[1]

(2) Sell or cause the motor vehicle to be sold, at public or private sale, pursuant to section 4 of this act;[2] or

(3) Cause a junk title certificate to be issued for the motor vehicle pursuant to section 5 of this act.[3]

b. No motor vehicle shall be sold and no junk title certificate shall be issued pursuant to this act where the cause for a motor vehicle being left in the possession of a motor vehicle repair facility for a period in excess of that set forth in section 1 of this act[4] is a dispute between the motor vehicle repair facility and the owner of the motor vehicle or other person having a legal right thereto regarding the amount to be paid in order to regain possession of the motor vehicle.

L.1983, c. 455, § 2.

[1] N.J.S.A. § 39:10A–10.
[2] N.J.S.A. § 39:10A–11.
[3] N.J.S.A. § 39:10A–12.
[4] N.J.S.A. § 39:10A–8.

39:10A–10. Notice to owner of intent to remove and store

Prior to the removal and storage of a motor vehicle pursuant to section 2a.(1) of this act,[1] an authorized representative of a motor vehicle repair facility shall give the owner of the motor vehicle or other person having a legal right thereto 30 days' notice of the intent to remove and store the motor vehicle.

L.1983, c. 455, § 3.

[1] N.J.S.A. § 39:10A–9.

39:10A–11. Notice of intent to and of date, time, place and manner of sale

Prior to the sale of a motor vehicle pursuant to section 2a.(2) of this act,[1] an authorized representative of a motor vehicle repair facility shall:

a. Give the owner of the motor vehicle or other person having a legal right thereto, the holder of any security interest in the motor vehicle filed with the Director of the Division of Motor Vehicles 30 days' notice of the intent to sell the motor vehicle or cause it to be sold; and

b. Give the owner of the motor vehicle or other person having a legal right thereto and the holder of any security interest in the motor vehicle filed with the Director of the Division of Motor Vehicles at least five days' notice of the date, time, place and manner of the proposed sale.

L.1983, c. 455, § 4.

[1] N.J.S.A. § 39:10A–9.

39:10A–12. Junk title certificate; issuance; notice

If a motor vehicle repair facility determines that a motor vehicle subject to the provisions of this act is incapable of being operated safely or of being put in safe operational condition except at a cost in excess of the value thereof, an authorized representative of the motor repair facility shall so certify to the Director of the Division of Motor Vehicles, on an application prescribed by him, and the Division of Motor Vehicles shall thereupon, without further certification or verification, issue to the motor vehicle repair facility, for a fee of $10.00, a junk title certificate for the vehicle; but no title certificate shall be issued unless the motor vehicle repair facility first gives 30 days' notice of its intention to obtain a junk title certificate to the owner of the motor vehicle or other person having a legal right thereto and to the holder of any security interest in the motor vehicle filed with the Director of the Division of Motor Vehicles.

L.1983, c. 455, § 5.

39:10A–13. Notices; writing; method of delivery; publication

Any notice required to be given by this act shall be in writing and sent by certified or registered mail, return receipt requested, to the last known address of the person to whom the notice is to be given. In the event that the notice is unclaimed by the addressee, or if the address of the person to whom the notice is to be given is unknown to the person giving the notice and cannot be ascertained from the records on file with the Division of Motor Vehicles, the notice shall be given by publishing it twice in at least one newspaper published in this State and circulating in the municipality in which the motor vehicle is left.

L.1983, c. 455, § 6.

39:10A–14. Reclamation of possession by owner prior to sale or issuance of junk title certificate

At any time prior to the sale of the motor vehicle or the issuance of a junk title certificate therefor, the owner of the motor vehicle may reclaim possession of the motor vehicle from the motor vehicle repair facility or other person with whom the motor vehicle is stored pursuant to this act, upon payment of the reasonable costs of removal and storage of the motor vehicle, the expenses incurred pursuant to the provisions of this act, and the charges for the servicing or repair of the motor vehicle.

L.1983, c. 455, § 7.

39:10A–15. Sale of motor vehicle; certificate of ownership; application; issuance; fee

Upon the sale of a motor vehicle for which no junk title certificate has been issued, an application for a certificate of ownership on a form prescribed by the Director of the Division of Motor Vehicles shall be submitted to the director. The application, in addition to containing any information required by the director, shall set forth the name and address, if known, of the former owner and shall contain a certification from the motor vehicle repair facility selling the motor vehicle that the sale was in conformity with the provisions of this act. The application shall be accepted by the director for issuance of a certificate of ownership for a fee of $10.00.

L.1983, c. 455, § 8.

39:10A–16. Bar of claims of former owner, other person formerly having legal right and holder of security interest

Upon the sale of a motor vehicle, or the issuance of a junk title certificate pursuant to the provisions of this act, all claims of interest in the motor vehicle of the former owner, any other person formerly having legal right thereto and any holder of a security interest shall be forever barred, except as provided for in section 10 of this act.[1]

L.1983, c. 455, § 9.

[1] N.J.S.A. § 39:10A–17.

39:10A–17. Claims allowable against repair facility in compliance with act only for balance of proceeds of sale

No claim of any kind may be asserted against a motor vehicle repair facility that complies with the provisions of this act by the owner of a motor vehicle for damages arising out of the storage, removal, sale or issuance of a junk title certificate for a motor vehicle except for the balance of the proceeds of the sale of the motor vehicle, if any, after deduction of the expenses of the sale, the costs and expenses incurred in the removal and storage of the motor vehicle and the charges of the motor

vehicle repair facility for the servicing and repair of the motor vehicle.

L.1983, c. 455, § 10.

39:10A–18. Pattern or practice of knowingly violating act or aids or advises such pattern or practice; penalty

A motor vehicle repair facility, or any employee, officer or agent thereof, which or who engages in a pattern or practice of knowingly violating any of the provisions of this act or aids or advises in such a pattern or practice is guilty of a crime of the third degree.

L.1983, c. 455, § 11.

39:10A–19. Rules and regulations

The Director of the Division of Motor Vehicles shall promulgate rules and regulations pursuant to the "Administrative Procedure Act," P.L.1968, c. 410 (C. 52:14B–1 et seq.), to implement the provisions of this act.

L.1983, c. 455, § 12.

39:10A–20. Act as additional remedy; priority of perfected lien or security interest

This act provides an additional remedy and shall not be construed to supersede procedures provided under any other act, and shall not be deemed to supersede or alter the priority of any perfected lien or security interest in an abandoned motor vehicle, which lien or security interest shall have priority over the amounts due to the motor vehicle repair facility.

L.1983, c. 455, § 13.

CHAPTER 10B

MOTOR VEHICLE COMPONENT PARTS

Section
39:10B–1. Definitions.
39:10B–2. Major component parts lacking manufacturer's part number; identification; records; exemption; production and examination; fines and penalties; seizure.
39:10B–3. Destroyed, removed, altered, defaced or obliterated manufacturer's part number or identification number; seizure or confiscation of vehicle; arrests; assigning and affixing new number; restoration of number.
39:10B–4. Violations; penalties; defenses; prima facie evidence; burden of proof.
39:10B–5. Inapplicability of act to scrap processors.
39:10B–6. Rules and regulations.

39:10B–1. Definitions

As used in this act:

a. "Director" means the Director of the Division of Motor Vehicles in the Department of Law and Public Safety.

b. "Major motor vehicle component part" or "component part" means the following parts of any motor vehicle:

(1) engine;

(2) cowl;

(3) transmission;

(4) frame;

(5) each door;

(6) third member or rear end assembly;

(7) each front fender or each rear fender of a rear panel;

(8) front end assembly;

(9) rear clip; and

(10) any other parts of a motor vehicle designated by the director.

c. "Manufacturer's part number" means the original manufacturer's number located on a major motor vehicle component part.

d. "Scrap processor" means a person who, from a fixed location, utilizes machinery and equipment for processing and manufacturing iron, steel, or nonferrous metallic scrap, which is or has been a motor vehicle or component part, into prepared grades for sale for remelting purposes, and who does not sell the materials as motor vehicles or major motor vehicle component parts.

L.1983, c. 368, § 1.

39:10B–2. Major component parts lacking manufacturer's part number; identification; records; exemption; production and examination; fines and penalties; seizure

a. All major motor vehicle component parts which do not contain a manufacturer's part number shall be identified by a person who deals in used motor vehicles, motor vehicle salvage or the component parts of motor vehicles. The identification shall be made in a manner to be determined by the director when the component part is removed from a motor vehicle.

b. A person who deals in used motor vehicles, motor vehicle salvage or the component parts of motor vehicles who purchases major motor vehicle component parts out of State shall identify the parts in the manner to be determined by the director.

c. A person authorized under this section to identify motor vehicle component parts shall maintain a record of all motor vehicles and component parts which come into that person's possession together with a record of the disposition of the motor vehicles or the component parts. The records shall be maintained in a manner and form prescribed by the director and shall include proof of ownership for the motor vehicles or the component parts in that person's possession.

The director may, by regulation, exempt motor vehicles or component parts from all or a portion of the record keeping requirements based upon the age of the motor vehicles or the component parts if the director finds that the record keeping serves no useful purpose.

Upon the request of an agent of the director or a law enforcement officer, a person shall produce the records and permit the agent or officer to examine them and the motor vehicle or component parts on the premises during business hours. For a failure to produce the records or to permit their inspection as required by this section, a person shall be subject to a fine of not less than $25.00 or more than $100.00 or imprisonment for not more than 90 days, or both. In addition, an agent of the director or a law enforcement officer may seize or take possession of the motor vehicles or component parts and hold and dispose of them in accordance with the rules and regulations adopted by the director.

L.1983, c. 368, § 2.

39:10B–3. Destroyed, removed, altered, defaced or obliterated manufacturer's part number or identification number; seizure or confiscation of vehicle; arrests; assigning and affixing new number; restoration of number

a. Members of the State and local law enforcement agencies or members of the division who are designated by the director for this function shall seize and confiscate a detached major motor vehicle component part if the manufacturer's part number, the identification number required by section 2 of this act,[1] or the identification number assigned by the division under subsection e. of this section has been destroyed, removed, altered, defaced, or obliterated.

b. The entire motor vehicle shall be seized and confiscated if the manufacturer's part number, the identification number required by section 2 of this act, or the identification number assigned by the division under subsection e. of this section of a major motor vehicle component part has been destroyed, removed, altered, defaced, or obliterated.

c. Members of the State and local law enforcement agencies shall arrest the alleged owner or custodian thereof. It shall be the duty of the police to retain the custody of each motor vehicle or major motor vehicle component part seized pending the prosecution of the person arrested, which shall remain in the custody of the police until the ownership thereof shall have been ascertained.

d. If a person other than the person arrested be the owner, the motor vehicle shall be returned to him as soon as he has arranged to have the division affix a new number to the major motor vehicle component part, and the division has done so, as provided in subsection e. of this section. No person other than an authorized member of the division shall assign and affix a new number to the motor vehicle or major motor vehicle component part. The division shall not release any vehicle or part so seized until it has affixed a new number to the part. At the time of the arrest the director shall be notified by the arresting officer.

e. If a detached major motor vehicle component part is seized and confiscated because it does not have a manufacturer's part number or the identification number required by section 2 of this act, or the appropriate number has been destroyed, removed, altered, defaced, or obliterated, or the entire vehicle has been seized because the appropriate number of a major motor vehicle component part has been destroyed, removed, altered, defaced, or obliterated, the number may be restored under the following conditions:

(1) If the owner or custodian of the motor vehicle or major motor vehicle component part can demonstrate that the damage to the manufacturer's part number or the number required by section 2 of this act was done without his knowledge, and can produce a bill of sale and, if applicable, title papers for the motor vehicle or major motor vehicle component part, the division shall return the motor vehicle or major motor vehicle part to him, provided that he arranges to have the division restore the damaged or obliterated number to the part, if possible, or affix a unique number to the part, as provided for in paragraph (2) of this subsection. The director is authorized to establish a reasonable fee for this service.

(2) If the owner or custodian of the motor vehicle or major motor vehicle component part cannot furnish title papers for the motor vehicle or a bill of sale for the major motor vehicle component part or if the alleged owner or custodian is arrested and convicted of the theft of the motor vehicle or major motor vehicle component part, an agent of the director or any police officer may seize and take possession of the vehicle or part and hold and dispose of it in accordance with rules and regulations adopted by the director, provided that the division first affixes a unique number to the major motor vehicle component part. The composition of this number shall indicate that it designates a used major motor vehicle component part. The director is authorized to establish a reasonable fee for this service, and this fee may be added to the price of the motor vehicle or major motor vehicle component part. The new number shall thereafter be used for identification, registration and all purposes of this act.

L.1983, c. 368, § 3.

1 N.J.S.A. § 39:10B–2.

39:10B–4. Violations; penalties; defenses; prima facie evidence; burden of proof

a. It shall be unlawful for a person to sell or offer for sale or transport a major motor vehicle component part or motor vehicle if a manufacturer's part number, an identification number required by section 2 of this act,[1] or a number assigned by the division under section

3 of this act [2] shall have been destroyed, removed, altered, defaced or so covered as to be concealed.

b. It shall be unlawful for a person to sell or offer for sale a component part from a motor vehicle less than three years old without providing the purchaser with an invoice indicating:

(1) The name and address of the seller and the purchaser;

(2) The price of the component part;

(3) The year, make, model and color of the motor vehicle from which the component part was removed; and

(4) The vehicle identification number of the motor vehicle from which the component part was removed.

c. It shall be unlawful for a person to purchase a major motor vehicle component part from a motor vehicle less than three years old without obtaining from the seller the invoice defined in subsection b. of this section.

d. It shall be unlawful for a person to transport a major motor vehicle component part unless that component part has been marked with an identification number as required by section 2 of this act or an identification number assigned by the division under subsection e. of section 3 of this act and the transporter has in his possession an invoice indicating:

(1) The name and address of the owner of the component part;

(2) The price of the component part;

(3) The year, make, model and color of the motor vehicle from which the component part was removed; and

(4) The vehicle identification number of the motor vehicle from which the component part was removed.

e. A person selling, offering to sell, transporting or purchasing a major motor vehicle component part or a motor vehicle in violation of the provisions of subsection a., b., c., or d. of this section is guilty of a crime of the fourth degree. A person who willfully removes, defaces, covers, alters or destroys a manufacturer's part number, an identification number required by section 2 of this act, or a number assigned by the division under section 3 of this act is guilty of a crime of the third degree.

A person having possession of a major motor vehicle component part or a motor vehicle of which a manufacturer's part number, an identification number required by section 2 of this act, or a number assigned by the division under section 3 of this act has been destroyed, removed, altered, defaced or so covered as to be concealed is guilty of a crime of the fourth degree. Upon prosecution under this section lack of knowledge of the condition of the number of the vehicle or part shall constitute a defense, but possession shall be prima facie evidence that the defendant had knowledge of the condition, and the burden of proof shall be upon him that he had no knowledge.

L.1983, c. 368, § 4.

₁ N.J.S.A. § 39:10B–2.
₂ N.J.S.A. § 39:10B–3.

39:10B–5. Inapplicability of act to scrap processors

The provisions of this act shall not apply to scrap processors as defined in section 1 of this act.[1]

L.1983, c. 368, § 5.

₁ N.J.S.A. § 39:10B–1.

39:10B–6. Rules and regulations

The director shall prescribe rules and regulations necessary to carry out the provisions of this act.

L.1983, c. 368, § 6.

CHAPTER 11

JUNK YARDS

Section
39:11–1.   Short title.
39:11–2.   Definitions.
39:11–3.   Repealed.
39:11–4.   Permit from municipality required.
39:11–5.   Municipal hearing; fee.
39:11–6.   Local hearing by commissioner.
39:11–7.   Examination of proposed location of business; recommendation of conditions.
39:11–8.   Fee for examination of proposed location of business.
39:11–9.   Certification of condition of motor vehicle sold.
39:11–10.   Review of action of governing body, zoning commission or director.
39:11–11.   Violation of R.S. 39:11–9; penalties; enforcement proceedings.

39:11–1. Short title

The short title of this chapter is the "motor vehicle junk law".

39:11–2. Definitions

The terms "motor vehicle junk business" or "motor vehicle junk yard" shall mean and describe any business and any place of storage or deposit of two or more unregistered motor vehicles which, in the opinion of the commission, are unfit for reconditioning for use for highway transportation, or used parts of motor vehicles or material which has been a part of a motor vehicle, the sum of which parts or material shall, in the opinion of the commission, be equal in bulk to two or more motor vehicles, but shall not include a salvage pool or auto auction whose primary business is the sale of total loss vehicles on behalf of insurance companies.

Amended by L.2003, c. 13, § 65; L.2009, c. 298, § 8, eff. Jan. 17, 2010.

39:11–3. Repealed by L.2009, c. 298, § 16, eff. Jan. 17, 2010

39:11–4. Permit from municipality required

A motor vehicle junk business or motor vehicle junk yard shall obtain a permit or certificate approving its proposed location from the governing body or zoning commission of the municipality in which it is proposed to establish or maintain the junk yard or business.

Amended by L.2003, c. 13, § 67; L.2009, c. 298, § 9, eff. Jan. 17, 2010.

39:11–5. Municipal hearing; fee

Upon receipt of an application for the local permit or certificate of approval, the governing body or zoning commission of the municipality in which the junk business or junk yard is proposed to be established or maintained, shall hold a public hearing upon the application, which hearing shall take place not less than two weeks nor more than four weeks from the date of the application. Notice of the hearing shall be given the applicant and be published once in a newspaper having a circulation in the municipality not less than seven days before the date thereof.

No permit or certificate of approval shall be granted unless the governing body or zoning commission, as the case may be, shall, after the hearing, find that no unreasonable depreciation of surrounding property would ensue from the establishment or maintenance of the motor vehicle junk yard or business and that the best interests of the community require the operation of the yard or business at the location designated. The proximity of schools, churches or other places of public gatherings, the sufficiency in number of other similar places in the vicinity and the suitability of the applicant to receive the license, shall be taken into consideration in considering the application.

Each applicant shall pay a fee of ten dollars, the costs of publication and expenses of the hearing to the treasurer of the municipality.

39:11–6. Local hearing by commissioner

Upon request of the governing body or zoning commission, as the case may be, of the municipality in which the yard or business is proposed to be located, the commission shall hold a public hearing within the municipality not less than three nor more than five weeks from the date of the application. Notice of the hearing shall be given to the applicant and to the council or mayor, by mail, postage prepaid, and be published once in a newspaper having a circulation within the municipality, not less than seven days before the date of the hearing. The hearing shall be conducted by the commission or its authorized representative, and the applicant shall pay to the commission or its representative a fee of twenty-five dollars, the costs of the notices and the expenses of the hearing. Upon the conclusion of the hearing, the commission shall, within five days, recommend in writing to the governing body or the zoning commission, as the case may be, the granting or refusal of the local permit or certificate of approval, giving its reasons for the recommendation.

Amended by L.2003, c. 13, § 68.

Historical and Statutory Notes

L.2003, c. 13, § 127, approved Jan. 28, 2003, provides:

"Sections 1, 2, 3, 12, 38, 109, 110 and 121 shall take effect immediately, sections 105, 106, 107, 108, and 120 shall take effect on July 1, 2003 and the remainder of this act shall take effect on the date the Commissioner of Transportation certifies to the Governor (hereinafter the "date of certification") that a majority of the members of the commission have been appointed or are in office and that all necessary anticipatory actions have been accomplished, provided, that the amount of revenues received pursuant to sections 109 and 110 prior to the date of certification are hereby appropriated to the division. Upon the date of certification, all such collected revenue shall be revenue of the commission. The Commissioner of Transportation, the Director of the Division of Motor Vehicles and the commission may take such anticipatory administrative action in advance as shall be necessary for the implementation of the act."

39:11–7. Examination of proposed location of business; recommendation of conditions

The commission or its representative, in connection with a request for a hearing made by a municipal governing body or zoning commission pursuant to R.S.39:11–6, may examine the location of the motor vehicle junk yard or business proposed to be established or maintained. The commission may recommend such conditions as it deems advisable, having regard to the depreciation of surrounding property and the health, safety, and general welfare of the public.

Amended by L.2003, c. 13, § 69; L.2009, c. 298, § 10, eff. Jan. 17, 2010.

39:11–8. Fee for examination of proposed location of business

A fee of $50 shall be paid by the applicant to the commission for the examination of the proposed location of each motor vehicle junk yard or business.

Amended by L.1975, c. 180, § 20, eff. Jan. 1, 1976; L.2003, c. 13, § 70; L.2009, c. 298, § 11, eff. Jan. 17, 2010.

39:11–9. Certification of condition of motor vehicle sold

Every person owning or operating a motor vehicle junk business or motor vehicle junk yard and who is also licensed as a motor vehicle dealer pursuant to the provisions of R.S.39:10–19 shall certify to the commission, upon the sale by him of a motor vehicle, that, at the time of the sale, the motor vehicle was or was not, as the case may be, in suitable condition to be operated on the highways.

Amended by L.2003, c. 13, § 71; L.2009, c. 298, § 12, eff. Jan. 17, 2010.

39:11–10. Review of action of governing body, zoning commission or director

A person aggrieved by the action of the governing body or zoning commission of a municipality under this chapter, or a person aggrieved by an action of the commission or its authorized representative under this chapter, may obtain a review in the Superior Court by a proceeding in lieu of prerogative writ.

Amended by L.1953, c. 36, p. 627, § 36; L.2003, c. 13, § 72.

Historical and Statutory Notes

L.2003, c. 13, § 127, approved Jan. 28, 2003, provides:

"Sections 1, 2, 3, 12, 38, 109, 110 and 121 shall take effect immediately, sections 105, 106, 107, 108, and 120 shall take effect on July 1, 2003 and the remainder of this act shall take effect on the date the Commissioner of Transportation certifies to the Governor (hereinafter the "date of certification") that a majority of the members of the commission have been appointed or are in office and that all necessary anticipatory actions have been accomplished, provided, that the amount of revenues received pursuant to sections 109 and 110 prior to the date of certification are hereby appropriated to the division. Upon the date of certification, all such collected revenue shall be revenue of the commission. The Commissioner of Transportation, the Director of the Division of Motor Vehicles and the commission may take such anticipatory administrative action in advance as shall be necessary for the implementation of the act."

39:11–11. Violation of R.S. 39:11–9; penalties; enforcement proceedings

A person who violates any provision of R.S.39:11–9 of this Title shall be fined not less than $25 nor more than $100 or be imprisoned not more than 90 days, or both.

The provisions of said section shall be enforced and all penalties for the violation thereof shall be recovered in accordance with the provisions of "The Penalty Enforcement Law of 1999," P.L.1999, c. 274 (C.2A:58–10 et seq.) and in addition to the provisions and remedies therein contained, the following provisions and remedies shall be applicable in any proceeding brought for a violation of any of the provisions of said sections:

a. The several municipal courts shall have jurisdiction of any such proceeding, in addition to the courts prescribed in "The Penalty Enforcement Law of 1999";

b. The complaint in any such proceeding may be made on information and belief by the commission, or any police or peace officer of any municipality, any county or the State;

c. A warrant may issue in lieu of summons;

d. Any police or peace officer shall be empowered to serve and execute process in any such proceeding;

e. The hearing in any such proceeding shall be without a jury;

f. Any such proceeding may be brought in the name of the commission or in the name of the State of New Jersey; and

g. Any sums received in payment of any fines imposed in any such proceeding shall be paid to the commission and shall be paid by it into the State treasury.

Amended by L.1954, c. 78, p. 450, § 1; L.1983, c. 403, § 34, eff. Dec. 23, 1983; L.2003, c. 13, § 73; L.2009, c. 298, § 13, eff. Jan. 17, 2010.

CHAPTER 12

DRIVING SCHOOLS

Section
39:12–1.   Definitions.
39:12–2.   License required; fee; exemption from fee; loss, mutilation or destruction of certificate.
39:12–2.1. Behind-the-wheel hourly instructional requirement; credit for hours as instructor in public or non-public secondary school.
39:12–2.2. Provision of list of licensed drivers' schools.
39:12–3.   Grounds for denial of application.
39:12–4.   Rules.
39:12–4.1. Inspection of premises of licensees; violations; fines.
39:12–5.   Instructor's license; motorcycle safety education endorsement.
39:12–6.   Grounds for denial of instructor's license or endorsement to license.
39:12–7.   Suspension or revocation of or refusal to issue renewal of school license, grounds for.
39:12–8.   Suspension, revocation or refusal to renew instructor's license or endorsement; grounds.
39:12–9.   Revocation or suspension of license or endorsement for violations during prior license period.
39:12–10.   Hearing on revocation or refusal of license or endorsement; notice; subpoena of witnesses.
39:12–11.   Records of licensee.
39:12–12.   Violations; punishment.
39:12–13.   Enforcement of act; jurisdiction of municipal courts.
39:12–14.   Effective date.
39:12–15.   Seat belts to be worn at all times; violations; penalties.

39:12–1. Definitions

As used in this act, the following words and terms shall have the following meanings:

a. "Drivers' school" means the business of giving instruction, for compensation, in the driving of motor vehicles and motorcycles;

b. "Person" includes an individual, corporation, and partnership;

c. "Place of business" means a designated location at which the business of a drivers' school is conducted; and

d. "Fraudulent practices" shall include, but shall not be limited to,

(1) any conduct or representation tending to give the impression that a license to operate a motor vehicle or motorcycle or any other license, registration or service granted by the Director of Motor Vehicles in the Department of Law and Public Safety may be obtained by any means other than the means prescribed by law or by furnishing or obtaining the same by illegal or by improper means or

(2) the requesting, accepting, exacting or collecting of money for such purpose.

L.1951, c. 216, p. 775, § 1.

39:12–2. License required; fee; exemption from fee; loss, mutilation or destruction of certificate

No person shall engage in the business of conducting a drivers' school without being licensed therefor by the Chief Administrator of the New Jersey Motor Vehicle Commission. Application therefor shall be in writing and contain such information therein as he shall require on initial and renewal applications, including the applicant's Federal Tax Identification number, State tax identification number and proof of workers' compensation insurance coverage by a mutual association or stock company authorized to write coverage on such risks in this State or written authorization by the Commissioner of Banking and Insurance to self-insure for workers' compensation pursuant to R.S.34:15–77. The applicant shall file a surety bond in the amount of $10,000 issued by a company authorized to transact surety business in this State and payable to the division. A license shall not be issued or renewed unless the applicant or an employee is a qualified supervising instructor. For purposes of this section, a "qualified supervising instructor" shall mean a drivers' school instructor who a. is currently licensed and has been licensed by the division for at least two years prior to submission of the initial or renewal application, b. has successfully provided a minimum of 500 hours of behind-the-wheel instruction, and c. has successfully completed a three credit New Jersey driver education college course offered by a college or university licensed by the New Jersey Commission on Higher Education. The applicant shall furnish, together with the application, satisfactory evidence that the applicant or an employee is a qualified supervising instructor as set forth herein, except that an applicant for license renewal shall have one year after the date this act becomes effective to furnish evidence of completion of a three credit New Jersey driver education college course to the division. If the application is approved, the applicant shall be granted a license to teach approved courses in classroom and behind-the-wheel driver education upon the payment of a fee of $250.00; provided, however, no license fee shall be charged for the issuance of a license to any board of education, school board, public, private or parochial school, which conducts a course in driver education, approved by the State Department of Education. A license so issued shall be valid during the calendar year. The annual fee for renewal shall be $200. The chief administrator shall issue a license certificate or license certificates to each licensee, one of which shall be displayed in each place of business of the licensee.

For the purposes of this section, each applicant for a license shall submit to the chief administrator the applicant's name, address, fingerprints and written consent for a criminal history record background check to be performed. The chief administrator is hereby authorized to exchange fingerprint data with and receive criminal history record information from the State Bureau of Identification in the Division of State Police and the Federal Bureau of Investigation consistent with applicable State and federal laws, rules and regulations, for purposes of facilitating determinations concerning licensure eligibility. The applicant shall bear the cost for the criminal history record background check, including all costs of administering and processing the check. The Division of State Police shall promptly notify the chief administrator in the event a current holder of a license or prospective applicant, who was the subject of a criminal history record background check pursuant to this section, is arrested for a crime or offense in this State after the date the background check was performed.

A public, parochial or private school or a drivers' school licensed by the chief administrator pursuant to this section shall be authorized to provide behind-the-wheel driving instruction.

Upon further application to the chief administrator, a drivers' school licensed by the chief administrator pursuant to this section may be approved by the chief administrator to conduct a State approved written drivers' examination, eye examination, or remedial training course, subject to a fee and annual renewal thereof in an amount which shall be determined by the chief administrator. The examinations and training course shall be administered pursuant to rules and regulations promulgated by the chief administrator and subject to oversight by the division. The authority of the chief administrator to suspend, revoke or deny issuance of an initial or renewal license to operate a drivers' school or an instructor's license, and to assess fines, pursuant to this chapter, shall apply to any violations related to the administration of a State approved written drivers' examination, eye examination or remedial training course.

In case of the loss, mutilation or destruction of a certificate, the chief administrator shall issue a duplicate upon proof of the facts and the payment of a fee of $5.

L.1951, c. 216, p. 776, § 2. Amended by L.1952, c. 196, p. 696, § 1; L.1975, c. 180, § 21, eff. Jan. 1, 1976; L.1994, c. 60, § 29, eff. July 1, 1994; L.2001, c. 420, § 9, eff. Jan. 8, 2002; L.2003, c. 199, § 23, eff. Dec. 24, 2003.

39:12–2.1. Behind-the-wheel hourly instructional requirement; credit for hours as instructor in public or non-public secondary school

Notwithstanding any law, rule or regulation to the contrary, a person who is employed as a driving instructor in a public or non-public secondary school shall receive hour-for-hour credit from the Division of Motor Vehicles for the person's behind-the-wheel instructional experience towards the fulfillment of any behind-the-wheel hourly instructional requirement necessary to obtain a drivers' school license. The principal of the high school or superintendent of the school district shall affirm, in the form of an affidavit, the person's total number of hours of behind-the-wheel instructional experience.

For the purposes of this act, behind-the-wheel instructional experience for courses taught only on public highways and streets is applicable to fulfillment of any behind-the-wheel hourly instructional requirement. Instructional experience using simulator devices and driving ranges shall not be applicable to the provisions of this act.

L.1998, c. 76, § 1, eff. Aug. 14, 1998.

39:12–2.2. Provision of list of licensed drivers' schools

The Director of the Division of Motor Vehicles shall, by January 31st of each year, provide to the Department of Education a list of all drivers' schools licensed by the director pursuant to section 2 of P.L.1951, c. 216 (C.39:12–2) and the department shall disseminate the list to all school districts in the State.

L.1999, c. 270, § 2, eff. Nov. 10, 1999.

39:12–3. Grounds for denial of application

The director may deny the application of any person for a license if, in his discretion, he determines that:

a. Such applicant has made a material false statement or concealed a material fact in connection with his application;

b. Such applicant, any officer, director, stockholder or partner, or any other person directly or indirectly interested in the business, was the former holder of a license under this act, or was an officer, director, stockholder or partner, in a corporation or partnership which held a license under this act and which license was revoked or suspended by the director;

c. Such applicant or any officer, director, stockholder, partner, employee, or any other person directly or indirectly interested in the business, has been convicted of a crime;

d. Such applicant has failed to furnish satisfactory evidence of good character, reputation and fitness;

e. Such applicant does not have a place of business as required by this act;

f. Such applicant is not the true owner of the drivers' school; or

g. The application is not accompanied by a copy of a standard liability insurance policy in the amount of $10,000.00 for personal injury to, or death of, any 1 person, $20,000.00 for personal injury to, or death of, any number of persons involved in any 1 accident, and

$5,000.00 for property damage in any 1 accident, suffered, or caused by reason of the negligence of the applicant or any agent or employee of the applicant, approved as to form and coverage by the director, and issued by a company duly licensed to transact business in this State under the insurance laws of this State.

L.1951, c. 216, p. 776, § 3. Amended by L.1959, c. 44, p. 149, § 1.

39:12–4. Rules

The director may make such rules as he deems reasonable for the conduct of drivers' schools.

L.1951, c. 216, p. 777, § 4.

39:12–4.1. Inspection of premises of licensees; violations; fines

The director shall make or cause to be made a full and complete inspection, at least annually, of the premises of each licensee at reasonable hours as the director may deem necessary to be assured that the licensee and the premises comply at all times with the provisions of this title governing drivers' schools, as well as the rules and regulations and the minimum standards established thereunder. A violation of such rules, regulations and standards sufficient to be considered more than de minimis shall result in a fine for the first violation of no less than $500 or more than $1,500; for a second violation, a fine of no less than $1,500 or more than $2,500; and for a third or subsequent violation, the suspension or revocation by the director of the license of any drivers' school.

L.2001, c. 420, § 10, eff. Jan. 8, 2002.

39:12–5. Instructor's license; motorcycle safety education endorsement

No person shall be employed by any such licensee to give instruction in driving a motor vehicle unless he shall be licensed to act as such instructor by the chief administrator. No person shall be employed by such licensee to instruct a motorcycle safety education course as established pursuant to section 1 of P.L.1991, c. 452 (C.27:5F–36) unless he has received from the chief administrator a motorcycle safety education instructor endorsement to his instructor's license. The chief administrator shall issue a motorcycle safety education instructor endorsement to an instructor's license if the person meets the requirements set forth in section 2 of P.L.1991, c. 452 (C.27:5F–37).

Application for an instructor's license or for a motorcycle safety education instructor endorsement to an instructor's license shall be in writing and shall contain such information as the chief administrator shall require.

The initial fee for an instructor's license shall be $75.00 and a fee for an annual renewal thereof shall be $50. No additional fee shall be charged by the chief administrator for a motorcycle safety education instructor endorsement. The license so issued shall be valid for the calendar year within which it is issued, and renewals shall be for succeeding calendar years.

For the purposes of this section, each applicant for a license shall submit to the chief administrator the applicant's name, address, fingerprints and written consent for a criminal history record background check to be performed. The chief administrator is hereby authorized to exchange fingerprint data with and receive criminal history record information from the State Bureau of Identification in the Division of State Police and the Federal Bureau of Investigation consistent with applicable State and federal laws, rules and regulations, for purposes of facilitating determinations concerning licensure eligibility. The applicant shall bear the cost for the criminal history record background check, including all costs of administering and processing the check. The Division of State Police shall promptly notify the chief administrator in the event a current holder of a license or prospective applicant, who was the subject of a criminal history record background check pursuant to this section, is arrested for a crime or offense in this State after the date the background check was performed.

L.1951, c. 216, p. 777, § 5. Amended by L.1952, c. 296, p. 997, § 1; L.1975, c. 180, § 22, eff. Jan. 1, 1976; L.1991, c. 452, § 8, eff. July 1, 1992; L.1994, c. 60, § 30, eff. July 1, 1994; L.2003, c. 199, § 24, eff. Dec. 24, 2003.

39:12–6. Grounds for denial of instructor's license or endorsement to license

The director may deny the application of any person for an instructor's license or for a motorcycle safety education instructor endorsement to an instructor's license if, in his discretion, he determines that:

    a.   the applicant has made a material false statement or concealed a material fact in connection with his application therefor;

    b.   the applicant has failed to furnish satisfactory evidence of the facts required of him in section five of this act [1]; or

    c.   the applicant for an instructor's license is not of good moral character; that he has not held a license to drive a motor vehicle within the State for the past three consecutive years; that he has not had a driving record satisfactory to the director; that he has been convicted of crime; that he is disqualified for a motorcycle safety education instructor endorsement for any reason set forth in section 2 of P.L.1991, c. 452 (C. 27:5F–37).

L.1951, c. 216, § 6. Amended by L.1952, c. 296, § 2; L.1991, c. 452, § 9, eff. July 1, 1992.

    1 N.J.S.A. § 39:12–5.

39:12–7. Suspension or revocation of or refusal to issue renewal of school license, grounds for

The director, or any employee of the Division of Motor Vehicles deputized by him, may suspend or revoke any school license issued under the provisions of this act or refuse to issue a renewal thereof if:

a. The licensee has made a material false statement or concealed a material fact in connection with the application for a license or the renewal thereof;

b. The licensee or any partner or officer of the licensee has been convicted of a crime;

c. The licensee has failed to comply with any of the provisions of this act or any of the rules and regulations of the director establishing instructional standards and procedures;

d. The licensee or any partner or officer of such licensee has been guilty of fraud or fraudulent practices in relation to the business conducted under the license, or guilty of inducing another person to resort to fraud or fraudulent practices in relation to securing for himself or another the license to drive a motor vehicle or motorcycle;

e. The licensee has knowingly employed, as an instructor, a person who has been convicted of a crime or has retained such a person in such employ after knowledge of his conviction; or

f. The licensee has failed to maintain satisfactory insurance to meet damage claims required by section three of this act.[1]

L.1951, c. 216, p. 778, § 7.

[1] N.J.S.A. § 39:12–3.

39:12–8. Suspension, revocation or refusal to renew instructor's license or endorsement; grounds

The director or any employee of the Division of Motor Vehicles deputized by him may suspend or revoke any instructor's license issued under the provisions of this act or refuse to issue renewal thereof if:

a. The licensee has made a material false statement or concealed a material fact in connection with his application for the license or any renewal thereof;

b. The licensee has been convicted of a crime;

c. The licensee has failed to comply with any of the provisions of this act or any of the rules and regulations of the director establishing instructional standards of procedure; or

d. The licensee has been guilty of fraud or fraudulent practices in relation to securing for himself or another a license to drive a motor vehicle or motorcycle.

The director or any employee of the Division of Motor Vehicles deputized by him may suspend or revoke a motorcycle safety education instructor endorsement to an instructor's license issued under section 5 of P.L.1951, c. 216 (C. 39:12–5) or refuse to issue renewal thereof if:

a. The licensee has made a material false statement or concealed a material fact in connection with his application for the endorsement or renewal thereof;

b. The licensee is disqualified under one of the provisions of section 2 of P.L.1991, c. 452 (C. 27:5F–37); or

c. The licensee has failed to comply with any of the provisions of this act or any of the rules and regulations of the director establishing instructional standards of procedure.

L.1951, c. 216, § 8. Amended by L.1991, c. 452, § 10, eff. July 1, 1992.

39:12–9. Revocation or suspension of license or endorsement for violations during prior license period

Notwithstanding the renewal of a license, the director may revoke or suspend such license or endorsement for causes and violations, as prescribed by this act, occurring during any prior license period.

L.1951, c. 216, § 9. Amended by L.1991, c. 452, § 11, eff. July 1, 1992.

39:12–10. Hearing on revocation or refusal of license or endorsement; notice; subpoena of witnesses

Every applicant or licensee shall be entitled to a hearing, before his application for a license, an endorsement or a renewal thereof is refused or his license or endorsement is revoked, and shall be given due notice thereof. The sending of a notice of a hearing by registered mail to the last known address of a licensee or applicant ten days prior to the date of the hearing shall be deemed due notice. The director, or the person deputized by him to conduct a hearing, shall have power to subpoena witnesses, administer oaths to witnesses and take testimony of any person or cause his deposition to be taken. A subpoena issued under the authority of this section shall be served in the same manner as a subpoena issued out of the Superior Court. Witnesses subpoenaed hereunder shall be entitled to the same fees and mileage as are allowed in civil actions in courts of record.

L.1951, c. 216, § 10. Amended by L.1991, c. 452, § 12, eff. July 1, 1992.

39:12–11. Records of licensee

Every licensee shall keep such records as the director may by regulation require. The records of the licensee shall be open to the inspection of the director or his representatives at all times during reasonable business hours.

L.1951, c. 216, p. 779, § 11.

39:12–12. Violations; punishment

A person who violates any of the provisions of this act shall be subject, for a first offense, to a fine of not less than one hundred dollars ($100.00) nor more than two hundred fifty dollars ($250.00) or imprisonment for a term of not less than ten days or more than thirty days, or both, in the discretion of the magistrate. For a subsequent violation, he shall be subject to a fine of not less than two hundred fifty dollars ($250.00) nor more than five hundred dollars ($500.00), or imprisonment for a period of not less than thirty days or more than three months, or ▄▄▄both, in the discretion of the magistrate.

L.1951, c. 216, p. 7⟍⟋9, § 12.

39:12–13. Enforcement of act; jurisdiction of municipal courts

The provisions of this act shall be enforced and all penalties for the violation thereof shall be recovered in accordance with the provisions of "the penalty enforcement law" (N.J.S. 2A:58–1 et seq.), and in addition to the provisions and remedies therein contained, the following provisions and remedies shall be applicable in any proceeding brought for a violation of any of the provisions of this act:

a. The several municipal courts shall have jurisdiction of such proceeding, in addition to the courts prescribed in said act;

b. The complaint in such proceeding may be made on information and belief by any member of the State Police, who hereby is designated for said purpose;

c. A warrant may issue in lieu of summons in such proceeding;

d. Any member of the State Police shall be empowered to serve and execute process in such proceeding;

e. The hearing in such proceeding shall be without a jury;

f. Such proceeding may be brought in the name of the Director of the Division of Motor Vehicles in the Department of Law and Public Safety or in the name of the State of New Jersey;

g. Any sums received in payment of any fines imposed in such proceeding shall be paid to the Director of the Division of Motor Vehicles and shall be paid by him into the State treasury.

L.1951, c. 216, p. 780, § 13. Amended by L.1983, c. 403, § 35, eff. Dec. 23, 1983.

39:12–14. Effective date

This act shall take effect July first, one thousand nine hundred and fifty-one.

L.1951, c. 216, p. 781, § 14.

39:12–15. Seat belts to be worn at all times; violations; penalties

No person shall give instruction in the operation of a motor vehicle at a drivers' school unless both the instructor and student wear seat belts at all times during a driving lesson, regardless of which person is operating the vehicle. A person who violates this act shall be subject to a fine of $25.00 for the first offense and $50.00 for a subsequent offense.

L.1984, c. 51, § 1, eff. June 14, 1984.

CHAPTER 13

AUTO BODY REPAIR FACILITIES

Section
39:13–1.   Definitions.
39:13–2.   License; application; fee; renewal.
39:13–2.1.   Auto body repair facility; full service license requirements.
313–2.2.   Automobile dealer sublet license.
313–2.3.   Review of full service auto body repair facility and motor vehicle dealer sublet license applications.
13–2.4.   Regulations.
13–3.   Investigations.
13–4.   Imposition of fine; refusal to grant, suspension or revocation of license.
3–5.   Notification of refusal to grant, suspension or revocation of license; hearing.
3–6.   Civil penalties.
3–7.   Rules and regulations.
3–8.   Damage repairs reimbursable under insurance policy by negotiable instrument payable to insured and lienholder or lessor; proof; inspection; priority of lien on sale; prohibition of payment of proceeds for delinquent amounts or outstanding installments.

3–1. Definitions

or the purposes of this act:

"Auto body repair facility" means a business or son who for compensation engages in the business of airing, removing, installing or painting integral component parts of a chassis or body of a motor vehicle naged as a result of a collision.

"Director" means the Director of the Division of tor Vehicles in the Department of Transportation.

Motor vehicle" means a vehicle as defined in R.S. 1–1 and which is required to be registered with the ision of Motor Vehicles, excluding motorcycles. 983, c. 360, § 1. Amended by L.1985, c. 148, § 22, April 24, 1985; L.2001, c. 53, § 1, eff. April 5, 2002.

13–2. License; application; fee; renewal

. The commission shall establish a system for the nsure of auto body repair facilities. This system y provide for licenses based upon the type or types of tor vehicles repaired by the facility and the equipent required for repair of the vehicles. At a minim, the commission shall provide for a full service to body repair facility license, the qualifications for ich are established under section 7 of this amendato- and supplementary act, and an automobile dealer blet license, the qualifications for which are established under section 8 of this amendatory and supplementary act. All facilities licensed pursuant to this ction may hold themselves out to the public as censed auto body repair facilities.

b. No person may engage in the business of an auto body repair facility unless it is licensed by the commission. An auto body repair facility shall be licensed by the commission upon submission and approval of an application and payment of a reasonable application fee sufficient to cover the cost of implementing the provisions of this act and to be prescribed by the commission. The commission may require biennial renewal of applications for licensure and may stagger the renewal dates and adjust the application fees accordingly.

L.1983, c. 360, § 2. Amended by L.1985, c. 148, § 23, eff. April 24, 1985; L.2001, c. 53, § 2, eff. April 5, 2002; L.2003, c. 13, § 74.

39:13–2.1. Auto body repair facility; full service license requirements

a. To qualify for a full service license an auto body repair facility shall:

(1) Have a building suitable for the conduct of all operations within the building, and a Certificate of Occupancy for an auto body repair facility issued by the applicable zoning authority. In the absence of evidence to the contrary, public operation as an auto body repair facility for a continuous period of five years shall create a presumption of compliance;

(2) Have all required licenses, permits and registrations required for the conduct of business including, but not limited to: a federal tax identification number; a New Jersey sales tax identification number; hazardous waste disposal systems that are in accordance with standards established by the State or federal government; stack permits; and any other licenses, permits and registrations as the director may find applicable;

(3) Maintain insurance coverage for damage to property and for liability arising from bodily injury, including, but not limited to: garage keepers' liability insurance in a minimum amount of $300,000 or a letter of credit in the amount of $300,000; workers' compensation insurance coverage in the amounts required pursuant to R.S.34:15–1 et seq.; fire insurance, and any other coverage required by the director;

(4) Possess and maintain an auto body repair facility reference source for estimating the cost of repairs, which reference source is generally accepted by the auto body repair industry. The reference source may be in either book or computerized form;

(5) Possess and maintain equipment to safely raise and support vehicles for inspection and repair;

(6) Possess and maintain a metal inert gas welder;

(7) Possess, maintain and utilize for all spray painting:

(a) an enclosed area for refinishing which complies with all applicable safety, fire, environmental and other regulations;

(b) the means to supply fresh air to workers within the spray area when using materials that require breathable air to be supplied; and

(c) a filtration method to reduce particles from the air exhausted from the spray area which is established in accordance with standards established by the State or federal government;

(8) Have equipment necessary to perform or the means for performing structural repair including, but not limited to: equipment to make multiple body and chassis pulls to straighten damaged vehicle components; equipment to anchor a unibody vehicle at four points; a three dimensional measuring device suitable to measure structural dimensions of symmetrical and non- symmetrical vehicles; and dimensional guides appropriate to the vehicles being repaired;

(9) Have equipment necessary to perform or the means for performing vehicle four-wheel alignment;

(10) Have (a) equipment necessary to perform or the means for performing vehicle air conditioner servicing including the means to evacuate, recycle, and recharge refrigerants and (b) a technician-employee certified to perform such repairs;

(11) Have equipment necessary to perform or the means for performing mechanical repairs necessitated by collision damage; and

(12) Provide evidence that at least one employee or ten (10%) percent, whichever is greater, of the employees performing repairs at the auto body repair facility have completed a recognized auto body repair related training course during the year immediately preceding the application for or renewal of licensure as a full service auto body repair facility. Training courses available through ICAR (Inter–Industry Conference on Auto Collision Repair), the manufacturer's representative or a generally recognized auto body repair training program shall qualify to satisfy the requirement.

b. An auto body repair facility may, however, qualify for a full service license if it meets all of the conditions established by paragraphs (1), (2), (3), (4), (5), (6), (7) and (12) of subsection a. of this section and has a written agreement to subcontract with another autobody repair facility licensee or other party to perform the work for which the equipment set forth in paragraph (8), (9), (10) or (11) of subsection a. of this section is required provided, however, that the other party meets the requirements set forth in those paragraphs with regard to equipment or the means for performing the required tasks and training.

L.2001, c. 53, § 7, eff. April 5, 2002.

39:13–2.2. Automobile dealer sublet license

A person which sells new automobiles under an agreement with an automobile manufacturer and does not satisfy the equipment requirements of section 7 of this amendatory and supplementary act may qualify for an automobile dealer sublet license provided that the automobile dealer agrees in the sublet license application to use only auto body repair facilities licensed pursuant to the provisions of section 7 of this amendatory and supplementary act to perform auto body repairs.

L.2001, c. 53, § 8, eff. April 5, 2002.

39:13–2.3. Review of full service auto body repair facility and motor vehicle dealer sublet license applications

Applications for a new or renewal full service auto body repair facility license or a motor vehicle dealer sublet license shall be reviewed by the director and a license issued or denied within 90 days following receipt by the director of the completed application and supporting documents. Applicants for renewal or initial licensure filed after the effective date of this amendatory and supplementary act shall certify that the applicant has met the requirements of the act. Auto body repair facilities holding a license issued prior to the effective date of this amendatory and supplementary act shall be subject to the provisions of the act on the first renewal date of the license established by the director. The director may extend licenses issued under the provisions of P.L.1983, c. 360 (C.39:13–1 et seq.), pending renewal of the licenses pursuant to the terms and conditions established by this amendatory and supplementary act. No later than the 45th day following the effective date of this amendatory and supplementary act, the director shall notify all licensed auto body repair facilities of the terms, conditions and requirements of the act.

L.2001, c. 53, § 9, eff. April 5, 2002.

39:13–2.4. Regulations

Within 360 days of the effective date of this amendatory and supplementary act the director shall promulgate regulations, in accordance with the provisions of the "Administrative Procedure Act," P.L.1968, c. 410 (C.52:14B–1 et seq.), to implement the provisions of this amendatory and supplementary act and to revise any existing regulations to make them consistent herewith.

L.2001, c. 53, § 10, eff. April 10, 2001.

39:13–3. Investigations

The director shall, on his own initiative or in response to complaints, investigate on a continuing basis and gather evidence of violations of this act and of any regulation adopted pursuant to this act by auto body repair facilities.

L.1983, c. 360, § 3. Amended by L.1985, c. 148, § 24, eff. April 24, 1985.

39:13–4. Imposition of fine; refusal to grant, suspension or revocation of license

The director may fine or refuse to grant or may suspend or revoke a license of an auto body repair facility for any of the following acts or omissions related to the conduct of the business of the auto body repair facility:

a. Making or authorizing any material written or oral statement which is known to be untrue or misleading;

b. Causing or allowing a customer to sign any estimate for repairs which does not state the repairs requested by the customer or the motor vehicle's odometer reading at the time of repair;

c. Failing to provide a customer with a copy of any estimate or document requiring his signature, as soon as a customer signs the estimate or document;

d. Making false promises or representations intended to influence, persuade, or induce a customer to authorize a repair of a motor vehicle which has been damaged as a result of a collision;

e. Giving an adjuster or appraiser directly or indirectly any gratuity or other consideration in connection with his appraisal service;

f. Making appraisals of the cost of repairing a motor vehicle which has been damaged as a result of a collision through the use of photographs, telephone calls, or any manner other than personal inspection;

g. Making an estimate for repairs or charging for repairs in such amount as to compensate the insured for the cost of the deductible applicable under an insurance policy;

h. A pattern of conduct which includes any of the acts or omissions prohibited in this section or any other unconscionable or fraudulent commercial practice prohibited by the director pursuant to regulations promulgated under the provisions of this act;

i. Failing to maintain its equipment and facilities in good operating condition, or failing to keep in force and effect any permits, accreditation, letter of credit or insurance required for licensure;

j. Operating an auto body repair facility without a license as required pursuant to section 2 of P.L.1983, c. 360 (C.39:13–2).

L.1983, c. 360, § 4. Amended by L.1985, c. 148, § 25, eff. April 24, 1985; L.2001, c. 53, § 3, eff. April 5, 2002.

39:13–5. Notification of refusal to grant, suspension or revocation of license; hearing

Upon refusal to grant a license or suspension or revocation of a license of an auto body repair facility, the director shall notify the auto body repair facility in writing by registered mail. The auto body repair facility shall be given a hearing by the director if, within 30 days thereafter, it files with the director a written request for a hearing concerning the refusal to grant a license or suspension or revocation of the license.

L.1983, c. 360, § 5. Amended by L.1985, c. 148, § 26, eff. April 24, 1985; L.2001, c. 53, § 4, eff. April 5, 2002.

39:13–6. Civil penalties

The director may issue and cause to be served, upon an auto body repair facility charged with a violation of P.L.1983, c. 360 (C.39:13–1 et seq.), an order requiring the auto body repair facility to cease and desist from the violation and the director may impose upon an auto body repair facility violating this act a civil penalty of not more than $5,000 for the first offense and not more than $20,000 for the second and each subsequent offense. The civil penalty shall be issued for and recovered by and in the name of the director and shall be collected and enforced by summary proceedings pursuant to the "Penalty Enforcement Law of 1999," P. L.1999, c. 274 (C.2A:58–10 et seq.). In the event of continued or serious violations, the director may suspend the license of the facility and require it to cease operations during the period of suspension.

L.1983, c. 360, § 6. Amended by L.1985, c. 148, § 27, eff. April 24, 1985; L.2001, c. 53, § 5, eff. April 5, 2002.

39:13–7.　Rules and regulations

The director shall promulgate rules and regulations necessary to effectuate the purposes of this act.

L.1983, c. 360, § 7. Amended by L.1985, c. 148, § 28, eff. April 24, 1985.

39:13–8.　Damage repairs reimbursable under insurance policy by negotiable instrument payable to insured and lienholder or lessor; proof; inspection; priority of lien on sale; prohibition of payment of proceeds for delinquent amounts or outstanding installments

a.　When a motor vehicle is repaired by an auto body repair facility as a result of damage to the vehicle and (1) the damage is reimbursable under a policy of insurance or is otherwise reimbursable by a third party; and (2) the proceeds of the reimbursement are in the form of a negotiable instrument issued by an insurer or other payer which is payable jointly to the owner or lessee of the vehicle and a lienholder or lessor, the auto body repair facility shall provide the lienholder or lessor with a statement of the repairs which have been made to the vehicle, which statement shall be attested by an authorized representative of the auto body repair facility. The statement shall constitute proof to the lienholder or lessor that all repairs have been made by an auto body repair facility. A color photograph of the repaired vehicle shall accompany the statement.

b.　In the event that any lienholder or lessor should wish to inspect any motor vehicle to which repairs have been made as provided in subsection a. of this section, the lienholder or lessor shall conduct the inspection upon the premises of the auto body repair facility within three business days after receipt of the notice by certified mail that the repair has been completed. If an inspection is not made by a lienholder or lessor within the three-day period provided herein, the lienholder or lessor shall forfeit the right to make an inspection.

c.　In the event a lienholder or lessor shall sell any motor vehicle to which repairs have been made as provided in subsection a. of this section prior to the payment or reimbursement of the auto body repair facility which repaired that motor vehicle, except for the amounts due that lienholder or lessor under the provisions of a perfected lien or security interest, the amount due the auto body repair facility for those repairs shall supersede and have priority over all other liens or outstanding interests, including those payable by an insurer to the owner or lessee of the repaired motor vehicle. In such cases, if the insurer or other payor has received a statement and request demanding payment from the auto body repair facility, the proceeds, or portion thereof, shall be directed by the insurer or other payor to that auto body repair facility.

d.　No lienholder or lessor shall deduct any amount from the aggregate proceeds of a negotiable instrument that was issued by an insurer or other payor to reimburse an auto body repair facility which, pursuant to the provisions of subsection a. of this section, repaired a damaged motor vehicle, but which is payable jointly to the owner or lessee and the lienholder or lessor, for the purpose of paying any delinquent amounts or outstanding installments that the owner or lessee may owe to the lienholder or lessor for the motor vehicle that has been repaired, nor shall any lienholder or lessor unreasonably withhold the endorsement of such instrument or, following endorsement, refuse to transmit the endorsed instrument to the owner or lessee.

For the purposes of this act, "auto body repair facility" shall mean an auto body repair facility as defined in section 1 of P.L.1983, c. 360 (C.39:13–1).

L.1987, c. 280, § 1, eff. Oct. 6, 1987. Amended by L.1989, c. 273, § 1, eff. Jan. 8, 1990; L.2001, c. 53, § 6, eff. April 5, 2002.

TITLE 2A

ADMINISTRATION OF CIVIL AND CRIMINAL JUSTICE

Subtitle
1. The Courts.
9. Evidence, Witnesses and Public Hearings.

Subtitle
10. Crimes.
11. Criminal Procedure.
12. Disorderly Persons.

SUBTITLE 1

THE COURTS

Chapter
4A. Family Court.

CHAPTER 4A

FAMILY COURT

ARTICLE 2. CODE OF JUVENILE JUSTICE

Section
2A:4A–20. Short title.
2A:4A–21. Purposes.
2A:4A–22. General definitions.
2A:4A–23. Definition of delinquency.
2A:4A–24. Exclusive jurisdiction of the court and nature of jurisdiction.
2A:4A–25. Transfer from other courts.
2A:4A–26. Referral to another court without juvenile's consent.
2A:4A–27. Referral to other court at election of juvenile.
2A:4A–28. Effect of referral to other court.
2A:4A–29. Use of juvenile's testimony at referral hearing.
2A:4A–30. Complaints and petitions.
2A:4A–31. Taking into custody.
2A:4A–32. Short-term custody.
2A:4A–33. Taking into custody; notice to parents.
2A:4A–34. Criteria for placing juvenile in detention.
2A:4A–35. Release of juvenile on own recognizance.
2A:4A–36. Detention of waiver cases.
2A:4A–37. Place of detention or shelter.
2A:4A–38. Detention hearing.
2A:4A–39. Right to counsel.
2A:4A–40. Rights of juveniles.
2A:4A–41. Dispositional hearing.
2A:4A–42. Predispositional evaluation.
2A:4A–43. Disposition of delinquency cases.
2A:4A–43.1. AIDS and HIV infection testing for juveniles charged with delinquency or adjudicated delinquent for acts constituting sexual assault or aggravated sexual assault.
2A:4A–43.2. Additional penalties for juvenile adjudicated delinquent.
2A:4A–43.3. Suspension or postponement of right to operate motor vehicle of person convicted of or adjudicated delinquent for certain violations.
2A:4A–43.4. AIDS and HIV infection testing ordered by court under certain circumstances.

Section
2A:4A–44. Incarceration—Aggravating and mitigating factors.
2A:4A–44.1. Agreements between department of corrections and county for incarceration of certain juveniles in county juvenile detention facility.
2A:4A–45. Retention of jurisdiction.
2A:4A–46. Disposition of juvenile-family crisis.
2A:4A–47. Termination of orders of disposition.
2A:4A–48. Effect of disposition.
2A:4A–49. Repealed.

ARTICLE 3. INFORMATION RELATING TO JUVENILES

2A:4A–60. Disclosure of juvenile information; penalties for disclosure.
2A:4A–60. Disclosure of juvenile information; penalties for disclosure.
2A:4A–60.1. Rules governing disclosure of juvenile records.
2A:4A–60.2. Limitation upon disclosure of statements made during a suicide or mental health screening.
2A:4A–60.3. Disclosure of reports or records relating to mental health services restricted prior to court's adjudication.
2A:4A–61. Fingerprint records; photographs of juveniles.
2A:4A–62. Sealing of records.

ARTICLE 4. COURT APPROVED JUVENILE SERVICES

2A:4A–70. County court intake services.
2A:4A–71. Review and processing of complaints.
2A:4A–72. Recommendation of diversion.
2A:4A–73. Diverting complaints.
2A:4A–74. Court intake service conference.
2A:4A–75. Juvenile conference committees.
2A:4A–76. Juvenile-family crisis intervention units established.
2A:4A–77. Call service to attend and stabilize juvenile-family crises; referrals; information; form.
2A:4A–78. Intervention unit response.
2A:4A–79. Intervention unit training and skills.
2A:4A–80. Law enforcement referral.
2A:4A–81. Other referrals.
2A:4A–82. Juvenile-family crisis stabilized.
2A:4A–83. Juvenile-family crisis referral to the court; continuing crisis.

Section

2A:4A–84. Juvenile-family crisis recommendations.

2A:4A–85. Alcoholic, drug-dependent parent; belief juvenile abused or neglected; juvenile with auditory or vision problem; examination, records and recommendations to court.

2A:4A–86. Juvenile-family crisis hearing; disposition.

2A:4A–87. Juvenile–family crisis referral to courts; out of home placement.

2A:4A–88. Temporary placement.

2A:4A–89. Out of home placement hearing.

2A:4A–90. Long-term placement.

2A:4A–91. Repealed.

2A:4A–92. "Court Appointed Special Advocate" defined; CASA program established; scope of program and advocate authority.

ARTICLE 2. CODE OF JUVENILE JUSTICE

2A:4A–20. Short title

This act shall be known and may be cited as the "New Jersey Code of Juvenile Justice."

L.1982, c. 77, § 1, eff. Dec. 31, 1983.

2A:4A–21. Purposes

This act shall be construed so as to effectuate the following purposes:

a. To preserve the unity of the family whenever possible and to provide for the care, protection, and wholesome mental and physical development of juveniles coming within the provisions of this act;

b. Consistent with the protection of the public interest, to remove from children committing delinquent acts certain statutory consequences of criminal behavior, and to substitute therefor an adequate program of supervision, care and rehabilitation, and a range of sanctions designed to promote accountability and protect the public;

c. To separate juveniles from the family environment only when necessary for their health, safety or welfare or in the interests of public safety;

d. To secure for each child coming under the jurisdiction of the court such care, guidance and control, preferably in his own home, as will conduce to the child's welfare and the best interests of the State; and when such child is removed from his own family, to secure for him custody, care and discipline as nearly as possible equivalent to that which should have been given by his parents;

e. To insure that children under the jurisdiction of the court are wards of the State, subject to the discipline and entitled to the protection of the State, which may intervene to safeguard them from neglect or injury and to enforce the legal obligations due to them and from them; and

f. Consistent with the protection of the public interest, to insure that any services and sanctions for juveniles provide balanced attention to the protection of the community, the imposition of accountability for offenses committed, fostering interaction and dialogue between the offender, victim and community and the development of competencies to enable children to become responsible and productive members of the community.

L.1982, c. 77, § 2, eff. Dec. 31, 1983. Amended by L.1995, c. 280, § 1, eff. Dec. 15, 1995; L.2001, c. 408, § 1, eff. Aug. 1, 2002.

2A:4A–22. General definitions

As used in this act:

a. "Juvenile" means an individual who is under the age of 18 years.

b. "Adult" means an individual 18 years of age or older.

c. "Detention" means the temporary care of juveniles in physically restricting facilities pending court disposition.

d. "Shelter care" means the temporary care of juveniles in facilities without physical restriction pending court disposition.

e. "Commit" means to transfer legal custody to an institution.

f. "Guardian" means a person, other than a parent, to whom legal custody of the child has been given by court order or who is acting in the place of the parent or is responsible for the care and welfare of the juvenile.

g. "Juvenile-family crisis" means behavior, conduct or a condition of a juvenile, parent or guardian or other family member which presents or results in (1) a serious threat to the well-being and physical safety of a juvenile, or (2) a serious conflict between a parent or guardian and a juvenile regarding rules of conduct which has been manifested by repeated disregard for lawful parental authority by a juvenile or misuse of lawful parental authority by a parent or guardian, or (3) unauthorized absence by a juvenile for more than 24 hours from his home, or (4) a pattern of repeated unauthorized absences from school by a juvenile subject to the compulsory education provision of Title 18A of the New Jersey Statutes.

h. "Repetitive disorderly persons offense" means the second or more disorderly persons offense committed by a juvenile on at least two separate occasions and at different times.

i. "Court" means the Superior Court, Chancery Division, Family Part unless a different meaning is plainly required.

j. "Commission" means the Juvenile Justice Commission established pursuant to section 2 of P.L.1995, c. 284 (C. 52:17B–170).

L.1982, c. 77, § 3, eff. Dec. 31, 1983. Amended by L.1991, c. 91, § 4, eff. April 9, 1991; L.1995, c. 280, § 2, eff. Dec. 15, 1995.

2A:4A–23. Definition of delinquency

As used in this act, "delinquency" means the commission of an act by a juvenile which if committed by an adult would constitute:

a. A crime;

b. A disorderly persons offense or petty disorderly persons offense; or

c. A violation of any other penal statute, ordinance or regulation.

But, the commission of (1) an act which constitutes a violation of chapter 3, 4, 6 or 8 of Title 39 of the Revised Statutes by a juvenile of any age; (2) an act relating to the ownership or operation of a motorized bicycle which constitutes a violation of chapter 3 or 4 of Title 39 of the Revised Statutes by a juvenile of any age; (3) an act which constitutes a violation of article 3 or 6 of chapter 4 of Title 39 of the Revised Statutes pertaining to pedestrians and bicycles, by a juvenile of any age; (4) the commission of an act which constitutes a violation of P.L.1981, c. 318 (C.26:3D–1 et seq.), P.L.1981, c. 319 (C.26:3D–7 et seq.), P.L.1981, c. 320 (C.26:3D–15 et seq.), P.L.1985, c. 185 (C.26:3E–7 et seq.), P.L.1985, c. 186 (C.26:3D–32 et seq.), N.J.S.2C:33–13, P.L.1985, c. 318 (C.26:3D–38 et seq.), P.L.1985, c. 381 (C.26:3D–46 et seq.), or of any amendment or supplement thereof, by a juvenile of any age; (5) an act which constitutes a violation of chapter 7 of Title 12 of the Revised Statutes relating to the regulation and registration of power vessels, by a juvenile of any age or section 2 of P.L.1987, c. 453 (C.12:7–61); or (6) an act which constitutes a violation of a municipal ordinance enacted pursuant to section 2 of P.L.1992, c. 132 (C.40:48–2.52) pertaining to curfew ordinances shall not constitute delinquency as defined in this act. The municipal court having jurisdiction over a case involving a violation by a juvenile of a section of Title 26 listed in this subsection, Title 40 listed in this subsection or N.J.S.2C:33–13, shall forward a copy of the record of conviction in that case to the Family Part intake service of the county where the municipal court is located. If a municipal court orders detention or imposes a term of imprisonment on a juvenile in connection with a violation of Title 39 of the Revised Statutes, chapter 7 of Title 12 of the Revised Statutes, Title 40 of the Revised Statutes or N.J.S.2C:33–13, that detention or term of imprisonment shall be served at a suitable juvenile institution and not at a county jail or county workhouse.

L.1982, c. 77, § 4, eff. Dec. 31, 1983. Amended by L.1983, c. 404, § 1, eff. Dec. 30, 1983; L.1986, c. 16, § 1, eff. May 20, 1986; L.1986, c. 39, § 5, eff. June 26, 1986; L.1987, c. 401, § 1, eff. Jan. 14, 1988; L.1987, c. 453, § 3, eff. Jan. 19, 1989; L.1989, c. 125, § 1, eff. July 3, 1989; L.1991, c. 96, § 1, eff. April 9, 1991; L.1997, c. 383, § 1, eff. Jan. 19, 1998.

2A:4A–24. Exclusive jurisdiction of the court and nature of jurisdiction

a. Except as otherwise provided by law, the court shall have exclusive jurisdiction in all cases where it is charged that a juvenile has committed an act of delinquency and over all matters relating to a juvenile-family crisis. Upon the determination that a juvenile has committed an act of delinquency or that a juvenile-family crisis exists, the court may impose such disposition or dispositions over those persons subject to its jurisdiction consistent with the purposes of this act.

Such jurisdiction shall extend in these matters over a juvenile and his parent, guardian or any family member found by the court to be contributing to a juvenile-family crisis. The court shall, in accordance with the Rules of Court, clearly specify the responsibilities of those subject to its jurisdiction with respect to the plan of rehabilitation for the juvenile.

b. The court shall have jurisdiction in respect to the custody of any juvenile who may be held as a material witness in any case pending in the court. Whenever a juvenile is a material witness in any other court, the procedures established by this act shall be followed.

c. Juveniles who appear before the court in any capacity shall be deemed to be wards of the court and protected accordingly.

d. Nothing in this act shall affect the jurisdiction of other courts over offenses committed after a juvenile under the jurisdiction of the court reaches the age of 18 years.

L.1982, c. 77, § 5, eff. Dec. 31, 1983.

2A:4A–25. Transfer from other courts

Except as provided in section 4 of P.L.1982, c. 77 (C. 2A:4A–23), and unless jurisdiction has been waived under section 7 of P.L.1982, c. 77 (C. 2A:4A–26), if during the pendency in any other court of a case charging a person with a crime, offense or violation, it is ascertained that such person was a juvenile at the time of the crime, offense or violation charged, such court shall immediately transfer such case to the Superior Court, Chancery Division, Family Part. The Family Part shall thereupon proceed in the same manner as if the case had been instituted under this chapter in the first instance.

L.1982, c. 77, § 6, eff. Dec. 31, 1983. Amended by L.1991, c. 91, § 5, eff. April 9, 1991; L.1995, c. 280, § 3, eff. Dec. 15, 1995.

2A:4A–26. Referral to another court without juvenile's consent

a. On motion of the prosecutor, the court shall, without the consent of the juvenile, waive jurisdiction over a case and refer that case from the Superior Court, Chancery Division, Family Part to the appropriate court and prosecuting authority having jurisdiction if it finds, after hearing, that:

(1) The juvenile was 14 years of age or older at the time of the charged delinquent act; and

(2) There is probable cause to believe that the juvenile committed a delinquent act or acts which if committed by an adult would constitute:

(a) Criminal homicide other than death by auto, strict liability for drug induced deaths, pursuant to N.J.S.2C:35–9, robbery which would constitute a crime of the first degree, carjacking, aggravated sexual assault, sexual assault, aggravated assault which would constitute a crime of the second degree, kidnapping, aggravated arson, or gang criminality pursuant to section 1 of P.L.2007, c. 341 (C.2C:33–29) where the underlying crime is enumerated in this subparagraph or promotion of organized street crime pursuant to section 2 of P.L.2007, c..341 (C.2C:33–30) which would constitute a crime of the first or second degree which is enumerated in this subparagraph; or

(b) A crime committed at a time when the juvenile had previously been adjudicated delinquent, or convicted, on the basis of any of the offenses enumerated in subsection a.(2)(a); or

(c) A crime committed at a time when the juvenile had previously been sentenced and confined in an adult penal institution; or

(d) An offense against a person committed in an aggressive, violent and willful manner, other than an offense enumerated in subsection a.(2)(a) of this section, or the unlawful possession of a firearm, destructive device or other prohibited weapon, arson or death by auto if the juvenile was operating the vehicle under the influence of an intoxicating liquor, narcotic, hallucinogenic or habit producing drug; or

(e) A violation of N.J.S.2C:35–3, N.J.S.2C:35–4, or N.J.S.2C:35–5; or

(f) Crimes which are a part of a continuing criminal activity in concert with two or more persons and the circumstances of the crimes show the juvenile has knowingly devoted himself to criminal activity as a source of livelihood; or

(g) An attempt or conspiracy to commit any of the acts enumerated in paragraph (a), (d) or (e) of this subsection; or

(h) Theft of an automobile pursuant to chapter 20 of Title 2C of the New Jersey Statutes; or

(i) Possession of a firearm with a purpose to use it unlawfully against the person of another under subsection a. of N.J.S.2C:39–4, or the crime of aggravated assault, aggravated criminal sexual contact, burglary or escape if, while in the course of committing or attempting to commit the crime including the immediate flight therefrom, the juvenile possessed a firearm; or

(j) Computer criminal activity which would be a crime of the first or second degree pursuant to section 4 or section 10 of P.L.1984. c.184 (C.2C:20–25 or C.2C:20–31); and

(3) Except with respect to any of the acts enumerated in subparagraph (a), (i) or (j) of paragraph (2) of subsection a. of this section, or with respect to any acts enumerated in subparagraph (e) of paragraph (2) of subsection a. of this section which involve the distribution for pecuniary gain of any controlled dangerous substance or controlled substance analog while on any property used for school purposes which is owned by or leased to any school or school board, or within 1,000 feet of such school property or while on any school bus, or any attempt or conspiracy to commit any of those acts, the State has shown that the nature and circumstances of the charge or the prior record of the juvenile are sufficiently serious that the interests of the public require waiver.

b. (Deleted by amendment, P.L.1999, c. 373).

c. An order referring a case shall incorporate therein not only the alleged act or acts upon which the referral is premised, but also all other delinquent acts arising out of or related to the same transaction.

d. A motion seeking waiver shall be filed by the prosecutor within 30 days of receipt of the complaint. This time limit shall not, except for good cause shown, be extended.

e. If the juvenile can show that the probability of his rehabilitation by the use of the procedures, services and facilities available to the court prior to the juvenile reaching the age of 19 substantially outweighs the reasons for waiver, waiver shall not be granted. This subsection shall not apply with respect to a juvenile 16 years of age or older who is charged with committing any of the acts enumerated in subparagraph (a), (i) or (j) of paragraph (2) of subsection a. of this section or with respect to a violation of N.J.S.2C:35–3, N.J.S.2C:35–4 or section 1 of P.L.1998, c. 26 (C. 2C:39–4.1).

f. The Attorney General shall develop for dissemination to the county prosecutors those guidelines or directives deemed necessary or appropriate to ensure the uniform application of this section throughout the State.

L.1982, c. 77, § 7, eff. Dec. 31, 1983. Amended by L.1987, c. 106, § 23, operative July 9, 1987; L.1991, c. 30, § 1, eff. Feb. 21, 1991; L.1991, c. 83, § 3, eff. April 2, 1991; L.1991, c. 91, § 6, eff. April 9, 1991; L.1999, c. 373, § 1; L.2003, c. 39, § 8, eff. April 14, 2003; L.2007, c. 341, § 3, eff. Jan. 13, 2008.

2A:4A–27. Referral to other court at election of juvenile

Any juvenile 14 years of age or older charged with delinquency may elect to have the case transferred to the appropriate court having jurisdiction. Any juvenile under 14 years of age charged with an offense which, if committed by an adult, would constitute murder under N.J.S. 2C:11–3 may elect to have the case transferred to the appropriate court having jurisdiction.

L.1982, c. 77, § 8, eff. Dec. 31, 1983.

2A:4A–28. Effect of referral to other court

Whenever a case is referred to another court as provided by section 7 of P.L.1982, c. 77 (C. 2A:4A–26) or section 8 of P.L.1982, c. 77 (C. 2A:4A–27), that case shall thereafter proceed in the same manner as if the case had been instituted in that court in the first instance.

L.1982, c. 77, § 9, eff. Dec. 31, 1983. Amended by L.1995, c. 280, § 4, eff. Dec. 15, 1995.

2A:4A–29. Use of juvenile's testimony at referral hearing

No testimony of a juvenile at a hearing pursuant to section 7 of P.L.1982, c. 77 (C. 2A:4A–26) or section 8 of P.L.1982, c. 77 (C. 2A:4A–27) shall be admissible for any purpose in any hearing to determine delinquency or guilt of any offense.

L.1982, c. 77, § 10, eff. Dec. 31, 1983. Amended by L.1995, c. 280, § 5, eff. Dec. 15, 1995.

2A:4A–30. Complaints and petitions

a. Complaints charging delinquency may be signed by any person who has knowledge of the facts alleged to constitute delinquency or is informed of such facts and believes that they are true. The complaint shall be filed with the clerk of the court and shall set forth:

(1) The name, address, and date of birth of the juvenile;

(2) The name and address of the juvenile's parents or guardian and, if the juvenile is in custody of some other person, the name and address of the custodian;

(3) The date, time, manner, and place of the acts alleged as the basis of the complaint;

(4) A citation of the law or ordinance allegedly violated by the juvenile; and

(5) The signature of the complainant.

b. Petitions alleging that a juvenile-family crisis exists shall be signed by court intake services pursuant to section 8 of P.L.1982, c. 80 (C. 2A:4A–83). The petition shall be filed with the clerk of the court and shall set forth:

(1) The name, address, and date of birth of the juvenile;

(2) The name and address of the juvenile's parents or guardian and, if the juvenile is in custody of some other person, the name and address of the custodian;

(3) The date, time, manner, and place of the behavior, conduct, or condition alleged as the basis of the petition; and

(4) The signature of the petitioner.

c. Complaints and petitions shall be in such form as prescribed by the Rules of Court.

L.1982, c. 77, § 11, eff. Dec. 31, 1983.

2A:4A–31. Taking into custody

a. A juvenile may be taken into custody:

(1) Pursuant to an order or warrant of any court having jurisdiction; or

(2) For delinquency, when there has been no process issued by a court, by a law enforcement officer, pursuant to the laws of arrest and the Rules of Court.

b. Except where delinquent conduct is alleged, a juvenile may be taken into short-term custody by a law enforcement officer without order of the court when:

(1) The officer has reasonable grounds to believe that the health and safety of the juvenile is seriously in danger and taking into immediate custody is necessary for his protection;

(2) The officer has reasonable grounds to believe the juvenile has left the home and care of his parents or guardian without the consent of such persons; or

(3) An agency legally charged with the supervision of a child has notified the law enforcement agency that the child has run away from out of home placement, provided, however, that in any case where the law enforcement officer believes that the juvenile is an "abused or neglected child" as defined in section 1 of P.L.1974, c. 119 (C. 9:6–8.21), the officer shall handle the case pursuant to the procedure set forth in that act.

c. The taking of a juvenile into custody shall not be construed as an arrest, but shall be deemed a measure to protect the health, morals and well-being of the juvenile.

L.1982, c. 77, § 12, eff. Dec. 31, 1983.

2A:4A–32. Short-term custody

a. Under no circumstances shall any juvenile taken into short-term custody under section 12 of P.L.1982, c. 77 (C. 2A:4A–31) be held more than six hours. A juvenile taken into short-term custody shall not be retained in a detention facility or jail. As used in this section, the juvenile-family crisis intervention unit means that unit established pursuant to P.L.1982, c. 80 (C. 2A:4A–76 et seq.).

b. An officer taking a juvenile into short-term custody shall inform the juvenile of the reason for custody and shall where possible transport, or arrange to have the juvenile transported to his home. The officer releasing a juvenile from such custody shall inform the juvenile's parents or guardian and the juvenile-family crisis intervention unit of the reason for taking the juvenile into custody and may, if he believes further services are needed, inform the juvenile and his parents of the nature and location of appropriate services.

c. A law enforcement officer taking a juvenile into short-term custody may transport the juvenile to the home of a relative of the juvenile or to the home of another responsible adult or make arrangement for such transportation where the officer reasonably believes that the child will be provided with adequate care and supervision and that the child will remain in custody of the adult until such time as the juvenile-family crisis intervention unit can bring about the child's return home or an alternative living arrangement or out of home placement. A law enforcement officer placing a juvenile with a relative or responsible adult shall immediately notify the juvenile-family crisis intervention unit of this fact and the reason for taking the juvenile into custody.

d. A law enforcement officer acting reasonably and in good faith pursuant to this section in releasing a juvenile to a person other than a parent of a juvenile is immune from civil or criminal liability for his action. A person other than a parent of the juvenile who receives a child pursuant to this section and who acts reasonably and in good faith in doing so is immune from civil or criminal liability for the act of receiving the child. Immunity shall not release a person from liability under any other laws, including the laws regulating licensed child care or prohibiting child abuse and neglect. *L.1982, c. 77, § 13, eff. Dec. 31, 1983. Amended by L.1995, c. 280, § 6, eff. Dec. 15, 1995.*

2A:4A-33. Taking into custody; notice to parents

a.[1] Any person taking a juvenile into custody shall immediately notify the parents, or the juvenile's guardian, if any, that the juvenile has been taken into custody. *L.1982, c. 77, § 14, eff. Dec. 31, 1983.*

[1] So in original, there is no subsection b.

2A:4A-34. Criteria for placing juvenile in detention

a. Except as otherwise provided in this section, a juvenile charged with an act of delinquency shall be released pending the disposition of a case, if any, to any person or agency provided for in this section upon assurance being received that such person or persons accept responsibility for the juvenile and will bring him before the court as ordered.

b. No juvenile shall be placed in detention without the permission of a judge or the court intake service.

c. A juvenile charged with delinquency may not be placed or retained in detention under this act prior to disposition, except as otherwise provided by law, unless:

(1) Detention is necessary to secure the presence of the juvenile at the next hearing as evidenced by a demonstrable record of recent willful failure to appear at juvenile court proceedings or to remain where placed by the court or the court intake service or the juvenile is subject to a current warrant for failure to appear at court proceedings which is active at the time of arrest; or

(2) The physical safety of persons or property of the community would be seriously threatened if the juvenile were not detained and the juvenile is charged with an offense which, if committed by an adult, would constitute a crime of the first, second or third degree or one of the following crimes of the fourth degree: aggravated assault; stalking; criminal sexual contact; bias intimidation; failure to control or report a dangerous fire; possession of a prohibited weapon or device in violation of N.J.S.2C:39-3; or unlawful possession of a weapon in violation of N.J.S.2C:39-5; or

(3) With respect to a juvenile charged with an offense which, if committed by an adult, would constitute a crime of the fourth degree other than those enumerated in paragraph (2) of this subsection, or a disorderly persons or petty disorderly persons offense, and with respect to a juvenile charged with an offense enumerated in subsection c. when the criteria for detention are not met, the juvenile may be temporarily placed in a shelter or other non-secure placement if a parent or guardian cannot be located or will not accept custody of the juvenile. Police and court intake personnel shall make all reasonable efforts to locate a parent or guardian to accept custody of the juvenile prior to requesting or approving the juvenile's placement in a shelter or other non-secure placement. If, after the initial detention hearing, continued placement is necessary, the juvenile shall be returned to a shelter or other non-secure placement.

d. The judge or court intake officer prior to making a decision of detention shall consider and, where appropriate, employ any of the following alternatives:

(1) Release to parents;

(2) Release on juvenile's promise to appear at next hearing;

(3) Release to parents, guardian or custodian upon written assurance to secure the juvenile's presence at the next hearing;

(4) Release into care of a custodian or public or private agency reasonably capable of assisting the juvenile to appear at the next hearing;

(5) Release with imposition of restrictions on activities, associations, movements and residence reasonably related to securing the appearance of the juvenile at the next hearing;

(6) Release with required participation in a home detention program;

(7) Placement in a shelter care facility; or

(8) Imposition of any other restrictions other than detention or shelter care reasonably related to securing the appearance of the juvenile.

e. In determining whether detention is appropriate for the juvenile, the following factors shall be considered:

(1) The nature and circumstances of the offense charged;

(2) The age of the juvenile;

(3) The juvenile's ties to the community;

(4) The juvenile's record of prior adjudications, if any; and

(5) The juvenile's record of appearance or nonappearance at previous court proceedings.

f. No juvenile 11 years of age or under shall be placed in detention unless he is charged with an offense which, if committed by an adult, would be a crime of the first or second degree or arson.

g. If the court places a juvenile in detention, the court shall state on the record its reasons for that detention.

h. For purposes of this section, a failure to appear at juvenile court proceedings or to remain where placed by the court or the court intake service shall be deemed recent if it occurred within the 12 months immediately preceding the detention hearing, or if it occurred within the period of 12 to 24 months preceding the detention hearing and the juvenile is unable to demonstrate a record of voluntary compliance with any subsequent court appearance and placement requirements.

L.1982, c. 77, § 15, eff. Dec. 31, 1983. Amended by L.1989, c. 306, § 1, eff. Jan. 12, 1990; L.2005, c. 361, § 1, eff. May 1, 2006.

2A:4A–35. Release of juvenile on own recognizance

A juvenile charged with delinquency may be released at either the police or court level on his own recognizance if all of the following circumstances have been met:

a. The nature of the offense charged is not such that a danger to the community would exist if the juvenile were released;

b. There is no parent, guardian or other appropriate adult custodian to whom the juvenile could be released and all reasonable measures have been exhausted by either police or court personnel to locate and contact any such person;

c. The juvenile is at least 14 years of age;

d. The identity and address of the juvenile are verified through a positive form of identification; and

e. Reasonable certainty exists on the part of the releasing authority that upon release, the juvenile will return to school or home safely and will appear at his hearing.

L.1982, c. 77, § 16, eff. Dec. 31, 1983.

2A:4A–36. Detention of waiver cases

a. If the court waives jurisdiction over a case and refers that case to the appropriate court and prosecuting authority, there shall be a hearing before the court waiving jurisdiction to decide whether to remand the juvenile to a juvenile or adult detention facility. The decision shall be based on the best interests of the juvenile and protection of the public, and shall take into account such factors as the juvenile's age and maturity, the nature and circumstances of the offense charged,

the juvenile's prior offense history, the programs at each of the detention facilities, and any other relevant factors.

b. No juvenile who has been waived to an appropriate adult court may be remanded to an adult detention facility prior to the hearing provided for in subsection a. L.1982, c. 77, § 17, eff. Dec. 31, 1983.

2A:4A–37. Place of detention or shelter

a. The Juvenile Justice Commission established pursuant to section 2 of P.L.1995, c. 284 (C.52:17B–170) shall specify the place where a juvenile may be detained; and the Department of Children and Families shall specify where a juvenile may be placed in shelter.

b. No juvenile shall be placed in detention or shelter care in any place other than that specified by the Juvenile Justice Commission or Department of Children and Families as provided in subsection a.

c. A juvenile being held for a charge under this act or for a violation of or contempt in connection with a violation of Title 39 of the Revised Statutes, chapter 7 of Title 12 of the Revised Statutes or N.J.S.2C:33–13, including a juvenile who has reached the age of 18 years after being charged, shall not be placed in any prison, jail or lockup nor detained in any police station, except that if no other facility is reasonably available a juvenile may be held in a police station in a place other than one designed for the detention of prisoners and apart from any adult charged with or convicted of a crime for a brief period if such holding is necessary to allow release to his parent, guardian, other suitable person, or approved facility. No juvenile shall be placed in a detention facility which has reached its maximum population capacity, as designated by the Juvenile Justice Commission.

d. No juvenile charged with delinquency shall be transferred to an adult county jail solely by reason of having reached age 18. The following standards shall apply to any juvenile who has been placed on probation pursuant to section 24 of P.L.1982, c. 77 (C.2A:4A–43) and who violates the conditions of that probation after reaching the age of 18; who has been placed on parole pursuant to the provisions of the "Parole Act of 1979," P. L.1979, c. 441 (C.30:4–123.45 et seq.) and who violates the conditions of that parole after reaching the age of 18;or who is arrested after reaching the age of 18 on a warrant emanating from the commission of an act of juvenile delinquency:

(1) In the case of a person 18 years of age but less than 20 years of age, the court, upon application by any interested party, shall determine the place of detention, taking into consideration the age and maturity of the person, whether the placement of the person in a juvenile detention facility would present a risk to the safety of juveniles residing at the facility, the likelihood that the person would influence in a negative manner juveniles incarcerated at the facility, whether the facility has sufficient space available for juveniles and any other

factor the court deems appropriate. Upon application at any time by the juvenile detention facility administrator or any other interested party, the court may order that the person be relocated to the county jail. The denial of an application shall not preclude subsequent applications based on a change in circumstances or information that was not previously made available to the court. The determination of the place of detention shall be made in a summary manner;

(2) In the case of a person 20 years of age or older, the person shall be incarcerated in the county jail unless good cause is shown.

e. (1) The Juvenile Justice Commission and the Department of Children and Families shall promulgate such rules and regulations from time to time as deemed necessary to establish minimum physical facility and program standards for juvenile detention facilities or shelters under their respective supervision.

(2) The Juvenile Justice Commission and the Department of Children and Families, in consultation with the appropriate county administrator of the county facility or shelter, shall assign a maximum population capacity for each juvenile detention facility or shelter based on minimum standards for these facilities.

f. (1) Where either the Juvenile Justice Commission or the Department of Children and Families determines that a juvenile detention facility or shelter under its control or authority is regularly over the maximum population capacity or is in willful and continuous disregard of the minimum standards for these facilities or shelters, the commission or department may restrict new admissions to the facility or shelter.

(2) Upon making such determination, the commission or department shall notify the governing body of the appropriate county of its decision to impose such a restriction, which notification shall include a written statement specifying the reasons therefor and corrections to be made. If the commission or department shall determine that no appropriate action has been initiated by the administrator of the facility or shelter within 60 days following such notification to correct the violations specified in the notification, it shall order that such juvenile detention facility or shelter shall immediately cease to admit juveniles. The county shall be entitled to a hearing where such a restriction is imposed by the commission or department.

(3) Any juvenile detention facility or shelter so restricted shall continue under such order until such time as the commission or department determines that the violation specified in the notice has been corrected or that the facility or shelter has initiated actions which will ensure the correction of said violations.

(4) Upon the issuance of an order to cease admissions to a juvenile detention facility or shelter, the commission or department shall determine whether other juvenile detention facilities or shelters have adequate room for admitting juveniles and shall assign the juveniles to the facilities or shelters on the basis of available space; provided that the department shall not assign the juvenile to a facility or shelter where such facility or shelter is at the maximum population. A juvenile detention facility or shelter ordered to accept a juvenile shall do so within five days following the receipt of an order to accept admission of such juvenile.

(5) A juvenile detention facility or shelter restricted by an order to cease admissions shall assume responsibility for the transportation of a juvenile sent to another juvenile detention facility or shelter so long as the order shall remain in effect.

(6) A facility or shelter receiving juveniles pursuant to paragraph (4) of this subsection shall receive from the sending county a reasonable and appropriate per diem allowance for each juvenile sent to the facility, such allowance to be used for the custody, care, maintenance, and any other services normally provided by the county to juveniles in the facility or shelter and which reflects all county expenditures in maintaining such juvenile, including a proportionate share of all buildings and grounds costs, personnel costs, including fringe benefits, administrative costs and all other direct and indirect costs.

(7) The governing body of a county whose juvenile detention facility or shelter has been prohibited from accepting new admissions, and whose juveniles have been assigned to other juvenile detention facilities or shelters, shall appropriate an amount to pay the county receiving such juveniles for all expenses incurred pursuant to paragraph (6) of this subsection.

L.1982, c. 77, § 18, eff. Dec. 31, 1983. Amended by L.1989, c. 125, § 2, eff. July 3, 1989; L.1995, c. 280, § 7, eff. Dec. 15, 1995; L.2003, c. 287, § 1, eff. Jan. 14, 2004; L.2006, c. 47, § 16, eff. July 1, 2006.

2A:4A–38. Detention hearing

a. When a juvenile is taken into custody and detained a complaint shall be filed forthwith as provided by the Rules of Court. The court shall determine whether detention is required pursuant to the criteria provided for in section 15 of P.L.1982, c. 77 (C. 2A:4A–34).

b. Notice of the detention hearing, either oral or written, stating the time, place, and purpose of the hearing shall be given to the juvenile and to the juvenile's parent or parents, or guardian, if any, if they can be contacted.

c. The detention hearing shall be conducted in accordance with the Rules of Court and shall be attended by the juvenile and one or both parents, or guardian, but may take place in the absence of parent or guardian if such notice or process fails to produce their attendance.

d. When the judge finds that detention is not necessary or required, the court shall order the juvenile's release and may place such conditions, if any, upon release as are consistent with the purposes of this act, the Rules of Court, and as are provided for in section 15 of P.L.1982, c. 77 (C. 2A:4A–34).

e. The initial detention hearing shall be held no later than the morning following the juvenile's placement in detention including weekends and holidays.

f. If a delinquency complaint has not been filed by the time the initial detention hearing has been held, the juvenile shall be released from custody immediately.

g. When the court determines that detention is necessary pursuant to section 15 of P.L.1982, c. 77 (C. 2A:4A–34), the court order continuing the juvenile's detention shall be supported by reasons and findings of fact on the record.

h. If the juvenile is not represented by counsel at the initial detention hearing and if the court continues the juvenile's detention after the hearing, the court shall forthwith schedule a second detention hearing to be held within two court days thereafter at which time the juvenile shall be represented by counsel as provided by the Rules of Court.

i. There shall be a probable cause determination where a juvenile has been charged with delinquency and has been placed in detention, within two court days after the initial hearing or, where a second detention hearing is necessary pursuant to subsection h. of this section, at that hearing.

j. A detention review hearing with counsel shall be held within 14 court days of the prior detention hearing and if detention is continued, detention review hearings shall be held thereafter at intervals not to exceed 21 court days.

k. When a juvenile is detained, an adjudicatory hearing shall be held no later than 30 days from the date of detention. If no adjudicatory hearing is held within 30 days, the court shall, within 72 hours of a motion by the juvenile, fix a date certain for the adjudicatory hearing unless an extension is granted by the court for good cause shown. Written notice of any application for a postponement shall be sent to the juvenile's counsel who shall have the right to be heard on the application.

l. When a juvenile has been adjudicated delinquent and is awaiting transfer to a dispositional alternative that does not involve a secure residential or out-of-home placement and continued detention is necessary, the juvenile shall be transferred to a non-secure facility.

L.1982, c. 77, § 19, eff. Dec. 31, 1983. Amended by L.1989, c. 306, § 2, eff. Jan. 12, 1990; L.1995, c. 280, § 8, eff. Dec. 15, 1995.

2A:4A–39. Right to counsel

a. A juvenile shall have the right, as provided by the Rules of Court, to be represented by counsel at every critical stage in the proceeding which, in the opinion of the court may result in the institutional commitment of the juvenile.

b. During every court proceeding in a delinquency case, the waiving of any right afforded to a juvenile shall be done in the following manner:

(1) A juvenile who is found to be competent may not waive any rights except in the presence of and after consultation with counsel, and unless a parent has first been afforded a reasonable opportunity to consult with the juvenile and the juvenile's counsel regarding this decision. The parent or guardian may not waive the rights of a competent juvenile.

(2) Any such waiver shall be executed in writing or recorded. Before the court may accept a waiver, the court shall question the juvenile and his counsel to determine if the juvenile is knowingly, willingly and voluntarily waiving his right. If the court finds after questioning the juvenile that the waiver is not being made voluntarily and intelligently, the waiver shall be denied.

(3) An incompetent juvenile may not waive any right. A guardian ad litem shall be appointed for the juvenile who may waive rights after consultation with counsel for the juvenile, and the juvenile.

(4) Waivers shall be executed in the language regularly spoken by the juvenile.

L.1982, c. 77, § 20, eff. Dec. 31, 1983.

2A:4A–40. Rights of juveniles

All defenses available to an adult charged with a crime, offense or violation shall be available to a juvenile charged with committing an act of delinquency.

All rights guaranteed to criminal defendants by the Constitution of the United States and the Constitution of this State, except the right to indictment, the right to trial by jury and the right to bail, shall be applicable to cases arising under this act.

L.1982, c. 77, § 21, eff. Dec. 31, 1983.

2A:4A–41. Dispositional hearing

Where a juvenile is adjudicated delinquent, the disposition of the case shall be entered within 30 days of such adjudication if the juvenile has been placed in a detention center or shelter-care facility. If the juvenile is so placed and no disposition of the case is made after 30 days, the court shall, upon motion of the juvenile, fix a date certain for the dispositional hearing which shall be within 10 days of the motion, unless an extension is granted by the court for good cause shown. Disposition shall be made in all other cases within 60 days unless an extension is granted by the court where good cause is shown. The court shall provide written notice to the proper parties as to the date, time and place of such hearing and do so sufficiently in advance of the hearing to allow adequate time for preparation.

L.1982, c. 77, § 22, eff. Dec. 31, 1983.

2A:4A–42. Predispositional evaluation

a. Before making a disposition, the court may refer the juvenile to an appropriate individual, agency or institution for examination and evaluation.

b. In arriving at a disposition, the court may also consult with such individuals and agencies as may be appropriate to the juvenile's situation, including the county probation division, the Department of Children and Families, the Juvenile Justice Commission established pursuant to section 2 of P.L.1995, c. 284 (C.52:17B–170), the county youth services commission, school personnel, clergy, law enforcement authorities, family members and other interested and knowledgeable parties. In so doing, the court may convene a predispositional conference to discuss and recommend disposition.

c. The predisposition report ordered pursuant to the Rules of Court may include a statement by the victim of the offense for which the juvenile has been adjudicated delinquent or by the nearest relative of a homicide victim. The statement may include the nature and extent of any physical harm or psychological or emotional harm or trauma suffered by the victim, the extent of any loss to include loss of earnings or ability to work suffered by the victim and the effect of the crime upon the victim's family. The probation division shall notify the victim or nearest relative of a homicide victim of his right to make a statement for inclusion in the predisposition report if the victim or relative so desires. Any statement shall be made within 20 days of notification by the probation division. The report shall further include information on the financial resources of the juvenile. This information shall be made available on request to the Victims of Crime Compensation Board established pursuant to section 3 of P.L.1971, c. 317 (C.52:4B–3) or to any officer authorized under section 3 of P.L.1979, c. 396 (C.2C:46–4) to collect payment of an assessment, restitution or fine. Any predisposition report prepared pursuant to this section shall include an analysis of the circumstances attending the commission of the act, the impact of the offense on the community, the offender's history of delinquency or criminality, family situation, financial resources, the financial resources of the juvenile's parent or guardian, and information concerning the parent or guardian's exercise of supervision and control relevant to commission of the act.

Information concerning financial resources included in the report shall be made available to any officer authorized to collect payment on any assessment, restitution or fine.

L.1982, c. 77, § 23, eff. Dec. 31, 1983. Amended by L.1986, c. 85, § 2, eff. Aug. 14, 1986; L.1995, c. 135, § 7; L.1995, c. 280, § 9, eff. Dec. 15, 1995; L.2001, c. 408, § 2, eff. Aug. 1, 2002; L.2004, c. 130, § 5, eff. Aug. 27, 2004; L.2006, c. 47, § 17, eff. July 1, 2006.

2A:4A–43. Disposition of delinquency cases

a. In determining the appropriate disposition for a juvenile adjudicated delinquent the court shall weigh the following factors:

(1) The nature and circumstances of the offense;

(2) The degree of injury to persons or damage to property caused by the juvenile's offense;

(3) The juvenile's age, previous record, prior social service received and out-of-home placement history;

(4) Whether the disposition supports family strength, responsibility and unity and the well-being and physical safety of the juvenile;

(5) Whether the disposition provides for reasonable participation by the child's parent, guardian, or custodian, provided, however, that the failure of a parent or parents to cooperate in the disposition shall not be weighed against the juvenile in arriving at an appropriate disposition;

(6) Whether the disposition recognizes and treats the unique physical, psychological and social characteristics and needs of the child;

(7) Whether the disposition contributes to the developmental needs of the child, including the academic and social needs of the child where the child has mental retardation or learning disabilities;

(8) Any other circumstances related to the offense and the juvenile's social history as deemed appropriate by the court;

(9) The impact of the offense on the victim or victims;

(10) The impact of the offense on the community; and

(11) The threat to the safety of the public or any individual posed by the child.

b. If a juvenile is adjudged delinquent, and except to the extent that an additional specific disposition is required pursuant to subsection e. or f. of this section, the court may order incarceration pursuant to section 25 of P.L.1982, c. 77 (C.2A:4A–44) or any one or more of the following dispositions:

(1) Adjourn formal entry of disposition of the case for a period not to exceed 12 months for the purpose of determining whether the juvenile makes a satisfactory adjustment, and if during the period of continuance the juvenile makes such an adjustment, dismiss the complaint; provided that if the court adjourns formal entry of disposition of delinquency for a violation of an offense defined in chapter 35 or 36 of Title 2C of the New Jersey Statutes the court shall assess the mandatory penalty set forth in N.J.S.2C:35–15 but may waive imposition of the penalty set forth in N.J.S.2C:35–16 for juveniles adjudicated delinquent;

(2) Release the juvenile to the supervision of the juvenile's parent or guardian;

(3) Place the juvenile on probation to the chief probation officer of the county or to any other suitable person who agrees to accept the duty of probation supervision for a period not to exceed three years upon such written conditions as the court deems will aid rehabilitation of the juvenile;

(4) Transfer custody of the juvenile to any relative or other person determined by the court to be qualified to care for the juvenile;

(5) Place the juvenile under the care and responsibility of the Department of Children and Families so that the commissioner may designate a division or organizational unit in the department pursuant to P.L.1951, c. 138 (C.30:4C–1 et seq.) for the purpose of providing services in or out of the home. Within 14 days, unless for good cause shown, but not later than 30 days, the Department of Children and Families shall submit to the court a service plan, which shall be presumed valid, detailing the specifics of any disposition order. The plan shall be developed within the limits of fiscal and other resources available to the department. If the court determines that the service plan is inappropriate, given existing resources, the department may request a hearing on that determination;

(6) Place the juvenile under the care and custody of the Commissioner of Human Services for the purpose of receiving the services of the Division of Developmental Disabilities of that department, provided that the juvenile has been determined to be eligible for those services under P.L.1965, c. 59, s.16 (C.30:4–25.4);

(7) Commit the juvenile, pursuant to applicable laws and the Rules of Court governing civil commitment, to the Department of Children and Families under the responsibility of the Division of Child Behavioral Health Services for the purpose of placement in a suitable public or private hospital or other residential facility for the treatment of persons who are mentally ill, on the ground that the juvenile is in need of involuntary commitment;

(8) Fine the juvenile an amount not to exceed the maximum provided by law for such a crime or offense if committed by an adult and which is consistent with the juvenile's income or ability to pay and financial responsibility to the juvenile's family, provided that the fine is specially adapted to the rehabilitation of the juvenile or to the deterrence of the type of crime or offense. If the fine is not paid due to financial limitations, the fine may be satisfied by requiring the juvenile to submit to any other appropriate disposition provided for in this section;

(9) Order the juvenile to make restitution to a person or entity who has suffered loss resulting from personal injuries or damage to property as a result of the offense for which the juvenile has been adjudicated delinquent. The court may determine the reasonable amount, terms and conditions of restitution. If the juvenile participated in the offense with other persons, the participants shall be jointly and severally responsible for the payment of restitution. The court shall not require a juvenile to make full or partial restitution if the juvenile reasonably satisfies the court that the juvenile does not have the means to make restitution and could not reasonably acquire the means to pay restitution;

(10) Order that the juvenile perform community services under the supervision of a probation division or other agency or individual deemed appropriate by the court. Such services shall be compulsory and reasonable in terms of nature and duration. Such services may be performed without compensation, provided that any money earned by the juvenile from the performance of community services may be applied towards any payment of restitution or fine which the court has ordered the juvenile to pay;

(11) Order that the juvenile participate in work programs which are designed to provide job skills and specific employment training to enhance the employability of job participants. Such programs may be without compensation, provided that any money earned by the juvenile from participation in a work program may be applied towards any payment of restitution or fine which the court has ordered the juvenile to pay;

(12) Order that the juvenile participate in programs emphasizing self-reliance, such as intensive outdoor programs teaching survival skills, including but not limited to camping, hiking and other appropriate activities;

(13) Order that the juvenile participate in a program of academic or vocational education or counseling, such as a youth service bureau, requiring attendance at sessions designed to afford access to opportunities for normal growth and development. This may require attendance after school, evenings and weekends;

(14) Place the juvenile in a suitable residential or nonresidential program for the treatment of alcohol or narcotic abuse, provided that the juvenile has been determined to be in need of such services;

(15) Order the parent or guardian of the juvenile to participate in appropriate programs or services when the court has found either that such person's omission or conduct was a significant contributing factor towards the commission of the delinquent act, or, under its authority to enforce litigant's rights, that such person's omission or conduct has been a significant contributing factor towards the ineffective implementation of a court order previously entered in relation to the juvenile;

(16) (a) Place the juvenile in a nonresidential program operated by a public or private agency, providing intensive services to juveniles for specified hours, which may include education, counseling to the juvenile and the juvenile's family if appropriate, vocational training, employment counseling, work or other services;

(b) Place the juvenile under the custody of the Juvenile Justice Commission established pursuant to section 2 of P.L.1995, c. 284 (C.52:17B–170) for placement with any private group home or private residential facility with which the commission has entered into a purchase of service contract;

(17) Instead of or in addition to any disposition made according to this section, the court may postpone, suspend, or revoke for a period not to exceed two years the driver's license, registration certificate, or both of any juvenile who used a motor vehicle in the course of committing an act for which the juvenile was adjudicated delinquent. In imposing this disposition and in deciding the duration of the postponement, suspension, or revocation, the court shall consider the severity of the delinquent act and the potential effect of the loss of driving privileges on the juvenile's ability to be rehabilitated. Any postponement, suspension, or revocation shall be imposed consecutively with any custodial commitment;

(18) Order that the juvenile satisfy any other conditions reasonably related to the rehabilitation of the juvenile;

(19) Order a parent or guardian who has failed or neglected to exercise reasonable supervision or control of a juvenile who has been adjudicated delinquent to make restitution to any person or entity who has suffered a loss as a result of that offense. The court may determine the reasonable amount, terms and conditions of restitution; or

(20) Place the juvenile, if eligible, in an appropriate juvenile offender program established pursuant to P.L. 1997, c. 81 (C.30:8–61 et al.).

c. (1) Except as otherwise provided in subsections e. and f. of this section, if the county in which the juvenile has been adjudicated delinquent has a juvenile detention facility meeting the physical and program standards established pursuant to this subsection by the Juvenile Justice Commission, the court may, in addition to any of the dispositions not involving placement out of the home enumerated in this section, incarcerate the juvenile in the youth detention facility in that county for a term not to exceed 60 consecutive days. Counties which do not operate their own juvenile detention facilities may contract for the use of approved commitment programs with counties with which they have established agreements for the use of pre-disposition juvenile detention facilities. The Juvenile Justice Commission shall promulgate such rules and regulations from time to time as deemed necessary to establish minimum physical facility and program standards for the use of juvenile detention facilities pursuant to this subsection.

(2) No juvenile may be incarcerated in any county detention facility unless the county has entered into an agreement with the Juvenile Justice Commission concerning the use of the facility for sentenced juveniles. Upon agreement with the county, the Juvenile Justice Commission shall certify detention facilities which may receive juveniles sentenced pursuant to this subsection and shall specify the capacity of the facility that may be made available to receive such juveniles; provided,

however, that in no event shall the number of juveniles incarcerated pursuant to this subsection exceed 50% of the maximum capacity of the facility.

(3) The court may fix a term of incarceration under this subsection where:

(a) The act for which the juvenile was adjudicated delinquent, if committed by an adult, would have constituted a crime or repetitive disorderly persons offense;

(b) Incarceration of the juvenile is consistent with the goals of public safety, accountability and rehabilitation and the court is clearly convinced that the aggravating factors substantially outweigh the mitigating factors as set forth in section 25 of P.L.1982, c. 77 (C.2A:4A–44); and

(c) The detention facility has been certified for admission of adjudicated juveniles pursuant to paragraph (2).

(4) If as a result of incarceration of adjudicated juveniles pursuant to this subsection, a county is required to transport a predisposition juvenile to a juvenile detention facility in another county, the costs of such transportation shall be borne by the Juvenile Justice Commission.

d. Whenever the court imposes a disposition upon an adjudicated delinquent which requires the juvenile to perform a community service, restitution, or to participate in any other program provided for in this section other than subsection c., the duration of the juvenile's mandatory participation in such alternative programs shall extend for a period consistent with the program goal for the juvenile and shall in no event exceed one year beyond the maximum duration permissible for the delinquent if the juvenile had been committed to a term of incarceration.

e. In addition to any disposition the court may impose pursuant to this section or section 25 of P.L.1982, c. 77 (C.2A:4A–44), the following orders shall be included in dispositions of the adjudications set forth below:

(1) An order of incarceration for a term of the duration authorized pursuant to this section or section 25 of P.L.1982, c. 77 (C.2A:4A–44) or an order to perform community service pursuant to paragraph (10) of subsection b. of this section for a period of at least 60 days, if the juvenile has been adjudicated delinquent for an act which, if committed by an adult, would constitute the crime of theft of a motor vehicle, or the crime of unlawful taking of a motor vehicle in violation of subsection c. of N.J.S.2C:20–10, or the third degree crime of eluding in violation of subsection b. of N.J.S.2C:29–2;

(2) An order of incarceration for a term of the duration authorized pursuant to this section or section 25 of P.L.1982, c. 77 (C.2A:4A–44) which shall include a minimum term of 60 days during which the juvenile shall be ineligible for parole, if the juvenile has been

adjudicated delinquent for an act which, if committed by an adult, would constitute the crime of aggravated assault in violation of paragraph (6) of subsection b. of N.J.S.2C:12–1, the second degree crime of eluding in violation of subsection b. of N.J.S.2C:29–2, or theft of a motor vehicle, in a case in which the juvenile has previously been adjudicated delinquent for an act, which if committed by an adult, would constitute unlawful taking of a motor vehicle or theft of a motor vehicle;

(3) An order to perform community service pursuant to paragraph (10) of subsection b. of this section for a period of at least 30 days, if the juvenile has been adjudicated delinquent for an act which, if committed by an adult, would constitute the fourth degree crime of unlawful taking of a motor vehicle in violation of subsection b. of N.J.S.2C:20–10;

(4) An order of incarceration for a term of the duration authorized pursuant to this section or section 25 of P.L.1982, c. 77 (C.2A:4A–44) which shall include a minimum term of 30 days during which the juvenile shall be ineligible for parole, if the juvenile has been adjudicated delinquent for an act which, if committed by an adult, would constitute the crime of unlawful taking of a motor vehicle in violation of N.J.S.2C:20–10 or the third degree crime of eluding in violation of subsection b. of N.J.S.2C:29–2, and if the juvenile has previously been adjudicated delinquent for an act which, if committed by an adult, would constitute either theft of a motor vehicle, the unlawful taking of a motor vehicle or eluding.

f. (1) The minimum terms of incarceration required pursuant to subsection e. of this section shall be imposed regardless of the weight or balance of factors set forth in this section or in section 25 of P.L.1982, c. 77 (C.2A:4A–44), but the weight and balance of those factors shall determine the length of the term of incarceration appropriate, if any, beyond any mandatory minimum term required pursuant to subsection e. of this section.

(2) When a court in a county that does not have a juvenile detention facility or a contractual relationship permitting incarceration pursuant to subsection c. of this section is required to impose a term of incarceration pursuant to subsection e. of this section, the court may, subject to limitations on commitment to State correctional facilities of juveniles who are under the age of 11 or developmentally disabled, set a term of incarceration consistent with subsection c. which shall be served in a State correctional facility. When a juvenile who because of age or developmental disability cannot be committed to a State correctional facility or cannot be incarcerated in a county facility, the court shall order a disposition appropriate as an alternative to any incarceration required pursuant to subsection e.

(3) For purposes of subsection e. of this section, in the event that a "boot camp" program for juvenile offenders should be developed and is available, a term of commitment to such a program shall be considered a term of incarceration.

g. Whenever the court imposes a disposition upon an adjudicated delinquent which requires the juvenile to perform a community service, restitution, or to participate in any other program provided for in this section, the order shall include provisions which provide balanced attention to the protection of the community, accountability for offenses committed, fostering interaction and dialogue between the offender, victim and community and the development of competencies to enable the child to become a responsible and productive member of the community.

L.1982, c. 77, § 24, eff. Dec. 31, 1983. Amended by L.1988, c. 44, § 16, eff. June 28, 1988; L.1988, c. 72, § 1, eff. July 21, 1988; L.1993, c. 133, § 1, eff. June 3, 1993; L.1995, c. 280, § 10, eff. Dec. 15, 1995; L.1997, c. 81, § 11, eff. Oct. 1, 1997; L.2001, c. 408, § 3, eff. Aug. 1, 2002; L.2004, c. 130, § 6, eff. Aug. 27, 2004; L.2006, c. 47, § 18, eff. July 1, 2006.

2A:4A–43.1.   AIDS and HIV infection testing for juveniles charged with delinquency or adjudicated delinquent for acts constituting sexual assault or aggravated sexual assault

In accordance with section 4 of P.L.1993, c. 364 (C.2C:43–2.2) and in addition to any other disposition authorized pursuant to N.J.S. 2A:4A–43, a court shall order a juvenile charged with delinquency or adjudicated delinquent for an act which if committed by an adult would constitute aggravated sexual assault or sexual assault as defined in subsection a. or c. of N.J.S.2C:14–2 to submit to an approved serological test for acquired immune deficiency syndrome (AIDS) or infection with the human immunodeficiency virus (HIV) or any other related virus identified as a probable causative agent of AIDS.

L.1993, c. 364, § 3, eff. Jan. 4, 1994.

2A:4A–43.2.   Additional penalties for juvenile adjudicated delinquent

In addition to any other penalty imposed by the court, any juvenile adjudicated delinquent for an offense which, if committed by an adult, would constitute criminal mischief pursuant to N.J.S. 2C:17–3, attempting to put another in fear of bodily violence pursuant to section 1 of P.L.1981, c. 282 (C. 2C:33–10), or defacement of private property pursuant to section 2 of P.L.1981, c. 282 (C. 2C:33–11), involving an act of graffiti, may be required either to pay to the owner of the damaged property monetary restitution in the amount of pecuniary damage caused by the act of graffiti or to perform community service, which shall include removing the graffiti from the property, if appropriate. If community service is ordered, it shall be for either not less than 20 days or not less than the number of days necessary to remove the graffiti from the property.

L.1995, c. 251, § 5, eff. Dec. 12, 1995.

2A:4A–43.3. Suspension or postponement of right to operate motor vehicle of person convicted of or adjudicated delinquent for certain violations

Instead of or in addition to any other disposition ordered by the court under section 24 of P.L.1982, c. 77 (C. 2A:4A–43) for an initial act of graffiti committed by a person at least 13 and under 18 years of age, the court, considering the factors provided in paragraph (17) of subsection b. of section 24 of P.L.1983, c. 77 (C. 2A:4A–43), may suspend or postpone for one year that person's right to operate a motor vehicle including a motorized bicycle. In the case of a person who at the time of the imposition of sentence is less than 17 years of age, the period of the suspension of driving privileges authorized herein, including a suspension of the privilege of operating a motorized bicycle, shall commence on the day the sentence is imposed and shall run for a period of one year after the day the person reaches the age of 17 years. If the driving privilege of any person is under revocation, suspension, or postponement for a violation of any provision of this Title or Title 39 of the Revised Statutes at the time of any conviction or adjudication of delinquency for a violation of any offense defined in this section, the revocation, suspension, or postponement period imposed herein shall commence as of the date of termination of the existing revocation, suspension, or postponement.

A second or subsequent offense may result in the suspension or postponement of the person's right to operate a motor vehicle for two years. If a second or subsequent offense occurs during a period when the person has had this right suspended or postponed, the person's right to operate a motor vehicle may be suspended or postponed for an additional two years to run consecutively.

The court before whom any person is convicted of or adjudicated delinquent for a violation shall collect forthwith the New Jersey driver's license or licenses of the person and forward such license or licenses to the Director of the Division of Motor Vehicles along with a report indicating the first and last day of the suspension or postponement period imposed by the court pursuant to this section. If the court is for any reason unable to collect the license or licenses of the person, the court shall cause a report of the conviction or adjudication of delinquency to be filed with the director. That report shall include the complete name, address, date of birth, eye color, and sex of the person and shall indicate the first and last day of the suspension or postponement period imposed by the court pursuant to this section. The court shall inform the person orally and in writing that if the person is convicted of personally operating a motor vehicle during the period of license suspension or postponement imposed pursuant to this section the person shall, upon conviction, be subject to the penalties set forth in R.S. 39:3–40. A person shall be required to acknowledge receipt of the written notice in writing. Failure to receive a written notice or failure to acknowledge in writing the receipt of a written notice

shall not be a defense to a subsequent charge of violation of R.S. 39:3–40. If the person is the holder of a driver's license from another jurisdiction, the court shall not collect the license but shall notify the director who shall notify the appropriate officials in the licensing jurisdiction. The court shall, however, in accordance with the provisions of this section, revoke the person's non-resident driving privileges in this State.

L.1995, c. 251, § 6, eff. Dec. 12, 1995.

2A:4A–43.4. AIDS and HIV infection testing ordered by court under certain circumstances

a. In addition to any other disposition made pursuant to law, a court shall order a juvenile charged with delinquency or adjudicated delinquent for an act which, if committed by an adult would constitute a crime, a disorderly persons offense or a petty disorderly persons offense, to submit to an approved serological test for acquired immune deficiency syndrome (AIDS) or infection with the human immunodeficiency virus (HIV) or any other related virus identified as a probable causative agent of AIDS if:

(1) in the course of the commission of the act, including the immediate flight thereafter or during any investigation or arrest related to that act, a law enforcement officer, the victim or other person suffered a prick from a hypodermic needle, provided there is probable cause to believe that the juvenile is an intravenous user of controlled dangerous substances; or

(2) in the course of the commission of the act, including the immediate flight thereafter or during any investigation or arrest related to that act, a law enforcement officer, the victim or other person had contact with the juvenile which involved or was likely to involve the transmission of bodily fluids.

The court may order a juvenile to submit to an approved serological test for AIDS or infection with the HIV or any other related virus identified as a probable causative agent of AIDS if in the course of the performance of any other law enforcement duties, a law enforcement officer suffers a prick from a hypodermic needle, provided that there is probable cause to believe that the defendant is an intravenous user of controlled dangerous substances, or had contact with the defendant which involved or was likely to involve the transmission of bodily fluids. The court shall issue such an order only upon the request of the law enforcement officer, victim of the offense or other affected person made at the time of indictment, charge or conviction. If a county prosecutor declines to make such an application within 72 hours of being requested to do so by the law enforcement officer, the law enforcement officer may appeal to the Division of Criminal Justice in the Department of Law and Public Safety for that officer to bring the application. The juvenile shall be ordered by the court to submit to such repeat or confirmatory tests as may be medically necessary.

b. A court order issued pursuant to subsection a. of this section shall require testing to be performed as soon as practicable by the Executive Director of the Juvenile Justice Commission pursuant to authority granted to the executive director by sections 6 and 10 of P.L.1976, c. 98 (C. 30:1B–6 and 30:1B–10) or by a provider of health care or at a health care facility licensed pursuant to section 12 of P.L.1971, c. 136 (C. 26:2H–12). The order shall also require that the results of the test be reported to the offender, the appropriate Office of Victim-Witness Advocacy if a victim of an offense is tested, and the affected law enforcement officer. Upon receipt of the result of a test ordered pursuant to subsection a. of this section, the Office of Victim–Witness Advocacy shall provide the victim with appropriate counseling, referral for counseling and if appropriate, referral for health care. The office shall notify the victim or make appropriate arrangements for the victim to be notified of the test result.

c. In addition to any other disposition authorized, a court may order a juvenile at the time of sentencing to reimburse the State for the costs of the tests ordered by subsection a. of this section.

d. The result of a test ordered pursuant to subsection a. of this section shall be confidential and health care providers and employees of the Juvenile Justice Commission, the Office of Victim-Witness Advocacy, a health care facility or counseling service shall not disclose the result of a test performed pursuant to this section except as authorized herein or as otherwise authorized by law or court order. The provisions of this section shall not be deemed to prohibit disclosure of a test result to the person tested.

e. Persons who perform tests ordered pursuant to subsection a. of this section in accordance with accepted medical standards for the performance of such tests shall be immune from civil and criminal liability arising from their conduct.

f. This section shall not be construed to preclude or limit any other testing for AIDS or infection with the HIV or any other related virus identified as a probable causative agent of AIDS which is otherwise permitted by statute, court rule or common law.

L.1996, c. 115, § 8, eff. Jan. 9, 1997.

2A:4A–44. Incarceration—Aggravating and mitigating factors

a. (1) Except as provided in subsections e. and f. of section 24 of P.L.1982, c. 77 (C.2A:4A–43), in determining whether incarceration is an appropriate disposition, the court shall consider the following aggravating circumstances:

(a) The fact that the nature and circumstances of the act, and the role of the juvenile therein, was committed in an especially heinous, cruel, or depraved manner;

(b) The fact that there was grave and serious harm inflicted on the victim and that based upon the juvenile's age or mental capacity the juvenile knew or reasonably should have known that the victim was particularly vulnerable or incapable of resistance due to advanced age, disability, ill-health, or extreme youth, or was for any other reason substantially incapable;

(c) The character and attitude of the juvenile indicate that the juvenile is likely to commit another delinquent or criminal act;

(d) The juvenile's prior record and the seriousness of any acts for which the juvenile has been adjudicated delinquent;

(e) The fact that the juvenile committed the act pursuant to an agreement that the juvenile either pay or be paid for the commission of the act and that the pecuniary incentive was beyond that inherent in the act itself;

(f) The fact that the juvenile committed the act against a policeman or other law enforcement officer, correctional employee or fireman, acting in the performance of his duties while in uniform or exhibiting evidence of his authority, or the juvenile committed the act because of the status of the victim as a public servant;

(g) The need for deterring the juvenile and others from violating the law;

(h) The fact that the juvenile knowingly conspired with others as an organizer, supervisor, or manager to commit continuing criminal activity in concert with two or more persons and the circumstances of the crime show that he has knowingly devoted himself to criminal activity as part of an ongoing business activity;

(i) The fact that the juvenile on two separate occasions was adjudged a delinquent on the basis of acts which if committed by an adult would constitute crimes;

(j) The impact of the offense on the victim or victims;

(k) The impact of the offense on the community; and

(*l*) The threat to the safety of the public or any individual posed by the child.

(2) In determining whether incarceration is an appropriate disposition the court shall consider the following mitigating circumstances:

(a) The child is under the age of 14;

(b) The juvenile's conduct neither caused nor threatened serious harm;

(c) The juvenile did not contemplate that the juvenile's conduct would cause or threaten serious harm;

(d) The juvenile acted under a strong provocation;

(e) There were substantial grounds tending to excuse or justify the juvenile's conduct, though failing to establish a defense;

(f) The victim of the juvenile's conduct induced or facilitated its commission;

(g) The juvenile has compensated or will compensate the victim for the damage or injury that the victim has sustained, or will participate in a program of community service;

(h) The juvenile has no history of prior delinquency or criminal activity or has led a law-abiding life for a substantial period of time before the commission of the present act;

(i) The juvenile's conduct was the result of circumstances unlikely to recur;

(j) The character and attitude of the juvenile indicate that the juvenile is unlikely to commit another delinquent or criminal act;

(k) The juvenile is particularly likely to respond affirmatively to noncustodial treatment;

(l) The separation of the juvenile from the juvenile's family by incarceration of the juvenile would entail excessive hardship to the juvenile or the juvenile's family;

(m) The willingness of the juvenile to cooperate with law enforcement authorities;

(n) The conduct of the juvenile was substantially influenced by another person more mature than the juvenile.

b. (1) There shall be a presumption of nonincarceration for any crime or offense of the fourth degree or less committed by a juvenile who has not previously been adjudicated delinquent or convicted of a crime or offense.

(2) Where incarceration is imposed, the court shall consider the juvenile's eligibility for release under the law governing parole.

c. The following juveniles shall not be committed to a State juvenile facility:

(1) Juveniles age 11 or under unless adjudicated delinquent for the crime of arson or a crime which, if committed by an adult, would be a crime of the first or second degree; and

(2) Juveniles who are developmentally disabled as defined in paragraph (1) of subsection a. of section 3 of P.L.1977, c. 82 (C.30:6D–3).

d. (1) When the court determines that, based on the consideration of all the factors set forth in subsection a., the juvenile shall be incarcerated, unless it orders the incarceration pursuant to subsection c. of section 24 of P.L.1982, c. 77 (C.2A:4A–43), it shall state on the record the reasons for imposing incarceration, including any findings with regard to these factors, and commit the juvenile to the custody of the Juvenile Justice Commission which shall provide for the juvenile's placement in a suitable juvenile facility pursuant to the conditions set forth in this subsection and for terms not to exceed the maximum terms as provided herein for what would constitute the following crimes if committed by an adult:

(a) Murder under 2C:11–3a(1) or (2) ..... 20 years

(b) Murder under 2C:11–3a(3) .... 10 years

(c) Crime of the first degree, except murder . 4 years

(d) Crime of the second degree .... 3 years

(e) Crime of the third degree .... 2 years

(f) Crime of the fourth degree .... 1 year

(g) Disorderly persons offense .... 6 months

(2) Except as provided in subsection e. of section 24 of P.L.1982, c. 77 (C.2A:4A–43), the period of confinement shall continue until the appropriate paroling authority determines that such a person should be paroled; except that in no case shall the period of confinement and parole exceed the maximum provided by law for such offense. However, if a juvenile is approved for parole prior to serving one-third of any term imposed for any crime of the first, second or third degree, including any extended term imposed pursuant to paragraph (3) or (4) of this subsection, or one-fourth of any term imposed for any other crime the granting of parole shall be subject to approval of the sentencing court. Prior to approving parole, the court shall give the prosecuting attorney notice and an opportunity to be heard. If the court denies the parole of a juvenile pursuant to this paragraph it shall state its reasons in writing and notify the parole board, the juvenile and the juvenile's attorney. The court shall have 30 days from the date of notice of the pending parole to exercise the power granted under this paragraph. If the court does not respond within that time period, the parole will be deemed approved.

Any juvenile committed under this act who is released on parole prior to the expiration of the juvenile's maximum term may be retained under parole supervision for a period not exceeding the unserved portion of the term and any term of post-incarceration supervision imposed pursuant to paragraph (5) of this subsection. The Parole Board, the juvenile, the juvenile's attorney, the juvenile's parent or guardian or, with leave of the court any other interested party, may make a motion to the court, with notice to the prosecuting attorney, for the return of the child from a juvenile facility prior to his parole and provide for an alternative disposition which would not exceed the duration of the original time to be served in the facility. Nothing contained in this paragraph shall be construed to limit the authority of the Parole Board as set forth in section 15 of P.L.1979, c. 441 (C.30:4–123.59).

(3) Upon application by the prosecutor, the court may sentence a juvenile who has been convicted of a crime of the first, second, or third degree if committed by an adult, to an extended term of incarceration beyond the maximum set forth in paragraph (1) of this subsection, if it finds that the juvenile was adjudged delinquent on at least two separate occasions, for offenses which, if committed by an adult, would constitute a crime of the first or second degree, and was previously committed to an adult or juvenile facility.

The extended term shall not exceed five additional years for an act which would constitute murder and shall not exceed two additional years for all other crimes of the first degree or second degree, if committed by an adult, and one additional year for a crime of the third degree, if committed by an adult.

(4) Upon application by the prosecutor, when a juvenile is before the court at one time for disposition of three or more unrelated offenses which, if committed by an adult, would constitute crimes of the first, second or third degree and which are not part of the same transaction, the court may sentence the juvenile to an extended term of incarceration not to exceed the maximum of the permissible term for the most serious offense for which the juvenile has been adjudicated plus two additional years.

(5) Every disposition that includes a term of incarceration shall include a term of post-incarceration supervision equivalent to one-third of the term of incarceration imposed. During the term of post-incarceration supervision the juvenile shall remain in the community and in the legal custody of the Juvenile Justice Commission established pursuant to section 2 of P.L.1995, c. 284 (C.52:17B–170) in accordance with the rules of the parole board, unless the appropriate parole board panel determines that post-incarceration supervision should be revoked and the juvenile returned to custody in accordance with the procedures and standards set forth in sections 15 through 21 of P.L.1979, c. 441 (C.30:4–123.59 through C.30:4–123.65). The term of post-incarceration supervision shall commence upon release from incarceration or parole, whichever is later. A term of post-incarceration supervision imposed pursuant to this paragraph may be terminated by the appropriate parole board panel if the juvenile has made a satisfactory adjustment in the community while on parole or under such supervision, if continued supervision is not required and if the juvenile has made full payment of any fine or restitution.

L.1982, c. 77, § 25, eff. Dec. 31, 1983. Amended by L.1993, c. 133, § 2, eff. June 3, 1993; L.1995, c. 280, § 11, eff. Dec. 15, 1995; L.2001, c. 408, § 4, eff. Aug. 1, 2002.

2A:4A–44.1. Agreements between department of corrections and county for incarceration of certain juveniles in county juvenile detention facility

The Juvenile Justice Commission established pursuant to section 2 of P.L.1995, c. 284 (C. 52:17B–170) may enter into an agreement with any county concerning the use of that county's juvenile detention facility for the housing of juveniles the court has placed under the custody of the commission for placement in State correctional facilities only if the county's juvenile detention facility is not over its maximum rated capacity.

Unless the contract otherwise provides or the commission so directs in order to provide for the secure and orderly operation of the facility, a juvenile placed in a county detention facility pursuant to the provisions of this act shall not be segregated from the juveniles otherwise placed in the county detention facility or excluded from any program or activity offered in that facility.

Any contract entered into pursuant to this section shall ensure that educational, vocational, mental health, health and rehabilitative services are provided to the juveniles and that these services are, at minimum, equivalent to those provided to adjudicated juveniles in State-operated facilities.

L.1992, c. 211, § 1, eff. April 1, 1993. Amended by L.1995, c. 280, § 12, eff. Dec. 15, 1995.

2A:4A–45. Retention of jurisdiction

a. The court shall retain jurisdiction over any case in which it has entered a disposition under paragraph 7 of subsection b. or subsection c. of section 24 of P.L.1982, c. 77 (C. 2A:4A–43) or under section 25 of P.L.1982, c. 77 (C. 2A:4A–44) for the duration of that disposition of commitment or incarceration and may substitute any disposition otherwise available to it under section 24 of P.L.1982, c. 77 (C. 2A:4A–43) other than incarceration.

b. Except as provided for in subsection a., the court shall retain jurisdiction over any case in which it has entered a disposition under section 24 of P.L.1982, c. 77 (C. 2A:4A–43) and may at any time for the duration of that disposition, if after hearing, and notice to the prosecuting attorney, it finds violation of the conditions of the order of disposition, substitute any other disposition which it might have made originally.

c. The court may by its order retain jurisdiction in any other case.

L.1982, c. 77, § 26, eff. Dec. 31, 1983. Amended by L.1995, c. 280, § 13, eff. Dec. 15, 1995.

2A:4A–46. Disposition of juvenile-family crisis

a. The court may order any disposition in a juvenile-family crisis provided for in paragraphs (2), (4), (5), (6), (7) and (13) of subsection b. of section 24 of P.L.1982, c. 77 (C.2A:4A–43) or other disposition specifically provided for in P.L.1982, c. 80 (C.2A:4A–76 et seq.).

b. No juvenile involved in a juvenile-family crisis shall be committed to or placed in any institution or facility established for the care of delinquent children or in any facility, other than an institution for the mentally retarded, a mental hospital or facility for the care of persons addicted to controlled dangerous substances, which physically restricts such juvenile committed to or placed in it.

L.1982, c. 77, § 27, eff. Dec. 31, 1983. Amended by L.1995, c. 280, § 14, eff. Dec. 15, 1995.

2A:4A–47. Termination of orders of disposition

a. Any order of disposition entered in a case under this act shall terminate when the juvenile who is the subject of the order attains the age of 18, or three years from the date of the order whichever is later unless such order involves incarceration or is sooner terminated by its terms or by order of the court.

b. Any agency providing services pursuant to any court ordered disposition shall give prior notice to the court at least 30 days before terminating these services which notice shall include the date of intended termination.

c. Upon termination of an order of disposition, maximum term, parole or community supervision the court shall enter an order requiring payment of any amounts owed by the juvenile or the parent or guardian of the juvenile pursuant to the court ordered disposition and shall file a copy of the order with the Clerk of the Superior Court who shall enter the following information upon the record of docketed judgments;

(1) the name of the juvenile or the juvenile's parent or guardian as judgment debtor;

(2) the amount of the assessment imposed pursuant to section 2 of P.L.1979, c. 396 (C. 2C:43–3.1) and the Victims of Crime Compensation Board as a judgment creditor in that amount;

(3) the amount of any restitution ordered and the name of any person entitled to receive payment as judgment creditors in the amount and according to the priority set by the court;

(4) the amount of any fine and the governmental entity entitled to receive payment pursuant to section 3 of P.L.1979, c. 396 (C. 2C:46–4.)

(5) the amount of the mandatory Drug Enforcement and Demand Reduction penalty imposed;

(6) the amount of the forensic laboratory fee imposed; and

(7) the date of the order.

Where there is more than one judgment creditor the creditors shall be given priority consistent with the provisions of section 13 of P.L.1991, c. 329 (C. 2C:46–4.1). These entries shall have the same force as a civil judgment docketed in the Superior Court. *L.1982, c. 77, § 28, eff. Dec. 31, 1983. Amended by L.1995, c. 281, § 1, eff. Dec. 15, 1995.*

2A:4A–48. Effect of disposition

No disposition under this act shall operate to impose any of the civil disabilities ordinarily imposed by virtue of a criminal conviction, nor shall a juvenile be deemed a criminal by reason of such disposition.

The disposition of a case under this act shall not be admissible against the juvenile in any criminal or penal case or proceeding in any other court except for consideration in sentencing, or as otherwise provided by law. *L.1982, c. 77, § 29, eff. Dec. 31, 1983.*

2A:4A–49. Repealed by L.1995, c. 284, § 11, eff. Dec. 15, 1995

ARTICLE 3. INFORMATION RELATING TO JUVENILES

2A:4A–60. Disclosure of juvenile information; penalties for disclosure

Text of section effective until November 1, 2010.

Disclosure of juvenile information; penalties for disclosure.

a. Social, medical, psychological, legal and other records of the court and probation division, and records of law enforcement agencies, pertaining to juveniles charged as a delinquent or found to be part of a juvenile-family crisis, shall be strictly safeguarded from public inspection. Such records shall be made available only to:

(1) Any court or probation division;

(2) The Attorney General or county prosecutor;

(3) The parents or guardian and to the attorney of the juvenile;

(4) The Department of Human Services or Department of Children and Families, if providing care or custody of the juvenile;

(5) Any institution or facility to which the juvenile is currently committed or in which the juvenile is placed;

(6) Any person or agency interested in a case or in the work of the agency keeping the records, by order of the court for good cause shown, except that information concerning adjudications of delinquency, records of custodial confinement, payments owed on assessments imposed pursuant to section 2 of P.L.1979, c. 396 (C.2C:43–3.1) or restitution ordered following conviction of a crime or adjudication of delinquency, and the juvenile's financial resources, shall be made available upon request to the Victims of Crime Compensation Agency established pursuant to section 2 of P.L.2007, c. 95 (C.52:4B–3.2), which shall keep such information and records confidential;

(7) The Juvenile Justice Commission established pursuant to section 2 of P.L.1995, c. 284 (C.52:17B–170);

(8) Law enforcement agencies for the purpose of reviewing applications for a permit to purchase a handgun or firearms purchaser identification card;

(9) Any potential party in a subsequent civil action for damages related to an act of delinquency committed by a juvenile, including the victim or a member of the victim's immediate family, regardless of whether the action has been filed against the juvenile; provided, however, that records available under this paragraph shall be limited to official court documents, such as complaints, pleadings and orders, and that such records may be disclosed by the recipient only in connection with asserting legal claims or obtaining indemnification on behalf of the victim or the victim's family and otherwise shall be safeguarded from disclosure to other members of the public. Any potential party in a civil action related to the juvenile offense may file a motion

with the civil trial judge seeking to have the juvenile's social, medical or psychological records admitted into evidence in a civil proceeding for damages;

(10) Any potential party in a subsequent civil action for damages related to an act of delinquency committed by a juvenile, including the victim or a member of the victim's immediate family, regardless of whether the action has been filed against the juvenile; provided, however, that records available under this paragraph shall be limited to police or investigation reports concerning acts of delinquency, which shall be disclosed by a law enforcement agency only with the approval of the County Prosecutor's Office or the Division of Criminal Justice. Prior to disclosure, all personal information regarding all individuals, other than the requesting party and the arresting or investigating officer, shall be redacted. Such records may be disclosed by the recipient only in connection with asserting legal claims or obtaining indemnification on behalf of the victim or the victim's family, and otherwise shall be safeguarded from disclosure to other members of the public;

(11) The Office of the Child Advocate established pursuant to P.L.2005, c. 155 (C.52:27EE–1 et al.). Disclosure of juvenile information received by the child advocate pursuant to this paragraph shall be in accordance with the provisions of section 76 of P.L.2005, c. 155 (C.52:27EE–76); and

(12) Law enforcement agencies with respect to information available on the juvenile central registry maintained by the courts pursuant to subsection g. of this section, including, but not limited to: records of official court documents, such as complaints, pleadings and orders for the purpose of obtaining juvenile arrest information; juvenile disposition information; juvenile pretrial information; and information concerning the probation status of a juvenile.

b. Records of law enforcement agencies may be disclosed for law enforcement purposes, or for the purpose of reviewing applications for a permit to purchase a handgun or a firearms purchaser identification card to any law enforcement agency of this State, another state or the United States, and the identity of a juvenile under warrant for arrest for commission of an act that would constitute a crime if committed by an adult may be disclosed to the public when necessary to execution of the warrant.

c. At the time of charge, adjudication or disposition, information as to the identity of a juvenile charged with an offense, the offense charged, the adjudication and disposition shall, upon request, be disclosed to:

(1) The victim or a member of the victim's immediate family;

(2) (Deleted by amendment P.L.2005, c. 165).

(3) On a confidential basis, the principal of the school where the juvenile is enrolled for use by the principal and such members of the staff and faculty of the school as the principal deems appropriate for maintaining order, safety or discipline in the school or to planning programs relevant to the juvenile's educational and social development, provided that no record of such information shall be maintained except as authorized by regulation of the Department of Education; or

(4) A party in a subsequent legal proceeding involving the juvenile, upon approval by the court.

d. A law enforcement or prosecuting agency shall, at the time of a charge, adjudication or disposition, send written notice to the principal of the school where the juvenile is enrolled of the identity of the juvenile charged, the offense charged, the adjudication and the disposition if:

(1) The offense occurred on school property or a school bus, occurred at a school-sponsored function or was committed against an employee or official of the school; or

(2) The juvenile was taken into custody as a result of information or evidence provided by school officials; or

(3) The offense, if committed by an adult, would constitute a crime, and the offense:

(a) resulted in death or serious bodily injury or involved an attempt or conspiracy to cause death or serious bodily injury; or

(b) involved the unlawful use or possession of a firearm or other weapon; or

(c) involved the unlawful manufacture, distribution or possession with intent to distribute a controlled dangerous substance or controlled substance analog; or

(d) was committed by a juvenile who acted with a purpose to intimidate an individual or group of individuals because of race, color, religion, sexual orientation or ethnicity; or

(e) would be a crime of the first, second, or third degree.

Information provided to the principal pursuant to this subsection shall be maintained by the school and shall be treated as confidential but may be made available to such members of the staff and faculty of the school as the principal deems appropriate for maintaining order, safety or discipline in the school or for planning programs relevant to a juvenile's educational and social development.

e. Nothing in this section prohibits a law enforcement or prosecuting agency from providing the principal of a school with information identifying one or more juveniles who are under investigation or have been taken into custody for commission of any act that would constitute an offense if committed by an adult when the law enforcement or prosecuting agency determines that the information may be useful to the principal in maintaining order, safety or discipline in the school or in planning programs relevant to the juvenile's educational and social development. Information provided to the principal pursuant to this subsection shall be treated as confidential but may be made available to such members of the staff and faculty of the school as the principal deems appropriate for maintaining order, safety or discipline in the school or for planning programs relevant to the juvenile's educational and social development. No information provided pursuant to this section shall be maintained.

f. Information as to the identity of a juvenile adjudicated delinquent, the offense, the adjudication and the disposition shall be disclosed to the public where the offense for which the juvenile has been adjudicated delinquent if committed by an adult, would constitute a crime of the first, second or third degree, or aggravated assault, destruction or damage to property to an extent of more than $500.00, unless upon application at the time of disposition the juvenile demonstrates a substantial likelihood that specific and extraordinary harm would result from such disclosure in the specific case. Where the court finds that disclosure would be harmful to the juvenile, the reasons therefor shall be stated on the record.

g. (1) Nothing in this section shall prohibit the establishment and maintaining of a central registry of the records of law enforcement agencies relating to juveniles for the purpose of exchange between State and local law enforcement agencies and prosecutors of this State, another state, or the United States. These records of law enforcement agencies shall be available on a 24–hour basis.

(2) Certain information and records relating to juveniles in the central registry maintained by the courts, as prescribed in paragraph (12) of subsection a. of this section, shall be available to State and local law enforcement agencies and prosecutors on a 24–hour basis.

h. Whoever, except as provided by law, knowingly discloses, publishes, receives, or makes use of or knowingly permits the unauthorized use of information concerning a particular juvenile derived from records listed in subsection a. or acquired in the course of court proceedings, probation, or police duties, shall, upon conviction thereof, be guilty of a disorderly persons offense.

i. Juvenile delinquency proceedings.

(1) Except as provided in paragraph (2) of this subsection, the court may, upon application by the juvenile or his parent or guardian, the prosecutor or any other interested party, including the victim or complainant or members of the news media, permit public attendance during any court proceeding at a delinquency case, where it determines that a substantial likelihood that specific harm to the juvenile would not result. The court shall have the authority to limit and control attendance in any manner and to the extent it deems appropriate;

(2) The court or, in cases where the county prosecutor has entered an appearance, the county prosecutor

shall notify the victim or a member of the victim's immediate family of any court proceeding involving the juvenile and the court shall permit the attendance of the victim or family member at the proceeding except when, prior to completing testimony as a witness, the victim or family member is properly sequestered in accordance with the law or the Rules Governing the Courts of the State of New Jersey or when the juvenile or the juvenile's family member shows, by clear and convincing evidence, that such attendance would result in a substantial likelihood that specific harm to the juvenile would result from the attendance of the victim or a family member at a proceeding or any portion of a proceeding and that such harm substantially outweighs the interest of the victim or family member to attend that portion of the proceeding;

(3) The court shall permit a victim, or a family member of a victim to make a statement prior to ordering a disposition in any delinquency proceeding involving an offense that would constitute a crime if committed by an adult.

j. The Department of Education, in consultation with the Attorney General, shall adopt, pursuant to the "Administrative Procedure Act," P.L.1968, c. 410 (C.52:14B–1 et seq.), rules and regulations concerning the creation, maintenance and disclosure of pupil records including information acquired pursuant to this section.

L.1982, c. 79, § 1, eff. Dec. 31, 1983. Amended by L.1994, c. 56, § 1, eff. June 29, 1994; L.1995, c. 135, § 8; L.1995, c. 280, § 15, eff. Dec. 15, 1995; L.2001, c. 3, § 2, eff. Jan. 16, 2001; L.2001, c. 191, § 1; L.2001, c. 407, § 1, eff. Jan. 8, 2002; L.2005, c. 155, § 106, eff. Jan. 17, 2006; L.2005, c. 165, § 1, eff. Aug. 5, 2005; L.2006, c. 47, § 19, eff. July 1, 2006; L.2009, c. 157, § 3, eff. Nov. 20, 2009.

2A:4A–60. Disclosure of juvenile information; penalties for disclosure

Text of section effective on November 1, 2010.

Disclosure of juvenile information; penalties for disclosure.

a. Social, medical, psychological, legal and other records of the court and probation division, and records of law enforcement agencies, pertaining to juveniles charged as a delinquent or found to be part of a juvenile-family crisis, shall be strictly safeguarded from public inspection. Such records shall be made available only to:

(1) Any court or probation division;

(2) The Attorney General or county prosecutor;

(3) The parents or guardian and to the attorney of the juvenile;

(4) The Department of Human Services or Department of Children and Families, if providing care or custody of the juvenile;

(5) Any institution or facility to which the juvenile is currently committed or in which the juvenile is placed;

(6) Any person or agency interested in a case or in the work of the agency keeping the records, by order of the court for good cause shown, except that information concerning adjudications of delinquency, records of custodial confinement, payments owed on assessments imposed pursuant to section 2 of P.L.1979, c. 396 (C.2C:43–3.1) or restitution ordered following conviction of a crime or adjudication of delinquency, and the juvenile's financial resources, shall be made available upon request to the Victims of Crime Compensation Agency established pursuant to section 2 of P.L.2007, c. 95 (C.52:4B–3.2), which shall keep such information and records confidential;

(7) The Juvenile Justice Commission established pursuant to section 2 of P.L.1995, c. 284 (C.52:17B–170);

(8) Law enforcement agencies for the purpose of reviewing applications for a permit to purchase a handgun or firearms purchaser identification card;

(9) Any potential party in a subsequent civil action for damages related to an act of delinquency committed by a juvenile, including the victim or a member of the victim's immediate family, regardless of whether the action has been filed against the juvenile; provided, however, that records available under this paragraph shall be limited to official court documents, such as complaints, pleadings and orders, and that such records may be disclosed by the recipient only in connection with asserting legal claims or obtaining indemnification on behalf of the victim or the victim's family and otherwise shall be safeguarded from disclosure to other members of the public. Any potential party in a civil action related to the juvenile offense may file a motion with the civil trial judge seeking to have the juvenile's social, medical or psychological records admitted into evidence in a civil proceeding for damages;

(10) Any potential party in a subsequent civil action for damages related to an act of delinquency committed by a juvenile, including the victim or a member of the victim's immediate family, regardless of whether the action has been filed against the juvenile; provided, however, that records available under this paragraph shall be limited to police or investigation reports concerning acts of delinquency, which shall be disclosed by a law enforcement agency only with the approval of the County Prosecutor's Office or the Division of Criminal Justice. Prior to disclosure, all personal information regarding all individuals, other than the requesting party and the arresting or investigating officer, shall be redacted. Such records may be disclosed by the recipient only in connection with asserting legal claims or obtaining indemnification on behalf of the victim or the victim's family, and otherwise shall be safeguarded from disclosure to other members of the public;

(11) The Office of the Child Advocate established pursuant to P.L.2005, c. 155 (C.52:27EE–1 et al.).

Disclosure of juvenile information received by the child advocate pursuant to this paragraph shall be in accordance with the provisions of section 76 of P.L.2005, c. 155 (C.52:27EE–76);

(12) Law enforcement agencies with respect to information available on the juvenile central registry maintained by the courts pursuant to subsection g. of this section, including, but not limited to: records of official court documents, such as complaints, pleadings and orders for the purpose of obtaining juvenile arrest information; juvenile disposition information; juvenile pretrial information; and information concerning the probation status of a juvenile; and

(13) A Court Appointed Special Advocate as defined in section 1 of P.L.2009 c. 217 (C.2A:4A–92).

b. Records of law enforcement agencies may be disclosed for law enforcement purposes, or for the purpose of reviewing applications for a permit to purchase a handgun or a firearms purchaser identification card to any law enforcement agency of this State, another state or the United States, and the identity of a juvenile under warrant for arrest for commission of an act that would constitute a crime if committed by an adult may be disclosed to the public when necessary to execution of the warrant.

c. At the time of charge, adjudication or disposition, information as to the identity of a juvenile charged with an offense, the offense charged, the adjudication and disposition shall, upon request, be disclosed to:

(1) The victim or a member of the victim's immediate family;

(2) (Deleted by amendment P.L.2005, c. 165).

(3) On a confidential basis, the principal of the school where the juvenile is enrolled for use by the principal and such members of the staff and faculty of the school as the principal deems appropriate for maintaining order, safety or discipline in the school or to planning programs relevant to the juvenile's educational and social development, provided that no record of such information shall be maintained except as authorized by regulation of the Department of Education; or

(4) A party in a subsequent legal proceeding involving the juvenile, upon approval by the court.

d. A law enforcement or prosecuting agency shall, at the time of a charge, adjudication or disposition, send written notice to the principal of the school where the juvenile is enrolled of the identity of the juvenile charged, the offense charged, the adjudication and the disposition if:

(1) The offense occurred on school property or a school bus, occurred at a school-sponsored function or was committed against an employee or official of the school; or

(2) The juvenile was taken into custody as a result of information or evidence provided by school officials; or

(3) The offense, if committed by an adult, would constitute a crime, and the offense:

(a) resulted in death or serious bodily injury or involved an attempt or conspiracy to cause death or serious bodily injury; or

(b) involved the unlawful use or possession of a firearm or other weapon; or

(c) involved the unlawful manufacture, distribution or possession with intent to distribute a controlled dangerous substance or controlled substance analog; or

(d) was committed by a juvenile who acted with a purpose to intimidate an individual or group of individuals because of race, color, religion, sexual orientation or ethnicity; or

(e) would be a crime of the first, second, or third degree.

Information provided to the principal pursuant to this subsection shall be maintained by the school and shall be treated as confidential but may be made available to such members of the staff and faculty of the school as the principal deems appropriate for maintaining order, safety or discipline in the school or for planning programs relevant to a juvenile's educational and social development.

e. Nothing in this section prohibits a law enforcement or prosecuting agency from providing the principal of a school with information identifying one or more juveniles who are under investigation or have been taken into custody for commission of any act that would constitute an offense if committed by an adult when the law enforcement or prosecuting agency determines that the information may be useful to the principal in maintaining order, safety or discipline in the school or in planning programs relevant to the juvenile's educational and social development. Information provided to the principal pursuant to this subsection shall be treated as confidential but may be made available to such members of the staff and faculty of the school as the principal deems appropriate for maintaining order, safety or discipline in the school or for planning programs relevant to the juvenile's educational and social development. No information provided pursuant to this section shall be maintained.

f. Information as to the identity of a juvenile adjudicated delinquent, the offense, the adjudication and the disposition shall be disclosed to the public where the offense for which the juvenile has been adjudicated delinquent if committed by an adult, would constitute a crime of the first, second or third degree, or aggravated assault, destruction or damage to property to an extent of more than $500.00, unless upon application at the time of disposition the juvenile demonstrates a substantial likelihood that specific and extraordinary harm would result from such disclosure in the specific case. Where the court finds that disclosure would be harmful to the juvenile, the reasons therefor shall be stated on the record.

g. (1) Nothing in this section shall prohibit the establishment and maintaining of a central registry of the records of law enforcement agencies relating to juveniles for the purpose of exchange between State and local law enforcement agencies and prosecutors of this State, another state, or the United States. These records of law enforcement agencies shall be available on a 24-hour basis.

(2) Certain information and records relating to juveniles in the central registry maintained by the courts, as prescribed in paragraph (12) of subsection a. of this section, shall be available to State and local law enforcement agencies and prosecutors on a 24-hour basis.

h. Whoever, except as provided by law, knowingly discloses, publishes, receives, or makes use of or knowingly permits the unauthorized use of information concerning a particular juvenile derived from records listed in subsection a. or acquired in the course of court proceedings, probation, or police duties, shall, upon conviction thereof, be guilty of a disorderly persons offense.

i. Juvenile delinquency proceedings.

(1) Except as provided in paragraph (2) of this subsection, the court may, upon application by the juvenile or his parent or guardian, the prosecutor or any other interested party, including the victim or complainant or members of the news media, permit public attendance during any court proceeding at a delinquency case, where it determines that a substantial likelihood that specific harm to the juvenile would not result. The court shall have the authority to limit and control attendance in any manner and to the extent it deems appropriate;

(2) The court or, in cases where the county prosecutor has entered an appearance, the county prosecutor shall notify the victim or a member of the victim's immediate family of any court proceeding involving the juvenile and the court shall permit the attendance of the victim or family member at the proceeding except when, prior to completing testimony as a witness, the victim or family member is properly sequestered in accordance with the law or the Rules Governing the Courts of the State of New Jersey or when the juvenile or the juvenile's family member shows, by clear and convincing evidence, that such attendance would result in a substantial likelihood that specific harm to the juvenile would result from the attendance of the victim or a family member at a proceeding or any portion of a proceeding and that such harm substantially outweighs the interest of the victim or family member to attend that portion of the proceeding;

(3) The court shall permit a victim, or a family member of a victim to make a statement prior to ordering a disposition in any delinquency proceeding involving an offense that would constitute a crime if committed by an adult.

j. The Department of Education, in consultation with the Attorney General, shall adopt, pursuant to the "Administrative Procedure Act," P.L.1968, c. 410 (C.52:14B–1 et seq.), rules and regulations concerning the creation, maintenance and disclosure of pupil records including information acquired pursuant to this section.

L.1982, c. 79, § 1, eff. Dec. 31, 1983. Amended by L.1994, c. 56, § 1, eff. June 29, 1994; L.1995, c. 135, § 8; L.1995, c. 280, § 15, eff. Dec. 15, 1995; L.2001, c. 3, § 2, eff. Jan. 16, 2001; L.2001, c. 191, § 1; L.2001, c. 407, § 1, eff. Jan. 8, 2002; L.2005, c. 155, § 106, eff. Jan. 17, 2006; L.2005, c. 165, § 1, eff. Aug. 5, 2005; L.2006, c. 47, § 19, eff. July 1, 2006; L.2009, c. 157, § 3, eff. Nov. 20, 2009; L.2009, c. 217, § 2, eff. Nov. 1, 2010.

2A:4A–60.1. Rules governing disclosure of juvenile records

The Supreme Court of New Jersey may adopt Rules of Court governing the disclosure to State and local law enforcement agencies and prosecutors of information and records relating to juveniles in the central registry maintained by the courts pursuant to paragraph (2) of subsection g. of section 1 of P.L.1982, c. 79 (C.2A:4A–60).

L.2001, c. 191, § 2, eff. Sept. 1, 2001.

2A:4A–60.2. Limitation upon disclosure of statements made during a suicide or mental health screening

Except as otherwise required by law, any statement made by a juvenile in the course of a suicide or mental health screening, conducted with or without the juvenile's consent, or reports or records produced pursuant to such suicide or mental health screening, shall not be:

a. disclosed, except by an attorney representing the juvenile and with the juvenile's consent, to the court, prosecutor, or any law enforcement officer; or

b. used in any investigation or delinquency or criminal proceeding involving the juvenile that is currently pending or subsequently initiated.

L.2007, c. 315, § 4, eff. Jan. 13, 2008.

2A:4A–60.3. Disclosure of reports or records relating to mental health services restricted prior to court's adjudication

Reports or records relating to mental health services provided to a juvenile prior to an adjudication of delinquency or a finding of guilt, regardless of whether such mental health services were provided with or without the consent of the juvenile, may be disclosed to the court only after an adjudication of delinquency or a finding of guilt has been entered; provided however, an attorney representing a juvenile, with the juvenile's consent, may disclose such reports or records prior to the adjudication of delinquency or finding of guilt. The provisions of this section shall not be construed to limit in any manner the applicability of any privilege or law

that otherwise prohibits disclosure of a juvenile's mental health records.

L.2007, c. 315, § 13, eff. Jan. 13, 2008.

2A:4A–61. Fingerprint records; photographs of juveniles

a. Fingerprints of a juvenile may be taken only in the following circumstances:

(1) Where latent fingerprints are found during the investigation of an offense and a law enforcement officer has reason to believe that they are those of a juvenile, he may, with the consent of the court or juvenile and his parent or guardian fingerprint the juvenile for the purpose of comparison with the latent fingerprints. Fingerprint records taken pursuant to this paragraph may be retained by the department or agency taking them and shall be destroyed when the purpose for the taking of fingerprints has been fulfilled.

(2) Where a juvenile is detained in or committed to an institution, that institution may fingerprint the juvenile for the purpose of identification. Fingerprint records taken pursuant to this paragraph may be retained by the institution taking them and shall be destroyed when the purpose for taking them has been fulfilled, except that if the juvenile was detained or committed as the result of an adjudication of delinquency, the fingerprint records may be retained by the institution.

(3) Where a juvenile 14 years of age or older is charged with delinquency on the basis of an act which, if committed by an adult, would constitute a crime, fingerprint records taken pursuant to this paragraph may be retained by a law enforcement agency for criminal identification purposes.

b. No juvenile under the age of 14 shall be photographed for criminal identification purposes without the consent of the court or of the juvenile and his parent or guardian.

c. Fingerprints of a juvenile shall be taken if the juvenile is adjudicated delinquent on the basis of an act which, if committed by an adult, would constitute a crime.

d. Fingerprints taken pursuant to subsection c. of this section shall be taken according to the fingerprint system of identification established by the Superintendent of State Police on the forms prescribed and shall be forwarded without delay to the State Bureau of Identification together with such information concerning the juvenile and the adjudication as the Superintendent may require. The State Bureau of Identification shall retain records received pursuant to this subsection for the sole purpose of exchange between State or local law enforcement agencies of this State, and law enforcement agencies of another state or the United States.

L.1982, c. 79, § 2, eff. Dec. 31, 1983. Amended by L.1994, c. 56, § 2, eff. June 29, 1994.

2A:4A–62. Sealing of records

a. On motion of a person who has been the subject of a complaint filed under this act or on its own motion, the court may vacate its order and findings and order the nondisclosure of social, medical, psychological, legal and other records of the court and probation services, and records of law enforcement agencies if it finds:

(1) Two years have elapsed since the final discharge of the person from legal custody or supervision, or two years have elapsed after the entry of any other court order not involving custody or supervision; and

(2) He has not been convicted of a crime, or a disorderly persons offense or adjudged delinquent, during the two years prior to the filing of the motion, and no proceeding or complaint is pending seeking such conviction or adjudication.

b. In any case wherein a juvenile has been adjudicated delinquent and said juvenile enlists in any branch of the Armed Forces of the United States, he may at any time after the date of such adjudication present a duly verified petition to the court where such adjudication was entered, setting forth all the facts in the matter, including proof of enlistment and acceptance in said armed forces, and praying for the relief provided in this section, and subject to the limitations hereinafter provided in this section, an order may be granted to seal all the records concerning such adjudication including records of the court, probation services and law enforcement agencies. Failure to enter the armed forces shall have the effect of nullifying the sealing order.

c. Reasonable written notice of the motion shall be given to:

(1) The Attorney General and the county prosecutor;

(2) The authority granting the discharge if the final discharge was from an institution, parole, or probation; and

(3) The law enforcement office, department, and central depository having custody of the files and records if such files and records are included in the motion.

d. Upon the entry of the order, the proceedings in the case shall be sealed and all index references shall be marked "not available" or "no record" and law enforcement officers and departments shall reply and the person may reply to any inquiry that there is no record with respect to such person, except that records may be maintained for purposes of prior offender status, identification and law enforcement purposes. Copies of the order shall be sent to each agency or official named therein.

Inspection of the files and records included in the order may thereafter be permitted by the court only upon motion and only to those persons named in the motion; provided, however, the court, in its discretion, may by special order in an individual case permit inspection by or release of information in the records to any clinic, hospital, or agency which has the person under care or treatment or to individuals or agencies engaged in fact-finding or research.

e. Any adjudication of delinquency or conviction of a crime subsequent to sealing shall have the effect of nullifying the sealing order.

f. Expungement of juvenile records shall be governed by the applicable provisions of chapter 52 of Title 2C [1] of the New Jersey Statutes.

L.1982, c. 79, § 3, eff. Dec. 31, 1983. Amended by L.1994, c. 56, § 3, eff. June 29, 1994.

[1] N.J.S.A. § 2C:52–1 et seq.

ARTICLE 4. COURT APPROVED JUVENILE SERVICES

2A:4A–70. County court intake services

a. Each county shall establish a court intake service which shall have among its responsibilities the screening of juvenile delinquency complaints and juvenile-family crisis referrals. The intake service shall operate in compliance with standards established by the Supreme Court, but in no instance shall the standards for personnel employed as counselors be less than a master's degree from an accredited institution in mental health or social or behavioral science discipline including degrees in social work, counseling, counseling psychology, mental health counseling or education. Equivalent experience is acceptable when it consists of a minimum of an associate's degree with a concentration in one of the behavioral sciences and a minimum of five years' experience working with troubled youth and their families or a bachelor's degree in one of the behavioral sciences and two year's experience working with troubled youth and their families. Intake personnel should also receive training in drug and alcohol abuse.

b. The court intake service shall make arrangements for the receipt of complaints, on a continuous basis, in situations where the subject of the complaint is a juvenile, or referrals through crisis intervention units where a juvenile-family crisis may exist. It shall assist the court in screening referrals for court intervention, making referrals to appropriate agencies, reviewing and approving alternative living arrangements as provided by law, determining that jurisdiction for juvenile-family crisis proceedings may exist prior to filing a petition, and in monitoring referrals for development and implementation of family service plans. Every complaint or juvenile-family crisis petition shall be reviewed by the court intake service unless otherwise ordered by the court.

c. The court intake service shall have the responsibility for monitoring, on a 24–hour a day, 7–day a week basis, the admission of alleged delinquents to the detention or shelter care facilities and no juvenile may be admitted to a detention or shelter care facility without its approval.

d. The Supreme Court shall have the authority to issue rules governing the duties, responsibilities, and practices of court intake services as it deems necessary to effectuate the purposes of this act; establish guidelines and procedures for the training of intake services staff; establish reporting procedures to be followed by court intake services in providing data for its evaluation; and conduct, at least annually, an evaluation of all intake services.

L.1982, c. 81, § 1, eff. Dec. 31, 1983. Amended by L.1991, c. 119, § 3, eff. April 25, 1991.

2A:4A–71. Review and processing of complaints

a. The jurisdiction of the court in any complaint filed pursuant to section 11 of P.L.1982, c. 77 (C. 2A:4A–30) shall extend to the juvenile who is the subject of the complaint and his parents or guardian.

b. Every complaint shall be reviewed by court intake services for recommendation as to whether the complaint should be dismissed, diverted, or referred for court action. Where the complaint alleges a crime which, if committed by an adult, would be a crime of the first, second, third or fourth degree, or alleges a repetitive disorderly persons offense or any disorderly persons offense defined in chapter 35 or chapter 36 of Title 2C, the complaint shall be referred for court action, unless the prosecutor otherwise consents to diversion. Court intake services shall consider the following factors in determining whether to recommend diversion:

(1) The seriousness of the alleged offense or conduct and the circumstances in which it occurred;

(2) The age and maturity of the juvenile;

(3) The risk that the juvenile presents as a substantial danger to others;

(4) The family circumstances, including any history of drugs, alcohol abuse or child abuse on the part of the juvenile, his parents or guardian;

(5) The nature and number of contacts with court intake services and the court that the juvenile or his family have had;

(6) The outcome of those contacts, including the services to which the juvenile or family have been referred and the results of those referrals;

(7) The availability of appropriate services outside referral to the court;

(8) Any recommendations expressed by the victim or complainant, or arresting officer, as to how the case should be resolved; and

(9) Any recommendation expressed by the county prosecutor.

L.1982, c. 81, § 2, eff. Dec. 31, 1983. Amended by L.1988, c. 44, § 17, eff. June 28, 1988.

2A:4A–72. Recommendation of diversion

a. Where court intake services recommends diverting the juvenile, the reasons for the recommendation shall be submitted by intake services and approved by the court before the case is deemed diverted.

b. Where, in determining whether to recommend diversion, court intake services has reason to believe that a parent or guardian is a drug dependent person, as defined in section 2 of the "New Jersey Controlled Dangerous Substances Act," P.L.1970, c. 226 (C. 24:21–2) or an alcoholic as defined by P.L.1975, c. 305 (C. 26:2B–8), the basis for this determination shall be stated in its recommendation to the court.

c. The county prosecutor shall receive a copy of each complaint filed pursuant to section 11 of P.L.1982, c. 77 [1] promptly after the filing of the complaint.

d. Within 5 days after receiving a complaint, the intake services officer shall advise the presiding judge and the prosecuting attorney of intake services' recommendation, as well as any other recommendations or objections received as to the complaint. In determining whether to divert, the court may hold a hearing to consider the recommendations and any objections submitted by court intake services in light of the factors provided in this section. The court shall give notice of the hearing to the juvenile, his parents or guardian, the prosecutor, arresting police officer and complainant or victim. Each party shall have the right to be heard on the matter. If the court finds that not enough information has been received to make a determination, a further hearing may be ordered. The court may dismiss the complaint upon a finding that the facts as alleged are not sufficient to establish jurisdiction, or that probable cause has not been shown that the juvenile committed a delinquent act.

L.1982, c. 81, § 3, eff. Dec. 31, 1983.

[1] N.J.S.A. § 2A:4A–30.

2A:4A–73. Diverting complaints

a. The court may divert a complaint filed pursuant to section 11 of P.L. 1982, c. 77 (C. 2A:4A–30), to intake conferences or juvenile conference committees. Where the complaint alleges a disorderly persons or petty disorderly persons offense the court may dispose of the case as a juvenile-family crisis pursuant to P.L. 1982, c. 80 (C. 2A:4A–76 et seq.). The county prosecutor shall be promptly notified of the diversion of a complaint.

b. The complainant or victim of any offense committed by a juvenile diverted by the court, which offense would be a crime if committed by an adult, shall receive a statement as to the reasons for the proposed diversion.

L.1982, c. 81, § 4, eff. Dec. 31, 1983.

2A:4A–74. Court intake service conference

a. Where the juvenile is diverted to a court intake service conference, notices of the conference shall be sent to the juvenile and his parents or guardian and to the complainant or victim. The parties may be requested to bring to the conference all pertinent documents in their possession, including medical, social, and school records.

b. In determining the appropriate resolution of a complaint, the following factors shall be considered by court intake services:

(1) The seriousness of the alleged offense or conduct and the circumstances in which it occurred;

(2) The age and maturity of the juvenile;

(3) The risk that the juvenile presents as a substantial danger to others;

(4) The family circumstances, including any history of drugs, alcohol abuse or child abuse on the part of the juvenile, his parents or guardian;

(5) The nature and number of contacts with court intake services and the court that the juvenile and his family have had;

(6) The outcome of those contacts, including the services to which the juvenile or family have been referred and the results of those referrals;

(7) The availability of appropriate services;

(8) Any recommendations expressed by the victim or complainant, or arresting officer, as to how the case should be disposed;

(9) Whether diversion can be accomplished in a manner that holds the juvenile accountable for the conduct;

(10) The impact of the offense on the victim or victims; and

(11) The impact of the offense on the community.

c. Each juvenile shall be reviewed without a presumption of guilt. The intake conference shall be concerned primarily with providing balanced attention to the protection of the community, the imposition of accountability for offenses committed, fostering interaction and dialogue between the offender, victim and community and the development of competencies to enable the juvenile offender to become a responsible and productive member of the community. In addition, the conference shall be concerned with preventing more serious future misconduct by the juvenile offender by obtaining the cooperation of the juvenile and his parents or guardian in complying with its recommendations. The court may schedule a hearing where the complainant or victim objects to the recommendations from the conference.

d. The resolution from the conference may include but shall not be limited to counseling, restitution, referral to appropriate community agencies, or any other community work programs or other conditions consistent with diversion that aids in providing balanced attention to the protection of the community, the imposition of accountability for offenses committed,

fostering interaction and dialogue between the offender, victim and community and the development of competencies to enable the juvenile offender to become a responsible and productive member of the community, provided that:

(1) Obligations imposed as a result of the intake conference shall be an order of the court approved by the presiding judge and shall be set forth in writing and may not exceed six months. The juvenile and his or her parents or guardian shall receive copies, as shall any agencies providing services under the agreement;

(2) The court intake service worker shall inform the juvenile and the juvenile's parents or guardian in writing of their right to object at any time prior to their written agreement to the facts or terms of the intake conference decision, and if objections arise, the intake service worker may alter the terms of the proposed agreement or refer the matter to the presiding judge who shall determine if the complaint will be heard in court or returned to intake conference for further action;

(3) Written agreement pursuant to intake conferences may be terminated at any time upon the request of the juvenile and the matter referred to the presiding judge;

(4) The court intake services conference may not order the confinement of a juvenile, place a juvenile on probation, or remove a juvenile from his family as a disposition; and

(5) If, at any time during the diversion period, the court intake service worker determines that the obligations imposed under the written agreement are not being met, the intake worker shall notify the presiding judge in writing. In the case of failure to comply with the obligations imposed under the agreement by the parents or guardian, the court may proceed against such persons for enforcement of the agreement. In the case of failure to comply by the juvenile, the matter shall be referred to the court for action.

e. At the end of the diversion period a second court intake services conference may be held with all parties to the written agreement present to ascertain if the terms of the agreement have been fulfilled. If all conditions have been met, the intake worker shall so inform the presiding judge in writing who shall order the complaint dismissed. A copy of the order dismissing the complaint shall be sent to the juvenile. If the conditions of the written agreement have not been met, the intake worker may refer the matter to the presiding judge who shall determine if the complaint will be heard in court or returned to court intake services for further action. Based on the evaluations required under this paragraph, the intake conference agreement may be extended beyond the six-month maximum if all parties agree. In no case shall an intake conference agreement exceed nine months.

f. All proceedings before the conference are confidential and they shall receive only those records which in the court's judgment are necessary to aid in making a recommendation.

L.1982, c. 81, § 5, eff. Dec. 31, 1983. Amended by L.1995, c. 280, § 16, eff. Dec. 15, 1995; L.2001, c. 408, § 5, eff. Aug. 1, 2002.

2A:4A–75. Juvenile conference committees

a. The court may appoint one or more juvenile conference committees for each county or municipality to hear and decide matters referred to it by the court.

b. The method of appointment and terms of membership to the committees shall be made pursuant to guidelines developed by the Supreme Court.

c. Where the juvenile is diverted to a juvenile conference committee, notices of the conference shall be sent to the juvenile and his parents or guardian and to the complainant or victim. The parties may be requested to bring to the conference all pertinent documents in their possession, including medical, social, and school records.

d. The committee shall serve under the authority of the court in hearing and deciding such matters involving alleged juvenile offenders as are specifically referred to it by the court. Each juvenile shall be reviewed without a presumption of guilt. The committee shall be concerned primarily with providing balanced attention to the protection of the community, the imposition of accountability for offenses committed, fostering interaction and dialogue between the offender, victim and community and the development of competencies to enable the juvenile offender to become a responsible and productive member of the community. In addition, the committee shall be concerned with preventing more serious future misconduct by the juvenile offender by obtaining the cooperation of the juvenile and his parents or guardian in complying with its recommendations. The court may schedule a hearing where the complainant or victim objects to the recommendations from the conference.

e. The committee shall provide for the resolution of the matter and shall supervise and follow up compliance with its recommendations in the same manner and under the same limitations and with the same sanctions as the court intake service conference.

f. All proceedings before the juvenile conference committee are confidential and include only those records which in the court's judgment are necessary to aid in making a recommendation.

L.1982, c. 81, § 6, eff. Dec. 31, 1983. Amended by L.2001, c. 408, § 6, eff. Aug. 1, 2002.

2A:4A–76. Juvenile-family crisis intervention units established

There shall be established in each county one or more juvenile-family crisis intervention units. Each unit shall operate either as a part of the court intake service, or where provided for by the county, through any other appropriate office or private service pursuant to an agreement with the Administrative Office of the Courts, provided that all such units shall be subject to the Rules of Court. In any county where a crisis intervention service system, designed to attend and stabilize juvenile and family problems on a county-wide basis, is in operation as of the effective date of this act, such service shall satisfy all the provisions of this act, and may continue in its present form and under its present procedures, provided that it is operating in substantial compliance with the specific requirements and goals set forth in this act.

L.1982, c. 80, § 1, eff. Dec. 31, 1983.

2A:4A–77. Call service to attend and stabilize juvenile-family crises; referrals; information; form

The purpose of the unit shall be to provide a continuous 24-hour on-call service designed to attend and stabilize juvenile-family crises as defined pursuant to section 3 of P.L. 1982, c. 77. [1] The juvenile-family crisis intervention unit shall respond immediately to any referral, complaint or information made pursuant to section 5 or 6 of this act,[2] except if, upon preliminary investigation, it appears that a juvenile-family crisis within the meaning of this act does not exist or that an immediate referral to another agency would be more appropriate.

Upon the receipt of any referral pursuant to section 5 and 6 of this act, the crisis intervention unit shall request information through the use of a form developed by the unit and approved by the Administrative Office of the Courts concerning the juvenile-family crisis. The form shall provide but shall not be limited to the following information:

a. The name, address, date of birth, and other appropriate personal data of the juvenile and parents or guardian;

b. Facts concerning the conduct of the juvenile or family which may contribute to the crisis, including evidence of alcoholism as defined in section 2 of P.L.1975, c. 305 (C. 26:2B–8), drug dependency as defined in section 2 of the "New Jersey Controlled Dangerous Substances Act," P.L.1970, c. 226 (C. 24:21–2) or that a juvenile is an "abused or neglected child" as defined in P.L.1974, c. 119 (C. 9:6–8.21).

L.1982, c. 80, § 2, eff. Dec. 31, 1983.

[1] N.J.S.A. § 2A:4A–22.
[2] N.J.S.A. § 2A:4A–80 or 2A:4A–81.

2A:4A–78. Intervention unit response

A crisis intervention response shall consist of immediate interviews with the parents and juvenile involved by one or more crisis intervention workers. Where the juvenile is not in the home, or in the custody of the police, the intervention workers shall attempt to interview the juvenile wherever the juvenile may be found. The juvenile and family shall be advised of the purpose of the unit and of the emphasis upon the voluntary exhaustion of community services prior to court involvement. The unit shall make all reasonable efforts to keep the family intact consistent with the physical safety and mental well-being of the juvenile by obtaining, where possible, written agreement of the family to accept recommendations which may include, but are not limited to, referral to appropriate services and agencies.

L.1982, c. 80, § 3, eff. Dec. 31, 1983.

2A:4A–79. Intervention unit training and skills

The juvenile-family crisis intervention unit shall have knowledge of community services and agencies and shall be specially trained in family counseling and crisis stabilization skills. The Supreme Court may issue rules concerning the duties, responsibilities, training and practices of the juvenile-family crisis intervention units consistent with the provisions of this act, but in no instance shall the minimum qualifications for personnel employed as counselors and hired after the effective date of this act be less than a master's degree from an accredited institution in a mental health or social or behavioral science discipline including degrees in social work, counseling, counseling psychology, mental health or education. Equivalent experience is acceptable when it consists of a minimum of an associate's degree with a concentration in one of the behavioral sciences and a minimum of 5 years' experience working with troubled youth and their families or a bachelor's degree in one of the behavioral sciences and 2 years' experience working with troubled youth and their families.

L.1982, c. 80, § 4, eff. Dec. 31, 1983.

2A:4A–80. Law enforcement referral

A law enforcement officer taking a juvenile into short-term custody pursuant to section 12 of P.L. 1982, c. 77 [1] shall immediately notify the juvenile-family crisis intervention unit and shall promptly bring the juvenile to the unit or place designated by the unit when:

a. The officer has reason to believe that it is not in the best interests of the juvenile or the family for the officer to return the juvenile to his home;

b. The juvenile resides in another county and the officer is unable to make arrangements to return the juvenile to his home;

c. The juvenile resides in another state;

d. The juvenile has run away from a placement and the juvenile refuses to return home or the juvenile, through his past behavior, has demonstrated an inability to remain at home;

e. The law enforcement officer is unable, by all reasonable efforts to identify or locate a parent, relative or other such appropriate person;

f. The juvenile requires immediate emergency services, such as medical or psychiatric care; or

g. No identification can be obtained from the juvenile.

L.1982, c. 80, § 5, eff. Dec. 31, 1983.

[1] N.J.S.A. § 2A:4A–31.

2A:4A–81. Other referrals

a. The juvenile-family crisis intervention unit shall also receive referrals on a continuous basis in situations where a juvenile-family crisis exists and there has been either:

(1) A request by a parent or juvenile for intervention; or

(2) A referral by a public or private agency, educational institution, or any other organization serving children, which has contact with the juvenile or family, and has reasonable cause to believe that a family crisis exists.

b. Any agency or organization making such a referral shall indicate whether their agency is capable of providing the appropriate services to the family or juvenile and indicate their present ability and willingness to do so in the particular case referred.

c. Any public agency making the referral which is under a legal obligation to provide services to the family or juvenile, shall, where it is unable to provide appropriate services in the particular case referred, state the reasons therefor.

L.1982, c. 80, § 6, eff. Dec. 31, 1983.

2A:4A–82. Juvenile-family crisis stabilized

When the juvenile-family crisis has been stabilized and the juvenile is residing in the home, the crisis intervention unit shall arrange a second interview session with the family as soon as practicable and preferably the day following the initial intervention, for the purpose of monitoring the family situation. The crisis intervention unit may, in appropriate cases, continue to work with the family on a short-term basis in order to stabilize the family situation.

L.1982, c. 80, § 7, eff. Dec. 31, 1983.

2A:4A–83. Juvenile-family crisis referral to the court; continuing crisis

When, in the judgment of the crisis intervention unit, a juvenile-family crisis continues to exist despite the provision of crisis intervention services and the exhaustion of appropriate community services, court intake services shall, by filing a petition, refer the case to the court. In counties where the crisis intervention units are not part of intake and a juvenile-family crisis continues to exist, the court shall immediately refer the case to intake for the filing of a petition pursuant to this section. Upon the filing of the petition, the jurisdiction of the court shall extend to the juvenile, parent or guardian, or other family member contributing to the crisis.

L.1982, c. 80, § 8, eff. Dec. 31, 1983.

2A:4A–84. Juvenile-family crisis recommendations

Court intake services shall submit with its petition facts as to the nature of the juvenile-family crisis and its recommendations for resolving the crisis, including recommendations as to community services or programs which are necessary to accomplish this purpose.

L.1982, c. 80, § 9, eff. Dec. 31, 1983.

2A:4A–85. Alcoholic, drug-dependent parent; belief juvenile abused or neglected; juvenile with auditory or vision problem; examination, records and recommendations to court

a. When a petition is filed and as a result of any information supplied on the family situation by the crisis intervention unit, court intake services has reason to believe that the parent or guardian is an alcoholic, as defined by P.L.1975, c. 305 (C.26:2B–8), or a drug-dependent person, as defined by section 2 of the "New Jersey Controlled Dangerous Substances Act," P.L. 1970, c. 226 (C.24:21–2), intake services shall state the basis for this determination and provide recommendations to the court.

b. When, as a result of any information supplied by the crisis intervention unit, court intake services has reason to believe that a juvenile is an "abused or neglected child," as defined in P.L.1974, c. 119 (C.9:6–8.21), they shall handle the case pursuant to the procedure set forth in that law. The Division of Youth and Family Services shall, upon disposition of any case originated pursuant to this subsection, notify court intake services as to the nature of the disposition.

c. (1) When, as a result of any information supplied with regard to any juvenile by the crisis intervention unit or from any other source, court intake services has reason to believe that the juvenile may have an auditory or vision problem, intake services shall state the basis for this determination and provide recommendations to the court. Before arriving at its determination, intake services may request the court to order any appropriate school medical records of the juvenile. On the basis of this recommendation or on its own motion, the court may order any juvenile concerning whom a complaint is filed to be examined by a physician, optometrist, audiologist, or speech language pathologist.

(2) Any examination shall be made and the findings submitted to the court within 30 days of the date the order is entered, but this period may be extended by the court for good cause.

(3) Copies of any reports of findings submitted to the court shall be available to counsel for all parties prior to an adjudication of whether or not the juvenile is delinquent.

L.1982, c. 80, § 10, eff. Dec. 31, 1983. Amended by L.1985, c. 437, § 1, eff. Jan. 13, 1986.

2A:4A–86. Juvenile-family crisis hearing; disposition

Whenever the court receives a petition from court intake services stating that a juvenile-family crisis may exist the court shall hold a hearing and consider the facts and recommendations submitted by intake services in order to determine the appropriate disposition to be made. The court shall notify the juvenile, his parent or guardian or other family member alleged in the petition as contributing to the family crisis that a juvenile-family crisis may exist. The juvenile, parent, guardian, or other family member may present witnesses and evidence to rebut the determination. If the court finds that there is not enough information to make a disposition it may continue the matter and hold one or more additional hearings. The court shall enter an order of disposition if it finds that a juvenile-family crisis exists as provided in section 27 of P.L. 1982, c. 77 (C. 2A:4A–46). In support of any such order, the court may require the juvenile, parent, guardian or family member contributing to the crisis, to participate in appropriate programs and services consistent with the disposition. The court may dismiss the petition upon a finding that based upon the preponderance of the evidence presented the petition is not sufficient to establish that a juvenile-family crisis exists. The court shall state the grounds for any disposition made pursuant to this section. In the case of failure of any person to comply with any orders entered pursuant to this section, the court may proceed against such person for the enforcement of litigants' rights.

L.1982, c. 80, § 11, eff. Dec. 31, 1983.

2A:4A–87. Juvenile–family crisis referral to courts; out of home placement

When, despite provision of crisis intervention services and the exhaustion of all alternative services, there is a refusal on the part of the juvenile to stay in or return to the home or a refusal on the part of the parents to allow the juvenile to stay in or return home, or the physical safety of the juvenile is threatened, or the juvenile is in need of immediate care such that it is necessary to make an out of home placement of the juvenile, court intake services shall:

a. Arrange, when agreed to by the parent or guardian and juvenile, alternate living arrangement for the juvenile with a relative, neighbor, or other suitable family setting. It shall not be necessary for a court hearing to approve the living arrangement and the arrangement may continue as long as there is agreement; or

b. Arrange, when no alternate living arrangement can be agreed to and when all possible resources for alternate living arrangements as set forth in subsection a. of this section have been exhausted, temporary out of home placement prior to the placement hearing. Court intake services shall immediately file a petition for out of home placement which shall include documentation of the attempts made to provide alternate living arrangements including, but not limited to, the names of persons contacted, their responses and the lack of agreement by the juvenile or the juvenile's parents if the persons contacted are willing to take the juvenile with the court. The crisis intervention unit shall inform the juvenile and parent or guardian that an out of home placement determination may be made by the court where an alternate living arrangement cannot be agreed to.

L.1982, c. 80, § 12, eff. Dec. 31, 1983. Amended by L.1989, c. 305, § 1, eff. Feb. 11, 1990.

2A:4A–88. Temporary placement

Placement of the juvenile prior to the placement hearing or pending determination by the court concerning placement under a family service plan, pursuant to section 14 of P.L.1982, c. 80 (C.2A:4A–89), shall be made in a host shelter, resource family or group home, a county shelter care facility as defined by law, or other suitable family setting. In no event shall such placement be arranged in a secure detention or other facility or in a secure correctional institution for the detention or treatment of juveniles accused of crimes or adjudged delinquent.

L.1982, c. 80, § 13, eff. Dec. 31, 1983. Amended by L.1995, c. 280, § 17, eff. Dec. 15, 1995; L.2004, c. 130, § 7, eff. Aug. 27, 2004.

2A:4A–89. Out of home placement hearing

When intake has filed with the court a petition for out of home placement, the court shall, within 24 hours, conduct a hearing on the petition. The court shall notify the parents, the juvenile and his counsel and, if indigent, have counsel appointed by the court. The hearing shall be conducted in accordance with the Rules of Court and shall be attended by the parents, the juvenile, and when requested by the court, a representative of the Department of Children and Families. The following procedure shall be followed for the hearing:

a. The court shall hold the hearing to consider the petition and may approve or disapprove the temporary out of home placement. The court may approve temporary out of home placement if either of the following factors exists:

(1) A serious conflict or other problem between the parent and the juvenile which cannot be resolved by delivery of services to the family during continued placement of the juvenile in the parental home; or

(2) The physical safety and well-being of the juvenile would be threatened if the juvenile were placed in the parental home.

b. If the court disapproves a petition for an out of home placement, a written statement of reasons shall be filed, and the court shall order that the juvenile is to remain at or return to the parental home.

c. Temporary out of home placement shall continue until otherwise provided by the court. The order approving the temporary out of home placement shall

direct the Department of Children and Families, or other service or agency to submit a family service plan that is designed to resolve the family crisis consistent with the well-being and physical safety of the juvenile. The court shall direct such department, service or agency to make recommendations as to which agency or person shall have physical custody of the child, the extent of the parental powers to be awarded to such agency or person and parental visitation rights.

d. Within 14 days of the date of the order approving the petition for temporary out of home placement is entered, unless for good cause shown, but no later than 30 days, the department, service or agency shall submit to the court a family service plan, which shall be presumed valid, detailing the specifics of the court order. The plan shall be developed within the limits of fiscal and other resources available to the department, service or agency. If the court determines that the service plan is inappropriate, given existing resources, the department, service or agency may request a hearing on that determination.

e. At the hearing held to consider the family service plan presented by the department or other service or agency, the court shall consider all such recommendations included therein. The court, consistent with this section, may modify such plan and shall make its dispositional order for the juvenile. The court's dispositional order shall specify the responsibility of the Department of Children and Families or other service with respect to the juvenile who shall be placed, those parental powers temporarily ordered to the department or service and parental visitation rights. Where placement cannot be immediately made, the department or other service or agency shall report to the court every 14 days on the status of the placement and progress toward implementation of the plan.

L.1982, c. 80, § 14, eff. Dec. 31, 1983. Amended by L.2006, c. 47, § 20, eff. July 1, 2006.

2A:4A–90. Long-term placement

In considering whether to approve or disapprove out of home placement under a family service plan on a long-term basis, the court shall consider whether placement in the home would fail to provide adequate physical protection, shelter or nutrition or would seriously obstruct the juvenile's medical care, education or physical and emotional development as determined according to the needs of the juvenile. Upon making an order approving a long-term out of home placement plan, the matter shall be reviewed pursuant to the provisions of the "Child Placement Review Act," P.L. 1977, c. 424 (C. 30:4C–50 et seq.).

L.1982, c. 80, § 15, eff. Dec. 31, 1983.

2A:4A–91. Repealed by L.1995, c. 284, § 11, eff. Dec. 15, 1995

2A:4A–92. "Court Appointed Special Advocate" defined; CASA program established; scope of program and advocate authority

Section effective on November 1, 2010.

a. As provided in this act,[1] a "Court Appointed Special Advocate" (CASA) shall mean a community volunteer who has been recruited, screened, trained, and supervised by a CASA program affiliated with Court Appointed Special Advocates of New Jersey or a similar organization as determined by the Administrative Office of the Courts. An affiliate CASA program shall meet all State Court Appointed Special Advocate and National Court Appointed Special Advocate standards, and shall be affiliated with Court Appointed Special Advocates of New Jersey and the National Court Appointed Special Advocates Association.

b. There shall be established in the State of New Jersey a Court Appointed Special Advocate program which shall serve as a resource to the courts in determining the best interests of any child less than 18 years of age who has been removed from his home due to abuse or neglect. A Court Appointed Special Advocate may continue to undertake activities in furtherance of the child's best interests, in appropriate cases, until the child who is the subject of the court appointment reaches 21 years of age.

c. Pursuant to the Rules of Court, the court may appoint a special advocate from the CASA program to act on behalf of the court. The special advocate shall undertake certain activities in furtherance of the child's interests, but shall not supplant or interfere with the role of counsel or guardian ad litem for that child. Any such special advocate shall be a volunteer associated with a court-authorized CASA program. The duties and activities of a CASA program and all of its volunteers shall be subject to guidelines and standards established by the Administrative Director of the Courts.

d. A person seeking to volunteer as a Court Appointed Special Advocate shall be subject to the following:

(1) a criminal history record background check submitted by the Administrative Office of the Courts or its designee to the appropriate authorities. A copy of the results shall be provided to the affiliate CASA program. A person shall not be approved as a Court Appointed Special Advocate if criminal history record information exists on file with the Federal Bureau of Investigation or the Division of State Police which would disqualify that person from serving in that capacity, as determined by the affiliate CASA program; and

(2) a child abuse record information check conducted by the Department of Children and Families to determine if an incident of child abuse or neglect has been substantiated, pursuant to section 4 of P.L.1971, c. 437 (C.9:6–8.11), against the prospective CASA volunteer. The department shall cooperate by conducting the child abuse record information check and providing the results to the affiliate CASA program.

If a prospective volunteer refuses to consent to, or cooperate in, the securing of a criminal history record background check or a child abuse record information check, the person shall not be appointed as a Court Appointed Special Advocate.

e. Upon presentation of an order of appointment, the special advocate shall be provided access to all information and records relevant to the child, including but not limited to: school records, child care records, medical records, mental health records, family court and juvenile court records, and records of the Division of Youth and Family Services in the Department of Children and Families.

f. Any special advocate or affiliate CASA program staff member acting in good faith within the scope of his appointment or employment shall have immunity from any civil or criminal liability that otherwise might result by reason of his actions or failure to act, except in cases of willful or wanton misconduct.

L.2009, c. 217, § 1, eff. Nov. 1, 2010.

[1] L.2009, c. 217 (N.J.S.A. §§ 2A:4A–92, 2A:4A–60).

SUBTITLE 9

EVIDENCE, WITNESSES AND PUBLIC HEARINGS

Chapter
84A. **Rules of Evidence.**

CHAPTER 84A

RULES OF EVIDENCE

For text of the New Jersey Rules of Evidence (N.J.R.E. 101 et seq.), adopted by the New Jersey Supreme Court, effective July 1, 1993, and table showing the disposition of the 1967 Rules of Evidence into N.J.R.E., see Appendix A following N.J.S.A. § 2A:84A–49.

ARTICLE I. GENERAL PROVISIONS

Section
2A:84A–1 to 2A:84A–16.   Repealed.
2A:84A–16.1.   Anatomically correct dolls or models; use in testimony of children.

ARTICLE II. PRIVILEGES

2A:84A–17.   Privilege of accused.
2A:84A–18.   Definition of incrimination.
2A:84A–19.   Self-incrimination; exceptions.
2A:84A–20.   Lawyer-client privilege.
2A:84A–21.   Newsperson's privilege.
2A:84A–21a.   Definitions; newsperson's privilege.
2A:84A–21.1.   Criminal proceeding; subpoena; application of newsperson's privilege.
2A:84A–21.2.   Time of proceedings.
2A:84A–21.3.   Prima facie showing subpenaed materials obtained during professional activities; waiver of newsperson's privilege or other grounds for disclosure; hearing.
2A:84A–21.4.   In camera inspection; hearing; determination of admissibility; order for production.
2A:84A–21.5.   Hearings; findings of fact and conclusions of law.
2A:84A–21.6.   Appeals; stay of penalty; sealing of record; return of privileged material.
2A:84A–21.7.   Co-defendants; notice of proceedings; right to intervene.
2A:84A–21.8.   Assessment of costs or counsel fee.
2A:84A–21.9.   News media person or entity; freedom from searches and seizures of documentary materials; exceptions.
2A:84A–21.10.   Applications for search warrant; approval.
2A:84A–21.11.   Civil cause of action for damages due to violations.
2A:84A–21.12.   Additional definitions; newsperson's privilege.

Section
2A:84A–21.13.   Inapplicability of act to rights of department of corrections.
2A:84A–22.   Marital privilege—Confidential communications.
2A:84A–22.1.   Definitions; patient-physician privilege.
2A:84A–22.2.   Patient and physician privilege.
2A:84A–22.3.   Mental incompetence; validity of will; nonprivileged communication.
2A:84A–22.4.   Contract of patient; condition of patient is element of claim; nonprivileged communications.
2A:84A–22.5.   Information reported to public official; nonprivileged communications.
2A:84A–22.6.   Obtaining physician to aid commission of crime or tort, or to escape detection or apprehension; nonprivileged communications.
2A:84A–22.7.   Testimony by physician on request of holder of privilege; termination of privilege.
2A:84A–22.8.   Utilization review committees of certified hospital or extended care facility; exceptions.
2A:84A–22.9.   Liability of member of utilization review committee for disclosure of information.
2A:84A–22.10.   Hospital or long-term health care facility committees; professional review committees; liability of members.
2A:84A–22.11, 2A:84A–22.12.   Repealed.
2A:84A–22.13.   Legislative findings and declarations.
2A:84A–22.14.   Definitions; victim counselor's privilege.
2A:84A–22.15.   Victim counselor's privilege.
2A:84A–22.16.   Disclosure to defendant in criminal action of information given to county victim-witness coordinator.
2A:84A–23.   Cleric-penitent privilege.
2A:84A–24.   Religious belief.
2A:84A–25.   Political vote.
2A:84A–26.   Trade secret.
2A:84A–27.   Official information.
2A:84A–28.   Identity of informer.
2A:84A–29.   Waiver of privilege by contract or previous disclosure; limitations.
2A:84A–30.   Admissibility of disclosure wrongfully compelled.
2A:84A–31.   Reference to exercise of privileges.
2A:84A–32.   Effect of error in overruling claim of privilege.
2A:84A–32a.   Post-conviction DNA testing; motion; determinations.
2A:84A–32b.   Rules.

Section

ARTICLE IIA. ADMISSIBILITY

2A:84A–32.1. Prosecutions involving rape; evidence of complaining witness' previous sexual conduct.
2A:84A–32.2. Conduct one year or more prior to date of offense; presumption of inadmissibility.
2A:84A–32.3. Complaining witness defined.
2A:84A–32.4. Prosecutions or actions for sexual assault, criminal sexual conduct, or child abuse or neglect; closed circuit testimony by minor.

ARTICLE III. ADOPTION OF RULES

2A:84A–33. Authority of Supreme Court.
2A:84A–34. Presentation of proposed rules at Judicial Conference.
2A:84A–35. Public announcement of proposed rules; delivery of copies.
2A:84A–36. Effective date of rules; rules subject to cancellation by joint resolution.
2A:84A–37. Change or cancellation of rules by statute or adoption of subsequent rules.
2A:84A–38. Adoption of rules at such time, or with such effective date, or without presentation at Judicial Conference, as may be provided in joint resolution.
2A:84A–39. Reduction or elimination of time during which rules may be canceled by joint resolution.
2A:84A–39.1 to 2A:84A–39.6. Repealed.
2A:84A–40. Effect of rules on conflicting laws.
2A:84A–41. Rules not to abridge, enlarge or modify substantive rights or eliminate right of trial by jury.
2A:84A–42. Applicability of rules to pending proceedings or existing rights or remedies.
2A:84A–43. Publication of compilations and restatements of rules.
2A:84A–44. Force and effect of existing rules dealing with admission or rejection of evidence.

ARTICLE IV. MISCELLANEOUS REVISIONS AND REPEALERS

2A:84A–45. Repeals.
2A:84A–46. Repealed.
2A:84A–47. Effect of repeals.
2A:84A–48. Short title.
2A:84A–49. Effective date.

ARTICLE I. GENERAL PROVISIONS

2A:84A–1 to 2A:84A–16. Repealed by L.1999, c. 319, § 2, eff. Jan. 6, 2000

2A:84A–16.1. Anatomically correct dolls or models; use in testimony of children

In prosecutions for those crimes described in sections 2C:14–2, 2C:14–3 and 2C:24–4 of the New Jersey Statutes, where the complaining witness is a child under the age of 16, the court shall permit the use of anatomically correct dolls, models or similar items of either or both sexes to assist the child's testimony.

L.1985, c. 205, § 1, eff. June 27, 1985.

ARTICLE II. PRIVILEGES

2A:84A–17. Privilege of accused

(1) Every person has in any criminal action in which he is an accused a right not to be called as a witness and not to testify. [1]

(2) The spouse or one partner in a civil union couple of the accused in a criminal action shall not testify in such action except to prove the fact of marriage or civil union unless (a) such spouse or partner consents, or (b) the accused is charged with an offense against the spouse or partner, a child of the accused or of the spouse or partner, or a child to whom the accused or the spouse or partner stands in the place of a parent, or (c) such spouse or partner is the complainant.

(3) An accused in a criminal action has no privilege to refuse when ordered by the judge, to submit his body to examination or to do any act in the presence of the judge or the trier of the fact, except to refuse to testify.

L.1960, c. 52, p. 454, § 17, eff. July 1, 1960. Amended Sept. 14, 1979, eff. July 1, 1980; L.1992, c. 142, § 1; L.2006, c. 103, § 90, eff. Feb. 19, 2007.

  [1] See, also, N.J.R.E. 501.

Historical and Statutory Notes

L.1992, c. 142, § 3, approved Nov. 17, 1992, provides:

"This act shall take effect immediately and, to the fullest extent consistent with constitutional restrictions, shall apply to all criminal actions regardless of the date on which the offense was committed or the action initiated."

2A:84A–18. Definition of incrimination

Rule 24.[1]

Within the meaning of this article,[2] a matter will incriminate (a) if it constitutes an element of a crime against this State, or another State or the United States, or (b) is a circumstance which with other circumstances would be a basis for a reasonable inference of the commission of such a crime, or (c) is a clue to the discovery of a matter which is within clauses (a) or (b) above; provided, a matter will not be held to incriminate if it clearly appears that the witness has no reasonable cause to apprehend a criminal prosecution. In determining whether a matter is incriminating under clauses (a), (b) or (c) and whether a criminal prosecution is to be apprehended, other matters in evidence, or disclosed in argument, the implications of the question, the setting in which it is asked, the applicable statute of limitations and all other factors, shall be taken into consideration.

L.1960, c. 52, p. 455, § 18, eff. July 1, 1960.

  [1] See, now, N.J.R.E. 502.
  [2] N.J.S.A. §§ 2A:84A–17 to 2A:84A–32.

2A:84A–19. Self-incrimination; exceptions

Rule 25.[1]

Subject to Rule 37,[2] every natural person has a right to refuse to disclose in an action or to a police officer or other official any matter that will incriminate him or expose him to a penalty or a forfeiture of his estate, except that under this rule:

(a) no person has the privilege to refuse to submit to examination for the purpose of discovering or recording his corporal features and other identifying characteristics or his physical or mental condition;

(b) no person has the privilege to refuse to obey an order made by a court to produce for use as evidence or otherwise a document, chattel or other thing under his control if some other person or a corporation or other association has a superior right to the possession of the thing ordered to be produced;

(c) no person has a privilege to refuse to disclose any matter which the statutes or regulations governing his office, activity, occupation, profession or calling, or governing the corporation or association of which he is an officer, agent or employee, require him to record or report or disclose except to the extent that such statutes or regulations provide that the matter to be recorded, reported or disclosed shall be privileged or confidential;

(d) subject to the same limitations on evidence affecting credibility as apply to any other witness, the accused in a criminal action or a party in a civil action who voluntarily testifies in the action upon the merits does not have the privilege to refuse to disclose in that action, any matter relevant to any issue therein.

L.1960, c. 52, p. 455, § 19, eff. July 1, 1960.

[1] See, now, N.J.R.E. 503.
[2] See, now, N.J.R.E. 530.

2A:84A–20. Lawyer-client privilege

Rule 26.[1]

(1) General rule. Subject to Rule 37[2] and except as otherwise provided by paragraph 2 of this rule communications between lawyer and his client in the course of that relationship and in professional confidence, are privileged, and a client has a privilege (a) to refuse to disclose any such communication, and (b) to prevent his lawyer from disclosing it, and (c) to prevent any other witness from disclosing such communication if it came to the knowledge of such witness (i) in the course of its transmittal between the client and the lawyer, or (ii) in a manner not reasonably to be anticipated, or (iii) as a result of a breach of the lawyer-client relationship, or (iv) in the course of a recognized confidential or privileged communication between the client and such witness. The privilege shall be claimed by the lawyer unless otherwise instructed by the client or his representative; the privilege may be claimed by the client in person, or if incompetent or deceased, by his guardian or personal representative. Where a corporation or association is the client having the privilege and it has been dissolved, the privilege may be claimed by its successors, assigns or trustees in dissolution.

(2) Exceptions. Such privilege shall not extend (a) to a communication in the course of legal service sought or obtained in aid of the commission of a crime or a fraud, or (b) to a communication relevant to an issue between parties all of whom claim through the client, regardless of whether the respective claims are by testate or intestate succession or by inter vivos transaction, or (c) to a communication relevant to an issue of breach of duty by the lawyer to his client, or by the client to his lawyer. Where 2 or more persons have employed a lawyer to act for them in common, none of them can assert such privilege as against the others as to communications with respect to that matter.

(3) Definitions. As used in this rule (a) "client" means a person or corporation or other association that, directly or through an authorized representative, consults a lawyer or the lawyer's representative for the purpose of retaining the lawyer or securing legal service or advice from him in his professional capacity; and includes an incompetent whose guardian so consults the lawyer or the lawyer's representative in behalf of the incompetent, (b) "lawyer" means a person authorized, or reasonably believed by the client to be authorized to practice law in any State or nation the law of which recognizes a privilege against disclosure of confidential communications between client and lawyer. A communication made in the course of relationship between lawyer and client shall be presumed to have been made in professional confidence unless knowingly made within the hearing of some person whose presence nullified the privilege.

L.1960, c. 52, p. 456, § 20, eff. July 1, 1960.

[1] See, now, N.J.R.E. 504.
[2] See, now, N.J.R.E. 530.

2A:84A–21. Newsperson's privilege

Rule 27.[1]

Subject to Rule 37,[2] a person engaged on, engaged in, connected with, or employed by news media for the purpose of gathering, procuring, transmitting, compiling, editing or disseminating news for the general public or on whose behalf news is so gathered, procured, transmitted, compiled, edited or disseminated has a privilege to refuse to disclose, in any legal or quasi-legal proceeding or before any investigative body, including, but not limited to, any court, grand jury, petit jury, administrative agency, the Legislature or legislative committee, or elsewhere.

a. The source, author, means, agency or person from or through whom any information was procured, obtained, supplied, furnished, gathered, transmitted, compiled, edited, disseminated, or delivered; and

b. Any news or information obtained in the course of pursuing his professional activities whether or not it is disseminated.

The provisions of this rule insofar as it relates to radio or television stations shall not apply unless the radio or television station maintains and keeps open for inspection, for a period of at least 1 year from the date of an actual broadcast or telecast, an exact recording, transcription, kinescopic film or certified written transcript of the actual broadcast or telecast.

L.1960, c. 52, p. 458, § 21, eff. July 1, 1960. Amended by L.1977, c. 253, § 1, eff. Oct. 5, 1977.

  [1] See, now, N.J.R.E. 508.

  [2] See, now, N.J.R.E. 530.

2A:84A–21a.   Definitions; newsperson's privilege

Unless a different meaning clearly appears from the context of this act, as used in this act:

a. "News media" means newspapers, magazines, press associations, news agencies, wire services, radio, television or other similar printed, photographic, mechanical or electronic means of disseminating news to the general public.

b. "News" means any written, oral or pictorial information gathered, procured, transmitted, compiled, edited or disseminated by, or on behalf of any person engaged in, engaged on, connected with or employed by a news media and so procured or obtained while such required relationship is in effect.

c. "Newspaper" means a paper that is printed and distributed ordinarily not less frequently than once a week and that contains news, articles of opinion, editorials, features, advertising, or other matter regarded as of current interest, has a paid circulation and has been entered at a United States post office as second class matter.

d. "Magazine" means a publication containing news which is published and distributed periodically, has a paid circulation and has been entered at a United States post office as second class matter.

e. "News agency" means a commercial organization that collects and supplies news to subscribing newspapers, magazines, periodicals and news broadcasters.

f. "Press association" means an association of newspapers or magazines formed to gather and distribute news to its members.

g. "Wire service" means a news agency that sends out syndicated news copy by wire to subscribing newspapers, magazines, periodicals or news broadcasters.

h. "In the course of pursuing his professional activities" means any situation, including a social gathering, in which a reporter obtains information for the purpose of disseminating it to the public, but does not include any situation in which a reporter intentionally conceals from the source the fact that he is a reporter, and does not include any situation in which a reporter is an eyewitness to, or participant in, any act involving physical violence or property damage.

L.1977, c. 253, § 2, eff. Oct. 5, 1977.

2A:84A–21.1.   Criminal proceeding; subpoena; application of newsperson's privilege

Where a newsperson is required to disclose information pursuant to a subpoena issued by or on behalf of a defendant in a criminal proceeding, not including proceedings before administrative or investigative bodies, grand juries, or legislative committees or commissions, the provisions and procedures in this act are applicable to the claim and exercise of the newsperson's privilege under Rule 27 (C. 2A:84A–21)[1].

L.1979, c. 479, § 1, eff. Feb. 27, 1980.

  [1] See, now, N.J.R.E. 508.

2A:84A–21.2.   Time of proceedings

Proceedings pursuant to this act shall take place before the trial, except that the court may allow a motion to institute proceedings pursuant to this act to be made during trial if the court determines that the evidence sought is newly discovered and could not have been discovered earlier through the exercise of due diligence.

L.1979, c. 479, § 2, eff. Feb. 27, 1980.

2A:84A–21.3.   Prima facie showing subpenaed materials obtained during professional activities; waiver of newsperson's privilege or other grounds for disclosure; hearing

a. To sustain a claim of the newsperson's privilege under Rule 27[1] the claimant shall make a prima facie showing that he is engaged in, connected with, or employed by a news media for the purpose of gathering, procuring, transmitting, compiling, editing or disseminating news for the general public or on whose behalf news is so gathered, procured, transmitted, compiled, edited or disseminated, and that the subpenaed[2] materials were obtained in the course of pursuing his professional activities.

b. To overcome a finding by the court that the claimant has made a prima facie showing under a. above, the party seeking enforcement of the subpena[2] shall show by clear and convincing evidence that the privilege has been waived under Rule 37 (C.2A:84A–29)[3] or by a preponderance of the evidence that there is a reasonable probability that the subpenaed materials are relevant, material and necessary to the defense, that they could not be secured from any less intrusive source, that the value of the material sought as it bears upon the issue of guilt or innocence outweighs the privilege against disclosure, and that the request is not overbroad, oppressive, or unreasonably burdensome which may be overcome by evidence that all or part of the information sought is irrelevant, immaterial, unnecessary to the defense, or that it can be secured from another source. Publication shall constitute a waiver only as to the specific materials published.

c. The determinations to be made by the court pursuant to this section shall be made only after a hearing in which the party claiming the privilege and the party seeking enforcement of the subpena shall have a full opportunity to present evidence and argument with respect to each of the materials or items sought to be subpenaed.

L.1979, c. 479, § 3, eff. Feb. 27, 1980.

  [1] See, now, N.J.R.E. 508.
  [2] So in original.
  [3] See, now, N.J.R.E. 530.

2A:84A–21.4. In camera inspection; hearing; determination of admissibility; order for production

Upon a finding by the court that there has been a waiver as to any of the materials sought or that any of the materials sought meet the criteria set forth in subsection 3.b.,[1] the court shall order the production of such materials, and such materials only, for in camera inspection and determination as to its probable admissibility in the trial. The party claiming the privilege and the party seeking enforcement of the subpoena shall be entitled to a hearing in connection with the in camera inspection of such materials by the court, during which hearing each party shall have a full opportunity to be heard. If the court, after its in camera review of the materials, determines that such materials are admissible according to the standards set forth in subsection 3.b., the court shall direct production of such materials, and such materials only.

L.1979, c. 479, § 4, eff. Feb. 27, 1980.

  [1] N.J.S.A. § 2A:84A–21.3(b).

2A:84A–21.5. Hearings; findings of fact and conclusions of law

After any hearing conducted by the court pursuant to section 3 or 4[1] hereof, the court shall make specific findings of fact and conclusions of law with respect to its rulings, which findings shall be in writing or set forth on the record.

L.1979, c. 479, § 5, eff. Feb. 27, 1980.

  [1] N.J.S.A. §§ 2A:84A–21.3, 2A:84A–21.4.

2A:84A–21.6. Appeals; stay of penalty; sealing of record; return of privileged material

An interlocutory appeal taken from a decision to uphold or quash a subpoena shall act as a stay of all penalties which may have been imposed for failure to comply with the court's order. The record on appeal shall be kept under seal until such time as appeals are exhausted. In the event that all material or any part thereof is found to be privileged, the record as to that privileged material shall remain permanently sealed. Any subpoenaed materials which shall, upon exhaustion and determination of such appeals, be found to be privileged, shall be returned to the party claiming the privilege.

L.1979, c. 479, § 6, eff. Feb. 27, 1980.

2A:84A–21.7. Co-defendants; notice of proceedings; right to intervene

Where proceedings are instituted hereunder by one of several co-defendants in a criminal trial, notice shall be provided to all of the co-defendants. Any co-defendant shall have the right to intervene if the co-defendant can demonstrate, pursuant to section 3,[1] that the materials sought by the issuance of the subpoena bear upon his guilt or innocence. Where such intervention is sought by a co-defendant, that co-defendant shall be required, prior to being permitted to participate in any in camera proceeding, to make that showing required of a defendant in section 3.

L.1979, c. 479, § 7, eff. Feb. 27, 1980.

  [1] N.J.S.A. § 2A:84A–21.3.

2A:84A–21.8. Assessment of costs or counsel fee

If the court finds no reasonable basis for requesting the information has been shown, costs, including counsel fee, may be assessed against the party seeking enforcement of the subpena.[1] Where an application for costs or counsel fee is made, the judge shall set forth his reasons for awarding or denying same.

L.1979, c. 479, § 8, eff. Feb. 27, 1980.

  [1] So in original.

2A:84A–21.9. News media person or entity; freedom from searches and seizures of documentary materials; exceptions

Any person, corporation, partnership, proprietorship or other entity engaged on, engaged in, connected with, or otherwise employed in gathering, procuring, transmitting, compiling, editing, publishing, or disseminating news for the public, or on whose behalf news is so gathered, procured, transmitted, compiled, edited, published or disseminated shall be free from searches and seizures, by State, county and local law enforcement officers with respect to any documentary materials obtained in the course of pursuing the aforesaid activities whether or not such material has been or will be disseminated or published.

This section shall not restrict or impair the ability of any law enforcement officer, pursuant to otherwise applicable law, to search for or seize such materials, if there is probable cause to believe that:

a. The person, corporation, partnership, proprietorship or other entity possessing the materials has committed or is committing the criminal offense for which the materials are sought; or

b. The immediate seizure of the materials is necessary to prevent the death of or serious bodily injury to a human being; or

c. The giving of notice pursuant to a subpena duces tecum would result in the destruction, alteration or deliberate concealment of the documentary materials other than work product; or

d. The documentary materials, other than work product, have not been produced in response to a court order directing compliance with a subpena duces tecum, and

(1) All appellate remedies have been exhausted by the party seeking to quash the subpena duces tecum; or

(2) There is a probability that the delay in an investigation or trial occasioned by further proceedings relating to the subpena would threaten the interests of justice. In the event a search warrant is sought pursuant to this subparagraph, the person, corporation, partnership, proprietorship or other entity possessing the materials shall be afforded adequate opportunity to submit an affidavit to the court setting forth the basis for any contention that the materials sought are not subject to seizure.

L.1979, c. 488, § 1, eff. Feb. 28, 1980.

2A:84A–21.10. Applications for search warrant; approval

In the event a search warrant is sought pursuant to Section 1 of this act,[1] all applications to the court for such warrants shall be approved in advance of their submission by the Attorney General or the prosecutor of the county in which execution of the warrant will take place.

L.1979, c. 488, § 2, eff. Feb. 28, 1980.

  [1] N.J.S.A. § 2A:84A–21.9.

2A:84A–21.11. Civil cause of action for damages due to violations

a. A person, corporation, partnership, proprietorship or other entity aggrieved by a search for or seizure of materials in violation of this act shall have a civil cause of action for damages for such search or seizure:

(1) Against the State of New Jersey, or against any other governmental unit, all of which shall be liable for violations of this act by their officers, employees or agents while acting within the scope or under color of their office, employment or agency.

(2) Against an officer, employee or agent of the State of New Jersey or any other governmental unit who has violated this act while acting other than within the scope or under color of his office, employment or agency. It shall be a complete defense to a civil action brought under this paragraph that the officer, employee or agent had a reasonable good faith belief in the lawfulness of his conduct unless his error is due to an ignorance of an official statement of the law.

b. The State of New Jersey or any other governmental unit, liable for violations of this act under paragraph 3 a. (1),[1] may not assert as a defense to a claim arising under this act the immunity of the officer, employee or agent whose violation is complained of or his reasonable good faith belief in the lawfulness of his conduct, except that such a defense may be asserted if the violation complained of is that of a judge.

c. The remedy provided by paragraph 3 a. (1) against the State of New Jersey or any other governmental unit is exclusive of any other civil action or proceeding for conduct constituting a violation of this act, against the officer, employee or agent whose violation gave rise to the claim, or against the estate of such officer, employee or agent.

d. A person, corporation, partnership, proprietorship or other entity having a cause of action under this section shall be entitled to recover actual damages but not less than liquidated damages of $1,000.00, such punitive damages as may be warranted, and such reasonable attorney's fee and other litigation costs reasonably incurred as the court, in its discretion, may award; provided, however, that the State of New Jersey or any other governmental unit shall not be liable for interest prior to judgment.

e. The Attorney General is authorized to settle a claim for damages brought against the State of New Jersey under this section and shall promulgate regulations to provide for the commencement of an administrative inquiry following a determination of a violation of this act by an officer, employee or agent of the State of New Jersey or any other governmental unit and for the imposition of administrative sanctions against such officer, employee or agent if warranted.

f. A county prosecutor may settle a claim for damages brought against the county of his jurisdiction or any other governmental unit under this section.

L.1979, c. 488, § 3, eff. Feb. 28, 1980.

  [1] N.J.S.A. § 2A:84A–21.11(a)(1).

2A:84A–21.12. Additional definitions; newsperson's privilege

As used in this act: a. "Documentary materials" means materials upon which information is recorded and includes, but is not limited to, written or printed materials, photographs, tapes, videotapes, negatives, films, outtakes and interview files.

b. "Work product" means any documentary materials created by or for a person in connection with his plans, or the plans of the person creating such materials, to gather, file procure, transmit, compile, edit, publish or disseminate news for the public, except such work product as constitutes contraband, or the fruits, instrumentalities or evidence of a crime.

c. "Any other governmental unit" includes any branch, subdivision or agency of the government of the State or any locality within it.

d. "Attorney General" means the Attorney General of the State of New Jersey, or his designee.

e. "County prosecutor" means the duly appointed prosecutor of a county, or his designee.

L.1979, c. 488, § 4, eff. Feb. 28, 1980.

2A:84A–21.13. Inapplicability of act to rights of department of corrections

Nothing contained in this act shall be construed to limit the right of the Department of Corrections to search the offices of inmate newspapers or the public information offices of any inmate organization located within a correctional facility.

L.1979, c. 488, § 5, eff. Feb. 28, 1980.

2A:84A–22. Marital privilege—Confidential communications

Rule 28.[1]

No person shall disclose any communication made in confidence between such person and his or her spouse unless both shall consent to the disclosure or unless the communication is relevant to an issue in an action between them or in a criminal action or proceeding in which either spouse consents to the disclosure, or in a criminal action or proceeding coming within Rule 23(2).[2] When a spouse is incompetent or deceased, consent to the disclosure may be given for such spouse by the guardian, executor or administrator. The requirement for consent shall not terminate with divorce or separation. A communication between spouses while living separate and apart under a divorce from bed and board shall not be a privileged communication.

L.1960, c. 52, p. 458, § 22, eff. July 1, 1960. Amended by L.1992, c. 142, § 2, eff. Nov. 17, 1992.

[1] See, now, N.J.R.E. 509.

[2] § 2A:84A–17.

Historical and Statutory Notes

L.1992, c. 142, § 3, approved Nov. 17, 1992, provides:

"This act shall take effect immediately and, to the fullest extent consistent with constitutional restrictions, shall apply to all criminal actions regardless of the date on which the offense was committed or the action initiated."

2A:84A–22.1. Definitions; patient-physician privilege

As used in this act, (a) "patient" means a person who, for the sole purpose of securing preventive, palliative, or curative treatment, or a diagnosis preliminary to such treatment, of his physical or mental condition, consults a physician, or submits to an examination by a physician; (b) "physician" means a person authorized or reasonably believed by the patient to be authorized, to practice medicine in the State or jurisdiction in which the consultation or examination takes place; (c) "holder of the privilege" means the patient while alive and not under the guardianship or the guardian of the person of an incompetent patient, or the personal representative of a deceased patient; (d) "confidential communication between physician and patient" means such information transmitted between physician and patient, including information obtained by an examination of the patient, as is transmitted in confidence and by a means which, so far as the patient is aware, discloses the information to no third persons other than those reasonably necessary for the transmission of the information or the accomplishment of the purpose for which it is transmitted.

L.1968, c. 185, § 1, eff. July 19, 1968.

2A:84A–22.2. Patient and physician privilege

Except as otherwise provided in this act, a person, whether or not a party, has a privilege in a civil action or in a prosecution for a crime or violation of the disorderly persons law or for an act of juvenile delinquency to refuse to disclose, and to prevent a witness from disclosing, a communication, if he claims the privilege and the judge finds that (a) the communication was a confidential communication between patient and physician, and (b) the patient or the physician reasonably believed the communication to be necessary or helpful to enable the physician to make a diagnosis of the condition of the patient or to prescribe or render treatment therefor, and (c) the witness (i) is the holder of the privilege or (ii) at the time of the communication was the physician or a person to whom disclosure was made because reasonably necessary for the transmission of the communication or for the accomplishment of the purpose for which it was transmitted or (iii) is any other person who obtained knowledge or possession of the communication as the result of an intentional breach of the physician's duty of nondisclosure by the physician or his agent or servant and (d) the claimant is the holder of the privilege or a person authorized to claim the privilege for him.

L.1968, c. 185, § 2, eff. July 19, 1968.

2A:84A–22.3. Mental incompetence; validity of will; nonprivileged communication

There is no privilege under this act as to any relevant communication between the patient and his physician (a) upon an issue of the patient's condition in an action to commit him or otherwise place him under the control of another or others because of alleged incapacity, or in an action in which the patient seeks to establish his competence or in an action to recover damages on account of conduct of the patient which constitutes a criminal offense other than a misdemeanor, or (b) upon an issue as to the validity of a document as a will of the patient, or (c) upon an issue between parties claiming by testate or intestate succession from a deceased patient.

L.1968, c. 185, § 3, eff. July 19, 1968. Amended by L.1997, c. 379, § 10, eff. Jan. 19, 1998.

2A:84A–22.4. Contract of patient; condition of patient is element of claim; nonprivileged communications

There is no privilege under this act in an action in which the condition of the patient is an element or factor of the claim or defense of the patient or of any party claiming through or under the patient or claiming as a beneficiary of the patient through a contract to which the patient is or was a party or under which the patient is or was insured.

L.1968, c. 185, § 4, eff. July 19, 1968.

2A:84A–22.5. Information reported to public official; nonprivileged communications

There is no privilege under this act as to information which the physician or the patient is required to report to a public official or as to information required to be recorded in a public office, unless the statute requiring the report or record specifically provides that the information shall not be disclosed.

L.1968, c. 185, § 5, eff. July 19, 1968.

2A:84A–22.6. Obtaining physician to aid commission of crime or tort, or to escape detection or apprehension; nonprivileged communications

No person has a privilege under this act if the judge finds that sufficient evidence, aside from the communication has been introduced to warrant a finding that the services of the physician were sought or obtained to enable or aid anyone to commit or to plan to commit a crime or a tort, or to escape detection or apprehension after the commission of a crime or a tort.

L.1968, c. 185, § 6, eff. July 19, 1968.

2A:84A–22.7. Testimony by physician on request of holder of privilege; termination of privilege

A privilege under this act as to a communication is terminated if the judge finds that any person while a holder of the privilege has caused the physician or any agent or servant of the physician to testify in any action to any matter of which the physician or his agent or servant gained knowledge through the communication.

L.1968, c. 185, § 7, eff. July 19, 1968.

2A:84A–22.8. Utilization review committees of certified hospital or extended care facility; exceptions

Information and data secured by and in the possession of utilization review committees established by any certified hospital or extended care facility in the performance of their duties shall not be revealed or disclosed in any manner or under any circumstances by any member of such committee except to: (a) a patient's attending physician, (b) the chief administrative officer of the hospital or extended care facility which it serves, (c) the medical executive committee, or comparable enforcement unit, of such hospital or extended care facility, (d) representatives of, including intermediaries or carriers for, government agencies in the performance of their duties, under the provisions of Federal and State law, or (e) any hospital service corporation, medical service corporation or insurance company with which said patient has pertinent coverage under a contract, policy or certificate, the terms of which authorize the carrier to request and be given such information and data.

L.1970, c. 313, § 1, eff. Dec. 21, 1970. Amended by L.1979, c. 68, § 1, eff. April 10, 1979.

2A:84A–22.9. Liability of member of utilization review committee for disclosure of information

No member of a utilization review committee may be held liable for damages or otherwise prejudiced in any manner by reason of recommendations or findings made by said committee or for furnishing information or data obtained in the course of his duties as a member of a committee to the persons and officials mentioned in section 1 hereof.[1]

L.1970, c. 313, § 2, eff. Dec. 21, 1970.

   1 N.J.S.A. § 2A:84A–22.8.

2A:84A–22.10. Hospital or long-term health care facility committees; professional review committees; liability of members

Any person who serves as a member of, is staff to, under a contract or other formal agreement with, participates with, or assists with respect to an action of:

    a. A hospital or long-term health care facility committee established to administer a utilization review plan for such hospital or long-term health care facility; or

    b. A hospital medical staff committee having the responsibility of evaluation and improvement of the quality of care rendered in such hospital; or

    c. (Deleted by amendment, P.L. 1985, c. 506.)

    d. A hospital peer-review committee having the responsibility for the review of the qualifications and credentials of physicians or dentists seeking appointment or reappointment to the medical or dental staff of a hospital, or of questions of the clinical or administrative competence of physicians or dentists so appointed, or of matters concerning limiting the scope of hospital privileges of physicians or dentists on the staff, or of matters concerning the dismissal or discharge of same; or

    e. A peer-review, ethics, grievance, judicial, quality assurance or professional relations committee or subcommittee thereof of a local, county or State medical, dental, podiatric, optometric, psychological, veterinary, chiropractic or pharmaceutical society or long-term health care facility association, of any such society or association itself, or of a health maintenance organization, when such society, association or organization or committee or subcommittee thereof is performing any peer-review, ethics, grievance, judicial, quality assurance or professional relations review function that

    (1) Is described in subsections a., b., and d., above of this section; or

    (2) Involves any controversy or dispute between (a) a physician, dentist, podiatrist, optometrist, psychologist, veterinarian, chiropractor, pharmacist, nurse, dietitian or licensed administrator and a patient or, in the case of a veterinarian, the patient's owner, concerning the diagnosis, treatment or care of such patient or the fees or charges therefor, (b) a physician, dentist, podiatrist, optometrist, psychologist, veterinarian, chiropractor, pharmacist, nurse, dietitian or licensed administrator and a provider of medical, dental, podiatric, veterinary, optometric, psychological, or pharmaceutical benefits concerning any medical or health charges or fees of such physician, dentist, podiatrist, optometrist, psychologist, veterinarian, chiropractor, pharmacist, nurse, dietitian or licensed administrator, or (c)

physicians, dentists, podiatrists, optometrists, psychologists, veterinarians, chiropractors, pharmacists, nurses, dietitians or licensed administrators:

shall not be liable in damages to any person for any action taken or recommendation made by him within the scope of his function with the committee, subcommittee or society in the performance of said peer-review, ethics, grievance, judicial, quality assurance or professional relations review functions, if such action or recommendation was taken or made without malice and in the reasonable belief after reasonable investigation that such action or recommendation was warranted upon the basis of facts disclosed.

L.1979, c. 128, § 1, eff. July 6, 1979. Amended by L.1985, c. 506, § 1, eff. Jan. 21, 1986; L.1987, c. 241, § 1, eff. Aug. 19, 1987; L.1989, c. 300, § 24, eff. Jan. 12, 1990.

2A:84A–22.11, 2A:84A–22.12. Repealed by L.1987, c. 169, § 6, eff. July 8, 1987

2A:84A–22.13. Legislative findings and declarations

The Legislature finds and declares that:

a. The emotional and psychological injuries that are inflicted on victims of violence are often more serious than the physical injuries suffered;

b. Counseling is often a successful treatment to ease the real and profound psychological trauma experienced by these victims and their families;

c. In the counseling process, victims of violence openly discuss their emotional reactions to the crime. These reactions are often highly intertwined with their personal histories and psychological profile;

d. Counseling of violence and victims is most successful when the victims are assured their thoughts and feelings will remain confidential and will not be disclosed without their permission; and

e. Confidentiality should be accorded all victims of violence who require counseling whether or not they are able to afford the services of private psychiatrists or psychologists.

Therefore, it is the public policy of this State to extend a testimonial privilege encompassing the contents of communications with a victim counselor and to render immune from discovery or legal process the records of these communications maintained by the counselor.

L.1987, c. 169, § 2, eff. July 8, 1987.

2A:84A–22.14. Definitions; victim counselor's privilege

As used in this act:

a. "Act of violence" means the commission or attempt to commit any of the offenses set forth in subsection b. of section 11 of P.L.1971, c. 317 (C.52:4B–11).

b. "Confidential communication" means any information exchanged between a victim and a victim counselor in private or in the presence of a third party who is necessary to facilitate communication or further the counseling process and which is disclosed in the course of the counselor's treatment of the victim for any emotional or psychological condition resulting from an act of violence. It includes any advice, report or working paper given or made in the course of the consultation and all information received by the victim counselor in the course of that relationship.

c. "Victim" means a person who consults a counselor for the purpose of securing advice, counseling or assistance concerning a mental, physical or emotional condition caused by an act of violence.

d. "Victim counseling center" means any office, institution, or center offering assistance to victims and their families through crisis intervention, medical and legal accompaniment and follow-up counseling.

e. "Victim counselor" means a person engaged in any office, institution or center defined as a victim counseling center by this act, who has undergone 40 hours of training and is under the control of a direct services supervisor of the center and who has a primary function of rendering advice, counseling or assisting victims of acts of violence. "Victim counselor" includes a rape care advocate as defined in section 4 of P.L.2001, c. 81 (C.52:4B–52).

L.1987, c. 169, § 3, eff. July 8, 1987. Amended by L.2001, c. 81, § 1, eff. May 4, 2001.

2A:84A–22.15. Victim counselor's privilege

Subject to Rule 37 of the Rules of Evidence,[1] a victim counselor has a privilege not to be examined as a witness in any civil or criminal proceeding with regard to any confidential communication. The privilege shall be claimed by the counselor unless otherwise instructed by prior written consent of the victim. When a victim is incompetent or deceased consent to disclosure may be given by the guardian, executor or administrator except when the guardian, executor or administrator is the defendant or has a relationship with the victim such that he has an interest in the outcome of the proceeding. The privilege may be knowingly waived by a juvenile. In any instance where the juvenile is, in the opinion of the judge, incapable of knowing consent, the parent or guardian of the juvenile may waive the privilege on behalf of the juvenile, provided that the parent or guardian is not the defendant and does not have a relationship with the defendant such that he has an interest in the outcome of the proceeding. A victim counselor or a victim cannot be compelled to provide testimony in any civil or criminal proceeding that would identify the name, address, location, or telephone number of a domestic violence shelter or any other facility that provided temporary emergency shelter to the victim of the offense or transaction that is the subject of the proceeding unless the facility is a party to the proceeding.

L.1987, c. 169, § 4, eff. July 8, 1987.

   1 See, now, N.J.R.E. 530.

2A:84A–22.16. Disclosure to defendant in criminal action of information given to county victim-witness coordinator

Nothing in this act shall be deemed to prevent the disclosure to a defendant in a criminal action of statements or information given by a victim to a county victim-witness coordinator, where the disclosure of the statements or information is required by the Constitution of this State or of the United States.

L.1987, c. 169, § 5, eff. July 8, 1987.

2A:84A–23. Cleric-penitent privilege

Rule 511.

Any communication made in confidence to a cleric in the cleric's professional character, or as a spiritual advisor in the course of the discipline or practice of the religious body to which the cleric belongs or of the religion which the cleric professes, shall be privileged. Privileged communications shall include confessions and other communications made in confidence between and among the cleric and individuals, couples, families or groups in the exercise of the cleric's professional or spiritual counseling role.

As used in this section, "cleric" means a priest, rabbi, minister or other person or practitioner authorized to perform similar functions of any religion.

The privilege accorded to communications under this rule shall belong to both the cleric and the person or persons making the communication and shall be subject to waiver only under the following circumstances:

(1) both the person or persons making the communication and the cleric consent to the waiver of the privilege; or

(2) the privileged communication pertains to a future criminal act, in which case, the cleric alone may, but is not required to, waive the privilege.

L.1960, c. 52, p. 458, § 23, eff. July 1, 1960. Amended by L.1981, c. 303, § 2, eff. Nov. 11, 1981; L.1994, c. 123, § 1, eff. Oct. 26, 1994.

2A:84A–24. Religious belief

Rule 30.[1]

Every person has a privilege to refuse to disclose his theological opinion or religious belief unless his adherence or nonadherence to such an opinion or belief is material to an issue in the action other than that of his credibility as a witness.

L.1960, c. 52, p. 458, § 24, eff. July 1, 1960.

   1 See, now, N.J.R.E. 512, 610.

2A:84A–25. Political vote

Rule 31.[1]

Every person has a privilege to refuse to disclose the tenor of his vote at a political election unless the judge finds that the vote was cast illegally.

L.1960, c. 52, p. 459, § 25, eff. July 1, 1960.

   1 See, now, N.J.R.E. 513.

2A:84A–26. Trade secret

Rule 32.[1]

The owner of a trade secret has a privilege, which may be claimed by him or his agent or employee, to refuse to disclose the secret and to prevent other persons from disclosing it if the judge finds that the allowance of the privilege will not tend to conceal fraud or otherwise work injustice.

L.1960, c. 52, p. 459, eff. July 1, 1960.

   1 See, now, N.J.R.E. 514.

2A:84A–27. Official information

Rule 34.[1]

No person shall disclose official information of this State or of the United States (a) if disclosure is forbidden by or pursuant to any Act of Congress or of this State, or (b) if the judge finds that disclosure of the information in the action will be harmful to the interests of the public.

L.1960, c. 52, p. 459, § 27, eff. July 1, 1960.

   1 See, now, N.J.R.E. 515.

2A:84A–28. Identity of informer

Rule 36.[1]

A witness has a privilege to refuse to disclose the identity of a person who has furnished information purporting to disclose a violation of a provision of the laws of this State or of the United States to a representative of the State or the United States or a governmental division thereof, charged with the duty of enforcing that provision, and evidence thereof is inadmissible, unless the judge finds that (a) the identity of the person furnishing the information has already been otherwise disclosed or (b) disclosure of his identity is essential to assure a fair determination of the issues.

L.1960, c. 52, p. 459, § 28, eff. July 1, 1960.

   1 See, now, N.J.R.E. 516.

2A:84A–29. Waiver of privilege by contract or previous disclosure; limitations

Rule 37.[1]

A person waives his right or privilege to refuse to disclose or to prevent another from disclosing a specified matter if he or any other person while the holder thereof has (a) contracted with anyone not to claim the right or privilege or, (b) without coercion and with knowledge of his right or privilege, made disclosure of any part of the privileged matter or consented to such a disclosure made by anyone.

A disclosure which is itself privileged or otherwise protected by the common law, statutes or rules of court of this State, or by lawful contract, shall not constitute a waiver under this section. The failure of a witness to claim a right or privilege with respect to 1 question shall not operate as a waiver with respect to any other question.

L.1960, c. 52, p. 459, § 29, eff. July 1, 1960.

[1] See, now, N.J.R.E. 530.

2A:84A–30. Admissibility of disclosure wrongfully compelled

Rule 38.[1]

Evidence of a statement or other disclosure is inadmissible against the holder of the privilege if the disclosure was wrongfully made or erroneously required.

L.1960, c. 52, p. 460, § 30, eff. July 1, 1960.

[1] See, now, N.J.R.E. 531.

2A:84A–31. Reference to exercise of privileges

Rule 39.[1]

If a privilege is exercised not to testify or to prevent another from testifying, either in the action or with respect to particular matters, or to refuse to disclose or to prevent another from disclosing any matter, the judge and counsel may not comment thereon, no presumption shall arise with respect to the exercise of the privilege, and the trier of fact may not draw any adverse inference therefrom. In those jury cases wherein the right to exercise a privilege, as herein provided, may be misunderstood and unfavorable inferences drawn by the trier of the fact, or be impaired in the particular case, the court, at the request of the party exercising the privilege, may instruct the jury in support of such privilege.

L.1960, c. 52, p. 460, § 31, eff. July 1, 1960. Amended Sept. 14, 1979, eff. July 1, 1980.

[1] See, now, N.J.R.E. 532.

2A:84A–32. Effect of error in overruling claim of privilege

Rule 40.[1]

(1) A party may predicate error on a ruling disallowing a claim of privilege only if he is the holder of the privilege.

(2) If a witness refuses to answer a question, under color of a privilege claimed pursuant to Rules 23 through 38,[2] after the judge has ordered the witness to answer, and a contempt proceeding is brought against the witness, the court hearing the same shall order it

dismissed if it appears that the order directing the witness to answer was erroneous.

L.1960, c. 52, p. 460, § 32, eff. July 1, 1960.

[1] See, now, N.J.R.E. 533.
[2] See, now, N.J.R.E. 501 to 509, 517.

2A:84A–32a. Post-conviction DNA testing; motion; determinations

a. Any person who was convicted of a crime and is currently serving a term of imprisonment may make a motion before the trial court that entered the judgment of conviction for the performance of forensic DNA testing.

(1) The motion shall be verified by the convicted person under penalty of perjury and shall do all of the following:

(a) explain why the identity of the defendant was a significant issue in the case;

(b) explain in light of all the evidence, how if the results of the requested DNA testing are favorable to the defendant, a motion for a new trial based upon newly discovered evidence would be granted;

(c) explain whether DNA testing was done at any prior time, whether the defendant objected to providing a biological sample for DNA testing, and whether the defendant objected to the admissibility of DNA testing evidence at trial. If evidence was subjected to DNA or other forensic testing previously by either the prosecution or the defense, the court shall order the prosecution or defense to provide all parties and the court with access to the laboratory reports, underlying data and laboratory notes prepared in connection with the DNA testing;

(d) make every reasonable attempt to identify both the evidence that should be tested and the specific type of DNA testing sought;and

(e) include consent to provide a biological sample for DNA testing.

(2) Notice of the motion shall be served on the Attorney General, the prosecutor in the county of conviction, and if known, the governmental agency or laboratory holding the evidence sought to be tested. Responses, if any, shall be filed within 60 days of the date on which the Attorney General and the prosecutor are served with the motion, unless a continuance is granted. The Attorney General or prosecutor may support the motion for DNA testing or oppose it with a statement of reasons and may recommend to the court that if any DNA testing is ordered, a particular type of testing be conducted.

b. The court, in its discretion, may order a hearing on the motion. The motion shall be heard by the judge who conducted the trial unless the presiding judge determines that judge is unavailable. Upon request of either party, the court may order, in the interest of justice, that the convicted person be present at the hearing of the motion.

c. The court shall appoint counsel for the convicted person who brings a motion pursuant to this section if that person is indigent.

d. The court shall not grant the motion for DNA testing unless, after conducting a hearing, it determines that all of the following have been established:

(1) the evidence to be tested is available and in a condition that would permit the DNA testing that is requested in the motion;

(2) the evidence to be tested has been subject to a chain of custody sufficient to establish it has not been substituted, tampered with, replaced or altered in any material aspect;

(3) the identity of the defendant was a significant issue in the case;

(4) the convicted person has made a prima facie showing that the evidence sought to be tested is material to the issue of the convicted person's identity as the offender;

(5) the requested DNA testing result would raise a reasonable probability that if the results were favorable to the defendant, a motion for a new trial based upon newly discovered evidence would be granted. The court in its discretion may consider any evidence whether or not it was introduced at trial;

(6) the evidence sought to be tested meets either of the following conditions:

(a) it was not tested previously;

(b) it was tested previously, but the requested DNA test would provide results that are reasonably more discriminating and probative of the identity of the offender or have a reasonable probability of contradicting prior test results;

(7) the testing requested employs a method generally accepted within the relevant scientific community; and

(8) the motion is not made solely for the purpose of delay.

e. If the court grants the motion for DNA testing, the court order shall identify the specific evidence to be tested and the DNA technology to be used. (1) If the parties agree upon a mutually acceptable laboratory that is accredited by the American Society of Crime Laboratory Directors Laboratory Accreditation Board or a laboratory that has a certificate of compliance with national standards issued pursuant to 42 U.S.C.A. § 14131 from the National Forensic Science Technology Center, the testing shall be conducted by that laboratory.

(2) If the parties fail to agree, the testing shall be conducted by the New Jersey State Police Forensic Science Laboratory. For good cause shown, however, the court may direct the evidence to an alternative laboratory that is accredited by the American Society of Crime Laboratory Directors Laboratory Accreditation Board or a laboratory that has a certificate of compli-

ance with national standards issued pursuant to 42 U.S.C.A. § 14131 from the National Forensic Science Technology Center.

f. The result of any testing ordered pursuant to this section shall be fully disclosed to the person filing the motion, the prosecutor and the Attorney General. If requested by any party, the court shall order production of the underlying laboratory data and notes.

g. The costs of the DNA testing ordered pursuant to this section shall be borne by the convicted person.

h. An order granting or denying a motion for DNA testing pursuant to this section may be appealed, pursuant to the Rules of Court.

i. DNA testing ordered by the court pursuant to this section shall be done as soon as practicable.

j. DNA profile information from biological samples taken from a convicted person pursuant to a motion for post-conviction DNA testing in accordance with the provisions of this section shall be treated as confidential and shall not be deemed a public record under P.L. 1963, c. 73 (C.47:1A–1 et seq.) or the common law concerning access to public records; except as provided in section 2 of P.L.2001, c. 377 (C.53:1–20.37).

k. As used in this act, the terms "DNA," "DNA sample," "DNA databank," "CODIS" and "FBI" shall have the meaning set forth in section 3 of P.L.1994, c. 136 (C.53:1–20.19).

L.2001, c. 377, § 1, eff. July 7, 2002.

2A:84A–32b.　Rules

The Supreme Court of New Jersey may adopt rules appropriate and necessary to effectuate the purpose of this act.

L.2001, c. 377, § 3.

ARTICLE IIA.　ADMISSIBILITY

2A:84A–32.1.　Prosecutions involving rape; evidence of complaining witness' previous sexual conduct

In prosecutions for the crime of rape, assault with intent to commit rape, and breaking and entering with intent to commit rape, evidence of the complaining witness' previous sexual conduct shall not be admitted nor reference made to it in the presence of the jury except as provided in this act. When the defendant seeks to admit the evidence for any purpose, he may apply for an order of the court at any time before or during the trial or preliminary hearing. After the application is made, the court shall conduct a hearing in camera to determine the admissibility of the evidence. If the court finds that evidence offered by the defendant regarding the sexual conduct of the complaining witness is relevant, and that the probative value of the evidence offered is not outweighed by the probability that its admission will create undue prejudice, confusion of the issues, or unwarranted invasion of the privacy of the complaining witness, the court shall make an order stating what evidence may be introduced and the nature of the questions which shall be permitted. The defendant may then offer evidence under the order of the court.

L.1976, c. 71, § 1, eff. Aug. 26, 1976.

2A:84A–32.2. Conduct one year or more prior to date of offense; presumption of inadmissibility

In the absence of clear and convincing proof to the contrary, evidence of the complaining witness' sexual conduct occurring more than 1 year before the date of the offense charged is presumed to be inadmissible under this act.

L.1976, c. 71, § 2, eff. Aug. 26, 1976.

2A:84A–32.3. Complaining witness defined

As used in this act "complaining witness" means the alleged victim of the crime charged, the prosecution of which is subject to this act.

L.1976, c. 71, § 3, eff. Aug. 26, 1976.

2A:84A–32.4. Prosecutions or actions for sexual assault, criminal sexual conduct, or child abuse or neglect; closed circuit testimony by minor

a. In prosecutions for aggravated sexual assault, sexual assault, aggravated criminal sexual contact, criminal sexual contact, or child abuse, or in any action alleging an abused or neglected child under P.L.1974, c. 119 (C.9:6–8.21 et seq.), the court may, on motion and after conducting a hearing in camera, order the taking of the testimony of a witness on closed circuit television at the trial, out of the view of the jury, defendant, or spectators upon making findings as provided in subsection b. of this section.

b. An order under this section may be made only if the court finds that the witness is 16 years of age or younger and that there is a substantial likelihood that the witness would suffer severe emotional or mental distress if required to testify in open court. The order shall be specific as to whether the witness will testify outside the presence of spectators, the defendant, the jury, or all of them and shall be based on specific findings relating to the impact of the presence of each.

c. A motion seeking closed circuit testimony under subsection a. of this section may be filed by:

(1) The victim or witness or the victim's or witness's attorney, parent or legal guardian;

(2) The prosecutor;

(3) The defendant or the defendant's counsel; or

(4) The trial judge on the judge's own motion.

d. The defendant's counsel shall be present at the taking of testimony in camera. If the defendant is not present, he and his attorney shall be able to confer privately with each other during the testimony by a separate audio system.

e. If testimony is taken on closed circuit television pursuant to the provisions of this act, a stenographic recording of that testimony shall also be required. A typewritten transcript of that testimony shall be included in the record on appeal. The closed circuit testimony itself shall not constitute part of the record on appeal except on motion for good cause shown.

L.1985, c. 126, § 1, eff. April 11, 1985.

ARTICLE III.   ADOPTION OF RULES

2A:84A–33. Authority of Supreme Court

The Supreme Court may adopt rules dealing with the admission or rejection of evidence, in accordance with the procedures set forth in this article.[1]

L.1960, c. 52, p. 461, § 33, eff. June 20, 1960.

[1] N.J.S.A. §§ 2A:84A–33 to 2A:84A–44.

2A:84A–34. Presentation of proposed rules at Judicial Conference

The subject matter and a tentative draft of a rule or rules proposed to be adopted pursuant to this article shall be entered upon the agenda and discussed at a Judicial Conference whose membership shall at least include delegates from the Supreme Court, the Appellate Division of the Superior Court, the judges of the Superior Court, the judges of the municipal courts, the surrogates, the State Bar Association, the county bar associations, the Senate and General Assembly, the Attorney General, the county prosecutors, the law schools of this State, and members of the public.

L.1960, c. 52, p. 461, § 34, eff. June 20, 1960. Amended by L.1991, c. 91, § 118, eff. April 9, 1991.

2A:84A–35. Public announcement of proposed rules; delivery of copies

The proposed rule or rules shall be publicly announced by the Supreme Court on September 15 next following such Judicial Conference (or, if such day be a Saturday, Sunday or legal holiday, on the first day thereafter that is not), and the court shall, on the same day, cause true copies thereof to be delivered to the President of the Senate, the Speaker of the General Assembly, and the Governor.

L.1960, c. 52, p. 461, § 35, eff. June 20, 1960.

2A:84A–36. Effective date of rules; rules subject to cancellation by joint resolution

The rule or rules so announced and delivered shall take effect on July 1 next following; provided, however, that all such rules shall remain subject to cancellation at any time up to such effective date by joint resolution to that effect adopted by the Senate and General Assembly and signed by the Governor.

L.1960, c. 52, p. 461, § 36, eff. June 20, 1960.

2A:84A–37. Change or cancellation of rules by statute or adoption of subsequent rules

Any rule or rules so proposed or adopted shall be subject to change or cancellation at any time by statute or by a subsequent rule adopted pursuant to this article.[1]

L.1960, c. 52, p. 462, § 37, eff. June 20, 1960.

1 N.J.S.A. §§ 2A:84A–33 to 2A:84A–44.

2A:84A–38. Adoption of rules at such time, or with such effective date, or without presentation at Judicial Conference, as may be provided in joint resolution

By joint resolution adopted by the Senate and General Assembly and signed by the Governor with respect to a particular rule or rules therein specified, the Supreme Court may adopt such rule or rules at such time or times, or with such effective date, or without presentation at a Judicial Conference, as may be provided in the joint resolution.

L.1960, c. 52, p. 462, § 38, eff. June 20, 1960.

2A:84A–39. Reduction or elimination of time during which rules may be canceled by joint resolution

By joint resolution adopted by the Senate and General Assembly and signed by the Governor with respect to a particular rule or rules therein specified, the period of time provided in section 36 [1] during which the same may be canceled by joint resolution may be reduced or eliminated.

L.1960, c. 52, p. 462, § 39, eff. June 20, 1960.

1 N.J.S.A. § 2A:84A–36.

2A:84A–39.1 to 2A:84A–39.6. Repealed by L.1978, c. 109, § 2, eff. July 1, 1978

2A:84A–40. Effect of rules on conflicting laws

All previous laws or parts of laws dealing with the admission or rejection of evidence which shall be expressly identified by footnote to any rule so adopted, and which shall be a conflict or inconsistent with such rule or rules, or included therein, revised or rendered obsolete thereby, shall be of no further force or effect after such rule or rules shall have taken effect.

L.1960, c. 52, p. 462, § 40, eff. June 20, 1960.

> *For table listing statutes superseded by the 1967 Rules of Evidence and continued to be superseded by the New Jersey Rules of Evidence, and for additional statutes superseded by said rules, see Official Note under N.J.R.E. 101, set out in Appendix A following this Chapter.*

2A:84A–41. Rules not to abridge, enlarge or modify substantive rights or eliminate right of trial by jury

No rule adopted pursuant to this article [1] shall abridge, enlarge or modify any substantive right or eliminate the right of trial by jury.

L.1960, c. 52, p. 462, § 41, eff. June 20, 1960.

1 N.J.S.A. §§ 2A:84A–33 to 2A:84A–44.

2A:84A–42. Applicability of rules to pending proceedings or existing rights or remedies

No rule adopted pursuant to this article [1] shall be made applicable to pending proceedings or to existing rights or remedies except to the extent that such application is fair and practicable, and does not impair the obligation of contracts or deprive a party of any remedy for enforcing a contract which existed when the contract was made.

L.1960, c. 52, p. 462, § 42, eff. June 20, 1960.

1 N.J.S.A. §§ 2A:84A–33 to 2A:84A–44.

2A:84A–43. Publication of compilations and restatements of rules

To the end that rules dealing with evidence may be conveniently presented and arranged, the Supreme Court may publish compilations and restatements thereof which may include, in addition to such rules as may be adopted pursuant to this article,[1] rules established by common law, statute, constitution or otherwise, together with editorial notes, tables and references, and with indications as to the source of each such rule. Where practicable or desirable, the numbering and arrangement of such publications shall conform to standard or uniform works on the subject, or provide cross-reference thereto.

L.1960, c. 52, p. 462, § 43, eff. June 20, 1960.

1 N.J.S.A. §§ 2A:84A–33 to 2A:84A–44.

2A:84A–44. Force and effect of existing rules dealing with admission or rejection of evidence

All rules of court heretofore promulgated and which may deal with the admission or rejection of evidence shall be deemed to have the same force and effect as though they had been adopted pursuant to this article.[1]

L.1960, c. 52, p. 463, § 44, eff. June 20, 1960.

1 N.J.S.A. §§ 2A:84A–33 to 2A:84A–44.

ARTICLE IV. MISCELLANEOUS REVISIONS AND REPEALERS

2A:84A–45. Repeals

The following acts and parts of acts and all amendments and supplements thereto are hereby repealed: Sections 2A:81–3, 2A:81–5, 2A:81–7, 2A:81–9 and 2A:81–10 of Title 2A of the New Jersey Statutes.

L.1960, c. 52, p. 465, § 49, eff. July 1, 1960.

2A:84A–46. Repealed by L.1999, c. 319, § 2, eff. Jan. 6, 2000

2A:84A–47. Effect of repeals

No repeal effected by this act [1] shall operate to revive any statute heretofore repealed nor to impair the obligation of contracts made before the effective date hereof, nor to deprive a party of any remedy for enforcing a contract which existed when the contract was made.

L.1960, c. 52, p. 465, § 51, eff. July 1, 1960.

[1] N.J.S.A. §§ 2A:84A–1 to 2A:84A–49.

2A:84A–48. Short title

This act [1] shall be known and may be cited as "The Evidence Act, 1960."

L.1960, c. 52, p. 465, § 52, eff. July 1, 1960.

[1] N.J.S.A. §§ 2A:84A–1 to 2A:84A–49.

2A:84A–49. Effective date

This act [1] shall take effect July 1, 1960, except that article III [2] shall take effect immediately.[3]

L.1960, c. 52, p. 465, § 53, eff. July 1, 1960.

[1] N.J.S.A. §§ 2A:81–2, 2A:81–17, 2A:82–16, 2A:82–27, 2A:84A–1 to 2A:84A–49.
[2] N.J.S.A. §§ 2A:84A–33 to 2A:84A–44.
[3] June 20, 1960.

CHAPTER 84A—NEW JERSEY RULES OF EVIDENCE

APPENDIX TO CHAPTER 84A

NEW JERSEY RULES OF EVIDENCE

This Appendix contains the New Jersey Rules of Evidence adopted by the Supreme Court of New Jersey on Sept. 15, 1992, as amended. See, also, Chapter 84A, Rules of Evidence, ante.

SUPREME COURT OF NEW JERSEY

IT IS ORDERED that the proposed *New Jersey Rules of Evidence* (*N.J.R.E.* 101 to 1103) contained in the June 1991 report of the Supreme Court Committee on the Rules of Evidence, as amended by the July 8, 1992, Supplement to the Report, are hereby approved and adopted to be effective July 1, 1993, subject to *N.J.S.A.* 2A:84A–36.

For the Court:
ROBERT N. WILENTZ
Chief Justice

Dated: September 15, 1992

REPORT OF THE NEW JERSEY SUPREME COURT COMMITTEE ON THE RULES OF EVIDENCE

To the Honorable Chief Justice Robert N. Wilentz and the Associate Justices of the Supreme Court of New Jersey

The task which you assigned to the Committee was to consider whether or to what extent New Jersey should adopt the Federal Rules of Evidence which are now followed by many states. You perceived that the bench and bar might benefit by this uniformity. New Jersey attorneys who appear in federal courts, and in the courts of sister states which have adopted the federal rules, would be conversant with a common body of law. In addition, judges and attorneys would gain insight and understanding in using the rules of evidence by the availability of a wider body of precedent. In considering the adoption of the federal rules, we were authorized to review their substance and to recommend appropriate changes.

The rules presented in this Report reflect what our Committee perceived as the best of the 1967 New Jersey Rules of Evidence and the 1975 Federal Rules of Evidence as amended. Both sets of rules have much in common; they both derived from the 1953 Uniform Rules of Evidence.

In working on this project the Committee examined in detail the New Jersey rules and the federal rules as a whole, the substance and wording of each individual rule, and issues in cases spawned by the rules. We considered the interplay between the rules of evidence and the Rules of Court, because the admissibility of evidence is affected occasionally by both sets of rules. For example, *R.* 4:16–1(c) provides for the use of testimony given in depositions. In general, these proposed rules of evidence do not address matters of practice and procedure, although

some rules may be said to fall into that category, such as Rule 615 dealing with sequestration of witnesses.

The Committee represented all segments of the profession. It was composed of practicing attorneys, prosecuting attorneys, public and private defense counsel, judges, and academics who teach evidence at law schools in this state. Many of the published opinions on our law of evidence were written by judges serving on the Committee. Several of our members had the advantage of having participated in the judicial conference which considered the 1963 report of the committee whose invaluable work, *Report of the Supreme Court Committee on Evidence,* was the foundation for the 1967 rules. Many members of the Committee had worked on the *ad hoc* committee whose recommendations for amending several evidence rules were previously adopted. See, for example, the amendments to *N.J.Evid.R.* 13 to 15, 20, 56, and 63(1)(a) and the commentary published in 108 *N.J.L.J.* 293, 301–302 (1981).

We did not have the services of an official reporter. As a result, this product represents the work of the Committee members themselves. The Committee took a practical approach based on the experience of its members in living with the 1967 rules. Nevertheless, our debates often returned to first principles.

The rules contained in this Report may be characterized broadly as follows. The organization essentially follows the format of the federal rules. Thus, the rules are divided into eleven articles. The number of each rule corresponds to the number of the federal rule with occasional deviations necessitated by some differences in approach, most noticeable in the organization of the hearsay exceptions in Article VIII. Those changes in organization, however, do not affect precepts of admissibility.

In general, we have adopted the substance and language of the federal rules when we considered them equal to or better than our present rules. However, in a number of instances we preferred the prevailing New Jersey law, especially when it reflected a resolution of previous controversy over important principles. For example, Rule 609 embodies the holding of *State v. Sands,* 76 *N.J.* 127 (1978), as to the use of prior convictions for impeachment purposes, and Rule 607 retains vestiges of the voucher rule found in *N.J.Evid.R.* 20. Frequently, language changes were made without intending any change in substance. The wording of some 1967 rules was retained when we considered it superior to the corresponding federal rules. The purpose was to improve the clarity of expression of numerous rules so that they could be better understood and applied.

These rules differ in many respects from the federal and 1967 New Jersey rules. We broadened some rules, tightened others, omitted some federal rules entirely, corrected aspects of the 1967 Rules to the extent that they conflicted with established practice (for example, *N.J.Evid.R.* 2 as to scope of application), and filled in gaps in the law not covered by the 1967 Rules. The overall effect, however, is neither startling nor radical and will not substantially alter prevailing practice, although there are some important changes which are noted in the Comments. The similarities between the federal rules and the 1967 New Jersey rules are far greater than their differences, and the perception of the Committee is that the New Jersey rules have worked well for the most part. Nevertheless, we endeavored to improve the substance and language of the rules. In the main, basic principles which served the interests of justice well in the past have been retained. We relied heavily on the valuable work of our colleagues and predecessors. With the adoption of this revision of the rules of evidence, New Jersey should continue to move forward in modernizing the law of evidence as was done in this state in 1967 and by the United States in 1975.

The law of evidence is not static. This is not the last word. But we hope to have contributed logic and good sense to this body of law and something to its beauty.

Respectfully submitted,

NEW JERSEY SUPREME COURT COMMITTEE ON RULES OF EVIDENCE

Hon. Theodore I. Botter, Chair

Jeffrey Blitz	Francis Hartman
Hon. Warren Brody	Hon. Michael P. King
John Cannel	Hon. Sylvia B. Pressler
Hon. Philip Carchman	Michael Risinger
Marina Corodemus	Robert E. Rochford
Richard Carley	Hon. Edwin H. Stern
Robert Carter	Harvey Weissbard
Alfred C. Clapp *	
Hon. Erminie L. Conley	Joyce Usiskin, Staff
Hon. William Dreier	Representatives of the
Zulima V. Farber	Administrative Office of
Hon. E. Stevenson Fluharty	the Courts
Hon. Myron Gottlieb	

* Deceased

June 1991

TABLE OF DISPOSITIONS

Showing where the subject matter of the 1967 Rules of Evidence can be found in the New Jersey Rules of Evidence (N.J.R.E.).

1967 Rules	N.J.R.E.
1(1)	Deleted. See Comment on Rule 101(b).
1(2)	401
1(3)	Deleted. See Comment on Rule 101(b).
1(4)	101(b)(1)
1(5)	101(b)(2)
1(6)	Deleted. See Comment on Rule 101(b).
1(7)	Deleted. See Comment on Rule 101(b).
1(8)	Deleted. See Comment on Rule 101(b).
1(9)	Deleted. See Comment on Rule 101(b).
1(10)	Deleted. See Comment on Rule 101(b).
1(11)	Deleted. See Comment on Rule 101(b).
1(12)	Deleted. See Comment on Rule 101(b).
1(13)	1001
1(14)	Deleted. See Comment on Rule 101(b).
2(1)	101(a)(1)
2(2)	101(a)(2) (first sentence) and 101(a)(2)(A)
2(3)	101(a)(3)
2(4) (first sentence)	101(c)
2(4) (second sentence)	no analogue
3	101(a)(4)
4	403
5	102
6	105
7(a)	601
7(b)	Deleted. See Comment on Rule 402.
7(c)	601
7(d)	Deleted. See Comment on Rule 402.
7(e)	Deleted. See Comment on Rule 402.
7(f)	402
8(1) (first sentence)	104(a)
8(1) (second sentence)	101(a)(2)(E), 104(a)
8(1) (third sentence)	104(a)
8(1) (fourth sentence)	104(e)
8(2)	104(b)
8(3)	104(c)
9(1)	201(a)(b)
9(2)	201(a)(b)
9(3)	201(c)(d)(e)
10(1)	201(e)
10(2)	201(f)
10(3)	Deleted. See Comment on Rule 201.
10(4)	Deleted. See Comment on Rule 201.
11	201(g)
12(1)	202
12(2)	202

1967 Rules	N.J.R.E.
12(3)	202
13	301
14	301
15	303
16 (not adopted)	
17 (first sentence) (a)	601(a)
17 (first sentence) (b)	601(b)
17 (second sentence)	604
18	603
19	602
20	607, 803(a)(2)
21 (not adopted)	609
22(a)	613(a)
22(b)	613(b)
22(c)	608
22(d)	608
23	501
24	502
25	503
26	504
26A–1	505
26A–2	506
26A–3	507
26A–4 (repealed L. 1987, c. 169, § 6)	
26A–5	517
27	508
28	509
28A–1	510
29	511
30	512, 610
31	513
32	514
33 (not enacted) (secret of state)	
34	515
35 (not enacted) (communication to grand jury)	
36	516
37	530
38	531
39	532
40	533
40A–1	See 412
41	Deleted. See Comment on Rule 606
42	605
43	606
44 (not adopted)	
45 (not adopted)	
46	405(a)
47	404(a)(1), 405
48	404(a)
49	406(a)
50	406(a)
51	407
52(1)	408
52(2)	408
53	411
54	411
55	404(b)
56(1)	701
56(2) (first sentence)	702
56(2) (second & third sentences)	703
56(3)	704

1967 Rules	N.J.R.E.		1967 Rules	N.J.R.E.
57	705		63(21)	803(c)(26)
58	705		63(22) (not adopted)	
59 (not adopted)			63(23)	804(b)(4)
60 (not adopted)			63(24)	804(b)(4)
61 (not adopted)			63(25)	804(b)(4)
62(1)	801(a)		63(26)	804(b)(4)
62(2)	801(b)		63(27)(a)	803(c)(20)
62(3)	801(f)		63(27)(b)	803(c)(20)
62(4)	Deleted as self-evident. See Comment on Rule 801.		63(27)(c)	803(c)(19)
			63(28)	803(c)(21)
62(5)	801(d)		63(29)	803(c)(15)
62(6)	804(a)		63(30)	803(c)(17)
63	801(c), 802		63(31) (not adopted)	See Rule 803(c)(18)
63(1)(a)	803(a)		63(32)	804(b)(6)
63(1)(b)	803(c)(5)		63(33)	804(b)(8)
63(1)(c)	803(c)		64	807
63(2) (not adopted)			65	806
63(3)	804(b)(1)		66	805
63(4)(a)	803(c)(1)		67	901
63(4)(b)	803(c)(2)		68(1)	902(a), (b), (e)
63(5)	804(b)(2)		68(2)	902(b)
63(6) (not adopted)			68(3)	902(c)
63(7)	803(b)(1)		68(4)	Deleted. See Comment on Rule 902.
63(8)	803(b)(2) & (3)			
63(9)(a)	803(b)(4)		69	902(k)
63(9)(b)	803(b)(5)		70(1) (Introductory Clause)	1002
63(10)	803(c)(25)		70(1)(a)	1004(a)
63(11)	804(b)(7)		70(1)(b)	1004(b)
63(12)(a)	803(c)(3)		70(1)(c)	1004(c)
63(12)(b)	803(c)(4)		70(1)(d)	1004(d)
63(12)(c)	803(c)(4)		70(1)(e)	1005
63(13)	803(c)(6)		70(1)(f)	1002
63(14)	803(c)(7)		70(1)(g)	1006
63(15)	803(c)(8)		70(1)(h)	1007
63(16)	803(c)(9)		70(2)	Deleted. See Comment on Rule 1004.
63(17)	803(c)(10)			
63(18)	803(c)(12)		70(3)	1008
63(19)	803(c)(14)		71	903
63(20)	803(c)(22)		72 (not adopted)	

TABLE OF CONTENTS

Rule

ARTICLE I.   GENERAL PROVISIONS

101.   Scope; definitions.
102.   Purpose and construction.
103.   Rulings.
104.   Preliminary questions.
105.   Limited admissibility.
106.   Remainder of or related writings or recorded statements.

ARTICLE II.   JUDICIAL NOTICE

201.   Judicial notice of law and adjudicative facts.
202.   Judicial notice in proceedings subsequent to trial.

ARTICLE III.   PRESUMPTIONS

301.   Effect of presumption.
302.   Choice of law.
303.   Presumptions against the accused in criminal cases.

ARTICLE IV.   RELEVANCY AND ITS LIMITS

401.   Definition of "relevant evidence".
402.   Relevant evidence generally admissible.

Rule

403.   Exclusion of relevant evidence on grounds of prejudice, confusion, or waste of time.
404.   Character evidence not admissible to prove conduct; exceptions; other crimes; evidence.
405.   Methods of proving character.
406.   Habit, routine practice.
407.   Subsequent remedial measures.
408.   Settlement offers and negotiations.
409.   Payment of medical and similar expenses.
410.   Inadmissibility of pleas, plea discussions and related statements.
411.   Liability insurance.
412.   Prosecutions.

ARTICLE V.   PRIVILEGES

500.   General rule.
501.   Privilege of accused.
502.   Definition of incrimination.
503.   Self-incrimination.
504.   Lawyer-client privilege.
505.   Psychologist privilege.
506.   Patient and physician privilege.
507.   Utilization review committees of certified hospital or extended care facility; exceptions.

Rule
508.   Newsperson's privilege.
509.   Marital privilege—confidential communications.
510.   Marriage counselor privilege.
511.   Priest-penitent privilege.
512.   Religious belief.
513.   Political vote.
514.   Trade secret.
515.   Official information.
516.   Identity of informer.
517.   Victim counselor privilege.
518.   Social worker privileges.
519.   Mediator Privilege.
520 to 529.   [Reserved].
530.   Waiver of privilege by contract or previous disclosure; limitations.
531.   Admissibility of disclosure wrongfully compelled.
532.   Reference to exercise of privileges.
533.   Effect of error in overruling claim of privilege.

ARTICLE VI.   WITNESSES

601.   General rule of competency.
602.   Lack of personal knowledge.
603.   Oath or affirmation.
604.   Interpreters.
605.   Restriction on judge as witness.
606.   Restriction on juror as witness.
607.   Credibility and neutralization.
608.   Evidence of Character for Truthfulness or Untruthfulness and Evidence of Prior False Accusation.
609.   Impeachment by evidence of conviction of crime.
610.   Religious beliefs or opinions.
611.   Mode and order of interrogation and presentation.
612.   Writing used to refresh memory.
613.   Prior statements of witnesses.
614.   Calling and interrogation of witnesses by judge.
615.   Sequestration of witnesses.

ARTICLE VII.   OPINIONS AND EXPERT TESTIMONY

701.   Opinion testimony of lay witnesses.
702.   Testimony by experts.
703.   Bases of opinion testimony by experts.
704.   Opinion on ultimate issue.
705.   Disclosure of facts or data underlying expert opinion; hypotheses not necessary.
706.   Court.

ARTICLE VIII.   HEARSAY

801.   Definitions.
802.   Hearsay rule.
803.   Hearsay exceptions not dependent on declarant's unavailability.
804.   Hearsay exceptions: declarant unavailable.
805.   Hearsay within hearsay.
806.   Attacking and supporting credibility of declarant.
807.   Discretion of judge to exclude evidence under certain exceptions.
808.   Expert opinion included in a hearsay statement admissible under an exception.

ARTICLE IX.   AUTHENTICATION AND IDENTIFICATION

901.   Requirement of authentication or identification.
902.   Self-authentication.

Rule
903.   Testimony of subscribing witness unnecessary.

ARTICLE X.   CONTENTS OF WRITINGS AND PHOTOGRAPHS

1001.   Definitions.
1002.   Requirement of original.
1003.   Admissibility of duplicates.
1004.   Admissibility of other evidence of contents.
1005.   Public records.
1006.   Summaries.
1007.   Testimony or written admission of party.
1008.   Functions of judge and jury.

ARTICLE XI.   MISCELLANEOUS

1101.   Applicability.
1102.   Amendment.
1103.   Title.

ARTICLE I.   GENERAL PROVISIONS

Rule 101.   Scope; definitions

(a) Applicability; exceptions.

(1) *Privileges.* The provisions of Rule 500 (privileges) shall apply, without relaxation, to all proceedings and inquiries, whether formal, informal, public or private, and to all branches and agencies of government.

(2) *Court proceedings; relaxation.* These rules of evidence shall apply in all proceedings, civil or criminal, conducted by or under the supervision of a court. Except as provided by paragraph (a)(1) of this rule, these rules may be relaxed in the following instances to admit relevant and trustworthy evidence in the interest of justice:

(A) actions within the cognizance of the Small Claims Section of the Special Civil Part of the Superior Court, Law Division, and the Small Claims Division of the Tax Court whether or not the action was instituted in a Small Claims Section or Division.

(B) in accordance with a statutory provision;

(C) proceedings in a criminal or juvenile delinquency action in which information is presented for the court's use in exercising a sentencing or other dispositional discretion, including bail and pretrial intervention and other diversionary proceedings;

(D) to the extent permitted by law, proceedings to establish probable cause, including grand jury proceedings, probable cause hearings, and *ex parte* applications;

(E) proceedings to determine the admissibility of evidence under these rules or other law.

(3) *Administrative proceedings.* Except as otherwise provided by paragraph (a)(1) of this rule, proceedings before administrative agencies shall not be governed by these rules.

(4) *Undisputed facts.* If there is no *bona fide* dispute between the parties as to a relevant fact, the judge may permit that fact to be established by stipulation or

binding admission. In civil proceedings the judge may also permit that fact to be proved by any relevant evidence, and exclusionary rules shall not apply, except Rule 403 or a valid claim of privilege.

(5) *Affidavit in lieu of testimony.* These rules shall not be construed to prohibit the use of an affidavit in lieu of oral testimony to the extent permitted by law.

(b) Definitions. As used in these rules, the following terms shall have the meaning hereafter set forth unless the context otherwise indicates:

(1) "Burden of persuasion" means the obligation of a party to meet the requirements of a rule of law that the fact be proved either by a preponderance of the evidence or by clear and convincing evidence or beyond a reasonable doubt, as the case may be.

(2) "Burden of producing evidence" means the obligation of a party to introduce evidence when necessary to avoid the risk of a judgment or peremptory finding against that party on an issue of fact.

(3) "Writing" has the meaning given in the definition contained in Rule 801(e).

(c) Repeal. The adoption of these rules of evidence shall not operate to repeal any existing statute by implication. However, where an existing statute has been expressly superseded pursuant to *N.J.S.A.* 2A:84A–40 by an official note heretofore or hereafter appended to a rule of evidence, such statute shall have no further force or effect.

Adopted eff. July 1, 1993. Amended September 15, 2004, eff. July 1, 2005.

Comment

Rule 101 is based on *N.J.Evid.R.* 1, 2, and 3 of the 1967 Rules of Evidence; *Fed.R.Evid.* 101 and 1101 deal with the scope and applicability of the federal rules.

Paragraph (a) of Rule 101 prescribes the scope of application of the evidence rules and organizes this material somewhat differently from both the 1967 New Jersey scope rule, *N.J.Evid.R.* 2, and *Fed.R.Evid.* 101 and 1101. The 1967 New Jersey scope rule is a four-part rule addressing both the general application of the rules of evidence and exceptions to their general application. The scheme of the federal rules is a general application provision, *Fed.R.Evid.* 101, and an additional rule, *Fed.R.Evid.* 1101, which addresses both applicability and exceptions to applicability. The scheme of the Rule 101(a) is to state in one rule the principles of application, relaxation and exception, although the rule incorporates by reference other rules which include exceptions to applicability, such as Rule 104(a) and Rule 201(f). Accordingly, there is no analogue to *Fed.R.Evid.* 1101 in these rules since its subject matter is covered by Rule 101.

With respect to the structure and specific provisions of paragraph (a) of this rule, subparagraph (1) provides that privileges shall apply without relaxation to all proceedings and inquiries, formal, informal, public or private, and to all branches and agencies of government. This provision follows both *N.J.Evid.R.* 2(1) and *Fed.R.Evid.* 1101(c) without substantive change.

Paragraph (a)(2) provides generally that the rules of evidence shall apply to all civil and criminal proceedings conducted by or under the supervision of a court. This provision corresponds to *N.J.Evid.R.* 2(2) and is the analogue of *Fed.R.Evid.* 101 and 1101(d). The second sentence of subsection (2), unlike *N.J.Evid.R.* 2(2), undertakes to enumerate those proceedings in which the rules of evidence, other than those relating to privileges, may be relaxed. These exceptions are limited to:

(A) Actions within the cognizance of the Small Claims Section of the Special Civil Part of the Law Division, the successor to the Small Claims Division of the County District Court. This exception reflects the amendment of *N.J.Evid.R.* 2(2), effective July 1, 1983. However, this rule clarifies that amendment by providing that the evidence rules may be relaxed in all cases within the small claims jurisdiction whether or not they are actually brought in a small claims section. This is consistent with the Rules of Court. This section also excepts the Small Claims Division of the Tax Court, whose procedure is also more informal. *See R.* 8:11 and *N.J.S.A.* 2A:3A–5.

(B) In accordance with a statutory provision. There is no analogue to this provision in the 1967 New Jersey rules. Under *N.J.Evid.R.* 2(3), provision for relaxation pursuant to statute applied only to administrative proceedings. *See* Comment on Rule 101(a)(3), replacing *N.J.Evid.R.* 2(3). While there is no direct analogue in the federal rules, the principle is reflected in *Fed.R.Evid.* 1101(e), which defers to specified federal statutes having particular evidential provisions for certain proceedings. Unlike the federal rule, this rule is drawn in general terms without enumeration of specific statutes.

(C) Sentencing and dispositional proceedings. The federal rule analogue to this provision is *Fed. R.Evid.* 1101(d)(3). It enumerates various miscellaneous proceedings to which the rules do not apply, including extradition or rendition proceedings, preliminary examination in criminal cases, sentencing, probation proceedings, issuance of warrants and summonses, and proceedings with respect to bail release. While there is no 1967 analogue to this rule, it is accepted practice in New Jersey not to apply the rules of evidence to these proceedings. *See, e.g., State v. Stewart,* 96 *N.J.* 596, 606 (1984); *State v. Kunz,* 55 *N.J.* 128 (1969).

Paragraph (a)(2)(C) of this rule generally follows the intent of the federal rule but is limited to those proceedings in which information is produced which forms the basis for the court's exercise of sentencing or dispositional discretion in criminal and juvenile delinquency actions. Such proceedings include final juvenile dispositions, pre-disposition detention determinations in juvenile delinquency actions, bail proceedings, pretrial intervention and other diversionary proceedings, and any other proceedings in which the exercise of judicial discretion determines the custodial status of or other restraints upon an accused or juvenile charged with delinquency.

Proceedings for the issuance of warrants or summonses are not covered by paragraph (a)(2)(C) but rather by paragraphs (a)(2)(D) and (a)(5) of this rule.

(D) Proceedings to establish probable cause. This paragraph of the rule covers proceedings in which the determination to be made is probable cause for taking an official action which constitutes a step in the criminal process. This rule includes grand jury proceedings, probable cause hearings conducted pursuant to *R.* 3:4–3, applications for search and arrest warrants, applications for wiretap orders, and proceedings under *R.* 3:5–7 challenging warrantless searches and seizures. In each of these proceedings substantive law governs both the extent to which the rules of evidence may be relaxed and the quantum of competent evidence that is required. This rule addresses only the character of the proof, not the form in which it is presented. The question of form is addressed by paragraph (a)(5) of this rule, which allows the use of affidavits to the extent permitted by substantive law.

The federal analogues of this rule are found in *Fed.R.Evid.* 1101(d)(2) (grand jury) and 1101(d)(3) (preliminary examinations and warrants). While there is no 1967 New Jersey analogue, these provisions do not modify New Jersey practice but merely codify it. *See, e.g., State v. Kasabucki,* 52 *N.J.* 110, 116–117 (1968) (search warrant); *State v. Fary,* 19 *N.J.* 431, 437 (1955) (grand jury proceedings).

Note that this rule does not refer to preliminary examination as does the federal rule, since the New Jersey court rules provide for a preliminary hearing (prior to the probable cause hearing) at which no factual findings are made. Compare *R.* 3:4–2 with *R.* 3:4–3.

(E) Admissibility hearings. Paragraph (a)(2)(E) is similar to *Fed.R.Evid.* 1101(d)(1). While the federal rule refers only to *Fed.R.Evid.* 104, this rule uses the phrase "under these rules or other law" in order to make clear that proceedings under Rule 104 are not the only proceedings to determine admissibility in which the rules of evidence may be relaxed. A relaxation provision is expressly included in Rule 201(f) dealing with judicial notice. Conditions for the admissibility of evidence are also imposed by other evidence rules, such as the qualifications to establish a business record under Rule 803(c)(6). *See Gunter v. Fischer Scientific American,* 193 *N.J.Super.* 688, 692 (App.Div.1984). As to conditions for admissibility imposed by case law, see *State v. Johnson,* 42 *N.J.* 146, 170–171 (1964) (criteria for admissibility of breathalyzer test results). *State v. Cardone,* 146 *N.J.Super.* 23 (App.Div.1976), *certif. denied,* 75 *N.J.* 3 (1977), dealing with admissibility of K–55 radar readings, illustrates this rule's application. *See also* Comment on Rule 104(a).

The rules of evidence have never been strictly applied in arbitration proceedings, although the parties might otherwise agree or stipulate. *See Local Union 560 v. Eazor Express, Inc.,* 95 *N.J.Super.* 219, 227 (App.Div.1967); *Livingston v. Combs & wife, Adm'rs,* 1 *N.J.L.* 50 (Sup.Ct.1790). *N.J.S.A.* 39:6A–24 to 35 and *N.J.S.A.* 2A:23A–20 to –30, respectively, provide for arbitration under court supervision of motor vehicle and personal injury claims of $15,000

or less. *See also R.* 4:21A. The provision for court supervision does not compel a change in this principle.

Paragraph (a)(3) of Rule 101 replaces *N.J.Evid.R.* 2(3), for which there is no federal analogue. While it changes the language of *N.J.Evid.R.* 2(3), it merely conforms the rule to established practice. *N.J.Evid.R.* 2(3) addressed only so-called formal hearings before administrative agencies and tribunals and provided that the rules of evidence were applicable to such hearings except as otherwise provided by statute. Since so-called informal hearings were not addressed, it appears that the 1967 rules of evidence were not intended to apply to those proceedings. The Administrative Procedure Act (APA), *N.J.S.A.* 52:14B–1, *et seq.,* enacted subsequent to the adoption of *N.J.Evid.R.* 2(3), replaced the former undefined formal and informal hearing dichotomy by creating the category of contested cases to which a variety of procedural consequences attach. *N.J.S.A.* 52:14B–2(b). The APA expressly provides that the rules of evidence do not apply to contested cases. *N.J.S.A.* 52:14B–10(a). This comports with pre-APA case law. *See, e.g., In re Plainfield–Union Water Co.,* 11 *N.J.* 382, 392 (1953). The requirement of *N.J.Evid.R.* 2(3) that the rules of evidence apply to formal hearings unless relaxed by statute was contrary to established case law and was not complied with in practice. Rule 101(a)(3) recognizes current practice and the codification of the common-law principle by the APA by making the rules of evidence inapplicable to all administrative proceedings. However, the law of privileges applies to all proceedings. That had been expressly provided for by *N.J.Evid.R.* 2(3) and is now repeated in Rule 101(a)(1) as well as in this paragraph. It is noted that neither this rule nor its predecessor addresses the question of the need for some residuum of competent evidence. That is a matter of substantive administrative law which these rules do not affect. *See, e.g., Weston v. State,* 60 *N.J.* 36, 50–52 (1972); *In re Cowan,* 224 *N.J.Super.* 737, 748–751 (App.Div.1988).

Paragraph (a)(4) of Rule 101 replaces *N.J.Evid.R.* 3, for which there is no federal analogue. *N.J.Evid.R.* 3 applied to civil proceedings only and permitted undisputed facts to be proved by any relevant evidence without reference to exclusionary rules. The provision is retained, nearly verbatim, by the second sentence of this rule. The first sentence is a new provision, applicable to both civil and criminal proceedings, which conforms with actual practice by permitting an undisputed fact to be established by stipulation or binding admission. *See State v. Mack,* 131 *N.J.Super.* 542 (App.Div.1974). This rule does not affect the scope of the jury function constitutionally required in criminal trials. It is intended only to relieve parties of the need for formal proof of specific facts. *See Horning v. District of Columbia,* 254 *U.S.* 135, 65 *L.Ed.*2d 185 (1920).

Paragraph (a)(5) has no analogue in the 1967 New Jersey rules or the federal rules. This paragraph codifies by reference the practice by which proofs are submitted by affidavit in lieu of oral testimony in *ex parte* matters, on motions, and in other proceedings. *See Gunter v. Fischer Scientific American, supra,* 193 *N.J.Super.* at 692; *State v. Cardone, supra,* 146 *N.J.Su-*

per. at 28–29. The rule refers only to the mode of presenting proof and not to its character or quality. It does not authorize relaxation of the rules of evidence but merely allows affidavits to be used as a vehicle for proof where permitted by law. *Cf. R.* 1:6–6, requiring the contents of affidavits to comply with the rules of evidence as to the competence of both the affiant and the evidence submitted. *See Patrolman's Benevolent Ass'n v. Montclair,* 70 *N.J.* 130, 134 n. 1 (1976).

Paragraph (b) of Rule 101 replaces *N.J.Evid.R.* 1, which contained the definition of 14 terms: evidence, relevant evidence, proof, burden of proof, burden of producing evidence, conduct, the hearing, finding of fact, guardian, judge, trier of fact, verbal, writing, and perceive. Paragraph (b) retains only three of these definitions, burden of proof (*N.J.Evid.R.* 1(4)), burden of producing evidence (*N.J.Evid.R.* 1(5)), and writing (*N.J.Evid.R.* 1(13)). Paragraph (b)(2) of this rule follows *N.J.Evid.R.* 1(5) almost verbatim. As to *N.J.Evid.R.* 1(4), the term "burden of proof" has been replaced in paragraph (b)(1) by the more accurate term "burden of persuasion." This obviates the need for the last sentence of *N.J.Evid.R.* 1(4) which provides that burden of proof is synonymous with burden of persuasion. The definition of writing, now contained in Rule 801(e) under the hearsay rules, is made applicable to all evidence rules by incorporation.

As to the remaining 11 terms defined in the 1967 rules, relevance is now defined in Rule 401, and the other 10 of the original 14 definitions of terms have been omitted because they are self-evident and have not proved useful. Note that definitions relating to the hearsay rule are included in Rule 801, and definitions relating to contents of writings and photographs are included in Rule 1001.

The first sentence of paragraph (c) of Rule 101 follows *N.J.Evid.R.* 2(4), making clear that the adoption of these rules should not be construed as an implied repeal of any presently existing statute. There is no federal analogue. The second sentence is a new provision intended to call attention to the supersession provision of *N.J.S.A.* 2A:84A–40, pursuant to which official footnotes were appended to specific 1967 rules to supersede existing statutes and pursuant to which footnotes may be appended to future rule amendments.

The Official Footnote to this rule catalogs all of the statutory provisions superseded by the 1962 rules and adds as well the statutory provisions superseded by these rules, namely, *N.J.S.A.* 2A:84A–1 to 2A:84A–15 inclusive (Definitions) and *N.J.S.A.* 2A:84A–16 (Scope). This constitutes a format change from the 1967 rules which appended the Official Footnote to each superseding rule rather than collecting them, as here, in a single catalog.

The 1967 Rules of Evidence, as amended, are referred to in these Comments either as the 1967 rule or rules or *N.J.Evid.R.* These rules are referred to as *N.J.R.E.* or Rule(s). *See* Rule 1103. The *Report of the New Jersey Supreme Court Committee on Evidence* (1963) is referred to in these comments as *The 1963 Report.*

Official Note

The statutes superseded by the 1967 Official Footnotes and which continue to be superseded by these Rules are as follows:

Superseded	By	N.J.R.E.
2A:81–1 and 8 19:34–26		601
2A:87–27 to 33		201, 202
2A:82–34 to 37		801(d)
2A:81–13 and 14		804(b)(1)
2A:82–34 to 37		803(c)(6), and (7)
2A:11–55		803(c)(8), (9), and (10)
2A:82–8 to 12 2A:82–14 to 16 2A:82–20 to 22 4:20–20 2A:82–22		803(c)(14) and (15)
2A:81–12, in part		803(c)(22)
2A:11–55 2A:82–8 to 12 2A:82–14 to 16 2A:82–25 45:6–30 and 31 45:9–20 45:14–28		902
2A:11–55 2A:82–8 to 12 2A:82–14 to 16 2A:82–20 to 23 4:20–20		1002, 1004, 1005
2A:82–2		903

These rules, in addition, supersede *N.J.S.A.* 2A:84A–1 to 2A:84A–15, inclusive (Definitions) and *N.J.S.A.* 2A:84A–16 (Scope). The statutory definitions are superseded by *N.J.R.E.* 101(b) and 801. The statutory provision as to scope is superseded by *N.J.R.E.*

Note: Adopted September 15, 1992 to be effective July 1, 1993; paragraph (b)(2) amended September 15, 2004 to be effective July 1, 2005.

Rule 102. Purpose and construction

These rules shall be construed to secure fairness in administration and elimination of unjustified expense and delay. The adoption of these rules shall not bar the growth and development of the law of evidence to the end that the truth may be ascertained and proceedings justly determined.

Adopted effective July 1, 1993.

Comment

This rule follows both *N.J.Evid.R.* 5 and *Fed.R.Evid.* 102, retaining the 1967 New Jersey formulation that the adoption of the evidence rules "shall not bar the growth and development of the law of evidence."

It should be noted that this rule is not intended as a rule authorizing the trial judge to relax the rules of evidence in a particular case. A proposed relaxation provision, *N.J.Evid.R.* 2(4), applicable to civil cases, was not adopted as part of the 1967 rules and has not been incorporated in these rules. *See The 1963 Report* at 9. *Cf.Fed.R.Evid.* 803(24) and 804(b)(5), not adopted in this revision, which allow for other exceptions to the hearsay rule if certain standards are satisfied. *See State v. D.R.* 109 *N.J.* 348, 371–377 (1988). *Cf. In re Baby M.,* 109 *N.J.* 396, 467 n. 20 (1988); *State v. Tirone,* 64 *N.J.* 222, 226–227 (1974); *State v. Kennedy,* 135 *N.J.Super.* 513, 521–525 (App. Div.1975).

Rule 103. Rulings on evidence
[Not Adopted]
Comment

Fed.R.Evid. 103 was not adopted. It provides for (1) the effect of erroneous rulings; (2) making a record of offers of proof and rulings thereon; (3) requiring that proceedings on evidential questions be held out of the hearing of the jury; and (4) notice of plain error. These matters are covered in the New Jersey Rules of Court and established case law and need not be repeated in the rules of evidence. *See R.* 1:7–2, *R.* 1:7–3 and *R.* 2:10–2.

Rule 104. Preliminary questions

(a) Questions of admissibility generally. When the qualification of a person to be a witness, or the admissibility of evidence, or the existence of a privilege is subject to a condition, and the fulfillment of the condition is in issue, that issue is to be determined by the judge. In making that determination the judge shall not apply the rules of evidence except for Rule 403 or a valid claim of privilege. The judge may hear and determine such matters out of the presence or hearing of the jury.

(b) Relevance conditioned on fact. Where evidence is otherwise admissible if relevant and its relevance is subject to a condition, the judge shall admit it upon or subject to the introduction of sufficient evidence to support a finding of the condition. In such cases the judge shall instruct the jury to consider the issue of the fulfillment of the condition and to disregard the evidence if it finds that the condition was not fulfilled. The jury shall be instructed to disregard the evidence if the judge subsequently determines that a jury could not reasonably find that the condition was fulfilled.

(c) Preliminary hearing on admissibility of defendant's statements. Where by virtue of any rule of law a judge is required in a criminal action to make a preliminary determination as to the admissibility of a statement by the defendant, the judge shall hear and determine the question of its admissibility out of the presence of the jury. In such a hearing the rules of evidence shall apply and the burden of persuasion as to the admissibility of the statement is on the prosecution. If the judge admits the statement the jury shall not be informed of the finding that the statement is admissible but shall be instructed to disregard the statement if it finds that it is not credible. If the judge subsequently determines from all of the evidence that the statement

is not admissible, the judge shall take appropriate action.

(d) Testimony by accused. By testifying upon a preliminary matter, the accused does not become subject to cross-examination as to other issues in the case.

(e) Weight and credibility. This rule does not limit the right of a party to introduce before the jury evidence relevant to weight or credibility.

Adopted effective July 1, 1993.

Comment

The subject matter covered by paragraph (a) of *Fed.R.Evid.* 104 is substantially the same as that covered by *N.J.Evid.R.* 8(1). Rule 104 uses the New Jersey formulation with some modifications. The phrase "stated in these rules" has been omitted, since the rules of evidence are not the only source of a condition imposed for the admissibility of evidence. *See* Comment on Rule 101(a)(2)(E). The last sentence of paragraph (1) of *N.J.Evid.R.* 8 is encompassed by paragraph (e) of the federal rule. Therefore, for purposes of consistency and uniformity, that sentence was moved from its location in the 1967 New Jersey rule to paragraph (e) of this rule. The provision requiring the judge to indicate to the parties which one has the burden of persuasion and the burden of producing evidence has been omitted. The next to the last sentence of paragraph (1) of *N.J.Evid.R.* 8(1), which provides that the admissibility hearing may be conducted outside the presence or hearing of the jury, is encompassed by paragraph (c) of the federal rule. That provision is retained in paragraph (a) of this rule. It should also be noted that the content of the second sentence of paragraph (a), making the rules of evidence inapplicable to hearings conducted thereunder, is also contained in Rule 101(a)(2)(E). Paragraph (c), discussed below, is reserved exclusively for hearings on the admissibility of confessions of a criminal defendant.

Paragraph (b) of *Fed.R.Evid.* 104 encompasses the same material as is contained in *N.J.Evid.R.* 8(2). See also *N.J.Evid.R.* 19. The 1967 New Jersey formulation has been retained, adding the phrase "subject to" which is in the federal rule and is implicit in the 1967 New Jersey rule. *Cf. N.J.Evid.R.* 19.

In lieu of paragraph (c) of *Fed.R.Evid.* 104, this rule retains virtually verbatim paragraph (3) of *N.J.Evid.R.* 8 as paragraph (c) of this rule dealing with conditions for the admissibility of a criminal defendant's statements, such as their voluntary nature. The 1967 New Jersey rule had been amended in 1976 in response to the holding of *State v. Hampton,* 61 *N.J.* 250 (1972), and continues to constitute an accurate and useful guide. Its application is limited to defendant's statements alone, and it does not purport to deal with the admissibility of other evidence such as identification evidence. Unlike paragraph (a), paragraph (c) provides that the rules of evidence do apply to hearings on the admissibility of defendant's statements. This follows *N.J.Evid.R.* 8(3). Note should also be taken of the 1979 adoption of *R.* 3:13–1(b), which permits pretrial hearings to determine admissibility of statements, identification evidence, and other evidence as well.

N.J.Evid.R. 8 does not have an analogue to paragraph (d) of the federal rule, which provides that by testifying upon a preliminary matter the accused does not subject himself to cross-examination as to other issues in the case. *Fed.R.Evid.* 104(d) is consistent with New Jersey practice and is, therefore, included as paragraph (d) of this rule.

As noted above, paragraph (e) of this rule is taken from the last sentence of *N.J.Evid.R.* 8(1). That sentence is placed in Rule 104(e) to correspond with its location in the federal rules.

Rule 105. Limited admissibility

When evidence is admitted as to one party or for one purpose but is not admissible as to another party or for another purpose, the judge, upon request, shall restrict the evidence to its proper scope and shall instruct the jury accordingly, but may permit a party to waive a limiting instruction.

Adopted effective July 1, 1993.

Comment

Rule 105, which replaces *N.J.Evid.R.* 6, follows *Fed.R.Evid.* 105, adding, however, the final proviso respecting waiver of the limiting instruction. This proviso has no analogue either in the 1967 New Jersey rules or the federal rules.

The only other difference between *N.J.Evid.R.* 6 and Rule 105 is that this rule requires that a request be made for a limiting instruction. Although the 1967 New Jersey rule appears to require the instruction whether or not a request is made, a number of cases have held that the failure to give a limiting instruction is not plain error unless the failure had the capacity to produce an unjust result. *See, e.g., State v. Lair,* 62 *N.J.* 388, 391–393 (1973); *Millison v. E.I. duPont de Nemours & Co.,* 226 *N.J.Super.* 572, 597–598 (App.Div.1988), *aff'd o.b.,* 115 *N.J.* 252 (1989); *State v. Rajnai,* 132 *N.J.Super.* 530, 537–539 (App.Div.1975). The trial judge should give a limiting instruction *sua sponte* where it appears necessary to avoid the potential for prejudice. See *State v. Cofield,* 127 *N.J.* 328 (1992), so holding in respect of other-crime evidence. Without a request, the failure to give a limiting instruction will be reviewed as plain error.

The second sentence of the rule was included in recognition of the practice that a party for whose benefit a limiting instruction may be given should have the right to expressly waive the instruction. This is often done for tactical reasons as, for example, to avoid emphasizing particular evidence.

Rule 106. Remainder of or related writings or recorded statements

When a writing or recorded statement or part thereof is introduced by a party, an adverse party may require the introduction at that time of any other part or any other writing or recorded statement which in fairness ought to be considered contemporaneously.

Adopted effective July 1, 1993.

Comment

This rule follows *Fed.R.Evid.* 106 almost verbatim. While there is no 1967 New Jersey analogue to this rule, the Rules of Court have similar provisions governing the use at trial of depositions and interrogatories. *See R.* 4:16–1(d); *R.* 4:17–8(a). The federal rule is adopted because it incorporates the prevailing practice in this state.

ARTICLE II. JUDICIAL NOTICE

Rule 201. Judicial notice of law and adjudicative facts

(a) Notice of law. Law which may be judicially noticed includes the decisional, constitutional and public statutory law, rules of court, and private legislative acts and resolutions of the United States, this state, and every other state, territory and jurisdiction of the United States as well as ordinances, regulations and determinations of all governmental subdivisions and agencies thereof. Judicial notice may also be taken of the law of foreign countries.

(b) Notice of facts. Facts which may be judicially noticed include (1) such specific facts and propositions of generalized knowledge as are so universally known that they cannot reasonably be the subject of dispute, (2) such facts as are so generally known or are of such common notoriety within the area pertinent to the event that they cannot reasonably be the subject of dispute, (3) specific facts and propositions of generalized knowledge which are capable of immediate determination by resort to sources whose accuracy cannot reasonably be questioned, and (4) records of the court in which the action is pending and of any other court of this state or federal court sitting for this state.

(c) When discretionary. A court may take judicial notice whether requested or not.

(d) When mandatory. A court shall take judicial notice if requested by a party on notice to all other parties and if supplied with the necessary information.

(e) Opportunity to be heard. Each party is entitled upon timely request to an opportunity to be heard as to the propriety of taking judicial notice and the tenor of the matter noticed. In the absence of prior notification, the request may be made after judicial notice has been taken.

(f) How taken. In determining the propriety of taking judicial notice of a matter or the tenor thereof, any source of relevant information may be consulted or used, whether or not furnished by a party, and the rules of evidence shall not apply except Rule 403 or a valid claim of privilege.

(g) Instructing the jury. In a civil action or proceeding, the judge shall instruct the jury to accept as conclusive any fact judicially noticed. In a criminal case, the judge shall instruct the jury that it may, but is not required to, accept as established any fact which has been judicially noticed.

Adopted effective July 1, 1993.

Comment

Rule 201 generally follows the format of *Fed. R.Evid.* 201 and replaces *N.J.Evid.R.* 9, 10, and 11.

The scheme of the federal analogue is to provide for a single rule addressing judicial notice of adjudicative facts. The 1967 New Jersey rules had four separate rules dealing with judicial notice of law and adjudicative facts. *N.J.Evid.R.* 9 to 12, inclusive. The structure of the federal analogue has been largely followed by these rules except that the first paragraph of this rule deals with judicial notice of law, and the content of *Fed.R.Evid.* 201(f) (time of taking notice) is addressed by Rule 202. Rules 201 and 202 embrace all of the material covered by *N.J.Evid.R.* 9 through 12.

Paragraph (a) of this rule deals with judicial notice of law. There is no analogue in the federal evidence rules because notice of law is addressed by the federal practice rules. *See Fed.R.Civ.P.* 44.1 and *Fed. R.Crim.P.* 26.1. This paragraph of Rule 201 collects the provisions of *N.J.Evid.R.* 9(1) and (2) as to judicial notice of law. New Jersey Rules of Court do not address this subject.

Paragraph (b) of this rule contains a more detailed definition of judicially noticeable fact than *Fed. R.Evid.* 201(b), embodying the notice of fact provisions of *N.J.Evid.R.* 9(1) and (2). It also provides for judicial notice of the records of the courts of New Jersey and of federal courts sitting in or for this state. While the federal rules of evidence contain no comparable provision, 28 *U.S.C.A.* § 1738 facilitates proof of the records and proceedings of any court of a state, territory or possession of the United States. *See also Fed.R.Evid.* 902 and 1005 dealing with authentication and admission of public records.

Paragraphs (c) and (d) of this rule follow *Fed. R.Evid.* 201(c) and (d), respectively, and replace the mandatory/discretionary provisions of *N.J.Evid.R.* 9(1), (2), and (3). Paragraph (d) does not contain a limitation as to the time when a request to take judicial notice must be made, as did *N.J.Evid.R.* 9(3). *N.J.Evid.R.* 10(3) provided that judicial notice need not be taken if the information available or supplied is insufficient or unconvincing. *N.J.Evid.R.* 10(4) provided that all matters pertaining to judicial notice are for the judge rather than the jury. Neither of these two provisions is expressly contained in *Fed. R.Evid.* 201, but they are implied by the language of this rule and the federal rule, particularly subsection (d).

Paragraph (e) of this rule follows *Fed.R.Evid.* 201(e), the only change being the substitution of the words "each party" for the words "a party" at the beginning of the sentence. With this change the paragraph incorporates the substance of *N.J.Evid.R.* 10(1) by permitting both the proponent and the adversary of the noticeable material to be heard.

Paragraph (f) of the rule follows *N.J.Evid.R.* 10(2). The substance of *Fed.R.Evid.* 201(f) is included in Rule 202.

Paragraph (g) of this rule is identical to *Fed.R.Evid.* 201(g) and replaces *N.J.Evid.R.* 11. It omits as unnecessary the provision of the New Jersey rule which required the judge to indicate to the jury the source of his information. The 1967 rule failed to distinguish between instructions to the jury in civil and criminal cases. This distinction is made in Rule 201(g). While the need to make this distinction has been debated, the rule takes the safer course in view of a defendant's sixth amendment right to trial by jury. However, the court retains the power to charge the jury on the legal significance of adjudicative facts which have been judicially noticed. *See* A.B.A. Section of Litigation, *Emerging Problems Under the Federal Rules of Evidence* 35–38 (1983).

Rule 202. Judicial notice in proceedings subsequent to trial

(a) Subsequent proceedings. The failure or refusal of the judge to take judicial notice of a matter or to instruct the trier of the fact with respect to it shall not preclude the judge from taking judicial notice of the matter in subsequent proceedings in the action.

(b) On appeal. The reviewing court in its discretion may take judicial notice of any matter specified in Rule 201, whether or not judicially noticed by the judge.

(c) Opportunity to be heard. A judge or a reviewing court taking judicial notice under paragraph (a) or (b) of this rule of a matter not previously noticed in the action may afford the parties the opportunity to present information relevant to the propriety of taking such judicial notice and to the tenor of the matter to be noticed.

Adopted effective July 1, 1993.

Comment

Rule 202 follows almost verbatim *N.J.Evid.R.* 12, whose federal analogue is *Fed.R.Evid.* 201(f). The federal rule provides merely that judicial notice may be taken at any stage of the proceeding. The 1967 New Jersey rule was preferred because its greater detail and specificity afford useful guidance in interpreting the scope and application of this rule, especially as to judicial notice on appeal.

ARTICLE III. PRESUMPTIONS

Rule 301. Effect of presumption

Except as otherwise provided in Rule 303 or by other law, a presumption discharges the burden of producing evidence as to a fact (the presumed fact) when another fact (the basic fact) has been established.

If evidence is introduced tending to disprove the presumed fact, the issue shall be submitted to the trier of fact for determination unless the evidence is such that reasonable persons would not differ as to the existence or nonexistence of the presumed fact. If no evidence tending to disprove the presumed fact is presented, the presumed fact shall be deemed established if the basic fact is found or otherwise established. The burden of persuasion as to the proof or disproof of the presumed fact does not shift to the party against whom the presumption is directed unless otherwise required by law. Nothing in this rule shall preclude the judge from commenting on inferences that may be drawn from the evidence.

Adopted effective July 1, 1993.

Comment

Rule 301 generally follows *Fed.R.Evid.* 301 as well as the principles of *N.J.Evid.R.* 13 and 14, which it replaces. The principle adopted reflects established New Jersey law. *Dwyer v. Ford Motor Co.,* 36 *N.J.* 487, 507 (1962); *Kirschbaum v. Metropolitan Life Ins. Co.,* 133 *N.J.L.* 5, 9–10 (E. & A. 1945); *Silver Lining Inc. v. Shein,* 37 *N.J.Super.* 206, 216–218 (App.Div. 1955). The principle is that a valid presumption can be used to establish a *prima facie* case, but the presumption normally disappears in the face of conflicting evidence. Nevertheless, any logical inference which can be drawn from the basic fact remains. Thus, the rule provides that the trial judge is not precluded from commenting on inferences that may be drawn from the evidence, even when conflicting evidence is presented. Note also that under Rule 301 the burden of persuasion is not shifted to a party against whom the presumption operates.

This rule does not concern conclusive presumptions, which are actually rules of substantive law. *See* Comment on Rule 13, *The 1963 Report* at 45–46.

Rule 302. Choice of law

In civil actions or proceedings, the existence and effect of a presumption respecting a fact which is an element of a claim or defense as to which federal law or the law of another jurisdiction supplies the rule of decision shall be determined in accordance with that federal or other law.

Adopted effective July 1, 1993.

Comment

Rule 302 is based on *Fed.R.Evid.* 302, which provides a choice of law rule for the effect of presumptions. There is no 1967 New Jersey rule analogue. This rule, like the federal rule, provides that when the law of another state or federal law supplies the rule of decision as to a fact which is an element of a claim or defense, the law of the same jurisdiction shall determine the effect of a presumption respecting that fact.

Rule 303. Presumptions against the accused in criminal cases

(a) Scope. Except as otherwise provided by law, in criminal cases presumptions against an accused, recognized at common law or created by statute, including statutory provisions that certain facts are prima facie evidence of other facts or of guilt, are governed by this rule. As used in this rule, the term "element of the offense" shall include any issue on which the prosecution bears the burden of persuasion beyond a reasonable doubt.

(b) Submission to jury. The judge may not direct the jury to find a presumed fact against the accused. If a presumed fact establishes an element of the offense, the judge may submit the question of the existence of the presumed fact to the jury upon proof of the basic fact but only if a reasonable juror on the evidence as a whole, including the evidence of the basic fact, could find the presumed fact beyond a reasonable doubt. If the presumed fact has a lesser effect, the question of its existence may be submitted to the jury provided the basic facts are supported by sufficient evidence or are otherwise established, unless the judge determines that reasonable jurors on the evidence as a whole could not find the existence of the presumed fact.

(c) Instructing the jury. Whenever the existence of a presumed fact against the accused is submitted to the jury, the judge may instruct the jury that it may regard the basic fact as sufficient evidence of the presumed fact but that it is not required to do so. In addition, if the presumed fact establishes guilt or is an element of the offense, the judge shall instruct the jury that its existence, on all of the evidence, must be proved beyond a reasonable doubt. The judge shall not use the word "presumed" or "presumption" in instructions to the jury.

Adopted eff. July 1, 1993. Amended September 15, 2004, eff. July 1, 2005.

Comment

Rule 303 states the effect of presumptions in criminal cases and embodies principles of constitutional law developed by both federal and New Jersey cases. *See County Court of Ulster County, New York v. Allen,* 442 *U.S.* 140, 60 *L.Ed.*2d 777 (1979); *State v. DiRienzo,* 53 *N.J.* 360, 369–382 (1969). *Cf. Tot v. United States,* 319 *U.S.* 463, 87 *L.Ed.* 1519 (1943). The provisions for instructing the jury are derived from *State v. DiRienzo, supra,* 53 *N.J.* at 381–382, and *State v. Humphreys,* 54 *N.J.* 406, 415–416 (1969). *See also State v. Ingram,* 98 *N.J.* 489 (1985), and *State v. Stasio,* 78 *N.J.* 467, 485 (1979).

A federal presumption rule for criminal cases, proposed as federal rule 303, was not adopted. However, that proposal was incorporated into rule 303 of the 1974 Uniform Rules of Evidence, which is the basis of this rule.

The 1967 New Jersey Rules of Evidence did not include a separate provision for presumptions against the accused in criminal cases. To distinguish between the effect of presumptions in civil cases and criminal cases, an interim rule, *N.J.Evid.R.* 15, was adopted effective July 1, 1982, to make clear that *N.J.Evid.R.* 13 and 14 did not apply against the accused in criminal cases. *See* the commentary published in 108 *N.J.L.J.* 301–302 (1981).

The 1979 New Jersey Code of Criminal Justice provided that presumptions established by statute with respect to any fact which is an element of an offense shall have the meaning accorded by the law of evidence. *N.J.S.A.* 2C:1–13(e).

ARTICLE IV. RELEVANCY AND ITS LIMITS

Rule 401. Definition of "relevant evidence"

"Relevant evidence" means evidence having a tendency in reason to prove or disprove any fact of consequence to the determination of the action.

Adopted effective July 1, 1993.

Comment

Rule 401 is similar to *N.J.Evid.R.* 1(2) in that it incorporates the phrase "evidence having a tendency in reason to prove," but it substitutes for the phrase, "any material fact," the phrase, "any fact of consequence to the determination of the action" which follows *Fed.R.Evid.* 401. Relevant evidence is evidence tending to prove or disprove a proposition about a matter of fact, or, as in the federal rule, evidence which has a tendency to make "more probable or less probable" a fact of consequence to the action.

Rule 402. Relevant evidence generally admissible

Except as otherwise provided in these rules or by law, all relevant evidence is admissible.

Adopted effective July 1, 1993.

Comment

Rule 402 is essentially the same as both *N.J.Evid.R.* 7(f) and *Fed.R.Evid.* 402. The subject of *N.J.Evid.R.* 7(a) and (c) (qualification of witnesses) is covered by Rule 601. *N.J.Evid.R.* 7(b), (d), and (e), which deal with witness privilege, were deleted as superfluous. However, this deletion should not be construed as a return to the common-law rules of witness disabilities. The provision in the federal rule that irrelevant evidence is inadmissible was omitted as self-evident.

Rule 403. Exclusion of relevant evidence on grounds of prejudice, confusion, or waste of time

Except as otherwise provided by these rules or other law, relevant evidence may be excluded if its probative value is substantially outweighed by the risk of (a) undue prejudice, confusion of issues, or misleading the jury or (b) undue delay, waste of time, or needless presentation of cumulative evidence.

Adopted effective July 1, 1993.

Comment

Rule 403 contains the principles established by both *N.J.Evid.R.* 4 and *Fed.R.Evid.* 403. Although the formulation is closer to the federal rule than the 1967 New Jersey rule, the intention was to retain the principles of *N.J.Evid.R.* 4 as construed by New Jersey courts. *See State v. Carter*, 91 *N.J.* 86, 105–107 (1982); *State v. Garfole*, 76 *N.J.* 445, 455–457 (1978); *State v. Reldan*, 185 *N.J.Super.* 494, 505 (App.Div.1982), *certif. denied*, 91 *N.J.* 543 (1982); *State v. Jackson*, 182 *N.J.Super.* 98 (App.Div.1981).

The opening phrase of this rule was added to accommodate certain exceptions to a trial judge's discretion. For example, Rule 404, like its predeces-

sor, *N.J.Evid.R.* 47, provides that evidence of good character offered by the defendant in a criminal proceeding cannot be excluded under this rule. *See also Chambers v. Mississippi*, 410 *U.S.* 284 (1972), holding that it is a denial of due process to exclude, under local evidence rules, the confession of another person to the crime charged against defendant.

Rule 404. Character evidence not admissible to prove conduct; exceptions; other crimes; evidence

(a) Character evidence generally. Evidence of a person's character or character trait, including a trait of care or skill or lack thereof, is not admissible for the purpose of proving that the person acted in conformity therewith on a particular occasion except:

(1) *Character of accused.* Evidence of a pertinent trait of the accused's character offered by the accused, which shall not be excluded under Rule 403, or by the prosecution to rebut the same;

(2) *Character of victim.* Evidence of a pertinent trait of character of the victim of the crime offered by an accused or by the prosecution to rebut the same, or evidence of a character trait of peacefulness of the victim offered by the prosecution in a homicide case to rebut evidence that the victim was the first aggressor;

(3) *Character of witness.* Evidence of the character of a witness as provided in Rule 608.

(b) Other Crimes, Wrongs, or Acts. Except as otherwise provided by Rule 608(b), evidence of other crimes, wrongs, or acts is not admissible to prove the disposition of a person in order to show that such person acted in conformity therewith. Such evidence may be admitted for other purposes, such as proof of motive, opportunity, intent, preparation, plan, knowledge, identity or absence of mistake or accident when such matters are relevant to a material issue in dispute.

(c) Character and character trait in issue. Evidence of a person's character or trait of character is admissible when that character or trait is an element of a claim or defense.

Adopted eff. July 1, 1993. Amended September 15, 2004, eff. July 1, 2005; September 12, 2006, eff. July 1, 2007.

Comment

Rule 404 generally follows *Fed.R.Evid.* 404 and replaces *N.J.Evid.R.* 46, 48, and 55. It also incorporates a portion of *N.J.Evid.R.* 47.

Paragraph (a) of Rule 404 is almost identical to *Fed.R.Evid.* 404(a). The introductory sentence of paragraph (a) adds to the federal formulation the phrase "including a trait of care or skill or lack thereof." This addition repeats the principle expressed by *N.J.Evid.R.* 48. Paragraph (a)(3) of this rule omits the cross references to Rule 607 and 609 appearing in the federal analogue. These references were deleted because only Rule 608 deals with character evidence offered to affect the credibility of a witness.

The formulation of paragraph (b) of this rule follows *Fed.R.Evid.* 404(b) rather than the New Jersey analogue, *N.J.Evid.R.* 55, except that it uses the word "disposition" contained in the New Jersey rule and it adds the final phrase "when such matters are relevant to a material issue in dispute." This addition was made to emphasize the provision of *N.J.Evid.R.* 55 that ordinarily other crimes evidence is admissible only to prove "some other fact in issue," and not a general disposition to commit crimes or other wrongs. In conformity with the federal rule, "opportunity" and "preparation" have been added to the *N.J.Evid.R.* 55 list of examples of other purposes for which other crimes evidence may be admitted.

This formulation is intended to encompass relevant New Jersey case law. See *e.g. State v. Cofield*, 127 *N.J.Super.* 328 (1992); *State v. Stevens*, 115 *N.J.* 289 (1989).

Paragraph (c) of this rule has no federal analogue although its principle is implicit in the federal practice. This paragraph is based on the general principle formerly expressed by *N.J.Evid.R.* 46, that evidence of character or a trait of character is admissible when that character or trait is an element of a claim or defense which is in issue.

As a result of adoption of Rule 404, evidence of a trait of character offered for the purpose of drawing inferences as to the conduct of a person on a specified occasion is no longer admissible in civil cases except as provided in Rule 404(c) (character and character trait in issue) and Rule 608 (trait of character for truthfulness/untruthfulness offered to affect the credibility of a witness).

Rule 405. Methods of proving character

(a) Reputation, opinion, or conviction of crime. When evidence of character or a trait of character of a person is admissible, it may be proved by evidence of reputation, evidence in the form of opinion, or evidence of conviction of a crime which tends to prove the trait. Specific instances of conduct not the subject of a conviction of a crime shall be inadmissible.

(b) Specific instances of conduct. When character or a trait of character of a person is an essential element of a charge, claim, or defense, evidence of specific instances of conduct may also be admitted.

Adopted effective July 1, 1993.

Comment

Rule 405(a) adopts the substance of *N.J.Evid.R.* 46 and 47 with changes in language and structure only. *Fed.R.Evid.* 405(a) does not provide for proof of character or a character trait by evidence of conviction of a crime and does not provide that specific instances of conduct not the subject of a crime are inadmissible. Rule 405(a), following *N.J.Evid.R.* 47, rejects the provision of the federal rule which permits inquiry on cross-examination into specific instances of conduct. This provision of *N.J.Evid.R.* 47 was originally designed to respond to the criticism of the common-law rule pursuant to which the prosecutor was permitted to impeach a defendant's character witness by inquiring of him on cross-examination whether he had heard rumors of "bad acts" by or

charges against the accused not evidenced by a judgment of conviction. See, *e.g., State v. La Porte*, 62 *N.J.* 312, 319–320 (1973); *cf. State v. Steensen*, 35 *N.J.Super.* 103, 108 (App.Div.1955). The Committee regards this principle of *N.J.Evid.R.* 47 as still valid. Note also the same prohibition imposed on "bad act" impeachment by *N.J.Evid.R.* 22(d), followed by Rule 608.

Rule 405(b) follows *Fed.R.Evid.* 405(b) with language changes, incorporating the principle of *N.J.Evid.R.* 46.

Rule 406. Habit, routine practice

(a) Evidence, whether corroborated or not, of habit or routine practice is admissible to prove that on a specific occasion a person or organization acted in conformity with the habit or routine practice.

(b) Evidence of specific instances of conduct is admissible to prove habit or routine practice if evidence of a sufficient number of such instances is offered to support a finding of such habit or routine practice.

Adopted effective July 1, 1993.

Comment

Paragraph (a) of Rule 406 follows *Fed.R.Evid.* 406 and replaces *N.J.Evid.R.* 49 without any change in substance. The term "routine practice" is taken from the federal rule and replaces the term "custom" contained in *N.J.Evid.R.* 49 and 50. The phrase, "regardless of the presence of eyewitnesses," contained in the federal analogue, was omitted from paragraph (a) as superfluous.

Paragraph (b), which follows *N.J.Evid.R.* 50 and is not contained in the federal rule, deals with one method of proving habit or routine practice, namely by proof of a sufficient number of specific instances of conduct. Habit or routine practice may also be proved by other competent evidence.

Rule 407. Subsequent remedial measures

Evidence of remedial measures taken after an event is not admissible to prove that the event was caused by negligence or culpable conduct. However, evidence of such subsequent remedial conduct may be admitted as to other issues.

Adopted effective July 1, 1993.

Comment

Rule 407 follows the principle stated by *N.J.Evid.R.* 51 and *Fed.R.Evid.* 407. The 1967 New Jersey rule did not have an express provision making evidence of subsequent remedial measures admissible for purposes other than proof of negligence. Nevertheless, the admissibility of such evidence for other purposes has been recognized by case law. See, *e.g., Brown v. Brown*, 86 *N.J.* 565, 580–582 (1981) (routine maintenance); *Shatz v. TEC Technical Adhesives*, 174 *N.J.Super.* 135, 141–142 (App.Div.1980) (change in warning on product before injury); *Lavin v. Fauci*, 170 *N.J.Super.* 403 (App.Div.1979) (feasibility and credibility); *Manieri v. Volkswagenwerk*, 151 *N.J.Super.* 422 (App.Div.1977), *certif. denied*, 75 *N.J.* 594 (1978) (control).

Rule 408.　Settlement offers and negotiations

When a claim is disputed as to validity or amount, evidence of statements or conduct by parties or their attorneys in settlement negotiations, with or without a mediator present, including offers of compromise or any payment in settlement of a related claim, shall not be admissible to prove liability for, or invalidity of, or amount of the disputed claim. Such evidence shall not be excluded when offered for another purpose; and evidence otherwise admissible shall not be excluded merely because it was disclosed during settlement negotiations.

Adopted eff. July 1, 1993. Amended September 15, 1998, eff. July 1, 1999.

Comment

Rule 408 generally follows *Fed.R.Evid.* 408 and replaces *N.J.Evid.R.* 52(1) and 53. The general principles of these rules have been retained, but the formulation has been simplified.

The reference to parties' attorneys was added to make it clear that the rule applies to their statements and conduct as well. The rule also follows the federal provision that evidence otherwise obtained is not rendered inadmissible because it was also the subject of settlement negotiations. For example, admissions of liability made at the scene of an accident may be admitted.

The rule permits the use of evidence arising out of settlement negotiations for purposes other than proving liability or the amount of damages. Such other purposes include, for example, proof of an accord and satisfaction (*N.J.Evid.R.* 53), proof of a debtor's promise to pay all or a portion of a preexisting debt (*N.J.Evid.R.* 52(1)(b)) and proof of bias or prejudice of a witness (*Fed.R.Evid.* 607). Evidence that a criminal defendant offered consideration for dropping or reducing a charge may also be admitted in appropriate circumstances. *See State v. Romero,* 95 *N.J.Super.* 482, 489–490 (App.Div.1967).

To the extent that statements of fact made during settlement negotiations are not expressly excluded by *N.J.Evid.R.* 52(1) or 53, Rule 408 follows the broader principle embodied in *Fed.R.Evid.* 408 which excludes such statements unless made outside of settlement negotiations.

Rule 409.　Payment of medical and similar expenses

Evidence of furnishing or offering or promising to pay medical, hospital, property damage, or similar expense occasioned by an injury or other claim is not admissible to prove liability for the injury.

Adopted eff. July 1, 1993. Amended September 15, 1998, eff. July 1, 1999.

Comment

Rule 409 follows *Fed.R.Evid.* 409 verbatim. Although there is no precise New Jersey analogue to this rule, it is partly encompassed by reference in *N.J.Evid.R.* 52(1) to furnishing consideration to a claimant "from humanitarian motives."

Rule 410.　Inadmissibility of pleas, plea discussions and related statements

Except as otherwise provided in this rule, evidence of a plea of guilty which was later withdrawn, of any statement made in the course of that plea proceeding, and of any statement made during plea negotiations when either no guilty plea resulted or a guilty plea was later withdrawn, is not admissible in any civil or criminal proceeding against the person who made the plea or statement or who was the subject of the plea negotiations. However, such a statement is admissible (1) in any proceeding in which another statement made in the course of the same plea or plea discussions has been introduced and the statement should in fairness be considered contemporaneously with it, or (2) in a criminal proceeding for perjury, false statement, or other similar offense, if the statement was made by the defendant under oath, on the record, and in the presence of counsel.

Adopted effective July 1, 1993.

Comment

Rule 410 generally follows *Fed.R.Evid.* 410. Deleted, however, are those provisions of the federal rule which are unique to the federal practice. In replacing the abbreviated statement of *N.J.Evid.R.* 52(2), this rule expands the exclusion to include not only an accused's offer to plead guilty but also any statements made during plea negotiations. The expanded scope of the exclusion is a change in current New Jersey practice. *See State v. Boyle,* 198 *N.J.Super.* 64, 69–73 (App.Div.1984), whose holding this rule effectively supersedes. Even under current practice, however, if a court refuses to accept a plea of guilty or permits the accused to withdraw his plea, no admission made by the accused in the plea proceedings may be admitted against him at his criminal trial. *State v. Boone,* 66 *N.J.* 38 (1974). *See R.* 3:9–2 and *R.* 5:22–2(d).

This rule does not preclude the admissibility of statements made during plea negotiations when an issue is later raised as to the terms of the plea offer or agreement. *See, e.g., State v. Kovack,* 91 *N.J.* 476, 479–484 (1982).

See also R. 3:9–2 which provides that in accepting a guilty plea, the judge, for good cause shown, may order that it not be admissible in a civil proceeding.

Rule 411.　Liability insurance

Evidence that a person was or was not insured against liability is not admissible on the issue of that person's negligence or other wrongful conduct. Subject to Rule 403, this rule does not require the exclusion of evidence of insurance against liability when offered for another purpose, such as proof of agency, ownership, control, bias, or prejudice of a witness.

Adopted effective July 1, 1993.

Comment

Rule 411 follows *Fed.R.Evid.* 411 with minor modification. It replaces *N.J.Evid.R.* 54, which was essentially the same as the first sentence of this rule.

While the 1967 New Jersey rule did not include the content of the second sentence of this rule, its import is consistent with current practice. The reference to Rule 403 has been added to the second sentence to emphasize the potential for prejudice of such evidence.

Rule 412. Prosecutions for rape and related offenses [Not Adopted]

Comment

Fed.R.Evid. 412 was not adopted since this subject is covered by *N.J.S.A.* 2C:14–7, the Rape–Shield Law, which provides:

a. In prosecutions for aggravated sexual assault, sexual assault, aggravated criminal sexual contact, criminal sexual contact, or endangering the welfare of a child in violation of N.J.S. 2C:24–4, evidence of the victim's previous sexual conduct shall not be admitted nor reference made to it in the presence of the jury except as provided in this section. When the defendant seeks to admit such evidence for any purpose, he must apply for an order of the court before the trial or preliminary hearing, except that the court may allow the motion to be made during trial if the court determines that the evidence is newly discovered and could not have been obtained earlier through the exercise of due diligence. After the application is made, the court shall conduct a hearing in camera to determine the admissibility of the evidence. If the court finds that evidence offered by the defendant regarding the sexual conduct of the victim is relevant and that the probative value of the evidence offered is not outweighed by its collateral nature or by the probability that its admission will create undue prejudice, confusion of the issue, or unwarranted invasion of the privacy of the victim, the court shall enter an order setting forth with specificity what evidence may be introduced and the nature of the questions which shall be permitted, and the reasons why the court finds that such evidence satisfies the standards contained in this section. The defendant may then offer evidence under the order of the court.

b. In the absence of clear and convincing proof to the contrary, evidence of the victim's sexual conduct occurring more than one year before the date of the offense charged is presumed to be inadmissible under this section.

c. Evidence of previous sexual conduct shall not be considered relevant unless it is material to negating the element of force or coercion or to proving that the source of semen, pregnancy or disease is a person other than the defendant. For the purpose of this section, "sexual conduct" shall mean any conduct or behavior relating to sexual activities of the victim, including but not limited to previous or subsequent experience of sexual penetration or sexual contact, use of contraceptives, living arrangement and life style.

Note that the two categories of admissible prior sexual conduct prescribed by *N.J.S.A.* 2C:14–7(c) have been held on sixth amendment confrontation grounds, to be illustrative rather than exclusive. *See State v. Budis,* 243 *N.J.Super.* 498 (App.Div.1990), *aff'd,* 125 *N.J.* 519 (1991), permitting evidence of the prior sexual abuse of the child victim by another in order to rebut her assumed naivete.

ARTICLE V. PRIVILEGES

Rule 500. General rule

Privileges as they now exist or may be modified by law shall be unaffected by the adoption of these rules. For convenience in reference certain existing provisions of law relating to privileges are enumerated in Article V.[1]

Adopted effective July 1, 1993.

[1] N.J.R.E. 500 et seq.

Comment

As a historical matter, New Jersey's statutory law governing testimonial privileges was adopted as part of L. 1960, c. 52, the same act by which some of the rules of evidence were adopted. At that time, however, the privilege provisions were not assigned rule numbers but were, rather, codified as part of *N.J.S.A.* 2A:84A, and were thereafter amended and supplemented from time to time. These proposed rules essentially follow that format but, as a matter of convenience, they assign a rule number to each of the statutory privileges, making no change in their present text. This approach is set forth in *N.J.R.E.* 500, a new provision, which states that the adoption of these rules do not affect "[p]rivileges as they now exist or may be modified by law."

Federal Rule 501 leaves the law of privilege to common-law development superseded only by the Constitution, Act of Congress, or Supreme Court rule. *Fed.R.Evid.* 501 also incorporates state privilege law when applicable in federal diversity actions. Thus *Fed.R.Evid.* 501 is, in that respect, not appropriate to a state code of evidence.

Rule 501. Privilege of accused

The text of Rule 501 does not conform with the text of § 2A:84A–17, as amended by L.1992, c. 142, § 1 and L.2006, c. 103, § 90.

N.J.S.A. 2A:84A–17 provides:

(1) Every person has in any criminal action in which he is an accused a right not to be called as a witness and not to testify.

(2) The spouse or one partner in a civil union couple of the accused in a criminal action shall not testify in such action except to prove the fact of marriage or civil union unless (a) such spouse or partner consents, or (b) the accused is charged with an offense against the spouse or partner, a child of the accused or of the spouse or partner, or a child to whom the accused or the spouse or partner stands in the place of a parent, or (c) such spouse or partner is the complainant.

(3) An accused in a criminal action has no privilege to refuse when ordered by the judge, to submit his body to examination or to do any act in the presence of the judge or the trier of the fact, except to refuse to testify.

Adopted effective July 1, 1993.

Comment

N.J.S.A. 2A:84A–17(4) which, as adopted in 1960, permitted adverse comment and inferences from a criminal defendant's failure to testify, in certain circumstances, was declared unconstitutional in *State v. Lanzo*, 44 *N.J.* 560, 562–564 (1965), citing *Griffin v. California*, 380 *U.S.* 609, 14 *L.Ed.*2d 106 (1965). Accordingly, *N.J.Evid.R.* 23(4) was deleted by amendment adopted by the New Jersey Supreme Court, effective July 1, 1980.

Rule 502. Definition of incrimination

N.J.S.A. 2A:84A–18 provides:

Within the meaning of this article, a matter will incriminate (a) if it constitutes an element of a crime against this State, or another State or the United States, or (b) is a circumstance which with other circumstances would be a basis for a reasonable inference of the commission of such a crime, or (c) is a clue to the discovery of a matter which is within clauses (a) or (b) above; provided, a matter will not be held to incriminate if it clearly appears that the witness has no reasonable cause to apprehend a criminal prosecution. In determining whether a matter is incriminating under clauses (a), (b) or (c) and whether a criminal prosecution is to be apprehended, other matters in evidence, or disclosed in argument, the implications of the question, the setting in which it is asked, the applicable statute of limitations and all other factors, shall be taken into consideration.

Adopted effective July 1, 1993.

Rule 503. Self-incrimination

N.J.S.A. 2A:84A–19 provides:

Subject to Rule 37 [Rule 530], every natural person has a right to refuse to disclose in an action or to a police officer or other official any matter that will incriminate him or expose him to a penalty or a forfeiture of his estate, except that under this rule:

(a) no person has the privilege to refuse to submit to examination for the purpose of discovering or recording his corporal features and other identifying characteristics or his physical or mental condition;

(b) no person has the privilege to refuse to obey an order made by a court to produce for use as evidence or otherwise a document, chattel or other thing under his control if some other person or a corporation or other association has a superior right to the possession of the thing ordered to be produced;

(c) no person has a privilege to refuse to disclose any matter which the statutes or regulations governing his office, activity, occupation, profession or calling, or governing the corporation or association of which he is an officer, agent or employee, require him to record or report or disclose except to the extent that such statutes or regulations provide that the matter to be recorded, reported or disclosed shall be privileged or confidential;

(d) subject to the same limitations on evidence affecting credibility as apply to any other witness, the accused in a criminal action or a party in a civil action who voluntarily testifies in the action upon the merits does not have the privilege to refuse to disclose in that action, any matter relevant to any issue therein.

Adopted effective July 1, 1993.

Rule 504. Lawyer-client privilege

N.J.S.A. 2A:84A–20 provides:

(1) General rule. Subject to Rule 37 [Rule 530] and except as otherwise provided by paragraph 2 of this rule communications between lawyer and his client in the course of that relationship and in professional confidence, are privileged, and a client has a privilege (a) to refuse to disclose any such communication, and (b) to prevent his lawyer from disclosing it, and (c) to prevent any other witness from disclosing such communication if it came to the knowledge of such witness (i) in the course of its transmittal between the client and the lawyer, or (ii) in a manner not reasonably to be anticipated, or (iii) as a result of a breach of the lawyer-client relationship, or (iv) in the course of a recognized confidential or privileged communication between the client and such witness. The privilege shall be claimed by the lawyer unless otherwise instructed by the client or his representative; the privilege may be claimed by the client in person, or if incompetent or deceased, by his guardian or personal representative. Where a corporation or association is the client having the privilege and it has been dissolved, the privilege may be claimed by its successors, assigns or trustees in dissolution.

(2) Exceptions. Such privilege shall not extend (a) to a communication in the course of legal service sought or obtained in aid of the commission of a crime or a fraud, or (b) to a communication relevant to an issue between parties all of whom claim through the client, regardless of whether the respective claims are by testate or intestate succession or by inter vivos transaction, or (c) to a communication relevant to an issue of breach of duty by the lawyer to his client, or by the client to his lawyer. Where 2 or more persons have employed a lawyer to act for them in common, none of them can assert such privilege as against the others as to communications with respect to that matter.

(3) Definitions. As used in this rule (a) "client" means a person or corporation or other association that, directly or through an authorized representative, consults a lawyer or the lawyer's representative for the purpose of retaining the lawyer or securing legal service or advice from him in his professional capacity; and includes an incompetent whose guardian so consults the lawyer or the lawyer's representative in behalf of the incompetent, (b) "lawyer" means a person authorized, or reasonably believed by the client to be authorized to practice law in any State or nation the law of which recognizes a privilege against disclosure of confidential communications between client and lawyer. A communication made in the course of relationship between lawyer and client shall be presumed to have been made in professional confidence unless knowingly made within the hearing of some person whose presence nullified the privilege.

Adopted effective July 1, 1993.

Rule 505. Psychologist privilege

The text of Rule 505 does not conform with the text of § 45:14B–28, as amended by L.1997, c. 379, § 11.

N.J.S.A. 45:14B–28 provides:

The confidential relations and communications between and among a licensed practicing psychologist and individuals, couples, families or groups in the course of the practice of psychology are placed on the same basis as those provided between attorney and client, and nothing in this act shall be construed to require any such privileged communications to be disclosed by any such person.

There is no privilege under this section for any communication: (a) upon an issue of the client's condition in an action to commit the client or otherwise place the client under the control of another or others because of alleged incapacity, or in an action in which the client seeks to establish his competence or in an action to recover damages on account of conduct of the client which constitutes a crime; or (b) upon an issue as to the validity of a document as a will of the client; or (c) upon an issue between parties claiming by testate or intestate succession from a deceased client.

Adopted effective July 1, 1993.

Rule 506. Patient and physician privilege

(a) *N.J.S.A.* 2A:84A–22.1 provides:

As used in this act, (a) "patient" means a person who, for the sole purpose of securing preventive, palliative, or curative treatment, or a diagnosis preliminary to such treatment, of his physical or mental condition, consults a physician, or submits to an examination by a physician; (b) "physician" means a person authorized or reasonably believed by the patient to be authorized, to practice medicine in the State or jurisdiction in which the consultation or examination takes place; (c) "holder of the privilege" means the patient while alive and not under the guardianship of the guardian of the person of an incompetent patient, or the personal representative of a deceased patient; (d) "confidential communication between physician and patient" means such information transmitted between physician and patient, including information obtained by an examination of the patient, as is transmitted in confidence and by a means which, so far as the patient is aware, discloses the information to no third persons other than those reasonably necessary for the transmission of the information or the accomplishment of the purpose for which it is transmitted.

(b) *N.J.S.A.* 2A:84A–22.2 provides:

Except as otherwise provided in this act, a person, whether or not a party, has a privilege in a civil action or in a prosecution for a crime or violation of the disorderly persons law or for an act of juvenile delinquency to refuse to disclose, and to prevent a witness from disclosing, a communication, if he claims the privilege and the judge finds that (a) the communication was a confidential communication between patient and physician, and (b) the patient or the physician reasonably believed the communication to be necessary or helpful to enable the physician to make a diagnosis of the condition of the patient or to prescribe or render treatment therefor, and (c) the witness (i) is the holder of the privilege or (ii) at the time of the communication was the physician or a person to whom disclosure was made because reasonably necessary for the transmission of the communication or for the accomplishment of the purpose for which it was transmitted or (iii) is any other person who obtained knowledge or possession of the communication as the result of an intentional breach of the physician's duty of nondisclosure by the physician or his agent or servant and (d) the claimant is the holder of the privilege or a person authorized to claim the privilege for him.

(c) *N.J.S.A.* 2A:84A–22.3 provides:

There is no privilege under this act as to any relevant communication between the patient and his physician (a) upon an issue of the patient's condition in an action to commit him or otherwise place him under the control of another or others because of alleged mental incompetence, or in an action in which the patient seeks to establish his competence or in an action to recover damages on account of conduct of the patient which constitutes a criminal offense other than a misdemeanor, or (b) upon an issue as to the validity of a document as a will of the patient, or (c) upon an issue between parties claiming by testate or intestate succession from a deceased patient.

(d) *N.J.S.A.* 2A:84A–22.4 provides:

There is no privilege under this act in an action in which the condition of the patient is an element or factor of the claim or defense of the patient or of any party claiming through or under the patient or claiming as a beneficiary of the patient through a contract to which the patient is or was a party or under which the patient is or was insured.

(e) *N.J.S.A.* 2A:84A–22.5 provides:

There is no privilege under this act as to information which the physician or the patient is required to report to a public official or as to information required to be recorded in a public office, unless the statute requiring the report or record specifically provides that the information shall not be disclosed.

(f) *N.J.S.A.* 2A:84A–22.6 provides:

No person has a privilege under this act if the judge finds that sufficient evidence, aside from the communication, has been introduced to warrant a finding that the services of the physician were sought or obtained to enable or aid anyone to commit or to plan to commit a crime or a tort, or to escape detection or apprehension after the commission of a crime or a tort.

(g) *N.J.S.A.* 2A:84A–22.7 provides:

A privilege under this act as to a communication is terminated if the judge finds that any person while a holder of the privilege has caused the physician or any agent or servant of the physician to testify in any action to any matter of which the physician or his agent or servant gained knowledge through the communication.

Adopted effective July 1, 1993.

Publisher's Note

L.1997, c. 379, § 10, amended N.J.S.A. 2A:84A–22.3, effective January 19, 1998, to read:

"There is no privilege under this act as to any relevant communication between the patient and his physician (a) upon an issue of the patient's condition in an action to commit him or otherwise place him under the control of another or others because of his alleged incapacity, or in an action to recover damages on account of conduct of the patient which constitutes a criminal offense other than a misdemeanor, or (b) upon an issue as to the validity of a document as a will of the patient, or (c) upon an issue between parties claiming by testate or intestate succession from a deceased patient."

Rule 507. Utilization review committees of certified hospital or extended care facility; exceptions

(a) *N.J.S.A.* 2A:84A–22.8 provides:

Information and data secured by and in the possession of utilization review committees established by any certified hospital or extended care facility in the performance of their duties shall not be revealed or disclosed in any manner or under any circumstances by any member of such committee except to: (a) a patient's attending physician, (b) the chief administrative officer of the hospital or extended care facility which it serves, (c) the medical executive committee, or comparable enforcement unit, of such hospital or extended care facility, (d) representatives of, including intermediaries or carriers for, government agencies in the performance of their duties, under the provisions of Federal and State law, or (e) any hospital service corporation, medical service corporation or insurance company with which said patient has pertinent coverage under a contract, policy or certificate, the terms of which authorize the carrier to request and be given such information and data.

(b) *N.J.S.A.* 2A:84A–22.9 provides:

No member of a utilization review committee may be held liable for damages or otherwise prejudiced in any manner by reason of recommendations or findings made by said committee or for furnishing information or data obtained in the course of his duties as a member of a committee to the persons and officials mentioned in section 1 [2A:84A–22.8] hereof.

Adopted effective July 1, 1993.

Rule 508. Newsperson's privilege

(a) *N.J.S.A.* 2A:84A–21 provides:

Subject to Rule 37 [Rule 530], a person engaged on, engaged in, connected with, or employed by news media for the purpose of gathering, procuring, transmitting, compiling, editing or disseminating news for the general public or on whose behalf news is so gathered, pro-

cured, transmitted, compiled, edited or disseminated has a privilege to refuse to disclose, in any legal or quasilegal proceeding or before any investigative body, including, but not limited to, any court, grand jury, petit jury, administrative agency, the Legislature or legislative committee, or elsewhere:

a. The source, author, means, agency or person from or through whom any information was procured, obtained, supplied, furnished, gathered, transmitted, compiled, edited, disseminated, or delivered; and

b. Any news or information obtained in the course of pursuing his professional activities whether or not it is disseminated.

The provisions of this rule insofar as it relates to radio or television stations shall not apply unless the radio or television station maintains and keeps open for inspection, for a period of at least 1 year from the date of an actual broadcast or telecast, an exact recording, transcription, kinescopic film or certified written transcript of the actual broadcast or telecast.

(b) *N.J.S.A.* 2A:84A–21a provides:

Unless a different meaning clearly appears from the context of this act, as used in this act:

a. "News media" means newspapers, magazines, press associations, news agencies, wire services, radio, television or other similar printed, photographic, mechanical or electronic means of disseminating news to the general public.

b. "News" means any written, oral or pictorial information gathered, procured, transmitted, compiled, edited or disseminated by, or on behalf of any person engaged in, engaged on, connected with or employed by a news media and so procured or obtained while such required relationship is in effect.

c. "Newspaper" means a paper that is printed and distributed ordinarily not less frequently than once a week and that contains news, articles of opinion, editorials, features, advertising, or other matter regarded as of current interest, has a paid circulation and has been entered at a United States post office as second class matter.

d. "Magazine" means a publication containing news which is published and distributed periodically, has a paid circulation and has been entered at a United States post office as second class matter.

e. "News agency" means a commercial organization that collects and supplies news to subscribing newspapers, magazines, periodicals and news broadcasters.

f. "Press association" means an association of newspapers or magazines formed to gather and distribute news to its members.

g. "Wire service" means a news agency that sends out syndicated news copy by wire to subscribing newspapers, magazines, periodicals or news broadcasters.

h. "In the course of pursuing his professional activities" means any situation, including a social gathering, in which a reporter obtains information for the purpose of disseminating it to the public, but does not include any situation in which a reporter intentionally conceals from the source the fact that he is a reporter, and does not include any situation in which a reporter is an eyewitness to, or participant in, any act involving physical violence or property damage.

(c) *N.J.S.A.* 2A:84A–21.1 provides:

Where a newsperson is required to disclose information pursuant to a subpoena issued by or on behalf of a defendant in a criminal proceeding, not including proceedings before administrative or investigative bodies, grand juries, or legislative committees or commissions, the provisions and procedures in this act are applicable to the claim and exercise of the newsperson's privilege under Rule 27[1] (C. 2A:84A–21).

(d) *N.J.S.A.* 2A:84A–21.2 provides:

Proceedings pursuant to this act shall take place before the trial, except that the court may allow a motion to institute proceedings pursuant to this act to be made during trial if the court determines that the evidence sought is newly discovered and could not have been discovered earlier through the exercise of due diligence.

(e) *N.J.S.A.* 2A:84A–21.3 provides:

a. To sustain a claim of the newsperson's privilege under Rule 27 [Rule 508(a)] the claimant shall make a prima facie showing that he is engaged in, connected with, or employed by a news media for the purpose of gathering, procuring, transmitting, compiling, editing or disseminating news for the general public or on whose behalf news is so gathered, procured, transmitted, compiled, edited or disseminated, and that the subpoenaed materials were obtained in the course of pursuing his professional activities.

b. To overcome a finding by the court that the claimant has made a prima facie showing under a. above, the party seeking enforcement of the subpoena shall show by clear and convincing evidence that the privilege has been waived under Rule 37 [Rule 530] (C. 2A:84A–29) or by a preponderance of the evidence that there is a reasonable probability that the subpoenaed materials are relevant, material and necessary to the defense, that they could not be secured from any less intrusive source, that the value of the material sought as it bears upon the issue of guilt or innocence outweighs the privilege against disclosure, and that the request is not overbroad, oppressive, or unreasonably burdensome which may be overcome by evidence that all or part of the information sought is irrelevant, immaterial, unnecessary to the defense, or that it can be secured from another source. Publication shall constitute a waiver only as to the specific materials published.

c. The determinations to be made by the court pursuant to this section shall be made only after a hearing in which the party claiming the privilege and the party seeking enforcement of the subpoena shall have a full opportunity to present evidence and argument with respect to each of the materials or items sought to be subpoenaed.

(f) *N.J.S.A.* 2A:84A–21.4 provides:

Upon a finding by the court that there has been a waiver as to any of the materials sought or that any of the materials sought meet the criteria set forth in subsection 3.b.,[2] the court shall order the production of such materials, and such materials only, for in camera inspection and determination as to its probable admissibility in the trial. The party claiming the privilege and the party seeking enforcement of the subpoena shall be entitled to a hearing in connection with the in camera inspection of such materials by the court, during which hearing each party shall have a full opportunity to be heard. If the court, after its in camera review of the materials, determines that such materials are admissible according to the standards set forth in subsection 3.b., the court shall direct production of such materials, and such materials only.

(g) *N.J.S.A.* 2A:84A–21.5 provides:

After any hearing conducted by the court pursuant to section 3 or 4 hereof,[3] the court shall make specific findings of fact and conclusions of law with respect to its rulings, which findings shall be in writing or set forth on the record.

(h) *N.J.S.A.* 2A:84A–21.6 provides:

An interlocutory appeal taken from a decision to uphold or quash a subpoena shall act as a stay of all penalties which may have been imposed for failure to comply with the court's order. The record on appeal shall be kept under seal until such time as appeals are exhausted. In the event that all material or any part thereof is found to be privileged, the record as to that privileged material shall remain permanently sealed. Any subpoenaed materials which shall, upon exhaustion and determination of such appeals, be found to be privileged, shall be returned to the party claiming the privilege.

(i) *N.J.S.A.* 2A:84A–21.7 provides:

Where proceedings are instituted hereunder by one of several co-defendants in a criminal trial, notice shall be provided to all of the co-defendants. Any co-defendant shall have the right to intervene if the co-defendant can demonstrate, pursuant to section 3, that the materials sought by the issuance of the subpoena bear upon his guilt or innocence. Where such intervention is sought by a co-defendant, that co-defendant shall be required, prior to being permitted to participate in any in camera proceeding, to make that showing required of a defendant in section 3.

(j) *N.J.S.A.* 2A:84A–21.8 provides:

If the court finds no reasonable basis for requesting the information has been shown, costs, including counsel fee, may be assessed against the party seeking enforcement of the subpoena. Where an application for costs or counsel fee is made, the judge shall set forth his reasons for awarding or denying same.

Adopted effective July 1, 1993.

1 Pub. Note: There is no bracketed reference to new rule in original Court copy.

2 N.J.S.A. § 2A:84A–21.3(b).

3 N.J.S.A. §§ 2A:84A–21.3, 2A:84A–21.4.

Rule 509.   Marital privilege—confidential communications

The text of Rule 509 does not conform with the text of § 2A:84A–22, as amended by L.1992, c. 142, § 2.

N.J.S.A. 2A:84A–22 provides:

No person shall disclose any communication made in confidence between such person and his or her spouse unless both shall consent to the disclosure or unless the communication is relevant to an issue in an action between them or in a criminal action or proceeding coming within Rule 23(2) [Rule 501(2)]. When a spouse is incompetent or deceased, consent to the disclosure may be given for such a spouse by the guardian, executor or administrator. The requirement for consent shall not terminate with divorce or separation. A communication between spouses while living separate and apart under a divorce from bed and board shall not be a privileged communication.

Adopted effective July 1, 1993.

Rule 510.   Marriage counselor privilege

N.J.S.A. 45:8B–29 provides:

Any communication between a marriage counselor and the person or persons counseled shall be confidential and its secrecy preserved. This privilege shall not be subject to waiver, except where the marriage counselor is a party defendant to a civil, criminal or disciplinary action arising from such counseling, in which case, the waiver shall be limited to that action.

Adopted effective July 1, 1993.

Rule 511.   Priest-penitent privilege

The text of Rule 511 does not conform with the text of § 2A:84A–23, as amended by L.1994, c. 123, § 1.

N.J.S.A. 2A:84A–23 provides:

Any communication made in confidence to a cleric in the cleric's professional character, or as a spiritual advisor in the course of the discipline or practice of the religious body to which the cleric belongs or of the religion which the cleric professes, shall be privileged. Privileged communications shall include confessions and other communications made in confidence between and among the cleric and individuals, couples, families or groups in the exercise of the cleric's professional or spiritual counseling role.

As used in this section, "cleric" means a priest, rabbi, minister or other person or practitioner authorized to perform similar functions of any religion.

The privilege accorded to communications under this rule shall belong to both the cleric and the person or persons making the communication and shall be subject to waiver only under the following circumstances:

(1) both the person or persons making the communication and the cleric consent to the waiver of the privilege; or

(2) the privileged communication pertains to a future criminal act, in which case, the cleric alone may, but is not required to, waive the privilege.

Adopted effective July 1, 1993.

Rule 512.   Religious belief

N.J.S.A. 2A:84A–24 provides:

Every person has a privilege to refuse to disclose his theological opinion or religious belief unless his adherence or nonadherence to such an opinion or belief is material to an issue in the action other than that of his credibility as a witness.

Adopted effective July 1, 1993.

Rule 513.   Political vote

N.J.S.A. 2A:84A–25 provides:

Every person has a privilege to refuse to disclose the tenor of his vote at a political election unless the judge finds that the vote was cast illegally.

Adopted effective July 1, 1993.

Rule 514.   Trade secret

N.J.S.A. 2A:84A–26 provides:

The owner of a trade secret has a privilege, which may be claimed by him or his agent or employee, to refuse to disclose the secret and to prevent other persons from disclosing it if the judge finds that the allowance of the privilege will not tend to conceal fraud or otherwise work injustice.

Adopted effective July 1, 1993.

Rule 515.   Official information

N.J.S.A. 2A:84A–27 provides:

No person shall disclose official information of this State or of the United States (a) if disclosure is forbidden by or pursuant to any Act of Congress or of this State, or (b) if the judge finds that disclosure of the information in the action will be harmful to the interests of the public.

Adopted effective July 1, 1993.

Rule 516.   Identity of informer

N.J.S.A. 2A:84A–28 provides:

A witness has a privilege to refuse to disclose the identity of a person who has furnished information purporting to disclose a violation of a provision of the laws of this State or of the United States to a representative of the State or the United States or a governmental division thereof, charged with the duty of enforcing that provision, and evidence thereof is inadmissible, unless the judge finds that (a) the identity of the person furnishing the information has already been otherwise disclosed or (b) disclosure of his identity is essential to assure a fair determination of the issues.

Adopted effective July 1, 1993.

Rule 517. Victim counselor privilege

(a) *N.J.S.A.* 2A:84A–22.13 provides:

The Legislature finds and declares that:

a. The emotional and psychological injuries that are inflicted on victims of violence are often more serious than the physical injuries suffered;

b. Counseling is often a successful treatment to ease the real and profound psychological trauma experienced by these victims and their families;

c. In the counseling process, victims of violence openly discuss their emotional reactions to the crime. These reactions are often highly intertwined with their personal histories and psychological profile;

d. Counseling of violence and victims is most successful when the victims are assured their thoughts and feelings will remain confidential and will not be disclosed without their permission; and

e. Confidentiality should be accorded all victims of violence who require counseling whether or not they are able to afford the services of private psychiatrists or psychologists.

Therefore, it is the public policy of this State to extend a testimonial privilege encompassing the contents of communications with a victim counselor and to render immune from discovery or legal process the records of these communications maintained by the counselor.

(b) *N.J.S.A.* 2A:84A–22.14 provides:

As used in this act:

a. "Act of violence" means the commission or attempt to commit any of the offenses set forth in subsection b. of section 11 of P.L. 1971, c. 317 (C. 52:4B–11).

b. "Confidential communication" means any information exchanged between a victim and a victim counselor in private or in the presence of a third party who is necessary to facilitate communication or further the counseling process and which is disclosed in the course of the counselor's treatment of the victim for any emotional or psychological condition resulting from an act of violence. It includes any advice, report or working paper given or made in the course of the consultation and all information received by the victim counselor in the course of that relationship.

c. "Victim" means a person who consults a counselor for the purpose of securing advice, counseling or assistance concerning a mental, physical or emotional condition caused by an act of violence.

d. "Victim counseling center" means any office, institution, or center offering assistance to victims and

their families through crisis intervention, medical and legal accompaniment and follow-up counseling.

e. "Victim counselor" means a person engaged in any office, institution or center defined as a victim counseling center by this act, who has undergone 40 hours of training and is under the control of a direct services supervisor of the center and who has a primary function of rendering advice, counseling or assisting victims of acts of violence.

(c) *N.J.S.A.* 2A:84A–22.15 provides:

Subject to Rule 37 [Rule 530] of the Rules of Evidence, a victim counselor has a privilege not to be examined as a witness in any civil or criminal proceeding with regard to any confidential communication. The privilege shall be claimed by the counselor unless otherwise instructed by prior written consent of the victim. When a victim is incompetent or deceased consent to disclosure may be given by the guardian, executor or administrator except when the guardian, executor or administrator is the defendant or has a relationship with the victim such that he has an interest in the outcome of the proceeding. The privilege may be knowingly waived by a juvenile. In any instance where the juvenile is, in the opinion of the judge, incapable of knowing consent, the parent or guardian of the juvenile may waive the privilege on behalf of the juvenile, provided that the parent or guardian is not the defendant and does not have a relationship with the defendant such that he has an interest in the outcome of the proceeding. A victim counselor or a victim cannot be compelled to provide testimony in any civil or criminal proceeding that would identify the name, address, location, or telephone number of a domestic violence shelter or any other facility that provided temporary emergency shelter to the victim of the offense or transaction that is the subject of the proceeding unless the facility is a party to the proceeding.

(d) *N.J.S.A.* 2A:84A–22.16 provides:

Nothing in this act shall be deemed to prevent the disclosure to a defendant in a criminal action of statements or information given by a victim to a county victim-witness coordinator, where the disclosure of the statements or information is required by the constitution of this State or of the United States.

Adopted effective July 1, 1993.

Rule 518. Social worker privileges

N.J.S.A. 45:15BB–13 provides:

A social worker licensed or certified pursuant to the provisions of this act shall not be required to disclose any confidential information that the social worker may have acquired from a client or patient while performing social work services for that client or patient unless:

a. Disclosure is required by other State law;

b. Failure to disclose the information presents a clear and present danger to the health or safety of an individual;

c. The social worker is a party defendant to a civil, criminal or disciplinary action arising from the social work services provided, in which case a waiver of the privilege accorded by this section shall be limited to that action;

d. The patient or client is a defendant in a criminal proceeding and the use of the privilege would violate the defendant's right to a compulsory process or the right to present testimony and witnesses on that person's behalf; or

e. A patient or client agrees to waive the privilege accorded by this section, and, in circumstances where more than one person in a family is receiving social work services, each such member agrees to the waiver. Absent a waiver from each family member, a social worker shall not disclose any information received from any family member.

Adopted September 15, 1998, to be effective July 1, 1999.

Rule 519. Mediator Privilege

(a) N.J.S. 2A:23C–4 provides:

a. Except as otherwise provided in section 6 of P.L. 2004, c. 157 (N.J.S. 2A:23C–6), a mediation communication is privileged as provided in subsection b. of this section and shall not be subject to discovery or admissible in evidence in a proceeding unless waived or precluded as provided by section 5 of P.L. 2004, c. 157 (N.J.S. 2A:23C–5).

b. In a proceeding, the following privileges shall apply:

(1) a mediation party may refuse to disclose, and may prevent any other person from disclosing, a mediation communication.

(2) a mediator may refuse to disclose a mediation communication, and may prevent any other person from disclosing a mediation communication of the mediator.

(3) a nonparty participant may refuse to disclose, and may prevent any other person from disclosing, a mediation communication of the nonparty participant.

c. Evidence or information that is otherwise admissible or subject to discovery shall not become inadmissible or protected from discovery solely by reason of its disclosure or use in a mediation.

(b) N.J.S. 2A:23C–5 provides:

a. A privilege under section 4 of P.L. 2004, c. 157 (N.J.S. 2A:23C–4) may be waived in a record or orally during a proceeding if it is expressly waived by all parties to the mediation and:

(1) in the case of the privilege of a mediator, it is expressly waived by the mediator; and

(2) in the case of the privilege of a nonparty participant, it is expressly waived by the nonparty participant.

b. A person who discloses or makes a representation about a mediation communication that prejudices another person in a proceeding is precluded from asserting a privilege under section 4 of P.L. 2004, c. 157 (N.J.S. 2A:23C–4), but only to the extent necessary for the person prejudiced to respond to the representation or disclosure.

c. A person who intentionally uses a mediation to plan, attempt to commit or commit a crime, or to conceal an ongoing crime or ongoing criminal activity is precluded from asserting a privilege under section 4 of P.L. 2004, c. 157 (N.J.S. 2A:23C–4).

(c) N.J.S. 2A:23C–6 provides:

a. There is no privilege under section 4 of P.L. 2004, c. 157 (N.J.S. 2A:23C–4) for a mediation communication that is:

(1) in an agreement evidenced by a record signed by all parties to the agreement;

(2) made during a session of a mediation that is open, or is required by law to be open, to the public;

(3) a threat or statement of a plan to inflict bodily injury or commit a crime;

(4) intentionally used to plan a crime, attempt to commit a crime, or to conceal an ongoing crime or ongoing criminal activity;

(5) sought or offered to prove or disprove a claim or complaint filed against a mediator arising out of a mediation;

(6) except as otherwise provided in subsection c., sought or offered to prove or disprove a claim or complaint of professional misconduct or malpractice filed against a mediation party, nonparty participant, or representative of a party based on conduct occurring during a mediation; or

(7) sought or offered to prove or disprove child abuse or neglect in a proceeding in which the Division of Youth and Family Services in the Department of Human Services is a party, unless the Division of Youth and Family Services participates in the mediation.

b. There is no privilege under section 4 of P.L. 2004, c. 157 (N.J.S. 2A:23C–4) if a court, administrative agency, or arbitrator finds, after a hearing in camera, that the party seeking discovery or the proponent of the evidence has shown that the evidence is not otherwise available, that there is a need for the evidence that substantially outweighs the interest in protecting confidentiality, and that the mediation communication is sought or offered in:

(1) a court proceeding involving a crime as defined in the "New Jersey Code of Criminal Justice," N.J.S. 2C:1–1 et seq.; or

(2) except as otherwise provided in subsection c., a proceeding to prove a claim to rescind or reform or a defense to avoid liability on a contract arising out of the mediation.

c. A mediator may not be compelled to provide evidence of a mediation communication referred to in paragraph (6) of subsection a. or paragraph (2) of subsection b.

d. If a mediation communication is not privileged under subsection a. or b., only the portion of the communication necessary for the application of the exception from nondisclosure may be admitted. Admission of evidence under subsection a. or b. does not render the evidence, or any other mediation communication, discoverable or admissible for any other purpose.

(d) N.J.S. 2A:23C–7 provides:

a. Except as required in subsection b., a mediator may not make a report, assessment, evaluation, recommendation, finding, or other oral or written communication regarding a mediation to a court, administrative agency, or other authority that may make a ruling on the dispute that is the subject of the mediation.

b. A mediator may disclose:

(1) whether the mediation occurred or has terminated, whether a settlement was reached, and attendance; or

(2) a mediation communication as permitted under section 6 of P.L. 2004, c. 157 (N.J.S. 2A:23C–6).

c. A communication made in violation of subsection a. may not be considered by a court, administrative agency, or arbitrator.

(e) N.J.S. 2A:23C–8 provides:

Unless made during a session of a mediation which is open, or is required by law to be open, to the public, mediation communications are confidential to the extent agreed by the parties or provided by other law or rule of this State.

Note: Adopted September 17, 2007 to be effective July 1, 2008.

Rules 520 to 529. [Reserved]

Rule 530. Waiver of privilege by contract or previous disclosure; limitations

N.J.S.A. 2A:84A–29 provides:

A person waives his right or privilege to refuse to disclose or to prevent another from disclosing a specified matter if he or any other person while the holder thereof has (a) contracted with anyone not to claim the right or privilege or, (b) without coercion and with knowledge of his right or privilege, made disclosure of any part of the privileged matter or consented to such a disclosure made by anyone.

A disclosure which is itself privileged or otherwise protected by the common law, statutes or rules of court of this State, or by lawful contract, shall not constitute a waiver under this section. The failure of a witness to claim a right or privilege with respect to one question

shall not operate as a waiver with respect to any other question.

Adopted effective July 1, 1993.

Rule 531. Admissibility of disclosure wrongfully compelled

N.J.S.A. 2A:84A–30 provides:

Evidence of a statement or other disclosure is inadmissible against the holder of the privilege if the disclosure was wrongfully made or erroneously required.

Adopted effective July 1, 1993.

Rule 532. Reference to exercise of privileges

N.J.S.A. 2A:84A–31 provides:

If a privilege is exercised not to testify or to prevent another from testifying, either in the action or with respect to particular matters, or to refuse to disclose or to prevent another from disclosing any matter, the judge and counsel may not comment thereon, no presumption shall arise with respect to the exercise of the privilege, and the trier of fact may not draw any adverse inference therefrom. In those jury cases wherein the right to exercise a privilege, as herein provided, may be misunderstood and unfavorable inferences drawn by the trier of the fact, or be impaired in the particular case, the court, at the request of the party exercising the privilege, may instruct the jury in support of such privilege.

Adopted effective July 1, 1993.

Rule 533. Effect of error in overruling claim of privilege

N.J.S.A. 2A:84A–32 provides:

(1) A party may predicate error on a ruling disallowing a claim of privilege only if he is the holder of the privilege.

(2) If a witness refuses to answer a question, under color of a privilege claimed pursuant to Rules 23 through 38 [Rules 501 through 531], after the judge has ordered the witness to answer, and a contempt proceeding is brought against the witness, the court hearing the same shall order it dismissed if it appears that the order directing the witness to answer was erroneous.

Adopted effective July 1, 1993.

ARTICLE VI. WITNESSES

Rule 601. General rule of competency

Every person is competent to be a witness unless (a) the judge finds that the proposed witness is incapable of expression concerning the matter so as to be understood by the judge and jury either directly or through interpretation, or (b) the proposed witness is incapable of understanding the duty of a witness to tell the truth, or (c) except as otherwise provided by these rules or by law.

Adopted effective July 1, 1993.

Comment

Rule 601 incorporates the substantive provisions of *N.J.Evid.R.* 7(a) and (c) and 17(a) and (b). The federal analogue, *Fed.R.Evid.* 601, is inapposite to the extent that it states a choice of law rule in federal proceedings. While the substantive provision of the federal rule is less specific than this rule, the federal rule is not inconsistent with this rule in principle. Subsection (c) was added to accommodate provisions of Rules 804(a)(5) and 805(b)(8)(B) regarding admissibility of a child's statements concerning sexual activity notwithstanding the child is not deemed competent as a witness under Rule 601.

Rule 602. Lack of personal knowledge

Except as otherwise provided by Rule 703 (bases of opinion testimony by experts), a witness may not testify to a matter unless evidence is introduced sufficient to support a finding that the witness has personal knowledge of the matter. Evidence to prove personal knowledge may, but need not, consist of the testimony of that witness.

Amended September 15, 2004, effective July 1, 2005.

Comment

Rule 602 follows *Fed.R.Evid.* 602 and part of *N.J.Evid.R.* 19. The provision contained in *N.J.Evid.R.* 19 which allowed evidence to be introduced conditionally is encompassed by Rule 104 and is therefore not repeated in this rule.

This rule should not be construed to deprive the judge of the inherent power to reject the testimony of a witness if he finds that no trier of fact could reasonably believe that the witness actually perceived the matter. The express provision to this effect contained in *N.J.Evid.R.* 19 was not included in this rule because it merely reflects a principle generally applicable to proof of all conditions for the admissibility of evidence which is embraced by Rule 104.

Rule 603. Oath or affirmation

Before testifying a witness shall be required to take an oath or make an affirmation or declaration to tell the truth under the penalty provided by law. No witness may be barred from testifying because of religious belief or lack of such belief.

Adopted effective July 1, 1993.

Comment

Rule 603 follows both *Fed.R.Evid.* 603 and *N.J.Evid.R.* 18 with minor language changes. As to the use of evidence respecting the religious belief of a witness, see Rule 610.

Although *N.J.S.A.* 41:1–6 prescribes a form of affirmation and declaration and *R.* 1:4–4(b) prescribes the form of certification in lieu of oath, no statute or rule of evidence or practice prescribes the form of witness oath. Consequently, although the so-called traditional form of oath is commonly used, it is not mandated and, especially in the case of children, any form will be acceptable if it satisfies the judge that it constitutes a commitment to speak the truth "on pain of future punishment of any kind." *State in Interest of R.R.,* 79 *N.J.* 97, 111 (1979).

See also Rule 610, which prohibits admissibility of a witness' beliefs or opinions to affect credibility.

Rule 604. Interpreters

The judge shall determine the qualifications of a person testifying as an interpreter. An interpreter shall be subject to all provisions of these rules relating to witnesses and shall take an oath or make an affirmation or declaration to interpret accurately.

Adopted effective July 1, 1993.

Comment

Rule 604 follows the current but presently uncodified practice of requiring an interpreter to take an oath or make an affirmation to interpret accurately and adopts the last sentence of *N.J.Evid.R.* 17 making the interpreter subject to rules relating to witnesses. While not inconsistent with *Fed.R.Evid.* 604, this rule avoids the potential for confusion in the federal rule's stipulation that an interpreter is subject to "qualification as an expert." Instead, this rule, filling a gap in the current New Jersey rules, simply leaves the qualification of a person to act as an interpreter to determination by the trial judge.

Because the use of an interpreter always presents some risk of distortion of the "message communicated by the primary witness," the use of an interpreter should be limited to those situations in which the trial judge is satisfied that the "witness' natural mode of expression is not intelligible to the tribunal." *State in Interest of R.R.,* 79 *N.J.* 97, 116 (1979).

To insure the integrity of the interpretation, the interpretation must be wholly impersonal, that is, an exact rendering of the witness' communication, neither paraphrased, summarized, expanded or otherwise modified. *Id.* at 117–118. More significantly, the interpreter must have no interest in the matter before the court; an interested interpreter may be allowed to act, if at all, only when there is no reasonable possibility of obtaining the services of a disinterested interpreter. *Ibid. See State v. Lee,* 211 *N.J.Super.* 590, 594–596 (App.Div.1986). In no circumstances may a primary witness act as interpreter for another primary witness. *State in the Interest of R.R., supra,* 79 *N.J.* at 119–120.

Rule 605. Restriction on judge as witness

The judge presiding at the trial may not testify as a witness in that trial. No objection need be made to preserve the point.

Adopted effective July 1, 1993.

Comment

Rule 605 follows *Fed.R.Evid.* 605 except that "in that trial" was moved to the end of the sentence. In principle the rule is the same as *N.J.Evid.R.* 42.

Note that a New Jersey judge may not testify as an expert witness on New Jersey law in a trial over which he is not presiding. *State v. Grimes,* 235 *N.J.Super.* 75, 79–81 (App.Div.1989), *certif. denied,* 118 *N.J.* 222 (1989).

Rule 606. Restriction on juror as witness

A member of the jury may not testify as a witness before the jury on which the juror is serving.

Adopted effective July 1, 1993.

Comment

Rule 606 follows the analogous provisions of both *Fed.R.Evid.* 606(a) and *N.J.Evid.R.* 43 with minor language changes only. The provision of the federal rule requiring objections to the testimony of a juror to be made outside the presence of the jury was deleted as self-evident.

Fed.R.Evid. 606(b) and *N.J.Evid.R.* 41 address the extent to which a juror may testify after the verdict with respect to factors influencing his vote. In general terms both prohibit such testimony unless it relates to improper outside influences. New Jersey case law on the subject is generally consistent with both rules. *See, e.g., State v. Athorn,* 46 *N.J.* 247 (1966), *cert. denied,* 384 *U.S.* 962 (1966); *State v. LaFera,* 42 *N.J.* 97, 105–111 (1964); *State v. Young,* 181 *N.J.Super.* 463, 466–472 (App.Div.1981); *R.* 1:16–1. *See also State v. Bey (I),* 112 *N.J.* 45, 86–92 (1988), prescribing standards for post-impanelment, pre-verdict interrogation of jurors respecting possible taint. The prohibition against testimony by jurors in the New Jersey analogue, *N.J.Evid.R.* 43, was intended only to prohibit a juror from testifying as a fact witness in the trial itself and does not address the question of testimony by a juror in a collateral hearing to determine whether improper influences upon him or the jury may have been exerted. *See* Comment on Rule 43, *The 1963 Report* at 83–84. Because New Jersey case law is comprehensive and the issue overlaps procedural concerns, it was deemed unnecessary to adopt an evidence rule dealing with juror misconduct, improper influence of jurors, and related matters. Consequently, no analogue to *N.J.Evid.R.* 41, or *Fed.R.Evid.* 606(b) was incorporated in this rule.

Rule 607. Credibility and neutralization

Except as otherwise provided by Rules 405 and 608, for the purpose of impairing or supporting the credibility of a witness, any party including the party calling the witness may examine the witness and introduce extrinsic evidence relevant to the issue of credibility, except that the party calling a witness may not neutralize the witness' testimony by a prior contradictory statement unless the statement is in a form admissible under Rule 803(a)(1) or the judge finds that the party calling the witness was surprised. A prior consistent statement shall not be admitted to support the credibility of a witness except to rebut an express or implied charge against the witness of recent fabrication or of improper influence or motive and except as otherwise provided by the law of evidence.

Adopted effective July 1, 1993.

Comment

Rule 607 follows almost verbatim *N.J.Evid.R.* 20 as amended effective July 1, 1982. That amendment, together with the contemporaneous amendment of *N.J.Evid.R.* 63(1)(a), substantially modified the so-called voucher rule as previously embraced in *N.J.Evid.R.* 20. *Fed.R.Evid.* 607, which abolished the voucher rule entirely, was rejected. Rule 607 also continues the neutralization provision embodied in *N.J.Evid.R.* 20, which is not contained in the federal analogue.

Fed.R.Evid. 607 was coupled in the original draft of the Federal Rules of Evidence with a hearsay exception providing for the substantive admissibility of all prior statements of a witness. *See Notes of Committee on the Judiciary, House Report No. 93–650,* Note to *Fed.R.Evid.* 801(d)(1), 28 *U.S.C.A.* (1984). When all prior statements of a witness are thus admissible, there is no longer the danger that a witness will be called solely to obtain forbidden hearsay benefits under the guise of impeachment, since the benefits are no longer forbidden. *See Notes of Advisory Committee on Proposed Rules,* Note to *Fed.R.Evid.* 607, 28 *U.S.C.A.* (1984). However, if some prior statements of a witness remain subject to hearsay restrictions on substantive use, restrictions on "impeaching" one's own witness should be retained, at least to some extent. This point was apparently overlooked by Congress when the wide open prior witness statement hearsay exception was narrowed, but a corresponding change was not made in the impeachment rule. Rule 607 reflects the properly tailored restrictions on impeachment of one's own witness contained in *N.J.Evid.R.* 20.

Prior to the adoption of the 1967 Rules of Evidence, it was recommended that Rule 20 take a form that "sweeps the decks clean as to impeachment." *The 1963 Report* at 59. It was argued that there should be no limitation on the right to impair the credibility of one's "own witness." *Ibid.* However, the proposed version of Rule 20, which mirrored the principle later embodied in Rule 607 of the Uniform Rules of Evidence, was rejected.

Instead a version incorporating the restrictive voucher rule was adopted.

The 1982 amendments to *N.J.Evid.R.* 20 broadened the right of a party to impeach a witness called by him by allowing him to use a prior inconsistent statement if in a form complying with *N.J.Evid.R.* 63(1)(a), as amended. Such a statement can also be used to neutralize the current testimony of the witness, whether or not the party calling the witness has been surprised by that testimony. A fuller statement of the purposes of the 1982 amendments to *N.J.Evid.R.* 20 and *N.J.Evid.R.* 63(1)(a) was given in the commentary to the proposed amendments to these rules published in 108 *N.J.L.J.* 301, 302 (1981).

Rule 607 permits the use of a prior consistent statement to rebut an express or implied charge of recent fabrication or of improper influence or motive. The phrase "improper influence or motive" has been added to the formulation in *N.J.Evid.R.* 20. It was taken from *Fed.R.Evid.* 801(d)(1)(B) and is repeated in Rule 803(a)(2). With respect to the provision dealing with the admissibility of prior consistent statements, the phrase "and except as otherwise provided by the law of evidence" refers to situations recognized by case law, such as the fresh complaint rule, which permits fresh complaint evidence to be offered to support the credibility of a witness. *State v. Balles*, 47 *N.J.* 331, 338 (1966), *cert. denied* and *appeal dismissed*, 388 *U.S.* 461 (1967); *State v. Bethune*, 232 *N.J.Super.* 532 (App.Div.1989), *aff'd*, 121 *N.J.* 137 (1990).

As to the use of extrinsic evidence other than prior statements to affect credibility, see generally *State v. Johnson*, 216 *N.J.Super.* 588, 603 (App.Div.1987). *See also* Rule 608 as to the use of character evidence of truthfulness to support the credibility of a witness.

Rule 608. Evidence of Character for Truthfulness or Untruthfulness and Evidence of Prior False Accusation

(a) The credibility of a witness may be attacked or supported by evidence in the form of opinion or reputation, provided, however, that the evidence relates only to the witness' character for truthfulness or untruthfulness, and provided further that evidence of truthful character is admissible only after the character of the witness for truthfulness has been attacked by opinion or reputation evidence or otherwise. Except as otherwise provided by Rule 609 and by paragraph (b) of this rule, a trait of character cannot be proved by specific instances of conduct.

(b) The credibility of a witness in a criminal case may be attacked by evidence that the witness made a prior false accusation against any person of a crime similar to the crime with which defendant is charged if the judge preliminarily determines, by a hearing pursuant to Rule 104(a), that the witness knowingly made the prior false accusation.

Note: Adopted September 15, 1992 to be effective July 1, 1993; caption amended, text redesignated as paragraph (a) and amended, and new paragraph (b) adopted September 12, 2006 to be effective July 1, 2007.

Comment

Rule 608 incorporates the limiting principles of *N.J.Evid.R.* 22(c) and (d) with respect to admission of evidence of a trait of character for truthfulness or untruthfulness when offered under *N.J.Evid.R.* 20 to affect the credibility of a witness. The form of language follows the federal analogue, *Fed.R.Evid.* 608, rather than the current New Jersey rule. The federal rule has the advantage of explicitly stating the mode of proof of character for veracity in its reference to "opinion or reputation" evidence. Although the current New Jersey rule does not specify the mode of proof, both opinion and reputation evidence were contemplated by *The 1963 Report* at 71. Rule 608 also incorporates expressly the provision found in the federal rule that evidence of truthful character is admissible only after the character of the witness for truthfulness has been attacked by opinion or reputation evidence or otherwise. This is consistent with established New Jersey law. *State v. Johnson*, 216 *N.J.Super.* 588, 605–607 (App.Div.1987); *The 1963 Report* at 64.

However, the 1982 amendment of *N.J.Evid.R.* 20 which amended the provision that "[n]o evidence to support the credibility of a witness shall be admitted except to meet a charge of recent fabrication of testimony" has been broadly interpreted to suggest that evidence of good character to support the credibility of a witness can be introduced without prior impeachment by character evidence. *See State v. Frost*, 242 *N.J.Super.* 601, 613 (App.Div.1990); *Cogdell v. Brown*, 220 *N.J.Super.* 330, 336 (Law Div.1987). This was not the intent of the 1982 amendment of *N.J.Evid.R.* 20. The provision which was changed was literally too restrictive; corroborating evidence which is admitted often has the incidental effect of supporting the credibility of a witness. What was intended by the 1967 version of Rule 20 was that, generally, credibility could not be supported by a prior consistent statement except to meet an express or implied charge of recent fabrication. The 1982 amendment revised the last sentence of this rule to express this principle more accurately. The revision was not intended to open the door to supporting character evidence of truthfulness when the character of the witness for truthfulness had not first been attacked. Rule 608 is intended to ratify the long-standing New Jersey rule in this respect.

Another change in the New Jersey rule is the express provision in the second sentence of the rule that the prohibition against proof of trait of character for truthfulness or untruthfulness does not apply to evidence of prior conviction admissible pursuant to Rule 609, which incorporates *N.J.S.A.* 2A:81–12 as interpreted by *State v. Sands*, 76 *N.J.* 127 (1978). Note further that the subject matter of *N.J.Evid.R.* 22(a) and (b) is dealt with in Rule 613.

Although this rule follows the formulation of *Fed.R.Evid.* 608, it retains present New Jersey practice by rejecting the provision of paragraph (b) of the federal rule which permits limited admissibility of specific instances of conduct on cross-examination. *N.J.Evid.R.* 22(d), followed by this rule, prohibited "specific instances of conduct" proof in any form if introduced to prove a trait of character. Thus, this rule is consistent in philosophy and effect with the choice made in respect of Rule 405(a), namely adopting the state rather than the federal analogue. It is the Committee's view that Rule 607 affords sufficient scope for the effective impeachment of credibility.

As to other rules dealing with proof of character traits for purposes other than impeaching credibility, see Rules 404 and 405 incorporating former *N.J.Evid.R.* 46, 47, 48 and 55.

Rule 609. Impeachment by evidence of conviction of crime

For the purpose of affecting the credibility of any witness, the witness' conviction of a crime shall be admitted unless excluded by the judge as remote or for other causes. Such conviction may be proved by examination, production of the record thereof, or by other competent evidence.

Adopted effective July 1, 1993.

Comment

Rule 609 is adopted in place of *Fed.R.Evid.* 609. The rule follows provisions contained in *N.J.S.A.* 2A:81–12 as interpreted by *State v. Sands*, 76 *N.J.* 127 (1978). There is no comparable 1967 rule, since the then proposed Rule 21, which contained restrictive provisions on the use of criminal convictions to impair credibility, was not adopted, the intention then being to leave *N.J.S.A.* 2A:81–12 in effect, except for the portion concerning the use in civil actions of judgments of conviction as substantive evidence of facts, which was superseded by virtue of the official note to *N.J.Evid.R.* 63(20). *See R.* 3:9–2 and *R.* 7:4–2(b).

The general rule stated by *Fed.R.Evid.* 609(a) limits the use of convictions to impeach the credibility of a witness to (1) crimes punishable by death or imprisonment in excess of a year and (2) all crimes involving dishonesty or false statement regardless of punishment. A further qualification in respect of the first category only is the determination by the judge that the probative value of admitting the evidence outweighs its prejudicial effect to the defendant. This rule makes no admissibility distinction in terms of the crime of which the witness has been convicted. Evidence of any conviction of crime is subject to exclusion if its probative value is outweighed by its prejudicial effect, but it is the defendant who bears the burden of proving the exclusion. *See State v. Kelly,* 97 *N.J.* 178, 217 n. 21 (1984); *State v. Balthrop,* 92 *N.J.* 542, 544–547 (1983). Paragraph (b) of the federal rule deals with the admissibility of convictions which are more than ten years old. This rule does not refer explicitly to the ten-year limitation and exceptions thereto. These are matters dealt with by *State v. Sands, supra,* whose principles, similar to those embodied by *Fed.R.Evid.* 609(b), should be deemed to have been incorporated in this rule.

While this rule draws no distinction between crimes of dishonesty or false statement and other crimes, it is clear that it applies only to indictable offenses which are the subject of valid convictions. Neither evidence of arrests for or charges of crime are admissible under this rule. *See, e.g., State v. McBride,* 213 *N.J.Super.* 255, 267 (App.Div.1986). Neither are convictions of disorderly persons offenses or traffic violations. *See, e.g., State v. Rowe,* 52 *N.J.* 293, 302 (1970). Nor are adjudications of juvenile delinquency. *See State in Interest of K.P.,* 167 *N.J.Super.* 290, 293–294 (App.Div. 1979), *certif. denied,* 87 *N.J.* 394 (1981). And, it has been held, uncounseled convictions are inadmissible. *State v. Rios,* 155 *N.J.Super.* 11, 15 (Law Div.1978). *See also State v. Koch,* 119 *N.J.Super.* 184 (App.Div. 1972).

As to the impeachment use of a prior conviction against a witness in a criminal trial rather than against the defendant himself and particularly against a prosecution witness, see *State v. Balthrop, supra,* 92 *N.J.* at 544–547, where the Court explained that while the same balancing test of probative value versus prejudicial effect applies to determine exclusion, nevertheless the prejudice to the defendant, not merely to the witness, must be a significant factor in the equation. In this regard, the federal rule is explicit, paragraph (a)(1) specifically defining prejudice as prejudice to the defendant.

As to the use of prior convictions for impeachment of witnesses in civil causes, see, *e.g., Tonsberg v. VIP Coach Lines, Inc.,* 216 *N.J.Super.* 522, 529 (App.Div. 1987); *Vartenissian v. Food Haulers, Inc.,* 193 *N.J.Super.* 603, 610–611 (App.Div.1984).

With respect to the mode of proof of prior convictions, *Fed.R.Evid.* 609(a) expressly requires proof by way of public record or admission by the witness. This rule incorporates both modes, which have been held to be acceptable. *See State v. H.G.G.,* 202 *N.J.Super.* 267 (App.Div.1985); *State v. Mazur,* 158 *N.J.Super.* 89, 106 (App.Div.1978), *certif. denied,* 75 *N.J.* 399 (1978). In addition, the rule also permits, without definition, proof by "other competent evidence." This provision may be deemed to incorporate *N.J.S.A.* 2C:44–4(d), which provides: "Any prior conviction may be proved by any evidence, including fingerprint records, made in connection with arrest, conviction or imprisonment, that reasonably satisfies the court that the defendant was convicted." *Cf. State v. Carey,* 232 *N.J.Super.* 553, 555–558 (App.Div. 1989) (holding a computer printout of defendant's driving record admissible to prove a prior driving-while-intoxicated conviction).

This rule contains no provisions comparable to *Fed.R.Evid.* 609(c), (d) and (e). Paragraph (c) of the federal rule deals with the effect of a pardon, annulment or other procedure upon the viability of the conviction. This subject is left for development by case law and the judicial interpretation of applicable statutes or other pertinent laws both of the jurisdiction in which the conviction was entered and in this jurisdiction. See, for example, *N.J.S.A.* 2C:52–27 which provides that, if an order of expungement is entered, the conviction "shall be deemed not to have occurred."

Paragraph (d) of the federal rule addresses juvenile adjudications. Since adjudications of juvenile delinquency are not convictions of crime in New Jersey, such adjudications do not come within this rule. *State in Interest of K.P., supra,* 167 *N.J.Super.* at 293–294. However, if a juvenile has been tried and convicted of a crime as an adult on a waiver of jurisdiction by the Chancery Division, Family Part, that conviction may be shown to impeach his credibility. *State v. Steffanelli,* 133 *N.J.Super.* 512 (App.Div. 1975).

Paragraph (e) of *Fed.R.Evid.* 609 deals with effect of a pending appeal on the use of a conviction to impeach credibility and provides that such pendency does not render evidence of the conviction inadmissible. New Jersey case law holds to the contrary. *See State v. Biegenwald,* 96 *N.J.* 630, 638 (1984), citing with approval *State v. Blue,* 129 *N.J.Super.* 8, 12 (App.Div. 1974), *certif. denied,* 66 *N.J.* 328 (1974). *See also State v. Eddy,* 189 *N.J.Super.* 22 (Law Div.1982). The conviction is, however, admissible pending appeal if the appeal challenges only the sentence and not the validity or integrity of the guilt adjudication. *See State v. Anderson,* 177 *N.J.Super.* 334 (App.Div.1981); *State v. Eddy, supra,* 189 *N.J.Super.* at 23. *Cf. State v. Rodriguez,* 202 *N.J.Super.* 543 (Law Div.1985).

This rule is not limited to convictions of crimes obtained in New Jersey. *See State v. Koch,* 118 *N.J.Super.* 421, 424–425 (App.Div.1972). *Cf. State v. Lueder,* 74 *N.J.* 62 (1977).

Note that New Jersey law permits a defendant who does not testify to appeal a trial court determination that a prior conviction could be used to impeach him if he were to testify at the trial. *See State v.*

Whitehead, 104 *N.J.* 353 (1986). This is contrary to the federal rule which requires the defendant to testify in order to preserve for appeal the claim that a prior conviction was improperly admitted for impeachment purposes. *See Luce v. United States,* 469 *U.S.* 38, 83 *L.Ed.*2d 443 (1984).

Rule 610. Religious beliefs or opinions

Evidence of the beliefs or opinions of a witness on matters of religion is not admissible for the purpose of showing that by reason of their nature the witness' credibility is impaired or enhanced.

Adopted effective July 1, 1993.

Comment

Rule 610 follows *Fed.R.Evid.* 610 verbatim. It is not inconsistent with *N.J.Evid.R.* 30, which cited the statutory privilege contained in *N.J.S.A.* 2A:84A–24. By virtue of that privilege a witness may "refuse to disclose his theological opinion or religious belief unless his adherence or nonadherence to such an opinion or belief is material to an issue in the action other than that of his credibility as a witness." Rule 610 makes inadmissible proof of the religious beliefs or opinions of a witness when offered through the testimony of that witness or by other evidence if the sole purpose is to affect the credibility of that witness by reason of the nature of those beliefs. Consistent with *N.J.S.A.* 2A:84A–24, this rule does not exclude proof of religious beliefs or opinions when offered for another purpose that is material to an issue in the action. *See, e.g., In re Conroy,* 98 *N.J.* 321, 361–362 (1985) (religious beliefs of an incompetent patient are admissible to determine the patient's prior intent to have life-sustaining medical intervention).

See also Rule 603 (oath or affirmation), which expressly permits a witness to testify irrespective of his religious belief or lack thereof.

Rule 611. Mode and order of interrogation and presentation

(a) Control by court. The court shall exercise reasonable control over the mode and order of interrogating witnesses and presenting evidence so as to (1) make the interrogation and presentation effective for the ascertainment of the truth, (2) avoid needless consumption of time, and (3) protect witnesses from harassment or undue embarrassment.

(b) Scope of cross-examination. Cross-examination should be limited to the subject matter of the direct examination and matters affecting the credibility of the witness. The court may, in the exercise of discretion, permit inquiry into additional matters as if on direct examination.

(c) Leading questions. Leading questions should not be used on the direct examination of a witness except as may be necessary to develop the witness' testimony. Ordinarily, leading questions should be permitted on cross-examination. When a party calls an adverse party or a witness identified with an adverse party, or when a witness demonstrates hostility or unresponsiveness, interrogation may be by leading questions, subject to the discretion of the court.

Adopted effective July 1, 1993.

Comment

Rule 611 follows *Fed.R.Evid.* 611 almost verbatim. Paragraph (c) was changed to add to the federal formulation "unresponsiveness" as a basis for permitting leading questions and to substitute "when a witness demonstrates hostility" for the term "hostile witness." While there is no 1967 New Jersey analogue, *N.J.S.A.* 2A:81–11 provides: "Except as otherwise provided by law, when any party is called as a witness by the adverse party he shall be subject to the same rules as to examination and cross-examination as other witnesses." *See Becker v. Eisenstodt,* 60 *N.J.Super.* 240, 248–249 (App.Div.1960).

Although the principles stated by Rule 611 have not heretofore been codified in this jurisdiction, they are nevertheless consistent with New Jersey practice. As to paragraph (a) of the Rule, see *Cestero v. Ferrara,* 110 *N.J.Super.* 264, 273 (App.Div.1970), *aff'd,* 57 *N.J.* 497 (1971), holding that "[t]he control of examination, both direct and cross, resides in [the trial judge], to the end that the proofs may be kept within reasonable bounds. His discretion in this respect is a broad one, and we will not interfere with its exercise absent a clear abuse of that discretion."

As to cross-examination, New Jersey courts have repeatedly held that while the scope of cross-examination is a matter within the trial judge's discretion and should ordinarily be restricted to the scope of the direct testimony, nevertheless, reasonable latitude should be permitted to assure its inclusion of relevant material, including matters relevant to showing the improbability of the direct evidence. *See, e.g., State v. Petillo,* 61 *N.J.* 165, 169 (1972), *cert. denied,* 410 *U.S.* 945 (1973); *State v. Pollack,* 43 *N.J.* 34, 39 (1964); *Singer Shop–Rite, Inc. v. Rangel,* 174 *N.J.Super.* 442, 448 (App.Div.1980), *certif. denied,* 85 *N.J.* 148 (1980); *State v. Mustacchio,* 109 *N.J.Super.* 257, 264 (App.Div. 1970), *aff'd,* 57 *N.J.* 265 (1970).

As to leading questions, see *Nobero Co. v. Ferro Trucking Inc.,* 107 *N.J.Super.* 394, 404 (App.Div.1969), noting that "[w]hile leading questions are generally not permitted on the direct examination of one's own witness, there is an area of permissible leading, within the discretion of the trial judge, to avoid confusion, to clarify testimony, or otherwise to bring out the truth in serving the cause of justice." *See also State v. Riley,* 28 *N.J.* 188, 204–205 (1958), *cert. denied,* 359 *U.S.* 313 (1959) and *cert. denied,* 361 *U.S.* 879 (1959), as to the propriety of a judge posing leading questions to a witness.

Rule 612. Writing used to refresh memory

Except as otherwise provided by law in criminal proceedings, if a witness while testifying uses a writing to refresh the witness' memory for the purpose of testifying, an adverse party is entitled to have the writing produced at the hearing for inspection and use in cross-examining the witness. The adverse party shall also be entitled to introduce in evidence those portions which relate to the testimony of the witness but only for the purpose of impeaching the witness. If it is claimed that the writing contains material not related to the subject of the testimony, the court shall examine the writing *in camera* and excise any unrelated portions. If the witness has used a writing to refresh the witness' memory before testifying, the court in its discretion and in the interest of justice may accord the adverse party the same right to the writing as that party would have if the writing had been used by the witness while testifying.

Adopted effective July 1, 1993.

Comment

Rule 612 generally follows the first two sentences of *Fed.R.Evid.* 612 with some language and technical changes. Although there is no 1967 New Jersey rule analogue, the provisions of this rule are consistent with accepted practice in this jurisdiction. *See State v. Carter,* 91 *N.J.* 86, 122–123 (1982); *State v. Bindhammer,* 44 *N.J.* 372, 385 (1965); *State v. Williams,* 226 *N.J.Super.* 94, 103 (App.Div.1988); *State v. Rajnai,* 132 *N.J.Super.* 530, 539–540 (App.Div.1975).

First, this rule makes clear that when a writing used by a witness to refresh his memory is offered in evidence by the adverse party, the purpose of the offer is limited to impeaching credibility. The writing itself does not constitute substantive evidence of the facts stated therein. While the federal rule is not explicit as to this limited purpose of the offer, that limitation is nevertheless implicit. *See State v. Carter, supra,* 91 *N.J.* at 123, explaining that "[t]he admissible evidence is the recollection of the witness, and not the extrinsic paper."

Second, the introductory phrase of the federal rule specifically excepts the provisions of 18 *U.S.C.A.* § 3500 (the Jencks Act), which accord defendants in criminal proceedings rights to discovery of any prior statement made by a prosecution witness. The evident purpose of this exception in the federal rule is to avoid the interpretation that it intends any curtailment of the discovery rights afforded by the Jencks Act. While New Jersey does not have a statutory analogue to the Jencks Act, its principles are embodied by rules of court. *See R.* 3:17–1 to 4. *See also* Comment on *R.* 3:17. Thus, the exception provision in the introductory phrase of Rule 612 is primarily intended as a reference to *R.* 3:17 and to the pertinent provisions of *R.* 3:13–3, which provide for pretrial discovery. Note that pretrial discovery in New Jersey, substantially broader than that available in the federal practice, has effectively eliminated the need of defendants to rely on *R.* 3:17, which is little used.

This rule retains the distinction made by the federal rule between statements used to refresh collection while the witness is testifying and statements used for that purpose before the testimony is given. When the statement is used during testimony, the adverse party is absolutely entitled to its production, inspection, use in cross-examination and introduction into evidence. Where, however, the writing is used by the witness to refresh his recollection before he testifies, the according of these rights to the adverse party is within the discretion of the court.

This rule omits the provisions of the last two sentences of the federal rule which require preservation of excised portions for appellate purposes and prescribe sanctions for violation of an order entered by the court pursuant to the rule. The first of these provisions is not necessary since it is a matter of well-established practice that any deleted portion of proffered evidence must be made available to the appellate court in the event of an appeal. *Cf. R.* 1:7–3, so providing in respect of excluded evidence. The sanction provision was omitted since sanctions generally are a matter within the sound discretion of the court.

The distinctions between a writing used to refresh memory offered under this rule and a statement of recorded recollection admissible as an exception to the hearsay rule under *R.* 803(c)(5) must be kept in mind. Under Rule 612 the offer may be made only by the adverse party, and when offered, the writing may be made only to impeach credibility. The substantive evidence is the testimony of the witness whose memory has been refreshed by recourse to the writing. The hearsay exception of *R.* 803(c)(5) is applicable when a witness is unable to recall even after recourse to the statement and, therefore, cannot give substantive testimony. Since the statement of recorded recollection can be offered by the proponent of the witness, it is subject to the further limitation that it may only be read to the jury and may not be introduced into evidence as an exhibit. This qualification is not made in the case of a writing used to refresh memory since that writing may be introduced only by an adverse party.

Note that a document used to refresh recollection under this rule need not have been authorized by the witness and may also be used pursuant to this rule even if obtained as the result of an unlawful search and seizure. *See State v. Carter, supra,* 91 *N.J.* at 122–123. The only relevant criteria governing the judge's exercise of discretion in allowing use of a document to refresh recollection are whether the witness' memory is actually impaired, whether the document does in fact fairly refresh recollection, and whether the value of the evidence outweighs any danger of undue suggestion. *Ibid.; State v. Williams, supra,* 226 *N.J.Super.* at 103.

As to the related problem of admitting testimony of recollection refreshed by hypnosis, see *State v. Hurd,* 86 *N.J.* 525 (1981), prescribing standards for the admission of such evidence.

Rule 613. Prior statements of witnesses

(a) Examining witness concerning prior statement. In examining a witness concerning a prior statement made by the witness, whether written or not, the statement need not be shown or its contents disclosed to the witness at that time. Upon request the statement shall be shown or disclosed to opposing counsel.

(b) Extrinsic evidence of prior inconsistent statement of witness. Extrinsic evidence of a prior inconsistent statement made by a witness may in the judge's discretion be excluded unless the witness is afforded an opportunity to explain or deny the statement and the opposing party is afforded an opportunity to interrogate on the statement, or the interests of justice otherwise require. This rule does not apply to admissions of a party opponent as defined in Rule 803(b).

Adopted effective July 1, 1993.

Comment

Rule 613 generally follows *Fed.R.Evid.* 613 with minor language changes only and is consistent with *N.J.Evid.R.* 22(a) and (b).

Note that while *N.J.Evid.R.* 22(b) is phrased in terms of the judge's discretion to exclude extrinsic evidence of the witness' prior inconsistent statement unless the preconditions for admissibility are met, this rule, following the federal formulation, provides that unless the preconditions are met, the evidence is not admissible except if "the interests of justice otherwise require." While the import of the two rules is thus essentially the same, this formulation is deemed preferable because of its emphasis on the general principle that absent some special reason, the evidence should not be admitted if the required explanatory opportunities were not afforded. *See generally State v. Conyers,* 58 *N.J.* 123, 132 (1971); *State v. Coruzzi,* 189 *N.J.Super.* 273, 305 (App.Div.1983), *certif. denied,* 94 *N.J.* 531 (1983).

Rule 614. Calling and interrogation of witnesses by judge

The judge, in accordance with law and subject to the right of a party to make timely objection, may call a witness and may interrogate any witness.

Adopted effective July 1, 1993.

Comment

Rule 614 generally follows *Fed.R.Evid.* 614. While there is no New Jersey rule analogue, this rule is consistent with current New Jersey practice. *See State v. Ross,* 80 *N.J.* 239, 248–249 (1979); *State v. Guido,* 40 *N.J.* 191, 207–208 (1963); *State v. Riley,* 28 *N.J.* 188, 200–201 (1958), *cert. denied* and *appeal dismissed,* 359 *U.S.* 313 (1959) and *cert. denied,* 361 *U.S.* 879 (1959). This case law establishes standards and limitations on the exercise of this authority. The phrase "in accordance with law" refers to such standards and limitations.

Rule 615. Sequestration of witnesses

At the request of a party or on the court's own motion, the court may, in accordance with law, enter an order sequestering witnesses.

Adopted effective July 1, 1993.

Comment

Rule 615 is a general statement incorporating by reference the body of New Jersey case law on witness sequestration. The formulation of *Fed.R.Evid.* 615 was therefore not adopted. There is no New Jersey rule analogue. Exercise of the inherent power to sequester witnesses is subject to the limitations and standards developed by judicial decision. *See, e.g., State v. Smith,* 55 *N.J.* 476, 484–485 (1970), *cert. denied,* 400 *U.S.* 949 (1970); *State v. DiModica,* 40 *N.J.* 404, 413–414 (1963); *State v. Williams,* 29 *N.J.* 27, 45–47 (1959). Note that the sequestration of juries during deliberations is dealt with by rule of court, *R.*

1:8–6. And see further as to witness sequestration, S. Pressler, *Current N.J. Court Rules, R.* 1:8–6 Comment 2 (1991).

ARTICLE VII. OPINIONS AND EXPERT TESTIMONY

Rule 701. Opinion testimony of lay witnesses

If a witness is not testifying as an expert, the witness' testimony in the form of opinions or inferences may be admitted if it (a) is rationally based on the perception of the witness and (b) will assist in understanding the witness' testimony or in determining a fact in issue.

Adopted effective July 1, 1993.

Comment

This rule follows both *Fed.R.Evid.* 701 and *N.J.Evid.R.* 56(1) in substance. Minor language changes have been made for clarity. The term "perception" is used in this rule in the sense as defined by *N.J.Evid.R.* 1(14), which has not been incorporated in these rules, namely, the acquisition of knowledge through one's own senses.

Rule 702. Testimony by experts

If scientific, technical, or other specialized knowledge will assist the trier of fact to understand the evidence or to determine a fact in issue, a witness qualified as an expert by knowledge, skill, experience, training, or education may testify thereto in the form of an opinion or otherwise.

Adopted effective July 1, 1993.

Comment

Rule 702 follows *Fed.R.Evid.* 702 verbatim and makes only minor language changes in the first sentence of *N.J.Evid.R.* 56(2). The foundation requirement set forth in *N.J.Evid.R.* 19 has been omitted as necessarily implied by the use in this rule of the generic word "witness" rather than the more limited word "expert" used in the 1967 New Jersey analogue. Note further for that reason, the applicability of the general conditional acceptance provision of Rule 104(b) to the proffered testimony of an expert witness. Consequently the similar provision of *N.J.Evid.R.* 19 is redundant.

This rule intends to incorporate New Jersey case law establishing the general criteria for admissibility of expert testimony articulated by *State v. Kelly,* 97 *N.J.* 178, 208 (1984). As restated by *Landrigan v. The Celotex Corporation,* ___ *N.J.* ___, ___ (1992), these criteria include the requirements that "(1) the intended testimony must concern a subject matter that is beyond the ken of the average juror; (2) the field testified to must be at a state of the act such that an expert's testimony could be sufficiently reliable; and (3) the witness must have sufficient expertise to offer the intended testimony."

Rule 703. Bases of opinion testimony by experts

The facts or data in the particular case upon which an expert bases an opinion or inference may be those perceived by or made known to the expert at or before the hearing. If of a type reasonably relied upon by experts in the particular field in forming opinions or inferences upon the subject, the facts or data need not be admissible in evidence.

Adopted effective July 1, 1993.

Comment

Rule 703 follows *Fed.R.Evid.* 703 verbatim and the last two sentences of *N.J.Evid.R.* 56(2). The New Jersey rule had been amended effective July 1, 1982, to conform to the federal rule. As to the purpose of that amendment, see the commentary published in 108 *N.J.L.J.* 301, 302 (1981). The term "perceived" as used in this rule means to have acquired knowledge through one's own senses. *See* Comment to Rule 701 above.

Rule 704. Opinion on ultimate issue

Testimony in the form of an opinion or inference otherwise admissible is not objectionable because it embraces an ultimate issue to be decided by the trier of fact.

Adopted effective July 1, 1993.

Comment

Rule 704 follows *Fed.R.Evid.* 704(a) and makes only minor language changes in *N.J.Evid.R.* 56(3). *State v. Odom*, 116 *N.J.* 65, 79 (1989).

Fed.R.Evid. 704 was amended by the Comprehensive Crime Control Act of 1984 (Pub.L. No. 98–473), to add subsection (b) to the rule, prohibiting expert witnesses testifying about the mental state of the defendant in a criminal case from giving an opinion as to whether or not defendant had the mental state or condition which constituted an element of the crime charged or a defense to the crime. The federal rule leaves that "ultimate issue" for the jury. This rule was not adopted; it is contrary to New Jersey law. *See Aponte v. State*, 30 *N.J.* 441, 446 (1959).

Rule 705. Disclosure of facts or data underlying expert opinion; hypotheses not necessary

The expert may testify in terms of opinion or inference and give reasons therefor without prior disclosure of the underlying facts or data, unless the court requires otherwise. The expert may in any event be required to disclose the underlying facts or data on cross-examination. Questions calling for the opinion of an expert witness need not be hypothetical in form unless in the judge's discretion it is so required.

Adopted eff. July 1, 1993. Amended September 15, 2004, eff. July 1, 2005.

Comment

The first sentence of Rule 705 follows *Fed.R.Evid.* 705 verbatim and makes only minor language changes in *N.J.Evid.R.* 57, which had been amended effective July 1, 1982, to conform to the federal rule. As to the purpose of that amendment, see the commentary published in 108 *N.J.L.J.* 301, 302 (1981).

The third sentence of Rule 705 follows *N.J.Evid.R.* 58 verbatim. There is no federal analogue.

Rule 706. Court appointed experts [Not Adopted]
Comment

Contrary to the recommendation of *The 1963 Report* at 115–121 (proposed *N.J.Evid.R.* 59, 60 and 61), the 1967 New Jersey rules did not include provisions for the court appointment of experts. The power of a court to appoint expert witnesses and to deal with related procedural matters may be viewed primarily as a matter of practice and procedure rather than as a part of the law of evidence. The court rules provide in detail for the appointment by the court of an impartial medical expert in personal injury and wrongful death actions. *R.* 4:20–1 *et seq.* The rules provide the method of appointment, disclosure to the jury of court appointment, and compensation. *R.* 4:20–3, 10 and 11. Court appointment of experts is also provided for in family actions. *R.* 5:3–3.

The power of the court to appoint experts is also established by the case law. *See Wayne Tp. v. Kosoff,* 73 *N.J.* 8, 13–15 (1977); *Handleman v. Marwen Stores Corp.,* 53 *N.J.* 404, 408–414 (1969). For related procedures, see *Kosoff,* 73 *N.J.* at 15.

ARTICLE VIII. HEARSAY
Rule 801. Definitions

For purposes of this article, the following definitions apply:

(a) Statement. A "statement" is (1) an oral or written assertion or (2) nonverbal conduct of a person if the person intends it as an assertion.

(b) Declarant. A "declarant" is a person who makes a statement.

(c) Hearsay. "Hearsay" is a statement, other than one made by the declarant while testifying at the trial or hearing, offered in evidence to prove the truth of the matter asserted.

(d) Business. A "business" includes every kind of business, institution, association, profession, occupation and calling, whether or not conducted for profit, and also includes activities of governmental agencies.

(e) Writing. A "writing" consists of letters, words, numbers, data compilations, pictures, drawings, photographs, symbols, sounds, or combinations thereof or their equivalent, set down or recorded by handwriting, typewriting, printing, photostating, photographing, magnetic impulse, mechanical or electronic recording, or by any other means, and preserved in a perceptible form, and their duplicates as defined by Rule 1001(d).

(f) Public Official. A "public official" includes an official of the United States, its territories, the District of Columbia and states, as well as political subdivisions, regional and other governmental agencies thereof.

Adopted eff. July 1, 1993. Amended September 15, 2004, eff. July 1, 2005.

Comment

The definitions of statement, declarant, and hearsay contained in Rule 801(a), (b), and (c), respectively, are identical to those of *Fed.R.Evid.* 801(a), (b), and (c), respectively. They replace without substantial change *N.J.Evid.R.* 62(1), 62(2), and 63, respectively.

The definition of business contained in Rule 801(d) follows *N.J.Evid.R.* 62(5). The federal analogue is the last sentence of *Fed.R.Evid.* 803(6), which, unlike this rule, does not include governmental activity within the definition of business. *See* Comment on Rules 803(c)(6) and 803(c)(8). However, *Fed.R.Evid.* 803(8), dealing with records of governmental activities, covers much of the material that would be admissible under the business record exception in Rule 803(c)(6) and the exception for public records, reports and findings in Rule 803(c)(8).

The definition of writing contained in Rule 801(e) follows *Fed.R.Evid.* 1001(1) and *N.J.Evid.R.* 1(13) in substance. The definition broadly includes records of all kinds. Nevertheless, some rules such as Rule 803(c)(5), (6) and (7) use both of the terms "writing" and "record" despite the redundancy.

Rule 801(e) includes provisions contained in both the federal and state analogues but is more comprehensive than *N.J.Evid.R.* 1(13) in enumerating forms of recording. It also includes duplicates as defined by Rule 1001(d), which follows the federal rule. *N.J.Evid.R.* 1(13) contains a number of specific forms of recorded expression requiring that the recording be reasonably permanent and readable by sight, a requirement incompatible with recordings of sound and electronic impulses. The requirement of permanency has been retained by this rule but the requirement of readability has been broadened to include all forms of perception. Thus, this rule includes recordings of writings, sounds, photographic images, x-rays, other images, data stored in computers, and electronic or other impulses in all forms of preservation that may be perceived by sight, sound or other senses directly or after retrieval. Photographs are not separately defined as in *Fed.R.Evid.* 1001(2) because photographs are included in the definition of a writing.

The definition of public official contained in Rule 801(f) follows *N.J.Evid.R.* 62(3) and 62(4), but broadens the definition to include officials of the United States and agencies of the United States and its territories. There is no federal analogue. However, federal agencies are included in the business record rule, Rule 803(c)(6) and *N.J.Evid.R.* 63(13), since "business" is defined by Rule 801(d) to include "activities of governmental agencies" as in *N.J.Evid.R.* 62(5). The definition of a public official is used primarily when applying Rule 803(c)(8), which refers to written records and reports of a public official. The federal version, *Fed.R.Evid.* 803(8), does not speak in terms of "public officials" but rather refers to records of public offices or agencies, as does *Fed.R.Evid.* 803(10) (absence of public record).

N.J.Evid.R. 62(4), which defined "State," was deleted as self-evident.

Rule 801 differs from *Fed.R.Evid.* 801 by omitting paragraph (d) of the federal rule. That paragraph excludes from the definition of hearsay prior statements of witnesses and party-opponents. The Advisory Committee's Note to *Fed.R.Evid.* 801(d) recognizes that these statements would "otherwise literally fall within the definition" of hearsay. *Notes of Advisory Committee on Proposed Rules,* Note to *Fed. R.Evid.* 801(d), 28 *U.S.C.A.* (1984). One reason for admitting certain extra-judicial statements of witnesses is that, because the declarant is a witness, he is subject to cross-examination and can normally affirm, deny, explain or otherwise qualify the statement. This special category of hearsay applies only to declarants who are witnesses. Like *N.J.Evid.R.* 63(1), these rules continue to treat prior extra-judicial statements of witnesses as hearsay statements which are admissible as exceptions to the hearsay rule in accordance with the provisions of Rule 803(a). The net effect is the same, that is to say, certain prior extra-judicial statements of witnesses are admitted either because they are deemed not hearsay under the federal formula or because they are an exception under the New Jersey formula. The same treatment is accorded to statements of a party-opponent. *Fed. R.Evid.* 801(d)(2) defines such extra-judicial statements as non-hearsay, whereas Rule 803(b) admits such statements as an exception to the hearsay rule, as in *N.J.Evid.R.* 63(7).

Because of this conceptual difference, the numbering of hearsay exceptions in these rules is somewhat different from the federal rules. The exceptions to the hearsay rule that do not depend on the declarant's unavailability as a witness are contained in *Fed. R.Evid.* 803(1) to (24). *Fed.R.Evid.* 804 contains hearsay exceptions that require proof of unavailability of the declarant. Similarly, in these rules all hearsay exceptions are contained in Rules 803 and 804. Rule 803(a) and (b) contain the exceptions for prior extra-judicial statements of witnesses and party-opponents, respectively, and Rule 803(c)(1) to (26) contain other specific exceptions not dependent upon the declarant's unavailability as a witness. Thus, Rules 803(c)(1) to (23) contain the parallel exceptions that are designated *Fed.R.Evid.* 803(1) to (23). No analogue to *Fed.R.Evid.* 803(24) (residual exceptions) was adopted. Rule 803(c)(25), which deals with statements against interest, corresponds to *Fed. R.Evid.* 804(b)(3), but unavailability of the declarant as a witness is not required under Rule 803(c)(25). There is no federal analogue for Rule 803(c)(26), which deals with judgments against persons entitled to indemnity, derived from *N.J.Evid.R.* 63(21). Rule 804, like *Fed.R.Evid.* 804, provides certain additional hearsay exceptions conditioned on the unavailability of the declarant as a witness.

As noted in the comment to Rule 802, neither the hearsay rule nor its exceptions address issues concerning a criminal defendant's right of confrontation under the sixth amendment. The right of confrontation was not the basis for the distinction between hearsay exceptions under Rules 803(c)(1) to (26), which do not depend on the unavailability of a witness, and hearsay exceptions under Rule 804(b), which do require proof of unavailability. See discussion of the confrontation clause, which normally requires a showing of witness unavailability, *Ohio v. Roberts,* 448 *U.S.* 56, 66, 65 *L.Ed.*2d 597, 608 (1980), under Comment, Rule 804(b)—Hearsay Exceptions, Introduction, *infra*.

Rule 802. Hearsay rule

Hearsay is not admissible except as provided by these rules or by other law.

Adopted effective July 1, 1993.

COMMENT

Rule 802 follows *Fed.R.Evid.* 802 in excluding hearsay subject to express exceptions provided by these rules or by law. The New Jersey analogue, *N.J.Evid.R.* 63, excluded hearsay subject to specific exceptions provided in *N.J.Evid.R.* 63(1) through 63(33). This rule allows for exceptions provided by law as well as specific exceptions contained in these rules. Rule 101(a)(2)(B) recognizes that hearsay evidence may be admitted in proceedings to which the rules of evidence are made inapplicable by statute. *See* Rule 101(a) and comments thereto. There is also the rare case in which statements which may be excluded as hearsay in some jurisdictions must be admitted as a matter of constitutional right. *See Chambers v. Mississippi,* 410 *U.S.* 284, 291–298, 35 *L.Ed.*2d 306–310 (1973).

As stated in the Advisory Committee's Note to *Fed.R.Evid.* 803, the exceptions "are phrased in terms of nonapplication of the hearsay rule, rather than in positive terms of admissibility, in order to repel any implication that other possible grounds for exclusion are eliminated from consideration." *Notes of Advisory Committee on Proposed Rules,* Note to *Fed.R.Evid.* 803, 28 *U.S.C.A.* (1984). To illustrate this point, lay opinion evidence that would not be admissible if the declarant were testifying in person does not become admissible because it is contained in business records that may be introduced as an exception to the hearsay rule. *See Brown v. Mortimer,* 100 *N.J.Super.* 395, 405–406 (App.Div.1968). Moreover, no attempt has been made to determine the extent to which hearsay exceptions may conflict with a criminal defendant's right of confrontation under the sixth amendment. *See Ohio v. Roberts,* 448 *U.S.* 56, 65–66, 65 *L.Ed.*2d 597, 607–608 (1980); *Dutton v. Evans,* 400 *U.S.* 74, 27 *L.Ed.*2d 213 (1970); *California v. Green,* 399 *U.S.* 149, 26 *L.Ed.*2d 489 (1970); *State v. Burgos,* 200 *N.J.Super.* 6, 12 (App.Div.1985), *certif. denied,* 101 *N.J.* 304 (1985).

Rule 803. Hearsay exceptions not dependent on declarant's unavailability

The following statements are not excluded by the hearsay rule:

(a) Prior statements of witnesses. A statement previously made by a person who is a witness at a trial or hearing, provided it would have been admissible if made by the declarant while testifying and the statement:

(1) is inconsistent with the witness' testimony at the trial or hearing and is offered in compliance with Rule 613. However, when the statement is offered by the party calling the witness, it is admissible only if, in addition to the foregoing requirements, it (A) is contained in a sound recording or in a writing made or

signed by the witness in circumstances establishing its reliability or (B) was given under oath subject to the penalty of perjury at a trial or other judicial, quasi-judicial, legislative, administrative or grand jury proceeding, or in a deposition; or

(2) is consistent with the witness' testimony and is offered to rebut an express or implied charge against the witness of recent fabrication or improper influence or motive; or

(3) is a prior identification of a person made after perceiving that person if made in circumstances precluding unfairness or unreliability.

(b) Statement by party-opponent. A statement offered against a party which is:

(1) the party's own statement, made either in an individual or in a representative capacity, or

(2) a statement whose content the party has adopted by word or conduct or in whose truth the party has manifested belief, or

(3) a statement by a person authorized by the party to make a statement concerning the subject, or

(4) a statement by the party's agent or servant concerning a matter within the scope of the agency or employment, made during the existence of the relationship, or

(5) a statement made at the time the party and the declarant were participating in a plan to commit a crime or civil wrong and the statement was made in furtherance of that plan.

In a criminal proceeding, the admissibility of a defendant's statement which is offered against the defendant is subject to Rule 104(c).

(c) Statements not dependent on declarant's availability. Whether or not the declarant is available as a witness:

(1) *Present sense impression.* A statement of observation, description or explanation of an event or condition made while or immediately after the declarant was perceiving the event or condition and without opportunity to deliberate or fabricate.

(2) *Excited utterance.* A statement relating to a startling event or condition made while the declarant was under the stress of excitement caused by the event or condition and without opportunity to deliberate or fabricate.

(3) *Then existing mental, emotional, or physical condition.* A statement made in good faith of the declarant's then existing state of mind, emotion, sensation or physical condition (such as intent, plan, motive, design, mental feeling, pain, or bodily health), but not including a statement of memory or belief to prove the fact remembered or believed unless it relates to the execution, revocation, identification, or terms of declarant's will.

(4) *Statements for purposes of medical diagnosis or treatment.* Statements made in good faith for purposes of medical diagnosis or treatment which describe medical history, or past or present symptoms, pain, or sensations, or the inception or general character of the cause or external source thereof to the extent that the statements are reasonably pertinent to diagnosis or treatment.

(5) *Recorded Recollection.* A statement concerning a matter about which the witness is unable to testify fully and accurately because of insufficient present recollection if the statement is contained in a writing or other record which (A) was made at a time when the fact recorded actually occurred or was fresh in the memory of the witness, and (B) was made by the witness or under the witness' direction or by some other person for the purpose of recording the statement at the time it was made, and (C) the statement concerns a matter of which the witness had knowledge when it was made, unless the circumstances indicate that the statement is not trustworthy; provided that when the witness does not remember part or all of the contents of a writing, the portion the witness does not remember may be read into evidence but shall not be introduced as an exhibit over objection.

(6) *Records of regularly conducted activity.* A statement contained in a writing or other record of acts, events, conditions, and, subject to Rule 808, opinions or diagnoses, made at or near the time of observation by a person with actual knowledge or from information supplied by such a person, if the writing or other record was made in the regular course of business and it was the regular practice of that business to make it, unless the sources of information or the method, purpose or circumstances of preparation indicate that it is not trustworthy.

(7) *Absence of an entry in records of regularly conducted activity.* Evidence that a matter is not included in a writing or other record kept in accordance with the provisions of Rule 803(c)(6), when offered to prove the nonoccurrence or nonexistence of the matter, if the matter was of a kind of which a writing or other record was regularly made and preserved, unless the sources of information or other circumstances indicate that the inference of nonoccurrence or nonexistence is not trustworthy.

(8) *Public records, reports, and findings.* Subject to Rule 807, (A) a statement contained in a writing made by a public official of an act done by the official or an act, condition, or event observed by the official if it was within the scope of the official's duty either to perform the act reported or to observe the act, condition, or event reported and to make the written statement, or (B) statistical findings of a public official based upon a report of or an investigation of acts, conditions, or events, if it was within the scope of the official's duty to make such statistical findings, unless the sources of information or other circumstances indicate that such statistical findings are not trustworthy.

(9) *Records of vital statistics.* Subject to Rule 807, a statement contained in any form such as records of births, fetal deaths, deaths, or marriages, if the report thereof was made to a public office pursuant to requirements of law.

(10) *Absence of public record or entry.* Subject to Rule 807, a certification in accordance with Rule 902 stating that diligent search failed to disclose a public record, report, writing, or entry when offered to prove (A) the absence of a public record, report, writing, or entry, or (B) the nonoccurrence or nonexistence of a matter of which a record, report, writing, or entry is regularly made and preserved by a public office or agency, unless the sources of information or other circumstances indicate that the inference of nonoccurrence or nonexistence is not trustworthy.

(11) *Records of religious organizations.* Subject to Rule 807, statements of births, marriages, divorces, deaths, legitimacy, ancestry, relationship by blood or marriage, or other similar facts of personal or family history, contained in a regularly kept record of a religious organization.

(12) *Marriage, baptismal, and similar certificates.* Subject to Rule 807, statements of fact contained in a certificate that the maker performed a marriage or other ceremony or administered a sacrament, made by a clergyman, public official, or other person authorized by the rules or practices of a religious organization or by law to perform the act certified, and purporting to have been issued at the time of the act or within a reasonable time thereafter.

(13) *Family records.* Subject to Rule 807, statements of fact concerning a personal or family history contained in family Bibles, genealogies, charts, engravings on rings, inscriptions on family portraits, engravings on urns, crypts, or tombstones, or the like.

(14) *Records of documents affecting an interest in property.* Subject to Rule 807, the record of a document purporting to establish or affect an interest in property, as proof of the content of the original recorded document and its execution and delivery by each person by whom it purports to have been executed, if the record is a record of a public office and an applicable statute authorized the recording of documents of that kind in that office.

(15) *Statements in documents affecting an interest in property.* Subject to Rule 807, a statement contained in a document purporting to establish or affect an interest in property if the matter stated was relevant to the purpose of the document, unless dealings with the property since the document was made have been inconsistent with the truth of the statement or the purport of the document.

(16) *Statements in ancient documents.* Statements in a document in existence 30 years or more whose authenticity is established.

(17) *Market reports, commercial publications.* Market quotations, tabulations, lists, directories, or other published compilations, generally used and relied upon by the public or by persons in particular occupations.

(18) *Learned treatises.* To the extent called to the attention of an expert witness upon cross-examination or relied upon by the expert in direct examination, statements contained in published treatises, periodicals, or pamphlets on a subject of history, medicine, or other science or art, established as a reliable authority by testimony or by judicial notice. If admitted, the statements may not be received as exhibits but may be read into evidence or, if graphics, shown to the jury.

(19) *Reputation concerning personal or family history.* Evidence of a person's reputation, among members of the person's family by blood, adoption, or marriage, or among that person's associates, or in the community, concerning a person's birth, adoption, marriage, divorce, death, legitimacy, ancestry, relationship by blood, adoption, or marriage, or other similar fact of the person's personal or family history.

(20) *Reputation concerning boundaries or general history.* Evidence of reputation in a community, arising before the controversy, as to boundaries of or customs affecting lands in the community, and as to events of general history important to the community or state or nation in which the community is located.

(21) *Reputation as to character.* Evidence of reputation of a person's character at a relevant time among the person's associates or in the community.

(22) *Judgments of Previous Conviction of Crime.* In a civil proceeding, except as otherwise provided by court order on acceptance of a plea, evidence of a final judgment against a party adjudging the party guilty of an indictable offense in New Jersey or of an offense which would constitute an indictable offense if committed in this state, as against that party, to prove any fact essential to sustain the judgment.

(23) *Judgment as to personal, family, or general history, or boundaries.* Judgments as proof of matters of personal, family or general history, or boundaries, essential to the judgment, if those matters would be provable by evidence of reputation.

(24) *Other exceptions.*

[Not Adopted]

(25) *Statement against interest.* A statement which was at the time of its making so far contrary to the declarant's pecuniary, proprietary, or social interest, or so far tended to subject declarant to civil or criminal liability, or to render invalid declarant's claim against another, that a reasonable person in declarant's position would not have made the statement unless the person believed it to be true. Such a statement is admissible against an accused in a criminal action only if the accused was the declarant.

(26) *Judgments Against Persons Entitled to Indemnity.* Subject to Rule 807 and except in a proceeding brought under the Joint Tortfeasors Contribution Law, N.J.S.A. 2A:53A–1 et seq., the record of a final judgment is admissible if offered by the judgment debtor in an action in which the debtor seeks to recover partial or total indemnity or exoneration for money paid or a liability incurred because of the judgment, as evidence of the liability of the judgment debtor, of the facts on which the judgment is based, and of the reasonableness of the damages recovered. If the defendant in the second action had notice of and opportunity to defend the first action, the judgment is conclusive evidence.

(27) *Statements by a Child Relating to a Sexual Offense.* A statement by a child under the age of 12 relating to sexual misconduct committed with or against that child is admissible in a criminal, juvenile, or civil proceeding if (a) the proponent of the statement makes known to the adverse party an intention to offer the statement and the particulars of the statement at such time as to provide the adverse party with a fair opportunity to prepare to meet it; (b) the court finds, in a hearing conducted pursuant to Rule 104(a), that on the basis of the time, content and circumstances of the statement there is a probability that the statement is trustworthy; and (c) either (i) the child testifies at the proceeding, or (ii) the child is unavailable as a witness and there is offered admissible evidence corroborating the act of sexual abuse; provided that no child whose statement is to be offered in evidence pursuant to this rule shall be disqualified to be a witness in such proceeding by virtue of the requirements of Rule 601.

Adopted eff. July 1, 1993. Amended September 15, 2004 eff. July 1, 2005.

Comment

Rule 803 Generally

Rule 803 states the hearsay exceptions whose application does not depend on the unavailability of the declarant. Rule 804 states the hearsay exceptions that apply only if the declarant is unavailable.

As noted in the Comment to Rule 801, Rule 803(a) treats certain prior extrajudicial statements of witnesses as an exception to the hearsay rule, and Rule 803(b) treats extrajudicial statements of party-opponents (admissions) as an exception to the hearsay rule. The result is consistent with that of *Fed.R.Evid.* 801(d)(1) and (2) which provide that such prior statements of witnesses and admissions of party-opponents are, by definition, not hearsay. Rules 803(c)(1) to (c)(26) collect the other general hearsay exceptions as to which the unavailability of the declarant is not a criterion for admissibility.

Rule 803(a)—Prior Statements

Rule 803(a)(1) follows almost verbatim *N.J.Evid.R.* 63(1)(a), as amended effective July 1, 1982. The words "sound recording" are omitted because they are contained in the definition of writing in Rule 801(e). The New Jersey formulation as to the substantive use of prior inconsistent statements of witnesses is less restrictive than the federal formulation in *Fed.R.Evid.* 801(d)(1)(A). The New Jersey rule permits the use of a prior inconsistent statement as substantive evidence when offered by a party other than the proponent of the witness, *State v. Provet*, 133 *N.J.Super.* 432, 435–439 (App.Div.1975), *certif. denied*, 68 *N.J.* 174 (1975), and also allows such use when offered by the party calling the witness if the inconsistent statement is in written or recorded form in circumstances bespeaking reliability, or was made under oath as specified by the rule. *State v. Mancine*, 124 *N.J.* 232, 236–256 (1991); *State v. Gross*, 121 *N.J.* 1, 7–15 (1990); *State v. Gross*, 121 *N.J.* 18 (1990). By contrast, *Fed.R.Evid.* 801(d)(1)(A) makes no distinction based upon which party called the witness and admits inconsistent statements as substantive evidence only if made under oath. Thus, the federal rule is much narrower than the New Jersey rule. For the history and application of the New Jersey rule and its relationship to Rule 607, see *State v. Hacker*, 177 *N.J.Super.* 533, 537 n. 2 (App.Div.), *certif. denied*, 87 *N.J.* 364 (1981), and commentary on the 1982 amendment published in 108 *N.J.L.J.* 302 (1981). *See also State v. Gross*, 121 *N.J.* 1 (1990), defining circumstantial reliability with regard to a prior inconsistent statement of an accomplice called by the prosecution as a witness.

Unlike Rule 803(a)(1), *Fed.R.Evid.* 801(d)(1) expressly requires that the declarant be a person who testifies at the trial or hearing "and is subject to cross-examination." While the "cross-examination" requirement is not explicitly stated in Rule 803(a)(1), it is implicit. The Rule requires that the statement be "inconsistent with [the witness'] testimony." The requirements that the statement be one which was previously made by "a witness at a trial or hearing" which is "inconsistent with his testimony" insure that the declarant is a witness who testifies, and is, therefore, subject to cross-examination. If the declarant is called as a witness and refuses to testify, his prior statement cannot be admitted as an inconsistent statement. *State v. Williams*, 182 *N.J.Super.* 427, 431–437 (App.Div.1982), holding that a prior signed statement by a witness who was charged with the same crimes could not be admitted as a prior inconsistent statement, since the witness refused to testify despite being granted immunity. The court reasoned that the statement was not inconsistent with the witness' testimony since he did not testify and could not be cross-examined. The court held that admission of the statement would violate defendant's sixth amendment confrontation rights, citing *Douglas v. Alabama*, 380 *U.S.* 415, 419–420, 13 *L.Ed.*2d 934, 937–938 (1965).

A more difficult issue arises when the statement was made by a witness who testifies that he cannot remember making the statement, or cannot remember the subject matter of the statement. Courts have admitted the prior statement as inconsistent with the witness' testimony where the trial judge finds that the witness' forgetfulness was feigned. *State v. Bryant*, 217 *N.J.Super.* 72, 75–79 (App.Div.1987), *certif. denied*, 108 *N.J.* 202 (1987), *cert. denied*, 484 *U.S.* 978 (1987); *State v. Burgos*, 200 *N.J.Super.* 6, 10–12 (App.Div.1985), *certif. denied*, 101 *N.J.* 304 (1985); *see California v. Green*, 399 *U.S.* 149, 168–169, 26 *L.Ed.*2d 489, 502–503 (1970), *on remand, People v. Green*, 3 *Cal.*3d 98, 92 *Cal.Rptr.* 494, 479 *P.*2d 998, 1000–1004 (1971); *but see United States v. Palumbo*, 639 *F.*2d 123, 128 n. 6 (3d Cir.1981), *cert. denied*, 454 *U.S.* 819 (1981), noting that a lack of memory as to the substance of the prior statement may not be inconsistent with the statement in various circumstances; 4 J. Weinstein & M. Berger, *Weinstein's Evidence* ¶ 801(d)(1)(A)[04] at 801–120 (1988), stating that the prior statement should not be admitted "if the judge finds that the witness genuinely cannot remember and the period of amnesia or forgetfulness is crucial as regards the facts in issue."

Rule 803(a)(2), dealing with prior consistent statements offered to rebut a charge of recent fabrication, has no direct New Jersey analogue located in the hearsay exception rules, but, rather, it repeats a portion of *N.J.Evid.R.* 20 which has been incorporated in Rule 607. The provision is included in this rule to allow such evidence to be used substantively. *See also* Comment on Rule 607. This rule follows *Fed.R.Evid.* 801(d)(1)(B) verbatim.

Rule 803(a)(3), dealing with evidence of prior identification, follows without substantial change the formulation of *N.J.Evid.R.* 63(1)(c). *See State v. Matlack*, 49 *N.J.* 491, 497–500 (1967), *cert. denied*, 389 *U.S.* 1009 (1967). It is consistent with *Fed.R.Evid.* 801(d)(1)(c), but adds criteria relating to reliability.

N.J.Evid.R. 63(1)(b), dealing with past recollection recorded, is now covered by Rule 803(c)(5).

Rule 803(b)—Party Admissions

Rule 803(b) follows the structure as well as the substantive content of *Fed.R.Evid.* 801(d)(2), while retaining some of the language of the 1967 New Jersey rule analogues. The last sentence of this rule was added to emphasize that the admissibility of statements by an accused is subject to Rule 104(c), formerly *N.J.Evid.R.* 8(3).

While Rule 803(b) changes some of the language of the 1967 New Jersey rule analogues, it makes no substantive change in current New Jersey practice. Paragraph (b)(1) replaces *N.J.Evid.R.* 63(7); paragraphs (b)(2) and (b)(3) replace *N.J.Evid.R.* 63(8); paragraph (b)(4) replaces *N.J.Evid.R.* 63(9)(a); and paragraph (b)(5) replaces *N.J.Evid.R.* 63(9)(b). As to paragraph (b)(5) (Statements of co-conspirators), See *Bourjaily v. United States*, 483 *U.S.* 171, 107 *S.Ct.* 22–15, 97 *L.Ed.* 144 (1987), construing the federal analogue broadly in favor of admissibility. The Committee takes no position on what are essentially policy issues and does not necessarily endorse *Bourjaily* by recommending the federal formulation. See as to the more restrictive New Jersey position, *State v. Phelps*, 96 *N.J.* 500 (1984).

Rule 803(c)—Other Statements

As stated above, Rule 803(c), following the federal format and the enumeration of *Fed.R.Evid.* 803, collects other hearsay exceptions which are not dependent upon the unavailability of the declarant as a witness. Unless excluded on other grounds, the hearsay exceptions contained in Rule 803(c) permit the admission of certain extra-judicial statements of a declarant as substantive evidence whether the declarant is available or unavailable as a witness. Unavailability as a witness is defined in Rule 804(a).

(1) Present sense impression. Rule 803(c)(1) is an amalgam of the content of *Fed.R.Evid.* 803(1) and *N.J.Evid.R.* 63(4)(a). It adds to the federal rule a provision found in *N.J.Evid.R.* 63(4)(a), making admissible statements of "observation" as well as statements "describing or explaining" an event or condition. It also incorporates a provision in the federal rule, which is not in the New Jersey rule, making admissible statements made immediately after declarant perceived an event or condition. As in the case of excited utterances, statements made immediately after the event must be so close to the event as to exclude the likelihood of fabrication or deliberation. This requirement is expressed by the phrase "without opportunity to deliberate or fabricate," which is not contained in the federal analogue.

(2) Excited utterance. Rule 803(c)(2) is identical to *Fed.R.Evid.* 803(2) except that it adds the phrase "without opportunity to deliberate or fabricate," taken from *N.J.Evid.R.* 63(4)(b), which this rule replaces without substantial change.

(3) Then existing mental, emotional, or physical condition. Rule 803(c)(3) follows *Fed.R.Evid.* 803(3) almost verbatim, adding the good faith requirement contained in *N.J.Evid.R.* 63(12). This rule replaces paragraph (a) of *N.J.Evid.R.* 63(12), first adding the term "physical condition" and, consistent with New Jersey law, the provision respecting declarant's will. *See Engle v. Siegel,* 74 *N.J.* 287, 293–294 (1977); *Wilson v. Flowers,* 58 *N.J.* 250, 261–264 (1971); *Fidelity Union Trust Co. v. Robert,* 36 *N.J.* 561 (1962). *See also N.J.S.A.* 3B:3–33, permitting proof of the testator's intent by way of extrinsic "relevant circumstances." The phrase "relevant circumstances" had been construed by *Engle v. Siegel, supra,* 74 *N.J.* at 291, as including testator's statements of intent.

With respect to conduct inferred from a declarant's statement of intent, there is some conflict among federal cases as to the viability of the *Hillmon* doctrine under *Fed.R.Evid.* 803(1). The United States Supreme Court held in *Mutual Life Ins. Co. v. Hillmon,* 145 *U.S.* 285, 295–300, 36 *L.Ed.* 706, 709–712 (1892), that letters of the declarant, Walters, to his family and his fiancee stating that he was leaving on a trip to Colorado with a man named Hillmon were admissible to prove from declarant's intention not only the likelihood that declarant went on the trip but also the likelihood that Hillmon went with declarant. Walters was never heard from again. The Advisory Committee on the Proposed [Federal] Rules stated that Rule 803(3) was intended to leave the *Hillmon* doctrine undisturbed. *Notes of Advisory Committee on Proposed Rules,* Note to *Fed.R.Evid.* 803(3), 28 *U.S.C.A.* (1984). However the House Committee on the Judiciary preferred to limit the *Hillmon* doctrine to permit statements of intent to show declarant's own future conduct, not the future conduct of another person. *Notes of Committee on the Judiciary, House Report No. 93–650,* Note to *Fed.R.Evid.* 803(3), 28 *U.S.C.A.* (1984).

With this background in mind, the court in *United States v. Pheaster,* 544 *F.2d* 353, 376–380 (9th Cir. 1976), *cert. denied,* 429 *U.S.* 1099 (1977), applied the

Hillmon doctrine; *see also United States v. Mangan,* 575 *F.2d* 32, 43 n. 12 (2d Cir.1978), *cert. denied,* 439 *U.S.* 931 (1978); but the limitation expressed by the House Committee was adopted in *Gual Morales v. Hernandez Vega,* 579 *F.2d* 677, 680 n. 2 (1st Cir.1978); *see also United States v. Jenkins,* 579 *F.2d* 840, 843 (4th Cir.1978), *cert. denied,* 439 *U.S.* 967 (1979).

The New Jersey law, as pronounced in *Hunter v. State,* 40 *N.J.L.* 495, 534–540 (E & A 1878), is the same as the *Hillmon* doctrine; in fact, the United States Supreme Court relied upon *Hunter* in the *Hillmon* decision. *Hillmon, supra,* 145 *U.S.* at 299–300, 36 *L.Ed.* at 712. *See also Brown v. Tard,* 552 *F.Supp.* 1341, 1351–1352 (D.N.J.1982). The "good faith" requirement carried over from *N.J.Evid.R.* 63(12) into this rule gives the trial judge discretion and responsibility in admitting statements of intent and other states of mind which would be particularly appropriate to apply in dealing with the problem posed by the *Hillmon* and *Hunter* cases.

(4) Statements for purposes of medical diagnosis or treatment. Rule 803(c)(4) follows *Fed.R.Evid.* 803(4) almost verbatim, adding the good faith requirement of *N.J.Evid.R.* 63(12). This rule replaces *N.J.Evid.R.* 63(12)(b) and (c) without substantive change except that the requirement of the New Jersey rule that the statement be made to a physician was omitted as too narrow since statements made for the purpose of diagnosis or treatment may be made to other health care professionals and paraprofessionals. For example, many psychotherapists are not MDs; they may be psychologists, social workers or practitioners of other disciplines.

(5) Recorded recollection. Rule 803(c)(5) generally follows both *Fed.R.Evid.* 803(5) and *N.J.Evid.R.* 63(1)(b), but it differs to some extent from both rules. The rule permits the exclusion of the recorded statement if circumstances indicate that the statement is untrustworthy. This provision is not contained in the federal or New Jersey analogues. It is substituted for the requirement in *Fed.R.Evid.* 803(5) that the statement be shown to reflect declarant's knowledge "correctly" and for the provision in *N.J.Evid.R.* 63(1)(b)(iii) that the witness must testify that his statement was true. These conditions cannot be realistically satisfied since the witness must also testify that he has insufficient recollection of the matter. *See State v. Wood,* 130 *N.J.Super.* 401, 408–410 (App.Div.1973), *aff'd,* 66 *N.J.* 8 (1974). Frequently a witness will say that the statement must have been true when made, but the trial judge should be permitted to exclude the statement if circumstances suggest that it was not trustworthy because of declarant's intention to lie or other reasons.

As to the distinction between a statement admissible under this rule and a writing used to refresh memory offered under Rule 612, see Comment on Rule 612.

(6) Records of regularly conducted activity. While Rule 803(c)(6) generally follows *Fed.R.Evid.* 803(6), its formulation is closer in some respects to *N.J.Evid.R.* 63(13). Rule 803(c)(6) follows the federal formulation by clearly requiring both that the records be made in the regular course of business and that it was the regular practice of that business to make those records. Although the "regular practice" condition was not expressly included in the 1967 New Jersey rule, its import is consistent with its judicial interpretation. *See Sas v. Strelecki,* 110 *N.J.Super.* 14, 19–22 (App.Div.1970).

Like the federal rule, Rule 803(c)(6) expressly permits the admission of opinions and diagnoses contained in business records. This provision was not contained in *N.J.Evid.R.* 63(13), but it is consistent with present practice. *Falcone v. New Jersey Bell Tel. Co.,* 98 *N.J.Super.* 138, 146–150 (App.Div.1967), *certif. denied,* 51 *N.J.* 190 (1968). The extent of admissibility of opinions contained in business records is qualified by Rule 808, a provision new to New Jersey practice and not included in the federal rules. As to the scope and intent of Rule 808, see the Comment on that rule.

In contrast to its federal counterpart, Rule 803(c)(6) follows the 1967 New Jersey rule in not requiring testimony of the custodian or other qualified witness as a condition for admission of business records. The requirement that a foundation be laid establishing the criteria for admissibility may be met by the kind of proof that would satisfy a trial judge in a hearing under Rule 104(a), including proof presented in affidavit form, such as in the case of hospital records. *Gunter v. Fischer Scientific American,* 193 *N.J.Super.* 688, 691–692 (App.Div.1984); *see The 1963 Report* at 186–187; *see also* Comment on Rule 101(a)(2)(E) and Rule 104(a).

This rule, like the federal rule and the 1967 New Jersey rule, contains a proviso that permits exclusion of the record if the sources of information or the method or circumstances of its preparation indicate that it is untrustworthy. This rule adds "purpose" of preparation as a factor of untrustworthiness to be considered. If the purpose for which the record was prepared was the anticipation of or the use in litigation, it should be subjected to special scrutiny for trustworthiness. *See Palmer v. Hoffman,* 318 *U.S.* 109, 111–116, 87 *L.Ed.* 645, 648–651 (1943); *but cf. Lewis v. Baker,* 526 *F.2d* 470, 472–473 (2d Cir.1975).

The admission of police reports as business records in criminal proceedings has been considered in a number of cases. Annotation, *Admissibility of Police Reports Under Federal Business Records Act (Federal Rules of Evidence, Rule 803, and Predecessor Amendments),* 31 *A.L.R.Fed.* 457 (1977); Annotation, *Admissibility in State Court Proceedings of Police Reports as Business Records,* 77 *A.L.R.3d* 115 (1977). *See United States v. Smith,* 521 *F.2d* 957, 962–969 (D.C.Cir.1975). *State v. McGeary,* 129 *N.J.Super.* 219, 223–229 (App.Div.1974), held that an inspection certificate as to the operating condition of a breathalyzer made in the regular course of a State Police employee's duties was sufficiently trustworthy to qualify as a business record admissible under *N.J.Evid.R.* 63(13). Test reports of unlawful drugs performed by State Police laboratory technicians may also be admitted. *See State v. Matulewicz,* 101 *N.J.* 27 (1985), and Comment to Rule 808. However, a report summarizing the observations of police officers in the course of a surveillance of an accused's activities may be excluded when offered against the accused on the ground that the purpose in preparing the report was to use it in litigation. *Cf. United States*

v. Smith, supra, 521 *F.2d* at 965–966. Such a report would be admissible, however, as a business record if offered by the accused against the prosecution. *Id.* at 965.

Police reports in civil cases in which the police officer making the report has no interest in the anticipated litigation are generally admissible under established law. *See Sas v. Strelecki, supra,* 110 *N.J.Super.* at 19–22; *Schneiderman v. Strelecki,* 107 *N.J.Super.* 113, 118–119 (App.Div.1969), *certif. denied,* 55 *N.J.* 163 (1969); *Brown v. Mortimer,* 100 *N.J.Super.* 395, 402–406 (App.Div.1968). The admissibility of a business record, however, does not mean that all parts of the record are necessarily admissible. For example, in *Sas* the court held inadmissible portions of a police report which contained statements given to a police officer because the statements were made by persons not under a "business duty" to render a truthful account of the automobile accident involved in the case. 110 *N.J.Super.* at 22. *See also State v. Lungsford,* 167 *N.J.Super.* 296, 309–310 (App.Div. 1979). Nevertheless, the rule does not condition admissibility of business records on proof that all information which they contain came from persons with a business duty to report the information accurately. The duty to report accurately may enhance the reliability of the business record. *See State v. Matulewicz, supra,* 101 *N.J.* at 30–31. But many business organizations regularly keep, use and rely upon information derived from sources without such a duty. Thus, to the extent that the holding in *Phoenix Associates, Inc. v. Edgewater Park Sewerage Auth.,* 178 *N.J.Super.* 109, 116 (App.Div.1981), *aff'd on other grounds sub nom. Phoenix Apartments, Inc. v. Edgewater Park Sewerage Auth.,* 89 *N.J.* 2 (1982), was based on the lack of a duty on the informant to report truthfully and accurately, it is not followed here. *See Matter of Ollag Constr. Equip. Corp.,* 665 *F.2d* 43, 46 (2d Cir.1981), which upheld the admissibility of financial statements prepared on a bank's form by the debtor, although the debtor was not under a business duty to supply the information.

As noted in the Comment on Rule 801(d), the definition of "business" under *Fed.R.Evid.* 803(6) does not expressly include activities of governmental agencies, in contrast to the definition in Rule 801(d) and *N.J.Evid.R.* 62(5). *See also* Comment on Rule 803(c)(8). The admissibility of reports of government agencies may also be governed by Rule 803(c)(8). *See State v. Matulewicz, supra,* 101 *N.J.* at 32; *State v. McGeary, supra,* 129 *N.J.Super.* at 227–228; *State v. Connors,* 129 *N.J.Super.* 476, 485 (App.Div.1974).

(7) Absence of an entry in records of regularly conducted activity. Rule 803(c)(7) follows both *Fed.R.Evid.* 803(7) and *N.J.Evid.R.* 63(14), with language changes that do not alter the basic principle of the rule. The "unless" clause at the end of the rule derives from the federal rule; it is not contained in *N.J.Evid.R.* 63(14).

As noted in the comment to Rule 803(c)(6), because governmental activity is included in the definition of business, Rule 803(c)(6) overlaps with 803(c)(8). Rule 803(c)(7) (absence of business record) is the converse of Rule 803(c)(6), and Rule 803(c)(10) (absence of public record) is the converse of Rule 803(c)(8). Thus, there is a corresponding overlap of Rules 803(c)(7) and 803(c)(10).

(8) Public records, reports, and findings. Rule 803(c)(8) follows *N.J.Evid.R.* 63(15) with minor language changes. The first portion of the rule deals with acts performed by or acts, conditions or events observed by, public officials within their duty to report upon. This portion of the rule corresponds to *Fed.R.Evid.* 803(8)(A) and (B) which make admissible records of "activities" of a public office or agency and of "matters observed" as to which there was a duty to report. However, the federal counterpart excludes from criminal cases matters observed by law enforcement personnel.

The second portion of the rule admits "statistical findings" of public officials. This is narrower than the term used in *Fed.R.Evid.* 803(8)(C), namely, "factual findings resulting from an investigation" authorized by law, except that such findings under the federal rule cannot be used against an accused in a criminal case.

The federal rule embodies the business record rule. Unlike the federal rules, these rules, like the New Jersey 1967 evidence rules, define the term "business" to include activities of governmental agencies. Thus, many records of governmental agencies can be admitted either under this rule or the traditional business record rule, Rule 803(c)(6). *See State v. Matulewicz,* 101 *N.J.* 27 (1985).

The extent to which opinions may be admitted as part of investigative records or evaluative reports of governmental agencies has caused difficulty under the federal rule. *Compare Baker v. Elcona Homes Corp.,* 588 *F.*2d 551, 556–559 (6th Cir.1978), *cert. denied,* 441 *U.S.* 933 (1979) (admitting a police report with the officer's conclusion from his investigation that plaintiff's vehicle entered the intersection against a red light, as a factual finding under federal Rule 803(8)) with *Smith v. Ithaca Corp.,* 612 *F.*2d 215, 220–223 (5th Cir.1980) (distinguishing "factual findings" in federal Rule 803(8)(C) from "opinions" and "diagnoses" in federal Rule 803(6) as to exclude "evaluative conclusions and opinions" of a Coast Guard agency investigation regarding liability and the cause of an accident, while admitting factual findings apparently based on objective data). *See Phillips v. Erie Lackawanna R.R. Co.,* 107 *N.J.Super.* 590 (App.Div.1969), *certif. denied,* 55 *N.J.* 444 (1970) (holding inadmissible the Board of Public Utility examiner's report of factual conclusions as to the hazardous condition of a railroad crossing, as well as the agency's order for corrective action); *but see State v. Matulewicz, supra,* 101 *N.J.* at 31–32.

Adjudicatory findings of the Division of Workers' Compensation, which can be judicially noticed under Rule 201(a), were held admissible as evidence in a "third party" Law Division negligence action in *Wunschel v. Jersey City,* 96 *N.J.* 651, 666–667 (1984), in pursuit of the policy of avoiding inconsistent adjudications. *See Alexander v. Gardner–Denver Co.,* 415 *U.S.* 36, 60 n. 21, 39 *L.Ed.*2d 147, 165 n. 21 (1974) (arbitral decision under collective bargaining agreement may be admitted as evidence in a District Court action for discrimination brought under Title VII of the 1964 Civil Rights Act, in furtherance of the dual federal policies favoring arbitration of labor disputes and preventing discrimination in employment). In other situations, however, arbitrators' decisions may be inadmissible in related litigation where policy reasons dictate that result. *See N.J.S.A.* 2A:23A–28 and *N.J.S.A.* 39:6A–33 making inadmissible arbitration decisions in non-automobile and automobile personal injury actions.

(9) Records of vital statistics. Rule 803(c)(9) follows *Fed.R.Evid.* 803(9) almost verbatim. *N.J.Evid.R.* 63(16), which is replaced by this rule, provided for the admissibility of "vital statistics," although not so designated in the rule, contained in a written "record, report or finding of fact" made and filed pursuant to statute if the maker of such record, report or finding was exclusively authorized by statute to perform the functions reflected in the writing and was required by statute to file in a designated public office a written report relating to the performance of such functions. As described in *The 1963 Report* at 193, the purpose of *N.J.Evid.R.* 63(16) was to admit "reports made by *ad hoc* public officials: physicians, undertakers, ministers, and the like, who are under a duty to file reports from time to time." Admissibility pursuant to *N.J.Evid.R.* 63(16) was subject to *N.J.Evid.R.* 64. This rule follows that scheme by making admissibility subject to *R.* 807, which replaces *N.J.Evid.R.* 64.

The first sentence of *N.J.Evid.R.* 63(17) provided for the admissibility of authenticated copies of official records or entries therein. This provision has been omitted since such a copy is normally a duplicate as defined by Rule 1001(d), and Rules 803(c)(8) and (9) provide for the admissibility of public records, reports and findings as well as records of reports of vital statistics to a public office.

(10) Absence of public record or entry. Rule 803(c)(10) generally follows *Fed.R.Evid.* 803(10) with changes in language and structure but not in substance. Section (A) of this rule replaces the second sentence of *N.J.Evid.R.* 63(17) without substantive change. There is no specific New Jersey rule analogue to section (B), the effect of which is to permit an inference of the nonoccurrence or nonexistence of a matter normally recorded to be drawn from proof of absence of the recording. Drawing such an inference is ordinarily the very purpose for which proof of the absence of a record would be made pursuant to *N.J.Evid.R.* 63(17). Thus, the federal formulation, which this rule follows, does not constitute a change in current New Jersey practice. *See N.J.Evid.R.* 63(14), now Rule 803(c)(7).

Testimony by a public official that his diligent search failed to disclose a particular record is not hearsay since that testimony is not offered to prove the contents of an extrajudicial statement. It is offered to prove the absence of any such report, from which an inference may be drawn that this act or event never occurred. Therefore, the use of the term "testimony" by the federal rule in this context was not followed, but such testimony is admissible.

(11) Records of religious organizations. Rule 803(c)(11) follows *Fed.R.Evid.* 803(11) almost verbatim. There is no 1967 New Jersey rule analogue. Religious records may be admitted as business records under Rule 803(c)(6) if made by an official of the religious organization who had a duty to make the record. Such records are also admissible under this rule even if the information contained in the record of the religious organization came from a person who had no duty to make the report, as is typically the case.

(12) Marriage, baptismal and similar certificates. Rule 803(c)(12) follows verbatim *Fed.R.Evid.* 803(12) except for the reference to Rule 807. The 1967 New Jersey analogue, *N.J.Evid.R.* 63(18), covered only certificates of marriage made by persons authorized by law to perform the marriage ceremony. The federal rule was adopted because of the high degree of reliability of the certificates it includes.

(13) Family records. Rule 803(c)(13) follows *Fed. R.Evid.* 803(13) almost verbatim, adding the reference to Rule 807. There is no 1967 New Jersey rule analogue. Frequently, authorities referred to in 5 J. Wigmore, *Evidence* §§ 1495–1496 (1974), are cited in support of the federal rule; *see Notes of Advisory Committee on Proposed Rules,* Note to *Fed.R.Evid.* 803(13), 28 *U.S.C.A.* (1984). The federal rule has some support in New Jersey law. *See In re Blau,* 4 *N.J.Super.* 343, 350–351 (App.Div.1949); *but cf. Supreme Council v. Conklin,* 60 *N.J.L.* 565, 569–571 (E & A 1897). As to the application of the rule, see 4 J. Weinstein & M. Berger, *Weinstein's Evidence* ¶ 803(13)[01] at 803–299 to 300 (1990). The cases usually look for some evidence of reliability of the source of the statement. Unavailability of the declarant is not required as under the common law rule.

(14) Records of documents affecting an interest in property. Rule 803(c)(14) follows *Fed.R.Evid.* 803(14) almost verbatim except for the reference to Rule 807. It makes no substantive change in *N.J.Evid.R.* 63(19), which it replaces. Note that the rule's reference to "public office" should be construed to include foreign as well as domestic public offices.

(15) Statements in documents affecting an interest in property. Rule 803(c)(15) follows *Fed.R.Evid.* 803(15) almost verbatim except for the reference to Rule 807. It makes no substantive change in *N.J.Evid.R.* 63(29), which it replaces.

(16) Statements in ancient documents. Rule 803(c)(16) follows *Fed.R.Evid.* 803(16) but substitutes a 30–year period for the 20–year period used by the federal rule. This is consistent with New Jersey law on the admissibility of ancient documents of apparent authenticity. *See Havens v. Sea Shore Land Co.,* 47 *N.J.Eq.* 365, 373–379 (Ch. 1890). There is no New Jersey rule analogue. For criteria used to authenticate ancient documents, see *Fed.R.Evid.* 901(b)(8). *See also* Comment to Rule 901. These rules do not establish particular criteria to satisfy the required proof of authenticity.

(17) Market reports, commercial publications. Rule 803(c)(17) follows *Fed.R.Evid.* 803(17) verbatim. While it changes the language of *N.J.Evid.R.* 63(30), it makes no substantial change in practice. The 1967 New Jersey rule analogue did not include documents relied on by the public but only those published for and used by persons in particular occupations. However, the same principle supports the admissibility of both categories of publications.

Although the formulation of this rule is somewhat broader than its predecessor, it is not intended to affect the holdings of *State v. McGee,* 131 *N.J.Super.* 292, 296–298 (App.Div.1974) (compilations of the National Crime Information Center not admissible) and *State v. Lungsford, supra,* 167 *N.J.Super.* at 301–306 (compilations of the National Automobile Theft Bureau not admissible), for reasons stated in these opinions.

(18) Learned treatises. Rule 803(c)(18) follows *Fed.R.Evid.* 803(18) almost verbatim, adding the proviso respecting the display of graphics to the jury. This formulation also substitutes the word "testimony" for the federal rule's use of the phrase "the testimony or admission of the witness or by other expert testimony." The intent of this formulation is to recognize that in some special instances, a lay witness may be able to testify as to the treatise's authoritativeness. Although a rule similar to this was proposed as *N.J.Evid.R.* 63(31) in *The 1963 Report* at 212, it was not adopted, and there is no 1967 New Jersey rule analogue. The adoption of this rule represents a change in practice by allowing the use of learned treatise evidence even if an expert witness fails to acknowledge that it is authoritative, so long as the reliability of the authority is established by other testimony or by judicial notice. The change has already been endorsed in concept by the Supreme Court in *Jacober v. St. Peter's Medical Center,* ___ *N.J.* ___ (1992).

(19) Reputation concerning personal or family history. Rule 803(c)(19) follows *Fed.R.Evid.* 803(19) almost verbatim. It combines *N.J.Evid.R.* 63(26) and 63(27)(c) with language changes but with no change in substance except for the omission of the phrase "resident in the community at the time of the reputation," a factor which would affect the weight of the evidence but not its admissibility.

(20) Reputation concerning boundaries or general history. Rule 803(c)(20) follows *Fed.R.Evid.* 803(20) almost verbatim and makes language changes but no substantive changes in *N.J.Evid.R.* 63(27)(a) and (b), which it replaces, except for broadening the condition that the event be "of importance to the community" to include "or state or nation" as well.

(21) Reputation as to character. Rule 803(c)(21) follows *Fed.R.Evid.* 803(21) almost verbatim. It incorporates the concept of "relevant time" included in *N.J.Evid.R.* 63(28), which this rule replaces with language changes but no substantive changes.

(22) Judgments of previous conviction of crime. Rule 803(c)(22) follows almost verbatim *N.J.Evid.R.* 63(20), which limits to civil proceedings the substantive use of judgments of convictions against a party. By contrast, the federal rule, *Fed.R.Evid.* 803(22), permits substantive use of prior convictions against the accused in criminal prosecutions. As to the difference between the 1967 New Jersey analogue, followed by this rule, and the federal rule, see *State v. Ingenito,* 87 *N.J.* 204, 222–224 (1981) (Schreiber, J., concurring), which notes that a prior conviction may be admitted in a criminal case if the fact of conviction constitutes an essential element of the subsequent offense. A prior conviction of a witness, whether or not a party, can also be used in both civil and criminal proceedings for impeachment purposes. *See id.* at 224, and *N.J.S.A.* 2A:81–12, to the extent that that statute was not superseded by the official footnote accompanying the 1967 adoption of *N.J.Evid.R.* 63(20). *See also* Rule 609 and Comment thereon. The provision in the federal rule allowing proof of convictions on appeal was not adopted as contrary to New Jersey law. *State v. Biegenwald,* 96 *N.J.* 630, 638 (1984) (citing with approval *State v. Blue,* 129 *N.J.Super.* 8, 11–12 (App.Div.1974), *certif. denied,* 66 *N.J.* 328 (1974)).

(23) Judgments as to personal, family, or general history, or boundaries. Rule 803(c)(23) follows *Fed.R.Evid.* 803(23). While there is neither a 1967 New Jersey rule analogue nor New Jersey case law on the subject, this exception has long been recognized by the general common law. *See City of London v. Clerke,* 90 *Eng.Rep.* 710 (K.B.1691); *Patterson v. Gaines,* 47 *U.S.* 550, 599, 12 *L.Ed.* 553, 573 (1848). The federal rule embodying the common law was adopted because judgments are ordinarily more reliable than the evidence of reputation concerning those matters admissible under Rules 803(c)(19) and (20).

(24) Other exceptions—not adopted. *Fed.R.Evid.* 803(24), which creates a general hearsay exception for statements not covered by a specific hearsay rule, provided they are attended by "equivalent circumstantial guarantees of trustworthiness" and are the most probative evidence reasonably available, and provided further that other stated criteria are met, was not adopted. The adoption of the federal rule was attended by substantial controversy and its application since its adoption has been disparate among the federal courts. *See* A.B.A. Section of Litigation, *Emerging Problems Under the Federal Rules of Evidence* 279–281 (1983). The adoption of *Fed.R.Evid.* 803(24), construable as a general relaxation rule, would represent a radical departure from New Jersey practice. The advantages and disadvantages of this departure are debatable. For the same reason, *Fed.R.Evid.* 804(b)(5) was not adopted. It should be noted that a broad relaxation rule proposed as Rule 2(4) in *The 1963 Report* at 9 was rejected.

(25) Statement against interest. Rule 803(c)(25) follows almost verbatim the first sentence of *Fed.R.Evid.* 804(b)(3) and replaces *N.J.Evid.R.* 63(10) without substantive change. The placement of this rule as a section of Rule 803 preserves the present New Jersey practice of permitting the use of declarations against interest irrespective of the declarant's availability as a witness. *See State v. Barry,* 86 *N.J.* 80, 91–92 (1981), *cert. denied,* 454 *U.S.* 1017 (1981); *Portner v. Portner,* 186 *N.J.Super.* 410, 416–418 (App. Div.1982), *rev'd on other grounds,* 93 *N.J.* 215 (1983). The federal rule, by placing this provision in Rule 804, conditions the use of such statements on the declarant's unavailability.

This rule follows the federal formulation by excluding statements against "social interest." That term is vague, and some declarations which are against social interest may also be against penal or other specified interest. *See, e.g., State v. West,* 145 *N.J.Super.* 226, 232–233 (App.Div.1976), *certif. denied,* 73 *N.J.* 67 (1977).

This rule also rejects the second sentence of the federal analogue which requires corroborating circumstances indicating trustworthiness as a condition for the admission of declarations against penal interest by another person exculpating an accused. *See Chambers v. Mississippi,* 410 *U.S.* 284, 299–302, 35 *L.Ed.*2d 297, 311–313 (1973).

Rule 803(c)(25), as originally proposed, had deleted as an admissible statement against interest a statement contrary to the declarant's social interest. The reason for this deletion was the committee's concurrence with the federal rule formulation which does not include statements against social interest and the committee's perception that the term is somewhat vague and that its content is probably encompassed by other interests specified by the rule. On reconsideration, the committee has concluded that social interest is a phrase which, particularly in view of its long-time inclusion in the New Jersey rules, has sufficient discrete content so as to justify retention in the revised rules.

(26) Judgments against persons entitled to indemnity. Rule 803(c)(26) follows *N.J.Evid.R.* 63(21) almost verbatim. The reference in the rule to the Joint Tortfeasors Contribution Law is intended to incorporate the modifying provision of the Comparative Negligence Law, *N.J.S.A.* 2A:15–5.3. While the rule does not so state in terms, it is clear that a judgment obtained by fraud is not admissible for the purposes stated by the rule. *Cf. Scaglione v. St. Paul–Mercury Indem. Co.,* 28 *N.J.* 88 (1958). There is no federal analogue.

(27) Statements by a child relating to a sexual offense. Following publication of the committee's original report and the adoption and transmission by the Supreme Court to the Legislature of the proposed Revised Rules of Evidence, some members of the law enforcement community objected to any change in Evid. R. 63(33) other than enlargement of its scope to include juvenile and civil actions. The committee was of the view that these objections had not been sufficiently aired as of this time and that there had not been an adequate opportunity for dialogue between the objecting members of the law enforcement community, supporters of the revised rule, and the committee, which, except for its members from the prosecutorial community, had been strongly in favor of the revised rule.

Since Evid. R. 63(33) has been in place for four years, the committee recommends that that rule be retained in its original form subject only to amendment to increase its scope, and that the committee, supporters of the revised rule, and objectors to the revised rule, undertake a dialogue and full reconsideration at a future time regarding the desirability for amending the rule.

Retention of Evid. R. 63(33) requires shifting of the rule from its present inclusion in Rule 804, which conditions admissibility on the declarant's unavailability, to Rule 803, which does not. Accordingly, New Jersey Evid. R. 63(33) is included in the Revised Rules as Rule 803(c)(27). Note further that the final proviso of Evid. R. 63(33) eliminates the necessity for proposed Rule 804(a)(5), which had provided a special unavailability definition for children's statements admissible under proposed Rule 804(d)(8). Proposed 804(a)(5) is therefore also to be deleted.

Rule 804. Hearsay exceptions: declarant unavailable

a. Definition of Unavailable. Except when the declarant's unavailability has been procured or wrongfully caused by the proponent of declarant's statement for the purpose of preventing declarant from attending or testifying, a declarant is "unavailable" as a witness if declarant:

(1) is exempted by ruling of the court on the ground of privilege from testifying concerning the subject matter of the statement; or

(2) persists in refusing to testify concerning the subject matter of the statement despite an order of the court to do so; or

(3) testifies to a lack of memory of the subject matter of the statement; or

(4) is absent from the hearing because of death, physical or mental illness or infirmity, or other cause, and the proponent of the statement is unable by process or other reasonable means to procure the declarant's attendance at trial, and, with respect to statements proffered under Rules 804(b)(4) and (7), the proponent is unable, without undue hardship or expense, to obtain declarant's deposition for use in lieu of testimony at trial.

b. Hearsay exceptions. Subject to Rule 807, the following are not excluded by the hearsay rule if the declarant is unavailable as a witness.

(1) *Testimony in prior proceedings.*

(A) Testimony given by a witness at a prior trial of the same or a different matter, or in a hearing or deposition taken in compliance with law in the course of the same or another proceeding, if the party against whom the testimony is now offered had an opportunity and similar motive in the prior trial, hearing or proceeding to develop the testimony by examination or cross-examination.

(B) In a civil action or proceeding, and only when offered by the defendant in a criminal action or proceeding, testimony given in a prior trial, hearing or deposition taken pursuant to law to which the party against whom the testimony is now offered was not a party, if the party who offered the prior testimony or against whom it was offered had an opportunity to develop the testimony on examination or cross-examination and had an interest and motive to do so which is the same or similar to that of the party against whom it is now offered.

Expert opinion testimony given in a prior trial, hearing, or deposition may be excluded, however, if the judge finds that there are experts of a like kind generally available within a reasonable distance from the place in which the action is pending and the interests of justice so require.

(2) *Statement under belief of imminent death.* In a criminal proceeding, a statement made by a victim unavailable as a witness is admissible if it was made voluntarily and in good faith and while the declarant believed in the imminence of declarant's impending death.

(3) [*Statement against interest*—adopted as Rule 803(c)(25)]

(4) *Statement of personal or family history.* A statement (A) concerning the declarant's own birth, adoption, marriage, divorce, legitimacy, ancestry, relationship by blood, adoption, or marriage, or other similar fact of personal or family history, even though declarant had no means of acquiring personal knowledge of the matter stated; or (B) concerning the foregoing matters, and the death also, of another person, if the declarant was related to the other by blood, adoption, or marriage or was so intimately associated with the other's family as to be likely to have accurate information concerning the matters declared.

(5) [*Other exceptions*—not adopted]

(6) *Trustworthy statements by deceased declarants.* In a civil proceeding, a statement made by a person unavailable as a witness because of death if the statement was made in good faith upon declarant's personal knowledge in circumstances indicating that it is trustworthy.

(7) *Voters' Statements.* A statement by a voter concerning the voter's qualifications to vote or the fact or content of the vote.

Adopted eff. July 1, 1993. Amended September 15, 2004, eff. July 1, 2005.

Comment

Rule 804(a)—Definition of "Unavailable"

Rule 804(a) specifies the circumstances in which a declarant will be deemed "unavailable" as a witness in order to satisfy this condition for admitting his prior statement in evidence under hearsay exceptions contained in Rule 804(b). In general, Rule 804(a) follows the provisions of the federal rule and incorporates some of the provisions of *N.J.Evid.R.* 62(6), which defines the terms "unavailable as a witness" for the purpose of certain hearsay exceptions.

Paragraphs (1), (2) and (3) of Rule 804(a) are identical to the federal rule. These provisions define unavailability to include (1) a declarant whose privilege not to testify has been upheld, (2) a declarant who refuses to testify despite a court order to do so, and (3) a declarant who testifies that he cannot recall the subject of his prior statement. These circumstances were not expressly included in *N.J.Evid.R.* 62(6). The issue raised in *State v. Wilson*, 57 *N.J.* 39, 47–48 (1970), that a declarant who can assert a privilege is not "unavailable" within the meaning of the hearsay exception for former testimony, will no longer present a problem under the expanded definition of "unavailable" contained in Rule 804(a). These new provisions are consistent with the principles underlying *N.J.Evid.R.* 62(6).

The contents of paragraphs (4) and (5) of *Fed. R.Evid.* 804(a) have been combined in paragraph (a)(4) of this rule, to which have been added principles embodied in *N.J.Evid.R.* 62(6) concerning the taking of a declarant's deposition with respect to only two Rule 804(b) exceptions, (b)(4) and (b)(7), applicable to statements of personal and family history and to voters' statements respectively. But see comment on Rule 804(b)(7).

Paragraph (4) of this rule does not specifically enumerate all possible causes for the inability to compel the appearance of the person whose prior statement will be offered. The rule expressly includes death of the declarant as well as mental or physical illness or infirmity. These terms are found in the federal rule and the 1967 New Jersey rule as well as in *R.* 4:16–1(c), dealing with use of depositions. The court rule also includes the terms "age" and "imprisonment". The provision for "other cause" in paragraph (4) would include imprisonment as well as all other circumstances resulting in the inability to produce the declarant as a witness at trial. Absence from the jurisdiction may be another cause. It was expressly included in *N.J.Evid.R.* 62(6) and *R.* 4:16–1(c). However, it was omitted from paragraph (4) because a person may be deemed available in certain circumstances despite absence from the jurisdiction if he or she is within the control of the proponent of the hearsay statement. As to the sufficiency of efforts to procure the witness' attendance at trial, see generally Annotation, "Sufficiency of Efforts to Procure Missing Witness' Attendance to Justify Admission of his Former Testimony—State Cases," 3 *A.L.R.*4th 87 (1981).

Federal Rule 804(a)(5) requires the attempt to depose an absent declarant whose hearsay statement is proffered under 804(b)(2) (statement under belief of impending death), (b)(3) (statement against interest) and (b)(4) (statement of personal or family history). As noted above this rule requires an attempt to depose a declarant only with respect to statements of personal or family history and voters' statements offered under Rules 804(b)(4) and (b)(7), respectively. This rule does not require an attempt to depose declarant in order to admit statements made under belief of impending death because the New Jersey rule, unlike the federal rule, permits admission of such statements only if the declarant is dead. Rule 804(b)(2), following *N.J.Evid.R.* 63(5). Nor does this rule require the deposition attempt for admission of statements against interest. Under New Jersey practice, the admissibility of declarations against interest is not dependent on the unavailability of the declarant. Rule 803(c)(25), following *N.J.Evid.R.* 63(10). In addition, this rule, like the federal rule, does not require the deposition attempt with respect to prior testimony. There is no reason to depose a declarant who has previously testified subject to cross-examination.

The federal rule has no counterpart to Rule 804(b)(7) (voter statements). Since the validity of an election may depend upon the content of the statement, the better practice is to require the deposition attempt, and this rule so provides. However, for self-evident reasons, the rule does not require deposition attempts for the two remaining "unavailability" exceptions, statements of deceased declarants and statements of children regarding sexual abuse, Rules 804(b)(6) and (b)(8), respectively.

Even where the deposition attempt is required, the failure to have made that attempt will not always preclude admissibility. The importance of the declarant's statement to the proceeding, the expectation that he would ordinarily be available at trial, the extent of the hardship and expense in taking the deposition, and other factors, may be considered in determining whether a declarant's deposition is required. Note that the additional provision in *N.J.Evid.R.* 62(6), "and the probable importance of the [declarant's] testimony is such as to justify the expense of taking such deposition" was omitted as embraced in the concept "without undue hardship or expense." Of course, if unavailability is disputed, the trial judge will be required to determine the issue pursuant to Rule 104(a). There are many factors that can be considered, and Rule 804(a) establishes general principles to guide the discretion of the court.

Rule 804(b)—Hearsay Exceptions

Introduction. Rule 804(b), like *Fed.R.Evid.* 804(b), provides certain hearsay exceptions if the declarant is unavailable as a witness. Under the 1967 New Jersey rules, the exceptions to the hearsay rule contained in *N.J.Evid.R.* 63 were not divided into categories according on the availability of the declarant as a witness. However, several exceptions were individually conditioned on the declarant's unavailability, namely, New Jersey Evidence Rules 63(3) (depositions and prior testimony), 63(5) (dying declarations), 63(23) and (24) (statements concerning one's own or another's family history), 63(32) (statements of declarants who have died), 63(11) (voters' statements), and to some extent, 63(33) (statements by a child relating to a sexual offense). These New Jersey evidence rules are the antecedents of Rules 804(b)(1), (2), (4), (6), (7) and (8), respectively. There are no federal counterparts to Rules 804(b)(6), (7), and (8). *Fed.R.Evid.* 804(b)(5), which contains a general exception for other trustworthy statements of unavailable declarants, was not adopted.

Like Rule 803, Rule 804(b) is phrased in the negative. It provides that certain statements are not excluded by the hearsay rule if the declarant is unavailable as a witness. However, statements of unavailable witnesses otherwise admissible under Rule 804(b) may be excluded under another rule of evidence, for example, in most instances when the statement is not based on the personal knowledge of the declarant or when the statement contains an opinion which the declarant is not qualified to give. On the other hand, statements of unavailable witnesses may also be admitted under any of the other hearsay exceptions contained in Rule 803(c).

Note that the admissibility of all hearsay offered pursuant to Rule 804(b) is subject to the notice requirements contained in Rule 807.

As a general caution, it must be noted that in criminal cases, "when a hearsay declarant is not present for cross-examination at trial, the Confrontation Clause normally requires a showing that he is unavailable." *Ohio v. Roberts,* 448 *U.S.* 56, 66, 65 *L.Ed.*2d 597, 608 (1980). Unavailability in the constitutional sense requires proof that the prosecutor has made a "good-faith effort" to produce the declarant at trial. 448 *U.S.* at 74, 65 *L.Ed.*2d at 613; *Barber v. Page,* 390 *U.S.* 719, 724–724, 20 *L.Ed.*2d 255, 260 (1968). When unavailability has been established, the *Roberts* court said: "Even then, [the] statement is admissible only if it bears adequate 'indicia of reliability'. Reliability can be inferred without more in a case where the evidence falls within a firmly rooted hearsay exception. In other cases, the evidence must be excluded, at least absent a showing of particularized guarantees of trustworthiness." *Roberts, supra,* 448 *U.S.* at 66, 65 *L.Ed.*2d at 608.

(1) Testimony in prior proceedings. Rule 804(b)(1), dealing with the admissibility of former testimony given at an earlier trial, hearing or proceeding or in a deposition in the same case or in another case, is similar to the federal rule and *N.J.Evid.R.* 63(3) in a number of respects, but differs in some respects from both rules. As for the use of depositions taken in the pending case, see generally *R.* 4:16 and, in particular, *R.* 4:16–1(c) with respect to unavailable witnesses and absent but not unavailable witnesses.

Rule 804(b)(1)(A) applies to testimony offered against a party who was a party to an earlier trial, hearing or proceeding involving the same or a different matter. Rule 804(b)(1)(B) applies to prior testimony which is offered against a party who was not a party to the prior action or proceeding in which the testimony was given.

Under Rule 804(b)(1)(A), testimony of a declarant who is unavailable as a witness is admissible against a party to the present civil or criminal case who was a party to the prior proceeding in which the testimony was given and had a similar motive and opportunity to develop the testimony as in the present case. *See State v. Wooters,* 228 *N.J.Super.* 171, 179 (App.Div. 1988). The term "develop the testimony by examination or cross-examination" is intended to include direct and redirect examination as well as cross-examination as in *Fed.R.Evid.* 804(b)(1). In some cases a party may not have had an opportunity or motive to develop the testimony on the earlier occasion, particularly if the issues were dissimilar. Examples in criminal cases include proceedings before a grand jury, where defendant does not have a right to appear and examine a witness, and in probable cause hearings where the motive to examine the witness extensively may be lacking or the opportunity curtailed. *See State v. Moody,* 169 *N.J.Super.* 177 (Law Div.1978); *but see State v. Ewings,* 154 *N.J.Super.* 472 (Law Div.1977); *cf. California v. Green,* 399 *U.S.* 149, 26 *L.Ed.*2d 489 (1970).

When testimony has been given in another proceeding in which the party against whom it is later offered was not a party, stricter rules apply. Rule 804(b)(1)(B). In criminal cases, such evidence cannot be admitted against a defendant because of his constitutional right to confront the declarant. In civil cases, or when offered by a defendant in a criminal proceeding, the former testimony may be admitted under this rule against a party who was not a party in the prior proceeding if a party in the prior proceeding had an interest substantially similar to that of the party against whom it is now being offered and also

had a similar motive and an opportunity to develop the testimony. By virtue of this rule, testimony given in a prior proceeding would be admissible against a present party if a party in the prior proceeding was a predecessor in interest or privy of the present party or one with a common interest, provided the issues in both proceedings are such that the party in the prior proceeding had an interest substantially similar to that of the present party and had a similar motive and opportunity to develop the testimony on direct, cross, or redirect examination.

Rule 804(b)(1)(B) is broader than a literal reading of its federal analogue with respect to testimony given in an earlier proceeding which is offered against a party who was not a party to that proceeding. Under the federal rule such former testimony is not admissible unless offered against a party whose "predecessor in interest" was a party to the proceeding in which the testimony was given. Rule 804(b)(1)(B) would admit such testimony in a civil case or in a criminal proceeding when offered by an accused if a party to the earlier proceeding had an interest similar to that of the party to the present proceeding against whom the testimony is offered and had a similar motive and an opportunity to develop the testimony.

The term "predecessor in interest" has caused difficulty in applying *Fed.R.Evid.* 804(b)(1). Some federal courts have given it an expansive reading comparable to the term "community of interest." *See Lloyd v. American Export Lines, Inc.,* 580 *F.*2d 1179, 1184–1187 (3d Cir.1978), *cert. denied,* 439 *U.S.* 969 (1978); *Clay v. Johns–Mansville Sales Corp.,* 722 *F.*2d 1289, 1293–1295 (6th Cir.1983), *cert. denied,* 467 *U.S.* 1253 (1984); *Carpenter v. Dizio,* 506 *F.Supp.* 1117, 1123–1124 (E.D.Pa.1981), *aff'd mem.,* 673 *F.*2d 1298 (3d Cir.1981). This interpretation is akin to the intent of Rule 804(b)(1)(B). *But see* cases cited in A.B.A. Section of Litigation, *Emerging Problems Under the Federal Rules of Evidence* 297 *et seq.* (1983).

Rule 804(b)(1) follows the substance of *N.J.Evid.R.* 63(3)(a) except that former deposition testimony under *N.J.Evid.R.* 63(3)(a) was limited to *de bene esse* depositions "for use as testimony in the trial" as distinguished from depositions taken for discovery purposes only. Rule 804(b)(1) makes admissible testimony of an unavailable witness, including a discovery deposition as well as a *de bene esse* deposition, if the other conditions of the rule are satisfied. The important safeguard is the inquiry into the motive, interest, and opportunity to examine the witness in the prior proceedings. For tactical reasons a party may not avail himself of the opportunity to fully examine or cross-examine a witness during a discovery deposition, preferring to retain an element of surprise for the actual trial. For this reason extra care should be taken in admitting deposition testimony taken for discovery purposes whether or not the present party against whom the testimony is offered was a party to the prior proceeding.

Rule 804(b)(1) contains a limitation on the admissibility of expert testimony given in a prior trial not found in either its federal or state analogues. *See Sacawa v. Polikoff,* 150 *N.J.Super.* 172, 177–179 (App. Div.1977).

(2) Statement under belief of impending death. Rule 804(b)(2) incorporates *N.J.Evid.R.* 63(5) verbatim, but like the other rules respecting statements of unavailable witnesses, it is made subject to the notice requirements of Rule 807 by virtue of the preamble in Rule 804(b).

Like its 1967 New Jersey Rule analogue, this rule is limited to criminal proceedings and covers all statements made by a declarant voluntarily and in good faith while believing his death is imminent, provided both that declarant is unavailable because of his death and was a victim of the crime. The federal rule analogue, Rule 804(b)(2), limits admissible dying declarations to statements concerning the cause or circumstances of declarant's perceived imminent death offered in all civil actions but restricts admission in criminal cases to prosecutions for homicide only. The New Jersey rule, applicable only to criminal actions, is not, however, limited to homicide cases. While the New Jersey rule is limited to criminal proceedings, any relevant statements made by a declarant who is dead may be admitted under Rule 804(b)(6) in civil actions if "made in good faith upon his personal knowledge in circumstances indicating that it is trustworthy." Thus, dying declarations may be admitted in civil actions if these conditions are met. Note, also, that unlike the New Jersey rule, the federal rule applies if the declaration was made while declarant believed his death was imminent, even if the declarant survived but is otherwise unavailable as a witness.

A dying declaration may include a conclusion or opinion, but before admitting such a statement the trial judge should determine in a preliminary hearing whether the inferences and conclusions were drawn from facts known or observed by the declarant, and whether, considering all the circumstances, the statement can be received without undue prejudice to the defendant. *State v. Hegel,* 113 *N.J.Super.* 193 (App. Div.1971), *certif. denied,* 58 *N.J.* 596 (1971).

The revised rule, as originally proposed, provided that a statement made under the belief of impending death by the victim in a criminal proceeding would be admissible only if the victim was unavailable by reason of death. Upon reconsideration at the request of the State Bar Association, the committee has concluded that a statement made by a victim which otherwise meets all of the stipulations of the rule is no less reliable and trustworthy because the victim has survived. The committee recognizes, moreover, that because of medical advances, victims may survive under physical disabilities precluding testimonial capacity.

(3) Statement against interest—adopted as Rule 803(c)(25). *Fed.R.Evid.* 804(b)(3), dealing with statements against interest, was not adopted as part of Rule 804(b) because such statements are made admissible under Rule 803(c)(25) regardless of declarant's availability. The inherent reliability of such statements was deemed sufficient to justify their admission even if the declarant is available as a witness. *See* Comment on Rule 63(10), *The 1963 Report* at 169. For other comment on *Fed.R.Evid.* 804(b)(3), see Rule 803(c)(25).

(4) Statement of personal or family history. Rule 804(b)(4) follows *Fed.R.Evid.* 804(4) almost verbatim. Section A replaces *N.J.Evid.R.* 63(23), and Section B replaces *N.J.Evid.R.* 63(24) with language changes only. *N.J.Evid.R.* 63(25) (statements concerning family history based on statement of another declarant) has not been separately adopted as its substance is comprehended by the formulation of Section A of this rule. However, this rule, unlike *N.J.Evid.R.* 63(25), does not require the unavailability of both declarants and is subject to the notice requirements of Rule 807.

(5) Other exceptions—not adopted. *Fed.R.Evid.* 804(b)(5), which provides for unspecified "other exceptions," has not been adopted. See Comment of Rule 803(c)(24) above explaining the failure to adopt a counterpart to *Fed.R.Evid.* 803(24) (other exceptions).

(6) Trustworthy statements by deceased declarants. Rule 804(b)(6) follows *N.J.Evid.R.* 63(32). While it makes some language changes, it does not change the substance of the New Jersey rule. There is no direct federal rule analogue to this rule, but such evidence may be admitted under the residual exception provisions of *Fed.R.Evid.* 804(b)(5) if the conditions of that rule are satisfied. The hearsay exception for dying declarations in civil proceedings, provided for by *Fed.R.Evid.* 804(b)(2), is encompassed by the broader terms of this rule.

Note that this rule is expressly limited to civil proceedings. However, statements of declarants who are dead may meet the requirements of other exceptions to the hearsay rule, such as Rules 803(c)(1) (present sense impression) and 803(c)(2) (excited utterances) and may be admitted in criminal as well as civil proceedings without violating a defendant's right of confrontation so long as adequate indicia of reliability inhere in the exception or are otherwise established. *Ohio v. Roberts, supra,* 448 *U.S.* at 66, 65 *L.Ed.*2d at 608.

(7) Voters' statements. Rule 804(b)(7) follows *N.J.Evid.R.* 63(11) verbatim, to which were added the notice requirements of Rule 807, which were not included in the 1967 New Jersey rule. There is no federal rule analogue. This rule is not inconsistent with *N.J.S.A.* 2A:84A–25 (*N.J.Evid.R.* 31) which accords a voter the privilege to refuse to disclose the tenor of his vote at a political election unless the judge finds that the vote was cast illegally. Clearly, the illegality of the vote must be determined before the hearsay statements provided for by this rule could be admitted. *See N.J.S.A.* 19:29–7, authorizing a judge to compel a voter, found to be unqualified, to disclose for whom he voted. *See also In re Mallon,* 232 *N.J.Super.* 249, 273 (App.Div.1989), *certif. denied,* 117 *N.J.* 166 (1989), where the court encouraged the "resourceful" procedure used by the trial judge and the attorneys in questioning unavailable voters by telephone conference. However, in a case where the illegal vote of a voter who is not available as a witness is critical to the outcome of the election, a judge may require the parties to take the deposition of the voter, if reasonable in the light of all circumstances, pursuant to the requirements of Rule 804(a)(4).

Rule 805. Hearsay within hearsay

A statement within the scope of an exception to Rule 802 shall not be inadmissible on the ground that it includes a statement made by another declarant which is offered to prove the truth of its contents if the included statement itself meets the requirements of an exception to Rule 802.

Adopted effective July 1, 1993.

Comment

Rule 805 follows *N.J.Evid.R.* 66 almost verbatim. *Fed.R.Evid.* 805 expresses the same principle in different language, providing that included hearsay is not excluded from an admissible hearsay statement if both hearsay statements conform with an exception to the hearsay rule.

Rule 806. Attacking and supporting credibility of declarant

When a hearsay statement has been admitted in evidence, the credibility of the declarant may be attacked, and if attacked may be supported, by any evidence which would be admissible for those purposes if the declarant had testified as a witness. Evidence of a statement or other conduct by a declarant, inconsistent with the declarant's hearsay statement received in evidence, is admissible although declarant had no opportunity to deny or explain it. If the party against whom a hearsay statement has been admitted calls the declarant as a witness, that party is entitled to examine the declarant on the statement as if under cross-examination.

Adopted effective July 1, 1993.

Comment

Rule 806 generally follows *Fed.R.Evid.* 806. Its first two sentences replace *N.J.Evid.R.* 65 without substantial change. The last sentence of this rule, which is taken from the federal rule, has no direct New Jersey analogue but was included here because it is consistent with current New Jersey practice.

Rule 807. Discretion of judge to exclude evidence under certain exceptions

Except if offered by an accused in a criminal proceeding, when any statement is admissible by reason of Rules 803(c)(8), 803(c)(9), 803(c)(10), 803(c)(11), 803(c)(12), 803(c)(13), 803(c)(14), 803(c)(15), 803(c)(26) or 804(b), the judge may exclude it at the trial if it appears that the proponent's intention to offer the statement in evidence was not made known to the adverse party at such time as to provide that party with a fair opportunity to meet it.

Adopted effective July 1, 1993.

Comment

Rule 807 follows *N.J.Evid.R.* 64 almost verbatim, with appropriate changes in the cross-references. There is no direct federal analogue. Although notice provisions are included in the residual exception rules, *Fed.R.Evid.* 803(24) and 804(b)(5), neither of

these rules has been adopted. Rule 807 is not intended to affect the notice requirements in the Rules of Court applicable to civil or criminal cases. *See, e.g., R.* 3:11–1; 3:13–3; 4:10 to 4:25, particularly 4:17–7, 4:23–2(b)(2), 4:23–4 and 4:23–5(b).

Rule 808. Expert opinion included in a hearsay statement admissible under an exception

Expert opinion which is included in an admissible hearsay statement shall be excluded if the declarant has not been produced as a witness unless the trial judge finds that the circumstances involved in rendering the opinion, including the motive, duty, and interest of the declarant, whether litigation was contemplated by the declarant, the complexity of the subject matter, and the likelihood of accuracy of the opinion, tend to establish its trustworthiness.

Adopted effective July 1, 1993.

Comment

Rule 808 deals with the admissibility of extra-judicial statements of expert opinion included in business records or other forms of admissible hearsay when the declarant of the expert opinion is not produced as a witness. There is no express counterpart in the federal or present New Jersey rules. However, *N.J.Evid.R.* 63(13) conditions the admission of a business record on proof that the "sources of information" and "the method and circumstances of its preparation were such to justify its admission." Relying on this language the Supreme Court in *State v. Matulewicz*, 101 *N.J.* 27, 30 (1985), held that the admissibility of a State Police chemist's laboratory report identifying a substance as marijuana would depend on the "method and circumstances" involved in preparing the report, such as the complexity or routine nature of the procedures used in making the analysis, the degree of objectivity and subjectivity involved, the existence of motive for untrustworthiness, and the responsibility of the declarant to be accurate and reliable.

The *Matulewicz* holding is consistent with the comment on proposed rule 63(13) contained in *The 1963 Report* at 185–186. *The 1963 Report* contemplated that opinions derived from a "relatively well-established" test, such as a "blood-grouping test, an alcoholism test, or the taking of an x-ray," and other "relatively simple" diagnostic tests contained in hospital records would be admitted in evidence. This approach has been followed. *State v. Martorelli*, 136 *N.J.Super.* 449 (App.Div.1975), *certif. denied*, 69 *N.J.* 445 (1976) (blood alcohol report in hospital record). *See also McCormick on Evidence* § 313 at 732 (Cleary 2d ed. 1972), § 313 at 732: "The admissibility of ordinary diagnostic findings customarily based on objective data and not usually presenting more than average difficulty of interpretation is usually conceded," but "diagnostic opinions which on their face are speculative are reasonably excluded." However, "under the Uniform Act, it would not be unreasonable ... to permit introduction of the record only if the declarant were produced for cross-examination," in those "borderline cases" of records with opinions "involving difficulty of interpretation," although "most courts favor admissibility." *Ibid. See also*

State in Interest of J.H., 244 *N.J.Super.* 207 (App.Div. 1990), holding that, to satisfy the confrontation clause requirement of particularized trustworthiness, a laboratory drug analysis certificate offered in evidence pursuant to *N.J.S.A.* 2C:35–19 must satisfy the *Matulewicz* criteria.

In dealing with the admissibility of diagnoses found in hospital records before adoption of *Fed.R.Evid.* 803(6), federal courts tended to admit entries relating to physical conditions and diagnoses as to which competent physicians would not differ and to exclude opinions based on conjecture or on an evaluation of subjective factors, such as psychiatric diagnoses. 4 J. Weinstein & M. Berger, *Weinstein's Evidence,* ¶ 803(6)[06], 803–199 to 200 (1990). Federal Rule 803(6) makes opinions and diagnoses contained in business records admissible without distinction but subject to exclusion by the trial judge where indicia of trustworthiness are lacking. *Id.* at 803–200 to 201. If the expert can be produced, the trial judge may require him to testify "to ensure trustworthiness through cross-examination," particularly when the issue is crucial and competent experts could disagree. *Ibid.*

The formulation of Rule 808 is intended to include in general terms all of the specific criteria discussed in *Matulewicz.*

ARTICLE IX. AUTHENTICATION AND IDENTIFICATION

Rule 901. Requirement of authentication or identification

The requirement of authentication or identification as a condition precedent to admissibility is satisfied by evidence sufficient to support a finding that the matter is what its proponent claims.

Adopted effective July 1, 1993.

Comment

Rule 901 generally follows *Fed.R.Evid.* 901 and replaces *N.J.Evid.R.* 67. The federal rule includes ten examples of authentication. These examples were not adopted because they are not exclusive nor is the proof set out in them necessarily sufficient in all cases. Rule 901 does not include the provision "or by any other means provided by law" found in the New Jersey rule analogue, *N.J.Evid.R.* 67, since that provision is clearly encompassed by the more inclusive "sufficient evidence" standard. The "law" incorporated by the source rule and still incorporated by this rule refers primarily to statutes which provide for authentication of various documents, such as recorded deeds or other instruments, and for their admission in evidence. *See, e.g., N.J.S.A.* 2A:82–17 and 18. The federal rule, which is followed by this rule, does not preclude proof of authenticity being furnished by operation of law; in fact, the illustration in *Fed. R.Evid.* 901(b)(10) expressly includes "authentication or identification" by any method provided by Act of Congress or Supreme Court rule. Rule 902(h), (i), and (j) provide that evidence of authenticity is satisfied by acknowledgment certificates on documents executed as provided by law, commercial paper

and signatures thereon as provided by applicable law, and documents, signatures and the like as declared by state or federal law.

Rule 902. Self-authentication

Extrinsic evidence of authenticity as a condition precedent to admissibility is not required with respect to the following:

(a) New Jersey public documents. A document purporting to bear a signature affixed in an official capacity by an officer or employee of the State of New Jersey or of a political subdivision, department, office, or agency thereof.

(b) Other domestic public documents. A document (1) bearing a seal purporting to be that of the United States, or of any state, district, commonwealth, territory, or possession thereof, or of a political subdivision, department, office, or agency thereof, and a signature purporting to be an attestation or execution, or (2) purporting to bear a signature affixed in an official capacity by an officer or employee of such an entity, having no seal, if a public officer having a seal and having official duties in the district or political subdivision of the officer or employee certifies under seal that the signer had the official capacity and that the signature is genuine.

(c) Foreign public documents. A document purporting to be executed or attested in an official capacity by a person authorized by the laws of a foreign country to make the execution or attestation, provided that either an apostille is affixed to the document certifying its genuineness pursuant to international agreement to which the United States is a party or the document is accompanied by a final certification as to the genuineness of the signature and official position (1) of the executing or attesting person, or (2) of any foreign official whose certificate of genuineness of signature and official position relates to the execution or attestation or is in a chain of certificates of genuineness of signature and official position relating to the execution or attestation. A final certification may be made by a secretary of embassy or legation, consul general, consul, vice consul, or consular agent of the United States, or a diplomatic or consular official of the foreign country assigned or accredited to the United States. If reasonable opportunity has been given to all parties to investigate the authenticity and accuracy of official documents, the court may, for good cause shown, order that they be treated as presumptively authentic without final certification or permit them to be evidenced by an attested summary with or without final certification.

(d) Certified copies of public records. A copy of an official record or report or entry therein, or of a document authorized by law to be recorded or filed and actually recorded or filed in a public office, including data compilations in any form, certified as correct by the custodian or other person authorized to make the certification, by certificate complying with paragraph (a), (b), or (c) of this rule or complying with any law or rule of court.

(e) Official publications. Books, pamphlets, or other publications purporting to be issued by public authority.

(f) Newspapers and periodicals. Printed materials purporting to be newspapers or periodicals.

(g) Trade inscriptions and the like. Inscriptions, signs, tags, or labels purporting to have been affixed in the course of business and indicating ownership, control, or origin.

(h) Acknowledged documents. Documents accompanied by a certificate of acknowledgment executed in the manner provided by law by a notary public or other officer authorized by law to take acknowledgments.

(i) Commercial paper and related documents. Commercial paper, signatures thereon, and documents relating thereto to the extent provided by applicable commercial law.

(j) Presumption under statute. Any signature, document, or other matter declared by state or federal law to be presumptively or prima facie genuine or authentic.

(k) Certificate of lack of record. A writing asserting the absence of an official record authenticated in the manner prescribed for public documents in paragraph (a), (b), or (c) of this rule.

Adopted effective July 1, 1993.

Comment

Rules 902(a) and (b) generally follow *Fed.R.Evid.* 902(1) and (2) and replace *N.J.Evid.R.* 68(1). These rules retain the distinction in *N.J.Evid.R.* 68(1) between New Jersey public documents and out-of-state public documents. Rule 902(a), which covers New Jersey documents, contains the former New Jersey provision that no seal be required. Rule 902(b), which covers out-of-state documents, does require a seal. The seal requirement for out-of-state documents is consistent with both the federal rule and the New Jersey analogue. Rule 902(b) is substantially the same as *Fed.R.Evid.* 902(1) and (2).

Rule 902(c) follows *Fed.R.Evid.* 902(3) and replaces *N.J.Evid.R.* 68(3). The only change from the federal rule is for the purpose of conforming this rule with the Hague Convention on Authentication of Foreign Documents. That convention allows authentication by apostille as an alternative to final certification by a consular official.

Rule 902(d) is substantially the same as *Fed.R.Evid.* 902(4) and is consistent with present New Jersey practice as generally expressed by *N.J.Evid.R.* 68.

Rule 902(e) follows *Fed.R.Evid.* 902(5) verbatim and makes no change in the substance of *N.J.Evid.R.* 68(1) which it replaces.

Rules 902(f) and (g) follow verbatim *Fed.R.Evid.* 902(6) and (7), respectively. There are no specific 1967 New Jersey rule analogues.

Rules 902(h), (i), and (j) generally follow *Fed. R.Evid.* 902(8), (9), and (10). The only change made in the federal rule is the substitution of the phrase "applicable commercial law" for "general commercial

law" in *Fed.R.Evid.* 902(9). This substitution is intended to make it clear that the law referred to is the law applicable to the specific document in question.

There are no express 1967 New Jersey rule analogues, but these sections would be covered by the provision in *N.J.Evid.R.* 67 for authentication "by any other means provided by law." *See* Comment to Rule 901 above.

Rule 902(k) follows *N.J.Evid.R.* 69. There is no specific federal analogue although the content of this rule is consistent with *Fed.R.Evid.* 902(4). *See* Rule 803(e)(10).

N.J.Evid.R. 68(4), providing prima facie indicia of genuineness, was not adopted since its substance is comprehended by the concept of self-authentication under this rule. Despite authentication under this rule, the genuineness of a document may always be challenged.

Rule 903. Testimony of subscribing witness unnecessary

The testimony of a subscribing witness is not necessary to authenticate a writing unless required by the law of the jurisdiction whose law governs the validity of the writing.

Adopted effective July 1, 1993.

Comment

Rule 903 follows *Fed.R.Evid.* 903 almost verbatim. It replaces *N.J.Evid.R.* 71 without any change in substance.

ARTICLE X. CONTENTS OF WRITINGS AND PHOTOGRAPHS

Rule 1001. Definitions

For purposes of this article the following definitions are applicable:

(a) Writings. "Writings," which include recordings, are defined in Rule 801(e).

(b) Photographs. "Photographs" include still photographs, X-ray films, video tapes, motion pictures and similar forms of reproduced likenesses.

(c) Original. An "original" of a writing is the writing itself or any counterpart intended by the person or persons executing or issuing it to have the same effect. An "original" of a photograph includes the negative or any print therefrom. If data are stored by means of a computer or similar device, any printout or other output readable by sight, shown to reflect the data accurately, is an "original."

(d) Duplicate. A "duplicate" is a counterpart produced by the same impression as the original, or from the same matrix, or by means of photography, including enlargements and reductions, or by mechanical or electronic re-recording, or by chemical reproduction, or by other equivalent technique which accurately reproduces the original.

Adopted effective July 1, 1993.

Rule 1001 generally follows *Fed.R.Evid.* 1001. The only New Jersey rule analogue, *N.J.Evid.R.* 1(13), which is replaced by Rule 801(e), contained a definition of writings and included in that definition reproductions of information and data which is recorded.

Rule 1001(a) merely incorporates the definition of writings in Rule 801(e). That definition was expanded expressly to include recordings.

Rule 1001(b) generally follows *Fed.R.Evid.* 1001(2) but adds the phrase "and similar forms of reproduced likenesses" in an attempt to include and anticipate technological developments.

Rule 1001(c) generally follows *Fed.R.Evid.* 1001(3), but it omits the word "recording" since Rule 1001(a) includes recordings within the definition of a writing. For the same reason the word "recording" has been omitted from Rules 1002, 1004, 1006, 1007, and 1008.

Rule 1001(d) follows *Fed.R.Evid.* 1001(4) almost verbatim. There is no 1967 New Jersey rule analogue. Rule 1003 provides for the admissibility of a duplicate as the equivalent of the original, subject to exceptions contained in that rule.

Rule 1002. Requirement of original

To prove the content of a writing or photograph, the original writing or photograph is required except as otherwise provided in these rules or by statute.

Adopted effective July 1, 1993.

Comment

Rule 1002 follows *Fed.R.Evid.* 1002. It is consistent with the preference for the original of a writing expressed by *N.J.Evid.R.* 70. However, the use of duplicates as authorized by Rule 1002 significantly diminishes the preference previously accorded originals under New Jersey law.

Rule 1003. Admissibility of duplicates

A duplicate as defined by Rule 1001(d) is admissible to the same extent as an original unless (a) a genuine question is raised as to the authenticity of the original, or (b) in the circumstances it would be unfair to admit the duplicate in lieu of the original.

Adopted effective July 1, 1993.

Comment

Rule 1003 follows *Fed.R.Evid.* 1003 almost verbatim. The concept of admitting a duplicate, defined by Rule 1001(d) as the equivalent of an original, is new to New Jersey practice. Rule 1003 provides that a duplicate is generally the equivalent of the original of a document for purposes of admissibility, subject to exceptions provided for in the rule. By contrast, *N.J.Evid.R.* 70 provides generally that no writing other than the "original writing itself is admissible" unless certain conditions are met, such as proof that the original is lost or cannot reasonably be procured.

Rule 1004. Admissibility of other evidence of contents

The original is not required and other evidence of the contents of a writing or photograph is admissible if:

(a) Originals lost or destroyed. All originals are lost or have been destroyed, unless the proponent lost or destroyed them in bad faith; or

(b) Original not obtainable. No original can be obtained by any available judicial process or procedure or by other available means; or

(c) Original in possession of opponent. At a time when an original was under the control of the party against whom offered, that party was put on notice by the pleadings or otherwise that the contents would be a subject of proof at the hearing, and that party does not produce the original at the hearing; or

(d) Collateral matters. The writing or photograph is not closely related to a controlling issue and it would not be expedient to require its production.

Adopted effective July 1, 1993.

Comment

Rule 1004 replaces *N.J.Evid.R.* 70(1)(a), (b), (c), and (d) without substantive change and follows *Fed.R.Evid.* 1004 almost verbatim.

Paragraphs (a) and (c) are identical to *Fed.R.Evid.* 1004(1) and (3), respectively.

The only change which paragraph (b) of this rule makes in *Fed.R.Evid.* 1004(2) is the retention of the provision contained in *N.J.Evid.R.* 70(1)(b) which makes clear that an original is not unavailable if a party can obtain it by other reasonable means in addition to judicial process or procedure.

The only change which paragraph (d) of this rule makes in *Fed.R.Evid.* 1004(4) is the addition of the final clause, taken from *N.J.Evid.R.* 70(1)(d), which requires the use of an original even for collateral matters unless it is not expedient to produce it.

This rule differs from *N.J.Evid.R.* 70 by eliminating the order of preference for secondary evidence provided for by *N.J.Evid.R.* 70(2). That rule placed "oral testimony of the content of the writing" after all "conveniently available written secondary evidence."

Rule 1005. Public records

The contents of an official record or of a writing authorized to be recorded or filed and actually recorded or filed, if otherwise admissible, may be proved by a copy, certified as correct in accordance with Rule 902, or testified to be correct by a witness who has compared it with the original. If a copy which complies with the foregoing cannot be obtained by the exercise of reasonable diligence, other evidence of the contents may be admitted.

Adopted effective July 1, 1993.

Rule 1005 follows *Fed.R.Evid.* 1005 almost verbatim and replaces *N.J.Evid.R.* 70(1)(e) without substantial change in current New Jersey practice.

Rule 1006.   Summaries

The contents of voluminous writings or photographs which cannot conveniently be examined in court may be presented by a qualified witness in the form of a chart, summary, or calculation. The originals, or duplicates, shall be made available for examination or copying, or both, by other parties at a reasonable time and place. The judge may order that they be produced in court.

Adopted effective July 1, 1993.

Comment

Rule 1006 generally follows *Fed.R.Evid.* 1006 and replaces *N.J.Evid.R.* 70(1)(g). The one change which this rule makes in the 1967 New Jersey rule analogue is the elimination of the general requirement that the writings be produced in court. Adopting the principles of the federal rules, this rule requires that the original or duplicates be made available to the other parties at a reasonable time and place. However, the judge may order their production in court.

This rule retains the requirement of *N.J.Evid.R.* 70(1)(g) that the summary be presented by a witness qualified to testify as to its contents. This provision is not contained in the federal rule.

Rule 1007.   Testimony or written admission of party

The contents of writings or photographs may be proved by the testimony or deposition of the party against whom offered or by that party's written admission, without accounting for the nonproduction of the original.

Adopted effective July 1, 1993.

Comment

Rule 1007 follows *Fed.R.Evid.* 1007 almost verbatim and replaces *N.J.Evid.R.* 70(1)(h) with no change in substance.

Rule 1008.   Functions of judge and jury

Ordinarily the judge shall determine the sufficiency of proof of a condition for the admission of evidence of the contents of a writing or photograph other than the original in accordance with Rule 104. However, when a party raises an issue as to (a) whether the asserted writing or photograph ever existed, or (b) whether another writing or photograph produced at the trial is the original, or (c) whether the evidence correctly reflects the content of the original writing or photograph, the issue shall be determined by the trier of fact as in the case of other issues of fact.

Adopted effective July 1, 1993.

Comment

Rule 1008 follows *Fed.R.Evid.* 1008 with language changes only and replaces *N.J.Evid.R.* 70(3) without change in substance.

ARTICLE XI.   MISCELLANEOUS

Rule 1101.   Applicability of rules
[Not Adopted]
Comment

Fed.R.Evid. 1101 was not adopted since the provisions relating to the applicability of these rules of evidence, including privileges, are covered by Rule 101.

Rule 1102.   Amendment of rules
[Not Adopted]
Comment

Fed.R.Evid. 1102, which deals with the procedure for amending the Federal Rules of Evidence, was not adopted. Amendment of the rules of evidence is governed by New Jersey law. *See, e.g., N.J.S.A.* 2A:84A–33 *et seq.*

Rule 1103.   Title

The title of these rules is the *New Jersey Rules of Evidence* and they may be cited as *N.J.R.E.*

Adopted effective July 1, 1993.

Comment

Rule 1103 is based on *Fed.R.Evid.* 1103 with the addition of an approved citation form. There is no 1967 New Jersey rule analogue. Illustratively, the proper citation of this rule is *N.J.R.E.* 1103.

Chapter
93. Bribery and Corruption.
102. Embezzlement, Conversion and Misappropriation.
123. Manufacture, Sale, Etc., of Certain Articles.
149. Unauthorized Use of Voting Machines or Electrical Voting Systems in Legislative or Public Bodies.

CHAPTER 93

BRIBERY AND CORRUPTION

Section
2A:93–5.1. Restitution to victim; hearing.

2A:93–5.1. Restitution to victim; hearing

A person who has been convicted of a violation of N.J.S. 2A:93–4, 2A:93–6, 2A:97–1, 2A:105–1 or 2A:105–2 from which there has occurred pecuniary gain to the offender or pecuniary loss to the victim may be ordered by the court to make restitution to the victim, in addition to paying any fine. In such a case the court shall, without a jury, conduct such hearing as is necessary to make findings as to the monetary amount of the pecuniary gain or pecuniary loss. For the purposes of this section, the term "gain" means the amount of money or the value of property derived by the offender, the term "loss" means the amount of money or the value of property separated from the victim, and the term "victim" includes the State or any of its political or administrative subdivisions. No restitution ordered paid to the victim shall exceed the victim's loss.

L.1977, c. 214, § 9, eff. Sept. 13, 1977.

CHAPTER 102

EMBEZZLEMENT, CONVERSION AND MISAPPROPRIATION

Section
2A:102–13. Advance funeral payments.
2A:102–14. Repayment on demand.
2A:102–15. Invalid advance funeral payment agreements.
2A:102–16. Violations.
2A:102–16.1. Irrevocable prepaid funeral trusts; qualifications of beneficiary or grantor of trust.
2A:102–16.2. Solicitation or inducement of irrevocable prepaid funeral trust with intent to collect or charge more than fair market value; expenditure of trust proceeds on other than funeral goods or services; crimes of fourth degree.
2A:102–17. Exceptions.
2A:102–18. Definitions.

2A:102–13. Advance funeral payments

Any and all moneys paid to a funeral director, undertaker, cemetery, or any other person, firm or corporation, under or in connection with an agreement for the sale of personal property to be used in connection with a funeral or burial, or for the furnishing of personal services of a funeral director, undertaker or cemetery, wherein the personal property is not to be delivered or the personal services are not to be rendered until the occurrence of the death of the person for whose funeral or burial such property or services are to be furnished, shall be trust funds in the possession of such funeral director, undertaker, cemetery, or other person, firm or corporation, and shall be deposited by him or it within 30 days after receipt thereof in a special account maintained exclusively for the deposit of such moneys in a federally insured State or federally chartered bank, savings bank or savings and loan association; or, if the person paying the moneys requests, in a pooled trust account established pursuant to P.L.1985, c. 147 (C.3B:11–16 et al.) and chosen by the person paying the moneys, and shall be so held on deposit, together with any interest thereon, until said personal property has been delivered and said personal services have been rendered, unless sooner repaid, in whole or in part. No depository institution shall be liable for the misuse, misapplication or improper withdrawal by any such funeral director, undertaker, cemetery or other person, firm or corporation, of any moneys deposited in such depository institution pursuant to this act.

Any agreement for funeral goods or funeral services, or both, executed on or after the effective date of P.L.1993, c. 147 by a provider shall comply with the provisions set forth in sections 1 through 13 of P.L.1993, c. 147 (C.45:7–82 to 45:7–94).

L.1957, c. 182, p. 632, § 1, eff. Aug. 15, 1957. Amended by L.1985, c. 147, § 4, eff. April 24, 1985; L.1993, c. 147, § 16, eff. Dec. 21, 1993; L.2009, c. 155, § 1, eff. Nov. 20, 2009.

2A:102–14. Repayment on demand

The amount of any and all moneys paid under or in connection with such an agreement, together with interest, if any, accrued thereon while on deposit as so required shall be repaid on demand at any time prior to the delivery of the personal property or the rendering of the personal services.

L.1957, c. 182, p. 633, § 2.

2A:102–15. Invalid advance funeral payment agreements

Any provision of any such agreement whereby a person who pays money under or in connection therewith waives any provision of this act shall be void.
L.1957, c. 182, p. 633, § 3.

2A:102–16. Violations

Any person, firm or corporation who or which, having received any moneys under or in connection with such an agreement, shall fail to deposit or keep on deposit, misapply or misappropriate or to repay any and all such moneys as provided in this act, is guilty of theft by failure to make the required disposition of property received pursuant to N.J.S.2C:20–9.

Any person, firm or corporation receiving moneys under P.L.1957, c. 182 (C. 2A:102–13 et seq.) is presumed:

a. to know his or its obligations relevant to criminal liability under this section; and

b. to have dealt with property as his or its own if he or it fails to pay or account upon lawful demand or if an audit reveals a shortage or falsification of accounts.
L.1957, c. 182, p. 633, § 4. Amended by L.1993, c. 147, § 17, eff. Dec. 21, 1993.

2A:102–16.1. Irrevocable prepaid funeral trusts; qualifications of beneficiary or grantor of trust

Notwithstanding the provisions of P.L.1957, c. 182 (C. 2A:102–13 et seq.) to the contrary, an agreement may provide that the trust shall be irrevocable during the lifetime of the beneficiary, if at the time of the signing of an agreement, the beneficiary or grantor of the trust is:

a. An aged, blind or disabled applicant for, or recipient of, benefits pursuant to the Supplemental Security Income Program under P.L.1973, c. 256 (C. 44:7–85 et seq.) or any Medicaid program under P.L. 1968, c. 413 (C. 30:4D–1 et seq.) utilizing the eligibility criteria of the Supplemental Security Income Program in regard to burial spaces and funds set aside for burial expenses; or

b. An aged, blind or disabled person who reasonably anticipates applying for, or receiving, the benefits provided for in subsection a. of this section within six months.

An irrevocable trust established pursuant to this section shall not affect the selection of funeral goods or services or the selection of the funeral home. If the beneficiary or grantor of the trust enters into an agreement, reasonably anticipating that the beneficiary or grantor will become an applicant for, or recipient of, these programs within six months from the execution of the agreement, the agreement shall provide that, in the event the beneficiary or grantor of the trust does not become an applicant for, or recipient of, any of these programs within the six month period, the trust shall revert to a revocable trust.

As used in this section "agreement" means an agreement for the sale of personal property to be used in connection with a funeral or burial, or for the furnishing of personal services of a funeral director or undertaker, wherein the personal property is not to be delivered or the personal services are not to be rendered until the occurrence of the death of the person for whose funeral or burial the property or services are to be furnished.
L.1991, c. 502, § 1, eff. Jan. 18, 1992.

2A:102–16.2. Solicitation or inducement of irrevocable prepaid funeral trust with intent to collect or charge more than fair market value; expenditure of trust proceeds on other than funeral goods or services; crimes of fourth degree

a. A person shall be guilty of a crime of the fourth degree if he knowingly or purposefully solicits or induces any person to execute an irrevocable trust pursuant to section 1 of P.L.1991, c. 502 (C. 2A:102–16.1) with an intent to collect or charge more than the fair market value for funeral goods or services.

b. A person shall be guilty of a crime of the fourth degree if the proceeds of the trust are expended on anything other than the fair market value of the funeral goods or services.
L.1991, c. 502, § 3, eff. Jan. 18, 1992.

2A:102–17. Exceptions

This act shall not apply to

a. the sale of lots or graves by a cemetery; or

b. the use of individually issued insurance policies as funding vehicles for prepaid funeral agreements.
L.1957, c. 182, p. 633, § 5. Amended by L.1993, c. 147, § 18, eff. Dec. 21, 1993.

2A:102–18. Definitions

As used in P.L.1957, c. 182 (C. 2A:102–13 et seq.):

"Assigned funeral insurance policy" means any insurance policy or annuity contract that is not a newly issued funeral insurance policy, but that, at the time an assignment was made of some or all of its proceeds, was intended to provide funds to the provider, whether directly or indirectly, at the time of the insured's death in connection with a prepaid funeral agreement.

"Deliver" or "delivery" means the conveyance of actual control and possession of prepaid funeral goods that have been permanently relinquished by a provider, or other person, firm or corporation, or an agent thereof, to the purchaser or person paying the moneys, or personal representative of the intended funeral recipient. Delivery has not been made if the provider, or other person, firm or corporation, or an agent thereof:

(1) Arranges or induces the purchaser or person paying the moneys to arrange for the storage or warehousing of prepaid funeral goods ordered pursuant to a prepaid funeral agreement, with or without evidence that legal title has passed; or

(2) Acquires or reacquires actual or constructive possession or control of prepaid funeral goods after their initial delivery to the purchaser or person paying the moneys or personal representative of the intended funeral recipient.

This definition of delivery shall apply to this term as used in P.L.1957, c. 182 (C. 2A:102–13 et seq.), notwithstanding the provisions set forth in the Uniform Commercial Code, Title 12A of the New Jersey Statutes.

"Funeral insurance policy" means any newly issued funeral insurance policy or assigned funeral insurance policy.

"Funeral trust" means a commingled or non-commingled account held in a pooled trust or P.O.D. account, established in accordance with P.L.1957, c. 182 (C. 2A:102–13 et seq.) or P.L.1985, c. 147 (C. 3B:11–16 et al.), which is intended as the depository for cash payments connected with a prepaid funeral agreement.

"Intended funeral recipient" means the person named in a prepaid funeral agreement for whose bodily disposition the prepaid funeral agreement is intended to provide. The intended funeral recipient may or may not be the purchaser.

"Newly issued funeral insurance policy" means any insurance policy or annuity contract that, at the time of issue, was intended to provide, or was explicitly marketed for the purpose of providing, funds to the provider, whether directly or indirectly, at the time of the insured's death in connection with a prepaid funeral agreement.

"Payable on death account" or "P.O.D. account" means an account payable on request to the purchaser or intended funeral recipient of a prepaid funeral agreement, during the lifetime of the intended funeral recipient and on his death, to a provider of funeral goods and services.

"Pooled trust" means a pooled trust account established pursuant to P.L.1985, c. 147 (C. 3B:11–16 et al.).

"Preneed funeral arrangements" means funeral arrangements made with an intended funeral recipient or his guardian, agent or next of kin, for the funeral of the intended funeral recipient.

"Prepaid funeral agreement" means a written agreement and all documents related thereto made by a purchaser with a provider prior to the death of the intended funeral recipient, with which there is connected a provisional means of paying for preneed funeral arrangements upon the death of the intended funeral recipient by the use of a funeral trust or funeral insurance policy, made payable to a provider and in return for which the provider promises to furnish, make

available or provide the prepaid funeral goods or services, or both, specified in the agreement, the delivery of which occurs after the death of the intended funeral recipient.

"Prepaid funeral goods" means personal property typically sold or provided in connection with a funeral, or the final disposition of human remains, including, but not limited to, caskets or other primary containers, cremation or transportation containers, outer burial containers, vaults, as defined in N.J.S.8A:1–2, memorials as defined in N.J.S.8A:1–2, funeral clothing or accessories, monuments, cremation urns, and similar funeral or burial items, which goods are purchased in advance of need and which will not be delivered until the death of the intended funeral recipient named in a prepaid funeral agreement. Prepaid funeral goods shall not mean the sale of interment spaces and related personal property offered or sold by a cemetery company as provided for in N.J.S.8A:1–1 et seq.

"Prepaid funeral services" means those services typically provided in connection with a funeral, or the final disposition of human remains, including, but not limited to, funeral directing services, embalming services, care of human remains, preparation of human remains for final disposition, transportation of human remains, use of facilities or equipment for viewing human remains, visitation, memorial services or services which are used in connection with a funeral or the disposition of human remains, coordinating or conducting funeral rites or ceremonies and similar funeral or burial services, including limousine services provided in connection therewith, which services are purchased in advance of need and which will not be provided or delivered until the death of the intended funeral recipient named in a prepaid funeral agreement. Prepaid funeral services shall not mean the sale of services incidental to the provision of interment spaces or any related personal services offered or sold by a cemetery company as provided for in N.J.S.8A:1–1 et seq.

"Provider" means a person, firm or corporation duly licensed and registered pursuant to the "Mortuary Science Act," P.L.1952, c. 340 (C. 45:7–32 et seq.) to engage in the business and practice of funeral directing or mortuary science, or an individual serving as an agent thereof and so licensed:

(1) Operating a duly registered mortuary in accordance with P.L.1952, c. 340 (C. 45:7–32 et seq.) and the regulations promulgated thereunder;

(2) Having his or its business and practice based within the physical confines of the registered mortuary; and

(3) Engaging in the practice of making preneed funeral arrangements, including, but not limited to, offering the opportunity to purchase or enroll in prepaid funeral agreements.

"Purchaser" means the person named in a prepaid funeral agreement who purchases the prepaid funeral goods and services to be provided thereunder. The purchaser may or may not be the intended funeral recipient. If the purchaser is different than the intended funeral recipient, it is understood that the relationship of the purchaser to the intended funeral recipient includes a means to provide administrative control over the agreement on behalf of the intended funeral recipient.

L.1993, c. 147, § 19, eff. Dec. 21, 1993.   Amended by L.1994, c. 163, § 3, eff. Dec. 20, 1994.

CHAPTER 123

MANUFACTURE, SALE, ETC., OF CERTAIN ARTICLES

Section
2A:123–3.   Definitions.
2A:123–4.   Short title.
2A:123–5.   Manufacture, sale or transportation of flammable wearing apparel forbidden.
2A:123–6.   Articles deemed highly flammable.
2A:123–7.   Enforcement of act; rules and regulations.
2A:123–8.   Filing of rules and regulations; amendment and revision.
2A:123–9.   Inspection of places where wearing apparel or fabrics are sold or manufactured.
2A:123–10. Injunction; confiscation proceedings; bond.
2A:123–11. Violations; penalty.
2A:123–12. Penalties inapplicable to person who furnishes guaranty.
2A:123–13. Exemptions from provisions of act.
2A:123–14. Wearing apparel or fabrics being transported or held for delivery.
2A:123–15. Effective date.
2A:123–16. Definitions.
2A:123–17. Nonflame resistant sleeping bags or tents; prohibition of sale, holding for sale or transportation for sale.
2A:123–18. Standards and regulations.
2A:123–19. Inspection of places for sale of articles.
2A:123–20. Violations; injunctions; confiscation of articles.
2A:123–21. Violations; penalties.
2A:123–22. Violations; inapplicability of penalty; guaranty of flame resistance by supplier or manufacturer of article.
2A:123–23. Exemptions from application of act.
2A:123–24. Inapplicability of act to articles in transit or being held for delivery.

2A:123–3.   Definitions

As used in this act the following words shall have the following meanings:

"Articles of wearing apparel" means any costume or article of clothing worn or intended to be worn by individuals except hats, gloves and footwear; provided, however, that such hats do not constitute, nor are part of a covering for the neck, face or shoulders when worn by individuals; and provided, further, that such gloves are not more than fourteen inches in length and are not affixed to or do not form an integral part of another garment; and provided, further, that such footwear does not consist of hosiery, in whole or in part, and is

not affixed to nor does not form an integral part of another garment.

"Fabric" means any material (other than a fiber, filament or yarn) woven, knitted, felted or otherwise produced from or in combination with any natural or synthetic filament or substitute therefor which is intended or sold for use in wearing apparel except that interlining fabrics, when intended or sold for use in wearing apparel, shall not be subject to this act.

"Interlining" means any fabric which is intended for incorporation into an article of wearing apparel as a layer between an outer shell and an inner lining.

"Commissioner" means the Commissioner of Labor and Industry of the State of New Jersey.

"Department" means the Department of Labor and Industry of the State of New Jersey.

"Sale," "sell" or "sold" means offering or exposing for sale or exchange or hire or lease, or consigning and delivering in consignment for sale, exchange, hire, or lease, or holding in possession with like intent. The possession of any article of wearing apparel or fabric, as herein defined, by any manufacturer or dealer, or his agent or servant in the course of business shall be presumptive evidence of intent to sell.

"Manufacture" means making, make or made, and includes converting, processing, altering, repairing, finishing, or preparing for sale any article of wearing apparel or fabric as wearing apparel and fabric are herein defined.

L.1953, c. 267, p. 1787, § 1, eff. Jan. 1, 1954.

2A:123–4.   Short title

This act shall be known and may be cited as the "Flammable Fabrics Act."

L.1953, c. 267, p. 1788, § 2, eff. Jan. 1, 1954.

2A:123–5.   Manufacture, sale or transportation of flammable wearing apparel forbidden

The manufacture for, or sale or offer for sale, transport or causing to be transported for the purpose of sale or delivery after sale within the State of New Jersey of any article of wearing apparel or fabric which, under the provisions of section four of this act,[1] is so highly flammable as to be dangerous when worn by individuals shall be unlawful.

L.1953, c. 267, p. 1788, § 3, eff. Jan. 1, 1954.

[1] N.J.S.A. § 2A:123–6.

2A:123–6.   Articles deemed highly flammable

Any article of wearing apparel or fabric shall be deemed so highly flammable, as to be dangerous when worn by individuals, within the meaning of this act, if any uncovered or exposed part of such article of wearing apparel or fabric exhibits rapid and intense combustion or burning when tested under the conditions and in the manner prescribed by rules and regulations adopted by the commissioner pursuant to section five of this act.[1]

L.1953, c. 267, p. 1788, § 4, eff. Jan. 1, 1954.

[1] N.J.S.A. § 2A:123–7.

2A:123–7. Enforcement of act; rules and regulations

This act, except as herein otherwise specifically provided, shall be enforced by the department, and the commissioner is hereby authorized and directed to adopt, amend and enforce rules and regulations establishing the conditions under which, and the manner in which, articles of wearing apparel or fabric shall be tested to determine whether or not they are so highly flammable, as to be dangerous when worn by individuals, within the meaning of this act, if any uncovered or exposed part of such article of wearing apparel or fabric exhibits rapid and intense burning when so tested, if such conditions and manner of testing shall, in all respects, from time to time, conform to the conditions and manner prescribed in the Commercial Standard promulgated by the Secretary of Commerce of the United States of America effective January 30, 1953, and identified as "Flammability of Clothing Textiles, Commercial Standard 191–53," or in the Commercial Standard promulgated by the Secretary of Commerce effective May 22, 1953, and identified as "General Purpose Vinyl Plastic Film, Commercial Standard 192–53," and modifications or supplements thereto enacted by the Congress of the United States or promulgated by the Secretary of Commerce of the United States of America which shall result from, and be developed under, the same procedures as were in use and effect in connection with the establishment of "Flammability of Clothing Textiles, Commercial Standard 191–53," or "General Purpose Vinyl Plastic Film, Commercial Standard 192–53," and also to adopt, amend and enforce rules and regulations designed and intended to effectuate the general purposes of this act and the specific objectives herein set forth, which said rules and regulations shall include the authorization to the commissioner to cause inspections, analyses, tests and examinations to be made of any article of wearing apparel or fabric which he has reason to believe falls within the prohibitions of this act.

L.1953, c. 267, p. 1788, § 5, eff. Jan. 1, 1954. Amended by L.1954, c. 210, p. 777, § 1, eff. Aug. 5, 1954.

2A:123–8. Filing of rules and regulations; amendment and revision

Such rules and regulations promulgated by the commissioner pursuant to this act shall be filed in the offices of the Secretary of State and of the department before becoming effective and may from time to time be amended and revised.

L.1953, c. 267, p. 1789, § 6, eff. Jan. 1, 1954.

2A:123–9. Inspection of places where wearing apparel or fabrics are sold or manufactured

Every place where articles of wearing apparel or fabrics are sold or manufactured shall be subject to inspection by the commissioner, who shall have power to inspect the manufacture or sale or delivery of all such articles of wearing apparel or fabrics covered by this act. The commissioner shall have power to cause examinations and tests to be made of such articles of wearing apparel or fabrics and to seize and hold as evidence any article of wearing apparel or fabric which is made or sold or held in possession in violation of this act or of the rules and regulations promulgated hereunder.

L.1953, c. 267, p. 1789, § 7, eff. Jan. 1, 1954.

2A:123–10. Injunction; confiscation proceedings; bond

Whenever the department has reason to believe that any article of wearing apparel has been manufactured or has been offered for sale in violation of the provisions of this act or of the rules and regulations promulgated hereunder, proceedings to enjoin such manufacture or sale or other disposition of such wearing apparel or fabrics may be instituted by the commissioner in the Superior Court of the State of New Jersey, and said commissioner may also institute proceedings for the confiscation of such article of wearing apparel or fabric in said Superior Court of the State of New Jersey and shall make such disposition of said wearing apparel or fabric as he shall be ordered so to do by said Superior Court of the State of New Jersey; provided, however, that said Superior Court may order the delivery of such condemned articles of wearing apparel or fabric to the owner or claimant thereof upon payment of legal costs and charges and upon the execution and deposit with said Superior Court of a good and sufficient bond conditioned upon said articles of wearing apparel or fabric not being disposed of until properly and adequately treated or processed so that such articles of wearing apparel or fabrics will comply with the provisions of this act and the rules and regulations promulgated pursuant thereto.

L.1953, c. 267, p. 1790, § 8, eff. Jan. 1, 1954.

2A:123–11. Violations; penalty

Any person who willfully violates this act shall forfeit and pay a penalty of not less than two hundred dollars ($200.00) and not more than five hundred dollars ($500.00) for the first offense, nor less than five hundred dollars ($500.00) or more than one thousand dollars ($1,000.00) for the second or any subsequent offense, to be sued for and recovered by and in the name of the department in a summary proceeding in accordance with the penalty enforcement law. (N.J.S. 2A:58–1 et seq.) Each article of wearing apparel or fabric made, sold or exposed for sale shall constitute a separate violation.

L.1953, c. 267, p. 1790, § 9, eff. Jan. 1, 1954.

2A:123–12. Penalties inapplicable to person who furnishes guaranty

The penalties provided for a violation of this act shall not apply to any person who establishes (1) a guaranty received in good faith, signed by and containing the name and address of the person by whom the fabric or wearing apparel covered by the guaranty was manufactured or from whom it was received, to the effect that reasonable and representative tests made under the rules and regulations in accordance with the procedures prescribed in this act show that the specific type of fabric covered by the guaranty and used in the wearing apparel or fabric covered by the guaranty when so tested was not highly flammable within the meaning of this act; and (2), that he has not, by further processing affected the flammability of the fabric or wearing apparel covered by the guaranty which he received. Such guaranty shall either be (1) a separate guaranty specifically designating the wearing apparel or fabric guaranteed, in which case it may be on the invoice or other paper relating to such wearing apparel or fabric; or (2) continuing guaranty filed with the commissioner or with the Federal Trade Commission applicable to any wearing apparel or fabric handled by the guarantor in such form as the commissioner or the Federal Trade Commission, as the case may be, by rules and regulations, may prescribe. It is provided, however, that a person furnishing such a guaranty (except a person relying upon a guaranty received in good faith to furnish a guaranty to the same effect, if he, by further processing, has not affected the flammability of the wearing apparel or fabric covered by the guaranty) shall not be relieved thereby from any of the penalties prescribed for the violations of this act.

L.1953, c. 267, p. 1791, § 10, eff. Jan. 1, 1954. Amended by L.1954, c. 210, p. 778, § 2, eff. Aug. 5, 1954.

2A:123–13. Exemptions from provisions of act

The provisions of this act shall not apply (a) to any common carrier, contract carrier or freight forwarder with respect to an article of wearing apparel or fabric shipped or delivered for shipment in the ordinary course of its business; or (b) to any person manufacturing, delivering for shipment, shipping, selling or offering for sale or export from the United States of America to any foreign country an article of wearing apparel or fabric made in accordance with the specifications of the purchaser; or (c) to any convertor, processor, or finisher in performing a contract or commission service for the account of a person subject to the provisions of this act; provided, however, that said convertor, processor, or finisher does not cause any article of wearing apparel or fabric to become subject to this act contrary to the terms of the contract or commission service; or (d) to any article of wearing apparel or fabric shipped or delivered for shipment into commerce for the purpose of finishing or processing to render article or fabric not highly flammable under the provisions of this act and to the rules and regulations promulgated pursuant thereto.

L.1953, c. 267, p. 1791, § 11, eff. Jan. 1, 1954.

2A:123–14. Wearing apparel or fabrics being transported or held for delivery

Nothing contained in this act shall apply to such wearing apparel or fabrics while being transported upon vessels, vehicles or railroad cars, or while being held for delivery; provided, such transport and delivery is subject to and in conformity with regulations now or hereafter prescribed by the Interstate Commerce Commission.

L.1953, c. 267, p. 1792, § 12, eff. Jan. 1, 1954.

2A:123–15. Effective date

This act shall take effect January first, one thousand nine hundred and fifty-four.

L.1953, c. 267, p. 1792, § 13.

2A:123–16. Definitions

As used in this act:

a. "Director" means the Director of the Division of Consumer Affairs and his designated representatives.

b. "Flame resistant" means the ability of a material to resist combustion and the conduction or continuation of fire when an ignition source is removed.

c. "Sale," "sell" or "sold" means offering or exposing for sale, or exchange or hire or lease, or consigning and delivering in consignment for sale, exchange, hire, or lease, or holding in possession with like intent. The possession of any tents or sleeping bags, as herein defined, by any dealer, or his agent or servant in the course of business shall be presumptive of intent to sell.

d. "Sleeping bag" means a bag that is usually lined or padded and normally designed for sleeping outdoors or in a camp or tent.

e. "Tent" means a collapsible shelter, for one or more persons, of canvas or other material, either natural or synthetic or any combination thereof, stretched and sustained by poles and used for camping outdoors or as a temporary building.

L.1975, c. 286, § 1, eff. Jan. 12, 1976.

2A:123–17. Nonflame resistant sleeping bags or tents; prohibition of sale, holding for sale or transportation for sale

It shall be unlawful for anyone to sell, hold for sale, or to cause the transportation for purposes of sale or delivery after sale within the State any sleeping bag or tent that is not classified by the Director of the Division of Consumer Affairs as being flame resistant according to the standards and regulations that the director shall promulgate pursuant to this act.

L.1975, c. 286, § 2, eff. Dec. 1, 1976.

2A:123–18. Standards and regulations

The director is authorized, empowered and directed, within 6 months of the effective date of this act, to establish and to promulgate pursuant to law, such standards and regulations necessary to implement and enforce this act; provided, however, that all such standards and regulations, including standards and facilities for testing material for its compliance with this act, shall be acceptable and safe standards for flame resistance.

L.1975, c. 286, § 3, eff. Jan. 12, 1976.

2A:123–19. Inspection of places for sale of articles

Every place where tents and sleeping bags are sold shall be subject to inspection by the director, or his agents who shall have power to inspect the sale or delivery of all such tents,[1] sleeping bags, covered by this act. The director shall have the power to cause examinations and tests to be made of such tents and sleeping bags and to seize and hold as evidence any such article sold or held in possession in violation of this act or of the rules and regulations promulgated hereunder.

L.1975, c. 286, § 4, eff. Jan. 12, 1976.

1 So in enrolled bill.

2A:123–20. Violations; injunctions; confiscation of articles

Whenever the director has reason to believe that any tent or sleeping bag has been offered for sale in violation of the provisions of this act or of the rules and regulations promulgated hereunder, proceedings to enjoin such sale or other disposition of such articles may be instituted by the director in the Superior Court, and said director may also institute proceedings for the confiscation of such tents or sleeping bags in said Superior Court and shall make such disposition of said tents or sleeping bags as he shall be ordered so to do by the court; provided, however, that the court may order the delivery or such confiscated articles to the owner or claimant thereof upon payment of legal costs and charges and upon the execution and deposit with the court of a good and sufficient bond conditioned upon said tents or sleeping bags not being disposed of until properly and adequately treated or processed so that such articles will comply with the provisions of this act and the rules and regulations promulgated pursuant thereto.

L.1975, c. 286, § 5, eff. Jan. 12, 1976.

2A:123–21. Violations; penalties

Any person who willfully violates this act shall forfeit and pay a penalty of not less than $200.00 nor more than $500.00 for the first offense, and not less than $500.00 nor more than $1,000.00 for the second or any subsequent offense, to be sued for and recovered by and in the name of the division in a summary proceeding in accordance with the penalty enforcement law (N.J.S. 2A:58–1 et seq.). Each tent or sleeping bag sold or exposed for sale shall constitute a separate violation.

L.1975, c. 286, § 6, eff. Jan. 12, 1976.

2A:123–22. Violations; inapplicability of penalty; guaranty of flame resistance by supplier or manufacturer of article

The penalties provided for a violation of this act shall not apply to any person who establishes a guaranty received in good faith, signed by and containing the name and address of the person by whom the tent or sleeping bag covered by the guaranty was manufactured or from whom it was received, to the effect that reasonable and representative tests made under the rules and regulations in accordance with the procedures prescribed in this act show that the specific type tent or sleeping bag covered by the guaranty when so tested was flame resistant within the meaning of this act; and that he has not, by further processing affected the flammability of the tent or sleeping bag covered by the guaranty which he received. Such guaranty shall either be a separate guaranty specifically designating the tent or sleeping bag guaranteed, in which case it may be on the invoice or other paper relating to such articles, or a continuing guaranty filed with the director or with the Federal Trade Commission applicable to any tent or sleeping bag handled by the guarantor in such form as the director or the Federal Trade Commission, as the case may be, by rules and regulations, may prescribe. It is provided, however, that a person furnishing such a guaranty, except a person relying upon a guaranty received in good faith to furnish a guaranty to the same effect, if he, by further processing, has not affected the flammability of the tent or sleeping bag covered by the guaranty, shall not be relieved thereby from any of the penalties prescribed for the violations of this act.

L.1975, c. 286, § 7, eff. Jan. 12, 1976.

2A:123–23. Exemptions from application of act

The provisions of this act shall not apply (a) to any common carrier, contract carrier or freight forwarder with respect to any tent or sleeping bag shipped or delivered for shipment in the ordinary course of its business; or (b) to any person manufacturing, delivering for shipment, shipping, selling or offering for sale or export any tent or sleeping bag from this State to any other state or foreign country, or (c) to any convertor, processor, or finisher in performing a contract or commission service for the account of a person subject to the provisions of this act; provided, however, that said convertor, processor, or finisher does not cause any tent or sleeping bag to become subject to this act contrary to the terms of the contract or commission service; or (d) to any tent or sleeping bag shipped or delivered for shipment into commerce for the purpose of finishing or processing to render the articles flame resistant under the provisions of this act or the rules and regulations promulgated pursuant thereto.

L.1975, c. 286, § 8, eff. Jan. 12, 1976.

2A:123–24. Inapplicability of act to articles in transit or being held for delivery

Nothing contained in this act shall apply to tents or sleeping bags being transported upon vessels, vehicles or railroad cars, or being held for delivery; provided, such transport and delivery is subject to and in conformity with regulations now or hereafter prescribed by the Interstate Commerce Commission.

L.1975, c. 286, § 9, eff. Jan. 12, 1976.

CHAPTER 149

UNAUTHORIZED USE OF VOTING MACHINES OR ELECTRICAL VOTING SYSTEMS IN LEGISLATIVE OR PUBLIC BODIES

Section
2A:149–1. Unauthorized use of voting machine or electrical voting system for recording votes.

2A:149–1. Unauthorized use of voting machine or electrical voting system for recording votes

Any person who uses a voting machine or electrical voting system of any legislative or other public body of this state for the purpose of recording a vote or votes thereon or thereby upon any matter or question being considered or voted upon by the members of such legislative or public body, and who is not entitled to use the same for those purposes, is guilty of a misdemeanor.

SUBTITLE 11

CRIMINAL PROCEDURE

Chapter
152. Definitions, Construction and General Provisions.
153. Rewards for Apprehension of Persons Accused of Crime.
154. Peace Officers.
155. Uniform Fresh Pursuit Law.
156. Uniform Act on Intrastate Fresh Pursuit.
156A. Wiretapping, Etc.
157. County Detectives and Investigators.
158. County Prosecutors.
158A. Public Defender.
159A. Interstate Agreement on Detainers.
160. Extradition.
161. Preliminary Proceedings in General.
161A. Personal Searches.
162. Bail and Recognizances.
163. Trial.
164. Sentence and Imprisonment.
166. Costs and Fines.
166A. Reimbursement to Counties for Criminal Prosecution Expenses.
167. Executive Clemency.
168. Probation and Parole.
168A. Rehabilitated Convicted Offenders.

CHAPTER 152

DEFINITIONS, CONSTRUCTION AND GENERAL PROVISIONS

Section
2A:152–1. Definitions.
2A:152–2. Forfeiture of estate and benefit of clergy abolished.
2A:152–3. Information not to lie.
2A:152–4. Laws relating to particular counties or localities not affected.
2A:152–5 to 2A:152–11. Repealed.
2A:152–12. Continued violations of criminal law in municipalities; notice to municipal authorities.
2A:152–13. Notice as authority to make complaint; warrants; absence of liability.
2A:152–14 to 2A:152–16. Repealed.
2A:152–17. Payment of transcripts for indigent defendants in criminal cases.
2A:152–18. Reimbursement.
2A:152–19. Effective date.

2A:152–1. Definitions

In the construction of this subtitle, the following words shall, unless repugnant to the context, or unless another and different definition or meaning is expressly given or stated, have the meaning herein given to them:

"Indictment" includes "accusation of crime."

"Property" shall include every matter or thing, whether real or personal, tangible or intangible, upon or with respect to which any offense may be committed.

"Prosecutor" includes "prosecutor of the pleas," "county prosecutor," "prosecuting officer" and "prosecuting attorney."

2A:152–2. Forfeiture of estate and benefit of clergy abolished

No conviction or judgment for any offense against this state, shall make or work corruption of blood, disinhersion of heirs, loss of dower, or forfeiture of estate.

The benefit of clergy is abolished.

2A:152–3. Information not to lie

No information for a matter merely criminal for which an indictment will lie, and in which no civil right is involved, or forfeiture or penalty given by law to any private person or common informer is prosecuted for, shall be exhibited or sustained in any court of this state.

2A:152–4. Laws relating to particular counties or localities not affected

R.S. 2:178–4 saved from repeal. (This section provides that nothing in this subtitle shall be construed to repeal or alter any law or part thereof which refers to particular counties or other localities.)

2A:152–5 to 2A:152–11. Repealed by L.1978, c. 95, § 2C:98–2, eff. Sept. 1, 1979

2A:152–12. Continued violations of criminal law in municipalities; notice to municipal authorities

Whenever the mayor or other chief executive, or the chief of police or other head officer of police, of any municipality, shall be notified by a written communication delivered to him personally, signed by the governor or attorney general, or by a judge of the Superior Court or the prosecutor of the county in which the municipality is situate, stating that it is alleged, and that there is reason to believe it to be true, that there exists in one or more places in such municipality, designated in the communication, open, continued or notorious violation of Title 2C of the New Jersey Statutes, which section or sections shall be stated in such communication, by any person occupying or carrying on business in such place or places, whether such person be known or unknown, the mayor or other chief executive or the chief of police or other head police officer so notified shall take immediate, proper and efficient measures, by complaint and arrest or by raid and arrest or otherwise, to prevent the further continuance of such illegal practices and to bring any person so alleged to be offending to justice. *Amended by L.1991, c. 91, § 119, eff. April 9, 1991.*

2A:152–13. Notice as authority to make complaint; warrants; absence of liability

The receipt of the communication mentioned in section 2A:152–12 of this title, by any officer named in said section, shall be sufficient warrant and authority for such officer to make a complaint upon information and belief founded thereon, charging that such person, known or unknown, is engaged in such illegal practices and violating the criminal laws of this state as in the communication stated, and any judge or magistrate having jurisdiction to issue criminal process may take and receive such complaint and issue a warrant for the arrest of such person, known or unknown, found upon the premises designated in the communication, and direct that such person be brought before such judge or magistrate to be dealt with as law and justice shall require.

The officer making any complaint hereunder shall not be liable to any action, civil or criminal, by any person taken upon or found in the place or places mentioned in the written communication.

2A:152–14 to 2A:152–16. Repealed by L.1978, c. 95, § 2C:98–2, eff. Sept. 1, 1979

2A:152–17. Payment of transcripts for indigent defendants in criminal cases

Any person convicted of any crime may make application under oath to any judge of the Law Division of the Superior Court of the county where the venue was laid showing that a copy of the transcript of the record, testimony and proceedings at the trial is necessary for the filing of any application with the trial court, and that he is unable, by reason of poverty, to defray the expense of procuring the same, and any such judge may, being satisfied of the facts stated and of the sufficiency thereof, certify the expense thereof to the county treasurer, who shall thereupon pay such expense, the amount thereof having been approved by the judge to whom such application was made. Where such person appeals to the Appellate Division of the Superior Court and copies of the transcript of the proceedings in the trial court are needed therefor he may make a similar application to such court which, being satisfied of the facts stated and the sufficiency thereof, may certify the expense and amount thereof to the county treasurer who shall thereupon pay such expense. *L.1956, c. 134, p. 555, § 1. Amended by L.1991, c. 91, § 120, eff. April 9, 1991.*

2A:152–18. Reimbursement

The county treasurer shall file a notice of said payment and the amount thereof with the institution in which said person, upon whose application the transcript of the record was prepared, is confined, and, to the extent of the expense incurred, the county treasurer shall be reimbursed from any institutional earnings of such person, in the event that the application for relief is denied by the trial court or an appellate court. *L.1956, c. 134, p. 555, § 2.*

2A:152–19. Effective date

This act [1] shall take effect January 1, 1957.

L.1956, c. 134, p. 556, § 3.

[1] N.J.S.A. §§ 2A:152–17 to 2A:152–19.

CHAPTER 153

REWARDS FOR APPREHENSION OF PERSONS ACCUSED OF CRIME

Section
2A:153–1.   Authority of governor in general.
2A:153–2.   Authority of chosen freeholders.
2A:153–3.   Escaped county prisoners; authority of chosen freeholders.
2A:153–4.   Apprehension of persons accused of crimes; authority of municipal governing body.
2A:153–4.1.   Apprehension of persons guilty of damaging property by acts of graffiti; ordinance; determination of recipients of reward.

2A:153–1. Authority of governor in general

The governor or person administering the government for the time being may issue a proclamation for apprehending and securing any person, known or unknown, charged, on oath of one or more credible witnesses, with having committed murder, kidnapping, burglary, robbery, arson or other heinous crime within this state, or for apprehending any person charged with aiding, abetting or concealing any such person, and in such proclamation may offer such reward as he may think proper, according to the nature and aggravation of the crime, not exceeding $25,000 for any 1 person. The reward shall be paid, on conviction of the party charged, to such person or persons as the governor or person administering the government for the time being may, in his discretion, deem entitled thereto. Such payment shall be made by the state treasurer, out of any public money in his hands unappropriated, on warrant of the comptroller under certification of the governor or person administering the government for the time being.

2A:153–2. Authority of chosen freeholders

The board of chosen freeholders of any county, on the recommendation and request in writing of the prosecutor of the county, approved by a judge of the Superior Court may offer a reward not exceeding $5,000 for the detection and apprehension of any person guilty of murder, kidnapping, burglary, robbery, arson or other heinous crime in such county, the reward to be payable after conviction out of such funds of the county as may be applicable thereto. The reward shall be paid to such person or persons as the board of chosen freeholders may, in its discretion, deem entitled thereto.

Amended by L.1991, c. 91, § 121, eff. April 9, 1991.

2A:153–3. Escaped county prisoners; authority of chosen freeholders

The board of chosen freeholders of any county may publicly advertise the escape of any prisoner or prisoners from any penal institution in such county, and may offer a reward not exceeding $300 for the detection and apprehension of each of such escaped prisoners. Any reward offered hereunder shall be payable only after the recapture and return of the prisoner or prisoners to the institution from which the escape was made. The amount of the reward and the expense of advertising shall be paid out of such funds of the county as may be applicable thereto. The reward shall be paid to such person or persons as the board of chosen freeholders may, in its discretion, deem entitled thereto.

2A:153–4. Apprehension of persons accused of crimes; authority of municipal governing body

The governing body of any municipality, on the recommendation and request in writing of the municipal police chief or principal law enforcement officer of such municipality, approved by a judge of the Superior Court may offer a reward not exceeding $3,000.00 for the detection and apprehension of any person guilty of murder, kidnapping, burglary, robbery, arson, or other heinous crime in such municipality; the reward is to be payable after conviction out of such funds of the municipality as may be applicable thereto. The reward shall be paid to such person or persons as the municipal governing body may, in its discretion, deem entitled thereto, but no such reward may be paid to any public employee, whose duty it is to investigate or to enforce the law.

L.1967, c. 171, § 1, eff. July 25, 1967. Amended by L.1991, c. 91, § 122, eff. April 9, 1991.

2A:153–4.1. Apprehension of persons guilty of damaging property by acts of graffiti; ordinance; determination of recipients of reward

The governing body of any municipality may, by ordinance, provide for the offering of rewards not exceeding $500.00 each, for the detection and apprehension of any person guilty of purposely or knowingly damaging tangible property of another by an act of graffiti in violation of N.J.S. 2C:17–3. A reward is to be payable after conviction out of those funds of the municipality made available therefor. The reward shall be paid to any person who the governing body, acting upon the recommendation of the municipal chief of police or other principal municipal law enforcement officer, may deem entitled thereto, but no reward shall be paid to any public employee whose duty it is to investigate or to enforce the law or to the employee's spouse, child or parent, living in the same household.

For the purposes of this act, "act of graffiti" means the drawing, painting or the making of any inscription on a bridge, building, public transportation vehicle, rock, wall, sidewalk, street or other exposed surface on public or private property without the permission of the owner.

L.1987, c. 45, § 1, eff. Feb. 19, 1987.

CHAPTER 154

PEACE OFFICERS

Section
2A:154–1. Conservators of the peace; powers and duties.
2A:154–2. Qualifications of peace officers.
2A:154–3. Court attendants, sheriff's officers and county correction officers as peace officers.
2A:154–4. Correction officers, parole officers and investigators in department of corrections as peace officers.
2A:154–5. Federal law enforcement officers empowered to arrest offenders against laws of state.
2A:154–6. Department of the Interior park police.

2A:154–1. Conservators of the peace; powers and duties

Any judge of the Superior Court, or of a municipal court shall have power to cause to be kept all laws made or to be made for the conservation of the peace and for the good government of the citizens and inhabitants of this State, within their respective counties, according to the force, form and effect of such laws, and to apprehend, and to cause to come before them, and imprison and punish all persons offending against such laws, or any of them, in their respective counties, in such manner as, according to such laws, shall be right and proper, and to perform and execute all such matters, acts and things as by law appertain to their office, and are or shall be enjoined upon them, or be committed to their charge and execution.

Amended by L.1991, c. 91, § 123, eff. April 9, 1991.

2A:154–2. Qualifications of peace officers

No sheriff or other person authorized to appoint special deputy sheriffs, constables, marshals, policemen or other peace officers in this state, for the purpose of preserving the public peace and preventing or quelling public disturbances, shall appoint as such any person who is not a qualified voter of this state.

2A:154–3. Court attendants, sheriff's officers and county correction officers as peace officers

a. All court attendants, sheriff's officers and county correction officers in the competitive class of civil service who have been or who may hereafter be appointed by the sheriff or board of chosen freeholders of any county in this State shall, by virtue of such appointment and in addition to any other power or authority, be empowered to act as officers for the detection, apprehension, arrest and conviction of offenders against the law.

b. In addition to the powers set forth in subsection a. of this section, any county correction officer who has satisfactorily completed a basic training course approved by the Police Training Commission, as provided by P.L.1961, c. 56 (C. 52:17B–66 et seq.), shall have full power of arrest for any crime committed in his presence anywhere within the territorial limits of the State of New Jersey.

c. A county correction officer who has full power of arrest pursuant to subsection b. of this section, and is acting under lawful authority beyond the territorial limits of his employing county, shall have all of the immunities from tort liability and shall have all of the pension, relief, disability, workers' compensation, insurance, and other benefits enjoyed while performing duties within the employing county.

Amended by L.1968, c. 326, § 1, eff. Nov. 4, 1968; L.1968, c. 398, § 1, eff. Jan. 10, 1969; L.1993, c. 248, § 1, eff. Aug. 9, 1993; L.1996, c. 40, § 1, eff. June 20, 1996.

2A:154–4. Correction officers, parole officers and investigators in department of corrections as peace officers

All correction officers of the State of New Jersey, parole officers employed by the State Parole Board and investigators in the Department of Corrections, who have been or who may hereafter be appointed or employed, shall, by virtue of such appointment or employment and in addition to any other power or authority, be empowered to act as officers for the detection, apprehension, arrest and conviction of offenders against the law.

L.1968, c. 427, § 1, eff. Jan. 27, 1969. Amended by L.1982, c. 230, § 2, eff. Dec. 31, 1982; L.1993, c. 246, § 1, eff. Aug. 9, 1993; L.2001, c. 79, § 14, eff. Sept. 1, 2001.

2A:154–5. Federal law enforcement officers empowered to arrest offenders against laws of state

The following persons employed as full-time law enforcement officers by the Federal Government, who are empowered to effect an arrest with or without a warrant for violations of the United States Code and who are authorized to carry firearms in the performance of their duties, shall be empowered to act as an officer for the arrest of offenders against the laws of this State where the person reasonably believes that a crime of the first, second or third degree is or is about to be committed or attempted in his presence:

Federal Bureau of Investigation special agents;

United States Secret Service special agents;

Immigration and Naturalization Service special agents, investigators and patrol officers;

United States Marshal Service deputies;

Drug Enforcement Administration special agents;

United States Postal inspectors;

United States Postal police officers while in the performance of their official duties;

United States Customs Service special agents, inspectors and patrol officers;

United States General Services Administration special agents;

United States Department of Agriculture special agents;

Bureau of Alcohol, Tobacco and Firearms special agents;

Internal Revenue Service special agents and inspectors;

Department of the Interior special agents, investigators, and park rangers;

Federal Reserve law enforcement officers while in the performance of their official duties; and

United States Department of Defense police officers.

L.1983, c. 268, § 1, eff. July 14, 1983. Amended by L.1999, c. 218, § 1, eff. Sept. 22, 1999; L.2003, c. 139, § 1, eff. Aug. 1, 2003; L.2004, c. 10, § 1, eff. May 5, 2004; L.2008, c. 42, § 2, eff. July 15, 2008.

2A:154–6. Department of the Interior park police

Full-time law enforcement officers employed by the Department of the Interior as park police who are empowered to effect an arrest with or without a warrant for violations of the United States Code and who are authorized to carry firearms in the performance of their duties shall be empowered to act as an officer for the arrest of offenders against the laws of this State:

a. where the person reasonably believes that a crime of the first, second, or third degree is or is about to be committed or attempted in his presence; and

b. where the person reasonably believes that a crime of the fourth degree, a disorderly persons offense, a petty disorderly persons offense, or a violation of Title 39 of the Revised Statutes is or is about to be committed or attempted in his presence on Ellis Island or in Liberty State Park within 500 feet of the ferry terminal serving passengers bound for the Statue of Liberty National Monument or Ellis Island or in Liberty State Park within 500 feet of the access bridge to Ellis Island while that officer is in performance of his official duties.

L.2008, c. 42, § 1, eff. July 15, 2008.

CHAPTER 155

UNIFORM FRESH PURSUIT LAW

Section
2A:155–1.   Short title.
2A:155–2.   Definitions.
2A:155–3.   Application and construction of chapter.

Section
2A:155–4. Officers of other states in fresh pursuit; authority to make arrests in this state.
2A:155–5. Hearing before magistrate; commitment or discharge.
2A:155–6. Lawfulness of arrest.
2A:155–7. Copies of chapter to other states.

2A:155–1. Short title

This chapter may be cited as the "uniform law on fresh pursuit."

2A:155–2. Definitions

As used in this chapter:

"State" shall include the District of Columbia.

"Fresh pursuit" shall include fresh pursuit as defined by the common law, and also the pursuit of a person who has committed a felony or who is reasonably suspected of having committed a felony. It shall also include the pursuit of a person suspected of having committed a supposed felony, though no felony has actually been committed, if there is reasonable ground for believing that a felony has been committed. Fresh pursuit as used herein shall not necessarily imply instant pursuit, but pursuit without unreasonable delay.

"Felony" shall include high misdemeanor.

2A:155–3. Application and construction of chapter

The provisions of this chapter shall be applicable only to such officers of a state which has enacted a statute similar to the provisions hereof, and this chapter shall be so interpreted and construed as to effectuate the general purpose of making uniform the laws of the states which enact it.

2A:155–4. Officers of other states in fresh pursuit; authority to make arrests in this state

Any member of a duly organized state, county or municipal peace unit of another state of the United States who enters this state in fresh pursuit, and continues within this state in such fresh pursuit, of a person in order to arrest him on the ground that he is believed to have committed a felony in such other state, shall have the same authority to arrest and hold such person in custody, as has any member of any duly organized state, county or municipal peace unit of this state, to arrest and hold in custody a person on the ground that he is believed to have committed a felony in this state.

2A:155–5. Hearing before magistrate; commitment or discharge

If an arrest is made in this state by an officer of another state in accordance with the provisions of section 2A:155–4 of this title, he shall, without unnecessary delay, take the person arrested before a neighboring magistrate, who shall conduct a hearing for the purpose of determining the lawfulness of the arrest. If the magistrate determines that the arrest was lawful he shall commit the person arrested to await for a reasonable time the issuance of an extradition warrant by the governor of this state or admit him to bail for such purpose. If the magistrate determines that the arrest was unlawful he shall discharge the person arrested.

2A:155–6. Lawfulness of arrest

Section 2A:155–4 of this title shall not be construed so as to make unlawful any arrest in this state which would otherwise be lawful.

2A:155–7. Copies of chapter to other states

It shall be the duty of the secretary of state to certify a copy of this chapter to the executive department of each of the states of the United States.

CHAPTER 156

UNIFORM ACT ON INTRASTATE FRESH PURSUIT

Section
2A:156–1. Peace officer in fresh pursuit may arrest anywhere in state.
2A:156–2. "Fresh pursuit" defined.
2A:156–3. Validity of arrest.
2A:156–4. Short title.

2A:156–1. Peace officer in fresh pursuit may arrest anywhere in state

Any peace officer of this state in fresh pursuit of a person who is reasonably believed by him to have committed a high misdemeanor in this state or has committed, or attempted to commit, any criminal offense in this state in the presence of such officer, or for whom such officer holds a warrant of arrest for a criminal offense, shall have the authority to arrest and hold in custody such person anywhere in this state.

2A:156–2. "Fresh pursuit" defined

The term "fresh pursuit" as used in this chapter shall include fresh pursuit as defined by the common law, and also the pursuit of a person who has committed a high misdemeanor or is reasonably suspected of having committed a high misdemeanor in this state, or who has committed or attempted to commit any criminal offense in this state in the presence of the arresting officer referred to in section 2A:156–1 of this title, or for whom such officer holds a warrant of arrest for a criminal offense. It shall also include the pursuit of a person suspected of having committed a supposed high misdemeanor in this state, though no high misdemeanor has actually been committed, if there is reasonable ground for so believing. Fresh pursuit as used herein shall not necessarily imply instant pursuit, but pursuit without unreasonable delay.

2A:156–3. Validity of arrest

Section 2A:156–1 of this title shall not make unlawful an arrest which would otherwise be lawful.

2A:156–4. Short title

This chapter may be cited as the "uniform act on intrastate fresh pursuit".

CHAPTER 156A

WIRETAPPING, ETC.

Section
2A:156A–1. Short title.
2A:156A–2. Definitions.
2A:156A–3. Interception, disclosure or use of wire or oral communications; violation; penalty.
2A:156A–4. Exceptions.
2A:156A–4.1. Exception for persons acting under color of law; "computer trespasser" defined; motions to suppress evidence; appeal.
2A:156A–5. Possession, sale, distribution, manufacture, or advertisement of intercepting devices; violation; penalty.
2A:156A–6. Exceptions.
2A:156A–7. Nuisance; seizure and forfeiture of intercepting devices.
2A:156A–8. Authorization for application for order to intercept communications.
2A:156A–9. Application for order; contents.
2A:156A–10. Grounds for entry of order.
2A:156A–11. Public facilities or facilities of persons entitled to privileged communications; additional grounds.
2A:156A–12. Order; contents; limitations; extensions and renewals; progress reports; assistance of communication common carrier.
2A:156A–13. Emergency situations; authority to grant verbal approval for interception without order.
2A:156A–14. Recording of intercepted communications; custody; destruction; duplicate tapes or wires.
2A:156A–15. Sealing of applications, orders and supporting papers; destruction; disclosure of contents; violations.
2A:156A–16. Service of inventory by judge; contents; inspection of intercepted communications, applications and orders.
2A:156A–17. Disclosure or use of contents of wire or oral communications or derivative evidence.
2A:156A–18. Interception of communications relating to other offenses; disclosure or use; application.
2A:156A–19. Unlawful use or disclosure of existence of order or information concerning intercepted communication or derivative evidence.
2A:156A–20. Service of copy of order and application before disclosure of intercepted communication in trial, hearing or proceeding.
2A:156A–21. Motion to suppress contents of intercepted communication or derivative evidence; grounds; appeal.
2A:156A–22. Report by issuing or denying judge to Administrative Director of courts; contents.

Section
2A:156A–23. Annual reports of Superior Court, Supreme Court and attorney general; records of attorney general and county prosecutors.
2A:156A–24. Civil action for unlawful interception, disclosure or use of wire or oral communication; damages; attorneys' fees.
2A:156A–25. Good faith reliance on court order as defense.
2A:156A–26. Partial invalidity.
2A:156A–27. Unlawful access to stored communications.
2A:156A–28. Disclosure of contents.
2A:156A–29. Requirements for access.
2A:156A–30. Backup preservation.
2A:156A–31. Cost reimbursement.
2A:156A–32. Civil action.
2A:156A–33. Good faith defenses to civil or criminal actions.
2A:156A–34. Exclusivity of remedies.

2A:156A–1. Short title

This act shall be known and may be cited as the "New Jersey Wiretapping and Electronic Surveillance Control Act."
L.1968, c. 409, § 1, eff. Jan. 1, 1969.

2A:156A–2. Definitions

As used in this act:

a. "Wire communication" means any aural transfer made in whole or in part through the use of facilities for the transmission of communications by the aid of wire, cable or other like connection between the point of origin and the point of reception, including the use of such connection in a switching station, furnished or operated by any person engaged in providing or operating such facilities for the transmission of intrastate, interstate or foreign communication. "Wire communication" includes any electronic storage of such communication, and the radio portion of a cordless telephone communication that is transmitted between the cordless telephone handset and the base unit;

b. "Oral communication" means any oral communication uttered by a person exhibiting an expectation that such communication is not subject to interception under circumstances justifying such expectation, but does not include any electronic communication;

c. "Intercept" means the aural or other acquisition of the contents of any wire, electronic or oral communication through the use of any electronic, mechanical, or other device;

d. "Electronic, mechanical or other device" means any device or apparatus, including an induction coil, that can be used to intercept a wire, electronic or oral communication other than:

(1) Any telephone or telegraph instrument, equipment or facility, or any component thereof, furnished to the subscriber or user by a provider of wire or electronic communication service in the ordinary course of its business and being used by the subscriber or user in the ordinary course of its business; or furnished by such subscriber or user for connection to the facilities of such

service and used in the ordinary course of its business; or being used by a provider of wire or electronic communication service in the ordinary course of its business, or by an investigative or law enforcement officer in the ordinary course of his duties; or

(2) A hearing aid or similar device being used to correct subnormal hearing to not better than normal;

e. "Person" means that term as defined in R.S.1:1–2 and includes any officer or employee of the State or of a political subdivision thereof;

f. "Investigative or law enforcement officer" means any officer of the State of New Jersey or of a political subdivision thereof who is empowered by law to conduct investigations of, or to make arrests for, any offense enumerated in section 8 of P.L.1968, c. 409 (C.2A:156A–8) and any attorney authorized by law to prosecute or participate in the prosecution of any such offense;

g. "Contents," when used with respect to any wire, electronic or oral communication, includes any information concerning the identity of the parties to such communication or the existence, substance, purport, or meaning of that communication, except that for purposes of sections 22, 23, 24 and 26 of P.L.1993, c. 29 (C.2A:156A–28, C.2A:156A–29, C.2A:156A–30, and C.2A:156A–32) contents, when used with respect to any wire, electronic, or oral communication means any information concerning the substance, purport or meaning of that communication;

h. "Court of competent jurisdiction" means the Superior Court;

i. "Judge," when referring to a judge authorized to receive applications for, and to enter, orders authorizing interceptions of wire, electronic or oral communications, means one of the several judges of the Superior Court to be designated from time to time by the Chief Justice of the Supreme Court to receive applications for, and to enter, orders authorizing interceptions of wire, electronic or oral communications pursuant to this act;

j. "Communication common carrier" means any person engaged as a common carrier for hire, in intrastate, interstate or foreign communication by wire or radio or in intrastate, interstate or foreign radio transmission of energy; but a person engaged in radio broadcasting shall not, while so engaged, be deemed a common carrier;

k. "Aggrieved person" means a person who was a party to any intercepted wire, electronic or oral communication or a person against whom the interception was directed;

l. "In-progress trace" means the determination of the origin of a telephonic communication to a known telephone during the communication;

m. "Electronic communication" means any transfer of signs, signals, writing, images, sounds, data, or intelligence of any nature transmitted in whole or in part by a wire, radio, electromagnetic, photoelectric or photo–optical system that affects interstate, intrastate or foreign commerce, but does not include:

(1) Any wire or oral communication;

(2) Any communication made through a tone–only paging device; or

(3) Any communication from a tracking device;

n. "User" means any person or entity who:

(1) Uses an electronic communication service; and

(2) Is duly authorized by the provider of such service to engage in such use;

o. "Electronic communication system" means any wire, radio, electromagnetic, photo–optical or photoelectronic facilities for the transmission of electronic communications, and any computer facilities or related electronic equipment for the electronic storage of such communications;

p. "Electronic communication service" means any service which provides to the users thereof the ability to send or receive wire or electronic communications;

q. "Electronic storage" means:

(1) Any temporary, intermediate storage of a wire or electronic communication incidental to the electronic transmission thereof; and

(2) Any storage of such communication by an electronic communication service for purpose of backup protection of the communication;

r. "Readily accessible to the general public" means, with respect to a radio communication, that such communication is not:

(1) Scrambled or encrypted;

(2) Transmitted using modulation techniques whose essential parameters have been withheld from the public with the intention of preserving the privacy of such communication;

(3) Carried on a subcarrier or other signal subsidiary to a radio transmission;

(4) Transmitted over a communication system provided by a common carrier, unless the communication is a tone–only paging system communication; or

(5) Transmitted on frequencies allocated under part 25, subpart D, E, or F of part 74, or part 94 of the Rules of the Federal Communications Commission, unless, in the case of a communication transmitted on a frequency allocated under part 74 that is not exclusively allocated to broadcast auxiliary services, the communication is a two-way voice communication by radio;

s. "Remote computing service" means the provision to the public of computer storage or processing services by means of an electronic communication system;

t. "Aural transfer" means a transfer containing the human voice at any point between and including the point of origin and the point of reception;

u. "Tracking device" means an electronic or mechanical device which permits the tracking of the movement of a person or device;

v. "Point of interception" means the site at which the investigative or law enforcement officer is located at the time the interception is made;

w. "Location information" means global positioning system data, enhanced 9–1–1 data, cellular site information, and any other information that would assist a law enforcement agency in tracking the physical location of a cellular telephone or wireless mobile device.

L.1968, c. 409, § 2, eff. Jan. 1, 1969. Amended by L.1978, c. 51, § 1, eff. June 23, 1978; L.1993, c. 29, § 1, eff. Jan. 28, 1993; L.1999, c. 151, § 2, eff. June 30, 1999; L.2009, c. 184, § 1, eff. Jan. 12, 2010.

2A:156A–3. Interception, disclosure or use of wire or oral communications; violation; penalty

Except as otherwise specifically provided in this act, any person who:

a. Purposely intercepts, endeavors to intercept, or procures any other person to intercept or endeavor to intercept any wire, electronic or oral communication; or

b. Purposely discloses or endeavors to disclose to any other person the contents of any wire, electronic or oral communication, or evidence derived therefrom, knowing or having reason to know that the information was obtained through the interception of a wire, electronic or oral communication; or

c. Purposely uses or endeavors to use the contents of any wire, electronic or oral communication, or evidence derived therefrom, knowing or having reason to know, that the information was obtained through the interception of a wire, electronic or oral communication;

shall be guilty of a crime of the third degree. Subsections b. and c. of this section shall not apply to the contents of any wire, electronic or oral communication, or evidence derived therefrom, that has become common knowledge or public information.

L.1968, c. 409, § 3, eff. Jan. 1, 1969. Amended by L.1989, c. 85, § 1, eff. June 1, 1989; L.1993, c. 29, § 2, eff. Jan. 28, 1993.

2A:156A–4. Exceptions

It shall not be unlawful under this act for:

a. An operator of a switchboard, or an officer, agent or employee of a provider of wire or electronic communication service, whose facilities are used in the transmission of a wire or electronic communication, to intercept, disclose or use that communication in the normal course of his employment while engaged in any activity which is a necessary incident to the rendition of his service or to the protection of the rights or property of the provider of that service. No provider of wire or electronic communication service shall utilize service observing or random monitoring except for mechanical or service quality control checks;

b. Any investigative or law enforcement officer to intercept a wire, electronic or oral communication, where such officer is a party to the communication or where another officer who is a party to the communication requests or requires him to make such interception;

c. Any person acting at the direction of an investigative or law enforcement officer to intercept a wire, electronic or oral communication, where such person is a party to the communication or one of the parties to the communication has given prior consent to such interception; provided, however, that no such interception shall be made without the prior approval of the Attorney General or his designee or a county prosecutor or his designee;

d. A person not acting under color of law to intercept a wire, electronic or oral communication, where such person is a party to the communication or one of the parties to the communication has given prior consent to such interception unless such communication is intercepted or used for the purpose of committing any criminal or tortious act in violation of the Constitution or laws of the United States or of this State or for the purpose of committing any other injurious act. The fact that such person is the subscriber to a particular telephone does not constitute consent effective to authorize interception of communications among parties not including such person on that telephone. Any person who unlawfully intercepts or uses such communication as provided in this paragraph shall be subject to the civil liability established in section 24 of P.L.1968, c. 409 (C.2A:156A–24), in addition to any other criminal or civil liability imposed by law;

e. Any person to intercept or access an electronic communication made through an electronic communication system that is configured so that such electronic communication is readily accessible to the general public;

f. Any person to intercept any radio communication which is transmitted:

(1) by any station for the use of the general public, or that relates to ships, aircraft, vehicles, or persons in distress;

(2) by any governmental, law enforcement, civil defense, private land mobile, or public safety communication system, including police and fire, readily accessible to the general public;

(3) by a station operating on an authorized frequency within the bands allocated to the amateur, citizens band, or general mobile radio services; or

(4) by any marine or aeronautical communications system;

g. Any person to engage in any conduct which:

(1) is prohibited by section 633 of the Communications Act of 1934; or

(2) is excepted from the application of section 705(a) of the Communications Act of 1934 by section 705(b) of that Act;

h. Any person to intercept any wire or electronic communication the transmission of which is causing harmful interference to any lawfully operating station or consumer electronic equipment, to the extent necessary to identify the source of such interference; or for other users of the same frequency to intercept any radio communication made through a system that utilizes frequencies monitored by individuals engaged in the provision or the use of such system, if such communication is not scrambled or encrypted; or

i. A provider of electronic communication service to record the fact that a wire or electronic communication was initiated or completed in order to protect such provider, another provider furnishing service toward the completion of the wire or electronic communication, or a user of that service, from fraudulent, unlawful or abusive use of such service.

L.1968, c. 409, § 4, eff. Jan. 1, 1969. Amended by L.1975, c. 131, § 1, eff. June 30, 1975; L.1978, c. 51, § 2, eff. June 23, 1978; L.1993, c. 29, § 3, eff. Jan. 28, 1993; L.1999, c. 151, § 3, eff. June 30, 1999.

2A:156A–4.1. Exception for persons acting under color of law; "computer trespasser" defined; motions to suppress evidence; appeal

a. It shall not be a violation of any provision of P.L.1968, c. 409 (C.2A:156A–1 et seq.) for a person acting under color of law to intercept the wire or electronic communications of a suspected computer trespasser transmitted to, through, or from a computer or any other device with Internet capability, if:

(1) the owner or operator of the computer or other device authorizes the interception of the computer trespasser's wire or electronic communications on the computer;

(2) the person acting under color of law is lawfully engaged in an investigation;

(3) the person acting under color of law has reasonable grounds to believe that the contents of the computer trespasser's wire or electronic communications will be relevant to the investigation; and

(4) such interception does not acquire communications other than those transmitted to or from the computer trespasser.

b. For purposes of this section, "computer trespasser" means a person who accesses a computer or any other device with Internet capability without authorization and thus has no reasonable expectation of privacy in any communication transmitted to, through, or from the computer or other device. The term "computer

trespasser" does not include a person known by the owner or operator of the computer or other device with Internet capability to have an existing contractual relationship with the owner or operator of the computer or other device for access to all or part of the computer or other device.

c. Any aggrieved person in any trial, hearing, or proceeding in or before any court or other authority of this State may move to suppress the contents of any wire or electronic communication intercepted in accordance with subsection a. of this section, or evidence derived therefrom, on the grounds that the communication was unlawfully intercepted or the interception was not made in conformity with the provisions of this section. The motion shall be made at least 10 days before the trial, hearing, or proceeding unless there was no opportunity to make the motion or the moving party was not aware of the grounds for the motion. Motions by coindictees are to be heard in a single consolidated hearing. The court, upon the filing of such motion by the aggrieved person, shall make available to the aggrieved person or his counsel for inspection such portions of the intercepted communication, or evidence derived therefrom, as the court determines to be in the interests of justice. If the motion is granted, the entire contents of all intercepted wire or electronic communications obtained during or after any interception which is determined to be in violation of P.L.1968, c. 409 (C.2A:156A–1 et seq.) or evidence derived therefrom, shall not be received in evidence in the trial, hearing or proceeding.

In addition to any other right to appeal, the State shall have the right to appeal from an order granting a motion to suppress upon certification to the court that the appeal is not taken for purposes of delay. The appeal shall be taken within the time specified by the Rules of Court and shall be diligently prosecuted.

L.2009, c. 142, § 1, eff. Oct. 19, 2009.

2A:156A–5. Possession, sale, distribution, manufacture, or advertisement of intercepting devices; violation; penalty

Except as otherwise specifically provided in section 6 of P.L.1968, c. 409 (C. 2A:156A–6), any person who:

a. Purposely possesses an electronic, mechanical or other device, knowing or having reason to know that the design of such device renders it primarily useful for the purpose of the surreptitious interception of a wire, electronic or oral communication;

b. Purposely sells an electronic, mechanical or other device, knowing or having reason to know that the design of such device renders it primarily useful for the purpose of the surreptitious interception of a wire, electronic or oral communication;

c. Purposely distributes an electronic, mechanical or other device, knowing or having reason to know that the design of such device renders it primarily useful for the purpose of the surreptitious interception of a wire, electronic or oral communication;

d. Purposely manufactures or assembles an electronic, mechanical or other device, knowing or having reason to know that the design of such device renders it primarily useful for the purpose of the surreptitious interception of a wire, electronic or oral communication; or

e. Purposely places in any newspaper, magazine, handbill, or other publication any advertisement of any electronic, mechanical or other device, knowing or having reason to know that the design of such device renders it primarily useful for the purpose of the surreptitious interception of a wire, electronic or oral communication or of any electronic, mechanical or other device where such advertisement promotes the use of such device for the purpose of the surreptitious interception of a wire, electronic or oral communication;

shall be guilty of a crime of the third degree.

L.1968, c. 409, § 5, eff. Jan. 1, 1969. Amended by L.1975, c. 131, § 2, eff. June 30, 1975; L.1989, c. 85, § 2, eff. June 1, 1989; L.1993, c. 29, § 4, eff. Jan. 28, 1993.

2A:156A–6. Exceptions

It shall not be unlawful under this act for:

a. A provider of wire or electronic communication service, or an officer, agent or employee of, or a person under contract with such a provider of wire or electronic communication service in the normal course of the business of providing that wire or electronic communication service; or

b. A person under contract with the United States, a state or a political subdivision thereof, or an officer, agent or employee of a state or a political subdivision thereof; to possess, sell, distribute, manufacture or assemble any electronic, mechanical or other device, while acting in furtherance of the appropriate activities of the United States, a state or a political subdivision thereof or a provider of wire or electronic communication service.

L.1968, c. 409, § 6, eff. Jan. 1, 1969. Amended by L.1975, c. 131, § 3, eff. June 30, 1975; L.1993, c. 29, § 5, eff. Jan. 28, 1993.

2A:156A–7. Nuisance; seizure and forfeiture of intercepting devices

Any electronic, mechanical or other device possessed, used, sent, distributed, manufactured, or assembled in violation of this act may be seized and forfeited to the State pursuant to chapter 64 of Title 2C of the New Jersey Statutes.

L.1968, c. 409, § 7, eff. Jan. 1, 1969. Amended by L.1993, c. 29, § 6, eff. Jan. 28, 1993.

2A:156A–8. Authorization for application for order to intercept communications

The Attorney General, county prosecutor or a person designated to act for such an official and to perform his duties in and during his actual absence or disability, may authorize, in writing, an ex parte application to a judge designated to receive the same for an order authorizing the interception of a wire, or electronic or oral communication by the investigative or law enforcement officers or agency having responsibility for an investigation when such interception may provide evidence of the commission of the offense of murder, kidnapping, gambling, robbery, bribery, a violation of paragraph (1) or (2) of subsection b. of N.J.S.2C:12–1, a violation of section 3 of P.L.1997, c. 353 (C.2C:21–4.3), a violation of N.J.S.2C:21–19 punishable by imprisonment for more than one year, a violation of P.L.1994, c. 121 (C.2C:21–23 et seq.),a violation of sections 1 through 5 of P.L.2002, c. 26 (C.2C:38–1 et seq.), a violation of N.J.S.2C:33–3, a violation of N.J.S.2C:17–2, a violation of sections 1 through 3 of P.L.1983, c. 480 (C.2C:17–7 through 2C:17–9), a violation of N.J.S.2C:12–3 (terroristic threats), violations of N.J.S.2C:35–3, N.J.S.2C:35–4 and N.J.S.2C:35–5, violations of sections 112 through 116, inclusive, of the "Casino Control Act," P.L.1977, c. 110 (C.5:12–112 through 5:12–116), arson, burglary, theft and related offenses punishable by imprisonment for more than one year, endangering the welfare of a child pursuant to N.J.S.2C:24–4, escape, forgery and fraudulent practices punishable by imprisonment for more than one year, alteration of motor vehicle identification numbers, unlawful manufacture, purchase, use, or transfer of firearms, unlawful possession or use of destructive devices or explosives, weapons training for illegal activities pursuant to section 1 of P.L.1983, c. 229 (C.2C:39–14), racketeering or a violation of subsection g. of N.J.S.2C:5–2, leader of organized crime, organized criminal activity directed toward the unlawful transportation, storage, disposal, discharge, release, abandonment or disposition of any harmful, hazardous, toxic, destructive, or polluting substance, or any conspiracy to commit any of the foregoing offenses or which may provide evidence aiding in the apprehension of the perpetrator or perpetrators of any of the foregoing offenses.

L.1968, c. 409, § 8. Amended by L.1975, c. 131, § 4, eff. June 30, 1975; L.1978, c. 51, § 3, eff. June 23, 1978; L.1989, c. 85, § 3, eff. June 1, 1989; L.1993, c. 29, § 7, eff. Jan. 28, 1993; L.1995, c. 119, § 1, eff. June 8, 1995; L.1999, c. 25, § 1, eff. Feb. 16, 1999; L.1999, c. 151, § 4, eff. June 30, 1999; L.2002, c. 26, § 6, eff. June 18, 2002.

2A:156A–9. Application for order; contents

Each application for an order of authorization to intercept a wire, electronic or oral communication shall be made in writing upon oath or affirmation and shall state:

a. The authority of the applicant to make such application;

b. The identity and qualifications of the investigative or law enforcement officers or agency for whom the authority to intercept a wire, electronic or oral communication is sought and the identity of whoever authorized the application.

c. A particular statement of the facts relied upon by the applicant, including: (1) The identity of the particular person, if known, committing the offense and whose communications are to be intercepted; (2) The details as to the particular offense that has been, is being, or is about to be committed; (3) The particular type of communication to be intercepted; and a showing that there is probable cause to believe that such communication will be communicated on the wire or electronic communication facilities involved or at the particular place where the oral communication is to be intercepted; (4) Except as provided in subsection g. of this section, the character and location of the particular wire or electronic communication facilities involved or the particular place where the oral communication is to be intercepted; (5) A statement of the period of time for which the interception is required to be maintained; if the character of the investigation is such that the authorization for interception should not automatically terminate when the described type of communication has been first obtained, a particular statement of facts establishing probable cause to believe that additional communications of the same type will occur thereafter; (6) A particular statement of facts showing that other normal investigative procedures with respect to the offense have been tried and have failed or reasonably appear to be unlikely to succeed if tried or to be too dangerous to employ;

d. Where the application is for the renewal or extension of an order, a particular statement of facts showing the results thus far obtained from the interception, or a reasonable explanation of the failure to obtain such results;

e. A complete statement of the facts concerning all previous applications, known to the individual authorizing and to the individual making the application, made to any court for authorization to intercept a wire, electronic or oral communication involving any of the same facilities or places specified in the application or involving any person whose communication is to be intercepted, and the action taken by the court on each such application; and

f. Such additional testimony or documentary evidence in support of the application as the judge may require.

g. An application need not meet the requirements of paragraph (4) of subsection c. of this section if:

(1) with respect to the application for an interception of an oral communication:

(a) the application is approved by the Attorney General or county prosecutor or a person designated to act for such an official and to perform his duties in and during his actual absence or disability; and

(b) the application contains a full and complete statement as to why specification is not practical and

identifies the person committing the offense and whose communications are to be intercepted; and

(c) the judge finds that such specification is not practical.

(2) with respect to the application for an interception of a wire or electronic communication:

(a) the application is approved by the Attorney General or county prosecutor or a person designated to act for such an official and to perform his duties in and during his actual absence or disability; and

(b) the application identifies the person believed to be committing the offense and whose communications are to be intercepted and the applicant makes a showing of a purpose, on the part of that person, to thwart interception by changing facilities; and

(c) the judge finds that such purpose has been adequately shown.

An interception of a communication under an order issued in conformity with this subsection shall not begin until the facilities from which, or the place where, the communication is to be intercepted is ascertained by the person implementing the interception order. A provider of wire or electronic communication service that has received an order as provided for in this subsection may make a motion that the court modify or quash the order on the ground that the provider's assistance with respect to the interception cannot be performed in a timely or reasonable fashion. The court upon notice to the Attorney General or county prosecutor shall decide such a motion expeditiously.

L.1968, c. 409, § 9, eff. Jan. 1, 1969. Amended by L.1975, c. 131, § 5, eff. June 30, 1975; L.1993, c. 29, § 8, eff. Jan. 28, 1993.

2A:156A–10. Grounds for entry of order

Upon consideration of an application, the judge may enter an ex parte order, as requested or as modified, authorizing the interception of a wire, electronic or oral communication, if the court determines on the basis of the facts submitted by the applicant that there is or was probable cause for belief that:

a. The person whose communication is to be intercepted is engaging or was engaged over a period of time as a part of a continuing criminal activity or is committing, has or had committed or is about to commit an offense as provided in section 8 of P.L.1968, c. 409 (C. 2A:156A–8);

b. Particular communications concerning such offense may be obtained through such interception;

c. Normal investigative procedures with respect to such offense have been tried and have failed or reasonably appear to be unlikely to succeed if tried or to be too dangerous to employ;

d. Except in the case of an application meeting the requirements of subsection g. of section 9 of P.L.1968, c. 409 (C. 2A:156A–9), the facilities from which, or the place where, the wire, electronic or oral communications are to be intercepted, are or have been used, or are about to be used, in connection with the commission of such offense, or are leased to, listed in the name of, or commonly used by, such individual;

e.　The investigative or law enforcement officers or agency to be authorized to intercept the wire, electronic or oral communication are qualified by training and experience to execute the interception sought; and

f.　In the case of an application, other than a renewal or extension, for an order to intercept a communication of a person or on a facility which was the subject of a previous order authorizing interception, the application is based upon new evidence or information different from and in addition to the evidence or information offered to support the prior order, regardless of whether such evidence was derived from prior interceptions or from other sources.

As part of the consideration of an application in which there is no corroborative evidence offered, the judge shall inquire in camera as to the identity of any informants or any other additional information concerning the basis upon which the investigative or law enforcement officer or agency has applied for the order of authorization which the judge finds relevant in order to determine if there is probable cause pursuant to this section.

L.1968, c. 409, § 10, eff. Jan. 1, 1969. Amended by L.1975, c. 131, § 6, eff. June 30, 1975; L.1993, c. 29, § 9, eff. Jan. 28, 1993.

2A:156A–11.　Public facilities or facilities of persons entitled to privileged communications; additional grounds

If the facilities from which a wire or electronic communication is to be intercepted are public, no order shall be issued unless the court, in addition to the matters provided in section 10 of P.L.1968, c. 409 (C. 2A:156A–10), determines that there is a special need to intercept wire or electronic communications over such facilities.

If the facilities from which, or the place where, the wire, electronic or oral communications are to be intercepted are being used, or are about to be used, or are leased to, listed in the name of, or commonly used by, a licensed physician, a licensed practicing psychologist, an attorney-at-law, a practicing clergyman, or a newspaperman, or is a place used primarily for habitation by a husband and wife, no order shall be issued unless the court, in addition to the matters provided in section 10 of P.L.1968, c. 409 (C. 2A:156A–10), determines that there is a special need to intercept wire, electronic or oral communications over such facilities or in such places.　Special need as used in this section shall require in addition to the matters required by section 10 of P.L.1968, c. 409 (C. 2A:156A–10), a showing that the licensed physician, licensed practicing psychologist, attorney-at-law, practicing clergyman or newspaperman is

personally engaging in or was engaged in over a period of time as a part of a continuing criminal activity or is committing, has or had committed or is about to commit an offense as provided in section 8 of P.L.1968, c. 409 (C. 2A:156A–8) or that the public facilities or the place used primarily for habitation by a husband and wife are being regularly used by someone who is personally engaging in or was engaged in over a period of time as a part of a continuing criminal activity or is committing, has or had committed or is about to commit such an offense.　No otherwise privileged wire, electronic or oral communication intercepted in accordance with, or in violation of, the provisions of this act, shall lose its privileged character.

L.1968, c. 409, § 11, eff. Jan. 1, 1969.　Amended by L.1975, c. 131, § 7, eff. June 30, 1975; L.1978, c. 51, § 4, eff. June 23, 1978; L.1993, c. 29, § 10, eff. Jan. 28, 1993.

2A:156A–12.　Order; contents; limitations; extensions and renewals; progress reports; assistance of communication common carrier

Each order authorizing the interception of any wire, electronic or oral communication shall state:

a.　The judge is authorized to issue the order;

b.　The identity of, or a particular description of, the person, if known, whose communications are to be intercepted;

c.　The character and location of the particular communication facilities as to which, or the particular place of the communication as to which, authority to intercept is granted, or, in the case of an application meeting the requirements of subsection g. of section 9 of P.L.1968, c. 409 (C.2A:156A–9) that specification is not practical or that the purpose to thwart interception by changing facilities has been shown;

d.　A particular description of the type of the communication to be intercepted and a statement of the particular offense to which it relates;

e.　The identity of the investigative or law enforcement officers or agency to whom the authority to intercept a wire, electronic or oral communication is given and the identity of whoever authorized the application; and

f.　The period of time during which such interception is authorized, including a statement as to whether or not the interception shall automatically terminate when the described communication has been first obtained.

No order entered under this section shall authorize the interception of any wire, electronic or oral communication for a period of time in excess of that necessary under the circumstances.　Every order entered under this section shall require that such interception begin and terminate as soon as practicable and be conducted in such a manner as to minimize or eliminate the interception of such communications not otherwise subject to interception under this act by making reasonable efforts, whenever possible, to reduce the hours of interception authorized by said order. In the event the intercepted communication is in a language other than English, or is in a code, and an interpreter or expert in that language or code is not reasonably available during the interception period or a portion of the interception period, minimization shall be accomplished as soon as practicable after the interception. Except as provided below in subsection g. of this section, no order entered under this section shall authorize the interception of wire, electronic or oral communications for any period exceeding 20 days. Extensions or renewals of such an order may be granted for two additional periods of not more than 10 days. No extension or renewal shall be granted unless an application for it is made in accordance with this section, and the court makes the findings required by sections 10 and 11 of P.L.1968, c. 409 (C.2A:156A–10 and 2A:156A–11) and by this section.

g. Orders entered under this section to provide evidence of racketeering in violation of N.J.S.2C:41–2, leader of organized crime in violation of subsection g. of N.J.S.2C:5–2, or leader of narcotics trafficking network in violation of N.J.S.2C:35–3, may authorize the interception of wire, electronic or oral communications for a period not to exceed 30 days and extensions or renewals of any order may be granted for additional periods of not more than 30 days, without limitation on the number of extension or renewal orders; provided, however, that orders authorized pursuant to this subsection shall not exceed six months.

h. Whenever an order authorizing an interception is entered, the order may require reports to be made to the judge who issued the order showing what progress has been made toward achievement of the authorized objective and the need for continued interception. Such reports shall be made at such intervals as the court may require.

An order authorizing the interception of a wire, electronic or oral communication shall, upon request of the applicant, direct that a provider of electronic communication service shall furnish the applicant forthwith all information, facilities and technical assistance necessary to accomplish the interception unobtrusively and with a minimum of interference with the services that such provider is affording the person whose communications are to be intercepted.

The obligation of a provider of electronic communication service under such an order shall include but is not limited to conducting an in-progress trace during an interception and shall also include the provision of technical assistance and equipment and utilization of any technological features which are available to the provider of electronic communication service. The obligation of the provider of electronic communication service to conduct an in-progress trace and provide other technical assistance may arise pursuant to court order based upon probable cause, under circumstances not involving an interception pursuant to this act. Any provider of electronic communication service furnishing

such facilities or assistance shall be compensated therefor by the applicant at the prevailing rates. Said provider shall be immune from civil liability for any assistance rendered to the applicant pursuant to this section.

An order authorizing the interception of a wire, electronic or oral communication may be executed at any point of interception within the jurisdiction of an investigative or law enforcement officer executing the order.

L.1968, c. 409, § 12, eff. Jan. 1, 1969. Amended by L.1975, c. 131, § 8, eff. June 30, 1975; L.1978, c. 51, § 5, eff. June 23, 1978; L.1989, c. 85, § 4, eff. June 1, 1989; L.1993, c. 29, § 11, eff. Jan. 28, 1993; L.1999, c. 151, § 5, eff. June 30, 1999.

2A:156A–13. Emergency situations; authority to grant verbal approval for interception without order

Whenever, upon informal application by an authorized applicant, a judge determines there are grounds upon which an order could be issued pursuant to this act, and that an emergency situation exists that involves: a. the investigation of conspiratorial activities of organized crime, related to an offense designated in section 8 of P.L.1968, c. 409 (C. 2A:156A–8); or b. immediate danger of death or serious bodily injury to any person, dictating authorization for immediate interception of wire, electronic or oral communication before an application for an order could with due diligence be submitted to him and acted upon, the judge may grant verbal approval for such interception without an order, conditioned upon the filing with him, within 48 hours thereafter, of an application for an order which, if granted, shall recite the verbal approval and be retroactive to the time of such verbal approval. Such interception shall immediately terminate when the communication sought is obtained or when the application for an order is denied. In the event no application for an order is made, the content of any wire, electronic or oral communication intercepted shall be treated as having been obtained in violation of this act.

In the event no application is made or an application made pursuant to this section is denied, the court shall require the wire, tape or other recording of the intercepted communication to be delivered to, and sealed by, the court and such evidence shall be retained by the court in accordance with section 14 of P.L.1968, c. 409 (C. 2A:156A–14) and the same shall not be used or disclosed in any legal proceeding except in a civil action brought by an aggrieved person pursuant to section 24 of P.L.1968, c. 409 (C. 2A:156A–24) or as otherwise authorized by court order. Failure to effect delivery of any such wire, tape or other recording shall be punishable as contempt by the court directing such delivery. Evidence of verbal authorization to intercept an oral, electronic or wire communication shall be a defense to any charge against the investigating or law enforcement officer for engaging in unlawful interception.

L.1968, c. 409, § 13, eff. Jan. 1, 1969. Amended by L.1993, c. 29, § 12, eff. Jan. 28, 1993.

2A:156A–14. Recording of intercepted communications; custody; destruction; duplicate tapes or wires

Any wire, electronic or oral communication intercepted in accordance with this act shall, if practicable, be recorded by tape, wire or other comparable method. The recording shall be done in such a way as will protect it from editing or other alteration. Immediately upon the expiration of the order or extensions or renewals thereof, the tapes, wires or other recordings shall be transferred to the judge issuing the order and sealed under his direction. Custody of the tapes, wires or other recordings shall be maintained wherever the court directs. They shall not be destroyed except upon an order of such court and in any event shall be kept for 10 years. Duplicate tapes, wires or other recordings may be made for disclosure or use pursuant to subsection a. of section 17 of P.L.1968, c. 409 (C. 2A:156A–17). The presence of the seal provided by this section, or a satisfactory explanation for its absence, shall be a prerequisite for the disclosure of the contents of any wire, electronic or oral communication, or evidence derived therefrom, under subsection b. of section 17 of P.L.1968, c. 409 (C. 2A:156A–17).

L.1968, c. 409, § 14, eff. Jan. 1, 1969. Amended by L.1993, c. 29, § 13, eff. Jan. 28, 1993.

2A:156A–15. Sealing of applications, orders and supporting papers; destruction; disclosure of contents; violations

Applications made and orders granted pursuant to this act and supporting papers shall be sealed by the court and shall be held in custody as the court shall direct and shall not be destroyed except on order of the court and in any event shall be kept for 10 years. They may be disclosed only upon a showing of good cause before a court of competent jurisdiction.

Any violation of the provisions of this section may be punished as contempt of the issuing or denying court.

L.1968, c. 409, § 15, eff. Jan. 1, 1969.

2A:156A–16. Service of inventory by judge; contents; inspection of intercepted communications, applications and orders

Within a reasonable time but not later than 90 days after the termination of the period of the order or of extensions or renewals thereof, or the date of the denial of an order applied for under section 13 of P.L.1968, c. 409 (C. 2A:156A–13), the issuing or denying judge shall cause to be served on the persons named in the order or application, persons arrested as a result of the interception of their conversations, persons indicted as a result of the interception of their conversations, persons whose conversations were intercepted and against whom indictments are likely to be returned, persons whose conversations were intercepted and who are potential witnesses to criminal activities, and such other parties to the intercepted communications as the judge may in his discretion determine to be in the interest of justice, an inventory which shall include:

a. Notice of the entry of the order or the application for an order denied under section 13 of P.L.1968, c. 409 (C. 2A:156A–13);

b. The date of the entry of the order or the denial of an order applied for under section 13 of P.L.1968, c. 409 (C. 2A:156A–13);

c. The period of authorized or disapproved interception; and

d. The fact that during the period wire, electronic or oral communications were or were not intercepted.

The court, upon filing of a motion, may in its discretion make available to such persons or their attorneys for inspection such portions of the intercepted communications, applications and orders as the court determines to be in the interest of justice. On an ex parte showing of good cause to the court the serving of the inventories required by this section may be postponed.

L.1968, c. 409, § 16, eff. Jan. 1, 1969. Amended by L.1978, c. 51, § 6, eff. June 23, 1978; L.1993, c. 29, § 14, eff. Jan. 28, 1993.

2A:156A–17. Disclosure or use of contents of wire or oral communications or derivative evidence

a. Any investigative or law enforcement officer or other person who, by any means authorized by this act, has obtained knowledge of the contents of any wire, electronic or oral communication, or evidence derived therefrom, may disclose or use such contents or evidence to investigative or law enforcement officers of this or another state, any of its political subdivisions, or of the United States to the extent that such disclosure or use is appropriate to the proper performance of the official duties of the officer making or receiving the disclosure.

b. Any person who, by any means authorized by this act, has obtained any information concerning any wire, electronic or oral communication or evidence derived therefrom intercepted in accordance with the provisions of this act, may disclose the contents of such communications or derivative evidence while giving testimony under oath or affirmation in any criminal proceeding in any court of this or another state or of the United States or before any Federal or State grand jury; provided, however, that the contents of any wire, electronic or oral communication may be initially disclosed solely through the use of the testimony of a witness to such communication or the actual recording of the communication.

c. The contents of any intercepted wire, electronic or oral communication, or evidence derived therefrom, may otherwise be disclosed or used only upon a showing of good cause before a court of competent jurisdiction.

L.1968, c. 409, § 17, eff. Jan. 1, 1969. Amended by L.1975, c. 131, § 9, eff. June 30, 1975; L.1993, c. 29, § 15, eff. Jan. 28, 1993.

2A:156A–18. Interception of communications relating to other offenses; disclosure or use; application

When an investigative or law enforcement officer, while engaged in intercepting wire, electronic or oral communications in the manner authorized herein, intercepts wire, electronic or oral communications relating to offenses other than those specified in the order of authorization, the contents thereof, and evidence derived therefrom, may be disclosed or used as provided in subsection a. of section 17 of P.L.1968, c. 409 (C. 2A:156A–17). Such contents and any evidence derived therefrom may be used under subsection b. of section 17 of P.L.1968, c. 409 (C. 2A:156A–17) when authorized or approved by a judge of competent jurisdiction where such judge finds on subsequent application that the contents were otherwise intercepted in accordance with the provisions of this act. Such application shall be made as soon as practicable.

L.1968, c. 409, § 18, eff. Jan. 1, 1969. Amended by L.1993, c. 29, § 16, eff. Jan. 28, 1993.

2A:156A–19. Unlawful use or disclosure of existence of order or information concerning intercepted communication or derivative evidence

Except as specifically authorized pursuant to this act any person who knowingly uses or discloses the existence of an order authorizing interception of a wire, electronic or oral communication or the contents of, or information concerning, an intercepted wire, electronic or oral communication or evidence derived therefrom, is guilty of a crime of the third degree.

L.1968, c. 409, § 19, eff. Jan. 1, 1969. Amended by L.1989, c. 85, § 5, eff. June 1, 1989; L.1993, c. 29, § 17, eff. Jan. 28, 1993.

2A:156A–20. Service of copy of order and application before disclosure of intercepted communication in trial, hearing or proceeding

The contents of any wire, electronic or oral communication intercepted in accordance with the provisions of this act, or evidence derived therefrom, shall not be disclosed in any trial, hearing, or proceeding before any court of this State unless not less than 10 days before the trial, hearing, or proceeding the parties to the action have been served with a copy of the order and accompanying application under which the interception was authorized.

The service of inventory, order, and application required by this section may be waived by the court where it finds that the service is not practicable and that the parties will not be prejudiced by the failure to make the service.

L.1968, c. 409, § 20, eff. Jan. 1, 1969. Amended by L.1993, c. 29, § 18, eff. Jan. 28, 1993.

2A:156A–21. Motion to suppress contents of intercepted communication or derivative evidence; grounds; appeal

Any aggrieved person in any trial, hearing, or proceeding in or before any court or other authority of this State may move to suppress the contents of any intercepted wire, electronic or oral communication, or evidence derived therefrom, on the grounds that:

a. The communication was unlawfully intercepted;

b. The order of authorization is insufficient on its face;

c. The interception was not made in conformity with the order of authorization or in accordance with the requirements of section 12 of P.L.1968, c. 409 (C. 2A:156A–12).

The motion shall be made at least 10 days before the trial, hearing, or proceeding unless there was no opportunity to make the motion or the moving party was not aware of the grounds for the motion. Motions by coindictees are to be heard in a single consolidated hearing.

The court, upon the filing of such motion by the aggrieved person, shall make available to the aggrieved person or his counsel for inspection such portions of the intercepted communication, or evidence derived therefrom, as the court determines to be in the interests of justice. If the motion is granted, the entire contents of all intercepted wire, electronic or oral communications obtained during or after any interception which is determined to be in violation of this act under subsections a., b., or c. of this section, or evidence derived therefrom, shall not be received in evidence in the trial, hearing or proceeding.

In addition to any other right to appeal, the State shall have the right to appeal from an order granting a motion to suppress if the official to whom the order authorizing the intercept was granted shall certify to the court that the appeal is not taken for purposes of delay. The appeal shall be taken within the time specified by the Rules of Court and shall be diligently prosecuted.

L.1968, c. 409, § 21, eff. Jan. 1, 1969. Amended by L.1975, c. 131, § 10, eff. June 30, 1975; L.1978, c. 51, § 7, eff. June 23, 1978; L.1993, c. 29, § 19, eff. Jan. 28, 1993.

2A:156A–22. Report by issuing or denying judge to Administrative Director of courts; contents

Within 30 days after the expiration of an order or an extension or renewal thereof entered under this act or the denial of an order confirming verbal approval of interception, the issuing or denying judge shall make a report to the Administrative Director of the courts stating that:

a. An order, extension or renewal was applied for;

b. The kind of order applied for;

c. The order was granted as applied for, was modified, or was denied;

d. The period of the interceptions authorized by the order, and the number and duration of any extensions or renewals of the order;

e. The offense specified in the order, or extension or renewal of an order;

f. The identify of the person authorizing the application and of the investigative or law enforcement officer and agency for whom it was made; and

g. The character of the facilities from which or the place where the communications were to be intercepted.

L.1968, c. 409, § 22, eff. Jan. 1, 1969.

2A:156A–23. Annual reports of Superior Court, Supreme Court and attorney general; records of attorney general and county prosecutors

a. In addition to reports required to be made by applicants pursuant to Federal law, all judges of the Superior Court authorized to issue orders pursuant to this act shall make annual reports on the operation of this act to the Administrative Director of the Courts. The reports by the judges shall contain (1) the number of applications made; (2) the number of orders issued; (3) the effective periods of such orders; (4) the number and duration of any renewals thereof; (5) the crimes in connection with which the conversations were sought; (6) the names of the applicants; and (7) such other and further particulars as the Administrative Director of the Courts may require.

b. In addition to reports required to be made by applicants pursuant to Federal Law, the Attorney General shall make annual reports on the operation of this act to the Administrative Director of the Courts. The reports by the Attorney General shall contain (1) the number of applications made; (2) the number of orders issued; (3) the effective periods of such orders; (4) the number and duration of any renewals thereof; (5) the crimes in connection with which the conversations were sought; (6) the name of the applicants; (7) the number of indictments resulting from each application; (8) the crime or crimes which each indictment charges; and (9) the disposition of each indictment.

c. In addition to reports required to be made by applicants pursuant to Federal law, the Attorney General shall receive and maintain records of all interceptions authorized pursuant to section 4 b. (C. 2A:156A–4) and shall include such information in his annual report to the Governor and the Legislature. It shall be the obligation of all law enforcement agencies in the State to file with the Attorney General on forms prescribed by the Attorney General information pertinent to the operation of section 4 b. The information on the forms shall include, but not be limited to (1) the name of the investigative or law enforcement officer making the interception; (2) the law enforcement agency employing the officer involved in the interception; (3) the character of the investigation or activity involved; and (4) the results of such activity.

d. In addition to reports and records otherwise required by law, the Attorney General and the county prosecutor shall maintain records of all interceptions authorized by them pursuant to section 4 c.,[1] on forms prescribed by the Attorney General. Such records shall include the name of the person requesting the authorization, the reasons for the request, and the results of any authorized interception. The Attorney General shall require that copies of such records maintained by county prosecutors be filed with him periodically and he shall report annually to the Governor and Legislature on the operation of section 4 c.

e. The Chief Justice of the Supreme Court and the Attorney General shall annually report to the Governor and the Legislature on such aspects of the operation of this act as they respectively deem appropriate including any recommendations they may care to make as to legislative changes or improvements to effectuate the purposes of this act and to assure and protect individual rights.

L.1968, c. 409, § 23, eff. Jan. 1, 1969. Amended by L.1975, c. 131, § 11, eff. June 30, 1975; L.1978, c. 51, § 8, eff. June 23, 1978.

[1] N.J.S.A. § 2A:156A–4.

2A:156A–24. Civil action for unlawful interception, disclosure or use of wire or oral communication; damages; attorneys' fees

Any person whose wire, electronic or oral communication is intercepted, disclosed or used in violation of this act shall have a civil cause of action against any person who intercepts, discloses or uses or procures any other person to intercept, disclose or use, such communication; and shall be entitled to recover from any such person:

a. Actual damages, but not less than liquidated damages computed at the rate of $100.00 a day for each day of violation, or $1,000.00, whichever is higher;

b. Punitive damages; and

c. A reasonable attorney's fee and other litigation costs reasonably incurred.

L.1968, c. 409, § 24, eff. Jan. 1, 1969. Amended by L.1993, c. 29, § 20, eff. Jan. 28, 1993.

2A:156A–25. Good faith reliance on court order as defense

A good faith reliance on a court order authorizing the interception shall constitute a complete defense to a civil or criminal action brought under this act or to administrative proceedings brought against a law enforcement officer.

L.1968, c. 409, § 25, eff. Jan. 1, 1969.

2A:156A-26. Partial invalidity

If any section, subsection or portion or provision of any section or sections of this act or the application thereof by or to any person or circumstances is declared invalid, the remainder of the section or sections or subsection of this act and the application thereof by or to other persons or circumstances shall not be affected thereby.

L.1968, c. 409, § 26, eff. Jan. 1, 1969.

2A:156A-27. Unlawful access to stored communications

a. A person is guilty of a crime of the fourth degree if he (1) knowingly accesses without authorization a facility through which an electronic communication service is provided or exceeds an authorization to access that facility, and (2) thereby obtains, alters, or prevents authorized access to a wire or electronic communication while that communication is in electronic storage.

b. A person is guilty of a crime of the third degree if, for the purpose of commercial advantage, private commercial gain, or malicious destruction or damage, he (1) knowingly accesses without authorization a facility through which an electronic communication service is provided or exceeds an authorization to access that facility, and (2) thereby obtains, alters, or prevents authorized access to a wire or electronic communication while that communication is in electronic storage.

c. This section does not apply to conduct authorized: (1) by the person or entity providing a wire or electronic communication service; or (2) by a user of that service with respect to a communication of or intended for that user; or (3) by section 10 of P.L.1968, c. 409 (C. 2A:156A-10), section 13 of P.L.1968, c. 409 (C. 2A:156A-13), or by section 23 or 24 of P.L.1993, c. 29 (C. 2A:156A-29 or C. 2A:156A-30).

L.1993, c. 29, § 21, eff. Jan. 28, 1993.

2A:156A-28. Disclosure of contents

a. (1) Except as provided in subsection b. of this section, a person or entity providing an electronic communication service to the public shall not knowingly divulge to any person or entity the contents of a communication while in electronic storage by that service; and

(2) Except as provided in subsection b. of this section, a person or entity providing remote computing service to the public shall not knowingly divulge to any person or entity the contents of any communication which is carried or maintained on that service:

(a) on behalf of, and received by means of electronic transmission from, or created by means of computer processing of communications received by means of

electronic transmission from, a subscriber or customer of the service; and

(b) solely for the purpose of providing storage or computer processing services to the subscriber or customer, if the provider is not authorized to access the contents of any such communication for the purpose of providing any services other than storage or computer processing.

b. A person or entity may divulge the contents of a communication:

(1) to an addressee or intended recipient of the communication or an agent of the addressee or intended recipient;

(2) as authorized or required by section 4 of P.L. 1968, c. 409 (C. 2A:156A-4), section 17 of P.L.1968, c. 409 (C. 2A:156A-17), section 18 of P.L.1968, c. 409 (C. 2A:156A-18) or section 23 of P.L.1993, c. 29 (C. 2A:156A-29);

(3) with the lawful consent of the originator or an addressee or intended recipient of the communication, or the subscriber in the case of a remote computing service;

(4) to a person employed or authorized or whose facilities are used to forward the communication to its destination;

(5) as may be necessarily incident to the rendition of the service or to the protection of the rights or property of the provider; or

(6) to a law enforcement agency, if the contents were inadvertently obtained by the provider and appear to pertain to the commission of a crime.

L.1993, c. 29, § 22, eff. Jan. 28, 1993.

2A:156A-29. Requirements for access

a. A law enforcement agency, but no other governmental entity, may require the disclosure by a provider of electronic communication service or remote computing service of the contents of an electronic communication without notice to the subscriber or the customer if the law enforcement agency obtains a warrant.

b. Except as provided in subsection c. of this section, a provider of electronic communication service or remote computing service may disclose a record or other information pertaining to a subscriber or customer of the service to any person other than a governmental entity. This subsection shall not apply to the contents covered by subsection a. of this section.

c. A provider of electronic communication service or remote computing service or a communication common carrier shall disclose a record, the location information for a subscriber's or customer's mobile or wireless communications device, or other information pertaining to a subscriber or customer of the service, other than contents covered by subsections a. and f. of this section, to a law enforcement agency under the following circumstances:

(1) the law enforcement agency has obtained a warrant;

(2) the law enforcement agency has obtained the consent of the subscriber or customer to the disclosure;

(3) the law enforcement agency has obtained a court order for such disclosure under subsection e. of this section; or

(4) with respect to only the location information for a subscriber's or customer's mobile or wireless communications device and not to a record or other subscriber or customer information, the law enforcement agency believes in good faith that an emergency involving danger of death or serious bodily injury to the subscriber or customer requires disclosure without delay of information relating to the emergency.

A law enforcement agency receiving records or information pursuant to this subsection is not required to provide notice to the customer or subscriber.

d.   Notwithstanding any other provision of law to the contrary, no service provider, its officers, employees, agents or other specified persons shall be liable in any civil action for damages as a result of providing information, facilities or assistance in accordance with the terms of a court order or warrant under this section.

e.   A court order for disclosure under subsection b. or c. may be issued by a judge of competent jurisdiction and shall issue only if the law enforcement agency offers specific and articulable facts showing that there are reasonable grounds to believe that the record or other information pertaining to a subscriber or customer of an electronic communication service or remote computing service or communication common carrier is relevant and material to an ongoing criminal investigation.   A judge who has issued an order pursuant to this section, on a motion made promptly by the service provider, may quash or modify such order, if the information or records requested are unusually voluminous in nature or compliance with such order otherwise would cause an undue burden on such provider.

f.   A provider of electronic communication service or remote computing service shall disclose to a law enforcement agency or to the State Commission of Investigation the:

(1) name;

(2) address;

(3) telephone or instrument number or other subscriber number or identity, including any temporarily assigned network address;

(4) local and long distance telephone connection records or records of session times and durations;

(5) length of service, including start date, and types of services utilized; and

(6) means and source of payment for such service, including any credit card or bank account number,

of a subscriber to or customer of such service when the law enforcement agency obtains a grand jury or trial subpoena or when the State Commission of Investigation issues a subpoena.

g.   Upon the request of a law enforcement agency, a provider of wire or electronic communication service or a remote computing service shall take all necessary steps to preserve, for a period of 90 days, records and other evidence in its possession pending the issuance of a court order or other legal process.   The preservation period shall be extended for an additional 90 days upon the request of the law enforcement agency.

L.1993, c. 29, § 23, eff. Jan. 28, 1993.   Amended by L.1994, c. 55, § 2, eff. June 28, 1994; L.1999, c. 151, § 6, eff. June 30, 1999; L.2005, c. 58, § 7, eff. March 28, 2005; L.2005, c. 270, § 1, eff. May 1, 2006; L.2009, c. 184, § 2, eff. Jan. 12, 2010.

2A:156A–30.   Backup preservation

a.   (1) A law enforcement agency acting pursuant to section 23 of P.L.1993, c. 29 (C. 2A:156A–29) may include in a court order a requirement that the service provider to whom the request is directed create a backup copy of the contents of the electronic communication sought in order to preserve those communications.   Without notifying the subscriber or customer of the court order, the service provider shall create the backup copy as soon as practicable, consistent with its regular business practices, but in no event later than within two business days after receipt by the provider of the court order and shall confirm to the law enforcement agency that the backup copy has been made.

(2) Notice to the subscriber or customer shall be made by the law enforcement agency within three days after receipt of confirmation that the backup copy has been made.

(3) The service provider shall not destroy or permit the destruction of the backup copy until either the delivery of the information or the resolution of all proceedings, including any appeals, concerning the court order, whichever is later.

(4) The service provider shall release the backup copy to the requesting law enforcement agency if, 14 days after the agency's notice to the subscriber or customer, the provider has not received written notice from the subscriber or customer that the subscriber or customer has filed a motion to vacate the order pursuant to subsection b. of this section or the provider has not initiated proceedings to challenge the request of the agency.

b.   Within 14 days after notice by the law enforcement agency to the subscriber or customer under paragraph (2) of subsection a. of this section the subscriber or customer may file a motion to vacate the court order, copies to be served upon the agency and written notice of the challenge to be given to the service provider.   A motion to vacate a court order shall be filed in the court which issued the order.   The motion or application shall contain an affidavit or sworn statement stating that the applicant is a customer of or subscriber to the service from which the contents of electronic communications maintained for the applicant have been sought and shall contain the applicant's reasons for believing that the records sought are not relevant to a legitimate law enforcement inquiry or that there has not been substantial compliance with the provisions of sections 21 through 26 of P.L.1993, c. 29, (C. 2A:156A–27 through C. 2A:156A–32).

c. Service shall be made upon the law enforcement agency by delivering or mailing by registered or certified mail a copy of the papers to the person, office or department specified in the notice which the customer received pursuant to paragraph (2) of subsection a. of this section.

d. If the court finds that the subscriber or customer has properly complied with subsections b. and c. of this section, the court shall order the law enforcement agency to file a sworn response, which may be filed in camera if it includes the reasons which make in camera review appropriate. If the court is unable to determine the motion or application on the basis of the initial allegations and responses, the court may conduct such additional proceedings as it deems appropriate. All such proceedings shall be completed and the motion or application decided as soon as practicable after the filing of the agency's response.

e. If the court finds that the applicant is not the subscriber or customer for whom the communications sought by the law enforcement agency are maintained, or that there is reason to believe that the law enforcement inquiry is legitimate and that the communications sought are relevant to that inquiry, it shall deny the motion or application and order the process enforced. If the court finds that the applicant is the subscriber or customer for whom the communications sought are maintained, and that there is no reason to believe that the communications sought are relevant to a legitimate law enforcement inquiry, or that there has not been substantial compliance with the provisions of sections 21 through 26 of P.L.1993, c. 29 (C. 2A:156A–27 through C. 2A:156A–32), it shall order the process quashed.
L.1993, c. 29, § 24.

2A:156A–31. Cost reimbursement

a. Except as otherwise provided in subsection c. of this section, a law enforcement agency obtaining the contents of communications, records or other information under sections 22, 23 or 24 of P.L.1993, c. 29 (C. 2A:156A–28, C. 2A:156A–29, or C. 2A:156A–30) shall reimburse the person or provider for such costs as are reasonably necessary and which have been directly incurred in searching for, assembling, reproducing and otherwise providing the information. Reimbursable costs shall include, but shall not be limited to, any costs due to necessary disruption of normal operations of any electronic communication service or remote computing service in which the information may be stored.

b. The amount of the reimbursement provided for in subsection a. of this section shall be as mutually agreed upon by a law enforcement agency and the service provider. In the absence of agreement, reimbursement shall be determined by the court which issued the order for production of the information or, if no court order was issued, then by the court before which a criminal prosecution relating to the information would be brought.

c. The requirement of subsection a. of this section does not apply with respect to records or other information maintained by a provider of wire or electronic communication service which relates to telephone toll records and telephone listings obtained under section 23 of P.L.1993, c. 29 (C. 2A:156A–29). The court may, however, order reimbursement as described in subsection a. of this section if the court determines the information required is voluminous or otherwise causes an undue burden on the provider.
L.1993, c. 29, § 25, eff. Jan. 28, 1993.

2A:156A–32. Civil action

a. Except as provided in subsection d. of section 23 of P.L.1993, c. 29 (C. 2A:156A–29), any service provider, subscriber or customer aggrieved by any violation of sections 21, 22, 23, or 24 of P.L.1993, c. 29 (C. 2A:156A–27, C. 2A:156A–28, C. 2A:156A–29, or C. 2A:156A–30) may recover, in a civil action, such relief as may be appropriate from the person or entity which knowingly or purposefully engaged in the conduct constituting the violation.

b. In a civil action under this section, appropriate relief may include:

(1) such preliminary and other equitable or declaratory relief as may be appropriate;

(2) damages under subsection c. of this section; and

(3) reasonable attorney fees and other litigation costs reasonably incurred.

c. The court may assess as damages in a civil action under this section the sum of the actual damages suffered by the plaintiff and any profits made by the violator as a result of the violation, but in no case shall a person entitled to recover receive less than the sum of $1,000.

d. A civil action under this section may not be commenced later than two years after the date upon which the claimant first discovered or had a reasonable opportunity to discover the violation.
L.1993, c. 29, § 26, eff. Jan. 28, 1993.

2A:156A–33. Good faith defenses to civil or criminal actions

It shall be a complete defense to any civil or criminal action brought pursuant to sections 21, 22, 23, 24 and 26 of P.L.1993, c. 29 (C. 2A:156A–27, C. 2A:156A–28, C. 2A:156A–29, C. 2A:156A–30, and C. 2A:156A–32) that the person made good faith reliance on:

a.   a court warrant or order, a legislative authorization or a statutory authorization;

b.   a request of an investigative or law enforcement officer under section 13 of P.L.1968, c. 409 (C. 2A:156A–13); or

c.   a good faith determination that section 4 of P.L.1968, c. 409 (C. 2A:156A–4) permitted the conduct which is the subject of the complaint.

L.1993, c. 29, § 27, eff. Jan. 28, 1993.

2A:156A–34.   Exclusivity of remedies

The remedies and sanctions described in sections 21 and 26 of P.L.1993, c. 29 (C. 2A:156A–27 and C. 2A:156A–32) are the only judicial remedies and sanctions for nonconstitutional violations of sections 21, 22, 23 and 24 of P.L.1993, c. 29 (C. 2A:156A–27, C. 2A:156A–28, C. 2A:156A–29 and C. 2A:156A–30).

L.1993, c. 29, § 28, eff. Jan. 28, 1993.

CHAPTER 157

COUNTY DETECTIVES AND INVESTIGATORS

Section
2A:157-1.   Short title.
2A:157-2.   County detectives generally; appointment; salary; duties.
2A:157-2.1.   Power of arrest for crime committed in presence of officer within territorial limits of state.
2A:157-3.   County detectives in first-class counties.
2A:157-4.   County detectives in second-class counties; appointment; minimum compensation.
2A:157-4.1.   Repealed.
2A:157-5.   County detectives in third-class counties of over 75,000 population.
2A:157-6.   County detectives in third-class counties of less than 75,000 population.
2A:157-7.   Repealed.
2A:157-8.   County detectives in fifth-class counties.
2A:157-9.   County detectives in sixth-class counties.
2A:157-10.   County investigators generally; appointment and removal; salary; duties.
2A:157-10.1.   County investigators; removal from office, employment or position; filing of complaints.
2A:157-10.2.   Subpoena of witnesses and evidence.
2A:157-10.3.   Suspension of county investigators; hearing requirements.
2A:157-10.4.   Suspension of county investigators; pay requirements.
2A:157-10.5.   County investigators; reinstatement; recovery of pay.
2A:157-10.6.   Illegal suspension or dismissal; recovery of pay.
2A:157-10.7.   Conviction of charges; right to review.
2A:157-10.8.   Defending actions arising from lawful exercise of police powers.
2A:157-11.   County investigators in first-class counties.
2A:157-12.   County investigators in second-class counties.
2A:157-13.   County investigators in third-class counties.
2A:157-14.   Repealed.
2A:157-15.   County investigators in counties of fifth class; compensation.
Section
2A:157-16.   County investigators in sixth-class counties.
2A:157-17.   Service of process; fees.
2A:157-18.   Payment of salaries; fixing salaries over minimum.
2A:157-19.   Power of prosecutor to incur expenses.
2A:157-20.   County detectives and special officers; status.
2A:157-21.   Saving clause.
2A:157-22.   Limitation on number.
2A:157-23.   Construction; "special officer" discontinued.

2A:157–1.   Short title

This chapter shall be known and may be cited as the "County Detectives and County Investigators Act (Revision of 1951)."

2A:157–2.   County detectives generally; appointment; salary; duties

The prosecutor in each of the several counties of this State may appoint such number of suitable persons, not in excess of the number, and at salaries not less than the minimum amounts, in this chapter provided, to be known as county detectives, to assist the prosecutor in the detection, apprehension, arrest and conviction of offenders against the law. Persons so appointed shall be in the classified service of the civil service and shall possess all the powers and rights and be subject to all the obligations of police officers, constables and special deputy sheriffs in criminal matters.

2A:157–2.1.   Power of arrest for crime committed in presence of officer within territorial limits of state

Notwithstanding the provisions of any other law to the contrary, any full-time, permanently appointed county detective, sheriff's officer and investigator sheriff's office shall have full power of arrest for any crime committed in his presence anywhere within the territorial limits of the State of New Jersey.

L.1977, c. 438, § 2, eff. March 2, 1978.

2A:157–3.   County detectives in first-class counties

In counties of the first class there may be appointed not in excess of 50 county detectives, of whom one may be designated chief of county detectives, two deputy chiefs of county detectives, four captains of county detectives, and not more than 12 lieutenants of county detectives; their annual salaries shall be fixed as follows: chief of county detectives, not less than $11,500.00; deputy chiefs of county detectives, not less than $11,000.00; captains of county detectives, not less than $9,500.00; lieutenants of county detectives, not less than $7,500.00; and other county detectives, not less than $6,500.00.

Amended by L.1959, c. 161, p. 635, § 1; L.1966, c. 266, § 1, eff. Sept. 6, 1966; L.1974, c. 171, § 1, eff. Dec. 10, 1974.

2A:157–4. County detectives in second-class counties; appointment; minimum compensation

a. In counties of the second class having a population in excess of 580,000 there may be appointed not in excess of 40 county detectives, of whom one may be designated chief of county detectives, one deputy chief of county detectives, one captain of county detectives, six lieutenants of county detectives and four sergeants of county detectives.

b. In counties of the second class having a population between 500,000 and 580,000 there may be appointed not in excess of 28 county detectives, of whom one may be designated chief of county detectives, one deputy chief of county detectives, one captain of county detectives, six lieutenants of county detectives and four sergeants of county detectives.

c. In counties of the second class having a population between 440,000 and 500,000, there may be appointed not in excess of 28 county detectives, of whom one may be designated chief of county detectives, one deputy chief of county detectives, four captains of county detectives and six lieutenants of county detectives.

d. In the counties of the second class having a population between 400,000 and 440,000, there may be appointed not in excess of 24 county detectives of whom one may be designated chief of county detectives, one captain of county detectives, four lieutenants of county detectives and two sergeants of county detectives.

e. In the counties of the second class having a population of 400,000 or under, there may be appointed not in excess of 12 county detectives of whom one may be designated chief of county detectives, one captain of county detectives, and three lieutenants of county detectives.

f. Their annual salaries shall be fixed as follows: chief of county detectives, not less than $9,500.00; deputy chief of county detectives, not less than $9,000.00; captain of county detectives, not less than $8,000.00; lieutenant of county detectives, not less than $7,000.00; sergeant of county detectives, not less than $6,500.00; and other county detectives, not less than $6,000.00.

Amended by L.1959, c. 161, § 2; L.1961, c. 97, p. 665, § 1; L.1967, c. 210, § 1, eff. Sept. 25, 1967; L.1970, c. 260, § 1, eff. Nov. 2, 1970; L.1973, c. 203, § 1, eff. July 31, 1973; L.1977, c. 79, § 1, eff. May 2, 1977; L.1978, c. 164, § 1, eff. Dec. 7, 1978; L.1980, c. 42, § 1, eff. June 20, 1980; L.1981, c. 462, § 8; L.1982, c. 142, § 1, eff. Sept. 20, 1982; L.1983, c. 433, § 1, eff. Jan. 5, 1984.

2A:157–4.1. Repealed by L.1973, c. 203, § 2, eff. July 31, 1973

2A:157–5. County detectives in third-class counties of over 75,000 population

In counties of the third class now or hereafter having a population in excess of 75,000 there may be appointed not in excess of 9 county detectives, of whom 1 may be designated chief of county detectives, 1 captain of county detectives; and 1 lieutenant of county detectives; their annual salaries shall be fixed as follows: chief of county detectives, not less than $7,500.00; captain of county detectives, not less than $7,000.00; lieutenant of county detectives, not less than $6,000.00; and other county detectives, not less than $5,500.00

Amended by L.1959, c. 161, p. 636, § 3.

2A:157–6. County detectives in third-class counties of less than 75,000 population

In counties of the third class now or hereafter having a population of less than 75,000 there may be appointed not in excess of five county detectives, of whom one may be designated chief of county detectives and of whom one may be designated as lieutenant of county detectives; their annual salaries shall be fixed as follows: chief of county detectives, not less than $6,500.00; lieutenant of county detectives, not less than $6,000.00; and other county detectives, not less than $5,500.00.

Amended by L.1959, c. 161, p. 636, § 4; L.1973, c. 278, § 1, eff. Nov. 29, 1973.

2A:157–7. Repealed by L.1981, c. 462, § 57

2A:157–8. County detectives in fifth-class counties

In counties of the fifth class with a population of 400,000 or less there may be appointed not in excess of 12 county detectives, and in counties of the fifth class with a population in excess of 400,000 there may be appointed not in excess of 15 county detectives, of whom one may be designated chief of county detectives, two captains of county detectives, and four lieutenants of county detectives.

Amended by L.1974, c. 5, § 1, eff. Feb. 15, 1974; L.1975, c. 234, § 1, eff. Oct. 24, 1975; L.1982, c. 187, § 1, eff. Dec. 1, 1982; L.1988, c. 65, § 1, eff. July 14, 1988.

2A:157–9. County detectives in sixth-class counties

In counties of the sixth class there may be appointed not in excess of six county detectives, of whom one may be designated chief of county detectives and one captain of county detectives; their annual salaries shall be fixed as follows: chief of county detectives, not less than $7,500.00; captain of county detectives, not less than $6,500.00; and other county detectives, not less than $5,500.00.

Amended by L.1959, c. 161, p. 637, § 6, eff. Sept. 17, 1959; L.1975, c. 280, § 1, eff. Jan. 12, 1976.

2A:157–10. County investigators generally; appointment and removal; salary; duties

In addition to the office of county detective, there is created in the office of the prosecutor, the office or position of county investigator which shall be in the unclassified service of the civil service. The prosecutor of each of the several counties of this state may appoint such number of suitable persons, not in excess of the number, and at salaries not less than the minimum amounts, in this act provided, to be known as county investigators, and to assist the prosecutor in the detection, apprehension, arrest and conviction of offenders against the law. Persons so appointed shall possess all the powers and rights and be subject to all the obligations of police officers, constables and special deputy sheriffs, in criminal matters.

Notwithstanding the provisions of this section, a single probationary or temporary appointment as a county investigator may be made for a total period not exceeding one year.

Amended by L.2003, c. 173, § 1, eff. Jan. 7, 2004.

2A:157–10.1. County investigators; removal from office, employment or position; filing of complaints

Except as otherwise provided by law, a county investigator employed by the county prosecutor shall not be removed from office, employment or position for political reasons or for any cause other than incapacity, misconduct, or disobedience of rules and regulations established by the prosecutor, nor shall such investigator be suspended, removed, fined or reduced in rank from or in office, employment, or position therein, except for just cause as hereinbefore provided and then only upon a written complaint setting forth the charge or charges against such investigator. The chief investigator and deputy chief investigator, however, may be removed or demoted by the prosecutor. The complaint shall be filed in the office having charge of the office wherein the complaint is made and a copy shall be served upon the investigator so charged, with notice of a designated hearing thereon by the proper authorities, which shall be not less than 10 or more than 30 days from the date of service of the complaint.

A complaint charging a violation of the internal rules and regulations established for the conduct of a prosecutor's office shall be filed no later than the 45th day after the date on which the person filing the complaint obtained sufficient information to file the matter upon which the complaint is based. The 45–day time limit shall not apply if an investigation of an investigator for a violation of the internal rules or regulations of the office is included directly or indirectly within a concurrent investigation of that office for a violation of the criminal laws of this State. The 45–day limit shall begin on the day after the disposition of the criminal investigation. The 45–day requirement of this paragraph for the filing of a complaint against an investigator shall not apply to a filing of a complaint by a private individual.

A failure to comply with these provisions as to the service of the complaint and the time within which a complaint is to be filed shall require a dismissal of the complaint.

The investigator may waive the right to a hearing and may appeal the charges directly to any available authority specified by law or regulation, or follow any other procedure recognized by a contract, as permitted by law.

For the purposes of this section, the transfer of an investigator from one section or unit to another section or unit within the office of the prosecutor shall not constitute a demotion, and the transferred investigator shall retain his rank, seniority, seniority-related privileges and salary.

L.2003, c. 173, § 2, eff. Jan. 7, 2004.

2A:157–10.2. Subpoena of witnesses and evidence

Except as otherwise provided by the law, the officer, board or authority empowered to hear and determine the charge or charges made against a county investigator shall have the power to subpoena witnesses and documentary evidence. The Superior Court shall have jurisdiction to enforce any such subpoena.

L.2003, c. 173, § 3, eff. Jan. 7, 2004.

2A:157–10.3. Suspension of county investigators; hearing requirements

If any county investigator shall be suspended pending a hearing as a result of charges made against him, such hearing, except as otherwise provided by law, shall be commenced within 30 days from the date of the service of the copy of the complaint upon him, in default of which the charges shall be dismissed and the investigator may be returned to duty.

L.2003, c. 173, § 4, eff. Jan. 7, 2004.

2A:157–10.4. Suspension of county investigators; pay requirements

Notwithstanding any other law to the contrary, whenever a county investigator is charged with an offense, under the laws of this State, another state, or the United States, the investigator may be suspended from performing his duties, with pay, until the case against the investigator is disposed of at trial, the complaint is dismissed, or the prosecution is terminated; provided, however, that if a grand jury returns an indictment against the investigator, or the investigator is charged with a crime of the first, second or third degree or which involves moral turpitude or dishonesty, the investigator may be suspended from his duties, without pay, until the case against him is disposed of at trial, the complaint is dismissed, or the prosecution is terminated.

L.2003, c. 173, § 5, eff. Jan. 7, 2004.

2A:157–10.5. County investigators; reinstatement; recovery of pay

If a suspended county investigator is found not guilty at trial, the charges are dismissed or the prosecution is terminated, the investigator shall be reinstated to his position and shall be entitled to recover all pay withheld during the period of suspension subject to any disciplinary proceedings or administrative action.

L.2003, c. 173, § 6, eff. Jan. 7, 2004.

2A:157–10.6. Illegal suspension or dismissal; recovery of pay

Whenever any county investigator shall be suspended or dismissed from his office, employment or position and that suspension or dismissal shall be judicially determined to be illegal, the investigator shall be entitled to recover his salary from the date of such suspension or dismissal, provided a written application therefor shall be filed with the prosecutor's office within 30 days after such judicial determination.

L.2003, c. 173, § 7, eff. Jan. 7, 2004.

2A:157–10.7. Conviction of charges; right to review

Any county investigator who has been tried and convicted of any charge or charges, and is employed by a prosecutor in a county where Title 11A (Civil Service) of the New Jersey Statutes is not in operation, may obtain a review thereof by the Superior Court. Such review shall be obtained by serving a written notice of an application therefor upon the party or board whose action is to be reviewed within 10 days after written notice to the investigator of the conviction. The party or board shall transmit to the court a copy of the record of such conviction, and of the charge or charges for which the applicant was tried. The court shall hear the cause de novo on the record below and may either affirm, reverse or modify such conviction. If the applicant was removed from his office, employment or position, the court may direct that he be restored to such office, employment or position, and to all his rights pertaining thereto, and may take such other order or judgement as the court deems proper. Either party may supplement the record with additional testimony subject to the rules of evidence.

L.2003, c. 173, § 8, eff. Jan. 7, 2004.

2A:157–10.8. Defending actions arising from lawful exercise of police powers

Whenever a county investigator is a defendant in any action or legal proceeding arising out of and directly related to the lawful exercise of police powers in the furtherance of his official duties, the prosecutor shall provide the investigator with the necessary means for the defense of such action or proceeding, but not for his defense in a disciplinary proceeding instituted against him by the prosecutor or in a criminal proceeding instituted as a result of a complaint on behalf of the prosecutor. If any such disciplinary or criminal proceeding instituted by or on complaint of the prosecutor shall be dismissed or finally determined in favor of the investigator, he shall be reimbursed for the expense of his defense.

L.2003, c. 173, § 9, eff. Jan. 7, 2004.

2A:157–11. County investigators in first-class counties

In counties of the first class there may be appointed not in excess of 30 county investigators, who shall be paid annual salaries of not less than $6,500.00

Amended by L.1959, c. 161, p. 637; L.1966, c. 265, § 1, eff. Sept. 6, 1966.

2A:157–12. County investigators in second-class counties

In counties of the second class there may be appointed not in excess of 9 county investigators, who shall be paid annual salaries of not less than $6,500.00.

Not more than 6 county investigators in counties of the second class with populations of 400,000 inhabitants or less, and not more than 21 county investigators in counties of the second class with populations in excess of 400,000 inhabitants, in addition to those provided for in this section may be appointed by the county prosecutor where there appears to be a reasonable necessity therefor, if approved by resolution of the board of chosen freeholders of the county.

Amended by L.1959, c. 161, p. 637, § 8; L.1966, c. 308, § 1, eff. Dec. 29, 1966; L.1970, c. 259, § 1, eff. Nov. 2, 1970.

2A:157–13. County investigators in third-class counties

In counties of the third class there may be appointed not in excess of 2 county investigators who shall be paid annual salaries of not less than $5,500.00.

Amended by L.1959, c. 161, p. 637, § 9.

2A:157–14. Repealed by L.1981, c. 462, § 57

2A:157–15. County investigators in counties of fifth class; compensation

In counties of the fifth class there may be appointed not in excess of 12 county investigators, who shall be paid annual salaries of not less than $5,500.00.

Amended by L.1959, c. 161, p. 637, § 11; L.1981, c. 462, § 9.

2A:157–16. County investigators in sixth-class counties

In counties of the sixth class there may be appointed not in excess of six county investigators, who shall be paid annual salaries of not less than $5,000.00.

Amended by L.1959, c. 161, p. 638, § 12; L.1975, c. 280, § 2, eff. Jan. 12, 1976.

2A:157–17. Service of process; fees

County detectives and county investigators may serve or execute for the sheriff any process or writ in any criminal proceeding and make return thereof. For every process or writ so served or executed by a county detective or county investigator, the sheriff shall be entitled to collect and receive the same fees, and to tax such fees in the bills of costs, as if the process or writ had been served by him.

2A:157–18. Payment of salaries; fixing salaries over minimum

Annual salaries of county detectives and county investigators shall be paid by the county treasurer upon the certification of the prosecutor out of funds of the county, in the same manner as other salaries are paid, and shall be not less than the minimum amounts in this act fixed. The prosecutor may, with the approval of the board of chosen freeholders, fix the salaries of county detectives and county investigators at amounts in excess of the minimum amounts in this chapter provided.

2A:157–19. Power of prosecutor to incur expenses

Nothing in this chapter shall be construed to limit the power of any prosecutor, duly conferred upon him by law, to incur expenses in the detection, arrest, indictment and conviction of offenders against the criminal laws of this state.

2A:157–20. County detectives and special officers; status

L.1951, c. 274, p. 946, section 20 of an act entitled "An Act to revise the law concerning county detectives and county investigators, and repealing sundry acts." (C. 2:181–51) saved from repeal.

2A:157–21. Saving clause

Notwithstanding any other provision of this chapter, nothing herein shall be construed to require an increase in any salaries heretofore paid or to be paid in any county, unless and until the salary schedules herein provided shall be adopted by resolution of the county board of chosen freeholders. Nothing in this chapter provided shall be construed to reduce the amount of salary now being paid to any person, to affect the pension rights of any person, to effect the transfer of the holder of any office or position from the classified to the unclassified service of the civil service, or to terminate tenure rights vested, by the provisions of any law repealed by this chapter, in any person continued in office or position in the unclassified service.

2A:157–22. Limitation on number

In any county in which the total number of county detectives and county investigators authorized by this chapter exceeds the total number of officers employed in the prosecutor's office of such county for the detection, apprehension, arrest, indictment and conviction of offenders against the law, as of the effective date of this chapter, no new appointments as county detective or county investigator shall be made, other than to fill vacancies hereafter occurring, without prior approval as to the number and salary thereof by the board of chosen freeholders or, in counties of the first class having a population of less than eight hundred thousand inhabitants, by order of the Superior Court Assignment Judge of the county.

Amended by L.1953, c. 385, p. 2004, § 1, eff. Aug. 14, 1953.

2A:157–23. Construction; "special officer" discontinued

It is the intention that this chapter be so construed as to make consistent throughout the state the law as it applies to the office or position of county detective and county investigator, to provide that county detectives shall be in the classified service of the civil service, and county investigators in the unclassified service and to discontinue the term "special officer" as the title of any office in the offices of prosecutors.

CHAPTER 158

COUNTY PROSECUTORS

Section

2A:158–1.   Appointment of county prosecutor; general duties.

2A:158–1.1.   Other gainful employment by prosecutor; prohibition; exception.

2A:158–1.2.   Repealed.

2A:158–2.   County prosecutor substituted for prosecutor of the pleas.

2A:158–3.   Oath of prosecutors.

2A:158–4.   Exclusive jurisdiction of prosecutors over criminal business; exceptions.

2A:158–5.   Powers, duties and liabilities of prosecutors.

2A:158–6.   Fees of prosecutors.

2A:158–7.   Expenses of prosecutors in enforcement of laws.

2A:158–8.   Expenses of prosecutors in enjoining nuisances under federal law.

2A:158–9.   Temporary prosecutors; appointment by court; powers; compensation.

2A:158–10.   Salaries of prosecutors.

2A:158–11 to 2A:158–12.1.   Repealed.

2A:158–12.2.   Repealed.

2A:158–13.   Payment of salaries of prosecutors; fees and costs paid to county.

2A:158–14.   Repealed.

2A:158–15.   Assistant prosecutors; number; appointment; designation; terms of office; oath of office.

2A:158–15.1, 2A:158–15.1a.   Repealed.

2A:158–15.1b.   Assistant prosecutors not to engage in practice of law or employment outside of prosecutor's office; exception.

2A:158–15.2.   Repealed.

2A:158–15.3.   Salaries of assistant prosecutors.

2A:158–16, 2A:158–16.1.   Repealed.

2A:158–17 to 2A:158–17.3.   Repealed.

2A:158–18.   Powers and duties of assistant prosecutors.

2A:158–18.1.   Legal assistant to county prosecutor in first class counties of 800,000 or less.

2A:158–18.2.   Approval of appointment of legal assistant.

2A:158–19.   Tenure of office of secretaries and stenographers in office of county prosecutor and office of county detective in certain counties.

2A:158–20.   Suspension, discharge or decrease of compensation of secretaries and stenographers.

2A:158–21.   Prohibited political activity of county prosecutors, assistant prosecutors or legal assistants.

2A:158–1. Appointment of county prosecutor; general duties

There shall be appointed, for each county, by the governor with the advice and consent of the senate to serve for a term of 5 years and until the appointment and qualification of his successor, some fit person who shall have been admitted to the practice of law in this state for at least 5 years, who shall be known as the county prosecutor and who, except as otherwise provided by law, shall prosecute the pleas of the state in such county and shall have all of the powers and perform all of the duties formerly had and performed by the prosecutor of the pleas of such county. As the term of the prosecutor of the pleas of any county shall expire there shall be appointed in his place and stead such county prosecutor.

2A:158–1.1. Other gainful employment by prosecutor; prohibition; exception

Any person appointed to the office of county prosecutor shall devote his entire time to the duties of his office and shall not engage in the practice of law or other gainful employment, except those appointed to that office in counties of the third class having a population between 65,000 and 85,000. No exception to the requirement that a prosecutor serve on a full-time basis shall be permitted on or after April 14, 1986.

L.1970, c. 6, § 1, eff. Feb. 9, 1970. Amended by L.1972, c. 33, § 1, eff. May 25, 1972; L.1975, c. 149, § 1, eff. July 9, 1975; L.1976, c. 15, § 1, eff. April 5, 1976; L.1976, c. 118, § 1, eff. Nov. 16, 1976; L.1978, c. 6, § 1, eff. March 17, 1978; L.1978, c. 24, § 1, eff. May 23, 1978; L.1980, c. 43, § 1, eff. June 23, 1980; L.1981, c. 462, § 10; L.1983, c. 288, § 2; L.1983, c. 300, § 1, eff. July 1, 1983.

2A:158–1.2. Repealed by L.1995, c. 424, § 5, eff. Jan. 10, 1996

2A:158–2. County prosecutor substituted for prosecutor of the pleas

In any statute in which the designation "prosecutor of the pleas" is used, it shall be construed to mean the county prosecutor. Until the term of any existing prosecutor of the pleas shall expire and a county prosecutor be appointed to succeed him as provided in this article, such prosecutor of the pleas shall have all of the powers, perform all of the duties and be entitled to the compensation of a county prosecutor for such county.

2A:158–3. Oath of prosecutors

Every person appointed county prosecutor shall, before entering upon the duties of his office, take and subscribe before the clerk of the county for which he has been appointed, or before a judge of the Superior Court, the following oath:

"I, , do solemnly promise and swear (or affirm), that I will faithfully, justly and impartially execute the duties of county prosecutor of this State, in and for the county of , to the best of my abilities and understanding. So help me God."

Amended by L.1991, c. 91, § 125, eff. April 9, 1991.

2A:158–4. Exclusive jurisdiction of prosecutors over criminal business; exceptions

The criminal business of the State shall be prosecuted by the Attorney General and the county prosecutors.

Amended by L.1970, c. 74, § 20, eff. May 21, 1970.

2A:158–5. Powers, duties and liabilities of prosecutors

Each prosecutor shall be vested with the same powers and be subject to the same penalties, within his county, as the attorney general shall by law be vested with or subject to, and he shall use all reasonable and lawful diligence for the detection, arrest, indictment and conviction of offenders against the laws.

2A:158–6. Fees of prosecutors

The same fees shall be payable for the services of prosecutors as are by law made payable for similar services of the attorney general.

2A:158–7. Expenses of prosecutors in enforcement of laws

All necessary expenses incurred by the prosecutor for each county in the detection, arrest, indictment and conviction of offenders against the laws shall, upon being certified to by the prosecutor and approved, under his hand, by a judge of the superior court, be paid by the county treasurer whenever the same shall be approved by the board of chosen freeholders of such county. The amount or amounts to be expended shall not exceed the amount fixed by the board of chosen freeholders in its regular or emergency appropriation, unless such expenditure is specifically authorized by order of the assignment judge of the superior court for such county.

Amended by L.1991, c. 91, § 126, eff. April 9, 1991.

2A:158–8. Expenses of prosecutors in enjoining nuisances under federal law

Whenever the prosecutor of any county shall bring an action, as authorized by the laws of the United States, to enjoin a nuisance as defined by the laws of the United States, all necessary expenses incurred thereby, certified to and approved under his hand by a judge of the superior court shall be paid by the county treasurer whenever the same shall be approved by the board of chosen freeholders of such county.

Amended by L.1991, c. 91, § 127, eff. April 9, 1991.

2A:158–9. Temporary prosecutors; appointment by court; powers; compensation

In the absence of the attorney general and of the county prosecutor, at any session of the Superior Court, the Assignment Judge of the Superior Court may appoint a fit person to prosecute the pleas of the State during that session. The person so appointed, on taking the oath or affirmation prescribed by N.J.S. 2A:158–3, shall be vested, during such session, with the powers of a prosecutor, and be entitled to the same compensation and subject to the same penalties.

Amended by L.1991, c. 91, § 128, eff. April 9, 1991.

2A:158–10. Salaries of prosecutors

County prosecutors shall receive annual salaries to be fixed by the governing body of the county at $153,000 beginning on January 1, 2008 and $165,000 beginning on January 1, 2009 and thereafter.

There shall be appropriated annually to the Department of Community Affairs for payment to each county for additional salary costs resulting from the increase in the salary of county prosecutors an amount equal to the amount by which the annual salary paid to the county prosecutor under this section exceeds $100,000.00.

Amended by L.1961, c. 41, p. 412, § 1; L.1968, c. 145, § 1, eff. July 12, 1968; L.1980, c. 45, § 1, eff. June 25, 1980; L.1981, c. 462, § 11; L.1983, c. 288, § 1, eff. July 29, 1983; L.1995, c. 424, § 2, eff. Jan. 10, 1996; L.1996, c. 99, § 1, eff. Aug. 12, 1996, retroactive to Jan. 1, 1996; L.1999, c. 380, § 5, eff. Jan. 14, 2000; L.2007, c. 350, § 2, eff. Jan. 14, 2008, retroactive to Jan. 1, 2008.

2A:158–11 to 2A:158–12.1. Repealed by L.1961, c. 41, § 4, eff. Sept. 1, 1961

2A:158–12.2. Repealed by L.1968, c. 145, § 2, eff. July 12, 1968

2A:158–13. Payment of salaries of prosecutors; fees and costs paid to county

The salaries of prosecutors shall be paid at the same times and in the same manner as other county salaries are paid, and shall be in lieu of all fees and costs or other compensation or allowances whatsoever.

All fees and costs allowed by law to the respective prosecutors shall be taxed in the bills of costs in the manner provided by law, and when collected in the manner provided by law, shall be paid into the treasury of the respective counties for the use thereof.

2A:158–14. Repealed by L.1970, c. 74, § 22, eff. May 21, 1970

2A:158–15. Assistant prosecutors; number; appointment; designation; terms of office; oath of office

Assistant prosecutors in and for the respective counties may be appointed by the prosecutors of such counties as hereinafter provided, who shall hold their appointments at the pleasure of the respective prosecutors, and shall, before entering upon the performance of the duties of their appointments, take, before a judge of the Superior Court or the Clerk of the Superior Court of the county in and for which they are appointed, an oath or affirmation to faithfully perform the duties of the office to the best of their ability.

a. In counties of the first class, the county prosecutor may appoint 15 assistant prosecutors, one of whom shall be designated as first assistant prosecutor.

b. In counties of the second class, the county prosecutor may appoint six assistant prosecutors, one of whom shall be designated as first assistant prosecutor.

c. In counties of the fifth class and counties of the third class having a population in excess of 120,000, the county prosecutor may appoint three assistant prosecutors, one of whom may be designated as first assistant prosecutor.

d. In all other counties the prosecutor may appoint one assistant prosecutor who may be designated first assistant prosecutor.

Creation of new or additional positions of assistant prosecutor as authorized by paragraphs a. through d. of this section, as hereby amended, shall require authorization by the governing body of the county.

Assistant prosecutors in addition to those provided for in paragraphs a. through d. of this section may be appointed by the county prosecutor in any county of the State where there appears to be a reasonable necessity therefor, if approved by order of the assignment judge and by resolution of the governing body of the county.

Amended by L.1961, c. 41, p. 413, § 2; L.1981, c. 462, § 12.

2A:158–15.1, 2A:158–15.1a. Repealed by L.2009, c. 285, §§ 1 and 2, eff. Jan. 17, 2010

2A:158–15.1b. Assistant prosecutors not to engage in practice of law or employment outside of prosecutor's office; exception

a. Except as provided in subsection b. of this section, assistant prosecutors shall devote their entire time to the duties of their office and shall not engage in the practice of law or other gainful employment.

b. Notwithstanding the provisions of subsection a. of this section, an assistant prosecutor may engage in limited outside employment or provide services as an independent contractor, under such terms and conditions as the county prosecutor deems appropriate, if:

(1) the county prosecutor has deemed the employment or services as not inconsistent with the duties of the office of assistant prosecutor;

(2) the employment or services do not involve the private practice of law or the provision of other legal services; and

(3) the employment or services do not qualify the assistant prosecutor for membership in any State-administered pension system.

c. Nothing in subsection b. of this section shall be construed to:

(1) limit the discretion of the county prosecutor to disapprove a request from an assistant prosecutor to engage in employment or services or to require an assistant prosecutor to terminate employment or services otherwise authorized under this subsection; or

(2) create an affirmative right for any assistant prosecutor to engage in employment or services without the approval of the county prosecutor.

L.2009, c. 285, § 3, eff. Jan. 17, 2010.

2A:158–15.2.   Repealed by L.1996, c. 99, § 4, eff. Aug. 12, 1996, retroactive to Jan. 1, 1996

2A:158–15.3.   Salaries of assistant prosecutors

a.   The annual salary of a first assistant prosecutor, a county prosecutor's principal assistant or an assistant prosecutor shall be determined by the board of chosen freeholders on recommendation of the county prosecutor.

b.   The salary of any person serving as a first assistant prosecutor, a county prosecutor's principal assistant or an assistant prosecutor prior to the effective date of P.L.1996, c. 99 (C. 2A:158–15.3 et al.) may not be reduced pursuant to the provisions of subsection a. of this section.

L.1996, c. 99, § 2, eff. Aug. 12, 1996, retroactive to Jan. 1, 1996.

2A:158–16, 2A:158–16.1.   Repealed by L.1996, c. 99, § 4, eff. Aug. 12, 1996, retroactive to Jan. 1, 1996

2A:158–17 to 2A:158–17.3.   Repealed by L.1961, c. 41, p. 415, § 4, eff. Sept. 1, 1961

2A:158–18.   Powers and duties of assistant prosecutors

In any county any of the assistant prosecutors of such county may attend the sessions of the grand jury of such county, and render therein any service or perform any duty that might be rendered or performed by the prosecutor of such county if he were present.

2A:158–18.1.   Legal assistant to county prosecutor in first class counties of 800,000 or less

In counties of the first class having a population not in excess of eight hundred thousand there is created in the office of the county prosecutor, the office or position of legal assistant to the county prosecutor which shall be in the unclassified service of the civil service.   The prosecutor of each of the said counties may appoint, subject to the approval hereinafter required, suitable persons to said office or position, not in excess of twelve and at salaries not less than six thousand dollars ($6,000.00) nor more than nine thousand dollars ($9,000.00) annually.   Every such legal assistant shall serve at the pleasure of the county prosecutor and be subject to removal by such prosecutor.   Before entering upon the performance of his duties every such legal assistant shall take and subscribe, before the county clerk of the county in and for which he is appointed, an oath to perform the duties of his office faithfully, impartially and justly to the best of his ability.

L.1953, c. 307, p. 1848, § 1, eff. July 28, 1953.

2A:158–18.2.   Approval of appointment of legal assistant

Every appointment of such a legal assistant and the amount of his salary shall be made subject to the approval of the board of chosen freeholders or the Superior Court assignment judge of the county.   Such approval shall not be required in the filling of vacancies.

L.1953, c. 307, p. 1848, § 2.

2A:158–19.   Tenure of office of secretaries and stenographers in office of county prosecutor and office of county detective in certain counties

L.1939, c. 271, p. 694, section 1 of an act entitled "An Act providing for and regulating tenure of office and service for persons holding secretarial and stenographic positions in the office of the prosecutor of the pleas and the office of county detectives in counties having a population of not less than eighty-two thousand nor more than one hundred and seventy-five thousand." saved from repeal.

2A:158–20.   Suspension, discharge or decrease of compensation of secretaries and stenographers

L.1939, c. 271, p. 694, section 2 of an act entitled "An Act providing for and regulating tenure of office and service for persons holding secretarial and stenographic positions in the office of the prosecutor of the pleas and the office of county detectives in counties having a population of not less than eighty-two thousand nor more than one hundred and seventy-five thousand." saved from repeal.

2A:158–21.   Prohibited political activity of county prosecutors, assistant prosecutors or legal assistants

No county prosecutor, assistant prosecutor or legal assistant to a prosecutor, while holding any such office or position, shall (1) be a candidate for election to, or hold, any elective public office or any office or position with any political party or club, or (2) in connection with the candidacy of any person for public office, sign or authorize the use of his name in connection with political or campaign literature or material, or print or publish in order to distribute such political or campaign literature or material;   provided, however, that the prohibition against holding office contained in this act shall not prevent any individual, holding or filling any such office as of the effective date of this act, from completing any term of office for which he has heretofore been elected or chosen;   and provided further that nothing herein contained shall be construed to prohibit any such prosecutor, assistant prosecutor or legal assistant from being a candidate for election to, or from holding, the office or position of delegate or alternate to the national convention of any political party.

L.1964, c. 168, § 1.

CHAPTER 158A

PUBLIC DEFENDER

Section

2A:158A–1.   Declaration of state policy.

2A:158A–2.   "Indigent defendant" defined.

2A:158A–3.   Establishment.

2A:158A–4.   Public defender; appointment; term; salary; vacancy.

2A:158A–5.   Duties of public defender.

2A:158A–5.1.   Repealed.

2A:158A–5.2.   Offenses and violations; legal representation.

2A:158A–6.   Deputy and assistant public defenders; appointment; salary.

2A:158A–7.   Powers of public defender.

2A:158A–8.   Lawyers to represent defendants on case basis; selection.

2A:158A–9.   Case workload; division; employment of counsel.

2A:158A–10.   Contracts authorizing private or public organizations to execute functions of public defender.

2A:158A–11.   Duties of staff members and others engaged on case basis.

2A:158A–12.   Attorney-client privilege.

2A:158A–13.   Standards and level of performance of attorneys providing legal services.

2A:158A–14.   Eligibility for services; determination.

2A:158A–15.   Repealed.

2A:158A–15.1.   Financial status of defendant; investigation by judge or court support office.

2A:158A–15.2.   Establishment of system in counties; responsibility for eligibility determinations; purpose of pilot project.

2A:158A–16.   Part payment of cost by defendant.

2A:158A–17.   Lien on property of defendant.

2A:158A–18.   Recording of liens; books provided; fees.

2A:158A–19.   Collections of moneys due.

2A:158A–20.   Compromise and settlement of claim for services.

2A:158A–21.   Repealed.

2A:158A–22.   Annual report.

2A:158A–23.   Oaths and affirmations.

2A:158A–24.   Juvenile delinquent or juvenile in need of supervision; legal representation.

2A:158A–25.   Minors; eligibility for services.

2A:158A–1. Declaration of state policy

It is hereby declared to be the policy of this State to provide for the realization of the constitutional guarantees of counsel in criminal cases for indigent defendants by means of the system and program established and authorized by this act to the end that no innocent person shall be convicted, and that the guilty, when convicted, shall be convicted only after a fair trial according to the due process of the law.

L.1967, c. 43, § 1, eff. July 1, 1967.

2A:158A–2. "Indigent defendant" defined

As used herein "indigent defendant" means a person who is formally charged with the commission of an indictable offense, and who does not have the present financial ability to secure competent legal representa-

tion, as determined by the factors in section 14 of P.L.1967, c. 43 (C. 2A:158A–14), and to provide all other necessary expenses of representation.

L.1967, c. 43, § 2, eff. July 1, 1967. Amended by L.1987, c. 170, § 1.

2A:158A–3. Establishment

There is hereby established in the Executive Branch of the State Government the Office of the Public Defender. For the purpose of complying with the provisions of Article V, Section IV, paragraph 1 of the New Jersey Constitution, the Office of the Public Defender is hereby allocated within the Department of State, but, notwithstanding said allocation, the office shall be independent of any supervision or control by the department or by any board or officer thereof.

L.1967, c. 43, § 3, eff. July l, 1967. Amended by L.1974, c. 27, § 9; L.1994, c. 58, § 7, eff. July 1, 1994.

2A:158A–4. Public defender; appointment; term; salary; vacancy

The head of the office shall be the Public Defender, who shall be an attorney-at-law of this State and experienced in the practice of law in this State. He shall be appointed by the Governor with the advice and consent of the Senate for a term of 5 years and until the appointment and qualification of his successor. He shall devote his entire time to the duties of his office and shall receive such salary as shall be provided by law. Any vacancy occurring in the office of the Public Defender shall be filled in the same manner as the original appointment, but for the unexpired term only.

L.1967, c. 43, § 4, eff. July 1, 1967.

2A:158A–5. Duties of public defender

It shall be the duty of the Public Defender to provide for the legal representation of any indigent defendant who is formally charged with the commission of an indictable offense.

All necessary services and facilities of representation (including investigation and other preparation) shall be provided in every case. The factors of need and real value to a defense may be weighed against the financial constraints of the Public Defender's office in determining what are the necessary services and facilities of representation.

Representation as herein provided for shall include any direct appeal from conviction and such post-conviction proceedings as would warrant the assignment of counsel pursuant to the court rules.

Representation for indigent defendants (a) may be provided in any federal court in any matter arising out of or relating to an action pending or recently pending in a court of criminal jurisdiction of this State and (b) may be provided in any federal court in this State where indigent defendants are charged with the commission of a federal criminal offense and where the representation is under a plan adopted pursuant to the Criminal Justice Act of 1964 (18 U.S.C. § 3006A).

L.1967, c. 43, § 5, eff. July 1, 1967. Amended by L.1987, c. 170, § 2.

2A:158A–5.1.　Repealed by L.1994, c. 58, § 70, eff. July 1, 1994

2A:158A–5.2.　Offenses and violations; legal representation

The Public Defender shall in the manner prescribed by P.L.1967, c. 43 (C. 2A:158A–1 et seq.) provide for the legal representation of any person charged with a disorderly persons offense or with the violation of any law, ordinance or regulation of a penal nature where there is a likelihood that the persons so charged, if convicted, will be subject to imprisonment or, in the opinion of the court, any other consequence of magnitude.

L.1974, c. 33, § 3.

2A:158A–6.　Deputy and assistant public defenders; appointment; salary

The Public Defender shall appoint deputy public defenders and assistant deputy public defenders in such number as he shall require to assist him in the performance of the duties of his office. Deputies and assistant deputies shall be attorneys-at-law of this State, shall serve at the pleasure of the Public Defender and shall receive such salaries as he shall from time to time designate.

L.1967, c. 43, § 6, eff. July 1, 1967.

2A:158A–7.　Powers of public defender

The Public Defender shall:

(a) Appoint such investigators, stenographic and clerical assistants and other personnel as may be required for the conduct of the office, subject to the provisions of Title 11A, Civil Service, of the New Jersey Statutes, and other applicable statutes;

(b) Establish and maintain suitable headquarters for the office and such regional quarters within the State as the Public Defender shall deem necessary for the proper functioning of the office;

(c) Maintain one or more trial pools of lawyers who shall be available to serve as counsel on a case basis as needed;

(d) Engage counsel from said trial pools on a case basis as may be necessary for the proper performance of the duties of the office and compensate them for their services;

(e) Accept the services of volunteer workers or consultants at no compensation or at nominal or token compensation and reimburse them for their proper and necessary expenses;

(f) (Deleted by amendment, P.L.1972, c. 168);

(g) Keep and maintain proper financial records and records in respect to particular cases handled and develop records for use in the calculation of direct and indirect costs of all or any aspect of the operation of the office;

(h) On the basis of available data or estimates to prepare schedules of rates from time to time of amounts to be paid for services rendered other than by the staff, taking into account the nature of the services, the time involved, trouble and risk, the skill and experience required, and other pertinent factors;

(i) Have a general responsibility for the operation of the office;

(j) Formulate and adopt rules and regulations as are necessary to effectuate the purposes of this act and for the efficient conduct of the work and general administration of the office, its professional staff and other employees;

(k) Be the request officer of the office within the meaning of such term as defined in P.L.1944, c. 112;[1]

(*l*) Have the authority to make all necessary arrangements to coordinate services to the office with any Federal program to provide counsel to the indigent, and to arrange for the receipt by the office, wherever possible, of sums allowable under such Federal program, whether by direct allowance, by assignment or transfer, or otherwise;

(m) Have the authority to solicit, apply for and expend grants, donations, or other funds available from the federal government or private foundations as may be available to support the programs of the office; and

(n) Assume responsibility for representation in litigation formerly handled by the Office of Inmate Advocacy in the Department of the Public Advocate that is pending on the effective date of P.L.1994, c. 58 (C. 52:27E–50 et al.).

L.1967, c. 43, § 7, eff. July 1, 1967. Amended by L.1970, c. 308, § 1, eff. Dec. 16, 1970; L.1972, c. 168, § 1, eff. Nov. 3, 1972; L.1994, c. 58, § 9, eff. July 1, 1994.

1 N.J.S.A. §§ 52:27B–1 to 52:27B–85.

2A:158A–8.　Lawyers to represent defendants on case basis; selection

In selecting deputy public defenders and assistant deputy public defenders or lawyers to be available to represent defendants on a case basis, the Public Defender shall make his selections on a basis calculated to provide the respective defendants with competent counsel in the light of the nature, complexity and other characteristics of the cases, the services to be performed, the status of the matters, and other relevant factors.

L.1967, c. 43, § 8, eff. July 1, 1967.

2A:158A–9. Case workload; division; employment of counsel

To achieve a proper balance between the services to be provided pursuant to this act and the efficiency of the operation as a whole, as well as to stimulate the continual development of professional experience and interest in the administration of criminal justice, the Public Defender shall divide the case workload of the office between the professional staff and the trial pool or pools. In any case where the matter involved requires some special experience or skill not available on the professional staff, the Public Defender shall engage counsel on a case basis, and shall assign a suitable member of the staff to the extent feasible to assist counsel so engaged. Counsel shall also be engaged on a case basis whenever needed to meet case load demands, or to provide independent counsel to multiple defendants whose interests may be in conflict.

L.1967, c. 43, § 9, eff. July 1, 1967.

2A:158A–10. Contracts authorizing private or public organizations to execute functions of public defender

The Public Defender is authorized to enter into contracts from time to time with private or public organizations that are equipped to provide legal services for indigent defendants or to execute any lawful functions of the office of the Public Defender, as occasion may require. Every such contract shall require that the level and quality of the work shall be at least equal to that of the office of the Public Defender, and that all services rendered thereunder shall be under the control and supervision of the Public Defender.

L.1967, c. 43, § 10, eff. July 1, 1967.

2A:158A–11. Duties of staff members and others engaged on case basis

The primary duty of all members of staff and of others engaged on a case basis shall be to the individual defendant, with like effect and to the same purpose as though privately engaged by him and without regard to the use of public funds to provide the service. This shall not preclude the designation or assignment of different individuals to perform various parts of the service from time to time, the duty in such cases to be the same as would exist in the case of a privately engaged law firm.

L.1967, c. 43, § 11, eff. July 1, 1967.

2A:158A–12. Attorney-client privilege

All communications between the individual defendant and any person in or engaged by the Office of the Public Defender whether on a case basis or by contract shall be fully protected by the attorney-client privilege to the same extent and degree as though counsel has been privately engaged. This shall in no way preclude the use by the office of material in its files, otherwise privileged, for the preparation and disclosure of statistical, case study and other sociological data, provided always that in any such use there shall be no disclosure of identity or of means for discovery of identity of particular defendants.

L.1967, c. 43, § 12, eff. July 1, 1967.

2A:158A–13. Standards and level of performance of attorneys providing legal services

In providing legal services to defendants pursuant to this act, the Office of the Public Defender and every attorney actually engaged in the performance of the same, whether as a member of the staff or engaged on a case basis or otherwise, shall adhere at all times to the standards and level of performance established from time to time by the Supreme Court of New Jersey in the execution of its duty to supervise the practice of law; and the office shall furnish to such court materials and data as may be requisite to the measurement of the adequacy of the performance hereunder.

L.1967, c. 43, § 13, eff. July 1, 1967.

2A:158A–14. Eligibility for services; determination

Eligibility for the services of the Office of the Public Defender shall be determined on the basis of the need of the defendant. Need shall be measured according to :

a. The financial ability of the defendant to engage and compensate competent private counsel ;

b. The current employment, salary and income of the defendant including prospects for continued employment if admitted to bail;

c. The liquid assets of the defendant, including all real and personal property and bank accounts;

d. The ability of the defendant to make bail and the source of bail posted;

e. Where appropriate the willingness and ability of the defendant's immediate family, friends or employer to assist the defendant in meeting defense costs;

f. Where appropriate an assessment of the probable and reasonable costs of providing a private defense, based upon the status of the defendant, the nature and extent of the charges and the likely issues;

g. Where appropriate, the ability of the defendant to demonstrate convincingly that he has consulted at least three private attorneys, none of whom would accept the case for a fee within his ability to pay; and

h. The ability of the defendant to provide all other necessary expenses of representation.

In the event that a determination of eligibility cannot be made before the time when the first services are to be rendered, or if an initial determination is found to be erroneous, the office shall undertake the same provisionally, and if it shall subsequently be determined that the defendant is ineligible it shall so inform the defendant, and the defendant shall thereupon be obliged to engage his own counsel and to reimburse the office for the cost of the services rendered to that time.

L.1967, c. 43, § 14, eff. July 1, 1967. Amended by L.1987, c. 170, § 3.

2A:158A–15. Repealed by L.1998, c. 77, § 3, eff. Aug. 14, 1998

2A:158A–15.1. Financial status of defendant; investigation by judge or court support office

In each county, the Assignment Judge shall designate a judge or court support office who shall make an investigation of the financial status of each defendant requesting the services of the Office of the Public Defender and make a determination whether to grant the request for an appointed attorney. A determination to grant or deny the services of the Public Defender shall be subject to final review by the Assignment Judge or his designated judge. The court, or a designated court support office shall make an investigation of the financial status of each defendant requesting an appointed attorney, which investigation shall include the factors enumerated in section 14 of P.L. 1967, c. 43 (C. 2A:158A–14). The court, in its discretion, may ask for the assistance of the Public Defender in conducting the investigation.

The judge or court support office is authorized to obtain information from any public record office of the State or of any subdivision or agency thereof on request and without payment of the fees ordinarily required by law.

Amended by L.1998, c. 77, § 1, eff. Aug. 14, 1998.

2A:158A–15.2. Establishment of system in counties; responsibility for eligibility determinations; purpose of pilot project

Within 30 days of the effective date of this section, the Administrative Office of the Courts shall establish a system in one or more counties and the Assignment Judge, through a designated judge or court support office shall be responsible for making eligibility determinations for the services of the Office of the Public Defender in that county. The purpose of the pilot project is to enable the Judiciary to develop a program for Statewide implementation and to gauge the fiscal impact of assuming responsibility for making eligibility determinations.

L.1987, c. 170, § 5, eff. July 8, 1987.

2A:158A–16. Part payment of cost by defendant

In all cases where it appears that the defendant has or reasonably expects to have means to meet some part, though not all, of the cost of the services rendered to him he shall be required to reimburse the office, either by a single payment or in installments, in such amounts as he can reasonably be expected to pay; but no default or failure in the making of any such payment shall in any wise affect or reduce the rendering of the services to him.

L.1967, c. 43, § 16, eff. July 1, 1967.

2A:158A–17. Lien on property of defendant

The reasonable value of the services rendered to a defendant pursuant to this act may in all cases be a lien on any and all property to which the defendant shall have or acquire an interest. The Public Defender shall effectuate such lien whenever the reasonable value of the services rendered to a defendant appears to exceed $150.00 and may effectuate such lien where the reasonable value of those services appears to be less than $150.00.

To effectuate such a lien, the Public Defender shall file a notice setting forth the services rendered to the defendant and the reasonable value thereof with the Clerk of the Superior Court. The filing of said notice with the Clerk of the Superior Court shall from the date thereof constitute a lien on said property for a period of 10 years, unless sooner discharged and except for such time limitations shall have the force and effect of a Judgment at Law. Within 10 days of the filing of the Notice of Lien, the Public Defender shall send by certified mail, or serve personally, a copy of such notice with a statement of the date of the filing thereof to or upon the defendant at his last known address. If the Public Defender shall fail to give notice, the lien shall be void.

L.1967, c. 43, § 17, eff. July 1, 1967. Amended by L.1968, c. 371, § 1, approved Dec. 27, 1968; L.1969, c. 29, § 1, eff. May 8, 1969.

2A:158A–18. Recording of liens; books provided; fees

The Clerk of the Superior Court shall provide separate books for the recording of said liens which books shall be properly indexed in the name of the judgment debtor. The Public Defender shall not be required to pay filing or recording fees.

L.1967, c. 43, § 18, eff. July 1, 1967.

2A:158A–19. Collections of moneys due

The Public Defender in the name of the State shall do all things necessary and proper to collect all moneys due to the State by way of reimbursement for services rendered pursuant to this act. He may enter into arrangements with one or more agencies of the State, including the comprehensive enforcement program established pursuant to the provisions of P.L.1995, c. 9 (C.2B:19–1 et seq.) or of the counties to handle said collections on a cost basis to the extent that such arrangements are calculated to simplify collection procedures. He shall have all the remedies and may take all of the proceedings for the collection thereof which may be had or taken for or upon the recovery of a judgment in a civil action and may institute and maintain any action or proceeding in the courts necessary therefor. In any such proceedings or action, the defendant may contest the value of the service rendered by the Public Defender.

L.1967, c. 43, § 19, eff. July 1, 1967. Amended by L.1969, c. 29, § 2, eff. May 8, 1969; L.2000, c. 120, § 1, eff. Dec. 13, 2000.

2A:158A–20. Compromise and settlement of claim for services

The Public Defender is authorized to compromise and make settlement of any claim for services performed for any person pursuant to this act whenever the financial circumstances of said person are such that in the judgment of the Public Defender the best interest of the State will be served by such compromise and settlement.

L.1967, c. 43, § 20, eff. July 1, 1967.

2A:158A–21. Repealed by L.1969, c. 305, § 1, eff. Jan. 19, 1970

2A:158A–22. Annual report

The Office of the Public Defender shall report annually to the Legislature, the Governor and the Supreme Court. Such report may be combined with that of any other body, agency or study group engaged in reviewing the administration of criminal justice. The report shall include all pertinent data on the operations of the office, the costs, projected needs, and to the extent experience may indicate, recommendations for statutory changes, including changes in the criminal law or changes in court rules, all as may be appropriate to the improvement of the system of criminal justice, the control of crime, the rehabilitation of offenders, and other related objectives.

L.1967, c. 43, § 22, eff. July 1, 1967.

2A:158A–23. Oaths and affirmations

The Public Defender, the deputy public defender, the assistant deputy public defenders and investigators attached to the Office of the Public Defender shall have the power to administer oaths and affirmations in relation to any matter within the jurisdiction of the Office of the Public Defender.

L.1968, c. 371, § 2.

2A:158A–24. Juvenile delinquent or juvenile in need of supervision; legal representation

Except as hereinafter provided, the Public Defender shall in the manner prescribed by P.L.1967, c. 43 (C. 2A:158A–1 et seq.) provide for the legal representation of any person who is charged as a juvenile delinquent or as a juvenile who is in need of supervision and where in the opinion of the juvenile judge the prosecution of the complaint may result in the institutional commitment of such person.

L.1968, c. 371, § 3. Amended by L.1974, c. 33, § 1, eff. May 31, 1974.

2A:158A–25. Minors; eligibility for services

Whenever a person formally charged with an indictable offense, or coming within this act, is under the age of 21 years, the question of eligibility for services shall be measured not only in terms of the financial circumstances of the individual, but also in terms of the financial circumstances of the individual's parents or legal guardians. The Office of the Public Defender shall be entitled to recover the cost of legal services from the parents or legal guardians of such persons to the same extent and in the same manner as is provided under P.L.1967, chapter 43,[1] and shall have authority to require parents or legal guardians of such to execute and deliver such written requests or authorization as may be requisite under applicable law in order to provide the office with access to records of public or private sources, otherwise confidential, as may be of aid to it in evaluating eligibility.

L.1968, c. 371, § 4.

[1] N.J.S.A. § 2A:158A–1 et seq.

CHAPTER 159A

INTERSTATE AGREEMENT ON DETAINERS

Section

2A:159A–1.   Agreement on detainers; findings of party states; purpose.

2A:159A–2.   Definitions.

2A:159A–3.   Request for final disposition of pending indictment, information or complaint; certificate of officer having custody; procedure; failure to commence trial; dismissal; waiver of extradition; escape.

2A:159A–4.   Request for temporary custody or availability of prisoner; procedure; time for commencing trial; failure to try; dismissal.

2A:159A–5.   Offer of temporary custody; procedure; duty of receiving state; nature of temporary custody; return of prisoner; running of sentence; custody of sending state; costs.

2A:159A–6.   Inability of prisoner to stand trial; tolling of time periods; inapplicability of agreement to mentally ill persons.

2A:159A–7.   Rules and regulations.

2A:159A–8.   Effective date of agreement; withdrawal of state; effect on status of proceedings.

2A:159A–9.   Liberal construction; severability of provisions.

2A:159A–10.   "Appropriate court," definition.

2A:159A–11.   Enforcement of agreement; co-operation.

2A:159A–12.   Delivery of prisoner.

2A:159A–13.   Escape from custody; offense; punishment.

2A:159A–14.   Central administrator and information officer; designation; powers; tenure.

2A:159A–15.   Transmittal of copies of act.

2A:159A–1. Agreement on detainers; findings of party states; purpose

The agreement on detainers is hereby enacted into law and entered into by this State with all other jurisdictions legally joining therein in the form substantially as follows:

AGREEMENT ON DETAINERS

The contracting States solemnly agree that:

ARTICLE I

The party States find that charges outstanding against a prisoner, detainers based on untried indictments, informations or complaints, and difficulties in securing speedy trial of persons already incarcerated in other jurisdictions, produce uncertainties which obstruct programs of prisoner treatment and rehabilitation. Accordingly, it is the policy of the party States and the purpose of this agreement to encourage the expeditious and orderly disposition of such charges and determination of the proper status of any and all detainers based on untried indictments, informations or complaints. The party States also find that proceedings with reference to such charges and detainers, when emanating from another jurisdiction, cannot properly be had in the absence of cooperative procedures. It is the further purpose of this agreement to provide such cooperative procedures.

L.1958, c. 12, p. 33, § 1 (Art. I), eff. April 18, 1958.

2A:159A–2. Definitions

ARTICLE II

As used in this agreement:

(a) "State" shall mean a State of the United States; the United States of America; a territory or possession of the United States; the District of Columbia; the Commonwealth of Puerto Rico.

(b) "Sending State" shall mean a State in which a prisoner is incarcerated at the time that he initiates a request for final disposition pursuant to Article III hereof or at the time that a request for custody or availability is initiated pursuant to Article IV hereof.[1]

(c) "Receiving State" shall mean the State in which trial is to be had on an indictment, information or complaint pursuant to Article III [2] or Article IV hereof.

L.1958, c. 12, p. 33, § 1 (Art. II).

[1] N.J.S.A. § 2A:159A–4.
[2] N.J.S.A. § 2A:159A–3.

2A:159A–3. Request for final disposition of pending indictment, information or complaint; certificate of officer having custody; procedure; failure to commence trial; dismissal; waiver of extradition; escape

ARTICLE III

(a) Whenever a person has entered upon a term of imprisonment in a penal or correctional institution of a party State, and whenever during the continuance of the term of imprisonment there is pending in any other party State any untried indictment, information or complaint on the basis of which a detainer has been lodged against the prisoner, he shall be brought to trial within 180 days after he shall have caused to be delivered to the prosecuting officer and the appropriate court of the prosecuting officer's jurisdiction written notice of the place of his imprisonment and his request for a final disposition to be made of the indictment, information or complaint: provided that for good cause shown in open court, the prisoner or his counsel being present, the court having jurisdiction of the matter may grant any necessary or reasonable continuance. The request of the prisoner shall be accompanied by a certificate of the appropriate official having custody of the prisoner, stating the term of commitment under which the prisoner is being held, the time already served, the time remaining to be served on the sentence, the amount of good time earned, the time of parole eligibility of the prisoner, and any decisions of the State parole agency relating to the prisoner.

(b) The written notice and request for final disposition referred to in paragraph (a) hereof shall be given or sent by the prisoner to the warden, commissioner of corrections or other official having custody of him, who shall promptly forward it together with the certificate to the appropriate prosecuting official and court by registered or certified mail, return receipt requested.

(c) The warden, commissioner of corrections or other official having custody of the prisoner shall promptly inform him of the source and contents of any detainer lodged against him and shall also inform him of his right to make a request for final disposition of the indictment, information or complaint on which the detainer is based.

(d) Any request for final disposition made by a prisoner pursuant to paragraph (a) hereof shall operate as a request for final disposition of all untried indictments, informations or complaints on the basis of which detainers have been lodged against the prisoner from the State to whose prosecuting official the request for final disposition is specifically directed. The warden, commissioner of corrections or other official having custody of the prisoner shall forthwith notify all appropriate prosecuting officers and courts in the several jurisdictions within the State to which the prisoner's request for final disposition is being sent of the proceeding being initiated by the prisoner. Any notification sent pursuant to this paragraph shall be accompanied by copies of the prisoner's written notice, request, and the certificate. If trial is not had on any indictment, information or complaint contemplated hereby prior to the return of the prisoner to the original place of imprisonment, such indictment, information or complaint shall not be of any further force or effect, and the court shall enter an order dismissing the same with prejudice.

(e) Any request for final disposition made by a prisoner pursuant to paragraph (a) hereof shall also be deemed to be a waiver of extradition with respect to any charge or proceeding contemplated thereby or included therein by reason of paragraph (d) hereof, and a waiver of extradition to the receiving State to serve any sentence there imposed upon him, after completion of his term of imprisonment in the sending State. The request for final disposition shall also constitute a consent by the prisoner to the production of his body in any court where his presence may be required in order to effectuate the purposes of this agreement and a further consent voluntarily to be returned to the original place of imprisonment in accordance with the provisions of this agreement. Nothing in this paragraph shall prevent the imposition of a concurrent sentence if otherwise permitted by law.

(f) Escape from custody by the prisoner subsequent to his execution of the request for final disposition referred to in paragraph (a) hereof shall void the request.

L.1958, c. 12, p. 33, § 1 (Art. III).

2A:159A–4. Request for temporary custody or availability of prisoner; procedure; time for commencing trial; failure to try; dismissal

ARTICLE IV

(a) The appropriate officer of the jurisdiction in which an untried indictment, information or complaint is pending shall be entitled to have a prisoner against whom he has lodged a detainer and who is serving a term of imprisonment in any party State made available in accordance with Article V(a) hereof [1] upon presentation of a written request for temporary custody or availability to the appropriate authorities of the State in which the prisoner is incarcerated: provided that the court having jurisdiction of such indictment, information or complaint shall have duly approved, recorded and transmitted the request: and provided further that there shall be a period of 30 days after receipt by the appropriate authorities before the request be honored, within which period the Governor of the sending State may disapprove the request for temporary custody or availability, either upon his own motion or upon motion of the prisoner.

(b) Upon receipt of the officer's written request as provided in paragraph (a) hereof, the appropriate authorities having the prisoner in custody shall furnish the officer with a certificate stating the term of commitment under which the prisoner is being held, the time already served, the time remaining to be served on the sentence, the amount of good time earned, the time of parole eligibility of the prisoner, and any decisions of the State parole agency relating to the prisoner. Said authorities simultaneously shall furnish all other officers and appropriate courts in the receiving State who have lodged detainers against the prisoner with similar certificates and with notices informing them of the request for custody or availability and of the reasons therefor.

(c) In respect of any proceeding made possible by this Article, trial shall be commenced within 120 days of the arrival of the prisoner in the receiving State, but for good cause shown in open court, the prisoner or his counsel being present, the court having jurisdiction of the matter may grant any necessary or reasonable continuance.

(d) Nothing contained in this Article shall be construed to deprive any prisoner of any right which he may have to contest the legality of his delivery as provided in paragraph (a) hereof, but such delivery may not be opposed or denied on the ground that the executive authority of the sending State has not affirmatively consented to or ordered such delivery.

(e) If trial is not had on any indictment, information or complaint contemplated hereby prior to the prisoner's being returned to the original place of imprisonment pursuant to Article V(e) hereof, such indictment, information or complaint shall not be of any further force or effect, and the court shall enter an order dismissing the same with prejudice.

L.1958, c. 12, p. 33, § 1 (Art. IV).

   [1] N.J.S.A. § 2A:159A–5.

2A:159A–5. Offer of temporary custody; procedure; duty of receiving state; nature of temporary custody; return of prisoner; running of sentence; custody of sending state; costs

ARTICLE V

(a) In response to a request made under Article III or Article IV hereof,[1] the appropriate authority in a sending State shall offer to deliver temporary custody of such prisoner to the appropriate authority in the State where such indictment, information or complaint is pending against such person in order that speedy and efficient prosecution may be had. If the request for final disposition is made by the prisoner, the offer of temporary custody shall accompany the written notice provided for in Article III of this agreement. In the case of a Federal prisoner, the appropriate authority in the receiving State shall be entitled to temporary custody as provided by this agreement or to the prisoner's presence in Federal custody at the place for trial, whichever custodial arrangement may be approved by the custodian.

(b) The officer or other representative of a State accepting an offer of temporary custody shall present the following upon demand:

(1) Proper identification and evidence of his authority to act for the State into whose temporary custody the prisoner is to be given.

(2) A duly certified copy of the indictment, information or complaint on the basis of which the detainer has been lodged and on the basis of which the request for temporary custody of the prisoner has been made.

(c) If the appropriate authority shall refuse or fail to accept temporary custody of said person, or in the event that an action on the indictment, information or complaint on the basis of which the detainer has been lodged is not brought to trial within the period provided in Article III or Article IV hereof, the appropriate court of the jurisdiction where the indictment, information or complaint has been pending shall enter an order dismissing the same with prejudice, and any detainer based thereon shall cease to be of any force or effect.

(d) The temporary custody referred to in this agreement shall be only for the purpose of permitting prosecution on the charge or charges contained in 1 or more untried indictments, informations or complaints which form the basis of the detainer or detainers or for prosecution on any other charge or charges arising out of the same transaction. Except for his attendance at court and while being transported to or from any place at which his presence may be required, the prisoner shall be held in a suitable jail or other facility regularly used for persons awaiting prosecution.

(e) At the earliest practicable time consonant with the purposes of this agreement, the prisoner shall be returned to the sending State.

(f) During the continuance of temporary custody or while the prisoner is otherwise being made available for trial as required by this agreement, time being served on the sentence shall continue to run but good time shall be earned by the prisoner only if, and to the extent that, the law and practice of the jurisdiction which imposed the sentence may allow.

(g) For all purposes other than that for which temporary custody as provided in this agreement is exercised, the prisoner shall be deemed to remain in the custody of and subject to the jurisdiction of the sending State and any escape from temporary custody may be dealt with in the same manner as an escape from the original place of imprisonment or in any other manner permitted by law.

(h) From the time that a party State receives custody of a prisoner pursuant to this agreement until such prisoner is returned to the territory and custody of the sending State, the State in which the 1 or more untried indictments, informations or complaints are pending or in which trial is being had shall be responsible for the prisoner and shall also pay all costs of transporting, caring for, keeping and returning the prisoner. The provisions of this paragraph shall govern unless the States concerned shall have entered into a supplementary agreement providing for a different allocation of costs and responsibilities as between or among themselves. Nothing herein contained shall be construed to alter or affect any internal relationship among the departments, agencies and officers of and in the government of a party State, or between a party State and its subdivisions, as to the payment of costs, or responsibilities therefor.

L.1958, c. 12, p. 33, § 1 (Art. V).

[1] N.J.S.A. §§ 2A:159A–3, 2A:159A–4.

2A:159A–6. Inability of prisoner to stand trial; tolling of time periods; inapplicability of agreement to mentally ill persons

ARTICLE VI

(a) In determining the duration and expiration dates of the time periods provided in Articles III and IV [1] of this agreement, the running of said time periods shall be tolled whenever and for as long as the prisoner is unable to stand trial, as determined by the court having jurisdiction of the matter.

(b) No provision of this agreement, and no remedy made available by this agreement, shall apply to any person who is adjudged to be mentally ill.

L.1958, c. 12, p. 33, § 1 (Art. VI).

[1] Sections 2A:159A–3, 2A:159A–4.

2A:159A–7. Rules and regulations

ARTICLE VII

Each State party to this agreement shall designate an officer who, acting jointly with like officers of other party States, shall promulgate rules and regulations to carry out more effectively the terms and provisions of this agreement, and who shall provide, within and without the State, information necessary to the effective operation of this agreement.

L.1958, c. 12, p. 33, § 1 (Art. VII).

2A:159A–8. Effective date of agreement; withdrawal of state; effect on status of proceedings

ARTICLE VIII

This agreement shall enter into full force and effect as to a party State when such State has enacted the same into law. A State party to this agreement may withdraw herefrom by enacting a statute repealing the same. However, the withdrawal of any State shall not affect the status of any proceedings already initiated by inmates or by State officers at the time such withdrawal takes effect, nor shall it affect their rights in respect thereof.

L.1958, c. 12, p. 33, § 1 (Art. VIII).

2A:159A–9. Liberal construction; severability of provisions

ARTICLE IX

This agreement shall be liberally construed so as to effectuate its purposes. The provisions of this agreement shall be severable and if any phrase, clause, sentence or provision of this agreement is declared to be contrary to the Constitution of any party State or of the United States or the applicability thereof to any government, agency, person or circumstance is held invalid, the validity of the remainder of this agreement and the applicability thereof to any government, agency, person or circumstance shall not be affected thereby. If this agreement shall be held contrary to the Constitution of any State party hereto, the agreement shall remain in full force and effect as to the remaining States and in full force and effect as to the State affected as to all severable matters.

L.1958, c. 12, p. 33, § 1 (Art. IX).

2A:159A–10. "Appropriate court," definition

The phrase "appropriate court" as used in the agreement on detainers shall, with reference to the courts of this State, mean any court with criminal jurisdiction.

L.1958, c. 12, p. 42, § 2.

2A:159A–11. Enforcement of agreement; co-operation

All courts, departments, agencies, officers and employees of this State and its political subdivisions are hereby directed to enforce the agreement on detainers and to co-operate with one another and with the other party States in enforcing the agreement and effectuating its purposes.

L.1958, c. 12, p. 42, § 3.

2A:159A–12. Delivery of prisoner

The warden or other official in charge of any penal or correctional institution in this State shall give over the person of any inmate thereof whenever so required by the operation of the agreement on detainers.

L.1958, c. 12, p. 42, § 4.

2A:159A–13. Escape from custody; offense; punishment

Escape from custody while in another State pursuant to the agreement on detainers shall constitute an offense against the laws of this State to the same extent and degree as an escape from the institution in which the prisoner was confined immediately prior to having been sent to another State pursuant to the provisions of the agreement on detainers and shall be punishable in the same manner as an escape from said institution.

L.1958, c. 12, p. 42, § 5.

2A:159A–14. Central administrator and information officer; designation; powers; tenure

Pursuant to said agreement, the Governor is hereby authorized and empowered to designate an officer or alternate who shall be the central administrator of and the information agent for the agreement on detainers and who, acting jointly with like officers of other party States, shall have power to formulate rules and regulations to carry out more effectively the terms of the agreement, and shall serve subject to the pleasure of the Governor.

L.1958, c. 12, p. 42, § 6.

2A:159A–15. Transmittal of copies of act

Duly authenticated copies of this act shall, upon its approval, be transmitted by the Secretary of State to the Governor of each State, the Attorney-General and the Administrator of the General Services Administration of the United States, and the Council of State Governments.

L.1958, c. 12, p. 43, § 7.

CHAPTER 160

EXTRADITION

ARTICLE 1. GENERAL PROVISIONS

Section
2A:160–1. Persons taken out of state to answer criminal charge; warrant of governor or waiver of extradition.
2A:160–2. Expenses of returning fugitives from justice.
2A:160–3. Advance of money to prosecutor for expenses of extradition; statement filed and approved by court.
2A:160–4. Accounting of expenditures; excess returned.
2A:160–5. Return of person extradited from and imprisoned in another state to such state in certain cases.

ARTICLE 2. UNIFORM CRIMINAL EXTRADITION LAW

A. DEFINITIONS, CONSTRUCTION AND SHORT TITLE

2A:160–6. Definitions.
2A:160–7. Construction of article.
2A:160–8. Effect of article as to waivers by and rights, powers and privileges of this state.
2A:160–9. Short title of article.

B. EXTRADITION FROM THIS STATE INTO OTHER STATES

2A:160–10. Fugitives from justice found in this state; arrest and delivery to demanding state; person charged with murder in demanding state and imprisoned in this state for term less than life; warrant of governor.
2A:160–11. Demand for extradition; form and contents; affidavit; copy of indictment or information; statement by executive authority of demanding state.
2A:160–12. Investigation by governor; duty of attorney general and prosecuting officers.
2A:160–13. Extradition of person leaving demanding state involuntarily.
2A:160–14. Extradition of persons not present in demanding state at time of commission of crime.
2A:160–15. Warrant of arrest; issue by governor; recitals.
2A:160–16. Execution of warrant of arrest.
2A:160–17. Authority of officer making arrest; assistance given.
2A:160–18. Rights of persons arrested; appearance before criminal court; habeas corpus; notice of and hearing on.
2A:160–19. Noncompliance with section 2A:160–18 a misdemeanor; punishment.
2A:160–20. Temporary confinement of persons arrested in county or municipal jail in this state; procedure; new requisition.
2A:160–21. Arrest of accused before requisition made; warrant for arrest.
2A:160–22. Arrest of accused without warrant.
2A:160–23. Commitment to jail of person arrested before requisition made, to await requisition; bail.
2A:160–24. Bail of accused for appearance, when authorized; bond or undertaking; surrender of accused to be arrested on warrant.

Section

2A:160–25. Discharge of accused; extension of time of commitment of accused; new bail for appearance.

2A:160–26. Forfeiture of bail; arrest of accused without warrant; recovery on bail bond.

2A:160–27. Extradition of persons pending outcome of criminal prosecution in this state.

2A:160–28. Inquiry into guilt or innocence of accused.

2A:160–29. Recall of warrant of arrest; alias warrant.

2A:160–30. Waiver of extradition proceedings; procedure; effect.

C. EXTRADITION FROM OTHER STATES OF PERSONS ACCUSED OF CRIME, ESCAPING FROM CONFINEMENT OR BREAKING TERMS OF BAIL, PROBATION OR PAROLE IN THIS STATE

2A:160–31. Demand for extradition; issue of warrant by governor.

2A:160–32. Application to governor for requisition; by whom made; contents; verification of application; execution in duplicate; certified copies of indictment, information and affidavit filed, or complaint to accompany application; copy filed with secretary of state; copy forwarded with requisition.

2A:160–33. Extradition of persons imprisoned or awaiting trial in another state; agreement to return to state from which extradited.

2A:160–34. Immunity from service of process in certain civil actions.

2A:160–35. No immunity from other criminal prosecution while in this state.

ARTICLE 1. GENERAL PROVISIONS

2A:160–1. Persons taken out of state to answer criminal charge; warrant of governor or waiver of extradition

It shall be unlawful to take, or cause or procure to be taken, or aid or abet in taking any person from out of this state, for the purpose of answering any criminal charge that may have been preferred against such person in any other state, except in the manner prescribed in this chapter, unless such person consents to his removal from this state by waiving extradition in the manner provided by section 2A:160–30 of this title.

2A:160–2. Expenses of returning fugitives from justice

Whenever any person charged in this State with any crime shall flee from justice and be found in another state, territory or district, and the attorney general or the prosecutor for any county where such person is so charged shall recommend to the governor or person administering the government of this State that he demand the fugitive, so that he may be brought into this State for trial, and the fugitive shall, on the demand of the executive authority of this State, be delivered up for removal to this State, the expense of such removal, being first ascertained to the satisfaction of the prosecutor of the county where such person is so charged, and being approved by a judge of the Superior Court, shall be paid by the county treasurer out of the funds of such county.

Amended by L.1991, c. 91, § 129, eff. April 9, 1991.

2A:160–3. Advance of money to prosecutor for expenses of extradition; statement filed and approved by court

The county treasurer of any county may advance to the prosecutor of the county, or to such person as the prosecutor shall designate, from the funds of such county appropriated, set aside and available for court expenses, money necessary to defray the expenses of the prosecutor or such person as he shall designate, to be used for the arrest, extradition and return from foreign jurisdictions of persons charged with violating the criminal laws of this State, and who are fugitives from justice. No such money shall be advanced by the county treasurer, except upon written order of the prosecutor with the approval of the Assignment Judge in such county indorsed thereon, and unless the prosecutor shall file with the county treasurer a statement of the purposes for which the money is to be used and an estimate, in reasonable detail, of the anticipated expenses.

Amended by L.1991, c. 91, § 130, eff. April 9, 1991.

2A:160–4. Accounting of expenditures; excess returned

Immediately after the person to whom the money has been advanced by the county treasurer, as provided by N.J.S. 2A:160–3, shall have completed the duties for which such money was advanced, he shall file with the county treasurer an itemized statement or account of the necessary expenses incurred in the performance of such duties, duly verified, certified to and approved under the hand of the prosecutor, and with the written approval of the Assignment Judge in such county. If the itemized statement or account so rendered and approved, as aforesaid, should exceed the sum of money so advanced to such person, the balance thereof shall be paid to such person by the county treasurer; and if the sum of money advanced to such person shall exceed the amount of his itemized statement or account of expenses, as the same shall be so certified and approved, such person shall forthwith return the excess money to the county treasurer.

Amended by L.1991, c. 91, § 131, eff. April 9, 1991.

2A:160–5. Return of person extradited from and imprisoned in another state to such state in certain cases

If any person charged with the crime of murder in this state is undergoing imprisonment in any other state, territory or district of the United States for a term less than imprisonment for life, and the governor of this state shall make demand for the return to this state of the person so charged, the governor may agree with the executive authority of such state, territory or district that, if the person so charged shall, on his trial in this state, be acquitted, or shall be convicted of the crime of manslaughter, or any degree of murder the punishment for which is less than death or imprisonment for life, such person shall be returned immediately to such other state, territory or district, at the expense of this state. The costs incident to the return of such person shall be borne by the county in which such person was tried for the crime of murder.

This section shall be subject to the provisions of the constitution of the United States controlling, and the acts of congress enacted in pursuance thereof.

ARTICLE 2.   UNIFORM CRIMINAL EXTRADITION LAW

A.   DEFINITIONS, CONSTRUCTION AND SHORT TITLE

2A:160–6.   Definitions

As used in this article, the term "governor" includes any person performing the functions of governor by authority of the law of this state. The term "executive authority" includes the governor and any person performing the functions of governor in a state other than this state. The term "state", referring to a state other than this state, includes any other state, territory or district, organized or unorganized, of the United States of America.

2A:160–7.   Construction of article

The provisions of this article shall be so interpreted and construed as to effectuate its general purposes to make uniform the law of those states which enact it.

2A:160–8.   Effect of article as to waivers by and rights, powers and privileges of this state

Nothing in this article contained shall be deemed to constitute a waiver by this state of its right, power or privilege to try such demanded person for crime committed within this state, or of its right, power or privilege to regain custody of such person by extradition proceedings or otherwise for the purpose of trial, sentence or punishment for any crime committed within this state, nor shall any proceedings had under this article which result in, or fail to result in, extradition be deemed a waiver by this state of any of its rights, privileges or jurisdiction in any way whatsoever.

2A:160–9.   Short title of article

This article may be cited as the "uniform criminal extradition law".

B.   EXTRADITION FROM THIS STATE INTO OTHER STATES

2A:160–10.   Fugitives from justice found in this state; arrest and delivery to demanding state; person charged with murder in demanding state and imprisoned in this state for term less than life; warrant of governor

Subject to the provisions of this article, the provisions of the constitution of the United States controlling, and

any and all acts of congress enacted in pursuance thereof, it is the duty of the governor of this state to have arrested and delivered up to the executive authority of any other state of the United States any person charged in that state with treason, felony or other crime, who has fled from justice and is found in this state; provided, if the executive authority of any other state or district requests the extradition of any person charged in that state with murder, and that person is imprisoned in a penal institution or jail of this state for a term less than imprisonment for life, the governor of this state may deliver him or her up to the executive authority of the demanding state or district for the purpose of trial in said state or district; provided, however, that prior to the removal of the person from this state, the executive authority of the demanding state or district shall have agreed that the person so delivered up is to be returned immediately to this state, at the cost of the demanding state or district, to serve the balance of his or her term of imprisonment in the event of his or her acquittal in the demanding state, or in the event of his or her conviction in such state of manslaughter or any degree of murder the punishment for which is less than death or imprisonment for life.

The warrant of the governor of this state shall be sufficient authority to the keeper of the New Jersey state prison or officer of any other institution to surrender the person named therein and for whom extradition is sought.

2A:160–11.   Demand for extradition; form and contents; affidavit; copy of indictment or information; statement by executive authority of demanding state

No demand for the extradition of a person charged with crime in another state shall be recognized by the governor unless in writing alleging that the accused was present in the demanding state at the time of the commission of the alleged crime, and that thereafter he fled from the state, except in cases arising under section 2A:160–14 of this title, and accompanied by a copy of an indictment found or by information supported by affidavit in the state having jurisdiction of the crime, or by a copy of an affidavit made before a magistrate there, together with a copy of any warrant which was issued thereon; or by a copy of a judgment of conviction or of a sentence imposed in execution thereof, together with a statement by the executive authority of the demanding state that the person claimed has escaped from confinement or has broken the terms of his bail, probation or parole. The indictment, information, or affidavit made before the magistrate must substantially charge the person demanded with having committed a crime under the law of that state; and the copy of the indictment, information, affidavit, judgment of conviction or sentence must be authenticated by the executive authority making the demand.

2A:160–12. Investigation by governor; duty of attorney general and prosecuting officers

When a demand shall be made upon the governor of this state by the executive authority of another state for the surrender of a person so charged with crime, the governor may call upon the attorney general or any prosecuting officer in this state to investigate or assist in investigating the demand, and to report to him the situation and circumstances of the person so demanded, and whether he ought to be surrendered.

2A:160–13. Extradition of person leaving demanding state involuntarily

The governor of this state may also surrender on demand of the executive authority of any other state any person in this state who is charged in the manner provided in section 2A:160–32 of this title with having violated the laws of the state whose executive authority is making the demand, even though such person left the demanding state involuntarily.

2A:160–14. Extradition of persons not present in demanding state at time of commission of crime

The governor of this state may also surrender, on demand of the executive authority of any other state, any person in this state charged in such other state in the manner provided in section 2A:160–11 of this title with committing an act in this state, or in a third state, intentionally resulting in a crime in the state whose executive authority is making the demand, and the provisions of this article not otherwise inconsistent shall apply to such cases, even though the accused was not in that state at the time of the commission of the crime, and has not fled therefrom.

2A:160–15. Warrant of arrest; issue by governor; recitals

If the governor decides that the demand should be complied with, he shall sign a warrant of arrest, which shall be sealed with the state seal, and be directed to any peace officer or other person whom he may think fit to entrust with the execution thereof. The warrant must substantially recite the facts necessary to the validity of its issuance.

2A:160–16. Execution of warrant of arrest

Such warrant shall authorize the peace officer or other person to whom directed to arrest the accused at any time and any place where he may be found within the state and to command the aid of all peace officers or other persons in the execution of the warrant, and to deliver the accused, subject to the provisions of this article, to the duly authorized agent of the demanding state.

2A:160–17. Authority of officer making arrest; assistance given

Every such peace officer or other person empowered to make the arrest, shall have the same authority, in arresting the accused, to command assistance therein, as peace officers have by law in the execution of any criminal process directed to them, with like penalties against those who refuse their assistance.

2A:160–18. Rights of persons arrested; appearance before criminal court; habeas corpus; notice of and hearing on

No person arrested upon such warrant shall be delivered over to the agent whom the executive authority demanding him shall have appointed to receive him, unless he shall first be taken forthwith before a judge of a criminal court of record in this state, who shall inform him of the demand made for his surrender and of the crime with which he is charged, and that he has the right to demand and procure legal counsel; and if the prisoner or his counsel shall state that he or they desire to test the legality of his arrest, the judge of such criminal court of record shall fix a reasonable time to be allowed him within which to apply for a writ of habeas corpus. When such writ is applied for, notice thereof, and of the time and place of hearing thereon, shall be given to the prosecuting officer of the county in which the arrest is made and in which the accused is in custody, and to the said agent of the demanding state.

2A:160–19. Noncompliance with section 2A:160–18 a misdemeanor; punishment

Any officer who shall deliver to the agent for extradition of the demanding state a person in his custody under the governor's warrant, in willful disobedience to section 2A:160–18 of this title, shall be guilty of a misdemeanor, and, on conviction, shall be fined not more than $1,000 or be imprisoned not more than 6 months, or both.

2A:160–20. Temporary confinement of persons arrested in county or municipal jail in this state; procedure; new requisition

The officer or persons executing the governor's warrant of arrest, or the agent of the demanding state to whom the prisoner may have been delivered may, when necessary, confine the prisoner in the jail of any county or municipality through which he may pass; and the keeper of such jail must receive and safely keep the prisoner until the officer or person having charge of him is ready to proceed on his route, such officer or person, however, being chargeable with the expense of keeping.

The officer or agent of a demanding state to whom a prisoner may have been delivered following extradition proceedings in another state, or to whom a prisoner may have been delivered after waiving extradition in such other state, and who is passing through this state with such a prisoner for the purpose of immediately returning such prisoner to the demanding state may, when necessary, confine the prisoner in the jail of any county or municipality through which he may pass; and the keeper of such jail must receive and safely keep the prisoner until the officer or agent having charge of him is ready to proceed on his route, such officer or agent, however, being chargeable with the expense of keeping; but such officer or agent shall produce and show to the keeper of such jail satisfactory written evidence of the fact that he is actually transporting such prisoner to the demanding state after a requisition by the executive authority of such demanding state. Such prisoner shall not be entitled to demand a new requisition while in this state.

2A:160–21. Arrest of accused before requisition made; warrant for arrest

Whenever any person within this state shall be charged on the oath of any credible person before any judge or magistrate of this state with the commission of any crime in any other state, and, except in cases arising under section 2A:160–14 of this title, with having fled from justice, or with having been convicted of a crime in that state and having escaped from confinement, or having broken the terms of his bail, probation or parole, or whenever complaint shall have been made before any judge or magistrate in this state setting forth on the affidavit of any credible person in another state that a crime has been committed in such other state and that the accused has been charged in such state with the commission of the crime, and, except in cases arising under said section 2A:160–14, has fled from justice, or with having been convicted of a crime in that state and having escaped from confinement, or having broken the terms of his bail, probation or parole, and is believed to be in this state, the judge or magistrate shall issue a warrant directed to any peace officer commanding him to apprehend the person named therein, wherever he may be found in this state, and to bring him before the same or any other judge, magistrate or court who or which may be available in or convenient of access to the place where the arrest may be made, to answer the charge or complaint and affidavit, and a certified copy of the sworn charge or complaint and affidavit upon which the warrant is issued shall be attached to the warrant.

2A:160–22. Arrest of accused without warrant

The arrest of a person may be lawfully made also by any peace officer or a private person, without a warrant, upon reasonable information that the accused stands charged in the courts of a state with a crime punishable by death or imprisonment for a term exceeding 1 year, but when so arrested the accused must be taken before a judge or magistrate with all practicable speed and complaint must be made against him under oath setting forth the ground for the arrest as in section 2A:160–21 of this title; and thereafter his answer shall be heard as if he had been arrested on a warrant.

2A:160–23. Commitment to jail of person arrested before requisition made, to await requisition; bail

If from the examination before the judge or magistrate it appears that the person held is the person charged with having committed the crime alleged, and, except in cases arising under section 2A:160–14 of this title, that he has fled from justice, the judge or magistrate must, by a warrant reciting the accusation, commit him to the county jail for such a time not exceeding 30 days and specified in the warrant, as will enable the arrest of the accused to be made under a warrant of the governor on a requisition of the executive authority of the state having jurisdiction of the offense, unless the accused give bail as provided in section 2A:160–24 of this title, or until he shall be legally discharged.

2A:160–24. Bail of accused for appearance, when authorized; bond or undertaking; surrender of accused to be arrested on warrant

Unless the offense with which the prisoner is charged is shown to be an offense punishable by death or life imprisonment under the laws of the state in which it was committed, a judge or magistrate in this state may admit the person arrested to bail by bond or undertaking, with sufficient sureties, and in such sum as he deems proper, conditioned for his appearance before him at a time specified in such bond or undertaking, and for his surrender, to be arrested upon the warrant of the governor of this state.

2A:160–25. Discharge of accused; extension of time of commitment of accused; new bail for appearance

If the accused is not arrested under warrant of the governor by the expiration of the time specified in the warrant, bond or undertaking, a judge may discharge him or may recommit him for a further period of 60 days, or a judge of the Superior Court may again take bail for his appearance and surrender, as provided in N.J.S. 2A:160–24, but within a period not to exceed 60 days after the date of such new bond or undertaking.
Amended by L.1991, c. 91, § 132, eff. April 9, 1991.

2A:160–26. Forfeiture of bail; arrest of accused without warrant; recovery on bail bond

If the prisoner is admitted to bail and fails to appear and surrender himself according to the conditions of his bond, the judge or magistrate, by proper order, shall declare the bond forfeited and order his immediate arrest without warrant if he be within this state. Recovery may be had on such bond in the name of the state as in the case of other bonds or undertakings given by the accused in criminal proceedings within this state.

2A:160–27. Extradition of persons pending outcome of criminal prosecution in this state

If a criminal prosecution has been instituted against such person under the laws of this state and is still pending, the governor, in his discretion, either may surrender him on demand of the executive authority of another state or hold him until he has been tried and discharged or convicted and punished in this state.

2A:160–28. Inquiry into guilt or innocence of accused

The guilt or innocence of the accused as to the crime of which he is charged may not be inquired into by the governor or in any proceeding after the demand for extradition, accompanied by a charge of crime in legal form as above provided, shall have been presented to the governor, except as it may be involved in identifying the person held as the person charged with the crime.

2A:160–29. Recall of warrant of arrest; alias warrant

The governor may recall his warrant of arrest or may issue another warrant whenever he deems proper.

2A:160–30. Waiver of extradition proceedings; procedure; effect

Any person arrested in this state charged with having committed any crime in another state or alleged to have escaped from confinement, or broken the terms of his bail, probation or parole, may waive the issuance and service of the warrant provided for in sections 2A:160–15 and 2A:160–16 of this title and all other procedure incidental to extradition proceedings, by executing or subscribing in the presence of a judge of any criminal court of record within this state a writing which states that he consents to return to the demanding state. Before such waiver shall be executed or subscribed by such person it shall be the duty of such judge to inform such person of his rights to the issuance and service of a warrant of extradition and to obtain a writ of habeas corpus as provided for in section 2A:160–18 of this title.

If and when such consent has been duly executed it shall forthwith be forwarded to the office of the governor of this state and filed therein. The judge shall direct the officer having such person in custody to deliver forthwith such person to the duly accredited agent or agents of the demanding state, and shall deliver or cause to be delivered to such agent or agents a copy of such consent. Nothing in this section shall be deemed to limit the rights of the accused person to return voluntarily and without formality to the demanding state, nor shall this waiver procedure be deemed to be an exclusive procedure or to limit the powers, rights or duties of the officers of the demanding state or of this state.

C. EXTRADITION FROM OTHER STATES OF PERSONS ACCUSED OF CRIME, ESCAPING FROM CONFINEMENT OR BREAKING TERMS OF BAIL, PROBATION OR PAROLE IN THIS STATE

2A:160–31. Demand for extradition; issue of warrant by governor

Whenever the governor of this state shall demand a person charged with crime or with escaping from confinement or breaking the terms of his bail, probation or parole in this state, from the executive authority of any other state, or from the chief justice or a judge of the district court of the United States for the District of Columbia authorized to receive such demand under the laws of the United States, he shall issue a warrant under the seal of this state, to some agent, commanding him to receive the person so charged if delivered to him and convey him to the proper officer of the county in this state in which the offense was committed.

2A:160–32. Application to governor for requisition; by whom made; contents; verification of application; execution in duplicate; certified copies of indictment, information and affidavit filed, or complaint to accompany application; copy filed with secretary of state; copy forwarded with requisition

1. When the return to this state of a person charged with crime in this state is required, the prosecuting attorney shall present to the governor his written application for a requisition for the return of the person charged, in which application shall be stated the name of the person so charged, the crime charged against him, the approximate time, place and circumstances of its commission, the state in which he is believed to be, including the location of the accused therein at the time the application is made and certifying that, in the opinion of the said prosecuting attorney, the ends of justice require the arrest and return of the accused to this state for trial and that the proceeding is not instituted to enforce a private claim.

2. When the return to this state is required of a person who has been convicted of a crime in this state and has escaped from confinement or broken the terms of his bail, probation or parole, the prosecuting attorney of the county in which the offense was committed, the parole board, or the warden of the institution or sheriff of the county from which escape was made, shall present to the governor a written application for a requisition for the return of such person, in which application shall be stated the name of the person, the crime of which he was convicted, the circumstances of his escape from confinement or of the breach of the terms of his bail, probation or parole, the state in which he is believed to be, including the location of the person therein at the time application is made.

3. The application shall be verified by affidavit, shall be executed in duplicate and shall be accompanied by 2 certified copies of the indictment returned, or information and affidavit filed, or of the complaint made to the judge or magistrate, stating the offense with which the accused is charged, or of the judgment of conviction or of the sentence. The prosecuting officer, parole board, warden or sheriff may also attach such further affidavits and other documents in duplicate as he or it shall deem proper to be submitted with such application. One copy of the application, with the action of the governor indicated by indorsement thereon, and 1 of the certified copies of the indictment, complaint, information, and

affidavits, or of the judgment of conviction or of the sentence shall be filed in the office of the secretary of state to remain of record in that office. The other copies of all papers shall be forwarded with the governor's requisition.

2A:160–33. Extradition of persons imprisoned or awaiting trial in another state; agreement to return to state from which extradited

When it is desired to have returned to this state a person charged in this state with a crime, and such person is imprisoned or is held under criminal proceedings then pending against him in another state, the governor of this state may agree with the executive authority of such other state for the extradition of such person before the conclusion of such proceedings or his term of sentence in such other state, upon condition that such person be returned to such other state at the expense of this state as soon as the prosecution in this state is terminated.

2A:160–34. Immunity from service of process in certain civil actions

A person brought into this state on, or after waiver of, extradition based on a criminal charge shall not be subject to service of personal process in civil actions arising out of the same facts as the criminal proceeding to answer which he is being or has been returned, until he has been convicted in the criminal proceeding, or, if acquitted, until he has had reasonable opportunity to return to the state from which he was extradited.

2A:160–35. No immunity from other criminal prosecution while in this state

After a person has been brought back to this state by extradition proceedings, he may be tried in this state for other crimes which he may be charged with having committed here as well as that specified in the requisition for his extradition.

CHAPTER 161

PRELIMINARY PROCEEDINGS IN GENERAL

Section
2A:161–1.   Appointment of citizen to make immediate arrest.

2A:161–1. Appointment of citizen to make immediate arrest

In all criminal complaints before a judge of the Superior Court or a municipal court, where in the opinion of such judge, public justice shall require that a warrant for the arrest of the alleged offender issue and be executed immediately, and no person authorized to make an arrest can be had in time, such judge may, by writing, under his hand and seal, appoint some fit person, who shall be a citizen of this State, to execute the warrant, who shall have the same authority in the

premises in all respects and be subject to the same liability as a constable.

Amended by L.1991, c. 91, § 133, eff. April 9, 1991.

CHAPTER 161A

PERSONAL SEARCHES

Section
2A:161A–1.   Strip search; prohibition; exceptions.
2A:161A–2.   Body cavity search; prohibition; exceptions.
2A:161A–3.   Strip search and body cavity search defined.
2A:161A–4.   Conduct of search by persons of same sex and at location without observation by unauthorized persons; permission of officer in charge of stationhouse; report on record of arrest; release of information; immediate action under emergency conditions.
2A:161A–5.   Conduct under sanitary conditions; conduct of body cavity search by physician or registered nurse; immunity from liability; certificate of search by requirements of act and in medically acceptable manner; inapplicability of physician and patient privilege.
2A:161A–6.   Failure to comply with act; subjection to administrative disciplinary action.
2A:161A–7.   Statutory or common law rights for purposes of civil action or injunctive relief.
2A:161A–8.   Regulations governing strip and body cavity searches; guidelines or directives for police; bail schedule for offenses other than crimes.
2A:161A–9.   Subordination of procedures established by this act to procedures of state's penal institutions.
2A:161A–10. Violations not to affect admissibility of evidence.

2A:161A–1. Strip search; prohibition; exceptions

A person who has been detained or arrested for commission of an offense other than a crime shall not be subjected to a strip search unless:

   a.   The search is authorized by a warrant or consent;

   b.   The search is based on probable cause that a weapon, controlled dangerous substance, as defined by the "Comprehensive Drug Reform Act of 1987," N.J.S. 2C:35–1 et al., or evidence of a crime will be found and a recognized exception to the warrant requirement exists; or

   c.   The person is lawfully confined in a municipal detention facility or an adult county correctional facility and the search is based on a reasonable suspicion that a weapon, controlled dangerous substance, as defined by the "Comprehensive Drug Reform Act of 1987," N.J.S. 2C:35–1 et al., or contraband, as defined by the Department of Corrections, will be found, and the search is authorized pursuant to regulations promulgated by the Commissioner of the Department of Corrections.

L.1985, c. 70, § 1, eff. June 5, 1985. Amended by L.1991, c. 305, § 1, eff. Nov. 7, 1991.

2A:161A–2. Body cavity search; prohibition; exceptions

A person who has been detained or arrested for commission of an offense other than a crime shall not be subjected to a body cavity search unless:

a. The search is authorized by a warrant or consent; or

b. The person is lawfully confined in an adult county correctional facility and the search is based on a reasonable suspicion that a weapon, controlled dangerous substance, as defined by the "Comprehensive Drug Reform Act of 1987," N.J.S. 2C:35–1 et al., or contraband, as defined by the Commissioner of the Department of Corrections, will be found, and the search is authorized pursuant to the regulations promulgated by the Commissioner of the Department of Corrections.

L.1985, c. 70, § 2, eff. June 5, 1985. Amended by L.1991, c. 305, § 2, eff. Nov. 7, 1991.

2A:161A–3. Strip search and body cavity search defined

a. For purposes of this act, a "strip search" means the removal or rearrangement of clothing for the purpose of visual inspection of the person's undergarments, buttocks, anus, genitals or breasts. The term does not include any removal or rearrangement of clothing reasonably required to render medical treatment or assistance or the removal of articles of outerclothing such as coats, ties, belts or shoelaces.

b. For purposes of this act, a "body cavity search" means the visual inspection or manual search of a person's anal or vaginal cavity.

L.1985, c. 70, § 3, eff. June 5, 1985. Amended by L.1991, c. 305, § 3, eff. Nov. 7, 1991.

2A:161A–4. Conduct of search by persons of same sex and at location without observation by unauthorized persons; permission of officer in charge of stationhouse; report on record of arrest; release of information; immediate action under emergency conditions

a. Any strip search or body cavity search conducted under this act shall be performed by persons of the same sex as the arrested person and at a location where the search cannot be observed by persons not physically conducting the search. The law enforcement officer or other person authorized to conduct a strip search or body cavity search shall obtain permission of the officer in charge of the station house to conduct the search and shall report the reason for the search on the record of arrest. Where emergency conditions require immediate action to prevent bodily harm to the officer or others, the requirements of this section shall not apply. In all cases where a strip search is conducted as an exception to the requirements of this section, the officer conducting the search shall file a separate written report setting forth the emergency conditions which required the immediate action. This written report shall be filed with and reviewed by the officer in charge who had the authority to authorize a strip search.

b. Reports required pursuant to this section shall not be deemed public records within the meaning of P.L.1963, c. 73 (C. 47:1A–1 et seq.) but, upon request, shall be made available to the person searched, the county prosecutor, the Attorney General or the Commissioner of the Department of Corrections.

c. Nothing in this section is intended to preclude lawful use of the report of a strip search or body cavity search by law enforcement officials, the county prosecutor or officials responsible for the administration of a county or State correctional facility.

L.1985, c. 70, § 4, eff. June 5, 1985. Amended by L.1991, c. 305, § 4, eff. Nov. 7, 1991.

2A:161A–5. Conduct under sanitary conditions; conduct of body cavity search by physician or registered nurse; immunity from liability; certificate of search by requirements of act and in medically acceptable manner; inapplicability of physician and patient privilege

a. Where it is determined that a strip search or body cavity search is necessary, it shall be performed under sanitary conditions. A body cavity search, pursuant to section 2 of this act,[1] shall be conducted by a licensed physician or registered professional nurse.

b. A physician or nurse who conducts a body cavity search pursuant to the requirements of this act and in a medically accepted manner shall be immune from civil or criminal liability for so acting, provided the skill and care given are those ordinarily required and exercised by others in the profession. Immunity from civil or criminal liability shall extend to the hospital or other medical facility on whose premises or under whose auspices the body cavity search is conducted, provided the skill, care and facilities provided are those ordinarily provided by similar medical facilities.

c. Any person conducting a body cavity search pursuant to this act shall, upon request, furnish to any law enforcement agency a certificate stating that the body cavity search was pursuant to the requirements of this act and performed in a medically acceptable manner. The certificate shall be signed under oath before a notary public or other person empowered to take oaths and shall be admissible in any proceeding as evidence of the statements contained therein.

d. No person may claim the physician and patient privilege under section 2 of P.L. 1968, c. 185 (C. 2A:84A–22.2) with respect to the conducting of a body cavity search pursuant to this act.

L.1985, c. 70, § 5, eff. June 5, 1985.

[1] N.J.S.A. § 2A:161A–2.

2A:161A–6. Failure to comply with act; subjection to administrative disciplinary action

Failure to comply with any provisions of this act shall subject the law enforcement officer or other authorized person to administrative disciplinary action. Nothing in this section shall be construed as limiting such person's criminal liability pursuant to the laws of this State.

L.1985, c. 70, § 6, eff. June 5, 1985.

2A:161A–7. Statutory or common law rights for purposes of civil action or injunctive relief

Nothing in this act shall be construed as limiting any statutory or common law rights of any person for purposes of any civil action or injunctive relief.

L.1985, c. 70, § 7, eff. June 5, 1985.

2A:161A–8. Regulations governing strip and body cavity searches; guidelines or directives for police; bail schedule for offenses other than crimes

a. The Commissioner of the Department of Corrections, after consultation with the Attorney General, pursuant to authority granted in sections 6 and 10 of P.L.1976, c. 98 (C. 30:1B–6 and 30:1B–10) and this section shall promulgate regulations governing strip and body cavity searches of persons detained in municipal detention or adult county correctional facilities. These regulations shall give full recognition to the rights of persons confined granted under the constitutions of the United States and this State.

b. The Attorney General shall issue guidelines or directives for police officers governing the release and confinement of persons who have been arrested for commission of an offense other than a crime and such guidelines governing the performance of strip and body cavity searches as he deems necessary to promote compliance with this act, the regulations promulgated by the Commissioner of the Department of Corrections, and with the constitutions of the United States and this State. The Attorney General may require law enforcement agencies to submit periodic reports providing data on all strip searches and body cavity searches conducted.

c. The Administrative Office of the Courts shall promulgate a bail schedule for all offenses other than crimes, and bail for a person arrested or detained on a warrant may be fixed and accepted by the law enforcement officer in charge of the station house.

L.1985, c. 70, § 8, eff. June 5, 1985. Amended by L.1991, c. 305, § 5, eff. Nov. 7, 1991.

2A:161A–9. Subordination of procedures established by this act to procedures of state's penal institutions

Notwithstanding any law, rule or regulation to the contrary, no procedures as set forth in this act shall supersede any procedures of the State's penal institutions.

L.1985, c. 70, § 9, eff. June 5, 1985.

2A:161A–10. Violations not to affect admissibility of evidence

A violation of the provisions of sections 4 and 5 of this act [1] shall not affect the admissibility of evidence seized pursuant to a strip search or body cavity search.

L.1985, c. 70, § 10, eff. June 5, 1985.

  [1] N.J.S.A. §§ 2A:161A–4 and 2A:161A–5.

CHAPTER 162

BAIL AND RECOGNIZANCES

Section
2A:162–1.   Record of recognizances in counties other than where taken; lien thereof.
2A:162–2 to 2A:162–4.   Repealed.
2A:162–5.   Duration of lien, upon any property, of forfeited recognizances not prosecuted to judgment; time limit after effective date for enforcement.
2A:162–6.   Revival of judgment on forfeited recognizances; limitation.
2A:162–7.   Money collected on forfeited recognizances paid to county treasurer.
2A:162–7.1.   Forfeiture of bail; procedures for disposition of amounts forfeited.
2A:162–8.   Return of amounts paid on forfeited recognizances.
2A:162–9.   Cash deposit; affidavit as to ownership.
2A:162–10.   Effective date.
2A:162–11.   Person convicted on disorderly person charge; bail or recognizance on appeal.
2A:162–12.   Crimes with bail restrictions.
2A:162–13.   Permissible court inquiry for bail.
2A:162–14.   Sufficiency of bail.

2A:162–1. Record of recognizances in counties other than where taken; lien thereof

When the real estate of the surety in a recognizance of bail is situate in a county other than the county where the recognizance is taken, the clerk of the court in which the bail is taken shall forthwith make and certify a copy of the recognizance and send the same to the county clerk or register of deeds of the county in which such real estate is situate, who shall record such certified copy in the same manner as if the recognizance had been taken in his county, and thereupon such recognizance shall constitute a lien upon such real estate and have the same force and effect as if taken in such county.

2A:162–2 to 2A:162–4. Repealed by L.1994, c. 126, § 2, eff. Oct. 26, 1994

2A:162–5. Duration of lien, upon any property, of forfeited recognizances not prosecuted to judgment; time limit after effective date for enforcement

All recognizances of bail made or entered into before any court, judge or magistrate having criminal jurisdiction, which have been or shall be forfeited, but upon which no writ of scire facias or other process to enforce or collect the same shall have been issued and prosecuted to final judgment within a period of 6 years after the same shall have been filed and recorded in the clerk's office, and all recognizances of bail which have not been forfeited, shall, after 6 years from the date of the filing and recording of any such recognizances of bail in the clerk's office, no longer be enforceable as a claim or as a lien or charge upon or against any property of which any principal or surety named in any such recognizance was or shall have been seized at the time of his entering into such recognizance or at any time thereafter; provided that any claim, lien, or charge against personal property affected by any of the provisions of this act may be prosecuted or enforced within 6 months from the effective date hereof.

Amended by L.1954, c. 233, p. 863, § 1, eff. Dec. 8, 1954.

2A:162–6. Revival of judgment on forfeited recognizances; limitation

Judgments in any court of record, entered upon forfeited recognizances in criminal cases, may be revived by scire facias, or a civil action may be brought thereon within 6 years next after the date of such judgment and not after.

2A:162–7. Money collected on forfeited recognizances paid to county treasurer

Every sheriff, prosecutor or clerk of any court who shall collect or receive any money on any forfeited recognizance, whether before or after execution, or from any amercement awarded by any court against any offender, shall, within 10 days after collecting or receiving the same, pay over the same to the treasurer of the county wherein such forfeiture was had or amercement awarded, for the use of the county.

2A:162–7.1. Forfeiture of bail; procedures for disposition of amounts forfeited

a.　If any bail deposited with a county clerk prior to January 1, 1995 shall be forfeited such forfeited bail and any interest thereon shall remain with the county.

b.　If any bail deposited on or after January 1, 1995 shall be forfeited, 50% of such bail and any interest thereon shall be paid to the county in which the bail was deposited.

L.1993, c. 275, § 22, eff. Dec. 6, 1993.

2A:162–8. Return of amounts paid on forfeited recognizances

When any court which has ordered or shall order the forfeiture of a recognizance, the amount whereof has been or shall be paid into the county treasury of any county in accordance with law, shall thereafter, in its discretion, order the return of the moneys so paid upon the forfeited recognizance, the treasurer of the county shall thereupon repay the amount of such recognizance, less the taxed costs on the proceedings to forfeit the same, to the recognizor or recognizors or the personal representatives of any deceased recognizor, who shall

have paid the same into the county treasury. Application for a return of moneys so paid shall be made to the court within 4 years after the recognizance shall have been declared forfeited.

2A:162–9. Cash deposit; affidavit as to ownership

Whenever cash money is deposited in any criminal case in lieu of bail and recognizance, the court accepting such deposit, or the judge or clerk of said court, shall require the person claiming the deposit to swear to and subscribe an affidavit as to the ownership of the said cash money, which affidavit shall become a part of the record of the case wherein the deposit is made. The form of such affidavits and the proceedings pertaining thereto shall be subject to the rules of the Supreme Court governing said courts.

L.1952, c. 163, p. 532, § 1, eff. May 1, 1952.

2A:162–10. Effective date

This act shall take effect May first, one thousand nine hundred and fifty-two.

L.1952, c. 163, p. 533, § 2, eff. May 1, 1952.

2A:162–11. Person convicted on disorderly person charge; bail or recognizance on appeal

In every case where a person has been convicted in a municipal court of a disorderly persons violation, and he has not violated or forfeited his bail or recognizance, such bail or recognizance shall continue in the same terms and effect pending appeal to the Superior Court in lieu of posting a new bond in connection with the appeal, or in the alternative the judge of the municipal court may discharge any such bail or recognizance and release the person on his own recognizance.

L.1974, c. 93, § 1, eff. Sept. 10, 1974. Amended by L.1991, c. 91, § 134, eff. April 9, 1991.

2A:162–12. Crimes with bail restrictions

a.　As used in this section:

"Crime with bail restrictions" means a crime of the first or second degree charged under any of the following sections:

(1) Murder 2C:11–3.

(2) Manslaughter 2C:11–4.

(3) Kidnapping 2C:13–1.

(4) Sexual Assault 2C:14–2.

(5) Robbery 2C:15–1.

(6) Carjacking P.L.1993, c. 221, s.1 (C.2C:15–2).

(7) Arson and Related Offenses 2C:17–1.

(8) Causing or Risking Widespread Injury or Damage 2C:17–2.

(9) Burglary 2C:18–2.

(10) Theft by Extortion 2C:20–5.

(11) Endangering the Welfare of Children 2C:24–4.

(12) Resisting Arrest; Eluding Officer 2C:29–2.

(13) Escape 2C:29–5.

(14) Corrupting or Influencing a Jury 2C:29–8.

(15) Possession of Weapons for Unlawful Purposes 2C:39–4.

(16) Weapons Training for Illegal Activities P.L. 1983, c. 229, s.1 (C.2C:39–14).

(17) Soliciting or Recruiting Gang Members P.L. 1999, c. 160, s.1 (C.2C:33–28).

"Crime with bail restrictions" also includes any first or second degree drug-related crimes under chapter 35 of Title 2C of the New Jersey Statutes and any first or second degree racketeering crimes under chapter 41 of Title 2C of the New Jersey Statutes.

b. Subject to the provisions of subsection c. of this section, a person charged with a crime with bail restrictions may post the required amount of bail only in the form of:

(1) Full cash;

(2) A surety bond executed by a corporation authorized under chapter 31 of Title 17 of the Revised Statutes; or

(3) A bail bond secured by real property situated in this State with an unencumbered equity equal to the amount of bail undertaken plus $20,000.

c. There shall be a presumption in favor of the court designating the posting of full United States currency cash bail to the exclusion of other forms of bail when a defendant is charged with an offense as set forth in subsection a. of this section and:

(1) has two other indictable cases pending at the time of the arrest; or

(2) has two prior convictions for a first or second degree crime or for a violation of section 1 of P.L.1987, c. 101 (C.2C:35–7) or any combination thereof; or

(3) has one prior conviction for murder, aggravated manslaughter, aggravated sexual assault, kidnapping or bail jumping;or

(4) was on parole at the time of the arrest,

unless the court finds on the record that another form of bail authorized in subsection b. of this section will ensure the defendant's presence in court when required.

d. When bail is posted in the form of a bail bond secured by real property, the owner of the real property, whether the person is admitted to bail or a surety, shall also file an affidavit containing:

(1) A legal description of the real property;

(2) A description of each encumbrance on the real property;

(3) The market value of the unencumbered equity owned by the affiant as determined in a full appraisal

conducted by an appraiser licensed by the State of New Jersey; and

(4) A statement that the affiant is the sole owner of the unencumbered equity.

e. Nothing herein is intended to preclude a court from releasing a person on the person's own recognizance when the court determines that such person is deserving.

L.1994, c. 144, § 1, eff. Feb. 14, 1994. Amended by L.2003, c. 177, § 1, eff. Sept. 12, 2003; L.2007, c. 46, § 1, eff. June 1, 2007.

2A:162–13. Permissible court inquiry for bail

a. When a person charged with a crime with bail restrictions, as defined in subsection a. of section 1 of P.L.1994, c. 144 (C.2A:162–12), posts cash bail or secures a bail bond, the person, no later than the time of posting bail or proffering the surety or bail bond, shall provide to the prosecutor, on a form promulgated by the Attorney General, relevant information under penalty of perjury about the obligor, indemnifier or person posting cash bail, the security offered, and the source of any money or property used to post the cash bail or secure the surety or bail bond, as the case may be. This required information shall include, but not be limited to, the defendant's employment history, the names and addresses of any persons who contributed money or pledged security for the proffered bail or toward a surety bond, the amount, nature and timing of such contributions, and the relationship to the defendant of any such persons contributing resources. Bail may not be accepted from a person subject to the requirements of this subsection until the prosecutor is provided the completed form required by this subsection.

b. When a person charged with an offense posts cash bail or secures a bail bond in any amount, the court may, upon the request of the prosecutor, conduct an inquiry to determine the reliability of the obligor or person posting cash bail, the value and sufficiency of any security offered, the relationship of the obligor or person posting cash bail to the defendant and the defendant's interest in ensuring that the bail is not forfeited, and whether the funds used to post the cash bail or secure the bail bond were acquired as a result of criminal or unlawful conduct. When the offense charged against such person is a crime with bail restrictions as defined in subsection a. of section 1 of P.L.1994, c.144 (C.2A:162-12), the court shall, upon the request of the prosecutor, conduct an inquiry pursuant to the provisions of this subsection. The court may examine, under oath or otherwise, any person who may possess relevant information, and may inquire into any matter appropriate to its determination, including, but not limited to, the following:

(1) The character, background and reputation of the person posting cash bail;

(2) The relationship of the person posting cash bail or securing a bail bond to the defendant;

(3) The source of any money posted as cash bail and whether any such money constitutes the fruits of criminal or unlawful conduct;

(4) The character, background and reputation of any person who has indemnified or agreed to indemnify an obligor on the bond;

(5) The character, background and reputation of any obligor, or, in the case of a surety bond, the qualifications of the surety and its executing agent;

(6) The source of any money or property deposited by any obligor as security and whether such money or property constitutes the fruits of criminal or unlawful conduct; and

(7) The source of any money or property delivered or agreed to be delivered by any obligor as indemnification on the bond and whether such money or property constitutes the fruits of criminal or unlawful conduct.

At the conclusion of the inquiry, the court shall issue an order either approving or disapproving the bail. The court shall not issue an order approving the bail unless it is satisfied that the evidence adduced in the inquiry establishes the reliability of the source of the funds used to post bail or security offered, that the relationship of the obligor or person posting cash bail is sufficient to ensure the defendant's presence in court when required, and that the funds used to post cash bail or secure a bail bond were not acquired as a result of criminal or unlawful conduct.

L.2003, c. 213, § 1, eff. Jan. 9, 2004. Amended by L.2007, c. 46, § 2, eff. June 1, 2007.

2A:162–14. Sufficiency of bail

The procedure to determine the sufficiency of bail shall be governed by rules adopted by the Supreme Court.

L.2003, c. 213, § 2, eff. Jan. 9, 2004.

CHAPTER 163

TRIAL

Section
2A:163–1.   Compensation of counsel assigned in murder cases.
2A:163–2, 2A:163–3.   Repealed.
2A:163–4.   Child and victim defined.
2A:163–5.   Criminal cases involving child victim; speedy trial.

2A:163–1. Compensation of counsel assigned in murder cases

Where counsel assigned by the court to represent a defendant in a murder case has been allowed compensation by the court for his services, the sum so fixed shall be paid by the county treasurer of the county where the indictment was found, upon presentation of a certificate of the judge, fixing and allowing such compensation.

2A:163–2, 2A:163–3. Repealed by L.1978, c. 95, § 2C:98–2, eff. Sept. 1, 1979

2A:163–4. Child and victim defined

As used in this act:

a. "Child" means a person 13 years of age or younger at the time a crime was committed against the child.

b. "Victim" means a child who suffers personal, physical, or psychological injury as a result of a crime committed against that child.

L.1987, c. 148, § 1, eff. June 24, 1987.

2A:163–5. Criminal cases involving child victim; speedy trial

In all criminal cases involving a child victim, the court shall take appropriate action to ensure a speedy trial in order to minimize the length of time the child must endure the stress of involvement in the proceedings. In ruling on any motion or other request for a delay or continuance of proceedings, the court shall consider and give weight to any adverse impact the delay or continuance may have on the well-being of a child victim.

L.1987, c. 148, § 2, eff. June 24, 1987.

CHAPTER 164

SENTENCE AND IMPRISONMENT

ARTICLE 1. CLINICS

Section
2A:164–1.   Clinics to study mental and physical conditions before sentence of convicted persons; organization; personnel; rules for conduct of; expenses.

ARTICLE 3. MISCELLANEOUS

2A:164–24.   Remission of sentence of prisoners confined in county jail or penitentiary for good conduct.

ARTICLE 1. CLINICS

2A:164–1. Clinics to study mental and physical conditions before sentence of convicted persons; organization; personnel; rules for conduct of; expenses

In order that judges conducting courts for the trial of criminal cases may have complete information for use in determining sentences to be imposed, there may be organized and operated in each county a clinic for the study of the mental and physical conditions of defendants to be sentenced and their environments.

Each assignment judge of the Superior Court shall have authority to organize a clinic in the county or counties in which he presides.

A clinic shall consist of any number of qualified persons, more than 3, as shall seem proper to the assignment judge organizing the same, 1 of which number shall be the county probation officer, 1 a physician licensed to practice in this state and 1 a psychologist.

Every clinic shall be conducted in accordance with rules prescribed by the courts which it shall serve and shall be operated without expense to the county in which it is organized unless the board of chosen freeholders thereof shall appropriate money to defray such expenses, which they are hereby authorized to do.

Amended by L.1991, c. 91, § 135, eff. April 9, 1991.

ARTICLE 3. MISCELLANEOUS

2A:164–24. Remission of sentence of prisoners confined in county jail or penitentiary for good conduct

The board of chosen freeholders of any county, or the committee on the discharge of prisoners of such board, may, upon the recommendation of the sheriff or jail warden of the county jail or penitentiary in whose custody any prisoner may be, remit for good conduct from the sentence of any person committed to such county jail or penitentiary, a term not exceeding 1 day for every 6 days of such sentence. If any such person shall be again convicted and sentenced to imprisonment in such county jail or penitentiary, he may, in addition to such new sentence, be required at the discretion of the court to serve out the number of days remitted to him on the previous term.

Amended by L.1968, c. 255, § 1, eff. Sept. 4, 1968.

CHAPTER 166

COSTS AND FINES

Section
2A:166–1 to 2A:166–7. Repealed.
2A:166–8.   Fees of witnesses and constables on acquittals; payment by and reimbursement of sheriff.
2A:166–9.   Fees of clerk and sheriff on acquittals; payment by county.
2A:166–10.   Repealed.
2A:166–11.   Repealed.
2A:166–12.   Execution against municipality for fines and costs returned unsatisfied.
2A:166–13.   Return of fine on reversal.
2A:166–14 to 2A:166–16. Repealed.
2A:166–17.   No fees or costs payable to judge or officer receiving salary.
2A:166–18.   No fees from parties applying to magistrate for services in criminal cases; payment by county.
2A:166–19.   Repealed.

2A:166–1 to 2A:166–7. Repealed by L.1978, c. 95, § 2C:98–2, eff. Sept. 1, 1979

2A:166–8. Fees of witnesses and constables on acquittals; payment by and reimbursement of sheriff

Whenever, on any indictment or accusation, there is an acquittal, the sheriff of the county in which the trial was had shall pay the fees of the witnesses and constables, taking receipts from them for such pay-ments. On the production of such receipts, or upon the oath of the sheriff, the amounts so paid shall, on demand, be repaid to the sheriff by the county treasurer from any moneys in his hand belonging to the county, and such payments shall be allowed to the county treasurer in the settlement of his accounts.

2A:166–9. Fees of clerk and sheriff on acquittals; payment by county

On the acquittal of any person indicted for crime the fees of the clerk and the sheriff shall be paid by the county treasurer, upon the taxed bill of costs, duly verified by the clerk and the sheriff, and certified to be correct by the prosecutor.

2A:166–10. Repealed by L.1979, c. 396, § 5, eff. Feb. 6, 1980

2A:166–11. Repealed by L.1978, c. 95, § 2C:98–2, eff. Sept. 1, 1979

2A:166–12. Execution against municipality for fines and costs returned unsatisfied

When any execution, issued against any municipality, for the amount of any fine and costs as provided in this subtitle shall be returned by the sheriff or other proper officer unsatisfied for want of goods and chattels or real estate of such municipality, the clerk of the court out of which the same issued shall make a copy thereof, with the indorsements thereon, and the return of the sheriff or other proper officer thereto, having added to the costs indorsed thereon $1, the fee of the clerk for the copy and a certificate thereof, and $2, the fee of the sheriff for the services hereinafter required of him, and certify the same under his hand and seal of office, and deliver it to the sheriff or other proper officer. Upon receiving such certified copy of the execution and return, the sheriff or other proper officer shall present the same to the county treasurer, who shall pay to the sheriff or other proper officer the amount of the costs indorsed, together with the interest due thereon, taking a receipt from the sheriff or other proper officer therefor, which certified copy and receipt shall be a sufficient voucher for the payment thereof, in the settlement of the accounts of the treasurer. The county treasurer, having paid the costs, shall thereupon charge the same, together with the amount of the fine, to the municipality against which such execution was issued, adding thereto interest up to the 15th day of December following the next annual levy of taxes in the county, and shall transmit a statement of the same to the county board of taxation on or before March 1st preceding such annual levy. Such sum shall be added to the proportion or quota of the tax next to be levied and collected in such municipality, and shall be assessed, levied, collected and paid over in the same manner and under the same penalties as the proportion or quota of tax is by law directed to be assessed, levied, collected and paid for.

2A:166–13. Return of fine on reversal

When a defendant has paid a fine upon being found guilty of an offense and has taken an appeal and obtained a decision in his favor terminating the case of the State against him, the treasury of the governmental entity which received the fine shall return to such person the amount of the fine so paid.

Amended by L.1979, c. 396, § 1, eff. Feb. 6, 1980.

2A:166–14 to 2A:166–16. Repealed by L.1978, c. 95, § 2C:98–2, eff. Sept. 1, 1979

2A:166–17. No fees or costs payable to judge or officer receiving salary

No fees or costs shall be paid by the county treasurer for the services of any judge, magistrate or officer of any criminal court, where such judge, magistrate or officer receives a salary.

2A:166–18. No fees from parties applying to magistrate for services in criminal cases; payment by county

In criminal cases no fees shall be demanded from parties applying to magistrates or constables for their services.

2A:166–19. Repealed by L.1979, c. 396, § 5, eff. Feb. 6, 1980

CHAPTER 166A

REIMBURSEMENT TO COUNTIES FOR CRIMINAL PROSECUTION EXPENSES

Section
2A:166A–1. Maximum amount of reimbursement.
2A:166A–2. Expenses allowable.
2A:166A–3. Claims; approval; certification; budget requests.
2A:166A–4. Effective date; applicability.

2A:166A–1. Maximum amount of reimbursement

Any county which incurs expense in connection with the prosecution and defense of a defendant charged with commission of a capital offense while confined to a State penal or correctional institution located in the county shall be entitled to reimbursement therefor by the State in amounts not to exceed the following:

a. $500.00 for any case, whether or not the same is brought to trial, plus

b. $750.00 for each trial day, plus

c. The actual expense of printing required in connection with any appeal from the judgment of the trial court.

L.1960, c. 24, p. 85, § 1.

2A:166A–2. Expenses allowable

The expenses for which a county shall be entitled to reimbursement shall be limited to fees allowed to counsel assigned by the trial court pursuant to section 2A:163–1 of the New Jersey Statutes, juror and expert witness fees, the costs of sequestering jurors and jury attendants, the cost of transcripts of court proceedings, and the costs of printing in connection with any appeal.

L.1960, c. 24, p. 85, § 2.

2A:166A–3. Claims; approval; certification; budget requests

Claims for reimbursement shall bear the approval of the trial judge and shall be certified to the administrative director of the courts by the assignment judge of the county for payment by the State Treasurer from funds appropriated for the administration of the courts. The administrative director of the courts shall formulate and include in annual budget requests sums necessary to carry out the provisions of this act.

L.1960, c. 24, p. 85, § 3.

2A:166A–4. Effective date; applicability

This act shall take effect immediately and shall apply to expenses incurred on and after September 1, 1959.

L.1960, c. 24, p. 86, § 4.

CHAPTER 167

EXECUTIVE CLEMENCY

Section
2A:167–1 to 2A:167–3. Repealed.
2A:167–3.1. Annual report by governor of each pardon, reprieve or commutation of sentence granted.
2A:167–4. Form of order; filing.
2A:167–5. Restoration of right of suffrage and other rights; suspension or remission of fine.
2A:167–6. Form of application.
2A:167–7. Investigation and report.
2A:167–8. Convicts having license to be at large; security; legal custody; return to place of punishment.
2A:167–9. Retaking and detention; warrant; credit for time spent in custody.
2A:167–10. Revocation of license or order.
2A:167–11. Investigation by state parole board.
2A:167–12. Order of revocation; arrest; detention; period of confinement.

2A:167–1 to 2A:167–3. Repealed by L.1978, c. 95, § 2C:98–2, eff. Sept. 1, 1979

2A:167–3.1. Annual report by governor of each pardon, reprieve or commutation of sentence granted

On or before March 1 of each year, the Governor shall report to the Legislature each reprieve, pardon and commutation granted, stating the name of the convicted person, the crime for which the person was convicted, the sentence imposed, its date, the date of the pardon, reprieve or commutation and the reasons for granting same.

L.1993, c. 26, § 1, eff. Jan. 25, 1993.

2A:167–4. Form of order; filing

The governor may, upon application for commutation of sentence of any person sentenced to imprisonment, order that such sentence be commuted upon such terms, conditions and limitations as the governor, in his discretion, may direct, as conditions precedent to the release of any such person from imprisonment; which terms, conditions and limitations shall be annexed to and form part of said order. Upon the filing of such order signed by the governor with the officer in whose custody such person may be, and after the acceptance by such person of the terms, conditions and limitations contained in said order, as evidenced by his signature affixed to the duplicate copy of such order to be kept in the files of the state parole board, such sentence shall thereupon be commuted in accordance with the terms, conditions and limitations of such order.

2A:167–5. Restoration of right of suffrage and other rights; suspension or remission of fine

Any person who has been convicted of a crime and by reason thereof has been deprived of the right of suffrage or of any other of his civil rights or privileges, or upon whom there has been imposed a fine or who has suffered a forfeiture, except disqualification to hold and enjoy any public office of honor, profit or trust in this state under judgment of impeachment, may make application for the restoration of the right of suffrage or of such other rights or privileges or for the suspension or remission of such fine or forfeiture, which application the governor may grant by order signed by him.

2A:167–6. Form of application

Applications for commutation of sentences, other than death sentences, or for the restoration of rights or privileges, or for the suspension or remission of any fine or forfeiture, shall be made upon forms prescribed by the governor.

2A:167–7. Investigation and report

The governor, in his discretion, may, prior to granting or denying any such application, refer the same to the state parole board for its investigation, and in such case the board shall make a full and complete investigation and report thereon in writing to the governor with its recommendation in the case.

2A:167–8. Convicts having license to be at large; security; legal custody; return to place of punishment

Any convict who was undergoing imprisonment in any of the penal institutions of this state and to whom was granted a license to be at large or at liberty by the court of pardons, or to whom was granted a commutation of sentence by order of the governor, shall remain subject to the security, terms, conditions and limitations, in all respects, upon which the same was granted. Any convict undergoing imprisonment in any of the penal institutions of this state and to whom may be granted a commutation of sentence by order of the governor shall remain subject to the security, terms, conditions and limitations, in all respects, upon which the same is granted.

Every convict at large or at liberty under any such license or order shall continue to be in the legal custody of the warden, keeper or chief executive officer of the institution from which such convict was or may be released under such license or order, and under immediate and constant supervision of the division of parole of the department of institutions and agencies in accordance with the rules and regulations of the state parole board approved by the governor, and until the expiration of the maximum term of the sentence imposed upon such person for the crime for which he or she was committed.

Every convict at large or at liberty under any such license or order shall be liable to be taken at any time and returned to the place of punishment to which he or she was originally sentenced, as hereinafter provided.

2A:167–9. Retaking and detention; warrant; credit for time spent in custody

If the parole officer having charge of any convict at large or at liberty under any such license or order shall have reasonable cause to believe that such person has resumed, or is about to resume, criminal conduct or associations, or has violated the terms, conditions or limitations of such license or order in any important respect, and the situation is one of immediate emergency, then such parole officer shall notify the division of parole which may, if the facts warrant, treat such convict as delinquent under such license or order. The division of parole shall immediately notify the governor and the state parole board of such action. By his own warrant the parole officer may apprehend any such delinquent person and cause his or her return to the institution from which released or cause such person's immediate confinement in an appropriate county or municipal jail, penitentiary or lockup. Such retaking and detention shall continue under authority of the parole officer's warrant until the determination by the governor as to the revocation of the license or order under which such convict is at large or at liberty, or his or her return to the community under such license or order. Such warrant shall be in the form prescribed by the state parole board and approved by the governor, and, when signed by the parole officer in charge of the case, shall be sufficient warrant and authority to all peace officers to assist in the apprehension of the convict and shall be also sufficient authority for the detention of the convict in the institution from which released or in a municipal or county jail, penitentiary or lockup. In such case, credit shall be given the convict on his or her sentence for time spent in such custody while awaiting the decision of the governor as to revocation of such license or order.

2A:167–10. Revocation of license or order

The governor may, at any time, in his discretion, revoke any such license or order, and shall revoke any such license or order whenever it shall come to his knowledge that the person to or for whom the same was granted has violated any of the terms, conditions or limitations thereof, or any penal law of this state, or of any other state, or of the United States.

2A:167–11. Investigation by state parole board

The governor, in his discretion, may, prior to determining whether to revoke any such license or order, refer the matter to the state parole board for its investigation, and in such case the board shall make a full and complete investigation and report thereon in writing to the governor with its recommendations in the case. The governor may also, by general rule or regulation, require the state parole board to investigate all such cases. In such event the board shall make a full and complete investigation and report in writing to the governor with its recommendations in each such case.

2A:167–12. Order of revocation; arrest; detention; period of confinement

When any such license or order is revoked it shall be done by an order in writing signed by the Governor and filed with the State Parole Board. The form of such order shall be prescribed by the Governor.

Upon the signing of such order, the Governor shall issue his warrant for the arrest of the convict to or for whom such license or order was granted, and his or her return to the place of confinement from which he or she was released thereunder. The warrant may be served by any person authorized to serve criminal process in any county in the State.

The convict to or for whom such license or order was or may be granted, when returned to the place of confinement from which he or she was released thereunder, shall be detained therein according to the terms of his or her original sentence; and, in computing the period of such convict's confinement, if it shall appear that such license or order was revoked because of conviction of crime of an indictable character committed while at liberty upon such license or order, the time between such person's release upon such license or order and return to confinement shall not be taken to be any part of the term of sentence. If the license or order is revoked for reasons other than such conviction of crime, then the holder of such license or order shall be required to serve the balance of time due on his or her sentence to be computed from the date of the violation of one or more of the terms, conditions or limitations which resulted in the revocation of such license or order. If the person for whose arrest such warrant is issued is confined in any prison or penal or correctional institution of this State, the officer to whom

the warrant shall be delivered, shall deliver the same to the warden, keeper or chief executive officer of such institution or prison, and the warden, keeper or chief executive officer shall, upon the expiration of the term of imprisonment or period of confinement then being served in that institution or prison, return the convict to the institution or prison from which such person was released under such license or order, or, if the release under such license or order was from the same institution or prison, he shall detain such convict therein according to the terms of his or her original sentence.

No part of a sentence imposed upon a convict, concerning which a license or order has been granted and revoked, shall be deemed to be served by such person while he or she is serving a sentence for an offense other than the one for which he or she was released under such license or order.

Amended by L.1953, c. 275, p. 1805, § 1, eff. July 25, 1953.

CHAPTER 168

PROBATION AND PAROLE

ARTICLE 1. GENERAL PROVISIONS

Section
2A:168–1 to 2A:168–4. Repealed.
2A:168–5. Probation officers; appointment; qualifications.
2A:168–6. Probation officers in counties of not less than 800,000; appointment of parole officers as; civil service; compensation.
2A:168–7. Powers and duties of chief probation officer; additional employees.
2A:168–8. Salaries and expenses of probation officers and employees.
2A:168–9. Temporary probation officers; appointment; compensation.
2A:168–10. Oath of probation officers; bond; accounts audited.
2A:168–11. Powers and duties of probation officers.
2A:168–12. Transfer of probationers.
2A:168–13. Investigations for superior court; financial status of persons seeking relief in forma pauperis; alimony or support payments.

ARTICLE 2. COMPACT BETWEEN STATES RELATING TO PERSONS CONVICTED OF CRIME ON PROBATION OR PAROLE

2A:168–14. Governor authorized to enter into compact with states; form; contents of compact; investigations; duties of receiving state; retaking of probationers or parolees by sending state; extradition waived; rules and regulations; compact operative on ratification; force and effect of compact; renunciation.
2A:168–15. Constitutionality.
2A:168–16. Compact deemed ratified, when.
2A:168–17. Citation.

Section

ARTICLE 3. RECIPROCAL LEGISLATION
UNDER COMPACT

2A:168–18. Incarceration of probationer or parolee in receiving state; receiving state as agent.
2A:168–19. "Receiving State" defined.
2A:168–20. Compact institutions; incarceration in; access to.
2A:168–21. Persons confined in compact institutions subject to jurisdiction of sending state.
2A:168–22. Rights of persons confined in compact institutions.
2A:168–23. Costs and expenses.
2A:168–24. Rules and regulations.
2A:168–25. Effective when other states enact similar legislation.

ARTICLE 4. INTERSTATE COMPACT FOR
ADULT OFFENDER SUPERVISION

2A:168–26. Interstate Compact for Adult Offender Supervision.
2A:168–27. Definitions.
2A:168–28. Interstate Commission for Adult Offender Supervision.
2A:168–29. Council.
2A:168–30. Powers and duties.
2A:168–31. By-laws; election of officers; records; qualified immunity.
2A:168–32. Actions; voting; public records; open meetings.
2A:168–33. Rulemaking.
2A:168–34. Oversight; mediation and binding dispute resolution; enforcement.
2A:168–35. Finance; expenses, annual assessment and budget.
2A:168–36. Eligibility; amendments to compact; effective date.
2A:168–37. Withdrawal from compact; default; enforcement and jurisdiction.
2A:168–38. Severability.
2A:168–39. Construction with other laws; binding effect.

ARTICLE 1. GENERAL PROVISIONS

2A:168–1 to 2A:168–4. Repealed by L.1978, c. 95, § 2C:98–2, eff. Sept. 1, 1979

2A:168–5. Probation officers; appointment; qualifications

The Assignment Judge of the Superior Court in each county may appoint a chief probation officer, and, on application of the chief probation officer, such men and women probation officers as may be necessary. Before any order is made by such judge appointing any additional probation officers, a notice of the time and place, when and where such order shall be considered, shall be given to the board of chosen freeholders of the county and they shall be given an opportunity to be heard as to the necessity of such additional probation officers. All probation officers who are to receive salaries shall be appointed in accordance with the rules and regulations of the Civil Service Commission. Or-

ders of appointment shall be in writing and be filed in the office of the county clerk.
Amended by L.1953, c. 311, p. 1851, § 1, eff. July 28, 1953; L.1991, c. 91, § 136, eff. April 9, 1991.

2A:168–6. Probation officers in counties of not less than 800,000; appointment of parole officers as; civil service; compensation

L.1940, c. 78, p. 202, an act entitled "An Act authorizing the appointment of persons employed as parole officers of a city home in cities of the first class to the position of probation officer in counties having a population as established by the 1930 census, of not less than 800,000, and supplementing article one of chapter one hundred and ninety-nine of Title 2 of the Revised Statutes." saved from repeal.

2A:168–7. Powers and duties of chief probation officer; additional employees

The chief probation officer shall have general supervision of the probation work under the direction of the court. He may appoint such other employees as may be necessary to carry out the purposes of this chapter, but the amount expended for this purpose shall not exceed the amount appropriated therefor in the annual county budget. The chief probation officer may make such necessary rules and regulations with respect to the management and conduct of the probation officers and other employees as may be authorized by the Assignment Judge of the Superior Court.
Amended by L.1991, c. 91, § 137, eff. April 9, 1991.

2A:168–8. Salaries and expenses of probation officers and employees

The judge authorized to appoint a chief probation officer or probation officers shall fix, by order under the hand of such judge, annual salaries to be paid such officers, and before any such order shall be made by such judge, notice of the time and place, when and where such order shall be considered, shall be given to the board of chosen freeholders of the county and such board shall be given an opportunity to be heard upon the same and such order shall be filed in the office of the County Clerk. The amounts so fixed shall be paid in equal semimonthly payments in the same manner as the salaries of other officers of the county.

The necessary and reasonable expenses of salaried probation officers incurred in the performance of their duties shall be paid out of the county treasury, after itemized statements of such expenses have been approved by the chief probation officer and the Assignment Judge of the Superior Court and filed in the office of the county treasurer. On request of the chief probation officer, the necessary traveling and maintenance expenses in attending probation officers' meetings and conferences of social work shall be included, when previously authorized by the judge authorized to appoint probation officers.

The salaries of employees appointed by the chief probation officer shall be fixed by the board of chosen freeholders in accordance with the schedules of the Civil Service Commission, and paid in the same manner as the salaries of probation officers.

Amended by L.1953, c. 311, p. 1858, § 2, eff. July 28, 1953; L.1991, c. 91, § 138, eff. April 9, 1991.

2A:168–9. Temporary probation officers; appointment; compensation

In case of the absence or disqualification of any probation officer for any cause, the Assignment Judge of the Superior Court may appoint some other person to serve temporarily as a probation officer, who shall receive as compensation for each day's service a sum determined by the court. The compensation so paid for any excess over 90 days' absence of any probation officer in any one year may be deducted from the salary of such probation officer.

Amended by L.1991, c. 91, § 139, eff. April 9, 1991.

2A:168–10. Oath of probation officers; bond; accounts audited

Each probation officer, before entering on the duties of his office, shall take an oath of office to be administered by one of the judges making the appointment. Each probation officer or employee who collects or has the custody of money shall execute a bond in a penal sum, to be fixed by the judges, with sufficient sureties approved by them, conditioned for the honest accounting of all money received by him as probation officer. The accounts of all probation officers shall be subject to audit at any time by the board of chosen freeholders.

2A:168–11. Powers and duties of probation officers

Probation officers shall have the powers of constables in the execution of their duties. The duties of probation officers shall be, among others:

a. To make such investigations and reports under sections 2A:168–3[1] and 2A:168–13 of this title as may be required by the judge or judges of any court having jurisdiction within the county for which the officer is appointed;

b. To receive under their supervision, on request of the court having jurisdiction, any person ordered to pay any sum for alimony or support in an order or judgment entered in a matrimonial action;

c. To receive under supervision any person placed on probation by any court within the county for which the officer is appointed;

d. To collect from persons under their supervision such payments as may be ordered by the court so to be made, and disburse the money so received under the direction of the court;

e. To furnish each person under their supervision with a statement of the conditions of his probation and to instruct him regarding them;

f. To keep detailed records of all the work done;

g. To keep accurate and complete accounts of all money collected and disbursed, and to give and obtain receipts therefor; and

h. To make such reports to the courts as they may require.

[1] Repealed; see, now, § 2C:44–6.

2A:168–12. Transfer of probationers

Probation officers may at any time, after approval by the court or chief probation officer, transfer any probationer under their care and supervision to the jurisdiction of any other probation officer. Whenever such transfer is made, the probation officer making the transfer shall send to the probation officer to whose care and supervision the probationer is being transferred, a copy of all the records of such officer as to the offense, criminal record and social history of the probationer.

Probation officers may accept under their care and supervision on transfer, any person placed on probation in any other jurisdiction, and shall, from time to time, report to the probation officer from whom the probationer was received under transfer as to the conduct and progress of the probationer. Probation officers shall, with respect to persons transferred to their supervision from any other jurisdiction, have all of the powers and be subject to all of the duties imposed by law upon them in regard to probationers received on probation in their own jurisdiction.

2A:168–13. Investigations for superior court; financial status of persons seeking relief in forma pauperis; alimony or support payments

The chief probation officer of each county shall, when requested by the superior court, immediately investigate and furnish to the court all necessary and available information and data concerning persons who may have become the subject of or legally interested in any matrimonial action in that court, or in any proceeding directly or indirectly involving the custody of infants, and who are residents of or are temporarily found within the county for which such probation officer was appointed.

When ordered by the superior court the chief probation officer shall cause to be investigated the financial status of applicants who are seeking relief through forma pauperis petitions.

The superior court may also order payments of alimony or support, or both, to be made in proper cases through the chief probation officer, who shall distribute such payments as directed by the court.

The superior court is empowered and authorized formally to request and require such investigations and information from any chief probation officer as may be necessary to effectuate the provisions of this section, and such requests may be made at any time and at any stage of any proceeding pending in the superior court. The court shall also have the discretionary power, in actions involving the custody of infants, to file a certified copy of its order or judgment with the chief probation officer of the county or counties where the child or children reside, with a direction therein to make periodic reports to the court as to the status of the custody.

ARTICLE 2. COMPACT BETWEEN STATES RELATING TO PERSONS CONVICTED OF CRIME ON PROBATION OR PAROLE

2A:168–14. Governor authorized to enter into compact with states; form; contents of compact; investigations; duties of receiving state; retaking of probationers or parolees by sending state; extradition waived; rules and regulations; compact operative on ratification; force and effect of compact; renunciation

The governor of this state is hereby authorized and directed to enter into a compact on behalf of the state of New Jersey with any of the states of the United States legally joining therein in the form substantially as follows:

A compact entered into by and among the contracting states, signatories hereto, with the consent of the congress of the United States of America, granted by an act entitled "An act granting the consent of congress to any 2 or more states to enter into agreements or compacts for co-operative effort and mutual assistance in the prevention of crime and for other purposes."[1]

The contracting states solemnly agree:

1. That it shall be competent for the duly constituted judicial and administrative authorities of a state party to this compact (herein called "sending state") to permit any person convicted of an offense within such state and placed on probation or released on parole to reside in any other state party to this compact (herein called "receiving state") while on probation or parole, if

a. Such person is in fact a resident of or has his family residing within the receiving state and can obtain employment there;

b. Though not a resident of the receiving state and not having his family residing there, the receiving state consents to such person being sent there.

Before granting such permission, opportunity shall be granted to the receiving state to investigate the home and prospective employment of such person.

A resident of the receiving state, within the meaning of this section, is one who has been an actual inhabitant of such state continuously for more than 1 year prior to his coming to the sending state and has not resided within the sending state more than 6 continuous months

immediately preceding the commission of the offense for which he has been convicted.

2. That each receiving state will assume the duties of visitation of and supervision over probationers or parolees of any sending state and in the exercise of those duties will be governed by the same standards that prevail for its own probationers and parolees.

3. That duly accredited officers of a sending state may at all times enter a receiving state and there apprehend and retake any person on probation or parole. For that purpose no formalities will be required other than establishing the authority of the officer and the identity of the person to be retaken. All legal requirements to obtain extradition of fugitives from justice are hereby expressly waived on the part of states party hereto, as to such persons. The decision of the sending state to retake a person on probation or parole shall be conclusive upon and not reviewable within the receiving state; provided, however, that if at the time when a state seeks to retake a probationer or parolee there should be pending against him within the receiving state any criminal charge, or he should be suspected of having committed within such state a criminal offense, he shall not be retaken without the consent of the receiving state until discharged from prosecution or from imprisonment for such offense.

4. That the duly accredited officers of the sending state will be permitted to transport prisoners being retaken through any and all states parties to this compact, without interference.

5. That the governor of each state may designate an officer who, acting jointly with like officers of other contracting states, if and when appointed, shall promulgate such rules and regulations as may be deemed necessary to more effectively carry out the terms of this compact.

6. That this compact shall become operative immediately upon its ratification by any state as between it and any other state or states so ratifying. When ratified it shall have the full force and effect of law within such state, the form of ratification to be in accordance with the laws of the ratifying state.

7. That this compact shall continue in force and remain binding upon each ratifying state until renounced by it. The duties and obligations hereunder of a renouncing state shall continue as to parolees or probationers residing therein at the time of withdrawal until retaken or finally discharged by the sending state. Renunciation of this compact shall be by the same authority which ratified it, by sending 6 months' notice in writing of its intention to withdraw from the compact to the other states party hereto.

[1] See 4 U.S.C.A. § 112.

2A:168–15. Constitutionality

If any section, sentence, subdivision or clause of this act is for any reason held invalid or to be unconstitutional, such decision shall not affect the validity of the remaining portions of this act.

2A:168–16. Compact deemed ratified, when

The aforesaid compact with any other states shall be deemed to have been ratified by this state when executed by the governor of this state and such other state.

2A:168–17. Citation

This article may be cited as the "uniform act for out-of-state parolee supervision."

ARTICLE 3. RECIPROCAL LEGISLATION UNDER COMPACT

2A:168–18. Incarceration of probationer or parolee in receiving state; receiving state as agent

Whenever the duly constituted judicial and administrative authorities in a sending State shall determine that incarceration of a probationer or reincarceration of a parolee is necessary or desirable, said officials may direct that the incarceration or reincarceration be in a prison or other correctional institution within the territory of the receiving State, such receiving State to act in that regard solely as agent for the sending State.

L.1953, c. 83, p. 1006, § 1.

2A:168–19. "Receiving State" defined

As used in this act, the term "receiving State" shall be construed to mean any State, other than the sending State, in which a parolee or probationer may be found; provided, that said State has enacted reciprocal legislation.

L.1953, c. 83, p. 1007, § 2.

2A:168–20. Compact institutions; incarceration in; access to

Every State which enacts a similar act to this act shall designate at least one of its correctional institutions as a "Compact Institution" and shall incarcerate persons therein as provided in such act, unless the sending and receiving State in question shall make specific contractual arrangements to the contrary. All such States shall have access to "Compact Institutions" at all reasonable hours for the purpose of inspecting the facilities thereof and for the purpose of visiting such of said State's prisoners as may be confined in the institution.

L.1953, c. 83, p. 1007, § 3.

2A:168–21. Persons confined in compact institutions subject to jurisdiction of sending state

Persons confined in "Compact Institutions" pursuant to the terms of the compact shall at all times be subject to the jurisdiction of the sending State and may at any time be removed from said "Compact Institution" for transfer to a prison or other correctional institution within the sending State, for return to probation or parole, for discharge, or for any other purpose permitted by the laws of the sending State.

L.1953, c. 83, p. 1007, § 4.

2A:168–22. Rights of persons confined in compact institutions

All persons who may be confined in a "Compact Institution" pursuant to the provisions of the compact shall be treated in a reasonable and humane manner. Incarceration or reincarceration in a receiving State shall not deprive any person so incarcerated or reincarcerated of any rights which said person would have had if incarcerated or reincarcerated in an appropriate institution of the sending State; nor shall any agreement to submit to incarceration or reincarceration pursuant to the terms of the compact be construed as a waiver of any rights which the prisoner would have had if he had been incarcerated or reincarcerated in any appropriate institution of the sending State, except that the hearing or hearings, if any, to which a parolee or probationer may be entitled, (prior to incarceration or reincarceration) by the laws of the sending State may be had before the appropriate judicial or administrative officers of the receiving State. In any such event, said judicial and administrative officers shall act as agents of the sending State after consultation with appropriate officers of the sending State.

L.1953, c. 83, p. 1007, § 5.

2A:168–23. Costs and expenses

Any receiving State incurring costs or other expenses under the compact shall be reimbursed in the amount of such costs or other expenses by the sending State unless the States concerned shall specifically otherwise agree. Any two or more States party to the compact may enter into supplementary agreements determining a different allocation of costs as among themselves.

L.1953, c. 83, p. 1008, § 6.

2A:168–24. Rules and regulations

Rules and regulations necessary to effectuate the purposes of this act may be promulgated by the appropriate officers of this State and of those States which have enacted substantially similar legislation.

L.1953, c. 83, p. 1008, § 7.

2A:168–25. Effective when other states enact similar legislation

This act shall take effect when any two or more States party to the compact shall enact substantially similar legislation to this act.

L.1953, c. 83, p. 1008, § 8.

ARTICLE 4. INTERSTATE COMPACT FOR ADULT OFFENDER SUPERVISION

2A:168–26. Interstate Compact for Adult Offender Supervision

a. The Interstate Compact for Adult Offender Supervision is hereby enacted into law and entered into with all other jurisdictions legally joining therein in the form substantially as follows:

INTERSTATE COMPACT FOR ADULT OFFENDER SUPERVISION

The Legislature hereby finds and declares the following:

The interstate compact for the supervision of Parolees and Probationers was established in 1937; it is the earliest corrections "compact" established among the states and has not been amended since its adoption for over 62 years;

This compact is the only vehicle for the controlled movement of adult parolees and probationers across state lines, and it currently has jurisdiction over more than a quarter of a million offenders;

The complexities of the compact have become more difficult to administer, and many jurisdictions have expanded supervision expectations to include currently unregulated practices such as victim input, victim notification requirements and sex offender registration;

After hearings, national surveys and a detailed study by a task force appointed by the National Institute of Corrections, the overwhelming recommendation has been to amend the document to bring about an effective management capacity that addresses public safety concerns and offender accountability; and

Upon the adoption of this Interstate Compact for Adult Offender Supervision by all states and territories of the United States, it is the intention of the Legislature to repeal the previous Interstate Compact for the Supervision of Parolees and Probationers.

b. This act shall be known and may be cited as the "Interstate Compact for Adult Offender Supervision."

c. Article I. Purpose. The compacting states to this Interstate Compact recognize that each state is responsible for the supervision of adult offenders in the community who are authorized pursuant to the bylaws and rules of this compact to travel across state lines both to and from each compacting state in such a manner as to track the location of offenders, transfer supervision authority in an orderly and efficient manner and when necessary return offenders to the originating jurisdictions.

The compacting states also recognize that Congress, by enacting the Crime Control Act, 4 U.S.C. § 112 (1965), has authorized and encouraged compacts for cooperative efforts and mutual assistance in the prevention of crime.

It is the purpose of this compact and the Interstate Commission created hereunder, through means of joint and cooperative action among the compacting states: to provide the framework for the promotion of public safety and protect the rights of victims through the control and regulation of the interstate movement of offenders in the community; to provide for the effective tracking, supervision and rehabilitation of these offenders by the sending and receiving states; and to equitably distribute the costs, benefits and obligations of the compact among the compacting states.

In addition, this compact will: create an Interstate Commission which will establish uniform procedures to manage the movement between states of adults placed under community supervision and released to the community under the jurisdiction of courts, paroling authorities, corrections or other criminal justice agencies which will promulgate rules to achieve the purpose of this compact; ensure an opportunity for input and timely notice to victims and to jurisdictions where defined offenders are authorized to travel or to relocate across state lines; establish a system of uniform data collection, access to information on active cases by authorized criminal justice officials, and regular reporting of compact activities to heads of state councils, state executive, judicial and legislative branches and criminal justice administrators; monitor compliance with rules governing interstate movement of offenders and initiate interventions to address and correct non-compliance; and coordinate training and education regarding regulations of interstate movement of offenders for officials involved in such activity.

The compacting states recognize that there is no "right" of any offender to live in another state and that duly accredited officers of a sending state may at all times enter a receiving state and there apprehend and retake any offender under supervision subject to the provisions of this compact and bylaws and rules promulgated hereunder.

It is the policy of the compacting states that the activities conducted by the Interstate Commission created herein are the formation of public policies and are therefore public business.

L.2002, c. 111, § 1, eff. Dec. 11, 2002.

2A:168–27. Definitions

Article II. Definitions.

As used in this compact, unless the context clearly requires a different construction:

"Adult" means a person who is 18 years of age or older or a person who is under 18 years of age who either by statute or court order is considered an adult.

"Bylaws" mean those bylaws established by the Interstate Commission for its governance, or for directing or controlling the Interstate Commission's actions or conduct.

"Compact administrator" means the individual in each compacting state appointed pursuant to the terms of this compact responsible for the administration and management of the State's supervision and transfer of offenders subject to the terms of this compact, the rules adopted by the Interstate Commission and policies adopted by the State Council under this compact.

"Compacting state" means any state which has enacted the enabling legislation for this compact.

"Commissioner" means the voting representative of each compacting state appointed pursuant to Article III of this compact.

"Interstate Commission" means the Interstate Commission for Adult Offender Supervision established by this compact.

"Member" means the commissioner of a compacting state or designee, who shall be a person officially connected with the commissioner.

"Non Compacting state" means any state which has not enacted the enabling legislation for this compact.

"Offender" means an adult placed under, or subject to, supervision as the result of the commission of a criminal offense and released to the community under the jurisdiction of courts, paroling authorities, corrections, or other criminal justice agencies.

"Person" means any individual, corporation, business enterprise, or other legal entity, either public or private.

"Rules" means acts of the Interstate Commission, duly promulgated pursuant to Article VIII of this compact, substantially affecting interested parties in addition to the Interstate Commission, which shall have the force and effect of law in the compacting states.

"State" means a state of the United States, the District of Columbia and any other territorial possessions of the United States.

"State Council" means the resident members of the State Council for Interstate Adult Offender Supervision created by each state under Article IV of this compact.

L.2002, c. 111, § 2, eff. Dec. 11, 2002.

2A:168–28. Interstate Commission for Adult Offender Supervision

Article III. The Compact Commission.

a. The compacting states hereby create the "Interstate Commission for Adult Offender Supervision." The Interstate Commission shall be a body corporate and joint agency of the compacting states. The Interstate Commission shall have all the responsibilities, powers and duties set forth herein, including the power to sue and be sued, and such additional powers as may be conferred upon it by subsequent action of the respective legislatures of the compacting states in accordance with the terms of this compact.

b. The Interstate Commission shall consist of Commissioners selected and appointed by resident members of a State Council for Interstate Adult Offender Supervision for each state. In addition to the Commissioners who are the voting representatives of each state, the Interstate Commission shall include individuals who are not commissioners but who are members of interested organizations. Such non-commissioner members shall include a member of the national organizations of governors, legislators, state chief justices, attorneys general and crime victims. All non-commissioner members of the Interstate Commission shall be ex-

officio (nonvoting) members. The Interstate Commission may provide in its by-laws for such additional, ex-officio, non-voting members as it deems necessary.

c. Each compacting state represented at any meeting of the Interstate Commission is entitled to one vote. A majority of the compacting states shall constitute a quorum for the transaction of business, unless a larger quorum is required by the by-laws of the Interstate Commission.

d. The Interstate Commission shall meet at least once each calendar year. The chairman may call additional meetings and, upon the request of 27 or more compacting states, shall call additional meetings. Public notice shall be given of all meetings and meetings shall be open to the public.

e. The Interstate Commission shall establish an Executive Committee which shall include commission officers, members and others as shall be determined by the by-laws. The Executive Committee shall have the power to act on behalf of the Interstate Commission during periods when the Interstate Commission is not in session, with the exception of rulemaking or amendment to the Compact. The Executive Committee shall oversee the day-to-day activities managed by the Executive Director and Interstate Commission staff, administer enforcement and compliance with the provisions of the compact, its by-laws and as directed by the Interstate Commission and perform other duties as directed by Commission or set forth in the by-laws.

L.2002, c. 111, § 3, eff. Dec. 11, 2002.

2A:168–29. Council

Article IV. The State Council.

a. There is hereby established the New Jersey State Council for Interstate Adult Offender Supervision which shall consist of the following members:

(1) two members of the General Assembly, no more than one of whom shall be of the same political party, appointed by the Speaker of the General Assembly;

(2) two members of the Senate, no more than one of whom shall be of the same political party, appointed by the President of the Senate;

(3) the Administrative Director of the Courts;

(4) the Commissioner of Corrections or his designee;

(5) a law enforcement officer and a representative from a crime victim's organization, each appointed by the Governor with the advice and consent of the Senate; and

(6) the Chairman of the State Parole Board.

b. The Governor shall appoint a compact administrator who shall serve at the pleasure of the Governor. The compact administrator may be a member of the State Council or a State government official with appropriate background and experience. The compact administrator shall be the compact commissioner and presiding officer of the council and shall serve as the

New Jersey Commissioner to the Interstate Commission.

c. Members of the Council shall be appointed for terms of four years and the terms of their successors shall be calculated from the expiration of the incumbent's term. Members shall serve until their successors are appointed and have qualified.

d. The State Council shall meet at least twice a year.

e. The State Council shall develop policies concerning the operation of the compact within this State. The State Council may adopt rules, including rules proposed by the commission for adoption by this state, to implement the compact.

f. The State Council shall report annually to the Legislature concerning the activities of the council and the Interstate Commission.

L.2002, c. 111, § 4, eff. Dec. 11, 2002.

2A:168–30. Powers and duties

Article V. Powers and Duties of the Interstate Commission.

The Interstate Commission shall have the following powers:

a. To adopt a seal and suitable by-laws governing the management and operation of the Interstate Commission;

b. To promulgate rules which shall have the force and effect of statutory law and shall be binding in the compacting states to the extent and in the manner provided in this compact;

c. To oversee, supervise and coordinate the interstate movement of offenders subject to the terms of this compact and any bylaws adopted and rules promulgated by the compact commission;

d. To enforce compliance with compact provisions, Interstate Commission rules, and by-laws, using all necessary and proper means, including but not limited to, the use of judicial process;

e. To establish and maintain offices;

f. To purchase and maintain insurance and bonds;

g. To borrow, accept, or contract for services of personnel, including, but not limited to, members and their staffs;

h. To establish and appoint committees and hire staff which it deems necessary for the carrying out of its functions including, but not limited to, an executive committee as required by Article III which shall have the power to act on behalf of the Interstate Commission in carrying out its powers and duties hereunder;

i. To elect or appoint such officers, attorneys, employees, agents, or consultants, and to fix their compensation, define their duties and determine their qualifications; and to establish the Interstate Commission's personnel policies and programs relating to, among other things, conflicts of interest, rates of compensation, and qualifications of personnel;

j. To accept any and all donations and grants of money, equipment, supplies, materials, and services, and to receive, utilize, and dispose of same;

k. To lease, purchase, accept contributions or donations of, or otherwise to own, hold, improve or use any property, real, personal, or mixed;

l. To sell, convey, mortgage, pledge, lease, exchange, abandon, or otherwise dispose of any property, real, personal or mixed;

m. To establish a budget and make expenditures and levy dues as provided in Article X of this compact;

n. To sue and be sued;

o. To provide for dispute resolution among compacting states;

p. To perform such functions as may be necessary or appropriate to achieve the purposes of this compact;

q. To report annually to the legislatures, governors, judiciary, and state councils of the compacting states concerning the activities of the Interstate Commission during the preceding year. Such reports shall also include any recommendations that may have been adopted by the Interstate Commission;

r. To coordinate education, training and public awareness regarding the interstate movement of offenders for officials involved in such activity; and

s. To establish uniform standards for the reporting, collecting, and exchanging of data.

L.2002, c. 111, § 5, eff. Dec. 11, 2002.

2A:168–31. By-laws; election of officers; records; qualified immunity

Article VI. Organization and Operation of the Interstate Commission.

a. By-laws. The Interstate Commission shall, by a majority of the Members, within twelve months of the first Interstate Commission meeting, adopt by-laws to govern its conduct as may be necessary or appropriate to carry out the purposes of the Compact, including, but not limited to:

(1) Establishing the fiscal year of the Interstate Commission.

(2) Establishing an executive committee and such other committees as may be necessary.

(3) Providing reasonable standards and procedures for the establishment of committees, and governing any general or specific delegation of any authority or function of the Interstate Commission.

(4) Providing reasonable procedures for calling and conducting meetings of the Interstate Commission, and ensuring reasonable notice of each such meeting.

(5) Establishing the titles and responsibilities of the officers of the Interstate Commission.

(6) Providing reasonable standards and procedures for the establishment of the personnel policies and programs of the Interstate Commission.

Notwithstanding any civil service or other similar laws of any Compacting State, the by-laws shall exclusively govern the personnel policies and programs of the Interstate Commission.

(7) Providing a mechanism for winding up the operations of the Interstate Commission and the equitable return of any surplus funds that may exist upon the termination of the Compact after the payment or reserving of all of its debts and obligations.

(8) Providing transition rules for "start up" administration of the compact.

(9) Establishing standards and procedures for compliance and technical assistance in carrying out the compact.

b. Officers and Staff. The Interstate Commission shall, by a majority of the members, elect from among its members a chairman and a vice chairman, each of whom shall have such authorities and duties as may be specified in the bylaws. The chairman, or in his absence or disability, the vice chairman, shall preside at all meetings of the Interstate Commission. The officers so elected shall serve without compensation or remuneration from the Interstate Commission; provided that, subject to the availability of budgeted funds, the officers shall be reimbursed for any actual and necessary costs and expenses incurred by them in the performance of their duties and responsibilities as officers of the Interstate Commission.

The Interstate Commission shall, through its executive committee, appoint or retain an executive director for such period, upon such terms and conditions and for such compensation as the Interstate Commission may deem appropriate. The executive director shall serve as secretary to the Interstate Commission, and hire and supervise such other staff as may be authorized by the Interstate Commission, but shall not be a member.

c. Corporate Records of the Interstate Commission. The Interstate Commission shall maintain its corporate books and records in accordance with the bylaws.

d. Qualified Immunity, Defense and Indemnification. The members, officers, executive director and employees of the Interstate Commission shall be immune from suit and liability, either personally or in their official capacity, for any claim for damage to or loss of property or personal injury or other civil liability caused or arising out of any actual or alleged act, error or omission that occurred within the scope of Interstate Commission employment, duties or responsibilities; provided, that nothing in this paragraph shall be construed to protect any such person from suit or liability for any damage, loss, injury or liability caused by the intentional or willful and wanton misconduct of any such person.

The Interstate Commission shall defend the Commissioner of a Compacting State, or his representatives or employees, or the Interstate Commission's representatives or employees, in any civil action seeking to impose liability, arising out of any actual or alleged act, error or omission that occurred within the scope of Interstate Commission employment, duties or responsibilities, or that the defendant had a reasonable basis for believing occurred within the scope of Interstate Commission employment, duties or responsibilities; provided, that the actual or alleged act, error or omission did not result from intentional wrongdoing on the part of such person.

The Interstate Commission shall indemnify and hold the Commissioner of a Compacting State, the appointed designee or employees, or the Interstate Commission's representatives or employees, harmless in the amount of any settlement or judgment obtained against such persons arising out of any actual or alleged act, error or omission that occurred within the scope of Interstate Commission employment, duties or responsibilities, or that such persons had a reasonable basis for believing occurred within the scope of Interstate Commission employment, duties or responsibilities, provided, that the actual or alleged act, error or omission did not result from gross negligence or intentional wrongdoing on the part of such person.

L.2002, c. 111, § 6, eff. Dec. 11, 2002.

2A:168–32. Actions; voting; public records; open meetings

Article VII. Activities of the Interstate Commission.

a. The Interstate Commission shall meet and take such actions as are consistent with the provisions of this Compact.

b. Except as otherwise provided in this Compact and unless a greater percentage is required by the bylaws, in order to constitute an act of the Interstate Commission, such act shall have been taken at a meeting of the Interstate Commission and shall have received an affirmative vote of a majority of the members present.

c. Each Member of the Interstate Commission shall have the right and power to cast a vote to which that Compacting State is entitled and to participate in the business and affairs of the Interstate Commission. A Member shall vote in person on behalf of the state and shall not delegate a vote to another member state. However, a State Council shall appoint another authorized representative, in the absence of the commissioner from that state, to cast a vote on behalf of the member state at a specified meeting. The By-laws may provide for Members' participation in meetings by telephone or other means of telecommunication or electronic communication. Any voting conducted by telephone, or other means of telecommunication or electronic communication shall be subject to the same quorum requirements of meetings where members are present in person.

d. The Interstate Commission shall meet at least once during each calendar year. The chairman of the Interstate Commission may call additional meetings at any time and, upon the request of a majority of the Members, shall call additional meetings.

e. The Interstate Commission's By-laws shall establish conditions and procedures under which the Interstate Commission shall make its information and official records available to the public for inspection or copying. The Interstate Commission may exempt from disclosure any information or official records to the extent they would adversely affect personal privacy rights or proprietary interests. In promulgating such Rules, the Interstate Commission may make available to law enforcement agencies records and information otherwise exempt from disclosure, and may enter into agreements with law enforcement agencies to receive or exchange information or records subject to nondisclosure and confidentiality provisions.

f. Public notice shall be given of all meetings and all meetings shall be open to the public, except as set forth in the Rules or as otherwise provided in the Compact. The Interstate Commission shall promulgate Rules consistent with the principles contained in the "Government in the Sunshine Act," 5 U.S.C. Section 552(b), as may be amended. The Interstate Commission and any of its committees may close a meeting to the public where it determines by two-thirds vote that an open meeting would be likely to:

(1) relate solely to the Interstate Commission's internal personnel practices and procedures;

(2) disclose matters specifically exempted from disclosure by statute;

(3) disclose trade secrets or commercial or financial information which is privileged or confidential;

(4) involve accusing any person of a crime, or formally censuring any person;

(5) disclose information of a personal nature where disclosure would constitute a clearly unwarranted invasion of personal privacy;

(6) disclose investigatory records compiled for law enforcement purposes;

(7) disclose information contained in or related to examination, operating or condition reports prepared by, or on behalf of or for the use of, the Interstate Commission with respect to a regulated entity for the purpose of regulation or supervision of such entity;

(8) disclose information, the premature disclosure of which would significantly endanger the life of a person or the stability of a regulated entity; or

(9) specifically relate to the Interstate Commission's issuance of a subpoena, or its participation in a civil action or proceeding.

g. For every meeting closed pursuant to this provision, the Interstate Commission's chief legal officer shall publicly certify that, in his opinion, the meeting may be closed to the public, and shall reference each relevant exemptive provision.

h. The Interstate Commission shall keep minutes which shall fully and clearly describe all matters discussed in any meeting and shall provide a full and accurate summary of any actions taken, and the reasons therefor, including a description of each of the views expressed on any item and the record of any roll call vote (reflected in the vote of each Member on the question). All documents considered in connection with any action shall be identified in such minutes.

i. The Interstate Commission shall collect standardized data concerning the interstate movement of offenders as directed through its bylaws and rules which shall specify the data to be collected, the means of collection and data exchange and reporting requirements.

L.2002, c. 111, § 7, eff. Dec. 11, 2002.

2A:168–33. Rulemaking

Article VIII. Rulemaking Functions of the Interstate Commission.

a. The Interstate Commission shall promulgate Rules in order to effectively and efficiently achieve the purposes of the Compact including transition rules governing administration of the compact during the period in which it is being considered and enacted by the states.

b. Rulemaking shall occur pursuant to the criteria set forth in this Article and the bylaws and Rules adopted pursuant thereto. Such rulemaking shall substantially conform to the principles of the federal Administrative Procedure Act, 5 U.S.C.A. section 551 et seq., and the federal Advisory Committee Act, 5 U.S.C.A. App. 2, section 1 et seq., as may be amended (hereinafter "APA").

c. All Rules and amendments shall become binding as of the date specified in each rule or amendment.

d. If a majority of the legislatures of the Compacting States rejects a rule, by enactment of a statute or resolution in the same manner used to adopt the compact, then such Rule shall have no further force and effect in any Compacting State.

e. When promulgating a rule, the Interstate Commission shall:

(1) publish the proposed rule stating with particularity the text of the Rule which is proposed and the reason for the proposed rule;

(2) allow persons to submit written data, facts, opinions and arguments, which information shall be publicly available;

(3) provide an opportunity for an informal hearing; and

(4) promulgate a final Rule and its effective date, if appropriate, based on the rulemaking record.

Not later than sixty days after a Rule is promulgated, any interested person may file a petition in the United States District Court for the District of Columbia or in the Federal District Court where the Interstate Commission's principal office is located for judicial review of such Rule. If the court finds that the Interstate Commission's action is not supported by substantial evidence (as defined in the APA) in the rulemaking record, the court shall hold the Rule unlawful and set it aside.

f. Subjects to be addressed within 12 months after the first meeting must at a minimum include:

(1) notice to victims and opportunity to be heard;

(2) offender registration and compliance;

(3) violations/returns;

(4) transfer procedures and forms;

(5) eligibility for transfer;

(6) collection of restitution and fees from offenders;

(7) data collection and reporting;

(8) the level of supervision to be provided by the receiving state;

(9) transition rules governing the operation of the compact and the Interstate Commission during all or part of the period between the effective date of the compact and the date on which the last eligible state adopts the compact; and

(10) Mediation, arbitration and dispute resolution.

g. The existing rules governing the operation of the previous compact superseded by this act shall be null and void twelve months after the first meeting of the Interstate Commission created hereunder.

h. Upon determination by the Interstate Commission that an emergency exists, it may promulgate an emergency rule which shall become effective immediately upon adoption, provided that the usual rulemaking procedures provided hereunder shall be retroactively applied to said rule as soon as reasonably possible, in no event later than 90 days after the effective date of the rule.

L.2002, c. 111, § 8, eff. Dec. 11, 2002.

2A:168–34. Oversight; mediation and binding dispute resolution; enforcement

Article IX. Oversight, Enforcement and Dispute Resolution by the Interstate Commission.

a. Oversight. The Interstate Commission shall oversee the interstate movement of adult offenders in the compacting states and shall monitor such activities being administered in Non-compacting States which may significantly affect Compacting States.

The courts and executive agencies in each Compacting State shall enforce this Compact and shall take all actions necessary and appropriate to effectuate the Compact's purposes and intent. In any judicial or administrative proceeding in a Compacting State pertaining to the subject matter of this Compact which may affect the powers, responsibilities or actions of the Interstate Commission, the Interstate Commission shall be entitled to receive all service of process in any such proceeding, and shall have standing to intervene in the proceeding for all purposes.

b. Dispute Resolution. The Compacting States shall report to the Interstate Commission on issues or activities of concern to them, and cooperate with and support the Interstate Commission in the discharge of its duties and responsibilities.

The Interstate Commission shall attempt to resolve any disputes or other issues which are subject to the Compact and which may arise among Compacting States and Non-compacting States.

The Interstate Commission shall enact a bylaw or promulgate a rule providing for both mediation and binding dispute resolution for disputes among the Compacting States.

c. Enforcement. The Interstate Commission, in the reasonable exercise of its discretion, shall enforce the provisions of this compact using any or all means set forth in Article XII, section b., of this compact.

L.2002, c. 111, § 9, eff. Dec. 11, 2002.

2A:168–35. Finance; expenses, annual assessment and budget

Article X. Finance.

a. The Interstate Commission shall pay or provide for the payment of the reasonable expenses of its establishment, organization and ongoing activities.

b. The Interstate Commission shall levy on and collect an annual assessment from each Compacting State to cover the cost of the internal operations and activities of the Interstate Commission and its staff which must be in a total amount sufficient to cover the Interstate Commission's annual budget as approved each year. The aggregate annual assessment amount shall be allocated based upon a formula to be determined by the Interstate Commission, taking into consideration the population of the state and the volume of interstate movement of offenders in each Compacting State and shall promulgate a rule binding upon all Compacting States which governs said assessment.

c. The Interstate Commission shall not incur any obligations of any kind prior to securing the funds adequate to meet the same; nor shall the Interstate Commission pledge the credit of any of the compacting states, except by and with the authority of the compacting state.

d. The Interstate Commission shall keep accurate accounts of all receipts and disbursements. The receipts and disbursements of the Interstate Commission shall be subject to the audit and accounting procedures established under its bylaws. However, all receipts and disbursements of funds handled by the Interstate Commission shall be audited yearly by a certified or licensed public accountant and the report of the audit shall be included in and become part of the annual report of the Interstate Commission.

e. (1) The Interstate compact for adult offender supervision fund is established as a special fund in the State Treasury. The fund consists of moneys appropriated for the purposes of meeting financial obligations imposed on the State of New Jersey as a result of the State's participation in this compact.

(2) An assessment levied or any other financial obligation imposed under this compact is effective against the State of New Jersey only to the extent that moneys to pay the assessment or meet the financial obligation have been appropriated and deposited in the fund established pursuant to paragraph (1) of this subsection.

L.2002, c. 111, § 10, eff. Dec. 11, 2002.

2A:168–36. Eligibility; amendments to compact; effective date

Article XI. Compacting States, Effective Date and Amendment.

a. Any state, as defined in Article II of this compact, is eligible to become a Compacting State.

b. The Compact shall become effective and binding upon legislative enactment of the Compact into law by no less than 35 of the States. The initial effective date shall be the later of July 1, 2001, or upon enactment into law by the 35th jurisdiction. Thereafter it shall become effective and binding, as to any other Compacting State, upon enactment of the Compact into law by that State. The governors of Non-member states or their designees will be invited to participate in Interstate Commission activities on a non-voting basis prior to adoption of the compact by all states and territories of the United States.

c. Amendments to the Compact may be proposed by the Interstate Commission for enactment by the Compacting States. No amendment shall become effective and binding upon the Interstate Commission and the Compacting States unless and until it is enacted into law by unanimous consent of the Compacting States.

L.2002, c. 111, § 11, eff. Dec. 11, 2002.

2A:168–37. Withdrawal from compact; default; enforcement and jurisdiction

Article XII. Withdrawal, Default, Termination and Judicial Enforcement.

a. Withdrawal. Once effective, the Compact shall continue in force and remain binding upon each and every Compacting State; provided, that a Compacting State may withdraw from the Compact ("Withdrawing State") by enacting a statute specifically repealing the statute which enacted the Compact into law.

The effective date of withdrawal is the effective date of the repeal.

The Withdrawing State shall immediately notify the Chairman of the Interstate Commission in writing upon the introduction of legislation repealing this Compact in the Withdrawing State.

The Interstate Commission shall notify the other Compacting States of the Withdrawing State's intent to withdraw within sixty days of its receipt thereof.

The Withdrawing State is responsible for all assessments, obligations and liabilities incurred through the effective date of withdrawal, including any obligations, the performance of which extend beyond the effective date of withdrawal.

Reinstatement following withdrawal of any Compacting State shall occur upon the Withdrawing State reenacting the Compact or upon such later date as determined by the Interstate Commission.

b. Default. If the Interstate Commission determines that any Compacting State has at any time defaulted ("Defaulting State") in the performance of any of its obligations or responsibilities under this Compact, the bylaws or any duly promulgated rules, the Interstate Commission may impose any or all of the following penalties:

Fines, fees and costs in such amounts as are deemed to be reasonable as fixed by the Interstate Commission;

Remedial training and technical assistance as directed by the Interstate Commission; and

Suspension and termination of membership in the compact. Suspension shall be imposed only after all other reasonable means of securing compliance under the By-laws and Rules have been exhausted. Immediate notice of suspension shall be given by the Interstate Commission to the Governor, the Chief Justice or Chief Judicial Officer of the state; the majority and minority leaders of the defaulting state's legislature, and the State Council.

The grounds for default include, but are not limited to, failure of a Compacting State to perform such obligations or responsibilities imposed upon it by this compact, Interstate Commission By-laws, or duly promulgated Rules. The Interstate Commission shall immediately notify the Defaulting State in writing of the penalty imposed by the Interstate Commission on the Defaulting State pending a cure of the default. The Interstate Commission shall stipulate the conditions and the time period within which the Defaulting State must cure its default. If the Defaulting State fails to cure the default within the time period specified by the Interstate Commission, in addition to any other penalties imposed herein, the Defaulting State may be terminated from the Compact upon an affirmative vote of a majority of the Compacting States and all rights, privileges and benefits conferred by this Compact shall be terminated from the effective date of suspension.

Within sixty days of the effective date of termination of a Defaulting State, the Interstate Commission shall notify the Governor, the Chief Justice or Chief Judicial

Officer and the Majority and Minority Leaders of the Defaulting State's legislature and the state council of such termination.

The Defaulting State is responsible for all assessments, obligations and liabilities incurred through the effective date of termination including any obligations, the performance of which extends beyond the effective date of termination.

The Interstate Commission shall not bear any costs relating to the Defaulting State unless otherwise mutually agreed upon between the Interstate Commission and the Defaulting State.

Reinstatement following termination of any Compacting State requires both a reenactment of the Compact by the Defaulting State and the approval of the Interstate Commission pursuant to the rules.

c. Judicial Enforcement. The Interstate Commission may, by majority vote of the Members, initiate legal action in the United States District Court for the District of Columbia or, at the discretion of the Interstate Commission, in the Federal District where the Interstate Commission has its offices to enforce compliance with the provisions of the Compact, its duly promulgated rules and bylaws, against any Compacting State in default. In the event judicial enforcement is necessary the prevailing party shall be awarded all costs of such litigation including reasonable attorneys fees.

d. Dissolution of Compact. The Compact dissolves effective upon the date of the withdrawal or default of the Compacting State which reduces membership in the Compact to one Compacting State.

Upon the dissolution of this Compact, the Compact becomes null and void and shall be of no further force or effect, and the business and affairs of the Interstate Commission shall be wound up and any surplus funds shall be distributed in accordance with the bylaws.

L.2002, c. 111, § 12, eff. Dec. 11, 2002.

2A:168–38. Severability

Article XIII. Severability and Construction. The provisions of this Compact shall be severable, and if any phrase, clause, sentence or provision is deemed unenforceable, the remaining provisions of the Compact shall be enforceable.

The provisions of this Compact shall be liberally constructed to effectuate its purposes.

L.2002, c. 111, § 13, eff. Dec. 11, 2002.

2A:168–39. Construction with other laws; binding effect

Article XIV. Binding Effect of Compact and Other Laws.

a. Other Laws. Nothing herein prevents the enforcement of any other law of a Compacting State that is not inconsistent with this Compact.

All Compacting States' laws conflicting with this Compact are superseded to the extent of the conflict.

b. Binding Effect of the Compact. All lawful actions of the Interstate Commission, including all rules and bylaws promulgated by the Interstate Commission, are binding upon the Compacting States.

All agreements between the Interstate Commission and the Compacting States are binding in accordance with their terms.

Upon the request of a party to a conflict over meaning or interpretation of Interstate Commission actions, and upon a majority vote of the Compacting States, the Interstate Commission may issue advisory opinions regarding such meaning or interpretation.

In the event any provision of this Compact exceeds the constitutional limits imposed on the legislature of any Compacting State, the obligations, duties, powers or jurisdiction sought to be conferred by such provision upon the Interstate Commission shall be ineffective and such obligations, duties, powers or jurisdiction shall remain in the Compacting State and shall be exercised by the agency thereof to which such obligations, duties, powers or jurisdiction are delegated by law in effect at the time this Compact becomes effective.

L.2002, c. 111, § 14, eff. Dec. 11, 2002.

CHAPTER 168A

REHABILITATED CONVICTED OFFENDERS

Section

2A:168A–1. Legislative findings.
2A:168A–2. Granting application for license or certificate or for admission to qualifying examination; grounds for refusal; written statement.
2A:168A–2. Granting application for license or certificate or for admission to qualifying examination; grounds for refusal; written statement.
2A:168A–3. Evidence of rehabilitation.
2A:168A–4. Addiction to drugs or intoxicating liquors within four months of application.
2A:168A–5. Regulated employment pursuant to approved program of vocational or educational rehabilitation.
2A:168A–6. Inapplicability of act to law enforcement agencies.
2A:168A–7. Certificates; relief from disabilities, forfeitures or bars; definitions.
2A:168A–7. Certificates; relief from disabilities, forfeitures or bars; definitions.
2A:168A–8. Certificate; issuance and application; eligibility.
2A:168A–9. Certificate as presumptive evidence of rehabilitation.
2A:168A–10. Supervising authority; notice to prosecutor of certificate or application for a certificate.
2A:168A–11. Revocation and reinstatement of certificate; disorderly persons offense.
2A:168A–12. Certificates; application to private employers.
2A:168A–13. Evaluation of effectiveness of implementation; system of recording certificates.

Section

2A:168A–14.   Report; impact of a prior criminal conviction on private employment opportunities.

2A:168A–15.   Pardons by governor.

2A:168A–16.   Promulgation of regulations, rules or guidelines.

2A:168A–1.   Legislative findings

The Legislature finds and declares that it is in the public interest to assist the rehabilitation of convicted offenders by removing impediments and restrictions upon their ability to obtain employment or to participate in vocational or educational rehabilitation programs based solely upon the existence of a criminal record.

Therefore, the Legislature finds and declares that notwithstanding the contrary provisions of any law or rule or regulation issued pursuant to law, a person shall not be disqualified or discriminated against by any licensing authority because of any conviction for a crime, unless N.J.S. 2C:51–2 is applicable or unless the conviction relates adversely to the occupation, trade, vocation, profession or business for which the license or certificate is sought.

L.1968, c. 282, § 2, eff. Sept. 4, 1968. Amended by L.1974, c. 161, § 2, eff. Nov. 15, 1974; L.1981, c. 487, § 3, eff. Jan. 12, 1982.

2A:168A–2.   Granting application for license or certificate or for admission to qualifying examination; grounds for refusal; written statement

Text of section effective until July 31, 2010.

Notwithstanding the contrary provisions of any law or rule or regulation issued pursuant to law, no State, county or municipal department, board, officer or agency, hereinafter referred to as "licensing authority" authorized to pass upon the qualifications of any applicant for a license or certificate of authority or qualification to engage in the practice of a profession or business or for admission to an examination to qualify for such a license or certificate may disqualify or discriminate against an applicant for a license or certificate or an application for admission to a qualifying examination on the grounds that the applicant has been convicted of a crime, or adjudged a disorderly person, except that a licensing authority may disqualify or discriminate against an applicant for a license or certificate if N.J.S. 2C:51–2 is applicable or if a conviction for a crime relates adversely to the occupation, trade, vocation, profession or business for which the license or certificate is sought. In determining that a conviction for a crime relates adversely to the occupation, trade, vocation, profession or business, the licensing authority shall explain in writing how the following factors, or any other factors, relate to the license or certificate sought:

a.   The nature and duties of the occupation, trade, vocation, profession or business, a license or certificate for which the person is applying;

b.   Nature and seriousness of the crime;

c.   Circumstances under which the crime occurred;

d.   Date of the crime;

e.   Age of the person when the crime was committed;

f.   Whether the crime was an isolated or repeated incident;

g.   Social conditions which may have contributed to the crime;

h.   Any evidence of rehabilitation, including good conduct in prison or in the community, counseling or psychiatric treatment received, acquisition of additional academic or vocational schooling, successful participation in correctional work-release programs, or the recommendation of persons who have or have had the applicant under their supervision.

L.1968, c. 282, § 2, eff. Sept. 4, 1968. Amended by L.1974, c. 161, § 3, eff. Nov. 15, 1974; L.1981, c. 487, § 4, eff. Jan. 12, 1982.

2A:168A–2.   Granting application for license or certificate or for admission to qualifying examination; grounds for refusal; written statement

Text of section effective on July 31, 2010.

Notwithstanding the contrary provisions of any law or rule or regulation issued pursuant to law, no State, county or municipal department, board, officer or agency, hereinafter referred to as "licensing authority" authorized to pass upon the qualifications of any applicant for a license or certificate of authority or qualification to engage in the practice of a profession or business or for admission to an examination to qualify for such a license or certificate may disqualify or discriminate against an applicant for a license or certificate or an application for admission to a qualifying examination on the grounds that the applicant has been convicted of a crime, or adjudged a disorderly person, except that a licensing authority may disqualify or discriminate against an applicant for a license or certificate if N.J.S.2C:51–2 or any disqualifying criminal activity set forth in subsection a. of section 7 of P.L.2009, c. 53 (C.17:11C–57) is applicable, or if a conviction for a crime relates adversely to the occupation, trade, vocation, profession or business for which the license or certificate is sought. In determining that a conviction for a crime relates adversely to the occupation, trade, vocation, profession or business, the licensing authority shall explain in writing how the following factors, or any other factors, relate to the license or certificate sought:

a.   The nature and duties of the occupation, trade, vocation, profession or business, a license or certificate for which the person is applying;

b.   Nature and seriousness of the crime;

c.   Circumstances under which the crime occurred;

d.   Date of the crime;

e. Age of the person when the crime was committed;

f. Whether the crime was an isolated or repeated incident;

g. Social conditions which may have contributed to the crime;

h. Any evidence of rehabilitation, including good conduct in prison or in the community, counseling or psychiatric treatment received, acquisition of additional academic or vocational schooling, successful participation in correctional work-release programs, or the recommendation of persons who have or have had the applicant under their supervision.

L.1968, c. 282, § 2, eff. Sept. 4, 1968. Amended by L.1974, c. 161, § 3, eff. Nov. 15, 1974; L.1981, c. 487, § 4, eff. Jan. 12, 1982; L.2009, c. 53, § 71.

Operative Date

For operative and effective date of L.2009, c. 53, see § 74 of that act.

2A:168A–3. Evidence of rehabilitation

The presentation to a licensing authority of evidence of a pardon or of the expungement of a criminal conviction, pursuant to N.J.S. 2A:164–28, or of a certificate of the Federal or State Parole Board, or of the Chief Probation Officer of a United States District Court or a county who has supervised the applicant's probation, that the applicant has achieved a degree of rehabilitation indicating that his engaging in the proposed employment would not be incompatible with the welfare of society shall preclude a licensing authority from disqualifying or discriminating against the applicant.

L.1968, c. 282, § 3, eff. Sept. 4, 1968. Amended by L.1974, c. 161, § 4, eff. Nov. 15, 1974.

2A:168A–4. Addiction to drugs or intoxicating liquors within four months of application

A licensing authority may disqualify or discriminate against an applicant for a license or certificate on the grounds that the applicant has within 4 months of the application for admission to a qualifying examination been addicted to the habitual use of drugs or intoxicating liquors.

L.1974, c. 161, § 5, eff. Nov. 15, 1974.

2A:168A–5. Regulated employment pursuant to approved program of vocational or educational rehabilitation

Notwithstanding the contrary provisions of any law or rule or regulation issued pursuant to law, any licensing authority may permit any person subject to correctional supervision in this State to engage in regulated employment pursuant to an approved program of vocational or educational rehabilitation.

L.1974, c. 161, § 6, eff. Nov. 15, 1974.

2A:168A–6. Inapplicability of act to law enforcement agencies

This act shall not be applicable to any law enforcement agency; however, nothing herein shall preclude a law enforcement agency in its discretion from adopting the policies and procedures set forth herein.

L.1974, c. 161, § 7, eff. Nov. 15, 1974.

2A:168A–7. Certificates; relief from disabilities, forfeitures or bars; definitions

Text of section effective until July 31, 2010.

a. Notwithstanding any law to the contrary, a certificate may be issued in accordance with the provisions of this act [1] that suspends certain disabilities, forfeitures or bars to employment or professional licensure or certification that apply to persons convicted of criminal offenses.

b. A certificate issued pursuant to this act shall have the effect of relieving disabilities, forfeitures or bars, except those established or required by federal law, to:

(1) public employment, as defined in this section;

(2) qualification for a license or certification to engage in the practice of a profession, occupation or business, except the practice of law; or

(3) admission to an examination to qualify for such a license or certification, except for the bar examination, or an examination for a law enforcement, homeland security, or emergency management position.

A certificate issued pursuant to this act may be limited to one or more enumerated disabilities, forfeitures or bars, or may relieve the subject of all disabilities, forfeitures or bars that may be affected by the act.

c. For purposes of this act:

(1) "Public employment" shall mean employment by a State, county, or municipal agency, but shall not include elected office, or employment in law enforcement, corrections, the judiciary, in a position related to homeland security or emergency management, or any position that has access to sensitive information that could threaten the public health, welfare, or safety.

(2) "Qualified offender" refers to a person who has one criminal conviction or who has convictions for more than one crime charged in separate counts of one indictment or accusation. Multiple convictions charged in two indictments or two accusations, or one indictment and one accusation filed in the same court prior to entry of judgment under any of them, shall be deemed to be one conviction. Convictions of crimes entered more than 10 years prior to an application for a certificate under this act shall not be considered in determining whether a person has one criminal conviction. In the case of a person seeking relief at the time of sentencing, qualified offender means a person who will have one conviction, as set forth in this paragraph, upon sentencing and issuance of the judgment of conviction.

(3) "Supervising authority" shall mean the court in the case of a person who was subject to probation or who was not required to serve a period of supervision, or the State Parole Board in the case of a person who was under parole supervision.

L.2007, c. 327, § 1, eff. Aug. 1, 2008.

1 L.2007, c. 327 (N.J.S.A. § 2A:168A–7 et seq.).

2A:168A–7. Certificates; relief from disabilities, forfeitures or bars; definitions

Text of section effective on July 31, 2010.

a. Notwithstanding any law to the contrary, a certificate may be issued in accordance with the provisions of this act [1] that suspends certain disabilities, forfeitures or bars to employment or professional licensure or certification that apply to persons convicted of criminal offenses.

b. A certificate issued pursuant to this act shall have the effect of relieving disabilities, forfeitures or bars, except those established or required by federal law, to:

(1) public employment, as defined in this section;

(2) qualification for a license or certification to engage in the practice of a profession, occupation or business, except the practice of law, or as a mortgage loan originator, or residential mortgage lender or residential mortgage broker as a qualified individual licensee, pursuant to the "New Jersey Residential Mortgage Lending Act," sections 1 through 39 of P.L.2009, c. 53 (C.17:11C–51 et seq.); or

(3) admission to an examination to qualify for that license or certification, except for the bar examination, a qualified written test for a mortgage loan originator, or residential mortgage lender or broker as a qualified individual licensee, or an examination for a law enforcement, homeland security, or emergency management position.

A certificate issued pursuant to this act may be limited to one or more enumerated disabilities, forfeitures or bars, or may relieve the subject of all disabilities, forfeitures or bars that may be affected by the act.

c. For purposes of this act:

(1) "Public employment" shall mean employment by a State, county, or municipal agency, but shall not include elected office, or employment in law enforcement, corrections, the judiciary, in a position related to homeland security or emergency management, or any position that has access to sensitive information that could threaten the public health, welfare, or safety.

(2) "Qualified offender" refers to a person who has one criminal conviction or who has convictions for more than one crime charged in separate counts of one indictment or accusation. Multiple convictions charged in two indictments or two accusations, or one indictment and one accusation filed in the same court prior to entry of judgment under any of them, shall be deemed to be one conviction. Convictions of crimes entered

more than 10 years prior to an application for a certificate under this act shall not be considered in determining whether a person has one criminal conviction. In the case of a person seeking relief at the time of sentencing, qualified offender means a person who will have one conviction, as set forth in this paragraph, upon sentencing and issuance of the judgment of conviction.

(3) "Supervising authority" shall mean the court in the case of a person who was subject to probation or who was not required to serve a period of supervision, or the State Parole Board in the case of a person who was under parole supervision.

L.2007, c. 327, § 1, eff. Aug. 1, 2008. Amended by L.2009, c. 53, § 72.

1 L.2007, c. 327 (N.J.S.A. § 2A:168A–7 et seq.).

Operative Date

For operative and effective date of L.2009, c. 53, see § 74 of that act.

2A:168A–8. Certificate; issuance and application; eligibility

A certificate may be issued pursuant to this act [1] as follows:

a. (1) A court, in its discretion, may issue a certificate at the time of sentencing if the applicant:

(a) is a qualified offender, who is being sentenced to a non-incarcerative sentence for a second, third or fourth degree crime;

(b) has established that a specific licensing or employment disqualification, forfeiture or bar, will apply to him, and may endanger his ability to maintain existing public employment or employment for which he has made application, or to engage in a business enterprise for which a license or certification is required;

(c) has no pending criminal charges, and there is no information presented that such a charge is imminent; and

(d) has established that the relief is consistent with the public interest.

(2) A certificate issued under this subsection shall apply only to the specific disability, forfeiture or bar that is affected, which must be specifically described in the certificate document.

b. (1) A supervising authority may issue a certificate in regard to a qualified offender who is, or had previously been, under supervision by the supervising authority if the supervising authority determines that:

(a) the applicant is convicted of a second, third or fourth degree offense and is eligible for relief under subsection c. of this section;

(b) the applicant has not been convicted of a crime since the conviction for which he is under supervision, has no pending criminal charge, and there is no information presented that such a charge is imminent;

(c) issuing the certificate will not pose a substantial risk to public safety; and

(d) issuing the certificate will assist in the successful reintegration of the offender and is consistent with the public interest.

(2) A certificate issued pursuant to this subsection may suspend disabilities, forfeitures and bars generally within the limits of this act, or only certain disabilities, forfeitures and bars, specifically named in the certificate document.

c. A qualified offender is eligible for relief under subsection b. of this section if the offender has not been convicted of:

(1) a first degree crime;

(2) an offense to which section 2 of P.L.1997, c. 117 (C.2C:43–7.2) applies;

(3) a second degree offense defined in chapters 13, 14, 15, 16, 24, 27, 30, 33, 38 of Title 2C of the New Jersey Statutes;

(4) a violation of subsection a. of N.J.S.2C:24–4 or paragraph (4) of subsection b. of N.J.S.2C:24–4;

(5) a crime requiring registration pursuant to section 2 of P.L.1994, c. 133 (C.2C:7–2);

(6) a crime committed against a public entity or against a public officer;

(7) a crime enumerated in subsection b. of section 2 of P.L.2007, c. 49 (C.43:1–3.1) committed by a public employee, which involves or touches upon the employee's office, position or employment, such that the crime was related directly to the person's performance in, or circumstances flowing from, the specific public office or employment held by the person;

(8) any crime committed against a person 16 years of age or younger, or a disabled or handicapped person; or

(9) a conspiracy or attempt to commit any of the crimes described in this subsection.

d. (1) A supervising authority may issue a certificate in regard to a qualified offender, when three years have passed since the applicant has completed the incarcerative or supervisory portion of his sentence, whichever is later, and the supervising authority finds that:

(a) the applicant is eligible for such relief as defined in subsection e. of this section;

(b) issuing the certificate does not pose a substantial risk to public safety; and

(c) issuing the certificate will assist in the successful reintegration of the offender and is consistent with the public interest.

(2) The certificate issued pursuant to this subsection may suspend disabilities, forfeitures and bars generally within the limits of this act, or only certain disabilities, forfeitures and bars specifically named in the certificate document.

e. A qualified offender is eligible for relief under subsection d. of this section if he has remained without criminal involvement since his conviction, including that he has not subsequently been convicted of a crime, has no pending charges for any crime, and there is no information presented that such a charge is imminent; and is applying for relief from a conviction other than:

(1) a first degree crime;

(2) any of the offenses to which section 2 of P.L.1997, c. 117 (C.2C:43–7. 2) applies;

(3) a violation of subsection a. of N.J.S.2C:24–4 or paragraph (4) of subsection b. of N.J.S.2C:24–4;

(4) a crime requiring registration pursuant to section 2 of P.L.1994, c. 133 (C.2C:7–2);

(5) a crime enumerated in subsection b. of section 2 of P.L.2007, c. 49 (C.43:1–3.1) committed by a public employee, which involves or touches upon the employee's office, position or employment, such that the crime was related directly to the person's performance in, or circumstances flowing from, the specific public office or employment held by the person;

(6) a crime committed against a person 16 years of age or younger, or a disabled or handicapped person; or

(7) a conspiracy or attempt to commit any offense described in this paragraph.

L.2007, c. 327, § 2, eff. Aug. 1, 2008.

[1] L.2007, c. 327 (N.J.S.A. § 2A:168A–7 et seq.).

2A:168A–9. Certificate as presumptive evidence of rehabilitation

A certificate issued pursuant to this act [1] shall be presumptive evidence of the subject's rehabilitation when considered in regard to public employment as defined in this act, or in conjunction with any licensing, or certification process to which this act applies, which in any particular case may or may not be overcome by other evidence or information. A certificate granted under this act shall not prevent any judicial, administrative, licensing or other body, board, authority or public official from relying on grounds other than the fact of the criminal conviction in exercising any discretionary authority, if any, to suspend, revoke, refuse to issue or refuse to renew any license, permit or other authority or privilege or to determine eligibility or suitability for employment.

L.2007, c. 327, § 3, eff. Aug. 1, 2008.

[1] L.2007, c. 327 (N.J.S.A. § 2A:168A–7 et seq.).

2A:168A–10. Supervising authority; notice to prosecutor of certificate or application for a certificate

In all cases, the applicant or the supervising authority shall provide notice to the prosecutor of either the issuance of a certificate or the pendency of an application for a certificate, or both, pursuant to procedures that shall be developed and published by the supervising authority within thirty days of the effective date of this act. [1]

L.2007, c. 327, § 4, eff. Aug. 1, 2008.

[1] L.2007, c. 327, eff. August 1, 2008.

2A:168A–11. Revocation and reinstatement of certificate; disorderly persons offense

a. A certificate granted pursuant to this act [1] shall no longer be valid if the person who is the subject of the certificate is indicted for a first or second degree crime or convicted of a crime.

b. Upon presentation of satisfactory proof that the criminal charges or indictment have been dismissed, or of an acquittal after trial, a certificate revoked under the circumstances described in subsection a. of this section may be reinstated by the issuing entity.

c. A certificate may be revoked at any time upon application of the prosecutor or on the supervising authority's own initiative when information is received that circumstances have materially changed such that the relief would not be authorized under this act or is no longer in the public interest. The supervising authority revoking such a certificate shall notify the subject of the certificate of the revocation.

d. In addition to any other offense that may apply, a person who knowingly uses or attempts to use a revoked certificate, or a certificate that is no longer valid, in order to obtain a benefit or avoid a disqualification shall be guilty of a disorderly persons offense. For the purposes of this subsection, "uses or attempts to use", shall include knowing failure to disclose to an employer or other affected public entity the revocation or invalidity of a certificate.

L.2007, c. 327, § 5, eff. Aug. 1, 2008.

[1] L.2007, c. 327 (N.J.S.A. § 2A:168A–7 et seq.).

2A:168A–12. Certificates; application to private employers

This act [1] shall not apply to private employers. A private employer may, in its sole and complete discretion, consider a certificate issued under this statute in making employment decisions. Nothing in this section shall be construed to create any right, privilege, or duty or to change any right, privilege, or duty existing under law.

L.2007, c. 327, § 6, eff. Aug. 1, 2008.

[1] L.2007, c. 327 (N.J.S.A. § 2A:168A–7 et seq.).

2A:168A–13. Evaluation of effectiveness of implementation; system of recording certificates

The State Parole Board and the Administrative Office of the Courts shall report to the Governor and the Legislature on or before the first day of the thirteenth month after the effective date of this act [1] an evaluation of the effectiveness of the implementation of this act, including the number of applications received, considered and granted under the act. Entities issuing certificates shall develop a system of recording the certificates and provide information to prospective employers regarding whether a certificate has been issued or is valid.

L.2007, c. 327, § 7, eff. Aug. 1, 2008.

[1] L.2007, c. 327, eff. August 1, 2008.

2A:168A–14. Report; impact of a prior criminal conviction on private employment opportunities

The Department of Labor and Workforce Development shall prepare a report detailing the impact of a prior criminal conviction on private employment opportunities for ex-offenders. The department shall consult with the State Parole Board, and may consult with and seek the assistance of other executive branch agencies, municipalities, agencies and any interested parties. The report shall include identification of barriers faced by ex-offenders seeking private employment, including those set forth in law, regulation and policies of private employers. The report shall analyze the effect of the hiring policies of employers with more than 100 employees on the employment of ex-offenders. In order to encourage cooperation, identities of employers and entities contacted in the course of preparing the report shall remain confidential. The results of this study shall be reported to the Governor and the Legislature within 180 days from the effective date of this act. [1]

L.2007, c. 327, § 8, eff. Jan. 13, 2008.

[1] L.2007, c. 327, eff. August 1, 2008.

2A:168A–15. Pardons by governor

Nothing in this act shall be deemed to alter, limit or affect the manner of applying for pardons to the Governor, and a certificate issued under this act [1] shall not be deemed or construed to be a pardon.

L.2007, c. 327, § 9, eff. Aug. 1, 2008.

[1] L.2007, c. 327 (N.J.S.A. § 2A:168A–7 et seq.).

2A:168A–16. Promulgation of regulations, rules or guidelines

The State Parole Board shall promulgate any regulations or issue guidelines necessary to effectuate the provisions of this act. The court may publish rules or guidelines to implement this act. [1]

L.2007, c. 327, § 10, eff. Aug. 1, 2008.

[1] L.2007, c. 327 (N.J.S.A. § 2A:168A–7 et seq.).

SUBTITLE 12

DISORDERLY PERSONS

Chapter
169. General Provisions.
170. Disorderly Persons Generally.

CHAPTER 169

GENERAL PROVISIONS

Section
2A:169–1, 2A:169–2. Repealed.
2A:169–3. Arrest of disorderly person without process.
2A:169–4 to 2A:169–11. Repealed.

2A:169–1, 2A:169–2. Repealed by L.1978, c. 95, § 2C:98–2, eff. Sept. 1, 1979

2A:169–3. Arrest of disorderly person without process

Whenever an offense is committed in his presence, any constable or police officer shall, and any other person may, apprehend without warrant or process any disorderly person, and take him before any magistrate of the county where apprehended.

2A:169–4 to 2A:169–11. Repealed by L.1978, c. 95, § 2C:98–2, eff. Sept. 1, 1979

CHAPTER 170

DISORDERLY PERSONS GENERALLY

ARTICLE 1. CERTAIN DISORDERLY PERSONS ENUMERATED

Section
2A:170–1 to 2A:170–7. Repealed.
2A:170–8. Repealed.
2A:170–9 to 2A:170–11. Repealed.
2A:170–12, 2A:170–13. Repealed.
2A:170–14. Repealed.
2A:170–15. Repealed.
2A:170–16 to 2A:170–19. Repealed.
2A:170–20. Repealed.
2A:170–20.1. Issuing honorary membership cards or courtesy cards on behalf of law enforcement organizations.
2A:170–20.2 to 2A:170–20.7. Repealed.
2A:170–20.8. Repealed.
2A:170–20.9 to 2A:170–20.12. Repealed.
2A:170–21. Repealed.
2A:170–22 to 2A:170–24. Repealed.
2A:170–25. Repealed.
2A:170–25.1. Repealed.
2A:170–25.2 to 2A:170–25.5. Repealed.
2A:170–25.6. Repealed.
2A:170–25.7, 2A:170–25.8. Repealed.
2A:170–25.9 to 2A:170–25.13. Repealed.
2A:170–25.14 to 2A:170–25.16. Repealed.
2A:170–25.17. Repealed.
2A:170–25.18 to 2A:170–25.20. Repealed.
2A:170–25.21 to 2A:170–25.23. Repealed.

ARTICLE 5. MINORS

2A:170–51. Repealed.
2A:170–51.1. Purchase of tobacco product by person 19 years of age or older for person under 19 years of age; petty disorderly person offense.
2A:170–51.2. Municipal vending machine ordinances not preempted.
2A:170–51.3. Repealed.
2A:170–51.4. Sale or distribution of tobacco or electronic smoking device products to persons under 19 years of age.
2A:170–51.5. Legislative findings and declaration; prohibition on sale of flavored cigarettes.
2A:170–51.6. Sale of flavored cigarettes prohibited; definitions; penalty; revocation of retail dealer license.
2A:170–52. Repealed.
2A:170–53. Repealed.
2A:170–54. Repealed.
2A:170–54.1, 2A:170–54.2. Repealed.

ARTICLE 7. SALES, PURCHASES, DISPLAYS AND UNAUTHORIZED ADVERTISEMENTS

2A:170–70 to 2A:170–76. Repealed.
2A:170–77. Repealed.
2A:170–77.1. Repealed.
2A:170–77.2 to 2A:170–77.2b. Repealed.
2A:170–77.3 to 2A:170–77.7. Repealed.
2A:170–77.8 to 2A:170–77.18. Repealed.

ARTICLE 9A. CERTAIN ACTS RELATING TO EMPLOYMENT AND EMPLOYERS

2A:170–90.1. Repealed.
2A:170–90.2 to 2A:170–90.5. Repealed.

ARTICLE 10. RENTALS OF PROPERTY AND INJURIES THERETO

2A:170–91. Repealed.
2A:170–92. Repealed.
2A:170–92.1. Repealed.
2A:170–93. Repealed.

ARTICLE 1. CERTAIN DISORDERLY PERSONS ENUMERATED

2A:170–1 to 2A:170–7. Repealed by L.1978, c. 95, § 2C:98–2, eff. Sept. 1, 1979

2A:170–8. Repealed by L.1970, c. 226, § 47

2A:170–9 to 2A:170–11. Repealed by L.1978, c. 95, § 2C:98–2, eff. Sept. 1, 1979

2A:170–12, 2A:170–13. Repealed by L.1971, c. 98, § 1, eff. April 16, 1971

2A:170–14. Repealed by L.1978, c. 95, § 2C:98–2, eff. Sept. 1, 1979

2A:170–15. Repealed by L.1971, c. 98, § 1, eff. April 16, 1971

2A:170–16 to 2A:170–19. Repealed by L.1978, c. 95, § 2C:98–2, eff. Sept. 1, 1979

2A:170–20. Repealed by L.1994, c. 16, § 24, eff. Aug. 9, 1994

2A:170–20.1. Issuing honorary membership cards or courtesy cards on behalf of law enforcement organizations

It shall be unlawful for any person, for or on behalf of any organization or association of law enforcement officers, or otherwise, to issue, offer, give, deliver or distribute any honorary membership card, courtesy card, or card of a similar nature, certificate, emblem, plaque, or article of a similar nature, of such organization or association, except to bona fide members or former members of the law enforcement agency represented by such organization or association or to such other persons who have performed outstanding or meritorious public service, and then only in accordance with formal authorization therefor prescribed by resolution duly adopted by such organization or association.

The term "outstanding or meritorious public service" as used in this section shall in no event be construed to mean or include the contribution or payment of money to such organization or association for any purpose whatsoever.

Any person who violates any provision of this section is a disorderly person.

L.1954, c. 181, p. 701, § 2.

2A:170–20.2 to 2A:170–20.7. Repealed by L.1994, c. 16, § 24, eff. Aug. 9, 1994

2A:170–20.8. Repealed by L.1978, c. 95, § 2C:98–2, eff. Sept. 1, 1979

2A:170–20.9 to 2A:170–20.12. Repealed by L.1994, c. 16, § 24, eff. Aug. 9, 1994

2A:170–21. Repealed by L.1978, c. 95, § 2C:98–2, eff. Sept. 1, 1979

2A:170–22 to 2A:170–24. Repealed by L.1977, c. 74, § 14

2A:170–25. Repealed by L.1978, c. 95, § 2C:98–2, eff. Sept. 1, 1979

2A:170–25.1. Repealed by L.1999, c. 90, § 19, eff. May 3, 1999

2A:170–25.2 to 2A:170–25.5. Repealed by L.1978, c. 95, § 2C:98–2, eff. Sept. 1, 1979

2A:170–25.6. Repealed by L.1971, c. 450, § 3, eff. Feb. 16, 1972

2A:170–25.7, 2A:170–25.8. Repealed by L.1978, c. 95, § 2C:98–2, eff. Sept. 1, 1979

2A:170–25.9 to 2A:170–25.13. Repealed by L.1999, c. 90, § 19, eff. May 3, 1999

2A:170–25.14 to 2A:170–25.16. Repealed by L.1978, c. 95, § 2C:98–2, eff. Sept. 1, 1979

2A:170–25.17. Repealed by L.1999, c. 90, § 19, eff. May 3, 1999

2A:170–25.18 to 2A:170–25.20. Repealed by L.1978, c. 95, § 2C:98–2, eff. Sept. 1, 1979

2A:170–25.21 to 2A:170–25.23. Repealed by L.1999, c. 90, § 19, eff. May 3, 1999

ARTICLE 5. MINORS

2A:170–51. Repealed by L.1999, c. 90, § 19, eff. May 3, 1999

2A:170–51.1. Purchase of tobacco product by person 19 years of age or older for person under 19 years of age; petty disorderly person offense

A person 19 years of age or older who purchases a tobacco product for a person who is under 19 years of age is a petty disorderly person.

L.1995, c. 304, § 3, April 4, 1996. Amended by L.2005, c. 384, § 3, eff. April 15, 2006.

2A:170–51.2. Municipal vending machine ordinances not preempted

Nothing in P.L.1995, c. 304 (C.2A:170–51.1 et al.) or section 1 of P.L.2000, c. 87 (C.2A:170–51.4) shall be construed to preempt the provisions of any municipal ordinance concerning vending machines that dispense tobacco products.

L.1995, c. 304, § 4, eff. April 4, 1996. Amended by L.2000, c. 87, § 2, eff. Aug. 14, 2000.

2A:170–51.3. Repealed by L.2000, c. 87, § 5, eff. Aug. 14, 2000

2A:170–51.4. Sale or distribution of tobacco or electronic smoking device products to persons under 19 years of age

a. No person, either directly or indirectly by an agent or employee, or by a vending machine owned by the person or located in the person's establishment, shall sell, offer for sale, distribute for commercial purpose at no cost or minimal cost or with coupons or rebate offers, give or furnish, to a person under 19 years of age:

(1) any cigarettes made of tobacco or of any other matter or substance which can be smoked, or any cigarette paper or tobacco in any form, including smokeless tobacco; or

(2) any electronic smoking device that can be used to deliver nicotine or other substances to the person inhaling from the device, including, but not limited to, an electronic cigarette, cigar, cigarillo, or pipe, or any cartridge or other component of the device or related product.

b. The establishment of all of the following shall constitute a defense to any prosecution brought pursuant to subsection a. of this section:

(1) that the purchaser of the tobacco product or electronic smoking device or the recipient of the promotional sample falsely represented, by producing either a driver's license or non-driver identification card issued by the New Jersey Motor Vehicle Commission, a similar card issued pursuant to the laws of another state or the federal government of Canada, or a photographic identification card issued by a county clerk, that the purchaser or recipient was of legal age to make the purchase or receive the sample;

(2) that the appearance of the purchaser of the tobacco product or electronic smoking device or the recipient of the promotional sample was such that an ordinary prudent person would believe the purchaser or recipient to be of legal age to make the purchase or receive the sample; and

(3) that the sale or distribution of the tobacco product or electronic smoking device was made in good faith, relying upon the production of the identification set forth in paragraph (1) of this subsection, the appearance of the purchaser or recipient, and in the reasonable belief that the purchaser or recipient was of legal age to make the purchase or receive the sample.

c. A person who violates the provisions of subsection a. of this section, including an employee of a retail dealer licensee under P.L.1948, c. 65 (C.54:40A–1 et seq.) who actually sells or otherwise provides a tobacco product to a person under 19 years of age, shall be liable to a civil penalty of not less than $250 for the first violation, not less than $500 for the second violation, and $1,000 for the third and each subsequent violation. The civil penalty shall be collected pursuant to the "Penalty Enforcement Law of 1999," P.L.1999, c. 274 (C.2A:58–10 et seq.), in a summary proceeding before the municipal court having jurisdiction. An official authorized by statute or ordinance to enforce the State or local health codes or a law enforcement officer having enforcement authority in that municipality may issue a summons for a violation of the provisions of subsection a. of this section, and may serve and execute all process with respect to the enforcement of this section consistent with the Rules of Court. A penalty recovered under the provisions of this subsection shall be recovered by and in the name of the State by the local health agency. The penalty shall be paid into the

treasury of the municipality in which the violation occurred for the general uses of the municipality.

d. In addition to the provisions of subsection c. of this section, upon the recommendation of the municipality, following a hearing by the municipality, the Division of Taxation in the Department of the Treasury may suspend or, after a second or subsequent violation of the provisions of subsection a. of this section, revoke the license issued under section 202 of P.L.1948, c. 65 (C.54:40A–4) of a retail dealer. The licensee shall be subject to administrative charges, based on a schedule issued by the Director of the Division of Taxation, which may provide for a monetary penalty in lieu of a suspension.

e. A penalty imposed pursuant to this section shall be in addition to any penalty that may be imposed pursuant to section 3 of P.L.1999, c. 90 (C.2C:33–13.1).

L.2000, c. 87, § 1, eff. Aug. 14, 2000. Amended by L.2003, c. 175, § 1, eff. Sept. 10, 2003; L.2005, c. 384, § 1, eff. April 15, 2006; L.2009, c. 182, § 3, eff. March 12, 2010.

2A:170–51.5. Legislative findings and declaration; prohibition on sale of flavored cigarettes

The Legislature finds and declares that:

a. There has been a proliferation of flavored cigarettes in recent years, and many of these products have fruit, chocolate or other flavors that are particularly attractive to children;

b. According to public health experts, the existence of these products increases the incidence of tobacco use among children;

c. The earlier a person begins using tobacco, the more likely the person will become addicted to tobacco products and continue to smoke throughout that person's life;

d. As a result, flavored cigarettes lead to increased tobacco use and addiction, higher health care costs, and a greater incidence of smoking-related illness and death; and

e. Therefore, flavored cigarettes pose a significant threat to the health of the general public, and the protection of the public health warrants that the sale and distribution of these products be prohibited in this State.

L.2008, c. 91, § 1, eff. Nov. 30, 2008.

2A:170–51.6. Sale of flavored cigarettes prohibited; definitions; penalty; revocation of retail dealer license

a. No person, either directly or indirectly by an agent or employee, or by a vending machine owned by the person or located in the person's establishment, shall sell, offer for sale, distribute for commercial purpose at no cost or minimal cost or with coupons or rebate offers, give or furnish, to a person a cigarette, or any component part thereof, which contains a natural or artificial constituent or additive that causes the cigarette or any smoke emanating from that product to have a characterizing flavor other than tobacco, clove or menthol. In no event shall a cigarette or any component part thereof be construed to have a characterizing flavor based solely on the use of additives or flavorings, or the provision of an ingredient list made available by any means.

As used in this section:

(1) "characterizing flavor other than tobacco, clove or menthol" means that: the cigarette, or any smoke emanating from that product, imparts a distinguishable flavor, taste or aroma other than tobacco, clove or menthol prior to or during consumption, including, but not limited to, any fruit, chocolate, vanilla, honey, candy, cocoa, dessert, alcoholic beverage, herb or spice flavoring; or the cigarette or any component part thereof is advertised or marketed as having or producing any such flavor, taste or aroma;

(2) "cigarette" means (a) any roll of tobacco wrapped in paper or in any substance not containing tobacco, and (b) any roll of tobacco wrapped in any substance containing tobacco which, because of its appearance, the type of tobacco used in the filler, or its packaging and labeling, is likely to be offered to, or purchased by, consumers as a cigarette as described in subparagraph (a) of this paragraph (2); and

(3) "component part thereof" includes, but is not limited to, the tobacco, paper, roll or filter, or any other matter or substance which can be smoked.

b. A person who violates the provisions of subsection a. of this section shall be liable to a civil penalty of not less than $250 for the first violation, not less than $500 for the second violation, and $1,000 for the third and each subsequent violation. The civil penalty shall be collected pursuant to the "Penalty Enforcement Law of 1999," P.L.1999, c. 274 (C.2A:58–10 et seq.), in a summary proceeding before the municipal court having jurisdiction. An official authorized by statute or ordinance to enforce the State or local health codes or a law enforcement officer having enforcement authority in that municipality may issue a summons for a violation of the provisions of subsection a. of this section, and may serve and execute all process with respect to the enforcement of this section consistent with the Rules of Court. A penalty recovered under the provisions of this subsection shall be recovered by and in the name of the State by the local health agency. The penalty shall be paid into the treasury of the municipality in which the violation occurred for the general uses of the municipality.

c. In addition to the provisions of subsection b. of this section, upon the recommendation of the municipality, following a hearing by the municipality, the Division of Taxation in the Department of the Treasury may suspend or, after a second or subsequent violation of the provisions of subsection a. of this section, revoke the license of a retail dealer issued under section 202 of

P.L.1948, c. 65 (C.54:40A–4). The licensee shall be subject to administrative charges, based on a schedule issued by the Director of the Division of Taxation, which may provide for a monetary penalty in lieu of a suspension.

L.2008, c. 91, § 2, eff. Nov. 30, 2008.

2A:170–52.   **Repealed by L.1971, c. 98, § 1 eff. April 16, 1971**

2A:170–53.   **Repealed by L.1978, c. 95, § 2C:98–2, eff. Sept. 1, 1979**

2A:170–54.   **Repealed by L.1971, c. 98, § 1 eff. April 16, 1971**

2A:170–54.1, 2A:170–54.2.   **Repealed by L.1978, c. 95, § 2C:98–2, eff. Sept. 1, 1979**

ARTICLE 7.   SALES, PURCHASES, DISPLAYS AND UNAUTHORIZED ADVERTISEMENTS

2A:170–70 to 2A:170–76.   **Repealed by L.1978, c. 95, § 2C:98–2, eff. Sept. 1, 1979**

2A:170–77.   **Repealed by L.1999, c. 90, § 19, eff. May 3, 1999**

2A:170–77.1.   **Repealed by L.1955, c. 277, p. 1000, § 5**

2A:170–77.2 to 2A:170–77.2b.   **Repealed by L.1999, c. 90, § 19, eff. May 3, 1999**

2A:170–77.3 to 2A:170–77.7.   **Repealed by L.1980, c. 133, § 9**

2A:170–77.8 to 2A:170–77.18.   **Repealed by L.1999, c. 90, § 19, eff. May 3, 1999**

ARTICLE 9A.   CERTAIN ACTS RELATING TO EMPLOYMENT AND EMPLOYERS

2A:170–90.1.   **Repealed by L.1981, c. 290, § 52, eff. Sept. 24, 1981**

2A:170–90.2 to 2A:170–90.5.   **Repealed by L.1999, c. 90, § 19, eff. May 3, 1999**

ARTICLE 10.   RENTALS OF PROPERTY AND INJURIES THERETO

2A:170–91.   **Repealed by L.1999, c. 90, § 19, eff. May 3, 1999**

2A:170–92.   **Repealed by L.1981, c. 323, § 4, eff. Dec. 9, 1981**

2A:170–92.1.   **Repealed by L.1970, c. 210, § 5, eff. Sept. 30, 1970**

2A:170–93.   **Repealed by L.1978, c. 95, § 2C:98–2, eff. Sept. 1, 1979**

P.L.1948, c.422 (C.54:40A-4). The license shall be subject to administrative charges based on a schedule issued by the Director of the Division of Taxation which may provide for a monetary penalty in lieu of a suspension.

L.2008, c. 20, s. 2, eff. Nov. 26, 2008.

2A:170-52. Repealed by L.1971, c. 98, § 1 eff. April 16, 1971.

2A:170-53. Repealed by L.1979, c. 95, § 2C:98-2, eff. Sept. 1, 1979.

2A:170-54. Repealed by L.1971, c. 98, § 1 eff. April 16, 1971.

2A:170-54.1, 2A:170-54.2. Repealed by L.1979, c. 95, § 2C:98-2, eff. Sept. 1, 1979.

ARTICLE 7. SALES, PURCHASES, DISPLAYS
AND UNAUTHORIZED
ADVERTISEMENTS.

2A:170-70 to 2A:170-76. Repealed by L.1979, c. 95, § 2C:98-2, eff. Sept. 1, 1979.

2A:170-77. Repealed by L.1999, c. 90, § 19, eff. May 3, 1999.

2A:170-77.1. Repealed by L.1955, c. 277, p. 1060, § 8.

2A:170-77.2 to 2A:170-77.2b. Repealed by L.1999, c. 90, § 19, eff. May 3, 1999.

2A:170-77.3 to 2A:170-77.7. Repealed by L.1986, c. 131, § 3.

2A:170-77.8 to 2A:170-77.18. Repealed by L.1999, c. 90, § 19, eff. May 3, 1999.

ARTICLE 9. CERTAIN ACTS RELATING
TO EMPLOYMENT AND EMPLOYERS.

2A:170-90.1. Repealed by L.1981, c. 290, § 32, eff. Sept. 24, 1981.

2A:170-90.2 to 2A:170-90.5. Repealed by L.1999, c. 90, § 19, eff. May 3, 1999.

ARTICLE 10. RENTALS OF PROPERTY
AND INJURIES THERETO.

2A:170-91. Repealed by L.1999, c. 90, § 19, eff. May 3, 1999.

2A:170-92. Repealed by L.1981, c. 325, § 4, eff. Dec. 9, 1981.

2A:170-92.1. Repealed by L.1979, c. 216, § 5, eff. Sept. 24, 1979.

2A:170-93. Repealed by L.1979, c. 95, § 2C:98-2, eff. Sept. 1, 1979.

TITLE 2B

COURT ORGANIZATION AND CIVIL CODE

Chapter
12. Municipal Courts.
19. Comprehensive Enforcement Program Fund.
20. Qualification and Selection of Jurors.
21. County Grand Juries.
22. State Grand Juries.
23. Petit Jurors.
25. Municipal Prosecutors.

CHAPTER 12

MUNICIPAL COURTS

Section
2B:12–1.   Establishment of municipal courts.
2B:12–2.   Name of court.
2B:12–3.   Place of court.
2B:12–4.   Judge of municipal court; term of office; appointment.
2B:12–5.   Additional municipal judges.
2B:12–6.   Designation of acting judges.
2B:12–7.   Qualifications of judges; compensation.
2B:12–8.   Chief judge.
2B:12–9.   Presiding judge of the municipal courts.
2B:12–10. Municipal court administrator and personnel.
2B:12–11. Certification of municipal court administrators; appointment of interim administrator.
2B:12–12. Bond or insurance.
2B:12–13. Powers of administrator.
2B:12–14. Officers empowered to execute process.
2B:12–15. Courtrooms and equipment.
2B:12–16. Territorial jurisdiction.
2B:12–17. Jurisdiction of specified offenses.
2B:12–17.1. Violations of Title 4 chapter 22, cruelty to animals; required notice.
2B:12–17.2. Death or serious bodily injury; jurisdiction of superior and municipal courts; procedural guidelines for prosecution of certain offenses.
2B:12–18. Jurisdiction of specified offenses where indictment and trial by jury are waived.
2B:12–19. Authority of municipal court judge prior to indictment; notice to county prosecutor.
2B:12–20. Municipal housing court; jurisdiction.
2B:12–21. Officials authorized to act for court.
2B:12–22. Periodic service of imprisonment.
2B:12–23. Default in payment of fine; community service.
2B:12–23.1. Inability to pay fine on date of court hearing; installment payments; alternative penalties.
2B:12–24. Costs charged to complainant in certain cases.
2B:12–25. Records and standards for municipal courts.
2B:12–26. Docketing judgment.
2B:12–27. County or municipality authorized to employ a prosecutor.
2B:12–28. Repealed.
2B:12–29. Blank.
2B:12–30. Automated Traffic System Fund.
2B:12–30.1. Automated Traffic System Statewide Modernization Fund.

Section
2B:12–31. Suspension of driving privileges.
2B:12–32. Municipal ordinances; court ruling as unconstitutional.
2B:12–33. Applicability.

2B:12–1.   Establishment of municipal courts

a. Every municipality shall establish a municipal court. If a municipality fails to maintain a municipal court or does not enter into an agreement pursuant to subsection b. or c. of this section, the Assignment Judge of the vicinage shall order violations occurring within its boundaries heard in any other municipal court in the county until such time as the municipality establishes and maintains a municipal court. The municipality without a municipal court shall be responsible for all administrative costs specified in the order of the Assignment Judge pending the establishment of its municipal court.

b. Two or more municipalities, by ordinance, may enter into an agreement establishing a single joint municipal court and providing for its administration. A copy of the agreement shall be filed with the Administrative Director of the Courts. As used in this act, "municipal court" includes a joint municipal court.

c. Two or more municipalities, by ordinance or resolution, may agree to provide jointly for courtrooms, chambers, equipment, supplies and employees for their municipal courts and agree to appoint judges and administrators without establishing a joint municipal court. Where municipal courts share facilities in this manner, the identities of the individual courts shall continue to be expressed in the captions of orders and process.

d. An agreement pursuant to subsection b. or c. of this section may be terminated as provided in the agreement. If the agreement makes no provision for termination, it may be terminated by any party with reasonable notices and terms as determined by the Assignment Judge of the vicinage.

e. Any county of the first class with a population of over 825,000 and a population density of less than 4,000 persons per square mile according to the latest federal decennial census, with a county police department and force established in accordance with N.J.S.40A:14–106 or a county park police system established in accordance with P.L.1960, c. 135 (C.40:37–261 et seq.), may establish, by ordinance, a central municipal court, which shall be an inferior court of limited jurisdiction, to adjudicate cases filed by agents of the county health department, members of the county police department and force or county park police system, or other cases within its jurisdiction referred by the vicinage Assignment Judge pursuant to the Rules of Court, and provide for its administration. A copy of that ordinance shall be filed with the Administrative Director of the Courts. As used in this act, "municipal court" includes a central municipal court.

L.1993, c. 293, § 1, eff. Feb. 15, 1994. Amended by L.1996, c. 95, § 1, eff. Oct. 24, 1996; L.2008, c. 2, § 1, eff. March 26, 2008.

2B:12–2. Name of court

The name of a municipal court of a single municipality shall be the "Municipal Court of (insert name of municipality)." The name of a joint municipal court shall be specified in the ordinances establishing the court. The name of a central municipal court shall be the "Central Municipal Court of the County of (insert name of county)" and shall be specified in the ordinance establishing the court.

L.1993, c. 293, § 1, eff. Feb. 15, 1994. Amended by L.1996, c. 95, § 2, eff. Oct. 24, 1996.

2B:12–3. Place of court

Courtrooms and sessions of a municipal court need not be in the municipality for which the court has jurisdiction. If the same person is serving as judge of more than one municipal court, sessions of the respective courts may be combined.

L.1993, c. 293, § 1, eff. Feb. 15, 1994.

2B:12–4. Judge of municipal court; term of office; appointment

a. Each judge of a municipal court shall serve for a term of three years from the date of appointment and until a successor is appointed and qualified. Any appointment to fill a vacancy not caused by the expiration of term shall be made for the unexpired term only. However, if a county or municipality requires by ordinance that the judge of the municipal court devote full time to judicial duties or limit the practice of law to non-litigated matters, the first appointment after the establishment of that requirement shall be for a full term of three years.

b. In municipalities governed by a mayor-council form of government, the municipal court judge shall be appointed by the mayor with the advice and consent of the council. Each judge of a joint municipal court shall be nominated and appointed by the Governor with the advice and consent of the Senate. In all other municipalities, the municipal judge shall be appointed by the governing body of the municipality.

c. In a county that has established a central municipal court, the judge of the central municipal court shall be nominated and appointed by the Governor with the advice and consent of the Senate. In those counties having a county executive, the county executive may submit the names of judicial candidates for judge of the central municipal court to the Governor. In all other counties, the governing body may submit the names of judicial candidates for judge of the central municipal court to the Governor.

L.1993, c. 293, § 1, eff. Feb. 15, 1994. Amended by L.1996, c. 95, § 3, eff. Oct. 24, 1996.

2B:12–5. Additional municipal judges

a. With the written consent of the Assignment Judge of the vicinage, a county or municipality may:

(1) increase the number of judgeships of the municipal court, or

(2) appoint one or more temporary municipal judges.

b. A temporary judge is an additional judge of the municipal court appointed to meet a special need of limited duration. The procedure for appointment of temporary municipal judges shall be the same as that for other municipal judges, but each term of a temporary judge shall not exceed one year.

L.1993, c. 293, § 1, eff. Feb. 15, 1994. Amended by L.1996, c. 95, § 4, eff. Oct. 24, 1996.

2B:12–6. Designation of acting judges

Subject to the Rules of Court, the Assignment Judge of the vicinage may appoint an acting judge of each of the municipal courts in the vicinage to serve as judge temporarily when the judge of that court is unable to hold the municipal court or for other cause. A person appointed as an acting judge shall be a judge of another municipal court or an attorney-at-law. A copy of the appointment of an acting judge for a municipal court shall be sent to the judge of that court and to the Administrative Director of the Courts.

L.1993, c. 293, § 1, eff. Feb. 15, 1994. Amended by L.1996, c. 95, § 5, eff. Oct. 24, 1996.

2B:12–7. Qualifications of judges; compensation

a. Every judge, temporary judge and acting judge of a municipal court shall be a resident of this State and an attorney-at-law admitted to practice in this State for at least five years provided, however, that this provision shall not apply to any attorney-at-law serving as a judge of a municipal court on the effective date of this act.

b. In lieu of any other fees, judges of municipal courts shall be paid annual salaries set by ordinance or resolution of the counties or municipalities establishing the court.

L.1993, c. 293, § 1, eff. Feb. 15, 1994. Amended by L.1996, c. 95, § 6, eff. Oct. 24, 1996.

2B:12–8. Chief judge

Where there is more than one judge of a municipal court, the county or municipality may designate one of the judges as the chief judge of the court. The chief judge shall designate the time and place of court and assign cases among the judges, pursuant to the Rules of Court.

L.1993, c. 293, § 1, eff. Feb. 15, 1994. Amended by L.1996, c. 95, § 7, eff. Oct. 24, 1996.

2B:12–9. Presiding judge of the municipal courts

If the Chief Justice designates a judge of the Superior Court or a judge of one of the municipal courts in a vicinage to serve as presiding judge of the municipal courts for that vicinage, that judge may exercise powers delegated by the Chief Justice or established by the Rules of Court.

If the presiding judge is a municipal court judge, the presiding judge shall be paid by the State for the time devoted to duties as Presiding Judge, unless that judge is also assigned duties at the request of a county, in which case compensation, pension and other benefits shall be as determined by the Assignment Judge and the governing body of the county, with the approval of the Chief Justice.

L.1993, c. 293, § 1, eff. Feb. 15, 1994. Amended by L.1996, c. 95, § 8, eff. Oct. 24, 1996.

2B:12–10. Municipal court administrator and personnel

a. A county or municipality shall provide for an administrator and other necessary employees for the municipal court and for their compensation. With approval of the Supreme Court, an employee of the county or municipality, in addition to other duties, may be designated to serve as administrator of the municipal court.

b. The judge of a municipal court may designate in writing an acting administrator or deputy administrator to serve temporarily for an absent administrator or deputy administrator until the absent administrator or deputy administrator returns or a new administrator or deputy administrator is appointed. The acting administrator or acting deputy administrator shall be paid at a rate established by the judge but not exceeding that established for the administrator or deputy administrator.

L.1993, c. 293, § 1, eff. Feb. 15, 1994. Amended by L.1996, c. 95, § 9, eff. Oct. 24, 1996.

2B:12–11. Certification of municipal court administrators; appointment of interim administrator

a. The Supreme Court may appoint a Municipal Court Administrator Certification Board. That board shall:

(1) Design examinations for certification of municipal court administrators;

(2) Establish courses satisfying training requirements in subjects closely related to the duties of a municipal court administrator; and

(3) Establish procedures and fees for certification.

b. A person shall be certified as a Municipal Court Administrator if the person:

(1) Is a high school graduate;

(2) Has a combination of two years of either full-time government employment performing duties related to those of a municipal court administrator, or higher education;

(3) Completes the training required by the board;

(4) Passes the examination held by the board, and

(5) Pays any required certification fee.

c. A person who is a municipal court administrator and has been serving in that position for five years on the effective date of this act[1] shall be certified as a municipal court administrator if the person passes the examination held by the board and pays any required certification fee. A person who is a municipal court administrator and has been serving in that position for three years on the effective date of this act shall be certified as a municipal court administrator if the person completes the training required by the board, passes the examination held by the board and pays any required certification fee.

d. Starting on the fifth anniversary of the effective date of P.L.2006, c. 20,[2] no person shall be appointed as a municipal court administrator unless that person holds a municipal court administrator certificate issued by the Supreme Court. Municipal court administrators hired in the interim between that effective date and the fifth anniversary following that effective date shall have five years from the date of hire to obtain certification.

e. Starting on the fifth anniversary of the effective date of P.L.2006, c. 20, after a vacancy in the office of municipal court administrator, the governing body may appoint a person who does not hold a municipal court administrator certificate to serve as a municipal court administrator, on an interim basis, for a period not to exceed one year commencing on the date of the appointment. Any person so appointed may, in consultation with the judge of the municipal court, be reappointed as a municipal court administrator, on an interim basis, for two subsequent one- year terms. The municipal court administrator appointed on an interim basis may be reappointed for a fourth, and, if necessary, a fifth additional one- year term, provided the municipal court administrator is currently enrolled in the certification program and needs additional time to complete that program.

(1) Time served as an interim municipal court administrator may be credited toward the experience authorized as a substitute for the college education requirement under paragraph (2) of subsection b. of this section.

(2) Time served as a municipal court administrator, on an interim basis, may not be credited as time served as a municipal court administrator for the purpose of acquiring tenure under section 1 of P.L.1953, c. 168

(C.2A:8–13.1) and section 1 of P.L.1975, c. 39 (C.2A:8–13.3).

f. Notwithstanding the provisions of P.L.2006, c. 20, a person who is serving as a municipal court administrator on the effective date of P.L.2006, c. 20, may continue to hold the position of municipal court administrator in that municipality, provided the person satisfactorily completes, within five years of the effective date of P.L.2006, c. 20, the training required by this section and thereafter satisfies the continuing education required of certified municipal court administrators. If a municipal court administrator qualified under this subsection transfers to a position as a municipal court administrator in another municipality, that administrator will be treated as a newly-hired administrator for purposes of this section.

g. The Supreme Court of New Jersey may adopt rules to implement the purposes of P.L.2006, c. 20.

h. A municipal court administrator certificate may be revoked or suspended by the board for dishonest practices or failure to perform, or neglect of, duties of a municipal court administrator.

L.1993, c. 293, § 1, eff. Feb. 15, 1994. Amended by L.2006, c. 20, § 1, eff. May 25, 2006.

1 L.1993, c. 293, § 1, eff. Feb. 15, 1994.
2 L.2006, c. 20, § 1, eff. May 25, 2006.

2B:12–12. Bond or insurance

Before assuming the duties of office, a judge or administrator of a municipal court, or person employed by the court who handles money in the scope of that employment, shall be covered by a bond or insurance against loss or misappropriation of funds payable to the municipality, county and State, in an amount and with terms set by the municipality.

L.1993, c. 293, § 1, eff. Feb. 15, 1994.

2B:12–13. Powers of administrator

Any process, order, warrant or judgment issued by a municipal court may be signed by the judge or be attested in the judge's name and signed by the municipal court administrator. The municipal court administrator shall have the authority granted by law and the Rules of Court to administrators and clerks of courts of record.

L.1993, c. 293, § 1, eff. Feb. 15, 1994.

2B:12–14. Officers empowered to execute process

Any law enforcement officer, or any other person authorized by law, may act in the service, execution and return of process, orders, warrants and judgments issued by any municipal court.

L.1993, c. 293, § 1, eff. Feb. 15, 1994.

2B:12–15. Courtrooms and equipment

Suitable courtrooms, chambers, offices, equipment and supplies for the municipal court, its administrator's office and its violations bureau shall be provided by the municipality or by a county that has established a central municipal court.

L.1993, c. 293, § 1, eff. Feb. 15, 1994. Amended by L.1996, c. 95, § 10, eff. Oct. 24, 1996.

2B:12–16. Territorial jurisdiction

a. A municipal court of a single municipality shall have jurisdiction over cases arising within the territory of that municipality except as provided in section 10 of P.L.1997, c. 357 (C.27:25–5.15). A joint municipal court shall have jurisdiction over cases arising within the territory of any of the municipalities which the court serves. The territory of a municipality includes any premises or property located partly in and partly outside of the municipality. A central municipal court shall have jurisdiction over cases arising within the territorial boundaries of the county.

b. A municipal court judge, serving as an acting judge in any other municipal court in the county, may also hear matters arising out of that other court, while sitting in the court where the acting judge holds a regular appointment.

L.1993, c. 293, § 1, eff. Feb. 15, 1994. Amended by L.1996, c. 95, § 11, eff. Oct. 24, 1996; L.1997, c. 357, § 13, eff. July 14, 1998.

2B:12–17. Jurisdiction of specified offenses

A municipal court has jurisdiction over the following cases within the territorial jurisdiction of the court:

a. Violations of county or municipal ordinances;

b. Violations of the motor vehicle and traffic laws;

c. Disorderly persons offenses, petty disorderly persons offenses and other non-indictable offenses except where exclusive jurisdiction is given to the Superior Court;

d. Violations of the fish and game laws;

e. Proceedings to collect a penalty where jurisdiction is granted by statute;

f. Violations of laws regulating boating; and

g. Any other proceedings where jurisdiction is granted by statute.

L.1993, c. 293, § 1, eff. Feb. 15, 1994. Amended by L.1996, c. 95, § 12, eff. Oct. 24, 1996.

2B:12–17.1. Violations of Title 4 chapter 22, cruelty to animals; required notice

As required pursuant to section 3 of P.L.2003, c.67 (C.4:22–57), a municipal court adjudging guilt or liability for a violation of any provision of chapter 22 of Title 4 of the Revised Statutes, shall charge the prosecutor, officer of the New Jersey Society for the Prevention of Cruelty to Animals or the district (county) society for the prevention of cruelty to animals, or other appropriate person, other than a certified animal control officer, with the responsibility to notify within 30 days the

Commissioner of Health and Senior Services, in writing, of the full name of the person found guilty of, or liable for, an applicable violation, and the violation for which or of which that person was found guilty or liable, and the person charged with the responsibility shall provide such notice.

L.2003, c. 67, § 4, eff. May 5, 2003.

2B:12–17.2. Death or serious bodily injury; jurisdiction of superior and municipal courts; procedural guidelines for prosecution of certain offenses

a. In any matter concerning Title 39 of the Revised Statutes where death or serious bodily injury has occurred, regardless of whether the death or serious bodily injury is an element of the offense or violation, the Superior Court shall have exclusive jurisdiction over the offense or violation until such time that the Superior Court transfers the matter to the municipal court. For the purposes of this section, the term "serious bodily injury" shall have the meaning set forth in subsection b. of N.J.S.2C:11–1.

b. The Attorney General may develop guidelines establishing procedures to be followed for prosecutions involving violations of N.J.S.2C:11–4, N.J.S.2C:11–5 or section 1 of P.L.1997, c. 111 (C.2C:11–5.1) or criminal offenses involving serious bodily injury and underlying motor vehicle offenses arising from the same incident consistent with the provisions of P.L.2006, c.28 (C.2B:12–17.2 et al.).

L.2006, c. 28, § 1, eff. June 29, 2006.

2B:12–18. Jurisdiction of specified offenses where indictment and trial by jury are waived

A municipal court has jurisdiction over the following crimes occurring within the territorial jurisdiction of the court, where the person charged waives indictment and trial by jury in writing and the county prosecutor consents in writing:

a. Crimes of the fourth degree enumerated in chapters 17, 18, 20 and 21 of Title 2C of the New Jersey Statutes; or

b. Crimes where the term of imprisonment that may be imposed does not exceed one year.

L.1993, c. 293, § 1, eff. Feb. 15, 1994.

2B:12–19. Authority of municipal court judge prior to indictment; notice to county prosecutor

a. A municipal court has authority to conduct proceedings in a criminal case within its territorial jurisdiction prior to indictment subject to the Rules of Court.

b. A municipal court shall not discharge a person charged with an indictable offense without first giving the county prosecutor notice and an opportunity to be heard in the case.

L.1993, c. 293, § 1, eff. Feb. 15, 1994.

2B:12–20. Municipal housing court; jurisdiction

A municipality in a county of the first class may establish, as a part of its municipal court, a full-time municipal housing court. Municipal housing courts shall have jurisdiction over actions for eviction involving property in the municipality which are transferred to the municipal housing court by the Special Civil Part of the Superior Court.

L.1993, c. 293, § 1, eff. Feb. 15, 1994. Amended by L.2003, c. 295, § 29, eff. July 12, 2004.

2B:12–21. Officials authorized to act for court

a. An administrator or deputy administrator of a municipal court, authorized by a judge of that court, may exercise the power of the municipal court to administer oaths for complaints filed with the municipal court and to issue warrants and summonses.

b. A police officer in charge of a police station, other than an officer who participated in the arrest of the defendant, may exercise the power of the municipal court to administer oaths for complaints filed with the municipal court. Any police officer may issue summonses related to such complaints and may as authorized by the Rules of the Court issue a summons in lieu of an arrest for an offense committed in the officer's presence.

c. The authority of the municipal court to set conditions of pre-trial release may be exercised by an administrator or deputy administrator of a municipal court who is authorized by the judge of that court, or by any police officer in charge of a police station, other than an officer who participated in the arrest of the defendant. The authority may be exercised only in accordance with bail schedules promulgated by the Administrative Office of the Courts or by the municipal court.

d. Except as otherwise provided by the Rules of Court, a person charged with a non-indictable offense shall be released on summons or personal recognizance without unnecessary delay and within 12 hours after arrest unless a judge or court administrator has set the conditions for pretrial release and the conditions remain unmet.

e. A person acting for a municipal court by authority of this section shall immediately file the complaint, warrant, summons or recognizance which was the subject of the action with the municipal court.

L.1993, c. 293, § 1, eff. Feb. 15, 1994.

2B:12–22. Periodic service of imprisonment

A court may order that a sentence of imprisonment be served periodically on particular days, rather than consecutively. The person imprisoned shall be given credit for each day or fraction of a day to the nearest hour actually served.

L.1993, c. 293, § 1, eff. Feb. 15, 1994.

2B:12–23. Default in payment of fine; community service

a. A person, sentenced by a municipal court to pay a fine, who defaults in payment may be ordered to perform community service in lieu of incarceration or other modification of the sentence with the person's consent.

b. The county or municipal official in charge of the community service program shall report to the municipal court any failure of a person subject to a court work order to report for work or to perform the assigned work. Upon receipt of the report, the court may revoke its community service order and impose any sentence consistent with the original sentence.

L.1993, c. 293, § 1, eff. Feb. 15, 1994. Amended by L.1996, c. 95, § 13, eff. Oct. 24, 1996.

2B:12–23.1. Inability to pay fine on date of court hearing; installment payments; alternative penalties

a. Notwithstanding any other provision of law to the contrary, if a municipal court finds that a person does not have the ability to pay a penalty in full on the date of the hearing or has failed to pay a previously imposed penalty, the court may order the payment of the penalty in installments for a period of time determined by the court. If a person defaults on any payment and a municipal court finds that the defendant does not have the ability to pay, the court may:

(1) reduce the penalty, suspend the penalty, or modify the installment plan;

(2) order that credit be given against the amount owed for each day of confinement, if the court finds that the person has served jail time for the default;

(3) revoke any unpaid portion of the penalty, if the court finds that the circumstances that warranted the imposition have changed or that it would be unjust to require payment;

(4) order the person to perform community service in lieu of payment of the penalty; or

(5) impose any other alternative permitted by law in lieu of payment of the penalty.

b. For the purposes of this section, "penalty" means any fine, statutorily-mandated assessment, surcharge or other financial penalty imposed by a municipal court, except restitution or a surcharge assessed pursuant to subsection f. of section 1 of P.L.2000, c. 75 (C.39:4–97.2).

L.2009, c. 317, § 1, eff. Jan. 18, 2010.

2B:12–24. Costs charged to complainant in certain cases

In cases where the judge of a municipal court dismisses the complaint or acquits the defendant and finds that the charge was false and not made in good faith, the judge may order that the complaining witness pay the costs of court established by law.

L.1993, c. 293, § 1, eff. Feb. 15, 1994.

2B:12–25. Records and standards for municipal courts

The Supreme Court may prescribe records to be maintained and reports to be filed by the municipal court and may promulgate standards for facilities and staff of municipal courts.

L.1993, c. 293, § 1, eff. Feb. 15, 1994.

2B:12–26. Docketing judgment

A judgment of a municipal court assessing a penalty, fine or restitution may be docketed in the Superior Court by the party recovering the judgment.

A judgment docketed in the Superior Court shall operate, from the time of the docketing, as though the judgment was obtained in an action originally commenced in the Superior Court.

After a judgment has been docketed in the Superior Court, the municipal court shall not issue an execution or hold proceedings in the case except that the municipal court may grant a new trial or process an appeal.

If a new trial is granted or an appeal taken after a judgment is docketed, the Superior Court shall not issue an execution on the judgment pending the final determination of the proceedings.

L.1993, c. 293, § 1, eff. Feb. 15, 1994.

2B:12–27. County or municipality authorized to employ a prosecutor

The governing body of the county or municipality may employ an attorney-at-law as a prosecutor, under the supervision of the Attorney General or county prosecutor, who may represent the State, county or municipality in any matter within the jurisdiction of the central municipal court or any other municipal court in accordance with the provisions of P.L.1999, c. 349 (C.2B:25–1 et al.).

L.1996, c. 95, § 14, eff. Oct. 24, 1996. Amended by L.1999, c. 349, § 11.

2B:12–28. Repealed by L.1997, c. 256, § 18, eff. Dec. 22, 1997

2B:12–29. Blank

2B:12–30. Automated Traffic System Fund

a. The Legislature finds and declares that there is a need to improve the management, efficiency and effectiveness of municipal court operations and quality of justice by providing funds:

(1) To be utilized by the Administrative Office of the Courts to design, equip, operate and maintain a standardized, Statewide computer system, including integrated traffic ticket control, court financial accounting, case processing, statistical reporting services and other

components necessary to automate municipal court operations; and

(2) To ensure the smooth exchange of automated information among the Judiciary, the Division of Motor Vehicles, law enforcement agencies, other public or quasi-public agencies, or those autonomous systems approved by the Administrative Office of the Courts pursuant to subsection d. of this section.

b. In order to accomplish these purposes, there is created the "Automated Traffic System Fund." The fund shall be a dedicated fund within the General Fund and administered by the Administrative Office of the Courts. The fund shall be the depository of moneys realized from the $1.00 surcharge imposed pursuant to section 6 of P.L.1990, c. 95 (C.2A:8–21.1), the $2.00 court cost assessment imposed pursuant to subsection a. of N.J.S. 22A:3–4 and any other moneys made available for the purposes of the fund.

c. The Supreme Court may issue Rules of Court to effectuate the purposes of this act.

d. Nothing in this section shall be deemed to prevent a municipality, at its own expense, from maintaining or obtaining and using an autonomous computer system for integrated traffic ticket control, court financial accounting, case processing, statistical reporting services and other components necessary to automate municipal court operations that interconnects with the Automated Traffic System, its components and computer network, upon the approval of the Administrative Office of the Courts, in accordance with the following:

(1) An autonomous system shall only be approved for interconnection with the Automated Traffic System (ATS) when it meets all technical interconnection requirements, standardized data definitions and functionality of the Automated Traffic System, including its criminal and ordinance violation components, necessary to: fully automate municipal court operations in accordance with law, court rule or administrative directive; maintain and update on-line the standardized Statewide data base and its electronic traffic and criminal warrant components; and provide for on-line inquiry and exchange of automated data, consistent with the purposes expressed in subsection a. of this section.

(2) A municipality that obtains and uses an autonomous system, approved for interconnection with the Automated Traffic System, shall retain, from the date of interconnection, one-half the full amount of that portion of the court cost assessment imposed and collected on and after that date for payment into the Automated Traffic System Fund, pursuant to subsection a. of N.J.S. 22A:3–4. The retained court cost assessment shall be used by the municipality to offset the operating costs of its autonomous system, including costs to maintain compliance with the interconnection requirements of the Automated Traffic System. A municipality shall be entitled only to retain those court cost assessments for as long as its autonomous system continues to meet the

update and other requirements of paragraph (1) of subsection d. of this section.

(3) That portion of the court cost assessment, imposed pursuant to subsection a. of N.J.S. 22A:3–4 and retained by the State, shall be used for the purposes described in subsection a. of this section including: the State's costs, within the Automated Traffic System, of developing and maintaining interconnection with an autonomous system; the maintenance, improvement and updating of the Automated Traffic System, its components and the standardized Statewide data base; and the procurement and maintenance of hand-held data entry devices and related equipment for use by parking authorities or parking agencies who choose to be directly serviced by the Automated Traffic System. The Administrative Office of the Courts may obtain either directly, through the Statewide master contract process, or as otherwise provided by law, automation services or equipment including hand-held, ticket-issuing devices and printers for use by those parking authorities or parking agencies to facilitate the exchange of automated information and maintain the efficiency of the standardized Statewide computer system.

(4) An autonomous computer system used by a municipality shall be interconnected with the Automated Traffic System and its components by January 1, 1997. The Administrative Office of the Courts shall, at no cost to the municipality, install and maintain the telecommunication line and the court's modem to permit the municipal court to provide for the on-line exchange of automated information with the Automated Traffic System and its components. The Administrative Office of the Courts shall maintain sufficient capacity on its mainframe computer to incorporate the standardized data of that municipal court into the Statewide record system, including the Statewide traffic and criminal warrant systems. Any municipality that fails to maintain and use an autonomous computer system that meets the requirements of this subsection by January 1, 1997 shall be implemented on ATS directly. After that date, municipal courts operating on ATS retain full discretion to either continue on ATS or subsequently obtain and use an autonomous system approved for interconnection.

(5) Nothing in this section shall preclude the Administrative Office of the Courts from immediately terminating, on an emergency basis, without notice, any interconnection with an autonomous system whose continued operation at any time immediately threatens or has compromised the security or data integrity of the Automated Traffic System, any of its components or any of the public and quasi-public agencies that exchange automated information with the Automated Traffic System, pursuant to paragraph (2) of subsection a. of this section. The municipality shall immediately be provided with written reasons for the termination, which shall continue until the threats to security and data integrity have been removed.

(6) If there is any disagreement between the municipality and the Administrative Office of the Courts concerning the standards for the exchange of automated information set forth in this section, the municipality or the Administrative Office of the Courts may seek the advice of the New Jersey Information Resources Management Commission established pursuant to P.L.1993, c. 199 (C.52:9XX–1 et seq.).

(7) Any municipal contract related to the operation of an autonomous computer system shall be subject to review, audit and the policies of the Division of Local Government Services in accordance with N.J.S. 40A:11–1 et seq. including the auditing standards of the Division of Local Government Services relating to the processing of transactions by servicing organizations pursuant to section 6 of P.L.1972, c. 112 (C.40A:11–12.6). All contracts between municipalities and private service providers shall require compliance with the provisions of this section.

(8) The Administrative Office of the Courts shall promulgate administrative procedures necessary to accomplish the purposes of this subsection.

e. By April 1, 1996, a special committee shall be established to review the adequacy of funding for the Automated Traffic System and the Automated Complaint System and the extent to which autonomous computer system interconnections have been requested and successfully completed. The committee may recommend to what extent, if any, the funding level should be adjusted and the need for any further legislative action. The special committee shall be comprised of seven members as follows: one Senator appointed by the President of the Senate; one member of the General Assembly appointed by the Speaker of the General Assembly; the Director of the Administrative Office of the Courts or his designee; the president of the New Jersey League of Municipalities or his designee; the president of the New Jersey Municipal Court Administrators Association or his designee; the president of the New Jersey Municipal Managers Association or his designee and the president of the New Jersey Association of Parking Authorities and Agencies or his designee. The committee shall report its findings to the Legislature by September 30, 1996.

L.1993, c. 293, § 1, eff. Feb. 15, 1994.

2B:12–30.1. Automated Traffic System Statewide Modernization Fund

a. There is established in the General Fund as separate, non-lapsing, dedicated account to be known as the Automated Traffic System Statewide Modernization Fund.

b. Each fiscal year, the State Treasurer shall credit all revenues derived from the offender assessment authorized under subsection c. of N.J.S. 22A:3–4 to the Automated Traffic System Statewide Modernization Fund established pursuant to subsection a. of this section.

c. Moneys in the Automated Traffic System Statewide Modernization Fund, including any interest accruing thereon, shall be utilized exclusively for the administration, operation and modernization of the Statewide Automated Traffic System.

L.2004, c. 62, § 1, eff. Sept. 1, 2004.

2B:12–31. Suspension of driving privileges

a. (1) If a defendant charged with a disorderly persons offense, a petty disorderly persons offense, a violation of a municipal ordinance, or a violation of any other law of this State for which a penalty may be imposed fails to appear at any scheduled court proceeding after written notice has been given to said defendant pursuant to the Rules of Court, a municipal court may order the suspension of the person's driving privileges or nonresident reciprocity privilege or prohibit the person from receiving or obtaining driving privileges until the pending matter is adjudicated or otherwise disposed of, except by dismissal for failure of defendant to appear.

(2) If a defendant sentenced to pay a fine or costs, make restitution, perform community service, serve a term of probation, or do any other act as a condition of that sentence fails to do so, a municipal court may order the suspension of the person's driving privileges or nonresident reciprocity privilege or prohibit the person from receiving or obtaining driving privileges until the terms and conditions of the sentence have been performed or modified.

b. Prior to any action being taken pursuant to the provisions of this section, the defendant shall be given notice of the proposed action and afforded an opportunity to appear before the court to contest the validity of the proposed action.

c. The municipal court shall notify the Division of Motor Vehicles of any action taken pursuant to the provisions of this section.

d. Any action taken by a municipal court pursuant to this section shall be in addition to any other remedies which are available to the court and in addition to any other penalties which may be imposed by the court.

e. (1) When a defendant whose license has been suspended pursuant to subsection a. of this section satisfies the requirements of that subsection, the municipal court shall forward to the Division of Motor Vehicles a notice to restore the defendant's driving privileges.

(2) There shall be included in the fines and penalties imposed by a court on a defendant whose license has been suspended pursuant to subsection a. of this section, the following:

(a) A fee of $3.00 which shall be transferred to the Division of Motor Vehicles;

(b) A penalty of $10.00 for the issuance of the failure to appear notice; and

(c) A penalty of $15.00 for the order of suspension of defendant's driving privileges.

L.1993, c. 293, § 1, eff. Feb. 15, 1994.

2B:12–32. Municipal ordinances; court ruling as unconstitutional

a. Upon a court ruling that a municipal ordinance is unconstitutional, or approving a settlement of a civil action contesting the constitutionality of a municipal ordinance and when the ruling is considered final because the time for appeal has expired:

(1) the municipality that enacted the ordinance and any judicial or law enforcement agency or agency in the criminal justice system that maintains a written or automated record or file concerning the subject of the order shall purge that record or file of all information identifying any person arrested, charged or convicted of violating the ordinance;

(2) the municipality shall notify any person arrested, charged or convicted of violating the ordinance that such record or file has been purged; and

(3) the municipality shall refund any fines, penalties or court costs paid by any person arrested, charged or convicted of violating the ordinance. The refund shall not be required in any case where, by settlement of a civil action contesting the constitutionality of the ordinance, the person has received or will receive monetary compensation in an amount equal to or greater than any fines, penalties or court costs the person paid.

b. Notwithstanding the provisions of any other law, purging of identifying information pursuant to this act shall not require any action by the defendant or the payment of any fee.

c. The Supreme Court of New Jersey may adopt rules and the Administrative Director of the Courts may issue directives and guidelines to be followed by municipal courts to implement the purposes of this act.

d. The Attorney General may issue any guidelines which may be necessary concerning procedures for law enforcement agencies or any agency in the criminal justice system for purging records or files of municipal ordinance violations as required by this act.

L.2000, c. 108, § 1, eff. Sept. 8, 2000.

2B:12–33. Applicability

a. This act shall apply to all rulings of unconstitutionality and all settlements dated on or after January 1, 1999.

b. In any case where a ruling of unconstitutionality or a settlement occurred on or after January 1, 1999 and prior to the enactment of this act, purging of identifying information pursuant to section 1 of this act shall be ordered by the court upon the ex parte application of any party.

L.2000, c. 108, § 2, eff. Sept. 8, 2000.

CHAPTER 19
COMPREHENSIVE ENFORCEMENT PROGRAM FUND

Section
2B:19–1.   Short title.
2B:19–2.   Legislative findings and declaration.
2B:19–3.   Comprehensive enforcement program fund established.
2B:19–4.   Deduction of money collected for deposit in comprehensive enforcement program fund.
2B:19–5.   Alternatives to direct incarceration; labor assistance program or enforced community service program; deposit of enrollment and daily fees in fund.
2B:19–6.   Transfer of collection matters to comprehensive enforcement program or private agencies; regulation of private collection agencies; disbursement of collections; public defender lien.
2B:19–7.   Transfer of community service matters to comprehensive enforcement program for compliance sanctions.
2B:19–8.   Alternatives to payment of remaining court ordered financial obligation; labor assistance program; enforced community service; term of imprisonment.
2B:19–9.   Recommendation of hearing officers to conform to court rules; approval by superior court judge required.
2B:19–10.   Referral of uncollected surcharges to the comprehensive enforcement program; development of procedures.
2B:19–11.   Additional duties.

2B:19–1. Short title

Sections 1 through 9 of this act[1] shall be known and may be cited as the "Comprehensive Enforcement Program Fund Act."

L.1995, c. 9, § 1, eff. Jan. 12, 1995.

[1] N.J.S.A. §§ 2B:19–1 to 2B:19–9.

2B:19–2. Legislative findings and declaration

The Legislature finds and declares that:

a. The Judiciary routinely enters judgments and court orders setting forth assessments, surcharges, fines and restitution against litigants pursuant to statutory law.

b. The enforcement of court orders is crucial to ensure respect for the rule of law and credibility of the court process.

c. Despite monitoring of judgments and court orders by probation divisions and other segments of the Judiciary responsible for doing so, many orders are not complied with because there is a lack of central coordination, funding, automation, and control.

d. The Judiciary has successfully developed a hearing officer program in child support enforcement and a pilot criminal enforcement court project, which is in the process of being expanded, that have demonstrated significant increases in collections and compliance.

e. The Governor's Management Review Commission has reviewed the collections process in New Jersey and made recommendations supporting the establishment and funding of a Statewide comprehensive enforcement program operated by the Judiciary.

f. Upon passage of this act, the Supreme Court and the Chief Justice will establish a Statewide comprehensive enforcement program which will provide for the enforcement of court orders and oversee collection of court-ordered fines, assessments, surcharges and judgments in the civil, criminal and family divisions, the Tax Court and in municipal court as provided in section 6 of P.L.1995, c. 9 (C.2B:19–6). The comprehensive enforcement program will provide for the collection of certain surcharges administratively imposed by the Division of Motor Vehicles as provided in section 6 of P.L.1995, c. 9 (C.2B:19–6). The comprehensive enforcement program will utilize the child support hearing officer model and the pilot project criminal enforcement court model, supported by a Statewide automation system designed to increase collections, compliance and accountability.

L.1995, c. 9, § 2, eff. Jan. 12, 1995. Amended by L.1997, c. 280, § 1, eff. April 6, 1998; L.2001, c. 421, § 1, eff. Jan. 8, 2002.

2B:19–3. Comprehensive enforcement program fund established

There is established as a separate fund in the General Fund, to be administered by the Administrative Office of the Courts, a "Comprehensive Enforcement Program Fund." This fund shall be the depository for the deductions from collections and the enforced community service fees described in sections 4 and 5 of this act [1] for the purpose of operating the comprehensive enforcement program, the computer system established pursuant to P.L.1992, c. 169, enforced community service and any subsequent programs or methodologies employed to enforce collection of court ordered financial obligations.

L.1995, c. 9, § 3, eff. Jan. 12, 1995.

[1] N.J.S.A. §§ 2B:19–4 and 2B:19–5.

2B:19–4. Deduction of money collected for deposit in comprehensive enforcement program fund

a. Subject to the approval of the Director of the Division of Budget and Accounting, the Administrative Office of the Courts is authorized to deduct an amount up to 25% of all moneys collected through the comprehensive enforcement program, except for victim restitution and for Victims of Crime Compensation Board assessments, for deposit in the "Comprehensive Enforcement Program Fund" established pursuant to section 3 of P.L.1995, c. 9 (C.2B:19–3) to fund the comprehensive enforcement program, the CAPS computer system, enforced community service, and other programs employed to collect court ordered financial obligations. The Administrative Office of the Courts shall promulgate a schedule for the deduction of

collections to be deposited in the "Comprehensive Enforcement Program Fund."

b. (Deleted by amendment, P.L.1997, c. 280).

L.1995, c. 9, § 4, eff. Jan. 12, 1995. Amended by L.1997, c. 280, § 2, eff. April 6, 1998.

2B:19–5. Alternatives to direct incarceration; labor assistance program or enforced community service program; deposit of enrollment and daily fees in fund

a. The governing body of each county, through the sheriff or such other authorized officer, may establish a labor assistance program as an alternative to direct incarceration to be utilized by the comprehensive enforcement program as a sentencing option. An enrollment fee of $25.00 shall be paid by each person who is sentenced to a labor assistance program. Additionally, each person so sentenced shall pay a fee of $8.00 per day for each day originally sentenced to the labor assistance program. Labor assistance program fees shall be paid to the county treasurer for use by the county.

b. In counties that do not establish a labor assistance program, the probation services division shall establish an enforced community service program as an alternative to direct incarceration, to be utilized by the comprehensive enforcement program as a sentencing option. An enrollment fee of $25.00 shall be paid by each person who is sentenced to the enforced community service program. Additionally, each person so sentenced shall pay a fee of $8.00 per day for each day originally sentenced to the enforced community service program. Enforced community service fees shall be deposited in the "Comprehensive Enforcement Program Fund" and specifically used to fund the enforced community service programs.

c. (1) As used in this section, "labor assistance program" means, a work program, established by the county under the direction of the sheriff or other authorized county officer, which rigorously supervises offenders providing physical labor as an alternative to incarceration. (2) As used in this section, "enforced community service" means a work program, established and supervised by the probation division, which directly and rigorously supervises offenders providing physical labor as an alternative to direct incarceration in those counties which have chosen not to create a labor assistance program.

L.1995, c. 9, § 5, eff. Jan. 12, 1995. Amended by L.2000, c. 120, § 2.

2B:19–6. Transfer of collection matters to comprehensive enforcement program or private agencies; regulation of private collection agencies; disbursement of collections; public defender lien

a. All matters involving the collection of monies in the Superior Court and Tax Court which have not been resolved in accordance with an order of the court may be transferred, pursuant to court rule, to the comprehensive enforcement program for such action as may be appropriate. As an alternative to, or in addition to, the use of the comprehensive enforcement program, the Administrative Director of the Courts may contract with a private agency or firm to collect any outstanding monies payable to the Superior Court, the Tax Court, or the municipal courts. Outstanding monies payable to a municipal court means monies owed after a final determination of guilt by a municipal court and only when the municipal court has exhausted all judicial enforcement remedies permitted by law or court rule. The use of private collection agencies to collect outstanding monies payable to the Superior Court, the Tax Court and municipal courts shall be governed by rules and procedures adopted by the Supreme Court. The Administrative Director of the Courts may authorize the assessment of and administrative fee by a private agency or firm not to exceed 22% of the amount collected to be paid by the defendant to the private collection agency to pay for the costs of collection.

b. (1) A municipal court may request that all matters which have not been resolved in accordance with an order of that court be transferred to the comprehensive enforcement program in accordance with the provisions of section 9 of P.L.1995, c. 9 (C.2B:19–9) for such action as may be appropriate. All monies collected through the comprehensive enforcement program which result from the enforcing of orders transferred from any municipal court shall be subject to the 25% deduction authorized pursuant to section 4 of P.L.1995, c. 9 (C.2B:19–4) except for monies collected in connection with the enforcement of orders related to parking violations.

(2) (Deleted by amendment, P.L.2009, c. 233)

c. The Chief Administrator of the New Jersey Motor Vehicle Commission may refer matters of surcharges imposed administratively under the New Jersey Merit Rating Plan in accordance with the provisions of section 6 of P.L.1983, c. 65 (C.17:29A–35) which have not been satisfied to the comprehensive enforcement program in accordance with the procedures established pursuant to section 4 of P.L.1997, c. 280 (C.2B:19–10) to be reduced to judgment and for such additional action as may be appropriate. All monies collected through the comprehensive enforcement program which result from the collection of these surcharge monies shall be subject to the 25% deduction authorized pursuant to section 4 of P.L.1995, c. 9 (C.2B:19–4).

d. (1) At the request of the Public Defender, the Clerk of the Superior Court shall refer every unsatisfied lien, filed by the Public Defender, to the comprehensive enforcement program for collection. All monies collected through the comprehensive enforcement program which result from the collection of these liens shall be subject to the deduction authorized pursuant to section 4 of P.L.1995, c. 9 (C.2B:19–4).

(2) Upon satisfaction of a public defender lien through the comprehensive enforcement program, the comprehensive enforcement program shall notify the Clerk of the Superior Court within 10 days of satisfaction and the satisfaction of the lien shall be entered in the Superior Court Judgment Index.

L.1995, c. 9, § 6, eff. Jan. 12, 1995. Amended by L.1997, c. 280, § 3, eff. April 6, 1998; L.2000, c. 120, § 3; L.2001, c. 421, § 2, eff. Jan. 8, 2002; L.2009, c. 233, § 1, eff. Jan. 16, 2010.

2B:19–7. Transfer of community service matters to comprehensive enforcement program for compliance sanctions

All matters involving the imposition of a sentence of community service by either the Superior Court or a municipal court which have not been complied with by the offender shall be transferred, by the sentencing judge to the comprehensive enforcement program for such suitable compliance sanctions as may be appropriate, including incarceration, participation in a labor assistance program, enforced community service, imposition of a financial sanction, or a combination of these sanctions or such other alternative as may be appropriate.

L.1995, c. 9, § 7, eff. Jan. 12, 1995.

2B:19–8. Alternatives to payment of remaining court ordered financial obligation; labor assistance program; enforced community service; term of imprisonment

a. At any time after a person has completed the total sentence to a labor assistance program or enforced community service program, the comprehensive enforcement hearing officer may determine that the payor is financially unable to comply with the financial obligations initially imposed by the sentencing court. The comprehensive enforcement hearing officer may then:

(1) Accept the participation in a labor assistance program or enforced community service in lieu of payment of the remaining court ordered financial obligations;

(2) Impose additional hours in a labor assistance program or enforced community service in lieu of payment of the remaining court ordered financial obligations;

(3) Impose a term of imprisonment in lieu of paying the remaining court ordered financial obligations; or

(4) Docket the total amount due as a judgment in the Superior Court.

b. When the comprehensive enforcement hearing officer has exhausted all of the steps enumerated in this section and any additional hours of a labor assistance program or enforced community service or any term of imprisonment have been completed, the person may be terminated from probation supervision and the total amount owed may be removed from probation records and deducted from outstanding and uncollectable amounts owed. These actions notwithstanding, whenever a judgment is docketed in the Superior Court, the person remains liable to pay the outstanding debt as originally imposed by the sentencing court.

c. Notwithstanding the foregoing, the comprehensive enforcement hearing officer may not relieve the person of the obligation to pay the VCCB assessment or restitution to a victim.

L.1995, c. 9, § 8, eff. Jan. 12, 1995.

2B:19–9. Recommendation of hearing officers to conform to court rules; approval by superior court judge required

Any recommendation by a comprehensive enforcement hearing officer shall be in conformity with court rules and shall be approved by:

a. a judge of the Superior Court for Superior Court matters and for any municipal court matters in which a final judgment has been docketed in the Superior Court; or

b. a judge of the municipal court, designated by the Assignment Judge of the vicinage, for municipal court matters in which a final judgment has not been docketed with the Superior Court.

L.1995, c. 9, § 9, eff. Jan. 12, 1995. Amended by L.2001, c. 421, § 3, eff. Jan. 8, 2002.

2B:19–10. Referral of uncollected surcharges to the comprehensive enforcement program; development of procedures

The Director of the Division of Motor Vehicles and the Administrative Office of the Courts shall develop procedures for the referral of uncollected surcharges imposed administratively by the Division of Motor Vehicles under the New Jersey Merit Rating Plan pursuant to section 6 of P.L.1983, c. 65 (C.17:29A–35). These procedures shall include, but shall not be limited to, the following:

a. The total dollar amount of uncollected surcharges imposed on a driver and the number of months of delinquency which may result in referral pursuant to section 6 of P.L.1995, c. 9 (C.2B:19–6) including procedures for installment payments, procedures for negotiating and implementing new schedules for installment payments and surcharges deferred until the end of a policy term of an automobile insurance policy as permitted by section 6 of P.L.1983, c. 65 (C.17:29A–35);

b. The interval of referral between the Division of Motor Vehicles and the comprehensive enforcement program such as monthly, quarterly or semi-annually and the method of referral such as through the municipal court where the Title 39 violation occurred or directly to the Superior Court;

c. The form of notice to be provided by the Division of Motor Vehicles when a surcharge is imposed indicat-

ing that an unpaid surcharge may be referred to the comprehensive enforcement program; and

d. Procedures for payment to the Division of Motor Vehicles of moneys collected and the billing and accounting methods to be used.

L.1997, c. 280, § 4, eff. Jan. 6, 1998.

2B:19–11. Additional duties

In addition to the duties set forth in P.L.1995, c. 9 (C.2B:19–1 et seq.), the comprehensive enforcement program shall provide for the collection of moneys due the State by way of reimbursement for services rendered by the Public Defender and filed as liens in the Office of the Clerk of the Superior Court.

L.2000, c. 120, § 4, eff. Dec. 13, 2000.

CHAPTER 20

QUALIFICATION AND SELECTION OF JURORS

Section
2B:20–1. Qualifications of jurors.
2B:20–2. Preparation of juror source list.
2B:20–3. Questionnaires concerning qualifications.
2B:20–4. Public and random selection of jurors.
2B:20–5. Certification, filing and posting of juror lists.
2B:20–6. Designation of period of service for petit jury panels.
2B:20–7. Summoning of jurors.
2B:20–8. Form and service of summons.
2B:20–9. Excuses and deferrals by Assignment Judge.
2B:20–10. Grounds for excuse from jury service.
2B:20–11. Deferral of jury service.
2B:20–12. Retention of records.
2B:20–13. Discharge of unneeded jurors.
2B:20–14. Failure to respond to questionnaire or summons.
2B:20–15. Notice and collection of fines.
2B:20–16. Excuse from employment for jury duty; compensation.
2B:20–17. Employment protection.
2B:20–18. Oath of allegiance.

2B:20–1. Qualifications of jurors

Every person summoned as a juror:

a. shall be 18 years of age or older;

b. shall be able to read and understand the English language;

c. shall be a citizen of the United States;

d. shall be a resident of the county in which the person is summoned;

e. shall not have been convicted of any indictable offense under the laws of this State, another state, or the United States;

f. shall not have any mental or physical disability which will prevent the person from properly serving as a juror.

L.1995, c. 44, § 1, eff. June 5, 1995. Amended by L.1997, c. 127, § 1, eff. June 23, 1997.

2B:20–2. Preparation of juror source list

a. The names of persons eligible for jury service shall be selected from a single juror source list of county residents whose names and addresses shall be obtained from a merger of the following lists: registered voters, licensed drivers, filers of State gross income tax returns and filers of homestead rebate or credit application forms. The county election board, the Division of Motor Vehicles and the State Division of Taxation shall provide these lists annually to the Assignment Judge of the county. The Assignment Judge may provide for the merger of additional lists of persons eligible for jury service that may contribute to the breadth of the juror source list. Merger of the lists of eligible jurors into a single juror source list shall include a reasonable attempt to eliminate duplication of names.

b. The juror source list shall be compiled once a year or more often as directed by the Assignment Judge.

c. The juror source list may be expanded by the Supreme Court as it deems appropriate.

L.1995, c. 44, § 1, eff. Jan. 1, 1995. Amended by L.2007, c. 62, § 41, eff. April 3, 2007.

2B:20–3. Questionnaires concerning qualifications

a. The Assignment Judge may direct that questionnaires be sent to potential jurors, requesting that they provide pertinent information concerning their qualifications for jury service, and any claims for exemption or deferral.

b. Questionnaires may be sent to all persons on the juror source list, or to persons randomly selected from the juror source list, either before or with the service of a summons for jury service.

L.1995, c. 44, § 1, eff. June 5, 1995.

2B:20–4. Public and random selection of jurors

a. Before each session of the Superior Court, the Assignment Judge shall provide for the drawing of names from the juror source list of persons to be summoned for service as grand and petit jurors.

b. The Assignment Judge shall specify the number of panels of grand and petit jurors to be drawn, the number of names to be drawn for each panel and the form and manner of preparation of the lists of names drawn. The lists shall state the name and address and, if available, occupation of each juror to be summoned.

c. The Assignment Judge shall provide for the selection of additional panels of grand and petit jurors from the juror source list at any time when it appears that additional panels of jurors will be required.

d. Both the drawing of names and the assignment of selected names to panels shall be public and random.

e. The Assignment Judge may provide for the random selection of jurors, and their assignment to panels, by the use of electronic devices, if:

(1) the method of random selection is specified with particularity in the instructions of the assignment judge; and

(2) the specification of the method and any programs and procedures used to implement the method, including any computer programs which are utilized, are available for public inspection upon request.

L.1995, c. 44, § 1, eff. June 5, 1995.

2B:20–5. Certification, filing and posting of juror lists

The list of names randomly selected from the juror source list shall be filed and publicly posted in the office of the County Clerk. The Assignment Judge shall certify on the list that the process specified for the selection of jurors and their assignment to panels has been followed.

L.1995, c. 44, § 1, eff. June 5, 1995.

2B:20–6. Designation of period of service for petit jury panels

a. The Assignment Judge shall designate the period of service of each panel of jurors selected from the juror source list.

b. A panel of jurors may be designated to serve during a portion of the then current session of the Superior Court, or during a portion of the next session of the Superior Court.

L.1995, c. 44, § 1, eff. June 5, 1995.

2B:20–7. Summoning of jurors

a. Upon receipt of a list of persons selected to serve on a panel of jurors, the sheriff shall, under the direction of the Assignment Judge, cause the persons to be summoned.

b. The sheriff shall make a return to the Assignment Judge of all of the jurors summoned.

L.1995, c. 44, § 1, eff. June 5, 1995.

2B:20–8. Form and service of summons

a. The summons for jury service shall be by written notice and shall state the date, time and place where the juror is to appear for service.

b. The summons shall be served at least 30 days prior to the date upon which the juror is to appear, by regular mail addressed to the juror's usual residence or business address unless service at another address is ordered by the Assignment Judge. Service of the summons shall be complete upon mailing.

c. If a sufficient number of jurors is unavailable due to a successful challenge or other unanticipated occurrence and new panels of jurors must be selected from the juror source list, the Assignment Judge may direct that the summons be served less than 30 days prior to the date upon which the jurors are to appear.

L.1995, c. 44, § 1, eff. June 5, 1995.

2B:20–9. Excuses and deferrals by Assignment Judge

a. A person may be excused from jury service or may have jury service deferred only by the Assignment Judge of the county in which the person was summoned, or by the Assignment Judge's designee.

b. The Assignment Judge may require verification of any of the facts supporting the grounds for a request for excuse or deferral. Records shall be kept of all requests for excuses and deferrals, and of the granting of excuses and deferrals.

L.1995, c. 44, § 1, eff. June 5, 1995.

2B:20–10. Grounds for excuse from jury service

An excuse from jury service shall be granted only if:

a. The prospective juror is 75 years of age or older;

b. The prospective juror has served as a juror within the last three years in the county to which the juror is being summoned;

c. Jury service will impose a severe hardship due to circumstances which are not likely to change within the following year. Severe hardship includes the following circumstances:

(1) The prospective juror has a medical inability to serve which is verified by a licensed physician.

(2) The prospective juror will suffer a severe financial hardship which will compromise the juror's ability to support himself, herself, or dependents. In determining whether to excuse the prospective juror, the Assignment Judge shall consider:

(a) the sources of the prospective juror's household income; and

(b) the availability and extent of income reimbursement; and

(c) the expected length of service.

(3) The prospective juror has a personal obligation to care for another, including a sick, aged or infirm dependent or a minor child, who requires the prospective juror's personal care and attention, and no alternative care is available without severe financial hardship on the prospective juror or the person requiring care.

(4) The prospective juror provides highly specialized technical health care services for which replacement cannot reasonably be obtained.

(5) The prospective juror is a health care worker directly involved in the care of a mentally or physically handicapped person, and the prospective juror's continued presence is essential to the regular and personal treatment of that person.

(6) The prospective juror is a member of the full-time instructional staff of a grammar school or high school, the scheduled jury service is during the school term, and a replacement cannot reasonably be obtained. In determining whether to excuse the prospective juror or grant a deferral of service, the Assignment Judge shall consider:

(a) the impact on the school considering the number and function of teachers called for jury service during the current academic year; and

(b) the special role of certified special education teachers in providing continuity of instruction to handicapped students;

d. The prospective juror is a member of a volunteer fire department or fire patrol; or

e. The prospective juror is a volunteer member of a first aid or rescue squad.

L.1995, c. 44, § 1, eff. June 5, 1995.

2B:20–11. Deferral of jury service

Upon a request for deferral of jury service or upon the denial of a request for an excuse from jury service, the Assignment Judge may direct that the jury service of a prospective juror be deferred to another time within the next twelve months.

L.1995, c. 44, § 1, eff. June 5, 1995.

2B:20–12. Retention of records

All records concerning the granting of excuses from and deferrals of jury service, and all juror questionnaires, shall be retained for a period of three years. All other records relating to the summoning, impaneling and charging of jurors shall be retained for five years.

L.1995, c. 44, § 1, eff. June 5, 1995.

2B:20–13. Discharge of unneeded jurors

If the number of jurors in attendance is greater than is necessary for the business of the court, the Assignment Judge may discharge the unneeded jurors before the expiration of the period for which they were summoned. The jurors discharged shall be selected randomly.

L.1995, c. 44, § 1, eff. June 5, 1995.

2B:20–14. Failure to respond to questionnaire or summons

a. Persons who are sent questionnaires concerning their qualifications for jury service who fail to respond to the questionnaire without reasonable excuse shall be liable for a fine not to exceed $500, payable to the county from which the questionnaire was sent, or may be punished for contempt of court.

b. Persons summoned as jurors who, without reasonable excuse, either fail to appear for jury service or refuse to serve, shall be liable for a fine not to exceed

$500, payable to the county in which the person was summoned, or may be punished for contempt of court.

L.1995, c. 44, § 1, eff. June 5, 1995.

2B:20–15. Notice and collection of fines

a. The Assignment Judge may direct the sheriff to send written notice to a person who has failed to respond to a questionnaire concerning jury service, or who has failed to appear for jury service or has refused to serve, that a fine has been imposed. The notice shall state the amount of the fine, the manner of payment to be made to the sheriff, and the consequences of failure to pay the fine within 30 days of the date specified in the notice. The notice shall be served in the same manner as a summons.

b. If a defaulting juror fails to pay the fine in response to the notice, the Assignment Judge may issue process directing the sheriff to recover the fine and costs by levy on the defaulting juror's personal property.

L.1995, c. 44, § 1, eff. June 5, 1995.

2B:20–16. Excuse from employment for jury duty; compensation.

Any person employed full-time by any agency, independent authority, instrumentality or entity of the State or of any political subdivision of the State shall be excused from employment at all times the person is required to be present for jury service in any court of this State, any court of another state, or any federal district court or in the United States District Court for New Jersey, and shall be entitled to receive from the employer the person's usual compensation for each day the person is present for jury service in lieu of any payment for juror service as provided in P.L.1993, c. 275 (C.22A:1–1.1).

L.1995, c. 44, § 1, eff. June 5, 1995. Amended by L.2001, c. 38, § 2, eff. March 23, 2001.

2B:20–17. Employment protection

a. An employer shall not penalize an employee with respect to employment, or threaten or otherwise coerce an employee with respect to that employment, because the employee is required to attend court for jury service.

b. An employer who violates subsection a. of this section is guilty of a disorderly persons offense.

c. If an employer penalizes an employee in violation of subsection a. of this section, the employee may bring a civil action for economic damages suffered as a result of the violation and for an order requiring the reinstatement of the employee. The action shall be commenced within 90 days from the date of the violation or the completion of jury service, whichever is later. If the employee prevails, the employee shall be entitled to a reasonable attorney's fee fixed by the court.

L.1995, c. 44, § 1, eff. June 5, 1995.

2B:20–18. Oath of allegiance

The following oath shall be administered to every person summoned for service as a juror who is not excused from service, before beginning service upon the panel:

"Do you swear or affirm that you will support the Constitution of the United States and the Constitution of this State?"

L.1995, c. 44, § 1, eff. June 5, 1995.

CHAPTER 21

COUNTY GRAND JURIES

Section
2B:21–1.   Number of grand juries.
2B:21–2.   Impaneling grand jury.
2B:21–3.   Oath of grand jurors.
2B:21–4.   Vacancies in grand jury.
2B:21–5.   Selection of foreperson and deputy foreperson.
2B:21–6.   Swearing of witnesses by foreperson.
2B:21–7.   Indictment.
2B:21–8.   Record of proceedings.
2B:21–9.   Statement of investigation.
2B:21–10.   Unauthorized disclosure of grand jury proceedings.

2B:21–1. Number of grand juries

The Assignment Judge for each county shall impanel one or more grand juries for that county, as the public interest requires. There shall be at least one grand jury serving in each county at all times.

L.1995, c. 44, § 1, eff. June 5, 1995.

2B:21–2. Impaneling grand jury

a. A grand jury shall consist of not more than 23 persons selected from the panel of jurors summoned for service as grand jurors. The grand jurors shall be selected publicly and randomly, in the same manner as is provided by statute for the impaneling of petit jurors.

b. The Assignment Judge, or a Superior Court judge designated by the Assignment Judge, shall conduct the voir dire of members of the grand jury panel and shall decide all requests for excuse or deferral of service on the grand jury.

c. The Assignment Judge, or a Superior Court judge designated by the Assignment Judge, shall excuse any person from service on the grand jury if the person is a federal, State or local government police officer or prosecutor.

d. The prosecutor may object to the selection of any person as a grand juror on the basis of the person's inability to be impartial or on the grounds that the person does not meet the qualifications specified in N.J.S. 2B:20–1. The objections by the prosecutor shall be made on the record and shall be decided by the Assignment Judge.

L.1995, c. 44, § 1, eff. June 5, 1995.

2B:21–3. Oath of grand jurors

The following oath shall be administered to all of the members of the grand jury:

"Do you as a member of this grand jury of the State of New Jersey and county of (county) swear or affirm that you will support the Constitution of the United States and the Constitution of this State; that you will diligently inquire into all matters brought before you to the best of your skill, knowledge and understanding; that you will take no action through envy, hatred or malice nor for fear, favor or affection, or for reward or the hope of reward; that you will make a true present-ment of all matters coming before you, and that you will keep secret the proceedings of the grand jury?"

L.1995, c. 44, § 1, eff. June 5, 1995.

2B:21–4. Vacancies in grand jury

A grand juror who becomes ill, dies or does not appear for service after having been sworn may be replaced at the direction of the Assignment Judge. The replacement grand juror shall be selected publicly and randomly and shall be sworn in the same manner as the grand juror being replaced.

L.1995, c. 44, § 1, eff. June 5, 1995.

2B:21–5. Selection of foreperson and deputy fore-person

The foreperson and the deputy foreperson of each grand jury shall be selected publicly and randomly from the persons impanelled as members of the grand jury. A person selected as the foreperson or deputy fore-person may freely decline to serve in the position, in which case another person shall be selected publicly and randomly to serve.

L.1995, c. 44, § 1, eff. June 5, 1995.

2B:21–6. Swearing of witnesses by foreperson

a. The foreperson of the grand jury shall administer the following oath to witnesses who give evidence before the grand jury:

"Do you swear or affirm that you will tell the truth, the whole truth, and nothing but the truth?"

b. The foreperson shall, before being discharged, certify to the court the names of the witnesses who have been sworn.

L.1995, c. 44, § 1, eff. June 5, 1995.

2B:21–7. Indictment

An indictment may be found only upon concurrence of 12 or more grand jurors who either were present during, or who have read or listened to the record of, all of the proceedings concerning the indictment and who have examined all exhibits presented with respect to the indictment.

L.1995, c. 44, § 1, eff. June 5, 1995.

2B:21–8. Record of proceedings

The testimony of witnesses, comments by the prose-cuting attorney, and colloquy between the prosecuting attorney and witnesses or members of the grand jury shall be recorded stenographically or electronically.

L.1995, c. 44, § 1, eff. June 5, 1995.

2B:21–9. Statement of investigation

a. A person who has been investigated by a grand jury and against whom no indictment has been returned, may request the grand jury to issue a statement indicating that a charge against the person was investi-gated and that the grand jury did not return an indictment from the evidence presented. The grand jury shall issue the statement upon the approval of the court which summoned the grand jury. The statement shall issue upon the completion of the investigation of the charge, but not beyond the end of the grand jury's term.

b. A person who has been called to appear before a grand jury for a purpose other than the investigation of a charge against the person, may request the grand jury to issue a statement indicating that the person was called only as a witness in an investigation, and that the investigation did not involve a charge against the person. The grand jury shall issue the statement upon the approval of the court which summoned the grand jury. The statement shall issue upon the completion of the investigation of the charge or a series of related charges, but not beyond the end of the grand jury's term.

L.1995, c. 44, § 1, eff. June 5, 1995.

2B:21–10. Unauthorized disclosure of grand jury pro-ceedings

a. Any person who, with the intent to injure anoth-er, purposely discloses any information concerning the proceedings of a grand jury, other than as authorized or required by law, commits a crime of the fourth degree. A public officer or employee who is convicted of a violation of this subsection shall be dismissed from public office or employment.

b. A person injured as a result of a violation of subsection a. of this section may bring a civil action against the person convicted of the violation. The person convicted shall be liable to the person injured for actual damages, punitive damages of not less than $1,000.00 or more than $100,000.00, reasonable litiga-tion costs and reasonable attorney fees.

L.1995, c. 44, § 1, eff. June 5, 1995.

CHAPTER 22

STATE GRAND JURIES

Section
2B:22–1. Impaneling State grand jury.
2B:22–2. Powers and duties of State grand jury.

Section
2B:22–3.   Selection of State grand jurors.
2B:22–4.   Summoning of State grand jurors.
2B:22–5.   Judicial supervision of State grand jury.
2B:22–6.   Presentation of evidence to State grand jury.
2B:22–7.   Return of indictment or presentment.
2B:22–8.   Expenses of State grand jury.
2B:22–9.   Instruction to grand jury; use of force by law
            enforcement officer.

2B:22–1.   Impaneling State grand jury

a.   There shall be at least one State grand jury with jurisdiction extending throughout the State serving at all times.

b.   The State grand jury shall be impaneled by a judge of the Superior Court designated for that purpose by the Chief Justice.

c.   The Attorney General or the Director of the Division of Criminal Justice may, when they determine it to be in the public interest, apply in writing to the designated judge requesting that one or more additional State grand juries be impaneled.   The judge may, for good cause shown, order the impaneling of additional State grand juries.

L.1995, c. 44, § 1, eff. June 5, 1995.

2B:22–2.   Powers and duties of State grand jury

a.   A State grand jury shall have the same powers and duties and shall function in the same manner as a county grand jury except that its jurisdiction shall extend throughout the State.   The law applicable to county grand juries shall apply to State grand juries to the extent that it is consistent with the specific provisions relating to State grand juries.

b.   The Supreme Court may promulgate rules to govern particularly the procedures of State grand juries.

L.1995, c. 44, § 1, eff. June 5, 1995.

2B:22–3.   Selection of State grand jurors

a.   The Administrative Director of the Courts, upon receipt of an order directing the impaneling of a State grand jury, shall prepare a list of prospective jurors randomly drawn from the current jurors lists of the several counties.   The list of prospective State grand jurors prepared by the Administrative Director of the Courts shall contain numbers of prospective jurors from each county in the same relative proportion as the population of each county bears to the total population of the State.

b.   The designated judge shall impanel a State grand jury from the prospective jurors on the list.   The selection of jurors for service on the State grand jury shall be public and random.

L.1995, c. 44, § 1, eff. June 5, 1995.

2B:22–4.   Summoning of State grand jurors

The Administrative Director of the Courts shall transmit the names of the prospective jurors selected for service on the State grand jury to the sheriffs of the counties in which the prospective jurors reside.   The sheriffs of the respective counties shall cause the prospective jurors resident in their counties to be summoned for service on the State grand jury.

L.1995, c. 44, § 1, eff. June 5, 1995.

2B:22–5.   Judicial supervision of State grand jury

The judge designated by the Chief Justice shall maintain judicial supervision over the grand jury.   All indictments, presentments and formal returns of any kind made by a State grand jury shall be returned to the designated judge.

L.1995, c. 44, § 1, eff. June 5, 1995.

2B:22–6.   Presentation of evidence to State grand jury

The Attorney General or the designee of the Attorney General shall present evidence to the State grand jury.

L.1995, c. 44, § 1, eff. June 5, 1995.

2B:22–7.   Return of indictment or presentment

The judge who issues an order impaneling a State grand jury shall designate the county of venue for the purpose of trial of an indictment returned by the State grand jury.   The judge may direct the consolidation of an indictment returned by a county grand jury with an indictment returned by a State grand jury and may fix the venue for trial of both indictments.

L.1995, c. 44, § 1, eff. June 5, 1995.

2B:22–8.   Expenses of State grand jury

a.   The State shall pay the expenses of impaneling and operating a State grand jury out of funds appropriated for this purpose to the Division of Criminal Justice in the Department of Law and Public Safety.

b.   The expenses incurred by a county for the prosecution and trial of a State grand jury indictment shall be paid by the State out of funds appropriated for this purpose to the Division of Criminal Justice in the Department of Law and Public Safety.   The county treasurer shall make application for payment of the expenses to the Assignment Judge of the county, and the Assignment Judge shall fix and certify the amount of the expenses.

L.1995, c. 44, § 1, eff. June 5, 1995.

2B:22–9.   Instruction to grand jury; use of force by law enforcement officer

a.   In a grand jury proceeding where the use of force by a law enforcement officer has been introduced as an issue, the prosecutor shall instruct the grand jury in the elements of justification for the use of force in law enforcement   pursuant   to   N.J.S.2C:3–7   and N.J.S.2C:3–9.

b.   The prosecutor shall specifically charge the grand jury as follows:

(1) Subject to the limitations set out below, the use of force upon or toward the person of another is justifiable when a law enforcement officer is making an arrest or assisting in making an arrest and the officer reasonably believes that such force is immediately necessary to effect a lawful arrest.

(2) The use of force is not justifiable unless:

(a) The officer makes known the purpose of the arrest or reasonably believes that it is otherwise known by or cannot reasonably be made known to the person to be arrested; and

(b) When the arrest is made under a warrant, the warrant is valid or reasonably believed by the officer to be valid.

(3) The use of deadly force is not justifiable unless:

(a) The officer effecting the arrest is authorized to act as a law enforcement officer; and

(b) The officer reasonably believes that the force employed creates no substantial risk of injury to innocent persons; and

(c) The officer reasonably believes that the crime for which the arrest is made was homicide, kidnapping, an offense under N.J.S.2C:14–2 or N.J.S.2C:14–3, arson, robbery, burglary of a dwelling, or an attempt to commit one of these crimes; and

(d) the officer reasonably believes:

(i) There is an imminent threat of deadly force to himself or to a third party; or

(ii) The use of deadly force is necessary to thwart the commission of a crime as set forth in subparagraph (c) of this paragraph; or

(iii) The use of deadly force is necessary to prevent an escape.

(4) The use of force to prevent the escape of an arrested person from custody is justifiable when the force could have been employed to effect the arrest under which the person is in custody under the provisions of this act. A correction officer or other person authorized to act as a law enforcement officer is, however, justified in using any force including deadly force, which he reasonably believes to be immediately necessary to prevent the escape of a person committed to a jail, prison, or other institution for the detention of persons charged with or convicted of an offense so long as the actor believes that the force employed creates no substantial risk of injury to innocent persons.

(5) The justification for the use of force afforded by this act is unavailable when:

(a) The officer's belief in the unlawfulness of the force or conduct against which he employs protective force or his belief in the lawfulness of an arrest which he endeavors to effect by force is erroneous; and

(b) His error is due to ignorance or mistake as to the provisions of the code, any other provisions of the criminal law or the law governing the legality of an arrest or search.

c. When the officer is justified under N.J.S.2C:3–3 to 2C:3–8 in using force upon or toward the person of another but he recklessly or negligently injures or creates a risk of injury to innocent persons, the justification afforded by those sections is unavailable in a prosecution for such recklessness or negligence towards innocent persons.

L.2001, c. 381, § 1, eff. Jan. 8, 2002.

CHAPTER 23

PETIT JURORS

Section
2B:23–1. Number of jurors.
2B:23–2. Selection of trial jury from panel.
2B:23–3. Impaneling of additional jurors.
2B:23–4. Names of selected trial jurors.
2B:23–5. Names of jurors drawn for trial jury replace in pool.
2B:23–6. Oath of jurors.
2B:23–7. Oath of officer attending jury.
2B:23–8. Jurors to serve beyond period for which drawn until completion of trial.
2B:23–9. Juries drawn from other counties.
2B:23–10. Examination of jurors.
2B:23–11. Challenge to qualifications of jurors.
2B:23–12. Interest in action by or against county or municipality.
2B:23–13. Peremptory challenges.
2B:23–14. Trial of challenges to jurors.
2B:23–15. Time for making challenges.
2B:23–16. Jury of view.
2B:23–17. Verdict by five-sixths of the jury.
2B:23–18. Disagreement of jurors.

2B:23–1. Number of jurors

a. Juries in criminal cases shall consist of 12 persons. Except in trials of crimes punishable by death, the parties in criminal cases may stipulate in writing, before the verdict and with court approval, that the jury shall consist of fewer than 12 persons.

b. Juries in civil cases shall consist of 6 persons unless the court shall order a jury of 12 persons for good cause shown.

L.1995, c. 44, § 1, eff. June 5, 1995.

2B:23–2. Selection of trial jury from panel

a. When a jury is required for trial, the names or identifying numbers of the jurors who constitute the panel or panels from which the jury is to be selected shall be placed on uniform pieces of paper or other uniform markers. The markers shall be deposited in a box.

b. The box containing the markers shall be shaken so as to mix the markers thoroughly and the officer designated by the court shall, at the direction of the court, publicly in open court, draw the markers from the box, one at a time, until the necessary number of persons is randomly selected. If any of the persons so selected is successfully challenged or excused from serving on that jury, the drawing shall be continued until the necessary number of persons is selected.

c. The Assignment Judge of the county may provide for the random selection of jurors for impaneling by the use of electronic or electro-mechanical devices, if:

(1) the method of random selection is specified with particularity in an order of the Assignment Judge; and

(2) the specification of the method and any programs and procedures used to implement the method, including the relevant computer programs or portions of computer programs which are utilized, are available for public inspection upon request.

L.1995, c. 44, § 1, eff. June 5, 1995.

2B:23–3.   Impaneling of additional jurors

The court may direct the impaneling of a jury with additional members having the same qualifications and impaneled and sworn in the same manner as a jury of 12 or 6. All the jurors shall hear the case, but the court for good cause may excuse any of them from service provided the number of jurors is not reduced to less than 12 or 6 in an appropriate civil case. If more than the prescribed number are left on the jury at the conclusion of the court's charge, the clerk of the court in its presence shall, by drawing names, randomly select that number of jurors' names as will reduce the jury to the required number.

L.1995, c. 44, § 1, eff. June 5, 1995.

2B:23–4.   Names of selected trial jurors

The names of the jurors selected and sworn to try a case shall be made a part of the record of the case.

L.1995, c. 44, § 1, eff. June 5, 1995.

2B:23–5.   Names of jurors drawn for trial jury replace in pool

After a jury has been selected and sworn, the names or identifying numbers of jurors not sworn to try the case shall be returned to the general pool of eligible jurors before the drawing of another jury. The names or identifying numbers of those jurors shall be returned to the general pool of eligible jurors unless the Assignment Judge directs otherwise.

L.1995, c. 44, § 1, eff. June 5, 1995.

2B:23–6.   Oath of jurors

The following oath shall be administered to each juror:

"Do you swear or affirm that you will try the matter in dispute and give a true verdict according to the evidence?"

L.1995, c. 44, § 1, eff. June 5, 1995.

2B:23–7.   Oath of officer attending jury

The following oath shall be administered to the officer appointed to attend the jury:

"Do you swear or affirm that you will do your best to keep every person sworn on this jury together in a private place, and that you will not allow any person to speak to them, nor speak to them yourself, except by order of the court, and except to ask them if they have agreed on a verdict, until they have so agreed?"

L.1995, c. 44, § 1, eff. June 5, 1995.

2B:23–8.   Jurors to serve beyond period for which drawn until completion of trial

When a jury does not complete its trial service during the session for which its members are to serve as jurors, the court may order that the jury shall serve until the completion of the trial even though such trial may extend into the next session or sessions.

L.1995, c. 44, § 1, eff. June 5, 1995.

2B:23–9.   Juries drawn from other counties

a. When a court orders a trial by a jury drawn from outside the county in which the court is sitting, the order shall specify the number of jurors to be returned and shall be directed, and made returnable, to the sheriff of the county from which the jury is to be taken. The jurors shall be competent jurors in the county from which they are to be taken and shall be selected in the same manner as the general panel of jurors is selected.

b. The county in which the trial will be held shall pay the expense of summoning and returning the jurors and of their attendance at the court.

L.1995, c. 44, § 1, eff. June 5, 1995.

2B:23–10.   Examination of jurors

a. In the discretion of the court, parties to any trial may question any person summoned as a juror after the name is drawn and before the swearing, and without the interposition of any challenge, to determine whether or not to interpose a peremptory challenge or a challenge for cause. Such examination shall be permitted in order to disclose whether or not the juror is qualified, impartial and without interest in the result of the action. The questioning shall be conducted in open court under the trial judge's supervision.

b. (Deleted by amendment, P.L.2007, c. 204).

L.1995, c. 44, § 1, eff. June 5, 1995. Amended by L.2007, c. 204, § 4, eff. Dec. 17, 2007.

2B:23–11.   Challenge to qualifications of jurors

It shall be good cause for challenge to any person summoned as a juror that the person does not possess the qualifications required by N.J.S. 2B:20–1 or that the person's name does not appear on the jury lists prepared pursuant to N.J.S. 2B:20–4. If the challenge is verified according to law or on the person's oath the person shall be discharged.

L.1995, c. 44, § 1, eff. June 5, 1995.

2B:23–12. Interest in action by or against county or municipality

In an action in which a county or municipality is or may be a party or otherwise has an interest in the action, it shall not be a ground for challenge to the jury panel that the court officers, court employees or jurors, solely because they are inhabitants of the county or municipality, are interested in the action or are taxed in the county.

L.1995, c. 44, § 1, eff. June 5, 1995.

2B:23–13. Peremptory challenges

Upon the trial of any action in any court of this State, the parties shall be entitled to peremptory challenges as follows:

a. In any civil action, each party, 6.

b. Upon an indictment for kidnapping, murder, aggravated manslaughter, manslaughter, aggravated assault, aggravated sexual assault, sexual assault, aggravated criminal sexual contact, aggravated arson, arson, burglary, robbery, forgery if it constitutes a crime of the third degree as defined by subsection b. of N.J.S.2C:21–1, or perjury, the defendant, 20 peremptory challenges if tried alone and 10 challenges if tried jointly and the State, 12 peremptory challenges if the defendant is tried alone and 6 peremptory challenges for each 10 afforded the defendants if tried jointly.

c. Upon any other indictment, defendants, 10 each; the State, 10 peremptory challenges for each 10 challenges allowed to the defendants. When the case is to be tried by a jury from another county, each defendant, 5 peremptory challenges, and the State, 5 peremptory challenges for each 5 peremptory challenges afforded the defendants.

L.1995, c. 44, § 1, eff. June 5, 1995. Amended by L.2007, c. 204, § 5, eff. Dec. 17, 2007.

2B:23–14. Trial of challenges to jurors

All challenges to panels of jurors or to individual jurors shall be decided by the court.

L.1995, c. 44, § 1, eff. June 5, 1995.

2B:23–15. Time for making challenges

a. Challenges to jurors may be made at any time before the juror is sworn to try the case.

b. No challenge to a juror may be made after the juror is sworn to try the case unless:

(1) the basis for the challenge could not reasonably have been known earlier to the person making the challenge; and

(2) the challenge is based upon the juror's inability to render a fair and impartial verdict.

L.1995, c. 44, § 1, eff. June 5, 1995.

2B:23–16. Jury of view

a. At any time during trial the court may order that the jury view the lands, places or personal property in question to understand the evidence better. The court shall direct the viewing procedure. The order shall be directed to the proper officer, specifying the day and place in question. Neither side shall give evidence when the jury is viewing. The officer who executes the order shall, by a special return, certify that the view has occurred according to the order.

b. In a civil case, the court shall determine which party shall bear the expense of a view.

c. The trial shall proceed even though a view which was ordered has not taken place.

L.1995, c. 44, § 1, eff. June 5, 1995.

2B:23–17. Verdict by five-sixths of the jury

In any civil trial by jury, at least five-sixths of the jurors shall render the verdict unless the parties stipulate that a smaller majority of jurors may render the verdict.

L.1995, c. 44, § 1, eff. June 5, 1995.

2B:23–18. Disagreement of jurors

If the jury does not agree on a verdict, the court may order a new trial.

L.1995, c. 44, § 1, eff. June 5, 1995.

CHAPTER 25

MUNICIPAL PROSECUTORS

Section
2B:25–1. Legislative findings.
2B:25–2. Definitions.
2B:25–3. Municipal prosecutors; exempt.
2B:25–4. Municipal courts; appointment of at least one municipal prosecutor.
2B:25–5. Municipal prosecutors; duties.
2B:25–5.1. Driving record abstract request.
2B:25–6. Appointments to fill vacancies.
2B:25–7. Attorney General or county prosecutor; superceding or intervening.
2B:25–8. Attorney General or county prosecutor; prosecution in municipal court; reimbursement for costs.
2B:25–9. Removal of municipal prosecutor.
2B:25–10. Curricula for training.
2B:25–11. Plea agreements.
2B:25–12. Amending original charge.

2B:25–1. Legislative findings

The Legislature finds and declares that municipal prosecutors are a critical component of New Jersey's system for the administration of justice, that the role of municipal prosecutor is not statutorily defined, and that in order to ensure the uniform and proper administration of justice in this State, it is necessary to define the duties of municipal prosecutors.

L.1999, c. 349, § 1, eff. April 13, 2000.

2B:25–2. Definitions

As used in this act:

a. "Municipal prosecutor" means a person appointed to prosecute all offenses over which the municipal court has jurisdiction.

b. "Governing body" of a county or municipality means the officer or body that is the appropriate appointing authority for county counsel, municipal attorney or corporation counsel under the laws applicable to the form of county or municipal government established in the county or municipality pursuant to law, provided that the municipal corporation counsel shall be the appointing authority in any city of the first class with a population greater than 270,000, according to the latest federal decennial census and in any city of the second class with a population of greater than 30,000 but less than 43,000, according to the latest decennial census, which city of the second class is located in a county of the first class with a population less than 600,000 according to the latest federal decennial census.

c. "Municipal court" means any municipal or joint municipal or central municipal court established pursuant to statute.

d. "Attorney General" includes the Attorney General of New Jersey and any assistants or deputies who may be designated to carry out the responsibilities conferred on the Attorney General by this act or the laws of this State.

e. "County prosecutor" shall mean the prosecutor of the county in which the municipal court is situated and any assistant prosecutors of that county who may be designated by this act.

L.1999, c. 349, § 2, eff. April 13, 2000.

2B:25–3. Municipal prosecutors; exempt

Any person serving as a municipal prosecutor on the effective date of this act shall be exempt from its requirements for a period of either one year or for the expiration of his or her current term of office, whichever is shorter, except that the provisions of the act pertaining to supersession (section 7) and removal (section 9) shall be in full force on the effective date of this act.

L.1999, c. 349, § 3, eff. April 13, 2000.

2B:25–4. Municipal courts; appointment of at least one municipal prosecutor

a. Each municipal court in this State shall have at least one municipal prosecutor appointed by the governing body of the municipality, municipalities or county in accordance with applicable laws, ordinances and resolutions.

b. A municipal prosecutor shall be an attorney-at-law of this State in good standing, and shall serve for a term of one year from the date of his or her appointment, except as determined by the governing body of a county or a city of the first class with a population greater than 270,000, according to the latest federal decennial census, or the governing body of a city of the second class with a population of greater than 30,000 but less than 43,000, according to the latest decennial census, which city of the second class is located in a county of the first class with a population less than 600,000 according to the latest federal decennial census, and may continue to serve in office pending reappointment or appointment of a successor. A municipal prosecutor may be appointed to that position in one or more municipal courts. The provisions of this act shall apply to each such position held.

c. (1) A municipal prosecutor of a joint municipal court shall be appointed upon the concurrence of the governing bodies of each of the municipalities in accordance with applicable laws, ordinances or resolutions.

(2) A municipal prosecutor of a central municipal court shall be appointed by the governing body of the county.

d. Municipal prosecutors shall be compensated either on an hourly, per diem, annual or other basis as the county, municipality or municipalities provide. In the case of a joint municipal court, municipalities shall, by similar ordinances, enter into an agreement fixing the compensation of the municipal prosecutor and providing for its payment. In the case of a central municipal court, the county shall fix the compensation of the municipal prosecutor and provide for its payment.

The compensation of municipal prosecutors shall be in lieu of any and all other fees; provided, however that when a municipal prosecutor is assigned to prosecute a de novo appeal in the Superior Court, the prosecutor shall be entitled to additional compensation unless the municipality expressly provides otherwise at the time the compensation is fixed.

e. In accordance with applicable laws, ordinances and resolutions, a municipality may appoint additional municipal prosecutors as necessary to administer justice in a timely and effective manner in its municipal court. Such appointments shall be subject to this act. This subsection also applies to joint municipal courts and central municipal courts.

f. Any municipal court having two or more municipal prosecutors shall have a "chief municipal prosecutor" who shall be appointed by the governing body of the county or the municipality. The chief municipal prosecutor of a joint municipal court shall be appointed upon the concurrence of the governing bodies of each municipality. The chief municipal prosecutor shall have authority over other prosecutors serving that court with respect to the performance of their duties.

g. (1) Nothing in this act shall affect the appointment of municipal attorneys in accordance with N.J.S.40A:9–139; provided, however, that a person appointed to the positions of both municipal prosecutor and municipal attorney shall be subject to all of the provisions of this act while serving in the capacity of municipal prosecutor.

(2) In addition to any other duties proscribed by the provisions of this act, a person serving as both a municipal prosecutor and a municipal attorney may prosecute county or municipal ordinance violations.

L.1999, c. 349, § 4, eff. April 13, 2000.

2B:25–5. Municipal prosecutors; duties

a. A municipal prosecutor, except as provided by subsection b. of this section and sections 6 and 7 of this act, shall represent the State, the county or the municipality in the prosecution of all offenses within the statutory jurisdiction of the municipal court as defined by law; including municipal ordinance and municipal code violations pertaining to zoning, land or property use regulation, property maintenance, building or construction. Such other local officials as may be deemed appropriate may be called by the municipal prosecutor in such prosecutions. Nothing contained herein shall prohibit a municipality from hiring special counsel to act as municipal prosecutor for these types of offenses. A municipal prosecutor shall be responsible for handling all phases of the prosecution of an offense, including but not limited to discovery, pretrial and post-trial hearings, motions, dismissals, removals to Federal District Court and other collateral functions authorized to be performed by the municipal prosecutor by law or Rule of Court. As used in this subsection, the term "post- trial hearing" shall not include de novo appeals in Superior Court.

b. A municipal prosecutor may, with the approval of the court and pursuant to the Rules of Court, authorize private attorneys to prosecute citizen complaints filed in the municipal court. A municipal prosecutor may, with the approval of the court, decline to participate in municipal court proceedings in which the defendant is not represented by counsel.

The court shall afford the citizen complainant an opportunity to be heard prior to determining whether to approve a municipal prosecutor's decision to authorize a private attorney to prosecute a citizen complaint or to decline to participate in a municipal court proceeding in which the defendant is not represented by counsel. When the municipal prosecutor declines to prosecute, the prevailing complainant may make an application to the court for counsel fee reimbursement to be paid out of applicable fines, but such reimbursement shall not exceed the amount of the applicable fines. Upon a finding that a conflict of interest precludes a municipal prosecutor from participating in a proceeding, the court

shall excuse the municipal prosecutor and may, in such a case, request the county prosecutor to provide representation in accordance with section 6 of this act unless the municipality has provided for alternative representation.

c. A municipal prosecutor may at any time move before the municipal court to amend or dismiss any complaint for good cause shown in accordance with the Rules of Court.

L.1999, c. 349, § 5, eff. April 13, 2000. Amended by L.2000, c. 178, § 1, eff. April 13, 2000.

2B:25–5.1. Driving record abstract request

Whenever a person is charged with a violation of R.S.39:3–40, R.S.39:4–50, section 2 of P.L.1981, c. 512 (C.39:4–50.4a) or R.S.39:4–129, a municipal prosecutor shall contact the New Jersey Motor Vehicle Commission by electronic or other means, for the purpose of obtaining an abstract of the person's driving record. In every such case, the prosecutor shall:

a. Determine, on the basis of the record, if the person shall be charged with enhanced penalties as a repeat offender; and

b. Transmit the abstract to the appropriate municipal court judge prior to the imposition of sentence.

L.2004, c. 95, § 1, eff. Oct. 1, 2004. Amended by L.2004, c. 185, § 1, eff. Dec. 30, 2004.

2B:25–6. Appointments to fill vacancies

a. Appointments to fill vacancies in the position of municipal prosecutor shall be made in accordance with the provisions of section 4 of this act as soon as practicable.

b. Unless the municipality has provided for alternative representation, the Attorney General or the county prosecutor, with notice to the Attorney General, may designate, at the request of the municipal prosecutor or municipal court, one or more assistant or deputy attorneys general or assistant prosecutors to prosecute the business of any municipal court if there is a vacancy in the office of the municipal prosecutor or the municipal prosecutor is temporarily unavailable and the municipal prosecutor or the municipal court has requested such designation.

L.1999, c. 349, § 6, eff. April 13, 2000.

2B:25–7. Attorney General or county prosecutor; superceding or intervening

Whenever in the opinion of the Attorney General or a county prosecutor the public interest of the State will be promoted by so doing, the Attorney General or county prosecutor, with notice to the Attorney General, may supersede a municipal prosecutor by prosecuting any offense against the laws of this State within the jurisdiction of a municipal court, or by intervening in any prosecution before a municipal court.

L.1999, c. 349, § 7, eff. April 13, 2000.

2B:25–8. Attorney General or county prosecutor; prosecution in municipal court; reimbursement for costs

Whenever the Attorney General or county prosecutor shall prosecute in a municipal court of this State pursuant to section 6 of this act, the Attorney General or county prosecutor shall, upon demand, be promptly reimbursed by the county, municipality or municipalities for costs, including the compensation of any assistants or deputies attorney general or assistant prosecutors.

L.1999, c. 349, § 8, eff. April 13, 2000.

2B:25–9. Removal of municipal prosecutor

In addition to any of the other means provided by law for the removal from office of a public official, a municipal prosecutor may be removed by the governing body of a county or municipality, or as provided by the agreement entered into between two or more municipalities participating in a joint municipal court, for good cause shown and after a public hearing, and upon due notice and an opportunity to be heard.

L.1999, c. 349, § 9, eff. April 13, 2000.

2B:25–10. Curricula for training

The Attorney General in consultation with the county and municipal prosecutors may develop curricula for training programs for all municipal prosecutors. Participation in such training programs shall be voluntary. An attorney successfully completing a training program shall receive such certification or recognition as deemed appropriate by the Attorney General.

L.1999, c. 349, § 10, eff. April 13, 2000.

2B:25–11. Plea agreements

In accordance with the Rules of Court adopted by the Supreme Court of New Jersey, a municipal prosecutor may recommend to the court to accept a plea to a lesser or other offense.

L.2000, c. 75, § 2, eff. July 24, 2000.

2B:25–12. Amending original charge

In accordance with the Rules of Court adopted by the Supreme Court of New Jersey, a municipal prosecutor may move before the municipal court to amend the original charge.

L.2000, c. 75, § 3, eff. July 24, 2000.

TITLE 4

AGRICULTURE AND DOMESTIC ANIMALS

Chapter
22.   Prevention of Cruelty to Animals.

CHAPTER 22

PREVENTION OF CRUELTY TO ANIMALS

ARTICLE 2.   PREVENTION OF CRUELTY

A.   DEFINITIONS; CONSTRUCTION

Section
4:22–15.   Definitions.
4:22–16.   Construction of article.
4:22–16.1.   Rules and regulations;   standards for humane treatment of domestic livestock.

B.   MISDEMEANORS AND FINES

4:22–17.   Cruelty;   disorderly persons offense.
4:22–18.   Carrying animal in cruel, inhumane manner;   disorderly persons offense.
4:22–19.   Failure to care for or destruction of impounded animals;   penalties;   collection.
4:22–19.1.   Chamber or device to induce hypoxia;   dismantlement and removal.
4:22–19.2.   Dismantlement and removal of decompression chamber or device;   offense.
4:22–19.3.   Prohibition of use of neuromuscular blocking agent to destroy domestic animal.
4:22–19.4.   Violations;   penalty.
4:22–20.   Abandoning disabled animal to die in public place;   abandoning domesticated animal;   disorderly persons offense.
4:22–21.   Sale of horses unfit for work;   disorderly persons offense.
4:22–22.   Use or disposal of animals having contagious diseases;   crime of the fourth degree.
4:22–23.   Use of live birds as targets;   disorderly persons offense.
4:22–24.   Fighting or baiting animals or creatures and related offenses.
4:22–25.   Repealed.
4:22–25.1.   Motorist hitting domestic animal to stop;   report.
4:22–25.2.   Punishment for violation.
4:22–25.3.   Prohibition of sale of dog or cat fur or hair.
4:22–25.4.   Prohibition of sale of dog or cat flesh.

ARTICLE 2.   PREVENTION OF CRUELTY

A.   DEFINITIONS; CONSTRUCTION

4:22–15.   Definitions

As used in this article:

"Animal" or "creature" includes the whole brute creation.

"Owner" or "person" includes a corporation, and the knowledge and acts of an agent or employee of a corporation in regard to animals transported, owned, employed or in the custody of the corporation shall be imputed to the corporation.

4:22–16.   Construction of article

Nothing contained in this article shall be construed to prohibit or interfere with:

a.   Properly conducted scientific experiments performed under the authority of the Department of Health or the United States Department of Agriculture. Those departments may authorize the conduct of such experiments or investigations by agricultural stations and schools maintained by the State or federal government, or by medical societies, universities, colleges and institutions incorporated or authorized to do business in this State and having among their corporate purposes investigation into the causes, nature, prevention and cure of diseases in men and animals;   and may for cause revoke such authority;

b.   The killing or disposing of an animal or creature by virtue of the order of a constituted authority of the State;

c.   The shooting or taking of game or game fish in such manner and at such times as is allowed or provided by the laws of this State;

d.   The training or engaging of a dog to accomplish a task or participate in an activity or exhibition designed to develop the physical or mental characteristics of that dog. These activities shall be carried out in accordance with the practices, guidelines or rules established by an organization founded for the purpose of promoting and enhancing working dog activities or exhibitions;   in a manner which does not adversely affect the health or safety of the dog;   and may include avalanche warning, guide work, obedience work, carting, dispatching, freight racing, packing, sled dog racing, sledding, tracking, and weight pull demonstrations;

e.   The raising, keeping, care, treatment, marketing, and sale of domestic livestock in accordance with the standards developed and adopted therefor pursuant to subsection a. of section 1 of P.L.1995, c. 311 (C. 4:22–16.1);   and

f.   The killing or disposing, by a reasonable or commercially acceptable method or means, of a Norway or brown rat (Rattus norvegicus), black rat (Rattus rattus), or house mouse (Mus musculus) by any person, or with the permission or at the direction of that person, while the animal is on property either owned or leased by, or otherwise under the control of, that person, provided that the animal is not a pet.

Amended by L.1985, c. 433, § 1, eff. Jan. 13, 1986; L.1995, c. 311, § 2, eff. Jan. 5, 1996; L.1997, c. 88, § 1, eff. May 8, 1997.

4:22–16.1. Rules and regulations; standards for humane treatment of domestic livestock

a. The State Board of Agriculture and the Department of Agriculture, in consultation with the New Jersey Agricultural Experiment Station and within six months of the date of enactment of this act, shall develop and adopt, pursuant to the "Administrative Procedure Act," P.L.1968, c. 410 (C. 52:14B–1 et seq.): (1) standards for the humane raising, keeping, care, treatment, marketing, and sale of domestic livestock; and (2) rules and regulations governing the enforcement of those standards.

b. Notwithstanding any provision in this title to the contrary:

(1) there shall exist a presumption that the raising, keeping, care, treatment, marketing, and sale of domestic livestock in accordance with the standards developed and adopted therefor pursuant to subsection a. of this section shall not constitute a violation of any provision of this title involving alleged cruelty to, or inhumane care or treatment of, domestic livestock;

(2) no person may be cited or arrested for a first offense involving a minor or incidental violation, as defined by rules and regulations adopted pursuant to subsection a. of this section, of any provision of this title involving alleged cruelty to, or inhumane care or treatment of, domestic livestock, unless that person has first been issued a written warning.

c. For the purposes of this act, "domestic livestock" means cattle, horses, donkeys, swine, sheep, goats, rabbits, poultry, fowl, and any other domesticated animal deemed by the State Board of Agriculture and the Department of Agriculture, in consultation with the New Jersey Agricultural Experiment Station, to be domestic livestock for such purposes, according to rules and regulations adopted by the department and the board pursuant to the "Administrative Procedure Act."

L.1995, c. 311, § 1, eff. Jan. 5, 1996.

B. MISDEMEANORS AND FINES

4:22–17. Cruelty; disorderly persons offense

a. A person who shall:

(1) Overdrive, overload, drive when overloaded, overwork, deprive of necessary sustenance, abuse, or needlessly kill a living animal or creature;

(2) Cause or procure, by any direct or indirect means, including but not limited to through the use of another living animal or creature, any such acts to be done; or

(3) Inflict unnecessary cruelty upon a living animal or creature, by any direct or indirect means, including but not limited to through the use of another living animal or creature; or unnecessarily fail to provide a living animal or creature of which the person has charge either as an owner or otherwise with proper food, drink, shelter or protection from the weather; or leave it unattended in a vehicle under inhumane conditions adverse to the health or welfare of the living animal or creature—

Shall be guilty of a disorderly persons offense, and notwithstanding the provisions of N.J.S.2C:43–3 to the contrary, for every such offense shall be fined not less than $250 nor more than $1,000, or be imprisoned for a term of not more than six months, or both, in the discretion of the court.   A violator of this subsection shall also be subject to the provisions of subsection c. and, if appropriate, subsection d. of this section.

b. A person who shall purposely, knowingly, or recklessly:

(1) Torment, torture, maim, hang, poison, unnecessarily or cruelly beat, or needlessly mutilate a living animal or creature; or

(2) Cause or procure, by any direct or indirect means, including but not limited to through the use of another living animal or creature, any such acts to be done—

Shall be guilty of a crime of the fourth degree.

If the animal or creature is cruelly killed or dies as a result of a violation of this subsection, or the person has a prior conviction for a violation of this subsection, the person shall be guilty of a crime of the third degree.

A violator of this subsection shall also be subject to the provisions of subsection c. and, if appropriate, subsection d. of this section.

c.   For a violation of subsection a. or b. of this section, in addition to imposing any other appropriate penalties established for a crime of the third degree, crime of the fourth degree, or disorderly persons offense, as the case may be, pursuant to Title 2C of the New Jersey Statutes, the court shall impose a term of community service of up to 30 days, and may direct that the term of community service be served in providing assistance to the New Jersey Society for the Prevention of Cruelty to Animals, a district (county) society for the prevention of cruelty to animals, or any other recognized organization concerned with the prevention of cruelty to animals or the humane treatment and care of animals, or to a municipality's animal control or animal population control program.   The court also may require the violator to pay restitution or otherwise reimburse any costs for food, drink, shelter, or veterinary care or treatment, or other costs, incurred by any agency, entity, or organization investigating the violation, including but not limited to the New Jersey Society for the Prevention of Cruelty to Animals, a district (county) society for the prevention of cruelty to animals, any other recognized organization concerned with the prevention of cruelty to animals or the humane treatment and care of animals, or a local or State governmental entity.

d. If a juvenile is adjudicated delinquent for an act which, if committed by an adult, would constitute a disorderly persons offense pursuant to subsection a. of this section or a crime of the third degree or crime of the fourth degree pursuant to subsection b. of this section, the court also shall order the juvenile to receive mental health counseling by a licensed psychologist or therapist named by the court for a period of time to be prescribed by the licensed psychologist or therapist.
Amended by L.1995, c. 355, § 2, eff. Jan. 5, 1996; L.1996, c. 64, § 1, eff. July 12, 1996; L.2000, c. 162, § 1, eff. Dec. 7, 2000; L.2001, c. 229, § 1, eff. Aug. 27, 2001; L.2003, c. 232, § 1, eff. Jan. 9, 2004; L.2005, c. 105, § 1, eff. June 29, 2005.

4:22–18. Carrying animal in cruel, inhumane manner; disorderly persons offense

A person who shall carry, or cause to be carried, a living animal or creature in or upon a vehicle or otherwise, in a cruel or inhumane manner, shall be guilty of a disorderly persons offense and punished as provided in subsection a. of R.S.4:22–17.
Amended by L.1995, c. 355, § 3, eff. Jan. 5, 1996; L.1996, c. 64, § 2, eff. July 12, 1996; L.2001, c. 229, § 2, eff. Aug. 27, 2001.

4:22–19. Failure to care for or destruction of impounded animals; penalties; collection

A person who shall:

a. Impound or confine, or cause to be impounded or confined, in a pound or other place, a living animal or creature, and shall fail to supply it during such confinement with a sufficient quantity of good and wholesome food and water; or

b. Destroy or cause to be destroyed any such animal by hypoxia induced by decompression or in any other manner, by the administration of a lethal gas other than an inhalant anesthetic, or in any other manner except by a method of euthanasia generally accepted by the veterinary medical profession as being reliable, appropriate to the type of animal upon which it is to be employed, and capable of producing loss of consciousness and death as rapidly and painlessly as possible for such animal shall, in the case of a violation of subsection a., be guilty of a disorderly persons offense and shall be punished as provided in subsection a. of R.S.4:22–17; or, in the case of a violation of subsection b., be subject to a penalty of $25 for the first offense and $50 for each subsequent offense. Each animal destroyed in violation of subsection b. shall constitute a separate offense. The penalty shall be collected in accordance with the "Penalty Enforcement Law of 1999," P.L.1999, c. 274 (C.2A:58–10 et seq.) and all money collected shall be remitted to the State.

This section shall apply to kennels, pet shops, shelters and pounds as defined and licensed pursuant to P.L. 1941, c. 151 (C.4:19–15.1 et seq.); to pounds and places of confinement owned and operated by municipalities, counties or regional governmental authorities; and to every contractual warden or impounding service, any provision to the contrary in this title notwithstanding.
Amended by L.1977, c. 231, § 1, eff. Sept. 20, 1977; L.1982, c. 76, § 1, eff. July 22, 1982; L.1982, c. 158, § 2, eff. Oct. 27, 1982; L.1996, c. 64, § 3, eff. July 12, 1996; L.2001, c. 229, § 3, eff. Aug. 27, 2001.

4:22–19.1. Chamber or device to induce hypoxia; dismantlement and removal

Within 30 days of the effective date of this act, any chamber or device used to induce hypoxia through decompression or in any other manner shall be dismantled and removed from the premises. The owner of any premises on which the chamber or device remains 30 days subsequent to the effective date of this act shall be guilty of a disorderly persons offense.
L.1982, c. 76, § 3, eff. July 22, 1982.

For similar section added by L. 1982, c. 158, § 3, eff. Oct. 27, 1982, see § 4:22–19.2, post.

4:22–19.2. Dismantlement and removal of decompression chamber or device; offense

Within 30 days of the effective date of this act, any chamber or device used to induce hypoxia through decompression or in any other manner and any gas chamber or similar device, except one which is used for the administration of an inhalant anesthetic, shall be dismantled and removed from the premises. The owner of any premises on which the chamber or device remains 30 days subsequent to the effective date of this act shall be guilty of a disorderly persons offense.
L.1982, c. 158, § 3, eff. Oct. 27, 1982.

For similar section added by L. 1982, c. 76, § 3, eff. July 22, 1982, see § 4:22–19.1, ante.

4:22–19.3. Prohibition of use of neuromuscular blocking agent to destroy domestic animal

Whenever any dog, cat, or any other domestic animal is to be destroyed, the use of succinylcholine chloride, curare, curariform drugs, or any other substance which acts as a neuromuscular blocking agent is prohibited.
L.1988, c. 160, § 1, eff. Nov. 16, 1988.

4:22–19.4. Violations; penalty

A person who violates this act shall be subject to a penalty of $25.00 for the first offense and $50.00 for each subsequent offense, to be collected in a civil action by a summary proceeding under "the penalty enforcement law" (N.J.S. 2A:58–1 et seq.). Each animal destroyed in violation of this act shall constitute a separate offense. The Superior Court shall have jurisdiction to enforce "the penalty enforcement law."
L.1988, c. 160, § 2, eff. Nov. 16, 1988.

4:22–20. Abandoning disabled animal to die in public place; abandoning domesticated animal; disorderly persons offense

a. A person who shall abandon a maimed, sick, infirm or disabled animal or creature to die in a public place, shall be guilty of a disorderly persons offense.

b. A person who shall abandon a domesticated animal shall be guilty of a disorderly persons offense. The violator shall be subject to the maximum $1,000 penalty.

Amended by L.1977, c. 229, § 1, eff. Sept. 20, 1977; L.1986, c. 176, § 1, eff. Dec. 8, 1986; L.1991, c. 108, § 1, eff. April 19, 1991.

4:22–21. Sale of horses unfit for work; disorderly persons offense

A person who shall receive or offer for sale a horse that is suffering from abuse or neglect, or which by reason of disability, disease, abuse or lameness, or for any other cause, could not be worked, ridden or otherwise used for show, exhibition, or recreational purposes, or kept as a domestic pet without violating the provisions of this article or any law of this State relating to cruelty to animals shall be guilty of a disorderly persons offense.

Amended by L.1995, c. 355, § 4, eff. Jan. 5, 1996; L.1998, c. 105, § 2, eff. Sept. 14, 1998.

4:22–22. Use or disposal of animals having contagious diseases; crime of the fourth degree

A person who shall:

a. Willfully sell, or offer to sell, use, expose, or cause or permit to be sold or offered for sale, used or exposed, any horse or other animal having the disease known as glanders or farcy, or other contagious or infectious disease dangerous to the health or life of human beings or animals; or

b. When any such disease is beyond recovery, refuse upon demand to deprive any such animal of life—

Shall be guilty of a crime of the fourth degree.

Amended by L.1995, c. 355, § 5, eff. Jan. 5, 1996.

4:22–23. Use of live birds as targets; disorderly persons offense

A person who shall:

a. Use a live pigeon, fowl or other bird for the purpose of a target, or to be shot at either for amusement or as a test of skill in marksmanship;

b. Shoot at a bird used as described in subsection a. of this section, or is a party to such shooting; or

c. Lease a building, room, field or premises, or knowingly permit the use thereof for the purpose of such shooting—

Shall be guilty of a disorderly persons offense, and shall, in addition to any penalty assessed therefor, be

fined $25 for each bird shot at or killed in violation of this section.

This section shall not apply to the shooting of game.

Amended by L.1995, c. 355, § 6, eff. Jan. 5, 1996; L.2003, c. 232, § 2, eff. Jan. 9, 2004.

4:22–24. Fighting or baiting animals or creatures and related offenses

A person who shall:

a. Keep, use, be connected with or interested in the management of, or receive money for the admission of a person to, a place kept or used for the purpose of fighting or baiting a living animal or creature;

b. Be present and witness, pay admission to, encourage or assist therein;

c. Permit or suffer a place owned or controlled by him to be so used;

d. For amusement or gain, cause, allow, or permit the fighting or baiting of a living animal or creature;

e. Own, possess, keep, train, promote, purchase, or knowingly sell a living animal or creature for the purpose of fighting or baiting that animal or creature; or

f. Gamble on the outcome of a fight involving a living animal or creature—

Shall be guilty of a crime of the third degree.

Amended by L.1989, c. 35, § 1, eff. March 7, 1989.

4:22–25. Repealed by L.1985, c. 433, § 3, eff. Jan. 13, 1986

4:22–25.1. Motorist hitting domestic animal to stop; report

Each person operating a motor vehicle who shall knowingly hit, run over, or cause injury to a cat, dog, horse or cattle shall stop at once, ascertain the extent of injury, report to the nearest police station, police officer, or notify the nearest Society for the Prevention of Cruelty to Animals and give his name, address, operator's license and registration number, and also give the location of the injured animal.

L.1939, c. 315, p. 762, § 1. Amended by L.1968, c. 39, § 1, eff. May 9, 1968.

4:22–25.2. Punishment for violation

Any person who shall violate any of the provisions of section 1 of P.L.1939, c. 315 (C. 4:22–25.1) shall be guilty of a petty disorderly persons offense.

L.1939, c. 315, p. 762, § 2. Amended by L.1953, c. 5, p. 47, § 62; L.1995, c. 355, § 7, eff. Jan. 5, 1996.

4:22–25.3. Prohibition of sale of dog or cat fur or hair

Any person who sells, barters, or offers for sale or barter, at wholesale or retail, the fur or hair of a domestic dog or cat or any product made in whole or in part from the fur or hair of a domestic dog or cat commits a crime of the fourth degree, provided that the person knew or reasonably should have known that the fur or hair was from a domestic dog or cat or that the product was made in whole or in part from the fur or hair of a domestic dog or cat. This section shall not apply to the sale or barter, or offering for sale or barter, of the fur or hair of a domestic dog or cat cut at a commercial grooming establishment or at a veterinary office or clinic or for scientific research purposes.

As used in this section, "domestic dog or cat" means a dog (*Canis familiaris*) or cat (*Felis catus* or *Felis domesticus*) that is generally recognized in the United States as being a household pet and shall not include coyote, fox, lynx, bobcat, or any other wild canine or feline species.

L.1999, c. 307, § 1, eff. Jan. 4, 2000.

4:22–25.4. Prohibition of sale of dog or cat flesh

Any person who sells, barters, or offers for sale or barter, at wholesale or retail, for human consumption, the flesh of a domestic dog or cat or any product made in whole or in part from the flesh of a domestic dog or cat commits a disorderly persons offense, provided that the person knew or reasonably should have known that the flesh was from a domestic dog or cat or the product was made in whole or in part from the flesh of a domestic dog or cat. Notwithstanding the provisions of Title 2C of the New Jersey Statutes to the contrary, any person found guilty of violating this section shall be subject to a fine of not less than $100 and a term of imprisonment of not less than 30 days.

As used in this section, "domestic dog or cat" means a dog (*Canis familiaris*) or cat (*Felis catus* or *Felis domesticus*) that is generally recognized in the United States as being a household pet and shall not include coyote, fox, lynx, bobcat, or any other wild canine or feline species.

L.1999, c. 307, § 2, eff. Jan. 4, 2000.

TITLE 9

CHILDREN—JUVENILE AND DOMESTIC RELATIONS COURTS

Subtitle
3. Protective Welfare Laws.

SUBTITLE 3

PROTECTIVE WELFARE LAWS

Chapter
6. Abandonment, Abuse, Cruelty and Neglect.

CHAPTER 6

ABANDONMENT, ABUSE, CRUELTY AND NEGLECT

ARTICLE 1. GENERAL PROVISIONS

A. ABUSE, ABANDONMENT, CRUELTY AND NEGLECT

Section
9:6–1. Abuse, abandonment, cruelty and neglect of child; what constitutes.
9:6–1.1. Treatment of ill children according to religious tenets of church.
9:6–2. "Parent" and "custodian" defined.
9:6–3. Cruelty and neglect of children; crime of fourth degree; remedies.
9:6–3.1. Institutional employee; temporary suspension of alleged offender; due process rights; single act; several incidents; remedial plan, changes, and sanctions.
9:6–4. Jurisdiction of complaints; immediate trial; procedure.
9:6–5. Complaints, who may prefer.
9:6–6. Disposition of fines, penalties and forfeitures.
9:6–7. Agents of societies for prevention of cruelty to children as police officers.
9:6–8. Warrant to enter place or house for supposed violations of chapter; arrest of violators.

B. ABUSED CHILD—REPORTS AND PROTECTIVE CUSTODY

9:6–8.1 to 9:6–8.7. Repealed.
9:6–8.8. Purpose.
9:6–8.9. Abused child; child abuse defined.
9:6–8.10. Reports of child abuse.
9:6–8.10a. Reports and information of child abuse reports; confidentiality; release.
9:6–8.10b. Permitting or encouraging release of record or report; penalty.
9:6–8.10c. Incarcerated persons and persons assuming care and custody of minor to undergo child abuse record information check.
9:6–8.10d. Rules and regulations.
9:6–8.10e. Child abuse registry check of applicant for professional guardian.

Section
9:6–8.11. Insuring safety of child upon receipt of report; report to central registry of bureau of children's services in Trenton; privacy of information.
9:6–8.12. Maintenance of 24 hour emergency telephone service for receipt of child abuse calls.
9:6–8.13. Person making report; immunity from liability; action for relief from discharge or discrimination.
9:6–8.14. Violations including failure to make report; disorderly person.
9:6–8.15. Rules and regulations.
9:6–8.16. Child taken to physician or hospital for treatment of serious physical injury; protective custody.
9:6–8.17. Report of action of taking protective custody.
9:6–8.18. Bureau of children's services or division of youth and family services; insuring safety of child; investigation; application for order placing child under protective custody.
9:6–8.19. Notice to parents or guardian; visitation rights; limitation on period.
9:6–8.19a. Notice and opportunity to be heard.
9:6–8.20. Physicians or directors of hospitals acting under this law; immunity from liability.

C. ADJUDICATION OF ALLEGED CHILD ABUSE OR NEGLECT

9:6–8.21. Definitions.
9:6–8.22. Superior Court, chancery division, family part; jurisdiction; duties; priority of cases.
9:6–8.23. Law guardian; representation of minor; appointment.
9:6–8.24. Jurisdiction.
9:6–8.25. Transfer to and from the Superior Court.
9:6–8.26. Venue.
9:6–8.27. Temporary removal with consent.
9:6–8.28. Preliminary orders of court before preliminary hearing held.
9:6–8.29. Emergency removal without court order.
9:6–8.30. Action by the division upon emergency removal.
9:6–8.31. Preliminary orders after filing of complaint.
9:6–8.32. Application to return child temporarily removed.
9:6–8.33. Originating proceeding to determine abuse or neglect.
9:6–8.34. Persons who may originate proceedings.
9:6–8.35. Preliminary procedure.
9:6–8.36. Admissibility of statements made during a preliminary conference.

Section

9:6–8.36a. Report of suspected child abuse and neglect by division to county prosecutor.
9:6–8.37. Issuance of summons.
9:6–8.38. Service of summons.
9:6–8.39. Issuance of warrant and reports.
9:6–8.40. Records involving abuse or neglect.
9:6–8.40a. Unfounded allegations of child abuse to be expunged from division's records.
9:6–8.41. Required findings concerning notice.
9:6–8.42. Effect of absence of parent or guardian.
9:6–8.43. Notice of rights.
9:6–8.44. Definition of "fact-finding hearing".
9:6–8.45. Definition of "dispositional hearing".
9:6–8.46. Evidence.
9:6–8.47. Sequence of hearings.
9:6–8.48. Adjournments.
9:6–8.49. Special consideration in certain cases.
9:6–8.50. Sustaining or dismissing complaint.
9:6–8.51. Disposition of adjudication.
9:6–8.52. Suspended judgment.
9:6–8.53. Release to custody of parent or guardian.
9:6–8.54. Placement.
9:6–8.55. Order of protection.
9:6–8.56. Probation supervision.
9:6–8.57. Abandoned child.
9:6–8.58. Provision for therapeutic services.
9:6–8.58a. Conditions on return of child to home; substance abuse assessment and treatment.
9:6–8.58b. Adoption of rules and regulations.
9:6–8.59. Staying, modifying, setting aside or vacating orders.
9:6–8.60. Petition to terminate placement.
9:6–8.61. Service of petition; answer.
9:6–8.62. Examination of petition and answer; hearing.
9:6–8.63. Orders on hearing.
9:6–8.64. Successive petitions.
9:6–8.65. Substitution for original placement.
9:6–8.66. Failure to comply with terms and conditions of suspended judgment.
9:6–8.67. Failure to comply with terms and conditions of order of probation or protection.
9:6–8.68. Effect of running away from place of placement.
9:6–8.69. Release from responsibility under order of placement.
9:6–8.70. Appealable orders.
9:6–8.71. Appropriations.
9:6–8.72. Rules and regulations.
9:6–8.72a. Rules and regulations; reporting and investigation of allegations of child abuse.
9:6–8.73. Severability.
9:6–8.74. New Jersey Task Force on Child Abuse and Neglect Act; short title.
9:6–8.75. New Jersey Task Force on Child Abuse and Neglect; grants from Children's Trust Fund; staffing and oversight review subcommittee.
9:6–8.76. Membership of task force; terms of office.
9:6–8.77. Procedure for filling vacancies; reimbursement of members for expenses.
9:6–8.78. Professional and clerical staff to be provided as needed.
9:6–8.79. Availability of services from other state entities; consultation with other organizations and associations.
9:6–8.80. Meetings; hearings.
9:6–8.81. Task force authorized to solicit, receive and disburse grants and donations.

Section

9:6–8.82. Report of findings and recommendations.
9:6–8.83. Short title; Comprehensive Child Abuse Prevention and Treatment Act.
9:6–8.84. Definitions.
9:6–8.85. Response to medical neglect reports.
9:6–8.86. Legal proceedings authorized; prevention or withholding or to provide medically indicated treatment.
9:6–8.87. Reunification of family; parent convicted of murder, manslaughter, assault or related crimes.
9:6–8.88. Child fatality and near fatality review board established.
9:6–8.89. Child fatality and near fatality review board; membership; terms; officers; authority.
9:6–8.90. Child fatality and near fatality review board; duties.
9:6–8.91. Community-based investigation teams.
9:6–8.92. Child fatality and near fatality review board; records.
9:6–8.93. Child fatality and near fatality review board; subpoenas; notice to prosecutors.
9:6–8.94. Child fatality and near fatality review board; member immunity.
9:6–8.95. Child fatality and near fatality review board; grants and funding.
9:6–8.96. Child fatality and near fatality review board; rules and regulations.
9:6–8.97. Citizen review panels.
9:6–8.98. Rules and regulations.
9:6–8.99. Regional diagnostic and treatment centers for child abuse and neglect established.
9:6–8.100. Center staff; intake, referral and tracking process.
9:6–8.101. Center duties.
9:6–8.102. Services provided by centers' staff.
9:6–8.103. Responsibility to ensure safety of child undergoing treatment.
9:6–8.104. Establishment and maintenance of county-based multidisciplinary teams.
9:6–8.105. Repealed.
9:6–8.106. Adoption of rules and regulations.

ARTICLE 1. GENERAL PROVISIONS

A. ABUSE, ABANDONMENT, CRUELTY AND NEGLECT

9:6–1. Abuse, abandonment, cruelty and neglect of child; what constitutes

Abuse of a child shall consist in any of the following acts: (a) disposing of the custody of a child contrary to law; (b) employing or permitting a child to be employed in any vocation or employment injurious to its health or dangerous to its life or limb, or contrary to the laws of this State; (c) employing or permitting a child to be employed in any occupation, employment or vocation dangerous to the morals of such child; (d) the habitual use by the parent or by a person having the custody and control of a child, in the hearing of such child, of profane, indecent or obscene language; (e) the performing of any indecent, immoral or unlawful act or deed, in the presence of a child, that may tend to debauch or endanger or degrade the morals of the child; (f) permitting or allowing any other person to perform any indecent, immoral or unlawful act in the presence of the child that may tend to debauch or endanger the morals of such child; (g) using excessive physical restraint on the child under circumstances which do not indicate that the child's behavior is harmful to himself, others or property; or (h) in an institution as defined in section 1 of P.L.1974, c. 119 (C. 9:6–8.21), willfully isolating the child from ordinary social contact under circumstances which indicate emotional or social deprivation.

Abandonment of a child shall consist in any of the following acts by anyone having the custody or control of the child: (a) willfully forsaking a child; (b) failing to care for and keep the control and custody of a child so that the child shall be exposed to physical or moral risk without proper and sufficient protection; (c) failing to care for and keep the control and custody of a child so that the child shall be liable to be supported and maintained at the expense of the public, or by child caring societies or private persons not legally chargeable with its or their care, custody and control.

Cruelty to a child shall consist in any of the following acts: (a) inflicting unnecessarily severe corporal punishment upon a child; (b) inflicting upon a child unnecessary suffering or pain, either mental or physical; (c) habitually tormenting, vexing or afflicting a child; (d) any willful act of omission or commission whereby unnecessary pain and suffering, whether mental or physical, is caused or permitted to be inflicted on a child; (e) or exposing a child to unnecessary hardship, fatigue or mental or physical strains that may tend to injure the health or physical or moral well-being of such child.

Neglect of a child shall consist in any of the following acts, by anyone having the custody or control of the child: (a) willfully failing to provide proper and sufficient food, clothing, maintenance, regular school education as required by law, medical attendance or surgical treatment, and a clean and proper home, or (b) failure to do or permit to be done any act necessary for the child's physical or moral well-being. Neglect also means the continued inappropriate placement of a child in an institution, as defined in section 1 of P.L.1974, c. 119 (C. 9:6–8.21), with the knowledge that the placement has resulted and may continue to result in harm to the child's mental or physical well-being.

Amended by L.1987, c. 341, § 1, eff. Dec. 24, 1987.

9:6–1.1. Treatment of ill children according to religious tenets of church

The article[1] to which this act is a supplement shall not be construed to deny the right of a parent, guardian or person having the care, custody and control of any child to treat or provide treatment for an ill child in accordance with the religious tenets of any church as authorized by other statutes of this State; *provided*, that the laws, rules, and regulations relating to communicable diseases and sanitary matters are not violated.

L.1950, c. 126, p. 236, § 1.

1 Article 1 of Chapter 6.

9:6–2. "Parent" and "custodian" defined

"Parent", as used in this chapter, shall include the stepfather and stepmother and the adoptive or resource family parent. "The person having the care, custody and control of any child", as used in this chapter, shall mean any person who has assumed the care of a child, or any person with whom a child is living at the time the offense is committed, and shall include a teacher, employee or volunteer, whether compensated or uncompensated, of an institution as defined in section 1 of P.L.1974, c. 119 (C.9:6–8.21) who is responsible for the child's welfare, and a person who legally or voluntarily assumes the care, custody, maintenance or support of the child. Custodian also includes any other staff person of an institution regardless of whether or not the person is responsible for the care or supervision of the child. Custodian also includes a teaching staff member or other employee, whether compensated or uncompensated, of a day school as defined in section 1 of P.L.1974, c. 119 (C.9:6–8.21).

Amended by L.1987, c. 341, § 2, eff. Dec. 24, 1987; L.2004, c. 130, § 20, eff. Aug. 27, 2004.

9:6–3. Cruelty and neglect of children; crime of fourth degree; remedies

Any parent, guardian or person having the care, custody or control of any child, who shall abuse, abandon, be cruel to or neglectful of such child, or any person who shall abuse, be cruel to or neglectful of any child shall be deemed to be guilty of a crime of the fourth degree. If a fine be imposed, the court may direct the same to be paid in whole or in part to the parent, or to the guardian, custodian or trustee of such minor child or children; provided, however, that whenever in the judgment of the court it shall appear to the best interest of the child to place it in the temporary care or custody of a society or corporation, organized or incorporated under the laws of this State, having as one of its objects the prevention of cruelty to children, and the society or corporation is willing to assume such custody and control, the court may postpone sentence and place the child in the custody of such society or corporation, and may place defendant on probation, either with the county probation officers or an officer of the society or corporation to which the child is ordered, and may order the parent, guardian or person having the custody and control of such child to pay to such society or corporation a certain stated sum for the maintenance of such child. When, however, a child is so placed in the custody of such society or corporation, and defendant fails to make the payments as ordered by the court, the court shall cause the arrest and arraignment before it of such defendant, and shall impose upon the defendant the penalty provided in this section.

Amended by L.1944, c. 196, p. 711, § 1; L.1990, c. 26, § 5, eff. Aug. 19, 1990.

9:6–3.1. Institutional employee; temporary suspension of alleged offender; due process rights; single act; several incidents; remedial plan, changes, and sanctions

a. A teacher, employee, volunteer or staff person of an institution as defined in section 1 of P.L.1974, c. 119 (C.9:6–8.21) who is alleged to have committed an act of child abuse or neglect as defined in R.S. 9:6–1, section 2 of P.L.1971, c. 437 (C.9:6–8.9) and section 1 of P.L. 1974, c. 119 (C.9:6–8.21) shall be temporarily suspended by the appointing authority from his position at the institution with pay, or reassigned to other duties which would remove the risk of harm to the child under the person's custody or control, if there is reasonable cause for the appointing authority to believe that the life or health of the alleged victim or other children at the institution is in imminent danger due to continued contact between the alleged perpetrator and a child at the institution.

A public employee suspended pursuant to this subsection shall be accorded and may exercise due process rights, including notice of the proposed suspension and a presuspension opportunity to respond and any other due process rights provided under the laws of this State governing public employment and under any applicable individual or group contractual agreement. A private employee suspended pursuant to this subsection shall be accorded and may exercise due process rights provided for under the laws of this State governing private employment and under any applicable individual or group employee contractual agreement.

b. If the child abuse or neglect is the result of a single act occurring in an institution, within 30 days of receipt of the report of child abuse or neglect, the Department of Children and Families may request that the chief administrator of the institution formulate a plan of remedial action. The plan may include, but shall not be limited to, action to be taken with respect to a teacher, employee, volunteer or staff person of the institution to assure the health and safety of the alleged victim and other children at the institution and to prevent future acts of abuse or neglect. Within 30 days of the date the department requested the remedial plan, the chief administrator shall notify the department in writing of the progress in preparing the plan. The chief administrator shall complete the plan within 90 days of the date the department requested the plan.

c. If the child abuse or neglect is the result of several incidents occurring in an institution, within 30 days of receipt of the report of child abuse or neglect, the department may request that the chief administrator of the institution make administrative, personnel or structural changes at the institution. Within 30 days of the date the department made its request, the chief

administrator shall notify the department of the progress in complying with the terms of the department's request. The department and chief administrator shall determine a time frame for completion of the terms of the request.

d. If a chief administrator of an institution does not formulate or implement a remedial plan or make the changes requested by the department, the department may impose appropriate sanctions or actions if the department licenses, oversees, approves or authorizes the operation of the institution. If the department does not license, oversee, approve or authorize the operation of the institution, the department may recommend to the authority which licenses, oversees, approves or authorizes the operation of the institution that appropriate sanctions or actions be imposed against the institution.

L.1987, c. 341, § 7, eff. Dec. 24, 1987. Amended by L.2004, c. 130, § 21, eff. Aug. 27, 2004; L.2006, c. 47, § 41, eff. July 1, 2006.

9:6–4. Jurisdiction of complaints; immediate trial; procedure

Complaints for violation of the provisions of this chapter may be made to the Superior Court or any municipal court. Whenever any person, who shall be charged with any such offense upon oath before any court or by indictment, shall, in writing signed by him and addressed to the county prosecutor of the county wherein the offense was committed, waive indictment and trial by jury, or trial by jury, as the case may be, and request to be tried immediately before the Superior Court without a jury, the county prosecutor shall report such fact to such court, which, unless it shall deem the public interest will be benefited by denying such request, shall with all due and reasonable speed, proceed to try the person so charged and determine and adjudge his guilt or innocence.

Amended by L.1944, c. 196, p. 712, § 2; L.1953, c. 9, p. 74, § 15; L.1991, c. 91, § 195, eff. April 9, 1991.

9:6–5. Complaints, who may prefer

Any board of education or police department of any municipality, township, towns and boroughs, its designated officers, members or agents, or any society, association or board incorporated or organized under the laws of this State, having as one of its objects the prevention of cruelty to children, its officers or agents, may prefer a complaint against and cause to be arrested and prosecuted any person who shall offend against the provisions of this chapter, and aid in prosecuting the complaint before the court.

Amended by L.1939, c. 277, § 1.

9:6–6. Disposition of fines, penalties and forfeitures

All fines, penalties and forfeitures imposed and collected in any case when any society, association or board incorporated or organized under the laws of this state having as one of its objects the prevention of cruelty to children, shall be complainant, shall inure to such society, to be used by it for the benefit of the children in its care. All other fines imposed by a court in accordance with the provisions of this chapter shall be paid to the overseer of the poor of the municipality where the defendant resided, to be used for the benefit of the poor of that municipality.

9:6–7. Agents of societies for prevention of cruelty to children as police officers

Any duly organized or incorporated humane society, having for one of its objects the protection of children from cruelty, may offer any agents or officers employed by such society to the mayor or other executive officer having authority to commission police officers of any municipality having a regularly organized police department, for the purpose of being commissioned to act as police officers through the limits of such municipality for the purpose of arresting all the offenders against this chapter or any of the provisions thereof, whereupon the mayor in such city shall, if such persons are proper and discreet persons, commission them to act as such police officers, with all the rights and powers appertaining thereto; but no such municipality shall be liable in any way for the salary or wages of such officers, or for any expense whatever in relation thereto, except for the detention of prisoners.

In any municipality not having a regularly organized police department, such humane society may offer similarly qualified persons to the Assignment Judge of the Superior Court for the county, whereupon such court shall, if they be fit persons, commission such persons to act as constables, with power to arrest all offenders against this chapter or any provisions thereof; but no municipality or county shall be in anywise liable for the salary or wages of any such officer, or for any expense in relation thereto, except for the detention of prisoners.

All persons thus qualified under this section shall be deemed to be constables and police officers, and the keepers of jails or lockups or station houses in any of such counties are required to receive all persons arrested by such policemen or constables.

Amended by L.1953, c. 9, p. 75, § 16; L.1991, c. 91, § 196, eff. April 9, 1991.

9:6–8. Warrant to enter place or house for supposed violations of chapter; arrest of violators

Whenever any person shall, before the Superior Court, or municipal court, make oath that the affiant believes that this chapter has been or is being violated in any place or house, such court shall forthwith issue a warrant to a constable or other authorized officer to enter such place or house and investigate the same, and such person may arrest or cause to be arrested all offenders and bring them before any court for a hearing of the case; and all constables and policemen shall aid

in bringing all such offenders before such authorities for a hearing.

Amended by L.1953, c. 9, p. 76, § 17; L.1991, c. 91, § 197, eff. April 9, 1991.

B.   ABUSED CHILD—REPORTS AND PROTECTIVE CUSTODY

9:6–8.1 to 9:6–8.7.   Repealed by L.1974, c. 119, § 54, eff. Oct. 10, 1974

9:6–8.8. Purpose

a. The purpose of this act is to provide for the protection of children under 18 years of age who have had serious injury inflicted upon them by other than accidental means. The safety of the children served shall be of paramount concern. It is the intent of this legislation to assure that the lives of innocent children are immediately safeguarded from further injury and possible death and that the legal rights of such children are fully protected.

b. (1) In accordance with the provisions of paragraphs (2), (3), and (4) of this subsection, when determining the reasonable efforts to be made and when making the reasonable efforts, the child's health and safety shall be of paramount concern.

(2) In any case in which the division accepts a child in care or custody, the division shall make reasonable efforts, prior to placement, to preserve the family in order to prevent the need for removing the child from his home. After placement, the division shall make reasonable efforts to make it possible for the child to safely return to his home.

(3) Reasonable efforts to place a child for adoption or with a legal guardian or in an alternative permanent placement may be made concurrently with reasonable efforts to preserve and reunify the child's family.

(4) In any case in which family reunification is not the permanency plan for the child, reasonable efforts shall be made to place the child in a timely manner and to complete the steps necessary to finalize the permanent placement of the child.

L.1971, c. 437, § 1, eff. Feb. 10, 1972. Amended by L.1999, c. 53, § 4, eff. March 31, 1999.

9:6–8.9. Abused child; child abuse defined

For purposes of this act:

"Abused child" means a child under the age of 18 years whose parent, guardian, or other person having his custody and control:

a. Inflicts or allows to be inflicted upon such child physical injury by other than accidental means which causes or creates a substantial risk of death, or serious or protracted disfigurement, or protracted impairment of physical or emotional health or protracted loss or impairment of the function of any bodily organ;

b. Creates or allows to be created a substantial or ongoing risk of physical injury to such child by other than accidental means which would be likely to cause death or serious or protracted disfigurement, or protracted loss or impairment of the function of any bodily organ; or

c. Commits or allows to be committed an act of sexual abuse against the child;

d. Or a child whose physical, mental, or emotional condition has been impaired or is in imminent danger of becoming impaired as the result of the failure of his parent or guardian, or such other person having his custody and control, to exercise a minimum degree of care (1) in supplying the child with adequate food, clothing, shelter, education, medical or surgical care though financially able to do so or though offered financial or other reasonable means to do so, or (2) in providing the child with proper supervision or guardianship, by unreasonably inflicting or allowing to be inflicted harm, or substantial risk thereof, including the infliction of excessive corporal punishment or using excessive physical restraint under circumstances which do not indicate that the child's behavior is harmful to himself, others or property; or by any other act of a similarly serious nature requiring the aid of the court;

e. Or a child who has been willfully abandoned by his parent or guardian, or such other person having his custody and control;

f. Or a child who is in an institution as defined in section 1 of P.L.1974, c. 119 (C. 9:6–8.21) and (1) has been so placed inappropriately for a continued period of time with the knowledge that the placement has resulted and may continue to result in harm to the child's mental or physical well-being or (2) has been willfully isolated from ordinary social contact under circumstances which indicate emotional or social deprivation.

A child shall not be considered abused pursuant to subsection f. of this section if the acts or omissions described therein occur in a day school as defined in section 1 of P.L.1974, c. 119 (C. 9:6–8.21).

L.1971, c. 437, § 2, eff. Feb. 10, 1972. Amended by L.1974, c. 119, § 53, eff. Oct. 10, 1974; L.1987, c. 341, § 3, eff. Dec. 24, 1987.

9:6–8.10. Reports of child abuse

Any person having reasonable cause to believe that a child has been subjected to child abuse or acts of child abuse shall report the same immediately to the Division of Youth and Family Services by telephone or otherwise. Such reports, where possible, shall contain the names and addresses of the child and his parent, guardian, or other person having custody and control of the child and, if known, the child's age, the nature and possible extent of the child's injuries, abuse or maltreatment, including any evidence of previous injuries, abuse or maltreatment, and any other information that the

person believes may be helpful with respect to the child abuse and the identity of the perpetrator.

L.1971, c. 437, § 3, eff. Feb. 10, 1972. Amended by L.1987, c. 341, § 4, eff. Dec. 24, 1987.

9:6–8.10a. Reports and information of child abuse reports; confidentiality; release

a. All records of child abuse reports made pursuant to section 3 of P.L.1971, c. 437 (C.9:6–8.10), all information obtained by the Department of Children and Families in investigating such reports including reports received pursuant to section 20 of P.L.1974, c. 119 (C.9:6–8.40), and all reports of findings forwarded to the child abuse registry pursuant to section 4 of P.L.1971, c. 437 (C.9:6–8.11) shall be kept confidential and may be disclosed only under the circumstances expressly authorized under subsections b., c., d., e., f. and g. herein. The department shall disclose information only as authorized under subsections b., c., d., e., f. and g. of this section that is relevant to the purpose for which the information is required, provided, however, that nothing may be disclosed which would likely endanger the life, safety, or physical or emotional well-being of a child or the life or safety of any other person or which may compromise the integrity of a department investigation or a civil or criminal investigation or judicial proceeding. If the department denies access to specific information on this basis, the requesting entity may seek disclosure through the Chancery Division of the Superior Court. This section shall not be construed to prohibit disclosure pursuant to paragraphs (2) and (7) of subsection b. of this section.

Nothing in this act shall be construed to permit the disclosure of any information deemed confidential by federal or State law.

b. The department may and upon written request, shall release the records and reports referred to in subsection a., or parts thereof, consistent with the provisions of P.L.1997, c. 175 (C.9:6–8.83 et al.) to:

(1) A public or private child protective agency authorized to investigate a report of child abuse or neglect;

(2) A police or other law enforcement agency investigating a report of child abuse or neglect;

(3) A physician who has before him a child whom he reasonably suspects may be abused or neglected or an authorized member of the staff of a duly designated regional child abuse diagnostic and treatment center which is involved with a particular child who is the subject of the request;

(4) A physician, a hospital director or his designate, a police officer or other person authorized to place a child in protective custody when such person has before him a child whom he reasonably suspects may be abused or neglected and requires the information in order to determine whether to place the child in protective custody;

(5) An agency, whether public or private, including any division or unit in the Department of Human Services or the Department of Children and Families, authorized to care for, treat, assess, evaluate or supervise a child who is the subject of a child abuse report, or a parent, guardian, resource family parent or other person who is responsible for the child's welfare, or both, when the information is needed in connection with the provision of care, treatment, assessment, evaluation or supervision to such child or such parent, guardian, resource family parent or other person and the provision of information is in the best interests of the child as determined by the Division of Youth and Family Services;

(6) A court or the Office of Administrative Law, upon its finding that access to such records may be necessary for determination of an issue before it, and such records may be disclosed by the court or the Office of Administrative Law in whole or in part to the law guardian, attorney or other appropriate person upon a finding that such further disclosure is necessary for determination of an issue before the court or the Office of Administrative Law;

(7) A grand jury upon its determination that access to such records is necessary in the conduct of its official business;

(8) Any appropriate State legislative committee acting in the course of its official functions, provided, however, that no names or other information identifying persons named in the report shall be made available to the legislative committee unless it is absolutely essential to the legislative purpose;

(9) (Deleted by amendment, P.L.1997, c. 175).

(10) A family day care sponsoring organization for the purpose of providing information on child abuse or neglect allegations involving prospective or current providers or household members pursuant to P.L.1993, c. 350 (C.30:5B–25.1 et seq.) and as necessary, for use in administrative appeals related to information obtained through a child abuse registry search;

(11) The Victims of Crime Compensation Board, for the purpose of providing services available pursuant to the "Criminal Injuries Compensation Act of 1971," P.L.1971, c. 317 (C.52:4B–1 et seq.) to a child victim who is the subject of such report;

(12) Any person appealing a department service or status action or a substantiated finding of child abuse or neglect and his attorney or authorized lay representative upon a determination by the department or the presiding Administrative Law Judge that such disclosure is necessary for a determination of the issue on appeal;

(13) Any person or entity mandated by statute to consider child abuse or neglect information when conducting a background check or employment-related screening of an individual employed by or seeking employment with an agency or organization providing services to children;

(14) Any person or entity conducting a disciplinary, administrative or judicial proceeding to determine terms of employment or continued employment of an officer, employee, or volunteer with an agency or organization providing services for children. The information may be disclosed in whole or in part to the appellant or other appropriate person only upon a determination by the person or entity conducting the proceeding that the disclosure is necessary to make a determination;

(15) The members of a county multi-disciplinary team, established in accordance with State guidelines, for the purpose of coordinating the activities of agencies handling alleged cases of child abuse and neglect;

(16) A person being evaluated by the department or the court as a potential care-giver to determine whether that person is willing and able to provide the care and support required by the child;

(17) The legal counsel of a child, parent or guardian, whether court-appointed or retained, when information is needed to discuss the case with the department in order to make decisions relating to or concerning the child;

(18) A person who has filed a report of suspected child abuse or neglect for the purpose of providing that person with only the disposition of the investigation;

(19) A parent, resource family parent or legal guardian when the information is needed in a department matter in which that parent, resource family parent or legal guardian is directly involved. The information may be released only to the extent necessary for the requesting parent, resource family parent or legal guardian to discuss services or the basis for the department's involvement or to develop, discuss, or implement a case plan for the child;

(20) A federal, State or local government entity, to the extent necessary for such entity to carry out its responsibilities under law to protect children from abuse and neglect;

(21) Citizen review panels designated by the State in compliance with the federal "Child Abuse Prevention and Treatment Act Amendments of 1996," Pub. L.104–235;

(22) The Child Fatality and Near Fatality Review Board established pursuant to P.L.1997, c. 175 (C.9:6–8.83 et al.); or

(23) Members of a family team or other case planning group formed by the Division of Youth and Family Services and established in accordance with regulations adopted by the Commissioner of Children and Families for the purpose of addressing the child's safety, permanency or well-being, when the provision of such information is in the best interests of the child as determined by the Division of Youth and Family Services.

Any individual, agency, board, court, grand jury, legislative committee, or other entity which receives from the department the records and reports referred to in subsection a., shall keep such records and reports, or parts thereof, confidential and shall not disclose such records and reports or parts thereof except as authorized by law.

c. The department may share information with a child who is the subject of a child abuse or neglect report, as appropriate to the child's age or condition, to enable the child to understand the basis for the department's involvement and to participate in the development, discussion, or implementation of a case plan for the child.

d. The department may release the records and reports referred to in subsection a. of this section to any person engaged in a bona fide research purpose, provided, however, that no names or other information identifying persons named in the report shall be made available to the researcher unless it is absolutely essential to the research purpose and provided further that the approval of the Commissioner of Children and Families or his designee shall first have been obtained.

e. For incidents determined by the department to be substantiated, the department shall forward to the police or law enforcement agency in whose jurisdiction the child named in the report resides, the identity of persons alleged to have committed child abuse or neglect and of victims of child abuse or neglect, their addresses, the nature of the allegations, and other relevant information, including, but not limited to, prior reports of abuse or neglect and names of siblings obtained by the department during its investigation of a report of child abuse or neglect. The police or law enforcement agency shall keep such information confidential.

f. The department may disclose to the public the findings or information about a case of child abuse or neglect which has resulted in a child fatality or near fatality. Nothing may be disclosed which would likely endanger the life, safety, or physical or emotional well-being of a child or the life or safety of any other person or which may compromise the integrity of a department investigation or a civil or criminal investigation or judicial proceeding. If the department denies access to specific information on this basis, the requesting entity may seek disclosure of the information through the Chancery Division of the Superior Court. No information may be disclosed which is deemed confidential by federal or State law. The name or any other information identifying the person or entity who referred the child to the department shall not be released to the public.

g. The department shall release the records and reports referred to in subsection a. of this section to a unified child care agency contracted with the department pursuant to N.J.A.C.10:15–2.1 for the purpose of providing information on child abuse or neglect allegations involving a prospective approved home provider or any adult household member pursuant to section 2 of

P.L.2003, c. 185 (C.30:5B–32) to a child's parent when the information is necessary for the parent to make a decision concerning the placement of the child in an appropriate child care arrangement.

The department shall not release any information that would likely endanger the life, safety, or physical or emotional well-being of a child or the life or safety of any other person.

L.1977, c. 102, § 1, eff. May 25, 1977. Amended by L.1993, c. 350, § 5, eff. June 29, 1995; L.1995, c. 135, § 9; L.1996, c. 32, § 1, eff. June 6, 1996; L.1997, c. 175, § 16, eff. July 31, 1997; L.2003, c. 185, § 1; L.2004, c. 130, § 22, eff. Aug. 27, 2004; L.2006, c. 47, § 42, eff. July 1, 2006.

9:6–8.10b. Permitting or encouraging release of record or report; penalty

Any person who willfully permits or encourages the release of the contents of any record or report in contravention of this act shall be guilty of a misdemeanor and subject to a fine of not more than $1,000.00, or to imprisonment for not more than 3 years, or both.

L.1977, c. 102, § 2, eff. May 25, 1977.

9:6–8.10c. Incarcerated persons and persons assuming care and custody of minor to undergo child abuse record information check

a. Upon receiving the presentencing investigation information from the court pursuant to section 1 of P.L.2003, c. 301 (C.2C:44–6.2) concerning a sole caretaker of a child who will be incarcerated and the person who will assume care and custody of the child during the period of incarceration, the Division of Youth and Family Services in the Department of Children and Families shall conduct a child abuse record information check of its child abuse records to determine if an incident of child abuse or neglect has been substantiated against the person who will be responsible for the child's care and custody or any adult and juvenile over 12 years of age in the person's household.

b. If, based on the information provided by the court and the check of its child abuse records, the division determines that the incarcerated person's minor child may be at risk for abuse or neglect or the child's emotional, physical, health care and educational needs will not be met during the period of incarceration, the division shall take appropriate action to ensure the safety of the child.

L.2003, c. 301, § 2, eff. April 13, 2004. Amended by L.2006, c. 47, § 43, eff. July 1, 2006.

9:6–8.10d. Rules and regulations

The Commissioner of Children and Families shall adopt rules and regulations pursuant to the "Administrative Procedure Act," P.L.1968, c. 410 (C.52:14B–1 et seq.) to carry out the purposes of sections 2 and 3 of this act.

L.2003, c. 301, § 4, eff. April 13, 2004. Amended by L.2006, c. 47, § 44, eff. July 1, 2006.

9:6–8.10e. Child abuse registry check of applicant for professional guardian

a. In accordance with the provisions of sections 6 and 7 of P.L.2005, c. 370 (C.52:27G–37 and C.52:27G–38), the Department of Children and Families shall conduct a check of its child abuse registry for each person seeking registration as a professional guardian who is required to undergo such a check pursuant to P.L.2005, c. 370 (C.52:27G–32 et al.). The department shall immediately forward the information obtained as a result of the check to the Office of the Public Guardian for Elderly Adults.

b. Subsequent to the initial registration of an individual as a professional guardian, the public guardian may submit the name of a registered professional guardian for an additional child abuse registry check. Upon receipt of a response from the department, the public guardian shall make a determination regarding the continuation of the registration of the person as a professional guardian.

L.2005, c. 370, § 9, eff. July 11, 2006. Amended by L.2006, c. 47, § 45, eff. July 1, 2006.

9:6–8.11. Insuring safety of child upon receipt of report; report to central registry of bureau of children's services in Trenton; privacy of information

Upon receipt of any such report, the Division of Youth and Family Services, or such another entity in the Department of Children and Families as may be designated by the Commissioner of Children and Families to investigate child abuse or neglect, shall immediately take such action as shall be necessary to insure the safety of the child and to that end may request and shall receive appropriate assistance from local and State law enforcement officials. A representative of the division or other designated entity shall initiate an investigation within 24 hours of receipt of the report, unless the division or other entity authorizes a delay based upon the request of a law enforcement official. The division or other entity shall also, within 72 hours, forward a report of such matter to the child abuse registry operated by the division in Trenton.

The child abuse registry shall be the repository of all information regarding child abuse or neglect that is accessible to the public pursuant to State and federal law. No information received in the child abuse registry shall be considered as a public record within the meaning of P.L.1963, c. 73 (C.47:1A–1 et seq.) or P.L.2001, c. 404 (C.47:1A–5 et al.).

L.1971, c. 437, § 4, eff. Feb. 10, 1972. Amended by L.2004, c. 130, § 23, eff. Aug. 27, 2004; L.2006, c. 47, § 46, eff. July 1, 2006.

9:6–8.12. Maintenance of 24 hour emergency telephone service for receipt of child abuse calls

The Division of Youth and Family Services shall maintain, at all times, an emergency telephone service for the receipt of calls involving a report, complaint or allegation of child abuse or neglect.

L.1971, c. 437, § 5, eff. Feb. 10, 1972. Amended by L.2004, c. 130, § 24, eff. Aug. 27, 2004.

9:6–8.13. Person making report; immunity from liability; action for relief from discharge or discrimination

Anyone acting pursuant to this act in the making of a report under this act shall have immunity from any liability, civil or criminal, that might otherwise be incurred or imposed. Any such person shall have the same immunity with respect to testimony given in any judicial proceeding resulting from such report.

A person who reports or causes to report in good faith an allegation of child abuse or neglect pursuant to section 3 of P.L.1971, c. 437 (C. 9:6–8.10) and as a result thereof is discharged from employment or in any manner discriminated against with respect to compensation, hire, tenure or terms, conditions or privileges of employment, may file a cause of action for appropriate relief in the family part of the Chancery Division of the Superior Court in the county in which the discharge or alleged discrimination occurred or in the county of the person's primary residence.

If the court finds that the person was discharged or discriminated against as a result of the person's reporting an allegation of child abuse or neglect, the court may grant reinstatement of employment with back pay or other legal or equitable relief.

L.1971, c. 437, § 6, eff. Feb. 10, 1972. Amended by L.1987, c. 341, § 5, eff. Dec. 24, 1987.

9:6–8.14. Violations including failure to make report; disorderly person

Any person knowingly violating the provisions of this act including the failure to report an act of child abuse having reasonable cause to believe that an act of child abuse has been committed, is a disorderly person.

L.1971, c. 437, § 7, eff. Feb. 10, 1972.

9:6–8.15. Rules and regulations

The Bureau of Children's Services[1] shall from time to time promulgate such rules and regulations as may be necessary to effectuate the provisions of this act.

L.1971, c. 437, § 8, eff. Feb. 10, 1972.

1 Now Division of Youth and Family Services, see § 30:4C–2.

9:6–8.16. Child taken to physician or hospital for treatment of serious physical injury; protective custody

Any physician examining or treating any child, or the director or his designate of any hospital or similar institution to which any child has been brought for care or treatment, is empowered to take the said child into protective custody when the child has suffered serious physical injury or injuries, and the most probable inference from the medical and factual information supplied, is that the said injury or injuries were inflicted upon the child by another person by other than accidental means, and the person suspected of inflicting, or permitting to be inflicted, the said injury upon the child, is a person into whose custody the child would normally be returned.

L.1973, c. 147, § 1, eff. May 24, 1973.

9:6–8.17. Report of action of taking protective custody

The physician or the director or his designate of a hospital or similar institution taking a child into such protective custody shall immediately report his action to the Division of Youth and Family Services by calling its emergency telephone service maintained pursuant to section 5 of P.L.1971, c. 437 (C.9:6–8.12).

L.1973, c. 147, § 2, eff. May 24, 1973. Amended by L.2004, c. 130, § 25, eff. Aug. 27, 2004.

9:6–8.18. Bureau of children's services or division of youth and family services; insuring safety of child; investigation; application for order placing child under protective custody

The Bureau of Children's Services or its successor, the Division of Youth and Family Services, shall upon receipt of such report, take action to insure the safety of the child under section 4 of P.L.1971, c. 437 (C. 9:6–8.11). The said report shall be deemed an oral complaint under section 12 of P.L.1951, c. 138 (C. 30:4C–12), and the Bureau of Children's Services or its successor, the Division of Youth and Family Services, shall investigate the circumstances under which the child was injured and may, after such investigation has been completed, apply for a court order placing the child under its care and supervision, pursuant to section 12 of P.L.1951, c. 138 (C. 30:4C–12).

L.1973, c. 147, § 3, eff. May 24, 1973.

9:6–8.19. Notice to parents or guardian; visitation rights; limitation on period

a. The Bureau of Children's Services or its successor, the Division of Youth and Family Services, shall immediately after the receipt of such report, and after making a determination to take the child into protective custody, shall serve or attempt to serve, written notice upon the parents or guardian that the said child has been taken into protective custody. The notice shall contain a statement of the maximum duration of the protective custody and the location of the child during protective custody.

b. The parents or guardian of a child in protective custody may, upon request and in the reasonable discretion of the physician, director, or his designate, or appropriate official of the Bureau of Children's Services, or its successor, the Division of Youth and Family Services, visit the said child, provided that the life or health of the child will not be endangered by such visit.

c. The entire period of protective custody shall not exceed 3 court days. The protective custody may be terminated earlier at the discretion of the reporting physician, director or appropriate official of the Bureau of Children's Services or its successor, the Division of Youth and Family Services, or upon order of the court.

L.1973, c. 147, § 4, eff. May 24, 1973.

9:6–8.19a. Notice and opportunity to be heard

In any case in which the Division of Youth and Family Services accepts a child in its care or custody, the child's resource family parent or relative providing care for the child, as applicable, shall receive written notice of and an opportunity to be heard at any review or hearing held with respect to the child, but the resource family parent or relative shall not be made a party to the review or hearing solely on the basis of the notice and opportunity to be heard.

L.1999, c. 53, § 5, eff. March 31, 1999. Amended by L.2004, c. 130, § 26, eff. Aug. 27, 2004.

9:6–8.20. Physicians or directors of hospitals acting under this law; immunity from liability

Any physician or director of a hospital or similar institution who takes a child into protective custody pursuant to this act shall have immunity from any civil and criminal liability that might otherwise be incurred or imposed. Any such person shall have the same immunity with respect to testimony given in any judicial proceeding resulting therefrom.

L.1973, c. 147, § 5, eff. May 24, 1973.

C. ADJUDICATION OF ALLEGED CHILD ABUSE OR NEGLECT

9:6–8.21. Definitions

As used in this act, unless the specific context indicates otherwise:

a. "Parent or guardian" means any natural parent, adoptive parent, resource family parent, stepparent, paramour of a parent or any person, who has assumed responsibility for the care, custody or control of a child or upon whom there is a legal duty for such care. Parent or guardian includes a teacher, employee or volunteer, whether compensated or uncompensated, of an institution who is responsible for the child's welfare and any other staff person of an institution regardless of whether or not the person is responsible for the care or supervision of the child. Parent or guardian also includes a teaching staff member or other employee, whether compensated or uncompensated, of a day school as defined in section 1 of P.L. 1974, c. 119 (C.9:6–8.21).

b. "Child" means any child alleged to have been abused or neglected.

c. "Abused or neglected child" means a child less than 18 years of age whose parent or guardian, as herein defined, (1) inflicts or allows to be inflicted upon such child physical injury by other than accidental means which causes or creates a substantial risk of death, or serious or protracted disfigurement, or protracted impairment of physical or emotional health or protracted loss or impairment of the function of any bodily organ; (2) creates or allows to be created a substantial or ongoing risk of physical injury to such child by other than accidental means which would be likely to cause death or serious or protracted disfigurement, or protracted loss or impairment of the function of any bodily organ; (3) commits or allows to be committed an act of sexual abuse against the child; (4) or a child whose physical, mental, or emotional condition has been impaired or is in imminent danger of becoming impaired as the result of the failure of his parent or guardian, as herein defined, to exercise a minimum degree of care (a) in supplying the child with adequate food, clothing, shelter, education, medical or surgical care though financially able to do so or though offered financial or other reasonable means to do so, or (b) in providing the child with proper supervision or guardianship, by unreasonably inflicting or allowing to be inflicted harm, or substantial risk thereof, including the infliction of excessive corporal punishment; or by any other acts of a similarly serious nature requiring the aid of the court; (5) or a child who has been willfully abandoned by his parent or guardian, as herein defined; (6) or a child upon whom excessive physical restraint has been used under circumstances which do not indicate that the child's behavior is harmful to himself, others or property; (7) or a child who is in an institution and (a) has been placed there inappropriately for a continued period of time with the knowledge that the placement has resulted or may continue to result in harm to the child's mental or physical well-being or (b) who has been willfully isolated from ordinary social contact under circumstances which indicate emotional or social deprivation.

A child shall not be considered abused or neglected pursuant to paragraph (7) of subsection c. of this section if the acts or omissions described therein occur in a day school as defined in this section.

No child who in good faith is under treatment by spiritual means alone through prayer in accordance with the tenets and practices of a recognized church or religious denomination by a duly accredited practitioner thereof shall for this reason alone be considered to be abused or neglected.

d. "Law guardian" means an attorney admitted to the practice of law in this State, regularly employed by the Office of the Public Defender or appointed by the court, and designated under this act to represent minors in alleged cases of child abuse or neglect and in termination of parental rights proceedings.

e. "Attorney" means an attorney admitted to the practice of law in this State who shall be privately retained; or, in the instance of an indigent parent or guardian, an attorney from the Office of the Public Defender or an attorney appointed by the court who shall be appointed in order to avoid conflict between the interests of the child and the parent or guardian in regard to representation.

f. "Division" means the Division of Youth and Family Services in the Department of Children and Families unless otherwise specified.

g. "Institution" means a public or private facility in the State which provides children with out of home care, supervision or maintenance. Institution includes, but is not limited to, a correctional facility, detention facility, treatment facility, day care center, residential school, shelter and hospital.

h. "Day school" means a public or private school which provides general or special educational services to day students in grades kindergarten through 12. Day school does not include a residential facility, whether public or private, which provides care on a 24–hour basis.

L.1974, c. 119, § 1, eff. Oct. 10, 1974. Amended by L.1977, c. 209, § 1, eff. Sept. 7, 1977; L.1987, c. 341, § 6, eff. Dec. 24, 1987; L.1994, c. 58, § 39, eff. July 1, 1994; L.1999, c. 53, § 55, eff. March 31, 1999; L.2004, c. 130, § 27, eff. Aug. 27, 2004; L.2005, c. 169, § 1, eff. Aug. 5, 2005; L.2006, c. 47, § 47, eff. July 1, 2006.

9:6–8.22. Superior Court, chancery division, family part; jurisdiction; duties; priority of cases

The Superior Court, Chancery Division, Family Part in each county shall have jurisdiction over all noncriminal proceedings involving alleged cases of child abuse or neglect, and shall be charged with the immediate protection of said children, whereby the safety of the children shall be of paramount concern. All noncriminal cases involving child abuse shall be commenced in or transferred to this court from other courts as they are made known to the other courts. Commencement of cases of child abuse or neglect must be the first order of priority in the Family Part.

L.1974, c. 119, § 2, eff. Oct. 10, 1974. Amended by L.1977, c. 209, § 2, eff. Sept. 7, 1977; L.1991, c. 91, § 198, eff. April 9, 1991; L.1999, c. 53, § 6, eff. March 31, 1999.

9:6–8.23. Law guardian; representation of minor; appointment

a. Any minor who is the subject of a child abuse or neglect proceeding under this act must be represented by a law guardian to help protect his interests and to help him express his wishes to the court. However, nothing in this act shall be construed to preclude any other interested person or agency from appearing by counsel.

b. The Superior Court, Chancery Division, Family Part, on its own motion, will make appointments of law guardians.

L.1974, c. 119, § 3, eff. Oct. 10, 1974. Amended by L.1991, c. 91, § 199, eff. April 9, 1991.

9:6–8.24. Jurisdiction

a. Notwithstanding any other law to the contrary, the Superior Court, Chancery Division, Family Part has exclusive original jurisdiction over noncriminal proceedings under this act alleging the abuse or neglect of a child.

b. In determining the jurisdiction of the court under this act, the age of the child at the time the proceedings are initiated is controlling.

c. In determining the jurisdiction of the court under this act, the child need not be currently in the care or custody of his parent or guardian, as defined herein.

d. If the matter in regard to the parent or guardian is referred to the county prosecutor by the Family Part or otherwise the Family Part may continue the proceeding under this act in regard to the child after such referral. If the proceeding in regard to the child is continued, the Family Part shall enter any preliminary order necessary to protect the interests of the child pending a final order from the criminal courts.

e. Any hearing held before the Family Part may serve as a permanency hearing to provide judicial review and approval of a permanency plan for the child if all the requirements of section 50 of P.L.1999, c. 53 (C.30:4C–61.2) are met.

L.1974, c. 119, § 4, eff. Oct. 10, 1974. Amended by L.1977, c. 209, § 3, eff. Sept. 7, 1977; L.1991, c. 91, § 200, eff. April 9, 1991; L.1999, c. 53, § 7, eff. March 31, 1999.

9:6–8.25. Transfer to and from the Superior Court

a. Notice to the prosecutor. Immediately upon receipt of a complaint, the Superior Court, Chancery Division, Family Part shall forward a copy of such complaint to the county prosecutor, after which the prosecutor shall take whatever action he deems necessary under all of the circumstances.

b. Any criminal complaint charging facts amounting to abuse or neglect under this act may be transferred by the county prosecutor or the criminal court in which the complaint was made, to the Family Part, in the county in which the former court is located. If any police officer, county prosecutor or criminal court receives a complaint which amounts to child abuse or neglect, the police officer, county prosecutor or criminal court shall report to the division pursuant to P.L.1971, c. 437, section 3 (C. 9:6–8.10). If any police officer, county prosecutor or the criminal court refers a matter with regard to the parent or guardian, or child, and there appears to be no basis for action in the Family Part, the proceeding may be terminated. If the Family Part

determines a complaint should be filed, proceedings under this act shall be commenced immediately.

c. Nothing in this act shall be interpreted to preclude the county prosecutor from bringing criminal action against the parent or guardian or any other person even though the child involved is initially or ultimately the subject of proceedings in the Family Part.

L.1974, c. 119, § 5, eff. Oct. 10, 1974. Amended by L.1977, c. 209, § 4, eff. Sept. 7, 1977; L.1991, c. 91, § 201, eff. April 9, 1991.

9:6–8.26. Venue

Proceedings under this act shall be brought in accordance with the Rules of Court.

L.1974, c. 119, § 6, eff. Oct. 10, 1974. Amended by L.1977, c. 209, § 5, eff. Sept. 7, 1977.

9:6–8.27. Temporary removal with consent

a. A police officer or an agency or institution or individual may temporarily remove a child from the place where he is residing with the consent of his parent or other person legally responsible for his care, if, there is reasonable cause to suspect that the child's life or health is in imminent danger. If the child is not returned within 3 working days from the date of removal, the procedure required pursuant to this act shall be applied immediately.

b. (Deleted by amendment, P.L.2006, c. 47).

L.1974, c. 119, § 7, eff. Oct. 10, 1974. Amended by L.1977, c. 209, § 6, eff. Sept. 7, 1977; L.2006, c. 47, § 48, eff. July 1, 2006.

9:6–8.28. Preliminary orders of court before preliminary hearing held

a. The Superior Court, Chancery Division, Family Part may enter an order, whereby the safety of the child shall be of paramount concern, directing the temporary removal of a child from the place where he is residing before a preliminary hearing under this act, if (1) the parent or other person legally responsible for the child's care was informed of an intent to apply for any order under this section; and (2) the child appears so to suffer from the abuse or neglect of his parent or guardian that his immediate removal is necessary to avoid imminent danger to the child's life, safety or health; and (3) there is not enough time to hold a preliminary hearing.

b. The order shall specify the facility to which the child is to be brought.

c. The Family Part may enter an order authorizing a physician or hospital to provide emergency medical or surgical procedures before a preliminary hearing is held under this act if (1) such procedures are necessary to safeguard the life or health of the child; and (2) there is not enough time to hold a preliminary hearing under section 11 hereof. [1]

d. Any person who originates a proceeding pursuant to section 14 of this act [2] may apply for through the division or the court on its own motion may issue, an order of temporary removal. The division shall make every reasonable effort to inform the parent or guardian of any such application, confer with a person wishing to make such an application and make such inquiries as will aid the court in disposing of such application. Within 24 hours the division shall report such application to the child abuse registry of the division.

e. Any person acting under the authority of this act may request and shall receive appropriate assistance from local and State law enforcement officials.

L.1974, c. 119, § 8, eff. Oct. 10, 1974. Amended by L.1977, c. 209, § 7, eff. Sept. 7, 1977; L.1991, c. 91, § 202, eff. April 9, 1991; L.1999, c. 53, § 8, eff. March 31, 1999; L.2004, c. 130, § 28, eff. Aug. 27, 2004.

  1 N.J.S.A. § 9:6–8.31.
  2 N.J.S.A. § 9:6–8.34.

9:6–8.29.   Emergency removal without court order

a. A police officer or a designated employee of the Probation Division or a designated employee of the division may remove a child from the place where he is residing, or any such person or any physician treating such child may keep a child in his custody without an order pursuant to section 8 of P.L.1974, c. 119 (C.9:6–8.28) and without the consent of the parent or guardian regardless of whether the parent or guardian is absent, if the child is in such condition that his continuance in said place or residence or in the care and custody of the parent or guardian presents an imminent danger to the child's life, safety or health, and there is insufficient time to apply for a court order pursuant to section 8 of P.L.1974, c. 119 (C.9:6–8.28), or any physician or hospital treating such child may keep a child in custody pursuant to P.L.1973, c. 147 (C.9:6–8.16 et seq.). The Division of Youth and Family Services shall not be required to provide reasonable efforts to prevent placement if removal of the child is necessary due to imminent danger to the child's life, safety or health in accordance with section 24 of P.L.1999, c. 53 (C.30:4C–11.2).

b. If a person authorized by this section removes or keeps custody of a child, he shall (1) inform the division immediately; (2) bring the child immediately to a place designated by the division for this purpose, and (3) make every reasonable effort to inform the parent or guardian of the facility to which he has brought the child.

c. Any person or institution acting in good faith in the removal or keeping of a child pursuant to this section shall have immunity from any liability, civil or criminal, that might otherwise be incurred or imposed as a result of such removal or keeping.

d. Any person acting under the authority of this act may request and shall receive appropriate assistance from local and State law enforcement officials.

L.1974, c. 119, § 9, eff. Oct. 10, 1974. Amended by L.1977, c. 209, § 8, eff. Sept. 7, 1977; L.1999, c. 53, § 9, eff. March 31, 1999.

9:6–8.30.   Action by the division upon emergency removal

a. The division when informed that there has been an emergency removal of a child from his home without court order shall make every reasonable effort to communicate immediately with the child's parent or guardian that such emergency removal has been made and the location of the facility to which the child has been taken, and advise the parent or guardian to appear in the appropriate Superior Court, Chancery Division, Family Part within two court days. The division shall make a reasonable effort, at least 24 hours prior to the court hearing, to: notify the parent or guardian of the time to appear in court; and inform the parent or guardian of his right to obtain counsel, and how to obtain counsel through the Office of the Public Defender if the parent or guardian is indigent. The division shall also advise the party making the removal to appear. If the removed child is returned to his home prior to the court hearing, there shall be no court hearing to determine the sufficiency of cause for the child's removal, unless the child's parent or guardian makes application to the court for review. For the purposes of this section, "facility" means a hospital, shelter or child care institution in which a child may be placed for temporary care, but does not include a resource family home.

b. The division shall cause a complaint to be filed under this act within two court days after such removal takes place.

c. Whenever a child has been removed pursuant to section 7[1] or 9[2] of P.L.1974, c. 119 (C.9:6–8.27 or 9:6–8.29), the division shall arrange for immediate medical screening of the child and shall have legal authority to consent to such screening. If necessary to safeguard the child's health or life, the division also is authorized to arrange for and consent to medical care or treatment of the child. Consent by the division pursuant to this subsection shall be deemed legal and valid for all purposes with respect to any person, hospital, or other health care facility screening, examining or providing care or treatment to a child in accordance with and in reliance upon such consent. Medical reports resulting from such screening, examination or care or treatment shall be released to the division for the purpose of aiding in the determination of whether the child has been abused or neglected. Any person or health care facility acting in good faith in the screening of, examination of or provision of care and treatment to a child or in the release of medical records shall have immunity from any liability, civil or criminal, that might otherwise be incurred or imposed as a result of such act.

L.1974, c. 119, § 10, eff. Oct. 10, 1974. Amended by L.1977, c. 209, § 9, eff. Sept. 7, 1977; L.1983, c. 290, § 1, eff. Aug. 4, 1983; L.1991, c. 91, § 203, eff. April 9, 1991; L.2004, c. 130, § 29, eff. Aug. 27, 2004; L.2006, c. 47, § 49, eff. July 1, 2006.

  1 N.J.S.A. § 9:6–8.27.
  2 N.J.S.A. § 9:6–8.29.

9:6–8.31. Preliminary orders after filing of complaint

a. In any case where the child has been removed without court order, except where action has been taken pursuant to P.L.1973, c. 147 (C.9:6–8.16 et seq.) the Superior Court, Chancery Division, Family Part shall hold a hearing on the next court day, whereby the safety of the child shall be of paramount concern, to determine whether the child's interests require protection pending a final order of disposition. In any other case under this act, any person who may originate a proceeding may apply for, or the court, on its own motion, may order a hearing at any time after the complaint is filed to determine, with the safety of the child of paramount concern, whether the child's interests require protection pending a final order of disposition.

b. Upon such hearing, if the court finds that continued removal is necessary to avoid an ongoing risk to the child's life, safety or health, it shall affirm the removal of the child to an appropriate place or place him in the custody of a suitable person.

If the court determines that removal of the child by a physician, police officer, designated employee of the Probation Division or designated employee of the Division of Youth and Family Services was necessary due to imminent danger to the child's life, safety or health, the court shall find that the Division of Youth and Family Services was not required to provide reasonable efforts to prevent placement of the child in accordance with section 24 of P.L.1999, c. 53 (C.30:4C–11.2).

c. Upon such hearing the court may, for good cause shown, issue a preliminary order of protection which may contain any of the provisions authorized on the making of an order of protection under section 35 of P.L.1974, c. 119 (C.9:6–8.55).

d. Upon such hearing, the court may, for good cause shown, release the child to the custody of his parent or guardian from whose custody or care the child was removed, pending a final order of disposition, in accord with section 33 of P.L.1974, c. 119 (C.9:6–8.53).

e. Upon such hearing, the court may authorize a physician or hospital to provide medical or surgical procedures if such procedures are necessary to safeguard the child's life or health.

f. If the court grants or denies a preliminary order requested pursuant to this section, it shall state the grounds for such decision.

g. In all cases involving abuse or neglect the court shall order an examination of the child by a physician appointed or designated for the purpose by the division. As part of such examination, the physician shall arrange to have color photographs taken as soon as practical of any areas of trauma visible on such child and may if indicated, arrange to have a radiological examination performed on the child. The physician, on the completion of such examination, shall forward the results thereof together with the color photographs to the court ordering such examination.

L.1974, c. 119, § 11, eff. Oct. 10, 1974. Amended by L.1977, c. 209, § 10, eff. Sept. 7, 1977; L.1991, c. 91, § 204, eff. April 9, 1991; L.1999, c. 53, § 10, eff. March 31, 1999.

9:6–8.32. Application to return child temporarily removed

Upon the application of the parent or guardian of a child temporarily removed under this act, the court shall hold a hearing, whereby the safety of the child shall be of paramount concern, to determine whether the child should be returned; a. if there has not been a hearing on the removal of the child at which the parent or guardian was present or had an adequate opportunity to be present; or b. upon good cause shown. Except for good cause shown, such hearing shall be held within 3 court days of the application. Upon such hearing, the court shall grant the application, unless it finds that such return presents an imminent risk to the child's life, safety or health.

L.1974, c. 119, § 12, eff. Oct. 10, 1974. Amended by L.1977, c. 209, § 11, eff. Sept. 7, 1977; L.1999, c. 53, § 11, eff. March 31, 1999.

9:6–8.33. Originating proceeding to determine abuse or neglect

a. A proceeding under this act is originated by the filing of a complaint in which facts sufficient to establish that a child is an abused or neglected child under this act are alleged.

b. Where more than one child is the responsibility of the parent or guardian it may be alleged in the same complaint that one or more children are abused or neglected children.

c. In cases of emergency, in addition to the removal of one child, any other child residing in the home may also be removed if his immediate removal is necessary to avoid imminent danger to his life or health.

L.1974, c. 119, § 13, eff. Oct. 10, 1974. Amended by L.1977, c. 209, § 12, eff. Sept. 7, 1977.

9:6–8.34. Persons who may originate proceedings

The following persons may originate a proceeding under this act:

a. A parent or other person interested in the child.

b. A duly authorized agency, association, society, institution or the division.

c. A police officer.

d. Any person having knowledge or information of a nature which convinces him that a child is abused or neglected.

e. A person on the court's direction.

f. The county prosecutor.

g. In cases where a private individual is unwilling or reluctant to file a complaint, he may request the division to initiate a complaint in his stead.

L.1974, c. 119, § 14, eff. Oct. 10, 1974. Amended by L.1977, c. 209, § 13, eff. Sept. 7, 1977.

9:6–8.35. Preliminary procedure

The division may, with the safety of the child of paramount concern:

a. Confer with any person seeking to file a complaint, the potential respondent, and other interested persons concerning the advisability of filing a complaint under this act; and

b. Attempt to adjust suitable cases before a complaint is filed over which the court apparently would have jurisdiction.

c. The division shall not prevent any person or agency who wishes to file a complaint under this act from having access to the court for that purpose.

d. Efforts at adjustment under this section may not extend for a period of more than 30 days without an order of a judge of the court, who may extend the period for an additional 30 days.

e. Such adjustment may include a preliminary conference held by the division at its discretion upon written notice to the parent or guardian and the potential complainant for the purpose of attempting such adjustment, provided however that the division shall not be authorized under this section to compel any person to appear at any conference, produce any papers, or visit any place.

f. The Superior Court, Chancery Division, Family Part and the division shall deal with cases involving imminent physical harm or actual physical harm on a priority basis.

L.1974, c. 119, § 15, eff. Oct. 10, 1974. Amended by L.1977, c. 209, § 14, eff. Sept. 7, 1977; L.1991, c. 91, § 205, eff. April 9, 1991; L.1999, c. 53, § 12, eff. March 31, 1999.

9:6–8.36. Admissibility of statements made during a preliminary conference

No statement made by the potential respondent during a preliminary conference held pursuant to section 15 [1] hereof may be admitted into evidence at a fact-finding hearing under this act or in a court of criminal jurisdiction at any time prior to conviction.

L.1974, c. 119, § 16, eff. Oct. 10, 1974. Amended by L.1977, c. 209, § 15, eff. Sept. 7, 1977.

  [1] N.J.S.A. § 9:6–8.35.

9:6–8.36a. Report of suspected child abuse and neglect by division to county prosecutor

The Department of Children and Families shall immediately report all instances of suspected child abuse and neglect, as defined by regulations, to the county prosecutor of the county in which the child resides. The regulations shall be developed jointly by the department and the county prosecutors, approved by the Attorney General, and promulgated by the Commissioner of Children and Families.

L.1977, c. 210, § 1, eff. Sept. 7, 1977. Amended by L.2004, c. 130, § 30, eff. Aug. 27, 2004; L.2006, c. 47, § 50, eff. July 1, 2006.

9:6–8.37. Issuance of summons

On the filing of a complaint involving abuse or neglect under this act, unless a warrant is issued pursuant to section 19 hereof,[1] the court shall cause a copy of the complaint and a summons to be issued forthwith, requiring the parent or guardian with whom the child is residing to appear at the court within 3 court days regarding the complaint. The court shall also, unless dispensed with for good cause shown, require the person thus summoned to produce the child at the time and place named.

L.1974, c. 119, § 17, eff. Oct. 10, 1974. Amended by L.1977, c. 209, § 16, eff. Sept. 7, 1977.

  [1] N.J.S.A. § 9:6–8.39.

9:6–8.38. Service of summons

a. In cases involving abuse, or neglect the complaint and summons shall be served within 2 court days after their issuance. If they cannot be served within that time, such fact shall be reported to the court with the reasons therefor within 3 court days after their issuance and the court shall thereafter issue a warrant in accordance with the provisions of section 19 of this act.[1] The court shall also, unless dispensed with for good cause shown, direct that the child be brought before the court.

b. Service of a summons and complaint shall be made by delivery of a true copy thereof to the person summoned at least 24 hours before the time stated therein for appearance.

c. If after reasonable effort, personal service is not made, the court may at any stage in the proceedings make an order providing for substituted service in the manner provided for substituted service in accordance with the Rules of Court.

L.1974, c. 119, § 18, eff. Oct. 10, 1974. Amended by L.1977, c. 209, § 17, eff. Sept. 7, 1977.

  [1] N.J.S.A. § 9:6–8.39.

9:6–8.39. Issuance of warrant and reports

a. The court may issue a warrant directing the parent or guardian with whom the child is residing to be brought before the court, when a complaint is filed with the court under this act and it appears that (1) the summons cannot be served; or (2) the summoned person has refused to obey the summons; or (3) the parent or guardian is likely to leave the jurisdiction; or (4) a summons, in the court's opinion, would be ineffectual; or (5) the safety of the child is endangered.

b. When issuing a warrant under this section, the court may also direct that the child be brought before the court.

c. If a warrant is not executed within 2 court days of its issuance such fact shall be reported to the court within 3 court days of its issuance.

L.1974, c. 119, § 19, eff. Oct. 10, 1974. Amended by L.1977, c. 209, § 18, eff. Sept. 7, 1977.

9:6–8.40. Records involving abuse or neglect

Records involving abuse or neglect. When the Department of Children and Families receives a report or complaint that a child may be abused or neglected; when the department provides services to a child; or when the department receives a request from the Superior Court, Chancery Division, Family Part to investigate an allegation of abuse or neglect, the department may request of any and all public or private institutions, or agencies including law enforcement agencies, or any private practitioners, their records past and present pertaining to that child and other children under the same care, custody and control. The department shall not be charged a fee for the copying of the records. Records kept pursuant to the "New Jersey Code of Juvenile Justice," P.L.1982, c. 77 (C.2A:4A–20 et seq.) may be obtained by the department, upon issuance by a court of an order on good cause shown directing these records to be released to the department for the purpose of aiding in evaluation to determine if the child is abused or neglected. In the release of the aforementioned records, the source shall have immunity from any liability, civil or criminal.

L.1974, c. 119, § 20, eff. Oct. 10, 1974. Amended by L.1977, c. 209, § 19, eff. Sept. 7, 1977; L.1991, c. 91, § 206, eff. April 9, 1991; L.1999, c. 53, § 13, eff. March 31, 1999; L.2004, c. 130, § 31, eff. Aug. 27, 2004; L.2006, c. 47, § 51, eff. July 1, 2006.

9:6–8.40a. Unfounded allegations of child abuse to be expunged from division's records

a. The Division of Youth and Family Services in the Department of Children and Families shall expunge from its records all information relating to a report, complaint or allegation of an incident of child abuse or neglect with respect to which the division or other entity designated by the Commissioner of Children and Families to investigate allegations of child abuse or neglect has determined, based upon its investigation thereof, that the report, complaint or allegation of the incident was unfounded.

b. (Deleted by amendment, P.L.2004, c. 130).

The definition of, and process for, making a determination of an unfounded report, complaint or allegation of an incident of child abuse or neglect shall be defined in regulations promulgated by the department pursuant to the "Administrative Procedure Act," P.L.1968, c. 410 (C.52:14B–1 et seq.).

L.1997, c. 62, § 1, eff. April 7, 1997. Amended by L.2004, c. 130, § 32, eff. Aug. 27, 2004; L.2006, c. 47, § 52, eff. July 1, 2006.

9:6–8.41. Required findings concerning notice

No hearing may commence under this act unless the court enters a finding:

a. That the parent or guardian is present at the hearing or has been served with a copy of the complaint; or

b. If the parent or guardian is not present, that every reasonable effort has been made to effect service under sections 18 and 19 hereof.[1]

L.1974, c. 119, § 21, eff. Oct. 10, 1974.

[1] N.J.S.A. §§ 9:6–8.38, 9:6–8.39.

9:6–8.42. Effect of absence of parent or guardian

If the parent or guardian is not present, the court may proceed to hear a complaint under this act only if the child is represented by a law guardian. If the parent or guardian thereafter makes a motion to the court that a resulting disposition be vacated and asks for a rehearing, the court shall grant the motion on an affidavit showing such relationship or responsibility unless the court finds that the parent or guardian willfully refused to appear at the hearing in which case the court may deny the motion.

L.1974, c. 119, § 22, eff. Oct. 10, 1974. Amended by L.1977, c. 209, § 20, eff. Sept. 7, 1977.

9:6–8.43. Notice of rights

a. The court shall advise the parent or guardian of his right to have an adjournment to retain counsel and consult with him. The court shall advise the respondent that if he is indigent, he may apply for an attorney through the Office of the Public Defender. In cases where the parent or guardian applies for an attorney through the Office of the Public Defender, the court may adjourn the case for a reasonable period of time for the parent or guardian to secure counsel; however, the adjournment shall not preclude the court from granting temporary relief as appropriate under the law. The court shall appoint a law guardian for the child as provided by this act.

b. The general public may be excluded from any hearing under this act, and only such persons and the representatives of authorized agencies may be admitted thereto as have an interest in the case.

L.1974, c. 119, § 23, eff. Oct. 10, 1974. Amended by L.1977, c. 209, § 21, eff. Sept. 7, 1977; L.1994, c. 58, § 40, eff. July 1, 1994; L.2004, c. 130, § 33, eff. Aug. 27, 2004.

9:6–8.44. Definition of "fact-finding hearing"

When used in this act the term "fact-finding hearing" means a hearing to determine whether the child is an abused or neglected child as defined herein.

L.1974, c. 119, § 24, eff. Oct. 10, 1974.

9:6–8.45. Definition of "dispositional hearing"

When used in this act the term "dispositional hearing" means a hearing to determine what order should be made.

L.1974, c. 119, § 25, eff. Oct. 10, 1974.

9:6–8.46. Evidence

a. In any hearing under this act, including an administrative hearing held in accordance with the "Administrative Procedure Act," P.L.1968, c. 410 (C.52:14B–1 et seq.), (1) proof of the abuse or neglect of one child shall be admissible evidence on the issue of the abuse or neglect of any other child of, or the responsibility of, the parent or guardian and (2) proof of injuries sustained by a child or of the condition of a child of such a nature as would ordinarily not be sustained or exist except by reason of the acts or omissions of the parent or guardian shall be prima facie evidence that a child of, or who is the responsibility of such person is an abused or neglected child, and (3) any writing, record or photograph, whether in the form of an entry in a book or otherwise, made as a memorandum or record of any condition, act, transaction, occurrence or event relating to a child in an abuse or neglect proceeding of any hospital or any other public or private institution or agency shall be admissible in evidence in proof of that condition, act, transaction, occurrence or event, if the judge finds that it was made in the regular course of the business of any hospital or any other public or private institution or agency, and that it was in the regular course of such business to make it, at the time of the condition, act, transaction, occurrence or event, or within a reasonable time thereafter, shall be prima facie evidence of the facts contained in such certification. A certification by someone other than the head of the hospital or agency shall be accompanied by a photocopy of a delegation of authority signed by both the head of the hospital or agency and by such other employees. All other circumstances of the making of the memorandum, record or photograph, including lack of personal knowledge of the making, may be proved to affect its weight, but they shall not affect its admissibility and (4) previous statements made by the child relating to any allegations of abuse or neglect shall be admissible in evidence; provided, however, that no such statement, if uncorroborated, shall be sufficient to make a fact finding of abuse or neglect.

b. In a fact-finding hearing (1) any determination that the child is an abused or neglected child must be based on a preponderance of the evidence and (2) only competent, material and relevant evidence may be admitted.

c. In a dispositional hearing and during all other stages of a proceeding under this act, only material and relevant evidence may be admitted.

L.1974, c. 119, § 26, eff. Oct. 10, 1974. Amended by L.1977, c. 209, § 22, eff. Sept. 7, 1977; L.2005, c. 169, § 2, eff. Aug. 5, 2005.

9:6–8.47. Sequence of hearings

a. Upon completion of the fact-finding hearing, the dispositional hearing may commence immediately after the required findings are made.

b. Reports prepared by the probation department or the division for use by the court at any time for the making of an order of disposition shall be deemed confidential information furnished to the court which the court in a proper case may, in its discretion, disclose in whole or in part to the law guardian, attorney as defined herein, or other appropriate person. Such reports may not be furnished to the court prior to the completion of a fact-finding hearing, but may be used in a dispositional hearing.

L.1974, c. 119, § 27, eff. Oct. 10, 1974. Amended by L.1977, c. 209, § 23, eff. Sept. 7, 1977.

9:6–8.48. Adjournments

a. The court may adjourn a fact-finding hearing or a dispositional hearing for good cause shown on its own motion or on the motion of the county prosecutor, the law guardian, or the respondent's attorney. If so requested, the court shall not proceed with a fact-finding hearing earlier than 3 days after service of summons and complaint, unless emergency medical or surgical procedures are necessary to safeguard the life and health of the child. Adjournment may not exceed 30 court days, without additional court appearance.

b. At the conclusion of a fact-finding hearing and after it has made findings required before a dispositional hearing may commence, the court may adjourn the proceedings to enable it to make inquiry into the surroundings, conditions, and capacities of the persons involved in the proceedings.

L.1974, c. 119, § 28, eff. Oct. 10, 1974.

9:6–8.49. Special consideration in certain cases

To ensure that the safety of children is of paramount concern, when scheduling hearings and investigations, the court shall give priority to proceedings under this act involving imminent or actual physical harm, or in which a child has been removed from home before a final order of disposition. Any adjournment granted in the course of such a proceeding should be for as short a time as possible.

L.1974, c. 119, § 29, eff. Oct. 10, 1974. Amended by L.1999, c. 53, § 14, eff. March 31, 1999.

9:6–8.50. Sustaining or dismissing complaint

a. If facts sufficient to sustain the complaint are established, the court shall enter an order finding that the child is an abused or neglected child and shall state the grounds for said findings.

b. If the proof does not conform to the specific allegations of the complaint, the court may amend the allegations to conform to the proof; provided, however, that in such case the respondent shall be given reasonable time to prepare to answer the amended allegations.

c. If facts sufficient to sustain the complaint under this act are not established, or the court concludes that its assistance is not required on the record before it, the court shall dismiss the complaint and shall state the grounds for the dismissal.

d. If the court makes a finding of abuse or neglect, it shall determine, based upon the facts adduced during the fact-finding hearing, and upon any other facts presented to it, whether a preliminary order pursuant to section 11 hereof[1] is required to protect the child's interests pending a final order of disposition. The court shall state the grounds for its determination. In addition, a child found to be abused or neglected may be removed and remanded to a place designated by the court or be placed in the custody of a suitable person, pending a final order of disposition, if the court finds that there is a substantial probability that the final order of disposition will be an order of placement under the section 34 hereof.[2]

e. If the court finds that the child is an abused or neglected child as defined in this act, it may refer any aspect of the matter, including anything related to the child and the parent or guardian, to the division, ordering that the division provide such services as are deemed appropriate to the ends of protecting the child and rehabilitating and improving family life, wherever possible. In the event of such referral, the court may suspend any dispositional hearing indefinitely. The division shall report the status of the case so referred to the court annually in writing, a copy to be served upon the parent or guardian and the law guardian. The division shall also report its intent to terminate services in a case so referred to the court in writing.

L.1974, c. 119, § 30, eff. Oct. 10, 1974. Amended by L.1977, c. 209, § 24, eff. Sept. 7, 1977.

[1] N.J.S.A. § 9:6–8.31.
[2] N.J.S.A. § 9:6–8.54.

9:6–8.51. Disposition of adjudication

a. At the conclusion of a dispositional hearing under this act, the court shall enter an order of disposition: (1) suspending judgment in accord with section 32 hereof;[1] (2) releasing the child to the custody of his parents or guardian in accord with section 33 hereof;[2] (3) placing the child in accord with section 34 hereof;[3] (4) making an order of protection in accord with section 35 hereof;[4] (5) placing the respondent on probation in accord with section 36 hereof;[5] (6) requiring that an individual found to have abused or neglected a child accept therapeutic services, and this order may be carried out in conjunction with any other order of disposition.

b. The court shall state the grounds for any disposition made under this section.

L.1974, c. 119, § 31, eff. Oct. 10, 1974.

[1] N.J.S.A. § 9:6–8.52.
[2] N.J.S.A. § 9:6–8.53.
[3] N.J.S.A. § 9:6–8.54.
[4] N.J.S.A. § 9:6–8.55.
[5] N.J.S.A. § 9:6–8.56.

9:6–8.52. Suspended judgment

a. The court shall define permissible terms and conditions of a suspended judgment. These terms and conditions shall relate to the acts of commission or omission of the parent or guardian.

b. The maximum duration of any term or condition of a suspended judgment shall be 1 year, unless the court finds at the conclusion of that period, upon a hearing, that exceptional circumstances required an extension thereof for an additional year.

L.1974, c. 119, § 32, eff. Oct. 10, 1974. Amended by L.1977, c. 209, § 25, eff. Sept. 7, 1977.

9:6–8.53. Release to custody of parent or guardian

a. If the order of disposition releases the child to the custody of his parent or guardian responsible for his care at the time of the filing of the complaint, the court may place the child under supervision of the division or may enter an order of protection under section 35 hereof.[1]

b. The court shall define permissible terms and conditions of supervision under this section. The maximum duration of any such term or condition shall not exceed a period of 1 year, unless the court finds at the conclusion of that period of 1 year, upon a hearing, that exceptional circumstances require an extension thereof for an additional year.

L.1974, c. 119, § 33, eff. Oct. 10, 1974.

[1] N.J.S.A. § 9:6–8.55.

9:6–8.54. Placement

a. For the purpose of section 31 of P.L.1974, c. 119 (C.9:6–8.51), the court may place the child in the custody of a relative or other suitable person or the division for the placement of a child after a finding that the division has made reasonable efforts to prevent placement or that reasonable efforts to prevent placement were not required in accordance with section 24 of P.L.1999, c. 53 (C.30:4C–11.2).

b. (1) Placements under this section may be for an initial period of 12 months and the court, in its discretion, may at the expiration of that period, upon a hearing make successive extensions for additional periods of up to one year each. The court on its own motion may, at the conclusion of any period of placement, hold a hearing concerning the need for continuing the placement.

(2) The court shall conduct a permanency hearing for the child no later than 30 days after placement in cases in which the court has determined that reasonable efforts to reunify the child with the parent or guardian are not required pursuant to section 25 of P.L.1999, c. 53 (C.30:4C–11.3), or no later than 12 months after placement in cases in which the court has determined that efforts to reunify the child with the parent or guardian are required. The hearing shall include, but not necessarily be limited to, consideration and evaluation of information provided by the division and other interested parties regarding such matters as those listed in subsection c. of section 50 of P.L.1999, c. 53 (C.30:4C–61.2).

(3) The court shall review the permanency plan for the child periodically, as deemed appropriate by the court, to ensure that the permanency plan is achieved.

c. No placement may be made or continued under this section beyond the child's eighteenth birthday without his consent.

d. If the parent or person legally responsible for the care of any such child or with whom such child resides receives public assistance and care, any portion of which is attributable to such child, a copy of the order of the court providing for the placement of such child from his home shall be furnished to the appropriate county welfare board, which shall reduce the public assistance and care furnished to such parent or other person by the amount attributable to such child.

L.1974, c. 119, § 34, eff. Oct. 10, 1974. Amended by L.1977, c. 209, § 26, eff. Sept. 7, 1977; L.1999, c. 53, § 15, eff. March 31, 1999; L.1999, c. 213, § 2, eff. Sept. 17, 1999.

9:6–8.55. Order of protection

The court may make an order of protection in assistance or as a condition of any other order made under this act. The order of protection may set forth reasonable conditions of behavior to be observed for a specified time by a person who is before the court and is a parent or guardian responsible for the child's care or the spouse of the parent or guardian, or both. Such an order may require any such person: a. To stay away from the home, the other spouse or the child; b. To permit a parent to visit the child at stated periods; c. To abstain from offensive conduct against the child or against the other parent or against any person to whom custody of the child is awarded; d. To give proper attention to the care of the home; and e. To refrain from acts of commission or omission that tend to make the home not a proper place for the child.

The court may also award custody of the child, during the term of the order of protection to either parent or to an appropriate relative; however, nothing in this section shall be construed to give the court power to place or board out any child or to commit a child to the custody

of an institution or agency. In making orders of protection, the court shall so act as to insure that in the care, protection, discipline and guardianship of the child, his religious faith shall be preserved and protected.

L.1974, c. 119, § 35, eff. Oct. 10, 1974.

9:6–8.56. Probation supervision

The court may place the respondent under the supervision of the probation department and the court shall define permissible terms and conditions of said supervision. The maximum duration of any such term or condition shall not exceed a period of 2 years, unless the court finds at the conclusion of that period that exceptional circumstances require an extension thereof for an additional year.

L.1974, c. 119, § 36, eff. Oct. 10, 1974. Amended by L.1977, c. 209, § 27, eff. Sept. 7, 1977.

9:6–8.57. Abandoned child

If the court finds that a child was abandoned by his parents or guardian, it may make an order so finding and may discharge the child to the custody of the Division which shall provide for such child as authorized by law.

L.1974, c. 119, § 37, eff. Oct. 10, 1974.

9:6–8.58. Provision for therapeutic services

In cases where, in the opinion of the court, an individual found to have abused or neglected a child appears to be in need of therapeutic services, the court may order the individual to accept such services or evaluation for such services, including, but not limited to, homemaker services, functional education, group self-help programs, and professional therapy; provided, however, that the court may not commit any person to any residential mental health facility without the consent of such person or after a hearing held pursuant to the requirements of R.S. 30:4–23 et seq.[1] The court shall determine the ability to pay and the method of payment for the care, as it orders.

L.1974, c. 119, § 38, eff. Oct. 10, 1974.

[1] Repealed. See, now, N.J.S.A. § 30:4–27.1 et seq.

9:6–8.58a. Conditions on return of child to home; substance abuse assessment and treatment

When a child is placed in the custody of a relative or other suitable person or the Division of Youth and Family Services pursuant to section 34 of P.L.1974, c. 119 (C.9:6–8.54), because of a finding of abuse or neglect, the Superior Court, Chancery Division, Family Part shall order the parent and, when appropriate, any other adult domiciled in the home to undergo substance abuse assessment, when necessary. If the assessment reveals positive evidence of substance abuse, the court shall require the parent and other adult, when appropriate, to demonstrate that he is receiving treatment and complying with the treatment program for the substance abuse problem before the child is returned to the parental home.

L.1998, c. 127, § 1, eff. Jan. 8, 1999.

9:6–8.58b. Adoption of rules and regulations

The Commissioner of Children and Families pursuant to the "Administrative Procedure Act," P.L.1968, c. 410 (C.52:14B–1 et seq.), shall adopt regulations to effectuate the purposes of this act.

L.1998, c. 127, § 2, eff. Jan. 8, 1999. Amended by L.2006, c. 47, § 53, eff. July 1, 2006.

9:6–8.59. Staying, modifying, setting aside or vacating orders

For good cause shown and after due notice, the court on its own motion, or that of the county prosecutor, the law guardian, the respondent's attorney, or the division may stay execution of arrest, set aside, modify or vacate any order issued in the course of a proceeding under this act. The court must state the grounds for this action.

L.1974, c. 119, § 39, eff. Oct. 10, 1974. Amended by L.1977, c. 209, § 28, eff. Sept. 7, 1977.

9:6–8.60. Petition to terminate placement

Any interested person acting on behalf of a child placed under section 34 hereof [1] or the child's parents or guardian may petition the court for any order terminating the placement. The petition must be verified and must show:

a. That an application for the child's return to his home was made to an appropriate person after expiration of the Order of Placement provided for in section 34 hereof;

b. That the application was denied or was not granted within 30 days from the day application was made; and

c. The grounds for the petition.

L.1974, c. 119, § 40, eff. Oct. 10, 1974.

[1] N.J.S.A. § 9:6–8.54.

9:6–8.61. Service of petition; answer

A copy of a petition under section 40 hereof [1] shall promptly be served pursuant to the Rules of Court upon the division or the individual having custody of the child under section 34 [2] whose duty it shall be to file an answer to the petition within 5 days.

L.1974, c. 119, § 41, eff. Oct. 10, 1974. Amended by L.1977, c. 209, § 29, eff. Sept. 7, 1977.

[1] N.J.S.A. § 9:6–8.60.
[2] N.J.S.A. § 9:6–8.54.

9:6–8.62. Examination of petition and answer; hearing

The court shall promptly examine the petition and answer. If the court concludes that a hearing should be held, it may proceed upon due notice to all concerned parties to hear the facts and determine whether continued placement serves the purposes of this act. If the court concludes that a hearing is not necessary, it shall enter an order granting or denying the petition.

L.1974, c. 119, § 42, eff. Oct. 10, 1974.

9:6–8.63. Orders on hearing

a. If the court determines after hearing that continued placement serves the purposes of this act, it shall deny the petition. The court may, on its own motion, reduce the duration of the placement, change the agency or institution in which the child is placed, or direct the division to make such other arrangements for the child's care and welfare as the facts of the case may require.

b. If the court determines, after hearing, that continued placement does not serve the purposes of this act, the court shall discharge the child from the custody of the division or person given custody under section 34 hereof. [1]

L.1974, c. 119, § 43, eff. Oct. 10, 1974.

[1] N.J.S.A. § 9:6–8.54.

9:6–8.64. Successive petitions

If a petition under section 40 hereof [1] is denied, it may not again be filed with the court for a period of 90 days after the denial, unless the order of denial permits refiling at an earlier time.

L.1974, c. 119, § 44, eff. Oct. 10, 1974.

[1] N.J.S.A. § 9:6–8.60.

9:6–8.65. Substitution for original placement

If under section 34, [1] custody of the child is given to a party other than the division, and that party is no longer able to continue custody of the child, the court may authorize the division to arrange for the child's care by another person or assume custody of the child.

L.1974, c. 119, § 45, eff. Oct. 10, 1974. Amended by L.1977, c. 209, § 30, eff. Sept. 7, 1977.

[1] N.J.S.A. § 9:6–8.54.

9:6–8.66. Failure to comply with terms and conditions of suspended judgment

If a parent or guardian responsible for a child's care is brought before the court for failing to comply with the terms and conditions of a suspended judgment issued under section 32 hereof, [1] and if, after hearing, the court is satisfied by competent proof that the parent or guardian did so, the court may revoke the suspension of judgment and enter any order that might have been made at the time judgment was suspended.

L.1974, c. 119, § 46, eff. Oct. 10, 1974.

[1] N.J.S.A. § 9:6–8.52.

9:6–8.67. Failure to comply with terms and conditions of order of probation or protection

If a parent or guardian is brought before the court for failing to comply with the terms and conditions of an order of probation issued under section 36 hereof,[1] or of an order of protection issued under section 35 [2] or section 11 [3] hereof, and if, after hearing, the court is satisfied by competent proof that the parent or guardian did so willfully and without just cause, the court may revoke the order of probation or of protection and enter any order that might have been made at the time the order of probation was made.

L.1974, c. 119, § 47, eff. Oct. 10, 1974.

[1] N.J.S.A. § 9:6–8.56.
[2] N.J.S.A. § 9:6–8.55.
[3] N.J.S.A. § 9:6–8.31.

9:6–8.68. Effect of running away from place of placement

If a child placed under section 34 hereof [1] runs away from the place of placement, the court may, after hearing, revoke the order of placement and may make any order, including an order of placement, that might have been made at the time the order of placement was made. The court may require that the child be present at such hearing and shall appoint a law guardian to represent him.

L.1974, c. 119, § 48, eff. Oct. 10, 1974.

[1] N.J.S.A. § 9:6–8.54.

9:6–8.69. Release from responsibility under order of placement

Those responsible for the operation of a place where a child has been placed under section 34 hereof [1] may petition the court for leave to return the child to the court and, for good cause shown, to be released from responsibility under the order of placement. After hearing the court may grant the petition and make any order, including an order of placement, that might have been made at the time the order of placement was made.

L.1974, c. 119, § 49, eff. Oct. 10, 1974.

[1] N.J.S.A. § 9:6–8.54.

9:6–8.70. Appealable orders

An appeal may be taken as of right from any final order of disposition and from any other final order made pursuant to this act. An appeal from a final order or decision in a case involving child abuse may be taken as of right to the Appellate Division of the Superior Court. Pending the determination of such appeal, such order or decision shall be stayed where the effect of such order or decision would be to discharge the child, if the Superior Court, Chancery Division, Family Part or the court before which such appeal is pending finds that such a stay is necessary to avoid imminent risk to the child's life or health.

L.1974, c. 119, § 50, eff. Oct. 10, 1974. Amended by L.1977, c. 209, § 31, eff. Sept. 7, 1977; L.1991, c. 91, § 207, eff. April 9, 1991.

9:6–8.71. Appropriations

There shall be appropriated from the general fund such funds as are necessary to implement the provisions and to effectuate the purposes of this act as shall be included in any general or supplemental appropriation act.

L.1974, c. 119, § 51, eff. Oct. 10, 1974.

9:6–8.72. Rules and regulations

The division shall promulgate such rules and regulations that will facilitate compliance with this act.

L.1974, c. 119, § 52, eff. Oct. 10, 1974.

9:6–8.72a. Rules and regulations; reporting and investigation of allegations of child abuse

The Commissioner of Education shall, in cooperation and consultation with the Commissioner of Children and Families, adopt rules and regulations, pursuant to the "Administrative Procedure Act," P.L. 1968, c. 410 (C.52:14B–1 et seq.), concerning the relationship, rights and responsibilities of the Department of Children and Families and local school districts regarding the reporting and investigation of allegations of child abuse.

L.1987, c. 341, § 8, eff. Dec. 24, 1987. Amended by L.2004, c. 130, § 34, eff. Aug. 27, 2004; L.2006, c. 47, § 54, eff. July 1, 2006.

9:6–8.73. Severability

If any provision of this act or the application thereof to any person or circumstances is held to be invalid, the remainder of the act and application of such provision to other persons or circumstances shall not be affected thereby.

L.1974, c. 119, § 55, eff. Oct. 10, 1974.

9:6–8.74. New Jersey Task Force on Child Abuse and Neglect Act; short title

This act shall be known and may be cited as the "New Jersey Task Force on Child Abuse and Neglect Act."

L.1994, c. 119, § 1, eff. Dec. 31, 1996.

9:6–8.75. New Jersey Task Force on Child Abuse and Neglect; grants from Children's Trust Fund; staffing and oversight review subcommittee

There is established the "New Jersey Task Force on Child Abuse and Neglect."

a. The purpose of the task force is to study and develop recommendations regarding the most effective means of improving the quality and scope of child protective and preventative services provided or supported by State government, including a review of the practices and policies utilized by the Division of Youth and Family Services and Division of Prevention and Community Partnerships in the Department of Children and Families in order to:

1. optimize coordination of child abuse-related services and investigations;

2. promote the safety of children at risk of abuse or neglect;

3. ensure a timely determination with regard to reports of alleged child abuse;

4. educate the public about the problems of, and coordinate activities relating to, child abuse and neglect;

5. develop a Statewide plan to prevent child abuse and neglect and mechanisms to facilitate child abuse and neglect prevention strategies in coordination with the Division of Prevention and Community Partnerships;

6. mobilize citizens and community agencies in a proactive effort to prevent and treat child abuse and neglect; and

7. foster cooperative working relationships between State and local agencies responsible for providing services to victims of child abuse and neglect and their families.

b. The task force shall receive, evaluate and approve applications of public and private agencies and organizations for grants from moneys annually appropriated from the 'Children's Trust Fund' established pursuant to section 2 of P.L.1985, c. 197 (C.54A:9–25.4). Any portion of the moneys actually appropriated which are remaining at the end of a fiscal year shall lapse to the "Children's Trust Fund."

Grants shall be awarded to public and private agencies for the purposes of planning and establishing or improving programs and services for the prevention of child abuse and neglect, including activities which:

(1) Provide Statewide educational and public informational seminars for the purpose of developing appropriate public awareness regarding the problems of child abuse and neglect;

(2) Encourage professional persons and groups to recognize and deal with problems of child abuse and neglect;

(3) Make information about the problems of child abuse and neglect available to the public and organizations and agencies which deal with problems of child abuse and neglect; and

(4) Encourage the development of community prevention programs, including:

(a) community-based educational programs on parenting, prenatal care, prenatal bonding, child development, basic child care, care of children with special needs, coping with family stress, personal safety and sexual abuse prevention training for children, and self-care training for latchkey children; and

(b) community-based programs relating to crisis care, aid to parents, child abuse counseling, peer support groups for abusive or potentially abusive parents and their children, lay health visitors, respite of crisis child care, and early identification of families where the potential for child abuse and neglect exists.

The task force shall, in awarding grants, establish such priorities respecting the programs or services to be funded and the amounts of funding to be provided as it deems appropriate, except that the task force shall place particular emphasis on community-based programs and services which are designed to develop and demonstrate strategies for the early identification, intervention and assistance of families and children at risk in order to prevent child abuse and neglect.

The task force shall adopt such rules and regulations pursuant to the "Administrative Procedure Act," P.L. 1968, c. 410 (C.52:14B–1 et seq.) to govern the awarding of grants pursuant to this subsection as may be necessary to establish adequate reporting requirements on the use of grant funds by recipient agencies and organizations and to permit the task force to evaluate the programs and services for which grants are awarded.

c. The task force shall establish a Staffing and Oversight Review Subcommittee to review staffing levels of the Division of Youth and Family Services in order to develop recommendations regarding staffing levels and the most effective methods of recruiting, hiring, and retaining staff within the division. In addition, the subcommittee shall review the division's performance in the achievement of management and client outcomes, and shall issue a preliminary report with its findings and recommendations no later than January 1, 2007, and subsequent reports annually thereafter with the first full report due no later than July 1, 2007. The subcommittee shall directly issue its reports to the Governor and, pursuant to section 2 of P.L. 1991, c. 164 (C.52:14–19.1), to the Legislature.

L.1994, c. 119, § 2, eff. Dec. 31, 1996. Amended by L.2006, c. 47, § 55, eff. July 1, 2006; L.2007, c. 130, § 1, eff. Aug. 6, 2007.

9:6–8.76. Membership of task force; terms of office

The task force shall consist of 30 members as follows: the Commissioners of Human Services, Children and Families, Education, Community Affairs, Corrections, and Health and Senior Services, the Attorney General, two judges of the Superior Court involved in both civil and criminal court proceedings related to child abuse and neglect as appointed by the Chief Justice of the Supreme Court, the Public Defender, the Child Advocate and the Superintendent of State Police, or their designees, as ex officio members; two members of the Senate and the General Assembly, respectively, no more than one of whom in each case shall be of the same political party; and a county prosecutor appointed by the Attorney General. The 13 public members shall be appointed by the Governor as follows: one member who is a director of a regional diagnostic and treatment center for child abuse and neglect; one member who represents the Association for Children of New Jersey; one member who represents Foster and Adoptive Family Services; one member who represents a faith-based organization; one member who is a director of a county department of human services; one member who is a youth 21 years of age or younger who is or has been placed under the care and custody of the Division of Youth and Family Services because of an allegation of child abuse or neglect; two members who represent service providers under contract with the Division of Youth and Family Services; and five members of the public who have an interest or expertise in issues concerning child welfare. The public members shall reflect the diversity of the residents of the State and the children and families served by the State's child welfare system.

The task force membership shall comply with the multidisciplinary requirements set forth in the "Child Abuse Prevention and Treatment Act," Pub.L.93–247 (42 U.S.C. s.5101 et seq.).

The task force shall be co-chaired, one co-chair shall be the Commissioner of Children and Families and the other shall be appointed by the Governor with the advice and consent of the Senate. The second co-chair shall be selected from among the public members and shall serve at the pleasure of the Governor. The public members shall serve for a term of three years.

L.1994, c. 119, § 3, eff. Dec. 31, 1996. Amended by L.2005, c. 155, § 107, eff. Jan. 17, 2006; L.2006, c. 47, § 56, eff. July 1, 2006; L.2009, c. 29, § 1, eff. March 21, 2009.

9:6–8.77. Procedure for filling vacancies; reimbursement of members for expenses

Vacancies in the membership of the task force shall be filled in the same manner provided for the original appointments. The members of the task force shall serve without compensation but may be reimbursed for traveling and other miscellaneous expenses necessary to perform their duties, within the limits of funds made available to the task force for its purposes.

L.1994, c. 119, § 4, eff. Dec. 31, 1996.

9:6–8.78. Professional and clerical staff to be provided as needed

The Department of Children and Families shall provide professional and clerical staff to the task force as necessary to effectuate the purposes of this act. *L.1994, c. 119, § 5, eff. Dec. 31, 1996. Amended by L.2006, c. 47, § 57, eff. July 1, 2006.*

9:6–8.79. Availability of services from other state entities; consultation with other organizations and associations

a. The task force shall be entitled to call upon the services of any State, county or municipal department, board, commission or agency, as may be available to it

for these purposes, and to incur such traveling and other miscellaneous expenses as it may deem necessary for the proper execution of its duties and as may be within the limit of funds appropriated or otherwise made available to it for these purposes.

b. The task force shall consult with such organizations and associations as the Association for Children of New Jersey, the New Jersey Association of Children's Residential Facilities, the New Jersey Chapter of the National Association of Social Workers, Inc., the Child Placement Advisory Council, the Medical Society of New Jersey, the New Jersey State Nurses Association, the New Jersey Education Association, the New Jersey Foster Parent Association, and the Graduate School of Social Work of Rutgers, The State University.

L.1994, c. 119, § 6, eff. Dec. 31, 1996.

9:6–8.80. Meetings; hearings

The task force may meet and hold hearings at such places as it shall designate during the sessions or recesses of the Legislature.

L.1994, c. 119, § 7, eff. Dec. 31, 1996.

9:6–8.81. Task force authorized to solicit, receive and disburse grants and donations

The task force may solicit, receive, disburse and monitor grants and other funds made available from any governmental, public, private, not-for-profit or for-profit agency, including funds made available under any federal or State law, regulation or program.

L.1994, c. 119, § 8, eff. Dec. 31, 1996.

9:6–8.82. Report of findings and recommendations

The task force shall present a report of its findings and recommendations to the Governor and the Legislature no later than one year after the organization of the task force.

L.1994, c. 119, § 9, eff. Dec. 31, 1996.

9:6–8.83. Short title; Comprehensive Child Abuse Prevention and Treatment Act

This act shall be known as and may be cited as the "Comprehensive Child Abuse Prevention and Treatment Act."

L.1997, c. 175, § 1, eff. July 31, 1997.

9:6–8.84. Definitions

As used in this act:

"Board" means the Child Fatality and Near Fatality Review Board established under P.L.1997, c. 175 (C.9:6–8.83 et al.).

"Child" means any person under the age of 18.

"Commissioner" means the Commissioner of Children and Families.

"Division" means the Division of Youth and Family Services in the Department of Children and Families.

"Near fatality" means a case in which a child is in serious or critical condition, as certified by a physician.

"Panel" means a citizen review panel as established under P.L.1997, c. 175 (C.9:6–8.83 et al.).

"Parent or guardian" means a person defined pursuant to section 1 of P.L.1974, c. 119 (C.9:6–8.21) who has the responsibility for the care, custody or control of a child or upon whom there is a legal duty for such care.

"Reasonable efforts" means attempts by an agency authorized by the Division of Youth and Family Services to assist the parents in remedying the circumstances and conditions that led to the placement of the child and in reinforcing the family structure, as defined in section 7 of P.L.1991, c. 275 (C.30:4C–15.1).

"Sexual abuse" means contacts or actions between a child and a parent or caretaker for the purpose of sexual stimulation of either that person or another person. Sexual abuse includes:

a. the employment, use, persuasion, inducement, enticement or coercion of any child to engage in, or assist any other person to engage in, any sexually explicit conduct or simulation of such conduct;

b. sexual conduct including molestation, prostitution, other forms of sexual exploitation of children or incest; or

c. sexual penetration and sexual contact as defined in N.J.S.2C:14–1 and a prohibited sexual act as defined in N.J.S.2C:24–4.

"Significant bodily injury" means a temporary loss of the functioning of any bodily member or organ or temporary loss of any one of the five senses.

"Withholding of medically indicated treatment" means the failure to respond to a child's life-threatening conditions by providing treatment, including appropriate nutrition, hydration, and medication which, in the treating physician's reasonable judgment, will most likely be effective in ameliorating or correcting all such conditions. The term does not include the failure to provide treatment, other than appropriate nutrition, hydration, or medication to a child when, in the treating physician's reasonable medical judgment:

a. the child is chronically and irreversibly comatose;

b. the provision of such treatment would merely prolong dying, not be effective in ameliorating or correcting all of the child's life-threatening conditions, or otherwise be futile in terms of the survival of the child; or

c. the provision of such treatment would be virtually futile in terms of the survival of the child and the treatment itself under such circumstances would be inhumane.

L.1997, c. 175, § 2, eff. July 31, 1997. Amended by L.1999, c. 53, § 16, eff. March 31, 1999; L.2006, c. 47, § 58, eff. July 1, 2006.

9:6–8.85. Response to medical neglect reports

The commissioner shall establish procedures for responding to the reporting of medical neglect, including instances of withholding of medically indicated treatment from disabled children with life-threatening conditions, to provide for: a. coordination and consultation with persons designated by and within appropriate health care facilities, and b. prompt notification by these persons of cases of suspected medical neglect, including withholding of medically indicated treatment from disabled children with life-threatening conditions.

L.1997, c. 175, § 3, eff. July 31, 1997.

9:6–8.86. Legal proceedings authorized; prevention or withholding or to provide medically indicated treatment

The division may pursue any legal remedies, including the initiation of legal proceedings in a court of competent jurisdiction, as may be necessary to: a. prevent the withholding of medically indicated treatment from disabled children with life-threatening conditions, or b. provide medical care or treatment for a child when such care or treatment is necessary to prevent or remedy serious harm to the child or to prevent the withholding of medically indicated treatment from disabled children with life-threatening conditions.

L.1997, c. 175, § 4, eff. July 31, 1997.

9:6–8.87. Reunification of family; parent convicted of murder, manslaughter, assault or related crimes

In any case in which the division accepts a child in care or custody, including placement, the division shall not be required to provide reasonable efforts to reunify the child with a parent if an exception to the requirement to provide reasonable efforts has been established in accordance with section 25 of P.L.1999, c. 53 (C.30:4C–11.3).

L.1997, c. 175, § 5, eff. July 31, 1997. Amended by L.1999, c. 53, § 17, eff. March 31, 1999.

9:6–8.88. Child fatality and near fatality review board established

There is established the Child Fatality and Near Fatality Review Board. For the purposes of complying with the provisions of Article V, Section IV, paragraph 1 of the New Jersey Constitution, the board is established within the Department of Children and Families, but notwithstanding the establishment, the board shall be independent of any supervision or control by the department or any board or officer thereof.

The purpose of the board is to review fatalities and near fatalities of children in New Jersey in order to identify their causes, their relationship to governmental support systems, and methods of prevention. The board shall describe trends and patterns of child fatalities and near fatalities in New Jersey; identify risk factors and their prevalence in these populations of children; evaluate the responses of governmental systems to children in families who are considered to be at high risk and to offer recommendations for improvement in those responses; characterize risk groups in terms that are compatible with the development of public policy; improve the sources of data collection by developing protocols for autopsies, death investigations, and complete recording of cause of death on the death certificate; and provide case consultation to individuals or agencies represented by the board.

L.1997, c. 175, § 6, eff. July 31, 1997. Amended by L.2006, c. 47, § 59, eff. July 1, 2006.

9:6–8.89. Child fatality and near fatality review board; membership; terms; officers; authority

a.   The board shall consist of 14 members as follows: the Commissioner of Children and Families, the Commissioner of Health and Senior Services, the Director of the Division of Youth and Family Services in the Department of Children and Families, the Attorney General, the Child Advocate and the Superintendent of State Police, or their designees, the State Medical Examiner, and the Chairperson or Executive Director of the New Jersey Task Force on Child Abuse and Neglect, who shall serve ex officio; and six public members appointed by the Governor, one of whom shall be a representative of the New Jersey Prosecutors' Association, one of whom shall be a Law Guardian, one of whom shall be a pediatrician with expertise in child abuse and neglect, one of whom shall be a psychologist with expertise in child abuse and neglect, one of whom shall be a social work educator with experience and expertise in the area of child abuse or a related field and one of whom shall have expertise in substance abuse.

b.   The public members of the board shall serve for three-year terms. Of the public members first appointed, three shall serve for a period of two years, and three shall serve for a term of three years. They shall serve without compensation but shall be eligible for reimbursement for necessary and reasonable expenses incurred in the performance of their official duties and within the limits of funds appropriated for this purpose. Vacancies in the membership of the board shall be filled in the same manner as the original appointments were made.

c.   The Governor shall appoint a public member to serve as chairperson of the board who shall be responsible for the coordination of all activities of the board and who shall provide the technical assistance needed to execute the duties of the board.

d.   The board is entitled to call to its assistance and avail itself of the services of employees of any State, county or municipal department, board, bureau, commission or agency as it may require and as may be available for the purposes of reviewing a case pursuant to the provisions of P.L.1997, c. 175 (C.9:6–8.83 et al.). The board may also seek the advice of experts, such as persons specializing in the fields of pediatric, radiological, neurological, psychiatric, orthopedic and forensic medicine; nursing; psychology; social work; edu-

cation; law enforcement; family law; substance abuse; child advocacy or other related fields, if the facts of a case warrant additional expertise.

L.1997, c. 175, § 7, eff. July 31, 1997. Amended by L.2005, c. 155, § 108, eff. Jan. 17, 2006; L.2006, c. 47, § 60, eff. July 1, 2006.

9:6–8.90.   Child fatality and near fatality review board; duties

The board shall:

a.   Identify the fatalities of children due to unusual circumstances according to the following criteria:

(1) The cause of death is undetermined;

(2) Death where substance abuse may have been a contributing factor;

(3) Homicide, child abuse or neglect;

(4) Death where child abuse or neglect may have been a contributing factor;

(5) Malnutrition, dehydration, or medical neglect or failure to thrive;

(6) Sexual abuse;

(7) Head trauma, fractures or blunt force trauma without obvious innocent reason such as auto accidents;

(8) Suffocation or asphyxia;

(9) Burns without obvious innocent reason such as auto accident or house fire; and

(10) Suicide.

b.   Identify fatalities and near fatalities among children whose family, currently or within the last 12 months, were receiving services from the division.

L.1997, c. 175, § 8, eff. July 31, 1997.

9:6–8.91.   Community-based investigation teams

a.   The board shall determine which fatalities shall receive full review. The board may establish local or regional community-based teams to review information regarding children identified by the board. At least one team shall be designated to review information regarding child fatalities due to unusual circumstances. At least one team shall be designated to review child fatalities and near fatalities identified pursuant to subsection b. of section 8 of P.L.1997, c.175 (C.9:6–8.90) as well as child fatalities where information available to the board indicates that child abuse or neglect may have been a contributing factor.

b.   Each team shall include, at a minimum, a person experienced in prosecution, a person experienced in local law enforcement investigation, a medical examiner, a public health advocate, a physician, preferably a pediatrician, and a casework supervisor from a division field office. As necessary to perform its functions, each team may add additional members or seek the advice of experts in other fields if the facts of a case warrant additional expertise.

c. Each team shall submit to the board chairperson a report of its findings and recommendations based upon its review of information regarding each child fatality or near fatality.

L.1997, c. 175, § 9, eff. July 31, 1997.

9:6–8.92. Child fatality and near fatality review board; records

a. The board shall record the name, age, date of birth, place of death or pronouncement of death, date and time of death, and circumstances surrounding the death in a confidential master file. Similar information shall be recorded for each near fatality reviewed by the board. The file shall serve as the minimum record of the case and shall be the only file that contains the name of the child and shall not be subject to discovery, but may be used by the chairperson of the board to refer an individual case, including the board's deliberations and conclusions, to the extent necessary for an appropriate agency to investigate or to provide services.

b. Except as provided in subsection a. of this section, the deliberations and conclusions of the board and of its teams, related to a specific case, shall be confidential. Summary records that are prepared by the board and the teams on each reported case shall be free of information that would identify the child.

c. The summary reports, deliberations and conclusions of the board or its teams shall not supersede or replace the conclusions or opinions of the agencies that contribute information from their own records.

d. The board shall review the reports submitted by each team and issue an annual report to the Governor and the Legislature which includes the number of cases reviewed and specific non-identifying information regarding cases of particular significance. The board shall also include in the report recommendations for achieving better coordination and collaboration among State and local agencies and recommendations for system-wide improvements in services to prevent fatalities and near fatalities among children.

L.1997, c. 175, § 10, eff. July 31, 1997.

9:6–8.93. Child fatality and near fatality review board; subpoenas; notice to prosecutors

a. The board may subpoena and review records that pertain to the child, except as provided in any statute, regulation or Executive Order relating to the confidentiality of criminal investigations and criminal investigative files. The records subject to subpoena and review shall include, but are not limited to, private medical and hospital records, school records, mental health records, and other records which may be deemed pertinent to the review process and necessary for the formulation of a conclusion by the board.

b. Records obtained by the board pursuant to subsection a. of this section shall not be subject to subpoena.

c. If, at the time of initial notification or during the subsequent review, the board has reasonable cause to believe that the death is the result of child abuse or neglect, or has reasonable cause to believe that the death is the result of an on-going hazard to other members of the household, then the board shall notify or shall verify that notification has been made to the county prosecutor of the county wherein the death occurred or was pronounced, and to the division.

L.1997, c. 175, § 11, eff. July 31, 1997.

9:6–8.94. Child fatality and near fatality review board; member immunity

A member of the board shall not be liable for any civil damages as a result of providing in good faith any reports, records, opinions or recommendations pursuant to P.L.1997, c. 175 (C.9:6–8.83 et al.).

L.1997, c. 175, § 12, eff. July 31, 1997.

9:6–8.95. Child fatality and near fatality review board; grants and funding

The board may solicit and receive grants and other funds made available from a governmental, public, private, nonprofit, or for-profit agency, including funds made available under any federal or State law, regulation or program.

L.1997, c. 175, § 13, eff. July 31, 1997.

9:6–8.96. Child fatality and near fatality review board; rules and regulations

The board shall adopt regulations pursuant to the "Administrative Procedure Act," P.L.1968, c. 410 (C.52:14B–1 et seq.) concerning the operation of the board, procedures for conducting reviews of cases involving child fatalities and near fatalities, and other matters necessary to effectuate the purposes of this act.

L.1997, c. 175, § 14, eff. July 31, 1997.

9:6–8.97. Citizen review panels

a. The commissioner shall designate three citizen review panels for the purpose of examining the policies and procedures of State and local agencies and, as appropriate, specific cases, and evaluating the extent to which the agencies are effectively discharging their child protection responsibilities.

b. The commissioner may designate as panels for the purposes of P.L.1997, c.175 (C.9:6–8.83 et al.), one or more existing entities established under federal or State law, if such entities have the capacity to satisfy the requirements of this act.

c. Each panel shall be composed of volunteer members who are broadly representative of the community in which the panel is established, including members who have expertise in the prevention and treatment of child abuse and neglect.

d. Each panel shall meet not less than once every three months.

e. The members of the panels:

(1) shall not disclose to any person or government official any identifying information about a specific child protection case with respect to which the panel is provided information; and

(2) shall not make public other information unless authorized by State statute.

f. Each panel shall have access to information as necessary to carry out its functions. Each panel is entitled to call to its assistance and avail itself of the services of employees of any State, county or municipal department, board, bureau, commission or agency as it may require and as may be available for the purposes of effectuating the provisions of P.L.1997, c. 175 (C.9:6–8.83 et al.). This subsection shall not be construed to permit access to information which may compromise the integrity of a division investigation or a civil or criminal investigation or judicial proceeding.

g. Each panel shall prepare and make available to the public on an annual basis, a report containing a summary of its activities.

h. A member of the panel shall not be liable for any civil damages as a result of providing, in good faith, a report, record, opinion or recommendation pursuant to P.L.1997, c. 175 (C.9:6–8.83 et al.).

i. A panel may receive grants and other funds made available from any governmental, public, private, non-profit or for-profit agency, including funds made available under any federal or State law, regulation or program.

L.1997, c. 175, § 15, eff. July 31, 1997.

9:6–8.98. Rules and regulations

The Department of Children and Families shall adopt rules and regulations pursuant to the "Administrative Procedure Act," P.L.1968, c. 410 (C.52:14B–1 et seq.) to effectuate the purposes of this act.

L.1997, c. 175, § 19, eff. July 31, 1997. Amended by L.2006, c. 47, § 61, eff. July 1, 2006.

9:6–8.99. Regional diagnostic and treatment centers for child abuse and neglect established

The Commissioner of Children and Families shall establish four regional diagnostic and treatment centers for child abuse and neglect affiliated with medical teaching institutions in the State that meet the standards adopted by the commissioner, in consultation with the New Jersey Task Force on Child Abuse and Neglect. The regional centers shall be located in the northern, north central, south central and southern regions of the State. Each center shall have experience in addressing the medical and mental health diagnostic and treatment needs of abused and neglected children in the region in which it is located.

L.1998, c. 19, § 1, eff. May 8, 1998. Amended by L.2006, c. 47, § 62, eff. July 1, 2006.

9:6–8.100. Center staff; intake, referral and tracking process

Each center shall demonstrate a multidisciplinary approach to identifying and responding to child abuse and neglect. The center staff shall include, at a minimum, a pediatrician, a consulting psychiatrist, a psychologist and a social worker who are trained to evaluate and treat children who have been abused or neglected and their families. Each center shall establish a liaison with the district office of the Division of Youth and Family Services in the Department of Children and Families and the prosecutor's office from the county in which the child who is undergoing evaluation and treatment resides. At least one member of the staff shall also have an appropriate professional credential or significant training and experience in the identification and treatment of substance abuse.

Each center shall develop an intake, referral and case tracking process which assists the division and prosecutor's office in assuring that child victims receive appropriate and timely diagnostic and treatment services.

L.1998, c. 19, § 2, eff. May 8, 1998. Amended by L.2006, c. 47, § 63, eff. July 1, 2006.

9:6–8.101. Center duties

The regional centers shall: evaluate and treat child abuse and neglect; be resources for the region and develop additional resources within the region; provide training and consultative services; and be available for emergency phone consultation 24 hours a day. The centers shall also be a source for research and training for additional medical and mental health personnel dedicated to the identification and treatment of child abuse and neglect.

The regional center may charge a sliding scale fee for services provided under this act.

L.1998, c. 19, § 3, eff. May 8, 1998.

9:6–8.102. Services provided by centers' staff

Services provided by the center's staff shall include, but not be limited to:

a. Providing psychological and medical evaluation and treatment of the child, counseling for family members and substance abuse assessment and mental health and substance abuse counseling for the parents or guardians of the child;

b. Providing referral for appropriate social services and medical care;

c. Providing testimony regarding alleged child abuse or neglect at judicial proceedings;

d. Providing treatment recommendations for the child and mental health and substance abuse treatment recommendations for his family, and providing mental health and substance abuse treatment recommendations for persons convicted of child abuse or neglect;

e. Receiving referrals from the Department of Children and Families and the county prosecutor's office and assisting them in any investigation of child abuse or neglect;

f. Providing educational material and seminars on child abuse and neglect and the services the center provides to children, parents, teachers, law enforcement officials, the judiciary, attorneys and other citizens.

L.1998, c. 19, § 4, eff. May 8, 1998. Amended by L.2004, c. 130, § 35, eff. Aug. 27, 2004; L.2006, c. 47, § 64, eff. July 1, 2006.

9:6–8.103. Responsibility to ensure safety of child undergoing treatment

The regional center shall ensure the safety of a child undergoing treatment while the child is at the regional center to the extent permitted by law. The appropriate law enforcement officials and protective services providers shall continue to ensure the safety of the child to the extent permitted by law.

L.1998, c. 19, § 5, eff. May 8, 1998.

9:6–8.104. Establishment and maintenance of county-based multidisciplinary teams

Regional centers shall act as a resource in the establishment and maintenance of county-based multidisciplinary teams which work in conjunction with the county prosecutor and the Department of Children and Families in the investigation of child abuse and neglect in the county in which the child who is undergoing evaluation and treatment resides. The Commissioner of Children and Families, in consultation with the New Jersey Task Force on Child Abuse and Neglect, shall establish standards for a county team. The county team shall consist of representatives of the following disciplines: law enforcement; child protective services;

mental health; substance abuse identification and treatment; and medicine; and, in those counties where a child advocacy center has been established, shall include a staff representative of a child advocacy center, all of whom have been trained to recognize child abuse and neglect. The county team shall provide: facilitation of the investigation, management and disposition of cases of criminal child abuse and neglect; referral services to the regional diagnostic center; appropriate referrals to medical and social service agencies; information regarding the identification and treatment of child abuse and neglect; and appropriate follow-up care for abused children and their families.

As used in this section, "child advocacy center" means a county-based center which meets the standards for a county team established by the commissioner pursuant to this section and demonstrates a multidisciplinary approach in providing comprehensive, culturally competent child abuse prevention, intervention and treatment services to children who are victims of child abuse or neglect.

L.1998, c. 19, § 6, eff. May 8, 1998. Amended by L.2001, c. 344, § 1, eff. Jan. 5, 2002; L.2004, c. 130, § 36, eff. Aug. 27, 2004; L.2006, c. 47, § 65, eff. July 1, 2006.

9:6–8.105. Repealed by L.2006, c.47, § 204, eff. July 1, 2006

9:6–8.106. Adoption of rules and regulations

The Commissioner of Children and Families shall adopt rules and regulations pursuant to the "Administrative Procedure Act," P.L.1968, c. 410 (C.52:14B–1 et seq.) necessary to effectuate the provisions of this act. [1]

L.1998, c. 19, § 8, eff. May 8, 1998. Amended by L.2006, c. 47, § 66, eff. July 1, 2006.

[1] P.L.1998, c. 19, § 8.

TITLE 13

CONSERVATION AND DEVELOPMENT—
PARKS AND RESERVATIONS

Chapter

1E. Solid Waste Management.
9.   State Forest Fire Service.

CHAPTER 1E

SOLID WASTE MANAGEMENT

Section

13:1E–9.   Codes, rules and regulations; enforcement;
             inspections; counsel; fees; remedies of and
             penalties for violations; order of abatement;
             hazardous wastes; forfeiture of conveyances;
             limitations of prosecution.
13:1E–48.2. Legislative findings.
13:1E–99.54. Violations; penalties.

13:1E–9. Codes, rules and regulations; enforcement; inspections; counsel; fees; remedies of and penalties for violations; order of abatement; hazardous wastes; forfeiture of conveyances; limitations of prosecution

a. All codes, rules and regulations adopted by the department related to solid waste collection and disposal shall have the force and effect of law. These codes, rules and regulations shall be observed throughout the State and shall be enforced by the department and by every local board of health, or county health department, as the case may be.

The department and the local board of health, or the county health department, as the case may be, shall have the right to enter a solid waste facility at any time in order to determine compliance with the registration statement and engineering design required pursuant to section 5 of P.L.1970, c. 39 (C.13:1E–5), and with the provisions of all applicable laws or rules and regulations adopted pursuant thereto.

The municipal attorney or an attorney retained by a municipality in which a violation of such laws or rules and regulations adopted pursuant thereto is alleged to have occurred shall act as counsel to a local board of health.

The county counsel or an attorney retained by a county in which a violation of such laws or rules and regulations adopted pursuant thereto is alleged to have occurred shall act as counsel to the county health department.

Any county health department may charge and collect from the owner or operator of any sanitary landfill facility within its jurisdiction such fees for enforcement activities as may be established by ordinance or resolution adopted by the governing body of any such county. The fees shall be established in accordance with a fee schedule regulation adopted by the department, pursuant to law, and shall be utilized exclusively to fund such enforcement activities.

All enforcement activities undertaken by county health departments pursuant to this subsection shall conform to all applicable performance and administrative standards adopted pursuant to section 10 of the "County Environmental Health Act," P.L.1977, c. 443 (C.26:3A2–28).

b. Whenever the commissioner finds that a person has violated any provision of P.L.1970, c. 39 (C.13:1E–1 et seq.), or any rule or regulation adopted, permit issued, or district solid waste management plan adopted pursuant to P.L.1970, c. 39, he shall:

(1) Issue an order requiring the person found to be in violation to comply in accordance with subsection c. of this section;

(2) Bring a civil action in accordance with subsection d. of this section;

(3) Levy a civil administrative penalty in accordance with subsection e. of this section;

(4) Bring an action for a civil penalty in accordance with subsection f. of this section; or

(5) Petition the Attorney General to bring a criminal action in accordance with subsection g. of this section.

c. Whenever the commissioner finds that a person has violated any provision of P.L.1970, c. 39, or any rule or regulation adopted, permit issued, or district solid waste management plan adopted pursuant to P.L.1970, c. 39, he may issue an order specifying the provision or provisions of P.L.1970, c. 39, or the rule, regulation, permit or district solid waste management plan of which the person is in violation, citing the action which constituted the violation, ordering abatement of the violation, and giving notice to the person of his right to a hearing on the matters contained in the order. The ordered party shall have 20 calendar days from receipt of the order within which to deliver to the commissioner a written request for a hearing. Such order shall be effective upon receipt and any person to whom such order is directed shall comply with the order immediately. A request for hearing shall not automatically stay the effect of the order.

d. The commissioner, a local board of health or county health department may institute an action or

953

proceeding in the Superior Court for injunctive and other relief, including the appointment of a receiver for any violation of this act, or of any code, rule or regulation adopted, permit issued, district solid waste management plan adopted or order issued pursuant to this act and said court may proceed in the action in a summary manner. In any such proceeding the court may grant temporary or interlocutory relief, notwithstanding the provisions of R.S.48:2–24.

Such relief may include, singly or in combination:

(1) A temporary or permanent injunction;

(2) Assessment of the violator for the costs of any investigation, inspection, or monitoring survey which led to the establishment of the violation, and for the reasonable costs of preparing and litigating the case under this subsection;

(3) Assessment of the violator for any cost incurred by the State in removing, correcting or terminating the adverse effects upon water and air quality resulting from any violation of any provision of this act or any rule, regulation or condition of approval for which the action under this subsection may have been brought;

(4) Assessment against the violator of compensatory damages for any loss or destruction of wildlife, fish or aquatic life, and for any other actual damages caused by any violation of this act or any rule, regulation or condition of approval established pursuant to this act for which the action under this subsection may have been brought. Assessments under this subsection shall be paid to the State Treasurer, or to the local board of health, or to the county health department, as the case may be, except that compensatory damages may be paid by specific order of the court to any persons who have been aggrieved by the violation.

If a proceeding is instituted by a local board of health or county health department, notice thereof shall be served upon the commissioner in the same manner as if the commissioner were a named party to the action or proceeding. The department may intervene as a matter of right in any proceeding brought by a local board of health or county health department.

e. The commissioner is authorized to assess a civil administrative penalty of not more than $50,000.00 for each violation provided that each day during which the violation continues shall constitute an additional, separate and distinct offense. The commission shall not assess a civil administrative penalty in excess of $25,000.00 for a single violation, or in excess of $2,500.00 for each day during which a violation continues, until the department has adopted, pursuant to the "Administrative Procedure Act," P.L.1968, c. 410 (C.52:14B–1 et seq.), regulations requiring the commissioner, in assessing a civil administrative penalty, to consider the operational history of the solid waste facility at which the violation occurred, the severity of the violation, the measures taken to mitigate or prevent further violations, and whether the penalty will maintain an appropriate deterrent. No assessment shall be levied pursuant to this section until after the violator has been notified by certified mail or personal service. The notice shall include a reference to the section of the statute, rule, regulation, order, permit condition or district solid waste management plan violated, a concise statement of the facts alleged to constitute a violation, a statement of the amount of the civil administrative penalties to be imposed, and a statement of the party's right to a hearing. The ordered party shall have 20 calendar days from receipt of the notice within which to deliver to the commissioner a written request for a hearing. After the hearing and upon finding that a violation has occurred, the commissioner may issue a final order after assessing the amount of the fine specified in the notice. If no hearing is requested, the notice shall become a final order after the expiration of the 20–day period. Payment of the assessment is due when a final order is issued or the notice becomes a final order. The authority to levy a civil administrative penalty is in addition to all other enforcement provisions in P.L.1970, c. 39, and the payment of any assessment shall not be deemed to affect the availability of any other enforcement provisions in connection with the violation for which the assessment is levied. The department may compromise any civil administrative penalty assessed under this section in an amount the department determines appropriate.

f. Any person who violates the provisions of P.L. 1970, c. 39, or any code, rule or regulation adopted pursuant thereto shall be liable to a penalty of not more than $50,000.00 per day, to be collected in a civil action commenced by a local board of health, a county health department, or the commissioner.

Any person who violates an administrative order issued pursuant to subsection c. of this section, or a court order issued pursuant to subsection d. of this section, or who fails to pay an administrative assessment in full pursuant to subsection e. of this section is subject upon order of a court to a civil penalty not to exceed $100,000.00 per day of such violations.

Of the penalty imposed pursuant to this subsection, 10% or $250.00, whichever is greater, shall be paid to the department from the General Fund if the Attorney General determines that a person is entitled to a reward pursuant to section 2 of P.L.1987, c. 158 (C.13:1E–9.2).

Any penalty imposed pursuant to this subsection may be collected with costs in a summary proceeding pursuant to "the penalty enforcement law" (N.J.S.2A:58–1 et seq.). The Superior Court and the municipal court shall have jurisdiction to enforce the provisions of "the penalty enforcement law" in connection with this act.

g. Any person who knowingly:

(1) Transports any hazardous waste to a facility or any other place which does not have authorization from the department to accept such waste;

(2) Generates and causes or permits to be transported any hazardous waste to a facility or any other place

which does not have authorization from the department to accept such waste;

(3) Disposes, treats, stores or transports hazardous waste without authorization from the department;

(4) Makes any false or misleading statement to any person who prepares any hazardous waste application, label, manifest, record, report, design or other document required to be submitted to the department; or

(5) Makes any false or misleading statement on any hazardous waste application, label, manifest, record, report, design or other document required to be submitted to the department shall, upon conviction, be guilty of a crime of the third degree and, notwithstanding the provisions of N.J.S.2C:43–3, shall be subject to a fine of not more than $50,000.00 for the first offense and not more than $100,000.00 for the second and each subsequent offense and restitution, in addition to any other appropriate disposition authorized by subsection b. of N.J.S.2C:43–2.

h.   Any person who recklessly:

(1) Transports any hazardous waste to a facility or any other place which does not have authorization from the department to accept such waste;

(2) Generates and causes or permits to be transported any hazardous waste to a facility or any other place which does not have authorization from the department to accept such waste;

(3) Disposes, treats, stores or transports hazardous waste without authorization from the department;

(4) Makes any false or misleading statement to any person who prepares any hazardous waste application, label, manifest, record, report, design or other document required to be submitted to the department; or

(5) Makes any false or misleading statement on any hazardous waste application, label, manifest, record, report, design or other document required to be submitted to the department, shall, upon conviction, be guilty of a crime of the fourth degree.

i.   Any person who, regardless of intent, generates and causes or permits any hazardous waste to be transported, transports, or receives transported hazardous waste without completing and submitting to the department a hazardous waste manifest in accordance with the provisions of this act or any rule or regulation adopted pursuant hereto shall, upon conviction, be guilty of a crime of the fourth degree.

j.   All conveyances used or intended for use in the willful discharge, in violation of the provisions of P.L.1970, c. 39 (C.13:1E–1 et seq.), of any solid waste, or hazardous waste as defined in P.L.1976, c. 99 (C.13:1E–38 et seq.) are subject to forfeiture to the State pursuant to the provisions of P.L.1981, c. 387 (C.13:1K–1 et seq.).

k.   (Deleted by amendment, P.L. 1997, c. 325)

l.   Pursuit of any remedy specified in this section shall not preclude the pursuit of any other remedy provided by any other law. Administrative and judicial remedies provided in this section may be pursued simultaneously.

L.1970, c. 39, § 9, eff. May 6, 1970. Amended by L.1975, c. 326, § 27, eff. July 1, 1976; L.1979, c. 395, § 1; L.1981, c. 438, § 1, eff. Jan. 9, 1982; L.1982, c. 123, § 1, eff. Sept. 1, 1982; L.1983, c. 68, § 1, eff. Feb. 17, 1983; L.1983, c. 569, § 1, eff. Jan. 17, 1984; L.1984, c. 240, § 1, eff. Dec. 28, 1984; L.1985, c. 348, § 2, eff. Nov. 1, 1985; L.1985, c. 483, § 1, eff. Jan. 17, 1986; L.1986, c. 170, § 1, eff. Dec. 4, 1986; L.1987, c. 158, § 1, eff. July 1, 1987; L.1990, c. 70, § 1; L.1997, c. 325, § 3, eff. Jan. 8, 1998.

13:1E–48.2.   Legislative findings

The Legislature finds that various human and animal health care centers and clinics, hospitals, laboratories, and other facilities generate substantial volumes of medical waste that must be transported and disposed in a sanitary and environmentally sound manner; that this waste poses both a potential threat to the health of those persons who handle, transport, dispose, or otherwise come into contact with it and to the public health; that, in addition to the actual and perceived risks associated with the management of medical waste, there are important aesthetic concerns that must be addressed; that the present regulatory scheme for medical waste is confusing and inadequate, and the enforcement thereof has been lacking and the penalties assessed for violations insufficient; and that the citizens of the State generally lack confidence that medical waste in the State is being managed in a proper and safe manner.

The Legislature therefore declares that it is appropriate to establish a comprehensive management system that provides for the proper and safe tracking, identification, packaging, storage, control, monitoring, handling, collection, and disposal of regulated medical waste; that monitoring of the regulated medical waste stream is best accomplished through the creation of a manifest tracking system for regulated medical waste; and that it is appropriate to provide for strict enforcement of the law concerning regulated medical waste and to establish substantial civil and criminal penalties for violations thereof.

L.1989, c. 34, § 2, eff. March 6, 1989.

13:1E–99.54.   Violations; penalties

a.   Whenever the commissioner finds that a person has violated any provision of this act, or any rule or regulation adopted pursuant thereto, the commissioner may:

(1) issue an order requiring the person found to be in violation to comply in accordance with subsection b. of this section;

(2) bring a civil action in accordance with subsection c. of this section;

(3) levy a civil administrative penalty in accordance with subsection d. of this section;

(4) bring an action for a civil penalty in accordance with subsection e. of this section; or

(5) petition the Attorney General to bring a criminal action in accordance with subsection g. of this section.

Pursuit of any of the remedies specified under this section shall not preclude the seeking of any other remedy specified.

b. Whenever the commissioner finds that a person has violated this act, or any rule or regulation adopted pursuant thereto, the commissioner may issue an order specifying the provision or provisions of this act, or the rule or regulation adopted pursuant thereto, of which the person is in violation, citing the action that constituted the violation, ordering abatement of the violation, and giving notice to the person of the person's right to a hearing on the matters contained in the order. The ordered person shall have 20 calendar days from receipt of the order within which to deliver to the commissioner a written request for a hearing. After the hearing and upon finding that a violation has occurred, the commissioner may issue a final order. If no hearing is requested, the order shall become final after the expiration of the 20–day period. A request for hearing shall not automatically stay the effect of the order.

c. The commissioner may institute an action or proceeding in the Superior Court for injunctive and other relief to enforce the provisions of this act and to prohibit and prevent a violation of this act, or of any rule or regulation adopted pursuant thereto, and the court may proceed in the action in a summary manner. In any such proceeding the court may grant temporary or interlocutory relief.

Such relief may include, singly or in combination:

(1) a temporary or permanent injunction;

(2) assessment of the violator for the reasonable costs of any inspection, including the costs of any sampling or testing of packages or packaging components that led to the establishment of the violation, and for the reasonable costs of preparing and litigating the case under this subsection.

d. (1) The commissioner may assess a civil administrative penalty of not more than $7,500.00 for a first offense, not more than $10,000.00 for a second offense and not more than $25,000.00 for a third and every subsequent offense. Each day that a violation continues shall constitute an additional, separate, and distinct offense.

No assessment may be levied pursuant to this section until after the violator has been notified by certified mail or personal service. The notice shall include a reference to the section of the statute, rule, regulation, or order violated, a concise statement of the facts alleged to constitute a violation, a statement of the amount of the civil administrative penalties to be imposed, and a statement of the person's right to a hearing. The ordered person shall have 20 calendar days from receipt of the notice within which to deliver to the commissioner a written request for a hearing.

After the hearing and upon finding that a violation has occurred, the commissioner may issue a final order after assessing the amount of the fine specified in the notice. If no hearing is requested, the notice shall become a final order after the expiration of the 20–day period. Payment of the assessment is due when a final order is issued or the notice becomes a final order. The authority to levy a civil administrative penalty is in addition to all other enforcement provisions in this act, and the payment of any assessment shall not be deemed to affect the availability of any other enforcement provisions in connection with the violation for which the assessment is levied. The department may compromise any civil administrative penalty assessed under this section in an amount the department determines appropriate.

(2) The commissioner may not assess a civil administrative penalty for a first offense for any violation of the provisions of this act, or of any rule or regulation adopted pursuant thereto, except in those instances where an ordered person violates an administrative order issued pursuant to subsection b. of section 10 of this act.[1]

e. (1) A person who violates this act, or any rule or regulation adopted pursuant thereto, shall be liable for a penalty of not more than $7,500.00 per day, to be collected in a civil action commenced by the commissioner.

(2) The commissioner may not bring an action for a civil penalty for a first offense for any violation of the provisions of this act, or of any rule or regulation adopted pursuant thereto, except in those instances where an ordered person violates an administrative order issued pursuant to subsection b. of section 10 of this act.

A person who violates an administrative order issued pursuant to subsection b. of this section, or a court order issued pursuant to subsection c. of this section, or who fails to pay an administrative assessment in full pursuant to subsection d. of this section is subject upon order of a court to a civil penalty not to exceed $50,000.00 per day of each violation.

Any penalty imposed pursuant to this subsection may be collected, with costs, in a summary proceeding pursuant to "the penalty enforcement law" (N.J.S.2A:58–1 et seq.). The Superior Court and the municipal court shall have jurisdiction to enforce the provisions of "the penalty enforcement law" in connection with this act.

f. Assessments and penalties under this section shall be paid to the department and deposited into the "Toxic Packaging Reduction Fund" established pursuant to section 12 of this act.[2]

g. Any person who purposely or knowingly:

(1) sells, offers for sale, or offers for promotional purposes any package or packaging component in violation of subsection a. of section 4 of this act,[3] or of any rule or regulation adopted pursuant thereto;

(2) sells, offers for sale, or offers for promotional purposes any product in violation of subsection b. of section 4 of this act, or of any rule or regulation adopted pursuant thereto; or

(3) sells, offers for sale, or offers for promotional purposes any package or packaging component that exceeds the maximum contaminant levels set forth in subsection c. of section 4 of this act; shall, upon conviction, be guilty of a crime of the third degree and, notwithstanding the provisions of N.J.S.2C:43–3, shall be subject to a fine of not less than $7,500.00 for a first offense, not more than $10,000.00 for a second offense and not more than $25,000.00 for a third and every subsequent offense. Each day during which the violation continues constitutes an additional, separate and distinct offense.

h. The provisions of N.J.S.2C:1–6 to the contrary notwithstanding, a prosecution for a violation of the provisions of subsection g. of this section shall be commenced within five years of the date of discovery of the violation.

i. No retailer shall be deemed to have violated the provisions of section 4 of this act, if the commissioner finds that the retailer can demonstrate that, in the purchase of a specified package or packaging component, the retailer relied in good faith on the written assurance of the product manufacturer or distributor that the package or packaging component complied with the provisions of this act. The written assurance shall state that a specified package or packaging component is in compliance with the provisions of this act, and shall be signed by an authorized representative of the package manufacturer or distributor. If an exemption is claimed for the package or packaging component pursuant to subsection b. of section 5 of this act,[4] the written assurance shall state the specific basis upon which the exemption is claimed.

L.1991, c. 520, § 11, eff. Jan. 20, 1992.

[1] N.J.S.A. § 13:1E–99.53.
[2] N.J.S.A. § 13:1E–99.55.
[3] N.J.S.A. § 13:1E–99.47.
[4] N.J.S.A. § 13:1E–99.48.

CHAPTER 9

STATE FOREST FIRE SERVICE

ARTICLE 1. GENERAL PROVISIONS

Section
13:9–44.10. Violations; injunction; penalties; criminal penalties; civil administrative remedy.

ARTICLE 1. GENERAL PROVISIONS

13:9–44.10. Violations; injunction; penalties; criminal penalties; civil administrative remedy

If any person violates any of the provisions of this act or any rule, regulation or order promulgated pursuant to provisions of this act, the department may:

(a) Institute a civil action in a court of competent jurisdiction for injunctive relief to prohibit and prevent such violation and the court may proceed in the action in a summary manner. Any person who violates the provisions of this act or any rule, regulation or order promulgated pursuant to this act shall be liable to a penalty of not more than $5,000.00 for each offense, to be collected in a civil action by a summary proceeding under "the penalty enforcement law" (N.J.S. 2A:58–1 et seq.) or in any case before a court of competent jurisdiction wherein injunctive relief has been requested. The Superior Court and municipal courts shall have jurisdiction to enforce "the penalty enforcement law." The Attorney General or the prosecuting attorney of the municipality or county in which the offense was committed may prosecute the case. If the violation is of a continuing nature, each day during which it continues shall constitute an additional, separate and distinct offense. The department is authorized to settle any claim for a penalty under this section in such amount in the discretion of the department as may appear appropriate and equitable under all of the circumstances;

(b) Petition the Attorney General to bring a criminal action against any person who knowingly violates any of the provisions of this act or any rule, regulation or order promulgated pursuant to the provisions of this act and thereby causes a wildfire. Such person shall, upon conviction, be guilty of a crime of the fourth degree and notwithstanding the provisions of N.J.S. 2C:43–3 shall be subject to a fine of not more than $100,000.00 for each offense; or

(c) Levy a civil administrative remedy of not more than $5,000.00 for each violation and additional penalties of not more than $500.00 for each day during which such violation continues after receipt of an order from the department. No penalty shall be levied pursuant to this section until the person has been notified by certified mail or personal service. The notice shall include a reference to the section of the statute violated; a concise statement of the facts alleged to constitute a violation; a statement of the person's right to a hearing. The person shall have 20 days from receipt of the notice within which to deliver to the commissioner a written request for a hearing. After the hearing and upon finding that a violation has occurred, the commissioner may issue a final order after assessing the amount of the fine specified in the notice. If no hearing is requested, then the notice shall become a final order after the expiration of the 20 day period. Payment is due when the final order is issued or the notice becomes a final order.

L.1981, c. 369, § 10, eff. Dec. 30, 1981. Amended by L.1991, c. 91, § 227, eff. April 9, 1991.

TITLE 15

CORPORATIONS AND ASSOCIATIONS NOT FOR PROFIT

Chapter
4. Detective Associations.

CHAPTER 4

DETECTIVE ASSOCIATIONS

Section
15:4–1. Pursuers may be appointed by private detective association; constabulary powers.
15:4–2. Fees and rewards for services as pursuers.
15:4–3. Insurance of members against loss by robbery.
15:4–4. Members may arrest and bring offenders before justice of peace.

15:4–1. Pursuers may be appointed by private detective association; constabulary powers

Where the certificate of incorporation of a corporation incorporated under chapter 1 of this title (§ 15:1–1 et seq.) or under an act entitled "An act to incorporate associations not for pecuniary profit," approved April twenty-first, one thousand eight hundred and ninety-eight, provides that the object of the corporation shall be the detection, pursuit, apprehension, arrest or prosecution of thieves, tramps, marauders, or other depredators on persons or property, or the recovery of stolen goods, the trustees of the corporation may appoint or elect, upon the authorization by resolution of the governing body of the municipality in which the principal office of such corporation is located, and the approval by the superintendent of state police, not more than twenty members of the corporation as pursuers, and give to each a badge of office. Such pursuers shall continue in office for one year, and during that time shall have the power and authority of constables, so far as may be necessary to carry out the objects of the corporation, and may execute warrants for that purpose in any part of the state, and shall have all the responsibilities and immunities of constables in the exercise of such power and authority. Such pursuers shall not be required to perform any service except as directed by the by-laws of the corporation.

Any person who shall act as such pursuer whose appointment has not been so made and approved shall be guilty of a misdemeanor.

For text of L.1871, c. 457, which created "The New Jersey Detective Agency", see Appendix following § 15:4–4.

15:4–2. Fees and rewards for services as pursuers

A pursuer may receive from any person who employs him such reasonable compensation as they may agree upon.

15:4–3. Insurance of members against loss by robbery

Any such corporation may provide for the indemnification of its members from loss in whole or in part by robbery, burglary, larceny or theft, may make by-laws, rules and regulations for the same, may fix the dues, fees and assessments of members and provide for the payment and collection thereof, and may sue for and recover the same in any court of competent jurisdiction.

15:4–4. Members may arrest and bring offenders before justice of peace

Every member of a thief-detecting society incorporated under the laws of this State may apprehend and arrest, upon view and without warrant, all persons committing breaches of the peace and all disorderly persons in any municipality in which the society is organized, and bring them before any court of competent jurisdiction, to be dealt with according to law. *Amended by L.1953, c. 15, p. 130, § 3, eff. March 19, 1953.*

APPENDIX

NEW JERSEY DETECTIVE ASSOCIATIONS

NEW JERSEY DETECTIVE ASSOCIATION—L.1871, c. 457

An Act to incorporate The New Jersey Detective Association.

1. Be it enacted by the Senate and General Assembly of the State of New Jersey, That Jacob Wambold, Edward L. McWilliams, Michael Kilcaulley, John M. Morris, Charles W. Mahon, Alexander H. Watkins, William O'Brien and Cornelius C. Martindale, and their successors be, and they are hereby constituted a body politic and corporate under the name and style of "The New Jersey Detective Agency," with power to purchase and hold real and personal property to an amount not to exceed five thousand dollars; to have a common seal; to elect a president and secretary, and such other officers and agents as they may deem necessary for the transaction of their business; and to sell and convey the said property at pleasure; to make such by-laws, rules and regulations as they may deem necessary for the transaction of their business; provided, the same do not conflict with the constitution or laws of this State or the constitution of the United States.

2. And be it enacted, That each of the above named incorporators, or a majority of them shall, on the first day of June next, file with the secretary of state a bond to the State of New Jersey, with two sureties, in the penal sum of one thousand dollars, conditioned for the faithful and bona fide perform-

ance of his duties and undertakings as a detective and police officer, when employed in that capacity by any person or persons, which said bond shall be executed and acknowledged in the same manner as deeds of conveyances of land are now required to be executed and acknowledged; and the sureties shall also each justify in the amount of the penalty thereof before a judge of the supreme court, or a supreme court commissioner, who shall certify his approval of said bond on the same.

3. And be it enacted, That when the said incorporators, or a majority of them, shall have filed a bond with the secretary of state in the manner prescribed in the next preceding section, the governor shall issue a commission to each of them who shall have filed a bond, empowering them to act as detectives or policemen in any part of this State, a copy of which commission shall be filed with the secretary of state.

4. And be it enacted, That it shall be lawful for the members of said agency to demand and receive reasonable fees and rewards as shall be agreed upon by the officer or officers and those who may employ them, for their services as such detectives or police officers from any person or persons who may employ them, to make contracts and agreements concerning such employment; to sue and be sued, implead and be impleaded, in any court of record in this State, in their corporate name.

5. And be it enacted, That the members of said agency shall have and possess the same powers and authority that constables and policemen have by law in the several cities, townships and counties, in which they may act in all criminal matters, and that it shall be lawful for them to serve any criminal process which constables and sheriffs may serve.

6. And be it enacted, That the said members of said agency shall have power to increase the number of their members by election in such manner as they may prescribe by their by-laws, to any number not exceeding twenty-five, a certificate of which election, signed by the president and attested by the secretary, shall be filed together with a bond, as prescribed in the second section of this act, with the secretary of state, and when so filed a commission shall issue to such members elect in the manner prescribed in the third section of this act.

7. And be it enacted, That the principle [1] office or place of business of said agency shall be in Jersey City, in the county of Hudson.

8. And be it enacted, That any person or persons, who shall or may feel himself or herself aggrieved or injured by any act or acts of any member or members of said agency, may petition the governor, setting forth the cause or causes of their grievance or injury, and pray an order for the prosecution of the bond or bonds of such member or members, and thereupon the governor may, at his discretion, order the said bond or bonds to be prosecuted at the expense of the petitioner, which order shall be filed with the secretary of state.

9. And be it enacted, That a certified copy of such bond and certificate under the hand and seal of the secretary of state, shall be received in evidence in all courts of record in this State.

10. And be it enacted, That each member of such detective agency when on duty shall wear a metallic shield or device, with the letters and words, "N.J. State Detective," in some convenient place upon the breast of his coat or vest, where it can be readily shown to any person demanding his authority.

11. And be it enacted, That it shall be lawful for the said agency to expel any member for such cause or causes as it shall prescribe by its by-laws.

12. And be it enacted, That when any member shall be expelled for cause, the said agency shall, within ten days from the time of such expulsion, file with the secretary of state, a certificate or notice of such expulsion, and thereupon the person so expelled shall cease to be a member of said agency, and shall no longer possess or exercise the powers or authority incident to such membership.

13. And be it enacted, That this act shall be deemed and taken to be a public act, and shall take effect immediately.

[1] So in original.

TITLE 21

EXPLOSIVES AND FIREWORKS

Subtitle
1. Explosives.
2. Fireworks.

SUBTITLE 1

EXPLOSIVES

Chapter
1A. Explosives Act.
1B. Liquefied Petroleum Gases.
1C. Model Rockets.

CHAPTER 1A

EXPLOSIVES ACT

Section
21:1A–1 to 21:1A–127. Repealed.
21:1A–128. Short title.
21:1A–129. Definitions.
21:1A–130. Enforcement.
21:1A–131. Rules and regulations.
21:1A–132. Prohibited acts; exceptions; permit required; records and reports of permittees; disposal of deteriorated or leaking explosives.
21:1A–133. Permits for manufacture, sale, storage, transportation or use of explosives.
21:1A–134. Investigation of applicants; qualifications, denial or revocation of permit; duration of permits; renewal; fee.
21:1A–135. Explosives manufacturing establishments; plan; intra-explosives plant quantity and distance table; distances for storage of explosives.
21:1A–136. Magazines; requirements.
21:1A–137. Transportation of explosives.
21:1A–138. Blasting operations.
21:1A–139. Jurisdiction of commissioner; law governing manufacture, sale, transportation, storage or use of explosives.
21:1A–140. Violations; penalties; revocation of permits; existing buildings and magazines.
21:1A–141. Exemptions.
21:1A–142. Possession of explosives or bombs for unlawful purpose.
21:1A–143. Partial invalidity.
21:1A–144. Repeals.

21:1A–1 to 21:1A–127. Repealed by L.1960, c. 55, § 17, eff. June 21, 1960

21:1A–128. Short title

This act [1] shall be known and may be cited as the "Explosives Act."

L.1960, c. 55, p. 468, § 1, eff. June 21, 1960.

[1] N.J.S.A. §§ 21:1A–128 to 21:1A–144.

21:1A–129. Definitions

As used in this act [1] unless the context clearly indicates otherwise:

(a) "Act" means this act and rules and regulations promulgated hereunder.

(b) "Commissioner" means the Commissioner of the Department of Labor and Industry or his authorized representative.

(c) "Barricaded" means that a building containing explosives is effectively screened from a magazine, inhabited building, railway or highway, either by a natural barricade or by an artificial barricade of such height that a straight line from the top of any sidewall of a building containing explosives to the eave line of any magazine or inhabited building or to a point 12 feet above the center of a railway or highway, will pass through such intervening natural or artificial barricade.

(d) "Artificial barricade" means an artificial mound or properly revetted wall of earth of a minimum thickness of 3 feet.

(e) "Natural barricade" means natural features of the ground including but not limited to hills, or timber of sufficient density so that the surrounding exposures which require protection cannot be seen from the magazine containing explosives when the trees are bare of leaves.

(f) "Explosives" means any chemical compound or mixture that is commonly used or intended for the purpose of producing an explosion, that contains any oxidizing and combustible materials or other ingredients, in such proportions, quantities or packing that an ignition by fire, by friction, by concussion or by detonation of any part of the compound or mixture may cause such a sudden generation of highly heated gases that the resultant gaseous pressures are capable of producing destructive effects on contiguous objects. The term "explosives" shall include, but is not limited to commercial explosives, propellants and nitro-carbo-nitrates. The term "explosives", except as specifically stated in this act, shall not include small arms ammunition, explosives in the forms prescribed by the official United States Pharmacopoeia, or fireworks regulated under Revised Statutes sections 21:2–1 through 21:2–7.

(g) "Commercial explosives" means all explosives except propellants and nitro-carbo-nitrates, including, but not limited to, dynamite, black blasting powder, pellet powder, initiating explosives, blasting caps, electric blasting caps, safety fuses, fuse igniters fuse lighters, squibs, cordeau detonant fuses, instantaneous fuses, igniter cord and igniters.

(h) "Propellants" means solid chemicals or solid chemical mixtures which function by rapid combustion of successive layers and include, but are not limited to, smokeless powder for small arms, smokeless powder for cannon, smokeless powder or solid propellants for rockets, jet thrust units, or other devices.

(i) "Nitro-carbo-nitrate" means a mixture intended for blasting consisting substantially of inorganic nitrates and carbonaceous combustibles in which none of the ingredients is a commercial explosive and the finished product, as mixed and packaged for use or shipment, cannot be detonated by the test procedure established by rules and regulations promulgated under this act.

(j) "Explosives manufacturing establishment" means all lands, and buildings situated thereon, used in connection with the manufacture of explosives.

(k) "Explosives manufacturing building" means any building or other structure, except magazines, in which the manufacture of explosives is carried on.

(*l*) "Magazine" means any building or structure used for the storage of explosives but shall not mean an explosives manufacturing building.

(m) "Inhabited building" means a building regularly occupied in whole or in part as a habitation for human beings, or any church, schoolhouse, railroad station, store or other structure where people are accustomed to assemble, except any building or structure occupied in connection with the manufacture, transportation, storage or use of explosives.

(n) "Highway" means any public street, road, highway, alley or those parts of navigable streams which are used as highways of commerce.

(*o*) "Public conveyance" means any transportation facility which is carrying passengers for hire.

(p) "Person" means any natural person, partnership, firm, association or corporation.

(q) "Railway" shall mean and include any steam, electric or other railroad or railway which carries passengers for hire on the particular line or branch in the vicinity where explosives storage magazines or explosives manufacturing buildings are situated, but shall not include auxiliary tracks, spurs and sidings installed and primarily used for transporting freight.

L.1960, c. 55, § 2, eff. June 21, 1960.

   1 N.J.S.A. §§ 21:1A–128 to 21:1A–144.

21:1A–130. Enforcement

The commissioner shall enforce the provisions of this act,[1] make complaints against persons violating its provisions, and prosecute violations of the same. The commissioner and any authorized person acting under him shall have authority to enter and inspect any place or establishment covered by this act. If upon inspection the commissioner discovers a condition which exists in violation of the provision of this act or if the commissioner determines that certain precautions are reasonably necessary for the safety of workers and the public and the protection of property, he shall be authorized to order such violation to cease or such precaution to be taken. The order shall state the items which are in violation of the provisions of the act or the precautions which he deems reasonably necessary to be taken, and shall provide a reasonable specified time within which the required action must be taken by the person responsible. If the violation or the lack of certain precautions constitutes an imminent hazard and the commissioner's order is not obeyed, the commissioner may apply for an injunction in the Superior Court of New Jersey. Nothing herein shall be deemed to prevent the commissioner from prosecuting any violation of this act, notwithstanding that such violations are corrected in accordance with his order.

The Division of State Police, Department of Law and Public Safety shall have concurrent enforcement power with regard to the transportation of explosives on any highway as defined in this act.

Any person aggrieved by an order or act of the commission under this act may, upon application made within 15 days after notice thereof, be entitled to a hearing before the commissioner who shall within 30 days after submission of the application hold a hearing of which at least 15 days written notice shall be given to all interested parties. The commissioner, upon application therefor, may stay the operation of the order complained of pending his final determination upon such terms and conditions as he may deem proper. Within 30 days after the said hearing the commissioner shall issue an appropriate order modifying, approving or disapproving his prior order or act. A copy of such order shall be served upon all interested parties.

L.1960, c. 55, § 3, eff. June 21, 1960.

   1 N.J.S.A. §§ 21:1A–128 to 21:1A–144.

21:1A–131. Rules and regulations

The commissioner may make and promulgate rules and regulations necessary to further the purposes of this act. The rules and regulations may include requirements that are not mentioned specifically in this act but which are reasonably necessary for the safety of workers and the public and the protection of property. Such rules and regulations shall have the force and effect of law and shall be enforced in the same manner. The procedure for the promulgation of rules and regulations under this section shall be as follows:

(a) Upon the completion of proposed rules and regulations by the commissioner notice of the proposed promulgation shall be given to all holders of explosive permits. This notice shall be in writing, shall state briefly the purpose of the proposed rules and regulations, shall state that a copy of the proposed rules and regulations may be obtained upon written request to the Department of Labor and Industry and shall state that upon written request to the Commissioner of Labor and Industry, a hearing will be held by the commissioner or his authorized representative for the purpose of hearing recommendations concerning the proposed rules and regulations.

(b) If no hearing is requested, the commissioner shall promulgate the rules and regulations within 60 days of the notice required by section 4(a) of this act.

(c) If a hearing is requested, notice of the hearing shall be sent to all holders of permits. The notice shall state the date, time and place of the hearing.

(d) Within 60 days after the hearing, the commissioner shall promulgate the rules and regulations as originally proposed or with such changes that he, in his discretion, decides to make in view of the recommendations offered at the hearing. No further hearings are required.

L.1960, c. 55, § 4, eff. June 21, 1960.

21:1A–132. Prohibited acts; exceptions; permit required; records and reports of permittees; disposal of deteriorated or leaking explosives

It is prohibited for any person to manufacture, store, sell, transport, use, dispose of, or possess explosives in any manner except as permitted under this act. Any person who is not engaged primarily in the manufacture, sale, storage, transportation or use of explosives but who in the course of activities engages in any of the above or uses explosives in any manufacturing process shall be required to comply with the provisions of this act.

A. No person shall sell, deliver, give away or otherwise dispose of any explosives to any persons not in possession of a permit as required by the provisions of this act. No person shall have any explosives in his possession or control without a permit required by this act.

B. Every person holding a permit to manufacture, sell, store or use explosives shall keep such records as may be required by the commissioner, and shall file reports monthly with the commissioner, on a date and in a form to be prescribed by the commissioner, listing amounts of explosives used, sold or otherwise disposed of, during the preceding month and showing inventories on hand, and shall be required to report immediately any loss, by theft or otherwise, of explosives in his possession to the commissioner, who shall immediately forward such information to the Attorney General of the State, provided, however, that where an employer is maintaining such records, his employees holding permits to use explosives, at the discretion of and with the written approval of the commissioner, shall not be required to maintain individual records. Records shall be retained at least until the end of the calendar year next following the year in which the record is made. All such records shall be open to inspection by the commissioner.

C. No person shall handle explosives while under the influence of narcotics or intoxicating liquors.

D. No person shall smoke or have open lights or fire- or flame-producing devices while handling or using explosives or when within 100 feet of any magazine or vehicle containing explosives; provided, however, that this prohibition shall not apply to the use of igniters when preparing to detonate an explosive charge.

E. When deteriorated or leaking explosives are found by the commissioner, he may order them disposed of in the manner he shall direct, at the expense of the possessor.

L.1960, c. 55, § 5, eff. June 21, 1960. Amended by L.1971, c. 35, § 1, eff. Feb. 25, 1971.

21:1A–133. Permits for manufacture, sale, storage, transportation or use of explosives

Any person who shall manufacture, sell, store, transport or use explosives first shall obtain a written or printed permit from the commissioner, which permit shall state specifically the use or uses authorized:

(a) To manufacture—authorizing the manufacture of explosives and storage of materials in process, developmental materials and finished products.

(b) To sell—authorizing the sale of explosives.

(c) To transport—authorizing the transportation of explosives; provided, however, that no permit will be required where such transportation is not on the highways nor where the articles being transported are of laboratory samples; however, such transportation shall otherwise be in conformity with the provisions of this act.

(d) To store—authorizing the purchase and storage of explosives in a specified magazine.

(e) To use—authorizing a person to use explosives for such purposes and under such conditions as are specified on the permit. The commissioner may establish classifications of use of explosives for blasting and other purposes, specifying the privileges and requirements of each classification. Persons holding, or employed by a person holding, a permit to manufacture explosives, and who are engaged in the testing of explosives incident to the manufacture or development thereof shall not be required to obtain a permit to use explosives.

A. No permit shall be required for the storage, transportation or use of smokeless powder which is used by private persons for the hand loading of small arms ammunition and which is not for resale. For this purpose not more than 36 lbs. of smokeless powder and not more than 5 pounds of black powder shall be stored or transported without a permit.

B. Permits shall at all times be readily available to inspection by the commissioner, State Police or local police and fire departments and shall be posted as directed by the commissioner.

C. Permits shall not be transferable.

D. Whenever a permanent storage magazine for which a permit has been issued is moved to a new location, or its physical surroundings are so changed that the magazine comes within the prohibited distances to a highway, railroad or inhabited building, the permit for said magazine shall become invalid and a new permit required.

E. No permittee shall manufacture, sell, transport, store or use explosives except in compliance with the limitations expressed on the permit.

L.1960, c. 55, § 6, eff. June 21, 1960. Amended by L.1971, c. 35, § 2, eff. Feb. 25, 1971.

21:1A–134. Investigation of applicants; qualifications, denial or revocation of permit; duration of permits; renewal; fee

Upon receipt of an application for a permit to manufacture, store, sell, transport or use explosives, and before the permit is issued, the commissioner shall make or cause to be made an investigation for the purpose of ascertaining if all applicable requirements of this act [1] have been met. The commissioner shall not issue a permit to manufacture, sell, store, transport or use explosives unless all the requirements of this act have been met. All permits issued in accordance with the provisions of this act shall be subject to any amendments hereafter made to this act.

A. An applicant for a permit shall, at his own expense, furnish whatever pertinent information the commissioner may require in addition to that specified herein. Application forms shall be furnished by the Department of Labor and Workforce Development.

B. An applicant for a permit to manufacture, sell, transport, store or use explosives must:

(a) be at least 21 years of age;

(b) have a reasonable understanding of the English language;

(c) present satisfactory evidence of experience in the manufacture, sale, transportation, storage or use of explosives;

(d) demonstrate by written, oral or field examination, as the commissioner may direct, adequate knowledge of the safe manufacture, sale, transportation, storage or use of explosives and of the provisions of this act; and

(e) be of good moral character and must never have been disloyal to the United States; and

it shall be within the sole discretion of the commissioner to determine whether an applicant who has been convicted of a crime involving moral turpitude has the good moral character necessary for a permit. It shall also be within the reasonable discretion of the commissioner to deny the issuance of a permit where he concludes, after a full examination of the qualifications of an applicant, that to grant a permit would be dangerous to the health, safety and welfare of the people of the State of New Jersey. The failure of a holder of a permit to maintain the qualifications stated herein shall be good cause for the revocation of the permit.

C. When the applicant for a permit to manufacture, sell, transport, store or use explosives is a firm, association or corporation, the applicant must demonstrate that such activities with regard to explosives will be under the direct supervision of a person who meets the qualifications stated above.

D. Permits shall be valid for one year unless sooner revoked. Permits which expire on July 1, 1960 may be renewed by the commissioner at his discretion for a period of not less than three months nor more than 15 months, and permits renewed after such a period shall thereafter be valid for one year unless sooner revoked. The fee for all permits shall be fixed by the commissioner on a yearly basis or, for periods of less than a year, in amounts proportionately less than the annual fee.

E. The application for any permit must be accompanied by a fee established by regulation in accordance with the following schedule:

(a) To manufacture—not less than $200 nor more than $2,000;

(b) To sell—not less than $25 nor more than $600;

(c) (Deleted by amendment, P.L.1991, c. 205).

(d) To store—not less than $25 nor more than $300; but if the explosives are in excess of 30,000 pounds, then the fee shall be not less than $150 nor more than $1,500;

(e) To use—not more than $400;

(f) For storage, transportation, and use of smokeless powder in amounts in excess of 36 pounds, but not in excess of 100 pounds and black powder in amounts in excess of 5 pounds but not in excess of 100 pounds which is used by private persons for the hand loading of small arms ammunition and which is not for resale—not less than $2 nor more than $20; where any such smokeless and black powder is in excess of 100 pounds, the fee shall be increased $20 for each additional 100 pounds, or fraction thereof.

All fees derived from the operation of this act shall be applied toward enforcement and administration costs of the Division of Workplace Standards in the Department of Labor and Workforce Development.

L.1960, c. 55, § 7, eff. June 21, 1960. Amended by L.1971, c. 35, § 3, eff. Feb. 25, 1971; L.1971, c. 154, § 4, eff. May 20, 1971; L.1991, c. 205, § 16, eff. July 12, 1991; L.2007, c. 274, § 1, eff. Jan. 13, 2008.

  1 N.J.S.A. §§ 21:1A–128 to 21:1A–144.

21:1A–135. Explosives manufacturing establishments; plan; intra-explosives plant quantity and distance table; distances for storage of explosives

All explosives manufacturing establishments shall come under the jurisdiction of the commissioner in accordance with the provisions of Title 34 of the Revised Statutes of the State of New Jersey.

A. A copy of the plan of the explosives manufacturing establishment shall be kept in the main office of the premises of every such establishment and shall be open to inspection by the commissioner. The said plan shall show the location of all explosives manufacturing buildings, the distance they are located from other buildings on the premises and from magazines. Before a permit to manufacture is issued by the commissioner, he may require that such a plan be submitted to him in triplicate for approval.

B. All commercial explosives manufacturing buildings shall be located one from the other and from other buildings of the explosives manufacturing establishment in which persons are regularly employed, and all commercial explosives magazines shall be located from explosives manufacturing buildings and other buildings of the explosives manufacturing establishment in which persons are regularly employed, in conformity with the Intra-Explosives Plant Quantity and Distance Table for commercial explosives set forth below.

INTRA EXPLOSIVES PLANT QUANTITY AND DISTANCE TABLE FOR COMMERCIAL EXPLOSIVES

Quantity of Explosives		Distance in Feet	
Pounds Over	Pounds Not Over	Unbarricaded	Barricaded
10	25	40	20
25	50	60	30
50	100	80	40
100	200	100	50
200	300	120	60
300	400	130	65
400	500	140	70
500	750	160	80
750	1,000	180	90
1,000	1,500	210	105
1,500	2,000	250	115
2,000	3,000	260	130
3,000	4,000	280	140
4,000	5,000	300	150
5,000	6,000	320	160
6,000	7,000	340	170
7,000	8,000	360	180
8,000	9,000	380	190
9,000	10,000	400	200
10,000	12,500	420	210

Quantity of Explosives		Distance in Feet	
Pounds Over	Pounds Not Over	Unbarricaded	Barricaded
12,500	15,000	450	225
15,000	17,500	470	235
17,500	20,000	490	245
20,000	25,000	530	265
25,000	30,000	560	280
30,000	35,000	590	295
35,000	40,000	620	310
40,000	45,000	640	320
45,000	50,000	660	330
50,000	55,000	680	340
55,000	60,000	700	350
60,000	65,000	720	360
65,000	70,000	740	370
70,000	75,000	770	385
75,000	80,000	780	390
80,000	85,000	790	395
85,000	90,000	800	400
90,000	95,000	820	410
95,000	100,000	830	415
100,000	125,000	900	450
125,000	150,000	950	475
150,000	175,000	1,000	500
175,000	200,000	1,050	525
200,000	225,000	1,100	550
225,000	250,000	1,150	575
250,000	275,000	1,200	600
275,000	300,000	1,270	635

Note: Ten (10) pounds or less may be stored in a separate building or in storage space properly separated by substantial dividing walls.

All explosives manufacturing buildings and magazines in which explosives are had, kept or stored must be located at distances from inhabited buildings, railways and public highways in conformity with the Tables of Distance established pursuant to section 9G of this act.[1]

L.1960, c. 55, § 8, eff. June 21, 1960.

  1 N.J.S.A. § 21:1A–136.

21:1A–136. Magazines; requirements

All explosives, except those in the process of manufacture or being transported or used as permitted by this act,[1] shall be stored in a magazine complying with the requirements of this act.

A. All magazines shall be in charge of a competent person who shall be at least 21 years of age. The holder of the storage permit shall be held responsible for compliance with all safety precautions.

B. All magazines shall be well ventilated, clean, dry and free of grit, paper, rubbish and any combustible material other than explosives or the cases containing them.

C. All magazines shall be kept closed and locked except when necessarily opened for the lawful purpose of storing or removing explosives, for inspections, or by persons lawfully entitled to enter same.

D. No container of explosives shall at any time be opened in or within 50 feet of any magazine, nor shall any explosives be kept in any magazine except in closed containers.

E. The commissioner is hereby authorized to deny a permit for a magazine which in his judgment is unsuited for the storage of explosives. The commissioner may require plans for magazines to be submitted for approval before the magazines are constructed and used.

F. Magazines shall not be provided with artificial heat or internal lighting except by approved portable electric safety battery lamps. Underground magazines may be provided with explosion proof lights where all wiring is in conduits and the switch is located outside of the magazine.

G. All magazines in which explosives are stored, except those in explosives manufacturing establishments, shall conform with the Tables of Distance for storage of explosives established by regulations promulgated under this act.

H. The commissioner shall state on each storage permit the maximum amount of explosives that may be stored under that permit. No quantity of explosives in excess of that amount shall be stored under the permit. In any event no quantity in excess of 300,000 pounds of commercial explosives and no quantity in excess of 20,000,000 blasting caps shall be kept or stored in any magazine.

I. Nitro-carbo-nitrates or propellants, or both, may be stored with commercial explosives in the same magazine, but when so stored, all commercial explosives magazine regulations apply, and the quantity of nitro-carbo-nitrate or propellant shall be taken into consideration in computing the total quantity in the magazine for compliance with the quantity and distance tables for commercial explosives established by regulation.

L.1960, c. 55, § 9, eff. June 21, 1960.

1 N.J.S.A. §§ 21:1A–128 to 20:1A–144.

21:1A–137. Transportation of explosives

A. The person using any vehicle for the transportation of explosives, whether he be the owner or lessee, shall be responsible for the keeping of inspection records required by the commissioner.

B. It is prohibited for any person to transport or carry explosives upon any public conveyance.

C. No explosives shall be transported in any form of full trailer, nor shall any trailer be attached to a vehicle transporting explosives.

D. Vehicles in which explosives are being transported shall be driven by and be under the control of a driver at least 21 years of age. Such a person shall be familiar with the New Jersey laws and rules and regulations pertaining to the transportation of explosives.

E. No quantity of explosives in excess of the quantity indicated upon the transportation permit shall be transported in a vehicle.

F. Blasting caps or electric blasting caps, or both, may be transported in the same vehicle with other commercial explosives only when the net weight of the other commercial explosives does not exceed 5,000 pounds.

G. When nitro-carbo-nitrates or propellants, or both, are transported in the same vehicle with commercial explosives, all requirements governing the transportation of commercial explosives must be followed. *L.1960, c. 55, § 10, eff. June 21, 1960.*

21:1A–138. Blasting operations

A. Persons authorized to conduct blasting operations and their employers or persons in charge of the operation shall comply with all provisions of this act and rules and regulations promulgated hereunder. No employer shall employ any person to prepare explosive charges or conduct blasting operations unless such person holds a valid permit to use explosives issued by the commissioner, provided however, that

(a) explosives may be used by a miner in underground mining operations without a permit to use explosives if the blasting operations are under the direct supervision of a person in possession of a valid permit.

(b) explosive charges may be prepared by a person at least 18 years of age without a permit to use explosives if such work is done under the direct supervision of a person in possession of a valid permit.

(c) persons not less than 15 years of age shall be permitted to assist in the preparation or use of propellants in amateur rocket experimentation when such work is done under the actual control and supervision of a person in possession of a valid permit to use explosives, and in such a manner and place as to insure the safety of persons and property where such work is performed, and in conformity with rules and regulations promulgated under this act.

B. The amount of explosives taken into a blast area shall never exceed the amount estimated by the blaster as necessary for the blast.

C. When commercial explosives are used in conjunction with nitro-carbo-nitrates, all safety precautions and rules and regulations for commercial explosives shall be observed.

D. Except when nitro-carbo-nitrates are mixed at the site of the blast for immediate use, any such mixing shall be deemed to be manufacturing of explosives and shall be subject to all applicable provisions relating thereto.

L.1960, c. 55, § 11, eff. June 21, 1960.

21:1A–139. Jurisdiction of commissioner; law governing manufacture, sale, transportation, storage or use of explosives

The commissioner shall have exclusive jurisdiction over the regulation of the manufacture, sale, transportation, storage and use of explosives. This act [1] shall supersede any existing ordinance, by-law or resolution of any municipality or other governmental subdivision pertaining to the manufacture, sale, transportation, storage or use of explosives.

L.1960, c. 55, § 12, eff. June 21, 1960.

1 N.J.S.A. §§ 21:1A–128 to 21:1A–144.

21:1A–140. Violations; penalties; revocation of permits; existing buildings and magazines

It shall be unlawful for any person, partnership, firm, association or corporation, and any officer, agent or employee thereof, to violate or proximately contribute to the violation of any of the provisions of this act [1] or of the regulations made hereunder. The violation of this act by an employee, acting within the scope of his authority, of any person, partnership, firm, association, or corporation shall be deemed also to be the violation of such person, partnership, firm, association or corporation. Violations of the provisions of this act or rules and regulations made hereunder shall be punishable for the first offense by a penalty of not less than $100 nor more than $5,000, for the second offense by a penalty of not less than $300 nor more than $10,000 and for the third and each succeeding offense by a penalty of not less than $500 nor more than $20,000. The penalties shall be collected by a summary proceeding pursuant to the "Penalty Enforcement Law of 1999," P.L.1999, c. 274 (C.2A:58–10 et seq.). Where the violation consists of a refusal to obey an order of the commissioner made under this act, each day during which the violation continues shall constitute a separate and distinct offense except during the time an appeal from said order may be taken or is pending.

Any sum collected as a penalty pursuant to this section shall be applied toward enforcement and administration costs of the Division of Workplace Standards in the Department of Labor and Workforce Development.

A. The Commissioner of Labor and Workforce Development, in his discretion, is hereby authorized and empowered to compromise and settle any claim for a penalty under this section for an amount that appears appropriate and equitable under all of the circumstances.

B. Permits to sell, transport, store or use explosives are revocable for cause by the commissioner. In any case where the commissioner revokes a permit, he shall notify the permittee of the revocation and shall provide, upon written request, for a hearing within 10 days of the date of the revocation. Within 30 days from the termination of the hearing, the commissioner shall issue an order approving, disapproving or modifying the revocation. Permits to manufacture are exempt from revocation, but the holders of such permits shall be subject in every other respect to the provisions of this act and the rules and regulations promulgated hereunder.

C. The requirements of this act concerning the distances of explosives manufacturing buildings and magazines from each other shall not be construed to apply to permanent buildings or magazines that exist at the time that this act becomes effective and which buildings and magazines have been used under authority of the laws formerly governing the manufacture and storage of explosives. This provision designating such explosives manufacturing buildings and magazines already existing at the effective date of this act as nonconforming uses shall not apply to any explosives manufacturing buildings or magazines constructed subsequent to the passage of this act nor to extensions or additions to such buildings and magazines that are made subsequent to the passage of this act.

L.1960, c. 55, § 13, eff. June 21, 1960. Amended by L.1991, c. 91, § 264, eff. April 9, 1991; L.1991, c. 205, § 17, eff. July 12, 1991; L.2007, c. 274, § 2, eff. Jan. 13, 2008.

1 N.J.S.A. § 21:1A–128 et seq.

21:1A–141. Exemptions

Nothing contained in this act [1] shall be construed as applying to the military or naval forces of the United States or its allies, or the duly authorized militia of any State, nor to the police or fire departments of this State, providing the same are acting in their official capacity and in the performance of their public duties.

A. Nothing contained in this act shall be construed as applying to explosives which are in transit upon vessels, railroad cars or vehicles or while being held for delivery, when such transportation and delivery are under the jurisdiction of and in conformity with regulations adopted by the Interstate Commerce Commission, the United States Coast Guard or the Civil Aeronautics Board, and provided, further, that nothing in this act shall be construed as applying to the receipt, possession, and use of signals required for the safe operation of vessels, motor vehicles, railroad cars, or aircraft by the operators of such vessels, motor vehicles, railroad cars or aircraft.

L.1960, c. 55, § 14, eff. June 21, 1960.

1 N.J.S.A. §§ 21:1A–128 to 21:1A–144.

21:1A–142. Possession of explosives or bombs for unlawful purpose

Any person who shall have in his possession or control any explosives, including any bomb, shell or similar device filled with one or more explosives, intending to use the same or cause the same to be used or who has used the same for an unlawful purpose shall be guilty of a high misdemeanor, and upon conviction shall be punished by imprisonment in a State prison for a term of not more than 25 years. The possession of explosives or any bomb, shell or similar device filled with explosives, without a permit as required by this act, shall be evidence of an intent to use the same or cause the same to be used for an unlawful purpose. Unlawful purpose shall mean a purpose that cannot be authorized under the provisions of this act.

L.1960, c. 55, § 15, eff. June 21, 1960. Amended by L.1971, c. 35, § 4, eff. Feb. 25, 1971.

21:1A–143. Partial invalidity

If any provision of this act [1] is adjudged unconstitutional or invalid for any reason, such adjudication shall not affect any of the other provisions of this act.

L.1960, c. 55, § 16, eff. June 21, 1960.

[1] N.J.S.A. §§ 21:1A–128 to 21:1A–144.

21:1A–144. Repeals

The following statutes are hereby repealed:

P.L.1941, c. 27 (approved March 28, 1941) and all amendments and supplements thereto.[1]

Sections 34:5–24 through 34:5–32 of the Revised Statutes.

Sections 21:1–41 through 21:1–44 of the Revised Statutes.

Sections 21:1–50 and 21:1–51 of the Revised Statutes.

The repeal of any statute herein shall not be deemed to revive any act previously repealed by any such statute.

L.1960, c. 55, § 17, eff. June 21, 1960.

[1] N.J.S.A. §§ 21:1A–1 to 21:1A–127.

CHAPTER 1B

LIQUEFIED PETROLEUM GASES

Section
21:1B–1. Definitions.
21:1B–2. Regulations.
21:1B–3. Equipment: Safety; propane gas installations; predominantly residential buildings; inspection; approval.
21:1B–4. Containers and receptacles.
21:1B–5. Violations; penalties; compromise and settlement of claims for penalties.
21:1B–6. Correction of violations; notice; orders.
21:1B–7. Ordinances not to conflict with regulations.
21:1B–8. Declaration of necessity.
21:1B–9. Transfer of powers, functions and duties of superintendent of state police to commissioner of labor and industry.
21:1B–10. Rules, regulations and orders of superintendent of state police; continuance.
21:1B–11. Method of transfer.
21:1B–12. Liquefied Petroleum Gas Education and Safety Board created.
21:1B–13. Powers of the board.
21:1B–14. Limitations on power.
21:1B–15. Assessment level recommendations.

21:1B–1. Definitions

As used in this chapter:

"Board" means the Liquefied Petroleum Gas Education and Safety Board;

"Bulk plant" means intermediate establishments or points of storage and distribution, as distinguished from terminals and refineries, from which liquefied petroleum gas is distributed to retail dealers and consumers;

"Commissioner" means the Commissioner of Community Affairs;

"Department" means the Department of Community Affairs; and

"Liquefied petroleum gas" means any material which is composed predominantly of any of the following hydrocarbons, or mixtures of the same: propane, propylene, butanes (normal butane or isobutane), and butylenes.

L.1950, c. 139, § 1, eff. May 25, 1950. Amended by L.1958, c. 43, p. 143, § 2, eff. May 20, 1958; L.1999, c. 109, § 5, eff. May 14, 1999.

21:1B–2. Regulations

(a) The Superintendent of State Police shall coordinate the implementation and enforcement of regulations adopted pursuant to P.L.1983, c. 401 (C.39:5B–25 et seq.) concerning the transporting of liquefied petroleum gases as required for compliance with the Code of Federal Regulations, Title 49.

(b) The Commissioner of Community Affairs shall make, promulgate and enforce regulations setting forth minimum standards covering the design, construction, location, installation and operation of equipment for storing, handling or utilizing liquefied petroleum gases at public utility establishments operated by public utilities as defined in section 48:2–13 of the Revised Statutes and at marine terminals, pipeline terminals, refineries and manufacturing establishments, which shall not be deemed to include bulk plants, and specifying the odorization of said gases and the degree thereof prior to sale by the manufacturer.

(c) All regulations promulgated under subsection (a) or (b) of this section shall be adopted only after a public hearing thereon and shall be such as are reasonably necessary for the protection of the health, welfare and safety of all persons and shall be in substantial conformity with the generally accepted and applicable standards of safety concerning the same subject matter.

L.1950, c. 139, § 2, eff. May 25, 1950. Amended by L.1958, c. 43, § 3, eff. May 20, 1958; L.1999, c. 109, § 6, eff. May 14, 1999.

21:1B–3. Equipment: Safety; propane gas installations; predominantly residential buildings; inspection; approval

All equipment shall be installed and maintained in a safe operating condition and in conformity with the rules and regulations adopted under section 2 of this act[1]; however, the inspection of propane gas equipment installations inside of predominantly residential buildings and those above ground installations which are on the outside of predominantly residential buildings may be made and approved or disapproved by the Construction Code official of the respective municipality pursuant to the standards promulgated by the Commissioner of Community Affairs. For purposes of this act "predominantly residential" means and includes buildings in which people reside or dwell as distinguished from buildings which are used entirely for commercial or business purposes. The term shall also include any building having 51% or more of its total floor space devoted to dwelling purposes.

L.1950, c. 139, § 3, eff. May 25, 1950. Amended by L.1958, c. 43, § 4, eff. May 20, 1958; L.1975, c. 165, § 1, eff. July 23, 1975; L.1999, c. 109, § 7, eff. May 14, 1999.

   1 N.J.S.A. § 21:1B–2.

21:1B–4. Containers and receptacles

No person, firm or corporation, other than the owner and those authorized by the owner so to do, shall sell, fill, refill, deliver or permit to be delivered, or use in any manner any liquefied petroleum gas container or receptacle for any gas, compound, or for any other purpose whatsoever.

L.1950, c. 139, § 4, eff. May 25, 1950.

21:1B–5. Violations; penalties; compromise and settlement of claims for penalties

It shall be unlawful for any person, firm, association, or corporation, on and after the effective date of this act to violate any of the provisions hereof or of the regulations made pursuant hereto. Any person, firm, association, or corporation violating any of the provisions of this act,[1] or said regulations made hereunder shall be liable to a penalty of not less than $50.00 nor more than $500.00 to be collected in a summary proceeding in any municipal court or in the Superior Court. Each day during which any violation of this act or of said regulations continues shall constitute a separate and distinct offense.

The Superintendent of State Police and the Commissioner of Community Affairs, according to the jurisdiction granted under section 2 of P.L.1950, c. 139 (C.21:1B–2), are hereby authorized and empowered to compromise and settle any claim for a penalty under this section in such amount, in the discretion of the Superintendent of State Police and the Commissioner of Community Affairs, respectively, as may appear appropriate and equitable under all of the circumstances.

L.1950, c. 139, § 5, eff. Sept. 1, 1951. Amended by L.1958, c. 43, § 5, eff. May 20, 1958; L.1991, c. 91, § 265, eff. April 9, 1991; L.1999, c. 109, § 8, eff. May 14, 1999.

   1 N.J.S.A. § 21:1B–1 et seq.

21:1B–6. Correction of violations; notice; orders

In addition to the penalties provided in section 5 of P.L.1950, c. 139 (C.21:1B–5), any person, firm or corporation who shall violate or remain in violation of any of the provisions hereof, or of any rule or regulation promulgated hereunder, may be directed and ordered by the Superintendent of State Police or the Commissioner of Community Affairs, according to their respective jurisdiction under section 2 of P.L.1950, c. 139 (C.21:1B–2), by notice in writing setting forth the facts relating to such violation to correct said violation. Such notice in writing shall be served personally upon said person or mailed by registered or certified mail to the principal office of said person, firm or corporation or if an individual or individuals, to his or their residence. If such order is not complied with and such violation not corrected within 20 days of the date of service of said order, the Superintendent of State Police or Commissioner of Community Affairs, as the case may be, may institute an action in the Superior Court for injunctive relief or an abatement. The court may proceed in the action in a summary manner or otherwise, and shall make such determination thereof as shall seem necessary and proper to correct the violation and secure enforcement of said order of the Superintendent of State Police or Commissioner of Community Affairs, as the case may be. Every such order issued by the Superintendent of State Police or Commissioner of Community Affairs under the provisions of this section shall be prima facie evidence of the truth of the matter and things therein set forth.

L.1950, c. 139, § 6, eff. May 25, 1950. Amended by L.1953, c. 21, § 3, eff. March 19, 1953; L.1958, c. 43, § 6, eff. May 20, 1958; L.1999, c. 109, § 9, eff. May 14, 1999.

21:1B–7. Ordinances not to conflict with regulations

No municipality or other political subdivision shall adopt or enforce any ordinance or regulation in conflict with the provisions of this act [1] or with the regulations promulgated under section two of this act.[2]

L.1950, c. 139, § 7, eff. Sept. 1, 1951.

   1 N.J.S.A. § 21:1B–5.
   2 N.J.S.A. § 21:1B–2.

21:1B–8. Declaration of necessity

The State of New Jersey hereby finds, determines and declares that this act [1] is necessary for the immediate preservation of the public peace, health and safety.

L.1950, c. 139, § 8, eff. May 25, 1950.

   1 N.J.S.A. §§ 21:1B–1 to 21:1B–8.

21:1B–9. Transfer of powers, functions and duties of superintendent of state police to commissioner of labor and industry

All the powers, functions and duties heretofore exercised by the Superintendent of State Police pursuant to the provisions of P.L.1950, c. 139, as amended (C. 21:1B–1 et seq.) and pertaining to the design, construction, location, installation and operation of equipment for storing, handling and utilizing liquefied petroleum

gases at places of employment are hereby transferred to and vested in the Commissioner of Labor and Industry.
L.1972, c. 107, § 1, eff. Oct. 25, 1972.

21:1B–10. Rules, regulations and orders of superintendent of state police; continuance

a. All rules and regulations promulgated by the Superintendent of State Police relating to such places of employment shall remain in full force and effect until they are superseded by rules and regulations promulgated by the Commissioner of Labor and Industry.

b. All orders of the Superintendent of State Police shall be continued in full force and effect unless modified or disapproved by the Commissioner of Labor and Industry; provided, however, that no order may be modified or disapproved with regard to an installation in existence on the effective date of this act except where such installation creates a hazardous condition that endangers the public.
L.1972, c. 107, § 2, eff. Oct. 25, 1972.

21:1B–11. Method of transfer

The transfer directed by this act shall be effected pursuant to the "State Agency Transfer Act," P.L.1971, c. 375 (C. 52:14D–1 et seq.).
L.1972, c. 107, § 3, eff. Oct. 25, 1972.

21:1B–12. Liquefied Petroleum Gas Education and Safety Board created

a. There is created within the Department of Community Affairs the Liquefied Petroleum Gas Education and Safety Board. This board shall be advisory in nature to the Commissioner of Community Affairs. The board shall be composed of 11 members: three public members appointed by the Governor on a nonpartisan basis, two of whom shall be professional firefighters or other fire safety professionals; one representative from the environmental community and one representative from a consumer group, appointed by the Governor; five members who are representatives of the liquefied petroleum gas industry appointed by the Governor upon recommendation by the Board of Directors of the New Jersey Propane Gas Association; and one representative of a gas public utility involved in the storage and distribution of liquefied petroleum gas, appointed by the Governor. Members of the board who are representatives of the liquefied petroleum gas industry and the gas public utility shall have been legal residents of the State for at least the five years prior to their appointment and have been actively engaged in the liquefied petroleum gas industry for at least five years. Members of the board shall be appointed within 90 days after the effective date of this act.

Of the members first appointed as public members, one shall serve for one year, one shall serve for two years, and one shall serve for three years. Of the members representing the liquefied petroleum gas industry, the first appointed shall serve for one year, the next appointed shall serve for two years, and the remainder shall serve for three years. The representative from the environmental community, the representative of the gas public utility and the representative from a consumer group shall each serve for three years.

Upon expiration of the terms of the members first appointed, the terms of all members shall be three years. Members may be reappointed. Members shall serve until a replacement is appointed. Vacancies shall be filled in the same manner as the original appointment. In the case of a vacancy occurring otherwise than by expiration of term, that vacancy shall be filled only for the unexpired term.

b. The board shall elect a chairman and vice-chairman from among its members at its first regular meeting each calendar year. All meetings of the board shall be held on a prescribed date, at least quarterly, and also at any time a majority of the board members requests a meeting in writing to the board chairman. Any six members shall constitute a quorum for the transaction of business. The board may adopt bylaws governing its procedures and method of operation.

c. The members of the board shall not receive compensation, but may receive an allowance for travel expenses as determined by the commissioner to the extent such funds are made available.
L.1999, c. 109, § 1, eff. May 14, 1999.

21:1B–13. Powers of the board

a. The Liquefied Petroleum Gas Education and Safety Board is empowered to:

(1) recommend to the Commissioner of Community Affairs for proposal and adoption rules and regulations:

(a) setting forth minimum general standards for the design, construction, location, installation, and operation of equipment for storing and handling of liquefied petroleum gas, and

(b) governing liquefied petroleum gas distributors and installers and the installation of liquefied petroleum gas systems, carburetion systems and fueling systems;

(2) make recommendations to the Commissioner of Community Affairs concerning:

(a) civil penalties for violation of any rule or order made under chapter 1B of Title 21 of the Revised Statutes;

(b) the method and form of application for a liquefied petroleum gas license or certification; the investigation of the experience, reputation and background of applicants; the issuance, suspension, revocation or denial of licenses; and the procedures for conducting hearings in connection with the applications for, or revocation of, licenses and certifications, including, but not limited to, compelling the attendance of witnesses by subpoena, requiring the production of any records or documents determined by it to be pertinent to the subject matter of the hearing, and applying to the

Superior Court for an order citing any applicant or witness for contempt, and for failure to attend, testify or produce required documents;

(c) procedures for the suspension or revocation of licenses or certifications and the denial of license or certification renewals when the applicant or licensee has been guilty of acts of conduct harmful to either the safety or protection of the public;

(d) the content of and procedures for administering examinations of every license applicant to determine the responsibility, ability, knowledge, experience or other qualification of the applicant for a license;

(e) competency testing for all employees and subcontractors of licensees engaged in transporting or dispensing liquefied petroleum gas or installing, servicing, or repairing a liquefied petroleum gas system, fueling system or carburetion system, as set forth in this chapter;

(f) procedures for the granting of exemptions from department rules and regulations to accommodate local needs as it determines to be in the best interest of the safety of the public or the persons using liquefied petroleum gas systems or services;

(g) the development of programs and projects, including educational programs for public safety officials and consumers, concerning safety and environmental advantages of liquefied petroleum gas, and safety and educational programs for the public and for industrial and emergency response personnel;

(h) procedures for entering into contracts or agreements to implement the provisions of this act; and

(i) a schedule of the fees and charges to cover all costs of administration of the provisions of this act as provided in this act.

b. (1) The board shall keep accurate records and minutes of all meetings, which shall be open to public inspection at all reasonable times, and keep a public record of all applications for licenses, and licenses issued by it.

(2) The board shall periodically report to the Commissioner of Community Affairs concerning its transactions and recommendations and the Commissioner of Community Affairs shall submit to the Governor a biennial report before September 1 of each even numbered year, covering its transactions during the biennium ending June 30 of that year, including a complete statement of the receipts and expenditures of the board during that period.

L.1999, c. 109, § 2, eff. May 14, 1999.

21:1B–14. Limitations on power

The board shall have no authority governing:

a. The production, refining or manufacture of liquefied petroleum gas;

b. The storage, sale, or transportation of liquefied petroleum gas by pipeline or railroad tank car by a pipeline company, producer, refiner or manufacturer;

c. The equipment used by a pipeline company, producer, refiner or manufacturer in a producing, refining or manufacturing process, or in the storage, sale or transportation by pipeline or railroad tank car;

d. Any deliveries of liquefied petroleum gas to another person at the place of production, refining, or manufacturing;

e. Regulations and requirements of liquefied petroleum gas transporters as covered by the Code of Federal Regulations, Title 49, as administered pursuant to P.L.1983, c. 401 (C.39:5B–25 et seq.); or

f. Those portions of the liquefied petroleum gas system operated by a gas public utility that are under the regulation and requirements of Title 49 of the Code of Federal Regulations, as administered by the New Jersey Board of Public Utilities.

L.1999, c. 109, § 3, eff. May 14, 1999.

21:1B–15. Assessment level recommendations

a. The board may recommend to the Commissioner of Community Affairs the level of an assessment to be levied on liquefied petroleum gas and the commissioner shall determine the level and may levy the assessment. The initial assessment shall be no greater than one-fifteenth of one cent per gallon. Thereafter, annual assessments shall be sufficient to cover the costs of the plans and programs developed by the board and approved by the commissioner, and the cost of administering the responsibilities of the department established pursuant to this act. The assessment shall not exceed one-half cent per gallon of odorized propane. The assessment may not be raised by more than one-tenth of one cent per gallon annually.

The owner of liquefied petroleum gas immediately prior to odorization shall be responsible for the payment of the assessment on the volume of liquefied petroleum gas at the time of import or odorization, whichever is earlier.

The commissioner may by regulation establish an alternative means for the department to collect the assessment if another means is found to be more efficient and effective. The commissioner may by regulation establish a late payment charge and rate of interest to be imposed on any person who fails to remit to the department any amount due.

b. Pending disbursement pursuant to a program, plan or project, the State Treasurer may invest funds collected through assessments and any other funds received by the department, only in obligations of the United States or any agency thereof, in general obligations of any state or any political subdivision thereof, in any interest-bearing account or certificate of deposit of a bank that is a member of the Federal Reserve

System, or in obligations fully guaranteed as to principal and interest by the United States.

c. There is established a "Liquefied Petroleum Gas Education and Safety Board Fund" as a non-lapsing revolving fund within the Department of Community Affairs. All assessments, fees and penalties collected by the department under this chapter shall be deposited in the fund. The fund shall be administered by the Commissioner of Community Affairs and shall be used exclusively to defray all expenses incurred by the department in operation of the board and the administration of the department's responsibilities under this act.

L.1999, c. 109, § 4, eff. May 14, 1999.

CHAPTER 1C

MODEL ROCKETS

Section
21:1C–1. Definitions.
21:1C–2. Examination, testing and certification of model rockets.
21:1C–3. Certificate required for sale; compliance with rules and regulations.
21:1C–4. Age of purchasers; permit for storage of solid propellant model rockets.
21:1C–5. Penalty for violation.
21:1C–6. Rules and regulations; compliance with Code for Unmanned Rockets of the National Fire Protection Association.

21:1C–1. Definitions

As used in this act:

"Model rocket" means a commercially made rocket that is propelled by a rocket motor; that contains a device for returning it to the ground in a condition to fly again; whose structural parts are made of paper, wood, or breakable plastic and contain no substantial metal parts; and whose primary use is for purposes of education, recreation, and sporting competition.

"Rocket motor" means a device that provides the necessary force or thrust to cause a rocket to move and the force or thrust is created by the discharge of gas generated by combustion, decomposition, change of state, or other operation of materials completely stored within the rocket motor during the commercial manufacturing process and requiring no mixing of propellants.

L.1991, c. 354, § 1, eff. July 17, 1992.

21:1C–2. Examination, testing and certification of model rockets

Model rockets offered for sale, sold, used, or made available to the public in this State shall be examined and tested by the Department of Labor to determine if they comply with the requirements of this act and with the rules and regulations promulgated thereto. The Commissioner of the Department of Labor shall certify

as acceptable for sale and use those products that do comply. At the discretion of the commissioner, the examination, testing, and certification may be carried out by an approved testing laboratory or an organization such as the National Association of Rocketry or an organization affiliated with the National Aeronautic Association.

The commissioner shall maintain a current and complete list of all model rockets which have received certification and shall make copies of this list available to any person upon request.

L.1991, c. 354, § 2, eff. Jan. 9, 1992.

21:1C–3. Certificate required for sale; compliance with rules and regulations

A model rocket shall not be sold, offered for sale, made available to the public, or used in this State unless it has been certified by the commissioner.

A model rocket shall not be used in this State except in accordance with this act and in compliance with the rules and regulations promulgated in accordance with section 6 of this act.[1]

L.1991, c. 354, § 3, eff. July 17, 1992.

[1] N.J.S.A. § 21:1C–6.

21:1C–4. Age of purchasers; permit for storage of solid propellant model rockets

a. A person at least 14 years of age, but less than 18 years of age, shall be eligible to purchase and use a model rocket bearing the standardized engine coding 1/4A, 1/2A, A, B, and C provided that the person has a consent form signed by a parent or legal guardian.

b. A person at least 18 years of age shall be permitted to purchase and use a model rocket of any type or size.

c. A person at least 12 years of age but less than 14 years of age who is a participant in a bona fide model rocket education program may fire a model rocket bearing the standardized engine coding 1/4A, 1/2A, A, B, and C only when under the direct supervision and control of a person who is at least 21 years of age and only during the course of the model rocket education program.

d. A person shall be required to obtain a permit for the storage of more than 100 kg (220 lbs.) of solid propellant model rockets. No other permit shall be required for the possession, use, purchase, transportation, or sale of model rockets.

L.1991, c. 354, § 4, eff. July 17, 1992.

21:1C–5. Penalty for violation

A person who violates any of the provisions of this act shall be fined $100.00 which shall be collected in a civil action by a summary proceeding under the "penalty enforcement law" (N.J.S. 2A:58–1 et seq.).

L.1991, c. 354, § 5, eff. July 17, 1992.

21:1C–6. Rules and regulations; compliance with Code for Unmanned Rockets of the National Fire Protection Association

The Commissioner of the Department of Labor shall establish rules and regulations pursuant to the "Administrative Procedure Act," P.L.1968, c. 410 (C. 52:14B–1 et seq.) which shall substantially comply with the NFPA 1122 Code for Unmanned Rockets of the National Fire Protection Association. The rules and regulations shall include, but need not be limited to, the procedures for obtaining the permit specified in subsection d. of section 4 of this act,[1] the procedures to be followed for the permitted use of model rockets, and the acceptable design, weight, and power of model rockets.

L.1991, c. 354, § 6, eff. Jan. 9, 1992.

[1] N.J.S.A. § 21:1C–4, subsec. d.

SUBTITLE 2

FIREWORKS

Chapter
2. Manufacture, Storage and Transportation.
3. Sale and Public Display.

CHAPTER 2

MANUFACTURE, STORAGE AND TRANSPORTATION

ARTICLE 1.　DEFINITIONS AND CONSTRUCTIONS

Section
21:2–1.　Short title of act.
21:2–2.　General definitions.
21:2–3.　"Dangerous fireworks" defined.
21:2–4.　Application of chapter.
21:2–5.　Explosives laws not repealed.

ARTICLE 2.　PROHIBITED FIREWORKS

21:2–6.　Dangerous fireworks prohibited.
21:2–7.　Fireworks showers in buildings unlawful; exception for theaters or public halls under certain circumstances.

ARTICLE 3.　MANUFACTURING

21:2–8.　Factory buildings; location of.
21:2–9.　Storage buildings; location of.
21:2–10.　Fences, gates and watchmen.
21:2–11.　Fire protection.
21:2–12.　Precautions against fire.
21:2–13.　Storage in factory buildings prohibited.
21:2–14.　Character of fireworks which may be manufactured.
21:2–15.　Marking packages.
21:2–16.　Uniforms of employees.
21:2–17.　Matches, liquor and narcotics.
21:2–18.　Smoking and carrying matches in fireworks plant.
21:2–19.　Warning signs.
21:2–20.　Containers for matches at entrances.
21:2–21.　Inspection.
21:2–22.　Certificate of registration; posting.
21:2–23.　Denial of certificate; reasons filed.
21:2–24.　Revocation of certificate.
21:2–25.　Statement of reasons for revocation.
21:2–26.　Records and duplicates of certificates.
21:2–27.　Indemnity bond.
21:2–28.　Exemption from filing bond.

ARTICLE 4.　STORAGE AND SALE

21:2–29.　Prohibited places of storage or sale.
21:2–29.1.　Permit to store or sell fireworks for use for agricultural purposes.
21:2–30.　Smoking not allowed in place of sale.

ARTICLE 5.　TRANSPORTATION

21:2–31 to 21:2–34.　Repealed.

Section

ARTICLE 6.　PENALTIES

21:2–35.　Violations; crime of fourth degree.
21:2–36.　Persons receiving fireworks required to show valid permit; permit number to be recorded and retained; violations.
21:2–37.　Annual registration with municipality where main office located or fireworks stored; identification number; denial of registration.

ARTICLE 1.　DEFINITIONS AND CONSTRUCTIONS

21:2–1.　Short title of act

This chapter may be cited as the "fireworks regulation law".

21:2–2.　General definitions

As used in this chapter:

"Fireworks" include any combustible or explosive composition, or any substance or combination of substances, or article prepared for the purpose of producing a visible or an audible effect by combustion, explosion, deflagration or detonation.

"Fireworks factory building" means any building or other structure in which the manufacture of fireworks, other than sparklers, or in which any processing involving fireworks other than sparklers, is carried on.

"Fireworks plant" means and includes all lands, with buildings thereon, used in connection with the manufacturing or processing of fireworks, as well as storehouses located thereon for the storage of finished fireworks.

"Highway" means any public street, public alley, public road, or navigable stream.

"Navigable streams" mean streams susceptible of being used, in their ordinary condition, as highways of commerce, over which trade and travel are or may be conducted in the customary modes, but shall not include streams which are not capable of navigation by barges, tugboats, and other large vessels.

"Railroad" means any steam, electric or other railroad which carries passengers for hire, but shall not include sidings or spur tracks installed primarily for the use of the fireworks plant.

21:2–3.　"Dangerous fireworks" defined

"Dangerous fireworks" mean and include the following:

Toy torpedoes containing more than 5 grains of an explosive composition.

Paper caps containing more than .35 grain of explosive composition.

Firecrackers or salutes exceeding 5 inches in length or ¾ inch in diameter.

Cannons, canes, pistols or other devices designed for use otherwise than with paper caps.

Any fireworks containing a compound or mixture of yellow or white phosphorous or mercury.

Any fireworks that contain a detonator or blasting cap.

Fireworks compositions that ignite spontaneously or undergo marked decomposition when subjected for 48 consecutive hours to a temperature of 167° Fahrenheit.

Fireworks that can be exploded en masse by a blasting cap placed in one of the units or by impact of a rifle bullet or otherwise.

Fireworks, such as sparklers or fusees, containing a match tip, or head, or similar igniting point or surface, unless each individual tip, head or igniting point or surface is thoroughly covered and securely protected from accidental contact or friction with any other surface.

Fireworks containing an ammonium salt and a chlorate.

21:2–4. Application of chapter

Nothing in this chapter shall be construed as applying to the transportation of any article or thing shipped in conformity with the regulations prescribed by the Interstate Commerce Commission, to the military or naval forces of the United States, to the duly authorized militia of the State, to the use and manufacture of signals and fusees necessary for the safe operation of railroads, steamboats or aircraft, or to the use of fireworks for agricultural purposes in connection with the raising of crops.
Amended by L.1938, c. 69, § 1; L.1954, c. 52, § 1, eff. July 22, 1954.

21:2–5. Explosives laws not repealed

Nothing in this chapter contained shall be deemed to repeal any of the provisions of chapter one of this title (§ 21:1–1 et seq.).

ARTICLE 2. PROHIBITED FIREWORKS

21:2–6. Dangerous fireworks prohibited

It shall be unlawful to manufacture, sell, transport or use dangerous fireworks within the state.

21:2–7. Fireworks showers in buildings unlawful; exception for theaters or public halls under certain circumstances

a. The use of what are technically known as fireworks showers, or of any composition containing potassium and sulphur, inside any building other than as

authorized in subsection b. of this section shall be unlawful. A violation of this section shall be subject to the provisions of R.S.21:3–8.

b. The use of what are technically known as fireworks showers, or of any composition containing potassium and sulphur, in theaters or public halls, shall be permitted but shall be subject to prior approval by the appropriate fire official according to the provisions of the "Uniform Fire Safety Act," P.L.1983, c. 383 (C.52:27D–192 et seq.).

No fire official shall approve any such use unless the premises have been designed and constructed to accommodate such activity in accordance with the applicable provisions of the Uniform Fire Safety Code adopted pursuant to the "Uniform Fire Safety Act," P.L.1983, c. 383 (C.52:27D–192 et seq.), the State Uniform Construction Code adopted pursuant to the "State Uniform Construction Code Act," P.L.1975, c. 217 (C.52:27D–119 et seq.), or both.
Amended by L.2005, c. 115, § 1, eff. June 29, 2005.

ARTICLE 3. MANUFACTURING

21:2–8. Factory buildings; location of

No factory building shall be situated nearer than two hundred feet from any inhabited building or to any highway or to any railroad, nor nearer than fifty feet from any building used for the storage of explosives or fireworks, nor nearer than twenty-five feet to any other factory building. This section shall not apply to factory buildings existing on March twenty-fifth, one thousand nine hundred and thirty, in fireworks plants then in operation.

21:2–9. Storage buildings; location of

No building in a fireworks plant used for the storage of finished fireworks, other than those containing only sparklers, shall be situated nearer than three hundred feet from any building not used in connection with the manufacture of fireworks, nor from any highway, railroad or navigable stream, nor within three hundred feet of the property line of the fireworks plant. This section shall not apply to such storehouses existing on March twenty-fifth, one thousand nine hundred and thirty.

21:2–10. Fences, gates and watchmen

All fireworks plants shall be inclosed on all sides by substantial fences and all openings to such inclosures shall be fitted with suitable gates, which, when not locked, shall be in charge of a competent watchman who shall have charge of the fireworks plant when it is not in operation.

21:2–11. Fire protection

Fireworks plants and all buildings situated within fireworks plant inclosures, shall be equipped with suitable fire protection, commensurate with the hazard involved, to protect life and property from direct burning and exposure. Such fire protection shall be installed as directed by the Commissioner of Labor or by the agency in the municipality wherein a plant is located which is authorized to enforce the "Uniform Fire Safety Act," P.L.1983, c. 383 (C.52:27D–192 et seq.).

Amended by L.1991, c. 55, § 9, eff. March 13, 1991.

21:2–12. Precautions against fire

No stoves, exposed flame or electrical heating devices shall be used in any part of any fireworks plant, except in the boiler room or machine shop if no fireworks or chemicals are stored therein. All parts of the buildings in fireworks plants shall be kept clean, orderly and free from accumulations of dust or rubbish.

21:2–13. Storage in factory buildings prohibited

Fireworks in the finished state shall not be stored in buildings where fireworks are in process of manufacture.

21:2–14. Character of fireworks which may be manufactured

No fireworks may be manufactured except such as shall be approved for transportation by the regulations of the interstate commerce commission.

21:2–15. Marking packages

The outside of each package of fireworks prepared by a manufacturer shall bear upon the outside thereof the words "Fireworks—Handle Carefully—Keep Fire Away" in letters not less than ⅞₆ inch in height, and in addition shall show the name of the fireworks manufacturer.

Amended by L.1991, c. 55, § 2, eff. March 13, 1991.

21:2–16. Uniforms of employees

All factory employees in fireworks plants employed in loading, filling or handling of charged fireworks in process of manufacture, or of explosive compositions, shall be clothed in suitable uniforms to be approved by the department of labor.

21:2–17. Matches, liquor and narcotics

No employee or other person shall enter or attempt to enter any fireworks plant with matches or other flame-producing devices, nor with liquor or narcotics in his or her possession or control, nor while under the influence of liquor or narcotics, nor partake of intoxicants or narcotics while in the plant.

21:2–18. Smoking and carrying matches in fireworks plant

No person shall smoke nor carry matches, a lighted cigar, cigarette or pipe within any room or inclosed place or upon any part of a fireworks plant.

21:2–19. Warning signs

All fireworks plants shall be properly posted with "Warning" and "No Smoking" signs.

21:2–20. Containers for matches at entrances

It shall be the duty of the superintendent, foreman or other person in charge of any fireworks plant to provide safety containers for matches at all main entrances of the plant, where all matches in the possession of all persons shall be deposited before entering the plant inclosure.

21:2–21. Inspection

On receipt of an application to operate a fireworks plant, the commissioner of labor shall cause an inspection to be made of the premises described in the application for the purpose of determining whether they conform to the provisions of this chapter.

21:2–22. Certificate of registration; posting

If the conditions in the fireworks plant conform to the provisions of this chapter, the commissioner of labor shall issue a certificate of registration which shall be protected under glass and posted in a conspicuous place near the entrance to the fireworks plant. The certificate shall continue in force until revoked.

21:2–23. Denial of certificate; reasons filed

If the commissioner denies an application for a certificate of registration, he shall file in his office a statement of the reasons therefor and furnish the applicant with a copy of the same.

21:2–24. Revocation of certificate

The commissioner may revoke a certificate of registration if the fireworks plant is not maintained in accordance with the provisions of this chapter applicable thereto.

21:2–25. Statement of reasons for revocation

If a certificate is revoked the commissioner shall file in his office a statement of the reasons therefor and furnish a copy of same to the owner and persons operating the fireworks plant. No fireworks plant shall be operated after revocation of its certificate of registration until such fireworks plant complies with this chapter, and a new certificate is issued.

21:2–26. Records and duplicates of certificates

A record of the certificates of registration issued and revoked shall be kept on file in the office of the commissioner, and a duplicate sent to the chief of the fire department of each community, in which a fireworks plant is located.

21:2–27. Indemnity bond

The owner or operator of any fireworks plant, within sixty days after demand therefor in writing by the commissioner of labor, unless exempted therefrom as hereinafter provided, shall file and keep on file with the department of banking and insurance of the state, an indemnity bond payable to the state of New Jersey in such sums as may be determined by the commissioner of labor and set forth in such demand, not in excess of fifty thousand dollars nor less than ten thousand dollars, with surety or sureties satisfactory to such department, conditioned for the payment of all final judgments that may be rendered against such owner or operator for damages caused to persons and property by reason of any explosion at such fireworks plant of the product or component part or parts thereof there manufactured, processed or handled.

21:2–28. Exemption from filing bond

Any fireworks plant owner or operator desiring to be exempted from filing such bond may make application to the state department of banking and insurance, showing his financial ability to discharge all such judgments to the amount of the bond required by the commissioner of labor that may be entered against him, whereupon such department, if satisfied with the financial ability of the applicant, shall, by written order, exempt the applicant from the filing of such bond, and the department of banking and insurance may from time to time require further statements from the applicant showing his financial ability and, if dissatisfied therewith, may in its discretion revoke such exemption, and require the filing of such bond.

ARTICLE 4. STORAGE AND SALE

21:2–29. Prohibited places of storage or sale

It shall be unlawful to store or sell fireworks:

a. In any building where paints, oils or varnishes are manufactured or kept for use or sale, unless paints, oils and varnishes are in original unbroken containers;

b. In any building where matches (other than approved safety matches), rosin, turpentine, gasoline, or other highly inflammable substances, or substances which may generate inflammable vapors are used, stored or kept for sale;

c. In any building where stoves or exposed flame are used in the part of the building where fireworks are stored or offered for sale.

21:2–29.1. Permit to store or sell fireworks for use for agricultural purposes

It shall be unlawful to store or sell fireworks, designed or intended to be used for agricultural purposes as pest-control bombs in connection with the raising of crops, without first obtaining from the Commissioner of Labor a permit to store or sell such fireworks.

The Commissioner of Labor is authorized to issue such permits subject to rules and regulations to be prescribed by him and upon the payment of the required fees.

The rules and regulations shall be such as will reasonably protect the safety of the public by limiting the quantities to be stored in any one place and by providing safeguards against the danger of explosion and damage thereby to persons and property.

In prescribing the rules and regulations, the commissioner shall consult and co-operate with the State Department of Agriculture.

The fee for issuing any such permit shall be fixed by the commissioner according to a scale of quantities and locations prescribed by him, but in no case shall such fee exceed $100.00.

L.1954, c. 52, p. 396, § 2. Amended by L.1955, c. 115, p. 586, § 1, eff. July 1, 1955; L.1991, c. 55, § 3, eff. March 13, 1991.

21:2–30. Smoking not allowed in place of sale

No smoking shall be allowed in any building where fireworks are offered for sale. Over each entrance to such a store a sign in large letters shall be displayed reading "Fireworks For Sale—No Smoking Allowed".

ARTICLE 5. TRANSPORTATION

21:2–31 to 21:2–34. Repealed by L.1991, c. 55, § 11, eff. March 13, 1991

ARTICLE 6. PENALTIES

21:2–35. Violations; crime of fourth degree

Any person who fails to comply with or violates any of the provisions of this chapter shall be guilty of a crime of the fourth degree.

Amended by L.1953, c. 21, p. 374, § 4, eff. March 19, 1953; L.1983, c. 561, § 1, eff. Jan. 17, 1984.

21:2–36. Persons receiving fireworks required to show valid permit; permit number to be recorded and retained; violations

a. A person shall not knowingly deliver fireworks to a person within this State unless the person to whom delivery is to be made is named on a valid permit obtained pursuant to R.S.21:3–1 et seq. as the person authorized to receive fireworks or unless the person is the owner, manager, or designated employee acting as the agent of the owner or manager, of a legally operated commercial enterprise registered pursuant to section 10 of P.L.1991, c. 55 (C.21:2–37). At the time of delivery, the person receiving the fireworks shall make the permit or registration available to the person making delivery for review and the number of the permit or registration held by the receiver shall be recorded on each bill of lading, manifest or invoice issued to cover the sale and shipment of the fireworks. A record of the bill of lading, manifest, or invoice shall be retained by the person making delivery for a period of three years and shall be available for inspection by municipal enforcement authorities, the Department of Labor, or other law enforcement authorities.

A package to be delivered to a person who does not have a valid permit or registration shall be turned over to the local municipal law enforcement authority who in turn shall notify the Office of Safety Compliance in the Department of Labor.

b. A package containing fireworks prepared by a manufacturer, supplier or seller for shipment or transportation into or within this State to a purchaser or receiver shall be labeled in accordance with the requirements of State and federal law, and the rules and regulations promulgated pursuant to those laws, concerning the transportation of hazardous materials.

Notwithstanding the penalty set forth in R.S.21:2–35, a violation of this section is a disorderly persons offense.

L.1991, c. 55, § 1, eff. March 13, 1991.

21:2–37. Annual registration with municipality where main office located or fireworks stored; identification number; denial of registration

A person who is the owner or manager of a legally operated commercial enterprise involving the manufacture, distribution, storage, or sale of fireworks shall, in addition to the certificate of registration issued pursuant to R.S.21:2–22 or a permit issued pursuant to section 2 of P.L.1954, c. 52 (C.21:2–29.1), annually register with the municipality in which the main office of the enterprise is located and with any municipality in which the enterprise stores fireworks, if fireworks are stored in a municipality other than the municipality in which the main office is located. The registration shall be filed with the agency authorized to enforce the "Uniform Fire Safety Act," P.L.1983, c. 383 (C.52:27D–192 et seq.) by submitting a letter of registration or by completing a form supplied by the agency.

An identification number for the registration shall be issued and a certified copy of the registration shall be returned to the owner or manager. The registration shall be available upon request for inspection by any person during normal business hours. A copy of each registration shall be forwarded to the Office of Safety Compliance in the Department of Labor.

The agency with which a registration is filed may deny the registration if it finds that the enterprise is not a legally operated commercial enterprise. Denial shall be in writing with the reasons for denial clearly stated. A copy of the letter of the denial shall immediately be forwarded to the Office of Safety Compliance in the Department of Labor.

L.1991, c. 55, § 10, eff. March 13, 1991.

CHAPTER 3

SALE AND PUBLIC DISPLAY

Section
21:3–1. Sale, use, etc., declared against public health, safety and welfare.
21:3–2. Sale, possession or use prohibited; exceptions.
21:3–3. Permits for public displays; application; restrictions.
21:3–4. Contents of applications for permits; approval of storage place; permit not transferable.
21:3–5. Surety by licensee.
21:3–6. Copy of application and permit forwarded to department of labor.
21:3–7. Effect on existing laws; exceptions.
21:3–8. Penalties for violations.
21:3–9. Enforcement by municipalities.

21:3–1. Sale, use, etc., declared against public health, safety and welfare

The sale, exposure for sale, use, distribution or possession of fireworks or pyrotechnics in the state of New Jersey, except as hereinafter provided, is hereby declared by the legislature to be against the public health, safety and welfare of the people of the state of New Jersey.

21:3–2. Sale, possession or use prohibited; exceptions

It shall be unlawful for any person to offer for sale, expose for sale, sell, possess or use, or explode any blank cartridge, toy pistol, toy cannon, toy cane or toy gun in which explosives are used; the type of balloon which requires fire underneath to propel the same; firecrackers; torpedoes; skyrockets, Roman candles, bombs, sparklers or other fireworks of like construction, or any fireworks containing any explosive or inflammable compound or any tablets or other device commonly used and sold as fireworks containing nitrates, chlorates, oxalates, sulphides of lead, barium, antimony, arsenic, mercury, nitroglycerine, phosphorus or any compound containing any of the same or other explosives, or any substance or combination of substances, or article prepared for the purpose of producing a visible or an audible effect by combustion, explosion, deflagration or detonation, other than aviation and railroad signal light flares, except (a) that it shall be lawful for any person to offer for sale, expose for sale, sell, possess or use, or explode any toy pistol, toy cane, toy gun, or other device in which paper or plastic caps containing .25 grain or less of explosive compound per cap are used, providing they are so constructed that the hand cannot come in contact with the cap when in place for use, and toy pistol paper or plastic caps which contain less than .20 grain of explosive mixture per cap and (b) as in this chapter further provided.

Except as otherwise may be provided in this chapter, it shall be lawful to sell fireworks to a person only if that person is named as the authorized purchaser in a valid permit issued pursuant to R.S.21:3–3 or that person is the owner, manager, or designated employee acting as the agent of the owner or manager, of a legally operated commercial enterprise registered pursuant to section 10 of P.L. 1991, c. 55 (C. 21:2–37), and the permit is presented to the manufacturer, seller or distributor at the time of purchase. If the manufacturer, seller or distributor is located in a state other than this State, a purchase shall be by mail order form and a photocopy of the valid permit or registration shall be submitted with the form to satisfy the requirement in this paragraph.

Amended by L.1962, c. 82, § 1, eff. June 18, 1962; L.1970, c. 220, § 1, eff. Oct. 16, 1970; L.1991, c. 55, § 4, eff. March 13, 1991.

21:3–3. Permits for public displays; application; restrictions

The governing body of any municipality, other than a county, notwithstanding any of the provisions of this chapter to the contrary, may, upon application in writing, upon the posting of a suitable bond, grant a permit for the purchase, possession and public display of fireworks by municipalities, religious, fraternal or civic organizations, fair associations, amusement parks, or other organizations or groups of individuals, approved by the governing body of such municipality to whom the application is made.

The governing body is authorized by resolution, to grant such permission when such display is to be handled by a competent operator, to be approved by the chiefs of the police and fire departments of the municipality. Such display shall be of such a character, and so located, discharged, or fired, as in the opinion of the chiefs of the police and fire departments, after proper inspection, shall not be hazardous to property or endanger any person or persons.

A permit issued pursuant to this section shall contain an identification number and the specific types or kinds of fireworks to be used. The permit shall name one person who shall be authorized to purchase, or otherwise order, and receive delivery of any fireworks. After such permit shall have been granted, sales, possession, and use of fireworks for such display shall be lawful for that purpose only.

Amended by L.1991, c. 55, § 5, eff. March 13, 1991.

21:3–4. Contents of applications for permits; approval of storage place; permit not transferable

All such applications for permits shall set forth the name of the person authorized to purchase, or otherwise order, and receive delivery of any fireworks, the specific types or kinds of fireworks to be obtained and used, the date, the hour, place of making such display, and place of storing fireworks prior to the display and, further, the name or names of the person, persons, firm, partnership, corporation, association or group of individuals making the display; the name of the person, or persons, in charge of the igniting, firing, setting-off, exploding or causing to be exploded such fireworks. The location of the storage place shall be subject to the approval of the chief of the fire department of the municipality. No permit granted hereunder shall be transferable.

Amended by L.1991, c. 55, § 6, eff. March 13, 1991.

21:3–5. Surety by licensee

The governing body of the municipality shall require surety which may be cash, government bonds, personal bond, or other form of insurance in a sum of not less than twenty-five hundred dollars ($2,500.00), conditioned for the payment of all damages, which may be caused either to a person or persons or to property, by reason of the display so as aforesaid licensed, and arising from any acts of the licensee, his agents, employees or subcontractors. Such surety shall run to the municipality in which the license is granted, and shall be for the use and benefit of any person, persons, or the owner or owners of any property so damaged, who is or are authorized to maintain an action thereon, or his or their heirs, executors, administrators, successors or assigns.

Amended by L.1946, c. 81, p. 287, § 1, eff. April 16, 1946.

21:3–6. Copy of application and permit forwarded to department of labor

A duplicate copy of the application and of the permit granted shall be forwarded to the Office of Safety Compliance in the Department of Labor by the governing body granting such permit and such copies shall be kept on file in the department, subject to public inspection.

Amended by L.1991, c. 55, § 7, eff. March 13, 1991.

21:3–7. Effect on existing laws; exceptions

Nothing in this chapter contained shall be construed to interfere with the provisions of chapter 2 of this title (§ 21:2–1 et seq.) where the provisions thereof are not inconsistent with the provisions of this chapter, nor shall anything in this chapter contained be construed to prohibit any manufacturer, wholesaler, dealer or jobber from selling at wholesale such fireworks to municipalities, religious, fraternal or civic organizations, fair associations, amusement parks, or other organizations or groups of individuals authorized to possess and use fireworks under this chapter; or the sale of any kind of fireworks, provided the same are to be shipped directly out of the state; or the sale or use of blank cartridges for a show or theater, or for signal purposes in athletic sports, or by railroads for signal purposes, or for the use by the militia, or construed to prohibit the manufacture and sale of aviation and railroad light flares. Any provision of any law in this state inconsistent with any provision of this chapter is hereby repealed.

21:3–8. Penalties for violations

Any person who sells, offers or exposes for sale, or possesses with intent to sell any fireworks as herein mentioned is guilty of a crime of the fourth degree. Any person who purchases, uses, discharges, causes to be discharged, ignites, fires, or otherwise sets in action, or possesses any fireworks is guilty of a petty disorderly persons offense.

Amended by L.1983, c. 561, § 2, eff. Jan. 17, 1984; L.1991, c. 55, § 8, eff. March 13, 1991.

21:3–9. Enforcement by municipalities

The municipalities of this State, and the Department of Labor and Industry, are hereby charged with the enforcement of all of the provisions of this chapter.

Amended by L.1955, c. 115, p. 587, § 2, eff. July 1, 1955.

TITLE 24

FOOD AND DRUGS

Subtitle
3. Narcotic Drugs and Other Dangerous Substances.

SUBTITLE 3

NARCOTIC DRUGS AND OTHER DANGEROUS SUBSTANCES

Chapter
21. Dangerous Substances Control Law.

CHAPTER 21

DANGEROUS SUBSTANCES CONTROL LAW

ARTICLE 1.   SHORT TITLE; DEFINITIONS

Section
24:21–1.   Short title.
24:21–2.   Definitions.

ARTICLE 2.   STANDARDS AND SCHEDULES

24:21–3.   Authority to control.
24:21–4.   Schedules of controlled substances.
24:21–5.   Schedule I.
24:21–6.   Schedule II.
24:21–7.   Schedule III.
24:21–8.   Schedule IV.
24:21–8.1.   Schedule V.
24:21–8.2.   Repealed.

ARTICLE 3.   REGULATION OF MANUFACTURE, DISTRIBUTION AND DISPENSING OF CONTROLLED DANGEROUS SUBSTANCES

24:21–9.   Rules and regulations.
24:21–10.   Registration requirements.
24:21–11.   Registration.
24:21–12.   Denial, revocation, or suspension of registration.

ARTICLE 4.   LABELS AND CONTAINERS

24:21–13.   Records of registrants.
24:21–14.   Order forms.
24:21–15.   Prescriptions.
24:21–16.   Form of label on containers of manufacturers and wholesalers; altering or removing label.
24:21–17.   Form of label to be used by pharmacists; altering or removing label.
24:21–18.   Repealed.

ARTICLE 5.   OFFENSES AND PENALTIES

24:21–19 to 24:21–20.   Repealed.
24:21–21.   Prohibited acts C.—Records and order forms of registered manufacturers and distributors—Penalties.

Section
24:21–22.   Prohibited acts D.—Fraud or misrepresentation by registered manufacturers or distributors—Penalties.
24:21–23.   General penalty.
24:21–24.   Attempt, endeavor and conspiracy.
24:21–25.   Additional penalties.
24:21–26, 24:21–27.   Repealed.
24:21–28.   Repealed.
24:21–29.   Second or subsequent offenses.
24:21–30.   Repealed.

ARTICLE 6.   ENFORCEMENT AND ADMINISTRATIVE PROVISIONS

24:21–31.   Powers of enforcement personnel.
24:21–32.   Administrative inspections and warrants.
24:21–33.   Injunctions.
24:21–34.   Cooperative arrangements.
24:21–35.   Nuisances.
24:21–36.   Reports of conviction of manufacturers and practitioners.
24:21–37.   Burden of proof; liabilities; immunity.
24:21–38.   Judicial review.

ARTICLE 7.   MISCELLANEOUS

24:21–39.   Reports by practitioners of drug dependent persons.
24:21–40.   Pending proceedings.
24:21–41.   Repealed.
24:21–42.   Uniformity of interpretation.
24:21–43.   Severability.
24:21–44.   Study of penalties relating to use and possession of marihuana.
24:21–45.   Repealer.

ARTICLE 8.   DRUG PARAPHERNALIA

24:21–46 to 24:21–50.   Repealed.
24:21–51.   Repealed.
24:21–52.   Seizure in violation of act.
24:21–53.   Severability.
24:21–54.   Controlled Dangerous Substances Administration and Enforcement Fund; appropriations.

ARTICLE 1. SHORT TITLE; DEFINITIONS

24:21–1. Short title

This act shall be known and may be cited as the "New Jersey Controlled Dangerous Substances Act."

L.1970, c. 226, § 1, eff. Jan. 17, 1971.

24:21–2. Definitions

As used in this act:

"Administer" means the direct application of a controlled dangerous substance, whether by injection, inhalation, ingestion, or any other means, to the body of a patient or research subject by: (1) a practitioner (or, in his presence, by his lawfully authorized agent), or (2) the patient or research subject at the lawful direction and in the presence of the practitioner.

"Agent" means an authorized person who acts on behalf of or at the direction of a manufacturer, distributor, or dispenser but does not include a common or contract carrier, public warehouseman, or employee thereof.

"Commissioner" means the Commissioner of Health and Senior Services.

"Controlled dangerous substance" means a drug, substance, or immediate precursor in Schedules I through V of article 2 of P.L.1970, c. 226 (C.24:21–1 et seq.), as amended and supplemented. The term shall not include distilled spirits, wine, malt beverages, as those terms are defined or used in R.S.33:1–1 et seq., or tobacco and tobacco products.

"Counterfeit substance" means a controlled dangerous substance which, or the container or labeling of which, without authorization, bears the trademark, trade name, or other identifying mark, imprint, number or device, or any likeness thereof, of a manufacturer, distributor, or dispenser other than the person or persons who in fact manufactured, distributed or dispensed such substance and which thereby falsely purports or is represented to be the product of, or to have been distributed by, such other manufacturer, distributor, or dispenser.

"Deliver" or "delivery" means the actual, constructive, or attempted transfer from one person to another of a controlled dangerous substance, whether or not there is an agency relationship.

"Director" means the Director of the Division of Consumer Affairs in the Department of Law and Public Safety.

"Dispense" means to deliver a controlled dangerous substance to an ultimate user or research subject by or pursuant to the lawful order of a practitioner, including the prescribing, administering, packaging, labeling, or compounding necessary to prepare the substance for that delivery. "Dispenser" means a practitioner who dispenses.

"Distribute" means to deliver other than by administering or dispensing a controlled dangerous substance. "Distributor" means a person who distributes.

"Division" means the Division of Consumer Affairs in the Department of Law and Public Safety.

"Drug Enforcement Administration" means the Drug Enforcement Administration in the United States Department of Justice.

"Drugs" means (a) substances recognized in the official United States Pharmacopoeia, official Homeopathic Pharmacopoeia of the United States, or official National Formulary, or any supplement to any of them; and (b) substances intended for use in the diagnosis, cure, mitigation, treatment, or prevention of disease in man or other animals; and (c) substances (other than food) intended to affect the structure or any function of the body of man or other animals; and (d) substances intended for use as a component of any article specified in subsections (a), (b) and (c) of this section; but does not include devices or their components, parts or accessories.

"Drug dependent person" means a person who is using a controlled dangerous substance and who is in a state of psychic or physical dependence, or both, arising from the use of that controlled dangerous substance on a continuous basis. Drug dependence is characterized by behavioral and other responses, including but not limited to a strong compulsion to take the substance on a recurring basis in order to experience its psychic effects, or to avoid the discomfort of its absence. "Hashish" means the resin extracted from any part of the plant Genus Cannabis L. and any compound, manufacture, salt, derivative, mixture, or preparation of such resin.

"Marihuana" means all parts of the plant Genus Cannabis L., whether growing or not; the seeds thereof; and every compound, manufacture, salt, derivative, mixture, or preparation of such plant or its seeds, except those containing resin extracted from such plant; but shall not include the mature stalks of such plant, fiber produced from such stalks, oil or cake made from the seeds of such plant, any other compound, manufacture, salt, derivative, mixture, or preparation of such mature stalks, fiber, oil, or cake, or the sterilized seed of such plant which is incapable of germination.

"Manufacture" means the production, preparation, propagation, compounding, conversion or processing of a controlled dangerous substance, either directly or by extraction from substances of natural origin, or independently by means of chemical synthesis, or by a combination of extraction and chemical synthesis, and includes any packaging or repackaging of the substance or labeling or relabeling of its container, except that this term does not include the preparation or compounding of a controlled dangerous substance by an individual for his own use or the preparation, compounding, packaging, or labeling of a controlled dangerous substance: (1) by a practitioner as an incident to his administering or dispensing of a controlled dangerous substance in the course of his professional practice, or (2) by a practitioner (or under his supervision) for the purpose of, or as an incident to, research, teaching, or chemical analysis and not for sale.

"Narcotic drug" means any of the following, whether produced directly or indirectly by extraction from substances of vegetable origin, or independently by means of chemical synthesis, or by a combination of extraction and chemical synthesis:

(a) Opium, coca leaves, and opiates;

(b) A compound, manufacture, salt, derivative, or preparation of opium, coca leaves, or opiates;

(c) A substance (and any compound, manufacture, salt, derivative, or preparation thereof) which is chemically identical with any of the substances referred to in subsections (a) and (b), except that the words "narcotic drug" as used in this act shall not include decocainized coca leaves or extracts of coca leaves, which extracts do not contain cocaine or ecgonine.

"Official written order" means an order written on a form provided for that purpose by the Attorney General of the United States or his delegate, under any laws of the United States making provisions therefor, if such order forms are authorized and required by the federal law, and if no such form is provided, then on an official form provided for that purpose by the division. If authorized by the Attorney General of the United States or the division, the term shall also include an order transmitted by electronic means.

"Opiate" means any dangerous substance having an addiction-forming or addiction-sustaining liability similar to morphine or being capable of conversion into a drug having such addiction-forming or addiction-sustaining liability. It does not include, unless specifically designated as controlled under section 3 of this act, [1] the dextrorotatory isomer of 3–methoxy-n-methylmorphinan and its salts (dextromethorphan). It does include its racemic and levorotatory forms.

"Opium poppy" means the plant of the species Papaver somniferum L., except the seeds thereof.

"Person" means any corporation, association, partnership, trust, other institution or entity or one or more individuals. "Pharmacist" means a registered pharmacist of this State.

"Pharmacy owner" means the owner of a store or other place of business where controlled dangerous substances are compounded or dispensed by a registered pharmacist; but nothing in this chapter contained shall be construed as conferring on a person who is not registered or licensed as a pharmacist any authority, right or privilege that is not granted to him by the pharmacy laws of this State.

"Poppy straw" means all parts, except the seeds, of the opium poppy, after mowing.

"Practitioner" means a physician, dentist, veterinarian, scientific investigator, laboratory, pharmacy, hospital or other person licensed, registered, or otherwise permitted to distribute, dispense, conduct research with respect to, or administer a controlled dangerous substance in the course of professional practice or research in this State.

(a) "Physician" means a physician authorized by law to practice medicine in this or any other state and any other person authorized by law to treat sick and injured human beings in this or any other state.

(b) "Veterinarian" means a veterinarian authorized by law to practice veterinary medicine in this State.

(c) "Dentist" means a dentist authorized by law to practice dentistry in this State.

(d) "Hospital" means any federal institution, or any institution for the care and treatment of the sick and injured, operated or approved by the appropriate State department as proper to be entrusted with the custody and professional use of controlled dangerous substances.

(e) "Laboratory" means a laboratory to be entrusted with the custody of narcotic drugs and the use of controlled dangerous substances for scientific, experimental and medical purposes and for purposes of instruction approved by the Department of Health and Senior Services.

"Production" includes the manufacture, planting, cultivation, growing, or harvesting of a controlled dangerous substance.

"Immediate precursor" means a substance which the division has found to be and by regulation designates as being the principal compound commonly used or produced primarily for use, and which is an immediate chemical intermediary used or likely to be used in the manufacture of a controlled dangerous substance, the control of which is necessary to prevent, curtail, or limit such manufacture.

"State" means the State of New Jersey.

"Ultimate user" means a person who lawfully possesses a controlled dangerous substance for his own use or for the use of a member of his household or for administration to an animal owned by him or by a member of his household.

L.1970, c. 226, § 2, eff. Jan. 17, 1971. Amended by L.1971, c. 3, § 1, eff. Jan. 17, 1971; L.1971, c. 367, § 1, eff. Dec. 28, 1971; L.1985, c. 134, § 1, eff. April 12, 1985; L.2007, c. 244, § 1, eff. Jan. 4, 2008.

[1] N.J.S.A. § 24:21–3.

ARTICLE 2. STANDARDS AND SCHEDULES

24:21–3. Authority to control

a. The director shall administer the provisions of P.L.1970, c. 226 (C.24:21–1 et seq.), as amended and supplemented, as provided herein. The director may add substances to or delete or reschedule all substances enumerated in the schedules in sections 5 through 8.1 of P.L.1970, c. 226, as amended and supplemented (C.24:21–5 through 24:21–8.1). In determining whether to control a substance, the director shall consider the following:

(1) Its actual or relative potential for abuse;

(2) Scientific evidence of its pharmacological effect, if known;

(3) State of current scientific knowledge regarding the substance;

(4) Its history and current pattern of abuse;

(5) The scope, duration, and significance of abuse;

(6) What, if any, risk there is to the public health;

(7) Its psychic or physiological dependence liability; and

(8) Whether the substance is an immediate precursor of a substance already controlled under this article.

After considering the above factors, the director shall make findings with respect thereto and shall issue an order controlling the substance if he finds that the substance has a potential for abuse.

b. If the director designates a substance as an immediate precursor, substances which are precursors of the controlled precursor shall not be subject to control solely because they are precursors of the controlled precursor.

c. If any substance is designated, rescheduled or deleted as a controlled dangerous substance under Federal law and notice thereof is given to the director, the director shall similarly control the substance under P.L.1970, c. 226, as amended and supplemented, after the expiration of 30 days from publication in the Federal Register of a final order designating a substance as a controlled dangerous substance or rescheduling or deleting a substance, unless within that 30–day period, the director objects to inclusion, rescheduling, or deletion. In that case, the director shall cause to be published in the New Jersey Register and made public the reasons for his objection and shall afford all interested parties an opportunity to be heard. At the conclusion of any such hearing, the director shall publish and make public his decision, which shall be final unless the substance is specifically otherwise dealt with by an act of the Legislature. Upon publication of objection to inclusion or rescheduling under P.L.1970, c. 226 (C.24:21–1 et seq.) by the director, control of such substance under this section shall automatically be stayed until such time as the director makes public his final decision.

The director may by regulation exclude any nonnarcotic substance from a schedule if such substance may, under the provisions of Federal or State law, be lawfully sold over the counter without a prescription, unless otherwise controlled pursuant to rules and regulations promulgated by the division.

d. The director shall update and republish the schedules in sections 5 through 8.1 of P.L.1970, c. 226, as amended and supplemented (C.24:21–5 through 24:21–8.1) periodically.

L.1970, c. 226, § 3, eff. Jan. 17, 1971. Amended by L.2007, c. 244, § 2, eff. Jan. 4, 2008.

24:21–4. Schedules of controlled substances

The schedules contained in sections 5 through 8 of this act [1] include the controlled dangerous substances listed or to be listed by whatever official name, common or usual name, chemical name, or trade name designated.

L.1970, c. 226, § 4, eff. Jan. 17, 1971.

[1] N.J.S.A. §§ 24:21–5 to 24:21–8.

24:21–5. Schedule I

a. Tests. The director shall place a substance in Schedule I if he finds that the substance: (1) has high potential for abuse; and (2) has no accepted medical use in treatment in the United States; or lacks accepted safety for use in treatment under medical supervision.

b. The controlled dangerous substances listed in this section are included in Schedule I, subject to any revision and republishing by the director pursuant to subsection d. of section 3 of P.L.1970, c. 226 (C.24:21–3), and except to the extent provided in any other schedule.

c. Any of the following opiates, including their isomers, esters, and ethers, unless specifically excepted, whenever the existence of such isomers, esters, ethers and salts is possible within the specific chemical designation:

(1) Acetylmethadol

(2) Allylprodine

(3) Alphacetylmethadol

(4) Alphameprodine

(5) Alphamethadol

(6) Benzethidine

(7) Betacetylmethadol

(8) Betameprodine

(9) Betamethadol

(10) Betaprodine

(11) Clonitazene

(12) Dextromoramide

(13) Dextrorphan

(14) Diampromide

(15) Diethylthiambutene

(16) Dimenoxadol

(17) Dimepheptanol

(18) Dimethylthiambutene

(19) Dioxaphetyl butyrate

(20) Dipipanone

(21) Ethylmethylthiambutene

(22) Etonitazene

(23) Etoxeridine

(24) Furethidine

(25) Hydroxypethidine

(26) Ketobemidone

(27) Levomoramide

(28) Levophenacylmorphan

(29) Morpheridine

(30) Noracymethadol

(31) Norlevorphanol

(32) Normethadone

(33) Norpipanone

(34) Phenadoxone

(35) Phenampromide

(36) Phenomorphan

(37) Phenoperidine

(38) Piritramide

(39) Proheptazine

(40) Properidine

(41) Racemoramide

(42) Trimeperidine.

d. Any of the following narcotic substances, their salts, isomers and salts of isomers, unless specifically excepted, whenever the existence of such salts, isomers and salts of isomers is possible within the specific chemical designation:

(1) Acetorphine

(2) Acetylcodone

(3) Acetyldihydrocodeine

(4) Benzylmorphine

(5) Codeine methylbromide

(6) Codeine–N–Oxide

(7) Cyprenorphine

(8) Desomorphine

(9) Dihydromorphine

(10) Etorphine

(11) Heroin

(12) Hydromorphinol

(13) Methyldesorphine

(14) Methylhydromorphine

(15) Morphine methylbromide

(16) Morphine methylsulfonate

(17) Morphine–N–Oxide

(18) Myrophine

(19) Nicocodeine

(20) Nicomorphine

(21) Normorphine

(22) Phoclodine

(23) Thebacon.

e. Any material, compound, mixture or preparation which contains any quantity of the following hallucinogenic substances, their salts, isomers and salts of isomers, unless specifically excepted, whenever the existence of such salts, isomers, and salts of isomers is possible within the specific chemical designation:

(1) 3,4–methylenedioxy amphetamine

(2) 5–methoxy–3,4–methylenedioxy amphetamine

(3) 3,4,5–trimethoxy amphetamine

(4) Bufotenine

(5) Diethyltryptamine

(6) Dimethyltryptamine

(7) 4–methyl–2,5–dimethoxylamphetamine

(8) Ibogaine

(9) Lysergic acid diethylamide

(10) Marihuana

(11) Mescaline

(12) Peyote

(13) N-ethyl–3–piperidyl benzilate

(14) N-methyl–3–piperidyl benzilate

(15) Psilocybin

(16) Psilocyn

(17) Tetrahydrocannabinols.

L.1970, c. 226, § 5, eff. Jan. 17, 1971. Amended by L.2007, c. 244, § 3, eff. Jan. 4, 2008.

24:21–6. Schedule II

a. Tests. The director shall place a substance in Schedule II if he finds that the substance: (1) has high potential for abuse; (2) has currently accepted medical use in treatment in the United States, or currently accepted medical use with severe restrictions; and (3) abuse may lead to severe psychic or physical dependence.

b. The controlled dangerous substances listed in this section are included in Schedule II, subject to any revision and republishing by the director pursuant to subsection d. of section 3 of P.L.1970, c. 226 (C.24:21–3), and except to the extent provided in any other schedule.

c. Any of the following substances except those narcotic drugs listed in other schedules whether produced directly or indirectly by extraction from substances of vegetable origin, or independently by means of chemical synthesis, or by combination of extraction and chemical synthesis:

(1) Opium and opiate, and any salt, compound, derivative, or preparation of opium or opiate.

(2) Any salt, compound, derivative, or preparation thereof which is chemically equivalent or identical with any of the substances referred to in clause 1, except that these substances shall not include the isoquinaline alkaloids of opium.

(3) Opium poppy and poppy straw.

(4) Coca leaves and any salt, compound, derivative, or preparation of coca leaves, and any salt, compound, derivative, or preparation thereof which is chemically equivalent or identical with any of these substances, except that the substances shall not include decocainized coca leaves or extractions which do not contain cocaine or ecogine.

d. Any of the following opiates, including their isomers, esters, ethers, salts, and salts of isomers, esters and ethers, unless specifically excepted, whenever the existence of such isomers, esters, ethers, and salts is possible within the specific chemical designation:

(1) Alphaprodine

(2) Anileridine

(3) Bezitramide

(4) Dihydrocodeine

(5) Diphenoxylate

(6) Fentanyl

(7) Isomethadone

(8) Levomethorphan

(9) Levorphanol

(10) Metazocine

(11) Methadone

(12) Methadone—Intermediate, 4–cyano–2–dimethylamino–4, 4–diphenyl butane

(13) Moramide—Intermediate, 2–methyl–3–morpholino–1, 1–diphenyl–propane–carboxylic acid

(14) Pethidine

(15) Pethidine—Intermediate—A, 4–cyano–1–methyl–4–phenylpiperidine

(16) Pethidine—Intermediate—B, ethyl–4–phenylpiperidine–4–carboxylate

(17) Pethidine—Intermediate—C, 1–methyl–4–phenylpiperidine–4–carboxylic acid

(18) Phenazocine

(19) Piminodine

(20) Racemethorphan

(21) Racemorphan.

L.1970, c. 226, § 6, eff. Jan. 17, 1971. Amended by L.2007, c. 244, § 4, eff. Jan. 4, 2008.

24:21–7. Schedule III

a. Tests. The director shall place a substance in Schedule III if he finds that the substance: (1) has a potential for abuse less than the substances listed in Schedules I and II; [1] (2) has currently accepted medical use in treatment in the United States; and (3) abuse may lead to moderate or low physical dependence or high psychological dependence.

b. The controlled dangerous substances listed in this section are included in Schedule III, subject to any revision and republishing by the director pursuant to subsection d. of section 3 of P.L.1970, c. 226 (C.24:21–3), and except to the extent provided in any other schedule.

c. Any material, compound, mixture, or preparation which contains any quantity of the following substances associated with a stimulant effect on the central nervous system:

(1) Amphetamine, its salts, optical isomers, and salts of its optical isomers.

(2) Phenmetrazine and its salts.

(3) Any substance which contains any quantity of methamphetamine, including its salts, isomers, and salts of isomers.

(4) Methylphenidate.

d. Any material, compound, mixture, or preparation which contains any quantity of the following substances having a potential for abuse associated with a depressant effect on the central nervous system:

(1) Any substance which contains any quantity of a derivative of barbituric acid, or any salt of a derivative of barbituric acid, except those substances which are specifically listed in other schedules

(2) Chlorhexadol

(3) Glutethimide

(4) Lysergic acid

(5) Lysergic acid amide

(6) Methyprylon

(7) Phencyclidine

(8) Sulfondiethylmethane

(9) Sulfonethylmethane

(10) Sulfonmethane

(11) Ketamine hydrochloride.

e. Nalorphine.

f. Any material, compound, mixture, or preparation containing limited quantities of any of the following narcotic drugs, or any salts thereof:

(1) Not more than 1.80 grams of codeine or any of its salts per 100 milliliters or not more than 90 milligrams per dosage unit, with an equal or greater quantity of an isoquinoline alkaloid of opium.

(2) Not more than 1.80 grams of codeine or any of its salts per 100 milliliters or not more than 90 milligrams per dosage unit, with one or more active, nonnarcotic ingredients in recognized therapeutic amounts.

(3) Not more than 300 milligrams of dihydrocodeinone or any of its salts per 100 milliliters or not more than 15 milligrams per dosage unit, with a four-fold or greater quantity of an isoquinoline alkaloid of opium.

(4) Not more than 300 milligrams of dihydrocodeinone or any of its salts per 100 milliliters or not more than 15 milligrams per dosage unit, with one or more active, nonnarcotic ingredients in recognized therapeutic amounts.

(5) Not more than 1.80 grams of dihydrocodeine or any of its salts per 100 milliliters or not more than 90 milligrams per dosage unit, with one or more active, nonnarcotic ingredients in recognized therapeutic amounts.

(6) Not more than 300 milligrams of ethylmorphine or any of its salts per 100 milliliters or not more than 15 milligrams per dosage unit, with one or more active, nonnarcotic ingredients in recognized therapeutic amounts.

(7) Not more than 500 milligrams of opium or any of its salts per 100 milliliters or per 100 grams, or not more than 25 milligrams per dosage unit, with one or more active, nonnarcotic ingredients in recognized therapeutic amounts.

(8) Not more than 50 milligrams of morphine or any of its salts per 100 milliliters or per 100 grams with one or more active, nonnarcotic ingredients in recognized therapeutic amounts.

g. The director may by regulation except any compound, mixture, or preparation containing any stimulant or depressant substance listed in subsections c. and d. of this schedule from the application of all or any part of this act if the compound, mixture, or preparation contains one or more active medicinal ingredients not having a stimulant or depressant effect on the central nervous system; provided, that such admixtures shall be included therein in such combinations, quantity, proportion, or concentration as to vitiate the potential for abuse of the substances which do have a stimulant or depressant effect on the central nervous system.

L.1970, c. 226, § 7, eff. Jan. 17, 1971. Amended by L.1971, c. 3, § 2, eff. Jan. 17, 1971; L.1971, c. 367, § 2, eff. Dec. 28, 1971; L.1997, c. 193, § 1, eff. Aug. 8, 1997; L.2007, c. 244, § 5, eff. Jan. 4, 2008.

1 N.J.S.A. §§ 24:21–5, 24:21–6.

24:21–8. Schedule IV

a. Tests. The director shall place a substance in Schedule IV if he finds that the substance: (1) has low potential for abuse relative to the substances listed in Schedule[1] III; (2) has currently accepted medical use in treatment in the United States; and (3) may lead to limited physical dependence or psychological dependence relative to the substances listed in Schedule III.

b. The controlled dangerous substances listed in this section are included in Schedule IV.

c. Any material, compound, mixture or preparation which contains any quantity of the following substances having a potential for abuse associated with a depressant effect on the central nervous system:

(1) Barbital

(2) Chloral betaine

(3) Chloral hydrate

(4) Ethchlorovynol

(5) Ethinamate

(6) Methohexital

(7) Meprobamate

(8) Methylphenobarbital

(9) Paraldehyde

(10) Petrichloral

(11) Phenobarbital.

d. The director may except by rule any compound, mixture, or preparation containing any depressant substance listed in subsection c. from the application of all or any part of this act if the compound, mixture or preparation contains one or more active medicinal ingredients not having a depressant effect on the central nervous system, and if the admixtures are included therein in combinations, quantity, proportion or concentration that vitiate the potential for abuse of the substances which have a depressant effect on the central nervous system.

L.1970, c. 226, § 8, eff. Jan. 17, 1971. Amended by L.1971, c. 3, § 3, eff. Jan. 17, 1971; L.2007, c. 244, § 6, eff. Jan. 4, 2008.

1 N.J.S.A. § 24:21–7.

24:21–8.1. Schedule V

a. Tests. The director shall place a substance in Schedule V if he finds that the substance: (1) has low potential for abuse relative to the substances listed in Schedule IV;[1] (2) has currently accepted medical use in treatment in the United States; and (3) has limited physical dependence or psychological dependence liability relative to the substances listed in Schedule IV.

b. The controlled dangerous substances listed in this section are included in Schedule V.

c. Any compound, mixture, or preparation containing limited quantities of any of the following narcotic drugs, which also contains one or more nonnarcotic active medicinal ingredients in sufficient proportion to confer upon the compound, mixture, or preparation, valuable medicinal qualities other than those possessed by the narcotic drug alone:

(1) Not more than 200 milligrams of codeine or any of its salts per 100 milliliters or per 100 grams;

(2) Not more than 100 milligrams of dihydrocodeine or any of its salts per 100 milliliters or per 100 grams;

(3) Not more than 50 milligrams of ethylmorphine or any of its salts per 100 milliliters or per 100 grams;

(4) Not more than 2.5 milligrams of diphenoxylate and not less than 25 micrograms of atropine sulfate per dosage unit;

(5) Not more than 100 milligrams of opium or any of its salts per 100 milliliters or per 100 grams.

L.1971, c. 3, § 4, eff. Jan. 17, 1971. Amended by L.2007, c. 244, § 7, eff. Jan. 4, 2008.

1 N.J.S.A. § 24:21–8.

24:21–8.2. Repealed by L.1992, c. 71, § 3, eff. July 30, 1992

ARTICLE 3. REGULATION OF MANUFACTURE, DISTRIBUTION AND DISPENSING OF CONTROLLED DANGEROUS SUBSTANCES

24:21–9. Rules and regulations

The director is authorized to promulgate rules and regulations and to charge reasonable fees relating to the registration and control of the manufacture, distribution, and dispensing of controlled dangerous substances within this State.

L.1970, c. 226, § 9, eff. Jan. 17, 1971. Amended by L.2007, c. 244, § 8, eff. Jan. 4, 2008.

24:21–10. Registration requirements

a. Every person who manufactures, distributes, or dispenses any controlled dangerous substance within this State or who proposes to engage in the manufacture, distribution, or dispensing of any controlled dangerous substance within this State, shall obtain a registration issued by the division in accordance with rules and regulations promulgated by it.

b. Persons registered by the director under this act to manufacture, distribute, dispense, or conduct research with controlled dangerous substances may possess, manufacture, distribute, dispense, or conduct research with those substances to the extent authorized by their registration and in conformity with the other provisions of this article.

c. The following persons shall not be required to register and may lawfully have under their control or possess controlled dangerous substances under the provisions of P.L.1970, c. 226 (C.24:21–1 et seq.), as amended and supplemented; provided, however, that nothing in this section shall be construed as conferring on a person who is not registered or licensed as a practitioner or as a pharmacist any authority, right or

privilege that is not granted him by the laws of this State:

(1) An agent, or an employee thereof, of any registered manufacturer, distributor, or dispenser of any controlled dangerous substance if such agent is acting in the usual course of his business or employment;

(2) A common carrier or warehouseman, or an employee thereof, whose possession of any controlled dangerous substance is in the usual course of his business or employment;

(3) An ultimate user or a person in possession of any controlled dangerous substance pursuant to a lawful order of a practitioner or in lawful possession of a Schedule V substance; 1

(4) Peace officers or employees in the performance of their official duties requiring possession or control of controlled dangerous substances; or to temporary incidental possession by employees or agents of persons lawfully entitled to possession, or by persons whose possession is authorized for the purpose of aiding peace officers in performing their official duties.

d. The director may, by regulation, waive the requirement for registration of certain manufacturers, distributors, or dispensers if he finds it consistent with the public health and safety.

e. A separate registration shall be required at each principal place of business or professional practice where the applicant manufactures, distributes, or dispenses controlled dangerous substances.

f. The director is authorized to inspect the establishment of a registrant or applicant for registration in accordance with the rules and regulations promulgated by him.

L.1970, c. 226, § 10, eff. Jan. 17, 1971. Amended by L.1971, c. 3, § 5, eff. Jan. 17, 1971; L.2007, c. 244, § 9, eff. Jan. 4, 2008.

1 N.J.S.A. § 24:21–8.1.

24:21–11. Registration

a. The division shall not register an applicant to manufacture or distribute controlled dangerous substances included in Schedules I through IV of article 2 of P.L.1970, c. 226 (C.24:21–3 et seq.), as amended and supplemented, unless it determines that the issuance of such registration is consistent with the public interest. In determining the public interest, the following factors shall be considered:

(1) Maintenance of effective controls against diversion of particular controlled dangerous substances into other than legitimate medical, scientific, or industrial channels;

(2) Compliance with applicable State and local laws;

(3) Any convictions of the applicant under any Federal and State laws relating to any controlled dangerous substance;

(4) Past experience in the manufacture of controlled dangerous substances, and the existence in the applicant's establishment of effective controls against diversion;

(5) Furnishing by the applicant false or fraudulent material in any application filed under this act;

(6) Suspension or revocation of the applicant's Federal registration to manufacture, distribute, or dispense controlled dangerous substances as authorized by Federal law; and

(7) Such other factors as may be relevant to and consistent with the public health and safety.

b. Registration granted under subsection a. of this section shall not entitle a registrant to manufacture and distribute controlled dangerous substances in Schedule I or II other than those specified in the registration.

c. Practitioners shall be registered to dispense substances in Schedules II through IV if they are authorized to dispense or conduct research under the law of this State. The director need not require separate registration under this article for practitioners engaging in research with nonnarcotic controlled dangerous substances in Schedules II through IV where the registrant is already registered under this article in another capacity. Practitioners registered under Federal law to conduct research in Schedule I substances are permitted to conduct research in Schedule I substances within this State upon furnishing the director evidence of that Federal registration.

d. Compliance by manufacturers and distributors with the provisions of the Federal law respecting registration (excluding fees) entitles them to be registered under P.L.1970, c. 226 (C.24:21–1 et seq.), as amended and supplemented.

e. The division shall initially permit persons to register who own or operate any establishment engaged in the manufacture, distribution or dispensing of any controlled dangerous substances prior to the effective date of P.L.1970, c. 226, as amended and supplemented, and who are registered or licensed by the State.

f. An incorporated humane society or a licensed animal control facility may designate an officer, a member of its board of trustees, the owner, the operator or the manager as its duly authorized agent. The division shall, consistent with the public interest, register such duly authorized agent for the limited purpose of buying, possessing, and dispensing to registered and certified personnel sodium pentobarbital to euthanize injured, sick, homeless and unwanted domestic pets or domestic or wild animals. The duly authorized agent shall file, on a quarterly basis, a report of any purchase, possession and use of sodium pentobarbital, which report shall be certified by the humane society or animal control facility as to its accuracy and validity. This report shall be in addition to any other recordkeeping and reporting requirements of State and Federal law and regulation.

The division shall adopt rules and regulations providing for the registration and certification of any individual who, under the direction of the duly authorized and registered agent of an incorporated humane society or licensed animal control facility, uses sodium pentobarbital to euthanize injured, sick, homeless and unwanted domestic pets or domestic or wild animals. The division may also adopt such other rules and regulations as shall provide for the safe and efficient use of sodium pentobarbital by animal control facilities and humane societies. Nothing herein shall be deemed to waive any other requirement imposed on animal control facilities and humane societies by State and Federal law and regulation.

L.1970, c. 226, § 11, eff. Jan. 17, 1971. Amended by L.1971, c. 3, § 6, eff. Jan. 17, 1971; L.1979, c. 204, § 1, eff. Sept. 20, 1979; L.2007, c. 244, § 10, eff. Jan. 4, 2008.

24:21–12. Denial, revocation, or suspension of registration

a. A registration pursuant to section 11 of P.L.1970, c. 226 (C.24:21–11) to manufacture, distribute, or dispense a controlled dangerous substance, may be suspended or revoked by the director upon a finding that the registrant:

(1) Has materially falsified any application filed pursuant to P.L.1970, c. 226 (C.24:21–1 et seq.), as amended and supplemented, or required by P.L.1970, c. 226, as amended and supplemented; or

(2) Has been convicted of an indictable offense under P.L.1970, c. 226, as amended and supplemented, or any law of the United States, or of any State, relating to any substance defined herein as a controlled dangerous substance; or

(3) Has violated or failed to comply with any duly promulgated regulation of the director and such violation or failure to comply reflects adversely on the licensee's reliability and integrity with respect to controlled dangerous substances; or

(4) Has had his Federal registration suspended or revoked by competent Federal authority and is no longer authorized by Federal law to engage in the manufacturing, distribution, or dispensing of controlled dangerous substances; or

(5) Has had his registration suspended or revoked by competent authority of another state for violation of its laws or regulations comparable to those of this State relating to the manufacture, distribution or dispensing of controlled dangerous substances.

b. The director may limit revocation or suspension of a registration to the particular controlled dangerous substance with respect to which grounds for revocation or suspension exist.

c. Before taking action pursuant to this section or pursuant to a denial of registration under section 11 of P.L.1970, c. 226 (C.24:21–11), the director shall serve upon the applicant or registrant an order to show cause why registration should not be denied, revoked, or suspended. The order to show cause shall contain a statement of the basis thereof and shall call upon the applicant or registrant to appear before the director at a time and place stated in the order, but in no event less than 30 days after the date of receipt of the order unless an earlier date is requested by the applicant or registrant and agreed to by the director. Proceedings to deny, revoke, or suspend shall be conducted pursuant to this section in accordance with the provisions of the "Administrative Procedure Act," P.L.1968, c. 410 (C. 52:14B–1 et seq.). Such proceedings shall be independent of, and not in lieu of, criminal prosecutions or other proceedings under P.L. 1970, c. 226, as amended and supplemented, or any law of the State.

d. The director may, in his discretion, suspend any registration simultaneously with the institution of proceedings under this section in cases where he finds that there is an imminent danger to the public health or safety. Such suspensions shall continue in effect until the conclusion of such proceedings, including judicial review thereof, unless sooner withdrawn by the director or dissolved by a court of competent jurisdiction.

e. In the event the director suspends or revokes a registration granted under section 11 of P.L.1970, c. 226 (C.24:21–11), all controlled dangerous substances owned or possessed by the registrant pursuant to such registration at the time of suspension or the effective date of the revocation order, as the case may be, may in the discretion of the director be placed under seal. No disposition may be made of substances under seal until the time for taking an appeal has elapsed or until all appeals have been concluded unless a court, upon application therefor, orders the sale of perishable substances and the deposit of the proceeds of the sale with the court. Upon a revocation order becoming final, all such controlled dangerous substances may be forfeited to the State.

f. The director shall promptly notify the Drug Enforcement Administration of all orders suspending or revoking registration and all forfeitures of controlled dangerous substances.

L.1970, c. 226, § 12, eff. Jan. 17, 1971. Amended by L.2007, c. 244, § 11, eff. Jan. 4, 2008.

ARTICLE 4. LABELS AND CONTAINERS

24:21–13. Records of registrants

Persons registered to manufacture, distribute, or dispense controlled dangerous substances under P.L. 1970, c. 226 (C.24:21–1 et seq.), as amended and supplemented, shall keep records and maintain inventories in conformance with the recordkeeping and inventory requirements of Federal law and with such additional rules as may be issued by the director.

L.1970, c. 226, § 13, eff. Jan. 17, 1971. Amended by L.2007, c. 244, § 12, eff. Jan. 4, 2008.

24:21–14. Order forms

a. Controlled dangerous substances in Schedules I and II [1] shall be distributed only by a registrant, pursuant to an official written order form, clearly identifying it as covering or relating to Schedule I and Schedule II, or either thereof, controlled dangerous substances and bearing the registration number of the registrant. Compliance with Federal law respecting order forms shall be deemed compliance with this section.

b. A pharmacist, only upon an official written order, may sell to a practitioner in quantities not exceeding one ounce at any one time, aqueous or oleaginous solutions compounded by him of which the content of narcotic drugs or other controlled dangerous substances does not exceed a proportion greater than 20% of the complete solution, to be used for medical purposes.

c. An official written order for any controlled dangerous substance in Schedule I or Schedule II shall be signed in triplicate by the person giving said order or by his duly authorized agent. The original and triplicate shall be presented to the person who sells or dispenses the controlled dangerous substance or substances named therein. In the event of the acceptance of such order by said person, except as may be otherwise required by rule, regulation, or order of the director, each party to the transaction shall preserve his copy of such order for a period of two years, in such a way as to be readily accessible for inspection by any public officer or employee engaged in the enforcement of this chapter.

d. Use of an official written order in electronic form shall comply with the requirements of State law and regulations.

L.1970, c. 226, § 14, eff. Jan. 17, 1971. Amended by L.2007, c. 244, § 13, eff. Jan. 4, 2008.

[1] N.J.S.A. §§ 24:21–5, 24:21–6.

24:21–15. Prescriptions

a. Except when dispensed directly in good faith by a practitioner, other than a pharmacist, in the course of his professional practice only, to an ultimate user, no controlled dangerous substance included in Schedule II, [1] which is a prescription drug as defined in section 2 of P. L.2003, c. 280 (C.45:14–41), may be dispensed without the written prescription of a practitioner; provided that in emergency situations, as prescribed by the division by regulation, such drug may be dispensed upon oral prescription reduced promptly to writing and filed by the pharmacist, if such oral prescription is authorized by Federal law. Prescriptions shall be retained in conformity with the requirements of section 13 of P.L.1970, c. 226 (C.24:21–13). No prescription for a Schedule II substance may be refilled.

b. Except when dispensed directly in good faith by a practitioner, other than a pharmacist, in the course of his professional practice only, to an ultimate user, no controlled dangerous substance included in Schedules

III and IV [2] which is a prescription drug as defined in section 2 of P.L.2003, c. 280 (C.45:14–41) may be dispensed without a written or oral prescription. Such prescription may not be filled or refilled more than six months after the date thereof or be refilled more than five times after the date of the prescription, unless renewed by the practitioner.

c. No controlled dangerous substance included in Schedule V [3] may be distributed or dispensed other than for a valid and accepted medical purpose.

d. A practitioner other than a veterinarian who prescribes a controlled dangerous substance in good faith and in the course of his professional practice may administer the same or cause the same to be administered by a nurse or intern under his direction and supervision.

e. A veterinarian who prescribes a controlled dangerous substance not for use by a human being in good faith and in the course of his professional practice may administer the same or cause the same to be administered by an assistant or orderly under his direction and supervision.

f. A person who has obtained a controlled dangerous substance from the prescribing practitioner for administration to a patient during the absence of the practitioner shall return to the practitioner any unused portion of the substance when it is no longer required by the patient or when its return is requested by the practitioner.

g. Whenever it appears to the division that a drug not considered to be a prescription drug under existing State law should be so considered because of its abuse potential, it shall so advise the New Jersey State Board of Pharmacy and furnish to it all available data relevant thereto.

L.1970, c. 226, § 15, eff. Jan. 17, 1971. Amended by L.1971, c. 3, § 7, eff. Jan. 17, 1971; L.2007, c. 244, § 14, eff. Jan. 4, 2008.

  [1] N.J.S.A. § 24:21–6.
  [2] N.J.S.A. §§ 24:21–7, 24:21–8.
  [3] N.J.S.A. § 24:21–8.1.

24:21–16. Form of label on containers of manufacturers and wholesalers; altering or removing label

Whenever a manufacturer sells or dispenses a controlled dangerous substance in a package prepared by him, he shall securely affix to each package in which that substance is contained a label showing in legible English the name and address of the vendor and the quantity, kind and form of the substance contained therein. Whenever a wholesaler sells or dispenses a controlled dangerous substance in any package or shipping container other than the package in which received from the manufacturer, he shall securely affix to such package a label showing in legible English his name and address.

No person except a pharmacist for the purpose of filling a prescription under this act, shall alter, deface or remove any label so affixed by the manufacturer. *L.1970, c. 226, § 16, eff. Jan. 17, 1971.*

24:21–17. Form of label to be used by pharmacists; altering or removing label

Whenever a pharmacist sells or dispenses any controlled dangerous substance on a prescription issued by a practitioner, he shall affix to the container in which such drug is sold or dispensed, a label showing his own name, address, and registry number, or the name, address, and registry number of the pharmacist or pharmacy owner for whom he is lawfully acting; the name of the patient or, if the patient is an animal, the name of the owner of the animal and the species of the animal; the name of the practitioner by whom the prescription was issued; the brand name or generic name of the drug dispensed unless the prescriber states otherwise on the prescription, such directions as may be stated on the prescription and such directions as may be required by rules or regulations promulgated by the director.

No person shall alter, deface, or remove any label so affixed as long as any of the original contents remain. *L.1970, c. 226, § 17, eff. Jan. 17, 1971. Amended by L.1979, c. 146, § 2, eff. Jan. 17, 1971; L.1986, c. 75, § 1, eff. Nov. 3, 1986; L.2007, c. 244, § 15, eff. Jan. 4, 2008.*

24:21–18. Repealed by L.1999, c. 90, § 19, eff. May 3, 1999

ARTICLE 5. OFFENSES AND PENALTIES

24:21–19 to 24:21–20. Repealed by L.1987, c. 106, § 25, operative July 9, 1987

24:21–21. Prohibited acts C.—Records and order forms of registered manufacturers and distributors—Penalties

a. It shall be unlawful for any person:

(1) Who is subject to the requirements of article 3 of this act to distribute or dispense a controlled dangerous substance in violation of section 14; [1]

(2) Who is a registrant, to manufacture, distribute, or dispense a controlled dangerous substance not authorized by his registration;

(3) To omit, remove, alter, or obliterate a symbol, label or mark required by Federal or State law;

(4) To refuse or fail to make, keep or furnish any record, notification, order form, statement, invoice or information required under this act;

(5) To refuse, any entry into any premises or inspection authorized by this act; or,

(6) Knowingly to keep or maintain any store, shop, warehouse, dwelling house, building, vehicle, boat, aircraft, or any place whatever, which is resorted to by

persons using controlled dangerous substances in violation of this act for the purpose of using such substances, or which is used for the keeping or selling of the same in violation of this act.

b. Any person who violates this section shall be subject to a fine of not more than $25,000.00; provided, that if the violation is prosecuted by an accusation or indictment which alleges that the violation was committed knowingly or intentionally, and the trier of fact specifically finds that the violation was committed knowingly or intentionally, such person is guilty of a high misdemeanor and shall be punished by imprisonment for not more than 3 years, or by a fine of not more than $25,000.00, or both.

L.1970, c. 226, § 21, eff. Jan. 17, 1971.

¹ N.J.S.A. § 24:21–14.

24:21–22. Prohibited acts D.—Fraud or misrepresentation by registered manufacturers or distributors—Penalties

a. It shall be unlawful for any person knowingly or intentionally:

(1) Who is a registrant to distribute a controlled dangerous substance classified in Schedule I or II,¹ in the course of his legitimate business, except pursuant to an order form as required by section 14 of this act; ²

(2) To use in the course of the manufacture or distribution of a controlled dangerous substance a registration number which is fictitious, revoked, suspended or issued to another person;

(3) (Deleted by amendment, P.L.1987, c. 106).

(4) To furnish false or fraudulent material information in, or omit any material information from, any application, report, or other document required to be kept or filed under this act, or any record required to be kept by this act; or

(5) To make, distribute, or possess any punch, die, plate, stone, or other thing designed to print, imprint, or reproduce the trademark, trade name, or other identifying mark, imprint, or device of another or any likeness of any of the foregoing upon any drug or container or labeling thereof so as to render such drug a counterfeit controlled dangerous substance.

b. Any person who violates this section shall be punished by imprisonment for not more than three years, or by a fine of not more than $30,000.00, or both.

L.1970, c. 226, § 22, eff. Jan. 17, 1971. Amended by L.1987, c. 106, § 18, operative July 9, 1987.

¹ N.J.S.A. §§ 24:21–5, 24:21–6.
² N.J.S.A. § 24:21–14.

24:21–23. General penalty

Any person who violates any provision of this act for which no specific penalty is provided shall be guilty of a disorderly persons offense.

L.1970, c. 226, § 23, eff. Jan. 17, 1971. Amended by L.1987, c. 106, § 19, operative July 9, 1987.

24:21–24. Attempt, endeavor and conspiracy

a. Any person who attempts, endeavors or conspires to commit any offense defined in this act is punishable by imprisonment or fine or both which may not exceed the maximum punishment prescribed for the offense, the commission of which was the object of the endeavor or conspiracy.

b. (Deleted by amendment, P.L.1987, c. 106.)

L.1970, c. 226, § 24, eff. Jan. 17, 1971. Amended by L.1987, c. 106, § 20, operative July 9, 1987.

24:21–25. Additional penalties

Any penalty imposed for violation of this act shall be in addition to, and not in lieu of, any civil or administrative penalty or sanction authorized by law. In any case where a violation of this act is violation of a Federal law or the law of another state, the conviction or acquittal under Federal law or the law of another state for the same act is a bar to prosecution in this State.

L.1970, c. 226, § 25, eff. Jan. 17, 1971.

24:21–26, 24:21–27. Repealed by L.1987, c. 106, § 25, operative July 9, 1987

24:21–28. Repealed by L.1979, c. 178, § 147, eff. Sept. 1, 1979

24:21–29. Second or subsequent offenses

a. Any person convicted of any offense under this act, if the offense is a second or subsequent offense, shall be punished by a term of imprisonment of up to twice that otherwise authorized, by up to twice the fine otherwise authorized, or by both.

b. For purposes of this section, an offense shall be considered a second or subsequent offense, if, prior to the commission of the offense, the offender has at any time been convicted of an offense or offenses under this act or under any law of the United States or of any state relating to narcotic drugs, marihuana, depressant, stimulant, or hallucinogenic drugs.

L.1970, c. 226, § 29, eff. Jan. 17, 1971. Amended by L.1979, c. 388, § 5, eff. Feb. 5, 1980; L.1987, c. 106, § 21, operative July 9, 1987.

24:21–30. Repealed by L.1987, c. 106, § 25, operative July 9, 1987

ARTICLE 6. ENFORCEMENT AND ADMINISTRATIVE PROVISIONS

24:21–31. Powers of enforcement personnel

a. It is hereby made the duty of the division, its officers, agents, inspectors and representatives, and of all peace officers within the State, and of the Attorney General and all county prosecutors, to enforce all provisions of P.L.1970, c. 226 (C.24:21–1 et seq.), as amended and supplemented, except those specifically delegated, and to cooperate with all agencies charged with the enforcement of the laws of the United States, of this State, and of all other states, relating to narcotic drugs or controlled dangerous substances, and it shall be the duty of the New Jersey Board of Pharmacy in the Division of Consumer Affairs in the Department of Law and Public Safety, its officers, agents, inspectors and representatives also to assist the division, peace officers and county prosecutors in the enforcement of all provisions of P.L.1970, c. 226, as amended and supplemented, relating to the handling of controlled dangerous substances by pharmacy owners and pharmacists.

b. Authority is hereby granted to the director:

(1) To promulgate all necessary rules and regulations for the efficient enforcement of P.L.1970, c. 226, as amended and supplemented;

(2) To promulgate, insofar as applicable, regulations from time to time promulgated by the Attorney General of the United States;

(3) To promulgate an order relative to any controlled dangerous substance under P.L.1970, c. 226, as amended and supplemented, when the delay occasioned by acting through promulgation of a regulation would constitute an imminent danger to the public health or safety.

(a) An order of the director shall take effect immediately, but it shall expire 270 days after promulgation thereof. Rules and regulations pursuant to such order may be adopted and promulgated by the director but they shall not take effect until he has given due notice of his intention to take such action and has held a public hearing.

(b) Any person who denies that a drug or pharmaceutical preparation is properly subject to an order by the director which applies the provisions of P.L.1970, c. 226, as amended and supplemented, to such drug or pharmaceutical preparation, may apply to the director for a hearing which must be afforded, except where a drug or pharmaceutical preparation has been the subject of a prior hearing or determination by the director, in which case a hearing shall be discretionary with the director. In such case a decision must be rendered by the director or his designee within 48 hours of the request for a hearing. If the petitioning party is aggrieved by the decision, he shall have the right to apply for injunctive relief against the order. Jurisdiction for such injunctive relief shall be in the Superior Court of New Jersey by way of summary proceedings.

c. In addition to the powers set forth in subsection a. of this section, any officer or employee of the division designated by the director may:

(1) Execute search warrants, arrest warrants, administrative inspection warrants, subpoenas, and summonses issued under the authority of this State;

(2) Make seizures of property pursuant to the provisions of this act; and

(3) Perform such other law enforcement duties as may be designated by the director with the approval of the Attorney General.

L.1970, c. 226, § 31, eff. Jan. 17, 1971. Amended by L.2007, c. 244, § 16, eff. Jan. 4, 2008.

24:21–32. Administrative inspections and warrants

a. Issuance and execution of administrative inspection warrants shall be as follows:

(1) Any judge of a court having jurisdiction in the municipality where the inspection or seizure is to be conducted, may, upon proper oath or affirmation showing probable cause, issue warrants for the purpose of conducting administrative inspections authorized P.L. 1970, c. 226 (C.24:21–1 et seq.), as amended and supplemented, or regulations thereunder, and seizures of property appropriate to such inspections. For the purposes of this section, "probable cause" means a valid public interest in the effective enforcement of P.L.1970, c. 226, as amended and supplemented, or regulations sufficient to justify administrative inspection of the area, premises, building or conveyance in the circumstances specified in the application for the warrant;

(2) A warrant shall issue only upon an affidavit of an officer or employee duly designated and having knowledge of the facts alleged, sworn to before the judge and establishing the grounds for issuing the warrant. If the judge is satisfied that grounds for the application exist or that there is probable cause to believe they exist, he shall issue a warrant identifying the area, premises, building, or conveyance to be inspected, the purpose of such inspection, and, where appropriate, the type of property to be inspected, if any. The warrant shall identify the item or types of property to be seized, if any. The warrant shall be directed to a person authorized by section 31 of P.L.1970, c. 226 (C.24:21–31) to execute it. The warrant shall state the grounds for its issuance and the name of the person or persons whose affidavit has been taken in support thereof. It shall command the person to whom it is directed to inspect the area, premises, building, or conveyance identified for the purpose specified, and where appropriate, shall direct the seizure of the property specified. The warrant shall direct that it be served during normal business hours. It shall designate the judge to whom it shall be returned;

(3) A warrant issued pursuant to this section must be executed and returned within 10 days of its date. If property is seized pursuant to a warrant, the person executing the warrant shall give to the person from whom or from whose premises the property was taken a copy of the warrant and a receipt for the property taken or shall leave the copy and receipt at the place from which the property was taken. The return of the warrant shall be made promptly and shall be accompanied by a written inventory of any property taken. The inventory shall be made in the presence of the person executing the warrant and of the person from whose possession or premises the property was taken, if they

are present, or in the presence of at least one credible person other than the person executing the warrant. The clerk of the court, upon request, shall deliver a copy of the inventory to the person from whom or from whose premises the property was taken and to the applicant for the warrant; and

(4) The judge who has issued a warrant under this section shall attach to the warrant a copy of the return and all papers filed in connection therewith and shall cause them to be filed with the court which issued such warrant.

b. The director is authorized to make administrative inspections of controlled premises in accordance with the following provisions:

(1) For the purposes of this article only, "controlled premises" means:

(a) Places where persons registered or exempted from registration requirements under P.L.1970, c. 226, as amended and supplemented, are required to keep records, and

(b) Places including factories, warehouses, establishments, and conveyances where persons registered or exempted from registration requirements under P.L. 1970, c. 226, as amended and supplemented, are permitted to hold, manufacture, compound, process, sell, deliver, or otherwise dispose of any controlled dangerous substance.

(2) When so authorized by an administrative inspection warrant issued pursuant to paragraph (1) of subsection a. of this section, an officer or employee designated by the director upon presenting the warrant and appropriate credentials to the owner, operator, or agent in charge, shall have the right to enter controlled premises for the purpose of conducting an administrative inspection.

(3) When so authorized by an administrative inspection warrant, an officer or employee designated by the director shall have the right:

(a) To inspect and copy records required by P.L. 1970, c. 226, as amended and supplemented, to be kept;

(b) To inspect, within reasonable limits and in a reasonable manner, controlled premises and all pertinent equipment, finished and unfinished material, containers and labeling found therein, and, except as provided in paragraph (5) of subsection b. of this section, all other things therein including records, files, papers, processes, controls, and facilities bearing on violation of P.L.1970, c. 226, as amended and supplemented; and

(c) To inventory any stock of any controlled dangerous substance therein and obtain samples of any such substance.

(4) This section shall not be construed to prevent entries and administrative inspections (including seizures of property) without a warrant:

(a) With the consent of the owner, operator or agent in charge of the controlled premises;

(b) In situations presenting imminent danger to health or safety;

(c) In situations involving inspection of conveyances where there is reasonable cause to believe that the mobility of the conveyance makes it impracticable to obtain a warrant;

(d) In any other exceptional or emergency circumstance where time or opportunity to apply for a warrant is lacking; and

(e) In all other situations where a warrant is not constitutionally required.

(5) Except when the owner, operator, or agent in charge of the controlled premises so consents in writing, no inspection authorized by this section shall extend to:

(a) Financial data;

(b) Sales data other than shipment data;

(c) Pricing data;

(d) Personnel data; or

(e) Research data.

L.1970, c. 226, § 32, eff. Jan. 17, 1971. Amended by L.2007, c. 244, § 17, eff. Jan. 4, 2008.

24:21–33. Injunctions

The Superior Court shall have jurisdiction in accordance with the rules of court to enjoin violations of this act.

L.1970, c. 226, § 33, eff. Jan. 17, 1977.

24:21–34. Cooperative arrangements

a. The director may cooperate with Federal and other State agencies in discharging his responsibilities concerning traffic in dangerous substances and in suppressing the abuse of dangerous substances. To this end, he is authorized to:

(1) Except as otherwise provided by law, arrange for the exchange of information between government officials concerning the use and abuse of dangerous substances; provided, however, that in no case shall any officer having knowledge by virtue of his office of any such prescription, order or record divulge such knowledge, except in connection with a prosecution or proceeding in court or before a licensing board or officer to which prosecution or proceeding the person to whom the records relate, is a party;

(2) Coordinate and cooperate in training programs on dangerous substances law enforcement at the local and State levels;

(3) Conduct programs of eradication aimed at destroying wild or illicit growth of plant species from which controlled dangerous substances may be extracted.

b. Results, information, and evidence received from the Drug Enforcement Administration relating to the regulatory functions of P.L.1970, c. 226 (C.24:21–1 et seq.), as amended and supplemented, including results of inspections conducted by that agency, may be relied upon and acted upon by the director in conformance with his regulatory functions under P.L.1970, c. 226, as amended and supplemented.

L.1970, c. 226, § 34, eff. Jan. 17, 1971. Amended by L.2007, c. 244, § 18, eff. Jan. 4, 2008.

24:21–35. Nuisances

The maintenance of any building, conveyance or premises whatever which is resorted to by persons for the unlawful manufacture, distribution, dispensing, administration or use of controlled dangerous substances shall constitute the keeping of a common nuisance.

L.1970, c. 226, § 35, eff. Jan. 17, 1971. Amended by L.1975, c. 42, § 1, eff. April 2, 1975; L.1979, c. 344, § 9, eff. Jan. 23, 1980.

24:21–36. Reports of conviction of manufacturers and practitioners

Whenever a manufacturer or practitioner is convicted of violating any provision of P.L.1970, c. 226 (C.24:21–1 et seq.), as amended and supplemented, or of a rule or regulation issued thereunder or of any offense defined in chapter 35 or 36 of Title 2C of the New Jersey Statutes, the court shall cause a copy of the judgment and sentence and opinion of the court, if any, to be sent to the division or professional board, as the case may be, by which the defendant was registered or licensed.

L.1970, c. 226, § 36, eff. Jan. 17, 1971. Amended by L.1987, c. 106, § 22, operative July 9, 1987; L.2007, c. 244, § 19, eff. Jan. 4, 2008.

24:21–37. Burden of proof; liabilities; immunity

a. It shall not be necessary for the State to negate any exemption or exception set forth in this act in any complaint, information, indictment or other pleading or in any trial, hearing, or other proceeding under this act, and the burden of proof of any such exemption or exception shall be upon the person claiming its benefit.

b. In the absence of proof that a person is the duly authorized holder of an appropriate registration or order form issued under this act, he shall be presumed not to be the holder of such registration or form, and the burden of proof shall be upon him to rebut such presumption.

c. No liability shall be imposed by virtue of this act upon any duly authorized State officer, engaged in the enforcement of this act, who shall be engaged in the enforcement of any law or municipal ordinance relating to controlled dangerous substances.

L.1970, c. 226, § 37, eff. Jan. 17, 1971.

24:21–38. Judicial review

All final determinations, findings and conclusions of the director under P.L.1970, c. 226 (C.24:21–1 et seq.), as amended and supplemented, shall be final and conclusive decisions of the matters involved, subject to the provisions for judicial review provided by the Rules of Court.

L.1970, c. 226, § 38, eff. Jan. 17, 1971. Amended by L.2007, c. 244, § 20, eff. Jan. 4, 2008.

ARTICLE 7. MISCELLANEOUS

24:21–39. Reports by practitioners of drug dependent persons

Every practitioner, within 24 hours after determining that a person is a drug dependent person by reason of the use of a controlled dangerous substance for purposes other than the treatment of sickness or injury prescribed and administered as authorized by law, shall report such determination verbally or by mail to the director. Such a report by a physician shall be confidential and shall not be admissible in any criminal proceeding. The director, in his discretion, may also treat any other reports submitted under this section as confidential if he determines that it is in the best interest of the drug dependent person and the public health and welfare. A practitioner who fails to make a report required by this section is a disorderly person.

L.1970, c. 226, § 39, eff. Jan. 17, 1971. Amended by L.2007, c. 244, § 21, eff. Jan. 4, 2008.

24:21–40. Pending proceedings

a. Prosecutions for any violation of law occurring prior to the effective date of this act shall not be affected or abated by the repealers contained in section 47 of this act.[1]

b. Civil seizures or forfeitures and injunctive proceedings commenced prior to the effective date of this act shall not be affected or abated by the repealers contained in section 47 of this act.

c. All administrative proceedings pending before any enforcing authority on the effective date of this act shall be continued and brought to final determination in accord with laws and regulations in effect prior to the effective date of this act. Such drugs placed under control prior to the effective date of this act which are not listed within Schedules I through IV[2] shall automatically be controlled and listed in the appropriate schedule.

d. The provisions of this act shall be applicable to violations of law, seizures and forfeiture, injunctive proceedings, administrative proceedings and investigations which occur following its effective date.

L.1970, c. 226, § 40, eff. Jan. 17, 1971.

[1] N.J.S.A. § 24:21–45.

[2] N.J.S.A. §§ 24:21–5 to 24:21–8.

24:21–41. Repealed by L.2007, c. 244, § 33, eff. Jan. 4, 2008

24:21–42. Uniformity of interpretation

This act shall be so construed as to effectuate its general purpose to make uniform the law of those states which enact it.

L.1970, c. 226, § 42, eff. Jan. 17, 1971.

24:21–43. Severability

If any clause, sentence, subdivision, paragraph, section or part of this act be adjudged to be unconstitutional or invalid, such judgment shall not affect, impair or invalidate the remainder thereof, but shall be confined in its operation to the clause, sentence, subdivision, paragraph, section or part thereof directly involved in the case in which said judgment shall have been rendered.

L.1970, c. 226, § 43, eff. Jan. 17, 1971.

24:21–44. Study of penalties relating to use and possession of marihuana

Within 1 year after the date the Federal Commission on Marihuana and Drug Abuse submits its report to the President and the United States Congress, the Legislature shall conduct a comprehensive study and review of the penalties established in this act concerning offenses relating to the use and possession of marihuana.

L.1970, c. 226, § 46, eff. Jan. 17, 1971.

24:21–45. Repealer

The following acts and parts of acts are repealed:

R.S. 24:18–1 to 24:18–7, 24:18–9 to 24:18–16, 24:18–18 to 24:18–28, 24:18–30 to 24:18–48 (constituting the remaining sections in chapter 18 of Title 24 of the Revised Statutes not previously repealed); P.L.1953, chapter 190 (C. 24:18–24.1, 24:18–24.2); P.L.1951, chapter 57 (C. 24:18–38.1 to 24:18–38.3); P.L.1966, chapter 314, sections 1–3 (C. 24:6C–1 to 24:6C–3); N.J.S. 2A:170–8.

L.1970, c. 226, § 47, eff. Jan. 17, 1971.

ARTICLE 8. DRUG PARAPHERNALIA

24:21–46 to 24:21–50. Repealed by L.1987, c. 106, § 25, operative July 9, 1987

24:21–51. Repealed by L.1999, c. 90, § 19, eff. May 3, 1999

24:21–52. Seizure in violation of act

Drug paraphernalia seized in violation of this act shall be subject to the forfeiture provisions of Chapter 64 of the "New Jersey Code of Criminal Justice" (N.J.S. 2C:64–1 et seq.).

L.1980, c. 133, § 7, eff. Feb. 24, 1981.

24:21–53. Severability

If any provisions of sections 2, 3, 4, 5, 6 and 7 [1] or the application thereof to any person or circumstance are held invalid, the invalidity shall not affect other provisions or applications of the sections which can be given effect without the invalid provision or application, and to this end the provisions of sections 2, 3, 4, 5, 6 and 7 are severable.

L.1980, c. 133, § 8, eff. Feb. 24, 1981.

[1] N.J.S.A. §§ 24:21–47 to 24:21–52, §§ 24:21–47 to 24:21–50 have been repealed.

24:21–54. Controlled Dangerous Substances Administration and Enforcement Fund; appropriations

a. There is established in the Department of the Treasury a special, dedicated nonlapsing fund to be known as the "Controlled Dangerous Substances Administration and Enforcement Fund." The fund shall be the depository for fees, cost recoveries and penalties collected in connection with the "New Jersey Controlled Dangerous Substances Act," P.L.1970, c. 226 (C.24:21–1 et seq.), as amended and supplemented, and the Prescription Monitoring Program established pursuant to section 25 of P.L.2007 c. 244 (C.45:1–45). Monies deposited in the fund and the interest earned thereon shall be used for the collection of information, administration and enforcement of laws relating to controlled dangerous substances.

b. The Legislature shall annually appropriate monies from the fund to the Division of Consumer Affairs in the Department of Law and Public Safety for the collection of information, administration, and enforcement of laws relating to controlled dangerous substances.

L.2007, c. 244, § 23, eff. Jan. 4, 2008.

TITLE 26

HEALTH AND VITAL STATISTICS

Chapter
2C. Air Pollution Control.
2D. Radiation Protection.

CHAPTER 2C

AIR POLLUTION CONTROL

AIR POLLUTION CONTROL ACT

Section
26:2C–19. Actions to prohibit and prevent violations; penalties; notice of release of air contaminants.

AIR POLLUTION CONTROL ACT

26:2C–19. Actions to prohibit and prevent violations; penalties; notice of release of air contaminants

a. If any person violates any of the provisions of P.L.1954, c. 212 (C. 26:2C–1 et seq.) or any code, rule, regulation or order adopted or issued pursuant thereto, the department may institute a civil action in a court of competent jurisdiction for injunctive or any other appropriate relief to prohibit and prevent such violation or violations and the court may proceed in the action in a summary manner.

b. Any person who violates the provisions of P.L. 1954, c. 212 (C. 26:2C–1 et seq.) or any code, rule, regulation or order adopted or issued pursuant thereto shall be liable to a civil administrative penalty of not more than $10,000 for the first offense, not more than $25,000 for the second offense, and not more than $50,000 for the third and each subsequent offense. If the violation is of a continuing nature, each day during which it continues shall constitute an additional, separate and distinct offense. No civil administrative penalty shall be levied except upon an administrative order issued pursuant to section 14 of P.L.1954, c. 212 (C. 26:2C–14).

c. The department is hereby authorized and empowered to compromise and settle any claim for a penalty under this section in such amount in the discretion of the department as may appear appropriate and equitable under all of the circumstances.

d. Any person who violates the provisions of P.L. 1954, c. 212 (C. 26:2C–1 et seq.) or any code, rule, regulation, or order adopted or issued pursuant thereto, or a court order issued pursuant to subsection a. of this section, or who fails to pay a civil administrative penalty in full pursuant to section 9 of P.L.1962, c. 215 (C. 26:2C–14.1), is subject, upon order of the court, to a civil penalty of not more than $10,000 for the first

offense, not more than $25,000 for the second offense, and not more than $50,000 for the third and each subsequent offense. If the violation is of a continuing nature, each day during which the violation continues, or each day in which the civil administrative penalty is not paid in full, constitutes an additional, separate and distinct offense. Any penalty imposed under this subsection may be recovered with costs in a summary proceeding pursuant to "the penalty enforcement law" (N.J.S. 2A:58–1 et seq.). The Law Division of the Superior Court has jurisdiction to enforce "the penalty enforcement law."

e. A person who causes a release of air contaminants in a quantity or concentration which poses a potential threat to public health, welfare or the environment or which might reasonably result in citizen complaints shall immediately notify the department. A person who fails to so notify the department is liable to the penalties and procedures prescribed in this section.

f. Any person who:

(1) purposely or knowingly violates the provisions of P.L.1954, c. 212 (C. 26:2C–1 et seq.), or any code, rule, regulation, administrative order, or court order adopted or issued pursuant thereto, is guilty of a crime of the third degree;

(2) purposely or knowingly violates any federally mandated air pollution control requirement, any operating permit condition, or any fee or filing requirement imposed in connection with an operating permit is guilty of a crime of the third degree, the sentence for which may include, notwithstanding the provisions of subsection b. of N.J.S. 2C:43–3, an enhanced fine of $10,000 per day per violation;

(3) purposely or knowingly makes any false material statement, representation, or certification in any form, notice, statement, or report required in connection with an operating permit, or who purposely or knowingly renders inaccurate any monitoring device or method required by an operating permit, is guilty of a crime of the third degree, the sentence for which may include, notwithstanding the provisions of subsection b. of N.J.S. 2C:43–3, an enhanced fine of $10,000 per day per violation;

(4) recklessly violates the provisions of P.L.1954, c. 212 (C. 26:2C–1 et seq.), or any code, rule, regulation, administrative order, or court order adopted or issued pursuant thereto, is guilty of a crime of the fourth degree.

g. In determining whether an odor unreasonably interferes with the enjoyment of life or property in violation of P.L.1954, c. 212 (C. 26:2C–1 et seq.) or any code, rule, regulation or order adopted or issued pursuant thereto, the department shall consider all of the relevant facts and circumstances, including, but not limited to, the character, severity, frequency, and duration of the odor, and the number of persons affected thereby. In considering these and other relevant facts and circumstances, no one factor shall be dispositive, but each shall be considered relevant in determining whether an odor interferes with the enjoyment of life or property, and, if so, whether such interference is unreasonable considering all of the circumstances.

The department shall publish in the New Jersey Register the guidelines and procedures utilized by the department for the investigation of citizen complaints regarding odors.

h. The department shall establish procedures for alternative dispute resolution as an option for settlement of contested cases. Alternative dispute resolution shall be voluntary and shall not be mandated by the department.

L.1954, c. 212, p. 786, § 19, eff. Sept. 16, 1954. Amended by L.1962, c. 215, § 11, eff. Jan. 8, 1963; L.1967, c. 105, § 1, eff. June 15, 1967; L.1985, c. 12, § 1, eff. Jan. 22, 1985; L.1989, c. 333, § 1, eff. Jan. 12, 1990; L.1995, c. 188, § 9, eff. Aug. 2, 1995.

CHAPTER 2D

RADIATION PROTECTION

I. RADIATION PROTECTION ACT

Section
26:2D–18. Radioactive materials; transportation or storage or detention pending transit; certificate of handling.
26:2D–19. Submission of information and issuance of certificate.
26:2D–22. Violations; penalties; crime of fourth degree; enforcement.

IV. RADON

26:2D–72. Necessity for certification; exemptions.
26:2D–73. Disclosure of address or owner of treated nonpublic building; prohibition; written waiver; exemptions; sale of building.
26:2D–74. Report of name of owner and address of treated building to state.
26:2D–77. Violations; penalty.

I. RADIATION PROTECTION ACT

26:2D–18. Radioactive materials; transportation or storage or detention pending transit; certificate of handling

No person shall transport into or through the State, or store, hold or detain pending or during such transit, any of the following materials without first having obtained a certificate of handling from the department:

a. Plutonium isotopes in any quantity and form exceeding two grams or 20 curies, whichever is less;

b. Uranium enriched in the isotope U–235 exceeding 25 atomic per cent of the total uranium content in quantities where the U–235 content exceeds one kilogram;

c. Any of the actinides the activity of which exceeds 20 curies;

d. Spent reactor fuel elements or mixed fission products associated with such spent fuel elements the activity of which exceeds 20 curies;

e. Any quantity of radioactive material which exceeds 20 curies; or

f. Any lesser quantity of radioactive material which, when combined with any other quantity of such material, exceeds 20 curies.

L.1977, c. 233, § 1, eff. Sept. 26, 1977.

26:2D–19. Submission of information and issuance of certificate

a. Any person seeking to obtain such a certificate shall submit to the department, not less than 7 business days prior to the storage or transporting of any of the materials specified in section 1 of this act,[1] the following information:

(1) Name of shipper, (2) Name of carrier, (3) Type and quantity of radioactive material, (4) Date and time of shipment, (5) Starting point, scheduled route, and destination, (6) Location and manner of storage, and (7) Other information required by the department.

b. The department, after consultation with the Chief of the State Police, shall issue the "certificate of handling" upon a finding that the storage or transporting of such material shall be accomplished in a manner necessary to protect public health and safety of the citizens of the State. The department, in its discretion, may require changes in the location or manner of storage or changes in dates, routes or time of transporting such material if necessary to maximize protection to public health and safety.

L.1977, c. 233, § 2, eff. Sept. 26, 1977.

1 N.J.S.A. § 26:2D–1.

26:2D–22. Violations; penalties; crime of fourth degree; enforcement

Any person who violates any provision of this act shall be liable to the penalties contained in P.L.1958, c. 116.[1] Any person who violates any provision of this act shall be guilty of a crime of the fourth degree. The State Police shall, and any local police department may, enforce the provisions of P.L.1977, c. 233 (C. 26:2D–18 et seq.).

L.1977, c. 233, § 5, eff. Sept. 26, 1977. Amended by L.1981, c. 296, § 6, eff. Oct. 9, 1981.

1 N.J.S.A. § 26:2D–1 et seq.

IV. RADON

26:2D–72. Necessity for certification; exemptions

Beginning 90 days after the establishment of the certification programs by the Department of Environmental Protection pursuant to sections 1 and 2 of this act,[1] no person who is not certified pursuant to section 1 or section 2 of this act, as appropriate, shall test for, or mitigate or safeguard a building from, the presence of radon gas and radon progeny. The provisions of this section shall not apply to a person performing this testing or mitigation on a building which he owns, or to a person performing testing or mitigation without remuneration.

L.1986, c. 83, § 3, eff. Aug. 14, 1986.

[1] N.J.S.A. §§ 26:2D–70 and 26:2D–71.

26:2D–73. Disclosure of address or owner of treated nonpublic building; prohibition; written waiver; exemptions; sale of building

No person shall disclose to any person, except to the Department of Environmental Protection or the Department of Health, the address or owner of a nonpublic building that the person tested or treated for the presence of radon gas and radon progeny, unless the owner of the building waives, in writing, this right of confidentiality.

The provisions of this section shall not apply to a person performing testing or treatment on a building which he owns, or to instances where disclosure is necessary to contract for further testing or to contract for the mitigating and safeguarding of a building from the presence of radon gas and radon progeny. In the case of a prospective sale of a building which has been tested for radon gas and radon progeny, the seller shall provide the buyer, at the time the contract of sale is entered into, with a copy of the results of that test and evidence of any subsequent mitigation or treatment, and any prospective buyer who contracts for the testing shall have the right to receive the results of that testing.

L.1986, c. 83, § 4, eff. Aug. 14, 1986.

26:2D–74. Report of name of owner and address of treated building to state

A person certified pursuant to section 1 or 2 of this act [1] to provide testing or mitigation services shall, within 30 days of the provision of these services, disclose to the Department of Environmental Protection the address or location of the building, the name of the owner of the building where the services were provided, and the results of any tests performed. The Department of Environmental Protection shall provide to the Department of Health this information upon the request of the Department of Health.

L.1986, c. 83, § 5, eff. Aug. 14, 1986.

[1] N.J.S.A. § 26:2D–70 or 26:2D–71.

26:2D–77. Violations; penalty

A person who violates the provisions of sections 3, 4, or 5 of this act,[1] or any rule or regulation adopted pursuant thereto, is guilty of a crime of the third degree.

L.1986, c. 83, § 8, eff. Aug. 14, 1986.

[1] N.J.S.A. §§ 26:2D–72, 26:2D–73, or 26:2D–74.

TITLE 27

HIGHWAYS

Subtitle
2. Public Roads and Highways in General.
3. State Highways.

Subtitle
5. County and Municipal Roads.
6. Turnpikes.

SUBTITLE 2

PUBLIC ROADS AND HIGHWAYS IN GENERAL

Chapter
5. Advertising Along Highways.
5I. Unattended Dumpsters.
5J. Archaeological Findings.

CHAPTER 5

ADVERTISING ALONG HIGHWAYS

Section
27:5–8. Roadside signs and outdoor advertising; license and permit required.
27:5–9. Sign permits; conditions and restrictions.
27:5–9.1. Signs on State right–of–way or real property; compliance with local zoning and building requirements.
27:5–10. Signs on right-of-way of Interstate and Primary Systems prohibited; exception.
27:5–16. Penalties.
27:5–23. Enforcement by state and local government; enforcement by police.

27:5–8. Roadside signs and outdoor advertising; license and permit required

a. A person shall not erect, maintain or make available to another a roadside sign, or engage in the business of outdoor advertising for profit through the rental or other compensation received for the erection, use or maintenance of signs or other objects upon real property for the display of advertising matter on any stationary object within public view without first obtaining from the commissioner a license to engage in that business, and a permit for the erection, use and maintenance of each sign or other object used for outdoor advertising, except as provided in this act. A permit issued to a person required to obtain a license under this act shall not be valid unless the person has obtained a license which is in full force and effect.

b. Notwithstanding any provision of law to the contrary, the commissioner shall not issue a permit, other than a conditional permit, for a new outdoor advertising sign required to be permitted pursuant to P.L.1991, c. 413 (C.27:5–7 et seq.) unless a public hearing has been held in accordance with the provisions of section 6 of P.L.1975, c. 291 (C.40:55D–10) and, where the permit applicant is a private entity, all relevant approvals required by the municipality have been received by the private entity seeking the permit.
L.1991, c. 413, § 4, eff. Jan. 17, 1992. Amended by L.2004, c. 42, § 4, eff. June 29, 2004.

27:5–9. Sign permits; conditions and restrictions

Signs permitted by this act shall be by permit from the commissioner pursuant to conditions consistent with the regulations of the commissioner, and the following:

a. A sign may not attempt or appear to attempt to direct the movement of traffic or interfere with, imitate, or resemble any official traffic sign, signal or device, or include or utilize flashing, intermittent or moving lights, or utilize lighting equipment or reflectorized materials which emit or reflect colors, including, but not limited to, red, amber or green, except as may be authorized by the commissioner or by agreement between the commissioner and the Secretary of Transportation of the United States.

b. A sign may not interfere or be likely to interfere with the ability of the operator of a motor vehicle to have a clear and unobstructed view of the highway ahead or of official signs, signals or traffic control devices.

c. Illumination of a sign shall be effectively shielded so as to prevent light from being directed at any portion of the main-traveled way of the highway, or, if not so shielded, be of a sufficiently low intensity or brilliance as not to cause glare or impair the vision of persons operating motor vehicles on that highway, or otherwise impair the operation of a motor vehicle.

d. Signs shall be maintained in a safe condition with due regard for conditions of climate, weather and terrain, and as a condition of continued use or permit renewal, unsafe signs shall be remediated by maintenance or repair.

e. A sign may not be of a type, size, or character so as to endanger or injure public safety, health or welfare, or be injurious to property in the vicinity thereof.

f. A sign may not be painted, drawn, erected or maintained upon trees, rocks, other natural features or public utility poles.

g. Signs for which a permit has been issued shall display in a conspicuous position on the sign or its supporting structure, the name of the person holding the permit.

h. A sign or other object shall not in any way simulate any official, directional, traffic control or warning signs erected or maintained by any governmental agency.

L.1991, c. 413, § 5, eff. Jan. 17, 1992.

27:5–9.1. Signs on State right–of–way or real property; compliance with local zoning and building requirements

Any billboard or outdoor advertising sign licensed and permitted pursuant to the "Roadside Sign Control and Outdoor Advertising Act," P.L.1991, c. 413 (C.27:5–5 et seq.), and proposed to be erected on or above any State right-of-way or any real property of the department shall be subject to local government zoning ordinances, applicable local government building permit requirements, and in the pinelands area, shall be subject to the provisions of the comprehensive management plan prepared and adopted by the Pinelands Commission pursuant to section 7 of P.L.1979, c. 111 (C.13:18A–8), and in the Highlands Region, shall be subject to the provisions of the "Highlands Water Protection and Planning Act," P.L.2004, c. 120 (C.13:20–1 et al.), any rules and regulations adopted pursuant thereto, and the Highlands regional master plan adopted by the Highlands Water Protection and Planning Council pursuant to section 8 of that act.

L.1997, c. 144, § 2, eff. June 27, 1997. Amended by L.2004, c. 120, § 57, eff. Aug. 10, 2004.

27:5–10. Signs on right-of-way of Interstate and Primary Systems prohibited; exception

No sign shall be erected or maintained within the right-of-way of any portion of the Interstate and Primary Systems within this State, except that this prohibition shall not apply to signs, public notices, or markers, erected or maintained by the department or with the approval of the department.

L.1991, c. 413, § 6, eff. Jan. 17, 1992.

27:5–16. Penalties

A person who erects or maintains a sign or other object for outdoor advertising, or authorizes his name to be used in connection therewith, without complying with the provisions of this act, or the regulations issued thereunder, shall be liable for a penalty in an amount not less than $50 or to exceed $500, for each offense. Each day of violation may be deemed to be a separate offense. The nature and circumstances of the violation, the conduct of the violator in connection with the violation and the revenue derived from the violation

shall be factors to be considered in the assessment of the amount and accrual of the penalty.

L.1991, c. 413, § 12, eff. Jan. 17, 1992.

27:5–23. Enforcement by state and local government; enforcement by police

a. It shall be the duty of all departments of State or local government and all county and municipal officers charged with the enforcement of State and municipal laws under the direction of the commissioner to assist in the enforcement of the provisions of this act and the orders issued, or rules or regulations adopted pursuant to this act.

b. The Superintendent of State Police in the Department of Law and Public Safety and the Chief of Police of any municipality are authorized and charged under the direction of the commissioner to enforce the provisions of this act and any rules or regulations adopted pursuant thereto.

L.1991, c. 413, § 19, eff. Jan. 17, 1992.

CHAPTER 5I

UNATTENDED DUMPSTERS

Section
27:5I–1.   Roll-off dumpsters and containers; consent to park or leave unattended along highway or public property; markers for warning; penalties.

27:5I–1. Roll-off dumpsters and containers; consent to park or leave unattended along highway or public property; markers for warning; penalties

a. No person shall park or leave unattended any waste or refuse container, commonly known as a roll-off dumpster or roll-off container, on or along any highway or public property, without the written consent of the appropriate municipal, county, or State authority having jurisdiction over the highway or public property. Consent shall be valid and remain in effect for a period of not more than 30 days, but may be renewed by the appropriate official upon application therefor.

To warn the operators of vehicles of the presence of a traffic hazard requiring the exercise of unusual care, any roll-off dumpster or roll-off container parked on or along any highway shall be equipped with and display markers consisting of all yellow reflective diamond-shaped panels having a minimum size of 18 inches by 18 inches. These panels shall be mounted at the edge of the dumpster or container at both ends nearest the path of passing vehicles and facing the direction of oncoming traffic. These markers shall have a minimum mounting height of three feet from the bottom of the panels to the surface of the roadway.

b. A person who is convicted of a violation of this section shall pay a fine of not more than $100.00 for each violation. In default of the payment of a fine, imprisonment in the county jail for a period of not more than 90 days may be imposed.

The fine shall be paid over to the board or body charged with the maintenance of the road or highway upon which the violation occurs.

L.1987, c. 403, § 1, eff. Jan. 14, 1988.

CHAPTER 5J

ARCHAEOLOGICAL FINDINGS

Section
27:5J–1.   Destruction, etc. of archaeological findings on lands or rights of way owned by certain transportation authorities; sale, etc. of archaeological findings; penalties, restitution, and damages; exceptions.

27:5J–1. Destruction, etc. of archaeological findings on lands or rights of way owned by certain transportation authorities; sale, etc. of archaeological findings; penalties, restitution, and damages; exceptions

a. (1) Except as may be provided pursuant to subsection c. of this section, no person may alter, deface, destroy, disturb, or remove any archaeological findings on any lands or rights of way owned by the Department of Transportation, the New Jersey Transit Corporation, the New Jersey Turnpike Authority, or the South Jersey Transportation Authority, without written permission from the respective administrative body as appropriate. As used in this section, "archaeological findings" shall include, but need not be limited to, relics, objects, fossils, or artifacts of an historical, prehistorical, geological, paleontological, archaeological or anthropological nature.

(2) As a condition of granting permission pursuant to paragraph (1) of this subsection, the owner of the property or right-of-way shall require that all excavation and exploration for archaeological findings be conducted in the least destructive manner possible. The owner of the property or right-of-way may also, in its discretion, require a person or persons granted such permission to consult with the owner of the property or right-of-way prior to undertaking an approved project to verify that the methods and techniques selected are the least destructive and most appropriate to the site.

(3) No person may sell, transfer, exchange, transport, purchase, receive or offer to sell, transfer, exchange, transport, purchase or receive any archaeological findings originating on any lands or right-of-ways owned by the Department of Transportation, the New Jersey Transit Corporation, the New Jersey Turnpike Authority or the South Jersey Transportation Authority without

the written permission of the owner of the property or right-of-way as appropriate.

b. A person who knowingly violates, or who solicits or employs any other person to violate, the provisions of subsection a. of this section shall be subject to the following penalties: a fine of not less than $750 nor more than $1,500 for the first offense; a fine of not less than $1,500 nor more than $3,000 for the second offense; and a fine of not less than $3, 000 nor more than $5,000 for any subsequent offense. Penalties assessed pursuant to this subsection shall be collected in a civil action by a summary proceeding. Any vessel, vehicle or equipment used in the commission of the violation shall be subject to confiscation and forfeiture to the owner of the property or right-of-way, if warranted, as determined by the courts. All fines collected shall be remitted to the Department of Environmental Protection to be used for Statewide preservation, remediation or protection of archaeological sites. Further, restitution and damages may be ordered to compensate the owner of the property or right-of-way for the cost of remediating any violation of this section and for the value of any lost, damaged, or destroyed archaeological findings. The owner of the property or right-of-way shall consult with the Department of Environmental Protection for proper remediation of affected lands. Any archaeological findings obtained as a result of a violation of this section shall be subject to confiscation, forfeiture, and return to the proper owner. Upon recovery, the archaeological findings shall be deposited with the Department of Environmental Protection for verification of ownership. The Department of Environmental Protection shall adopt, pursuant to the "Administrative Procedure Act," P.L.1968, c. 410 (C.52:14B–1 et seq.), rules and regulations to ensure the appropriate disposition of any confiscated, forfeited, or returned archaeological findings. The return of archaeological findings to the owner of the property or right-of-way shall be made upon verification of ownership by the Department of Environmental Protection that the owner of the property or right-of-way owns the archaeological findings.

c. The owner of the property or right-of-way shall provide for exceptions to the prohibitions set forth in subsection a. of this section for archaeological findings of de minimis value innocently discovered on any lands or rights-of-way.

d. Notwithstanding any provision of this section to the contrary, examination or retrieval of artifacts, or scientific research, conducted by a State department, agency, commission, authority or corporation otherwise required or permitted by federal or State law are exempt from the provisions of this section.

L.2004, c. 170, § 7, eff. Dec. 7, 2004.

SUBTITLE 3

STATE HIGHWAYS

Chapter

7. Acquisition, Construction and Maintenance by the State.

CHAPTER 7

ACQUISITION, CONSTRUCTION AND MAINTENANCE BY THE STATE

Section

27:7–44. Injurious substances on highway forbidden; protection of property; penalties.

27:7–44. Injurious substances on highway forbidden; protection of property; penalties

No person shall place or allow to fall upon a state highway any broken glass, pottery or sharp object, or any substance injurious to the surface of the road or to the person, health or property of those using the highway or residing along the line thereof nor shall any person interfere with or injure any tree, handrail, wall, bridge, culvert or other public property within the lines of a state highway.

A person who violates any of the provisions of this section or who willfully damages, injures or destroys any such highway or its appurtenances shall be liable to a fine of not less than ten dollars nor more than twenty dollars for each offense together with the costs of prosecution, to be recovered by the department in the name of the state in an action at law in any court of competent jurisdiction.

The fines collected shall be paid into the state treasury to the credit of the funds available for the construction, maintenance and repair of roads.

SUBTITLE 5

COUNTY AND MUNICIPAL ROADS

Chapter
19. County Bridges and Viaducts.

CHAPTER 19

COUNTY BRIDGES AND VIADUCTS

ARTICLE 1.   BRIDGES AND VIADUCTS
IN GENERAL

Section
27:19–13.   Regulations for bridges and viaducts; bridge tenders; police powers.

ARTICLE 2.   SELF–LIQUIDATING BRIDGES

27:19–36.3.   Appointment of bridge police; authority; procedure on arrest.

ARTICLE 1.   BRIDGES AND VIADUCTS IN GENERAL

27:19–13. Regulations for bridges and viaducts; bridge tenders; police powers

The board of chosen freeholders shall make rules and regulations for the protection and use of the viaducts and bridges in the county under its care and control, and may place any viaduct or bridge in the special care or charge of such person as it may appoint for that purpose. Where there are one or more viaducts or bridges connecting two or more counties, the board of chosen freeholders of those counties or any joint committee having charge thereof, shall make rules and regulations for the protection and use thereof, and may place them in the special care or charge of such person or persons as they may appoint for that purpose. The person so appointed shall have the same powers as policemen in cities of the first class in respect to such viaduct, bridge or roads or its approaches for the enforcement of all laws, rules and regulations.

Amended by L.1953, c. 289, p. 1793, § 1.

ARTICLE 2.   SELF–LIQUIDATING BRIDGES

27:19–36.3. Appointment of bridge police; authority; procedure on arrest

Notwithstanding any of the provisions of the article of which this act is a supplement,[1] any county bridge commission created pursuant to said article may appoint policemen and all policemen so appointed are hereby authorized and empowered to make arrests on view and without warrant on Sunday or any other day for crimes, misdemeanors and offenses of any character, or for disorder or breach of the peace or violations of any rules and regulations adopted by such county bridge commissions, committed within the jurisdiction of this State on any bridge owned by or under the control of such county bridge commission, or at the approaches thereof, or on any other property owned by or under the control of such commission. In addition, such policemen shall have all the powers conferred by law on police officers or constables in the enforcement of laws in this State and the apprehension of violators.

Any person so arrested shall be conducted by the officer to a municipal magistrate of the political subdivision in which the arrest is made or, if there is no such available magistrate, to the nearest available magistrate in any other political subdivision.

Any policeman may, instead of arresting an offender as herein provided, serve upon him a summons.

L.1960, c. 168, p. 709, § 1.

[1] N.J.S.A. § 27:19–26 et seq.

SUBTITLE 6

TURNPIKES

Chapter
23. New Jersey Turnpike Authority.

CHAPTER 23

NEW JERSEY TURNPIKE AUTHORITY

Section
27:23–1.   Transportation projects.
27:23–2.   Credit of State not pledged.
27:23–3.   New Jersey Turnpike Authority.
27:23–3.1.   Repealed.
27:23–3.2.   Reports.
27:23–4.   Definitions.
27:23–5.   General grant of powers.
27:23–5.1.   Repealed.
27:23–5.2.   Feeder roads authorized.
27:23–5.3.   Existing roads as feeder roads.
27:23–5.4.   New alignment, feeder road constructed over.
27:23–5.5.   Repealed.
27:23–5.6.   Turning back roads to local authorities.
27:23–5.6a. Discretionary transfer of project to the Department of Transportation.
27:23–5.7.   Repealed.
27:23–5.8.   Advancements or contributions to federal or state governments; contracts with state or New Jersey transportation trust fund authority for payment of revenues; agreements with department of transportation for funding of I–95 extension.
27:23–5.9.   Limitation of power.
27:23–5.10. Proposed tolls; hearing.
27:23–5.11. Notice of hearings.
27:23–6.   Incidental powers.
27:23–6.1.   Contracts; standing operating rules and procedures; bids; threshold amount.
27:23–6.2.   Registration with New Jersey Turnpike Authority; display of decals; schedule of fees; fines.
27:23–6.3.   Contracts for roadway construction and maintenance; partial payments.
27:23–6.4.   Obligations and powers of the authority with respect to bonds and bondholders.
27:23–7.   Bonds.
27:23–7a.   Savings provisions.
27:23–7.1.   Notes.
27:23–8.   Trust agreement.
27:23–9.   Revenues.
27:23–10.   Trust funds.
27:23–11.   Remedies.
27:23–12.   Exemption from taxation.
27:23–13.   Bonds eligible for investment.
27:23–14.   Miscellaneous.
27:23–14.1. Use of reclaimed asphalt pavement; New Jersey Turnpike Authority.
27:23–15.   Refunding bonds.
27:23–16.   Operation as toll roads.
27:23–17.   Preliminary expenses.
27:23–18.   Additional method.
27:23–19.   Act liberally construed.

Section
27:23–20.   Severability.
27:23–21.   Inconsistent laws inapplicable.
27:23–22.   Short title.
27:23–23.   Turnpike project authorized; combining projects; Legislature must designate direction; consent of Highway Commissioner.
27:23–23a. Legislative findings.
27:23–23.1. Project addition authorized.
27:23–23.2. Project addition authorized.
27:23–23.3. Toms River extension.
27:23–23.4. Approval of governor.
27:23–23.5. Environmental impact statement.
27:23–23.6. Route 295 interchange.
27:23–23.7. I–95 addition and extension; conveyance and transfer to authority; agreement between state and authority.
27:23–23.8. New Jersey Turnpike addition and extension at Interchange 8A.
27:23–24.   State Highway Department's jurisdiction over route to cease.
27:23–24a. Jurisdiction and control over I–95 extension.
27:23–24.1. Repeal.
27:23–24.2. Partial invalidity; severability.
27:23–25.   Tolls; payment required.
27:23–26.   Operation of vehicles on turnpike project; care required.
27:23–27.   Speed of vehicles on turnpike project.
27:23–28.   Traffic control; signals.
27:23–29.   Compliance with regulations; authority to make regulations.
27:23–30.   Stopping in case of accident; report.
27:23–31.   Transportation of explosives and products likely to endanger persons or property.
27:23–32.   Violation constituting violation of law or ordinance if committed in municipality.
27:23–33.   Violation resulting in injury or death or property damage over $5000 a high misdemeanor.
27:23–34.   Violations of regulations; trial; practice and procedure.
27:23–34.1. Definitions; toll collection monitoring by turnpike authority.
27:23–34.2. Adoption of toll collection monitoring system regulations.
27:23–34.3. Violations; advisory and payment request sent to owner; enforcement; penalties.
27:23–34.4. Power of authority to enforce toll collection regulations and traffic laws not limited.
27:23–34.5. Power of authority to establish and assess tolls unaffected.
27:23–35.   Repealed.
27:23–36.   Partial invalidity.
27:23–37.   Regulations of counties or municipalities inapplicable to vehicles upon turnpike project.
27:23–38.   Suspension or revocation of registration and license certificates for violations; nonresidents.
27:23–39.   Requirements of Title 39; applicability.

Section

27:23–40.   Tolls; exemption of emergency and other vehicles.

27:23–41.   Legislative findings.

27:23–42.   Transfer of powers, rights and duties from the Highway Authority to the Turnpike Authority.

27:23–43.   Management of the Garden State Parkway and other projects.

27:23–44.   Counties and municipalities; funding non-highway transportation projects.

27:23–45.   Acquisition of roadside areas.

27:23–46.   Authority to lend, lease, grant or convey park or recreational areas.

27:23–47.   Maintenance of Vietnam Veterans' Memorial.

27:23–48.   Regulations for sale of agricultural products labeled "Jersey Fresh" at service areas.

27:23–49.   Snow and ice removal; equipment necessary to remove from commercial motor vehicles.

27:23–1. Transportation projects

In order to facilitate vehicular traffic and remove the present handicaps and hazards on the congested highways in the State, and to provide for the acquisition and construction of modern express highways embodying every known safety device including center divisions, ample shoulder widths, long sight distances, multiple lanes in each direction and grade separations at all intersections with other highways and railroads, and for the purposes enumerated in section 1 of P.L.2003, c.79 (C.27:23–41), the New Jersey Turnpike Authority is hereby authorized and empowered to acquire, construct, maintain, improve, manage, repair and operate transportation projects (as hereinafter defined) or any part thereof at such locations as shall be established by the authority in its discretion or by law, and to issue transportation revenue bonds of the Authority, payable from tolls, other revenues, proceeds of bonds and other available sources to finance such projects.

L.1948, c. 454, p. 1856, § 1. Amended by L.1950, c. 1, p. 12, § 2; L.1991, c. 183, § 3, eff. June 30, 1991; L.2003, c. 79, § 2.

Historical and Statutory Notes

L.2003, c. 79, § 50, approved May 27, 2003, provides:

"This act shall take effect on the Transfer Date, except that section 3 [27:23–42], section 8 [27:23–4] and the amendment of section 5 of P.L.1948, c. 454 (C.27:23–5) adding a new subsection (t), as provided in section 9 of this act, shall take effect immediately, provided that the authority shall be granted such powers as are contained herein which shall be necessary or appropriate for it to issue bonds and to take such other actions to effectuate the transfer of the Highway Authority and its projects and functions to the authority as soon as practicable after the date of enactment. The authority may take such anticipatory action in advance as shall be necessary for the implementation of this act."

27:23–2. Credit of State not pledged

Transportation revenue bonds issued under the provisions of this act shall not be deemed to constitute a debt or liability of the State or of any political subdivision thereof or a pledge of the faith and credit of the State or of any such political subdivision, but such bonds, unless refunded by bonds of the Authority created in this act, shall be payable from funds pledged or available for their payment as authorized herein. All such transportation revenue bonds shall contain on the face thereof a statement to the effect that the Authority is obligated to pay the same or the interest thereon only from the tolls, other revenues, proceeds of bonds and other available sources, and that, except as provided in section 41of P.L.2003, c.79 (C.27:23–41), neither the State nor any political subdivision thereof is obligated to pay the principal thereof, premium or the interest thereon and that neither the faith and credit nor the taxing power of the State or any political subdivision thereof is pledged to the payment of the principal of, premium or the interest on such bonds.

All expenses incurred in carrying out the provisions of this act shall be payable solely from funds provided under the authority of this act and, except as provided in section 41 of P.L.2003, c.79 (C.27:23–44), nothing in this act contained shall be construed to authorize the Authority to incur indebtedness or liability on behalf of or payable by the State or any political subdivision thereof.

L.1948, c. 454, p. 1857, § 2. Amended by L.1950, c. 1, p. 13, § 3; L.2003, c. 79, § 5.

Historical and Statutory Notes

L.2003, c. 79, § 50, approved May 27, 2003, provides:

"This act shall take effect on the Transfer Date, except that section 3 [27:23–42], section 8 [27:23–4] and the amendment of section 5 of P.L.1948, c. 454 (C.27:23–5) adding a new subsection (t), as provided in section 9 of this act, shall take effect immediately, provided that the authority shall be granted such powers as are contained herein which shall be necessary or appropriate for it to issue bonds and to take such other actions to effectuate the transfer of the Highway Authority and its projects and functions to the authority as soon as practicable after the date of enactment. The authority may take such anticipatory action in advance as shall be necessary for the implementation of this act."

27:23–3. New Jersey Turnpike Authority

(A) There is hereby established in the State Department of Transportation a body corporate and politic, with corporate succession, to be known as the "New Jersey Turnpike Authority." The authority is hereby constituted an instrumentality exercising public and essential governmental functions, and the exercise by the authority of the powers conferred by this act in the acquisition, construction, operation, improvement, management, repair and maintenance of transportation projects or any part thereof shall be deemed and held to be an essential governmental function of the State.

(B) The New Jersey Turnpike Authority shall consist of eight members, as follows: the Commissioner of Transportation, ex officio, or his designee; five members appointed by the Governor, with the advice and consent of the Senate, and two members appointed by the Governor, one upon recommendation of the President of the Senate and the other upon recommendation of the Speaker of the General Assembly, each of whom shall be a resident of the State and shall have been a qualified elector therein for a period of at least one year next preceding his appointment. Each appointed member of the authority shall serve for a term of five years and until his successor is appointed and has qualified; except that of the first appointments hereunder, one shall be for a term of two years and one for a term of three years, and they shall serve until their respective successors are appointed and have qualified. The term of each of the first appointees hereunder shall be designated by the Governor. Each appointed member of the authority may be removed from office by the Governor, for cause, after a public hearing. Each member of the authority before entering upon his duties shall take and subscribe an oath to perform the duties of his office faithfully, impartially and justly to the best of his ability. A record of such oaths shall be filed in the office of the Secretary of State. Any vacancies in the appointed membership of the authority occurring other than by expiration of term shall be filled in the same manner as the original appointment, but for the unexpired term only.

(C) The Governor shall designate one of the members of the authority as chairman thereof and another member as vice chairman thereof. The chairman and vice chairman of the authority so designated shall serve as such at the pleasure of the Governor and until their respective successors have been designated. The authority shall elect a secretary and a treasurer who need not be members. At the option of the authority the same person may be elected to serve both as secretary and treasurer. Five members of the authority shall constitute a quorum and the vote of five members shall be necessary for any action taken by the authority. No vacancy in the membership of the authority shall impair the right of a quorum to exercise all the rights and perform all the duties of the authority.

(D) Each member of the authority shall execute a surety bond in the penal sum of $25,000.00 and the treasurer shall execute a surety bond in the penal sum of $50,000.00, each such surety bond to be conditioned upon the faithful performance of the duties of the office of such member or treasurer, as the case may be, to be executed by a surety company authorized to transact business in the State of New Jersey as surety and to be approved by the Attorney General and filed in the office of the Secretary of State.

(E) The members of the authority shall not receive compensation for their services as members of the authority. Each member shall be reimbursed by the authority for his actual expenses necessarily incurred in the performance of his duties. Notwithstanding the provisions of any other law, no member shall be deemed to have forfeited, nor shall the member forfeit, the member's office or employment or any benefits or emoluments thereof by reason of the member's accep-

tance of the office of ex officio member of the authority or the member's services therein.

(F) No resolution or other action of the authority providing for the issuance of bonds, refunding bonds or other obligations or for the fixing, revising or adjusting of tolls for the use of any transportation project or parts or sections thereof shall be adopted or otherwise made effective by the authority without the prior approval in writing of the Governor and at least one of the following: the State Treasurer and the Director of the Division of Budget and Accounting in the Department of the Treasury. A true copy of the minutes of every meeting of the authority shall be forthwith delivered by and under the certification of the secretary thereof, to the Governor. No action taken at such meeting by the authority shall have force or effect until 10 days, exclusive of Saturdays, Sundays and public holidays, after such copy of the minutes shall have been so delivered. If, in said 10–day period, the Governor returns such copy of the minutes with veto of any action taken by the authority or any member thereof at such meeting such action shall be null and of no effect. The Governor may approve all or part of the action taken at such meeting prior to said 10–day period. The powers conferred in this subsection (F) upon the Governor, the State Treasurer and the Director of the Division of Budget and Accounting in the Department of the Treasury shall be exercised with due regard for the rights of the holders of bonds of the authority at any time outstanding, and nothing in, or done pursuant to, this subsection (F) shall in any way limit, restrict or alter the obligation or powers of the authority or any representative or officer of the authority to carry out and perform in every detail each and every covenant, agreement or contract at any time made or entered into by or on behalf of the authority with respect to its bonds or for the benefit, protection or security of the holders thereof.

(G) The ex officio member of the authority may designate an employee of his department to represent him at meetings of the authority. A designee may lawfully vote and otherwise act on behalf of the member for whom he constitutes the designee. The designations shall be in writing and delivered to the authority and shall be effective until revoked or amended by a writing delivered to the authority.

L.1948, c. 454, p. 1858, § 3. Amended by L.1952, c. 35, p. 125, § 1; L.1963, c. 76, § 1; L.1970, c. 15, § 1; L.1973, c. 38, § 1, eff. Feb. 21, 1973; L.1988, c. 177, § 8, eff. Dec. 27, 1988; L.1991, c. 183, § 4, eff. June 30, 1991; L.2003, c. 79, § 6.

Historical and Statutory Notes

L.2003, c. 79, § 50, approved May 27, 2003, provides:

"This act shall take effect on the Transfer Date, except that section 3 [27:23–42], section 8 [27:23–4] and the amendment of section 5 of P.L.1948, c. 454 (C.27:23–5) adding a new subsection (t), as provided in section 9 of this act, shall take effect immediately, provided that the authority shall be granted such powers as are contained herein which shall be necessary or appropriate for it to issue bonds and to take such other actions to effectuate the transfer of the Highway Authority and its projects and functions to the authority as soon as practicable after the date of enactment. The authority may take such anticipatory action in advance as shall be necessary for the implementation of this act."

27:23–3.1. Repealed by L.1970, c. 15, § 3, eff. Feb. 20, 1970

27:23–3.2. Reports

Notwithstanding any inconsistent provisions of the act hereby supplemented or any other law, the New Jersey Turnpike Authority shall submit to the Governor, the Chairs of the Appropriations Committees of the Senate and General Assembly, and the Director of the Division of Budget and Accounting of the Department of the Treasury, the following reports:

a. Within 90 days after the end of each of its fiscal years, a complete and detailed report of (1) its operations and accomplishments during said year; (2) its receipts and disbursements, or revenues and expenses, during said year in accordance with the categories or classifications established by the authority for its own operating and capital outlay purposes and in accordance with such other categories and classifications as may be designated by any of the persons enumerated in section 1 of this act;[1] (3) its assets and liabilities at the end of said year, including the status of reserve, depreciation, special or other funds and including the receipts and payments of these funds; (4) a schedule of its bonds outstanding at the end of said year, together with a statement of the amounts redeemed, authorized, issued and defeased during that year; and (5) a listing of all contracts exceeding $100,000.00 entered into during said year;

b. Before the close of each of its fiscal years, a complete and detailed report of its operating and capital construction budget, in the form and detail established by the authority for its own operating and capital outlay budget and in such form and detail as may be designated by any of the persons enumerated in section 1 of this act for the next succeeding fiscal year, including its receipts and disbursements or revenues and expenses, for the prior fiscal year and its estimated receipts and disbursements, or revenues and expenses, for said year and for the succeeding fiscal year;

c. Prior to December 1 of each year, the authority shall prepare and file with the commissioner a Capital Project and Investment Plan that details proposed transportation projects and proposed work on existing transportation projects that further the goals of attaining coordinated and integrated Statewide and regional transportation systems. The plan shall address, among other matters, the interconnection of the New Jersey Turnpike and the Garden State Parkway with other transportation systems. The plan should also consider the impact of an improved transportation system on the State's economy. The commissioner is authorized to appoint a five-member advisory committee composed of persons with experience in transportation planning, finance, or economics to review and make recommendations to the commissioner as to the plan.

The commissioner shall include as part of the Annual Transportation Capital Program, submitted pursuant to section 22 of P.L.1984,c.73 (C.27:1B–22), the Capital Project and Investment Plan for review by the Legislature, but no authorization or approval by the Legislature shall be required for the authority to undertake the projects proposed in the plan or to undertake work on existing transportation projects.

L.1970, c. 184, § 1, eff. Aug. 19, 1970. Amended by L.2003, c. 79, § 7.

    [1] N.J.S.A. § 27:32–1.

Historical and Statutory Notes

L.2003, c. 79, § 50, approved May 27, 2003, provides:

"This act shall take effect on the Transfer Date, except that section 3 [27:23–42], section 8 [27:23–4] and the amendment of section 5 of P.L.1948, c. 454 (C.27:23–5) adding a new subsection (t), as provided in section 9 of this act, shall take effect immediately, provided that the authority shall be granted such powers as are contained herein which shall be necessary or appropriate for it to issue bonds and to take such other actions to effectuate the transfer of the Highway Authority and its projects and functions to the authority as soon as practicable after the date of enactment. The authority may take such anticipatory action in advance as shall be necessary for the implementation of this act."

27:23–4. Definitions

As used in this act, the following words and terms shall have the following meanings, unless the context shall indicate another or different meaning or intent:

"Act" means P.L.1948, c. 454 (C.27:23–1 et seq.), as amended and supplemented.

"Authority" means the New Jersey Turnpike Authority, created by section 3 of this act,[1] or, if said authority shall be abolished, the board, body or commission succeeding to the principal functions thereof or to whom the powers given by this act to the authority shall be given by law.

"Bonds" or "transportation revenue bonds" means any bonds, refunding bonds, notes or other obligations issued by the authority authorized under the provisions of this act or issued by or for the Highway Authority.

"Commissioner" means the Commissioner of Transportation.

"Construction" or "construct" means the planning, designing, construction, development, reconstruction, rehabilitation, redevelopment, replacement, repair, extension, enlargement, improvement and betterment of highway and transportation projects, and includes the demolition, clearance and removal of buildings or structures on land acquired, held, leased or used for those projects.

"Cost" means all or any part of the expenses incurred in connection with the acquisition, construction, operation, management and maintenance of any real property, lands, structures, real or personal property rights, rights-of-way, franchises, easements, and interests acquired or used for a project; any financing charges and reserves for the payment of principal, premium and interest on bonds; the expenses of engineering, appraisal, architectural, accounting, financial, legal and other consulting services; and other expenses as may be necessary, desirable, convenient, or incident to the financing, acquisition, construction, operation, improvement, management, repair and maintenance of a project.

"Credit Agreement" means loan agreement, lease agreement, revolving credit agreement, agreement establishing a line of credit, letter of credit, reimbursement to purchase bonds, purchase or sale agreements, or commitments or other contracts or agreements authorized and approved by the authority in connection with the authorization, issuance, security, purchase, tender, redemption, or payment of bonds.

"Department" means the Department of Transportation.

"Feeder road" means any road or highway project that in the determination of the authority is necessary, desirable or convenient to create or facilitate access to a transportation project.

"Garden State Arts Center" means the Garden State Arts Center, sometimes referred to as the PNC Bank Arts Center, a highway project of the authority.

"Highway project" means the acquisition, operation, improvement, management, repair, construction, including express E–ZPass where determined by the authority, and maintenance of the New Jersey Turnpike and of the Garden State Parkway, including the demolition and removal of toll houses and toll barriers, and of the Garden State Arts Center, as transferred to the authority pursuant to P.L.2003, c.79 (C.27: 23–41 et al.), and of any other highway or feeder road at the locations and between the termini as may hereafter be established by the authority or by law and acquired or constructed under the provisions of this act by the authority, and shall include but not be limited to all bridges, parking facilities, public highways, feeder roads, tunnels, overpasses, underpasses, interchanges, traffic circles, grade separations, entrance and exit plazas, approaches, toll houses, service areas, stations and facilities, communications facilities, administration, storage and other buildings and facilities, and other structures directly or indirectly related to a transportation project, intersecting highways and bridges and feeder roads which the authority may deem necessary, desirable, or convenient in its discretion for the operation, maintenance or management, either directly or indirectly, of a transportation project, and includes any planning, design or other preparation work necessary for the execution of any highway project, and adjoining park or recreational areas and facilities, directly or indirectly related to the use of a transportation project as the authority shall find

to be necessary and desirable, and the costs associated therewith.

"Land and improvements" means any area or lands, any interest, right or title in land, including but not limited to, any reversionary right, fee, license or leasehold interest and any real or personal property, structure, facility, building or equipment.

"Owner" means all individuals, copartnerships, associations, private or municipal corporations and all political subdivisions of the State having any title or interest in any property, rights, easements and interests authorized to be acquired by this act.

"Parking facility" means any area or place, garage, building, or other improvement or structure for the parking or storage of motor or other vehicles, including but not limited to all real property and personal property, driveways, roads and other structures or areas necessary, useful or convenient for access to a facility from a public street, road or highway, or from any project; meters, mechanical equipment necessary, useful or convenient for or in connection with that parking or storage; and any structures, buildings, space or accommodations, whether constructed by the authority or by the lessee, to be leased for any business, commercial or other use, including the sale of gasoline or accessories for, or the repair or other servicing of automobiles and other motor vehicles, or motorist services, if, in the opinion of the authority, the inclusion, provision and leasing is necessary, desirable or convenient to assist in defraying the expenses of the authority and make possible the operation of the parking facility at reasonable rates.

"Public highway" means all public highways, roads and streets in the State, whether maintained by the State or by any county, city, borough, town, township, village or other political subdivision.

"Real property" means lands within the State, above or below water, and improvements thereof or thereon, or any riparian or other rights or interests therein.

"Transfer Date" means, with respect to the assumption by the authority of the powers, duties, assets and responsibilities of the New Jersey Highway Authority, the date on which the Chair of the authority and the commissioner certify to the Governor that: (i) all bonds issued by the New Jersey Highway Authority cease to be outstanding within the meaning of the resolutions pursuant to which those bonds were issued; and (ii) upon which the authority assumes all debts, and statutory responsibilities and obligations of the New Jersey Highway Authority.

"Transportation project" or "project" means, in addition to highway projects, any other transportation facilities or activities determined necessary or appropriate by the authority in its discretion to fulfill the purposes of the authority, and the costs associated therewith.

L.1948, c. 454, p. 1859, § 4. Amended by L.1950, c. 1, p. 13, § 4; L.1969, c. 197, § 1, eff. Dec. 1, 1969; L.1991, c. 183, § 5, eff. June 30, 1991; L.2003, c. 79, § 8, eff. May 27, 2003.

1 N.J.S.A. § 27:23–3.

27:23–5. General grant of powers

The authority shall be a body corporate and politic and shall have perpetual succession and shall have the following powers:

(a) To adopt bylaws for the regulation of its affairs and the conduct of its business;

(b) To adopt an official seal and alter the same at pleasure;

(c) To maintain an office at such place or places within the State as it may designate and to organize itself into such sub-departments, operating divisions or units as it deems appropriate;

(d) To sue and be sued in its own name;

(e) To acquire, improve, construct, maintain, repair, manage, and operate transportation projects or any part thereof at such locations as shall be established by law or by the authority;

(f) To borrow money and issue negotiable bonds for any of its corporate purposes, and to secure the same through the pledging of tolls and other revenues and proceeds of such bonds, or other available sources, and to refund its bonds, and to enter into any credit agreement, all as provided in this act;

(g) In the exercise of any of its powers, by resolution to fix and revise from time to time and charge and collect tolls, fees, licenses, rents, concession charges and other charges for each transportation project or any part thereof constructed or acquired by it. No toll revenues derived from the New Jersey Turnpike or the Garden State Parkway shall be used or available for any transportation project other than a highway project and all transportation projects other than highway projects shall be self-sustaining; provided however that such toll revenues may be used to finance or support the costs of non-highway transportation projects on an interim basis according to such terms, with or without interest, as the authority shall establish;

(h) To establish rules and regulations for the use of any project including restrictions on the type, weight and size of vehicles utilizing transportation projects, and also including the power to exclude from any part of a highway project any traffic other than passenger automobiles if the authority finds that such part is not suitable or sufficient as a highway to carry mixed traffic;

(i) To acquire, hold and dispose of real and personal property in the exercise of its powers and the performance of its duties under this act;

(j) To acquire in the name of the authority by purchase or otherwise, on such terms and conditions and in such manner as it may deem proper, or by the exercise of the power of eminent domain, except as against the State of New Jersey, any land and other property, which it may determine is reasonably necessary for any transportation project or feeder road or for the relocation or reconstruction of any highway by the authority under the provisions of this act and any and all rights, title and interest in such land and other property, including public lands, parks, playgrounds, reservations, highways or parkways, owned by or in which the State of New Jersey or any county, city, borough, town, township, village, or other political subdivision of the State of New Jersey has any right, title or interest, or parts thereof or rights therein and any fee simple absolute or any lesser interest in private property, and any fee simple absolute in, easements upon, or the benefit of restrictions upon, abutting property to preserve and protect transportation projects. Upon the exercise of the power of eminent domain, the compensation to be paid thereunder shall be ascertained and paid in the manner provided in the " Eminent Domain Act of 1971," P.L.1971, c. 361 (C.20:3–1 et seq.), insofar as the provisions thereof are applicable and not inconsistent with the provisions contained in this act. The authority may join in separate subdivisions in one petition or complaint the descriptions of any number of tracts or parcels of land or property to be condemned and the names of any number of owners and other parties who may have an interest therein and all such land or property included in said petition or complaint may be condemned in a single proceeding; provided, however, that separate awards be made for each tract or parcel of land or property; and provided, further, that each of said tracts or parcels of land or property lies wholly in or has a substantial part of its value lying wholly within the same county.

Upon the filing of such petition or complaint or at any time thereafter the authority may file with the clerk of the county in which such property is located and also with the Clerk of the Superior Court a declaration of taking, signed by the authority, declaring that possession of one or more of the tracts or parcels of land or property described in the petition or complaint is thereby being taken by and for the use of the authority. The said declaration of taking shall be sufficient if it sets forth: (1) a description of each tract or parcel of land or property to be so taken sufficient for the identification thereof, to which there may or may not be attached a plan or map thereof; (2) a statement of the estate or interest in the said land or property being taken; and (3) a statement of the sum of money estimated by the authority by resolution to be just compensation for the taking of the estate or interest in each tract or parcel of land or property described in said declaration.

Upon the filing of the said declaration, the authority shall deposit with the Clerk of the Superior Court the amount of the estimated compensation stated in said declaration.

Upon the filing of the said declaration as aforesaid and depositing with the Clerk of the Superior Court the amount of the estimated compensation stated in said declaration, the authority, without other process or proceedings, shall be entitled to the exclusive possession and use of each tract of land or property described in said declaration and may forthwith enter into and take possession of said land or property, it being the intent of this provision that the proceedings for compensation or any other proceedings relating to the taking of said land or interest therein or other property shall not delay the taking of possession thereof and the use thereof by the authority for the purpose or purposes for which the authority is authorized by law to acquire or condemn such land or other property or interest therein.

The authority shall cause notice of the filing of said declaration and the making of said deposit to be served upon each party in interest named in the petition residing in this State, either personally or by leaving a copy thereof at his residence, if known, and upon each party in interest residing out of the State, by mailing a copy thereof to him at his residence, if known. In the event that the residence of any such party or the name of such party is unknown, such notice shall be published at least once in a newspaper published or circulating in the county or counties in which the land is located. Upon the application of any party in interest and after notice to other parties in interest, including the authority, any judge of the Superior Court assigned to sit for said county may order that the money deposited with the Clerk of the Superior Court or any part thereof be paid forthwith to the person or persons entitled thereto for or on account of the just compensation to be awarded in said proceeding; provided, that each such person shall have filed with the Clerk of the Superior Court a consent in writing that, in the event the award in the condemnation proceeding shall be less than the amount deposited, the court, after notice as herein provided and hearing, may determine his liability, if any, for the return of such difference or any part thereof and enter judgment therefor. If the amount of the award as finally determined shall exceed the amount so deposited, the person or persons to whom the award is payable shall be entitled to recover from the authority the difference between the amount of the deposit and the amount of the award, with interest at the rate of six per centum (6%) per annum thereon from the date of making the deposit. If the amount of the award shall be less than the amount so deposited, the Clerk of the Superior Court shall return the difference between the amount of the award and the deposit to the authority, unless the amount of the deposit or any part thereof shall have theretofore been distributed, in which event the court, on petition of the authority and notice to all persons interested in the award and affording them an opportunity to be heard, shall enter judgment in favor of the authority for such difference against the party or parties liable for the return thereof. The authority shall cause notice of the date fixed for such hearing to be served upon each party thereto residing in this State, either personally or by leaving a copy thereof at his residence, if known, and upon each party residing out of the State, by mailing a copy to him at his residence, if known. In the event that the residence of any party or the name of such party is unknown, such notice shall be published at least once in a newspaper published or circulating in the county or counties in which the land is located. Such service, mailing or publication shall be made at least 10 days before the date fixed for such hearing.

Whenever under the "Eminent Domain Act of 1971" the amount of the award may be paid into court, payment may be made into the Superior Court and may be distributed according to law;

(k) To designate the locations, and establish, limit and control such points of ingress to and egress from each highway or transportation project as may be necessary or desirable in the judgment of the authority to insure the proper operation and maintenance of such project, and to prohibit entrance to such project from any point or points not so designated;

(*l*) To make and enter into all contracts and agreements necessary or incidental to the performance of its duties and the execution of its powers under this act and to enter into contracts with federal, State and local governments and private entities for the financing, administration, operation, management and construction of transportation projects;

(m) To appoint such additional officers, who need not be members of the authority, as the authority deems advisable, and to employ consulting engineers, attorneys, accountants, construction and financial experts, superintendents, managers, and such other similarly situated employees and agents as may be necessary in its judgment; to fix their compensation; and to promote and discharge such officers, employees and agents, all without regard to the provisions of Title 11A of the New Jersey Statutes;

(n) To receive and accept from any federal agency, subject to the approval of the Governor, grants for or in aid of the acquisition or construction of any transportation project or any part thereof, and to receive and accept aid or contributions, from any source, of either money, property, labor or other things of value, to be held, used and applied only for the purposes for which such grants and contributions may be made;

(*o*) To do all acts and things necessary or convenient to carry out the powers expressly or impliedly granted in this act;

(p) Subject to any agreement with the bondholders, to invest moneys of the authority not required for immediate use, including proceeds from the sale of any bonds, in such obligations, securities and other investments as the authority shall deem prudent;

(q) To apply for, receive and accept from any federal agency, any bistate agency, or the State and any subdivision thereof, grants for or in aid of the planning, acquisition, management, maintenance, operation or construction of any project, and to receive and accept aid or contributions from any other public or private source, of either money, property, labor or other things of value, to be held, used and applied only for the purposes for which those grants and contributions may be made;

(r) To procure and enter into contracts for any type of insurance and to indemnify against loss or damage to property from any cause, including the loss of use and occupancy and business interruption, death or injury of any person, employee liability, any act of any member, officer, employee or servant of the authority, whether part-time, compensated or uncompensated, in the performance of the duties of office or employment or any other insurable risk or any other losses in connection with property, operations, assets or obligations in any amounts and from any insurers as are deemed desirable. In addition, the authority may carry its own liability insurance;

(s) To adopt regulations, pursuant to the "Administrative Procedure Act," P.L.1968, c. 410 (C.52:14B–1 et seq.), to provide open and competitive procedures for awarding contracts for towing and storage services. Towing and storage services on a highway project may be provided on a rotating basis, provided that the authority determines that there would be no additional cost to the authority, excepting administrative costs, as a result of those services being provided on a rotating basis. The regulations shall fix maximum towing and storage fees, and establish objective criteria to be considered in awarding a contract for towing and storage services which shall include, but shall not be limited to, reliability, experience, response time, acceptance of credit cards and prepaid towing contracts, adequate equipment to safely handle a sufficient volume of common vehicle types under a variety of traffic and weather conditions, location of storage and repair facilities, security of vehicles towed or stored, financial return to the authority, maintenance of adequate liability insurance and appropriate safeguards to protect the personal safety of customers, including considerations related to the criminal background of employees. The Division of Consumer Affairs in the Department of Law and Public Safety shall provide, at the authority's request, a report to the authority on any prospective contractor for which the division has information relevant to the prospective contractor's service record, subject to the provisions of the New Jersey consumer fraud act, P.L.1960, c. 39 (C.56:8–1 et seq.). The Division of Insurance Fraud Prevention in the Department of Banking and Insurance also shall provide, at the authority's request, a report to the authority on any prospective contractor for which the division has information relevant to the prospective contractor's service record, subject to the "New Jersey Insurance Fraud Prevention Act," P.L.1983, c. 320 (C.17:33A–1 et seq.);

(t) To adopt, prior to the Transfer Date and notwithstanding any other provision of law to the contrary, a resolution authorizing the issuance of bonds, notes or other obligations on such terms as otherwise provided for in this act for the retirement by defeasance, redemption, secondary market purchase, tender payment at maturity or otherwise, of all of the New Jersey Highway Authority's outstanding bonds, notes or other obligations, as if the Transfer Date transferring to the authority the rights, duties and obligations to operate, maintain and manage the Garden State Parkway had already occurred; and

(u) To transfer, sell, dispose of, or otherwise relinquish all right, title, or interest in the Garden State Arts Center, and any related or auxiliary facilities, to the New Jersey Sports and Exposition Authority, established by P.L.1971, c. 137 (C.5:10–1 et seq.), or to any other entity, according to such terms and process as the authority may establish in its discretion.

L.1948, c. 454, p. 1860, § 5. Amended by L.1950, c. 1, p. 14, § 5; L.1984, c. 73, § 41, eff. July 10, 1984; L.1991, c. 183, § 6, eff. June 30, 1991; L.2003, c. 79, § 9.

27:23–5.1.　Repealed by L.2003, c. 79, § 49

Historical and Statutory Notes

L.2003, c. 79, § 49, approved May 27, 2003, provides:

"The repeal of any statute herein shall not be deemed to revive any act previously repealed by any such statute."

L.2003, c. 79, § 50, approved May 27, 2003, provides:

"This act shall take effect on the Transfer Date, except that section 3 [27:23–42], section 8 [27:23–4] and the amendment of section 5 of P.L.1948, c. 454 (C.27:23–5) adding a new subsection (t), as provided in section 9 of this act, shall take effect immediately, provided that the authority shall be granted such powers as are contained herein which shall be necessary or appropriate for it to issue bonds and to take such other actions to effectuate the transfer of the Highway Authority and its projects and functions to the authority as soon as practicable after the date of enactment. The authority may take such anticipatory action in advance as shall be necessary for the implementation of this act."

27:23–5.2.　Feeder roads authorized

The New Jersey Turnpike Authority is authorized to acquire, construct, reconstruct, repair and maintain any feeder road.

L.1949, c. 40, p. 119, § 2. Amended by L.1991, c. 183, § 8, eff. June 30, 1991; L.2003, c. 79, § 10.

Historical and Statutory Notes

L.2003, c. 79, § 50, approved May 27, 2003, provides:

"This act shall take effect on the Transfer Date, except that section 3 [27:23–42], section 8 [27:23–4] and the amendment of section 5 of P.L.1948, c. 454 (C.27:23–5) adding a new subsection (t), as provided in section 9 of this act, shall take effect immediately, provided that the authority shall be granted such powers as are contained herein which shall be necessary or appropriate for it to issue bonds and to take such other actions to effectuate the transfer of the Highway Authority and its projects and functions to the authority as soon as practicable after the date of enactment. The authority may take such anticipatory action in advance as shall be necessary for the implementation of this act."

27:23–5.3.   Existing roads as feeder roads

The Turnpike Authority is authorized to take over for reconstruction, maintenance and repair any existing road which is needed as a feeder road. Before exercising the powers contained in this section, the consent of the local authorities, then exercising jurisdiction over the said existing road, must be obtained. The Turnpike Authority is authorized to realign any such existing road and to build additional sections of road over new alignment in connection with such existing road or roads.

L.1949, c. 40, p. 119, § 3. Amended by L.1991, c. 183, § 9, eff. June 30, 1991.

27:23–5.4.   New alignment, feeder road constructed over

In any case where a feeder road is constructed over new alignment, the Turnpike Authority is granted the same powers concerning the construction thereof as is granted in connection with the construction of the highway project by the terms of the act to which this act is a supplement.[1] Any feeder road, eighty per centum (80%) or more of which is built over new alignment, shall for the purposes of this act be deemed to be a "new feeder road."

L.1949, c. 40, p. 120, § 4. Amended by L.2003, c. 79, § 11.

[1] N.J.S.A. § 27:23–1 et seq.

Historical and Statutory Notes

L.2003, c. 79, § 50, approved May 27, 2003, provides:

"This act shall take effect on the Transfer Date, except that section 3 [27:23–42], section 8 [27:23–4] and the amendment of section 5 of P.L.1948, c. 454 (C.27:23–5) adding a new subsection (t), as provided in section 9 of this act, shall take effect immediately, provided that the authority shall be granted such powers as are contained herein which shall be necessary or appropriate for it to issue bonds and to take such other actions to effectuate the transfer of the Highway Authority and its projects and functions to the authority as soon as practicable after the date of enactment. The authority may take such anticipatory action in advance as shall be necessary for the implementation of this act."

27:23–5.5.   Repealed by L.2003, c. 79, § 49

Historical and Statutory Notes

L.2003, c. 79, § 49, approved May 27, 2003, provides:

"The repeal of any statute herein shall not be deemed to revive any act previously repealed by any such statute."

L.2003, c. 79, § 50, approved May 27, 2003, provides:

"This act shall take effect on the Transfer Date, except that section 3 [27:23–42], section 8 [27:23–4] and the amendment of section 5 of P.L.1948, c. 454 (C.27:23–5) adding a new subsection (t), as provided in section 9 of this act, shall take effect immediately, provided that the authority shall be granted such powers as are contained herein which shall be necessary or appropriate for it to issue bonds and to take such other

actions to effectuate the transfer of the Highway Authority and its projects and functions to the authority as soon as practicable after the date of enactment. The authority may take such anticipatory action in advance as shall be necessary for the implementation of this act."

27:23–5.6.   Turning back roads to local authorities

The Turnpike Authority is authorized to turn back to local authorities any road or portions of road taken over from such local authorities in connection with the establishing of a feeder road.

L.1949, c. 40, p. 120, § 6. Amended by L.1991, c. 183, § 10, eff. June 30, 1991; L.2003, c. 79, § 13.

Historical and Statutory Notes

L.2003, c. 79, § 50, approved May 27, 2003, provides:

"This act shall take effect on the Transfer Date, except that section 3 [27:23–42], section 8 [27:23–4] and the amendment of section 5 of P.L.1948, c. 454 (C.27:23–5) adding a new subsection (t), as provided in section 9 of this act, shall take effect immediately, provided that the authority shall be granted such powers as are contained herein which shall be necessary or appropriate for it to issue bonds and to take such other actions to effectuate the transfer of the Highway Authority and its projects and functions to the authority as soon as practicable after the date of enactment. The authority may take such anticipatory action in advance as shall be necessary for the implementation of this act."

27:23–5.6a.   Discretionary transfer of project to the Department of Transportation

The authority may in its discretion turn over to the Department of Transportation any highway project or part thereof and provide by agreement with the department for its continued maintenance and repair by the authority.

L.2003, c. 79, § 12.

Historical and Statutory Notes

L.2003, c. 79, § 50, approved May 27, 2003, provides:

"This act shall take effect on the Transfer Date, except that section 3 [27:23–42], section 8 [27:23–4] and the amendment of section 5 of P.L.1948, c. 454 (C.27:23–5) adding a new subsection (t), as provided in section 9 of this act, shall take effect immediately, provided that the authority shall be granted such powers as are contained herein which shall be necessary or appropriate for it to issue bonds and to take such other actions to effectuate the transfer of the Highway Authority and its projects and functions to the authority as soon as practicable after the date of enactment. The authority may take such anticipatory action in advance as shall be necessary for the implementation of this act."

27:23–5.7.   Repealed by L.2003, c. 79, § 49

L.2003, c. 79, § 49, approved May 27, 2003, provides:

"The repeal of any statute herein shall not be deemed to revive any act previously repealed by any such statute."

L.2003, c. 79, § 50, approved May 27, 2003, provides:

"This act shall take effect on the Transfer Date, except that section 3 [27:23–42], section 8 [27:23–4] and the amendment of section 5 of P.L.1948, c. 454 (C.27:23–5) adding a new subsection (t), as provided in section 9 of this act, shall take effect immediately, provided that the authority shall be granted such powers as are contained herein which shall be necessary or appropriate for it to issue bonds and to take such other actions to effectuate the transfer of the Highway Authority and its projects and functions to the authority as soon as practicable after the date of enactment. The authority may take such anticipatory action in advance as shall be necessary for the implementation of this act."

27:23–5.8. Advancements or contributions to federal or state governments; contracts with state or New Jersey transportation trust fund authority for payment of revenues; agreements with department of transportation for funding of I–95 extension

The New Jersey Turnpike Authority shall have, in addition to the powers heretofore granted to it, power:

a. To pay or make any advance or contribution to the United States Government or the State of New Jersey or any agency thereof for the purpose of paying the State's share or any portion thereof under the federal aid highway laws of the cost of construction of any transportation improvement determined by the authority to be a major improvement necessary to restore or prevent physical damage to any transportation project or any feeder roads, for the safe or efficient operation of such project, or to prevent loss of revenues therefrom.

b. Subject to the rights and security interests of the holders from time to time of bonds or notes heretofore or hereafter issued by the New Jersey Turnpike Authority, to enter into contracts with the State or the New Jersey Transportation Trust Fund Authority established by section 4 of the "New Jersey Transportation Trust Fund Authority Act of 1984," P.L.1984, c. 73 (C. 27:1B–4), providing for the payment from the revenues of the New Jersey Turnpike Authority to the State or to the New Jersey Transportation Trust Fund Authority of the amount or amounts of revenues that may be set forth in or determined in accordance with the contracts. Any contracts authorized pursuant to this section may include conditions and covenants necessary and desirable to facilitate the issuance and sale of bonds, notes and other obligations of the New Jersey Transportation Trust Fund Authority. Any agreements entered into between the State and the Turnpike Authority pursuant to this subsection shall terminate upon the effective date of any agreement entered into between the Turnpike Authority and the New Jersey Transportation Trust Fund Authority providing for the payment of revenues of the Turnpike Authority directly from the Turnpike Authority to the New Jersey Transportation Trust Fund Authority.

c. To enter into agreements with the Department of Transportation with respect to the funding of the resurfacing, restoring, rehabilitation and reconstruction of the I–95 Extension of the New Jersey Turnpike through the allocation of monies apportioned by the United States Department of Transportation pursuant to 23 U.S.C. s.119 or a successor program. Any such

agreement shall be subject to the continued eligibility of the I–95 Extension for federal aid, the availability of funds appropriated by Congress and the appropriation of funds by the Legislature for that purpose. No such agreement shall constitute or create a debt or liability of the State within the meaning of any constitutional or statutory limitation nor shall any such agreement constitute a pledge of either the faith and credit or the taxing power of the State. Funds payable or paid to the authority pursuant to any such agreement shall not be pledged as security for any indebtedness of the authority.

L.1966, c. 8, § 1, eff. Feb. 16, 1966. Amended by L.1984, c. 73, § 30, eff. July 10, 1984; L.1991, c. 183, § 11, eff. June 30, 1991; L.2003, c. 79, § 14.

Historical and Statutory Notes

L.2003, c. 79, § 50, approved May 27, 2003, provides:

"This act shall take effect on the Transfer Date, except that section 3 [27:23–42], section 8 [27:23–4] and the amendment of section 5 of P.L.1948, c. 454 (C.27:23–5) adding a new subsection (t), as provided in section 9 of this act, shall take effect immediately, provided that the authority shall be granted such powers as are contained herein which shall be necessary or appropriate for it to issue bonds and to take such other actions to effectuate the transfer of the Highway Authority and its projects and functions to the authority as soon as practicable after the date of enactment. The authority may take such anticipatory action in advance as shall be necessary for the implementation of this act."

27:23–5.9. Limitation of power

The authority shall not engage in the acquisition, construction or operation of any facility or activity not directly or indirectly related to the use of a transportation project except as may be specially authorized by law.

L.1969, c. 197, § 2, eff. Dec. 1, 1969. Amended by L.1991, c. 183, § 12, eff. June 30, 1991; L.2003, c. 79, § 15.

Historical and Statutory Notes

L.2003, c. 79, § 50, approved May 27, 2003, provides:

"This act shall take effect on the Transfer Date, except that section 3 [27:23–42], section 8 [27:23–4] and the amendment of section 5 of P.L.1948, c. 454 (C.27:23–5) adding a new subsection (t), as provided in section 9 of this act, shall take effect immediately, provided that the authority shall be granted such powers as are contained herein which shall be necessary or appropriate for it to issue bonds and to take such other actions to effectuate the transfer of the Highway Authority and its projects and functions to the authority as soon as practicable after the date of enactment. The authority may take such anticipatory action in advance as shall be necessary for the implementation of this act."

27:23–5.10. Proposed tolls; hearing

The authority shall, whenever it desires to increase any existing toll or establish any new toll for the use of any highway project and the different parts or sections thereof, hold a public hearing on such proposed toll at least 45 days prior to the date on which such toll is proposed to become effective.

L.1977, c. 230, § 1, eff. Sept. 20, 1977. Amended by L.2003, c. 79, § 16.

Historical and Statutory Notes

L.2003, c. 79, § 50, approved May 27, 2003, provides:

"This act shall take effect on the Transfer Date, except that section 3 [27:23–42], section 8 [27:23–4] and the amendment of section 5 of P.L.1948, c. 454 (C.27:23–5) adding a new subsection (t), as provided in section 9 of this act, shall take effect immediately, provided that the authority shall be granted such powers as are contained herein which shall be necessary or appropriate for it to issue bonds and to take such other actions to effectuate the transfer of the Highway Authority and its projects and functions to the authority as soon as practicable after the date of enactment. The authority may take such anticipatory action in advance as shall be necessary for the implementation of this act."

27:23–5.11. Notice of hearings

The authority shall cause to be published notice of such hearing at least 10 days prior to such hearing in at least 10 newspapers with a daily circulation in this State.

L.1977, c. 230, § 2, eff. Sept. 20, 1977.

27:23–6. Incidental powers

The authority shall have power to construct grade separations at intersections of any highway project with public highways and to change and adjust the lines and grades of such highways so as to accommodate the same to the design of such grade separation. The cost of such grade separations and any damage incurred in changing and adjusting the lines and grades of such highways shall be ascertained and paid by the authority as a part of the cost of such highway project.

If the authority shall find it necessary to change the location of any portion of any public highway, it shall cause the same to be reconstructed at such location as the authority shall deem most favorable and of substantially the same type and in as good condition as the original highway. The cost of such reconstruction and any damage incurred in changing the location of any such highway shall be ascertained and paid by the authority as a part of the cost of such highway project.

Any public highway affected by the construction of any highway project may be vacated or relocated by the authority in the manner now provided by law for the vacation or relocation of public roads, and any damages awarded on account thereof shall be paid by the authority as a part of the cost of such project.

In addition to the foregoing powers the authority and its authorized agents and employees may enter upon any lands, waters and premises in the State for the purpose of making surveys, soundings, drillings and examinations as it may deem necessary or convenient for the purposes of this act, and such entry shall not be deemed an entry under any condemnation proceedings which may be then pending. The authority shall make reimbursement for any actual damages resulting to such lands, waters and premises as a result of such activities.

The authority shall also have power to make reasonable regulations for the installation, construction, maintenance, repair, renewal, relocation and removal of tracks, pipes, mains, conduits, cables, wires, towers, poles and other equipment and appliances (herein called "public utility facilities") of any public utility as defined in section 27:7–1 of the Revised Statutes, in, on, along, over or under any highway project. Whenever the authority shall determine that it is necessary that any such public utility facilities which now are, or hereafter may be, located in, on, along, over or under any highway project, shall be relocated in such highway project, or should be removed from such highway project, the public utility owning or operating such facilities shall relocate or remove the same in accordance with the order of the authority; provided, however, that the cost and expenses of such relocation or removal, including the cost of installing such facilities in a new location, or new locations, and the cost of any lands, or any rights or interests in lands, and any other rights, acquired to accomplish such relocation or removal, shall be ascertained and paid by the authority as a part of the cost of such highway project. In case of any such relocation or removal of facilities, as aforesaid, the public utility owning or operating the same, its successors or assigns, may maintain and operate such facilities, with the necessary appurtenance, in the new location or new locations, for as long a period, and upon the same terms and conditions, as it had the right to maintain and operate such facilities in their former location or locations.

In case of any such relocation or removal of facilities, as aforesaid, the authority shall own and maintain, repair and renew structures within the rights of way of railroad companies carrying highway projects or feeder roads over railroads, and the authority shall bear the cost of maintenance, repair and renewal of structures within the rights of way of railroad companies carrying railroads over highway projects or feeder roads, but this provision shall not relieve any railroad company from responsibility for damage caused to any authority or railroad structure by the operation of its railroad. Such approaches, curbing, sidewalk paving, guard rails on approaches and surface paving on turnpike projects or feeder roads as shall be within the rights of way of a railroad company or companies shall be owned and maintained, repaired and renewed by the authority; rails, pipes and lines shall be owned and maintained, repaired and renewed by the railroad company or companies.

L.1948, c. 454, p. 1862, § 6. Amended by L.1961, c. 141, p. 811, § 1; L.2003, c. 79, § 17.

Historical and Statutory Notes

L.2003, c. 79, § 50, approved May 27, 2003, provides:

"This act shall take effect on the Transfer Date, except that section 3 [27:23–42], section 8 [27:23–4] and the amendment of section 5 of P.L.1948, c. 454 (C.27:23–5) adding a new subsection (t), as provided in section 9 of this act, shall take effect immediately, provided that the authority shall be granted such powers as are contained herein which shall be necessary or appropriate for it to issue bonds and to take such other actions to effectuate the transfer of the Highway Authority and its projects and functions to the authority as soon as practicable after the date of enactment. The authority may take such anticipatory action in advance as shall be necessary for the implementation of this act."

27:23–6.1. Contracts; standing operating rules and procedures; bids; threshold amount

a. The New Jersey Turnpike Authority, in the exercise of its authority to make and enter into contracts and agreements necessary or incidental to the performance of its duties and the execution of its powers, shall adopt standing operating rules and procedures providing that, except as hereinafter provided, no contract on behalf of the authority shall be entered into for the doing of any work, or for the hiring of equipment or vehicles, where the sum to be expended exceeds the sum of $25,000 or, after the effective date of P.L.1999, c. 440, the amount determined pursuant to subsection b. of this section unless the authority shall first publicly advertise for bids therefor, and shall award the contract to the lowest responsible bidder; provided, however, that such advertising shall not be required where the contract to be entered into is one for the furnishing or performing services of a professional or consultative nature, or for the supplying of any product or the rendering of any service by a public utility subject to the jurisdiction of the Board of Public Utilities of this State and tariffs and schedules of the charges, made, charged, or exacted by the public utility for any such products to be supplied or services to be rendered are filed with the said board, or when the purchase is to be made through or by the Director of the Division of Purchase and Property pursuant to section 1 of P.L.1959, c. 40 (C.52:27B–56.1), or through a contract made by any of the following: the New Jersey Sports and Exposition Authority established under section 4 of P.L.1971, c. 137 (C.5:10–4); the New Jersey Meadowlands Commission established under section 5 of P.L.1968, c. 404 (C.13:17–5); the New Jersey Water Supply Authority established under section 4 of P.L.1981, c. 293 (C.58:1B–4); the South Jersey Transportation Authority established under section 4 of P.L.1991, c. 252 (C.27:25A–4); the Port Authority of New York and New Jersey established under R.S.32:1–4; the Delaware River Port Authority established under R.S.32: 3–2; the Higher Education Student Assistance Authority established under N.J.S.18A:71A–3. Any purchase, contract or agreement may be made, negotiated or awarded by the authority without public bid or advertising when the authority has advertised for bids on two occasions and has received no bids on both occasions in response to its advertisements, or received no responsive bids. Any purchase, contract or agreement may then be negotiated and may then be awarded to any contractor or supplier determined to be responsible except that the

terms, conditions, restrictions and specifications set forth in the negotiated contract agreement shall not be substantially different from those which were the subject of competitive bidding.

This subsection shall not prevent the authority from having any work done by its own employees, nor shall it apply to repairs, or to the furnishing of materials, supplies or labor, or the hiring of equipment or vehicles, when the safety or protection of its or other public property or the public convenience require, or the exigency of the authority's service will not admit of such advertisement. In such case the authority shall, by resolution, passed by the affirmative vote of a majority of its members, declare the exigency or emergency to exist, and set forth in the resolution the nature thereof and the approximate amount to be so expended.

b. Commencing in the fifth year after the year in which P.L.1999, c. 440 takes effect, and every five years thereafter, the Governor, in consultation with the Department of the Treasury, shall adjust the threshold amount set forth in subsection a. of this section, or after the effective date of P.L.1999, c. 440, the threshold amount resulting from any adjustment under this subsection, in direct proportion to the rise and fall of the index rate as that term is defined in section 2 of P.L.1971, c. 198 (C.40A: 11–2), and shall round the adjustment to the nearest $1,000. The Governor shall, no later than June 1 of every fifth year, notify the authority of the adjustment. The adjustment shall become effective on July 1 of the year in which it is made.

L.1968, c. 461, § 1, eff. Feb. 21, 1969. Amended by L.1984, c. 128, § 5, eff. Aug. 8, 1984; L.1999, c. 440, § 86; L.2003, c. 79, § 18.

Historical and Statutory Notes

L.2003, c. 79, § 50, approved May 27, 2003, provides:

"This act shall take effect on the Transfer Date, except that section 3 [27:23–42], section 8 [27:23–4] and the amendment of section 5 of P.L.1948, c. 454 (C.27:23–5) adding a new subsection (t), as provided in section 9 of this act, shall take effect immediately, provided that the authority shall be granted such powers as are contained herein which shall be necessary or appropriate for it to issue bonds and to take such other actions to effectuate the transfer of the Highway Authority and its projects and functions to the authority as soon as practicable after the date of enactment. The authority may take such anticipatory action in advance as shall be necessary for the implementation of this act."

27:23–6.2. Registration with New Jersey Turnpike Authority; display of decals; schedule of fees; fines

a. An operator awarded a contract for towing and storage services by the New Jersey Turnpike Authority shall register with the authority. Upon issuance of the registration, the authority shall provide the operator with two decals and accompanying notices for each tow truck owned or leased by that operator and to be used under the terms of the contract. The decals and the accompanying notices, which shall be of a distinctive design and color, shall be conspicuously displayed on the exterior of each such tow truck in a manner and location prescribed by the authority.

The decals shall set forth a specific registration number for each registered tow truck. The notices shall include a statement indicating substantially the following: "This tow truck is registered with the New Jersey Highway Authority. The driver is required to provide you with a written schedule of the fees charged for towing and storage services before providing that service to you, including those services for which there is no fee. If the fee charged is in excess of the fee listed on the schedule, please notify the authority or the New Jersey Division of Consumer Affairs." An operator shall file a copy of the schedule of fees with the authority. Upon request of the Division of Consumer Affairs in the Department of Law and Public Safety, the authority shall provide a list of the registered tow trucks to the division, in addition to a copy of the schedule of fees.

b. Prior to providing any towing services, a driver of a tow truck shall provide the person whose vehicle is to be towed a written schedule of fees and shall recite the information contained in the notice.

c. An operator who fails to display the decals and notices required by subsection a. of this section or the driver of a tow truck who fails to provide a person to be towed the written schedule of fees or recite the information contained in the notice prior to providing a towing service as required by subsection b. of this section shall be subject to a fine of $300 for the first offense. For the second and any subsequent offense the operator or the driver, as the case may be, shall be subject to a fine of $600.

d. It shall be an unlawful practice and a violation of P.L.1960, c. 39 (C. 56:8–1 et seq.) for any person to charge a fee in excess of the fee listed in the written schedule of fees provided pursuant to subsection a. of this section.

e. If an operator or the driver of an operator's tow truck is convicted a third time for violation of any provisions of this section, the authority may, in its discretion, terminate the operator's contract for towing and storage services with the authority.

L.2002, c. 77, § 2, eff. Sept. 5, 2002. Amended by L.2007, c. 193, § 16, eff. Oct. 18, 2008; L.2009, c. 39, § 11, eff. April 15, 2009.

27:23–6.3. Contracts for roadway construction and maintenance; partial payments

Contracts entered into by the New Jersey Turnpike Authority for roadway construction and maintenance shall provide for partial payments at least once each month or from time to time as the work progresses on work of construction or maintenance. Two per centum of the amount due on partial payments of the total contract price shall be withheld from the contractor pending completion of the contract, but upon substantial completion of the contract, as defined by rules or regulations of the authority, 1% shall be withheld. At any time during the performance of the work, if work is not progressing, as defined by the "New Jersey Turnpike Authority Standard Specifications," the authority may, in its discretion, increase the withholding to 4% of the payment due. No retainage shall be withheld on service contracts including, but not limited to, mowing, sweeping, tree trimming and similar contracts. Any partial payments made after substantial completion of the contract shall be made only upon certification by the general contractor to the authority that all subcontractors have been paid in the same proportion that he has been paid; however, should the amount owed by a general contractor to a subcontractor be in dispute the authority shall be empowered to advance to the general contractor the amount in dispute after a determination by the authority.

Contracts may also provide for partial payments at least once in each month or from time to time as the work progresses on all materials placed along or upon the site, or stored at locations approved by the authority, which are suitable for the use and execution of the contract, provided the contractor furnishes releases of liens for all materials furnished at the time each estimate of work is submitted for payment, but such partial payments shall not exceed the cost of material.

When the contract provides that a portion of the work may be deferred with the approval of the authority, the sum withheld from the contractor may not be less than 25% of the value of the work.

Any money heretofore or hereafter withheld from contract payments as provided for herein shall be paid by the authority to any contractor entitled thereto who shall deposit under terms of an escrow agreement, in a banking institution located in this State and approved by the authority, negotiable bonds, acceptable to the authority, issued by the State or any political subdivision thereof, the bonds having value equal to the amount of money to be paid to any such contractor. For purposes of this section, value shall mean par value or market value, whichever is lower.

L.2007, c. 180, § 1, eff. Jan. 1, 2008.

27:23–6.4. Obligations and powers of the authority with respect to bonds and bondholders

The provisions of this act [1] shall not modify, limit, or restrict in any manner the obligations and powers of the New Jersey Turnpike Authority to comply with, carry out, and perform each and every covenant, agreement, or contract heretofore made or entered into by the authority with respect to the authority's bonds or for the benefit, protection, or security of the bondholders.

L.2007, c. 180, § 2, eff. Jan. 1, 2008.

[1] L.2007, c. 180 (N.J.S.A. §§ 27:23–6.3 and 27:23–6.4).

27:23–7. Bonds

The authority is hereby authorized to provide by resolution, at one time or from time to time, for the issuance of bonds of the authority for any of its corporate purposes, including the refunding of its bonds. The principal of and the interest on any issue of such bonds shall be payable solely from and may be secured by a pledge of tolls and other revenues of all or any part of the transportation projects. The proceeds of any such bonds may be used or pledged for the payment or security of the principal of or interest on bonds and for the establishment of any or all reserves for such payment or security or for other corporate purposes as the authority may authorize in the resolution authorizing the issuance of bonds or in the trust agreement securing the same. The bonds of each issue shall be dated, shall bear interest at such rate or rates, shall mature at such time or times not exceeding 40 years from their date or dates, as may be determined by the authority, and may be made redeemable before maturity, at the option of the authority, at such price or prices and under such terms and conditions as may be fixed by the authority prior to the issuance of the bonds. The authority shall determine the form of the bonds including any interest coupons to be attached thereto, and shall fix the denomination or denominations of the bonds and the place or places of payment of principal and interest, which may be at any bank or trust company within or without the State. The bonds shall be signed by the chairman of the authority or shall bear his facsimile signature and the official seal of the authority or a facsimile thereof shall be impressed, imprinted, engraved or otherwise reproduced thereon. The official seal or facsimile thereof shall be attested by the secretary and treasurer of the authority, or by such other officer or agent as the authority shall appoint and authorize and any coupons attached to such bonds shall bear the facsimile signature of the chairman of the authority. In case any officer whose signature or a facsimile of whose signature shall appear on any bonds or coupons shall cease to be such officer before the delivery of such bonds, such signature or such facsimile shall nevertheless be valid and sufficient for all purposes the same as if he had remained in office until such delivery. All bonds issued under the provisions of this act shall have and are hereby declared to have all the qualities and incidents of negotiable instruments under the negotiable instruments law of the State. The bonds may be issued in coupon or in registered form, or both, as the authority may determine, and provision may be made for the registration of any coupon bonds as to principal alone and also as to both principal and interest, and for the reconversion into coupon bonds of any bonds registered as to both principal and interest. The authority may sell such bonds in such manner and for such price, as it may determine to be for the best interests of the authority. Neither the members of the authority nor any person executing the bonds shall be personally liable on the bonds or be accountable by reason of the issuance thereof in accordance with the provisions of this act.

The proceeds of the bonds of each issue shall be disbursed in such manner and under such restrictions, if any, as the authority may provide in the resolution authorizing the issuance of such bonds or in the trust agreement hereinafter mentioned securing the same.

Prior to the preparation of definitive bonds, the authority may, under like restrictions, issue interim receipts or temporary bonds, with or without coupons, exchangeable for definitive bonds when such bonds shall have been executed and are available for delivery. The authority may also provide for the replacement of any bonds which shall become mutilated or shall be destroyed or lost. Bonds may be issued under the provisions of this act without obtaining the consent of any department, division, commission, board, bureau or agency of the State, and without any other proceedings or the happening of any other conditions or things than those proceedings, conditions or things which are specifically required by this act.

The State of New Jersey does pledge to and agree with the holders of the bonds issued pursuant to authority contained in this act, that the State will not limit or restrict the rights hereby vested in the authority to acquire, maintain, construct, improve, manage, repair, reconstruct, and operate any projects as defined in this act, or to establish and collect such charges and tolls as may be convenient or necessary to produce sufficient revenue to meet the expenses of maintenance and operation thereof and to fulfill the terms of any agreements made with the holders of bonds authorized by this act or in any way impair the rights or remedies of the holders of such bonds until, the bonds, together with interest thereon, are fully paid and discharged.

L.1948, c. 454, p. 1864, § 7. Amended by L.1950, c. 1, p. 20, § 6; L.1966, c. 8, § 2; L.1991, c. 183, § 13, eff. June 30, 1991; L.2003, c. 79, § 19.

Historical and Statutory Notes

L.2003, c. 79, § 50, approved May 27, 2003, provides:

"This act shall take effect on the Transfer Date, except that section 3 [27:23–42], section 8 [27:23–4] and the amendment of section 5 of P.L.1948, c. 454 (C.27:23–5) adding a new subsection (t), as provided in section 9 of this act, shall take effect immediately, provided that the authority shall be granted such powers as are contained herein which shall be necessary or appropriate for it to issue bonds and to take such other actions to effectuate the transfer of the Highway Authority and its projects and functions to the authority as soon as practicable after the date of enactment. The authority may take such anticipatory action in advance as shall be necessary for the implementation of this act."

27:23–7a. Savings provisions

Nothing in or done pursuant to the powers and obligations set forth in this amendatory and supplementary act (P.L.1991, c. 183) shall in any way limit or restrict the obligations or powers of the New Jersey Turnpike Authority to carry out and perform each and

every covenant, agreement or contract heretofore made or entered into by the Authority or the New Jersey Highway Authority with respect to its bonds or for the benefit, protection or security of the holders thereof.
L.1991, c. 183, § 21, eff. June 30, 1991. Amended by L.2003, c. 79, § 20.

Historical and Statutory Notes

L.2003, c. 79, § 50, approved May 27, 2003, provides:

"This act shall take effect on the Transfer Date, except that section 3 [27:23–42], section 8 [27:23–4] and the amendment of section 5 of P.L.1948, c. 454 (C.27:23–5) adding a new subsection (t), as provided in section 9 of this act, shall take effect immediately, provided that the authority shall be granted such powers as are contained herein which shall be necessary or appropriate for it to issue bonds and to take such other actions to effectuate the transfer of the Highway Authority and its projects and functions to the authority as soon as practicable after the date of enactment. The authority may take such anticipatory action in advance as shall be necessary for the implementation of this act."

27:23–7.1. Notes

The authority is hereby authorized from time to time to issue its notes for any of its corporate purposes and renew from time to time any notes by the issuance of new notes, whether the notes to be renewed have or have not matured. The authority may issue notes partly to renew notes or to discharge other obligations then outstanding and partly for any other purpose and may issue bonds to redeem or pay the principal of and interest on notes. The notes may be authorized, sold, executed and delivered in the same manner as bonds and shall be exempt from taxation and eligible for investment and negotiable in the same manner as bonds under the provisions of this act. Subject to agreements with bondholders and noteholders, the authority may pledge tolls and other revenues for the payment of the notes and may in addition secure the notes in the same manner and with the same effect as herein provided for bonds. Any resolution or resolutions authorizing notes of the authority or any issue thereof may contain any provisions which the authority is authorized to include in any resolution or trust agreement authorizing or securing bonds of the authority or any issue thereof, and the authority may include in any notes any terms, covenants or conditions which it is authorized to include in any bonds. In case of default on its notes, or violation of any of the obligations of the authority to the noteholders, the noteholders shall have all the remedies provided herein for the bondholders.

L.1967, c. 150, § 2, eff. July 10, 1967.

27:23–8. Trust agreement

In the discretion of the Authority any bonds issued under the provisions of this act may be secured by a trust agreement by and between the Authority and a corporate trustee, which may be any trust company or bank having the powers of a trust company within or without the State. Such trust agreement or the resolu-

tion providing for the issuance of such bonds (subject to the provisions of section 7 of this act[1]) may pledge or assign tolls or other revenues to which the Authority's right then exists or may thereafter come into existence, and the moneys derived therefrom, and the proceeds of such bonds, but shall not convey or mortgage any transportation project or any part thereof. Such trust agreement or resolution providing for the issuance of such bonds may contain such provisions for protecting and enforcing the rights and remedies of the bondholders as may be reasonable and proper and not in violation of law, including covenants setting forth the duties of the Authority in relation to the acquisition of property and the acquisition, construction, improvement, maintenance, repair, operation and insurance of the transportation project or projects or any part thereof, the rates of tolls and revenues to be charged, the payment, security or redemption of bonds, and the custody, safeguarding and application of all moneys, and provisions for the employment of consulting engineers in connection with the acquisition, construction or operation of such transportation project or projects or any part thereof. It shall be lawful for any bank or trust company incorporated under the laws of the State which may act as depository of the proceeds of bonds or of revenues to furnish such indemnifying bonds or to pledge such securities as may be required by the Authority. Any such trust agreement or resolution may set forth the rights and remedies of the bondholders and of the trustee, and may restrict the individual rights of action by bondholders. In addition to the foregoing, any such trust agreement or resolution may contain such other provisions as the Authority may deem reasonable and proper for the security of the bondholders. All expenses incurred in carrying out the provisions of such trust agreement may be treated as a part of the cost of the operation of the transportation project or projects.

Any pledge of tolls or other revenues or other moneys made by the Authority shall be valid and binding from the time when the pledge is made; the tolls or other revenues or other moneys so pledged and thereafter received by the Authority shall immediately be subject to the lien of such pledge without any physical delivery thereof or further act, and the lien of any such pledge shall be valid and binding as against all parties having claims of any kind in tort, contract or otherwise against the Authority, irrespective of whether such parties have notice thereof. Neither the resolution nor any trust agreement by which a pledge is created need be filed or recorded except in the records of the Authority.

L.1948, c. 454, p. 1865, § 8. Amended by L.1991, c. 183, § 14, eff. June 30, 1991; L.2003, c. 79, § 21.

[1] N.J.S.A. § 27:23–7.

Historical and Statutory Notes

L.2003, c. 79, § 50, approved May 27, 2003, provides:

"This act shall take effect on the Transfer Date, except that section 3 [27:23–42], section 8 [27:23–4] and the amendment of section 5 of P.L.1948, c. 454 (C.27:23–5) adding a new subsection (t), as provided in section 9 of this act, shall take effect immediately, provided that the authority shall be granted such powers as are contained herein which shall be necessary or appropriate for it to issue bonds and to take such other actions to effectuate the transfer of the Highway Authority and its projects and functions to the authority as soon as practicable after the date of enactment. The authority may take such anticipatory action in advance as shall be necessary for the implementation of this act."

27:23–9. Revenues

(A) The authority is hereby authorized by resolution to fix, revise, charge and collect tolls, fees, licenses, rents, concession charges and other charges for the use of each project and the different parts or sections thereof, and to contract with any person, partnership, association or corporation desiring the use of any part thereof, including the right-of-way adjoining the paved portion, for placing thereon telephone, telegraph, electric light or power lines, gas stations, garages, stores, hotels, and restaurants, offices, entertainment facilities, or for any other purpose, and to fix the terms, conditions, rents and rates of charges for such use; provided, that a sufficient number of gas stations may be authorized to be established in each service area along any such highway to permit reasonable competition by private business in the public interest. Such tolls shall be so fixed and adjusted as to carry out and perform the terms and provisions of any contract with or for the benefit of bondholders. Such tolls shall not be subject to supervision or regulation by any other commission, board, bureau or agency of the State. The use and disposition of tolls and revenues shall be subject to the provisions of the resolution authorizing the issuance of such bonds or of the trust agreement securing the same.

(B) (Deleted by amendment, P.L.2003, c.79).

(C) All revenues and other funds of the authority not pledged or otherwise required to pay or secure the payment of principal and interest on any indebtedness of the authority existing from time to time under, and not otherwise required for the purpose of, this act and not pledged under a contract providing for payment of funds to the State or New Jersey Transportation Trust Fund Authority created pursuant to P.L.1984, c. 73 (C.27:1B–1 et seq.) shall be applied to the authority's corporate purposes or as hereafter provided by law.

L.1948, c. 454, p. 1867, § 9. Amended by L.1963, c. 76, § 2; L.1964, c. 56, § 1; L.1984, c. 73, § 31, eff. July 10, 1984; L.1991, c. 183, § 15, eff. June 30, 1991; L.2003, c. 79, § 22.

Historical and Statutory Notes

L.2003, c. 79, § 50, approved May 27, 2003, provides:

"This act shall take effect on the Transfer Date, except that section 3 [27:23–42], section 8 [27:23–4] and the amendment of section 5 of P.L.1948, c. 454 (C.27:23–5) adding a new subsection (t), as provided in section 9 of this act, shall take effect immediately, provided that the authority shall be granted such powers as are contained herein which shall be necessary or appropriate for it to issue bonds and to take such other actions to effectuate the transfer of the Highway Authority and its projects and functions to the authority as soon as practicable

after the date of enactment. The authority may take such anticipatory action in advance as shall be necessary for the implementation of this act."

27:23–10. Trust funds

All moneys received pursuant to the authority of this act, whether as proceeds from the sale of bonds or as revenues, shall be deemed to be trust funds, to be held and applied solely as provided in this act. The resolution authorizing the bonds of any issue or the trust agreement securing such bonds shall provide that any officer with whom, or any bank or trust company with which, such moneys shall be deposited shall act as trustee of such moneys and shall hold and apply the same for the purposes hereof, subject to such regulations as this act and such resolution or trust agreement may provide.

L.1948, c. 454, p. 1868, § 10.

27:23–11. Remedies

Any holder of bonds issued under the provisions of this act or any of the coupons appertaining thereto, and the trustee under any trust agreement, except to the extent the rights herein given may be restricted by such trust agreement, may, by civil action or proceeding, protect and enforce any and all rights under the laws of the State or granted hereunder or under such trust agreement or the resolution authorizing the issuance of such bonds, and may enforce and compel the performance of all duties required by this act or by such trust agreement or resolution to be performed by the Authority or by any officer thereof, including the fixing, charging and collecting of tolls.

L.1948, c. 454, p. 1868, § 11.

27:23–12. Exemption from taxation

The exercise of the powers granted by this act will be in all respects for the benefit of the people of the State, for the increase of their commerce and prosperity, and for the improvement of their health and living conditions, and as the operation and maintenance of transportation projects and other property by the Authority will constitute the performance of essential governmental functions, the Authority shall not be required to pay any taxes or assessments upon any transportation project or any property acquired or used by the Authority under the provisions of this act or upon the income therefrom, and any transportation project and any property acquired or used by the Authority under the provisions of this act and the income therefrom, and the bonds issued under the provisions of this act, their transfer and the income therefrom (including any profit made on the sale thereof) shall be exempt from taxation. The Legislature reaffirms that all existing facilities and property, and their operations, and management, of the authority and of the New Jersey Highway Authority, as transferred to the authority, are deemed public and essential governmental functions and are exempt from local taxes or assessments.

L.1948, c. 454, p. 1869, § 12. Amended by L.2003, c. 79, § 23.

Historical and Statutory Notes

L.2003, c. 79, § 50, approved May 27, 2003, provides:

"This act shall take effect on the Transfer Date, except that section 3 [27:23–42], section 8 [27:23–4] and the amendment of section 5 of P.L.1948, c. 454 (C.27:23–5) adding a new subsection (t), as provided in section 9 of this act, shall take effect immediately, provided that the authority shall be granted such powers as are contained herein which shall be necessary or appropriate for it to issue bonds and to take such other actions to effectuate the transfer of the Highway Authority and its projects and functions to the authority as soon as practicable after the date of enactment. The authority may take such anticipatory action in advance as shall be necessary for the implementation of this act."

27:23–13. Bonds eligible for investment

Bonds issued by the Authority under the provisions of this act are hereby made securities in which the State and all political subdivisions of this State, their officers, boards, commissions, departments or other agencies, all banks, bankers, savings banks, trust companies, savings and loan associations, investment companies and other persons carrying on a banking business, all insurance companies, insurance associations, and other persons carrying on an insurance business, and all administrators, executors, guardians, trustees and other fiduciaries, and all other persons whatsoever who now are or may hereafter be authorized to invest in bonds or other obligations of the State, may properly and legally invest any funds, including capital belonging to them or within their control; and said bonds or other securities or obligations are hereby made securities which may properly and legally be deposited with and received by any State or municipal officers or agency of the State for any purpose for which the deposit of bonds or other obligations of the State is now or may hereafter be authorized by law.

L.1948, c. 454, p. 1869, § 13.

27:23–14. Miscellaneous

Each highway project when constructed and opened to traffic shall be maintained and kept in good condition and repair by the Authority. Each such project shall also be policed and operated by such force of police, toll-takers and other operating employees as the Authority may in its discretion employ, unless the Authority provides otherwise by agreement with any federal, state or local entity. The expenses for this maintenance and operation shall be paid by the authority from its own funds or from funds made available to the authority, unless the authority provides otherwise by agreement with any federal, state or local entity.

All counties, cities, boroughs, towns, townships, villages, and other political subdivisions and all public departments, agencies and commissions of the State of New Jersey, notwithstanding any contrary provision of law, are hereby authorized and empowered to sell, lease, lend, grant or otherwise convey to the Authority at its request upon such terms and conditions as the proper authorities of such counties, cities, boroughs, towns, townships, villages, and political subdivisions and departments, agencies or commissions of the State may deem reasonable and fair and without the necessity for any advertisement, order of court or other action or formality, other than the regular and formal action of the authorities concerned, any real property which may be necessary or convenient to the effectuation of the authorized purposes of the Authority, including public roads and other real property already devoted to public use.

The Authority shall cause an audit of its books and accounts to be made at least once in each year by certified public accountants and the cost thereof may be treated as a part of the cost of construction or of operation of the project.

Any member, agent or employee of the Authority who is interested, either directly or indirectly, in any contract of another with the Authority, or in the sale of any property, either real or personal, to the Authority shall be guilty of a crime of the fourth degree.

L.1948, c. 454, p. 1870, § 14. Amended by L.1991, c. 183, § 16, eff. June 30, 1991; L.2003, c. 79, § 24.

Historical and Statutory Notes

L.2003, c. 79, § 50, approved May 27, 2003, provides:

"This act shall take effect on the Transfer Date, except that section 3 [27:23–42], section 8 [27:23–4] and the amendment of section 5 of P.L.1948, c. 454 (C.27:23–5) adding a new subsection (t), as provided in section 9 of this act, shall take effect immediately, provided that the authority shall be granted such powers as are contained herein which shall be necessary or appropriate for it to issue bonds and to take such other actions to effectuate the transfer of the Highway Authority and its projects and functions to the authority as soon as practicable after the date of enactment. The authority may take such anticipatory action in advance as shall be necessary for the implementation of this act."

27:23–14.1. Use of reclaimed asphalt pavement; New Jersey Turnpike Authority

a. Notwithstanding any law, rule or regulation to the contrary, the New Jersey Turnpike Authority shall permit for a turnpike project under the jurisdiction of the authority the use of reclaimed asphalt pavement that constitutes a maximum of 25 percent by weight of the total pavement mixture for base and intermediate pavement courses and a maximum of 15 percent by weight of the total pavement mixture for surface pavement courses.

b. The authority shall permit for turnpike projects under its jurisdiction the use of reclaimed asphalt pavement that constitutes from 25 to 50 percent by weight of the total pavement mixture for base and intermediate pavement courses, after an evaluation of the material properties of the reclaimed asphalt pavement in a "closed system" project. A "closed system" project is defined as a project on which the asphalt millings from the project are recycled back into the hot mix asphalt on that same project.

c. Reclaimed asphalt pavement shall not be used for bridge decking and elevated approaches, open-graded and modified open-graded friction courses, or any other special purpose or premium asphalt mix required in specific projects to increase pavement skid resistance.

L.2002, c. 114, § 3, eff. Dec. 11, 2002.

27:23–15. Refunding bonds

The Authority is hereby authorized to provide by resolution for the issuance of refunding bonds of the Authority for the purpose of refunding any bonds then outstanding which shall have been issued under the provisions of this act, including the payment of any redemption premium thereon and any interest accrued or to accrue to the date of redemption or maturity of such bonds, and, if deemed advisable by the Authority, for the additional purpose of constructing improvements, extensions, or enlargements of the transportation project or projects in connection with which the bonds to be refunded shall have been issued. The Authority is further authorized to provide by resolution for the issuance of its bonds for the combined purpose of (a) refunding any bonds then outstanding which shall have been issued under the provisions of this act, including the payment of any redemption premium thereon and any interest accrued or to accrue to the date of redemption of such bonds, and (b) paying all or any part of the cost of any additional project or projects or feeder roads. The issuance of such bonds, the maturities and other details thereof, the rights of the holders thereof, and the rights, duties and obligations of the Authority in respect of the same, shall be governed by the provisions of this act insofar as the same may be applicable.

L.1948, c. 454, p. 1871, § 15. Amended by L.1991, c. 183, § 17, eff. June 30, 1991; L.2003, c. 79, § 25.

Historical and Statutory Notes

L.2003, c. 79, § 50, approved May 27, 2003, provides:

"This act shall take effect on the Transfer Date, except that section 3 [27:23–42], section 8 [27:23–4] and the amendment of section 5 of P.L.1948, c. 454 (C.27:23–5) adding a new subsection (t), as provided in section 9 of this act, shall take effect immediately, provided that the authority shall be granted such powers as are contained herein which shall be necessary or appropriate for it to issue bonds and to take such other actions to effectuate the transfer of the Highway Authority and its projects and functions to the authority as soon as practicable after the date of enactment. The authority may take such anticipatory action in advance as shall be necessary for the implementation of this act."

27:23–16. Operation as toll roads

When all bonds issued under the provisions of this act to finance any highway project or projects and the interest thereon shall have been paid or a sufficient

amount for the payment of all such bonds and the interest thereon to the maturity thereof shall have been set aside in trust for the benefit of the bondholders, all such projects shall become part of the State highway system and shall thereafter be operated and maintained by the authority.

L.1948, c. 454, p. 1871, § 16. Amended by L.1963, c. 76, § 3; L.1964, c. 56, § 2; L.2003, c. 79, § 26.

Historical and Statutory Notes

L.2003, c. 79, § 50, approved May 27, 2003, provides:

"This act shall take effect on the Transfer Date, except that section 3 [27:23–42], section 8 [27:23–4] and the amendment of section 5 of P.L.1948, c. 454 (C.27:23–5) adding a new subsection (t), as provided in section 9 of this act, shall take effect immediately, provided that the authority shall be granted such powers as are contained herein which shall be necessary or appropriate for it to issue bonds and to take such other actions to effectuate the transfer of the Highway Authority and its projects and functions to the authority as soon as practicable after the date of enactment. The authority may take such anticipatory action in advance as shall be necessary for the implementation of this act."

27:23–17. Preliminary expenses

The Department of Transportation is hereby authorized in its discretion to expend out of any funds available for the purpose such moneys as may be necessary for the study of any transportation project or projects and to use its engineering and other forces, including consulting engineers and traffic engineers, for the purpose of effecting such study and to pay for such additional engineering and traffic and other expert studies as it may deem expedient, and all such expenses incurred by the department shall be paid by the department and charged to the appropriate transportation project or projects, and the department shall keep proper records and accounts showing each amount so charged. Upon the sale of transportation revenue bonds for any project or projects, the funds so expended by the department in connection with such project or projects shall be reimbursed by the Authority to the department from the proceeds of such bonds.

Any obligation or expense hereafter incurred by the Department of Transportation with the approval of the Authority for traffic surveys, borings, preparation of plans and specifications, and other engineering services in connection with the construction of a project shall be regarded as a part of the cost of such project and shall be reimbursed to the State out of the proceeds of bonds herein authorized.

L.1948, c. 454, p. 1872, § 17. Amended by L.2003, c. 79, § 27.

Historical and Statutory Notes

L.2003, c. 79, § 50, approved May 27, 2003, provides:

"This act shall take effect on the Transfer Date, except that section 3 [27:23–42], section 8 [27:23–4] and the amendment of section 5 of P.L.1948, c. 454 (C.27:23–5) adding a new subsection (t), as provided in section 9 of this act, shall take effect immediately, provided that the authority shall be granted such powers as are contained herein which shall be necessary or appropriate for it to issue bonds and to take such other actions to effectuate the transfer of the Highway Authority and its projects and functions to the authority as soon as practicable after the date of enactment. The authority may take such anticipatory action in advance as shall be necessary for the implementation of this act."

27:23–18. Additional method

The foregoing sections of this act shall be deemed to provide an additional and alternative method for the doing of the things authorized thereby, and shall be regarded as supplemental and additional to powers conferred by other laws, and shall not be regarded as in derogation of any powers now existing; provided, however, that the issuance of transportation revenue bonds or refunding bonds under the provisions of this act need not comply with the requirements of any other law applicable to the issuance of bonds.

L.1948, c. 454, p. 1873, § 18. Amended by L.2003, c. 79, § 28.

Historical and Statutory Notes

L.2003, c. 79, § 50, approved May 27, 2003, provides:

"This act shall take effect on the Transfer Date, except that section 3 [27:23–42], section 8 [27:23–4] and the amendment of section 5 of P.L.1948, c. 454 (C.27:23–5) adding a new subsection (t), as provided in section 9 of this act, shall take effect immediately, provided that the authority shall be granted such powers as are contained herein which shall be necessary or appropriate for it to issue bonds and to take such other actions to effectuate the transfer of the Highway Authority and its projects and functions to the authority as soon as practicable after the date of enactment. The authority may take such anticipatory action in advance as shall be necessary for the implementation of this act."

27:23–19. Act liberally construed

This act, being necessary for the welfare of the State and its inhabitants, shall be liberally construed to effect the purposes thereof.

L.1948, c. 454, p. 1873, § 19.

27:23–20. Severability

If any provision of this act or the application thereof to any person or circumstance is held invalid, such invalidity shall not affect other provisions or applications of the act which can be given effect without the invalid provisions or application and to this end the provisions of this act are declared to be severable.

L.1948, c. 454, p. 1873, § 20.

27:23–21. Inconsistent laws inapplicable

All other general or special laws, or parts thereof, inconsistent herewith are hereby declared to be inapplicable to the provisions of this act.

L.1948, c. 454, p. 1873, § 21.

27:23–22. Short title

This act shall be known as, and may be cited as the "New Jersey Turnpike Authority Act of 1948."

L.1948, c. 454, p. 1873, § 22.

27:23–23. Turnpike project authorized; combining projects; Legislature must designate direction; consent of Highway Commissioner

The New Jersey Turnpike Authority, created pursuant to the provisions of chapter four hundred fifty-four of the laws of one thousand nine hundred and forty-eight [1] is hereby authorized to construct, maintain, repair and operate turnpike projects at all or any of the following locations: (a) Beginning at a point to be selected by the Authority at State Highway Route No. 6 approximately three miles westerly from the westerly end of George Washington Bridge, and thence in a general southerly direction through the counties of Bergen, Hudson or Passaic or both, Essex and Union to Middlesex county, and thence in a generally southerly and westerly direction through the counties of Middlesex, Monmouth or Mercer or both, Burlington, Camden, Gloucester and into the county of Salem to connection with a proposed new bridge across the Delaware river at or near Deepwater, Lower Penns Neck township, Salem county; (b) Beginning at the aforesaid point as selected by the Authority at State Highway Route No. 6, and thence in such general northerly direction as shall hereafter be specifically designated by the Legislature, through the county of Bergen to the boundary line between the State of New Jersey and the State of New York at a point which will connect with the proposed New York State Thruway or with a suitable connection to said Thruway; (c) Beginning at such point as the Authority may select as most feasible and practicable at or in the vicinity of Port street in the city of Newark, on the New Jersey turnpike which is now under construction and thence in a general easterly direction across Newark bay to such point in Hudson county on or adjacent to the easterly shore of Newark bay as the Authority may select as most feasible and practicable, and thence across Hudson county along such route as the Authority may select as most feasible and practicable to connection with the Holland tunnel; (d) Beginning in the general vicinity of the interchange of the New Jersey turnpike which is now under construction in Bordentown township, Burlington county, or southward thereof at or near a new interchange at a point on the New Jersey turnpike now under construction which the Authority may select as most feasible and practicable, and thence in a general westerly direction to a point on or near the Delaware river and across the Delaware river, to provide a connection with the Pennsylvania Turnpike System, by means of a bridge which the Authority is hereby authorized to construct, operate and maintain, either alone or in conjunction with the Pennsylvania Turnpike Commission, or for the construction, operation and maintenance of which the Authority is hereby authorized to contract with said commission, pursuant to such compact as may be entered into between the State of New Jersey and the Commonwealth of Pennsylvania; and (e) Beginning at a point to be selected by the Authority at the presently constructed New Jersey Turnpike in the county of Hudson, Union or Essex which the Authority may select as most feasible and practicable, and thence in a general westerly direction through the counties of Hudson, Union or Essex, or one or more of said counties, Morris and Warren, to a point on or near the Delaware river, at or near Phillipsburg or at or near Columbia, to be selected by the Authority, and across the Delaware river, to provide a connection with the Pennsylvania Highway System by means of a proposed new or then existing bridge; provided, however, that the New Jersey Turnpike Authority may, for purposes of financing, construction, operation and maintenance, combine with the turnpike project now under construction at the location described above in subdivision (a) of this section one or more of the turnpike projects at the locations described above in subdivisions (b), (c), (d) and (e) of this section, and combine any two or more of the turnpike projects at the locations described above in said subdivisions (b), (c), (d) and (e), if said Authority shall by resolution or resolutions determine one or more of such combinations to be desirable; and provided further, that no construction shall be commenced at the location described above in subdivision (b) of this section until the Legislature shall first specifically designate the direction thereof and until the State Highway Commissioner of this State shall have first filed with the New Jersey Turnpike Authority his consent in writing to the construction of a turnpike project at such location; and provided further, that no construction shall be commenced at the location described above in subdivisions (c) or (e) of this section until the State Highway Commissioner of this State shall have first filed with the New Jersey Turnpike Authority his consent in writing to the construction of a turnpike project at such location.

L.1949, c. 41, p. 121, § 1.　Amended by L.1950, c. 2, p. 23, § 1; L.1951, c. 286, p. 1030, § 1; L.1952, c. 334, p. 1072, § 1.

1 N.J.S.A. §§ 27:23–1 to 27:23–22.

27:23–23a.　Legislative findings

The Legislature finds and declares that the highway corridor between the Delaware Memorial Bridge and the George Washington Bridge is the main artery of the State's integrated highway system and of vital importance to the economy and vitality of the State and the region; that both the Department of Transportation and the New Jersey Turnpike Authority have mutually consistent and coordinate responsibilities within the corridor for the planning, construction and maintenance of highway projects; that it is in the public interest that the Department of Transportation and the New Jersey Turnpike Authority be authorized to enter into agreements to provide for an enhanced coordination and unification of responsibilities for the planning, acquisition, construction, operation and maintenance of high-

way projects in order to ensure a safe, effective and efficient highway system; and that any such agreements shall acknowledge the obligation of the New Jersey Turnpike Authority to the holders of its covenants, contracts and agreements.

L.1991, c. 183, § 1, eff. June 30, 1991.

27:23–23.1.　Project addition authorized

The New Jersey Turnpike Authority is authorized to construct, maintain, repair and operate a project addition to the New Jersey Turnpike consisting of a highway at the following location or such part or parts thereof as the New Jersey Turnpike Authority may determine to be suitable for a project as contemplated by this act: Beginning at Route 33 between the City of Trenton and Mercerville in Hamilton Township on the west, from thence easterly to an interchange with the New Jersey Turnpike between Allentown and Robbinsville, thence easterly south of State Highway 33 to, and to connect with or intersect, the Garden State Parkway at one or more locations between the intersection of said parkway with State Highway No. 33 in the vicinity of its intersection with State Highway No. 66 and the intersection of said parkway with State Highway No. 37, in such manner as may be determined by the New Jersey Turnpike Authority to be the most practical route in order to afford convenient access to the New Jersey seashore area.

L.1964, c. 175, § 1.

27:23–23.2.　Project addition authorized

The New Jersey Turnpike Authority is authorized to construct, maintain, repair and operate a project addition to the New Jersey Turnpike consisting of a highway at the following location or such part or parts thereof as the New Jersey Turnpike Authority may determine to be suitable for a project as contemplated by this act: Beginning at or near present interchange 15 of the New Jersey Turnpike situate in the city of Newark, county of Essex, and thence in a general northeasterly direction through Hudson and Bergen counties west of the Hackensack river and through the Hackensack meadows west of the Hackensack river and, after crossing the Hackensack river, to the general vicinity of the existing turnpike at U.S. Highway No. 46 in the village of Ridgefield Park, county of Bergen.

L.1966, c. 6, § 1, eff. Feb. 16, 1966.

27:23–23.3.　Toms River extension

The New Jersey Turnpike Authority is authorized to construct, maintain, repair and operate a project addition and extension to the New Jersey Turnpike consisting of a highway, or such part or parts thereof as the New Jersey Turnpike Authority may determine to be suitable for a project as contemplated by this act, at the following location:

　Beginning at a point south of but near present New Brunswick Interchange 9 of the New Jersey Turnpike, and thence in a general southeasterly direction through Middlesex, Monmouth and Ocean counties, with the terminus being in the vicinity of the river known as Toms River, adjacent to the present Garden State Parkway, which said terminus shall have the concurrence of the New Jersey Highway Authority and the Commissioner of Transportation of the State of New Jersey.

L.1972, c. 28, § 1, eff. May 25, 1972.

27:23–23.4. Approval of governor

The authority may not acquire any land, erect any structure, nor alter the landscape for the purpose of carrying out the project described in section 1 [1] unless and until the Governor, upon reviewing the environmental impact statement described in section 3 [2] and upon consulting with the Commissioner of Environmental Protection, shall declare that such statement adequately provides for the minimization of any adverse environmental impact of such project and that such project is in the best interests of the people of this State.

L.1972, c. 28, § 2, eff. May 25, 1972.

  [1] N.J.S.A. § 27:23–23.3.
  [2] N.J.S.A. § 27:23–23.5.

27:23–23.5. Environmental impact statement

The authority shall submit to the Governor an environmental impact statement on the project described in section 1 [1] in accordance with guidelines to be established by the Commissioner of Environmental Protection. The authority shall include in this statement the records of a public hearing to be held at such time and place as shall be convenient for residents of the area through which the project is proposed to pass. The authority shall make available prior to such hearing information concerning such project to any interested party who wishes to submit comments at such public hearing.

L.1972, c. 28, § 3, eff. May 25, 1972.

  [1] N.J.S.A. § 27:23–23.3.

27:23–23.6. Route 295 interchange

Subject to the findings of a feasibility study, the New Jersey Turnpike Authority may construct, maintain and repair an interchange connecting Route 295 with the New Jersey Turnpike—Pennsylvania Extension in Burlington county.

L.1985, c. 517, § 1, eff. Jan. 21, 1986.

27:23–23.7. I–95 addition and extension; conveyance and transfer to authority; agreement between state and authority

a. The New Jersey Turnpike Authority is authorized and directed to acquire, maintain, repair and operate a project addition and extension to the New Jersey Turnpike consisting of a 4.4 mile section of high-speed limited access superhighway being that portion of Interstate Highway 95 under the jurisdiction of the Department of Transportation beginning at the existing

northern terminus of the New Jersey Turnpike and thence in a general northerly direction to the vicinity of the George Washington Bridge (and hereinafter referred to as the "I–95 Extension."). Notwithstanding any other provision of law to the contrary, the I–95 Extension shall remain forever free of toll.

b. The State shall sell, convey and transfer to the authority all rights of way, property, easements or interests and other rights with respect to the project addition and extension and the authority shall pay to the State in consideration therefor the sum of $400,000,000. The State shall deposit that sum in the General Fund.

The State and the authority are authorized, in connection with this transfer, to enter into an agreement containing indemnification and defense provisions which the State and the authority agree are necessary or advisable to protect the interests of the State, or the authority, or both, as they determine.

L.1991, c. 183, § 19, eff. June 30, 1991.

27:23–23.8. New Jersey Turnpike addition and extension at Interchange 8A

The New Jersey Turnpike authority is authorized to acquire, construct, maintain, repair and operate a project addition and extension to the New Jersey Turnpike consisting of a high speed limited-access superhighway beginning at or near Interchange 8A of the New Jersey Turnpike and thence in a general westerly direction through Middlesex County to an interchange with U.S. Route 1 in the general vicinity of the intersection of U.S. Route 1 and Ridge Road (County Road 522) or U.S. Route 27 as the authority, after study, deems appropriate.

L.1991, c. 474, § 1, eff. Jan. 18, 1992.

27:23–24. State Highway Department's jurisdiction over route to cease

At such time as the New Jersey Turnpike Authority shall undertake to construct this turnpike project, the jurisdiction and authority of the State Highway Department over such route shall cease except as otherwise provided by law.

L.1949, c. 41, p. 121, § 2.

27:23–24a. Jurisdiction and control over I–95 extension

At such time as the New Jersey Turnpike Authority shall acquire the I–95 Extension, the jurisdiction and control of the Department of Transportation over that route shall cease except as otherwise provided by law.

L.1991, c. 183, § 20, eff. June 30, 1991.

27:23–24.1. Repeal

Any provision of law heretofore enacted (except laws authorizing interstate compacts or agreements) which restricts, prohibits, or limits the construction or acquisition of any bridge or tunnel over or under the Delaware river within any distance from any bridge at any time authorized, owned, held, operated or maintained by any county or municipality of this State, or any bridge commission, bridge authority, public officer, board, commission or agency or other public body created by or in this State or any county or municipality thereof, is hereby repealed.

L.1951, c. 286, p. 1032, § 3.

27:23–24.2. Partial invalidity; severability

If any provision of this act or the application thereof to any person or circumstance is held invalid, such invalidity shall not affect other provisions or applications of the act which can be given effect without the invalid provision or application and to this end the provisions of this act are declared to be severable.

L.1951, c. 286, p. 1032, § 4.

27:23–25. Tolls; payment required

No vehicle shall be permitted to make use of any highway project or part thereof operated by the New Jersey Turnpike Authority created pursuant to P.L. 1948, c. 454 (C.27:23–1 et seq.) (hereinafter called the "Authority") except upon the payment of such tolls, if any, as may from time to time be prescribed by the Authority. It is hereby declared to be unlawful for any person to refuse to pay, or to evade or to attempt to evade the payment of such tolls.

L.1951, c. 264, p. 915, § 1. Amended by L.1991, c. 183, § 18, eff. June 30, 1991; L.2003, c. 79, § 29.

Historical and Statutory Notes

L.2003, c. 79, § 50, approved May 27, 2003, provides:

"This act shall take effect on the Transfer Date, except that section 3 [27:23–42], section 8 [27:23–4] and the amendment of section 5 of P.L.1948, c. 454 (C.27:23–5) adding a new subsection (t), as provided in section 9 of this act, shall take effect immediately, provided that the authority shall be granted such powers as are contained herein which shall be necessary or appropriate for it to issue bonds and to take such other actions to effectuate the transfer of the Highway Authority and its projects and functions to the authority as soon as practicable after the date of enactment. The authority may take such anticipatory action in advance as shall be necessary for the implementation of this act."

27:23–26. Operation of vehicles on turnpike project; care required

No vehicle shall be operated on any such highway project carelessly or recklessly, or in disregard of the rights or safety of others, or without due caution or prudence, or in a manner so as to endanger unreasonably or to be likely to endanger unreasonably persons or property, or while the operator thereof is under the influence of intoxicating liquors or any narcotic or habit-forming drug, nor shall any vehicle be so constructed, equipped, lacking in equipment, loaded or operated in such a condition of disrepair as to endanger

unreasonably or to be likely to endanger unreasonably persons or property.

L.1951, c. 264, p. 915, § 2. Amended by L.2003, c. 79, § 30.

Historical and Statutory Notes

L.2003, c. 79, § 50, approved May 27, 2003, provides:

"This act shall take effect on the Transfer Date, except that section 3 [27:23–42], section 8 [27:23–4] and the amendment of section 5 of P.L.1948, c. 454 (C.27:23–5) adding a new subsection (t), as provided in section 9 of this act, shall take effect immediately, provided that the authority shall be granted such powers as are contained herein which shall be necessary or appropriate for it to issue bonds and to take such other actions to effectuate the transfer of the Highway Authority and its projects and functions to the authority as soon as practicable after the date of enactment. The authority may take such anticipatory action in advance as shall be necessary for the implementation of this act."

27:23–27. Speed of vehicles on turnpike project

A person operating a vehicle on any such highway project shall operate it at a careful and prudent speed, having due regard to the rights and safety of others and to the traffic, surface and width of the highway, and any other conditions then existing; and no person shall operate a vehicle on any such highway project at such a speed as to endanger life, limb or property; provided, however, that it shall be prima facie lawful for a driver of a vehicle to operate it at a speed not exceeding a speed limit which is designated by the Authority as a reasonable and safe speed limit, when appropriate signs giving notice of such speed limit are erected at the roadside or otherwise posted for the information of operators of vehicles.

No person shall operate a vehicle on any such highway project at such a slow speed as to impede or block the normal and reasonable movement of traffic except when reduced speed is necessary for safe operation thereof.

No person shall operate a vehicle on any such highway project in violation of any speed limit designated by regulation adopted by the Authority as hereinafter provided.

L.1951, c. 264, p. 915, § 3. Amended by L.2003, c. 79, § 31.

Historical and Statutory Notes

L.2003, c. 79, § 50, approved May 27, 2003, provides:

"This act shall take effect on the Transfer Date, except that section 3 [27:23–42], section 8 [27:23–4] and the amendment of section 5 of P.L.1948, c. 454 (C.27:23–5) adding a new subsection (t), as provided in section 9 of this act, shall take effect immediately, provided that the authority shall be granted such powers as are contained herein which shall be necessary or appropriate for it to issue bonds and to take such other actions to effectuate the transfer of the Highway Authority and its projects and functions to the authority as soon as practicable after the date of enactment. The authority may take such anticipatory action in advance as shall be necessary for the implementation of this act."

27:23–28. Traffic control; signals

All persons operating vehicles upon any such highway project must at all times comply with any lawful order, signal or direction by voice or hand of any police officer engaged in the direction of traffic upon such project. When traffic is controlled by traffic lights, signs or by mechanical or electrical signals, such lights, signs and signals shall be obeyed unless a police officer directs otherwise.

L.1951, c. 264, p. 916, § 4. Amended by L.2003, c. 79, § 32.

Historical and Statutory Notes

L.2003, c. 79, § 50, approved May 27, 2003, provides:

"This act shall take effect on the Transfer Date, except that section 3 [27:23–42], section 8 [27:23–4] and the amendment of section 5 of P.L.1948, c. 454 (C.27:23–5) adding a new subsection (t), as provided in section 9 of this act, shall take effect immediately, provided that the authority shall be granted such powers as are contained herein which shall be necessary or appropriate for it to issue bonds and to take such other actions to effectuate the transfer of the Highway Authority and its projects and functions to the authority as soon as practicable after the date of enactment. The authority may take such anticipatory action in advance as shall be necessary for the implementation of this act."

27:23–29. Compliance with regulations; authority to make regulations

All persons operating vehicles upon any such highway project, or seeking to do so, must at all times comply with regulations, not inconsistent with the other sections of this act, adopted by the New Jersey Turnpike Authority concerning types, weights and sizes of vehicles permitted to use any such highway project, and with regulations adopted by the Authority for or prohibiting the parking of vehicles, concerning the making of turns and the use of particular traffic lanes, together with any and all other regulations adopted by the Authority to control traffic and prohibit acts hazardous in their nature or tending to impede or block the normal and reasonable flow of traffic upon any highway project; provided, however, that prior to the adoption of any regulation for the control of traffic on any such highway project, including the designation of any speed limits, the Authority shall investigate and consider the need for and desirability of such regulation for the safety of persons and property, including the Authority's property, and the contribution which any such regulation would make toward the efficient and safe handling of traffic and use of such highway project, and shall determine that such regulation is necessary or desirable to accomplish such purposes or one or some of them, and that upon or prior to the effective date of any such regulation and during its continuance, notice thereof shall be given to the drivers of vehicles by appropriate signs erected at the roadside or otherwise posted.

The Authority is hereby authorized and empowered to make, adopt and promulgate regulations referred to in this section in accordance with the provisions hereof.

Regulations adopted by the Authority pursuant to the provisions of this section shall insofar as practicable, having due regard to the features of any such highway project and the characteristics of traffic thereon, be consistent with the provisions of Title 39 of the Revised Statutes applicable to similar subjects.

The Authority shall have power to amend, supplement or repeal any regulation adopted by it under the provisions of this section.

L.1951, c. 264, p. 916, § 5. Amended by L.2003, c. 79, § 33.

Historical and Statutory Notes

L.2003, c. 79, § 50, approved May 27, 2003, provides:

"This act shall take effect on the Transfer Date, except that section 3 [27:23–42], section 8 [27:23–4] and the amendment of section 5 of P.L.1948, c. 454 (C.27:23–5) adding a new subsection (t), as provided in section 9 of this act, shall take effect immediately, provided that the authority shall be granted such powers as are contained herein which shall be necessary or appropriate for it to issue bonds and to take such other actions to effectuate the transfer of the Highway Authority and its projects and functions to the authority as soon as practicable after the date of enactment. The authority may take such anticipatory action in advance as shall be necessary for the implementation of this act."

27:23–30. Stopping in case of accident; report

The operator of any vehicle involved in an accident resulting in injury or death to any person or damage to any property shall immediately stop such vehicle at the scene of the accident, render such assistance as may be needed, and give his name, address, and operator's license and registration number to the person injured or to any officer or witness of the injury. The operator of such vehicle shall make a report of such accident in accordance with the law of the State of New Jersey.

L.1951, c. 264, p. 917, § 6.

27:23–31. Transportation of explosives and products likely to endanger persons or property

No person shall transport in or upon any such highway project, any dynamite, nitroglycerin, black powder, fireworks, blasting caps or other explosives, gasoline, alcohol, ether, liquid shellac, kerosene, turpentine, formaldehyde or other inflammable or combustible liquids, ammonium nitrate, sodium chlorate, wet hemp, powdered metallic magnesium, nitro-cellulose film, peroxides or other readily inflammable solids or oxidizing materials, hydrochloric acid, sulfuric acid or other corrosive liquids, prussic acid, phosgene, arsenic, carbolic acid, potassium cyanide, tear gas, lewisite or any other poisonous substances, liquids or gases, or any compressed gas, or any radioactive article, substance or material, at such time or place or in such manner or condition as to endanger unreasonably or as to be likely to endanger unreasonably persons or property.

L.1951, c. 264, p. 918, § 7. Amended by L.2003, c. 79, § 34.

Historical and Statutory Notes

L.2003, c. 79, § 50, approved May 27, 2003, provides:

"This act shall take effect on the Transfer Date, except that section 3 [27:23–42], section 8 [27:23–4] and the amendment of section 5 of P.L.1948, c. 454 (C.27:23–5) adding a new subsection (t), as provided in section 9 of this act, shall take effect immediately, provided that the authority shall be granted such powers as are contained herein which shall be necessary or appropriate for it to issue bonds and to take such other actions to effectuate the transfer of the Highway Authority and its projects and functions to the authority as soon as practicable after the date of enactment. The authority may take such anticipatory action in advance as shall be necessary for the implementation of this act."

27:23–32. Violation constituting violation of law or ordinance if committed in municipality

If the violation of any provision of this act, or the violation of any regulation adopted by the Authority under the provisions of this act, would have been a violation of law or ordinance if committed on any public road, street or highway in the municipality in which such violation occurred, it shall be tried and punished in the same manner as if it had been committed in such municipality.

L.1951, c. 264, p. 918, § 8.

27:23–33. Violation resulting in injury or death or property damage over $5000 a high misdemeanor

Notwithstanding the provisions of section eight hereof,[1] if the violation within the State of the provisions of section seven hereof[2] shall result in injury or death to a person or persons or damage to property in excess of the value of five thousand dollars ($5,000.00), such violation shall constitute a high misdemeanor.

L.1951, c. 264, p. 918, § 9.

[1] N.J.S.A. § 27:23–32.
[2] N.J.S.A. § 27:23–31.

27:23–34. Violations of regulations; trial; practice and procedure

Except as provided in sections eight and nine of this act,[1] any violation of any of the provisions hereof, including but not limited to those regarding the payment of tolls, and any violation of any regulation adopted by the Authority under the provisions of this act shall be punishable by a fine not exceeding five hundred dollars ($500) or by imprisonment not exceeding thirty days or by both such fine and imprisonment. Such a violation shall be tried in a summary way and shall be within the jurisdiction of and may be brought in the Superior Court or any municipal court where the offense was committed. The rules of the Supreme Court shall govern the practice and procedure in such proceedings. Proceedings under this section may be instituted on any day of the week, and the institution of the proceedings on a Sunday or a holiday shall be no bar to the successful prosecution thereof. Any process served on a Sunday or a holiday shall be as valid as if served on any other day of the week.

When imposing any penalty under the provisions of this section the court having jurisdiction shall be guided by the appropriate provisions of any statute adopted at the current session of the Legislature, or hereafter, fixing uniform penalties for violation of certain provisions of the motor vehicle and traffic laws contained in Title 39 of the Revised Statutes.

L.1951, c. 264, p. 918, § 10. Amended by L.1991, c. 91, § 306, eff. April 9, 1992; L.2003, c. 79, § 35.

[1] N.J.S.A. §§ 27:23–32, 27:23–33.

Historical and Statutory Notes

L.2003, c. 79, § 50, approved May 27, 2003, provides:

"This act shall take effect on the Transfer Date, except that section 3 [27:23–42], section 8 [27:23–4] and the amendment of section 5 of P.L.1948, c. 454 (C.27:23–5) adding a new subsection (t), as provided in section 9 of this act, shall take effect immediately, provided that the authority shall be granted such powers as are contained herein which shall be necessary or appropriate for it to issue bonds and to take such other actions to effectuate the transfer of the Highway Authority and its projects and functions to the authority as soon as practicable after the date of enactment. The authority may take such anticipatory action in advance as shall be necessary for the implementation of this act."

27:23–34.1. Definitions; toll collection monitoring by turnpike authority

As used in sections 6 through 10 of P.L.1997, c. 59 (C.27:23–34.1 through C.27:23–34.5):

"Authority" means the New Jersey Turnpike Authority established by section 3 of P.L.1948, c. 454 (C.27:23–3).

"Lessee" means any person, corporation, firm, partnership, agency, association or organization that rents, leases or contracts for the use of a vehicle and has exclusive use of the vehicle for any period of time.

"Lessor" means any person, corporation, firm, partnership, agency, association or organization engaged in the business of renting or leasing vehicles to any lessee under a rental agreement, lease or other contract that provides the lessee with the exclusive use of the vehicle for any period of time.

"Operator" means the term "operator" as defined in R.S.39:1–1.

"Owner" means the term "owner" as defined in R.S.39:1–1.

"Toll collection monitoring system" means a vehicle sensor, placed in a location to work in conjunction with a toll collection facility, that produces one or more photographs, one or more microphotographs, a videotape or other recorded images, or a written record, of a vehicle at the time the vehicle is used or operated in a violation of the toll collection monitoring system regulations. The term shall also include any other process that identifies a vehicle by photographic, electronic or other method.

"Toll collection monitoring system regulations" means the regulations authorized and adopted pursuant to section 7 of P.L.1997, c. 59 (C.27:23–34.2) that prohibit a vehicle from making use of any project except upon the payment of such tolls as may from time to time be prescribed by the authority and that further makes it a violation subject to a civil penalty for any person to refuse to pay, to evade, or to attempt to evade the payment of such tolls, if the violation is recorded by a toll collection monitoring system as defined in this section.

"Vehicle" means the term "vehicle" as defined in R.S.39:1–1.

L.1997, c. 59, § 6, eff. April 2, 1997. Amended by L.2003, c. 79, § 36.

Historical and Statutory Notes

L.2003, c. 79, § 50, approved May 27, 2003, provides:

"This act shall take effect on the Transfer Date, except that section 3 [27:23–42], section 8 [27:23–4] and the amendment of section 5 of P.L.1948, c. 454 (C.27:23–5) adding a new subsection (t), as provided in section 9 of this act, shall take effect immediately, provided that the authority shall be granted such powers as are contained herein which shall be necessary or appropriate for it to issue bonds and to take such other actions to effectuate the transfer of the Highway Authority and its projects and functions to the authority as soon as practicable after the date of enactment. The authority may take such anticipatory action in advance as shall be necessary for the implementation of this act."

27:23–34.2. Adoption of toll collection monitoring system regulations

a. The authority may, in accordance with the "Administrative Procedure Act," P.L.1968, c. 410 (C.52:14B–1 et seq.), adopt toll collection monitoring system regulations. The regulations shall include a procedure for processing toll violations and for the treatment of inadvertent violations. A person who violates the regulations shall be liable to a civil penalty in an amount not to exceed $500 to be established by the authority. The penalty shall be enforced pursuant to the "Penalty Enforcement Law of 1999," P.L.1999, c. 274 (C.2A:58–10 et seq.).

b. Except as provided in subsection b. of section 8 of P.L.1997, c. 59 (C. 27:23–34.3), an owner of a vehicle shall be jointly and severally liable for the failure of an operator of the vehicle to comply with the toll collection monitoring system regulations. The owner of a vehicle shall be liable if such vehicle was used or operated by the operator with the express or implied permission of the owner when the violation of the toll collection monitoring system regulations was committed, and the evidence of the violation is obtained by a toll collection monitoring system. An owner of a vehicle shall not be liable if the operator of the vehicle has been identified and charged with a violation of section 10 of P.L.1951, c. 264 (C. 27:23–34) for the same incident.

c. A toll collection monitoring system acquired or operated by, or under contract to, the authority shall be so designed that it does not produce one or more photographs, microphotographs, a videotape or other recorded image or images of the face of the operator or any passenger in a motor vehicle.

L.1997, c. 59, § 7, eff. April 2, 1997. Amended by L.2003, c. 79, § 37.

Historical and Statutory Notes

L.2003, c. 79, § 50, approved May 27, 2003, provides:

"This act shall take effect on the Transfer Date, except that section 3 [27:23–42], section 8 [27:23–4] and the amendment of section 5 of P.L.1948, c. 454 (C.27:23–5) adding a new subsection (t), as provided in section 9 of this act, shall take effect immediately, provided that the authority shall be granted such powers as are contained herein which shall be necessary or appropriate for it to issue bonds and to take such other actions to effectuate the transfer of the Highway Authority and its projects and functions to the authority as soon as practicable after the date of enactment. The authority may take such anticipatory action in advance as shall be necessary for the implementation of this act."

27:23–34.3. Violations; advisory and payment request sent to owner; enforcement; penalties

a. If a violation of the toll collection monitoring system regulations is committed as evidenced by a toll collection monitoring system, the authority or the agent of the authority may send an advisory and payment request within 60 days of the date of the violation to the owner of the vehicle by regular mail at the address of record for that owner with the New Jersey Motor Vehicle Commission or with any other motor vehicle licensing authority of another jurisdiction, providing the owner with the opportunity to resolve the matter prior to the issuance of a summons and complaint that charges a violation of the toll collection monitoring system regulations. The advisory and payment request shall contain sufficient information to inform the owner of the nature, date, time and location of the alleged violation. The authority or its agent may require as part of the advisory and payment request that the owner pay to the agent the proper toll and a reasonable administrative fee established by the authority and based upon the actual cost of processing and collecting the violation. If the owner fails to pay the required toll and fee within 30 days of the date the advisory and payment request was sent, the owner shall be subject to liability on the 31st day following the date the advisory and payment request was sent for the violation of the toll collection monitoring system regulations by the vehicle operator pursuant to the issuance of a complaint and summons.

b. An owner of a vehicle who is a lessor of the vehicle used in violation of the toll collection monitoring system regulations of the authority shall not be liable for the violation of the regulations if the lessor submits to the authority, in a timely manner, a copy of the rental agreement, lease or other contract document covering that vehicle on the date of the violation, with the name and address of the lessee clearly legible to the authority and to the court having jurisdiction over the violation. If the lessor fails to provide the information in a timely manner, the lessor shall be held liable for the violation of the regulations. If the lessor provides the required information to the authority, the lessee of the vehicle on the date of the violation shall be deemed to be the owner of the vehicle for the purposes of sections 6 through 10 of P.L.1997, c. 59 (C.27:23–34.1 through C.27:23–34.5) and the toll collection monitoring system regulations and shall be subject to liability for the violation of the regulations.

c. Except as otherwise provided in this subsection, a certified report of an employee or agent of the authority reporting a violation of the toll collection monitoring system regulations and any information obtained from a toll collection monitoring system shall be available for the exclusive use of the authority and any law enforcement official for the purposes of discharging their duties pursuant to sections 6 through 10 of P.L.1997, c. 59 (C.27:23–34.1 through C.27:23–34.5) and the toll collection monitoring system regulations. Any such report or information shall not be deemed a public record under P.L.1963, c. 73 (C.47:1A–1 et seq.) or the common law concerning access to public records. The certified reports and information, including but not limited to, any recorded image of any motor vehicle, the license plate of any motor vehicle or the operator or any passenger in any motor vehicle, shall not be discoverable as a public record by any person, entity or governmental agency, except upon a subpoena issued by a grand jury or a court order in a criminal matter, nor shall they be offered in evidence in any civil or administrative proceeding, not directly related to a violation of the toll collection monitoring system regulations, or in any municipal court prosecution for a violation of any of the provisions of Title 39 of the Revised Statutes. However, in the event that, notwithstanding the provisions of subsection c. of section 7 of this act, [1] a recorded image of the face of the operator or any passenger in a motor vehicle is produced by the toll collection monitoring system, that image shall not be used by the authority for any purpose nor shall the image or any record or copy thereof be transmitted or communicated to any person, governmental, non-governmental, or judicial or administrative entity.

d. A complaint and summons charging a violation of the toll collection monitoring system regulations shall be on a form prescribed by the Administrative Director of the Courts pursuant to the Rules Governing the Courts of the State of New Jersey. The authority may authorize by regulation an employee or agent to be a complaining witness to make, sign, and initiate complaints and to issue summonses in the name of the authority on behalf of the State of New Jersey, pursuant to the Rules Governing the Courts of the State of New Jersey. The complaints and summonses may be made on information based upon evidence obtained by a toll collection monitoring system, the toll collection monitoring system record and the records of the New Jersey Motor Vehicle Commission or of any other state, province, or motor vehicle licensing authority.

Service may be made by means provided by the Rules Governing the Courts of the State of New Jersey.

Except as provided in subsection c. of this section, the recorded images produced by a toll collection monitoring system shall be considered an official record kept in the ordinary course of business and shall be admissible in a proceeding for a violation of any toll collection monitoring system regulations.

e. The municipal court of the municipality wherein a toll collection monitoring system record was made shall have jurisdiction to hear violations of the toll collection monitoring system regulations. Violations shall be enforced and penalties collected pursuant to the "Penalty Enforcement Law of 1999," P.L.1999, c. 274 (C.2A:58–10 et seq.). A proceeding and a judgment arising therefrom shall be pursued and entered in accordance with the provisions of N.J.S.2B:12–1 et seq. and the Rules Governing the Courts of the State of New Jersey.

In addition to the civil penalty that may be assessed by a court having jurisdiction for a violation of the toll collection monitoring system regulations, a court shall require the defendant to pay the proper toll and shall require the defendant to pay a reasonable administrative fee as determined by the authority. Following collection and distribution of the fees set forth in section 11 of P.L.1953, c. 22 (C.22A:3–4), any tolls and administrative fees imposed and collected by the court for a violation of the toll collection monitoring system regulations shall be promptly remitted to the authority by the court. The civil penalty shall be distributed pursuant to the "Penalty Enforcement Law of 1999," P.L.1999, c. 274 (C.2A:58–10 et seq.).

L.1997, c. 59, § 8, eff. April 2, 1997. Amended by L.2003, c. 79, § 38; L.2005, c. 62, § 1, eff. April 7, 2005.
   [1] N.J.S.A. § 27:23–34.2.

Historical and Statutory Notes

L.2003, c. 79, § 50, approved May 27, 2003, provides:

"This act shall take effect on the Transfer Date, except that section 3 [27:23–42], section 8 [27:23–4] and the amendment of section 5 of P.L.1948, c. 454 (C.27:23–5) adding a new subsection (t), as provided in section 9 of this act, shall take effect immediately, provided that the authority shall be granted such powers as are contained herein which shall be necessary or appropriate for it to issue bonds and to take such other actions to effectuate the transfer of the Highway Authority and its projects and functions to the authority as soon as practicable after the date of enactment. The authority may take such anticipatory action in advance as shall be necessary for the implementation of this act."

27:23–34.4. Power of authority to enforce toll collection regulations and traffic laws not limited

Nothing in sections 6 through 10 of P.L.1997, c. 59 (C. 27:23–34.1 through C. 27:23–34.5) shall be construed as limiting the power of the authority as provided in P.L.1951, c. 264 (C. 27:23–25 et seq.) to proceed against an operator of a vehicle for a violation of the authority's toll collection regulations, or as prohibiting or limiting the enforcement of a violation of the motor vehicle and traffic laws as set forth in Title 39 of the Revised Statutes except that an operator of a vehicle charged with a violation of section 10 of P.L. 1951, c. 264 (C. 27:23–34) shall not be liable for the civil penalty provided in subsection a. of section 7 of this act for the same incident.

L.1997, c. 59, § 9, eff. April 2, 1997.

27:23–34.5. Power of authority to establish and assess tolls unaffected

Nothing in sections 6 through 10 of P.L.1997, c. 59 (C. 27:23–34.1 through C. 27:23–34.5) shall be construed as extending or diminishing the power of the authority to establish and assess tolls on turnpike projects of the authority.

L.1997, c. 59, § 10, eff. April 2, 1997.

27:23–35. Repealed by L.1999, c. 319, § 2, eff. Jan. 6, 2000

27:23–36. Partial invalidity

If any term or provision of this act shall be declared unconstitutional or ineffective in whole or in part by a court of competent jurisdiction, then to the extent that it is not unconstitutional or ineffective such term or provision shall be enforced, nor shall such determination be deemed to invalidate the remaining terms or provisions of this act.

L.1951, c. 264, p. 919, § 12.

27:23–37. Regulations of counties or municipalities inapplicable to vehicles upon turnpike project

No resolution or ordinance heretofore or hereafter adopted by the governing body of any county or municipality for the control and regulation of traffic shall be applicable to vehicles while upon any turnpike project operated by the Authority.

L.1951, c. 264, p. 920, § 13.

27:23–38. Suspension or revocation of registration and license certificates for violations; nonresidents

In addition to any punishment or penalty provided by other sections of this act, every registration certificate and every license certificate to drive motor vehicles may be suspended or revoked and any person may be prohibited from obtaining a driver's license or a registration certificate and the reciprocity privileges of a nonresident may be suspended or revoked by the Director of the Division of Motor Vehicles for a violation of any of the provisions of this act, after due notice in writing of such proposed suspension, revocation or prohibition and the ground thereof, and otherwise in accordance with the powers, practice and procedure established by those provisions of Title 39 of the Revised Statutes applicable to such suspension, revocation or prohibition.

L.1951, c. 264, p. 920, § 14.

27:23–39. Requirements of Title 39; applicability

Except as otherwise provided by this act or by any regulation of the New Jersey Turnpike Authority made in accordance with the provisions hereof, the requirements of Title 39 of the Revised Statutes applicable to persons using, driving or operating vehicles on the public highways of this State and to vehicles so used, driven or operated shall be applicable to persons using, driving or operating vehicles on any turnpike project referred to herein and to vehicles so used, driven or operated.

L.1951, c. 264, p. 920, § 15.

27:23–40. Tolls; exemption of emergency and other vehicles

No toll shall be charged for the passage of any ambulance, first-aid or emergency-aid vehicle or of any vehicular fire-fighting apparatus or police vehicle operated for the benefit of the public by the State of New Jersey, or by any county or municipal corporation, or nonprofit corporation or organization, first-aid squad, emergency squad, or fire or police department, of New Jersey through or over the facilities of the New Jersey Turnpike Authority, or any part thereof, and any such vehicle or apparatus shall be entitled to pass through or over without the payment of any toll for such passage. The authority may in its discretion establish other categories of public safety related free passage with due consideration of the rights of bondholders.

L.1961, c. 134, p. 802, § 1. Amended by L.2003, c. 79, § 39.

Historical and Statutory Notes

L.2003, c. 79, § 50, approved May 27, 2003, provides:

"This act shall take effect on the Transfer Date, except that section 3 [27:23–42], section 8 [27:23–4] and the amendment of section 5 of P.L.1948, c. 454 (C.27:23–5) adding a new subsection (t), as provided in section 9 of this act, shall take effect immediately, provided that the authority shall be granted such powers as are contained herein which shall be necessary or appropriate for it to issue bonds and to take such other actions to effectuate the transfer of the Highway Authority and its projects and functions to the authority as soon as practicable after the date of enactment. The authority may take such anticipatory action in advance as shall be necessary for the implementation of this act."

27:23–41. Legislative findings

The Legislature finds and declares:

a. Increasing traffic and related congestion are impairing the quality of life and economy of the State. In order to deal with the problems of increasing traffic and congestion, it is necessary to provide for a more coordinated and rational organization of the State's two major toll roads by abolishing the New Jersey Highway Authority and providing for the acquisition by the New Jersey Turnpike Authority of the Garden State Parkway and all other projects of the New Jersey Highway Authority.

b. The abolishment of the New Jersey Highway Authority and the transfer of its functions to the New Jersey Turnpike Authority will permit improved transportation planning, facilitate more efficient operations, improve the capital budget process and achieve administrative economies.

c. Joining the two highways under one umbrella will maintain the historic integrity and separate identities of each roadway while bringing to each economies of scale and financial savings in operations, purchasing, maintenance and administration. These economies and the ability to pool capital resources will create a safer, less congested, better maintained and improved road network. Doing so is vital to fostering a strong State economy and achieving the high quality of life we derive from it.

d. The abolishment and transfer will also permit implementation of effective remedies to address the financial, operational and administrative problems that have hitherto plagued the E–ZPass system. This enactment will stem the brewing E–ZPass crisis threatening the very success of the E–ZPass system now enjoyed by nearly 60% of the drivers on the two roadways for its convenience and easing of congestion by permitting a repayment of over $300 million in E–ZPass debt and cost overruns without a toll increase.

L.2003, c. 79, § 1.

Historical and Statutory Notes

L.2003, c. 79, § 50, approved May 27, 2003, provides:

"This act shall take effect on the Transfer Date, except that section 3 [27:23–42], section 8 [27:23–4] and the amendment of section 5 of P.L.1948, c. 454 (C.27:23–5) adding a new subsection (t), as provided in section 9 of this act, shall take effect immediately, provided that the authority shall be granted such powers as are contained herein which shall be necessary or appropriate for it to issue bonds and to take such other actions to effectuate the transfer of the Highway Authority and its projects and functions to the authority as soon as practicable after the date of enactment. The authority may take such anticipatory action in advance as shall be necessary for the implementation of this act."

27:23–42. Transfer of powers, rights and duties from the Highway Authority to the Turnpike Authority

a. Until the Transfer Date, the New Jersey Turnpike Authority (hereinafter the "authority") shall not exercise any powers, rights or duties conferred by this act or by any other law in any way which will interfere with the powers, rights and duties of the New Jersey Highway Authority (hereinafter the "Highway Authority"). The authority shall not before the Transfer Date exercise any powers of the Highway Authority. The authority and the Highway Authority are directed to cooperate with each other so that the Transfer Date shall occur as soon as practicable after the date of enactment of this act, and both authorities shall make available information concerning their property and assets, outstanding bonds and other debts, obligations, liabilities and contracts, operations and finances as the authority may require to provide for the retirement of any outstanding bonds, notes or other obligations of either authority and the efficient exercise by the authority of all powers, rights and duties conferred upon it by this act.

b. On the Transfer Date: (1) The authority shall assume all of the powers, rights, assets and duties of the Highway Authority to the extent provided by this act, and such powers shall then and thereafter be vested in and shall be exercised by the authority.

(2) The terms of office of the members of the Highway Authority shall terminate, the officers having custody of the funds of the Highway Authority shall deliver those funds into the custody of the chief financial officer of the authority, the property and assets of the Highway Authority shall, without further act or deed, become the property and assets of the authority, and the Highway Authority shall cease to exist.

(3) The officers and employees of the Highway Authority are transferred to the authority and shall become employees of the authority until determined otherwise by the authority.

Nothing in this act shall be construed to deprive any officers or employees of the Highway Authority of their rights, privileges, obligations or status with respect to any pension or retirement system. The employees shall retain all of their rights and benefits under existing collective negotiation agreements or contracts until such time as new or revised agreements or contracts are agreed to. All existing employee representatives shall be retained to act on behalf of those employees until such time as the employees shall, pursuant to law, elect to change those representatives. Nothing in this act shall affect the civil service status, if any, of those officers or employees.

(4) All debts, liabilities, obligations and contracts of the Highway Authority, except to the extent specifically provided or established to the contrary in this act, are imposed upon the authority, and all creditors of the Highway Authority and persons having claims against or contracts with the Highway Authority of any kind or character may enforce those debts, claims and contracts against the authority as successor to the Highway Authority in the same manner as they might have had against the Highway Authority, and the rights and remedies of those holders, creditors and persons having claims against or contracts with the Highway Authority shall not be limited or restricted in any manner by this act.

(5) In continuing the functions, contracts, obligations and duties of the Highway Authority, the authority is authorized to act in its own name or in the name of the Highway Authority as may be convenient or advisable under the circumstances from time to time.

(6) Any references to the Highway Authority in any other law or regulation shall be deemed to refer and apply to the authority.

(7) All rules and regulations of the Highway Authority shall continue in effect as the rules and regulations of the authority until amended, supplemented or rescinded by the authority in accordance with law. Notwithstanding any requirements of the "Administrative Procedure Act," P. L.1968, c. 410 (C.52:14B–1 et seq.) to the contrary, the authority may adopt regulations, after notice and an opportunity for public comment, amending, supplementing, modifying or repealing the regulations of both authorities or either of them. Such regulations shall be effective immediately upon filing with the Office of Administrative Law and shall be effective for a period not to exceed 18 months from the Transfer Date and they may, thereafter, be amended, adopted or readopted in accordance with the "Administrative Procedure Act." Regulations of the Highway Authority inconsistent with the provisions of this act or of regulations of the authority shall be deemed void if so judged by the authority acting pursuant to the provisions of this paragraph.

(8) All operations of the Highway Authority shall continue as operations of the authority until altered by the authority as may be permitted pursuant to this act.

(9) The powers vested in the authority by this act shall be construed as being in addition to and not in diminution of the powers heretofore vested by law in the Highway Authority to the extent not otherwise altered or provided for in this act.

c. As soon as practicable after the Transfer Date, the authority shall notify the Governor and the presiding officers of each house of the Legislature that the transfer has occurred, the date of the transfer and any other information concerning the transfer the authority deems appropriate.

d. On and after the Transfer Date, no officer or employee of the authority shall be granted permanent tenure at the authority.

L.2003, c. 79, § 3, eff. May 27, 2003.

27:23–43. Management of the Garden State Parkway and other projects

The authority, pursuant to the provisions of this act, is hereby authorized to construct, maintain, improve, manage, repair and operate a project known as the "Garden State Parkway," authorized pursuant to section 20 of P.L.1952, c. 16 (C.27:12B–20), repealed by this act, and any other existing project or facility of the Highway Authority.

L.2003, c. 79, § 4.

Historical and Statutory Notes

L.2003, c. 79, § 50, approved May 27, 2003, provides:

"This act shall take effect on the Transfer Date, except that section 3 [27:23–42], section 8 [27:23–4] and the amendment of section 5 of P.L.1948, c. 454 (C.27:23–5) adding a new subsection (t), as provided in section 9 of this act, shall take effect immediately, provided that the authority shall be granted such powers as are contained herein which shall be necessary or appropriate for it to issue bonds and to take such other actions to effectuate the transfer of the Highway Authority and its projects and functions to the authority as soon as practicable after the date of enactment. The authority may take such anticipatory action in advance as shall be necessary for the implementation of this act."

27:23–44. Counties and municipalities; funding non-highway transportation projects

For the purpose of aiding and cooperating in the acquisition, construction, or operation of any non-highway transportation project of the authority, any county or municipality may, upon agreement with the authority and in the manner provided by law:

a. Appropriate moneys for the purposes of the authority and loan or donate the money to the authority in the installments and upon the terms as may be agreed upon by the authority;

b. Perform any act for the authority which it is empowered by law to perform;

c. Incur indebtedness, borrow money and issue bonds or notes for the purpose of financing a project pursuant to the provisions of the "Local Bond Law," (N.J.S.40A:2–1 et seq.); and

d. Unconditionally guarantee the punctual payment of the principal of and interest on any bonds or notes of the authority.

L.2003, c. 79, § 41.

Historical and Statutory Notes

L.2003, c. 79, § 50, approved May 27, 2003, provides:

"This act shall take effect on the Transfer Date, except that section 3 [27:23–42], section 8 [27:23–4] and the amendment of section 5 of P.L.1948, c. 454 (C.27:23–5) adding a new subsection (t), as provided in section 9 of this act, shall take effect immediately, provided that the authority shall be granted such powers as are contained herein which shall be necessary or appropriate for it to issue bonds and to take such other actions to effectuate the transfer of the Highway Authority and its projects and functions to the authority as soon as practicable after the date of enactment. The authority may take such anticipatory action in advance as shall be necessary for the implementation of this act."

27:23–45. Acquisition of roadside areas

Subject to the terms of any agreement by the authority with the holders of bonds, the authority is authorized to acquire in cooperation with the Department of Environmental Protection limited roadside areas adjoining highway projects and transfer any or all such areas to the Department of Environmental Protection for maintenance as roadside parks.

L.2003, c. 79, § 42.

Historical and Statutory Notes

L.2003, c. 79, § 50, approved May 27, 2003, provides:

"This act shall take effect on the Transfer Date, except that section 3 [27:23–42], section 8 [27:23–4] and the amendment of section 5 of P.L.1948, c. 454 (C.27:23–5) adding a new subsection (t), as provided in section 9 of this act, shall take effect immediately, provided that the authority shall be granted such powers as are contained herein which shall be necessary or appropriate for it to issue bonds and to take such other actions to effectuate the transfer of the Highway Authority and its projects and functions to the authority as soon as practicable after the date of enactment. The authority may take such anticipatory action in advance as shall be necessary for the implementation of this act."

27:23–46. Authority to lend, lease, grant or convey park or recreational areas

Subject to the terms of any agreement by the authority with the holders of bonds, the authority shall have power to lend, lease, grant or convey to the Department of Environmental Protection at its request upon such terms and conditions and with such reservations as the authority shall deem reasonable and fair, any park or recreational areas or facilities owned by the authority, and after such loan, lease, grant or conveyance the park or recreational areas or facilities so loaned, leased, granted or conveyed shall no longer constitute part of a project.

L.2003, c. 79, § 43.

Historical and Statutory Notes

L.2003, c. 79, § 50, approved May 27, 2003, provides:

"This act shall take effect on the Transfer Date, except that section 3 [27:23–42], section 8 [27:23–4] and the amendment of section 5 of P.L.1948, c. 454 (C.27:23–5) adding a new subsection (t), as provided in section 9 of this act, shall take effect immediately, provided that the authority shall be granted such powers as are contained herein which shall be necessary or appropriate for it to issue bonds and to take such other actions to effectuate the transfer of the Highway Authority and its projects and functions to the authority as soon as practicable after the date of enactment. The authority may take such anticipatory action in advance as shall be necessary for the implementation of this act."

27:23–47. Maintenance of Vietnam Veterans' Memorial

The authority, as the successor to the Highway Authority, may provide for the perpetual maintenance of the Vietnam Veterans' Memorial in accordance with the agreement executed by the Highway Authority, pursuant to section 2 of P.L.1991, c. 70 (C.27:12B–5.4), repealed by this act, and the Legislature shall appropriate to the Department of Military and Veterans' Affairs for payment to the authority such funds from the Vietnam Veterans' Memorial Fund, created under section 4 of P.L.1985, c. 494 (C.52:18A–208), and any other source of available revenue, as may be necessary for the authority to carry out its responsibilities under this section.

L.2003, c. 79, § 44.

Historical and Statutory Notes

L.2003, c. 79, § 50, approved May 27, 2003, provides:

"This act shall take effect on the Transfer Date, except that section 3 [27:23–42], section 8 [27:23–4] and the amendment of section 5 of P.L.1948, c. 454 (C.27:23–5) adding a new subsection (t), as provided in section 9 of this act, shall take

effect immediately, provided that the authority shall be granted such powers as are contained herein which shall be necessary or appropriate for it to issue bonds and to take such other actions to effectuate the transfer of the Highway Authority and its projects and functions to the authority as soon as practicable after the date of enactment. The authority may take such anticipatory action in advance as shall be necessary for the implementation of this act."

27:23–48. Regulations for sale of agricultural products labeled "Jersey Fresh" at service areas

a. The New Jersey Turnpike Authority shall adopt, in consultation with the Department of Agriculture and pursuant to the "Administrative Procedure Act," P.L. 1968, c. 410 (C.52:14B–1 et seq.), rules and regulations to provide for and encourage the sale of agricultural products labeled "Jersey Fresh" and other agricultural or horticultural products grown and raised in the State, at service areas along the Garden State Parkway and the New Jersey Turnpike. These rules and regulations shall include, but need not be limited to, provisions allowing for:

(1) the selection of appropriate service areas;

(2) the designation of locations for such sales at selected service areas;

(3) procedures for growers and sellers of agricultural or horticultural products to use these designated sales locations; and

(4) compliance with the rules and regulations adopted by the State Board of Agriculture pursuant to section 3 of P.L.2008, c. 40 (C.4:1–11.2).

b. To the extent necessary, appropriate, and practicable, the New Jersey Turnpike Authority shall initiate discussions with contracted vendors at service areas concerning the promotion and sale of agricultural products labeled "Jersey Fresh" and other agricultural or horticultural products at service areas and shall incorporate any necessary provisions in the contracts of the vendors to allow for the promotion and sale of these products at service areas along the Garden State Parkway and the New Jersey Turnpike.

L.2008, c. 40, § 1, eff. July 15, 2008.

27:23–49. Snow and ice removal; equipment necessary to remove from commercial motor vehicles

Section effective on October 19, 2010.

Subject to the rights and security interests of the holders from time to time of bonds or notes heretofore or hereafter issued by the New Jersey Turnpike Authority, the authority shall purchase, install, and maintain, or enter into contracts or agreements providing for the purchase, installation, and maintenance of, equipment and technology to be used to remove snow and ice from commercial motor vehicles, as the term is defined in R.S.39:1–1, at locations along the New Jersey Turnpike and Garden State Parkway that are convenient and easily accessible to such commercial motor vehicles, including, but not limited to, service areas, weigh stations, and inspection facilities.

L.2009, c. 138, § 3, eff. Oct. 19, 2010.

TITLE 33

INTOXICATING LIQUORS

Chapter
1. **Alcoholic Beverage Law.**
2. **Stills and Distilling Apparatus.**
3. **Other Laws relating to Intoxicating Liquors.**
4. **Commission on Alcoholism and Promotion of Temperance.**

CHAPTER 1

ALCOHOLIC BEVERAGE LAW

For Administrative Regulations related to this Chapter, see Appendix to Chapter 1, following Title 33.

Section
33:1–1.   Definitions.
33:1–1.1.   Presumption as to fitness for beverage purposes and alcoholic content.
33:1–2.   Unlawful manufacture, sale, etc.; personal use; special permit.
33:1–3.   Director of division of alcoholic beverage control; duties.
33:1–3.1.   Citation of title; legislative findings and declarations.
33:1–4.   Director's powers as to quarters, organization and appointment of deputies, employees, inspectors, experts and counsel.
33:1–4.1.   Deposit of fees and penalties in special nonlapsing fund; use of monies.
33:1–5.   Boards of alcoholic beverage control in municipalities of 15,000 inhabitants or more, appointment, term, etc.
33:1–5.1 to 33:1–5.3.   Repealed.
33:1–5.4.   Secretary to board of alcoholic beverage control.
33:1–6.   Only eligible persons to be appointed.
33:1–7.   Officers and employees not to be interested in liquor industry; acceptance of gifts.
33:1–8.   Form of official bonds; force and effect.
33:1–9.   Classes of licenses.
33:1–10.   Class A licenses; subdivisions; fees.
33:1–11.   Class B licenses; subdivisions; fees.
33:1–11.1.   Sales by Class A or Class B licensees to organizations of army, navy or air force personnel.
33:1–11.2.   Definitions.
33:1–11.3.   Foreign persons holding Class B licenses; sales to resident retail licensees prohibited; exception.
33:1–11.4.   Inapplicability to foreigners who also hold Class A license.
33:1–11.5.   Revocation or suspension of license.
33:1–11.6.   State beverage distributor's license; denial of renewal; failure to use within 2 year period; limitation on number; filing fee.
33:1–12.   Class C licenses; subdivisions; fees.
33:1–12.   Class C licenses; subdivisions; fees.
33:1–12a.   Posting of fetal alcohol syndrome warning notices required.

Section
33:1–12b.   Fine imposed for failure to comply with posting requirements.
33:1–12c.   Sample, sampling and tasting event, defined.
33:1–12d.   Samplings and tasting events on the premises of certain license holders; applicable terms and conditions; penalties.
33:1–12.1.   Repealed.
33:1–12.2 to 33:1–12.12.   Void.
33:1–12.13.   Renewal licenses; new licenses.
33:1–12.14.   Limitation on number of new retail licenses in municipality.
33:1–12.15.   Municipalities under 1000, licenses in.
33:1–12.16.   Renewal or transfer of existing licenses.
33:1–12.17.   Seasonal retail consumption licenses to persons who had licenses in previous season; transfer.
33:1–12.18.   New license on failure to renew; filing fee.
33:1–12.19.   New license where licensee served in armed forces.
33:1–12.20.   Hotel or motel operator, new license to.
33:1–12.20a.   Licenses contingent on completion of construction; rights of holder.
33:1–12.21.   Municipal regulations limiting number of license, act is in addition to.
33:1–12.22.   Effective date.
33:1–12.22a.   License transferred to spouse and surrendered during licensee's service in armed forces; new license.
33:1–12.22b.   Sixth class counties; retail licensees who served in armed forces and permitted license to lapse; issuance of license.
33:1–12.23.   Sale and display for off-premises consumption.
33:1–12.24.   Municipalities in which sale for consumption on premises is prohibited, effect of act in.
33:1–12.25.   Hotel guests, sale and delivery to.
33:1–12.26.   Renewal of expired or expiring license, what is; new licenses.
33:1–12.27.   New limited retail distribution license; issuance.
33:1–12.28.   Renewal of existing limited retail distribution licenses.
33:1–12.29.   New limited retail distribution license within 60 days after expiration of renewal period.
33:1–12.30.   Death of licensee and cessation of business; issuance of new license in place of voided license.
33:1–12.31.   Acquisition of beneficial interest in more than two retail licenses prohibited.
33:1–12.32.   Exceptions.
33:1–12.33.   Inheritance of beneficial interest in retail license; time within which to comply with act.
33:1–12.34.   Membership in organization holding club license.
33:1–12.35.   Right to continue to hold, use and renew existing licenses.
33:1–12.36.   Corporate licenses.
33:1–12.37.   Violation; penalty.
33:1–12.38.   Rules and regulations.
33:1–12.39.   Class C license; renewal if not actively used within period of 2 years; filing fee.

Section

33:1–12.40. Legislative findings.

33:1–12.41. Definitions.

33:1–12.42. Persons required to complete educational program.

33:1–12.43. Educational programs for plenary and limited retail distribution licensees; certificate of completion.

33:1–12.44. Requirements of educational program.

33:1–12.45. Contract with non-profit education organization to conduct educational program.

33:1–12.46. Time to complete educational program.

33:1–12.47. Presentation of certificate of completion required upon renewal of license.

33:1–12.48. Rules and regulations.

33:1–12.49. Special permit for plenary retail consumption license; certain businesses in a qualifying development project; requirements.

33:1–13. Class D licenses; transportation license; fees.

33:1–14. Class E licenses; subdivisions; fees.

33:1–15. Separate license for each warehouse, salesroom or office.

33:1–16. One license for premises located in more than one municipality; division of fee; number of licenses.

33:1–17. Licensee to give bond; custody of bonds.

33:1–17.1. Issuance, renewal or transfer when licensee subject to review.

33:1–18. Commissioner to administer issuance of certain licenses.

33:1–19. Municipal board or body to administer issuance of certain licenses; "other issuing authority" construed.

33:1–19.1. New or additional retail licenses; issuance by municipality; procedure; notice.

33:1–19.2. Issuance of license after publication of notice.

33:1–19.3. Issuance to highest qualified bidder; public sale; qualifications.

33:1–19.4. Bids; notice and invitation; publication; contents; announcement of qualified applicants.

33:1–19.5. Issuance of license or rejection of all bids; postponement or cancellation of sale; disposition of funds.

33:1–19.6. Inapplicability of act to powers of issuing authority; appeals.

33:1–19.7. Plenary retail consumption license for nonprofit musical or theatrical corporations.

33:1–20. License to member of issuing authority issued only by director; additional fee.

33:1–21 to 33:1–21.15. Repealed.

33:1–22. Appeal to director from action of issuing authority respecting license; procedure.

33:1–23. Enumeration of duties of commissioner.

33:1–23.1. Regulation by Commissioner of sales in violation of fair trade contract.

33:1–24. Duties of municipal authorities issuing licenses.

33:1–24.1. Legislative findings and declarations; issuance of special licenses within a smart growth communities.

33:1–24.2. Definitions; director authority to issue additional special licenses; licensee qualifications; application fees.

33:1–24.3. Urban enterprise zones; sale or transfer of inactive plenary retail consumption licenses.

33:1–25. Licensees; qualifications; applications; contents; corporations; partnerships; clubs; notice; publication.

Section

33:1–25.1. Peace officers; right to leadership or titular position in nonprofit organization with club license.

33:1–25.2. Nonprofit organization; use of name other than peace officer as licensee.

33:1–26. Term of license; prorated fee; separate licenses; license restrictions; extension of license; procedure on transfer of license; employment regulations; filing fee.

33:1–26.1. Peace officers; employment in business licensed to sell alcoholic beverages.

33:1–27. Payment of license fee required; exceptions.

33:1–28. Transportation of beverages by licensees in their own vehicles; transit insignia.

33:1–28a. Special permit for temporary or emergency transportation of alcoholic beverages.

33:1–28.1 to 33:1–28.4. Repealed.

33:1–29. Regulation of use of alcoholic beverages by druggists and hospitals; sales to.

33:1–30. Sale of alcohols unfit for use as beverages; preparations and products excepted; violations; misdemeanor.

33:1–31. Suspension or revocation of license; grounds; procedure; effect of revocation; refund of fees; surrender of license; appeal to commissioner.

33:1–31.1. Automatic suspension of license upon conviction of violation; effect of appeal.

33:1–31.2. Removal of disqualification to hold license because of conviction of crime; application to commissioner; order of removal; effect; filing fee.

33:1–32. Conditions to issuance of license.

33:1–33. Refusal of license to persons failing to pay tax or license fee; bond or cash deposit.

33:1–34. Notice of change in facts set forth in application; corporations.

33:1–35. Investigations, inspections, searches and examinations; examination of witnesses; subpoenas; procedure on failure to obey; powers of deputy directors.

33:1–36. Service of subpoenas.

33:1–37. Seal; authentication; fee; inspection of records; certification of facts and findings.

33:1–38. Commissioner to hear appeals; powers on appeal; execution of orders.

33:1–39. Rules and regulations by commissioner; subjects covered.

33:1–39.1. Reciprocal rules and regulations with other states.

33:1–39.2. Rules and regulations with respect to consumer sales.

33:1–40. Municipal regulation of number of retail licenses, hours of sale, etc.

33:1–40.3. Sale for consumption off-premises of wine and malt alcoholic beverages in original container by retail consumption or distribution licensee; limitation for cities of first class.

33:1–41. Appeal from limitation of number of retail licenses or hours of sale.

33:1–42. Sale in public buildings of state or political subdivisions prohibited; exceptions.

33:1–43. Interest in both brewery, distillery or wholesaling, etc., and in retailing; prohibition.

33:1–43a. Limited right of wholesaler to acquire interest in corporation.

Section

33:1–43.1. Loans or furnishing of fixtures to retail licensee by brewer prohibited; exceptions.

33:1–43.2. Providing of services, items or equipment to retailers to enhance or protect products; conditions; licensee entertainment.

33:1–44. Municipal referendum on retail sales of alcoholic beverages except brewed malt and fermented wine.

33:1–45. Municipal referendum on retail sales of all kinds of alcoholic beverages.

33:1–45.1. Club license where vote was "No" in referendum; duration of act.

33:1–45.2 to 33:1–45.4. Inoperative.

33:1–46. Municipal referendum on retail sales of alcoholic beverages, except for consumption on trains, airplanes and boats.

33:1–46.1. Club license; authority to issue after municipal referendum.

33:1–46.2. Special permits to golf and country clubs; license fee.

33:1–46.3. Powers granted director cumulative.

33:1–47. Municipal referendum on Sunday sales.

33:1–47.1. Municipal referendum on hours of retail sales.

33:1–48. Municipal boards certified to commissioner.

33:1–49. Purchase of illicit beverage; misdemeanor.

33:1–50. Manufacture, sale, possession, etc., in violation of chapter; misdemeanor.

33:1–51. Other violations of chapter; misdemeanor.

33:1–52. Aiding in violations; misdemeanor.

33:1–53. Conviction of second offense.

33:1–54. Violation upon leased premises; termination of lease; notice; summary proceedings.

33:1–55. Maintenance of place where unlawful property is kept, manufactured or sold.

33:1–56. Issuing search warrant; private dwellings.

33:1–57. Prerequisites to issuance of search warrant; contents; service.

33:1–58. Breaking and entry in execution of warrant.

33:1–59. Service of warrant in nighttime.

33:1–60. Execution and return of warrant; time limit.

33:1–61. Receipt for and inventory of property seized.

33:1–62. Return of illegally seized property.

33:1–63. Resisting officer serving or executing search warrant; misdemeanor.

33:1–64. Procuring search warrant without probable cause; misdemeanor.

33:1–65. Search without warrant; misdemeanor.

33:1–66. Seizure of unlawful property; bond or cash for return; replevin; forfeiture, sale, etc., of unclaimed property; hearing; certain property subject to seizure; manufacture, sale, etc., of unlawful property; return of seized property; liens upon seized property.

33:1–67. Solicitor's permit required; exceptions; issuance; fee; violations; penalty.

33:1–68. Detention of evidence.

33:1–69. Place of sale; determination.

33:1–70. Each violation separate offense; name of purchaser unnecessary in affidavits, indictments, etc.

33:1–71. Officers to use diligence; arrests.

33:1–72. Sale of warehouse receipts; license required; fee.

33:1–73. Intention and construction of law.

Section

33:1–74. Temporary contingency permits; fees; designated premises; number; ordinances or resolutions prohibiting sales.

33:1–75. Special permits for home manufacture of wines for personal consumption; fee.

33:1–76. Sales within 200 feet of church or school prohibited; waiver; exceptions.

33:1–76.1. Renewal or reissuance of club or Class B wholesale license granted on waiver.

33:1–76.2. Plenary or limited retail distribution licenses; renewal on annual waivers for 15 or more years; effect.

33:1–77. Sale to person under legal age; penalty; defenses.

33:1–78. Bottling without license; misdemeanor.

33:1–79. Licenses to purchase and sell alcoholic beverages of certain manufacturers only.

33:1–80. Issue of stamps, labels, etc.; fees.

33:1–81. Purchase of alcoholic beverages; unlawful acts by persons under legal age; purchases by another for minor; disorderly persons; suspension of driver's license; alcohol education and treatment program.

33:1–81.1. Hearing; attendance by parent or guardian; subpoena.

33:1–81.1a. Notification of parent or guardian of conviction of juvenile under § 33:1–81 or § 2C:33–15; parent or guardian subject to fine for failure to exercise reasonable supervision.

33:1–81.2. Identification card; contents.

33:1–81.3 to 33:1–81.6. Repealed.

33:1–81.7. Transfer of card; penalty.

33:1–81.8. Alcoholic beverage licensee not relieved from liabilities by presentation.

33:1–81.9. Repealed.

33:1–82 to 33:1–84. Repealed.

33:1–85. Retail licensees to sell or possess alcohol only pursuant to special permit.

33:1–86. Punishment for violating section 33:1–85.

33:1–87. Exemptions from provisions of act.

33:1–88. Alcoholic beverage deemed prima facie illicit; no label; false label; no indicia of tax payment.

33:1–89. Discrimination in price to retailers prohibited.

33:1–90. Discounts, rebates or other allowances to retailers.

33:1–91. Participation in unlawful transactions prohibited.

33:1–92. Penalties.

33:1–93. Rules and regulations for supervising alcoholic beverage industry.

33:1–93.1 to 33:1–93.5. Repealed.

33:1–93.6. Discrimination in sales to wholesalers.

33:1–93.7. Refusal to sell to wholesaler; petition for hearing; filing fee.

33:1–93.8. Order to complete sale to wholesaler.

33:1–93.9. Noncompliance with director's order.

33:1–93.10. Rules and regulations.

33:1–93.11. Repeal.

33:1–93.12. Short title.

33:1–93.13. Legislative findings and declarations.

33:1–93.14. Definitions.

33:1–93.15. Contract between brewer and wholesaler for supply, distribution and sale of products; applicability; prohibited and conforming contact terms; violations.

Section

33:1–93.16. Immediate termination of contract between brewer and wholesaler; conditions.

33:1–93.17. Proper representation of brewer by wholesaler.

33:1–93.18. Action against brewer for violation; remedies; third party action limited.

33:1–93.19. Invalidity; applicability of Franchise Practices Act; severability.

33:1–93.20. Input by brewer into operations of wholesaler; conditions; contract terms.

33:1–94. Retail regulations by municipalities to be governed by ordinance only.

33:1–95. Repealed.

33:1–96. Licenses for new license terms deemed renewals.

33:1–97. Special auction permit; alcoholic beverages.

33:1–1. Definitions

For the purpose of this chapter, the following words and terms shall be deemed to have the meanings herein given to them:

a. "Alcohol." Ethyl alcohol, hydrated oxide of ethyl or neutral spirits from whatever source or by whatever process produced.

b. "Alcoholic beverage." Any fluid or solid capable of being converted into a fluid, suitable for human consumption, and having an alcohol content of more than one-half of one per centum (½ of 1%) by volume, including alcohol, beer, lager beer, ale, porter, naturally fermented wine, treated wine, blended wine, fortified wine, sparkling wine, distilled liquors, blended distilled liquors and any brewed, fermented or distilled liquors fit for use for beverage purposes or any mixture of the same, and fruit juices.

c. "Building." A structure of which licensed premises are or may be a part, including all rooms, cellars, outbuildings, passageways, closets, vaults, yards, attics, and every part of the structure of which the licensed premises are a part, and of any other structure to which there is a common means of access, and any other appurtenances.

d. "Commissioner." The Director of the Division of Alcoholic Beverage Control.

e. "Container." Any glass, can, bottle, vessel or receptacle of any material whatsoever used for holding alcoholic beverages, which container is covered, corked or sealed in any manner whatsoever.

f. "Eligible." The status of a person who is a citizen of the United States, a resident of this State, of good moral character and repute, and of legal age.

g. "Governing board or body." The board or body which governs a municipality, including a board of aldermen in municipalities so governed; but in every municipality having a board of public works which exercises general licensing powers such board shall be considered as the governing board or body.

h. "Importing." The act of bringing or causing to be brought any alcoholic beverage into this State.

i. "Illicit beverage." Any alcoholic beverage manufactured, distributed, bought, sold, bottled, rectified, blended, treated, fortified, mixed, processed, warehoused, possessed or transported in violation of this chapter, or on which any federal tax or tax imposed by the laws of this State has not been paid; and any alcoholic beverage possessed, kept, stored, owned or imported with intent to manufacture, sell, distribute, bottle, rectify, blend, treat, fortify, mix, process, warehouse or transport in violation of the provisions of this chapter.

j. "Licensed building." Any building containing licensed premises.

k. "Licensed premises." Any premises for which a license under this chapter is in force and effect.

l. "Magistrate." The Superior Court or municipal court.

m. "Manufacturer." Any person who, directly or indirectly, personally or through any agency whatsoever, engages in the making or other processing whatsoever of alcoholic beverages.

n. "Municipality." Any city, town, township, village, or borough, including a municipality governed by a board of commissioners or improvement commission, but excluding a county.

o. "Municipal board." The municipal board of alcoholic beverage control as established by this chapter.

p. "Officer." Any sheriff, deputy sheriff, constable, police officer, member of the Division of State Police, or any other person having the power to execute a warrant for arrest, or any inspector or investigator of the Division of Alcoholic Beverage Control.

q. "Original container." Any container in which an alcoholic beverage has been delivered to a retail licensee.

r. "Person." Any natural person or association of natural persons, association, trust company, partnership, corporation, organization, or the manager, agent, servant, officer, or employee of any of them.

s. "Premises." The physical place at which a licensee is or may be licensed to conduct and carry on the manufacture, distribution or sale of alcoholic beverages, but not including vehicular transportation.

t. "Restaurant." An establishment regularly and principally used for the purpose of providing meals to the public, having an adequate kitchen and dining room equipped for the preparing, cooking and serving of food for its customers and in which no other business, except such as is incidental to such establishment, is conducted.

u. "Retailer." Any person who sells alcoholic beverages to consumers.

v. "Rules and regulations." The rules and regulations established from time to time by the director.

w. "Sale." Every delivery of an alcoholic beverage otherwise than by purely gratuitous title, including deliveries from without this State and deliveries by any person without this State intended for shipment by carrier or otherwise into this State and brought within this State, or the solicitation or acceptance of an order for an alcoholic beverage, and including exchange, barter, traffic in, keeping and exposing for sale, serving with meals, delivering for value, peddling, possessing with intent to sell, and the gratuitous delivery or gift of any alcoholic beverage by any licensee.

x. "Unlawful alcoholic beverage activity." The manufacture, sale, distribution, bottling, rectifying, blending, treating, fortifying, mixing, processing, warehousing or transportation of any alcoholic beverage in violation of this chapter, or the importing, owning, possessing, keeping or storing in this State of alcoholic beverages with intent to manufacture, sell, distribute, bottle, rectify, blend, treat, fortify, mix, process, warehouse or transport alcoholic beverages in violation of this chapter, or the owning, possessing, keeping or storing in this State of any implement or paraphernalia for the manufacture, sale, distribution, bottling, rectifying, blending, treating, fortifying, mixing, processing, warehousing or transportation of alcoholic beverages with intent to use the same in the manufacture, sale, distribution, bottling, rectifying, blending, treating, fortifying, mixing, processing, warehousing or transportation of alcoholic beverages in violation of this chapter, or to aid or abet another in the manufacture, sale, distribution, bottling, rectifying, blending, treating, fortifying, mixing, processing, warehousing or transportation of alcoholic beverages in violation of this chapter, or the aiding or abetting of another in any of the foregoing activities.

y. "Unlawful property." All illicit beverages and all implements, vehicles, vessels, airplanes, and paraphernalia for the manufacture, sale, distribution, bottling, rectifying, blending, treating, fortifying, mixing, processing, warehousing or transportation of illicit beverages used in the manufacture, sale, distribution, bottling, rectifying, blending, treating, fortifying, mixing, processing, warehousing or transportation of illicit beverages or owned, possessed, kept or stored with intent to use the same in the manufacture, sale, distribution, bottling, rectifying, blending, treating, fortifying, mixing, processing, warehousing or transportation of illicit beverages, whether such use be by the person owning, possessing, keeping, or storing the same, or by another with the consent of such person; and all alcoholic beverages, fixtures and personal property located in or upon any premises, building, yard or inclosure connected with a building, in which an illicit beverage is found, possessed, stored or kept.

z. "Wholesaler." Any person who sells an alcoholic beverage for the purpose of resale either to a licensed wholesaler or to a licensed retailer, or both.

aa. "Limousine." A motor vehicle used in the business of carrying passengers for hire to provide prearranged passenger transportation at a premium fare on a dedicated, nonscheduled, charter basis that is not conducted on a regular route, or is furnished without fare as an accommodation for a patron in connection with other business purposes, and with a seating capacity in no event of more than 14 passengers, not including the driver, provided, that such a motor vehicle shall not have a seating capacity in excess of four passengers, not including the driver, beyond the maximum passenger seating capacity of the vehicle, not including the driver, at the time of manufacture. This shall not include taxicabs, hotel or airport shuttles and buses, buses employed solely in transporting schoolchildren or teachers to and from school, vehicles owned and operated directly or indirectly by businesses engaged in the practice of mortuary science when those vehicles are used exclusively for providing transportation related to the provision of funeral services or vehicles owned and operated without charge or remuneration by a business entity for its own purposes.

bb. "Entertainment facility" is a privately-owned facility in which athletic, commercial, cultural, or artistic events are featured.

Any definition herein contained shall apply to the same word in any form. Thus "sell" means to make a "sale" as above defined.

Amended by L.1953, c. 32, p. 571, § 1, eff. March 19, 1953; L. 1985, c. 157, § 1, eff. April 26, 1985; L.1991, c. 91, § 342, eff. April 9, 1991; L.1997, c. 8, § 1, eff. Jan. 24, 1997; L.1999, c. 356, § 1; L.2000, c. 83, § 5, eff. Aug. 14, 2000; L.2001, c. 416, § 1, eff. Jan. 8, 2002.

33:1–1.1. Presumption as to fitness for beverage purposes and alcoholic content

In any proceeding for any violation of this chapter, or any ordinance or resolution enacted pursuant thereto, any alcohol, beer, lager beer, ale, porter, naturally fermented wine, treated wine, blended wine, fortified wine, sparkling wine, distilled liquors, blended distilled liquors and any brewed, fermented or distilled liquors, shall be presumed to be fit and intended for use for beverage purposes and to contain more than one-half of one per cent of alcohol by volume.

33:1–2. Unlawful manufacture, sale, etc.; personal use; special permit

a. It shall be unlawful to manufacture, sell, possess with intent to sell, transport, warehouse, rectify, blend, treat, fortify, mix, process, bottle or distribute alcoholic beverages in this State, except pursuant to and within the terms of a license, or as otherwise expressly authorized, under this chapter; but any drink actually intended for immediate personal use may be mixed by any person. Except as hereinafter provided, a person may, without limitation, purchase any amount of alcoholic beverages intended in good faith to be used solely for personal use and may personally transport those alcoholic beverages so purchased for personal use in any vehicle from a point within this State. Alcoholic beverages intended in good faith solely for personal use may be transported, by the owner thereof, in a vehicle other than that of the holder of a transportation license, from a point outside this State to the extent of, not exceeding 1/4 barrel or one case containing not in excess of 12 quarts in all, of beer, ale or porter, and one gallon of wine and two quarts of other alcoholic beverages within any consecutive period of 24 hours; provided, however, that except pursuant to and within the terms of a license or permit issued by the director, no person shall transport into this State or receive from without this State into this State, alcoholic beverages where the alcoholic beverages are transported or received from a state which prohibits the transportation into that state of alcoholic beverages purchased or otherwise obtained in the State of New Jersey. If any person or persons desire to transport alcoholic beverages intended only for personal use in quantities in excess of those above-mentioned, an application may be made to the director who may, upon being satisfied of the good faith of the applicant, and upon payment of a fee of $25.00 issue a special permit limited by such conditions as the director may impose, authorizing the transportation of alcoholic beverages in quantities in excess of those above-mentioned.

b. A holder of a Class B license under R.S. 33:1–11 shall not sell or deliver for sale in New Jersey any brand of alcoholic beverage for resale in this State unless the alcoholic beverage is acquired from the brand owner, or his authorized agent, or a wholesale licensee designated as the registered distributor by the brand owner, or his authorized agent.

c. No licensee shall knowingly sell, offer for sale, deliver, receive or purchase, for resale in this State, any alcoholic beverage, including private label brands owned by a retailer and exclusive brands owned by a manufacturer or wholesaler and offered for sale or sold by such manufacturer or wholesaler exclusively to one New Jersey retailer or affiliated retailer, unless the brand owner or his authorized agent files with the Director of the Division of Alcoholic Beverage Control a brand registration schedule containing such information as the director shall by rule or regulation require. Each brand registration schedule must be renewed annually by January 1 of each year.

d. Each person who files a brand registration schedule and amendments thereto shall pay a filing fee of $23 per filing for each initial brand registration and annual renewal and $10 for each amendment. All wines shall be subject to the initial brand registration and annual renewal filings and fees, except that different vintages of the same wine shall not require separate brand registrations or renewals. Any registration may be suspended or revoked in the same manner as an alcoholic beverage license for any violation of Title 33 of the Revised Statutes and the rules and regulations promulgated thereto.

e. Nothing contained in this section shall be deemed to limit or modify the prohibition against discrimination

in the sale of any nationally advertised brand of alcoholic beverages to currently authorized wholesalers as set forth in P.L.1966, c. 59 (C. 33:1–93.6 et seq.) nor shall this section be deemed to require the sale to anyone other than authorized retailers of private label brands which are owned by a retailer or exclusive brands which are owned by a manufacturer or wholesaler and offered for sale or sold by the manufacturer or wholesaler exclusively to one retailer or affiliated retailer, in this State.

Amended by L.1938, c. 79, § 1, eff. April 4, 1938; L.1963, c. 100, § 1, eff. June 13, 1963; L.1968, c. 298, § 1, approved Sept. 9, 1968; L.1984, c. 233, § 1, eff. Jan. 27, 1985; L.1991, c. 402, § 1, eff. Jan. 17, 1992; L.1992, c. 188, § 1, eff. Dec. 16, 1992; L.1996, c. 152, § 1, eff. Dec. 27, 1996.

33:1–3. Director of division of alcoholic beverage control; duties

It shall be the duty of the Director of the Division of Alcoholic Beverage Control in the Department of Law and Public Safety to supervise the manufacture, distribution and sale of alcoholic beverages in such a manner as to fulfill the public policy and legislative purpose of this act as expressed in section 4 of P.L.1985, c. 258 (C. 33:1–3.1).

Amended by L.1985, c. 258, § 1, eff. July 31, 1985.

33:1–3.1. Citation of title; legislative findings and declarations

a. Title 33 of the Revised Statutes (R.S. 33:1–1 et seq.) shall be known and may be cited as the "New Jersey Alcoholic Beverage Control Act."

b. The Legislature hereby finds and declares as the public policy of this State and the legislative purpose of Title 33 the following:

(1) To strictly regulate alcoholic beverages to protect the health, safety and welfare of the people of this State.

(2) To foster moderation and responsibility in the use and consumption of alcoholic beverages.

(3) To protect the collection of State taxes imposed upon alcoholic beverages.

(4) To protect the interests of consumers against fraud and misleading practices in the sale of alcoholic beverages.

(5) To protect against the infiltration of the alcoholic beverage industry by persons with known criminal records, habits or associations. Participation in the industry as a licensee under this act shall be deemed a revocable privilege conditioned upon the proper and continued qualification of the licensee.

(6) To provide a framework for the alcoholic beverage industry that recognizes and encourages the beneficial aspects of competition.

(7) To maintain trade stability.

(8) To maintain a three-tier (manufacturer, wholesaler, retailer) distribution system.

(9) To maintain primary municipal control over the retailing of alcoholic beverages.

(10) To prohibit discrimination in the sale of alcoholic beverages to retail licensees.

L.1985, c. 258, § 4, eff. July 31, 1985.

33:1–4. Director's powers as to quarters, organization and appointment of deputies, employees, inspectors, experts and counsel

The director is hereby empowered:

a. To maintain suitable headquarters for said division and such other offices and establishments within the State as he may determine necessary; to organize said division, creating such bureaus and altering them in such manner and at such times as he considers advisable.

b. To appoint and have at all times five deputy directors who shall each receive such salary as shall be approved by the director and the president of the Civil Service Commission, subject to availability of funds and who shall be removable by the director for cause, and who shall be respectively in charge of the bureaus assigned to them by the director. Each such deputy shall, before entering upon the duties of his office, if required by the director, give bond, to be approved by the director, in the sum of $12,000.00. Deputy directors shall not be subject to the provisions of Title 11,[1] Civil Service.

c. To appoint such clerical force and employees as he may deem necessary and to fix their duties, all of whom shall be subject to the provisions of Title 11, Civil Service.

d. To appoint such investigators and executive assistants as he may deem necessary and to fix their duties and compensation. Investigators and executive assistants shall (1) not be subject to the provisions of Title 11, Civil Service, and (2) shall be removable by the director at will; provided, however, that any person who has been employed as such investigator or executive assistant for a period of three years shall serve during good behavior and shall not be removed except for cause. The director, deputies, executive assistants and investigators shall have authority to investigate, and to arrest, without warrant, for violations of this chapter committed in their presence, and shall have all the authority and powers of peace officers to enforce this chapter.

e. To appoint for short-time employment or for the purpose of performing specified expert or specialist service such experts and specialists as from time to time he shall deem necessary to carry out the provisions of this chapter, and to determine the specified duty, salary or fee and term of service. Such experts or specialists shall not be subject to the provisions of Title 11, Civil Service.

f. To appoint such counsel and other legal assistants as he shall deem necessary to carry out the provisions of this chapter and to fix their powers, duties, salaries and terms of office. Such counsel and assistants shall not be subject to the provisions of Title 11, Civil Service.

Amended by L.1942, c. 155, p. 458, § 1; L.1944, c. 216, p. 755, § 1; L.1945, c. 229, p. 743, § 1; L.1962, c. 65, § 7, eff. July 1, 1962; L.1973, c. 139, § 1, eff. May 17, 1973; L.1985, c. 76, § 9, eff. March 14, 1985.

[1] Repealed; now, Title 11A.

33:1–4.1. Deposit of fees and penalties in special nonlapsing fund; use of monies

All fees and penalties collected by the Director of the Division of Alcoholic Beverage Control pursuant to the provisions of Title 33 of the Revised Statutes shall be forwarded to the State Treasurer for deposit in a special nonlapsing fund. Monies in the fund shall be used exclusively for the operation of the Alcoholic Beverage Control Enforcement Bureau in the Division of State Police and the Division of Alcoholic Beverage Control and for reimbursement of all additional costs of enforcement of the provisions of Title 33 incurred by the Department of Law and Public Safety.

L.1992, c. 188, § 14.

33:1–5. Boards of alcoholic beverage control in municipalities of 15,000 inhabitants or more, appointment, term, etc.

Each municipality now or hereafter having a population of fifteen thousand or more, according to Federal or State census, may establish in and for such municipality, by resolution or ordinance of the governing board or body now established by law in respect to such municipality, a municipal board of alcoholic beverage control, which shall consist of three persons, no more than two of whom shall be of the same political party, who shall be chosen and appointed by the governing board or body of such municipality, for a term of three years; but one of the initial appointments shall be for one year, another for two years, and the third for three years. In the case of any vacancy occurring before the expiration of any term, the appointment to fill such vacancy shall be only for the unexpired term.

The members of such municipal board shall receive no salaries, except in counties of the first class, in which such members may be paid salaries not to exceed three thousand dollars ($3,000.00) per annum, and they shall be removable by the appointing authority for cause. Such members shall not be subject to the provisions of Title 11,[1] Civil Service, and may be members of said governing board or body of said municipality.

No salaried member of such municipal board of alcoholic beverage control may be an official, officer or employee of the State of New Jersey, or any county or municipality therein.

Amended by L.1942, c. 143, p. 437, § 1, eff. July 4, 1942.

[1] Repealed; see now, Title 11A.

33:1–5.1 to 33:1–5.3. Repealed by L.1981, c. 462, § 57, eff. Jan. 1, 1982

33:1–5.4. Secretary to board of alcoholic beverage control

Any board of alcoholic beverage control established pursuant to section 33:1–5 of the Revised Statutes may, with the approval of the governing board or body of the municipality, appoint a secretary, who shall receive such annual salary as shall be fixed by such governing board or body of the municipality; but any person now serving any such board with the title of clerk to the chairman shall be designated as secretary to such board.

L.1947, c. 269, p. 971, § 1, eff. June 11, 1947.

33:1–6. Only eligible persons to be appointed

No person shall be appointed to any office, position or employment under this chapter unless he is eligible as hereinbefore defined but clerical employees need not be of legal age.

33:1–7. Officers and employees not to be interested in liquor industry; acceptance of gifts

No person appointed to any office, position or employment under this chapter while holding said office, position or employment, shall directly or indirectly, individually or as a member of a partnership or as a stockholder of a corporation or any other association have any interest whatsoever in the manufacture, sale or distribution of alcoholic beverages, or in any enterprise or industry dealing or connected with alcoholic beverages or kindred or cognate thereto; nor shall any such person accept any gift, gratuity, or anything of value whatsoever from any licensee or applicant for a license, directly or indirectly; but it shall not be a violation of this chapter for such person to purchase or possess for consumption and not for resale any alcoholic beverages.

33:1–8. Form of official bonds; force and effect

All bonds made or furnished by any person appointed to any office, position or employment under this chapter, except the commissioner, shall be given to the commissioner and are to be approved as to form and sufficiency by the commissioner and be conditioned for the proper accounting of public funds intrusted to the care of said person and shall remain in force and effect notwithstanding expiration of office or appointment or employment or removal therefrom.

33:1–9. Classes of licenses

Licenses shall be of the following classes:

Class A—Manufacturer's license.

Class B—Wholesaler's license.

Class C—Retailer's license.

Class D—Transportation license.

Class E—Public warehouse license.

33:1–10. Class A licenses; subdivisions; fees

Class A licenses shall be subdivided and classified as follows:

Plenary brewery license. 1a. The holder of this license shall be entitled, subject to rules and regulations, to brew any malt alcoholic beverages and to sell and distribute his products to wholesalers and retailers licensed in accordance with this chapter, and to sell and distribute without this State to any persons pursuant to the laws of the places of such sale and distribution, and to maintain a warehouse. The fee for this license shall be $10,625.

Limited brewery license. 1b. The holder of this license shall be entitled, subject to rules and regulations, to brew any malt alcoholic beverages in a quantity to be expressed in said license, dependent upon the following fees and not in excess of 300,000 barrels of 31 fluid gallons capacity per year and to sell and distribute this product to wholesalers and retailers licensed in accordance with this chapter, and to sell and distribute without this State to any persons pursuant to the laws of the places of such sale and distribution, and to maintain a warehouse. The fee for this license shall be graduated as follows: to so brew not more than 50,000 barrels of 31 fluid gallons capacity per annum, $1,250; to so brew not more than 100,000 barrels of 31 fluid gallons capacity per annum, $2,500; to so brew not more than 200,000 barrels of 31 fluid gallons capacity per annum, $5,000; to so brew not more than 300,000 barrels of 31 fluid gallons capacity per annum, $7,500.

Restricted brewery license. 1c. The holder of this license shall be entitled, subject to rules and regulations, to brew any malt alcoholic beverages in a quantity to be expressed in such license not in excess of 3,000 barrels of 31 fluid gallons capacity per year. Notwithstanding the provisions of R.S.33:1–26, the director shall issue a restricted brewery license only to a person or an entity which has identical ownership to an entity which holds a plenary retail consumption license issued pursuant to R. S.33:1–12, provided that such plenary retail consumption license is operated in conjunction with a restaurant regularly and principally used for the purpose of providing meals to its customers and having adequate kitchen and dining room facilities, and that the licensed restaurant premises is immediately adjoining the premises licensed as a restricted brewery. The holder of this license shall only be entitled to sell or deliver the product to that restaurant premises. The fee for this license shall be $1,250, which fee shall entitle the holder to brew up to 1,000 barrels of 31 fluid gallons per annum. The licensee also shall pay an additional $625 for every additional 1,000 barrels of 31 fluid gallons produced. No more than two restricted brewery licenses shall be issued to a person or entity which holds an interest in a plenary retail consumption license. If the governing body of the municipality in which the licensed premises will be located should file a written objection, the director shall hold a hearing and may issue the license only if the director finds that the issuance of the license will not be contrary to the public interest. All fees related to the issuance of both licenses shall be paid in accordance with statutory law.

Plenary winery license. 2a. Provided that the holder is engaged in growing and cultivating grapes or fruit used in the production of wine on at least three acres on, or adjacent to, the winery premises, the holder of this license shall be entitled, subject to rules and regulations, to produce any fermented wines, and to blend, fortify and treat wines, and to sell and distribute his products to wholesalers and retailers licensed in accordance with this chapter and to churches for religious purposes, and to sell and distribute without this State to any persons pursuant to the laws of the places of such sale and distribution, and to maintain a warehouse, and to sell his products at retail to consumers on the licensed premises of the winery for consumption on or off the premises and to offer samples for sampling purposes only. The fee for this license shall be $938. The holder of this license shall also have the right to sell such wine at retail in original packages in six salesrooms apart from the winery premises for consumption on or off the premises and for sampling purposes for consumption on the premises, at a fee of $250 for each salesroom. Additionally, subject to rules and regulations, one salesroom per county may be jointly controlled and operated by at least two plenary or farm winery licensees for the sale of the products of any plenary or farm winery licensee for consumption on or off the premises and for consumption on the licensed premises for sampling purposes at an additional fee of $625 per county salesroom. For the purposes of this subsection, "sampling" means the selling at a nominal charge or the gratuitous offering of an open container not exceeding one and one-half ounces of any wine.

For the purposes of this subsection, "product" means any wine that is produced, blended, fortified, or treated by the licensee on its licensed premises situated in the State of New Jersey.

Any holder of a plenary winery license who sold wine which was produced, bottled, and labelled by that holder in a place other than its licensed New Jersey premises between July 1, 1992 and June 30, 1993, may continue to sell that wine provided no more than 25,000 cases, each case consisting of 12 750 milliliter bottles or the equivalent, are sold in any single license year. This privilege shall terminate upon, and not survive, any transfer of the license to another person or entity subsequent to the effective date of this 1993 amendatory act or any transfer of stock of the licensed corporation other than to children, grandchildren, parents, spouses or siblings of the existing stockholders.

Farm winery license. 2b. The holder of this license shall be entitled, subject to rules and regulations, to manufacture any fermented wines and fruit juices in a quantity to be expressed in said license, dependent upon the following fees and not in excess of 50,000 gallons per year and to sell and distribute his products to wholesalers and retailers licensed in accordance with this chapter

and to churches for religious purposes and to sell and distribute without this State to any persons pursuant to the laws of the places of such sale and distribution, and to maintain a warehouse and to sell at retail to consumers for consumption on or off the licensed premises and to offer samples for sampling purposes only. The license shall be issued only when the winery at which such fermented wines and fruit juices are manufactured is located and constructed upon a tract of land exclusively under the control of the licensee, provided that the licensee is actively engaged in growing and cultivating an area of not less than three acres on or adjacent to the winery premises and on which are growing grape vines or fruit to be processed into wine or fruit juice; and provided, further, that for the first five years of the operation of the winery such fermented wines and fruit juices shall be manufactured from at least 51% grapes or fruit grown in the State and that thereafter they shall be manufactured from grapes or fruit grown in this State at least to the extent required for labeling as "New Jersey Wine" under the applicable federal laws and regulations. The containers of all wine sold to consumers by such licensee shall have affixed a label stating such information as shall be required by the rules and regulations of the Director of the Division of Alcoholic Beverage Control. The fee for this license shall be graduated as follows: to so manufacture between 30,000 and 50,000 gallons per annum, $375; to so manufacture between 2,500 and 30,000 gallons per annum, $250; to so manufacture between 1,000 and 2,500 gallons per annum, $125; to so manufacture less than 1,000 gallons per annum, $63. No farm winery license shall be held by the holder of a plenary winery license or be situated on a premises licensed as a plenary winery.

The holder of this license shall also have the right to sell his products in original packages at retail to consumers in six salesrooms apart from the winery premises for consumption on or off the premises, and for sampling purposes for consumption on the premises, at a fee of $250 for each salesroom. Additionally, subject to rules and regulations, one salesroom per county may be jointly controlled and operated by at least two plenary or farm winery licensees for the sale of the products of any plenary or farm winery licensee for consumption on or off the premises and for consumption on the licensed premises for sampling purposes only, at an additional fee of $625 per county salesroom. For the purposes of this subsection, "sampling" means the selling at a nominal charge or the gratuitous offering of an open container not exceeding one and one-half ounces of any wine.

Unless otherwise indicated, for the purposes of this subsection, with respect to farm winery licenses, "manufacture" means the vinification, aging, storage, blending, clarification, stabilization and bottling of wine or juice from New Jersey fruit to the extent required by this subsection.

Wine blending license. 2c. The holder of this license shall be entitled, subject to rules and regulations, to blend, treat, mix, and bottle fermented wines and fruit juices with non-alcoholic beverages, and to sell and distribute his products to wholesalers and retailers licensed in accordance with this chapter, and to sell and distribute without this State to any persons pursuant to the laws of the places of such sale and distribution, and to maintain a warehouse. The fee for this license shall be $625.

Instructional winemaking facility license. 2d. The holder of this license shall be entitled, subject to rules and regulations, to instruct persons in and provide them with the opportunity to participate directly in the process of winemaking and to directly assist such persons in the process of winemaking while in the process of instruction on the premises of the facility. The holder of this license also shall be entitled to manufacture wine on the premises not in excess of an amount of 10% of the wine produced annually on the premises of the facility, which shall be used only to replace quantities lost or discarded during the winemaking process, to maintain a warehouse, and to offer samples produced by persons who have received instruction in winemaking on the premises by the licensee for sampling purposes only on the licensed premises for the purpose of promoting winemaking for personal or household use or consumption. Wine produced on the premises of an instructional winemaking facility shall be used, consumed or disposed of on the facility's premises or distributed from the facility's premises to a person who has participated directly in the process of winemaking for the person's personal or household use or consumption. The holder of this license may sell mercantile items traditionally associated with winemaking and novelty wearing apparel identified with the name of the establishment licensed under the provisions of this section. The holder of this license may use the licensed premises for an event or affair, including an event or affair at which a plenary retail consumption licensee serves alcoholic beverages in compliance with all applicable statutes and regulations promulgated by the director. The fee for this license shall be $1,000. For the purposes of this subsection, "sampling" means the gratuitous offering of an open container not exceeding one and one-half ounces of any wine.

Plenary distillery license. 3a. The holder of this license shall be entitled, subject to rules and regulations, to manufacture any distilled alcoholic beverages and rectify, blend, treat and mix, and to sell and distribute his products to wholesalers and retailers licensed in accordance with this chapter, and to sell and distribute without this State to any persons pursuant to the laws of the places of such sale and distribution, and to maintain a warehouse. The fee for this license shall be $12,500.

Limited distillery license. 3b. The holder of this license shall be entitled, subject to rules and regulations, to manufacture and bottle any alcoholic beverages distilled from fruit juices and rectify, blend, treat, mix, compound with wine and add necessary sweetening and flavor to make cordial or liqueur, and to sell and

distribute to wholesalers and retailers licensed in accordance with this chapter, and to sell and distribute without this State to any persons pursuant to the laws of the places of such sale and distribution and to warehouse these products. The fee for this license shall be $3,750.

Supplementary limited distillery license. 3c. The holder of this license shall be entitled, subject to rules and regulations, to bottle and rebottle, in a quantity to be expressed in said license, dependent upon the following fees, alcoholic beverages distilled from fruit juices by such holder pursuant to a prior plenary or limited distillery license, and to sell and distribute his products to wholesalers and retailers licensed in accordance with this chapter, and to sell and distribute without this State to any persons pursuant to the laws of the places of such sale and distribution, and to maintain a warehouse. The fee for this license shall be graduated as follows: to so bottle and rebottle not more than 5,000 wine gallons per annum, $313; to so bottle and rebottle not more than 10,000 wine gallons per annum, $625; to so bottle and rebottle without limit as to amount, $1,250.

Rectifier and blender license. 4. The holder of this license shall be entitled, subject to rules and regulations, to rectify, blend, treat and mix distilled alcoholic beverages, and to fortify, blend, and treat fermented alcoholic beverages, and prepare mixtures of alcoholic beverages, and to sell and distribute his products to wholesalers and retailers licensed in accordance with this chapter, and to sell and distribute without this State to any persons pursuant to the laws of the places of such sale and distribution, and to maintain a warehouse. The fee for this license shall be $7,500.

Bonded warehouse bottling license. 5. The holder of this license shall be entitled, subject to rules and regulations, to bottle alcoholic beverages in bond on behalf of all persons authorized by federal and State law and regulations to withdraw alcoholic beverages from bond. The fee for this license shall be $625. This license shall be issued only to persons holding permits to operate Internal Revenue bonded warehouses pursuant to the laws of the United States.

The provisions of section 21 of P.L.2003, c. 117 amendatory of this section shall apply to licenses issued or transferred on or after July 1, 2003, and to license renewals commencing on or after July 1, 2003.

Amended by L.1938, c. 30, p. 103, § 1; L.1938, c. 296, p. 685, § 1; L.1938, c. 429, p. 1243, § 1; L.1939, c. 235, p. 635, § 1; L.1940, c. 83, p. 208, § 1; L.1942, c. 154, p. 454, § 1; L.1949, c. 276, p. 849, § 1; L.1950, c. 340, p. 1127, § 1; L.1954, c. 26, p. 88, § 1; L.1964, c. 228, § 1; L.1965, c. 208, § 1; L.1969, c. 100, § 1, eff. June 26, 1969; L.1970, c. 78, § 1, eff. May 29, 1970; L.1976, c. 44, § 1, eff. June 30, 1976; L.1981, c. 280, § 1, eff. Sept. 10, 1981; L.1985, c. 130, § 1, eff. April 12, 1985; L.1985, c. 131, § 1, eff. April 12, 1985; L.1989, c. 209, § 1, eff. Dec. 29, 1989; L.1993, c. 216, § 1, eff. July 30, 1993; L.1993, c. 372, § 1, eff. Jan. 10, 1994; L.2003, c. 117, § 21, eff. July 1, 2003; L.2004, c. 102, § 1, eff. July 14, 2004; L.2007, c. 329, § 1, eff. April 1, 2008.

33:1–11. Class B licenses; subdivisions; fees

Class B licenses shall be subdivided and classified as follows:

Plenary wholesale license. 1. The holder of this license shall be entitled, subject to rules and regulations, to sell and distribute alcoholic beverages to retailers and wholesalers licensed in accordance with this chapter, and to sell and distribute without this State to any persons pursuant to the laws of the places of such sale and distribution, and to maintain a warehouse and salesroom; provided, however, that the delivery of such alcoholic beverages by the holder of this license to retailers licensed under this Title shall be from inventory in a warehouse located in New Jersey which is operated under a plenary wholesale license. The fee for this license shall be $8,750.

Limited wholesale license. 2a. The holder of this license shall be entitled, subject to rules and regulations, to sell and distribute brewed malt alcoholic beverages and naturally fermented wines to retailers and wholesalers licensed in accordance with this chapter, and to sell and distribute without this State to any persons pursuant to the laws of the places of such sale and distribution, and to maintain a warehouse and salesroom. The fee for this license shall be $1,875.

Wine wholesale license. 2b. The holder of this license shall be entitled, subject to rules and regulations, to sell and distribute any naturally fermented, treated, blended, fortified and sparkling wines to retailers and wholesalers licensed in accordance with this chapter, and to sell and distribute without this State to any persons pursuant to the laws of the places of such sale and distribution, and to maintain a warehouse and salesroom; provided, however, that the delivery of such wines by the holder of this license to retailers licensed under this Title shall be from inventory in a warehouse located in New Jersey which is operated under a wine wholesale license. The fee for this license shall be $3,750.

State beverage distributor's license. 2c. (1) The holder of this license shall be entitled, subject to rules and regulations, to sell and distribute unchilled, brewed, malt alcoholic beverages in original containers only, in quantities of not less than 144 fluid ounces and chilled draught malt alcoholic beverages in kegs, barrels or other similar containers of at least one fluid gallon in capacity, to retailers licensed in accordance with this chapter, and to sell and distribute without this State to any person pursuant to the laws of the places of such sale and distribution, and to maintain a warehouse and salesroom. The holder of this license may sell unchilled, brewed, malt alcoholic beverages in original containers only, in quantities of not less than 144 fluid ounces and chilled draught malt alcoholic beverages in kegs, barrels or other similar containers of at least 7.75 fluid gallons in capacity, at retail; provided, however, that such sales shall be made only for consumption off the licensed premises. This license shall not be issued to any person holding a plenary or limited brewery license, nor shall it be issued to any person directly or indirectly interested in any brewery within or without this State. This license shall not be issued for premises in or upon which any retail business, except the sale of malt alcoholic beverages and nonalcoholic beverages, is carried on. The fee for this license shall be $1,031.

(2) After the effective date of P.L.1995, c. 309 any license issued or transferred pursuant to this subsection for a premises located in a municipality in a county of the fifth or sixth class shall be limited to prohibit retail sales.

(3) The holder of a license issued pursuant to this subsection shall not be entitled to sell malt alcoholic beverages at retail as provided in paragraph (1) of this subsection, at hours of the day or on days of the week during which sales by holders of plenary retail distributors licenses are prohibited in the municipality in which the licensed premises is located or in a municipality which, in accordance with the provisions of this title, prohibits all retail sales of wine and malt alcoholic beverages in original bottle or can containers.

The provisions of section 22 of P.L.2003, c. 117 (C.33:1–11) amendatory of this section shall apply to licenses issued or transferred on or after July 1, 2003, and to license renewals commencing on or after July 1, 2003.

Amended by L.1942, c. 158, p. 464, § 1; L.1954, c. 26, p. 92, § 2; L.1964, c. 170, § 1, approved Aug. 19, 1964; L.1970, c. 78, § 2; L.1976, c. 44, § 2, eff. June 30, 1976; L.1982, c. 166, § 1, eff. Nov. 1, 1982; L.1995, c. 309, § 1, eff. Jan. 5, 1996; L.2003, c. 117, § 22, eff. July 1, 2003.

33:1–11.1. Sales by Class A or Class B licensees to organizations of army, navy or air force personnel

The holder of any valid and unrevoked Class A or Class B license, as defined in sections 33:1–10 and 33:1–11 of the Revised Statutes, except the holder of a bonded warehouse bottling license, shall be entitled, subject to rules and regulations, to distribute and sell alcoholic beverages within the limits of his license to any voluntary unincorporated organization of army, navy or air force personnel for consumption on the military installation whereon such organization is established pursuant to regulations promulgated by the Secretary of War, the Secretary of the Navy or the Secretary of the Air Force, or, if the consent of the State Department of Defense shall have first been obtained, under the State National Guard regulations.

L.1941, c. 326, p. 868, § 1. Amended by L.1950, c. 26, p. 55, § 1, eff. April 11, 1950.

33:1–11.2. Definitions

For the purposes of this act,[1] the following phrases shall be deemed to have the meanings herein given to them:

(a) Foreign person—a person resident in or incorporated under the laws of any State other than the State of New Jersey.

(b) Resident person—a person resident in or incorporated under the laws of the State of New Jersey.

L.1956, c. 110, p. 495, § 1, eff. July 1, 1956.

[1] N.J.S.A. §§ 33:1–11.2 to 33:1–11.5, 33:1–39.2.

33:1–11.3. Foreign persons holding Class B licenses; sales to resident retail licensees prohibited; exception

No foreign person holding a Class B license in this State shall sell or distribute alcoholic beverages directly to any retail licensee within this State unless a resident person is permitted to sell and distribute alcoholic beverages directly to all persons licensed to sell the same at retail in the State or nation in which such foreign person is resident or incorporated on the same terms and conditions as such foreign person enjoys such privilege in such State or nation.

L.1956, c. 110, p. 495, § 2.

33:1–11.4. Inapplicability to foreigners who also hold Class A license

The provisions of this act [1] shall not apply to any foreign person holding a Class B license who also holds a Class A license.

L.1956, c. 110, p. 495, § 3.

[1] N.J.S.A. §§ 33:1–11.2 to 33:1–11.5, 33:1–39.2.

33:1–11.5. Revocation or suspension of license

If, in the opinion of the director, privileges conferred by any Class B license, whether held by a resident person or a foreign person, are being used to circumvent or evade the provisions of this act,[1] the director may revoke such Class B license, or suspend the same until such time as the holder thereof satisfies the director that such license, or the privileges conferred thereby, will not be used to circumvent or evade the provisions of this act.

L.1956, c. 110, p. 495, § 4.

[1] N.J.S.A. §§ 33:1–11.2 to 33:1–11.5, 33:1–39.2.

33:1–11.6. State beverage distributor's license; denial of renewal; failure to use within 2 year period; limitation on number; filing fee

No State beverage distributor's license, as defined in subsection c. of section 2 of R.S. 33:1–11, shall be renewed if it has not been actively used in connection with the operation of a licensed premises within a period of two years prior to the commencement date of the license period for which the renewal application is filed, unless the director, for good cause and after a hearing, authorizes a further application for renewal; provided, however, that, if the licensee has been deprived of the use of the licensed premises as a result of eminent domain, fire or other casualty, and establishes

by affidavit filed with the director that he is making a good faith effort to resume active use of the license in connection with the operation of a licensed premises, then the period of two years provided for in this section shall be automatically extended for an additional two years. Commencing on the effective date of this act, no additional State beverage distributors' licenses shall be issued to exceed the number in existence on the date this act takes effect.

Any request for relief under this section shall be accompanied by a nonreturnable filing fee of $100.00 payable to the director.

L.1982, c. 166, § 2, eff. Nov. 1, 1982. Amended by L.1992, c. 188, § 6, eff. Dec. 16, 1992.

33:1–12. Class C licenses; subdivisions; fees

Class C licenses shall be subdivided and classified as follows:

Plenary retail consumption license. 1. The holder of this license shall be entitled, subject to rules and regulations, to sell any alcoholic beverages for consumption on the licensed premises by the glass or other open receptacle, and also to sell any alcoholic beverages in original containers for consumption off the licensed premises; but this license shall not be issued to permit the sale of alcoholic beverages in or upon any premises in which a grocery, delicatessen, drug store or other mercantile business is carried on, except as hereinafter provided. The holder of this license shall be permitted to conduct consumer wine, beer and spirits tasting events and samplings for a fee or on a complimentary basis pursuant to conditions established by rules and regulations of the Division of Alcoholic Beverage Control, provided however, that the holder of this license complies with the terms and conditions set forth in section 3 of P.L.2009, c. 216 (C.33:1–12d). Subject to such rules and regulations established from time to time by the director, the holder of this license shall be permitted to sell alcoholic beverages in or upon the premises in which any of the following is carried on: the keeping of a hotel or restaurant including the sale of mercantile items incidental thereto as an accommodation to patrons; the sale, at an entertainment facility as defined in R.S.33:1–1, having a seating capacity for no less than 4,000 patrons, of mercantile items traditionally associated with the type of event or program held at the site; the sale of distillers', brewers' and vintners' packaged merchandise prepacked as a unit with other suitable objects as gift items to be sold only as a unit; the sale of novelty wearing apparel identified with the name of the establishment licensed under the provisions of this section; the sale of cigars, cigarettes, packaged crackers, chips, nuts and similar snacks and ice at retail as an accommodation to patrons, or the retail sale of nonalcoholic beverages as accessory beverages to alcoholic beverages; or, in commercial bowling establishments, the retail sale or rental of bowling accessories and the retail sale from vending machines of candy, ice cream and nonalcoholic beverages. The fee for this license shall be fixed by the governing board or body of the municipality in which the licensed premises are situated, by ordinance, at not less than $250 and not more than $2,500. No ordinance shall be enacted which shall raise or lower the fee to be charged for this license by more than 20% from that charged in the preceding license year or $500.00, whichever is the lesser. The governing board or body of each municipality may, by ordinance, enact that no plenary retail consumption license shall be granted within its respective municipality.

The holder of this license shall be permitted to obtain a restricted brewery license issued pursuant to subsection 1c. of R.S.33:1–10 and to operate a restricted brewery immediately adjoining the licensed premises in accordance with the restrictions set forth in that subsection. All fees related to the issuance of both licenses shall be paid in accordance with statutory law.

Seasonal retail consumption license. 2. The holder of this license shall be entitled, subject to rules and regulations, to sell any alcoholic beverages for consumption on the licensed premises by the glass or other open receptacle, and also to sell any alcoholic beverages in original containers for consumption off the licensed premises, during the summer season from May 1 until November 14, inclusive, or during the winter season from November 15 until April 30, inclusive; but this license shall not be issued to permit the sale of alcoholic beverages in or upon any premises in which a grocery, delicatessen, drug store or other mercantile business is carried on, except as hereinafter provided. Subject to such rules and regulations established from time to time by the director, the holder of this license shall be permitted to sell alcoholic beverages in or upon the premises in which any of the following is carried on: the keeping of a hotel or restaurant including the sale of mercantile items incidental thereto as an accommodation to patrons; the sale of distillers', brewers' and vintners' packaged merchandise prepacked as a unit with other suitable objects as gift items to be sold only as a unit; the sale of novelty wearing apparel identified with the name of the establishment licensed under the provisions of this section; the sale of cigars, cigarettes, packaged crackers, chips, nuts and similar snacks and ice at retail as an accommodation to patrons; or the retail sale of nonalcoholic beverages as accessory beverages to alcoholic beverages. The fee for this license shall be fixed by the governing board or body of the municipality in which the licensed premises are situated, by ordinance, at 75% of the fee fixed by said board or body for plenary retail consumption licenses. The governing board or body of each municipality may, by ordinance, enact that no seasonal retail consumption license shall be granted within its respective municipality.

Plenary retail distribution license. 3. a. The holder of this license shall be entitled, subject to rules and regulations, to sell any alcoholic beverages for consumption off the licensed premises, but only in original containers; except that licensees shall be permitted to conduct consumer wine, beer, and spirits tasting events and samplings on a complimentary basis pursuant to conditions established by rules and regulations of the Division of Alcoholic Beverage Control, provided however

, that the holder of this license complies with the terms and conditions set forth in section 3 of P.L.2009, c. 216 (C.33:1–12d).

The governing board or body of each municipality may, by ordinance, enact that this license shall not be issued to permit the sale of alcoholic beverages in or upon any premises in which any other mercantile business is carried on, except that any such ordinance, heretofore or hereafter adopted, shall not prohibit the retail sale of distillers', brewers' and vintners' packaged merchandise prepacked as a unit with other suitable objects as gift items to be sold only as a unit; the sale of novelty wearing apparel identified with the name of the establishment licensed under the provisions of this act; cigars, cigarettes, packaged crackers, chips, nuts and similar snacks, ice, and nonalcoholic beverages as accessory beverages to alcoholic beverages. The fee for this license shall be fixed by the governing board or body of the municipality in which the licensed premises are situated, by ordinance, at not less than $125 and not more than $2,500. No ordinance shall be enacted which shall raise or lower the fee to be charged for this license by more than 20% from that charged in the preceding license year or $500.00, whichever is the lesser. The governing board or body of each municipality may, by ordinance, enact that no plenary retail distribution license shall be granted within its respective municipality.

Limited retail distribution license. 3. b. The holder of this license shall be entitled, subject to rules and regulations, to sell any unchilled, brewed, malt alcoholic beverages in quantities of not less than 72 fluid ounces for consumption off the licensed premises, but only in original containers; provided, however, that this license shall be issued only for premises operated and conducted by the licensee as a bona fide grocery store, meat market, meat and grocery store, delicatessen, or other type of bona fide food store at which groceries or other foodstuffs are sold at retail; and provided further that this license shall not be issued except for premises at which the sale of groceries or other foodstuffs is the primary and principal business and at which the sale of alcoholic beverages is merely incidental and subordinate thereto. The fee for this license shall be fixed by the governing body or board of the municipality in which the licensed premises are situated, by ordinance, at not less than $31 and not more than $63. The governing board or body of each municipality may, by ordinance, enact that no limited retail distribution license shall be granted within its respective municipality.

Plenary retail transit license. 4. The holder of this license shall be entitled, subject to rules and regulations, to sell any alcoholic beverages, for consumption only, on railroad trains, airplanes, limousines and boats, while in transit. The fee for this license for use by a railroad or air transport company shall be $375, for use by the owners of limousines shall be $31 per vehicle, and for use on a boat shall be $63 on a boat 65 feet or less in length, $125 on a boat more than 65 feet in length but not more than 110 feet in length, and $375 on a boat more than 110 feet in length; such boat lengths shall be determined in the manner prescribed by the Bureau of Customs of the United States Government or any federal agency successor thereto for boat measurement in connection with issuance of marine documents. A license issued under this provision to a railroad or air transport company shall cover all railroad cars and planes operated by any such company within the State of New Jersey. A license for a boat or limousine issued under this provision shall apply only to the particular boat or limousine for which issued, and shall permit the purchase of alcoholic beverages for sale or service in a boat or limousine to be made from any Class A and B licensee or from any Class C licensee whose license privilege permits the sale of alcoholic beverages in original containers for off-premises consumption. An interest in a plenary retail transit license issued in accordance with this section shall be excluded in determining the maximum number of retail licenses permitted under P.L.1962, c. 152 (C.33:1–12.31 et seq.).

Club license. 5. The holder of this license shall be entitled, subject to rules and regulations, to sell any alcoholic beverages but only for immediate consumption on the licensed premises and only to bona fide club members and their guests. The fee for this license shall be fixed by the governing board or body of the municipality in which the licensed premises are situated, by ordinance, at not less than $63 and not more than $188. The governing board or body of each municipality may, by ordinance, enact that no club licenses shall be granted within its respective municipality. Club licenses may be issued only to such corporations, associations and organizations as are operated for benevolent, charitable, fraternal, social, religious, recreational, athletic, or similar purposes, and not for private gain, and which comply with all conditions which may be imposed by the Director of the Division of Alcoholic Beverage Control by rules and regulations.

The provisions of section 23 of P.L.2003, c. 117 amendatory of this section shall apply to licenses issued or transferred on or after July 1, 2003, and to license renewals commencing on or after July 1, 2003.

Amended by L.1942, c. 156, p. 460, § 1; L.1946, c. 272, p. 932, § 1; L.1951, c. 163, p. 632, § 1; L.1956, c. 215, p. 772, § 1; L.1957, c. 179, p. 620, § 1; L.1966, c. 180, § 1, eff. June 22, 1966; L.1967, c. 296, § 1, eff. Feb. 15, 1968; L.1968, c. 335, § 1, eff. Nov. 13, 1968; L.1969, c. 183, § 1, eff. Nov. 5, 1969; L.1976, c. 44, § 3, eff. June 30, 1976; L.1976, c. 54, § 1, eff. July 26, 1976; L.1985, c. 157, § 2, eff. April 26, 1985; L.1993, c. 198, § 1, eff. July 23, 1993; L.1993, c. 216, § 2, eff. July 30, 1993. Amended by L.1996, c. 83, § 1, eff. July 25, 1996; L.1997, c. 8, § 2, eff. Jan. 24, 1997; L.2003, c. 117, § 23, eff. July 1, 2003; L.2003, c. 279, § 1, eff. June 1, 2004; L.2009, c. 216, § 1, eff. May 1, 2010.

33:1–12a. Posting of fetal alcohol syndrome warning notices required

A person who holds a Class C license, except a plenary retail transit license, or a club license shall ensure that a warning notice prepared by the Department of Health is posted prominently in any service area as well as on a wall, towel dispenser or other appropriate location in any public rest room for women patrons on the licensed premises. The notice shall warn patrons that alcohol consumption during pregnancy has been determined to be harmful to the fetus and can cause birth defects, low birth weight and Fetal Alcohol Syndrome, which is one of the leading causes of mental retardation.

L.1993, c. 43, § 1, eff. Aug. 1, 1993.

33:1–12b. Fine imposed for failure to comply with posting requirements

A person who fails to comply with the provisions of this act may be subject to a fine of $50.

L.1993, c. 43, § 3, eff. Aug. 1, 1993.

33:1–12c. Sample, sampling and tasting event, defined

As used in this act:

"Sample" means a small amount of an alcoholic beverage.

"Sampling" means a licensee or permittee offering a sample to a consumer for the purpose of inducing or promoting a sale.

"Tasting event" means a scheduled event hosted by a licensee or permittee, at which samples may be provided, that may be open to the general public or limited by invitation.

L.2009, c. 216, § 2, eff. May 1, 2010.

33:1–12d. Samplings and tasting events on the premises of certain license holders; applicable terms and conditions; penalties

The following terms and conditions shall apply to consumer wine, beer, and spirits tasting events and samplings conducted by or on the premises of the holder of a plenary retail consumption license or plenary retail distribution license:

a. Samples shall not be offered to, or allowed to be consumed by, any person under the legal age for consuming alcoholic beverages or an intoxicated person;

b. Tasting events and samplings shall not be conducted when the sale of alcoholic beverages is otherwise prohibited;

c. Tasting events and samplings shall be confined to the licensed premises;

d. In any one calendar day, each consumer shall be limited to no more than four one-and-one-half ounce samples of wine, four three ounce samples of beer, or three one-half ounce samples of spirits;

e. Any supplier, manufacturer, importer, wholesaler, solicitor, or an authorized representative licensed or permitted by the division may participate in, assist with, and promote consumer wine, beer, and spirits tasting events up to two times per month at the licensed premises, but samples shall not be served by any employee of a wholesaler. A solicitor employed by a supplier, manufacturer or importer who holds a wholesale license, or an authorized representative licensed or permitted by the division, may serve samples at a tasting event;

f. Wine, beer, and spirits used in tasting events and samplings shall be owned by the plenary retail consumption or plenary retail distribution licensee;

g. Tasting events may be advertised in any type of media, including, but not limited to, print, radio, television, Internet, and signs, and these advertisements may include the date, time, and location of the event, such as the name and address of the licensed premises and other information regarding the event; and

h. A supplier, manufacturer, importer, wholesaler, solicitor, or authorized representative licensed or permitted by the division may provide the licensee upon whose premises the tasting event will be held with permissible advertising and promotional materials for use at the event and permissible consumer novelties for distribution to the consumer attending the event.

Notwithstanding any other penalty that may be lawfully imposed, a person who violates subsections a. through h. of this section shall be fined an amount to be established by the director.

L.2009, c. 216, § 3, eff. May 1, 2010.

33:1–12.1. Repealed by L.1943, c. 47, § 1, eff. March 27, 1943

33:1–12.2 to 33:1–12.12. Void

33:1–12.13. Renewal licenses; new licenses

For the purposes of this act [1] any license for a new license term, which is issued to replace a license which expired on the last day of the license term which immediately preceded the commencement of said new license term or which is issued to replace a license which will expire on the last day of the license term which immediately precedes the commencement of said new license term, shall be deemed to be a renewal of the expired or expiring license; *provided*, that said license is of the same class and type as the expired or expiring license, covers the same licensed premises, is issued to the holder of the expired or expiring license and is issued pursuant to an application therefor which shall have been filed with the proper issuing authority prior to the commencement of said new license term or not later than thirty days after the commencement thereof. Licenses issued otherwise than as above herein provided shall be deemed to be new licenses.

L.1947, c. 94, p. 501, § 1.

[1] N.J.S.A. §§ 33:1–12.13 to 33:1–12.22.

33:1–12.14. Limitation on number of new retail licenses in municipality

Except as otherwise provided in this act, no new plenary retail consumption or seasonal retail consumption license shall be issued in a municipality unless and until the combined total number of such licenses existing in the municipality is fewer than one for each 3,000 of its population according to the most recent estimates issued by the U.S. Bureau of the Census; provided, however, in the year that the official federal decennial counts are received by the Governor, those federal decennial counts shall be used. No new plenary retail distribution license shall be issued in a municipality unless and until the number of such licenses existing in the municipality is fewer than one for each 7,500 of its population according to the most recent estimates issued by the U.S. Bureau of the Census; provided, however, in the year that the official federal decennial counts are received by the Governor, those federal decennial counts shall be used.

L.1947, c. 94, p. 502, § 2. Amended by L.1960, c. 72, p. 514, § 1, eff. June 23, 1960; L.1969, c. 170, § 1; L.1971, c. 196, § 1; L.1999, c. 189, § 1, eff. Aug. 31, 1999.

33:1–12.15. Municipalities under 1000, licenses in

Nothing in this act shall prevent the issuance and existence of one plenary or seasonal retail consumption license and one plenary retail distribution license in a municipality whose population as shown by the last then preceding Federal census is less than one thousand.

L.1947, c. 94, p. 502, § 3.

33:1–12.16. Renewal or transfer of existing licenses

Nothing in this act shall prevent the renewal of licenses existing on the effective date of this act, or the transfer of such licenses or the renewal of licenses so transferred.

L.1947, c. 94, p. 502, § 4.

33:1–12.17. Seasonal retail consumption licenses to persons who had licenses in previous season; transfer

Nothing in this act [1] shall be deemed to prevent the issuance of a new seasonal retail consumption license to a person who held such a license in the municipality for the same premises, and for the same seasonal period, during the then next preceding summer or winter season, nor shall anything in this act prevent the transfer of such a license so issued.

L.1947, c. 94, p. 502, § 5.

[1] N.J.S.A. §§ 33:1–12.13 to 33:1–12.22.

33:1–12.18. New license on failure to renew; filing fee

Nothing in this act shall be deemed to prevent the issuance of a new license to a person who files application therefor within 60 days following the expiration of the license renewal period if the director shall determine in writing that the applicant's failure to apply for a renewal of his license was due to circumstances beyond his control.

Any request for relief under this section shall be accompanied by a nonreturnable filing fee of $100.00 payable to the director.

L.1947, c. 94, p. 502, § 6. Amended by L.1992, c. 188, § 7, eff. Dec. 16, 1992.

33:1–12.19. New license where licensee served in armed forces

Nothing in this act shall prevent the issuance, in a municipality, of a new license to a person who, having held a license of the same class in the municipality, surrendered his license or permitted it to expire because of his induction into or service in the armed forces of the United States; *provided, however,* that such ex-licensee shall have filed the application for a new license within one year from the completion of his active service in said armed forces.

L.1947, c. 94, p. 502, § 7.

33:1–12.20. Hotel or motel operator, new license to

a. Nothing in this act shall prevent the issuance, in a municipality, of a new license to a person who operates a hotel or motel containing 100 guest sleeping rooms or who may hereafter construct and establish a new hotel or motel containing at least 100 guest sleeping rooms.

b. A person who holds a license issued pursuant to subsection a. of this section and who has been required by law to reduce the number of sleeping rooms in the hotel may continue to hold the license if the hotel has at least 75 sleeping rooms, has been in continuous operation for at least 120 years in the same building, and is listed in the National Register of Historic Places.

c. (1) After the effective date of P.L.2009, c. 83, a minimum bid not to exceed $25,000 plus $50 per sleeping room may be required for the issuance of a license pursuant to the provisions of this section if the dining facilities of the hotel or motel are regularly and principally used to provide only meals for catered events and breakfast for guests of the hotel or motel.

(2) This subsection shall not be construed to prohibit a municipality from requiring a minimum bid for any license issued under the provisions of this section to a hotel or motel that does not meet the criteria set forth in paragraph (1) of this subsection.

L.1947, c. 94, p. 502, § 8. Amended by L.1968, c. 359, § 1, eff. Jan. 1, 1969; L.2000, c. 160, § 1, eff. Dec. 1, 2000; L.2009, c. 83, § 1, eff. July 2, 2009.

33:1–12.20a. Licenses contingent on completion of construction; rights of holder

Nothing in this act shall affect the right of the holder of any license issued or approved for issuance, contingent on completion of construction for a hotel or motel premises to use and to renew such license.

L.1968, c. 359, § 2, eff. Jan. 1, 1969.

33:1–12.21. Municipal regulations limiting number of license, act is in addition to

This act is in addition to and not in exclusion of municipal regulations, limiting the number of licenses to sell alcoholic beverages at retail, duly adopted pursuant to the authority granted by section 33:1–40 of the Revised Statutes.

L.1947, c. 94, p. 503, § 9.

33:1–12.22. Effective date

This act shall take effect May fifteenth, one thousand nine hundred and forty-seven.

L.1947, c. 94, p. 503, § 10.

33:1–12.22a. License transferred to spouse and surrendered during licensee's service in armed forces; new license

Nothing in the act [1] to which this act is a supplement shall prevent the issuance, in a municipality, of a new license to sell alcoholic beverages at retail, to a person who, having served honorably in the armed forces of the United States and having held a license of the same class in the municipality, transferred said license to his spouse within the last past fifteen years and having served some time during said fifteen years in the armed forces of the United States, and whose spouse, during his service in the armed forces of the United States, surrendered said license or permitted it to expire; *provided,* that no license of the same class has been issued in said municipality since the surrender or expiration of said license; *and provided further,* that such person has filed or shall file his application for a new license within one year from the effective date of this act.

L.1950, c. 145, p. 298, § 1, eff. May 26, 1950.

   [1] N.J.S.A. §§ 33:1–1 to 33:1–96.

33:1–12.22b. Sixth class counties; retail licensees who served in armed forces and permitted license to lapse; issuance of license

In any county of the sixth class, any person who held a license to sell alcoholic beverages at retail for a period of two years prior to serving in the armed forces of the United States and who permitted said license to lapse, may apply for such license from the municipality originally issuing the same, and such municipality may, if the applicant is otherwise eligible for such license, issue the same regardless of any jurisdictional dispute between such municipality and an adjoining municipality as to boundary lines; *provided,* that application for said license is made or has been made within six months of the honorable discharge of the applicant from the armed forces of the United States.

L.1950, c. 145, p. 298, § 2.

33:1–12.23. Sale and display for off-premises consumption

The holder of a plenary retail consumption license or a seasonal retail consumption license, after the effective date of this act, may sell and display for sale alcoholic beverages in original containers for consumption off the licensed premises only in the public barroom of the licensed premises, such barroom being a room containing a public bar, counter or similar piece of equipment designed for and used to facilitate the sale and dispensing of alcoholic beverages by the glass or other open receptacle for consumption on the licensed premises; *provided, however*, that where, prior to the effective date of this act, alcoholic beverages in original containers for off-premises consumption were sold and displayed for sale by the holder of such license, either to the exclusion of sale for consumption on the licensed premises or upon a portion of the licensed premises other than the public barroom, such sale and display shall be permitted as heretofore and notwithstanding renewal or transfer of the license either from person to person or place to place, subject to rules and regulations to be promulgated by the commissioner.

L.1948, c. 98, p. 552, § 1, eff. May 28, 1948.

33:1–12.24. Municipalities in which sale for consumption on premises is prohibited, effect of act in

Nothing in this act shall be deemed to limit the sale and display for sale of alcoholic beverages in original containers for consumption off the licensed premises to the public barroom on premises licensed under plenary retail consumption license or seasonal retail consumption license in any municipality in which the sale of alcoholic beverages by the glass or other open receptacle for consumption on the licensed premises is prohibited by law notwithstanding that, prior to such prohibition, such sale and display for sale was required to be limited to the public barroom.

L.1948, c. 98, p. 552, § 2.

33:1–12.25. Hotel guests, sale and delivery to

Nothing in this act shall be deemed to prohibit the lawful sale and delivery of alcoholic beverages in original containers by the holder of a plenary retail consumption license or seasonal retail consumption license issued for hotel premises to guests of the hotel in the regular course of business.

L.1948, c. 98, p. 553, § 3.

33:1–12.26. Renewal of expired or expiring license, what is; new licenses

For the purposes of this act [1] any license for a new license term, which is issued to replace a license which expired on the last day of the license term which immediately preceded the commencement of said new license term or which is issued to replace a license which will expire on the last day of the license term which immediately precedes the commencement of said new

license term, shall be deemed to be a renewal of the expired or expiring license; *provided*, that said license is of the same class and type as the expired or expiring license, covers the same licensed premises, is issued to the holder of the expired or expiring license and is issued pursuant to an application therefor which shall have been filed with the proper issuing authority prior to the commencement of said new license term or not later than thirty days after the commencement thereof. Licenses issued otherwise than as above herein provided shall be deemed to be new licenses.

L.1952, c. 284, p. 970, § 1, eff. May 23, 1952.

[1] N.J.S.A. §§ 33:1–12.26 to 33:1–12.29.

33:1–12.27. New limited retail distribution license; issuance

No new limited retail distribution license shall be issued in any municipality after this act becomes effective, except as provided in section four of this act.[1]

L.1952, c. 284, p. 970, § 2.

[1] N.J.S.A. § 33:1–12.29.

33:1–12.28. Renewal of existing limited retail distribution licenses

Nothing in this act shall prevent the renewal of limited retail distribution licenses existing on the effective date of this act, or the transfer of such licenses or the renewal of licenses so transferred.

L.1952, c. 284, p. 970, § 3.

33:1–12.29. New limited retail distribution license within 60 days after expiration of renewal period

Nothing in this act shall be deemed to prevent the issuance of a new limited retail distribution license to a person who files application therefor within sixty days following the expiration of the license renewal period if the State director shall determine in writing that the applicant's failure to apply for a renewal of his license was due to circumstances beyond his control.

L.1952, c. 284, p. 971, § 4.

33:1–12.30. Death of licensee and cessation of business; issuance of new license in place of voided license

In any municipality wherein not more than one retail consumption license and not more than one plenary retail distribution license may be issued pursuant to State law and wherein one license of either type or of each type is issued, if the holder of either type of license dies or shall have died and operation of the business ceases or shall have ceased during the license term and if no application for extension or transfer of the license is or shall have been filed within ninety days following the decease, the municipal issuing authority may by resolution void said license and thereafter it shall be lawful to issue in such municipality a new license of the same type as that of the license so voided.

L.1953, First Sp.Sess., c. 437, p. 2403, § 1, eff. Dec. 21, 1953.

33:1–12.31. Acquisition of beneficial interest in more than two retail licenses prohibited

On and after the effective date of this act no person, as the same is defined in R.S. 33:1–1, shall, except as hereinafter provided, acquire a beneficial interest in more than a total of two alcoholic beverage retail licenses, but nothing herein shall require any such person who has, on August 3, 1962, such an interest in more than two such licenses to surrender, dispose of, or release his interest in any such license or licenses.

L.1962, c. 152, § 1, eff. Aug. 3, 1962. Amended by L.1971, c. 217, § 1, eff. June 17, 1971.

33:1–12.32. Exceptions

The provisions of this act shall not apply to the acquisition of an additional license or licenses or an interest therein, when such license is issued to a person for use in connection with the operation of a hotel containing at least 50 sleeping rooms, for use in connection with the operation of a restaurant, for use in connection with the operation of a bowling establishment consisting of more than 20 lanes, but only so long as the person uses the license in connection with the operation of that bowling establishment, or for use on premises within the grounds of an international airport, nor shall the provisions of this act affect the right of any person to dispose of an interest in a license or licenses by will or to the transfer of such an interest by descent and distribution.

Any additional license acquired for use in connection with a restaurant or bowling establishment consisting of more than 20 lanes or for use on premises within the grounds of an international airport, as herein authorized, shall be limited, however, to the sale of alcoholic beverages for consumption on the licensed premises only.

L.1962, c. 152, § 2. Amended by L.1964, c. 220, § 1; L.1983, c. 91, § 1, eff. March 11, 1983; L.1985, c. 65, § 1, eff. March 5, 1985.

33:1–12.33. Inheritance of beneficial interest in retail license; time within which to comply with act

Whenever a person shall acquire a beneficial interest in a retail license from the estate of a decedent which results in such person having a beneficial interest in more than 2 licenses, the Director of Alcoholic Beverage Control shall, by order, prescribe a reasonable time within which such person shall comply with the provisions of this act and the holding of any such license or interest during the time permitted under such an order shall not constitute a violation of this act.

L.1962, c. 152, § 3.

33:1–12.34. Membership in organization holding club license

Membership in any organization which is or may become the holder of a club license shall not constitute acquisition of an interest in a retail license.

L.1962, c. 152, § 4.

33:1–12.35. Right to continue to hold, use and renew existing licenses

Nothing in this act shall affect the right of any holder of retail licenses heretofore acquired to continue to hold, use and renew such licenses.

L.1962, c. 152, § 5.

33:1–12.36. Corporate licenses

Nothing in this act shall affect (a) the right of any person having a beneficial interest in a retail license or licenses to hold or acquire an interest of not more than 10% of any corporation the shares of which are traded on a national securities exchange or regularly traded in an over-the-counter market by one or more members of a national or affiliated securities association or (b) the right of any person to hold or acquire an interest in a corporation from his parent or grandparent provided such child or grandchild does not have a beneficial interest in any retail license or licenses other than those held by the corporation.

L.1962, c. 152, § 6. Amended by L.1965, c. 197, § 1, eff. Dec. 17, 1965.

33:1–12.37. Violation; penalty

Any person violating any provision of this act or of any rule or regulation issued pursuant to this act shall be punished by a fine of not less than $50.00 and not more than $250.00 and such person shall also be subject to the penalties and provisions of chapter 1 of Title 33 [1] which are applicable thereto by virtue of such violation.

L.1962, c. 152, § 7. Amended by L.1964, c. 220, § 2.

[1] N.J.S.A. § 33:1–1 et seq.

33:1–12.38. Rules and regulations

The Director of the Division of Alcoholic Beverage Control may adopt from time to time such rules and regulations as shall be necessary or desirable to carry out the provisions of this act and of the act to which this act is a supplement.

L.1964, c. 220, § 3.

33:1–12.39. Class C license; renewal if not actively used within period of 2 years; filing fee

No Class C license, as the same is defined in R.S.33:1–12, shall be renewed if the same has not been actively used in connection with the operation of a licensed premises within a period of two years prior to the commencement date of the license period for which the renewal application is filed unless the director, for good cause and after a hearing, authorizes a further application for one or more renewals within a stated period of years; provided, however that, if the licensee has been deprived of the use of the licensed premises as a result of eminent domain, fire or other casualty, and establishes by affidavit filed with the director that he is making a good faith effort to resume active use of the license in connection with the operation of a licensed premise then the period of two years provided for in this section shall be automatically extended for an additional period of two years.

Any request for relief under this section shall be accompanied by a nonreturnable filing fee of $100.00 payable to the director.

L.1977, c. 246, § 1, eff. Oct. 3, 1977. Amended by L.1992, c. 188, § 8, eff. Dec. 16, 1992; L.1996, c. 127, § 1, eff. Nov. 20, 1996.

33:1–12.40. Legislative findings

The Legislature finds and declares that:

a. The retail alcoholic beverage industry is one of the most highly regulated industries of the State, controlled by a broad array of laws enacted by the Legislature and regulations promulgated by the Director of the Division of Alcoholic Beverage Control.

b. It is the public policy of this State, as set forth in section 4 of P.L.1985, c. 258 (C. 33:1–3.1), to strictly regulate alcoholic beverages to protect the health, safety and welfare of its citizens, to foster moderation and responsibility in the use and consumption of alcoholic beverages, to protect the collection of State taxes imposed upon alcoholic beverages, and to protect the interest of consumers against fraud and misleading practices in the sale of alcoholic beverages.

c. Participation in the alcoholic beverage industry as a licensee under Title 33 of the Revised Statutes is deemed a revocable privilege conditioned upon the proper and continued qualification of the licensee.

d. Notwithstanding the degree to which retail licensees are regulated, licensees are not required to demonstrate knowledge and understanding of the laws and regulations or their social responsibilities, for the purpose of obtaining or renewing the privilege to hold a retail alcoholic beverage license.

e. Since the alcoholic beverage industry was deregulated in 1980, market forces have impacted the retail industry to such an extent that a significant number of licenses have changed, and continue to change, hands and a large segment of new licensees have insufficient knowledge of their legal and social responsibilities.

f. These disruptive market forces and the numerous transfers of license ownership have occurred during a period of intensive legislative scrutiny of the industry, the enactment of many new laws and regulations, and the development of programs directed at the responsible sale and consumption of alcoholic beverages.

g. Retail alcoholic beverage licensees should be required to periodically demonstrate a knowledge and

understanding of the regulations, laws, and public policies of the State impacting upon their industry before their license privileges are renewed.

L.1991, c. 9, § 1, eff. Jan. 22, 1991.

33:1–12.41. Definitions

As used in this act:

"Division" means the Division of Alcoholic Beverage Control in the Department of Law and Public Safety.

"Director" means the Director of the Division of Alcoholic Beverage Control in the Department of Law and Public Safety.

L.1991, c. 9, § 2, eff. Jan. 22, 1991.

33:1–12.42. Persons required to complete educational program

If the Director determines to establish an educational program pursuant to section 4 [1] of this act, all holders of a plenary retail or limited retail distribution license issued under R.S. 33:1–12, or their designees pursuant to section 5 [2] of this act, shall be required to successfully complete the educational program prescribed in section 4 of P.L.1991, c. 9 (C. 33:1–12.43).

L.1991, c. 9, § 3, eff. Jan. 22, 1991.

[1] N.J.S.A. § 33:1–12.43.
[2] N.J.S.A. § 33:1–12.44.

33:1–12.43. Educational programs for plenary and limited retail distribution licensees; certificate of completion

The director may, in the director's discretion, establish initial and supplemental educational programs for plenary retail and limited retail distribution licensees and shall grant a certificate of completion when a licensee satisfactorily completes each program.

L.1991, c. 9, § 4, eff. Jan. 22, 1991.

33:1–12.44. Requirements of educational program

If an educational program is established by the director pursuant to section 4 of this act [1], the director shall by regulation determine:

a. The person or persons who may attend the educational programs as designees of the licensee;

b. The dates and geographic locations at which the programs shall be offered;

c. The penalties for failure to successfully complete the educational requirements;

d. The curriculum for the educational programs and the instructors or lecturers who shall conduct the programs; and

e. Registration fees to be charged licensees for attending initial and supplemental training programs.

L.1991, c. 9, § 5, eff. Jan. 22, 1991.

[1] N.J.S.A. § 33:1–12.43.

33:1–12.45. Contract with non-profit education organization to conduct educational program

In order to meet the requirements and intent of this act on the most cost effective basis, the director may contract with a non-profit educational organization chartered in this State to conduct all or part of the educational program. The registration fees collected may be used by the division to defray the cost of the programs. If the director contracts with a non-profit organization to conduct the educational programs, the programs shall be made available and reasonably accessible to all licensees.

L.1991, c. 9, § 6, eff. Jan. 22, 1991.

33:1–12.46. Time to complete educational program

All plenary retail and limited retail distribution licensees shall be required to successfully complete the initial educational program within nine months of the effective date of regulations establishing any educational program. The director shall determine the time schedule for successful completion of supplemental training programs.

L.1991, c. 9, § 7, eff. Jan. 22, 1991.

33:1–12.47. Presentation of certificate of completion required upon renewal of license

Upon application for renewal of any plenary retail or limited retail distribution license, the licensee shall present to the licensing authority the certificate of completion of the initial educational program and any supplemental programs which may have been required by the director under the time schedule established pursuant to section 7[1] of this act. The director shall determine penalties for failure to comply with this section.

L.1991, c. 9, § 8, eff. Jan. 22, 1991.

[1] N.J.S.A. § 33:1–12.46.

33:1–12.48. Rules and regulations

The director shall promulgate rules and regulations necessary to effectuate the purposes of this act pursuant to the "Administrative Procedure Act," P.L.1968, c. 410 (C. 52:14B–1 et seq.).

L.1991, c. 9, § 9, eff. Jan. 22, 1991.

33:1–12.49. Special permit for plenary retail consumption license; certain businesses in a qualifying development project; requirements

a. The Director of the Division of Alcoholic Beverage Control may issue one or more special permits to one or more individual corporations or other types of legal entities operating a restaurant on any premises located in a qualifying development project, as defined in subsection g. of this section.

b. Each permit may authorize the sale of alcoholic beverages on the operator's premises in accordance with an agreement, approved by the director, between the holder of a plenary retail consumption license pursuant to R.S.33:1–12 and the operator of those premises, which may provide for the terms and conditions of the management and operation of the premises and may establish legal liability and responsibility between the licensee and the operator for any violation of Title 33 of the Revised Statutes, provided that the licensee primarily shall be responsible for ensuring compliance with the terms and conditions of the permit and applicable statutes and regulations on the premises of the permit holders. In the case of a serious violation or a series of violations by an operator, the director also may impose penalties against the licensee which would result in a substantial revocation or suspension of the license.

c. The permits and plenary retail consumption license under which the permits were issued shall be subject to all the provisions of Title 33 of the Revised Statutes, rules and regulations promulgated by the director and municipal ordinances. Any violation by an operator may result in the denial of the renewal of the operator's permit. Any series of violations by multiple operators within the qualifying development project may result in the denial of the issuance of future permits or the renewal of existing permits.

d. No person who would fail to qualify as a licensee under Title 33 of the Revised Statutes shall be permitted to operate a licensed premises holding a special permit under this act.

e. Application for each permit shall be made on an annual basis and the administrative fee for the permit shall be fixed by the director. One–half of the administrative fee shall be allocated to the director and one-half of the administrative fee shall be allocated to the municipality in which the licensed premises is located. In addition, the initial administrative fee for a permit shall be based upon the average sales price for plenary retail consumption licenses recently sold in the county where the permit is being issued, reduced by the fair market value of the limitation on transferability, as set forth in subsection f. of this section.

f. No permit issued pursuant to this section shall be transferred to any premises other than a premises located within the same qualifying development project.

g. As used in this act, a "qualifying development project" means a real estate development project that:

(1) Is located in a municipality which lacks the anticipated number of plenary retail consumption licenses to be utilized within the real estate development project, as determined by the Director of the Division of Alcoholic Beverage Control;

(2) Is expected to generate directly or indirectly at least $250 million of private investments and more than $7.5 million annually in new sales and use tax revenue or hotel and motel occupancy fee revenue;

(3) Consists of at least 200 contiguous acres of land approved as a single unitary development by the planning board or zoning board of adjustment of the

municipality where the real estate development project is located;

(4) Is contiguous to a minimum 1,500 acres of land which, in the aggregate, have been either preserved by the operator of the real estate development project or sold or donated by the operator or adjacent landowners to the State for a public use purpose;

(5) Includes a ski area as defined in section 2 of P.L.1979, c. 29 (C.5:13–2); and

(6) Holds, through any entity having an interest in all or a part of the real estate development project, a plenary retail consumption license.

L.2006, c. 17, § 1, eff. Aug. 1, 2006.

33:1–13. Class D licenses; transportation license; fees

Class D licenses shall be as follows:

Transportation license. The holder of this license shall be entitled, subject to rules and regulations, to transport alcoholic beverages into, out of, through and within the State of New Jersey and to maintain a warehouse. The fee for this license shall be $625.

The provisions of section 24 of P.L.2003, c. 117 amendatory of this section shall apply to licenses issued or transferred on or after July 1, 2003, and to license renewals commencing on or after July 1, 2003.

Amended by L.1970, c. 78, § 3; L.2003, c. 117, § 24, eff. July 1, 2003.

33:1–14. Class E licenses; subdivisions; fees

Class E licenses shall be subdivided and classified as follows:

Public warehouse license. 1. The holder of this license shall be entitled, subject to rules and regulations, to receive for purposes of storing and warehousing and to store and warehouse alcoholic beverages in the licensed public warehouse; but this license shall not authorize the transportation of alcoholic beverages. The fee for this license shall be $500.

Broker's license. 2. The holder of this license shall be entitled, subject to rules and regulations, to act as a broker in the purchase and sale of alcoholic beverages for a fee or commission, for or on behalf of a person authorized to manufacture or sell at wholesale alcoholic beverages within or without the State. Such license shall not entitle the holder to buy or sell any alcoholic beverages for his own account, or take or deliver title to such alcoholic beverages, or receive or store any alcoholic beverages in his own name in this State, or offer, negotiate for the sale of or sell any alcoholic beverages to any wholesaler or retailer within this State; but such licensee shall be permitted, subject to rules and regulations, to use samples of alcoholic beverages in connection with the exercise of the privileges of such license. Such licensee's activities hereunder shall not be deemed to constitute a sale within the meaning of paragraph

"w" of section 33:1–1 of the Revised Statutes. The fee for this license shall be $500.

The provisions of section 25 of P.L.2003, c. 117 amendatory of this section shall apply to licenses issued or transferred on or after July 1, 2003, and to license renewals commencing on or after July 1, 2003.

Amended by L.1954, c. 26, p. 93, § 3; L.1955, c. 101, p. 560, § 1, eff. June 28, 1955; L.1970, c. 78, § 4; L.2003, c. 117, § 25, eff. July 1, 2003.

33:1–15. Separate license for each warehouse, salesroom or office

Any licensee entitled to maintain a warehouse or salesroom shall, if approved by the commissioner, secure a separate license for each additional warehouse or salesroom or separate office desired, and pay as a fee therefor twenty-five per cent of the fee paid for his license, each additional warehouse or salesroom or separate office being deemed a separate place of business.

33:1–16. One license for premises located in more than one municipality; division of fee; number of licenses

Whenever it shall appear that a building or premises to be licensed is located in more than 1 municipality, whether originally so constructed or whether resulting from enlargement or addition to the building or premises, it shall not be necessary to secure more than 1 license of the same class for the building or premises. Application may be made in 1 of the municipalities having jurisdiction over any part of the building or premises and said municipalities shall agree upon a satisfactory division of the fee. If the municipalities cannot agree upon a satisfactory division of the fee it shall then be the duty of the commissioner to determine the proportionate amount of the fee to be paid to each of the municipalities; but in no case shall the total fee to be paid exceed the higher license fee as fixed in any of the municipalities in which part of the building or premises is located. For the purpose of any statute fixing limits on the number of licenses which may be issued in a municipality, any license issued in compliance with this section shall be charged only to the municipality in whose name the same is issued.

Amended by L.1959, c. 67, p. 183, § 1, eff. June 3, 1959.

33:1–17. Licensee to give bond; custody of bonds

Before any Class A, Class B, Class D or Class E license shall be issued, each such licensee shall give a bond to the state of New Jersey, to be approved by the state tax commissioner as to form and amount, conditioned for the payment of all taxes, penalties and interest imposed by the laws of this state upon the sale or delivery of alcoholic beverages. Such bonds shall be transmitted to and be held by the state tax commissioner, and all such bonds heretofore received and now held by the commissioner of the department of alcoholic beverage control shall be transmitted forthwith to the state tax commissioner.

33:1–17.1. Issuance, renewal or transfer when licensee subject to review

An alcoholic beverage retail license or license that confers the right to sell alcoholic beverages to consumers shall not be issued, renewed or transferred unless the licensee, if subject to review in the prior calendar year pursuant to section 3 of P.L.1995, c. 161 (C. 54:50–28), or prospective licensee, if subject to review pursuant to section 3 of P.L.1995, c. 161 (C. 54:50–28), shall have been issued an alcoholic beverage retail licensee clearance certificate for the review period pursuant to section 3 of P.L.1995, c. 161 (C. 54:50–28).

L.1995, c. 161, § 2.

33:1–18. Commissioner to administer issuance of certain licenses

It shall be the duty of the commissioner to administer the issuance of manufacturers', wholesalers', plenary retail transit, transportation and public warehouse licenses, in accordance with this chapter.

33:1–19. Municipal board or body to administer issuance of certain licenses; "other issuing authority" construed

It shall be the duty of the governing board or body of each municipality, except in such municipalities as shall have created municipal boards pursuant to this chapter, in which latter event it shall be the duty of such respective municipal boards, to administer the issuance of all other licenses within their respective municipalities, in accordance with this chapter, and forthwith to report the issuance of all such licenses to the commissioner. The issuing authorities constituted by this section are sometimes hereinafter referred to as "other issuing authority".

33:1–19.1. New or additional retail licenses; issuance by municipality; procedure; notice

Whenever a municipality is authorized to issue one or more new or additional plenary retail consumption, seasonal retail consumption or plenary retail distribution licenses or a plenary retail consumption license acquired pursuant to section 3 of P.L.2007, c. 351 (C.33:1–24.3) and the governing body by resolution determines to permit the issuance thereof, the governing body shall cause to be published a notice of the proposed issuance of said license or licenses and that applications therefor will be accepted by the governing body or in municipalities having a municipal board of alcoholic beverage control or municipal excise commission, by the board or commission, as the case may be. The notice shall specify a time and date after which no further applications will be accepted. The notice shall be published in a newspaper circulating generally in the municipality by not less than two insertions, 1 week apart, the second of which shall be made not less than

30 days prior to the time and date specified in the notice as the time and date after which no further applications will be accepted.

L.1975, c. 275, § 1, eff. Jan. 12, 1976. Amended by L.2007, c. 351, § 4, eff. April 1, 2008.

33:1–19.2. Issuance of license after publication of notice

The provisions of this act shall not be construed to require the issuance of any license or licenses with respect to which a notice has been published pursuant to this act, but in any case in which any such license or licenses have not been issued within 6 months after the closing time and date for acceptance of applications specified in the notice, no such license or licenses shall be issued without again complying with the provisions of this act.

L.1975, c. 275, § 2, eff. Jan. 12, 1976.

33:1–19.3. Issuance to highest qualified bidder; public sale; qualifications

Whenever a municipality is authorized to issue one or more plenary retail consumption, seasonal retail consumption or plenary retail distribution licenses and the governing body determines to permit the issuance thereof, the governing body by resolution may authorize that such license or licenses be issued to the highest qualified bidder therefor and shall conduct a public sale for such purpose or direct that such a sale be conducted by the municipal board of alcoholic beverage control or municipal excise commission in a municipality where such board or commission exists. The governing body by resolution may also prescribe qualifications for prospective bidders including the requirement that a licensee, as a condition of the award of the license, shall operate a restaurant, public accommodation or other facility; provided, however, that no municipal license requirement is contrary or inconsistent with law, rule or regulation. The governing body may, by resolution, fix a minimum bid and conditions of sale with the reservation of the right to reject all bids where the highest bid is not accepted.

L.1981, c. 416, § 1, eff. Jan. 9, 1982.

33:1–19.4. Bids; notice and invitation; publication; contents; announcement of qualified applicants

If a governing body determines to conduct a sale pursuant to this act notice thereof and an invitation to bid shall be published in a newspaper circulating generally in the municipality by not less than two insertions, to be published not less than 1 week apart, and none to be published less than 30 days prior to the date of the sale. The notice shall also specify that any prospective bidder shall apply and qualify for a license prior to the sale, that proof of qualification for a license shall be included with the bid, and that all bids shall be sealed. The notice shall also specify, as determined by governing body resolution, the minimum acceptable bid, any special requirements for prospective licensees, general conditions of sale including the statement that the municipality reserves the right to reject all bids where the highest bid is not accepted. The notice shall specify the time and place at which bids shall be received and opened and that all prospective bidders shall qualify no later than 5 business days prior to the opening of bids. The agent for the municipal governing body, municipal board of alcoholic beverage control, or municipal excise commission, as the case may be, shall 5 days prior to opening the bids, publicly announce those applicants who meet the qualifications for bidding as fixed by law, rules and regulations, and resolution. No bid shall be opened from or on behalf of any prospective bidder who does not qualify. No bid shall be considered which does not contain proof of qualification.

L.1981, c. 416, § 2, eff. Jan. 9, 1982.

33:1–19.5. Issuance of license or rejection of all bids; postponement or cancellation of sale; disposition of funds

Upon the conclusion of a sale the issuing authority shall issue a license to the highest qualified bidder therefor upon payment of his bid and the license fee, or shall reject all bids if the highest bid is not accepted. A sale may be postponed or canceled at any time prior to the opening of the bids. Funds derived from the conduct of a sale shall be remitted to the municipal treasurer for the general use of the municipality.

L.1981, c. 416, § 3, eff. Jan. 9, 1982.

33:1–19.6. Inapplicability of act to powers of issuing authority; appeals

Nothing in this act shall limit or restrict any issuing authority in the reasonable exercise of any of its powers over the issuance of alcoholic beverage licenses and no appeal shall lie from any action of the issuing authority under the provisions of this act except where the ground for such appeal is that the appellant had qualified as a bidder and submitted a higher bid than the successful applicant.

L.1981, c. 416, § 4, eff. Jan. 9, 1982.

33:1–19.7. Plenary retail consumption license for nonprofit musical or theatrical corporations

It shall be lawful for the governing board or body of any municipality, upon the approval of the Director of the Division of Alcoholic Beverage Control, to issue a plenary retail consumption license to a nonprofit corporation, which conducts musical or theatrical performances or concerts on premises with a seating capacity of 1,000 persons or more, authorizing the sale of alcoholic beverages by the nonprofit corporation or its restaurant operator who has been approved pursuant to procedures established by the Division of Alcoholic Beverage Control for consumption on the licensed premises only during performances and the two hours immediately preceding and the two hours immediately following performances.

For the purposes of this section, "licensed premises" shall include the premises where the musical or theatrical performance or concert is held and any adjacent premises owned and operated by the licensee.

A license issued under the provisions of this act shall not be counted in determining the number of licenses under P.L.1947, c. 94 (C.33:1–12.13 et seq.) or under P.L.1968, c. 277 (C.40:48–2.40 et seq.).

L.1985, c. 151, § 1, eff. April 25, 1985. Amended by L.1994, c. 18, § 1, eff. April 11, 1994.

33:1–20. License to member of issuing authority issued only by director; additional fee

No license other than a club license shall be issued under this chapter by any issuing authority to any member thereof or to any corporation, organization or association in which any member thereof is interested directly or indirectly; but in any such case application for such license may be made by such member, corporation, organization or association directly to the director who is hereby authorized to issue such license, subject to rules and regulations, upon the same terms and conditions and for the same fee as other licenses of the same class are issued or are issuable by the said governing board or body. In addition to the fee for such license, which shall be payable to the municipality, a fee of $50.00 shall be payable to the director to be accounted for by him as are license fees.

Amended by L.1970, c. 77, § 1, eff. May 29, 1970; L.1976, c. 44, § 4, eff. June 30, 1976.

33:1–21 to 33:1–21.15. Repealed by L.1942, c. 159, § 1, eff. May 6, 1942

33:1–22. Appeal to director from action of issuing authority respecting license; procedure

If the other issuing authority shall refuse to issue any license, or if the other issuing authority shall refuse to extend the license for a limited time not exceeding its term, to the executor or administrator of a deceased licensee, or to a person who shall be appointed by the courts having jurisdiction, in the event of the incompetency of any licensee, the applicant shall be notified forthwith of the refusal by a notice served personally upon the applicant, or sent to him by registered mail addressed to him at the address stated in the application. The applicant may within 30 days after the date of service or of mailing of the notice, upon payment to the director of a nonreturnable filing fee of $100.00, appeal to the director from the action of the issuing authority. If the other issuing authority shall issue a license, or grant an extension of the license for a limited time not exceeding its term, to the executor or administrator of a deceased licensee, or to a person who shall be appointed by the courts having jurisdiction, in the event of the incompetency of any licensee, any taxpayer or other aggrieved person opposing the issuance of the license may, within 30 days after the issuance of the license, upon payment to the director of a nonreturnable filing fee of $100.00, appeal to the director from the action of the issuing authority. The director shall fix a time for the hearing of the appeal and before hearing the same, shall give at least five days' notice of the time so fixed to the applicant, taxpayer, or other aggrieved person and other issuing authority.

Where an appeal is taken from the denial of an application for a renewal of a license, the director may, in his discretion, issue an order upon the respondent issuing authority to show cause why the term of the license should not be extended pending the determination of the appeal, together with ad interim relief extending the term of the license pending the return of the order to show cause. If it shall appear upon the return of the order to show cause that the action of the respondent issuing authority is prima facie erroneous and that irreparable injury to the appellant would otherwise result, the director may, subject to conditions as he may impose, order that the term of the license be extended pending a final determination of the appeal.

Amended by L.1946, c. 316, p. 1028, § 1, eff. May 6, 1946; L.1971, c. 9, § 1, eff. Jan. 18, 1971; L.1992, c. 188, § 2, eff. Dec. 16, 1992.

33:1–23. Enumeration of duties of commissioner

It shall be the duty of the commissioner to administer and enforce this chapter and administer the department of alcoholic beverage control; to make an annual report to the governor of the activities of his department; to investigate applicants for Class A, Class B, Class D, Class E, and plenary retail transit licenses, and all licensees, and to inspect all licensed premises; to conduct hearings in accordance with this chapter; to make and conduct searches, seizures and forfeitures in accordance with this chapter; to dispose of articles seized and forfeited; to maintain proper records; to maintain a petty cash fund not in excess of one thousand dollars; to requisition the purchase of necessary supplies and equipment; to co-operate with municipalities and municipal boards in enforcing this chapter; to keep full and correct minutes; to publish lists of all licenses issued; and to do, perform, take and adopt all other acts, procedures and methods designed to insure the fair, impartial, stringent and comprehensive administration of this chapter.

The enumeration of the above specific duties shall not be construed to limit or restrict in any way the general authority given by this chapter to the commissioner.

33:1–23.1. Regulation by Commissioner of sales in violation of fair trade contract

The State Commissioner of Alcoholic Beverage Control is hereby vested with the following powers to be exercised in such manner as will assist in properly supervising the liquor industry and promoting temperance: The commissioner may, in his discretion, by rule or regulation, prohibit or regulate the sale of alcoholic beverages within this State in violation of any fair trade contract entered into pursuant to the legislative sanction afforded by Revised Statutes, Title 56, chapter four.

L.1938, c. 208, p. 492, § 1.

33:1–24. Duties of municipal authorities issuing licenses

It shall be the duty of each other issuing authority to receive applications for such licenses as such other issuing authority is authorized to issue; to investigate applicants and to inspect premises sought to be licensed; to conduct public hearings on applications and revocations; to enforce primarily the provisions of this chapter and the rules and regulations so far as the same pertain or refer to or are in any way connected with retail licenses, except plenary retail transit licenses; to maintain proper records; to keep full and correct minutes; and to do, perform, take and adopt all other acts, procedures and methods designed to insure the fair, impartial, stringent and comprehensive administration of this chapter. The enumeration of the above specific duties shall not be construed to limit or restrict in any way the general authority given by this chapter to each said other issuing authority.

33:1–24.1. Legislative findings and declarations; issuance of special licenses within a smart growth communities

The Legislature finds and declares that:

a.   Smart growth is an innovative approach to land use planning that directs the State's resources and funding to projects that enhance the quality of life for New Jersey residents;

b.   Smart growth encourages the development of distinctive, attractive communities with mixed use development, walkable town centers and neighborhoods, a range of housing options, and a variety of transportation modes;

c.   Small businesses, including restaurants and other establishments that serve alcoholic beverages, enhance the economic viability of a smart growth community and the quality of life for residents and visitors;

d.   Many municipalities in New Jersey do not have a sufficient number of liquor licenses for all the establishments that wish to serve alcoholic beverages to patrons; and

e.   In order to foster and encourage development in smart growth communities, it is appropriate to create special licenses to serve alcoholic beverages for establishments located in smart growth projects and to provide financial compensation to alcoholic beverage licensees in those communities who already have established businesses and paid market value for their licenses.

L.2007, c. 351, § 1, eff. April 1, 2008.

33:1–24.2. Definitions; director authority to issue additional special licenses; licensee qualifications; application fees

a. As used in this act:

"Smart growth development project" or "project" means a development project that:

(1) Is located in smart growth area as defined in section 1 of P.L.2004, c. 89 (C.52:27D–10.2); is expected to generate, directly or indirectly, at least $50 million of private investments and more than $25 million annually in new sales and use tax revenue; and consists of at least five acres of land under the control of a developer; or

(2) Is expected to increase the value of all taxable property in a municipality by not less than 40% over the value of that property for the previous tax year as shown in column six of the abstract of ratables.

b. The Director of the Division of Alcoholic Beverage Control, upon approval of the municipality, may issue one or more special licenses to one or more individual corporations or other types of legal entities operating a premises where alcoholic beverages are intended to be served that is located in a smart growth development project. The license shall authorize the sale of alcoholic beverages for immediate consumption on the operator's premises. If the project is located within the boundaries of two or more municipalities, each municipality shall approve the issuance of the license or licenses. The director may issue not more than 566 such licenses.

c. No person who would fail to qualify as a licensee under Title 33 of the Revised Statutes shall be permitted to hold an interest in a special license under the provisions of this section.

d. Licenses shall be subject to all the provisions of Title 33 of the Revised Statutes, rules and regulations promulgated by the director and municipal ordinances.

e. No license issued pursuant to this section shall be transferred to any premises other than a premises located within the same smart growth development project.

f. Application for the initial issuance and renewal of each license shall be made to the director on an annual basis. The fee for the initial issuance of the license shall be two and one half times the average sale price for the three most recent sales of plenary retail consumption licenses in the municipality where the license is being issued during the preceding five years. If the project is located within the boundaries of two or more municipalities, the highest average sale price of the two or more municipalities shall be used. If less than three plenary retail consumption licenses have been sold in the municipality or municipalities, as the case may be, within the previous five years, the municipality or municipalities, as the case may be, shall obtain an appraisal, at the applicant's expense, to determine the appropriate fee for the license. The appraisal process shall include an examination of previous transactions in the municipality or municipalities, as the case may be, and shall reflect what a willing buyer, under no pressure to buy, would pay a willing seller, under no pressure to sell, for a plenary retail consumption license in that municipality or municipalities, as the case may be. One half of the amount of the application fee for the initial issuance of the license shall be paid upon the issuance of the license and the other half of that amount shall be paid one year later. The director shall establish an annual fee for the license which shall not exceed the fee which may be imposed by a municipality for a plenary retail consumption license pursuant to R.S.33:1–12.

g. The fee for the initial issuance of the license shall be distributed in the following manner:

(1) Twenty-five percent shall be paid to the municipality wherein the smart growth development project is located and if the project is located within the boundaries of two or more municipalities, the fee shall be divided equally among those municipalities;

(2) Twenty-five percent shall be paid to the Director of the Division of Alcoholic Beverage Control;

(3) Fifty percent shall be divided equally among and paid to the plenary retail consumption licensees in the municipality or municipalities where the licensed premises will be located.

h. If the individual corporation or entity holding the license determines to sell a license issued pursuant to this section, the license shall be sold for the sum paid pursuant to paragraph (3) of subsection g. of this section.

i. The director shall not issue a special concessionaire permit for any location or premises which is eligible to obtain a license to serve alcoholic beverages under the provisions of this act. [1]

j. Pursuant to the "Administrative Procedure Act," P.L.1968, c. 410 (C.52:14B–1 et seq.), the director shall adopt rules and regulations to effectuate the purposes of this act.

L.2007, c. 351, § 2, eff. April 1, 2008.

[1] L.2007, c. 351, (N.J.S.A. § 33:1–24.1 to 33:1–24.3).

33:1–24.3. Urban enterprise zones; sale or transfer of inactive plenary retail consumption licenses

a. Notwithstanding the provisions of section 1 of P.L.1977, c. 246 (C.33:1–12.39), a municipality in which is located an urban enterprise zone as designated pursuant to P.L.1983, c. 303 (C.52:27H–60 et al.) or any supplement thereto, and a Planning Area 1 (Metropolitan), as designated pursuant to the "State Planning Act," sections 1 through 12 of P.L.1985, c. 398 (C.52:18A–196 et seq.), may acquire any existing plenary retail consumption licenses within the municipality that are inactive and retain any such licenses in an inactive status for a period of up to five years.

b. A municipality subject to the provisions of subsection a. of this section may issue at public sale one or more of any such inactive plenary retail consumption licenses in a manner consistent with the provisions of P.L.1975, c. 275 (C.33:1–19.1 et seq.), to no more than one corporation or legal entity for each such plenary retail consumption license for use only at a licensed premises that shall be located in a development project within a smart growth area, as defined in section 1 of P.L.2004, c. 89 (C.52:27D–10.2), in the municipality. The use of any such plenary retail consumption license shall be an a manner consistent with the provisions of Title 33 of the Revised Statutes and any regulations promulgated thereunder by the director.

L.2007, c. 351, § 3, eff. April 1, 2008.

33:1–25. Licensees; qualifications; applications; contents; corporations; partnerships; clubs; notice; publication

No license of any class shall be issued to any person under the age of 18 years or to any person who has been convicted of a crime involving moral turpitude. A beneficiary of a trust who is not otherwise disqualified to hold an interest in a license may qualify regardless of age so long as the trustee of the trust qualifies and the trustee shall hold the beneficiary's interest in trust until the beneficiary is at least the age of majority.

Each applicant shall submit to the director the applicant's name, address, fingerprints and written consent for a criminal history record background check to be performed. The director is authorized to receive criminal history record information from the State Bureau of Identification in the Division of State Police and the Federal Bureau of Investigation consistent with applicable State and federal laws, rules and regulations. The applicant shall bear the cost for the criminal history record background check, including all costs of administering and processing the check. The Division of State Police shall promptly notify the director in the event a current holder of a license or prospective applicant, who was the subject of a criminal history record background check pursuant to this section, is arrested for a crime or offense in this State after the date the background check was performed.

In applications by corporations, except for club licenses, the names and addresses of, and the amount of stock held by, all stockholders holding 1% or more of any of the stock thereof, and the names and addresses of all officers and of all members of the board of directors must be stated in the application, and if one or more of the officers or members of the board of directors or one or more of the owners, directly or indirectly, of more than 10% of the stock would fail to qualify as an individual applicant in all respects, no license of any class shall be granted.

In applications for club licenses, the names and addresses of all officers, trustees, directors, or other governing official, together with the names and addresses of all members of the corporation, association or organization, must be stated in the application.

In applications by partnerships, the application shall contain the names and addresses of all the partners. No license shall be issued unless all of the partners would qualify as individual applicants.

A photostatic copy of all federal permits necessary to the lawful conduct of the business for which a State license is sought and which relate to alcoholic beverages, or other evidence in lieu thereof satisfactory to the director, must accompany the license application, together with a deposit of the full amount of the required license fee, which deposit to the extent of 90% thereof shall be returned to the applicant by the director or other issuing authority if the application is denied, and the remaining 10% shall constitute an investigation fee and be accounted for as other license fees.

Every applicant for a license that is not a renewal of an annual license shall cause a notice of the making of the application to be published in a form prescribed by rules and regulations, once per week for two weeks successively in a newspaper printed in the English language, published and circulated in the municipality in which the licensed premises are located; but if there shall be no such newspaper, then the notice shall be published in a newspaper, printed in the English language, published and circulated in the county in which the licensed premises are located. No publication shall be required with respect to applications for transportation or public warehouse licenses or with respect to applications for renewal of licenses.

The Division of Alcoholic Beverage Control shall cause a general notice of the making of annual renewal applications and the manner in which members of the public may object to the approving of the applications to be published in a form prescribed by rules and regulations, once per week from the week of April 1 through the week of June 1 in a newspaper printed in the English language published and circulated in the counties in which the premises of applicants for renewals of annual licenses are located. Any application for the renewal of an annual license shall be made by May 1, and none shall be approved before May 1.

Every person filing an application for license, renewal of license or transfer of license with a municipal issuing authority shall, within 10 days of such filing, file with the director a copy of the application together with a nonreturnable filing fee of $200.

Applicants for licenses shall answer questions as may be asked and make declarations as shall be required by the form of application for license as may be promulgated by the director from time to time. All applications shall be duly sworn to by each of the applicants, except in the case of applicants in the military service of the United States whose applications may be signed in their behalf by an attorney-in-fact holding a power of attorney in form approved by the director, and except in cases of applications by corporations which shall be duly sworn to by the president or vice-president. All statements in the applications required to be made by law or by rules and regulations shall be deemed material, and any person who shall knowingly misstate any material fact, under oath, in the application shall be guilty of a misdemeanor. Fraud, misrepresentation, false statements, misleading statements, evasions or suppression of material facts in the securing of a license are grounds for suspension or revocation of the license.

The provisions of section 26 of P.L.2003, c. 117 amendatory of this section shall apply to licenses issued or transferred on or after July 1, 2003, and to license renewals commencing on or after July 1, 2003.

Amended by L.1941, c. 97, p. 220, § 1; L.1942, c. 249, p. 676, § 1; L.1943, c. 46, p. 88, § 1; L.1960, c. 117, p. 614, § 1, eff. Aug. 23, 1960; L.1970, c. 77, § 2, eff. May 29, 1970; L.1973, c. 14, § 1, eff. Jan. 31, 1973; L.1975, c. 99, § 1, eff. July 1, 1975; L.1976, c. 44, § 5, eff. June 30, 1976; L.1992, c. 188, § 3, eff. Dec. 16, 1992; L.2003, c. 117, § 26, eff. July 1, 2003; L.2003, c. 199, § 18, eff. Dec. 24, 2003; L.2008, c. 56, § 1, eff. Aug. 5, 2008.

33:1–25.1. Peace officers; right to leadership or titular position in nonprofit organization with club license

Nothing within the provisions of Title 33 of the Revised Statutes or any regulation promulgated by the Division of Alcoholic Beverage Control in the Department of Law and Public Safety shall prohibit any regular police officer, peace officer or any other person whose powers or duties include the enforcement of the alcoholic beverage laws or regulations from assuming any leadership or titular position in any fraternal, veterans', religious, or similar type of nonprofit organization that is a club licensee.

L.1981, c. 267, § 1, eff. Aug. 24, 1981.

33:1–25.2. Nonprofit organization; use of name other than peace officer as licensee

Any nonprofit organization holding a club license shall name as the licensee a person other than a regular police officer, peace officer or any other person whose powers or duties include the enforcement of the alcoholic beverage laws or regulations.

L.1981, c. 267, § 2, eff. Aug. 24, 1981.

33:1–26. Term of license; prorated fee; separate licenses; license restrictions; extension of license; procedure on transfer of license; employment regulations; filing fee

All licenses shall be for a term of one year from July 1 in each year. The respective fees for any such license shall be prorated according to the effective date of the license and based on the respective annual fee as in this chapter provided. Where the license fee deposited with the application exceeds the prorated fee, a refund of the excess shall be made to the licensee. Licenses are not transferable except as hereinafter provided. A separate license is required for each specific place of business and the operation and effect of every license is confined to the licensed premises. No retail license of any class

shall be issued to any holder of a manufacturer's or wholesaler's license, and no manufacturer's or wholesaler's license shall be issued to the holder of a retail license of any class. Any person who shall exercise or attempt to exercise, or hold himself out as authorized to exercise, the rights and privileges of a licensee except the licensee and then only with respect to the licensed premises, shall be guilty of a misdemeanor.

In case of death, bankruptcy, receivership or incompetency of the licensee, or if for any other reason whatsoever the operation of the business covered by the license shall devolve by operation of law upon a person other than the licensee, the director or the issuing authority may, in his or its discretion, extend the license for a limited time, not exceeding its term, to the executor, administrator, trustee, receiver or other person upon whom the same has devolved by operation of law as aforesaid. Under no circumstances, however, shall a license, or rights thereunder, be deemed property, subject to inheritance, sale, pledge, lien, levy, attachment, execution, seizure for debts, or any other transfer or disposition whatsoever, except for payment of taxes, fees, interest and penalties imposed by any State tax law for which a lien may attach pursuant to R.S.54:49–1 or pursuant to the State Tax Uniform Procedure Law, R.S.54:48–1 et seq., or any similar State lien of tax, except to the extent expressly provided by this chapter.

On application made therefor setting forth the same matters and things with reference to the premises to which a transfer of license is sought as are required to be set forth in connection with an original application for license, as to the premises, and after publication of notice of intention to apply for transfer, in the same manner as is required in case of an application for license as to the premises, the director or other issuing authority may transfer, upon payment of a fee of 10% of the annual license fee for the license sought to be transferred, any license issued by him or it respectively to a different place of business than that specified therein, by endorsing permission upon the license.

On application made therefor setting forth the same matters and things with reference to the person to whom a transfer of license is sought as are required to be set forth in connection with an original application for license, which application for transfer shall be signed and sworn to by the person to whom the transfer of license is sought and shall bear the consent in writing of the licensee to the transfer, and after publication of notice of intention by the person to whom the transfer of license is sought, to apply for transfer in the same manner as is required in the case of an original application for license, the director or other issuing authority, as the case may be, may transfer any license issued by him or it respectively to the applicant for transfer by endorsing the license. The application and the applicant shall comply with all requirements of this chapter pertaining to an original application for license and shall be accompanied, in lieu of the license fee required on the original application, by a fee of 10% of the annual license fee for the license sought to be transferred, which 10% shall be retained by the director or other issuing authority, as the case may be, whether the transfer be granted or not, and accounted for as other license fees.

If the other issuing authority shall refuse to grant a transfer the applicant shall be notified forthwith of the refusal by a notice served personally upon the applicant, or sent to him by registered mail addressed to him at the address stated in the application, and the applicant may, within 30 days after the date of service or mailing of the notice, appeal to the director from the action of the issuing authority. If the other issuing authority shall grant a transfer, any taxpayer or other aggrieved person opposing the grant of the transfer may, within 30 days after the grant of the transfer, appeal to the director from the action of the issuing authority.

No person who would fail to qualify as a licensee under this chapter shall be knowingly employed by or connected in any business capacity whatsoever with a licensee. A person failing to qualify as to age or by reason of conviction of a crime involving moral turpitude may, with the approval of the director, and subject to rules and regulations, be employed by any licensee, but the employee if disqualified by age shall not, in any manner whatsoever serve, sell or solicit the sale or participate in the manufacture, rectification, blending, treating, fortification, mixing, processing or bottling of any alcoholic beverage; and further provided, that no permit shall be necessary for the employment in a bona fide hotel or restaurant of any person failing to qualify as to age so long as the person shall not in any manner whatsoever serve, sell or solicit the sale of any alcoholic beverage, or participate in the mixing, processing or preparation thereof. Each person seeking to be employed or connected in any business capacity whatsoever with a licensee shall submit to the director the applicant's name, address, fingerprints and written consent for a criminal history record background check to be performed. The director is authorized to receive criminal history record information from the State Bureau of Identification in the Division of State Police and the Federal Bureau of Investigation consistent with applicable State and federal laws, rules and regulations. The applicant shall bear the cost for the criminal history record background check, including all costs of administering and processing the check. The Division of State Police shall promptly notify the director in the event a current holder of a license or prospective applicant, who was the subject of a criminal history record background check pursuant to this section, is arrested for a crime or offense in this State after the date the background check was performed.

Any request for relief under this section shall be accompanied by a nonreturnable filing fee of $100.00 payable to the director.

Amended by L.1938, c. 297, p. 688, § 1; L.1941, c. 295, p. 431, § 1; L.1941, c. 405, p. 1035, § 1; L.1943, c. 152, p. 431, § 1; L.1955, c. 43, p. 157, § 1, eff. June 2, 1955; L.1970, c. 78, § 5; L.1973, c. 14, § 2, eff. Jan. 31, 1973; L.1973, c. 285, § 1, eff. Dec. 4, 1973; L.1992, c. 188, § 4, eff. Dec. 16, 1992; L.1993, c. 232, § 1, eff. Aug. 6, 1993; L.2003, c. 199, § 19, eff. Dec. 24, 2003.

33:1–26.1. Peace officers; employment in business licensed to sell alcoholic beverages

Nothing within the provisions of Title 33 of the Revised Statutes or any regulation promulgated pursuant thereto by the Division of Alcoholic Beverage Control in the Department of Law and Public Safety shall prohibit permanent, full-time members of municipal police departments or of county police departments from being employed, other than in the municipality, or in the county, as the case may be, for which they serve as police officers, by a business licensed to sell alcoholic beverages in this State.

A police officer so employed shall not, while engaged in the selling, serving, possessing or delivering of any alcoholic beverages:

a. Have in his possession any firearm; or

b. Wear or display any uniform, badge or insignia which would identify him as a police officer.

No police officer so employed shall be permitted to work in excess of 24 hours a week in any such establishment.

L.1982, c. 84, § 1, eff. July 23, 1982.

33:1–27. Payment of license fee required; exceptions

Any statute or exemption to the contrary notwithstanding, no license shall be issued to any person except upon payment of the full fee therefor or as above prorated; but no license shall be required and no fee charged in connection with the retail sale of alcoholic beverages for consumption on the premises where sold, when sold at any camp, post or regimental exchange duly organized under the regulations of the United States Army or Navy or Marine Corps or Coast Guard or when sold by any voluntary unincorporated organization of the Armed Forces operating a place for the sale of goods pursuant to the regulations promulgated by the Secretaries of the respective Departments of National Government under which the Armed Services operate or, if the consent of the State Military Board shall have been first obtained, under the State National Guard regulations.

Amended by L.1951, c. 74, p. 463, § 1; L.1952, c. 126, p. 472, § 1, eff. May 6, 1952; L.1992, c. 188, § 10, eff. Dec. 16, 1992.

33:1–28. Transportation of beverages by licensees in their own vehicles; transit insignia

Licensees, except public warehouse licensees, may transport alcoholic beverages in their own vehicles, solely, however, for their own respective business in connection with and as defined in their respective licenses, without possessing a transportation license; provided, however, that such vehicles while so used shall be marked in the manner prescribed for all vehicles authorized to transport alcoholic beverages as shall be provided in rules and regulations. Each vehicle so used shall bear a transit insignia to be furnished by the director at a fee of $50.00 each.

Amended by L.1942, c. 157, p. 463, § 1; L.1954, c. 26, p. 94, § 4; L.1959, c. 174, p. 709, § 1, eff. Dec. 1, 1959; L.1970, c. 78, § 6; L.1976, c. 44, § 6, eff. June 30, 1976; L.1992, c. 188, § 12, eff. Dec. 16, 1992.

33:1–28a. Special permit for temporary or emergency transportation of alcoholic beverages

The Director of the Division of Alcoholic Beverage Control or, pursuant to rules and regulations, any designated agent of the director, may issue a special permit for the temporary or emergency transportation of alcoholic beverages into or out of the State in any vehicle which is not otherwise so authorized in accordance with R.S. 33:1–28. The fee for these permits shall be $25.00 and, where a designated agent issues the permit, the agent may receive an additional surcharge in an amount to be fixed by the director.

L.1988, c. 67, § 1, eff. Nov. 1, 1988.

33:1–28.1 to 33:1–28.4. Repealed by L.2004, c. 102, § 2, eff. July 14, 2004

33:1–29. Regulation of use of alcoholic beverages by druggists and hospitals; sales to

Druggists and pharmacists duly registered under the laws of this state as such may, upon their respective registered premises as aforesaid, without license hereunder, purchase and use alcoholic beverages for the compounding of physicians' prescriptions and for the preparation of mixtures and medicines, unfit for use as beverages, and sell same after being so compounded or prepared, subject to rules and regulations; but they may not sell alcoholic beverages otherwise than as aforesaid and particularly shall not sell the same in either original containers or by glass or other open containers, except under a license obtained under this chapter permitting the same.

Hospitals may purchase and use alcoholic beverages for the compounding of physicians' prescriptions, and for the preparation of mixtures and medicines unfit for use as beverages, and for dispensing to patients in accordance with physicians' orders and prescriptions, without license therefor, subject to rules and regulations.

Wholesale licensees may sell alcoholic beverages, directly to druggists and pharmacists, registered as aforesaid, and to hospitals, for use as herein authorized, subject to rules and regulations.

The commissioner shall have and exercise the same powers of investigation and of prescribing rules and regulations with regard to the alcoholic beverages purchased, used, mixed, compounded or dispensed pursuant to this section as are by this chapter accorded to him in connection with the sale, distribution, rectification, blending, treating, fortifying, mixing, processing, warehousing and transportation of all alcoholic beverages.

33:1–30. Sale of alcohols unfit for use as beverages; preparations and products excepted; violations; misdemeanor

This chapter is not designed to prohibit sales of denatured alcohol and alcoholic mixtures or composition or articles of commerce containing alcohol which are unfit for use as beverages without license hereunder.

No provision of this chapter shall apply to alcohol intended for and actually used in the manufacture and sale of any of the following when they are unfit in fact for beverage purposes, namely:

a. Denatured alcohol produced and used pursuant to acts of congress and regulations promulgated thereunder.

b. Patent, proprietary, medicinal, pharmaceutical, antiseptic and toilet preparations.

c. Flavoring extracts, syrups and food products.

d. Scientific, chemical, mechanical and industrial products.

Any person who shall knowingly sell, use or transport any of the products enumerated in paragraphs "a", "b", "c" or "d" for beverage purposes, or who shall use, sell or transport any of the same under circumstances from which he might reasonably deduce the intention of the purchaser or consignee to use them for such purposes shall be guilty of a misdemeanor.

The commissioner shall have the power to investigate the sale, purchase, use and transportation of industrial alcohol as set forth above to the extent reasonably necessary to prevent conversion into alcoholic beverages fit for consumption.

33:1–31. Suspension or revocation of license; grounds; procedure; effect of revocation; refund of fees; surrender of license; appeal to commissioner

Any license, whether issued by the director or any other issuing authority, may be suspended or revoked by the director, or the other issuing authority may suspend or revoke any license issued by it, for any of the following causes:

a. Violation of any of the provisions of this chapter;

b. Manufacture, transportation, distribution or sale of alcoholic beverages in a manner or to an extent not permitted by the license or by law;

c. Nonpayment of any excise tax or other payment required by law to be paid to the State Tax Commissioner;

d. Failure to comply with any of the provisions of subtitle 8 of the Title Taxation (§ 54:41–1 et seq.);

e. Failure to have at all times a valid, unrevoked permit, license or special tax stamp, or other indicia of payment, of all fees, taxes, penalties and payments required by any law of the United States;

f. Failure to have at all times proper stamps or other proper evidence of payment of any tax required to be paid by any law of this State;

g. Any violation of rules and regulations;

h. Any violation of any ordinance, resolution or regulation of any other issuing authority or governing board or body;

i. Any other act or happening, occurring after the time of making of an application for a license which if it had occurred before said time would have prevented the issuance of the license; or

j. For any other cause designated by this chapter.

No suspension or revocation of any license shall be made until a five–day notice of the charges preferred against the licensee shall have been given to him personally or by mailing the same by registered mail addressed to him at the licensed premises and a reasonable opportunity to be heard thereon afforded to him.

A suspension or revocation of license shall be effected by a notice in writing of such suspension or revocation, designating the effective date thereof, and in case of suspension, the term of such suspension, which notice may be served upon the licensee personally or by mailing the same by registered mail addressed to him at the licensed premises. Such suspension or revocation shall apply to the licensee and to the licensed premises.

A revocation shall render the licensee and the officers, directors and each owner, directly or indirectly, of more than 10% of the stock of a corporate licensee ineligible to hold or receive any other license, of any kind or class under this chapter, for a period of two years from the effective date of such revocation and a second revocation shall render the licensee and the officers, directors and each owner, directly or indirectly, of more than 10% of the stock of a corporate licensee ineligible to hold or receive any such license at any time thereafter. Any revocation may, in the discretion of the director or other issuing authority as the case may be, render the licensed premises ineligible to become the subject of any further license, of any kind or class under this chapter, during a period of two years from the effective date of the revocation.

The director may, in his discretion and subject to rules and regulations, accept from any licensee an offer in compromise in such amount as may in the discretion of the director be proper under the circumstances in lieu of any suspension of any license by the director or any other issuing authority.

No refund, except as expressly permitted by section 33:1–26 of this Title, shall be made of any portion of a license fee after issuance of a license; but if any licensee, except a seasonal retail consumption licensee, shall voluntarily surrender his license, there shall be returned to him, after deducting as a surrender fee 50% of the license fee paid by him, the prorated fee for the unexpired term; provided, that such licensee shall not

have committed any violation of this chapter or of any rule or regulation or done anything which in the fair discretion of the director or other issuing authority, as the case may be, should bar or preclude such licensee from making such claim for refund and that all taxes and other set-offs or counterclaims which shall have accrued and shall have become due and payable to this State or any municipality, or both, have been paid. Such refund, if any, shall be made as of the date of such surrender. The surrender of a license shall not bar proceedings to revoke such license. The refusal of the other issuing authority to grant any refund hereunder shall be subject to appeal to the director within 30 days after notice of such refusal is mailed to or served upon the licensee. Surrenders of retail licenses shall be promptly certified by the issuing authority to the director. Surrender fees shall be accounted for as are investigation fees. If any licensee to whom a refund shall become due under the provisions of this section shall be indebted to the State of New Jersey for any taxes, penalties or interest by virtue of the provisions of subtitle 8 of the Title Taxation (§ 54:41–1 et seq.), it shall be the duty of the issuing authority before making any such refund, upon receipt of a certificate of the State Tax Commissioner evidencing the said indebtedness to the State of New Jersey, to deduct therefrom, and to remit forthwith to the State Tax Commissioner the amount of such taxes, penalties and interest.

In the event of any suspension or revocation of any license by the other issuing authority, the licensee may, within 30 days after the date of service or of mailing of said notice of suspension or of revocation, upon payment to the director of a nonreturnable filing fee of $100.00, appeal to the director from the action of the other issuing authority in suspending or revoking such license which appeal shall act as a stay of such suspension or revocation pending the determination thereof unless the director shall otherwise order. When any person files with any other issuing authority written complaint against a licensee specifying charges and requesting that proceedings be instituted to revoke or suspend such license, he may appeal to the director from its refusal to revoke or suspend such license or other action taken by it in connection therewith within 30 days from the time of service upon or mailing of notice to him of such refusal or action. The director shall thereupon fix a time for the hearing of the appeal and before hearing the same shall give at least five days' notice of the time so fixed to such licensee, other issuing authority and appellant.

Amended by L.1955, c. 80, p. 250, § 1, eff. June 17, 1955; L.1971, c. 9, § 2, eff. Jan. 18, 1971; L.1992, c. 188, § 11, eff. Dec. 16, 1992.

33:1–31.1. Automatic suspension of license upon conviction of violation; effect of appeal

Upon conviction of violation of any of the provisions of this chapter, any license held at the time of said conviction pursuant to this chapter by the person convicted or by any partnership of which he is then a member, or by any corporation of which he was a director or officer or stockholder owning ten per cent or more of the stock either at the time of the conviction or the violation resulting therein, shall suspend automatically and without notice. The pendency of an appeal from the conviction shall not affect the suspension which shall continue for the balance of the term of the license unless the commissioner, in his discretion and for good cause shown, shall otherwise order. Nothing herein contained shall bar proceedings pursuant to this chapter to revoke or suspend any license.

33:1–31.2. Removal of disqualification to hold license because of conviction of crime; application to commissioner; order of removal; effect; filing fee

Any person convicted of a crime involving moral turpitude may, after the lapse of five years from the date of conviction, apply to the commissioner for an order removing the resulting statutory disqualification from obtaining or holding any license or permit under this chapter. Whenever any such application is made and it appears to the satisfaction of the commissioner that at least five years have elapsed from the date of conviction, that the applicant has conducted himself in a law-abiding manner during that period and that his association with the alcoholic beverage industry will not be contrary to the public interest, the commissioner may, in his discretion and subject to rules and regulations, enter an order removing the applicant's disqualification from obtaining or holding a license or permit because of the conviction.

On and after the date of the entry of the order, the person therein named shall be qualified to obtain and hold a license or permit under this chapter, notwithstanding the conviction therein referred to, provided he is, in all other respects, qualified under this chapter.

Any request for relief under this section shall be accompanied by a nonreturnable filing fee of $100.00 payable to the director. Each applicant shall submit to the director the applicant's name, address, fingerprints and written consent for a criminal history record background check to be performed. The director is authorized to receive criminal history record information from the State Bureau of Identification in the Division of State Police and the Federal Bureau of Investigation consistent with applicable State and federal laws, rules and regulations. The applicant shall bear the cost for the criminal history record background check, including all costs of administering and processing the check. The Division of State Police shall promptly notify the director in the event a current holder of a license or employee or prospective applicant, who was the subject of a criminal history record background check pursuant to this section, is arrested for a crime or offense in this State after the date the background check was performed.

Amended by L.1938, c. 350, p. 878, § 1; L.1992, c. 188, § 5, eff. Dec. 16, 1992; L.2003, c. 199, § 20, eff. Dec. 24, 2003.

33:1–32. Conditions to issuance of license

Subject to rules and regulations, each issuing authority by resolution, first approved by the commissioner, may impose any condition or conditions to the issuance of any license deemed necessary and proper to accomplish the objects of this chapter and secure compliance with the provisions hereof, and all such licenses shall become effective only upon compliance with the conditions so stated and shall be revocable for subsequent violation thereof.

33:1–33. Refusal of license to persons failing to pay tax or license fee; bond or cash deposit

No license shall be issued to any person to whom a license shall have been issued under an act entitled "An act concerning the manufacture, distribution and sale of certain beverages having an alcoholic content and providing for licenses, regulations and fees in connection therewith and penalties for violations thereof," approved April twelfth, one thousand nine hundred and thirty-three (L.1933, c. 85, p. 176),[1] as amended and supplemented, or under this chapter, and who shall have failed to pay to this state or to any municipality of this state any tax, license fee or penalty which shall have accrued pursuant to the provisions of said act and of this chapter and of subtitle 8 of the title Taxation (§ 54:41–1 et seq.), unless such person shall have posted with the state tax commissioner, or the municipality, as the case may be, a cash deposit in an amount, or a bond in form, with sureties and in an amount satisfactory to the state tax commissioner, or the municipality, as the case may be, to secure the payment of said tax, license fee or penalty, and this provision shall remain in force and effect notwithstanding the repeal of any of the aforesaid laws.

1 Repealed by L.1934, c. 32.

33:1–34. Notice of change in facts set forth in application; corporations

Whenever any change shall occur in the facts as set forth in any application for license, the licensee shall file with the director and the other issuing authority, where applicable, a notice in writing of such change within 10 days after the occurrence thereof; said change, when so notified, shall thereupon become part of said application for license to the end that subsequent changes must likewise be so notified; but no notice need be given by corporate licensees of changes in stockholdings therein unless and until the aggregate of such changes, if made before the time of said application, would have prevented the issuance of the license.

Amended by L.1970, c. 77, § 3, eff. May 29, 1970.

33:1–35. Investigations, inspections, searches and examinations; examination of witnesses; subpoenas; procedure on failure to obey; powers of deputy directors

The Director of the Division of Alcoholic Beverage Control and each other issuing authority may make, or cause to be made, such investigations as he or it shall deem proper in the administration of this chapter and of any and all other laws now or which may hereafter be in force and effect concerning alcoholic beverages, or the manufacture, distribution or sale thereof, or the collection of taxes thereon, including the inspection and search of premises for which the license is sought or has been issued, of any building containing the same, of licensed buildings, examination of the books, records, accounts, documents and papers of the licensees or on the licensed premises.

Every applicant for a license, and every licensee, and every director, officer, agent and employee of every licensee, shall, on demand, exhibit to the director or other issuing authority, as the case may be, or to his or its deputies or investigators, or inspectors or agents all of the matters and things which the director of the division or other issuing authority, as the case may be, is hereby authorized or empowered to investigate, inspect or examine, and to facilitate, as far as may be in their power so to do, in any such investigation, examination or inspection, and they shall not in any way hinder or delay or cause the hindrance or delay of same, in any manner whatsoever. Investigations, inspections and searches of licensed premises may be made without search warrant by the director, his deputies, inspectors or investigators, by each other issuing authority and by any officer.

For the purpose of any investigation, examination or inspection, revocation, rule to show cause and every other proceeding authorized under this chapter or appropriate for its enforcement, the director, his deputy directors, attorneys and legal assistants designated to act on his behalf, and each other issuing authority may examine, under oath, any and all persons whatsoever and compel by subpoena the attendance of witnesses and the production of books, records, accounts, papers and documents of any person or persons and the director, his deputy directors, inspectors and investigators and each other issuing authority may take any oath or affirmation of any person to any deposition, statement, report or application required in the administration of this chapter, or of any and all other laws now or which may hereafter be in force and effect concerning alcoholic beverages, or the manufacture, distribution and the sale thereof, or the collection of taxes thereon.

The fees of witnesses required to attend before the director or other issuing authority shall be the same as those allowed to witnesses in the Superior Court.

The above enumerations of purposes and powers shall not be construed as exclusive and shall not limit such power to investigate, examine and subpoena for any purpose consonant with the administration and enforcement of this chapter.

If a person subpoenaed to attend any hearing refuses or fails to appear or to be examined, or to answer any question or to produce any books, records, accounts, papers and documents when ordered so to do by the director, the director or other issuing authority, as the case may be, may apply to the Superior Court to compel the person to comply forthwith with the subpoena, direction or order of the director or the other issuing authority, as the case may be.

Each deputy director shall have and exercise all the powers conferred by this chapter upon the director to the extent that the same shall be delegated to him by the director by rules and regulations.

One of such deputy directors shall be designated by the director with power to perform all of the duties of the director in case of his absence or inability to act for any cause and who shall also have authority to so act in the event of the death of the director until a successor has been appointed and qualified.

Amended by L.1943, c. 37, p. 74, § 1; L.1953, c. 32, p. 575, § 2, eff. March 19, 1953.

33:1–36. Service of subpoenas

Each chief of police, or other official who for the time being shall exercise the functions of the office of chief of police, of each municipality, shall, upon request of the commissioner, cause to be served any subpoena which may be directed to any person residing or being within such municipality. No fee shall be charged for this service by such chief of police or by the members of any municipal police department.

Subpoenas may also be served by any officer as hereinbefore defined, or by any deputy, agent or employee of the commissioner, or of the issuing authority, as the case may be.

33:1–37. Seal; authentication; fee; inspection of records; certification of facts and findings

The commissioner shall adopt an official seal. Copies of any act, rule, regulation, order or decision made by him and of any paper or papers filed in any office maintained by him, may be authenticated under said seal and when so authenticated shall be evidenced in all courts of this state of the same weight and force as the originals thereof. For authenticating any such copy he shall receive such fees as are fixed by him, commensurate with the reasonable cost of the services rendered, to be accounted for by him as in case of license fees, as hereinbefore provided. All records and files of the department shall be open for inspection, pursuant to rules and regulations.

The commissioner may certify under said seal any facts concerning the records and files of the department and said certificates shall be received as evidence in all courts of this state to prove the facts contained therein. The commissioner may certify under said seal any findings with respect to the physical properties, nature, flavor, specific gravity, purity, ingredients, proof and alcoholic content of any alcoholic beverage and that such findings are in an analysis made by a graduate chemist regularly employed by the department of alcoholic beverage control and said certificate shall be received as evidence to prove the facts contained therein.

33:1–38. Commissioner to hear appeals; powers on appeal; execution of orders

The commissioner is hereby empowered and it is his duty to hear and conduct all appeals provided for by this chapter and thereupon to render written decisions stating conclusions and reason therefor upon each matter so appealed, and enter orders pursuant thereto. Said decisions and orders shall be binding upon all persons and shall be honored and forthwith executed by the other issuing authority.

The commissioner is hereby authorized to order the other issuing authority to issue a license when and if, after a hearing on the appeal of an applicant therefor, the commissioner shall decide that a license was improperly refused or improperly revoked by the other issuing authority; to order the other issuing authority to suspend or revoke a license, or to forthwith terminate the suspension or cancel the revocation of a license, when and if, after a hearing on appeal, the commissioner shall reverse the decision of the other issuing authority; to establish procedure and rules; and to make all findings, rulings, decisions and orders as may be right and proper and consonant with the spirit of this chapter.

Where any order entered by the commissioner pursuant to any appeal taken under this chapter, except from the denial of a refund, is not honored and executed within ten days after the date thereof, it shall be deemed self-executed and shall have the same force and effect as though actually complied with by the other issuing authority.

33:1–39. Rules and regulations by commissioner; subjects covered

The commissioner may make such general rules and regulations and such special rulings and findings as may be necessary for the proper regulation and control of the manufacture, sale and distribution of alcoholic beverages and the enforcement of this chapter, in addition thereto, and not inconsistent therewith, and may alter, amend, repeal and publish the same from time to time.

Such rules and regulations may cover the following subjects: Specification of duties of holders of any office, position or employment in the department of alcoholic beverage control; instructions for municipalities and municipal boards; all forms necessary or convenient in the administration of this chapter; tax paid, licensed vehicle and other insignia; inspections, investigations, searches, seizures, findings and such activities as may become necessary from time to time; hours of sale; sales on credit; sales to defectives and habitual drunkards; out-of-door sales; limitation of sales, limitation of the quantity to be sold to a consumer for off-premises consumption, unfair competition; racketeering; prostitution; solicitation; disorderly houses; criminals; dis-

reputable characters; gambling, slot machines and gambling devices; control of signs and other displays on licensed premises; use of screens; identification of licensees and their employees; employment of aliens, minors and females; storage; warehouses; transportation; health and sanitary requirements; standards of cleanliness, orderliness and decency; sampling and analysis of products; standards of purity and labeling; records to be kept by licensees and availability thereof; practices unduly designed to increase consumption of alcoholic beverages; gifts of equipment, products and things of value; and such other matters whatsoever as are or may become necessary in the fair, impartial, stringent and comprehensive administration of this chapter.

Amended by L.1943, c. 154, p. 435, § 1, eff. April 8, 1943.

33:1–39.1. Reciprocal rules and regulations with other states

The commissioner may make such reciprocal rules and regulations and special rulings pertaining to any one or more states designated therein as may be necessary for the proper regulation and control of the manufacture, sale and distribution of alcoholic beverages and the enforcement of this chapter, in addition thereto and not inconsistent therewith, and alter, amend, repeal and publish the same from time to time.

33:1–39.2. Rules and regulations with respect to consumer sales

The Director of the Division of Alcoholic Beverage Control shall, in accordance with R.S. 33:1–39, make and promulgate such rules and regulations with respect to sales by licensees selling to consumers relative to the following subjects as will assist in properly supervising the alcoholic beverage industry and preventing discrimination in the alcoholic beverage industry:

(a) Gifts of things of value in connection with or as an inducement to the purchase of malt alcoholic beverages,

(b) Combination sales of malt alcoholic beverages of different brands, of different manufacturers, of different names or trade names, or combination sales of any alcoholic beverages and other merchandise,

(c) Publication and maintenance of prices at which malt alcoholic beverages may be sold within recognized trading areas or below which malt alcoholic beverages may not be sold within such areas.

L.1956, c. 110, p. 496, § 5, eff. July 1, 1956. Amended by L.1985, c. 258, § 2, eff. July 31, 1985.

33:1–40. Municipal regulation of number of retail licenses, hours of sale, etc.

The governing board or body of each municipality may, as regards said municipality, by ordinance, limit the number of licenses to sell alcoholic beverages at retail, but any such limitation adopted by ordinance or resolution prior to July first, one thousand nine hundred and thirty-seven, shall continue in full force and effect until repealed, amended or otherwise altered by ordinance. The governing board or body of each municipality may, as regards said municipality, by ordinance or resolution, limit the hours between which the sale of alcoholic beverages at retail may be made, prohibit the retail sale of alcoholic beverages on Sunday, and, subject to the approval of the commissioner first obtained, regulate the conduct of any business licensed to sell alcoholic beverages at retail and the nature and condition of the premises upon which any such business is to be conducted. The aforesaid limitations of number of licenses and of hours of sale shall be subject respectively to appeal to the commissioner, as hereinafter provided.

The governing board or body of each municipality may make, enforce, amend and repeal such ordinances as it may deem necessary to prevent the possession, sale, distribution and transportation of alcoholic beverages within its municipality in violation of this chapter.

The governing board or body of each municipality may, by ordinance, enact that no more than one retail license shall be granted to any person in said municipality and that said license shall cover only the licensed premises; but nothing herein contained shall operate to disqualify a guardian, executor, administrator, trustee, receiver, or any other fiduciary or court officer from obtaining or from holding more than one such license in different official capacities.

33:1–40.3. Sale for consumption off-premises of wine and malt alcoholic beverages in original container by retail consumption or distribution licensee; limitation for cities of first class

Whenever the sale of alcoholic beverages for consumption on the premises and off the premises or either thereof is authorized in any municipality by ordinance or rule or regulation of the Division of Alcoholic Beverage Control, by the holder of a retail consumption or retail distribution license, such ordinance or rule shall authorize the sale of wine and malt alcoholic beverages in original bottle or can containers for consumption off the premises on the same days and during the same hours as the sale of alcoholic beverages for consumption on the premises is permitted and authorized in the municipality. If a municipality has no ordinance or local law that authorizes the sale of alcoholic beverages for consumption on the premises, then the municipality may by ordinance authorize the sale of wine and malt alcoholic beverages in original bottle or can containers by retail distribution licensees any time between the hours of 12:30 p.m. and 6:30 p.m. on Sunday, in addition to such weekday hours as may be authorized by ordinance.

Notwithstanding the provisions of this section or any other law to the contrary, a city of the first class may establish by ordinance separate hours for:

(1) sales by each type of retail license set forth in R.S.33:1–12, and

(2) sales by such licensees for consumption on the premises and consumption off the premises.

All parts of ordinances and regulations of the Director of the Division of Alcoholic Beverage Control inconsistent with the provisions of this act are superseded to the extent of such inconsistency.

L.1971, c. 184, § 1. Amended by L.1973, c. 287, § 1; L.1981, c. 69, § 1; L.1991, c. 370, § 1, eff. Jan. 10, 1992; L.1997, c. 54, § 1, eff. April 1, 1997.

33:1–41. Appeal from limitation of number of retail licenses or hours of sale

If any person affected or who might be affected by any limitation of the number of licenses or of the hours between which sales of alcoholic beverages at retail may be made shall consider himself aggrieved thereby, he may appeal to the commissioner in respect thereto and thereupon the commissioner, after public hearing, may set aside, vacate and repeal the limitation complained of or change, alter, amend or otherwise modify the same.

33:1–42. Sale in public buildings of state or political subdivisions prohibited; exceptions

No sales of alcoholic beverages shall be made in any public buildings belonging to or under the control of the state or any political subdivision thereof except as to the national guard as hereinbefore provided, and except as permitted by the commissioner in specified cases and subject to rules and regulations.

33:1–43. Interest in both brewery, distillery or wholesaling, etc., and in retailing; prohibition

a. It shall be unlawful for any owner, part owner, stockholder or officer or director of any corporation, or any other person whatsoever interested in any way whatsoever in any brewery, winery, distillery or rectifying and blending plant, or any wholesaler of alcoholic beverages, to conduct, own either in whole or in part, or be directly or indirectly interested in the retailing of any alcoholic beverages in New Jersey except as provided in this chapter, and such interest shall include any payments or delivery of money or property by way of loan or otherwise accompanied by an agreement to sell the product of said brewery, winery, distillery, rectifying and blending plant or wholesaler.

b. It shall be unlawful for any owner, part owner, stockholder or officer or director of any corporation, or any other person whatsoever, interested in any way whatsoever in the retailing of alcoholic beverages to conduct, own either in whole or in part, or to be a shareholder, officer or director of a corporation or association, directly or indirectly, interested in any brewery, winery, distillery, rectifying and blending plant, or wholesaling or importing interest of any kind whatsoever.

No interest in the retailing of alcoholic beverages shall be deemed to exist by reason of the ownership, delivery or loan of interior signs designed for and exclusively used for advertising the product of or product offered for sale by such brewery, winery, distillery or rectifying and blending plant or wholesaler.

c. Nothing in this section shall prohibit:

(1) The exercise of limited retail privileges by Class A or Class B licensees conferred pursuant to R.S. 33:1–10, R.S. 33:1–11, by rule or regulation or by special permit issued by the director;

(2) Any owner, part owner, stockholder, officer or director of any corporation, or any other person whatsoever interested in any way whatsoever in any brewery, winery, distillery, rectifying and blending plant or any wholesaler of alcoholic beverages, from conducting, owning, either in whole or in part, or being directly or indirectly interested in the retailing of any alcoholic beverages, under any retail consumption license or State issued permit, in conjunction with and as a part of the operations of a hotel or motel;

(3) Any owner, part owner, stockholder or officer or director of any corporation, or any other person or corporation interested in any way whatsoever in the retailing of alcoholic beverages, under a retail consumption license or State issued permit, in conjunction with and as a part of the operations of a hotel or motel from conducting, owning, either in whole or in part, or being a shareholder, officer or director of a corporation or association, directly or indirectly interested in any brewery, winery, distillery, rectifying and blending plant, or wholesaling or importing interest of any kind whatsoever; or

(4) The exercise of a restricted brewery license privilege by an immediately adjoining restaurant having a plenary retail consumption license issued under R.S. 33:1–12.

No more than 20% of the total gross annual revenues of a hotel or motel described in paragraphs (2) and (3) shall be derived from the sale of alcoholic beverages by the hotel or motel. A retail licensee described in paragraphs (2) and (3) shall not purchase or sell any alcoholic beverage product produced or sold by the brewery, winery, distillery, rectifying and blending plant, wholesaler or importer that has any interest in the retail license of the hotel or motel, unless the total of all such products is 5% or less of the total volume of alcoholic beverage products purchased and sold annually by the hotel or motel holding the retail license. The retail licensee shall, within 30 days following the effective date of this act, file with the Division of Alcoholic Beverage Control a list of all alcoholic beverage products which shall not be purchased or sold by the hotel or motel except to the extent permitted herein. Thereafter, the retail licensee shall file a new or amended list with the division within 30 days of any changed circumstances which affect the information on the list. This list shall be made available to the public upon request.

For purposes of this subsection "hotel" or "motel" means an establishment containing at least 100 guest room accommodations where the relationship between the occupants thereof and the owner or operator of the establishment is that of innkeeper and guest.

Amended by L.1938, c. 147, p. 304, § 1; L.1939, c. 225, p. 622, § 1; L.1940, c. 234, p. 919, § 1; L.1966, c. 58, § 1, eff. June 2, 1966; L.1983, c. 572, § 1, eff. Jan. 17, 1984; L.1987, c. 433, § 1, eff. Jan. 15, 1988; L.1993, c. 216, § 3, eff. July 30, 1993.

33:1–43a. Limited right of wholesaler to acquire interest in corporation

Nothing in this act shall affect the right of any person having any interest whatsoever in the wholesaling in this State of alcoholic beverages, other than malt alcoholic beverages, to hold or acquire an interest of not more than 10% of any corporation, the shares of which are traded on a national securities exchange or regularly traded in an over-the-counter market by one or more members of a national or affiliated securities association.

L.1966, c. 58, § 2, eff. June 2, 1966.

33:1–43.1. Loans or furnishing of fixtures to retail licensee by brewer prohibited; exceptions

No owner, part owner, stockholder, officer or director of any corporation or any other person whatsoever interested in any way whatsoever in any brewery shall make any loan, directly or indirectly, to any retail licensee; but the foregoing shall not prohibit the extension, subject to rules and regulations, of reasonable credit in respect to ordinary current sales of brewery products.

No owner, part owner, stockholder, officer or director of any corporation or any other person whatsoever interested in any way whatsoever in any brewery shall furnish, repair or replace fixtures in any licensed retail business, except that the cleaning and repairing of pipes and similar matters may be permitted by rules and regulations.

33:1–43.2. Providing of services, items or equipment to retailers to enhance or protect products; conditions; licensee entertainment

a. Manufacturers, importing entities or wholesalers, as these terms are defined in R.S.33:1–1, or third parties at the direction of manufacturers, importing entities or wholesalers, may sell, lease or provide services, items or equipment to retailers that are intended to enhance or protect the quality, display, availability or marketing of their products to consumers, including:

(1) Cleaning and needed repairs of dispensing systems for alcoholic beverage products, including draught systems for malt alcoholic beverages, powered decanter systems for wine and pouring systems, and decanter racks or blending machines for distilled spirits.

(2) Certain equipment, such as tap handles, filters, faucets, tavern heads, regulators, and similar ancillary equipment, that protects the quality or taste of the alcoholic beverage products produced or supplied by

the appropriate licensee, subject to the provisions of R.S.33:1–43.1. Substantial equipment such as complete draught or refrigeration systems, or coolant shall only be sold at no less than fair market value; however nothing in this subsection shall be construed to prevent a licensee from renting or providing such substantial equipment to a retailer on a short-term temporary basis for special events.

(3) Delivery of alcoholic beverages into a retail account at the number of locations as mutually agreed upon by the wholesaler and the retailer.

(4) Occasional, unscheduled placing, and stocking of alcoholic beverages sold by the wholesaler within a retail accounts' premises, to ensure the alcoholic beverages will be available for consumers to purchase, as mutually agreed upon by the wholesaler and retailer, and regular rotation of alcoholic beverages sold by the wholesaler as necessary to ensure the freshness of those products with a limited shelf life.

(5) Shelf management, marketing and pricing recommendations, and implementation of shelf management decisions and resets of a manufacturer's supplier's, wholesaler's, or third party's own products as mutually agreed upon by the wholesaler and the retailer.

(6) Building product displays, including price signs denoting prices established by the retailer, sweepstakes prizes for customers as part of a display and advertising items such as point of sale advertising and consumer novelties, as mutually agreed upon by the wholesaler and retailer.

b. A licensee may provide reasonable entertainment to another licensee, such as engaging in sporting activities, taking a licensee to an entertainment or sports event, or providing meals and beverages to the licensee. The licensee shall not condition the provision of such services, equipment, consumer sweepstakes prizes or entertainment on an agreement to sell the alcoholic beverage products of a manufacturer, supplier or wholesaler. A retailer shall not request the provision of such services, equipment, consumer sweepstakes prizes or entertainment as a condition for selling the alcoholic beverage products of a manufacturer, supplier or wholesaler.

L.2005, c. 243, § 10, eff. March 1, 2006.

33:1–44. Municipal referendum on retail sales of alcoholic beverages except brewed malt and fermented wine

Whenever a petition, signed by at least fifteen per centum (15%) of the qualified electors of any municipality as evidenced by the total number of votes cast for members of the General Assembly, at the then next preceding general election held for the election of all of the members of the General Assembly, in such municipality, shall be presented to the governing board or body thereof, requesting a referendum on the question hereinafter stated, such governing board or body shall adopt forthwith a resolution directing the clerk of the county

in which such municipality is situated to print, pursuant to Title 19, Elections, hereinafter referred to as the "general election law," upon the official ballot to be used in such municipality at the next ensuing general election a question to read: "Shall the retail sale of alcoholic beverages other than brewed malt alcoholic beverages and naturally fermented wine, for consumption on the licensed premises by the glass or other open receptacle pursuant to chapter one of the Title Intoxicating Liquors of the Revised Statutes (s. 33:1–1 et seq.), be permitted in this municipality?" Thereupon the clerk or secretary of said governing board or body shall forthwith deliver to the county clerk a certified copy of such resolution. If the copy shall be delivered to the county clerk not less than thirty days before such general election, he shall cause such question to be printed in an appropriate place on the ballot to be used in such municipality at the next ensuing general election pursuant to the general election law and thereupon all proceedings with respect to the referendum on such question shall be subject to and governed by the general election law as in other cases of the submission of public questions to the electorate.

If a majority of the legal voters voting upon the question shall vote "Yes," the clerk of the governing board or body of such municipality shall forthwith in writing notify the commissioner and municipal board, if any, having authority to issue such licenses, of the action taken by the legal voters of such municipality and the retail sales as aforesaid of such alcoholic beverages and the issuing of licenses pursuant to this chapter shall be permitted in such municipality.

If a majority of the legal voters voting upon the question shall vote "No," then the clerk of the governing board or body of the municipality shall forthwith in writing notify the commissioner and municipal board, if any, having authority to issue such licenses, of the action taken by the legal voters of the municipality, and after thirty days have elapsed after the date of such vote the retail sale of alcoholic beverages, other than brewed malt alcoholic beverages and naturally fermented wines, for consumption on the licensed premises by the glass or other open receptacle (such retail sale being sometimes hereinafter called "prohibited sale"), shall be unlawful in such municipality and constitute a violation of this chapter, and it shall forthwith upon such vote be unlawful for the other issuing authority of the municipality, having authority to issue licenses, to issue any license in respect to such municipality which shall permit such prohibited sale, and all licenses theretofore issued in respect to such municipality which shall have licensed such prohibited sale shall, to the extent that they permitted such prohibited sale, become void and inoperative thirty days after the date of such vote.

Whenever a referendum shall have been had in any municipality pursuant to this section, no further referendum on the same question shall be held therein prior to the general election to be held in such municipality in the fifth year thereafter and so long as such referendum remains effective, all ordinances, resolutions or regulations inconsistent with the result of such referendum shall have no effect within such municipality.

Amended by L.1948, c. 20, p. 71, § 1; L.1949, c. 296, p. 898, § 1, eff. June 14, 1949.

33:1–45. Municipal referendum on retail sales of all kinds of alcoholic beverages

Whenever a petition signed by at least fifteen per centum (15%) of the qualified electors of any municipality as evidenced by the total number of votes cast for members of the General Assembly, at the then next preceding general election held for the election of all of the members of the General Assembly, in such municipality, shall be presented to the governing board or body thereof, requesting a referendum on the question hereinafter stated, such governing board or body shall adopt forthwith a resolution directing the clerk of the county in which such municipality is situated to print, pursuant to Title 19, Elections, hereinafter referred to as the "general election law," upon the official ballot to be used in such municipality at the next ensuing general election a question to read: "Shall the retail sale of all kinds of alcoholic beverages, for consumption on the licensed premises by the glass or other open receptacle pursuant to chapter one of the Title Intoxicating Liquors of the Revised Statutes (s. 33:1–1 et seq.), be permitted in this municipality?" Thereupon the clerk or secretary of such governing board or body shall forthwith deliver to such county clerk a certified copy of the resolution. If the copy shall be delivered to the county clerk not less than thirty days before such general election, he shall cause such question to be printed in an appropriate place on the ballot to be used in such municipality at the next ensuing general election pursuant to the general election law and thereupon all proceedings with respect to the referendum on such question shall be subject to and governed by the general election law as in other cases of the submission of public questions to the electorate.

If a majority of the legal voters voting upon the question shall vote "Yes," the clerk of the governing board or body of such municipality shall forthwith in writing notify the commissioner and municipal board, if any, having authority to issue such licenses, of the action taken by the legal voters of such municipality and the retail sales as aforesaid of such alcoholic beverages and the issuing of licenses pursuant to this chapter shall be permitted in such municipality.

If a majority of the legal voters voting upon the question shall vote "No," then the clerk of the governing board or body of such municipality shall forthwith in writing notify the commissioner and municipal board, if any, having authority to issue such licenses, of the action taken by the legal voters of the municipality, and after thirty days have elapsed after the date of such vote, the retail sale of all kinds of alcoholic beverages for consumption on the licensed premises by the glass or other open receptacle (such retail sale being sometimes hereinafter called "prohibited sale"), shall be unlawful in such municipality and constitute a violation of this chapter, and it shall forthwith upon such vote be unlawful for the other issuing authority of such municipality having authority to issue licenses to issue any license in respect to such municipality which shall permit such prohibited sale and all licenses theretofore issued in respect to such municipality which shall have licensed such prohibited sale shall, to the extent that they permitted such prohibited sale, become void and inoperative thirty days after the date of such vote.

Whenever a referendum shall have been had in any municipality pursuant to this section, no further referendum on the same question shall be held therein prior to the general election to be held in such municipality in the fifth year thereafter and so long as such referendum remains effective, all ordinances, resolutions or regulations inconsistent with the result of such referendum shall have no effect within such municipality.

Amended by L.1948, c. 20, p. 73, § 2; L.1949, c. 296, p. 900, § 2.

33:1–45.1. Club license where vote was "No" in referendum; duration of act

It shall be lawful for the municipal issuing authority of any municipality in which a referendum has been held pursuant to the provisions of Revised Statutes, section 33:1–45, wherein a majority of the legal voters of said municipality voted "No," to issue a club license as defined in and regulated by subparagraph five of section 33:1–12 of the Revised Statutes, to any constituent unit, chartered or otherwise duly enfranchised chapter or member club of a national organization or association which is in possession of suitable premises and which is operated for benevolent, charitable, fraternal, social, religious, recreational, athletic, or similar purposes, and not for private gain, and which comply with all conditions which may be imposed by the director of the division of alcoholic beverage control in the department of law and public safety.

This law shall not be effective after August first, one thousand nine hundred and forty-nine, except, however, that any national club, organization, or association, or any constituent unit chartered or otherwise duly enfranchised chapter thereof holding a license issued by said municipality previous to August first, one thousand nine hundred and forty-nine, shall be entitled to retain said license and any renewals thereof regardless of the provisions of this act.

L.1949, c. 255, p. 819, § 1, eff. May 25, 1949.

33:1–45.2 to 33:1–45.4. Inoperative

33:1–46. Municipal referendum on retail sales of alcoholic beverages, except for consumption on trains, airplanes and boats

Whenever a petition, signed by at least fifteen per centum (15%) of the qualified electors of any municipality as evidenced by the total number of votes cast for members of the General Assembly, at the then next preceding general election held for the election of all of the members of the General Assembly, in such municipality, shall be presented to the governing board or body thereof, requesting a referendum on the question hereinafter stated, such governing board or body shall adopt forthwith a resolution directing the clerk of the county in which such municipality is situated to print, pursuant to Title 19, Elections, hereinafter referred to as the "general election law," upon the official ballot to be used in such municipality at the next ensuing general election, a question to read: "Shall the sale of all alcoholic beverages at retail, except for consumption on railroad trains, airplanes and boats, and the issuance of any retail licenses, except as aforesaid, pursuant to chapter one of the Title Intoxicating Liquors of the Revised Statutes (§ 33:1–1 et seq.), be permitted in this municipality?" Thereupon the clerk or secretary of the governing board or body of such municipality shall forthwith deliver to such county clerk a certified copy of such resolution. If the copy shall be delivered to the county clerk not less than thirty days before such general election, he shall cause such question to be printed in an appropriate place on the ballot to be used in such municipality at the next ensuing general election, pursuant to the general election law and thereupon all proceedings with respect to the referendum on such question shall be subject to and governed by the general election law as in other cases of the submission of public questions to the electorate.

If a majority of the legal voters voting upon the question shall vote "Yes," the clerk of the governing board or body of such municipality shall forthwith in writing notify the commissioner and municipal board, if any, having authority to issue such licenses, of the action taken by the legal voters of such municipality and retail sales of alcoholic beverages and the issuing of retail licenses pursuant to this chapter shall be permitted in such municipality.

If a majority of the legal voters voting upon the question shall vote "No," then the clerk of the governing board or body of such municipality shall forthwith in writing notify the commissioner and municipal board, if any, having authority to issue such licenses, of the action taken by the legal voters of such municipality and thereupon it shall be unlawful for the other issuing authority of such municipality, having authority to issue plenary retail consumption, plenary retail distribution and limited retail consumption licenses, to issue any such licenses in respect to such municipality, and all such licenses theretofore issued in respect to such municipality shall become void and inoperative thirty days after the date of such vote, and thereupon the municipal board of such municipality shall be dissolved, and the offices of its members shall terminate and all its activities hereunder shall cease; but if in a later referendum held pursuant to this chapter a majority of the legal voters voting upon the same question last above stated shall vote "Yes," a municipal board for such municipality may forthwith be appointed in the

same manner and with the same effect as when this chapter first became effective. Whenever any such license shall become void and inoperative by virtue of such referendum there shall be returned to the licensee the prorated license fee for the unexpired term.

Whenever a referendum shall have been had in any municipality pursuant to this section, no further referendum on the same question shall be held therein prior to the general election to be held in such municipality in the fifth year thereafter and so long as such referendum remains effective, all ordinances, resolutions or regulations inconsistent with the result of such referendum shall have no effect within such municipality.

Amended by L.1948, c. 20, p. 75, § 3; L.1949, c. 296, p. 902, § 3.

33:1–46.1. Club license; authority to issue after municipal referendum

It shall be lawful for the governing board or body of any municipality in which a referendum has been held pursuant to the provisions of R.S. 33:1–45 or R.S. 33:1–46, wherein a majority of the legal voters of said municipality voted "No," to issue a club license as defined in and regulated by subsection 5 of R.S. 33:1–12, to any constituent unit, chartered or otherwise duly enfranchised chapter or member club of a national or state order, organization or association, or to a bona fide golf and country club in said municipality, incorporated not for pecuniary gain, and which is in possession of a suitable premises and to adopt an enabling ordinance therefor.

L.1945, c. 55, p. 321, § 1. Amended by L.1953, c. 367, p. 1954, § 1, eff. Aug. 11, 1953; L.1983, c. 365, § 1, eff. Oct. 13, 1983.

33:1–46.2. Special permits to golf and country clubs; license fee

The director may, subject to rules and regulations, issue special permits to a constituent unit, chartered or otherwise duly enfranchised chapter or member club of a national or state order, organization or association, or to a bona fide golf and country club in the event that the said municipality has failed or neglected to adopt an enabling ordinance as aforesaid, or has failed or neglected to properly act upon an application by such a constituent unit, chartered or otherwise duly enfranchised chapter or member club or a bona fide golf and country club for a club license, as aforesaid; the fee for the same shall be determined in each case by the director and shall not be less or more than the fee provided for by subsection 5 of R.S. 33:1–12.

L.1945, c. 55, p. 321, § 2. Amended by L.1983, c. 365, § 2, eff. Oct. 13, 1983.

33:1–46.3. Powers granted director cumulative

Nothing in this act shall be deemed to limit or modify any powers otherwise granted by law to the director.

L.1945, c. 55, p. 321, § 3. Amended by L.1983, c. 365, § 3, eff. Oct. 13, 1983.

33:1–47. Municipal referendum on Sunday sales

Whenever a petition, signed by at least fifteen per centum (15%) of the qualified electors of any municipality as evidenced by the total number of votes cast for members of the General Assembly, at the then next preceding general election held for the election of all of the members of the General Assembly, in such municipality, shall be presented to the governing board or body thereof, requesting a referendum on the question hereinafter stated, such governing board or body shall adopt forthwith a resolution directing the clerk of the county in which such municipality is situated to print, pursuant to Title 19, Elections, hereinafter referred to as the "general election law," upon the official ballot to be used in such municipality at the next ensuing general election, a question to read: "Shall the sale of alcoholic beverages be permitted on Sundays in this municipality?" Thereupon the clerk or secretary of the governing board or body of such municipality shall forthwith deliver to such county clerk a certified copy of such resolution. If such copy shall be delivered to the county clerk not less than thirty days before such general election, he shall cause such question to be printed in an appropriate place on the ballot to be used in such municipality at the next ensuing general election, pursuant to the general election law and thereupon all proceedings with respect to the referendum on such question shall be subject to and governed by the general election law as in other cases of the submission of public questions to the electorate.

If a majority of the legal voters voting upon the question shall vote "Yes," the clerk of the governing board or body of such municipality shall forthwith in writing notify the commissioner and municipal board, if any, having authority to issue such licenses, of the action taken by the legal voters of such municipality and the sale of alcoholic beverages on Sundays pursuant to the provisions of this chapter shall be permitted in such municipality.

If a majority of the legal voters voting upon the question shall vote "No," then the clerk of the governing board or body of such municipality shall forthwith in writing notify the commissioner and municipal board, if any, as the case may be, having authority to issue such licenses of the action taken by the legal voters of such municipality, and thereupon it shall be unlawful for any person to sell alcoholic beverages in such municipality on Sundays and such sale shall constitute a violation of this chapter.

Whenever a referendum shall have been had in any municipality pursuant to this section, no further referendum on the same question shall be held therein prior to the general election to be held in such municipality in the fifth year thereafter and so long as such referendum remains effective, all ordinances, resolutions or regulations inconsistent with the result of such referendum shall have no effect within such municipality.

Amended by L.1948, c. 20, p. 77, § 4; L.1949, c. 296, p. 904, § 4.

33:1–47.1. Municipal referendum on hours of retail sales

Whenever a petition, signed by at least fifteen per centum (15%) of the qualified electors of any municipality as evidenced by the total number of votes cast at the then next preceding general election, held for the election of all of the members of the General Assembly in such municipality, shall be presented to the governing board or body thereof, requesting a referendum on any proposed questions as to whether the hours between which the sale of alcoholic beverages at retail may be made in such municipality on week days, Sundays, either or both, shall be fixed as provided in such petition, which questions shall be specifically and separately set forth in the petition, such governing board or body shall adopt forthwith a resolution directing the clerk of the county in which such municipality is situated to print such question or questions stated in the petition pursuant to Title 19, Elections, hereinafter referred to as the "general election law," upon the official ballot to be used in such municipality at the next ensuing general election. Thereupon the clerk or secretary of such governing board or body shall forthwith deliver to such county clerk a certified copy of such resolution. If such copy shall be delivered to such county clerk not less than thirty days before such general election, he shall cause such question or questions to be printed in an appropriate place on the ballot to be used in such municipality at the next ensuing general election, pursuant to the general election law, and shall cause to be printed on the ballot immediately below the printed question or questions the following:

"Explanatory Statement—A 'Yes' is a vote to permit sales only within the hours set forth in the question or questions printed above. A 'No' vote is a vote against changing the hours during which sales of alcoholic beverages are now permitted in this municipality," and thereupon all proceedings with respect to the referendum on such question or questions shall be subject to and governed by the general election law as in other cases of the submission of public questions to the electorate.

If a majority of the legal voters shall vote affirmatively on the question of whether the hours of sale shall be fixed in the manner set forth in such question or questions, the clerk of the governing board or body of such municipality shall forthwith in writing notify the commissioner and municipal board, if any, of the action taken by the legal voters of such municipality and thereafter the retail sale of alcoholic beverages may be made only within the hours fixed by such referendum. Such sale at any other time within such municipality shall be unlawful and constitute a violation of this chapter.

If a majority of legal voters voting upon such question or questions shall vote in the negative on the question of whether the hours of sale shall be fixed in the manner set forth in such question or questions, the clerk of the governing board or body of such municipality shall forthwith in writing notify the commissioner and municipal board, if any, of the action taken by the legal voters of such municipality and thereafter the hours between which the sale of alcoholic beverages at retail may be made may be regulated as theretofore in such municipality.

No petition under this section shall be received by the governing board or body while any other petition covering the same subject matter which has theretofore been presented hereunder has not been voted upon.

Whenever a referendum shall have been had in any municipality pursuant to this section, no further referendum on the same question shall be held therein prior to the general election to be held in such municipality in the fifth year thereafter and so long as such referendum remains effective, all ordinances, resolutions or regulations inconsistent with the result of such referendum shall have no effect within such municipality.

Amended by L.1945, c. 259, p. 786, § 1; L.1948, c. 20, p. 79, § 5; L.1949, c. 296, p. 905, § 5.

33:1–48. Municipal boards certified to commissioner

All municipal boards created under this chapter shall be certified to the commissioner in writing under seal of the municipality, if any, and attested by the clerk thereof, or person performing for the time being the duties of clerk, and all appointments thereto shall become effective upon filing of a certificate of an acceptance thereof by each member thereof with the commissioner.

33:1–49. Purchase of illicit beverage; misdemeanor

No person, except an officer, or other person authorized by and acting pursuant to instructions from such officer, so doing in the course of and for the purpose of enforcing this chapter shall knowingly purchase, receive or procure any illicit beverage. Any person who shall violate this provision shall be guilty of a misdemeanor and punished by a fine of not less than ten dollars and not more than one hundred dollars, or imprisonment for not less than two days and not more than ten days, or both.

33:1–50. Manufacture, sale, possession, etc., in violation of chapter; misdemeanor

Any person who shall:

a. Manufacture, sell, distribute, bottle, rectify, blend, treat, fortify, mix, process, warehouse or transport any alcoholic beverage in violation of this chapter; or

b. Import, own, possess, keep or store in this state alcoholic beverages with intent to manufacture, sell, distribute, bottle, rectify, blend, treat, fortify, mix, process, warehouse or transport alcoholic beverages in violation of the provisions of this chapter; or

c. Own, possess, keep or store in this state any implement or paraphernalia for the manufacture, sale,

distribution, bottling, rectifying, blending, treating, fortifying, mixing, processing, warehousing or transportation of alcoholic beverages with intent to use the same in the manufacture, sale, distribution, bottling, rectifying, blending, treating, fortifying, mixing, processing, warehousing or transportation of alcoholic beverages in violation of this chapter; or

d. Aid or abet another in the manufacture, sale, distribution, bottling, rectifying, blending, treating, fortifying, mixing, processing, warehousing or transportation of alcoholic beverages in violation of this chapter; or

e. Possess, have custody of, offer for sale or sell any illicit beverage—

Shall be guilty of a misdemeanor, and punished by a fine of not less than one hundred dollars and not more than one thousand dollars, or imprisonment for not less than thirty days and not more than three years, or both.

33:1–51. Other violations of chapter; misdemeanor

Any person who shall knowingly violate any of the other provisions of this chapter shall be guilty of a misdemeanor and punished by a fine of not less than fifty dollars and not more than two hundred fifty dollars, or imprisonment for not less than ten days and not more than ninety days, or both.

33:1–52. Aiding in violations; misdemeanor

Any person who shall knowingly aid or abet another in the violation of this chapter shall be guilty of a misdemeanor punishable in the same manner as the violation aided or abetted.

33:1–53. Conviction of second offense

In case any person shall, after conviction of an offense under this chapter, be convicted of another offense under this chapter, such other and subsequent offense shall be punishable by a fine or imprisonment, the maximum and minimum limits of which shall be twice the limits otherwise by this chapter imposed, or by both such fine and imprisonment, in the discretion of the court.

33:1–54. Violation upon leased premises; termination of lease; notice; summary proceedings

Any violation of this chapter upon any leased premises by any lessee or sublessee, or by any other person with the knowledge and consent of the lessee, or sublessee, shall, at the option of lessor, immediate or remote, upon five days' written notice to such lessee or sublessee of the exercise of such option and the cause therefor, cause the term of the lease forthwith, at the expiration of such five days, to cease and come to an end, and the right to possession of the leased premises shall thereupon revert to the lessor, together with such further rights in the lessor as may be reserved to him by the terms of said lease or by law, or by both, noncompliance with this chapter and the exercise of lessor's option being a limitation upon the term of the lease. The lessor may enforce his right of possession hereunder by summary proceedings as for term ended, as prescribed by article 5 of chapter 58 of the title Administration of Civil and Criminal Justice (§ 2:58–16 et seq.). This section shall not affect any lease made and entered into prior to the sixth day of December, one thousand nine hundred and thirty-three.

33:1–55. Maintenance of place where unlawful property is kept, manufactured or sold

No person shall knowingly keep, occupy or maintain any premises, building, vehicle or place whatsoever wherein unlawful property is owned, possessed, kept, stored, manufactured, sold, distributed or transported, and all unlawful property may be seized by any officer and be confiscated and disposed of as in this chapter provided.

33:1–56. Issuing search warrant; private dwellings

Any magistrate, hereinafter termed the "issuing magistrate", may issue a search warrant in the manner hereinafter provided, to search any premises, building, vehicle or place whatsoever containing, or believed upon probable cause, to contain unlawful property; but no search warrant shall issue to search any private dwelling, occupied exclusively as such, unless there is probable cause to believe it is being used for, or in connection with, unlawful alcoholic beverage activity and provided that such use be evidenced by oath of some person, on his own knowledge.

33:1–57. Prerequisites to issuance of search warrant; contents; service

A search warrant shall only issue after (1) proof under oath, which may be by written affidavit or deposition, has been produced before the issuing magistrate setting forth facts tending to establish the grounds of the application, or probable cause for believing that such grounds exist, and (2) naming or describing the person or describing the premises, building, vehicle or other place to be searched.

If the issuing magistrate is satisfied of the existence of the grounds of the application, or that there is probable cause to believe their existence, he must issue a search warrant, signed by him with the title of his office, to any officer, or officers, stating the particular grounds, or probable cause, for its issuance, and the name or names of the person or persons sworn in support thereof, and commanding him forthwith to search the person, or the premises, building, vehicle or place to be searched.

A search warrant shall be served by the officer, or any of the officers, to whom the same is directed, but by no other person excepting in aid of said officer, he being present and acting in its execution.

33:1–58. Breaking and entry in execution of warrant

The officer or officers to whom the search warrant is directed may break open any outer or inner door or window of any premises, building, vehicle or other place, or anything contained therein, to execute the warrant if, after pronouncement of his authority and purpose, he does not receive admission, and also when necessary for his own liberation or that of any person aiding him in the execution of the warrant.

33:1–59. Service of warrant in nighttime

No search warrant shall be served in the nighttime except for special cause shown to the satisfaction of the issuing magistrate and upon insertion in the warrant of a direction that it may be served in the nighttime.

33:1–60. Execution and return of warrant; time limit

Every search warrant shall be executed and returned to the issuing magistrate within forty-eight hours after its issuance, after which time, unless executed, it shall be void.

33:1–61. Receipt for and inventory of property seized

Any officer who shall seize any property under a search warrant shall give a copy of the warrant, together with an itemized receipt for the property, to the person from whom it was taken or in whose possession it was found or, in the absence of any person, such officer shall leave said copy and receipt in the place where he found the property. The officer who executes a search warrant shall return the same to the issuing magistrate, together with a written inventory of the property taken, made in the presence of at least one credible person other than the officer. The magistrate shall, upon request, exhibit the inventory to any person claiming the property and to the applicant for the warrant and allow copies to be made thereof.

33:1–62. Return of illegally seized property

In case any person shall be deprived of any property, or the possession of any property, under color of any search warrant, except substantially in accordance with the procedure herein set forth, the issuing magistrate, upon timely application therefor, shall require the return of said property, except such property as shall be proven beyond a reasonable doubt to be unlawful property.

33:1–63. Resisting officer serving or executing search warrant; misdemeanor

Any person who shall knowingly and willfully obstruct, resist or oppose any officer or person assisting an officer, in serving or executing, or attempting to serve or execute, any search warrant authorized by this chapter shall be guilty of a misdemeanor.

33:1–64. Procuring search warrant without probable cause; misdemeanor

Any person who shall maliciously and without probable cause procure a search warrant to be issued and executed shall be guilty of a misdemeanor.

33:1–65. Search without warrant; misdemeanor

Any person who shall intentionally search any private dwelling occupied exclusively for dwelling purposes, without a warrant therefor, or who shall maliciously and without probable cause, and without a warrant therefor, search any other building, premises, vehicle or place, shall be guilty of a misdemeanor.

33:1–66. Seizure of unlawful property; bond or cash for return; replevin; forfeiture, sale, etc., of unclaimed property; hearing; certain property subject to seizure; manufacture, sale, etc., of unlawful property; return of seized property; liens upon seized property

a. Any officer knowing, or having reasonable cause to believe, that any person is engaged in unlawful alcoholic beverage activity, it shall be his duty to investigate, under proper search warrant when necessary, which it shall be his further duty to apply for, and to seize all property which he shall know, or have reasonable ground to believe is unlawful property, including in the case of illicit alcoholic beverages within any vehicle, the vehicle containing the same, and to arrest all persons whom he shall know, or have reasonable ground to believe, are committing, or have committed, a misdemeanor under this chapter and to make complaint against such persons as in other cases of misdemeanors. All property when seized shall be under the jurisdiction of the Director of the Division of Alcoholic Beverage Control subject to this chapter.

Any seized property shall be returned to any person claiming the same upon execution and delivery by him to the director of a bond in a form and with sureties satisfactory to the director in a sum double the retail value of the property, as appraised by the director, conditioned, (1) to pay to the director for the use of the State the full retail value of such property in case the same shall appear to have been unlawful property, and (2) in case it shall appear that said property was not unlawful property, to pay such part of the retail value thereof as may represent the value of the outstanding right, title, interest, lien or claim of any other person, to such other person, which bond shall be enforceable, as other obligations for payment of money, by civil action in any court of competent jurisdiction, first by the director, to be instituted within one year from the date thereof, and, secondly, by such other person as third party beneficiaries, at any time after final judgment in such action by the director, or after the expiration of said year in case no such action shall have been instituted by the director in the meantime.

In lieu of such bond, the claimant to the seized property may pay to the director for the use of the State the retail value thereof in cash, as appraised by the director, under protest, subject to the right of the person making the payment to recover such sum upon establishing that the property was not unlawful property by an action to be commenced within one year from the date of such payment, and not thereafter, in any court of competent jurisdiction.

Such claimant may, in lieu of either remedy, bring an action for the replevin of the property against the director in any court of competent jurisdiction according to the forms and procedure including the delivery of a bond, of such court, such action to be commenced within thirty days from the seizure of such property and not thereafter.

If the director shall be satisfied that property seized was not unlawful property he may return the same to the person from whom or the place from which the same was taken. If any seized property shall not be reclaimed within thirty days, after determination by him that such property is unlawful property, and subject to rules and regulations, the director shall forfeit such property and may, in his discretion, order that the seized property in whole or in part be sold, destroyed or retained for the use of hospitals and State, county and municipal institutions. The forfeiture of any seized property shall terminate all property interests therein and in any proceeds therefrom, including the interests of the owner, any conditional vendor, chattel mortgagee or other lienor and all other persons.

No such forfeiture, sale, destruction or retention for use of hospitals and State, county and municipal institutions shall be had except after hearing, of which notice, of not less than fifteen nor more than thirty days, shall be given by mail to all persons known or believed by the director to have an interest in the seized property and by publication twice in a newspaper to be designated by the director and circulating in the county where the property was seized, once in each of the two consecutive calendar weeks preceding such hearing. After such hearing, the director shall file his determination in the form of an order which shall be subject to review by the Superior Court in a proceeding in lieu of prerogative writ.

All moneys received by the director hereunder shall be reserved during the time allowed any person an opportunity of establishing a right thereto and shall immediately thereafter be accounted for by the director as in the case of license fees received hereunder.

All sales by the director shall convey the director's right, title and interest which shall be that of sole and absolute ownership, free and clear of all outstanding title, rights, interest and liens.

Property seized and released shall thereafter be subject to further seizure because of ownership, possession or use thereof in connection with further unlawful alcoholic beverage activities.

b. All alcoholic beverages, fixtures and personal property located in or upon any premises, building, yard or inclosure connected with a building, in which an illicit beverage is found, possessed, stored or kept, are hereby declared unlawful property and shall be seized, forfeited and disposed of in the same manner as other unlawful property seized under this section.

c. All alcoholic beverages manufactured, sold, imported or transported in violation of rules and regulations, together with any vehicle containing the same, are hereby declared unlawful property and shall be seized, forfeited and disposed of in the same manner as other unlawful property seized under this section.

d. Any contrivance, preparation, compound, tablet, substance or recipe advertised, designed or intended for use in the manufacture of alcoholic beverages for personal consumption or otherwise in violation of this chapter is hereby declared unlawful property and shall be seized, forfeited and disposed of in the same manner as other unlawful property seized under this section. Any person who shall advertise, manufacture, sell or possess for sale, or cause to be advertised, manufactured, sold or possessed for sale property declared unlawful under this paragraph, shall be guilty of a misdemeanor and punished by a fine of not less than one hundred dollars ($100.00) and not more than five hundred dollars ($500.00), or imprisonment for not less than thirty days and not more than six months, or both.

e. The director upon being satisfied that a person whose property has been seized or forfeited pursuant to the provisions of this section has acted in good faith and has unknowingly violated the provisions thereof, may order that such property be returned upon payment of the reasonable costs incurred in connection with the seizure, such costs to be determined by the director.

The director may, upon being satisfied that a common carrier, whose vehicle has been seized under the provisions of this chapter, has acted in good faith and had no knowledge at the time of the seizure, that the vehicle contained illicit alcoholic beverages, order that the seized vehicle be returned to the common carrier.

f. The director, upon being satisfied that a person having a bona fide and valid lien upon or interest in property seized or forfeited pursuant to the provisions of this section has acted in good faith and had no knowledge of the unlawful use to which the property was put or of such facts as would have led a person of ordinary prudence to discover such use, may, in his discretion and subject to rules and regulations, recognize the validity and priority of such claim or interest. Where the validity and priority of a lien or interest have been so recognized by the director, he may (1) order, where it appears that the amount or value of such lien or interest exceeds the value of the property plus costs, that the property be returned to the innocent claimant upon payment of the reasonable costs incurred in connection with the seizure, such costs to be determined by the director, or (2) order that the property be sold and that the amount of the lien or value of the interest, which amount or value shall be established to the satisfaction of the director, be paid out of the proceeds of sale after having deducted therefrom the reasonable costs incurred in connection with the seizure, such costs to be determined by the director.

Amended by L.1953, c. 32, p. 577, § 3, eff. March 19, 1953.

33:1–67. Solicitor's permit required; exceptions; issuance; fee; violations; penalty

No individual shall offer for sale or solicit any order in the State for the purchase or sale of any alcoholic beverage, whether such sale is to be made within or without this State, unless such person shall have a solicitor's permit issued by the director hereunder.

Nothing contained in this section shall prohibit such offer or solicitation by any licensee himself or any employee of any retail licensee in connection with and in the course of the licensed business.

The director is empowered to issue, subject to rules and regulations, solicitor's permits, which shall set forth such facts as may be prescribed by the director and shall authorize the permittee to make offers for such sales and solicit orders for such sales of alcoholic beverages as are in accordance with this chapter, and any rules and regulations promulgated thereunder, on behalf of any vendor or vendors represented by the solicitor and designated in the permit. The fee for such permits shall be $15.00 per annum or any part thereof for solicitors employed exclusively by licensees whose licenses permit sale of malt alcoholic beverages only, and $25.00 per annum or any part thereof for solicitors employed by other licensees. A separate fee shall be paid for each vendor designated in the permit. Such permits shall expire on June 30 following their issuance, except as otherwise specified therein.

Any person who violates any provisions of this section shall be guilty of a misdemeanor and punished by a fine of not less than $50.00 and not more than $200.00 or imprisonment for not less than 10 days or not more than 3 months, or both.

Amended by L.1954, c. 26, p. 94, § 5, eff. May 11, 1954; L.1970, c. 78, § 7.

33:1–68. Detention of evidence

Nothing in this chapter contained shall prohibit the detention of evidence pursuant to law.

33:1–69. Place of sale; determination

In case of sale of an alcoholic beverage in which a delivery is accompanied by transportation, whether by a common carrier or otherwise, the sale shall be deemed to be made in the county wherein the delivery was made or in the county where the transfer of title, or agreement for sale, was made, or in the county from or to which the shipment was made, and prosecution for such sale may be had in any one of such counties.

33:1–70. Each violation separate offense; name of purchaser unnecessary in affidavits, indictments, etc.

Every violation of this chapter shall constitute a separate offense. In any affidavit, information, complaint or indictment for a violation of this chapter, separate offenses may be united, and the defendant may be tried on one or more counts at one trial, and the penalty for each separate offense may be imposed.

It shall not be necessary in any affidavit, information, complaint or indictment involving a sale of alcoholic beverages to give the name of the purchaser thereof, and it shall not in any affidavit, information, complaint or indictment be necessary to include any defensive negative averments, but it shall be sufficient to state the act or acts constituting the violation and that the same was or were then and there prohibited by law, saving, however, to all defendants the right to require a bill of particulars as in other cases.

33:1–71. Officers to use diligence; arrests

To the end that local police and other enforcing agencies shall enforce this chapter in the interest of economy and effective control, all officers shall use all due diligence to detect violations of this chapter and shall apprehend the offenders and make a proper complaint before a magistrate. Arrests may be made as in other cases of misdemeanors.

33:1–72. Sale of warehouse receipts; license required; fee

The sale of receipts, certificates, contracts or other documents given upon the storage of alcoholic beverages is prohibited, except under and pursuant to the provisions of a warehouse receipts license issued by the director. The holder of such license shall be entitled to sell such warehouse receipts subject to rules and regulations and the fee therefor shall be $375. No publication shall be required with respect to applications for warehouse receipts licenses.

The provisions of section 27 of P.L.2003, c. 117 amendatory of this section shall apply to licenses issued or transferred on or after July 1, 2003, and to license renewals commencing on or after July 1, 2003.

Amended by L.1954, c. 26, p. 95, § 6, eff. May 11, 1954; L.1970, c. 78, § 8; L.2003, c. 117, § 27, eff. July 1, 2003.

33:1–73. Intention and construction of law

This chapter is intended to be remedial of abuses inherent in liquor traffic and shall be liberally construed.

33:1–74. Temporary contingency permits; fees; designated premises; number; ordinances or resolutions prohibiting sales

a. To provide for contingencies where it would be appropriate and consonant with the spirit of this chapter to issue a license but the contingency has not been expressly provided for, the director of the division may for special cause shown, subject to rules and regulations, issue temporary permits. The fee for a one-day permit authorizing the sale of alcoholic beverages for consumption on a designated premises by a civic, religious, educational or veterans organization shall be $100 and for a one-day permit authorizing such sale by any other organization, $150. The fee for any other type of temporary permit shall be determined in each case by the director of the division and shall not be less than $10

nor more than $2,000, payable to the director of the division and to be accounted for by the director as are license fees.

b. As to any designated premises such temporary permits shall not exceed in the aggregate 25 in any one calendar year, but the director of the division may by said rules and regulations provide for a lesser number in the aggregate for any such designated premises in any one calendar year.

c. The issuance of temporary permits to authorize the sale of alcoholic beverages by the glass or other open receptacle by civic, religious, educational, veterans or other qualified organizations shall be permissible, notwithstanding that the sale of alcoholic beverages has otherwise been prohibited by referendum under R.S. 33:1–44 through R.S. 33:1–47 or municipal ordinance or resolution.

Amended by L.1960, c. 92, p. 578, § 1, eff. July 7, 1960; L.1976, c. 44, § 7, eff. June 30, 1976; L.1982, c. 37, § 1, eff. June 14, 1982; L.1991, c. 334, § 1, eff. Jan. 6, 1992; L.1992, c. 188, § 13, eff. Dec. 16, 1992; L.2003, c. 117, § 28, eff. July 1, 2003.

33:1–75. Special permits for home manufacture of wines for personal consumption; fee

a. The director may, subject to rules and regulations, issue special permits authorizing the manufacture by a person who is 21 years of age or older, within a home or other noncommercial premises, of wines or malt alcoholic beverages in quantities not exceeding 200 gallons per calendar year for the person's personal or household use or consumption.

b. The director may, subject to rules and regulations, issue special permits authorizing the manufacture of wines in an instructional winemaking facility by a person who is 21 years of age or older, residing within or without this State, in quantities not exceeding 200 gallons per calendar year for the person's personal or household use or consumption.

c. The director shall, by regulation, establish a reasonable fee to cover the costs incurred in issuing the special permits required by this section.

d. A person manufacturing wines or malt alcoholic beverages pursuant to this section shall not be liable for any tax imposed under the "Alcoholic beverage tax law," R.S.54:41–1 et seq.

Amended by L.1954, c. 26, p. 95, § 7, eff. May 11, 1954; L.1991, c. 302, § 1, eff. Nov. 7, 1991; L.2007, c. 329, § 2, eff. April 1, 2008.

33:1–76. Sales within 200 feet of church or school prohibited; waiver; exceptions

Anything to the contrary hereinbefore notwithstanding, and for the benefit not of property but of persons attendant therein, no license shall be issued for the sale of alcoholic beverages within two hundred feet of any church or public schoolhouse or private schoolhouse not conducted for pecuniary profit, except to manufacturers, wholesalers, hotels, clubs and fraternal organizations which owned or were actually in possession of the licensed premises on December sixth, one thousand nine hundred and thirty-three. The protection of this section may be waived at the issuance of the license and at each renewal thereafter, by the duly authorized governing body on authority of such church or school, such waiver to be effective until the date of the next renewal of the license. Said two hundred feet shall be measured in the normal way that a pedestrian would properly walk from the nearest entrance of said church or school to the nearest entrance of the premises sought to be licensed.

The prohibition contained in this section shall not apply to the renewal of any license where no such church or schoolhouse was located within two hundred feet of the licensed premises as aforesaid at the time of the issuance of the license, nor to the issuance or renewal, or both, of any license where such premises have been heretofore licensed for the sale of alcoholic beverages or intoxicating liquors, and such church or schoolhouse was constructed or established, or both, during the time said premises were operated under said previous license.

33:1–76.1. Renewal or reissuance of club or Class B wholesale license granted on waiver

Notwithstanding the provisions of section 33:1–76 of the Revised Statutes if a club or Class B (wholesale) license has been or shall be granted on a waiver of its protection granted on authority of a church or school, the holder of such license shall be entitled to apply for renewal thereof without further or renewed authority, or waiver, of the church or school; but the renewal or reissuance of such license after a revocation, or subsequent transfer of such license, shall not be permitted without a new waiver granted on authority of the church or school.

L.1961, c. 83, p. 632, § 1. Amended by L.1965, c. 188, § 2, eff. Dec. 14, 1965.

33:1–76.2. Plenary or limited retail distribution licenses; renewal on annual waivers for 15 or more years; effect

Notwithstanding the provisions of Revised Statutes 33:1–76 if a plenary or limited retail distribution license has been or shall be granted on a waiver of its protection granted on authority of a church or school, and such license has been, or shall have been renewed on authority of annual waivers by the church or school for 15 or more consecutive years, the holder of such license shall thereafter be entitled to apply for renewal or reissuance thereof without further or renewed authority, or waiver, of the church or school; but the renewal or reissuance of such license after a revocation, shall not be permitted without a new waiver granted on authority of the church or school.

L.1967, c. 152, § 1, eff. July 10, 1967.

33:1–77. Sale to person under legal age; penalty; defenses

Anyone who sells any alcoholic beverage to a person under the legal age for purchasing alcoholic beverages is a disorderly person; provided, however, that the establishment of all of the following facts by a person making any such sale shall constitute a defense to any prosecution therefor: (a) that the purchaser falsely represented in writing, or by producing a driver's license bearing a photograph of the licensee, or by producing a photographic identification card issued pursuant to section 2 of P.L.1980, c. 47 (C.39:3–29.3), or a similar card issued pursuant to the laws of this State, another state or the federal government that he or she was of legal age to make the purchase, (b) that the appearance of the purchaser was such that an ordinary prudent person would believe him or her to be of legal age to make the purchase, and (c) that the sale was made in good faith relying upon such written representation, or production of a driver's license bearing a photograph of the licensee, or production of a photographic identification card issued pursuant to section 2 of P.L.1980, c. 47 (C.39:3–29.3), or a similar card issued pursuant to the laws of this State, another state or the federal government and appearance and in the reasonable belief that the purchaser was actually of legal age to make the purchase.

Amended by L.1939, c. 228, p. 625, § 1, eff. July 18, 1939; L.1971, c. 54, § 1, eff. March 19, 1971; L.1982, c. 61, § 1, eff. July 9, 1982; L.1983, c. 565, § 2, eff. Jan. 17, 1984; L.1985, c. 503, § 1, eff. Jan. 21, 1986; L.2003, c. 175, § 3, eff. Sept. 10, 2003.

33:1–78. Bottling without license; misdemeanor

Any person, except a person holding a brewery, distillery, winery or rectifier's license under this chapter, who shall bottle alcoholic beverages for sale or resale shall be guilty of a misdemeanor.

33:1–79. Licenses to purchase and sell alcoholic beverages of certain manufacturers only

No licensee hereunder may purchase or sell any alcoholic beverages unless the same shall have been manufactured by manufacturers licensed as such hereunder, or, if manufactured by foreign manufacturers not licensed as such hereunder, unless said foreign manufacturers shall have complied with the same standards and requirements as are or shall be prescribed by rules and regulations for manufacturers licensed as such under this chapter.

33:1–80. Issue of stamps, labels, etc.; fees

Subject to rules and regulations, the commissioner may issue to foreign manufacturers and to persons licensed under this chapter, stamps, labels and other indicia evidencing compliance with prescribed standards upon payment of fees to be fixed by him commensurate with the reasonable cost of the services involved and to be accounted for by him as are license fees.

33:1-81. Purchase of alcoholic beverages; unlawful acts by persons under legal age; purchases by another for minor; disorderly persons; suspension of driver's license; alcohol education and treatment program

It shall be unlawful for:

(a) A person under the legal age for purchasing alcoholic beverages to enter any premises licensed for the retail sale of alcoholic beverages for the purpose of purchasing, or having served or delivered to him or her, any alcoholic beverage; or

(b) A person under the legal age for purchasing alcoholic beverages to consume any alcoholic beverage on premises licensed for the retail sale of alcoholic beverages, or to purchase, attempt to purchase or have another purchase for him any alcoholic beverage; or

(c) Any person to misrepresent or misstate his age, or the age of any other person for the purpose of inducing any licensee or any employee of any licensee, to sell, serve or deliver any alcoholic beverage to a person under the legal age for purchasing alcoholic beverages; or

(d) Any person to enter any premises licensed for the retail sale of alcoholic beverages for the purpose of purchasing, or to purchase alcoholic beverages, for another person who does not because of his age have the right to purchase and consume alcoholic beverages.

Any person who shall violate any of the provisions of this section shall be deemed and adjudged to be a disorderly person, and upon conviction thereof, shall be punished by a fine of not less than $500.00. In addition, the court shall suspend or postpone the person's license to operate a motor vehicle for six months.

Upon the conviction of any person under this section, the court shall forward a report to the Division of Motor Vehicles stating the first and last day of the suspension or postponement period imposed by the court pursuant to this section. If a person at the time of the imposition of a sentence is less than 17 years of age, the period of license postponement, including a suspension or postponement of the privilege of operating a motorized bicycle, shall commence on the day the sentence is imposed and shall run for a period of six months after the person reaches the age of 17 years.

If a person at the time of the imposition of a sentence has a valid driver's license issued by this State, the court shall immediately collect the license and forward it to the division along with the report. If for any reason the license cannot be collected, the court shall include in the report the complete name, address, date of birth, eye color, and sex of the person as well as the first and last date of the license suspension period imposed by the court.

The court shall inform the person orally and in writing that if the person is convicted of operating a motor vehicle during the period of license suspension or postponement, the person shall be subject to the penalties set forth in R.S. 39:3-40. A person shall be required to acknowledge receipt of the written notice in writing. Failure to receive a written notice or failure to acknowledge in writing the receipt of a written notice shall not be a defense to a subsequent charge of a violation of R.S. 39:3-40.

If the person convicted under this section is not a New Jersey resident, the court shall suspend or postpone, as appropriate given the age at the time of sentencing, the non-resident driving privilege of the person and submit to the division the required report. The court shall not collect the license of a non-resident convicted under this section. Upon receipt of a report by the court, the division shall notify the appropriate officials in the licensing jurisdiction of the suspension or postponement.

In addition to the general penalties prescribed for an offense, the court may require any person under the legal age to purchase alcoholic beverages who violates this act to participate in an alcohol education or treatment program authorized by the Department of Health for a period not to exceed the maximum period of confinement prescribed by law for the offense for which the individual has been convicted.

Amended by L.1946, c. 246, p. 867, § 1; L.1953, c. 32, p. 581, § 4; L.1964, c. 40, § 1; L.1979, c. 265, § 1, eff. Jan. 2, 1980; L.1983, c. 574, § 1, eff. July 1, 1985; L.1985, c. 113, § 1; L.1991, c. 169, § 1, eff. June 19, 1991.

33:1-81.1. Hearing; attendance by parent or guardian; subpoena

In any hearing for a violation of section 33:1-81 of the Revised Statutes the court in its discretion may require the attendance at such hearing of a parent or guardian, if there be no parent, of the minor charged with such violation if such parent or guardian is a resident of the State and may, in its discretion, compel such attendance by subpoena.

L.1956, c. 52, p. 104, § 1, eff. May 22, 1956.

33:1-81.1a. Notification of parent or guardian of conviction of juvenile under § 33:1-81 or § 2C:33-15; parent or guardian subject to fine for failure to exercise reasonable supervision

A parent, guardian or other person having legal custody of a person under 18 years of age found in violation of R.S. 33:1-81 or section 1 of P.L.1979, c. 264 (C.2C:33-15) shall be notified of the violation in writing. The parent, guardian or other person having legal custody of a person under 18 years of age shall be subject to a fine in the amount of $500.00 upon any subsequent violation of R.S. 33:1-81 or section 1 of P.L.1979, c. 264 (C.2C:33-15) on the part of such person if it is shown that the parent, guardian or other person having legal custody failed or neglected to exercise reasonable supervision or control over the conduct of the person under 18 years of age.

L.1991, c. 169, § 3, eff. June 19, 1991.

33:1–81.2. Identification card; contents

The county clerk in any county shall before the effective date of P.L.2003, c. 175 issue, upon application of any resident of that county who shall have attained the age of 21 years, and who shall have supplied the clerk with the necessary information required by rules and regulations made by the Director of Alcoholic Beverage Control, an identification card bearing the applicant's date of birth, physical description, photograph, signature, and such other information, as said regulation may require, attesting to the age of the applicant. The identification card shall be signed by the applicant in the clerk's presence. Such cards shall be numbered and a permanent record thereof maintained by the clerk. No further cards shall be issued on or after the effective date of P.L.2003, c. 175 and cards issued prior to that date shall have no validity on or after the effective date of P.L.2003, c. 175; provided however, that the county clerk shall continue to maintain the permanent record of each card previously issued pursuant to the authority of this section.

L.1968, c. 313, § 1, eff. Sept. 26, 1968. Amended by L.2003, c. 175, § 4, eff. Sept. 10, 2003.

33:1–81.3 to 33:1–81.6. Repealed by L.2003, c. 175, § 5, eff. Sept. 10, 2003

33:1–81.7. Transfer of card; penalty

It shall be unlawful for the owner of an identification card, as defined by this act, to transfer said card to any other person for the purpose of aiding such person to secure alcoholic beverages. Any person who shall transfer such identification card for the purpose of aiding such transferee to obtain alcoholic beverages shall be guilty of a misdemeanor and, upon conviction thereof, shall be sentenced to pay a fine of not more than $300.00, or undergo imprisonment for not more than 60 days. Any person not entitled thereto who shall have unlawfully procured or have issued or transferred to him, as aforesaid, identification card or any person who shall make any false statement on any card required by subsection (c) hereof to be signed by him shall be guilty of a misdemeanor and, upon conviction thereof, shall be sentenced to pay a fine of not more than $300.00, or undergo imprisonment for not more than 60 days.

L.1968, c. 313, § 6, eff. Sept. 26, 1968.

33:1–81.8. Alcoholic beverage licensee not relieved from liabilities by presentation

The fact of the possession or presentation of the identification card prescribed by this act by any person in connection with the purchase or attempted purchase, of any alcoholic beverage from any alcoholic beverage licensee shall not be deemed to relieve such licensee of the obligations, responsibilities, or liabilities imposed by law upon such licensee.

L.1968, c. 313, § 7, eff. Sept. 26, 1968.

33:1–81.9. Repealed by L.1985, c. 503, § 2, eff. Jan. 21, 1986

33:1–82 to 33:1–84. Repealed by L.1943, c. 153, § 1, eff. April 8, 1943

33:1–85. Retail licensees to sell or possess alcohol only pursuant to special permit

No retail licensee shall sell, offer for sale or possess in or upon the licensed premises nor shall any person sell or offer for sale at retail to consumers any alcohol for any purpose, except pursuant to and within the limitations of a special permit issued by the State Commissioner of Alcoholic Beverage Control.

L.1939, c. 173, p. 523, § 1.

33:1–86. Punishment for violating section 33:1–85

Any person who sells or offers for sale, or any retail licensee who sells, offers for sale or possesses alcohol in violation of this act shall be punished by a fine of not less than one hundred dollars ($100.00) and not more than one thousand dollars ($1,000.00), or by imprisonment of not less than thirty (30) days and not more than three (3) years, or by both fine and imprisonment in the discretion of the court.

L.1939, c. 173, p. 524, § 2.

33:1–87. Exemptions from provisions of act

Nothing herein contained shall apply to the sale or possession of alcohol which is not intended for beverage purposes and has been denatured or otherwise rendered unfit in fact for beverage purposes, nor with the possession of alcohol for the actual manufacture of United States Pharmacopoeia and National Formulary preparations and for the compounding of physicians' original prescriptions by pharmacists registered by the Board of Pharmacy of the State of New Jersey under the laws of the State of New Jersey, who are owners or managers of pharmacies registered with the Board of Pharmacy and operated under unlimited permits issued by the Board of Pharmacy of the State of New Jersey.

L.1939, c. 173, p. 524, § 3.

33:1–88. Alcoholic beverage deemed prima facie illicit; no label; false label; no indicia of tax payment

Any alcoholic beverage in any keg, barrel, can, bottle, flask or similar container shall, in any proceeding under the chapter which this act supplements, be deemed prima facie an illicit beverage where the container (1) does not bear any label describing its contents, or (2) bears a label which does not truly describe its contents, or (3) does not bear such indicia of payment of tax as is required by the laws of the United States and the State of New Jersey.

L.1939, c. 177, p. 530, § 1, eff. July 11, 1939.

33:1–89. Discrimination in price to retailers prohibited

It shall be unlawful for any manufacturer, wholesaler, or other person privileged to sell to retailers to discriminate in price, directly or indirectly, between different retailers purchasing alcoholic beverages other than malt beverages bearing the same brand or trade name and of like age and quality.

L.1939, c. 87, p. 174, § 1, eff. June 12, 1939.

33:1–90. Discounts, rebates or other allowances to retailers

It shall be unlawful for any manufacturer, wholesaler, or other person privileged to sell to retailers to grant, directly or indirectly, to any retailer purchasing alcoholic beverages other than malt beverages, any discount, rebate, free goods, allowance or other inducement over and above any discount, rebate, free goods, allowance or other inducement available to any other retailer purchasing from him alcoholic beverages bearing the same brand or trade name and of like age, quality and quantity.

L.1939, c. 87, p. 175, § 2, eff. June 12, 1939.

33:1–91. Participation in unlawful transactions prohibited

It shall be unlawful for any manufacturer, wholesaler, retailer and for any of their stockholders, officers, directors and employees, to participate, directly or indirectly, in any transactions which are declared unlawful by the preceding paragraphs of this act.

L.1939, c. 87, p. 175, § 3, eff. June 12, 1939.

33:1–92. Penalties

Violation of this act shall be punished by a fine of not more than five hundred dollars ($500.00) or by imprisonment of not more than thirty (30) days or by both such fine and imprisonment in the discretion of the court.

L.1939, c. 87, p. 175, § 4, eff. June 12, 1939.

33:1–93. Rules and regulations for supervising alcoholic beverage industry

The Director of the Division of Alcoholic Beverage Control is hereby vested with power to promulgate such rules and regulations on the following subjects as will assist in properly supervising the alcoholic beverage industry: (a) maximum discounts, rebates, free goods, allowances and other inducements to retailers by manufacturers, wholesalers and other persons privileged to sell to retailers; (b) gifts and deliveries of money, products and other things of value by manufacturers, wholesalers, other persons privileged to sell to retailers, their stockholders, officers, directors and employees, to retailers, their stockholders, directors, officers and employees; (c) maintenance and publication of invoice prices, discounts, rebates, free goods, allowances and other inducements; and (d) such other matters as may be necessary to fulfill the restrictions embodied in this act.

L.1939, c. 87, p. 175, § 5, eff. June 12, 1939. Amended by L.1985, c. 258, § 3, eff. July 31, 1985.

33:1–93.1 to 33:1–93.5. Repealed by L.1966, c. 59, § 6, eff. June 2, 1966

33:1–93.6. Discrimination in sales to wholesalers

There shall be no discrimination in the sale of any nationally advertised brand of alcoholic beverage other than malt alcoholic beverage, by importers, blenders, distillers, rectifiers and wineries, to duly licensed wholesalers of alcoholic beverages who are authorized by such importers, blenders, distillers, rectifiers and wineries to sell such nationally advertised brand in New Jersey.

L.1966, c. 59, § 1, eff. June 2, 1966.

33:1–93.7. Refusal to sell to wholesaler; petition for hearing; filing fee

In the event any such importer, blender, distiller, rectifier or winery shall refuse to sell alcoholic beverages, other than malt alcoholic beverages, to any such individual wholesaler or comply with the provisions of this act, then the wholesaler shall petition the director setting forth the facts and demanding a hearing thereon to determine whether or not the refusal to sell was discriminatory.

Any petition under this section shall be accompanied by a nonreturnable filing fee of $100.00 payable to the director.

L.1966, c. 59, § 2. Amended by L.1992, c. 188, § 9, eff. Dec. 16, 1992.

33:1–93.8. Order to complete sale to wholesaler

If the director shall determine that said refusal to sell is discriminatory and shall be satisfied with the ability of the wholesaler to pay for such merchandise as ordered, he shall order the importer, blender, distiller, rectifier or winery to complete said sale of alcoholic beverages other than malt alcoholic beverages, to the wholesaler.

L.1966, c. 59, § 3.

33:1–93.9. Noncompliance with director's order

In the event said importer, blender, distiller, rectifier or winery refuses to complete said sale or to comply with the terms of the director's order, the director shall issue an order to every licensed wholesaler prohibiting purchase by such wholesaler of any alcoholic beverages other than malt alcoholic beverages, of said importer, blender, distiller, rectifier or winery directly or indirectly until there is strict compliance by said importer, blender, distiller, rectifier or winery with the order of the director.

L.1966, c. 59, § 4.

33:1–93.10. Rules and regulations

The director shall adopt and promulgate such rules and regulations as may be necessary to carry out and insure compliance with the provisions of this act.

L.1966, c. 59, § 5.

33:1–93.11. Repeal

"An act concerning alcoholic beverages, and supplementing chapter 1 of Title 33 of the Revised Statutes," approved June 25, 1942,[1] is repealed.

L.1966, c. 59, § 6.

[1] N.J.S.A. §§ 33:1–93.1 to 33:1–93.5.

33:1–93.12. Short title

Sections 1 through 9 of this act [1] shall be known and may be cited as the "Malt Alcoholic Beverage Practices Act."

L.2005, c. 243, § 1, eff. March 1, 2006.

[1] N.J.S.A. §§ 33:1–93.12 through 33:1–93.20.

33:1–93.13. Legislative findings and declarations

The Legislature finds and declares that:

a. The distribution and sale of malt alcoholic beverages in this State vitally affects the general economy and revenues of the State, as well as the public interest and public welfare.

b. It is appropriate to recognize the guiding characteristics regarding the distribution of malt alcoholic beverages to foster responsible industry practices involving the moderate and responsible use of these beverages, to provide a framework for the malt alcohol beverage industry that recognizes and encourages the beneficial aspects of competition, to provide trade stability, to maintain the three-tier distribution system, to protect the interests of the consumer regarding product quality and freshness and to achieve all facets of the legislatively declared public policy of this State as set forth in section 4 of P.L.1985, c. 258 (C.33:1–3.1).

c. It is therefore fitting and proper to regulate the business relationship between brewers and wholesalers of malt alcoholic beverages and set forth their respective responsibilities to further the public policy of this State and protect beer wholesalers from unreasonable demands and requirements by brewers, while devoting sufficient efforts and resources to the distribution and sale of malt alcoholic beverages.

d. The Legislature also finds and declares that nothing in sections 1 through 9 of this act [1] shall be construed in any manner whatsoever to apply to wholesalers of wines and spirits and that sections 1 through 9 of the act shall be strictly limited to the responsibilities of brewers and wholesalers. But section 10 of this act [2] shall apply to wholesalers of beer, wine and spirits alike.

L.2005, c. 243, § 2, eff. March 1, 2006.

[1] N.J.S.A. §§ 33:1–93.12 through 33:1–93.20.
[2] N.J.S.A. § 33:1–43.2.

33:1–93.14. Definitions

As used in sections 1 through 9 of this act: [1]

"Base product" is a malt alcoholic beverage product distributed by a wholesaler.

"Brand extension" means any malt alcoholic beverage product offered for sale in the State, other than on a test market basis in a defined market area, that uses as part of its brand name, logo, packaging or trade dress, including but not limited to, the name of the brewer if the brewer's name is a part of the product name, or that is sold or marketed to the beer trade or to the consumer substantially in association with, a brand name, logo, packaging or trade dress, including, but not limited to, the name of the brewer if the brewer's name is a part of the product name, of a malt alcoholic beverage product then distributed by a wholesaler.

"Brewer" means any person, whether located within or outside the State who:

a. brews, manufactures, imports, markets or supplies malt alcoholic beverages and sells malt alcoholic beverages to a plenary wholesale licensee or a limited wholesale licensee for the purpose of resale;

b. is an agent or broker of such a person who solicits orders for or arranges sales of such person's malt alcoholic beverages to a plenary wholesale licensee or a limited wholesale licensee for the purpose of resale; or

c. is a successor brewer.

"Fair market value" of an asset means the price at which the asset would change hands between a willing seller and a willing buyer when neither is acting under compulsion and when both have knowledge of the relevant facts.

"Good cause" means and is limited to a failure to substantially comply with reasonable terms contained in a contract or agreement between a brewer and wholesaler that contains the same terms as the brewer's contract with similarly situated United States, not including United States territories or possessions, distributors.

"Person" means a natural person, corporation, partnership, trust, or other entity and, in case of an entity, it shall include any other entity, except a natural person, which has a majority interest in such entity or effectively controls such entity.

"Sale or transfer" means any disposition of a contract, agreement or relationship between a brewer and a wholesaler or of any rights to acquire and distribute products of a brewer, or any interest therein, with or without consideration, including, but not limited to, bequest, inheritance, gift, exchange, lease or license.

"Successor brewer" means any person, not under common control with the predecessor brewer, who by any means, including, without limitation, by way of purchase, assignment, transfer, lease, license, appointment, contract, agreement, joint venture, merger, or other disposition of all or part of the business, assets, including trademarks, brands, distribution rights and other intangible assets, or ownership interests of a brewer, acquires the business or malt alcoholic beverage brands of another brewer, or otherwise succeeds to a brewer's interest with respect to any malt alcoholic beverage brands.

"Wholesaler" means a plenary wholesale licensee or a limited wholesale licensee who purchases malt alcoholic beverages from a brewer for the purpose of resale to Class C licensees or State Beverage Distributor Licensees.

L.2005, c. 243, § 3, eff. March 1, 2006.

1 N.J.S.A. §§ 33:1–93.12 through 33:1–93.20.

33:1–93.15. Contract between brewer and wholesaler for supply, distribution and sale of products; applicability; prohibited and conforming contact terms; violations

a. Every brewer shall contract and agree in writing with a wholesaler for all supply, distribution and sale of the products of the brewer in this State, and each contract shall provide and specify the rights and duties of the brewer and the wholesaler with regard to such supply, distribution and sale. The terms and provisions of such contracts shall be reasonable, reflect the parties' mutuality of purpose and community of interest in the responsible sale and marketing of their products, and shall comply with and conform to State law and the terms of this act. The provisions of this act may not be waived or modified by written or oral agreement, estoppel or otherwise, and any provision of a contract or ancillary agreement that directly or indirectly requires or amounts to a waiver of any provision of this act, or that would relieve any person of any obligation or liability under this act, or that imposes unreasonable standards of performance on a wholesaler, shall be a violation of this act and shall be null, void and of no effect.

b. This act shall apply to all contracts, agreements and relationships among any brewers and wholesalers, including contracts, agreements or relationships entered into, renewed, extended or modified after the effective date of this act. Contracts, agreements and relationships existing prior to the effective date of this act that are continuing in nature, have an indefinite term or have no specific duration shall be deemed for purposes of this act to have been renewed 60 days after the effective date of this act. 1

c. The terms or provisions of a contract or agreement between a brewer and wholesaler shall not permit a brewer, and it shall be a violation of this act for a brewer:

(1) to terminate, cancel or refuse to renew a contract, agreement or relationship with a wholesaler, or to fail or refuse to grant to a wholesaler the right to purchase and resell any brand extension under the same form of agreement as the base product, in part or in whole,

except where the brewer establishes that it has acted for good cause and in good faith;

(2) to terminate, cancel or refuse to renew a contract, agreement or relationship with a wholesaler, in part or in whole, because the wholesaler refuses or fails to accept an unreasonable amendment to the contract, agreement or relationship;

(3) to terminate, cancel or refuse to renew a contract, agreement or relationship with a wholesaler, in part or in whole, without first giving the wholesaler written notice setting forth all of the alleged deficiencies on the part of the wholesaler and giving the wholesaler a reasonable opportunity of not more than 120 days to cure the alleged deficiencies; provided, however, that such period for cure may be increased or reduced to a commercially reasonable period by an order of a court in this State in a proceeding in which each party shall bear its own costs and expenses;

(4) to require the brewer's consent to the acquisition, sale or transfer of distribution rights for products other than those of the brewer or of assets unrelated to the distribution of the brewer's products;

(5) to unreasonably withhold consent to a proposed sale or transfer of any ownership interests in the wholesaler to the spouse, children or heirs of existing holders of such ownership interests or to employees of the wholesaler, or to trusts for the benefit of such persons, except upon a statement of reasonable grounds, provided such transfer does not result in a sale or transfer of effective control, including but not limited to a change in the persons holding the majority voting power, of the wholesaler; or to take more than 30 days to approve or disapprove the proposed sale or transfer after the brewer has received written notice of the proposal from the wholesaler and received all reasonably requested information from the wholesaler to enable the brewer to pass upon the proposed sale or transfer.

(6) to unreasonably withhold consent to a proposed sale or transfer, in part or in whole, of any ownership interests in the wholesaler or the distribution rights for the brewer's products, assets of the wholesaler related to the distribution of the brewer's products, or of ownership interests in the wholesaler to other parties, except upon a statement of reasonable grounds that are based upon reasonable, previously announced, in an agreement with its wholesalers or otherwise, standards of the brewer, relating to the qualifications of such transferee relating to the character, financial ability or business experience of the proposed transferee, or relating to the resulting market combinations or territory to be serviced by the transferee; or to take more than 30 days to approve or disapprove the proposed sale or transfer after the brewer has received written notice of the proposal from the wholesaler and received all reasonably requested information from the wholesaler to enable the brewer to pass upon the proposed sale or transfer, provided that such period may be extended by

agreement of the parties; provided, however, that at any time within such 30–day period prior to the date on which the brewer approves or disapproves such a proposed sale or transfer, the brewer shall have the right and option to purchase, and in the event of a brewer's disapproval relating to the resulting market combinations or territory to be serviced by the transferee, the wholesaler shall have the right and option to require the brewer to purchase at the price and on the terms and conditions set forth in the agreement between the wholesaler and the proposed transferee, all of the distribution rights, assets or ownership interest that are the subject of the proposed sale or transfer, at the price and on the terms and conditions set forth in the agreement between the wholesaler and the proposed transferee, subject to the following:

(a) if the proposed transferee is the spouse, children or heirs of existing holders of ownership interests in the wholesaler, then the brewer shall not have the right and option to purchase such ownership interest;

(b) if the proposed transferee is an existing holder of ownership interests in the wholesaler, or is the manager or the successor manager of the wholesaler, then if the brewer exercises its option to purchase under this section, the wholesaler may, instead of selling or transferring to the brewer, rescind the proposed sale or transfer by notice to the brewer; and

(c) the brewer shall complete such purchase within 60 days of its exercise of its right to do so.

(7) to allow more than one wholesaler to sell any of the brewer's product lines or brands within the same territory or area at the same time. This paragraph shall not apply to contracts or agreements entered into prior to the effective date of this act, or future renewals of such contracts or agreements, to the extent that, as permitted under the existing contract or agreement and the future renewals allow, as of the effective date of this act, different wholesalers to sell certain but not all of the brewer's brands or brand extensions within the same territory or area at the same time;

(8) to unreasonably fail to consent to the wholesaler's designation of an individual as the wholesaler's manager or successor-manager in accordance with previously announced non-discriminatory and reasonable qualifications and standards;

(9) to withdraw approval of an individual as the wholesaler's manager or successor-manager unless in good faith and with just cause based upon deficiencies in the performance of the manager or successor-manager, which in the case of the manager shall be material deficiencies;

(10) to prohibit, directly or indirectly, the right of free association among wholesalers for any lawful purpose; or

(11) to fail to act, during the term of the contract, agreement or relationship between them in a manner

consistent with the covenant of good faith and fair dealing implicit in State contract law.

A wholesaler also shall act in a manner consistent with the covenant of good faith and fair dealing implied in State contract.

d. It shall not be a violation of this act for a successor brewer to:

(1) terminate, in whole or in part, its contract, agreement or relationship with a wholesaler, or the contract, agreement or relationship with a wholesaler of the brewer it succeeded, for the purpose of transferring the distribution rights in the wholesaler's territory for the malt alcoholic beverage brands to which the successor brewer succeeded, to a wholesaler or wholesalers that then distributes other products of the successor brewer in such territory, provided that the successor brewer or the second wholesaler or wholesalers first pays to the first wholesaler the fair market value of the first wholesaler's business with respect to the terminated brand or brands; provided, however, that such termination shall not be permitted, and may be enjoined, where it may cause irreparable injury to the first wholesaler and the standards for injunctive relief are otherwise met; and provided further that a rebuttable presumption of such irreparable injury shall be inferred when the terminated brand or brands represent 20% or more of the first wholesaler's gross sales; or

(2) to assume and continue the contract, agreement or relationship of the brewer it succeeded with a wholesaler in the wholesaler's territory for the malt alcoholic beverage brands to which it succeeded, notwithstanding that the successor brewer distributes other products in such territory through another wholesaler.

e. Whether the terms of a contract, agreement or relationship conform with the provisions of this section shall be determined by a court of this State in the context of a specific case or controversy among wholesalers and brewers only, and not by generally applicable rule, regulation or otherwise. In any such determination proper consideration should be given to relevant precedents provided under the "Franchise Practices Act," P.L.1971, c. 356 (C.56:10–1 et seq.), and the fact that a term of a contract, agreement or relationship may be a term of the kind described in section 9 of this act [2] shall not be considered in making such determination.

L.2005, c. 243, § 4, eff. March 1, 2006.

[1] L.2005, c. 243, eff. March 1, 2006.
[2] N.J.S.A. § 33:1–93.20.

33:1–93.16. Immediate termination of contract between brewer and wholesaler; conditions

Notwithstanding the provisions of paragraphs (1) through (3) of subsection c. of section 4 of this act, [1] a brewer may immediately terminate a contract or agreement with a wholesaler, to the extent provided in reasonable terms of the contract or agreement that contains the same terms as the brewer's contract with similarly situated United States, not including United

States territories or possessions, distributors, if any of the following occur:

a. The assignment or attempted assignment by the wholesaler for the benefit of creditors, the institution of proceedings in bankruptcy by or against the wholesaler, the dissolution or liquidation of the wholesaler, the insolvency of the wholesaler or the wholesaler's failure to pay for malt alcoholic beverages in accordance with the agreed terms;

b. Failure of any owner to sell his ownership interest in a wholesaler within 120 days after the:

(1) owner has been convicted of a felony or crime of the third degree or higher which, in the reasonable judgment of the brewer, may adversely affect the goodwill or interests of the wholesaler or the brewer and the brewer notifies the wholesaler that it requires such sale; or

(2) brewer learns of such conviction and notifies the wholesaler that it requires such sale because, in the reasonable judgment of the brewer, it may adversely affect the goodwill or interests of the wholesaler or the brewer and the brewer notifies the wholesaler that it requires such sale;

c. Fraudulent conduct of the wholesaler, in any of its dealings with the brewer or the brewer's products, that is known to, or should have been known to the senior management or the owners of the wholesaler;

d. Revocation or suspension for more than 31 days of the wholesaler's federal basic permit or of any state or local license required of a wholesaler for the normal operation of its business;

e. Intentional sale, directly or indirectly, of malt alcoholic beverages by a wholesaler outside the sales territory prescribed by the brewer; or

f. Without brewer consent, the wholesaler engages in changes in ownership, the establishment of trusts or other ownership interests, enters into buy-sell agreements, or grants an option to purchase an ownership interest; this provision will not apply if the wholesaler establishes that the brewer's failure to consent, after having received notice as provided in paragraph (5) or (6) of subsection c. of section 4 of this act, was in violation of this act.

L.2005, c. 243, § 5, eff. March 1, 2006.

[1] N.J.S.A. § 33:1–93.15.

33:1–93.17. Proper representation of brewer by wholesaler

During the term of a contract or agreement between a brewer and a wholesaler subject to this act, the wholesaler shall, in accordance with the reasonable standards of such contract or agreement, as reasonably relied upon by the wholesaler, enforced without discriminatory intent and in good faith, and uniformly applicable to similarly situated distributors, maintain physical facilities, equipment and personnel so that the product and brand of the brewer are properly represent-

ed in the territory of the wholesaler, the reputation and trade name of the brewer are reasonably protected, and the public is served.

L.2005, c. 243, § 6, eff. March 1, 2006.

33:1–93.18. Action against brewer for violation; remedies; third party action limited

a. Any brewer or wholesaler may bring an action against a brewer for violation of this act, or against a successor brewer in connection with a termination pursuant to paragraph (1) of subsection d. of section 4 of this act, [1] in the Superior Court of the State of New Jersey. Any brewer who violates any provision of this act, and any successor brewer who terminates a contract, agreement or relationship with a wholesaler pursuant to paragraph (1) of subsection d. of section 4 of this act, shall pay the injured wholesaler all reasonable damages sustained by it as a result of the brewer's violations. Injunctive and other equitable relief also shall be available in appropriate circumstances under the applicable standards for such relief under State law. Injunctive equitable relief shall be granted against an actual or threatened unlawful failure or refusal to grant a wholesaler the right to purchase and resell a brand extension. The wholesaler or brewer who sues alleging a violation of this act shall, if successful, also be entitled to the costs of the action including, but not limited to, reasonable attorney's fees.

b. Without limiting the provisions of subsection a. of this section, if a brewer violates paragraph (1), (2) or (3) of subsection c. of section 4 of this act, the injured wholesaler's reasonable damages shall include the fair market value of the wholesaler's business with respect to the terminated brand or brands.

c. If a brewer terminates or fails to renew, in whole or in part, a contract, agreement or relationship with a wholesaler for good cause and in good faith, other than terminations or failures to renew properly based upon grounds for immediate termination under section 5 of this act, [2] the brewer shall pay to the wholesaler reasonable compensation, which may be established by a reasonable liquidated damages provision in a written contract or written agreement between the brewer and the wholesaler. Payment for inventory and other tangible assets owned and used by the wholesaler in its operation as a wholesaler for the brewer's products as provided for under the standards of a written contract or written agreement, as well as a payment determined by multiplying by two the wholesaler's pre-tax net income attributable to the sale of the brewer's brand or brands for the wholesaler's most recently completed fiscal year preceding the year in which the termination occurs, is deemed to be a reasonable liquidated damages provision under this act for such a termination of the right to distribute brands representing more than 20% of the wholesaler's revenues. This payment shall not be deemed reasonable compensation in any other circumstance or to represent a basis for calculating fair market value. In particular and without limitation, in the case of brands representing 20% or less of a wholesaler's revenues, which may not require significant incremental expenses for delivery, sales and service, making a net income standard inappropriate, such payment shall not be deemed to be a reasonable liquidated damages provision under this act.

d. In the event of a termination under section 5 of this act, payment for inventory in the manner prescribed under the reasonable standards of a contract or agreement is reasonable compensation under this act.

e. Nothing in this act shall be deemed to give a right of action for violation of this act to any third party to the relationship between a brewer and a wholesaler, except for a brewer adversely affected by another brewer's violation of this act with respect to a common wholesaler.

L.2005, c. 243, § 7, eff. March 1, 2006.

   1 N.J.S.A. § 33:1–93.15.
   2 N.J.S.A. § 33:1–93.16.

33:1–93.19. Invalidity; applicability of Franchise Practices Act; severability

If any material provision within any section of this act is held invalid, the remainder of this act and the act as a whole shall be held invalid; provided that if the application of any material provision within any section of this act to any person or circumstance is held invalid, then the remainder of this act and the act as a whole shall be held invalid as to such person or circumstance. The "Franchise Practices Act," P.L.1971, c. 356 (C.56:10–1 et seq.) shall not apply to those agreements subject to this act; provided, however, that as the material provisions of this act are not severable, this section shall not be severable from the provisions of sections 3, 4 and 7 of this act, 1 and in the event that any provision thereof is held invalid, then the "Franchise Practices Act" shall be fully applicable to the extent it would otherwise apply as if this act had not been enacted, and if the application of any provision thereof to any person or circumstance is held invalid, then the "Franchise Practices Act" shall be fully applicable to such person or circumstance to the extent it would otherwise apply as if this act had not been enacted with respect to such person or circumstance.

L.2005, c. 243, § 8, eff. March 1, 2006.

   1 N.J.S.A. §§ 33:1–93.14, 33:1–93.15, and 33:1–93.18.

33:1–93.20. Input by brewer into operations of wholesaler; conditions; contract terms

The Legislature finds that where a brewer's products represent more than 20% of a wholesaler's gross sales and the brewer and wholesaler have a community of interest in the marketing of the brewer's products, there is a justification for certain input by the brewer into the operations of the wholesaler, but that such input from numerous brewers representing smaller percentages of a wholesaler's gross sales might subject wholesalers to inconsistent obligations, create uncertainty as to those

obligations, and interfere unreasonably with the wholesaler's ability to operate its business. Accordingly, consistent with the legislatively declared public policy of this State in section 4 of P.L.1985, c. 258 (C.33:1–3.1), the use of the following terms in any agreement or contract, including agreements or contracts existing on the effective date of this act, 1 between manufacturers of malt alcoholic beverages and wholesalers, shall not be construed to grant such manufacturer or wholesaler an interest in another manufacturer or wholesaler under the relevant provisions of Title 33 of the Revised Statutes or any rule or regulation promulgated thereunder provided that the brewer's products represent more than 20% of the wholesaler's gross sales and the brewer and wholesaler have a community of interest in the marketing of the brewer's products:

a. Terms providing brewers the ability to give reasonable consent to wholesaler ownership and management changes, including successor management;

b. Terms setting forth quality, operational, marketing and sales standards designed to properly represent the products, brands, reputation and trade name of the brewer, in the territory and at retail, including terms under which a wholesaler commits to provide certain efforts and resources toward a brewer's products;

c. Terms concerning ordering and inventory methods with respect to the brewer's products; and

d. Terms requiring wholesalers to provide financial information to a brewer related to sales and operations of the brewer's products, and reasonable aggregated financial information related to the sales and operations of all other malt alcoholic beverage products distributed by the wholesaler.

L.2005, c. 243, § 9, eff. March 1, 2006.

   1 L.2005, c. 243, eff. March 1, 2006.

33:1–94. Retail regulations by municipalities to be governed by ordinance only

No regulation concerning the sale, transportation, delivery, serving, mixing, distribution, storing or possession of alcoholic beverages at retail, or the conduct of any business licensed to sell alcoholic beverages at retail, or the nature and condition of the premises upon which the sale of alcoholic beverages at retail may be made, or the retail sale of alcoholic beverages on Sunday, or the fixing of license fees, shall hereafter be adopted by the governing board or body of any municipality except by ordinance; provided, however, all such regulations heretofore adopted by the governing board or body of any municipality whether by ordinance or resolution shall continue in full force and effect until repealed, amended or otherwise altered or changed by ordinance.

L.1939, c. 234, p. 634, § 1, eff. July 18, 1939.

33:1–95. Repealed by L.1942, c. 159, § 1, eff. May 6, 1942

33:1–96. Licenses for new license terms deemed renewals

Any license for a new license term, which is issued to replace a license which expired on the last day of the license term which immediately preceded the commencement of said new license term or which is issued to replace a license which will expire on the last day of the license term which immediately precedes the commencement of said new license term shall be deemed to be a renewal of the expired or expiring license; *provided*, that said license is of the same class and type as the expired or expiring license, covers the same licensed premises, is issued to the holder of the expired or expiring license and is issued pursuant to an application therefor which shall have been filed with the proper issuing authority prior to the commencement of said new license term or not later than thirty days after the commencement thereof. Licenses issued otherwise than as above herein provided shall be deemed to be new licenses.

L.1939, c. 281, p. 702, § 1, eff. Aug. 2, 1939. Amended by L.1944, c. 187, p. 695, § 1, eff. April 20, 1944.

33:1–97. Special auction permit; alcoholic beverages

a. The director may issue a special auction permit to any nonprofit organization operating solely for civic, religious, educational, charitable, fraternal, social or recreational purposes. The fee for the license shall be $100.

b. The permit shall only entitle the permittee to sell at auction alcoholic beverages donated to the organization. A person licensed under Title 33 of the Revised Statutes may in any calendar year donate alcoholic beverages to a maximum of three nonprofit organizations which have been issued a permit under this section, provided such donations are not made in connection with a sale of an alcoholic beverage.

c. The permit shall be valid only for the date specified. Only one such permit shall be issued to a nonprofit organization in any calender [1] year.

d. Pursuant to the provisions of the "Administrative Procedure Act," P.L.1968, c. 410 (C.52:14B–1 et seq.), the director shall promulgate regulations to effectuate the provisions of this act.

L.2001, c. 115, § 1, eff. Sept. 1, 2001.

[1] So in original. Probably should be "calendar".

CHAPTER 2

STILLS AND DISTILLING APPARATUS

Section
33:2–1.   Stills and distilling apparatus registered with commissioner; powers of commissioner; definitions.
33:2–2.   Stills not registered declared unlawful property.
33:2–3.   Seizure of unregistered stills; search warrant; arrest of offenders.
33:2–4.   Hearing by commissioner; notice.

Section
33:2–5.   Forfeiture and sale of seized property; padlocking premises.
33:2–6.   Director's determination in form of order; review.
33:2–7.   Return of seized property; costs.
33:2–8.   Accounting for moneys.
33:2–9.   Violating padlocking order; misdemeanor.
33:2–10.   Failure to register still; misdemeanor.
33:2–11.   Unregistered stills in actual operation declared nuisance; destruction.

33:2–1. Stills and distilling apparatus registered with commissioner; powers of commissioner; definitions

Every person having in his possession or custody or under his control any still or any distilling apparatus set up, dismantled or in the process of construction or parts thereof, shall register the same with the commissioner of alcoholic beverage control, hereinafter in this chapter called the "commissioner".

The commissioner shall have and exercise the same powers of investigation and of prescribing rules and regulations with respect to such stills and distilling apparatus and parts thereof as are accorded to him by chapter 1 of this title (§ 33:1–1 et seq.), in connection with the manufacture of alcoholic beverages.

The definitions set forth in section 33:1–1 of this title shall also apply to this chapter.

33:2–2. Stills not registered declared unlawful property

Any such still or distilling apparatus or parts thereof not registered pursuant to section 33:2–1 of this title, together with all articles, implements or paraphernalia used or adaptable for use in connection therewith and all personal property of whatsoever kind, found in a building or in any yard or inclosure connected with a building or on the premises in which such still or distilling apparatus or parts thereof are found, are declared to be unlawful property.

33:2–3. Seizure of unregistered stills; search warrant; arrest of offenders

Any officer knowing or having reasonable cause to believe that any still or distilling apparatus or any parts thereof constitute such unlawful property, it shall be his duty to investigate, under proper search warrant when necessary, which it shall be his further duty to apply for, and to seize such still or distilling apparatus or parts thereof, together with all articles, implements or paraphernalia used or adaptable for use in connection therewith and all personal property of whatsoever kind, found in a building or in any yard or inclosure connected with a building or on the premises in which such still or distilling apparatus or parts thereof are found, and to arrest all persons whom he shall know, or have reasonable ground to believe, are committing, or have committed, a misdemeanor under this chapter and to make complaint against such persons as in other cases of misdemeanors. All property when seized shall be under the jurisdiction of the commissioner.

33:2–4. Hearing by commissioner; notice

When any property is seized pursuant to section 33:2–3 of this title, the commissioner within fifteen days of such seizure shall cause to be posted at the place of seizure a notice that a hearing will be held by the commissioner at a place and time named in such notice which time shall not be less than five nor more than thirty days after the posting of such notice, to determine whether the seized property constitutes such unlawful property.

At least three days prior to the date of hearing a notice thereof shall be published in a newspaper printed and circulating in the county where the property was seized and shall be mailed to any person known or believed by the commissioner to have an interest in the seized property and to the record owner of and any person known or believed to have an interest in any building or premises in or on which the seized property was located when seized.

33:2–5. Forfeiture and sale of seized property; padlocking premises

If after such hearing the commissioner determines that the seized property constitutes such unlawful property he shall declare such property forfeited and may, in his discretion, order that the seized property, in whole or in part, be sold, destroyed or retained for the use of hospitals, and state, county and municipal institutions and that the building or premises in or on which such unlawful property was located when seized shall not be occupied or used for any purpose whatsoever for such period, not exceeding one year, as shall be fixed by the commissioner.

33:2–6. Director's determination in form of order; review

The determination of the director shall be in the form of an order which shall be subject to review by the Superior Court by a proceeding in lieu of prerogative writ.

Amended by L.1953, c. 32, p. 582, § 5, eff. March 19, 1953.

33:2–7. Return of seized property; costs

The commissioner, upon being satisfied that the seized property does not constitute unlawful property, shall return the same to the person or place from whom or which the same was taken. The commissioner, upon being satisfied that a person whose property has been seized or forfeited pursuant to the provisions of this chapter has acted in good faith and has unknowingly violated the provisions of this chapter, may order that such property be returned upon payment of the reasonable costs incurred in connection with the seizure, such costs to be determined by the commissioner.

33:2–8. Accounting for moneys

All moneys received by the commissioner under this chapter shall be accounted for as in the case of license fees.

33:2–9. Violating padlocking order; misdemeanor

Any person who shall knowingly violate any order of the commissioner that a building or premises shall not be occupied or used for any purpose whatsoever shall be guilty of a misdemeanor, and punished by a fine of not less than one hundred dollars and not more than five hundred dollars, or imprisonment for not less than thirty days and not more than six months, or both.

33:2–10. Failure to register still; misdemeanor

Any person who shall have in his possession or custody or under his control any still or distilling apparatus set up, dismantled, or in the process of construction, or parts thereof without having registered same in accordance with the provisions of this chapter shall be guilty of a misdemeanor, and punished by a fine of not less than one hundred dollars and not more than one thousand dollars or imprisonment for not less than thirty days and not more than three years, or both.

33:2–11. Unregistered stills in actual operation declared nuisance; destruction

Any still not registered pursuant to this chapter in actual operation in the manufacture of illicit beverages or set up for such purpose, is hereby declared to be a nuisance per se and such still, parts thereof and all other property actually used in connection therewith when seized may be destroyed at the direction of the commissioner at the time of the seizure or thereafter, without notice or hearing, anything in this chapter to the contrary notwithstanding.

CHAPTER 3

OTHER LAWS RELATING TO INTOXICATING LIQUORS

Section
33:3–1 to 33:3–8. Repealed.
33:3–9.   Manufacture, sale, etc., of poisoned liquors; penalty.
33:3–10. Sale, etc. of poisoned liquors causing serious injury or death; penalty; certain laws unaffected.

33:3–1 to 33:3–8. Repealed by L.1938, c. 285, § 1, eff. May 31, 1938

33:3–9. Manufacture, sale, etc., of poisoned liquors; penalty

Any person, corporation, partnership or member of any association or any agent, servant or employee of any person, corporation, partnership or member of any association who shall manufacture, transport, possess, sell, barter, give away, furnish or otherwise dispose of any alcohol for internal consumption, any whiskey, gin, brandy, wine or any other alcoholic beverage of any nature whatsoever containing any poisonous chemical or chemicals or any poisonous ingredients of any description whatsoever which, if taken internally, will injuriously affect the health or bodily condition of any person or which will cause the death of any person shall be guilty of a misdemeanor.

33:3–10. Sale, etc. of poisoned liquors causing serious injury or death; penalty; certain laws unaffected

Any person, corporation, partnership or member of any association or any agent, servant or employee of any person, corporation, partnership or member of any association who shall have sold, bartered, given away, furnished or otherwise disposed of to any person whatsoever any alcohol for internal consumption, whiskey, gin, brandy, wine or any other alcoholic beverage of any nature whatsoever containing any poisonous chemical or chemicals or any poisonous ingredients of any description whatsoever which shall have caused serious injury to the health or bodily condition of any person or shall have caused the death of any person shall be guilty of a high misdemeanor and shall be punishable by a fine of not exceeding two thousand dollars ($2,000.00), or imprisonment at hard labor or otherwise not exceeding ten years, or both.

Nothing in this section is intended to diminish, alter or in anywise change or in anywise affect the provisions

of sections 2A:113–1 to 2A:113–5 of the New Jersey Statutes.

Amended by L.1953, c. 32, p. 582, § 6, eff. March 19, 1953.

CHAPTER 4

COMMISSION ON ALCOHOLISM AND PROMOTION OF TEMPERANCE

Section
33:4–1.   Commission created; purpose and powers.

33:4–1.   Commission created; purpose and powers

The Commissioner of Alcoholic Beverage Control, the Commissioner of Institutions and Agencies, the Commissioner of Education and the Director of Health, are hereby constituted a commission, to be known as the Commission on Alcoholism and Promotion of Temperance, and empowered to prepare and administer a program for the rehabilitation of alcoholics and the promotion and furtherance of temperance and temperance education in this State; to utilize such facilities in this State, including equipment, and professional and other personnel, as may be made available for said purposes; and to expend such sums for said purposes as may, from time to time, be appropriated therefor by the Legislature.

L.1945, c. 94, p. 435, § 1, eff. April 4, 1945.

APPENDIX to Chapter 1
NEW JERSEY ADMINISTRATIVE CODE

TITLE 13

LAW AND PUBLIC SAFETY

CHAPTER 2

DIVISION OF ALCOHOLIC BEVERAGE CONTROL

CHAPTER EXPIRATION NOTE

Chapter 2, Division of Alcoholic Beverage Control, expires on January 19, 2011.

SUBCHAPTER 8.   CLUB LICENSES

Section
13:2–8.1.	Definitions.
13:2–8.2.	Bona fide clubs.
13:2–8.3.	Previous period of continuous, active operation.
13:2–8.4.	Previous period of possession and use of club quarters.
13:2–8.5.	Exceptions to eligibility requirements.
13:2–8.6.	Qualifications of officers and members.
13:2–8.7.	Submission of club member list and club charter.
13:2–8.8.	Sales restricted to club members.
13:2–8.9.	Sales for on-premises consumption only.
13:2–8.10.	Hours of permissible sale and consumption.
13:2–8.11.	Social affairs permittees.
13:2–8.12.	Advertising prohibition.
13:2–8.13.	Advertising prohibition.
13:2–8.14.	Violations.

SUBCHAPTER 10.   PLENARY AND FARM WINERY LICENSES; WINE BLENDING LICENSES; RETAIL PRIVILEGES.

13:2–10.1.	Application for plenary and farm winery licenses; statement of intent.
13:2–10.2.	License certificate endorsement.
13:2–10.3.	Labeling wine sold at retail.
13:2–10.4.	Hours of retail sales.
13:2–10.5.	Application for wine blending license; form.
13:2–10.6.	Joint retail salesroom.

SUBCHAPTER 12.   SPECIAL PERMITS FOR HOME MANUFACTURE OF MALT ALCOHOLIC BEVERAGES AND WINES FOR PERSONAL OR HOUSEHOLD USE OR CONSUMPTION

13:2–12.1.	Special malt alcoholic beverage and wine permits.
13:2–12.2.	(Reserved).
13:2–12.3.	Ineligibility of premises.
13:2–12.4.	Ineligibility of persons under the legal age.
13:2–12.5.	Other disqualification.
13:2–12.6.	Number of permits per year.
13:2–12.7.	Transfer of permits.
13:2–12.8.	Revocation of permit.

Section

SUBCHAPTER 14.   EMPLOYMENT BY LICENSEES OF A PERSON FAILING TO QUALIFY AS A LICENSEE

13:2–14.1.	Restriction upon a minor's employment activities on a licensed premises.
13:2–14.2.	Minor's employment permit; fees.
13:2–14.3.	Permit; age restrictions.
13:2–14.4.	Blanket minors' employment permit.
13:2–14.5.	Restrictions upon employing criminally disqualified persons.
13:2–14.6.	Application for a rehabilitation employment permit; temporary work letter.
13:2–14.7.	Rehabilitation employment permit; duration; types; fees.
13:2–14.8.	Restrictions upon limited rehabilitation employment permittee.
13:2–14.9.	Termination of employment of disqualified person.
13:2–14.10.	Nontransferability of permits; term of permit; applicant's photograph and fingerprints.
13:2–14.11.	Amendment of application.
13:2–14.12.	Prohibited conduct of permittee.
13:2–14.13.	Cancellation, suspension and revocation of permit.

SUBCHAPTER 16.   SOLICITOR'S PERMIT

13:2–16.1.	Necessity of permit.
13:2–16.2.	Privileges of permit.
13:2–16.3.	Eligibility for permit.
13:2–16.4.	Permits to enforcement officers or municipal officials.
13:2–16.5.	Permit fees.
13:2–16.6.	Application for permit; photograph and fingerprints; affidavit of compliance with the Alcoholic Beverage Control Act.
13:2–16.7.	Term of permit.
13:2–16.8.	Nontransferability of permit.
13:2–16.9.	Amendment of application.
13:2–16.10.	Surrender of permit upon termination of employment.
13:2–16.11.	Restrictions on permittee.
13:2–16.12.	Interest of permittee in retail business.
13:2–16.13.	Search of permittee's vehicle.
13:2–16.14.	Responsibilities of employer.
13:2–16.15.	Solicitor's contracts.
13:2–16.16.	Filing of statement of compensation with Director.
13:2–16.17.	Suspension or revocation of solicitor's permit.

Section

SUBCHAPTER 20. TRANSPORTATION OF ALCOHOLIC
BEVERAGES BY LICENSEES; INSIGNIA

13:2–20.1. Transit insignia; transportation of alcoholic beverages.

13:2–20.2. Transportation by retail licensee; delivery slip; emergency delivery.

13:2–20.3. Transportation by State licensee with retail privileges; delivery slip or route card.

13:2–20.4. Transportation by other State licensees, importers and manufacturers; delivery documents.

13:2–20.5. Eligibility for transit insignia or transportation license insignia.

13:2–20.6. Application; fees.

13:2–20.7. Term of transit insignia or transportation license insignia; renewal.

13:2–20.8. Location of transit insignia or transportation license insignia.

13:2–20.9. Restrictions applicable to vehicles bearing transit insignia or transportation license insignia.

13:2–20.10. Search of licensed vehicle.

13:2–20.11. Duty of personnel delivering alcoholic beverages to consumers.

SUBCHAPTER 21. TRANSPORTATION OF ALCOHOLIC
BEVERAGES INTO, THROUGH OR OUT OF THE
STATE

13:2–21.1. Delivery into or out of the State.

13:2–21.2. Interstate transportation for personal use; amount limitation; permit.

13:2–21.3. Transportation through New Jersey.

13:2–21.4. Limited transportation permit.

13:2–21.5. Emergency trip permit.

13:2–21.6. Prohibited transportation; seizure of unlawful property.

13:2–21.7. Search of vehicle.

SUBCHAPTER 23. CONDUCT OF LICENSEES
AND PERMITTEES AND USE OF
LICENSED PREMISES

13:2–23.1. Prohibition against serving persons under the legal age and intoxicated persons.

13:2–23.2. Prohibiting sales or consumption of alcoholic beverages during elections; municipal option.

13:2–23.3. Closing premises during public emergency or crime investigation.

13:2–23.4. House-to-house solicitation forbidden.

13:2–23.5. Prohibited patrons; narcotics or other unlawful drugs; illegal activity or enterprise.

13:2–23.6. Prohibition against immoral activities; disturbance; nuisance on premises.

13:2–23.7. Prohibition against lottery and gambling; exceptions.

13:2–23.8. Eastern Standard Time change.

13:2–23.9. Prohibition against adulterated alcoholic beverages.

13:2–23.10. Restriction upon receiving prohibited deliveries of alcoholic beverages.

13:2–23.11. Consumption of alcoholic beverages and possession of open containers prohibited upon retail distribution licensee's premises; exception.

13:2–23.12. Receiving alcoholic beverages from prohibited source.

13:2–23.13. Maintaining copies of current license certificate; application; list of employees on the licensed premises.

Section

13:2–23.14. Prohibition against indecent matter upon licensed premises.

13:2–23.15. Possession of container mislabeled as to fill prohibited; exception.

13:2–23.16. Prohibited promotions.

13:2–23.17. Restriction upon limited retail distribution licensee possessing chilled malt alcoholic beverages.

13:2–23.18. Solicitation prohibited.

13:2–23.19. Prohibition against offering substitute beverages; exception.

13:2–23.20. Intoxicated workers prohibited.

13:2–23.21. Restrictions upon storage of alcoholic beverages.

13:2–23.22. Requirement for labeled tap markers; provision for electronic systems.

13:2–23.23. Requirements concerning labels; tax payment indicia.

13:2–23.24. Restrictions upon placing of orders.

13:2–23.25. Restrictions upon retail/manufacturer or wholesaler relationships.

13:2–23.26. Fingerprinting requirements.

13:2–23.27. Prohibited activities during license suspension.

13:2–23.28. Standard of liability.

13:2–23.29. Detention of evidence; search of licensed premises.

13:2–23.30. Prohibition against hindering an investigation.

13:2–23.31. Law enforcement officers; ownership prohibition; employment restrictions.

13:2–23.32. Records to be maintained on the licensed premises; other required records.

13:2–23.33. Dishonored checks; unpaid fees.

SUBCHAPTER 38. LIMITATION OF HOURS FOR SALE AND
DELIVERY AT RETAIL OF ALCOHOLIC BEVERAGES IN
ORIGINAL CONTAINERS FOR OFF–PREMISES CONSUMPTION

13:2–38.1. Retail package sales hours.

13:2–38.2. Sunday sales hours for retail distribution licensees and state beverage distributors; effect of municipal ordinances and State statute on sale for off-premises consumption.

SUBCHAPTER 8. CLUB LICENSES

13:2–8.1 Definitions

The following words and terms when used in this subchapter shall have the following meanings unless the context clearly indicates otherwise.

'Club' means an organization, corporation or association controlled by and consisting of 60 or more persons, of legal drinking age, operating solely for benevolent, charitable, fraternal, social, religious, recreational, athletic or similar purposes and not for private gain.

'Club member' means any individual in good standing who has been admitted to voting membership in the manner regularly prescribed by the bylaws of a club, and who maintains such membership in a bona fide manner and whose name and address are entered on the list of members. No individual shall be eligible for such club membership unless he has filed written application with the appropriate body, as set forth in the club bylaws, and such application is approved by said body at least three days subsequent to the filing thereof. Persons holding limited or auxiliary club membership shall not be deemed to be club members.

'Guest of club member' means an individual who is expressly invited to the club licensed premises by an individual member of the club and who is sponsored by and personally attended by the member at such premises. An individual club member may have as his guest no more than nine individuals on any one occasion unless such individuals are attending a private affair, such as a wedding, anniversary, confirmation, bar mitzvah or birthday party, honoring a spouse, child, parent, brother or sister of a club member.

Administrative Correction:
See: 15 N.J.R. 1876(b).
Amended by R.1990 d.412, effective August 20, 1990.
See: 22 N.J.R. 1811(a), 22 N.J.R. 2508(c).
Amended by R.1995 d.450, effective August 21, 1995.
See: 27 N.J.R. 2051(a), 27 N.J.R. 3177(a).

13:2–8.2   Bona fide clubs

Club licenses shall be issued only to bona fide clubs.

13:2–8.3   Previous period of continuous, active operation

Except as provided in N.J.A.C. 13:2-8.5, no license shall be issued to any club unless it shall have been in active operation in the State of New Jersey for at least three years continuously immediately prior to the submission of its application for a license.

13:2–8.4   Previous period of possession and use of club quarters

Except as provided herein or in N.J.A.C. 13:2-8.5, no license shall be issued to any club unless it shall have been in exclusive possession and use of a clubhouse or club quarters for at least three years continuously immediately prior to the submission of its application for a license. A bona fide club which has been in active operation in this State for the period of time required as aforesaid, but which has been deprived of continuous possession and use of its clubhouse or club quarters by reasons of foreclosure, loss of lease, eminent domain, fire, casualty or other removal for a cause other than the violation of the laws of the State or of municipal ordinance, shall not be prevented thereby from obtaining a club license upon presenting to the satisfaction of the issuing authority proof of said facts and proof that possession of suitable premises has been obtained.

Amended by R.1990 d.412, effective August 20, 1990.
See: 22 N.J.R. 1811(a), 22 N.J.R. 2508(c).

13:2–8.5   Exceptions to eligibility requirements

(a) Any constituent unit, chartered or otherwise duly enfranchised chapter or member club of a national or state order, organization or association, which is in possession of suitable premises, shall not be prevented from obtaining a club license by reason of the fact that the unit, chapter or member club has not been in active operation in this State for at least three years continuously or has not been in exclusive continuous possession and use of a clubhouse or club quarters for the same period of time, provided said unit, chapter or member club obtains from the Director, and presents to the issuing authority at or before the issuance of the license, a certificate stating that satisfactory proof has been submitted to the Director that said unit, chapter or member club has been duly credentialed by a national or state order, organization or association which has been in active operation in this State for at least three years continuously immediately prior to submission of the application for a license.

(b) Nothing in N.J.A.C. 13:2-8.3 or 8.4 shall prevent the issuance of a club license to a bona fide club provided that special cause for such issuance is shown in writing to the Director and provided that the Director's written approval of such issuance is first obtained.

Amended by R.1990 d.412, effective August 20, 1990.
See: 22 N.J.R. 1811(a), 22 N.J.R. 2508(c).
Amended by R.2000 d.342, effective August 21, 2000.
See: 32 N.J.R. 1717(a), 32 N.J.R. 3162(a).

13:2–8.6   Qualifications of officers and members

(a) No club license shall be used nor renewal granted to any corporation, association or organization in which an officer or member of the governing body has been convicted of a disqualifying offense pursuant to Title 33 unless the statutory disqualification resulting from such conviction has been removed by order of the Director. Application for removal of the disqualification may be made by verified petition to the Director when the unlawful situation is corrected.

(b) No application shall be approved or renewed unless the issuing authority affirmatively finds and reduces to resolution that:

1. The submitted application form is complete in all respects, including the requirements of N.J.A.C. 13:2-8.7;

2. The officers and directors of applicant club are qualified to be licensed according to all standards established by Title 33 of the New Jersey statutes, regulations promulgated thereunder as well as pertinent local ordinances or conditions consistent with Title 33;

3. The club maintains all records required pursuant to N.J.A.C. 13:2-8.7 and 8.8; and

4. The officers and directors of the applicant club have certified, on a form prescribed by the Director, that they have read and understand all their legal responsibilities pertaining to the operation of a club license.

Amended by R.1979 d.138, effective May 1, 1979.
See: 11 N.J.R. 143(a), 11 N.J.R. 257(c).
Amended by R.1990 d.412, effective August 20, 1990.
See: 22 N.J.R. 1811(a), 22 N.J.R. 2508(c).
Amended by R.1995 d.450, effective August 21, 1995.
See: 27 N.J.R. 2051(a), 27 N.J.R. 3177(a).

13:2–8.7 Submission of club member list and club charter

(a) A printed or typewritten list containing the names and addresses of all members of the club as of date of filing a club license application shall be submitted with the initial application as well as with each subsequent renewal application. No club license shall be renewed unless the club consists of at least 60 members at the time of renewal. The charter or articles of association of the club shall also be presented for inspection or certified copy of the same submitted with the initial application.

(b) Nothing in this section shall prevent the renewal of a license to a club not qualified by reason of a lack of requisite number of members, provided that special cause of such renewal is shown in writing to the Director and further provided that the Director's written approval for such renewal is first obtained.

Amended by R.1990 d.412, effective August 20, 1990.
See: 22 N.J.R. 1811(a), 22 N.J.R. 2508(c).

13:2–8.8 Sales restricted to club members

(a) No club licensee shall sell, serve or deliver, or allow, permit or suffer the sale, service or delivery of any alcoholic beverage to any person not a bona fide member of the club or a bona fide guest of such member.

(b) All club licensees shall have and keep on the licensed premises a true record, on the form prescribed by the Director (set forth below), of all scheduled dinners, luncheons, receptions, dances, parties, catered events and similar affairs held at the club licensed premises and attended by non-club members.

Date of affair _____

Type of affair _____

Sponsored by _____

Was affair conducted under authority of a special permit? _____

If so, give number of permit _____

Were alcoholic beverages supplied by the club licensee? _____

(Signature of authorized officer)

(c) No club licensee shall allow, permit or suffer any such affair to be held at the club licensed premises at which any charge is made to a non-club member or non-bona fide guest in connection with the affair, whether the charge be a direct one for drinks, imposed through the sales of tickets or charging of admission, requiring donation or special assessments, or where the charge is made ostensibly for food, entertainment or anything

else unless a special permit is first obtained from the Director.

Amended by R.1990 d.412, effective August 20, 1990.
See: 22 N.J.R. 1811(a), 22 N.J.R. 2508(c).
Amended by R.1995 d.450, effective August 21, 1995.
See: 27 N.J.R. 2051(a), 27 N.J.R. 3177(a).

13:2–8.9 Sales for on-premises consumption only

No club licensee shall sell, serve or deliver, or allow, permit or suffer the sale, service or delivery of any alcoholic beverages in original containers for off-premises consumption.

Amended by R.1990 d.412, effective August 20, 1990.
See: 22 N.J.R. 1811(a), 22 N.J.R. 2508(c).

13:2–8.10 Hours of permissible sale and consumption

No club licensee shall sell, serve or deliver, or allow, permit or suffer the sale, service, delivery or consumption of any alcoholic beverage on the licensed premises during hours or on days when plenary or seasonal retail consumption licensees in the same municipality are prohibited from such activity by municipal regulation or referendum.

13:2–8.11 Social affairs permittees

No club licensee shall sell, serve or deliver any alcoholic beverages to the holder of any special permit authorizing sale of alcoholic beverages at a social affair to be conducted by a permittee other than the club licensee itself, or to any person attending such social affair on the club licensed premises unless such person is, in fact, a bona fide member of the licensee-club or a bona fide guest of such member.

Amended by R.1990 d.412, effective August 20, 1990.
See: 22 N.J.R. 1811(a), 22 N.J.R. 2508(c).

13:2–8.12 (Reserved)

Amended by R.1990 d.412, effective August 20, 1990.
See: 22 N.J.R. 1811(a), 22 N.J.R. 2508(c).
Repealed by R.1995 d.450, effective August 21, 1995.
See: 27 N.J.R. 2051(a), 27 N.J.R. 3177(a).

13:2–8.13 Advertising prohibition

No club licensee shall advertise, directly or indirectly, or allow, permit or suffer any advertising to non-club members the availability of alcoholic beverages at its licensed premises; provided, however, that the prohibition here in shall not apply to the holder of any special permit issued by the director and authorizing the sale of alcoholic beverages at a social affair to be conducted at the club's licensed premises, with respect to such particular affair providing the social affair permit number is indicated in the advertisement.

Amended by R.1990 d.412, effective August 20, 1990.
See: 22 N.J.R. 1811(a), 22 N.J.R. 2508(c).

13:2–8.14 Violations

A club license is restricted type of retail license and therefore its holder must comply with not only the rules set forth in this subchapter, but with all the relevant provisions applicable to retail licenses. In disciplinary proceedings brought pursuant to the alcoholic beverage law, it shall be sufficient, in order to establish the guilt of the club licensee, to show the violation was committed by an agent, servant or employee of the club licensee or a member of the club. The fact that the licensee did not participate in the violation or that its agent, servant, employee or member acted contrary to instructions given to him by the club licensee or that the violation did not occur in the presence of the licensee's agent, servant, employee or member shall constitute no defense to the charges preferred in such disciplinary proceedings.

Amended by R.1990 d.412, effective August 20, 1990.
See: 22 N.J.R. 1811(a), 22 N.J.R. 2508(c).

SUBCHAPTER 10.   PLENARY AND FARM WINERY LICENSES; WINE BLENDING LICENSES; RETAIL PRIVILEGES

13:2–10.1 Application for plenary and farm winery licenses; statement of intent

(a) All applicants for plenary winery licenses shall comply with the application, advertising and hearing provisions of this chapter. The application shall be filed on a form prescribed by the Director in which the applicant shall demonstrate its ability to comply with the requirements of N.J.S.A. 33:1-10.2a. The applicant shall file a statement of intent which shall include the following information: number of acres engaged in cultivating grapes or growing fruit; location of acreage in respect to the proposed licensed premises; type of products to be produced (for example, naturally fermented wines, fortified wines, treated wines); intent to sell products to wholesalers, retailers, or consumers; and intent to utilize other premises for retail sales.

(b) All applicants for a farm winery license shall comply with the application, advertising and hearing provisions of this chapter. The application shall be filed on a form prescribed by the Director in which the applicant shall demonstrate its ability to comply with the requirements of N.J.S.A. 33:1-10.2b. The applicant shall file a statement of intent which shall include the following information: number of acres engaged in cultivating grapes or growing fruit; location of acreage with respect to the proposed licensed premises; means by which acreage is under the applicant's control; plan under which New Jersey grown fruit will constitute at least 51 percent of wine product initially with plans to increase that percentage over five years; intent to sell products to wholesalers, retailers, and/or consumers; number of gallons projected to be produced annually; and intent for off winery premises retail sales locations.

(c) Any winery licensee who seeks permission for additional retail sales premises shall file an application on a form prescribed by the Director which shall be accompanied by a sketch of the proposed licensed premises which depicts the area to be included under the license and includes the perimeter measurements. If the additional sales location is to be within a premises where another mercantile business is operating, the application shall be accompanied by a description of the business relationship with the other mercantile business and shall include, a copy of the lease agreement; a statement of how the winery will maintain separate accounting for sales; a description of how the applicant will compensate its sales employees, and shall identify whether any consumption or sampling will take place, and if so, how this will be controlled, and will state its plan for demarcating the licensed premises.

Repeal and New Rule, R.1990 d.412, effective August 20, 1990.
See: 22 N.J.R. 1811(a), 22 N.J.R. 2508(c).
Amended by R.1995 d.450, effective August 21, 1995.
See: 27 N.J.R. 2051(a), 27 N.J.R. 3177(a).

13:2–10.2 License certificate endorsement

Whenever the holder of a plenary or farm winery license is granted the privilege of selling its wine products at retail at a premises other than the winery licensed premises, the license certificate shall be appropriately endorsed by the Director and will set forth the retail privileges conferred thereunder, and no plenary or farm winery licensee whose certificate does not bear such endorsement shall sell or deliver or allow, permit or suffer the sale or delivery at retail of wine at other than the winery licensed premises.

Amended by R.1990 d.412, effective August 20, 1990.
See: 22 N.J.R. 1811(a), 22 N.J.R. 2508(c).
Amended by R.1995 d.450, effective August 21, 1995.
See: 27 N.J.R. 2051(a), 27 N.J.R. 3177(a).

13:2–10.3 Labeling wine sold at retail

(a) Unless the container in which the wine product is sold shall bear a label approved pursuant to the provisions of the Federal Alcoholic Administration Act, each plenary winery licensee having the privilege of selling wine at retail shall attach a label to each container in which wine is sold to consumers, which label shall bear the brand name, type, alcoholic content of the wine stated in percentage of alcohol by volume within an accuracy of one percent, net contents of the container, and name or trade name and address of the licensee.

(b) Unless the container in which the wine is sold shall bear a label approved pursuant to the provisions of the Federal Alcoholic Ad-ministration Act, each farm winery licensee shall attach a label to each container in which wine is sold to consumers, which label shall bear the brand name, type, alcoholic content of the wine stated in percentage of alcohol by volume within an accuracy of one percent, net contents of the container, and the name and address of the licensee. Every container's label must indicate that it is 'New Jersey Wine' and its wine contents shall comply with the requirements of N.J.S.A. 33:1-10.2b.

(c) All wine products which a plenary or farm winery license shall offer for resale to another authorized New Jersey licensee or to sell to consumers at retail shall be brand registered pursuant to the provisions of N.J.A.C. 13:2-33.1.

Amended by R.1990 d.412, effective August 20, 1990.
See: 22 N.J.R. 1811(a), 22 N.J.R. 2508(c).
Amended by R.1995 d.450, effective August 21, 1995.
See: 27 N.J.R. 2051(a), 27 N.J.R. 3177(a).

13:2–10.4 Hours of retail sales

No plenary or farm winery licensee privileged to sell at retail shall sell, serve or deliver, or allow, permit or suffer the sale, service or delivery of any wine at retail during any hours where the retail sale of alcoholic beverages is prohibited in the municipality where the winery retail sale would occur.

Amended by R.1990 d.412, effective August 20, 1990.
See: 22 N.J.R. 1811(a), 22 N.J.R. 2508(c).
Amended by R.1995 d.450, effective August 21, 1995.
See: 27 N.J.R. 2051(a), 27 N.J.R. 3177(a).

13:2–10.5 Application for wine blending license; form

All applicants for a wine blending license shall comply with the application, advertising and hearing provisions of this chapter. The application shall be filed on a form prescribed by the Director in which the applicant shall demonstrate its ability to comply with the requirements of N.J.S.A. 33:1-10.2c. The applicant shall file a statement of intent which shall include the following information: type of process to be implemented, for example, blending, treating, mixing, or bottling; products to result from process; and intended sales to wholesalers or retailers.

Repeal and New Rule, R.1990 d.412, effective August 20, 1990.
See: 22 N.J.R. 1811(a), 22 N.J.R. 2508(c).
Amended by R.1995 d.450, effective August 21, 1995.
See: 27 N.J.R. 2051(a), 27 N.J.R. 3177(a).

13:2–10.6 Joint retail salesroom

(a) A 'joint retail salesroom' is defined as a jointly controlled and operated retail salesroom by at least two plenary or farm winery licensees. Products of any plenary or farm winery licensee may be sold at retail in joint retail salesrooms for consumption on and off the joint licensed salesroom premises and for sampling purposes on the joint licensed salesroom premises.

(b) Applicants for a joint retail salesroom permit shall comply with the application, advertising, and hearing provisions of this chapter. The application shall also be accompanied by a sketch of the proposed joint salesroom premises depicting the area to be included within the scope of the license and the perimeter measurements. If the sales location is to be within another mercantile business operation, the application shall be accompanied by a description of the business relationship with the other business and shall include at a minimum, a copy of the lease agreement; a statement of how the winery sales outlet will maintain separate accounting for sales; a description of how the applicant will compensate the sales employees; and a description of any consumption or sampling to take place including how this will be controlled, and will state its plan for demarcating the licensed premises.

New Rule, R.1990 d.412, effective August 20, 1990.
See: 22 N.J.R. 1811(a), 22 N.J.R. 2508(c).
Amended by R.1995 d.450, effective August 21, 1995.
See: 27 N.J.R. 2051(a), 27 N.J.R. 3177(a).

SUBCHAPTER 12. SPECIAL PERMITS FOR HOME MANUFACTURE OF MALT ALCOHOLIC BEVERAGES AND WINES FOR PERSONAL OR HOUSEHOLD USE OR CONSUMPTION

13:2–12.1 Special malt alcoholic beverage and wine permits

(a) Malt alcoholic beverages and wines for personal or household use or consumption may be manufactured only under the provisions of a special permit, issued by the Director. This permit allows the manufacture within the home of the permittee or other authorized premises used in connection therewith, during the permit period, malt alcoholic beverages and wines in quantities of not more than 200 gallons.

(b) Malt alcoholic beverages and wines manufactured under the authority of such permit may not be sold under any circumstances, nor may it be used for any purpose other than for personal or household use or consumption of the permittee. The fee for this permit is $15.00.

Amended by R.1990 d.412, effective August 20, 1990.
See: 22 N.J.R. 1811(a), 22 N.J.R. 2508(c).
Amended by R.1995 d.450, effective August 21, 1995.
See: 27 N.J.R. 2051(a), 27 N.J.R. 3177(a).
Special amendment, R.2003 d.311, effective July 3, 2003 (to expire January 3, 2004).
See: 35 N.J.R. 3707(a).
Adopted concurrent amendment, R.2003 d.470, effective November 5, 2003.
See: 35 N.J.R. 3707(a), 35 N.J.R. 5427(a).

13:2–12.2 (Reserved)

Amended by R.1990 d.412, effective August 20, 1990.
See: 22 N.J.R. 1811(a), 22 N.J.R. 2508(c).
Repealed by R.1995 d.450, effective August 21, 1995.
See: 27 N.J.R. 2051(a), 27 N.J.R. 3177(a).

13:2–12.3 Ineligibility of premises

(a) No permit shall be issued for the manufacture of malt alcoholic beverages or wines on premises that are also licensed for the retailing, wholesaling or manufacturing of alcoholic beverages.

(b) 'Non-commercial premises' referenced in N.J.S.A. 33:1-75 and as used in this section shall include premises in which equipment and space are leased to a permittee for the purpose of brewing malt alcoholic beverages or fermenting wines for personal or household use or consumption.

(c) Nothing contained within this section shall prohibit the issuance of a special permit for home manufacture of malt alcoholic beverages and wines to a permittee who utilizes an authorized non-commercial premises offering the use of space, equipment, ingredients, bottling supplies, advice and expertise exclusively for the production of the permittee's malt alcoholic beverage or wine. No operation as described in this section shall be permitted unless:

1. The non-commercial premises shall obtain a public warehouse license in accordance with N.J.S.A. 33:1-14.1;

2. The owner of the non-commercial premises shall provide written notice of the proposed operation to, and shall receive written approval from the Director. The Director shall advise the appropriate municipality of any pending applications. Upon timely receipt of a duly signed written objection to the operation of the non-commercial premises, which must be received within 30 days of the notification to the municipality, the Director will afford a hearing to all parties and notify the owner of the non-commercial premises and the objector of the date, hour and place thereof;

3. The owner of the non-commercial premises shall keep records of permittees using the facility to produce malt alcoholic beverages and wines. These records are to be retained for a period of two years and must be available for inspection by the Director, the Director's authorized deputies, inspectors and investigators, and by any officer defined by N.J.S.A. 33:1-1p; and

4. Representatives of the non-commercial premises shall not provide physical assistance to, or on the behalf of, permittees in the production or bottling of malt alcoholic beverages and wines, nor storage other than that necessary to manufacture the malt alcoholic beverages or wines.

Amended by R.1990 d.412, effective August 20, 1990.
See: 22 N.J.R. 1811(a), 22 N.J.R. 2508(c).
Amended by R.1995 d.450, effective August 21, 1995.
See: 27 N.J.R. 2051(a), 27 N.J.R. 3177(a).

13:2–12.4 Ineligibility of persons under the legal age

No permit shall be issued to any person under 21 years of age.

Amended by R.1990 d.412, effective August 20, 1990.
See: 22 N.J.R. 1811(a), 22 N.J.R. 2508(c).
Amended by R.1995 d.450, effective August 21, 1995.
See: 27 N.J.R. 2051(a), 27 N.J.R. 3177(a).

13:2–12.5 Other disqualification

No permit shall be issued to any person who has been convicted of an offense involving 'unlawful alcoholic beverage activity', as defined in N.J.S.A. 33:1-1(x), subject to a waiver of this prohibition in the discretion of the Director after the lapse of 12 months from the date of such conviction.

Amended by R.1990 d.412, effective August 20, 1990.
See: 22 N.J.R. 1811(a), 22 N.J.R. 2508(c).

13:2–12.6 Number of permits per year

No more than one malt alcoholic beverage and one wine permit shall be issued to any individual during any calendar year.

Amended by R.1990 d.412, effective August 20, 1990.
See: 22 N.J.R. 1811(a), 22 N.J.R. 2508(c).
Amended by R.1995 d.450, effective August 21, 1995.
See: 27 N.J.R. 2051(a), 27 N.J.R. 3177(a).

13:2–12.7 Transfer of permits

No permit shall be transferable from person to person, and transfer from premises to premises may only be made with the written permission of the Director.

Amended by R.1990 d.412, effective August 20, 1990.
See: 22 N.J.R. 1811(a), 22 N.J.R. 2508(c).

13:2–12.8 Revocation of permit

Violation of the provisions of the permit shall be grounds for revocation.

Amended by R.1990 d.412, effective August 20, 1990.
See: 22 N.J.R. 1811(a), 22 N.J.R. 2508(c).

SUBCHAPTER 14.   EMPLOYMENT BY LICENSEES OF A PERSON FAILING TO QUALIFY AS A LICENSEE

13:2–14.1 Restriction upon a minor's employment activities on a licensed premises

(a) No licensee shall allow, permit or suffer any person under the age of 18 years to sell, serve or solicit the sale of any alcoholic beverage, or to participate in the manufacture, rectification, blending, treating, fortification, mixing, processing, preparing or bottling of any alcoholic beverage. It shall not constitute a defense to any prosecution for violation of this rule that the employment of a person under the age of 18 years is permitted under N.J.A.C. 13:2-14.2.

(b) No licensee shall allow, permit or suffer any person under 18 years of age to be employed as an entertainer on any premises where the consumption of alcoholic beverages is permitted unless such minor's employment shall be authorized pursuant to N.J.S.A. 34:2-21.1 et seq. of the New Jersey Child Labor Law and the rules and regulations established thereunder.

Amended by R.1973 d.234, effective August 30, 1973.
See: 5 N.J.R. 356(a).
Amended by R.1990 d.412, effective August 20, 1990.
See: 22 N.J.R. 1811(a), 22 N.J.R. 2508(c).

13:2–14.2   Minor's employment permit; fees

(a) No licensee, except a retail licensee operating in conjunction with a bona fide hotel or public restaurant, shall allow, permit or suffer the employment of any person under the age of 18 years, in or upon the licensed premises, unless such person obtains an employment permit from the Director of the Division of Alcoholic Beverage Control no later than 10 days from commencement of employment or unless the licensee holds a blanket employment permit issued by the Director pursuant to N.J.A.C. 13:2-14.4.

(b) The fee for an individual permit is $15.00 per calendar year.

Amended by R.1971 d.24, effective March 1, 1971.
See: 2 N.J.R. 75(d), 3 N.J.R. 65(a).
Amended by R.1973 d.234, effective August 30, 1973.
See: 5 N.J.R. 356(a).
Amended by R.1975 d.237, effective August 8, 1975.
See: 7 N.J.R. 336(a), 7 N.J.R. 436(b).
Amended by R.1990 d.412, effective August 20, 1990.
See: 22 N.J.R. 1811(a), 22 N.J.R. 2508(c).
Amended by R.1993 d.288, effective June 7, 1993.
See: 25 N.J.R. 1340(a), 25 N.J.R. 2485(a).
Amended by R.1995 d.450, effective August 21, 1995.
See: 27 N.J.R. 2051(a), 27 N.J.R. 3177(a).
Special amendment, R.2003 d.311, effective July 3, 2003 (to expire January 3, 2004).
See: 35 N.J.R. 3707(a).
Adopted concurrent amendment, R.2003 d.470, effective November 5, 2003.
See: 35 N.J.R. 3707(a), 35 N.J.R. 5427(a).

13:2–14.3   Permit; age restrictions

(a) No individual permit shall be issued to and no blanket permit shall cover any person under the age of 16 years except:

1. caddies, pinsetters or similar temporary or seasonal type employees as the Director may deem appropriate upon a showing of good cause and

2. Persons employed by a plenary or limited retail distribution licensee; such licensee may not employ any person under 15 years of age.

Amended by R.1990 d.412, effective August 20, 1990.
See: 22 N.J.R. 1811(a), 22 N.J.R. 2508(c).
Amended by R.1995 d.450, effective August 21, 1995.
See: 27 N.J.R. 2051(a), 27 N.J.R. 3177(a).

13:2–14.4   Blanket minors' employment permit

(a) A blanket minors' employment permit may be issued by the Director to a licensee to authorize the employment of persons disqualified by reasons of age, who are employed by the licensee as caddies, pinsetters, similar temporary or seasonal employees as the Director may deem appropriate upon a showing of good cause, and such persons covered by the licensee's blanket minors' employment permit need not hold or apply for individual employment permits.

(b) The fee for the blanket employment permit shall be based upon the number of anticipated employees to be hired under the permit, but shall not exceed $1,000 per calendar year.

New Rule, R.1990 d.412, effective August 20, 1990.
See: 22 N.J.R. 1811(a), 22 N.J.R. 2508(c).
Amended by R.1995 d.450, effective August 21, 1995.
See: 27 N.J.R. 2051(a), 27 N.J.R. 3177(a).
Special amendment, R.2003 d.311, effective July 3, 2003 (to expire January 3, 2004).
See: 35 N.J.R. 3707(a).
Adopted concurrent amendment, R.2003 d.470, effective November 5, 2003.
See: 35 N.J.R. 3707(a), 35 N.J.R. 5427(a).

13:2–14.5   Restrictions upon employing criminally disqualified persons

No licensee shall knowingly employ or have connected with him in any business capacity any person who has been convicted of a crime involving moral turpitude unless the statutory disqualification resulting from such conviction has been removed by order of the Director, in accordance with N.J.A.C. 13:2-15, or such person has first obtained the appropriate rehabilitation employment permit or temporary work letter from the Director.

New Rule R.1990 d.412, effective August 20, 1990.
See: 22 N.J.R. 1811(a), 22 N.J.R. 2508(c).

13:2–14.6   Application for a rehabilitation employment permit; temporary work letter

(a) Any person convicted of a crime involving moral turpitude may apply to the Director, in the manner and form prescribed by the Director, for a rehabilitation employment permit. Whenever that application is made and it appears to the satisfaction of the Director that such person's employment in the alcoholic beverage industry will not be contrary to the public interest, the

Director may, in the exercise of sound discretion, issue such employment permit.

(b) Upon the proper filing of an application and proof of promised employment, the Director may, in the exercise of sound discretion, issue the applicant temporary work letters not to exceed 90 days at any one time, authorizing employment upon a specified licensed premises pending determination on the application for a permit.

(c) A Temporary Work Letter may be issued if the applicant demonstrates to the Director's satisfaction, that the applicant has behaved in a law abiding manner and has not engaged in and will not participate in any conduct detrimental to the integrity of the alcoholic beverage industry or the public interest. The final determination shall be in the sole discretion of the Director.

As amended, R.1971 d.24, effective March 1, 1971.
See: 2 N.J.R. 75(d), 3 N.J.R. 65(a).
As amended, R.1973 d.234, effective August 30, 1973.
See: 5 N.J.R. 356(a).
As amended, R.1974 d.40, effective February 15, 1974.
See: 6 N.J.R. 17(a), 6 N.J.R. 119(c).
As amended, R.1975 d.237, effective August 8, 1975.
See: 7 N.J.R. 336(a), 7 N.J.R. 436(b).
Amended by R.1990 d.412, effective August 20, 1990.
See: 22 N.J.R. 1811(a), 22 N.J.R. 2508(c).
Amended by R.1995 d.450, effective August 21, 1995.
See: 27 N.J.R. 2051(a), 27 N.J.R. 3177(a).
Amended by R.2006 d.67, effective February 21, 2006.
See: 37 N.J.R. 3221(a), 38 N.J.R. 1193(a).
Inserted the last sentence of (c) which reads: 'The final determination shall be in the sole discretion of the Director.'.

13:2–14.7 Rehabilitation employment permit; duration; types; fees

(a) A rehabilitation employment permit shall be issued for a one year period, and shall be renewable annually for the term of disqualification, as set forth in N.J.S.A. 33:1-31.2.

(b) Rehabilitation employment permits shall consist of the following types:

1. Unlimited employment permit: This permit shall allow the holder thereof to be employed by any class license, without restriction as to type of employment. Such permits may not be issued to persons who have been convicted of crimes which, in the opinion of the Director, present a special risk to the alcoholic beverage industry.

2. Limited employment permit: This permit shall allow the holder thereof to be employed by any class license in any non-managerial capacity, and may allow the holder to sell, serve or deliver alcoholic beverages.

(c) The fee for either type of rehabilitation employment permit shall be $ 125.00 per year, payable on the date of application.

As amended, R.1971 d.24, effective March 1, 1971.
See: 2 N.J.R. 75(d), 3 N.J.R. 65(a).
As amended, R.1973 d.234, effective August 30, 1973.
See: 5 N.J.R. 356(a).
As amended, R.1974 d.40, effective February 15, 1974.
See: 6 N.J.R. 17(a), 6 N.J.R. 119(c).
Amended by R.1990 d.412, effective August 20, 1990.
See: 22 N.J.R. 1811(a), 22 N.J.R. 2508(c).
Amended by R.1993 d.288, effective June 7, 1993.
See: 25 N.J.R. 1340(a), 25 N.J.R. 2485(a).
Amended by R.1995 d.450, effective August 21, 1995.
See: 27 N.J.R. 2051(a), 27 N.J.R. 3177(a).
Special amendment, R.2003 d.311, effective July 3, 2003 (to expire January 3, 2004).
See: 35 N.J.R. 3707(a).
Adopted concurrent amendment, R.2003 d.470, effective November 5, 2003.
See: 35 N.J.R. 3707(a), 35 N.J.R. 5427(a).
Amended by R.2006 d.67, effective February 21, 2006.
See: 37 N.J.R. 3221(a), 38 N.J.R. 1193(a).
Lowered the fee for either type of rehabilitation employment permit from $150.00 to $125.00.

13:2–14.8 Restrictions upon limited rehabilitation employment permittee

No licensee shall allow, permit or suffer the holder of limited rehabilitation employment permit to act in a managerial capacity with respect to the licensed business or to sell, serve or deliver any alcoholic beverage if the limited permit so prohibits; nor shall the holder of a limited rehabilitation permit engage in any activity prohibited by the permit.

Amended by R.1990 d.412, effective August 20, 1990.
See: 22 N.J.R. 1811(a), 22 N.J.R. 2508(c).
Amended by R.1995 d.450, effective August 21, 1995.
See: 27 N.J.R. 2051(a), 27 N.J.R. 3177(a).

13:2–14.9 Termination of employment of disqualified person

No licensee shall employ in any manner whatsoever on the licensed premises any criminally disqualified person upon the withdrawal or denial of the application of such person for a Rehabilitation Employment Permit or upon the cancellation, suspension, revocation or expiration of a Rehabilitation Employment Permit or a Temporary Work Letter.

As amended, R.1975 d.237, effective August 8, 1975.
See: 7 N.J.R. 336(a), 7 N.J.R. 436(b).
Amended by R.1990 d.412, effective August 20, 1990.
See: 22 N.J.R. 1811(a), 22 N.J.R. 2508(c).
Amended by R.1995 d.450, effective August 21, 1995.
See: 27 N.J.R. 2051(a), 27 N.J.R. 3177(a).
Amended by R.2006 d.67, effective February 21, 2006.
See: 37 N.J.R. 3221(a), 38 N.J.R. 1193(a).

13:2–14.10 Nontransferability of permits; term of permit; applicant's photograph and fingerprints

(a) Employment permits are not transferable from person to person.

(b) All individual permits, except rehabilitation permits, expire on March 31st following their issuance unless otherwise specified therein.

(c) Each applicant for his first permit shall submit with the application four color passport-type photographs, two inches by two inches, taken not more than 30 days prior to the date of application.

(d) Applications for a rehabilitation employment permit shall require fingerprinting of the applicant and payment of the necessary fingerprinting processing fees attendant thereto.

As amended, R.1975 d.237, effective August 8, 1975.
See: 7 N.J.R. 336(a), 7 N.J.R. 436(b).
Amended by R.1990 d.412, effective August 20, 1990.
See: 22 N.J.R. 1811(a), 22 N.J.R. 2508(c).
Amended by R.2006 d.67, effective February 21, 2006.
See: 37 N.J.R. 3221(a), 38 N.J.R. 1193(a).
Substituted 'four' for 'one' in (c).

13:2–14.11 Amendment of application

Whenever any change shall occur in any of the facts set forth in the application for a permit, the permittee shall file with the Director a notice in writing of the change within 10 days after its occurrence.
Amended by R.1990 d.412, effective August 20, 1990.
See: 22 N.J.R. 1811(a), 22 N.J.R. 2508(c).
Amended by R.1995 d.450, effective August 21, 1995.
See: 27 N.J.R. 2051(a), 27 N.J.R. 3177(a).

13:2–14.12 Prohibited conduct of permittee

No permittee shall engage in any conduct which is prohibited to his employer by the Alcoholic Beverage Control Act, N.J.S.A. 33:1-1 et seq. or any regulation adopted thereunder, or by any valid municipal ordinance or regulation pertaining to employment upon licensed premises.
Amended by R.1990 d.412, effective August 20, 1990.
See: 22 N.J.R. 1811(a), 22 N.J.R. 2508(c).

13:2–14.13 Cancellation, suspension and revocation of permit

(a) Any employment permit may be canceled or suspended or revoked by the Director for cause, including, but not limited to, any of the following:

1. Violation by the holder of any provision of the alcoholic beverage law or any regulation adopted thereunder;

2. For any fraud, misrepresentation, false statement, misleading statement, evasion or suppression of a material fact in the application for the permit;

3. Proof that the holder has a prohibited interest in any license issued by the Director or any other issuing authority;

4. The permit holder is disqualified from being employed by a licensee for reasons other than the disqualification referred to in the employment permit;

5. Any other act or happening, occurring after the time of making an application for an employment permit which, if it had occurred before said time, would have prevented issuance of the permit; and

6. With respect to rehabilitation employment permits or temporary work letters issued pursuant to N.J.A.C. 13:2-14.6, proof of arrest or conviction of the permit holder of any crime or disorderly persons offense.

Amended by R.1974 d.46, effective February 15, 1974.
See: 6 N.J.R. 17(a), 6 N.J.R. 119(c).
Amended by R.1990 d.412, effective August 20, 1990.
See: 22 N.J.R. 1811(a), 22 N.J.R. 2508(c).

SUBCHAPTER 16. SOLICITOR'S PERMIT

13:2–16.1 Necessity of permit

No individual shall offer for sale or solicit any order in this State for the purchase or sale of any alcoholic beverage, whether such sale is to be made within or without this State, unless such individual holds a solicitor's permit and has such permit upon his person at the time of such solicitation. This, however, does not prohibit such offer or solicitation by any individual licensee himself or by the individual members of a licensed partnership or by any employee of any retail licensee in connection with and in the course of the licensed business.

13:2–16.2 Privileges of permit

A solicitor's permit, issuable by the Director of the Division of Alcoholic Beverage Control, authorizes the permittee to make offers and solicit for such sales of alcoholic beverages on behalf of the licensee represented by the solicitor and designated in the permit.
Amended by R.1973 d.234, effective August 30, 1973.
See: 5 N.J.R. 356(a).
Amended by R.1990 d.412, effective August 20, 1990.
See: 22 N.J.R. 1811(a), 22 N.J.R. 2508(c).

13:2–16.3 Eligibility for permit

Solicitor's permits may be issued only to bona fide employees of Class A (N.J.S.A. 33:1-10) or Class B (N.J.S.A. 33:1-11) licensees with the exception that no solicitor's permits shall be issued to employees of a bonded warehouse bottling licensee which holds no other type of Class A or Class B license.
Amended by R.1990 d.412, effective August 20, 1990.
See: 22 N.J.R. 1811(a), 22 N.J.R. 2508(c).

13:2–16.4   Permits to enforcement officers or municipal officials

No solicitor's permit shall be issued to or held by any person charged or entrusted with the enforcement of the laws concerning alcoholic beverages in any manner whatsoever, except that nothing herein shall prohibit a member of a municipal governing body or municipal issuing authority from being issued or holding a solicitor's permit, provided, however, that no holder of a solicitor's permit shall, directly or indirectly, offer for sale or solicit any order for the purchase or sale of any alcoholic beverages in any municipality in which he is a member of the municipal governing body or municipal issuing authority.

Amended by R.1990 d.412, effective August 20, 1990.
See: 22 N.J.R. 1811(a), 22 N.J.R. 2508(c).

13:2–16.5   Permit fees

The fee for a solicitor's permit is $15.00 per annum for solicitors employed exclusively by licensees whose license permits the sale of malt alcoholic beverages only, and $25.00 per annum for solicitors employed by all other eligible licensees. A separate fee shall be paid for each licensee designated in the permit.

Repeal and New Rule, R.1990 d.412, effective August 20, 1990.
See: 22 N.J.R. 1811(a), 22 N.J.R. 2508(c).

13:2–16.6   Application for permit; photograph and fingerprints; affidavit of compliance with the Alcoholic Beverage Control Act

(a) Each applicant for the issuance or renewal of a solicitor's permit shall make application on a form promulgated by the Director accompanied with the appropriate fee.

(b) Applications for the issuance of a solicitor's permit shall be accompanied by one passport type color photograph of the applicant, two inches by two inches, taken not more than 30 days prior to the date of the application.

(c) Applications for the issuance of a solicitor's permit shall require the fingerprinting of the applicant and the payment of the finger-printing processing fees attendant thereto.

(d) Applications for the issuance of a solicitor's permit shall be accompanied by the applicant's affidavit, on a form prescribed by the Director, attesting to compliance with the Alcoholic Beverage Control Act. Such affidavit shall specifically state that the applicant has read, understands and promises not to violate the Alcoholic Beverage Control laws and regulations, including those which relate to:

1. Tied House Restrictions (pursuant to N.J.S.A. 33:1-43 and N.J.A.C. 13:2-23.25);

2. The Retail Cooperative Purchase Regulation (pursuant to N.J.A.C. 13:2-26); and

3. The Trade Member Discrimination, Marketing, and Advertising Regulation (pursuant to N.J.A.C. 13:2-24.)

Repeal and New Rule, R.1990 d.412, effective August 20, 1990.
See: 22 N.J.R. 1811(a), 22 N.J.R. 2508(c).
Amended by R.1995 d.450, effective August 21, 1995.
See: 27 N.J.R. 2051(a), 27 N.J.R. 3177(a).

13:2–16.7   Term of permit

All solicitors' permits shall expire on May 31st following their issuance, unless otherwise specified therein, as provided in N.J.S.A. 33:1-67.

Repeal and New Rule, R.1990 d.412, effective August 20, 1990.
See: 22 N.J.R. 1811(a), 22 N.J.R. 2508(c).

13:2–16.8   Nontransferability of permit

Each solicitor's permit covers only the employment designated therein and is not transferable as to employer or employee or employment.

Recodified from 13:2-16.9 by R.1990 d.412, effective August 20, 1990.
See: 22 N.J.R. 1811(a), 22 N.J.R. 2508(c).

13:2–16.9   Amendment of application

Whenever any change shall occur in any of the facts set forth in the application for a solicitor's permit, the permittee shall file with the Director a notice in writing of such change within 10 days after its occurrence.

Recodified from 13:2-16.10 by R.1990 d.412, effective August 20, 1990.
See: 22 N.J.R. 1811(a), 22 N.J.R. 2508(c).

13:2–16.10   Surrender of permit upon termination of employment

Upon the termination of any employment for which a solicitor's permit has been granted, the employer named therein shall file with the Director a notice in writing of such termination and the permittee shall surrender for cancellation to the Director the permit covering such employment within 10 days after its occurrence.

Recodified from 13:2-16.11 by R.1990 d.412, effective August 20, 1990.
See: 22 N.J.R. 1811(a), 22 N.J.R. 2508(c).

13:2–16.11   Restrictions on permittee

(a) No holder of a solicitor's permit shall, in the State of New Jersey, offer for sale or solicit any order for the purchase or sale of any alcoholic beverage other than to the extent duly allowed and permitted by law and by the New Jersey license of his or her employer.

(b) No holder of a solicitor's permit shall directly or indirectly engage in any conduct prohibited its employer by the provision of Title 33 or any regulations promulgated thereunder, nor shall such person sell, solicit, or deliver alcoholic beverages at a price or upon terms or conditions or under promotions or contests not contained in his or her employer's 'Marketing Manual' and 'Current Price List' kept pursuant to N.J.A.C. 13:2-24 for the operative period.

(c) As of February 16, 1999, no holder of a solicitor's permit shall offer for sale or solicit any order for the purchase or sale of any alcoholic beverage to any retail licensee in which an immediate family member of the solicitor has any direct or indirect financial interest or participates in the operation of the retail licensee.

(d) The term immediate family member as used in this chapter means husband, wife, son, daughter, grandson, granddaughter, brother, sister, father, mother, brother-in-law, sister-in-law, father-in-law, mother-in-law, son-in-law, or daughter-in-law.

(e) The provisions of (c) and (d) above do not apply to any solicitor who has been issued a solicitor's permit on or before February 16, 1999.

New Rule, R.1990 d.412, effective August 20, 1990.
See: 22 N.J.R. 1811(a), 22 N.J.R. 2508(c).
Amended by R.1999 d.57, effective February 16, 1999.
See: 30 N.J.R. 4316(a), 31 N.J.R. 545(a).
Amended by R.2005 d.212, effective July 5, 2005.
See: 36 N.J.R. 4211(a), 37 N.J.R. 2544(a).

13:2–16.12   Interest of permittee in retail business

No holder of a solicitor's permit shall be interested, directly or indirectly, in any retail license or any business conducted thereunder, nor shall the holder of a solicitor's permit be employed by or connected in any business capacity with any retail licensee.

Repeal and New Rule, R.1990 d.412, effective August 20, 1990.
See: 22 N.J.R. 1811(a), 22 N.J.R. 2508(c).

13:2–16.13   Search of permittee's vehicle

By the acceptance of a solicitor's permit, the permittee consents to inspection and search of any vehicle owned or being driven by him, without search warrant, by the Director, his or her deputies, inspectors and investigators and by any officer as defined by N.J.S.A. 33:1-1(p).

Amended by R.1990 d.412, effective August 20, 1990.
See: 22 N.J.R. 1811(a), 22 N.J.R. 2508(c).

13:2–16.14   Responsibilities of employer

No holder of a Class A (N.J.S.A. 33:1-10) or Class B (N.J.S.A. 33:1-11) license shall allow, permit or suffer, in his behalf, any individual to offer for sale or solicit any order in the State of New Jersey for the purchase or sale of any alcoholic beverage, whether such sale is to be made within or without the State, unless such person has a solicitor's permit.

New Rule, R.1990 d.412, effective August 20, 1990.
See: 22 N.J.R. 1811(a), 22 N.J.R. 2508(c).

13:2–16.15   Solicitor's contracts

All contracts of employment between Class A (N.J.S.A. 33:1-10) or Class B (N.J.S.A. 33:1-11) licenses and their solicitors shall be in writing and shall set forth the salary, commission or other compensation of any kind agreed to be paid to such solicitor. Contracts shall be maintained by the employer for a period of three years from the date of execution and shall be available for inspection by the Director, his or her deputies, inspectors, investigators and agents and other officers as defined by N.J.S.A. 33:1-1(p).

New Rule, R.1990 d.412, effective August 20, 1990.
See: 22 N.J.R. 1811(a), 22 N.J.R. 2508(c).

13:2–16.16   Filing of statement of compensation with Director

On or before May 31 of each year, each holder of a Class A (N.J.S.A. 33:1-10) or Class B (N.J.S.A. 33:1-11) license employing any solicitor during the preceding calendar year shall file with the Director a true statement listing all compensation, itemized as to salary, commission, reimbursed expenses, prizes, awards, bonuses, or otherwise, paid to each such solicitor by such manufacturer or wholesaler during that calendar year.

New Rule, R.1990 d.412, effective August 20, 1990.
See: 22 N.J.R. 1811(a), 22 N.J.R. 2508(c).

13:2–16.17   Suspension or revocation of solicitor's permit

If a solicitor holds more than one solicitor's permit and one of the solicitor's permits is suspended or revoked, all of the solicitor's permits shall be suspended or revoked unless the solicitor demonstrates good cause why the solicitor's other permits should not be suspended or revoked.

New Rule, R.2005 d.212, effective July 5, 2005.
See: 36 N.J.R. 4211(a), 37 N.J.R. 2544(a).

SUBCHAPTER 20.   TRANSPORTATION
OF ALCOHOLIC BEVERAGES BY
LICENSEES; INSIGNIA

13:2–20.1   Transit insignia; transportation of alcoholic beverages

No licensee shall transport alcoholic beverages into, out of, or within the State of New Jersey in any vehicle unless it is owned, leased or contracted for by the licensee. Such vehicle, while so used, shall first have issued therefor a transit insignia, or transportation license insignia issued pursuant to the provisions of this subchapter, or a limited transportation permit or emergency trip permit issued pursuant to the provisions of N.J.A.C. 13:2-21.

Amended by R.1985 d.333, effective July 1, 1985.
See: 17 N.J.R. 1054(a), 17 N.J.R. 1662(a).
Amended by R.1989 d.372, effective July 17, 1989.
See: 21 N.J.R. 1300(a), 21 N.J.R. 2045(a).
Amended by R.2006 d.67, effective February 21, 2006.
See: 37 N.J.R. 3221(a), 38 N.J.R. 1193(a).
Deleted a reference to special transit insignia.

13:2–20.2   Transportation by retail licensee; delivery slip; emergency delivery

(a) No retail licensee shall deliver or transport any alcoholic beverages into, out of, or within the State of New Jersey in any vehicle unless the driver of the vehicle has in his or her possession a bona fide, authentic and accurate delivery slip, invoice, manifest, waybill, or similar document stating the date of delivery, the bona fide name and address of the purchaser or consignee, and the brand, size of container, quantity and price of each item of the alcoholic beverages being delivered or transported. The original or true copy of such delivery slip, invoice, manifest, waybill or similar document shall be retained by the licensee at his licensed premises for a period of one year from the date of delivery and shall be available for inspection by any person authorized to enforce the provisions of the New Jersey Alcoholic Beverage Control Act, N.J.S.A. 33:1-1 et seq., unless the Director shall have granted to the licensee written permission to keep such documents at another designated place.

(b) No such licensee shall peddle, barter, or otherwise sell any alcoholic beverages from any vehicle.

(c) It shall be an affirmative defense, to a charge of violating N.J.A.C. 13:2-20.1, where the licensee satisfactorily demonstrates that:

1. The licensee owned or leased a properly permitted vehicle;

2. An emergency situation arose which prevented the delivery from being made in the properly permitted vehicle; and

3. The delivery was, in all other respects, made in accordance with the provisions of N.J.A.C. 13:2-20.2(a).

Amended by R. 1985 d.333, effective July 1, 1985.
See: 17 N.J.R. 1054(a), 17 N.J.R. 1662(a).
Amended by R.1989 d.372, effective July 17, 1989.
See: 21 N.J.R. 1300(a), 21 N.J.R. 2045(a), 21 N.J.R. 2385(c).
Amended by R.1995 d.450, effective August 21, 1995.
See: 27 N.J.R. 2051(a), 27 N.J.R. 3177(a).

13:2–20.3   Transportation by State licensee with retail privileges; delivery slip or route card

(a) No State licensee privileged to sell alcoholic beverages at retail shall deliver or transport any alcoholic beverages in any vehicle, unless:

1. The driver of the vehicle has in his or her possession a bona fide, authentic and accurate delivery slip, invoice, manifest, waybill, or similar document stating the bona fide name and address of the purchaser or consignee, and the brand, size of container, quantity and price of each item of the alcoholic beverages being delivered or transported; or

2. The driver of the vehicle has in his or her possession a route card which shall contain the name, address and standing order of the customer, and the

entry at the time of delivery of the date of delivery, the brand, size of container, quantity delivered and the price charged. In addition to such route cards, there must be carried in the vehicle a loading list setting forth the total quantity of alcoholic beverages loaded for delivery, indicating as to each brand loaded the total quantity of each size of container; and

3. The original or true copy of such delivery slip, invoice, manifest, waybill, route card or similar document shall be retained by the licensee at his licensed premises for a period of one year from the date of delivery, and shall be available for inspection by any person authorized to enforce the provisions of the New Jersey Alcoholic Beverage Control Act, N.J.S.A. 33:1-1 et seq., unless the Director shall have granted to the licensee written permission to keep such documents at another designated place.

(b) No such licensee shall peddle, barter, or otherwise sell any alcoholic beverage from any vehicle to any consumer.

Amended by R.1985 d.333, effective July 1, 1985.
See: 17 N.J.R. 1054(a), 17 N.J.R. 1662(a).
Amended by R.1989 d.372, effective July 17, 1989.
See: 21 N.J.R. 1300(a), 21 N.J.R. 2045(a).
Amended by R.1995 d.450, effective August 21, 1995.
See: 27 N.J.R. 2051(a), 27 N.J.R. 3177(a).
Amended by R.2006 d.67, effective February 21, 2006.
See: 37 N.J.R. 3221(a), 38 N.J.R. 1193(a).
Deleted (b) and relettered former (c) as (b).

13:2–20.4   Transportation by other State licensees, importers and manufacturers; delivery documents

(a) No manufacturer, importer or wholesaler shall deliver or transport, directly or indirectly, any alcoholic beverages into, out of, or within the State of New Jersey in any vehicle, nor shall any transportation licensee so deliver or transport alcoholic beverages for any licensee, unless the driver of the vehicle has in his possession a bona fide, authentic and accurate delivery slip, invoice, manifest, waybill or similar document stating the name, address and New Jersey State assigned license number (if applicable) of the purchaser or consignee, the brand, size of container, terms of sale, quantity and price of each kind of alcoholic beverages being delivered or transported. Such document shall further bear a printed or stamped legend reading substantially as follows:

"The undersigned licensee hereby acknowledges that all of the alcoholic beverages itemized above have been ordered and were received on _____

                         (Date)

_____ "

           (Signature by or for licensee)

(b) Two copies of such delivery slip, invoice, manifest, waybill or similar document shall be truly dated and signed by the licensee or his agent at the time and on the date of actual delivery of any alcoholic beverage. One copy shall be retained for a period of one year from the date thereof by the manufacturer, importer or wholesaler and the other by the purchasing licensee for a like period at its respective licensed premises, and shall be available for inspection by any person authorized to enforce the provisions of the New Jersey Alcoholic Beverage Control Act, N.J.S.A. 33:1-1 et seq., unless the Director shall have granted written permission to the manufacturer, importer, wholesaler or retailer to keep its copies at another designated place.

(c) Except that with regard to the following:

1. Sales or transfers from manufacturers or importers to wholesalers or distributors, when the nature of the documentation and transaction precludes the immediate availability of all documents required in (a) and (b) above, compliance shall be deemed to have occurred when all such records are available within a reasonable time following the sale, transfer, delivery and receipt; and

2. Sales or deliveries of keg beer or ale only to retail licensees, when the nature of the documentation and transaction precludes the immediate availability of all documents required in (a) and (b) above, compliance shall be deemed to have occurred when all such records are available upon completion of the operative period of the terms of such sales which shall have been set forth and shall be consistent with the seller's Marketing Manual and Current Price List pursuant to N.J.A.C. 13:2-24.

Amended by R.1985 d.333, effective July 1, 1985.
See: 17 N.J.R. 1054(a), 17 N.J.R. 1662(a).
Amended by R.1989 d.372, effective July 17, 1989.
See: 21 N.J.R. 1300(a), 21 N.J.R. 2045(a).

13:2–20.5   Eligibility for transit insignia or transportation license insignia

(a) No transit insignia or transportation license insignia shall be issued:

1. To a bonded warehouse bottling licensee, public warehouse licensee, or warehouse receipts licensee, unless such licensee also holds a license of some type which authorizes the transportation of alcoholic beverages.

2. For any motor vehicle unless it is properly registered in New Jersey or authorized to utilize New Jersey roads in accordance with State law applicable to such vehicle.

3. For any leased vehicle or other vehicle not owned by the licensee unless said lease or other document by its terms transfers to the licensee exclusive possession, control and operation of such vehicle when utilized in connection with the licensed business. A copy of the lease or other document must be furnished with any application.

(b) No transit insignia shall be issued for any solicitor's vehicle unless an agreement exists authorizing

utilization of the solicitor's vehicle for purposes in furtherance of the business of the solicitor's employer.

Amended by R.1985 d.333, effective July 1, 1985.
See: 17 N.J.R. 1054(a), 17 N.J.R. 1662(a).
Amended by R.1989 d.372, effective July 17, 1989.
See: 21 N.J.R. 1300(a), 21 N.J.R. 2045(a).
Amended by R.2005 d.212, effective July 5, 2005.
See: 36 N.J.R. 2411(a), 37 N.J.R. 2544(a).

13:2–20.6   Application; fees

(a) Application for transit insignia shall be filed with the Director upon a prescribed form accompanied by the full fee of $75.00 for each insignia payable to the order of the Division of Alcoholic Beverage Control.

(b) Application for transportation license insignia shall be filed with the Director upon a prescribed form and shall be issued at a cost of $30.00 for each insignia payable to the order of the Division of Alcoholic Beverage Control.

1. No transportation license insignia shall be required for any vehicle operated by a parcel delivery service holding a transportation license for delivery of alcoholic beverages purchased at retail to consumers unless the vehicle is primarily and substantially used at any time for transport or delivery of alcoholic beverages.

2. The parcel delivery service must first be licensed by the Director. Application for licensure shall be made on a form to be provided by the Division.

3. An invoice must be attached to every package stating the purchaser's name, address, destination, quantity of wine being shipped and place of purchase. A copy of the original invoice must be made available for inspection by any person authorized to enforce the provisions of the New Jersey Alcoholic Beverage Control Act, N.J.S.A. 33:1-1 et seq. for a period of one year at the office of the licensee.

Amended by R.1973 d.234, effective August 30, 1973.
See: 5 N.J.R. 356(a).
Amended by R.1978 d.75, effective March 1, 1978.
See: 9 N.J.R. 482(a), 10 N.J.R. 170(a).
Amended by R.1985 d.333, effective July 1, 1985.
See: 17 N.J.R. 1054(a), 17 N.J.R. 1662(a).
Amended by R.1989 d.372, effective July 17, 1989.
See: 21 N.J.R. 1300(a), 21 N.J.R. 2045(a).
Amended by R.1993 d.288, effective June 7, 1993.
See: 25 N.J.R. 1340(a), 25 N.J.R. 2485(a).
Amended by R.1995 d.450, effective August 21, 1995.
See: 27 N.J.R. 2051(a), 27 N.J.R. 3177(a).
Amended by R.2000 d.342, effective August 21, 2000.
See: 32 N.J.R. 1717(a), 32 N.J.R. 3162(a).
Special amendment, R.2003 d.311, effective July 3, 2003 (to expire January 3, 2004).
See: 35 N.J.R. 3707(a).
Adopted concurrent amendment, R.2003 d.470, effective November 5, 2003.
See: 35 N.J.R. 3707(a), 35 N.J.R. 5427(a).
Amended by R.2005 d.212, effective July 5, 2005.
See: 36 N.J.R. 4211(a), 37 N.J.R. 2544(a).

13:2–20.7   Term of transit insignia or transportation license insignia; renewal

(a) All transit insignia expire on August 31 following their issuance unless sooner terminated by order of the Director or by surrender or termination of the basic license under which the insignia was issued.

(b) All transportation license insignia expire on June 30 following their issuance or upon sooner termination of the underlying transportation license.

(c) Renewals must be applied for in the same manner as a new insignia.

Amended by R.1985 d.333, effective July 1, 1985.
See: 17 N.J.R. 1054(a), 17 N.J.R. 1662(a).
Amended by R.1989 d.372, effective July 17, 1989.
See: 21 N.J.R. 1300(a), 21 N.J.R. 2045(a).
Amended by R.2005 d.212, effective July 5, 2005.
See: 36 N.J.R. 4211(a), 37 N.J.R. 2544(a).

13:2–20.8   Location of transit insignia or transportation license insignia

(a) Transit insignia must be directly affixed to the exterior of the vehicle, on the driver side front bumper, so as to be clearly visible at all times.

(b) Transportation license insignia shall be affixed to the vehicle body exterior on the left driver's side of the vehicle and shall be clearly visible at all times in the same manner as a transit insignia or otherwise visibly displayed as may be determined by the Director.

Amended by R.1985 d.333, effective July 1, 1985.
See: 17 N.J.R. 1054(a), 17 N.J.R. 1662(a).
Amended by R.1989 d.372, effective July 17, 1989.
See: 21 N.J.R. 1300(a), 21 N.J.R. 2045(a).
Amended by R.2005 d.212, effective July 5, 2005.
See: 36 N.J.R. 4211(a), 37 N.J.R. 2544(a).
Amended by R.2006 d.67, effective February 21, 2006.
See: 37 N.J.R. 3221(a), 38 N.J.R. 1193(a).
Substituted 'on the driver side front bumper' for 'on the left side thereof' in (a).

13:2–20.9   Restrictions applicable to vehicles bearing transit insignia or transportation license insignia

(a) No licensee shall allow, permit or suffer any vehicle for which a transit insignia, or transportation license insignia is issued to be used to transport alcoholic beverages except solely for the licensee's own business.

(b) When any transit insignia, or transportation license insignia shall become marred, defaced or damaged, the licensee shall forthwith notify the Director in writing, so that there may be appropriate replacement, if necessary, of such insignia.

(c) Transit insignia may be used only for the vehicle for which issued, provided, however, that nothing herein contained shall prohibit the transportation of alcoholic beverages by a transferee of a license in a vehicle for which a transit insignia was issued to his transferor for a period not exceeding seven days subsequent to the effective date of the transfer of license to such transferee.

(d) A transportation license insignia is issued to the holder of a transportation license and may be used for any eligible vehicle under N.J.A.C. 13:2-20.5, provided the identity of the transportation license holder is indicated on the vehicle.

(e) Except as provided in (c) above, no licensee shall sell or otherwise dispose of any vehicle to which a transit insignia is affixed, without having first removed said insignia.

Amended by R.1985 d.333, effective July 1, 1985.
See: 17 N.J.R. 1054(a), 17 N.J.R. 1662(a).
Amended by R.1989 d.372, effective July 17, 1989.
See: 21 N.J.R. 1300(a), 21 N.J.R. 2045(a).
Amended by R.2006 d.67, effective February 21, 2006.
See: 37 N.J.R. 3221(a), 38 N.J.R. 1193(a).
Deleted references to special transit insignia throughout; and deleted 'and having notified the Director of such removal' in (e).

13:2–20.10   Search of licensed vehicle

By acceptance of a transit insignia, or transportation license insignia, the licensee consents to the inspection and search of the vehicle for which such insignia is issued, without search warrant, by any person authorized to enforce the provisions of the New Jersey Alcoholic Beverage Control Act, N.J.S.A. 33:1-1 et seq.

Amended by R.1985 d.333, effective July 1, 1985.
See: 17 N.J.R. 1054(a), 17 N.J.R. 1662(a).
Amended by R.1989 d.372, effective July 17, 1989.
See: 21 N.J.R. 1300(a), 21 N.J.R. 2045(a).
Amended by R.2006 d.67, effective February 21, 2006.
See: 37 N.J.R. 3221(a), 38 N.J.R. 1193(a).
Deleted a reference to special transit insignia.

13:2–20.11   Duty of personnel delivering alcoholic beverages to consumers

It is the duty of personnel delivering alcoholic beverages to consumers to seek to determine that, at the time of delivery of product, the party signing a delivery receipt is of legal age to purchase and consume alcoholic beverages. Failure to carry out this duty by the employee shall be considered a violation and is grounds for the suspension or revocation of the employer's license.

New Rule, R.1995 d.450, effective August 21, 1995.
See: 27 N.J.R. 2051(a), 27 N.J.R. 3177(a).

SUBCHAPTER 21.   TRANSPORTATION OF ALCOHOLIC BEVERAGES INTO, THROUGH OR OUT OF THE STATE

13:2–21.1   Delivery into or out of the State

Delivery of alcoholic beverages into or shipment of alcoholic beverages out of New Jersey is prohibited unless the beverages are transported by a licensee pursuant to N.J.A.C. 13:2-20 or in a vehicle bearing or carrying a permit issued in accordance with this subchapter.

Repeal and New Rule, R.1989 d.371, effective July 17, 1989.
See: 21 N.J.R. 1304(a), 21 N.J.R. 2047(a).

13:2–21.2   Delivery into or out of the State

(a) Alcoholic beverages intended in good faith for personal use and not for sale may be transported into this State from a point outside New Jersey by any person in a vehicle under his control, without any transportation license or permit, to the extent permitted by N.J.S.A. 33:1-2 that is, not exceeding one-fourth barrel or one case containing not in excess of 12 quarts in all, of beer, ale or porter, and one gallon of wine, and two quarts of other alcoholic beverages within any consecutive period of 24 hours.

(b) Interstate transportation of alcoholic beverages intended in good faith for personal use in excess of the limits set forth in this section is prohibited; unless the consumer:

1. Has the alcoholic beverages transported by a New Jersey licensed alcoholic beverage transporter; or

2. Acquires from the Division a special permit to authorize the interstate transportation for a fee of $ 50.00 as set forth in N.J.S.A. 33:1-2. No such permit shall be issued until the applicant establishes that there has been payment of all applicable New Jersey Alcoholic Beverage taxes.

Repealed by R.1989 d.371, effective July 17, 1989.
See: 21 N.J.R. 1304(a), 21 N.J.R. 2047(a).
Amended by R.1995 d.450, effective August 21, 1995.
See: 27 N.J.R. 2051(a), 27 N.J.R. 3177(a).
Amended by R.2006 d.67, effective February 21, 2006.
See: 37 N.J.R. 3221(a), 38 N.J.R. 1193(a).
Increased the fee in (b)2 from $ 25.00 to $ 50.00.

13:2–21.3   Transportation through New Jersey

(a) Alcoholic beverages may be transported through the State of New Jersey in any vehicle provided the following terms and conditions are met:

1. No delivery is made in New Jersey;

2. The alcoholic beverages may lawfully be sold and transported from the state of origin;

3. The driver of the vehicle possesses a bona fide, accurate waybill, bill of sale, invoice, receipt or similar document stating the name and address of the seller and buyer, the type and quantity of alcoholic beverages being transported and the places of origin and destination; and

4. The alcoholic beverages may lawfully be delivered to and received in the state of destination.

Repeal and New Rule, R.1989 d.371, effective July 17, 1989.
See: 21 N.J.R. 1304(a), 21 N.J.R. 2047(a).

13:2–21.4   Limited transportation permit

(a) Alcoholic beverages not intended for delivery, sale or use in New Jersey may be transported from the licensed premises in this State of a manufacturer, wholesaler or public warehouse licensee, to points outside this State; or between points outside this State and piers of import or export located within the State by the holder of a New Jersey transportation license or a limited transportation permit.

(b) Application for a limited transportation permit shall be made to the Division on a form prescribed by the Director accompanied by a fee of $ 500.00.

(c) A limited transportation permit has a term of one year terminating on September 30, unless sooner canceled by the Director.

(d) The holder of a limited transportation permit cannot transport alcoholic beverages unless the vehicles have affixed thereto a limited transportation permit insignia.

(e) Limited transportation permit insignia are obtainable from the Division in the same manner, with the same eligibility requirements, transfer restrictions and insignia location as a transit insignia as set forth in N.J.A.C. 13:2-20. The cost for this limited transportation permit insignia is $75.00 per vehicle.

Amended by R.1989 d.371, effective July 17, 1989.
See: 21 N.J.R. 1304(a), 21 N.J.R. 2047(a).
Amended by R.1993 d.288, effective June 7, 1993.
See: 25 N.J.R. 1340(a), 25 N.J.R. 2485(a).
Amended by R.1995 d.450, effective August 21, 1995.
See: 27 N.J.R. 2051(a), 27 N.J.R. 3177(a).
Special amendment, R.2003 d.311, effective July 3, 2003 (to expire January 3, 2004).
See: 35 N.J.R. 3707(a).
Adopted concurrent amendment, R.2003 d.470, effective November 5, 2003.
See: 35 N.J.R. 3707(a), 35 N.J.R. 5427(a).
Amended by R.2005 d.212, effective July 5, 2005.
See: 36 N.J.R. 4211(a), 37 N.J.R. 2544(a).
Amended by R.2006 d.67, effective February 21, 2006.
See: 37 N.J.R. 3221(a), 38 N.J.R. 1193(a).

13:2–21.5   Emergency trip permit

(a) The Director, Division of Alcoholic Beverage Control, or any designated agent of the Director may issue a special emergency trip permit for the temporary or emergency transportation of alcoholic beverages into or out of the State in any vehicle not otherwise authorized by license or permit issued pursuant to N.J.A.C. 13:2-20 or this subchapter.

(b) An emergency trip permit shall authorize the delivery into or out of the State for a particular singular shipment identified in the permit from a specified source of origin to a specified destination. The permit shall remain in effect for the duration of the trip, or for 24 hours from the time of issuance, whichever period is longer.

(c) Applications for an emergency trip permit shall be on a form prescribed by the Director and may be issued by the Director or his designated agent for such purpose.

(d) The fee for an emergency trip permit is $25.00, which shall be deposited in the State Treasury. A surcharge in an amount allowed by the Director may be collected and retained by the agent when the permit is issued by that designated agent.

(e) A designated agent shall maintain true and accurate books of account, electronically transmit to the Division at time of issuance a copy of the issued permit, remit emergency trip permit fees to the Division within seven business days after issuance, and post an adequate performance bond if required.

(f) A designated agent serves at the will of the Director and may be dismissed without cause upon 30 days notice.

Repeal and New Rule, R.1989 d.371, effective July 17, 1989.
See: 21 N.J.R. 1304(a), 21 N.J.R. 2047(a).
Amended by R.1995 d.450, effective August 21, 1995.
See: 27 N.J.R. 2051(a), 27 N.J.R. 3177(a).

13:2–21.6 Prohibited transportation; seizure of unlawful property

No alcoholic beverages shall be transported into, through or out of the State except in accordance with this subchapter. Alcoholic beverages transported in violation of this subchapter and the vehicle containing the same, are unlawful property and are subject to seizure and forfeiture by the Director in accordance with N.J.S.A. 33:1-66.

Repealed by R.1989 d.371, effective July 17, 1989.
See: 21 N.J.R. 1304(a), 21 N.J.R. 2047(a).

13:2–21.7 Search of vehicle

By acceptance of a special permit issued pursuant to this subchapter for the transportation of alcoholic beverages in excess of the quantities authorized by law, or a limited transportation permit, or an emergency trip permit, the holder of the permit consents to the inspection and search of the vehicle for which such permit is issued, without search warrant, by any person authorized to enforce the provisions of the New Jersey Alcoholic Beverage Control Act, N.J.S.A. 33:1-1 et seq.

New Rule, R.1989 d.371, effective July 17, 1989.
See: 21 N.J.R. 1304(a), 21 N.J.R. 2047(a).

SUBCHAPTER 23. CONDUCT OF LICENSEES AND PERMITTEES AND USE OF LICENSED PREMISES

13:2–23.1 Prohibition against serving persons under the legal age and intoxicated persons

(a) No licensee shall sell, serve or deliver or allow, permit or suffer the sale, service or delivery of any alcoholic beverage, directly or indirectly, to any person under the legal age to purchase or consume alcoholic beverages, or allow, permit or suffer the consumption of any alcoholic beverage by any such person in or upon the licensed premises.

(b) No licensee shall sell, serve or deliver or allow, permit or suffer the sale, service or delivery of any alcoholic beverage, directly or indirectly, to any person actually or apparently intoxicated, or permit or suffer the consumption of any alcoholic beverage by any such person in or upon the licensed premises.

Amended by R.1973 d.234, effective August 30, 1973.
See: 5 N.J.R. 356(a).
Amended by R.1980 d.304, effective July 3, 1980.
See: 12 N.J.R. 343(b), 12 N.J.R. 494(b).
Amended by R.1990 d.412, effective August 20, 1990.
See: 22 N.J.R. 1811(a), 22 N.J.R. 2508(c).

13:2–23.2 Prohibiting sales or consumption of alcoholic beverages during elections; municipal option

No licensee shall sell or offer for sale at retail or deliver to any consumer any alcoholic beverage, or allow, permit or suffer the consumption of any alcoholic beverage in or upon the licensed premises while the polls are open for voting in any municipality in which an election is being held and the sale of alcoholic beverages is prohibited during such election by municipal ordinance.

Amended by R.1970 d.101, effective August 24, 1970.
See: 2 N.J.R. 76(a).
Amended by R.1990 d.412, effective August 20, 1990.
See: 22 N.J.R. 1811(a), 22 N.J.R. 2508(c).

13:2–23.3 Closing premises during public emergency or crime investigation

No licensee shall sell, serve or deliver or allow, permit or suffer the sale, service or delivery of any alcoholic beverage, at retail, or allow, permit or suffer the consumption of any alcoholic beverage on the licensed premises, or allow, permit or suffer the retail licensed premises to be open, during any period for which any duly constituted State, county or municipal law enforcement authority, because of a public emergency or investigation of crime, has ordered the licensed premises to be closed, unless excepted by such authority to permit continuing conduct of business other than the sale of alcoholic beverages.

13:2–23.4 House-to-house solicitation forbidden

No licensee shall solicit from house-to-house, personally or by telephone, the purchase of any alcoholic beverage, or allow, permit or suffer such solicitation.

Amended by R.1990 d.412, effective August 20, 1990.
See: 22 N.J.R. 1811(a), 22 N.J.R. 2508(c).

13:2–23.5 Prohibited patrons; narcotics or other unlawful drugs; illegal activity or enterprise

(a) No licensee shall allow, permit or suffer in or upon the licensed premises the habitual presence of any known prostitute, gangster, racketeer, notorious criminal, or other person of ill repute.

(b) No licensee shall allow, permit or suffer in or upon the licensed premises any unlawful possession of or any unlawful activity pertaining to:

1. Narcotic drugs;

2. Controlled dangerous substances as defined by the New Jersey Controlled Dangerous Substances Act (N.J.S.A. 24:21-1 et seq.);

3. Controlled dangerous analogs as defined by the Comprehensive Drug Reform Act of 1987 (N.J.S.A. 2C:35-1 et seq.);

4. Any prescription legend drug, in any form, which is not a narcotic drug or a controlled dangerous substance or analog, as so defined; or

5. Drug paraphernalia as defined by N.J.S.A. 2C:36-1.

(c) No licensee shall allow, permit or suffer the licensed premises to be accessible to any premises upon which any illegal activity or enterprise is carried on, or the licensed premises or business to be used in furtherance or aid of or accessible to any illegal activity or enterprise.

Amended by R.1972 d.67, effective April 6, 1972.
See: 4 N.J.R. 50(a), 4 N.J.R. 105(c).
Amended by R.1990 d.412, effective August 20, 1990.
See: 22 N.J.R. 1811(a), 22 N.J.R. 2508(c).

13:2–23.6 Prohibition against immoral activities; disturbance; nuisance on premises

(a) No licensee shall engage in or allow, permit or suffer on or about the licensed premises:

1. Any lewdness or immoral activity or

2. Any brawl, act of violence, disturbance, or unnecessary noise.

(b) Every licensee shall operate its business in an orderly and lawful fashion, so as not to constitute a nuisance. A licensee's responsibility under this subsection includes the conduct of the licensee, its employees and patrons, if such conduct is contrary to the public health, safety and welfare.

Amended by R.1990 d.412, effective August 20, 1990.
See: 22 N.J.R. 1811(a), 22 N.J.R. 2508(c).
Amended by R.2005 d.212, effective July 5, 2005.
See: 36 N.J.R. 4211(a), 37 N.J.R. 2544(a).

13:2–23.7 Prohibition against lottery and gambling; exceptions

(a) No licensee shall engage in or allow, permit or suffer on or about the licensed premises:

1. The conduct of any lottery;

2. Any ticket or participation right in any lottery to be sold or offered for sale;

3. Any pool-selling, bookmaking or any unlawful game or gambling of any kind;

4. Any slot machine or device in the nature of a slot machine or any other gambling device which may be used for the purpose of playing for money or other valuable thing;

5. Any gambling paraphernalia including, but not limited to, any slip, ticket, book, record, document, memorandum or other writing pertaining in any way to any lottery, pool-selling, bookmaking or unlawful game or gambling of any kind;

6. Any video device, which resembles a game of cards, dice, roulette, or any other game of chance or crane device, which device has not been approved by the Director. In approving a device, the Director must be satisfied that the specific device is an entertainment device and not a gambling device. In reaching this determination, the Director shall consider all factors relating to the operation of the device, including, but not limited to, whether the device can easily be used for or adapted to gambling. A licensee wishing to place such a device on a licensed premises shall request written confirmation from the Director, prior to placement, that the specific device has been previously approved or, if the specific device has not been previously approved, shall request that the Director make such a determination. The approval letter shall be kept on the licensed premises at all times or the device may be deemed to be unapproved; or

7. Any raffle, drawing, lottery or contest, etc., the prize for which is an alcoholic beverage, without the appropriate permit.

(b) This rule shall not apply to bingo, raffles or New Jersey State Lottery, or tickets or participation rights therein, being conducted pursuant to appropriate license under the Bingo Licensing Law (N.J.S.A. 5:8-24), Raffles Licensing Law (N.J.S.A. 5:8-50), State Lottery Law (N.J.S.A. 5:9-11) or other activity authorized by State law. However, in any instance of bingo at licensed premises, no licensee, during the period between the commencement of the first and the conclusion of the last game, shall sell, serve, or deliver or allow, permit or suffer the sale, service, delivery or consumption of any alcoholic beverage in or upon any part of the licensed premises where the bingo or any part thereof is being conducted.

(c) All licensees which have approved video games on their licensed premises shall notify the Division within 48 hours of the placement thereof.

Amended by R.1990 d.412, effective August 20, 1990.
See: 22 N.J.R. 1811(a), 22 N.J.R. 2508(c).
Amended by R.1995 d.450, effective August 21, 1995.
See: 27 N.J.R. 2051(a), 27 N.J.R. 3177(a).
Amended by R.2005 d.212, effective July 5, 2005.
See: 36 N.J.R. 4211(a), 37 N.J.R. 2544(a).

13:2–23.8   Eastern Standard Time change

(a) On the first Sunday of April of each year, at 2:00 A.M., the clocks in each licensed premises will be advanced one hour in observance of Eastern Daylight Savings Time. The official time will then become 3:00 A.M., and in any municipality having a closing time later than 2:00 A.M., the remaining hours of sale will be calculated accordingly.

(b) On the last Sunday of October of each year, at 2:00 A.M., the clocks in each licensed premises will be turned one hour back in observance of Eastern Standard Time. The official time will be 1:00 A.M., and in any municipality having a closing hour later than 2:00 A.M., remaining hours of sale will be calculated accordingly.

(c) In either case, (a) or (b) above, licensed premises having closing hours of 2:00 A.M. or earlier, will be unaffected.

Amended by R.1980 d.304, effective July 3, 1980.
See: 12 N.J.R. 343(b), 12 N.J.R. 494(b).
Amended by R.1990 d.412, effective August 20, 1990.
See: 22 N.J.R. 1811(a), 22 N.J.R. 2508(c).
Amended by R.1995 d.450, effective August 21, 1995.
See: 27 N.J.R. 2051(a), 27 N.J.R. 3177(a).

13:2–23.9   Prohibition against adulterated alcoholic beverages

(a) No licensee shall manufacture, transport, possess, sell, barter, give away, offer for sale or furnish any alcoholic beverages adulterated with any foreign or harmful substance or containing any visible fruit flies or other insect matter. Notwithstanding, to the extent permitted by Federal law, tequila containing the agave worm shall not be deemed in violation of this provision.

(b) If, at the time that a violation of (a) above is discovered by an enforcing agency, the violative container is either sealed or equipped with a pouring spout containing a screen designed to prevent the ability of fruit flies and/or other insects from entering the container, then the enforcing agency shall direct the licensee to empty the violative container. Licensees shall immediately comply with this directive. Compliance

with the directive shall result in no administrative charges for this violation.

(c) Nothing in this section shall prohibit licensees from storing and temporarily retaining such beverages for purposes of returning same to a manufacturer or wholesaler provided the container is immediately resealed and labeled with the name and address of the customer and the date of return by the customer.

Amended by R.1990 d.412, effective August 20, 1990.
See: 22 N.J.R. 1811(a), 22 N.J.R. 2508(c).
Amended by R.2000 d.342, effective August 21, 2000.
See: 32 N.J.R. 1717(a), 32 N.J.R. 3162(a).

13:2–23.10   Restriction upon receiving prohibited deliveries of alcoholic beverages

No licensee shall receive, possess or sell any alcoholic beverage transported into this State in violation of N.J.A.C. 13:2-20 and 13:2-21.

Amended by R.1990 d.412, effective August 20, 1990.
See: 22 N.J.R. 1811(a), 22 N.J.R. 2508(c).

13:2–23.11   Consumption of alcoholic beverages and possession of open containers prohibited upon retail distribution licensee's premises; exception

(a) No retail distribution licensee shall allow, permit or suffer any alcoholic beverage to be consumed in or upon the licensed premises nor shall such licensee possess or allow, permit or suffer any open containers of alcoholic beverage in or upon the licensed premises.

(b) Nothing in this provision shall prohibit opened bottles of alcoholic beverages returned by a customer as allegedly defective from being possessed by such licensee pending return to the manufacturer or wholesaler; provided the container is immediately resealed and labeled with the name and address of the customer and the date of return by the customer.

Amended by R.1990 d.412, effective August 20, 1990.
See: 22 N.J.R. 1811(a), 22 N.J.R. 2508(c).

13:2–23.12   Receiving alcoholic beverages from prohibited source

(a) No retail licensee shall purchase or obtain any alcoholic beverage except from the holder of a New Jersey manufacturer's or wholesaler's license or pursuant to a special permit first obtained from the Director.

(b) The purchase of alcoholic beverages by one retailer from another and sale of alcoholic beverages by one retailer to another are prohibited; provided, however, that the passage of title in any alcoholic beverages from transferor to transferee of a license may be authorized by special permit obtained from the Director.

Amended by R.1990 d.412, effective August 20, 1990.
See: 22 N.J.R. 1811(a), 22 N.J.R. 2508(c).
Amended by R.1995 d.450, effective August 21, 1995.
See: 27 N.J.R. 2051(a), 27 N.J.R. 3177(a).

13:2–23.13　Maintaining copies of current license certificate; application; list of employees on the licensed premises

(a) No licensee holding a Class C license shall conduct the licensed business unless:

1. The current license certificate is at all times conspicuously displayed on the retail licensed premises in such plain view as to be easily read by all persons visiting such premises, with Permit for Off-Premises Storage of Business Records sticker affixed, if applicable;

2. A photostatic or other true copy of the application for the current license as well as the last filed long-form application (if current application is the short form), is kept on the licensed premises; and

3. A list, on a form prescribed by the Director, containing the names and addresses of, and required information with respect to, all persons currently employed on retail licensed premises, is kept on the licensed premises. A licensee shall be deemed to have complied with this requirement if this information is contained in a computer system, accessible from the licensed premises, and the information can be immediately produced.

(b) Such application copy and such list shall be available for inspection by the Director, the Director's deputies, inspectors and investigators, and by any officer defined by N.J.S.A. 33:1-1(p).

Amended by R.1990 d.412, effective August 20, 1990.
See: 22 N.J.R. 1811(a), 22 N.J.R. 2508(c).
Amended by R.1995 d.450, effective August 21, 1995.
See: 27 N.J.R. 2051(a), 27 N.J.R. 3177(a).
Amended by R.2005 d.212, effective July 5, 2005.
See: 36 N.J.R. 4211(a), 37 N.J.R. 2544(a).

13:2–23.14　Prohibition against indecent matter upon licensed premises

No licensee shall allow, permit or suffer in or upon the licensed premises or have in his possession or distribute or cause to be distributed any obscene, indecent, filthy, lewd, lascivious or disgusting recording, printing, writing, picture or other matter.

Amended by R.1990 d.412, effective August 20, 1990.
See: 22 N.J.R. 1811(a), 22 N.J.R. 2508(c).

13:2–23.15　Possession of container mislabeled as to fill prohibited; exception

No licensee shall knowingly display, sell or deliver any alcoholic beverage in an original container having a content of fill less than that stated on the container or label thereof, subject to such tolerance as permitted by Federal law and regulation; and no licensee shall possess such a container except for the sole purpose of

return for credit or replacement consistent with N.J.A.C. 13:2-23.11 and 39.1.

Amended by R.1979 d.138, effective May 1, 1979.
See: 11 N.J.R. 143(a), 11 N.J.R. 257(c).
Amended by R.1990 d.412, effective August 20, 1990.
See: 22 N.J.R. 1811(a), 22 N.J.R. 2508(c).

13:2–23.16　Prohibited promotions

(a) Except for consumer alcoholic beverage tasting events conducted in accordance with N.J.A.C. 13:2-37, and promotions permitted in this section, no licensee, permittee or brand registrant shall, directly or indirectly, allow, permit or suffer any practice or promotion that:

1. Offers unlimited availability of any alcoholic beverage for consumption on a licensed premises, for a set price, except for:

i. Private parties, not sponsored by the licensee, such as wedding and birthday parties, and events held by social affair permittees; or

ii. New Year's Eve parties sponsored by a licensee where a set price for attendance includes an open bar;

2. Offers to a patron or consumer a free drink, gift, prize or anything of value, conditioned upon the purchase of an alcoholic beverage or product, except for:

i. Branded or unique glassware or souvenirs in connection with a single purchase;

ii. Consumer mail-in rebates offered in accordance with N.J.A.C. 13:2-24.11;

iii. Manufacturer's sweepstakes and contests, not prohibited by law, where entry or opportunity to win is open to the public without a requirement that a purchase be made;

iv. Discounts offered by retailers to consumers on the purchase of alcoholic beverages for off premises consumption;

v. Offers of not more than one free drink per patron, as a gesture of good will, in a 24 hour period, by an on-premise consumption licensee;

vi. Offers of not more than one free drink coupon, ticket, or token redeemable by a patron, once in a 24 hour period;

vii. Offers of a set price for a meal that includes a single alcoholic beverage drink; or

viii. Offers of a single bottle of wine or champagne to guests staying at a licensed hotel or motel, as part of a specialty package, provided that the primary guests are of legal drinking age;

3. Requires or allows a consumer to prepurchase more than one drink or product at a time via tickets, tokens, admission fees, or the like, as a condition for entry into a licensed premises or as a requirement for service or entertainment thereon;

4. Offers any prize, gift or award which consists of alcoholic beverages or coupons or gift certificates which

may be redeemed for alcoholic beverages, such as two for one, and the like, except for a prize consisting of alcoholic beverages in sealed containers offered in a raffle licensed pursuant to N.J.S.A. 5:8-50. A coupon or gift certificate, other than a certificate purchased by a consumer for an amount equal to the dollar value of the certificate, shall expressly state that the certificate shall not be applied toward the purchase or consumption of alcoholic beverages; or

    5. Contains an instant win coupon, ticket, cap, game card or the like.

    (b) No prize or promotion shall be given to, nor shall any contest for consumers be open to, any person under the legal age to purchase or consume alcoholic beverage, any supplier, wholesaler, distributor or retailer; or affiliates, employees or members of the immediate family or household of any such persons or entities.

New Rule, R.1980 d.304, effective July 3, 1980.
See: 12 N.J.R. 343(b), 12 N.J.R. 494(b).
Amended by R.1983 d.527, effective November 21, 1983.
See: 15 N.J.R. 1558(a), 15 N.J.R. 1946(a).
Amended by R.1995 d.450, effective August 21, 1995.
See: 27 N.J.R. 2051(a), 27 N.J.R. 3177(a).
Amended by R.1996 d.271, effective June 17, 1996.
See: 27 N.J.R. 2051(a), 28 N.J.R. 3177(a).
Amended by R.2000 d.342, effective August 21, 2000.
See: 32 N.J.R. 1717(a), 32 N.J.R. 3162(a).
Amended by R.2006 d.67, effective February 21, 2006.
See: 37 N.J.R. 3221(a), 38 N.J.R. 1193(a).
Substituted 'beverage tasting events' for 'beverage tastings' in the introductory paragraph of (a), and added (a)5.

13:2–23.17   Restriction upon limited retail distribution licensee possessing chilled malt alcoholic beverages

No limited retail distribution licensee shall possess or allow, permit or suffer any chilled malt alcoholic beverages other than chilled draught malt alcoholic beverages in kegs, barrels or similar containers of at least 7.75 fluid gallons in capacity, in or upon the licensed premises.

Amended by R.1990 d.412, effective August 20, 1990.
See: 22 N.J.R. 1811(a), 22 N.J.R. 2508(c).

13:2–23.18   Solicitation prohibited

No plenary or seasonal retail consumption licensee shall allow, permit or suffer any person employed on the licensed premises to solicit any beverage, alcoholic or otherwise, at the expense of or as a gift from any customer or patron.

13:2–23.19   Prohibition against offering substitute beverages; exception

No licensee privileged to sell alcoholic beverages for consumption on the licensed premises shall serve or allow, permit or suffer the service of any alcoholic beverage other than ordered or substitute a nonalcohol-

ic beverage when an alcoholic beverage has been ordered, unless agreed to by the customer.

Amended by R.1990 d.412, effective August 20, 1990.
See: 22 N.J.R. 1811(a), 22 N.J.R. 2508(c).

13:2–23.20   Intoxicated workers prohibited

No licensee shall work in any capacity in or upon the licensed premises while actually or apparently intoxicated, or allow, permit or suffer any actually or apparently intoxicated person to work in any capacity in or upon the licensed premises.

Amended by R.1990 d.412, effective August 20, 1990.
See: 22 N.J.R. 1811(a), 22 N.J.R. 2508(c).

13:2–23.21   Restrictions upon storage of alcoholic beverages

No licensee shall store any alcoholic beverage except at his licensed premises, or at a public warehouse licensed under the alcoholic beverage law, or at other premises pursuant to special permit first obtained from the Director. Nothing herein shall prohibit the storage of alcoholic beverages by a licensee upon the formerly licensed premises for a period not exceeding five days after the effective date of the transfer of the license to other premises or for a period not to exceed 72 hours following delivery at the licensed premises of alcoholic beverages purchased, as part of a cooperative order by a fellow member of a cooperative purchasing agreement made pursuant to N.J.A.C. 13:2-26.

Amended by R.1980 d.304, effective July 3, 1980.
See: 12 N.J.R. 343(b), 12 N.J.R. 494(b).
Amended by R.1990 d.412, effective August 20, 1990.
See: 22 N.J.R. 1811(a), 22 N.J.R. 2508(c).
Amended by R.1995 d.450, effective August 21, 1995.
See: 27 N.J.R. 2051(a), 27 N.J.R. 3177(a).

13:2–23.22   Requirement for labeled tap markers; provision for electronic systems

    (a) No licensee privileged to sell alcoholic beverages for consumption on the licensed premises shall allow, permit or suffer any tap on the licensed premises to be connected with any barrel or other container of a malt alcoholic beverage unless such tap bears a marker which truly indicates the name or brand of the manufacturer of such malt alcoholic beverage, and unless such name or brand is in full view of the purchaser when the tap is located at a bar at which consumers are served.

    (b) On premises where either an electronic or automatic system is being used, which provides for the dispensing of distilled alcoholic beverages in a barroom, and the label on the container from which the beverage is drawn is not visible to a consumer at the bar, then some alternate device must be used to indicate to the consumer the brand being dispensed.

Amended by R.1990 d.412, effective August 20, 1990.
See: 22 N.J.R. 1811(a), 22 N.J.R. 2508(c).

13:2–23.23 Requirements concerning labels; tax payment indicia

(a) No retail licensee shall possess, have custody of, or allow, permit or suffer in or upon the licensed premises any alcoholic beverage manufactured, distributed, bought, sold, bottled, rectified, blended, treated, fortified, mixed, processed, warehoused, possessed or transported in violation of the alcoholic beverage law, or any alcoholic beverage in any keg, barrel, can, bottle, flask or similar container which:

1. Does not bear any label describing its contents; or

2. Bears a label which does not truly describe its contents; or

3. Does not bear any indicia of tax payment as required by the laws of the United States.

Amended by R.1990 d.412, effective August 20, 1990.
See: 22 N.J.R. 1811(a), 22 N.J.R. 2508(c).

13:2–23.24 Restrictions upon placing of orders

No licensee shall place any order within this State for the purchase of any alcoholic beverage or allow, permit or suffer any of his employees to place any order for the purchase of any alcoholic beverage, with any individual soliciting in violation of N.J.A.C. 13:2-16.

Amended by R.1990 d.412, effective August 20, 1990.
See: 22 N.J.R. 1811(a), 22 N.J.R. 2508(c).

13:2–23.25 Restrictions upon retail/manufacturer or wholesaler relationships

No retail licensee shall employ or have connected with him in any business capacity whatsoever any person interested, directly or indirectly, in the manufacturing or wholesaling of any alcoholic beverage within or without this State, nor shall any retail licensee be employed by or connected in any business capacity whatsoever with any person interested, directly or indirectly, in the manufacturing or wholesaling of any alcoholic beverage within or without this State.

Amended by R.1990 d.412, effective August 20, 1990.
See: 22 N.J.R. 1811(a), 22 N.J.R. 2508(c).

13:2–23.26 Fingerprinting requirements

No licensee shall employ or have connected with him in any business capacity whatsoever any person who refuses to submit himself for fingerprinting when required to do so by the Director or the municipal license issuing authority concerned.

Amended by R.1990 d.412, effective August 20, 1990.
See: 22 N.J.R. 1811(a), 22 N.J.R. 2508(c).
Amended by R.1995 d.450, effective August 21, 1995.
See: 27 N.J.R. 2051(a), 27 N.J.R. 3177(a).

13:2–23.27 Prohibited activities during license suspension

(a) No licensee, during the suspension of license, shall:

1. Allow, permit, or suffer the sale, service, delivery or consumption of any alcoholic beverage, or any other alcoholic beverage activity in or upon the licensed premises, except the storage of alcoholic beverages on hand or (with the permission of the Director) the return of alcoholic beverages to wholesalers or manufacturers; or

2. Deliver any alcoholic beverage to any consumer; or

3. Receive delivery of any alcoholic beverage at the licensed premises; or

4. Advertise that the licensed premises is closed or the licensed business stopped because of repairs or alterations or for any reason other than the suspension.

Amended by R.1990 d.412, effective August 20, 1990.
See: 22 N.J.R. 1811(a), 22 N.J.R. 2508(c).

13:2–23.28 Standard of liability

(a) Unless otherwise specified by statute or rule, a licensee is guilty of a violation of the Alcoholic Beverage Control Act if it allows, permits or suffers the violative act on or about its licensed premises.

(b) When knowledge is required to establish a violation of the Alcoholic Beverage Control Act, knowledge is established if:

1. The licensee itself committed the violative act;

2. The licensee had actual knowledge or was on notice that the violative activity was taking place, or about to take place, on or about the licensed premises; or

3. The licensee could have discovered violative activity was taking place, or about to take place, on or about the licensed premises through reasonable inquiry and had notice of circumstances which gave rise to a duty to inquire regarding same.

(c) In disciplinary proceedings brought pursuant to the alcoholic beverage law, it shall be sufficient, in order to establish the guilt of the licensee, to show that the violation was committed by an agent, servant, employee or patron or the licensee. The fact that the licensee did not participate in the violation or that his agent, servant or employee acted contrary to instructions given by him by the licensee or that the violation did not occur in the licensee's presence shall constitute no defense to the charges preferred in such disciplinary proceedings.

(d) No licensee shall commit any act which gives rise to a violation which is chargeable against any other licensee. The licensee committing such violation may be administratively charged for same even if the other licensee is not charged.

(e) The provisions of this section apply to all classes of alcoholic beverage licenses.

Amended by R.1990 d.412, effective August 20, 1990.
See: 22 N.J.R. 1811(a), 22 N.J.R. 2508(c).
Amended by R.2005 d.212, effective July 5, 2005.
See: 36 N.J.R. 4211(a), 37 N.J.R. 2544(a).

13:2–23.29   Detention of evidence; search of licensed premises

By the acceptance of the license, the licensee consents to the detention, as and for evidence, of any physical matter, including alcoholic beverages, found on the licensed premises or during the course of any investigation, inspection or search of the licensed premises being conducted by the Director, the Director's deputies, inspectors or investigators or by any officer as defined by N.J.S.A. 33:1-1(p).

Amended by R.1990 d.412, effective August 20, 1990.
See: 22 N.J.R. 1811(a), 22 N.J.R. 2508(c).
Amended by R.1995 d.450, effective August 21, 1995.
See: 27 N.J.R. 2051(a), 27 N.J.R. 3177(a).

13:2–23.30   Prohibition against hindering an investigation

(a) Every license and every person with an ownership interest therein and every director, officer, agent and employee of every licensee shall facilitate any investigation or inspection of the licensed premises conducted by, or on behalf of the Division, or other issuing authority. The failure of any of the foregoing persons or entities, either directly or indirectly, to answer any question, to produce any document in the time, place and manner requested or to facilitate in any way whatsoever the inspection of the licensed business or premises shall constitute a violation of this section.

(b) A refusal by any licensee, or any of the persons identified in (a) above, to comply with an investigatory subpoena or request combined with a prompt legal challenge thereto shall constitute a defense if the refusal and legal challenge are based upon a legally cognizable privilege or claim for which the licensee has an objectively reasonable basis to believe applies to its circumstances, as determined by the Director or a court of law with competent jurisdiction. A legal challenge to an investigatory subpoena shall be prompt if a motion to quash the subpoena is filed with either the Director or a court of law before the return date of the subpoena.

(c) Every person identified in (a) above shall accept service of any investigatory request, including requests for documents or testimony or subpoena issued by the Director. If service of an investigatory request cannot be made due to the refusal of the licensee or any such person identified in (a) above to accept service of same, the licensee may be considered in violation of N.J.S.A. 33:1-35 and N.J.A.C. 13:2-23.30.

(d) No licensee, permittee or any shareholder, partner or other person having an interest in a license or permit shall refuse to submit to fingerprinting when so required by the Director or the local issuing authority.

(e) No licensee, permittee or any shareholder, partner or other person having an interest in a license or permit shall refuse to submit full disclosure in a financial investigation, including but not limited to all savings, checking, or other bank or financial accounts held by or for such person or entity individually, jointly, or in trust (for himself, herself or another person or entity), when so required by the Director or the local issuing authority.

Amended by R.1990 d.412, effective August 20, 1990.
See: 22 N.J.R. 1811(a), 22 N.J.R. 2508(c).
Amended by R.1995 d.450, effective August 21, 1995.
See: 27 N.J.R. 2051(a), 27 N.J.R. 3177(a).
Amended by R.2000 d.342, effective August 21, 2000.
See: 32 N.J.R. 1717(a), 32 N.J.R. 3162(a).
Amended by R.2005 d.212, effective July 5, 2005.
See: 36 N.J.R. 4211(a), 37 N.J.R. 2544(a).

13:2–23.31   Law enforcement officers; ownership prohibition; employment restrictions

(a) No license shall be held by any regular police officer, any peace officer or any other person whose powers or duties include the enforcement of the alcoholic beverage law or regulations, or by any profit corporation or association in which any such officer or person is interested, directly or indirectly.

(b) No licensee shall employ or have connected with him in any business capacity whatsoever any such officer or person, except that:

1. Nothing herein shall prohibit a licensee from employing in a non-managerial capacity a special law enforcement officer; and

2. A licensee, upon prior written application to and written approval by the Director, may employ a regular police officer, peace officer or other person whose powers and duties include the enforcement of the Alcoholic Beverage Law (other than an officer employed by the Division of State Police) provided that such officer shall not be employed in a jurisdiction in which the officer is officially employed and further provided:

i. Written application pursuant to (b)2 above shall include prior written approval of such employment by the chief law enforcement officer of the jurisdiction which employs said officer or person and proof that written notice of the application has been provided to the chief law enforcement officer of the jurisdiction where the licensee is located.

ii. In the case of the chief law enforcement officer seeking such employment, the prior written approval must be from the chief executive officer of the governing body of the jurisdiction which employs said chief officer;

iii. A police officer so employed shall not, while engaged in the selling, serving, possessing or delivering of any alcoholic beverages;

(1) Have in his or her possession any firearm; or

(2) Wear or display any uniform, badge or insignia which would identify him or her as a police officer; and

iv. No police officer so employed shall be permitted to work in excess of 24 hours a week in any such establishment.

(c) The Director may authorize, upon prior application, the employment of regular police officers, peace officers, or other persons whose powers and duties include the enforcement of the alcoholic beverage laws and regulations, by licensees who operate racetracks, stadiums, auditoriums, theatres and other such establishments whose primary business does not consist of the sale or service of alcoholic beverages, where the use of trained police officers may be required to provide crowd control, traffic control or security for large sums of money located at such establishments. Persons employed in such capacity may not distribute, possess or sell alcoholic beverages and may only accept such employment with the consent of their governmental employer.

(d) Nothing contained in this section shall prohibit any regular police officer, peace officer or any other person whose powers and duties include the enforcement of the alcoholic beverage control laws or regulations from assuming any leadership or titular position in any fraternal, veterans', religious or similar type of nonprofit organization that is a club licensee; provided, however that:

1. The actual licensee of the organization is not a police officer or a person whose duties include enforcement of the alcoholic beverage control laws and regulations; and

2. No police officer or person whose duties include enforcement of the alcoholic beverage control laws and regulations shall be involved in the alcoholic beverage operations of the club licensee.

Amended by R.1974 d.341, effective December 16, 1974.
See: 6 N.J.R. 439(a), 7 N.J.R. 13(a).
Amended by R.1979 d.67, effective February 15, 1979.
See: 10 N.J.R. 557(a), 11 N.J.R. 146(a).
Amended by R.1980 d.526, effective December 4, 1980.
See: 12 N.J.R. 605(b), 13 N.J.R. 41(c).
Amended by R.1990 d.412, effective August 20, 1990.
See: 22 N.J.R. 1811(a), 22 N.J.R. 2508(c).
Amended by R.1995 d.450, effective August 21, 1995.
See: 27 N.J.R. 2051(a), 27 N.J.R. 3177(a).
Amended by R.2006 d.67, effective February 21, 2006.
See: 37 N.J.R. 3221(a), 38 N.J.R. 1193(a).
Substituted 'law enforcement' for 'police' in (b)1.

13:2–23.32 Records to be maintained on the licensed premises; other required records

(a) Unless a licensee has obtained a permit for the off-premises storage of certain records, pursuant to N.J.A.C. 13:2-29.4, each licensee holding a Class C license must keep and maintain the following documents and records on its licensed premises:

1. The current license certificate;

2. A copy of the current license application with any amendments filed, if applicable, together with a copy of the last long-form retail licensee application filed by the licensee;

3. A fully completed up-to-date list of all persons currently working on the licensed premises (commonly known as Form E-141A);

4. The current Federal special tax stamp, or proof of proper filing for such annual stamp;

5. Copies of all delivery slips, invoices or similar documents for such transactions made within the past year;

6. Records of transactions with or placements by a registered display service;

7. New Jersey Sales Tax Certificate of Authority; and

8. Records set forth in (b) and (c) below.

(b) All licensees shall maintain, for a period of five years, a record of all money or any other thing of value received in the ordinary course of business or received outside the ordinary course of business, including, but not limited to, alcoholic beverage sales, food sales, rebates, including payments from any Retail Incentive Program 'RIPs,' and miscellaneous income.

(c) All licensees shall maintain, for a period of five years, records which show the payment of all expenses. The records shall indicate the name of the person or entity receiving such payment, the amount of the payment and the reason that the payment was made. Payment records shall include payments made for:

1. The purchase of alcoholic beverages;

2. The purchase of food items;

3. The purchase of supplies and use of utilities;

4. The purchase or lease of equipment;

5. The payment of employees' compensation, including all required withholding;

6. The payment of all local, state and Federal taxes and license fees;

7. The payments of rents, mortgages, loans and/or a reduction of an owner's equity; and

8. All other disbursements.

(d) All licensees shall produce the above-enumerated records for inspection immediately upon request by the Director, the issuing authority or the agents or representatives thereof and any other law enforcement officer, peace officer or any other person whose powers or duties include the enforcement of the Alcoholic Beverage Control Act and officers as defined by N.J.S.A. 33:1-1(p), unless a different time period is prescribed in N.J.A.C. 13:2-29.4, at a location designated by the requester. The failure to comply with this subsection shall be considered a violation of N.J.S.A. 33:1-35 and N.J.A.C. 13:2-23.30.

(e) All licensees shall have and keep, for an unlimited period of time, permanent records of account which shall truly and accurately contain a record of all moneys invested in the licensed business, including loans, the source of all such investments and the disposition of such investments for an unlimited period of time. Such documents may be stored on or off the licensed premises and shall be produced within seven days of a request from by the Director, the issuing authority or the agents or representatives thereof and any other law enforcement officer, peace officer or any other person whose powers or duties include the enforcement of the Alcoholic Beverage Control Act and officers as defined by N.J.S.A. 33:1-1(p) at a location designated by the requester.

(f) All records required to be maintained by a licensee shall be in the English language.

Amended by R.1990 d.412, effective August 20, 1990.
See: 22 N.J.R. 1811(a), 22 N.J.R. 2508(c).
Amended by R.1995 d.450, effective August 21, 1995.
See: 27 N.J.R. 2051(a), 27 N.J.R. 3177(a).
Amended by R.2005 d.212, effective July 5, 2005.
See: 36 N.J.R. 4211(a), 37 N.J.R. 2544(a).

13:2–23.33 Dishonored checks; unpaid fees

If a check submitted by a licensee, permittee or applicant is returned unpaid to the Division or other issuing authority or if all or any portion of any fee required is unpaid, the licensee, permittee or applicant shall be subject to disciplinary action or denial of current and future applications.

New Rule, R.2005 d.212, effective July 5, 2005.
See: 36 N.J.R. 4211(a), 37 N.J.R. 2544(a).

SUBCHAPTER 38. LIMITATION OF HOURS FOR SALE AND DELIVERY AT RETAIL OF ALCOHOLIC BEVERAGES IN ORIGINAL CONTAINERS FOR OFF-PREMISES CONSUMPTION

13:2–38.1 Retail package sales hours

(a) Subject to local options as expressed in the New Jersey Alcoholic Beverage Control Act, N.J.S.A. 33:1-1 et seq. and except as further specified in (b) below, no licensee shall allow, permit or suffer the sale, service or delivery of any alcoholic beverage at retail in its original container for consumption off the licensed premises, or the removal of any alcoholic beverage in its original container from retail licensed premises, before 9:00 A.M. or after 10:00 P.M. on any day of the week.

(b) However, if the sale of alcoholic beverages for consumption on the premises is authorized in a municipality, the sale, service or delivery of wine and malt alcoholic beverages in original containers for consumption off the premises shall be authorized on the same days and during the same hours.

(c) Cities of the first class may establish by ordinance separate hours of sale for each type of retail license, and separate hours for each type of retail license for sales by such licenses of alcoholic beverages for on-premises and off-premises consumption.

Amended by R.1973 d.234, effective August 30, 1973.
See: 5 N.J.R. 356(a).
Amended by R.1981 d.71, effective May 1, 1981.
See: 13 N.J.R. 37(b), 13 N.J.R. 238(b).
Amended by R.1990 d.412, effective August 20, 1990.
See: 22 N.J.R. 1811(a), 22 N.J.R. 2508(c).
Amended by R.1995 d.450, effective August 21, 1995.
See: 27 N.J.R. 2051(a), 27 N.J.R. 3177(a).
Amended by R.2000 d.342, effective August 21, 2000.
See: 32 N.J.R. 1717(a), 32 N.J.R. 3162(a).

13:2–38.2 Sunday sales hours for retail distribution licensees and state beverage distributors; effect of municipal ordinances and State statute on sale for off-premises consumption

(a) If a municipality has no ordinance or local law that authorizes the sale of alcoholic beverages for consumption on the premises on Sunday, then except as provided in (b) below, a municipality may by ordinance authorize the sale of wine and malt alcoholic beverages in original containers for consumption off-premises by retail distribution licensees and State beverage distributor's licensees any time between the hours of 12:30 P.M. and 6:30 P.M. on Sunday, in addition to such weekday hours as may be authorized by ordinance.

(b) However, in any city of the first class which prohibits the Sunday sale of alcoholic beverages for consumption on the premises, no licensee shall allow, permit or suffer the sale, service or delivery of any alcoholic beverage at retail in its original container for consumption off the licensed premises or the removal of any alcoholic beverage in its original container from retail licensed premises, at any hour on any Sunday.

Amended by R.1990 d.412, effective August 20, 1990.
See: 22 N.J.R. 1811(a), 22 N.J.R. 2508(c).
Amended by R.1995 d.450, effective August 21, 1995.
See: 27 N.J.R. 2051(a), 27 N.J.R. 3177(a).

13:2–38.3 (Reserved)

Amended by R.1990 d.412, effective August 20, 1990.
See: 22 N.J.R. 1811(a), 22 N.J.R. 2508(c).
Repealed by R.1995 d.450, effective August 21, 1995.
See: 27 N.J.R. 2051(a), 27 N.J.R. 3177(a).

TITLE 40A

MUNICIPALITIES AND COUNTIES

Chapter
14. Fire and Police.

CHAPTER 14

FIRE AND POLICE

D. POLICE—MUNICIPALITIES

Section
40A:14–152. Members and officers shall have powers of peace officers and constables.
40A:14–152.1. Municipal police officer; power of arrest for crime committed in his presence anywhere within state.

D. POLICE—MUNICIPALITIES

40A:14–152. Members and officers shall have powers of peace officers and constables

The members and officers of a police department and force, within the territorial limits of the municipality, shall have all the powers of peace officers and upon view may apprehend and arrest any disorderly person or any person committing a breach of the peace. Said members and officers shall have the power to serve and execute process issuing out of the courts having local criminal jurisdiction in the municipality and shall have the powers of a constable in all matters other than in civil causes arising in such courts.

L.1971, c. 197, § 1, eff. July 1, 1971.

40A:14–152.1. Municipal police officer; power of arrest for crime committed in his presence anywhere within state

Notwithstanding the provisions of N.J.S. 40A:14–152 or any other law to the contrary, any full-time, permanently appointed municipal police officer shall have full power of arrest for any crime committed in said officer's presence and committed anywhere within the territorial limits of the State of New Jersey.

L.1977, c. 436, § 1, eff. March 2, 1978.

TITLE 48

PUBLIC UTILITIES

Chapter
13A. Solid Waste Collection and Disposal.

CHAPTER 13A

SOLID WASTE COLLECTION AND DISPOSAL

Section
48:13A–12.   Violations; penalty.
48:13A–12.1. Vehicles used to transport food not to be used
              to transport solid waste; exceptions.
48:13A–12.2. Violations; penalties.

48:13A–12. Violations; penalty

a. Any person or any officer or agent thereof who shall knowingly violate any of the provisions of this act or aid or advise in such violation, or who, as principal, manager, director, agent, servant or employee knowingly does any act comprising a part of such violation, is guilty of a crime of the fourth degree and shall be punished by imprisonment for not more than 18 months or, notwithstanding the provisions of N.J.S. 2C:43–3, by a fine of not more than $50,000.00, or both; and if a corporation by a fine of not more than $100,000.00. Each day during which the violation continues constitutes an additional, separate and distinct offense.

b. Any person who shall violate any provision of P.L.1970, c. 40 (C. 48:13A–1 et seq.) or P.L.1991, c. 381 (C.48:13A–7.1 et al.) or any rule, regulation or administrative order adopted or issued pursuant thereto, including an interdistrict, intradistrict or interstate waste flow order issued in conjunction with the Department of Environmental Protection, or under any applicable provision of Title 48 of the Revised Statutes, or who shall engage in the solid waste collection business or solid waste disposal business without having been issued a certificate of public convenience and necessity, shall be liable to a penalty of not more than $10,000.00 for a first offense, not more than $25,000.00 for a second offense and not more than $50,000.00 for a third and every subsequent offense. Each day during which the violation continues constitutes an additional, separate and distinct offense. The penalties herein provided shall be enforced by summary proceedings instituted by the board under "the penalty enforcement law" (N.J.S. 2A:58–1 et seq.). The Superior Court and the municipal courts shall all have jurisdiction to enforce "the penalty enforcement law" in connection with this act.

c. Whenever it shall appear to the board, a municipality, local board of health, or county health department, as the case may be, that any person has violated, intends to violate, or will violate any provision of P.L.1970, c. 40 (C. 48:13A–1 et seq.) or P.L.1991, c. 381 (C.48:13A–7.1 et al.) or any rule, regulation or administrative order adopted or issued pursuant thereto, or under any applicable provision of Title 48 of the Revised Statutes, the board, the municipality, local board of health or county health department may institute a civil action in the Superior Court for injunctive relief and for such other relief as may be appropriate in the circumstances, and the court may proceed in any such action in a summary manner.

Notwithstanding the provisions of any other law, or any rule or regulation adopted pursuant thereto to the contrary, all penalties recovered pursuant to actions brought by the board under this section shall be paid to the "Solid Waste Enforcement Fund" established pursuant to section 21 of P.L.1991, c. 381 (C. 48:13A–21). If a money judgment is rendered against a defendant pursuant to subsections a. or b. of this section, the payment made to the court shall be remitted to the fund.

L.1970, c. 40, § 13. Amended by L.1987, c. 149, § 1, eff. June 24, 1987; L.1989, c. 95, § 1, eff. June 14, 1989; L.1989, c. 118, § 1, eff. June 29, 1989; L.1991, c. 381, § 34.

48:13A–12.1. Vehicles used to transport food not to be used to transport solid waste; exceptions

a. Except as provided in subsections b., c. or d., no vehicle, including any truck, trailer or other haulage vehicle other than a truck tractor, utilized for the transportation of solid waste in this State shall be subsequently utilized for the transportation of fresh food or fresh food products, including meat, poultry, produce or other non-processed fresh food products intended for sale for human consumption. The presence of refrigeration equipment in a vehicle shall be prima facie evidence that the vehicle is used for the transportation of fresh food or fresh food products, unless the vehicle is lawfully registered, equipped and operated for the transportation of medical waste.

b. No vehicle which is registered pursuant to State solid waste laws and regulations for lawful solid waste transportation activities in this State shall be utilized for the transportation of fresh food or fresh food products, including meat, poultry, produce or other non-processed fresh food products intended for sale for human consumption, unless that vehicle has been appropriately cleaned and sanitized in accordance with rules and regulations adopted by the Department of Environmental Protection, after consultation with the Department of Health, prior to any use for the transportation of fresh food or fresh food products. The Department of Environmental Protection may adopt rules and regulations requiring notification, recordkeeping or reporting of the use of registered vehicles for the transportation of fresh food or fresh food products.

c. The provisions of this section shall not apply to any vehicles utilized for the transportation of source separated recyclable materials as defined in section 2 of P.L.1987, c. 102 (C. 13:1E–99.12).

d. A vehicle, including any truck, trailer or other haulage vehicle other than a truck tractor, owned or operated by any person engaging in the transportation of fresh produce intended for human consumption, may be utilized for the transportation of vegetative waste material generated from the fresh produce that was transported in that vehicle if the vegetative waste material is transported without delay to a vegetative waste composting facility.

L.1991, c. 214, § 1, eff. July 24, 1991.

48:13A–12.2. Violations; penalties

a. Any owner or operator who knowingly violates the provisions of section 1 of P.L.1991, c. 214 (C.48:13A–12.1) is guilty of a crime of the third degree.

b. The provisions of N.J.S. 2C:43–3 to the contrary notwithstanding, any person convicted of a violation of the provisions of section 1 of P.L.1991, c. 214 (C. 48:13A–12.1) is subject to a fine of not less than $7,500.00 for a first offense, not more than $10,000.00 for a second offense and not more than $25,000.00 for a third and every subsequent offense. Each day during which the violation continues constitutes an additional, separate and distinct offense.

c. If a person is convicted of a violation of the provisions of section 1 of P.L.1991, c. 214 (C. 48:13A–12.1), the court shall, in addition to the penalties provided under this section, require the person to perform community service for a term of not more than 90 days, and the person shall forthwith forfeit his right to operate a motor vehicle over the highways of this State for a period of not less than six months nor more than one year.

d. All conveyances used or intended for use in the unlawful transportation of solid waste in violation of the provisions of section 1 of P.L.1991, c. 214 (C. 48:13A–12.1) are subject to forfeiture to the State pursuant to the provisions of P.L.1981, c. 387 (C. 13:1K–1 et seq.).

L.1991, c. 214, § 2, eff. July 24, 1991.

TITLE 53

STATE POLICE

Chapter

1. Organization and Personnel.
2. Powers and Duties.
3. Housing, Equipment, and Expenses.

CHAPTER 1

ORGANIZATION AND PERSONNEL

ARTICLE 1B. ALCOHOLIC BEVERAGE CONTROL ENFORCEMENT BUREAU

Section

53:1–11.3. Establishment.
53:1–11.6. Investigation relating to enforcement of Title 33; request.

ARTICLE 2. STATE BUREAU OF IDENTIFICATION

53:1–13. Fingerprints and other records filed; information furnished by state institutions.
53:1–14. Record of fingerprints, etc., of persons confined in penal institutions; penal institutions to furnish.
53:1–15. Fingerprinting; forwarding copies.
53:1–15.1. Crime related to criminal street gang activity; designation on fingerprinting form.
53:1–16. Comparison of all records received.
53:1–17. Supervisor to instruct, assist and co-operate with local police officials.
53:1–18. Report of criminal charges or disorderly offenses; duty of clerks of courts.
53:1–18.1. Fingerprints of persons arrested for or charged with narcotic or dangerous drug offenses.
53:1–18.2. Reports on narcotic or dangerous drug cases; duty of clerks of court.
53:1–18.5. "Dangerous drugs" defined.
53:1–20. Failure of officers to perform duties; misdemeanor; removal.
53:1–20.2. Duty of law enforcement officers and public officers and employees to supply information; county bureau of identification defined.
53:1–20.3. Release of prisoners from penal or other institutions; notice to bureau; photographs.
53:1–20.4. Department originally arresting prisoner to be notified of his release.
53:1–20.17. DNA Database and Databank Act of 1994; short title.
53:1–20.18. Legislative findings and declaration.
53:1–20.19. Definitions.
53:1–20.20. Persons convicted of sexual offenses to provide blood specimen for DNA testing.
53:1–20.21. Nature of DNA testing; use of test results.
53:1–20.22. Procedures for obtaining blood specimen; persons authorized to draw blood.
53:1–20.23. Rules and regulation; quality assurance guidelines.
53:1–20.24. Inclusion of results in state database; use of data.
53:1–20.25. Expungement of DNA record from state database; conditions.
53:1–20.26. Wrongful disclosure of DNA information; disorderly persons offense.
53:1–20.27. Confidentiality.
53:1–20.28. Funding.
53:1–20.29. Sexual offender liable for costs of DNA testing.
53:1–20.37. Retention and maintenance of DNA information.

ARTICLE 11. NATIONAL CRIME PREVENTION AND PRIVACY COMPACT

53:1–32. National Crime Prevention and Privacy Compact.
53:1–33. Removal or suspension of certain State Police members; written complaint required.

ARTICLE 1B. ALCOHOLIC BEVERAGE CONTROL ENFORCEMENT BUREAU

53:1–11.3. Establishment

There is established in the Division of State Police in the Department of Law and Public Safety an Alcoholic Beverage Control Enforcement Bureau under the supervision of the Superintendent of State Police.

L.1985, c. 76, § 1, eff. March 14, 1985.

53:1–11.6. Investigation relating to enforcement of Title 33; request

The Director of the Division of Alcoholic Beverage Control in the Department of Law and Public Safety may request the bureau to conduct an investigation relating to the enforcement of Title 33 of the Revised Statutes or any supplement thereto.

L.1985, c. 76, § 4, eff. March 14, 1985.

ARTICLE 2. STATE BUREAU OF IDENTIFICATION

53:1–13. Fingerprints and other records filed; information furnished by state institutions

The supervisor of the state bureau of identification shall procure and file for record, fingerprints, plates, photographs, pictures, descriptions, measurements and such other information as may be pertinent, of all persons who have been or may hereafter be convicted of an indictable offense within the state, and also of all well known and habitual criminals wheresoever the same may be procured.

The person in charge of any state institution shall furnish any such information to the supervisor of the state bureau of identification upon request of the superintendent of state police.

53:1–14. Record of fingerprints, etc., of persons confined in penal institutions; penal institutions to furnish

The supervisor of the state bureau of identification may procure and file for record, fingerprints, photographs and other identification data of all persons confined in any workhouse, jail, reformatory, penitentiary or other penal institution and shall file for record such other information as he may receive from the law enforcement officers of the state and its subdivisions.

The wardens, jailers or keepers of workhouses, jails, reformatories, penitentiaries or other penal institutions shall furnish the state bureau of identification with fingerprints and photographs of all prisoners who are or may be confined in the respective institutions, and shall also furnish such other information respecting such prisoners as may be requested.

53:1–15. Fingerprinting; forwarding copies

The sheriffs, chiefs of police, members of the State Police and any other law enforcement agencies and officers shall, immediately upon the arrest of any person for an indictable offense, or for any of the grounds specified in paragraph (1), (2), (3) or (4) of subsection a. of section 5 of P.L.1991, c. 261 (C.2C:25–21) or of any person believed to be wanted for an indictable offense, or believed to be an habitual criminal, or within a reasonable time after the filing of a complaint by a law enforcement officer charging any person with an indictable offense, or upon the arrest of any person for shoplifting, pursuant to N.J.S.2C:20–11, or upon the arrest of any person for prostitution, pursuant to N.J.S.2C:34–1, or the conviction of any other person charged with a nonindictable offense, where the identity of the person charged is in question, take the fingerprints of such person, according to the fingerprint system of identification established by the Superintendent of State Police and on the forms prescribed, and forward without delay two copies or more of the same, together with photographs and such other descriptions as may be required and with a history of the offense committed, to the State Bureau of Identification.

Such sheriffs, chiefs of police, members of the State Police and any other law enforcement agencies and officers shall also take the fingerprints, descriptions and such other information as may be required of unknown dead persons and as required by section 2 of P.L.1982, c. 79 (C.2A:4A–61) of juveniles adjudicated delinquent and shall forward same to the State Bureau of Identification.

Any person charged in a complaint filed by a law enforcement officer with an indictable offense, who has not been arrested, or any person charged in an indictment, who has not been arrested, or any person

convicted of assault or harassment constituting domestic violence as defined in section 3 of P.L.1991, c. 261 (C.2C:25–19), or any person against whom a final order has been entered in any domestic violence matter pursuant to the provisions of section 13 of P.L.1991, c. 261 (C.2C:25–29) shall submit himself to the identification procedures provided herein either on the date of any court appearance or upon written request of the appropriate law enforcement agency within a reasonable time after the filing of the complaint. Any person who refuses to submit to such identification procedures shall be a disorderly person.

Amended by L.1952, c. 93, p. 427, § 1; L.1981, c. 411, § 1, eff. Jan. 7, 1982; L.1982, c. 219, § 1, eff. Dec. 29, 1982; L.1994, c. 56, § 4, eff. June 29, 1994; L.1997, c. 93, § 2, eff. May 8, 1997; L.1999, c. 288, § 1, eff. Dec. 20, 1999.

53:1–15.1. Crime related to criminal street gang activity; designation on fingerprinting form

a. Upon the arrest of any person for a crime or offense for which fingerprinting is required, the arresting officer shall designate whether the crime or offense was related to criminal street gang activity on the form used for the collection of fingerprints pursuant to R.S. 53:1–15. For the purposes of this section, a crime is related to criminal street gang activity if the crime was committed for the benefit of, at the direction of, or in association with a criminal street gang as defined in subsection h. of N.J.S.2C:44–3.

b. The form used for the collection of fingerprints pursuant to R.S.53:1–15 shall include a place for the arresting officer to designate whether the crime or offense was related to criminal street gang activity.

L.2005, c. 332, § 2, eff. Aug. 1, 2006.

53:1–16. Comparison of all records received

The supervisor of the state bureau of identification shall compare all records received with those already on file in such bureau, and whether or not he finds that the person arrested has a criminal record or is a fugitive from justice, he shall at once inform the requesting agency or arresting officer of such fact.

53:1–17. Supervisor to instruct, assist and co-operate with local police officials

The supervisor of the state bureau of identification shall co-operate with, afford instruction and offer assistance to sheriffs, chiefs of police and other law enforcement officers in the establishment and operation of their local systems of criminal identification and in obtaining fingerprints and other means of identification of all persons arrested on a complaint of an indictable offense, to assure co-ordination with the system of identification conducted by the state bureau. The superintendent of state police shall arrange for such co-operation, instruction and assistance by the supervisor.

53:1–18. Report of criminal charges or disorderly offenses; duty of clerks of courts

For the purpose of submitting to the Governor and the Legislature a report of statistics on crime conditions in the annual report of the Division of State Police, the clerk of every court before which a person appears on any criminal charge or disorderly persons offense shall within 30 days report to the State Bureau of Identification the sentence of the court or other disposition of the case.

Amended by L.1967, c. 284, § 1, eff. Jan. 23, 1968.

53:1–18.1. Fingerprints of persons arrested for or charged with narcotic or dangerous drug offenses

Every law enforcement officer designated in R.S. 53:1–15 shall, immediately upon the arrest of any person for or within a reasonable time after the filing of a complaint by a law enforcement officer charging any person with any offense against the laws of the United States, or any offense against the laws of this State, relating to narcotic or dangerous drugs, whether the same shall be indictable or otherwise, take the fingerprints of such person and forward copies thereof together with photographs and such other description and information as is required by such section in the case of the arrest of persons for any offense indictable under the laws of this State.

L.1952, c. 92, p. 426, § 1. Amended by L.1967, c. 298, § 3, eff. Feb. 15, 1968; L.1981, c. 411, § 2, eff. Jan. 7, 1982.

53:1–18.2. Reports on narcotic or dangerous drug cases; duty of clerks of court

The clerk of every court of this State in which any person is prosecuted for an offense under the laws of this State relating to narcotic or dangerous drugs, whether the same be indictable or otherwise, shall promptly report to the State Bureau of Identification the sentence of the court or other disposition of the case.

L.1952, c. 92, p. 427, § 2. Amended by L.1967, c. 298, § 4, eff. Feb. 15, 1968.

53:1–18.5. "Dangerous drugs" defined

As used in this act of which this act is amendatory and supplementary "dangerous drugs, substances or compounds" means and includes any of the following in any form: any depressant, stimulant or hallucinogenic drug, substance or compound as defined pursuant to section 1 of chapter 314 of the laws of 1966 (C. 24:6C–1) or the New Jersey Controlled Dangerous Substances Act or any prescription legend drug which is not a narcotic drug within the meaning of chapter 18 of Title 24 of the Revised Statutes or the New Jersey Controlled Dangerous Substances Act, unless obtained from, or on a valid

prescription of, and used as prescribed by, a duly licensed physician, veterinarian or dentist.

Added by L.1967, c. 298, § 2, eff. Feb. 15, 1968. Amended by L.1970, c. 227, § 7, eff. Oct. 19, 1970.

53:1–20. Failure of officers to perform duties; misdemeanor; removal

Any officer mentioned in this article who shall neglect or refuse to make any report or to do any act required by any provision of this article shall be guilty of a misdemeanor and punished by a fine not exceeding one hundred dollars. Such neglect or refusal shall also constitute nonfeasance in office and subject the officer to removal therefrom.

53:1–20.2. Duty of law enforcement officers and public officers and employees to supply information; county bureau of identification defined

To the end that the county bureaus of identification in each of the counties of this State and the bureau of identification of the Department of the State Police [1] may have available the requisite information for the keeping of such records, it shall be the duty of sheriffs, members of the State Police, county detectives, chiefs of police and other law enforcement officers, immediately upon the receipt of a complaint that an indictable offense has been committed, to forward to the county bureau of identification and the bureau of identification of the State Police Department all of such information which can at that time be obtained, on forms to be provided for that purpose by the head of the office in which such county bureau of identification is established.

It shall also be the duty of such officers, from time to time, upon receipt of additional information, to forward the same to the county bureau of identification and to the bureau of identification of the State Police Department, on forms to be provided for that purpose by the head of the office in which such county bureau of identification is established.

It shall also be the duty of the prosecutor of the pleas, the county clerks, and the probation office in the various counties of this State to supply to the county bureau of identification and to the bureau of identification in the Department of State Police all information on record in their respective offices which may be necessary to complete the records in the prescribed form, as set forth in section one hereof.

The duties herein prescribed to be performed by the public officers and employees herein referred to shall be additional to the duties now prescribed by law to be performed by such public officers and employees.

The words "The County Bureau of Identification," as used in this act, shall be taken to mean the bureau of identification as now established in the office of the sheriff or in the office of the prosecutors of the pleas in the respective counties in this State.

L.1939, c. 78, p. 131, § 2.

1 Now division of state police in department of law and public safety, see §§ 52:17B–6, 52:17B–51.

53:1–20.3. Release of prisoners from penal or other institutions; notice to bureau; photographs

It shall be the duty of the wardens of the county jail in the various counties, of the wardens of the county penitentiaries and workhouses in the various counties of the State and of the Principal Keeper of the State Prison and of the wardens or superintendents of the other State institutions to which prisoners are or may be committed upon the release of any prisoner in their respective charges to notify the Bureau of Identification of the county from which that prisoner was committed and the Bureau of Identification of the State Police of the fact of such prisoner's release and the date of such release.

In the case of any such prisoner who was committed for a term of 5 years or more, it shall also be the duty of the Principal Keeper of the State Prison to forward to the Bureau of Identification of the county from which the prisoner was committed and to the Bureau of Identification of the State Police, at the time of giving the said notification, a photograph of the said prisoner taken within the 30-day period immediately preceding his release.

L.1940, c. 65, § 1. Amended by L.1956, c. 45, p. 93, § 1.

53:1–20.4. Department originally arresting prisoner to be notified of his release

It shall be the duty of the County Bureau of Identification in the several counties of the State immediately upon receipt of such information concerning the release of a prisoner to notify the head of the police department or other law enforcement department which made the original arrest of said prisoner that the said prisoner has been released and the date of his release.

L.1940, c. 65, § 2.

53:1–20.17. DNA Database and Databank Act of 1994; short title

This act shall be known and may be cited as the "DNA Database and Databank Act of 1994."

L.1994, c. 136, § 1, eff. Oct. 31, 1994.

53:1–20.18. Legislative findings and declaration

The Legislature finds and declares that DNA databanks are an important tool in criminal investigations and in deterring and detecting recidivist acts. It is the policy of this State to assist federal, state and local criminal justice and law enforcement agencies in the identification and detection of individuals who are the subjects of criminal investigations. It is therefore in the best interest of the State of New Jersey to establish a DNA database and a DNA databank containing blood or other biological samples submitted by every person convicted or found not guilty by reason of insanity of a crime. It is also in the best interest of the State of New Jersey to include in this DNA database and DNA databank blood or other biological samples submitted by juveniles adjudicated delinquent or adjudicated not delinquent by reason of insanity for acts, which if committed by an adult, would constitute a crime.

L.1994, c. 136, § 2, eff. Oct. 31, 1994. Amended by L.1997, c. 341, § 1, eff. Jan. 12, 1998; L.2003, c. 183, § 1, eff. Sept. 22, 2003.

53:1–20.19. Definitions

As used in this act:

"CODIS" means the FBI's national DNA identification index system that allows the storage and exchange of DNA records submitted by State and local forensic laboratories.

"DNA" means deoxyribonucleic acid.

"DNA Record" means DNA identification information stored in the State DNA database or CODIS for the purpose of generating investigative leads or supporting statistical interpretation of DNA test results.

"DNA Sample" means a blood or other biological sample provided by any person convicted of any offense enumerated in section 4 of P.L.1994, c. 136 (C.53:1–20.20) or provided by any juvenile adjudicated delinquent for an act which, if committed by an adult, would constitute any offense enumerated in section 4 of P.L.1994, c. 136 (C.53:1–20.20) or submitted to the division for analysis pursuant to a criminal investigation.

"Division" means the Division of State Police in the Department of Law and Public Safety.

"FBI" means the Federal Bureau of Investigation.

"State DNA Database" means the DNA identification record system to be administered by the division which provides DNA records to the FBI for storage and maintenance in CODIS.

"State DNA Databank" means the repository of DNA samples collected under the provisions of this act.

L.1994, c. 136, § 3, eff. Oct. 31, 1994. Amended by L.1997, c. 341, § 2, eff. Jan. 12, 1998; L.2003, c. 183, § 2, eff. Sept. 22, 2003.

53:1–20.20. Persons convicted of sexual offenses to provide blood specimen for DNA testing

a. On or after January 1, 1995 every person convicted of aggravated sexual assault and sexual assault under N.J.S.2C:14–2 or aggravated criminal sexual contact and criminal sexual contact under N.J.S.2C:14–3 or any attempt to commit any of these crimes and who is sentenced to a term of imprisonment shall have a blood sample drawn or other biological sample collected for purposes of DNA testing upon commencement of the period of confinement.

In addition, every person convicted on or after January 1, 1995 of these offenses, but who is not sentenced to a term of confinement, shall provide a DNA sample as a condition of the sentence imposed. A person who has been convicted and incarcerated as a result of a conviction of one or more of these offenses prior to January 1, 1995 shall provide a DNA sample before parole or release from incarceration.

b. On or after January 1, 1998 every juvenile adjudicated delinquent for an act which, if committed by an adult, would constitute aggravated sexual assault or sexual assault under N.J.S.2C:14–2 or aggravated criminal sexual contact or criminal sexual contact under N.J.S.2C:14–3, or any attempt to commit any of these crimes, shall have a blood sample drawn or other biological sample collected for purposes of DNA testing.

c. On or after January 1, 1998 every person found not guilty by reason of insanity of aggravated sexual assault or sexual assault under N.J.S.2C:14–2 or aggravated criminal sexual contact or criminal sexual contact under N.J.S.2C:14–3, or any attempt to commit any of these crimes, or adjudicated not delinquent by reason of insanity for an act which, if committed by an adult, would constitute one of these crimes, shall have a blood sample drawn or other biological sample collected for purposes of DNA testing.

d. On or after January 1, 2000 every person convicted of murder pursuant to N.J.S.2C:11–3, manslaughter pursuant to N.J.S.2C:11–4, aggravated assault of the second degree pursuant to paragraph (1) or (6) of subsection b. of N.J.S.2C:12–1, kidnapping pursuant to N.J.S.2C:13–1, luring or enticing a child in violation of P.L.1993, c. 291 (C.2C:13–6), engaging in sexual conduct which would impair or debauch the morals of a child pursuant to N.J.S.2C:24–4, or any attempt to commit any of these crimes and who is sentenced to a term of imprisonment shall have a blood sample drawn or other biological sample collected for purposes of DNA testing upon commencement of the period of confinement.

In addition, every person convicted on or after January 1, 2000 of these offenses, but who is not sentenced to a term of confinement, shall provide a DNA sample as a condition of the sentence imposed. A person who has been convicted and incarcerated as a result of a conviction of one or more of these offenses prior to January 1, 2000 shall provide a DNA sample before parole or release from incarceration.

e. On or after January 1, 2000 every juvenile adjudicated delinquent for an act which, if committed by an adult, would constitute murder pursuant to N.J.S.2C:11–3, manslaughter pursuant to N.J.S.2C:11–4, aggravated assault of the second degree pursuant to paragraph (1) or (6) of subsection b. of N.J.S. 2C:12–1, kidnapping pursuant to N.J.S.2C:13–1, luring or enticing a child in violation of P.L.1993, c. 291 (C.2C:13–6), engaging in sexual conduct which would impair or

debauch the morals of a child pursuant to N.J.S.2C:24–4, or any attempt to commit any of these crimes, shall have a blood sample drawn or other biological sample collected for purposes of DNA testing.

f. On or after January 1, 2000 every person found not guilty by reason of insanity of murder pursuant to N.J.S.2C:11–3, manslaughter pursuant to N.J.S. 2C:11–4, aggravated assault of the second degree pursuant to paragraph (1) or (6) of subsection b. of N.J.S.2C:12–1, kidnapping pursuant to N.J.S.2C:13–1, luring or enticing a child in violation of P.L.1993, c. 291 (C.2C:13–6), engaging in sexual conduct which would impair or debauch the morals of a child pursuant to N.J.S.2C:24–4, or any attempt to commit any of these crimes, or adjudicated not delinquent by reason of insanity for an act which, if committed by an adult, would constitute one of these crimes, shall have a blood sample drawn or other biological sample collected for purposes of DNA testing.

g. Every person convicted or found not guilty by reason of insanity of a crime shall have a blood sample drawn or other biological sample collected for purposes of DNA testing. If the person is sentenced to a term of imprisonment or confinement, the person shall have a blood sample drawn or other biological sample collected for purposes of DNA testing upon commencement of the period of imprisonment or confinement. If the person is not sentenced to a term of imprisonment or confinement, the person shall provide a DNA sample as a condition of the sentence imposed. A person who has been convicted or found not guilty by reason of insanity of a crime prior to the effective date of P.L.2003, c. 183 and who, on the effective date, is serving a sentence of imprisonment, probation, parole or other form of supervision as a result of the crime or is confined following acquittal by reason of insanity shall provide a DNA sample before termination of imprisonment, probation, parole, supervision or confinement, as the case may be.

h. Every juvenile adjudicated delinquent, or adjudicated not delinquent by reason of insanity, for an act which, if committed by an adult, would constitute a crime shall have a blood sample drawn or other biological sample collected for purposes of DNA testing. If under the order of disposition the juvenile is sentenced to some form of imprisonment, detention or confinement, the juvenile shall have a blood sample drawn or other biological sample collected for purposes of DNA testing upon commencement of the period of imprisonment, detention or confinement. If the order of disposition does not include some form of imprisonment, detention or confinement, the juvenile shall provide a DNA sample as a condition of the disposition ordered by the court. A juvenile who, prior to the effective date of P.L.2003, c. 183, has been adjudicated delinquent, or adjudicated not delinquent by reason of insanity for an act which, if committed by an adult, would constitute a crime and who on the effective date is under some form of imprisonment, detention, confinement, probation, parole or any other form of supervision as a result of the offense or is confined following an adjudication of not delinquent by reason of insanity shall provide a DNA sample before termination of imprisonment, detention, supervision or confinement, as the case may be.

i. Nothing in this act shall be deemed to limit or preclude collection of DNA samples as authorized by court order or in accordance with any other law.

L.1994, c. 136, § 4, eff. Oct. 31, 1994. Amended by L.1997, c. 341, § 3, eff. Jan. 12, 1998; L.2000, c. 118, § 1, eff. Sept. 13, 2000; L.2003, c. 183, § 3, eff. Sept. 22, 2003.

53:1–20.21. Nature of DNA testing; use of test results

Tests shall be performed on each blood or other biological sample submitted pursuant to section 4 of P.L.1994, c. 136 (C.53:1–20.20) in order to analyze and type the genetic markers contained in or derived from the DNA. Except insofar as the use of the results of these tests for such purposes would jeopardize or result in the loss of federal funding, the results of these tests shall be used for the following purposes:

a. For law enforcement identification purposes;

b. For development of a population database;

c. To support identification research and protocol development of forensic DNA analysis methods;

d. To assist in the recovery or identification of human remains from mass disasters or for other humanitarian purposes;

e. For research, administrative and quality control purposes;

f. For judicial proceedings, by order of the court, if otherwise admissible pursuant to applicable statutes or rules;

g. For criminal defense purposes, on behalf of a defendant, who shall have access to relevant samples and analyses performed in connection with the case in which the defendant is charged; and

h. For such other purposes as may be required under federal law as a condition for obtaining federal funding.

The DNA record of identification characteristics resulting from the DNA testing conducted pursuant to this section shall be stored and maintained in the State DNA database and forwarded to the FBI for inclusion in CODIS. The DNA sample itself will be stored and maintained in the State DNA databank.

L.1994, c. 136, § 5, eff. Oct. 31, 1994. Amended by L.2003, c. 183, § 4, eff. Sept. 22, 2003.

53:1–20.22. Procedures for obtaining blood specimen; persons authorized to draw blood

Each blood sample required to be drawn or biological sample collected pursuant to section 4 of P.L.1994, c. 136 (C.53:1–20.20) from persons who are incarcerated shall be drawn or collected at the place of incarceration. DNA samples from persons who are not sentenced to a term of confinement shall be drawn or collected at a prison or jail unit to be specified by the sentencing court. DNA samples from persons who are adjudicated delinquent shall be drawn or collected at a prison or jail identification and classification bureau specified by the family court. Only a correctional health nurse technician, physician, registered professional nurse, licensed practical nurse, laboratory or medical technician, phlebotomist or other health care worker with phlebotomy training shall draw any blood sample to be submitted for analysis, and only a correctional health nurse technician, physician, registered professional nurse, licensed practical nurse, laboratory or medical technician or person who has received biological sample collection training in accordance with protocols adopted by the Attorney General,in consultation with the Department of Corrections, shall collect or supervise the collection of any other biological sample to be submitted for analysis. No civil liability shall attach to any person authorized to draw blood or collect a biological sample by this section as a result of drawing blood or collecting the sample from any person if the blood was drawn or sample collected according to recognized medical procedures. No person shall be relieved from liability for negligence in the drawing or collecting of any DNA sample. No sample shall be drawn or collected pursuant to section 4 of P.L.1994, c. 136 (C.53:1–20.20) if the division has previously received a blood or biological sample from the convicted person or the juvenile adjudicated delinquent which was adequate for successful analysis and identification.

L.1994, c. 136, § 6, eff. Oct. 31, 1994. Amended by L.1997, c. 341, § 4, eff. Jan. 12, 1998; L.2003, c. 183, § 5, eff. Sept. 22, 2003.

53:1–20.23. Rules and regulation; quality assurance guidelines

The division shall adopt rules governing the procedures to be used in the submission, identification, analysis and storage of DNA samples and typing results of DNA samples submitted under this act. The DNA sample shall be securely stored in the State databank. The typing results shall be securely stored in the State database. These procedures shall also include quality assurance guidelines to insure that DNA identification records meet audit standards for laboratories which submit DNA records to the State database. The DNA identification system established pursuant to this act shall be compatible with that utilized by the FBI.

L.1994, c. 136, § 7, eff. Oct. 31, 1994.

53:1–20.24. Inclusion of results in state database; use of data

a. It shall be the duty of the division to store, analyze, classify and file in the State database and with the FBI for inclusion in CODIS the DNA record of identification characteristic profiles of DNA samples submitted pursuant to section 4 of this act [1] and to make such information available from the State database as provided in this section. The division may contract out DNA typing analysis to a qualified DNA laboratory that meets established guidelines. The results of the DNA profile of individuals in the State database shall be made available to local, State or federal law enforcement agencies, and approved crime laboratories which serve these agencies, upon written or electronic request and in furtherance of an official investigation of a criminal offense. These records shall also be available upon receipt of a valid court order issued by a judge of the Superior Court directing the division to release these results to appropriate parties not listed above. The division shall maintain a file of such court orders.

b. The division shall adopt rules governing the methods of obtaining information from the State database and CODIS and procedures for verification of the identity and authority of the requester.

c. The division shall create a separate population database comprised of records obtained pursuant to this act after all personal identification is removed. Nothing shall prohibit the division from sharing or disseminating population databases with other law enforcement agencies, and crime laboratories that serve these agencies, upon written or electronic request and in furtherance of an official investigation of a criminal offense, or other third parties deemed necessary to assist with statistical analysis of the population databases. The population database may be made available to and searched by other agencies participating in the CODIS system.

L.1994, c. 136, § 8, eff. Oct. 31, 1994.

[1] N.J.S.A. § 53:1–20.20.

53:1–20.25. Expungement of DNA record from state database; conditions

a. (1) Any person whose DNA record or profile has been included in the State DNA database and whose DNA sample is stored in the State DNA databank may apply for expungement on the grounds that the conviction that resulted in the inclusion of the person's DNA record or profile in the State database or the inclusion of the person's DNA sample in the State databank has been reversed and the case dismissed. The person, either individually or through an attorney, may apply to the court for expungement of the record. A copy of the application for expungement shall be served on the prosecutor for the county in which the conviction was obtained not less than 20 days prior to the date of the hearing on the application. A certified copy of the order reversing and dismissing the conviction shall be

attached to an order expunging the DNA record or profile insofar as its inclusion rests upon that conviction.

(2) Any juvenile adjudicated delinquent whose DNA record or profile has been included in the State DNA database and whose DNA sample is stored in the State DNA databank may apply for expungement on the grounds that the adjudication that resulted in the inclusion of the juvenile's DNA record or profile in the State database or the inclusion of the juvenile's DNA sample in the State databank has been reversed and the case dismissed. The juvenile adjudicated delinquent, either individually or through an attorney, may apply to the court for expungement of the record. A copy of the application for expungement shall be served on the prosecutor for the county in which the conviction was obtained not less than 20 days prior to the date of the hearing on the application. A certified copy of the order reversing and dismissing the adjudication shall be attached to an order expunging the DNA record or profile insofar as its inclusion rests upon that conviction.

(3) Any person found not guilty by reason of insanity, or adjudicated not delinquent by reason of insanity, whose DNA record or profile has been included in the State DNA database and whose DNA sample is stored in the State DNA databank may apply for expungement on the grounds that the judgment that resulted in the inclusion of the person's DNA record or profile in the State database or the inclusion of the person's DNA sample in the State databank has been reversed and the case dismissed. The person, either individually or through an attorney, may apply to the court for expungement of the record. A copy of the application of expungement shall be served on the prosecutor for the county in which the judgment was obtained not less than 20 days prior to the date of the hearing on the application. A certified copy of the order reversing and dismissing the judgment shall be attached to an order expunging the DNA record or profile insofar as its inclusion rests upon that conviction.

b. Upon receipt of an order of expungement and unless otherwise provided, the division shall purge the DNA record and all other identifiable information from the State database and the DNA sample stored in the State databank covered by the order. If the entry in the database reflects more than one conviction or adjudication, that entry shall not be expunged unless and until the person or the juvenile adjudicated delinquent has obtained an order of expungement for each conviction or adjudication on the grounds contained in subsection a. of this section. If one of the bases for inclusion in the DNA database was other than conviction or adjudication, that entry shall not be subject to expungement.

L.1994, c. 136, § 9, eff. Oct. 31, 1994. Amended by L.1997, c. 341, § 5, eff. Jan. 12, 1998.

53:1–20.26. Wrongful disclosure of DNA information; disorderly persons offense

Any person who by virtue of employment, or official position, has possession of, or access to, individually identifiable DNA information contained in the State DNA database or databank and who purposely discloses it in any manner to any person or agency not entitled to receive it is guilty of a disorderly person's offense.

L.1994, c. 136, § 10, eff. Oct. 31, 1994.

53:1–20.27. Confidentiality

All DNA profiles and samples submitted to the division pursuant to this act shall be treated as confidential except as provided in section 8 of this act.[1]

L.1994, c. 136, § 11, eff. Oct. 31, 1994.

1 N.J.S.A. § 53:1–20.24.

53:1–20.28. Funding

The Attorney General shall use funds obtained through seizure, forfeiture or abandonment pursuant to any federal or State statutory or common law, and the proceeds of the sale of any such confiscated property or goods, as may be available and appropriate for the costs of implementing P.L.1994, c. 136 (C. 53:1–20.17 et seq.) during the first year following enactment.

L.1994, c. 136, § 12, eff. Oct. 31, 1994.

53:1–20.29. Sexual offender liable for costs of DNA testing

Any person required pursuant to the provisions of P.L.1994, c. 136 (C.53:1–20.17 et seq.) to have a blood sample drawn or other biological sample collected for purposes of DNA testing shall be liable for the costs of such testing.

L.1997, c. 51, § 1, eff. April 1, 1997. Amended by L.2000, c. 118, § 2, eff. Sept. 13, 2000.

53:1–20.37. Retention and maintenance of DNA information

a. Notwithstanding any other provision of law to the contrary, the Division of State Police in the Department of Law and Public Safety shall retain all DNA profile information from biological samples taken from a convicted person pursuant to the provisions of section 1 of P.L.2001, c. 377 (C.2A:84A–32a) and may use the profile information in the investigation and prosecution of other crimes. The DNA profile information shall be added to, stored and maintained in the State DNA databank established pursuant to the "DNA Database and Databank Act of 1994," P.L.1994, c. 136 (C.53:1–20.17 et seq.) and shall be forwarded to the FBI for inclusion in CODIS.

b. The Attorney General shall adopt rules governing the procedures to be used in the analysis and storage of DNA profile information obtained in accordance with the provisions of P.L.2001, c. 377 (C.2A:84A–32a et al.).

L.2001, c. 377, § 2, eff. July 7, 2002.

ARTICLE 11. NATIONAL CRIME PREVENTION AND PRIVACY COMPACT

53:1–32. National Crime Prevention and Privacy Compact

The Contracting Parties agree to the following:

OVERVIEW

(a) IN GENERAL.—This Compact organizes an electronic information sharing system among the Federal Government and the States to exchange criminal history records for noncriminal justice purposes authorized by Federal or State law, such as background checks for governmental licensing and employment.

(b) OBLIGATIONS OF PARTIES.—Under this Compact, the FBI and the Party States agree to maintain detailed databases of their respective criminal history records, including arrests and dispositions, and to make them available to the Federal Government and to Party States for authorized purposes. The FBI shall also manage the Federal data facilities that provide a significant part of the infrastructure for the system.

ARTICLE I—DEFINITIONS

In this Compact:

(1) ATTORNEY GENERAL.—The term "Attorney General" means the Attorney General of the United States.

(2) COMPACT OFFICER.—The term "Compact officer" means—

(A) with respect to the Federal Government, an official so designated by the Director of the FBI; and

(B) with respect to a Party State, the chief administrator of the State's criminal history record repository or a designee of the chief administrator who is a regular full-time employee of the repository.

(3) COUNCIL.—The term "Council" means the Compact Council established under Article VI.

(4) CRIMINAL HISTORY RECORDS.—The term "criminal history records"—

(A) means information collected by criminal justice agencies on individuals consisting of identifiable descriptions and notations of arrests, detentions, indictments, or other formal criminal charges, and any disposition arising therefrom, including acquittal, sentencing, correctional supervision, or release; and

(B) does not include identification information such as fingerprint records if such information does not indicate involvement of the individual with the criminal justice system.

(5) CRIMINAL HISTORY RECORD REPOSITORY.—The term "criminal history record repository" means the State agency designated by the Governor or other appropriate executive official or the legislature of

a State to perform centralized recordkeeping functions for criminal history records and services in the State.

(6) CRIMINAL JUSTICE.—The term "criminal justice" includes activities relating to the detection, apprehension, detention, pretrial release, post-trial release, prosecution, adjudication, correctional supervision, or rehabilitation of accused persons or criminal offenders. The administration of criminal justice includes criminal identification activities and the collection, storage, and dissemination of criminal history records.

(7) CRIMINAL JUSTICE AGENCY.—The term "criminal justice agency"—

(A) means—

(i) courts; and

(ii) a governmental agency or any subunit thereof that—

(I) performs the administration of criminal justice pursuant to a statute or Executive order; and

(II) allocates a substantial part of its annual budget to the administration of criminal justice; and

(B) includes Federal and State inspectors general offices.

(8) CRIMINAL JUSTICE SERVICES.—The term "criminal justice services" means services provided by the FBI to criminal justice agencies in response to a request for information about a particular individual or as an update to information previously provided for criminal justice purposes.

(9) CRITERION OFFENSE.—The term "criterion offense" means any felony or misdemeanor offense not included on the list of nonserious offenses published periodically by the FBI.

(10) DIRECT ACCESS.—The term "direct access" means access to the National Identification Index by computer terminal or other automated means not requiring the assistance of or intervention by any other party or agency.

(11) EXECUTIVE ORDER.—The term "Executive order" means an order of the President of the United States or the chief executive officer of a State that has the force of law and that is promulgated in accordance with applicable law.

(12) FBI.—The term "FBI" means the Federal Bureau of Investigation.

(13) INTERSTATE IDENTIFICATION SYSTEM.—The term "Interstate Identification Index System" or "III System"—

(A) means the cooperative Federal–State system for the exchange of criminal history records; and

(B) includes the National Identification Index, the National Fingerprint File and, to the extent of their participation in such system, the criminal history record repositories of the States and the FBI.

(14) NATIONAL FINGERPRINT FILE.—The term "National Fingerprint File" means a database of fingerprints, or other uniquely personal identifying information, relating to an arrested or charged individual maintained by the FBI to provide positive identification of record subjects indexed in the III System.

(15) NATIONAL IDENTIFICATION INDEX.—The term "National Identification Index" means an index maintained by the FBI consisting of names, identifying numbers, and other descriptive information relating to record subjects about whom there are criminal history records in the III System.

(16) NATIONAL INDICES.—The term "National indices" means the National Identification Index and the National Fingerprint File.

(17) NONPARTY STATE.—The term "Nonparty State" means a State that has not ratified this Compact.

(18) NONCRIMINAL JUSTICE PURPOSES.—The term "noncriminal justice purposes" means uses of criminal history records for purposes authorized by Federal or State law other than purposes relating to criminal justice activities, including employment suitability, licensing determinations, immigration and naturalization matters, and national security clearances.

(19) PARTY STATE.—The term "Party State" means a State that has ratified this Compact.

(20) POSITIVE IDENTIFICATION.—The term "positive identification" means a determination, based upon a comparison of fingerprints or other equally reliable biometric identification techniques, that the subject of a record search is the same person as the subject of a criminal history record or records indexed in the III System. Identifications based solely upon a comparison of subjects names or other nonunique identification characteristics or numbers, or combinations thereof, shall not constitute positive identification.

(21) SEALED RECORD INFORMATION.—The term "sealed record information" means—

(A) with respect to adults, that portion of a record that is—

(i) not available for criminal justice uses;

(ii) not supported by fingerprints or other accepted means of positive identification; or

(iii) subject to restrictions on dissemination for non-criminal justice purposes pursuant to a court order related to a particular subject or pursuant to a Federal or State statute that requires action on a sealing petition filed by a particular record subject; and

(B) with respect to juveniles, whatever each State determines is a sealed record under its own law and procedure.

(22) STATE.—The term "State" means any State, territory, or possession of the United States, the District of Columbia, and the Commonwealth of Puerto Rico.

ARTICLE II—PURPOSES

The purposes of this Compact are to—

(1) provide a legal framework for the establishment of a cooperative Federal–State system for the interstate and Federal–State exchange of criminal history records for noncriminal justice uses;

(2) require the FBI to permit use of the National Identification Index and the National Fingerprint File by each Party State, and to provide, in a timely fashion, Federal and State criminal history records to requesting States, in accordance with the terms of this Compact and with rules, procedures, and standards established by the Council under Article VI;

(3) require Party States to provide information and records for the National Identification Index and the National Fingerprint File and to provide criminal history records, in a timely fashion, to criminal history record repositories of other States and the Federal Government for noncriminal justice purposes, in accordance with the terms of this Compact and with rules, procedures, and standards established by the Council under Article VI;

(4) provide for the establishment of a Council to monitor III System operations and to prescribe system rules and procedures for the effective and proper operation of the III System for noncriminal justice purposes; and

(5) require the FBI and each Party State to adhere to III System standards concerning record dissemination and use, response times, system security, data quality, and other duly established standards, including those that enhance the accuracy and privacy of such records.

ARTICLE III—RESPONSIBILITIES OF COMPACT PARTIES

(a) FBI RESPONSIBILITIES.—The Director of the FBI shall—

(1) appoint an FBI Compact officer who shall—

(A) administer this Compact within the Department of Justice and among Federal agencies and other agencies and organizations that submit search requests to the FBI pursuant to Article V(c);

(B) ensure that Compact provisions and rules, procedures, and standards prescribed by the Council under Article VI are complied with by the Department of Justice and the Federal agencies and other agencies and organizations referred to in Article III(1)(A); and

(C) regulate the use of records received by means of the III System from Party States when such records are supplied by the FBI directly to other Federal agencies;

(2) provide to Federal agencies and to State criminal history record repositories, criminal history records maintained in its database for the noncriminal justice purposes described in Article IV, including—

(A) information from Nonparty States; and

(B) information from Party States that is available from the FBI through the III System, but is not available from the Party State through the III System;

(3) provide a telecommunications network and maintain centralized facilities for the exchange of criminal history records for both criminal justice purposes and the noncriminal justice purposes described in Article IV, and ensure that the exchange of such records for criminal justice purposes has priority over exchange for noncriminal justice purposes; and

(4) modify or enter into user agreements with Nonparty State criminal history record repositories to require them to establish record request procedures conforming to those prescribed in Article V.

(b) STATE RESPONSIBILITIES.—Each Party State shall—

(1) appoint a Compact officer who shall—

(A) administer this Compact within that State;

(B) ensure that Compact provisions and rules, procedures, and standards established by the Council under Article VI are complied with in the State; and

(C) regulate the in-State use of records received by means of the III System from the FBI or from other Party States;

(2) establish and maintain a criminal history record repository, which shall provide—

(A) information and records for the National Identification Index and the National Fingerprint File; and

(B) the State's III System-indexed criminal history records for noncriminal justice purposes described in Article IV;

(3) participate in the National Fingerprint File; and

(4) provide and maintain telecommunications links and related equipment necessary to support the services set forth in this Compact.

(c) COMPLIANCE WITH III SYSTEM STANDARDS.—In carrying out their responsibilities under this Compact, the FBI and each Party State shall comply with III System rules, procedures, and standards duly established by the Council concerning record dissemination and use, response times, data quality, system security, accuracy, privacy protection, and other aspects of III System operation.

(d) MAINTENANCE OF RECORD SERVICES.—

(1) Use of the III System for noncriminal justice purposes authorized in this Compact shall be managed so as not to diminish the level of services provided in support of criminal justice purposes.

(2) Administration of Compact provisions shall not reduce the level of service available to authorized noncriminal justice users on the effective date of this Compact.

ARTICLE IV—AUTHORIZED RECORD DISCLOSURES

(a) STATE CRIMINAL HISTORY RECORD RE-POSITORIES.—To the extent authorized by section 552a of title 5, United States Code (commonly known as the "Privacy Act of 1974"), the FBI shall provide on request criminal history records (excluding sealed records) to State criminal history record repositories for noncriminal justice purposes allowed by Federal statute, Federal Executive order, or a State statute that has been approved by the Attorney General and that authorizes national indices checks.

(b) CRIMINAL JUSTICE AGENCIES AND OTHER GOVERNMENTAL OR NONGOVERNMENTAL AGENCIES.—The FBI, to the extent authorized by section 552a of title 5, United States Code (commonly known as the "Privacy Act of 1974"), and State criminal history record repositories shall provide criminal history records (excluding sealed records) to criminal justice agencies and other governmental or nongovernmental agencies for noncriminal justice purposes allowed by Federal statute, Federal Executive order, or a State statute that has been approved by the Attorney General, that authorizes national indices checks.

(c) PROCEDURES.—Any record obtained under this Compact may be used only for the official purposes for which the record was requested. Each Compact officer shall establish procedures, consistent with this Compact, and with rules, procedures, and standards established by the Council under Article VI, which procedures shall protect the accuracy and privacy of the records, and shall—

(1) ensure that records obtained under this Compact are used only by authorized officials for authorized purposes;

(2) require that subsequent record checks are requested to obtain current information whenever a new need arises; and

(3) ensure that record entries that may not legally be used for a particular noncriminal justice purpose are deleted from the response and, if no information authorized for release remains, an appropriate "no record" response is communicated to the requesting official.

ARTICLE V—RECORD REQUEST PROCEDURES

(a) POSITIVE IDENTIFICATION.—Subject fingerprints or other approved forms of positive identification shall be submitted with all requests for criminal history record checks for noncriminal justice purposes.

(b) SUBMISSION OF STATE REQUESTS.—Each request for a criminal history record check utilizing the national indices made under any approved State statute shall be submitted through that State's criminal history record repository. A State criminal history record repository shall process an interstate request for non-criminal justice purposes through the national indices only if such request is transmitted through another State criminal history record repository or the FBI.

(c) SUBMISSION OF FEDERAL REQUESTS.—Each request for criminal history record checks utilizing the national indices made under Federal authority shall be submitted through the FBI or, if the State criminal history record repository consents to process fingerprint submissions, through the criminal history record repository in the State in which such request originated. Direct access to the National Identification Index by entities other than the FBI and State criminal history records repositories shall not be permitted for noncriminal justice purposes.

(d) FEES.—A State criminal history record repository or the FBI—

(1) may charge a fee, in accordance with applicable law, for handling a request involving fingerprint processing for noncriminal justice purposes; and

(2) may not charge a fee for providing criminal history records in response to an electronic request for a record that does not involve a request to process fingerprints.

(e) ADDITIONAL SEARCH.—

(1) If a State criminal history record repository cannot positively identify the subject of a record request made for noncriminal justice purposes, the request, together with fingerprints or other approved identifying information, shall be forwarded to the FBI for a search of the national indices.

(2) If, with respect to a request forwarded by a State criminal history record repository under paragraph (1), the FBI positively identifies the subject as having a III System-indexed record or records-

(A) the FBI shall so advise the State criminal history record repository; and

(B) the State criminal history record repository shall be entitled to obtain the additional criminal history record information from the FBI or other State criminal history record repositories.

ARTICLE VI—ESTABLISHMENT OF COMPACT COUNCIL

(a) ESTABLISHMENT.—

(1) IN GENERAL.—There is established a council to be known as the "Compact Council", which shall have the authority to promulgate rules and procedures governing the use of the III System for noncriminal justice purposes, not to conflict with FBI administration of the III System for criminal justice purposes.

(2) ORGANIZATION.—The Council shall—

(A) continue in existence as long as this Compact remains in effect;

(B) be located, for administrative purposes, within the FBI; and

(C) be organized and hold its first meeting as soon as practicable after the effective date of this Compact.

(b) MEMBERSHIP.—The Council shall be composed of 15 members, each of whom shall be appointed by the Attorney General, as follows:

(1) Nine members, each of whom shall serve a two–year term, who shall be selected from among the Compact officers of Party States based on the recommendation of the Compact officers of all Party States, except that, in the absence of the requisite number of Compact officers available to serve, the chief administrators of the criminal history record repositories of Nonparty States shall be eligible to serve on an interim basis.

(2) Two at-large members, nominated by the Director of the FBI, each of whom shall serve a three–year term, of whom—

(A) One shall be a representative of the criminal justice agencies of the Federal Government and may not be an employee of the FBI; and

(B) One shall be a representative of the noncriminal justice agencies of the Federal Government.

(3) Two at-large members, nominated by the Chairman of the Council, once the Chairman is elected pursuant to Article VI(c), each of whom shall serve a three–year term, of whom—

(A) One shall be a representative of State or local criminal justice agencies; and

(B) One shall be a representative of State or local noncriminal justice agencies.

(4) One member, who shall serve a three–year term, and who shall simultaneously be a member of the FBI's advisory policy board on criminal justice information services, nominated by the membership of that policy board.

(5) One member, nominated by the Director of the FBI, who shall serve a three–year term, and who shall be an employee of the FBI.

(c) CHAIRMAN AND VICE CHAIRMAN.—

(1) IN GENERAL.—From its membership, the Council shall elect a Chairman and a Vice Chairman of the Council, respectively. Both the Chairman and Vice Chairman of the Council—

(A) shall be a Compact officer, unless there is no Compact officer on the Council who is willing to serve, in which case the Chairman may be an at-large member; and

(B) shall serve a two–year term and may be reelected to only one additional two–year term.

(2) DUTIES OF VICE CHAIRMAN.—The Vice Chairman of the Council shall serve as the Chairman of the Council in the absence of the Chairman.

(d) MEETINGS.—

(1) IN GENERAL.—The Council shall meet at least once each year at the call of the Chairman. Each meeting of the Council shall be open to the public. The Council shall provide prior public notice in the Federal Register of each meeting of the Council, including the matters to be addressed at such meeting.

(2) QUORUM.—A majority of the Council or any committee of the Council shall constitute a quorum of the Council or of such committee, respectively, for the conduct of business. A lesser number may meet to hold hearings, take testimony, or conduct any business not requiring a vote.

(e) RULES, PROCEDURES, AND STANDARDS.—The Council shall make available for public inspection and copying at the Council office within the FBI, and shall publish in the Federal Register, any rules, procedures, or standards established by the Council.

(f) ASSISTANCE FROM FBI.—The Council may request from the FBI such reports, studies, statistics, or other information or materials as the Council determines to be necessary to enable the Council to perform its duties under this Compact. The FBI, to the extent authorized by law, may provide such assistance or information upon such a request.

(g) COMMITTEES.—The Chairman may establish committees as necessary to carry out this Compact and may prescribe their membership, responsibilities, and duration.

ARTICLE VII—RATIFICATION OF COMPACT

This Compact shall take effect upon being entered into by two or more States as between those States and the Federal Government. Upon subsequent entering into this Compact by additional States, it shall become effective among those States and the Federal Government and each Party State that has previously ratified it. When ratified, this Compact shall have the full force and effect of law within the ratifying jurisdictions. The form of ratification shall be in accordance with the laws of the executing State.

ARTICLE VIII—MISCELLANEOUS PROVISIONS

(a) RELATION OF COMPACT TO CERTAIN FBI ACTIVITIES.—Administration of this Compact shall not interfere with the management and control of the Director of the FBI over the FBI's collection and dissemination of criminal history records and the advisory function of the FBI's advisory policy board chartered under the Federal Advisory Committee Act (5 U.S.C. App.) for all purposes other than noncriminal justice.

(b) NO AUTHORITY FOR NONAPPROPRIATED EXPENDITURES.—Nothing in this Compact shall require the FBI to obligate or expend funds beyond those appropriated to the FBI.

(c) RELATING TO PUBLIC LAW 92–544.—Nothing in this Compact shall diminish or lessen the obligations, responsibilities, and authorities of any

State, whether a Party State or a Nonparty State, or of any criminal history record repository or other subdivision or component thereof, under the Departments of State, Justice, and Commerce, the Judiciary, and Related Agencies Appropriation Act, 1973 (Public Law 92–544), or regulations and guidelines promulgated thereunder, including the rules and procedures promulgated by the Council under Article VI(a), regarding the use and dissemination of criminal history records and information.

ARTICLE IX—RENUNCIATION

(a) IN GENERAL.—This Compact shall bind each Party State until renounced by the Party State.

(b) EFFECT.—Any renunciation of this Compact by a Party State shall—

(1) be effected in the same manner by which the Party State ratified this Compact; and

(2) become effective 180 days after written notice of renunciation is provided by the Party State to each other Party State and to the Federal Government.

ARTICLE X—SEVERABILITY

The provisions of this Compact shall be severable, and if any phrase, clause, sentence, or provision of this Compact is declared to be contrary to the constitution of any participating State, or to the Constitution of the United States, or the applicability thereof to any government, agency, person, or circumstance is held invalid, the validity of the remainder of this Compact and the applicability thereof to any government, agency, person, or circumstance shall not be affected thereby. If a portion of this Compact is held contrary to the constitution of any Party State, all other portions of this Compact shall remain in full force and effect as to the remaining Party States and in full force and effect as to the Party State affected, as to all other provisions.

ARTICLE XI—ADJUDICATION OF DISPUTES

(a) IN GENERAL.—The Council shall—

(1) have initial authority to make determinations with respect to any dispute regarding—

(A) interpretation of this Compact;

(B) any rule or standard established by the Council pursuant to Article V; and

(C) any dispute or controversy between any parties to this Compact; and

(2) hold a hearing concerning any dispute described in paragraph (1) at a regularly scheduled meeting of the Council and only render a decision based upon a majority vote of the members of the Council. Such decision shall be published pursuant to the requirements of Article VI(e).

(b) DUTIES OF FBI.—The FBI shall exercise immediate and necessary action to preserve the integrity of the III System, maintain system policy and standards, protect the accuracy and privacy of records, and to

prevent abuses, until the Council holds a hearing on such matters.

(c) RIGHT OF APPEAL.—The FBI or a Party State may appeal any decision of the Council to the Attorney General, and thereafter may file suit in the appropriate district court of the United States, which shall have original jurisdiction of all cases or controversies arising under this Compact. Any suit arising under this Compact and initiated in a State court shall be removed to the appropriate district court of the United States in the manner provided by section 1446 of title 28, United States Code, or other statutory authority.

L.2001, c. 331, § 1, eff. Jan. 5, 2002.

53:1–33. Removal or suspension of certain State Police members; written complaint required

Except as otherwise provided by law, no permanent officer or trooper of the New Jersey State Police shall be removed from his office, employment or position for political reasons or for any cause other than incapacity, misconduct, or disobedience of rules and regulations established for the State Police, nor shall an officer or trooper be suspended, removed, fined or reduced in rank from or in office, employment, or position therein, except for just cause as hereinbefore provided and then only upon a written complaint setting forth the charge or charges against the officer or trooper. The complaint shall be filed in the office of the Superintendent or with the officer or officers having charge of the unit of the State Police wherein the complaint is made and a copy shall be served upon the officer or trooper so charged, with notice of a designated hearing thereon by the proper authorities, which shall be not less than 10 or more than 30 days from date of service of the complaint.

A complaint charging a violation of the internal rules and regulations established for the conduct of the State Police shall be filed no later than the 45th day after the date on which the person filing the complaint obtained sufficient information to file the matter upon which the complaint is based, except that a complaint charging a violation of the internal rules and regulations established for the conduct of the State Police involving (1) prohibited discrimination, (2) unreasonable use of force or threat of force, or (3) an intentional constitutional violation shall be filed no later than the 120th day after the date on which the person filing the complaint obtained sufficient information to file the matter upon which the complaint is based, until such time as the consent decree entered into between the United States and this State in Civil No. 99–5970 (MLC), ordered by United States District Court Judge Mary Cooper on December 30, 1999, has expired on such matter and all discipline issues will be governed by the 45–day limit thereafter. The applicable time limit shall not apply if an investigation of an officer or trooper for a violation of the internal rules or regulations of the law enforcement unit is included directly or indirectly within a concurrent investigation of that person for a violation of the criminal laws of this State. The applicable time limit shall begin on the day after the disposition of the criminal investigation. The time requirement of this section for the filing of a complaint against an officer or trooper shall not apply to a filing of a complaint by a private individual.

A failure to comply with the provisions of this section concerning the service of the complaint and the time within which a complaint is to be filed shall require a dismissal of the complaint.

The officer or trooper may waive the right to a hearing and may appeal the charges directly to any available authority specified by law or regulation, or follow any other procedure recognized by a contract, as permitted by law.

L.2001, c. 380, § 1.

Historical and Statutory Notes

L.2001, c. 380, § 2, approved Jan. 8, 2002, provides:

"This act shall take effect immediately as to any complaint pending at the time of enactment of this act which charges a member of the State Police with a violation of the internal rules and regulations established for the conduct of the State Police involving prohibited discrimination, unreasonable use of force or threat of force, or an intentional constitutional violation which complaint, if unresolved, will result in the delay of a listed promotional opportunity for that member, and shall take effect on the 75th day after enactment as to any complaint pending at the time of enactment of this act which charges a member of the State Police with a violation of the internal rules and regulations established for the conduct of the State Police which does not involve prohibited discrimination, unreasonable use of force or threat of force, or an intentional constitutional violation which complaint, if unresolved, will result in the delay of a listed promotional opportunity for that member, and shall take effect on the 120th day after enactment as to all other complaints against a member of the State Police."

CHAPTER 2

POWERS AND DUTIES

Section
53:2–1. Powers and duties in general; co-operation with other authorities.

53:2–1. Powers and duties in general; co-operation with other authorities

The members of the State Police shall be subject to the call of the Governor. They shall be peace officers of the State, shall primarily be employed in furnishing adequate police protection to the inhabitants of rural sections, shall give first aid to the injured and succor the helpless, and shall have in general the same powers and authority as are conferred by law upon police officers and constables.

They shall have power to prevent crime, to pursue and apprehend offenders and to obtain legal evidence necessary to insure the conviction of such offenders in the courts. They shall have power to execute any lawful warrant or order of arrest issued against any person, and to make arrests without warrant for violations of the law

committed in their presence, and for felonies committed the same as are or may be authorized by law for other peace officers.

They may co-operate with any other State department, or any State or local authority in detecting crime, apprehending criminals and preserving law and order; but the State Police shall not be used as a posse in any municipality except upon order of the Governor when requested by the governing body of such municipality; provided, however, that the Superintendent of State Police, or the person in charge thereof, shall, upon request made to him by the superintendent of elections of any county of this State, assign for use on any election day officers and troopers, not to exceed fifteen in number in any one county, to aid such superintendents of elections in the enforcement of the election laws of this State.

They may act as inspectors of motor vehicles and as wardens in the protection of the forests, and the fish and game of the State. With respect to enforcement of the provisions of the "New Jersey Alcoholic Beverage Control Act," Title 33 of the Revised Statutes, they shall have all the powers conferred upon "officers" pursuant to that title. They shall have the authority to investigate any offenses or violations occurring on the waters of this State, as defined in section 1 of P.L.1986, c. 150 (C.53:1–11. 10), and to stop and board a vessel in the waters of the State to determine whether the vessel complies with State and federal boating safety laws and shall have the power to order a vessel that does not comply with these laws to return immediately to shore. They shall have the authority, in accordance with applicable State and federal laws, rules and regulations, to take appropriate action as authorized by the United States Coast Guard to assist the United States Coast Guard in the enforcement of any safety and security zone established by the United States Coast Guard Captain of the Port for the Port of New York and New Jersey or the Port of Philadelphia. They shall have the authority to perform all of the duties of members of the State Capitol Police Force as defined in section 2 of P.L.1977, c. 135 (C.52:17B–9.2).

Amended by L.1940, c. 198, p. 848, § 1; L.1997, c. 19, § 3; L.2004, c. 82, § 2, eff. July 2, 2004.

CHAPTER 3

HOUSING, EQUIPMENT, AND EXPENSES

ARTICLE 2. EQUIPMENT, AND DAMAGES TO PROPERTY

Section
53:3–6. Penalty for wearing or imitating uniform.

ARTICLE 2. EQUIPMENT, AND DAMAGES TO PROPERTY

53:3–6. Penalty for wearing or imitating uniform

No person other than a member of the department of state police [1] shall, directly or indirectly, wear, use, or order to be worn or used, copy or imitate in any respect or manner the standard uniforms specified in section 53:3–5 of this title. Any person who shall violate any provision of this section shall be guilty of a misdemeanor, and punished by a fine not exceeding two hundred and fifty dollars, or by imprisonment in the county jail for a term not exceeding one year, or both, at the discretion of the court.

The term "person" as used herein shall include individuals, associations, corporations, or agents, officers or officials elected or appointed by any municipality or county.

[1] Now division of state police in department of law and public safety, see §§ 52:17B–6, 52:17B–51.

TITLE 56

TRADE NAMES, TRADE–MARKS AND UNFAIR TRADE PRACTICES

Chapter
9. Antitrust Act.

CHAPTER 9

ANTITRUST ACT

Section
56:9–1.   Short title.
56:9–2.   Definitions.
56:9–3.   Contracts and combinations in restraint of trade.
56:9–4.   Monopolies; unlawful acquisitions.
56:9–5.   Exempt organizations and activities.
56:9–6.   Duties of attorney general.
56:9–7.   Violations; dissolution and other relief.
56:9–8.   Foreign corporations; violations; relief.
56:9–9.   Investigations; subpoenas.
56:9–10.   Injunctions and other relief; jurisdiction.
56:9–11.   Violations; punishment.
56:9–12.   Treble damages suit.
56:9–13.   Final judgment in civil or criminal proceeding as prima facie evidence.
56:9–14.   Limitation period.
56:9–15.   Suspension of limitations period.
56:9–16.   Cumulative remedies.
56:9–17.   Cooperation with Federal Government and with other states.
56:9–18.   Uniform construction.
56:9–19.   Appropriation.

56:9–1.   Short title

This act may be known and shall be cited as the "New Jersey Antitrust Act."

L.1970, c. 73, § 1, eff. May 21, 1970.

56:9–2.   Definitions

a.   As used in this act, unless the context otherwise requires "person" shall mean any natural person or persons, or any corporation, partnership, company, trust or association of persons.

b.   "Trade or commerce" shall include all economic activity involving or relating to any commodity or service.

c.   "Commodity" shall mean any kind of real or personal property.

d.   "Service" shall mean any activity which is performed in whole or in part for the purpose of financial gain, including but not limited to sale, rental, leasing or licensing for use.

L.1970, c. 73, § 2, eff. May 21, 1970.

56:9–3.   Contracts and combinations in restraint of trade

Every contract, combination in the form of trust or otherwise, or conspiracy in restraint of trade or commerce, in this State, shall be unlawful.

L.1970, c. 73, § 3, eff. May 21, 1970.

56:9–4.   Monopolies; unlawful acquisitions

a.   It shall be unlawful for any person to monopolize, or attempt to monopolize, or to combine or conspire with any person or persons, to monopolize trade or commerce in any relevant market within this State.

b.   No corporation engaged in commerce shall acquire, directly or indirectly, the whole or any part of the stock or other share capital of another corporation engaged also in commerce, where the effect of such acquisition may be to substantially lessen competition within this State between the corporation whose stock is so acquired and the corporation making the acquisition, or to restrain such commerce in any section or community of this State, or tend to create a monopoly of any line of commerce within this State.

c.   No corporation shall acquire, directly or indirectly, the whole or any part of the stock or other share capital of two or more corporations engaged in commerce where the effect of such acquisition, or the use of such stock by the voting or granting of proxies or otherwise, may be to substantially lessen competition within this State between such corporations, or any of them, or to restrain such commerce in any section or community of this State, or tend to create a monopoly of any line of commerce within this State.

d.   This section shall not apply to corporations purchasing such stock solely for investment and not using the same by voting or otherwise to bring about, or in attempting to bring about, the substantial lessening of competition.   Nor shall anything contained in this section prevent a corporation engaged in commerce from causing the formation of subsidiary corporations for the actual carrying on of their immediate lawful business, or the natural and legitimate branches or extensions thereof, or from owning and holding all or a part of the stock of such subsidiary corporations, when the effect of such formation is not to substantially lessen competition.

e.   Nothing contained in this section shall be held to affect or impair any right heretofore legally acquired.

L.1970, c. 73, § 4, eff. May 21, 1970.

56:9–5. Exempt organizations and activities

a. This act shall not forbid the existence of trade and professional organizations created for the purpose of mutual help, and not having capital stock, nor forbid or restrain members of such organizations from lawfully carrying out the legitimate objects thereof not otherwise in violation of this act; nor shall those organizations or members per se be illegal combinations or conspiracies in restraint of trade under the provisions of this act.

b. No provisions of this act shall be construed to make illegal:

(1) The activities of any labor organization or of individual members thereof which are directed solely to labor objectives which are legitimate under the laws of either the State of New Jersey or the United States;

(2) The activities of any agricultural or horticultural cooperative organization, whether incorporated or unincorporated, or of individual members thereof, which are directed solely to objectives of such cooperative organizations which are legitimate under the laws of either the State of New Jersey or the United States;

(3) The activities of any public utility, as defined in R.S.48:2–13 to the extent that such activities are subject to the jurisdiction of the Board of Public Utilities, the Department of Transportation, the Federal Energy Regulatory Commission, the Federal Communications Commission, the Federal Department of Transportation or the Interstate Commerce Commission, except that this exemption, and that of subsection c. of this section, shall apply to the activities of any electric public utility or gas public utility or any related competitive business segment of an electric public utility or related competitive business segment of a gas public utility, or any public utility holding company or related competitive business segment of a public utility holding company as those terms are defined in section 3 of P.L.1999, c. 23 (C.48:3–51) (now before the Legislature as this bill), only to the extent such activities are expressly required by and supervised pursuant to State regulation or are required by federal or State law;

(4) The activities, including, but not limited to, the making of or participating in joint underwriting or joint reinsurance arrangements, of any insurer, insurance agent, insurance broker, independent insurance adjuster or rating organization to the extent that such activities are subject to regulation by the Commissioner of Banking and Insurance of this State under, or are permitted, or are authorized by, the "Department of Banking and Insurance Act of 1948," P.L.1948, c. 88 (C.17:1–1.1 et al.) and the "Department of Insurance Act of 1970," P.L.1970, c. 12 (C.17:1C–1 et seq.), provided, however, the provisions of this paragraph (4) shall not apply to private passenger automobile insurance business, except as provided in section 69 of P.L.1990, c. 8 (C.17:33B–31);

(5) The bona fide religious and charitable activities of any not for profit corporation, trust or organization established exclusively for religious or charitable purposes, or for both purposes;

(6) The activities engaged in by securities dealers, issuers or agents who are (I) a. licensed by the State of New Jersey under the "Uniform Securities Law (1967)," P.L.1967, c. 93 (C.49:3–47 et seq.); or (ii) members of the National Association of Securities Dealers, or (iii) members of any National Securities Exchange registered with the Securities and Exchange Commission under the "Securities Exchange Act of 1934," as amended,[1] in the course of their business of offering, selling, buying and selling, or otherwise trading in or underwriting securities, as agent, broker, or principal, and activities of any National Securities Exchange so registered, including the establishment of commission rates and schedules of charges;

(7) The activities of any State or national banking institution to the extent that such activities are regulated or supervised by officers of the State government under the "Department of Banking and Insurance Act of 1948," P.L.1948, c. 88 (C.17:1–1.1 et al.) or P.L.1970, c. 11 (C.17:1B–1 et seq.), or the federal government under the banking laws of the United States;

(8) The activities of any state or federal savings and loan association to the extent that such activities are regulated or supervised by officers of the State government under the "Department of Banking and Insurance Act of 1948," P.L.1948, c. 88 (C.17:1–1.1 et al.) or P.L.1970, c. 11 (C.17:1B–1 et seq.), or the federal government under the banking laws of the United States;

(9) The activities of any bona fide not for profit professional association, society or board, licensed and regulated by the courts or any other agency of this State, in recommending schedules of suggested fees, rates or commissions for use solely as guidelines in determining charges for professional and technical services; or

(10) The activities permitted under the provisions of chapter 4 of Title 56 of the Revised Statutes, "An act to regulate the retail sale of motor fuels," P.L.1938, c. 163 (C.56:6–1 et seq.), the "Unfair Motor Fuels Practices Act," P.L.1953, c. 413 (C.56:6–19 et seq.) and the "Unfair Cigarette Sales Act of 1952," P.L.1952, c. 247 (C.56:7–18 et seq.).

c. This act shall not apply to any activity directed, authorized or permitted by any law of this State that is in conflict or inconsistent with the provisions of this act, and the enactment of this act shall not be deemed to repeal, either expressly or by implication, any such other law in effect on the date of its enactment.

L.1970, c. 73, § 5, eff. May 21, 1970. Amended by L.1990, c. 8, § 70, eff. March 12, 1990; L.1994, c. 188, § 2, eff. Dec. 23, 1994; L.1999, c. 23, § 61, eff. Feb. 9, 1999.

[1] 15 U.S.C.A. § 78a et seq.

56:9–6. Duties of attorney general

The Attorney General shall investigate suspected violations of, and institute such proceedings as are hereinafter provided for violation of the provisions of this act. The Attorney General may direct the county prosecutor of any county in which such proceedings may be brought to aid and assist him in the conduct of such investigations and proceedings.

L.1970, c. 73, § 6, eff. May 21, 1970.

56:9–7. Violations; dissolution and other relief

Upon a violation of this act by any corporation or association organized under the laws of this State, or upon failure to comply with the terms of a final judgment or decree rendered by a court of this State for a violation of the provisions of this act, or to comply with a consent judgment or decree rendered by a court of this State concerning an alleged violation of this act, the Attorney General may institute proper proceedings in a court of competent jurisdiction for the forfeiture of charter rights, franchises, privileges and powers, and for the dissolution of the corporation or association, or for the suspension of the privilege to conduct business within the State. The court, in its discretion, and with due consideration of all relevant factors, including relevant public interests and competitive and economic factors, may order the dissolution, suspend the privilege to conduct business for a specific period, deny such relief, or provide other appropriate relief. A dissolution shall be conducted in accordance with the procedures specified by law for either voluntary or involuntary dissolution of the particular type of corporation or association.

L.1970, c. 73, § 7, eff. May 21, 1970.

56:9–8. Foreign corporations; violations; relief

Upon a violation of this act by a foreign corporation or association exercising the privilege of conducting business within this State, or upon a failure to comply with the terms of a final judgment or decree rendered by a court of this State issued for a violation of the provisions of this act, or to comply with a consent judgment or decree rendered by a court of this State concerning an alleged violation of this act, the Attorney General may institute appropriate proceedings for the revocation or suspension of franchises, privileges, and powers connected with doing business within the State. The court, in its discretion, and with due consideration of all relevant factors, including relevant public interests and competitive and economic factors, may order the revocation, suspend the privilege to conduct business for a specified period, deny relief, or provide other appropriate relief. A revocation shall have the same effect as a failure to qualify to do business in this State.

L.1970, c. 73, § 8, eff. May 21, 1970.

56:9–9. Investigations; subpoenas

a. (1) Whenever the Attorney General, by his own inquiry or as the result of a complaint, suspects that a violation of this act or of the federal antitrust laws is occurring, has occurred or is about to occur, or, whenever the Attorney General believes it to be in the public interest that an investigation be made, the Attorney General or his designee may, prior to the institution of a criminal or civil action thereon, issue in writing and cause to be served upon any person who may have information relevant to such investigation a subpena to appear and be examined under oath before the Attorney General, his designee or a court of record; answer written interrogatories under oath; or produce documents or any other information or materials for inspection or copying.

(2) Any subpena issued pursuant to this subsection shall:

(a) Contain a general statement concerning the subject matter of the investigation;

(b) Contain a statement advising the person subpenaed that he has the right, at any time before the return date of the subpena, to seek a court order determining the validity of the subpena;

(c) Contain a statement advising the person subpenaed that he may have an attorney present when he appears and testifies or otherwise responds to the subpena;

(d) Describe the classes of documentary material to be produced thereunder with sufficient particularity to permit such materials to be reasonably identified;

(e) Prescribe a date and time at which the person subpenaed shall appear to testify, under oath, or by which the person shall answer written interrogatories or produce the documents or other information or materials for inspection or copying; provided that such date shall not be less than 15 days from the date of service of the subpena; and

(f) Specify a place for the taking of testimony or for the submission of answers or for the production of documents or other information or materials and identify the persons who are authorized to receive the return of the subpena.

(3) The powers of subpena and examination contained in this subsection shall not abate or terminate by reason of any action or proceeding brought by the Attorney General under this act.

b. (1) If a person in attendance upon such investigation pursuant to subpena, or if a person required to provide the Attorney General answers in writing under oath or otherwise, personally refuses to answer a question or produce evidence of any other kind or make the required answers on the ground that he may be incriminated thereby, and if the Attorney General or his designee, in a writing directed to the person, orders that person to answer the question or produce the evidence, that person shall comply with the order. After complying therewith, and if but for this section he would have been privileged to withhold the answer given or the evidence produced, such answer, testimony or evidence or any evidence directly or indirectly derived therefrom may not be used against the person in any prosecution for a crime or offense concerning which he gave answer or produced evidence; provided that the answer, testimony or evidence is responsive to the question propounded. However, he may nevertheless be prosecuted or subject to penalty or forfeiture for any perjury, false swearing or contempt committed in answering, or failing to answer, or in producing evidence or failing to produce evidence in accordance with the order.

(2) Any person who fails to obey the command of a subpena, after being ordered to do so by a court of competent jurisdiction, is guilty of a crime of the fourth degree. In the alternative, if a person fails to obey a subpena after being ordered to do so by a court of competent jurisdiction, the Attorney General may apply to that court to have that person adjudged in contempt and to commit him to jail until such time as he purges himself of contempt by responsively answering, testifying or producing evidence as ordered.

(3) A person shall not be excused from complying with the terms of a subpena on the ground of failure to tender or pay a witness fee for mileage, unless demand therefor is made at the time compliance is about to be made. Payment of a witness fee or mileage shall not apply to any officer, director or person in the employ of any person whose conduct or practices are being investigated.

c. (1) Except as otherwise provided in this subsection, no material produced pursuant to this section or information derived therefrom shall be available for examination, without the consent of the person who produced the material, by any person other than the Attorney General or his designee in connection with the enforcement of this act. However, nothing contained herein shall prevent the legitimate use of such information or materials by the Attorney General or his designee, without the consent of the person who produced the materials, for investigational purposes.

(2) The Attorney General or his designee may disclose, without the consent of the person who produced the material, the material produced pursuant to this section or information derived therefrom to officers and employees of appropriate federal or State law enforcement agencies upon the prior certification of an officer of the federal or State law enforcement agency that the information will be maintained in confidence and will be used only for official law enforcement purposes; provided, however, the Attorney General or his designee shall advise such person of his intent to disclose such material or information derived therefrom 10 days prior to the disclosure.

(3) The Attorney General or his designee may disclose, without the consent of the person who produced

the material, material produced pursuant to this section or information derived therefrom to any court or grand jury.

d. Service of a subpena pursuant to this section shall be by any of those methods specified in the New Jersey Rules of Court for service of a summons and complaint in a civil action.

L.1970, c. 73, § 9, eff. May 21, 1970. Amended by L.1983, c. 25, § 1, eff. Jan. 25, 1983.

56:9–10. Injunctions and other relief; jurisdiction

a. The Superior Court shall have jurisdiction to prevent and restrain violations of this act. The Attorney General may institute proceedings to prevent and restrain violations. In addition to granting prohibitory injunctions and other restraints for a period and upon terms and conditions necessary to deter the defendant from, and insure against, the committing of a future violation of this act, the court may grant mandatory injunctions reasonably necessary to restore and preserve competition in the trade or commerce affected by the violation. The court may issue temporary restraining orders or prohibitions and the court may proceed in a summary manner.

b. Any person may institute proceedings for injunctive relief, temporary or permanent in the Superior Court against threatened loss or damage to his property or business by a violation of this act, when and under the same conditions and principles as injunctive relief against threatened conduct that will cause loss or damage is granted by courts of equity, under the rules governing such proceedings, and upon the execution of proper bond against damages for an injunction improvidently granted and a showing that the danger of irreparable loss or damage is immediate, a preliminary injunction may issue. If the court issues a permanent injunction, the plaintiff shall be awarded reasonable attorneys' fees, filing fees and reasonable costs of suit. Reasonable costs of suit may include, but shall not be limited to the expenses of discovery and document reproduction.

c. In addition to injunctive relief authorized pursuant to subsection a of this section, any person who violates the provisions of this act shall be liable to a penalty of not more than the greater of $100,000.00 or $500.00 per day for each and every day of said violation. *L.1970, c. 73, § 10, eff. May 21, 1970.*

56:9–11. Violations; punishment

a. Any person who shall knowingly violate any of the provisions of P.L.1970, c. 73 (C.56:9–1 et seq.) or knowingly aid or advise in such violation is guilty of a crime.

b. Any person convicted pursuant to the provisions of subsection a. of this section of a violation involving or affecting trade or commerce of a value less than $1,000,000.00 shall be guilty of a crime of the third degree. Any person convicted pursuant to the provisions of subsection a. of this section of a violation involving or affecting trade or commerce of a value equal to or greater than $1,000,000.00 shall be guilty of a crime of the second degree. Any person convicted pursuant to the provisions of subsection a. of this section of a violation involving bid rigging on public contracts, regardless of the value of trade or commerce involved or affected, shall be guilty of a crime of the second degree.

c. Notwithstanding the provisions of subsections a. and b. of N.J.S.2C:43–3, a person convicted of a crime of the second degree under this section shall be subject to a fine of not less than $50,000.00 nor more than $300,000.00, or, in the case of a corporation, partnership, or other business entity, be subject to a fine of not less than $250,000.00 nor more than $1,000,000.00, or imprisonment, or both, and a person convicted of a crime of the third degree under this section shall be subject to a fine of not less than $25,000.00 nor more than $150,000.00, or, in the case of a corporation, partnership, or other business entity, be subject to a fine of not less than $100,000.00 nor more than $300,000.00, or imprisonment, or both.

L.1970, c. 73, § 11, eff. May 21, 1970. Amended by L.1999, c. 440, § 104.

56:9–12. Treble damages suit

a. Any person who shall be injured in his business or property by reason of a violation of the provisions of this act may sue therefor and shall recover threefold the damages sustained by him, together with reasonable attorneys' fees, filing fees and reasonable costs of suit. Reasonable costs of suit may include, but shall not be limited to the expenses of discovery and document reproduction.

b. The State and any of its political subdivisions and public agencies shall be deemed a person within the meaning of this section. The Attorney General, on behalf of the State or any of its political subdivisions or public agencies, or the political subdivision or public agency at the direction of or with the permission of the Attorney General, may institute an action to recover the damages provided for by this section or by any comparable provisions of Federal law.

L.1970, c. 73, § 12, eff. May 21, 1970.

56:9–13. Final judgment in civil or criminal proceeding as prima facie evidence

A final judgment heretofore or hereafter rendered in any civil or criminal proceeding brought by the State for violation of this act to the effect that a defendant has violated said act shall be prima facie evidence against such defendant in any proceeding brought by any other party against such defendant pursuant to section 12 of this act,[1] as to all matters with respect to which said judgment or decree would be an estoppel as between the parties thereto; provided, that this section shall not apply to consent judgments or decrees entered before any testimony has been taken, or to judgments or

decrees entered in actions brought under section 12 of this act.

L.1970, c. 73, § 13, eff. May 21, 1970. Amended by L.1972, c. 37, § 1, eff. May 25, 1972.

     [1] N.J.S.A. § 56:9–12.

56:9–14. Limitation period

Any action brought to enforce the provisions of this act shall be barred unless commenced within 4 years after the cause of action arose, or if the cause of action is based upon a conspiracy in violation of this act, within 4 years after the plaintiff discovered, or by the exercise of reasonable diligence should have discovered the facts relied upon for proof of the conspiracy. No cause of action barred on the effective date of this act shall be revived by this act. For the purpose of this section, a cause of action for a continuing violation is deemed to arise at any time during the period of such violation.

L.1970, c. 73, § 14, eff. May 21, 1970.

56:9–15. Suspension of limitations period

Whenever any civil or criminal proceeding shall be commenced by the State to prevent, restrain or punish a violation of this act, but not including an action brought by the State under section 12 of this act,[1] the running of the statute of limitations in respect of every private right of action arising under this act and based in whole or in part on any matter complained of in said proceeding shall be suspended during the pendency thereof and for 1 year thereafter; provided that whenever the running of the statute of limitations in respect of a cause of action arising under section 12 shall be suspended hereunder, any action to enforce such cause of action shall be forever barred unless commenced either within the period of suspension or within 4 years after the cause of action accrued, whichever is later.

L.1970, c. 73, § 15, eff. May 21, 1970.

     [1] N.J.S.A. § 56:9–12.

56:9–16. Cumulative remedies

The remedies provided in this act shall be cumulative.

L.1970, c. 73, § 16, eff. May 21, 1970.

56:9–17. Cooperation with Federal Government and with other states

The Attorney General may cooperate with officials of the Federal Government and the several states in the enforcement of this act.

L.1970, c. 73, § 17, eff. May 21, 1970.

56:9–18. Uniform construction

This act shall be construed in harmony with ruling judicial interpretations of comparable Federal antitrust statutes and to effectuate, insofar as practicable, a uniformity in the laws of those states which enact it.

L.1970, c. 73, § 18, eff. May 21, 1970.

56:9–19. Appropriation

There is hereby appropriated out of the General State Fund to the Department of Law and Public Safety for the purpose of this act the sum of $100,000.00 for the period ending June 30, 1971, which sum shall be returned to the General State Fund from the sums derived from litigation instituted by the Attorney General under this act or the antitrust laws of the United States, as determined by the Director of the Division of Budget and Accounting. In addition to the sum hereinabove appropriated, there are hereby appropriated as a revolving fund the sums derived as aforesaid for the purpose of paying any additional expenses incurred by the Attorney General in the administration of this act or litigation instituted under the antitrust laws of the United States, provided, however, that the expenditure of such additional sums shall first be approved by the Director of the Division of Budget and Accounting and the Legislative Budget and Finance Director in the same manner as transfers of appropriations are approved.

L.1970, c. 73, § 19, eff. May 21, 1970.

TITLE 58

WATERS AND WATER SUPPLY

Chapter
10.   Pollution of Waters.
10A. Water Pollution Control.

CHAPTER 10

POLLUTION OF WATERS

ARTICLE 6A. DISCHARGE OF PETROLEUM PRODUCTS, DEBRIS AND HAZARDOUS SUBSTANCES INTO WATERS

Section
58:10–23.11u.   Giving or causing to be given false information or other violations; penalty; enforcement; forfeiture of conveyances.

ARTICLE 6A. DISCHARGE OF PETROLEUM PRODUCTS, DEBRIS AND HAZARDOUS SUBSTANCES INTO WATERS

58:10–23.11u.   Giving or causing to be given false information or other violations; penalty; enforcement; forfeiture of conveyances

a.   (1) Whenever, on the basis of available information, the department determines that a person is in violation of a provision of P.L.1976, c. 141 (C. 58:10–23.11 et seq.), including any rule, regulation, plan, information request, access request, order or directive promulgated or issued pursuant thereto, or that a person knowingly has given false testimony, documents or information to the department, the department may:

(a) bring a civil action in accordance with subsection b. of this section;

(b) levy a civil administrative penalty in accordance with subsection c. of this section; or

(c) bring an action for a civil penalty in accordance with subsection d. of this section.

Use of any remedy specified in this section shall not preclude use of any other remedy. The department may simultaneously pursue administrative and judicial remedies provided in this section.

b.   The department may commence a civil action in Superior Court for, singly or in combination:

(1) a temporary or permanent injunction;

(2) the costs of any investigation, cleanup or removal, and for the reasonable costs of preparing and successfully litigating an action under this subsection;

(3) the cost of restoring, repairing, or replacing real or personal property damaged or destroyed by a discharge, any income lost from the time the property is damaged to the time it is restored, repaired or replaced, and any reduction in value of the property caused by the discharge by comparison with its value prior thereto;

(4) the cost of restoration and replacement, where practicable, of any natural resource damaged or destroyed by a discharge; and

(5) any other costs incurred by the department pursuant to P.L.1976, c. 141.

Compensatory damages for damages awarded to a person other than the State shall be paid to the person injured by the discharge.

c.   (1) The department may assess a civil administrative penalty of not more than $50,000 for each violation, and each day of violation shall constitute an additional, separate and distinct violation. A civil administrative penalty shall not be levied until a violator has been notified by certified mail or personal service of:

(a) the statutory or regulatory basis of the violation;

(b) the specific citation of the act or omission constituting the violation;

(c) the amount of the civil administrative penalty to be imposed;

(d) the right of the violator to a hearing on any matter contained in the notice and the procedures for requesting a hearing.

(2)(a) A violator shall have 20 calendar days following receipt of notice within which to request a hearing on any matter contained in the notice, and shall comply with all procedures for requesting a hearing. Failure to submit a timely request or to comply with all departmental procedures shall constitute grounds for denial of a hearing request. After a hearing and upon a finding that a violation has occurred, the department shall issue a final order assessing the amount of the civil administrative penalty specified in the notice. If a violator does not request a hearing or fails to satisfy the statutory and administrative requirements for requesting a hearing, the notice of assessment of a civil administrative penalty shall become a final order on the 21st calendar day following receipt of the notice by the violator. If the department denies a hearing request, the notice of denial shall become a final order upon receipt of the notice by the violator.

(b) A civil administrative penalty may be settled by the department on such terms and conditions as the department may determine.

(c) Payment of a civil administrative penalty shall not be deemed to affect the availability of any other enforcement remedy in connection with the violation for which the penalty was levied.

(3) If a civil administrative penalty imposed pursuant to this section is not paid within 30 days of the date that the penalty is due and owing, and the penalty is not contested by the person against whom the penalty has been assessed, or the person fails to make a payment pursuant to a payment schedule entered into with the department, an interest charge shall accrue on the amount of the penalty from the 30th day that amount was due and owing. In the case of an appeal of a civil administrative penalty, if the amount of the penalty is upheld, in whole or in part, the rate of interest shall be calculated on that amount as of the 30th day from the date the amount was due and owing under the administrative order. The rate of interest shall be that established by the New Jersey Supreme Court for interest rates on judgments, as set forth in the Rules Governing the Courts of the State of New Jersey.

(4) The department may assess and recover, by civil administrative order, the costs of any investigation, cleanup or removal, and the reasonable costs of preparing and successfully enforcing a civil administrative penalty pursuant to this subsection. The assessment may be recovered at the same time as a civil administrative penalty, and shall be in addition to the penalty assessment.

d. Any person who violates a provision of P.L.1976, c. 141 (C. 58:10–23.11 et seq.), or a court order issued pursuant thereto, or who fails to pay a civil administrative penalty in full or to agree to a schedule of payments therefor, shall be subject to a civil penalty not to exceed $50,000.00 per day for each violation, and each day's continuance of the violation shall constitute a separate violation. Any penalty incurred under this subsection may be recovered with costs in a summary proceeding pursuant to "the penalty enforcement law" (N.J.S. 2A:58–1 et seq.) in the Superior Court or a municipal court.

e. All conveyances used or intended for use in the willful discharge of any hazardous substance are subject to forfeiture to the State pursuant to the provisions of P.L.1981, c. 387 (C. 13:1K–1 et seq.).

L.1976, c. 141, § 22, eff. April 1, 1977. Amended by L.1979, c. 346, § 7, eff. Jan. 23, 1980; L.1984, c. 240, § 2, eff. Dec. 28, 1984; L.1986, c. 170, § 2, eff. Dec. 4, 1986; L.1990, c. 75, § 1, eff. July 1, 1990.

CHAPTER 10A

WATER POLLUTION CONTROL

Section
58:10A–3. Definitions.
58:10A–10. Violations; remedies, fines and penalties; enforcement; forfeiture of conveyances.

Section
58:10A–49. Intentionally dumping material into or which comes into ocean waters within jurisdiction of state; penalty; reward for information leading to imposition or collection of criminal penalty.

58:10A–3. Definitions

As used in this act, unless the context clearly requires a different meaning, the following words and terms shall have the following meanings:

a. "Administrator" means the Administrator of the United States Environmental Protection Agency or his authorized representative;

b. "Areawide plan" means any plan prepared pursuant to section 208 of the Federal Act; [1]

c. "Commissioner" means the Commissioner of Environmental Protection or his authorized representative;

d. "Department" means the Department of Environmental Protection;

e. "Discharge" means an intentional or unintentional action or omission resulting in the releasing, spilling, leaking, pumping, pouring, emitting, emptying, or dumping of a pollutant into the waters of the State, onto land or into wells from which it might flow or drain into said waters or into waters or onto lands outside the jurisdiction of the State, which pollutant enters the waters of the State. "Discharge" includes the release of any pollutant into a municipal treatment works;

f. "Effluent limitation" means any restriction on quantities, quality, rates and concentration of chemical, physical, thermal, biological, and other constituents of pollutants established by permit, or imposed as an interim enforcement limit pursuant to an administrative order, including an administrative consent order;

g. "Federal Act" means the "Federal Water Pollution Control Act Amendments of 1972" (Public Law 92–500; 33 U.S.C. § 1251 et seq.);

h. "Municipal treatment works" means the treatment works of any municipal, county, or State agency or any agency or subdivision created by one or more municipal, county or State governments and the treatment works of any public utility as defined in R.S.48:2–13;

i. "National Pollutant Discharge Elimination System" or "NPDES" means the national system for the issuance of permits under the Federal Act;

j. "New Jersey Pollutant Discharge Elimination System" or "NJPDES" means the New Jersey system for the issuance of permits under this act;

k. "Permit" means a NJPDES permit issued pursuant to section 6 of this act.[2] "Permit" includes a letter of agreement entered into between a delegated local agency and a user of its municipal treatment works, setting effluent limitations and other conditions on the user of the agency's municipal treatment works;

l. "Person" means any individual, corporation, company, partnership, firm, association, owner or operator of a treatment works, political subdivision of this State and any state or interstate agency. "Person" shall also mean any responsible corporate official for the purpose of enforcement action under section 10 of this act; [3]

m. "Point source" means any discernible, confined and discrete conveyance, including but not limited to, any pipe, ditch, channel, tunnel, conduit, well, discrete fissure, container, rolling stock, concentrated animal feeding operation, or vessel or other floating craft, from which pollutants are or may be discharged;

n. "Pollutant" means any dredged spoil, solid waste, incinerator residue, sewage, garbage, refuse, oil, grease, sewage sludge, munitions, chemical wastes, biological materials, radioactive substance, thermal waste, wrecked or discarded equipment, rock, sand, cellar dirt, and industrial, municipal or agricultural waste or other residue discharged into the waters of the State. "Pollutant" includes both hazardous and nonhazardous pollutants;

o. "Pretreatment standards" means any restriction on quantities, quality, rates, or concentrations of pollutants discharged into municipal or privately owned treatment works adopted pursuant to P.L.1972, c. 42 (C.58:11–49 et seq.);

p. "Schedule of compliance" means a schedule of remedial measures including an enforceable sequence of actions or operations leading to compliance with water quality standards, an effluent limitation or other limitation, prohibition or standard;

q. "Substantial modification of a permit" means any significant change in any effluent limitation, schedule of compliance, compliance monitoring requirement, or any other provision in any permit which permits, allows, or requires more or less stringent or more or less timely compliance by the permittee;

r. "Toxic pollutant" means any pollutant identified pursuant to the Federal Act, or any pollutant or combination of pollutants, including disease causing agents, which after discharge and upon exposure, ingestion, inhalation or assimilation into any organism, either directly or indirectly by ingestion through food chains, will, on the basis of information available to the commissioner, cause death, disease, behavioral abnormalities, cancer, genetic mutations, physiological malfunctions, including malfunctions in reproduction, or physical deformation, in such organisms or their offspring;

s. "Treatment works" means any device or systems, whether public or private, used in the storage, treatment, recycling, or reclamation of municipal or industrial waste of a liquid nature including intercepting sewers, outfall sewers, sewage collection systems, cooling towers and ponds, pumping, power and other equipment and their appurtenances; extensions, improvements, remodeling, additions, and alterations thereof; elements essential to provide a reliable recycled supply such as standby treatment units and clear well facilities; and any other works including sites for the treatment process or for ultimate disposal of residues resulting from such treatment. "Treatment works" includes any other method or system for preventing, abating, reducing, storing, treating, separating, or disposing of pollutants, including storm water runoff, or industrial waste in combined or separate storm water and sanitary sewer systems;

t. "Waters of the State" means the ocean and its estuaries, all springs, streams and bodies of surface or ground water, whether natural or artificial, within the boundaries of this State or subject to its jurisdiction;

u. "Hazardous pollutant" means:

(1) Any toxic pollutant;

(2) Any substance regulated as a pesticide under the Federal Insecticide, Fungicide, and Rodenticide Act, Pub.L.92–516 (7 U.S.C. § 136 et seq.);

(3) Any substance the use or manufacture of which is prohibited under the federal Toxic Substances Control Act, Pub.L.94–469 (15 U.S.C. § 2601 et seq.);

(4) Any substance identified as a known carcinogen by the International Agency for Research on Cancer;

(5) Any hazardous waste as designated pursuant to section 3 of P.L.1981, c. 279 (C.13:1E–51) or the "Resource Conservation and Recovery Act," Pub. L.94–580 (42 U.S.C. § 6901 et seq.); or

(6) Any hazardous substance as defined pursuant to section 3 of P.L.1976, c. 141 (C.58:10–23.11b);

v. "Serious violation" means an exceedance of an effluent limitation for a discharge point source set forth in a permit, administrative order, or administrative consent agreement, including interim enforcement limits, by 20 percent or more for a hazardous pollutant, or by 40 percent or more for a nonhazardous pollutant, calculated on the basis of the monthly average for a pollutant for which the effluent limitation is expressed as a monthly average, or, in the case of an effluent limitation expressed as a daily maximum and without a monthly average, on the basis of the monthly average of all maximum daily test results for that pollutant in any month; in the case of an effluent limitation for a pollutant that is not measured by mass or concentration, the department shall prescribe an equivalent exceedance factor therefor. The department may utilize, on a case-by-case basis, a more stringent factor of exceedance to determine a serious violation if the department states the specific reasons therefor, which may include the potential for harm to human health or the environment. "Serious violation" shall not include a violation of a permit limitation for color;

w. "Significant noncomplier" means any person who commits a serious violation for the same hazardous pollutant or the same nonhazardous pollutant, at the same discharge point source, in any two months of any six-month period, or who exceeds the monthly average or, in a case of a pollutant for which no monthly average has been established, the monthly average of the daily maximums for an effluent limitation for the same pollutant at the same discharge point source by any amount in any four months of any six-month period, or who fails to submit a completed discharge monitoring report in any two months of any six-month period. The department may utilize, on a case-by-case basis, a more stringent frequency or factor of exceedance to determine a significant noncomplier, if the department states the specific reasons therefor, which may include the potential for harm to human health or the environment. A local agency shall not be deemed a "significant noncomplier" due to an exceedance of an effluent limitation established in a permit for flow;

x. "Local agency" means a political subdivision of the State, or an agency or instrumentality thereof, that owns or operates a municipal treatment works;

y. "Delegated local agency" means a local agency with an industrial pretreatment program approved by the department;

z. "Upset" means an exceptional incident in which there is unintentional and temporary noncompliance with an effluent limitation because of an event beyond the reasonable control of the permittee, including fire, riot, sabotage, or a flood, storm event, natural cause, or other act of God, or other similar circumstance, which is the cause of the violation. "Upset" also includes noncompliance consequent to the performance of maintenance operations for which a prior exception has been granted by the department or a delegated local agency;

aa. "Bypass" means the anticipated or unanticipated intentional diversion of waste streams from any portion of a treatment works;

bb. "Major facility" means any facility or activity classified as such by the Administrator of the United States Environmental Protection Agency, or his representative, in conjunction with the department, and includes industrial facilities and municipal treatment works;

cc. "Significant indirect user" means a discharger of industrial or other pollutants into a municipal treatment works, as defined by the department, including, but not limited to, industrial dischargers, but excluding the collection system of a municipal treatment works;

dd. "Violation of this act" means a violation of any provisions of this act, and shall include a violation of any rule or regulation, water quality standard, effluent limitation or other condition of a permit, or order adopted, issued, or entered into pursuant to this act;

ee. "Aquaculture" means the propagation, rearing, and subsequent harvesting of aquatic organisms in controlled or selected environments, and the subsequent processing, packaging and marketing, and shall include, but need not be limited to, activities to intervene in the rearing process to increase production such as stocking, feeding, transplanting, and providing

for protection from predators. "Aquaculture" shall not include the construction of facilities and appurtenant structures that might otherwise be regulated pursuant to any State or federal law or regulation;

ff. "Aquatic organism" means and includes, but need not be limited to, finfish, mollusks, crustaceans, and aquatic plants which are the property of a person engaged in aquaculture.

L.1977, c. 74, § 3, eff. July 24, 1977. Amended by L.1990, c. 28, § 1; L.1997, c. 236, § 26, eff. Aug. 31, 1997.

[1] 33 U.S.C.A. § 1288.
[2] N.J.S.A. § 58:10A–6.
[3] N.J.S.A. § 58:10A–10.

58:10A–10. Violations; remedies, fines and penalties; enforcement; forfeiture of conveyances

a. Whenever the commissioner finds that any person is in violation of any provision of this act, he shall:

(1) Issue an order requiring any such person to comply in accordance with subsection b. of this section; or

(2) Bring a civil action in accordance with subsection c. of this section; or

(3) Levy a civil administrative penalty in accordance with subsection d. of this section; or

(4) Bring an action for a civil penalty in accordance with subsection e. of this section; or

(5) Petition the Attorney General to bring a criminal action in accordance with subsection f. of this section.

Use of any of the remedies specified under this section shall not preclude use of any other remedy specified.

In the case of one or more pollutants for which interim enforcement limits have been established pursuant to an administrative order, including an administrative consent order, by the department or a local agency, the permittee shall be liable for the enforcement limits stipulated therein.

b. Whenever the commissioner finds that any person is in violation of any provision of this act, he may issue an order (1) specifying the provision or provisions of this act, or the rule, regulation, water quality standard, effluent limitation, or permit of which he is in violation, (2) citing the action which caused such violation, (3) requiring compliance with such provision or provisions, and (4) giving notice to the person of his right to a hearing on the matters contained in the order.

c. The commissioner is authorized to commence a civil action in Superior Court for appropriate relief for any violation of this act or of a permit issued hereunder. Such relief may include, singly or in combination:

(1) A temporary or permanent injunction;

(2) Assessment of the violator for the reasonable costs of any investigation, inspection, or monitoring

survey which led to the establishment of the violation, and for the reasonable costs of preparing and litigating the case under this subsection;

(3) Assessment of the violator for any reasonable cost incurred by the State in removing, correcting or terminating the adverse effects upon water quality resulting from any unauthorized discharge of pollutants for which the action under this subsection may have been brought;

(4) Assessment against the violator of compensatory damages for any loss or destruction of wildlife, fish or aquatic life, or other natural resources, and for any other actual damages caused by an unauthorized discharge;

(5) Assessment against a violator of the actual amount of any economic benefits accruing to the violator from a violation. Economic benefits may include the amount of any savings realized from avoided capital or noncapital costs resulting from the violation; the return earned or that may be earned on the amount of avoided costs; any benefits accruing to the violator as a result of a competitive market advantage enjoyed by reason of the violation; or any other benefits resulting from the violation.

Assessments under paragraph (4) of this subsection shall be paid to the State Treasurer, except that compensatory damages shall be paid by specific order of the court to any persons who have been aggrieved by the unauthorized discharge. Assessments pursuant to actions brought by the commissioner under paragraphs (2), (3) and (5) of this subsection shall be paid to the "Clean Water Enforcement Fund," established pursuant to section 12 of P.L.1990, c. 28 (C.58:10A–14.4).

d. (1)(a) The commissioner is authorized to assess, in accordance with a uniform policy adopted therefor, a civil administrative penalty of not more than $50,000.00 for each violation and each day during which such violation continues shall constitute an additional, separate, and distinct offense. Any amount assessed under this subsection shall fall within a range established by regulation by the commissioner for violations of similar type, seriousness, and duration. The commissioner shall adopt, by regulation, a uniform assessment of civil penalties policy by January 1, 1992.

(b) In adopting rules for a uniform penalty policy for determining the amount of a penalty to be assessed, the commissioner shall take into account the type, seriousness, including extent, toxicity, and frequency of a violation based upon the harm to public health or the environment resulting from the violation, the economic benefits from the violation gained by the violator, the degree of cooperation or recalcitrance of the violator in remedying the violation, any measures taken by the violator to avoid a repetition of the violation, any unusual or extraordinary costs directly or indirectly imposed on the public by the violation other than costs recoverable pursuant to paragraph (3) or (4) of subsection c. of this section, and any other pertinent factors

that the commissioner determines measure the seriousness or frequency of the violation, or conduct of the violator.

(c) In addition to the assessment of a civil administrative penalty, the commissioner may, by administrative order and upon an appropriate finding, assess a violator for costs authorized pursuant to paragraphs (2) and (3) of subsection c. of this section.

(2) No assessment shall be levied pursuant to this subsection until after the discharger has been notified by certified mail or personal service. The notice shall include a reference to the section of the statute, regulation, order or permit condition violated; a concise statement of the facts alleged to constitute a violation; a statement of the amount of the civil penalties to be imposed; and a statement of the party's right to a hearing. The ordered party shall have 20 days from receipt of the notice within which to deliver to the commissioner a written request for a hearing. After the hearing and upon finding that a violation has occurred, the commissioner may issue a final order after assessing the amount of the fine specified in the notice. If no hearing is requested, then the notice shall become a final order after the expiration of the 20–day period. Payment of the assessment is due when a final order is issued or the notice becomes a final order.

(3) If a civil administrative penalty imposed pursuant to this subsection is not paid within 30 days of the date that the penalty is due and owing, and the penalty is not contested by the person against whom the penalty has been assessed, or the person fails to make a payment pursuant to a payment schedule entered into with the department, an interest charge shall accrue on the amount of the penalty due and owing from the 30th day after the date on which the penalty was due and owing. The rate of interest shall be that established by the New Jersey Supreme Court for interest rates on judgments, as set forth in the Rules Governing the Courts of the State of New Jersey.

(4) The authority to levy a civil administrative penalty is in addition to all other enforcement provisions in this act, and the payment of any assessment shall not be deemed to affect the availability of any other enforcement provisions in connection with the violation for which the assessment is levied. Any civil administrative penalty assessed under this section may be compromised by the commissioner upon the posting of a performance bond by the violator, or upon such terms and conditions as the commissioner may establish by regulation, except that the amount compromised shall not be more than 50% of the assessed penalty, and in no instance shall the amount of that compromised penalty be less than the statutory minimum amount, if applicable, prescribed in section 6 of P.L.1990, c. 28 (C.58:10A–10.1). In the case of a violator who is a local agency that enters into an administrative consent order, the terms of which require the local agency to take prescribed measures to comply with its permit, the commissioner shall have full discretion to compromise

the amount of penalties assessed or due for violations occurring during a period up to 24 months preceding the entering into the administrative consent order; except that the amount of the compromised penalty may not be less than the statutory minimum amount, if applicable, prescribed in section 6 of P.L.1990, c. 28 (C.58:10A–10.1). A civil administrative penalty assessed against a local agency for a violation of an administrative consent order may not be compromised by more than 50% of the assessed penalty. In no instance shall the amount of a compromised penalty assessed against a local agency be less than the statutory minimum amount, if applicable, prescribed in section 6 of P.L.1990, c. 28 (C.58:10A–10.1). The commissioner shall not compromise the amount of any component of a civil administrative penalty which represents the economic benefit gained by the violator from the violation.

(5) A person, other than a local agency, appealing a penalty assessed against that person in accordance with this subsection, whether contested as a contested case pursuant to P.L.1968, c. 410 (C.52:14B–1 et seq.) or by appeal to a court of competent jurisdiction, shall, as a condition of filing the appeal, post with the commissioner a refundable bond, or other security approved by the commissioner, in the amount of the civil administrative penalty assessed. If the department's assessed penalty is upheld in full or in part, the department shall be entitled to a daily interest charge on the amount of the judgment from the date of the posting of the security with the commissioner and until paid in full. The rate of interest shall be that established by the New Jersey Supreme Court for interest rates on judgments, as set forth in the Rules Governing the Courts of the State of New Jersey. In addition, if the amount of the penalty assessed by the department is upheld in full in an appeal of the assessment at an administrative hearing or at a court of competent jurisdiction, the person appealing the penalty shall reimburse the department for all reasonable costs incurred by the department in preparing and litigating the imposition of the assessment, except that no litigation costs shall be imposed where the appeal ultimately results in a reduction or elimination of the assessed penalty.

(6) A civil administrative penalty imposed pursuant to a final order:

(a) may be collected or enforced by summary proceedings in a court of competent jurisdiction in accordance with "the penalty enforcement law," N.J.S.2A:58–1 et seq.; or

(b) shall constitute a debt of the violator or discharger and the civil administrative penalty may be docketed with the clerk of the Superior Court, and shall have the same standing as any judgment docketed pursuant to N.J.S.2A:16–1; except that no lien shall attach to the real property of a violator pursuant to this subsection if the violator posts a refundable bond or other security with the commissioner pursuant to an appeal of a final

order to the Appellate Division of the Superior Court. No lien shall attach to the property of a local agency.

(7) The commissioner shall refer to the Attorney General and the county prosecutor of the county in which the violations occurred the record of violations of any permittee determined to be a significant noncomplier.

e. Any person who violates this act or an administrative order issued pursuant to subsection b. or a court order issued pursuant to subsection c., or who fails to pay a civil administrative penalty in full pursuant to subsection d., or to make a payment pursuant to a payment schedule entered into with the department, shall be subject upon order of a court to a civil penalty not to exceed $50,000.00 per day of such violation, and each day's continuance of the violation shall constitute a separate violation. Any penalty incurred under this subsection may be recovered with costs, and, if applicable, interest charges, in a summary proceeding pursuant to "the penalty enforcement law" (N.J.S.2A:58–1 et seq.). In addition to any civil penalties, costs or interest charges, the court, in accordance with paragraph (5) of subsection c. of this section, may assess against a violator the amount of any actual economic benefits accruing to the violator from the violation. The Superior Court shall have jurisdiction to enforce "the penalty enforcement law" in conjunction with this act.

f. (1)(a) Any person who purposely, knowingly, or recklessly violates this act, and the violation causes a significant adverse environmental effect, shall, upon conviction, be guilty of a crime of the second degree, and shall, notwithstanding the provisions of subsection a. of N.J.S.2C:43–3, be subject to a fine of not less than $25,000 nor more than $250,000 per day of violation, or by imprisonment, or by both.

(b) As used in this paragraph, a significant adverse environmental effect exists when an action or omission of the defendant causes: serious harm or damage to wildlife, freshwater or saltwater fish, any other aquatic or marine life, water fowl, or to their habitats, or to livestock, or agricultural crops; serious harm, or degradation of, any ground or surface waters used for drinking, agricultural, navigational, recreational, or industrial purposes; or any other serious articulable harm or damage to, or degradation of, the lands or waters of the State, including ocean waters subject to its jurisdiction pursuant to P.L.1988, c. 61 (C.58:10A–47 et seq.).

(2) Any person who purposely, knowingly, or recklessly violates this act, including making a false statement, representation, or certification in any application, record, or other document filed or required to be maintained under this act, or by falsifying, tampering with, or rendering inaccurate any monitoring device or method required to be maintained pursuant to this act, or by failing to submit a monitoring report, or any portion thereof, required pursuant to this act, shall, upon conviction, be guilty of a crime of the third degree, and shall, notwithstanding the provisions of subsection

b. of N.J.S.2C:43–3, be subject to a fine of not less than $5,000 nor more than $75,000 per day of violation, or by imprisonment, or by both.

(3) Any person who negligently violates this act, including making a false statement, representation, or certification in any application, record, or other document filed or required to be maintained under this act, or by falsifying, tampering with, or rendering inaccurate any monitoring device or method required to be maintained pursuant to this act, or by failing to submit a discharge monitoring report, or any portion thereof, required pursuant to this act, shall, upon conviction, be guilty of a crime of the fourth degree, and shall, notwithstanding the provisions of subsection b. of N.J.S.2C:43–3, be subject to a fine of not less than $5,000 nor more than $50,000 per day of violation, or by imprisonment, or by both.

(4) Any person who purposely or knowingly violates an effluent limitation or other condition of a permit, or who discharges without a permit, and who knows at that time that he thereby places another person in imminent danger of death or serious bodily injury, as defined in subsection b. of N.J.S.2C:11–1, shall, upon conviction, be guilty of a crime of the first degree, and shall, notwithstanding the provisions of subsection a. of N.J.S.2C:43–3, be subject to a fine of not less than $50,000 nor more than $250,000, or, in the case of a corporation, a fine of not less than $200,000 nor more than $1,000,000, or by imprisonment or by both.

(5) As used in this subsection, "purposely," "knowingly," "recklessly," and "negligently" shall have the same meaning as defined in N.J.S.2C:2–2.

g. All conveyances used or intended for use in the purposeful or knowing discharge, in violation of the provisions of P.L.1977, c. 74 (C.58:10A–1 et seq.), of any pollutant or toxic pollutant are subject to forfeiture to the State pursuant to the provisions of P.L.1981, c. 387 (C.13:1K–1 et seq.).

h. The amendatory portions of this section, as set forth in P.L.1990, c. 28 (C.58:10A–10.1 et al.), except for subsection f. of this section, shall not apply to violations occurring prior to July 1, 1991.

L.1977, c. 74, § 10, eff. July 24, 1977. Amended by L.1984, c. 240, § 3, eff. Dec. 28, 1984; L.1986, c. 170, § 3, eff. Dec. 4, 1986; L.1990, c. 28, § 5, eff. July 1, 1991.

58:10A–49. Intentionally dumping material into or which comes into ocean waters within jurisdiction of state; penalty; reward for information leading to imposition or collection of criminal penalty

a. A person who intentionally dumps any material into the ocean waters within the jurisdiction of this State, or into the waters outside the jurisdiction of this State, which material enters the ocean waters within the jurisdiction of this State, is guilty of a crime of the third degree.

b. Of the monetary penalty imposed pursuant to this section, 10% shall be paid to the Department of Environmental Protection from the General Fund if the Attorney General determines that a person or persons are entitled to a reward pursuant to subsection c. of this section.

c. Any person who provides information to an enforcing authority concerning a violation of this act that proximately results in the imposition and collection of a criminal penalty as the result of a criminal action brought pursuant to this act shall be entitled to a reward of 10% of the penalty collected. The reward shall be paid by the department from moneys received pursuant to subsection b. of this section. If more than one person is entitled to a reward, the Attorney General shall determine the percentage of the reward that each person shall receive. The Attorney General shall adopt, pursuant to the "Administrative Procedure Act," P.L. 1968, c. 410 (C. 52:14B–1 et seq.), rules and regulations necessary to implement this section, including procedures to assure the anonymity of the person or persons providing the information to the enforcing authority when appropriate.

L.1988, c. 61, § 3, eff. July 11, 1988.

RULES GOVERNING THE COURTS OF THE STATE OF NEW JERSEY

PART I.   RULES OF GENERAL APPLICATION

Research Note

For a comprehensive treatment of practice and procedure under these Rules, see Klock, New Jersey Court Rules Annotated (Practice Series Volumes 1 through 2A), *and Walzer,* New Jersey Civil Practice Forms (Practice Series Volumes 3–4C).

Use WESTLAW ®*to find cases citing a rule.* WESTLAW *may also be used to search for specific terms or to update a rule; see the scope screens in NJ–RULES and NJ–RULESUPDATES for further information.*

Amendments to these rules are published, as received, in Atlantic Reporter 2d *and* New Jersey Reports *advance sheets.*

CHAPTER I.   PROCEDURE.

Rule

1:1.   APPLICABILITY, SCOPE, CONSTRUCTION, RELAXATION AND CITATION OF RULES.
1:1–1.   Applicability; Scope.
1:1–2.   Construction and Relaxation; References to Marriage, Spouse and Related Terms.
1:1–3.   Citation of Rules.
1:2.   CONDUCT OF PROCEEDINGS GENERALLY.
1:2–1.   Proceedings in Open Court; Robes.
1:2–2.   Trial Courts; Verbatim Record of Proceedings.
1:2–3.   Exhibits.
1:2–4.   Sanctions: Failure to Appear; Motions and Briefs.
1:2–5.   Advancement.
1:2–6.   Case Management Conference; Orders.
1:3.   TIME.
1:3–1.   Computation of Time.
1:3–2.   Time Unaffected by Expiration of Term.
1:3–3.   Additional Time After Service by Ordinary Mail.
1:3–4.   Enlargement of Time.
1:4.   FORM AND EXECUTION OF PAPERS.
1:4–1.   Caption: Name and Addresses of Party and Attorney; Format.
1:4–2.   Paragraphs.
1:4–3.   Adoption by Reference; Exhibits.
1:4–4.   Affidavits.
1:4–5.   Signing and Dating of Pleadings; Motions.
1:4–6.   Typewritten Names.
1:4–7.   Verification of Pleadings.
1:4–8.   Frivolous Litigation.
1:4–9.   Size, Weight and Format of Filed Papers.
1:5.   SERVICE AND FILING OF PAPERS.
1:5–1.   Service: When Required.
1:5–2.   Manner of Service.
1:5–3.   Proof of Service.

Rule

1:5–4.   Service by Mail or Courier: When Complete.
1:5–5.   Service; Numerous Defendants.
1:5–6.   Filing.
1:5–7.   Non-military Affidavit.
1:6.   MOTIONS AND BRIEFS IN THE TRIAL COURTS.
1:6–1.   Applicability of Rule.
1:6–2.   Form of Motion; Hearing.
1:6–3.   Filing and Service of Motions and Cross–Motions.
1:6–4.   Superior Court; Place for Filing Motions, Orders to Show Cause and Orders.
1:6–5.   Briefs.
1:6–6.   Evidence on Motions; Affidavits.
1:6–7.   Reading of Moving Papers and Briefs in Advance.
1:6–8.   Issuance of Process and Entry of Judgment.
1:7.   GENERAL PROVISIONS FOR TRIALS.
1:7–1.   Opening and Closing Statement.
1:7–2.   Objections.
1:7–3.   Record of Excluded Evidence.
1:7–4.   Findings by the Court in Non-jury Trials and on Motions.
1:7–5.   Trial Errors.
1:7–6.   Non-public Business Records.
1:8.   JURY.
1:8–1.   Trial by Jury.
1:8–2.   Number of Jurors.
1:8–3.   Examination of Jurors; Challenges.
1:8–4.   Foreperson.
1:8–5.   Availability of Petit Jury List.
1:8–6.   Sequestration of Juries.
1:8–7.   Requests to Charge the Jury.
1:8–8.   Materials to be Submitted to the Jury; Note-taking; Juror Questions.
1:8–9.   Return of Verdict.
1:8–10.   Polling of Jury.
1:9.   SUBPOENAS.
1:9–1.   For Attendance of Witnesses; Forms; Issuance; Notice in Lieu of Subpoena.

Rule

1:9–2. For Production of Documentary Evidence and Electronically Stored Information; Notice in Lieu of Subpoena.

1:9–3. Service.

1:9–4. Place of Service.

1:9–5. Failure to Appear.

1:9–6. Enforcement of Subpoena of Public Officer or Agency.

1:10. CONTEMPT OF COURT; ENFORCEMENT OF LITIGANT'S RIGHTS.

1:10–1. Summary Contempt in Presence of Court.

1:10–2. Summary Contempt Proceedings on Order to Show Cause or Order for Arrest.

1:10–3. Relief to Litigant.

1:11. WITHDRAWAL, SUBSTITUTION, TERMINATION OF RESPONSIBILITY OF ATTORNEY.

1:11–1. Death, Removal or Disbarment of Attorney.

1:11–2. Withdrawal or Substitution.

1:11–3. Termination of Responsibility in the Trial Court; Responsibility on Appeal.

1:12. DISQUALIFICATION AND DISABILITY OF JUDGES.

1:12–1. Cause for Disqualification; on the Court's Motion.

1:12–2. Disqualification on Party's Motion.

1:12–3. Proceedings in the Trial Courts in the Event of Disqualification or Inability.

1:13. MISCELLANEOUS RULES AS TO PROCEDURE.

1:13–1. Clerical Mistakes.

1:13–2. Proceedings by Indigents.

1:13–3. Approval and Filing of Surety Bond; Judgment Against Principal and Surety.

1:13–4. Transfer of Actions.

1:13–5. Tables of Mortality and Life Expectancy.

1:13–6. Military Lists.

1:13–7. Dismissal of Civil Cases for Lack of Prosecution.

1:13–8. Priorities of Liens and Encumbrances Determined as of Commencement of Action.

1:13–9. Amicus Curiae; Motion; Grounds for Relief; Briefs.

1:13–10. Payment of Fees, Penalties, and Sanctions.

CHAPTER II. CONDUCT OF LAWYERS, JUDGES AND COURT PERSONNEL.

1:14. CODES OF ETHICS.

1:15. LIMITATION ON PRACTICE OF ATTORNEYS.

1:15–1. Limitation on Practice of Attorneys Serving as Judges and Surrogates.

1:15–2. Limitations on Practice of Attorneys Serving as Clerks and Employees of Courts and Judges.

1:15–3. Limitations on Practice of Other Attorneys.

1:15–4. Limitations Extended to Partners, etc.; Municipal Court Judges; Municipal Prosecutors.

1:15–5. Application of Rule.

1:16. MISCELLANEOUS LIMITATIONS ON ATTORNEYS AND PARTIES.

1:16–1. Interviewing Jurors Subsequent to Trial.

1:16–2. Prohibition as to Gratuities.

1:17. JUDGES AND COURT PERSONNEL: LIMITATION ON POLITICAL ACTIVITY, HOLDING OF OTHER PUBLIC OFFICE

OR POSITION AND OTHER GAINFUL PURSUIT.

1:17–1. Persons Prohibited.

1:17–2. Judges.

1:17–3. Non-judge Employees.

1:17–4. Non-applicability.

1:17–5. Ineligibility of Judicial Employees for Appointments.

1:17–6. Other Employment of Judicial Employees.

1:17A. ADVISORY COMMITTEE ON OUTSIDE ACTIVITIES OF JUDICIARY EMPLOYEES.

1:17A–1. Appointment and Organization.

1:17A–2. Jurisdiction.

1:17A–3. Scope of Review.

1:17A–4. Form of Inquiry.

1:17A–5. Disposition of Inquiries.

1:17A–6. Inquiries From Supreme Court.

1:17A–7. Procedure.

1:17A–8. Petitions for Review.

1:17A–9. Reports.

1:18. DUTY OF JUDGES.

1:18A. ADVISORY COMMITTEE ON EXTRAJUDICIAL ACTIVITIES.

1:18A–1. Appointment and Organization.

1:18A–2. Jurisdiction.

1:18A–3. Form of Inquiry.

1:18A–4. Disposition of Inquiries.

1:18A–5. Inquiries From Supreme Court.

1:18A–6. Procedure.

1:18A–7. Petitions for Review.

1:18B. JUDICIAL FINANCIAL REPORTING.

1:18B–1. Obligation to Report.

1:18B–2. Advisory Committee on Judicial Financial Reporting.

1:18B–3. Retention and Disclosure of Statements.

1:19. ADVISORY COMMITTEE ON PROFESSIONAL ETHICS.

1:19–1. Appointment and Organization.

1:19–2. Jurisdiction.

1:19–3. Form of Inquiry.

1:19–4. Disposition of Inquiries.

1:19–5. Inquiries From Supreme Court.

1:19–6. Effect of Published Opinions.

1:19–7. Procedure.

1:19–8. Petitions for Review.

1:19–9. Ethics Telephone Research Service.

1:19A. COMMITTEE ON ATTORNEY ADVERTISING.

1:19A–1. Appointment and Organization.

1:19A–2. Jurisdiction.

1:19A–3. Advisory Opinions.

1:19A–4. Ethics Grievances.

1:19A–5. Records; Confidentiality.

1:19A–6. Immunity.

1:19A–7. Referral to Office of Attorney Ethics.

1:19A–8. Telephone Inquiries.

1:20. DISCIPLINE OF MEMBERS OF THE BAR.

1:20–1. Disciplinary Jurisdiction; Annual Fee and Registration.

1:20–2. Office of Attorney Ethics.

1:20–3. District Ethics Committees; Investigations.

1:20–4. Formal Pleadings.

1:20–5. Prehearing Procedures.

1:20–6. Hearings.

1:20–7. Additional Rules of Procedure.

1:20–8. Time Goals; Accountability; Priority.

Rule

1:20–9.	Confidentiality; Access to and Dissemination of Disciplinary Information.
1:20–10.	Discipline by Consent.
1:20–11.	Temporary Suspension.
1:20–11A.	Suspension of License to Practice Law for Failure to Support Dependents.
1:20–11B.	Suspension of License to Practice Law for Failure to Repay Student Loans.
1:20–12.	Incapacity and Disability.
1:20–13.	Attorneys Charged with or Convicted of Crimes.
1:20–14.	Reciprocal Discipline and Disability Proceedings.
1:20–15.	Disciplinary Review Board.
1:20–15A.	Final Disciplinary Determinations; Sanctions.
1:20–16.	Action by the Supreme Court.
1:20–17.	Reimbursement of Disciplinary Costs.
1:20–18.	Supervision of Disciplined Attorney.
1:20–19.	Appointment of Attorney–Trustee to Protect Clients' Interest.
1:20–20.	Future Activities of Attorney Who Has Been Disciplined or Transferred to Disability Inactive Status.
1:20–21.	Reinstatement After Final Discipline.
1:20–22.	Resignation Without Prejudice.
1:20–23.	Release of Restrained Funds in Attorney Accounts.
1:20A.	DISTRICT FEE ARBITRATION COMMITTEES.
1:20A–1.	Appointment and Organization.
1:20A–2.	Jurisdiction.
1:20A–3.	Arbitration.
1:20A–4.	Referral to Office of Attorney Ethics.
1:20A–5.	Records; Confidentiality; Immunity.
1:20A–6.	Pre–action Notice to Client.
1:20B.	DISCIPLINARY OVERSIGHT COMMITTEE.
1:20B–1.	Disciplinary Oversight Committee.
1:20B–2.	Appointment.
1:20B–3.	Organization; Officers; Quorum; Meetings.
1:20B–4.	Powers; Confidentiality.

CHAPTER III. PRACTICE OF LAW AND ADMISSION TO PRACTICE.

1:21.	PRACTICE OF LAW.
1:21–1.	Who May Practice; Appearance in Court.
1:21–1A.	Professional Corporations for the Practice of Law.
1:21–1B.	Limited Liability Companies for the Practice of Law.
1:21–1C.	Limited Liability Partnerships for the Practice of Law.
1:21–2.	Appearances Pro Hac Vice.
1:21–3.	Appearance by Law Graduates and Students; Special Permission for Out-of-State Attorneys.
1:21–4.	Attorneys for Consuls of Any Government not Recognized.
1:21–5.	Counsellors; Masters Abolished.
1:21–6.	Recordkeeping; Sharing of Fees; Examination of Records.
1:21–7.	Contingent Fees.
1:21–7A.	Retainer.
1:21–8.	[Deleted].
1:21–9.	Certification and Practice of Foreign Legal Consultants.
1:21–10.	Provision of Legal Services Following Determination of Major Disaster.

Rule

1:22.	COMMITTEE ON THE UNAUTHORIZED PRACTICE OF LAW.
1:22–1.	Appointment; Membership; Administration.
1:22–1A.	Organization; Quorum.
1:22–2.	Jurisdiction.
1:22–3.	Procedure: Advisory Opinions.
1:22–3A.	Petitions for Review.
1:22–4.	Complaints: Preliminary Investigation.
1:22–5.	Complaints: Informal Disposition.
1:22–6.	Complaints: Referrals.
1:22–7.	Immunity From Suit.
1:22–8.	Subpoena:.
1:22–9.	Prosecution.
1:22–10.	Legal.
1:23.	BOARD OF BAR EXAMINERS.
1:23–1.	Appointment; Organization.
1:23–2.	Duties; Procedure.
1:23–3.	Confidentiality; Immunity.
1:23–4.	Funds.
1:23–5.	Bar Examination Test–Taking Improprieties.
1:24.	BAR EXAMINATIONS; QUALIFICATIONS FOR ADMISSION TO EXAMINATION.
1:24–1.	Bar Examinations.
1:24–2.	Qualification for Admission to Examination.
1:25.	COMMITTEE ON CHARACTER.
1:26.	SKILLS AND METHODS COURSE [DELETED].
1:27.	ADMISSION TO PRACTICE.
1:27–1.	Plenary Admission.
1:27–2.	Limited License; In–House Counsel.
1:27–3.	Admission of Law School Teachers.
1:27–4.	Oath or Affirmation on Admission.
1:27A.	ADVISORY COMMITTEE ON BAR ADMISSIONS.
1:27A–1.	Establishment of Committee; Duties.
1:27A–2.	Committee Membership.
1:27B.	BAR ADMISSIONS FINANCIAL COMMITTEE.
1:27B–1.	Bar Admissions Financial Committee.
1:27B–2.	Appointment.
1:27B–3.	Organization; Officers; Quorum; Meetings.
1:27B–4.	Powers.
1:28.	NEW JERSEY LAWYERS' FUND FOR CLIENT PROTECTION.
1:28–1.	Purpose; Administration; Appointments.
1:28–2.	Payment to the Fund; Enforcement.
1:28–3.	Payment of Claims.
1:28–4.	Duties of Trustees and Officers.
1:28–5.	General Powers of Trustees.
1:28–6.	Subpoenas; Notice in Lieu of Subpoena; Non-compliance.
1:28–7.	Administration.
1:28–8.	Custodial Receivers.
1:28–9.	Confidentiality.
1:28A.	INTEREST ON LAWYERS TRUST ACCOUNTS (IOLTA) FUND.
1:28A–1.	Purpose; Administration; Appointments.
1:28A–2.	Attorney IOLTA Trust Accounts.
1:28A–3.	Duties of Trustees and Officers.
1:28A–4.	General Powers of Trustees.
1:28A–5.	Confidentiality.
1:28B.	NEW JERSEY LAWYERS ASSISTANCE PROGRAM.

Rule

1:28B–1.   Board of Trustees; Purpose; Administration; Annual Assessment.
1:28B–2.   Duties of Trustees and Treasurer.
1:28B–3.   Confidentiality.
1:28B–4.   Immunity.
1:29.   CERTIFICATES OF ADMISSION AND GOOD STANDING; CHANGE OF NAME; CONFIRMATORY CERTIFICATES.
1:29–1.   Certificates of Admission and Good Standing; Fees.
1:29–2.   Change of Name.
1:29–3.   Confirmatory Certificates; Fee.

CHAPTER IV.   ADMINISTRATION.

1:30.   COURT SCHEDULES.
1:30–1.   Courts Always Open.
1:30–2.   Terms of Court; Stated Sessions of Superior Court.
1:30–3.   Sittings of Courts.
1:30–4.   Clerks' Offices.
1:30–5.   Vacations.
1:31.   PLACES FOR TRANSACTION OF COURT BUSINESS.
1:31–1.   Location of Courtrooms; Judges' Chambers; Clerks' Offices.
1:31–2.   Inadequate Court Facilities.
1:32.   REPORTS BY COURTS AND PERSONNEL; RECORDS; FORMS AND PROCESS PRESCRIBED BY ADMINISTRATIVE DIRECTOR.
1:32–1.   Reports by Judges; Court Clerks; Court Reporters.
1:32–2.   Books and Records.
1:32–3.   Process; Forms.
1:33.   ADMINISTRATIVE RESPONSIBILITY.
1:33–1.   The Chief Justice of the Supreme Court; Acting Chief Justice.
1:33–2.   Court Managerial Structure.
1:33–3.   The Administrative Director of the Courts.
1:33–4.   Assignment Judges; Presiding Judge for Administration of the Appellate Division.
1:33–5.   Trial Court Administrators—Case Coordinators.
1:33–6.   Presiding Judges of Functional Units.
1:33–6A.   Supervising Judges of the Special Civil Part.
1:33–7.   Division Managers.
1:33–8.   Probation Services.
1:33–9.   Review of Administratively Recommended Facilities Disputes Dispositions.
1:34.   SUPPORTING PERSONNEL OF THE COURTS.
1:34–1.   Standing.
1:34–2.   Clerks of Court.
1:34–3.   Reserved.
1:34–4.   Probation Officers and Volunteers in Probation.
1:34–5.   Court Reporters.
1:34–6.   Office of Foreclosure.
1:34–7.   Interpreters, Transliterators, and Translators.
1:35.   JUDICIAL CONFERENCES.
1:35–1.   The Judicial Conference of New Jersey.

Rule

1:35–2.   Conference of Judges.
1:35A.   JUDICIAL PERFORMANCE PROGRAM.
1:35A–1.   Judicial Performance Committee.
1:35A–2.   Judicial Performance Program.
1:35A–3.   Records.
1:35A–4.   Judicial Evaluation Commission.
1:36.   OPINIONS; FILING; PUBLICATION.
1:36–1.   Filing of Opinions.
1:36–2.   Publication.
1:36–3.   Unpublished Opinions.
1:37.   COURT TITLES; SEALS; ABBREVIATIONS.
1:37–1.   Title of Courts.
1:37–2.   Seal of Courts.
1:37–3.   Abbreviations; Title on Temporary Assignment.
1:38.   PUBLIC ACCESS TO COURT RECORDS AND ADMINISTRATIVE RECORDS.
1:38–1.   Policy.
1:38–2.   Definition of Court Records.
1:38–3.   Court Records Excluded from Public Access.
1:38–4.   Definition of Administrative Records.
1:38–5.   Administrative Records Excluded from Public Access.
1:38–6.   Intergovernmental Exchanges.
1:38–7.   Confidential Personal Identifiers.
1:38–8.   Documents Improperly Submitted to Court.
1:38–9.   Fees.
1:38–10.   Determinations; Appeal Process.
1:38–11.   Sealing of Court Records.
1:38–12.   Unsealing of Court Records.
1:39.   CERTIFICATION OF ATTORNEYS.
1:39–1.   Board on Attorney Certification.
1:39–1A.   Certification Committees.
1:39–2.   Eligibility.
1:39–3.   Written Examination.
1:39–4.   Decision by Board.
1:39–5.   Grant; Duration; Withholding of Certification.
1:39–6.   Effect of Certification.
1:39–7.   Renewal of Certification.
1:39–8.   Termination of Certification.
1:39–9.   Review of Action of Board.
1:40.   COMPLEMENTARY DISPUTE RESOLUTION PROGRAMS.
1:40–1.   Purpose, Goals.
1:40–2.   Modes and Definitions of Complementary Dispute Resolution.
1:40–3.   Organization and Management.
1:40–4.   Mediation—General Rules.
1:40–5.   Mediation in Family Part Matters.
1:40–6.   Mediation of Civil, Probate, and General Equity Matters.
1:40–7.   Complementary Dispute Resolution Programs in the Special Civil Part.
1:40–8.   Mediation of Minor Disputes in Municipal Court Actions.
1:40–9.   Civil Arbitration.
1:40–10.   Relaxation of Court Rules and Program Guidelines.
1:40–11.   Non-Court Dispute Resolution.
1:40–12.   Mediators and Arbitrators in Court–Annexed Programs.

CHAPTER I. PROCEDURE
RULE 1:1. APPLICABILITY, SCOPE, CONSTRUCTION, RELAXATION AND CITATION OF RULES

1:1–1. Applicability; Scope

Unless otherwise stated, the rules in Part I are applicable to the Supreme Court, the Superior Court, the Tax Court, the surrogate's courts, and the municipal courts.

Note: Amended November 22, 1978 to be effective December 7, 1978; amended June 20, 1979 to be effective July 1, 1979; amended December 20, 1983 to be effective December 31, 1983.

1:1–2. Construction and Relaxation; References to Marriage, Spouse and Related Terms

(a) The rules in Part I through Part VIII, inclusive, shall be construed to secure a just determination, simplicity in procedure, fairness in administration and the elimination of unjustifiable expense and delay. Unless otherwise stated, any rule may be relaxed or dispensed with by the court in which the action is pending if adherence to it would result in an injustice. In the absence of rule, the court may proceed in any manner compatible with these purposes and, in civil cases, consistent with the case management/trial management guidelines set forth in Appendix XX of these rules.

(b) As used in Part I through Part VIII of these rules and appendices, references to "marriage," "husband," "wife," "spouse," "family," "immediate family," "dependent," "next of kin," "widow," "widower," "widowed," or another word that in a specific context denotes a marital or spousal relationship shall include a civil union, as established by N.J.S.A. 37:1–28 to –36, and a registered domestic partnership, as established by N.J.S.A. 26:8A–1 to –13, and the persons in those relationships.

Note: Source—R.R. 1:27A, 3:1–2, 3:11–9, 4:1–2, 4:121, 6:1–1 (second sentence), 6:1–2, 8:1–2. Amended June 20, 1979 to be effective July 1, 1979; amended July 5, 2000 to be effective September 5, 2000; caption amended, former text designated as paragraph (a), and new paragraph (b) adopted July 16, 2009 to be effective September 1, 2009.

1:1–3. Citation of Rules

These rules shall be referred to as "N.J. Court Rules, 1969" and may be cited as, e.g., "R. 1:1–3."

Note: Source—R.R. 1:1–10(a).

RULE 1:2. CONDUCT OF PROCEEDINGS GENERALLY

1:2–1. Proceedings in Open Court; Robes

All trials, hearings of motions and other applications, pretrial conferences, arraignments, sentencing conferences (except with members of the probation department) and appeals shall be conducted in open court unless otherwise provided by rule or statute. If a proceeding is required to be conducted in open court, no record of any portion thereof shall be sealed by order of the court except for good cause shown, as defined by R. 1:38–11(b), which shall be set forth on the record. Settlement conferences may be heard at the bench or in chambers. Every judge shall wear judicial robes during proceedings in open court.

Note: Source—R.R. 1:28–6, 3:5–1 (first clause), 4:29–5, 4:118–5, 7:7–1, 8:13–7(c); amended July 14, 1992 to be effective September 1, 1992; amended July 16, 2009 to be effective September 1, 2009.

1:2–2. Trial Courts; Verbatim Record of Proceedings

In the trial divisions of the Superior Court and in the Tax Court, all proceedings in court shall be recorded verbatim except, unless the court otherwise orders, settlement conferences, case management conferences, calendar calls, and ex parte motions. Unless a transcript thereof is marked into evidence, a verbatim record shall also be made of the content of an audio or video tape played during the proceedings and the tape itself shall be marked into evidence as a court's exhibit and retained by the court. Ex parte proceedings pursuant to R. 4:52 and R. 4:67 shall, however, be recorded verbatim subject to the availability of either a court reporter or a recording device. In the municipal courts, the taking of a verbatim record of the proceedings shall be governed by R. 7:8–8. Charge conferences, whether conducted in open court or in chambers, shall be recorded verbatim as required by R. 1:8–7(a).

Note: Source—R.R. 3:7–5 (first sentence), 3:7–10(d) (fifth sentence), 4:44–2 (first sentence), 4:44–5, 4:61–1(b). Amended June 20, 1979 to be effective July 1, 1979; amended December 20, 1983 to be effective December 31, 1983; amended July 26, 1984 to be effective September 10, 1984; amended January 5, 1998, to be effective February 1, 1998; amended July 10, 1998 to be effective September 1, 1998; amended July 5, 2000 to be effective September 5, 2000; amended July 12, 2002 to be effective September 3, 2002; amended July 28, 2004 to be effective September 1, 2004.

1:2–3. Exhibits

The verbatim record of the proceedings shall include references to all exhibits and, as to each, the offering party, a short description of the exhibit stated by the offering party or the court, and the marking directed by the court. Following the conclusion of trial, evidence shall be returned to the proponent and so acknowledged on the record unless the court otherwise orders. The record shall note any exhibits retained by the court. All evidence shall be preserved pending direct appeal and proceedings on certification, and shall be made available for inclusion by any party in the record on appeal.

Note: Source—R.R. 3:7–5A, 4:45B; amended November 2, 1987 to be effective January 1, 1988; amended July 13, 1994 to be effective September 1, 1994.

1:2–4. Sanctions: Failure to Appear; Motions and Briefs

(a) Failure to Appear. If without just excuse or because of failure to give reasonable attention to the matter, no appearance is made on behalf of a party on the call of a calendar, on the return of a motion, at a pretrial conference, settlement conference, or any other proceeding scheduled by the court, or on the day of trial, or if an application is made for an adjournment, the court may order any one or more of the following: (a) the payment by the delinquent attorney or party or by the party applying for the adjournment of costs, in such amount as the court shall fix, to the Clerk of the Court made payable to "Treasurer, State of New Jersey," or to the adverse party; (b) the payment by the delinquent attorney or party or the party applying for the adjournment of the reasonable expenses, including attorney's fees, to the aggrieved party; (c) the dismissal of the complaint, cross- claim, counterclaim or motion, or the striking of the answer and the entry of judgment by default, or the granting of the motion; or (d) such other action as it deems appropriate.

(b) Motions; Briefs. For failure to comply with the requirements of R. 1:6–3, 1:6–4 and 1:6–5 for filing motion papers and briefs and for failure to submit a required brief, the court may dismiss or grant the motion or application, continue the hearing to the next motion day or take such other action as it deems

appropriate. If the hearing is continued, the court may impose sanctions as provided by paragraph (a) of this rule.

Note: Source–R.R. 1:8–5, 4:5–5(b) (second sentence), 4:5–10(e), 4:6–3(b), 4:29–1(c), 4:41–6. Amended June 20, 1979 to be effective July 1, 1979; paragraph (a) amended November 7, 1988 to be effective January 2, 1989; paragraph (a) amended June 28, 1996 to be effective September 1, 1996; paragraph (a) amended July 27, 2006 to be effective September 1, 2006.

1:2–5. Advancement of Cases for Trial or Argument [Deleted]

Note: Source–R.R. 1:8–1(b), 3:11–5 (second sentence), 4:41–4(b) (second sentence), 4:88–6, 7:7–6. Amended July 14, 1972 to be effective September 5, 1972; amended July 24, 1978 to be effective September 11, 1978; amended December 20, 1983 to be effective December 31, 1983; deleted June 28, 1996 to be effective September 1, 1996.

Official Comment to Deleted R. 1:2–5

The deleted rule attempted to accord preference in the scheduling of cases for trial, hearing or argument across trial court and Appellate Division lines. The rule was deleted as the Supreme Court takes the position that the issue of calendar preference is best addressed administratively rather than in the context of court rules. Nonetheless, as a matter of policy, the preferences enumerated in the rule should be looked to as guidelines in determining priority of cases scheduled for trial, hearing or argument in the trial courts and the Appellate Division. These preferences include: (1) all contested matters where a principal issue is the custody, status, welfare and protection of minors; criminal and quasi-criminal cases, election actions, actions (except negligence actions) to which the State, a county, municipality or other public or quasi-public agency is a party; (2) if the action is in a trial court, all cases to be tried without a jury; (3) appeals on leave granted pending in the appellate courts; (4) workers' compensation appeals; and (5) such other cases as any court may from time to time order.

1:2–6. Case Management Conference; Orders

All dispositions made and directives issued by the court at a case management conference shall be memorialized by order.

Note: Adopted June 28, 1996 to be effective September 1, 1996.

RULE 1:3. TIME

1:3–1. Computation of Time

In computing any period of time fixed by rule or court order, the day of the act or event from which the designated period begins to run is not to be included. The last day of the period so computed is to be included, unless it is a Saturday, Sunday or legal holiday, in which event the period runs until the end of the next day which is neither a Saturday, Sunday nor legal holiday. In computing a period of time of less than 7 days, Saturday, Sunday and legal holidays shall be excluded.

Note: Source—R.R. 1:27, 8:12–4.

1:3–2. Time Unaffected by Expiration of Term

The period of time provided for the doing of any act is not affected or limited by the continued existence or expiration of a term of court.

Note: Source—R.R. 4:6–2 (first sentence).

1:3–3. Additional Time After Service by Ordinary Mail

When service of a notice or paper is made by ordinary mail, and a rule or court order allows the party served a period of time after the service thereof within which to take some action, 3 days shall be added to the period.

Note: Source—R.R. 4:6–4; amended June 28, 1996 to be effective September 1, 1996.

1:3–4. Enlargement of Time

(a) Enlargement by Order or Consent. Unless otherwise expressly provided by rule, a period of time thereby fixed for the doing of an act may be enlarged before or after its expiration by court order on notice or (unless a court has otherwise ordered) by consent of the parties in writing.

(b) Enlargement for Appeal and Review. Enlargement of time for appeal and review shall be governed by the following rules: appeals to the Supreme Court and Superior Court, Appellate Division, by R. 2:4–4; actions in lieu of prerogative writs in the Superior Court, Law Division, by R. 4:69–6(c); appeals to the Superior Court, Law Division from reports of condemnation commissioners, by R. 4:73–6(a); civil appeals to the Superior Court, Law Division, by R. 4:74–2(b); and review of ex parte probate actions, by R. 4:85–2.

(c) Enlargements Prohibited. Neither the parties nor the court may, however, enlarge the time specified by R. 1:7–4 (motion for amendment of findings); R. 3:18–2 (motion for judgment of acquittal after discharge of jury); R. 3:20–2, R. 4:49–1(b) and (c) and R. 7:10–1 (motion for new trial); R. 3:21–9 (motion in arrest of judgment); R. 3:21–10(a); R. 3:22–12 (petitions for post-conviction relief); R. 3:23–2 (appeals to the Law Division from judgments of conviction in courts of limited criminal jurisdiction); R. 3:24 (appeals to the Law Division from interlocutory orders and orders dismissing the complaint entered by courts of limited criminal jurisdiction); R. 4:40–2(b) (renewal of motion for judgment); R. 4:49–2 (motion to alter or amend a judgment); and R. 4:50–2 (motion for relief from judgment or order).

Note: Source—R.R. 1:27B(a) (b) (c) (d) (e), 4:6–1, 8:12–5(a)(b). Paragraph (c) amended July 7, 1971, effective September 13, 1971; paragraph (b) amended November 27, 1974 to be effective April 1, 1975; paragraph (b) amended July 22, 1983 to be effective September 12, 1983; paragraph (c) amended July 26, 1984 to be effective September 10, 1984; paragraphs (b) and (c) amended July 14, 1992 to be effective September 1, 1992; paragraph (c) amended January 5, 1998 to be effective February 1, 1998; paragraph (c) amended July 10, 1998 to be effective September 1, 1998; paragraph (c) amended July 28, 2004 to be effective September 1, 2004; paragraph (c) amended July 16, 2009 to be effective September 1, 2009.

RULE 1:4. FORM AND EXECUTION OF PAPERS

1:4–1. Caption: Name and Addresses of Party and Attorney; Format

(a) Caption.

Every paper to be filed shall contain a caption setting forth the name, division and part thereof, if any, of the court, the county in which the venue in a Superior Court action is laid, the title of the action, the docket number except in the case of a complaint, the designation "Civil Action" or "Criminal Action", as appropriate, and a designation such as "complaint", "order", or the like. In a complaint in a civil action, the title of the action shall include the names of all the parties, but in other papers it need state only the name of the first party on each side with an appropriate indication that there are other parties. Except as otherwise provided by R. 5:4–2(a), the first pleading of any party shall state the party's residence address, or, if not a natural person, the address of its principal place of business.

(b) Format; Addresses. At the top of the first page of each paper filed, a blank space of approximately 3 inches shall be reserved for notations of receipt and filing by the clerk. Above the caption at the left-hand margin of the first sheet of every paper to be filed there shall be printed or typed the name of the attorney filing the paper, office address and telephone number or, if a party is appearing pro se, the name of such party, residence address and telephone number. No paper shall bear an attorney's post office box number in lieu of a street address. An attorney or pro se party shall advise the court and all other parties of a change of address or telephone number if such occurs during the pendency of an action.

Note: Source—R.R. 4:5–8, 4:10–1, 5:5–1(e), 7:5–2(a) (first two sentences); paragraph (a) amended December 20, 1983 to be effective December 31, 1983; paragraph (a) redesignated as paragraph (a)(1) and paragraph (a)(2) added November 7, 1988 to be effective January 2, 1989; paragraph (b) amended July 14, 1992 to be effective September 1, 1992; paragraph (a)(1) amended July 13, 1994 to be effective September 1, 1994; paragraph (b) amended July 28, 2004 to be effective September 1, 2004; paragraph (a)(2) caption and text deleted, paragraph (a)(1) caption deleted, and paragraph (b) amended July 9, 2008 to be effective September 1, 2008.

1:4–2. Paragraphs

Allegations of claim or defense in a civil action shall be made in numbered paragraphs, each limited as far as practicable to a single set of circumstances. A paragraph may be referred to by number in the same or succeeding pleadings. Each claim founded upon a separate transaction or occurrence and each defense other than denials shall be stated in a separate count or defense whenever a separation facilitates the clear presentation of the matter.

Note: Source—R.R. 4:10–2.

1:4–3. Adoption by Reference; Exhibits

Statements in a pleading and exhibits to a pleading may be adopted by reference in a different part of the same pleading or in another pleading or in any motion. A copy of a document which is an exhibit to a pleading is a part thereof. Copies of bonds, mortgages, tax sale certificates, and assignments thereof shall not be annexed to complaints in actions for the foreclosure of a mortgage or a tax sale certificate.

Note: Source—R.R. 4:10–3.

1:4–4. Affidavits

(a) Form. Every affidavit shall run in the first person and be divided into numbered paragraphs as in pleadings. The caption shall include a designation of the particular proceeding the affidavit supports or opposes and the original date, if any, fixed for hearing. Ex parte affidavits may be taken outside the State by a person authorized to take depositions under R. 4:12–2 and R. 4:12–3.

(b) Certification in Lieu of Oath. In lieu of the affidavit, oath or verification required by these rules, the affiant may submit the following certification which shall be dated and immediately precede the affiant's signature: "I certify that the foregoing statements made by me are true. I am aware that if any of the foregoing statements made by me are wilfully false, I am subject to punishment."

(c) Facsimile Signature. If the affiant is not available to sign an affidavit or certification, it may be filed with a facsimile of the original signature provided the attorney offering the document certifies that the affiant acknowledged the genuineness of the signature and that the document or a copy with an original signature affixed will be filed if requested by the court or a party.

Note: Source—R.R. 1:27F, 4:10–4; paragraph (c) adopted June 29, 1990 to be effective September 4, 1990; paragraph (b) amended July 13, 1994 to be effective September 1, 1994.

Publisher's Note

On March 27, 2000 the New Jersey Supreme Court issued the following order:

WHEREAS the Judiciary has successfully tested the use of electronic filing technology in the Judiciary Electronic Filing and Imaging System (JEFIS) pilot project in the Special Civil Part of the Superior Court, Law Division, Monmouth County, pursuant to orders of this Court dated December 10, 1996 and February 1, 1999; and

WHEREAS the Judiciary is preparing to implement the electronic filing component of JEFIS in all of the Special Civil Part offices in the other twenty counties, while continuing to operate the pilot project in Monmouth County;

Pursuant to N.J. Const. (1947), Art. VI, § 2, par. 3, IT IS ORDERED, effective September 1, 2000 and until further Order of the Court, that the Rules of Court be relaxed and supplemented, as set forth below, so as to permit the Judiciary to establish and operate a statewide program in the Special Civil Part of the Superior Court, Law Division, in which attorneys who meet the requirements established by the Administrative Office of the Courts and are registered with the Superior Court Clerk's Office may, in civil actions in which the amount in controversy does not exceed the Part's monetary limit and where the actions are filed in that court pursuant to Rule 6:1-2(a)(1), electronically file pleadings and other papers in a

prescribed format via the Internet with the Clerk of the Superior Court, with computers capable of electronically managing documents and images of documents to be used to process and distribute those documents and images of documents to the office of the Special Civil Part Clerk in the county of venue for printing, processing, and storage in paper form (except in Monmouth County, where the documents will continue to be processed and stored in electronic form as part of the JEFIS project):

1. Rule 1:4–4(c) is relaxed so as to permit an attorney participating in the program and electronically filing an affidavit or certification to use a facsimile of the original signature regardless of the affiant's availability; the original signature of an affiant who is an attorney may be typed or digitized if the affiant is the individual attorney filing the document electronically; the remaining requirements of the rule remain in effect.

2. Rule 1:4–5 is relaxed so as to permit the use of the individual attorney's typed or digitized signature on all electronically filed documents that would otherwise require the attorney's handwritten signature.

3. Rule 1:4–8 is supplemented so [sic] to impose its obligations on an attorney who uses a typed or digitized signature on a document that is filed electronically.

4. Rule 1:4–9 is relaxed so as to permit attorneys participating in the program to file all pleadings and other papers in an electronic format prescribed by the Administrative Office of the Courts that will produce, as needed, printed paper copies that meet the requirements of the rule. Pleadings and papers subsequent to the complaint may be filed electronically only in those cases that were commenced by electronic filing of the complaint.

* * *

On April 4, 2000 the New Jersey Supreme Court issued the following order:

Pursuant to *N.J. Const.* Art. VI, § 2, ¶ 3, it is ORDERED that the Rules of Court be relaxed, as set forth below, to permit attorneys to file electronically with the Appellate Division Clerk's Office and to serve electronically the trial court and trial judge, via the Internet, notices of appeal and accompanying required documents in cases where the filing fee is waived or the attorney has a collateral account with the Finance Section of the Superior Court.

1. Rule 1:4–4 is relaxed to permit an original signature otherwise required by the rule to be typed, and if possible digitized, if the document is electronically filed with the Appellate Division Clerk's Office and electronically served on the trial court and trial judge.

2. Rule 1:4–5 is relaxed to permit the use of the individual attorney's typed, and if possible digitized, signature on all documents electronically filed with the Appellate Division Clerk's Office and electronically served on the trial court and trial judge that would otherwise require the attorney's handwritten signature.

3. Rule 1:4–9 is relaxed to permit attorneys to file papers in an electronic format prescribed by the Appellate Division and to so serve the trial court and trial judge.

* * *

It is further ORDERED that notices of appeal transmitted electronically before 5:00 p.m. on an Appellate Division regular business day will be deemed received as of the time sent by the attorney's Internet Service Provider; and

Notices of appeal transmitted electronically after 5:00 p.m., on holidays or weekends will be deemed received on the next business day; and

Except for electronically providing copies of the appeal documents to the trial court and trial judge, nothing herein relieves attorneys from the non-electronic service and notice requirements otherwise set forth in Rule 2:5–1.

The terms of this Order become effective May 1, 2000 and will remain in effect until further Order of the Court.

* * *

On October 7, 2003, the New Jersey Supreme Court issued the following order:

WHEREAS the Judiciary has successfully tested the use of electronic filing technology in the Judiciary Electronic Filing and

Imaging System (JEFIS) pilot project in the Special Civil Part of the Superior Court, Law Division, Monmouth County, pursuant to orders of this Court dated December 10, 1996 and February 1, 1999; and

WHEREAS the Judiciary has implemented the electronic filing component of JEFIS in all of the Special Civil Part offices in the other twenty counties pursuant to an Order of this Court dated March 27, 2000, while continuing to operate the pilot project in Monmouth County;

Pursuant to N.J. Const. (1947), Art. VI, sec. 2, par. 3, IT IS ORDERED, effective November 3, 2003 and until further Order of the Court, that the Rules of Court be relaxed and supplemented, as specified in the Court's Order dated March 27, 2000, to permit the Judiciary to expand the imaging component of JEFIS to civil actions filed in the Special Civil Part in Mercer and Ocean Counties pursuant to Rule 6:1–2(a)(1), so that documents filed in those cases, whether electronically or on paper, can be processed and stored in electronic form as part of the JEFIS project.

This Order supplements, where appropriate, the Court's Orders of December 10, 1996 and February 1, 1999 with regard to the JEFIS project in Monmouth County and the Court's Order of March 27, 2000 permitting the statewide expansion of the electronic filing component of JEFIS.

* * *

On February 2, 2004, the New Jersey Supreme Court issued the following order:

WHEREAS N.J.S.A. 2B:12–30(d)(3) authorizes the Administrative Office of the Courts to obtain hand-held, ticket-issuing, data entry devices and related equipment for use by approved parking authorities or parking agencies to facilitate the exchange of automated information and maintain the efficiency of the standardized statewide computer system; and the Administrative Office of the Courts has developed such devices and equipment under a program entitled the Parking Authority Ticket System;

Pursuant to N.J. Const. (1947), Art. VI, sec. 2, par. 3, it is ORDERED that, effective immediately and until further Order, Rules 1:4–4 and 7:2–1 of the Rules Governing the Courts of the State of New Jersey, are hereby relaxed and supplemented so as to permit the use of an electronic signature by any law enforcement officer or other person authorized to issue a parking ticket through the Parking Authority Ticket System in those municipalities that have implemented the Parking Authority Ticket System; and

It is FURTHER ORDERED that such electronic signature on a parking ticket issued under the Parking Authority Ticket System shall be equivalent to an original signature.

* * *

On April 27, 2004, the New Jersey Supreme Court issued the following order to be effective on May 3, 2004:

WHEREAS the Judiciary has successfully tested the use of electronic filing technology in the Judiciary Electronic Filing and Imaging System (JEFIS) pilot project in the Special Civil Part of the Superior Court, Law Division, Monmouth County, pursuant to orders of this Court dated December 10, 1996 and February 1, 1999; and

WHEREAS the Judiciary has implemented the electronic filing component of JEFIS in all of the Special Civil Part offices in the other twenty counties pursuant to an Order of this Court dated March 27, 2000, while continuing to operate the pilot project in Monmouth County; and

WHEREAS the Judiciary has expanded the imaging component of JEFIS to civil actions filed in the Special Civil Part in Mercer and Ocean Counties pursuant to an Order of this Court dated October 7, 2003;

Pursuant to N.J. Const. (1947), Art. VI, sec. 2, par. 3, IT IS ORDERED, effective May 3, 2004 and until further Order of the Court, that the Rules of Court be relaxed and supplemented, as specified in the Court's Order dated March 27, 2000, to permit the Judiciary to expand the imaging component of JEFIS to civil actions filed in the Special Civil Part in Bergen, Burlington, Camden, Cumberland, Gloucester, Morris, Salem, Somerset and Union Counties pursuant to *Rule* 6:1–2(a)(1), so that documents filed in those cases, whether electronically or on paper, can be processed and stored in electronic form as part of the JEFIS project.

This Order supplements, where appropriate, the Court's Orders of December 10, 1996 and February 1, 1999 with regard to the JEFIS project in Monmouth County, the Court's Order of March 27, 2000 permitting the statewide expansion of the electronic filing component of JEFIS, and the Court's Order of October 7, 2003 permitting expansion of the imaging component of JEFIS to Mercer and Ocean Counties.

* * *

On July 7, 2005, the New Jersey Supreme Court issued the following order to be effective on July 7, 2005:

Pursuant to N.J. Const. (1947), Art. VI, sec. 2, par. 3, IT IS ORDERED, effective immediately and until further Order of the Court, that the Rules of Court be relaxed and supplemented as specified in the Court's Order dated March 27, 2000, to permit the Judiciary to further expand the imaging component of JEFIS to Atlantic, Cape May, Essex, Hudson, Hunterdon, Middlesex, Passaic, Sussex and Warren Counties for actions filed pursuant to Rule 6:1–2(a)(1), so that documents in those Special Civil Part cases, whether filed electronically or on paper, can be processed and stored in electronic form as part of the JEFIS project.

* * *

On June 5, 2007, the New Jersey Supreme Court issued the following order to be effective on June 5, 2007:

It is ORDERED, pursuant to N.J. Const., Art. VI, sec. 2, par. 3, that effective immediately and until further Order the provisions of the following Rules Governing the Courts of the State of New Jersey are supplemented and relaxed on a statewide basis in connection with program utilizing the electronic transmission and filing of domestic violence complaints and temporary restraining orders with the Family Division of Superior Court (the "E–TRO Project"), as indicated:

1. Rule 1:4–4(c) is relaxed and supplemented so that an electronic signature in typewritten form on a domestic violence complaint has the same effect as the faxed signature authorized by this rule. Notwithstanding this provision, a copy of the document with the original signature must be retained at the police department. Additionally, the confirmatory order subsequently signed by the Municipal Court judge or Superior Court judge must be transmitted to the police department for retention as well.

2. Rule 5:7A(b) is relaxed and supplemented so as to give electronic entry of the judge's name in typewritten form by the law enforcement officer on the temporary restraining order the same effect as the officer's printing of the judge's name that is expressly authorized by that rule. Also, the signature of the applicant on the certification portion of the domestic violence complaint and temporary restraining order may be entered electronically in typewritten form subsequent to the applicant taking the oath and giving sworn testimony.

3. Rule 4:42–1(e) is relaxed and supplemented so as to authorize the use of electronic signatures for Superior Court or Municipal Court judges for temporary restraining orders issued under this pilot program.

The process will be used in the participating municipalities in connection with domestic violence complaints and temporary restraining orders from a Municipal Court judge or Superior Court judge after regular Superior Court hours. The program will permit law enforcement officers to prepare domestic violence complaints and temporary restraining orders in electronic form on personal computers and then transmit those complaints/TROs electronically to the Judiciary for filing and entry in the Judiciary's Family automated case system (FACTS), including automatic updating of the Domestic Violence Central Registry.

The provisions of this Order shall be in effect pending adoption of conforming amendments to the Rules of Court. This Order supersedes all Orders previously issued in connection with the pilot test of the E–TRO Project, including the December 10, 2002 initial rule relaxation order as to Burlington County; the April 28, 2003 order extending the pilot project to Camden, Cape May, Essex, and Somerset Counties; and the July 7, 2005 order extending it to Passaic County.

* * *

On December 2, 2008, the New Jersey Supreme Court issued the following order to be effective on December 2, 2008:

WHEREAS the New Jersey Judiciary has been working closely with the Executive Branch to implement a new automated child support enforcement system, known as NJKiDS (New Jersey Kids Deserve Support), to replace the current system, known as ACSES (Automated Child Support Enforcement System); and

WHEREAS NJKiDS will electronically generate child support orders, which the court will use to establish, modify or enforce child support; and NJKiDS will permit the electronic filing of child support complaints and post-judgment applications, which will require the moving party to enter a digital signature in order to complete the filing transaction;

IT IS ORDERED, pursuant to N.J. Const. (1947), Art. VI, § 2, ¶ 3, that, effective immediately and until further order, the following Rules of Court are relaxed and supplemented as they relate to child support matters as indicated:

1. Rule 1:4–4 is relaxed so as to permit an electronic or digital signature to have the same effect as a facsimile signature authorized by this rule;

2. Rule 1:4–5 is relaxed so as to permit an electronic or digital signature to have the same effect as an original signature required by this rule;

3. Rule 1:4–9 is relaxed so as to permit the filing of all pleadings and other papers in an electronic format prescribed by the Administrative Office of the Courts that will produce, as needed, printed paper copies that meet the requirements of the rule;

4. Rule 1:5–2 is relaxed so as to permit electronic service of copies of all papers referred to in Rule 1:5–1 through the Judiciary's computer system, if service is available in this manner;

5. Rule 1:5–3 is relaxed so as to permit an electronic or digital signature to have the same effect as an original signature required by this rule;

6. Rule 4:42–1(e) is relaxed and supplemented so as to authorize the use of electronic or digital signatures for judges of the Superior Court to sign child support orders;

7. Rule 5:5–4 is relaxed so as to permit an electronic or digital signature to have the same effect as an original signature on an order entered after a motion;

8. Rule 5:6 is relaxed so as to permit an electronic or digital signature to have the same effect as an original signature for summary actions for support;

9. Rule 5:6B is relaxed so as to permit an electronic or digital signature to have the same effect as an original signature for an order granting a child support cost-of-living adjustment; and

10. Rule 5:25–3 is relaxed so as to permit an electronic or digital signature to have the same effect as an original signature for an order entered resulting from the recommendations of a Child Support Hearing Officer.

1:4–5. Signing and Dating of Pleadings; Motions

Pleadings (other than indictments), motions and briefs shall be signed by the attorney of record or the attorney's associate or by a pro se party. Signatures of a firm may be typed, followed by the signature of an attorney of the firm. Signatures on any duplicate original or carbon copy required to be filed may be typed. Every paper to be filed shall bear the date on which it was signed.

Note: Source—R.R. 4:5–6(a) (third sentence), 4:7–2(b), 4:11 (first three sentences); caption and text amended to be effective September 11, 1978; amended July 16, 1981 to be effective September 14, 1981; amended July 13, 1994 to be effective September 1, 1994.

Publisher's Note

For text of the New Jersey Supreme Court orders issued on March 27, 2000, April 4, 2000, and December 2, 2008, see note following Rule 1:4–4

1:4–6. Typewritten Names

Names shall be typed or stamped beneath all signatures on papers to be filed or served.

Note: Source—R.R. 4:5–9.

1:4–7. Verification of Pleadings

Pleadings need not be verified unless ex parte relief is sought thereon or a rule or statute otherwise provides. The verification shall not repeat the allegations of the pleadings but may incorporate them by reference if made on personal knowledge and so stated, and the allegations are of facts admissible in evidence to which the affiant is competent to testify.

Note: Source—R.R. 4:11 (fourth and fifth sentences).

1:4–8. Frivolous Litigation

(a) Effect of Signing, Filing or Advocating a Paper. The signature of an attorney or pro se party constitutes a certificate that the signatory has read the pleading, written motion or other paper. By signing, filing or advocating a pleading, written motion, or other paper, an attorney or pro se party certifies that to the best of his or her knowledge, information, and belief, formed after an inquiry reasonable under the circumstances:

(1) the paper is not being presented for any improper purpose, such as to harass or to cause unnecessary delay or needless increase in the cost of litigation;

(2) the claims, defenses, and other legal contentions therein are warranted by existing law or by a non-frivolous argument for the extension, modification, or reversal of existing law or the establishment of new law;

(3) the factual allegations have evidentiary support or, as to specifically identified allegations, they are either likely to have evidentiary support or they will be withdrawn or corrected if reasonable opportunity for further investigation or discovery indicates insufficient evidentiary support; and

(4) the denials of factual allegations are warranted on the evidence or, as to specifically identified denials, they are reasonably based on a lack of information or belief or they will be withdrawn or corrected if a reasonable opportunity for further investigation or discovery indicates insufficient evidentiary support.

If the pleading, written motion or other paper is not signed or is signed with intent to defeat the purpose of this rule, it may be stricken and the action may proceed as though the document had not been served. Any adverse party may also seek sanctions in accordance with the provisions of paragraph (b) of this rule.

(b) Motions for Sanctions.

(1) *Contents of Motion, Certification.* An application for sanctions under this rule shall be by motion made

separately from other applications and shall describe the specific conduct alleged to have violated this rule. No such motion shall be filed unless it includes a certification that the applicant served written notice and demand pursuant to R. 1:5–2 to the attorney or pro se party who signed or filed the paper objected to. The certification shall have annexed a copy of that notice and demand, which shall (i) state that the paper is believed to violate the provisions of this rule, (ii) set forth the basis for that belief with specificity, (iii) include a demand that the paper be withdrawn, and (iv) give notice, except as otherwise provided herein, that an application for sanctions will be made within a reasonable time thereafter if the offending paper is not withdrawn within 28 days of service of the written demand. If, however, the subject of the application for sanctions is a motion whose return date precedes the expiration of the 28–day period, the demand shall give the movant the option of either consenting to an adjournment of the return date or waiving the balance of the 28–day period then remaining. A movant who does not request an adjournment of the return date as provided herein shall be deemed to have elected the waiver. The certification shall also certify that the paper objected to has not been withdrawn or corrected within the appropriate time period provided herein following service of the written notice and demand.

No motion shall be filed if the paper objected to has been withdrawn or corrected within 28 days of service of the notice and demand or within such other time period as provided herein.

(2) *Time for Filing; Attorney's Fees.* A motion for sanctions shall be filed with the court no later than 20 days following the entry of final judgment. If warranted, the court may award to the party prevailing on the motion the reasonable expenses and attorneys' fees incurred in presenting or opposing the motion. For purposes of this rule, the term "final judgment" shall include any order deciding a post-judgment motion whether or not that order is directly appealable.

(3) *Scope of Responsibility.* Except in extraordinary circumstances, a law firm shall be jointly responsible for violations committed by its partners, shareholders, associates and employees.

(c) Sanction on Court's Initiative. On its own initiative, the court may enter an order describing the specific conduct that appears to violate this rule and directing the attorney or pro se party to show cause why he or she has not violated the rule. The order to show cause shall issue before a voluntary dismissal or settlement of the claims made by or against the pro se party or the attorney who is the subject of the order to show cause.

(d) Order for Sanctions. A sanction imposed for violation of paragraph (a) of this rule shall be limited to a sum sufficient to deter repetition of such conduct. The sanction may consist of (1) an order to pay a penalty into court, or (2) an order directing payment to the movant of some or all of the reasonable attorneys' fees and other expenses incurred as a direct result of the violation, or both. Among the factors to be considered by the court in imposing a sanction under (2) is the timeliness of the movant's filing of the motion therefor. In the order imposing sanctions, the court shall describe the conduct determined to be a violation of this rule and explain the basis for the sanction imposed.

(e) Exceptions. This rule does not apply to disclosures and discovery requests, responses, objections, and discovery motions that are subject to the provisions of R. 4:23.

(f) Applicability to Parties. To the extent practicable, the procedures prescribed by this rule shall apply to the assertion of costs and fees against a party other than a pro se party pursuant to N.J.S.A. 2A:15–59.1.

Note: Source—R.R. 4:11 (seventh through tenth sentences); amended July 13, 1994 to be effective September 1, 1994; amended June 28, 1996 to be effective September 1, 1996; paragraph (b)(2) amended July 12, 2002 to be effective September 3, 2002; paragraph (b)(2) amended and paragraph (g) deleted July 28, 2004 to be effective September 1, 2004.

Publisher's Note

For text of the New Jersey Supreme Court orders issued on March 27, 2000, see note following Rule 1:4–4

1:4–9. Size, Weight and Format of Filed Papers

Except as otherwise provided by R. 2:6–10, pleadings and other papers filed with the court, including letter briefs and memoranda but excluding preprinted legal forms and documentary exhibits, shall be prepared on letter size (approximately 8.5 × 11 inches) paper of standard weight and quality for copy paper and shall be double spaced with no smaller than 10–pitch or 12–point type. Both sides of the paper may be used and recycled paper should be used, provided legibility is maintained.

Note: Source—R.R. 1:27C; caption and text amended June 29, 1990 to be effective September 4, 1990; amended July 13, 1994 to be effective September 1, 1994; amended June 28, 1996 to be effective September 1, 1996; amended July 27, 2006 to be effective September 1, 2006; amended July 9, 2008 to be effective September 1, 2008.

Publisher's Note

For text of the New Jersey Supreme Court orders issued on March 27, 2000, April 4, 2000, and December 2, 2008, see note following Rule 1:4–4

RULE 1:5. SERVICE AND FILING OF PAPERS

1:5–1. Service: When Required

(a) Civil Actions. In all civil actions, unless otherwise provided by rule or court order, orders, judgments, pleadings subsequent to the original complaint, written motions (not made ex parte), briefs, appendices, petitions and other papers except a judgment signed by the clerk shall be served upon all attorneys of record in the action and upon parties appearing pro se; but no service need be made on parties who have failed to appear except that pleadings asserting new or additional claims for relief against such parties in default shall be served upon them in the manner provided for service of original process. The party obtaining an order or judgment shall serve it as herein prescribed within 7 days after the date it was signed unless the court otherwise orders therein.

(b) Criminal Actions. In criminal actions, unless otherwise provided by rule or court order, written motions (not made ex parte), briefs, appendices, petitions, memoranda and other papers shall be served upon all attorneys of record in the action, upon parties appearing pro se and upon such other agencies of government as may be affected by the relief sought.

Note: Source—R.R. 3:11–4(a), 4:5–1. Paragraph (a) amended July 16, 1979 to be effective September 10, 1979; paragraph (b) amended July 13, 1994 to be effective September 1, 1994.

1:5–2. Manner of Service

Service upon an attorney of papers referred to in R. 1:5–1 shall be made by mailing a copy to the attorney at his or her office by ordinary mail, by handing it to the attorney, or by leaving it at the office with a person in the attorney's employ, or, if the office is closed or the attorney has no office, in the same manner as service is made upon a party. Service upon a party of such papers shall be made as provided in R. 4:4–4 or by registered or certified mail, return receipt requested, and simultaneously by ordinary mail to the party's last known address; or if no address is known, despite diligent effort, by ordinary mail to the clerk of the court. Mail may be addressed to a post office box in lieu of a street address only if the sender cannot by diligent effort determine the addressee's street address or if the post office does not make street-address delivery to the addressee. The specific facts underlying the diligent effort required by this rule shall be recited in the proof of service required by R. 1:5–3. If, however, proof of diligent inquiry as to a party's whereabouts has already been filed within six months prior to service under this rule, a new diligent inquiry need not be made provided the proof of service required by R. 1:5–3 asserts that the party making service has no knowledge of any facts different from those recited in the prior proof of diligent inquiry.

Note: Source—R.R. 1:7–12(d), 1:10–10(b), 1:11–2(c), 2:11–2(c), 3:11–1(b), 4:5–2(a) (first four sentences); amended July 16, 1981 to be effective September 14, 1981; amended July 13, 1994 to be effective September 1, 1994; amended July 28, 2004 to be effective September 1, 2004.

Publisher's note

For text of the New Jersey Supreme Court orders, issued on March 27, 2000, see note following Rule 1:5–3

On November 17, 2009, the New Jersey Supreme Court issued the following order:

It is ORDERED, pursuant to N.J. Const. Art. VI, sec. 2, par. 3, that the provisions of Rule 1:5–2 ("Manner of Service") of the Rules Governing the Court of the State of New Jersey are supplemented and relaxed so as to provide that where service of papers referred to in Rule 1:5–1(a) ("Service; When Required - Civil Actions") is required to be made upon the clerk of the court because, despite diligent effort, no address for the party is known, the filing of the papers with the clerk shall be deemed to satisfy that service requirement and there need be no separate service upon the clerk.

1:5–3. Proof of Service

Proof of service of every paper referred to in R. 1:5–1 may be made (1) by an acknowledgment of service, signed by the attorney for a party or signed and acknowledged by the party, or (2) by an affidavit of the person making service, or (3) by a certification of service appended to the paper to be filed and signed by the attorney for the party making service. If service has been made by mail the affidavit or certification shall state that the mailing was to the last known address of the person served. A proof of service made by affidavit or certification shall state the name and address of each attorney served, identifying the party that attorney represents, and the name and address of any *pro se* party. The proof shall be filed with the court promptly and in any event before action is to be taken on the matter by the court. Where service has been made by registered or certified mail, filing of the return receipt card with the court shall not be required. Failure to make proof of service does not affect the validity of the service, and the court at any time may allow the proof to be amended or supplied unless an injustice would result.

Note: Source—R.R. 4:5–2(b), 4:88–10 (fifth sentence); amended July 17, 1975 to be effective September 8, 1975; amended July 29, 1977 to be effective September 6, 1977; amended June 29, 1990 to be effective September 4, 1990; amended July 12, 2002 to be effective September 3, 2002.

Publisher's Note

On March 27, 2000 the New Jersey Supreme Court issued the following order:

WHEREAS the Judiciary has successfully tested the use of electronic filing technology in the Judiciary Electronic Filing and Imaging System (JEFIS) pilot project in the Special Civil Part of the Superior Court, Law Division, Monmouth County, pursuant to orders of this Court dated December 10, 1996 and February 1, 1999; and

WHEREAS the Judiciary is preparing to implement the electronic filing component of JEFIS in all of the Special Civil Part offices in the other twenty counties, while continuing to operate the pilot project in Monmouth County;

Pursuant to N.J. Const. (1947), Art. VI, § 2, par. 3, IT IS ORDERED, effective September 1, 2000 and until further Order of the Court, that the Rules of Court be relaxed and supplemented, as set forth below, so as to permit the Judiciary to establish and operate a statewide program in the Special Civil Part of the Superior Court, Law Division, in which attorneys who meet the requirements established by the Administrative Office of the Courts and are registered with the Superior Court Clerk's Office may, in civil actions in which the amount in controversy does not exceed the Part's monetary limit and where the actions are filed in that court pursuant to Rule 6:1-2(a)(1), electronically file pleadings and other papers in a prescribed format via the Internet with the Clerk of the Superior Court, with computers capable of electronically managing documents and images of documents to be used to process and distribute those documents and images of documents to the office of the Special Civil Part Clerk in the county of venue for printing, processing, and storage in paper form (except in Monmouth County, where the documents will continue to be processed and stored in electronic form as part of the JEFIS project):

* * *

5. Rule 1:5–2 is relaxed so as to permit attorneys participating in the program to serve copies of all papers referred to in Rule 1:5–1 on each other electronically through the program's computer system, if it provides this service.

6. Rule 1:5–3 is supplemented so as to permit the use of the individual attorney's typed or digitized signature in lieu of a handwritten signature on a certification of service appended to a document that the attorney files electronically.

7. Rule 1:5–6(b) is supplemented and paragraph 7 of the Court's December 10, 1996 Order is superseded to the effect that documents transmitted electronically to the court after 4:30 p.m. shall be deemed received on the next court day.

8. Rule 1:5–6(c) is relaxed and supplemented so as to permit the clerk to reject a document presented electronically for filing as part of a batch of electronic documents, or to reject the entire batch, if the document is not presented in accordance with the standards for batch filing prescribed by the Administrative Office of the Courts.

* * *

On April 4, 2000, the New Jersey Supreme Court issued the following order:

Pursuant to *N.J. Const.* Art. VI, § 2, ¶ 3, it is ORDERED that the Rules of Court be relaxed, as set forth below, to permit attorneys to file electronically with the Appellate Division Clerk's Office and to serve electronically the trial court and trial judge, via the Internet, notices of appeal and accompanying required documents in cases where the filing fee is waived or the attorney has a collateral account with the Finance Section of the Superior Court.

* * *

4. Rule 1:5–3 is relaxed to permit an original signature otherwise required by the rule to be typed, and if possible digitized, if the document is electronically filed with the Appellate Division Clerk's Office and electronically served on the trial court and trial judge.

* * *

It is further ORDERED that notices of appeal transmitted electronically before 5:00 p.m. on an Appellate Division regular business day will be deemed received as of the time sent by the attorney's Internet Service Provider; and

Notices of appeal transmitted electronically after 5:00 p.m., on holidays or weekends will be deemed received on the next business day; and

Except for electronically providing copies of the appeal documents to the trial court and trial judge, nothing herein relieves attorneys from the non-electronic service and notice requirements otherwise set forth in Rule 2:5–1.

The terms of this Order become effective May 1, 2000 and will remain in effect until further Order of the Court.

* * *

On January 16, 2001, the New Jersey Supreme Court issued the following order:

It is ORDERED, pursuant to N.J. Const. Art. VI, § 2, par. 3, that effective immediately and until further order, Rule 1:5–3 ("Proof of Service") of the Rules Governing the Courts of the State of New Jersey is hereby relaxed so as to require that proofs of service of all papers served pursuant to Rule 1:5–1 specifically list the names and addresses of all attorneys served and the parties they represent, as well as the names and addresses of all pro se parties served.

* * *

On October 7, 2003, the New Jersey Supreme Court issued the following order:

WHEREAS the Judiciary has successfully tested the use of electronic filing technology in the Judiciary Electronic Filing and Imaging System (JEFIS) pilot project in the Special Civil Part of the Superior Court, Law Division, Monmouth County, pursuant to orders of this Court dated December 10, 1996 and February 1, 1999; and

WHEREAS the Judiciary has implemented the electronic filing component of JEFIS in all of the Special Civil Part offices in the other twenty counties pursuant to an Order of this Court dated March 27, 2000, while continuing to operate the pilot project in Monmouth County;

Pursuant to N.J. Const. (1947), Art. VI, sec. 2, par. 3, IT IS ORDERED, effective November 3, 2003 and until further Order of the Court, that the Rules of Court be relaxed and supplemented, as specified in the Court's Order dated March 27, 2000, to permit the Judiciary to expand the imaging component of JEFIS to civil actions filed in the Special Civil Part in Mercer and Ocean Counties pursuant to Rule 6:1–2(a)(1), so that documents filed in those cases, whether electronically or on paper, can be processed and stored in electronic form as part of the JEFIS project.

This Order supplements, where appropriate, the Court's Orders of December 10, 1996 and February 1, 1999 with regard to the JEFIS project in Monmouth County and the Court's Order of March 27, 2000 permitting the statewide expansion of the electronic filing component of JEFIS.

* * *

On April 27, 2004, the New Jersey Supreme Court issued the following order to be effective on May 3, 2004:

WHEREAS the Judiciary has successfully tested the use of electronic filing technology in the Judiciary Electronic Filing and Imaging System (JEFIS) pilot project in the Special Civil Part of the Superior Court, Law Division, Monmouth County, pursuant to orders of this Court dated December 10, 1996 and February 1, 1999; and

WHEREAS the Judiciary has implemented the electronic filing component of JEFIS in all of the Special Civil Part offices in the other twenty counties pursuant to an Order of this Court dated March 27, 2000, while continuing to operate the pilot project in Monmouth County; and

WHEREAS the Judiciary has expanded the imaging component of JEFIS to civil actions filed in the Special Civil Part in Mercer and Ocean Counties pursuant to an Order of this Court dated October 7, 2003;

Pursuant to N.J. Const. (1947), Art. VI, sec. 2, par. 3, IT IS ORDERED, effective May 3, 2004 and until further Order of the Court, that the Rules of Court be relaxed and supplemented, as specified in the Court's Order dated March 27, 2000, to permit the Judiciary to expand the imaging component of JEFIS to civil actions filed in the Special Civil Part in Bergen, Burlington, Camden, Cumberland, Gloucester, Morris, Salem, Somerset and Union Counties pursuant to Rule 6:1–2(a)(1), so that documents filed in those cases, whether electronically or on paper, can be processed and stored in electronic form as part of the JEFIS project.

This Order supplements, where appropriate, the Court's Orders of December 10, 1996 and February 1, 1999 with regard to the JEFIS project in Monmouth County, the Court's Order of March 27, 2000 permitting the statewide expansion of the electronic filing component of JEFIS, and the Court's Order of October 7, 2003 permitting expansion of the imaging component of JEFIS to Mercer and Ocean Counties.

* * *

On July 7, 2005, the New Jersey Supreme Court issued an order to be effective on July 7, 2005, see Publisher's Note following Rule 1:4-4 for contents of that order.

1:5–4. Service by Mail or Courier: When Complete

(a) Service by Ordinary Mail if Registered or Certified Mail Is Required and Is Refused. Where under any rule, provision is made for service by certified or registered mail, service may also be made by ordinary mail simultaneously or thereafter, unless simultaneous service is required under these rules.

(b) Service Complete on Mailing. Except for motions that are governed by R. 1:6–3(c), service by mail of any paper referred to in R. 1: 5–1, when authorized by rule or court order, shall be complete upon mailing of the ordinary mail. If no ordinary mailing is made, service shall be deemed complete upon the date of acceptance of the certified or registered mail. If service is simultaneously made by ordinary mail and certified or registered mail, service shall be deemed complete on mailing of the ordinary mail. If service is not made simultaneously and the addressee accepts the certified or registered mail, service shall be deemed complete on the date of the acceptance. If the addressee fails to claim or refuses to accept delivery of certified or registered mail, service shall be deemed complete on mailing of the ordinary mail.

(c) Service by Commercial Courier. Service by a commercial courier of a paper referred to in R. 1:5–1, except for motions, which are governed by R. 1:6–3, shall be complete upon the courier's receipt of the paper from the sender, provided the courier's regular business is delivery service, and provided further that it guarantees delivery to the addressee by the end of the next business day following the courier's receipt from the sender.

Note: Source — R.R. 4:5–2(a) (fifth sentence). Paragraph (a) adopted and former rule designated (b) June 29, 1973 to be effective September 10, 1973; amended November 1, 1985 to be effective January 2, 1986; paragraph (b) amended and paragraph (c) added July 13, 1994 to be effective September 1, 1994; paragraph (b) amended July 10, 1998 to be effective September 1, 1998; paragraph (a) amended July 28, 2004 to be effective September 1, 2004; paragraphs (a) and (b) amended July 27, 2006 to be effective September 1, 2006.

1:5–5. Service; Numerous Defendants

In any civil action in which there are unusually large numbers of defendants, the court, upon motion or on its own initiative, may order that service of the pleadings of the defendants and replies thereto need not be made as between the defendants and that any cross-claim, counterclaim, or matter constituting an avoidance or affirmative defense contained therein shall be deemed to be denied or avoided by all other parties and that the filing of any such pleadings and service thereof upon the plaintiff, or an adverse party in a cross-claim, constitutes due notice of it to the parties. In any such action the court may designate certain parties as representatives for receipt of service for all defendants similarly situated and may order that service of pleadings, motions and other papers filed in the action may be served upon such representatives with the same effect as if all such defendants had been served. A copy of every such order shall be served upon the parties in interest in such manner and form as the court directs.

Note: Source—R.R. 4:5–3.

1:5–6. Filing

(a) Time for Filing. In any trial court, unless otherwise stated, all papers required to be served by R. 1:5–1 shall be filed with the court either before service or promptly thereafter, unless the rule requiring service or filing provides otherwise. Whenever in these rules provision is made for the publication, mailing or posting of notice, proof thereof shall be filed with the court within 20 days after the publication or mailing or posting.

(b) What Constitutes Filing With the Court. Except as otherwise provided by R. 1:6–4 (motion papers), R. 1:6–5 (briefs), R. 4:42–1(e) (orders and judgments), and R. 5:5–4 (motions in Family actions), a paper is filed with the trial court if the original is filed as follows:

(1) In civil actions in the Superior Court, Law Division, and in actions in the Superior Court, Chancery Division, General Equity, except mortgage and tax foreclosure actions, with the deputy clerk of the Superior Court in the county of venue;

(2) In criminal actions in the Superior Court, Law Division, with the Criminal Division Manager in the county of venue, as designee of the deputy clerk of the Superior Court;

(3) In mortgage and tax foreclosure actions, with the Clerk of the Superior Court, unless and until the action is deemed contested and the papers have been sent by the Clerk to the county of venue, in which event subsequent papers shall be filed with the deputy clerk of the Superior Court in the county of venue;

(4) In actions in the Chancery Division, Family Part, with the deputy clerk of the Superior Court in the county of venue if the action is for dissolution of marriage, with the Surrogate of the county of venue if the action is for adoption, and in all other actions, with the Family Division Manager in the county of venue, as designee of the deputy clerk of the Superior Court;

(5) In probate matters in the Surrogate's Court, with the Surrogate, and in actions in the Chancery Division, Probate Part, with the Surrogate of the county of venue as deputy clerk of the Superior Court;

(6) In actions of the Special Civil Part, as provided by Part VI of these rules;

(7) In actions in the Tax Court, as provided by Part VIII of these rules.

The foregoing notwithstanding, in any case the judge or, at the judge's chambers, a member of the staff may accept papers for filing if they show the filing date and the judge's name and office. The filed papers shall be forwarded forthwith to the appropriate office.

(c) Nonconforming Papers. The clerk shall file all papers presented for filing and may notify the person filing if such papers do not conform to these rules, except that

(1) the paper shall be returned stamped "Received but not Filed (date)" if it is presented for filing unaccompanied by any of the following:

(A) the required filing fee; or

(B) a completed Case Information Statement as required by R. 4:5–1 in the form set forth in Appendices XII–B1 or XII–B2 to these rules; or

(C) in Family Part actions, the affidavit of insurance coverage required by R. 5:4–2(f), the Parents Education Program registration fee required by N.J.S.A. 2A:34–12.2, the Confidential Litigant Information Sheet as required by R. 5:4–2(g) in the form prescribed in Appendix XXIV, or the Affidavit or Certification of Notification of Complementary Dispute Resolution Alternatives as required by R. 5:4–2(h) in the form prescribed in Appendix XXVII–A or XXVII–B of these rules; or

(D) the signature of an attorney permitted to practice law in this State pursuant to R. 1:21–1 or the signature of a party appearing *pro se*, provided, however, that a *pro se* appearance is provided for by these rules; or

(E) a certification of title search as required by R. 4:64–1(a).

If a paper is returned under this rule, it shall be accompanied by a notice advising that if the paper is retransmitted together with the required signature, document or fee, as appropriate, within ten days after the date of the clerk's notice, filing will be deemed to have been made on the stamped receipt date.

(2) if an answer is presented by a defendant against whom default has been entered other than in a mortgage or tax foreclosure action, the clerk shall return the same stamped "Received but not Filed (date)" with notice that the defendant may move to vacate the default.

(3) a demand for trial de novo may be rejected and returned if not filed within the time prescribed in R. 4:21A–6 or if it is submitted for filing by a party in default or whose answer has been suppressed.

(4) a paper shall be returned stamped "Received but not Filed (date)" if it does not conform to the requirements of R. 1:4–9 with notice that if the document is retransmitted on conforming paper within 10 days after the date of the clerk's notice, filing will be deemed to have been made on the stamped receipt date.

(d) Misfiled Papers. If papers are sent to the wrong filing office, they shall be stamped "Received but not Filed (date)" and transmitted by that office to the proper filing office and a notice shall be sent by the transmitting office to the filer of the paper advising of the transmittal. The stamped received date shall be deemed to be the date of filing.

(e) Attorneys Answerable for Clerk's Fees. The attorney of record in every action shall be answerable for the clerk's lawful fees and charges.

Note: Source—R. R.1:7–11, 1:12–3(b), 2:10, 3:11–4(d), 4:5–5(a), 4:5–6(a) (first and second sentence), 4:5–7 (first sentence), 5:5–1(a). Paragraphs (b) and (c) amended July 14, 1972 to be effective September 5, 1972; paragraph (c) amended November 27, 1974 to be effective April 1, 1975; paragraph (b) amended November 7, 1988 to be effective January 2, 1989; paragraph (b) amended June 29, 1990 to be effective September 4, 1990; paragraph (c) amended November 26, 1990 to be effective April 1, 1991; paragraphs (b) and (c) amended, new text substituted for paragraph (d) and former paragraph (d) redesignated paragraph (e) July 13, 1994 to be effective September 1, 1994; paragraph (b)(1) amended, new paragraph (b)(2) adopted, paragraphs (b)(2), (3), (4), (5) and (6) redesignated paragraphs (b)(3), (4), (5), (6) and (7), and newly designated paragraph (b)(4) amended July 13, 1994 to be effective January 1, 1995; paragraphs (b)(1),(3) and (4) amended June 28, 1996 to be effective September 1, 1996; paragraph (b)(4) amended July 10, 1998 to be effective September 1, 1998; paragraph (c) amended July 5, 2000 to be effective September 5, 2000; paragraphs (c)(1) and (c)(3) amended July 28, 2004 to be effective September 1, 2004; subparagraph (c)(1)(E) adopted, paragraphs (c)(2) and (c)(3) amended, and paragraph (c)(4) adopted July 27, 2006 to be effective September 1, 2006; paragraph (b) amended June 15, 2007 to be effective September 1, 2007; subparagraph (c)(1)(C) amended July 16, 2009 to be effective September 1, 2009.

Publisher's Note

On August 22, 2000, the New Jersey Supreme Court issued the following Order:

It is ORDERED that the Court's April 29, 1997 order relaxing Rule 1:5–6 regarding the captioning and filing of adoption matters is hereby vacated, the substance of said Order having been incorporated in Rule 1:5–6 through subsequent rule amendment.

* * *

On January 3, 2002, the New Jersey Supreme Court issued the following Order:

IT IS ORDERED that pursuant to *N.J. Const.* Art. VI, § 2, par. 3, effective January 1, 2002 *nunc pro tunc* and until further order, the provisions of *Rule* 1:5–6(c)(1) of the Rules Governing the Courts of the State of New Jersey are relaxed and supplemented so as to provide that if a party petitioning for Kinship Legal Guardianship pursuant to *N.J.S.A.* 2B:12A–1 to –6 and *N.J.S.A.* 30:4C–84 to –88 submits a petition for filing without including the statutorily required Kinship Caregiver Assessment, the clerk shall return the pleading stamped "Received but not Filed [date]" with a notice that if the pleading is resubmitted together with the Kinship Caregiver Assessment within ten days after the date of the clerk's notice, the pleading will be deemed to have been filed on the stamped receipt date.

1:5–7. Non-military Affidavit

Before entry of judgment by default, an affidavit, which may be filed as part of the affidavit of proof, shall be filed as required by law setting forth facts showing that the defendant is not in military service. Unless based on facts admissible in evidence, the affidavit shall have attached to it a statement from the Department of Defense or from each branch of the armed forces that the defendant is not in the military service. If the plaintiff is unable to determine whether the defendant is in military service, the affidavit shall so state, and the court, before entering judgment, may require the plaintiff to post a bond in an amount approved by the court to indemnify the defendant, if later found to have been in military service, against any loss or damage resulting from the judgment should it be set aside. The bond shall remain in effect until expiration of the time for appeal and setting aside of the judgment.

Note: Source — R.R. 7:9–3; amended July 28, 2004 to be effective September 1, 2004; amended July 27, 2006 to be effective September 1, 2006.

RULE 1:6. MOTIONS AND BRIEFS IN THE TRIAL COURTS

1:6–1. Applicability of Rule

Rule 1:6 shall apply to all trial courts, except the municipal courts and except as otherwise provided by R. 3:26–2(d) (motions for bail reductions), R. 5:5–4 (motions in civil family actions), and R. 6:3–3 (motions in the Special Civil Part).

Note: Amended November 7, 1988 to be effective January 2, 1989; amended July 13, 1994 to be effective January 1, 1995; amended January 21, 1999 to be effective April 5, 1999.

1:6–2. Form of Motion; Hearing

(a) Generally. An application to the court for an order shall be by motion, or in special cases, by order to show cause. A motion, other than for bail pursuant to R. 3:26–2(d) or one made during a trial or hearing, shall be by notice of motion in writing unless the court permits it to be made orally. Every motion shall state the time and place when it is to be presented to the court, the grounds upon which it is made and the nature of the relief sought, and, as to motions filed in the Law Division–Civil Part only, the discovery end date or a statement that no such date has been assigned. The motion shall be accompanied by a proposed form of order in accordance with R. 3:1–4(a) or R. 4:42–1(e), as applicable. The form of order shall note whether the motion was opposed or unopposed. If the motion or response thereto relies on facts not of record or not subject of judicial notice, it shall be supported by affidavit made in compliance with R. 1:6–6. The motion shall be deemed uncontested and there shall be no right to argue orally in opposition unless responsive papers are timely filed and served stating with particularity the basis of the opposition to the relief sought. If the motion is withdrawn or the matter settled, counsel shall forthwith inform the court.

(b) Civil Motions in Chancery Division and Specially Assigned Cases; Affidavit of Non–Involvement in Medical Malpractice Action.

(1) *Generally.* When a civil action has been specially assigned to an individual judge for case management and disposition of all pretrial and trial proceedings and in all cases pending in the Superior Court, Chancery Division, the judge, on receipt of motion papers, shall determine the mode and scheduling of the disposition of the motion. Except as provided in R. 5:5–4, motions filed in causes pending in the Superior Court, Chancery Division, Family Part, shall be governed by this paragraph.

(2) *Motion for Dismissal Pursuant to N.J.S.A. 2A:53A–40.* A party moving for dismissal of the action on the ground of non-involvement in the cause of action pursuant to N.J.S.A. 2A:53A–40 of the New Jersey Medical Care Access and Responsibility and Patients First Act, N.J.S.A. 2A:53A–37 to 42, shall annex to the notice of motion an affidavit of non-involvement that complies with Rule 1:6–6. In the absence of opposition filed in accordance with Rule 1:6–3, the court shall enter an order dismissing the action as to the moving party. If opposition is filed, the court shall proceed in accordance with this rule.

(c) Civil and Family Part Discovery and Calendar Motions. Every motion in a civil case or a case in the Chancery Division, Family Part, not governed by paragraph (b), involving any aspect of pretrial discovery or the calendar, shall be listed for disposition only if accompanied by a certification stating that the attorney for the moving party has either (1) personally conferred orally or has made a specifically described good faith attempt to confer orally with the attorney for the opposing party in order to resolve the issues raised by the motion by agreement or consent order and that such effort at resolution has been unsuccessful, or (2) advised the attorney for the opposing party by letter, after the default has occurred, that continued non-compliance with a discovery obligation will result in an appropriate motion being made without further attempt to resolve the matter. A motion to extend the time for discovery shall have annexed thereto either a copy of all prior orders extending the discovery period or a certification that there have been no such prior orders. The moving papers shall also set forth the date of any scheduled pretrial conference, arbitration proceeding scheduled pursuant to R. 4:21A, calendar call or trial, or state that no such dates have been fixed. Discovery and calendar motions shall be disposed of on the papers unless, on at least two days notice, the court specifically directs oral argument on its own motion or, in its discretion, on a party's request. A movant's request for oral argument shall be made either in the moving papers or reply; a respondent's request for oral argument shall be made in the answering papers.

(d) Civil and Family Part Motions—Oral Argument. Except as otherwise provided by R. 5:5–4 (family actions), no motion shall be listed for oral argument unless a party requests oral argument in the moving papers or in timely-filed answering or reply papers, or unless the court directs. A party requesting oral argument may, however, condition the request on the motion being contested. If the motion involves pretrial discovery or is directly addressed to the calendar, the request shall be considered only if accompanied by a statement of reasons and shall be deemed denied unless the court otherwise advises counsel prior to the return day. As to all other motions, the request shall be granted as of right.

(e) Oral Argument—Mode. The court in civil matters, on its own motion or on a party's request, may direct argument of any motion by telephone conference without court appearance. A verbatim record shall be made of all such telephone arguments and the rulings thereon.

(f) Order; Record Notation. If the court has made findings of fact and conclusions of law explaining its disposition of the motion, the order shall indicate whether the findings and conclusions were written or oral and the date on which they were rendered. However, if the motion was argued and the court intends to place its findings on the record at a later date, it shall give all parties one day's notice, which may be telephonic, of the time and place it shall do so. If no such findings have been made, the court shall append to the order a statement of reasons for its disposition if it concludes that explanation is either necessary or appropriate. If the order directs a plenary or other evidential hearing, it shall specifically describe the issues to be so tried. A written order or record notation shall be entered by the court memorializing the disposition made on a telephone motion.

Note: Source—R.R. 3:11–2, 4:8–5(a) (second sentence). Amended July 14, 1972 to be effective September 5, 1972; amended November 27, 1974 to be effective April 1, 1975; amended July 24, 1978 to be effective September 11, 1978; former rule amended and redesignated as paragraph (a) and paragraphs (b), (c), (d), and (e) adopted July 16, 1981 to be effective September 14, 1981; paragraph (c) amended July 15, 1982 to be effective September 13, 1982; paragraph (c) amended July 22, 1983 to be effective September 12, 1983; paragraph (b) amended December 20, 1983 to be effective December 31, 1983; paragraphs (a) and (c) amended and paragraph (f) adopted November 1, 1985 to be effective January 2, 1986; paragraph (a) amended November 7, 1988 to be effective January 2, 1989; paragraph (c) amended and paragraph (d) caption and text amended June 29, 1990 to be effective September 4, 1990; paragraph (d) amended July 14, 1992 to be effective September 1, 1992; paragraph (c) amended July 13, 1994 to be effective September 1, 1994; paragraph (a) amended July 13, 1994 to be effective January 1, 1995; paragraphs (a) and (f) amended January 21, 1999 to be effective April 5, 1999; paragraphs (c) and (d) amended July 5, 2000 to be effective September 5, 2000; paragraph (a) amended July 28, 2004 to be effective September 1, 2004; paragraphs (b), (c), and (f) amended July 27, 2006 to be effective September 1, 2006; paragraph (b) caption amended, former text of paragraph (b) captioned and redesignated as paragraph (1), and new paragraph (2) adopted July 9, 2008 to be effective September 1, 2008.

Publisher's Note

On July 8, 2004, the New Jersey Supreme Court issued the following Order:

It is ORDERED, pursuant to N.J. Const. Art. VI, sec. 2, par. 3, that effective immediately and until further Order, Rule 1:6–2 ("Form of Motion; Hearing") of the Rules Governing the Courts of the State of New Jersey is hereby relaxed and supplemented as follows:

(1) A party filing an affidavit of non-involvement pursuant to the New Jersey Medical Care Access and Responsibility and Patients First Act (L.2004, c. 17) shall do so by annexing the affidavit, which shall comply with Rule 1:6–6, to a notice of motion for dismissal of the action as to that party; and

(2) If no opposition to the motion is filed in accordance with Rule 1:6–3, an order shall be entered dismissing the action as to the moving party; and

(3) If no opposition to the motion is filed, the court shall proceed in accordance with Rule 1:6–2.

1:6–3. Filing and Service of Motions and Cross–Motions

(a) Motions Generally. Other than an ex parte motion and except as otherwise provided by R. 4:46–1 (summary judgment) and R. 5:5–4 (c) (post judgment motions), a notice of motion shall be filed and served not later than 16 days before the specified return date unless otherwise provided by court order, which may be applied for ex parte. Thus, for example, if the return date of the motion is a Friday, the motion must be filed and served not later than the Wednesday, 16 days prior. If a motion is supported by affidavit or certification, the affidavit or certification shall be filed and served with the motion. Except as provided by R. 4:49–1(b) (motion for new trial), any opposing affidavits, certifications or objections filed pursuant to R. 1:6–2 shall be filed and served not later than 8 days before the return date unless the court relaxes that time. Thus, for example, if the return date is on a Friday, any response must be filed and served no later than Thursday of the prior week. Reply papers responding to opposing affidavits or certifications shall be filed and served not later than 4 days before the return date unless the court otherwise orders. Thus, for example, such papers must be filed and served on Monday for a return date of the following Friday. No other papers may be filed without leave of court.

(b) Cross–Motions. A cross-motion may be filed and served by the responding party together with that party's opposition to the motion and noticed for the same return date only if it relates to the subject matter of the original motion, except in Family Part motions brought under Part V of these Rules where a notice of cross-motion may seek relief unrelated to that sought in the original motion. A cross-motion relating to the subject matter of the original motion shall, if timely filed pursuant to this rule, relate back to the date of the filing of the original motion. The original moving party's response to the cross-motion shall be filed and served as provided by paragraph (a) for reply papers. The court may, however, on request of the original moving party, or on its own motion, enlarge the time for filing an answer to the cross-motion, or fix a new return date for both. No reply papers may be served or filed by the cross-movant without leave of court.

(c) Completion of Service. For purposes of this rule, service of motion papers is complete only on receipt at the office of adverse counsel or the address of a pro se party. If service is by ordinary mail, receipt will be presumed on the third business day after mailing.

Note: Source—R.R. 3:11–1, 4:6–3(a); amended July 24, 1978 to be effective September 11, 1978; amended July 16, 1979 to be effective September 10, 1979; amended July 16, 1981 to be effective September 14, 1981; amended November 1, 1985 to be effective January 2, 1986; amended June 29, 1990 to be effective September 4, 1990; amended July 13, 1994 to be effective September 1, 1994; amended and paragraphs (a), (b) and (c) designated July 10, 1998 to be effective September 1, 1998; paragraph (a) amended July 5, 2000 to be effective September 5, 2000; paragraph (b) amended July 12, 2002 to be effective September 3, 2002; paragraph (b) amended June 15, 2007 to be effective September 1, 2007; paragraph (b) amended July 16, 2009 to be effective September 1, 2009.

1:6–4. Superior Court; Place for Filing Motions, Orders to Show Cause and Orders

The original of all motion papers, orders to show cause and orders in civil actions in the Superior Court shall be filed in accordance with R. 1:5–6(b), except that in all actions in the Chancery Division or specially assigned to a judge of the Law Division or, if the judge to whom the motion is assigned is known, a copy of all motion papers shall also be simultaneously submitted to the judge.

Note: Source — R.R. 3:11–1, 4:5–5(b) (first sentence), 4:5–6(b); amended July 16, 1981 to be effective September 14, 1981; caption amended and paragraphs (a) and (b) adopted November 7, 1988 to be effective January 2, 1989; paragraph (a) amended June 29, 1990 to be effective September 4, 1990; former caption and text replaced July 13, 1994 to be effective September 1, 1994; amended June 28, 1996 to be effective September 1, 1996; amended July 27, 2006 to be effective September 1, 2006.

1:6–5. Briefs

The moving party's brief in support of a motion shall, pursuant to R. 1:6–3, be served and submitted to the court with the moving papers. The respondent shall serve and submit an answering brief at least 8 days before the return date. A reply brief, if any, shall be served and submitted at least 4 days before the return date. Briefs may not be submitted after the time fixed by this rule or by court order, including the pretrial order, without leave of court, which may be applied for ex parte.

Note: Source—R.R. 4:5–5(b) (first sentence), 4:5–10(a)(b)(c)(e); paragraph (a) amended July 16, 1979 to be effective September 10, 1979; paragraphs (a) and (b) amended July 13, 1994 to be effective September 1, 1994; amended July 10, 1998 to be effective September 1, 1998; amended July 5, 2000 to be effective September 5, 2000.

1:6–6. Evidence on Motions; Affidavits

If a motion is based on facts not appearing of record, or not judicially noticeable, the court may hear it on affidavits made on personal knowledge, setting forth only facts which are admissible in evidence to which the affiant is competent to testify and which may have annexed thereto certified copies of all papers or parts thereof referred to therein. The court may direct the affiant to submit to cross-examination, or hear the matter wholly or partly on oral testimony or depositions.

Note: Source—R.R. 4:44–4 (second sentence), 4:58–6.

1:6–7. Reading of Moving Papers and Briefs in Advance

Insofar as possible judges shall read moving papers and briefs in advance of the hearing and to this end, when briefs are submitted in the trial courts, the matter shall be assigned insofar as possible to the judge in advance of the hearing. The parties shall promptly advise the court if a motion is withdrawn or the matter settled prior to the hearing date.

Note: Source — R.R. 1:30–1; amended July 27, 2006 to be effective September 1, 2006.

1:6–8. Issuance of Process and Entry of Judgment

All motions and applications in the clerk's office for issuing original and mesne process, for issuing final process to enforce and execute judgments, for entering defaults and for other proceedings which do not require allowance or order of the court, are grantable of course by the clerk, whose action may be suspended or altered or rescinded by the court for good cause.

Note: Source—R.R. 4:118–7, 7:19–6; amended July 13, 1994 to be effective September 1, 1994.

RULE 1:7. GENERAL PROVISIONS FOR TRIALS

1:7–1. Opening and Closing Statement

(a) Opening Statement. Before any evidence is offered at trial, the State in a criminal action or the plaintiff in a civil action, unless otherwise provided in the pretrial order, shall make an opening statement. A defendant who chooses to make an opening statement shall do so immediately thereafter.

(b) Closing Statement. After the close of the evidence and except as may be otherwise ordered by the court, the parties may make closing statements in the reverse order of opening statements. In civil cases any party may suggest to the trier of fact, with respect to any element of damages, that unliquidated damages be calculated on a time-unit basis without reference to a specific sum. In the event such comments are made to a jury, the judge shall instruct the jury that they are argument only and do not constitute evidence.

Note: Source — R.R. 3:7–3, 4:44–1, 7:8–4; former rule redesignated as paragraph (a), paragraph (b) adopted and caption amended July 15, 1982 to be effective September 13, 1982; paragraph (a) amended July 13, 1994 to be effective September 1, 1994; paragraph (b) amended July 12, 2002 to be effective September 3, 2002; paragraph (b) amended July 27, 2006 to be effective September 1, 2006.

1:7–2. Objections

For the purpose of reserving questions for review or appeal relating to rulings or orders of the court or instructions to the jury, a party, at the time the ruling or order is made or sought, shall make known to the court specifically the action which the party desires the court to take or the party's objection to the action taken and the grounds therefor. Except as otherwise provided by R. 1:7–5 and R. 2:10–2 (plain error), no party may urge as error any portion of the charge to the jury or omissions therefrom unless objections are made thereto before the jury retires to consider its verdict, but opportunity shall be given to make the objection in open court, in the absence of the jury. A party shall only be prejudiced by the absence of an objection if there was an opportunity to object to a ruling, order or charge.

Note: Source—R.R. 3:7–7(b), 3:7–8, 4:47, 4:52–1 (third and fourth sentences); amended July 13, 1994 to be effective September 1, 1994.

1:7–3. Record of Excluded Evidence

If an objection to a question propounded to a witness is sustained by the court, the examining attorney may, out of the hearing of the jury (if there is a jury), make a specific offer of what is expected to be proved by the answer of the witness, and the court may add such other and further statement as clearly shows the character of the evidence, the form in which it was offered, and the ruling thereon. In actions tried without a jury the court shall upon request permit the evidence and any cross-examination relating thereto or evidence in rebuttal thereof to be taken down by the court reporter in full, or otherwise preserved, unless it clearly appears to the court that the evidence is not admissible on any ground or that the witness is privileged or unless the interest of justice otherwise requires. In actions tried with a jury the court may, in its discretion and in the absence of the jury, permit such taking and preservation of the excluded evidence.

Note: Source—R.R. 4:44–3; amended July 13, 1994 to be effective September 1, 1994.

1:7–4. Findings by the Court in Non-jury Trials and on Motions

(a) Required Findings. The court shall, by an opinion or memorandum decision, either written or oral, find the facts and state its conclusions of law thereon in all actions tried without a jury, on every motion decided by a written order that is appealable as of right, and also as required by R. 3:29. The court shall thereupon enter or direct the entry of the appropriate judgment.

(b) Motion for Amendment. On motion made not later than 20 days after service of the final order or judgment upon all parties by the party obtaining it, the court may grant a rehearing or may, on the papers submitted, amend or add to its findings and may amend the final order or judgment accordingly, but the failure of a party to make such motion or to object to the findings shall not preclude that party's right thereafter to question the sufficiency of the evidence to support the findings. The motion to amend the findings, which may be made with a motion for a new trial, shall state with specificity the basis on which it is made, including a statement of the matters or controlling decisions that counsel believes the court has overlooked or on which it has erred. Motions for reconsideration of interlocutory orders shall be determined pursuant to R. 4:42–2.

Note: Source—R.R. 3:7–1(c), 4:53–1, 4:53–2, 8:7–2(c); caption and text amended November 1, 1985 to be effective January 2, 1986; caption and text amended November 5, 1986 to be effective January 1, 1987; amended November 7, 1988 to be effective January 2, 1989; caption and text amended July 14, 1992 to be effective September 1, 1992; amended and paragraphs (a) and (b) designated July 10, 1998 to be effective September 1, 1998; paragraph (a) amended July 5, 2000 to be effective September 5, 2000.

1:7–5. Trial Errors

Any error or omission which does not prejudice a substantial right shall be disregarded by the trial court before, during and after trial. The trial court, however, at every stage of the action, including a timely application after trial, may notice any error of such a nature as to have been clearly capable of producing an unjust result, even though such error was not brought to its attention by a party.

Note: Source—R.R. 4:63–1, 4:63–2.

1:7–6. Non-public Business Records

Where the original of a non-public business record has been produced at trial and a clear copy thereof is certified and offered to the court, the court, except for good cause shown, shall permit the copy to be marked into evidence and the original to be returned to its custodian. The parties may stipulate in advance as to the admissibility of such copy.

Note: Adopted November 27, 1974 to be effective April 1, 1975.

RULE 1:8.　JURY

1:8–1.　Trial by Jury

(a) Criminal Actions. Criminal actions required to be tried by a jury shall be so tried unless the defendant, in writing and with the approval of the court, after notice to the prosecuting attorney and an opportunity to be heard, waives a jury trial. In sentencing proceedings conducted pursuant to N.J.S.A. 2C:11–3(c)(1), the consent of prosecutor shall be required for such waiver.

(b) Civil Actions. Issues in civil actions triable of right by a jury shall be so tried only if a jury trial is demanded by a party in accordance with R. 4:35–1 or R. 6:5–3, as applicable, and is not thereafter waived. If a jury of twelve is requested, that request shall be included in the jury demand.

Note: Source—R.R. 3:7–1(a), 4:40–3; paragraph (a) amended September 28, 1982 to be effective immediately; paragraph (a) amended July 13, 1994 to be effective September 1, 1994; captions added to paragraphs (a) and (b) and paragraph (b) amended July 10, 1998 to be effective September 1, 1998.

1:8–2.　Number of Jurors

(a) Number Deliberating in Criminal Actions. A deliberating jury in a criminal action shall consist of 12 persons, but at any time before verdict the parties may stipulate that the jury shall consist of any number less than 12 except in the trials of crimes punishable by death. Such stipulations shall be in writing and with the approval of the court.

(b) Number Deliberating in Civil Actions. A deliberating jury in a civil action shall consist of six persons unless:

(1) for good cause shown the court orders a jury of 12 persons pursuant to a demand made in accordance with R. 1:8–1(b); or

(2) fewer than six jurors remain prior to commencement of deliberations and the parties then agree on the record to submit the case to the remaining jurors; or

(3) more than six jurors remain prior to the commencement of deliberations and the parties then agree on the record that all remaining jurors shall deliberate.

(c) Verdict in Civil Actions.

(1) Unless the parties have agreed on the record prior to commencement of deliberations to accept a verdict or finding by a lesser number, the verdict or finding shall be by agreement of five jurors when six jurors deliberate, and by 10 jurors when 12 jurors deliberate.

(2) If the parties have agreed on the record to submit the case to fewer than six jurors, pursuant to paragraph (b)(2) of this rule, the verdict or finding shall be unanimous, unless the parties have also agreed on the record prior to commencement of deliberations to a verdict or finding by a lesser number.

(3) If the parties have agreed on the record to more than six jurors pursuant to paragraph (b)(3) of this rule, the verdict or finding shall be by agreement of five-sixths of the deliberating jurors, unless the parties have otherwise agreed on the record prior to commencement of deliberations.

(d) Alternate Jurors;　Civil and Criminal Actions.

(1) *All Actions.* The court in its discretion may direct the impanelling of a jury of such number as it deems necessary to ensure that a sufficient number of jurors will remain to deliberate. If a juror is excused after being sworn but before opening statements begin, another juror may be impanelled and sworn, but no juror may be empaneled and sworn thereafter. All the jurors shall sit and hear the case, but the court for good cause shown may excuse any of them from service provided the number of jurors is not reduced to less than 12 or 6 as the case may be or such other number as may be stipulated. If more than such number are left on the jury at the conclusion of the court's charge, the clerk of the court in the jury's presence shall randomly draw such number of names as will reduce the jury to the number required to determine the issues. Following the drawing of the names of jurors to determine the issues, the court may in its discretion order that the alternate jurors not be discharged, in which event the alternate jurors shall be sequestered apart from the other jurors and shall be subject to the same orders and instructions of the court, with respect to sequestration and other matters, as the other jurors. If the alternate jurors are not discharged and if at any time after submission of the case to the jury, a juror dies or is discharged by the court because of illness or other inability to continue, the court may direct the clerk to draw the name of an alternate juror to take the place of the juror who is deceased or discharged. When such a substitution of an alternate juror is made, the court shall instruct the jury to recommence deliberations and shall give the jury such other supplemental instructions as may be appropriate.

(2) *Civil Actions.* In civil actions, instead of selecting alternate jurors, the parties may agree on the record, pursuant to paragraph (b)(3) of this rule, that all remaining jurors shall deliberate and that the verdict or finding shall be returned by such number as is provided by paragraph (c)(3) of this rule.

Note:　Source—R.R.　3:7–1(b),　3:7–2(d),　4:48–2, 4:49–1(a)(b).　Amended July 7, 1971 to be effective September 13, 1971; paragraph (d) amended July 14, 1972 to be effective September 5, 1972; paragraph (d) amended June 29, 1973 to be effective September 10, 1973; paragraph (b) amended July 17, 1975 to be effective September 8, 1975; paragraph (d) amended July 29, 1977 to be effective September 6, 1977; paragraph (d) amended July 21, 1980 to be effective September 8, 1980; paragraph (a) amended September 28, 1982 to be effective immediately; paragraph (d) amended July 13, 1994 to be effective September 1, 1994; amended July 10, 1998 to be effective September 1, 1998.

1:8–3. Examination of Jurors; Challenges

(a) Examination of Jurors. For the purpose of determining whether a challenge should be interposed, the court shall interrogate the prospective jurors in the box after the required number are drawn without placing them under oath. The parties or their attorneys may supplement the court's interrogation in its discretion. At trials of crimes punishable by death, the examination shall be made of each juror individually, as his name is drawn, and under oath.

(b) Challenges in the Array; Challenges for Cause. Any party may challenge the array in writing on the ground that the jurors were not selected, drawn or summoned according to law. A challenge to the array shall be decided before any individual juror is examined. A challenge to any individual juror which by law is ground of challenge for cause must be made before the juror is sworn to try the case, but the court for good cause may permit it to be made after the juror is sworn but before any evidence is presented. All challenges shall be tried by the court.

(c) Peremptory Challenges in Civil Actions. In civil actions each party shall be entitled to 6 peremptory challenges. Parties represented by the same attorney shall be deemed 1 party for the purposes of this rule. Where, however, multiple parties having a substantial identity of interest in one or more issues are represented by different attorneys, the trial court in its discretion may, on application of counsel prior to the selection of the jury, accord the adverse party such additional number of peremptory challenges as it deems appropriate in order to avoid unfairness to the adverse party.

(d) Peremptory Challenges in Criminal Actions. Upon indictment for kidnapping, murder, aggravated manslaughter, manslaughter, aggravated assault, aggravated sexual assault, sexual assault, aggravated criminal sexual contact, aggravated arson, arson, burglary, robbery, forgery if it constitutes a crime of the third degree as defined by N.J.S.A. 2C:21–1b, or perjury, the defendant shall be entitled to 20 peremptory challenges if tried alone and to 10 such challenges when tried jointly; and the State shall have 12 peremptory challenges if the defendant is tried alone and 6 peremptory challenges for each 10 afforded defendants when tried jointly. In other criminal actions each defendant shall be entitled to 10 peremptory challenges and the State shall have 10 peremptory challenges for each 10 challenges afforded defendants. The trial judge shall have the discretionary authority to increase proportionally the number of peremptory challenges available to the defendant and the State in any case in which the sentencing procedure set forth in subsection c. of N.J.S. 2C:11–3 might be utilized. When the case is to be tried by a foreign jury, each defendant shall be entitled to 5 peremptory challenges, and the State 5 peremptory challenges for each 5 peremptory challenges afforded defendants.

(e) Order of Exercising of Peremptory Challenges.

(1) In any case in which each side is entitled to an equal number of challenges, those challenges shall alternate one by one, with the State in a criminal case and the plaintiff in a civil case exercising the first challenge.

(2) In any case in which there is more than one defendant and/or an uneven number of peremptory challenges, the court shall establish the order of challenge, which shall be set forth on the record prior to the commencement of the jury selection process.

(3) The passing of a peremptory challenge by any party shall not constitute a waiver of the right thereafter to exercise the same against any juror, unless all parties pass successive challenges.

(f) Conference Before Examination. Prior to the examination of the prospective jurors, the court shall hold a conference on the record to determine the areas of inquiry during voir dire. Attorneys shall submit proposed voir dire questions in writing in advance. If requested, the court shall determine whether the attorneys may participate in the questioning of the prospective jurors and, if so, to what extent. During the course of the questioning, additional questions of prospective jurors may be requested and asked as appropriate under the circumstances. The judge shall rule on the record on the proposed voir dire questions and on any requested attorney participation.

Note: Source — R.R. 3:7–2(b)(c), 4:48–1, 4:48–3. Paragraphs (c) and (d) amended July 7, 1971 to be effective September 13, 1971; paragraph (d) amended July 21, 1980 to be effective September 8, 1980; paragraph (a) amended September 28, 1982 to be effective immediately; paragraph (d) amended July 22, 1983 to be effective September 12, 1983; paragraph (d) amended July 26, 1984 to be effective September 10, 1984; paragraph (d) amended November 5, 1986 to be effective January 1, 1987; paragraph (c) amended November 7, 1988 to be effective January 2, 1989; paragraph (e) added July 14, 1992 to be effective September 1, 1992; paragraph (b) amended July 13, 1994 to be effective September 1, 1994; paragraph (f) added July 5, 2000 to be effective September 5, 2000; paragraph (f) amended July 27, 2006 to be effective September 1, 2006.

1:8–4. Foreperson

Juror number one shall be the foreperson; but if that juror is thereafter selected as an alternate juror or otherwise discharged, then the juror next drawn on the impanelling of a jury, who remains on the jury for the determination of the issues, shall be the foreperson.

Note: Source—R.R. 3:7–2(e), 4:48–2 (last phrase). Amended July 7, 1971 to be effective September 13, 1971; former rule deleted and new rule adopted June 29, 1973 to be effective September 10, 1973; caption and text amended June 29, 1990 to be effective September 4, 1990.

1:8–5. Availability of Petit Jury List

The list of the general panel of petit jurors shall be made available by the clerk of the court to any party requesting the same at least ten days prior to the date fixed for trial. In cases where the death penalty may be imposed, the list shall be made available to any party requesting it at least twenty days prior to the date fixed for trial.

Note: Source—R.R. 3:7–2(a). Amended July 16, 1979 to be effective September 10, 1979; amended September 28, 1982 to be effective immediately.

1:8–6.　Sequestration of Juries

(a) **Prior to Instructing of Jury.** The jury shall not be sequestered in any action, civil or criminal, prior to the instructing of the jury by the court, unless the court, in its discretion so orders on its finding that there are extraordinary circumstances requiring sequestration for the protection of the jurors or in the interests of justice.

(b) **Following Instructing of Jury.** Following the instructing of the jury by the court and during the course of deliberations, the court may, in its discretion, in both civil and criminal actions, permit the dispersal of the jury for the night, for meals, and during other authorized intermissions in the deliberations.

Note: Source—R.R. 3:7–2(f). Amended July 14, 1972 to be effective September 5, 1972.

1:8–7.　Requests to Charge the Jury

(a) **Generally.** Either within the time provided by R. 4:25–7 or thereafter but before the close of the evidence, as to issues not anticipated prior to trial, any party may submit written requests that the court instruct the jury on the law as set forth in the requests. The requests shall make specific reference to the Model Civil Jury Charges, if applicable, or to applicable law. Copies of the requests shall be furnished all parties at the time they are submitted to the court. The court shall, on the record, rule on the requests prior to closing arguments to the jury. A verbatim record shall be made of any charge conference the court holds. Objections to the instructions to the jury shall be in accordance with R. 1:7–2.

(b) **In Criminal Cases.** Prior to closing arguments, the court shall hold a charge conference on the record in all criminal cases. At the conference the court shall advise counsel of the offenses, defenses and other legal issues to be charged and shall rule on requests made by counsel.

Note: Source—R.R. 3:7–7(a), 4:52–1 (first and second sentences); amended July 21, 1980 to be effective September 8, 1980; paragraph (a) caption and new paragraph (b) added July 13, 1994 to be effective September 1, 1994; paragraph (a) amended July 10, 1998 to be effective September 1, 1998; paragraph (a) amended July 5, 2000 to be effective September 5, 2000.

1:8–8.　Materials to be Submitted to the Jury; Note–taking; Juror Questions

(a) **Materials.** The jury may take into the jury room the exhibits received in evidence, and if the court so directs in a civil action, a list of the claims made by the parties and of the defenses to such claims, a list of the various items of damage upon which proof was submit-

ted at the trial and a list of the verdicts that may be properly found by the jury. Any such list may be prepared by an attorney or the court, but before delivery to the jury, it shall be submitted to all parties. The court, in its discretion, may submit a copy of all or part of its instructions to the jury for its consideration in the jury room. The court may also, in its discretion and at such time and in such format as it shall determine, permit the submission to the jury of individual copies of any exhibit provided an appropriate request to employ that technique was made prior to trial on notice to all parties and provided further that the court finds that no party will be unduly prejudiced by the procedure.

(b) **Juror Note-taking.** Prior to opening statements, the attorneys or any party may request that the jury be permitted to take notes during the trial or portion thereof, including opening and closing statements. If the court determines to permit note-taking after all parties have had an opportunity to be heard, it shall provide the jurors with note-taking materials and shall take such steps as will ensure the security and confidentiality of each juror's notes.

(c) **Juror Questions.** Prior to the commencement of the *voir dire* of prospective jurors in a civil action, the court shall determine whether to allow jurors to propose questions to be asked of the witnesses. The court shall make its determination after the parties have been given an opportunity to address the issue, but they need not consent. If the court determines to permit jurors to submit proposed questions, it shall explain to the jury in its opening remarks that subject to the rules of evidence and the court's discretion, questions by the jurors will be allowed for the purpose of clarifying the testimony of a witness. The jurors' questions shall be submitted to the court in writing at the conclusion of the testimony of each witness and before the witness is excused. The court, with counsel, shall review the questions out of the presence of the jury. Counsel shall state on the record any objections they may have, and the court shall rule on the permissibility of each question. The witness shall then be recalled, and the court shall ask the witness those questions ruled permissible. Counsel shall, on request, be permitted to reopen direct and cross-examination to respond to the jurors' questions and the witness's answers. A witness who has been excused shall not be recalled to respond to juror questions unless all counsel and the court agree or unless the court otherwise orders for good cause shown.

Note: Source — R.R. 4:52–2; caption and text amended July 15, 1982 to be effective September 13, 1982; amended and paragraphs (a) and (b) designated July 10, 1998 to be effective September 1, 1998; new paragraph (c) added July 12, 2002 to be effective September 3, 2002; caption amended July 28, 2004 to be effective September 1, 2004; paragraph (c) amended July 27, 2006 to be effective September 1, 2006.

1:8–9. Return of Verdict

In every trial by jury the verdict shall be returned by the jury to the judge in open court. The verdict shall be unanimous in all criminal actions and shall be rendered in civil actions by the number required by R. 1:8–2(c).

Note: Source—R.R. 3:7–9(a), 4:40–4, 7:8–6; amended July 10, 1998 to be effective September 1, 1998.

1:8–10. Polling of Jury

Before the verdict is recorded, the jury shall be polled at the request of any party or upon the court's motion, and it shall be polled in every civil action if the verdict is not unanimous. If the poll discloses that there is not unanimous concurrence in a criminal action or concurrence by the number required by R. 1:8–2(c) in a civil action, the jury may be directed to retire for further deliberations or discharged.

Note: Source—R.R. 3:7B9(d), 4:49B2; amended July 10, 1998 to be effective September 1, 1998.

RULE 1:9. SUBPOENAS

1:9–1. For Attendance of Witnesses; Forms; Issuance; Notice in Lieu of Subpoena

A subpoena may be issued by the clerk of the court or by an attorney or party in the name of the clerk or as provided by R. R. 7:7–8 (subpoenas in certain cases in the municipal court). It shall state the name of the court and the title of the action and shall command each person to whom it is directed to attend and give testimony at the time and place specified therein. If the witness is to testify in a criminal action for the State or an indigent defendant, the subpoena shall so note, and shall contain an order to appear without the prepayment of any witness fee. The testimony of a party who could be subpoenaed may be compelled by a notice in lieu of subpoena served upon the party's attorney demanding that the attorney produce the client at trial. If the party is a corporation or other organization, the testimony of any person deposable on its behalf, under R. 4:14–2, may be compelled by like notice. The notice shall be served in accordance with R. 1:5–2 at least 5 days before trial. The sanctions of R. 1:2–4 shall apply to a failure to respond to a notice in lieu of a subpoena.

Note: Source—R.R. 3:5–10(a)(b), 4:46–1, 6:3–7(a), 7:4–3 (second paragraph), 8:4–9(a)(b); caption and text amended November 27, 1974 to be effective April 1, 1975; amended July 13, 1994 to be effective September 1, 1994; amended January 5, 1998 to be effective February 1, 1998.

1:9–2. For Production of Documentary Evidence and Electronically Stored Information; Notice in Lieu of Subpoena

A subpoena or, in a civil action, a notice in lieu of subpoena as authorized by R. 1:9–1 may require production of books, papers, documents, electronically stored information, or other objects designated therein. The court on motion made promptly may quash or modify the subpoena or notice if compliance would be unreasonable or oppressive and, in a civil action, may condition denial of the motion upon the advancement by the person in whose behalf the subpoena or notice is issued of the reasonable cost of producing the objects subpoenaed. The court may direct that the objects designated in the subpoena or notice be produced before the court at a time prior to the trial or prior to the time when they are to be offered in evidence and may upon their production permit them or portions of them to be inspected by the parties and their attorneys and, in matrimonial actions and juvenile proceedings, by a probation officer or other person designated by the court. Except for pretrial production directed by the court pursuant to this rule, subpoenas for pretrial production shall comply with the requirements of R. 4:14–7(c).

Note: Source — R.R. 3:5–10(c), 4:46–2, 6:3–7(b), 7:4–3 (second paragraph), 8:4–9(c); amended November 27, 1974 to be effective April 1, 1975; amended June 29, 1990 to be effective September 4, 1990; caption and text amended July 27, 2006 to be effective September 1, 2006.

1:9–3. Service

A subpoena may be served by any person 18 or more years of age. Service of a subpoena shall be made by delivering a copy thereof to the person named together with tender of the fee allowed by law, except that if the person is a witness in a criminal action for the State or an indigent defendant, the fee shall be paid before leaving the court at the conclusion of the trial by the sheriff or, in the municipal court, by the clerk thereof.

Note: Source—R.R. 3:5–10(b) (last sentence), 3:5–10(d), 4:46–3, 5:2–2, 6:3–7(c), 7:4–6(a) (last sentence), 8:4–9(d); amended July 13, 1994 to be effective September 1, 1994.

1:9–4. Place of Service

A subpoena requiring the attendance of a witness at a hearing in any court may be served at any place within the State of New Jersey.

Note: Source—R.R. 3:5–10(e), 6:3–7(d), 7:4–6(b), 8:4–9(e).

1:9–5. Failure to Appear

Failure without adequate excuse to obey a subpoena served upon any person may be deemed a contempt of the court from which the subpoena issued.

Note: Source—R.R. 3:5–10(f), 6:3–7(e), 8:4–9(f); amended July 13, 1994 to be effective September 1, 1994.

1:9–6. Enforcement of Subpoena of Public Officer or Agency

(a) Ex Parte Application for Compliance. Where by statute a public officer or agency may apply ex parte to the court to compel a person to testify or to produce or file books, papers, documents or other objects in accordance with the subpoena or direction of the officer or agency, or to refrain from certain misconduct, the application may be made by motion supported by affidavit. The court may order the person to appear before the officer or agency and there to proceed as may be directed in the order.

(b) Application for Compliance on Notice. If in such a case the statute does not provide for an application ex parte, an order to show cause may issue on the motion and supporting affidavit. The order shall be made returnable in not less than 2 nor more than 10 days, requiring such person to show cause before the court why the subpoena or other direction should not be complied with or such misconduct refrained from, and upon the return of the order the court shall afford the person an opportunity to be heard under oath. The court may order a person determined by it to have failed, without justification, to obey the subpoena or other direction, answer a proper question, produce any such thing, or to have been guilty of misconduct, to appear before the officer or agency at a time or times and place mentioned in the order and there to proceed as may be directed in the order.

(c) Application for Sanctions. Where a statute provides that failure of a person to obey a subpoena or order of a public officer or administrative agency or a receiver, to testify, to answer a proper question, or to produce books, papers, documents or other objects, or that misconduct on the part of a person attending a hearing, shall be punishable by the court in the same manner as like failure or misconduct is punishable in an action pending in the court, the matter shall be brought before the court by motion supported by affidavit stating the circumstances. Upon the motion the court may issue an order to show cause, returnable in not less than 2 nor more than 10 days, requiring the person to show cause before the court why punishment should not be ordered; or the court may issue an attachment. If the court determines that the failure or misconduct above mentioned was without justification, it may punish as for a contempt of court.

Note: Source—R.R. 4:46–5(a)(b)(c); paragraphs (b) and (c) amended July 13, 1994 to be effective September 1, 1994.

RULE 1:10. CONTEMPT OF COURT; ENFORCEMENT OF LITIGANT'S RIGHTS

1:10–1. Summary Contempt in Presence of Court

A judge conducting a judicial proceeding may adjudicate contempt summarily without an order to show cause if:

(a) the conduct has obstructed, or if continued would obstruct, the proceeding;

(b) the conduct occurred in the actual presence of the judge, and was actually seen or heard by the judge;

(c) the character of the conduct or its continuation after an appropriate warning unmistakably demonstrates its willfulness;

(d) immediate adjudication is necessary to permit the proceeding to continue in an orderly and proper manner; and

(e) the judge has afforded the alleged contemnor an immediate opportunity to respond.

The order of contempt shall recite the facts and contain a certification by the judge that he or she saw or heard the conduct constituting the contempt and that the contemnor was willfully contumacious. Punishment may be determined forthwith or deferred. Execution of sentence shall be stayed for five days following imposition and, if an appeal is taken, during the pendency of the appeal, provided, however, that the judge may require bail if reasonably necessary to assure the contemnor's appearance.

Note: Source—R.R. 4:87–1, 8:8; amended July 13, 1994 to be effective September 1, 1994.

1:10–2. Summary Contempt Proceedings on Order to Show Cause or Order for Arrest

(a) Institution of Proceedings. Every summary proceeding to punish for contempt other than proceedings under R. 1:10–1 shall be on notice and instituted only by the court upon an order for arrest or an order to show cause specifying the acts or omissions alleged to have been contumacious. The proceedings shall be captioned "In the Matter of _____ Charged with Contempt of Court."

(b) Release Pending Hearings. A person charged with contempt under R. 1:10–2 shall be released on his or her own recognizance pending the hearing unless the judge determines that bail is reasonably necessary to assure appearance. The amount and sufficiency of bail shall be reviewable by a single judge of the Appellate Division.

(c) Prosecution and Trial. A proceeding under R. 1:10–2 may be prosecuted on behalf of the court only by the Attorney General, the County Prosecutor of the county or, where the court for good cause designates an attorney, then by the attorney so designated. The matter shall not be heard by the judge who instituted the prosecution if the appearance of objectivity requires trial by another judge. Unless there is a right to a trial by jury, the court in its discretion may try the matter without a jury. If there is an adjudication of contempt, the provisions of R. 1:10–1 as to stay of execution of sentence shall apply.

Note: Source—R.R. 4:87–2; former R. 1:10–2 redesignated R. 1:10–2(a), former R. 1:10–3 amended, recaptioned and redesignated R. 1:10–2(b) and former R. 1:10–4 amended, recaptioned and redesignated R. 1:10–2(c) July 13, 1994 to be effective September 1, 1994.

1:10–3. Relief to Litigant

Notwithstanding that an act or omission may also constitute a contempt of court, a litigant in any action may seek relief by application in the action. A judge shall not be disqualified because he or she signed the order sought to be enforced. If an order entered on such an application provides for commitment, it shall specify the terms of release provided, however, that no order for commitment shall be entered to enforce a judgment or order exclusively for the payment of money, except for orders and judgments based on a claim for equitable relief including orders and judgments of the Family Part and except if a judgment creditor demonstrates to the court that the judgment debtor has assets that have been secreted or otherwise placed beyond the reach of execution. The court in its discretion may make an allowance for counsel fees to be paid by any party to the action to a party accorded relief under this rule. In family actions, the court may also grant additional remedies as provided by R. 5:3–7. An application by a litigant may be tried with a proceeding under R. 1:10–2(a) only with the consent of all parties and subject to the provisions of R. 1:10–2(c).

Note: Source—R.R. 4:87–5; amended July 26, 1984 to be effective September 10, 1984; former R. 1:10–3 recaptioned and redesignated R. 1:10–2(b), former R. 1:10–4 recaptioned and redesignated R. 1:10–2(c), and former R. 1:10–5 amended and redesignated R. 1:10–3 July 13, 1994 to be effective September 1, 1994; amended July 10, 1998 to be effective September 1, 1998; amended January 21, 1999 to be effective April 5, 1999.

RULE 1:11. WITHDRAWAL, SUBSTITUTION, TERMINATION OF RESPONSIBILITY OF ATTORNEY

1:11–1. Death, Removal or Disbarment of Attorney

In the event an attorney dies, or ceases to be authorized by R. 1:21–1 to practice in this State, or is disbarred, suspended or resigns, any party to a pending action may notify the client in the manner prescribed by R. 1:5–2 to appoint another attorney and, if the client fails to do so within 20 days after the notice, any party may proceed with the action. A new attorney retained by the client shall file an appearance promptly.

Note: Source—R.R. 1:12–7; amended July 13, 1994 to be effective September 1, 1994.

1:11–2. Withdrawal or Substitution

(a) Generally. Except as otherwise provided by R. 5:3–5(d) (withdrawal in a civil family action),

(1) prior to the entry of a plea in a criminal action or prior to the fixing of a trial date in a civil action, an attorney may withdraw upon the client's consent provided a substitution of attorney is filed naming the substituted attorney or indicating that the client will appear pro se. If the client will appear pro se, the withdrawing attorney shall file a substitution. An attorney retained by a client who had appeared pro se shall file a substitution, and

(2) after the entry of a plea in a criminal action or the fixing of a trial date in a civil action, an attorney may withdraw without leave of court only upon the filing of the client's written consent, a substitution of attorney executed by both the withdrawing attorney and the substituted attorney, a written waiver by all other parties of notice and the right to be heard, and a certification by both the withdrawing attorney and the substituted attorney that the withdrawal and substitution will not cause or result in delay.

(b) Professional Associations. If a partnership or attorney assumes the status of a professional corporation, or limited liability entity, pursuant to Rules 1:21-1A, 1:21-1B or 1:21-1C, respectively, or if a professional corporation or a limited liability entity for the practice of law dissolves and reverts to an unincorporated status, it shall not be necessary for the firm to file substitutions of attorney in its pending matters provided that the firm name, except for the addition or deletion of the entity designation, is not changed as a result of the change in status.

Note: Source — R.R. 1:12–7A; amended July 16, 1981 to be effective September 14, 1981; amended November 7, 1988 to be effective January 2, 1989; amended June 28, 1996 to be effective September 1, 1996; amended July 10, 1998 to be effective September 1, 1998; amended and paragraph designations and captions added January 21, 1999 to be effective April 5, 1999; paragraphs (a)(1) and (a)(2) amended July 27, 2006 to be effective September 1, 2006.

1:11–3. Termination of Responsibility in the Trial Court; Responsibility on Appeal

The responsibility of an attorney of record in any trial court with respect to the further conduct of the proceedings shall terminate upon the expiration of the time for appeal from the final judgment or order entered therein. For purposes of appeal or certification, however, the attorney of record for the adverse party in the court below shall be considered as attorney for the respondent, and notice and papers served upon that attorney shall be deemed good service until the appellant or petitioner is notified of an appearance entered by a new attorney or is given written notice by the respondent naming another attorney.

Note: Source—R.R. 1:12–3(a), 2:10; amended July 13, 1994 to be effective September 1, 1994.

RULE 1:12. DISQUALIFICATION AND DISABILITY OF JUDGES

1:12–1. Cause for Disqualification; on the Court's Motion

The judge of any court shall be disqualified on the court's own motion and shall not sit in any matter, if the judge

(a) is by blood or marriage the second cousin of or is more closely related to any party to the action;

(b) is by blood or marriage the first cousin of or is more closely related to any attorney in the action. This proscription shall extend to the partners, employers, employees or office associates of any such attorney except where the Chief Justice for good cause otherwise permits;

(c) has been attorney of record or counsel in the action; or

(d) has given an opinion upon a matter in question in the action; or

(e) is interested in the event of the action; or

(f) when there is any other reason which might preclude a fair and unbiased hearing and judgment, or which might reasonably lead counsel or the parties to believe so.

Paragraphs (c), (d) and (e) shall not prevent a judge from sitting because of having given an opinion in another action in which the same matter in controversy came in question or given an opinion on any question in controversy in the pending action in the course of previous proceedings therein, or because the board of chosen freeholders of a county or the municipality in which the judge resides or is liable to be taxed are or may be parties to the record or otherwise interested.

Note: Source—R.R. 1:25B(a); introductory paragraph, paragraph (d), and concluding paragraph amended July 13, 1994 to be effective September 1, 1994.

1:12–2. Disqualification on Party's Motion

Any party, on motion made to the judge before trial or argument and stating the reasons therefor, may seek that judge's disqualification.

Note: Source—R.R. 1:25B(b); amended June 28, 1996 to be effective September 1, 1996.

1:12–3. Proceedings in the Trial Courts in the Event of Disqualification or Inability

(a) Before or After Trial; Designation. In the event of the disqualification or inability for any reason of a judge to hear any pending matter before or after trial, another judge of the court in which the matter is pending or a judge temporarily assigned to hear the matter shall be designated by the Chief Justice or by the Assignment Judge of the county where the matter is pending except that in the municipal court the Assignment Judge shall designate the acting judge and in the Tax Court the Chief Justice or the Presiding Judge of the Tax Court shall designate another Tax Court judge.

(b) During Trial. If a judge is prevented during a trial from continuing to preside therein, another judge may be designated to complete the trial as if having presided from its commencement, provided, however, that the substituted judge is able to become familiar with the proceedings and all of the testimony therein through a complete transcript thereof.

(c) Disposition in the Interest of Justice. No substituted judge shall continue the trial in any matter pursuant to this rule unless satisfied, under the circumstances, that the judicial duties can fairly be discharged. If not so satisfied, the substituted judge shall make such disposition as the circumstances warrant, as where trial has taken place, by ordering a new trial or, in a case tried without a jury, by directing the recall of any witness.

Note: Source—R.R. 3:7–4(a), (b), (c), 4:65, 6:2–1(b), 8:7–9, 8:13–2; paragraph (a) amended November 27, 1974 to be effective April 1, 1975; paragraph (a) amended June 20, 1979 to be effective July 1, 1979; paragraphs (b) and (c) amended July 13, 1994 to be effective September 1, 1994.

RULE 1:13. MISCELLANEOUS RULES AS TO PROCEDURE

1:13–1. Clerical Mistakes

Clerical mistakes in judgments, orders or other parts of the record and errors therein arising from oversight and omission may at any time be corrected by the court on its own initiative or on the motion of any party, and on such notice and terms as the court directs, notwithstanding the pendency of an appeal.

Note: Source—R.R. 3:7–14, 4:62–1, 8:7–12.

1:13–2. Proceedings by Indigents

(a) **Waiver of Fees.** Except when otherwise specifically provided by these rules, whenever any person by reason of poverty seeks relief from the payment of any fees provided for by law which are payable to any court or clerk of court including the office of the surrogate or any public officer of this State, any court upon the verified application of such person, which application may be filed without fee, may in its discretion order the payment of such fees waived. In any case in which a person is represented by a legal aid society, a Legal Services project, private counsel representing indigents in cooperation with any of the preceding entities, the Office of the Public Defender, or counsel assigned in accordance with these rules, all such fees and any charges of public officers of this State for service of process shall be waived without the necessity of a court order.

(b) **Compensation of Attorneys.** Except as provided by any order of the court, no attorney assigned to represent a person by reason of poverty shall take or agree to take or seek to obtain from the client, payment of any fee, profit or reward for the conduct of such proceedings for office or other expenses; but no attorney shall be required to expend any personal funds in the prosecution of the cause.

Note: Source—R.R. 1:27E, 4:98–2(c). Paragraph (a) amended and paragraph (b) adopted July 7, 1971 to be effective September 13, 1971; paragraph (a) amended July 29, 1977 to be effective September 6, 1977; amended May 3, 1982 to be effective immediately; paragraph (a) amended July 22, 1983 to be effective September 12, 1983; paragraph (b) amended July 13, 1994 to be effective September 1, 1994.

1:13–3. Approval and Filing of Surety Bond; Judgment Against Principal and Surety

(a) **Approval by the Court.** Neither the clerk of the court, the sheriff, nor any other person shall accept a surety bond in any action or proceeding pending in the court, other than a bond for costs given by a non-resident claimant, unless the same has been approved as to form and sufficiency by a judge of any court of this State except that a surrogate may approve and accept a bond, and in the absence of a judge the clerk may approve and accept a bail bond. Bonds need not be filed in duplicate.

(b) **Contents.** All surety and bail bonds given in any court shall provide that the principal and surety thereby submit themselves to the jurisdiction of the court (or to the jurisdiction of the trial court, if the bond is given in an appellate court); that they irrevocably appoint the clerk of the court having jurisdiction as their agent upon whom papers affecting their liability on the bond may be served; that they waive any right to a jury trial; that the liability of the principal and surety may be enforced by motion in the action, if one is pending, without the necessity of an independent action; and that the motion may be served on the principal and surety by mailing it, by ordinary mail, to the clerk of the court, or to the surrogate in the case of a bond approved by the Chancery Division, Probate Part or the surrogate, who shall forthwith mail copies thereof by ordinary mail to the principal and surety at the addresses stated in the bond.

(c) **Cash Deposit.** Whenever a bond with sureties is required, the court, including the Surrogate, may by order allow a cash deposit in lieu thereof.

(d) **Registry of Insurers.** No surety bond for purposes of bail shall be accepted by any court unless the insurer has first filed with the Clerk of the Superior Court a Bail Program Registration Form in the form prescribed by Appendix XXI to these rules. Said form shall include the insurer's certification that it is authorized or admitted to transact surety business by the New Jersey Department of Banking and Insurance and shall include the name and address of each of its bail agents and agencies, any other person or entity who has provided it with a guarantee to satisfy forfeited bail or a bail forfeiture judgment, and any other person or entity authorized by the insurer to administer or manage its bail bond business. The bail agents and agencies so registered by the insurer shall be licensed as insurance producers or limited lines insurance producers. The insurer shall have a continuing obligation to update its Bail Program Registration Form as changes occur in order to assure that the information is complete and accurate.

(e) **Removal from Bail Registry.**

(1) *Licensure.* A registered insurer shall be removed from the Bail Registry on 30 days notice if it fails to provide complete and accurate information as required by the Bail Program Registration Form. A registered insurer who fails to maintain its authorization or admission to transact surety business in this State or a registered bail agent or agency, guarantor, or other person administering or managing an insurer's bail bond business if it fails to maintain any license required by the Department of Banking and Insurance shall be forthwith removed from the Bail Registry.

(2) *Failure to Satisfy Judgment.* If a registered insurer fails to satisfy a judgment entered pursuant to R.

3:26–6(c) or R. 7:4–5(c), the Clerk of the Superior Court shall forthwith send the insurer a notice informing it that if it fails to satisfy the judgment within fifteen days of the notice, it shall be removed from the Bail Registry until satisfaction is made. Further, the insurer's bail agents and agencies, guarantors, and other persons or entities authorized to administer or manage its bail bond business in this State will have no further authority to act for it. Their names, as acting for the insurer, will be removed from the Bail Registry. In addition, the bail agent or agency, guarantor, or other person or entity authorized by the insurer to administer or manage its bail bond business in this State who acted in such capacity with respect to the forfeited bond will be precluded, by removal from the Bail Registry, from so acting for any other insurer until the judgment has been satisfied.

(3) *Habitual Noncompliance.* Unless the court orders otherwise, nothing herein shall preclude the Clerk of the Superior Court, on 30 days' notice, from removing from the Bail Registry any person or entity habitually failing to perform the obligations imposed by the bail bonds.

(4) *Notice.* All notices required by this rule shall be sent by certified mail, return receipt requested, to the address listed on the Bail Program Registration Form.

Note: Source—R.R. 1:4–8(b), 1:4–9, 3:9–7(c) (second, third and fourth sentences), 4:72–2, 4:118–6(a)(b). Paragraph (a) amended July 7, 1971 to be effective September 13, 1971; paragraph (b) amended July 14, 1972 to be effective September 5, 1972; paragraphs (a) and (b) amended July 13, 1994 to be effective September 1, 1994; paragraph (c) amended June 28, 1996 to be effective September 1, 1996; new sections (d) and (e) added July 5, 2000 to be effective September 5, 2000; paragraph (d) amended May 20, 2003 to be effective immediately; paragraph (a) amended, former paragraph (d) deleted and new paragraph (d) adopted, text of paragraph (e) deleted and new text adopted July 28, 2004 to be effective September 1, 2004.

Publisher's Note

On August 31, 2004, the New Jersey Supreme Court issued the following Order

IT IS ORDERED, that the Court's November 1, 2000 Order, which set out the notice and procedural requirements to be followed in bail forfeitures and judgments, and the amendatory Orders dated June 11, 2002 (to modify the time permitted to file an objection to set aside a bail forfeiture preclusion) and May 20, 2003 (to conform to statutory changes effected by the New Jersey Insurance Producer Act of 2001 (L.2001, c. 210) are hereby terminated effective September 1, 2004, the effective date of the July 28, 2004 amendments to Rules 1:13–3, 2:9–6, 3:26–6, 7:4–3 and 7:4–5.

1:13–4.　Transfer of Actions

(a) **On Motion.** Subject to the right to be prosecuted by indictment, if any court is without jurisdiction of the subject matter of an action or issue therein or if there has been an inability to serve a party without whom the action cannot proceed as provided by R. 4:28–1, it shall, on motion or on its own initiative, order the action, with the record and all papers on file,

transferred to the proper court or administrative agency, if any, in the State. The action shall then be proceeded upon as if it had been originally commenced in that court or agency.

(b) **After Appeal.** If any action transferrable under paragraph (a) because of lack of jurisdiction over the subject matter is appealed without having been transferred, the appellate court may decide the appeal and direct the appropriate judgment or decision to be entered in the court or agency to which the action should have been transferred.

(c) **Payment of Fees.** Where pursuant to this rule an action is ordered transferred to or judgment or decision ordered entered in the proper court or agency, the order shall be conditioned upon the payment by the parties to the clerk of such court or to such agency of the fees that would have been payable had the action originally been instituted in such court or agency. Payments to the clerk of any court shall be made payable to the "Treasurer, State of New Jersey."

Note: Source — R.R. 1:27D; paragraphs (a), (b) and (c) amended July 24, 1978 to be effective September 11, 1978; paragraph (c) amended July 27, 2006 to be effective September 1, 2006.

Publisher's Note

On March 27, 2000 the New Jersey Supreme Court issued the following order:

WHEREAS the Judiciary has successfully tested the use of electronic filing technology in the Judiciary Electronic Filing and Imaging System (JEFIS) pilot project in the Special Civil Part of the Superior Court, Law Division, Monmouth County, pursuant to orders of this Court dated December 10, 1996 and February 1, 1999; and

WHEREAS the Judiciary is preparing to implement the electronic filing component of JEFIS in all of the Special Civil Part offices in the other twenty counties, while continuing to operate the pilot project in Monmouth County;

Pursuant to N.J. Const. (1947), Art. VI, § 2, par. 3, IT IS ORDERED, effective September 1, 2000 and until further Order of the Court, that the Rules of Court be relaxed and supplemented, as set forth below, so as to permit the Judiciary to establish and operate a statewide program in the Special Civil Part of the Superior Court, Law Division, in which attorneys who meet the requirements established by the Administrative Office of the Courts and are registered with the Superior Court Clerk's Office may, in civil actions in which the amount in controversy does not exceed the Part's monetary limit and where the actions are filed in that court pursuant to Rule 6:1-2(a)(1), electronically file pleadings and other papers in a prescribed format via the Internet with the Clerk of the Superior Court, with computers capable of electronically managing documents and images of documents to be used to process and distribute those documents and images of documents to the office of the Special Civil Part Clerk in the county of venue for printing, processing, and storage in paper form (except in Monmouth County, where the documents will continue to be processed and stored in electronic form as part of the JEFIS project):

* * *

9. Rule 1:13–4 is supplemented so as to provide that the papers transferred to another court or agency may be printed paper copies of the documents that have been filed electronically.

* * *

On October 7, 2003, the New Jersey Supreme Court issued the following order:

WHEREAS the Judiciary has successfully tested the use of electronic filing technology in the Judiciary Electronic Filing and Imaging System (JEFIS) pilot project in the Special Civil Part of the

Superior Court, Law Division, Monmouth County, pursuant to orders of this Court dated December 10, 1996 and February 1, 1999; and

WHEREAS the Judiciary has implemented the electronic filing component of JEFIS in all of the Special Civil Part offices in the other twenty counties pursuant to an Order of this Court dated March 27, 2000, while continuing to operate the pilot project in Monmouth County;

Pursuant to N.J. Const. (1947), Art. VI, sec. 2, par. 3, IT IS ORDERED, effective November 3, 2003 and until further Order of the Court, that the Rules of Court be relaxed and supplemented, as specified in the Court's Order dated March 27, 2000, to permit the Judiciary to expand the imaging component of JEFIS to civil actions filed in the Special Civil Part in Mercer and Ocean Counties pursuant to Rule 6:1–2(a)(1), so that documents filed in those cases, whether electronically or on paper, can be processed and stored in electronic form as part of the JEFIS project.

This Order supplements, where appropriate, the Court's Orders of December 10, 1996 and February 1, 1999 with regard to the JEFIS project in Monmouth County and the Court's Order of March 27, 2000 permitting the statewide expansion of the electronic filing component of JEFIS.

* * *

On April 27, 2004, the New Jersey Supreme Court issued the following order to be effective May 3, 2004:

WHEREAS the Judiciary has successfully tested the use of electronic filing technology in the Judiciary Electronic Filing and Imaging System (JEFIS) pilot project in the Special Civil Part of the Superior Court, Law Division, Monmouth County, pursuant to orders of this Court dated December 10, 1996 and February 1, 1999; and

WHEREAS the Judiciary has implemented the electronic filing component of JEFIS in all of the Special Civil Part offices in the other twenty counties pursuant to an Order of this Court dated March 27, 2000, while continuing to operate the pilot project in Monmouth County; and

WHEREAS the Judiciary has expanded the imaging component of JEFIS to civil actions filed in the Special Civil Part in Mercer and Ocean Counties pursuant to an Order of this Court dated October 7, 2003;

Pursuant to N.J. Const. (1947), Art. VI, sec. 2, par. 3, IT IS ORDERED, effective May 3, 2004 and until further Order of the Court, that the Rules of Court be relaxed and supplemented, as specified in the Court's Order dated March 27, 2000, to permit the Judiciary to expand the imaging component of JEFIS to civil actions filed in the Special Civil Part in Bergen, Burlington, Camden, Cumberland, Gloucester, Morris, Salem, Somerset and Union Counties pursuant to Rule 6:1–2(a)(1), so that documents filed in those cases, whether electronically or on paper, can be processed and stored in electronic form as part of the JEFIS project.

This Order supplements, where appropriate, the Court's Orders of December 10, 1996 and February 1, 1999 with regard to the JEFIS project in Monmouth County, the Court's Order of March 27, 2000 permitting the statewide expansion of the electronic filing component of JEFIS, and the Court's Order of October 7, 2003 permitting expansion of the imaging component of JEFIS to Mercer and Ocean Counties.

* * *

On July 7, 2005, the New Jersey Supreme Court issued the following order to be effective on July 7, 2005:

Pursuant to N.J. Const. (1947), Art. VI, sec. 2, par. 3, IT IS ORDERED, effective immediately and until further Order of the Court, that the Rules of Court be relaxed and supplemented as specified in the Court's Order dated March 27, 2000, to permit the Judiciary to further expand the imaging component of JEFIS to Atlantic, Cape May, Essex, Hudson, Hunterdon, Middlesex, Passaic, Sussex and Warren Counties for actions filed pursuant to Rule 6:1–2(a)(1), so that documents in those Special Civil Part cases, whether filed electronically or on paper, can be processed and stored in electronic form as part of the JEFIS project.

1:13–5. Tables of Mortality and Life Expectancy

The tables of mortality and life expectancy printed as an Appendix to these rules shall be admissible in evidence as prima facie proof of the facts therein contained.

Note: Source—R.R. 4:45A.

1:13–6. Military Lists

If it appears by affidavit or other competent proof that a party to an action pending on the trial calendar in any court is in the military service of the United States, and if in the opinion of the court the party's ability to prosecute the action or conduct a defense is materially affected by reason of the military service and the party's attendance may not be secured within a reasonable time without undue inconvenience, the action shall be placed on the Military List. The affidavit or other proof shall show the place where the party is stationed and, upon information and belief, the duration of that assignment and shall establish that the party cannot be available for the trial of the action within a reasonable time and without undue inconvenience. Such actions shall be automatically returned to the active trial calendar by the court at the end of 6 months unless it is made to appear by further affidavit or other competent proof that the ability of the party to prosecute the action or to conduct the defense continues to be materially affected by reason of the party's military service. A similar procedure shall be followed at the expiration of every 6–month period until the action is restored to the active trial calendar.

Note: Source—R.R. 1:31–2(a)(b); amended July 13, 1994 to be effective September 1, 1994; amended July 10, 1998 to be effective September 1, 1998.

1:13–7. Dismissal of Civil Cases for Lack of Prosecution

(a) Except in receivership and liquidation proceedings and in condemnation and foreclosure actions governed by R. 4:64–8 and except as otherwise provided by rule or court order, whenever an action has been pending for four months or, if a general equity action, for two months, without a required proceeding having been taken therein as hereafter defined in subsection (b), the court shall issue written notice to the plaintiff advising that the action as to any or all defendants will be dismissed without prejudice 60 days following the date of the notice or 30 days thereafter in general equity cases unless, within said period, action specified in subsection (c) is taken. If no such action is taken, the court shall enter an order of dismissal without prejudice as to any named defendant and shall furnish the plaintiff with a copy thereof. After dismissal, reinstatement of an action against a single defendant may be permitted on submission of a consent order vacating the dismissal and allowing the dismissed defendant to file an answer, provided the proposed consent order is accompanied by the answer for filing, a case information statement, and the requisite fee. If the defendant has been properly served but declines to execute a consent order, plaintiff shall move on good cause shown for vacation of the dismissal. In multi-defendant actions in which at least one defendant has been properly served, the consent order shall be submitted within 60 days of the order of dismissal, and if not so submitted, a motion for reinstatement shall be required. The motion shall be granted on good cause shown if filed within 90 days of the order of dismissal, and thereafter shall be granted only on a showing of exceptional circumstances. In multi-defendant actions, if an order of dismissal pursuant to this rule is vacated and an answering pleading is filed by the restored defendant during or after the discovery period, the restored defendant shall be considered an added party, and discovery shall be extended pursuant to Rule 4:24–1(b). Nothing in this rule precludes the court with respect to a particular defendant from imposing reasonable additional or different procedures to facilitate the timely occurrence of the next required proceeding to be taken in the case with respect to that defendant.

(b) The following events constitute required proceedings that must be timely taken to avoid the issuance by the court of a written notice of dismissal as set forth in subsection (a):

(1) proof of service or acknowledgment of service filed with the court; or

(2) filing of answer; or

(3) entry of default; or

(4) entry of default judgment. However, in any case involving multiple defendants in which at least one defendant has answered, no defaulted defendant will be noticed for dismissal due to the plaintiff's failure to timely convert a default into a default judgment as required by R. 4:43–2.

In the event the answer of any defendant is suppressed under R. 4:23–5(a) or otherwise and the plaintiff takes no further action, the court will place the defendant on the dismissal list 120 days from the date of the order of suppression.

No defendant will be automatically noticed for dismissal if a motion has been filed by or with respect to that defendant during the four-month period, unless the court in a particular case directs otherwise.

(c) An order of dismissal will enter 60 days from the date of the notice referred to in subsection (a) unless one of the following actions is taken within said 60–day period:

(1) a proof of service or acknowledgment of service is filed, if the required action not timely taken was failure to file proof of service or acknowledgment of service with the court;

(2) an answer is filed or a default is requested, if the required action not timely taken was failure to answer or enter default;

(3) a default judgment is obtained, if the required action not timely taken was failure to convert a default request into a default judgment;

(4) a motion is filed by or with respect to a defendant noticed for dismissal. If a motion to remove the defendant from the dismissal list is denied, the defendant will be dismissed without further notice.

(d) Special Civil Part. If original process in an action filed in the Special Civil Part has not been served within 60 days after the date of the filing of the complaint, the clerk of the court shall dismiss the action as to any unserved defendant and notify plaintiff that it has been marked "dismissed subject to automatic reinstatement within one year as to the non-answering defendant or defendants." The action shall be reinstated without motion or further order of the court if the complaint and summons are served within one year from the date of the dismissal. A case dismissed pursuant to this rule may be restored after one year only by order upon application, which may be made *ex parte*, and a showing of good cause for the delay in making service and due diligence in attempting to serve the summons and complaint. The entry of such an order shall not prejudice any right the defendant has to raise a statute of limitations defense in the restored action.

Note: Source—R.R. 1:30–3(a) (b) (c) (d), 1:30–4. Amended July 7, 1971 to be effective September 13, 1971; former rule redesignated as paragraph (a) and paragraph (b) adopted July 15, 1982 to be effective September 13, 1982; paragraph (b) amended November 5, 1986 to be effective January 1, 1987; paragraph (a) amended June 28, 1996 to be effective September 1, 1996; caption and paragraph (a) amended July 5, 2000 to be effective September 5, 2000; paragraphs (a) and (b) amended July 12, 2002 to be effective September 3, 2002; paragraph (a) amended, former paragraph (b) deleted, and new paragraphs (b), (c), and (d) adopted July 28, 2004 to be effective September 1, 2004; paragraph (a) amended July 9, 2008 to be effective September 1, 2008.

1:13–8. Priorities of Liens and Encumbrances Determined as of Commencement of Action

The priorities of parties' liens and encumbrances are fixed and determined as of the date of the commencement of the action, unless the parties otherwise agree or it is otherwise adjudicated in the action or any other action.

Note: Source—R.R. 4:64–2(b). Adopted July 7, 1971 to be effective September 13, 1971.

1:13–9. Amicus Curiae; Motion; Grounds for Relief; Briefs

An application for leave to appear as amicus curiae in any court shall be made by motion in the cause stating with specificity the identity of the applicant, the issue intended to be addressed, the nature of the public interest therein and the nature of the applicant's special interest, involvement or expertise in respect thereof. The court shall grant the motion if it is satisfied under all the circumstances that the motion is timely, the applicant's participation will assist in the resolution of an issue of public importance, and no party to the litigation will be unduly prejudiced thereby. The order granting the motion shall define with specificity the permitted extent of participation by the amicus and shall, where appropriate, fix a briefing schedule. An amicus curiae who has been granted leave to appear in a cause may, without seeking further leave, file a brief in an appeal taken to any court from the judgment therein entered. Briefs filed by an amicus curiae in any court shall comply with all applicable rules.

Note: Adopted July 16, 1979 to be effective September 10, 1979; caption and text amended July 13, 1994 to be effective September 1, 1994.

1:13–10. Payment of Fees, Penalties, and Sanctions

Checks in payment of any fees, penalties, and sanctions required by these rules to be paid directly to the court shall be made payable to Treasurer, State of New Jersey.

Note: Adopted July 27, 2006 to be effective September 1, 2006.

CHAPTER II. CONDUCT OF LAWYERS, JUDGES AND COURT PERSONNEL
RULE 1:14. CODES OF ETHICS

The Rules of Professional Conduct and the Code of Judicial Conduct of the American Bar Association, as amended and supplemented by the Supreme Court and included as an Appendix to Part I of these Rules, and the Code of Conduct for Judiciary Employees, also included as an Appendix to Part I of these Rules, shall govern the conduct of the members of the bar and the judges and employees of all courts of this State.

When appropriate, the words "partnership," "attorney," and "lawyer" shall be construed to include professional corporations and limited liability entities for the practice of law, as well as attorney employees, agents, shareholders and members thereof, and attorneys acting as "of counsel" thereto.

The Code of Professional Conduct for Interpreters, Transliterators, and Translators, also included as an Appendix to Part I of these Rules, shall govern the conduct of persons who are employed by or under contract to the Judiciary to interpret, transliterate, or translate.

Note: Source—R.R. 1:25. Canons of Professional Ethics of the American Bar Association deleted July 7, 1971 and the Code of Professional Responsibility, as amended and supplemented, adopted July 7, 1971 to be effective September 13, 1971; amended November 27, 1974 to be effective April 1, 1975, amended July 16, 1981 to be effective September 14, 1981; Disciplinary Rules of the Code of Professional Responsibility deleted and Rules of Professional Conduct, as amended and supplemented, adopted July 12, 1984, to be effective September 10, 1984; amended December 7, 1993, to be effective immediately; amended October 24, 1994 to be effective December 1, 1994; amended July 10, 1998 to be effective September 1, 1998.

RULE 1:15. LIMITATION ON PRACTICE OF ATTORNEYS

1:15–1. Limitation on Practice of Attorneys Serving as Judges and Surrogates

(a) Full Time Judges. An attorney who is a judge required by law to devote full time to judicial duties shall not practice law.

(b) Judges of Municipal Courts. An attorney who is a judge or acting judge of a municipal court shall not practice in any criminal, quasi-criminal or penal matter, whether judicial or administrative in nature, except to perform the official duties of a municipal attorney of another municipality. Nor shall a municipal court judge act as attorney for the municipality or any of the municipalities served by that court or as attorney for any agency or officer thereof; nor practice before the governing body or any agency or officer thereof; nor be associated in the practice of law, either as "of counsel"

to or as partner, employer, employee or agent of, or office associate, with an attorney who is a member of such governing body.

An attorney who is a judge of a municipal court shall be subject to the terms of that section of the New Jersey Conflicts of Interest Law which restricts involvement with specific casino industry activities (N.J.S.A. 52:13D–17.2).

(c) Surrogates. An attorney who is a surrogate or deputy surrogate in any county, or who is in the employ of any such official, shall not practice law in any estate or trust matter, including the preparation of wills, trust documents, or any other probate documents, in or out of court. Furthermore, a surrogate or deputy surrogate shall not practice law in any criminal, quasi-criminal or penal matter, whether judicial or administrative in nature, in that county, nor in the Superior Court, Chancery Division, Probate Part in any county.

Note: Source—R.R. 1:26–1(a)(b)(c)(d)(e)(f), 8:13–7(b). Paragraph (d) amended November 22, 1978 to be effective December 7, 1978; paragraph (c) amended July 16, 1981 to be effective September 14, 1981, except that, as to part-time municipal court judges outside of Atlantic City, the last sentence shall be effective December 26, 1981; paragraph (d) amended February 17, 1983 to be effective immediately; former paragraph (b) deleted and former paragraphs (c) and (d) redesignated to paragraphs (b) and (c) July 26, 1984 to be effective September 10, 1984; paragraphs (a) and (b) amended July 13, 1994 to be effective September 1, 1994; paragraph (c) amended July 12, 2002 to be effective September 3, 2002; paragraph (c) amended July 9, 2008 to be effective September 1, 2008.

1:15–2. Limitations on Practice of Attorneys Serving as Clerks and Employees of Courts and Judges

An attorney who is a clerk or deputy clerk of any court, other than a surrogate or deputy surrogate, or who is, or is in the employ of or regularly assigned to a court, judge, or court clerk, shall not practice in any court, but the limitation so imposed upon him shall not be greater than the limitation on the practice of the judge of such court. An attorney who is, or is regularly assigned to, a jury commissioner, grand jury or probation department shall not practice in any court in that county.

Note: Source—R.R. 1:26–2. As to a surrogate or deputy surrogate, see R. 1:15–1(d).

1:15–3. Limitations on Practice of Other Attorneys

(a) Sheriffs and County Prosecutors. An attorney who is a sheriff or county prosecutor, or is in the employ or service of such an official, shall not practice on behalf of any defendant in any criminal, quasi-criminal or penal matter, whether judicial or administrative in nature. Nor shall an attorney who is a sheriff of any county or in the sheriff's employ practice in any court in that county.

(b) Municipal Attorneys and Members of Governing Bodies. A municipal attorney of any municipality shall not represent any defendant in the municipal court thereof, except to perform official duties, but may represent a defendant in a joint municipal court if the defendant resides and the offense was allegedly committed in a municipality for which the attorney is not the municipal attorney. A municipal prosecutor shall not represent a defendant in any other municipal court in that county or in a criminal proceeding in the Superior Court in that county but may represent a defendant in a municipal court or in a criminal proceeding in the Superior Court in a county other than the one in which he or she serves as a municipal prosecutor. An attorney who is a member of the governing body of a municipality shall not practice in the municipal court of that municipality. For purposes of this rule, a municipal public defender shall not be deemed a municipal attorney.

(c) Other Attorneys Representing Public Bodies. Paragraphs (a) and (b) of the rule shall not be deemed to exhaust the limitations on practice necessitated by a conflict of interest on the part of an attorney representing a public body, agency or officer.

Note: Source—R.R. 1:26–3(a)(b)(c)(d); paragraphs (a) and (b) amended July 13, 1994 to be effective September 1, 1994; paragraph (b) amended January 19, 2000 to be effective immediately; paragraph (b) amended July 5, 2000 to be effective September 5, 2000.

1:15–4. Limitations Extended to Partners, etc.; Municipal Court Judges; Municipal Prosecutors

(a) General Application. Subject to paragraphs (b) and (c), whenever R. 1:15 imposes limitations on the practice of law by an attorney, such limitations shall also extend to the attorney's partners, employers, employees, office associates, shareholders in a professional corporation or members in a limited liability entity in which the attorney practices. The limitations imposed by R. 1:15 on attorneys shall not preclude assignments of partners, employers, employees, office associates or shareholders by a court for the representation of indigents.

(b) Municipal Court Judges. As applied to partners, employers, employees, office associates, shareholders, and members, the limitations imposed on the practice of law by judges of municipal courts by R. 1:15–1(b) shall extend only to the county in which the court of the judge or acting judge is located. Except for full-time municipal court judges and all judges appointed to the municipal court of the City of Atlantic City, this rule shall not apply to the two-year post-employment restrictions on casino industry related activities referred to in N.J.S.A. 52:13D–17.2(c) and imposed on municipal court judges by R. 1:15–1(b).

(c) Municipal Prosecutors. As applied to partners, employers, employees, office associates, shareholders, and members, the limitations imposed on the practice of law by municipal prosecutors by R. 1:15–3(b) shall extend only to matters that have occurred in the municipality in which the prosecutor serves and any matters that involve law enforcement personnel or other material witnesses from that municipality.

Note: Source—R.R. 1:26–4; amended July 16, 1981 to be effective September 14, 1981; amended November 1, 1985 to be effective January 2, 1986; amended July 13, 1994 to be effective September 1, 1994; amended July 10, 1998 to be effective September 1, 1998; caption amended, text amended and redesignated as paragraphs (a) and (b), and new paragraph (c) added November 17, 2003 to be effective January 1, 2004.

Publisher's Note

On May 3, 2000, the New Jersey Supreme Court issued the following Order:

The Court having determined that the limitations on municipal prosecutors imposed by *State v. Clark*, 162 N.J. 201 (2000), should not be extended to the partners, shareholders, associates, employers, or members of a limited liability entity of a municipal prosecutor pending the issuance of the final report of the American Bar Association's Commission on the Evaluation of the Rules of Professional Conduct (the "Ethics 2000 Commission") and its review by the Court,

IT IS ORDERED that *Rule* 1:15–4 is relaxed to exempt from its terms the limitations imposed on municipal prosecutors in *State v. Clark, supra*, effective January 1, 2001, through December 31, 2002, and until the further Order of the Court.

1:15–5. Application of Rule

(a) Limitations under R. 1:15 upon the practice in criminal, quasi-criminal or penal matters, whether judi-

cial or administrative in nature, shall extend to proceedings before courts and agencies or officers established under the laws of the United States, but in all other respects R. 1:15 shall not apply to such courts and agencies.

(b) The term "office associates" as used in R. 1:15 includes attorneys who share common office facilities.

Note: Source—R.R. 1:26–5(a)(c).

RULE 1:16. MISCELLANEOUS LIMITATIONS ON ATTORNEYS AND PARTIES

1:16–1. Interviewing Jurors Subsequent to Trial

Except by leave of court granted on good cause shown, no attorney or party shall directly, or through any investigator or other person acting for the attorney, interview, examine, or question any grand or petit juror with respect to any matter relating to the case.

Note: Source—R.R. 1:25A. Amended July 16, 1979 to be effective September 10, 1979; amended December 7, 1993, to be effective immediately.

1:16–2. Prohibition as to Gratuities

No attorney or party shall give either directly or indirectly any gratuity or gift to any employee of any

court, or of any officer serving a court, or of any other governmental agency or officer, when such attorney has had or is likely to have any professional or official transaction with such court, office or agency; nor shall an employee of any court, or of any office serving a court, accept any gratuity, gift, loan, discount, favor, hospitality, or service either directly or indirectly from any attorney or other person who has had or is likely to have any professional or official transaction with the employee or with the employee's court or office.

Note: Source—R.R. 1:34(a)(b). Amended December 7, 1993, to be effective immediately.

RULE 1:17. JUDGES AND COURT PERSONNEL: LIMITATION ON POLITICAL ACTIVITY, HOLDING OF OTHER PUBLIC OFFICE OR POSITION AND OTHER GAINFUL PURSUIT

1:17–1. Persons Prohibited

The following persons in or serving the judicial branch of government shall not hold any elective public office nor be a candidate therefor, nor engage in partisan political activity:

(a) Judges;

(b) The Administrative Director of the Courts, the Clerk of the Supreme Court, the Clerk of the Appellate Division of the Superior Court, the Clerk of the Superior Court, the Administrator of the Tax Court, and all employees of their respective offices, and official court reporters;

(c) Probation officers and all employees of county probation divisions;

(d) Clerks to grand juries, assistants to clerks of grand juries, and all employees regularly assigned to attend or serve grand or petit juries;

(e) Law secretaries, administrative assistants to judges, stenographers, sergeants-at-arms, assignment clerks, courtroom clerks, court attendants, court aides, court interpreters, sound recording operators, and all

public employees regularly assigned to a judge or court, except those employees of county sheriffs who provide only security services;

(f) Surrogates, except such political activity as is permitted under the Code of Conduct for Judiciary Employees, included as an Appendix to Part I of these Rules. A person elected to the office of Surrogate shall, prior to taking the oath of office, resign from any other public office, position or employment, elected or appointed, held by such person;

(g) Deputy surrogates and all persons employed by or regularly assigned to a surrogate's office;

(h) Directors, administrators, deputy administrators, violations clerks, and all persons employed by or regularly assigned to a municipal court.

Note: Source—R.R. 1:25C(a); paragraph (b) amended November 27, 1974 to be effective April 1, 1975; paragraph (b) amended July 15, 1982 to be effective September 13, 1982; paragraph (g) amended June 15, 1983 to be effective immediately; paragraph (i) amended July 26, 1984 to be effective September 10, 1984; paragraph (g) amended June 29, 1990 to be effective September 4, 1990; caption amended, paragraphs (b) and (c) amended, paragraph (d) deleted, former paragraph (e) redesignated paragraph (d), former paragraph (f) amended and redesignated paragraph (e), former paragraph (g) amended and redesignated paragraph (f), former paragraph (h) redesignated paragraph (g), and former paragraph (i) amended and redesignated paragraph (h) December 7, 1993, to be effective immediately; paragraph (b) amended July 28, 2004 to be effective September 1, 2004.

1:17–2. Judges

Judges may not engage in non-partisan political activity. Without prior written approval of the Supreme Court, requested through the Administrative Director of the Courts, judges may not hold any other public office, position, or employment.

Note: Former Rule 1:17–2 redesignated as Rule 1:17–4; new Rule 1:17–2 adopted December 7, 1993, to be effective immediately.

1:17–3. Non-judge Employees

Whether non-judge employees may participate in non-partisan political activity or hold any other public office, position or employment shall be determined according to the Code of Conduct for Judiciary Employees, included as an Appendix to Part I of these Rules, as that Code is interpreted and applied by the Advisory Committee on Outside Activities of Judiciary Employees, established under Rule 1:17A.

Note: Former Rule 1:17–3 redesignated as Rule 1:17–5; new Rule 1:17–3 adopted December 7, 1993, to be effective immediately.

1:17–4. Non-applicability

Rule 1:17–1 shall not apply to county clerks, county prosecutors, sheriffs, or employees of their respective offices except as such employees are specifically referred to therein and except as otherwise provided by N.J.S. 2A:158–21 (proscribed political activity of county prosecutors and their staffs).

Note: Source—R.R. 1:25C(b); amended June 15, 1983 to be effective immediately. Former Rule 1:17–4 redesignated as Rule 1:17–6; Rule 1:17–4, formerly Rule 1:17–2, amended December 7, 1993, to be effective immediately.

1:17–5. Ineligibility of Judicial Employees for Appointments

(a) No person in or serving the judicial branch of government full time including any person in the employ of a surrogate shall be eligible for appointment as or serve as an appraiser, receiver, commissioner, guardian ad litem, administrator, or other appointment for which a fee may be allowed in any matter pending in any court unless he or she agrees in advance to waive such fee.

(b) The foregoing applies to situations in which the appointment is made by a court. It shall not apply when an employee may be named outside of court to serve for a fee in one of the enumerated capacities, e.g., an employee named in a will to execute a decedent's estate, in which event the employee may accept an executor's commission. See Canon 5.B.7. of the Code of Conduct for Judiciary Employees, included as an Appendix to Part I of these Rules.

Note: Source—R.R. 5:5–4. Rule 1:17–5, formerly Rule 1:17–3, former text amended and designated as paragraph (a) and paragraph (b) adopted December 7, 1993, to be effective immediately.

1:17–6. Other Employment of Judicial Employees

No public officer or employee employed by or regularly assigned to a judge shall hold any position or employment in private business or engage in other gainful pursuit except as the same may be permitted under the Code of Conduct for Judiciary Employees, included as an Appendix to Part I of these Rules.

Note: Source—R.R. 1:25C(c). Rule 1:17–6, formerly Rule 1:17–4, amended December 7, 1993, to be effective immediately.

RULE 1:17A. ADVISORY COMMITTEE ON OUTSIDE ACTIVITIES OF JUDICIARY EMPLOYEES

1:17A–1. Appointment and Organization

The Supreme Court shall appoint an Advisory Committee on Outside Activities of Judiciary Employees consisting of at least 16 members serving for terms of two years with the terms of approximately one half of the members expiring each year. No member who has served five full two-year terms shall be eligible for immediate reappointment. The Committee shall include at least six judges (at least one from the Appellate Division), one Surrogate, four judiciary employees, two practicing attorneys, and three public members. A vacancy occurring during a term shall be filled for the unexpired portion thereof. The Court shall annually designate a member of the Committee to serve as Chairperson and another member to serve as Vice Chairperson. The Administrative Director of the Courts or designee shall serve as secretary of the Committee.

Note: Adopted December 7, 1993, to be effective immediately. Amended December 6, 2005 to be effective immediately.

1:17A–2. Jurisdiction

The Committee shall have jurisdiction to interpret the Code of Conduct for Judiciary Employees. In particular, the Committee shall have jurisdiction to issue advisory opinions and to render decisions as follows:

(a) The Committee shall render advisory opinions concerning employees' outside activities when such opinions are requested by any judiciary employee or supervisor.

(b) The Committee shall decide whether to permit employees who are subject to Canon 5.C.1 of the Code of Conduct to accept appointments to public positions or to undertake community activities. Such employees are required to obtain the consent of the Committee before beginning any of those activities.

(c) The Committee shall decide appeals from any judiciary employee who has been informed of an adverse decision:

(1) regarding outside employment by a supervisor or other person named in Canon 5.B.14.a.(2)(a)–(f) of the Code of Conduct;

(2) regarding appointment to a public position by a supervisor or other person named in Canon 5.C.2.e.(2)(a)–(f) of the Code of Conduct;

(3) regarding participation in non-partisan political activities by a supervisor or other person named in Canon 6.H.2.(a)–(f) of the Code of Conduct.

(d) The Committee shall render advisory opinions in any matter when requested to do so by the Supreme Court.

Note: Adopted December 7, 1993, to be effective immediately.

1:17A–3. Scope of Review

(a) In rendering its decisions and in issuing its advisory opinions, the Committee shall determine whether the activities that are the subject of the inquiry would violate, contravene, or conflict either with specific provisions of the Code or with the principles, goals, or standards of the Code.

(b) All decisions rendered and advisory opinions issued by the Committee shall be based on the facts presented pursuant to Rule 1:17A–4.

(c) In all matters in which a decision or advisory opinion of the Committee would depart from the Code of Conduct or involve a policy decision that is beyond the scope of the Code of Conduct, the Committee shall refer such matters to the Supreme Court for review, with such recommendation as the Committee may wish to make.

Note: Adopted December 7, 1993, to be effective immediately.

1:17A–4. Form of Inquiry

All inquiries, whether requesting a decision or an advisory opinion, as applicable, shall be addressed to the secretary, who shall transmit them to the Committee. They shall be in writing, shall set out the factual situation in detail, and shall be accompanied by a short memorandum citing the relevant section(s) of the Code of Conduct.

Note: Adopted December 7, 1993, to be effective immediately.

1:17A–5. Disposition of Inquiries

Except as may otherwise be determined by the Committee in the case of routine inquiries that require a response before the Committee can act, no decision or advisory opinion shall be given or made by the Committee unless concurred in by a majority thereof. The Committee shall render its decision or advisory opinion within 30 days of its receipt of the written inquiry. In every matter the secretary shall convey the Committee's response in writing to the person making the inquiry. When the Committee determines, in its discretion, that a determination is of statewide importance, it may in addition file a formal opinion and make suitable arrangements for its publication. Formal opinions shall not, insofar as practicable, identify the employee making the inquiry.

Note: Adopted December 7, 1993, to be effective immediately.

1:17A–6. Inquiries From Supreme Court

The Committee shall consider and advise the Supreme Court or render opinions on such matters as the Supreme Court may submit to it from time to time. Those opinions shall not be published without prior approval of the Court.

Note: Adopted December 7, 1993, to be effective immediately.

1:17A–7. Procedure

The Committee shall prescribe the methods and procedure to be followed in considering inquiries, expressing advisory opinions, and rendering decisions.

Note: Adopted December 7, 1993, to be effective immediately.

1:17A–8. Petitions for Review

(a) Review on Leave Granted by the Supreme Court. The determination of the Committee shall be final unless the Supreme Court grants a petition for review filed pursuant to this Rule, or unless the Court in its sole discretion decides to review the matter.

(b) Notice. Within 30 days after an employee is notified in writing of the response to the inquiry, or, if a formal opinion has been rendered, within 20 days after its publication, the employee, if aggrieved thereby, may seek review thereof by filing a notice of petition for review with the Clerk of the Supreme Court.

(c) Application for Waiver of Filing Fee for Petition for Review. At the time of filing of the notice of petition for review, an employee may file with the clerk of the Supreme Court an application for waiver of the filing fee set forth in N.J.S.A. 22A:2–1. Such application may be granted based on the employee's certification that the matter presented for review pertains to the interpretation or administration of the Code of Conduct for Judiciary Employees.

(d) Record on Petition for Review. If the petition for review is granted, the record on review shall be the formal opinion, if any, or the Committee's written response to the employee issued pursuant to Rule 1:17A–5, the inquiry or memorandum submitted, and any documents relied on by the Committee in arriving at its determination.

(e) Form of Petition for Review. A petition for review shall contain a short statement of the matter involved, the question presented, the errors complained of, and the arguments in support of petitioner's position.

(f) Service and Filing of Petition for Review. Within 10 days after filing of the notice of petition for review, the employee shall serve 2 copies of the petition on the Secretary of the Committee and shall file 9 copies thereof with the Clerk of the Supreme Court.

(g) Final Determination. The final determination of a petition for review may be either by written opinion or by order of the Supreme Court and shall state whether the opinion or other action of the Committee is affirmed, reversed, or modified, or shall provide for such other disposition as is appropriate.

Note: Adopted December 7, 1993 to be effective immediately; former paragraph (c) redesignated paragraph (d), paragraph (d) redesignated paragraph (e), paragraph (e) redesignated paragraph (f), paragraph (f) redesignated paragraph (g), new paragraph (c) adopted February 3, 1997 to be effective March 1, 1997.

1:17A–9. Reports

From time to time the Committee shall evaluate its operations in reports to the Supreme Court. Such reports shall include any recommendations the Committee may wish to make regarding amendments either to the Code of Conduct, to the procedures whereunder the Code of Conduct is administered, or to this Rule.

Note: Adopted December 7, 1993, to be effective immediately.

RULE 1:18. DUTY OF JUDGES

It shall be the duty of every judge to abide by and to enforce the provisions of the Rules of Professional Conduct, the Code of Judicial Conduct and the provisions of R. 1:15 and R. 1:17.

Note: Source—R.R. 1:26–6, 8:13–7(a); amended July 29, 1977 to be effective September 6, 1977; amended July 14, 1992 to be effective September 1, 1992.

RULE 1:18A. ADVISORY COMMITTEE ON EXTRAJUDICIAL ACTIVITIES

1:18A–1. Appointment and Organization

The Supreme Court shall appoint an Advisory Committee on Extrajudicial Activities consisting of at least 9 members serving for terms of 2 years with the terms of approximately one half of the members expiring each year. No member who has served five full two-year terms shall be eligible for immediate reappointment. The Committee shall include one practicing attorney and one public member. A vacancy occurring during a term shall be filled for the unexpired portion thereof. The Court shall annually designate a member of the Committee to serve as Chair and another member to serve as Vice-Chair. The Administrative Director of the Courts or designee shall serve as secretary of the Committee.

Note: Adopted November 29, 1988, to be effective January 2, 1989; amended May 1, 2006 to be effective immediately.

1:18A–2. Jurisdiction

The Committee shall accept inquiries concerning extrajudicial activities only from a judge or the Supreme Court.

Note: Adopted November 29, 1988, to be effective January 2, 1989.

1:18A–3. Form of Inquiry

All inquiries shall be addressed to the secretary, who shall transmit them to the Committee. They shall be in writing, shall set out the factual situation in detail, and shall be accompanied by a short memorandum citing the relevant Code of Judicial Conduct or Guidelines for Extrajudicial Activities.

Note: Adopted November 29, 1988, to be effective January 2, 1989.

1:18A–4. Disposition of Inquiries

Except as may otherwise be determined by the Committee in the case of routine inquiries that require a response before the Committee can act, no opinion shall be given by the Committee unless concurred in by a majority thereof. In every matter, the secretary shall convey the Committee's response in writing to the judge making the inquiry. The Committee may, in its discretion, issue, in addition, a formal opinion for distribution to all judges and make suitable arrangements for its publication. Formal opinions shall not, insofar as practicable, identify the judge making the inquiry.

Note: Adopted November 29, 1988, to be effective January 2, 1989.

1:18A–5. Inquiries From Supreme Court

The Committee shall consider and advise the Supreme Court or render opinions on such matters as the Supreme Court may submit to it from time to time. Those opinions shall not be published without prior approval of the Court.

Note: Adopted November 29, 1988, to be effective January 2, 1989.

1:18A–6. Procedure

The Committee shall prescribe the methods and procedure to be followed in considering inquiries and expressing opinions.

Note: Adopted November 29, 1988, to be effective January 2, 1989.

1:18A–7. Petitions for Review

(a) Notice. Within 30 days after a judge is notified in writing of the response to the inquiry, or, if a formal opinion has been rendered, within 20 days after its publication, the judge, if aggrieved thereby, may seek review thereof by filing a notice of petition for review with the Clerk of the Supreme Court.

(b) Record on Petition for Review. If the petition for review is granted, the record on review shall be the formal opinion, if any, or the Committee's written response to the judge issued pursuant to R. 1:18A–4, the inquiry or memorandum submitted, and any documents relied on by the Committee in arriving at its determination.

(c) Form of Petition for Review. A petition for review shall contain a short statement of the matter involved, the question presented, the errors complained of, and the arguments in support of the petitioner's position.

(d) Service and Filing of Petition for Review. Within 10 days after filing of the notice of petition for review 2 copies of the petition shall be served on the secretary of the Committee and 9 copies thereof shall be filed with the Clerk of the Supreme Court.

(e) Final Determination. The final determination of a petition for review may be either by written opinion or by order of the Supreme Court and shall state whether the opinion or other action of the Committee is affirmed, reversed, or modified, or shall provide for such other final disposition as is appropriate.

Note: Adopted November 29, 1988, to be effective January 2, 1989.

RULE 1:18B. JUDICIAL FINANCIAL REPORTING

1:18B–1. Obligation to Report

(a) General. Every Supreme Court justice, Superior Court judge, Tax Court judge, and Municipal Court judge shall annually submit a financial reporting statement to the Supreme Court. This reporting requirement applies to both sitting judges and retired judges who have been recalled to active judicial service.

(b) Form of Report. The annual judicial financial reporting statement shall be in a form promulgated by the Administrative Director and approved by the Supreme Court. It shall cover the judge, the judge's spouse, and the judge's dependent children residing in the same domicile.

(c) To Whom to Submit Report. The annual judicial financial reporting statements are to be submitted to the Supreme Court in care of the Administrative Director of the Courts. Supreme Court justices, Superior Court judges, and Tax Court judges shall submit their reporting statements directly to the Administrative Director. Municipal Court judges shall submit their reporting statements to their Assignment Judge, who in turn will forward the reporting statements to the Administrative Director.

(d) Date By Which to Submit Report. The annual judicial financial reporting statements for each calendar year must be submitted to the Administrative Director, or in the case of a Municipal Court judge to his or her Assignment Judge, no later than May 15 of the following year.

(e) Requests for Extension of Time to Submit Report. A judge may for good cause request an extension of time, not to exceed sixty days, within which to submit a judicial financial reporting statement. Such requests shall be in writing to the Administrative Director of the Courts, or in the case of a Municipal Court judge to his or her Assignment Judge.

(f) Failure to Submit Report or to Submit Complete Report. If by May 15 a judge has not submitted either a fully completed judicial financial reporting statement for the preceding calendar year or a written request for an extension pursuant to paragraph (e), the Administrative Director, or in the case of a Municipal Court judge his or her Assignment Judge, shall inform the judge in writing that he or she has not satisfied the requirements of this Rule. In the case of a Municipal Court judge the Assignment Judge shall forward a contemporaneous copy of that notice to the Administrative Director. If the judge does not submit the required reporting statement within fifteen days of such notice, the Administrative Director shall refer the matter to the Advisory Committee on Judicial Conduct.

Note: Adopted January 15, 2002 to be effective immediately; paragraphs (a), (c), (d), (e) and (f) amended January 6, 2003 to be effective immediately; paragraphs (d) and (f) amended December 9, 2009, to be effective immediately.

1:18B–2. Advisory Committee on Judicial Financial Reporting

(a) Appointment and Organization. The Supreme Court shall appoint a three-member Advisory Committee on Judicial Financial Reporting to respond to inquiries from judges concerning interpretations of the judicial financial reporting requirements. The members will serve staggered three-year terms, with the term of one member expiring each year on December 31. The Supreme Court will annually designate one of the members to serve as chair of the Advisory Committee. The Administrative Director of the Courts will designate a staff person from the Administrative Office of the Courts to serve as Secretary of the Advisory Committee.

(b) Jurisdiction. The Advisory Committee shall accept inquiries only from a judge or from the Supreme Court.

(c) Form of Inquiry. All inquiries shall be in writing and addressed to the Secretary of the Advisory Committee, who shall transmit them to the Advisory Committee. Inquiries must set out the specific question in detail, including all pertinent facts.

(d) Disposition of Inquiries. Except in the case of routine inquiries that require a response before the full committee can act, the Advisory Committee shall not issue an opinion unless concurred in by a majority thereof. In every matter, the Secretary shall convey the Advisory Committee's response in writing to the judge making the inquiry. In its discretion, the Advisory Committee may also issue a formal opinion for distribution to all judges, with suitable arrangements for its publication. Formal opinions shall not identify the judge making the inquiry.

(e) Inquiries from Supreme Court. The Advisory Committee shall consider and advise the Supreme Court or render opinions on such matters as the Supreme Court may submit to it from time to time. Such opinions shall not be published without the prior approval of the Supreme Court.

(f) Procedures. The Advisory Committee shall promulgate in writing the procedures to be followed in considering and responding to inquiries.

(g) Petitions for Review.

(1) Notice. Within thirty days after a judge has been notified in writing of the Advisory Committee's response to his or her inquiry, or if a formal opinion has been rendered, within twenty days after its publication, the judge may seek review thereof by filing a notice of petition for review with the Clerk of the Supreme Court. The Clerk shall not impose a fee for the filing of the notice.

(2) Record on Petition for Review. If the petition for review is granted, the record on review shall be the formal opinion, if any, or the Advisory Committee's written response to the judge issued pursuant to Rule 1:18B–2(d), the inquiry submitted, and any documents relied on by the Advisory Committee in arriving at its determination.

(3) Form of Petition for Review. A petition for review shall contain a short statement of the matter involved, the question presented, the errors complained of, and the arguments in support of the petitioner's position.

(4) Service and Filing of Petition for Review. Within ten days after filing of the notice of petition for review, four copies of the petition shall be served on the secretary of the Committee and nine copies thereof shall be filed with the Clerk of the Supreme Court.

(5) Final Determination. The final determination of a petition for review may be either by written opinion or by order of the Supreme Court and shall state whether the opinion or other action of the Advisory Committee is affirmed, reversed, or modified, or shall provide for such other final disposition as is appropriate.

Note: Adopted January 15, 2002 to be effective immediately.

1:18B–3. Retention and Disclosure of Statements

(a) Retention. The submitted reports shall be maintained by the Administrative Director of the Courts on behalf of the Supreme Court.

(b) Disclosure. The reports shall be available to the public upon request. Requests must be in writing addressed to the Administrative Director of the Courts and must set forth in detail the specific reporting statement sought and the requesting party's name and address. The Administrative Director may promulgate a standard form for such requests, in which case every request must be submitted using that standard form. Absent extraordinary circumstances, the Administrative Director shall provide the requesting party with a copy of the specific reporting statement sought.

Note: Adopted January 15, 2002 to be effective immediately.

RULE 1:19. ADVISORY COMMITTEE ON PROFESSIONAL ETHICS

1:19–1. Appointment and Organization

The Supreme Court shall appoint an Advisory Committee on Professional Ethics consisting of fifteen members of the bar and three lay members. Members shall serve for terms of three years with the terms of six such members expiring each year. No member who has served four full three-year terms shall be eligible for immediate reappointment. A vacancy occurring during a term shall be filled for the unexpired portion thereof. The Court shall annually designate a member of the committee to serve as Chairperson and another member to serve as Vice Chairperson. The Administrative Director of the Courts shall serve as secretary of the committee.

Note: Source—R.R. 1:26A(a). Amended June 29, 1990 to be effective September 4, 1990; amended November 7, 2005 to be effective immediately.

1:19–2. Jurisdiction

The committee shall accept inquiries only from the state bar association, from any county or local bar association, or from any member of the New Jersey bar, concerning proper conduct for a member of the legal profession under the Rules of Professional Conduct of the American Bar Association as amended by the Supreme Court (except for inquiries relating to advertisements and other communications arising under Rules of Professional Conduct 7.1 through 7.5, exclusive of 7.3(c), (d), (e) and (f)) and other Rules of this Court governing the practice of attorneys. It shall not consider an inquiry involving a pending action where its opinion might affect the interests of the parties, and it may decline to accept any inquiry without stating its reasons therefor.

Note: Source—R.R. 1:26A(b) (first sentence), (c) (third sentence), (d); amended April 4, 1977, effective immediately; first sentence amended June 26, 1987 to be effective July 1, 1987.

1:19–3. Form of Inquiry

All inquiries shall be addressed to the secretary who shall transmit them to the committee. They shall be in writing, shall set out the factual situation in detail, shall be accompanied by a short brief or memorandum citing the rules of court or canons of ethics involved and any other pertinent authorities, and shall contain a certificate that any opinion of the committee will not affect the interests of the parties to any pending action.

Note: Source—R.R. 1:26A(b) (second and third sentences).

1:19–4. Disposition of Inquiries

The committee may act through parts consisting of not fewer than six members, but if the opinion of any such part is not unanimous the inquiry shall be referred to the committee as a whole. No opinion shall be given by the committee as a whole unless concurred in by eleven members thereof. The opinion of the committee on any inquiry accepted for consideration shall be in writing and shall be filed with the secretary, who shall transmit a copy to the person making the inquiry and, where the committee so requests, make suitable arrangements for its publication. Published opinions shall not, insofar as practicable, identify the party or parties making the inquiry. The committee, in its discretion, may conduct a hearing on any inquiry.

Note: Source—R.R. 1:26A(c) (first, second and fourth sentences), (e). Amended June 29, 1990 to be effective September 4, 1990.

1:19–5. Inquiries From Supreme Court

The committee as a whole shall consider and render opinions on such matters as the Supreme Court may from time to time submit to it. Such opinions shall not be published without prior approval of the court.

Note: Source—R.R. 1:26A(f).

1:19–6. Effect of Published Opinions

Published opinions of the committee shall be binding upon the Ethics Committee in their disposition of all matters.

1:19–7. Procedure

The committee shall, subject to the approval of the Supreme Court, determine the methods and procedure to be followed in considering inquiries and expressing opinions.

Note: Source—R.R. 1:26A(g).

1:19–8. Petitions for Review

(a) Notice. Within 20 days after an opinion is published, or within 30 days after any final action of the Advisory Committee on Professional Ethics other than the publication of an opinion, any aggrieved member of the bar, bar association or ethics committee may seek review thereof by serving on the Attorney General a notice of petition for review by the Supreme Court and by filing the original notice with the Clerk of the Supreme Court. The notice shall set forth the petitioner's name and address and the name and address of counsel, if any. The notice shall designate the action of the Advisory Committee on Professional Ethics sought to be reviewed and shall concisely state the manner in which the petitioner is aggrieved.

(b) Deposit for Costs. Deposit for costs shall be made in accordance with R. 2:12–5.

(c) Record on Petition for Review. If the petition for review is granted, the record on review shall be the formal opinion, if any, issued pursuant to R. 1:19–4 or R. 1:19–5, the inquiry, brief or memorandum submitted, and any documents or other evidence or proof relied upon by the Advisory Committee on Professional Ethics in arriving at its determination.

(d) Form of Petition for Review. A petition for review shall be in the form of a brief, conforming to the applicable provisions of R. 2:6 and not exceeding 15 pages if printed or 20 pages if otherwise reproduced or typed, exclusive of tables of contents, citations and appendix. It shall contain a short statement of the matter involved, the question presented, the errors complained of and the arguments in support of the petitioner's position. It shall also contain a certification by the petitioner or counsel, if any, that the petition presents a substantial question and is filed in good faith and not for purposes of delay.

(e) Service and Filing of Petition for Review. Within 10 days after filing of the notice of petition for review, 2 copies of the petition shall be served on the Attorney General and the Secretary of the Advisory Committee on Professional Ethics and 9 copies thereof shall be filed with the Clerk of the Supreme Court.

(f) Response to Petition for Review. The Attorney General shall, within 30 days of the service of the petition, serve 2 copies of a brief in opposition to the petition and file 9 copies thereof with the Clerk of the Supreme Court. The brief shall be direct and concise, shall conform to the applicable provisions of R. 2:6 and shall not exceed 15 pages if printed or 20 pages if otherwise reproduced or typed, exclusive of table of contents, citations and appendix. Within 10 days of such service, petitioner may serve 2 copies and file 9 copies of a reply brief not exceeding 9 pages if printed or 10 pages if otherwise reproduced or typed, exclusive of tables of contents, citations or appendix.

(g) Final Determination. The final determination of a petition for review may be either by written opinion or by order of the Supreme Court and shall state whether the opinion or other action of the Advisory Committee on Professional Ethics is affirmed, reversed or modified or shall provide for such other final disposition as is appropriate.

Note: Adopted April 4, 1977 to be effective immediately; paragraphs (a) and (f) amended July 13, 1994 to be effective September 1, 1994.

1:19–9. Ethics Telephone Research Service

(a) Generally. The Advisory Committee on Professional Ethics shall operate a telephone ethics hotline to provide, with respect to issues of legal ethics within its jurisdiction, and issues of advertising and solicitation within the jurisdiction of the Committee on Attorney Advertising, general information and research assistance, but not legal advice or advisory opinions, to members of the bar of this state in good standing. The existence and limited nature of this ethics telephone research service shall be advertised regularly as a notice

to the bar in the official publication designed by the Supreme Court. The Chair of the Advisory Committee, in consultation with the Chair of the Advertising Committee, shall hire and direct one full-time attorney and one secretary to provide this service. Staff shall assist attorneys requesting information to the extent that time and resources permit and to render general assistance and information to an inquiring attorney.

(b) Form of Inquiry and Certification. An attorney requesting information and research assistance on issues of legal ethics may communicate with the Ethics Research Assistance Service either by phone or in writing. At the time the initial inquiry is made, the attorney shall provide identification as a qualified member of the bar, shall certify that the facts presented concern his or her prospective ethical conduct and shall certify that the inquirer is not the subject of a disciplinary grievance or proceeding. The inquirer shall provide in good faith all material facts bearing on the ethical issue presented. Where the inquiry would require resolution of questions concerning substantive law, the inquiry shall be declined.

(c) Disclaimer. Before rendering assistance to an inquirer, the Ethics Research Assistance Service staff shall advise each inquirer that (1) only legal research assistance is being furnished and no legal opinion is being rendered and (2) the inquirer is responsible for making his or her own final judgment on the ethical issue presented.

(d) Inadmissibility of Inquiry Results. Neither the fact that an inquiry has been made nor the results thereof, shall be admissible in any legal proceeding, including an attorney or judicial discipline proceeding.

(e) Records; Disclosure. The Ethics Research Assistance Service shall keep records of the number of inquiries and the nature and type of inquiries, but shall not reveal the name of the inquirer, the substance of a specific inquiry, or the specific response thereto. All information provided to, and all records maintained by, the Ethics Research Assistance Service shall be confidential and shall not be disclosed, except as authorized by the Supreme Court. All such information shall be immune from subpoena in any civil, disciplinary or administrative matter.

Note: Adopted January 31, 1995 to be effective March 1, 1995; paragraph (a) amended July 10, 1998 to be effective September 1, 1998; paragraph (a) amended October 9, 2007, to be effective immediately.

RULE 1:19A. COMMITTEE ON ATTORNEY ADVERTISING

1:19A–1. Appointment and Organization

(a) Appointment. The Supreme Court shall appoint a Committee on Attorney Advertising (hereinafter the Advertising Committee) consisting of seven members,

five of whom shall be members of the bar and two of whom shall be public members. The initial members shall be appointed to terms of one, two, or three years. At the expiration of such terms all subsequent reappointments shall be for a term of three years. No member who has served four full three-year terms shall be eligible for immediate reappointment. A vacancy occurring during a term shall be filled for the unexpired portion thereof.

(b) Meetings; Quorum. A majority of the members of the Advertising Committee shall constitute a quorum, but no decision shall be made unless concurred in by a majority of those present. The Chair may designate subpanels of not fewer than three members, at least one of whom is a public member and a majority of whom shall be attorneys, in order to consider any matter and hold hearings, if necessary, and to report to the Advertising Committee. All final decisions shall be made by the Advertising Committee in accordance with these rules. The Advertising Committee shall meet at such times as directed by the Chair or the Supreme Court.

(c) Officers. The Court shall annually designate a member of the Advertising Committee to serve as Chair. A staff member of the Administrative Office of the Courts shall serve as Secretary.

Note: Adopted June 26, 1987, to be effective July 1, 1987; paragraph (a) amended July 10, 1998 to be effective September 1, 1998.

1:19A–2. Jurisdiction

(a) Advisory Opinions and Ethics Grievances. The Advertising Committee shall have the exclusive authority to consider requests for advisory opinions and ethics grievances concerning the compliance of advertisements and other related communications with Rules of Professional Conduct 7.1 "Communications Concerning a Lawyer's Service," 7.2 "Advertising," 7.3 "Personal Contact with Prospective Clients" (excluding subsections (c), (d), (e) and (f)), 7.4 "Communication of Fields of Practice," and 7.5 "Firm Names and Letterheads," and with any duly approved advertising guidelines promulgated by the Advertising Committee with the approval of the Supreme Court.

(b) Rules of Procedure. The Advertising Committee shall, consistent with these Rules, establish procedures, publish forms and maintain records as required for its conduct.

(c) Advertising Guidelines. The Advertising Committee may adopt advertising guidelines consistent with the Rules of Professional Conduct set forth in section (a) and with these Rules, after affording the bar an opportunity to comment and after approval by the Supreme Court. Advertising guidelines may include by way of example, but not by way of limitation, disclosure requirements, restrictions beyond those set forth in RPC 7.2(a), time, place, and manner regulations, guidelines for determining the application of the "predominantly informational" and "extreme portrayal" requirements, and, generally, any guideline that the Advertising Committee deems either necessary or desirable in clarifying the application of the Rules governing advertisements and other communications within its jurisdic-

tion. Upon adoption all advertising guidelines shall be published initially in the New Jersey Law Journal and New Jersey Lawyer.

(d) Pre-publication Review. The Advertising Committee may, in its discretion, require any attorney or firm or association of attorneys that has hired an advertising agency, public relations counsel, or entity providing assistance in connection with advertising or other related communications within the jurisdiction of the Advertising Committee, to submit to the Advertising Committee before publication for its approval, disapproval, or modification any series of advertisements or other communications within its jurisdiction, any advertising program, or any general public relations program.

(e) Education. The Advertising Committee may undertake such action as it deems necessary (1) to educate the public concerning rational means of selecting counsel and of determining whether counsel is needed, and (2) to educate the bar concerning the ethical limitations of attorney advertising.

(f) Reports. The Advertising Committee shall monitor the impact of all advertising and other communications within its jurisdiction to determine the extent to which existing Rules and guidelines achieve their goals and the extent to which there is any need for revision. Without limiting the Advertising Committee's observations in any way, it should specifically monitor the impact of all rules and advertising guidelines, as they exist from time to time, to determine if consumers are obtaining enough information about their need for lawyers and to aid them in the selection of lawyers, if price competition is being achieved, if damage to the qualities of the profession that serve society is occurring, and if consumers are being damaged through non-rational appeals.

The Advertising Committee shall submit to the Supreme Court an annual report, the first of which shall be filed on January 1, 1988. The first report of the Advertising Committee should report on the experience of New Jersey, as well as other states concerning attorney advertising. Prior to submitting its first annual report, the Advertising Committee shall conduct at least one public hearing on the desirability of retaining, revising, or repealing the then-existing advertising Rules or guidelines, or adopting any other proposed Rule on attorney advertising. Public hearings shall be held in subsequent years in the discretion of the Advertising Committee or as directed by the Supreme Court.

Note: Adopted June 26, 1987 to be effective July 1, 1987; paragraph (c) amended July 10, 1998 to be effective September 1, 1998.

1:19A–3. Advisory Opinions

(a) Form of Inquiry. All inquiries shall be addressed to the Secretary. The Advertising Committee shall accept inquiries from any member of the New Jersey bar. Inquiries shall be in writing and shall have appended to them a copy of the questioned advertisement or other related communication and shall contain a certificate that any opinion of the Advertising Committee will not affect the interests of the parties to any pending action. The inquiry shall be accompanied by a letter brief or brief citing the Rules of Court, Rules of Professional Conduct or Advertising Guidelines, if any, that are applicable, and shall state clearly the factual situation in detail and the inquirer's position as to the propriety of the advertisement or other related communication.

(b) Disposition of Inquiries. The Advertising Committee shall, so far as practical, act on an inquiry at its next meeting following receipt of the inquiry, provided that the inquiry is received by the Secretary at least ten business days prior to the Advertising Committee's meeting. In its discretion the Advertising Committee may authorize oral argument, which shall be electronically or stenographically recorded and may be transcribed. The Advertising Committee may, in its discretion, reconsider a prior decision (provided that the same is final) at any time, but a reversal or modification of a prior decision shall have prospective effect only.

All advisory opinions shall be given in writing to the inquirer. The decision shall state the Advertising Committee's determination as to whether the advertisement or other related communication is proper; it shall also briefly state the rationale that supports it and the rule or rules relied upon. The Advertising Committee may condition its approval by requiring any reasonable changes that are, in its opinion, necessary to conform with the Rules of Court, Rules of Professional Conduct or Advertising Guidelines, including, but not limited to, disclosure requirements, and time, place, and manner regulations.

(c) Effect of Opinions; Publication. An opinion approving an advertisement or other communication shall, until and unless revised in accordance with section (d) or reconsidered, be a bar to prosecution of ethical charges against the lawyer or law firm, except for a prosecution based on a charge that it is false or misleading in violation of RPC 7.1(a)(1). An opinion disapproving an advertisement or other related communication shall, until and unless revised in accordance with section (d) or reconsidered, be binding upon the inquirer and anyone with actual or constructive knowledge thereof so that such use of a disapproved advertisement or other related communication shall be per se unethical conduct.

When the Advertising Committee believes it to be in the best interest of the bar or the public, it may publish its opinion in the New Jersey Law Journal and New Jersey Lawyer. Published opinions shall constitute constructive notice to, and shall be binding on, all members of the bar and in connection with any ethics proceedings, unless revised pursuant to section (d) or reconsidered.

(d) Petition for Review. Any aggrieved member of the New Jersey bar may seek review of any final action

of the Advertising Committee relating to requests for advisory opinions in accordance with R. 1:19–8.

Note: Adopted June 26, 1987 to be effective July 1, 1987; paragraphs (a) and (c) amended July 10, 1998 to be effective September 1, 1998.

1:19A–4. Ethics Grievances

(a) Procedure for Considering Grievances. All ethics grievances alleging unethical conduct with respect to advertisements and other related communications set forth in Rule 1:19A–2(a) shall be considered solely by the Advertising Committee. Except as expressly stated herein, no District Ethics Committee shall take any action on such a grievance received by it, but shall forward it to the Secretary of the Advertising Committee for review and action.

An ethics grievance concerning advertising or other related communications by an attorney shall be filed with the Secretary of the Advertising Committee. Grievances shall be accepted from members of the public and the bar. The Advertising Committee may on its own motion initiate an ethics grievance. Upon receipt of an ethics grievance alleging unethical conduct the Secretary of the Advertising Committee shall acknowledge receipt to the grievant and may forward a copy of the grievance to the attorney or law firm responsible for an initial written response, provided that if the Secretary concludes that even if true the alleged facts show beyond debate no violation of the Rules, the grievance may be dismissed. If the Secretary requests a response, the lawyer or law firm shall file with the Secretary and serve (personally or by mail) upon the grievant a responding letter brief or brief within fourteen (14) days after service. Such lawyer or law firm shall also file with the Secretary a true copy of the advertisement, tape recording, video tape, or other related communication for the Advertising Committee's use, provided that no such filing shall be required for any advertisement or other related communication that was disseminated more than three years prior to receipt of the grievance by the Advertising Committee. The failure of an attorney or law firm to file and serve a response together with a true copy of the advertisement or other related communication as set forth above may, in the Advertising Committee's discretion, be taken as an adverse inference of an ethical violation.

(b) Initial Review and Dismissal by Advertising Committee. At the conclusion of the expiration of time provided for the attorney's filing of any initial response the Advertising Committee shall review the matter. If it concludes there is a need for further investigation, the Advertising Committee shall direct the Secretary to proceed accordingly and it shall reconsider the matter following such further investigation. Upon any matter within its jurisdiction coming to its attention, the Advertising Committee may arrange an informal conference with the lawyer or law firm. If the Advertising Committee concludes that there is no unethical conduct, it shall dismiss the grievance and so notify the parties in writing, briefly stating the reasons therefor.

An appeal from the decision of the Advertising Committee to dismiss a grievance shall be available in accordance with Rule 1:20–15(e), but the Disciplinary Review Board shall be limited in its review to the legal conclusion of the Advertising Committee as to whether there is unethical conduct.

(c) **Formal Complaint and Answer.** In all other cases where the Advertising Committee concludes that the facts may demonstrate by clear and convincing evidence that unethical conduct has occurred, it shall direct the Secretary to file a formal complaint in accordance with Rule 1:20–4(d). The Secretary shall serve the formal complaint upon the original grievant, if any, and upon the respondent, who shall be required to file a formal answer within ten days of service of the formal complaint, all in accordance with Rule 1:20–4(e).

(d) **Hearing Where Material Facts Not Disputed.** Where in the opinion of the Advertising Committee there are no material controverted issues of fact, it shall bring the matter on for oral argument (which shall be electronically or stenographically recorded) on notice to the respondent. The Advertising Committee shall designate a presenter. The sole issue before the Advertising Committee shall be whether, and the extent to which, discipline is required. The Advertising Committee shall prepare a written dated report containing its findings of fact on each issue presented in accordance with Rule 1:20–6(c)(2)(E). If public discipline is recommended, the report shall also contain a specific recommendation as to the extent thereof. Unless it dismisses the matter, the Advertising Committee shall promptly file its report and recommendation with the Disciplinary Review Board, which shall proceed in accordance with Rule 1:20–15(f). Dismissals shall be appealable and notice thereof given, as set forth in section (b) above.

(e) **Hearings Where Material Facts Are Disputed.** Where in the opinion of the Advertising Committee there are material controverted issues of fact (including, but not limited to, instances of alleged false, fraudulent, misleading, or deceptive advertisements or other communications), it may, after the filing of a formal complaint and answer, (1) hear and determine the matter itself in accordance with Rule 1:20–6(a) and (c) (in which case the hearing shall be electronically or stenographically transcribed), or (2) refer the matter to the appropriate District Ethics Committee for hearings in accordance with Rule 1:20–6 and the filing of a report with the Advertising Committee, which report shall be limited to findings of fact on the issues presented, in accordance with Rule 1:20–6(c)(2)(E). In either event the Advertising Committee shall, unless it dismisses the matter, render its report and recommendation to the Disciplinary Review Board in accordance with Rule 1:20–6(c)(2)(E). If public discipline is recommended, the report shall also contain a specific recommendation as to the extent thereof. If the matter is dismissed, notification of parties and appeal shall be the same as set forth in section (b) above.

(f) **Action by Disciplinary Review Board on Reports Recommending Discipline.** Where the Advertising Committee files with the Board a report recommending discipline, the Board shall, except as stated below, proceed in accordance with Rule 1:20–15(f). In considering a report and recommendation of the Advertising Committee the Board shall accept the facts found as conclusive. The sole issues to be determined shall be the legal conclusion reached by the Advertising Committee as to whether there is unethical conduct and the extent of final discipline to be imposed.

(g) **Attorney for Respondent; Subpoenas.** Insofar as necessary, Rules 1:20–4(g)(2) and 1:20–7(i) shall be applicable to proceedings by the Advertising Committee. Subpoenas may be signed either by any member of the Advertising Committee, or by its Secretary.

(h) **Dual Grievances.** When the ethical issues presented in a grievance involve both aspects of advertising and other related communications within the jurisdiction of the Advertising Committee and also other ethical issues not ordinarily within its jurisdiction, the Advertising Committee shall take jurisdiction of the entire matter if the grievance is predominantly related to advertising and other related communications within its jurisdiction. In all other cases of dual grievances, the Advertising Committee may accept such grievances. If it accepts such grievances the Advertising Committee shall, to the extent necessary to conclude all aspects of the grievance, exercise all the jurisdiction and functions of a District Ethics Committee. Otherwise, the Advertising Committee may decline jurisdiction in writing and refer its entire file in the matter to the appropriate District Ethics Committee. A District Ethics Committee to whom a dual ethics grievance has been referred in accordance with this section shall take jurisdiction over the entire matter and proceed in accordance with Rule 1:20–3(g). To the extent necessary to conclude all aspects of the grievance so referred, a District Ethics Committee shall exercise all the jurisdiction and functions of the Advertising Committee.

Note: Adopted June 26, 1987 to be effective July 1, 1987; paragraph (b) amended November 7, 1988 to be effective January 2, 1989; paragraphs (b), (c), (d), (e), (f), (g) and (h) amended July 10, 1998 to be effective September 1, 1998.

1:19A–5. Records; Confidentiality

The Advertising Committee shall maintain such records and file such reports as shall be required by the Administrative Director of the Courts or the Supreme Court. With respect to requests for advisory opinions, both the request and the advisory opinion shall be available to the public; otherwise proceedings concerning advisory opinions shall be confidential except as ordered by the Supreme Court. With respect to ethics grievances, confidentiality shall be maintained in accordance with Rule 1:20–9.

Note: Adopted June 26, 1987 to be effective July 1, 1987; amended July 10, 1998 to be effective September 1, 1998.

1:19A–6. Immunity

The Rules governing immunity of ethics and fee arbitration committee members and the Secretary thereof, as well as grievants, clients, and witnesses as set forth in R. 1:20–7(e) and (f), shall apply to all proceedings of the Advertising Committee. This immunity shall not, however, extend to any publication or distribution of information in violation of the confidentiality provisions of Rule 1:19A–5.

Note: Adopted June 26, 1987 to be effective July 1, 1987; amended July 10, 1998 to be effective September 1, 1998.

1:19A–7. Referral to Office of Attorney Ethics

Wherever appropriate the Advertising Committee may bring to the attention of the Director of the Office of Attorney Ethics facts that it believes may constitute cause for temporary suspension, including, but not limited to, an attorney's use of a disapproved advertisement or other related communication. The Director may take such action as appropriate, including an emergent application for temporary suspension pursuant to Rule 1:20–11.

Note: Adopted June 26, 1987 to be effective July 1, 1987; amended July 13, 1994 to be effective September 1, 1994; amended July 10, 1998 to be effective September 1, 1998.

1:19A–8. Telephone Inquiries

Telephone inquiries to the Committee on Attorney Advertising shall be made in accordance with R. 1:19–9.

Note: Adopted July 10, 1998 to be effective September 1, 1998.

RULE 1:20. DISCIPLINE OF MEMBERS OF THE BAR

Glossary of Attorney Discipline Terms

Agreement in Lieu of Discipline—the vehicle used to accomplish diversion of "minor" unethical conduct matters where an attorney admits "minor" unethical conduct has been committed and that attorney qualifies for diversionary treatment. See R. 1:20–3(i)(2)(B).

Board or Disciplinary Review Board—the intermediate appellate tribunal in disciplinary matters.

Complaint—the written document formally charging the respondent with specific violations of unethical conduct. A complaint is issued after completion of an investigation if it meets the standard of R. 1:20–4(a).

Consent Matter—the appellate process before the Disciplinary Review Board and the Supreme Court by which the extent of discipline to be imposed as the result of discipline by consent is reviewed, without oral argument. See R. 1:20–15(g) and R. 1:20–16(e).

Director—the Director of the Office of Attorney Ethics, who administers the Office of Attorney Ethics, Ethics Committees, Fee Committees, the Random Audit Program, the Annual Attorney Registration Statement, and the Trust Overdraft Notification Program.

Disciplinary Oversight Committee—the Disciplinary Oversight Committee reviews the annual disciplinary system budget and makes recommendations to the Supreme Court concerning the disciplinary system.

Discipline by Consent—a procedure whereby a respondent may agree with an investigator, presenter or ethics counsel to admit facts constituting unethical conduct and recommend specific discipline or a range of specific discipline, subject to review by the Disciplinary Review Board. See R. 1:20–10(b).

Diversion—a non-disciplinary treatment by consent for attorneys who admit they have committed "minor" unethical conduct and who otherwise qualify for diversionary treatment. Diversion is accomplished through an "Agreement In Lieu of Discipline." See R. 1:20–3(i)(2)(A) and (B).

Ethics Committee(s)—one or more district ethics committees throughout the state that screen, investigate, prosecute, and hear disciplinary and disability-inactive matters.

Ethics Counsel—an attorney of the Office of Attorney Ethics. See R. 1:20–2(a).

Fee Committee(s)—one or more district fee arbitration committees throughout the state that screen, hear, and decide disputes by clients over legal fees.

Grievance—any allegation of unethical conduct made against an attorney. A grievance, if docketed, is assigned for investigation by the Director or by an Ethics Committee.

Minor Unethical Conduct—minor types of unethical conduct which, if proved, would not warrant discipline greater than an admonition. Minor unethical conduct matters are eligible for diversionary treatment. R. 1:20–3(i)(2).

Presenter—the attorney who is appointed to prosecute a complaint. R. 1:20–4(g)(1).

Respondent—the attorney who is the subject of disciplinary charges.

Trier of Fact—refers to an ethics committee hearing panel or single member adjudicator or special ethics master.

Unethical Conduct—all ethics violations that would subject an attorney to discipline are referred to as unethical conduct. R. 1:20–3(i)(1).

Note: Adopted January 31, 1995 to be effective March 1, 1995; "Agreement In Lieu of Discipline," "Complaint," "Discipline By Consent," "Diversion," "Ethics Counsel," "Grievance," "Minor Misconduct," and "Presenter" modified, "Misconduct" deleted, and "Board or Disciplinary Review Board," "Director," "Disciplinary Oversight Committee," "Ethics Committee(s)," "Fee Committee(s)," "Respondent," and "Unethical Conduct" added July 28, 2004 to be effective September 1, 2004.

1:20–1. Disciplinary Jurisdiction; Annual Fee and Registration

(a) Generally. Every attorney and business entity authorized to practice law in the State of New Jersey, including those attorneys specially authorized for a limited purpose or in connection with a particular proceeding, shall be subject to the disciplinary jurisdiction of the Supreme Court as set forth in the Constitution of 1947, Article 6, Section 2, Paragraph 3. Attorneys who have resigned without prejudice pursuant to Rule 1:20–22 shall also be subject to such jurisdiction in respect of conduct undertaken prior to the acceptance of the resignation by the Court.

To assist in the administration of its disciplinary function, the Supreme Court shall establish, in accordance with these Rules, district ethics committees (hereinafter referred to as the Ethics Committees or the Ethics Committee), district fee arbitration committees (hereinafter referred to as the Fee Committee or the Fee Committees), a Disciplinary Review Board (hereinafter referred to as the Board or Disciplinary Review Board), a Disciplinary Oversight Committee (hereinafter referred to as the Oversight Committee), and an Office of Attorney Ethics and a Director thereof (hereinafter referred to as the Director).

(b) Annual Fee. Every attorney admitted to practice law in the State of New Jersey, including all persons holding a plenary license, those admitted pro hac vice in accordance with Rule 1:21–2, those holding a limited license as in-house counsel under Rule 1:27–2, those registered as multijurisdictional practitioners under RPC 5.5(b), and those certified as Foreign Legal Consultants under Rule 1:21–9, shall pay annually to the Oversight Committee a sum that shall be determined each year by the Supreme Court. All sums so paid shall be used for the attorney-discipline and fee-arbitration systems. This assessment shall be collected administratively in the same manner as and subject to the same exemptions provided under Rule 1:28–2, except that plenary-licensed attorneys who are in their second calendar year of admission shall pay a partial fee, as determined by the Supreme Court. The names of all persons failing to comply with the provisions of this Rule shall be reported to the Supreme Court for inclusion on its Ineligible to Practice Law List.

(c) Annual Registration Statement. To facilitate the collection of the annual fee provided for in paragraph (b), every attorney admitted to practice law in this state, including all persons holding a plenary license, those admitted pro hac vice, those holding a limited license as in-house counsel, those registered as multijurisdictional practitioners, and those certified as Foreign Legal Consultants, shall, on or before February 1 of every year, or such other date as the Court may determine, pay the annual fee and file a registration statement with the New Jersey Lawyers' Fund for Client Protection (hereinafter referred to as the Fund). The registration statement shall be in a form prescribed by the Administrative Director of the Courts with the approval of the Supreme Court. As part of the annual registration process, each attorney shall certify compliance with Rule 1:28A. All registration statements shall be filed by the Fund with the Office of Attorney Ethics, which may destroy the registration statements after one year. Each lawyer shall file with the Fund a supplemental statement of any change in the attorney's billing address and shall file with the Office of Attorney Ethics a supplemental statement of any change in the home and primary bona fide law office addresses, as well as the main law office telephone number previously submitted and the financial institution or the account numbers for the primary trust and business accounts, either prior to such change or within thirty days thereafter. All persons first becoming subject to this rule shall file the statement required by this rule prior to or within thirty days of the date of admission.

The information provided on the registration statement shall be confidential except as otherwise directed by the Supreme Court.

(d) Remedies for Failure to Pay or File. Any person who fails to complete and file the annual registration statement required by paragraph (c) on or before February 1 of each year or such other date as the Court may determine, or to make payment as required by paragraph (b) within 30 days after the due date each year shall be declared to be ineligible to practice law and shall be included on the Ineligible To Practice Law List of the Supreme Court. A person who makes payment after February 1 of the billing year, or such other due date as the Court may establish, but before being placed on the Ineligible List, shall be subject to a late fee of $40. These late fees shall be shared equally between the Oversight Committee and the Fund. Such person shall be reinstated automatically to the practice of law without further order of the Court on filing with the Fund the completed annual registration statement for the current year together with the annual payment, the late fee, any arrears due from prior years, and full compliance with the Rule 1:28–2 requirements of the Fund. Pursuant to Rule 1:28–2(c), failure to complete and file the annual registration statement for seven consecutive years shall result in the administrative revocation of the attorney's license to practice in this State.

Note: Adopted February 23, 1978, to be effective April 1, 1978. Any matter pending unheard before a County Ethics Committee as of April 1, 1978 shall be transferred, as appropriate, to the District Ethics Committee or the District Fee Arbitration Committee having jurisdiction. Any matter heard or partially heard by a County Ethics Committee by April 1, 1978 shall be concluded by such Ethics Committee and shall be reported on in accordance with these rules; amended July 16, 1981 to be effective September 14, 1981. Caption amended and first two paragraphs amended and redesignated as paragraph (a); new paragraphs (b), (c) and (d) adopted January 31, 1984 to be effective February 15, 1984; paragraph (c) amended November 5, 1986 to be effective January 1, 1987; paragraph (d) amended June 29, 1990 to be effective September 4, 1990; paragraph (c) amended July 14, 1992 to be effective September 1, 1992; paragraph (c) amended September 15, 1992, to be effective January 1, 1993; caption added to all paragraphs and paragraphs (a), (b), (c), and (d) amended February 8, 1993 to be effective immediately; paragraphs (a), (b) and (c) amended January 31, 1995, to be effective March 1, 1995; paragraph (a) amended July 10, 1998, to be effective September 1, 1998; paragraph (b) amended July 12, 2002 to be effective September 3, 2002; paragraphs (a), (b), (c) and (d) amended July 28, 2004 to be effective September 1, 2004; paragraph (c) amended July 9, 2008 to be effective September 1, 2008.

1:20–2. Office of Attorney Ethics

(a) Appointment. The Supreme Court shall appoint a Director of the Office of Attorney Ethics and such assistant and deputy ethics counsel and staff as it may from time to time determine are necessary to perform properly the functions prescribed by these rules. Neither the Director, ethics counsel nor staff shall be permitted to otherwise engage in the practice of law nor to be otherwise employed except as may be provided by the Code of Conduct for Judiciary Employees, these rules and R. 1:17.

(b) Authority. The Director shall have the discretion and the authority to:

(1) exercise exclusive jurisdiction over the investigation and prosecution of the following:

(A) any case in which the Director determines the matter involves serious or complex issues that must be immediately addressed or one that requires emergent action;

(B) all cases in which an attorney is a defendant in any criminal proceedings;

(C) any case in which the Ethics Committee requests intervention;

(D) any case in which an Ethics Committee has not resolved a matter within one year of the filing of a grievance;

(E) any case in which the Board or the Supreme Court determines the matter should be assigned to the Director;

(F) any case involving multijurisdictional practice or practice as in-house counsel.

(2) investigate any information coming to the Director's attention, whether by grievance or otherwise, which, in the Director's judgment, may be grounds for discipline or transfer to disability-inactive status;

(3) dispose of, by investigation or dismissal, all matters involving alleged unethical conduct, by transfer to disability-inactive status, by agreement in lieu of discipline in minor unethical conduct cases, or by the prosecution of formal charges before a duly constituted hearing panel or special ethics master, all in accordance with these Rules;

(4) prosecute ethics proceedings before the Disciplinary Review Board;

(5) prosecute all ethics proceedings before the Supreme Court, unless the Court or the Director requests the assistance of Board Counsel to do so;

(6) seek from the Supreme Court judicial review of any final determination of the Board within the time and in the manner prescribed by the Rules of the Court;

(7) transfer any matter pending before an Ethics Committee or Fee Committee to another district;

(8) maintain records of all ethics and fee arbitration matters;

(9) administer the programs of the Fee Committees in accordance with R. 1:20A–1 et seq., of the Ethics Committees in accordance with R. 1:20–3 et seq., and to render to both of them appropriate legal and administrative advice;

(10) administer the Random Audit Compliance Program in accordance with R. 1:21–6(c);

(11) prepare annually, jointly with Counsel for the Disciplinary Review Board, a proposed budget for the attorney disciplinary system of the state;

(12) hire and discharge secretaries of Ethics Committees and Fee Committees and recommend and pay their compensation;

(13) recommend to the Supreme Court the appointment and replacement of members of Ethics Committees and Fee Committees;

(14) recommend the creation of new Ethics Committees and Fee Committees and the reorganization and termination of existing Ethics Committees and Fee Committees;

(15) recommend to the Supreme Court rules and guidelines governing the procedures to be followed in all ethics and fee arbitration proceedings in this state;

(16) hire and discharge all staff of the Office of Attorney Ethics consistent with personnel policies of the judiciary and subject to the approval of the Chief

Justice, and to recommend the hiring of all ethics counsel to the Supreme Court;

(17) select attorneys and non-attorneys from among former Ethics and Fee Committee members to act as hearing panel members; and

(18) approve additional volunteer attorneys who are not members of an Ethics Committee to act as investigators or presenters.

In all actions the Director shall exercise all of the investigative and prosecutorial authority of an Ethics Committee in addition to any authority invested in the Director under these rules.

(c) Advisory Opinions Prohibited. The Office of Attorney Ethics shall not render advisory opinions of any kind, either orally or in writing.

(d) Exemption From Costs. As an agency of the Supreme Court, the Office of Attorney Ethics and any lawfully appointed designee shall be exempt from the payment of any Court costs required by rule of law of the State of New Jersey including, but not limited to, the filing or docketing of any document, deposit for costs or service of process.

Note: Former rule redesignated R. 1:20–3 and new rule adopted January 31, 1984 to be effective February 15, 1984; paragraph (b)(15) amended and new paragraph (16) adopted November 5, 1986 to be effective January 1, 1987; paragraph (b)(8) amended June 29, 1990 to be effective September 4, 1990; paragraphs (a) and (b) amended, subparagraphs (b)(1) (i) (ii) (iii) (iv) (v) amended and redesignated (b)(1) (A) (B) (C) (D) and (E), new subparagraph (b)(17) added, paragraphs (c) and (d) adopted January 31, 1995 to become effective March 1, 1995; paragraph (b)(1) amended, subparagraph (b)(1)(E) amended, new subparagraph (b)(1)(F) adopted, new subparagraph (b)(2) added, former subparagraphs (b)(2) and (b)(3) renumbered as (b)(3) and (b)(4) and amended, former subparagraphs (b)(4) to (b)(9) renumbered as (b)(5) to (b)(10), former subparagraphs (b)(10) and (b)(11) renumbered as (b)(11) and (b)(12) and amended, former subparagraph (b)(12) renumbered as (b)(13), former subparagraph (b)(13) renumbered as (b)(14) and amended, former subparagraphs (b)(14) to (b)(17) renumbered as (b)(15) to (b)(18), and new last sentence added to paragraph (b) July 28, 2004 to be effective September 1, 2004; subparagraphs (b)(16) and (b)(17) amended July 9, 2008 to be effective September 1, 2008.

1:20–3. District Ethics Committees; Investigations

(a) Disciplinary Districts. The Supreme Court shall establish, and may from time to time alter, disciplinary districts consisting of defined geographical areas and shall appoint in each such district a District Ethics Committee which shall consist of such number of members, not fewer than eight, as the Court may determine, at least four of whom shall be attorneys of this state, at least two of whom shall not be attorneys, all of whom shall either reside or work in the district or county in which the district is located.

(b) Appointments. Members of Ethics Committees shall be appointed by, and shall serve at the pleasure of the Supreme Court for a term of four years. With the approval of the Supreme Court, a member who has served a full term may be reappointed to one successive term. A member serving in connection with an investigation pending at the time the member's term expires may continue to serve in such matter until its conclusion. In order that, as nearly as possible, the terms of one-quarter of the members shall expire each year, the Supreme Court may, when establishing a new Ethics Committee, appoint members for terms of less than four years and members so appointed shall be eligible for reappointment to a full successive term.

(c) Officers; Organization. The Supreme Court shall annually designate a member of each Ethics Committee to serve at its pleasure as chair and another member to serve as vice-chair. Whenever the chair is absent or unable to act or disqualified from acting due to a conflict, the vice-chair shall perform the duties of the chair. The chair shall be responsible for administering the Ethics Committee. Under the chair's direction, the vice-chair, or another Ethics Committee member designated by the chair, shall be responsible for administering all matters where a complaint has been filed.

Each Ethics Committee shall hold an organization meeting in September of each year and shall meet thereafter at least monthly except that, with the approval of the Director, an Ethics Committee may meet less frequently. The Ethics Committee shall also meet at the call of the Supreme Court, the chair, the Board or the Director.

The Director shall, after consultation with the chair, appoint a secretary who shall not be a member of the Ethics Committee but who shall be a member of the bar maintaining an office within the district or county in which the district is located. The secretary shall continue to serve at the pleasure of the Director and shall be paid an amount annually set by the Supreme Court to reimburse the secretary for costs and expenses. The secretary shall keep full and complete records of all Ethics Committee proceedings, shall maintain files with respect to all inquiries and grievances received and investigations undertaken, shall transmit copies of all documents filed immediately on receipt thereof to the Director and shall promptly notify the latter of each final disposition. Reports with respect to the work of the Ethics Committee shall be filed by the secretary with the Director as instructed by the Director.

(d) Office. Each Ethics Committee shall receive grievances at the office of its secretary and at such additional places as shall be designated by the Director.

(e) Screening; Docketing.

The secretary shall evaluate inquiries and grievances in accordance with this rule and shall docket, decline, or dismiss the matters within 45 days of their receipt. The secretary shall not conduct an investigation of a grievance.

(1) The secretary shall evaluate all information received by inquiry, grievance or from other sources alleging attorney unethical conduct or incapacity by an attorney maintaining an office in that district. If the attorney is subject to the jurisdiction of the Court and the grievance alleges facts which, if true, would constitute unethical conduct as defined by the Rules of Professional Conduct, case law or other authority, or incapacity, the matter shall be docketed and investigated.

(2) The secretary shall decline jurisdiction if:

(A) the attorney is not subject to the jurisdiction of the Supreme Court of New Jersey, in which case the matter shall be declined and referred to the appropriate entity in any jurisdiction in which the attorney is admitted;

(B) the matter involves an inquiry or grievance regarding advertising or other related communications within the jurisdiction of the Committee on Attorney Advertising (R. 1:19A–2(a)), in which case the matter shall be sent to that committee unless the matter has been referred by the Advertising Committee in accordance with R. 1:19A–4(e) or (h);

(C) the facts stated in the inquiry or grievance involve circumstances which the Supreme Court has determined through the adoption of court rules or administrative guidelines will not be entertained, in which case the matter shall be declined;

(D) the grievance involves aspects of a substantial fee dispute and a charge of unethical conduct, unless so directed by the Director or unless the matter is referred by the Fee Committee in accordance with Rule 1:20A–4.

(3) The secretary, with concurrence by a designated public member, shall decline jurisdiction if the facts stated in the inquiry or grievance, if true, would not constitute unethical conduct or incapacity.

(4) If a grievance is not in writing and if the secretary concludes that the grievance must be declined under subsection (e)(2) or that the grievant alleges facts that, even if true, would not constitute unethical conduct or incapacity, the secretary shall so advise the grievant and that if the grievant wishes further consideration the secretary will provide a written attorney grievance form for completion. Unless declination is mandatory under subparagraph (e)(2), on receipt of a properly completed attorney grievance form the secretary will have the grievance reviewed by one or more public members of the Ethics Committee designated by the secretary. If a designated public member agrees with the secretary, the matter shall be declined. Otherwise, the matter shall be docketed and assigned for investigation.

(5) If a matter is declined, the secretary shall furnish a concise written statement to the grievant of the reasons therefor and shall enclose a copy of the court rule or written guideline for declination approved by the Supreme Court.

(6) There shall be no appeal from a decision to decline a grievance made in accordance with this rule. An appeal may be taken from dismissal of a grievance after docketing in accordance with R. 1:20–3(h).

(f) Related Pending Litigation. If a grievance alleges facts that, if true, would constitute unethical conduct and if those facts are substantially similar to the material allegations of pending civil or criminal litigation, the grievance shall be docketed and investigated if, in the opinion of the secretary or Director, the facts alleged clearly demonstrate provable ethical violations or if the facts alleged present a substantial threat of imminent harm to the public. All other grievances involving such related pending civil and criminal litigation may be declined and not docketed. If the matter has already been docketed when the related pending litigation is discovered, the matter may be administratively dismissed, provided the matter is still in the investigative stage. The grievant shall be informed in writing of any decision, together with a brief statement of the reasons therefor and a copy of any Court Rule or written guideline supporting declination. Once a formal complaint has been filed, the matter shall not be dismissed nor held in abeyance pending completion of the related litigation, unless so authorized by the Director. Whenever an attorney is a defendant in any criminal proceeding, the Director shall docket the matter and may, in the Director's discretion, investigate and prosecute the disciplinary case.

(g) Investigation.

(1) *Generally.* Except in those districts in which the Director assigns investigators, the chair of the Ethics Committee shall assign an attorney member to each docketed case to conduct such investigation as may be necessary in order to determine whether unethical conduct has occurred or whether the respondent is disabled or incapacitated from practicing law.

(2) *Notice to Respondent.* No disposition other than dismissal, declination or designation as untriable shall be taken without first notifying the respondent in writing of the substance of the matter and affording the respondent an opportunity to respond in writing. Notice to the respondent shall be given by mail addressed to the address listed either in the current edition of the New Jersey Lawyer's Diary and Manual or with the Lawyers' Fund for Client Protection.

(3) *Duty to Cooperate.* Every attorney shall cooperate in a disciplinary investigation and reply in writing within ten days of receipt of a request for information. Such reply may include the assertion of any available constitutional right, together with the specific factual and legal basis therefor. Attorneys shall also produce the original of any client or other relevant law office file for inspection and review, if requested, as well as all accounting records required to be maintained in accor-

dance with R. 1:21–6. Where an attorney is unable to provide the requested information in writing within ten days, the attorney shall, within that time, inform the investigator in writing of the reason that the information cannot be so provided and give a date certain when it will be provided.

(4) *Failure to Cooperate.* If a respondent fails to cooperate either by not replying in writing to a request for information or by not producing the attorney's client and/or business file or accounting records for inspection and review, the Office of Attorney Ethics may file and serve a motion for temporary suspension with the Supreme Court, together with proof of service. The failure of a respondent to file a response in opposition to the motion may result in the entry of an order of temporary suspension without oral argument until further order of the Court. An attorney temporarily suspended under this rule may apply to the Court for reinstatement on proof of compliance with subsection (3) of this paragraph on notice to the Office of Attorney Ethics.

(5) *Notice to Grievant.* The substance of respondent's written response shall be communicated to the grievant, who shall be afforded an opportunity to respond in writing within 14 days of receipt of the communication.

(6) *Investigative Subpoena.* During the investigation of any matter, a subpoena may be issued in accordance with R. 1:20–7(i) in the name of the Supreme Court of New Jersey.

(h) Dismissal and Appeal; Administrative Dismissal. The investigator shall report in writing to the chair, providing a copy to the secretary. The report shall set forth the facts, together with a recommendation for action. If the chair concludes that there is no reasonable prospect of proving unethical conduct or incapacity by clear and convincing evidence, the matter shall be dismissed. Written notice of the facts and reasons for dismissal shall be provided to the respondent, the Director, and the grievant, who shall be advised of the right of appeal to the Board within 21 days as provided by Rule 1:20–15(e)(2).

The Director may authorize that a grievance be declined or administratively dismissed where either the attorney has been disciplined and the Director determines that the processing of additional matters against the respondent would not likely result in the imposition of substantially different discipline, or the attorney, although not yet disciplined, is already the subject of disciplinary proceedings and the nature or time periods covered by the additional grievances are similar to other unethical conduct already being pursued, so that the results would be likely to be merely cumulative. If so approved, the secretary shall give notice of declination or administrative dismissal to any grievant, together with an explanation of the reasons supporting the action.

(i) Determination of Unethical Conduct.

(1) *Generally.* If the chair determines that there is a reasonable prospect of a finding of unethical conduct by clear or convincing evidence, a further determination shall be made as to whether such conduct is either unethical conduct or minor unethical conduct.

(2) *Minor Unethical Conduct.*

(A) Defined. Minor unethical conduct is conduct, which, if proved, would not warrant a sanction greater than a public admonition. Unethical conduct shall not be considered minor if any of the following considerations apply: (i) the unethical conduct involves the knowing misappropriation of funds; (ii) the unethical conduct resulted in or is likely to result in substantial prejudice to a client or other person and restitution has not been made; (iii) the respondent has been disciplined in the previous five years; (iv) the unethical conduct involves dishonesty, fraud or deceit; (v) or the unethical conduct constitutes a crime as defined by the New Jersey Code of Criminal Justice (N.J.S.A. 2C:1–1, et seq.). Classification of unethical conduct as minor unethical conduct shall be in the sole discretion of the Director.

(B) Agreements in Lieu of Discipline.

(i) If, as a result of investigation, the chair concludes that minor unethical conduct has occurred, the chair may request that the Director, or his designee, divert the matter and approve an agreement in lieu of discipline. Such request shall be accompanied by any initial grievance, the respondent's response, an investigative report, the written agreement signed by the respondent, and a letter to any grievant enclosing a copy of the agreement. The letter shall give ten days notice to the grievant that the Director is being asked to approve the disposition and that any comments must be sent to the Director within that time. Diversion shall not be available subsequent to the filing of a complaint.

(ii) There shall be no appeal from the Director's decision.

(iii) An agreement in lieu of discipline may contain an agreement to meet, within a specified period (usually no more than six months), stated conditions addressed, to the extent practicable, to the remediation of the cause of the unethical conduct. Such conditions may include, but are not limited to, reimbursement of fees or costs, completion of legal work, participation in alcohol or drug rehabilitation program, psychological counseling or satisfactory completion of a course of study and such other programs as are developed. If approved, the Director shall monitor the terms of agreement. If the respondent fulfills the terms, the matter shall be dismissed.

(C) Other Process. If an attorney declines to agree to divert a matter to administrative disposition under subparagraph (B), or if the Director determines, as a matter of exclusive discretion, that the attorney does not qualify for diversion or has failed to comply with the terms of the diversion agreement, the matter shall proceed in accordance with subparagraph (i)(3)(A) of these rules.

(3) *Unethical Conduct.*

(A) Defined. All ethical violations of the Rules of Professional Conduct, case law, or other authority not determined in accordance with these rules to be minor unethical conduct shall be processed as unethical conduct.

(B) Process. Unethical conduct may be prosecuted by the filing of a complaint under R. 1:20–4 or through Discipline by Consent under R. 1:20–10.

(j) Incapacity. If the Director or the chair conclude that there is a reasonable prospect of proving incapacity by clear and convincing evidence, the matter shall proceed as provided under R. 1:20–12.

Note: Former Rule redesignated as Rule 1:20–4 January 31, 1984 to be effective February 15, 1984. Source- Former Rule 1:20–2 adopted February 23, 1978, to be effective April 1, 1978; paragraphs (a), (h), (l) and (m) amended January 17, 1979, which were superseded on March 2, 1979, to be effective April 1, 1979; and paragraphs (n) and (o) restored on March 22, 1979, to be effective April 1, 1979; subparagraph (l)(3) deleted and new paragraph (p) adopted June 19, 1981, to be effective immediately; paragraphs (c), (h), (j) and (l)(1)(i) amended July 16, 1981, to be effective September 14, 1981; Rule redesignated as Rule 1:20–3; paragraphs (a) through (e) amended; paragraphs (f), (g) and part of (k) deleted; paragraphs (h), (i), (j), (k), (l), (m), (n), (o) and (p) amended and redesignated (f), (h), (i), (j), (k), (l), (m), (n) and (o) and new paragraphs (g)and (p) adopted January 31, 1984, to be effective February 15, 1984; paragraphs (f), (g), (h), (i), (l), (n), (o) and (p) amended November 5, 1986, to be effective January 1, 1987; paragraphs (e) and (m) amended June 26, 1987 to be effective July 1, 1987; paragraphs (i), (j) and (o) amended November 7, 1988 to be effective January 2, 1989; paragraphs (f) and (i) amended, and paragraph (n)(3) caption and text amended June 29, 1990 to be effective September 4, 1990; paragraph (f) amended July 13, 1994 to be effective September 1, 1994; paragraph (g) and (n)(2) captions and text amended August 8, 1994 to be effective immediately; paragraphs (a), (b), (c) and (d) amended, paragraphs (e) through (p) deleted and new paragraphs (e) through (j) adopted January 31, 1995 to be effective March 1, 1995; paragraphs (f), (g)(5), and (h) amended July 5, 2000 to be effective September 5, 2000; paragraph (g)(1) amended July 12, 2002 to be effective September 3, 2002; paragraphs (a), (b), (c), (e), (f), (g), (h), (i) (text and caption), and (j) amended July 28, 2004 to be effective September 1, 2004; paragraph (b) amended June 15, 2007 to be effective September 1, 2007.

1:20–4. Formal Pleadings

(a) Complaint Determination. Where the chair or Director, in his or her sole discretion, determines that there is a reasonable prospect of a finding of unethical conduct by clear and convincing evidence and where the matter is not diverted pursuant to R. 1:20–3(i)(2), a complaint shall issue.

(b) Contents of Complaint. Every complaint shall be in writing, designated as such in the caption, and brought against the respondent in the name of either the District Ethics Committee or the Office of Attorney Ethics. The complaint shall be signed by the chair, secretary or any Ethics Committee member, the Director, or the Director's designee. The complaint shall state the name of the grievant, if any, and the name, year of admission, law office or other address, and county of practice of the respondent, and shall set forth sufficient facts to constitute fair notice of the nature of the alleged unethical conduct, specifying the ethical rules alleged to have been violated. It shall also state above the caption the name, address and phone number of the presenter assigned to handle the matter.

(c) Consolidation of Charges and Respondents. A complaint may include any number of charges against a respondent. A consolidated complaint may be filed against two or more respondents if they are members of the same law firm or if the allegations are based on the same general conduct or arise out of the same transaction or series of transactions.

(d) Filing and Service. The original complaint shall be filed with the secretary of the Ethics Committee or the designated special ethics master to whom the case is assigned. If the matter will be determined by an Ethics Committee, service of the complaint shall be made by the secretary; otherwise service shall be made by the Director. A copy of the complaint shall be served on the respondent and respondent's attorney, if known, in accordance with R. 1:20–7(h), together with written notice advising the respondent of the requirements of R. 1:20–4(e) and (f), the name and address of the secretary or the Director as appropriate, as well as the address and telephone number of the vice chair of the Ethics Committee or special ethics master to whom all questions and requests for extension of time to file answers shall be directed. In appropriate circumstances, the secretary or the Director shall forward a copy of every complaint to the respondent's law firm or public agency employer in accordance with R. 1: 20–9(k).

(e) Answer. Within twenty-one days after service of the complaint, the respondent shall file with and serve on the secretary the original and one copy of a written, verified answer designated as such in the caption. The respondent shall also file a copy with the presenter, the vice chair or special ethics master and, in cases prosecuted by the Director, two copies with that office. The verification shall be made in the following form:

"Verification of Answer

I, (insert respondent's name), am the respondent in the within disciplinary action and hereby certify as follows:

(1) I have read every paragraph of the foregoing Answer to the Complaint and verify that the statements therein are true and based on my personal knowledge.

(2) I am aware that if any of the foregoing statements made by me are willfully false, I am subject to punishment."

An answer that has not been verified within ten days after the respondent is given notice of the defect shall be deemed a failure to answer as defined within these Rules.

For good cause shown, the vice chair or the special ethics master, if one has been appointed, may, on written application made within twenty-one days after service of the complaint, extend the time to answer. The Director shall be notified of any extension granted in cases prosecuted by that office. The secretary shall forward one copy of all answers to the Director. The respondent's answer shall set forth (1) a full, candid, and complete disclosure of all facts reasonably within the scope of the formal complaint; (2) all affirmative defenses, including any claim of mental or physical disability and whether it is alleged to be causally related to the offenses charged; (3) any mitigating circumstances; (4) a request for a hearing either on the charges or in mitigation, and (5) any constitutional challenges to the proceedings. All constitutional questions shall be held for consideration by the Supreme Court as part of its review of any final decision of the Board. Interlocutory relief may be sought only in accordance with R. 1:20–16(f)(1). Failure to request a hearing shall be deemed a waiver thereof. A respondent is required to file an answer even if the respondent does not wish to contest the complaint.

(f) Failure to Answer.

(1) *Admission.* The failure of a respondent to file a verified answer within the prescribed time shall be deemed an admission that the allegations of the complaint are true and that they provide a sufficient basis for the imposition of discipline. No further proof hearing shall be required.

(2) *Certification to Disciplinary Review Board.* If a respondent has been duly served with a complaint, but has failed to file a verified answer within the prescribed time, a certification detailing that failure may be filed with the Director by the secretary or special ethics master, or, in cases prosecuted by the Director, by ethics counsel. The Director may thereafter file that certification with the Board, which shall treat the matter as a default. A copy of the certification shall be mailed to the respondent.

(g) Counsel.

(1) *Presenter.* All disciplinary and disability proceedings shall be prosecuted by an attorney presenter designated by the Director or chair.

(2) *Respondent's Counsel; Assignment for Indigents.* A respondent may be represented by counsel admitted to practice law in New Jersey or admitted pro hac vice by the Board, or may appear pro se. A respondent desiring representation but claiming inability to retain counsel by reason of indigency, shall promptly so notify the vice chair and special ethics master, if one is appointed, and shall, within 14 days after service of the complaint, make written application to the Assignment Judge of the vicinage in which respondent practices or formerly practiced, simultaneously serving the application on the vice chair and special ethics master, if one has been assigned, and on the presenter. The application shall be supported by a certification complying with R. 1:4–4(b), which shall contain a current statement of all assets and liabilities, any bankruptcy petition and orders, and copies of the respondent's state and federal income and business tax returns for the prior three-year period. For good cause shown, the Assignment Judge shall assign an attorney to represent the respondent without compensation, so notifying the respondent, the secretary, the vice chair and special ethics master, if one has been assigned, and the Office of Attorney Ethics of any decision.

(3) *Grievant's Counsel.* A grievant may be represented by a retained attorney. Such attorney shall be limited to consulting with the grievant and may not be designated as the presenter in the matter.

Note: Text and former R. 1:20–4 redesignated R. 1:20–15. New text to R. 1:20–4, adopted January 31, 1995 to be effective March 1, 1995; paragraph (e) amended July 5, 2000 to be effective September 5, 2000; paragraphs (e) and (f)(2) amended July 12, 2002 to be effective September 3, 2002; paragraphs (a), (b), (d), (e), (f), and (g) amended July 28, 2004 to be effective September 1, 2004; paragraph (d) amended August 1, 2006 to be effective September 1, 2006; paragraph (b) amended July 9, 2008 to be effective September 1, 2008.

1:20–5.   Prehearing Procedures

(a) Discovery.

(1) *Generally.* Discovery shall be available to the presenter. Discovery shall also be available to the respondent, provided that a verified answer in compliance with R. 1:20–4(e) has been filed. All such requests shall be in writing.

(2) *Scope.* On written request the following information, if relevant to the investigation, prosecution, or defense of a matter, and if within the possession, custody or control of the presenter, the respondent or counsel, is subject to discovery and shall be made available for inspection and copying as set forth in this rule:

(A) a writing as defined by N.J.R.E. 801(e) or any other tangible object, including those obtained from or belonging to the respondent;

(B) written statements, if any, including any memoranda reporting or summarizing oral statements, made by any witness, including the respondent;

(C) results or reports of mental or physical examinations and of scientific tests or experiments made in connection with the matter;

(D) names, addresses and telephone numbers of all persons known to have relevant knowledge or information about the matter, including a designation by the presenter and respondent as to which of those persons will be called as witnesses;

(E) police reports and any investigation reports;

(F) name and address of each person expected to be called as an expert witness, the expert's qualifications, the subject matter on which the expert will testify, a copy of all written reports submitted by the expert or, if none, a statement of the facts and opinions to which the expert will testify and a summary of the grounds for each opinion; and

(G) any final disciplinary investigative report.

(3) *Documents Not Subject to Discovery.* This rule does not require discovery of a party's work product consisting of internal reports, memoranda or documents made by that party or that party's attorney or agents in connection with the investigation, prosecution or defense of the matter. Nor does it require discovery of statements, signed or unsigned, made by respondent to respondent's attorney or that attorney's agents. Any materials relating to any matter deemed "confidential" under R. 1:20–9, including dismissals and diversions, are not discoverable. This rule does not authorize discovery of any internal manuals or materials prepared by the Office of Attorney Ethics or the Disciplinary Review Board.

(4) *Type of Discovery Not Permitted.* Neither written interrogatories, nor requests for admissions, nor oral depositions shall be permitted in any matter, except that depositions to preserve the testimony of a witness likely to be unavailable for hearing due to death, incapacity or otherwise, may be taken in accordance with the procedure (modified as appropriate to disciplinary proceedings) set forth in R. 3:13–2.

(5) *Timeliness of Discovery; Continuing Duty.* Initial discovery shall be made available within 20 days after receipt of a written request therefor. A party's obligation to provide discovery is a continuing one. If, subsequent to compliance with a request for discovery, a party discovers additional names or statements of witnesses or other information reasonably encompassed by the initial request for discovery, the original discovery response shall be promptly supplemented accordingly.

(6) *Failure to Make Discovery.* Any discoverable information that is not timely furnished either by original or supplemental response to a discovery request may, on application of the aggrieved party, be excluded from evidence at hearing. The failure of the presenter or respondent to disclose the name and provide the report or summary of any expert who will be called to testify at least 20 days prior to the hearing date shall result in the exclusion of the witness, except on good cause shown.

(7) *Discovery Applications.* All discovery applications shall be made on notice to the hearing panel chair or special ethics master, if one has been appointed. An interlocutory appeal may be sought only pursuant to R. 1:20–16(f)(1).

(b) Prehearing Conference.

(1) *Attendance.* A prehearing conference may be held in standard unethical conduct cases in the discretion of the trier of fact if requested by the presenter, the respondent, or the trier of fact. A prehearing conference shall be held in all complex cases alleging unethical conduct at the request of the presenter, the respondent, or the trier of fact. The prehearing conference shall be held by the hearing panel chair, sitting alone or, if assigned, a special ethics master, within 45 days after the time within which an answer to a complaint is due. At least 14 days written notice of the date of the conference shall be given. Attendance at the conference is mandatory by all parties. A prehearing conference may be held by telephone call where appropriate. No transcript shall be made of the prehearing conference, except in unusual circumstances.

(2) *Prehearing Report.* At least five business days before the date scheduled for the prehearing conference, both the presenter and the respondent shall file a report with the hearing panel chair or special ethics master, and with the adversary, disclosing the name, address and telephone numbers of each person expected to be called at hearing, including any person who will testify as to the character or reputation of the respondent, and all experts. With respect to an expert witness, the report shall state the person's name, address, qualifications, and the subject matter on which the expert is expected to testify. A copy of the expert's report, if any, or, if no written report is prepared, a statement of the facts and opinions to which the expert is expected to testify and a summary of the grounds for each opinion, shall be attached. Every respondent shall also include his or her own office and home address (including a street address) and telephone number where the attorney can be reached at all times. The respondent shall have a continuing duty to promptly advise the hearing panel chair, special ethics master, presenter, secretary of any district committee and the Director of any changes in any of the items required above.

(3) *Objectives.* At the prehearing conference, the hearing panel chair or special ethics master shall address the following matters:

(A) the formulation and simplification of issues;

(B) admissions and stipulations of the parties with respect to allegations, defenses and any aggravation or mitigation;

(C) the factual and legal contentions of the parties;

(D) the identification and limitation of witnesses, including character and expert witnesses;

(E) deadlines for the completion of discovery, including the timely exchange of expert reports;

(F) the hearing date and its estimated length;

(G) issuance of any subpoenas necessary to presentation of the case;

(H) premarking of all exhibits into evidence to which the parties consent;

(I) the priority of disciplinary proceedings under R. 1:20–8 and any known trial commitments by the presenter, respondent, and respondent's counsel that could conflict with the scheduling of the matter. Counsel shall be under a continuing duty to promptly notify the hearing panel chair or the special ethics master of any such trial dates assigned as soon as known; and

(J) any other matters which may aid in the disposition of the case.

(4) *Case Management Order.* Within seven days following the prehearing conference, the hearing panel chair or special ethics master shall issue a case management order, designated as such in the caption, memorializing any agreements by the parties and any determinations made respecting any matters considered at the conference. That order shall set forth the time period within which all discovery shall be completed. The case management order, which constitutes part of the record, shall be served on the presenter and the respondent and filed with the vice chair and the Director.

(5) *Setting Hearing Date and Conclusion.* At the prehearing conference the hearing panel chair or special ethics master shall schedule dates for the hearing of the case within 60 days after the date of the conference, except in extraordinary circumstances, which hearing dates shall be promptly reported to the vice chair and Director. The hearing shall be concluded within 45 days after its commencement and a hearing report shall be filed with the Board and served on the parties within 60 days after the hearing's conclusion, except in extraordinary circumstances.

(c) Sanctions. The hearing panel chair or special ethics master shall make and enforce all rules and orders necessary to compel compliance with this rule and may suppress an answer, bar defenses, or bar the admissibility of any evidence offered that is in substantial violation of the case management order, discovery obligations, or any other order.

(d) Motion to Dismiss. No motion to dismiss a complaint shall be entertained except:

(1) a prehearing motion addressed either to the legal sufficiency of a complaint to state a cause of action as a matter of law or to jurisdiction;

(2) a motion to dismiss at the conclusion of the presenter's case in chief; and

(3) a motion by the presenter to dismiss the complaint, in whole or in part, when

(A) an essential witness becomes unavailable or

(B) as a result of newly discovered or newly disclosed evidence, one or more counts of the complaint cannot be proven by clear and convincing evidence. Such motion shall be supported by the presenter's certification of the facts supporting the motion and any relevant exhibits, and shall be decided by the trier of fact.

Note: Former R. 1:20–5 redesignated R. 1:20–16 adopted January 31, 1995 to be effective March 1, 1995; paragraph (b)(6) amended July 5, 2000 to be effective September 5, 2000; paragraph (a)(7) amended July 12, 2002 to be effective September 3, 2002; paragraphs (a) and (b) amended, former subparagraph (b)(c) redesignated as paragraph (c), former paragraph (c) redesignated as paragraph (d) and amended July 28, 2004 to be effective September 1, 2004; subparagraphs (a)(3) and (b)(2) amended July 9, 2008 to be effective September 1, 2008.

1:20–6. Hearings

(a) Hearing Panels.

(1) *Hearing Panel Designations; Oversight.* The chair shall annually determine the composition of hearing panels which shall be administered and advised by the vice chair. Each hearing panel shall consist of only three members, one of whom shall be a public member. The chair shall designate an attorney member as the chair of each panel. An additional attorney member and an additional public member may be designated as alternates to remain available but not to sit and hear the matter unless one of the attorney members or the public member is unable to do so. An attorney member involved in the investigation of a matter shall not serve as a hearing panel member on that matter.

The vice chair shall designate a hearing panel to hear the matter after the time prescribed for the filing of an answer and shall notify the presenter and respondent of the designation.

(2) *Quorum.* A quorum shall consist of two attorney members and one public member. The hearing panel shall act only with the concurrence of two. When by reason of absence, disability or disqualification the number of members of the hearing panel able to act is fewer than a quorum, the following procedures will apply:

(A) if the hearing has not commenced, the attorney alternate or another attorney member shall be substituted for the absent attorney or the public member alternate or another public member shall be substituted for the absent public member;

(B) if the hearing has commenced but all evidence has not been received, the vice chair shall designate the attorney alternate or another attorney member or the public member alternate or another public member to permit the orderly conclusion of the proceedings, provided that the member so designated shall have the opportunity to review the entire record including the transcript of the proceedings to date;

(C) if all the evidence has been received, the matter may be determined by the remaining two hearing panel members, provided their decision is unanimous. In the event of disagreement, the vice chair shall designate the attorney alternate or another attorney member or the public member alternate or another public member who, on review of the entire record including the transcript of the proceedings, shall be eligible to vote thereon.

(3) *Powers and Duties.* Hearing panels shall have the following powers and duties:

(A) to conduct hearings on formal charges of unethical conduct and petitions for reinstatement where requested by the Board or the Court;

(B) to submit to the Board written findings or fact, conclusions of law and recommendations, together with the record of the hearing; and

(C) to determine issues of unethical conduct by majority vote, provided a quorum is present.

(4) *Powers and Duties of Hearing Panel Chair.* Each hearing panel chair shall have the following powers and duties:

(A) to conduct prehearing conferences in accordance with R. 1:20–5(b);

(B) to entertain prehearing motions;

(C) to preside at all hearings; and

(D) to perform such other functions as provided for by these rules or assigned by the Director with the approval of the Supreme Court.

Unless relieved by the Supreme Court, a member serving as a trier of fact where testimony has begun at the time the member's term expires shall continue in such matter until its conclusion and the filing of a report.

(b) Special Ethics Masters.

(1) *Qualifications.* A retired or recalled judge of this state, a former member of the Disciplinary Review Board, a former member of the Disciplinary Oversight Committee, a former officer of a district ethics committee, or a former chair of a hearing panel may be appointed, with his or her consent, to serve as a special ethics master.

(2) *Appointment; Compensation.* Special ethics masters shall be appointed by, and shall serve at the pleasure of, the Supreme Court under the administration of the Director. Attorneys shall be paid the per diem rate in effect for single arbitrators under R. 4:21A–2(d)(1). The full per diem rate shall be paid for each day of a prehearing conference or hearing, or part thereof, but shall not be paid for separate days for opinion preparation. A reasonable additional amount may be paid for actual typing expenses. Retired judges may serve pro bono or with compensation or, if they are on recall, shall be paid at the rate in effect for judges on recall service.

(3) *Designation; Oversight.* When, in the judgment of the Director, a hearing may reasonably be expected

to take three days or more, or where the case should be heard continuously from day to day until conclusion, or when the Director believes it is in the interest of justice to do so, the Director may request designation of a special ethics master to try the case. An Ethics Committee chair may request the Director to appoint a special ethics master. The Director shall determine the appropriateness of such an appointment pursuant to the above criteria and other relevant considerations. The Director shall render appropriate administrative and legal services to special ethics masters.

(4) *Powers and Authority.* A special ethics master shall have the full power and authority of a hearing panel.

(c) Hearings Involving Unethical Conduct; When Required.

(1) *When Required.* A hearing shall be held only if the pleadings raise genuine disputes of material fact, if the respondent's answer requests an opportunity to be heard in mitigation, or if the presenter requests to be heard in aggravation. In all other cases the pleadings, together with a statement of procedural history, shall be filed by the trier of fact directly with the Board for its consideration in determining the appropriate sanction to be imposed.

(2) *Notice and Conduct of Hearings.*

(A) Generally. At least 25 days prior to the initial scheduled hearing date, a written notice of hearing shall be served on the presenter, the respondent, and any counsel of record, stating the date, time and place of hearing. Subsequent days of hearing may be scheduled orally or in writing. Prior to the hearing the respondent will be advised of the right to be represented by counsel, to cross-examine witnesses and to present evidence. Arrangements for the hearing, including location of hearing, recording, interpreters and transcripts, shall be made by the Ethics Committee or special ethics master, if one has been appointed. A complete stenographic record of the hearing shall be made by an official court reporter or by a court reporter designated by the Director. Each trier of fact shall be obligated to inform every court reporter, witness and party of any protective order that has been issued and the effect thereof. All witnesses shall be duly sworn. If special circumstances dictate, the trier of fact may accept testimony of a witness by telephone and/or video conference.

(B) Standard of Proof. Formal charges of unethical conduct, medical defenses, and reinstatement proceedings shall be established by clear and convincing evidence.

(C) Burden of Proof; Burden of Going Forward. The burden of proof in proceedings seeking discipline or demonstrating aggravating factors relevant to unethical conduct charges is on the presenter. The burden of going forward regarding defenses or demonstrating mitigating factors relevant to charges of unethical conduct shall be on the respondent. The burden of proof in proceedings seeking reinstatement shall be on the petitioner.

(D) Respondent's Presence and Testimony; Presence and Sequestration of Witnesses. Respondent's appearance at all hearings is mandatory. In accordance with R. 1:20–7(*l*), however, a respondent's absence shall not delay the orderly processing of the case. The grievant, if any, the grievant's attorney, if any, and respondent's attorney, if any, and administrative staff assisting in the prosecution of the matter shall have the right to be present at all times during the hearing. Any other witnesses may be sequestered during their testimony on reasonable terms on timely application and a showing of good cause.

(E) Findings and Report. The trier of fact shall submit to the Board written findings of fact and conclusions of law on each issue presented, together with the record of the hearing, and shall take one of the following actions:

(i) Dismissal. If the trier of fact finds that there has been no unethical conduct, the secretary or special ethics master shall send to the presenter, the respondent, the grievant, if any, the Director and the vice chair, a letter of dismissal in a form approved by the Director, together with a copy of the hearing panel's report. The original report and record shall be filed with the Director. The hearing panel or special ethics master shall not order any transcript without the prior approval of the Director or the Board. Appeals may be taken in accordance with R. 1:20–15(e)(2).

(ii) Admonition Recommendation. If the hearing panel or special ethics master finds that there has been unethical conduct for which an admonition constitutes adequate discipline, the panel chair or special ethics master shall submit the original hearing panel report stating the specific discipline recommended and the record of all proceedings before it to the Director for transmittal to the Board. The hearing panel or special ethics master shall not order any transcript without the prior approval of either the Director or the Board. A copy of the hearing panel's report shall be served on the presenter, the respondent, the grievant, if any, the vice chair and secretary. The Board shall proceed pursuant to R. 1:20–15(f).

(iii) Reprimand, Censure, Suspension or Disbarment Recommendations. If the hearing panel or special ethics master finds that there has been unethical conduct that requires the imposition of a reprimand, censure, suspension or disbarment, the panel chair or special ethics master shall submit the original hearing panel report stating the specific nature of the discipline recommended and the record of all proceedings, including the original transcript, to the Director for transmittal to the Board. A copy of the hearing panel's report shall be served on the presenter, the respondent, the

grievant, if any, the vice chair and secretary. The Board shall proceed pursuant to R. 1:20–15(f).

(F) Public Hearings. Unless a protective order has been issued in accordance with R. 1:20–9(h), all hearings shall be open to the public in accordance with R. 1:20–9(c).

(d) Abstention and Request For Disqualification. A trier of fact shall refrain from taking part in any proceeding in which a judge, similarly situated, would be required to abstain under R. 1:12–1. It shall not be cause for disqualification that the trier of fact has heard or decided other cases involving the same respondent. Requests to disqualify a trier of fact shall, where possible, be made in advance of any prehearing conference; otherwise, it shall be made in advance of the initial day of hearing. The request shall be decided initially by the trier of fact, whose decision may be superseded by the vice chair or, in the event of a conflict, the chair, or, in matters handled by the Office of Attorney Ethics, by the Director.

(e) Withdrawal By Respondent's Counsel; When Permitted. After the date of the pretrial conference or fixing of the first trial date, respondent' s counsel may withdraw without leave of the trier of fact only upon the filing of the respondent's written consent, a substitution of attorney executed by both the withdrawing respondent's attorney and the substituted respondent's attorney, a written waiver by all other parties of notice and the right to be heard, and a certification by both the withdrawing respondent' s attorney and the substituted respondent's attorney (or respondent pro se) that the withdrawal and substitution will not cause or result in delay.

Note: Adopted January 31, 1995 to be effective March 1, 1995; paragraph (c) amended July 25, 1995 to be effective immediately; paragraph (b)(2) amended July 5, 2000 to be effective September 5, 2000; paragraphs (a)(1), (a)(2), and (c)(2)(E)(i) amended July 12, 2002 to be effective September 3, 2002; paragraphs (a) and (b) amended, paragraph (c) caption and text amended, former paragraph (d) deleted and new paragraph (d) adopted July 28, 2004 to be effective September 1, 2004; new paragraph (e) adopted July 27, 2006 to be effective September 1, 2006; subparagraph (c)(2)(F) amended August 1, 2006 to be effective September 1, 2006; subparagraphs (b)(1) and (c)(2)(A) amended July 9, 2008 to be effective September 1, 2008.

1:20–7.   Additional Rules of Procedure

(a) Nature of Proceedings. Discipline and disability proceedings are neither civil nor criminal in nature.

(b) Evidence Rules Relaxed. The rules of evidence may be relaxed in all disciplinary proceedings, but the residuum evidence rule shall apply.

(c) Time Limitations. There are no time limitations with respect to the initiation of any discipline or disability matter.

(d) Delay Caused by Grievant. Neither unwillingness nor neglect by the grievant to sign a grievance or prosecute a charge, nor settlement or compromise between the grievant and the respondent or restitution by the respondent, shall, in itself, justify abatement of the processing of any grievance.

(e) Immunity of Disciplinary and Fee Authorities. Members of the Office of Attorney Ethics, the Disciplinary Review Board, Disciplinary Oversight Committee, Ethics Committees, Fee Committees, their secretaries, special ethics masters and their lawfully appointed designees and staff, shall be absolutely immune from suit, whether legal or equitable in nature, based on their respective conduct in performing their official duties. The Supreme Court shall request the Attorney General to represent disciplinary authorities in all civil or criminal litigation in state or federal courts.

(f) Immunity of Grievants, Witnesses and Others. Grievants in ethics matters, clients in fee arbitration cases and witnesses and potential witnesses in both ethics and fee matters shall be absolutely immune from suit, whether legal or equitable in nature, for all communications, including testimony, only to the Office of Attorney Ethics, the Disciplinary Review Board, Disciplinary Oversight Committee, Ethics Committees, Fee Committees, their secretaries, special ethics masters and their lawfully appointed designees and staff.

(g) Immunity From Criminal Prosecution. With the consent of the Attorney General, the Director, in a discipline or disability proceeding, may apply to the Supreme Court, or to an Assignment Judge designated by it, for a grant of immunity to a witness from criminal prosecution in accordance with N.J.S.A. 2A:81–17.3.

(h) Service. Service on the respondent of any pleading, motion, or other document required by these rules to be served in a disciplinary or disability proceeding may be made by personal service, or by certified mail (return receipt requested) and regular mail, at the address listed in the New Jersey Lawyers' Diary and Manual or the address shown on the records of the Lawyers' Fund for Client Protection. Service on a respondent may also be made by serving respondent's counsel, if any, by regular mail or by facsimile transmission.

(i) Subpoena Power.

(1) *Oaths.* In discipline and disability matters, members of a hearing panel, special ethics masters, court reporters or ethics counsel may administer oaths and affirmations.

(2) *Investigative and Hearing Subpoenas.* During the investigation or hearing of a matter, a subpoena may be issued in the name of the Supreme Court to compel the appearance of any person for questioning or testimony or to compel the production of books, records, documents or other items designated therein. A showing of relevance or materiality may be required before the issuance of any subpoena. The subpoena shall issue in a form approved by the Supreme Court. Investigative

and hearing subpoenas may be signed by any Ethics Committee member, the presenter, ethics counsel or by the Board or its legal staff. Hearing subpoenas may also be issued by a hearing panel member, special ethics master or by the Board or its staff.

(3) *Service; Fees.* Subpoenas shall be served within the State of New Jersey by any person 18 or more years of age by delivering a copy thereof to the person named, except that subpoenas may be served on an attorney who is a witness or a party, by certified mail, return receipt requested. No attendance fee need be paid. Service on a respondent may also be made by serving respondent's counsel, if any, by regular mail.

(4) *Enforcement; Contempt.* Subpoenas issued under this rule may be enforced pursuant to R. 1:9–6.

(5) *Standards; Quashing Subpoena; Appeals.*

(A) Generally. The Board chair, during the investigation stage of a matter, or the hearing panel chair or special ethics master, after the filing of a complaint, may, on motion made promptly, quash or modify a subpoena if the subject testimony or documentation is patently irrelevant or if compliance would be unreasonable or oppressive.

(B) Interlocutory Appeals. The determination on a challenge to a subpoena shall not be subject to interlocutory appeal, but any objection thereto will be preserved for review on appeal, if any, or on an authorized review under R. 1:20–15 and 16.

(6) *Subpoena Pursuant to Law of Another Jurisdiction.* Whenever a subpoena is sought in this state by a foreign disciplinary authority pursuant to the law of that jurisdiction for use in a discipline or disability proceeding, and where the foreign disciplinary counsel certifies that the issuance of the subpoena has been duly approved under the law of the other jurisdiction, the Disciplinary Review Board, on petition for good cause, on notice to the Director, may issue a subpoena as provided in this rule to compel the attendance of witnesses and production of documents in this state.

(j) Grievances Against Disciplinary Agency Members.

(1) *Grievances Alleging Improper Processing.* Any grievance against Ethics Committee or Fee Committee members and secretaries, members of the Office of Attorney Ethics, hearing panels, special ethics masters or the Board, their lawfully appointed designees and staff, arising out of their processing of an ethics grievance or fee arbitration request shall be filed with and considered exclusively by the Board in connection with any appeal or other authorized review of a matter in the normal course under R. 1:20–15(e). After review, the Board shall make any appropriate direction regarding the grievance. Nothing herein shall preclude introduction of the facts which underlie the grievance in evidence in any ethics proceeding if relevant.

(2) *Other Grievances.* Except as provided in section (1), if a grievance is filed against the Director, Office of

Attorney Ethics, ethics counsel or staff, or a member of the Board or Board Counsel or staff, the matter shall be transmitted to the Clerk of the Supreme Court, who shall make any appropriate direction for processing the matter.

(k) Extension of Time; Adjournments. Reasonable extensions of time and adjournments may be granted for good cause. Such requests shall be made by writing, stating with specificity the facts on which the request is based. Such requests shall be either granted or denied in writing; if granted they shall be only for a definite and reasonably short interval. The vice chair or special ethics master may grant extensions for the filing of an answer to a complaint. After the parties have been notified of the date of hearing, requests for adjournments shall be directed to the hearing panel chair or special ethics master. If such request is based on an attorney's scheduling conflict, the hearing panel chair or special ethics master should communicate with the appropriate assignment judge in order to accommodate the priority accorded disciplinary proceedings by R. 1:20–8(g).

(*l*) Absent or Non–responding Respondent. A respondent's absence, non-responsiveness or other failure to reply or to file any document or to attend any required conference or hearing shall not delay the orderly processing of a case, provided the respondent has been properly served.

(m) Transcripts. Where in a pending matter a respondent is found guilty of unethical conduct warranting reprimand, censure, suspension or disbarment, the trier of fact shall order the original transcript and shall file it, together with its report and the record of the matter, with the Board. If no finding of unethical conduct is made, the trier of fact may order the transcript only with prior permission of the Director or the Board. Where a matter is pending, a respondent may, at personal expense, order a transcript of the hearing, provided that the respondent also directs the reporter to furnish a copy of the transcript to the trier of fact. Where a matter is concluded the respondent may, at personal expense, order a transcript of the hearing. Except where a protective order has been issued pursuant to R. 1:20–9(h), any other person may order all or any part of a transcript at the individual's prepaid expense. Either the Board or the Director shall have the right to order a transcript wherever necessary.

(n) Prior Discipline or Disability. Information concerning prior final discipline or disability of the respondent shall not be a matter for consideration by the trier of fact until a finding of unethical conduct has first been made, unless such information is probative of issues pending before the trier of fact. On a finding of unethical conduct the trier of fact shall request the Office of Attorney Ethics to disclose to it and to the presenter and to the respondent a summary of any orders, letters or opinions imposing temporary or final discipline or disability on the respondent. Within five days of receipt of the submission of any prior discipline

or disability, either the presenter or ethics counsel or respondent may submit written argument on the issue of the effect to be given thereto.

Note: Adopted January 31, 1995 to be effective March 1, 1995; paragraphs (h), (i), (m), and (n) amended July 28, 2004 to be effective September 1, 2004; paragraph (m) amended August 1, 2006 to be effective September 1, 2006.

1:20–8. Time Goals; Accountability; Priority

(a) Investigations. The Disciplinary system shall endeavor to complete all investigations of standard matters within six months, and of complex matters within nine months, the time period commencing on the date a written grievance is docketed and concluding on the date a formal complaint is filed, the grievance is dismissed or other authorized disposition is made.

(b) Formal Hearings. The disciplinary system shall endeavor to complete formal hearings within six months from the expiration of the time for filing an answer to a complaint until a report is filed with the Director for transmittal to the Disciplinary Review Board.

(c) Appellate Review. The disciplinary system shall endeavor to complete all recommendations for discipline filed with the Disciplinary Review Board within six months from the date of docketing by the Office of Board Counsel until the issuance of the Board's decision. All ethics and fee arbitration appeals should be completed and a decision issued within three months of docketing the appeal by the Board.

(d) Supreme Court Review. The disciplinary system shall endeavor to complete matters (except emergent actions) filed with the Supreme Court within six months from the date of docketing by the Office of the Clerk of the Court until issuance of the Court's order or opinion.

(e) Effect of Goals. The time periods herein prescribed are not jurisdictional and shall not serve as a bar or defense to any disciplinary investigation or proceeding.

(f) Accountability. Analysis of compliance by the disciplinary system of the time periods herein prescribed shall be made annually and at such intervals as the Disciplinary Oversight Committee may direct, and an analysis published showing how the respective caseloads compare with these goals.

(g) Priority of Disciplinary Matters. Generally, disciplinary matters shall take precedence over administrative, civil and criminal cases. All courts and tribunals shall make reasonable accommodations for the attendance of counsel, witnesses, and other participants. Every participant in a disciplinary proceeding shall be obligated to give reasonable advance notice of potential litigation conflicts to the assignment judge or to the particular judge or officer in charge of the litigation. The same advance notice also shall be given to the presenter, respondent, counsel, and the panel chair or special ethics master in the disciplinary matter.

Note: Former R. 1:20–8 deleted, new text adopted January 31, 1995 to be effective March 1, 1995; paragraph (a) amended July 10, 1998 to be effective September 1, 1998; paragraphs (a), (b), (c), and (g) amended July 28, 2004 to be effective September 1, 2004.

1:20–9. Confidentiality; Access to and Dissemination of Disciplinary Information

(a) Confidentiality by the Director. Prior to the filing and service of a complaint, a disciplinary stipulation waiving the filing of a formal complaint, a motion for final or reciprocal discipline, or the approval of a motion for discipline by consent, the disciplinary matter and all written records gathered and made pursuant to these rules shall be kept confidential by the Director, except that the pendency, subject matter, and status of a grievance may be disclosed by the Director if:

(1) the respondent has waived or breached confidentiality; or

(2) the proceeding is based on allegations of reciprocal discipline, a pending criminal charge, or a guilty plea or conviction of a crime, either before or after sentencing; or

(3) there is a need to notify another person or organization, including the Lawyers' Fund for Client Protection, in order to protect the public, the administration of justice, or the legal profession; or

(4) the Supreme Court has granted an emergent disciplinary application for relief; or

(5) the matter has become common knowledge to the public.

(b) Disclosure by Grievant. For grievances pending on, or filed after, October 19, 2005, the grievant may make public statements regarding the disciplinary process, the filing and content of the grievance, and the result, if any, of the grievance. If the grievant makes a public statement, respondent may reply publicly to any matter revealed by the grievant.

(c) Public Proceedings. All proceedings shall be public except:

(1) as otherwise provided by paragraph (a); or

(2) prehearing conferences; or

(3) deliberations of the trier of fact, Board or Supreme Court; or

(4) information subject to a protective order; or

(5) proceedings alleging disability in accordance with paragraph (g).

(d) Public Records.

(1) Subject to paragraphs (a) and (c), on the filing and service of a complaint, a disciplinary stipulation waiving the filing of a formal complaint, a motion for final or reciprocal discipline or the approval of a motion for discipline by consent (except for documents submitted in connection with confidential prehearing conferences), those documents, as well as the documents and records filed subsequent thereto, shall be available for public inspection and copying. Inspection and copying shall be available by appointment at the office of the body where the matter is then pending. Transcripts shall be available to the public in accordance with R. 1:20–7(m) at their pre-paid expense. Where, in the opinion of the district secretary or the Director, the documentation to be copied is voluminous, a commercial photocopy service may be used for reproduction at the prepaid expense of the person requesting them.

(2) In the event an attorney has been temporarily suspended for disciplinary reasons, the motion papers, any response and any orders issued by the Board or the Court shall be available to the public by their respective offices. Unless the Court otherwise orders, all other records regarding emergent applications, including but not limited to those for temporary suspension (either for disciplinary reasons, failure to pay disciplinary costs, failure to pay fee arbitration determinations or settlements or otherwise), license restrictions, conditions of practice, transfer to temporary disability-inactive status, shall be confidential, except for orders issued by the Supreme Court.

(3) There shall be no private discipline. Private reprimands issued prior to the effective date of this rule shall remain confidential.

(4) Ethics Committees, Office of Attorney Ethics or the Board may impose a reasonable charge for the actual cost of reproducing public documents.

(5) The following records are also public for purpose of inspection: District Ethics Committee Manual and District Fee Arbitration Manual. These manuals may be inspected at the Office of Attorney Ethics, the Disciplinary Review Board and the secretaries of the respective Ethics Committees and Fee Committees.

(e) Referral to Admissions/Disciplinary Agencies. Whenever an attorney-at-law of this state is also admitted, or has applied for admission, to another jurisdiction, the Director may refer information concerning a pending or completed investigation or proceeding regarding that attorney to such admission or disciplinary agency. Such transmittal by the Director shall be made on notice to the attorney and, if the information submitted is confidential, shall be accompanied by a directive that the information submitted remain confidential and be used solely for admissions or disciplinary purposes in that jurisdiction.

In those cases in which an admission or disciplinary agency in another jurisdiction initiates a request for information, that agency shall certify that its request for information is made in furtherance of an ongoing investigation or proceeding involving that attorney.

(f) Disclosure of Evidence of Criminal Conduct; All Other Disclosure Including Subpoenas.

(1) Subsequent to the filing of a complaint, a disciplinary stipulation waiving the filing of a formal complaint, a motion for final or reciprocal discipline, or the approval of a motion for discipline by consent, the Director may refer any matter to law enforcement authorities without prior notice to respondent if criminal conduct may be involved. Prior to the filing and service of a complaint, the Director may refer a matter to law enforcement authorities if criminal conduct may be involved and the respondent has been temporarily suspended. In both cases, a copy of the letter of referral shall be sent to the respondent and any known counsel. Where criminal conduct may be involved but where the respondent has not been temporarily suspended or served with a complaint, the Director shall, prior to such referral, give ten days written notice to the respondent and any known counsel of the intention to make a referral. The respondent may, within said period, apply to the Board for a protective order based on good cause shown.

(2) In all other cases, including cases where civil or criminal subpoenas have been issued to disciplinary personnel, the Board may authorize the referral of any confidential documentary information to the appropriate authority only for good cause shown. When a requesting authority shall seek such information, it shall issue its subpoena, which shall be transmitted to the Board or shall file a motion seeking disclosure with the Board, on ten days notice to the respondent and any known counsel, and the Director, both of whom shall be given an opportunity to be heard.

(g) Proceedings Alleging Disability. Proceedings for transfer to or from disability-inactive status are confidential. All orders transferring an attorney to or from disability-inactive status are public.

(h) Protective Orders. In exceptional cases, protective orders may be sought to prohibit the disclosure of specific information to protect the interests of a grievant, witness, third party or respondent. The presenter or respondent shall make any application for a protective order. On application or on its own motion, and for good cause shown, the Supreme Court, the Board, or the trier of fact may issue the protective order. A copy of any protective order entered shall be sent promptly to the Director, the secretary of any appropriate Ethics Committee, all parties, Board Counsel and the Clerk of the Supreme Court. The trier of fact or the Board may also direct that implementation of the protective order include a requirement that any hearing on the matter be conducted in such a manner as to preserve the confidentiality of the information that is the subject of the order.

(i) Duty to Maintain Confidentiality. All disciplinary system officials, employees and all participants in a proceeding under these rules shall maintain the confidentiality provided by this rule, including compliance with any protective order.

(j) Records Retention, Expungement and Reporting. The Clerk of the Supreme Court shall maintain permanently all disciplinary and disability files processed by the Supreme Court for decision including, but not limited to, all files resulting in the imposition of final or temporary discipline or the transfer to disability-inactive status, and all applications for reinstatement or restoration. Chief Counsel to the Disciplinary Review Board shall permanently maintain all ethics files previously resulting in private reprimands and admonitions issued by the Board, and shall maintain files of all ethics and fee arbitration appeals processed to the Board for a period of three years after the matter is terminated or for one year after the date of death of the attorney, whichever is earlier. All Ethics Committees shall maintain files for one year after the date a matter is terminated or after the attorney's death. All files maintained by the Office of Attorney Ethics and all other files maintained by the Disciplinary Review Board may be destroyed after five years following the date the matter is terminated or after one year following the date of the attorney's death. However, Chief Counsel to the Disciplinary Review Board and the Director of the Office of Attorney Ethics shall permanently maintain a summary of all docketed matters processed by each office containing the name of the respondent and any grievant or client, a brief summary of the nature and disposition of the matter and the date the case was opened and closed by their respective offices.

Except with respect to any application by an attorney for appointment to or employment by a judicial branch of government or a law enforcement or corrections agency, the matter shall, after the time herein specified for destruction of the file, be deemed expunged and any agency response to an inquiry requiring a reference to such matter shall state that there is no record of the filing of cases that are over five years old where the matter is dismissed or terminated other than by discipline or transfer to disability-inactive status. Except with respect to inquiries by the judicial branch of government, or a law enforcement or corrections agency, the respondent may answer any inquiry requiring a reference to a destroyed file by stating that the grievance was dismissed and thereafter expunged pursuant to court rule.

(k) Law Firm/Public Agency Notice of Public Action. Unless the respondent is the sole proprietor of a law firm, an Ethics Committee or the Office of Attorney Ethics shall send promptly to the law firm of which the respondent is known to be a member or by which the respondent is known to be employed, or the public agency by which the respondent is known to be employed, a copy of every complaint filed and served by that entity, disciplinary stipulation waiving the filing of a formal complaint, motion for final or reciprocal discipline or approved motion for discipline by consent.

(l) Notice to National Lawyer Regulatory Data Bank. The Clerk of the Supreme Court shall transmit promptly notice of all discipline, whether temporary or final, imposed on an attorney, transfers to or from disability-inactive status, and reinstatements to the National Lawyer Regulatory Data Bank maintained by the American Bar Association.

(m) Public Notice of Discipline Imposed. The Clerk of the Supreme Court shall cause promptly notices of all discipline, whether temporary or final, imposed against an attorney, transfers to or from disability-inactive status and reinstatements to be published in the official newspaper designated by the Supreme Court.

(n) Notice to the Courts. The Clerk of the Supreme Court shall promptly transmit a copy of all orders of discipline, whether temporary or final, transfers to or from disability-inactive status and reinstatements to all Assignment Judges, to the Presiding Judge for Administration of the Appellate Division, the Presiding Judge of the Tax Court of New Jersey, and to the Clerk of the United States District Court for the District of New Jersey. If a respondent has been suspended, disbarred or the subject of an equivalent sanction or transferred to disability-inactive status and fails to or is unable to comply with the requirement of R. 1:20–20, the Office of Attorney Ethics or the County Bar Association may, where necessary, request the Assignment Judge of the county in which the respondent practiced law to designate a practicing attorney member of the bar of that county to take such action pursuant to R. 1:20–19 as may be necessary to protect the interests of the respondent and the respondent's clients.

(o) Notice to Disciplinary Agencies. The Office of Attorney Ethics shall promptly transmit notice of final discipline and transfers to disability-inactive status to the disciplinary enforcement agency of every other jurisdiction in which the respondent is known to have been admitted.

(p) Annual Reports. The Office of Attorney Ethics and the Board shall each annually publish reports to the Supreme Court concerning their respective activities.

Note: Former R. 1:20–9 redesignated R. 1:20–12, new text adopted January 31, 1995 to be effective March 1, 1995; paragraph (k) amended July 10, 1998 to be effective September 1, 1998; paragraphs (d) and (g) amended July 5, 2000 to be effective September 5, 2000; paragraphs (a), (b), (c), (f), (g), (i), (k), (l), (m), and (n) amended, and paragraphs (e) and (j) caption and text amended July 28, 2004 to be effective September 1, 2004; paragraph (a) caption and text amended, new paragraph (b) adopted, former paragraphs (b), (c), and (h) amended and redesignated as paragraphs (c), (d), and (i), former paragraphs (d), (e), (f), (g), (i), (j), (k), (l), (m), (n), and (o) redesignated as paragraphs (e), (f), (g), (h), (j), (k), (l), (m), (n), (o), and (p) July 27, 2006 to be effective September 1, 2006; corrective amendment to paragraph (b) adopted September 26, 2006, to be retroactive to September 1, 2006; paragraph (a), subparagraphs (d)(1) and (f)(1), and paragraph (k) amended July 9, 2008 to be effective September 1, 2008.

Publisher's Note

The Supreme Court of New Jersey, in R.M. v. Supreme Court of New Jersey, 185 N.J. 208, 883 A.2d 369 (2005), held unconstitutional and invalidated the confidentiality provisions of Rule 1:20–9.

1:20–10. Discipline by Consent

(a) Disbarment by Consent.

(1) *General Procedure.* An attorney against whom a grievance has been filed may submit a consent to disbarment as a member of the bar to the Supreme Court through the Director, who shall transmit the consent in due form together with a report and recommendation. If accepted, the disbarment by consent shall be equivalent to disbarment, and the order accepting it shall be published as in cases of disbarments.

(2) *Affidavit of Consent.* Consents to disbarment shall be by affidavit in the form approved by the Supreme Court in which the respondent asserts:

(A) the respondent has consulted with an attorney; and

(B) the respondent's consent is freely and voluntarily given; the respondent has not been subjected to coercion or duress; the respondent is fully aware of the implications of submitting the consent; and

(C) the respondent is not under any disability, mental or physical, nor under the influence of any medication, intoxicants or other substances that would impair the respondent's ability to knowingly and voluntarily execute the disbarment by consent; and

(D) the respondent is aware that there is presently pending an investigation or proceeding involving allegations of unethical conduct, which allegations are set forth in the consent form; and

(E) an acknowledgement that the material facts so alleged are true; and

(F) an acknowledgement that the allegations of unethical conduct could not be successfully defended against; and

(G) the understanding that the disbarment by consent, if accepted by the Supreme Court, is tantamount to disbarment and constitutes an absolute bar to reinstatement to the practice of law; and

(H) the understanding that disciplinary costs will be assessed by the Supreme Court in accordance with R. 1:20–17.

The affidavit of consent to disbarment shall not be received by the Director unless accompanied by a letter from the respondent's attorney certifying that an attorney has consulted with respondent and that, in so far as the attorney is able to determine, respondent's consent is knowingly and voluntarily given and that respondent is not under any disability affecting respondent's capacity knowingly and voluntarily to consent to disbarment.

(3) *Action by Supreme Court.* The Supreme Court may either reject the tendered consent or accept it and enter an order of disbarment. Otherwise, the Court

shall reject the consent. If rejected, the disciplinary proceeding shall resume as if no consent had been submitted, and the consent to disbarment shall not thereafter be admitted into evidence.

(b) Other Discipline by Consent.

(1) *Timeliness and Form of Petition.* At any time during the investigation of a disciplinary matter or within 60 days after the time prescribed for the filing of any answer to a complaint, the respondent may agree with the investigator or presenter to submit an affidavit of discipline by consent in exchange for a specific recommendation for discipline. Following approval by the chair or Director, the matter shall be submitted to the Board as an agreed matter by way of a motion to impose discipline on consent in accordance with R. 1:20–15(g). A copy of the motion shall be provided to the Director.

(2) *Contents of Motion.* The motion, which shall be filed by the investigator or presenter shall certify the concurrence of the chair or the Director, and shall be supported by a signed stipulation setting forth in detail the admitted facts regarding the unethical conduct, the specific ethical rules violated, a specific recommendation for, or range of, discipline, together with a brief analysis of the legal precedent therefore. The stipulation shall attach the respondent's affidavit of consent in the form approved by the Supreme Court and containing the assertions set forth in paragraph (a)(2)(B),(C),(E) and (H).

(3) *Action by Board.* Pursuant to R. 1:20–15(g), the perfected motion shall be submitted to the Board. The Board may allow the motion and accept the discipline recommended. The Board shall either deny the motion in which case the disciplinary proceeding shall resume as if no motion had been made or the Board shall grant the motion. If accepted by the Board, it shall submit the record of the proceedings to the Clerk of the Supreme Court for entry of a consent order of discipline in accordance with R. 1:20–16(e). If the motion is denied, no admissions made therein shall be admitted into evidence.

Note: Former R. 1:20–10 text deleted, new text adopted January 31, 1995 to be effective March 1, 1995; paragraph (a)(2)(H) amended July 10, 1998 to be effective September 1, 1998; paragraphs (a) and (b) amended July 28, 2004 to be effective September 1, 2004.

1:20–11. Temporary Suspension

(a) Standard. An attorney may be subject to immediate temporary suspension by the Supreme Court if it finds that by reason of a violation of the Rules of Professional Conduct, caselaw or other authority, or a disability as defined by R. 1:20–12, the attorney poses a substantial threat of serious harm to an attorney, a client or the public. An attorney may also be immediately temporarily suspended as otherwise authorized by these rules.

(b) Procedure. A temporary suspension proceeding shall be initiated by the Director which shall:

(1) transmit the evidence to the Court by motion for immediate temporary suspension with supporting affidavit, together with proof of service; and

(2) contemporaneously make a reasonable attempt to provide the respondent with notice, including telephone notice, of the transmittal of the motion to the Court.

(c) Order. On review of the evidence transmitted by the Director and of rebuttal evidence, if any, which the respondent has filed prior to the Court's ruling, the Court may enter an order immediately suspending the respondent pending final disposition of a disciplinary proceeding or may take such other action as it deems appropriate.

(d) Notice to Clients. A respondent suspended pursuant to paragraph (b) shall comply with the notice requirements in R. 1:20–20.

(e) Motion for Reinstatement. On two days notice to the Director, a respondent suspended pursuant to paragraph (b) may move for reinstatement or modification of the order of suspension, and in that event the motion shall be heard and determined as expeditiously as the ends of justice require.

(f) Recommendation by Disciplinary Review Board. The Supreme Court may also order the temporary suspension of any attorney where so recommended by the Disciplinary Review Board in accordance with R. 1:20–15(i) and (k).

Note: Former R. 1:20–11 deleted, new text adopted January 31, 1995 to be effective March 1, 1995.

1:20–11A. Suspension of License to Practice Law for Failure to Support Dependents

(a) Suspension and Reinstatement of License. Upon receipt of an order issued pursuant to R. 5:7–5(e), that calls for the suspension of a license to practice law in New Jersey, the Supreme Court shall enter an order suspending the attorney from the practice of law. The Supreme Court shall enter an order reinstating the license to practice law, without the need for the attorney to file a verified petition for reinstatement or publish a notice as required by R. 1:20–21, upon receipt of an order issued by the Chancery Division, Family Part calling for the reinstatement of the license.

(b) Release of Attorney Information to Probation Division. The Office of Attorney Ethics and the New Jersey Lawyer's Fund for Client Protection shall, upon request, provide the Probation Division of the Superior Court with, if available, an attorney's social security number, home address and primary law office address when the basis for such a request is a license revocation proceeding in accordance with R. 5:7–5(e).

Note: Adopted March 15, 1996, to be effective immediately.

1:20–11B. Suspension of License to Practice Law for Failure to Repay Student Loans

(a) Certification; Contents. An entity seeking the suspension of an attorney's license to practice law pursuant to *N.J.S.A.* 2A:13–12 shall file with the Clerk of the Supreme Court and serve on the attorney a certification that (1) identifies the attorney, the attorney's last known home and law office addresses, and the date of the attorney's admission to the New Jersey bar; (2) states the amount currently owed by the attorney on the loan and attests that the loan is in default pursuant to state or federal law; and (3) certifies that the entity has complied with all of the regulations, approved by the Supreme Court, that govern the temporary suspension of attorney licenses for failure to repay student loans. Proof of service on the attorney at his or her last known home and office addresses, by regular and certified mail, return receipt requested, shall be filed with the entity's certification.

(b) Supreme Court Action. On receipt of the entity's certification pursuant to paragraph (a), the Court shall direct the Clerk to enter an Order temporarily suspending the license of the attorney until the further Order of the Court.

(c) Reinstatement. An attorney temporarily suspended from the practice of law pursuant to this Rule may seek reinstatement by filing a certification with the Supreme Court. The certification must confirm, in detail, that the attorney is meeting all current requirements for the repayment of his or her outstanding loans. The attorney must attach a copy of a repayment agreement to the certification, along with proof either that payments have begun in accordance with the agreement or that there is other evidence sufficient to demonstrate repayment. Proof of service on the entity by regular and certified mail, return receipt requested, shall be filed with the attorney's certification. If the attorney has continued to meet all other requirements for licensing during his or her suspension, the Court shall direct the Clerk to enter an Order reinstating the attorney to the practice of law.

(d) Release of Attorney Information to Lenders or Guarantors. At the request of an entity seeking the suspension of an attorney's license to practice law pursuant this Rule, the Clerk of the Supreme Court shall provide the entity with an attorney's last known home address and law office address. The information that is provided may be used only in connection with an application pursuant to paragraph (a) of this Rule.

Adopted March 5, 2002, to be effective May 1, 2002.

1:20–12. Incapacity and Disability

(a) Disability Inactive Status; Effect of Judicial Determination of Mental Incapacity or on Involuntary Commitment. When an attorney who is admitted to practice in this state has been judicially declared mentally incapacitated or involuntarily committed to a mental hospital, the Supreme Court, on proof of the fact, shall enter an order transferring the attorney to disability inactive status, effective immediately and until further order of the Court. Such transfer shall stay any pending disciplinary proceedings. When an attorney who has been transferred to disability inactive status is thereafter, in proceedings duly taken, judicially declared to be competent, the Court may dispense with the need

for further evidence that the disability has been removed and may direct reinstatement on such terms as are deemed proper and advisable. Any judge sitting in a court in this state who declares an attorney admitted to practice in this state mentally incapacitated, or who commits such attorney to a mental hospital, or who thereafter declares the attorney to be competent shall, on entry of the final order, promptly forward a copy to the Director.

(b) Request for Medical Examination. Whenever the Director presents evidence which reasonably brings into question the capacity of an attorney to practice law, whether by reason of mental or physical infirmity or illness, or because of addiction to drugs or intoxicants, the Board shall direct that the attorney submit to such medical examination as may be appropriate to enable the Director to determine whether the attorney is so incapacitated. Such action shall be taken on an expedited basis. Thereafter the Director may request the Board to recommend to the Supreme Court that the attorney be immediately transferred to Disability Inactive Status. If the Board concludes that the attorney lacks the capacity to practice law, it shall forthwith recommend to the Supreme Court that the attorney be transferred to disability inactive status until the further order of the Court. No pending disciplinary proceeding against the attorney shall be held in abeyance unless the Court shall additionally find that the respondent is incapable of assisting counsel in defense of any ethics proceedings.

(c) Assignment of Counsel; Notice of Proceedings. Either the Court or the Board may order the assignment of counsel for an attorney during any proceeding under this rule if it is in the interest of justice to do so. A copy of all applications and orders made pursuant to this rule shall be served on the attorney or counsel, any guardian, or the director of any institution to which the attorney has been committed.

(d) Proceedings to Determine Incapacity. Information relating to an attorney's physical or mental condition that adversely affects the capacity to practice law may be investigated and, where warranted, shall be the subject of a hearing to determine whether the attorney shall be transferred to disability inactive status. In conjunction with any such investigation the Director may also request the Board to direct the attorney to submit to an appropriate medical examination. All proceedings and any formal hearing shall be conducted in the same manner as disciplinary proceedings. The issue before the hearing panel or special ethics master, the Board and the Court shall be whether the attorney lacks the capacity to practice law. If on due consideration of the matter the Court concludes that the attorney lacks the capacity to practice law, it shall enter an order transferring the attorney to disability inactive status for an indefinite period and until the further order of the Court.

(e) Inability to Properly Defend. If, during the course of a disciplinary proceeding, the respondent is unable to assist counsel in defense of the matter due to mental or physical incapacity, the Court shall immediately transfer the respondent to disability inactive status pending determination of the incapacity.

If the Court determines that the attorney is unable to defend against the charges or complaint because of mental or physical incapacity, the disciplinary proceeding shall be deferred and the respondent retained on "disability inactive" status until the Court subsequently considers a petition for restoration of the respondent to active status. On application of the Director, the Court may also make such order for the perpetuation of testimony in the disciplinary proceedings as may be appropriate. If the Court considering a petition for restoration determines to grant the petition, any deferred disciplinary proceedings shall be reactivated.

If the Court determines that the attorney is able to defend against the charges or complaint, the disciplinary proceeding shall resume.

(f) Transfer to Active Status on Termination of Disability. Any attorney transferred to disability inactive status under the provisions of this rule shall be ineligible to practice law and shall comply with R. 1:20–20 governing suspended attorneys. Such attorney may apply for transfer to active status on notice to the Director. No such attorney shall be eligible to practice law until transferred to active status by order of the Supreme Court. Such application may be granted by the Court or referred by the Court for hearing in accordance with paragraph (d) above.

(g) Burden of Proof. In a proceeding seeking an order of transfer to disability inactive status, the burden of proof by clear and convincing evidence shall rest with the petitioner. In a proceeding seeking an order revoking the disability inactive status, the burden of proof by clear and convincing evidence shall rest with the attorney.

(h) Waiver of Doctor–Patient Privilege. Either the filing of an application by an attorney for transfer to disability inactive status or the filing of an application by an attorney for transfer from disability inactive to active status shall be deemed to constitute a waiver of any doctor-patient privilege. The attorney shall be required to disclose the name of every psychiatrist, psychologist, physician and hospital or other institution or facility by whom or at which the attorney has been examined, evaluated or treated. The attorney shall furnish to the Director written consent to the release of such information and records as requested.

Note: Adopted January 31, 1984 to be effective February 15, 1984; paragraph (g) amended November 5, 1986 to be effective January 1, 1987; paragraphs (a) and (b) caption and text amended, paragraphs (c) and (d) deleted, new paragraphs (c), (d) and (e) added and former paragraphs (e), (f) and (g) amended and redesignated (f), (g) and (h) November 7, 1988 to be effective January 2, 1989; paragraph (d) amended July 13, 1994 to be effective September 1, 1994; former R. 1:20–9 redesignated as R. 1:20–12, paragraphs (a) through (h) amended January 31, 1995 to be effective March 1, 1995; caption and text of paragraph (a) amended July 12, 2002 to be effective September 3, 2002.

1:20–13. Attorneys Charged with or Convicted of Crimes

(a) Reporting Criminal Matters.

(1) *Duty of Attorney Charged.* An attorney who has been charged with an indictable offense in this state or with an equivalent offense in any other state, territory, commonwealth, or possession of the United States or in any federal court of the United States or the District of Columbia shall promptly inform the Director of the Office of Attorney Ethics in writing of the charge. The attorney shall thereafter promptly inform the Director of the disposition of the matter.

(2) *Cooperation of Law Enforcement.* The Director may request the principal law enforcement officer of every law enforcement agency having jurisdiction within the State of New Jersey (including municipal and county prosecutors, the Attorney General and the United States Attorney) to promptly notify the Director of the Office of Attorney Ethics of any criminal charge filed against a New Jersey attorney, including all disorderly, petty disorderly or any second or subsequent motor vehicle charges involving the use of drugs or alcohol and to provide relevant information.

(b) Automatic Temporary Suspension.

(1) *Procedure.* On the filing with the Supreme Court of the Director's certification that any attorney authorized to practice law in the State of New Jersey has been determined to be guilty (whether sentenced or not) in any court of the United States or the District of Columbia or of any state, territory, commonwealth or possession of the United States of a serious crime as hereinafter defined, the Supreme Court shall enter an order immediately suspending that attorney from the practice of law until final disposition of a disciplinary proceeding to be commenced at the conclusion of the criminal proceeding, whether the determination resulted from a plea of guilty, no contest, or nolo contendere, or from a verdict after trial or otherwise, and regardless of the pendency of any appeal. A copy of the order of suspension shall immediately be served on the attorney. On good cause shown, the Supreme Court may set aside the order when it appears in the interest of justice to do so. Nothing herein shall be construed to preclude the application for a temporary suspension otherwise allowable by court rule, of any attorney determined to be guilty of any other crime.

(2) *Serious Crimes Defined.* The term "serious crime" shall include any crime of the first or second degree as defined by the New Jersey Code of Criminal Justice (N.J.S.A.2C:1–1 et seq.); or any felony of the United States or the District of Columbia or of any state, territory, commonwealth or possession of the United States; or any other crime of this state or of the United States or the District of Columbia or of any state, territory, commonwealth or possession of the United States, a necessary element of which, as determined by the statutory or common law definition of such crime in the jurisdiction where the judgment was

entered, involves interference with the administration of justice, false swearing, misrepresentation, fraud, deceit, bribery, extortion, misappropriation, theft; or any attempt or a conspiracy or solicitation of another to commit a "serious crime;" or violations involving criminal drug offenses, excluding solely minor possessory offenses.

(3) *Reinstatement.* An attorney suspended under the provisions of paragraph (1) may apply to the Court, on notice to the Director, for reinstatement immediately on the filing of a certificate demonstrating that the underlying conviction of or plea to a serious crime has been reversed. An order of reinstatement will not terminate any disciplinary proceeding then pending against the attorney.

(c) Final Discipline.

(1) *Conclusive Evidence.* In any disciplinary proceeding instituted against an attorney based on criminal or quasi-criminal conduct, the conduct shall be deemed to be conclusively established by any of the following: a certified copy of a judgment of conviction, the transcript of a plea of guilty to a crime or disorderly persons offense, whether the plea results either in a judgment of conviction or admission to a diversionary program, a plea of no contest, or nolo contendere, or the transcript of the plea.

(2) *Procedure.* At the conclusion of all criminal matters, including disorderly persons offenses, involving findings or admissions of guilt that are not the subject of a direct appeal, or at the conclusion of all direct appeals from all such matters, the Director may file directly with the Board and serve on the respondent or counsel, if any, a motion for final discipline based on a criminal conviction or admission of guilt specifying the sanction requested. Within 21 days after service of such motion the respondent shall file with the Board and serve on the Director a brief together with any other permissible filings. The Director may within 21 days thereafter file and serve any responding brief. If the respondent either fails to file a timely brief or timely files a brief which does not disagree with the sanction requested, no oral argument is required and the Board may decide the matter on the record. In all other cases the Board shall notify the parties of a date for oral argument. Following oral argument, the Board shall issue its decision and recommendation for final discipline to the Supreme Court.

The sole issue to be determined shall be the extent of final discipline to be imposed. The Board and Court may consider any relevant evidence in mitigation that is not inconsistent with the essential elements of the criminal matter for which the attorney was convicted or has admitted guilt as determined by the statute defining the criminal matter. No witnesses shall be allowed and no oral testimony shall be taken; however, both the Board and the Court may consider written materials otherwise allowed by this rule that are submitted to it. Either the Board or the Court, on the showing of good

cause therefore or on its own motion, may remand a case to a trier of fact for a limited evidentiary hearing and report consistent with this subsection.

Nothing in this rule shall be construed to preclude the Office of Attorney Ethics from filing a complaint and proceeding by hearing where the Director determines that procedure to be appropriate.

Note: Source—Former Rule 1:20–6 adopted January 31, 1984 to be effective February 15, 1984; paragraph (a)(1) amended November 1, 1985 to be effective January 2, 1986; paragraphs (a) and (b) amended November 5, 1986 to be effective January 1, 1987; new paragraph (a) adopted and paragraphs (a) and (b) redesignated (b) and (c) November 7, 1988 to be effective January 2, 1989; former R. 1:20–6 redesignated as R. 1:20–13, captions added, former text of paragraph (a) redesignated (a)(1); new paragraph (a)(2) adopted, paragraph (b) and (c) amended January 31, 1995 to be effective March 1, 1995; paragraph (b) amended July 28, 2004 to be effective September 1, 2004.

1:20–14. Reciprocal Discipline and Disability Proceedings

(a) Reciprocal Attorney Discipline and Disability.

(1) *Reporting Duty.* An attorney admitted to practice in this state, including those attorneys specially authorized for a limited purpose or in connection with a particular proceeding, shall promptly inform the Director in writing on transfer to disability-inactive status or on imposition of discipline as an attorney or otherwise in connection with the practice of law in another jurisdiction, including any federal court of the United States or the District of Columbia, a state or federal administrative agency or other tribunal, a court of any state, territory, commonwealth or possession of the United States.

(2) *Procedure.* On the filing with the Board and service on the respondent by the Director of a motion for reciprocal discipline or disability attaching a certified or exemplified copy of a judgment or order that demonstrates that an attorney admitted to practice in this state, including those attorneys specially authorized for a limited purpose or in connection with a particular proceeding, has been transferred to disability-inactive status or disciplined as an attorney or otherwise in connection with the practice of law by another court, agency or tribunal, the respondent shall have 21 days after service of that motion to file and serve any brief containing any claim predicated on the grounds set forth in subsection (4) hereof that the recommendation to the Supreme Court of the imposition of the identical action or discipline by the Board would be unwarranted, together with the reasons therefor. The attorney shall have the burden of establishing by clear and convincing evidence the grounds asserted. The Director shall prosecute these proceedings and may submit a reply brief within 21 days after the expiration of the attorney's time for filing.

(3) *Stay of Foreign Proceedings*. In the event the discipline or disability imposed in the other jurisdiction has been stayed there, proceedings under this rule shall be deferred until such stay expires unless good cause appears to the contrary.

(4) *Board Decision*. On the expiration of the time allowed for the Director's filing of a reply brief, the matter shall be set down before the Board. If the respondent either fails to file a timely brief or timely files a brief that does not contest the sanction requested by the Director, no oral argument is required and the Board may decide the matter on the record. The Board shall recommend the imposition of the identical action or discipline unless the respondent demonstrates, or the Board finds on the face of the record on which the discipline in another jurisdiction was predicated that it clearly appears that:

(A) the disciplinary or disability order of the foreign jurisdiction was not entered;

(B) the disciplinary or disability order of the foreign jurisdiction does not apply to the respondent;

(C) the disciplinary or disability order of the foreign jurisdiction does not remain in full force and effect as the result of appellate proceedings;

(D) the procedure followed in the foreign disciplinary matter was so lacking in notice or opportunity to be heard as to constitute a deprivation of due process; or

(E) the unethical conduct established warrants substantially different discipline.

When the Board determines that any of said elements exists, it shall make such recommendation to the Court as it deems appropriate. The Director may argue that the law of this state or the facts of the case do or should warrant the imposition of greater discipline than that imposed in other jurisdictions, but in such event the Director shall bear the burden of establishing such contentions by clear and convincing evidence. In the event that the Board determines that the Director has met the burden in this regard, the Board shall recommend the imposition of such greater discipline as it deems appropriate.

(5) *Conclusive Evidence*. In all other respects, a final adjudication in another court, agency or tribunal, that an attorney admitted to practice in this state, including those attorneys specially authorized for a limited purpose or in connection with a particular proceeding, has been transferred to "disability-inactive" status or is guilty of unethical conduct in another jurisdiction as an attorney or otherwise in connection with the practice of law, shall establish conclusively the facts on which it rests for purposes of a disciplinary proceeding in this state.

(b) **Reciprocal Judicial Discipline.**

(1) *Reporting Duty*. Any attorney admitted to practice in this state shall promptly inform the Director in writing on being subjected to discipline as a judge in any other jurisdiction including any federal court of the United States or the District of Columbia, a state or federal administrative agency or other tribunal, a court of any state, territory, commonwealth or possession of the United States.

(2) *Procedures for Foreign Judicial Determination*. On the filing with the Board and service on the respondent by the Director of a motion for final discipline attaching a certified or exemplified copy of a judgment or order that demonstrates that an attorney admitted to practice in this state has been disciplined as a judge by another court, agency or tribunal, the matter shall proceed in accordance with subsections (a)(2) through (5).

(3) *Procedure for New Jersey Judicial Determination*. If a motion for final discipline is based on a final determination of unethical judicial conduct by the Supreme Court of New Jersey, that determination shall conclusively establish the facts on which it rests for purposes of an attorney disciplinary proceeding. In such case the Director may file directly with the Board and serve on the respondent or counsel, if any, a motion for reciprocal discipline. Within 21 days after service of such motion the respondent shall file with the Board and serve on the Director a brief together with any other permissible filings. The Director may within 21 days thereafter file and serve any responding brief. If the respondent either fails to file a timely brief or timely files a brief that does not disagree with the sanction requested; no oral argument is required and the Board may decide the matter on the record. In all other cases the Board shall notify the parties of a date for oral argument, following which the Board shall issue its decision and recommendation for final discipline to the Supreme Court.

The sole issue to be determined under this section shall be the extent of final discipline to be imposed. The Board and Court may consider any relevant evidence in mitigation that is not inconsistent with the findings of fact and determinations of the Supreme Court of New Jersey in the judicial proceeding. No witnesses shall be allowed and no oral testimony shall be taken; however, both the Board and the Court may consider written materials otherwise allowed by this rule that are submitted to it. Either the Board or the Court, on the showing of good cause therefore or on its own motion, may remand a case to a special ethics master for a limited evidentiary hearing and report consistent with this subsection.

(c) **Attorney Discipline Based on New Jersey Judicial Discipline.** Where a judge has been removed or disciplined pursuant to R. 2:14 or 2:15, respectively, those proceedings shall be conclusive of the conduct on which that discipline was based in any subsequent disciplinary proceeding brought against the judge arising out of the same conduct. Attorney disciplinary proceedings may be taken in accordance with R. 1:20–14(b)(2).

(d) **Alternative Procedure; Complaint.** Nothing in this rule shall be construed to preclude the Director from filing a complaint pursuant to R. 1:20–4 where the Director determines that procedure to be appropriate.

Note: Adopted January 31, 1984 to be effective February 15, 1984; paragraphs (a), (b), (d) and (e) amended November 5, 1986 to be effective January 1, 1987; paragraph (d)(5) amended July 13, 1994 to be effective September 1, 1994; former R. 1:20–7 redesignated as R. 1:20–14, captions added, subsections (a)(b)(c)(d) and (e) amended and renumbered (a)(1) through (5), and new subsections (b) and (c) added January 31, 1995 to be effective March 1, 1995; paragraphs (a) and (b) amended and new paragraph (d) adopted July 28, 2004 to be effective September 1, 2004.

1:20–15. Disciplinary Review Board

(a) Appointment; Officers. The Supreme Court shall appoint a Disciplinary Review Board consisting of nine members, at least five of whom shall be attorneys of this state and at least three of whom shall not be attorneys. Members shall be appointed for three-year terms and may be reappointed in the Supreme Court's discretion. The Supreme Court shall annually designate a chair and vice chair of the Board from among its members.

(b) Office of Counsel. The Supreme Court shall establish an Office of Disciplinary Review Board Counsel and shall, with the advice of the Board, appoint a counsel who shall be a member of the bar of the State of New Jersey. Neither counsel, assistant counsel nor staff shall be permitted to otherwise engage in the practice of law nor to be otherwise employed except as may be provided by these rules and R. 1:17. Counsel for the Board shall have the authority to:

(1) provide legal counsel and advice to the Board;

(2) represent the Board before the Supreme Court when so requested by the Court or the Director;

(3) serve as the secretariat for the Board;

(4) maintain permanent records of all matters considered by the Board;

(5) prepare annually, jointly with the Director, a proposed budget for the attorney disciplinary system of the state;

(6) recommend to the Board, for its adoption, subject to approval of the Supreme Court, regulations governing its own administrative procedures;

(7) hire and discharge all staff of the Office of Disciplinary Review Board Counsel consistent with personnel policies of the judiciary and subject to the approval of the Chief Justice, and recommend the hiring of assistant and deputy counsel subject to the advice of the Board chair and approval of the Supreme Court;

(8) perform such other duties as may be specifically assigned by the Disciplinary Review Board or the Supreme Court.

(c) Quorum; Dissenting Report. Five members of the Board shall constitute a quorum and all determinations shall be made by a majority of a quorum, provided however that a determination that discipline be imposed

or a recommendation for temporary suspension shall have the concurrence of at least five members of the Board who have considered the record and briefs, if any; and provided further that at least three of them were present at any oral argument. Any Board member not concurring in a majority decision may file a separate report.

(d) Regulations. The Board may, subject to the prior approval of the Supreme Court, promulgate rules governing proceedings before it.

(e) Review of Final Action.

(1) *Ethics Actions Subject to Review.* The Board shall review, upon the filing of an ethics appeal by the original grievant or the Director, the following actions taken by an Ethics Committee, a special ethics master or by the Committee on Attorney Advertising:

(i) a determination to dismiss after investigation on the basis that there is no unethical conduct.

(ii) a determination to dismiss made after hearing on the basis that there has been no unethical conduct.

(2) *Perfection of Review.* The original grievant or the Director may, within 21 days after receipt of notice of the action, file with the Board a notice of appeal in the form prescribed by the Board and shall serve a copy thereof by regular mail upon the respondent, and, where appropriate, the presenter and the secretary of the Ethics Committee, the Director or the Committee on Attorney Advertising. The notice of appeal shall have attached a complete copy of the investigation report. The secretary of the Ethics Committee or of the Committee on Attorney Advertising or the Director, as appropriate, shall provide the record of its proceedings to the Board within ten days after its request. Within 21 days after receipt of the notice of appeal the respondent, the Ethics Committee, the Director, or the Committee on Attorney Advertising, as appropriate, may file a response with the Board.

(3) *Review; Disposition.* The review by the Board shall be de novo on the record with or without oral argument as it shall in its discretion determine. It shall by written determination affirm, modify, or reverse the action appealed from and may remand the matter for such further proceedings as it may direct. Review by the Board of decisions by the Committee on Attorney Advertising shall be limited as set forth in Rule 1:19A–4(b) and (d).

(f) Recommendations for Discipline.

(1) *Generally.* All recommendations for discipline received by the Board, except for admonitions and those consent matters that are reviewable only as to the recommended sanction, shall be promptly heard de novo on the record on notice to all parties. Recommendations for discipline filed by the Committee on Attorney Advertising shall be reviewed in accordance with Rule 1:19A–4(f). The Board's review shall include any portion of the charges dismissed by the trier of fact.

(2) *Procedure; Waiver of Hearing.* The notice of Board hearing shall contain a briefing schedule for the parties. Within ten days after receipt of that notice, the

respondent and the presenter shall enter an appearance with the Office of Disciplinary Review Board Counsel. At that time, respondent may agree in writing to proceed on the record and waive oral argument. The waiver shall specify whether or not respondent agrees with the conclusions and recommendation of the trier of fact. Neither the presenter nor assigned ethics counsel may elect to waive oral argument but if respondent has filed a complete waiver, the Board may elect to review the matter without argument.

(3) *Disposition.* The Board shall render a formal decision including findings of fact and conclusions of law as to each issue presented, and shall make a specific determination as to the appropriate disciplinary sanction, if any, to be imposed, except in those matters in which a reprimand has been recommended and the Board determines to impose an admonition. When the Board determines to impose an admonition rather than a reprimand, it shall promptly issue a letter in accordance with paragraph (4) of this Rule. The letter shall include a statement of reasons for the Board's conclusion that a lesser sanction is warranted. The Board's disposition shall require respondent to make reimbursement of disciplinary costs in accordance with R. 1:20–17. The Board's decision shall be promptly filed with the Clerk of the Supreme Court and served on the Director and the parties by regular mail.

(4) *Admonitions.* All post-hearing recommendations for admonitions received by the Board shall be considered promptly de novo on the record below on notice to all parties. Admonitions recommended by the Committee on Attorney Advertising shall be reviewed in accordance with Rule 1:19A–4(f). In its discretion the Board may direct that the transcript be produced, briefs be filed, or that oral argument be held. Except in minor unethical conduct matters the Board, in its discretion, may direct that a panel report recommending an admonition be treated as a recommendation for greater discipline. In that event, all proceedings shall be held in conformance with paragraph (1) above. The Board shall have the authority to impose an admonition together with a direction for reimbursement of costs. When the Board determines that an admonition should be imposed, including admonition by consent, it shall issue the letter of admonition. When the Board determines that no ethics violation has occurred, it shall dismiss the charges. The Board's determination, in letter form, shall be sent promptly to the respondent by certified mail. Copies shall be forwarded by regular mail to the Clerk of the Supreme Court, the Director, the Ethics Committee, the Committee on Attorney Advertising, if applicable, and the original grievant, if any. The Supreme Court may review admonitions in accordance with Rule 1:20–16(b).

(g) **Consent Matters.** On its review of a motion for imposition of discipline by consent pursuant to R. 1:20–10(b), the Board may either grant the motion and accept the recommendation, or deny the motion. If denied, the disciplinary proceeding shall resume as if no motion had been submitted and no such submission shall be evidentiary.

(h) **Constitutional Challenges.** Constitutional challenges to the proceedings raised before the trier of fact shall be preserved, without Board action, for Supreme Court consideration as a part of its review of the matter on the merits. Interlocutory relief may be sought only in accordance with Rule 1:20–16(f)(1).

(i) **Temporary Suspension.** On receipt of evidence demonstrating that an attorney subject to the disciplinary jurisdiction of this state has committed a violation of the Rules of Professional Conduct, caselaw or other authority, or is under a disability as herein defined, and poses a substantial threat of serious harm to the public or, where necessary to protect the interests of an attorney, a client or the public, or where otherwise authorized by these rules, the Board may, on the motion of the Director, or on its own motion, recommend to the Supreme Court that an attorney be suspended temporarily from practice upon such terms and conditions as it deems appropriate.

(j) **Imposition of Sanctions.** In addition to any other authority granted by these Rules to impose or recommend the imposition of costs incurred in the prosecution of disciplinary proceedings, the Board may impose appropriate sanctions, including monetary sanctions as a form of discipline. The Board shall limit the imposition of such sanctions to those exceptional circumstances in which other forms of discipline are not appropriate to accomplish the purposes of attorney discipline.

(k) **Enforcement of Fee Arbitration Committee Determination or Stipulation.** When a matter involving a determination by a Fee Committee or a signed Stipulation of Settlement is referred to the Director because of the attorney's failure to comply within 30 days of receipt of the arbitration determination, or of the date set forth in the stipulation, the Board, upon motion of the Director and after affording the attorney an opportunity to be heard, may recommend to the Supreme Court that the attorney be temporarily suspended until compliance with the determination or stipulation.

(*l*) **Fee Arbitration Appeals.** The Board shall review an appeal from a determination of a fee arbitration committee in accordance with R. 1:20A–3(c).

(m) **Exemption From Costs.** As an agency of the Supreme Court, the Disciplinary Review Board and any lawfully appointed designee shall be exempt from the payment of any court costs required by rule of law of the State of New Jersey including, but not limited to, the filing or docketing of any document, deposit for costs or service of process.

(n) **Committee on Disciplinary Decisions; Publication of Disciplinary Dispositions.** The Chief Justice shall appoint a Committee on Disciplinary Decisions to review Disciplinary Review Board decisions to determine which should be published. Decisions of the Board shall be published only after entry of a dispositional Supreme Court Order and only if so directed by the Supreme Court or if approved for publication by the Committee on Disciplinary Decisions. Any person or entity may seek publication of a disciplinary decision by submitting to the Committee a written request explaining the basis for the request and identifying in what way the decision: (1) determines a new and important question of professional conduct, or (2) alters an established principle of professional conduct, or (3) establishes or changes a practice or procedure, or (4) is of continuing public or professional interest and importance, or (5) clarifies a principle or procedure.

Note: Former Rule redesignated as Rule 1:20–5 January 31, 1984 to be effective February 15, 1984. Source— Former Rule 1:20–3 adopted February 23, 1978, to be effective April 1, 1978; paragraphs (a), (e), (g), (h) and (I) amended July 16, 1981, to be effective September 14, 1981; paragraph (f) (g), and (h) deleted; paragraph (a) amended; paragraphs (b), (c), (d), (e), (I) and (j) amended and redesignated (c), (d), (e), (f), (g) and (I); new paragraphs (b) and (h) adopted January 31, 1984, to be effective February 15, 1984; paragraph (I) amended November 1, 1985, to be effective January 2, 1986; paragraphs (e) and (f) amended November 5, 1986, to be effective January 1, 1987; paragraphs (e) and (f) amended June 26, 1987, to be effective July 1, 1987; paragraph (I) caption and text amended November 7, 1988 to be effective January 2, 1989; paragraph (f)(2) amended November 6, 1989, to be effective January 2, 1990; paragraph (f) amended June 29, 1990 to be effective September 4, 1990; paragraph (e)(2) amended July 13, 1994 to be effective September 1, 1994; paragraph (f)(2) caption and text amended August 8, 1994 to be effective immediately; R. 1:20–4 redesignated R. 1:20–15, paragraphs (a), (b), (c), (d) and (e) amended, former text of paragraph (f)(1) and (2) amended and incorporated into new (f)(1)(2)(3) and (4), and former paragraphs (f)(3), (g),(h) and (I) amended and redesignated paragraphs (h)(i)(j) and (k), new paragraphs (g), (l) and (m) adopted January 31, 1995 to be effective March 1, 1995; paragraph (j) amended July 10, 1998 to be effective September 1, 1998; paragraph (f)(3) amended and new paragraph (n) adopted March 20, 2003, to be effective immediately; paragraphs (a), (c), (e), (f), (i), and (l) amended July 28, 2004 to be effective September 1, 2004.

1:20–15A. Final Disciplinary Determinations; Sanctions

(a) Categories of Discipline. The imposition of final discipline may include any of the following sanctions, all of which shall be public:

(1) Disbarment. An attorney who is disbarred shall have his or her name permanently stricken from the roll of attorneys.

(2) Indeterminate Suspension. Unless the Court's Order provides otherwise, an indeterminate suspension shall prohibit the attorney from seeking reinstatement for a minimum of five years.

(3) Term of Suspension. Absent special circumstances, a suspension for a term shall be for a period that is no less than three months and no more than three years.

(4) Censure.

(5) Reprimand.

(6) Admonition.

(b) Conditions. The Supreme Court's Order may provide for one or more of the following, either as a part of a sanction imposed pursuant to paragraph (a) or as a condition to reinstatement:

(1) Financial controls including, but not limited to, a designated co-signatory for all attorney trust and business account checks;

(2) Restrictions on the ability to practice including, but not limited to, the use of a supervising attorney approved by the Office of Attorney Ethics as a prerequisite to engaging in the private practice of law;

(3) Substance abuse control including, but not limited to, requiring abstinence, testing, and an identifiable commitment to appropriate support groups;

(4) Mental health treatment and counseling, together with a finding of fitness to practice by a mental health professional approved by the Office of Attorney Ethics;

(5) Taking and passing the New Jersey bar examination, as well as meeting all other qualifications for admission including, but not limited to, a certification of the attorney's good character by the Supreme Court after review by the Committee on Character; and

(6) Such other conditions as may be deemed appropriate in the light of the circumstances presented including, but not limited to, probation or a suspended suspension.

Note: Adopted July 30, 2002, to be effective September 3, 2002.

1:20–16. Action by the Supreme Court

(a) Review of Recommendations for Disbarment. The Supreme Court shall review all decisions of the Board that recommend disbarment. The review shall be on the basis of the decision, the transcript of the hearing before the Board, any briefs filed with the Board, and the record of the proceedings before the Ethics Committee, if any. The record shall be supplemented by the filing of briefs and by oral argument before the Supreme Court in accordance with R. 2:5, 2:6 and 2:11, insofar as applicable.

(b) Review of Other Final Disciplinary Determinations. In all matters other than those in which disbarment has been recommended, the Board's decision shall become final on the entry of an appropriate Order by the Clerk of the Supreme Court. Unless the Court otherwise orders, entry of a final Order of discipline shall be stayed by the filing of a timely petition for review of the Board's decision by the respondent or the Office of Attorney Ethics or by the entry of an Order scheduling the matter for briefing and, where appropriate, oral argument on the Court's own motion.

The Court may, on its own motion, decide to review any determination of the Board where disbarment has not been recommended.

Either respondent or the Office of Attorney Ethics may seek review by filing a notice of petition for review within twenty days of the filing of the Board's decision with the Court. The notice shall be accompanied by nine copies of a petition for review, which shall be a brief that meets the format requirements of Rule 2:12–7(a). The responding party shall serve and file a responding brief within ten days of the filing of the petition for review. A reply brief, if any, shall be served and filed within seven days thereafter.

If the Court grants the petition for review, the record before it shall consist of the briefs filed on the petition and the record developed below, consistent with paragraph (a) of this Rule.

The Court may, in its discretion, elect to determine any matter on the papers submitted to it, without oral argument.

Unless the Court otherwise directs, the entry of its disposition shall vacate any stay in effect.

(c) De Novo Review. Supreme Court review shall be de novo on the record.

(d) Non–appealable Matters. The Board's decision shall be final and not subject to further review by the Court, whether by appeal by leave or in any other manner, in all matters considered by the Board pursuant to R. 1:20–15(e)(1)(i) and R. 1:20A–3(c).

(e) Consent Orders. Except for admonition by consent, on acceptance by the Disciplinary Review Board pursuant to R. 1:20–15(g) of a motion for imposition of discipline by consent, the record of the proceedings shall be filed with the Clerk of the Court for entry of an order of discipline in conformance therewith. The order shall be entered within 30 days after filing of the record.

(f) Constitutional Issues.

(1) *Interlocutory Review.* An aggrieved party may file with the Supreme Court a motion for leave to appeal to seek interlocutory review of a constitutional challenge to proceedings pending before the trier of fact or the Board. The motion papers shall conform to R. 2:8–1. Leave to appeal may be granted only when necessary to prevent irreparable injury. If leave to appeal is granted, the record below may, in the discretion of the Court, be supplemented by the filing of briefs and oral argument. The filing of any motion to the Supreme Court for interlocutory review authorized by these rules shall not automatically stay disciplinary proceedings unless the Court enters an order specifically granting a stay pending its resolution of the request.

(2) *Final Review.* In any case in which a constitutional challenge to the proceedings has been properly raised below and preserved pending review of the merits of the disciplinary matter by the Supreme Court, the aggrieved party may seek the review of the Court by proceeding in accordance with the applicable provisions of paragraph (b) of this rule.

(g) Review of Other Matters. All recommendations of the Board other than those otherwise referred to in this rule shall be reviewed by the Supreme Court on the full record below, supplemented as it may order on its own or a party's motion.

(h) Restraint on Attorney Accounts. A Supreme Court order imposing interim or final discipline may include a restraint on the disbursement of funds from accounts maintained by the respondent pursuant to Rule 1:21–6 or from other appropriate accounts. Applications for release of those funds shall be governed by Rule 1:20–23.

(i) Practice of Law Prohibited. No attorney who has been ordered disbarred, suspended, or transferred to disability-inactive status shall practice law after such disbarment or during the period of such suspension or disability, and every order of disbarment shall include a permanent injunction from such practice.

(j) Practicing Law in Violation of Supreme Court Order. Whenever there is reason to believe that an attorney may have violated an Order of the Supreme Court prohibiting that attorney from practicing law in this state, the Director may refer the underlying facts to the appropriate law enforcement agency. The Director also may file and prosecute an action for contempt under R. 1:10–2. Any action under R. 1:10–2 shall be instituted on order to show cause to the Assignment Judge of the vicinage in which the respondent is alleged to have engaged in the prohibited practice of law.

(k) Advice to Suspended and Disbarred Attorneys; Supreme Court Order. An order of the Supreme Court suspending an attorney shall contain a provision specifically advising the attorney of the requirements of R.1:20–20(b)(15) for filing an affidavit of compliance within 30 days with the Director, the Clerk of the Supreme Court, and the Board; and of the serious consequences for failure to fully and timely comply with those requirements as provided in R.1:20–20(c).

Note: Former rule redesignated as R. 1:20–8, R. 1:20–10 and R. 1:20–11. Source—Former Rule 1:20–4 adopted February 23, 1978, to be effective April 1, 1978; paragraph (a) amended January 10, 1979 to be effective immediately; new paragraph (d) adopted and paragraphs (d) and (e) redesignated (e) and (f) July 16, 1981 to be effective September 14, 1981; paragraphs (a) and (b) amended; paragraph (c) deleted; paragraphs (d), (e) and (f) amended and redesignated (c), (d) and (e) January 31, 1984 to be effective February 15, 1984; new paragraph (d) adopted and former paragraphs (d) and (e) redesignated (e) and (f) November 6, 1989, to be effective January 2, 1990; paragraph (a) amended June 29, 1990 to be effective September 4, 1990; paragraph (d) amended August 8, 1994 to be effective immediately; former R. 1:20–5 redesignated R. 1:20–16, caption and text of paragraph (a) amended, paragraphs (b) and (d) deleted, new paragraphs (b)(c)(d)(e) and (i) adopted, former paragraphs (c)(e)(f) amended and redesignated (f)(g) and (h) January 31, 1995 to be effective March 1, 1995; paragraph (b) amended March 24, 1995, to be effective immediately; former paragraphs (h) and (i) redesignated as paragraphs (i) and (j) and new paragraph (h) adopted July 10, 1998 to be effective September 1, 1998; paragraphs (f), (i), and (j) amended and new paragraph (k) adopted July 28, 2004 to be effective September 1, 2004; paragraph (i) amended July 9, 2008 to be effective September 1, 2008.

1:20–17. Reimbursement of Disciplinary Costs

(a) Generally. Except in extraordinary cases, the final order of discipline or final order of transfer to disability-inactive status shall impose costs as recommended by the Disciplinary Review Board.

(b) Amount and Nature of Costs Assessed. In calculating its recommendation the Disciplinary Review Board shall assess both basic administrative costs and disciplinary expenses actually incurred.

(1) *Basic Administrative Costs.* Basic administrative costs shall be assessed as follows:

(A) For final Discipline by Consent (including Disbarment by Consent, if tendered prior to hearing), $650.

(B) For a Motion for Final Discipline or a Motion for Reciprocal Discipline, $1,000.

(C) For other final discipline or transfer to disability-inactive status ordered by the Board or the Court, including Admonition, Reprimand, Censure, Suspension, Transfer to Disability–Inactive Status, Disbarment and Disbarment by Consent (if tendered after the commencement of hearing), $2,000.

(2) *Disciplinary Expenses Actually Incurred.* Disciplinary expenses actually incurred shall be separately assessed, including, but not limited to, the following:

(A) Costs of any outside experts, such as accountants, auditors, interpreters, physicians, and other consultants;

(B) Charges for service of process and notice by publication;

(C) Transcript and recording or court reporter costs;

(D) Costs of a special ethics master;

(E) Disciplinary Review Board reproduction costs at 15 cents per page;

(F) Costs and fees paid to witness;

(c) Disputes; Procedure. On the entry of an order imposing final discipline or final transfer to disability-inactive status by the Supreme Court that includes an authorization for imposition of costs, Counsel to the Board shall promptly furnish the respondent with a statement of disciplinary costs. Within 20 days thereafter the respondent shall reimburse in full all basic administrative costs and such disciplinary expenses actually incurred as to which there is no dispute. A respondent disputing any included actually-incurred disciplinary expense shall, within that time, specifically detail in writing the items disputed and the factual basis for the dispute. The Board shall review a timely filed letter of dispute without oral argument. Board Counsel shall notify respondent of the Board's decision, which shall be final and not subject to appeal. Respondent shall remit full payment of any balance due within 20 days after receipt of said notice.

Interest shall be charged on the unpaid balance of costs assessed beginning ten days after the date the assessment becomes final. The rate of interest charged shall be 10% per annum, or such other rate established by the Supreme Court from time to time.

(d) Claims of Extraordinary Financial Hardship. Service on respondent of the statement of disciplinary costs shall be accompanied by a notice advising that, in the event of inability to make payment by reason of extraordinary financial hardship, an installment payment schedule may be requested in writing. The request shall be made in writing within 20 days after service of the statement on respondent and shall include a proposed payment plan and be supported by a detailed statement of reasons together with such information specified in the notice. Respondent shall certify the truth of the information provided in accordance with R. 1:4–4.

The Board shall review a timely request under this section. The Board's decision shall be final and not subject to appeal. On respondent's failure to comply with the schedule of payments, the entire unpaid balance of disciplinary costs shall become immediately due and payable. Board Counsel may, in the exercise of discretion, decline to enter into further installment agreements with a respondent who has already defaulted on an agreed installment plan.

(e) Failure to Pay Disciplinary Costs.

(1) *Temporary Suspension.* On a default in payment required by this rule, Board Counsel, on ten days notice to the respondent, may file with the Supreme Court a certification of the default. The Supreme Court shall forthwith enter an order temporarily suspending the attorney from the practice of law until payment is made and until further order of the Court.

(2) *Denial of Reinstatement.* The Supreme Court shall not consider a recommendation for reinstatement unless accompanied by a Board certification that all assessed disciplinary costs have been paid.

(3) *Docketing Judgment.* Upon certification of the amount of disciplinary costs assessed and due, the Clerk of the Superior Court shall, without fee, enter on the civil judgment and order docket both the order authorizing costs and Board Counsel's certification of the amount due. Upon payment, Board Counsel shall execute a warrant for satisfaction.

Note: Adopted January 31, 1995 to be effective March 15, 1995; paragraph (f) deleted July 10, 1998 to be effective September 1, 1998; paragraphs (a), (b), (c), (d), and (e) amended July 28, 2004 to be effective September 1, 2004.

1:20–18. Supervision of Disciplined Attorney

(a) Generally. An order of discipline or reinstatement entered by the Supreme Court may require the respondent to practice law under supervision by a practicing attorney. Such order shall include the general conditions prescribed by this rule and such specific additional conditions as the Director may require with the approval of the Supreme Court.

(b) Violation of Supervision or RPC's. The supervisor and the respondent shall report promptly to the Director any facts that appear to constitute a violation by the respondent of the Rules of Professional Conduct or the conditions of supervision.

(c) Mental or Physical Disability. The supervisor and the respondent shall report promptly to the Director any facts that appear to demonstrate alcohol or substance abuse by the respondent, or that indicate that the respondent may be incapacitated from practicing law by reason of mental or physical infirmity or illness.

(d) Weekly Conferences. The supervisor shall confer in person with the respondent at least weekly to review the status of all matters being handled.

(e) Time Records. The respondent shall maintain contemporaneous time records on all legal matters, which shall be retained for a minimum of one year after termination of the supervisory period.

(f) New Cases. The respondent shall not accept any cases without the prior approval of the supervisor.

(g) Respondent's Monthly Reports. The respondent shall provide monthly Case Listing Reports to the supervisor by the fifth business day of each month, listing for each case assigned to the respondent: (1) the case caption, (2) the full name and address of the client(s), (3) a brief description of the nature of the case, (4) a brief narrative of its current status, (5) the name of all opposing attorneys, and (6) in all litigated matters, the name of the court and docket number, as well as the names of all judges before whom the attorney appeared during that month. The respondent shall certify all monthly reports in accordance with Rule 1:4–4(b). Reports shall be submitted in a form acceptable to the Director.

(h) Supervisor's Quarterly Reports. The supervisor shall provide to the Director the supervisor's Quarterly Reports in a form acceptable to the Director beginning on the tenth business day of the third month following respondent's order of discipline or of reinstatement by the Supreme Court of New Jersey imposing Conditions of Supervision. Reports shall be made quarterly thereafter on the tenth business day of the month. The quarterly report shall be certified in accordance with Rule 1:4–4(b) and shall have appended to it a copy of each monthly Case Listing Report submitted by the respondent during the quarter. The quarterly report shall set forth the supervisor's overall analysis of the handling of all legal matters entrusted to the respondent and shall indicate specifically whether, in the supervisor's judgment, the respondent's handling of any matter is unsatisfactory. The supervisor shall support his or her conclusions by a brief statement of facts and reasons.

(i) Financial Record Keeping Instructions. During the term of this supervision, the supervisor shall instruct the respondent as to the proper maintenance of trust and business accounts and records in accordance with RPC 1.15 and Rule 1:21–6.

(j) Selection of Supervisor. The respondent shall submit the name of a proposed supervisor to the Director for approval.

(k) Termination of Supervision. After the expiration of time set forth in the order of discipline or reinstatement imposing the Conditions of Supervision, the respondent shall apply to the Supreme Court for termination of the conditions on notice to the Director, who shall file a report and recommendation with the Court.

(l) Failure to Comply. If during the term of the supervision, the Director becomes aware of facts that should be brought to the Court's attention, such as a respondent's failure to comply with the conditions of supervision or a supervisor's failure to comply therewith or a request to be relieved, the Director shall petition the Court for an appropriate order on notice to the supervisor and the respondent.

Note: Adopted January 31, 1995 to be effective March 1, 1995; paragraphs (a), (b), (c), (f), (g), (h), (i), (j), (k), and (l) amended July 28, 2004 to be effective September 1, 2004.

1:20–19. Appointment of Attorney–Trustee to Protect Clients' Interest

(a) Jurisdiction; Appointment.

(1) *Regular Attorney–Trustee.* If an attorney has been suspended or disbarred or transferred to disability-inactive status and has not complied with R. 1:20–20 (future activities of disciplined or disability-inactive attorneys), or has abandoned the law practice, or cannot be located, or has died, and no partner, shareholder, executor, administrator or other responsible party capable of conducting the respondent's affairs as stated hereinafter is known to exist, the Assignment Judge, or designee, in the vicinage in which the attorney maintained a practice may, on proper proof of the fact and on the application of any interested party, appoint one or more members of the bar of the vicinage where the law practice is situate as attorney-trustee. Where a responsible party capable of conducting respondent's affairs is known to exist, and where that person is a New Jersey attorney or has retained a New Jersey attorney, that attorney may be appointed and directed to take appropriate action. Notice of an order of appointment shall be given to the Director of the Office of Attorney Ethics and the secretaries of the appropriate Ethics Committee and Fee Committee and county bar association in the vicinage.

(2) *Temporary Attorney–Trustee.* When, in the opinion of the Assignment Judge, an attorney is otherwise unable to carry on the attorney's practice temporarily so that clients' matters are at risk, the Assignment Judge, or designee, in the vicinage in which the attorney maintained a practice may, on proper proof of the fact

and on the application of any interested party, appoint a temporary attorney-trustee for a period of up to six months following the same conditions and procedures set forth in subparagraph (a)(1) of this Rule. The purposes of the temporary attorney-trustee shall be to preserve, in so far as practical, the practice of the attorney and all attorney-client relationships pending a report to the Assignment Judge at 150 days after appointment as to the attorney's condition and ability to resume the practice. The Assignment Judge may then either dissolve the temporary attorney-trusteeship or convert it to a regular attorney-trusteeship as if created under subparagraph (a)(1) of this Rule.

The temporary attorney-trustee shall have the powers and responsibilities authorized by the Assignment Judge, as well as those specifically granted above and those in paragraphs (c), (e) and (h). The temporary attorney-trustee shall not have the powers granted under paragraphs (d), (f) and (g), except that the reports required by paragraph (d) shall be filed.

The temporary attorney-trustee shall not apply for legal fees within the first thirty days after appointment, but may at any time be awarded reasonable costs and expenses as stated under paragraph (h), including the right to satisfy those costs and expenses from the attorney's business or personal accounts as directed by the Assignment Judge. After thirty days from appointment, the temporary attorney-trustee may apply to the Assignment Judge for reduced legal fees below the normal hourly rate in accordance with paragraph (h).

The attorney whose practice is subjected to a temporary trusteeship shall have the right to make application at any time for an order vacating the temporary trusteeship on notice to all interested parties.

(b) Purposes; Inventory of Files, Trust and Other Assets. The purposes of the appointment shall be (1) to inventory active files and make reasonable efforts to distribute them to clients, (2) to take possession of the attorney trust and business accounts, (3) to make reasonable efforts to distribute identified trust funds to clients or other parties (other than the attorney), and (4) after obtaining an order of the court, to dispose of any remaining funds and assets as directed by the court. The attorney-trustee shall have no obligation or liability to the attorney. The attorney-trustee may take possession of the attorney's law practice and, in accordance with R.1:20–20(b)(13), all monies and fees due the attorney for the sole purpose of creating a fund for payment of reasonable fees, costs and expenses of the trusteeship as ordered by the court under paragraph (h).

(c) Protection of Client Information. Any attorney-trustee shall not disclose any information contained in any files under this rule without the consent of the client to whom the file relates, except as necessary to carry out the order of appointment or to comply with any request from an Ethics Committee or the Director.

(d) Reports; Instructions. The attorney-trustee shall file an initial report with the Assignment Judge or designee within 120 days after appointment and a final report prior to being discharged. The reports shall describe the nature and scope of the work accomplished and to be accomplished under this rule and the significant activities of the attorney-trustee in meeting the obligations under the rule. The final report must include accountings for any trust and business accounts, the disposition of active case files and any requests for disposition of remaining files and property. The attorney-trustee may apply to the Assignment Judge, or such other Judge as may be designated, for instructions whenever necessary to carry out or conclude the duties and obligations imposed by this rule.

(e) Immunity. All attorney-trustees appointed pursuant to this rule shall be immune from liability for conduct in the performance of their official duties in accordance with R. 1:20–7(e). This immunity shall not extend to employment under section (f).

(f) Acceptance of Clients. With the consent of any client, the attorney-trustee may, but need not, accept employment to complete any legal matter.

(g) Legal Responsibility of Attorney. The attorney for whom an attorney-trustee has been appointed is liable to the attorney-trustee for all fees, costs, and expenses reasonably incurred by the attorney-trustee as approved by the court under paragraph (h).

(h) Legal Fees, Costs, and Expenses. The attorney-trustee shall be entitled to reimbursement from the attorney for (1) actual expenses incurred by the attorney-trustee for costs, including, but not limited to, reasonable secretarial, paralegal, legal, accounting, telephone, postage, moving and storage expenses, and (2) reasonable hourly attorneys' fees. Application for allowance of fees, costs, and expenses shall be made by affidavit to the appointing judge, or designee, who may enter a judgment in favor of the attorney-trustee against the attorney. The application shall be accompanied by an accounting in a form and substance acceptable to the court. The application shall be made on notice to the attorney or, if deceased, to the attorney's personal representative, or heirs. For good cause shown, an interim application for costs and legal fees may be made. The attorney-trustee shall be accorded a priority as an administrative expense for all attorney fees, costs, and expenses awarded by the court. If, after paying the attorney-trustee, there are funds or assets remaining, the Assignment Judge or designee may make such order of disposition as may be appropriate.

Note: Adopted November 5, 1986 to be effective January 1, 1987; former R. 1:20–12 redesignated 1:20–19, paragraphs (a) and (b) amended and paragraph (f) adopted January 31, 1995 to be effective March 1, 1995; paragraph (a) amended, former paragraphs (b), (c), and (f) redesignated as (c), (d), and (h) and captions and text amended, former paragraphs (d) and (e) redesignated as (e) and (f) and amended, and new paragraphs (b) and (g) adopted July 28, 2004 to be effective September 1, 2004; paragraph (a) amended July 27, 2006 to be effective September 1, 2006; paragraph (a) text redesignated as subparagraph (a)(1), subparagraph (a)(1) caption adopted, new subparagraph (a)(2) caption and text adopted July 9, 2008 to be effective September 1, 2008.

1:20–20. Future Activities of Attorney Who Has Been Disciplined or Transferred to Disability Inactive Status

(a) Prohibited Association. No attorney or other entity authorized to practice law in the State of New Jersey shall, in connection with the practice of law, employ, permit or authorize to perform services for the attorney or other entity, or share or use office space with, another who has been disbarred, resigned with prejudice, transferred to disability- inactive status, or is under suspension from the practice of law in this or any other jurisdiction.

(b) Notice to Clients, Adverse Parties and Others. An attorney who is suspended, transferred to disability-inactive status, disbarred, or disbarred by consent or equivalent sanction:

(1) shall not practice law in any form either as principal, agent, servant, clerk or employee of another, and shall not appear as an attorney before any court, justice, judge, board, commission, division or other public authority or agency;

(2) shall not occupy, share or use office space in which an attorney practices law;

(3) shall not furnish legal services, give an opinion concerning the law or its application or any advice with relation thereto, or suggest in any way to the public an entitlement to practice law, or draw any legal instrument;

(4) shall not use any stationery, sign or advertisement suggesting that the attorney, either alone or with any other person, has, owns, conducts, or maintains a law office or office of any kind for the practice of law, or that the attorney is entitled to practice law;

(5) shall, except for the purposes of disbursing trust monies for the 30–day period stated in this subparagraph, cease to use any bank accounts or checks on which the attorney's name appears as a lawyer or attorney-at-law or in connection with the words "law office". If the suspension is for a period greater than six months, or involves a temporary suspension that lasts for more than six months, or involves transfer to disability-inactive status, disbarment, disbarment by consent or their equivalent sanction, the attorney shall, within the 30 day period prescribed in subparagraph (15), disburse all attorney trust account monies that are appropriate to be disbursed and shall arrange to transfer the balance of any trust monies to an attorney admitted to practice law in this state and in good standing for appropriate disbursement, on notice to all interested parties, or dispose of the balance of funds in accordance with R. 1:21–6(j), "Unidentifiable and Unclaimed Trust Fund Accumulations and Trust Funds Held for Missing Owners"; however, it shall not be a violation of this subparagraph for an attorney to take appropriate action to comply after the stated 30–day period;

(6) shall, from the date of the order imposing discipline (regardless of the effective date thereof), not solicit or procure any legal business or retainers for the disciplined attorney or for any other attorney;

(7) shall promptly request the telephone company to remove any listing in the telephone directory indicating that the attorney is a lawyer, or holds a similar title;

(8) shall promptly request the publishers of Martindale–Hubbell Law Directory, the New Jersey Lawyers Diary and Manual, and any other law list in which the attorney's name appears, including all websites on which the attorney's name appears, to remove any listing indicating that that attorney is a member of the New Jersey Bar in good standing;

(9) shall notify the admitting authority in any jurisdiction to whose bar the attorney has been admitted of the disciplinary action taken in the State of New Jersey;

(10) shall, except as otherwise provided by paragraph (d) of this rule, promptly notify all clients in pending matters, other than litigation or administrative proceedings, of the attorney's suspension, transfer to disability-inactive status, disbarment, or disbarment by consent, and of the attorney's consequent inability to act as an attorney due to disbarment, suspension, or disability-inactive status, and shall advise said clients to seek legal advice elsewhere and to obtain another attorney to complete their pending matters. Even if requested by a client, the attorney may not recommend another attorney to complete a matter. When a new attorney is selected by a client, the disciplined or former attorney shall promptly deliver the file and any other paper or property of the client to the new attorney or to the client if no new attorney is selected, without waiving any right to compensation earned as provided in paragraph (13) below;

(11) shall, except as otherwise provided by paragraph (d) of this rule, as to litigated or administrative proceedings pending in any court or administrative agency, promptly give notice of the suspension, transfer to disability-inactive status, disbarment, or disbarment by consent and of the consequent inability to act as an attorney due to disbarment, suspension, or disability-inactive status, to: (1) each client; (2) the attorney for each adverse party in any matter involving any clients; and (3) the Assignment Judge with respect to any action pending in any court in that vicinage, or the clerk of the appropriate appellate court or administrative agency in which a matter is pending. The notice to clients shall advise them to obtain another attorney and promptly to substitute that attorney for the disciplined or former attorney. Even if requested by a client, the disciplined or former attorney may not recommend an attorney to continue the action. The notices to opposing attorneys and the Assignment Judge or Court Clerk shall clearly indicate the caption and docket number of the case or cases and name and place of residence of each client involved. In the event a client involved in litigation or a pending proceeding does not obtain a substitute attor-

ney within 20 days of the mailing of said notice, the disciplined or former attorney shall move pro se in the court or administrative tribunal in which the action or proceeding is pending for leave to withdraw therefrom. When a client selects a new attorney, the disciplined or former attorney shall promptly deliver the file and any other paper or property of the client to the new attorney or to the client if no attorney is selected, without waiving any right to compensation earned, as provided in paragraph (13), below;

(12) shall, in all cases in which the attorney is then acting, or who thereafter attempts to obtain letters of appointment from a Surrogate to act, in any specified fiduciary capacity, including, but not limited to, executor, administrator, guardian, receiver or conservator, promptly notify in writing all (1) co-fiduciaries, (2) beneficiaries, (3) Assignment Judges and Surrogates of any vicinage and county out of which the matter arose, of the attorney's suspension, transfer to disability-inactive status, disbarment, or disbarment by consent. Such notice shall clearly state the name of the matter, any caption and docket number, and, if applicable, the name and date of death or current residence of the decedent, settlor, individual or entity with respect to whose assets the attorney is acting as a fiduciary;

(13) shall not share in any fee for legal services performed by any other attorney following the disciplined or former attorney's prohibition from practice, but may be compensated for the reasonable value of services rendered and disbursements incurred prior to the effective date of the prohibition, provided the attorney has fully complied with the provisions of this rule and has filed the required affidavit of compliance under subparagraph (b)(15). The reasonable value of services for the disciplined or former attorney and the substituted attorney shall not exceed the amount the client would have had to pay had no substitution been required. If an attorney-trustee has been appointed under R. 1:20–19, all fees for legal services and other compensation due the attorney shall be paid solely to the attorney-trustee for disbursement as directed by the court in accordance with the provisions of that rule. Compensation shall include any monies or other thing of value paid for legal services due or that is related to any agreement, sale, assignment or transfer of any aspect of the attorney's share of a law firm;

(14) shall maintain:

(A) files, documents, and other records relating to any matter that was the subject of a disciplinary investigation or proceeding;

(B) files, documents, and other records relating to all terminated matters in which the disciplined or former attorney represented a client prior to the imposition of discipline;

(C) files, documents, and other records of pending matters in which the disciplined or former attorney had responsibility on the date of, or represented a

client during the year prior to, the imposition of discipline or resignation;

(D) all financial records related to the disciplined or former attorney's practice of law during the seven years preceding the imposition of discipline, including but not limited to bank statements, time and billing records, checks, check stubs, journals, ledgers, audits, financial statements, tax returns, and tax reports; and

(E) all records relating to compliance with this rule.

(15) shall within 30 days after the date of the order of suspension (regardless of the effective date thereof) file with the Director the original of a detailed affidavit specifying by correlatively numbered paragraphs how the disciplined attorney has complied with each of the provisions of this rule and the Supreme Court's order. Signed copies of that affidavit shall be provided at the same time to the Clerk of the Supreme Court and to the Disciplinary Review Board. The affidavit shall be accompanied by a copy of all correspondence sent pursuant to this rule and shall also set forth the current residence or other address and telephone number of the disciplined or former attorney to which communications may be directed. The disciplined or former attorney shall thereafter inform the Director of any change in such residence, address, or telephone number. The affidavit shall also set forth whether the attorney maintained malpractice insurance coverage for the past five years and, for each policy maintained, the name of the carrier, the carrier's address, the policy number, and the dates of coverage. The affidavit shall also attach an alphabetical list of the names, addresses, telephone numbers, and file numbers of all clients whom the attorney represented on the date of discipline or transfer to disability-inactive status.

(c) Failure to Comply. Failure to comply fully and timely with the obligations of this rule and file the affidavit of compliance required by paragraph (b)(15) within the 30–day period, unless extended by the Director for good cause, shall, in the case of a suspension, preclude the Board from considering any petition for reinstatement until the expiration of six months from the date of filing proof of compliance in accordance with R.1:20–21(i)(A). Such failure shall also constitute a violation of RPC 8.1(b) (failure to cooperate with ethics authorities) and RPC 8.4(d) (conduct prejudicial to the administration of justice). The Director also may file and prosecute an action for contempt pursuant to R. 1:10–2.

(d) Definite Suspension of Six Months or Less. A lawyer who has been suspended for a definite period of six months or less is exempt from the requirements of paragraph (b)(7) and (b)(8).

(e) Responsibility of Partners and Shareholders. An attorney who is affiliated with the disciplined or former attorney as a partner, shareholder, or member shall take reasonable actions to ensure that the attorney complies with this rule. In lieu of compliance by the attorney with the requirement of paragraph (b)(10) and (b)(11), the firm, corporation, or limited liability entity may promptly notify all clients represented by the disciplined or former attorney of the attorney's inability to act due to disbarment, suspension, or disability-inactive status and that the firm will continue to represent the client unless the client requests in writing that the firm withdraw from the matter and substitute a new attorney.

If the disciplined or former attorney fails to comply with this rule within 30 days of the date of suspension, transfer, or disbarment, the law firm shall do so. Proof of compliance shall be by verified affidavit of a member of the firm, shareholder, or member filed with the Director within 30 days of the date of suspension, transfer, or disbarment. The affidavit shall be accompanied by a copy of all notices sent to clients pursuant to this paragraph.

Note: Adopted February 23, 1978, to be effective April 1, 1978; amended January 31, 1984 to be effective February 15, 1984; amended July 13, 1994 to be effective September 1, 1994; paragraph (a) was former R. 1:21–8, new paragraphs (b), (c) and (d) adopted January 31, 1995 to be effective March 1, 1995; paragraph (d) amended July 10, 1998 to be effective September 1, 1998; paragraphs (a), (b)(10), (b)(11) and (d) amended, paragraphs (b)(12), (b)(13), and (b)(14) amended and redesignated as paragraphs (b)(13), (b) (14), and (b)(15), and new paragraph (b)(12) adopted July 5, 2000 to be effective September 5, 2000; caption of rule amended, paragraphs (a) and (b) amended, former paragraph (c) redesignated as (d), former paragraph (d) redesignated as (e) and amended, and new paragraph (c) adopted July 28, 2004 to be effective September 1, 2004; subparagraphs (b)(5), (b)(7), and (b)(8) amended July 9, 2008 to be effective September 1, 2008.

1:20–21. Reinstatement After Final Discipline

(a) Definite Suspension of More Than Six Months and Indefinite Suspensions. After the expiration of a definite suspension of more than six months or at any time after an indefinite suspension has been ordered, an attorney may file a verified petition for reinstatement with the Disciplinary Review Board pursuant to this rule.

(b) Definite Suspension of Six Months or Less. A lawyer who has been suspended for a definite period of six months or less may file a petition for reinstatement and publish notice of reinstatement forty days prior to the expiration of the period of suspension. All other procedures specified by this rule shall apply, except that the petition need not contain responses to paragraphs (f)(6), and (f)(8) to (f)(10), inclusive.

(c) Filing and Service of Petition. The petitioner shall file an original and 12 copies of the verified petition with the Board and shall serve two copies on the Director.

(d) Costs. Petitions for reinstatement shall be accompanied by a non-refundable check payable to the Disciplinary Oversight Committee in the amount of $750 to cover the reasonable administrative costs of processing the petition. Either the Board or the Court may also direct the petitioner to pay such additional sum during the processing of a petition as it deems appropriate to meet the cost of actual out-of-pocket expenses, including, but not limited to, medical or psychiatric examinations, transcripts and other investigatory and review expenses deemed necessary to a proper evaluation of the reinstatement petition.

(e) Publication of Notice. Contemporaneously with the filing of the petition for reinstatement, or within twenty-one days prior thereto, the petitioner shall publish a notice of application for reinstatement in bold-faced type in all official newspapers designated by the Supreme Court and in a newspaper of general circulation in each county in which the respondent last maintained a law office and in the county in which respondent resided at the time of the imposition of discipline. Publication of a notice shall be sufficient if in the following language: NOTICE TO THE PUBLIC. John Doe, who was admitted to the bar of the State of New Jersey on . . . ., 20.. and who was thereafter suspended from the practice of law by the Supreme Court, is applying to be reinstated to the practice. Objections or relevant information concerning this application for reinstatement should be forwarded immediately to Chief Counsel, Disciplinary Review Board, P.O. Box 962, Trenton, New Jersey 08625–0962.

(f) Contents of Petition. The petitioner shall provide a certified petition for reinstatement setting forth all material facts on which the petitioner relies to establish fitness to resume the practice of law. The petition shall in the discretion of the Board considering the nature of the disciplinary offense contain, in correlatively numbered paragraphs, the following information:

(1) the name of the petitioner and a copy of a current photograph of petitioner, not smaller than three inches by three inches showing front and side views;

(2) the date on which the suspension was imposed and the citation of the reported opinion, if any;

(3) the age, current residence address and telephone number of the petitioner, the address of all residences maintained during the suspension period and the date of each residence;

(4) the nature of petitioner's occupation during the suspension, including the name and address of each employer, the dates of each employment, the positions occupied and titles held, the name, address and telephone of the immediate supervisor, and the reason for leaving the employment;

(5) the case caption, general nature, dates and disposition of every civil, criminal, administrative or disciplinary action which was pending during the period of suspension to which petitioner was either a party or claimed an interest;

(6) petitioner's written consent to the Board and to the Director to examine and secure copies of any records relating to any criminal investigation of or action against petitioner;

(7) a statement of the monthly earnings and other income of the petitioner and the sources from which all earnings and income were derived during the period of suspension;

(8) a statement of assets and financial obligations of the petitioner as of the date of the original suspension and at the time of the reinstatement application, the dates when acquired or incurred, and the names and addresses of all creditors;

(9) the names and addresses of all financial institutions at which petitioner had, or was signatory to, accounts, safety deposit boxes, deposits or loans during the period of suspension, the number of each account, box, deposit or loan; the date each account, box, deposit or loan was opened, approved or made; and the date each account, box, deposit or loan was closed, discharged or paid;

(10) copies of petitioner's federal and state income tax returns and any business tax returns for each of the three years immediately preceding the date the petition is filed and for each year, or part of a year, during the period of suspension and, in an appropriate form, petitioner's written consent to the Board and the Director to secure copies of the original returns;

(11) a statement of restitution made for any and all obligations to all former clients and the Lawyers' Fund for Client Protection and the source and amount of funds used for this purpose;

(12) whether the petitioner, during the period of suspension, sought or obtained assistance, consultation or treatment, whether as an in- or out-patient, for a mental or emotional disorder or for addiction to drugs or alcohol, if such services relate to the disciplinary offenses or the Board determines that such information is relevant to the petitioner's present ability to practice law. The name, address and telephone of each provider of these services, the services rendered, their duration and purpose and a copy of all medical records shall be provided to the Board;

(13) whether the petitioner, during the period of suspension, applied for admission or reinstatement to practice as an attorney in this state or any other state and the caption and details of the application;

(14) whether the petitioner has ever applied for or been granted a license or certificate relating to any business or occupation and whether that license or certificate has ever been the subject of any disciplinary action and the details thereof;

(15) a statement as to whether or not any applications were made during the period of suspension for a license requiring proof of good character, the dates, name, address and telephone of the authority to whom

such applications were addressed and the disposition thereof;

(16) whether petitioner, during the period of suspension, engaged in the practice of law in any jurisdiction and all material facts relating thereto;

(17) a statement of any procedure or inquiry during the period of suspension, relating to petitioner's standing as a member of any other profession or organization, or holder of any license or office, which involved the censure, removal, suspension, revocation of license, or discipline of petitioner, and, as to each, the dates, facts, and the disposition thereof and the name, address and telephone of the authority in possession of the record thereof;

(18) a written representation of petitioner's intentions concerning the practice of law, if reinstated;

(19) a newly completed Annual Attorney Registration Statement;

(20) a copy of the detailed affidavit required to be filed in accordance with R. 1:20–20;

(21) such other information as the Director, the Board or the Supreme Court may from time to time require.

(g) Objections by Director; Recommendation by the Board. Within 21 days following receipt of the petition or 14 days if the period of suspension was six months or less, the Director shall file an original and 12 copies of a response with the Board either objecting or not objecting to the petition. The Director shall serve the respondent with a copy of the response. If the Director consents or fails to file objections, the Board may submit its findings and recommendations to the Supreme Court. If the Director files objections, the Board may set the matter down for oral argument on notice to the parties or may, after considering the objections, submit its findings and recommendations as to the attorney's fitness to practice law to the Supreme Court without argument. The Board may recommend and the Court may impose conditions on the attorney's reinstatement deemed necessary to protect the lawyer, clients or the public.

(h) Referral to Trier of Fact. In an appropriate case, the Board may refer specific issues regarding reinstatement to a trier of fact, which shall then hold a hearing and furnish the Board with a report of findings and recommendations.

(i) Consideration of Petition for Reinstatement. No petition for reinstatement shall be considered by the Board unless:

(A) the respondent first affirmatively demonstrates full and timely compliance with R. 1:20–20. If compliance has not occurred, and if the required affidavit of compliance has not been timely filed, the Board shall not consider the petition until the expiration of six months from the date of filing of that proof of compliance.

(B) all disciplinary costs assessed have been paid, unless an extraordinary financial hardship claim has been timely requested and granted and unless respondent is current in the schedule of payments thereunder;

(C) all orders for restitution have been paid;

(D) the respondent has reimbursed or has reached agreement in writing with the Lawyers' Fund for Client Protection to reimburse it in full for all sums paid or authorized to be paid as a result of the respondent's conduct;

(E) all annual registration fees and charges for ethics and the Lawyers' Fund for Client Protection have been paid.

(j) Successive Petitions. Except as otherwise ordered by the Supreme Court, a petitioner may not file a subsequent petition for reinstatement until six months after the Supreme Court has adversely decided the prior petition.

(k) Public Proceedings and Records. All reinstatement records and proceedings shall be considered public in accordance with R. 1:20–9.

(*l*) Standard of Proof. The standard of proof in reinstatement proceedings shall be by clear and convincing evidence.

(m) Burden of Proof; Burden of Going Forward. The burden of proof in proceedings seeking reinstatement shall be on the petitioner.

Note: Adopted January 31, 1995 to be effective March 1, 1995; paragraph (e) amended July 12, 2002 to be effective September 3, 2002; paragraphs (c), (d), (e), (f), (g), (h), and (i) amended and new paragraphs (l) and (m) adopted July 28, 2004 to be effective September 1, 2004.

1:20–22. Resignation Without Prejudice

(a) Generally. A resignation without prejudice from the bar of this state of a member in good standing shall be submitted through the Director and may be accepted by the Supreme Court, provided that at the time of its submission, the member presents satisfactory proof that no disciplinary or criminal proceedings are pending in any jurisdiction and that, if the attorney has actively engaged in the practice of law in this state in the preceding two years, all clients for whom the attorney has performed any professional services or by whom the attorney has been retained during that time in this state have been notified of the resignation.

(b) Form. A resignation without prejudice submitted pursuant to this rule shall be in a form approved by the Director, Office of Attorney Ethics, and shall set forth the reason for the resignation. It shall be accompanied by an affidavit in the form approved by the Director.

(c) Effect. On acceptance of the resignation, which shall be by order of the Supreme Court, the membership in the bar of this state shall cease, and any subsequent application for membership shall be in accordance with the provisions of R. 1:24. An attorney whose resignation without prejudice from the bar is accepted by the Supreme Court shall cease the practice of law in this state as of the effective date of the order of acceptance. A resignation shall not affect the jurisdiction of the disciplinary system with regard to any unethical conduct that occurred prior to resignation.

Note: Adopted January 31, 1995 to be effective March 1, 1995; paragraphs (a) and (c) amended July 28, 2004 to be effective September 1, 2004; paragraph (a) amended July 9, 2008 to be effective September 1, 2008.

1:20–23. Release of Restrained Funds in Attorney Accounts

(a) Petition for Release of Funds. A party claiming a right to attorney trust or business account funds or to other funds that have been restrained from disbursement by Supreme Court Order shall make any application for release of those funds to the Supreme Court. The petitioning party shall file an original plus eight copies of a verified petition setting forth the standing of the petitioner to make the application and the factual basis for the claim that the funds sought are the property of the petitioner. Relevant documentation shall be appended to the petition. Legal argument, if any, in support of the petitioner's contentions shall be submitted separately in the form of a brief.

(b) Notice. Two copies of the petition shall be served on the disciplined attorney, the Disciplinary Review Board, the Office of Attorney Ethics, the Lawyers' Fund for Client Protection, any attorney-trustee appointed pursuant to Rule 1:20–19, and any other parties in interest. Proof of service shall be filed with the petition.

(c) Response to Petition. Parties served with the petition shall have ten days within which to file and serve nine copies of a response.

(d) Supreme Court Action; Publication. If the Court determines the claimed funds are the property of the petitioner or of any other claimant, it shall enter an appropriate Order directing disbursement. The Court may make the release of funds subject to prior general notice by publication.

(e) Priority Over Remaining Funds. If the actual ownership of the funds cannot be established by clear and convincing evidence, the Lawyers' Fund for Client Protection shall have priority over the funds to the extent it has been subrogated to the rights of claimants against the Fund. If the Fund does not make a claim or if satisfaction of its claim does not exhaust the funds that have been restrained, the Disciplinary Oversight Committee shall have priority over the remaining funds to satisfy unpaid costs assessed against the disciplined attorney.

Note: Adopted July 10, 1998 to be effective September 1, 1998; paragraph (b) amended July 28, 2004 to be effective September 1, 2004.

RULE 1:20A.　DISTRICT FEE ARBITRATION COMMITTEES

1:20A–1.　Appointment and Organization

(a) Fee Arbitration Districts. The Supreme Court shall establish, and may from time to time alter, fee arbitration districts consisting of defined geographical areas and shall appoint in each district a District Fee Arbitration Committee which shall consist of such number of members, not fewer than 8, as the Court may determine, at least 4 of whom shall be attorneys of this state and at least 2 of whom shall not be attorneys. Any person appointed shall either reside or work in the district or county in which the district is located.

(b) Appointments. Members of Fee Committees shall be appointed by and shall serve a term of 4 years. A member who has served a full term shall not be eligible for reappointment to a successive term but a member appointed to fill an unexpired term shall be eligible for reappointment to a full successive term. A member serving in connection with a proceeding in which testimony has begun at the time the member's term expires shall continue in such matter until its conclusion and the filing of an arbitration determination or stipulation of settlement unless relieved by the Supreme Court. In order that, as nearly as possible, the terms of one-quarter of the members shall expire each year, the Supreme Court may, when establishing a new fee committee, appoint members for terms of less than 4 years and members so appointed shall be eligible for reappointment to a full successive term.

(c) Officers; Organization. The Supreme Court shall annually designate a member of each Fee Committee to serve as chair and another member to serve as vice chair. When the chair is absent or unable to act or is disqualified from acting due to a conflict, the vice chair shall perform the duties of the chair. Each Fee Committee shall hold an organization meeting in September of each year and shall meet regularly, except when there is no business to be conducted. The Fee Committee shall also meet at the call of the Supreme Court, the Chair, the Board or the Director.

The Director shall, after consultation with the chair, appoint a secretary who shall not be a member of the Fee Committee but who shall be a member of the bar maintaining an office in the district or county in which the district is located. The secretary shall serve at the pleasure of the Director and be paid an amount annually set by the Supreme Court to reimburse the secretary for costs and expenses. The secretary shall keep full and complete records of all Fee Committee proceedings, shall maintain files with respect to all fee disputes received, shall transmit copies of all documents filed immediately on receipt thereof to the Director, and shall promptly notify the Director of each final disposition. Reports with respect to the work of the Fee Committee shall be filed by the secretary with the Director, as instructed by the Director.

(d) Office. Each Fee Committee shall receive fee dispute inquiries at the office of its secretary and at such additional places as shall be designated by the Director.

(e) Filing; Transfer. Unless specifically directed to the contrary by the Board or by the Director, a fee committee shall not act on fee arbitration requests involving an attorney who does not maintain an office within the district but shall refer that information to the Director for appropriate referral. A fee committee shall not render advisory opinions. On request of a fee committee or sua sponte, the Director may transfer any matter to another fee committee and may, on direction of the Supreme Court or sua sponte, supersede the functions of a fee committee.

Note: Adopted February 23, 1978 to be effective April 1, 1978; amended January 31, 1984 to be effective February 15, 1984; text of R. 1:20A–1 amended and incorporated into 1:20A–1(e), new paragraphs (a)(b)(c) and (d) adopted January 31, 1995 to be effective March 1, 1995; paragraph (c) amended July 28, 2004 to be effective September 1, 2004.

1:20A–2.　Jurisdiction

(a) Generally. Each Fee Committee shall, pursuant to these rules, have jurisdiction to arbitrate fee disputes between clients and attorneys, including pro hac vice attorneys, multijurisdictional practitioners, and Foreign Legal Consultants. Fee Committees shall also have jurisdiction to arbitrate disputes in which a person other than the client is legally bound to pay for the legal services, except that Fee Committees shall not have jurisdiction of such cases if the obligation arises out of the settlement of a legal action. A fee arbitration determination is final and binding upon the parties except as provided by R. 1:20A–3(c).

(b) Discretionary Jurisdiction. A Fee Committee may, in its discretion, decline to arbitrate fee disputes:

(1) in which persons who are not parties to the arbitration have an interest that would be substantially affected by the arbitration;

(2) in which the primary issues in dispute raise substantial legal questions in addition to the basic fee dispute;

(3) in which the total fee charged exceeds $100,000, excluding out-of-pocket costs and disbursements;

(4) involving multijurisdictional practitioners where it appears that substantial services involving the practice of law in New Jersey have not been rendered in the matter.

(c) Absence of Jurisdiction. A Fee Committee shall not have jurisdiction to decide:

(1) a fee which is allowed or allowable as of right by a court or agency pursuant to any applicable rule or statute.

(2) claims for monetary damages resulting from legal malpractice, although a fee committee may consider the quality of services rendered in assessing the reasonableness of the fee pursuant to RPC 1.5.

(A) Submission of a matter to fee arbitration shall not bar the client from filing an action in a court of competent jurisdiction for legal malpractice.

(B) No submission, testimony, decision or settlement made in connection with a fee arbitration proceeding shall be admissible evidence in a legal malpractice action.

(3) a fee for legal services rendered by the Office of the Public Defender, pursuant to N.J.S.A. 2A:158A–1 et seq.; and

(4) a fee in which no attorney's services have been rendered for more than six years from the last date services were rendered.

(d) Procedure for Determining Jurisdiction. All questions of jurisdiction shall be resolved initially by the secretary or, if a hearing panel has already been appointed, by the panel chair.

Note: Adopted February 23, 1978 to be effective April 1, 1978; amended January 31, 1984 to be effective February 15, 1984; amended June 29, 1990 to be effective September 4, 1990; text deleted, new paragraphs (a)(b)(c) and (d) adopted January 31, 1995 to be effective March 1, 1995; new paragraph (c)(3) added July 12, 2002 to be effective September 3, 2002; paragraphs (a) and (b) amended July 28, 2004 to be effective September 1, 2004; paragraph (b)(1) deleted, paragraphs (b)(2) through (b)(5) renumbered as paragraphs (b)(1) through (b)(4), paragraph (c)(3) amended, and new paragraph (c)(4) adopted July 9, 2008 to be effective September 1, 2008.

1:20A–3. Arbitration

(a) Submission.

(1) *Request Form.* A fee dispute shall be arbitrated only on the written request of a client or a third party defined by Rule 1:20A–2. Fee committees shall have authority to consider such a request whether or not the attorney has already received the fee in dispute and regardless of whether the attorney has been suspended, resigned, disbarred or transferred to disability inactive status since the fee was incurred. All requests for fee arbitration shall be made on forms approved by the Director, and a copy of each request so filed shall be promptly transmitted to the Office of Attorney Ethics. The filing of a Fee Arbitration Request Form with the secretary shall constitute a stay of all pending court actions for the collection of the fee. The secretary shall notify the appropriate court clerk when any pending proceeding is stayed by this rule.

(2) *Administrative Filing Fee.* All requests for arbitration and all attorney responses must be accompanied by a non-refundable administrative filing fee of $50. Filing fees shall be paid only by check or money order payable to "Disciplinary Oversight Committee."

(i) Non-Payment. If the party making the fee arbitration request fails to submit the filing fee, the secretary shall not docket the matter and shall so inform the parties, who shall have no more than twenty days from the date of notification in writing to correct the deficiency. If the attorney fails to submit the fee, the secretary shall inform the attorney that unless payment is made within twenty days from the date the attorney is notified in writing, the attorney shall be barred from further participation, and the matter will proceed uncontested.

(ii) Dishonored Instruments. If a negotiable instrument submitted by a party is returned unpaid for any reason, the matter shall be stayed pending the resubmission of a certified or cashier's check in double the amount of the original filing fee within twenty days of the date the party is notified in writing by the secretary of the return. Failure of the party filing the fee request to make a timely resubmission shall result in dismissal of the matter with prejudice. If a resubmitted instrument is returned unpaid for any reason, the matter shall be dismissed with prejudice. Failure of a responding attorney to make a timely resubmission shall be a bar to the attorney's further participation, and the fee arbitration shall proceed uncontested.

(b) Procedure.

(1) *Hearing Panel; Burden of Proof.* All arbitration proceedings shall be heard before a hearing panel of at least three (3) members of the fee committee, a majority of whom shall be attorneys, except that in all cases in which the amount of the total fee charged is less than $3,000, the hearing may be held before a single attorney member at the direction of the chair. A quorum for the hearing of any matter in which the fee charged is $3,000 or more shall consist of at least three (3) members of the fee committee. The determination of a matter shall be made by a majority of the membership sitting on the hearing panel, provided a quorum is present. When by reason of absence, disability, or disqualification the number of members of the panel able to act is fewer than a quorum, with the consent of the client and the attorney the hearing may proceed before two members of the panel. The secretary of the Fee Committee shall not be eligible to sit on any hearing panel. The determination of a matter shall be made in accordance with R.P.C. 1.5. The burden of proof shall be on the attorney to prove the reasonableness of the fee in accordance with R.P.C. 1.5 by a preponderance of the evidence. Within thirty (30) days after the docketing of a request for fee arbitration a client may, in writing, notify the secretary of a withdrawal from the proceeding; thereafter a client shall have no right of withdrawal. After a matter has been withdrawn by the client, the client shall not be permitted to resubmit it to fee arbitration.

(2) *Notice; Attorney Response.* The Fee Committee shall notify the parties at least 10 days in advance, in writing, of the time and place of hearing, and shall have

the power, at a party's request and for good cause shown, or on its own motion, to compel the attendance of witnesses and the production of documents by the issuance of subpoenas in accordance with R. 1:20–7(i). All parties shall promptly report changes of address to the secretary of the Fee Committee, the hearing panel chair or single member arbitrator, and other parties. All service on attorneys required by fee arbitration rules shall be made in accordance with Rule 1:20–7(h), except that service by mail may be made by regular mail, unless the letter will result in barring an attorney from further participation or unless the attorney updates an address as stated above in which event service will be made at that address. Service on non-attorney parties shall be made at their last known address by regular mail, unless the address has been updated as stated above, in which event it shall be sent to the updated address.

The secretary of the Fee Committee shall serve on the attorney a copy of the client's written request for fee arbitration, and any supplemental documentation supplied to the panel; the secretary shall also forward to the attorney for completion an Attorney Fee Response form in a form approved by the Director. The secretary shall also serve a copy of the client's request for fee arbitration and an Attorney Fee Response on the law firm, if any, of which the original attorney is a member. The attorney shall specifically set forth in the Attorney Fee Response the name of any other third party attorney or law firm which the original attorney claims is liable for all or a part of the client's claim. The attorney shall file with the secretary the completed Attorney Fee Response, together with any supplemental documentation, within 20 days of receipt of the client's written request for fee arbitration; the attorney shall certify that a true copy of the Attorney Fee Response has been served on the client. Failure to file the Attorney Fee Response shall not delay the scheduling of a hearing. If the attorney fails to timely file an attorney fee response, the secretary shall inform the attorney that unless an attorney fee response is filed, and the filing fee paid, within 20 days of the date that the attorney is notified in writing, the attorney shall be barred from further participation, and the matter will proceed uncontested. Nothing in this section shall preclude the panel or arbitrator in its discretion from refusing to consider evidence offered by the attorney which would reasonably be expected to have been disclosed on the Attorney Fee Response.

(3) *Third Party Practice.* In the event that the attorney has named a third party attorney or law firm as potentially liable in whole or part for the fee, the original attorney shall, within the time for filing the Attorney Fee Response with the secretary, serve a copy of the client's Request For Fee Arbitration and a copy of the Attorney Fee Response on the third party attorney or law firm, stating clearly in a cover letter that a third party fee dispute claim is being made against them. A copy of such letter shall be filed with the secretary, who shall forward to the third party attorney or law firm for completion an Attorney Fee Response form, which shall be filed with the secretary and served by the third party attorney on the client and the original attorney as provided for in the case of the original attorney. A third party attorney or law firm so noticed shall be deemed a party with all of the rights of and obligations of the original attorney.

(4) *Conduct of Hearing; Determination.* All arbitration hearings shall be conducted formally and in private, but the strict rules of evidence need not be observed. All witnesses including all parties to the proceeding shall be duly sworn, and no stenographic or other similar record shall be made except in exceptional circumstances at the direction of the Board or the Director. Both the client and the attorney whose fee is questioned shall have the right to be present at all times during the hearing with their attorneys, if any. If special circumstances dictate, the trier of fact may accept testimony of a witness by telephone or video conference. The written determination of the hearing panel or the single member arbitrator shall be in the form approved by the Director and shall have annexed a brief statement of reasons therefor. If a stay of a proceeding pending in court has been entered prior to the Fee Committee's determination, when the determination is rendered the secretary of the Fee Committee shall, if requested by either party, send a copy of the determination to the Clerk of the Court who is to vacate the stay and relist the matter. Where a third party attorney or law firm has been properly joined the arbitration determination shall clearly state the individuals or entities liable for the fee, or to whom the fee is due and owing. It shall be served on the parties and filed with the Director by ordinary mail within thirty (30) days following the conclusion of the hearing or from the end of any time period permitted for the supplemental briefs or other materials. Both the attorney and the client shall have 30 days from receipt to comply with the determination of the Fee Committee. Enforcement of arbitration determinations and stipulations of settlement shall be governed by paragraph (e).

(c) Appeal. No appeal from the determination of a Fee Committee may be taken by the client or the attorney to the Disciplinary Review Board except where facts are alleged that:

(1) any member of the Fee Committee hearing the fee dispute failed to be disqualified in accordance with the standards set forth in R. 1:12–1; or

(2) the Fee Committee failed substantially to comply with the procedural requirements of R. 1:20A, or there was substantial procedural unfairness that led to an unjust result; or

(3) there was actual fraud on the part of any member of the Fee Committee; or

(4) there was a palpable mistake of law by the fee committee which on its face was gross, unmistakable, or in manifest disregard of the applicable law, which mistake has led to an unjust result.

(d) Procedure on Appeal. The party taking an appeal shall file a notice of appeal in the form prescribed by the Board within twenty-one days after the parties' receipt of the Fee Committee's written arbitration determination. The notice of appeal shall be filed with the Board and shall include a statement of the ground for appeal and an affidavit or certification stating the factual basis therefor. Copies of the notice of appeal shall be served on the other parties, the secretary of the Fee Committee and the hearing panel chair by the party appealing who shall certify such service in the notice of appeal. The filing of a notice of appeal from a Fee Committee determination shall act as a stay of execution of any judgment obtained as a result of a fee arbitration process. That stay shall not be lifted until final conclusion of the fee arbitration proceedings. The hearing panel chair of the Fee Committee shall, within twenty-one days of receipt of the notice of appeal, furnish to the Board a specific reply to the facts in the notice of appeal, setting forth the alleged grounds for appeal and shall serve a copy of the reply on all other parties. The Board may, in its discretion, decide an appeal without a response from the hearing panel chair. Within the same twenty-one day time period, the secretary of the Fee Committee or the Office of Attorney Ethics shall file with the Board the record of proceedings before the Fee Committee and any briefs or other papers filed with the Fee Committee. Subject to the same time limitations, any other party to the fee proceedings may file a response with the Board and shall certify service on all other parties, the secretary, and the hearing panel chair.

The Board shall dismiss the appeal on notice to the parties if it determines that the notice of appeal fails to state a ground for appeal specified in paragraph (c) of this rule or that the affidavit or certification fails to state a factual basis for such ground. If the notice of appeal and supporting affidavit or certification comply with these rules, the Board shall review the challenge to the arbitration. If it finds that there has been a violation of Rule 1:20A–3(c), the Board shall remand the fee dispute to a Fee Committee for a new arbitration hearing, or determine the matter itself if it deems such action appropriate.

(e) Enforcement. Whenever a Fee Committee determines, or the parties by signed stipulation of settlement agree, that a refund of all or part of the fee paid by a client should be made and the attorney fails to appeal or to comply with such determination or stipulation within thirty (30) days of receipt thereof, the matter shall be referred to the Director for such action as may be appropriate, in accordance with R. 1:20–15(k). In the event of an appeal, no enforcement of the Fee Committee's determination will occur while that appeal is pending before the Board.

If an action for collection of the fee is pending when the client's written request for arbitration is filed under Rule 1:20A–3(a) and is stayed thereby pending a determination by the Fee Committee, the amount of the fee or refund as so determined may be entered as a judgment in the action unless the full balance due is paid within 30 days of receipt of the arbitration determination. If no such action is pending, the attorney or client may, by summary action brought pursuant to Rule 4:67, obtain judgment in the amount of the fee or refund as determined by the Fee Committee. In any application for the entry of a judgment in accordance with this rule, no court shall have jurisdiction to review a fee arbitration committee determination. Said review is reserved exclusively to the Disciplinary Review Board under R.1:20–15(1).

On payment and collection of any balance due from a client or third party under an arbitration determination or stipulation of settlement, the attorney shall promptly prepare, execute and provide the client or third party with a warrant for satisfaction of any judgment entered, if requested or, if a civil action for the fee is pending, shall cause it to be dismissed. The client or third party shall bear the cost of filing any warrant for satisfaction.

Note: Adopted February 23, 1978 to be effective April 1, 1978; paragraph (c) amended, new paragraph (d) adopted and paragraph (d) redesignated (e) July 15, 1982 to be effective September 13, 1982; paragraphs (a) through (e) amended January 31, 1984 to be effective February 15, 1984; paragraph (b) amended November 1, 1985 to be effective January 2, 1986; paragraphs (a) and (b) amended November 5, 1986 to be effective January 1, 1987; paragraphs (d) and (e) amended November 7, 1988 to be effective January 2, 1989; paragraphs (a) and (b) amended and subheadings (1), (2), (3) and (4) added June 29, 1990 to be effective September 4, 1990; paragraph (a)(1) amended and subparagraph (a)(2) added February 8, 1993 to be effective March 1, 1993; paragraphs (a)(b)(c)(d) and (e) amended, new paragraph (c)(4) adopted January 31, 1995 to be effective March 1, 1995; paragraph (e) amended June 28, 1996 to be effective September 1, 1996; paragraph (d) amended July 10, 1998 to be effective September 1, 1998; paragraphs (a)(1), (a)(2), (b)(2), (b)(3), (d), and (e) amended July 5, 2000 to be effective September 5, 2000; paragraph (c) amended July 28, 2004 to be effective September 1, 2004; subparagraphs (b)(2) and (b)(4) amended July 9, 2008 to be effective September 1, 2008.

1:20A–4. Referral to Office of Attorney Ethics

When a grievance involves aspects of both a fee dispute and a charge of ethical misconduct, the Fee Committee shall first determine the propriety of the fee charged unless it clearly appears to the Fee Committee, or to the Director, that there is presented an ethical question of a serious or emergent nature, in which event the Fee Committee shall administratively dismiss the matter and transmit the file to the Director for processing. In all cases it shall be the duty of each Fee Committee, after hearing and determination of the fee, to refer any matter that it concludes may involve ethical misconduct that raises a substantial question as to the attorney's honesty, trustworthiness or fitness as a lawyer in other respects (including overreaching) to the Director for investigation. Such referrals shall be made in letter form detailing the facts known to the Fee

Committee and shall include a complete copy of the Fee Committee's file. Nothing in this rule shall preclude a client from filing an independent grievance with an Ethics Committee at the conclusion of a fee dispute proceeding.

Note: Adopted February 23, 1978 to be effective April 1, 1978; amended January 31, 1984 to be effective February 15, 1984; amended November 5, 1986 to be effective January 1, 1987; caption and text amended January 31, 1995 to be effective March 1, 1995.

1:20A–5. Records; Confidentiality; Immunity

Each Fee Committee shall maintain such records and file such reports as shall be required by the Director. Except as may be otherwise necessary for compliance with these rules or to take ancillary legal action in respect thereof, all records, documents, files, hearings, transcripts or recordings of hearings, if any, and proceedings made and conducted in accordance with these rules shall be confidential. They shall not be disclosed to or attended by anyone unless (1) the Board so directs following written application to the Board with notice to the Director and the attorney whose fee was questioned; or (2) on order of the Supreme Court. Fee Committee members, secretaries and their lawfully appointed designees and staff shall be entitled to the immunity as provided by Rule 1:20–7(e).

Note: Adopted February 23, 1978 to be effective April 1, 1978; amended January 31, 1984 to be effective February 15, 1984; caption and text amended January 31, 1995 to be effective March 1, 1995.

1:20A–6. Pre–action Notice to Client

No lawsuit to recover a fee may be filed until the expiration of the 30 day period herein giving Pre–action Notice to a client; however, this shall not prevent a lawyer from instituting any ancillary legal action. Pre–action Notice shall be given in writing, which shall be sent by certified mail and regular mail to the last known address of the client, or, alternatively, hand delivered to the client, and which shall contain the name, address and telephone number of the current secretary of the Fee Committee in a district where the lawyer maintains an office. If unknown, the appropriate Fee Committee secretary listed in the most current New Jersey Lawyers Diary and Manual shall be sufficient. The notice shall specifically advise the client of the right to request fee arbitration and that the client should immediately call the secretary to request appropriate forms; the notice shall also state that if the client does not promptly communicate with the Fee Committee secretary and file the approved form of request for fee arbitration within 30 days after receiving pre-action notice by the lawyer, the client shall lose the right to initiate fee arbitration. The attorney's complaint shall allege the giving of the notice required by this rule or it shall be dismissed.

Note: Adopted November 1, 1985 to be effective January 2, 1986; amended June 29, 1990 to be effective September 4, 1990; amended January 31, 1995 to be effective March 1, 1995.

RULE 1:20B. DISCIPLINARY OVERSIGHT COMMITTEE

1:20B–1. Disciplinary Oversight Committee

The Supreme Court shall establish a Disciplinary Oversight Committee (hereinafter referred to as the Oversight Committee) consisting of 11 members to assist it as an advisory body in administering the attorney disciplinary system and the financial aspects thereof.

Adopted Jan. 31, 1995, effective March 1, 1995.

1:20B–2. Appointment

The Supreme Court shall appoint the members of the Oversight Committee; five shall be lawyers or sitting or retired judges, one shall be an annual designee of the New Jersey State Bar Association, and five shall be members of the public. The Administrative Director of the Courts, or the Administrative Director's designee, shall serve as a non-voting member of the Committee.

Other than the designee of the New Jersey State Bar Association and the Administrative Director or the Administrative Director's designee, each member shall be appointed for a term of three years, and may be reappointed to three successive full terms. A vacancy occurring during a term shall be filled for the unexpired portion thereof.

Note: Adopted January 31, 1995, effective March 1, 1995; amended July 12, 2002 to be effective September 3, 2002; amended March 20, 2003, to be effective immediately; amended January 10, 2006 to be effective immediately.

1:20B–3. Organization; Officers; Quorum; Meetings

The Oversight Committee shall organize annually. The Supreme Court shall annually appoint a Chair and Vice Chair. The Oversight Committee shall elect a Treasurer and Assistant Treasurer. The Administrative Director of the Courts shall designate a staff member with fiscal responsibilities to provide assistance. Meetings shall be held at the call of the Chair or any four members of the Committee. Seven voting members shall constitute a quorum for the transaction of business.

Note: Adopted January 31, 1995, effective March 1, 1995; amended March 20, 2003, to be effective immediately.

1:20B–4. Powers; Confidentiality

(a) The Oversight Committee shall have the following specific powers:

(1) to evaluate the efficiency and effectiveness of the attorney disciplinary system and to report to the Supreme Court quarterly and at such other times as the Supreme Court and the Oversight Committee deem appropriate, making whatever recommendations it believes would improve the quality and efficiency of the disciplinary system and strengthen adherence to high ethical standards. It shall be the responsibility of the Office of Attorney Ethics and the Disciplinary Review Board to provide the Oversight Committee with all relevant information so as to enable it properly and thoroughly to perform its evaluating and reporting functions. The Oversight Committee shall also be entitled to any information it may request from any person or entity within the disciplinary system;

(2) to receive annually from the Director and Board Counsel, on or before August 15, a proposed budget for the attorney disciplinary system in a form agreed to by the Oversight Committee; to review the same and to make a written recommendation to the Supreme Court concerning that budget each year; and to respond and make further recommendations as necessary to any written comments received from the Bar and the public after Supreme Court approval for publication of a summary of the proposed budget and the Oversight Committee's recommendation;

(3) to receive quarterly from the Director and Board Counsel a report, in a form agreed to by the Oversight Committee, detailing the expenditures incurred by the disciplinary system and revenues received for that quarter;

(4) to receive, hold, manage, distribute and invest the fund received pursuant to R. 1:20–1(b) and any other funds it may receive, all in accordance with these rules and policies approved by the Supreme Court;

(5) to establish necessary bank accounts and to require an independent annual financial audit of its accounts, which shall be submitted to the Supreme Court;

(6) to employ and compensate consultants, agents, and such other persons as it deems necessary and appropriate in the performance of its functions and responsibilities consistent with policies of the Judiciary;

(7) to establish procedures and maintain records required for the performance of its responsibilities consistent with these rules and subject to the approval of the Supreme Court; and

(8) to provide the Supreme Court with information and recommendations on personnel and other operational matters that affect the budget as such matters arise throughout the fiscal year, and to act on such matters as are within the range of discretion accorded the Oversight Committee by the Supreme Court.

(b) a Minutes of meetings and the Oversight Committee's synopsis of the budget recommended by the Director, Office of Attorney Ethics, and Counsel to the Disciplinary Review Board shall be public. All other records, documents, and proceedings are confidential.

Note: Adopted January 31, 1995, to be effective March 1, 1995; paragraph (a) amended, paragraph (b) deleted, and paragraph (c) redesignated as paragraph (b) March 20, 2003, to be effective immediately.

CHAPTER III. PRACTICE OF LAW AND ADMISSION TO PRACTICE
RULE 1:21. PRACTICE OF LAW

1:21–1. Who May Practice; Appearance in Court

(a) **Qualifications.** Except as provided below, no person shall practice law in this State unless that person is an attorney holding a plenary license to practice in this State, has complied with the Rule 1:26 skills and methods course requirement in effect on the date of the attorney's admission, is in good standing, and, except as provided in paragraph (d) of this Rule, maintains a *bona fide* office for the practice of law. For the purpose of this section, a *bona fide* office is a place where clients are met, files are kept, the telephone is answered, mail is received and the attorney or a responsible person acting on the attorney's behalf can be reached in person and by telephone during normal business hours to answer questions posed by the courts, clients or adversaries and to ensure that competent advice from the attorney can be obtained within a reasonable period of time. For the purpose of this section, a *bona fide* office may be located in this or any other state, territory of the United States, Puerto Rico, or the District of Columbia

(hereinafter "a United States jurisdiction"). An attorney who practices law in this state and fails to maintain a *bona fide* office shall be deemed to be in violation of RPC 5.5(a). An attorney who is not domiciled in this State and does not have a *bona fide* office in this State, but who meets all the qualifications for the practice of law set forth herein must designate the Clerk of the Supreme Court as agent upon whom service of process may be made for all actions, including disciplinary actions, that may arise out of the practice of law and activities related thereto, in the event that service cannot otherwise be effectuated pursuant to the appropriate Rules of Court. The designation of the Clerk as agent shall be made on a form approved by the Supreme Court.

A person not qualifying to practice pursuant to the first paragraph of this rule shall nonetheless be permitted to appear and prosecute or defend an action in any court of this State if the person (1) is a real party in interest to this action or the guardian of the party; or (2) has been admitted to speak *pro hac vice* pursuant to

R. 1:21–2; (3) is a law student or law graduate practicing within the limits of R. 1:21–3; or (4) is an in-house counsel licensed and practicing within the limitations of R. 1:27–2.

Attorneys admitted to the practice of law in another United States jurisdiction may practice law in this state in accordance with RPC 5.5(b) and (c) as long as they maintain a bona fide office.

No attorney authorized to practice in this State shall permit another person to practice in this State in the attorney's name or as the attorney's partner, employee or associate unless such other person satisfies the requirements of this rule.

(b) Appearance. All attorneys and pro se parties appearing in any action shall be under the control of the court in which they appear and subject to appropriate disciplinary action. An attorney admitted in another jurisdiction shall not be deemed to be making an appearance in this State by reason of taking a deposition pursuant to R. 4:11–4.

(c) Prohibition on Business Entities. Except as otherwise provided by paragraph (d) of this rule and by R. 1:21–1A (professional corporations), R. 1:21–1B (limited liability companies), R. 1:21–1C (limited liability partnerships), R. 6:10 (appearances in landlord-tenant actions), R. 6:11 (appearances in small claims actions), R. 7:6–2(a) (pleas in municipal court), R. 7:8–7(a) (presence of defendant in municipal court) and by R. 7:12–4(d) (municipal court violations bureau), a business entity other than a sole proprietor shall neither appear nor file any paper in any action in any court of this State except through an attorney authorized to practice in this State.

(d) Federal Government Agencies. Staff attorneys employed full time by agencies of the federal government that have an office in New Jersey may represent the interests of that agency in federal and state courts in New Jersey without maintaining a bona fide law office in this state.

(e) Legal Assistance Organizations. Nonprofit organizations incorporated in this or any other state for the purpose of providing legal assistance to the poor or functioning as a public interest law firm, and other federally tax exempt legal assistance organizations or trusts, such as those defined by 26 U.S.C.A. 120(b) and 501(c)(20), that provide legal assistance to a defined and limited class of clients, may practice law in their own names through staff attorneys who are members of the bar of the State of New Jersey, provided that: (1) the legal work serves the intended beneficiaries of the organizational purpose, (2) the staff attorney responsible for the matter signs all papers prepared by the organization, and (3) the relationship between staff attorney and client meets the attorney's professional responsibilities to the client and is not subject to interference, control, or direction by the organization's board or employees except for a supervising attorney who is a member of the New Jersey bar.

(f) Appearances Before Office of Administrative Law and Administrative Agencies. Subject to such limitations and procedural rules as may be established by the Office of Administrative Law, an appearance by a non-attorney in a contested case before the Office of Administrative Law or an administrative agency may be permitted, on application, in any of the following circumstances:

(1) where required by federal statute or regulation;

(2) to represent a state agency if the Attorney General does not provide representation in the particular matter and the non-attorney representative is an employee of the agency with special expertise or experience in the matter in controversy;

(3) to represent a county welfare agency if County Counsel does not provide representation in the particular matter and the non-attorney representative is an employee of the agency with special expertise or experience in the matter in controversy;

(4) to assist in providing representation to an indigent as part of a Legal Services program if the non-attorney is a paralegal or legal assistant employed by that program;

(5) to represent a state, county or local government employee in Civil Service proceedings, provided (i) the non-attorney making such appearance is an authorized representative of a labor organization and (ii) the labor organization is the duly authorized representative of the employee for collective bargaining purposes;

(6) to represent a close corporation provided the non-attorney is a principal of the corporation;

(7) to assist an individual who is not represented by an attorney provided (i) the presentation appears likely to be enhanced by such assistance, (ii) the individual certifies that he or she lacks the means to retain an attorney and that representation is not available through a Legal Services program and (iii) the conduct of the proceeding by the Office of Administrative Law will not be impaired by such assistance;

(8) to represent parents or children in special education proceedings, provided the non-attorney has knowledge or training with respect to handicapped pupils and their educational needs so as to enable the non-attorney to facilitate the presentation of the claims or defenses of the parent or child;

(9) to represent union members and employees entitled to union representation in public employment relations proceedings, provided the appearance is by a union representative;

(10) to represent a county or local government appointing authority in Civil Service proceedings, provided the non-attorney representative is an employee of the appointing authority with special expertise or experience in the matter in controversy and the legal representative for the county or municipality does not provide representation in the particular matter; or

(11) to represent a claimant or employer before the Appeal Tribunals or Board of Review of the Department of Labor.

No representation or assistance may be undertaken pursuant to subsection (f) by any disbarred or suspended attorney or by any person who would otherwise receive a fee for such representation.

(g) Appearances at Personal Injury Protection Arbitrations. A non-attorney may represent an insurance company employer at a Personal Injury Protection (PIP) arbitration.

Note: Source—R.R. 1:12–4(a) (b) (c) (d) (e) (f). Paragraph (c) amended by order of December 16, 1969 effective immediately; paragraphs (a) and (c) amended July 29, 1977 to be effective September 6, 1977; paragraph (a) amended July 24, 1978 to be effective September 11, 1978; paragraph (a) amended September 21, 1981 to be effective immediately; paragraph (c) amended and paragraph (d) adopted July 15, 1982 to be effective September 13, 1982; paragraph (a) amended August 13, 1982 to be effective immediately; paragraph (e) adopted July 22, 1983 to be effective September 12, 1983; paragraph (c) amended November 1, 1985 to be effective January 2, 1986; paragraph (a) amended November 5, 1986 to be effective January 1, 1987; paragraph (a) amended November 7, 1988 to be effective January 2, 1989; paragraph (b) amended and paragraph (d) caption and text amended June 29, 1990 to be effective September 4, 1990; paragraph (c) amended and paragraph (e)(8) adopted July 14, 1992 to be effective September 1, 1992; paragraphs (c), (e), and (e)(7) amended, and paragraph (e)(9) added July 13, 1994 to be effective September 1, 1994; paragraphs (a) and (e) amended June 28, 1996 to be effective September 1, 1996; paragraph (c) amended November 18, 1996 to be effective January 1, 1997; paragraph (c) amended January 5, 1998 to be effective February 1, 1998; paragraph (a) amended, former paragraphs (d) and (e) redesignated as paragraphs (e) and (f), and new paragraph (d) adopted July 10, 1998 to be effective September 1, 1998; closing paragraph amended July 5, 2000 to be effective September 5, 2000; paragraph (f) amended and new paragraph (f)(11) added July 12, 2002 to be effective September 3, 2002; paragraph (a) amended November 17, 2003 to be effective January 1, 2004; paragraph (a) amended July 28, 2004 to be effective September 1, 2004; paragraph (e) caption and text amended July 27, 2006 to be effective September 1, 2006; paragraph (f) amended and paragraph (g) adopted July 16, 2009 to be effective September 1, 2009.

Official Comment by Supreme Court (November 17, 2003)

The Court has directed that the Clerk of the Supreme Court, the attorney disciplinary system, the Lawyers' Fund for Client Protection, and the Administrative Office of the Courts monitor the experience gained under this amended rule (Rule 1:21–1). Three years from the January 1, 2004 effective date of the amended rule, the Administrative Office of the Courts will coordinate and present to the Court an evaluation of its effects based on the collected data, as supplemented by the comments of the bench, the bar, and the public. At that time the Court will determine whether the amended rule should be retained permanently, modified, or rescinded.

**1:21–1A.   Professional Corporations
for the Practice of Law**

(a) Attorneys may engage in the practice of law as professional corporations in the same manner as an individual or a partnership may engage in the practice of law, provided that:

(1) All provisions of the "Professional Service Corporation Act" (N.J.S.A. 14A:17–1 through 18) shall be complied with.

(2) The professional corporation shall comply with and be subject to all rules governing the practice of law by attorneys and it shall do nothing which, if done by an individual attorney would violate the standards of professional conduct applicable to attorneys licensed to practice law in this State. Any violation of this rule by the professional corporation shall be grounds for the Supreme Court to terminate or suspend the professional corporation's right to practice law or otherwise to discipline it.

(3) The professional corporation shall obtain and maintain in good standing one or more policies of lawyers' professional liability insurance which shall insure the corporation against liability imposed upon it by law for damages resulting from any claim made against the corporation by its clients arising out of the performance of professional services by attorneys employed by the corporation in their capacities as attorneys. The insurance shall be in an amount for each claim of at least $100,000 multiplied by the number of attorneys employed by the corporation, provided that the maximum coverage shall not be required to exceed $5,000,000 for each claim, and further provided that the deductible portion to such insurance shall not exceed $10,000 multiplied by the number of attorneys employed by the corporation or $500,000, whichever is less. The corporation may enter into an indemnity agreement with its insurer under which the corporation agrees to indemnify the insurer for losses in excess of the amount of the permitted deductible, provided that the insurer remains liable to pay all judgments against the corporation up to the policy limits regardless whether the corporation indemnifies the insurer as required under the indemnity agreement.

(b) Within 30 days after filing its certificate of incorporation or, in the case of a foreign professional legal corporation, the filing of its registration with the Secretary of State, each professional corporation formed to engage in the practice of law shall file with the Clerk of the Supreme Court a certificate of insurance, issued by the insurer, setting forth the name and address of the insurance company writing the insurance policies required by paragraph (a)(3) of this rule and the policy number and policy limits. The professional corporation shall also file such other information as the Supreme court may from time to time prescribe.

Amendments to and renewals of the certificate of insurance shall be filed with the Clerk of the Supreme

Court within 30 days after the date on which such amendments or renewals become effective.

(c) The corporate name of the professional corporation shall comply with the provisions of RPC 7.5 and shall contain only the full or last names of one or more of its shareholders or members of a predecessor firm, whether the shareholder or member be living, deceased or retired. Wherever the corporate name of the professional corporation is used it shall be followed by the phrase "A professional corporation," or by any other phrase or abbreviation authorized by N.J.S.A. 14A:17–14 to indicate that it is a professional corporation. When the professional corporation is a foreign professional legal corporation, the phrase shall also identify the state of incorporation (e.g., "A professional corporation incorporated in the State of New York"). The corporate name shall be used on all pleadings, correspondence or other documents. Correspondence, pleadings and other documents executed in connection with the practice of law shall be executed on behalf of the corporation by one of its attorney employees. Corporate documents executed other than in connection with the practice of law may be executed on behalf of the corporation by an authorized employee who is not licensed to practice law.

(d) No person shall hold any shares of stock in any professional corporation engaged in the practice of law unless actually and actively engaged in the practice of law as an employee or agent of, or "of counsel" to such corporation, except for leave of absence not to exceed one year and for absences on account of illness, accident, time spent in the armed services and vacation, and except that the legal representative of the estate of a deceased shareholder and a shareholder disqualified from the practice of law may continue to hold shares of stock in the professional corporation for the period provided for in the Professional Service Corporation Act, as amended and supplemented, but without the right to receive as a shareholder any portion of the earnings or profits of the corporation derived from professional services rendered by the corporation subsequent to the date of death of the deceased shareholder or the date of disqualification of the disqualified shareholder, as the case may be. A professional corporation actually and actively engaged in the practice of law may hold shares of stock in another professional corporation covered by this rule.

(e) The Board of Directors of a professional corporation for the practice of law shall consist of one or more persons, all of whom shall be licensed to practice law, and at least one of whom shall be licensed to practice in New Jersey. Such directors need not be shareholders. Officers of the professional law corporation need not be licensed members of the New Jersey bar unless the corporation is a domestic professional legal corporation, in which case the president shall be so licensed.

(f) A professional corporation may engage in the practice of law in partnership with another professional corporation or corporations, or with an attorney or partnership of attorneys. The partnership name shall, in addition to meeting the requirements of Rule 1:21–1A(c), be followed by the designation "a partnership of professional corporations" or "a partnership including professional corporations." When any member of a partnership is a foreign professional legal corporation that is incorporated in a state other than New Jersey, the required designation shall also state this fact. When the professional corporation is engaged in the practice of law in partnership with another corporation, partnership, or attorney, all disciplinary rules and rules of practice applicable to partnerships of attorneys will apply.

Note: Adopted December 16, 1969 effective immediately; paragraph (a) amended July 7, 1971 to be effective September 13, 1971; paragraph (c) amended June 29, 1973 to be effective September 10, 1973; paragraphs (a), (b), (c), (d) and (e) amended and paragraph (f) adopted July 16, 1981 to be effective September 14, 1981; paragraph (c) amended January 16, 1984 to be effective immediately; paragraph (c) amended July 14, 1992 to be effective September 1, 1992; paragraph (d) amended July 13, 1994 to be effective September 1, 1994; paragraph (a) amended December 9, 1994 to be effective January 2, 1995; paragraphs (a), (b), (c), (e), and (f) amended April 30, 1996 to be effective immediately.

1:21–1B. Limited Liability Companies for the Practice of Law

(a) Attorneys may engage in the practice of law as limited liability companies in the same manner as an individual or a partnership may engage in the practice of law, provided that:

(1) All provisions of the "New Jersey Limited Liability Company Act," N.J.S.A. 42:2B–1 through 70, shall be complied with, except where inconsistent with these rules.

(2) Any attorney who is a member, employee, agent, or representative of the limited liability company shall remain personally liable for his or her own negligence, omissions, malpractice, wrongful acts, or misconduct, and that of any person under his or her direct supervision and control while rendering professional services on behalf of the limited liability company.

(3) The limited liability company shall comply with and be subject to all rules governing the practice of law by attorneys and it shall do nothing which, if done by an individual attorney would violate the standards of professional conduct applicable to attorneys licensed to practice law in this State. Any violation of this rule by the limited liability company shall be grounds for the Supreme Court to terminate or suspend the limited liability company's right to practice law or otherwise to discipline it.

(4) The limited liability company shall obtain and maintain in good standing one or more policies of lawyers' professional liability insurance which shall insure the limited liability company against liability imposed upon it by law for damages resulting from any claim made against the limited liability company by its clients arising out of the performance of professional services by attorneys employed by the limited liability company in their capacities as attorneys. The insurance shall be in the amount for each claim of at least $100,000 multiplied by the number of attorneys employed by the limited liability company, provided that the maximum coverage shall not be required to exceed $5,000,000 for each claim, and further provided that the deductible portion of such insurance shall not exceed $10,000 multiplied by the number of attorneys employed by the limited liability company or $500,000, whichever is less. The limited liability company may enter into an indemnity agreement with its insurer under which the limited liability company agrees to indemnify the insurer for losses in excess of the amount of the permitted deductible provided that the insurer remains liable to pay all judgments against the limited liability company up to the policy limits regardless whether the limited liability company indemnifies the insurer as required under the indemnity agreement.

(5) The limited liability company shall not engage in any business other than the rendering of professional legal services of the type provided by attorneys-at-law, except that a limited liability company shall not be prohibited from investing its funds in real estate, mortgages, stocks, bonds or any other type of investments, or from owning real or personal property necessary for, or appropriate or desirable in, the fulfillment or rendering of its professional legal services.

(6) No limited liability company may render legal services in this State except through its members, employees or agents who are duly licensed and otherwise qualified to render legal services under these rules.

(b) Within 30 days after filing its certificate of formation or, in the case of a foreign limited liability company, the filing of its application for registration with the Secretary of State, each limited liability company engaged in the practice of law shall file with the Clerk of the Supreme Court a certificate of insurance, issued by the insurer, setting forth the name and address of the insurance company writing the insurance policies required by paragraph (a)(4) of this rule and the policy number and policy limits. The limited liability company shall also file such other information as the Supreme Court may from time to time prescribe.

Amendments to and renewals of the certificate of insurance shall be filed with the Clerk of the Supreme Court within 30 days after the date on which such amendments or renewals become effective.

(c) The name of the limited liability company shall comply with the provisions of RPC 7.5 and shall contain only the full or last names of one or more of its present members, or one or more of the members, partners, or shareholders of a predecessor firm, whether living, deceased or retired. Wherever the name of the limited liability company is used it shall be followed by the phrase "A limited liability company," or by any other

phrase or abbreviation authorized by N.J.S.A. 42:2B–3 to indicate that it is a limited liability company. In the case of a foreign limited liability company, the phrase shall also identify the jurisdiction of formation (e.g., "A limited liability company formed in the State of New York"). The limited liability company name shall be used on all pleadings, correspondence or other documents. Correspondence, pleadings and other documents executed in connection with the practice of law shall be executed on behalf of the limited liability company by one of its members, employees, agents or representatives who is an attorney licensed to practice law. Limited liability company documents executed other than in connection with the practice of law may be executed on behalf of the limited liability company by an authorized employee who is not licensed to practice law.

(d) No person shall hold any interest in any limited liability company engaged in the practice of law unless licensed to practice law and actually and actively engaged in the practice of law as a member, employee or agent of, or "of counsel" to the limited liability company, except for leave of absence not to exceed one year and for absences on account of illness, accident, time spent in the armed services and vacation. The legal representative of the estate of a deceased member, a member disqualified from the practice of law, or a member who is withdrawing from membership in the limited liability company or whose employment with the limited liability company is being terminated for any reason whatsoever, may continue to hold an interest in the limited liability company for the following periods and under the following conditions:

(1) Within 375 days following the date of death of a member or within 90 days following the member's disqualification from the practice of law, or the member's withdrawal from membership or termination of employment, all of the interest of the member shall be transferred to, and acquired by the limited liability company or attorneys qualified to own the interest. If the transfer and acquisition is not otherwise effected within the specified period, the limited liability company shall forthwith purchase and redeem all of the member's interest at the value established in the operating agreement or other agreement, if any. If the method of valuation is not established by agreement, redemption shall be at the book value of the shares, determined as of the end of the month immediately preceding death, disqualification, withdrawal or termination. For this purpose, the book value shall be determined by an independent certified public accountant employed by the limited liability company from the books and records of the limited liability company in accordance with the regular methods of accounting used by it. Nothing contained herein shall prevent the parties from agreeing, either through the operating agreement or otherwise, to another arrangement for the transfer of a member's interest to the limited liability company or persons qualified to own the interest, provided that

within the periods specified, all of the interest involved shall have been so transferred.

(2) The continued interest of a member as described in (1) above during the period specified shall not include the right to participate in any decisions concerning the rendering of professional legal services by the limited liability company, nor the right to receive any portion of the earnings or profits of the limited liability company derived from legal services rendered by the limited liability company subsequent to the date of death, disqualification, or withdrawal from membership or termination of employment.

(3) Notwithstanding the foregoing, if any member, employee, agent or representative of the limited liability company becomes legally disqualified to engage in the practice of law, he or she shall forthwith sever all employment with the limited liability company.

A limited liability company actually and actively engaged in the practice of law may hold shares of stock in a professional corporation covered by R. 1:21–1A, and may hold interests in another limited liability company covered by this rule.

(e) At least one member of the limited liability company shall be licensed to practice law in New Jersey. In addition, if the limited liability company has an operating agreement that provides for the management of the limited liability company by managers, at least one of the managers shall be a member who is licensed to practice law in New Jersey.

(f) A limited liability company may engage in the practice of law in partnership with another limited liability company or companies, professional corporation or corporations covered by Rule 1:21–1A, or with any attorney or partnership of attorneys, including limited liability partnerships covered by Rule 1:21–1C. The partnership name shall, in addition to meeting the requirements of Rule 1:21–1B(c), clearly designate that it is a partnership of or including other limited liability companies, professional corporations, partnerships, limited liability partnerships, or attorneys, as applicable. When any member of a partnership is a foreign limited liability company, foreign professional corporation, or foreign partnership or attorney, the required designation shall also state this fact. When the limited liability company is engaged in the practice of law in partnership with another limited liability company, corporation, partnership, or attorney, all disciplinary rules and rules of practice applicable to partnerships of attorneys will apply.

Note: Adopted November 18, 1996 to be effective January 1, 1997.

1:21–1C. Limited Liability Partnerships for the Practice of Law

(a) Attorneys may engage in the practice of law as limited liability partnerships in the same manner as an individual or a partnership may engage in the practice of law, provided that:

(1) All provisions of the Uniform Partnership Act, N.J.S.A. 42:1A–1 through 56, shall be complied with, except where inconsistent with these rules. For a limited liability partnership that is a foreign limited liability partnership, N.J.S.A. 42:1A–50 through 54 shall apply, except where inconsistent with these rules and except that an attorney practicing in this State who is a member, employee, agent, or representative of such a limited liability partnership shall not be shielded from personal liability for his or her own negligence, omissions, malpractice, wrongful acts, or misconduct, and that of any person under his or her direct supervision and control while rendering professional services on behalf of the limited liability partnership.

(2) The limited liability partnership shall comply with and be subject to all rules governing the practice of law by attorneys and it shall do nothing which, if done by an individual attorney would violate the standards of professional conduct applicable to attorneys licensed to practice law in this State. Any violation of this rule by the limited liability partnership shall be grounds for the Supreme Court to terminate or suspend the limited liability partnership's right to practice law or otherwise to discipline it.

(3) The limited liability partnership shall obtain and maintain in good standing one or more policies of lawyers' professional liability insurance which shall insure the limited liability partnership against liability imposed upon it by law for damages resulting from any claim made against the limited liability partnership by its clients arising out of the performance of professional services by attorneys employed by the limited liability partnership in their capacities as attorneys. The insurance shall be in the amount for each claim of at least $100,000 multiplied by the number of attorneys employed by the limited liability partnership, provided that the maximum coverage shall not be required to exceed $5,000,000 for each claim, and further provided that the deductible portion of such insurance shall not exceed $10,000 multiplied by the number of attorneys employed by the limited liability partnership or $500,000, whichever is less. The limited liability partnership may enter into an indemnity agreement with its insurer under which the limited liability partnership agrees to indemnify the insurer for losses in excess of the amount of the permitted deductible provided that the insurer remains liable to pay all judgments against the limited liability partnership up to the policy limits regardless whether the limited liability partnership indemnifies the insurer as required under the indemnity agreement.

(b) Within 30 days after filing its application, or in the case of a foreign limited liability partnership, the filing of its registration with the Secretary of State, each limited liability partnership engaged in the practice of law shall file with the Clerk of the Supreme Court a certificate of insurance, issued by the insurer, setting forth the name and address of the insurance company writing the insurance policies required by paragraph (a)(3) of this rule and the policy number and policy limits. The limited liability partnership shall also file such other information as the Supreme Court may from time to time prescribe.

Amendments to and renewals of the certificate of insurance shall be filed with the Clerk of the Supreme Court within 30 days after the date on which such amendments or renewals become effective.

(c) The name of the limited liability partnership shall comply with the provisions of RPC 7.5 and shall contain only the full or last names of one or more of its partners or partners of a predecessor firm, whether the partner be living, deceased or retired. Wherever the name of the limited liability partnership is used it shall be followed by the phrase "A limited liability partnership," or by any other phrase or abbreviation authorized by N.J.S.A. 42:1A–48 to indicate that it is a limited liability partnership. In the case of a foreign limited liability partnership, the phrase shall also identify the jurisdiction of formation (e.g., "A limited liability partnership formed in the State of New York"). The limited liability partnership name shall be used on all pleadings, correspondence or other documents. Correspondence, pleadings and other documents executed in connection with the practice of law shall be executed on behalf of the limited liability partnership by one of its attorney partners or employees. Partnership documents executed other than in connection with the practice of law may be executed on behalf of the limited liability partnership by an authorized employee who is not licensed to practice law.

(d) A limited liability partnership actually and actively engaged in the practice of law may hold shares of stock in a professional corporation covered by Rule 1:21–1A, and may hold an interest in a limited liability company covered by Rule 1:21–1B.

(e) A limited liability partnership may engage in the practice of law in partnership with another partnership of attorneys, including a limited liability partnership, with a professional corporation or corporations covered by Rule 1:21–1A, with a limited liability company or companies covered by Rule 1:21–1B, or with an attorney or partnership of attorneys. The limited liability partnership name shall, in addition to meeting the requirements of Rule 1:21–1C(c), clearly designate that it is a partnership of or including other partnerships, limited liability partnerships, professional corporations, limited liability companies, or attorneys, as applicable. When any member of a limited liability partnership is a foreign partnership, foreign professional corporation, foreign limited liability company, or foreign attorney, the required designation shall also state this fact.

Note: Adopted November 18, 1996 to be effective January 1, 1997; paragraphs (a)(1) and (c) amended July 28, 2004 to be effective September 1, 2004.

1:21–2. Appearances Pro Hac Vice

(a) Conditions for Appearance. An attorney of any other jurisdiction, of good standing there, whether practicing law in such other jurisdiction as an individual or a member or employee of a partnership or an employee of a professional corporation or limited liability entity authorized to practice law in such other jurisdiction, or an attorney admitted in this state, of good standing, may, at the discretion of the court in which any matter is pending, be permitted, *pro hac vice*, to speak in such matter in the same manner as an attorney of this state who maintains a *bona fide* office for the practice of law in this state and who is therefore, pursuant to R. 1:21B1(a), authorized to practice in this state. Except for attorneys who are employees of and are representing the United States of America or a sister state, no attorney shall be admitted under this rule without annually complying with R. 1:20–1(b), R. 1:28–2, and R. 1:28B–1(e) during the period of admission. An attorney granted admission *pro hac vice* in accordance with this rule must include a copy of the order granting such permission when submitting to the New Jersey Lawyers' Fund for Client Protection the annual fee provided for by R. 1:20–1 and the other rules referred to herein. An attorney admitted both in this state and any other jurisdiction shall not, however, be permitted to appear *pro hac vice* if for any reason disqualified from practice in this state.

(b) Application for Admission. An application for admission *pro hac vice* shall be made on motion to all parties in the matter; which shall contain the following:

(1) In both civil and criminal actions, the motion shall be supported by an affidavit or certification of the attorney stating that:

(A) the attorney is a member in good standing of the bar of the highest court of the state in which the attorney is domiciled or principally practices law;

(B) the attorney is associated in the matter with New Jersey counsel of record qualified to practice pursuant to R. 1:21–1;

(C) the client has requested to be represented by said attorney; and

(D) no disciplinary proceedings are pending against the attorney in any jurisdiction and no discipline has previously been imposed on the attorney in any jurisdiction. If discipline has previously been imposed, the certification shall state the date, jurisdiction, nature of the ethics violation and the penalty imposed. If proceedings are pending, the certification shall specify the jurisdiction, the charges and the likely time of their disposition. An attorney admitted pro hac vice shall have the continuing obligation during the period of such admission promptly to advise the court of a disposition made of pending charges or of the institution of new disciplinary proceedings.

(2) In criminal actions a motion so supported shall be granted unless the court finds, for specifically stated

reasons, that there are supervening considerations of judicial administration.

(3) In civil actions the motion shall be granted only if the court finds, from the supporting affidavit, that there is good cause for such admission, which shall include at least one of the following:

(A) the cause in which the attorney seeks admission involves a complex field of law in which the attorney is a specialist, or

(B) there has been an attorney-client relationship with the client for an extended period of time, or

(C) there is a lack of local counsel with adequate expertise in the field involved, or

(D) the cause presents questions of law involving the law of the foreign jurisdiction in which the applicant is licensed, or

(E) there is need for extensive discovery or other proceedings in the foreign jurisdiction in which the applicant is licensed, or

(F) such other reason similar to those set forth in this subsection as would present good cause for the *pro hac vice* admission.

(c) Contents of Order. The order granting admission *pro hac vice* shall require the attorney to:

(1) abide by these rules, including all disciplinary rules;

(2) consent to the appointment of the Clerk of the Supreme Court as agent upon whom service of process may be made for all actions against the attorney or the attorney's firm that may arise out of the attorney's participation in the matter;

(3) notify the court immediately of any matter affecting the attorney's standing at the bar of any other court; and

(4) have all pleadings, briefs and other papers filed with the court signed by an attorney of record authorized to practice in this State, who shall be held responsible for them and for the conduct of the cause and of the admitted attorney therein. The order may contain further requirements concerning the participation of New Jersey counsel as the court from time to time deems necessary.

(d) Appearances in Subsequent Courts. An attorney permitted to speak *pro hac vice* by order entered by the trial court may speak in the cause on appeal by filing with the clerk of the appellate court a copy of the trial court's order together with a certification stating that all the conditions of the order have been complied with and, to the extent applicable, will continue to be complied with in the appellate court.

(e) Revocation of Permission to Appear. The court may, on its own or a party's motion, withdraw the permission to appear granted pursuant to this rule for good cause shown. In the event of said revocation, the court shall make such further order respecting the further progress of the litigation as the circumstances may require.

Note: Source—R.R. 1:12–8. Amended December 16, 1969 effective immediately; caption and text amended November 27, 1974 to be effective April 1, 1975; amended January 10, 1979 to be effective immediately; former rule amended and redesignated as paragraphs (a) and (b) and paragraph (c) adopted July 22, 1983 to be effective September 12, 1983; paragraph (a) amended January 31, 1984 to be effective February 15, 1984; new paragraph (c) adopted and former paragraph (c) redesignated as paragraph (d) November 1, 1985 to be effective January 2, 1986; paragraph (a) amended November 5, 1986 to be effective January 1, 1987; paragraph (a) amended July 14, 1992 to be effective September 1, 1992; paragraphs (b)(2) and (3) amended July 13, 1994 to be effective September 1, 1994; paragraph (a)(1)(iv) added June 28, 1996 to be effective September 1, 1996; paragraph (a) amended July 10, 1998 to be effective September 1, 1998; paragraphs (a)(1)(i), (a)(1)(ii), (a)(1)(iii), and (a)(1)(iv) amended and redesignated as (a)(1)(A), (a)(1)(B), (a)(1)(C), and (a)(1)(D) July 5, 2000 to be effective September 5, 2000; paragraph (a) amended and subsections of paragraph (a)(3) redesignated from (i) through (vi) to (A) through (F) July 12, 2002 to be effective September 3, 2002; paragraph (a) amended, portion of paragraph (a) redesignated as new paragraph (b), and former paragraphs (b), (c), and (d) redesignated as (c), (d), and (e) July 28, 2004 to be effective September 1, 2004.

1:21–3. Appearance by Law Graduates and Students; Special Permission for Out-of-State Attorneys

(a) Appearance Prior to Passing Bar Examination. A graduate of a law school approved by the American Bar Association who has successfully completed an approved skills and methods course may, before passing the bar examination, appear in any court for the purpose of answering the calendar call in an action in which the attorney or firm employing the graduate is the attorney of record.

(b) Appearance by Law Students and Graduates. A third year law student at, or graduate of, a law school approved by the American Bar Association may appear before a trial court or agency in accordance with a program approved by the Supreme Court on submission by such law school, a legal aid society, legal services project, or an agency of municipal, county or state government. A program once approved, need not be resubmitted to the Supreme Court provided that reports are filed listing the participants and the nature of their assignments, as required by the Administrative Office of the Courts. Participation in a program pursuant to this paragraph by a law graduate who has not passed the New Jersey bar examination shall terminate upon the graduate's failure to pass the bar examination for the third time, or after two years of employment following graduation, whichever is sooner.

(c) Permission for Out–of–State Attorneys to Practice in This State. A graduate of an approved law school who is a member of the bar of another state or of the District of Columbia and is employed by, associated with, or serving as a volunteer pro bono attorney with an organization described in R. 1:21–1(e) and approved by the Supreme Court, shall be permitted to practice, under the supervision of a member of the bar of the State, before all courts of this State in all causes in which the attorney is associated or serving pro bono with such legal services program, subject to the following conditions:

(1) Permission for an out-of-state attorney to practice under this rule shall become effective on filing with the Clerk of the Supreme Court evidence of graduation from an approved law school, a certificate of any court of last resort certifying that the out-of-state attorney is a member in good standing of the bar of another state or of the District of Columbia, and, (a) in the case of attorneys employed by or associated with an approved R. 1:21–1(e) organization, a statement signed by the President, Legal Services of New Jersey, that the out-of-state attorney is currently employed by or associated with such organization; or (b) in the case of a pro bono attorney with an approved R. 1:21–1(e) organization, on the filing of a statement by the executive director of that organization certifying that the attorney is serving on a voluntary pro bono basis with the organization;

(2) Permission to practice under this rule shall cease whenever the out- of-state attorney ceases to be employed by, associated with, or serving as a volunteer pro bono attorney with an approved R. 1: 21–1(e) organization in this State;

(3) Notice of said cessation shall be filed with the Clerk of the Supreme Court by the President, Legal Services of New Jersey, within five days after being notified of the cessation of the out-of-state attorney's employment or association; or by the executive director of the organization, in the case of a volunteer pro bono attorney;

(4) Permission to practice in this State under this rule shall remain in effect no longer than 2 1/2 years, except that there is no time limit on volunteer pro bono service with an approved R. 1:21–1(e) organization;

(5) Permission to practice in this State under this rule may be revoked or suspended by the Supreme Court, in its discretion, at any time either by written notice to the

out-of-state attorney or by amendment or deletion of this rule; and

(6) Out–of–state attorneys permitted to practice under this rule are not, and shall not represent themselves to be, members of the bar of this State.

Note: Source — R.R. 1:12–8A(a)(b)(c). Caption amended and paragraph (d) adopted July 1, 1970 effective immediately; paragraph (c) amended July 7, 1971 to be effective September 13, 1971; paragraph (a) amended April 2, 1973 to be effective immediately; paragraph (c) amended July 17, 1975 to be effective September 8, 1975; caption and paragraph (a) amended July 29, 1977 to be effective September 6, 1977; paragraph (c) amended July 16, 1979 to be effective September 10, 1979; paragraph (c) amended October 9, 1979 to be effective immediately but amendment stayed October 31, 1979; paragraph (c) amended July 21, 1980 to be effective September 8, 1980; paragraph (d) amended July 16, 1981 to be effective September 14, 1981; former paragraph (b) deleted and former paragraphs (c) and (d) redesignated as (b) and (c) November 1, 1985 to be effective January 2, 1986; paragraphs (a), (b) and (c) amended July 13, 1994 to be effective September 1, 1994; paragraph (c) amended July 12, 2002 to be effective September 3, 2002; paragraph (c) amended July 27, 2006 to be effective September 1, 2006.

1:21–4. Attorneys for Consuls of Any Government not Recognized

Attorneys for consuls-general or consular officers of any government not recognized by the United States of America shall have no authority, as such, to appear in any action or proceedings in court or to receive distribution of any estate or other fund.

Note: Source—R.R. 4:118–9.

1:21–5. Counsellors; Masters Abolished

The titles of Counsellor-at-law of this State, Master of the Superior Court, and Special Master, Commissioner or Examiner of the Superior Court are abolished.

Note: Source—R.R. 1:21–1, 1:21–2, 1:21–3.

1:21–6. Recordkeeping; Sharing of Fees; Examination of Records

(a) Required Trust and Business Accounts. Every attorney who practices in this state shall maintain in a financial institution in New Jersey, in the attorney's own name, or in the name of a partnership of attorneys, or in the name of the professional corporation of which the attorney is a member, or in the name of the attorney or partnership of attorneys by whom employed:

(1) a trust account or accounts, separate from any business and personal accounts and from any fiduciary accounts that the attorney may maintain as executor, guardian, trustee, or receiver, or in any other fiduciary capacity, into which trust account or accounts funds entrusted to the attorney's care shall be deposited; and

(2) a business account into which all funds received for professional services shall be deposited.

One or more of the trust accounts shall be the IOLTA account or accounts required by Rule 1:28A.

Other than fiduciary accounts maintained by an attorney as executor, guardian, trustee, or receiver, or in any other similar fiduciary capacity, all attorney trust accounts, whether general or specific, as well as all deposit slips and checks drawn thereon, shall be prominently designated as an "Attorney Trust Account." Nothing herein shall prohibit any additional descriptive designation for a specific trust account. All business accounts, as well as all deposit slips and all checks drawn thereon, shall be prominently designated as an "Attorney Business Account," an "Attorney Professional Account," or an "Attorney Office Account." The IOLTA account or accounts shall each be designated "IOLTA Attorney Trust Account."

The names of institutions in which such primary attorney trust and business accounts are maintained and identification numbers of each account shall be recorded on the annual registration form filed with the annual payment, pursuant to Rule 1:20–1(b) and Rule 1:28–2, to the Disciplinary Oversight Committee and the New Jersey Lawyers' Fund for Client Protection. Such information shall be available for use in accordance with paragraph (h) of this rule. For all IOLTA accounts, the account numbers, the name the account is under, and the depository institution shall be indicated on the registration statement. The signed annual registration statement required by Rule 1:20–1(c) shall constitute authorization to depository institutions to convert an existing non-interest bearing account to an IOLTA account.

(b) Account Location; Financial Institution's Reporting Requirements. An attorney trust account shall be maintained only in New Jersey financial institutions approved by the Supreme Court, which shall annually publish a list of such approved institutions. A financial institution shall be approved if it shall file with the Supreme Court an agreement, in a form provided by the Court, to report to the Office of Attorney Ethics in the event any properly payable attorney trust account instrument is presented against insufficient funds, irrespective of whether the instrument is honored; any such agreement shall apply to all branches of the financial institution and shall not be canceled except on thirty days' notice in writing to the Office of Attorney Ethics. The agreement shall further provide that all reports made by the financial institution shall be in the following format: (1) in the case of a dishonored instrument, the report shall be identical to the overdraft notice customarily forwarded to the depositor; (2) in the case of instruments that are presented against insufficient funds but which instruments are honored, the report shall identify the financial institution, the attorney or

law firm, the account number, the date of presentation for payment, and the date paid, as well as the amount of the overdraft created thereby. Such reports shall be made simultaneously with, and within the time provided by law for, notice of dishonor, if any; if an instrument presented against insufficient funds is honored, then the report shall be made within five banking days of the date of presentation for payment against insufficient funds.

In addition, each financial institution approved by the Supreme Court must co-operate with the IOLTA Program, and must offer an IOLTA account to any attorney who wishes to open one, and must from its income on such IOLTA accounts remit to the Fund the amount remaining after providing such institution a just and reasonable return equivalent to its return on similar non–IOLTA interest-bearing deposits. These remittances shall be monthly unless otherwise authorized by the Fund.

Nothing herein shall prevent an attorney from establishing a separate interest-bearing account for an individual client in accordance with these rules, providing that all interest earned shall be the sole property of the client and may not be retained by the attorney.

In addition to the reports specified above, approved financial institutions shall agree to cooperate fully with the Office of Attorney Ethics and to produce any attorney trust account or attorney business account records on receipt of a subpoena therefor.

Digital images of these records may be maintained by financial institutions provided that: (a) imaged copies of checks shall, when printed (including, but not limited to, when images are provided to the attorney with a monthly statement or otherwise or when subpoenaed by the Office of Attorney Ethics), be limited to no more than two checks per page (showing the front and back of each check) and (b) all digital records shall be maintained for a period of seven years. Nothing herein shall preclude a financial institution from charging an attorney or law firm for the reasonable cost of producing the reports and records required by this Rule. Every attorney or law firm in this state shall be conclusively deemed to have consented to the reporting and production requirements mandated by this Rule.

(c) Required Bookkeeping Records.

(1) Attorneys, partnerships of attorneys and professional corporations who practice in this state shall maintain in a current status and retain for a period of seven years after the event that they record:

(A) appropriate receipts and disbursements journals containing a record of all deposits in and withdrawals from the accounts specified in paragraph (a) of this rule and of any other bank account which concerns or affects their practice of law, specifically identifying the date, source and description of each item deposited as well as the date, payee and purpose of each disbursement. All trust account receipts shall be deposited intact and the duplicate deposit slip shall be sufficiently detailed to identify each item. All trust account withdrawals shall be made only by attorney authorized financial institution transfers as stated below or by check payable to a named payee and not to cash. Each electronic transfer out of an attorney trust account must be made on signed written instructions from the attorney to the financial institution. The financial institution must confirm each authorized transfer by returning a document to the attorney showing the date of the transfer, the payee, and the amount. Only an attorney admitted to practice law in this state shall be an authorized signatory on an attorney trust account, and only an attorney shall be permitted to authorize electronic transfers as above provided; and

(B) an appropriate ledger book, having at least one single page for each separate trust client, for all trust accounts, showing the source of all funds deposited in such accounts, the names of all persons for whom the funds are or were held, the amount of such funds, the description and amounts of charges or withdrawals from such accounts, and the names of all persons to whom such funds were disbursed. A regular trial balance of the individual client trust ledgers shall be maintained. The total of the trial balance must agree with the control figure computed by taking the beginning balance, adding the total of moneys received in trust for the client, and deducting the total of all moneys disbursed; and

(C) copies of all retainer and compensation agreements with clients; and

(D) copies of all statements to clients showing the disbursement of funds to them or on their behalf; and

(E) copies of all bills rendered to clients; and

(F) copies of all records showing payments to attorneys, investigators or other persons, not in their regular employ, for services rendered or performed; and

(G) originals of all checkbooks with running balances and check stubs, bank statements, prenumbered cancelled checks and duplicate deposit slips, except that, where the financial institution provides proper digital images or copies thereof to the attorney, then these digital images or copies shall be maintained; all checks, withdrawals and deposit slips, when related to a particular client, shall include, and attorneys shall complete, a distinct area identifying the client's last name or file number of the matter; and

(H) copies of all records, showing that at least monthly a reconciliation has been made of the cash balance derived from the cash receipts and cash disbursement journal totals, the checkbook balance, the bank statement balance and the client trust ledger sheet balances; and

(I) copies of those portions of each client's case file reasonably necessary for a complete understanding of the financial transactions pertaining thereto.

(2) ATM or cash withdrawals from all attorney trust accounts are prohibited.

(3) No attorney trust account shall have any agreement for overdraft protection.

(d) **Type and Availability of Bookkeeping Records.** The financial books and other records required by paragraphs (a) and (c) of this rule shall be maintained in accordance with generally accepted accounting practice. Bookkeeping records may be maintained by computer provided they otherwise comply with this rule and provided further that printed copies and computer files in industry-standard formats can be made on demand in accordance with this section or section (h). They shall be located at the principal New Jersey office of each attorney, partnership or professional corporation and shall be available for inspection, checks for compliance with this Rule and copying at that location by a duly authorized representative of the Office of Attorney Ethics. When made available pursuant to this rule, all such books and records shall remain confidential except for the purposes thereof or by direction of the Supreme Court, and their contents shall not be disclosed by anyone in such a way as to violate the attorney-client privilege.

(e) **Dissolutions.** Upon the dissolution of any partnership of attorneys or of any professional corporation, the former partners or shareholders shall make appropriate arrangements for the maintenance by one of them or by a successor firm of the records specified in paragraph (c) of this rule.

(f) **Attorneys Practicing With Foreign Attorneys or Firms.** All of the requirements of this rule shall be applicable to every attorney rendering legal services in this state regardless whether affiliated with or otherwise related in any way to an attorney, partnership, legal corporation, limited liability company, or limited liability partnership formed or registered in another state.

(g) **Attorneys Associated With Out of State Attorneys.** An attorney who practices in this state shall maintain and preserve for seven years a record of all fees received and expenses incurred in connection with any matter in which the attorney was associated with an attorney of another state.

(h) **Availability of Records.** Any of the records required to be kept by this rule shall be produced in response to a subpoena duces tecum issued in connection with an ethics investigation or hearing pursuant to R. 1:20–1 to 1:20–11, or shall be produced at the direction of the Disciplinary Review Board or the Supreme Court. They shall be available upon request for review and audit by the Office of Attorney Ethics. Every attorney shall be required to cooperate and to respond completely to questions by the Office of Attorney Ethics regarding all transactions concerning records required to be kept under this rule. When so produced, all such records shall remain confidential except for the purposes of the particular proceeding and their contents shall not be disclosed by anyone in such a way as to violate the attorney-client privilege. When produced or examined during the course of a disciplinary or random audit, both the attorney or law firm and the producers and licensors of computerized software shall be conclusively deemed to have consented to the use of said software by disciplinary authorities as evidence during the course of the disciplinary proceeding.

(i) Disciplinary Action. An attorney who fails to comply with the requirements of this rule in respect of the maintenance, availability and preservation of accounts and records or who fails to produce or to respond completely to questions regarding such records as required shall be deemed to be in violation of R.P.C. 1.15(d) and R.P.C. 8.1(b).

(j) Unidentifiable and Unclaimed Trust Fund Accumulations and Trust Funds Held for Missing Owners. When, for a period in excess of two years, an attorney's trust account contains trust funds which are either unidentifiable, unclaimed, or which are held for missing owners, such funds shall be so designated. A reasonable search shall then be made by the attorney to determine the beneficial owner of any unidentifiable or unclaimed accumulation, or the whereabouts of any missing owner. If the beneficial owner of an unidentified or unclaimed accumulation is determined, or if the missing beneficial owner is located, the funds shall be delivered to the beneficial owner when due. Trust funds which remain unidentifiable or unclaimed, and funds which are held for missing owners, after being designated as such, may, after the passage of one year during which time a diligent search and inquiry fails to identify the beneficial owner or the whereabouts of a missing owner, be paid to the Clerk of the Superior Court for deposit with the Superior Court Trust Fund. The Clerk shall hold the same in trust for the beneficial owners or for ultimate disposition as provided by order of the Supreme Court. All applications for payment to the Superior Court Clerk under this section shall be supported by a detailed affidavit setting forth specifically the facts and all reasonable efforts of search, inquiry and notice. The Clerk of the Superior Court may decline to accept funds where the petition does not

evidence diligent search and inquiry or otherwise fails to conform with this section.

Note: Source—R.R. 1:12–5A(a)(b)(c). Caption amended and paragraph (d) adopted July 1, 1970 effective immediately; paragraph (c) amended July 7, 1971 to be effective September 13, 1971; paragraph (a) amended April 2, 1973 to be effective immediately; paragraph (c) amended July 17, 1975 to be effective September 8, 1975; caption and paragraph (a) amended July 29, 1977 to be effective September 6, 1977. Paragraphs (a) and (b) amended, new paragraph (c) adopted and former paragraphs (c), (d), (e), (f) and (g) redesignated and amended February 23, 1978 to be effective April 1, 1978; paragraphs (b), (c) and (h) amended November 22, 1978 to be effective January 1, 1979; paragraph (a) amended July 16, 1979 to be effective September 10, 1979; paragraph (b) amended July 16, 1981 to be effective September 14, 1981; paragraphs (a), (b), (c), (g) and (h) amended January 31, 1984 to be effective February 15, 1984 except that the amendments to paragraph (a)(2) regarding designations to be placed on trust and business accounts shall not be effective until July 1, 1984; effective date of amendment to paragraph (a)(2) deferred on June 15, 1984 from July 1, 1984 to September 1, 1984; paragraphs (a)(1) and (2), (e)(1) and (h) amended July 26, 1984 to be effective September 10, 1984; paragraphs (a), (e) and (f) amended November 1, 1984 to be effective March 1, 1985; paragraphs (b) and (c) amended and paragraph (i) adopted November 5, 1986 to be effective January 1, 1987; paragraph (a) amended July 14, 1992 to be effective September 1, 1992; paragraph (a)(2) amended September 15, 1992, to be effective January 1, 1993; former paragraph (e) deleted and new paragraph (e) adopted November 18, 1996, to be effective January 1, 1997; paragraph (a) amended, new paragraph (b) added, former paragraphs (b) through (i) redesignated as paragraphs (c) through (j), and redesignated paragraphs (c), (d), (e), (h), and (i) amended July 12, 2002 to be effective September 3, 2002; caption of Rule and paragraphs (a) and (b) amended February 6, 2003 to be effective March 1, 2003; paragraph (c), (e), (f), (g), and (j) amended July 28, 2004 to be effective September 1, 2004; paragraph (b) amended July 9, 2008 to be effective September 1, 2008.

1:21–7. Contingent Fees

(a) As used in this rule the term "contingent fee arrangement" means an agreement for legal services of an attorney or attorneys, including any associated or forwarding counsel, under which compensation, contingent in whole or in part upon the successful accomplishment or disposition of the subject matter of the agreement, is to be in an amount which either is fixed or is to be determined under a formula.

(b) An attorney shall not enter into a contingent fee arrangement without first having advised the client of the right and afforded the client an opportunity to retain the attorney under an arrangement for compensation on the basis of the reasonable value of the services.

(c) In any matter where a client's claim for damages is based upon the alleged tortious conduct of another, including products liability claims and claims among family members that are subject to Part V of these Rules but excluding statutorily based discrimination and employment claims, and the client is not a subrogee, an attorney shall not contract for, charge, or collect a contingent fee in excess of the following limits:

(1) 33 1/3 % on the first $500,000 recovered;

(2) 30% on the next $500,000 recovered;

(3) 25% on the next $500,000 recovered;

(4) 20% on the next $500,000 recovered; and

(5) on all amounts recovered in excess of the above by application for reasonable fee in accordance with the provisions of paragraph (f) hereof; and

(6) where the amount recovered is for the benefit of a client who was a minor or mentally incapacitated when the contingent fee arrangement was made, the foregoing limits shall apply, except that the fee on any amount recovered by settlement without trial shall not exceed 25%.

(d) The permissible fee provided for in paragraph (c) shall be computed on the net sum recovered after deducting disbursements in connection with the institution and prosecution of the claim, whether advanced by the attorney or by the client, including investigation expenses, expenses for expert or other testimony or evidence, the cost of briefs and transcripts on appeal, and any interest included in a judgment pursuant to R. 4:42–11(b); but no deduction need be made for post-judgment interest or for liens, assignments or claims in favor of hospitals or for medical care and treatment by doctors and nurses, or similar items. The permissible fee shall include legal services rendered on any appeal or review proceeding or on any retrial, but this shall not be deemed to require an attorney to take an appeal. When joint representation is undertaken in both the direct and derivative action, or when a claim for wrongful death is joined with a claim on behalf of a decedent, the contingent fee shall be calculated on the aggregate sum of the recovery.

(e) Paragraph (c) of this rule is intended to fix maximum permissible fees and does not preclude an attorney from entering into a contingent fee arrangement providing for, or from charging or collecting a

contingent fee below such limits. In all cases contingent fees charged or collected must conform to RPC 1.5(a).

(f) If at the conclusion of a matter an attorney considers the fee permitted by paragraph (c) to be inadequate, an application on written notice to the client may be made to the Assignment Judge for the hearing and determining of a reasonable fee in light of all the circumstances. This rule shall not preclude the exercise of a client's existing right to a court review of the reasonableness of an attorney's fee.

(g) Where the amount of the contingent fee is limited by the provisions of paragraph (c) of this rule, the contingent fee arrangement shall be in writing, signed both by the attorney and the client, and a signed duplicate shall be given to the client. Upon conclusion of the matter resulting in a recovery, the attorney shall prepare and furnish the client with a signed closing statement.

(h) Calculation of Fee in Structured Settlements. As used herein the term "structured settlement" refers to the payment of any settlement between the parties or judgment entered pursuant to a proceeding approved by the Court, the terms of which provide for the payment of the funds to be received by the plaintiff on an installment basis. For purposes of paragraph (c), the basis for calculation of a contingent fee shall be the value of the structured settlement as herein defined. Value shall consist of any cash payment made upon consummation of the settlement plus the actual cost to the party making the settlement of the deferred payment aspects thereof. In the event that the party paying the settlement does not purchase the deferred payment component, the actual cost thereof shall be the actual cost assigned by that party to that component. For further purposes of this rule, the party making the settlement offer shall, at the time the offer is made, disclose to the party receiving the settlement offer its actual cost and, if it does not purchase the deferred payment aspect of the settlement, the factors and assumptions used by it in assigning actual cost.

(i) Calculation of Fee in Settlement of Class or Multiple Party Actions. When representation is undertaken on behalf of several persons whose respective claims, whether or not joined in one action, arise out of the same transaction or set of facts or involve substantially identical liability issues, the contingent fee shall be calculated on the basis of the aggregate sum of all recoveries, whether by judgment, settlement or both, and shall be charged to the clients in proportion to the recovery of each. Counsel may, however, make application for modification of the fee pursuant to paragraph (f) of this rule in appropriate cases.

Note: Source—R. 1:21–6(f), as adopted July 7, 1971 to be effective September 13, 1971 and deleted December 21, 1971 to be effective January 31, 1972. Adopted December 21, 1971 to be effective January 31, 1972. Amended June 29, 1973 to be effective September 10, 1973. Paragraphs (c) and (e) amended October 13, 1976, effective as to contingent fee arrangements entered into on November 1, 1976 and thereafter. Closing statements on all contingent fee arrangements filed as previously required between January 31, 1972 and January 31, 1973 shall be filed with the Administrative Office of the Courts whenever the case is closed; paragraph (c) amended July 29, 1977 to be effective September 6, 1977; paragraph (d) amended July 24, 1978 to be effective September 11, 1978; paragraph (c) amended and new paragraphs (h) and (i) adopted January 16, 1984, to be effective immediately; paragraph (d) amended July 26, 1984 to be effective September 10, 1984; paragraph (e) amended June 29, 1990 to be effective September 4, 1990; paragraphs (b) and (c)(5) amended July 13, 1994 to be effective September 1, 1994; paragraph (c) amended June 28, 1996 to be effective September 1, 1996; paragraph (c) amended January 21, 1999 to be effective April 5, 1999; paragraphs (g) and (h) amended July 5, 2000 to be effective September 5, 2000; paragraph (c) amended July 12, 2002 to be effective September 3, 2002; paragraphs (d) and (f) amended July 9, 2008 to be effective September 1, 2008.

1:21–7A. Retainer Agreements in Family Actions [Deleted]

Rule 1:21–7A deleted in its entirety January 21, 1999 effective April 5, 1999.

1:21–8. [Deleted]

Note: R. 1:21–8 redesignated as paragraph (a) in R. 1:20–20 effective March 1, 1995.

1:21–9. Certification and Practice of Foreign Legal Consultants

(a) Certification of Foreign Legal Consultants. No person who is admitted to practice in a foreign country as an attorney or counselor at law or the equivalent may render legal services in this State unless and until that person complies with the provisions in this rule and becomes certified by the Supreme Court as a foreign legal consultant. In that capacity, such person may render legal services within this State to the extent permitted by this rule.

(b) Conditions of Representation. A foreign legal consultant may, at the discretion of the Supreme Court, be permitted to represent New Jersey clients for the sole purpose of rendering professional legal advice on the laws, rules, regulations or any other matters involving the foreign country in which the foreign legal consultant is licensed. The foreign legal consultant shall associate and consult with a New Jersey attorney and the associating New Jersey attorney shall assume full responsibility for the conduct of the foreign legal consultant.

(c) Eligibility. In its discretion the Supreme Court may certify as a foreign legal consultant an applicant who:

(1) for a period of not less than 5 of the 7 years immediately preceding the date of application has been admitted to practice and has been in good standing as an attorney or counselor at law or the equivalent in a foreign country and has engaged either (A) in the practice of law in such country or (B) in a profession or occupation which requires as a prerequisite admission to practice and good standing as an attorney or counselor at law or the equivalent in such country; and

(2) possesses the good moral character customarily required for admission to the practice of law in this State; and

(3) intends to maintain, within this State, a bona fide office for practice as a foreign legal consultant.

(d) Applications.

(1) Application for admission under this rule shall be made to the Clerk of the Supreme Court. The application shall be supported by an affidavit of the applicant, which shall provide: (A) the applicant's name and age; (B) the applicant's last place of residence; (C) the character and duration of the applicant's formal legal education or training; (D) the name of and date of attendance at each university or post graduate level educational institution which the applicant has attended and/or graduated from, and the degree conferred, if any; (E) the names of all courts or other licensing authorities to which the applicant has applied for admission to the practice of law or certification or licensure as a foreign legal consultant; (F) the names of all courts or other licensing authorities under the auspices of which the applicant has taken any bar or equivalent examinations, the dates upon which said examinations were taken and the results thereof; (G) the names of all courts and other licensing authorities by which the applicant has actually been licensed to practice as an attorney or counselor at law or equivalent or certified or licensed as a foreign legal consultant and the dates of each licensure or certification; (H) a statement that the applicant is admitted to practice and is in good standing as an attorney or counselor at law or the equivalent in a foreign country and has maintained that status for a period of not less than five of the seven years immediately prior to the date of the application; (I) a statement that the applicant possesses the good moral character customarily required for admission to the practice of law in New Jersey; (J) the identity of a New Jersey attorney holding a plenary license to practice law in this State who is in good standing with the Supreme Court with whom the applicant shall associate; and (K) a statement advising whether the applicant is currently or has ever been the subject of any investigation or proceeding for professional misconduct and whether the applicant has ever been rejected upon

an application for admission to practice before any court or by any other licensing authority. If the applicant has been the subject of any investigation or proceeding for professional misconduct or has been rejected for admission to practice, the applicant shall state the date, jurisdiction, nature of the violation, and penalty imposed and may set forth a brief explanation of the disposition and any extenuating or mitigating circumstances. An applicant admitted under this rule shall have a continuing obligation to advise the Court of a disposition made of a pending charge or the institution of new disciplinary proceedings. A filing fee, set by order of the Supreme Court, shall accompany each application.

(2) The application shall be accompanied by the following documents, together with duly authenticated English translations of each document that is not in English:

(A) Duly executed certificates and/or documents from the authority having final jurisdiction over professional discipline in the foreign country in which the applicant is admitted to practice attesting to:

(i) the authority's jurisdiction in such matters;

(ii) the applicant's admission to practice in such foreign country, the date thereof and the applicant's current good standing as an attorney or counselor at law or the equivalent therein; and

(iii) whether any charge or complaint has ever been filed against the applicant with such authority, and, if so, the nature and substance of the allegations of each such charge or complaint and the disposition thereof.

(B) A letter of recommendation from one of the members of the executive body of such authority or from one of the judges of a court of general original or appellate jurisdiction within such foreign country, setting forth the applicant's professional qualifications, together with a certificate from the clerk of such authority or of such court, as the case may be, attesting to the office held by the person signing the letter and the genuineness of the person's signature.

(C) Letters of recommendation from at least two attorneys or counselors at law or the equivalent admitted to practice and practicing in such foreign country, setting forth the length of time and circumstances under which they have come to know the applicant, and their appraisal of the applicant's moral character.

(D) Letters of recommendation from at least two attorneys admitted to the practice of law in this State, setting forth the length of time and circumstances under which they have come to know the applicant, and their appraisal of the applicant's moral character.

(E) An affidavit of the New Jersey attorney with whom the foreign legal consultant will associate in which the New Jersey counsel agrees to the association and acknowledges that he or she will be responsible for the conduct of the foreign legal consultant.

An associating attorney is one who voluntarily agrees to assume full responsibility for the foreign legal consultant as described in sections (b), (d), (e) and (f) of this rule.

(F) Such other relevant documents or information as may be requested by the Supreme Court.

(3) The statements contained in the application and supporting documents shall be investigated by the Supreme Court or its designee. Prior to granting certification as a foreign legal consultant, the Supreme Court shall be satisfied that the applicant is of the good moral character. The application shall be granted by the Court unless there is a finding of good cause for denying the application.

(e) Contents of Order. The order granting admission shall require that:

(1) the foreign legal consultant shall:

(A) abide by this rule; and

(B) consent to the appointment of the Clerk of the Supreme Court as agent upon whom service of process may be made for all actions against the foreign legal consultant or the New Jersey attorney with whom such person has associated that may arise out of the foreign legal consultant's participation in a matter; and

(C) notify the Supreme Court immediately of any matter affecting the foreign legal consultant's standing at the bar of any other court; and

(2) the associating New Jersey attorney shall assume full responsibility for the conduct of the foreign legal consultant.

(f) Advertising of Foreign Legal Consultant's Practice.

(1) A foreign legal consultant and the associating New Jersey attorney may advertise the admission of the foreign legal consultant and permitted scope of practice consistent with this rule and the laws and regulations of this State;

(2) A foreign legal consultant shall be listed and identified on the letterhead of the associating New Jersey attorney with appropriate designation and limitation of practice as a foreign legal consultant under this rule.

(g) Scope of Practice. A person licensed as a foreign legal consultant under this rule may render and be compensated for the performance of legal services within the State, but specifically shall not:

(1) appear for another person as attorney in any court or before any other judicial officer or administrative agency in the State, or sign or file in the capacity of a lawyer or legal advisor any pleadings or any other papers in any action or proceeding brought in any such court or before any judicial officer or administrative agency; or

(2) prepare any deed, mortgage, assignment, discharge, lease, agreement or contract of sale or any other instrument for purposes of recordation which may affect title to real estate located in the United States of America, its territories, districts or possessions; or

(3) prepare:

(A) any will or trust instrument effecting the disposition of any property located in the United States of America, its territories, districts or possessions and owned by a resident thereof; or

(B) any instrument relating directly to the primary administration of a decedent's estate in the United States of America, its territories, districts or possessions; or

(4) prepare any instrument in respect of the marital relations, rights or duties of a resident of the United States of America, its territories, districts or possessions or the custody or care of the children of such a resident; or

(5) render professional legal advice on the laws of this State or the United States of America or any other state, territory, district or possession of the United States of America or any foreign country other than a country to the bar of which the foreign legal consultant is admitted as an attorney or counselor at law or the equivalent (whether rendered incident to the preparation of legal instruments or otherwise), except on the basis of advice from a person admitted to the practice of law as an attorney of this State or such other state, territory, district or possession or as an attorney or counselor at law or the equivalent in such other foreign country, who has been consulted by the foreign legal consultant in the particular matter at hand and who has been identified to the client by name; or

(6) in any way represent that such person is licensed as an attorney at law of this State, or as an attorney at law or foreign legal consultant of another state territory or district, or as an attorney or counselor at law or the equivalent of a foreign country, unless so licensed; or

(7) use any title other than "foreign legal consultant"; provided that such person's authorized title and firm name in the foreign country in which such person is admitted to practice as an attorney or counselor at law or the equivalent may be used, provided that the title, firm name, and the name of such foreign country are stated together with the title "foreign legal consultant" and further provided that such use does not create the impression that the foreign legal consultant holds a plenary license to practice law in this State.

(h) Conduct and Discipline.

(1) The professional conduct of foreign legal consultants, as limited by section (g) of this rule, shall be governed in all respects by the Rules of Professional Conduct of the American Bar Association, as amended and supplemented by the Supreme Court and included as an Appendix to Part I of these rules.

(2) For purposes of Rules 1:14, 1:16, 1:19, 1:20, 1:20A, 1:21–6, 1:21–7, 1:22, 1:25, 1:27–3, 1:28 and 1:29, a foreign legal consultant shall be deemed a member of the legal profession and shall be subject to the same requirements and procedures as an attorney and member of the bar holding a plenary license to practice law in the State of New Jersey. However, nothing in this subsection shall be construed as expanding the scope of practice authorized by section (g) of this rule. No foreign legal consultant shall be admitted under this rule without annually complying with R. 1:20–1(b) and R. 1:28–2 during the period of admission.

(3) All admissions under this rule shall be valid for a period of 12 months and may be renewed annually.

Note: Adopted November 7, 1988 to be effective January 2, 1989; paragraph (a) amended, new paragraph (b) added, former paragraph (b) amended and redesignated as paragraph (c), former paragraph (c) amended and redesignated as paragraph (d), former paragraph (d) deleted, new paragraphs (e) and (f) added, former paragraph (e) amended and redesignated as paragraph (g), and former paragraph (f) amended and redesignated as paragraph (h) July 12, 2002 to be effective September 3, 2002.

1:21–10. Provision of Legal Services Following Determination of Major Disaster

(a) Determination of Existence of Major Disaster. Solely for purposes of this Rule, the Supreme Court shall determine when an emergency affecting the justice system, as a result of a natural or other major disaster, has occurred:

(1) in New Jersey and whether the emergency caused by the major disaster affects all or only a part of the State, or

(2) in another jurisdiction, but only after such a determination and its geographical scope have been made by the highest court of that jurisdiction. The authority to engage in the temporary practice of law in New Jersey pursuant to paragraph (c) of this Rule shall extend only to lawyers who principally practice in the area of such other jurisdiction determined to have suffered a major disaster causing an emergency affecting the justice system and the provision of legal services.

(b) Temporary Practice in New Jersey Following Major Disaster. Following the determination of an emergency affecting the justice system in New Jersey pursuant to paragraph (a) of this Rule, or a determination that persons displaced by a major disaster in another jurisdiction and residing in New Jersey are in need of pro bono services and the assistance of lawyers from outside of New Jersey is required to help provide such assistance, a lawyer authorized to practice law in another United States jurisdiction, and not disbarred, suspended from practice or otherwise restricted from practice in any jurisdiction, may provide legal services in this jurisdiction on a temporary basis. Such legal services must be provided on a pro bono basis without compensation, expectation of compensation or other direct or indirect pecuniary gain to the lawyer. Such legal services shall be assigned and supervised through an established not-for-profit bar association, pro bono program or legal services program or through such organization(s) specifically designated by the Court.

(c) Temporary Practice in New Jersey Following Major Disaster in Another Jurisdiction. Following the determination of a major disaster in another United States jurisdiction, a lawyer who is authorized to practice law and who principally practices in that affected jurisdiction, and who is not disbarred, suspended from practice or otherwise restricted from practice in any jurisdiction, may provide legal services in New Jersey on a temporary basis. Those legal services must arise out of and be reasonably related to that lawyer's practice of law in the jurisdiction, or area of such other jurisdiction, where the major disaster occurred.

(d) Duration of Authority for Temporary Practice.

(1) The authority to practice law in New Jersey granted by paragraph (b) of this Rule shall end when the Supreme Court determines that the conditions caused by the major disaster in New Jersey have ended, except that a lawyer then representing clients in New Jersey pursuant to paragraph (b) of this Rule is authorized to continue the provision of legal services for such time as is reasonably necessary to complete the representation, but the lawyer shall not thereafter accept new clients.

(2) The authority to practice law in New Jersey granted by paragraph (c) of this Rule shall end 60 days after the Supreme Court declares that the conditions caused by the major disaster in the affected jurisdiction have ended.

(e) Court Appearances. The authority granted by this Rule does not include appearances in court except:

(1) pursuant to R. 1:21–2 (appearances pro hac vice) and, if such admission is granted, the fees for such admission shall be waived; or

(2) if the Supreme Court, in any determination made under paragraph (a) of this Rule, grants blanket permission to appear in all or designated courts of this jurisdiction to lawyers providing legal services pursuant to paragraph (b) of this Rule. If such permission is granted, any pro hac vice admission fees shall be waived.

(f) Disciplinary Authority, Registration, Lawful Practice of Law. Lawyers providing legal services in New Jersey pursuant to this Rule:

(1) are subject to the Supreme Court's disciplinary authority and the Rules of Professional Conduct;

(2) shall, within 30 days from the commencement of the provision of legal services in New Jersey, file a registration statement with the Clerk of the Supreme Court. The registration statement shall be in a form prescribed by the Supreme Court;

(3) shall not be considered to be engaged in the unlawful practice of law in New Jersey; and

(4) shall not be required to comply with R. 1:20–1(b) or (c), R. 1:28–2 or R. 1:28B–1 (payment of annual assessments and filing of annual registration statement with New Jersey Lawyers' Fund for Client Protection).

(g) Notification to Clients. Lawyers who provide legal services pursuant to this Rule shall inform clients in New Jersey of the jurisdiction in which they are authorized to practice law, any limits of that authorization, and that they are not authorized to practice law in New Jersey except as permitted by this Rule. They shall not state or imply to any person that they are otherwise authorized to practice law in New Jersey.

Note: Adopted July 9, 2008 to be effective September 1, 2008.

RULE 1:22.   COMMITTEE ON THE UNAUTHORIZED PRACTICE OF LAW

1:22–1.   Appointment; Membership; Administration

(a) Appointment. The Supreme Court shall appoint a committee on the unauthorized practice of law consisting of 21 attorneys of this State and four lay members. The members shall be appointed for staggered terms of three years and no member who has served four full three-year terms shall be eligible for reappointment. Any vacancy shall be filled for the unexpired term. The Supreme Court shall annually designate a chair and vice-chair, who shall be members of the committee.

(b) Staff. The Administrative Director of the Courts shall provide the committee with a secretary, who shall be responsible for day-to-day coordination of staff support to the committee. The secretary shall file with the Administrative Director a copy of (1) the minutes of

every meeting; (2) every advisory opinion; and (3) every recommendation for the institution of litigation.

(c) Records; Confidentiality. All records of the committee shall be filed and maintained by the secretary at the principal office of the committee which shall be located at the Administrative Office of the Courts. All records, files, meetings and proceedings of the committee or of a part thereof shall be confidential and shall not be disclosed to or attended by anyone except as authorized by these rules or by the Supreme Court.

Note: Source—R.R. 1:12A–1(a) (b) (c) (d) (e) (f); caption to rule and text of paragraph (a) amended, paragraphs (b) (c) (d) and (e) deleted, and new paragraphs (b) and (c) with new captions adopted June 29, 1990 to be effective September 4, 1990; paragraph (a) amended June 28, 1996 to be effective September 1, 1996.

1:22–1A. Organization; Quorum

(a) Parts. The Supreme Court shall divide the committee into parts consisting of not less than six members each, one of whom shall be a lay member, and shall assign to each part a designated area of the State. The chair of the committee shall appoint an attorney member as chair of each part.

(b) Quorum. A majority of the committee, or of a part, shall constitute a quorum. No action may be taken by less than a majority of the committee or of a part except as expressly provided by this rule. At the request of the chair, the Supreme Court may appoint temporary members of the committee or a part. The committee and its parts shall meet at the call of their respective chairs.

(c) Action by Committee. The full jurisdiction and authority of the committee, as provided in these rules, may be exercised by a part thereof, except that (1) no advisory opinion shall be given, as provided in R. 1:22–3, without the approval of a majority of the committee; (2) no determination of the unauthorized practice of law by a respondent and referral of a matter to a law enforcement or other agency shall be made, as provided in R. 1:22–6, without the approval of a majority of the committee; and (3) the action of a part on any matter shall be subject to review and the approval or disapproval of the committee.

Note: Adopted June 29, 1990 to be effective September 4, 1990; paragraphs (a) and (c) amended June 28, 1996, to be effective September 1, 1996.

1:22–2. Jurisdiction

(a) Advisory Opinions. On request of any person, or in connection with the consideration of any complaint or any investigation made on its own initiative, the committee may render advisory opinions relating to the unauthorized practice of law and arrange for their publication.

(b) Complaints. The committee shall have jurisdiction over and shall inquire into and consider complaints alleging the unauthorized practice of law by any natural or other persons or entity.

(c) Investigation. The committee may, on its own initiative, and without any complaint being made to it, investigate any condition or situation of which it becomes aware that may involve the unauthorized practice of law.

Note: Source—R.R. 1:12A–2(a) (b) (c); paragraph (a) amended, paragraphs (b) and (c) deleted, and new paragraphs (b) and (c) with new captions adopted June 29, 1990 to be effective September 4, 1990.

1:22–3. Procedure: Advisory Opinions

(a) Receipt of Request. Upon receipt of a request for an advisory opinion, the secretary shall make a written acknowledgement thereof to the person or persons bringing the matter to the committee's attention. The secretary shall promptly forward a copy of the inquiry and other information to the chair of the committee and to the chair of the part of the area of the State from which the inquiry originates. If the request for an advisory opinion originates outside of New Jersey, the matter may be referred to any part by the secretary.

(b) Pending Controversy. No opinion shall be rendered if, to the committee's knowledge, the subject matter either involves or might affect a case or controversy pending in any court.

(c) Technical Requirements. In accordance with R. 1:22–2(a), an advisory opinion shall be issued by the committee in writing and shall be filed with the secretary, who shall transmit a copy to the person making the inquiry. Where the committee so instructs, the secretary shall make suitable arrangements for publication. Published opinions shall not, insofar as practicable, identify the party or parties making an inquiry, or the complainant or respondent.

(d) Form of Opinion. Upon the conclusion of a review by the committee or a part of a request for an advisory opinion, a report shall be made to the whole committee. The committee shall determine the form in which the advisory opinion is to be promulgated, in accordance with R. 1:22–3.

(e) Rules and Procedures. The committee may adopt such additional rules, subject to approval by the Supreme Court, as it may deem appropriate for prescribing the methods and procedures to be followed in considering requests and expressing opinions.

Note: Source—R.R. 1:12A–3(a) (b) (c); caption to rule amended, paragraph (a) deleted and new paragraph (a) with new caption adopted, caption and text of paragraph (b) amended, and paragraphs (c)(d) and (e) adopted June 29, 1990 to be effective September 4, 1990; paragraph (c) amended June 28, 1996 to be effective September 1, 1996.

1:22–3A. Petitions for Review

(a) Notice. Within 20 days after an opinion is published, or within 30 days after any final action of the Committee on the Unauthorized Practice of Law other than the publication of any opinion, any aggrieved member of the bar, bar association, person or entity may seek review thereof by serving on the Attorney General a notice of petition for review by the Supreme Court and by filing the original notice with the Clerk of the Supreme Court. The notice shall set forth the petitioner's name and address and, if represented, the name and address of counsel. The notice shall designate the action of the Committee on the Unauthorized Practice of Law sought to be reviewed and shall concisely state the manner in which the petitioner is aggrieved.

(b) Deposit for Costs. Deposit for costs shall be made in accordance with R. 2:12–5.

(c) Record on Petition for Review. If the petition for review is granted, the record on review shall be the formal opinion, if any, issued pursuant to R. 1:22–3; the inquiry; brief or memorandum of law, if any; and any documents or other evidence or proof relied upon by the committee in arriving at its determination.

(d) Form of Petition for Review. A petition for review shall be in the form of a brief, conforming to the applicable provisions of R. 2:6 and not exceeding 15 pages if printed or 20 pages if otherwise reproduced or typed, exclusive of tables of contents, citations and appendix. It shall contain a short statement of the matter involved, the question presented, the errors complained of and the arguments in support of the petitioner's position. It shall also contain a certification by the petitioner or counsel, if any, that the petition presents a substantial question and is filed in good faith and not for purposes of delay.

(e) Service and Filing of Petition for Review. Within 10 days after filing of the notice of petition for review, two copies of the petition shall be served on the Attorney General and the Secretary of the Committee on the Unauthorized Practice of Law and nine copies thereof shall be filed with the Clerk of the Supreme Court.

(f) Response to Petition for Review. The Attorney General shall, within 30 days of the service of the petition, serve two copies of the brief in opposition to the petition and file nine copies thereof with the Clerk of the Supreme Court. The brief shall be direct and concise, shall conform to the applicable provisions of R. 2:6 and shall not exceed 15 pages if printed or 20 pages if otherwise reproduced or typed, exclusive of table of contents, citations and appendix. Within 10 days of such service, petitioner may serve two copies and file nine copies of a reply brief not exceeding nine pages if printed or 10 pages if otherwise reproduced or typed, exclusive of tables of contents, citations or appendix.

(g) Final Determination. The final determination of a petition for review may be either by written opinion or by order of the Supreme Court and shall state whether the opinion or other action of the Committee on the Unauthorized Practice of Law is affirmed, reversed or modified or shall provide for such other final disposition as is appropriate.

Note: Adopted June 28, 1996 to be effective September 1, 1996.

1:22–4. Complaints: Preliminary Investigation

(a) Receipt of Complaint. Upon receipt of a complaint or any other matter within the committee's jurisdiction, the secretary shall make written acknowledgement thereof to the person bringing the matter to the committee's attention.

(b) Referral to Part. The secretary shall promptly forward a copy of the complaint and other information to the chair of the committee and to the chair of the part in the area of the State in which the respondent's activities occur. If the person, persons or entity alleged to be engaged in such unauthorized practice is located outside of New Jersey, the matter may be referred to any part by the secretary.

(c) Investigation. The investigation or review shall be promptly instituted by the part or by a member thereof designated by the chair of the part. If a complaint has been filed, the investigating member shall interview the complainant and respondent and shall conduct such further investigation as is deemed appropriate. At the discretion of the committee, the respondent may be informed of the identity of the complainant.

(d) Report. Upon the conclusion of an investigation of a complaint, a report shall be made to the committee and recorded in the minutes. If, after consideration of the report, the committee concludes that there has been no unauthorized practice of law, the complaint shall be dismissed and the secretary shall so notify the complainant and the respondent in writing and shall close the file in the matter. If the committee concludes that there has been unauthorized practice of law, the committee shall attempt to persuade the respondent to enter into a written agreement to refrain from such conduct in the future, in accordance with R. 1:22–5.

(e) Pending Controversy. No complaint shall be investigated if, to the committee's knowledge, the conduct complained of is the subject matter of or might affect a case or controversy pending in any court. *Note: Source—R.R. 1:12A–4(a) (b) (c); caption and text of rule deleted, and new caption and paragraphs (a) (b) (c) and (d) adopted June 29, 1990 to be effective September 4, 1990; paragraph (e) adopted June 28, 1996 to be effective September 1, 1996.*

1:22–5. Complaints: Informal Disposition

(a) Informal Review; Conference. The committee may attempt to arrive at an amicable disposition of any matter within its jurisdiction with the person, persons or entity concerned. At any time during the pendency of a matter before it, the committee may conduct an informal conference with the person, persons or entity that is the subject of a committee inquiry or investigation. At the committee's discretion, an electronic recording or written transcription of the proceeding may be made. No oath shall be administered. A person or entity subject to an informal conference may be represented by counsel.

(b) Disposition. If it appears that the conduct in question involves the unauthorized practice of law, the committee shall endeavor to have the person, persons or entity enter into a written agreement to refrain in the future from such conduct. The informal disposition of matters as provided in this rule is encouraged. If, after a finding by the committee of the unauthorized practice of law, a person or entity declines to enter into a written agreement pursuant to this rule, the committee shall refer the matter to an appropriate law enforcement or other agency in accordance with R. 1:22–6.

Note: Source—R.R. 1:12A–5(a) (b) (c) (d) (e) (f); caption and text of rule deleted, and new caption and paragraphs (a) and (b) adopted June 29, 1990 to be effective September 4, 1990; paragraph (b) amended June 28, 1996 to be effective September 1, 1996.

1:22–6. Complaints: Referrals

(a) Referral to Enforcement Agency. When the committee concludes from its preliminary investigation or from the failure of an informal conference as provided in R. 1:22–5 that an amicable disposition of any matter within its jurisdiction with the person, persons or entity concerned cannot be effected, it shall, based upon the nature of the complaint, the relief sought, and the facts as then known, refer the matter to the law enforcement or other agency the committee determines is best suited to conduct an investigation and any prosecution of such matter.

(b) Contents of File. Upon making a determination that an amicable disposition of a matter cannot be effected, and that the matter should be referred to a particular law enforcement or other agency, the committee shall send such agency the original complaint, response, evidence or other proof, investigative report and, if an informal conference has been conducted, a transcript of such proceedings. The committee shall retain copies of all such documents for its file.

(c) Notice to Complainant. Upon referring a matter to a law enforcement or other agency, the secretary shall notify the complainant of such action in writing.

Note: Source—R.R. 1:12A–6(a) (b); caption and text of rule deleted, and new caption and paragraphs (a) (b) (c) (d) (e) (f) (g) (h) (i) (j) and (k) adopted June 29, 1990 to be effective September 4, 1990; caption of rule and caption and text of paragraph (a) amended, caption and text of paragraphs (b) and (c) deleted, new caption and text of paragraphs (b) and (c) adopted, and caption and text of paragraphs (d)(e)(f)(g)(h)(i)(j) and (k) deleted June 28, 1996 to be effective September 1, 1996.

RULE 1:23. BOARD OF BAR EXAMINERS

1:23–1. Appointment; Organization

The Supreme Court shall appoint a Board of Bar Examiners consisting of such number of attorneys of this State as it shall from time to time determine. Each member shall serve for a term of three years, and may be reappointed to three successive full terms. A vacancy occurring during a term shall be filled for the unexpired portion thereof. The Supreme Court shall designate one of the members of the Board as its Chair and shall appoint a secretary to the Board who shall not be a member.

Note: Source—R.R. 1:19–1(a) (b) (e). Amended July 7, 1971, to be effective September 13, 1971; amended October 1, 1992, to be effective January 1, 1993; amended July 5, 2000 to be effective September 5, 2000.

1:23–2. Duties; Procedure

Subject to the approval of the Supreme Court, the Board shall prepare and conduct examinations for

1:22–7. Immunity From Suit

(a) The members and staff of the committee shall be absolutely immune from suit, whether legal or equitable in nature, for any conduct in the performance of their official duties.

(b) Persons who bring allegations concerning any individual or entity to the committee shall be immune from suit, whether legal or equitable in nature, for all communications to the committee or to its staff. This immunity shall not extend to any other publication or communication of such information.

Note: Adopted June 29, 1990 to be effective September 4, 1990; R. 1:22–11 amended and redesignated as R. 1:22–7 June 28, 1996 to be effective September 1, 1996.

1:22–8. Subpoena: Authority of Committee; Service [Deleted]

Note: Source—R.R. 1:12A–8; caption and text of rule deleted, and new caption and paragraphs (a) (b) and (c) adopted June 29, 1990 to be effective September 4, 1990; deleted June 28, 1996 to be effective September 1, 1996.

1:22–9. Prosecution of Disorderly Persons Offense [Deleted]

Note: Source—R.R. 1:12A–9; caption and text of rule deleted, and new caption and text adopted June 29, 1990 to be effective September 4, 1990; deleted June 28, 1996 to be effective September 1, 1996.

1:22–10. Legal Assistance [Deleted]

Note: Adopted June 29, 1990 to be effective September 4, 1990; deleted June 28, 1996 to be effective September 1, 1996.

applicants for admission as attorneys, prescribe rules, forms and procedures relating thereto and state the topics upon which applicants will be examined.

Note: Source—R.R. 1:19–1(c) (d).

1:23–3. Confidentiality; Immunity

(a) The files and records maintained by the Board of Bar Examiners and the Committee on Character shall be confidential, subject to the rules and regulations of the Board and the Committee and unless otherwise ordered by the Supreme Court.

(b) Members of the Board of Bar Examiners, the Committee on Character, and their lawfully appointed designees and staff shall be absolutely immune from suit, whether legal or equitable in nature, based on their respective conduct in performing their official duties. The Supreme Court shall request the Attorney General to represent bar admission authorities in all civil or criminal litigation in state or federal courts.

Note: Adopted November 7, 1988 to be effective January 2, 1989; title amended, former text amended and designated as paragraph (a), and new paragraph (b) added July 10, 1998 to be effective September 1, 1998.

1:23–4. Funds

The operations of the Board of Bar Examiners and the committee on character shall be supported by the fees paid by candidates for admission to the bar, as set forth in rules and regulations approved by the Supreme Court. To the extent that the Board of Bar Examiners and committee on character are not self-supporting, funds necessary for their operation shall be provided by the Administrative Office of the Courts.

Note: Adopted March 15, 1989, to be effective immediately.

1:23–5. Bar Examination Test– Taking Improprieties

(a) All allegations of impropriety in the taking of a bar examination by a bar applicant who has not been admitted to practice law in this state shall be investigated and prosecuted by the Director, Office of Attorney Ethics in accordance with the applicable provisions of R. 1:20–1 et. seq., except that:

(1) the burden of proving the charges shall be by a preponderance of the credible evidence;

(2) the Supreme Court shall appoint a special master to make findings of fact and recommended conclusions;

(3) the special master's report shall be forwarded to the Board of Bar Examiners for appellate review on the record, including oral argument, before a three-member panel of the Board appointed by the Chair;

(4) the decision of the Board of Bar Examiners shall be submitted to the Supreme Court for such final action as it deems appropriate, including oral argument if directed by the Court; and

(5) issues of confidentiality, access to and dissemination of information in these cases shall be governed by R. 1:20–9.

(b) If such allegations of impropriety arise after the bar applicant has been admitted to the bar of this state, the matter shall proceed as any other attorney disciplinary matter in accordance with R. 1:20–1 et. seq.

Note: Adopted July 28, 2004 to be effective September 1, 2004.

RULE 1:24. BAR EXAMINATIONS; QUALIFICATIONS FOR ADMISSION TO EXAMINATION

1:24–1. Bar Examinations

(a) **Time and Place.** Two examinations shall be held annually at such times and places and of such duration as the Board shall determine, subject to the approval of the Supreme Court.

(b) **Application; Fee; Fingerprints.** Each applicant shall give written notice to the Board of the applicant's intention to sit for a bar examination. The Board shall, subject to the approval of the Supreme Court, establish deadlines for the filing of notices of intention and all application materials. Each applicant shall be fingerprinted prior to taking the examination in accordance with rules prescribed by the Board and shall pay the required fees established by the Board, with the approval of the Supreme Court, to the secretary.

Note: Source—R.R. 1:19–2(a) (c), 1:19–4. Paragraph (b) amended April 2, 1973 to be effective immediately; paragraph (c) adopted July 24, 1978 to be effective September 11, 1978; paragraphs (b) and (c) amended October 18, 1979 to be effective immediately; paragraph (c) deleted September 21, 1981 to be effective immediately; paragraph (b) caption and text amended November 7, 1988 to be effective January 2, 1989; paragraph (b) amended March 15, 1989, to be effective immediately.

1:24–2. Qualification for Admission to Examination

No person shall be admitted to the bar examination without first presenting to the Board, in the manner prescribed by its rules:

(a) Satisfactory evidence that the applicant is more than 18 years of age;

(b) Certification by a duly authorized officer of the applicant's law school that it is approved by the American Bar Association and that it has awarded the applicant a Juris Doctor degree or its equivalent.

(c) Satisfactory evidence that the applicant is a member of the bar in good standing in every other jurisdiction which has ever admitted the applicant to practice.

Note: Source—R.R. 1:20–1, 1:20–1A, 1:20–2(a), 1:20–3, 1:20–4, 1:22–2. Paragraph (b) amended and paragraph (e) adopted April 2, 1973 to be effective immediately; paragraph (a) amended September 19, 1973 to be effective immediately; former paragraph (b) deleted, former paragraphs (c), (d) and (e) redesignated (b), (c) and (d) and paragraph (d) amended July 24, 1978 to be effective September 11, 1978; paragraph (d) deleted September 21, 1981 to be effective immediately; (d) deleted September 21, 1981 to be effective immediately; introductory paragraph and paragraphs (a), (b) and (c) amended July 13, 1994; paragraph (b) amended July 10, 1998 to be effective September 1, 1998.

RULE 1:25. COMMITTEE ON CHARACTER

The Supreme Court shall appoint a committee on character comprised of such number of attorneys as it may determine. It shall be the duty of the committee on character to determine the fitness to practice law of each candidate for admission to the bar of the State of New Jersey on the basis of and by reviewing the personal record and reputation of each candidate and, following such review, to certify as to such fitness to the Supreme Court or withhold such certification. Subject

to the approval of the Supreme Court, the committee shall prescribe such rules governing its procedures as may be deemed necessary and desirable.

Note: Source—R.R. 1:20–6. R. 1:25–1, 1:25–2, 1:25–3 and 1:25–4 deleted and R. 1:25 adopted July 7, 1971 to be effective September 13, 1971. R. 1:25 amended April 2, 1973 to be effective immediately; caption and text amended November 7, 1988 to be effective January 2, 1989.

RULE 1:26. SKILLS AND METHODS COURSE [DELETED]

Note: Source—R.R. 1:20–7A(a), (b). Paragraph (b) adopted April 2, 1973 to be effective immediately. Paragraph (a) amended and paragraph (b) deleted September 13, 1976 to be effective September 13, 1976; paragraph (a) deleted and new rule adopted November 5, 1986 to be effective January 1, 1987. Deleted December 18, 2009 to be effective immediately.

RULE 1:27. ADMISSION TO PRACTICE

1:27–1. Plenary Admission

(a) Qualification for Licensure. No person shall be admitted to the bar of this State unless the following shall first have successfully occurred in a manner prescribed by the rules of the Board of Bar Examiners:

(1) Passage of the bar examination;

(2) Certification of good character by the Committee on Character pursuant to R. 1:25 and the regulations of that body; and

(3) Attainment of a qualifying score on the Multi-State Professional Responsibility Examination or passage of an approved course on professional ethics given by an American Bar Association-accredited law school.

(b) Report to Supreme Court. The Board of Bar Examiners shall report to the Supreme Court the names of those applicants whose qualifications accord with these Rules. The Supreme Court may then authorize the administration of the oaths prescribed by Rule 1:27–4 in such manner as the Court shall deem appropriate.

(c) Roll of Attorneys; Oath Card. Within thirty days of taking the attorney's oath, attorneys must file the completed Roll of Attorneys oath card with the Clerk of the Supreme Court. If the oath card is not properly filed within that period, the attorney's admission shall not be effective. Subject to paragraph (d) of this Rule, an attorney who has not timely filed an oath card must re-take the oath of admission and complete a new card. Except by leave of the Supreme Court, the date of admission to the bar of such an attorney shall not relate back to the original administration of the oaths.

(d) Time limit on admission. Admission to practice must occur no more than ninety days after the date the candidate has become eligible for the administration of the attorney's oaths.

(e) Registration Statement. Failure to file the registration statement required by Rule 1:20–1(c) within thirty days of its receipt shall cause the name of the delinquent attorney to be included in an Order of the Supreme Court declaring him or her ineligible to practice law until such statement is filed.

Note: Source—R.R. 1:22–1(a) (b); paragraph (b) amended July 29, 1977 to be effective September 6, 1977; paragraph (a) amended and paragraph (d) adopted July 24, 1978 to be effective September 11, 1978; caption amended and paragraph (d) deleted September 21, 1981 to be effective immediately; caption amended and new paragraph (a) adopted, former paragraph (a) amended and redesignated (b) and former paragraphs (b) and (c) deleted September 21, 1981 to be effective February 1, 1982; paragraph (b) amended January 31, 1984 to be effective February 15, 1984; paragraph (b) amended July 26, 1984 to be effective September 10, 1984; paragraph (a)(4) deleted November 5, 1986 to be effective January 1, 1987; paragraph (b) caption and text amended and last sentence redesignated paragraph (c) and caption adopted November 7, 1988 to be effective January 2, 1989; paragraph (b) amended and redesignated as paragraphs (b) and (d), former paragraph (c) amended and redesignated as paragraph (e), and new paragraph (c) adopted July 10, 1998 to be effective September 1, 1998; paragraph (d) amended July 5, 2000 to be effective September 5, 2000; paragraph (b) amended November 8, 2004 to be effective immediately.

1:27–2. Limited License; In–House Counsel

To be eligible to practice law in New Jersey as an in-house counsel, a lawyer must comply with the provisions of this Rule. A limited license issued by the Supreme Court pursuant to this Rule shall authorize the lawyer to practice solely for the designated employer in New Jersey or eligible constituents of the designated employer as set forth in subparagraph (b)(iii) of this rule. Except as specifically limited herein, the rules, rights and privileges governing the practice of law in this State shall be applicable to a lawyer admitted under this Rule.

(a) In–House Counsel Defined. In–House Counsel is a lawyer who is employed in New Jersey for a corporation, a partnership, association, or other legal entity (taken together with its respective parents, subsidiaries, and affiliates) authorized to transact business in this State that is not itself engaged in the practice of law or the rendering of legal services outside such organization, whether for a fee or otherwise, and does not charge or collect a fee for the representation or advice other than to entities comprising such organization.

(b) Requirements. All applications under this Rule are to be submitted to the Secretary to the Board of Bar Examiners. An in-house counsel who is admitted to practice law before the highest court of any other state, territory of the United States, Puerto Rico, or the District of Columbia (hereinafter a United States jurisdiction) may receive a limited license to practice law in this State under the following conditions:

(i) The applicant certifies that he or she is a member in good standing of the bar of the highest court of each United States jurisdiction in which the applicant is licensed to practice law and provides a certificate of good standing from each United States jurisdiction in which the applicant is admitted;

(ii) The applicant certifies that: (a) no disciplinary proceedings are pending against the applicant and that no discipline has previously been imposed on the applicant in any jurisdiction; or (b) if discipline has been previously imposed, the certification shall state the date, jurisdiction, nature of the violation, and the sanction imposed. If proceedings are pending, the certification shall specify the jurisdiction, the charges, and the likely time of their disposition. A lawyer admitted under this Rule shall have the continuing obligation during the period of such admission promptly to inform the Director of the Office of Attorney Ethics pursuant to Rule 1:20–14(a) of a disposition made of disciplinary proceedings. Any questions concerning the character or fitness of a lawyer may be referred to the Supreme Court Committee on Character for review and recommendation (Rule 1:25). The submission of an application for an In–House Limited License shall be a consent to such investigation as the Committee on Character deems appropriate;

(iii) The applicant certifies that he or she performs legal services in this State solely for the identified employer, or that he or she performs legal services in this State solely for the identified employer and its constituents (employees, directors, officers, members, partners, shareholders) in respect of the same proceeding or claim as the employer, provided that the performance of such services is consistent with RPC 1.13 and RPC 1.7; and

(iv) The employer certifies through an officer, director or general counsel that the applicant is employed as a lawyer for said employer, that the applicant is of good moral character, and that the nature of the employment conforms to the requirements of this Rule.

(c) Compliance. A lawyer admitted pursuant to this Rule shall comply with the annual assessments pursuant to R. 1:20–1(b) (Disciplinary Oversight Committee), R. 1:28–2 (New Jersey Lawyers' Fund for Client Protection), and R.1:28B–1(e) (Lawyers Assistance Program).

(d) Limitation. In–house counsel shall not appear as Attorney of Record for his or her employer, its parent, subsidiary, affiliated entities or any of their constituents in any case or matter pending before the courts of this State, except pursuant to R. 1:21–1(c) and R. 1:21–2.

(e) Duration. The limited license to practice law in this State shall expire if such lawyer is admitted to the Bar of this State under any other rule of this Court, or if such lawyer ceases to be an employee for the employer or its parent, subsidiary, or affiliated entities, listed on such lawyer's application, whichever shall first occur; provided, however, that if such lawyer, within ninety days of ceasing to be an employee for the employer or its parent, subsidiary, or affiliated entities listed on such lawyer's application, becomes employed by another employer for which such lawyer shall perform legal services as in-house counsel, such lawyer may maintain his or her admission under this Rule by promptly filing with the Secretary to the Board of Bar Examiners a certification to such effect, stating the date on which his or her prior employment ceased and his/her new employment commenced, identifying his or her new employer and reaffirming that he or she shall not provide legal services, in this State, to any individual or entity other than as described in (b)(iii). The lawyer shall also file a certification of the new employer as described in (b)(iv). In the event that the employment of a lawyer admitted under this Rule shall cease with no subsequent employment by a successor employer within ninety days, such lawyer shall promptly file with the Secretary to the Board of Bar Examiners a statement to such effect, stating the date that such employment ceased.

(f) Fee. Each applicant for a limited license shall pay the required fees as established by the Board of Bar Examiners and approved by the Supreme Court.

Note: New R. 1:27–2 adopted November 17, 2003 to be effective January 1, 2004; paragraph (e) amended November 29, 2006 to be effective immediately; first paragraph and subparagraph (b)(iii) and paragraphs (d) and (e) amended July 9, 2008 to be effective September 1, 2008.

1:27–3. Admission of Law School Teachers

An applicant for admission who has been engaged full time in the teaching of law at an approved law school in the State for 5 years immediately preceding the application may be admitted as an attorney of this State, without examination or completion of a skills and methods course, provided the applicant has been admitted, after examination, as an attorney of another state whose educational qualifications for admission to the bar are equal to those of this State. In determining the 5 year period the Supreme Court may grant credit for time spent on leave of absence from such law school. The application shall be made to the Board of Bar Examiners, in accordance with its rules, and the Board shall expeditiously investigate the application and file its report and recommendations thereon to the Supreme Court for appropriate action by it.

Note: Source—R.R. 1:20–2(b), adopted as R. 1:27–2; amended July 29, 1977 to be effective September 6, 1977; amended November 7, 1988 to be effective January 2, 1989; renumbered as R. 1:27–3 November 17, 2003 to be effective January 1, 2004.

1:27–4. Oath or Affirmation on Admission

No person shall be admitted as an attorney of this State without first taking the oath to support the Constitution of the United States and the Constitution of New Jersey, the oath of allegiance to this State, and the oath of office as an attorney. An affirmation may be given in lieu of oath.

Note: Source—R.R. 1:22–3; adopted as R. 1:27–3; amended July 13, 1994 to be effective September 1, 1994; renumbered as R. 1:27–4 November 17, 2003 to be effective January 1, 2004.

RULE 1:27A. ADVISORY COMMITTEE ON BAR ADMISSIONS

1:27A–1. Establishment of Committee; Duties

There is hereby established an Advisory Committee on Bar Admissions. It shall be the duty of this Committee to consider issues related to legal education, eligibility and admission to the bar and report its conclusions and recommendations to the Supreme Court.

Note: Adopted September 21, 1981 to be effective immediately.

1:27A–2. Committee Membership

The Committee shall be comprised of the following ex officio members in addition to such other members as the Court shall appoint for a term of years: the Board of Bar Examiners; the deans of the American Bar Association-approved law schools located in New Jersey; the Chair of the Supreme Court Committee on Character; the President of the New Jersey State Bar Association; the President of the Garden State Bar Association; and the Director of Legal Services of New Jersey. The Chair shall be so designated by the Supreme Court annually.

Note: Adopted September 21, 1981 to be effective immediately; amended June 28, 1996 to be effective September 1, 1996.

RULE 1:27B. BAR ADMISSIONS FINANCIAL COMMITTEE

1:27B–1. Bar Admissions Financial Committee

The Supreme Court shall establish a Bar Admissions Financial Committee (hereinafter referred to as the Financial Committee) to assist it in administering the financial aspects of the attorney admission system.

Note: Adopted March 15, 1989, to be effective immediately.

1:27B–2. Appointment

The Supreme Court shall appoint the members of the Financial Committee. The membership shall include the Chief Justice of the Supreme Court, the Administrative Director of the Courts, the Chair of the Board of Bar Examiners, the Statewide Chair of the Committee on Character, the Chair of the Advisory Committee on Bar Admissions, and the President of the New Jersey State Bar Association, or a designee of such members, each of whom shall serve without specified term at the pleasure of the Supreme Court.

Note: Adopted March 15, 1989, to be effective immediately.

1:27B–3. Organization; Officers; Quorum; Meetings

The Financial Committee shall organize annually and shall elect from among its members a Chair and a Treasurer. The Administrative Director of the Courts shall designate a staff member with fiscal responsibilities to serve as Assistant Treasurer. The Secretary to the Board of Bar Examiners shall provide appropriate assistance to the Financial Committee in furtherance of its designated responsibilities.

Meetings shall be held at the call of the Chair. Four voting members shall constitute a quorum for the transaction of business.

Note: Adopted March 15, 1989, to be effective immediately; amended July 13, 1994 to be effective September 1, 1994.

1:27B–4. Powers

The Financial Committee shall have the following general powers:

(a) to receive annually from the Secretary a budget for the attorney admission system of the state; to review the same and to recommend to the Supreme Court a proposed budget subject to public comment thereon;

(b) to receive, hold, manage, distribute, and invest the funds it may receive, all in accordance with these rules and policies approved by the Supreme Court;

(c) to establish necessary bank accounts and approve and monitor expenditures based on the budget annually adopted by the Supreme Court.

Note: Adopted March 15, 1989, to be effective immediately.

RULE 1:28. NEW JERSEY LAWYERS' FUND FOR CLIENT PROTECTION

1:28–1. Purpose; Administration; Appointments

(a) Administration. The Supreme Court shall appoint seven trustees to administer and operate, in accordance with these rules, the New Jersey Lawyers' Fund for Client Protection, whose purpose is the reimbursement, to the extent and in the manner provided by these rules, of losses caused by the dishonest conduct of members of the bar of this State.

(b) Qualification, Terms of Trustees. The original appointment shall be of one trustee for a one-year term, one for a 2-year term, one for a 3-year term, one for a 4-year term and one for a 5-year term. At the expiration of such terms all subsequent appointments shall be for a term of 5 years, and no trustee who has served a full 5-year term shall be eligible for immediate reappointment. A vacancy occurring during a term shall be filled for the unexpired portion thereof. Five trustees shall be members of the bar of this State; and two members shall not be an attorneys.

(c) Organization; Meetings. The trustees shall organize annually and shall then elect from among their number a chair and a treasurer to serve for a one-year term and such other officers for such terms as they deem necessary or appropriate. Meetings thereafter shall be held at the call of the chair. Four trustees shall constitute a quorum and may transact all business except as may be otherwise provided by this rule or by the rules and regulations promulgated by the trustees.

(d) Regulations. The trustees shall adopt rules and regulations, consistent with these rules and subject to the approval of the Supreme Court, governing the administration of the Fund, the procedures for the presentation, consideration and payment of claims, and the exercise of their investment powers.

(e) Reimbursement. The trustees shall serve without compensation but shall be entitled to reimbursement from the Fund for their expenses reasonably incurred in the performance of their duties.

(f) Immunity. The Board of Trustees, Director and Counsel, Deputy Counsel, Secretary and all staff personnel shall be absolutely immune from suit, whether legal or equitable in nature, for any conduct in the performance of their official duties.

Note: Source—R.R. 1:22A–1(a) (b) (c) (d) (e); paragraphs (a) (b), and (c) amended and paragraph (f) adopted June 29, 1990 to be effective September 4, 1990; paragraph (a) amended July 14, 1992 to be effective September 1, 1992; paragraphs (a) and (b) amended May 3, 1994 to be effective immediately; paragraph (c) amended June 28, 1996 to be effective September 1, 1996.

1:28–2. Payment to the Fund; Enforcement

(a) Generally. Except as hereinafter provided, each holder of a plenary license to practice law in the State of New Jersey shall pay annually to the treasurer of the Fund a sum that shall be determined each year by the Supreme Court. An attorney who makes payment after February 1 of the billing year, or such other date as the Court may determine, but before being placed on the Ineligible List shall be subject to a late fee as set forth in Rule 1:20–1(d), which shall be shared equally with the Disciplinary Oversight Committee. The treasurer shall annually report the names of all attorneys failing to comply with the provisions of this Rule to the Supreme Court for inclusion on the list of those attorneys deemed ineligible to practice law in New Jersey by order of the Court. An attorney shall be reinstated automatically to the practice of law without further order of the Court on filing with the Fund the annual registration statement for the current year together with the annual payment, the late fee, any arrears due from prior years, and a reinstatement fee of $50 if the attorney's name is being removed from one calendar year's Ineligible List or $100 if the attorney's name is being removed from two or more calendar year's Lists.

All persons admitted pro hac vice in accordance with Rule 1:21–2, those holding limited licenses as in-house counsel under R. 1:27–2, those registered as multijurisdictional practitioners under RPC 5.5(b), and those certified as Foreign Legal Consultants under R. 1:21–9, shall also make the same annual payment described above subject to the same late fees and reinstatement from ineligible list fees. However, such persons shall not be entitled to the exemptions provided hereinafter.

For the purpose of annual assessment all members of the Bar, including those admitted pro hac vice, those holding limited licenses as in-house counsel, those registered as multijurisdictional practitioners, and those certified as Foreign Legal Consultants, shall report changes of address as they occur and thus keep their billing address current with the Fund at all times.

Any member of the Bar who receives a billing notice addressed to another member of the Bar shall either forward the notice to the intended recipient or return it to the Fund.

(b) Exceptions. The following categories of plenary license holders shall be exempt from payment to the Fund:

(1) Newly admitted attorneys, for the balance of the calendar year of their plenary admission and for the next succeeding calendar year;

(2) Attorneys who have been admitted to practice for fifty years or more;

(3) Attorneys on full-time active duty with the armed forces, VISTA, or the Peace Corps and not engaging in any way in private practice, but they shall be considered in all respects inactive New Jersey attorneys; and

(4) Attorneys who have retired completely from the practice of law, but they shall be considered in all respects inactive New Jersey attorneys.

(c) License Revocation for Repeated Non–Compliance. Any attorney who, at the time of the publication of the Fund's Ineligible Attorneys List for 2005 and thereafter, has been declared ineligible for seven or more consecutive years shall have his or her license to practice in this State administratively revoked by Order of the Supreme Court.

On the entry of a license revocation Order pursuant to this Rule, the attorney's membership in the Bar of this State shall cease. Any subsequent application for membership shall be in accordance with the provisions of Rule 1:24. An Order of revocation shall not, however, preclude the exercise of jurisdiction by the disciplinary system in respect of any misconduct that occurred prior to Order's effective date.

Note: Source—R.R. 1:22A–2; amended July 17, 1975 to be effective September 8, 1975; amended January 31, 1984 to be effective February 15, 1984; amended June 29, 1990 to be effective September 4, 1990; redesignated paragraph (a) amended and paragraph (b) adopted July 14, 1992 to be effective September 1, 1992; paragraphs (a) and (b) amended February 8, 1993, to be effective immediately; paragraph (a) amended and new paragraph (c) added July 28, 2004 to be effective September 1, 2004.

1:28–3. Payment of Claims

(a) Eligible Claims. The Trustees may consider for payment all claims resulting from the dishonest conduct of a member of the bar of this state or an attorney admitted pro hac vice acting either as an attorney or fiduciary, provided that:

(1) Said conduct was engaged in while the attorney was a practicing member of the Bar of this State or admitted Pro Hac Vice in a matter pending in this State;

(2) On or after January 1, 1969, the attorney has been suspended, disbarred or placed in disability inactive status, has resigned with prejudice or has pleaded guilty to, or been convicted of embezzlement or misappropriation of money or other property; or an ethics committee has certified a claim to the trustees as an appropriate matter for their consideration. Where an ethics committee does not act and an attorney cannot be located, is deceased or incapacitated, the trustees may consider timely application directly provided that the trustees find that the claim is an appropriate matter for their consideration;

(3) The claim is filed within one year of the earliest of an event set forth in subparagraph (2) above. The time limitation set forth in this subparagraph may be extended by the trustees in their discretion;

(4) The claim is made directly by or on behalf of the injured client or the client's personal representative or, if a corporation, by or on behalf of itself or its successors in interest; and

(5) The claimant certifies that the relevant facts have been fully disclosed in writing to the appropriate law enforcement and disciplinary authorities. A willfully false certification in this regard shall be an absolute bar to any award.

(b) Consideration of Claims. The trustees in their sole discretion but on the affirmative vote of 4 of them shall determine which eligible claims merit reimbursement from the Fund and the amount, time, manner, conditions and order of payment of reimbursement. In making such determinations the trustees shall consider, among other appropriate factors, the following:

(1) The amounts available and likely to become available to the Fund for the payment of claims and the size and number of claims which are likely to be presented;

(2) The amount of the claimant's loss as compared with the amount of losses sustained by other eligible claimants;

(3) The degree of hardship suffered by the claimant as a result of the loss;

(4) The degree of negligence, if any, of the claimant which may have contributed to the loss;

(5) The potential for recovery from a collateral source.

(c) Limitation on Payments. The trustees shall, by regulation, fix the maximum amount which any one claimant may recover from the Fund and the aggregate maximum amount which may be recovered because of the dishonest conduct of any one attorney.

(d) Rights to Fund. No claimant or any other person or organization shall have any right in the Fund as beneficiary or otherwise.

(e) Conditions of Payment. The trustees may require as a condition to payment that the claimant execute such instruments, take such action or enter into such agreements as the trustees require, including assignments, subrogation agreements, trust agreements, and promises to cooperate with the trustees in making or prosecuting claims or charges against any person.

(f) Attorney's Fee. No attorney representing a claimant shall receive a fee for services unless authorized by the rules and regulations of the trustees and upon their express direction.

Note: Source—R.R. 1:22A–3(a) (b) (c) (d) (e) (f). Paragraph (a)(2) amended June 24, 1974 to be effective immediately; paragraph (a) amended and paragraph (a)(5) adopted January 31, 1984 to be effective February 15, 1984; paragraph (a)(1), (2), and (5) amended, former paragraph (a)(4) deleted, paragraph (a)(3) redesignated as paragraph (a)(4), new paragraph (a)(3) adopted; paragraph (b) amended and paragraph (b)(5) adopted June 29, 1990 to be effective September 4, 1990; paragraphs (a) and (a)(1) amended July 14, 1992 to be effective September 1, 1992; introductory paragraph and paragraphs (a)(4) and (f) amended July 13, 1994 to be effective September 1, 1994.

1:28–4. Duties of Trustees and Officers

(a) Audit and Report. The Fund shall be audited by state or private auditors annually and at such other times as the Supreme Court shall direct, such audits to be at the expense of the Fund. The annual audit shall be included in a report to be submitted annually by the trustees to the Supreme Court reviewing in detail the administration of the Fund during the preceding year.

(b) Applications to the Supreme Court. The trustees may apply to the Supreme Court for interpretations of these rules and of the extent of their powers thereunder and for advice regarding the proper administration of the Fund.

(c) Treasurer's Duties. The treasurer shall maintain the assets of the Fund in a separate account and shall disburse monies therefrom only upon the action of the trustees pursuant to these rules. Said treasurer shall file a bond annually with the trustees with such surety as may be approved by them and in such amount as they may fix.

Note: Source—R.R.1:22A–4; paragraph (c) amended June 29, 1990 to be effective September 4, 1990.

1:28–5. General Powers of Trustees

In addition to the powers conferred by these rules upon the trustees, they shall have the following general powers:

(a) to receive, hold, manage, distribute and invest the funds received by the Fund pursuant to R. 1:28–2 and such other funds as it may receive by voluntary contribution or otherwise;

(b) to enforce claims which the Fund may have for reimbursements, including utilization of the Comprehensive Enforcement Program;   pursuant to N.J.S.A. 22A:2–23, the Fund shall not be liable for the payment of any fee provided for by N.J.S.A. 22A:2–1 et seq.;

(c) to employ and compensate consultants, agents, legal counsel and such other employees as they deem necessary and appropriate consistent with personnel policies of the judiciary.

Note: Source—R.R. 1:22A–5, amended January 31, 1984 to be effective February 15, 1984; paragraphs (b) and (c) amended June 29, 1990 to be effective September 4, 1990; paragraph (b) amended July 12, 2002 to be effective September 3, 2002.

1:28–6. Subpoenas; Notice in Lieu of Subpoena; Noncompliance

(a) Issuance; Service. The trustees or an individual trustee or the Director or an attorney designated to act on behalf of the trustees, upon determining that any person has knowledge or is in possession or custody of books, papers, documents or other objects relevant to the disposition of a claim, may issue a subpoena or a notice in lieu of subpoena in the name of the Clerk of the Superior Court requiring such person to appear and testify or to produce such books, papers, documents or other objects before the trustees or an individual trustee, or the Director or an attorney designated to act on behalf of the trustees, at the time and place specified therein.

Subpoenas and notices in lieu of subpoena shall be served in the manner prescribed by R. 1:9, except that subpoenas may be served upon an attorney who is a witness or a party, by certified mail, return receipt requested and simultaneously by first class mail. No attendance fee need be paid.

(b) Noncompliance. If any person, without adequate excuse, shall fail to obey a subpoena, the trustees, or an individual trustee or an attorney designated to act on their behalf, may file with the Superior Court a verified statement setting forth the facts establishing such disobedience, and the court may then, in its discretion, institute contempt proceedings pursuant to R. 1:10–2. If such person is found guilty of contempt, the court may compel payment of the costs of the contempt proceedings to be taxed by the court.

Note: Adopted July 14, 1972 to be effective September 5, 1972; caption and paragraph (a) amended June 29, 1990 to be effective September 4, 1990; paragraph (b) amended July 13, 1994 to be effective September 1, 1994.

1:28–7. Administration

The Administrative Office of the Courts shall provide supporting services as requested by the Board of

Trustees. Trustees, from funds available, shall reimburse the Administrative Office of the Courts for the salaries and benefits of Fund staff and for other expenses which may be incurred on the behalf of the Fund.

Note: Adopted June 29, 1973 to be effective September 10, 1973; amended June 29, 1990 to be effective September 4, 1990.

1:28–8. Custodial Receivers

Upon approval of the Board of Trustees pursuant to R. 1:28–1(c), the Director or an attorney designated to act on behalf of the Trustees may, upon the occasions set forth below, make application to an appropriate court for the appointment of a custodial receiver to take possession of the property of an attorney, including, but not limited to, property incident to the attorney's law practice. Provided the Trustees first find a reasonable probability that a claim or claims will be presented to the Fund on account of the alleged misconduct of the attorney, such application may be made in any of the following instances:

(a) Where an attorney has been disbarred or suspended by the Supreme Court, or where the attorney's resignation has been accepted by it, with prejudice.

(b) Where the Trustees have received notice that a presentment has been or is about to be submitted against an attorney by a county ethics committee.

(c) Where the Trustees have received notice that a criminal charge, whether by way of indictment or otherwise, has been or is about to be laid against an attorney.

(d) Where an attorney shall admit the existence of defalcations with respect to clients' property, for which defalcations the attorney's misconduct shall have been responsible.

(e) Where credible evidence of such misconduct reaches the Trustees otherwise than as set forth above.

Note: Adopted May 8, 1975, effective immediately; first paragraph amended and last paragraph deleted June 29, 1990 to be effective September 4, 1990; introductory paragraph and paragraphs (a) and (d) amended July 13, 1994 to be effective September 1, 1994.

1:28–9. Confidentiality

(a) All proceedings conducted and records made or maintained by the Fund in connection with the filing or consideration of claims shall be confidential and shall not be disclosed except as follows:

(1) Once a claim has been approved for payment, the Fund may, upon written request, make available the following information:

(a) name and address according to Fund records of the respondent attorney;

(b) name and city of residence of the claimant;

(c) the amount claimed;

(d) the amount awarded; and

(e) a summary of the factual basis for the claim.

(2) Nothing herein shall preclude the release of information to the respondent and claimant or their attorneys or to the authorities specified in R. 1:28–3(a)(5), nor shall it preclude use of such information by the Fund pursuant to its rights under R. 1:28–3(e).

(3) Nothing herein shall preclude the inclusion of statistical information regarding claims in the annual report prepared pursuant to R. 1:28–4(a).

(b) Information received and maintained by the Fund in connection with the annual billing and registration of attorneys pursuant to R. 1:28–2 shall be made available to the Supreme Court and the Administrative Office of the Courts upon request and may be made available to the public in accordance with such policies as the Trustees may adopt subject to approval of the Supreme Court. Copies of such records, including computer generated information, may be made available upon written request and upon such terms and conditions as the Trustees and the Supreme Court may in their discretion direct.

Note: Adopted June 29, 1990 to be effective September 4, 1990.

RULE 1:28A. INTEREST ON LAWYERS TRUST ACCOUNTS (IOLTA) FUND

1:28A–1. Purpose; Administration; Appointments

(a) Administration. The Supreme Court shall appoint six Trustees to administer and operate, in accordance with these Rules, the IOLTA Fund of the Bar of New Jersey, whose purpose is to provide a means of using the return to IOLTA on income earned by depository institutions from funds held in IOLTA accounts to fund law-related, public-interest programs. In addition to the Trustees appointed by the Supreme Court, the following shall be ex officio members and will

have the right to vote on all matters except grant applications made to the Board of Trustees, but they may participate in Board discussions of the grant applications: the President of the New Jersey State Bar Association; the First Vice President of the New Jersey State Bar Foundation; and the President of Legal Services of New Jersey, Inc.

(b) Qualification, Terms of Trustees. The original appointment shall be of two Trustees for a one-year term, one for a two-year term, one for a three-year term, one for a four-year term and one for a five-year term. At the expiration of such terms all subsequent appointments shall be for a term of five years, and no Trustee who has served a full five-year term shall be eligible for immediate reappointment. A vacancy occurring during a term shall be filled for the unexpired portion thereof. At least four of the Trustees appointed by the Supreme Court shall be members of the bar of this State.

(c) Organization; Meetings. The Trustees shall organize annually and shall then elect from among their number a chairperson and a treasurer to serve for a one-year term and such other officers for such terms as they deem necessary or appropriate. Meetings thereafter shall be held at the call of the chairperson. Except as may be otherwise provided by this rule or by regulations promulgated by the Trustees, five of the nine trustees, including the ex officio members, shall constitute a quorum and may transact all business not involving grants. Four of the six Trustees appointed by the Supreme Court shall constitute a quorum for all decisions concerning grants.

(d) Regulations. The Trustees shall adopt regulations, consistent with these rules and subject to the approval of the Supreme Court, governing the administration of the Fund, the procedures for the presentation, consideration, and payment of grants, and the exercise of their investment powers.

(e) Reimbursement. The Trustees shall serve without compensation.

Note: Adopted February 23, 1988, to be effective March 1, 1988; paragraphs (a), (b), (c) and (d) amended September 15, 1992, to be effective January 1, 1993; paragraph (a) amended July 10, 1998, to be effective September 1, 1998; caption of Rule 1:28A and paragraphs (a) and (b) of Rule 1:28A–1 amended February 6, 2003 to be effective March 1, 2003.

1:28A–2. Attorney IOLTA Trust Accounts

(a) Attorney Participation. Commencing on the date established by regulations to be adopted by the Board of Trustees pursuant to Rule 1:28A–1(d), every attorney who practices in this State shall maintain in a financial institution in New Jersey, in the attorney's own name or in the name of a partnership of attorneys, or in the name of the professional corporation or limited liability entity of which the attorney is a member, or in the name of the attorney or partnership of attorneys by whom employed, an IOLTA non-interest-bearing trust account or accounts for all clients' funds that are not placed at interest for the benefit of the client.

(1) The IOLTA non-interest-bearing trust account may be established with any financial institution approved by the Supreme Court to hold attorney trust funds under R. 1:21–6(a) and insured by the Federal Deposit Insurance Corporation or an analogous federal government agency. Funds in each IOLTA non-interest-bearing trust account will be subject to withdrawal on request and without delay.

(2) Funds shall be deposited in an IOLTA non-interest-bearing trust account authorized by this Rule when an attorney determines that a trust account deposit will not be placed at interest for a client. Such a determination shall be made whenever an attorney determines that either (A) the amount of the funds or the period of time that the funds are held, if deposited in an interest-bearing account, would not earn interest in excess of the cost incurred to secure such interest, or (B) because of particular costs in accounting, administration, or attribution of income, as may occur when multiple parties or clients pool advance payments against the costs of litigation in a single fund, a client's funds should not be deposited in an interest-bearing account because they will not realize income. No ethical impropriety will attend an attorney's depositing such funds in an IOLTA non-interest-bearing trust account in accordance with this Rule.

(3) An attorney or law firm shall maintain one or more IOLTA non-interest-bearing trust accounts and shall submit to the approved financial institutions in which such accounts are maintained such forms as may be necessary to establish and maintain such accounts, on forms prescribed by the Trustees, and provide a copy of such form to the IOLTA Fund Trustees. If such a form is not filed, the signed registration statement required by Rule 1:20–1 and Rule 1:21–6 shall constitute such authorization.

(b) Deposit of Funds in IOLTA Account. An attorney will exercise good-faith judgment in determining initially whether the funds of a client are of a nominal amount, are expected to be held by the attorney for a short period of time, or otherwise fall within the circumstances described in (a) above.

In exercising that judgment, the attorney will also consider such other factors as:

(1) the cost of establishing and maintaining a separate non-IOLTA, interest-bearing trust account, including service charges, bookkeeping and accounting and tax-reporting procedures;

(2) the nature of the transaction(s) involved;

(3) the likelihood of delay in the matter for which the funds are held;

(4) whether the funds received by an attorney in a fiduciary capacity from a client or beneficial owner will generate less than $150 of interest, provided that that $150 figure may be used by an attorney as a minimum threshold indicating whether monies received in a fiduciary capacity should be placed in an IOLTA trust account, but shall not preclude the use of a higher figure if the costs or circumstances warrant; and

(5) the other circumstances described in (a) above.

(c) Periodic Review of Deposits. At reasonable intervals, an attorney should consider whether changed circumstances require different action respecting the deposit of client funds.

(d) Registration; Enforcement. The accounts required by this Rule shall be registered annually with the IOLTA Fund in the manner prescribed by the IOLTA Fund Trustees. The Trustees shall annually report the names of all attorneys failing to comply with the provisions of this Rule to the Supreme Court for inclusion on a list of those attorneys deemed ineligible to practice law in New Jersey by Order of the Court. An attorney shall be removed from the Ineligible List without further Order of the Court on submission to the Trustees of the prescribed forms.

(e) Duties of Financial Institution. The financial institution must:

(1) from its income on such IOLTA accounts remit to the Fund the amount remaining after providing such institutions a just and reasonable return equivalent to their return on similar non–IOLTA interest-bearing deposits. These remittances shall be monthly unless otherwise authorized by the Fund. And

(2) report in the form provided by the Fund.

Note: Adopted February 23, 1988, to be effective March 1, 1988; former rule deleted and R. 1:28A–3 renumbered as 1:28A–2 September 15, 1992, to be effective January 1, 1993; paragraph (a)(1) of former R. 1:28A–3 amended November 7, 1988, to be effective January 2, 1989; rule amended September 15, 1992, to be effective January 1, 1993; new paragraph (d) adopted and former paragraph (d) redesignated as paragraph (e) December 13, 1993, to be effective January 3, 1994; paragraph (a) amended July 10, 1998 to be effective September 1, 1998; paragraphs (a) and (e) amended February 6, 2003 to be effective March 1, 2003.

1:28A–3. Duties of Trustees and Officers

(a) Audit and Report. The Trustees shall arrange for an independent audit annually and at such other times as the Supreme Court shall direct, such audits to be at the expense of the Fund. The annual audit shall be included in a report to be submitted annually by the Trustees to the Supreme Court, reviewing in detail the administration of the Fund during the preceding year.

(b) Applications to the Supreme Court. The Trustees may apply to the Supreme Court for interpretations of these Rules and of the extent of their powers thereunder and for advice regarding the proper administration of the Fund.

(c) Treasurer's Duties. The treasurer shall maintain the assets of the Fund in separate accounts and shall disburse monies therefrom only on the action of the Trustees pursuant to these Rules. He or she shall file a bond annually with the Trustees with such surety as may be approved by them and in such amount as they may fix.

Note: Adopted as R. 1:28A-4 February 23, 1988, to be effective March 1, 1988; renumbered as R. 1:28A–3 and paragraphs (b) and (c) amended September 15, 1992, to be effective January 1, 1993.

1:28A–4. General Powers of Trustees

(a) Reserve Fund. The Trustees of the Fund are authorized to maintain a reasonable reserve fund. At least annually, after a reasonable reserve fund has been created, the Trustees will solicit applications for grants and award grants to those entities deemed to be meritorious under the regulations of the Fund. Grant-making decisions of the Board are final and are not subject to appeal or judicial review.

(b) Grants. Grants will be made only for the following purposes:

(1) legal aid to the poor;

(2) improvement of the administration of justice;

(3) education of lay persons in legal and justice-related areas; or

(4) such other programs for the benefit of the public as are specifically approved by the New Jersey Supreme Court from time to time.

(c) Awards. The Board of Trustees shall award:

(1) to Legal Services of New Jersey, Inc., not less than 75% of the funds available annually for grants, to be used directly by itself and, through subgrants, by its local member Legal Services programs, in conducting legal assistance activities on behalf of the poor throughout New Jersey;

(2) to the New Jersey State Bar Foundation, not less than 12.5% of the funds available annually for grants to be used for the purposes enumerated in R. 1:28A–4(b)(1)–(4) above; and

(3) to other entities deemed to be meritorious under the regulations of the Fund, the balance of the funds available annually for grants to be used for the purposes enumerated in R. 1:28A–4(b)(1)–(4) above.

The foregoing may be amended by the Supreme Court from time to time in the public interest.

(d) General Powers. In addition to the powers conferred by these Rules on the Trustees, they shall have the following general powers:

(1) to receive, hold, manage, distribute, and invest the funds received by the Fund and such other funds as it may receive by voluntary contribution or otherwise;

(2) to employ and compensate consultants, agents, legal counsel, and such other employees as they deem necessary and appropriate consistent with personnel policies of the Judiciary; and

(3) to monitor and insure compliance with the provisions of this Rule.

Note: Adopted as R. 1:28A-5 February 23, 1988, to be effective March 1, 1988; renumbered as R. 1:28A–4 and amended September 15, 1992, to be effective January 1, 1993.

1:28A–5. Confidentiality

All activities conducted and records made or maintained by the IOLTA Fund in connection with its operations under this rule shall not be disclosed, except that the IOLTA Board is authorized to:

(a) Release such information as it may deem necessary to carry out its responsibilities as prescribed by this rule, including the identity of recipients and amounts and purposes of grant awards, and data concerning participating financial institutions; and

(b) Release statistical and other information in its annual report to the Supreme Court or as requested by the Supreme Court.

Note: Former Rule 1:28A–5 redesignated as Rule 1:28A–4 September 15, 1992 to be effective January 1, 1993. New Rule 1:28A–5 adopted July 12, 2002 to be effective September 3, 2002.

RULE 1:28B.   NEW JERSEY LAWYERS ASSISTANCE PROGRAM

1:28B–1.   Board of Trustees; Purpose; Administration; Annual Assessment

(a) **Appointments.** A Board of Trustees shall oversee the financial operation and administration of the New Jersey Lawyers Assistance Program (LAP) by the New Jersey State Bar Association (NJSBA). The Supreme Court shall appoint eight of the nine members of the Board. At least five of the Trustees appointed by the Supreme Court shall be members of the bar of this State. The initial Trustees shall be appointed to terms of one, two, or three years. At the expiration of such terms, all subsequent appointments and reappointments shall be for a term of three years. No Trustee who has served four full three-year terms shall be eligible for immediate reappointment. A vacancy occurring during a term shall be filled for the unexpired portion thereof. The Court shall annually designate members of the Board of Trustees to serve as Chair and Vice-Chair.

In addition to the Trustees appointed by the Supreme Court, the President of the New Jersey State Bar Association or a designee shall serve as an *ex officio* member of the Board. The Administrative Director of the Courts, or a designee, shall serve, *ex officio*, as Treasurer of the LAP.

(b) **Purpose; Administration.** The purpose of the New Jersey Lawyers' Assistance Program is to provide assistance to attorneys, full-time members of the State Judiciary, law students, and law school graduates with alcohol, drug, gambling, emotional, behavioral, or other personal problems that affect well-being and professional performance. NJSBA shall operate LAP through a Director and appropriate staff pursuant to a contract with the Judiciary that is subject to the review and approval of the Supreme Court.

(c) **Meetings.** The Board of Trustees shall conduct meetings at the call of the Chair. Except as may be otherwise provided by this Rule or by regulations promulgated by the Trustees, five of the nine Trustees shall constitute a quorum and may transact all business of the Board. In the Chair's absence or inability to serve, the Vice–Chair shall preside.

(d) **Compensation.** The Trustees shall serve without compensation.

(e) **Annual Assessment.** Every attorney admitted to practice law in the State of New Jersey, including those holding a plenary license and those admitted pro hac vice in accordance with Rule 1:21–2, shall be assessed and shall pay annually to the Lawyers Assistance Program a fee in a sum that shall be determined each year by the Supreme Court. All fees so paid shall be used for the administration of the Lawyers Assistance Program. This assessment shall be collected administratively in the same manner as and subject to the same exemptions as provided under Rule 1:28–2, except that no such fee shall be assessed to attorneys during the first calendar year of their admission. The fee shall be assessed to all attorneys in their second through forty-ninth calendar year of admission. The names of any and all attorneys failing to comply with the provisions of this rule shall be reported to the Supreme Court for inclusion on its Ineligible to Practice Law List. Any attorney who fails to pay the annual assessment for seven consecutive years shall be subject to the license revocation procedures contained in Rule 1:28–2(c).

Note: Adopted July 15, 1999, to be effective September 1, 1999; caption amended and new paragraph (e) added July 12, 2002 to be effective September 3, 2002; paragraph (b) amended February 4, 2003 to be effective immediately; paragraph (e) amended July 28, 2004 to be effective September 1, 2004; paragraph (a) amended December 5, 2006 to be effective immediately; paragraph (e) amended November 27, 2007 to be effective immediately.

1:28B–2.   Duties of Trustees and Treasurer

(a) **Regulations.** The Board of Trustees shall adopt regulations governing the Board's oversight of the administration of LAP. The regulations shall be consistent with these Rules and be subject to the approval of the Supreme Court.

(b) **Annual Budget.** The NJSBA shall, on or before September 30 of each year, present to the Board of Trustees a proposed budget for LAP in a form approved by the Board. The Board shall review the proposal, make such modifications as it deems necessary or appropriate, and forward the recommended budget to the Supreme Court for its review and approval no later than November 15. As approved, the budget shall cover the fiscal year beginning each July 1.

(c) **Quarterly Reimbursement of Expenses.** The NJSBA shall submit to the Board of Trustees quarterly reports seeking reimbursement of expenses incurred on behalf of LAP. The Board shall make recommendations on the NJSBA reports to the Supreme Court, which shall direct the payment to the NJSBA of all appropriate expenses.

(d) Audit and Report. The Board of Trustees shall arrange for an independent financial audit annually and at such other times as the Supreme Court shall direct, such audits to be at the expense of LAP. The annual financial audit shall be included in a report to be submitted annually by the Board to the Supreme Court, reviewing in detail the administration of LAP during the preceding year.

(e) Reports from LAP Director. On a quarterly basis, the Director of LAP shall file a report with the Board of Trustees in a form approved by the Board. The report shall cover LAP operations but shall neither identify program clients nor otherwise disclose information that is confidential under the regulations of the program.

(f) Applications to the Supreme Court. The Board of Trustees may apply to the Supreme Court for interpretations of these Rules and of the extent of their powers thereunder and for advice regarding the proper administration of LAP.

(g) Treasurer's Duties. The Treasurer shall maintain the assets of LAP in one or more separate accounts and shall disburse monies from them only at the direction of the Supreme Court pursuant to these Rules.

Note: Adopted July 15, 1999, to be effective September 1, 1999.

1:28B–3. Confidentiality

The records, documents, and meetings of LAP and the Board of Trustees are confidential, with the following exceptions:

(a) Annual Audit Reports;

(b) Annual reports of the Board of Trustees to the Supreme Court;

(c) Quarterly reports to the Board of Trustees from the LAP Director; and

(d) All materials relating to the budget process that do not identify clients of the program or otherwise disclose information that would compromise the confidentiality of the program as detailed in regulations adopted by the Board of Trustees and approved by the Supreme Court.

In no event, however, shall the identity of program clients be disclosed in the above reports.

Note: Adopted July 15, 1999, to be effective September 1, 1999.

1:28B–4. Immunity

Members of the LAP Board of Trustees, program employees and other staff, agents, program volunteers, attorney peer counselors, and attorneys providing practice assistance shall be absolutely immune from suit, whether legal or equitable in nature, based on their respective conduct in performing their official LAP duties. The Supreme Court shall request the Attorney General to represent those covered by this Rule in all civil or criminal litigation in any court or tribunal.

Note: Adopted July 15, 1999, to be effective September 1, 1999; amended July 12, 2002 to be effective September 3, 2002.

RULE 1:29. CERTIFICATES OF ADMISSION AND GOOD STANDING; CHANGE OF NAME; CONFIRMATORY CERTIFICATES

1:29–1. Certificates of Admission and Good Standing; Fees

(a) Certificate of Admission. Each attorney admitted to the bar of this State shall be eligible to receive a formal certificate of admission. Effective with the administration of the February 1994 bar examination, all successful applicants shall pay a certificate fee established by the Board of Bar Examiners and approved by the Supreme Court.

(b) Certificate of Good Standing. An attorney in good standing at the bar of this State may obtain a certificate so stating under seal from the Clerk of the Supreme Court. Attorneys seeking a Certificate of Good Standing shall pay a fee established by the Board of Bar Examiners and approved by the Supreme Court.

Note: Former Rule deleted July 29, 1977, to be effective September 6, 1977. Rule title amended and new Rule adopted on October 19, 1993, to be effective January 3, 1994.

1:29–2. Change of Name

If an attorney changes his or her name after admission to practice in this State, the attorney shall file with the Clerk of the Supreme Court an affidavit stating the name under which the attorney was admitted, the new name, the facts pertaining to the change of name, and the name under which the attorney wishes to continue to practice.

Note: Source—R.R. 1:14; caption amended July 29, 1977, to be effective September 6, 1977; text amended July 29, 1977, to be effective September 6, 1977; amended October 19, 1993, to be effective January 3, 1994.

1:29–3. Confirmatory Certificates; Fee

Whenever an affidavit pertaining to change of name is filed indicating a desire to continue practice under a new name, or whenever an attorney declares that the certificate of admission originally issued to the attorney has been lost or destroyed, the Clerk of the Supreme Court, on payment by the attorney of a fee to be established with the approval of the Supreme Court, shall issue a confirmatory certificate in the appropriate name.

Note: Source—R.R. 1:15–1. Amended July 7, 1971 to be effective September 13, 1971; amended July 29, 1977 to be effective September 6, 1977; caption and text amended October 19, 1993, to be effective January 3, 1994.

CHAPTER IV. ADMINISTRATION
RULE 1:30. COURT SCHEDULES

1:30–1. Courts Always Open

The courts shall be deemed always open for filing any proper paper, the issuance and return of process, the making of motions, the entering of orders and judgments, and the transaction of all judicial business.

Note: Source—R.R. 3:11–8, 4:118–4, 6:2–4, 8:12–7.

1:30–2. Terms of Court; Stated Sessions of Superior Court

(a) Terms. All courts shall hold one term annually, commencing on such date as shall be fixed by the Chief Justice. Matters not concluded in a term shall be carried to the succeeding term, but the continued existence or expiration of a term of court in no way affects the power of the court to do any act or take any proceeding in any action which has been pending before it.

(b) Sessions. Within each term of the Superior Court, Law Division there shall be 3 stated sessions commencing at times fixed by the Chief Justice.

Note: Source—R.R. 1:1–3, 1:28A, 2:1–2, 3:1–4, 4:6–2 (second sentence), 4:118–3. Paragraph (a) amended December 21, 1971 to be effective January 31, 1972; amended July 13, 1994 to be effective September 1, 1994; caption amended July 28, 2004 to be effective September 1, 2004.

1:30–3. Sittings of Courts

(a) Court Hours. Court hours for all trial courts, except the municipal courts, shall be fixed by the Chief Justice. Court hours for each municipal court shall be fixed by the judge or presiding judge thereof, subject to the approval of the Administrative Director of the Courts.

(b) Court Days. When not in recess, all courts shall sit Monday to Friday, inclusive; except that the appellate courts shall sit on days fixed by the Chief Justice and municipal courts shall sit on days fixed by the judge or presiding judge thereof, subject to the approval of the Administrative Director of the Courts.

(c) Motion Days. Motions shall be heard in all trial courts as scheduled from time to time by the Chief Justice.

(d) Court Recesses. All courts shall be in recess on Saturdays, Sundays, legal holidays and such other days as the Chief Justice shall order.

(e) Special Sittings. Nothing in this rule shall preclude the Chief Justice, the presiding judge of an appellate court, the Assignment Judge, or the judge presiding in any court from directing that any matter be heard at such other hours or on such other days as the judge may deem necessary or appropriate.

Note: Source—R.R. 1:28–1, 1:28–2, 1:28–3, 1:28–4, 1:28–5, 4:119–1 (first sentence), 6:2–5(a), 8:2–2; paragraph (e) amended July 13, 1994 to be effective September 1, 1994.

Publisher's Note

On December 9, 2009, the New Jersey Supreme Court issued the following order:

Pursuant to N.J. Const. Art. VI, sec. 2, par. 3, it is ORDERED that the relaxation of Rule 1:30–3(d) of the Rules Governing the Courts of the State of New Jersey so as to authorize the Newark Municipal Court to hold court sessions on Saturdays and Sundays for the limited purpose of conducting first appearances for incarcerated defendants, as effected by the Court's Order of March 15, 2004 and extended by the Court's Orders of March 14, 2005; December 6, 2005; December 5, 2006; November 27, 2007; and December 2, 2008, is hereby further extended through December 31, 2010 or until further order of the Court.

1:30–4. Clerks' Offices

The office of the clerk of every court, except the municipal courts, shall be open to the public for the transaction of all business of the court for such hours and on such days as shall be fixed by the Chief Justice. The office of the clerk of every municipal court shall be open to the public for the transaction of all business of the court on days and during hours fixed by the judge or presiding judge thereof, subject to the approval of the Administrative Director of the Courts.

Note: Source—R.R. 7:19–4. Amended December 21, 1971 to be effective January 31, 1972.

1:30–5. Vacations

(a) Judges. Vacations of judges of all appellate courts shall be scheduled by the Chief Justice. Vacations of judges of all trial courts, except the Tax Court and the municipal courts, shall be scheduled by the Assignment Judge, subject to the approval of the Chief Justice. Judges of the municipal courts shall schedule their own vacations, subject to the approval of the presiding judge of such court and the Administrative Director of the Courts, but shall make provision where necessary for other judges to sit in their stead. The presiding judge of the Tax Court shall schedule vacations of the judges thereof, subject to the approval of the Chief Justice.

(b) Supporting Personnel. Vacations of persons in the judicial branch of government shall be scheduled insofar as practicable during times when the courts are in recess or at such other times as shall least inconvenience the work of the courts. The amount of vacation time allowed shall be commensurate with that allowed other public employees holding comparable positions.

The vacations of all persons assigned to or employed by a judge shall be subject to the approval of such judge and the Assignment Judge.

Note: Source—R.R. 1:28–5, 6:2–7. Paragraph (a) amended June 20, 1979 to be effective July 1, 1979; paragraph (a) amended July 22, 1983 to be effective September 12, 1983.

RULE 1:31. PLACES FOR TRANSACTION OF COURT BUSINESS

1:31–1. Location of Courtrooms; Judges' Chambers; Clerks' Offices

All courtrooms, judges' chambers and clerks' offices shall be located in public buildings, except that where adequate facilities are not available in public buildings, conveniently located, the Administrative Director of the Courts may approve their location in some other appropriate place.

Note: Source—R.R. 1:28–7, 6:2–3(b)(d), 8:2–1, 8:13–6.

1:31–2. Inadequate Court Facilities

The Administrative Director of the Courts, upon determining that the facilities provided for any court, judge or clerk are inadequate, even though the facilities are located in a public building, may, after giving a reasonable opportunity for adequate facilities to be provided, direct the court, judge or clerk to cease using the same.

Note: Amended July 13, 1994 to be effective September 1, 1994.

RULE 1:32. REPORTS BY COURTS AND PERSONNEL; RECORDS; FORMS AND PROCESS PRESCRIBED BY ADMINISTRATIVE DIRECTOR

1:32–1. Reports by Judges; Court Clerks; Court Reporters

(a) Trial Judges Generally. On or before Monday of each week, every trial judge, except municipal court judges, shall submit to the Administrative Director of the Courts, on prescribed and supplied forms, a report containing such information as the Administrative Director of the Courts, with the approval of the Chief Justice, prescribes. Each judge shall forward a copy of such weekly report to the Assignment Judges of each county in which the judge was sitting during the week covered by such report except that the judges of the Tax Court shall submit such weekly report to the Administrative Director of the Courts and forward a copy of such weekly report to the Presiding Judge of the Tax Court.

(b) Judges of Municipal Courts. Every judge of a municipal court shall, on or before the 10th day of each month, submit to the Administrative Director of the Courts, on prescribed and supplied forms, a report for the preceding month and at other times shall submit such other reports all as the Administrative Director of the Courts, with the approval of the Chief Justice, requests.

(c) Clerks and Reporters. The clerks of all courts and all official court reporters and reporter supervisors shall submit to the Administrative Director of the Courts such reports at such times as are requested.

Note: Source—R.R. 1:30–5, 8:13–10(b). Paragraph (a) amended June 20, 1979 to be effective July 1, 1979; paragraphs (a), (b) and (c) amended July 13, 1994 to be effective September 1, 1994.

1:32–2. Books and Records

(a) Recordkeeping by Clerk. The clerks of all courts shall keep such books and records and may microfilm or electronically retain or destroy the same as the Administrative Director of the Courts with the approval of the Chief Justice may prescribe.

(b) Municipal Court Books and Records. Judges or presiding judges of the municipal court shall be responsible for the keeping of such prescribed books and records for the municipal courts.

(c) Retention Schedules and Purging Lists. Retention schedules identifying the length of time court records must be kept prior to destruction and purging lists identifying documents to be removed from case files before storage or replication shall be adopted by administrative directive. For purpose of this rule, "purging" means the removal and destruction of documents in the case file which have no legal, administrative or historical value.

(d) Reproduction of Original as Evidence. In the event of any destruction or other disposition of court records pursuant to this rule, the photographic or electronic reproduction or image of the original or a certified copy of same shall be receivable in evidence in any court or proceeding and shall have the same force and effect as though the original public record had been there produced and proved.

Note: Source—R.R. 3:11–7, 4:120–3, 4:120–4, 4:120–8, 4:120–9, 4:120–10, 4:120–11, 4:120–12, 5:5–3, 6:2–8(a)(b), 7:23, 7:24, 8:12–6, 8:13–8(e), 8:13–10(c). Amended July 22, 1983 to be effective September 12, 1983; text amended and designated as paragraphs (a) and (b) and paragraphs (c) and (d) added July 13, 1994 to be effective September 1, 1994; paragraphs (a), (b) and (c) amended June 28, 1996 to be effective September 1, 1996.

Publisher's Note

On April 30, 2002, the New Jersey Supreme Court issued the following order:

It is ORDERED, pursuant to *N.J. Const.* Art. VI, sec. 2 part. 3, that effective immediately and until further order the provisions of Rule 1:32–2(b) of the Rules Governing the Courts of the State of New Jersey and the provisions of Directive #3–01 are supplemented and relaxed with regard to the certain damaged and/or contaminated original records in the Mount Olive Township Municipal Court so as to permit the substitution where necessary of photocopied reproductions or electronically retained information residing on the Automated Traffic System (ATS) for those damaged and/or contaminated original documents.

1:32–3. Process; Forms

The Administrative Director of the Courts may, subject to the approval of the Supreme Court, prescribe forms of process and such other forms for the implementation of these rules as shall be necessary from time to time.

Note: Source—R.R. 8:3–2(b)(2) (last sentence), 8:10–1(a).

RULE 1:33. ADMINISTRATIVE RESPONSIBILITY

1:33–1. The Chief Justice of the Supreme Court; Acting Chief Justice

The Chief Justice of the Supreme Court shall be responsible for the administration of all courts in the State. To assist in those duties the Chief Justice shall appoint an Administrative Director of the Courts who shall serve at the pleasure of and report directly to the Chief Justice. A full-time judge of any court of this State may be designated to serve temporarily as Acting Administrative Director, in which event such judge shall continue to hold, and shall only be paid the salary of such judicial office. If there is a vacancy in the office of Chief Justice, the senior justice shall serve temporarily as Acting Chief Justice. Seniority shall be determined by order of taking of oath as a member of the court. If the Chief Justice is absent or unable to serve, the senior justice shall serve temporarily as Acting Chief Justice.

Note: Source—R.R. 6:2–1A(b), 7:20–2(b), 8:13–3A, Const. of 1947, Art. VI, Sec. VII, par. 1; amended June 5, 1973, effective immediately; 5th, 6th and 7th sentences adopted October 30, 1973, to be effective immediately; amended January 16, 1975 to be effective April 1, 1975; amended June 20, 1979 to be effective July 1, 1979; amended October 26, 1983 to be effective immediately; amended June 29, 1990 to be effective September 4, 1990.

1:33–2. Court Managerial Structure

(a) The Chief Justice shall divide the State into such geographical divisions as appropriate to facilitate the efficient administration of the courts. Such geographical divisions shall be known as "vicinages."

(b) For each vicinage, the Chief Justice shall designate a judge of the Superior Court to serve as Assignment Judge. Each such Assignment Judge shall serve at the pleasure of and report directly to the Chief Justice.

(c) Within each vicinage, the Chief Justice shall organize the trial court system into four functional units to facilitate the management of the trial court system within that vicinage. These units shall be: Civil, Criminal, Family and General Equity.

(d)(1) Each functional unit shall be supervised by a Presiding Judge who shall be appointed by the Chief Justice, after consultation with the Assignment Judge, and who shall serve at the pleasure of the Chief Justice. A Presiding Judge may supervise more than one functional unit. The Presiding Judge shall report directly and be responsible to the Assignment Judge.

(2) The Chief Justice may appoint the Assignment Judge to serve as the Presiding Judge for one or more functional units within the vicinage.

(e) The Chief Justice shall designate a judge of the Tax Court as presiding judge, to serve at the pleasure of the Chief Justice.

Note: Former rule redesignated R. 1:33–3 and new rule adopted October 26, 1983 to be effective immediately; paragraphs (a) (b) (d) and (e) amended June 29, 1990 to be effective September 4, 1990; paragraph (c) amended June 28, 1996 to be effective September 1, 1996.

1:33–3. The Administrative Director of the Courts

The Administrative Director of the Courts shall be generally responsible for the enforcement of the rules, policies and directives of the Supreme Court and the Chief Justice relating to matters of administration. At the direction of the Chief Justice and the Supreme Court, the Administrative Director shall promulgate a compilation of administrative rules and directives relating to case processing, records and management information services, personnel, budgeting and such other matters as the Chief Justice and Supreme Court shall direct. The Administrative Director also shall perform such other functions and duties as may be assigned by the Chief Justice or by rule of the Supreme Court.

Note: Former rule redesignated as R. 1:33–4 October 26, 1983 to be effective immediately. Source (Current Rule)—Formerly R. 1:33–2 redesignated as R. 1:33–3 and amended October 26, 1983 to be effective immediately; amended June 29, 1990 to be effective September 4, 1990.

1:33–4. Assignment Judges; Presiding Judge for Administration of the Appellate Division

(a) The Assignment Judge shall be the chief judicial officer within the vicinage and shall have plenary responsibility for the administration of all courts therein, subject to the direction of the Chief Justice and the rules of the Supreme Court. The Assignment Judge shall be responsible for the implementation and enforcement of the rules, policies and directives of the Supreme Court, the Chief Justice and the Administrative Director.

(b) The Assignment Judge shall be the authorized representative of the Chief Justice for the efficient and economic management of all courts within the vicinage. The responsibilities of the Assignment Judge also shall include all such matters affecting county and municipal governments, including but not limited to budgets, personnel, and facilities.

(c) The Assignment Judge shall be responsible for the supervision and efficient management of all court matters filed in the vicinage and for the supervision, superintendence and allocation of all judges and personnel having a judicial support function within the vicinage.

(d) The Assignment Judge shall have full responsibility for the administration of all court units within the vicinage, including those of the Surrogate and the Deputy Clerk of the Superior Court.

(e) Subject to uniform minimum standards and conditions promulgated by the Administrative Director, the Assignment Judge may appoint and discharge judicial support personnel within the vicinage.

(f) The Assignment Judge shall perform such additional duties as shall be assigned by the Chief Justice or by rule of the Supreme Court.

(g) The Presiding Judge for Administration of the Appellate Division shall have responsibility for the administration of the Appellate Division subject to the direction of the Chief Justice and the rules of the Supreme Court. The Presiding Judge shall be responsible for the implementation and enforcement of the rules, policies and directives of the Supreme Court, the Chief Justice and the Administrative Director; the responsibilities of the Presiding Judge shall include all personnel and management matters as are assigned by the Chief Justice or by rule of the Supreme Court, and the Presiding Judge shall perform such additional duties as may be assigned.

Note: Former rule redesignated R. 1:33–6 October 26, 1983, to be effective immediately. Source (Current Rule)—R.R. 1:29–1, 1:29–1A, 1:29–2, 1:31–1, 3:11–5 (first sentence), 4:41–4(b) (first sentence); caption amended and paragraph (g) adopted November 1, 1985 to be effective January 2, 1986; paragraphs (a) (b) (e) and (f) amended June 29, 1990 to be effective September 4, 1990.

1:33–5. Trial Court Administrators— Case Coordinators

(a) The Trial Court Administrator shall be the administrative arm of the courts within the vicinage, under the direction of the Assignment Judge and the Administrative Director. The Trial Court Administrator shall be appointed by the Administrative Director, after consultation with the Assignment Judge, subject to the approval of the Chief Justice. The responsibilities of the Trial Court Administrator shall include the provision of technical and managerial support to the Assignment Judge and Administrative Director with respect to budget development and expenditures, the supervision of all judicial support personnel, program development and analysis, facilities and resource management, the provision of such assistance as shall be necessary to such advisory committees to the courts as shall be appointed, and such additional administrative duties as shall be designated by the Administrative Director.

(b) After consultation with the Assignment Judge, the Administrative Director may appoint such Assistant Trial Court Administrators as are deemed necessary. The Assistant Trial Court Administrators shall report to and be supervised by the Trial Court Administrator.

(c) For each vicinage there shall be a Case Coordinator who shall be responsible for the efficient movement of cases within the vicinage, subject to the direction of the Assignment Judge.

(d) The Trial Court Administrator shall serve as the Case Coordinator for the vicinage, provided, however, that the Administrative Director may designate, after consultation with the Assignment Judge, an Assistant Trial Court Administrator to serve as Case Coordinator.

Note: Former rule redesignated as R. 1:33–9 and new rule adopted October 26, 1983 to be effective immediately; paragraphs (a) and (b) amended June 29, 1990 to be effective September 4, 1990.

1:33–6. Presiding Judges of Functional Units

(a) Except as provided by the Chief Justice or by the Supreme Court, the Assignment Judge may delegate to the Presiding Judge of each functional unit within the vicinage, judicial duties and responsibilities allocated to the Assignment Judge by these rules.

(b) In addition to judicial duties, the Presiding Judge of each functional unit within the vicinage shall be responsible for the expeditious processing to disposition of all matters filed within that unit.

(c) The Presiding Judge annually shall submit to the Trial Court Administrator and Assignment Judge, budget and personnel needs and recommendations for the unit at such times and in such format and in accordance with such procedures as shall be prescribed by the Administrative Director.

(d) The Presiding Judge shall perform such additional administrative duties as shall be assigned by the

Assignment Judge and shall be responsible for the implementation and enforcement within the court of all administrative rules, policies and directives of the Supreme Court, the Chief Justice, the Administrative Director and the Assignment Judge.

Note: Source—R.R. 1:31–1, 6:2–1A, 7:7–2, 7:7–8, 7:7–9, 7:19–2 (first sentence), 7:20–2(a), 8:7–1 (third and fourth sentences), 8:13–3A. Formerly R. 1:33–4, redesignated and amended October 26, 1983 to be effective immediately; new paragraph (a) adopted and paragraphs (a), (b), and (c) redesignated (b), (c), and (d), respectively November 1, 1985 to be effective January 2, 1986; paragraphs (b) (c) and (d) amended June 29, 1990 to be effective September 4, 1990.

1:33–6A. Supervising Judges of the Special Civil Part

The Assignment Judge in each vicinage shall designate a Supervising Judge of the Special Civil Part, who shall be responsible for such supervisory and administrative duties for that Part as may be assigned by the Civil Presiding Judge. The Supervising Judge shall serve at the pleasure of the Assignment Judge and the Assignment Judge may designate the Civil Presiding Judge to be the Supervising Judge.

Note: New R. 1:33–6A adopted July 13, 1994 to be effective September 1, 1994.

1:33–7. Division Managers

There shall be on the staff of the Trial Court Administrator a Division Manager for each court-support unit within the vicinage who shall be appointed by the Administrative Director after consultation with the Assignment Judge. The Division Manager's responsibilities shall include the management, under the direction of the Presiding Judge and Trial Court Administrator, of such judicial-support personnel and resources as have been allocated to the Division Manager's functional unit by the Assignment Judge and Trial Court Administrator.

Note: Adopted October 26, 1983, to be effective immediately; amended June 29, 1990, to be effective September 4, 1990; amended July 14, 1992 to be effective September 1, 1992.

1:33–8. Probation Services

(a) For each vicinage, there shall be a Vicinage Chief Probation Officer who shall be appointed by the Administrative Director after consultation with the Assignment Judge, subject to the approval of the Chief Justice and who shall serve at the pleasure of the Administrative Director.

(b) The Vicinage Chief Probation Officer shall be the supervisor of probation services. The responsibilities of said officer shall include the supervision and management of the delivery of probation services as part of a statewide system as organized and directed as to programmatic and statewide policy matters by the authority of the Administrative Director. In the performance of professional duties over probation services, the Vicinage Chief Probation Officer shall report to the Assignment Judge. In the performance of administrative duties, the Vicinage Chief Probation Officer shall report to the Trial Court Administrator.

(c) The Vicinage Chief Probation Officer annually shall submit to the Trial Court Administrator the budget and personnel needs of the Probation Department and recommendations for probation services at such times, in such format and in accordance with such procedures as shall be prescribed by the Administrative Director.

(d) The Vicinage Chief Probation Officer shall assign to each functional unit such staff as may be required. The staff so assigned shall be directly responsible to the Presiding Judge with regard to their day-to-day functions.

(e) The Vicinage Chief Probation Officer shall perform such additional duties as shall be assigned by the Assignment Judge.

Note: Adopted October 26, 1983 to be effective immediately; paragraphs (b) (c) and (e) amended June 29, 1990 to be effective September 4, 1990.

1:33–9. Review of Administratively Recommended Facilities Disputes Dispositions

Any dispute between the county governing body and the Assignment Judge concerning the location, size, or other physical characteristics of courtrooms, chambers, office space or related facilities shall, at the request of either party, be resolved by submission of the dispute to arbitration. The number or selection of arbitrators may be stipulated by mutual consent of both parties to the dispute. If the parties fail to stipulate the names or number of arbitrators, the county governing body shall select one arbitrator, the Assignment Judge a second arbitrator, and the two arbitrators thus selected shall pick a third. In the event said two arbitrators are unable to agree upon a third arbitrator, the third arbitrator shall be selected by the American Arbitration Association in accordance with its procedures. The arbitrators' jurisdiction shall be limited to the consideration of disputes concerning the location, size, or other physical characteristics of courtrooms, chambers, office space or related facilities. The decision of the arbitrators is subject to review by the Supreme Court pursuant to the standards set forth in N.J.S.A. 2A:24–8 and –9 but, otherwise, shall be final, binding, and not subject to review unless the Supreme Court, on petition by the county or by the Assignment Judge, finds by clear and convincing evidence that the decision fails to balance the needs and interests of the county and the Judiciary in a fair manner.

Note: Adopted March 11, 1981 to be effective immediately. Formerly R. 1:33–5, redesignated October 26, 1983, to be effective immediately; paragraph (a) amended, new paragraph (b) adopted, former paragraphs (b), (c), (d), (e), (f), (g) redesignated as paragraphs (c), (d), (e), (f), (g) and (h) and amended December 31, 1987 to be effective December 31, 1987; paragraph (a) and former paragraphs (c) and (d) amended, paragraphs (b), (c), (d) and (e) adopted, and former paragraphs (b), (c), (d), (e), (f), (g) and (h) redesignated paragraphs (f), (g), (h), (i), (j), (k) and (l), respectively, July 14, 1992 to be effective September 1, 1992; new paragraph (m) adopted February 28, 1995 to be effective March 1, 1995; paragraphs (a), (b), (c), (d), (e), (f), (g), (h), (i), (j), (k) and (l) deleted and paragraph designation (m) deleted and amended June 28, 1996 to be effective September 1, 1996.

RULE 1:34. SUPPORTING PERSONNEL OF THE COURTS

1:34–1. Standing Masters of the Supreme Court [Deleted]

Note: Source—R.R. 1:1–7. Amended June 29, 1973 to be effective September 10, 1973. Deleted November 27, 1974 to be effective April 1, 1975.

1:34–2. Clerks of Court

The clerk of every court, except the Supreme Court, the Appellate Division, the Superior Court and the Tax Court, shall be responsible to and under the supervision of the judge or presiding judge of the court that the clerk serves, the Assignment Judge of the county, and the Administrative Director of the Courts. The clerks of the Supreme and Superior Courts shall be responsible to and under the supervision of the Administrative Director of the Courts and the Chief Justice. The clerk of the Appellate Division shall be responsible to and under the supervision of the Administrative Director of the Courts, the Chief Justice, and the Presiding Judge for Administration of the court. The clerk of the Tax Court shall be responsible to and under the supervision of the presiding judge of the court and the Administrative Director of the Courts. Each county shall have one or more deputy clerks of the Superior Court with respect to Superior Court matters filed in that county; deputy clerks may issue writs out of the Superior Court. The Surrogate of the county shall be the deputy clerk of the Superior Court, Chancery Division, Probate Part, with respect to probate matters pending in that county. The Vicinage Chief Probation Officer shall be the deputy clerk of the Superior Court for the purpose of certifying child support judgments and orders as required by R. 4:101, and with respect to writs of execution as provided by R. 4:59–1(b). All employees serving as deputy clerks of the Superior Court shall be, in that capacity, responsible to the clerk of the Superior Court.

Note: Source—R.R. 6:2–7, 7:21–1, 7:21–2, 8:13–4. Amended July 14, 1972 to be effective September 5, 1972; amended June 20, 1979 to be effective July 1, 1979; amended June 29, 1990 to be effective September 4, 1990; amended July 14, 1992 to be effective September 1, 1992; amended June 28, 1996 to be effective June 28, 1996; amended July 28, 2004 to be effective September 1, 2004.

1:34–3. Reserved.

(Former Rule 1:34–3 deleted July 12, 2002 to be effective September 3, 2002.)

Note: Source—R.R. 1:29–2. Cf. N.J.S. 2A:68–1, as amended.

1:34–4. Probation Officers and Volunteers in Probation

Probation officers and volunteers in probation shall be appointed in accordance with standards fixed by the Supreme Court. All probation officers and volunteers in probation shall be responsible to and under the supervision of the Chief Probation Officer of the county who shall be responsible to and under the supervision of the judge designated by the Assignment Judge to be responsible for the administration of the probation department in the county in accordance with applicable statutes, rules of the Supreme Court, and directives of the Chief Justice, the Administrative Director of the Courts, and the Assignment Judge of the County.

Note: Cf. N.J.S. 2A:168–5, N.J.S.A., as amended; amended November 27, 1974 to be effective April 1, 1975; amended July 21, 1980 to be effective September 8, 1980.

1:34–5. Court Reporters

Court reporters shall be appointed by the Supreme Court or the Administrative Director of the Courts as provided by law and shall be subject to assignment by the Administrative Director of the Courts. They shall be responsible to and under the supervision of the reporter supervisor of the county, the judge of the court to which assigned, the Assignment Judge of the county, and the Administrative Director of the Courts. The Administrative Director of the Courts shall promulgate regulations which shall govern all court reporters and the preparation and filing of transcripts of all court and related proceedings, including depositions in pending actions.

Note: Source—R.R. 1:30–6.

1:34–6. Office of Foreclosure

There shall be an Office of Foreclosure within the Administrative Office of the Courts. This office shall be responsible for recommending the entry of orders or judgments in uncontested foreclosure matters pursuant to R. 4:64–1 and R. 4:64–7 subject to the approval of a Superior Court Judge designated by the Chief Justice. The Office of Foreclosure may also recommend the entry of the following orders in uncontested actions:

(1) correcting a clerical error in orders or judgments;

(2) correcting the defendant's name;

(3) correcting venue;

(4) substituting the plaintiff if, during the course of the foreclosure action, the original plaintiff reorganizes, merges with another entity, is acquired by another entity, or assigns the mortgage to another entity;

(5) entering default;

(6) extending time to answer;

(7) filing an amended complaint, provided no new cause of action or claim for relief is set forth in the amended complaint;

(8) vacating a default entered by the clerk;

(9) vacating judgment and execution, reinstating a bond or note and mortgage and, with the consent of the answering defendants, dismissing the proceedings;

(10) authorizing the sheriff to collect additional lawful sums;

(11) dismissing the tax foreclosure action as to any parcel redeemed;

(12) vacating an *in rem* foreclosure judgment upon application of the municipality owner;

(13) correcting minor technical irregularities in the mortgage, note or legal description, if a substantial right of a party is not prejudiced;

(14) substituting heirs and personal representative for deceased defendants; and

(15) disbursing surplus foreclosure money.

Note: Adopted July 22, 1983 to be effective September 12, 1983; subparagraphs (1) and (2) amended, subparagraphs (3) through (7) renumbered as (8) through (12), subparagraphs (9) through (12) amended, new subparagraphs (3) through (7) and (13) through (15) adopted July 9, 2008 to be effective September 1, 2008.

1:34–7. Interpreters, Transliterators, and Translators

Interpreters, transliterators, and translators shall be appointed and perform their duties in the manner established by the Chief Justice and shall serve at the pleasure of the appointing authority.

Note: Adopted February 3, 1997 to be effective March 1, 1997.

RULE 1:35. JUDICIAL CONFERENCES

1:35–1. The Judicial Conference of New Jersey

(a) **Function.** There shall be a judicial conference, to be known as "The Judicial Conference of New Jersey," to assist the Supreme Court in the consideration of improvements in the practice and procedure in the courts and in the administration and organization of the judicial branch of government.

(b) **Membership.** The membership of the conference shall be as follows:

(1) The Chief Justice and Associate Justices of the Supreme Court, the presiding judges of the Appellate Division of the Superior Court, the Assignment Judges, the Presiding Judge of the Tax Court and the Chief Judge of the United States District Court for the District of New Jersey.

(2) Not more than 50 judges of the Superior Court, the Tax Court, and the municipal courts, to be selected by the Supreme Court.

(3) The President of the Senate, the Speaker of the General Assembly, and the majority and minority leaders and assistant leaders, and the chairmen of the Judiciary Committees of the Senate and General Assembly.

(4) The Attorney General, the Public Defender, the Administrative Director of the Courts, the clerks of the Supreme, Superior and Tax Courts, the chair of the Board of Bar Examiners, the chair of the Committee on Character, the chair of the Advisory Committee on Professional Ethics, the chair of the Committee on the Unauthorized Practice of Law, the chair of the trustees of the New Jersey Lawyers' Fund for Client Protection, the chair of the Ethics Financial Committee, 3 trial court administrators to be selected by the Supreme Court, and the deans of all accredited law schools in New Jersey.

(5) Three county prosecutors, 3 surrogates, 3 county clerks, 3 probation officers, and 3 representatives of agencies providing legal services for the poor, to be selected by the Supreme Court.

(6) The officers of the State Bar Association, and the president of each county bar association, or, if unable to attend, another officer of the county bar association to be designated by the president, plus one additional representative of each county bar association or designated alternate, to be selected by the president thereof, for each 200,000 persons in the county according to the last census.

(7) Not more than 15 representatives of the general public to be selected by the Supreme Court.

(8) Other persons selected by the Supreme Court because they have professional responsibilities, interests or other qualifications which relate to particular topics to be considered.

(c) Term. All members, except those serving ex-officio, shall serve for a term of one year commencing January 1. A vacancy occurring during a term shall be filled for the unexpired portion thereof.

(d) Committees. The Supreme Court shall appoint such committees as it shall deem necessary or desirable, but the members of such committees need not be members of the conference. Each committee shall meet at such times and places as its chair shall designate.

(e) Meetings. The conference shall meet in general session at least once each year at such times and places as the Supreme Court shall designate. In the ordinary course the Supreme Court will consider for adoption only those proposed amendments to the rules that have been reported on by the appropriate committee and published for comment.

(f) Secretariat. The Administrative Office of the Courts shall serve as secretariat for the conference and for all committees.

Note: Source—R.R. 1:23–1(a) (b) (c) (d) (f) (g); paragraph (b) amended November 27, 1974 to be effective April 1, 1975; paragraphs (b)(1), (2), and (4) and paragraph (b)(8) adopted April 2, 1980 to be effective immediately; paragraphs (b)(1), (2), and (4) amended July 8, 1980 to be effective July 15, 1980; paragraph (e) amended July 22, 1983 to be effective September 12, 1983; paragraph (b)(2) amended July 26, 1984 to be effective September 10, 1984; paragraph (b)(4) amended November 5, 1986 to be effective January 1, 1987; paragraph (b) amended July 14, 1992 to be effective September 1, 1992; paragraph (b)(6) amended July 13, 1994 to be effective September 1, 1994; paragraph (b)(4) and paragraph (d) amended June 28, 1996 to be effective September 1, 1996.

1:35–2.　Conference of Judges

At least once each year there shall be a conference of all justices and judges in the State, except the judges of the municipal courts, held at such times and places as the Chief Justice shall designate, and at which the Administrative Office of the Courts shall serve as secretariat. At least once each year there shall be a conference in each county of all municipal court judges in the county to be held at such times and places as the Assignment Judge of the county shall designate. The purpose of these conferences is to raise the standards of judicial performance and to make more uniform the operation and administration of the courts of the State.

Note: Source—R.R. 1:23–2(a) (b), 8:13–5(a) (b). Amended June 29, 1973 to be effective September 10, 1973.

RULE 1:35A.　JUDICIAL PERFORMANCE PROGRAM

1:35A–1.　Judicial Performance Committee

The Supreme Court shall appoint a Judicial Performance Committee to develop and administer, under the Court's direction and supervision, a program for the continuing improvement of judicial performance. The Supreme Court shall appoint the Committee and designate one member to serve as Chairperson. No less than six members shall be judges from the Superior Court, with representation from the Appellate Division, Civil Division, Criminal Division, Family Division, General Equity Division, and Assignment Judges. No less than three members shall be members of the Bar, no less than two members shall be representatives of the general public, and such number of other members as determined by the Supreme Court. The members shall be appointed by the Supreme Court for terms of three years and may be reappointed for such additional term or terms as the Supreme Court shall determine. The Committee shall report periodically to the Supreme Court concerning the Judicial Performance Program.

Note: Adopted June 2, 1988 to be effective immediately; amended March 28, 1994 to be effective September 1, 1994.

1:35A–2.　Judicial Performance Program

The Supreme Court shall establish a program for the continuing improvement of judicial performance to be known as the Judicial Performance Program. The Judicial Performance Program shall be administered so that there is no interference with the performance of the regular duties of judges and no infringement on judicial independence and integrity or on the prerogatives of an individual judge in deciding cases and discharging judicial responsibilities. The primary objective of the Judicial Performance Program shall be the improvement of the judicial system through the improvement of the performance of judges on an individual and institutional basis. The Judicial Performance Program shall include the regular evaluation of the performance of judges and educational programs to enable judges to improve their performance. Evaluation information that is obtained under the program shall be considered personnel records of individual judges and shall be used solely to further the objectives of the program and judicial management. In the evaluation of judicial performance under the program, the Committee shall use professionally accepted methods to provide to the extent possible objective and reliable evaluations and to reduce the risk of unfair ratings and statistical comparisons.

Note: Adopted June 2, 1988 to be effective immediately.

1:35A–3. Records

(a) Confidentiality. All records and information obtained and maintained by the Committee concerning judicial performance shall be confidential and shall not be disclosed except in accordance with this Rule. The Committee shall ensure the confidentiality of information received under the evaluation program regarding the performance of judges, and shall ensure the confidentiality of the identity and preserve the anonymity of responding individuals and other persons who may be requested to furnish evaluation information.

(b) Disclosure. Individual records and information pertaining to the performance and evaluation of judges shall not be disclosed except as follows:

(1) A judge may obtain summaries of responses to questionnaires or other information concerning the judge's own performance, provided that the summaries are presented in a manner that will not disclose the identity of any person furnishing such responses or information. Such responses or information shall be disclosed only if based on sufficient data to ensure the statistical reliability of the evaluation information.

(2) Records or information of the Committee concerning the performance of a judge may be disclosed to the Supreme Court, the Assignment Judge of that judge's vicinage, and the Judicial Evaluation Commission established pursuant to Rule 1:35A–4.

(3) Information of the Committee concerning the performance of a judge who is under consideration for reappointment may be disclosed to the Governor and the Senate Judiciary Committee, under such conditions as the Court may deem appropriate. Such information shall be presented in the form of summaries of aggregate data of performance evaluation pertaining to the judge being considered for reappointment. A copy of such information shall be furnished to the judge, who may present to the Supreme Court written objections to or comments thereto prior to its disclosure.

(4) Notwithstanding these restrictions and conditions on disclosure, upon the written request of a judge, and for good cause, the Supreme Court may release evaluation information relating to the performance of the judge. The manner and content of any such disclosure shall be consistent with the objectives of the Judicial Performance Program, shall not reveal the names of responding individuals or specific court matters involved, and shall comport with notions of fairness to the judge and the preservation of the independence and integrity of the Judiciary.

Note: Adopted June 2, 1988 to be effective immediately.

1:35A–4. Judicial Evaluation Commission

The Supreme Court shall appoint a Judicial Evaluation Commission of at least three retired judges for terms of three years, who may be reappointed for such additional term or terms as the Court shall determine. The Court shall designate one member to chair the Commission. The Commission shall assist the Committee generally, shall assist in the review of evaluation information, shall provide consultation and assistance to individual judges, shall assist in the development and administration of instructional and judicial performance improvement programs in cooperation with the Judicial College and other judicial education programs, and shall perform such other functions as may be assigned to it by the Committee.

Note: Adopted June 2, 1988 to be effective immediately; amended March 28, 1994 to be effective September 1, 1994.

RULE 1:36. OPINIONS; FILING; PUBLICATION

1:36–1. Filing of Opinions

The original of each written opinion handed down in each court, including letter opinions and memorandum decisions, shall be filed with the clerk of the court in which rendered and copies thereof shall be sent to counsel and, on all appeals, to the court or agency below. Opinions of the Appellate Division shall have typed or stamped thereon the following notice: "Not for Publication Without the Approval of the Appellate Division." Opinions of the trial courts shall have typed or stamped thereon the following notice: "Not for

Publication Without the Approval of the Committee on Opinions."

Note: Source—R.R. 1:32(a)(b); amended July 13, 1994 to be effective September 1, 1994.

1:36–2. Publication

(a) Appellate Opinions. All opinions of the Supreme Court shall be published except where otherwise directed by the Court. Opinions of the Appellate Division shall be published only upon the direction of the panel issuing the opinion.

(b) Committee on Opinions; Trial Court Opinions. The Chief Justice shall appoint a Committee on Opinions to review formal written opinions submitted for publication by a trial judge. Except in extraordinary circumstances, the Committee shall not review a trial court opinion until the time for appeal from the final judgment in the cause has expired. If an appeal has not been taken, the Committee shall determine whether to approve publication of the trial court opinion. If an appeal has been taken, the Appellate Division panel shall determine, when it decides the appeal, whether the trial court opinion shall be published. A trial judge submitting an opinion for review for publication shall file it with the Administrative Office of the Courts in triplicate with the notation on its face that it is being submitted for publication.

(c) Request for Publication. Any person may request publication of an opinion by letter to the Committee on Opinions explaining the basis of the request with specificity and with reference to the guidelines prescribed by paragraph (d). In the case of Appellate Division opinions, the Committee shall transmit the request to the presiding judge of the panel together with its recommendation, but the court shall retain the publication decision.

(d) Guidelines for Publication. An opinion in appropriate form, excluding letter opinions and transcripts of oral opinions, shall be published where the decision (1) involves a substantial question under the United States or New Jersey Constitution, or (2) determines a new and important question of law, or (3) changes, reverses, seriously questions or criticizes the soundness of an established principle of law, or (4) determines a substantial question on which the only case law in this State antedates September 15, 1948, or (5) is based upon a matter of practice and procedure not theretofore authoritatively determined, or (6) is of continuing public interest and importance, or (7) resolves an apparent conflict of authority, or (8) although not otherwise meriting publication, constitutes a significant and nonduplicative contribution to legal literature by providing an historical review of the law, or describing legislative history, or containing a collection of cases that should be of substantial aid to the bench and bar.

Note: Source—R.R. 1:32(c) (d); amended July 29, 1977, to be effective September 6, 1977; text deleted and paragraphs (a)(b)(c) and (d) substituted July 13, 1994 to be effective September 1, 1994.

1:36–3. Unpublished Opinions

No unpublished opinion shall constitute precedent or be binding upon any court. Except for appellate opinions not approved for publication that have been reported in an authorized administrative law reporter, and except to the extent required by res judicata, collateral estoppel, the single controversy doctrine or any other similar principle of law, no unpublished opinion shall be cited by any court. No unpublished opinion shall be cited to any court by counsel unless the court and all other parties are served with a copy of the opinion and of all other relevant unpublished opinions known to counsel including those adverse to the position of the client.

Note: Adopted July 16, 1981 to be effective September 14, 1981; caption and rule amended July 13, 1994 to be effective September 1, 1994; amended July 12, 2002 to be effective September 3, 2002.

RULE 1:37. COURT TITLES; SEALS; ABBREVIATIONS

1:37–1. Title of Courts

The titles of the courts of this State shall be as follows:

(a) "Supreme Court of New Jersey"

(b) "Superior Court of New Jersey, _____" (here state Law, Chancery or Appellate Division, as appropriate and the part thereof, if any)

(c) "Tax Court of New Jersey"

(d) "Municipal Court of _____" (here state the name of the municipality)

Note: Source—R.R. 1:1–1, 2:1–1, 4:118–1, 5:1–1. Amended June 20, 1979 to be effective July 1, 1979; amended December 20, 1983 to be effective December 31, 1983.

1:37–2. Seal of Courts

The seal of each court shall be in the form prescribed by the Administrative Director of the Courts with the approval of the Supreme Court and shall be kept in the custody of the clerk of the court.

Note: Source—R.R. 1:1–2, 4:118–2, 7:19–1.

Publisher's Note

On March 27, 2000 the New Jersey Supreme Court issued the following order:

WHEREAS the Judiciary has successfully tested the use of electronic filing technology in the Judiciary Electronic Filing and Imaging System (JEFIS) pilot project in the Special Civil Part of the Superior Court, Law Division, Monmouth County, pursuant to orders of this Court dated December 10, 1996 and February 1, 1999; and

WHEREAS the Judiciary is preparing to implement the electronic filing component of JEFIS in all of the Special Civil Part offices in the other twenty counties, while continuing to operate the pilot project in Monmouth County;

Pursuant to N.J. Const. (1947), Art. VI, § 2, par. 3, IT IS ORDERED, effective September 1, 2000 and until further Order of the Court, that the Rules of Court be relaxed and supplemented, as set forth below, so as to permit the Judiciary to establish and operate a statewide program in the Special Civil Part of the Superior Court, Law Division, in which attorneys who meet the requirements established by the Administrative Office of the Courts and are registered with the Superior Court Clerk's Office may, in civil actions in which the amount in controversy does not exceed the Part's monetary limit and where the actions are filed in that court pursuant to Rule 6:1–2(a)(1), electronically file pleadings and other papers in a prescribed format via the Internet with the Clerk of the Superior Court, with computers capable of electronically managing documents and images of documents to be used to process and distribute those documents and images of documents to the office of the Special Civil Part Clerk in the county of venue for printing, processing, and storage in paper form (except in Monmouth County, where the documents will continue to be processed and stored in electronic form as part of the JEFIS project):

* * *

10. Rule 1:37–2 is supplemented so as to permit the printed reproduction of the court's seal on all papers that require a seal under the Rules of Court.

* * *

On October 7, 2003, the New Jersey Supreme Court issued the following order:

WHEREAS the Judiciary has successfully tested the use of electronic filing technology in the Judiciary Electronic Filing and Imaging System (JEFIS) pilot project in the Special Civil Part of the Superior Court, Law Division, Monmouth County, pursuant to orders of this Court dated December 10, 1996 and February 1, 1999; and

WHEREAS the Judiciary has implemented the electronic filing component of JEFIS in all of the Special Civil Part offices in the other twenty counties pursuant to an Order of this Court dated March 27, 2000, while continuing to operate the pilot project in Monmouth County;

Pursuant to N.J. Const. (1947), Art. VI, sec. 2, par. 3, IT IS ORDERED, effective November 3, 2003 and until further Order of the Court, that the Rules of Court be relaxed and supplemented, as specified in the Court's Order dated March 27, 2000, to permit the Judiciary to expand the imaging component of JEFIS to civil actions filed in the Special Civil Part in Mercer and Ocean Counties pursuant to Rule 6:1–2(a)(1), so that documents filed in those cases, whether electronically or on paper, can be processed and stored in electronic form as part of the JEFIS project.

This Order supplements, where appropriate, the Court's Orders of December 10, 1996 and February 1, 1999 with regard to the JEFIS project in Monmouth County and the Court's Order of March 27, 2000 permitting the statewide expansion of the electronic filing component of JEFIS.

* * *

On April 27, 2004, the New Jersey Supreme Court issued the following order to be effective May 3, 2004:

WHEREAS the Judiciary has successfully tested the use of electronic filing technology in the Judiciary Electronic Filing and Imaging System (JEFIS) pilot project in the Special Civil Part of the Superior Court, Law Division, Monmouth County, pursuant to orders of this Court dated December 10, 1996 and February 1, 1999; and

WHEREAS the Judiciary has implemented the electronic filing component of JEFIS in all of the Special Civil Part offices in the other twenty counties pursuant to an Order of this Court dated March 27, 2000, while continuing to operate the pilot project in Monmouth County; and

WHEREAS the Judiciary has expanded the imaging component of JEFIS to civil actions filed in the Special Civil Part in Mercer and Ocean Counties pursuant to an Order of this Court dated October 7, 2003;

Pursuant to N.J. Const. (1947), Art. VI, sec. 2, par. 3, IT IS ORDERED, effective May 3, 2004 and until further Order of the Court, that the Rules of Court be relaxed and supplemented, as specified in the Court's Order dated March 27, 2000, to permit the Judiciary to expand the imaging component of JEFIS to civil actions filed in the Special Civil Part in Bergen, Burlington, Camden, Cumberland, Gloucester, Morris, Salem, Somerset and Union Counties pursuant to Rule 6:1–2(a)(1), so that documents filed in those cases, whether electronically or on paper, can be processed and stored in electronic form as part of the JEFIS project.

This Order supplements, where appropriate, the Court's Orders of December 10, 1996 and February 1, 1999 with regard to the JEFIS project in Monmouth County, the Court's Order of March 27, 2000

permitting the statewide expansion of the electronic filing component of JEFIS, and the Court's Order of October 7, 2003 permitting expansion of the imaging component of JEFIS to Mercer and Ocean Counties.

* * *

On July 7, 2005, the New Jersey Supreme Court issued the following order to be effective on July 7, 2005:

Pursuant to N.J. Const. (1947), Art. VI, sec. 2, par. 3, IT IS ORDERED, effective immediately and until further Order of the Court, that the Rules of Court be relaxed and supplemented as specified in the Court's Order dated March 27, 2000, to permit the Judiciary to further expand the imaging component of JEFIS to Atlantic, Cape May, Essex, Hudson, Hunterdon, Middlesex, Passaic, Sussex and Warren Counties for actions filed pursuant to Rule 6:1–2(a)(1), so that documents in those Special Civil Part cases, whether filed electronically or on paper, can be processed and stored in electronic form as part of the JEFIS project.

1:37–3. Abbreviations; Title on Temporary Assignment

The following abbreviations may be used in orders, judgments, opinions and memoranda:

C.J.	for Chief Justice of the Supreme Court
J.	for Associate Justice of the Supreme Court
P.J.A.D.	for Presiding Judge of a Part of the Appellate Division
J.A.D.	for Judge of the Appellate Division
A.J.S.C.	for Assignment Judge
J.S.C.	for Judge of the Superior Court
P.J.Ch.	for Presiding Judge of the Superior Court, Chancery Division
P.J.F.P.	for Presiding Judge of the Family Part, Chancery Division
P.J.Cv.	for Presiding Judge of the Civil Part, Law Division
P.J.Cr.	for Presiding Judge of the Criminal Part, Law Division
P.J.T.C.	for Presiding Judge of the Tax Court
J.T.C.	for Judge of the Tax Court
P.J.M.C.	for Presiding Judge–Municipal Courts
J.M.C.	for Judge of the Municipal Court

If a judge is temporarily assigned to a court, that judge's permanent title followed by the words "(temporarily assigned)" shall be used.

If a retired judge is recalled and assigned pursuant to N.J.S. 43:6A–13, that judge's permanent title at the time of retirement followed by the phrase "(retired and temporarily assigned on recall)" shall be used.

Note: Source—R.R. 1:33; amended November 27, 1974 to be effective April 1, 1975; amended July 29, 1977, to be effective September 6, 1977; amended June 20, 1979 to be effective July 1, 1979; amended December 20, 1983 to be effective December 31, 1983; amended July 13, 1994 to be effective September 1, 1994; amended July 28, 2004 to be effective September 1, 2004.

RULE 1:38. PUBLIC ACCESS TO COURT RECORDS AND ADMINISTRATIVE RECORDS

1:38–1. Policy

Court records and administrative records as defined by R. 1:38–2 and R. 1:38–4 respectively and within the custody and control of the judiciary are open for public inspection and copying except as otherwise provided in this rule. Exceptions enumerated in this rule shall be narrowly construed in order to implement the policy of open access to records of the judiciary.

Note: New caption for Rule 1:38 adopted July 16, 2009 to be effective September 1, 2009. New Rule 1:38–1 adopted July 16, 2009 to be effective September 1, 2009.

1:38–2. Definition of Court Records

(a) "Court record" includes:

(1) any information maintained by a court in any form in connection with a case or judicial proceeding, including but not limited to pleadings, motions, briefs and their respective attachments, evidentiary exhibits, indices, calendars, and dockets;

(2) any order, judgment, opinion, or decree related to a judicial proceeding;

(3) any official transcript or recording of a public judicial proceeding, in any form;

(4) any information in a computerized case management system created or prepared by the court in connection with a case or judicial proceeding;

(5) any record made or maintained by a Surrogate as a judicial officer.

(b) "Court record" does not include:

(1) information gathered, maintained or stored by a governmental agency or other entity to which the court has access but which is not part of the court record as defined by this rule;

(2) unfiled discovery materials in any action.

Note: New Rule 1:38–2 adopted July 16, 2009 to be effective September 1, 2009.

1:38–3. Court Records Excluded from Public Access

The following court records are excluded from public access:

(a) General. Records required to be kept confidential by statute, rule, or prior case law consistent with this rule, unless otherwise ordered by a court. These records remain confidential even when attached to a non-confidential document.

(b) Internal Records.

(1) Notes, memoranda, draft opinions, or other working papers maintained in any form by or for the use of a justice, judge, or judiciary staff member in the course of performing official duties, except those notes, not otherwise excluded from public access under this rule, that are required by rule or law, e.g., R. 7:2–1(e), to be taken as part of the record of the proceeding;

(2) Records of consultative, advisory, or deliberative discussions pertaining to the rendering of decisions or the management of cases.

(c) Records of Criminal and Municipal Court Proceedings.

(1) Discovery materials provided to the Criminal Division Manager's office by the prosecutor pursuant to R. 3:9–1 and R. 3:13–3;

(2) Writs to produce prisoners pending execution of the writ;

(3) Indictments sealed pursuant to R. 3:6–8(a);

(4) Records relating to grand jury proceedings pursuant to R. 3:6–7 except as provided by R. 3:6–6(b) and R. 3:6–9(d);

(5) Records relating to participants in drug court programs and programs approved for operation under R. 3:28 (Pre-trial Intervention), and reports made for a court or prosecuting attorney pertaining to persons enrolled in or applications for enrollment in such programs, but not the fact of enrollment and the enrollment conditions imposed by the court;

(6) Victim statements unless placed on the record at a public proceeding;

(7) Expunged records pursuant to N.J.S.A. 2C:52–15;

(8) Reports of the Diagnostic Center to the extent provided under R. 3:21–3;

(9) Records relating to child victims of sexual assault or abuse pursuant to N.J.S.A. 2A:82–46;

(10) Search warrants pursuant to Rule 3:5–4 and the affidavit or testimony upon which a warrant is based, except as provided in Rules 3:5–6(c) and 3:13–3;

(11) Documents, records and transcripts related to proceedings and hearings required by the Supreme Court pursuant to *Doe v. Poritz*, 142 *N.J.* 1, 39 (1995), or subsequent orders of the Court;

(12) Names and addresses of victims or alleged victims of domestic violence or sexual offenses.

(d) Records of Family Part Proceedings.

(1) Family Case Information Statements required by R. 5:5–2 including all attachments;

(2) Confidential Litigant Information Sheets pursuant to R. 5:4–2(g);

(3) Medical, psychiatric, psychological, and alcohol and drug dependency records, reports, and evaluations in matters related to child support, child custody, or parenting time determinations;

(4) Documents, records and transcripts related to proceedings and hearings required by the Supreme Court pursuant to Doe v. Poritz, 142 N.J. 1, 39 (1995), or subsequent orders of the Court;

(5) Juvenile delinquency records and reports pursuant to R. 5:19–2 and N.J.S.A. 2A:4A–60;

(6) Records of Juvenile Conference Committees to the extent provided under R. 5:25–1(e);

(7) Expunged juvenile records pursuant to N.J.S.A. 2A:4A–62f and 2C:52–15;

(8) Sealed juvenile records pursuant to N.J.S.A. 2A:4A–62;

(9) Domestic violence records and reports pursuant to N.J.S.A. 2C:25–33;

(10) Names and addresses of victims or alleged victims of domestic violence or sexual offenses;

(11) Records relating to child victims of sexual assault or abuse pursuant to N.J.S.A. 2A:82–46;

(12) Records relating to Division of Youth and Family Services proceedings held pursuant to R. 5:12;

(13) Child custody evaluations, reports, and records pursuant to R. 5:8–4, R. 5:8B, N.J.S.A. 9:2–1, or N.J.S.A. 9:2–3;

(14) Paternity records and reports, except for the final judgments or birth certificates pursuant to N.J.S.A. 9:17–42;

(15) Records and reports relating to child placement matters pursuant to R. 5:13–8(a);

(16) Adoption records and reports pursuant to N.J.S.A. 9:3–52;

(17) Records of hearings on the welfare or status of a child, to the extent provided under R. 5:3–2.

(e) Records of Guardianship Proceedings.

Guardianship records and reports maintained by the Surrogate and by the Chancery Division, Probate Part, except that such records will be made available to the spouse or family members to the third degree of consanguinity of the ward. Any other individual or entity seeking such records must demonstrate before a Superior Court judge a special interest in the matter.

(f) Records of Other Proceedings.

(1) Records pertaining to mediation sessions and complementary dispute resolution proceedings pursuant to R. 1:40–4(d) and R. 7:8–1, but not the fact that mediation has occurred;

(2) Records and transcripts of civil commitment proceedings, pursuant to N.J.S.A. 30:4–24.3, N.J.S.A. 30:4–27.27(c), N.J.S.A. 30:4–82.4h, R. 4:74–7, and R.4:74–7A;

(3) Police investigative reports, unless admitted into evidence or submitted to the court in support of a motion, brief, or other pleading;

(4) Records that are impounded, sealed pursuant to R. 1:38–11, or subject to a protective order pursuant to R. 4:10–3;

(5) Criminal, Family, and Probation Division records pertaining to any investigations and reports made by court staff or pursuant to court order for a court or pertaining to persons on probation;

(6) Family, Finance and Probation Division records containing information pertaining to persons receiving or ordered to pay child support, including the child(ren); custodial parents; non–custodial parents; legal guardians; putative fathers; family members and any other individuals for whom information may be collected and retained by the court in connection with child support cases subject to Title IV–D of the Social Security Act, 42 U.S.C. § 651 et seq. and applicable state and federal statutes, but not the complaint or orders in such cases;

(7) Records maintained by the Judiciary that contain identifying information about a person who has or is suspected of having AIDS or HIV infection, pursuant to N.J.S.A. 26:5C–7, except as provided in N.J.S.A. 26:5C–8 and –9;

(8) Records of appeals from the Division of Developmental Disabilities in accordance with N.J.S.A. 30:4–24.3.

Note: New Rule 1:38–3 adopted July 16, 2009 to be effective September 1, 2009; subparagraph (b)(1) amended December 9, 2009 to be effective immediately; paragraphs (e) and (f) amended January 5, 2010 to be effective immediately; subparagraph (c)(11) amended, subparagraph (c)(12) adopted, and subparagraph (d)(10) amended February 16, 2010 to be effective immediately.

1:38–4. Definition of Administrative Records

An "administrative record" is any information maintained in any form by the judiciary that is not associated with any particular case or judicial proceeding.

Note: New Rule 1:38–4 adopted July 16, 2009 to be effective September 1, 2009.

1:38–5. Administrative Records Excluded from Public Access

The following administrative records are excluded from public access:

(a) Records required to be kept confidential by statute, rule, or prior case law consistent with this rule, unless otherwise ordered by a court;

(b) Notes, memoranda, or other working papers maintained in any form by or for the use of a justice, judge or judiciary staff member in the course of his or her official duties, including administrative duties;

(c) Minutes, reports, memoranda, notes, and correspondence in any form pertaining to the development and implementation of judiciary rules and policies, including draft versions of rules, policies and procedures, self-critical analysis reports, and peer review reports;

(d) Reports, memoranda, and other records pertaining to policies and procedures for court security and data security;

(e) Personnel records, except for an employee's name, title, position, salary, compensation, dates of service, and date and type of separation;

(f) Records concerning volunteers, except for a volunteer's name, title, if any, program to which assigned, and dates of service;

(g) Juror source lists prepared pursuant to N.J.S.A. 2B:20–2, jury questionnaires completed pursuant to N.J.S.A. 2B:20–3, and preliminary lists prepared pursuant to N.J.S.A. 2B:20–4 of persons to be summoned for possible service as grand or petit jurors, which shall remain confidential, except as provided in Rule 1:8–5, unless otherwise ordered by the Assignment Judge;

(h) Reports required to be prepared by trial court judges on a weekly, monthly, or other basis and submitted to the Administrative Director of the Courts pursuant to R. 1:32–1;

(i) Records and information obtained and maintained by the Judicial Performance Committee pursuant to R. 1:35A, except as otherwise provided in that rule;

(j) Records of the Ethics Telephone Research Service to the extent provided under R. 1:19–9;

(k) Records of proceedings concerning advisory opinions of the Committee on Attorney Advertising to the extent provided under R. 1:19A–5;

(l) Records relating to attorney discipline to the extent provided under R. 1:20–9;

(m) Records of District Fee Arbitration Committees to the extent provided under R. 1:20A–5;

(n) Records of the Attorney Disciplinary Oversight Committee to the extent provided under R. 1:20B–4;

(o) Records of the Lawyers' Fund for Client Protection to the extent provided under R. 1:28–9;

(p) Records of the Advisory Committee on Judicial Conduct to the extent provided under R. 2:15–20.

Note: New Rule 1:38–5 adopted July 16, 2009 to be effective September 1, 2009; paragraph (g) amended January 5, 2010 to be effective immediately.

1:38–6. Intergovernmental Exchanges

The Supreme Court may authorize the exchange of information, otherwise excluded from public access, with other branches of state government, with other state governments, and with the federal government when the public benefit of such disclosure outweighs the need for confidentiality. Child support information may be exchanged only to the extent allowed by federal law and regulations.

Note: New Rule 1:38–6 adopted July 16, 2009 to be effective September 1, 2009.

1:38–7. Confidential Personal Identifiers

(a) Definition of Confidential Personal Identifiers. A confidential personal identifier is a Social Security number, driver's license number, vehicle plate number, insurance policy number, active financial account number, or active credit card number.

(b) Prohibition on Submission of Confidential Personal Identifiers to the Court. A party shall not set forth confidential personal identifiers as defined in R. 1:38–7(a) in any document or pleading submitted to the court unless otherwise required by statute, rule, administrative directive, or court order; provided, however, that an active financial account number may be identified by the last four digits when the financial account is the subject of the litigation and cannot otherwise be identified.

(c) Compliance.

(1) In every trial Division of the Superior Court where a Case Information Statement is required, parties shall certify in the Case Information Statement that all confidential personal identifiers have been redacted and that subsequent papers submitted to the court will not contain confidential personal identifiers in accordance with the provisions of this rule.

(2) In General Equity and Special Civil Part matters, where no Case Information Statement is required, parties shall include the following language in the first filed pleading as provided in R. 4:5–1(b)(3), "I certify that confidential personal identifiers have been redacted from documents now submitted to the court, and will be redacted from all documents submitted in the future in accordance with Rule 1:38–7(b)."

(3) In all criminal matters, the judge shall inform both parties at the time of the defendant's arraignment

status conference that confidential personal identifiers must be redacted from any documents submitted to the court as provided in R. 1:38–7(b) and R. 3:9–1(c).

(d) Judgment Debtors. Applications for any writ, order, or judgment issued by the court involving a judgment debtor may include the judgment debtor's name(s), address, date of birth, the last four digits of active financial account numbers, and the last four digits of the individual's Social Security number. No other personal identifiers shall be included.

(e) Redaction of Required Personal Identifiers. When confidential personal identifiers as defined in R. 1:38–7(a) are required by statute, rule, or court order to be included in documents or pleadings, such identifiers shall be redacted before public inspection is permitted. This redaction requirement, however, does not apply to driver's license numbers that the New Jersey Motor Vehicle Commission requires in documents pertaining to the suspension and reinstatement of licenses.

(f) Redaction of Social Security Numbers from Records in Bulk. Any request for the mass release, in bulk, of electronically stored or microfilmed records containing Social Security numbers must be submitted to the Administrative Director of the Courts. A fee may be charged for the cost of redacting Social Security numbers from such records.

Note: New Rule 1:38–7 adopted July 16, 2009 to be effective September 1, 2009; paragraph (e) amended September 22, 2009 to be effective immediately.

1:38–8. Documents Improperly Submitted to Court

A party or other interested person may request that the court remove from its file an improperly submitted document upon application to the court and notice to all parties. A document is deemed improperly submitted to the court if the person who submitted the document had no legitimate basis in rule or law for doing so and if the document is not an evidentiary exhibit or part of a motion, brief, or other pleading. The party or interested person seeking to have a document removed from a court file bears the burden of proving by a preponderance of the evidence that it was improperly submitted.

Note: New Rule 1:38–8 adopted July 16, 2009 to be effective September 1, 2009.

1:38–9. Fees

The Supreme Court shall establish a schedule of fees for copies of records.

Note: New Rule 1:38–9 adopted July 16, 2009 to be effective September 1, 2009.

1:38–10. Determinations; Appeal Process

(a) Requests for court records or administrative records to be inspected or copied under this rule shall be directed to the following officers or their designees:

(1) Supreme Court records (including committees and offices reporting to the Supreme Court): Clerk of the Supreme Court

(2) Superior Court records, Clerk's office, including Foreclosure Unit: Clerk of the Superior Court

(3) Superior Court records, Appellate Division: Clerk of the Appellate Division

(4) Superior Court records, Law and Chancery Divisions (other than Clerk's office and Probate Part): Trial Court Administrator of appropriate vicinage

(5) Superior Court records, Chancery Division, Probate Part, and Surrogate's Court records: Surrogate of appropriate county

(6) Tax Court records: Clerk of the Tax Court

(7) Municipal Court records: Municipal Court Director or Administrator of appropriate municipal court

(8) Administrative Office of the Courts records and all other judiciary records: Deputy Administrative Director of the Courts

(b) Any person denied access to a court record or administrative record by one of the above officers or their designees may seek review by the Administrative Director of the Courts under procedures established by the Supreme Court, except that an appeal regarding a municipal court record shall first be filed with the Trial Court Administrator of the appropriate vicinage. An appeal from the decision of the Administrative Director shall be filed in the Appellate Division in accordance with R. 2:2–3(a)(2).

Note: New Rule 1:38–10 adopted July 16, 2009 to be effective September 1, 2009.

1:38–11. Sealing of Court Records

(a) Information in a court record may be sealed by court order for good cause as defined in this section. The moving party shall bear the burden of proving by a preponderance of the evidence that good cause exists.

(b) Good cause to seal a record shall exist when:

(1) Disclosure will likely cause a clearly defined and serious injury to any person or entity; and

(2) The person's or entity's interest in privacy substantially outweighs the presumption that all court and administrative records are open for public inspection pursuant to R. 1:38.

(c) The provisions of this rule do not apply to actions required to be sealed pursuant to the New Jersey False Claims Act (N.J.S.A. 2A:32C–5(c)).

Note: New Rule 1:38–11 adopted July 16, 2009 to be effective September 1, 2009; new paragraph (c) adopted January 5, 2010 to be effective immediately.

1:38–12. Unsealing of Court Records

A record that has been sealed by order of the court may be unsealed upon motion by any person or entity. The proponent for continued sealing shall bear the burden of proving by a preponderance of the evidence that good cause continues to exist for sealing the record.

Note: New Rule 1:38–12 adopted July 16, 2009 to be effective September 1, 2009.

RULE 1:39. CERTIFICATION OF ATTORNEYS

An attorney of the State of New Jersey may be certified as a civil trial attorney, a criminal trial attorney, a matrimonial law attorney, or a workers' compensation law attorney, or in more than one designated area of practice, but only on establishing eligibility and satisfying requirements regarding education, experience, knowledge, and skill for each designated area of practice as set forth below.

To assist in the administration of the certification function, the Supreme Court shall establish, in accordance with these rules, a Board on Attorney Certification.

Note: Adopted January 26, 1979 to be effective April 1, 1979; amended May 15, 1980 to be effective September 8, 1980; amended June 28, 1996 to be effective September 1, 1996.

1:39–1. Board on Attorney Certification

(a) Appointment; Officers. The Supreme Court shall appoint a Board on Attorney Certification consisting of not more than eleven members of the bar of the State of New Jersey. Members shall be appointed for three-year terms. No member who has served four full three-year terms successively shall be eligible for immediate reappointment. Members appointed to fill unexpired terms may be reappointed to four successive terms. The Supreme Court shall annually designate a Chair and a Vice Chair from among the members of the Board. The Secretary of the Board of Bar Examiners shall serve as Secretary. The Administrative Director of the Courts shall designate a member of the Administrative Director's staff with fiscal responsibilities to serve as Treasurer.

(b) Quorum. One more than half of the number of members sitting on the Board shall constitute a quorum and all determinations shall be made by a majority of a quorum except that a decision to grant certification or recertification shall have the concurrence of at least one more than half the members sitting on the Board.

(c) Regulations. The Board on Attorney Certification shall, subject to the prior approval of the Supreme Court, promulgate, and amend Regulations governing the certification program and providing that the proceedings and files shall be confidential and shall not be disclosed to or attended by anyone except as authorized by these rules, the Regulations, or upon the direction of the Court.

(d) Operations. The Board shall, consistent with these rules and its Regulations, establish procedures, publish forms and maintain records as required for the conduct of the Board's operations and the certification of attorneys. The Board shall function as an appellate arm for Certification Committee decisions. The Board will be responsible for the financial and administrative operations of the certification program. The Board will maintain responsibility for policy, for making recommendations to the Court in respect of Rule and Regulation amendments, and for accrediting continuing legal education courses.

(e) Legal Education. The Board shall cooperate with law schools in this State, the Institute for Continuing Legal Education, and other recognized continuing legal education sponsors in developing and maintaining courses, clinics and other offerings by such institutions to enhance the skills and increase the knowledge of attorneys who seek to be certified by the Supreme Court. The Board may also cooperate with other law schools, bar associations and agencies interested in legal education.

(f) Reports. Reports as to the activities of the Board may be submitted to the Supreme Court from time to time. An annual report shall be submitted by February 15th of each year as to the status of the certification program.

(g) Funds. To the extent that the Board is not self-supporting, funds necessary for the operation of the certification program for attorneys shall be provided by the Administrative Office of the Courts.

(h) Fees. Each applicant for certification and recertification shall pay required fees to the Secretary for the use of the Board. The fees shall be established in amounts to be set from time to time by the Board, subject to the approval of the Supreme Court, and, to the extent possible, so as to enable the program to be self-supporting.

(i) Effect of Board Membership. During service with the Board on Attorney Certification, no member shall apply for or be examined for certification in this State. A Certified Board Member may be recertified during the term of service on the Board.

Note: Adopted January 26, 1979 to be effective April 1, 1979; paragraphs (a), (b), (c), (d), (g), (h), and (i) amended May 15, 1980 to be effective September 8, 1980; paragraph (i) amended November 5, 1986 to be effective January 1, 1987; paragraph (a) amended February 8, 1993 to be effective immediately; paragraphs (a), (b), (c), (d), (e), (g), (h), and (i) amended June 28, 1996, to take effect September 1, 1996; paragraphs (a), (b), (c), (d), (e), and (f) amended July 5, 2000 to be effective September 5, 2000.

1:39–1A. Certification Committees

(a) **Appointment; Officer.** The Supreme Court shall appoint a Civil Trial Law Committee, a Criminal Trial Law Committee, a Matrimonial Law Committee, and a Workers' Compensation Law Committee. The Court shall appoint no fewer than four and no more than eleven members of the bar to serve on each Committee. Committee members shall be appointed for three-year terms. No member who has served four full three-year terms successively shall be eligible for immediate reappointment. Members appointed to fill unexpired terms may be reappointed to four successive full terms. The Supreme Court shall designate one member of each Committee to serve as Chair of that Committee. The Chairs shall serve, ex officio, as members of the Board on Attorney Certification.

(b) **Quorum.** For each Committee, one more than half the number of members shall constitute a quorum.

(c) **Operations.** The Committees shall, consistent with the Regulations of the Board, draft applications for certification and recertification, review applications to determine eligibility for certification and recertification, create and grade examinations, and undertake such other tasks as may be assigned by the Board. In accordance with these Rules and the Board's Regulations, adverse decisions by a Certification Committee in respect of eligibility or examination are reviewable by the Board or the Supreme Court.

(d) **Effect of Committee Membership.** During service on a Certification Committee, no Committee member shall apply for or be examined for certification in this State. A Committee member who is not yet certified and who has served his or her full term on the Committee may apply for certification at the conclusion of his or her term on the Committee. Once making application, the former Committee member, if otherwise eligible for certification, will not have to take the appropriate certification examination. A previously-certified Committee member may be recertified during his or her term of service on the Committee. An attorney who sits on a Certification Committee who is not yet certified may offer a referral fee pursuant to RG. 402:6 so long as a referral fee is permitted.

Note: Adopted June 28, 1996, to be effective September 1, 1996; paragraphs (a) and (c) amended and new paragraph (d) adopted July 5, 2000 to be effective September 5, 2000.

1:39–2. Eligibility

Subject to the specific requirements contained in the Regulations of the Board, an attorney shall be eligible to apply for certification in a designated area of practice on demonstrating to the Board on Attorney Certification the following:

(a) **Minimum Admission Period; Practice of Law.** Membership in good standing with a plenary license at the bar of the State of New Jersey for at least five years. Applicants for certification must be (1) engaged in the private practice of law, wherein the applicant represents and gives legal advice to clients, and maintains the appropriate bank accounts pursuant to Rule 1:21–6; or (2) employed by State, county, or municipal government representing and giving legal advice to clients.

(b) **Professional Experience.** Extensive and substantial experience as an attorney in the designated area of practice as set forth in the Board's Regulations.

(c) **Professional Reputation.** The Board shall require each applicant to establish his or her professional competence in the designated area of practice. Pursuant to the Regulations of the Board, the applicant shall submit to the Board the names of a specified number of peer references of whom the Board may inquire with regard to the applicant's competence as an attorney within the designated area of practice. The Board may inquire of other attorneys or judges with respect to the professional qualifications and reputation of the applicant.

(d) **Educational Experience.** An applicant must demonstrate to the Board satisfactory and substantial educational involvement within the three years immediately preceding his or her application. The Board will evaluate the nature, sponsorship, faculty, content and duration of educational involvements submitted by applicants on a case by case basis. The Board shall adopt Regulations governing the number of credits of continuing legal education required for certification and the approval of continuing legal education courses, and shall impose such fees as it determines are appropriate, subject to the approval of the Supreme Court.

(e) **Ongoing Obligation.** Each applicant has an ongoing responsibility to report to the Board any malpractice actions brought, disciplinary complaints filed, fee arbitrations filed, or any discipline imposed on him or her during the pendency of the application. In addition, each applicant has an ongoing obligation to notify the Board during the pendency of the application process of any additional information that relates to the requirements for certification.

Note: Adopted January 26, 1979 to be effective April 1, 1979; paragraph (a) amended, former paragraph (b) deleted and former paragraph (c) redesignated as (b) and amended, former paragraph (d) redesignated as (c) and amended, and new paragraph (d) adopted May 15, 1980 to be effective September 8, 1980; paragraph (a) amended November 1, 1985 to be effective January 2, 1986; paragraph (d) amended November 7, 1988 to be effective January 2, 1989; paragraphs (b)(2) and (c) amended July 13, 1994 to be effective September 1, 1994; introduction and paragraphs (b), (c), and (d) amended June 28, 1996, to be effective September 1, 1996; corrective amendment to paragraph (c) adopted August 1, 1996 to be effective September 1, 1996; paragraphs (a), (b), (c), and (d) amended and new paragraph (e) adopted July 5, 2000 to be effective September 5, 2000; paragraph (a) amended July 28, 2004 to be effective September 1, 2004.

1:39–3. Written Examination

An attorney shall be eligible for certification in a designated area of practice upon successful completion of a written examination on that area of practice within 18 months of the notification by the Board that the qualification requirements of R. 1:39–2 have been met. Admission to each written examination shall be upon payment of the examination fee to be set from time to time by the Board, subject to approval by the Supreme Court. The Board shall adopt Regulations governing the format and content of the examination and grading procedures to be followed.

Note: Former rule adopted January 26, 1979 to be effective April 1, 1979; former rule deleted and present rule adopted May 15, 1980 to be effective September 8, 1980; amended June 28, 1996 to be effective September 1, 1996; corrective amendment adopted August 1, 1996 to be effective September 1, 1996; amended July 5, 2000 to be effective September 5, 2000.

1:39–4. Decision by Board

(a) Ineligible Applicants. An applicant who is found ineligible to sit for the examination shall be notified of those areas in which he or she did not meet the program's requirements. An applicant may supplement his or her application to correct deficiencies, but such supplemental materials must be submitted within fourteen days of the date of notification of ineligibility. Should a Certification Committee determine that an applicant is ineligible to sit for the examination, that applicant has fourteen days to apply to the Board for de novo review pursuant to the Board's Regulations.

(b) Duration of Eligibility; Qualified Applicants. An applicant found eligible must successfully complete the examination requirements as found in Part Two and Three of the Board's Regulations within eighteen months of notification of eligibility to sit for the examination. If eligibility expires, the applicant must file a new application for certification. When an applicant has complied with the requirements of Rule 1:39–2 and 3 and the Board's Regulations, the Certification Committee shall forward the file to the Board, which shall review the file and make such further inquiry, pursuant to its Regulations, as it deems necessary and appropriate. Thereafter, the Board shall determine within a reasonable time whether the applicant is qualified for certification in the designated area of practice.

Note: Former rule adopted January 26, 1979 to be effective April 1, 1979; former rule deleted and former Rule 1:39–5 redesignated Rule 1:39–4 and amended May 15, 1980 to be effective September 8, 1980; new paragraph (a) adopted and former rule amended and designated paragraph (b) June 28, 1996, to be effective September 1, 1996; paragraphs (a) and (b) amended July 5, 2000 to be effective September 5, 2000.

1:39–5. Grant; Duration; Withholding of Certification

(a) Grant of Certification. If upon due consideration the Board determines that an applicant is quali-

fied for certification as a civil or a criminal trial attorney, a matrimonial law attorney, or a workers' compensation law attorney, it shall so report to the Supreme Court, which shall direct the making of an appropriate entry on the roll of attorneys and shall cause to be issued an appropriate document attesting thereto.

(b) Duration of Certification. A grant of certification shall be effective for five years from the date of entry on the roll of attorneys. Subject to the approval of the Supreme Court, the Board may adopt regulations authorizing a tolling of the duration period of certification under specific circumstances, such as government employment or appointment to the judiciary.

(c) Withholding of Certification. If upon due consideration the Board determines that an applicant is not qualified for certification in a designated area of practice, it shall so notify the applicant, advising as to the procedure for reapplication in accordance with its regulations.

Note: Adopted January 26, 1979 as Rule 1:39–6 to be effective April 1, 1979; redesignated Rule 1:39–5 and paragraphs (a) and (c) amended and paragraph (d) deleted May 15, 1980 to be effective September 8, 1980; paragraph (c) amended July 13, 1994 to be effective September 1, 1994; paragraphs (a) and (c) amended June 28, 1996, to be effective September 1, 1996; paragraph (b) amended July 5, 2000 to be effective September 5, 2000.

1:39–6. Effect of Certification

(a) Not Exclusive. The standards and systems adopted herein shall in no way limit the right of a certified attorney to practice law in any respect nor shall any attorney-at-law of this State be barred from engaging in a designated area of practice by reason of lack of eligibility or certification.

(b) Use of Designation. An attorney who has satisfied the requirements of this rule and who has been certified may make dignified use of the area of practice designation as provided in the Regulations of the Board.

(c) Restrictions on Designation Use. No use may be made of the designations set forth in the Regulations of the Board except as therein provided, nor may other words or combination of words be used by a certified attorney in place of such designations.

(d) Division of Fees. A certified attorney who receives a case referral from a lawyer who is not a partner in or associate of that attorney's law firm or law office may divide a fee for legal services with the referring attorney or the referring attorney's estate. The fee division may be made without regard to services performed or responsibility assumed by the referring attorney, provided that the total fee charged the client relates only to the matter referred and does not exceed reasonable compensation for the legal services rendered therein. The provisions of this paragraph shall not apply to matrimonial law matters that are referred to certified attorneys.

(e) Obligation of Certified Attorneys. A certified attorney is under a continuing obligation, during the duration of the certification period, to notify the Board of any malpractice action brought, fee arbitrations filed, disciplinary complaints filed, or discipline imposed.

Note: Adopted January 26, 1979 as Rule 1:39–7 to be effective April 1, 1979; amended and redesignated Rule 1:39–6 May 15, 1980 to be effective September 8, 1980; amended December 13, 1983 to be effective January 3, 1984; paragraph (d) adopted November 1, 1985 to be effective January 2, 1986; paragraph (b) amended November 7, 1988 to be effective January 2, 1989; paragraph (d) amended July 13, 1994 to be effective September 1, 1994; paragraphs (a), (b), (c), and (d) amended June 28, 1996, to be effective September 1, 1996; corrective amendment adopted August 1, 1996 to be effective September 1, 1996; new paragraph (e) adopted July 5, 2000 to be effective September 5, 2000.

1:39–7. Renewal of Certification

A member of the bar of this State who has been certified pursuant to these rules and the Regulations of the Board, may apply for a renewal of such certification during the last twelve months of the five year period for which the attorney had received certification. The application for renewal shall include information specified in the Regulations of the Board, which will set forth the substantive and educational requirements for recertification. The appropriate Certification Committee and the Board shall render a decision regarding the application for renewal of certification in the same manner as provided by these rules and Regulations for initial certification.

Note: Adopted January 26, 1979, as Rule 1:39–8 to be effective April 1, 1979; amended and redesignated Rule 1:39–7 May 15, 1980 to be effective September 8, 1980; amended November 2, 1987 to be effective January 1, 1988; amended June 28, 1996, to be effective September 1, 1996; amended July 5, 2000 to be effective September 5, 2000.

1:39–8. Termination of Certification

(a) Basis for Termination.   Certification may be terminated after a finding by the Board that a certified attorney no longer demonstrates continuing competence or has engaged in conduct or omissions to discharge responsibility that are not acceptable on the part of a certified attorney.

(b) Procedures to Follow. In all cases a complaint, notice, and opportunity to be heard shall be given in accordance, so far as applicable, with the rules and administrative guidelines governing plenary ethics hearings (Rule 1:20–3(h) to –3(m), –3(o)).

(c) Effect of Determination of Unethical Conduct. Whenever an attorney has been found guilty, either as an attorney or a judge, of unethical conduct in a disciplinary proceeding in this state resulting in public discipline, a copy of the decision or opinion in that matter shall be conclusive evidence of the facts established there. The sole issue to be determined by the

Board shall be the extent of the sanction to be imposed. However, a respondent may introduce relevant evidence in mitigation that is not inconsistent with the essential facts established in the disciplinary decision or opinion.

(d) Hearing Panels; Recommendation to Court. In all cases hearings may be held before a panel of three members of the Board, which shall render a report to the full Board. In appropriate circumstances, the matter may be referred for consideration to the District Ethics Committee. The Board shall recommend to the Supreme Court the sanction to be imposed, which may include either termination or suspension for a stated period. Should the Supreme Court approve the Board's recommendation to terminate certification, the Board shall notify other certifying agencies to which the attorney holds a certification of that termination.

(e) Burden of Proofs; Effect of Termination. In proceedings under this Rule, the presenter shall have the burden of proof. The respondent shall have the burden of proving all affirmative defenses, constitutional challenges, and mitigating circumstances, if any. The standard of proof for the presenter and the respondent shall be clear and convincing evidence on all issues. No person whose certification has been terminated pursuant to this Rule may be thereafter again certified except in accordance with the procedure set forth in Rule 1:39–1 to –9 and the Regulations of the Board.

(f) Lapsing of Certification. An attorney who allows his or her certification to lapse and thereafter seeks to be certified shall be required to comply with all of the requirements for making an initial application for certification. The Board shall notify other certifying organizations to which the certified attorney holds a certification that his or her certification by the Supreme Court has lapsed.

Note: Adopted January 26, 1979, as Rule 1:39–9 to be effective April 1, 1979; amended and redesignated Rule 1:39–8 May 15, 1980 to be effective September 8, 1980; amended November 2, 1987 to be effective January 1, 1988; amended and rule designated as paragraphs (a), (b), (c), (d), and (e) June 28, 1996, to be effective September 1, 1996; paragraph (d) amended and new paragraph (f) adopted July 5, 2000 to be effective September 5, 2000.

1:39–9. Review of Action of Board

Within 30 days after final action of the Board on Attorney Certification with respect to an application for certification, recertification, or termination of certification, an aggrieved member of the bar may seek review thereof by serving on the Secretary of the Board a notice of petition for review and by filing the original notice with the Clerk of the Supreme Court. The notice shall set forth the petitioner's name and address and, if he or she is represented, the name and address of counsel. The notice shall designate the action of the Board sought to be reviewed and shall concisely state the manner in which the petitioner is aggrieved. It shall be accompanied by the required filing fee. Thereafter, deposit for costs, filings and proceedings shall be as set forth in R. 1:19–8, Petition for Review, except that the record on review shall be the Board's entire file with respect to the applicant or respondent as to whom review is sought.

The applicant shall not have access to the materials in the file submitted by another person.

Note: Adopted January 26, 1979, as Rule 1:39–10 to be effective April 1, 1979; amended and redesignated Rule 1:39–9 May 15, 1980 to be effective September 8, 1980; amended November 2, 1987 to be effective January 1, 1988; amended July 13, 1994 to be effective September 1, 1994; amended June 28, 1996, to be effective September 1, 1996; amended July 5, 2000 to be effective September 5, 2000.

RULE 1:40. COMPLEMENTARY DISPUTE RESOLUTION PROGRAMS

1:40–1. Purpose, Goals

Complementary Dispute Resolution Programs (CDR) provided for by these rules are available in the Superior Court and Municipal Courts and constitute an integral part of the judicial process, intended to enhance its quality and efficacy. Attorneys have a responsibility to become familiar with available CDR programs and inform their clients of them.

Note: Adopted July 14, 1992 to be effective September 1, 1992; amended July 5, 2000 to be effective September 5, 2000.

1:40–2. Modes and Definitions of Complementary Dispute Resolution

Complementary Dispute Resolution Programs (CDR) conducted under judicial supervision in accordance with these rules, as well as guidelines and directives of the Supreme Court, and the persons who provide the services to these programs are as follows:

(a) "Adjudicative Processes" means and includes the following:

(1) *Arbitration:* A process by which each party and/or its counsel presents its case to a neutral third party, who then renders a specific award. The parties may stipulate in advance of the arbitration that the award shall be binding. If not so stipulated, the provisions of Rule 4:21A–6 (Entry of Judgment; Trial De Novo) shall be applicable.

(2) *Settlement Proceedings:* A process by which the parties appear before a neutral third party or panel of such neutrals, who assists them in attempting to resolve their dispute by voluntary agreement.

(3) *Summary Jury Trial:* A process by which the parties present summaries of their respective positions to a panel of jurors, which may then issue a non-binding advisory opinion as to liability, damages, or both.

(b) "Evaluative Processes" means and includes the following:

(1) *Early Neutral Evaluation (ENE):* A pre-discovery process by which the attorneys, in the presence of their respective clients, present their factual and legal conten-

tions to a neutral evaluator, who then provides an assessment of the strengths and weaknesses of each position and, if settlement does not ensue, assists in narrowing the dispute and proposing discovery guidelines.

(2) *Neutral Fact Finding:* A process by which a neutral, agreed upon by the parties, investigates and analyzes a dispute involving complex or technical issues, and who then makes non-binding findings and recommendations.

(c) "Facilitative Process" means and includes mediation, which is a process by which a mediator facilitates communication between parties in an effort to promote settlement without imposition of the mediator's own judgment regarding the issues in dispute.

(d) "Hybrid Process" means and includes:

(1) *Mediation-arbitration:* A process by which, after an initial mediation, unresolved issues are then arbitrated.

(2) *Mini-trial:* A process by which the parties present their legal and factual conditions to either a panel of representatives selected by each party, or a neutral third party, or both, in an effort to define the issues in dispute and to assist settlement negotiations. A neutral third party may issue an advisory opinion, which shall not, however, be binding, unless the parties have so stipulated in writing in advance.

(e) "Other CDR Programs" means and includes any other method or technique of complementary dispute resolution permitted by guideline or directive of the Supreme Court.

(f) "Neutral": A "neutral" is an individual who provides a CDR process. A "qualified neutral" is an individual included on any roster of neutrals maintained by the Administrative Office of the Courts or an Assignment Judge. Neutral evaluators, neutral fact finders, and settlement program panelists are not required to comply with the training requirements of Rule 1:40–12 or to be on any roster of neutrals maintained by the Administrative Office of the Courts or an Assignment Judge.

Note: Adopted July 14, 1992 to be effective September 1, 1992; caption and text amended, paragraphs (a) through (d) deleted, new paragraphs (a) through (f) adopted July 5, 2000 to be effective September 5, 2000; corrective amendment to paragraph (a)(3) adopted November 8, 2000 to be effective immediately.

1:40–3. Organization and Management

(a) **Vicinage Organization and Management.** Pursuant to these rules and Supreme Court guidelines, the Assignment Judge of each vicinage shall have overall responsibility for CDR programs, including their development and oversight, continuing relations with the Bar to secure the effectiveness of these programs, and mechanisms to educate judges, attorneys, staff, and the public on the benefits of CDR. The assignment judge shall appoint a CDR coordinator to assist in the oversight, coordination and management of the vicinage CDR programs. The Assignment Judge shall maintain, pursuant to these rules, all required rosters of neutrals except the roster of statewide civil, general equity, and probate action mediators.

(b) **Statewide Organization and Management.** The Administrative Office of the Courts shall have the responsibility (1) to promote uniformity and quality of CDR programs in all vicinages; (2) to monitor and evaluate vicinage CDR programs and assist CDR Coordinators in implementing them; (3) to serve as a clearinghouse for ideas, issues, and new trends relating to CDR, both in New Jersey and in other jurisdictions; (4) to develop CDR pilot projects to meet new needs; (5) to monitor training and continuing education programs for neutrals; and (6) to institutionalize relationships relating to CDR with the bar, universities, the Marie L. Garibaldi ADR Inn of Court, and private providers of CDR services. The Administrative Office of the Courts shall maintain the statewide roster of civil, general equity, and probate action mediators.

Note: Adopted July 14, 1992 to be effective September 1, 1992; caption amended, text amended and designated as paragraph (a), and new paragraph (b) adopted July 5, 2000 to be effective September 5, 2000.

1:40–4. Mediation—General Rules

(a) **Referral to Mediation.** Except as otherwise provided by these rules, a Superior Court or Municipal Court judge may require the parties to attend a mediation session at any time following the filing of a complaint.

(b) **Compensation and Payment of Mediators.** Parties in Superior Court, except in the Special Civil Part, assigned to mediation pursuant to this rule shall equally share the fees and expenses of the mediator on an ongoing basis, subject to court review and allocation to create equity. Any fee or expense of the mediator shall be waived in cases, as to those parties exempt, pursuant to Rule 1:13-2(a). A party may opt out of the mediation process after the mediator has expended two hours of service, which shall be allocated equally between preparation and the first mediation session, and which shall be at no cost to the parties. Fees shall be as determined by the mediator and the parties. Failure to pay the mediator may result in an order by the court to pay the fees and costs of the mediator including any additional costs and fees incurred due to the non-payment and imposing appropriate sanctions.

(c) **Evidentiary Privilege.** A mediation communication is not subject to discovery or admissible in evidence in any subsequent proceeding except as provided by the New Jersey Uniform Mediation Act, N.J.S.A. 2A:23C–1 to –13. A party may, however, establish the substance of the mediation communication in any such proceeding by independent evidence.

(d) **Confidentiality.** Unless the participants in a mediation agree otherwise or to the extent disclosure is permitted by this rule, no party, mediator, or other participant in a mediation may disclose any mediation communication to anyone who was not a participant in the mediation. A mediator may disclose a mediation communication to prevent harm to others to the extent such mediation communication would be admissible in a court proceeding. A mediator has the duty to disclose to a proper authority information obtained at a mediation session if required by law or if the mediator has a reasonable belief that such disclosure will prevent a participant from committing a criminal or illegal act likely to result in death or serious bodily harm. No mediator may appear as counsel for any person in the same or any related matter. A lawyer representing a client at a mediation session shall be governed by the provisions of RPC 1.6.

(e) **Limitations on Service as a Mediator.**

(1) Mediators shall be qualified and trained in accordance with the provisions of Rule 1:40– 12.

(2) No one holding a public office or position or any candidate for a public office or position shall serve as a court- approved mediator in a matter directly or indirectly involving the governmental entity in which that individual serves or is seeking to serve.

(3) The approval of the Assignment Judge is required for service as a mediator by any of the following: (A) police or other law enforcement officers employed by the State or any local unit of government; (B) employees of any court; or (C) government officials or employees whose duties involve regular contact with the court in which they serve E.

(4) The Assignment Judge shall also have the discretion to require prior review and approval of the Supreme Court of prospective mediators whose employment or position appears to the Assignment Judge to require such review and approval.

(f) **Mediator Disclosure of Conflict of Interest.**

(1) Before accepting a mediation, a person who is requested to serve as a mediator shall:

(A) make an inquiry that is reasonable under the circumstances to determine whether there are any known facts that a reasonable person would consider likely to affect the impartiality of the mediator, including a financial or personal interest in the outcome of the mediation or an existing or past relationship with a mediation party or foreseeable participant in the mediation; and

(B) disclose any such known fact to the mediation parties as soon as is practicable before accepting a mediation.

(2) If a mediator learns any fact described in subparagraph (f)(1)(A) after accepting a mediation, the mediator shall disclose it as soon as is practicable.

(3) After entry of the order of referral in an economic mediation, if the court is advised by the mediator, counsel, or one of the parties that a conflict of interest exists, the court shall reassign the case to a different mediator. The parties shall have the opportunity to select a replacement mediator from the roster or the court may appoint one. An amended order of referral shall then be prepared and provided to the parties. All data shall be entered into the Family Automated Case Tracking System (FACTS).

(g) Conduct of Mediation Proceedings. Mediation proceedings shall commence with an opening statement by the mediator describing the purpose and procedures of the process. Mediators may require the participation of persons with negotiating authority. An attorney or other individual designated by a party may accompany the party to and participate in a mediation. A waiver of representation or participation given before the mediation may be rescinded. Non–party witnesses may be heard in the discretion of the mediator, and other non-parties shall be permitted to attend only with the consent of the parties and the mediator. Multiple sessions may be scheduled. Attorneys and parties have an obligation to participate in the mediation process in good faith in accordance with program guidelines.

(h) Termination of Mediation.

(1) The mediator or a participant may terminate the session if (A) there is an imbalance of power between the parties that the mediator cannot overcome, (B) a party challenges the impartiality of the mediator, (C) there is abusive behavior that the mediator cannot control, or (D) a party continuously resists the mediation process or the mediator.

(2) The mediator shall terminate the session if (A) there is a failure of communication that seriously impedes effective discussion, (B) the mediator believes a party is under the influence of drugs or alcohol, or (C) the mediator believes continued mediation is inappropriate or inadvisable for any reason.

(i) Final Disposition. If the mediation results in the parties' total or partial agreement, it shall be reduced to writing and a copy thereof furnished to each party. The agreement need not be filed with the court, but if formal proceedings have been stayed pending mediation, the mediator shall report to the court whether agreement has been reached. If an agreement is not reached, the matter shall be referred back to court for formal disposition.

Note: Adopted July 14, 1992 to be effective September 1, 1992; paragraph (c)(3) amended and paragraph (c)(4) adopted June 28, 1996 to be effective September 1, 1996; paragraphs (a) and (c)(2) amended and paragraph (c)(3)(v) adopted July 10, 1998 to be effective September 1, 1998; caption amended, paragraph (a) amended and redesignated as paragraphs (a) and (b), paragraphs (b), (c), (d), (e), and (f) amended and redesignated as paragraphs (c), (d), (e), (f), and (g) July 5, 2000 to be effective September 5, 2000; paragraphs (d)(2) and (d)(3) amended July 28, 2004 to be effective September 1, 2004; paragraph (b) amended July 27, 2006 to be effective September 1, 2006; new paragraph (c) adopted, former paragraph (c) redesignated as paragraph (d) and amended, former paragraph (d) redesignated as paragraph (e), new paragraph (f) adopted, former paragraph (e) redesignated as paragraph (g) and amended, former paragraph (f) redesignated as paragraph (h), and former paragraph (g) redesignated as paragraph (i) June 15, 2007 to be effective September 1, 2007; paragraph (b) amended and new subparagraph (f)(3) adopted July 16, 2009 to be effective September 1, 2009.

1:40–5. Mediation in Family Part Matters

(a) Mediation of Custody and Parenting Time Actions

(1) Screening and Referral. All complaints or motions involving a custody or parenting time issue shall be screened to determine whether the issue is genuine and substantial, and if such a determination is made, the matter shall be referred to mediation for resolution in the child's best interests. However, no matter shall be referred to mediation if there is in effect a preliminary or final order of domestic violence entered pursuant to the Prevention of Domestic Violence Act (N.J.S.A. 2C:25–17 et seq.). In matters involving domestic violence in which no order has been entered or in cases involving child abuse or sexual abuse, the custody or parenting time issues shall be referred to mediation provided that the issues of domestic violence, child abuse or sexual abuse shall not be mediated in the custody mediation process. The mediator or either party may petition the court for removal of the case from mediation based upon a determination of good cause.

(2) Conduct of Mediation. In addition to the general requirements of Rule 1:40–4, the parties shall be required to attend a mediation orientation program and may be required to attend an initial mediation session. Mediation sessions shall be closed to the public. The mediator and the parties should consider whether it is appropriate to involve the child in the mediation process. The mediator or either party may terminate a mediation session in accordance with the provisions of Rule 1:40–4(h).

(3) Mediator Not to Act as Evaluator. The mediator may not subsequently act as an evaluator for any court-ordered report nor make any recommendation to the court respecting custody and parenting time.

(b) Mediation of Economic Aspects of Divorce.

(1) *Referral to MESP.* The CDR program of each vicinage shall include a post-Matrimonial Early Settlement Panel (MESP) program for the mediation of the economic aspects of divorce or for the conduct of a post-MESP alternate Complementary Dispute Resolution (CDR) event consistent with the provisions of this rule and R. 5:5–6. However, no matter shall be referred to mediation if a temporary or final restraining order is in effect in the matter pursuant to the Prevention of Domestic Violence Act (*N.J.S.A.* 2C:25-17 et seq.).

(2) *Designation of Mediator of Economic Aspects of Family Law Matters.* A credentials committee comprised of representatives from the Supreme Court Committee on Complementary Dispute Resolution shall be responsible for reviewing and approving all mediator applications. Applicants must complete an application form posted on the Judiciary's Internet web site (www.judiciary.state.nj.us or www.njcourtsonline.com). Mediators who meet the training requirements set forth in this rule, and any other approved criteria developed by the Family Court Programs Subcommittee of the Committee on Complementary Dispute Resolution shall be added to the Roster of Approved Mediators. The roster shall be maintained by the Administrative Office of the Courts and shall be posted on the Judiciary's Internet web site.

(3) *Exchange of Information.* In mediation of economic aspects of Family actions, parties are required to provide accurate and complete information to the mediator and to each other, including but not limited to tax returns, Case Information Statements, and appraisal reports. The court may, in the Mediation Referral Order, stay discovery and set specific times for completion of mediation.

(4) *Timing of Referral.* Parties shall be referred to economic mediation or other alternate CDR event following the unsuccessful attempt to resolve their issues through MESP. At the conclusion of the MESP process, parties shall be directed to confer with appropriate court staff to expedite the referral to economic mediation in accordance with the following procedures:

A. Parties may conference with the judge or the judge's designee.

B. Court staff shall explain the program to the parties and/or their attorneys.

C. Parties shall be provided with the roster of approved mediators for selection.

D. After a mediator has been selected, court staff shall attempt immediate contact to secure the mediator's acceptance and the date of initial appointment. If court staff is unable to contact the mediator for

confirmation, the order of referral shall state that the mediator and the date of initial appointment remain tentative until confirmation is secured. Staff will attempt to confirm within 24 hours and send an amended order to the parties and/or their attorneys.

E. If a mediator notifies the court that he or she cannot take on any additional cases, court staff will so advise the parties at the time of selection so that an alternate mediator can be selected.

F. The court shall enter an Economic Mediation Referral Order stating the name of the mediator, listing the financial documents to be shared between the parties and with the mediator, indicating the allocation of compensation by each party if mediation extends beyond the initial two hours, stating the court's expectation that the parties will mediate in good faith, defining the mediation time frame, and identifying the next court event and the date of that event.

G. The referral order, signed by the judge, shall be provided to the parties before they leave the courthouse. Amended orders with confirmed appointments shall be faxed to the parties and/or their attorneys the next day, replacing the tentative orders.

H. If the parties are unable to agree upon and select a mediator, the judge will appoint one. Staff shall then follow the above procedures as applicable.

I. Referral to economic mediation shall be recorded in the Family Automated Case Tracking System (FACTS).

(5) *Adjournments.* Adjournment of events in the mediation process shall be determined by the mediator after conferring with the parties and/or attorneys, provided that any such adjournment will not result in the case exceeding the return date to the court. If an adjournment would cause delay of the return date to the court, a written adjournment request must be made to the judge who has responsibility for the case or the judge's designee.

Note: Adopted July 14, 1992 to be effective September 1, 1992; new paragraph (c) adopted January 21, 1999 to be effective April 5, 1999; caption and paragraphs (a) and (b) amended July 5, 2000 to be effective September 5, 2000; caption amended, former paragraphs (a), (b), and (c) redesignated as paragraphs (a)(1), (a)(2), and (a)(3), new paragraph (a) caption adopted, and new paragraph (b) adopted July 27, 2006 to be effective September 1, 2006; paragraph (a)(2) amended July 31, 2007 to be effective September 1, 2007; paragraph (b) amended and redesignated as paragraph (b)(1), caption for paragraph (b)(1) added, and new paragraphs (b)(2), (b)(3), (b)(4), and (b)(5) adopted July 16, 2009 to be effective September 1, 2009.

1:40–6. Mediation of Civil, Probate, and General Equity Matters

The CDR program of each vicinage shall include mediation of civil, probate, and general equity matters, pursuant to rules and guidelines approved by the Supreme Court.

(a) Referral to Mediation. The court may, sua sponte and by written order, refer any civil, general equity, or probate action to mediation for an initial two hours, which shall include an organizational telephone conference, preparation by the mediator, and the first mediation session. In addition, the parties to an action may request an order of referral to mediation and may either select the mediator or request the court to designate a mediator from the court-approved roster.

(b) Designation of Mediator. If the parties have not selected the mediator prior to entry of the mediation referral order, the court shall in its referral order designate a mediator from the court-approved roster. The parties may, however, within 14 days after entry of the mediation referral order stipulate in writing to the designation of a different mediator. Within that fourteen-day period, the stipulation shall be filed with the Civil CDR Coordinator and a copy thereof served upon the mediator designated by the mediation referral order. A mediator designated by such stipulation shall comply with all terms and conditions set forth in the mediation referral order.

(c) Stay of Proceedings. The court may, in the mediation referral order, stay discovery for a specific or an indeterminate period.

(d) Withdrawal and Removal from Mediation. A motion for removal from mediation shall be filed and served upon all parties within 10 days after the entry of the mediation referral order and shall be granted only for good cause. Any party may withdraw from mediation after the initial two hours provided for by paragraph (a) of this rule. The mediation may, however, continue with the consent of the mediator and the remaining parties if they determine that it may be productive even without participation by the withdrawing party.

(e) Mediation Statement. The mediator shall fix a date following the telephonic conference for the exchange by the parties and service upon the mediator of a brief statement of facts and proposals for settlement not exceeding ten pages. At the discretion of the mediator, each party's statement of facts may be prepared and submitted to the mediator for review without service of the statement of facts on the other party. All documents prepared for mediation shall be confidential and subject to Rule 1:40–4(c) and (d).

(f) Procedure Following Mediation. Promptly upon termination of the mediation process, the mediator shall report to the court in writing as to whether or not the action or any severable claim therein has been settled.

(g) Compensation of Mediators. Mediators shall be compensated as provided by Rule 1:40–4(b) and Appen-

dix XXVI ("Guidelines for the Compensation of Mediators Serving in the Civil Mediation Program").

Note: Adopted July 5, 2000 to be effective September 5, 2000 (and former Rule 1:40–6 redesignated as Rule 1:40–7); paragraph (b) amended July 12, 2002 to be effective September 3, 2002; paragraphs (e) and (g) amended July 27, 2006 to be effective September 1, 2006; paragraph (a) amended September 11, 2006 to be effective immediately; paragraph (d) amended July 9, 2008 to be effective September 1, 2008; paragraph (e) amended July 31, 2007 to be effective September 1, 2007; paragraph (e) amended July 16, 2009 to be effective September 1, 2009.

1:40–7.   Complementary Dispute Resolution Programs in the Special Civil Part

(a) Small Claims. Each vicinage shall provide a small claims settlement program in which (1) law clerks from all the divisions who have been trained in settlement techniques and as mediators pursuant to R. 1:40–12(b)(5), and other employees and volunteers who have been trained in settlement techniques and as mediators pursuant to R. 1:40–12(b)(1), serve as trained neutrals who help litigants settle their cases, and (2) cases that are not settled are tried on the same day, if possible. The training requirements apply to law clerks but not to other attorneys.

(b) Tenancy Actions. If complementary dispute resolution programs are used for tenancy actions, cases that are not settled shall be tried on the same day, if possible.

(c) Other Actions for Damages. For other Special Civil Part actions for damages each vicinage shall establish a settlement program that does not include arbitration in which there is one settlement event scheduled to occur on the trial date.

Note: Adopted July 14, 1992 as Rule 1:40–6 to be effective September 1, 1992; amended and redesignated as Rule 1:40-7 July 5, 2000 to be effective September 5, 2000; caption and text deleted, new caption and new paragraphs (a), (b), and (c) adopted July 12, 2002 to be effective September 3, 2002; paragraph (a) amended July 16, 2009 to be effective September 1, 2009.

1:40–8.   Mediation of Minor Disputes in Municipal Court Actions

(a) Referral. A mediation notice may issue pursuant to Rule 7:8–1 requiring the parties to appear at a mediation session to determine whether mediation pursuant to these rules is an appropriate method for resolving the minor dispute. No referral to mediation shall be made if the complaint involves (1) serious injury, (2) repeated acts of violence between the parties, (3) clearly demonstrated psychological or emotional disability of a party, (4) incidents involving the same persons who are already parties to a Superior Court action between them, (5) matters arising under the Prevention of Domestic Violence Act (N.J.S.A. 2C:25–17 et seq.), or (6) a violation of the New Jersey Motor Vehicle Code (Title 39).

(b) Appointment of Mediators. A municipal court mediator shall be appointed by the Assignment Judge who may, either sua sponte or on request of the municipal court judge, remove a mediator upon the determination that the individual is unable properly to perform the mediator's functions.

Note: Adopted July 14, 1992 as Rule 1:40–7 to be effective September 1, 1992; paragraph (a) amended January 5, 1998 to be effective February 1, 1998; redesignated as Rule 1:40–8, paragraph (a) amended, and caption and text of paragraph (b) amended July 5, 2000 to be effective September 5, 2000.

1:40–9. Civil Arbitration

The CDR program of each vicinage shall include arbitration of civil actions in accordance with Rule 4:21A.

Note: Adopted July 5, 2000 to be effective September 5, 2000 (and former Rule 1:40–9 redesignated as Rule 1:40–11).

1:40–10. Relaxation of Court Rules and Program Guidelines

These rules, and any program guidelines may be relaxed or modified by the court in its discretion if it determines that injustice or inequity would otherwise result. Factors to be considered in making that determination include but are not limited to

(1) the incapacity of one or more parties to participate in the process, (2) the unwillingness of one or more parties to participate in good faith, (3) the previous participation by the parties in a CDR program involving the same issue, and (4) any factor warranting termination of the program pursuant to Rule 1:40–4(h).

Note: Adopted July 14, 1992 as Rule 1:40–8 to be effective September 1, 1992; caption and text amended and redesignated as Rule 1:40–10 July 5, 2000 to be effective September 5, 2000; amended July 31, 2007, to be effective September 1, 2007.

1:40–11. Non-Court Dispute Resolution

With the approval of the Assignment Judge or the Assignment Judge's designee, the court, while retaining jurisdiction, may refer a matter to a non-court administered dispute resolution process on the condition that any such mediation process will be subject to the confidentiality provisions of Rule 1:40-4(c) and (d). The Assignment Judge or designee may approve such referral upon the finding that it will not prejudice the interests of the parties.

Note: Adopted July 14, 1992 as Rule 1:40–9 to be effective September 1, 1992; redesignated as Rule 1:40–11 July 5, 2000 to be effective September 5, 2000; amended July 12, 2002 to be effective September 3, 2002; amended July 31, 2007, to be effective September 1, 2007.

1:40–12. Mediators and Arbitrators in Court–Annexed Programs

(a) Mediator Qualifications.

(1) *Generally.* Unless otherwise specified by these rules, no special occupational status or educational degree is required for mediator service and mediation training. An applicant for listing on a roster of mediators maintained by either the Administrative Office of the Courts or the Assignment Judge shall, however, certify to good professional standing. An applicant whose professional license has been revoked shall not be placed on the roster, or if already on the roster shall be removed therefrom.

(2) *Custody and Parenting Time Mediators.* The Assignment Judge, upon recommendation of the Presiding Judge of the Family Part, may approve persons or agencies to provide mediation services in custody and parenting time disputes if the mediator meets the following minimum qualifications: (A) a graduate degree or certification of advanced training in a behavioral or social science; (B) training in mediation techniques and practice as prescribed by these rules; and (C) supervised clinical experience in mediation, preferably with families. In the discretion of the Assignment Judge relevant experience may be substituted for either a graduate degree or certification, or clinical experience, or both.

(3) *Civil, General Equity, and Probate Action Mediators.* Mediator applicants for civil, general equity, and probate actions shall have at least five years of professional experience in the field of their expertise, as well as either an advanced degree or an undergraduate degree, coupled in both cases with mediation experience. For purposes of this rule, an advanced degree means a juris doctor or equivalent; an advanced degree in business, finance, or accounting, an advanced degree in the field of expertise in which the applicant will practice mediation, for example, engineering, architecture, or mental health; or state licensure in the field of expertise, for example, certified public accountant, architect, or engineer. For purposes of this rule, mediation experience which, together with an advanced degree, will qualify an applicant means evidence of successful mediation of a minimum of two cases within the last year, provided however that mediation experience is waived if mediation training was completed within the last five years. For purposes of this rule, mediation experience which, together with an undergraduate degree, will qualify an applicant means evidence of successful mediation of a minimum of ten cases involving subject matter otherwise cognizable in the Superior Court within the last five years.

(4) *Special Civil Part Mediators/Settlors.* In addition to qualified neutrals on the civil roster, those judicial law clerks, court staff, and volunteers who have completed a course of mediation training approved by the Administrative Office of the Courts may mediate/settle Small Claims actions. In the discretion of the Assignment Judge, such persons may also mediate/settle landlord-tenant disputes and other Special Civil Part actions, provided that they complete additional substantive and procedural training in landlord-tenant law of at

least three and one-half hours for law clerks and attorneys and at least seven hours for all others, with such training to be approved by the Administrative Office of the Courts.

(5) *Municipal Court Mediators.* Municipal Court mediators shall be approved for that position by the Assignment Judge for the vicinage in which they intend to serve on recommendation of the Municipal Court judge, stating the applicant's qualifications. In considering the recommendation, the Assignment Judge shall review the applicant's general background, suitability for service as a mediator, and any mediation training the applicant may have completed.

(6) *Family Part Economic Mediators.* Mediators of economic issues in family disputes shall meet the applicable requirements herein set forth for attorneys and non-attorneys and shall complete the required training set forth in paragraph (b) of this Rule:

(i) Attorneys

   a. Juris Doctor (or equivalent law degree)
   b. Admission to the bar for at least seven years
   c. Licensed to practice law in the state of New Jersey
   d. Practice substantially devoted to matrimonial law

(ii) Non-Attorneys

   a. Advanced degree in psychology, psychiatry, social work, business, finance, or accounting, or a CPA or other relevant advanced degree deemed appropriate by the credentials committee,
   b. At least seven years experience in the field of expertise, and
   c. Licensed in New Jersey if required in the field of expertise

(iii) Any retired Superior Court judge with experience in handling dissolution matters.

(b) Mediator Training Requirements.

(1) *General Provisions.* All persons serving as mediators shall have completed the basic dispute resolution training course as prescribed by these rules and approved by the Administrative Office of the Courts. Volunteer mediators in the Special Civil Part and Municipal Court mediators shall have completed 18 classroom hours of basic mediation skills complying with the requirements of subparagraph (3) of this rule. Mediators on the civil, general equity, and probate roster of the Superior Court shall have completed 18 classroom hours of basic mediation skills complying with the requirements of subparagraph (3) of this rule and at least five hours being mentored by an experienced mediator on the roster in accordance with guidelines promulgated by the Administrative Office of the Courts in at least two cases in the Superior Court. Individuals may obtain a waiver of the mentoring requirement from the Administrative Office of the

Courts on the successful demonstration that they have previously served as a mediator in at least five cases under R. 1:40–4 or comparable mediation program or have satisfactorily completed at least 10 hours in an approved advanced mediation course. Family Part mediators shall have completed a 40-hour training program complying with the requirements of subparagraph (4) of this rule; and judicial law clerks shall have successfully completed 12 classroom hours of basic mediation skills complying with the requirements of subparagraph (5) of this rule.

(2) *Continuing Training.* Commencing in the year following the completion of the basic training course or the waiver thereof, all mediators shall annually attend four hours of continuing education and shall file with the Administrative Office of the Courts or the Assignment Judge, as appropriate, an annual certification of compliance. To meet the requirement, this continuing education should cover at least one of the following: (A) reinforcing and enhancing mediation and negotiation concepts and skills, (B) ethical issues associated with mediation practice, or (C) other professional matters related to mediation. Mediators who have been approved to serve as mentors under subsection (b)(1) of this Rule may apply the time spent mentoring to satisfy this requirement.

(3) *Mediation Course Content—Basic Skills.* The 18-hour classroom course in basic mediation skills shall, by lectures, demonstrations, exercises and role plays, teach the skills necessary for mediation practice, including but not limited to conflict management, communication and negotiation skills, the mediation process, and addressing problems encountered in mediation.

(4) *Mediation Course Content-Family Part Actions.* The 40-hour classroom course for family action mediators shall include basic mediation skills as well as at least 22 hours of specialized family mediation training, which should cover family and child development, family law, divorce procedures, family finances, and community resources. In special circumstances and at the request of the Assignment Judge, the Administrative Office of the Courts may temporarily approve for a one-year period an applicant who has not yet completed the specialized family mediation training, provided the applicant has at least three years of experience as a mediator or a combination of mediation experience and service in the Family Part, has co-mediated in a CDR program with an experienced family mediator, and certifies to the intention to complete the specialized training within one year following the temporary approval. Economic mediators in family disputes: (1) shall have completed 40 hours of training in family mediation in accordance with this rule, or (2) shall have completed a minimum of 25 hours of mediation training with a commitment to complete the remaining 15 hours of specialized training within one year following their

addition to the roster of mediators consistent with the requirements of this subparagraph.

(5) *Training Requirements for Judicial Law Clerks.* Judicial law clerks serving as mediators shall first have completed either a 12-hour training course prescribed by the Administrative Office of the Courts, an approved course conducted by another institution or agency, or other comparable training. Proof of completion of any training other than the prescribed 12-hour course shall be submitted to the Administrative Office of the Courts for a determination of suitability. The Administrative Office of the Courts shall work with other institutions and agencies to encourage their provision of judicial law clerk mediation training and shall either approve or evaluate that training.

(6) *Co-mediation; mentoring; training evaluation.* In order to reinforce mediator training, the vicinage CDR coordinator shall, insofar as practical and for a reasonable period following initial training, assign any new mediator who is either an employee or a volunteer to co-mediate with an experienced mediator and shall assign an experienced mediator to mentor a new mediator. Using evaluation forms prescribed by the Administrative Office of the Courts, the vicinage CDR coordinator shall also evaluate the training needs of each new mediator during the first year of the mediator's qualifications and shall periodically assess the training needs of all mediators.

(c) Arbitrator Qualification and Training. Arbitrators serving in judicial arbitration programs shall have the minimum qualifications prescribed by Rule 4:21A–2 and must be annually recommended for inclusion on the approved roster by the local arbitrator selection committee and approved by the Assignment Judge or designee. All arbitrators shall attend initial training of at least three classroom hours and continuing training every two years of at least two hours in courses approved by the Administrative Office of the Courts.

(1) *Arbitration Course Content—Initial Training.* The three-hour classroom course shall teach the skills necessary for arbitration, including applicable statutes, court rules and administrative directives and policies, the standards of conduct, applicable uniform procedures as reflected in the approved procedures manual and other relevant information.

(2) *Arbitration Course Content—Continuing Training.* The two-hour biennial training course should cover at least one of the following: (a) reinforcing and enhancing relevant arbitration skills and procedures, (b) ethical issues associated with arbitration, or (c) other matters related to court-annexed arbitration.

(d) Training Program Evaluation. The Administrative Office of the Courts shall conduct periodic assessments and evaluations of the CDR training programs to ensure their continued effectiveness and to identify any needed improvements.

Note: Adopted July 14, 1992 as Rule 1:40–10 to be effective September 1, 1992; caption amended, former text redesignated as paragraphs (a) and (b), paragraphs (a)3.1 and (b)4.1 amended June 28, 1996 to be effective September 1, 1996; redesignated as Rule 1:40–12, caption amended and first sentence deleted, paragraph (a)1.1 amended and redesignated as paragraph (a)(1), paragraph (a)2.1 amended and redesignated as paragraph (a)(2), paragraph (a)2.2 amended and redesignated as paragraph (b)(5), new paragraphs (a)(3) and (a)(4) adopted, paragraph (a)3.1 redesignated as paragraph (a)(5), paragraph (a)3.2 amended and incorporated in paragraph (b)(1), paragraph (a)4.1 amended and redesignated as paragraph (b)(6), paragraph (b)1.1 amended and redesignated as paragraph (b)(1), paragraphs (b)2.1 and (b)3.1 amended and redesignated as paragraphs (b)(2) and (b)(3), paragraph (b)4.1 redesignated as paragraph (b)(4) with caption amended, paragraph (b)5.1 amended and redesignated as paragraph (b)(7) with caption amended, new section (c) adopted, and paragraph (b)5.1(d) amended and redesignated as new section (d) with caption amended July 5, 2000 to be effective September 5, 2000; paragraphs (a)(3) and (b)(1) amended July 12, 2002 to be effective September 3, 2002; paragraphs (b)(1), (b)(3), and (c) amended July 28, 2004 to be effective September 1, 2004; caption amended and paragraph (a) (4) caption and text amended June 15, 2007 to be effective September 1, 2007; new paragraph (a)(6) caption and text adopted, paragraph (b)(1) amended, paragraph (b)(2) deleted, paragraphs (b)(3) and (b)(4) redesignated as paragraphs (b)(2) and (b)(3), paragraph (b)(5) amended and redesignated as paragraph (b)(4), and paragraphs (b)(6) and (b)(7) redesignated as paragraphs (b)(5) and (b)(6) July 16, 2009 to be effective September 1, 2009.

PART III. RULES GOVERNING CRIMINAL PRACTICE

Research Note

For a comprehensive treatment of practice and procedure under these Rules, see Klock, New Jersey Court Rules Annotated *(Practice Series Volumes 1 through 2A),* and Arnold, New Jersey Criminal Practice and Procedure *(Practice Series Volumes 31 and 32).*

Use WESTLAW ® *to find cases citing a rule.* WESTLAW *may also be used to search for specific terms or to update a rule; see the Scope Screens in NJ–RULES and NJ–RULESUPDATES for further information.*

Amendments to these rules are published, as received, in Atlantic Reporter 2d *and* New Jersey Reports *advance sheets.*

Table of Rules

CHAPTER I. SCOPE; PRELIMINARY PROCEEDINGS.

Rule
3:1.   GENERAL PROVISIONS.
3:1–1.   Scope.
3:1–2.   Territorial Limits.
3:1–3.   Effect.
3:1–4.   Orders; Form; Entry.
3:1–5.   Indictable Offenses in the Superior Court; Transfer.
3:1–6.   Trial of Non-Indictables in Superior Court.
3:2.   CONTENTS OF COMPLAINT, ARREST WARRANT AND SUMMONS.
3:2–1.   Contents of Complaint; Forwarding of Indictable Complaints to Prosecutor and Criminal Division Manager.
3:2–2.   Summons.
3:2–3.   Arrest Warrant.
3:3.   SUMMONS OR WARRANT UPON COMPLAINT.
3:3–1.   Issuance of an Arrest Warrant or Summons.
3:3–2.   [Reserved].
3:3–3.   Execution or Service; Return.
3:3–4.   Defective Warrant or Summons.
3:4.   PROCEEDINGS BEFORE THE COMMITTING JUDGE; PRETRIAL RELEASE.
3:4–1.   Procedure After Arrest.
3:4–2.   First Appearance After Filing Complaint.
3:4–3.   Hearing as to Probable Cause on Indictable Offenses.
3:4–4.   Proceedings in Arrest Under Uniform Fresh Pursuit Law.
3:4–5.   Effect of Technical Insufficiency or Irregularity in the Proceedings.
3:5.   SEARCH WARRANTS.
3:5–1.   Authority to Issue.
3:5–2.   Grounds for Issuance.
3:5–3.   Issuance and Contents.
3:5–4.   Secrecy.
3:5–5.   Execution and Return with Inventory.
3:5–6.   Filing; Confidentiality.
3:5–7.   Motion to Suppress Evidence and for Return of Property.
3:5–8.   Search and Seizure Without Search Warrant.
3:5A.   INVESTIGATIVE DETENTION.

Rule
3:5A–1.   Authority to Issue.
3:5A–2.   Application.
3:5A–3.   Notice and Return.
3:5A–4.   Grounds for Issuance.
3:5A–5.   Contents of Order for Investigative Detention.
3:5A–6.   Emergent Application.
3:5A–7.   Service.
3:5A–8.   Filing.
3:5A–9.   Definition.
3:6.   THE GRAND JURY.
3:6–1.   Summoning the Grand Jury.
3:6–2.   Objections to Grand Jury and Grand Jurors.
3:6–3.   Supervising and Charging the Grand Jury.
3:6–4.   Foreperson; Deputy Foreperson.
3:6–5.   Clerk.
3:6–6.   Who May be Present; Record and Transcript.
3:6–7.   Secrecy of Proceedings.
3:6–8.   Finding and Return of Indictment; No Bill.
3:6–9.   Finding and Return of Presentment.
3:6–10.   Discharge; Continuance of Term.
3:6–11.   Impanelment and Judicial Supervision of State Grand Jury.
3:7.   INDICTMENT AND ACCUSATION.
3:7–1.   Entitling of Papers.
3:7–2.   Use of Indictment or Accusation.
3:7–3.   Nature and Contents of Indictment or Accusation; Timing of Supplemental Indictment.
3:7–4.   Amendment of Indictment or Accusation.
3:7–5.   Bill of Particulars.
3:7–6.   Joinder of Offenses.
3:7–7.   Joinder of Defendants.
3:7–8.   Issuance of Warrant or Summons Upon Indictment or Accusation.
3:7–9.   Form of Warrant and Summons.
3:7–10.   Execution of Service; Return.
3:8.   APPEARANCE OF COUNSEL.
3:8–1.   Filing Appearance.
3:8–2.   Joint Representation.
3:8–3.   Representation by Public Defender.

CHAPTER II. ARRAIGNMENT; PLEAS; MOTIONS; PRETRIAL; DISCOVERY.

3:9.   PRETRIAL PROCEDURE.

Rule

3:9–1. Prearraignment Conference; Plea Offer; Arraignment/Status Conference; Pretrial Hearings; Pretrial Conference.
3:9–2. Pleas.
3:9–3. Plea Discussions; Agreements; Withdrawals.
3:10. PLEADINGS AND MOTIONS BEFORE TRIAL; DEFENSES AND OBJECTIONS.
3:10–1. Pleadings and Motions.
3:10–2. Time and Manner of Making Motion; Hearing on Motion.
3:10–3. [Reserved].
3:10–4. [Reserved].
3:10–5. [Reserved].
3:10–6. [Reserved].
3:10–7. Effect of Determination of Motion.
3:11. [RESERVED].
3:12. DEFENDANT'S OBLIGATION TO PROVIDE NOTICE.
3:12–1. Notice Under Specific Criminal Code Provisions.
3:12–2. Notice of Alibi; Failure to Furnish.
3:12A. [DELETED].
3:13. DEPOSITIONS; DISCOVERY.
3:13–1. [Deleted].
3:13–2. Depositions.
3:13–3. Discovery and Inspection.
3:13–4. Additional Discovery in Capital Cases.

CHAPTER III. VENUE; TRIAL.

3:14. PLACE OF TRIAL; FOREIGN JURIES.
3:14–1. Venue.
3:14–2. Motion for Change of Venue or Foreign Jury.
3:14–3. Foreign Juries; Order and Selection.
3:14–4. Order for Change of Venue; Costs.
3:15. JOINDER AND SEVERANCE.
3:15–1. Trial of Indictments or Accusations Together.
3:15–2. Relief From Prejudicial Joinder.
3:15–3. Trial of Criminal Offenses and Lesser, Related Infractions.
3:16. PRESENCE OF THE DEFENDANT.
3:17. ELECTRONIC RECORDATION.
3:18. MOTION FOR JUDGMENT OF ACQUITTAL.
3:18–1. Motion Before Submission to Jury.
3:18–2. Motion After Discharge of Jury.
3:19. VERDICT.
3:19–1. Several Defendants or Counts; Written Verdict Sheets.
3:19–2. Acquittal by Reason of Insanity.

CHAPTER IV. PROCEEDINGS AFTER VERDICT OR FINDING.

3:20. NEW TRIAL.
3:20–1. Trial by Court or Jury.
3:20–2. Time for Making Motion.
3:21. SENTENCE AND JUDGMENT; WITHDRAWAL OF PLEA; PRESENTENCE INVESTIGATION; PROBATION.
3:21–1. Withdrawal of Plea.
3:21–2. Presentence Procedure.
3:21–3. Diagnostic Center Report.
3:21–4. Sentence.
3:21–4A. Sentence, Murder Under N.J.S.A. 2C:11–3(a)(1) or N.J.S.A. 2C:11–3(a)(2).
3:21–5. Judgment.
3:21–6. Conviction of a Corporation.

Rule

3:21–7. Probation and Suspended Sentence.
3:21–8. Credit for Confinement Pending Sentence.
3:21–9. Arrest of Judgment.
3:21–10. Reduction or Change of Sentence.
3:22. POST–CONVICTION RELIEF.
3:22–1. Petition for Relief.
3:22–2. Grounds.
3:22–3. Exclusiveness of Remedy; not Substitute for Appeal or Motion.
3:22–4. Bar of Grounds Not Raised in Prior Proceedings; Bar of Second or Subsequent Petitions; Exceptions.
3:22–5. Bar of Ground Expressly Adjudicated.
3:22–6. Indigents; Waiver of Fees; Assignment of Counsel, and Grant of Transcript; Assigned Counsel May not Withdraw.
3:22–6A. Notifying Court of Assignment; Filing of Appearance.
3:22–7. Docketing; Service on Prosecutor; Assignment for Disposition.
3:22–8. Contents of Petition; Verification.
3:22–9. Amendments of Pleadings; Answer by Prosecutor.
3:22–10. Presence of Defendant at Hearing.
3:22–11. Determination; Findings and Conclusions; Judgment; Supplementary Orders.
3:22–12. Limitations.

CHAPTER V. APPEALS FROM COURTS OF LIMITED CRIMINAL JURISDICTION.

3:23. APPEALS FROM JUDGMENTS OF CONVICTION IN COURTS OF LIMITED CRIMINAL JURISDICTION.
3:23–1. Exclusive Method of Review.
3:23–2. Appeal; How Taken; Time.
3:23–3. Notice of Appeal; Contents.
3:23–4. Duties of Clerks of the Trial Court and Superior Court, Law Division.
3:23–5. Relief Pending Appeal.
3:23–6. Transmittal of Recognizance or Cash Deposit.
3:23–7. Dismissal of Appeal.
3:23–8. Hearing on Appeal.
3:23–9. Prosecuting Attorney Defined.
3:24. APPEALS FROM ORDERS IN COURTS OF LIMITED CRIMINAL JURISDICTION.
3:24. Appeals from Orders in Courts of Limited Criminal Jurisdiction.

CHAPTER VI. SUPPLEMENTARY AND SPECIAL PROCEEDINGS.

3:25. DISMISSAL.
3:25–1. Upon Motion of the Prosecutor Before or During Trial.
3:25–2. Order for Trial.
3:25–3. Dismissal for Delay.
3:25A. CONSOLIDATED DISPOSITIONS.
3:25A–1. Application for Disposition.
3:25A–2. Order of Disposition; Filing.
3:26. BAIL.
3:26–1. Right to Bail Before Conviction.
3:26–2. Authority to Set Bail.
3:26–3. Bail for Witness.

Rule

3:26–4.   Form and Place of Deposit; Location of Real Estate; Record of Recognizances, Discharge and Forfeiture Thereof.

3:26–5.   Justification of Sureties.

3:26–6.   Forfeiture.

3:26–7.   Exoneration.

3:26–8.   Bail Sufficiency; Source Hearing.

3:27.   [RESERVED].

3:28.   PRETRIAL INTERVENTION PROGRAMS.

GUIDELINES FOR OPERATION OF PRETRIAL INTERVENTION IN NEW JERSEY.

Rule

Guideline 1.

Guideline 2.

Guideline 3.

Guideline 4.

Guideline 5.

Guideline 6.

Guideline 7.

Guideline 8.

3:29.   STATEMENT OF REASONS FOR DISPOSITION OF MOTION OR APPLICATION.

3:30.   FEES FOR EXPUNGEMENT OF RECORDS.

CHAPTER I. SCOPE; PRELIMINARY PROCEEDINGS
RULE 3:1. GENERAL PROVISIONS

3:1–1. Scope

The rules in Part III govern the practice and procedure in all indictable and non-indictable proceedings in the Superior Court Law Division, and, insofar as they are applicable, the practice and procedure on indictable offenses in all other courts, including the municipal courts, and the practice and procedure in juvenile delinquency proceedings in the Chancery Division, Family Part except as otherwise provided for in Part V.

Note: Source—R.R. 3:1–1. Amended December 20, 1983 to be effective December 31, 1983, amended January 5, 1998 to be effective February 1, 1998.

3:1–2. Territorial Limits

The writs and processes of the Superior Court may be directed anywhere within the jurisdiction of this State.

Note: Source—R.R. 3:11–4(e). Amended December 20, 1983 to be effective December 31, 1983.

3:1–3. Effect of Prosecutor's Election to Waive Death Penalty [Deleted]

Note: Source—R.R. 3:1–3A; deleted September 28, 1982 to be effective immediately.

3:1–4. Orders; Form; Entry

(a) **Time.** Except for judgments to be prepared by the court and entered pursuant to R. 3:21–5, formal written orders shall be presented to the court in accordance with R. 4:42–1(e) except that only the original of the signed order shall be filed. The court may also issue and transmit to the Department of Corrections electronic Orders to Produce inmates, with those orders or writs containing an electronically affixed signature of a Superior Court judge. Such orders shall have the same authority as orders that contain a judge's original signature.

(b) **Settlement by Motion or Consent.** Except as otherwise provided by paragraph (c) of this rule, by other rule or by law, and except for ex parte matters and for judgments entered pursuant to R. 3:21–5, no judgment or order shall be signed by the court unless the form thereof has been settled on motion on notice to all parties affected thereby or unless the written approval of such attorneys or parties to the form thereof is endorsed thereon.

(c) **Settlement on Notice.** In lieu of settlement by motion or consent, the party proposing the form of judgment or order may forward the original thereof to the judge who heard the matter and shall serve a copy thereof on every other party not in default together with a notice that unless the judge and the proponent of the judgment or order are notified in writing of specific objections thereto within 5 days after such service, the judgment or order may be signed in the judge's discretion. If no such objection is timely made, the judge may forthwith sign the judgment or order. If objection is made, the matter may be listed for hearing in the discretion of the court.

Note: Adopted July 29, 1977 to be effective September 6, 1977. Paragraph (c) amended July 24, 1978 to be effective September 11, 1978; paragraph (a) amended July 16, 1981 to be effective September 14, 1981; paragraph (a) amended November 7, 1988 to be effective January 2, 1989; paragraph (c) amended July 13, 1994 to be effective September 1, 1994; paragraph (a) amended July 28, 2004 to be effective September 1, 2004.

3:1–5. Indictable Offenses in the Superior Court; Transfer

(a) **Generally.** All indictable offenses shall be prosecuted in the Superior Court, Law Division, except that an action brought pursuant to N.J.S. 2C:24–5 (Willful Nonsupport) shall be prosecuted in the Superior Court, Chancery Division, Family Part.

(b) **Transfer From Family Part to Law Division.** An action initially prosecuted in the Family Part pursuant to paragraph (a) of this rule shall be transferred to the Law Division for trial if the defendant is entitled to and demands trial by jury.

(c) **Transfer From Law Division to Family Part.** Upon defendant's waiver of trial by jury pursuant to R. 1:8–1 and upon the written consent of the defendant and prosecutor, the Assignment Judge may, on motion of any party, transfer any indictable offense pending in the Superior Court to the Family Part for trial and disposition provided that the gravamen of the offense charged arises out of a family or a family type relationship between the defendant and the victim.

Note: Former rule redesignated as R. 3:1–6(a), December 20, 1983 to be effective December 31, 1983. Source— new; paragraph (a) amended July 14, 1992 to be effective September 1, 1992.

3:1–6. Trial of Non-Indictables in Superior Court

(a) Generally. Proceedings involving charges constituting disorderly persons offense or a petty disorderly

persons offense shall be heard in Superior Court as required by law, and shall be governed by the rules in Part III insofar as applicable.

(b) Transfer From the Municipal Court to the Superior Court, Chancery Division, Family Part. An offense or violation pending in municipal court may be transferred for trial and disposition to the Chancery Division, Family Part pursuant to R. 5:1–3.

Note: Adopted August 28, 1979 to be effective September 1, 1979. Formerly designated as R. 3:1–5(a), redesignated and new paragraph (b) added December 20, 1983 to be effective December 31, 1983; paragraph (a) amended July 28, 2004 to be effective September 1, 2004.

RULE 3:2. CONTENTS OF COMPLAINT, ARREST WARRANT AND SUMMONS

3:2–1. Contents of Complaint; Forwarding of Indictable Complaints to Prosecutor and Criminal Division Manager

(a) Complaint. The complaint shall be a written statement of the essential facts constituting the offense charged made on a form approved by the Administrative Director of the Courts. All complaints except complaints for traffic offenses, as defined in R. 7:2–1 where made on Uniform Traffic Tickets and complaints for non-indictable offenses made on the Special Form of Complaint and Summons, shall be by certification or on oath before a judge or other person authorized by N.J.S.A. 2B:12–21 to take complaints. The clerk or deputy clerk, municipal court administrator or deputy court administrator shall accept for filing any complaint made by any person.

(b) Forwarding of Indictable Complaints to Prosecutor and Criminal Division Manager. Where the complaint alleges an indictable offense, the complaint, and all available investigative reports, shall be forwarded to the prosecutor within 48 hours. The complaint shall be forwarded by the municipal court to the criminal division manager's office within 48 hours.

Note: Source—R.R. 3:2–1(a)(b); amended July 26, 1984 to be effective September 10, 1984; main caption amended, caption added, former text amended and redesignated paragraph 3:2–1(a), paragraph (b) adopted July 13, 1994 to be effective January 1, 1995; paragraph (a) amended January 5, 1998 to be effective February 1, 1998.

3:2–2. Summons

A summons shall be made on a Complaint–Summons (CDR–1) form, a Uniform Traffic Ticket, or a Special Form of Complaint and Summons. The summons shall be directed to the person named in the complaint, requiring that person to appear before the court in which the complaint is made at a stated time and place and shall inform the person that an arrest warrant will be issued for failure to appear. The summons shall be

signed by the judicial or law enforcement officer issuing it. An electronic entry of the signature of the law enforcement officer shall be equivalent to and have the same force and effect as an original signature.

Note: Adopted July 13, 1994 to be effective January 1, 1995; amended July 27, 2006 to be effective September 1, 2006.

3:2–3. Arrest Warrant

(a) An arrest warrant shall be made on a Complaint–Warrant (CDR2) form. The warrant shall contain the defendant's name or if that is unknown, any name or description that identifies the defendant with reasonable certainty, and shall be directed to any officer authorized to execute it, ordering that the defendant be arrested and brought before the court that issued the warrant. Except as provided in paragraph (b), the warrant shall be signed by the judge, clerk, deputy clerk, municipal court administrator, or deputy court administrator.

(b) A judge may issue an arrest warrant on sworn oral testimony of a law enforcement applicant who is not physically present. Such sworn oral testimony may be communicated by the applicant to the judge by telephone, radio or other means of electronic communication.

The judge shall administer the oath to the applicant. Subsequent to taking the oath, the applicant must identify himself or herself, and read verbatim the Complaint–Warrant (CDR2) and any supplemental affidavit that establishes probable cause for the issuance of an arrest warrant. If the facts necessary to establish probable cause are contained entirely on the Complaint–Warrant (CDR2) and/or supplemental affidavit, the judge need not make a contemporaneous written or electronic recordation of the facts in support of probable cause. If the law enforcement officer provides additional sworn oral testimony in support of probable cause, the judge shall contemporaneously record such sworn oral testimony by means of a tape-recording device or stenographic machine, if such are available; otherwise, adequate longhand notes summarizing the contents of the law enforcement applicant's testimony shall be made by the judge. This sworn testimony shall be deemed to be an affidavit, or a supplemental affidavit, for the purposes of issuance of an arrest warrant.

An arrest warrant may issue if the judge is satisfied that probable cause exists for issuing the warrant. On approval, the judge shall memorialize the date, time, defendant's name, complaint number, the basis for the probable cause determination and any other specific terms of the authorization. That memorialization shall be either by means of a tape-recording device, steno-graphic machine, or by adequate longhand notes. Thereafter, the judge shall direct the applicant to print his or her name, the date and time of the warrant, followed by the phrase "By Officer _____ , per telephonic authorization by _____ " on the Complaint/Warrant (CDR–2) form. Within 48 hours the applicant shall deliver to the judge, either in person or via facsimile transmission, the signed Complaint–Warrant (CDR–2) and any supporting affidavit. The judge shall verify the accuracy of these documents by affixing his or her signature to the Complaint–Warrant (CDR–2).

Note: Adopted July 13, 1994 to be effective January 1, 1995; original text of rule amended and designated as paragraph (a) and new paragraph (b) added July 28, 2004 to be effective September 1, 2004.

RULE 3:3. SUMMONS OR WARRANT
UPON COMPLAINT

3:3–1. Issuance of an Arrest Warrant or Summons

(a) Issuance of a Warrant. An arrest warrant may be issued on a complaint only if:

(1) a judge, clerk, deputy clerk, municipal court administrator or deputy municipal court administrator finds from the complaint or an accompanying affidavit or deposition, that there is probable cause to believe that an offense was committed and that the defendant committed it and notes that finding on the warrant; and

(2) a judge, clerk, deputy clerk, municipal court administrator or deputy municipal court administrator finds that subsection (c) of this rule allows a warrant rather than a summons to be issued.

(b) Issuance of a summons. A summons may be issued on a complaint only if:

(1) a judge, clerk, deputy clerk, municipal court administrator or deputy municipal court administrator finds from the complaint or an accompanying affidavit or deposition, that there is probable cause to believe that an offense was committed and that the defendant committed it and notes that finding on the summons; or

(2) the law enforcement officer who made the complaint, issues the summons.

(c) Determination of Whether to Issue a Summons or Warrant. A summons rather than an arrest warrant shall be issued unless:

(1) the defendant is charged with murder, kidnapping, aggravated manslaughter, manslaughter, robbery, aggravated sexual assault, sexual assault, aggravated criminal sexual contact, criminal sexual contact, second degree aggravated assault, aggravated arson, arson, burglary, violations of Chapter 35 of Title 2C that constitute first or second degree crimes, any crime involving the possession or use of a firearm, or conspiracies or attempts to commit such crimes;

(2) the defendant has been served with a summons and has failed to appear;

(3) there is reason to believe that the defendant is dangerous to self, other persons, or property;

(4) there is an outstanding warrant for the defendant;

(5) the defendant's identity or address is not known and a warrant is necessary to subject the defendant to the jurisdiction of the court; or

(6) there is reason to believe that the defendant will not appear in response to a summons.

(d) Finding of No Probable Cause. If a judicial officer finds that there is no probable cause to believe that an offense was committed or that the defendant committed it, the officer shall not issue a warrant or summons on the complaint. If the finding is made by an officer other than a judge, the finding shall be reviewed by a judge. If the judge finds no probable cause, the judge shall dismiss the complaint.

(e) Additional warrants or summonses. More than one warrant or summons may issue on the same complaint.

(f) Process Against Corporations. A summons rather than an arrest warrant shall issue if the defendant is a corporation. If a corporation fails to appear in response to a summons, the court shall proceed as if the corporation appeared and entered a plea of not guilty.

Note: Source—R.R. 3:2–2 (a) (1) (2) (3) and (4); paragraph (a) amended, new paragraph (b) adopted and former paragraphs (b) and (c) redesignated as (c) and (d) respectively July 21, 1980 to be effective September 8, 1980; paragraph (b) amended and paragraph (e) adopted July 16, 1981 to be effective September 14, 1981; paragraph (b) amended July 22, 1983 to be effective September 12, 1983; caption and paragraph (a) amended and paragraph (f) adopted July 26, 1984 to be effective September 10, 1984; paragraph (b) amended January 5, 1988 to be effective February 1, 1988; captions and text amended to paragraphs (a), (b), (c), (e) and (f), paragraph (g) adopted July 13, 1994, text of paragraph (a) amended December 9, 1994, to be effective January 1, 1995; paragraphs (a), (c), (e), (f), and (g) deleted, paragraph (b) amended and redesignated as paragraph (c), paragraph (d) amended and redesignated as paragraph (e), new paragraphs (a), (b), (d), and (f) adopted July 5, 2000 to be effective September 5, 2000.

3:3–2. [Reserved]

Note: Source—R.R. 3:2–2(b); deleted July 13, 1994 to be effective January 1, 1995.

3:3–3. Execution or Service; Return

(a) By Whom. The warrant shall be executed and the summons served by any officer authorized by law.

(b) Territorial Limits. The warrant may be executed and the summons served at any place within this State. An officer arresting a defendant in a county other than the one in which the warrant was issued shall take the defendant, without unnecessary delay, before the nearest available committing judge authorized to admit to bail in accordance with R. 3:26–2, who may admit to bail conditioned on the defendant's appearance before the court issuing the warrant. Nothing in this rule shall affect the provisions of N.J.S. 2A:156–1 to 2A:156–4 (Uniform Act on Intrastate Fresh Pursuit).

(c) Execution of Warrant. The warrant shall be executed by the arrest of the defendant. The warrant need not be in the possession of the officer at the time of the arrest, but upon request, the officer shall show the warrant to the defendant as soon as possible. If the warrant is not in the possession of the officer at the time of the arrest, the officer shall inform the defendant of the offense charged and of the fact that a warrant has been issued.

(d) Service of Summons. The summons shall be served in accordance with R. 4:4–4.

(e) Return. The officer executing a warrant shall make prompt return thereof to the court which issued the warrant. The officer serving a summons shall make return thereof to the court before whom the summons is returnable on or before the return day.

Note: Source—R.R. 3:2–2(c); paragraphs (b) and (c) amended July 13, 1994 to be effective September 1, 1994.

3:3–4. Defective Warrant or Summons

(a) Amendment. No person arrested under a warrant or appearing in response to a summons shall be discharged from custody or dismissed because of any technical insufficiency or irregularity in the warrant or summons, but the warrant or summons may be amended to remedy any such technical defect.

(b) Issuance of New Warrant or Summons. If prior to or during the hearing as to probable cause, it appears that the warrant executed or summons issued does not properly name or describe the defendant, or the offense with which the defendant is charged, or that although not guilty of the offense specified in the warrant or summons there is reasonable ground to believe that the defendant is guilty of some other offense, the court shall not discharge or dismiss the defendant but shall forthwith cause a new complaint to be filed and thereupon issue a new warrant or summons.

Note: Source—R.R. 3:2–2(d); paragraph (b) amended July 13, 1994 to be effective September 1, 1994.

RULE 3:4. PROCEEDINGS BEFORE THE COMMITTING JUDGE; PRETRIAL RELEASE

3:4–1. Procedure After Arrest

(a) Arrest Without Warrant.

(1) *Preparation of Complaint.* A law enforcement officer shall take a person who was arrested without a warrant to a police station where a complaint shall be prepared immediately. If it appears that issuance of a warrant is authorized by Rule 3:3–1(c) or the prosecution of the person would be jeopardized by immediate release, the complaint may be prepared on a Complaint–Warrant (CDR2) form. Otherwise, the complaint shall be prepared on a Complaint–Summons (CDR1) form.

(2) *Issuance of Process.* If a Complaint–Summons (CDR1) has been prepared, the law enforcement officer may serve the summons and release the defendant. If a Complaint–Warrant (CDR2) has been prepared, without unnecessary delay, and no later than 12 hours after arrest, the matter shall be presented to a judge, or, in the absence of a judge, to a judicial officer who has the authority to set bail for the offense charged. The judicial officer shall determine whether to issue a warrant or summons as provided in Rule 3:3–1, and if a warrant is issued, shall set bail immediately.

(b) Arrest on Warrant. If bail was not set when an arrest warrant was issued, the person who is arrested on that warrant shall have bail set without unnecessary delay, and no later than 12 hours after arrest.

(c) Identification procedures. If the defendant has been released on a summons, any post-arrest identification procedures required by N.J.S.A. 53:1–15 or otherwise required by law, shall be completed on the return date of the summons.

Note: Source—R.R. 3:2–3(a), 8:3–3(a). Amended July 7, 1971 to be effective September 13, 1971; caption amended, former rule redesignated as paragraph (a) and paragraphs (b) and (c) adopted July 21, 1980 to be effective September 8, 1980; paragraph (b) amended July 16, 1981 to be effective September 14, 1981; paragraphs (a) and (b) amended, new paragraph (c) adopted and former paragraph (c) redesignated paragraph (d) and paragraph (d)(7) deleted November 5, 1986 to be effective January 1, 1987; paragraphs (b) and (c) amended April 10, 1987 to be effective immediately; paragraph (b) amended January 5, 1988 to be effective February 1, 1988; captions added to paragraphs (a)(b) and (c), new paragraph (c) adopted, paragraph (d) introductory text deleted and paragraphs (d)(1)(2)(3)(4)(5) and (6) redesignated as paragraphs (b)(1)(a)(b)(c)(d) and (f) and paragraph (1)(e) amended and paragraphs (b)(2) and (3) adopted, July 13, 1994 to be effective January 1, 1995; paragraph (a) amended and redesignated as paragraph (b), paragraph (b) amended and redesignated as paragraph (a), paragraph (c) deleted, and new paragraph (c) adopted July 5, 2000 to be effective September 5, 2000.

3:4–2. First Appearance After Filing Complaint

(a) Time of First Appearance. Without unnecessary delay, following the filing of a complaint the defendant shall be brought before a judge for a first appearance as provided in this Rule. If the defendant remains in custody, the first appearance shall occur within 72 hours after arrest, excluding holidays, and shall be before a judge with authority to set bail for the offenses charged.

(b) Procedure in Indictable Offenses. At the defendant's first appearance before a judge, if the defendant is charged with an indictable offense, the judge shall:

(1) give the defendant a copy of the complaint and inform the defendant of the charge;

(2) inform the defendant of the right to remain silent and that any statement may be used against the defendant;

(3) inform the defendant of the right to retain counsel and, if indigent, the right to be represented by the public defender;

(4) ask the defendant specifically whether he or she wants counsel and record the defendant's answer on the complaint;

(5) if the defendant asserts indigence, and does not affirmatively, and with understanding, waive the right to counsel, assure that the defendant completes the appropriate application form for public defender services and files it with the criminal division manager's office;

(6) inform the defendant that there is a pretrial intervention program and where and how an application to it may be made;

(7) inform the defendant of his or her right to have a hearing as to probable cause and of his or her right to indictment by the grand jury and trial by jury, and if the offense charged may be tried by the court upon waiver of indictment and trial by jury, the court shall so inform the defendant. All such waivers shall be in writing, signed by the defendant, and shall be filed and entered on the docket. If the complaint charges an indictable offense which cannot be tried by the court on waiver, it shall not ask for or accept a plea to the offense; and

(8) admit the defendant to bail as provided in Rule 3:26.

(c) Procedure in Non–Indictable Offenses. At the defendant's first appearance before a judge, if the defendant is charged with an non-indictable offense, the judge shall:

(1) give the defendant a copy of the complaint and inform the defendant of the charge;

(2) inform the defendant of the right to remain silent and that any statement may be used against the defendant;

(3) inform the defendant of the right to retain counsel and, if indigent and entitled by law to the appointment of counsel, the right to be represented by a public defender or assigned counsel; and

(4) assign counsel, if the defendant is indigent and entitled by law to the appointment of counsel, and does not affirmatively, and with understanding, waive the right to counsel.

(d) Trial of Indictable Offenses in Municipal Court. If a defendant who is charged with an indictable offense that may be tried in Municipal Court is brought before a Municipal Court, that court may try the matter provided that the defendant waives the rights to indictment and trial by jury. The waivers shall be in writing, signed by the defendant, and approved by the county prosecutor, and retained by the Municipal Court.

Note: Source—R.R. 3:2–3(b), 8:4–2 (second sentence). Amended July 7, 1971 effective September 13, 1971; amended April 1, 1974 effective immediately; text of former Rule 3:4–2 amended and redesignated paragraphs (a) and (b) and text of former Rules 3:27–1 and –2 amended and incorporated into Rule 3:4–2, July 13, 1994 to be effective January 1, 1995; paragraphs (a) and (b) amended June 28, 1996 to be effective September 1, 1996; paragraph (b) amended January 5, 1998 to be effective February 1, 1998; caption amended, paragraphs (a) and (b) deleted, new paragraphs (a), (b), (c), and (d) adopted July 5, 2000 to be effective September 5, 2000.

3:4–3. Hearing as to Probable Cause on Indictable Offenses

(a) If the defendant does not waive indictment and trial by jury but does waive a hearing as to probable cause, the court shall forthwith bind the defendant over to await final determination of the cause. If the defendant does not waive a hearing as to probable cause and if before the hearing an indictment has not been returned against the defendant with respect to the offense charged, after notice to the county prosecutor a judge of the Superior Court shall hear the evidence offered by the State within a reasonable time and the defendant may cross-examine witnesses offered by the State. If, from the evidence, it appears to the court that there is probable cause to believe that an offense has been committed and the defendant has committed it, the court shall forthwith bind the defendant over to await final determination of the cause; otherwise, the court shall discharge the defendant from custody if the defendant is detained. Notice to the county prosecutor may be oral or in writing. An entry shall be made on the docket as to when and how such notice was given.

(b) After concluding the proceeding the court shall transmit, forthwith, to the county prosecutor all papers in the cause. Whether or not the court finds probable cause, it shall continue in effect any bail previously posted in accordance with R. 3:26 or any other condition of pretrial release not involving restraints on liberty; and any bail taken by the court shall be transmitted to the financial division manager's office. If the defendant is discharged for lack of probable cause and an indictment is not returned within 120 days, the bail shall thereafter be returned and conditions of pretrial release, if any, terminated.

Note: Source—R.R. 3:2–3(c). Paragraph designations added and paragraphs (a) and (b) amended July 16, 1979 to be effective September 10, 1979; paragraph (a) amended July 13, 1994 to be effective September 1, 1994; paragraph (b) amended July 5, 2000 to be effective September 5, 2000; paragraph (a) amended June 15, 2007 to be effective September 1, 2007.

3:4–4. Proceedings in Arrest Under Uniform Fresh Pursuit Law

If an arrest is made in this State by an officer of another state in accordance with the provisions of N.J.S. 2A:155–1 to N.J.S. 2A:155–7, inclusive (Uniform Law on Fresh Pursuit), the officer shall take the arrested person, without unnecessary delay, before the nearest available judge who shall conduct a hearing for the purpose of determining the lawfulness of the arrest. If the judge determines that the arrest was lawful, the judge shall commit the person to await, for a reasonable time, the issuance of an extradition warrant by the Governor of this State, or admit the person to bail for such purpose. If the court determines that the arrest was unlawful it shall discharge the person arrested.

Note: Source—R.R. 3:2–3(d), 8:3–3(d); amended July 13, 1994 to be effective September 1, 1994.

3:4–5. Effect of Technical Insufficiency or Irregularity in the Proceedings

A defendant held in custody under a commitment after a hearing as to probable cause shall not be discharged nor shall such hearing be deemed invalid because of any technical insufficiency or irregularity in the commitment or prior proceedings not prejudicial to the defendant, or because the offense for which the defendant is held to answer is other than that stated in the complaint or arrest warrant.

Note: Source—R.R. 3:2–3(e), 8:3–3(e).

RULE 3:5. SEARCH WARRANTS

3:5–1. Authority to Issue

A search warrant may be issued by a judge of a court having jurisdiction in the municipality where the property sought is located.

Note: Source—R.R. 3:2A–1.

3:5–2. Grounds for Issuance

A search warrant may be issued to search for and seize any property, including documents, books, papers and any other tangible objects, obtained in violation of the penal laws of this State or any other state; or possessed, controlled, designed or intended for use or which has been used in connection with any such violation; or constituting evidence of or tending to show any such violation.

Note: Source—R.R. 3:2A–2, 3:2A–7.

3:5–3. Issuance and Contents

(a) An applicant for a search warrant shall appear personally before the judge, who must take the applicant's affidavit or testimony before issuing the warrant. The judge may also examine, under oath, any witness the applicant produces, and may require that any person upon whose information the applicant relies appear personally and be examined under oath concerning such information. If the judge is satisfied that grounds for granting the application exist or that there is probable cause to believe they exist, the judge shall date and issue the warrant identifying the property to be seized, naming or describing the person or place to be searched and specifying the hours when it may be executed. The warrant shall be directed to any law enforcement officer, without naming an officer, and it shall state the basis for its issuance and the names of the persons whose affidavits or testimony have been taken in support thereof. The warrant shall direct that it be returned to the judge who issued it.

(b) A Superior Court judge may issue a search warrant upon sworn oral testimony of an applicant who is not physically present. Such sworn oral testimony may be communicated to the judge by telephone, radio or other means of electronic communication. The judge shall contemporaneously record such sworn oral testimony by means of a tape-recording device or stenographic machine if such are available; otherwise, adequate longhand notes summarizing what is said shall be made by the judge. Subsequent to taking the oath, the applicant must identify himself or herself, specify the purpose of the request and disclose the basis of his or her information. This sworn testimony shall be deemed to be an affidavit for the purposes of issuance of a search warrant. A warrant may issue if the judge is satisfied that exigent circumstances exist sufficient to excuse the failure to obtain a written warrant, and that sufficient grounds for granting the application have been shown. Upon approval, the judge shall memorialize the specific terms of the authorization to search and shall direct the applicant to enter this authorization verbatim on a form, or other appropriate paper, designated the duplicate original search warrant. This warrant shall be deemed a search warrant for the purpose of R. 3:5. The judge shall direct the applicant to print the judge's name on the warrant. The judge shall also contemporaneously record factual determinations as to exigent circumstances. If a recording is made, the judge shall direct that the testimony be transcribed as soon as practicable. This transcribed record shall be certified by the judge. The judge shall promptly issue a written confirmatory search warrant and shall enter thereon the exact time of issuance of the duplicate original warrant. In all other respects, the method of issuance and contents of the warrant shall be that required by subsection (a) of this rule.

Note: Source—R.R. 3:2A–3, 3:2A–4 (second sentence); former rule redesignated paragraph (a) and paragraph (b) adopted July 26, 1984 to be effective September 10, 1984; paragraphs (a) and (b) amended July 13, 1994 to be effective September 1, 1994.

3:5–4. Secrecy

A search warrant shall be issued with all practicable secrecy and the affidavit or testimony upon which it is based shall not be filed with the criminal division manager's office or made public in any way prior to execution. The disclosure, prior to its execution, that a warrant has been applied for or issued, except as necessary for its execution, may constitute a contempt. After execution a warrant and accompanying papers shall remain confidential except as provided in R. 3:5–6(c)

Note: Source—R.R. 3:2A–9 (first paragraph); amended July 13, 1994 to be effective January 1, 1995; amended July 12, 2002 to be effective September 3, 2002.

3:5–5. Execution and Return with Inventory

(a) A search warrant may be executed by any law enforcement officer, including the Attorney General or county prosecutor or sheriff or members of their staffs. The warrant must be executed within 10 days after its issuance and within the hours fixed therein by the judge issuing it, unless for good cause shown the warrant provides for its execution at any time of day or night. The officer taking property under the warrant shall give to the person from whom or from whose premises the property is taken a copy of the warrant and a receipt for the property taken or shall leave the copy and receipt at the place from which the property is taken. The return shall be made promptly and shall be accompanied by a written inventory of any property taken. The inventory shall be made and verified by the officer executing the warrant in the presence of the person from whom or from whose premises the property is taken or, if such person is not present, in the presence of some other person. The judge shall upon request deliver a copy of the inventory to the person from whom or from whose premises the property was taken and to the applicant for the warrant.

(b) If a duplicate original search warrant has been executed, the person who executed the warrant shall enter the exact time of its execution on its face. If a tape or stenographic record of the oral testimony has been made, the judge shall require the applicant to sign a transcript of that record. In all other respects, execution and return of the duplicate original search warrant shall be that required by paragraph (a) of this rule.

Note: Source—R.R. 3:2A–4; former rule redesignated as paragraph (a) and paragraph (b) adopted July 26, 1984 to be effective September 10, 1984.

3:5–6. Filing; Confidentiality

(a) Except as provided in subsection b, the judge who issued the warrant shall attach thereto the return, inventory, and all other papers in connection therewith, including the affidavits and a transcript or summary of any oral testimony and, where applicable, a duplicate original search warrant, and shall file them with the criminal division manager's office of the county wherein the property was seized. When a tape or stenographic record has been made, it shall also be filed by the judge.

(b) In the event a search warrant is issued based in whole or in part on oral, wire, or electronic communications authorized by a wiretap judge under the provisions of the New Jersey Wiretapping and Electronic Surveillance Control Act, N.J.S.A. 2A:156A–1 et seq., the judge who issued the warrant shall file only with the wiretap judge the application for the search warrant and all other affidavits, documents and exhibits submitted in connection therewith, as well as any tape or stenographic record of oral testimony taken by the wiretap judge.

The judge who issued the warrant shall file a notice of such filing with the wiretap judge, as aforesaid, together with the warrant and, where applicable, a duplicate original search warrant and inventory with the criminal division manager's office of the county wherein the property was seized.

(c) All warrants that have been completely executed and the papers accompanying them, including the affidavits, transcript or summary of any oral testimony, duplicate original search warrant, return and inventory, and any original tape or stenographic recording shall be confidential except that the warrant and accompanying papers shall be available for inspection and copying by the defendant as provided in R. 3:13–3 and by any person claiming to be aggrieved by an unlawful search and seizure upon notice to the county prosecutor for good cause shown.

Note: Source—R.R. 3:2A–5, 3:2A–9 (second paragraph). Amended June 29, 1973 to be effective September 10, 1973; amended July 26, 1984 to be effective September 10, 1984; paragraph designations and text of paragraph (b) adopted and paragraph (a) amended November 7, 1988 to be effective January 2, 1989; paragraphs (a) and (b) amended July 13, 1994, paragraph (c) amended December 9, 1994, to be effective January 1, 1995; paragraph (b) amended June 28, 1996 to be effective September 1, 1996; caption amended and paragraph (c) amended July 12, 2002 to be effective September 3, 2002.

3:5–7.   Motion to Suppress Evidence and for Return of Property

(a) **Notice; Time.** On notice to the prosecutor of the county in which the matter is pending or threatened, to the applicant for the warrant if the search was with a warrant, and to co-indictees, if any, and in accordance with the applicable provisions of R. 1:6–3 and R. 3:10, a person claiming to be aggrieved by an unlawful search and seizure and having reasonable grounds to believe that the evidence obtained may be used against him or her in a penal proceeding, may apply to the Superior Court only and in the county in which the matter is pending or threatened to suppress the evidence and for the return of the property seized even though the offense charged or to be charged may be within the jurisdiction of a municipal court. Such motion shall be made pursuant to R. 3:10–2.

(b) **Briefs.** If the search was made with a warrant, a brief stating the facts and arguments in support of the motion shall be submitted with the notice of motion. The State shall, within ten days thereafter, submit a brief stating the facts and arguments in support of the search to which the movant may reply by brief submitted no later than three days before the hearing. If the

search was made without a warrant, the State shall, within 15 days of the filing of the motion, file a brief, including a statement of the facts as it alleges them to be, and the movant shall file a brief and counter statement of facts no later than three days before the hearing.

(c) **Hearing.** All such motions by co-indictees shall be consolidated for determination in a single hearing, except for good cause shown. If material facts are disputed, testimony thereon shall be taken in open court.

(d) **Appellate Review.** Denial of a motion made pursuant to this rule may be reviewed on appeal from a judgment of conviction notwithstanding that such judgment is entered following a plea of guilty.

(e) **Return of Property.** If a motion made pursuant to this rule is granted, the property shall be delivered to the person entitled thereto, unless otherwise subject to lawful detention, and shall not be admissible in evidence in any court. Delivery of the property need not be made, however, until the expiration of the time within which the State may obtain leave to appeal pursuant to R. 2:5–6.

(f) **Consequences of Failure to Move.** If a timely motion is not made in accordance with this rule, the defendant shall be deemed to have waived any objection during trial to the admission of evidence on the ground that such evidence was unlawfully obtained.

(g) **Effect of Irregularity in Warrant.** In the absence of bad faith, no search or seizure made with a search warrant shall be deemed unlawful because of technical insufficiencies or irregularities in the warrant or in the papers or proceedings to obtain it, or in its execution.

Note: Source—R.R. 3:2A–6(a)(b). Paragraph (a) amended, paragraphs (b), (c), (d) adopted and former paragraphs (b), (c), (d) redesignated as (e), (f), (g) respectively January 28, 1977 to be effective immediately; paragraphs (a) and (c) amended July 16, 1979 to be effective September 10, 1979; paragraph (a) amended July 16, 1981 to be effective September 14, 1981; paragraph (a) amended June 9, 1989 to be effective June 19, 1989; paragraph (a) amended July 13, 1994 to be effective January 1, 1995; paragraph (a) amended January 5, 1998 to be effective February 1, 1998.

3:5–8.   Search and Seizure Without Search Warrant

Rule 3:5 shall not be construed to make illegal a lawful search and seizure made without a search warrant.

Note: Source—R.R. 3:2A–8.

RULE 3:5A. INVESTIGATIVE DETENTION

3:5A–1. Authority to Issue

Prior to the filing of a formal criminal charge against a person, an order authorizing the temporary detention of that person and compelling that person to submit to non-testimonial identification procedures for the purpose of obtaining evidence of that person's physical characteristics may be issued by a judge of the Superior Court pursuant to this Rule, on an application authorized in writing by the Attorney General or the Attorney General's designee or by the County Prosecutor or designated Assistant Prosecutor.

Note: Adopted July 26, 1984 to be effective September 10, 1984; amended July 14, 1992 to be effective September 1, 1992; amended July 13, 1994 to be effective September 1, 1994.

3:5A–2. Application

The application and any subsequent pleadings shall be captioned in the Superior Court of New Jersey and entitled, "In the Matter of the Investigation of (description of crime)." The application shall contain affidavits forming a factual basis for the findings required by R. 3:5A–4. In addition, the application shall state:

(a) The name or description of the individual sought to be detained for investigation.

(b) The specific type of identifying physical characteristic sought.

(c) The place and time at which the evidence sought is to be obtained.

(d) The method by which the evidence sought is to be obtained.

(e) The period of the detention, not to exceed five hours, during which the physical characteristic sought is to be obtained.

Note: Adopted July 26, 1984 to be effective September 10, 1984.

3:5A–3. Notice and Return

Unless the judge finds the application to be of emergent nature, as set forth below, the judge shall not consider it unless written notice shall have been given personally to the person, at least 36 hours before the time the application is to be made, that on a specific date and at a specific time application for an order of temporary detention will be made to the named judge. The notice shall advise the individual that counsel may accompany him or her at the hearing on the application.

Note: Adopted July 26, 1984 to be effective September 10, 1984; amended July 13, 1994 to be effective September 1, 1994.

3:5A–4. Grounds for Issuance

An order for investigative detention shall be issued only if the judge concludes from the application that:

(a) a crime has been committed and is under active investigation, and

(b) there is a reasonable and well-grounded basis from which to believe that the person sought may have committed the crime, and

(c) the results of the physical characteristics obtained during the detention will significantly advance the investigation and determine whether or not the individual probably committed the crime, and

(d) the physical characteristics sought cannot otherwise practicably be obtained.

Note: Adopted July 26, 1984 to be effective September 10, 1984.

3:5A–5. Contents of Order for Investigative Detention

(a) The order shall command the named person to appear at a specified time and place for the taking of evidence of specified physical characteristics. It shall advise the person that on failure to do so, an arrest warrant will issue for the identification procedure. The order shall specify the length of the detention, the identification methods to be used, and, where necessary, the medical safeguards to be observed. The date and time of its signing shall be entered thereon.

(b) The terms of any order for investigative detention shall be the least onerous on the named person consistent with the investigative need.

Note: Adopted July 26, 1984 to be effective September 10, 1984; paragraph (a) amended July 13, 1994 to be effective September 1, 1994.

3:5A–6. Emergent Application

If, without notice to the person, an application is made to a judge, and the judge is satisfied from it that its underlying purpose would be frustrated were notice to be given, the judge may sign an order for investigative detention with provisions appropriate to the investigative need and certify therein a finding that the matter is emergent. That order, directed to the person, may authorize the police officers executing it to use reasonable force in effectuating the detention of the person and in effectuation of identification procedures set forth therein.

Note: Adopted July 26, 1984 to be effective September 10, 1984; amended July 13, 1994 to be effective September 1, 1994.

3:5A–7. Service

An order for investigative detention shall be served within five days of its signing; otherwise it shall be void.

Note: Adopted July 26, 1984 to be effective September 10, 1984.

3:5A–8. Filing

The judge shall impound the original application and order. Upon receipt of the certification of test results, the judge shall cause the application, order, and certification to be impounded under seal with the criminal division manager as designee of the deputy clerk of the Superior Court.

Upon obtaining test results of the physical characteristic specified, the applicant shall, within two days, file with the judge, and deliver to the person, a certification of the date, time and place of detention, the length of the detention, and the testing or procedures used to obtain the physical characteristic evidence. The results of those tests, as they bear on the identification of the person detained as the perpetrator of the crime under investigation, shall be included in the certification, unless the court rules for good cause that they shall not be.

Note: Adopted July 26, 1984 to be effective September 10, 1984; amended July 13, 1994 to be effective January 1, 1995.

3:5A–9. Definition

"Evidence of physical characteristics" shall include fingerprints, palm prints, footprints, physical measurements, handwriting and handprinting samples, blood samples, urine samples, saliva samples, fingernail scrapings, hair samples, photographs, voice exemplars, display of designated portions of the body, the taking of photographs, and appearance in a lineup.

Note: Adopted July 26, 1984 to be effective September 10, 1984.

RULE 3:6. THE GRAND JURY

3:6–1. Summoning the Grand Jury

The Assignment Judge of each county shall order and organize according to law one or more grand juries for the county not exceeding 23 members each to be summoned at such times as the public interest requires. At least one grand jury shall be serving in each county at all times.

Note: Source—R.R. 3:3–1.

3:6–2. Objections to Grand Jury and Grand Jurors

The prosecuting attorney or a defendant, after being held to answer a complaint charging an indictable offense or after indictment, may, in writing, challenge the array of the grand jury which has returned or is expected to return the indictment on the ground that it was not selected, drawn or summoned according to law, and may challenge an individual juror on the ground that the juror is not legally qualified. All such challenges shall be made within 30 days of the service of the complaint or no later than at the arraignment/status conference. For good cause shown, the court may allow the motion to be brought at any time. Such challenges shall be tried by a judge designated by the Assignment Judge. If a defendant has already been indicted, such challenges may be the basis of a motion to dismiss the indictment.

Note: Source—R.R. 3:3–2(a)(b); amended July 13, 1994 to be effective January 1, 1995.

3:6–3. Supervising and Charging the Grand Jury

(a) Potential Bias. When appropriate, the Assignment Judge shall inquire of potential grand jurors about such aspects of their background as may reveal possible bias or interest in a matter to come before the grand jury. The Assignment Judge shall instruct the grand jury that without the Assignment Judge's approval no grand juror shall participate in any matter in which that juror has a bias or a financial, proprietary, or personal interest; and if that juror wishes to participate, the juror shall forthwith so inform the prosecutor. The prosecutor shall forthwith inform the Assignment Judge, who shall determine, in camera, whether such bias or interest exists and whether it justifies excusal.

(b) Copy of Charge. When the judge designated by the Assignment Judge charges the grand jury, that judge shall cause a copy of the charge to be promptly furnished to each juror.

Note: Source—R.R. 3:3–3; caption amended paragraph (a) adopted, and former rule captioned and redesignated paragraph (b) June 29, 1990 to be effective September 4, 1990; paragraph (b) amended July 13, 1994 to be effective September 1, 1994.

3:6–4. Foreperson; Deputy Foreperson

The Assignment Judge shall appoint one of the jurors to be foreperson and another to be deputy foreperson. The foreperson shall have power to administer oaths and shall endorse all indictments. During the absence of the foreperson, the deputy foreperson shall act as foreperson.

Note: Source—R.R. 3:3–4; amended July 14, 1992, to be effective September 1, 1992.

3:6–5. Clerk

The clerk of the grand jury shall make and keep minutes of the proceedings of the grand jury as well as a record of the vote of each juror, by name, on each considered matter. If there is no clerk of the grand jury, the foreperson or another juror designated by the foreperson shall keep such a record. The record of the vote on every count of every indictment and on every presentment shall be filed with the clerk of the grand jury. The record shall not be made public except on order of the Assignment Judge.

Note: Source—R.R. 3:3–5. Amended July 14, 1972 to be effective September 5, 1972; amended July 29, 1977 to be effective September 6, 1977; amended July 13, 1994 to be effective September 1, 1994.

3:6–6. Who May be Present; Record and Transcript

(a) Attendance at Session. No person other than the jurors, the prosecuting attorney, the clerk of the grand jury, the witness under examination, interpreters when needed and, for the purpose of recording the proceedings, a stenographer or operator of a recording device may be present while the grand jury is in session. No person other than the jurors, the clerk, the prosecuting attorney and the stenographer or operator of the recording device may be present while the grand jury is deliberating. The grand jury, however, may request either (1) the prosecuting attorney and the stenographer or operator or (2) the clerk to leave the jury room during its deliberations.

(b) Record; Transcript. A stenographic record or sound recording shall be made of all testimony of witnesses, comments by the prosecuting attorney, and colloquy between the prosecuting attorney and witnesses or members of the grand jury, before the grand jury.

After an indictment has been returned, at the request of the defendant, a transcript of the grand jury proceedings shall be made. The request shall designate the portion or portions of the proceedings to be transcribed and the person or persons to whom the transcript is to be furnished. A copy of the request for a transcript will be served contemporaneously by the defendant upon the prosecutor, who may move for a protective order pursuant to R. 3:13–3(f). The prosecutor may request a copy of the transcript at any time.

(c) Retention of Records. If no request has been made or order entered directing a transcript of the grand jury proceedings to be made within six months after their termination, the stenographic record or sound recording shall be sealed and deposited with the operations division manager's office who shall retain it subject to the directions of the Administrative Director of the Courts.

Note: Source—R.R. 3:3–6(a)(b)(c); paragraphs (a) and (b) amended July 15, 1982 to be effective September 13, 1982; paragraph (b) amended and second paragraph added to paragraph (b) July 13, 1994, new text in paragraph (b) amended December 9, 1994, to be effective January 1, 1995; paragraph (c) amended July 5, 2000 to be effective September 5, 2000.

3:6–7. Secrecy of Proceedings

Except as otherwise provided by R. 3:13–3, the requirement as to secrecy of proceedings of the grand jury shall remain as heretofore, and all persons other than witnesses, permitted by R. 3:6–6 to be present while the grand jury is in session, shall be required to take an oath of secrecy before their admission thereto. Such oath shall also be taken by typists making transcripts of testimony given before the grand jury.

Note: Source—R.R. 3:3–7; amended July 13, 1994 and December 9, 1994, to be effective January 1, 1995.

3:6–8. Finding and Return of Indictment; No Bill

(a) Return; Secrecy. An indictment may be found only upon the concurrence of 12 or more jurors and shall be returned in open court to the Assignment Judge or, in the Assignment Judge's absence, to any Superior Court judge assigned to the Law Division in the county. With the approval of the Assignment Judge, an indictment may be returned to such judge by only the foreperson or the deputy foreperson rather than with all other members of the grand jury. Such judge may direct that the indictment shall be kept secret until the defendant is in custody or has given bail and in that event it shall be sealed by the clerk, and no person shall disclose its finding except as necessary for the issuance and execution of a warrant or summons.

(b) No Bill. If the defendant has been held to answer a complaint and, after submission to the grand jury, no indictment has been found, the foreperson shall forthwith so report in writing to the court, who shall forthwith order the defendant's release unless the defendant's detention is required by other pending proceedings. Notice of the action of the grand jury shall also be mailed by the clerk of the court to the defendant's attorney, a defendant not in custody, and the defendant's sureties if bail has been posted.

Note: Source–R.R. 3:3–8(a)(b); paragraph (a) amended July 16, 1981 to be effective September 14, 1981; paragraph (a) amended July 26, 1984 to be effective September 10, 1984; paragraphs (a) and (b) amended July 13, 1994 to be effective September 1, 1994; paragraph (a) amended June 15, 2007 to be effective September 1, 2007.

3:6–9. Finding and Return of Presentment

(a) Finding. A presentment may be made only upon the concurrence of 12 or more jurors. It may refer to public affairs or conditions, but it may censure a public official only where that public official's association with the deprecated public affairs or conditions is intimately and inescapably a part of them.

(b) Return. A presentment shall be returned in open court to the Assignment Judge, who shall be notified in advance thereof by the foreperson so that the judge may arrange to be available in court to receive it.

(c) Examination; Reference Back; Striking. Promptly and before the grand jury is discharged, the Assignment Judge shall examine the presentment. If it appears that a crime has been committed for which an indictment may be had, the Assignment Judge shall refer the presentment back to the grand jury with appropriate instructions. If a public official is censured the proof must be conclusive that the existence of the condemned matter is inextricably related to non-criminal failure to discharge that public official's public duty. If it appears that the presentment is false, or is based on partisan motives, or indulges in personalities without basis, or if other good cause appears, the Assignment Judge shall strike the presentment either in full or in part. As an aid in examining the presentment the Assignment Judge may call for and examine the minutes and records of the grand jury, with or without the aid of the foreperson or the prosecuting attorney, to determine if a substantial foundation exists for the public report. If the presentment censures a public official and the Assignment Judge determines not to strike, a copy of the presentment shall forthwith be served upon the public official who may, within 10 days thereafter, move for a hearing, which shall be held in camera. The public official may examine the grand jury minutes fully, under such reasonable supervision as the court deems advisable, and be permitted to introduce additional evidence to expose any deficiency.

(d) Filing and Publication. Such portions of the presentment as are not referred back to the grand jury for further action or are not stricken in accordance with paragraph (c) of this rule shall be filed and made public, and the Assignment Judge shall instruct the clerk of the grand jury to send copies thereof to such public bodies or officials as may be concerned with the criticisms and recommendations made therein and to the Administrative Director of the Courts. The presentment or any portion thereof shall not be made public by any person except the Assignment Judge. The Assignment Judge shall withhold publication of the presentment until the expiration of the time for the making of a motion for a hearing by a public official pursuant to R. 3:6–9(c), and if such motion is made, shall withhold publication of the presentment pending the judge's determination.

(e) Review. The action taken by the Assignment Judge pursuant to this rule is judicial in nature and is subject to review for abuse of discretion by the State or by any aggrieved person, including any member of the grand jury making the presentment.

Note: Source—R.R. 3:3–9(a)(b)(c)(d)(e); paragraphs (a), (b), (c) and (d) amended July 13, 1994 to be effective September 1, 1994.

3:6–10. Discharge; Continuance of Term

(a) Term. A grand jury shall serve until discharged by the Assignment Judge, but not longer than 20 weeks unless the Assignment Judge shall order it continued as

hereinafter provided. A grand jury shall not be discharged before the expiration of its term of service except for good cause. The continuance of such grand jury shall not affect the usual drawing, selecting and serving of further grand juries.

(b) Order for Continuance. Whenever it appears to the Assignment Judge that the grand jury has not completed its labors, although its ordinary term is about to expire, the Assignment Judge may, if satisfied of the necessity therefor, order that its term be continued. The order shall be made and filed within the session of court for which such grand jury shall have been drawn, and shall provide a continuance for a definite period of time not exceeding 3 calendar months, provided, however, that the Assignment Judge may make a further order, or orders, continuing such grand jury in office for a further term or terms of 3 calendar months each.

Note: Source—R.R. 3:3–10(a)(b)(c); paragraph (b) amended July 13, 1994 to be effective September 1, 1994.

3:6–11. Impanelment and Judicial Supervision of State Grand Jury

(a) Generally. All rules relating to grand juries shall apply to the State Grand Jury except as otherwise specifically provided by statute or rule.

(b) Designation of Assignment Judge. The Chief Justice shall designate an Assignment Judge of the Superior Court to impanel and supervise the State Grand Jury or Grand Juries. The Chief Justice may also designate one or more Judges of the Superior Court to assist said Assignment Judge with regard to impanelment and supervision of the State Grand Jury or Grand Juries and to perform such other duties and responsibilities with regard thereto as ordered by the Chief Justice or the designated Assignment Judge.

Note: Adopted July 17, 1975 to be effective September 8, 1975.

RULE 3:7.   INDICTMENT AND ACCUSATION

3:7–1.   Entitling of Papers

The indictment and all subsequent papers in connection therewith shall be entitled in the Superior Court.

Note: Source—R.R. 3:4–1(b).

3:7–2.   Use of Indictment or Accusation

A crime punishable by death shall be prosecuted by indictment. Every other crime shall be prosecuted by indictment unless the defendant, after having been advised of the right to indictment, shall waive the right in a signed writing, in which case the defendant may be tried on accusation. Such accusation shall be prepared by the prosecuting attorney and entitled and proceeded upon in the Superior Court. Nothing herein contained, however, shall be construed as limiting the criminal

jurisdiction of a municipal court over indictable offenses provided by law and these rules.

Note: Source—R.R. 3:4–2(a)(b). Amended August 28, 1979 to be effective September 1, 1979; amended July 13, 1994 to be effective September 1, 1994.

3:7–3.   Nature and Contents of Indictment or Accusation; Timing of Supplemental Indictment

(a) Nature and Contents Generally. The indictment or accusation shall be a written statement of the essential facts constituting the crime charged, need not contain a formal commencement and shall be signed by the prosecuting attorney. The indictment shall be endorsed as a true bill by the foreperson and conclude: "against the peace of this State, the government and dignity of the same." Allegations made in one count of the indictment or accusation may be incorporated by reference in another count. It may be alleged in a single count either that the means by which the defendant committed the offense are unknown or that the defendant committed it by one or more specified means. An indictment or accusation or any count thereof charging the violation of a statute or statutes shall state the official or customary citation thereof, but error in the citation or its omission shall not be ground for dismissal of the indictment or accusation or for reversal of a conviction if the error or omission did not prejudicially mislead the defendant. Surplusage in the indictment or accusation may be stricken by the court on defendant's motion.

(b) Indictment for Murder. Every indictment for murder shall specify whether the act is murder as defined by N.J.S.A. 2C:11-3(a)(1), (2) or (3) and whether the defendant is alleged: (1) to have committed the act by his or her own conduct or (2) to have procured the commission of the offense by payment or promise of payment, of anything of pecuniary value or (3) to be the leader of a drug trafficking network, as defined in N.J.S.A.2C:35-3, and who, in furtherance of a conspiracy enumerated in N.J.S.A. 2C:35-3, commanded or by threat or promise solicited the commission of the offense.

(c) Specification of Aggravating Factors. In addition to the requirements in paragraph (b) of this rule, every indictment or supplemental indictment for a crime punishable by death shall specify any aggravating factors as set forth in N.J.S.A. 2C:11-3(c)(4) that the State intends to prove at the penalty phase.

(d) Timing of Supplemental Indictments. Any supplemental indictment specifying aggravating factors set forth in N.J.S.A. 2C:11-3(c)(4) shall be returned no later than 90 days after the return or unsealing of the original indictment, which period shall be enlarged only for good cause shown.

Note: Source—R.R. 3:4-3(a)(b)(c), 3:4-4. Paragraphs (a) and (b) amended August 28, 1979 to be effective September 1, 1979; paragraph (b) amended September 28, 1982 to be effective immediately; paragraph (b) amended July 13, 1993 to be effective immediately; paragraphs (a) and (b) amended July 13, 1994 to be effective September 1, 1994; caption amended and new paragraphs (c) and (d) adopted March 14, 2005 to be effective immediately; paragraph (b) text and caption amended June 15, 2007 to be effective September 1, 2007.

3:7-4. Amendment of Indictment or Accusation

The court may amend the indictment or accusation to correct an error in form or the description of the crime intended to be charged or to charge a lesser included offense provided that the amendment does not charge another or different offense from that alleged and the defendant will not be prejudiced thereby in his or her defense on the merits. Such amendment may be made on such terms as to postponing the trial, to be had

before the same or another jury, as the interest of justice requires.

Note: Source—R.R. 3:4-5. Amended August 28, 1979 to be effective September 1, 1979; amended July 13, 1994 to be effective September 1, 1994.

3:7-5. Bill of Particulars

A bill of particulars shall be ordered by the court if the indictment or accusation is not sufficiently specific to enable the defendant to prepare a defense. The defendant shall move therefore pursuant to Rule 3:10-2. The application shall point out clearly the particulars sought by the defense. The prosecutor shall furnish the bill of particulars within 10 days after the order of the court. Further particulars may be ordered when a demand therefor is promptly made. A bill of particulars may be amended at any time, subject to such conditions as the interest of justice requires. Any particulars that have been furnished to the defendant pursuant to R. 3:13-3 and 4 shall not be subject to an application pursuant to this rule.

Note: Source—R.R. 3:4-6; amended June 29, 1990, to be effective September 4, 1990; amended July 13, 1994 and December 9, 1994, to be effective January 1, 1995.

3:7-6. Joinder of Offenses

Two or more offenses may be charged in the same indictment or accusation in a separate count for each offense if the offenses charged are of the same or similar character or are based on the same act or transaction or on 2 or more acts or transactions connected together or constituting parts of a common scheme or plan. Relief from prejudicial joinder shall be afforded as provided by R. 3:15-2.

Note: Source—R.R. 3:4-7; amended August 28, 1979 to be effective September 1, 1979.

3:7-7. Joinder of Defendants

Two or more defendants may be charged in the same indictment or accusation if they are alleged to have participated in the same act or transaction or in the same series of acts or transactions constituting an offense or offenses. Such defendants may be charged in one or more counts together or separately and all of the defendants need not be charged in each count. The disposition of the indictment or accusation as to one or more of several defendants joined in the same indictment or accusation shall not affect the right of the State to proceed against the other defendants. Relief from prejudicial joinder shall be afforded as provided by R. 3:15-2.

Note: Source—R.R. 3:4-8.

3:7-8. Issuance of Warrant or Summons Upon Indictment or Accusation

Upon the return of an indictment or the filing of an accusation a summons or warrant shall be issued in accordance with R. 3:3-1 by the criminal division manager as designee of the deputy clerk of the Superior Court in the manner provided by law for each defendant named in the indictment or accusation who is not under bail. The criminal division manager as designee of the deputy clerk of the Superior Court, upon request, shall issue more than one warrant or summons for the same defendant. If the defendant fails to appear in response to a summons, a warrant shall issue.

If a summons is issued upon indictment to a defendant who has not been previously held to answer a complaint, the defendant shall undergo all post-arrest identification procedures that are required by law upon arrest, on the return date of the summons, or upon written request of the appropriate law enforcement agency.

Note: Source—R.R. 3:4–9. Amended July 22, 1983 to be effective September 12, 1983; amended July 13, 1994 to be effective January 1, 1995.

3:7–9. Form of Warrant and Summons

The warrant shall contain the name of the defendant or, if the defendant's name is unknown, any name or description by which the defendant can be identified with reasonable certainty, shall describe the offense charged in the indictment or accusation and shall command that the defendant be arrested and brought before the court. Conditions of pretrial release shall be fixed by the court and endorsed thereon, and in such case the sheriff or warden may take any bail. The summons shall be in the same form as the warrant except that it shall be directed to the defendant and require the defendant to appear to plead before the court at a stated time and place. The summons shall also state that if the defendant fails to so appear, a warrant for defendant's arrest shall issue.

Note: Source—R.R. 3:4–10(a)(b); amended July 13, 1994 to be effective January 1, 1995.

3:7–10. Execution of Service; Return

(a) Execution of Warrant. The warrant shall be executed in accordance with R. 3:3–3.

(b) Summons to an Individual. The summons shall be served upon an individual in accordance with R. 4:4–4.

(c) Summons to a Corporation. Service of a summons upon a defendant corporation, municipal or otherwise, shall be made in accordance with R. 4:4–2. If the defendant corporation does not appear, the court shall order the clerk to enter an appearance for said corporation and endorse the plea of not guilty on the indictment or accusation, and further proceedings may then be had thereon in the same manner as if the corporation had appeared and so pleaded. A plea to an indictment or accusation by a defendant corporation shall be made by an attorney of this State.

(d) Service Upon a Corporation by Publication. If the summons directed to a corporation is returned "not served" and it appears to the satisfaction of the court that the summons could not be served, the court shall by order direct the corporation to cause its appearance and plea to be entered by a day certain. A copy of such order shall within 5 days after the date thereof be published in a newspaper in this State once, at least 2 weeks preceding the day certain so specified. If the defendant corporation does not appear within the time specified by the order, the court, if satisfied that publication has been duly made, shall direct the clerk to enter an appearance and a plea of "not guilty" for the defendant corporation, and thereupon further proceedings may be had on the indictment or accusation as provided by these rules.

(e) Return. The officer executing a warrant shall make prompt return thereof to the court, and at the request of the prosecuting attorney any unexecuted warrant shall be returned and cancelled. The officer serving a summons shall make return thereof on or before the return day. At the request of the prosecuting attorney made at any time while the indictment or accusation is pending, a warrant returned unexecuted and not cancelled or a summons returned unserved or a duplicate thereof may be delivered by the clerk to the sheriff or other authorized officer for execution or service.

Note: Source—R.R. 3:4–11, 3:4–12(a)(b), 3:4–13. Paragraph (d) amended July 7, 1971 to be effective September 13, 1971.

RULE 3:8. APPEARANCE OF COUNSEL

3:8–1. Filing Appearance

The attorney for a defendant in a criminal action shall forthwith file an appearance with the criminal division manager's office of the county wherein venue is laid.

Note: Source—R.R. 3:5–4(b). Rule designation and caption adopted and text formerly designated R. 3:8 redesignated R. 3:8–1 July 16, 1979 to be effective September 10, 1979; amended July 13, 1994 and December 9, 1994, to be effective January 1, 1995.

3:8–2. Joint Representation

No attorney or law firm shall be permitted to enter an appearance for or represent more than one defendant

in a multi-defendant indictment without securing permission of the court.

Such motion shall be made in the presence of the defendants sought to be represented as early as practicable in the proceedings but no later than the arraignment/status conference so as to avoid delay of the trial. For good cause shown, the court may allow the motion to be brought at any time.

Note: Source—R.R. 3:5–4(b). Adopted July 16, 1979 to be effective September 10, 1979; amended July 13, 1994 to be effective January 1, 1995.

3:8–3. Representation by Public Defender

The criminal division manager's office shall receive applications for services of the Public Defender and shall determine indigence. A defendant who qualifies for service shall be referred to the Office of the Public Defender no later than the pre-arraignment interview. The defense counsel appointed by the Office of the

Public Defender shall promptly file an appearance. Representation of a defendant by the Office of the Public Defender shall continue through direct appeal from conviction, post-conviction proceedings for which the Rules of Court provide assigned counsel, and appeals from those proceedings.

Note: Adopted July 5, 2000 to be effective September 5, 2000.

CHAPTER II. ARRAIGNMENT; PLEAS; MOTIONS; PRETRIAL; DISCOVERY
RULE 3:9. PRETRIAL PROCEDURE

3:9–1. Prearraignment Conference; Plea Offer; Arraignment/Status Conference; Pretrial Hearings; Pretrial Conference

(a) **Prearraignment Conference.** After an indictment has been returned, or an indictment sealed pursuant to R. 3:6–8 has been unsealed, a copy of the indictment, together with the discovery for each defendant named therein, shall be either delivered to the criminal division manager's office, or be available at the prosecutor's office, within 14 days of the return or unsealing of the indictment. After the return or unsealing of the indictment the defendant shall be notified in writing by the criminal division manager's office to appear for a prearraignment conference which shall occur within 21 days of indictment. At the prearraignment conference the defendant shall be: informed of the charges; notified in writing of the date, place and time for the arraignment/status conference; and, if the defendant so requests, be allowed to apply for pretrial intervention. The criminal division manager's office shall not otherwise advise the defendant regarding the case. The criminal division manager's office, shall ascertain whether the defendant is represented by counsel and, if not, whether the defendant can afford counsel. If indicated that the defendant cannot afford counsel, the defendant shall be required to fill out the Uniform Defendant Intake Report. If a defendant does not appear for a prearraignment conference, the criminal division manager shall notify the criminal presiding judge who may issue a bench warrant. A defendant's attorney seeking discovery shall obtain a copy of the indictment and discovery from either the criminal division manager's office, or the prosecutor's office, no later than 28 days after the return or unsealing of the indictment. No prearraignment conference shall be required where the defendant has counsel and the criminal division manager's office has established to its satisfaction: (1) that an appearance has been filed under Rule 3:8–1; (2) that discovery, if requested, has been obtained; and (3) that defendant and counsel have obtained a date, place and time for the arraignment/status conference.

(b) **Plea Offer.** Prior to the arraignment/status conference the prosecutor and the defense attorney shall discuss the case, including any plea offer, and any outstanding or anticipated motions and discovery issues and report thereon at the arraignment/status conference. Any plea offer to be made by the prosecutor shall be in writing and forwarded to the defendant's attorney.

(c) **Arraignment/Status Conference; In Open Court.** The arraignment/status conference shall be conducted in open court no later than 50 days after indictment. The judge shall advise the defendant of the substance of the charge and confirm that the defendant has reviewed with counsel the indictment and the discovery. The judge shall inform all parties of their obligation to redact confidential personal identifiers from any documents submitted to the court in accordance with Rule 1:38–7(b). The defendant shall enter a plea to the charges. If the plea is not guilty counsel shall report on the results of plea negotiations, and such other matters, discussed pursuant to R. 3:9–1(b), which shall promote a fair and expeditious disposition of the case. At that time, the dates for hearing of motions and a further status conference, if necessary shall be scheduled according to the differentiated needs of each case. Each status conference shall be held in open court with the defendant present.

(d) **Pretrial Hearings.** Hearings to resolve issues relating to the admissibility of statements by defendant, pretrial identifications of defendant, sound recordings, and motions to suppress shall, unless otherwise ordered by the court, be held prior to the pretrial conference and, upon a showing of good cause, hearings as to admissibility of other evidence may also be held pretrial.

(e) **Pretrial Conference.** If the court determines that discovery is complete; that all motions have been decided or scheduled in accordance with paragraph (d); and that all reasonable efforts to dispose of the case without trial have been made and it appears that further negotiations or an additional status conference will not result in disposition of the case, or progress toward disposition of the case, the judge shall conduct a pretrial conference. The conference shall be conducted in open court with the prosecutor, defense counsel and the defendant present. Unless objected to by a party, the court shall ask the prosecutor to describe, without prejudice, the case including the salient facts and anticipated proofs and shall address the defendant to determine that the defendant understands: (1) the State's final plea offer, if one exists; (2) the sentencing exposure for the offenses charged, if convicted; (3) that ordinarily a negotiated plea will not be accepted after the pretrial conference and a trial date has been set; (4) the nature, meaning and consequences of the fact that a negotiated plea will not be accepted after the pretrial conference has been conducted and a trial date has been set and (5) that the defendant has a right to reject the plea offer and go to trial and that if the defendant goes to trial the State must prove the case beyond a reasonable doubt. If the case is not otherwise disposed of, a pretrial memorandum shall be prepared in a form prescribed by the Administrative Director of the Courts. The pretrial memorandum shall be reviewed on the record with counsel and the defendant present and shall be signed by the judge who, in consultation with counsel, shall fix the trial date. No admissions made by the defendant or defendant's attorney at the conference shall be used against the defendant unless the admissions are reduced to writing and signed by the defendant and defendant's attorney. The court shall also inform the defendant of the right to be present at trial, the trial date set, and the consequences of a failure to appear for trial, including the possibility that the trial will take place in defendant's absence.

Note: Source—R.R. 3:5–1. Paragraph (b) deleted and new paragraph (b) adopted July 7, 1971, to be effective September 13, 1971; paragraph (b) amended July 29, 1977 to be effective September 6, 1977; paragraph (a) amended and paragraph (b) deleted July 21, 1980 to be effective September 8, 1980; paragraph (a) amended July 14, 1992 to be effective September 1, 1992; first three sentences of former paragraph (a) amended and redesignated paragraph (c), last sentence of former paragraph (a) amended and moved to new paragraph (e), new paragraphs (a), (b), (d) and (e) adopted July 13, 1994 to be effective January 1, 1995; paragraph (e) amended July 12, 2002 to be effective September 3, 2002; paragraph (c) amended July 16, 2009 to be effective September 1, 2009.

3:9–2. Pleas

A defendant may plead only guilty or not guilty to an offense. The court, in its discretion, may refuse to accept a plea of guilty and shall not accept such plea without first questioning the defendant personally, under oath or by affirmation, and determining by inquiry of the defendant and others, in the court's discretion, that there is a factual basis for the plea and that the plea is made voluntarily, not as a result of any threats or of any promises or inducements not disclosed on the record, and with an understanding of the nature of the charge and the consequences of the plea. In addition to its inquiry of the defendant, the court may accept a written stipulation of facts, opinion, or state of mind that the defendant admits to be true, provided the stipulation is signed by the defendant, defense counsel, and the prosecutor. When the defendant is charged with a crime punishable by death, no factual basis shall be required from the defendant before entry of a plea of guilty to a capital offense or to a lesser included offense,

provided the court is satisfied from the proofs presented that there is a factual basis for the plea. For good cause shown the court may, in accepting a plea of guilty, order that such plea not be evidential in any civil proceeding. If a plea of guilty is refused, no admission made by the defendant shall be admissible in evidence against the defendant at trial. If a defendant refuses to plead or stands mute, or if the court refuses to accept a plea of guilty, a plea of not guilty shall be entered. Before accepting a plea of guilty, the court shall require the defendant to complete, insofar as applicable, and sign the appropriate form prescribed by the Administrative Director of the Courts, which shall then be filed with the criminal division manager's office.

Note: Source—R.R. 3:5–2 (a)(b). Amended July 14, 1972 to be effective September 5, 1972. Amended July 17, 1975 to be effective September 8, 1975. Amended September 28, 1982 to be effective immediately; amended July 13, 1994 to be effective January 1, 1995; amended July 28, 2004 to be effective September 1, 2004.

3:9–3. Plea Discussions; Agreements; Withdrawals

(a) Plea Discussions Generally. The prosecutor and defense attorney may engage in discussions relating to pleas and sentences and shall engage in discussions about such matters as will promote a fair and expeditious disposition of the case, but except as hereinafter authorized the judge shall take no part in such discussions.

(b) Entry of Plea. When the prosecutor and defense counsel reach an agreement concerning the offense or offenses to which a defendant will plead on condition that other charges pending against the defendant will be dismissed or an agreement concerning the sentence that the prosecutor will recommend, or when pursuant to paragraph (c) the defendant pleads guilty based on indications by the court of the maximum sentence to be imposed, such agreement and such indications shall be placed on the record in open court at the time the plea is entered.

(c) Disclosure to Court. On request of the prosecutor and defense counsel, the court in the presence of both counsel may permit the disclosure to it of the tentative agreement and the reasons therefor in advance of the time for tender of the plea or, if no tentative agreement has been reached, the status of negotiations toward a plea agreement. The court may then indicate to the prosecutor and defense counsel whether it will concur in the tentative agreement or, if no tentative agreement has been reached and with the consent of both counsel, the maximum sentence it would impose in the event the defendant enters a plea of guilty, assuming, however, in both cases that the information in the presentence report at the time of sentence is as has been represented to the court at the time of the disclosure and supports its determination that the interests of justice would be served thereby. If the agreement is reached without such disclosure or if the court agrees conditionally to accept the plea agreement as set forth above, or if the plea is to be based on the court's conditional indication about the sentence, all the terms of the plea, including the court's concurrence or its indication concerning sentence, shall be placed on the record in open court at the time the plea is entered. Nothing in this Rule shall be construed to authorize the court to dismiss or downgrade any charge without the consent of the prosecutor.

(d) Agreements Involving the Right to Appeal. Whenever a plea agreement includes a provision that defendant will not appeal, the court shall advise the defendant that notwithstanding the inclusion of this provision, the defendant has the right to take a timely appeal if the plea agreement is accepted, but that if the defendant does so, the plea agreement may be annulled at the option of the prosecutor, in which event all charges shall be restored to the same status as immediately before the entry of the plea. In the event the defendant files an appeal in a case in which the plea agreement included a provision that the defendant will not appeal, the State must exercise its right to annul the plea agreement no later than seven days prior to the date scheduled for oral argument or submission without argument.

(e) Withdrawal of Plea. If at the time of sentencing the court determines that the interests of justice would not be served by effectuating the agreement reached by the prosecutor and defense counsel or by imposing sentence in accordance with the court's previous indications of sentence, the court may vacate the plea or the defendant shall be permitted to withdraw the plea.

(f) Conditional Pleas. With the approval of the court and the consent of the prosecuting attorney, a defendant may enter a conditional plea of guilty reserving on the record the right to appeal from the adverse determination of any specified pretrial motion. If the defendant prevails on appeal, the defendant shall be afforded the opportunity to withdraw his or her plea. Nothing in this rule shall be construed as limiting the right of appeal provided for in R. 3:5–7(d).

(g) Plea Cut Off. After the pretrial conference has been conducted and a trial date set, the court shall not accept negotiated pleas absent the approval of the Criminal Presiding Judge based on a material change of circumstance, or the need to avoid a protracted trial or a manifest injustice.

Note: Adopted July 17, 1975 to be effective September 8, 1975. Paragraph (d) adopted July 29, 1977 to be effective September 6, 1977; paragraph (d) redesignated as (e); paragraph (f) adopted July 21, 1980 to be effective September 8, 1980; paragraphs (b), (c) and (e) and captions for paragraphs (b) and (c) amended May 23, 1989 to be effective June 15, 1989; paragraph (d) amended June 29, 1990 to be effective September 4, 1990; paragraphs (a) and (f) amended, paragraph (g) adopted July 13, 1994 to be effective January 1, 1995; caption to paragraph (g) amended July 5, 2000 to be effective September 5, 2000.

Supreme Court Commentary

A "material change of circumstance" means a change occurring after the pretrial conference that strengthens or weakens the case of either the prosecution or the defense sufficiently to warrant a change in their plea-bargaining position. It may be either a change in fact or in the knowledge of counsel. Some typical examples that may constitute material change of circumstance are when new charges are filed after the plea cut-off has been imposed, a justifiable change of attorney has occurred, a witness becomes no longer available, a mistrial or hung jury occurs, or some evidence is newly discovered. However, a change that would ordinarily have been anticipated by a reasonably competent prosecutor or defense attorney, including some of the foregoing examples, is not material, nor is a change that results from counsel's lack of ordinary diligence. A "protracted trial" is one that will probably last two weeks or more. One example of manifest injustice is a sexual assault case in which the victim is a child: if the trial is likely to have a substantial adverse impact on the child, the court may grant waiver. "Manifest injustice" does not exist simply because the parties are able and willing to enter into a plea bargain on or before the date of trial.

A plea cut-off rule was recommended by twelve members of the Supreme Court Criminal Practice Committee in a dissent filed with the 1992–94 Criminal Practice Committee Recommendations on Rules Necessary to Implement the Criminal Division Operating Standards. See 137 *N.J.L.J.* 54, 76–77. That recommendation was adopted and further modified by the Supreme Court as set forth above.

RULE 3:10. PLEADINGS AND MOTIONS BEFORE TRIAL; DEFENSES AND OBJECTIONS

3:10–1. Pleadings and Motions

Pleadings in criminal actions shall consist only of the complaint, the indictment or accusation, and the plea. Any defense or objection capable of determination without trial of the general issue may be raised before trial by motion to dismiss or for other appropriate relief.

Note: Source—R.R. 3:5–5(a)(b)(1).

3:10–2. Time and Manner of Making Motion; Hearing on Motion

(a) Time and Manner of Making Motion. Unless otherwise required by law, pre-indictment motions shall be heard by the judge to whom the case is assigned. If the case has not been assigned to a judge pre-indictment motions shall be made to the Criminal Presiding Judge or designee, except as otherwise provided by law. Unless otherwise required by law, or ordered by the Criminal Presiding Judge, post-indictment motions shall be made to the judge to whom the indictment has been assigned. At the arraignment/status conference counsel shall advise the court of their intention to make motions. The dates for filing, briefing and for the hearing of such motions shall be set by the court at the arraignment/status conference. Unless otherwise ordered by the court, motions and status conferences shall be scheduled on the same day. The court may for good cause shown and in the interest of justice permit additional motions to be made thereafter. A motion shall include all defenses and objections then available to the defendant.

(b) Hearing on Motion. A motion made before trial shall be determined before the trial memorandum is prepared and the trial date fixed, unless the court, for good cause, orders it deferred for determination at or after trial.

(c) Defenses and Objections Which Must Be Raised Before Trial. The defense of double jeopardy and all other defenses and objections based on defects in the institution of the prosecution or in the indictment or accusation, except as otherwise provided by R. 3:10–2(d) (defenses which may be raised only before or after trial) and R. 3:10–2(e) (lack of jurisdiction), must be raised by motion before trial. Failure to so present any such defense constitutes a waiver thereof, but the court for good cause shown may grant relief from the waiver.

(d) Defenses and Objections Which May Only Be Raised Before or After Trial. The defense that the indictment or accusation fails to charge an offense and the defense that the charge is based on a statute or regulation promulgated pursuant to statute which is unconstitutional or invalid in whole or in part may only be raised by motion either before trial or within 10 days after a verdict of guilty or within such further time as the court may fix during such 10–day period, or on appeal. Such defenses shall not be considered during trial.

(e) Lack of Jurisdiction. The court shall notice the defense of lack of jurisdiction in the court at any time during the pendency of the proceeding except during trial.

Note: Source—R.R. 3:5-5(b)(2)(3) and (4); caption amended, former Rules 3:10–2, –3, –4, –5 and –6 amended, redesignated and incorporated into R. 3:10–2 as paragraphs (c), (d), (e), (a), and (b) July 13, 1994 to be effective January 1, 1995.

3:10–3.　[Reserved]

Note: Source—R.R. 3:5–5(b)(2) (first sentence); former R. 3:10–3 redesignated R. 3:10–2(d) July 13, 1994 to be effective January 1, 1995.

3:10–4.　[Reserved]

Note: Source—R.R. 3:5–5(b)(2) (fifth sentence); former R. 3:10–4 redesignated R. 3:10–2(e) July 13, 1994 to be effective January 1, 1995.

3:10–5.　[Reserved]

Note: Source—R.R. 3:5–5(b)(2) (third sentence), 3:5–5(b)(3); former R. 3:10–5 amended and redesignated R. 3:10–2(a) July 13, 1994 to be effective January 1, 1995.

3:10–6.　[Reserved]

Note: Source—R.R. 3:5–5(b)(4); former R. 3:10–6 amended and redesignated R. 3:10–2(b) July 13, 1994 to be effective January 1, 1995.

3:10–7.　Effect of Determination of Motion

Except as provided in R. 3:9–3(f), if a motion is determined adversely to the defendant, the defendant shall be permitted to plead if the defendant has not previously pleaded but a plea previously entered shall stand. If an objection or defense specified in R. 3:10–2 is sustained and is not otherwise remediable the court shall order the indictment or accusation dismissed. If the court grants a motion to dismiss an indictment or accusation, it may also order that the defendant be held in custody or that bail be continued for a specified time pending the filing of a new indictment or accusation.

Note: Source—R.R. 3:5–5(b)(2) (sixth sentence), 3:5–5(b)(5). Amended July 21, 1980 to be effective September 8, 1980; amended July 13, 1994 to be effective September 1, 1994; amended July 13, 1994 to be effective January 1, 1995.

RULE 3:11.　[RESERVED]

[R. 3:11–1 and R. 3:11–2 revised and redesignated as R. 3:12–2(a) and (b) July 13, 1994 to be effective January 1, 1995.]

RULE 3:12.　DEFENDANT'S OBLIGATION TO PROVIDE NOTICE

3:12–1.　Notice Under Specific Criminal Code Provisions

A defendant shall serve written notice on the prosecutor if the defendant intends to rely on any of the following sections of the Code of Criminal Justice: Ignorance or Mistake, 2C:2–4(c); Accomplice: Renunciation Terminating Complicity, 2C:2–6(e)(3); Intoxication, 2C:2–8(d); Duress, 2C:2–9(a); Entrapment, 2C:2–12(b); General Principles of Justification, 2C:3–1 to 2C:3–11; Insanity, 2C:4–1; Lack of Requisite State of Mind, 2C:4–2; Criminal Attempt (renunciation of criminal purpose), 2C:5–1(d); Conspiracy (renunciation of criminal purpose), 2C:5–2(e); Murder (affirmative defense, felony murder), 2C:11–3(a)(3); Criminal Restraint, 2C:13–2(b); Theft by Extortion, 2C:20–5; Perjury (retraction), 2C:28–1(d); False Swearing (retraction), 2C:28–2(b); and Controlled Dangerous Substances Near or On School Property, 2C:35–7; and

Distributing, Dispensing or Possessing Controlled Substances Within 500 Feet of Public Housing Facilities, Parks or Buildings, 2C:35–7.1.

No later than seven days before the arraignment/status conference the defendant shall serve on the prosecutor a notice of intention to claim any of the defenses listed herein; and if the defendant requests or has received discovery pursuant to R. 3:13–3(c), the defendant shall, pursuant to R. 3:13–3(d), furnish the prosecutor with discovery pertaining to such defenses at the time the notice is served. The prosecutor shall, within 14 days after receipt of such discovery, comply with R. 3:13–3(c) and (g) with respect to any defense for which the prosecutor has received notice.

For good cause shown the court may extend the time of service of any of the foregoing, or make such other orders as the interest of justice requires. If a party fails to comply with this Rule, the court may take such action as the interest of justice requires. The action taken may include refusing to allow the party in default to present witnesses in support or in opposition of that defense at the trial or to allow the granting of an adjournment or delay during trial as the interest of justice demands.

Note: Source—R.R. 3:5–9A. Former Rule 3:12 amended August 28, 1979 to be effective September 1, 1979; main caption amended and former Rules 3:12 and 3:12A amended, combined and redesignated as Rule 3:12–1, July 13, 1994, second paragraph amended December 9, 1994, to be effective January 1, 1995; amended July 12, 2002 to be effective September 3, 2002.

3:12–2. Notice of Alibi; Failure to Furnish

(a) Alibi. If a defendant intends to rely in any way on an alibi, within 10 days after a written demand by the prosecutor the defendant shall furnish a signed alibi, stating the specific place or places at which the defendant claims to have been at the time of the alleged offense and the names and addresses of the witnesses upon whom the defendant intends to rely to establish such alibi. Within 10 days after receipt of such alibi, the prosecutor shall, on written demand, furnish the defendant or defendant's attorney with the names and addresses of the witnesses upon whom the State intends to rely to establish defendant's presence at the scene of the alleged offense. The trial court may order such amendment or amplification as the interest of justice requires.

(b) Failure to Furnish. If the information required in paragraph (a) is not furnished, the court may refuse to allow the party in default to present witnesses at trial as to defendant's absence from or presence at the scene of the alleged offense, or make such other order or grant such adjournment, or delay during trial, as the interest of justice requires.

Note: Former Rules 3:11–1 and –2 amended and redesignated R. 3:12–2 July 13, 1994 to be effective January 1, 1995.

RULE 3:12A.   [DELETED]

Note: Adopted July 26, 1984 to be effective September 10, 1984; amended July 14, 1992 to be effective September 1, 1992; R. 3:12A combined with R. 3:12 and redesignated as R. 3:12–1 July 13, 1994, to be effective January 1, 1995.

RULE 3:13.   DEPOSITIONS; DISCOVERY

3:13–1. [Deleted]

Note: Source—R.R. 3:5–3(a)(b). Paragraph designations and paragraph (b) adopted July 16, 1979 to be effective September 10, 1979; paragraph (a) amended July 21, 1980 to be effective immediately; paragraph (b) amended July 15, 1982 to be effective September 13, 1982; Rule deleted and redesignated as R. 3:9–1(e) and (d) July 13, 1994 to be effective January 1, 1995.

3:13–2. Depositions

(a) When Authorized. If it appears to the judge of the court in which a complaint, indictment or accusation is pending that a material witness is likely to be unable to testify at trial because of death or physical or mental incapacity, the court, upon motion and notice to the parties, and after a showing that such action is necessary to prevent manifest injustice, may order that a deposition of the testimony of such witness be taken and that any designated books, papers, documents or tangible objects, not privileged, be produced at the same time and place. If a witness is committed for failure to give bail to appear to testify at a trial or hearing, on written motion of the witness and upon notice to the parties, the court may direct that the witness's deposition be taken, and after the deposition has been subscribed the court may discharge the witness.

(b) Procedure. The deposition shall be videotaped unless the court orders otherwise. The deposition shall be taken before the judge at such location as will be convenient to all parties. If, because the deposition is to be taken outside of the State, the judge is unable to preside, the deposition shall be taken before a person designated by the judge to perform that function. All parties and counsel shall have a right to be present at the deposition. Examination, cross-examination and determination of admissibility of evidence, shall proceed in the same manner as at trial. Videotaping shall be done by a person independent of both prosecution and defense and chosen by the judge.

(c) Use. Depositions taken pursuant to this rule may be used at trial in lieu of live testimony of the witness in open court if the witness is unable to testify because of death or physical or mental incapacity. In the case of a witness deposed to allow discharge from commitment for failure to give bail as provided in paragraph (a) above, the deposition may be used, in addition, if the court finds that the party offering the deposition has been unable to procure the attendance of the witness by subpoena or otherwise. The deposition shall be admissible insofar as allowable under the Rules of Evidence applied as though the witness were then present and testifying. The deposition shall not be used unless the court finds that the circumstances surrounding its taking allowed full preparation and cross-examination by all parties. A record of the videotaped testimony, which shall be part of the official record of the court proceedings, shall be made in the same manner as if the witness were present and testifying, but, in addition, the videotape shall be retained by the court. If the judge finds that use of the videotaped testimony would be unfairly prejudicial to a party, the judge may order that only the audiotape of the testimony be used or that the transcript of the witness's testimony be read to the jury if either of these limitations would prevent such prejudice.

(d) Jury Instruction. In any case where a deposition is used in any form, the court shall instruct the jury that this procedure is employed for the convenience of the witness and that the jury should draw no inference from its use.

Note: Source—R.R. 3:5–8(a)(b)(c)(d)(e). Text of former rule deleted and new rule adopted November 5, 1986 to be effective January 1, 1987; paragraphs (a) and (c) amended July 13, 1994 to be effective January 1, 1995; rule redesignation of July 13, 1994 eliminated December 9, 1994 to be effective January 1, 1995.

3:13–3. Discovery and Inspection

(a) Pre–indictment Discovery. Where the prosecutor has made a pre-indictment plea offer, the prosecutor shall upon request permit defense counsel to inspect and copy or photograph any relevant material which would be discoverable following an indictment pursuant to section (b) or (c).

(b) Post Indictment Discovery. A copy of the prosecutor's discovery shall be delivered to the criminal division manager's office, or shall be available at the prosecutor's office, within 14 days of the return or unsealing of the indictment. Defense counsel shall obtain a copy of the discovery from the criminal division manager's office, or the prosecutor's office, no later than 28 days after the return or unsealing of the indictment. A defendant who does not seek discovery from the State shall so notify the criminal division manager's office and the prosecutor, and the defendant need not provide discovery to the State pursuant to sections (d) or (g), except as required by Rule 3:12–1 or

otherwise required by law. Defense counsel will forward a copy of discovery materials to the prosecuting attorney no later than 7 days before the arraignment/status conference.

(c) Discovery by the Defendant. The prosecutor shall permit defendant to inspect and copy or photograph the following relevant material if not given as part of the discovery package under section (b):

(1) books, tangible objects, papers or documents obtained from or belonging to the defendant;

(2) records of statements or confessions, signed or unsigned, by the defendant or copies thereof, and a summary of any admissions or declarations against penal interest made by the defendant that are known to the prosecution but not recorded;

(3) results or reports of physical or mental examinations and of scientific tests or experiments made in connection with the matter or copies thereof, which are within the possession, custody or control of the prosecutor;

(4) reports or records of prior convictions of the defendant;

(5) books, papers, documents, or copies thereof, or tangible objects, buildings or places which are within the possession, custody or control of the prosecutor;

(6) names, addresses, and birthdates of any persons whom the prosecutor knows to have relevant evidence or information including a designation by the prosecutor as to which of those persons may be called as witnesses;

(7) record of statements, signed or unsigned, by such persons or by co-defendants which are within the possession, custody or control of the prosecutor and any relevant record of prior conviction of such persons;

(8) police reports which are within the possession, custody, or control of the prosecutor;

(9) names and addresses of each person whom the prosecutor expects to call to trial as an expert witness, the expert's qualifications, the subject matter on which the expert is expected to testify, a copy of the report, if any, of such expert witness, or if no report is prepared, a statement of the facts and opinions to which the expert is expected to testify and a summary of the grounds for each opinion. Except in the penalty phase of a capital case if this information is requested and not furnished 30 days in advance of trial, the expert witness may, upon application by the defendant, be barred from testifying at trial.

(d) Discovery by the State. A defendant shall permit the State to inspect and copy or photograph the following relevant material if not given as part of the discovery package under section (b):

(1) results or reports of physical or mental examinations and of scientific tests or experiments made in connection with the matter or copies thereof, which are

within the possession, custody or control of defense counsel;

(2) any relevant books, papers, documents or tangible objects, buildings or places or copies thereof, which are within the possession, custody or control of defense counsel;

(3) the names, addresses, and birthdates of those persons known to defendant who may be called as witnesses at trial and their written statements, if any, including memoranda reporting or summarizing their oral statements;

(4) written statements, if any, including any memoranda reporting or summarizing the oral statements, made by any witnesses whom the State may call as a witness at trial;

(5) names and address of each person whom the defense expects to call to trial as an expert witness, the expert's qualifications, the subject matter on which the expert is expected to testify, and a copy of the report, if any, of such expert witness, or if no report is prepared, a statement of the facts and opinions to which the expert is expected to testify and a summary of the grounds for each opinion. Except in the penalty phase of a capital case if this information is requested and not furnished 30 days in advance of trial the expert may, upon application by the prosecutor, be barred from testifying at trial.

(e) Documents Not Subject to Discovery. This rule does not require discovery of a party's work product consisting of internal reports, memoranda or documents made by that party or the party's attorney or agents, in connection with the investigation, prosecution or defense of the matter nor does it require discovery by the State of records or statements, signed or unsigned, of defendant made to defendant's attorney or agents.

(f) Protective Orders.

(1) *Grounds.* Upon motion and for good cause shown the court may at any time order that the discovery or inspection sought pursuant to this rule be denied, restricted, or deferred or make such other order as is appropriate. In determining the motion, the court may consider the following: protection of witnesses and others from physical harm, threats of harm, bribes, economic reprisals and other intimidation; maintenance of such secrecy regarding informants as is required for effective investigation of criminal activity; protection of confidential relationships and privileges recognized by law; any other relevant considerations.

(2) *Procedure.* The court may permit the showing of good cause to be made, in whole or in part, in the form of a written statement to be inspected by the court alone, and if the court thereafter enters a protective order, the entire text of the statement shall be sealed and preserved in the records of the court, to be made available only to the appellate court in the event of an appeal.

(g) Continuing Duty to Disclose; Failure to Comply. If subsequent to the compliance with a request by the prosecuting attorney or defense counsel or with an order issued pursuant to the within rule and prior to or during trial a party discovers additional material or witnesses previously requested or ordered subject to discovery or inspection, that party shall promptly notify the other party or that party's attorney of the existence thereof. If at any time during the course of the proceedings it is brought to the attention of the court that a party has failed to comply with this rule or with an order issued pursuant to this rule, it may order such party to permit the discovery or inspection of materials not previously disclosed, grant a continuance or delay during trial, or prohibit the party from introducing in evidence the material not disclosed, or it may enter such other order as it deems appropriate.

Note: Source–R.R. 3:5–11(a)(b)(c)(d)(e)(f)(g)(h). Paragraphs (b)(c)(f) and (h) deleted; paragraph (a) amended and paragraphs (d)(e)(g) and (i) amended and redesignated June 29, 1973 to be effective September 10, 1973. Paragraph (b) amended July 17, 1975 to be effective September 8, 1975; paragraph (a) amended July 15, 1982 to be effective September 13, 1982; paragraphs (a) and (b) amended July 22, 1983 to be effective September 12, 1983; new paragraphs (a) and (b) added, former paragraphs (a), (b), (c), (d) and (f) amended and redesignated paragraphs (c), (d), (e), (f) and (g) respectively and former paragraph (e) deleted July 13, 1994, to be effective January 1, 1995; Rule redesignation of July 13, 1994 eliminated December 9, 1994, to be effective January 1, 1995; paragraphs (c)(6) and (d)(3) amended June 15, 2007 to be effective September 1, 2007.

3:13–4. Additional Discovery in Capital Cases

(a) In addition to any discovery provided pursuant to R. 3:13–3, the prosecuting attorney shall provide the defendant with the indictment containing the aggravating factors that the State intends to prove at the penalty phase together with all discovery bearing on these factors. The prosecuting attorney shall provide the defendant with any discovery in the possession of the prosecution that is relevant to the existence of any mitigating factors. Such discovery shall be transmitted at the arraignment/status conference unless the time to do so is enlarged for good cause. If the aggravating factors are not contained in the original indictment, but are contained in a supplemental indictment, the prosecuting attorney shall provide the defendant with any discovery bearing on these factors immediately upon return of the supplemental indictment, unless the time to do so is enlarged for good cause shown.

(b) The defendant shall provide the prosecuting attorney with an itemization setting forth the mitigating factors the defendant intends to rely on at the sentencing hearing together with any discovery in the possession of the defendant in support of those factors. Such discovery shall be transmitted to the prosecuting attorney forthwith upon a verdict of guilty, or plea of guilty, to a crime punishable by death.

(c) The duty to disclose the discovery relevant to the existence of aggravating and mitigating factors shall be a continuing one.

Note: Adopted September 28, 1982 to be effective immediately; paragraphs (a) and (b) amended July 13, 1994 to be effective September 1, 1994; paragraph (a) amended July 13, 1994 and December 9, 1994, to be effective January 1, 1995; paragraph (a) amended March 14, 2005 to be effective immediately.

CHAPTER III. VENUE; TRIAL
RULE 3:14. PLACE OF TRIAL; FOREIGN JURIES

3:14–1. Venue

An offense shall be prosecuted in the county in which it was committed, except that

(a) If it is uncertain in which one of 2 or more counties the offense has been committed or if an offense is committed in several counties prosecution may be had in any of such counties.

(b) If a person dies in one county as a result of an offense committed in any other county or counties, the prosecution may be had in any of such counties.

(c) Whenever the body of any person who died as a result of an offense is found in any county, prosecution may be had in such county, regardless of where the offense was committed.

(d) Whenever a person dies within the jurisdiction of this State as a result of an offense committed outside the jurisdiction of this State, or dies outside the jurisdiction of this State as a result of an offense committed within the jurisdiction of this State, the prosecution shall be had in the county in which the death occurred or the offense was committed.

(e) Prosecution for acts of treason against this State which were committed outside the jurisdiction of this State shall be had in any county designated by the Chief Justice.

(f) Prosecutions for libel shall be had either in the county in which the publication was made or the county in which the libeled person resided at the time of the publication.

(g) An accessory may be prosecuted as such either in the county in which the offense to which he or she is an accessory is triable or the county in which he or she became such accessory.

(h) Any person who steals the property of another, outside this State, or receives such property knowing it to have been stolen, and brings it into this State, may be prosecuted in any county into or through which the stolen property is brought.

(i) Prosecutions for acts of forgery, embezzlement, conversion or misappropriation may be had either in the county in which such offense was committed or in the county in which the offender last resided.

(j) Prosecutions for desertion may be had either in the county in which the wife or any child resided at the time of the desertion or in the county in which the wife resides when the prosecution is begun.

(k) The county of venue for purposes of trial of indictments returned by a State Grand Jury shall be designated by the Assignment Judge appointed to impanel and supervise the State Grand Jury or Grand Juries pursuant to R. 3:6–11(b).

Note: Source—R.R. 3:6–1; paragraph (k) adopted July 17, 1975 to be effective September 8, 1975; paragraph (g) amended July 13, 1994 to be effective September 1, 1994.

3:14–2. Motion for Change of Venue or Foreign Jury

A motion for change of venue may be made only by a defendant. A motion for trial by a foreign jury may be made by any party. Such motions shall be made to the judge assigned to try the case or to the Assignment Judge of the county in which the indictment was found or the accusation filed on notice to the other party or parties on such proofs as the court directs and shall be granted if the court finds that a fair and impartial trial cannot otherwise be had.

Note: Source—R.R. 3:6–2(a)(b). Amended July 22, 1983 to be effective September 12, 1983.

3:14–3. Foreign Juries; Order and Selection

If a foreign jury is ordered, the order shall specify the number of jurors to be returned and a venire directed to the sheriff of the county from which such jury shall be taken, which shall be returnable to the court in the county in which the matter is to be tried. The jurors shall be selected in the same manner as the general panel of jurors is selected in the county from which they are taken.

Note: Source—R.R. 3:6–2(c).

3:14–4. Order for Change of Venue; Costs

If a change of venue is ordered, the criminal division manager's office in which the indictment or accusation is pending shall transmit to the criminal division manager's office to which the matter is transferred all papers filed therein or duplicates thereof, and the prosecution shall continue in that county. The costs of trial shall be certified to the Assignment Judge of the county in which the indictment was found or the accusation was filed.

Note: Source—R.R. 3:6–2(d); amended July 13, 1994 to be effective January 1, 1995.

RULE 3:15. JOINDER AND SEVERANCE

3:15–1. Trial of Indictments or Accusations Together

(a) Permissible Joinder. The court may order 2 or more indictments or accusations tried together if the offenses and the defendants, if there are 2 or more, could have been joined in a single indictment or accusation. The procedure shall be the same as if the prosecution were under such single indictment or accusation.

(b) Mandatory Joinder. Except as provided by R. 3:15–2(b), a defendant shall not be subject to separate trials for multiple criminal offenses based on the same conduct or arising from the same episode, if such offenses are known to the appropriate prosecuting officer at the time of the commencement of the first trial and are within the jurisdiction and venue of a single court.

Note: Source—R.R. 3:5–6. Paragraph (a) amended and paragraph (b) adopted July 29, 1977 to be effective September 6, 1977; paragraph (b) revised November 2, 1987 to be effective January 1, 1988.

3:15–2. Relief From Prejudicial Joinder

(a) Motion by State Before Trial. If two or more defendants are to be jointly tried and the prosecuting attorney intends to introduce at trial a statement, confession or admission of one defendant involving any other defendant, the prosecuting attorney shall move before trial on notice to all defendants for a determination by the court as to whether such portion of the statement, confession, or admission involving such other defendant can be effectively deleted therefrom. The court shall direct the specific deletions to be made, or, if it finds that effective deletions cannot practically be made, it shall order separate trials of the defendants. Upon failure of the prosecuting attorney to so move before trial, the court may refuse to admit such statement, confession or admission into evidence at trial, or take such other action as the interest of justice requires.

(b) Motion by Defendant and State. If for any other reason it appears that a defendant or the State is prejudiced by a permissible or mandatory joinder of offenses or of defendants in an indictment or accusation the court may order an election or separate trials of counts, grant a severance of defendants, or direct other appropriate relief.

(c) Time. A motion for separate trial of counts of an indictment or accusation must be made pursuant to R. 3:10–2, unless the court, for good cause shown, enlarges the time.

Note: Source—R.R. 3:5–7. Paragraph (b) amended July 29, 1977 to be effective September 6, 1977; paragraph (a) amended July 16, 1981 to be effective September 14, 1981; paragraph (c) adopted July 26, 1984 to be effective September 10, 1984; paragraphs (a) and (c) amended July 13, 1994 to be effective January 1, 1995.

3:15–3. Trial of Criminal Offenses and Lesser, Related Infractions

(a) Joinder of Criminal Offense and Lesser Related Infraction.

(1) Except as provided in paragraph (b), the court shall join any pending non-indictable complaint for trial with a criminal offense based on the same conduct or arising from the same episode.

(2) Regardless of whether a jury sits as the finder of facts with respect to the criminal offense, and unless the complaint charges a disorderly persons offense or a petty disorderly persons offense that must be submitted to the jury in accordance with the provisions of N.J.S.A. 2C:1–8(e), the Superior Court judge shall sit as a municipal court judge on the complaint and shall render the verdict with respect to the complaint on the proofs adduced in the course of trial.

(3) If evidence is held to be admissible with respect to the trial of the complaint but inadmissible with respect to the trial of the criminal offense, the court shall hear that evidence outside of the jury's presence and may, in its discretion, postpone such hearing until the jury has retired to deliberate. The court shall not render its verdict on the complaint until the jury has rendered its verdict or until the jury has been dismissed.

(b) Relief From Joinder. If for any reason it appears that a defendant or the State is prejudiced by the joinder required by paragraph (a), the court may decline to join or may grant other appropriate relief. A defendant's request to avoid joinder shall constitute a waiver of any claim against twice being placed in jeopardy that would not have arisen had the defendant's request been denied.

(c) Consequence of Failure to Join. In no event shall failure to join as required in paragraph (a) be deemed to constitute grounds for barring a subsequent prosecution of the complaint except as required by statute or by the Federal or State Constitutions.

Note: Adopted January 14, 1991 to be effective September 1, 1992.

RULE 3:16. PRESENCE OF THE DEFENDANT

(a) Pretrial. The defendant must be present for every scheduled event unless excused by the court for good cause shown.

(b) At Trial or Post-conviction Proceedings. The defendant shall be present at every stage of the trial, including the impaneling of the jury and the return of the verdict, and at the imposition of sentence, unless otherwise provided by Rule. Nothing in this Rule, however, shall prevent a defendant from waiving the right to be present at trial. A waiver may be found either from (a) the defendant's express written or oral waiver placed on the record, or (b) the defendant's conduct evidencing a knowing, voluntary, and unjustified absence after (1) the defendant has received actual notice in court or has signed a written acknowledgment of the trial date, or (2) trial has commenced in defendant's presence. A corporation shall appear by its attorney for all purposes. The defendant's presence is not required at a reduction of sentence under R. 3:21–10 or, except as provided in R. 3:22–10, at a hearing on a petition for post conviction relief.

Note: Source—R.R. 3:5–4(a); amended July 14, 1992 to be effective September 1, 1992; captions added, new paragraph (a) adopted, former text amended and redesignated paragraph (b) July 13, 1994 to be effective January 1, 1995, caption to paragraph (b) amended December 9, 1994 to be effective January 1, 1995; paragraph (b) amended July 12, 2002 to be effective September 3, 2002.

RULE 3:17. ELECTRONIC RECORDATION

(a) Unless one of the exceptions set forth in paragraph (b) are present, all custodial interrogations conducted in a place of detention must be electronically recorded when the person being interrogated is charged with murder, kidnapping, aggravated manslaughter, manslaughter, robbery, aggravated sexual assault, sexual assault, aggravated criminal sexual contact, criminal sexual contact, second degree aggravated assault, aggravated arson, burglary, violations of Chapter 35 of Title 2C that constitute first or second degree crimes, any crime involving the possession or use of a firearm, or conspiracies or attempts to commit such crimes. For purposes of this rule, a "place of detention" means a building or a police station or barracks that is a place of operation for a municipal or state police department, county prosecutor, sheriff or other law enforcement agency, that is owned or operated by a law enforcement agency at which persons are or may be detained in connection with criminal charges against those persons. Place of detention shall also include a county jail, county workhouse, county penitentiary, state prison or institution of involuntary confinement where a custodial interrogation may occur.

(b) Electronic recordation pursuant to paragraph (a) must occur unless: (i) a statement made during a custodial interrogation is not recorded because electronic recording of the interrogation is not feasible, (ii) a spontaneous statement is made outside the course of an interrogation, (iii) a statement is made in response to questioning that is routinely asked during the processing of the arrest of the suspect, (iv) a statement is made during a custodial interrogation by a suspect who indicated, prior to making the statement, that he/she would participate in the interrogation only if it were not recorded; provided however, that the agreement to participate under that condition is itself recorded, (v) a statement is made during a custodial interrogation that is conducted out-of-state, (vi) a statement is given at a time when the accused is not a suspect for the crime to which that statement relates while the accused is being interrogated for a different crime that does not require recordation, (vii) the interrogation during which the statement is given occurs at a time when the interrogators have no knowledge that a crime for which recording is required has been committed. The State shall bear the burden of proving, by a preponderance of the evidence, that one of the exceptions is applicable.

(c) If the State intends to rely on any of the exceptions set forth in paragraph (b) in offering a defendant's unrecorded statement into evidence, the State shall furnish a notice of intent to rely on the unrecorded statement, stating the specific place and time at which the defendant made the statement and the specific exception or exceptions upon which the State intends to rely. The prosecutor shall, on written demand, furnish the defendant or defendant's attorney with the names and addresses of the witnesses upon whom the State intends to rely to establish one of the exceptions set forth in paragraph (b). The trial court shall then hold a hearing to determine whether one of the exceptions apply.

(d) The failure to electronically record a defendant's custodial interrogation in a place of detention shall be a factor for consideration by the trial court in determining the admissibility of a statement, and by the jury in determining whether the statement was made, and if so, what weight, if any, to give to the statement.

(e) In the absence of an electronic recordation required under paragraph (a), the court shall, upon request of the defendant, provide the jury with a cautionary instruction.

Note: Adopted October 14, 2005, to be effective in respect of all homicide offenses as of January 1, 2006, and as of January 1, 2007, in respect of the other offenses specified in paragraph (a) of the Rule.

RULE 3:18. MOTION FOR JUDGMENT OF ACQUITTAL

3:18–1. Motion Before Submission to Jury

At the close of the State's case or after the evidence of all parties has been closed, the court shall, on defendant's motion or its own initiative, order the entry of a judgment of acquittal of one or more offenses charged in the indictment or accusation if the evidence is insufficient to warrant a conviction. A defendant may offer evidence after denial of a motion for judgment of acquittal made at the close of the State's case without having reserved the right.

Note: Source—R.R. 3:7–6; amended July 13, 1994 to be effective September 1, 1994.

3:18–2. Motion After Discharge of Jury

If the jury returns a verdict of guilty or is discharged without having returned a verdict, a motion for judgment of acquittal may be made, even if not earlier made pursuant to R. 3:18–1 or it may be renewed within 10 days after the jury is discharged or within such further time as the court fixes during the 10-day period. The court on such motion may set aside a verdict of guilty and order the entry of a judgment of acquittal and may so order if no verdict has been returned.

RULE 3:19. VERDICT

3:19–1. Several Defendants or Counts; Written Verdict Sheets

(a) Several Defendants or Counts. If there are 2 or more counts of an indictment or 2 or more defendants tried together, the jury may return a verdict or verdicts with respect to a defendant or defendants as to whom it has agreed, specifying the counts on which it has agreed; the defendant or defendants may be tried again on the count or counts as to which it has not agreed.

(b) Written Verdict Sheets. In the discretion of the court, a written verdict sheet may be submitted to the jury in conjunction with a general verdict to facilitate the determination of the grade of the offense under the Code of Criminal Justice or otherwise simplify the determination of a verdict when multiple charges are submitted to the jury. A written verdict sheet shall be used in those cases in which the jury must find the factual predicate for an enhanced sentence or the existence of a fact relevant to sentencing unless that factual predicate or fact is an element of the offense.%

The verdict sheet shall be marked as a court exhibit and retained by the court pursuant to Rule 1:2–3.

Note: Source—R.R. 3:7–9(b); former rule redesignated as paragraph (a), paragraph (b) adopted and caption amended July 16, 1981 to be effective September 14, 1981; paragraph (b) amended July 10, 1998 to be effective September 1, 1998; paragraph (b) amended June 19, 2001 to be effective immediately.

3:19–2. Acquittal by Reason of Insanity

If a defendant interposes the defense of insanity and is acquitted after trial on that ground, the verdict and judgment shall so state.

The procedure for disposition of the defendant shall be as provided by N.J.S.A. 2C:4–8 and 2C:4–9 and by R. 4:74–7, except that in the case of defendants acquitted of murder by reason of insanity all hearings pursuant to R. 4:74–7(e) shall be in open court unless good cause is shown for a hearing in camera.

Note: Source—R.R. 3:7–9(e); amended August 28, 1979 to be effective September 1, 1979; amended July 14, 1992 to be effective September 1, 1992.

CHAPTER IV. PROCEEDINGS AFTER VERDICT OR FINDING

RULE 3:20. NEW TRIAL

3:20–1. Trial by Court or Jury

The trial judge on defendant's motion may grant the defendant a new trial if required in the interest of justice. If trial was by the judge without a jury, the judge may, on defendant's motion for a new trial, vacate the judgment if entered, take additional testimony and direct the entry of a new judgment. The trial judge shall not, however, set aside the verdict of the jury as against the weight of the evidence unless, having given due regard to the opportunity of the jury to pass upon the credibility of the witnesses, it clearly and convincing-ly appears that there was a manifest denial of justice under the law.

Note: Source—R.R. 3:7–11(a) (first and second sentences), 3:7–11(b); amended July 13, 1994 to be effective September 1, 1994.

3:20–2. Time for Making Motion

A motion for a new trial based on the ground of newly-discovered evidence may be made at any time, but if an appeal is pending, the court may grant the motion only on remand of the case. A motion for a new trial based on a claim that the defendant did not waive his or her appearance for trial shall be made prior to sentencing. A motion for a new trial based on any other ground shall be made within 10 days after the verdict or finding of guilty, or within such further time as the court fixes during the 10–day period.

Note: Source—R.R. 3:7–11(a) (third and fourth sentences); amended July 14, 1992, to be effective September 1, 1992.

RULE 3:21.   SENTENCE AND JUDGMENT; WITHDRAWAL OF PLEA; PRESENTENCE INVESTIGATION; PROBATION

3:21–1.   Withdrawal of Plea

A motion to withdraw a plea of guilty or non vult shall be made before sentencing, but the court may permit it to be made thereafter to correct a manifest injustice.

Note: Source—R.R. 3:7–10(a).

3:21–2.   Presentence Procedure

(a) **Investigation.** Before the imposition of a sentence or the granting of probation court support staff shall make a presentence investigation in accordance with N.J.S.A. 2C:44–6 and report to the court. The report shall contain all presentence material having any bearing whatever on the sentence and shall be furnished to the defendant and the prosecutor. On counts on which the death penalty is to be imposed, a presentence report shall not be prepared.

(b) **Examination.** After the presentence investigation and before imposing sentence, the court may order, pursuant to N.J.S.A. 2C:44–6c, a physical or mental examination of the defendant provided that the defendant may not be committed to an institution for the purpose of that examination. The examination report shall be furnished to the defendant and the prosecuting attorney.

(c) **Transmittal of Reports.** If a custodial sentence is imposed, court staff shall, within fifteen days thereafter, transmit a copy of the presentence report and the examination report, if any, to the person in charge of the institution to which the defendant has been committed.

Note: Source—R.R. 3:7–10(b). Amended July 7, 1971 to be effective September 13, 1971; amended June 29, 1973 to be effective September 10, 1973; amended August 27, 1974 to be effective September 9, 1974; amended July 29, 1977 to be effective September 6, 1977; amended July 16, 1979 to be effective September 10, 1979; paragraph designations and new paragraph (b) adopted and paragraph (c) amended August 28, 1979, to be effective September 1, 1979; paragraph (a) amended September 28, 1982, to be effective immediately; paragraphs (a) and (c) amended July 14, 1992 to be effective September 1, 1992; paragraphs (a) and (b) amended July 13, 1994 to be effective January 1, 1995; paragraph (a) amended July 28, 2004 to be effective September 1, 2004.

3:21–3.   Diagnostic Center Report

Whenever the defendant is convicted of an offense enumerated in N.J.S.A. 2C:47–1 et seq., the court, before imposing sentence or making disposition of the offender under the provisions of said chapter, shall furnish to the prosecutor, defendant or defendant's attorney a copy of the report of the Diagnostic Center, shall advise defendant of the opportunity to be heard thereon, and shall afford the defendant such hearing. The report of the Diagnostic Center shall be confidential unless otherwise provided by rule, statute or court order.

Note: Adopted February 25, 1969 to be effective September 8, 1969. Amended August 28, 1979 to be effective September 1, 1979; amended July 13, 1994 to be effective January 1, 1995.

3:21–4.   Sentence

(a) **Imposition of Sentence; Bail.** Sentence shall be imposed without unreasonable delay. Pending sentence the court may commit the defendant or continue or alter the bail.

(b) **Presence of Defendant; Statement.** Sentence shall not be imposed unless the defendant is present or has filed a written waiver of the right to be present. Before imposing sentence the court shall address the defendant personally and ask the defendant if he or she wishes to make a statement in his or her own behalf and to present any information in mitigation of punishment. The defendant may answer personally or by his or her attorney.

(c) **Sentence to Probation.** The court, at time of sentence, shall inform defendants sentenced to probation what penalties might be imposed on revocation should they not adhere to the conditions of their probation.

(d) **Extradition.** Nothing herein contained shall be construed as affecting the provisions of N.J.S. 2A:160–5 (relating to extradition) or the power of the court to resentence a defendant after reversal of the judgment by reason of error in the sentence.

(e) **Extended or Enhanced Term of Imprisonment; Sentence Pursuant to N.J.S.A. 2C:35–8.** A motion pursuant to N.J.S.A. 2C:44–3 or N.J.S.A. 2C:43–6f for the imposition of an extended term of imprisonment, or a motion for enhanced sentence pursuant to N.J.S.A. 2C:35–8, shall be filed with the court by the prosecutor within 14 days of the entry of the defendant's guilty plea or the return of the verdict. Where the defendant is pleading guilty pursuant to a negotiated disposition, the prosecutor shall make the motion at or prior to the plea. If the negotiated disposition includes the recommendation of an extended term, the prosecutor's oral notice and the recordation of the extended term exposure in the plea form completed by defendant and reviewed on the record shall serve as the State's motion. For good cause shown the court may extend the time for filing the motion. The sentence shall include a determination as to whether the defendant was convicted and sentenced to an extended term of imprisonment as provided in N.J.S.A. 2C:43–7, 2C:44–3 and 2C:44–6e, N.J.S.A. 2C:43–6f or whether the defendant was being sentenced pursuant to N.J.S.A. 2C:35–8, and the commitment or order of sentence which directs the defendant's confinement shall so specify.

(f) Sentence Pursuant to N.J.S.A. 2C:43–7.1, 2C:43–7.2, or 2C:44–5.1. A notice to impose sentence pursuant to N.J.S.A. 2C:43–7.1, N.J.S.A. 2C:43–7.2, or 2C:44–5.1 shall be filed with the court and served upon the defendant by the prosecutor within 14 days of the entry of the defendant's guilty plea or return of the verdict. Where the defendant is pleading guilty pursuant to a negotiated disposition, the prosecutor shall file and serve the notice at or prior to the plea. If the negotiated disposition includes the recommendation of an extended term, the prosecutor's oral notice and the recordation of the extended term exposure in the plea form completed by defendant and reviewed on the record shall serve as the State's notice. For good cause shown the court may extend the time for filing the notice. The sentence shall include a determination as to whether the defendant was convicted and sentenced pursuant to N.J.S.A. 2C:43–7.1, N.J.S.A. 2C:43–7.2, or 2C:44–5.1 and the judgment and commitment shall so specify.

(g) Reasons for Sentence. At the time sentence is imposed the judge shall state reasons for imposing such sentence including findings pursuant to the criteria for withholding or imposing imprisonment or fines under N.J.S.A. 2C:44–1 to 2C:44–3 and the factual basis supporting a finding of particular aggravating or mitigating factors affecting sentence.

(h) Notification of Right to Appeal and to File Petitions for Post-Conviction Relief. After imposing sentence, whether following the defendant's plea of guilty or a finding of guilty after trial, the court shall advise the defendant of the right to appeal and, if the defendant is indigent, of the right to appeal as an indigent. The court shall also inform the defendant of the time limitations in which to file petitions for post-conviction relief.

(i) Sentence Imposed Pursuant to N.J.S.A. 2C:44–1(f)(2). In the event the court imposes sentence pursuant to N.J.S.A. 2C:44–1(f)(2), such sentence shall not become final until 10 days after the date sentence was pronounced.

(j) Statement of Estimated Real Time to Be Served. If defendant is sentenced to prison or jail, at the time sentence is imposed the judge shall state the approximate period of time defendant will actually serve in custody according to the then current State Parole Board "Parole Eligibility Tables." The statement should also consider the impact of jail credits, and should indicate that it is made for the benefit of the public, including those in attendance at the proceedings, and cannot be relied upon by the defendant for purposes of proceedings before the Parole Board or any direct or collateral appeal.

Note: Source—R.R. 3:7–10(d). Paragraph (f) amended September 13, 1971, paragraph (c) deleted and paragraphs (d), (e) and (f) redesignated as (c), (d) and (e) July 14, 1972 to be effective September 5, 1972; paragraph (e) adopted and former paragraph (e) redesignated as (f) August 27, 1974 to be effective September 9, 1974; paragraph (b) amended July 17, 1975 to be effective September 8, 1975; paragraphs (d) and (e) amended August 28, 1979 to be effective September 1, 1979; paragraph (d) amended December 26, 1979 to be effective January 1, 1980; paragraph (g) adopted July 26, 1984 to be effective September 10, 1984; paragraph (d) caption and text amended November 5, 1986 to be effective January 1, 1987; paragraph (d) amended November 2, 1987 to be effective January 1, 1988; paragraph (d) amended January 5, 1988 to be effective February 1, 1988; new paragraph (c) adopted and former paragraphs (c), (d), (e), (f), and (g) redesignated (d), (e), (f), (g), and (h) respectively June 29, 1990 to be effective September 4, 1990; paragraph (b) amended July 14, 1992 to be effective September 1, 1992; paragraph (I) adopted April 21, 1994 to be effective June 1, 1994; paragraphs (b), (e), (f) and (g) amended July 13, 1994 to be effective January 1, 1995; former paragraphs (f), (g), (h), and (I) redesignated as paragraphs (g), (h), (I), and (j) and new paragraph (f) adopted July 10, 1998 to be effective September 1, 1998; paragraph (j) amended July 5, 2000 to be effective September 5, 2000; paragraph (e) caption and text amended, and paragraph (f) amended June 15, 2007 to be effective September 1, 2007; paragraph (h) caption and text amended July 16, 2009 to be effective September 1, 2009.

Court Comment to April 21, 1994 Amendment
Effective June 1, 1994

When defendants are sentenced to a period of incarceration, whether committed to the custody of the Commissioner of the Department of Corrections or to a county institution, including incarceration as a condition of probation, the sentence generally does not suggest what the actual period of time in custody will be as a result of the parole statutes. The Court believes that the public is entitled to that information and that the Code contemplates that it will be given. See N.J.S.A. 2C:43–2e and 2C:44–1c(2). In order to avoid the many complexities and contingencies that surround that determination, the Court has opted to provide the public with the information contained in the State Parole Board's Eligibility Tables as being a fair and practical indicator of the likely actual custodial time for those defendants who get full credit for good time, work time, and minimum custody time. The Rule (Rule 3:21–4(i)) is intended solely to inform the public, and not the defendant, who presumably will have been informed of parole considerations by his or her attorney. Defendants will be told that they cannot rely in any way on the judge's statement, that it is intended solely to inform the public. Rule 3:21–4(i) is not intended to apply to sentences for disorderly persons offenses.

3:21–4A. Sentence, Murder Under N.J.S.A. 2C:11–3(a)(1) or N.J.S.A. 2C:11–3(a)(2)

Where the defendant has been convicted of, or has entered a plea of guilty to, N.J.S.A. 2C:11–3(a)(1) or N.J.S.A. 2C:11–3(a)(2) and where the provisions of N.J.S.A. 2C:11–3(c) apply, a separate sentencing hearing shall be conducted pursuant to N.J.S.A. 2C:11–3(c) immediately thereafter, except for good cause shown. At the sentencing hearing the jury, or the court if there is no jury, shall complete a special verdict form.

Note: Adopted September 28, 1982 to be effective immediately.

3:21–5. Judgment

(a) **Capital Convictions.** On the imposition of a sentence of death, the court shall immediately enter the judgment of conviction and the Criminal Division Manager shall transmit it within two days to the Clerk of the Supreme Court, all parties, and their counsel. If a defendant sentenced to death is later sentenced for non-capital offenses, the court shall prepare an amended judgment containing all convictions. A copy of such amended judgment shall be provided to the Clerk of the Supreme Court.

(b) **Non–Capital Convictions.** The judgment shall be signed by the judge and entered by the clerk. A judgment of conviction shall set forth the plea, the verdict or findings, the adjudication and sentence, a statement of the reasons for such sentence, and a statement of credits received pursuant to R. 3:21–8. If the defendant is found not guilty or for any other reason is entitled to be discharged, judgment shall be entered accordingly. The Criminal Division Manager shall forward a copy of the judgment forthwith to all parties and their counsel.

Note: Source—R.R. 3:7–10(e); amended August 27, 1974 to be effective September 9, 1974; amended July 29, 1977 to be effective September 6, 1977; amended November 1, 1985 effective January 2, 1986; new paragraph (a) added, and former text amended, caption added, and designated as paragraph (b) July 12, 2002 to be effective September 3, 2002.

3:21–6. Conviction of a Corporation

If a corporation is convicted of an offense the court shall give judgment thereon and shall cause such judgment to be enforced in the same manner as a judgment in a civil action.

Note: Source—R.R. 3:7–10(f).

3:21–7. Probation and Suspended Sentence

After conviction, unless otherwise provided by law, the court may suspend the imposition of a sentence or the defendant may be placed on probation.

(a) **Conditions.** The order shall require the defendant to comply with standard conditions adopted by the court and filed by counsel with the criminal division manager as designee of the deputy clerk of the Superior Court (except as otherwise ordered), as well as such special conditions, including a term of imprisonment pursuant to N.J.S.A. 2C:45–1c, as the court imposes. As a condition of probation the court may impose a term of community-related service to be performed by the defendant under such terms and conditions as the court may determine. A copy of the order, together with the standard and special conditions, shall be furnished to the defendant, and read and explained to the defendant by the probation officer, whereupon the defendant and the probation officer shall sign a joint statement, to be filed with the criminal division manager as designee of the deputy clerk of the Superior Court, as to the officer's compliance with such reading and explanation requirement. If the defendant refuses to sign such statement, the defendant shall be resentenced.

(b) **Detention.** The court may, pursuant to N.J.S.A. 2C:45–3a(3), upon a showing of probable cause that the defendant has committed another offense, detain without bail pending determination of the charge, a defendant who was sentenced to probation or whose sentence was suspended.

(c) **Revocation.** At any time before termination of the period of suspension or probation, the court may revoke a suspension or probation pursuant to N.J.S.A. 2C:45–3.

Note: Source—R.R. 3:7–10(g). Amended July 16, 1979 to be effective September 10, 1979; amended August 28, 1979 to be effective September 1, 1979; paragraphs (a) and (b) amended July 13, 1994 to be effective January 1, 1995.

3:21–8. Credit for Confinement Pending Sentence

The defendant shall receive credit on the term of a custodial sentence for any time served in custody in jail or in a state hospital between arrest and the imposition of sentence.

Note: Source—R.R. 3:7–10(h) (first sentence); amended July 13, 1994 to be effective September 1, 1994.

3:21–9. Arrest of Judgment

The court on a defendant's motion shall arrest judgment if the indictment or accusation does not charge an offense or if the charge is based on an invalid or unconstitutional statute or regulation promulgated pursuant to a statute or if the court was without jurisdiction of the offense charged. The motion in arrest of judgment shall be made within 10 days after verdict of guilt or the entry of a plea of guilty or non vult, or within such further time as the court fixes during such 10-day period.

Note: Source—R.R. 3:7–12.

3:21–10. Reduction or Change of Sentence

(a) Time. Except as provided in paragraph (b) hereof, a motion to reduce or change a sentence shall be filed not later than 60 days after the date of the judgment of conviction. The court may reduce or change a sentence, either on motion or on its own initiative, by order entered within 75 days from the date of the judgment of conviction and not thereafter.

(b) Exceptions. A motion may be filed and an order may be entered at any time (1) changing a custodial sentence to permit entry of the defendant into a custodial or non-custodial treatment or rehabilitation program for drug or alcohol abuse, or (2) amending a custodial sentence to permit the release of a defendant because of illness or infirmity of the defendant, or (3) changing a sentence for good cause shown upon the joint application of the defendant and prosecuting attorney, or (4) changing a sentence as authorized by the Code of Criminal Justice, or (5) correcting a sentence not authorized by law including the Code of Criminal Justice, or (6) changing a custodial sentence to permit entry into the Intensive Supervision Program, or (7) changing or reducing a sentence when a prior conviction has been reversed on appeal or vacated by collateral attack.

(c) Procedure. A motion filed pursuant to paragraph (b) hereof shall be accompanied by supporting affidavits and such other documents and papers as set forth the basis for the relief sought. A hearing need not be conducted on a motion filed under paragraph (b) hereof unless the court, after review of the material submitted with the motion papers, concludes that a hearing is required in the interest of justice. All changes of sentence shall be made in open court upon notice to the defendant and the prosecutor. An appropriate order setting forth the revised sentence and specifying the change made and the reasons therefor shall be entered on the record. On any motion filed pursuant to this rule, upon a showing of good cause, the court may assign the Office of the Public Defender to represent the defendant.

(d) Consideration During Appeal. Notwithstanding R. 2:9–1(a), the trial court may reconsider a sentence pursuant to this Rule during the pendency of an appeal upon notice to the Appellate Division.

(e) Intensive Supervision. Motions for change of custodial sentence and entry into the Intensive Supervision Program, as provided for in paragraph (b) of this rule, shall be addressed entirely to the sound discretion of the three-judge panel assigned to hear them. Because of the nature of the program, there shall be no administrative or judicial review at the several levels of eligibility established under the program. No further appellate review of the panel's substantive decision shall be afforded. The three-judge panel shall have the authority to resentence offenders, in accordance with applicable statutes, in the event they fail to perform satisfactorily following entry into the program.

Source—R.R. 3:7–13(a)(b); paragraph (b) amended and redesignated as (c) and new paragraph (b) adopted July 17, 1975 to be effective September 8, 1975; paragraph (b) amended August 28, 1979 to be effective September 1, 1979; new paragraph (d) adopted July 16, 1981 to be effective September 14, 1981; paragraph (a) amended July 15, 1982 to be effective September 13, 1982; paragraph (b) amended and paragraph (e) adopted July 22, 1983 to be effective September 12, 1983; paragraph (c) amended July 13, 1994 to be effective January 1, 1995; paragraph (b) amended June 28, 1996 to be effective September 1, 1996; paragraphs (b) and (c) amended July 16, 2009 to be effective September 1, 2009.

RULE 3:22. POST–CONVICTION RELIEF

3:22–1. Petition for Relief

Any person convicted of a crime may, pursuant to this rule, file with the criminal division manager's office of the county in which the conviction took place a petition for post-conviction relief captioned in the action in which the conviction was entered.

Note: Source—R.R. 3:10A–1. Amended July 5, 2000 to be effective September 5, 2000.

3:22–2. Grounds

A petition for post-conviction relief is cognizable if based upon any of the following grounds:

(a) Substantial denial in the conviction proceedings of defendant's rights under the Constitution of the United States or the Constitution or laws of the State of New Jersey;

(b) Lack of jurisdiction of the court to impose the judgment rendered upon defendant's conviction;

(c) Imposition of sentence in excess of or otherwise not in accordance with the sentence authorized by law if raised together with other grounds cognizable under paragraph (a), (b), or (d) of this rule. Otherwise a claim alleging the imposition of sentence in excess of or otherwise not in accordance with the sentence authorized by law shall be filed pursuant to R. 3:21–10(b)(5).

(d) Any ground heretofore available as a basis for collateral attack upon a conviction by habeas corpus or any other common-law or statutory remedy.

Note: Source—R.R. 3:10A–2; paragraph (c) amended July 16, 2009 to be effective September 1, 2009.

3:22–3. Exclusiveness of Remedy; not Substitute for Appeal or Motion

Except as otherwise required by the Constitution of New Jersey, a petition pursuant to this rule is the exclusive means of challenging a judgment rendered upon conviction of a crime. It is not, however, a substitute for appeal from conviction or for motion incident to the proceedings in the trial court, and may not be filed while such appellate review or motion is pending.

Note: Source—R.R. 3:10A–3; amended July 16, 2009 to be effective September 1, 2009.

Rule 3:22–4.　Bar of Grounds Not Raised in Prior Proceedings; Bar of Second or Subsequent Petitions; Exceptions

(a) First Petition for Post–Conviction Relief. Any ground for relief not raised in the proceedings resulting in the conviction, or in a post-conviction proceeding brought and decided prior to the adoption of this rule, or in any appeal taken in any such proceedings is barred from assertion in a proceeding under this rule unless the court on motion or at the hearing finds:

(1) that the ground for relief not previously asserted could not reasonably have been raised in any prior proceeding; or

(2) that enforcement of the bar to preclude claims, including one for ineffective assistance of counsel, would result in fundamental injustice; or

(3) that denial of relief would be contrary to a new rule of constitutional law under either the Constitution of the United States or the State of New Jersey.

A ground could not reasonably have been raised in a prior proceeding only if defendant shows that the factual predicate for that ground could not have been discovered earlier through the exercise of reasonable diligence.

A denial of relief would be contrary to a new rule of constitutional law only if the defendant shows that the claim relies on a new rule of constitutional law, made retroactive to defendant's petition by the United States Supreme Court or the Supreme Court of New Jersey, that was unavailable during the pendency of any prior proceedings.

(b) Second or Subsequent Petition for Post–Conviction Relief. A second or subsequent petition for post-conviction relief shall be dismissed unless:

(1) it is timely under R. 3:22–12(a)(2); and

(2) it alleges on its face either:

(A) that the petition relies on a new rule of constitutional law, made retroactive to defendant's petition by the United States Supreme Court or the Supreme Court of New Jersey, that was unavailable during the pendency of any prior proceedings; or

(B) that the factual predicate for the relief sought could not have been discovered earlier through the exercise of reasonable diligence, and the facts underlying the ground for relief, if proven and viewed in light of the evidence as a whole, would raise a reasonable probability that the relief sought would be granted; or

(C) that the petition alleges a prima facie case of ineffective assistance of counsel that represented the defendant on the first or subsequent application for post-conviction relief.

Note: Source—R.R. 3:10A–4; caption amended, introductory paragraph amended and designated as paragraph (a), former paragraphs (a), (b), and (c) redesignated as subparagraphs (a)(1), (a)(2), and (a)(3), and new paragraph (b) adopted January 14, 2010 to be effective February 1, 2010.

3:22–5.　Bar of Ground Expressly Adjudicated

A prior adjudication upon the merits of any ground for relief is conclusive whether made in the proceedings resulting in the conviction or in any post-conviction proceeding brought pursuant to this rule or prior to the adoption thereof, or in any appeal taken from such proceedings.

Note: Source—R.R. 3:10A–5.

3:22–6.　Indigents; Waiver of Fees; Assignment of Counsel, and Grant of Transcript; Assigned Counsel May not Withdraw

(a) Waiver of Fees; Assignment on First Petition. At the time of filing of a petition under this Rule, a defendant who wants to be represented by the Office of the Public Defender may annex thereto a sworn statement alleging indigency in the form prescribed by the Administrative Director of the Courts, which form shall be furnished to the defendant by the criminal division manager's office. The criminal division manager's office shall determine whether the defendant is indigent and screen the petition to determine whether the petition is cognizable under R. 3:22–2 and, if so, whether the requirements of R. 3:22–8 have been met. The Criminal Division Manager shall thereafter forthwith submit the same to the Criminal Presiding Judge who, if satisfied therefrom that the defendant is indigent, shall order the criminal division manager's office to file the petition without payment of filing fees. At the same time, and without separate petition therefor, if the petition is the first one filed by the defendant attacking the conviction pursuant to this rule, the court shall as of course, unless defendant affirmatively states an intention to proceed pro se, by order assign the matter to the Office of the Public Defender if the defendant's conviction was for an indictable offense, or assign counsel in accordance with R. 3:4–2 if the defendant's conviction was for a non-indictable offense. All orders of assignment pursuant to this section shall contain the name of the judge to whom the case is assigned and shall set a place and date for a case management conference.

If the petition is not cognizable under R. 3:22–2, or if the petition does not meet the requirements of R. 3:22–8, the court shall set forth the reasons that the petition is not cognizable under R. 3:22–2, or fails to meet the requirements of R. 3:22–8.

(b) Assignment of Counsel on Cause Shown. Upon any second or subsequent petition filed pursuant to this

Rule attacking the same conviction, the matter shall be assigned to the Office of the Public Defender only upon application therefor and showing of good cause. For purposes of this section, good cause exists only when the court finds that a substantial issue of fact or law requires assignment of counsel and when a second or subsequent petition alleges on its face a basis to preclude dismissal under R. 3:22–4.

(c) Transcript. After assignment of counsel, or if the indigent defendant proceeds without counsel, the court may grant an application for the transcript of testimony of any proceeding shown to be necessary in establishing the grounds of relief asserted.

(d) Substitution; Withdrawal of Assigned Counsel. The court shall not substitute new assigned counsel at the request of defendant while assigned counsel is serving, except upon a showing of good cause and notice to the Office of the Public Defender. Assigned counsel may not seek to withdraw on the ground of lack of merit of the petition. Counsel should advance all of the legitimate arguments requested by the defendant that the record will support. If defendant insists upon the assertion of any grounds for relief that counsel deems to be without merit, counsel shall list such claims in the petition or amended petition or incorporate them by reference. Pro se briefs can also be submitted.

Note: Source—R.R. 3:10A–6(a)(b)(c)(d). Paragraph (b) amended July 14, 1972 to be effective September 5, 1972; paragraphs (a) and (d) amended July 13, 1994 to be effective January 1, 1995; paragraphs (a), (b), (c) and (d) amended July 16, 2009 to be effective September 1, 2009.

3:22–6A. Notifying Court of Assignment; Filing of Appearance

(1) Within ninety days of receipt of an order of assignment on a filed petition for post-conviction relief, the Public Defender shall provide the court with the name of the attorney assigned to represent the defendant. That attorney shall, within ten days, file an appearance with the judge.

(2) If a direct appeal, including a petition for certification, is pending, the Public Defender shall notify the court, and the petition shall be dismissed without prejudice. If the defendant refiles the petition within 90 days of the date of the judgment on direct appeal, including consideration of a petition for certification, or within five years after the date of the entry pursuant to Rule 3:21–5 of the judgment of conviction being challenged, it shall be considered a first petition for post-conviction relief.

(3) Where the order of assignment sets forth reasons that the petition is not cognizable under R. 3:22–2, or does not contain the requirements of R. 3:22–8, or the Office of the Public Defender determines that such deficiencies exist and so notifies the court, the attorney assigned to represent the defendant shall, within 120 days of assignment, file an amended petition or new application that is cognizable under R. 3:22–2 and which meets the requirements contained in R. 3:22–8, or shall

seek other relief as may be appropriate. In the absence of an amended petition, the court may dismiss the petition without prejudice.

(4) In all other cases in which an attorney is representing the defendant, the attorney shall file an appearance contemporaneously with the filing of a petition for post-conviction relief.

Note: Adopted July 16, 2009 to be effective September 1, 2009; paragraph (2) amended January 14, 2010 to be effective February 1, 2010.

3:22–7. Docketing; Service on Prosecutor; Assignment for Disposition

The criminal division manager shall make an entry of the filing of the petition in the proceedings in which the conviction took place, and, if it is filed pro se, shall forthwith transmit a copy thereof to the prosecutor of the county. If an attorney files the petition, that attorney shall serve a copy thereof on the prosecutor before filing and shall file proof, certification or acknowledgment of service with the petition. The criminal division manager shall promptly notify the Criminal Presiding Judge of the filing of the petition, and the Criminal Presiding Judge shall forthwith refer the matter for disposition to a trial judge.

Note: Source—R.R. 3:10A–7; amended July 13, 1994 to be effective September 1, 1994; amended July 16, 2009 to be effective September 1, 2009.

3:22–8. Contents of Petition; Verification

The petition shall be verified by defendant and shall set forth with specificity the facts upon which the claim for relief is based, the legal grounds of complaint asserted, and the particular relief sought. The petition shall include the following information: (a) the date, docket number, and content of the indictment or accusation upon which the conviction was based and the county where filed; (b) the date and content of the sentence or judgment complained of and the name of the presiding judge; (c) any appellate proceedings brought from the conviction, attaching a copy of opinions therein; (d) any previous post-conviction proceedings relating to the same conviction, giving date and nature of claim and date and nature of disposition, and concerning any appeal therefrom, together with copies of opinions therein, trial and appellate; (e) whether petitioner was represented by counsel in any of the proceedings aforementioned, naming the counsel in each such proceeding, and stating whether counsel was in each instance retained or assigned; (f) whether and where defendant is presently confined. Argument, citations and discussion of authorities shall be omitted from the petition, but may be submitted in a separate memorandum of law.

Note: Source—R.R. 3:10A–8.

3:22–9. Amendments of Pleadings; Answer by Prosecutor

Amendments of pleadings shall be liberally allowed. For all petitions assigned to the Office of the Public

Defender pursuant to R. 3:22–6(a), assigned counsel may as of course serve and file an amended petition within 90 days after assignment. Except as provided in R. 3:22–6A(3), if assigned counsel determines that no amended petition is warranted, counsel must serve and file notice of that determination within 90 days after assignment. For all petitions assigned to the Office of the Public Defender, the prosecutor shall, within 60 days after service of a copy of the amended petition or the notice that no amended petition will be filed, serve and file an answer to the petition or amended petition. For all other petitions for post-conviction relief, within 60 days after service of a copy of the petition or amended petition, the prosecutor shall serve and file an answer thereto. The court may make such other orders with respect to pleadings, as it deems appropriate.

Note: Source—R.R. 3:10A–9; caption and text amended July 16, 2009 to be effective September 1, 2009.

3:22–10. Presence of Defendant at Hearing

(a) A defendant in custody may be present in court in the court's discretion. The defendant shall be entitled to be present when oral testimony is adduced. However, the defendant's presence may be waived by counsel upon request of the defendant.

(b) A defendant shall be entitled to an evidentiary hearing only upon the establishment of a prima facie case in support of post-conviction relief, a determination by the court that there are material issues of disputed fact that cannot be resolved by reference to the existing record, and a determination that an evidentiary hearing is necessary to resolve the claims for relief. To establish a prima facie case, defendant must demonstrate a reasonable likelihood that his or her claim, viewing the facts alleged in the light most favorable to the defendant, will ultimately succeed on the merits.

(c) Any factual assertion that provides the predicate for a claim of relief must be made by an affidavit or certification pursuant to Rule 1:4–4 and based upon personal knowledge of the declarant before the court may grant an evidentiary hearing.

(d) The scope of an evidentiary hearing shall be limited to the issue of whether the defendant was improperly convicted.

(e) A court shall not grant an evidentiary hearing:

(1) if an evidentiary hearing will not aid the court's analysis of the defendant's entitlement to post-conviction relief;

(2) if the defendant's allegations are too vague, conclusory or speculative; or

(3) for the purpose of permitting a defendant to investigate whether additional claims for relief exist for

which defendant has not demonstrated a reasonable likelihood of success as required by R. 3:22–10(b).

Note: Source—R.R. 3:10A–11; amended July 13, 1994 to be effective September 1, 1994; caption amended, first sentence of former rule deleted, remaining text of former rule retained as introductory language, and new paragraphs (a), (b), (c), and (d) adopted July 16, 2009 to be effective September 1, 2009; introductory paragraph of rule amended and designated as new paragraph (a), former paragraphs (a), (b), and (c) redesignated as paragraphs (b), (c), and (d), and former paragraph (d) amended and redesignated as paragraph (e) January 14, 2010 to be effective February 1, 2010.

3:22–11. Determination; Findings and Conclusions; Judgment; Supplementary Orders

The court shall make its final determination not later than 60 days after the hearing or, if there is no hearing, not later than 60 days after the filing of the last amended petition or answer, with discretion to extend the final determination an additional 30 days, if approved by the Criminal Presiding Judge. In making final determination upon a petition, the court shall state separately its findings of fact and conclusions of law, and shall enter a judgment, which shall include an appropriate order or direction with respect to the judgment or sentence in the conviction proceedings and any appropriate provisions as to rearraignment, retrial, custody, bail, discharge, correction of sentence, or as may otherwise be required.

Note: Source—R.R. 3:10A–11; amended July 13, 1994 to be effective September 1, 1994; caption amended, first sentence of former rule deleted, remaining text of former rule retained as introductory language, and new paragraphs (a), (b), (c), and (d) adopted July 16, 2009 to be effective September 1, 2009; introductory paragraph of rule amended and designated as new paragraph (a), former paragraphs (a), (b), and (c) redesignated as paragraphs (b), (c), and (d), and former paragraph (d) amended and redesignated as paragraph (e) January 14, 2010 to be effective February 1, 2010.

3:22–12. Limitations

(a) General Time Limitations.

(1) *First Petition For Post–Conviction Relief.* Except as provided in paragraphs (a)(2), (a)(3), and (a)(4) of this rule, no petition shall be filed pursuant to this rule more than 5 years after the date of entry pursuant to Rule 3:21–5 of the judgment of conviction that is being challenged unless it alleges facts showing that the delay beyond said time was due to defendant's excusable neglect and that there is a reasonable probability that if the defendant's factual assertions were found to be true enforcement of the time bar would result in a fundamental injustice.

(2) *Second or Subsequent Petition for Post–Conviction Relief.* Notwithstanding any other provision in this rule, no second or subsequent petition shall be filed more than one year after the latest of:

(A) the date on which the constitutional right asserted was initially recognized by the United States Supreme Court or the Supreme Court of New Jersey, if that right has been newly recognized by either of those Courts and made retroactive by either of those Courts to cases on collateral review; or

(B) the date on which the factual predicate for the relief sought was discovered, if that factual predicate could not have been discovered earlier through the exercise of reasonable diligence; or

(C) the date of the denial of the first or subsequent application for post-conviction relief where ineffective assistance of counsel that represented the defendant on the first or subsequent application for post-conviction relief is being alleged.

(3) *Dismissal Without Prejudice When Direct Appeal Is Pending.* A petition dismissed without prejudice pursuant to R. 3:22–6A(2) because a direct appeal, including a petition for certification, is pending, shall be treated as a first petition for purposes of these rules if refiled within 90 days of the date of the judgment on direct appeal, including consideration of a petition for certification, or within five years after the date of the entry pursuant to Rule 3:21–5 of the judgment of conviction that is being challenged.

(4) *Dismissal Without Prejudice As Not Cognizable or For Insufficient Verification or Contents.* A petition dis-missed pursuant to R. 3:22–6A(3) without prejudice as not cognizable under R. 3:22–2, or for failing to meet the requirements of R. 3:22–8, shall be treated as a first petition for purposes of these rules if amended and refiled within 90 days after the date of dismissal, or within five years after the date of the entry pursuant to Rule 3:21–5 of the judgment of conviction that is being challenged.

(b) Capital Causes; Petition. In cases in which the death penalty has been imposed, defendant's petition for post-conviction relief must be filed within thirty days of the denial of *certiorari* or other final action by the United States Supreme Court in respect of defendant's direct appeal.

(c) These time limitations shall not be relaxed, except as provided herein.

Note: Source—R.R. 3:10A–13. Caption added and text designated as paragraph (a), and new paragraph (b) added July 12, 2002 to be effective September 3, 2002; paragraph (a) amended and new paragraph (c) adopted July 16, 2009 to be effective September 1, 2009; former paragraph (a) amended and allocated into subparagraphs (a)(1), (a)(3), and (a)(4), captions adopted for subparagraphs (a)(1), (a)(3), and (a)(4), and new subparagraph (a)(2) caption and text adopted January 14, 2010 to be effective February 1, 2010.

CHAPTER V. APPEALS FROM COURTS OF LIMITED CRIMINAL JURISDICTION
RULE 3:23. APPEALS FROM JUDGMENTS OF CONVICTION IN COURTS OF LIMITED CRIMINAL JURISDICTION

3:23–1. Exclusive Method of Review

Except as provided by R. 2:2–3(b), review of a judgment of conviction in a criminal action or proceeding in a court of limited criminal jurisdiction shall be by appeal as provided by R. 3:23.

Note: Source—R.R. 3:10–1.

3:23–2. Appeal; How Taken; Time

The defendant, a defendant's legal representative, or other person aggrieved by a judgment of conviction, or the defendant or State, if aggrieved by a final post-judgment order entered by a court of limited jurisdiction, shall appeal therefrom by filing a notice of appeal with the clerk of the court below within 20 days after the entry of judgment. Within five days after the filing of the notice of appeal, one copy thereof shall be served on the prosecuting attorney, as hereinafter defined, and one copy thereof shall be filed with the Criminal Division Manager's office together with the filing fee therefor and an affidavit of timely filing of said notice with the clerk of court below and service on the prosecuting attorney (giving the prosecuting attorney's name and address). On failure to comply with each of the foregoing requirements, the appeal shall be dis-missed by the Superior Court, Law Division without further notice or hearing. However, if the appeal is from a final judgment of the Superior Court arising out of a municipal court matter heard by a Superior Court judge sitting as a municipal court judge, the appeal shall be to the Appellate Division in accordance with R. 2:2–3(a)(1) and the time limits of R. 2:4–1(a) shall apply.

Note: Source—R.R. 1:3–1(c), 1:27B(d), 3:10–2, 3:10–5. Amended November 22, 1978 to be effective December 7, 1978; amended July 11, 1979 to be effective September 10, 1979; amended November 5, 1986 to be effective January 1, 1987; amended July 13, 1994 to be effective September 1, 1994; amended July 5, 2000 to be effective September 5, 2000; amended July 12, 2002 to be effective September 3, 2002; amended July 28, 2004 to be effective September 1, 2004.

3:23–3. Notice of Appeal; Contents

The notice of appeal shall set forth the title of the action; the name and the address of the appellant and appellant's attorney, if any; a general statement of the nature of the offense; the date of the judgment; the sentence imposed; whether the defendant is in custody;

and if a fine was imposed; whether it was paid or suspended; and the name of the court from which the appeal is taken. There shall be included in the notice of appeal a statement as to whether or not a stenographic record or sound recording was made pursuant to R. 7:8–8 in the court from which the appeal is taken. Where a verbatim record of the proceeding was taken, the notice of appeal shall also contain the attorney's certification of compliance with R. 2:5–3(a) (request for transcript) and R. 2:5–3(d) (deposit for transcript) or certification of the filing and service of a motion for abbreviation of transcript pursuant to R. 2:5–3(c).

Note: Source—R.R. 3:10–3. Amended July 7, 1971 to be effective September 13, 1971; amended July 13, 1994 to be effective September 1, 1994; amended January 5, 1998 to be effective February 1, 1998.

3:23–4.　Duties of Clerks of the Trial Court and Superior Court, Law Division

(a) **Preparation of Transcript.** Upon the filing of the notice of appeal, the clerk of the court below shall forthwith deliver to the criminal division manager's office the complaint, the judgment of conviction, the exhibits retained by the clerk, and a transcript of the entire docket in the action, and the criminal division manager's office shall deliver copies thereof to the prosecuting attorney on request.

(b) **Docketing; Hearing Date.** Upon the filing of a copy of the notice of appeal, the affidavit and the payment of the filing fees, as provided by R. 3:23–2, the criminal division manager's office shall docket the appeal and shall thereafter fix a date for the hearing of the appeal and mail written notice thereof to the prosecuting attorney and the appellant, or, if the appellant is represented, the appellant's attorney.

Note: Source—R.R. 3:10–4. Caption amended November 22, 1978 to be effective December 7, 1978; paragraphs (a) and (b) amended July 13, 1994 to be effective September 1, 1994; paragraphs (a) and (b) amended July 5, 2000 to be effective September 5, 2000.

3:23–5.　Relief Pending Appeal

(a) **Relief From Custodial Sentence.** If a custodial sentence has been imposed, and an appeal from the judgment of conviction has been taken, the defendant shall be admitted to bail by a judge of the Superior Court in accordance with the standards set forth in R. 3:26–1a.

(b) **Relief From Fine.** A sentence to pay a fine, a fine and costs, or a forfeiture may be stayed by the court in which the conviction was had or to which the appeal is taken upon such terms as the court deems appropriate.

(c) **Relief From Order for Probation.** An order for probation may be stayed if an appeal is taken.

Note: Source—R.R. 3:10–6. Paragraph (c) amended July 24, 1978 to be effective September 11, 1978; paragraph (a) amended January 5, 1998 to be effective February 1, 1998.

3:23–6.　Transmittal of Recognizance or Cash Deposit

The judge or clerk of the court below shall transmit to the finance division manager's office any recognizance taken in accordance herewith or cash deposited in lieu of such recognizance.

Note: Source—R.R. 3:10–7. Amended July 13, 1994 to be effective September 1, 1994; amended July 5, 2000 to be effective September 5, 2000; corrective amendment adopted November 8, 2000 to be effective immediately.

3:23–7.　Dismissal of Appeal

If the appeal shall be dismissed for failure to comply with the requirements of R. 3:23–2 or 3:23–8(a) or (b) or for failure to prosecute, the matter and the record therein shall forthwith be remanded to the court from which the appeal was taken for execution of the judgment therein.

Note: Source—R.R. 3:10–9.

3:23–8.　Hearing on Appeal

(a) **Plenary Hearing; Hearing on Record; Correction or Supplementation of Record; Transcript for Indigents.** If a verbatim record or sound recording was made pursuant to R. 7:8–8 in the court from which the appeal is taken, the original transcript thereof duly certified as correct shall be filed by the clerk of the court below with the criminal division manager's office, and a certified copy served on the prosecuting attorney by the clerk of the court below within 20 days after the filing of the notice of appeal or within such extension of time as the court permits. In such cases the trial of the appeal shall be heard de novo on the record unless it shall appear that the rights of either party may be prejudiced by a substantially unintelligible record or that the rights of defendant were prejudiced below in which event the court to which the appeal has been taken may either reverse and remand for a new trial or conduct a plenary trial de novo without a jury. The court shall provide the municipal court with reasons for the remand. The court may also supplement the record and admit additional testimony whenever (1) the municipal court erred in excluding evidence offered by the defendant, (2) the state offers rebuttal evidence to discredit supplementary evidence admitted hereunder, or (3) the record being reviewed is partially unintelligible or defective. If the appellant, upon application to the court appealed to, is found to be indigent, the court may order the transcript of the proceedings below furnished at the county's expense if the appeal involves violation of a statute and at the municipality's expense if the appeal involves violation of an ordinance. If no such record was made in the court from which the appeal is taken, the appeal shall operate as an application for a plenary trial de novo without a jury in the court to which the appeal is taken.

(b) **Briefs.** Briefs shall be required only if questions of law are involved on the appeal or if ordered by the court and shall be filed and served prior to the date fixed for hearing or such other date as the court fixes.

(c) Waiver; Exception. The appeal shall operate as a waiver of all defects in the record including any defect in, or the absence of, any process or charge laid in the complaint, and as a consent that the court may, during or before the hearing of the appeal, amend the complaint by making the charge more specific, definite or certain, or in any other manner, including the substitution of any charge growing out of the act or acts complained of or the surrounding circumstances of which the court from whose judgment or sentence the appeal is taken had jurisdiction, except that if the appeal is from a conviction for an indictable offense, the appeal shall not operate as a consent that the complaint may be amended so as to charge such an offense or a new or different indictable offense, unless the defendant agrees to such amendment.

(d) Defenses Which Must Be Raised Before Trial. The defenses of double jeopardy, lack of jurisdiction in the court, failure of the complaint to charge an offense, the unconstitutionality of the statute, regulation promulgated pursuant to statute or ordinance under which the complaint is made and all other defenses and objections based on defects in the institution of the prosecution or in the complaint must be raised by motion and determined in accordance with R. 3:10.

(e) Disposition by Superior Court, Law Division. If the defendant is convicted, the court shall impose sentence as provided by law. If the defendant is acquitted, the court shall order the defendant discharged, the conviction in the court below set aside, and the return of all fines and costs paid by the defendant. An appropriate judgment shall be entered and a copy thereof transmitted to the court below.

(f) Appearance by Prosecuting Attorney. The prosecuting attorney shall appear and act on behalf of the respondent at the hearing.

Note: Source—R.R. 3:10–13. Paragraph (b) amended by order of September 5, 1969 effective September 8, 1969; paragraph (a) amended June 29, 1973 to be effective September 10, 1973; paragraph (a) amended July 29, 1977 to be effective September 6, 1977; paragraphs (a), (b) and (e) amended November 22, 1978 to be effective December 7, 1978; paragraphs (a), (b) and (e) amended July 11, 1979 to be effective September 10, 1979; paragraph (a) amended February, 1983 to be effective immediately; paragraph (a) amended January 5, 1998 to be effective February 1, 1998; paragraph (a) amended July 5, 2000 to be effective September 5, 2000; paragraph (a) amended July 16, 2009 to be effective September 1, 2009.

3:23–9. Prosecuting Attorney Defined

In all appeals under R. 3:23 the prosecuting attorney shall be:

(a) The Attorney General, where required by law.

(b) The municipal attorney, in a case involving a violation of a municipal ordinance.

(c) The county prosecutor, in all other cases.

(d) With the assent of the prosecuting attorney and the consent of the court, the attorney for a complaining witness or other person interested in the prosecution may be permitted to act for the prosecuting attorney; provided, however, that the court has first reviewed the attorney certification submitted on a form prescribed by the Administrative Director of the Courts, ruled on the contents of the certification, and granted the attorney's motion to act as private prosecutor for good cause shown. The finding of good cause shall be made on the record.

Note: Source—R.R. 3:10–13. Paragraph (b) amended September 5, 1969 to be effective September 8, 1969; paragraph (d) amended November 22, 1978 to be effective December 7, 1978; paragraph (d) amended July 11, 1979 to be effective September 10, 1979; amended July 28, 2004 to be effective September 1, 2004.

RULE 3:24.   APPEALS FROM ORDERS IN COURTS OF LIMITED CRIMINAL JURISDICTION

3:24. Appeals from Orders in Courts of Limited Criminal Jurisdiction

(a) Either the prosecuting attorney or the defendant may seek leave to appeal to the Superior Court, Law Division from an interlocutory order entered before trial by a court of limited criminal jurisdiction.

(b) The prosecuting attorney may appeal, as of right, a pre-trial or post-trial judgment dismissing a complaint and, notwithstanding the provisions of paragraph (a), an order suppressing evidence entered in a court of limited criminal jurisdiction.

(c) Appeals pursuant to this rule shall be taken within 20 days after the entry of such order by filing with

the Superior Court, Law Division in the county of venue a notice of motion for leave to appeal under paragraph (a) or the notice of appeal under paragraph (b), except that an appeal from the grant of a motion to suppress shall be taken within 30 days after the entry of the order. A copy of the notice shall be filed with the clerk of the court below, and a copy thereof shall be served on the prosecuting attorney as defined by R. 3:23–9 or on the defendant or defendant's attorney, as appropriate, at least 10 days prior to the return date fixed therein. The original filed with the court and the copy served shall have annexed thereto copies of all papers of record and any affidavits essential to the determination of the motion and shall be accompanied by a brief. The respondent shall file and serve any answering brief and other papers in opposition at least 3 days before the hearing. With respect to interlocutory applications, the court may grant or deny leave to appeal on terms and may elect simultaneously to grant the motion and decide the appeal on the merits on the papers before it, or it may direct the filing of additional briefs or make such other order as it deems appropriate for the expeditious disposition of the matter. A copy of any order or judgment entered by it shall be promptly transmitted to the clerk of the court below.

(d) On appeal by the State from the grant of a motion to suppress the matter shall be tried de novo on the record. In cases in which the Attorney General or county prosecutor did not appear in the municipal

court, the State shall be permitted to supplement the record and to present any evidence or testimony concerning the legality of the contested search and seizure. The defendant shall be permitted to offer related evidence in opposition to the supplementary evidence offered by the State.

Note: Adopted February 25, 1969 to be effective September 8, 1969. Caption amended, paragraph designation added, former rule amended and designated as paragraphs (a) and (c), and new paragraph (b) adopted July 16, 1979 to be effective September 10, 1979; paragraphs (b) and (c) amended, paragraph (d) added June 9, 1989 to be effective June 19, 1989; paragraph (c) amended July 10, 1998 to be effective September 1, 1998.

CHAPTER VI. SUPPLEMENTARY AND SPECIAL PROCEEDINGS
RULE 3:25. DISMISSAL

3:25–1. Upon Motion of the Prosecutor Before or During Trial

(a) Pre-indictment. A complaint may be administratively dismissed by the prosecutor without presentation to the grand jury in which event said prosecutor shall report the dismissal and the basis therefor to the Assignment Judge and shall notify the defendant.

(b) Post-indictment. Upon motion by the prosecuting attorney, an indictment, accusation or complaint, or any count thereof, may be dismissed prior to trial by order of the judge to whom the same has been assigned for trial. During trial an indictment or accusation, or any count thereof may be dismissed by the trial judge on motion by the prosecuting attorney with the consent of the defendant.

Note: Source—R.R. 3:11–3(a); amended July 17, 1975 to be effective September 8, 1975, amended July 29, 1977 to be effective September 6, 1977; caption amended, captions added and former text amended and redesignated paragraphs (a) and (b) July 13, 1994 to be effective January 1, 1995.

3:25–2. Order for Trial

A defendant who has remained in custody awaiting trial on an indictment, other than for a capital offense, for at least 90 consecutive days after the return of that indictment may move for a trial date. The motion shall be on notice to the prosecutor and shall be accompanied by a certification that the defense is ready to

proceed to trial. The court shall, after affording the prosecutor an opportunity to be heard, fix a date for trial. In the event the prosecutor is unable to proceed on the trial date, the court shall take such action and enter such orders as the interest of justice requires, which may include pretrial release.

Note: Source—R.R. 3:11–3(b); amended July 17, 1975 to be effective September 8, 1975; former Rule redesignated paragraph (a) and paragraph (b) adopted November 2, 1987 to be effective January 1, 1988; paragraph (a) deleted, paragraph (b) amended and paragraph designation removed July 13, 1994 to be effective January 1, 1995.

3:25–3. Dismissal for Delay

If there is an unreasonable delay in presenting the charge to a grand jury or in filing an accusation against a defendant who has been held to answer upon a complaint, the Assignment Judge, or the Assignment Judge's designee, may dismiss the matter *sua sponte* or on motion of the defendant. If there is unreasonable delay in the disposition of an indictment or accusation, the judge to whom the case has been assigned may dismiss the matter *sua sponte* or on motion of the defendant.

Note: Source—R.R. 3:11–3(c); amended July 17, 1975 to be effective September 8, 1975; amended July 13, 1994 to be effective January 1, 1995; amended July 12, 2002 to be effective September 3, 2002.

RULE 3:25A. CONSOLIDATED DISPOSITIONS

3:25A–1. Application for Disposition

Notwithstanding the provisions of Rule 3:14, when a defendant has charges pending in more than one county at any stage prior to sentencing, either the defendant, or the prosecutor in any such county with the consent of

the defendant, may move before the presiding judge of the criminal part in the county in which consolidation is sought, or before any judge designated to hear such motion, for consolidation for purposes of entering a plea or for sentencing. Written notice of such motion and an opportunity to be heard shall be given to the prosecutor in each county in which such a charge is pending. The motion shall be supported by certification that includes the information the court is required to consider under this Rule.

In deciding whether to order consolidation and, if so, the county to be the forum for the consolidated charges, the judge shall consider: (1) the nature, number, and comparative gravity of crimes committed in each of the respective counties; (2) the similarity or connection of the crimes committed including the time span within which the crimes were committed; (3) the county in which the last crime was committed; (4) the county in which the most serious crime was committed; (5) the defendant's sentencing status; (6) the rights of the victims and the impact on any victim's opportunity to be heard; and (7) any other relevant factor.

Each county prosecutor of the county in which a charge is pending shall be allowed to participate fully in the disposition of that charge after consolidation is ordered. If a plea agreement is entered that resolves less than all of the consolidated charges, the judge in the

forum county shall order each unresolved charge to be returned immediately to the originating county. In the event that the consolidated charges have not been resolved within a reasonable period after consolidation, the judge in the forum county shall order each charge to be returned immediately to the originating county.

Note: Adopted July 17, 1975 to be effective September 8, 1975; amended July 14, 1992 to be effective September 1, 1992.

3:25A–2.   Order of Disposition; Filing

Every disposition made pursuant to R. 3:25A–1 shall be set forth in an order or judgment which shall be filed in the county where such disposition is made and the county where the matter was pending. Unless the disposition is set aside, all subsequent proceedings shall be had in the county where such disposition was made, and copies of all orders and judgments entered in connection therewith shall be filed there.

Note: Adopted July 17, 1975 to be effective September 8, 1975.

RULE 3:26.   BAIL

3:26–1.   Right to Bail Before Conviction

(a) Persons Entitled; Standards for Fixing. All persons, except those charged with crimes punishable by death when the prosecutor presents proof that there is a likelihood of conviction and reasonable grounds to believe that the death penalty may be imposed, shall be bailable before conviction on such terms as, in the judgment of the court, will ensure their presence in court when required. The factors to be considered in setting bail are: (1) the seriousness of the crime charged against defendant, the apparent likelihood of conviction, and the extent of the punishment prescribed by the Legislature; (2) defendant's criminal record, if any, and previous record on bail, if any; (3) defendant's reputation, and mental condition; (4) the length of defendant's residence in the community; (5) defendant's family ties and relationships; (6) defendant's employment status, record of employment, and financial condition; (7) the identity of responsible members of the community who would vouch for defendant's reliability; (8) any other factors indicating defendant's mode of life, or ties to the community or bearing on the risk of failure to appear, and, particularly, the general policy against unnecessary sureties and detention. In its discretion the court may order the release of a person on that person's own recognizance. The court may also impose terms or conditions appropriate to the defendant's release including conditions necessary to protect persons in the community.

(b) Restrictions on Contact. If the court imposes conditions of bail that include restrictions on contact

between the defendant and defendant's minor child, (1) a copy of the order imposing the restrictions shall be transmitted to the Family Part, and (2) such restrictions shall not affect contact authorized by an order of the Family Part in a child abuse/neglect case entered after any restriction on contact was imposed as part of a bail order.

(c) Crimes with Bail Restrictions Defined in N.J.S.A. 2A:162–12. If a defendant is charged with a crime with bail restrictions as defined in N.J.S.A. 2A:162–12, no later than the time of posting bail or proffering the surety or bail bond, the defendant shall provide to the prosecutor, on the Bail Source Inquiry Questionnaire promulgated by the Attorney General, relevant information about the obligor, indemnifier or person posting cash bail, the security offered, and the source of any money or property used to post the cash bail or secure the surety or bail bond.

(d) On Failure to Indict. If a person committed for a crime punishable by death is not indicted within 3 months after commitment, a judge of the Superior Court, for good cause shown, may admit the person to bail.

(e) On Failure to Move Indictment. If an indictment or accusation is not moved for trial within 6 months after arraignment, a judge of the Superior Court, for cause shown, may discharge the defendant upon the defendant's own recognizance.

(f) Extradition Proceedings. Where a person has been arrested in any extradition proceeding, that person may be admitted to bail except where that person is charged with a crime punishable by death.

Note: Source–R.R. 3:9–1(a)(b)(c)(d); paragraph (a) amended September 28, 1982 to be effective immediately; paragraphs (a), (b), (c) and (d) amended July 13, 1994 to be effective January 1, 1995; paragraph (a) amended July 10, 1998 to be effective September 1, 1998; new paragraph (b) adopted, and former paragraphs (b), (c), and (d) redesignated as paragraphs (c), (d), and (e) June 15, 2007 to be effective September 1, 2007; new paragraph (c) adopted and former paragraphs (c), (d), and (e) redesignated as paragraphs (d), (e), and (f) July 9, 2008 to be effective September 1, 2008.

3:26–2. Authority to Set Bail

(a) Authority to Set Initial Bail. A Superior Court judge may set bail for a person charged with any offense. Bail for any offense except murder, kidnapping, manslaughter, aggravated manslaughter, aggravated sexual assault, sexual assault, aggravated criminal sexual contact, a person arrested in any extradition proceeding or a person arrested under N.J.S.A. 2C:29–9b for violating a restraining order may be set by any other judge, or in the absence of a judge, by a municipal court administrator or deputy court administrator.

(b) Initial Bail Set. Initial bail shall be set pursuant to R. 3:4–1(a) or (b) on indictable or non-indictable offenses.

(c) Review of Initial Set. Any person unable to post bail shall have his or her bail reviewed by a Superior Court judge no later than the next day which is neither a Saturday, Sunday nor a legal holiday.

Except in those indictable cases in which a Superior Court judge has set bail, a municipal court judge has the authority to make bail revisions up to and including the time of the defendant's first appearance before the court. A municipal court judge has the authority to make bail revisions on any non-indictable offense at any time during the course of the proceedings.

(d) Bail Reductions. A first motion for bail reduction shall be heard by the court no later than seven days after it is filed.

Note: Source—R.R. 3:9–3(a)(b)(c); amended July 24, 1978 to be effective September 11, 1978; amended May 21, 1979 to be effective June 1, 1979; amended August 28, 1979 to be effective September 1, 1979; amended July 26, 1984 to be effective September 10, 1984; caption amended, former text amended and redesignated paragraph (a) and new paragraphs (b), (c) and (d) adopted July 13, 1994 to be effective January 1, 1995; paragraph (b) amended January 5, 1998 to be effective February 1, 1998.

3:26–3. Bail for Witness

(a) Authority to Issue. A Superior Court judge may, on application, conduct proceedings under N.J.S.A. 2C:104–1 et seq. as to any person who can give testimony relevant to the prosecution or defense of a pending indictment, accusation, or complaint for a crime or a criminal investigation before a grand jury.

(b) Application. The application shall be captioned in Superior Court and entitled "In the Matter of (name of person alleged to be a material witness)". The application shall include a copy of the pending indictment, complaint, or accusation and an affidavit containing: (1) the name and address of the person alleged to be a material witness, (2) a summary of the facts believed to be known by the alleged material witness and the relevance to the criminal action or investigation, (3) the grounds for belief that the person has material and necessary information concerning the pending criminal action or investigation, and (4) the reasons why the alleged material witness is unlikely to respond to a subpoena. If the application requests an arrest warrant, the affidavit shall set forth why immediate arrest is necessary.

(c) Order to Appear. If there is probable cause to support issuance of a material-witness order against the person named in the application, the court may order the person to appear at a hearing to determine whether the person should be adjudged a material witness. The order and a copy of the application shall be served personally on the alleged material witness at least 48 hours before the hearing, unless the judge adjusts the time period for good cause, and shall advise the person of: (1) the time and place of the hearing, and (2) the right to be represented by an attorney and to have an attorney appointed if the person cannot afford one.

(d) Warrant for Immediate Detention. If there is clear and convincing evidence that the person will not be available as a witness unless immediately detained, the court may issue an order requiring that the person be brought before the court immediately. If the detention does not take place during regular court hours, the person shall be brought to the emergency-duty Superior Court judge. The judge shall inform the person: (1) the reason for detention, (2) the time and place of the hearing to determine whether the person is a material witness, and (3) that the person has a right to an attorney and to have an attorney appointed if the person cannot afford one. The judge shall set conditions for release, or, if there is clear and convincing evidence that the person will not be available as a witness unless detention is continued, the judge may order the person held until the material-witness hearing, which shall take place as soon as practicable but no later than 48 hours after detention.

(e) Detention Without Prior Court Authorization. Where a law enforcement officer has detained an alleged material witness without prior court authorization, the law enforcement officer shall immediately bring the person before a Superior Court judge. If the detention does not take place during regular court hours, the person shall be brought to the emergent duty Superior Court judge. The judge shall determine whether there is probable cause to believe that the person is a material witness of a crime and, if an indictment, accusation, or complaint for that crime has not issued or if a grand jury has not commenced a criminal investigation of that crime, the judge shall determine whether there is probable cause to believe that, within 48 hours of the detention, an indictment, accusation, or complaint will issue or a grand jury investigation will commence. The judge will then proceed as if an application for an order had been made under paragraph (b).

(f) Material Witness Hearing. At the material-witness hearing, the person shall have the rights: (1) to be represented by an attorney and to have an attorney appointed if the person cannot afford one, (2) to be heard and to present witnesses and evidence, and (3) unless otherwise sealed by the court for exceptional circumstances, to have all of the evidence in support of the application, and (4) to confront and cross-examine witnesses. If there is probable cause to believe that the person possesses information material to the prosecution of a defense of a pending indictment, accusation or complaint for a crime, or a criminal investigation before a grand jury and is unlikely to respond to subpoena, the judge shall: (1) set forth findings of facts on the record, and (2) set the conditions of release of the material witness.

(g) Conditions of Release or Detention. Conditions of release for a material-witness or for a person held on an application for a material-witness order shall be the least restrictive to effect the order of the court including but not limited to: (1) placing the witness in the custody of a designated person or organization agreeing to supervise the person; (2) restricting the travel, association, or place of abode of the person during the period of detention; (3) requiring the person to report; (4) setting bail, or (5) imposing other reasonable restrictions on the material witness. No person may be detained unless the judge finds, by clear and convincing evidence, that detention is the only method that will secure the appearance of the material witness. A person detained as a material witness or pending a material-witness hearing shall be lodged in appropriate quarters and shall not be held in a jail or prison.

(h) Deposition. The prosecutor, defendant, or material witness may apply to the Superior Court for an order directing that a deposition be taken to preserve the witness's testimony, for use at trial if the witness becomes unavailable, as provided by R. 3:13–2. After a deposition has been taken, the judge shall vacate the material-witness order and impose the least restrictive conditions to secure the appearance of the material witness.

(i) Reconsideration of Material Witness Order. On motion of the material witness, prosecutor, or defendant, a material witness order may be reconsidered at any time by the court that entered the order.

Note: Source—R.R. 3:9–4; first paragraph re-designated paragraph (a) and paragraphs (b), (c) (d), (e), (f) and (g) added July 14, 1992 to be effective September 1, 1992; paragraph (g) amended July 13, 1994 and December 9, 1994, to be effective January 1, 1995; paragraphs (a), (b), (c) and (d) amended, former paragraphs (e), (f), and (g) amended and redesignated as paragraphs (f), (g), and (h), and new paragraphs (e) and (i) adopted July 10, 1998 to be effective September 1, 1998.

3:26–4. Form and Place of Deposit; Location of Real Estate; Record of Recognizances, Discharge and Forfeiture Thereof

(a) Deposit of Bail. A person admitted to bail shall, together with that person's sureties, sign and execute a recognizance before the person authorized to take bail or, if the defendant is in custody, the person in charge of the place of confinement. The recognizance shall contain the terms set forth in R. 1:13–3(b) and shall be conditioned upon the defendant's appearance at all stages of the proceedings until final determination of the matter, unless otherwise ordered by the court. One or more sureties may be required. Cash may be accepted, and in proper cases no security need be required. A corporate surety shall be one approved by the Commissioner of Insurance and shall execute the recognizance under its corporate seal, cause the same to be duly acknowledged and shall annex thereto proof of authority of the officers or agents executing the same and of corporate authority and qualification. Bail given in the Superior Court shall be deposited with the Finance Division Manager in the county in which the offense was committed, provided that upon order of the court bail shall be transferred from the county of deposit to the county in which defendant is to be tried. Real estate offered as bail for indictable and non-indictable offenses shall be approved by and deposited with the clerk of the county in which the offense occurred and not with the Municipal Court clerk. In any county, with the approval of the Assignment Judge, a program may be instituted for the deposit in court of cash in the amount of 10 percent of the amount of bail fixed.

(b) Limitation on Individual Surety. Unless the court for good cause otherwise permits, no surety, other than an approved corporate surety, shall enter into a recognizance or undertaking for bail if there remains undischarged any previous recognizance or bail undertaken by that surety.

(c) Real Estate in Other Counties. Real estate owned by a surety located in a county other than the one in which the bail is taken may be accepted, in which case the clerk of the court in which the bail is taken shall forthwith transmit a copy of the recognizance certified by that clerk to the clerk of the county in which the real estate is situated, who shall record it in the same manner as if the recognizance had been taken in that clerk's county.

(d) Record of Recognizance. The clerk of every court, except the municipal court, before which any recognizance shall be entered into shall record immediately into the Central Automated Bail System (CABS), the names of the persons entering into the recognizance, the amount thereof and the date of its acknowledgment. The Central Automated Bail System shall be kept in the clerk's office of the county of which such court shall be held, and be open for public inspection. In municipal court proceedings the record of the recognizance shall be entered in the docket book maintained by the clerk.

(e) Record of Discharge; Forfeiture. When any recognizance shall be discharged by court order upon proof of compliance with the conditions thereof or by reason of the judgment in any matter, the clerk of the court shall enter the word "discharged" and the date of discharge at the end of the record of such recognizance. When any recognizance is forfeited, the Finance Division Manager shall enter the word "forfeited", and the date of forfeiture at the end of the record of such recognizance, and shall give notice of such forfeiture to the county counsel. When real estate of the surety located in a county other than the one in which the bail was taken is affected, the clerk of the court in which such recognizance is given shall forthwith send notice of the discharge or forfeiture and the date thereof to the clerk of the county where such real estate is situated, who shall make the appropriate entry at the end of the record of such recognizance.

(f) Cash Deposit. When a person other than the defendant deposits cash in lieu of bond the person making the deposit shall file an affidavit or certification concerning the lawful ownership thereof, and on discharge such cash may be returned to the owner named in the affidavit or certification.

(g) Ten Percent Cash Bail. Except in first or second degree cases as set forth in N.J.S.A. 2A:162–12 and unless the order setting bail specifies to the contrary, whenever bail is set pursuant to Rule 3:26–1, bail may be satisfied by the deposit in court of cash in the amount of ten-percent of the amount of bail fixed and defendant's execution of a recognizance for the remaining ninety percent. No surety shall be required unless the court fixing bail specifically so orders. When cash equal to ten-percent of the bail fixed is deposited pursuant to this Rule, if the cash is owned by someone other than the defendant, the owner shall charge no fee for the deposit other than lawful interest and shall submit an affidavit or certification with the deposit so stating and also listing the names of any other persons for whom the owner has deposited bail. The person making the deposit authorized by this subsection shall file an affidavit or certification concerning the lawful ownership thereof, and on discharge such cash may be returned to the owner named in the affidavit or certification.

Note: Source–R.R. 3:9–5(a)(b)(c)(d)(e)(f)(g). Paragraph (a) amended June 29, 1973 to be effective September 10, 1973; paragraph (a) amended July 16, 1979 to be effective September 10, 1979; paragraph (g) adopted November 5, 1986 to be effective January 1, 1987; paragraph (a) amended November 7, 1988 to be effective January 2, 1989; paragraphs (f) and (g) amended July 14, 1992 to be effective September 1, 1992; paragraphs (a), (b) and (c) amended July 13, 1994 to be effective September 1, 1994; paragraph (g) amended February 27, 1995 to be effective immediately; paragraphs (a), (d), (e),(f) and (g) amended June 15, 2007 to be effective September 1, 2007.

3:26–5. Justification of Sureties

Every surety, except an approved corporate surety, shall justify by affidavit and be required to describe therein the property by which the surety proposes to justify and the encumbrances thereon, the number and amount of other recognizances and undertakings for bail entered into by the surety and remaining undischarged, if any, and all the surety's other liabilities. No recognizance shall be approved unless the surety thereon shall be qualified.

Note: Source—R.R. 3:9–6; amended July 13, 1994 to be effective September 1, 1994.

3:26–6. Forfeiture

(a) Declaration; Notice. Upon breach of a condition of a recognizance, the court on its own motion shall order forfeiture of the bail, and the finance division manager shall forthwith send notice of the forfeiture, by ordinary mail, to county counsel, the defendant, and any surety or insurer, bail agent or agency whose names appear on the bail recognizance. Notice to any insurer, bail agent or agency shall be sent to the address recorded in the Bail Registry maintained by the Clerk of the Superior Court pursuant to R. 1:13–3. The notice shall direct that judgment will be entered as to any outstanding bail absent a written objection seeking to set aside the forfeiture, which must be filed within 75 days of the date of the notice. The notice shall also advise the insurer that if it fails to satisfy a judgment entered pursuant to paragraph (c), and until satisfaction is made, it shall be removed from the Bail Registry and its bail agents and agencies, guarantors, and other persons or entities authorized to administer or manage its bail bond business in this State will have no further authority to act for it, and their names, as acting for the insurer, will be removed from the Bail Registry. In addition the bail agent or agency, guarantor or other person or entity authorized by the insurer to administer or manage its bail bond business in this State who acted in such capacity with respect to the forfeited bond will be precluded, by removal from the Bail Registry, from so acting for any other insurer until the judgment has been satisfied. The court shall not enter judgment until the merits of any objection are determined either on the papers filed or, if the court so orders for good cause, at a hearing. In the absence of objection, judgment shall be entered as provided in paragraph (c), but the court may thereafter remit it, in whole or part, in the interest of justice.

(b) Setting Aside. The court may, either before or after the entry of judgment, direct that an order of forfeiture or judgment be set aside, in whole or in part, if its enforcement is not required in the interest of justice upon such conditions as it imposes.

(c) Enforcement; Remission. In the absence of a motion, when a forfeiture is not set aside or satisfied, the court shall, upon expiration of the 75 days provided for in paragraph (a), summarily enter a judgment of default for any outstanding bail and execution may issue thereon. After entry of such judgment, the court may remit it in whole or in part in the interest of justice. If, following the court's decision on an objection pursuant to paragraph (a) of this rule, the forfeiture is not set aside or satisfied in whole or part, the court shall enter judgment for any outstanding bail and, in the absence of satisfaction thereof, execution may issue thereon.

Judgments entered pursuant to this rule shall also advise the insurer that if it fails to satisfy a judgment, and until satisfaction is made, it shall be removed from the Bail Registry and its bail agents and agencies, guarantors, and other persons or entities authorized to administer or manage its bail bond business in this State will have no further authority to act for it, and their names, as acting for the insurer, will be removed from the Bail Registry, as provided in paragraph (a). A copy of the judgment entered pursuant to this rule is to be served by ordinary mail to county counsel, and on any surety or any insurer, bail agent or agency named in the judgment. Notice to any insurer, bail agent or agency shall be sent to the address recorded in the Bail Registry. In any contested proceeding, county counsel shall appear on behalf of the government. County counsel shall be responsible for collection of forfeited amounts.

Note: Source—R.R. 3:9–7 (a)(b)(c) (first sentence) (d); paragraphs (a) and (c) amended July 10, 1998 to be effective September 1, 1998; paragraphs (a), (b) and (c) amended July 28, 2004 to be effective September 1, 2004.

Publisher's Note

On August 31, 2004, the New Jersey Supreme Court issued the following Order

IT IS ORDERED, that the Court's November 1, 2000 Order, which set out the notice and procedural requirements to be followed in bail forfeitures and judgments, and the amendatory Orders dated June 11, 2002 (to modify the time permitted to file an objection to set aside a bail forfeiture preclusion) and May 20, 2003 (to conform to statutory changes effected by the New Jersey Insurance Producer Act of 2001 (L.2001, c. 210) are hereby terminated effective September 1, 2004, the effective date of the July 28, 2004 amendments to Rules 1:13–3, 2:9–6, 3:26–6, 7:4–3 and 7:4–5.

3:26–7. Exoneration

When the condition of the recognizance has been satisfied or the forfeiture thereof has been set aside or remitted, the court shall exonerate the obligors and release any bail. A surety may be exonerated by a deposit of cash in the amount of the recognizance or by a timely surrender of the defendant into custody.

Note: Source—R.R. 3:9–8.

3:26–8. Bail Sufficiency; Source Hearing

(a) Time and Notice. The State may request either orally or in writing, at any time prior to the commencement of trial, a hearing pursuant to N.J.S.A. 2A:162–13. The request shall be made on notice to the defendant's counsel, or on notice to the defendant if he or she is unrepresented at the time the request is made.

(b) Request for Hearing. If the State requests a hearing pursuant to N.J.S.A. 2A:162–13 and the defendant is charged with a crime enumerated in paragraph

(a) of N.J.S.A. 2A:162–12, the court shall conduct a hearing within the time prescribed by section (c) hereof. If the State requests a hearing pursuant to N.J.S.A. 2A:162–13 and the defendant is not charged with a crime enumerated in paragraph (a) of N.J.S.A. 2A:162–12, the State must demonstrate a reasonable and well grounded basis to warrant an inquiry by the court regarding:

(1) the reliability of the obligor or person posting cash bail, the value and sufficiency of any security offered, the relationship of the obligor or person posting cash bail to the defendant, and the defendant's interest in ensuring that the bail is not forfeited, or

(2) whether the funds used to post the cash bail or secure the bail bond were acquired as a result of criminal or unlawful conduct.

If the court grants the State's request for a hearing as to a defendant who is not charged with a crime enumerated in paragraph (a) of N.J.S.A. 2A:162–12, the court shall set forth on the record and in the bail order the reasons for granting the request.

(c) Time of Hearing. The court shall conduct a hearing required or authorized pursuant to N.J.S.A. 2A:162–13 within three (3) business days after bail is posted or proffered if defendant is incarcerated, or within a reasonable period of time after granting the request if the defendant has been released on bail.

(d) Release of Defendant; Failure to Appear. If the defendant has not yet been released when the State requests a hearing for a person charged with a crime enumerated in N.J.S.A. 2A:162–12 or when the court grants a request for a hearing for any other offense, the defendant shall remain in custody until further order of the court. If the defendant has already been released after posting bail, the defendant's bail status shall be maintained until the completion of the hearing and the defendant will be notified when to appear in court for the hearing. Should the defendant fail to appear for the hearing the bail shall be forfeited and a warrant shall issue for the arrest of the defendant.

(e) Hearing. At the hearing pursuant to N.J.S.A. 2A:162–13, the court may order the examination, under oath or otherwise, of any person who may possess relevant information, and may inquire into any matter appropriate to its determination, including, but not limited to, the following:

(1) The character, background and reputation of the person posting cash bail;

(2) The relationship of the person posting cash bail or securing a bail bond to the defendant;

(3) The source of any money posted as cash bail and whether any such money constitutes the fruits of criminal or unlawful conduct;

(4) The character, background and reputation of any person who has indemnified or agreed to indemnify an obligor on the bond;

(5) The character, background, and reputation of any obligor, or, in the case of a surety bond, the qualifications of the surety and its executing agent;

(6) The source of any money or property deposited by any obligor as security and whether such money or property constitutes the fruits of criminal or unlawful conduct; and

(7) The source of any money or property delivered or agreed to be delivered by any obligor as indemnification on the bond and whether such money or property constitutes the fruits of criminal or unlawful conduct.

(f) Order. At the conclusion of the hearing, the court shall make specific findings of fact and issue an order complying with N.J.S.A. 2A:162–13(b) regarding the person posting or proffering cash bail or serving as obligor on any bond, the sufficiency and value of the security for bail posted or proffered by the defendant, the source of funds used to post cash bail or secure a bail bond and identifying the approved source(s) of bail. The defendant shall not be released from custody unless he or she complies with the conditions of the court's order. If the defendant has already been released, he or she shall be returned to custody, immediately, and not be released until the conditions of the court order regarding the bail are satisfied.

(g) Nothing herein shall prevent the court from otherwise setting bail, or altering bail on motion therefor, in accordance with the rules of court.

Note: Adopted July 9, 2008 to be effective September 1, 2008.

RULE 3:27.   [RESERVED]

[R. 3:27–1 and R. 3:27–2 deleted July 13, 1994 to be effective January 1, 1995.]

RULE 3:28.   PRETRIAL INTERVENTION PROGRAMS

(a) Each Assignment Judge shall designate a judge or judges to act on all matters pertaining to pretrial intervention programs in the vicinage in accordance with N.J.S.A. 2C:43–12 and –13.

(b) Where a defendant charged with a penal or criminal offense has been accepted by the program, the designated judge may, on the recommendation of the criminal division manager and with the consent of the prosecutor and the defendant, postpone all further proceedings against said defendant on such charges for a period not to exceed thirty-six months.

(c) At the conclusion of the period set forth in paragraph (b) or earlier upon motion of the criminal division manager, the designated judge shall make one of the following dispositions:

(1) On recommendation of the criminal division manager and with the consent of the prosecutor and the defendant, dismiss the complaint, indictment or accusation against the defendant, such a dismissal to be designated "matter adjusted—complaint (or indictment or accusation) dismissed"; or

(2) On recommendation of the criminal division manager and with the consent of the prosecutor and the defendant, further postpone all proceedings against such defendant on such charges for an additional period of time as long as the aggregate of postponement periods under the rule does not exceed thirty-six months; or

(3) On the written recommendation of the criminal division manager or the prosecutor or on the court's own motion order the prosecution of the defendant to proceed in the ordinary course. Where a recommendation for such an order is made by the criminal division manager or the prosecutor, such person shall, before submitting such recommendation to the designated judge, provide the defendant or defendant's attorney with a copy of such recommendation, shall advise the defendant of the opportunity to be heard thereon, and the designated judge shall afford the defendant such a hearing.

(4) During the conduct of hearings subsequent to an order returning the defendant to prosecution in the ordinary course, no program records, investigative reports, reports made for a court or prosecuting attorney, or statements made by the defendant to program staff shall be admissible in evidence against such defendant.

(5) No statement or other disclosure regarding the charge or charges against the participant made or disclosed by a participant in pretrial intervention to a person designated to provide supervisory treatment shall be disclosed by such person at any time, to the prosecutor, nor shall any such statement or disclosure be admitted as evidence in any civil or criminal proceeding against the participant, provided that the criminal division manager shall not be prevented from informing the prosecutor, or the court, on request or otherwise, whether the participant is satisfactorily responding to supervisory treatment.

(d) Where proceedings have been postponed against a defendant for an additional period as provided in paragraph (c)(2), at the conclusion of such period the designated judge may not again postpone proceedings but shall make a disposition in accordance with paragraph (c)(1) or (3). The aggregate of postponement periods under this rule shall in no case exceed thirty-six months.

(e) The Administrative Director of the Courts shall establish and maintain a Pretrial Intervention Registry for the purpose of determining applications, enrollments and the degree of completion thereof by a defendant in a program approved by the Supreme Court in accordance with paragraph (a). The Pretrial Intervention Registry shall contain such information and material as directed by the Supreme Court. No order to expunge or seal records of arrest after dismissal of a complaint, indictment or accusation under paragraph (c) or (d) shall bar the retention of material and information in the Pretrial Intervention Registry for the purposes of determining a defendant's prior applications to, enrollments in and the degree of completion of a Pretrial Intervention Program or for statistical reports required of the Administrative Director of the Courts, by law or the Supreme Court.

(f) When the criminal division manager and prosecutor reject an application for participation in the pretrial intervention program, there shall be no pretrial review by an appellate court if the rejection is upheld by the designated judge or the Assignment Judge. An order enrolling a defendant into the pretrial intervention program over the prosecutor's objection shall be deemed final for purposes of appeal, as of right, and shall be automatically stayed for fifteen days following its entry and thereafter pending appellate review.

(g) Denial of acceptance pursuant to this rule may be reviewed on appeal from a judgment of conviction notwithstanding that such judgment is entered following a plea of guilty.

(h) Application for pretrial intervention shall be made at the earliest possible opportunity, including before indictment, but in any event no later than twenty-eight days after indictment. The criminal division manager shall complete the evaluation and make a recommendation within twenty-five days of the filing of the application. The prosecutor shall complete a review of the application and inform the court and defendant within fourteen days of the receipt of the criminal division manager's recommendation.

An appeal by the defendant shall be made on motion to the Presiding Judge of the Criminal Division or to the judge to whom the case has been assigned within ten days after the rejection and shall be made returnable at the next status conference or at such time as the judge determines will promote an expeditious disposition of the case.

Where application is made pre-indictment, the prosecutor may withhold action on the application until the matter has been presented to the grand jury.

Note: Adopted October 7, 1970, effective immediately. Paragraphs (a)(b)(c)(d) amended June 29, 1973, to be effective September 10, 1973; caption and paragraphs (a)(b)(c)(d) amended April 1, 1974 effective immediately; paragraph (e) adopted January 10, 1979 to be effective January 15, 1979; paragraphs (a)(b)(c)(d) amended August 28, 1979 to be effective September 1, 1979; paragraphs (f) and (g) adopted October 25, 1982 to be effective December 1, 1982; paragraphs (a) (b) (c) (d) and (f) amended and paragraph (h) added July 13, 1994, to be effective January 1, 1995; paragraph (f) amended June 28, 1996 to be effective September 1, 1996; paragraph (f) amended July 12, 2002 to be effective September 3, 2002; paragraph (c)(4) amended June 15, 2007 to be effective September 1, 2007.

GUIDELINES FOR OPERATION OF PRETRIAL INTERVENTION IN NEW JERSEY
As Amended Effective September 1, 1996.

SUPREME COURT OF NEW JERSEY

ORDERED that the attached revised guidelines governing pretrial intervention programs are approved for implementation as applicable in counties where such programs have been authorized by the Supreme Court pursuant to R. 3:28; and

FURTHER ORDERED that the guidelines approved by the order of January 10, 1979 are hereby superceded.

For the Court,

Robert N. Wilentz

C.J.

Dated: July 13, 1994

Guideline 1

The purposes of pretrial intervention are:

(a) To provide defendants with opportunities to avoid ordinary prosecution by receiving early rehabilitative services, when such services can reasonably be expected to deter future criminal behavior by the defendant, and when there is an apparent causal connection between the offense charged and the rehabilitative need, without which cause both the alleged offense and the need to prosecute might not have occurred.

(b) To provide an alternative to prosecution for defendants who might be harmed by the imposition of criminal sanctions as presently administered, when such an alternative can be expected to serve as sufficient sanction to deter criminal conduct.

(c) To provide a mechanism for permitting the least burdensome form of prosecution possible for defendants charged with "victimless" offenses.

(d) To assist in the relief of presently overburdened criminal calendars in order to focus expenditure of criminal justice resources on matters involving serious criminality and severe correctional problems.

(e) To deter future criminal or disorderly behavior by a defendant/participant in pretrial intervention.

Comment

Guideline 1(a) states a rehabilitative model on which PTI programs in New Jersey are based. The rehabilitative model emphasizes that social, cultural and economic conditions often result in a defendant's choice of environmental compulsion to commit crime. PTI seeks to solve personal problems which tend to result from the conditions that appear to cause crime.

Guideline 1(b) recognizes that diversion in appropriate circumstances can serve as sufficient sanction to deter future criminal conduct.

Guideline 1(c) provides for the use of PTI as a mechanism for minimizing penetration into the criminal process for broad categories of offenders accused of "victimless crimes," without relinquishing criminal justice control over such persons while statutes proscriptive of such behavior remain in force.

Guideline 1(d) provides for removing from ordinary prosecution those who can be deterred from criminal behavior by short term rehabilitative work or supervision. It is to be emphasized that the potential for rehabilitation must be considered in light of the time periods embodied in Rule 3:28(b), (c), (d).

The deterrence of criminal behavior in many cases requires intensive work: counseling, psychotherapy, drug-abuse prevention and control, employment placement. Programs in these cases should be measured against available treatment facilities and the time constraints of PTI. For other defendants, however, no more than a supervised pretrial probationary period may be necessary when no extensive need for rehabilitative services can be discerned.

Guideline 1(e) acknowledges that pre-conviction rehabilitation can be in the public interest when it results in the deterrence of future misconduct.

Guideline 2

Eligibility for PTI is broad enough to include all defendants who demonstrate sufficient effort to effect necessary behavioral change and show that future criminal behavior will not occur. Any defendant accused of crime shall be eligible for admission into a PTI program. When the application indicates factors which would ordinarily lead to exclusion under the guidelines established hereinafter, the applicant nevertheless shall have the opportunity to present to the criminal division manager, and through the criminal division manager to the prosecutor, any facts or materials demonstrating the defendant's amenability to the rehabilitative process, showing compelling reasons justifying the defendant's admission, and establishing that a decision against enrollment would be arbitrary and unreasonable.

Comment

Guideline 2 provides that each applicant for a PTI program is entitled to full and fair consideration of his or her application. When the application indicates factors that cause either the criminal division manager to reject the application or the prosecutor to deny consent to an enrollment, a statement particularizing the reasons for the rejection or the withholding of consent by the prosecutor must be furnished to the defendant. If the defendant wishes to challenge a rejection by the criminal division manager, or the prosecutor's denial of consent to enrollment, the defendant may do so in accordance with the procedures set forth in guidelines 6 and 8. It is the duty of the applicant to allege and present any facts and materials to the criminal division manager for reconsideration either by the criminal division manager or prosecutor, if the prosecutor has denied consent, showing compelling reasons justify-

ing admission, and establishing that a decision against enrollment would be arbitrary and unreasonable. The presentation of this material should be done concurrently with the filing of a motion under guideline 8 for review of a decision by a criminal division manager not to recommend or of a prosecutor not to consent to enrollment.

Guideline 3

In evaluating a defendant's application for participation in a pretrial intervention program, consideration shall be given to the criteria set forth in N.J.S.A. 2C:43–12(e). In addition thereto, the following factors shall also be considered together with other relevant circumstances:

(a) Age. Pretrial intervention is designed to deal only with adult defendants who, in accordance with New Jersey law, are those persons above the age of 18. Also included are those juveniles between the ages of 16 and 18 who are treated as adults under R. 5:9–5.

(b) Residence. New Jersey's PTI program is designed to deal with the problem of crime in New Jersey. Only those defendants are ineligible who reside such distances from New Jersey as to bar effective counseling or supervisory procedures.

(c) Jurisdiction. Only defendants charged with criminal or penal offenses in the criminal or municipal courts of the State of New Jersey may be enrolled pursuant to R. 3:28.

(d) Minor Violations. Defendants should not be eligible for enrollment if the likely disposition would result in a suspended sentence without probation or a fine. Those charged with ordinance, health code and other similar violations are not eligible.

(e) Prior Record of Convictions. While the pretrial intervention program is not limited to "first offenders", defendants who have been previously convicted of a criminal offense should ordinarily be excluded. Such defendants who have at any prior time been convicted of a first or second degree crime or who irrespective of the degree of the crime have completed a term of probation, incarceration or parole within five years prior to the date of application for diversion shall ordinarily not be considered for enrollment in PTI except on joint application by the defendant and the prosecutor. Defendants charged with more than one offense may be considered for enrollment.

(f) Parolees and Probationers. Defendants who, at the time of arrest, are probationers or parolees should be considered for enrollment under R. 3:28 only after consultation with the Chief Probation Officer or District Parole Supervisor whose departments supervise the defendants, and only after they have agreed that revocation of probation or parole need not be recommended or after the appropriate authority has made the decision not to revoke probation or parole.

(g) Defendants Previously Diverted. Supervisory treatment may occur only once with respect to any defendant who has previously been enrolled in a program of pretrial intervention or conditionally discharged pursuant to N.J.S.A. 24:21–27 or N.J.S.A.

2C:36A–1. All applications for enrollment in a PTI program must proceed in accordance with the rules of the Supreme Court and these guidelines after reference to the Pretrial Intervention Registry established pursuant to R. 3:28(e) and N.J.S.A. 2C:43–21(a). No order to expunge or seal records of arrest after dismissal of a complaint, indictment or accusation under paragraph (c) or (d) shall bar the retention of material and information in the Pretrial Intervention Registry for the purposes of determining a defendant's prior applications to, enrollments in, and the degree of completion of a Pretrial Intervention Program or for statistical reports required of the Administrative Director of the Courts, by law or the Supreme Court.

(h) Eligibility Under N.J.S.A. 24:21–27 or N.J.S.A. 2C:36A–1. The statutes set forth the criteria for eligibility and guidelines for exclusion. Defendants eligible for pretrial intervention or conditional discharge pursuant to N.J.S.A. 2C:36A–1 or § 27 of the Controlled Dangerous Substances Act may be placed under the supervision of a pretrial intervention program.

(i) Assessment of the Nature of the Offense. Any defendant charged with crime is eligible for enrollment in a PTI program, but the nature of the offense is a factor to be considered in reviewing the application. If the crime was (1) part of organized criminal activity; or (2) part of a continuing criminal business or enterprise; or (3) deliberately committed with violence or threat of violence against another person; or (4) a breach of the public trust where admission to a PTI program would deprecate the seriousness of defendant's crime, the defendant's application should generally be rejected. A defendant charged with a first or second degree offense or sale or dispensing of Schedule I or II narcotic drugs as defined in L.1970, c. 226 (N.J.S.A. 24:21–1 et seq.) by persons not drug dependent, should ordinarily not be considered for enrollment in a PTI program except on joint application by the defendant and the prosecutor. However, in such cases, the applicant shall have the opportunity to present to the criminal division manager, and through the criminal division manager to the prosecutor, any facts or materials demonstrating the applicant's amenability to the rehabilitative process, showing compelling reasons justifying the applicant's admission and establishing that a decision against enrollment would be arbitrary and unreasonable.

(j) Co-defendants. The impact of diversion on the prosecution of co-defendants is a factor to be considered.

(k) Restitution and Community Service. A restitution or community service requirement, or both, may be included as part of an individual's service plan when such a requirement promises to aid the rehabilitation of the offender. Any such requirement and its terms shall be judicially determined at the time of enrollment following recommendation by the criminal division manager and consent by the Prosecutor. Evidence of the restitution condition is not admissible against defendant in any subsequent civil or criminal proceeding.

Admission to the program shall not be denied solely on the basis of anticipated inability to meet a restitution requirement. Where appropriate to further rehabilitation, symbolic or partial restitution may be included in the service.

Comment

Guideline 3, in its introductory statement, requires that the statutory criteria of N.J.S.A. 2C:43–12(e) be considered in the evaluation of a defendant's application for pretrial intervention. That statutory provision requires consideration of those criteria "among others." Accordingly, the original criteria of this guideline have also been retained as explanatory of and supplemental to the statutory criteria. For convenience in reference, the statutory criteria are as follows:

(1) The nature of the offense;

(2) The facts of the case;

(3) The motivation and age of the defendant;

(4) The desire of the complainant or victim to forego prosecution;

(5) The existence of personal problems and character traits which may be related to the applicant's crime and for which services are unavailable within the criminal justice system, or which may be provided more effectively through supervisory treatment and the probability that the causes of criminal behavior can be controlled by proper treatment;

(6) The likelihood that the applicant's crime is related to a condition or situation that would be conducive to change through his participation in supervisory treatment;

(7) The needs and interests of the victim and society;

(8) The extent to which the applicant's crime constitutes part of a continuing pattern of anti-social behavior;

(9) The applicant's record of criminal and penal violations and the extent to which he may present a substantial danger to others;

(10) Whether or not the crime is of an assaultive or violent nature, whether in the criminal act itself or in the possible injurious consequences of such behavior;

(11) Consideration of whether or not prosecution would exacerbate the social problem that led to the applicant's criminal act;

(12) The history of the use of physical violence toward others;

(13) Any involvement of the applicant with organized crime;

(14) Whether or not the crime is of such a nature that the value of supervisory treatment would be outweighed by the public need for prosecution;

(15) Whether or not the applicant's involvement with other people in the crime charged or in other crime is such that the interest of the State would be best served by processing his case through traditional criminal justice system procedures;

(16) Whether or not applicant's participation in pretrial intervention will adversely affect the prosecution of co-defendants; and

(17) Whether or not the harm done to society by abandoning criminal prosecution would outweigh the benefits to society from channeling an offender into a supervisory treatment program.

Guideline 3(a) indicates that the services of PTI programs may, in appropriate instances and at the request of juvenile authorities and programs, be made available to juvenile defendants when the need for inter-program cooperative work is indicated.

Under Guideline 3(b), residents of other States, charged with offenses in New Jersey counties in which there exist pretrial intervention programs may, with the approval of the prosecuting attorney, the designated judge, and Administrative Office of the Courts, be permitted to participate in such out-of-state program while enrolled pursuant to R. 3:28.

Regardless of the New Jersey jurisdiction in which the complaint, indictment or accusation has been filed, defendants or participants may, with the agreement of the PTI coordinators involved, be transferred for participation among the various county or vicinage programs.

Guideline 3(c) establishes jurisdictional requirements. However, defendants charged in other States or in the Federal Courts, may in appropriate instances and with the permission of the Administrative Office of the Court, be permitted to participate in the counseling or supervision regimes of the county or vicinage PTI programs on request of the Federal Authorities or a PTI program in another State.

Guideline 3(d) sets forth the policy that those charged with minor violations should not be admitted to a PTI program. It is felt that while no per se exclusion of non-indictable offenses is appropriate, the PTI process is not appropriate for such cases which do not involve a potential sentence of consequence. Rodriguez v. Rosenblatt, 58 N.J. 281, 277 A.2d 216 (1971).[1]

1. Of course all defendants charged with an indictable offense are eligible for PTI.

Guideline 3(e) makes it clear that a prior criminal record may be indicative of a behavioral pattern not conducive to short term rehabilitation. Therefore, pretrial intervention should ordinarily be limited to persons who have not previously been convicted of a crime and hence a rebuttable presumption against enrollment is created by the fact of a prior conviction. An even heavier onus is placed upon defendants whose prior conviction is of a first or second degree crime or who have completed a term of imprisonment, probation or parole within the five-year period immediately preceding the application for diversion. As to those defendants, admission to the program is ordinarily dependent upon the prosecutor joining in the PTI application.

Guideline 3(f) sets forth a policy permitting probationers and parolees to enter PTI programs. Since the parolee/probationer is under the supervision of the District Parole Supervisor or Chief Probation Officer, consultation should be sought prior to recommending enrollment of the defendant into a PTI program.

Guideline 3(g) creates a bar against admission into a PTI program for those defendants who have previously been diverted under N.J.S.A. 2C:43–12 et seq. or conditionally discharged pursuant to N.J.S.A. 24:21–27 or N.J.S.A. 2C:36A–1. The Pretrial Intervention Registry established pursuant to N.J.S.A. 2C:43–21(a) and R. 3:28 serves as the means of identifying defendants previously diverted through a PTI program. This registry is designed to complement the Controlled Dangerous Substance Registry Act of 1970, pursuant to N.J.S.A. 26:2G–17 et seq.

Guideline 3(h) deems it appropriate that PTI programs may assume the supervision of N.J.S.A. 24:21–27 or N.J.S.A. 2C:36A–1 cases.

Guideline 3(i) recognizes that consistent with State v. Leonardis, 71 N.J. 85, 363 A.2d 321 (1976) and 73 N.J. 360, 375 A.2d 607 (1977), there must be a balance struck between a defendant's amenability to correction, responsiveness to rehabilitation and the nature of the offense. It is to be emphasized that while all persons are eligible for pretrial intervention programs, those charged with offenses encompassed within certain enumerated categories must bear the burden of presenting compelling facts and materials justifying admission. First and second degree crimes (and their Title 2A cognates) and the sale or dispensing of Schedule I and II narcotics by persons not drug dependent are specific categories of offenses that establish a rebuttable presumption against admission of defendants into a PTI program. This presumption reflects the public policy of PTI. PTI programs should ordinarily reject applications by defendants who fall within these categories unless the prosecutor has affirmatively joined in the application. A heavy burden rests with the defendant to present to the criminal division manager at the time of application (a) proof that the prosecutor has joined in the application and (b) any material that would otherwise rebut the presumption against enrollment. When a defendant charged with a first or second degree crime or the sale or dispensing of Schedule I or II narcotics has been rejected because the prosecutor refuses to consent to the filing of the application, or because in the sound discretion of the criminal division manager the defendant has not rebutted the presumption against admission, the burden lies with the defendant upon appeal to the court to show that the prosecutor or criminal division manager abused such discretion. When an application is rejected because the defendant is charged with a crime of the first or second degree or sale or dispensing of Schedule I or II narcotics, and the prosecutor refuses to join affirmatively in the filing of an application or later refuses to consent to enrollment, such refusal should create a rebuttable presumption against enrollment.

Guideline 3(k) recognizes that the use of restitution and community service may play an integral role in rehabilitation. Requiring either is strongly consonant with the individual approach defined in State v. Leonardis, 71 N.J. 85, 363 A.2d 321 (1976) and 73 N.J. 360, 375 A.2d 607 (1977), which emphasized the needs of the offender. In determin-

ing the restitution requirement and its terms including ability of the offender to pay, the Court should rely on the procedures outlined in State in Interest of DGW, 70 N.J. 488, 361 A.2d 513 (1976) and State v. Harris, 70 N.J. 586 (1976).

Full restitution need not be completed during participation in the program. In determining whether a restitution requirement has been fulfilled, the designated judge shall consider good-faith efforts by the defendant. In appropriate cases, at the conclusion of participation, a civil judgment by confession may be entered by the court. However, restitution should never be used in PTI for the sole purpose of collecting monies for victims.

Guideline 4

Enrollment in PTI programs should be conditioned upon neither informal admission nor entry of a plea of guilty. Enrollment of defendants who maintain their innocence should be permitted unless the defendant's attitude would render pretrial intervention ineffective.

Comment

A PTI program is presented to defendants as an opportunity to earn a dismissal of charges for social reasons and reasons of present and future behavior, legal guilt or innocence notwithstanding. This stance produces a relation of trust between counselor and defendant. Within the context of pretrial intervention when and whether guilt should be admitted is a decision for counselors. Counselors should be free to handle each case individually according to their best judgment.

Neither admission of guilt nor acknowledgment of responsibility is required. Steps to bar participation solely on such grounds would be an unwarranted discrimination.

Nevertheless, many guilty defendants blame their behavior on society, family, friends or circumstance, and avoid recognition of the extent of their own role and responsibility. While such an attitude continues, it is unlikely that behavioral change can occur as a result of short-term rehabilitative work. An understanding and acceptance of responsibility for behavior achieved through counseling, can and often does, result in the beginnings of the defendant's ability to control his/her acts and is an indication that rehabilitation may, in large measure, have been achieved.

Guideline 5

Effective operation of pretrial intervention programs requires that a relationship of confidence and trust be initiated and maintained between participating defendants and staff. No information, therefore, obtained as a result of a defendant's application to or participation in a pretrial intervention program should be used, in any subsequent proceeding, against his or her advantage.

Comment

That a relationship based on trust is necessary for the rehabilitation/attitude change process to operate cannot seriously be doubted, and the policy reflected in the admissibility and defendant protection provisions of R. 3:28 and R. 1:38 recognizes such a need. The priority of the maintenance of the counselor-participant relation over the need for disclosures resulting from this relationship is the same, of course, as the priority for the maintenance of, for example, the confidentiality of lawyer-client, physician/psychologist-patient communications. (Counselors should feel free to shroud their association in an air of confidentiality. Use of information gathered in this process would most likely be barred from future proceedings "as contrary to basic standards of due process and fundamental fairness." See In the Interest of J.P.B., 143 N.J.Super. 96, 362 A.2d 1183 (App.Div.1976). Of course, defendants who give false information on PTI applications may subject themselves to charges of perjury or false swearing in instances where supporting affidavits may be required by the criminal division manager. Affidavits relating to the facts and circumstances of the underlying offense shall not be required.)

The essential PTI format is to give participating defendants a true second chance to accomplish rehabilitation or to show otherwise that criminal conduct is not likely to occur in the future; and if the defendant fails in this effort, to return him or her to that stage of ordinary prosecution at which proceedings had been stopped under R. 3:28, and to the extent possible, enable prosecution to take place as if such defendants had not participated in the PTI program so that defendants will not be prejudiced by an unsuccessful attempt to earn a R. 3:28 dismissal.

Guideline 6

Application for PTI should be made as soon as possible after commencement of proceedings, but, where an indictable offense is charged, not later than 28 days after indictment. All applications for PTI should be processed in the order of their filing. However, where the application is filed after an indictment has been returned, the PTI Program should complete its evaluation and make its recommendation thereon within 25 days after filing. The prosecutor should complete a review and advise the defendant within 14 days thereafter. An appeal by defendant to the trial court shall be brought within 10 days after the rejection notice and should be determined either before or at the pretrial conference.

Comment

To relieve defendants from the anxiety of facing prosecution, to apply appropriate rehabilitative measures at an early date, and to effect savings in criminal justice resources, PTI programs should endeavor to divert qualified defendants from the ordinary course of prosecution as soon as possible after the filing of a complaint. The court must advise defendant of the opportunity to be considered for PTI at the first appearance before the court. See R. 3:4–2. While a PTI application should be made before indictment, there are nevertheless problems involved in securing public defender counsel before arraignment. Thus, while pre-indictment filing is encouraged, the application may be made no later than 28 days after indictment, but not thereafter. This time requirement should permit all defendants sufficient opportunity to make a voluntary and informed choice concerning enrollment in a PTI program.

The time requirements set forth in the guidelines for evaluation, recommendation and review are intended to enable complete processing of a defendant's application before the pretrial conference. See R. 3:9–1e. Early filing as encouraged by this guideline, will afford PTI programs and prosecutors the opportunity to manage their resources better by providing them sufficient time to make informed evaluations. The time limits for processing applications are designed to facilitate speedy trials and are realistic in view of the limited scope of review following rejection.

Guideline 7

Where application is made in an indictable offense, the prosecutor may withhold action on the application until the matter has been presented to the grand jury.

Comment

Guideline 7 recognizes that at times it may be in the public interest to have a particular defendant screened out of the criminal justice system, either by administrative decision or grand jury action, rather than diverted into a PTI program. Thus, the prosecutor is given the discretion to choose an appropriate route and the court will not be burdened by hearing challenges if no indictment is to be returned. However, the option of delaying action until the grand jury has voted on the case should be considered only in rare instances. Generally, expeditious handling of PTI applications is in consonance with the purpose of diversion. Of course, if the prosecutor consents to the application, enrollment into a PTI program should not be delayed and the defendant should generally be enrolled before indictment.

Guideline 8

The decisions and reasons therefor made by the designated judges (or Assignment Judges), prosecutors and criminal division managers in granting or denying defendants' applications for PTI enrollment, in recommending and ordering termination from the program or dismissal of charges, in all cases must be reduced to writing and disclosed to defendant.

A defendant may be accepted into a PTI program by the designated judge (or the Assignment Judge) on recommendation of the criminal division manager, and with the consent of the prosecuting attorney and the defendant. Applications that are recommended for enrollment by the criminal division manager and consented to by the prosecutor must be presented to the designated judge (or Assignment Judge) authorized to enter orders. If a defendant desires to challenge the decision of a criminal division manager not to recommend enrollment or of a prosecutor refusing to consent to enrollment into a PTI program, a motion must be filed before the designated judge (or the Assignment Judge) authorized to enter orders under R. 3:28. The challenge is to be based upon alleged arbitrary or capricious action, and the defendant has the burden of showing that the criminal division manager or prosecutor abused discretion in processing the application. No direct appeal can be filed to the Appellate Division challenging the actions of the criminal division manager or the prosecutor. The decision of the criminal division manager or prosecutor may be challenged at a hearing on defendant's motion before the designated judge (or Assignment Judge) and, thereafter, defendant or prosecutor can seek leave to appeal from the court's decision denying or permitting enrollment.

A defendant shall also be entitled to a hearing challenging a criminal division manager or prosecutor's recommendation (following an initial or subsequent adjournment under Rule 3:28) that the prosecution of defendant proceed in the normal course. The decision of the court shall be appealable by the defendant or the prosecutor as in the case of any interlocutory order.

A defendant aggrieved by the decision of the designated judge or assignment judge respecting the joint decision of the criminal division manager and prosecutor to deny an application for participation in a pretrial intervention program may not seek appellate review thereof until after entry of judgment of conviction. A defendant may then seek such review even if the judgment was entered following a plea of guilty. However, a prosecutor whose denial of consent has been reversed by the designated judge or assignment judge may seek leave to appeal pursuant to R. 2:2.

Guidelines 2, 3, 6 and 8 and Comments to Guidelines 2, 3, 5 and 6 amended July 13, 1994 to be effective January 1, 1995; Guidelines 3(g) and (h) and Comments to Guidelines 3(g) and (h) amended June 28, 1996 to be effective September 1, 1996.

RULE 3:29. STATEMENT OF REASONS FOR DISPOSITION OF MOTION OR APPLICATION

The court shall place on the record the reasons supporting its decision on a motion to dismiss an indictment, accusation or complaint, or on an applica-

tion for diversion, change or reduction of sentence, or other disposition of a criminal matter.

Note: Adopted July 29, 1977 to be effective September 6, 1977.

RULE 3:30. FEES FOR EXPUNGEMENT OF RECORDS

Any person who files an application for an expungement of records, pursuant to N.J.S.A. 2C:52–1 to –32,

shall pay filing fees as required by N.J.S.A. 2C:52–29 and N.J.S.A. 22A:2–25.

Note: Adopted July 16, 2009 to be effective September 1, 2009.

PART V.   RULES GOVERNING PRACTICE IN THE CHANCERY DIVISION, FAMILY PART

Research Note

For a comprehensive treatment of practice and procedure under these Rules, see Klock, New Jersey Court Rules Annotated (Practice Series Volumes 1 through 2A), *Walzer,* New Jersey Civil Practice Forms (Practice Series Volumes 3–4C), *and Winters and Baldwin,* New Jersey Family Law and Practice, With Forms (Practice Series Volumes 10–12).

Use Westlaw *to find cases citing a rule.* Westlaw *may also be used to search for specific terms or to update a rule; see the Scope Screens in NJ–RULES and NJ–RULESUPDATES for further information.*

Amendments to these rules are published, as received, in Atlantic Reporter 2d *and* New Jersey Reports *advance sheets.*

Table of Rules

CHAPTER III.   FAMILIES IN CRISIS.

Rule
5:15.   PETITION: CONTENTS; FILING; SERVICE.
5:15–1.   When and by Whom Filed.
5:15–2.   Form and Contents of Petition.
5:15–3.   Filing and Service, Notice of Hearing.
5:16.   SHORT–TERM CUSTODY.
5:16–1.   Standards for Taking Into Custody.
5:16–2.   Procedure Following Custody.
5:17.   JUVENILE–FAMILY CRISIS HEARING.
5:17–1.   Appearances.
5:17–2.   Finding.
5:17–3.   Disposition.
5:17–4.   Closed Hearings; Records.
5:18.   OUT–OF–HOME PLACEMENT.
5:18–1.   Petition for Out-of-Home Placement; Temporary
              Placement.
5:18–2.   Temporary Out-of-Home Placement; Hearing.
5:18–3.   Long-Term Placement.

CHAPTER IV.   JUVENILE DELINQUENCY ACTIONS.

5:19.   GENERAL PROVISIONS.
5:19–1.   Establishment of Venue; Change of Venue.
5:19–2.   Confidentiality of Hearing and Records.
5:19–3.   Individual Hearings.
5:20.   COMPLAINT; PROCESS.
5:20–1.   Complaint.
5:20–2.   Summons.
5:20–3.   Warrant.
5:20–4.   Necessary Parties.
5:21.   CUSTODY, PRETRIAL DETENTION.

Rule
5:21–1.   Taking Into Custody, Initial Procedure.
5:21–2.   Release.
5:21–3.   Detention Hearings.
5:21–4.   Place of Detention or Shelter Care.
5:21–5.   Standards for Detention.
5:21–6.   Post-complaint Detention.
5:21–7.   Adjudicatory Hearing.
5:21–8.   Custody and Detention of Material Witness.
5:21A.   JUVENILE PLEA FORM.
5:22.   REFERRAL TO OTHER COURTS.
5:22–1.   Referral at Election of Juvenile.
5:22–2.   Referral Without Juvenile's Consent.
5:22–3.   Detention Hearing After Referral.
5:22–4.   Proceedings After Transfer.
5:23.   TRANSFER OF CAUSES FROM OTHER
              COURTS.
5:23–1.   Transfer Generally.
5:23–2.   Proceedings After Transfer.
5:24.   DISPOSITION.
5:24–1.   Disposition Hearing.
5:24–2.   Predisposition Evaluation.
5:24–3.   Manner of Disposition.
5:24–4.   Order of Disposition.
5:24–5.   Retention of Jurisdiction.
5:24–6.   Modification of Order of Disposition: Post-disposi-
              tion Relief.
5:25.   JUVENILE CONFERENCE COMMITTEES;
              REFEREES.
5:25–1.   Juvenile Conference Committees.
5:25–2.   Referees.
5:25–3.   Child Support Hearing Officers.
5:25–4.   Domestic Violence Hearing Officers.

CHAPTER III. FAMILIES IN CRISIS
RULE 5:15. PETITION: CONTENTS; FILING; SERVICE

5:15–1. When and by Whom Filed

A petition referring a juvenile-family crisis to the court shall be filed by Court Intake Services pursuant to N.J.S. 2A:4A–83 when, in the judgment of a crisis intervention unit, a juvenile-family crisis, as defined by N.J.S. 2A:4A–22(g), continues to exist despite the provision of crisis intervention services and the exhaustion of appropriate community services. Where, however, the facts alleged are primarily governed by other specific statutes a petition shall not be filed pursuant to this rule but rather Court Intake Services shall proceed as otherwise required by law.

Note: Source—new. Adopted December 20, 1983, to be effective December 31, 1983; amended November 5, 1986 to be effective January 1, 1987.

5:15–2. Form and Contents of Petition

A petition alleging the existence of a juvenile-family crisis shall be captioned "The State of New Jersey in the Interest of the Family of _____," shall be made on oath by a Court Intake Services officer, shall be in the form prescribed by the Administrative Director of the Courts and shall include the following:

(a) The name, address and date of birth of the juvenile.

(b) The name, address and date of birth of the juvenile's parents, guardian or custodian and any other family member believed to be contributing to the juvenile-family crisis.

(c) A statement of facts describing the nature of the juvenile-family crisis.

(d) The recommendations of Court Intake Services for resolving the crisis, including recommendations regarding community services or programs necessary to implement the recommendations.

(e) The services, if any, previously provided by the Crisis Intervention Unit, the community services to which the family has previously been referred, if any, and a statement that these services have not resolved or stabilized the crisis.

(f) If Court Intake Services has reason to believe that a parent or guardian of the juvenile is an alcoholic, as defined by N.J.S. 26:2B–8, or drug dependent, as defined by N.J.S. 24:21–2, the petition shall state the basis for this determination and provide recommendations to the court.

Note: Source—new. Adopted December 20, 1983, to be effective December 31, 1983.

5:15–3. Filing and Service, Notice of Hearing

The petition shall be filed with the clerk of the court who shall, to the extent possible, notify by telephone all persons listed in the petition of the date, time and place of hearing. In addition to the telephone notice, a copy of the petition together with a summons in the form prescribed by R. 4:4–2 shall be served on all parties named in the petition in accordance with R. 4:4–4 as soon after filing as is practicable.

Note: Source—new. Adopted December 20, 1983, to be effective December 31, 1983.

RULE 5:16. SHORT–TERM CUSTODY

5:16–1. Standards for Taking Into Custody

Except where delinquent conduct is alleged, a law enforcement officer may take any juvenile into short-term custody, not to exceed six hours, when:

(a) there are reasonable grounds to believe that the health and safety of the juvenile is seriously in danger and that immediate custody is necessary for the juvenile's protection;

(b) there are reasonable grounds to believe that the juvenile has left the home and care of parents or guardian without their consent; or

(c) an agency legally charged with supervision of the juvenile has notified the law enforcement agency that the juvenile has run away from out-of-home placement; except where there are reasonable grounds to believe that the juvenile is an "abused or neglected child" within the meaning of N.J.S. 9:6–8.21 in which case the provisions of said law shall govern.

The taking of a juvenile into custody shall not be construed as an arrest but shall be deemed a measure to protect the juvenile's health, morals and well-being. Nor shall a juvenile taken into short-term custody be detained in a detention facility or jail.

Note: Source—new. Adopted December 20, 1983, to be effective December 31, 1983.

5:16–2. Procedure Following Custody

(a) Notification of Parents. An officer taking a juvenile into short-term custody shall immediately notify the juvenile's parents or guardian thereof.

(b) Release to Juvenile's Home. An officer taking a juvenile into short-term custody shall inform the juvenile of the reason for custody and shall where possible transport or arrange for transport to the juvenile's home. The officer so releasing a juvenile shall inform the juvenile's parents or guardian and the juvenile-family crisis intervention unit of the reason for taking the juvenile into custody and may, if the officer believes further services are needed, inform the juvenile and the juvenile's parents of the nature and location of appropriate services.

(c) Release of the Juvenile to Another's Home. An officer taking a juvenile into short-term custody may transport the juvenile to the home of a relative of the juvenile or to the home of another responsible adult or make arrangements for such transportation where the officer reasonably believes that the child will be provided with adequate care and supervision and that the child will remain in custody of the adult until such time as the juvenile-family crisis intervention unit can bring about the child's return home or an alternative living arrangement or out-of-home placement. A law enforcement officer placing a juvenile with a relative or responsible adult shall immediately notify the juvenile-family crisis intervention unit thereof and of the reason for taking the juvenile into custody.

(d) Transfer of Custody to Crisis Intervention Unit. A law enforcement officer taking a juvenile into short-term custody shall immediately notify the juvenile-family crisis intervention unit and shall promptly bring the juvenile to the unit or such other place as is designated by the unit when:

(1) The officer has reason to believe that it is not in the best interests of the juvenile or the family for the officer to return the juvenile home;

(2) The juvenile resides in another county and the officer is unable to make arrangements to return the juvenile home;

(3) The juvenile resides in another state;

(4) The juvenile has run away from a placement and the juvenile refuses to return home or the juvenile, through past behavior, has demonstrated an inability to remain at home;

(5) The law enforcement officer is unable by all reasonable efforts to identify or locate a parent, relative or other such appropriate person;

(6) The juvenile requires immediate emergency services, such as medical or psychiatric care; or

(7) No identification can be obtained from the juvenile.

Note: Source—new. Adopted December 20, 1983, to be effective December 31, 1983; paragraphs (b) and (d)(1), (d)(2), and (d)(4) amended July 13, 1994 to be effective September 1, 1994.

RULE 5:17. JUVENILE–FAMILY CRISIS HEARING

5:17–1. Appearances

The juvenile, the juvenile's parents or guardian, and each family member alleged in the petition as contributing to the family crisis, shall appear at the initial hearing. A warrant may issue to compel the appearance of any such person who fails to appear. However, no warrant shall be issued for failure to appear pursuant to telephonic notification. Any warrant issued pursuant to this rule shall be limited to arrest during hours that the court is in session and shall state that the non-appearing party be brought directly to court and not incarcerated prior to court appearance. Each of said persons may present evidence regarding the existence of a juvenile-family crisis.

Note: Source—new. Adopted December 20, 1983, to be effective December 31, 1983; caption amended and former rule redesignated paragraph (a) and paragraph (b) adopted November 5, 1986 to be effective January 1, 1987; paragraph (a) amended and paragraph (b) deleted July 13, 1994 to be effective September 1, 1994.

5:17–2. Finding

When court intake service determines in accordance with R. 5:15–1 that a juvenile-family crisis may exist and that appropriate community services have been exhausted, it shall file a petition with the court for hearing. The court shall review the petition and either schedule a hearing or take other appropriate action. At the hearing the court shall consider all evidence presented by any family member and by the court intake service and shall determine whether a juvenile-family crisis as defined by law exists by a preponderance of evidence. If the court finds that there is insufficient information to allow a determination, it may continue the matter and hold one or more additional hearings.

Note: Source—new. Adopted December 20, 1983, to be effective December 31, 1983; amended November 5, 1986 to be effective January 1, 1987.

5:17–3. Disposition

If it finds that juvenile-family crisis exists, the court shall continue the hearing to determine the appropriate disposition, and shall consider the recommendations submitted by intake services, family members and any other interested parties. The court shall make such disposition as it deems appropriate, including requiring the juvenile, parent, guardian or family member contributing to the crisis to participate in appropriate programs and services consistent with the disposition. If the court, however, concludes that an out-of-home placement is necessary, further proceedings shall be taken pursuant to R. 5:18 insofar as applicable. The court shall state its reasons for any disposition made and in the event of the failure of any person to comply with a dispositional order, it may proceed against such person for the enforcement of litigant's rights.

Note: Source—new. Adopted December 20, 1983, to be effective December 31, 1983.

5:17–4. Closed Hearings; Records

(a) Hearings. Every hearing shall be conducted in private with only such persons in attendance as have a direct involvement in the proceeding, except as hereinafter provided. At the judge's discretion, attendance may also be permitted at any private hearing of any person who has an interest in the work of the court; provided, however, that such person shall agree not to record, disclose or publish the names, photographs or other identifying data with respect to any of the participants in the hearing. Upon objection by any family member involved in the hearing or by the attorney of any family member, any person seeking permission to attend because of interest in the work of the court may be excluded from any hearing involving said juvenile.

(b) Records. Social, medical, psychological, legal, and other records of the court or family intake services, and records of law enforcement agencies, found to be part of a juvenile-family crisis matter, shall be strictly safeguarded from public inspection and shall be made available only pursuant to N.J.S.A. 2A:4A–60 to –62. Any application for such records shall be made by motion to the court.

Note: Source—R. (1969) 5:9–1. Adopted December 20, 1983, to be effective December 31, 1983; amended July 13, 1994 to be effective September 1, 1994; caption amended, text of rule redesignated as paragraph (a), and new paragraph (b) added July 12, 2002 to be effective September 3, 2002.

RULE 5:18. OUT–OF–HOME PLACEMENT

5:18–1. Petition for Out-of-Home Placement; Temporary Placement

(a) When Petition May Be Filed. The Court Intake Services may petition the court for out-of-home placement where, after exhaustion of crisis intervention services and appropriate community services, the juvenile refuses to stay or return home, or the juvenile's parents or guardians refuse to permit the juvenile to stay or return home, or the physical safety of the juvenile is threatened, or the juvenile is in need of immediate care available only by a use of out-of-home placement and in addition to any one of the foregoing, the juvenile's parents or guardians do not agree to an alternate living arrangement for the juvenile in a suitable family setting which is proposed by the Court Intake Services. The petition shall state what appropriate community services have been attempted and the reasons why such services have not proved successful.

(b) Temporary Placement. Prior to the court's disposition of an out-of-home placement petition, the Court Intake Services may make a temporary out-of-home placement of the juvenile pursuant to and in accordance with N.J.S. 2A:4A–88.

(c) Form of Petition. The petition in out-of-home placement actions shall be captioned "The State of New Jersey in the Interest of the Family of _____," and shall be made under oath and in the form prescribed by the Administrative Director of the Courts.

Note: Source—new. Adopted December 20, 1983, to be effective December 31, 1983; paragraph (a) amended and paragraph (c) adopted November 5, 1986 to be effective January 1, 1987; paragraphs (a) and (c) amended July 13, 1994 to be effective September 1, 1994.

5:18–2. Temporary Out-of-Home Placement; Hearing

(a) Time; Appearances. The court shall hold a hearing on an out-of-home placement petition within 24 hours after it has been filed. All necessary parties shall be notified of the hearing pursuant to R. 5:15–3 and their presence secured, if necessary, by warrant pursuant to R. 5:17–1. The juvenile shall be represented by counsel and if indigent, counsel shall be appointed by the court. The court may request attendance at the hearing of a representative of the Division of Youth and Family Services.

(b) Hearing; Disposition. Based on the evidence adduced at the hearing, the court shall either approve or disapprove the temporary out-of-home placement. Approval of temporary out-of-home placement shall be made only if either serious conflict or other problem between the parent or guardian and the juvenile exists which cannot be resolved by the delivery of services to the family while the juvenile is residing at home; or the physical safety and well-being of the juvenile would be threatened if the juvenile resided at the parental home. The order approving the temporary placement shall direct the Division of Youth and Family Services or other service or agency to submit a family service plan and to make custodial recommendations pursuant to N.J.S. 2A:4A–89(c) and (d). The order shall set a specific date when the plan is due and shall also instruct the agency to transmit the family service plan to all counsel or parties appearing pro se no later than 3 court days prior to the due date of the hearing. If the court disapproves a petition for temporary out-of-home placement, it shall file a written statement of its reasons therefor and order the juvenile to remain at or return to the parental home.

(c) Family Service Plan. Following the submission to the court of the family service plan herein provided for and on notice to all parties, the court shall consider the plan and all evidence adduced with respect thereto and may approve, reject or modify the plan in its dispositional order. The order shall specify the agency responsible for the juvenile, the parental rights temporarily transferred to such agency and the parenting time or visitation rights accorded to the juvenile's parents. If placement cannot be immediately made, the responsible agency shall report to the court every 14 days on the status of the placement plan. In such event, when the agency has completed the plan it should transmit it to all counsel or parties appearing pro se no later than three court days prior to the new date of the hearing.

Note: Source—new. Adopted December 20, 1983, to be effective December 31, 1983; paragraphs (b) and (c) amended November 5, 1986 to be effective January 1, 1987; paragraphs (a) and (b) amended July 13, 1994 to be effective September 1, 1994; paragraph (c) amended July 5, 2000 to be effective September 5, 2000.

5:18–3. Long-Term Placement

In considering whether to approve or disapprove out-of-home placement under a family service plan on a long-term basis, the court shall consider whether placement in the home would fail to provide adequate physical protection, shelter or nutrition or would seriously obstruct the juvenile's medical care, education, or physical and emotional development. Upon entry of an order approving a long-term out-of-home placement plan, the matter shall be reviewed pursuant to the provisions of the Child Placement Review Act, P.L. 1977, c. 424 (N.J.S. 30:4C–50 et seq.).

Note: Source—new. Adopted December 20, 1983, to be effective December 31, 1983.

CHAPTER IV. JUVENILE DELINQUENCY ACTIONS
RULE 5:19. GENERAL PROVISIONS

5:19–1. Establishment of Venue; Change of Venue

(a) Establishment of Venue.

(1) Juvenile delinquency complaints are filed in the county where the incident giving rise to the complaint allegedly occurred. However, when the juvenile charged is domiciled in a county other than the county of the alleged occurrence, venue shall be laid in the county of the juvenile's domicile unless the court finds good cause for venue to be retained in the county where the incident allegedly occurred.

(2) If there are multiple defendants, juvenile or adult, the Family Division Manager or designee in the county where the complaint was filed shall immediately notify the county prosecutor and any attorney of record of an intent to transfer the juvenile matter to the county of domicile. Any objection to the transfer of venue to the county where the juvenile is domiciled shall be made to the court in the county where the complaint was filed, within five days of such notice.

(b) Change of Venue. Except when venue has been established by a court pursuant to an objection raised in paragraph (a)(2), a motion for change of venue may be made at any time. Such motion shall be made to the Family Presiding Judge or designee in the county where the matter is currently venued on notice to the other party. Venue shall be retained unless the court determines that good cause exists to change venue.

Note: Source — R. (1969) 5:3–1(a) and (b). Adopted December 20, 1983, to be effective December 31, 1983; amended June 29, 1990 to be effective September 4, 1990; amended and redesignated as paragraphs (a), (b), and (c) July 10, 1998 to be effective September 1, 1998; caption amended, former text deleted in full, and new captions and text adopted for paragraphs (a) and (b) July 27, 2006 to be effective September 1, 2006.

5:19–2. Confidentiality of Hearing and Records

(a) Hearing.

(1) The court may upon application by the juvenile or the juvenile's parent or guardian, the prosecutor or any other interested party, including the victim or complainant or members of the news media, permit public attendance during any court proceeding in a delinquency case, where it determines that there is no substantial likelihood of specific harm to the juvenile.

(2) Unless such application is made and granted, every hearing shall be conducted in private with only such persons in attendance as have a direct involvement in the proceeding, except as hereinafter provided. At the judge's discretion, attendance may also be permitted at such private hearing by any person who has an interest in the work of the court, provided, however, that such person shall agree not to record, disclose or publish the names, photographs or other identifying data with respect to any of the participants in the hearing except as expressly authorized by the judge. Upon objection by the juvenile, the juvenile's attorney, or the juvenile's parents, guardian or custodian, any person seeking permission to attend because of interest in the work of the court may be excluded from any hearing involving that juvenile.

(3) The court shall permit a victim or a family member of a victim to make a statement prior to ordering a disposition in any delinquency proceeding involving an offense that would constitute a crime if committed by an adult, subject to a court determination that exigent circumstances exist that require an immediate disposition.

(b) Confidentiality of Records. Social, medical, psychological, legal and other records of the Court, Probation Division and law enforcement agencies pertaining to juveniles charged as delinquents shall be strictly safeguarded from public inspection and shall be made available only pursuant to N.J.S.A. 2A:4A–60 to –62.

Any application for such records shall be made by motion to the court.

Note: Source—R. (1969) 5:9–1(a), 5:10–7. Adopted December 20, 1983, to be effective December 31, 1983; paragraph (a) amended July 13, 1994 to be effective September 1, 1994; paragraph (a) amended and redesignated as paragraphs (a)(1) and (a)(2), new paragraph (a)(3) added, and paragraph (b) amended July 12, 2002 to be effective September 3, 2002.

5:19–3. Individual Hearings

Each juvenile brought before the court may receive an individual hearing even though the conduct alleged may have been performed in association with other juveniles.

Note: Source—R. (1969) 5:9–2. Adopted December 20, 1983, to be effective December 31, 1983.

RULE 5:20. COMPLAINT; PROCESS

5:20–1. Complaint

(a) How Made, Contents. The complaint in juvenile delinquency actions shall be captioned "The State of New Jersey in the Interest of _____", shall be made on oath and in the form prescribed by the Administrative Director of Court and shall include:

(1) The name, address and date of birth of the juvenile;

(2) The names and addresses of the juvenile's parents or guardian or custodian;

(3) The date, time, place and nature of the conduct alleged as the basis of the complaint; a citation of the law or ordinance allegedly violated by the juvenile, but error in citation shall not be grounds for dismissal if the juvenile has not been misled thereby to the juvenile's prejudice;

(4) The signature of the complainant, who may be any person having knowledge of the facts alleged to constitute delinquency or who is informed of such facts and has reason to believe they are true; and

(5) Where practicable, a statement of the names and addresses of all other persons having knowledge of relevant facts concerning the acts alleged in the complaint, but failure to include this statement shall not be grounds for dismissal of the complaint.

(b) Filing and Service. The complaint shall be filed with the clerk of the court who shall promptly refer it to court intake services and the county prosecutor. A copy of the complaint shall be served with the summons or, whenever practicable, at the time of the execution of the warrant.

(c) Court Intake Services Referral. Every complaint alleging juvenile delinquency shall be reviewed by court intake services in the manner provided by law for recommendation as to whether the complaint should be dismissed, diverted or referred for further court action. Where the complaint alleges conduct which, if committed by an adult, would constitute a crime as defined by N.J.S. 2C:1–4a or a repetitive disorderly persons offense as defined by N.J.S. 2A:4A–22(h), the matter shall not be diverted by the court unless the prosecutor consents thereto.

(d) Amendment. The court may amend the complaint to correct an error in form or the description of the offense intended to be charged or to charge a lesser included offense provided that the amendment does not charge another or different offense from that alleged and the defendant will not be prejudiced thereby in the defense on the merits.

(e) Consolidation. If two or more complaints are filed alleging separate acts constituting delinquency, hearing of the several complaints may be consolidated and a single disposition made of the combined causes.

Note: Source—R. (1969) 5:8–1(a), (b), (c), and (d); R. (1969) 5:9–3(a) and (b). Adopted December 20, 1983, to be effective December 31, 1983; paragraphs (a)(3) and (d) amended July 13, 1994 to be effective September 1, 1994.

5:20–2. Summons

(a) Issuance. If it appears from the complaint that there is probable cause to believe that a juvenile is delinquent and after review of the complaint by the court intake service it recommends court action, a summons shall issue to the juvenile and the juvenile's parents, guardians or custodian.

(b) Form. The summons shall be signed by the judge, or by the clerk of the court if authorized by the judge and shall have affixed thereto a copy of the complaint. It shall set forth the name of the juvenile and the names of the parents, guardian, or custodian of the juvenile; shall command the juvenile and the juvenile's parents, guardian, or custodian to appear before the court at a stated time and place; shall advise that the juvenile and the juvenile's parents, guardian, or custodian have the right to be represented by counsel at every stage of the proceeding and that if unable to afford counsel, upon application to the court counsel will be assigned if in the opinion of the court the proceedings may result in the institutional commitment of the juvenile or other consequences of magnitude; and shall advise the juvenile and the juvenile's parents that all witnesses reasonably necessary for the defense of the juvenile will be subpoenaed by the court on request. In lieu of summons the judge may issue a warrant if the nature of the case requires the immediate custody of the juvenile. The warrant shall be substantially in the same form as the summons except that it shall command that the person or persons named therein be taken into custody and placed in detention or shelter care, or brought before the court.

(c) Service. The summons shall be served in the manner provided by R. 4:4–4 upon the juvenile and the juvenile's parents or either of them, or the juvenile's guardian or custodian, or by mailing it to their last known address.

Note: Source—R. (1969) 5:8–4(a)(b)(c); 5:8–5(a)(b). Adopted December 20, 1983, to be effective December 31, 1983; paragraph (b) amended November 7, 1988 to be effective January 2, 1989; paragraphs (a), (b) and (c) amended July 13, 1994 to be effective September 1, 1994.

5:20–3. Warrant

(a) When Issued. In lieu of summons the judge may issue a warrant if the nature of the case requires the immediate custody of the juvenile. A warrant may also issue if any person or persons fail to appear as required by summons.

(b) Execution. The warrant shall be executed in accordance with R. 3:3–3(c), and upon execution the procedures of R. 5:21, to the extent applicable, shall govern.

Note: Source—R. (1969) 5:8–5(a) and (c). Adopted December 20, 1983, to be effective December 31, 1983.

5:20–4. Necessary Parties

The parents, guardians or other person having custody, control and supervision over the juvenile shall be necessary parties to every proceeding in all juvenile delinquency actions.

Note: Source—R. (1969) 5:8–8. Adopted December 20, 1983, to be effective December 31, 1983.

RULE 5:21. CUSTODY, PRETRIAL DETENTION

5:21–1. Taking Into Custody, Initial Procedure

A law enforcement officer may take into custody without process a juvenile who the officer has probable cause to believe is delinquent as defined by N.J.S. 2A:4A–23. When a juvenile has been taken into custody for delinquency, a complaint, if not already filed, shall immediately be filed as provided by R. 5:20–1. The taking of a juvenile into custody shall not be construed as an arrest but shall be deemed a measure to protect the health, morals and well-being of the juvenile, and the person taking the juvenile into custody shall immediately notify the juvenile's parents, guardian or other custodian.

Note: Source—R. (1969) 5:8–2(a) (first and second sentence), (e). Adopted December 20, 1983, to be effective December 31, 1983; amended July 13, 1994 to be effective September 1, 1994.

5:21–2. Release

(a) Pre-hearing Release. Whenever it will not adversely affect the health, safety or welfare of a juvenile, the juvenile shall be released pending disposition to an authorized person or agency upon written assurance that such person or agency shall assume responsibility for the juvenile subject to conditions which may be imposed by the court and shall bring the juvenile before the court at all scheduled hearings or as otherwise ordered. In any event no juvenile shall be placed in detention without the permission of a judge or the court intake service.

(b) Judicial Release. At any time between the filing of the complaint and the disposition, the judge may order the release of any juvenile from detention or shelter care facility and fix the terms of such release pursuant to N.J.S. 2A:4A–34(d).

(c) Release on Own Recognizance. A law enforcement officer may and the judge or court intake officer shall, where appropriate, release the juvenile on his or her own recognizance on terms and conditions prescribed if: (a) The nature of the offense charged is such that the juvenile's release would not constitute a danger to the community; (b) There is no parent, guardian or other appropriate adult custodian to whom the juvenile could be released and all reasonable measures have been exhausted by either police or court personnel to locate and contact any such person; (c) The juvenile is at least 14 years of age; (d) The identity and address of the juvenile are verified; and (e) Reasonable certainty exists on the part of the releasing authority that upon release, the juvenile will return to school or home safely and will appear at the hearing.

Note: Source—R. (1969) 5:8–2(a) and (d) (third and fourth sentence), R. (1969) 5:8–6(b). Adopted December 20, 1983, to be effective December 31, 1983; paragraph (c) amended June 29, 1990 to be effective September 4, 1990; paragraph (c) amended July 13, 1994 to be effective September 1, 1994.

5:21–3. Detention Hearings

(a) Initial Detention Hearing. If the juvenile has not been released pursuant to R. 5:21–2, an initial hearing to determine whether pretrial detention is required pursuant to the standards of R. 5:21–5 shall be held no later than the morning following the juvenile's placement in custody, including holidays and weekends. Said hearing shall be on oral or written notice to the juvenile and the juvenile's parents or guardian, all of whom shall be present at the hearing. The hearing, however, shall not be adjourned if such notice or process fails to produce the attendance of the parents or guardian. If a complaint has not been filed by the time the initial hearing is held, the juvenile shall be immediately released from custody. If the juvenile is not represented by counsel at the initial hearing and if the court determines that the juvenile should be detained, a second detention hearing shall be held within two court days after the initial hearing at which the juvenile shall be represented by assigned or retained counsel or by the Public Defender as the circumstances require.

(b) Probable Cause Hearing. If the juvenile is detained following the initial detention hearing, the court shall conduct a probable cause hearing within two court days after the initial hearing. Where a second detention hearing is required by paragraph (a), it shall be held with the probable cause hearing. If the prosecutor has filed a motion seeking waiver of jurisdiction pursuant to Rule 5:22-2 or indicates an intention to file such a motion, or the court determines based on the circumstances that such a motion is likely, the court shall permit the parties to present evidence regarding the issues of age of the juvenile and other standards for referral which may be addressed at the time of the probable cause hearing. If the court determines that there is no probable cause to believe that the juvenile has committed the conduct alleged in the complaint, the juvenile shall be forthwith released. If probable cause is found, detention review hearings shall be conducted as provided in paragraph (c).

(c) Detention Review Hearing. If the court determines that the juvenile should continue to be detained, a detention review hearing shall be held within 14 court days after the prior detention hearing. If detention is again continued, review hearings shall be held thereafter at intervals not to exceed 21 court days. The juvenile shall be represented by counsel at all such hearings.

(d) Findings. Whenever the court places a juvenile in detention, it shall state the reasons therefor on the record, giving consideration to the following factors among others:

(1) The nature and circumstances of the offense charged;

(2) The age of the juvenile;

(3) The juvenile's ties to the community;

(4) The juvenile's record of prior adjudications, if any; and

(5) The juvenile's record of appearance or non-appearance at previous court proceedings.

(e) Credit for Time Served. A juvenile shall receive credit on the term of a custodial sentence for any time served in detention or court-ordered shelter care between apprehension and disposition.

Note: Source—R. (1969) 5:8-2(c) and (d); R. (1969) 5:8-6(d). Adopted December 20, 1983, to be effective December 31, 1983; paragraph (e) adopted November 1, 1985 to be effective January 2, 1986; paragraph (b) amended July 14, 1992 to be effective September 1, 1992; paragraphs (a) and (e) amended July 13, 1994 to be effective September 1, 1994.

5:21-4. Place of Detention or Shelter Care

No juvenile shall be placed in detention or shelter care in any place other than that specified by the State Juvenile Justice Commission or Department of Children and Families as provided by law. No juvenile shall be detained or placed in any prison, jail, lockup, or police station. If however, no other facility is reasonably available and if a brief holding is necessary to allow the release of the juvenile to the juvenile's parent, or guardian, or other suitable person, or approved facility, a juvenile may be held in a police station in a place other than one designed for the detention of prisoners and apart from any adult charged with or convicted of crime. Nor shall a juvenile be placed in a detention facility which has reached its maximum population capacity as determined by the Juvenile Justice Commission.

Note: Source—R. (1969) 5:8-6(a). Adopted December 20, 1983, to be effective December 31, 1983; amended July 13, 1994 to be effective September 1, 1994; amended July 10, 1998 to be effective September 1, 1998; amended July 16, 2009 to be effective September 1, 2009.

5:21-5. Standards for Detention

(a) Juveniles Over the Age of 11. The court shall only order pretrial detention of a juvenile over the age of 11 if it finds, pursuant to subparagraphs (1) and (2) hereof, either that detention is necessary to secure the presence of the juvenile at the next hearing or that the physical safety of persons or property of the community would be seriously threatened if a juvenile, charged with an offense as hereafter set forth, were not detained.

(1) The necessity of detention to secure the presence of a juvenile at the next hearing may be demonstrated by the juvenile's record of recent willful failure to appear at juvenile court proceedings or the juvenile's unauthorized departure from a placement made by the court or the court intake service.

(2) For purposes of this rule a juvenile may be detained to protect the physical safety of persons or property only if the juvenile is charged with an offense which, if committed by an adult, would constitute a crime. If the charge would constitute a repetitive disorderly persons offense, the juveniles shall be detained only if the judge determines that there is a likelihood that upon adjudication of delinquency a custodial disposition will be ordered.

(3) When the criteria for detention are met and the juvenile is charged with an offense which, if committed by an adult, would constitute a disorderly persons or petty disorderly persons offense, the juvenile may be placed in detention temporarily. Police and court intake personnel shall make all reasonable efforts to locate a parent or guardian to accept custody of the juvenile prior to requesting or approving the juvenile's placement in detention. If, after the initial detention hearing, continued detention is necessary, the juvenile shall not be detained in a secure facility but shall be transferred to a shelter or other non-secure placement.

(b) Juvenile Not Over the Age of 11. The court may order pretrial detention of a juvenile not over the age of 11 only if the juvenile is charged with an offense which, if committed by an adult, would constitute a crime of the first or second degree or arson and provided further that the juvenile otherwise meets either of the detention criteria of paragraph (a) of this rule.

Note: Source—R. (1969) 5:8–6(e). Adopted December 20, 1983, to be effective December 31, 1983; paragraphs (a)(1), (a)(2), and (b) amended July 13, 1994 to be effective September 1, 1994; paragraphs (a)(1) and (a)(2) amended and paragraph (a)(3) adopted July 10, 1998 to be effective September 1, 1998.

5:21–6. Post-complaint Detention

At any time after the filing of a complaint the court may, after a detention or shelter care hearing and pursuant to these rules, direct that a juvenile be placed in an appropriate facility.

Note: Source—R. (1969) 5:8–6(c). Adopted December 20, 1983, to be effective December 31, 1983.

5:21–7. Adjudicatory Hearing

If a juvenile has been detained the adjudicatory hearing shall be held within 30 days after the date of initial detention. If the adjudicatory hearing is not held within said time, the court shall, within 72 hours after a motion by the juvenile so requesting, fix a date certain for the adjudicatory hearing unless an extension is granted by the court for good cause shown. Written notice of any application for a postponement shall be furnished the juvenile's counsel, who shall have a right to be heard on the application.

Note: Source—new. Adopted December 20, 1983, to be effective December 31, 1983.

5:21–8. Custody and Detention of Material Witness

The judge of the Family Part shall be notified when any juvenile under 18 years of age has been taken into custody or detained as a material witness. The custody and conditions of detention of such juvenile material witness, pending the arraignment and the trial of the adult involved, shall be determined by the court upon notice to the prosecutor and other proper parties. If a juvenile is held in detention as a material witness, the trial for which the juvenile is held shall be brought on with all possible dispatch. The court may, in a proper case, dismiss a complaint for juvenile delinquency and designate the juvenile a material witness. Insofar as applicable, the provisions of R. 5:21 apply to the detention of a juvenile as a material witness.

Note: Source—R. (1969) 5:8–7. Adopted December 20, 1983, to be effective December 31, 1983; amended July 13, 1994 to be effective September 1, 1994.

RULE 5:21A. JUVENILE PLEA FORM

A juvenile's plea of guilty is subject to the requirements of Rule 3:9–2. Before accepting a plea of guilty, the court may require a juvenile to complete, insofar as applicable, and sign the appropriate plea form prescribed by the Administrative Director of the Courts. The form shall then be filed with the Family Division Manager. The use of this form does not eliminate the obligation of the court to determine by inquiry of defendant and others, in the court's discretion, that a factual basis exists for the plea and that the plea is being made voluntarily, not as the result of any threats or of any promises or inducements not disclosed on the record, and with an understanding of the nature of the charge and the consequences of the plea.

Note: Adopted July 10, 1998 to be effective September 1, 1998.

RULE 5:22. REFERRAL TO OTHER COURTS

5:22–1. Referral at Election of Juvenile

Any competent juvenile 14 years of age or older charged with delinquency may elect to have the action transferred to the appropriate court and prosecuting authority having jurisdiction. Any competent juvenile under 14 years of age charged with an offense which if committed by an adult would constitute murder as defined by N.J.S. 2C:11–3 may elect to have the case transferred to the appropriate court and prosecuting authority. The judge shall inform the juvenile of the right to elect such referral at the initial detention or probable cause hearing. The judge shall determine that such election, if requested, has been made knowingly, willingly, voluntarily and after consultation with counsel.

Note: Source—R. (1969) 5:9–5(a). Adopted December 20, 1983, to be effective December 31, 1983.

5:22–2. Referral Without Juvenile's Consent

(a) Motion for Referral. A motion seeking waiver of jurisdiction by the Family Part shall be filed by the prosecutor within 30 days after the receipt of the complaint, which time shall not be extended except for good cause shown.

(b) Probable Cause; Evidence. At the referral hearing, the court shall receive the evidence offered by the State and by the juvenile, limited to the issue of probable cause. The court also shall permit cross-examination of any witnesses.

(c) Standards for Referral. The court shall waive jurisdiction of a juvenile delinquency action without the juvenile's consent and shall refer the action to the appropriate court and prosecuting authority having jurisdiction under the following circumstances:

(1) *Judicial Discretion for Juveniles Age 14 or Older and Charged with a Chart 2 Offense.* The juvenile must have been 14 years of age or older at the time of the alleged delinquent act and there must be probable cause to believe that he or she committed a delinquent act which if committed by an adult would constitute:

(A) a crime committed at a time when the juvenile had previously been adjudicated delinquent, or convicted of:

   1. criminal homicide, other than death by auto; or

   2. strict liability for drug-induced deaths (N.J.S.A. 2C:35–9); or

   3. first degree robbery; or

   4. carjacking; or

   5. aggravated sexual assault; or

   6. sexual assault; or

   7. second degree aggravated assault; or

   8. kidnapping; or

   9. aggravated arson; or

(B) crime committed at a time when the juvenile had previously been sentenced to and confined in an adult penal institution; or

(C) an offense against a person committed in an aggressive, violent, and willful manner, other than a Chart 1 offense enumerated in N.J.S.A. 2A:4A–26a(2)(a); or the unlawful possession of a firearm, destructive device or other prohibited weapon; or arson; or death by auto if the juvenile was operating the vehicle under the influence of an intoxicating liquor, narcotic, hallucinogenic, or habit-producing drug; or an attempt or conspiracy to commit any of these crimes; or

(D) a violation of N.J.S.A. 2C:35–3 (Leader of a Narcotics Trafficking Network), N.J.S.A. 2C:35–4 (Maintaining and Operating a CDS Production Facility), N.J.S.A. 2C:35–5 (Manufacturing, Distributing or Dispensing Narcotics), or an attempt or conspiracy to commit any of these crimes, other than where the violation, attempt or conspiracy involves the distribution for pecuniary gain of any controlled dangerous substance or controlled substance analog while on any school property or within 1000 feet of such school property; or

(E) a crime or crimes that are part of a continuing criminal activity in concert with two or more persons, when the circumstances show that the juvenile has knowingly devoted himself or herself to criminal activity as a source of livelihood; or

(F) theft of an automobile.

On a finding of probable cause for any of the offenses enumerated above, the burden is on the prosecution to show that the nature and circumstances of the charge or the juvenile's prior record are sufficiently serious that the interests of the public require waiver. Waiver shall not be granted, however, if the juvenile can show that the probability of his or her rehabilitation prior to reaching the age of 19 by use of the procedures, services, and facilities available to the court substantially outweighs the reasons for waiver.

(2) *Judicial Discretion for Juveniles Age 14 or 15 and Charged with a Chart 1 Offense or with Certain Drug Offenses Committed Within a School Zone.* The juvenile must have been 14 or 15 years old at the time of the alleged delinquent act and there must be probable cause to believe that he or she committed a delinquent act that if committed by an adult would constitute:

(A) criminal homicide, other than death by auto; or strict liability for drug-induced deaths; or first degree robbery; or carjacking; or aggravated sexual assault; or sexual assault; or second degree aggravated assault; or kidnapping; or aggravated arson; or an attempt or conspiracy to commit any of these crimes; or

(B) possession of a firearm with a purpose to use it unlawfully against the person of another under subsection (a) of N.J.S.A. 2C:39–4, or possession of a firearm while committing or attempting to commit, including the immediate flight therefrom, aggravated assault, aggravated criminal sexual contact, burglary or escape; or

(C) a violation of N.J.S.A. 2C:35–3 (Leader of a Narcotics Trafficking Network), N.J.S.A. 2C:35–4 (Maintaining and Operating a CDS Production Facility), N.J.S.A. 2C:35–5 (Manufacturing, Distributing or Dispensing Narcotics), or an attempt or conspiracy to commit any of these crimes; and which violation, attempt or conspiracy involves the distribution for pecuniary gain of any controlled dangerous substance or controlled substance analog while on any school property or within 1000 feet of such school property; or

(D) computer activity that would be a crime of the first or second degree pursuant to section 4 or section 10 of P.L.1984, c.184 (N.J.S.A. 2C:20–25 or 2C:20–31).

On a finding of probable cause for any of these enumerated offenses, there is a rebuttable presumption that waiver will occur. The juvenile can rebut this presumption only by demonstrating that the probability of his or her rehabilitation prior to reaching the age of 19 by use of the procedures, services or facilities available to the court substantially outweighs the reasons for waiver.

(3) *Prosecutorial Discretion for Juveniles Age 16 or Older and Charged with a Chart 1 Offense or Certain Other Enumerated Offenses.* The juvenile must have been 16 years of age or older at the time of the alleged delinquent act and there must be probable cause to believe that he or she committed a delinquent act that if committed by an adult would constitute:

(A) criminal homicide, other than death by auto; or strict liability for drug-induced deaths; or first degree robbery; or carjacking; or aggravated sexual assault; or sexual assault; or second degree aggravated assault; or kidnapping; or aggravated arson; or

(B) possession of a firearm with a purpose to use it unlawfully against the person of another under subsection (a) of N.J.S.A. 2C:39–4, or possession of a firearm while committing or attempting to commit, including the immediate flight therefrom, aggravated assault, aggravated criminal sexual contact, burglary or escape; or

(C) a violation of N.J.S.A. 2C:35–3 (Leader of a Narcotics Trafficking Network), N.J.S.A. 2C:35–4 (Maintaining and Operating a CDS Production Facility), or N.J.S.A. 2C:39–4.1 (Weapons Possession While Committing Certain CDS Offenses); or

(D) computer activity that would be a crime of the first or second degree pursuant to section 4 or section 10 of P.L.1984, c.184 (N.J.S.A. 2C:20–25 or C.2C:20–31).

On a finding of probable cause for any of these enumerated offenses, no additional showing is required for waiver to occur. Jurisdiction of the case shall be transferred immediately.

(4) *Judicial Discretion for Juveniles Age 16 or 17 and Charged with Certain Drug Offenses Committed Within a School Zone.* The juvenile must have been 16 years of age or older at the time of the alleged delinquent act and there must be probable cause to believe that he or she committed a delinquent act that if committed by an adult would constitute:

(A) a violation of N.J.S.A. 2C:35–5 (Manufacturing, Distributing or Dispensing Narcotics), or an attempt or conspiracy to commit this crime; and which violation, attempt or conspiracy involves the distribution for pecuniary gain of any controlled dangerous substance or controlled substance analog while on school property or within 1000 feet of such school property.

On a finding of probable cause for any such offense, there is a rebuttable presumption that waiver will occur. The juvenile can rebut this presumption only by demonstrating that the probability of his or her rehabilitation prior to reaching the age of 19 by use of the procedures, services and facilities available to the court substantially outweighs the reasons for waiver.

(d) Order of Reference. An order referring a case shall incorporate therein not only the alleged act or acts upon which the referral is based but all other delinquent acts charged against the juvenile arising out of or related to the same transaction.

(e) Admissibility of Testimony Given at Referral Hearing. No testimony of a juvenile at a hearing to determine referral by this rule shall be admissible for any purpose in any subsequent hearing to determine delinquency or guilt of any offense.

Note: Source—R. (1969) 5:9–5(b), (c). Adopted December 20, 1983, to be effective December 31, 1983; paragraph (b)(2)(E) amended July 14, 1992 to be effective September 1, 1992; paragraphs (a), (b)(2)(F) and (b)(4) amended July 13, 1994 to be effective September 1, 1994; paragraphs (a) and (b)(2)(D), (E) and (F) amended, paragraph (b)(2)(G) adopted June 28, 1996 to be effective September 1, 1996; paragraphs (b) and (b)(1) amended, former paragraphs (b)(2), (b)(3), and (b)(4) deleted, new paragraphs (b)(2), (b)(3), and (b)(4) added July 10, 2002 to be effective September 3, 2002; paragraphs (b)(2)(B) and (b)(2)(C) amended, new paragraph (b)(2)(D) adopted, paragraph (b)(3) caption amended, paragraphs (b)(3)(B) and (b)(3)(C) amended, new paragraph (b)(3)(D) adopted July 28, 2004 to be effective September 1, 2004; new paragraph (b) added, and former paragraphs (b), (c), (d) redesignated as paragraphs (c), (d), (e) June 15, 2007 to be effective September 1, 2007.

5:22–3. Detention Hearing After Referral

When a case is referred to another court as provided by R. 5:22–1 or R. 5:22–2, the court waiving jurisdiction shall, on hearing, determine pursuant to the criteria set forth in N.J.S. 2A:4A–36(a) whether the juvenile, if in custody pending trial, shall be confined in an adult or juvenile detention facility. In no case shall a juvenile be remanded to an adult detention facility prior to the hearing provided for herein.

Note: Source—R. (1969) 5:9–5(d). Adopted December 20, 1983, to be effective December 31, 1983; caption and text amended November 5, 1986 to be effective January 1, 1987.

5:22–4. Proceedings After Transfer

Whenever a case is referred to another court as provided by R. 5:22–1 or R. 5:22–2, the action shall proceed in the same manner as if it has been instituted in that court in the first instance.

Note: Source—R. (1969) 5:9–5(e). Adopted December 20, 1983, to be effective December 31, 1983.

RULE 5:23. TRANSFER OF CAUSES FROM OTHER COURTS

5:23–1. Transfer Generally

Except as herein otherwise provided, if during the pendency of any matter in any other court in which a person is charged with a crime, offense or violation, it is discovered that such person was a juvenile at the time of the commission of the conduct charged, such court shall immediately transfer the action to the Family Part. The action shall not, however, be transferred if it involves any violation by a juvenile of Title 39 of the Revised Statutes (motor vehicles) enumerated by N.J.S. 2A:4A–23.

Note: Source—R. (1969) 5:9–6 (first sentence). Adopted December 20, 1983, to be effective December 31, 1983; amended January 10, 1984, to be effective immediately.

5:23–2. Proceedings After Transfer

Upon transfer of an action to the Family Part, a new complaint shall be filed therein and the matter shall thereafter proceed as if the action had been instituted in that court.

Note: Source—R. (1969) 5:9–6 (second sentence). Adopted December 20, 1983, to be effective December 31, 1983.

RULE 5:24. DISPOSITION

5:24–1. Disposition Hearing

(a) Time for Hearing: Detention Cases. If a juvenile is in a detention center or shelter care facility when adjudicated delinquent, the disposition hearing shall be conducted, on notice to the juvenile and all other proper parties, within 30 days after the adjudication. If, after 30 days, no order of disposition has been entered, the court shall, upon motion of the juvenile, fix a date certain for a dispositional hearing which shall be within 10 days of the motion unless an extension is granted by the court for good cause shown.

(b) Time for Hearing: Non-detention Cases. If the juvenile is not in a detention center or shelter care facility when adjudicated delinquent, the disposition hearing shall be conducted, on notice to the juvenile and all other proper parties, within 60 days after the adjudication, which time may be extended by the court on good cause shown.

Note: Source—new. Adopted December 20, 1983, to be effective December 31, 1983.

5:24–2. Predisposition Evaluation

(a) Before disposition of any matter but only after an adjudication of delinquency or a determination by the court that the evidence is sufficient to support such an adjudication, the court may refer the juvenile to an appropriate individual, agency or institution on such terms as may be appropriate for examination and evaluation. Before the juvenile may be referred to any institution as an in-patient for such purpose, the court must first provide for the representation of the juvenile, the juvenile's parents, guardian or custodians by counsel as the circumstances require. The court may also confer and consult with such individuals and agencies as may be appropriate to the juvenile's situation and may convene a predisposition conference to discuss and recommend a disposition. Any such reports shall be filed with the court no later than five court days before the dispositional hearing date.

(b) Any predispositional reports filed with the court shall be made available to counsel or parties appearing pro se no later than three court days before the dispositional hearing date, or as determined by the court.

Note: Source—R. (1969) 5:9–1(d); R. (1969) 5:9–7; R. (1969) 5:9–8. Adopted December 20, 1983, to be effective December 31, 1983; former rule redesignated paragraph (a) and paragraph (b) adopted November 5, 1986 to be effective January 1, 1987; paragraph (a) amended July 13, 1994 to be effective September 1, 1994; paragraph (a) amended June 15, 2007 to be effective September 1, 2007.

5:24–3. Manner of Disposition

If the evidence supports the charge made in the complaint beyond a reasonable doubt, the court may make any custodial or non-custodial disposition on such terms and conditions as it may impose in accordance with the provisions of N.J.S. 2A:4A–43 and 2A:4A–44.

Note: Source—R. (1969) 5:9–9. Adopted December 20, 1983, to be effective December 31, 1983.

5:24–4. Order of Disposition

(a) Filing of Order. An order shall be filed in every case indicating the disposition thereof.

(b) Order of Probation or Commitment. If a juvenile is placed on probation or is committed, the order of the court shall have attached thereto a memorandum containing such information as may assist the receiving agency or institution in the treatment of the juvenile. Before a juvenile is committed to a correctional institution a pre-disposition investigation and report or other functional equivalent (such as a Juvenile Intensive Supervision Program (JISP) report or a Violation of Probation summary) shall be made and considered by the court. If the court commits a juvenile to a correctional institution and the maximum authorized term is less than three years the commitment order shall state what the degree of the offense and the sentence maximum would have been had the juvenile committed the offense as an adult.

(c) Expense of Commitment Proceedings and Board. If a juvenile is committed to any institution or referred to the State Diagnostic Center, the judge shall make inquiry as to the ability of the parent or guardian to pay the expense of commitment proceedings and the board of the juvenile, and the judge shall endorse on the order of commitment a statement of the findings in that regard.

Note: Source—R. (1969) 5:9–10(a), (b), (c). Adopted December 20, 1983, to be effective December 31, 1983; paragraph (c) amended July 13, 1994 to be effective September 1, 1994; paragraph (b) amended July 28, 2004 to be effective September 1, 2004.

5:24–5. Retention of Jurisdiction

(a) Mandatory Retention of Jurisdiction. The court shall retain jurisdiction over every action in which it has entered an order of disposition for the duration of the dispositional terms and conditions. If the court finds at any time during the duration of the disposition, on notice and hearing, that the conditions of the order of disposition have been violated, it may substitute any other disposition which it might originally have made.

If the disposition was an order of commitment or incarceration the court may, during the duration of that disposition, substitute any other disposition otherwise available to it.

(b) Discretionary Retention of Jurisdiction. Where retention of jurisdiction is not mandatory pursuant to paragraph (a) hereof, the order of disposition may provide for the retention of the court's jurisdiction over a juvenile for a term not exceeding that specified therein.

Note: Source—R. (1969) 5:9–10(d). Adopted December 20, 1983, to be effective December 31, 1983.

5:24–6. Modification of Order of Disposition: Post-disposition Relief

In addition to the modification of order of disposition provided for by R. 5:24–5, the court may correct, change or modify an order of disposition at any time pursuant to law and may entertain an application for post-disposition relief, which shall be made and determined in accordance with the provisions of R. 3:22, insofar as applicable.

Note: Source—R. (1969) 5:9–10(e). Adopted December 20, 1983, to be effective December 31, 1983.

RULE 5:25. JUVENILE CONFERENCE COMMITTEES; REFEREES

5:25–1. Juvenile Conference Committees

(a) Appointment; Jurisdiction. The court may appoint one or more Juvenile Conference Committees for the county. If only one committee is appointed for the entire county, it shall sit at such times and places in the county as it shall determine with a view, wherever feasible, to holding hearings in or near the municipality where the juvenile involved resides. If more than one committee is appointed, each committee shall serve a single municipality or 2 or more adjacent municipalities where feasible and all municipalities so served shall have at least one representative on such committee.

(b) Membership. A committee shall consist of not less than 6 nor more than 9 members. Members of a committee, to the maximum feasible extent, shall represent the various socio-economic, racial and ethnic groups in the community or communities to be served by it. The term of each member appointed to the committee shall be for 3 years, and shall terminate on December 31, provided, however, that appointments shall be made so that the terms of one-third of the members of a committee expire each year. Vacancies shall be filled for the unexpired term.

(c) Duties. The committee shall serve as an arm of the court in hearing and deciding such matters involving alleged juvenile offenders as are specifically referred to it by the court. Its function shall be to set limits upon the behavior of the juvenile offenders before it by expressing, through its disposition of each case, the

community disapproval of the behavior with which it deals. It shall be concerned primarily with providing balanced attention to the protection of the community, the imposition of accountability for offenses committed, fostering interaction and dialogue between the offender, victim and community, and the development of competencies to enable the juvenile offender to become a responsible and productive member of the community. In addition, the committee shall be concerned with endeavoring to forestall more serious future misconduct by the juvenile offender before it by obtaining the voluntary cooperation of the juvenile and the juvenile's parents or guardians with its recommendations for disciplinary or corrective action. The committee shall supervise and follow up compliance with its recommendations and keep the court advised thereof.

(d) Appearance; Compliance. No person shall be compelled to appear before, or comply with any recommendations of, a committee. If voluntary appearance or compliance cannot be attained, or if any person interested in a committee proceeding is not satisfied therewith, the matter shall be referred by the committee to the court.

(e) Confidentiality. All matters coming before a committee shall be held in strict confidence and under no circumstances made public. Every committee member shall be duly sworn by the judge to observe the confidential nature of committee proceedings. A committee member, however, when authorized by the entire committee, may publicize in general terms the duties of the committee, the kinds and numbers of cases it hears (without in any way revealing the names or identities of persons involved or the action taken in any specific case), or any community conditions which the committee's work indicates may require correction to prevent future delinquency.

Note: Source—R. (1969) 5:10–2. Adopted December 20, 1983, to be effective December 31, 1983; paragraph (c) amended July 13, 1994 to be effective September 1, 1994; paragraph (c) amended July 12, 2002 to be effective September 3, 2002.

5:25–2. Referees

The judge of the Family Part may with the approval of the Chief Justice appoint a suitable person to act as referee. The recommendations of the referee shall be without effect unless approved by the court and incorporated in an appropriate order or judgment of the court.

Note: Source—R. (1969) 5:10–3. Adopted December 20, 1983, to be effective December 31, 1983.

5:25–3. Child Support Hearing Officers

(a) Appointment. There shall be established within the Family Part of the Chancery Division an Office of the Child Support Hearing Officer. The Office of the Child Support Hearing Officer shall consist of a Chief Child Support Hearing Officer, and as many other Child Support Hearing Officers as may be determined appropriate by the Supreme Court. The Chief Child Support Hearing Officer and other Child Support Hearing Officers shall be appointed by the Chief Justice and shall be under the direct supervision of the Family Part Presiding Judge of the county in which the Child Support Hearing Officer is assigned. The administrative supervision of the Child Support Hearing Officers shall be vested in the Administrative Director of the Courts.

(b) Jurisdiction. The Child Support Hearing Officer shall hear and make recommendations that the court enter orders based thereon in all Title IV–D, Federal Social Security Act, cases concerning:

(1) Establishment of Paternity or the Parent/Child relationship only when the matter is uncontested. When the issue of paternity is contested, the Child Support Hearing Officer shall refer the paternity issue to the court.

(2) Establishment of the obligation and amount of child support.

(3) Establishment of any other financial obligation regarding the care and maintenance of children as well as an obligation to provide medical coverage.

(4) Modification of the obligation of child support.

(5) Enforcement of the obligation of child support or any other support order.

(6) The establishment, modification and enforcement of support pursuant to N.J.S.A. 2A:4–30.65 to–30.123, the Uniform Interstate Family Support Act.

(7) If any establishment case involves a complex issue requiring judicial resolution, the Child Support Hearing Officer shall recommend a temporary order establishing the obligation of child support pending referral of the matter to the court.

(8) Advanced written and oral notice shall be given to the parties that their case will be heard by a Child Support Hearing Officer, and they may object to the recommendation of the Child Support Hearing Officer, which will result in an immediate hearing before a Superior Court Judge pursuant to Rule 5:25–3(d)(2).

(c) Duties, Powers, and Responsibilities. The Child Support Hearing Officer shall be responsible to the Presiding Judge in the establishment, modification, and enforcement of all Title IV–D child-support actions. Such Child Support Hearing Officers shall serve at the pleasure of the Chief Justice and his/her powers and duties shall be prescribed in the order appointing him/her or in the Rules of Procedure of the Family Part. Such Child Support Hearing Officers shall:

(1) regulate all proceedings before him/her;

(2) take testimony and establish a record;

(3) do all acts and take all measures necessary or proper for the efficient performance of his/her duties;

(4) recommend that the court order the production before him/her of books, papers, vouchers, documents, and writings;

(5) rule upon the admissibility of evidence;

(6) recommend the issuance of summonses or subpoenas for the appearance of parties or witnesses, administer oaths, examine parties and witnesses under oath;

(7) accept voluntary acknowledgment of support liability and stipulations or agreements setting the amount of child support to be paid and/or admitting paternity;

(8) evaluate evidence and make recommendations as to the establishment and enforcement of child-support orders;

(9) recommend entry of default judgments in appropriate cases;

(10) in appropriate cases and with the immediate review by the court, make written findings, and based thereon may:

(A) recommend that the court adjudicate that a person has failed to comply with an order in violation of litigant's rights, and recommend incarceration for failure to comply with an order of the court that provided for the payment of support or the performance of any other act;

(B) request that a witness or party be brought directly before the court for a judicial hearing;

(11) recommend that the court issue a warrant upon the failure of a party or a witness to appear after having been properly served, and recommend a release amount to satisfy full arrears;

(12) recommend that the court order a party to participate in blood or genetic tests for the purpose of establishing paternity.

(d) Review by Presiding Judge or Designee; Appeal; Time; Record.

(1) The Presiding Judge of the Family Part or a Judge designated by the Presiding Judge shall immediately review all recommendations of a Child Support Hearing Officer. Appropriate recommendations shall be signed and ratified by the Judge.

(2) A party not accepting a recommendation entered by the Child Support Hearing Officer shall be entitled to an immediate appeal of the recommendation to the Presiding Judge of the Family Part or a Judge designated by the Presiding Judge who shall conduct a hearing forthwith. The appeal may be made by either party, and shall be heard de novo not on the record below. Failure of a party to request a de novo appeal on the day of the hearing shall require the filing of a motion before further relief can be considered.

(3) Orders of the Family Part entered as a result of a Child Support Hearing Officer's recommendation shall be recognized as a final order of the Superior Court. Copies of the orders shall be provided to the parties or their attorneys. Orders may be appealed to the Appellate Division of the Superior Court within the time and according to the procedures prescribed by the Rules for appeals to the Appellate Division. The time for appeal shall run from the date of the signing of the order by a Judge of the Superior Court.

(e) Service. All rules concerning service of notice and due process rights applicable to the Family Part shall be applicable to the Child Support Hearing Officer hearings.

(f) Standards and Guidelines. The Child Support Hearing Officer shall use any support-setting guidelines that may be approved by the Supreme Court.

(g) Qualifications and Compensation. The qualifications and compensation for the Chief Child Support Hearing Officer and other Child Support Hearing Officers shall be established by the Administrative Director of the Courts, subject to the approval of the Supreme Court.

Note: Source-new. Adopted September 24, 1985 to be effective October 1, 1985; paragraph (c)(12) adopted June 28, 1996 to be effective September 1, 1996; paragraph (b)(6) amended May 25, 1999 to be effective July 1, 1999; paragraphs (c)(10) and (c)(11) amended June 15, 2007 to be effective September 1, 2007; paragraph (d)(2) amended July 16, 2009 to be effective September 1, 2009.

5:25–4. Domestic Violence Hearing Officers

Domestic Violence Hearing Officers may be appointed by the Judiciary to handle and make recommendations in matters under the Prevention of Domestic Violence Act (N.J.S.A. 2C:25–17 et seq.) in accordance with the provisions of that Act, Rule 5:7A ("Domestic Violence: Restraining Orders"), and such other policies and procedures as are applicable.

Note: Adopted July 28, 2004 to be effective September 1, 2004.

PART VII.   RULES GOVERNING PRACTICE IN THE MUNICIPAL COURTS

Research Note

For a comprehensive treatment of practice and procedure under these Rules, see Klock, New Jersey Court Rules Annotated (Practice Series Volumes 1 through 2A) *and Ramsey,* New Jersey Municipal Court Practice (Practice Series Volumes 17 and 17A).

Use Westlaw *to find cases citing a rule.* Westlaw *may also be used to search for specific terms or to update a rule; see the Scope Screens in NJ–RULES and NJ–RULESUPDATES for further information.*

Amendments to these rules are published, as received, in Atlantic Reporter 2d *and* New Jersey Reports *advance sheets.*

Table of Rules

Rule

7:1.	SCOPE.
7:2.	PROCESS.
7:2–1.	Contents of Complaint, Arrest Warrant and Summons.
7:2–2.	Issuance of Arrest Warrant or Summons.
7:2–3.	Arrest Warrant: Execution and Service: Return.
7:2–4.	Summons: Execution and Service; Return.
7:2–5.	Defective Warrant or Summons; Amendment.
7:2–6.	Fax Transmission of Complaint–Warrants.
7:3.	PROCEEDINGS BEFORE THE COMMITTING JUDGE; PRETRIAL RELEASE.
7:3–1.	Procedure After Arrest.
7:3–2.	Hearing on First Appearance; Right to Counsel.
7:4.	BAIL.
7:4–1.	Right to Bail Before Conviction.
7:4–2.	Authority to Set Bail.
7:4–3.	Form and Place of Deposit; Location of Real Estate; Record of Recognizances, Discharge and Forfeiture.
7:4–4.	Justification of Sureties.
7:4–5.	Forfeiture.
7:4–6.	Exoneration.
7:4–7.	Place of Deposit.
7:4–8.	Bail After Conviction.
7:5.	SEARCH WARRANTS; SUPPRESSION.
7:5–1.	Filing.
7:5–2.	Motion to Suppress Evidence.
7:5–3.	Search and Seizure Without a Warrant.
7:6.	ARRAIGNMENT, PLEAS.
7:6–1.	Arraignment.
7:6–2.	Pleas, Plea Agreements.
7:6–3.	Guilty Plea by Mail in Non–Traffic Offenses.
7:7.	PRETRIAL PROCEDURES.
7:7–1.	Pleadings; Objections.
7:7–2.	Motions.
7:7–3.	Notice of Alibi; Failure to Furnish.
7:7–4.	Notice of Defense of Insanity; Evidence of Mental Disease or Defect.
7:7–5.	Pretrial Procedure.
7:7–6.	Depositions.
7:7–7.	Discovery and Inspection.
7:7–8.	Subpoenas.
7:7–9.	Filing Appearance.

Rule

7:7–10.	Joint Representation.
7:8.	TRIAL.
7:8–1.	Mediation of Minor Disputes in Municipal Court Actions.
7:8–2.	Place of Trial; Disqualification.
7:8–3.	Adjournment.
7:8–4.	Trial of Complaints Together.
7:8–5.	Dismissal.
7:8–6.	Transfer to the Chancery Division, Family Part.
7:8–7.	Appearances; Exclusion of the Public.
7:8–8.	Record of Proceedings; Transcripts.
7:8–9.	Procedures on Failure to Appear.
7:8–10.	Waiver of Right to Counsel at Trial.
7:9.	SENTENCE AND JUDGMENT.
7:9–1.	Sentence.
7:9–2.	Judgment.
7:9–3.	Credit for Confinement Pending Sentence.
7:9–4.	Reduction or Change of Sentence.
7:10.	POST–TRIAL PROCEEDINGS.
7:10–1.	New Trial.
7:10–2.	Post–Conviction Relief.
7:11.	SUMMARY PROCEEDINGS FOR COLLECTION OF STATUTORY PENALTIES [DELETED].
7:11–1.	Applicability.
7:11–2.	Complaint;.
7:11–3.	Process.
7:11–4.	Penalties;.
7:11–5.	Judgment;.
7:12.	TRIAL OF TRAFFIC OFFENSES.
7:12–1.	Trial Date; Adjournment.
7:12–2.	Calendar Parts; Sessions.
7:12–3.	Pleas of Not Guilty and Pleas of Guilty by Mail in Certain Traffic or Parking Offenses.
7:12–4.	Violations Bureau; Designation; Functions.
7:13.	APPEALS.
7:13–1.	Appeals.
7:13–2.	Stay.
7:13–3.	Reversal; Remission of Fine and Costs.
7:14.	GENERAL PROVISIONS; ADMINISTRATION.
7:14–1.	Opening Statement.
7:14–2.	Amendment of Process or Pleading.
7:14–3.	Court Calendar; Attorneys.
7:14–4.	Financial Control.

Rule
7:14–5.   Oath of Municipal Court Judge.

APPENDIX TO PART VII.   GUIDELINES FOR OPER-
ATION OF PLEA AGREEMENTS IN THE MU-
NICIPAL COURTS OF NEW JERSEY

GUIDELINE 1.   PURPOSE.

Rule
GUIDELINE 2.   DEFINITIONS.
GUIDELINE 3.   PROSECUTOR'S RESPONSIBILITIES.
GUIDELINE 4.   LIMITATION.

RULE 7:1.   SCOPE

The rules in Part VII govern the practice and procedure in the municipal courts in all matters within their statutory jurisdiction, including disorderly and petty disorderly persons offenses; other non-indictable offenses not within the exclusive jurisdiction of the Superior Court; violations of motor vehicle and traffic, fish and game, and boating laws; proceedings to collect penalties where jurisdiction is granted by statute; violations of county and municipal ordinances; and all other proceedings in which jurisdiction is granted by statute. The rules in Part III govern the practice and procedure in indictable actions, and Rule 5:7A governs the practice and procedure in the issuance of temporary restraining orders pursuant to the Prevention of Domestic Violence Act of 1990.

Note: Source—R. (1969) 7:1.   Adopted October 6, 1997 to be effective February 1, 1998.

RULE 7:2.   PROCESS

7:2–1.   Contents of Complaint, Arrest Warrant and Summons

(a) Complaint: General. The complaint shall be a written statement of the essential facts constituting the offense charged made on a form approved by the Administrative Director of the Courts.   Except as otherwise provided by paragraphs (f) (Traffic Offenses), (g) (Special Form of Complaint and Summons), and (h) (Use of Special Form of Complaint and Summons in Penalty Enforcement Proceedings), the complaining witness shall attest to the facts contained in the complaint by signing a certification or signing an oath before a judge or other person so authorized by N.J.S.A. 2B:12–21.

If the complaining witness is a law enforcement officer, the complaint may be signed by an electronic entry secured by a Personal Identification Number (hereinafter referred to as an electronic signature) on the certification, which shall be equivalent to and have the same force and effect as an original signature.

(b) Acceptance of Complaint. The municipal court administrator or deputy court administrator shall accept for filing every complaint made by any person.

(c) Summons: General. The summons shall be on a Complaint-Summons form (CDR-1) or other form prescribed by the Administrative Director of the Courts and shall be signed by the officer issuing it.   An electronic signature of any law enforcement officer or any other person authorized by law to issue a Complaint-Summons shall be equivalent to and have the same force and effect as an original signature.   The summons shall be directed to the defendant named in the complaint, shall require defendant's appearance at a stated time and place before the court in which the complaint is made, and shall inform defendant that an arrest warrant may be issued for a failure to appear.

(d) Arrest Warrant: General. The arrest warrant shall be made on a Complaint-Warrant form (CDR-2) or other form prescribed by the Administrative Director of the Courts and shall be signed by the judge or, when authorized by the judge, by the municipal court administrator or deputy court administrator after a determination of probable cause.   An electronic signature by the judge, authorized municipal court administrator, or deputy court administrator shall be equivalent to and have the same force and effect as an original signature. The warrant shall contain the defendant's name or, if unknown, any name or description that identifies the defendant with reasonable certainty.   It shall be directed to any officer authorized to execute it and shall order that the defendant be arrested and brought before the court issuing the warrant.   The judicial officer issuing a warrant may specify therein the amount and conditions of bail, consistent with R. 7:4, required for defendant's release.

(e) Arrest Warrant: By Telephone. A judge may issue an arrest warrant upon sworn oral testimony of a law enforcement applicant who is not physically present. Such sworn oral testimony may be communicated by the applicant to the judge by telephone, radio or other means of electronic communication.

The judge shall administer the oath to the applicant. Subsequent to taking the oath, the applicant must identify himself or herself and read verbatim the Complaint-Warrant (CDR-2) and any supplemental affidavit that establishes probable cause for the issuance of an arrest warrant.   If the facts necessary to establish probable cause are contained entirely on the Complaint-Warrant (CDR-2) and/or supplemental affidavit, the judge need not make a contemporaneous written or electronic recordation of the facts in support of probable cause. If the law enforcement applicant provides additional sworn oral testimony in support of probable cause, the judge shall contemporaneously record such sworn oral testimony by means of a tape-recording device or stenographic machine, if such is available; otherwise, adequate longhand notes summarizing the contents of the law enforcement applicant's testimony shall be made by the judge. This sworn testimony shall be deemed to be an affidavit or a supplemental affidavit for the purposes of issuance of an arrest warrant.

An arrest warrant may issue if the judge is satisfied that probable cause exists for issuing the warrant. Upon approval, the judge shall memorialize the date, time, defendant's name, complaint number, the basis for the probable cause determination, and any other specific terms of the authorization. That memorialization shall be either by means of a tape-recording device, stenographic machine or by adequate longhand notes. Thereafter, the judge shall direct the applicant to print his or her name, the date and time of the warrant, followed by the phrase "By Officer ----------------, per telephonic authorization by ----------------" on the Complaint-Warrant (CDR-2) form. Within 48 hours, the applicant shall deliver to the judge, either in person or via facsimile transmission, the signed Complaint-Warrant (CDR-2) and supporting affidavit. The judge shall verify the accuracy of these documents by affixing his or her signature to the Complaint-Warrant (CDR-2).

(f) Traffic Offenses

(1) *Form of Complaint and Process.* The Administrative Director of the Courts shall prescribe the form of Uniform Traffic Ticket to serve as the complaint, summons or other process to be used for all parking and other traffic offenses. On a complaint and summons for a parking or other non-moving traffic offense, the defendant need not be named. It shall be sufficient to set forth the license plate number of the vehicle, and its owner or operator shall be charged with the violation.

(2) *Issuance.* The complaint may be made and signed by any person, but the summons shall be signed and issued only by a law enforcement officer or other person authorized by law to issue a Complaint-Summons, the municipal court judge, municipal court administrator or deputy court administrator of the court having territorial jurisdiction. An electronic signature of any law enforcement officer or other person authorized by law to issue a Complaint-Summons shall be equivalent to and have the same force and effect as an original signature.

(3) *Records and Reports.* Each court shall be responsible for all Uniform Traffic Tickets printed and distributed to law enforcement officers or others in its territorial jurisdiction, for the proper disposition of Uniform Traffic Tickets and for the preparation of such records and reports as the Administrative Director of the Courts prescribes. The provisions of this subparagraph shall apply to the Chief Administrator of the Motor Vehicle Commission, the Superintendent of State Police in the Department of Law and Public Safety, and to the responsible official of any other agency authorized by the Administrative Director of the Courts to print and distribute the Uniform Traffic Ticket to its law enforcement personnel.

(g) Special Form of Complaint and Summons. A special form of complaint and summons for any action, as prescribed by the Administrative Director of the Courts, shall be used in the manner prescribed in place of any other form of complaint and process.

(h) Use of Special Form of Complaint and Summons in Penalty Enforcement Proceedings. The Special Form of Complaint and Summons, as prescribed by the Administrative Director of the Courts, shall be used for all penalty enforcement proceedings in the municipal court, including those that may involve the confiscation and/or forfeiture of chattels. If the Special Form of Complaint and Summons is made by a governmental body or officer, it may be certified or verified on information and belief by any person duly authorized to act on its or the State's behalf.

Note: Source—Paragraph (a): R. (1969) 7:2, 7:3–1, 3:2–1; paragraph (b): R. (1969) 7:2, 7:3–1, 7:6–1, 3:2–2; paragraph (c): R. (1969) 7:2, 7:3–1, 7:6–1, 3:2–3; paragraph (d): R. (1969) 7:6–1; paragraph (e): R. (1969) 4:70–3(a); paragraph (f): new. Adopted October 6, 1997 to be effective February 1, 1998; paragraph (a) caption added, former paragraph (a) amended and redesignated as paragraph (a)(1), former paragraph (b) amended and redesignated as paragraph (a)(2), former paragraph (c) redesignated as paragraph (a)(3), former paragraph (d) redesignated as paragraph (b), former paragraph (e) caption and text amended and redesignated as paragraph (c), and former paragraph (f) redesignated as paragraph (d) July 12, 2002 to be effective September 3, 2002; caption for paragraph (a) deleted, former paragraphs (a)(1) and (a)(2) amended and redesignated as paragraphs (a) and (b), former paragraph (a)(3) redesignated as paragraph (c), new paragraph (d) adopted, former paragraph (b) amended and redesignated as paragraph (e), former paragraph (c) deleted, former paragraph (d) amended and redesignated as paragraph (f), and new paragraph (g) adopted July 28, 2004 to be effective September 1, 2004; paragraph (a) amended, new paragraph (b) adopted, former paragraphs (b), (c), (d), and (e) amended and redesignated as paragraphs (c), (d), (e), and (f), former paragraphs (f) and (g) redesignated as paragraphs (g) and (h) July 16, 2009 to be effective September 1, 2009.

Publisher's Note:

On February 2, 2004, the New Jersey Supreme Court issued the following order:

WHEREAS N.J.S.A. 2B:12–30(d)(3) authorizes the Administrative Office of the Courts to obtain hand-held, ticket-issuing, data entry devices and related equipment for use by approved parking authorities or parking agencies to facilitate the exchange of automated information and maintain the efficiency of the standardized statewide computer system; and the Administrative Office of the Courts has developed such devices and equipment under a program entitled the Parking Authority Ticket System;

Pursuant to N.J. Const. (1947), Art. VI, sec. 2, par. 3, it is ORDERED that, effective immediately and until further Order, Rules 1:4–4 and 7:2–1 of the Rules Governing the Courts of the State of New Jersey, are hereby relaxed and supplemented so as to permit the use of an electronic signature by any law enforcement officer or other person authorized to issue a parking ticket through the Parking Authority Ticket System in those municipalities that have implemented the Parking Authority Ticket System; and

It is FURTHER ORDERED that such electronic signature on a parking ticket issued under the Parking Authority Ticket System shall be equivalent to an original signature.

7:2–2. Issuance of Arrest Warrant or Summons

(a) Authorization for Process.

(1) *Citizen Complaint.* An arrest warrant or a summons on a complaint charging any offense made by a private citizen may be issued only by a judge or, if authorized by the judge, by a municipal court administrator or deputy court administrator of a court with jurisdiction in the municipality where the offense is alleged to have been committed within the statutory time limitation. The arrest warrant or summons may be issued only if it appears to the judicial officer from the complaint, affidavit, certification or testimony that there is probable cause to believe that an offense was committed, the defendant committed it, and an arrest warrant or summons can be issued. The judicial officer's finding of probable cause shall be noted on the face of the summons or warrant and shall be confirmed by the judicial officer's signature issuing the arrest warrant or summons. If, however, the municipal court administrator or deputy court administrator finds that no probable cause exists to issue an arrest warrant or summons, or that the applicable statutory time limitation to issue the arrest warrant or summons has expired, that finding shall be reviewed by the judge. A judge finding no probable cause to believe that an offense occurred or that the statutory time limitation to issue an arrest warrant or summons has expired shall dismiss the complaint.

(2) *Complaint by Law Enforcement Officer or Other Statutorily Authorized Person.* A summons on a complaint made by a law enforcement officer charging any offense may be issued by a law enforcement officer or by any person authorized to do so by statute without a finding by a judicial officer of probable cause for issuance. A law enforcement officer may personally serve the summons on the defendant without making a custodial arrest.

(3) *Complaint by Code Enforcement Officer.* A summons on a complaint made by a Code Enforcement Officer charging any offense within the scope of the Code Enforcement Officer's authority and territorial jurisdiction may be issued without a finding by a judicial officer of probable cause for issuance. A Code Enforcement Officer may personally serve the summons on the defendant. Otherwise, service shall be in accordance with these rules. For purposes of this rule, a "Code Enforcement Officer" is a public employee who is responsible for enforcing the provisions of any state, county or municipal law, ordinance or regulation which the public employee is empowered to enforce.

(b) Determination Whether to Issue a Summons or Warrant. A summons rather than an arrest warrant shall issue if the defendant is a corporation, partnership or unincorporated association. If the defendant is an individual, a summons rather than an arrest warrant shall issue unless the judge or duly authorized municipal court administrator or deputy court administrator finds that:

(1) the defendant has failed to respond to a summons; or

(2) there is reason to believe that the defendant is dangerous to himself or herself, to others, or to property; or

(3) there is one or more outstanding arrest warrants for the defendant; or

(4) the address of the defendant is not known, and an arrest warrant is necessary to subject the defendant to the jurisdiction of the court; or

(5) the defendant cannot be satisfactorily identified; or

(6) there is reason to believe that the defendant will not appear in response to a summons.

(c) Failure to Appear After Summons. If a defendant who has been served with a summons fails to appear on the return date, an arrest warrant may issue pursuant to law and Rule 7:8–9 (Procedures on Failure to Appear). If a corporation, partnership or unincorporated association has been served with a summons and has failed to appear on the return date, the court shall proceed as if the corporation had appeared and entered a plea of not guilty.

(d) Additional Arrest Warrants or Summonses. More than one arrest warrant or summons may issue on the same complaint.

(e) Identification Procedures. If a summons has been issued or an arrest warrant executed on a complaint charging either the offense of shoplifting or prostitution or on a complaint charging any non-indictable offense where the identity of the person charged is in question, the defendant shall submit to the identification procedures prescribed by N.J.S.A. 53:1–15. Upon the defendant's refusal to submit to any required identification procedures, the court may issue an arrest warrant.

Note: Source—R. (1969) 7:2, 7:3–1, 3:3–1. Adopted October 6, 1997 to be effective February 1, 1998; paragraphs (b) and (c) amended July 10, 1998 to be effective September 1, 1998; paragraph (a)(1) amended July 5, 2000 to be effective September 5, 2000; paragraph (a)(1) amended, new paragraph (b)(5) added, and former paragraph (b)(5) redesignated as paragraph (b)(6) July 12, 2002 to be effective September 3, 2002; paragraph (a)(1) amended, and paragraph (a)(2) caption and text amended July 28, 2004 to be effective September 1, 2004; paragraph (a)(1) amended and new paragraph (a)(3) adopted July 16, 2009 to be effective September 1, 2009.

7:2–3. Arrest Warrant: Execution and Service: Return

(a) By Whom Executed; Territorial Limits. An arrest warrant shall be executed by any officer authorized by law. The arrest warrant may be executed at any place within this State. A law enforcement officer arresting a defendant outside the territorial jurisdiction of the court that issued the warrant shall take the defendant, without unnecessary delay, before the nearest committing judge authorized to admit to bail in accordance with R. 7:4–2(a) and any other applicable rule of court.

(b) How Executed. The arrest warrant shall be executed by the arrest of the defendant. The law enforcement officer need not possess the warrant at the time of the arrest, but upon request, the officer shall show the warrant or a copy of an Automated Traffic System/Automated Complaint System (ATS/ACS) electronic record evidencing its issuance to the defendant as soon as possible. If the law enforcement officer does not have the actual warrant to show or does not have access to an ATS/ACS printer to produce a copy of the electronic record at the time of the arrest, the officer shall inform the defendant of the offense charged and that an arrest warrant has been issued.

(c) Return. The law enforcement officer executing an arrest warrant shall make prompt return of the arrest warrant to the court that issued the warrant. If the arrested defendant is not admitted to bail, the arresting officer shall notify the court issuing the arrest warrant by telephone or other electronic means of communication of the date and time of the arrest and the place of the defendant's incarceration.

Note: Source—Paragraph (a): R.(1969) 7:2; 7:3–1, 3:3–3(a), (b), (c), (e); Paragraphs (b)(1), (2), (3): R. (1969) 7:3–1: Paragraph (b)(4): R.(1969) 7:2, 7:3–1, 3:3–3(e). Adopted October 6, 1997 to be effective February 1, 1998; caption amended, caption of former paragraph (a) deleted, caption and text of former paragraph (b) deleted and relocated to new Rule 7:2–4, former paragraphs (a)(1), (a)(2), and (a)(3) redesignated as paragraphs (a), (b), and (c) July 28, 2004 to be effective September 1, 2004.

7:2–4. Summons: Execution and Service; Return

(a) Summons; Personal Service Under R. 4:4–4 or By Ordinary Mail.

(1) The Complaint–Summons shall be served personally in accordance with R. 4:4–4(a), by ordinary mail or by simultaneous mailing in accordance with paragraph (b) of this rule. Service of the Complaint–Summons by ordinary mail may be attempted by the court, by the law enforcement agency that prepared the complaint or by an agency or individual authorized by law to serve process.

(2) Service by ordinary mail shall have the same effect as personal service if the defendant contacts the court orally or in writing in response to or in acknowledgment of the service of the Complaint–Summons. Service by ordinary mail shall not be attempted until a court date for the first appearance has been set by the municipal court administrator, deputy court administrator, or other authorized court employee.

(3) If the court is provided with a different, updated address for the defendant, along with a postal verification or other proof satisfactory to the court that the defendant receives mail at that address, service of the Complaint–Summons may be re-attempted.

(b) Simultaneous Service by Mail.

(1) If service is attempted by ordinary mail and the defendant does not appear in court on the first appearance date or does not contact the court orally or in writing by that date, the court subsequently shall send the Complaint–Summons simultaneously by ordinary mail and certified mail with return receipt requested to the defendant's last known mailing address. Service by simultaneous mailing shall not be attempted until a new court date for the first appearance has been set by the municipal court administrator, deputy court administrator, or other authorized court employee.

(2) When the Complaint–Summons is addressed and mailed to the defendant at a place of business or employment with postal instructions to deliver to addressee only, service will be deemed effective only if the signature on the return receipt appears to be that of the defendant to whom the Complaint–Summons was mailed.

(3) Consistent with due process of law, service by simultaneous mailing, as provided in Section (b)(1) of this rule, shall constitute effective service unless the mail is returned to the court by the postal service marked "Moved, Left No Address", "Attempted—Not Known", "No Such Number", "No Such Street", "Insufficient Address", "Not Deliverable as Addressed—Unable to Forward" or the court has other reason to believe that service was not effected. However, if the certified mail is returned to the court marked "Refused" or "Unclaimed," service is effective providing that the ordinary mail has not been returned.

(4) Process served by ordinary or certified mail with return receipt requested may be addressed to a post office box.

(c) Notice to Prosecuting Attorney and Complaining Witness; Dismissal of Complaint.

(1) If the court has not obtained effective service over the defendant after attempting service by simultaneous mailing under section (b)(1) of this rule, the court shall provide written notice of that fact to the prosecuting attorney and the complaining witness.

(2) he case shall be eligible for dismissal unless within 45 days of the receipt of the written notice, the prosecuting attorney or the complaining witness provides the court with a different, updated address for the defendant, along with a postal verification or other

proof satisfactory to the court that the defendant receives mail at that address.

(3) Notwithstanding the provisions of this rule, nothing shall preclude the prosecuting attorney or other authorized person from attempting service in any lawful manner.

(4) If the prosecuting attorney and complaining witness do not respond to the court's written notice within 45 days or if the defendant is not otherwise served, the court may dismiss the case pursuant to R. 7:8–5.

(d) Parking Offenses. A copy of the Uniform Traffic Ticket prepared and issued out of the presence of the defendant charging a parking offense may be served by affixing it to the vehicle involved in the violation.

(e) Corporations, Partnerships and Unincorporated Associations. A copy of the Uniform Traffic Ticket charging a corporation, partnership or unincorporated association with a violation of a statute or ordinance relating to motor vehicles may be served on the operator of the vehicle.

(f) Return. The law enforcement officer serving a summons shall make return of the summons on or before the return date to the court before whom the summons is returnable.

Note: Former Rule 7:2–4 redesignated as Rule 7:2–5 and new Rule 7:2–4 (incorporating portions of former Rule 7:2–3) adopted July 28, 2004 to be effective September 1, 2004.

7:2–5. Defective Warrant or Summons; Amendment

No person arrested under a warrant or appearing in response to a summons shall be discharged from custody or dismissed because of any technical insufficiency or irregularity in the warrant or summons, but the warrant or summons may be amended to remedy any such technical defect.

Note: Source—R. (1969) 7:2, 7:3–1, 3:3–4(a). Adopted October 6, 1997 as Rule 7:2–4 to be effective February 1, 1998; redesignated as Rule 7:2–5 July 28, 2004 to be effective September 1, 2004.

7:2–6. Fax Transmission of Complaint–Warrants

During off-business hours, a law enforcement officer may submit a Complaint–Warrant (CDR–2) and any supporting documentation by facsimile (fax) transmission to the municipal court judge or to the authorized court administrator or deputy court administrator (judicial officer) to obtain a signature if probable cause is found, as follows:

(a) The law enforcement officer seeking the issuance of a Complaint–Warrant shall prepare a CDR–2 and contact a judicial officer.

(b) The law enforcement officer shall fax the CDR–2 to the judicial officer for a determination of probable cause. The fax machine must be capable of printing on each transmitted document the time and date of the fax transmission.

(c) If the judicial officer makes any corrections to the transmitted fax document, the law enforcement officer shall make those corrections on the original document. The officer shall then retransmit the corrected document to the judicial officer for signature.

(d) On the next business day, the judicial officer shall conform the original CDR–2 and shall attach the signed fax copy to the original. If the judicial officer who signed the fax copy is the municipal court judge, the original CDR–2 may be signed by the judge or be attested in the judge's name and signed by the municipal court administrator.

Note: Adopted July 28, 2004 to be effective September 1, 2004.

RULE 7:3. PROCEEDINGS BEFORE THE COMMITTING JUDGE; PRETRIAL RELEASE

7:3–1. Procedure After Arrest

(a) First Appearance; Time. Following the filing of a complaint and service of process upon the defendant, the defendant shall be brought, without unnecessary delay, before the court for a first appearance. If the defendant remains in custody, the first appearance shall be conducted within 72 hours after arrest by a judge with authority to set bail for the offenses charged in the complaint. If the defendant's bail was not set when the arrest warrant on a complaint was issued, bail or other conditions of release shall be set without unnecessary delay, but in no event later than 12 hours after arrest.

(b) Custodial Arrest Without Warrant.

(1) *Preparation of a Complaint and Summons or Warrant.* A law enforcement officer making a custodial arrest without a warrant shall take the defendant to the police station where a complaint shall be immediately prepared. The complaint shall be prepared on a complaint-summons form (CDR–1 or Special Form of Complaint and Summons), unless the law enforcement officer determines that one or more of the factors in R. 7:2–2(b) applies. Upon such determination, the law enforcement officer shall prepare a complaint-warrant form (CDR–2).

(2) *Probable Cause; Issuance of Process; Bail.* If a complaint-warrant form (CDR–2) is prepared, the law enforcement officer shall, without unnecessary delay, but in no event later than 12 hours after arrest, present the matter to a judge, or in the absence of a judge, to a municipal court administrator or deputy court administrator who has been granted authority to set bail for the

offense charged. The judicial officer shall determine whether there is probable cause to believe that the defendant has committed an offense. If probable cause is found, a summons or warrant may issue, but if the judicial officer determines that the defendant will appear in response to a summons, a summons shall be issued consistent with the standard prescribed by R. 7:2–2(b). If a warrant is issued, bail shall be set without unnecessary delay, but in no event later than 12 hours after arrest. The finding of probable cause shall be noted on the face of the summons or warrant. If no probable cause is found, no process shall issue and the complaint shall be dismissed by the judge.

(3) *Summons.* If a complaint-summons form (CDR–1 or Special Form of Complaint and Summons) has been prepared, or if a judicial officer has determined that a summons shall issue, the summons shall be served and the defendant shall be released after completion of post-arrest identification procedures required by law and pursuant to R. 7:2–2(e).

(c) **Non–Custodial Arrest.** A law enforcement officer charging any offense may personally serve a complaint-summons (Special Form of Complaint and Summons) at the scene of the arrest without taking the defendant into custody.

Note: Source—R. (1969) 7:2, 7:3–1, 3:4–1. Adopted October 6, 1997 to be effective February 1, 1998; paragraphs (b)(1) and (b)(2) amended July 12, 2002 to be effective September 3, 2002; paragraph (b) caption amended, paragraphs (b)(1) and (b)(2) amended, and new paragraph (c) adopted July 28, 2004 to be effective September 1, 2004.

7:3–2. Hearing on First Appearance; Right to Counsel

(a) **Hearing on First Appearance.** At the defendant's first appearance, the judge shall inform the defendant of the charges and shall furnish the defendant with a copy of the complaint or copy of the electronic ATS/ACS record of the complaint, if not previously provided to the defendant. The judge shall also inform the defendant of the range of penal consequences for each offense charged, the right to remain silent and that any statement made may be used against the defendant. The judge shall inform the defendant of the right to retain counsel or, if indigent, to have counsel assigned pursuant to paragraph (b) of this rule. The defendant shall be specifically asked whether legal representation is desired and defendant's response shall be recorded on

the complaint. If the defendant is represented at the first appearance or then affirmatively states the intention to proceed without counsel, the court may, in its discretion, immediately arraign the defendant pursuant to R. 7:6–1.

(b) **Assignment of Counsel.** If the defendant asserts indigency but does not affirmatively state an intention to proceed without counsel, the court shall order defendant to complete an appropriate application and other forms prescribed by the Administrative Director of the Courts. Pursuant to law, the judge shall either order defendant to pay any application fee or shall waive its payment. If the court is satisfied that the defendant is indigent and that the defendant faces a consequence of magnitude or is otherwise constitutionally or by law entitled to counsel, the court shall assign the municipal public defender to represent the defendant. The "Guidelines for Determining a Consequence of Magnitude" are contained in the Appendix to Part VII of the Rules of Court. The court may, however, excuse the municipal public defender for cause and assign counsel to represent the defendant, without cost to the defendant from, insofar as practicable, a list of attorneys maintained by the Assignment Judge. Assigned counsel shall promptly file an appearance pursuant to R. 7:7–9. The court shall allow the defendant a reasonable time and opportunity to consult trial defense counsel before proceeding further. Assigned counsel shall represent the defendant through trial and, in the event of a conviction, through sentencing, including advising the defendant of the right to appeal. If the defendant elects to appeal, assigned counsel or the municipal public defender shall prepare and file the notice of appeal and an application for the assignment of appellate counsel, but neither assigned counsel nor the municipal public defender shall act as appellate counsel or represent defendant on any subsequent application for post-conviction relief unless specifically so assigned by the court. Assigned counsel shall, however, be responsible for the representation of the defendant on the appeal upon failure to file either the notice of appeal or the application for the assignment of counsel on appeal.

Note: Source—R. (1969) 7:2, 7:3–1, 3:4–2(b). Adopted October 6, 1997 to be effective February 1, 1998; paragraph (b) amended July 10, 1998, to be effective September 1, 1998; paragraph (b) amended July 28, 2004 to be effective September 1, 2004; paragraph (a) amended July 16, 2009 to be effective September 1, 2009.

RULE 7:4. BAIL

7:4–1. Right to Bail Before Conviction

Every defendant shall have a right to bail before conviction on such terms as, in the judgment of the court, will insure the defendant's presence when required, having regard for the defendant's background,

residence, employment and family status and, particularly, the general policy against unnecessary sureties and detention. In its discretion, the court may order defendant's release on defendant's own recognizance and may impose terms or conditions appropriate to such release.

Note: Source—R. (1969) 7:5–1, 3:26–1(a). Adopted October 6, 1997 to be effective February 1, 1998.

7:4–2. Authority to Set Bail

(a) Authority to Admit to Initial Bail. Conditions of pre-trial release, including bail, may be set by a judge sitting regularly in or as acting or temporary judge of the jurisdiction in which the offense was committed, or by a vicinage Presiding Judge of the Municipal Courts, or as authorized by any other rule of court. A judge who has fixed the amount of bail may designate the taking of the recognizance by the municipal court administrator or any other person authorized by law to take recognizances, other than the law enforcement arresting officer. In the absence of the judge, and to the extent consistent with N.J.S.A. 2B:12–21, a defendant, arrested and charged with a non-indictable offense that may be tried by the judge, may be admitted to bail by the duly authorized municipal court administrator or deputy court administrator. In the absence of the judge, the municipal court administrator, and deputy court administrator, the defendant may be admitted to bail by any other person authorized by law to admit to bail. The authority of the municipal court administrator, deputy court administrator or other authorized persons shall, however, be exercised only in accordance with bail schedules promulgated by the Administrative Office of the Courts or the municipal court judge.

(b) Bail Revisions. A municipal court judge may modify bail or any other condition of pre-trial release on any non-indictable offense at any time during the course of the municipal court proceedings.

Note: Source—Paragraph (a): R. (1969) 7:5–3; paragraph (b): R. (1969) 7:5–1, 3:26–2(c). Adopted October 6, 1997 to be effective February 1, 1998; paragraphs (a) and (b) amended July 10, 1998, to be effective September 1, 1998.

7:4–3. Form and Place of Deposit; Location of Real Estate; Record of Recognizances, Discharge and Forfeiture

(a) Deposit of Bail. A defendant admitted to bail shall, together with the sureties, if any, sign and execute a recognizance before the person authorized to take bail or, if the defendant is in custody, the person in charge of the place of confinement. The recognizance shall contain the terms set forth in R. 1:13–3(b) and shall be conditioned upon the defendant's appearance at all stages of the proceedings until the final determination of the matter, unless otherwise ordered by the court. The total recognizance may be satisfied by more than one surety, if necessary. Cash may be accepted, and in proper cases, within the court's discretion, the posting of security may be waived. A corporate surety shall be one approved by the Commissioner of Insurance. A corporate surety shall execute the recognizance under its duly acknowledged corporate seal, and shall attach to its bond written proof of the corporate authority and

qualifications of the officers or agents executing the recognizance. Real estate offered as security for bail for non-indictable offenses shall be approved by and deposited with the clerk of the county in which the offense occurred and not with the municipal court administrator.

(b) Limitation on Individual Surety. Unless the court for good cause otherwise permits, no surety, other than an approved corporate surety, shall enter into a recognizance if there remains any previous undischarged recognizance or bail that was undertaken by that surety.

(c) Real Estate in Other Counties. Real estate owned by a surety located in a county other than the one in which the bail is taken may be accepted, in which case the municipal court administrator of the court in which the bail is taken shall certify and transmit a copy of the recognizance to the clerk of the county in which the real estate is situated, and it shall be there recorded in the same manner as if taken in that county.

(d) Record of Recognizance. In municipal court proceedings, the record of the recognizance shall be entered by the municipal court administrator or designee in the manner required by the Administrative Director of the Courts to be maintained for that purpose.

(e) When any recognizance shall be discharged by court order on proof of compliance with the conditions thereof or by reason of the judgment in any matter, the municipal court administrator or deputy court administrator shall enter the word "discharged" and the date of discharge at the end of the record of such recognizance. When any recognizance is forfeited, the municipal court administrator or deputy court administrator shall enter the word "forfeited" and the date of forfeiture at the end of the record of such recognizance and shall give notice of such forfeiture by ordinary mail to the municipal attorney, the defendant and any surety or insurer, bail agent or agency whose names appear in the bail recognizance. Notice to any insurer, bail agent or agency shall be sent to the address recorded in the Bail Registry maintained by the Clerk of the Superior Court pursuant to R. 1:13–3. When real estate of the surety located in a county other than the one in which the bail was taken is affected, the municipal court administrator or deputy court administrator in which such recognizance is given shall immediately send notice of the discharge or forfeiture and the date thereof to the clerk of the county where such real estate is situated, who shall make the appropriate entry at the end of the record of such recognizance.

(f) Cash Deposit. When a person other than the defendant deposits cash in lieu of bond, the person making the deposit shall file an affidavit or certification explaining the lawful ownership thereof, and on discharge, such cash shall be returned to the owner named in the affidavit or certification, unless otherwise ordered by the court.

(g) Ten Percent Cash Bail. Unless otherwise specified in the order setting the bail, bail may be satisfied by the deposit in court of cash in the amount of ten percent of the amount of bail fixed together with defendant's executed recognizance for the remaining ninety percent. No surety shall be required, unless specifically ordered by the court. If a ten percent bail is made by cash owned by one other than the defendant, the owner shall charge no fee for the cash deposited, other than lawful interest, and shall submit an affidavit or certification with the deposit detailing the rate of interest, confirming that no other fee is being charged, and listing the names of any other persons for whom the owner has deposited bail. A person making the ten percent deposit who is not the owner, shall file an affidavit or certification identifying the lawful owner of the cash, and, on discharge, the cash deposit shall be returned to the owner named in the affidavit or certification, unless otherwise ordered by the court.

Note: Source—R. (1969) 7:5–1, 3:26–4. Adopted October 6, 1997 to be effective February 1, 1998; subsection (e) amended December 8, 1998 to be effective January 15, 1999; caption amended, and paragraphs (e), (f), and (g) amended July 28, 2004 to be effective September 1, 2004.

Publisher's Note

For text of the New Jersey Supreme Court order issued on August 31, 2004, see note following Rule 7:4–5

7:4–4. Justification of Sureties

Every surety, except an approved corporate surety, shall justify the proposed property by affidavit, which shall include a description of the property, any encumbrances, the number and amount of other recognizances and undertakings for bail entered into by the surety and remaining undischarged, if any, and all of the surety's other liabilities. No recognizance shall be approved unless the surety thereon shall be qualified.

Note: Source—R. (1969) 7:5–1, 3:26–5. Adopted October 6, 1997 to be effective February 1, 1998.

7:4–5. Forfeiture

(a) Declaration; Notice. On breach of a condition of a recognizance, the court may forfeit the bail on its own or on the prosecuting attorney's motion. If the court orders bail to be forfeited, the municipal court administrator or deputy court administrator shall immediately forfeit the bail pursuant to R. 7:4–3(e) and shall send notice of the forfeiture by ordinary mail to the municipal attorney, the defendant, and any non-corporate surety or insurer, bail agent, or bail agency whose names appear on the bail recognizance. Notice to any insurer, bail agent, or bail agency shall be sent to the address recorded in the Bail Registry maintained by the Clerk of the Superior Court pursuant to R. 1:13–3. The notice shall direct that judgment will be entered as to any outstanding bail absent a written objection seeking to set aside the forfeiture, which must be filed within 75 days of the date of the notice. The notice shall also advise the insurer that if it fails to satisfy a judgment entered pursuant to paragraph (c) of this rule, and until satisfaction is made, it shall be removed from the Bail Registry and its bail agents and agencies, guarantors, and other persons or entities authorized to administer or manage its bail bond business in this State will have no further authority to act for it, and their names, as acting for the insurer, will be removed from the Bail Registry. In addition, the bail agent or agency, guarantor, or other person or entity authorized by the insurer to administer or manage its bail bond business in this State who acted in such capacity with respect to the forfeited bond will be precluded, by removal from the Bail Registry, from so acting for any other insurer until the judgment has been satisfied. The court shall not enter judgment until the merits of any objection are determined either on the papers filed or, if the court so orders, for good cause, at a hearing. In the absence of a written objection, judgment shall be entered as provided in paragraph (c) of this rule, but the court may thereafter remit it, in whole or part, in the interest of justice.

(b) Setting Aside. The court may, upon such conditions as it imposes, direct that an order of forfeiture or judgment be set aside in whole or in part, if required in the interest of justice.

(c) Enforcement; Remission. If a forfeiture is not set aside, the court shall, on motion, enter a judgment of default for any outstanding bail, and execution may issue on the judgment. After entry of the judgment, the court may remit the forfeiture in whole or in part in the interest of justice. If, following the court's decision on an objection pursuant to paragraph (a) of this rule, the forfeiture is not set aside or satisfied in whole or in part, the court shall enter judgment for any outstanding bail and, in the absence of satisfaction thereof, execution may issue thereon.

Judgments entered pursuant to this rule shall also advise the insurer that if it fails to satisfy a judgment, and until satisfaction is made, it shall be removed from the Bail Registry and its bail agents and agencies, guarantors, and other persons or entities authorized to administer or manage its bail bond business in this State will have no further authority to act for it, and their names, as acting for the insurer, will be removed from the Bail Registry as provided in paragraph (a) of this rule. A copy of the judgment entered pursuant to this rule is to be served by ordinary mail on the municipal attorney, and on any surety or any insurer, bail agent, or bail agency named in the judgment. Notice to any surety or insurer, bail agent, or bail agency shall be sent to the address recorded in the Bail Registry. In any contested proceeding, the municipal attorney shall appear on behalf of the government. The municipal attorney shall be responsible for the collection of forfeited amounts.

Note: Source—R. (1969) 7:5–1, 3:26–6. Adopted October 6, 1997 to be effective February 1, 1998; paragraph (a) caption and text amended, and paragraphs (b) and (c) amended July 28, 2004 to be effective September 1, 2004.

Publisher's Note

On August 31, 2004, the New Jersey Supreme Court issued the following Order

  IT IS ORDERED, that the Court's November 1, 2000 Order, which set out the notice and procedural requirements to be followed in bail forfeitures and judgments, and the amendatory Orders dated June 11, 2002 (to modify the time permitted to file an objection to set aside a bail forfeiture preclusion) and May 20, 2003 (to conform to statutory changes effected by the New Jersey Insurance Producer Act of 2001 (L.2001, c. 210) are hereby terminated effective September 1, 2004, the effective date of the July 28, 2004 amendments to Rules 1:13–3, 2:9–6, 3:26–6, 7:4–3 and 7:4–5.

7:4–6. Exoneration

When the condition of the recognizance has been satisfied or its forfeiture has been set aside or remitted, the court shall exonerate the obligors and release any bail. A surety may be exonerated by a deposit of cash in the amount of the recognizance or by a timely surrender of the defendant into custody.

Note: Source—R. (1969) 7:5–1, 3:26–7. Adopted October 6, 1997 to be effective February 1, 1998.

7:4–7. Place of Deposit

Bail in non-indictable matters given in the municipal court shall be deposited with the municipal court administrator or deputy court administrator. At the surety's discretion, bail may also be deposited with the person in charge of the place of confinement where the defendant is in custody, and that person shall then transmit the bail to the appropriate municipal court administrator or deputy court administrator for deposit in accordance with this rule.

Note: Source—R. (1969) 7:5–2. Adopted October 6, 1997 to be effective February 1, 1998.

7:4–8. Bail After Conviction

When a sentence has been imposed and an appeal from the judgment of conviction has been taken, the trial judge may admit the appellant to bail within 20 days from the date of conviction or sentence, whichever occurs later. Bail after conviction may be imposed only if the trial judge has significant reservations about the appellant's willingness to appear before the appellate court. The bail or other recognizance shall be of sufficient surety to guarantee the appellant's appearance before the appellate court and compliance with the court's judgment. Once the appellant has placed bail or filed a recognizance, if the a appellant is in custody, the trial court shall immediately discharge the appellant from custody. The court shall transmit to the vicinage Criminal Division Manager any cash deposit and any recognizance submitted.

Note: Source—R. (1969) 7:5–4. Adopted October 6, 1997 to be effective February 1, 1998; amended July 5, 2000 to be effective September 5, 2000.

RULE 7:5. SEARCH WARRANTS; SUPPRESSION

7:5–1. Filing

(a) By Whom; Documents to be Filed. The judge issuing a search warrant shall attach to it the return, inventory, and all other papers related to the warrant, including affidavits and a transcript or summary of any oral testimony and, if applicable, a duplicate original search warrant. The judge shall promptly deliver these documents to the municipal court administrator, who shall file them with the vicinage Criminal Division Manager of the county in which the property was seized. The municipal court administrator shall retain in a confidential file copies of all papers filed with the Criminal Division Manager. If a tape or transmitted recording has been made, the municipal court administrator shall also send them to the Criminal Division Manager, but shall not retain a copy.

(b) Inspection. All completely executed warrants, together with the supporting papers and recordings described in paragraph (a) of this rule, shall be available for inspection and copying by the defendant pursuant to R. 7:7–7 and, upon notice to the county prosecutor and for good cause shown, by any other person claiming to be aggrieved by the search and seizure.

Note: Source—R. (1969) 3:5–6(a), (c). Adopted October 6, 1997 to be effective February 1, 1998.

7:5–2. Motion to Suppress Evidence

(a) Jurisdiction. The municipal court shall entertain motions to suppress evidence seized without a warrant in matters within its trial jurisdiction on notice to the prosecuting attorney and, if the county prosecutor is not the prosecuting attorney, also to the county prosecutor. A motion to suppress evidence seized pursuant to a warrant and motions to suppress evidence seized without a warrant, but in matters beyond the trial jurisdiction of the municipal court, shall be made and heard in the Superior Court.

(b) Procedure. Written briefs in support of and opposition to the motion to suppress shall be filed only in the discretion of the judge, who shall determine the briefing schedule, if briefs are permitted. All motions to suppress shall be heard before the start of the trial.

(c) Order; Stay.

(1) *Order Granting Suppression.* An order granting a motion to suppress evidence shall be entered immediately upon decision of the motion. Within ten days after its entry, the municipal court administrator shall provide a copy of the order to all parties and, if the county prosecutor is not the prosecuting attorney, also to the county prosecutor. All further proceedings in the municipal court shall be stayed pending a timely appeal by the State, pursuant to R. 3:24. The property that is the subject of the suppression order shall, if not otherwise subject to lawful detention, be returned to the person entitled to it only after exhaustion by the State of its right to appeal.

(2) *Order Denying Suppression.* An order denying suppression may be reviewed on appeal from an ensuing judgment of conviction pursuant to R. 3:23 whether the judgment was entered on a guilty plea or on a finding of guilt following trial.

(d) Waiver. Unless otherwise ordered by the court for good cause, defendant's failure to make a pretrial motion to the municipal court pursuant to this rule shall constitute a waiver of any objection during trial to the admission of the evidence on the ground that the evidence was unlawfully obtained.

Note: Source—Paragraphs (a), (b), (c): R. (1969) 7:4–2(f); paragraph (d): R. (1969) 3:5–7(f). Adopted October 6, 1997 to be effective February 1, 1998.

7:5–3. Search and Seizure Without a Warrant

R. 7:5 shall not be construed to make illegal a lawful search and seizure executed without a warrant.

Note: Source—R. (1969) 3:5–8. Adopted October 6, 1997 to be effective February 1, 1998.

RULE 7:6. ARRAIGNMENT, PLEAS

7:6–1. Arraignment

(a) Conduct of Arraignment. Except as otherwise provided by paragraph (b) of this rule, the arraignment shall be conducted in open court and shall consist of reading the complaint to the defendant or stating to the defendant the substance of the charge and calling upon the defendant, after being given a copy of the complaint, to plead thereto. The defendant may waive the reading of the complaint.

(b) Written Statement. A defendant who is represented by an attorney and desires to plead not guilty may do so, unless the court otherwise orders, by the filing, at or before the time fixed for arraignment, of a written statement, signed by the attorney, certifying that the defendant has received a copy of the complaint and has read it or the attorney has read it and explained it to the defendant, that the defendant understands the substance of the charge, and that the defendant pleads not guilty to the charge.

Note: Source—R. (1969) 7:4–2(a). Adopted October 6, 1997 to be effective February 1, 1998.

7:6–2. Pleas, Plea Agreements

(a) Pleas Allowed, Guilty Plea.

(1) *Generally.* A defendant may plead not guilty or guilty, but the court may, in its discretion, refuse to accept a guilty plea. Except as otherwise provided by Rules 7:6–2, 7:6–3, and 7:12–3, the court shall not, however, accept a guilty plea without first addressing the defendant personally and determining by inquiry of the defendant and, in the court's discretion, of others, that the plea is made voluntarily with understanding of the nature of the charge and the consequences of the plea and that there is a factual basis for the plea. Prior to accepting a guilty plea when an unrepresented defendant faces a consequence of magnitude, the judge shall make a finding on the record that the court is satisfied that the defendant's waiver of the right to counsel is knowing and intelligent. On the request of the defendant, the court may, at the time of the acceptance of a guilty plea, order that the plea shall not be evidential in any civil proceeding. If a defendant refuses to plead or stands mute or if the court refuses to accept a guilty plea, the court shall enter a plea of not guilty. If a guilty plea is entered, the court may hear the witnesses in support of the complaint prior to judgment and sentence and after such hearing may, in its discretion, refuse to accept the plea.

(2) *Corporate Defendants.* A defendant that is a corporation, partnership or unincorporated association may enter a plea by an authorized officer or agent and may appear by an officer or agent provided the appearance is consented to by the named party defendant and the court finds that the interest of justice does not require the appearance of counsel. If a defendant that is a corporation, partnership, or unincorporated association fails to appear or answer, the court, if satisfied that service was duly made, shall enter an appearance and a plea of not guilty for the defendant and thereupon proceed to hear the complaint.

(b) Withdrawal of Plea. A motion to withdraw a plea of guilty shall be made before sentencing, but the court may permit it to be made thereafter to correct a manifest injustice.

(c) Conditional Pleas. With the approval of the court and the consent of the prosecuting attorney, a defendant may enter a conditional plea of guilty, reserving on the record the right to appeal from the adverse determination of any specified pretrial motion. A defendant who prevails on appeal shall be afforded the opportunity to withdraw the guilty plea. Nothing in this rule shall be construed as limiting the right to appeal provided by R. 7:5–2(c)(2).

(d) Plea Agreements. Plea agreements may be entered into only pursuant to the Guidelines and accompanying Comment issued by the Supreme Court, both of which are annexed as an Appendix to Part VII, provided, however, that:

(1) the complaint is prosecuted by the municipal prosecutor, the county prosecutor, or the Attorney General; and

(2) the defendant is either represented by counsel or knowingly waives the right to counsel on the record; and

(3) the prosecuting attorney represents to the court that the victim, if the victim is present at the hearing, has been consulted about the agreement; and

(4) the plea agreement involves a matter within the jurisdiction of the municipal court and does not result in the downgrade or disposition of indictable offenses without the consent of the county prosecutor, which consent shall be noted on the record; and

(5) the sentence recommendations, if any, do not circumvent minimum sentences required by law for the offense.

Pursuant to paragraph (a)(1) of this rule, when a plea agreement is reached, its terms and the factual basis that supports the charge(s) shall be fully set forth on the record personally by the prosecutor, except as provided in Guideline 3 for Operation of Plea Agreements. If the judge determines that the interests of justice would not be served by accepting the agreement, the judge shall so state, and the defendant shall be informed of the right to withdraw the plea if already entered.

Note: Source-Paragraph (a): R. (1969) 7:4–2(b); paragraph (b): R. (1969) 3:21–1; paragraph (c): R. (1969) 3:9–3(f); paragraph (d): R. (1969) 7:4–8. Adopted October 6, 1997 to be effective February 1, 1998; paragraph (d) amended July 12, 2002 to be effective September 3, 2002; paragraph (d) amended July 28, 2004 to be effective September 1, 2004; paragraph (a)(1) amended June 15, 2007 to be effective September 1, 2007; paragraph (d)(3) amended July 16, 2009 to be effective September 1, 2009.

7:6–3. Guilty Plea by Mail in Non–Traffic Offenses

(a) Entry of Guilty Plea by Mail. In all non-traffic and non-parking offenses, except as limited below, on consideration of a written application, supported by certification, with notice to the complaining witness and prosecutor, and at the time and place scheduled for trial, the judge may permit the defendant to enter a guilty plea by mail if the court is satisfied that a personal appearance by the defendant would constitute an undue hardship such as illness, physical incapacity, substantial distance to travel, or incarceration. The guilty plea by mail form may also include a statement for the court to consider when determining the appropriate sentence. A guilty plea by mail shall not be available for the following:

(1) cases involving the imposition of a mandatory term of incarceration on conviction, unless defendant is currently incarcerated and the mandatory term of incarceration would be served concurrently and would not extend the period of incarceration;

(2) cases involving an issue of the identity of the defendant;

(3) cases involving acts of domestic violence;

(4) cases where the prosecution intends to seek the imposition of a custodial term in the event of a conviction, unless defendant is currently incarcerated and the proposed term of incarceration would not extend the period of incarceration and would be served concurrently; and

(5) any other case where excusing the defendant's appearance in municipal court would not be in the interest of justice.

(b) Plea Form–Certification. The Guilty Plea by Mail shall be submitted on a form approved by the Administrative Director of the Courts.

(c) Judgment. The court shall send the defendant and complaining witness a copy of its decision by ordinary mail.

Note: Adopted June 15, 2007 to be effective September 1, 2007.

RULE 7:7. PRETRIAL PROCEDURES

7:7–1. Pleadings; Objections

Pleadings in municipal court actions shall consist only of the complaint. A defense or objection capable of determination without trial of the general issue shall be raised before trial by motion to dismiss or for other appropriate relief, except that a motion to dismiss based upon lack of jurisdiction or the unconstitutionality of a municipal ordinance may be made at any time.

Note: Source—R. (1969) 7:4–2(e), 3:10–1. Adopted October 6, 1997 to be effective February 1, 1998.

7:7–2. Motions

(a) How Made. Except as otherwise provided by R. 7:5–2 (motion to suppress), motions in the municipal court and answers to motions, if any, shall be made orally, unless the court directs that the motion and answer be in writing. Oral testimony or affidavits in support of or in opposition to the motion may be required by the court in its discretion.

(b) Hearings. A motion made before trial shall be determined before trial unless the court, in the interest of justice, directs that it be heard during or after trial.

(c) Effect of Determination of Motion. Except as otherwise provided by R. 7:6–2(c) (conditional pleas), if a motion is determined adversely to the defendant, the defendant shall be permitted to plead, if a plea has not already been entered. If a plea has been entered, the defendant may be permitted to stand trial as soon as the adverse determination on the motion is made. If an objection or defense specified in R. 7:7–1 is sustained and is not otherwise remediable, the court shall order the complaint dismissed. If the court dismisses the complaint and the defendant is held in custody on that complaint, the court shall order the defendant released.

Note: Source—Paragraph (a): R. (1969) 7:4–2(e); paragraph (b): R. (1969) 7:4–2(e), 3:10–2(b); paragraph (c): R. (1969) 3:10–7. Adopted October 6, 1997 to be effective February 1, 1998.

7:7–3. Notice of Alibi; Failure to Furnish

(a) Alibi. A defendant who intends to rely on an alibi shall, within 10 days after a written demand by the prosecuting attorney, furnish the prosecuting attorney with a signed statement of alibi, specifying the specific place or places at which the defendant claims to have been at the time of the alleged offense and the names and addresses of the witnesses upon whom the defendant intends to rely to establish the alibi. Within 10 days after receipt of the statement of alibi, the prosecuting attorney shall, on written demand, furnish the defendant or defendant's attorney with the names and addresses of the witnesses upon whom the State intends to rely to establish defendant's presence at the scene of the alleged offense. The court may order any amendment to or amplification of the alibi statement as required in the interest of justice.

(b) Failure to Furnish. If the information required by paragraph (a) of this rule is not furnished, the court may refuse to permit the party in default to present witnesses at trial as to defendant's presence at or absence from the scene of the alleged offense or may make any other order or grant any adjournment or continuance as may be required in the interest of justice.

Note: Source—R. (1969) 3:12–2. Adopted October 6, 1997 to be effective February 1, 1998.

7:7–4. Notice of Defense of Insanity; Evidence of Mental Disease or Defect

(a) Insanity as a Defense. A defendant who intends to claim insanity as a defense, pursuant to N.J.S.A. 2C:4–1, or a lack of the requisite state of mind, pursuant to N.J.S.A. 2C:4–2, shall serve a written notice of that intention upon the prosecuting attorney prior to trial. For good cause shown, the court may extend the time for service of the notice or make such other order as the interest of justice requires. If the defendant fails to comply with this rule, the court may take such action as the interest of justice requires.

(b) Acquittal by Reason of Insanity. If a defendant interposes the defense of insanity and is acquitted after trial on that ground, the decision and judgment shall include a statement of those facts and the procedure for referral of the defendant as provided by N.J.S.A. 2C:4–8 and 2C:4–9 and R. 4:74–7 shall apply.

(c) Involuntary Civil Commitments. Rule 4:74–7 shall govern the practice and procedure in the municipal court for the disposition of involuntary civil commitment matters, pursuant to N.J.S.A. 30:4–27.1 et seq.

Note: Source—Paragraph (a): R. (1969) 3:12–1; paragraph (b): R. (1969) 3:19–2; paragraph (c): new. Adopted October 6, 1997 effective February 1, 1998; paragraph (b) amended July 5, 2000 to be effective September 5, 2000.

7:7–5. Pretrial Procedure

(a) Pretrial Conference. At any time after the filing of the complaint, the court may order one or more conferences with the parties to consider the results of negotiations between them relating to a proposed plea or to other matters that will promote a fair and expeditious disposition or trial. With the consent of the parties or counsel for the parties, the court may permit any pretrial conference to be conducted by means of telephone or video link.

(b) Pretrial Hearings. The court may conduct hearings to resolve issues relating to the admissibility of statements by defendant, pretrial identifications of defendant, and sound recordings at any time prior to trial. Upon a showing of good cause, hearings as to the admissibility of other evidence may also be conducted at any time prior to trial.

Note: Source—Paragraph (a): new; paragraph (b): R. (1969) 7:4–2(d), 3:9–1(d). Adopted October 6, 1997 to be effective February 1, 1998; paragraph (a) amended July 16, 2009 to be effective September 1, 2009.

7:7–6. Depositions

(a) When Authorized. If it appears to the judge of the court in which a complaint is pending that a witness is likely to be unable to testify at trial because of impending death or physical or mental incapacity, the court, upon motion and notice to the parties, and after a showing that such action is necessary to prevent manifest injustice, may order that a deposition of the testimony of that witness be taken and that any designated books, papers, documents or tangible objects, not privileged, be produced at the same time and place.

(b) Procedure. The deposition shall be videotaped, unless the court otherwise orders. The deposition shall be taken before the judge at a location convenient to all parties. If the judge is unable to preside because the deposition is to be taken outside of the State, the deposition shall be taken before a person designated by the judge. All parties and counsel shall have a right to be present at the deposition. Examination, cross-examination, and determination of admissibility of evidence shall proceed in the same manner as at trial. Videotaping shall be done by a person chosen by the judge who is independent of both prosecution and defense.

(c) Use. Depositions taken pursuant to paragraph (a) of this rule may be used at trial instead of the testimony of the witness if the witness is unable to testify in court because of impending death or physical or mental incapacity, or if the judge finds that the party offering the deposition has been unable to procure the attendance of the witness by subpoena or otherwise, the deposition shall be admissible pursuant to the Rules of Evidence applied as though the witness were then present and testifying. The deposition shall not be admissible, however, unless the court finds that the circumstances surrounding its taking allowed adequate preparation and cross-examination by all parties. A record of the videotaped testimony, which shall be part of the official record of the court proceedings, shall be made in the same manner as if the witness were present and testifying. On conclusion of the trial, the videotape shall be retained by the court.

Note: Source—R. (1969) 7:4–2(h), 3:13–2(a), (b), (c). Adopted October 6, 1997 to be effective February 1, 1998.

7:7–7. Discovery and Inspection

(a) **Scope.** If the government is represented by the municipal or a private prosecutor, discovery shall be available to the parties only as provided by this rule, unless the court otherwise orders. In the absence of a municipal or private prosecutor, discovery shall be available to the parties in the manner directed by the court. All discovery requests by defendant shall be served on the municipal prosecutor, who shall be responsible for making government discovery available to the defendant. If the matter is, however, not being prosecuted by the municipal prosecutor, the municipal prosecutor shall transmit defendant's discovery requests to the prosecutor, or, if there is no prosecutor, the municipal prosecutor shall transmit defendant's court ordered discovery requests to the complaining witness.

(b) **Discovery by Defendant.** In all cases involving a consequence of magnitude or when ordered by the court, the defendant, on written notice to the municipal prosecutor or private prosecutor, shall be allowed to inspect, copy, and photograph or to be provided with copies of any relevant:

(1) books, tangible objects, papers or documents obtained from or belonging to the defendant;

(2) records of statements or confessions, signed or unsigned, by the defendant or copies thereof, and a summary of any admissions or declarations against penal interest made by the defendant that are known to the prosecution but not recorded;

(3) grand jury proceedings recorded pursuant to R. 3:6–6;

(4) results or reports of physical or mental examinations and of scientific tests or experiments made in connection with the matter or copies of these results or reports, that are within the possession, custody or control of the prosecuting attorney;

(5) reports or records of defendant's prior convictions;

(6) books, originals or copies of papers and documents, or tangible objects, buildings or places that are within the possession, custody or control of the government;

(7) names and addresses of any persons whom the prosecuting attorney knows to have relevant evidence or information, including a designation by the prosecuting attorney as to which of those persons the prosecuting attorney may call as witnesses;

(8) record of statements, signed or unsigned, by the persons described by subsection (7) of this rule or by co-defendants within the possession, custody or control of the prosecuting attorney, and any relevant record of prior conviction of those persons;

(9) police reports that are within the possession, custody or control of the prosecuting attorney;

(10) warrants, that have been completely executed, and any papers accompanying them, as described by R. 7:5–1(a);

(11) the names and addresses of each person whom the prosecuting attorney expects to call to trial as an expert witness, the expert's qualifications, the subject matter on which the expert is expected to testify, a copy of the report, if any, of the expert witness, or if no report was prepared, a statement of the facts and opinions to which the expert is expected to testify and a summary of the grounds for each opinion. If this information is requested and not furnished, the expert witness may, upon application by the defendant, be barred from testifying at trial.

(c) **Discovery by the State.** In all cases involving a consequence of magnitude or when ordered by the court, the municipal prosecutor or private prosecutor, on written notice to the defendant, shall be allowed to inspect, copy, and photograph or to be provided with copies of any relevant:

(1) results or reports of physical or mental examinations and of scientific tests or experiments made in connection with the matter or copies of these results or reports within the possession, custody or control of the defendant or defense counsel;

(2) any relevant books, originals or copies of papers and other documents or tangible objects, buildings or places within the possession, custody or control of the defendant or defense counsel;

(3) the names and addresses of those persons known to defendant who may be called as witnesses at trial and their written statements, if any, including memoranda reporting or summarizing their oral statements;

(4) written statements, if any, including any memoranda reporting or summarizing the oral statements, made by any witnesses whom the government may call as a witness at trial; and

(5) the names and addresses of each person whom the defense expects to call to trial as an expert witness, the expert's qualifications, the subject matter on which the expert is expected to testify, and a copy of the report, if any, of such expert witness, or if no report is prepared, a statement of the facts and opinions to which the expert is expected to testify and a summary of the

grounds for each opinion. If this information is requested and not furnished, the expert may, upon application by the prosecuting attorney, be barred from testifying at trial.

(d) Documents Not Subject to Discovery. This rule does not require discovery of a party's work product, consisting of internal reports, memoranda or documents made by that party or by that party's attorney or agents, in connection with the investigation, prosecution or defense of the matter. Nor does it require discovery by the government of records or statements, signed or unsigned, by defendant made to defendant's attorney or agents.

(e) Protective Orders.

(1) *Grounds.* Upon motion and for good cause shown, the court may at any time order that the discovery or inspection, copying or photographing sought pursuant to this rule be denied, restricted, or deferred or make such other order as is appropriate. In determining the motion, the court may consider the following: protection of witnesses and others from physical harm, threats of harm, bribes, economic reprisals and other intimidation; maintenance of such secrecy regarding informants as is required for effective investigation of criminal activity; protection of confidential relationships and privileges recognized by law; and any other relevant considerations.

(2) *Procedures.* The court may permit the showing of good cause to be made, in whole or in part, in the form of a written statement to be inspected by the court alone. If the court enters a protective order, the entire text of the statement shall be sealed and preserved in the court's records, to be made available only to the appellate court in the event of an appeal.

(f) Time and Procedure. A defense request for discovery shall be made contemporaneously with the entry of appearance by the defendant's attorney, who shall submit a copy of the appearance and demand for discovery directly to the municipal prosecutor. If the defendant is not represented, any requests for discovery shall be made in writing and submitted by the defendant directly to the municipal prosecutor. The municipal prosecutor shall respond to the discovery request in accordance with paragraph (b) of this rule within 10 days after receiving the request. Unless otherwise ordered by the judge, the defendant shall provide the prosecutor with discovery, as provided by paragraph (c) of this rule, within 20 days of the prosecuting attorney's compliance with the defendant's discovery request. Unless otherwise ordered by the judge, the parties may exchange discovery through the use of e-mail, internet or other electronic means.

(g) Continuing Duty to Disclose; Failure to Comply. If a party who has complied with this rule discovers, either before or during trial, additional material or names of witnesses previously requested or ordered subject to discovery or inspection, that party shall promptly notify the other party or that party's attorney

of the existence of these additional materials and witnesses. If at any time during the course of the proceedings it is brought to the attention of the court that a party has failed to comply with this rule or with an order issued pursuant to this rule, the court may order that party to permit the discovery, inspection, copying or photographing of materials not previously disclosed, grant a continuance, prohibit the party from introducing in evidence the material not disclosed or enter such other order as it deems appropriate.

Note: source-Paragraph (a): new; paragraph (b): R. (1969) 7:4–2(h), 3:13–3(c); paragraph (c): R. (1969) 7:4–2(h), 3:13–3(d); paragraph (d): R. (1969) 7:4–2(h), 3:13–3(e); paragraph (e): R. (1969) 7:4–2(h), 3:13–3(f); paragraph (f) new; paragraph (g): R. (1969) 7:4-2(h), 3:13–3(g). Adopted October 6, 1997 effective February 1, 1998; paragraph (c) amended July 5, 2000 to be effective September 5, 2000; paragraph (f) amended July 16, 2009 to be effective September 1, 2009.

7:7–8. Subpoenas

(a) Issuance. Except as otherwise provided in paragraph (d), upon the issuance of process on a complaint within the trial jurisdiction of the municipal court, a subpoena may be issued by a judicial officer, by an attorney in the name of the court administrator, or, in cases involving a non-indictable offense, by a law enforcement officer or other authorized person. The subpoena shall be in the form approved by the Administrative Director of the Courts. In cases involving non-indictable offenses, the law enforcement officer may issue subpoenas to testify in the form prescribed by the Administrative Director of the Courts. Courts having jurisdiction over such offenses, the Division of State Police, the Motor Vehicle Commission, and any other agency so authorized by the Administrative Director of the Courts may supply subpoena forms to law enforcement officers.

(b) Subpoena to Testify. A subpoena to testify shall state the name of the municipal court and the title of the action. It shall contain the appropriate case docket number and shall command each natural person or authorized agent of an entity to whom it is directed to attend and give testimony at a specific time and date when the court will be in session. The subpoena may also specify that the specific time and date to attend court will be established at a later time by the court. If the witness is to testify in an action for the State or for an indigent defendant, the subpoena shall so note and shall contain an order to appear without the prepayment of any witness fee as otherwise required under N.J.S.A. 22A:1–4.

(c) Subpoena to Produce Documents or Electronically Stored Information. A subpoena may require the production of books, papers, documents, electronically stored information or other items on the date of the scheduled court appearance. The court may enter a supplemental order directing that the items designated in the subpoena be produced in court at a time prior to the scheduled court appearance or at another location.

The order of the court may also specify that the designated items may, upon their production, be inspected by the parties and their attorneys.

(d) Investigative Subpoenas in Operating While Under the Influence Cases. When the State demonstrates to the court through sworn testimony and/or supporting documentation that there is a reasonable basis to believe that a person has operated a motor vehicle in violation of N.J.S.A. 39:4–50 or N.J.S.A. 39:3–10.13, a vessel in violation of N.J.S.A. 12:7–46, or an aircraft in violation of N.J.S.A. 6:1–18, a municipal court judge with jurisdiction over the municipality where the alleged offense occurred may issue an investigative subpoena directing an authorized agent of a medical facility located in New Jersey to produce medical records related to the presence of alcohol, narcotics, hallucinogens, habit-producing drugs or chemical inhalants in the operator's body. If no case is pending, the subpoena may be captioned "In the Matter" under investigation.

(e) Personal Service. A subpoena may be served at any place within the State of New Jersey by any person 18 or more years of age. Service of a subpoena shall be made by personally delivering a copy to the person named, together with the fee allowed by law, except that if the person is a witness in an action for the State or an indigent defendant, the fee shall be paid before leaving the court at the conclusion of the trial by the municipal court administrator as otherwise required by N.J.S.A. 22A:1–4. After service of a subpoena, the person serving the subpoena shall promptly file a copy of the subpoena and proof of service with the court.

(f) Continuing Duty to Appear. A witness who has been personally served with a subpoena shall remain under a continuing obligation to appear until released by the court.

(g) Failure to Appear. In the absence of an adequate excuse, any person who fails to obey a personally served subpoena, as evidenced by an executed return of service, is subject to punishment for contempt of court. The court may issue a warrant for the arrest of the person subject to contempt as authorized by N.J.S.A. 2A:10–8.

(h) Motion to Quash. The court, on motion made prior to the scheduled court date, may quash or modify a subpoena to testify or a subpoena to produce writings or electronically stored information if compliance would be unreasonable, oppressive or not in compliance with the procedures required under this rule.

Note: Source—R. (1969) 7:3–3. Adopted October 6, 1997 to be effective February 1, 1998; caption amended, former text deleted, captions and text for new paragraphs (a) through (h) adopted July 16, 2009 to be effective September 1, 2009.

7:7–9. Filing Appearance

The attorney for the defendant in an action before the municipal court shall immediately file an appearance with the municipal court administrator of the court having jurisdiction over the matter and shall serve a copy on the appropriate prosecuting attorney or other involved party, as identified by the municipal court administrator.

Note: Source—R. (1969) 3:8–1. Adopted October 6, 1997 to be effective February 1, 1998.

7:7–10. Joint Representation

No attorney or law firm shall enter an appearance for or represent more than one defendant in a multi-defendant trial or enter a plea for any defendant without first securing the court's permission by motion made in the presence of the defendants who seek joint representation. The motion shall be made as early as practicable in the proceedings in order to avoid delay of the trial. For good cause shown, the court may allow the motion to be brought at any time.

Note: Source—R. (1969) 3:8–2. Adopted October 6, 1997 to be effective February 1, 1998.

RULE 7:8. TRIAL

7:8–1. Mediation of Minor Disputes in Municipal Court Actions

If a person seeks to file or has filed a complaint charging an offense that may constitute a minor dispute, the court may issue a notice to the person making the charge and the person charged, requiring their appearance before the court or before a person or program designated by the court and approved by the Assignment Judge pursuant to R. 1:40–8 (Mediation of Minor Disputes in Municipal Court Actions). If on the return date of a summons, it appears to the court that the offense charged may constitute a minor dispute, the court may order the persons involved to participate in mediation in accordance with R. 1:40–8. No referral to mediation shall be made, however, if the complaint involves (1) serious injury, (2) repeated acts of violence between the parties, (3) clearly demonstrated psychological or emotional disability of a party, (4) incidents involving the same persons who are already parties to a Superior Court action between them, (5) matters arising under the Prevention of Domestic Violence Act (N.J.S.A. 2C:25–17 et seq.), (6) a violation of the New Jersey Motor Vehicle Code (Title 39), or (7) matters involving penalty enforcement actions.

Note: Source—R. (1969) 7:3–2. Adopted October 6, 1997 to be effective February 1, 1998; amended July 5, 2000 to be effective September 5, 2000; caption and text amended June 15, 2007 to be effective September 1, 2007.

7:8–2. Place of Trial; Disqualification

(a) Generally. Except as otherwise provided by law, the prosecution for an offense shall take place in the jurisdiction in which the offense was committed.

(b) Disqualification of Judge. In the event of the judge's disqualification or inability for any reason to hear a pending matter, the judge, in addition to the provisions of R. 1:12–3(a), may either refer the matter to the Assignment Judge for designation of an acting judge pursuant to N.J.S.A. 2B:12–6 or transfer the matter to a judge sitting in another municipality within the vicinage. The transferee judge may, however, accept the transfer only if:

(1) the transferee judge has been designated as an acting judge of the court of origin by the Assignment Judge of the vicinage, pursuant to N.J.S.A. 2B:12–6 and R. 1:12–3(a); and

(2) the transferring judge has found that transfer of the matter will not substantially inconvenience any party.

Upon completion of the trial, the transferee court shall immediately advise the court of origin of the disposition made and shall remit to it the complaint, judgment, all records, and any fines and costs collected. The court of origin shall retain jurisdiction and shall maintain all necessary records as though the matter had been tried in the court of origin, which shall be responsible for effecting final disposition of the matter. The municipality of the court of origin shall bear the costs of prosecution of the matter.

Note: Source—R. (1969) 7:4–3. Adopted October 6, 1997 to be effective February 1, 1998.

7:8–3. Adjournment

On or before the first scheduled trial date, the court may adjourn the trial for not more than fourteen days, except that an adjournment for a longer period or additional adjournments may be granted if the court deems postponement of the trial to be reasonably necessary in the interest of justice. In contested matters, the court shall specify the new trial date in granting the adjournment and shall cause the complaining witness, all defendants, and all other known witnesses to be notified of the adjournment and of the new trial date.

Note: Source—R. (1969) 7:4–2(c). Adopted October 6, 1997 to be effective February 1, 1998.

7:8–4. Trial of Complaints Together

The court may order two or more complaints to be tried together if the offenses arose out of the same facts and circumstances, regardless of the number of defendants. In all other matters, the court may consolidate complaints for trial with the consent of the persons charged. A party seeking consolidation Complaints originating in two or more municipalities may be consolidated for trial only with the approval of the appropriate Assignment Judge, who shall designate the municipal court in which trial is to proceed. A party seeking consolidation of complaints originating in dif-

ferent municipalities shall file a written motion for that relief directly with the Assignment Judge.

Note: Source—R. (1969) 7:4–2(g). Adopted October 6, 1997 to be effective February 1, 1998.

7:8–5. Dismissal

If the complaint is not moved on the day for trial, the court may direct that it be heard on a specified return date and a notice thereof be served on the complaining witness, all defendants and all other known witnesses. If the complaint is not moved on that date, the court may order the complaint dismissed. A complaint may also be dismissed by the court for good cause at any time on its own motion, on the motion of the State, county or municipality or on defendant's motion. On dismissal, any warrant issued shall be recalled, and the matter shall not be reopened on the same complaint except to correct a manifest injustice.

Note: Source—R. (1969) 7:4–2(i). Adopted October 6, 1997 to be effective February 1, 1998; amended July 28, 2004 to be effective September 1, 2004.

7:8–6. Transfer to the Chancery Division, Family Part

An action pending in a municipal court may be transferred to the Superior Court, Chancery Division, Family Part pursuant to R. 5:1–2(c)(3) and R. 5:1–3(b)(2).

Note: Source—R. (1969) 7:4–2(j). Adopted October 6, 1997 to be effective February 1, 1998.

7:8–7. Appearances; Exclusion of the Public

(a) Presence of Defendant. Except as otherwise provided by Rules 7:6–1(b), 7:6–3, or 7:12–3, the defendant shall be present, either in person, or by means of a video link as approved by the Administrative Office of the Courts, at every stage of the proceeding and at the imposition of sentence. If, however, defendant is voluntarily absent after the proceeding has begun in the defendant's presence or the defendant fails to appear at the proceeding after having been informed in open court of the time and place of the proceeding, the proceeding may continue to and including entry of judgment. A corporation, partnership or unincorporated association shall appear by its attorney unless an appearance on its behalf by an officer or agent has been permitted pursuant to R. 7:6–2(a)(2). The defendant's presence is not, however, required at a hearing on a motion for reduction of sentence.

(b) Appearance for the Prosecution. The municipal prosecutor, municipal attorney. Attorney General, county prosecutor, or county counsel, as the case may be, may appear in any municipal court in any action on behalf of the State and conduct the prosecution either on the court's request or on the request of the respective public official. The court may also, in its discretion and in the interest of justice, direct the municipal prosecutor to represent the State. The court may permit an attorney to appear as a private prosecutor to represent the State in cases involving cross-complaints. Such private prosecutors may be permitted to appear on behalf of the State only if the court has first reviewed the private prosecutor's motion to so appear and an accompanying certification submitted on a form approved by the Administrative Director of the Courts. The court may grant the private prosecutor's application to appear if it is satisfied that a potential for conflict exists for the municipal prosecutor due to the nature of the charges set forth in the cross-complaints. The court shall place such a finding on the record.

(c) Exclusion of the Public. In matters involving domestic relations, sex offenses, school truancy, parental neglect, and as may be otherwise provided by law, the court, in its discretion and with defendant's consent, may exclude from the courtroom any person not directly interested in the matter during the conduct of the trial or hearing.

Note: Source — R. (1969) 7:4–2(g). Adopted October 6, 1997 to be effective February 1, 1998; paragraph (a) amended July 5, 2000 to be effective September 5, 2000; paragraphs (a) and (b) amended June 15, 2007 to be effective September 1, 2007.

7:8–8. Record of Proceedings; Transcripts

(a) Record. If required by order of the Supreme Court, the municipal court shall cause all proceedings to be recorded by sound recording equipment approved by the Administrative Office of the Courts. If not so required, the court may, at its own expense, cause proceedings to be recorded either by sound recording equipment or by a court reporter. If sound recording equipment is used, or if the proceedings are not otherwise recorded, the court shall permit a record of the proceedings to be made by a certified shorthand reporter at the request and expense of any party. Every sound recording and stenographic record of proceedings made pursuant to this rule shall be retained by the municipal court administrator or by the reporter, as the case may be, for 5 years.

(b) Transcript. If the proceedings have been sound recorded, any person may order a transcript from the municipal court administrator, and if the proceedings have been recorded stenographically, any person may order a transcript from the court reporter. The charge shall not exceed the rates as provided by law. The person preparing the transcript shall certify to its accuracy.

(c) Supervision. The recording of proceedings and the preparation of transcripts thereof, whether by sound recording or reporters, shall be subject to the supervision and control of the Administrative Director of the Courts.

Note: Source—R. (1969) 7:4–5. Adopted October 6, 1997 to be effective February 1, 1998.

7:8–9. Procedures on Failure to Appear

(a) Warrant or Notice.

(1) *Non–Parking Motor Vehicle Cases.* If a defendant in any non-parking case before the court fails to appear or answer a complaint, the court may either issue a warrant for the defendant's arrest in accordance with R. 7:2–2(c) or issue and mail a failure to appear notice to the defendant on a form approved by the Administrative Director of the Courts. If a failure to appear notice is mailed to the defendant and the defendant fails to comply with its provisions, a warrant may be issued in accordance with R. 7:2–2(c).

(2) *Parking Cases.* In all parking cases, an arrest warrant shall only be issued if the defendant has failed to respond to two or more pending parking tickets within the jurisdiction. A warrant shall not issue when the pending tickets have been issued on the same day or otherwise within the same 24–hour period.

(b) Driving Privileges; Report to Motor Vehicle Commission.

(1) *Non-Parking Motor Vehicle Cases.* If the court has not issued an arrest warrant upon the failure of the defendant to comply with the court's failure to appear notice, the court shall report the failure to appear or answer to the Chief Administrator of the Motor Vehicle Commission on a form approved by the Administrative Director of the Courts within 30 days of the defendant's failure to appear or answer. The court shall then mark the case as closed on its records, subject to being reopened pursuant to subparagraph (e) of this rule. If the court elects, however, to issue an arrest warrant, it may simultaneously report the failure to appear or answer to the Motor Vehicle Commission on a form approved by the Administrative Director of the Courts. If the court does not simultaneously notify the Motor Vehicle Commission and the warrant has not been executed within 30 days, the court shall report the failure to appear or answer to the Motor Vehicle Commission on a form approved by the Administrative Director of the Courts. Upon the notification to the Motor Vehicle Commission, the court shall then mark the case as closed on its records subject to being reopened pursuant to subparagraph (e) of this rule.

(2) *All Other Cases.* In all other cases, whether or not an arrest warrant is issued, the court may order the suspension of the defendant's driving privileges or of defendant's nonresident reciprocity privileges or prohibit the person from receiving or obtaining driving privileges until the pending matter is adjudicated or otherwise disposed of. The court shall then mark the case as closed on its records, subject to being reopened pursuant to subparagraph (e) of this rule.

(c) Unexecuted Arrest Warrant. If an arrest warrant is not executed, it shall remain open and active until the court either recalls, withdraws or discharges it. If bail has been posted after the issuance of the arrest warrant and the defendant fails to appear or answer, the court may declare a forfeiture of the bail, report a motor vehicle bail forfeiture to the Motor Vehicle Commission and mark the case as closed on its records subject to being reopened pursuant to subparagraph (e) of this rule. The court may set aside any bail forfeiture in the interest of justice.

(d) Parking Cases; Unserved Notice. In parking cases, no arrest warrant may be issued if the initial failure to appear notice is returned to the court by the Postal Service marked to indicate that the defendant cannot be located. The court then may order a suspension of the registration of the motor vehicle or of the defendant's driving privileges or defendant's nonresident reciprocity privileges or prohibit the person from receiving or obtaining driving privileges until the pending matter is adjudicated or otherwise disposed of. The court shall forward the order to suspend to the Motor Vehicle Commission on a form approved by the Administrative Director of the Courts. The court shall then mark the case as closed on its records, subject to being reopened pursuant to subparagraph (e) of this rule.

(e) Reopening. A case marked closed shall be reopened upon the request of the defendant, the prosecuting attorney or on the court's own motion.

(f) Dismissal of Parking Tickets. In any parking case, if the municipal court fails, within three years of the date of the violation, to either issue a warrant for the defendant's arrest or to order a suspension of the registration of the vehicle or the defendant's driving privileges or the defendant's non-resident reciprocity privileges or prohibit the person from receiving or obtaining driving privileges, the matter shall be dismissed and shall not be reopened.

Note: Source—Paragraphs (a), (b), (c), (d), (e): R. (1969) 7:6–3; paragraph (f): new. Adopted October 6, 1997 to be effective February 1, 1998; paragraph (a) text deleted, and new paragraphs (a)(1) and (a)(2) adopted July 28, 2004 to be effective September 1, 2004; paragraph (b) caption amended, paragraphs (b)(1), (c), (d) and (f) amended July 16, 2009 to be effective September 1, 2009.

7:8–10.   Waiver of Right to Counsel at Trial

In all cases other than parking cases, a request by a defendant to proceed to trial without an attorney shall not be granted until the judge is satisfied from an inquiry on the record that the defendant has knowingly and voluntarily waived the right to counsel following an explanation by the judge of the range of penal consequences and an advisement that the defendant may have defenses and that there are dangers and disadvantages inherent in defending oneself.

Note: Adopted July 16, 2009 to be effective September 1, 2009.

RULE 7:9.   SENTENCE AND JUDGMENT

7:9–1.   Sentence

(a) Imposition of Sentence; Bail. If the defendant has been convicted of or pleaded guilty to a nonindictable offense, sentence shall be imposed immediately, unless the court postpones sentencing in order to obtain a presentence report or for other good cause. Pending sentence, the court may commit the defendant or continue or modify the bail. Before imposing sentence the court shall afford the defendant and defense counsel an opportunity to make a statement on defendant's behalf and to present any information in mitigation of punishment. Where a sentence has been opened and vacated, the defendant shall be resentenced immediately, except where a new trial is granted.

(b) Statement of Reasons. At the time sentence is imposed, the court shall state its reasons for imposing the sentence, including its findings respecting the criteria prescribed by N.J.S.A. 2C:44–1 to 2C:44–3 for withholding or imposing imprisonment, fines or restitution. The court shall also state its factual basis for its finding of particular aggravating or mitigating factors affecting sentence.

(c) Probation. The court, at the time of sentencing, shall inform a defendant sentenced to probation of the penalties that may be imposed upon revocation of probation for failure to adhere to the conditions of probation.

(d) Probation and Suspended Sentence. After conviction, unless otherwise provided by law, the court may suspend the imposition of a sentence or place the defendant on probation. The order shall require the defendant to comply with standard conditions of probation adopted by the court and filed with the municipal court administrator, as well as such special conditions, including a term of imprisonment pursuant to N.J.S.A. 2C:45–1(c), as the court imposes. As a condition of probation the court may also impose a term of community-related service to be performed by the defendant under such terms and conditions as the court may determine. A copy of the order, together with the standard and special conditions, shall be furnished to the defendant and read and explained to the defendant by the probation officer. The defendant and the probation officer shall sign a joint statement, to be filed with the municipal court administrator, as to the officer's compliance with the reading and explanation requirements of this rule. If the defendant refuses to sign the statement, the defendant shall be resentenced. At any time before termination of the period of suspension or probation, the court may revoke a suspension or probation pursuant to N.J.S.A. 2C:45–3.

Note: Source—Paragraph (a): R. (1969) 7:4–6(a); paragraph (b): R. (1969) 7:4–6(c); paragraph (c): R. (1969) 3:21–4(c); paragraph (d): R. (1969) 7:4–6(e) and R. (1969) 3:21–7. Adopted October 6, 1997 to be effective February 1, 1998.

7:9–2. Judgment

(a) Generally. A judgment of conviction shall set forth the complaint, the plea, the findings, the adjudication and the sentence. It shall cite with specificity the statute or ordinance section to which the conviction relates or a short description of the statute or ordinance, the names and addresses of the witnesses sworn, and a list of exhibits produced at the trial. If the defendant is found not guilty or for any other reason is entitled to be discharged, a judgment shall be entered accordingly. The judgment shall be signed by the court and entered by the municipal court administrator. If at the time of hearing, judgment was reserved, the court upon the entry of judgment of acquittal shall immediately mail a copy of the judgment to the defendant by ordinary mail; if convicted, however, the defendant shall be notified to appear in court for entry of judgment and sentencing.

(b) Conviction of a Corporation. If a corporation is convicted of an offense, the court shall give judgment on the conviction and shall cause the judgment to be enforced in the same manner as a judgment in a civil action.

Note: Source—Paragraph (a): R. (1969) 7:4–6(b); paragraph (b): R. (1969) 7:4–6(d), 3:21–6. Adopted October 6, 1997 to be effective February 1, 1998.

7:9–3. Credit for Confinement Pending Sentence

The defendant shall receive credit on the term of custodial sentence for any time served in custody, either in jail or in a state hospital, between the arrest and the imposition of a sentence.

Note: Source—R. (1969) 7:4–6(f), 3:21–8. Adopted October 6, 1997 to be effective February 1, 1998.

7:9–4. Reduction or Change of Sentence

(a) Time. The court, in its discretion, may reduce or change a sentence, either on its own motion or on the motion of defendant, which may be either oral or written, at any time during which the court retains jurisdiction over the matter.

(b) Procedure. All changes of sentence shall be made in open court upon notice to the defendant and the prosecuting attorney. An appropriate order setting forth the revised sentence and specifying the change made and the reasons for the change shall be entered on the record.

Note: Source—R. (1969) 7:4–6(g), 3:21–10(a), (c). Adopted October 6, 1997 to be effective February 1, 1998.

RULE 7:10. POST–TRIAL PROCEEDINGS

7:10–1. New Trial

On defendant's motion, the court may, pursuant to the time limitations of this rule, grant the defendant a new trial if required in the interest of justice. The court may vacate the judgment if already entered, take additional testimony, and direct the entry of a new judgment. A motion for a new trial, based on the ground of newly discovered evidence, shall be made within two years after entry of a final judgment. A motion for a new trial on the grounds of fraud or lack of jurisdiction may be made at any time. A motion for a new trial, based on any other grounds, shall be made within twenty days after the entry of judgment of conviction or within such further time as the court fixes during the twenty-day period.

Note: Source–R. (1969) 7:4–7. Adopted October 6, 1997 to be effective February 1, 1998; amended June 15, 2007 to be effective September 1, 2007.

7:10–2. Post–Conviction Relief

(a) Petition for Relief. A person convicted of an offense may, pursuant to this rule, file with the municipal court administrator of the municipality in which the conviction took place, a petition for post-conviction relief captioned in the action in which the conviction was entered.

(b) Limitations and Exclusiveness.

(1) A petition to correct an illegal sentence may be filed at any time.

(2) A petition based on any other grounds shall not be accepted for filing more than five years after entry of the judgment of conviction or imposition of the sentence sought to be attacked, unless it alleges facts showing that the delay in filing was due to defendant's excusable neglect.

(3) A petition for post-conviction relief shall be the exclusive means of challenging a judgment of conviction, except as otherwise required by the Constitution of New Jersey, but it is not a substitute for appeal from a conviction or for a motion incident to the proceedings in the trial court, and may not be filed while appellate review or the filing of a motion in the municipal court is available.

(c) Grounds. A petition for post-conviction relief is cognizable if based on any of the following grounds:

(1) substantial denial in the conviction proceedings of defendant's rights under the Constitution of the United States or the Constitution or laws of New Jersey;

(2) lack of jurisdiction of the court to impose the judgment rendered on defendant's conviction;

(3) imposition of sentence in excess of or otherwise not in accordance with the sentence authorized by law; or

(4) any ground previously available as a basis for collateral attack on a conviction by habeas corpus or any other common law or statutory remedy.

(d) Bar of Grounds Not Raised in Prior Proceedings; Exceptions.

(1) The defendant is barred from asserting in a proceeding under this rule any grounds for relief not raised in a prior proceeding under this rule, or in the proceedings resulting in the conviction, or in a post-conviction proceeding brought and decided prior to the adoption of R. 3:22–4, or in any appeal taken in any of those proceedings, unless the court on motion or at the hearing finds that:

(A) the grounds for relief not previously asserted could not reasonably have been raised in any prior proceeding;

(B) enforcement of the bar would result in fundamental injustice; or

(C) denial of relief would be contrary to the Constitution of the United States or of New Jersey.

(2) A prior adjudication on the merits of any grounds for relief asserted in the petition is conclusive, whether made in the proceedings resulting in the conviction or any prior post-conviction proceeding, or in any appeal taken from those proceedings.

(e) Assignment of Counsel. A defendant may annex to the petition a sworn statement asserting indigency in the form (Form 5A) prescribed by the Administrative Director of the Courts, which form shall be furnished by the municipal court administrator. If the court finds that the defendant is indigent as herein provided, and that the original conviction involved a consequence of magnitude, it shall order counsel assigned to represent defendant and shall further order a transcript of testimony of any proceeding shown to be necessary in establishing the grounds of relief asserted. Absent a showing of good cause, which shall not include lack of merit of the petition, the court shall not substitute new assigned counsel. If counsel is assigned, the court shall not thereafter substitute new assigned counsel absent a showing of good cause, which shall not, however, include lack of merit of the petition.

(f) Procedure.

(1) The municipal court administrator shall make an entry of the filing of the petition in the proceedings in which the conviction took place, and if it is filed pro se, shall forthwith transmit a copy to the municipal prosecutor. An attorney filing the petition shall serve a copy on the municipal prosecutor before filing.

(2) The petition shall be verified by defendant and shall set forth with specificity the facts upon which the claim for relief is based, the legal grounds of the complaint asserted and the particular relief sought. The petition shall include the following information:

(A) the date, docket number and contents of the complaint upon which the conviction is based and the municipality where filed;

(B) the sentence or judgment complained of, the date it was imposed or entered, and the name of the municipal court judge then presiding;

(C) any appellate proceedings brought from the conviction, with copies of the appellate opinions attached;

(D) any prior post-conviction relief proceedings relating to the same conviction, including the date and nature of the claim and the date and nature of disposition, and whether an appeal was taken from those proceedings and, if so, the judgment on appeal;

(E) the name of counsel, if any, representing defendant in any prior proceeding relating to the conviction, and whether counsel was retained or assigned; and

(F) whether and where defendant is presently confined. A separate memorandum of law may be submitted.

(G) In addition, the moving papers in support of such an application shall include, if available, records related to the underlying conviction, including, but not limited to, copies of all complaints, applications for assignment of counsel, waiver forms and transcripts of the defendant's first appearance, entry of guilty plea and all other municipal court proceedings related to the conviction sought to be challenged. The petitioner shall account for any unavailable records by way of written documentation from the municipal court administrator or the custodian of records, as the case may be.

(3) Amendments of the petitions shall be liberally allowed. Assigned counsel may, as a matter of course, serve and file an amended petition within 25 days after assignment. Within 30 days after service of a copy of the petition or amended petition, the municipal prosecutor shall serve and file an answer to the petition or move on ten days' notice for dismissal. If the motion for dismissal is denied, the government's answer shall be filed within fifteen days after entry of the order denying the dismissal.

(4) A defendant in custody shall be present in court if oral testimony is adduced on a material issue of fact within the defendant's personal knowledge. A defendant in custody may otherwise be present in court only in the judge's discretion.

(5) In making a final determination on a petition, either on motion for dismissal or after hearing, the court shall state separately its findings of fact and conclusions of law and shall enter judgment or sentence in the conviction proceedings and any appropriate provisions as to rearraignment, retrial, custody, bail, discharge, correction of sentence or as may otherwise be required.

(g) Petition to Obtain Relief from an Enhanced Custodial Term Based on a Prior Conviction

(1) *Venue.* A post-conviction petition to obtain relief from an enhanced custodial term based on a prior conviction shall be brought in the court where the prior conviction was entered.

(2) *Time Limitations.* The time limitations for filing petitions for post-conviction relief under this section shall be the same as those set forth in R. 7:10–2(b)(2).

(3) *Procedure.* A petition for post-conviction relief sought under this section shall be in writing and shall conform to the requirements of Rule 7:10–2(f). In addition, the moving papers in support of such an application shall include, if available, records related to the underlying conviction, including, but not limited to, copies of all complaints, applications for assignment of counsel, waiver forms and transcripts of the defendant's first appearance, entry of guilty plea and all other municipal court proceedings related to the conviction sought to be challenged. The petitioner shall account for any unavailable records by way of written documentation from the municipal court administrator or the custodian of records, as the case may be.

(4) *Appeal.* Appeals from a denial of post-conviction relief from the effect of a prior conviction shall be combined with any appeal from proceedings involving the repeat offense. Appeals by the State may be taken under R. 3:23–2(a).

Note: Source—Paragraph (a): R. (1969) 3:22–1; paragraph (b)(1),(2): R. (1969) 3:22–12; paragraph (b)(3): R (1969) 3:22–3; paragraph (c): R. (1969) 7:8–1, 3:22–2; paragraph (d)(1): R. (1969) 3:22–4; paragraph (d)(2): R. (1969) 3:22-5; paragraph (e): R. (1969) 3:22–6(a),(c),(d); paragraph (f)(1): R. (1969) 3:22–7; paragraph (f)(2): R. (1969) 3:22–8; paragraph (f)(3): R. (1969) 3:22–9; paragraph (f)(4): R. (1969) 3:22–10; paragraph (f)(5): R. (1969) 3:22–11. Adopted October 6, 1997 to be effective February 1, 1998; new subparagraph (f)(2)(G) and new paragraph (g) adopted June 15, 2007 to be effective September 1, 2007; paragraph (g)(2) amended July 16, 2009 to be effective September 1, 2009.

RULE 7:11. SUMMARY PROCEEDINGS FOR COLLECTION OF STATUTORY PENALTIES [DELETED]

7:11–1. Applicability of Rule [Deleted]

Note: Source—R. (1969) 7:9, 4:70–1(a). Adopted October 6, 1997 to be effective February 1, 1998; rule deleted July 28, 2004 to be effective September 1, 2004.

7:11–2. Complaint; Verification [Deleted]

Note: Source—R.(1969) 7:9, 4:70–2. Adopted October 6, 1997 to be effective February 1, 1998; rule deleted July 28, 2004 to be effective September 1, 2004.

7:11–3. Process [Deleted]

Note: Source—R. (1969) 7:9, 4:70–3. Adopted October 6, 1997 to be effective February 1, 1998; paragraph (a) amended July 5, 2000 to be effective September 5, 2000; rule deleted July 28, 2004 to be effective September 1, 2004.

7:11–4. Penalties; Payment; Hearing [Deleted]

Note: Source—R. (1969) 7:9, 4:70–4. Adopted October 6, 1997 to be effective February 1, 1998; paragraph (a) amended July 5, 2000 to be effective September 5, 2000; rule deleted July 28, 2004 to be effective September 1, 2004.

7:11–5. Judgment; Commitment [Deleted]

Note: Source—R.(1969) 7:9, 4:70–5. Adopted October 6, 1997 to be effective February 1, 1998; rule deleted July 28, 2004 to be effective September 1, 2004.

RULE 7:12. TRIAL OF TRAFFIC OFFENSES

7:12–1. Trial Date; Adjournment

The date fixed for the trial of any traffic offense shall be not less than five days from the date of its commission unless the defendant, having been informed of the right to such trial date, waives it and the court in its discretion fixes an earlier date. If a hearing is adjourned, the court may detain the defendant in safe custody, unless the defendant makes a cash deposit or gives a recognizance in accordance with R. 7:4 in an amount not exceeding $500, or qualifies and justifies in real estate security situated in this State in twice the amount fixed for the bail.

Note: Source—R. (1969) 7:6–4. Adopted October 6, 1997 to be effective February 1, 1998.

7:12–2. Calendar Parts; Sessions

Insofar as practicable, traffic offenses shall be tried separate and apart from other offenses. Except for good cause shown, if a court sits in parts and one part sits in daily session and has been designated as a traffic court, traffic offenses shall be tried in that part only, or if a court has designated a particular session, which may be an evening session, as the traffic session, traffic offenses shall be tried in that session. If there is neither a special part nor a special session, the court shall designate the time for a trial of traffic offenses. The Administrative Director of the Courts may, where necessary, direct a court to hold more frequent traffic sessions or to coordinate the sessions held by the court with those regularly scheduled by any other municipal court judges in the county.

Note: Source—R. (1969) 7:6–5. Adopted October 6, 1997 to be effective February 1, 1998.

7:12–3. Pleas of Not Guilty and Pleas of Guilty by Mail in Certain Traffic or Parking Offenses

(a) Use of Pleas by Mail; Limitations. In all traffic or parking offenses, except as limited below, the judge may permit the defendant to enter a guilty plea by mail, or to plead not guilty by mail and submit a written defense for use at trial, if a personal appearance by the defendant would constitute an undue hardship such as illness, physical incapacity, substantial distance to travel, or incarceration. This procedure shall not be available in the following types of cases:

(1) traffic offenses or parking offenses that require the imposition of a mandatory loss of driving privileges on conviction;

(2) traffic offenses or parking offenses involving an accident that resulted in personal injury to anyone other than the defendant;

(3) traffic offenses or parking offenses that are related to non-traffic matters that are not resolved;

(4) any other traffic offense or parking offense when excusing the defendant's appearance in municipal court would not be in the interest of justice.

(b) Plea of Guilty by Mail.

(1) In those cases where a defendant may enter a plea of guilty to a traffic offense or parking offense by mail, such plea shall include:

(A) an acknowledgement that defendant committed the traffic violation or parking offense set forth in the complaint(s);

(B) a waiver of the defendant's right to contest the case at a trial, the right to appear personally in court and, if unrepresented by an attorney, the right to be represented by an attorney;

(C) an acknowledgement by the defendant that the plea of guilty is being entered voluntarily;

(2) A plea of guilty to a traffic offense or parking offense by mail may also include a statement for the court to consider when determining the appropriate sentence.

(c) Plea of Not Guilty by Mail

(1) In those cases where a defendant may enter a plea of not guilty to a traffic offense or parking offense and submit any defense to the charge(s) by mail, such not guilty plea and defense shall include the following:

(A) A waiver of the defendant's right to appear personally in court to contest the charge(s) and, if unrepresented by an attorney, a waiver of the right to be represented by an attorney;

(B) Any factual or legal defenses that the defendant would like the court to consider;

(2) A defense to a traffic offense or parking offense submitted by mail may also include a statement for the court to consider when deciding on the appropriate sentence in the event of a finding of guilty.

(d) Forms. Any forms necessary to implement the provisions of this rule shall be approved by the Administrative Director of the Courts.

(e) Judgment. If a defendant elects to enter a plea of guilty or to enter a plea of not guilty under the procedures set forth in this rule, the court shall send the defendant a copy of the judgment by ordinary mail. *Source—R. (1969) 7:7–6. Adopted October 6, 1997 to be effective February 1, 1998; caption amended, paragraph (a) caption and text amended, former paragraph (b) amended and redesignated as paragraph (c), and new paragraph (b) adopted July 28, 2004 to be effective September 1, 2004; caption of rule amended, captions and text of former paragraphs (a) and (b) deleted, former paragraph (c) redesignated as paragraph (e) and amended, and new paragraphs (a), (b), (c), and (d) adopted June 15, 2007 to be effective September 1, 2007; paragraph (a) amended July 16, 2009 to be effective September 1, 2009.*

7:12–4. Violations Bureau; Designation; Functions

(a) Establishment. If the court determines that the efficient disposition of its business and the convenience of defendants so requires, it may establish a violations bureau and designate the violations clerk. The violations clerk may be the municipal court administrator, the deputy court administrator, other employee of the court, or, with the prior approval of the Supreme Court, any other appropriate official or employee of the municipality, except any elected official or any officer or employee of a police department in the municipality in which the court is held. If no municipal official or employee of the municipality is available, any other suitable and responsible person may be appointed subject to the prior approval of the Supreme Court. The judge designated to preside over a joint or central municipal court may establish a violations bureau. The violations clerk may be the municipal court administrator, the deputy court administrator, other employee of the joint or central municipal court, or, with the prior approval of the Supreme Court, any other appropriate official or employee of the municipality in the instance of a central municipal court or of any of the municipalities comprising the joint municipal court, except any elected official or any officer or employee of a police department in the municipality in which the court is held. If no such municipal official or employee is available, any other suitable and responsible person may be appointed subject to the prior approval of the Supreme Court. The violations clerk shall accept appearances, waiver of trial, pleas of guilty and payments of fines and costs in non-indictable offenses, subject to the limitations as provided by law or Part VII of the Rules of Court or the Statewide Violations Bureau Schedule approved by the Supreme Court. The violations clerk shall serve under the direction and control of the designating court.

(b) Location. Whenever practical, the violations bureau shall be in a public building. The location shall be designated by the court subject to the approval of the Administrative Director of the Courts, and the violations clerk shall take pleas and accept payment of fines and costs only at such location. An appropriate sign reading "Violations Bureau, _____ Municipal Court" shall be posted at the entrance to the violations bureau.

(c) Designated Offenses; Schedule of Penalties. The court shall establish by order a "Local Supplemental Violations Bureau Schedule", which may from time to time be amended, supplemented or repealed, designating the non-indictable offenses within the authority of the violations clerk, provided that such offenses shall not include:

(1) non-parking traffic offenses requiring an increased penalty for a subsequent violation;

(2) offenses involving traffic accidents resulting in personal injury;

(3) operation of a motor vehicle while under the influence of intoxicating liquor or a narcotic or habit-producing drug or permitting another person who is under such influence to operate a motor vehicle owned by the defendant or in his or her custody or control;

(4) reckless driving;

(5) careless driving where there has been an accident resulting in personal injury;

(6) leaving the scene of an accident;

(7) driving while on the revoked list; or

(8) driving without a valid driver's license.

The Local Supplemental Violations Bureau Schedule shall be submitted to and approved by the Assignment Judge of the county in which the court is located. It shall specify the amount of fines, costs and statutory

penalties to be imposed for each offense within the authority of the violations clerk, including, in the discretion of the court, higher fines, costs and penalties for second and subsequent offenses, provided such fines, costs and penalties are within the limits declared by statute or ordinance. The Statewide Violations Bureau Schedule and the Local Supplemental Violations Bureau Schedule shall be posted for public view at the violations bureau.

(d) Plea and Payment of Fines, Costs and Penalties. A person charged with an offense within the authority of the violations clerk, may, upon ascertaining the fines, costs and penalties established by the Statewide Violations Bureau Schedule or Local Supplemental Violations Bureau Schedule for the offense charged, pay the same, either by mail or in person, to the violations clerk on or before the return date of the summons, provided that when the summons is marked to indicate that a court appearance is required, payment may not be made to the violations clerk even though the offense is on the Statewide Violations Bureau Schedule or Local Supplemental Violations Bureau Schedule. The tender of payment for an offense to the Violations Bureau, without a signed guilty plea and waiver, may be accepted by the clerk, and shall have the effect of a guilty plea. The court may process the payment and enter a guilty finding to the offense on its records. That finding shall be subject to being reopened subject to R. 7:10–1, in the court's discretion, on motion by either the court or the defendant. If the defendant is a corporation, partnership, or unincorporated association, the plea and waiver may be signed or payment may be made on its behalf by any of its agents or employees. The court in its discretion may authorize the violations clerk to accept such plea and payment after the return date of the summons.

Note: Source–Paragraph (a): R. (1969) 7:7–1; paragraph (b): R. (1969) 7:7–2; paragraph (c): R. (1969) 7:7–3; paragraph (d): R. (1969) 7:7–4. Adopted October 6, 1997 to be effective February 1, 1998; paragraph (d) amended July 5, 2000 to be effective September 5, 2000; paragraph (a) amended June 15, 2007 to be effective September 1, 2007.

RULE 7:13. APPEALS

7:13–1. Appeals

Appeals shall be taken in accordance with R. 3:23, 3:24, and 4:74–3, and in extraordinary cases and in the interest of justice, in accordance with R. 2:2–3(b). Appeals from judgments of conviction and interlocutory orders in municipal court actions heard in the Law Division, Special Civil Part, pursuant to R. 6:1–2(a)(5),

shall be taken to the Appellate Division pursuant to Rules 2:2–3(a)(1) and 2:2–4, respectively.

Note: Source—R. (1969) 7:8–1. Adopted October 6, 1997 to be effective February 1, 1998; amended July 28, 2004 to be effective September 1, 2004.

7:13–2. Stay

Notwithstanding R. 3:23–5, a sentence or a portion of a sentence may be stayed by the court in which the conviction was had or to which the appeal is taken on such terms as the court deems appropriate.

Note: Source–R. (1969) 7:8–2. Adopted October 6, 1997 to be effective February 1, 1998; amended June 15, 2007 to be effective September 1, 2007.

7:13–3. Reversal; Remission of Fine and Costs

A fine or a fine and costs paid pursuant to a judgment of conviction and disbursed by the court in accordance with R. 7:14–4(a) shall be remitted by the recipient of that money to the defendant or defendant's attorney upon service on the recipient of a copy of the order reversing the judgment.

Note: Source—R. (1969) 7:8–3. Adopted October 6, 1997 to be effective February 1, 1998.

RULE 7:14. GENERAL PROVISIONS; ADMINISTRATION

7:14–1. Opening Statement

(a) Required Opening Statement. The judge shall give an opening statement prior to the commencement of the court session concerning court procedures and rights of defendants. This statement shall not, however, be a substitute for the judge advising individual defendants of their rights prior to their respective hearings.

(b) Notice to Defendant on Guilty Plea. Before accepting a plea of guilty to a traffic offense, other than a parking offense, and as part of the opening statement, the court shall inform the defendant that a record of the conviction will be sent to the Director of the Division of Motor Vehicles of this State or the Commissioner of Motor Vehicles of the state issuing defendant's license to drive, to become a part of the defendant's driving record.

(c) Notification of Right to Appeal. Regardless of whether the defendant pleads guilty or is found guilty after a trial, the court, as part of the opening statement, shall advise each defendant of the right to appeal and, if indigent, of the right to appeal as an indigent.

Note: Source—Paragraph (a): R. (1969) 7:4–4(d); paragraph (b): R. (1969) 7:6–7; paragraph (c): R. (1969) 3:21–4(g). Adopted October 6, 1997 to be effective February 1, 1998.

7:14–2. Amendment of Process or Pleading

The court may amend any process or pleading for any omission or defect therein or for any variance between the complaint and the evidence adduced at the trial, but no such amendment shall be permitted which charges a different substantive offense, other than a lesser included offense. If the defendant is surprised as a result of such amendment, the court shall adjourn the hearing to a future date, upon such terms as the court deems appropriate.

Note: Source—R. (1969) 7:10–2. Adopted October 6, 1997 to be effective February 1, 1998.

7:14–3. Court Calendar; Attorneys

(a) Court Calendar. On each hearing day, the court shall follow as closely as possible, the following order:

(1) applications for adjournment;

(2) unlitigated motions;

(3) arraignments;

(4) guilty pleas;

(5) litigated motions;

(6) contested matters with an attorney;

(7) other contested matters.

(b) Appearances of Attorneys. Appearances by attorneys shall be entered promptly with the court or municipal court administrator. Unless the appearance is entered, the attorney shall not receive priority on the trial list.

Note: Source—R. (1969) 7:10–3. Adopted October 6, 1997 to be effective February 1, 1998.

7:14–4. Financial Control

(a) Fines and Forfeitures. Moneys received by a court as fines or forfeitures, together with the financial reports covering such funds, shall be forwarded by the court on or before the fifteenth day of each month as follows:

(1) To the custodian of the funds of the municipality where such moneys were received in the course of enforcing municipal ordinances or local regulations, if assessed and collected by the municipal court or to the custodian of the funds of the municipality in which the violation occurred, if assessed and collected by the Special Civil Part of the Superior Court.

(2) To the custodian of the funds of the municipality or of the county, or to such state agency or officer, as the case may be, where the money was collected in the course of enforcing state laws and regulations, as provided by law.

(b) Receipts and Disbursements. The court shall keep an accurate account of all fees, costs and moneys received, as well as of any money disbursed and to whom disbursed. Receipts shall be turned over to the appropriate municipal, county or state finance officer, or deposited as soon after receipt as practical, in a bank or banks authorized to do business in this State. No disbursement shall be made except by check drawn on such bank. The court shall issue or cause to be issued and shall obtain a receipt in the form and manner prescribed by the Administrative Director of the Courts in every instance where money is received or disbursed.

(c) Electronic Payments of Court Fees and Financial Obligations. The various municipal, central and joint municipal courts may accept electronic payments for fees, costs, fines, penalties, service charges or other judicially imposed financial obligations pursuant to conditions and administrative procedures established by the Administrative Director of the Courts.

(d) Payment of Moneys Due. No moneys due the court, its employees, or any persons attending upon it, for salaries, fees, costs or other charges shall be deducted from receipts, but shall be paid only on a voucher submitted by the court to the appropriate finance officer.

(e) Docket: Fiscal Forms and Procedures: Record–Keeping. The court shall maintain such separate dockets in such form as the Administrative Director of the Courts prescribes. All fiscal forms, procedures and record-keeping shall conform to the requirements of the Administrative Director of the Courts.

Note: Source—R. (1969) 7:10–4. Adopted October 6, 1997 to be effective February 1, 1998.

7:14–5. Oath of Municipal Court Judge

Before entering upon the duties of the office, the oath of office of a municipal court judge shall be taken before a judge of the Superior Court. The original shall be filed with the municipal court administrator and a copy of the original filed with the Administrative Director of the Courts.

Note: Source—R. (1969) 7:10–5. Adopted October 6, 1997 to be effective February 1, 1998.

APPENDIX TO PART VII. GUIDELINES FOR OPERATION OF PLEA AGREEMENTS IN THE MUNICIPAL COURTS OF NEW JERSEY

GUIDELINE 1. PURPOSE

The purpose of these Guidelines is to allow for flexibility in the definitions and exclusions relating to the plea agreement process as that process evolves and certain offenses come to demand lesser or greater scrutiny.

GUIDELINE 2. DEFINITIONS

For the purpose of these Guidelines, a plea agreement occurs in a Municipal Court matter whenever the prosecutor and the defense agree as to the offense or offenses to which a defendant will plead guilty on condition that any or all of the following occur:

(a) the prosecutor will recommend to the court that another offense or offenses be dismissed,

(b) the prosecutor will recommend to the court that it accept a plea to a lesser or other offense (whether included or not) than that originally charged,

(c) the prosecutor will recommend a sentence(s), not to exceed the maximum permitted, to the court or remain silent at sentencing,

GUIDELINE 3. PROSECUTOR'S RESPONSIBILITIES

Nothing in these Guidelines should be construed to affect in any way the prosecutor's discretion in any case to move unilaterally for an amendment to the original charge or a dismissal of the charges pending against a defendant if the prosecutor determines and personally represents on the record the reasons in support of the motion. The prosecutor shall also appear in person to set forth any proposed plea agreement on the record. However, with the approval of the municipal court judge, in lieu of appearing on the record, the prosecutor may submit to the court a Request to Approve Plea Agreement, on a form approved by the Administrative Director of the Courts, signed by the prosecutor and by the defendant. Nothing in this Guideline shall be construed to limit the court's ability to order the prosecutor to appear at any time during the proceedings.

GUIDELINE 4. LIMITATION

No plea agreements whatsoever will be allowed in drunken driving or certain drug offenses. Those offenses are:

A. Driving while under the influence of liquor or drugs (N.J.S.A. 39:4–50) and

B. Possession of marijuana or hashish (N.J.S.A. 2C:35–10a(4)), being under the influence of a controlled dangerous substance or its analog (N.J.S.A. 2C:35–10b), and use, possession or intent to use or possess drug paraphernalia, etc. (N.J.S.A. 2C:36–2).

No plea agreements will be allowed in which a defendant charged for a violation of N.J.S.A. 39:4–50 with a blood alcohol concentration of 0.10% or higher seeks to plead guilty and be sentenced under section a(1)(i) of that statute (blood alcohol concentration of .08% or higher, but less than 0.10%).

If a defendant is charged with a second or subsequent offense of driving while under the influence of liquor or drugs (N.J.S.A. 39:4–50) and refusal to provide a breath sample (N.J.S.A. 39:4–50.4a) arising out of the same factual transaction, and the defendant pleads guilty to the N.J.S.A. 39:4–50 offense, the judge, on recommendation of the prosecutor, may dismiss the refusal charge. A refusal charge in connection with a first offense N.J.S.A. 39:4–50 charge shall not be dismissed by a plea agreement, although a plea to a concurrent sentence for such charges is permissible.

Except in cases involving an accident or those that occur when school properties are being utilized, if a defendant is charged with driving while under the influence of liquor or drugs (N.J.S.A. 39:4–50(a)) and a school zone or school crossing violation under N.J.S.A. 39:4–50(g), arising out of the same factual transaction, and the defendant pleads guilty to the N.J.S.A. 39:4–50(a) offense, the judge, on the recommendation of the prosecutor, may dismiss the N.J.S.A. 39:4–50(g) charge.

If a defendant is charged with more than one violation under Chapter 35 or 36 of the Code of Criminal Justice arising from the same factual transaction and pleads guilty to one charge or seeks a conditional discharge under N.J.S.A. 2C:36A–1, all remaining Chapter 35 or 36 charges arising from the same factual transaction may be dismissed by the judge on the recommendation of the prosecutor.

Nothing contained in these limitations shall prohibit the judge from considering a plea agreement as to the collateral charges arising out of the same factual transaction connected with any of the above enumerated offenses in sections A and B of this Guideline.

The judge may, for certain other offenses subject to minimum mandatory penalties, refuse to accept a plea agreement unless the prosecuting attorney represents that the possibility of conviction is so remote that the interests of justice requires the acceptance of a plea to a lesser offense.

SUPREME COURT COMMENT

Over the years, various unique practices and procedures have evolved in connection with the disposition of Municipal Court cases. Thus, it is the intent of these Guidelines to define regulated plea agreements as including every common practice that has evolved as a subterfuge for plea agreements. Therefore, for the purpose of these Guidelines, a plea agreement shall include all of those traditional practices, utilized by prosecutors and defense counsel, including "merger", "dismissal", "downgrade" or "amendment." Generally, "mergers" involve the dismissal of lesser-included or related offenses when a defendant pleads to the most serious offense. "Dismissals" involve motions to dismiss a pending charge or plea agreement when the municipal prosecutor determines, for cause (usually for insufficient evidence), that the charge should be dismissed. "Downgrades" or "amendments" involve the taking of a plea to a lesser or included offense to that originally charged.

Plea agreements are to be distinguished from the discretion of a prosecutor to charge or unilaterally move to dismiss, amend or otherwise dispose of a matter. It is recognized that it is not the municipal prosecutor's function merely to seek convictions in all cases. The prosecutor is not an ordinary advocate. Rather, the prosecutor has an obligation to defendants, the State and the public to see that justice is done and truth is revealed in each individual case. The goal should be to achieve individual justice in individual cases.

In discharging the diverse responsibilities of that office, a prosecutor must have some latitude to exercise the prosecutorial discretion demanded of that position. It is well established, for example, that a prosecutor should not prosecute when the evidence does not support the State's charges. Further, the prosecutor

should have the ability to amend the charges to conform to the proofs.

Note: Guidelines and Comment adopted June 29, 1990, simultaneously with former Rule 7:4–8 ("Plea Agreements") to be effective immediately; as part of 1997 recodification of Part VII rules, re-adopted without change as Appendix to Part VII and referenced by Rule 7:6–2 ("Pleas, Plea Agreements"), October 6, 1997 to be effective February 1, 1998; Guideline 4 amended July 5, 2000 to be effective September 5, 2000; Guidelines 3 and 4 amended July 28, 2004 to be effective September 1, 2004; Guideline 4 amended June 15, 2007 to be effective September 1, 2007; Guideline 3 amended July 16, 2009 to be effective September 1, 2009.

SECOND APPENDIX TO PART VII. GUIDELINES FOR DETERMINATION OF CONSEQUENCE OF MAGNITUDE (SEE RULE 7:3–2)

On October 6, 1997, the Supreme Court adopted the Comprehensive Revision of Part VII of the Rules of Court to be effective on February 1, 1998. R. 7:3–2 of that Comprehensive Revision provides for the assignment of counsel "[i]f the court is satisfied that the defendant is indigent and that the defendant faces a consequence of magnitude or is otherwise constitutionally or by law entitled to counsel ..." The Supreme Court directed that guidelines for the determination of a consequence of magnitude be developed by the Supreme Court Municipal Court Practice Committee to assist municipal court judges in deciding what factors should be considered when determining a consequence of magnitude.

In response to this direction, the Supreme Court Municipal Court Practice Committee developed the following set of guidelines. The Supreme Court, as recommended by the Committee, has included the guidelines as an Appendix to the Part VII Rules.

In determining if an offense constitutes a consequence of magnitude in terms of municipal court sentencing, the judge should consider the following:

(1) Any sentence of imprisonment;

(2) Any period of (a) driver's license suspension, (b) suspension of the defendant's non-resident reciprocity privileges or (c) driver's license ineligibility; or

(3) Any monetary sanction imposed by the court of $750 or greater in the aggregate, except for any public defender application fee. A monetary sanction is defined as the aggregate of any type of court imposed financial obligation, including fines, costs, restitution, penalties and/or assessments.

It should be noted that if a defendant is alleged to have a mental disease or defect, and the judge, after examination of the defendant on the record, agrees that the defendant may have a mental disease or defect, the judge shall appoint the municipal public defender to represent that defendant, if indigent, regardless of whether the defendant is facing a consequence of magnitude, if convicted.

Note: Guidelines adopted July 28, 2004 to be effective September 1, 2004.

COMBINED INDEX

References are to Title, Chapter, Section and Rules

ABANDON
Definitions, vulnerable adults, crimes and offenses, 2C:24–8

ABANDONED OR UNCLAIMED PROPERTY
Aged persons, crimes and offenses, 2C:24–8
Attorneys, trust funds, **Rule 1:21–6**
Building or occupied structure, criminal trespass, 2C:18–3
Motor Vehicles, this index
School buses, repainting, 39:3–77.1
Stolen property, procedure for disposition, 2C:65–1 et seq.

ABANDONMENT
Animals, 4:22–20
Attorneys, practice, protecting clients interest, **Rule 1:20–19**
Conspiracy, 2C:5–2
Crimes and offenses, commission, 2C:5–1
Disabled animals, misdemeanor, 4:22–20
Grade Crossings, this index
Handicapped persons, crimes and offenses, 2C:24–8

ABATEMENT AND SURVIVAL
Liquefied petroleum gases, crimes and offenses, 21:1B–6
Nuisance, this index

ABDUCTION
Kidnapping, generally, this index

ABETTORS
Accomplices and Accessories, generally, this index

ABODE
Residence and Residents, generally, this index

ABOLITION
Common law crimes, 2C:1–5
Husband coercing wife, presumption, 2C:2–9
Motor vehicles division, inspectors, 39:2–9.1, 39:2–9.2

ABSCONDING
Parolees, criminal prosecutions, 2C:29–5

ABSENCE AND ABSENTEES
Juvenile delinquents and dependents, detention hearings, 2A:4A–38

ABSTRACTS
Definitions, commercial motor vehicles, 39:10–2

ABUSE OF PROCESS
Human trafficking, 2C:13–8

ABUSE OR NEGLECT
Aged Persons, this index
Child Abuse, generally, this index

ABUSE OR NEGLECT—Cont'd
Domestic Violence, generally, this index

ABUSIVE LANGUAGE
Disorderly conduct, 2C:33–2
Harassment, 2C:33–4

ACCESS
Definitions, computer related offenses, 2C:20–23

ACCESS DEVICES
Computers, this index
Definitions, theft, 2C:20–1
Telecommunications, this index

ACCESSORIES
Accomplices and Accessories, generally, this index

ACCIDENT INSURANCE
Health and Accident Insurance, generally, this index

ACCIDENTS
Attorneys, solicitation, crimes and offenses, 2C:40A–5
Automobiles. Traffic Accidents, generally, this index
Commercial drivers licenses, fatalities, suspension or revocation, 39:3–10.20
Crimes and offenses, health care professionals, solicitation, 2C:40A–4
Drivers Licenses, this index
Health and Accident Insurance, generally, this index
Health care professionals, solicitation, crimes and offenses, 2C:40A–4
Insurance. Health and Accident Insurance, generally, this index
Motor Vehicle Insurance, generally, this index
Motor vehicles. Traffic Accidents, generally, this index
Reports,
  Motorized bicycles, 39:4–14.3f
  Traffic Accidents, this index
Snowmobiles, reports, 39:3C–21
Traffic Accidents, generally, this index

ACCOMPLICES AND ACCESSORIES
Generally, 2C:5–1
Acquittal, conviction of, 2C:2–6
Aggravated criminal sexual contact, 2C:14–3
Aggravated sexual assault, 2C:14–2
Aiding another in commission of offense, accomplice status, 2C:2–6
Alcoholic beverage law violations, 33:1–50, 33:1–52
Bigamy, 2C:24–1
Conduct of another, criminal liability, 2C:2–6
Conviction, evidence, **Rule 3:12–1**
Defenses, notice, **Rule 3:12–1**

ACCOMPLICES AND ACCESSORIES
—Cont'd
Definitions, Code of Criminal Justice, 2C:2–6
Duty to prevent commission of offense, failure, accomplice status, 2C:2–6
Escape, sentence and punishment, 2C:29–6
Evidence, criminal prosecutions, 2C:2–6
Facilitating commission of offense, accomplice status, 2C:2–6
Hindering apprehension or prosecution, 2C:29–3
Homicide, 2C:11–3
Immunity from criminal prosecution, conviction of accomplice, 2C:2–6
Liability, conduct of another, 2C:2–6
Promoting commission of offense, accomplice status, 2C:2–6
Public officers and employees, official actions or information, speculating or wagering, 2C:30–3
Solicitation of another to commit offense, accomplice status, 2C:2–6
Speculating or wagering on official action or information, 2C:30–3
Status as accessory, 2C:2–6
Suicide, aiding suicide, 2C:11–6
Terrorism, this index
Transporting persons, foreign state, criminal charges, 2A:160–1
Venue, **Rule 3:14–1**

ACCOUNTANTS
Commercial bribery and breach of duty, 2C:21–10

ACCOUNTS AND ACCOUNTING
Attorneys, this index
Banks and Banking, this index
Criminal history record information fund, 53:1–20.7
Interest on lawyers trust accounts, **Rules 1:21–6, 1:28A–2**
Municipal courts, fees, costs and monies received, **Rule 7:14–4**

ACCUSATION OF CRIME
Indictment, Information or Presentment, generally, this index

ACCUSED PERSONS
Privileges and immunities, witnesses, 2A:84A–17

ACETORPHINE
Controlled substances, 24:21–1 et seq.

ACETYLCODONE
Controlled substances, 24:21–1 et seq.

ACETYLDIHYDROCODEINE
Controlled substances, 24:21–1 et seq.

I–1

ACETYLMETHADOL
Controlled substances, **24:21–1 et seq.**

ACID
Golf balls, **2C:12–2**
Poisons, generally, this index
Turnpike projects, transportation regulations, **27:23–31**

ACKNOWLEDGMENTS
Motor vehicle title papers, **39:10–8**
Process, this index

ACQUIRED IMMUNE DEFICIENCY SYN-DROME
AIDS (Acquired Immune Deficiency Syndrome), generally, this index

ACQUITTAL
Accomplice conviction, **2C:2–6**
Costs,
　Fees of clerk and sheriff, **2A:166–9**
　Payment of fees, witnesses and constables, **2A:166–8**
Double Jeopardy, generally, this index
Entrapment defense, **2C:2–12**
Insanity Defense, this index
Judgments and decrees, motions, **Rules 3:18–1, 3:18–2**
　After discharge of jury, enlargement of time, **Rule 1:3–4**
Mentally ill defendant, **2C:4–3 et seq.**

ACT OF GRAFFITI
Definitions, criminal mischief, **2C:17–3, 2C:17–3.1**

ACTIONS AND PROCEEDINGS
　See, also, Hearings, generally, this index
Accused, privilege not to be called as witness or to testify, **2A:84A–17**
Administrative Law and Procedure, generally, this index
Adult offender supervision interstate commission, defenses, **2A:168–31**
Age, this index
Air pollution, **26:2C–19**
Alcoholic Beverages, this index
Appeal and Review, generally, this index
Arbitration and Award, generally, this index
Associations and societies, racketeering, **2C:41–4**
Attachment, generally, this index
Attorney General, generally, this index
Award. Arbitration and Award, generally, this index
Bribery and Corruption, generally, this index
Burden of Proof, generally, this index
Child Abuse, this index
Children and Minors, this index
Complaints, generally, this index
Compromise and Settlement, generally, this index
Contempt, generally, this index
Controlled substances, dealers, liability, **2C:35B–1 et seq.**
Corporations, this index
Corrupt influence. Bribery and Corruption, generally, this index
Costs, generally, this index
Counties, this index
Court records. Records of Court, generally, this index
Courts, generally, this index
Damages, generally, this index
Decrees. Judgments and Decrees, generally, this index

ACTIONS AND PROCEEDINGS—Cont'd
Defenses, generally, this index
Definitions, motor vehicle insurance, valid diagnostic tests, lists, **39:6A–4.7**
Dentists review committees, immunity from liability, **2A:84A–22.10**
Discovery, generally, this index
Dismissal and Nonsuit, generally, this index
Dockets, generally, this index
Domestic violence, weapons seizure, **2C:25–21**
Drivers privacy protection, **39:2–3.6**
Evidence, generally, this index
Expungement, records, **2C:52–7 et seq.**
Extradition, action on bond or forfeiture of bail, **2A:160–26**
Foreign Jury, generally, this index
Forests, fire prevention and control, fines and penalties, **13:9–44.10**
Forfeitures, generally, this index
Health care professionals, review committees, immunity from liability, **2A:84A–22.10**
Hearings, generally, this index
Hospitals, this index
Identity theft, **2C:21–17.4**
Immunity, child abuse, reports, **9:6–8.13**
Injunctions, generally, this index
Judgment creditors. Debtors and Creditors, generally, this index
Judgments and Decrees, generally, this index
Judicial Notice, generally, this index
Judicial review. Appeal and Review, generally, this index
Jurisdiction, generally, this index
Jury and Jurors, generally, this index
Jury Lists, generally, this index
Justification, effect on civil remedies, **2C:3–1**
Limitation of Actions, generally, this index
Liquefied petroleum gas, violations, **21:1B–6**
Liquidated damages. Damages, generally, this index
Local Health Boards, this index
Money laundering and illegal investments, **2C:21–28**
Monopolies and unfair trade, hearings or inquiries, **56:9–9**
Motor vehicle commission, chief administrator, powers and duties, **39:2A–28**
Motor Vehicles, this index
Negligence, generally, this index
Nonsuit. Dismissal and Nonsuit, generally, this index
Nuisance, generally, this index
Oaths and Affirmations, generally, this index
Orders, generally, this index
Partnerships, this index
Personal Injuries, generally, this index
Petit jurors, number, **2B:23–1**
Physicians and Surgeons, this index
Police and Police Departments, this index
Presumptions, generally, this index
Privileged communications, physician and patients, **2A:84A–22.1 et seq.**
Probate Proceedings, generally, this index
Process, generally, this index
Production of Books and Papers, generally, this index
Racketeering activities, civil remedies, **2C:41–4**
Records of Court, generally, this index
Review. Appeal and Review, generally, this index
Settlement. Compromise and Settlement, generally, this index
Solid Waste, this index
Spouses, testifying as witness, **2A:84A–17**
Statute of limitations. Limitation of Actions, generally, this index

ACTIONS AND PROCEEDINGS—Cont'd
Stolen property,
　Disposition after final determination, **2C:65–3**
　Persons receiving, actions against, **2C:20–20**
Subpoenas, generally, this index
Summary Proceedings, generally, this index
Summons, generally, this index
Superior Court, generally, this index
Testimony,
　Evidence, generally, this index
　Witnesses, generally, this index
Theft, this index
Third Parties, generally, this index
Torts, generally, this index
Toxic packaging reduction, **13:1E–99.54**
Transcripts, generally, this index
Transportation Department, this index
Trespass, generally, this index
Trial, generally, this index
Witnesses, generally, this index

ACTOR
Definitions, sexual offenses, **2C:14–1**

ACUTE CARE
Hospitals, this index

AD VALOREM TAXES
Taxation, generally, this index

ADDICTS
Alcoholics and Alcoholism, generally, this index
Drug Abuse, generally, this index

ADDRESS
Crimes and offenses, discovery, **Rule 3:13–3**
Victims of crime, confidential or privileged information, **Rule 1:38–3**

ADHESIVES
Glues, inhalants, **2C:35–10.4**

ADJOURNMENT
Application, expenses, **Rule 1:2–4**
Municipal courts, **Rule 7:8–3**

ADJUDICATION
Juvenile Delinquents, this index

ADMINISTERS
Definitions, controlled substances, **2C:35–2**

ADMINISTRATION
Oaths and Affirmations, generally, this index

ADMINISTRATIVE DIRECTOR OF THE COURTS
Generally, **Rule 1:33–3**
Acting director, **Rule 1:33–1**
Appointment, **Rule 1:33–1**
Candidate for public office, limitations, **Rule 1:17–1**
Compilation of administrative rules and directives, **Rule 1:33–3**
Political activity, **Rule 1:17–1**
Powers and duties, **Rule 1:33–3**
Professional ethics, advisory committee on, secretary, **Rule 1:19–1**
Public office, holding, **Rule 1:17–1**
Reports, trial judges, **Rule 1:32–1**
Seal of courts, **Rule 1:37–2**
Trial court administrators, **Rule 1:33–5**

ADMINISTRATIVE DISMISSAL
Criminal procedure, complaint, **Rule 3:25–1**

**ADMINISTRATIVE INSPECTION WAR-
RANTS**
Controlled substances, 24:21–31, 24:21–32

ADMINISTRATIVE LAW AND PROCEDURE
See, also, Rules and Regulations, generally,
this index
Adult offender supervision interstate commis-
sion, 2A:168–33
Air pollution, civil administrative penalties,
26:2C–19
Appearance, nonattorneys, **Rule 1:21–1**
Application of rules, **Evidence Rule 101**
Child abuse, records and recordation, identifi-
cation check, conviction of crime, sole
caretaker, presentence investigations,
9:6–8.10d
Definitions, bribery and corruption, 2C:27–1
Domestic livestock, humane treatment,
4:22–16.1
Domestic violence, weapons, 2C:25–21.1
Hearings, medical advisory panel, 39:2–15
Law graduates and students, appearance, **Rule
1:21–3**
Medical advisory panel, 39:2–15
Motor vehicle commission, 39:2A–21
Motor vehicle offenses, penalty points,
39:5–30.5
Nonattorney, appearance, **Rule 1:21–1**
Orders, air pollution, civil administrative penal-
ties, 26:2C–19
Penalty points, traffic offenses, 39:5–30.5
Points, penalty points, traffic offenses,
39:5–30.5
Records and recordation, correctional institu-
tions, identification check, conviction of
crime, sole caretaker, presentence investi-
gations, 9:6–8.10d
Traffic offenses, penalty points, 39:5–30.5
Turnpike authority, highway authority, transfer
of powers and duties, 27:23–42

ADMINISTRATIVE LAW OFFICE
Child abuse reports, release, access to,
9:6–8.10a

**ADMINISTRATIVE OFFICE OF THE
COURTS**
Automated traffic system fund, administration,
promulgation of procedures, 2B:12–30
Client protection fund, administration, **Rule
1:28–7**
Courts computerized collection fund, 2C:46–1.1
Directors,
Jury lists, state grand jurors, powers and
duties, 2B:22–3
Municipal courts, designation of acting
judges, 2B:12–6
State grand jurors, transmittal of names to
sheriff, 2B:22–4
Domestic violence, prevention and treatment,
Records, relief applications, 2C:25–33
Training courses, development and approval,
2C:25–20
Foreclosure office, **Rule 1:34–6**
Motor vehicles, tort claims, arbitration,
39:6A–35
Records, domestic violence prevention, relief
applications, 2C:25–33
Released prisoners, registration and notifica-
tion procedures, 2C:7–2 et seq.
Reports, motor vehicles, tort claims arbitration,
39:6A–35
Sex offenses, released offenders, registration
and notification procedures, 2C:7–2 et seq.

ADMINISTRATIVE PROCEDURE ACT
Administrative Law and Procedure, generally,
this index

ADMISSIBILITY OF EVIDENCE
Evidence, generally, this index

ADMISSION TO INSTITUTIONS
Commitment and Admission to Institutions,
generally, this index

ADMISSIONS
Application of law, **Evidence Rule 101**
Commitment and Admission to Institutions,
generally, this index
Crimes and Offenses, this index
Joint defendants, notice of use, **Rule 3:15–2**

ADOLESCENTS
Children and Minors, generally, this index

ADOPTION
Adults,
Crimes and offenses, unlawful adoptions,
2C:24–6
Unlawful adoptions, 2C:24–6
Child abuse,
Placement, priorities and preferences,
9:6–8.8
Priorities and preferences, placement,
9:6–8.8
Confidential or privileged information, **Rule
1:38–3**
Crimes and offenses,
Adults, unlawful adoptions, 2C:24–6
Unlawful adoptions, 2C:24–6
Criminal history record information, agencies,
53:1–20.9d
Filing, **Rule 1:5–6**
Labor and employment, criminal history record
information, agencies, 53:1–20.9d
Placement, priorities and preferences, abuse or
neglect, 9:6–8.8
Priorities and preferences, children and minors,
abuse or neglect, placement, 9:6–8.8
Unlawful adoptions, 2C:24–6

**ADULT DIAGNOSTIC AND TREATMENT
CENTER**
Commitment, sex and violent offenders,
2C:47–1
Reductions, 2C:47–8
Costs, maintenance, sex and violent offenders,
2C:47–7
Disposition, sex and violent offenders, 2C:47–3
Inmates, sexually oriented materials, posses-
sion, distribution or exhibition, 2C:47–10
Maintenance, costs, sex and violent offenders,
2C:47–7
Parole, revocation, confinement, 2C:47–5.1
Reductions, imprisonment term, sex and vio-
lent offenders, 2C:47–8
Referral, sex and violent offenders, 2C:47–1
Reports, transfers, offenders, 2C:47–3
Sanctions, inmates, sexually oriented materials,
possession, distribution or exhibition,
2C:47–10
Sexually oriented materials, possession, distri-
bution or exhibition, inmates, 2C:47–10
Transfers, 2C:47–4.1
Examinations, 2C:47–3
Parole violations, 2C:47–5.1

**ADULT OFFENDER SUPERVISION INTER-
STATE COMPACT**
Generally, 2A:168–26 et seq.

ADULTERATION
Adulterated, definitions, deceptive business
practices, 2C:21–7
Food, this index

ADULTS
Adoption, this index
Definitions,
Adult offender supervision, interstate com-
pacts, 2A:168–27
Juvenile justice, 2A:4A–22
Domestic Violence, generally, this index

ADVERSE OR PECUNIARY INTEREST
Attorneys, limitation on practice, **Rule 1:15–1
et seq.**
Commercial bribery, 2C:21–10
County officers and employees, 2C:27–9
Crimes and offenses, 2C:21–10, 2C:44–1,
2C:44–2
Grand jury members, **Rule 3:6–3**
Intoxicating liquor officers or employees,
33:1–7
Judges and Justices, this index
Mediation, disclosure, **Rule 1:40–4**
Motor vehicle commission, board, application
of law, 39:2A–18
Municipal officers and employees, 2C:27–9
Municipal prosecutors, 2B:25–5
Professional criminals, 2C:44–3
Property interest, acquisition, 2C:30–3
Public officers and employees, property inter-
est, acquisition, 2C:30–3
Public servants, 2C:27–9
State Officers and Employees, this index

ADVERTISEMENTS
Alcoholic beverages,
Misdemeanor by advertising unlawful prop-
erty, 33:1–66
Seizure, property used in unlawful activity,
33:1–66
Assault firearms, disorderly persons, 2C:39–15
Attorneys, this index
Cigarettes and cigars, promotional gifts, chil-
dren and minors, crimes and offenses,
2A:170–51.4
Crimes and offenses, electronic, mechanical or
other devices, wiretapping and electronic
surveillance, 2A:156A–5
Disorderly Persons, this index
Drugs and Medicine, this index
Kosher food, 2C:21–7.2 et seq.
Machine guns, disorderly persons, 2C:39–15
Motor vehicle master keys or devices, 2C:5–6
Motor Vehicles, this index
Noncommercial trucks, 39:3–8.1
Outdoor Advertising, generally, this index
Packages, consumer products, crimes and of-
fenses, 2C:40–19
Promotional gifts, cigarettes and cigars, chil-
dren and minors, crimes and offenses,
2A:170–51.4
Roadside advertising. Outdoor Advertising,
generally, this index
Semiautomatic rifles, disorderly persons,
2C:39–15
Traffic signs bearing advertising prohibited,
39:4–183.3

ADVISORY COMMITTEES
See, also, Advisory Councils, generally, this
index
Bar admissions advisory committee, **Rules
1:27A–1, 1:27A–2**

ADVISORY COMMITTEES—Cont'd
Complementary dispute resolution programs, **Rule 1:40–3**
Extrajudicial activities, **Rule 1:18A–1 et seq.**
Judicial financial reporting, **Rule 1:18B–2**
Judiciary employees, outside activities of, **Rule 1:17A–1 et seq.**
Professional ethics, **Rule 1:19–1 et seq.**
Turnpike authority, capital project and investment plan, annual, **27:23–3.2**

ADVISORY COUNCILS
Business advisory council, motor vehicle commission, **39:2A–26**
Customer service advisory council, motor vehicle commission, **39:2A–26**
Internet registry, sex offenses, **2C:7–18**
Motor vehicle commission, **39:2A–26**
Notification advisory council, sex offenders, community notification, establishment, **2C:7–11**
Safety advisory council, motor vehicle commission, **39:2A–26**
Security and privacy advisory council, motor vehicle commission, **39:2A–26**
Sex offenses, internet registry, **2C:7–18**
Technology advisory council, motor vehicle commission, **39:2A–26**

ADVISORY OPINIONS
Attorney advertising committee, **Rules 1:19A–2, 1:19A–3**
Attorney ethics, office of, prohibition, **Rule 1:20–2**
Judiciary employees, outside activities of, **Rule 1:17A–2**
Unauthorized practice of law, committees, **Rules 1:22–2, 1:22–3**

ADVISORY PANELS
See, also, Advisory Councils, generally, this index
Medical advisory panel, **39:2–13 et seq.**

ADVOCATES
Attorneys, generally, this index

AFFECTIONAL ORIENTATION
Discrimination, generally, this index

AFFIDAVITS
Alcoholic Beverages, this index
Arrest of fugitive before requisition made, **2A:160–21**
Attorneys, this index
Bail, cash deposit in lieu of, **2A:162–9; Rule 3:26–4**
Caption, **Rule 1:4–4**
Certification in lieu of oath or verification, **Rule 1:4–4**
Complementary dispute resolution, service of notices, filing, **Rule 1:5–6**
Default judgment, nonmilitary service affidavit, **Rule 1:5–7**
Dismissal and nonsuit, inactive cases, **Rule 1:13–7**
Evidence, application of law, **Evidence Rule 101**
Ex parte affidavits, **Rule 1:4–4**
Extradition, this index
Facsimile signatures, **Rule 1:4–4**
Family actions, complaint, nonconforming papers, **Rule 1:5–6**
Format, **Rule 1:4–4**
Insurance, coverage, filing, **Rule 1:5–6**
Investigative detention, applications, **Rule 3:5A–2**

AFFIDAVITS—Cont'd
Military list, inability to prosecute or defend action, **Rule 1:13–6**
Motions, **Rule 1:6–6**
  Manner of filing, **Rule 1:6–4**
  Response relying on fact not of record or subject to judicial notice, **Rule 1:6–2**
  Service and filing, **Rule 1:6–3**
Motor vehicle title papers, loss of, **39:10–12**
Motorized bicycles, ownership proof, bicycles purchased before registration statute effective, **39:4–14.3p**
Noninvolvement, medical malpractice, motions, dismissal, **Rule 1:6–2**
Paragraphs, **Rule 1:4–4**
Preliminary hearings, driver license or motor vehicle registration, suspension or revocation, **39:5–30**
Pro hac vice appearances, motion for admission, **Rule 1:21–2**
Searches and Seizures, this index
Service, process on nonresidents, **39:7–3**
Subpoenas, request of public officer or agency supporting motion, **Rule 1:9–6**
Trust funds, unidentifiable or unclaimed funds held by attorneys, deposits in court, applications for payment, **Rule 1:21–6**

AFFINITY
Judges, disqualification, **Rule 1:12–1**

AFFIRMATIONS
Oaths and Affirmations, generally, this index

AFFIRMATIVE DEFENSES
Defenses, this index

AFRICAN AMERICANS
Discrimination, generally, this index

AGE
  See, also, Aged Persons, generally, this index
Abuse of children, jurisdiction, superior court, chancery division, family part, **9:6–8.24**
Actions and proceedings, abuse of children, superior court, chancery division, family part, jurisdiction, **9:6–8.24**
Alcoholic Beverages, this index
Bicycles, helmet requirements, **39:4–10.1**
Children and Minors, this index
Crimes and Offenses, this index
Drivers Licenses, this index
Electric personal assistive mobility devices, operation, **39:4–14.10**
Explosives,
  Blasting operations, **21:1A–138**
  Permit qualifications, **21:1A–134**
False representations, defense to sale of alcoholic beverages, **33:1–77**
Jurisdiction, superior court, chancery division, family part, abuse of children, **9:6–8.24**
Jury and Jurors, this index
Juvenile Delinquents, this index
Mistake as to age, sexual offenses, **2C:14–5**
Motor Vehicles, this index
Motorized bicycles,
  Operators, **39:4–14.3**
  Owners, registration of bicycles, **39:4–14.3i**
Physical appearance, defense to sale of alcoholic beverages, **33:1–77**
Probationary licenses, drivers licenses, **39:3–13.4**
Rockets, **21:1C–4**
School buses, termination of use, **39:3B–5.1 et seq.**
Sexual offenses,
  Assault, victim, accused, **2C:14–2**

AGE—Cont'd
Sexual offenses—Cont'd
  Capability, presumption, **2C:14–5**
Special learners permit, behind the wheel automobile driving education, eligibility, permit, **39:3–13.1**
Verification, documents or forms, simulation, crimes and offenses, **2C:21–2.1**
Young adult offenders, **2C:43–5**

AGED PERSONS
Abandonment, crimes and offenses, **2C:24–8**
Abuse or neglect,
  Judges and justices, education, **2C:25–20**
  Legally responsible parties, **2C:24–8**
  Prevention and treatment, training, **2C:25–20**
Commitment and Admission to Institutions, generally, this index
Crimes and offenses,
  Neglect or failure to care for, **2C:24–8**
  Presentence reports, **2C:44–6**
  Sentence, reduction, change, **Rule 3:21–10**
Criminal history record information,
  Assisted living facilities, **53:1–20.9c**
  Homemaker home health aides, certificates, **53:1–20.9a**
  Nurses aides or personal care assistants, certificates, **53:1–20.9a**
Crosswalks, older and walking impaired persons crossing, designation of areas and erection of signs, **39:4–183.1b**
Drivers licenses, color photographs, exceptions, **39:3–10f**
Failure to care for, legally responsible parties, **2C:24–8**
Homemaker home health aides, criminal history record checks, certificates, **53:1–20.9a**
Hospitals, this index
Institutionalized elderly persons, assault, **2C:12–1**
Judges and justices, abuse or neglect, education, **2C:25–20**
Mentally Deficient and Mentally Ill Persons, this index
Nurses aides, criminal history record checks, certificates, **53:1–20.9a**
Personal care assistants, criminal history record checks, certificates, **53:1–20.9a**
Rehabilitation, institutionalized elderly persons, assault, **2C:12–1**
Retired law enforcement officers, firearms, possession, **2C:39–6, 2C:39–6.1**
Victims of crime, **2C:44–1**
  Aggravating circumstance, **2C:44–1**
  Presentence investigations and reports, **2C:44–6**

AGENTS AND AGENCIES
Alcoholic Beverage Law, service of subpoenas, **33:1–36**
Commercial bribery and breach of duty, **2C:21–10**
Controlled substances, registered manufacturer, distributor or dispenser, **24:21–10**
Corporations, generally, this index
Definitions,
  Code of Criminal Justice, **2C:2–7**
  Controlled substances, **2C:35–2, 24:21–2**
Entrapment, **2C:2–12**
Evidence, requiring agents to produce evidence, **2A:84A–19**
Expungement, records, use by, pending petition, **2C:52–17**
Fiduciaries, generally, this index
Forfeitures, rights of owners, **2C:64–5**
High managerial agent, definitions, **2C:2–7**

AGENTS AND AGENCIES—Cont'd
Home Health Care Services, this index
Process, this index
State Agencies, generally, this index
Trade secrets, compelling disclosure,
2A:84A–26
Weapons, wholesale dealers, 2C:58–1

AGGRAVATED ARSON
Generally, 2C:17–1 et seq.
Jury, number of peremptory challenges,
2B:23–13

AGGRAVATED ASSAULT
Generally, 2C:12–1
Aggravated Criminal Sexual Contact, generally,
this index
Aggravated Sexual Assault, generally, this index
Arrest warrant, issuance, **Rule 3:3–1**
Arrest without warrant, release, **Rule 3:4–1**
Correctional institutions, inmates, throwing
bodily fluids, 2C:12–12, 2C:12–13
Extended term of imprisonment, 2C:43–7,
2C:43–7.1
Hit and run drivers, 2C:12–1.1
Jury, peremptory challenges, **Rule 1:8–3**
Juvenile delinquents and dependents, jurisdiction,
waiver, 2A:4A–26
Law enforcement officers,
Throwing bodily fluids, 2C:12–13
Weapons, 2C:12–1
Weapons, possession, 2C:39–7
Mandatory sentence, 2C:43–6

AGGRAVATED CRIMINAL SEXUAL CONTACT
Generally, 2C:14–3
Adult Diagnostic and Treatment Center, generally,
this index
Appeal and review, record, closed circuit testimony
of children, 2A:84A–32.4
Arrest warrant, issuance, **Rule 3:3–1**
Arrest without warrant, release, **Rule 3:4–1**
Bail, authority to admit to, **Rule 3:26–2**
Children and minors, closed circuit testimony,
2A:84A–32.4
Closed circuit testimony, sexual abuse, children,
2A:84A–32.4
Community notification. Sex Offenses, this index
Diagnostic center report, presentence investigation,
Rule 3:21–3
Evidence,
Closed circuit testimony, children,
2A:84A–32.4
Previous sexual conduct of victim, 2C:14–7
Expungement, record, 2C:52–2
Indigent, neglected or abandoned children,
closed circuit testimony, 2A:84A–32.4
Jury, number of peremptory challenges,
2B:23–13
Motions, closed circuit testimony, children and
minors, 2A:84A–32.4
Offenders, registration. Sex Offenses, this index
Records and recordation, expungement,
2C:52–2
Transcripts, record, closed circuit testimony of
children, 2A:84A–32.4
Videotaped testimony, children and minors,
2A:84A–32.4
Weapons, possession, mandatory sentence,
2C:43–6
Witnesses, children and minors, closed circuit
testimony, 2A:84A–32.4

AGGRAVATED HAZING
Generally, 2C:40–3

AGGRAVATED MANSLAUGHTER
Arrest warrant, issuance, **Rule 3:3–1**
Arrest without warrant, release, **Rule 3:4–1**
Bail, authority to admit to, **Rule 3:26–2**
Death by auto or vessel, charge not precluded,
2C:11–5
Extended term of imprisonment, 2C:43–7,
2C:43–7.1
Jury, number of peremptory challenges,
2B:23–13
Vehicular homicide, charge not precluded by,
2C:11–5

AGGRAVATED RAPE
Generally, 2C:14–2

AGGRAVATED SEXUAL ASSAULT
Generally, 2C:14–2
Adult Diagnostic and Treatment Center, generally,
this index
Appeal and review, record, closed circuit testimony
of children, 2A:84A–32.4
Arrest warrant, issuance, **Rule 3:3–1**
Arrest without warrant, release, **Rule 3:4–1**
Bail, authority to admit to, **Rule 3:26–2**
Children and minors, closed circuit testimony,
2A:84A–32.4
Closed circuit testimony, sexual abuse, children,
2A:84A–32.4
Community notification. Sex Offenses, this index
Diagnostic center report, presentence investigation,
Rule 3:21–3
Evidence,
Closed circuit testimony, children,
2A:84A–32.4
Previous sexual conduct of victim, 2C:14–7
Expungement, record, 2C:52–2
Extended term of imprisonment, 2C:43–7,
2C:43–7.1
Fines and penalties, surcharges, 2C:43–3.7
Indigent, neglected or abandoned children,
closed circuit testimony, 2A:84A–32.4
Jury, number of peremptory challenges,
2B:23–13
Motions, closed circuit testimony, children and
minors, 2A:84A–32.4
Offenders, registration. Sex Offenses, this index
Parole supervision for life, special sentence,
Violent Predator Incapacitation Act of
1994, 2C:43–6.4
Records and recordation, expungement,
2C:52–2
Surcharges, 2C:43–3.7
Transcripts, record, closed circuit testimony of
children, 2A:84A–32.4
Videotaped testimony, children and minors,
2A:84A–32.4
Weapons, possession, person convicted of,
2C:39–7
Witnesses, children and minors, closed circuit
testimony, 2A:84A–32.4

AGGRAVATED SODOMY
Generally, 2C:14–2

AGGRAVATING CIRCUMSTANCES
Crimes and offenses, 2C:44–1 et seq.

AGGRIEVED PERSON
Definitions, wiretapping and electronic surveillance,
2A:156A–2

AGREEMENTS
Contracts, generally, this index
Plea agreements, crimes and offenses, **Rule
3:9–3**

AGRICULTURAL COMMODITIES
Agricultural Products, generally, this index

AGRICULTURAL CROPS
Agricultural Products, generally, this index

AGRICULTURAL EXPERIMENT STATION
Appropriations, center for agricultural molecular
biology, satellite field testing facility,
39:4–103.1
Center for agricultural molecular biology, satellite
field testing facility, 39:4–103.1

AGRICULTURAL FAIRS AND EXHIBITIONS
Cannons, antique cannons, possession, 2C:39–6
Firearms, unlawful possession exemption,
2C:39–6
Rigging publicly exhibited contests, 2C:21–11
Snowmobiles, 39:3C–1 et seq.
Theft of services, 2C:20–8

AGRICULTURAL LAND
Destruction by operation of motor vehicles,
39:4–97a
Point system, assessment against drivers license,
39:5–30.5a
Dirt bikes, registration, 39:3C–6
Motor Vehicles, this index
Trespass, damages, 2C:18–4 et seq.

**AGRICULTURAL MACHINERY AND
EQUIPMENT**
Application of law, 39:3–45
Brakes, 39:3–68
Commercial drivers licenses, exemption,
39:3–10j et seq.
Exemptions, commercial drivers licenses,
39:3–10j et seq.
Farm tractor, definitions, 39:1–1
Feed impregnating machines, licenses, 39:3–26
Length and weight, 39:3–84
Licenses and permits, 39:3–24
License plates for trucks engaged in transportation
of farm products, 39:3–25
Lights, 39:3–65
Applicability of statute, 39:3–45
Maximum weight and length, 39:3–84
Plates or markers, 39:3–27.116 et seq.
Registration, operation on highways, 39:3–24
Transfer of titles and perfection of security
interests, 39:10–2
Trucks, width, maximum width, 39:3–84
Weight and length, 39:3–84
Width and length, 39:3–84

AGRICULTURAL PRODUCTS
Agricultural products to be used for food,
39:3–25
Crimes and offenses, stealing produce, 39:5–46
Definitions, 39:3–25
Drivers licenses, stealing produce, reports,
39:5–46
Food, generally, this index
Jersey Fresh, sales, 27:23–48
Motor vehicles, operators, stealing produce,
39:5–46
Pest control bombs, storage or sale, 21:2–29.1
Reports, licensed vehicle operators, stealing
produce, 39:5–46
Sales, highways and roads, 27:23–48
Stealing, farm produce, 39:5–46
Vandalism, 2C:18–5

AGRICULTURAL SCHOOLS
Vocational Education, generally, this index

AGRICULTURE
Agricultural Products, generally, this index
Animals, generally, this index
Diseases of animals. Animals, generally, this index
Farm winery license, **33:1–10**
Fireworks,
  Exceptions, application of law, **21:2–4**
  Storage and sale, permits, **21:2–29.1**
Food, generally, this index
Horses, generally, this index
Implements. Agricultural Machinery and Equipment, generally, this index
License plates for farmers trucks, **39:3–25**
Machinery and equipment. Agricultural Machinery and Equipment, generally, this index
Motor vehicles,
  Drivers licenses, persons under age 17 and over 16, **39:3–11.1 et seq.**
  Plates or markers, **39:3–27.116 et seq.**
Pest control bombs, storage or sale, **21:2–29.1**
Wineries. Wine, this index

AGRICULTURE DEPARTMENT
Agricultural Products, generally, this index

AID
Public officers, justification defense, criminal prosecutions, **2C:3–3**

AIDING AND ABETTING
Accomplices and Accessories, generally, this index

AIDS (ACQUIRED IMMUNE DEFICIENCY SYNDROME)
Consent, sexual penetration, informed consent, **2C:34–5**
Crimes and offenses,
  Sexual penetration, knowledge, **2C:34–5**
  Testing,
    Disorderly persons, **2A:4A–43.4, 2C:43–2.3**
    Sex offenders, **2C:43–2.2**
Disorderly Persons, this index
Records and recordation, confidential or privileged information, **Rule 1:38–3**
Sexual penetration, crimes and offenses, knowledge, **2C:34–5**

AIDS ASSISTANCE ACT
AIDS (Acquired Immune Deficiency Syndrome), generally, this index

AIR FORCE
Armed Forces, generally, this index
Veterans, generally, this index

AIR POLLUTION
See, also, Environmental Protection, generally, this index
Alternative dispute resolution, contested cases, **26:2C–19**
Buses, this index
Codes, rules and regulations,
  Injunction against violation, **26:2C–19**
  Penalty for violation, **26:2C–19**
Crimes and offenses, **26:2C–19**
Emissions. Motor Vehicles, this index
Fines and penalties, **26:2C–19**
  Motor vehicles, standards, **39:3–70.2**
Hearings, clean air council, injunctive relief, **26:2C–19**
Injunctions, **26:2C–19**

AIR POLLUTION—Cont'd
Notice,
  Injunctive relief, **26:2C–19**
  Release of contaminants, **26:2C–19**
Odors, investigation, procedure, publication, **26:2C–19**
Orders,
  Preventive or corrective measures, **26:2C–19**
  Violations, **26:2C–19**
Regional air pollution control agency, motor vehicle registration fee exemption, **39:3–27**
Rules and regulations. Codes, ante
School Buses, this index
Second and subsequent offenses, **26:2C–19**
Settlement of claims, **26:2C–19**

AIR TRAFFIC
Airports and Landing Fields, generally, this index

AIRCRAFT
See, also, Airports and Landing Fields, generally, this index
Alcoholic beverages,
  Municipal referendum on retail sales, **33:1–46**
  Plenary retail transit license, **33:1–12**
Safety, devices and facilities, damage or impairment, criminal mischief, **2C:17–3.1**

AIRPORT SECURITY OFFICERS
Weapons, unlawful possession, exemption, **2C:39–6**

AIRPORTS AND LANDING FIELDS
Air traffic safety devices, damage or impairment, criminal mischief, **2C:17–3.1**
Crimes and Offenses, this index
Criminal mischief, damage or interference with facilities or equipment, **2C:17–3.1**
Facilities, criminal mischief, tampering, **2C:17–3.1**
Fireworks, exceptions, application of law, **21:2–4**
Heliports and helistops, criminal mischief, tampering, **2C:17–3.1**
International airports, intoxicating liquors, licenses and permits, Chain Store Liquor License Act, **33:1–12.32**
Intoxicating liquors, licenses and permits, international airports, Chain Store Liquor License Act, **33:1–12.32**
Safety, air traffic safety devices, damage or impairment, criminal mischief, **2C:17–3.1**

ALARMS
Drivers licenses, suspension or revocation, juvenile delinquents and dependents, false alarms, **2C:33–3.1**
False alarms,
  Drivers licenses, suspension or revocation, juvenile delinquents and dependents, **2C:33–3.1**
  Fines and penalties, **2C:33–3.2**
Fines and penalties, false alarms, **2C:33–3.2**
Juvenile delinquents and dependents, drivers licenses, suspension or revocation, false alarms, **2C:33–3.1**

ALCOHOL
Alcoholic Beverages, generally, this index

ALCOHOLIC BEVERAGE CONTROL ACT
Generally, **33:1–1 et seq.**

ALCOHOLIC BEVERAGE CONTROL DIVISION
Directors,
  Administration, issuance of licenses, **33:1–18**
  Approval, bonds (officers and fiduciaries), **33:1–8**
  Authentication of copies of rules, orders, **33:1–37**
  Authority to make rules and regulations, **33:1–39**
  Certification of facts and findings, **33:1–37**
  Cumulative powers, **33:1–46.3**
  Definitions, **33:1–1**
  Educational program, laws, regulations and social responsibilities of package store owners, **33:1–12.40 et seq.**
  Enumeration of duties, **33:1–23**
  Licenses,
    Adverse or pecuniary interest, **33:1–20**
    Applications by corporations, **33:1–25**
    Automatic suspension on conviction, **33:1–31.1**
    Division of fees, premises located in multiple municipalities, **33:1–16**
  Official seal, **33:1–37**
  Orders, sales to wholesalers, **33:1–93.8, 33:1–93.9**
  Permission for sale in public buildings of state or political subdivisions, **33:1–42**
  Powers, investigations, inspections, **33:1–35**
  Reciprocal rules and regulations with other states, **33:1–39.1**
  Records of, **33:1–23**
  Reports, **33:1–23**
    Municipal boards, issuance of licenses, **33:1–19**
  Rules and regulations, **33:1–29, 33:1–39, 33:1–93**
    Licenses, **33:1–12.38**
  Suspension or revocation of license, **33:1–31**
Duty to administer, **33:1–23**
Records and files open for inspection, **33:1–37**
Seal, **33:1–37**

ALCOHOLIC BEVERAGE CONTROL ENFORCEMENT BUREAU
Generally, **53:1–11.3 et seq.**
Inspection and inspectors, unlawful possession of weapons, exemption, **2C:39–6**
Investigations, **53:1–11.6**
State police, powers and duties, **53:2–1**
Weapons, unlawful possession, exemption, **2C:39–6**

ALCOHOLIC BEVERAGE TAX
Bonded warehouses, bottling license, **33:1–10**
Collections, policy, **33:1–3.1**
Container, indicia of payment, beverage deemed prima facie illicit, **33:1–88**
Deduction of taxes due state on refund of license fee, **33:1–31**
Exemptions, beverages manufactured for personal consumption, **33:1–75**
Refunds, license fee on surrender of license where taxes paid, **33:1–31**
Refusal of license to persons failing to pay tax, **33:1–33**
Suspension or revocation of license for failure to pay, **33:1–31**

ALCOHOLIC BEVERAGES
Generally, **33:1–1 et seq.**
Actions and proceedings,
  Bond for return of seized property, **33:1–66**
  Recover cash paid for return of seized property, **33:1–66**

ALCOHOLIC BEVERAGES—Cont'd
Actions and proceedings—Cont'd
Replevin by claimant of seized property,
   33:1–66
Wholesalers, contracts, breweries, malt bev-
   erages, **33:1–93.18**
Address, licenses and permits, **33:1–25**
Adverse or pecuniary interest,
Brewery, distillery, or wholesaler, retailing,
   33:1–43
Officers or employees, **33:1–7**
Advertisements, this index
Affidavits,
Defensive negative averments, **33:1–70**
Joinder of separate offenses, **33:1–70**
Name of purchaser, **33:1–70**
Search warrants, **33:1–57**
Age,
Identification card, **33:1–81.2**
Licenses, persons under legal age, **33:1–25**
Misrepresenting or misstating age, inducing
   sale to minor, **33:1–81**
Persons under legal age, possession,
   2C:33–15
Sale to persons under legal age, **33:1–77**
Agents,
Aid to investigation, director, **33:1–35**
Person under Alcoholic Beverage Law,
   33:1–1
Aircraft, this index
Alcohol concentration, definitions, Commercial
   Driver License Act, **39:3–10.11**
Alcoholic Beverage Control Division, generally,
   this index
Alcoholic Beverage Tax, generally, this index
Alcoholics and Alcoholism, generally, this in-
   dex
Aliens,
Class A licensee, **33:1–11.4**
Definitions, **33:1–11.2**
Rules, employment, **33:1–39**
Sale of alcoholic beverages, Class B licenses,
   33:1–11.3
Alteration,
Limitation of number of licenses or hours of
   sale, **33:1–41**
Rules and regulations, **33:1–39, 33:1–39.1**
Amendments,
Limitation of number of licenses or hours of
   sale, **33:1–41**
Ordinances to prevent possession, sale,
   33:1–40
Rules and regulations, **33:1–39, 33:1–39.1**
Analysis,
Certification of findings by chemist, **33:1–37**
Rules and regulations, **33:1–39**
Appeal and review,
Action of issuing authority respecting license,
   33:1–22
Bids for licenses, **33:1–19.6**
Hours of sale, limitations, **33:1–41**
Licenses, issuance, renewal or transfer,
   33:1–17.1
Limitation of number of licenses or hours of
   sale, **33:1–41**
Number of licenses, limitations, **33:1–41**
Power and duty to hear and conduct appeals,
   33:1–38
Refusal of refund of license fee, **33:1–31**
Refusal to extend license to executor or ad-
   ministrator, **33:1–22**
Refusal to revoke or suspend license,
   33:1–31
Suspension or revocation of license, **33:1–31,**
   33:1–31.1

ALCOHOLIC BEVERAGES—Cont'd
Appointment,
Certificate of acceptance by member of mu-
   nicipal board, **33:1–48**
Clerical force and employees by director,
   33:1–4
Counsel and other legal assistants, **33:1–4**
Deputies, **33:1–4**
Eligible persons, **33:1–6**
Executive assistants by director, **33:1–4**
Experts and specialists, **33:1–4**
Municipal board of alcoholic beverage con-
   trol, **33:1–5**
Municipalities, post
Position, **33:1–6**
Appraisal and appraisers, smart growth devel-
   opment projects, licenses and permits,
   33:1–24.2
Approval, bonds (officers and fiduciaries),
   33:1–17
Armed Forces, this index
Arrest, **33:1–66, 33:1–71**
Director, deputies, investigators, **33:1–4**
Assignments, wholesalers, termination, con-
   tracts, breweries, malt beverages,
   33:1–93.16
Associations and Societies, this index
Attachment of license, **33:1–26**
Auctions and auctioneers, nonprofit corpora-
   tions and associations, licenses and per-
   mits, **33:1–97**
Authentication under seal of copies of rules,
   orders, **33:1–37**
Barrels, distributors license, chilled draught
   malt beverages, **33:1–11**
Barroom, definitions, **33:1–12.23**
Beer,
On and off premises consumption, sale, time,
   33:1–40.3
Presumption, fitness for beverage purposes
   and alcoholic content, **33:1–1.1**
Sampling parties, **33:1–12**
Tasting parties, **33:1–12**
Bids and bidding. Licenses and permits, post
Blending. Rectifying and blending, generally,
   post
Bonds (officers and fiduciaries),
Action of replevin for seized property,
   33:1–66
Custody of licensees bond, **33:1–17**
Deputy directors, **33:1–4**
Issuance of license, condition precedent,
   33:1–33
Officers and employees, **33:1–8**
Persons appointed to office, **33:1–8**
Return of seized property, **33:1–66**
Warehouses, bottling licenses, **33:1–10**
Bottling,
Misdemeanor, **33:1–50**
Without license, **33:1–78**
Bowling alleys,
Licenses, additional licenses, Chain Store Li-
   quor License Act, **33:1–12.32**
Plenary retail consumption license, **33:1–12**
Brands, labels and marks,
Absence or falsity of, **33:1–88**
Containers without, **33:1–88**
Issuance, **33:1–80**
Registration, schedules, filing, **33:1–2**
Wine, **33:1–10**
Breaking and entry in execution of search war-
   rant, **33:1–58**
Breweries,
Actions and proceedings, wholesalers, con-
   tracts, malt beverages, **33:1–93.18**
Bottling without license, **33:1–78**

ALCOHOLIC BEVERAGES—Cont'd
Breweries—Cont'd
Construction of law, wholesalers, contracts,
   malt beverages, **33:1–93.19**
Contracts, wholesalers, malt beverages,
   33:1–93.15 et seq.
Crimes and offenses, persons interested in
   retailing or wholesaling, **33:1–43**
Good faith, wholesalers, malt beverages, con-
   tracts, **33:1–93.15**
Licenses and permits, **33:1–10**
Loans or furnishing of fixtures, to retail li-
   censee by brewery, **33:1–43.1**
Operation by retailers, **33:1–12, 33:1–43**
Persons interested in retailing, **33:1–43**
Repairs of fixtures and pipes by brewer for
   retail licensee, **33:1–43.1**
Sales, wholesalers, malt beverages, contracts,
   33:1–93.15
Termination, contracts, wholesalers, malt
   beverages, **33:1–93.16**
Wholesaling, interest in, **33:1–43**
Brokers license, fee, **33:1–14**
Buildings,
Breaking and entry in execution of search
   warrant, **33:1–58**
Definitions, **33:1–1**
License fees, building located in more than
   one municipality, **33:1–16**
Order of director, occupied or used for cer-
   tain period, stills and distilling appara-
   tus, **33:2–5, 33:2–9**
Personal property in building in which unreg-
   istered still, found as unlawful property,
   33:2–2
Property in or upon building, seizure, forfei-
   ture, **33:1–66**
Sales, **33:1–42**
Search warrant, **33:1–56, 33:1–57**
Seizure of personal property, unregistered
   still, found, **33:2–3**
Unlawful property, **33:1–55**
Cash,
Deposit, condition precedent to issuance of
   license, **33:1–33**
Return of seized property, **33:1–66**
Certificates and certification,
Facts and findings, certification by director
   of alcoholic beverage control division,
   33:1–37
Municipal boards, **33:1–48**
Resolutions, copies, **33:1–45**
Sale of certificates given on storage of bever-
   ages, **33:1–72**
Chain Store Liquor Licenses, generally, this
   index
Change, limitation of number of licenses or
   hours of sale, **33:1–41**
Children and minors,
Convictions, unlawful purchases, notice to
   parent or guardian, **33:1–81.1a**
Emergencies, consumption, privileges and
   immunities, **2C:33–15**
Fine, failure to supervise, juvenile convicted
   for unlawful purchases, **33:1–81.1a**
Hearings, **33:1–81.1**
Licenses and permits, **33:1–25**
Misrepresenting or misstating age to induce
   sale, **33:1–81**
Notice, **33:1–81.1a**
Possession, **2C:33–15**
Privileges and immunities, consumption,
   emergencies, **2C:33–15**
Purchase or consumption in retail outlets,
   33:1–81
Hearings, **33:1–81.1**

ALCOHOLIC BEVERAGES—Cont'd

Children and minors—Cont'd

Retail licenses transfer of interest to child in corporation, Chain Store Liquor License Act, **33:1–12.36**

Rules and regulations, employment of minors, **33:1–39**

Sale to minors, **33:1–77, 33:1–81**

Serving or making available, **2C:33–17**

Transfer of interest in corporation by parent, Chain Store Liquor License Act, **33:1–12.36**

Chilled draught malt alcoholic beverages, distributors license, **33:1–11**

Church, sales within 200 feet, **33:1–76**

Waiver of protection, **33:1–76.1, 33:1–76.2**

Civic organizations, temporary permits, fees, **33:1–74**

Class A licenses, **33:1–9, 33:1–10**

Bonds (officers and fiduciaries), **33:1–17**

Foreign person, **33:1–11.4**

Investigations, applicants, **33:1–23**

Operation or ownership of manufacturing or wholesaling entities, **33:1–43**

Sale to voluntary unincorporated organization of army or navy personnel, **33:1–11.1**

Class B licenses, **33:1–9, 33:1–11**

Bonds (officers and fiduciaries), **33:1–17**

Foreign person, sale of beverages, **33:1–11.3**

Investigations of applicants, **33:1–23**

Operation or ownership of manufacturing or wholesale entities, **33:1–43**

Revocation, **33:1–11.5**

Sale to voluntary unincorporated organization of army or navy personnel, **33:1–11.1**

Suspension, **33:1–11.5**

Wholesale license,

Acquisition of brand liquors from authorized agent, **33:1–2**

Renewal, waiver or protection, **33:1–76.1**

Class C licenses, **33:1–9, 33:1–12**

Holders of, warning notices, harmful effects, drinking during pregnancy, posting requirements, **33:1–12a**

Renewal, **33:1–12.39**

Warning notices, pregnant women, harmful effects, **33:1–12a**

Fines, **33:1–12b**

Class D licenses, **33:1–9, 33:1–13**

Investigations of applicants, **33:1–23**

Class E licenses, **33:1–9, 33:1–14**

Bonds (officers and fiduciaries), **33:1–17**

Investigations of applicants, **33:1–23**

Classes of licenses, **33:1–9 et seq.**

Cleaning of pipes by owner, brewery for retail licensee, **33:1–43.1**

Clerical force and employees,

Appointment and fixing duties, **33:1–4**

Eligible persons, **33:1–6**

Clubs, this index

Combination sales, control, **33:1–39.2**

Commercial bowling establishments, plenary retail consumption license, **33:1–12**

Compensation and salaries,

Clerical force employees, **33:1–4**

Counsel and other legal assistants, **33:1–4**

Deputies, **33:1–4**

Deputy directors, **33:1–4**

Experts and specialists, **33:1–4**

Members of municipal board of alcoholic beverage control, **33:1–5**

Complaints,

Defensive negative averments, **33:1–70**

Joinder of separate offenses, **33:1–70**

ALCOHOLIC BEVERAGES—Cont'd

Complaints—Cont'd

Name of purchaser, **33:1–70**

Officers duty to make complaint before magistrate, **33:1–71**

Compromise and settlement, suspension of license, **33:1–31**

Conflict of interest, officers or employees, **33:1–7**

Constables, nonprofit organizations, licenses and permits, **33:1–25.1, 33:1–25.2**

Construction of law, **33:1–73**

Consumption,

Club license, **33:1–12**

License on fee exemption, sale or consumption on premises, **33:1–27**

Limited retail distribution license, **33:1–12**

Municipal referendum on retail sales, **33:1–46**

All kinds of beverages for consumption on licensed premises, **33:1–45**

Beverages except brewed malt and fermented wine for consumption on licensed premises, **33:1–44**

Plenary retail consumption license, **33:1–12**

Municipal referendum on retail sales, **33:1–46**

Nonprofit corporation, musical or theatrical performances, **33:1–19.7**

Plenary retail distribution license, **33:1–12**

Plenary retail transit license, **33:1–12**

Plenary winery license, **33:1–10**

Restricted brewery license, **33:1–10**

Seasonal retail consumption license, **33:1–12**

Special permits, manufacture for personal consumption, **33:1–75**

Containers,

Definitions, **33:1–1**

Illicit beverages, containers without labels, **33:1–88**

Limited retail distribution license, **33:1–12**

Plenary retail consumption license, **33:1–12, 33:1–12.23**

Certain municipalities, **33:1–12.24**

Plenary retail distribution license, **33:1–12**

Seasonal retail consumption license, **33:1–12, 33:1–12.23**

Certain municipalities, **33:1–12.24**

State beverage distributors license, **33:1–11**

Contracts,

Breweries, wholesalers, malt beverages, **33:1–93.15 et seq.**

Sale of contracts given on storage of beverages, **33:1–72**

Conviction of crime,

Crime involving moral turpitude as affecting issuance of license, **33:1–25**

Rehabilitation complete, habitual use of, professional and occupational licenses, disqualification, **2A:168A–4**

Removal of disqualification to hold license, **33:1–31.2**

Second offense, **33:1–53**

Violation of liquor laws as affecting issuance of license, **33:1–25**

Costs,

Fees for issuance of stamps, labels, commensurate with cost of services, **33:1–80**

Return of seized property to good faith claimant on payment, **33:1–66**

Sale of seized property in which bona fide lien or interest exists, **33:1–66**

Counties of sixth class, license, lapse because of military service, **33:1–12.22b**

Crimes and offenses, **33:1–49 et seq., 33:1–91**

Adverse or pecuniary interest, **33:1–43**

ALCOHOLIC BEVERAGES—Cont'd

Crimes and offenses—Cont'd

Affecting issuance of license, **33:1–25**

Aiding and abetting, **33:1–52**

Blending, **33:1–50**

Bottling, **33:1–50**

Without license, **33:1–78**

Breweries, persons interested in retailing or wholesaling, **33:1–43**

Confiscation and disposition, **33:1–55**

Conflict of interest, **33:1–43**

Containers without labels, **33:1–88**

Contrivance for use and manufacture, **33:1–66**

Custody of illicit beverage, **33:1–50**

Definitions, **33:1–1**

Destruction of seized property, **33:1–66**

Discounts to retailers, **33:1–90**

Discrimination, sales to retailers, **33:1–89**

Discriminatory practices, **33:1–91**

Distribution, **33:1–50**

Employees, moral turpitude, **33:1–26**

Forfeiture of seized property, **33:1–66**

Fortifying, **33:1–50**

Identification cards, transfers, **33:1–81.7**

Implements, possession or ownership, **33:1–50**

Importing, **33:1–50**

Investigation by officer on belief person is engaged in, **33:1–66**

Issuance of warrant to search private dwelling, **33:1–56**

Keeping intoxicating liquors, **33:1–50**

Keeping unlawful property, **33:1–55**

Leased premises, violation upon, **33:1–54**

Magistrates authority to issue warrant to search premises, **33:1–56**

Maintenance of premises, unlawful, **33:1–55**

Malicious procurement of search warrant, **33:1–64**

Manufacturers and manufacturing, post

Misdemeanor by purchasing, receiving or procuring, **33:1–49**

Misrepresentation of age to induce sale, minors, **33:1–81**

Mixing, **33:1–50**

Obstruction, search warrant service or execution, **33:1–63**

Occupying premises, unlawful, **33:1–55**

Opposing officer, search warrant service or execution, **33:1–63**

Paraphernalia, ownership or possession, **33:1–50**

Persons under legal age, retail sales, **33:1–81**

Poisoned liquors, **33:3–9, 33:3–10**

Possession, **33:1–50**

Children and minors, **2C:33–15**

Custody or sale, **33:1–50**

Sale, misdemeanor, **33:1–50**

Unlawful property, **33:1–55, 33:1–66**

Processing intoxicating liquors, **33:1–50**

Procurement of illicit beverage, **33:1–49**

Property subject to seizure, **33:1–66**

Purchase, receipt or procurement, **33:1–49**

Receiving illicit beverage, **33:1–49**

Removal of disqualification to hold license, **33:1–31.2**

Resale, bottling for resale without license, **33:1–78**

Resistance of officer, search warrant service or execution, **33:1–63**

Retailers, persons interested in distilleries, breweries, or wholesaling, **33:1–43**

Return of seized vehicle to carrier who acted in good faith, **33:1–66**

Sales, post

ALCOHOLIC BEVERAGES—Cont'd
Crimes and offenses—Cont'd
  Search without warrant, **33:1–65**
  Second or subsequent offenses, **33:1–53**
  Seizure, **33:1–55, 33:1–66**
  Serving or making available to minors,
    2C:33–17
  Solicitors permits, violation, **33:1–67**
  Storage, **33:1–50, 33:1–55**
  Title, unlawful property, **33:1–55**
  Transportation, **33:1–50, 33:1–55**
  Wholesalers,
    Persons interested in retailing, **33:1–43**
    Stock investment, **33:1–43a**
  Wineries,
    Interest by wholesaler, **33:1–43a**
    Persons interested in retailing or wholesal-
      ing, **33:1–43**
Criminal history record information,
  Licenses and permits, **33:1–25, 33:1–26**
  Removal of disqualification to hold license,
    33:1–31.2
Decisions,
  Authentication, copies of decision, **33:1–37**
  Hearing appeals, **33:1–38**
Definitions, **33:1–1**
  Malt beverages, **33:1–93.14**
Delicatessen stores,
  Limited retail distribution license, **33:1–12**
  Packaged merchandise, sale, **33:1–12**
Delivery,
  Beverage by licensees without transportation
    license, **33:1–28**
  Certified copy of resolution for municipal
    referendum to county clerk, **33:1–45**
  Misrepresenting age to induce delivery to
    minor, **33:1–81**
Deposit of fee to accompany license applica-
  tion, **33:1–25**
Deposition to secure issuance of search war-
  rant, **33:1–57**
Deputy directors, **33:1–4**
  Powers with respect to investigations, inspec-
    tions, **33:1–35**
  Service of subpoenas, **33:1–36**
Descent of licenses, **33:1–26**
Destruction of seized property, **33:1–66**
Detention of evidence, **33:1–68**
Development projects, licenses and permits,
  plenary licenses, retail consumption li-
  cense, municipalities, **33:1–12.49**
Diligence of officers in detection of violation,
  33:1–71
Discounts to retailers, **33:1–90**
Discrimination. Wholesalers, post
Disorderly Persons, this index
Disposition of seized or unlawful property,
  33:1–55, 33:1–66
Distillers, brewers and vintners package mer-
  chandise, sale, **33:1–12**
Distillery licenses, **33:1–10**
Distilling apparatus. Stills and Distilling Ap-
  paratus, generally, this index
Distribution,
  Causes for suspension or revocation of li-
    cense, **33:1–31**
  Class B licenses, **33:1–11**
    Acquisition of brand liquor from author-
      ized agent, **33:1–2**
  Directors,
    Authority to make rules and regulations,
      33:1–39
    Duty to supervise, **33:1–3**
  Interest of officers or employees, **33:1–7**
  Licenses, **33:1–11**
    Renewal, **33:1–11.6**

ALCOHOLIC BEVERAGES—Cont'd
Distribution—Cont'd
  Misdemeanor, **33:1–50**
  Municipal regulation, **33:1–40**
  Plenary retail distribution license, **33:1–12,
    33:1–46**
  Reciprocal rules and regulations with other
    states, **33:1–39.1**
  Retailers license, **33:1–12**
  Supervision, **33:1–3**
  Unlawful property, **33:1–55**
  Wholesalers license, **33:1–11**
Division of alcoholic beverage control. Alco-
  holic Beverage Control Division, generally,
  this index
Documents,
  Compelling production by subpoena, **33:1–35**
  Sale of documents given on storage of bever-
    ages, **33:1–72**
Door, breaking in execution of search warrant,
  33:1–58
Drivers Licenses, this index
Drug stores, packaged merchandise, sale,
  33:1–12
Drunkards. Alcoholics and Alcoholism, gener-
  ally, this index
Earnings. Compensation and salaries, general-
  ly, ante
Education,
  Director, definitions, plenary or limited retail
    distribution licenses, **33:1–12.41**
  Division, definitions, plenary or limited retail
    distribution licenses, **33:1–12.41**
  Legislative findings, plenary or limited retail
    distribution licenses, **33:1–12.40**
  Persons under legal age, **33:1–81**
  Possession, **2C:33–15**
Educational organizations, temporary permits,
  fees, **33:1–74**
Effective date, **33:1–22**
Eligible, definitions, **33:1–1**
Emergency transportation, permit, **33:1–28a**
Eminent domain, class C license, renewal,
  33:1–12.39
Employees. Officers and employees, generally,
  post
Entertainment facilities, plenary retail con-
  sumption licenses, **33:1–12**
Entry in execution of search warrant, **33:1–58**
Evidence,
  Authenticated copies of acts, rules, orders,
    33:1–37
  Certificate of facts and findings, **33:1–37**
  Detention of evidence, **33:1–68**
  Illicit beverages, **33:1–88**
  License application, **33:1–25**
Examination of books, records, **33:1–35**
Excise tax, nonpayment, suspension or revoca-
  tion of license, **33:1–31**
Execution of license, **33:1–26**
Executions, order by director on appeal,
  33:1–38
Executors and administrators, license,
  Extension to, **33:1–22**
  More than one license in different capacities,
    33:1–40
Exemptions, fees, **33:1–27**
Expiration of solicitors permit, **33:1–67**
Extension of term of license pending appeal
  from denial of renewal of license, **33:1–22**
Fees,
  Accounting for surrender fee, **33:1–31**
  Appeals,
    Refusal to issue license, **33:1–22**
    Revocation or suspension of license,
      33:1–31

ALCOHOLIC BEVERAGES—Cont'd
Fees—Cont'd
  Brand registration schedule, **33:1–2**
  Brokers license, **33:1–14**
  Class C licenses, **33:1–12**
    Renewal, **33:1–12.39**
  Class D licenses, **33:1–13**
  Class E licenses, **33:1–14**
  Corporations, in which member is interested,
    33:1–20
  Deposit into fund, **33:1–4.1**
  Deposit of fee to accompany license applica-
    tion, **33:1–25**
  Director, authenticated copy of rules, orders,
    33:1–37
  Division of license fee, premises located in
    more than one municipality, **33:1–16**
  Exemptions, **33:1–27**
  Experts and specialists appointed by director,
    33:1–4
  Issuance of stamps, labels, **33:1–80**
  Manufacturing license fees, **33:1–10**
  New licenses, issuance upon failure to renew,
    33:1–12.18
  Prorated fee, exemption from payment,
    33:1–27
  Refund on voluntary surrender of license,
    33:1–31
  Refusal of license to persons failing to pay
    license fee, **33:1–33**
  Remittance of deduction for taxes, refund of
    license fee, **33:1–31**
  Retailers license, **33:1–12**
  Separate license for each warehouse, sales-
    room, or office, **33:1–15**
  Solicitors permits, **33:1–67**
  Special permits, manufacture for personal
    consumption, **33:1–75**
  Temporary contingency permits, **33:1–74**
  Transit insignia for delivery by licensees
    without transportation license, **33:1–28**
  Warehouse receipts license, **33:1–72**
  Wholesalers license, **33:1–11**
  Witnesses before director or other issuing
    authority, **33:1–35**
Fermented liquors,
  Municipal referendum on retail sales,
    33:1–44
  Naturally fermented wine,
    Presumption, fitness for beverage purposes
      and alcoholic content, **33:1–1.1**
    Wholesalers license, **33:1–11**
  Presumption, fitness for beverage purposes
    and alcoholic content, **33:1–1.1**
Fetal alcohol syndrome, drinking during preg-
  nancy, warning notices, posting require-
  ments, class C license holders, **33:1–12a**
  Violation of provisions, fines, penalties,
    33:1–12b
Fines and penalties, **33:1–50, 33:1–51, 33:1–86**
  Advertising, manufacturing, unlawful proper-
    ty, **33:1–66**
  Age, sale to persons under legal age, **33:1–77**
  Aiding or abetting another in violation of
    law, **33:1–52**
  Arrest by officers for misdemeanors, **33:1–66**
  Bottling without license, **33:1–78**
  Discriminatory practices, **33:1–92**
  Disorderly conduct, **33:1–81**
  Identification cards, **33:1–81.7**
  Illicit beverages, purchase, receipt or pro-
    curement, **33:1–49**
  Licenses, fines and penalties, Chain Store
    Liquor License Act, **33:1–12.37**
  Malicious procurement of search warrant,
    33:1–64

ALCOHOLIC BEVERAGES—Cont'd
Fines and penalties—Cont'd
Manufacture, sale, possession, **33:1–50**
Poisoned liquors, **33:3–9, 33:3–10**
Misrepresenting age to induce sale or delivery to minor, **33:1–81**
Parents, failure to supervise, conviction of juvenile, unlawful purchases, **33:1–81.1a**
Possession, children and minors, **2C:33–15**
Procurement of search warrant without probable cause, **33:1–64**
Purchasing, receiving or procuring illicit beverage, **33:1–49**
Resisting, officer, serving or executing warrant, **33:1–63**
Search without warrant, **33:1–65**
Second or subsequent offense, **33:1–53**
Tasting events, sampling, **33:1–12d**
Violations of law, **33:1–51**
Concerning solicitors permits, **33:1–67**
Warning notices, pregnant women, harmful effects, class C licenses, **33:1–12b**
Fireworks, manufacturers and manufacturing, entry, **21:2–17**
Fixtures,
Forfeiture, **33:1–66**
Replacement, retail licenses, **33:1–43.1**
Forfeitures, **33:1–23**
Property as subject to forfeiture, **33:1–66**
Unclaimed seized property, **33:1–66**
Forms,
Bonds (officers and fiduciaries), **33:1–8**
Licensees, **33:1–17**
Return of seized property, **33:1–66**
Director, authority to make rules and regulations, **33:1–39**
Notice of intention to make application for license, **33:1–25**
Fortified wines,
Presumption, fitness for beverage purposes and alcoholic content, **33:1–1.1**
Wholesalers license, **33:1–11**
Fortifying as misdemeanor, **33:1–50**
Fraternal organizations, licenses and permits, law enforcement personnel, **33:1–25.1, 33:1–25.2**
Fraud,
Revocation of license, **33:1–25**
Wholesalers, termination, contracts, breweries, malt beverages, **33:1–93.16**
Free goods, discriminatory allowances to retailers, **33:1–90**
Fund, deposit of fees and penalties, use of monies, **33:1–4.1**
Gifts,
Acceptance by person appointed to office, **33:1–7**
Inducement to purchase, control, **33:1–39.2**
Rules and regulations by director, **33:1–39**
Wholesalers, to retailers, **33:1–93**
Glass, sale by the glass, temporary permits, **33:1–74**
Good faith, wholesalers,
Breweries, malt beverages, contracts, **33:1–93.15**
Contracts, breweries, malt beverages, **33:1–93.17**
Governing board or body, definitions, **33:1–1**
Grocery stores,
Limited retail distribution license, **33:1–12**
Package merchandise, sale, **33:1–12**
Guardian of minor,
Attendance at hearing, **33:1–81.1**
Notice, conviction of juvenile for unlawful purchases, **33:1–81.1a**

ALCOHOLIC BEVERAGES—Cont'd
Habitual drunkards. Alcoholics and Alcoholism, generally, this index
Health, sale, poisoned liquors, **33:3–9, 33:3–10**
Hearings,
Appeals, **33:1–38**
Action of issuing authority respecting license, **33:1–22**
Enumeration of duties, **33:1–23**
Forfeiture, sale, seized property, **33:1–66**
Issuance of licenses, municipal authorities, **33:1–24**
Minor, attendance of parent or guardian, **33:1–81.1**
Notice, appeal from refusal of issuing authority to revoke or suspend license, **33:1–31**
Historical sites and property, licenses and permits, hotels and motels, **33:1–12.20**
Home manufacture for personal consumption, special permits, **33:1–75, 33:1 App.**
Hospitals, regulation of use, **33:1–29**
Hours of sale, **33:1 App.**
Appeal from limitation of hours of sale, **33:1–41**
Municipal referendum on hours of retail sales, **33:1–47.1**
Municipal regulation, **33:1–40**
Rules and regulations by director, **33:1–39**
Identification cards, **33:1–81.2 et seq.**
Identity and identification, sales, theft of identity, exceptions, **2C:21–17**
Identity theft, personal identifying information, obtaining, **2C:21–17.2**
Implement for manufacture, owning, possessing, **33:1–50**
Imports and exports, **33:1 App.**
Beverages as misdemeanor, **33:1–50**
Definitions, **33:1–1**
Markets and marketing, retailers, products, **33:1–43.2**
Indicia of compliance with standards, issuance, **33:1–80**
Indictment, information or presentment,
Defensive negative averments, **33:1–70**
Joinder of separate offenses, **33:1–70**
Name of purchaser, **33:1–70**
Infants. Children and minors, generally, ante
Inheritance of licenses, **33:1–26**
Initiative and referendum. Municipalities, post
Insignia,
Rules and regulations by director, **33:1–39**
Transit insignia for delivery by licensees without transportation license, **33:1–28**
Inspection and inspectors,
Director or other issuing authority, **33:1–35**
Licensed premises, **33:1–23**
Municipal authorities, **33:1–24**
Records and files of department, **33:1–37**
Rules and regulations by director, **33:1–39**
Instructional winemaking facilities, licenses and permits, **33:1–10, 33:1–75**
Intent, misdemeanor by owning, possessing, beverages or paraphernalia for manufacture, **33:1–50**
Intention of law, **33:1–73**
Interest,
Brewery, distillery or wholesaler, retail, **33:1–43**
Crimes and offenses, adverse or pecuniary interest, **33:1–43**
Deduction of interest due state on refund of license fee, **33:1–31**
Good faith in property seized or forfeited, **33:1–66**
Liquor industry, **33:1–7**

ALCOHOLIC BEVERAGES—Cont'd
International airports, licenses, Chain Store Liquor License Act, **33:1–12.32**
Inventories, property seized under warrant, **33:1–61**
Investigations, **33:1–35**
Appointment, compensation, **33:1–4**
License applicants, **33:1–23**
Municipal authorities, **33:1–24**
Officer on belief person is engaged in unlawful activity, **33:1–66**
Officers, **33:1–1**
Rules and regulations by director, **33:1–39**
Sale, purchase, industrial alcohol, **33:1–30**
Stills and distilling apparatus, **33:2–1**
Use by druggists and hospitals, **33:1–29**
Issuance,
Licenses and permits, post
Stamps, labels, **33:1–80**
Temporary contingency permits, **33:1–74**
Issuance of search warrant, **33:1–56, 33:1–57**
Joinder of separate offenses in affidavit, information, **33:1–70**
Jurisdiction, property seized under Alcoholic Beverage Law, **33:1–66**
Keeping,
Misdemeanor, **33:1–50**
Unlawful property, **33:1–55**
Kegs, distributors license, chilled draught malt beverages, **33:1–11**
Labor and employment, licenses and permits, **33:1 App.**
Lager beer, presumption, fitness for beverage purposes and alcoholic content, **33:1–1.1**
Law enforcement officers, nonprofit organizations, licenses and permits, **33:1–25.1, 33:1–25.2**
Leased premises, violation upon, **33:1–54**
Legal age, persons under legal age, possession, **2C:33–15**
Liberal construction of law, **33:1–73**
Licensed building, definitions, **33:1–1**
Licenses and permits,
Acceptance, officers or employees of gift, from licensee or applicant, **33:1–7**
Additional licenses,
Bowling alleys, Chain Store Liquor License Act, **33:1–12.32**
Hotel operation, Chain Store Liquor License Act, **33:1–12.32**
International airports, Chain Store Liquor License Act, **33:1–12.32**
Notice of issuance, publication, **33:1–19.1, 33:1–19.2**
Administration, issuance, **33:1–18**
Applications, **33:1–25**
License to member of issuing authority or corporation, in which member is interested, **33:1–20**
Photostatic copy, accompanying application, **33:1–25**
Armed forces,
Lapses, counties of sixth class, **33:1–12.22b**
New licenses,
Exlicensees entitled to, **33:1–12.19**
Transfer to spouse, surrender or expiration, **33:1–12.22a**
Associations and societies, club licenses, municipalities rejecting referendum, **33:1–46.1**
Attachment of licenses, **33:1–26**
Bankruptcy of licensee, extension to trustee, **33:1–26**
Bids and bidding,
Appeals, **33:1–19.6**
Notice, announcements, **33:1–19.4**

ALCOHOLIC BEVERAGES—Cont'd
Licenses and permits—Cont'd
Bids and bidding—Cont'd
  Qualifications, **33:1–19.3**
  Rejection, **33:1–19.5**
Bonded warehouse bottling license, **33:1–10**
Bonds (officers and fiduciaries), **33:1–17**
Bowling alleys, additional licenses, Chain Store Liquor License Act, **33:1–12.32**
Brokers license, fee, **33:1–14**
Class A licenses, generally, ante
Class B licenses, generally, ante
Class C licenses, generally, ante
Classes of licenses, **33:1–9 et seq.**
Classification and subdivision, **33:1–10**
Conditions to issuance, **33:1–32**
Conviction of crime as disqualification for license, **33:1–25**
Crimes and offenses, **33:1–25**
Criminal history record information, background check, **33:1–25, 33:1–26**
Death of licensee,
  Extension to executor or administrator, **33:1–22, 33:1–26**
  Issuance of new license, **33:1–12.30**
Definitions, **33:1–1**
Delivery by licensees without transportation license, **33:1–28**
Descent and distribution, **33:1–26**
Development projects, plenary licenses, retail consumption license, municipalities, **33:1–12.49**
Distilleries,
  Bottling without license, **33:1–78**
  Classification of, **33:1–10**
Distributors licenses, **33:1–11**
  Renewal, **33:1–11.6**
Evidence to accompany application, **33:1–25**
Exceptions to provision for solicitors permits, **33:1–67**
Execution of licenses, **33:1–26**
Exemption, retail sale for consumption on premises, **33:1–27**
Exemption from payment of fees, **33:1–27**
Extension of term pending appeal from denial of renewal, **33:1–22**
Fees, smart growth development projects, **33:1–24.2**
Furnishing, repair or replacement of fixtures for retail licensee by owner, brewery, **33:1–43.1**
Golf and country club license in municipalities rejecting referendum, **33:1–46.1 et seq.**
Historical sites and property, hotels and motels, **33:1–12.20**
Incompetency of licensee, extension, **33:1–22, 33:1–26**
Inheritance of licenses, **33:1–26**
Inspection, **33:1–23**
  By director or other issuing authority, **33:1–35**
Instructional winemaking facilities, **33:1–10, 33:1–75**
International airports, Chain Store Liquor License Act, **33:1–12.32**
Investigations by director or other issuing authority, **33:1–35**
Issuance, **33:1–32**
  New license, fees, failure to renew, **33:1–12.18**
  Notice of issuance of new licenses, publication, **33:1–19.1, 33:1–19.2**
  Review, **33:1–17.1**
  Sales within 200 feet of church or school, **33:1–76**

ALCOHOLIC BEVERAGES—Cont'd
Licenses and permits—Cont'd
Issuance—Cont'd
  Temporary contingency permits, **33:1–74**
Labor and employment, **33:1 App.**
Law enforcement officers, nonprofit organizations, **33:1–25.1, 33:1–25.2**
Levies against licenses, **33:1–26**
Licenses, death of licensee, issuance, **33:1–12.30**
Liens against licenses, **33:1–26**
Limited licenses,
  Brewery license, **33:1–10**
  Distillery license, **33:1–10**
  Export wholesale license, **33:1–11**
  Retail consumption license, municipal referendum, **33:1–46**
  Retail distribution licenses, **33:1–12**
    New license, **33:1–12.27, 33:1–12.29**
    Renewal, **33:1–12.28, 33:1–76.2**
  Supplementary limited distillery license, **33:1–10**
  Wholesale license, **33:1–11**
Loans to retail licensee by owner, brewery, **33:1–43.1**
Manufacturers and manufacturing, post
Members of issuing authority, adverse or pecuniary interest, **33:1–20**
Motels, **33:1–12.20**
  Contingent on completion of new construction, **33:1–12.20a**
Municipal board to administer issuance, **33:1–19**
New licenses, **33:1–12.18, 33:1–12.26**
  Armed forces, transfer to spouse, surrender or expiration, **33:1–12.22a**
  Exlicensee entitled to, **33:1–12.19**
  Limited retail distribution license, **33:1–12.27, 33:1–12.29**
  Term, **33:1–12.26**
Nonprofit corporations and associations, post
Nonprofit organizations, law enforcement officers, **33:1–25.1, 33:1–25.2**
Number of retail licenses, limitation, Chain Store Liquor License Act, **33:1–12.14**
Other issuing authority, construed, **33:1–19**
Photostatic copy of permits, to accompany license application, **33:1–25**
Pledges of licenses, **33:1–26**
Plenary licenses,
  Brewery license, **33:1–10**
  Development projects, retail consumption license, municipalities, **33:1–12.49**
  Distillery license, **33:1–10**
  Education,
    Certificate, **33:1–12.43**
    Renewal, certificate of completion, **33:1–12.47**
    Requirements, **33:1–12.42, 33:1–12.44**
    Rules and regulations, **33:1–12.48**
    Time, **33:1–12.46**
  Export wholesale license, **33:1–11**
  Musical or theatrical performances or concerts, nonprofit corporations, **33:1–19.7**
  Nonprofit corporations, musical or theatrical performances or concerts, **33:1–19.7**
  Retail consumption license, **33:1–12 et seq.**
    Additional licenses, notice of issuance, publication, **33:1–19.1, 33:1–19.2**
    Death of licensee, issuance, new license, **33:1–12.30**
    Hotels and motels, sales and delivery to guests, **33:1–12.25**

ALCOHOLIC BEVERAGES—Cont'd
Licenses and permits—Cont'd
Plenary licenses—Cont'd
  Retail consumption license—Cont'd
    Municipal referendum, except for consumption on trains, airplanes and boats, **33:1–46**
    Municipalities under 1000, **33:1–12.15**
    Off premises consumption, sales and displays, **33:1–12.23**
      Certain municipalities, **33:1–12.24**
    Sale, qualifications, **33:1–19.3**
  Retail distribution licenses, **33:1–10, 33:1–12**
    Additional licenses, notice of issuance, publication, **33:1–19.1, 33:1–19.2**
    Death of licensee, issuance, new license, **33:1–12.30**
    Municipal referendum on retail sales, **33:1–46**
    Municipalities under 1000, **33:1–12.15**
    Number, **33:1–12.14**
    Renewal, **33:1–76.2**
    Sale, qualifications, **33:1–19.3**
  Retail transit licenses, **33:1–12**
    Issuance, **33:1–18**
  Sale, qualifications, **33:1–19.3**
  Wholesale license, **33:1–11**
  Winery license, **33:1–10**
Plenary retail,
  Consumption license, **33:1–12**
  Distribution license, **33:1–12**
Plenary retail distribution licenses, sale, qualifications, **33:1–19.3**
Possession, **33:1–2**
Premises located in more than one municipality, **33:1–16**
Publication of notice of intention to apply for license, **33:1–25**
Publication of notice of intention to make application, **33:1–25**
Purchasing and selling beverages of certain manufacturers, **33:1–79**
Receivership of licensee, extension to receiver, **33:1–26**
Rectifier and blender, **33:1–10**
  Bottling without rectifiers license, **33:1–78**
Refund of license fee after issuance of license, **33:1–31**
Refusal to issue,
  Appeals, fees, **33:1–22**
  Failing to pay tax, license fee or penalty, **33:1–33**
Regulation, **33:1–26, 33:1–40**
Removal of disqualification to hold, lapse of five years from conviction, **33:1–31.2**
Renewal, **33:1–12.13, 33:1–12.16**
  Class C license, nonuse, **33:1–12.39**
  Continuing right of retail license holder, Chain Store Liquor License Act, **33:1–12.35**
  Distributors license, **33:1–11.6**
  Eminent domain, distributors license, **33:1–11.6**
  Fires, distributors license, **33:1–11.6**
  Limited retail distribution license, **33:1–12.28**
  New license term, **33:1–12.26, 33:1–96**
  Notice, publication, **33:1–25**
  Review, **33:1–17.1**
  Sales within 200 feet of church or school, **33:1–76**
  Waiver of protection, **33:1–76.1, 33:1–76.2**
Replacement of license expiring on last day of license term, **33:1–12.26**

ALCOHOLIC BEVERAGES—Cont'd
Licenses and permits—Cont'd
  Requirement for, 33:1–2
  Restaurant operation, Chain Store Liquor
    License Act, 33:1–12.32
  Restricted brewery license, 33:1–10
  Retailers, post
  Rules and regulations,
    Displays, 33:1–39
    Identification of licensees and their em-
      ployees, 33:1–39
  Sales, post
  Searches by director or other issuing authori-
    ty, 33:1–35
  Seasonal retail consumption licenses, 33:1–12
    Hotels and motels, sales and delivery to
      guests, 33:1–12.25
    Issuance procedure, notice, 33:1–19.1,
      33:1–19.2
    Limitation, number, 33:1–12.14
    Municipalities under 1000, 33:1–12.15
    Off premises consumption, sales or dis-
      plays, 33:1–12.23
    Certain municipalities, 33:1–12.24
    Persons having in previous season,
      33:1–12.17
    Sales, qualifications, 33:1–19.3
  Seizure for debts, 33:1–26
  Separate license for each warehouse, sales-
    room or office, 33:1–15
  Smart growth development projects,
    33:1–24.1 et seq.
  Solicitors permits, 33:1–67, 33:1 App.
  Special permits,
    Clubs, 33:1–46.2
    Manufacturing, personal consumption,
      33:1–75
    Smart growth development projects,
      33:1–24.2
    Temporary or emergency transportation,
      33:1–28a
  Subjects of rules and regulations, 33:1–39
  Surrender,
    Accounting for surrender fees, 33:1–31
    Effect on proceedings to revoke license,
      33:1–31
    Issuing authority to certify to commission-
      er, 33:1–31
    Refund of license fee, 33:1–31
  Suspension or revocation, 33:1–31
    Automatic upon conviction of violation,
      33:1–31.1
    Class B license, 33:1–11.5
    Compromise and settlement, 33:1–31
    Failure to have unrevoked permit, 33:1–31
    Fees, appeals, 33:1–31
    Fraud, evasions, 33:1–25
    Hearings, 33:1–24
    Order by director after hearing on appeal,
      33:1–38
    Violation of conditions to issuance of li-
      cense, 33:1–32
  Suspension or revocation of license, 33:1–31
  Tasting events, sampling, 33:1–12d
  Temporary or emergency transportation,
    33:1–28a
  Transfer, 33:1–12.16, 33:1–26
    Review, 33:1–17.1
    Seasonal retail consumption license,
      33:1–12.17
  Transportation, post
  Warehouse receipts license, 33:1–72
  Warning notices, pregnant women, harmful
    effects, 33:1–12a
    Fines, 33:1–12b
  Wholesalers, post

ALCOHOLIC BEVERAGES—Cont'd
Limited licenses. Licenses and permits, ante
Limited retail distribution license, 33:1–12
Limousine or livery service, passengers,
  39:4–51a
Limousines, definitions, 33:1–1
Local Option Act, 33:1–44 et seq.
Magistrate, definitions, 33:1–1
Maintenance of premises, unlawful property,
  33:1–55
Maintenance of prices, 33:1–39.2
Malicious procurement of search warrant,
  33:1–64
Malt beverages, 33:1–93.12 et seq., 33:1 App.
  Actions and proceedings, wholesalers, con-
    tracts, breweries, 33:1–93.18
  Construction of law, breweries, wholesalers,
    contracts, 33:1–93.19
  Contracts, breweries, wholesalers, 33:1–93.15
    et seq.
  Good faith,
    Breweries, wholesalers, contracts,
      33:1–93.15
    Wholesalers, contracts, breweries,
      33:1–93.17
  Licenses,
    Brewing, 33:1–10
    Distribution, chilled draught malt alcoholic
      beverages, 33:1–11
  On and off premise consumption, sale,
    33:1–40.3
  Termination, breweries, wholesalers, con-
    tracts, 33:1–93.16
Manufacturers and manufacturing, 33:1–50
  Causes for suspension or revocation of li-
    cense, 33:1–31
  Crimes and offenses, 33:1–50
    Interest by wholesaler, 33:1–43a
    Unlawful property, 33:1–66
    Wholesalers interest, 33:1–43
  Definitions, 33:1–1
    Class A licenses, 33:1–10
  Director,
    Authority to make rules and regulations,
      33:1–39
    Duty to supervise, 33:1–3
    Interest by wholesaler, 33:1–43, 33:1–43a
    Interest of officers or employees, 33:1–7
    Issuance of license, 33:1–18
    Licenses and permits, 33:1–2, 33:1–9,
      33:1–10, 33:1–79
      Bonds (officers and fiduciaries), 33:1–17
      Eligibility to hold retail license, 33:1–26
      Investigation of applicants, 33:1–23
      Sale to voluntary unincorporated organiza-
        tion of army or navy personnel,
        33:1–11.1
  Markets and marketing, retailers, products,
    33:1–43.2
  Personal consumption, special permits,
    33:1–75
  Reciprocal rules and regulations with other
    states, 33:1–39.1
  Sales,
    Church or school, 33:1–76
      Waiver of protection, 33:1–76.1,
        33:1–76.2
    Poisoned liquors, 33:3–9, 33:3–10
  Search and seizure, 33:1–66
  Special permits, manufacture for personal
    consumption, 33:1–75
  Supervision, 33:1–3
  Unlawful property, 33:1–55
  Wholesaling, interest in, 33:1–43
Markets and marketing, retailers, products,
  wholesalers, 33:1–43.2

ALCOHOLIC BEVERAGES—Cont'd
Meat markets, limited retail distribution li-
  cense, 33:1–12
Mentally deficient and mentally ill persons,
  Extension of license to person appointed by
    court, 33:1–22
  Warning notices, pregnant women, harmful
    effects, class C licenses, 33:1–12a
    Fines, 33:1–12b
Mercantile business, packaged merchandise,
  sale, 33:1–12
Military service, license application by attorney
  in fact, 33:1–25
Minors. Children and minors, generally, ante
Minutes, municipal authorities issuing licenses,
  33:1–24
Misrepresenting or misstating age to induce
  sale, minor, 33:1–81
Mixing as misdemeanor, 33:1–50
Modification, limitation of number of licenses
  or hours of sale, 33:1–41
Monopolies, 33:1–23.1
Motor Vehicles, this index
Municipalities, 33:1–40
  Addition to regulations, 33:1–12.21
  Administration, issuance of licenses, 33:1–19
  Appeal to director from action respecting
    license, 33:1–22
  Appointment, referendum on retail sales,
    33:1–46
  Cash deposit or bond, condition to issuance
    of license, 33:1–33
  Certification, 33:1–48
  Conditions to issuance of license, 33:1–32
  Cooperation, 33:1–23
  Definitions, 33:1–1
  Development projects, licenses and permits,
    plenary licenses, retail consumption li-
    cense, 33:1–12.49
  Dissolution after municipal referendum on
    retail sales, 33:1–46
  Enumeration of duties, issuing licenses,
    33:1–24
  Establishment of municipal board of alcohol-
    ic beverage control, 33:1–5
  Examination,
    Books, records, 33:1–35
    Witnesses, 33:1–35
  Fee for retailers license, 33:1–12
  Hours of retail sales, 33:1–47.1
  Initiative and referendum,
    Ballots, 33:1–45, 33:1–46
      Except brewed malt and fermented
        wine, 33:1–44
      Hours of retail sales, 33:1–47.1
      Sunday sales, 33:1–47
    Hours of retail sales, 33:1–47.1
    Licenses and permits,
      Retail sales, 33:1–46
      All kinds of alcoholic beverages,
        33:1–45
      Beverages except brewed malt and
        fermented wine, 33:1–44
    Sunday sales, 33:1–47
    Notice,
      Hours of retail sales, 33:1–47.1
      Retail sales, 33:1–44 et seq.
      All kinds of alcoholic beverages,
        33:1–45
      Consumption on trains, airplanes and
        boats, 33:1–46
      Sunday sales, 33:1–47
    Retail sales, 33:1–46
      All kinds of alcoholic beverages, 33:1–45
      Brewed malt and fermented wine,
        33:1–44

ALCOHOLIC BEVERAGES—Cont'd
Municipalities—Cont'd
  Initiative and referendum—Cont'd
    Sunday sales, **33:1–47**
  Inspections and investigations in administration of law, **33:1–35**
  Instructions for boards as subject of rules and regulations, **33:1–39**
  Instructions for municipalities as subject of rules and regulations, **33:1–39**
  Investigations in administration of law, **33:1–35**
  Licenses and permits,
    Additions to, **33:1–12.21**
    Fees, premises located in multiple municipalities, **33:1–16**
    Number of retail licenses, **33:1–40**
  Limitation of number of retail licenses, **33:1–12.14**
  Municipalities of 15,000 inhabitants or more, **33:1–5**
  Notice,
    Change in facts set forth in application for license, **33:1–34**
    Vote on municipal referendum on,
      Retail sales, **33:1–44 et seq.**
      Sunday sales, **33:1–47**
  Number of members, **33:1–5**
  Order by director to board or body after hearing on appeal, **33:1–38**
  Public employment of salaried member forbidden, **33:1–5**
  Publication of notice of intention to make application for license, **33:1–25**
  Referendum, sales, **33:1–44**
  Regulation of number of retail licenses, hours of sale, **33:1–40**
  Retail sales,
    All kinds of alcoholic beverages, **33:1–45**
    Beverages except brewed malt and fermented wine, **33:1–44**
  Return of deposit on denial of application for license, **33:1–25**
  Search of premises, **33:1–35**
  Secretary, **33:1–5.4**
  Sunday sales, **33:1–47**
  Suspension or revocation of license, **33:1–31**
  Vacancies in board, **33:1–5**
Name of purchaser, affidavits, indictments, **33:1–70**
New licenses, fees, issuance upon failure to renew, **33:1–12.18**
Nighttime, service of search warrant in, **33:1–59**
Nonprofit corporations and associations, licenses and permits,
  Auctions and auctioneers, **33:1–97**
  Law enforcement personnel, **33:1–25.1, 33:1–25.2**
  Plenary retail consumption license, musical or theatrical performances, **33:1–19.7**
Notice,
  Applicant of refusal to issue license, **33:1–22**
  Change in facts set forth in application for license, **33:1–34**
  Hearing,
    By director after seizure of stills, distilling apparatus, **33:2–4**
    Seized property, forfeiture, sale, **33:1–66**
  Intention to make application for license, **33:1–25**
  Lessee or sublessee of lessors exercise of option for violation on leased premises, **33:1–54**
  Licenses, issuance of additional licenses, publication, **33:1–19.1, 33:1–19.2**
  Municipalities, ante

ALCOHOLIC BEVERAGES—Cont'd
Notice—Cont'd
  Parent or guardian, conviction of juvenile for unlawful purchases, **33:1–81.1a**
  Refusal of,
    Issuing authority to revoke or suspend license, **33:1–31**
    Refund of license fee, **33:1–31**
  Renewal of licenses, publication, **33:1–25**
  Suspension or revocation of license, **33:1–31**
  Time of hearing appeal from refusal of issuing authority to revoke or suspend license, **33:1–31**
  Warning notices, pregnant women, harmful effects, class C licenses, **33:1–12a**
  Fines, **33:1–12b**
Nuisances, seizure, forfeiture, **2C:33–12.1**
Numbers and numbering,
  Appeal from limitation of number of retail licenses, **33:1–41**
  Members of municipal board of alcoholic beverage control, **33:1–5**
  Municipal regulation of number of retail licenses, **33:1–40**
Oaths and affirmations,
  Applications, **33:1–25**
  Applications for alcoholic beverage licenses, **33:1–25**
  Power of director, to examine witnesses, **33:1–35**
  Proof under oath of grounds of application for search warrant, **33:1–57**
  Use of private dwelling for unlawful alcoholic beverage activity, basis for issuing search warrant, **33:1–56**
Obstructing officer, serving or executing search warrant, **33:1–63**
Occupying premises, unlawful property, **33:1–55**
Offenses. Crimes and offenses, generally, ante
Officers and employees,
  Acceptance of gifts, **33:1–7**
  Aid to investigation, **33:1–35**
  Appointment, **33:1–4**
  Arrest of person for misdemeanor, **33:1–66**
  Breaking and entry in execution of search warrant, **33:1–58**
  Definitions, **33:1–1**
  Diligence to detect violations, **33:1–71**
  Eligible persons to be employed, **33:1–6**
  Interest in liquor industry, **33:1–7**
  Investigation on belief person engaged in unlawful activity, **33:1–66**
  Manufacture, sale, poisoned liquors, **33:3–9, 33:3–10**
  Moral turpitude, employment affected by conviction of crime, **33:1–26**
  Obstructing, resisting, officer serving or executing search warrant, **33:1–63**
  Person under Alcoholic Beverage Law, **33:1–1**
  Receipt for and inventory of property seized under warrant, **33:1–61**
  Retail licensees employees as unaffected by provision for solicitors permits, **33:1–67**
  Service of,
    Search warrant, **33:1–57**
    Subpoenas, employees of director or of issuing authority, **33:1–36**
Offices, separate license for each office maintained by licensee, **33:1–15**
Opposing officer, serving or executing search warrant, **33:1–63**
Option of lessor to terminate lease for violation, **33:1–54**

ALCOHOLIC BEVERAGES—Cont'd
Order to show cause,
  Director,
    Appeal from denial of application for renewal of alcoholic beverage license, **33:1–22**
    Power to compel attendance of witnesses and production of documents, **33:1–35**
    Failure of person subpoenaed by director or other issuing authority to obey, **33:1–35**
Orders,
  Authentication under seal of copies of orders, **33:1–37**
  Director,
    Hearing appeals, **33:1–38**
    Relative to forfeiture, sale, property seized, **33:1–66**
  Sale of seized property, **33:1–66**
  Solicitors permit, **33:1–67**
Ordinances, **33:1–94**
  License may be suspended or revoked for violation, **33:1–31**
  Ordinances inconsistent with municipal referendum, **33:1–45**
  Prevention of possession, sale, distribution and transportation, **33:1–40**
  Regulation of number of retail licenses, hours of sale, **33:1–40**
Organization as person under Alcoholic Beverage Law, **33:1–1**
Out of door sales, rules and regulations, **33:1–39**
Paraphernalia for manufacture, owning, possessing, **33:1–50**
Partnerships, this index
Penalties. Fines and penalties, generally, ante
Permits. Licenses and permits, generally, ante
Personal consumption, manufacturing, special permit, **33:1–75**
Personal property subject to seizure, forfeiture, **33:1–66**
Personal use, manufacture, sale, possession, **33:1–2**
Petty cash fund, **33:1–23**
Pharmacists,
  Packaged merchandise, sale, **33:1–12**
  Regulation of use, **33:1–29**
Photographs, identification card, **33:1–81.2**
Photostatic copy of licenses, to accompany license application, **33:1–25**
Pledge of license, **33:1–26**
Plenary licenses. Licenses and permits, ante
Poisoned liquors, manufacture, transportation or sale, **33:3–9, 33:3–10**
Police,
  Employment, **33:1–26.1**
  Nonprofit organizations, licenses and permits, **33:1–25.1, 33:1–25.2**
Possession,
  Alcohol by retail licensee, **33:1–85**
    Exemption, **33:1–87**
  Consumption by officers and employees, **33:1–7**
  Intended for personal use, **33:1–2**
  License, **33:1–2**
  Misdemeanor, **33:1–50**
  Municipal regulations of retailed transactions, **33:1–40, 33:1–94**
  Persons under legal age, **2C:33–15**
  Return of property illegally seized under color of search warrant, **33:1–62**
  Unlawful property, **33:1–55**
Pregnancy, this index
Presumption, fitness for beverage purposes and alcoholic content, **33:1–1.1**

ALCOHOLIC BEVERAGES—Cont'd
Price,
  Discriminations on sales to retailers, 33:1–89
  Publication and maintenance, 33:1–39.2
Priority of claim or interest in property seized or forfeited, 33:1–66
Private dwelling, issuance of warrant to search, 33:1–56
Probable cause. Search warrants, post
Processing as misdemeanor, 33:1–50
Procurement of illicit beverage as misdemeanor, 33:1–49
Product, definitions, Class A licenses, 33:1–10
Publications,
  Applications for warehouse receipts licenses, 33:1–72
  Hearing relative to forfeiture, sale, property seized, 33:1–66, 33:2–4
  Intention to make application for license, 33:1–25
  Prices, 33:1–39.2
  Renewal of licenses, 33:1–25
  Rules and regulations, 33:1–39, 33:1–39.1
Purchases,
  Druggists and hospitals, 33:1–29
  Illicit beverage as misdemeanor, 33:1–49
  Industrial alcohol, 33:1–30
  Licensed manufacturers, 33:1–79
  Officers or employees, 33:1–7
Rape, impairing resistance of victim with intoxicants, 2C:14–1
Rebated to retailers, 33:1–90
Receiving illicit beverage as misdemeanor, 33:1–49
Reciprocity, 33:1–39.1
Records and recordation,
  Compelling production, investigation, 33:1–35
  Director, 33:1–23
  License issuance, municipal authorities, 33:1–24
Rectifying and blending,
  Crimes and offenses, 33:1–50
    Interest of wholesaler, 33:1–43a
    Persons interested in wholesaling or retailing, 33:1–43
  Interest of wholesaler, 33:1–43, 33:1–43a
  License, 33:1–10
    Bottling without license, 33:1–78
  Misdemeanor, 33:1–50
  Plants, persons interested in retailing, 33:1–43
  Wholesaling, interest in, 33:1–43
Refund of license fee after issuance of license, 33:1–31
Regulations. Rules and regulations, generally, post
Rehabilitated convicted offenders, habitual use of, professional and occupational licenses, disqualification, 2A:168A–4
Religious corporations and associations,
  Licenses and permits, law enforcement personnel, 33:1–25.1, 33:1–25.2
  Temporary permits, fees, 33:1–74
Removal from office,
  Deputy directors, 33:1–4
  Disqualification to hold license, 33:1–31.2
  Members of municipal board of alcoholic beverage control, 33:1–5
Repair of fixtures and pipes by owner, brewery for retail licensee, 33:1–43.1
Repeal,
  Prevention of possession, sale, 33:1–40
  Rules and regulations, 33:1–39, 33:1–39.1
Replacement of fixtures for retail licensee by owner, brewery, 33:1–43.1

ALCOHOLIC BEVERAGES—Cont'd
Reports,
  Director to governor, 33:1–23
  Municipal boards to director, issuance of licenses, 33:1–19
Requisition for purchase of supplies, director, 33:1–23
Resale, bottling for resale without license, 33:1–78
Resident person, definitions, 33:1–11.2
Resisting officer, serving or executing search warrant, 33:1–63
Resolutions,
  Conditions to issuance of license, 33:1–32
  Hours of retail sales, 33:1–47.1
  Inconsistent with municipal referendum, 33:1–45
  Municipal regulation of hours of sale, 33:1–40
  Sales, 33:1–46
    All kinds of alcoholic beverages, 33:1–45
    Beverages except brewed malt and fermented wine, 33:1–44
  Sunday sales, 33:1–47
  Suspension or revocation of license for violation, 33:1–31
Responsibility in consumption of alcoholic beverages, 33:1–3.1
Restaurants,
  Disorderly persons, unlicensed premises, 2C:33–27
  Licenses and permits, Chain Store Liquor License Act, 33:1–12.32
Restricted brewery license, 33:1–10
Retail license, eligibility to hold manufacturers or wholesalers license, 33:1–26
Retailers,
  Application for license, 33:1–25
  Brewery operation, 33:1–12, 33:1–43
  Crimes and offenses, persons interested in distilleries, breweries, or wholesaling, 33:1–43
  Definitions, 33:1–1
  Discounts to retailers, 33:1–90, 33:1–93
  Discriminatory practices on sales to retailers, penalties, 33:1–92
  Distilleries, persons interested in retailing, 33:1–43
  Distillers and vintners packaged merchandise, 33:1–12
  Exceptions to provision for solicitors permits, 33:1–67
  Free goods, discriminatory allowances to retailers, 33:1–90
  Identification cards, liabilities, sale, 33:1–81.8
  Licenses and permits, 33:1–9, 33:1–12
    Additional license, hotels, restaurants, Chain Store Liquor License Act, 33:1–12.32
    Club license, membership in organization holding, Chain Store Liquor License Act, 33:1–12.34
    Continuing right of holder to use and renew license, Chain Store Liquor License Act, 33:1–12.35
    Descent and distribution, transfer of interest by, Chain Store Liquor License Act, 33:1–12.32, 33:1–12.33
    Fines and penalties, Chain Store Liquor License Act, 33:1–12.37
    Limitation on number held by one person, Chain Store Liquor License Act, 33:1–12.31

ALCOHOLIC BEVERAGES—Cont'd
Retailers—Cont'd
  Licenses and permits—Cont'd
    Shares of corporation traded on national securities exchange, acquiring interest in, Chain Store Liquor License Act, 33:1–12.36
    Wills, disposing of interest by will, Chain Store Liquor License Act, 33:1–12.32
  Limited retail distribution license,
    New license, 33:1–12.27, 33:1–12.29
    Renewal, 33:1–12.28
  Malt beverages, time periods, 33:1–40.3
  Municipal regulations to be by ordinance only, 33:1–94
  Price discriminations on sales to retailers, 33:1–89
  Products, markets and marketing, wholesalers, 33:1–43.2
  Prohibition, state beverage distributors license, 33:1–11
  Rebates to retailers, 33:1–90
  Special permits, 33:1–85
    Exemption, 33:1–87
  Surrender of license, 33:1–31
  Wholesaler, brewery, 33:1–43
Retention of seized property for use of hospitals, 33:1–66
Return,
  Property illegally seized under color of warrant, 33:1–62
  Property seized to claimant, 33:1–66
  Search warrant, 33:1–60, 33:1–61
Reversion to lessor of right to possession for violation, 33:1–54
Review. Appeal and review, generally, ante
Rules and regulations, 33:1–12.38
  Application for licenses, 33:1–25
  Authentication of copies under seal, 33:1–37
  Authority of director, 33:1–39
  Cleaning and repairing of pipes, brewery for retail licensee, 33:1–43.1
  Definitions, 33:1–1
  Director of alcoholic beverage control, 33:1–39.2
  Educational programs, plenary or limited retail distribution licenses, 33:1–12.48
  Hours of sale, 33:1–39
  Inconsistent with municipal referendum, 33:1–45
  Inspections, 33:1–39
  Issuance of licenses, municipal authorities, 33:1–24
  Issuance of stamps, labels, 33:1–80
  Municipal regulation of number of retail licenses, hours of sale, 33:1–40
  Municipalities, development projects, licenses and permits, plenary licenses, retail consumption license, 33:1–12.49
  Purchase and use by druggists, pharmacists, and hospitals, 33:1–29
  Reciprocal rules and regulations with other states, 33:1–39.1
  Sale of warehouse receipts, 33:1–72
  Solicitors permits, 33:1–67
  Special permits, manufacture for personal consumption, 33:1–75
  Statements in applications for licenses, 33:1–25
  Suspension or revocation of license for violation, 33:1–31
  Temporary contingency permits, 33:1–74
Salaries. Compensation and salaries, generally, ante
Sale of beverage in which delivery is accomplished by transportation, 33:1–69

ALCOHOLIC BEVERAGES—Cont'd
Sales,
　Alcohol at retail, special permits, **33:1–85**
　　Exemption, **33:1–87**
　Alcohols unfit for use as beverages, **33:1–30**
　Authority to make rules and regulations,
　　33:1–39
　Beverages to druggists and hospitals, **33:1–29**
　Bottling for sale or resale without license,
　　33:1–78
　Breweries, wholesalers, malt beverages, con-
　　tracts, **33:1–93.15**
　Causes for suspension or revocation of li-
　　cense, **33:1–31**
　Children and minors, **33:1–77**
　Church, sales within 200 feet of, **33:1–76**
　　Waiver of protection, **33:1–76.1, 33:1–76.2**
　Class B licenses, **33:1–11**
　　Acquisition of brand liquors from author-
　　　ized agent, **33:1–2**
　Crimes and offenses, **33:1–50**
　　Bottling without a license, **33:1–78**
　　Children and minors, **33:1–77**
　　Medicinal preparations, industrial prod-
　　　ucts, **33:1–30**
　　Minors, **33:1–77**
　　Theft of identity, exceptions, **2C:21–17**
　　Unlawful property, **33:1–55, 33:1–66**
　Definitions, **33:1–1**
　Director, duty to supervise, **33:1–3**
　Discrimination, wholesalers, **33:1–93.6**
　Fee exemption, **33:1–27**
　Fermented wines and fruit juices, plenary
　　winery license holders, **33:1–10**
　Glass, sale by the glass, temporary permits,
　　33:1–74
　Identification cards, **33:1–81.2 et seq.**
　Identity and identification, theft of identity,
　　exceptions, **2C:21–17**
　Interest of officers or employees in sale,
　　33:1–7
　Investigations, inspections, administration of
　　law, **33:1–35**
　Licenses and permits, **33:1–2, 33:1–26**
　　Alcohols unfit for use as beverages,
　　　33:1–30
　　Exemption, **33:1–27**
　　Manufacturers, **33:1–79**
　　Notice, announcements, **33:1–19.4**
　　Postponement or cancellation, **33:1–19.5**
　Malt beverages, on and off premise con-
　　sumption, **33:1–40.3**
　Manufacturers and manufacturing, ante
　Minors, misdemeanor, **33:1–77**
　Misrepresenting age to induce sale to minor,
　　33:1–81
　Municipal regulations,
　　By ordinance only, **33:1–94**
　　Hours of sale, sale on Sunday, **33:1–40**
　Name of purchaser, affidavits, indictments,
　　33:1–70
　Nonalcoholic beverages as accessory to alco-
　　holic beverages, **33:1–12**
　Off premises,
　　Plenary retail consumption licensee or sea-
　　　sonal retail consumption licenses,
　　　33:1–12.23
　　Certain municipalities, **33:1–12.24**
　　Plenary winery licenses, other alcoholic
　　　beverages, **33:1–10**
　Persons under legal age, **33:1–81**
　Place of sale of beverage in which delivery is
　　accompanied by transportation, **33:1–69**
　Plenary retail consumption licensee,
　　33:1–19.3 et seq.
　　Certain municipalities, **33:1–12.24**

ALCOHOLIC BEVERAGES—Cont'd
Sales—Cont'd
　Plenary retail consumption licensee—Cont'd
　　Hotels and motels, **33:1–12.25**
　Poisoned liquors, **33:3–9, 33:3–10**
　Property seized, **33:1–66**
　Public buildings of state or political subdivi-
　　sions, **33:1–42**
　Public policy, **33:1–3.1**
　Receipts, certificates, given on storage of
　　beverages, **33:1–72**
　Reciprocal rules and regulations with other
　　states, **33:1–39.1**
　School, sales within 200 feet of, **33:1–76**
　　Waiver of protection, **33:1–76.1, 33:1–76.2**
　Seasonal retail consumption licensee,
　　33:1–12, 33:1–12.23
　　Certain municipalities, **33:1–12.24**
　　Hotels and motels, **33:1–12.25**
　Sell, definitions, **33:1–1**
　Solicitors permit, **33:1–67**
　Supervision, **33:1–3**
　Unlawful property, **33:1–55**
　Warehouse receipts, **33:1–72**
　Wholesalers, generally, post
Salesroom, **33:1–11**
　Separate license for each salesroom, **33:1–15**
Sampling,
　Parties, **33:1–12**
　Tasting events, **33:1–12d**
　Winery service, **33:1–10**
Schools and School Districts, this index
Search warrants, **33:1–56, 33:1–57, 33:1–60,**
　33:1–61
　Breaking and entry in execution of warrant,
　　33:1–58
　Contents of warrant, **33:1–57**
　Copy to be given person from whom proper-
　　ty taken, **33:1–61**
　Execution and return, **33:1–60, 33:1–61**
　　Breaking and entering, execution of war-
　　　rant, **33:1–58**
　Inventory of property seized, **33:1–61**
　Investigation by officer on belief person en-
　　gaged in unlawful activity, **33:1–66**
　Issuance, **33:1–56, 33:1–57**
　Magistrates authority to issue, **33:1–56,**
　　33:1–57
　Malicious procurement of warrant, **33:1–64**
　Obstruction, **33:1–63**
　Prerequisites to issuance, **33:1–57**
　Probable cause,
　　Issuance of warrant, **33:1–56, 33:1–57**
　　Procuring warrant without probable cause,
　　　33:1–64
　　Search without probable cause and with-
　　　out warrant, **33:1–65**
　Receipt for and inventory of property seized,
　　33:1–61
　Resisting officer, **33:1–63**
　Return,
　　Property illegally seized under warrant,
　　　33:1–62
　　Warrant, **33:1–60, 33:1–61**
　Search without warrant, **33:1–65**
　Service, **33:1–57**
　　Crimes and offenses, resisting officer,
　　　33:1–63
　　Nighttime, **33:1–59**
　　Obstruction, **33:1–63**
　Warrantless search, director, **33:1–35**
Search without warrant, **33:1–65**
Searches and seizures, **33:1–55**
　Enumeration of commissioners duties,
　　33:1–23

ALCOHOLIC BEVERAGES—Cont'd
Searches and seizures—Cont'd
　Personal property, yard where unregistered
　　still found, **33:2–3**
　Receipt for and inventory of property seized,
　　33:1–61
　Return of seized property, **33:1–66**
　　Property illegally seized, **33:1–62**
　Rules and regulations by director, **33:1–39**
　Searches by director or other issuing authori-
　　ty, **33:1–35**
　Unlawful property, **33:1–55**
　Seizure of, **33:1–66**
　Warrants. Search warrants, generally, ante
Seasonal retail consumption licenses. Licenses
　and permits, ante
Secretary of municipal board, **33:1–5.4**
Separate offenses by violations of law, **33:1–70**
Service,
　Applicant for alcoholic beverage license of
　　refusal to issue license, **33:1–22**
　Refusal of issuing authority to grant refund
　　of license fee, **33:1–31**
　Search warrants, ante
　Subpoenas, **33:1–36**
　Suspension or revocation of license, **33:1–31**
Shares and Shareholders, this index
Sheriffs, this index
Signatures,
　Identification card, **33:1–81.2**
　Search warrant, **33:1–57**
Sixth class counties, license, lapse because of
　military service, **33:1–12.22b**
Smart growth development projects, licenses
　and permits, **33:1–24.1 et seq.**
Societies, licenses and permits, law enforce-
　ment personnel, **33:1–25.1, 33:1–25.2**
Sodomy, impairing resistance of victim with
　intoxicants, **2C:14–1**
Solicitors permits, **33:1–67, 33:1 App.**
Special permits. Licenses and permits, ante
Stamps,
　Issuance, **33:1–80**
　License suspended or revoked for failure to
　　have tax stamp, **33:1–31**
　Photostatic copy to accompany license appli-
　　cation, **33:1–25**
State beverage distributors license, **33:1–11**
Stay, suspension or revocation of license pend-
　ing appeal, **33:1–31**
Stills and Distilling Apparatus, generally, this
　index
Storage,
　Misdemeanor, **33:1–50**
　Paraphernalia, manufacture, misdemeanor,
　　33:1–50
　Rules and regulations, **33:1–39**
　Sale of receipts, certificates, given on storage
　　of beverages, **33:1–72**
　Unlawful property, **33:1–55**
Subdivisions, class C licenses, **33:1–12**
Subpoenas, director, power to issue, **33:1–35**
Summary proceedings on violation, **33:1–54**
Sunday,
　Municipal referendum, hours of retail sales,
　　33:1–47.1
　Retail sale on Sunday, **33:1–40**
　Sale of malt beverages, **33:1–40.3**
Supplementary limited distillery license,
　33:1–10
Suppliers, markets and marketing, retailers,
　products, **33:1–43.2**
Sureties on bond for return of seized property,
　33:1–66
Tasting events, sampling, **33:1–12d**
Tasting parties, **33:1–12**

ALCOHOLIC BEVERAGES—Cont'd

Taxation. Alcoholic Beverage Tax, generally, this index

Temporary contingency permits, **33:1–74**

Temporary transportation, permit, **33:1–28a**

Term of office,
Counsel and other legal assistants, **33:1–4**
Experts or specialists, **33:1–4**
Municipal board of alcoholic beverage control, **33:1–5**

Termination, identification card, contents, **33:1–81.2**

Third party beneficiaries action on bond for return of seized property, **33:1–66**

Time,
Action on bond for return of seized property, **33:1–66**
Appeal to director from action of issuing authority respecting license, **33:1–22**
Execution and return of search warrant, **33:1–60**
Malt beverages on and off premises consumption, sales, **33:1–40.3**
Replevin action for seized property, **33:1–66**

Title to property,
Conveyed by sale of seized property, **33:1–66**
Loans or furnishing of fixtures, to retail licensee by owner of brewery, **33:1–43.1**
Unlawful property, **33:1–55**

Transfer. Licenses and permits, ante

Transit insignia, **33:1–28**

Transportation,
Causes for suspension or revocation of license, **33:1–31**
Crimes and offenses, medicinal preparations, industrial products, **33:1–30**
Industrial alcohol, **33:1–30**
Licensees own vehicles, **33:1–28**
Licenses and permits, **33:1–9, 33:1–13, 33:1 App.**
Bonds (officers and fiduciaries), **33:1–17**
Delivery by licensees without transportation license, **33:1–28**
Investigations of applicants, **33:1–23**
Issuance, **33:1–18**
Publication of notice of intention to apply for license, **33:1–25**
Temporary or emergency, permits, **33:1–28a**
Misdemeanor, **33:1–50**
Municipal referendum on retail sales, exception, **33:1–46**
Municipal regulation, **33:1–40**
Retail transactions to be by ordinance only, **33:1–94**
Place of sale of beverage in which delivery is accompanied by transportation, **33:1–69**
Poisoned liquors, **33:3–9**
Rules and regulations, **33:1–39**
Violation of rules and regulations as subject to seizure, **33:1–66**

Turnpike project, transportation regulations, **27:23–31**

Unfair competition, **33:1–23.1**

Unlawful property, **33:1–55**

Urban enterprise zones, licenses and permits, smart growth development projects, **33:1–24.3**

Vacancies on municipal board of alcoholic beverage control, **33:1–5**

Vessel, operating under influence, homicide, sentence and punishment, **2C:11–5**

Veterans, this index

ALCOHOLIC BEVERAGES—Cont'd

Veterans associations and organizations, licenses and permits,
Law enforcement personnel, **33:1–25.1, 33:1–25.2**
Temporary permits, fees, **33:1–74**

Wages. Compensation and salaries, generally, ante

Warehouse license, **33:1–9, 33:1–14, 33:1–23**
Bonds (officers and fiduciaries), **33:1–17**

Warehouses,
Bonded warehouses, bottling license, **33:1–10**
Issuance of public warehouse license, **33:1–18**
Maintenance by holder of transportation license, **33:1–13**
Misdemeanor by violation of Alcoholic Beverage Law, **33:1–50**
Public warehouse license, **33:1–9, 33:1–14**
Publication, notice of intention to apply for public warehouse license, **33:1–25**
Right of holder of class B license to maintain, **33:1–11**
Rules and regulations by director, **33:1–39**
Sale of warehouse receipts, **33:1–72**
Separate license for each warehouse, **33:1–15**
Warehouse receipts license, **33:1–72**

Wholesalers,
Actions and proceedings, contracts, breweries, malt beverages, **33:1–93.18**
Assignments, termination, contracts, breweries, malt beverages, **33:1–93.16**
Breweries, malt beverages, contracts, **33:1–93.15**
Contracts, breweries, malt beverages, **33:1–93.15 et seq.**
Crimes and offenses,
Persons interested in retailing, **33:1–43**
Stock investment, **33:1–43a**
Definitions, **33:1–1**
Discrimination, distillers, importers, **33:1–93.6 et seq.**
Order to complete sale, **33:1–93.8**
Noncompliance, **33:1–93.9**
Petition for hearing, filing fee, **33:1–93.7**
Refusal to sell, **33:1–93.7**
Rules and regulations, **33:1–93.10**
Fraud, termination, contracts, breweries, malt beverages, **33:1–93.16**
Good faith,
Breweries, malt beverages, contracts, **33:1–93.15**
Contracts, breweries, malt beverages, **33:1–93.17**
Interested in retailing, **33:1–43**
Licenses and permits, **33:1–9, 33:1–11**
Administration, issuance, **33:1–18**
Bonds (officers and fiduciaries), **33:1–17**
Class B,
Acquisition of brand liquor from authorized agent, **33:1–2**
Renewal or transfer, waiver of protection, **33:1–76.1**
Eligibility to hold retail license, **33:1–26**
Foreign persons, **33:1–11.3, 33:1–11.4**
Investigation of applicants, **33:1–23**
Revocation, **33:1–11.5**
Sale by licensees to druggists and pharmacists, **33:1–29**
Sale to voluntary unincorporated organization of army or navy personnel, **33:1–11.1**
Suspension, **33:1–11.5**
Wine wholesale license, **33:1–11**
Markets and marketing, retailers, products, **33:1–43.2**

ALCOHOLIC BEVERAGES—Cont'd

Wholesalers—Cont'd
Refusal to sell to, discrimination, **33:1–93.7**
Sales to retailers, **33:1–89 et seq.**
Sales within 200 feet of church or school, **33:1–76**
Waiver of protection, **33:1–76.1**
Stock investment, **33:1–43a**
Termination, contracts, breweries, malt beverages, **33:1–93.16**

Window, breaking in execution of search warrant, **33:1–58**

Wine, generally, this index

Yards, this index

ALCOHOLICS AND ALCOHOLISM

Attorneys, disability inactive status, **Rule 1:20–12**

Basis for criminal liability, **2C:2–8**

Child abuse, alcoholic parent, juvenile family crisis, **2A:4A–85**

Commitment and admission to institutions, treatment, probation and probation officers, **2C:35–14**

Consent, victim of crime, **2C:2–10**

Convicted offenders, rehabilitation, **2A:168A–4**

Crimes and offenses, **2C:2–8**
Consent of victim, **2C:2–10**
Defenses, notice, **Rule 3:12–1**
Food, adulteration, **2C:12–2**
Sentence,
Change, **Rule 3:21–10**
Illness, infirmity, reduction, change, **Rule 3:21–10**

Defense of intoxication, criminal liability, **2C:2–8**

Definitions, Code of Criminal Justice, **2C:2–8**

Dependent or neglected children, juvenile family crisis, **2A:4A–85**

Driving while intoxicated, intoxication of driver. Motor Vehicles, this index

Evidence, clear and convincing, criminal liability, **2C:2–8**

Fines and penalties,
Food, adulteration, **2C:12–2**
Treatment, probation and probation officers, **2C:35–14**

Firearms, permits, obtaining, **2C:58–3**

Food, adulteration, crimes and offenses, **2C:12–2**

Hazardous substances and waste, inhalants, **2C:35–10.4**

Homicide, **2C:11–3**

Hospitals, this index

Judicial notice, treatment, probation and probation officers, **2C:35–14**

Juvenile Delinquents, this index

Moderation in consumption of alcoholic beverages, Alcoholic Beverage Control Act, **33:1–3.1**

Murder, mitigating factors, **2C:11–3**

Probation and probation officers, commitment and admission to institutions, treatment, **2C:35–14**

Public policy, moderation and responsibility in consumption of alcoholic beverages, Alcoholic Beverage Control Act, **33:1–3.1**

Regulation of sales to, **33:1–39**

Rehabilitated convicted offenders, **2A:168A–4**

Treatment,
Juvenile delinquents and dependents, probation and probation officers, **2C:35–14**
Probation and probation officers, **2C:35–14**

Weapons, permits, obtaining, **2C:58–3**

ALCOHOLISM AND PROMOTION OF TEM-PERANCE COMMISSION
Generally, **33:4–1**

ALE
Presumption, fitness for beverage purposes and alcoholic content, **33:1–1.1**

ALIAS WARRANTS
Arrest of fugitive from justice, **2A:160–29**

ALIBI
Crimes and offenses, defense, notice, **Rules 3:12–2, 7:7–3**

ALIENS
Alcoholic Beverages, this index
Authorized presence in U.S., proof, requirement,
Identification card for nondrivers, **39:3–29.3**
Special learners permit, motor vehicles, **39:3–13.1**
Drivers licenses, authorized presence in U.S., **39:3–10**
Examination permits, **39:3–13**
Human trafficking, **2C:13–8**
Immigration and Naturalization, generally, this index
Naturalization. Immigration and Naturalization, generally, this index
Weapons violations, convictions, reports, **2C:58–9**

ALIMONY
Probation officers,
Payment of alimony to, **2A:168–13**
Supervision of persons required to pay, **2A:168–11**

ALL TERRAIN VEHICLES
Generally, **39:3C–1 et seq.**
Accidents, reports, **39:3C–21**
Agricultural land, operation on, registration exemption, **39:3C–6**
Animals, harassment, **39:3C–19**
Brakes, **39:3C–19, 39:3C–24**
Certificates and certification, fees, **39:3C–3**
Children and minors, operation, **39:3C–16**
Crossing highways, **39:3C–17**
Application of law, **39:3C–30**
Definitions, registration and regulation of snowmobiles and all terrain vehicles, **39:3C–1**
Environmental rules and regulations, **39:3C–14**
Exemptions, registration, **39:3C–6**
Fees, registration, **39:3C–3**
Fines and penalties,
Crossing highway, **39:3C–30**
Disposition of funds, **39:3C–9**
Insurance, **39:3C–20**
Public lands, **39:3C–33**
Races, **39:3C–22**
Forfeitures, public lands, **39:3C–34**
Freeways, operation, **39:3C–17**
Golf courses, operation on, **39:3C–30.1**
Helmets, **39:3C–19**
Highways and roads, application of law, **39:3C–30**
Impounding, public lands, **39:3C–34**
Inspection, **39:3C–25**
Insurance, **39:3C–20**
Lights and Lighting, this index
Limited access highways, rules and regulations, **39:3C–17**
Mufflers, this index
Nighttime, operation, **39:3C–19**
Nonresidents, registration fees, **39:3C–3**

ALL TERRAIN VEHICLES—Cont'd
Passengers, helmets, **39:3C–19**
Protective helmets, **39:3C–19**
Public lands, operation, **39:3C–32 et seq.**
Railroads, trespass, **39:3C–19**
Reciprocity, **39:3C–7**
Reckless driving, **39:3C–19**
Registration, **39:3C–3**
Display of number, **39:3C–8**
Exclusive registration, **39:3C–13**
Exemptions, **39:3C–6, 39:3C–23**
Fees, disposition of funds, **39:3C–29**
Issuance, **39:3C–5**
Permanent number, **39:3C–4**
Police identification, **39:3C–9**
Racing, exemptions, **39:3C–23**
Reciprocity, **39:3C–7**
Removal from state, **39:3C–12**
Transfer of ownership, **39:3C–11**
Removal from state, notification, **39:3C–12**
Rules and regulations, **39:3C–2**
Environmental protection, **39:3C–14**
Races, **39:3C–22**
Safety education and training program, **39:3C–9, 39:3C–14, 39:3C–15, 39:3C–16, 39:3C–23, 39:3C–26, 39:3C–29, 39:3C–30.1**
Safety equipment, **39:3C–15**
Sales, equipment, **39:3C–26**
Speed, **39:3C–19**
Theft, notification, **39:3C–12**
Traffic rules and regulations, **39:3C–19**
Transfer of ownership, registration, **39:3C–5, 39:3C–11**
Trespass, **39:3C–18**
Permit, **39:3C–19**

ALLEGIANCE
Oaths and Affirmations, this index

ALLEYS
Streets and Alleys, generally, this index

ALLYLPRODINE
Controlled substances, **24:21–1 et seq.**

ALPHACETYLMETHADOL
Controlled substances, **24:21–1 et seq.**

ALPHAMEPRODINE
Controlled substances, **24:21–1 et seq.**

ALPHAMETHADOL
Controlled substances, **24:21–1 et seq.**

ALPHAPRODINE
Controlled substances, **24:21–1 et seq.**

AMATEUR RADIO LICENSES
Motor vehicle registration plates, **39:3–27.5 et seq.**

AMATEUR ROCKET EXPERIMENTATION
Supervision, **21:1A–138**

AMBASSADORS
Traffic rules and regulations, privileges and immunities, records and recordation, **39:5–53 et seq.**

AMBULANCES
Automobile insurance, no fault insurance, application of law, **39:6A–1 et seq.**
Brands, marks and labels, sales, removal, **39:10–9.4**
Commercial drivers licenses, exemption, **39:3–10j, 39:3–10k**

AMBULANCES—Cont'd
Crimes and offenses, sales, removal, brands, marks and labels, **39:10–9.4**
Destruction of agricultural or recreational property by operation of vehicle, exception, **39:4–97a**
No fault insurance, application of law, **39:6A–1 et seq.**
Registration, fees, exemption, **39:3–27**
Removal, brands, marks and labels, sales, **39:10–9.4**
Sales, markings, removal, **39:10–9.4**
Turnpikes, tolls, **27:23–40**

AMENDMENTS
Accusation, indictment, **Rule 3:7–4**
Alcoholic Beverages, this index
Arrest warrant, **Rule 3:3–4**
Findings, this index
Indictment, accusation, **Rule 3:7–4**
Judgments and decrees, motion, enlargement of time, **Rule 1:3–4**
Nonresident Violator Compact, motor vehicles, **39:5F–26 et seq.**
Pleadings, municipal courts, **Rule 7:14–2**
Summons, crimes and offenses, **Rule 3:3–4**

AMERCEMENT
County treasurer, money collected from amercement award paid to, **2A:162–7**

AMICUS CURIAE
Generally, **Rule 1:13–9**

AMMONIUM NITRATE
Turnpike project, transportation regulation, **27:23–31**

AMMUNITION
Generally, **2C:39–1 et seq.**
Armor penetrating ammunition,
Person convicted of crime involving, possession of any weapon prohibited, **2C:39–7**
Possession, **2C:39–3, 2C:39–9**
Children and minors, transfers, **2C:58–3.3**
Crimes and offenses, transfers, **2C:58–3.3**
Discharge, incendiary or tracer, **2C:58–10**
Dum dum bullets,
Person convicted of crime involving, possession of any weapon prohibited, **2C:39–7**
Prohibited weapons, **2C:39–3**
Firearms and weapons, **2C:39–1 et seq.**
Large capacity ammunition magazine, possession, crime of fourth degree, exception for certain shooting matches, **2C:39–3**
Possession, **2C:58–7**
Regulatory provisions, violations, **2C:39–10**
Reports, motor vehicles apparently struck by bullet, duty of garageman or repairman, **39:4–132**
Smokeless powder, small arms, necessity of permit, **21:1A–133**
Transfers, **2C:58–3.3**

AMPHETAMINES
Generally, **24:21–1 et seq.**
Phenylalanine, possession, manufacturing, **2C:35–28**

AMUSEMENTS
Roller skating safety, amusements. Roller Skates, generally, this index

ANAL INTERCOURSE
Generally, **2C:14–1 et seq.**
Children and minors, pornography, second degree crime, **2C:24–4**

ANALYSIS
Alcoholic Beverages, this index

ANARCHY
Expungement of record, 2C:52–2

ANATOMICAL GIFTS
Crimes and offenses, human body parts, purchases, sales, 2C:22–2
Donate Life NJ Registry, 39:3–12.3 et seq.
Donor,
   Designation, drivers license, 39:3–10, 39:3–12.2
   Organ and tissue donor awareness education fund, 39:3–12.3
   Registration, 39:3–12.3 et seq.
Drivers licenses,
   Donors, 39:3–12.4
   Examination, Anatomical Gift Act, questions, 39:3–10
Drivers manuals, information explaining provisions of anatomical gift act, 39:3–10
Education, organ and tissue donor awareness education fund, 39:3–12.3
Fraud, human body parts, sales, purchases, 2C:22–2
Funds,
   Organ and tissue donor awareness education fund, 39:3–12.3
   Registration, 39:3–12.3, 39:3–12.5
Grants, registration, 39:3–12.5
Human body parts, crimes and offenses, purchases, sales, 2C:22–2
Identification cards, donors, 39:3–12.4
Internet, registration, donors, 39:3–12.3 et seq.
Motor vehicles, special plates, 39:3–27.127 et seq.
Organ and tissue donor awareness education fund, 39:3–12.3
Purchases, human body parts, crimes and offenses, 2C:22–2
Records and recordation, disclosure, 39:3–12.2
Registration, donor, 39:3–12.3 et seq.
Sales, human body parts, crimes and offenses, 2C:22–2
Special plates, motor vehicles, 39:3–27.127 et seq.

ANCESTORS OR ANCESTRY
Discrimination, generally, this index

ANCHORAGE UNITS
Motor vehicles,
   Child passenger restraint systems, 39:3–76.2a et seq.
   Seat safety belts, 39:3–76.2

ANCIENT DOCUMENTS
Hearsay exception, **Evidence Rule 803**

ANGLE PARKING
Parking, this index

ANHYDROUS AMMONIA
Possession, methamphetamine, manufacturing, 2C:35–28
Theft, methamphetamine, manufacturing, 2C:20–2

ANILERIDINE
Controlled substances, 24:21–1 et seq.

ANIMAL CONTROL OFFICERS
Notice, cruelty to animals, convictions, disqualification, 2B:12–17.1

ANIMAL DISEASES
Diseases. Animals, this index

ANIMAL DRAWN VEHICLES
Horse Drawn Vehicles, generally, this index

ANIMAL POPULATION CONTROL FUND
Animal welfare license plates,
   Costs reimbursed from fund, 39:3–27.56
   Fees deposited into fund, 39:3–27.56

ANIMALS
Abandonment, this index
Animal welfare license plates, population control program, 39:3–27.55 et seq.
Baiting animals, cruelty to animals, 4:22–24
Cats, generally, this index
Confined animals, cruelty, offenses, 4:22–19
Control facilities, controlled substances, 24:21–11
Controlled substances, registration, 24:21–11
Crimes and offenses, destruction, 4:22–19
Cruelty to Animals, generally, this index
Decompression, destruction of animal, penalties, 4:22–19, 4:22–19.2
Definitions, prevention of cruelty, 4:22–15
Destruction,
   Neuromuscular blocking agents, 4:22–19.3, 4:22–19.4
   Penalties, 4:22–19
Disabled animals. Abandonment, this index
Diseases,
   Refusal to kill diseased animals, 4:22–22
   Sale or exposure of diseased animals, 4:22–22
Disorderly persons,
   Abandonment, 4:22–20
   Decompression or gas chambers, removal, 4:22–19, 4:22–19.2
   Hypoxia, destruction, 4:22–19, 4:22–19.1
   Law enforcement officers animals, killing, maiming or harming, 2C:29–3.1
Dogs, generally, this index
Euthanasia, offenses, 4:22–19
Farm products, cattle, 39:3–25
Fighting animals, cruelty to animals, 4:22–24
Fines and penalties,
   Destruction, 4:22–19
   Law enforcement officers, ownership, killing or harming, 2C:29–3.1
   Motorists, hitting or injuring animals, failure to stop and report, 4:22–25.2
Fish and Game, generally, this index
Gas chambers, destruction of animals, penalties, 4:22–19, 4:22–19.2
Guide dogs. Blind Persons, this index
Harming, law enforcement officers animals, disorderly persons, 2C:29–3.1
Horses, generally, this index
Hypoxia,
   Chambers or devices to induce, dismantling, 4:22–19.1
   Destruction of animal, penalties, 4:22–19, 4:22–19.2
Impounded animals, cruelty, 4:22–19
Killing, law enforcement officers animal, disorderly persons, 2C:29–3.1
Law enforcement officers, animals used or owned by, killing or harming, disorderly persons, 2C:29–3.1
Marine mammals, marine mammal stranding center fund, wildlife conservation license plate renewal fees, 39:3–33.11
Motor Vehicles, this index

ANIMALS—Cont'd
Population control program, dogs and cats, animal welfare license plates, 39:3–27.55 et seq.
Public utilities employees, protective devices, 2C:39–6
Reports, motorist hitting or injuring domestic animal, 4:22–25.1
   Penalty for violation, 4:22–25.2
Riders rights and duties, 39:4–25.1
Seals, marine mammal stranding center fund, wildlife conservation license plate renewal fees, 39:3–33.11
Shelters, destruction of animals, 4:22–19, 4:22–19.2
Sodium pentobarbital, registration and certification, 24:21–11
Spaying and neutering, population control program, dogs and cats, animal welfare license plates, 39:3–27.55 et seq.
Traffic accidents, 4:22–25.1, 4:22–25.2
Veterinarians, generally, this index
Whales, marine mammal stranding center, moneys from wildlife conservation license plate renewal fees, 39:3–33.11
Wildlife conservation license plate renewal fees, 39:3–33.11

ANNOYANCE
Harassment, 2C:33–4

ANSWER
Attorney disciplinary proceedings, complaints, **Rule 1:20–4**
Case information statement, filing with, **Rule 1:5–6**
Motions, opposing affidavits and cross motions, service and filing, **Rule 1:6–3**
Striking answer, failure to appear, **Rule 1:2–4**

ANTIPIRACY ACT
Generally, 2C:21–21

ANTIPOVERTY PROGRAM
Indigent Persons, generally, this index

ANTIQUE CANNONS
Generally, 2C:39–1 et seq.

ANTIQUE FIREARMS
Cannons, possession, exemption, 2C:39–6
Defaced firearms, possession, 2C:39–9
Definitions, 2C:39–1
Personalized handguns, exemptions, 2C:58–2.4, 2C:58–2.5
Possession, 2C:39–5
   Exemptions, 2C:39–6
Rifles or shotguns, retail delivery, 2C:58–2
Unlawful possession, exemption, 2C:39–6

ANTIQUE SLOT MACHINES
Definitions, 2C:37–7

ANTISHOPLIFTING OR INVENTORY CONTROL DEVICE COUNTERMEASURE
Crimes and offenses, 2C:20–11

ANTITERRORISM
Generally, 2C:38–1 et seq.
Terrorism, generally, this index

ANTITRUST LAWS
Monopolies, generally, this index

ANYTHING OF VALUE
Definitions, theft, 2C:20–1

APARTMENTS AND APARTMENT HOUSES
Roads and streets, owner of apartment building, motor vehicle and traffic laws, **39:5A–1 et seq.**

APPARATUS
Distilling apparatus. Stills and Distilling Apparatus, generally, this index
Fire Engines, Apparatus and Equipment, generally, this index
Moving Heavy Machinery, generally, this index

APPEAL AND REVIEW
Abuse of children, **9:6–8.70**
Record, closed circuit testimony, **2A:84A–32.4**
Aggravated sexual assault, children and minors, closed circuit testimony, **2A:84A–32.4**
Aggravated sexual contact, children and minors, closed circuit testimony, **2A:84A–32.4**
Alcoholic Beverages, this index
Amicus curiae, **Rule 1:13–9**
Assault firearms, licenses, **2C:58–5**
Attorney fees, arbitration and award, **Rule 1:20A–3**
Attorneys, this index
Bail,
Disorderly persons, **2A:162–11**
Postconviction bail, **Rule 7:4–8**
Briefs, this index
Child Abuse, this index
Child support hearing officers, **Rule 5:25–3**
Children and Minors, this index
Constitutional issues,
Attorney disciplinary proceedings, **Rule 1:20–3 et seq.**
Questioning validity of provisions, withholding for consideration by supreme court, **Rule 1:20–3**
Construction of law, Criminal Justice Code, **2C:1–2**
Controlled substances, **24:21–38**
Fines and penalties, **2C:35–7a**
Costs, deposits, unauthorized practice of law decisions, **Rule 1:22–3A**
County detectives and investigators, convictions, **2A:157–10.7**
Crimes and offenses. Appeals In Criminal Prosecutions, generally, this index
De minimis infractions, dismissal, **2C:2–11**
Defendant adjudicated guilty, reversal on appeal, return of fine, **2A:166–13**
Disciplinary review board, attorneys, **Rules 1:20–1, 1:20–15**
Disorderly persons, bail or recognizances, **2A:162–11**
Domestic violence, weapons seizure, **2C:25–21**
Drunken driving,
Revoked license not restored pending appeal, **39:5–22**
Statute requiring term of imprisonment to be served not to interfere with appeal, **39:4–51**
Evidence, this index
Explosives, orders, **21:1A–130**
Extension of time, **Rule 1:3–4**
Extrajudicial activities advisory committee decisions, **Rule 1:18A–7**
Fee arbitration, attorneys, **Rule 1:20A–3**
Fines, return of fine, reversal of guilty adjudication, **2A:166–13**
Firearms, registration, manufacturers or wholesale dealers, **2C:58–1**
Handgun permits,
Denial of permits to carry, **2C:58–4**

APPEAL AND REVIEW—Cont'd
Handgun permits—Cont'd
Purchase permits or identification cards, denial, **2C:58–3**
Health and Accident Insurance, this index
Health care claims fraud, licenses and permits, suspension or revocation, **2C:51–5**
Homicide, sentence, **2C:11–3**
Indigent Persons, this index
Indigents,
Neglected or abandoned children, juvenile family crisis, long term out of home placement, **2A:4A–90**
Payment of transcripts, **2A:152–17, 2A:152–18**
Judges and justices, financial statements and reports, **Rule 1:18B–2**
Judicial notice, **Evidence Rule 202**
Juvenile delinquents and dependents,
Detention, **2A:4A–38**
Juvenile family crisis, long term out of home placement, **2A:4A–90**
Leave to appeal, attorney disciplinary proceedings, constitutional issues, **Rule 1:20–16**
Machine guns, licenses, **2C:58–5**
Material witness order, **2C:104–9**
Motor vehicle and traffic law violations, appeal from conviction, **39:5–11**
Motor vehicle division, directors, **39:5–2**
Motor vehicle junk yard, appeal from decisions or orders relating to, **39:11–10**
Motor Vehicles, this index
Municipal Courts, this index
Murder, sentence, **2C:11–3**
Narcotics and dangerous substances, controlled dangerous substances, **24:21–38**
Newspersons, information disclosure privilege exercise, **2A:84A–21.6**
Notice of appeal,
Attorney fee arbitration, **Rule 1:20A–3**
Attorney of record, **Rule 1:11–3**
Judiciary employees, advisory committee on outside activities of, **Rule 1:17A–8**
Professional ethics, advisory committee on, **Rule 1:19–8**
Open court proceedings, **Rule 1:2–1**
Oral argument, attorney disciplinary proceedings, **Rules 1:20–15, 1:20–16**
Petitions,
Judiciary employees, advisory committee, **Rule 1:17A–8**
Professional ethics, advisory committee, **Rule 1:19–8**
Postconviction bail, **Rule 7:4–8**
Pro hac vice appearances, **Rule 1:21–2**
Probate proceedings, ex parte actions, enlargement of time, **Rule 1:3–4**
Process,
Attorney of record, **Rule 1:11–3**
Professional ethics, advisory committee on, petition for review, **Rule 1:19–8**
Professional ethics, advisory committee on, **Rule 1:19–8**
Public admonitions, attorneys, **Rules 1:20–15, 1:20–16**
Public defenders, poor persons, **2A:158A–5**
Recognizances or bail, disorderly persons, **2A:162–11**
Record on appeal, professional ethics, advisory committee on, opinion, **Rule 1:19–8**
Records and recordation, abuse of children, closed circuit testimony, **2A:84A–32.4**
Reserving questions for review, objections to rulings, orders or instructions to jury, **Rule 1:7–2**

APPEAL AND REVIEW—Cont'd
Reversal, return of fine to defendant, **2A:166–13**
Sex offenses, children and minors, closed circuit testimony, **2A:84A–32.4**
State police, complaints, **53:1–33**
Stay, this index
Stills and distilling apparatus, directors orders, **33:2–6**
Termination of attorneys responsibility in trial court, **Rule 1:11–3**
Time,
Attorney disciplinary proceedings, **Rule 1:20–3**
Expiration of time, termination of attorneys responsibility in trial court, **Rule 1:11–3**
Transcripts, this index
Transfer of actions, **Rule 1:13–4**
Weapons, handguns, licenses and permits, **2C:58–3**

APPEALS IN CRIMINAL PROSECUTIONS
Generally, **Rule 3:22–1 et seq.**
Appearance,
Prosecuting attorney, **Rule 3:23–8**
Public defenders, **Rule 3:8–3**
Attorneys, this index
Bail, custodial sentence, relief pending appeal, **Rule 3:23–5**
Briefs, this index
Cash deposit, transmittal, **Rule 3:23–6**
Change of sentence, consideration by trial court, **Rule 3:21–10**
Collateral attacks of conviction or sentence, postconviction proceedings, reduction or change in sentence, **Rule 3:21–10**
Constitutional law, defenses, raising before trial, **Rule 3:23–8**
Courts of limited criminal jurisdiction, **Rule 3:22–1 et seq.**
Criminal sexual contact, children and minors, closed circuit testimony, **2A:84A–32.4**
De novo hearing, **Rule 3:23–8**
Defects, record, **Rule 3:23–8**
Dismissal and Nonsuit, this index
Dismissal of de minimis infractions, **2C:2–11**
Disposition, **Rule 3:23–8**
DNA database and databank, motions, **2A:84A–32a**
Docketing, **Rule 3:23–4**
Double jeopardy, motion, **Rule 3:23–8**
Enlargement of time, **Rule 1:3–4**
Exclusive method of review, courts of limited jurisdiction, **Rule 3:23–1**
Exhibits, delivery, **Rule 3:23–4**
Extended terms, **2C:44–7**
Failure to charge offense, raising, **Rule 3:23–8**
Filing,
Briefs, **Rule 3:23–8**
Notice, **Rule 3:23–2**
Time, **Rule 3:21–4**
Fines and penalties, relief pending appeal, **Rule 3:23–5**
Forfeiture, relief pending appeal, **Rule 3:23–5**
Grand jury presentment, **Rule 3:6–9**
Hearing, **Rule 3:23–8**
Date, **Rule 3:23–4**
Indigent defendants,
Right to appeal, notification, **Rule 3:21–4**
Transcripts, **Rule 3:23–8**
Intensive supervision program, entry, effect, **Rule 3:21–10**
Jurisdiction, lack, motion, **Rule 3:23–8**
Lack, jurisdiction, motion, **Rule 3:23–8**
Limitation, notice of appeal, filing, **Rule 3:23–2**

APPEALS IN CRIMINAL PROSECUTIONS
—Cont'd
Limited criminal jurisdiction, courts of, **Rule 3:24**
Judgments of conviction, **Rule 3:23–1 et seq.**
Motions, defenses raised before trial, **Rule 3:23–8**
Nature of offense, notice of appeal, statement, **Rule 3:23–3**
Notice,
Contents, **Rule 3:23–3**
Filing, **Rule 3:23–2**
Right to, sentence, **Rule 3:21–4**
Sentence reduction, change, consideration, **Rule 3:21–10**
Objections, raising before trial, **Rule 3:23–8**
Offenses committed before effective date of code, **2C:1–1**
Orders of court, limited criminal jurisdiction, courts of, **Rule 3:24**
Plea agreements, right to appeal, **Rule 3:9–3**
Plenary hearing, **Rule 3:23–8**
Postconviction relief, **Rule 3:22–1 et seq.**
Enlargement of time, **Rule 1:3–4**
Exclusive remedy, **Rule 3:22–3**
Municipal courts, **Rule 7:10–2**
Preparation, transcript, **Rule 3:23–4**
Pretrial intervention program,
Applications, rejection, **Rule 3:28**
Order enrolling over prosecutors objection, **Rule 3:28**
Probation, order for, relief pending appeal, **Rule 3:23–5**
Process,
Briefs, **Rule 3:23–8**
Notice of appeal, **Rule 3:23–2**
Prosecuting attorney,
Appearance, **Rule 3:23–8**
Defined, **Rule 3:23–9**
Public defenders, **Rule 3:8–3**
Recognizance, transmittal, **Rule 3:23–6**
Records and recordation,
Correction, supplementation, transcript for indigents, **Rule 3:23–8**
Notice of appeal, statement, **Rule 3:23–3**
Waiver, defects, **Rule 3:23–8**
Reduction of sentence, consideration by trial court, **Rule 3:21–10**
Relief pending appeal, **Rule 3:23–5**
Reversal of conviction, reduction or change in sentence, **Rule 3:21–10**
Right to counsel, indigent persons, continuing representation, **Rule 3:4–2**
Searches and seizures, motions, suppressing evidence, returning property, **Rule 3:5–7**
Sentence,
Custodial, relief pending appeal, **Rule 3:23–5**
Notice of appeal,
Right to, **Rule 3:21–4**
Statement, **Rule 3:23–3**
Reduction, change, consideration by trial court, **Rule 3:21–10**
Sound recording, record, **Rules 3:23–3, 3:23–4, 3:23–8**
Stay of sentence pending review, **Rule 3:23–5**
Stenographic record, **Rules 3:23–3, 3:23–4, 3:23–8**
Suppression of evidence, **Rule 3:24**
Municipal courts, **Rule 7:5–2**
Time,
Enlargement of time, **Rule 1:3–4**
Filing, notice, **Rule 3:21–4**
Notice of appeal, filing, **Rule 3:23–2**
Transcripts,
Indigents, **Rule 3:23–8**
Preparation, **Rule 3:23–4**

APPEARANCE
Generally, **Rule 1:21–1**
Administrative law and procedure, nonattorneys, **Rule 1:21–1**
Appointment of new attorney, death, removal or disbarment, **Rule 1:11–1**
Business entities, **Rule 1:21–1**
Consuls general, attorneys, **Rule 1:21–4**
Corporations, **Rule 1:21–1**
Crimes and Offenses, this index
Criminal defendants, **Rule 3:8–1**
Failure to appear, sanctions, **Rule 1:2–4**
Foreign practitioners, taking deposition not deemed an appearance, **Rule 1:21–1**
Guardian and ward, parties, **Rule 1:21–1**
Juvenile conference committees, **Rule 5:25–1**
Juvenile family crisis, **Rule 5:17–1**
Temporary out of home placement, **Rule 5:18–2**
Law graduates and students, **Rules 1:21–1, 1:21–3**
Limited admission certification, attorneys, **Rule 1:21–3**
Limited liability companies and partnerships, **Rule 1:21–1**
Material witness. Witnesses, this index
Municipal courts, **Rules 7:7–9, 7:8–7, 7:14–3**
Nonattorneys, administrative agencies, **Rule 1:21–1**
Notice, entry by new attorney, **Rule 1:11–3**
Pro hac vice, **Rules 1:21–1, 1:21–2**
Public defenders, **Rule 3:8–3**
Real party in interest, **Rule 1:21–1**
Sanctions, failure to appear, **Rule 1:2–4**
Special education proceedings, nonattorneys, **Rule 1:21–1**
Temporary practice of law, major disasters, foreign states, **Rule 1:21–10**

APPELLATE DIVISION
Superior Court, this index

APPENDICES
Crimes and offenses, service, **Rule 1:5–1 et seq.**
Service, **Rule 1:5–1 et seq.**

APPLICATION OF RULES
Generally, **Evidence Rule 101; Rule 1:1–1**

APPOINTMENTS
County Detectives and Investigators, this index
County Prosecutors, this index
Governor, this index
Senate, this index

APPRAISAL AND APPRAISERS
Alcoholic beverages, licenses and permits, smart growth development projects, **33:1–24.2**
Commercial bribery and breach of duty, **2C:21–10**
Judicial employees, appointment, **Rule 1:17–3**
Motor vehicles, body repair facilities, fine or license refusal, revocation, or suspension, **39:13–4**
Smart growth development projects, alcoholic beverages, licenses and permits, **33:1–24.2**

APPROPRIATE IDENTIFICATION
Definitions, handicapped parking, **39:4–207.6**

APPROPRIATE VICTIM
Definitions, intoxication of driver, **39:4–50**

APPROPRIATION OF PROPERTY
Justification, **2C:3–10**

APPROPRIATIONS
Agricultural Experiment Station, this index
Coastal protection trust fund, **39:3–27.52**
Counties, this index
Environmental Protection Department, this index
Handicapped parking enforcement units, **39:4–197.14**
Municipalities, this index

AQUACULTURE
Definitions, water pollution, **58:10A–3**

ARBITRATION AND AWARD
Attorney Fees, this index
Bribery and Corruption, generally, this index
Commercial bribery and breach of duty, arbitrators, **2C:21–10**
Compensation and salaries, motor vehicles, tort claims, **39:6A–28**
Complementary dispute resolution programs, **Rule 1:40–1 et seq.**
Confirmation, motor vehicle tort claims, **39:6A–31**
Corrupt influence. Bribery and Corruption, generally, this index
District fee arbitration committees, attorneys, **Rules 1:20–1, 1:20A–1 et seq.**
Facilities disputes, **Rule 1:33–9**
Motions, discovery and calendar motions, **Rule 1:6–2**
Motor vehicle insurance, no fault insurance, **39:6A–24 et seq.**
Insurers claim against insured tort feasor, **39:6A–9.1**
Motor Vehicles, this index
Naming of arbitrators or umpire, motor vehicles, tort claims, **39:6A–27**
Number of arbitrators, motor vehicles, tort claims, **39:6A–27**
Personal injury actions, representation, insurance companies, **Rule 1:21–1**
Rules of court, compensation for arbitrators, motor vehicle tort claims, **39:6A–28**
Stipulations, number or names of arbitrators, motor vehicles, torts, **39:6A–27**
Subpoenas, this index
Training, arbitrators, **Rule 1:40–12**

ARCHAEOLOGY AND ARCHAEOLOGISTS
Transportation, state property, archaeological findings, alteration, **27:5J–1**

ARGUMENT AND CONDUCT OF COUNSEL
Closing argument, **Rule 1:7–1**
Opening argument, **Rule 1:7–1**

ARMED FORCES
Alcoholic beverages, licenses and permits,
Application by attorney in fact, **33:1–25**
Fee exemption, retail sale, **33:1–27**
Issuance to one,
Permitting lapse while in military service, **33:1–12.22b**
Surrendering license while in service, **33:1–12.22a**
Manufacturers license, **33:1–11.1**
Wholesalers license, **33:1–11.1**
Attorneys, client protection fund, exemption from payment, **Rule 1:28–2**
Battleship U.S.S. New Jersey license plates, **39:3–27.67 et seq.**
Bomb, exemption from law prohibiting possession or carrying, **21:1A–141**
Commercial drivers licenses, exemption, **39:3–10j, 39:3–10k**

ARMED FORCES—Cont'd
Default judgment, nonmilitary service affidavit,
    Rule 1:5–7
Drivers licenses,
    Fee, **39:3–11.5**
    Temporary licenses, **39:3–10n**
Explosives Law, application, **21:1A–141**
Fireworks, exceptions, application of law,
    21:2–4
Intoxicating liquors. Alcoholic beverages, gen-
    erally, ante
Justification defense, criminal prosecutions,
    2C:3–3
Juvenile delinquents and dependents, enlist-
    ment, sealing of records, **2A:4A–62**
License plates, motor vehicles, reserves,
    39:3–27.33, 39:3–27.34
Licenses and permits. Alcoholic beverages,
    ante
Military list, inability to prosecute or defend
    action, **Rule 1:13–6**
Motor Vehicles, this index
National Guard, generally, this index
Prohibited weapons, exceptions, **2C:39–3**
Reserves, motor vehicles, license plates,
    39:3–27.33, 39:3–27.34
Southeast Asia, drivers license, waiver of fee,
    39:3–11.5
Speed law, applicability to military vehicles,
    39:4–103
Veterans, generally, this index
Weapons, unlawful possession, exemptions,
    2C:39–6

ARMS
Weapons, generally, this index

ARMY
Armed Forces, generally, this index
Veterans, generally, this index

ARRAIGNMENT
Capital cases, additional discovery, **Rule 3:13–4**
Conferences, prearraignment and arraignment
    status, **Rule 3:9–1**
Motor vehicle and traffic laws, power of clerk
    or deputy clerk, **39:5–6**
Municipal courts, **Rule 7:6–1**
Pretrial conference, **Rule 3:9–1**

ARREST
    Generally, **Rule 3:4–1 et seq.**
Advising rights, **Rule 3:4–1**
Affidavits, arrest of fugitive before requisition
    made, **2A:160–21**
Alcoholic Beverages, this index
Arson and Other Burnings, this index
Auto bus operator driving while intoxicated or
    under influence of narcotics, **39:5–25**
Bail, generally, this index
Breach of Peace, this index
Burglary, this index
Child Abuse, this index
Citizen appointed to make arrest, **2A:161–1**
Complaint warrant or complaint summons,
    procedure after arrest, **Rule 3:4–1**
Contempt, institution of proceedings, **Rule**
    1:10–2
Controlled Substances, this index
Correction officers, **2A:154–3, 2A:154–4**
County bridge police, **27:19–36.3**
County detectives and investigators, powers
    and duties, **2A:157–2, 2A:157–2.1**
Court attendants power to make, **2A:154–3**
Credit, confinement pending sentence, **Rule**
    3:21–8

ARREST—Cont'd
Deadly force, grand jury, instructions to jury,
    2B:22–9
Definitions, juvenile delinquents and depen-
    dents, taking into custody, **2A:4A–31**
Denial, record expungement, **2C:52–14**
Destructive devices, **2C:39–14**
Detective associations, members, powers,
    15:4–4
Disclosure, expungement order, **2C:52–30**
Diversion programs, record expungement,
    2C:52–20
Exemptions, record expungement, **2C:52–2**
Expungement, records, **2C:52–1 et seq.**
Extradition, this index
Federal officers,
    Powers, state law violation, **2A:154–5**
    State law violation, **2A:154–5**
Fees, record expungement, **2C:52–29**
Fines, nonpayment, **2C:46–2**
Fingerprints and photographs of arrested per-
    son,
    Compared by bureau of identification with
        records on file, **53:1–16**
    Sent to bureau of identification, **53:1–15**
Force or violence, **2C:3–9**
    Grand jury, instructions to jury, **2B:22–9**
Fresh Pursuit Law, **2A:155–1 et seq.**
Fugitive from justice found in New Jersey,
    2A:160–10
Grade and degree of offenses, hindering appre-
    hension or prosecution, **2C:29–3**
Grand jury, justifiable force, instructions to
    jury, **2B:22–9**
Hearings, record expungement, **2C:52–9 et seq.**
Hindering apprehension or prosecution,
    2C:29–3
    Terrorism, **2C:38–4**
Indictable offenses, record expungement,
    2C:52–2
Indictment, Information or Presentment, this
    index
Inspectors and inspection, records, expunge-
    ment, **2C:52–19**
Investigative detention, **Rule 3:5A–1 et seq.**
    Applications, emergent application, **Rule**
        3:5A–6
    Contents, orders, **Rule 3:5A–5**
    Evidence of physical characteristics, defined,
        Rule 3:5A–9
    Filing, order, application, **Rule 3:5A–8**
    Fingerprints, **Rule 3:5A–1 et seq.**
    Grounds, orders, issuance, **Rule 3:5A–4**
    Notice, application, **Rule 3:5A–3**
    Service, orders, **Rule 3:5A–7**
Justifiable force, grand jury, instructions to
    jury, **2B:22–9**
Juvenile delinquents,
    Appearance at hearings, **Rule 5:20–2**
    Custody, **2A:4A–31; Rule 5:21–1**
    Warrants, issuance, **Rule 5:20–3**
Juvenile family crisis, appearance, **Rule 5:17–1**
Law enforcement officer, without warrant or
    process, violation of motor vehicle or traf-
    fic law in presence of, **39:5–25**
Library theft, **2C:20–14**
Material witness. Witnesses, this index
Motor Vehicles, this index
Motorman operating vehicle while intoxicated
    or under influence of narcotics, **39:5–25**
Nonresidents, traffic violations, **39:5F–1 et seq.**
Notice, records and recordation, expungement,
    2B:12–32
Orders of court, record expungement,
    2C:52–11 et seq.
Ordinances, unconstitutionality, **2B:12–32**

ARREST—Cont'd
Parole officers, **2A:154–4**
Person by officer of another state in fresh
    pursuit, **2A:155–6**
Petitions, record expungement, **2C:52–7 et seq.**
Piracy, sound recordings, audiovisual works,
    2C:21–21
Presentence report, record expungement,
    2C:52–21
Probable cause, domestic violence, **2C:25–21**
Probation and probation officers, **2C:45–3**
Procedure after, **Rule 3:4–1**
Process, record expungement, **2C:52–10**
Records and recordation,
    Expungement, **2C:52–1 et seq.**
        Ordinances, unconstitutionality, **2B:12–32**
    Pretrial intervention programs, expunging,
        sealing, **Rule 3:28**
Release, record expungement, **2C:52–19**
Removal, records, **2C:52–15**
Resisting arrest, **2C:29–2**
    Unlawful arrest, use of force, **2C:3–4**
Restitution, nonpayment, **2C:46–2**
Sealing, record expungement, **2C:52–26**
Search Warrants, generally, this index
Searches and Seizures, generally, this index
Sex offenses, repetitive or compulsive sex of-
    fenders, recidivism, monitoring, **2C:47–9**
Sheriffs,
    Officers, **2A:154–3**
    Powers, **2A:157–2.1**
Shoplifting, powers, **2C:20–11**
State Police, this index
Statements, record expungement petition,
    2C:52–8
Stills and distilling apparatus, offenders, **33:2–3**
Street gangs, fingerprints and fingerprinting,
    53:1–15.1
Streetcar operators under influence of alcohol
    or drugs, **39:5–25**
Summons. Crimes and Offenses, this index
Sunday, generally, this index
Supervisory treatment programs, record ex-
    pungement, **2C:52–20**
Suspended sentence, defendant under, **2C:45–3**
Taking before judge, **Rule 3:4–1**
Telecommunications, witnesses, warrants, **Rule**
    3:2–3
Television and radio, witnesses, warrants, **Rule**
    3:2–3
Temporary detention, investigation, **Rule**
    3:5A–1 et seq.
Traffic rules and regulations, records and re-
    cordation, expungement, **2C:52–28**
Uniform Fresh Pursuit Law, **2A:155–1 et seq.;**
    Rule 3:4–4
United States law enforcement officers, state
    law, special agents, **2A:154–5**
Use of force, **2C:3–7**
    Unlawful arrest, **2C:3–9**
Warrants, **Rule 3:3–1 et seq.**
    Abuse of children, **9:6–8.39**
    Accusation, indictment, issuance, **Rules**
        3:7–8, 3:7–9
    Additional warrants, **Rule 3:3–1**
    Amendment, defect, **Rule 3:3–4**
    Bail, fixing, **Rule 3:7–9**
    Citizen appointed to execute, **2A:161–1**
    Complaint after notice of violation of laws,
        2A:152–13
    Complaint warrant, procedure after arrest,
        Rule 3:4–1
    Controlled substances, **24:21–31**
    Crimes required, **Rule 3:3–1**
    Defect, **Rule 3:3–4**

ARREST—Cont'd
Warrants—Cont'd
Defendants under suspended sentence or probation, 2C:45–3
Discovery, **Rule 3:13–3**
Execution,
Return, **Rule 3:3–3**
Service, return, **Rule 3:7–10**
Expungement, records, 2C:52–1 et seq.
Federal officers, powers, state law violation, 2A:154–5
Forms, **Rule 3:2–3**
Indictment, accusation, **Rule 3:7–9**
Issuance, **Rules 3:3–1, 7:2–2**
Indictment, accusation, **Rule 3:7–8**
Municipal Courts, this index
New warrant issued, **Rule 3:3–4**
Person arrested without, issuance, **Rule 3:4–1**
Records, expungement, 2C:52–1 et seq.
Return, **Rule 3:3–3**
Service, execution, **Rule 3:7–10**
Service, execution, return, **Rule 3:7–10**
State polices authority to execute, 53:2–1
Taking before court, **Rule 3:4–1**
Territorial limits, **Rule 3:3–3**
Without warrant,
Federal officers, state law violation, 2A:154–5
Library theft, 2C:20–14
Piracy, sound recordings, audiovisual works, 2C:21–21

ARREST OF JUDGMENT
Crimes and offenses, **Rule 3:21–9**
Motions, enlargement of time, **Rule 1:3–4**

ARSENIC
Poisons, this index

ARSON AND OTHER BURNINGS
Generally, 2C:17–1 et seq.
Aggravated arson, 2C:17–1 et seq.
Aggravated criminal sexual contact, 2C:14–3
Aggravated sexual assault, 2C:14–2
Arrest,
Force or violence, 2C:3–7
Grand jury, instructions to jury, 2B:22–9
Warrants, issuance, **Rule 3:3–1**
Without warrant, release, **Rule 3:4–1**
Assault, emergency services personnel, 2C:12–1
Attempts, body vests, 2C:39–13
Body vests, 2C:39–13
Burns, injuries, reports, 2C:58–8
Expungement of record, 2C:52–2
Force or violence, 2C:3–6
Arrest, grand jury, instructions to jury, 2B:22–9
Homicide, 2C:11–3
Investigations, weapons possession, exemption, 2C:39–6
Jury, peremptory challenges, 2B:23–13; **Rule 1:8–3**
Juvenile delinquents and dependents,
Jurisdiction, waiver, 2A:4A–26
Referral to other courts without juveniles consent, **Rule 5:22–2**
Murder, 2C:11–3
Places of worship, 2C:17–1
Records and recordation, expungement, 2C:52–2
Reward for apprehension and conviction, 2A:153–1 et seq.
Terrorism, 2C:38–2
Weapons, persons convicted of, possession, 2C:39–7
Zoning, avoidance, 2C:17–1

ARTIFICIAL BARRICADE
Definitions, Explosives Act, 21:1A–129

ARTIFICIALLY SWEETENED ICE CREAM
Frozen Desserts and Dietary Foods, generally, this index

ASHES
Number of motor drawn vehicles used in collection, 39:4–54

ASSAULT AND BATTERY
Generally, 2C:12–1
Aggravated Assault, generally, this index
Aggravated criminal sexual contact, 2C:14–3
Aggravated Sexual Assault, generally, this index
Assault by auto or vessel, 2C:12–1
Attempts, body vests, 2C:39–13
Body vests, 2C:39–13
Cable television, officers and employees, 2C:12–1
Correctional institutions, officers and employees, consecutive sentences, 2C:44–5
Domestic Violence, generally, this index
Emergency services personnel, 2C:12–1
Harassment, 2C:33–4
Hit and run drivers, assault by auto or vessel, 2C:12–1, 2C:12–1.1
Institutionalized elderly persons, 2C:12–1
Intimidation based on bias, fourth degree crime, extended term of imprisonment, 2C:43–7, 2C:43–7.1
Juvenile delinquents and dependents,
Jurisdiction, waiver, 2A:4A–26
Referral to other courts without juveniles consent, **Rule 5:22–2**
Law enforcement officers, weapons, aggravated assault, 2C:12–1
Motor vehicles, 2C:12–1
Prevention of domestic violence, 2C:25–17 et seq.
Public utilities, officers and employees, 2C:12–1
Racketeering, 2C:41–1 et seq.
Rape, generally, this index
Schools and School Districts, this index
Sexual Assault, generally, this index
Sports, schools and school districts, events, 2C:12–1
Vessel, operation of, 2C:12–1

ASSAULT FIREARMS
See, also, Machine Guns, generally, this index
Advertisements, violation of provisions, disorderly persons, 2C:39–15
Conviction, crime involving use of,
Extended term of imprisonment,
Criteria for sentence of, 2C:44–3
Eligibility for parole, 2C:43–7
Term of imprisonment, 2C:43–6
Definitions, 2C:39–1
False information, application for permit, third degree crime, 2C:39–10
Inoperable, definitions, legally owned firearm rendered inoperable, certification, 2C:58–13
Large capacity ammunition magazine,
Person convicted of crime involving, possession of any weapon prohibited, 2C:39–7
Possession, participation in certain shooting matches, 2C:39–3
Legitimate target shooting purposes, assault firearms used for, list, registration, 2C:58–12

ASSAULT FIREARMS—Cont'd
Licenses and permits, 2C:58–5
Purchase of, condition of registration, 2C:58–12
Violation of regulatory provisions, crime of fourth degree, 2C:39–10
Manufacture, sale, without registration or license,
Person convicted of crime involving, possession of any weapon prohibited, 2C:39–7
Third degree crime, 2C:39–9
Previous conviction, crime involving use of, term of imprisonment, 2C:43–6
Registration statement, contents, return, 2C:58–12
Report by attorney general to legislature, 2C:58–14
Rifle or pistol club engaged in legitimate target shooting matches, membership, condition of registration, 2C:58–12
Surrender of legally owned firearm, 2C:58–13
Transfer, legally owned firearm, 2C:58–13
Unlawful possession, 2C:39–5
Use in commission of crime,
Civil liability of owner, 2C:58–12
License holder, civil liability for damages, 2C:58–5

ASSEMBLY
General Assembly, generally, this index

ASSESSMENTS
Adult offender supervision interstate commission, 2A:168–35
Crimes and offenses,
Collection and enforcement, 2C:46–4
Law enforcement officers training and equipment fund, 2C:43–3.3
Conviction, victims of crime compensation board, 2C:43–3.1
Transaction fee, 2C:46–1 et seq.
Satisfaction of claims, 2C:46–4.1
Exemptions, New Jersey turnpike authority, 27:23–12
Lawyers assistance program, **Rule 1:28B–1**
Probation, crimes and offenses, conditions, 2C:45–1
Solid Waste, this index
Solid Waste Management Act, 13:1E–9
Supervisory treatment procedure, crimes and offenses, 2C:43–13
Suspended sentences, crimes and offenses, conditions, 2C:45–1

ASSIGNATION AND ASSIGNATION HOUSES
Prostitution, generally, this index

ASSIGNMENT JUDGE
Generally, **Rules 1:33–2, 1:33–4**
Facilities disputes, arbitration, **Rule 1:33–9**
Grand jury, **Rule 3:6–11**
Superior Court Judges, this index
Trial court administrators, **Rule 1:33–5**

ASSIGNMENT OF COUNSEL
Attorneys, this index

ASSIGNMENTS
Definitions, Certificate of Motor Vehicle Ownership Law, 39:10–2
Foreclosure actions, copies annexed to complaints, **Rule 1:4–3**
Judgments and decrees, motor vehicle accident cases, state treasurer, 39:6–77

ASSIGNMENTS—Cont'd

Motor vehicle insurance, no fault insurance, personal injuries, **39:6A–4**
  Medical expense benefits, **39:6A–3.1**

ASSISTANCE

Indigent Persons, generally, this index

Public officers, justification defense, criminal prosecutions, **2C:3–3**

ASSOCIATIONS AND SOCIETIES

Actions and proceedings, racketeering, **2C:41–4**

Alcoholic beverages,
  Club licenses, **33:1–12, 33:1–46.1**
  Law enforcement officers, licenses and permits, **33:1–25.1**
  Licenses and permits,
    Law enforcement personnel, **33:1–25.1, 33:1–25.2**
    Member of issuing authority interested in association, **33:1–20**
    Police, **33:1–25.1**
  Poisoned liquors, manufacture or sale, **33:3–9, 33:3–10**
  Special permits, **33:1–46.2**

Automobile full insurance underwriting association. Motor Vehicle Insurance, this index

Badges, emblems and insignia, registration of badges. Badges, Emblems and Insignia, generally, this index

Bribery and corruption, effect of conviction, **2C:51–2**

Cease and desist orders, racketeering, **2C:41–4**

Charitable Organizations and Associations, generally, this index

Chiropractic associations, review committees, immunity from liability, **2A:84A–22.10**

Club officers, intoxicating liquors, law enforcement personnel, **33:1–25.1**

Confidential or privileged information, racketeering investigations, **2C:41–5**

Constables, intoxicating liquors, licenses and permits, **33:1–25.1**

Crimes and offenses, racketeering, **2C:41–1 et seq.**

Debtors and creditors, racketeering, **2C:41–1 et seq.**

Definitions,
  Racketeering, **2C:41–1**
  Unsatisfied claim and judgment fund, **39:6–62**

Dental associations, review committees, immunity from liability, **2A:84A–22.10**

Detectives, this index

Discovery, racketeering investigations, **2C:41–5**

Examinations and examiners, racketeering, **2C:41–5**

Fines and penalties, racketeering, **2C:41–1 et seq.**

Forfeitures, racketeering, **2C:41–3 et seq.**

Fraternal Benefit Societies, generally, this index

Fraternal Organizations, generally, this index

Indebtedness, racketeering, **2C:41–1 et seq.**

Inspections and inspectors, racketeering investigations, **2C:41–5**

Interrogatories, racketeering, investigations, **2C:41–5**

Intoxicating liquors. Alcoholic beverages, generally, ante

Investigations and investigators, racketeering, **2C:41–5**

Investments, racketeering, **2C:41–1 et seq.**

Judgments and decrees, racketeering, **2C:41–4**

ASSOCIATIONS AND SOCIETIES—Cont'd

Law enforcement officers, intoxicating liquors, licenses and permits, **33:1–25.1**

Licenses and permits,
  Alcoholic beverages, ante
  Racketeering, revocation or suspension, **2C:41–4**

Medical associations, review committees, immunity from liability, **2A:84A–22.10**

Monopolies and unfair trade, exemptions, **56:9–5**

Municipal courts, traffic tickets, service, **Rule 7:2–4**

Nonprofit Corporations and Associations, generally, this index

Officers and employees,
  Commercial bribery and breach of duty, **2C:21–10**
  Intoxicating liquors, law enforcement personnel, **33:1–25.1**

Optometric associations, review committees, immunity from liability, **2A:84A–22.10**

Partnerships, generally, this index

Person, Alcoholic Beverage Law, **33:1–1**

Pleas, criminal causes, **Rule 7:6–2**

Podiatric associations, review committees, immunity from liability, **2A:84A–22.10**

Police and police departments, intoxicating liquors, licenses and permits, **33:1–25.1**

Process, racketeering, **2C:41–5**

Production of books and papers, racketeering, **2C:41–5**

Psychological associations, review committees, immunity from liability, **2A:84A–22.10**

Racketeering, **2C:41–1 et seq.**

Records and recordation, racketeering, investigations, **2C:41–5**

Registration of badges. Badges, Emblems and Insignia, generally, this index

Religious Corporations and Associations, generally, this index

Restitution, racketeering, **2C:41–4**

Securities, racketeering, **2C:41–1 et seq.**

Sheriffs, intoxicating liquors, licenses and permits, **33:1–25.1**

Society for prevention of cruelty to children. Child Abuse, this index

Society for the prevention of cruelty to animals. Cruelty to Animals, this index

Summons, municipal court issuance, **Rule 7:2–2**

Veterans Associations and Organizations, generally, this index

Veterinarian associations, review committees, immunity from liability, **2A:84A–22.10**

ASYMMETRIC HEADLAMPS

Definitions, Motor Vehicle Law, **39:3–46**

ATHLETICS

Aggravated assault, schools and school districts, **2C:12–1**

Assault and battery, schools and school districts, events, **2C:12–1**

Children and minors, sex offenders, participation, **2C:7–22, 2C:7–23**

Coaches and officials, victims of crime, **2C:44–1**

Gambling, presumptions, proof of occurrence, **2C:37–5**

Managers, victims of crime, **2C:44–1**

Schools and School Districts, this index

Sports officials, victims of crime, **2C:44–1**

Volunteer coaches and officials, victims of crime, **2C:44–1**

ATLANTIC CITY

Casinos, generally, this index

ATLANTIC OCEAN

Coastal protection license plate program, **39:3–27.47 et seq.**

ATM MACHINES

Electronic Fund Transfers, generally, this index

ATOMIC ENERGY

Crimes and offenses, release, radiation, **2C:17–7 et seq.**

Power plants, guards, weapons, possession, **2C:39–3, 2C:39–6**

ATP CARD

Definitions, food stamps, crimes and offenses, **2C:20–35**

ATROPINE SULPHATE

Controlled substances, **24:21–1 et seq.**

ATTACHABLE AUXILIARY MOTOR VEHICLE AXLE

Definitions, **39:4–54**

ATTACHMENT

Alcoholic beverage licenses, **33:1–26**

Controlled substances, ex parte proceedings, dealers, liability, **2C:35B–13**

Exemptions, motor vehicle insurance, no fault benefits, **39:6A–4**

Funeral expense benefits, motor vehicle insurance, exemptions, **39:6A–4**

Intoxicating liquor licenses, **33:1–26**

Motor vehicle insurance, no fault benefits, exemptions, **39:6A–4**

Motor vehicles, surrender of title papers, **39:10–15**

Subpoenas, public officers or agencies, enforcement, **Rule 1:9–6**

ATTEMPTS

Generally, **2C:5–1**

Aggravated assault, **2C:12–1**

Arrest warrant, issuance, **Rule 3:3–1**

Arrest without warrant, release, **Rule 3:4–1**

Assault, **2C:12–1**
  Intimidation based on bias, fourth degree crime, **2C:12–1**
    Extended term of imprisonment, **2C:43–7, 2C:43–7.1**

Bias intimidation, **2C:16–1**

Body vests, **2C:39–13**

Burglary, **2C:18–2**

Conspiracy, **2C:5–2**

Controlled substances, commission of offense, **24:21–24**

Defenses, notice, **Rule 3:12–1**

Definitions, **2C:5–1**

Fines and penalties, **2C:5–4**

Grade and degree of offense, **2C:5–4**

Homicide, **2C:11–3**
  Multiple victims, fines and penalties, **2C:5–4**

Included offenses, **2C:1–8**

Limitation of criminal prosecutions, **2C:1–6**

Murder, **2C:11–3**

Radio, interception of police, fire or emergency medical communication, used to commit crime, fourth degree crime, **2C:33–21 et seq.**

Territorial applicability of code of criminal justice, **2C:1–3**

Terrorism, fines and penalties, **2C:5–4**

Victim of crime, accomplice, **2C:2–6**

ATTESTATION
Certificates and certification, alcoholic beverage control division director, municipal boards, **33:1–48**

ATTORNEY ETHICS OFFICE
Generally, **Rules 1:20–1, 1:20–2**

ATTORNEY FEES
Action to recover, notice to client, option to pursue fee arbitration remedy, **Rule 1:20A–6**
Administrative filing fee, arbitration, **Rule 1:20A–3**
Appeal and review, arbitration and award, **Rule 1:20A–3**
Arbitration and award, **Rule 1:20A–1 et seq.**
  Annual assessment, **Rule 1:20–1**
  Clients, immunity from liability, **Rule 1:20–7**
  District committees, **Rule 1:20A–1 et seq.**
  Establishment, **Rule 1:20–1**
  Enforcement of decision, **Rule 1:20–15**
  Oversight committee, **Rule 1:20–1**
Attorney trustee, **Rule 1:20–19**
Bar examinations, **Rule 1:24–1**
Certificates of admission and good standing, **Rule 1:29–1**
Certified attorneys, division of fees, **Rule 1:39–6**
Class actions, contingent fees, **Rule 1:21–7**
Clients security fund claimants, **Rule 1:28–3**
Closing statements, contingent fees, **Rule 1:21–7**
Confirmation of admission, certificates, **Rule 1:29–3**
Contempt hearings, **Rule 1:10–3**
Contingent fees, **Rule 1:21–7**
Controlled substances, dealers, liability, **2C:35B–5, 2C:35B–6**
Copies of client agreements, bill, **Rule 1:21–6**
Credit, history, identity theft, **2C:21–17.4**
Default judgment, arbitration hearing requested, **Rule 1:20A–3**
Depositions, criminal proceedings, **Rule 3:13–2**
Disability inactive status, **Rule 1:20–12**
Disciplinary oversight committee, **Rule 1:20–1**
District fee arbitration committees, **Rules 1:20–1, 1:20A–1 et seq.**
Division of fees, certified attorneys, **Rule 1:39–6**
Failure to appear, sanctions, **Rule 1:2–4**
Frivolous litigation, **Rule 1:4–8**
Identity theft, **2C:21–17.4**
Indigent persons, **Rule 1:13–2**
Jury service, employment protection, employer violations, civil action, award of reasonable fees, **2B:20–17**
Late fees,
  Registration, **Rule 1:20–1**
  Tardy payment to client protection fund, **Rule 1:28–2**
Limited certificate holders, **Rule 1:21–3**
Limits, contingent fees, **Rule 1:21–7**
Major disasters, temporary practice of law, foreign states, **Rule 1:21–10**
Monopolies and unfair trade, **56:9–10**
Motor Vehicles, this index
Multiple party actions, contingent fees, **Rule 1:21–7**
Murder prosecution, compensation of counsel assigned in, **2A:163–1**
Newspersons privilege, enforcement of subpoena against, **Evidence Rule 508**
Out of state attorneys, **Rule 1:21–6**
Recovery, action, notice of option to pursue fee arbitration remedy, **Rule 1:20A–6**

ATTORNEY FEES—Cont'd
Refund, arbitration, **Rule 1:20A–3**
Reinstatement fee, **Rule 1:28–2**
Rules of court, fee schedule, motor vehicle tort claim arbitrations, **39:6A–28**
Sharing, out of state firms, **Rule 1:21–6**
Structured settlements, contingent fees, **Rule 1:21–7**
Third party attorneys or law firms, arbitration of disputes, liability, **Rule 1:20A–3**
Trusts and trustees, disbursement, disciplined attorneys, **Rule 1:20–20**
Unsatisfied claim and judgment law, fees in defending actions or claims under law, **39:6–67**

ATTORNEY GENERAL
Colleges and Universities, generally, this index
Commercial motor vehicle, consent, taking samples of breath, chemical analyses performed under methods approved by, **39:3–10.25**
Commitment and Admission to Institutions, generally, this index
Consent, wiretapping and electronic surveillance, **2A:156A–4**
Contempt, prosecuting, **Rule 1:10–2**
County Prosecutors, generally, this index
Crimes and offenses,
  Money laundering and illegal investments, **2C:21–24, 2C:21–28, 2C:21–29**
  Process, service of petition, **2C:52–10**
Criminal business of state, **2A:158–4**
Definitions,
  Municipal prosecutors, **2B:25–2**
  Racketeering, **2C:41–1**
  Searches and seizures, news organizations, **2A:84A–21.12**
  Theft, **2C:20–1**
Deputies, weapons, possession, exemption, **2C:39–6**
Domestic violence, prevention and treatment,
  Courses, police officers, **2C:25–20**
  Records, relief applications, **2C:25–33**
Extradition, investigation of demand for extradition of fugitive in New Jersey, **2A:160–12**
Intervention, municipal prosecutors, **2B:25–7**
Judicial conference,
  Membership, **Rule 1:35–1**
  Rules of evidence, **2A:84A–34**
Monopolies and unfair trade,
  Investigations, **56:9–9**
  Proceedings against violators, **56:9–6**
Motor vehicle commission, board, members and membership, **39:2A–12**
Motor vehicles, representation of complainant on appeal from conviction, **39:5–20**
Municipal prosecutors, **2B:25–7**
  Intervention, **2B:25–7**
  Training, **2B:25–10**
  Vacancies in office, assistants, **2B:25–6**
  Reimbursement, **2B:25–8**
Notice, mayor or chief of police of continued violation of criminal laws, **2A:152–12, 2A:152–13**
Powers and duties, criminal business of state, **2A:158–4**
Reports,
  Assault firearms, **2C:58–14**
  Juvenile delinquents and dependents, jurisdiction waivers, **2A:4A–26**
Searches and seizures, warrants, execution, **Rule 3:5–5**
Sex offenders, registration, verification, **2C:7–2**
State grand juries,
  Presentation of evidence, **2B:22–6**

ATTORNEY GENERAL—Cont'd
State grand juries—Cont'd
  Written request for impaneling, **2B:22–1**
Subpoenas, disobedience, suspension or revocation of motor vehicle registration or drivers license, recovery, **39:5–30**
Terrorism, wiretapping and electronic surveillance, applications, **2A:156A–8**
Traffic congestion, emergency conditions, authority for removing, **39:4–213 et seq.**
Traffic law violations, representation of complainant on appeal from conviction, **39:5–20**
Turnpike authority members and treasurer, approval of bonds, **27:23–3**
Wiretapping and electronic surveillance,
  Application for order, **2A:156A–8 et seq.**
  Consent, **2A:156A–4**

ATTORNEY TRUST ACCOUNTS
Generally, **Rule 1:21–6**

ATTORNEYS
Abandoned or unclaimed property, trust funds, **Rule 1:21–6**
Abandonment of practice, appointment of attorney trustee, protection of clients interest, **Rule 1:20–19**
Abolished title, **Rule 1:21–5**
Acceptance of employment, attorney trustee, appointed to protect clients interest following death, disbarment, suspension, **Rule 1:20–19**
Accidents, solicitation, crimes and offenses, **2C:40A–5**
Accounts and accounting, **Rule 1:21–6**
  Interest on lawyers trust accounts, **Rules 1:21–6, 1:28A–2**
  Restraint on, disciplinary proceedings, **Rules 1:20–16, 1:20–23**
Acting judge, municipal courts, practicing, **Rule 1:15–1**
Addiction, drugs or alcohol, disability inactive status, **Rule 1:20–12**
Address,
  Change, notice to court, **Rule 1:4–1**
  Pleadings, **Rule 1:4–1**
Administration filing fee, arbitration of attorney fees, **Rule 1:20A–3**
Admission to practice, **Rule 1:27–1 et seq.**
  Advisory committee, **Rules 1:27A–1, 1:27A–2**
  Bar examinations, **Rules 1:24–1, 1:24–2**
    Certification, **Rule 1:39–3**
    Passage, qualifications for licensure, **Rule 1:27–1**
    Preparation and conducting, **Rule 1:23–2**
    Reinstatement to practice, **Rule 1:20–15A**
    Tests and testing, improprieties, **Rule 1:23–5**
  Board of bar examiners, **Rules 1:23–1, 1:23–2**
    Immunity from liability, **Rule 1:23–3**
    Reports, persons passing examination, **Rule 1:27–1**
  Certificate of admission, **Rule 1:29–1**
  Character and reputation, **Rules 1:25, 1:27–1**
  Cheating, tests and testing, **Rule 1:23–5**
  Confirmation, change of name or loss or destruction of original certificate, **Rule 1:29–3**
  Degree requirement, **Rule 1:24–2**
  Ethics course, passage, **Rule 1:27–1**
  Fees, **Rule 1:23–4**
  Improprieties, tests and testing, **Rule 1:23–5**
  In house counsel, limited licenses, **Rule 1:27–2**
  Law school teachers, **Rule 1:27–3**

ATTORNEYS—Cont'd

Admission to practice—Cont'd
Multistate professional responsibility examination, **Rule 1:27–1**
Notice, intention to take bar examination, **Rule 1:24–1**
Oaths, **Rules 1:27–1, 1:27–4**
Authorization of administration, **Rule 1:27–1**
Pro hac vice appearance, **Rule 1:21–2**
Professional responsibility examination, **Rule 1:27–1**
Qualifications, **Rules 1:24–2, 1:27–1**
Skills and methods course, **Rule 1:27–1**
Tests and testing, improprieties, **Rule 1:23–5**
Admonition, **Rule 1:20–15A**
Public, **Rule 1:20–3 et seq.**
Appeal and review, **Rules 1:20–15, 1:20–16**
Adverse or pecuniary interest, limitation on practice, **Rule 1:15–1 et seq.**
Advertisements,
Committee on attorney advertising, **Rule 1:19A et seq.**
Confidential or privileged information, **Rule 1:38–5**
Disciplinary review board, **Rule 1:20–15**
District ethics committees, acting on advertising grievances, **Rule 1:20–3**
Advisory committees,
Bar admissions, **Rules 1:27A–1, 1:27A–2**
Professional ethics, **Rule 1:19–1 et seq.**
Advisory opinions,
Attorney advertising committee, **Rules 1:19A–2, 1:19A–3**
Unauthorized practice of law committee, **Rules 1:22–2, 1:22–3**
Affidavits,
Change of name, **Rules 1:29–2, 1:29–3**
Fee arbitration, notice of appeal, **Rule 1:20A–3**
Pro hac vice appearance, **Rule 1:21–2**
Age, admission to practice, **Rule 1:24–2**
Agent for service of process,
Nonresidents, **Rule 1:21–1**
Pro hac vice appearance, **Rule 1:21–2**
Alcoholism,
Disability inactive status, **Rule 1:20–12**
Treatment, reinstatement to practice, **Rule 1:20–15A**
Answer, complaint, discipline, **Rule 1:20–4**
Appeal and review,
Advertising committee advisory opinions, **Rule 1:19A–3**
Attorney of record, **Rule 1:11–3**
Certificate holders, withholding or termination of certification, **Rule 1:39–9**
Certification committee ineligibility determinations, **Rule 1:39–4**
Contingent fees, **Rule 1:21–7**
Disciplinary review board, **Rules 1:20–1, 1:20–15**
Discipline, post
Fee arbitration, **Rule 1:20A–3**
Petitions, final actions of advisory committee on professional ethics, **Rule 1:19–8**
Public admonitions, **Rules 1:20–15, 1:20–16**
Unauthorized practice of law decisions, **Rule 1:22–3A**
Appeals in criminal prosecutions,
Name and address, notice of appeal, **Rule 3:23–3**
Postconviction relief, **Rule 7:10–2**
Responsibility for prosecution of appeal, failure to file notice of application for assignment of counsel, **Rule 3:4–2**
Appearance, generally, this index

ATTORNEYS—Cont'd

Arbitration and award. Attorney Fees, this index
Armed forces duty, client protection fund, exemption from payment, **Rule 1:28–2**
Assessments,
Costs, disciplinary proceedings, **Rule 1:20–17**
Discipline and fee arbitration system, **Rule 1:20–1**
Lawyers assistance program, **Rule 1:28B–1**
Assignment of counsel,
Attorney incapacity and disability, **Rule 1:20–12**
Indigent persons, **Rule 3:4–2**
Attorney disciplinary proceedings, **Rule 1:20–4**
Postconviction relief, **Rule 7:10–2**
Attorney client privilege, **2A:84A–20**
Public defenders, **2A:158A–12**
Attorney ethics office, **Rules 1:20–1, 1:20–2**
Referrals from advertising committee, **Rule 1:19A–7**
Audits and auditors,
Advertising, grievance hearings, **Rule 1:19A–4**
Client protection fund, **Rule 1:28–4**
Financial records, **Rule 1:21–6**
Random audit compliance program, office of attorney ethics, **Rule 1:20–2**
Bank accounts, required accounts, **Rule 1:21–6**
Bar admissions financial committee, **Rule 1:27B–1 et seq.**
Bar examinations. Admission to practice, ante
Bar membership, resignation without prejudice, **Rule 1:20–22**
Boards and commissions,
Attorney certification, **Rule 1:39–1**
Board of bar examiners. Admission to practice, ante
Lawyers assistance program, trusts and trustees, **Rule 1:28B–1 et seq.**
Bookkeeping records, **Rule 1:21–6**
Bribery, conviction, discipline, **Rule 1:20–13**
Briefs, signatures, **Rules 1:4–5, 1:4–8**
Budgets,
Disciplinary system, **Rule 1:20–2**
Preparation, **Rule 1:20–15**
Lawyers assistance program, **Rule 1:28B–2**
Burden of proof,
Disability inactive status, **Rule 1:20–12**
Disciplinary proceedings,
Hearings involving misconduct, **Rule 1:20–6**
Incapacity and disability, **Rule 1:20–12**
Fee arbitration, proving reasonableness, **Rule 1:20A–3**
Reciprocal discipline, **Rule 1:20–14**
Termination of certification, **Rule 1:39–8**
Business accounts, appointment of attorney trustee to protect clients interest, suspension, disbarment, death, **Rule 1:20–19**
Business entity, practicing law, **Rule 1:21–1**
Calendar call, answering by law students or graduates, **Rule 1:21–3**
Case management order, **Rule 1:20–5**
Casinos, limitation on practice, industry related activities, **Rule 1:15–4**
Censure, **Rule 1:20–15A**
Certificates and certification, **Rule 1:39–1 et seq.**
Admission, **Rule 1:29–1**
Confirmatory certificates, **Rule 1:29–3**
Ethics, advertising and solicitation, telephone research service, **Rule 1:19–9**
Good standing, **Rule 1:29–1**
Out of state attorneys, **Rule 1:21–3**

ATTORNEYS—Cont'd

Certificates and certification—Cont'd
Insurance, professional corporations, **Rule 1:21–1A**
Pro hac vice appearance, **Rule 1:21–2**
Signature on pleadings and motions, **Rule 1:4–8**
Unauthorized practice of law, appeal of decisions, **Rule 1:22–3A**
Changes,
Address, phone number,
Filing supplemental statement, **Rule 1:20–1**
Notice to court, **Rule 1:4–1**
Name, **Rules 1:29–2, 1:29–3**
Character and Reputation, this index
Cheating, admission to practice, tests and testing, **Rule 1:23–5**
Child Abuse, this index
Children and minors, contingent fee arrangements, **Rule 1:21–7**
Civil trial attorneys, certification, **Rule 1:39–1 et seq.**
Claims, client protection fund, **Rule 1:28–3**
Class actions, contingent fees, **Rule 1:21–7**
Clerks fees, liability, **Rule 1:5–6**
Client, definitions, lawyer client privilege, **2A:84A–20**
Client protection fund, **Rule 1:28–1 et seq.**
Confidential or privileged information, **Rule 1:38–5**
Filing of registration statement, **Rule 1:20–1**
Clients funds,
Interest on lawyers trust accounts, **Rules 1:21–6, 1:28A–2**
Restraint on, disciplinary proceedings, **Rules 1:20–16, 1:20–23**
Commercial bribery and breach of duty, **2C:21–10**
Commissions. Boards and commissions, generally, ante
Commitment, mental hospital, disability inactive status, **Rule 1:20–12**
Committees,
Advertising, **Rule 1:19A–1 et seq.**
Bar admissions,
Advisory committee, **Rules 1:27A–1, 1:27A–2**
Financial committee, **Rule 1:27B–1 et seq.**
Certification, **Rule 1:39–1A**
Character, **Rule 1:25**
Funding, **Rule 1:23–4**
Disciplinary oversight committee, **Rule 1:20–1**
District ethics committees, **Rules 1:20–1, 1:20–3**
District fee arbitration committees, **Rules 1:20–1, 1:20A–1 et seq.**
Judicial conference, membership, **Rule 1:35–1**
Unauthorized practice of law, **Rule 1:22–1 et seq.**
Complaints,
Advertising, ethics grievance, **Rule 1:19A–4**
Discipline, **Rule 1:20–4**
Pending actions and proceedings, **Rule 1:20–3**
Termination of certification, **Rule 1:39–8**
Unauthorized practice of law, **Rules 1:22–2, 1:22–5**
Compliance, suspension, disciplined attorneys, future activities, **Rule 1:20–20**
Compromise and settlement, contingent fees, structured settlements, **Rule 1:21–7**
Computers, bookkeeping records, use to maintain, **Rule 1:21–6**

ATTORNEYS—Cont'd

Conduct of proceedings, termination of responsibility, **Rule 1:11–3**

Conferences,
  Attorney discipline, prehearing conference, **Rule 1:20–5**
  Pretrial conference, withdrawal, **Rule 1:11–2**

Confidential or privileged information, **2A:84A–20; Evidence Rule 504**
  Advertising committee, **Rule 1:19A–5**
  Attorney trustee, protecting clients interest, suspension or death of attorney, **Rule 1:20–19**
  Bookkeeping records, **Rule 1:21–6**
  Client protection fund, claim information, **Rule 1:28–9**
  Client security fund, claim information, **Rule 1:28–9**
  Disciplinary proceedings, **Rule 1:20–9**
  Fee arbitration records, **Rule 1:20A–5**
  Financial records, production for audit or inspection, **Rule 1:21–6**
  Interest on lawyers trust accounts, **Rule 1:21–5**
  Lawyers assistance program, **Rule 1:28B–3**
  Public defenders, attorney client privilege, **2A:158A–12**
  Registration information, **Rule 1:20–1**
  Unauthorized practice of law committee, **Rule 1:22–1**

Confirmation of admission, **Rule 1:29–3**

Conflict of interest, limitation on practice, **Rule 1:15–1 et seq.**

Consent of client, withdrawal or substitution, **Rule 1:11–2**

Conspiracy, conviction, discipline, **Rule 1:20–13**

Constitutional challenges, disciplinary proceedings, **Rule 1:20–15**
  Review, **Rule 1:20–16**

Constructive notice, advisory opinions, advertising committee, **Rule 1:19A–3**

Consuls general or consular officers, **Rule 1:21–4**

Consultants, foreign countries, **Rule 1:21–9**

Contempt,
  Client protection fund, subpoena, noncompliance, **Rule 1:28–6**
  Subpoena, disciplinary proceedings, **Rule 1:20–3**

Contingent fees, **Rule 1:21–7**

Controlled dangerous substances,
  Conviction of crime, automatic temporary suspension, **Rule 1:20–13**
  Treatment, reinstatement to practice, **Rule 1:20–15A**

Conviction of crime, disciplinary proceedings, **Rule 1:20–16**

Corporations,
  In house counsel, limited licenses, admission to practice, **Rule 1:27–2**
  Practicing law, **Rule 1:21–1**
  Professional corporations, generally, post

Costs,
  Attorney Fees, generally, this index
  Disciplinary proceedings, **Rule 1:20–17**

Costs of disciplinary proceedings,
  Attorney trustee, **Rule 1:20–19**
  Reinstatement petition, **Rule 1:20–21**

Counsellor at law, abolishment of title, **Rule 1:21–5**

County Prosecutors, generally, this index

Court claims, contingent fees, **Rule 1:21–7**

Crimes and offenses,
  Appearance, **Rules 3:8–1, 3:8–2**
  Assignment of counsel, **Rule 3:4–2**

ATTORNEYS—Cont'd

Crimes and offenses—Cont'd
  Assignment of counsel—Cont'd
    Indigents, postconviction relief, **Rules 3:22–6, 3:22–6A**
  Compensation and expenses, **Rule 1:13–2**
  Conviction of crime, **Rule 1:20–13**
  Corporation, appearance by, **Rule 3:16**
  Documents, discovery, **Rule 3:13–3**
  Fees, depositions, **Rule 3:13–2**
  Filing appearance, **Rule 3:8–1**
  Health care claims fraud, **2C:21–4.2, 2C:21–4.3**
    Licenses and permits, suspension or revocation, **2C:51–5**
      Rehabilitation, order of debarment, rescission, **2C:27–1**
  Informing defendant of rights, **Rule 3:4–2**
  Joint representation, **Rule 3:8–2**
  Multidefendant representation, **Rule 3:8–2**
  Municipal judges or acting judges, practicing in criminal matters, **Rule 1:15–1**
  Notice, attorneys charged with crimes, **Rule 1:20–13**
  Plea discussion, **Rule 3:9–3**
  Pro hac vice appearances, foreign attorneys, **Rule 1:21–2**
  Right to counsel, generally, post
  Solicitation, disasters or accidents, **2C:40A–5**
  Surrogates, practice of law in criminal matters, **Rule 1:15–1**
  Unauthorized practice, **2C:21–22**
  Withdrawal or substitution, **Rule 1:11–2**
    Postconviction relief, assigned counsel, **Rule 3:22–6**
  Work product, discovery, **Rule 3:13–3**

Criminal trial attorneys, certification, **Rule 1:39–1 et seq.**

Custodial receivers, client protection fund, attorney misconduct, **Rule 1:28–8**

Damages,
  Contingent fees, **Rule 1:21–7**
  Lawyers fund for client protection, **Rule 1:28–1 et seq.**

Death,
  Appointment of attorney trustee to protect clients interest, **Rule 1:20–19**
  Limited liability company members, disposition of interest, **Rule 1:21–1B**
  Pending actions, notice to appoint another attorney, **Rule 1:11–1**

Default, student loans, **Rule 1:20–11B**

Default judgments, fees, arbitration hearing requested, **Rule 1:20A–3**

Defendants in criminal proceedings, investigation, office of attorney ethics, **Rule 1:20–2**

Defenses, disciplinary proceedings, answer to complaint, **Rule 1:20–4**

Definitions,
  Abuse of children, **9:6–8.21**
  Attorney client privilege, **Evidence Rule 504**
  Lawyer client privilege, **2A:84A–20**

Delegation of powers and duties, municipal prosecutors, private attorneys, **2B:25–5**

Deposits, bookkeeping records, **Rule 1:21–6**

Derivative actions, contingent fees, **Rule 1:21–7**

Directors,
  Office of attorney ethics, **Rules 1:20–1, 1:20–2**
  Professional corporations, **Rule 1:21–1A**

Disability inactive status, **Rule 1:20–12**
  Appointment of attorney trustee to protect clients interest, **Rule 1:20–19**
  Foreign states, reciprocal action, **Rule 1:20–14**
  Future activities, **Rule 1:20–20**

ATTORNEYS—Cont'd

Disability inactive status—Cont'd
  Practice of law prohibited, **Rule 1:20–16**
  Prohibited associations, **Rule 1:20–20**

Disasters,
  Solicitation, crimes and offenses, **2C:40A–5**
  Temporary practice of law, foreign states, **Rule 1:21–10**

Disbarment, **Rule 1:20–15A**
  Appointment of attorney trustee, protection of clients interest, **Rule 1:20–19**
  Client protection fund, **Rule 1:28–3**
    Custodial receivers, **Rule 1:28–8**
  Client representation or assistance, **Rule 1:21–1**
  Consent, **Rule 1:20–10**
  Noncompliance with determination or stipulation of settlement, **Rule 1:20–15**
  Pending proceedings, notice to appoint another attorney, **Rule 1:11–1**
  Practice of law prohibited, **Rule 1:20–16**
  Prohibited associations, **Rule 1:20–20**
  Review, **Rule 1:20–16**

Disbursement, trust accounts, suspension, disciplined attorneys, **Rule 1:20–20**

Disciplinary oversight committee, **Rules 1:20, 1:20B–1 et seq.**
  Establishment, **Rule 1:20–1**

Disciplinary review board, **Rules 1:20, 1:20–15**
  Establishment, **Rule 1:20–15**

Discipline, **Rule 1:20–1 et seq.**
  Advertising, grievances, **Rules 1:19A–2, 1:19A–4**
  Agreements in lieu of, **Rule 1:20–3**
  Annual fee, **Rule 1:20–1**
  Appeal and review,
    Action by supreme court, **Rule 1:20–16**
    Office of attorney ethics, **Rule 1:20–2**
    Petitions, **Rule 1:19–8**
    Review Board, **Rule 1:20–15**
    Right of appeal, time, **Rule 1:20–3**
  Categories, **Rule 1:20–15A**
  Censure, **Rule 1:20–15A**
  Certification, pro hac vice appearance, **Rule 1:21–2**
  Certified attorneys, **Rule 1:39–8**
  Complaints, **Rule 1:20–4**
  Confidential or privileged information, **Rules 1:20–9, 1:38–5**
  Consent, **Rule 1:20–10**
  Constitutional challenges, **Rule 1:20–15**
  Constitutional issues, review, **Rule 1:20–16**
  Conviction of crimes, **Rule 1:20–13**
  Disbarment, generally, ante
  Dismissal, **Rule 1:20–3**
  Financial records, failure to comply with requirements, **Rule 1:21–6**
  Findings, hearings involving misconduct, **Rule 1:20–6**
  Fines and penalties, **Rule 1:20–15**
  Future activities, **Rule 1:20–20**
  Glossary of terms, **Rule 1:20**
  Hearings, **Rule 1:20–6**
    Review Board, **Rule 1:20–15**
  Immunity from liability, participants in proceedings, **Rule 1:20–7**
  Interlocutory relief, **Rule 1:20–15**
  Investigations, office of attorney ethics, **Rule 1:20–2**
  Major disasters, temporary practice of law, foreign states, **Rule 1:21–10**
  Miscellaneous procedures, **Rule 1:20–7**
  Oral argument, post
  Pending proceedings, incapacity or disability, **Rule 1:20–12**

ATTORNEYS—Cont'd

Discipline—Cont'd

Pleadings,

Disciplinary proceedings, **Rule 1:20–4**

Frivolous litigation, **Rule 1:4–8**

Prehearing procedures, **Rule 1:20–5**

Priorities and preferences, **Rule 1:20–8**

Professional corporations, **Rule 1:21–1A**

Public discipline recommendation, **Rule 1:20–15**

Reciprocal discipline, **Rule 1:20–14**

Referral of matters by fee arbitration committee, **Rule 1:20A–4**

Reinstatement after, **Rule 1:20–21**

Reports, post

Resignation, continuing jurisdiction, **Rule 1:20–1**

Restraint on accounts, **Rules 1:20–16, 1:20–23**

Right to counsel, **Rule 1:20–4**

Sanctions, **Rule 1:20–15A**

Suspension from practice, generally, post

Temporary suspension, generally, post

Time limitations, initiation, **Rule 1:20–7**

Disclosure,

Attorney trustee, protection of clients interest following suspension, disbarment, death, **Rule 1:20–19**

Confidential information, disciplinary proceedings, **Rule 1:20–9**

Fee arbitration records, **Rule 1:20A–5**

Unauthorized practice of law committee, record, **Rule 1:22–1**

Discovery, disciplinary proceedings, **Rule 1:20–5**

Dishonest conduct, client protection fund, **Rule 1:28–1 et seq.**

Dishonored checks,

Administrative filing fee, arbitration of attorney fees, **Rule 1:20A–3**

Trust accounts, **Rule 1:21–6**

Disorderly persons, **2A:158A–5.2**

Dissenting reports, disciplinary review board, **Rule 1:20–15**

Dissolution, partnerships or professional corporations, maintenance of records, **Rule 1:21–6**

District ethics committees, **Rule 1:20–3**

Establishment, **Rule 1:20–1**

District fee arbitration committees, **Rule 1:20A–1 et seq.**

Establishment, **Rule 1:20–1**

DNA database and databank, right to counsel, motions, **2A:84A–32a**

Doctor patient privilege, waiver, disability inactive status, **Rule 1:20–12**

Drug addiction, disability inactive status, **Rule 1:20–12**

Drugs, conviction of crime, automatic temporary suspension, **Rule 1:20–13**

Education, attorney advertising, **Rule 1:19A–2**

Educational experience, certification, **Rule 1:39–2**

Embezzlement, lawyers fund for client protection, **Rule 1:28–1 et seq.**

Emergencies, temporary practice of law, foreign states, **Rule 1:21–10**

Employees, limitation on practice, exemptions, **Rule 1:15–4**

Ethics, **Rule 1:14**

Advertising committee, **Rule 1:19A–1 et seq.**

Courses of study, requirement for admission, **Rule 1:27–1**

Disciplinary oversight committee, **Rule 1:20–1**

District ethics committees, **Rule 1:20–3**

ATTORNEYS—Cont'd

Ethics—Cont'd

District ethics committees—Cont'd

Establishment, **Rule 1:20–1**

Gratuities, court officers and other public officials, **Rule 1:16–2**

Grievances, advertisements, **Rule 1:19A–4**

Jurors, interviewing subsequent to trial, **Rule 1:16–1**

Office of attorney ethics, **Rule 1:20–2**

Establishment, **Rule 1:20–1**

Referral, advertisements, **Rule 1:19A–7**

Professional ethics, advisory committee on, **Rule 1:19–1 et seq.**

Final actions, petitions for review of, **Rule 1:19–8**

Telephone research service, **Rule 1:19–9**

Special ethics masters, **Rule 1:20–6**

Evidence, standards, reinstatement, discipline, **Rule 1:20–21**

Expenses and expenditures,

Attorney trustee, reimbursement, **Rule 1:20–19**

Client protection fund trustees, **Rule 1:28–1**

Contingent fee arrangements, **Rule 1:21–7**

Lawyers assistance program, **Rule 1:28B–2**

Personal funds, indigent clients, **Rule 1:13–2**

Experience requirements, certification, **Rule 1:39–2**

Extortion, conviction, discipline, **Rule 1:20–13**

Failure to appear, sanctions, **Rule 1:2–4**

False swearing, conviction, discipline, **Rule 1:20–13**

Federal courts or agencies, limitation on practice, **Rule 1:15–5**

Fees. Attorney Fees, generally, this index

Fiduciaries, this index

Fiduciary accounts, maintaining separate accounts, **Rule 1:21–6**

Files and filing,

Appointment of attorney trustee, protection of clients interest, **Rule 1:20–19**

Criminal cases, appearance, **Rule 3:8–1**

Registration statements, **Rule 1:20–1**

Financial committee, **Rules 1:20–1, 1:27B–1 et seq.**

Financial records and accounts, **Rule 1:21–6**

Fines and penalties,

Disciplinary proceedings, **Rule 1:20–15**

Health care claims fraud, **2C:21–4.2, 2C:21–4.3**

Licenses and permits, suspension or revocation, **2C:51–5**

Rehabilitation, order of debarment, rescission, **2C:27–1**

Fingerprinting, bar examination applicants, **Rule 1:24–1**

Foreign legal consultants, **Rule 1:21–9**

Discipline, annual fee, **Rule 1:20–1**

Foreign states,

Deposition, taking not deemed making appearance, **Rule 1:21–1**

Major disasters, temporary practice of law, **Rule 1:21–10**

Practice of law, office, **Rule 1:21–1**

Pro hac vice appearance, **Rule 1:21–2**

Reciprocal discipline, **Rule 1:20–14**

Forfeitures, licenses and permits, health care claims fraud, **2C:51–5**

Fraud,

Conviction, discipline, **Rule 1:20–13**

Health care claims fraud, generally, post

Full time judges, practicing, **Rule 1:15–1**

Fund for client protection, fees, pro hac vice appearance, **Rule 1:21–2**

Grand Jury, this index

ATTORNEYS—Cont'd

Gratuities, court officers and employees or other governmental agency officials, **Rule 1:16–2**

Grievance,

Attorney advertising committee, **Rules 1:19A–2, 1:19A–4**

District ethics committee, **Rule 1:20–3**

Guardian and Ward, this index

Guidelines, advertising committee, **Rule 1:19A–2**

Health care claims fraud, **2C:21–4.2, 2C:21–4.3**

Licenses and permits, suspension or revocation, **2C:51–5**

Rehabilitation, order of debarment, rescission, **2C:27–1**

Hearings,

Advertising, grievance complaints, **Rule 1:19A–4**

Attorney discipline, **Rule 1:20–6**

Disciplinary review board, **Rule 1:20–15**

Fee arbitration, **Rule 1:20A–3**

Termination of certification, **Rule 1:39–8**

Illness, disability inactive status, **Rule 1:20–12**

Immigration and naturalization, unauthorized practice, **2C:21–31**

Immunities. Privileges and immunities, generally, post

Improprieties, admission to practice, tests and testing, **Rule 1:23–5**

In house counsel,

Admission to practice, limited licenses, **Rule 1:27–2**

Discipline, annual fee, **Rule 1:20–1**

Incapacity and disability, **Rule 1:20–12**

District ethics committees, investigation, **Rule 1:20–3**

Incompetent persons,

Contingent fee arrangements, **Rule 1:21–7**

Disability inactive status, **Rule 1:20–12**

Indemnity, professional corporations, **Rule 1:21–1A**

Indigent, neglected or abandoned children, appointment of counsel, juvenile family crisis, out of home placement hearings, **2A:4A–89**

Indigent persons, **Rule 3:4–2**

Complaints, discipline, **Rule 1:20–4**

Fees, waiver, **Rule 1:13–2**

Personal funds, expenditure, **Rule 1:13–2**

Representation by paralegals or legal assistants, **Rule 1:21–1**

Ineligibility to practice, list, lawyers client protection fund violations, **Rule 1:28–2**

Ineligible to practice law list, failure to pay discipline and fee arbitration assessment or file registration statement, **Rule 1:20–1**

Infants, contingent fee arrangements, **Rule 1:21–7**

Informal disposition, unauthorized practice of law, **Rule 1:22–5**

Injunctions, practice of law, disbarment, **Rule 1:20–16**

Injured clients, lawyers fund for client protection, **Rule 1:28–1 et seq.**

Interest on lawyers trust accounts fund, **Rules 1:21–6, 1:28A–1 et seq.**

Interference with administration of justice, conviction, discipline, **Rule 1:20–13**

Interlocutory review, disciplinary proceedings, **Rule 1:20–15**

Constitutional challenge, **Rule 1:20–16**

Interviewing jurors subsequent to trial, **Rule 1:16–1**

ATTORNEYS—Cont'd

Inventory, files, trust assets, attorney trustee, appointment to protect clients interest, suspension, disbarment, death, **Rule 1:20–19**

Investigations,
Advertising, grievances, **Rule 1:19A–4**
Defendants in criminal proceedings, **Rule 1:20–13**
District ethics committees, **Rule 1:20–3**
Incapacity and disability of attorney, **Rule 1:20–12**
Interviewing jurors subsequent to trial, **Rule 1:16–1**
Office of attorney ethics, **Rule 1:20–2**
Committee, **Rule 1:22–2**
Involuntary commitment, mental hospital, disability inactive status, **Rule 1:20–12**

IOLTA trust accounts, **Rules 1:21–6, 1:28A–2**
Registration statement, certification of compliance, **Rule 1:20–1**
Restraint on accounts, disciplinary proceedings, **Rules 1:20–16, 1:20–23**

Joinder, third party attorney or law firm, arbitration determination, **Rule 1:20–3**

Joint and several liability, frivolous litigation, **Rule 1:4–8**

Joint representation, criminal defendants, **Rules 3:8–2, 7:7–10**

Judges and Justices, generally, this index

Judicial conference, membership, **Rule 1:35–1**

Jurisdiction,
Attorney advertising committee, **Rule 1:19A–2**
District fee arbitration committees, **Rule 1:20A–2**

Jurors, interviewing subsequent to trial, **Rule 1:16–1**

Jury commissioners, attorneys assigned to, practice of law, **Rule 1:15–2**

Juvenile Delinquents, this index

Lapse, certificates and certification, **Rule 1:39–8**

Late fee,
Client protection fund, **Rule 1:28–2**
Registration, **Rule 1:20–1**

Law, unauthorized practice, crimes and offenses, **2C:21–22**

Law school teachers, admission to practice, **Rule 1:27–3**

Law students, appearance, **Rules 1:21–1, 1:21–3**

Lawyers assistance program, **Rule 1:28B–1 et seq.**

Lawyers fund for client protection, **Rule 1:28–1 et seq.**

Leave of court, withdrawal or substitution, **Rule 1:11–2**

Ledger books, **Rule 1:21–6**

Legal aid societies, appearance by law graduates or students, **Rule 1:21–3**

Legal assistants, representation of indigents, **Rule 1:21–1**

Legal services corporations or projects,
Appearance by law students or graduates, **Rule 1:21–3**
Practicing law, **Rule 1:21–1**

Liability insurance,
Limited liability companies, **Rule 1:21–1B**
Limited liability partnerships, **Rule 1:21–1C**
Professional corporations, **Rule 1:21–1A**

Licenses and permits,
Health care claims fraud, suspension or revocation, **2C:51–5**
Rehabilitation, order of debarment, rescission, **2C:27–1**
Requirement for practice, **Rule 1:21–1**

ATTORNEYS—Cont'd

Licenses and permits—Cont'd
Revocation or suspension, registration, filing, **Rule 1:20–1**
Suspension from practice, generally, post

Limitation on practice, **Rule 1:15–1 et seq.**

Limited certification, effect, **Rule 1:21–3**

Limited liability entities,
IOLTA accounts, **Rule 1:28A–2**
Practice of law, **Rules 1:21–1, 1:21–1B, 1:21–1C**
Limitation on practice, exemptions, **Rule 1:15–4**
Pro hac vice appearances, **Rule 1:21–2**

Limited licenses, in house counsel, admission to practice, **Rule 1:27–2**

List, attorneys ineligible to practice, lawyer client protection fund violations, **Rule 1:28–2**

Loans, student loans, suspension from practice, default, **Rule 1:20–11B**

Major disasters, temporary practice of law, foreign states, **Rule 1:21–10**

Malfeasance, lawyers fund for client protection, **Rule 1:28–1 et seq.**

Malpractice insurance, professional corporations, **Rule 1:21–1A**

Master of superior court, abolishment of title, **Rule 1:21–5**

Matrimonial law attorneys, certification, **Rule 1:39–1 et seq.**

Mentally deficient and mentally ill persons,
Contingent fee arrangements, **Rule 1:21–7**
Disability inactive status, **Rule 1:20–12**
Treatment, reinstatement to practice, **Rule 1:20–15A**

Military forces duty, client protection fund, exemption from payment, **Rule 1:28–2**

Minor misconduct, hearings involving, **Rule 1:20–6**

Minor unethical conduct, determination, **Rule 1:20–3**

Minors, contingent fee arrangements, **Rule 1:21–7**

Misappropriation of funds,
Conviction, discipline, **Rule 1:20–13**
Lawyers fund for client protection, **Rule 1:28–1 et seq.**

Misrepresentation,
Conviction, discipline, **Rule 1:20–13**
Immigration and naturalization, unauthorized practice, **2C:21–31**

Missing owners, trust funds, **Rule 1:21–6**

Monopolies and unfair trade, hearings and inquiries, right to attorney, **56:9–9**

Motions,
Criminal defendants, joint representation, **Rule 3:8–2**
Signatures, **Rules 1:4–5, 1:4–8**

Motor vehicle commission, legal representation, **39:2A–25**

Multijurisdictional practice,
Discipline, annual fee, **Rule 1:20–1**
Office of attorney ethics, **Rule 1:20–2**

Multiple party actions, contingent fees, **Rule 1:21–7**

Municipal court judges, practicing, **Rule 1:15–1**

Municipal Courts, this index

Names,
Change of name, **Rules 1:29–2, 1:29–3**
Limited liability companies and partnerships, **Rules 1:21–1B, 1:21–1C**
Professional corporations, **Rule 1:21–1A**

Naturalization and immigration, unauthorized practice, **2C:21–31**

ATTORNEYS—Cont'd

Negligence, lawyers fund for client protection, **Rule 1:28–1 et seq.**

Newly admitted attorneys, exception from client protection fund, **Rule 1:28–2**

Nonattorneys, appearances, **Rule 1:21–1**

Nonresidents,
Practice of law, **Rules 1:21–1, 1:21–3**
Pro hac vice appearance, **Rule 1:21–2**

Notice,
Application for reinstatement, **Rule 1:20–21**
Appointment of another attorney, death, removal or disbarment, **Rule 1:11–1**
Certification,
Denial or termination of certification, review, **Rule 1:39–9**
Termination of certification, **Rule 1:39–8**
Withholding, **Rule 1:39–5**
Change of address or telephone number, **Rule 1:4–1**
Crimes and offenses, charging attorney with, **Rule 1:20–13**
Disciplinary proceedings, **Rule 1:20–9**
Fee arbitration committee, reactivation of fee disputes, **Rule 1:20A–4**
Hearings involving misconduct, **Rule 1:20–6**
Disciplined attorneys, future activities, **Rule 1:20–20**
Dismissal, inactive cases, **Rule 1:13–7**
Fee arbitration hearings, **Rule 1:20A–3**
Naming new attorney, **Rule 1:11–3**
Nonresidents practicing in state, revocation or suspension of permission, **Rule 1:21–3**
Recovery of fee from client, option to pursue fee arbitration remedy, **Rule 1:20A–6**
Referral to enforcement agency, unauthorized practice of law, **Rule 1:22–6**
Temporary practice of law, foreign states, major disasters, **Rule 1:21–10**
Unauthorized practice of law decisions, appeals from, **Rule 1:22–3A**
Withdrawal or substitution, **Rule 1:11–2**

Oaths and affirmations, admission to practice, **Rule 1:27–4**
Authorization of administration, **Rule 1:27–1**

Office, maintaining, requirement for practice, **Rule 1:21–1**

Office of attorney ethics, **Rules 1:20–1, 1:20–2**

Office of disciplinary review board counsel, **Rule 1:20–15**

Opinions, advisory opinions, unauthorized practice of law committee, **Rules 1:22–2, 1:22–3**

Oral argument, discipline,
Conviction of crime, **Rule 1:20–13**
Disciplinary review board, **Rule 1:20–15**
Supreme court review, **Rule 1:20–16**

Orders, pro hac vice appearance, **Rule 1:21–2**

Out of state address, appearing on pleadings, **Rule 1:4–1**

Out of state attorneys, certificates of good standing, **Rule 1:21–3**

Paralegals, representation of indigents, **Rule 1:21–1**

Partnerships,
Certified attorneys, use of designation, **Rule 1:39–6**
Disciplined attorneys, **Rule 1:20–20**
Dissolution, maintenance of records, **Rule 1:21–6**
IOLTA accounts, **Rule 1:28A–2**
Limitation on practice, exemptions, **Rule 1:15–4**
Limited liability entities, generally, ante

ATTORNEYS—Cont'd
Partnerships—Cont'd
Professional corporations with other professional corporations or attorneys, **Rule 1:21–1A**
Relationship of judge, disqualification, **Rule 1:12–1**
Peace corps, client protection fund, exemption from payment, **Rule 1:28–2**
Pending Actions and Proceedings, this index
Personal service, **Rule 1:5–2**
Petitions,
Reinstatement after final discipline, **Rule 1:20–21**
Review, final actions of advisory committee on professional ethics, **Rule 1:19–8**
Physical incapacity, **Rule 1:20–12**
Physician patient privilege, waiver, application for transfer to disability inactive status, **Rule 1:20–12**
Pleadings,
Addresses, **Rule 1:4–1**
Signatures, post
Poor persons, public defenders, **2A:158A–1 et seq.**
Practice of law, **Rule 1:21–1 et seq.**
Admission to practice, generally, ante
Clerks of court, **Rule 1:15–2**
County prosecutors, **Rule 1:15–3**
Deputy clerks of court, **Rule 1:15–2**
Disbarment, generally, ante
Judges, **Rule 1:15–1**
Limitation on practice, **Rule 1:15–1 et seq.**
Office of attorney ethics, **Rule 1:20–2**
Reinstatement to practice, generally, post
Sheriffs, **Rule 1:15–3**
Surrogates, **Rule 1:15–1**
Prehearing procedures, attorney discipline, **Rule 1:20–5**
Preliminary investigations, unauthorized practice of law, **Rule 1:22–4**
Prepublication review, advertising, **Rule 1:19A–2**
Pretrial Conferences, this index
Priorities and preferences, discipline, **Rule 1:20–8**
Privileged information. Confidential or privileged information, generally, ante
Privileges and immunities,
Advertising committee, **Rule 1:19A–6**
Attorney client privilege, **2A:84A–20**
Attorney trustee, appointment to protect clients interest following death, suspension, disbarment, **Rule 1:20–19**
Bar examiners board, **Rule 1:23–3**
Character committee, **Rule 1:23–3**
Client protection fund, trustees, **Rule 1:28–1**
Disciplinary proceedings, participants, **Rule 1:20–7**
Fee arbitration authorities, **Rule 1:20A–5**
Lawyers assistance program, **Rule 1:28B–4**
Unauthorized practice of law committee proceedings, **Rule 1:22–7**
Pro hac vice, **Rule 1:21–2**
Payment, client protection fund, **Rule 1:28–2**
Probation departments, attorneys assigned to, practice of law, **Rule 1:15–2**
Process, generally, this index
Production of books and papers,
Client protection fund, **Rule 1:28–6**
Fee arbitration hearings, **Rule 1:20A–3**
Financial records, **Rule 1:21–6**
Products liability claims, contingent fees, **Rule 1:21–7**

ATTORNEYS—Cont'd
Professional conduct rules, **Rule 1:14**
Foreign legal consultants, application, **Rule 1:21–9**
Professional corporations, **Rule 1:21–1A**
Dissolution, maintenance of records, **Rule 1:21–6**
Financial records and accounts, **Rule 1:21–6**
IOLTA accounts, **Rule 1:28A–2**
Limitation on practice, exemptions, **Rule 1:15–4**
Pending proceedings, assumption of status of corporation or dissolution of corporation, substitution of attorney, **Rule 1:11–2**
Pro hac vice appearance, **Rule 1:21–2**
Professional ethics, advisory committee, **Rule 1:19–1 et seq.**
Telephone research service, **Rule 1:19–9**
Prohibited associations, **Rule 1:20–20**
Proof of service, **Rule 1:5–3**
Public Defenders, generally, this index
Public discipline recommendations, **Rules 1:20–3, 1:20–15**
Publication, disciplinary proceedings, **Rule 1:20–15**
Published opinions, advertising committee advisory opinions, **Rule 1:19A–3**
Qualifications, certification, **Rule 1:39–2**
Random audit compliance program, office of attorney ethics, **Rule 1:20–2**
Receipts and disbursements journals, required bookkeeping records, **Rule 1:21–6**
Receivers, this index
Reciprocal discipline, **Rule 1:20–14**
Records and recordation,
Bookkeeping records, **Rule 1:21–6**
Confidentiality,
Advertising committee, **Rule 1:19A–5**
Disciplinary proceedings, **Rule 1:20–9**
Disciplinary hearings, review by Supreme court, **Rule 1:20–16**
Disciplinary review board, **Rule 1:20–15**
Ethics, advertising and solicitation, telephone research service, **Rule 1:19–9**
Fee arbitration, confidentiality, **Rule 1:20A–5**
Financial records and accounts, **Rule 1:21–6**
Office of attorney ethics, **Rule 1:20–2**
Out of state attorneys, association with, fees and expenses, **Rule 1:21–6**
Unauthorized practice of law, committees, **Rule 1:22–1**
Referral to enforcement agency, unauthorized practice of law, **Rule 1:22–6**
Registration,
Disciplinary oversight committee, furnishing financial account information, **Rule 1:21–6**
Filing, **Rule 1:20–1**
Financial committee, failure to file, **Rule 1:27–1**
Major disasters, temporary practice of law, foreign states, **Rule 1:21–10**
Regulations, disciplinary review board, recommendation, **Rule 1:20–15**
Reimbursement, costs, disciplinary proceedings, **Rule 1:20–17**
Reinstatement to practice,
After final discipline, **Rule 1:20–21**
Conditions, **Rule 1:20–15A**
Disability inactive status, **Rule 1:20–12**
Nonsupport of dependents, suspension for, **Rule 1:20–11A**
Student loans, default, **Rule 1:20–11B**
Tardy client protection fund payment, **Rule 1:28–2**

ATTORNEYS—Cont'd
Renewal of certification, **Rule 1:39–7**
Reports,
Admission to practice, persons passing bar exam, **Rule 1:27–1**
Advertising committee, **Rule 1:19A–2**
Attorney certification board, grant of certification, **Rule 1:39–5**
Client protection fund, attorneys failing to comply, **Rule 1:28–2**
Discipline,
Certificates and certification, **Rule 1:39–6**
Applicants, **Rule 1:39–2**
Hearings involving misconduct, **Rule 1:20–6**
Investigation, **Rule 1:20–3**
Prehearing report, **Rule 1:20–5**
Supervisors of disciplined attorneys, **Rule 1:20–18**
Lawyers assistance program, **Rules 1:28B–2, 1:28B–3**
Trust accounts, instruments presented against insufficient funds, **Rule 1:21–6**
Trusts and trustees, suspension, disbarment, death, protection of clients interest, **Rule 1:20–19**
Reprimand, **Rule 1:20–15A**
Private reprimand, **Rule 1:20–2**
Resignation,
Client protection fund, **Rule 1:28–3**
Custodial receivers, **Rule 1:28–8**
Disciplinary jurisdiction, **Rule 1:20–1**
Pending proceedings, notice to appoint another attorney, **Rule 1:11–1**
Without prejudice, **Rule 1:20–22**
Restoration to practice. Reinstatement to practice, generally, ante
Restraint on accounts, disciplinary proceedings, **Rules 1:20–16, 1:20–23**
Retention of another attorney, **Rule 1:11–3**
Review. Appeal and review, generally, ante
Revocation or suspension, licenses and permits, registration, filing, **Rule 1:20–1**
Right to counsel,
Abuse of children proceedings, **9:6–8.23, 9:6–8.43**
Assignment, **Rule 3:4–2**
Postconviction relief, **Rules 3:22–6, 3:22–6A**
Attorney disciplinary proceedings, **Rule 1:20–4**
Depositions, attorney fees, **Rule 3:13–2**
DNA database and databank, motions, **2A:84A–32a**
Informing defendant, **Rule 3:4–2**
Investigative detention, orders, hearings, **Rule 3:5A–3**
Juvenile Delinquents, this index
Lie detector tests, employees, **2C:40A–1**
Municipal courts,
First appearance, **Rule 7:3–2**
Waiver, **Rule 7:8–10**
Municipal prosecutors, **2B:25–5**
Postconviction relief, assignment, **Rules 3:22–6, 3:22–6A**
Withdrawal, assigned counsel, postconviction relief, **Rule 3:22–6**
Rule of professional conduct, **Rule 1:14**
Rules of court, fee schedule, motor vehicle tort claim arbitrations, **39:6A–28**
Sanctions, **Rule 1:20–15A**
Screening, district ethics committees, **Rule 1:20–3**
Settlement, contingent fees in structured settlements, **Rule 1:21–7**

ATTORNEYS—Cont'd

Shares and shareholders,
    Disciplined attorneys, **Rule 1:20–20**
    Professional corporations, **Rule 1:21–1A**
Sheriffs, practice of law, **Rule 1:15–3**
Signatures,
    Pleadings, motions and briefs, **Rule 1:4–5**
        Effect of signature, **Rule 1:4–8**
        Proof of service, **Rule 1:5–3**
        Typing or stamping name beneath signature, **Rule 1:4–6**
    Trust accounts, authorized signatory, **Rule 1:21–6**
Skills and methods course, requirement for admission, **Rule 1:21–1**
Soliciting disorderly persons, **2A:158A–5.2**
Special master, commissioner or examiner of Superior court, abolishment of title, **Rule 1:21–5**
Standards, evidence, reinstatement, discipline, **Rule 1:20–21**
Stipulations, fee arbitration, **Rule 1:20A–3**
Structured settlements, contingent fees, **Rule 1:21–7**
Student loans, suspension from practice, default, **Rule 1:20–11B**
Subpoenas,
    Advertising, grievance hearings, **Rule 1:19A–4**
    Client protection fund, **Rule 1:28–6**
    Disciplinary proceedings, **Rule 1:20–7**
        Investigation, **Rule 1:20–3**
    Fee arbitration hearings, **Rule 1:20A–3**
    Financial records, **Rule 1:21–6**
    Inspection of objects designated in subpoena, **Rule 1:9–2**
    Issuance in name of clerk, **Rule 1:9–1**
Substitution of attorney, **Rule 1:11–2**
    Death, removal, disbarment or withdrawal, **Rule 1:11–1**
Summary actions, fee arbitration, stipulations, **Rule 1:20A–3**
Supersedeas or stay, interlocutory review, disciplinary proceedings, constitutional challenge, **Rule 1:20–16**
Supervision, disciplined attorneys, **Rules 1:20–15A, 1:20–18**
Support of persons, failure to maintain, disciplinary action, **Rule 1:20–11A**
Supreme court review, disciplinary recommendations, **Rule 1:20–16**
Suspension from practice, **Rule 1:20–15A**
    Appointment of attorney trustee, protection of clients interest, **Rule 1:20–19**
    Certified attorneys, **Rule 1:39–8**
    Client protection fund, **Rule 1:28–3**
    Client representation or assistance, **Rule 1:21–1**
        Custodial receivers, **Rule 1:28–8**
    Conviction of crime, **Rule 1:20–13**
    Indeterminate suspension, **Rule 1:20–15A**
    Noncompliance with determination or stipulation of settlement, **Rule 1:20–15**
    Nonsupport of dependents, **Rule 1:20–11A**
    Pending proceedings, notice to appoint another attorney, **Rule 1:11–1**
    Prohibited associations, **Rule 1:20–20**
    Reinstatement after, **Rule 1:20–21**
    Review, **Rule 1:20–16**
    Student loans, default, **Rule 1:20–11B**
    Temporary suspension, generally, post
Term, **Rule 1:20–15A**
Telephone inquiries, supervisory committee, **Rules 1:19–9, 1:19A–8**
Telephone number, change, notice to court, **Rule 1:4–1**

ATTORNEYS—Cont'd

Temporary attorney trustees, **Rule 1:20–19**
Temporary practice of law, major disasters, foreign states, **Rule 1:21–10**
Temporary suspension, **Rule 1:20–11**
    Conviction of crime, **Rule 1:20–13**
    Disciplinary review board, **Rule 1:20–15**
    Failure to pay disciplinary costs, **Rule 1:20–17**
    Review of recommendation, **Rule 1:20–16**
    Student loans, default, **Rule 1:20–11B**
Termination of certification, **Rule 1:39–8**
Termination of responsibility, trial, **Rule 1:11–3**
Tests and testing, admission to practice, improprieties, **Rule 1:23–5**
Theft, conviction, discipline, **Rule 1:20–13**
Third party attorney or law firm, fee dispute arbitration, potential liability, **Rule 1:20A–3**
Time,
    Certificates and certification, tolling, **Rule 1:39–5**
    Discipline, **Rule 1:20–8**
Transcripts, disciplinary proceedings, **Rule 1:20–7**
Trial attorneys, certification, **Rule 1:39–1 et seq.**
Trust accounts, **Rule 1:21–6**
    Banks, record keeping, **Rule 1:21–6**
    Client funds, interest, **Rule 1:28A–2**
    Disbursement, suspension, disciplined attorneys, **Rule 1:20–20**
    Restraint on, disciplinary proceedings, **Rules 1:20–15A, 1:20–16, 1:20–23**
Trusts and trustees,
    Appointment of attorney trustee, protection of clients interest, **Rule 1:20–19**
    Client protection fund, **Rule 1:28–1**
    Duties, **Rules 1:28–4, 1:28–5**
    Lawyers assistance program, **Rule 1:28B–1 et seq.**
    Unidentifiable and unclaimed funds, **Rule 1:21–6**
Unauthorized practice,
    Committees, **Rule 1:22–1 et seq.**
    Crimes and offenses, **2C:21–22**
    Immigration and naturalization, **2C:21–31**
Unethical conduct,
    Determination, **Rule 1:20–3**
    Hearings involving, **Rule 1:20–6**
Unidentifiable and unclaimed trust funds, **Rule 1:21–6**
United States courts or agencies,
    Limitation on practice, **Rule 1:15–5**
    Staff attorneys, practice of law, **Rule 1:21–1**
Verification, answer, complaint, discipline, **Rule 1:20–4**
Vista, client protection fund, exemption from payment, **Rule 1:28–2**
Voir dire examination, **Rule 1:8–3**
Waiver, doctor patient privilege, disability inactive status, request for restoration, **Rule 1:20–12**
Withdrawal, **Rule 1:11–2**
    Assigned counsel, postconviction relief, **Rule 3:22–6**
    Client from fee arbitration proceeding, **Rule 1:20A–3**
    Disciplinary proceedings, **Rule 1:20–6**
    Notice to appoint new attorney, **Rule 1:11–1**
Witnesses, disciplinary hearings, immunity from liability, **Rule 1:20–7**
Work product, discovery, crimes and offenses, **Rule 3:13–3**
Workers Compensation Law, certification, **Rule 1:39–1 et seq.**

ATTORNEYS—Cont'd

Wrongful death claims, joinder with claim on behalf of decedent, contingent fees, **Rule 1:21–7**

AUCTIONS AND AUCTIONEERS
Motor Vehicles, this index

AUDIOVISUAL MATERIALS
Piracy, **2C:21–21**

AUDITS AND AUDITORS
Attorneys, this index
Client protection fund, **Rule 1:28–4**
Interest on lawyers trust account fund, **Rule 1:28A–3**
Motor carriers,
    Intermodal transportation, chassis, facilities, **39:3–79.18**
    Operational accounts, **39:3–6.18**
Motor vehicle commission, **39:2A–22**
Motor vehicles, apportioned vehicle and International Registration Plan, supersedure, **39:3–6.19**

AURAL TRANSFER
Definitions, wiretapping and electronic surveillance, **2A:156A–2**

AUTHENTICATION OF EVIDENCE
Generally, **Evidence Rules 901, 902**

AUTHORITIES
Definitions,
    Speed, sixty five mph, implementation, **39:4–98.4**
    Toll collection monitoring system, turnpike authority, **27:23–34.1**
Highway authority. Turnpike Authority, generally, this index
Motor vehicles, sale of abandoned and unclaimed vehicles, **39:10A–1 et seq.**
Turnpike Authority, generally, this index

AUTHORIZED EMERGENCY VEHICLES
Definitions, traffic laws, **39:1–1**

AUTHORSHIP
Criminal simulation, **2C:21–2**

AUTO BODY REPAIR FACILITIES
Generally, **39:13–1 et seq.**
Definitions, proof of repair, **39:13–8**

AUTO OR VESSEL
Definitions, vehicular homicide, **2C:11–5**

AUTO THEFT
Theft, this index

AUTOBUSES
Buses, generally, this index

AUTOMATED TRAFFIC SYSTEM
Autonomous computer system, interconnection, use by municipality, **2B:12–30**
Fund,
    Court cost assessments, deposit, use by municipality, **2B:12–30, 2B:12–31**
    Creation, **2B:12–30**
    Legislative declaration and purpose, **2B:12–30**

AUTOMATED TRAFFIC SYSTEM STATEWIDE MODERNIZATION FUND
Generally, **2B:12–30.1**

AUTOMATIC RIFLES
Weapons, generally, this index

AUTOMOBILE FULL INSURANCE UNDER-WRITING ASSOCIATION
Motor Vehicle Insurance, this index

AUTOMOBILE INSURANCE
Motor Vehicle Insurance, generally, this index

AUTOMOBILE INSURANCE COST REDUCTION ACT
Generally, 39:6A–1.1 et seq.
Motor Vehicle Insurance, this index

AUTOMOBILE INSURANCE RISK EXCHANGE
Generally, 39:6A–21, 39:6A–22

AUTOMOBILE REPARATION REFORM ACT
Generally, 39:6A–1 et seq.

AUTOMOBILES
Motor Vehicles, generally, this index

AVALANCHES
Causing or risking widespread injury or damage, 2C:17–2
Criminal mischief, 2C:17–3

AVIATION
Credit card offenses, tickets, 2C:21–6
Interference with transportation, 2C:33–14
Landing fields. Airports and Landing Fields, generally, this index
Theft, 2C:20–2
Unlawful taking, 2C:20–10
Visual distress signaling devices on aircraft, 2C:39–6, 2C:58–3, 2C:58–10
Weapons exemption, 2C:39–6
Weapons on aircraft, visual distress signaling devices, 2C:39–6, 2C:58–3, 2C:58–10

AVIATION FIELDS
Airports and Landing Fields, generally, this index

AVIGATION AND AVIGATION FACILITIES
Airports and Landing Fields, generally, this index

AWARDS
Arbitration and Award, generally, this index
Chosen freeholders authority to offer, criminal procedure, 2A:153–2, 2A:153–3

BABIES
Children and Minors, generally, this index

BACCARAT
Casinos, generally, this index

BACK UP LAMPS
Motor vehicles, 39:3–52
Color, 39:3–50

BACKGROUND CHECKS
Criminal History Record Information, generally, this index

BACKING VEHICLES
Traffic Rules and Regulations, this index

BAD CHECKS
Generally, 2C:21–5

BADGES, EMBLEMS AND INSIGNIA
Animal welfare license plates, 39:3–27.55
Battleship U.S.S. New Jersey license plates, 39:3–27.67 et seq.
Coastal protection license plates, 39:3–27.48
Emergency medical technician ambulance, special license plates, 39:3–27.59
Identification Cards, generally, this index
Law enforcement officers, unauthorized transfer, 2C:21–2.2
Silver star medal recipients special registration plates, 39:3–27.45
Transfer, law enforcement officers, 2C:21–2.2
Tree of life, special license plates, emergency medical technician ambulance, 39:3–27.59

BAIL
See, also, Recognizances, generally, this index
Generally, Rule 3:26–1 et seq.
Acceptance, Rule 1:13–3
Affidavits,
Cash bail submitted by person other than defendant, Rule 3:26–4
Cash deposit in lieu of, 2A:162–9
Agents and agencies, service of process, Rule 1:13–3
Appeals in criminal prosecutions, custodial sentence, relief pending appeal, Rule 3:23–5
Approval, Rule 1:13–3
Arrest on warrant, Rule 3:4–1
Authority to admit to or set, Rule 3:26–2
Municipal courts, Rule 7:4–2
Before conviction, Rule 3:26–1 et seq.
Body cavity searches, persons unable to post bail, 2C:161A–8
Bonds (officers and fiduciaries), acceptance, Rule 1:13–3
Bonds secured by real property, requirements, crime with bail restrictions, 2A:162–12
Capital punishment,
Failure to indict, admitting to bail, Rule 3:26–1
Person punishable by, failure to indict, Rule 3:26–1
Cash deposit, Rule 3:26–4
Affidavit, 2A:162–9
Crime with bail restrictions, 2A:162–12
Municipal courts, Rule 7:4–3
Central automated bail system, Rule 3:26–4
Character and reputation, obligor, hearings, sufficiency, 2A:162–13
Clerks of court, bond, acceptance, Rule 1:13–3
Conditions,
Release of nonresident driver of motor vehicle involved in accident, 39:7–7
Satisfaction, exoneration, satisfaction, Rule 3:26–7
Contact, children and minors, conditions, Rule 3:26–1
Contempt,
Jumping, 2C:29–7
Persons charged, Rule 1:10–2
Continuance, probable cause hearing, Rule 3:4–3
Controlled dangerous substances, revocation, injunctions, 2C:35–5.8
Crime with bail restrictions, definitions, certain offenses, 2A:162–12
Crimes committed during release on, notice to impose sentence, Rule 3:21–4
Deposits,
Municipal courts, Rule 7:4–3
Place, form, Rule 3:26–4
Ten percent cash bail, Rule 3:26–4

BAIL—Cont'd
Deputy clerk, taking of bail under motor vehicle and traffic laws, 39:5–6
Director of division of motor vehicles, enforcement of bail bond by, 39:5–9
Discharge,
Forfeiture, Rule 3:26–4
Municipal courts, Rule 7:4–3
Probable cause, hearing, Rule 3:4–3
Disorderly Persons, this index
Domestic violence, release before trial, bail, 2C:25–26
Evidence,
Application of rules, Evidence Rule 101
Jumping, 2C:29–7
Exoneration, Rule 3:26–7
Municipal courts, Rule 7:4–6
Expunged records, use in setting, 2C:52–21
Extradition, this index
Failure to indict, Rule 3:26–1
Fines and penalties, defendant released on bail, 2C:44–5.1
Forfeitures, Rule 3:26–6
Deduction of costs and fees, motor vehicle violations, 39:5–9
Discharge, Rule 3:26–4
Fugitive arrested before requisition made, 2A:160–26
Motor vehicle and traffic violation prosecutions, 39:5–9
Municipal courts, Rules 7:4–3, 7:4–5
Disposition, 2C:46–4
Recognizances, Rule 3:26–5
Forms,
Crime with bail restrictions, cash, surety bond, 2A:162–12
Information, money, source, 2A:162–13
Place of deposit, Rule 3:26–4
Registration, insurers, Rule 1:13–3
Fresh pursuit, person arrested by officer of another state, 2A:155–5
Hearings,
Source, Rule 3:26–8
Sufficiency, 2A:162–13
Homicide, cash, crime with bail restrictions, 2A:162–12
Imposition of sentence, pending, Rule 3:21–4
Individual surety, limitation, Rule 3:26–4
Information, money, source, 2A:162–13
Initial set, Rule 3:26–2
Indictable offenses, Rule 3:4–1
Judgments and decrees,
Forfeitures, municipal courts, Rule 7:4–5
Registry, insurers, removal, Rule 1:13–3
Jumping bail, 2C:29–7
Jury trial, waiver, Rule 1:13–3
Justification, sureties, Rule 3:26–5
Municipal courts, Rule 7:4–4
Juvenile delinquents and dependents, 2A:4A–40
Kidnapping, cash, crime with bail restrictions, 2A:162–12
Minor offenses, 2C:6–1
Money, source, hearings, sufficiency, 2A:162–13
Motions,
Enforcement, bond, Rule 1:13–3
Reduction of bail, first motion, Rule 3:26–2
Municipal Courts, this index
Notice,
Forfeiture, Rule 3:26–6
Municipal courts, Rule 7:4–5
Removal, registry, insurers, Rule 1:13–3
Sentence and punishment, crimes committed while out on bail, Rule 3:21–4
Objections and exceptions, forfeitures, municipal courts, Rule 7:4–5
Obligors, reliability, hearings, 2A:162–13

BAIL—Cont'd
Other counties, real estate, **Rule 3:26–4**
Parole, cash, crime with bail restrictions,
 2A:162–12
Petty offenses, **2C:6–1**
Place of deposit, **Rule 3:26–4**
 Municipal courts, **Rule 7:4–7**
Postconviction, municipal courts, **Rule 7:4–8**
Probable cause hearing, continuance, **Rule 3:4–3**
Real estate,
 Location, **Rule 3:26–4**
 Municipal courts, **Rule 7:4–3**
Recognizances, record of, **Rule 3:26–4**
Records,
 Municipal courts, **Rule 7:4–3**
 Recognizance, discharge, forfeiture, **Rule 3:26–4**
Reduction, first motion, **Rule 3:26–2**
Registration,
 Forms, insurers, **Rule 1:13–3**
 Removal, forfeitures, **Rule 3:26–6**
Relationships, obligors, reliability, hearings,
 2A:162–13
Release,
 Exoneration, **Rule 3:26–7**
 Recognizance, **Rule 3:26–1**
Reliability, obligors, hearings, **2A:162–13**
Relief pending appeal, custodial sentence, **Rule 3:23–5**
Removal, registry, insurers, **Rule 1:13–3**
Revision, municipal courts, **Rule 7:4–2**
Sentence and punishment, defendant released on bail, **2C:44–5.1**
Service of process, bonds, agent for service, **Rule 1:13–3**
Sex offenses, victims of crime, injunctions, **2C:14–12**
Sexual assault, cash, restrictions, **2A:162–12**
Signature, execution, recognizance, **Rule 3:26–4**
Source,
 Disclosure, **Rule 3:26–1**
 Hearings, **Rule 3:26–8**
Strip searches, persons unable to post bail, **2A:161A–8**
Sufficiency, hearings, **2A:162–13; Rule 3:26–8**
Sureties, justification, **Rule 3:26–5**
Suspended sentence or probation, new offenses, **2C:45–3**
Ten percent cash bail, **Rule 3:26–4**
Traffic rules and regulations,
 Forfeiture of bail, **39:5–9**
 Nonresident drivers, release, **39:7–7**
 Taking of bail by clerk or deputy clerk authorized, **39:5–6**
Vacating or setting aside, forfeitures, **Rule 3:26–6**
Witnesses, **Rule 3:26–3**
 Commitment, failure to appear, deposition, **Rule 3:13–2**

BAILMENT
Commercial motor vehicle, violation of weights and measurements law, fines, **39:3–84.3**

BAITING ANIMALS
Cruelty to animals, **4:22–24**

BALLISTIC KNIVES
Definitions, **2C:39–1**
Manufacturer, transport, disposition and defacement, **2C:39–9**
Person convicted of crime involving, possession of any weapon prohibited, **2C:39–7**
Prohibited weapons, **2C:39–3**

BALLOTS
County clerks, municipal referendum on hours of retail sales, **33:1–44 et seq.**

BANK DEPOSITS AND COLLECTIONS
Currency transactions, reports, money laundering and illegal investments, **2C:21–25**
Money Laundering and Illegal Investments, generally, this index
Receiving deposits in failing institutions, **2C:21–14**
Reports, cash transactions, money laundering and illegal investments, **2C:21–25**

BANKING DIRECTOR
Insurance, generally, this index

BANKRUPTCY
Fraud in insolvency, **2C:21–13**
Unsatisfied Claim and Judgment Fund Law, discharge in bankruptcy as not relieving person from penalties and liabilities under act, **39:6–87**

BANKS AND BANKING
Accounts and accounting, terrorism, freezing, **2C:66–1 et seq.**
Bonds. Investments, post
Cash transactions, reports, money laundering and illegal investments, **2C:21–25**
Contests, hearings, terrorism, funds, freezing, **2C:66–5**
Crimes and offenses, tear gas, **2C:39–6**
Currency, transactions, reports, money laundering and illegal investments, **2C:21–25**
Debit cards. Electronic Fund Transfers, generally, this index
Electronic Fund Transfers, generally, this index
Forfeitures, state, terrorism, funds, freezing, **2C:66–6**
Freezing, funds, terrorism, **2C:66–1 et seq.**
Funds, freezing, terrorism, **2C:66–1 et seq.**
Hearings, contests, terrorism, funds, freezing, **2C:66–5**
Investments, bonds, turnpike authority, **27:23–13**
Misapplication of entrusted property, **2C:21–15**
Money Laundering and Illegal Investments, generally, this index
Monopolies and unfair trade, exemptions, **56:9–5**
Motor vehicle insurance, impounded vehicles, release, **39:3–40.6**
Motor vehicles, impounding, release, **39:3–40.6**
Notice, terrorism, funds, freezing, **2C:66–8**
Orders of court, terrorism, funds, freezing, **2C:66–3**
Person, Alcoholic Beverage Law, **33:1–1**
Port authority of New York and New Jersey, bonds. Investments, ante
Privileges and immunities, terrorism, funds, freezing, **2C:66–10**
Receiving deposits in failing institution, **2C:21–14**
Reports, cash transactions, money laundering and illegal investments, **2C:21–25**
State, forfeiture, terrorism, funds, freezing, **2C:66–6**
Tear gas, unlawful possession, exemptions, **2C:39–6**
Teller machines. Electronic Fund Transfers, generally, this index
Terrorism, accounts and accounting, freezing, **2C:66–1 et seq.**
Weapons, security guards, possession, **2C:39–6**

BAPTISMAL CERTIFICATES
Hearsay exception, **Evidence Rule 803**

BAR
Attorneys, generally, this index

BAR ADMISSIONS ADVISORY COMMITTEE
Generally, **Rules 1:27A–1, 1:27A–2**

BAR ADMISSIONS FINANCIAL COMMITTEE
Generally, **Rule 1:27B–1 et seq.**

BAR ASSOCIATIONS AND LAWYERS CLUBS
Judicial conference, rules of evidence, membership, **2A:84A–34**

BAR EXAMINATIONS
Attorneys, this index

BAR EXAMINERS BOARD
Generally, **Rules 1:23–1, 1:23–2**
Confidential or privileged information, files and records, **Rule 1:23–3**
Funding, **Rule 1:23–4**

BARBITAL
Generally, **24:21–1 et seq.**

BARBITURIC ACID
Controlled substances, **24:21–1 et seq.**

BARGES
Vessels, generally, this index

BARNEGAT BAY DECOY AND BAYMENS MUSEUM
Special licenses plates, funding, **39:3–27.86 et seq.**

BARRELS
Intoxicating liquors, distributors license, **33:1–11**

BARRICADED
Definitions, Explosives Act, **21:1A–129**

BARROOM
Definitions, **33:1–12.23**

BARTER
Poisoned liquors, **33:3–9, 33:3–10**

BASIC AUTOMOBILE INSURANCE POLICY
Definitions, no fault insurance, **39:6A–2**

BATTERED CHILDREN
Child Abuse, generally, this index

BATTERED PERSONS
Domestic Violence, generally, this index

BATTERY
Assault and Battery, generally, this index

BEACHES AND BEACH FRONTS
Adopt a beach program, appropriations, **39:3–27.52**
Coastal protection license plate program, **39:3–27.47 et seq.**

BEACONS
Traffic signals, **39:4–118, 39:4–119**

BEER
Alcoholic Beverages, this index

BELLS
Sleighbells, **39:4–15**
Vehicles, use on other than emergency vehicles prohibited, **39:3–69**

BENEFIT CARD
Definitions, food stamps, crimes and offenses, **2C:20–35**

BENEFIT DERIVED
Definitions, crimes and offenses, **2C:21–8.1**

BENEFIT OF CLERGY
Abolished, **2A:152–2**

BENEVOLENT ORGANIZATIONS AND IN-STITUTIONS
Fraternal Organizations, generally, this index

BENZETHIDINE
Controlled substances, **24:21–1 et seq.**

BENZYLMORPHINE
Controlled substances, **24:21–1 et seq.**

BERM
Definitions, traffic regulations, **39:1–1**

BEST EVIDENCE
Generally, **Evidence Rule 1001 et seq.**

BESTIALITY
Children and minors, second degree crime, **2C:24–4**

BETACETYLMETHADOL
Controlled substances, **24:21–1 et seq.**

BETAMEPRODINE
Controlled substances, **24:21–1 et seq.**

BETAMETHADOL
Controlled substances, **24:21–1 et seq.**

BETAPRODINE
Controlled substances, **24:21–1 et seq.**

BETTING
Gambling, generally, this index

BEVERAGES
Alcoholic Beverage Tax, generally, this index
Alcoholic Beverages, generally, this index
Motor vehicle commission, concessions, contracts, **39:2A–33**

BEZITRAMIDE
Controlled substances, **24:21–1 et seq.**

BIAS
Discrimination, generally, this index

BIAS INTIMIDATION
Crimes and offenses, **2C:16–1**

BICYCLE PATHS
Electric personal assistive mobility devices, operation, **39:4–14.10**

BICYCLES
Arrest, equipment violations, **39:4–14.9**
Brake, **39:4–11.1**
Carrying another person prohibited, **39:4–12**
Children and minors,
　Fines and penalties, **39:4–203.3, 39:4–203.4**
　Pedestrian violations, fines and penalties, **39:4–203.3, 39:4–203.4**

BICYCLES—Cont'd
Definitions, **39:4–14.5**
　Helmet requirements, **39:4–10.1**
Drivers licenses, motorized bicycles, **39:4–14.3**
　Suspension or revocation of license, **39:5–30**
　Minors, **39:4–14.3h**
Equipment,
　Application of law, **39:4–14.6**
　Definitions, **39:4–14.5**
　Enforcement of act, **39:4–14.9**
　Fines and penalties, **39:4–14.8**
　Rules and regulations, **39:4–14.7**
Exemptions, sale or rental, **39:4–14.6**
Fines and penalties,
　Collection, **39:4–14.9**
　Equipment, **39:4–14.8**
　Helmets,
　　Failure to wear, **39:4–10.2**
　　Notification violations, **39:4–10.3**
　Violation of statute, **39:4–203**
　　Minors, **39:4–203.3, 39:4–203.4**
Funds, bicycle and skating safety fund, **39:4–10.2**
Hands or feet of rider not to be removed from bicycle, **39:4–12**
Helmets, **39:4–10.1 et seq.**
　Notice, affixation to bicycle, **39:4–14.7a**
　Requirements,
　　Notice, **39:4–10.3**
　　Violations, **39:4–10.2**
　Rules and regulations, promotion, **39:4–14.4a**
　Statement promoting use, **39:4–14.4a, 39:4–14.7a**
Hitching on to vehicles, prohibited, **39:4–14**
Law enforcement officers, **39:4–14.1**
Left turns, **39:4–14.2**
Lights, **39:4–10, 39:4–14.4**
　Application of law, **39:4–14.6**
Motorized Bicycles, generally, this index
Nighttime, lights and reflectors, **39:4–10**
Operation, roadways, **39:4–14.2**
Passing vehicle, **39:4–14.2**
Penalties.　Fines and penalties, generally, ante
Process, equipment violations, **39:4–14.9**
Reflectors, **39:4–10, 39:4–14.4**
Rentals,
　Exemptions, **39:4–14.6**
　Lights, **39:4–14.4**
Right side of roadway, **39:4–14.2**
Rights and duties of bicycle rider, **39:4–14.1**
Rules and regulations, **39:4–10.4**
　Bicycles helmets, promotion, **39:4–14.4a**
Sales,
　Exemptions, **39:4–14.6**
　Lights, **39:4–14.4**
Second and subsequent offenses, equipment violations, **39:4–14.8**
Signals, audible signal required, **39:4–11**
　Sirens or whistles on prohibited, **39:3–69**
Special bicycle paths, use, **39:4–14.2**
Summary proceedings, equipment, enforcement of law, **39:4–14.9**
Trick or fancy riding prohibited, **39:4–12**
Two abreast, **39:4–14.2**
Unlawful taking, **2C:20–10**
Venue, equipment, enforcement of law, **39:4–14.9**
Wrong side of roadway, operating on, **39:4–14.2**

BIDS AND BIDDING
Bribery and corruption, effect of conviction, **2C:51–2**
Government contracts, conviction of crime, **2C:51–2**

BIDS AND BIDDING—Cont'd
Motor vehicle commission, ancillary services, contracts, **39:2A–33**
Turnpike authority, contracts, **27:23–6.1**

BIG SIX WHEEL
Casinos, generally, this index

BIGAMY
Generally, **2C:24–1**

BIKES
Bicycles, generally, this index
Motorcycles, generally, this index

BILL OF PARTICULARS
Generally, **Rule 3:7–5**
Alibi defense, crimes and offenses, **Rule 3:12–2**

BILLBOARDS
Outdoor Advertising, generally, this index

BILLIES
Weapons, generally, this index

BILLS
Statutes, generally, this index

BINDERS
Motor vehicle liability policy issued under motor vehicle security responsibility law, **39:6–48**

BIOLOGICAL WARFARE AND WEAPONS
Terrorism, **2C:38–2, 2C:38–3**

BIRDS
Fish and Game, generally, this index
Shooting at, crimes and offenses, **4:22–23**

BIRTH CERTIFICATES
Crimes and offenses, false certificates, **2C:21–2.1, 2C:21–17.2**
False certificates, crimes and offenses, **2C:21–2.1, 2C:21–17.2**
Immigration and naturalization, improper retention, crimes and offenses, **2C:21–31**
Sales, false certificates, crimes and offenses, **2C:21–2.1**

BIRTHDATES
Crimes and offenses, discovery, **Rule 3:13–3**

BIRTHS
Certificates and certification.　Birth Certificates, generally, this index
Records and recordation.　Birth Certificates, generally, this index

BISEXUALITY
Discrimination, generally, this index

BISQUE TORTONI
Frozen Desserts and Dietary Foods, generally, this index

BLACK POWDER
Turnpike project, transportation regulation, **27:23–31**

BLACKJACK
Casinos, generally, this index
Weapons, generally, this index

BLACKMAIL
Generally, **2C:20–2, 2C:20–5**

BLANKS
Application for registration for private utility and house type semitrailers and trailers, **39:3–8**

BLASTING
Explosives, generally, this index

BLENDED DISTILLED LIQUORS
Presumption, fitness for beverage purposes and alcoholic content, **33:1–1.1**

BLENDED WINE
Presumption, fitness for beverage purposes and alcoholic content, **33:1–1.1**
Wholesalers license, **33:1–11**

BLENDING
Crimes and offenses, alcoholic beverages, **33:1–50**

BLIND PERSONS
Guide dogs, right of way, **39:4–37.1**
Identification cards for nondrivers, **39:3–29.3**
Validity for life, **39:3–29.5**
Motor Vehicles, this index
Right of way, crossing highways or intersections, **39:4–37.1**

BLOCKS
Motor vehicle tire projections, **39:3–81**

BLOOD
DNA Database and Databank, generally, this index

BLUDGEONS
Weapons, generally, this index

BOARD OF CHOSEN FREEHOLDERS
Chosen Freeholders, generally, this index

BOARD OF COMPACT ADMINISTRATORS
Nonresident Violator Compact, motor vehicles, **39:5F–15 et seq.**

BOARD OF DIRECTORS
Directors, generally, this index

BOARDING SCHOOL
Child Care Centers, generally, this index

BOARDS AND COMMISSIONS
Administrative Law and Procedure, generally, this index
Adult offender supervision interstate commission, **2A:168–28 et seq.**
Alcoholism and promotion of temperance, **33:4–1**
Attorneys, this index
Boards of education. Schools and School Districts, this index
Child fatality and near fatality review board, **9:6–8.88 et seq.**
Chosen Freeholders, generally, this index
Criminal sentencing and disposition commission, **2C:48A–1 et seq.**
Definitions,
Adult offender supervision, interstate compacts, **2A:168–27**
Comprehensive Child Abuse Prevention and Treatment Act, **9:6–8.84**
Controlled substances, **24:21–2**
Explosives Act, **21:1A–129**
Flammable fabrics, **2A:123–3**
Intoxicating liquor law, **33:1–1**
Juvenile justice, **2A:4A–22**

BOARDS AND COMMISSIONS—Cont'd
Definitions—Cont'd
Liquefied petroleum gas education and safety board, **21:1B–1**
Motor vehicles, **39:1–1**
Unsatisfied claim and judgment fund, **39:6–62**
Registration and regulation of snowmobiles and all terrain vehicles, **39:3C–1**
Unsatisfied claim and judgment fund, **39:6–62**
Unsatisfied Claim and Judgment Fund Law, **39:6–62**
Water pollution control, **58:10A–3**
Directors, professional corporations, **Rule 1:21–1A**
Disciplinary review board, attorneys, **Rule 1:20**
Higher education. Colleges and Universities, generally, this index
Interstate compacts, Nonresident Violator Compact, motor vehicles, board of compact administrators, **39:5F–15 et seq.**
Judicial evaluation commission, **Rule 1:35A–4**
Juvenile justice commission, contracts, use of countys juvenile detention facility, **2A:4A–44.1**
Liquefied petroleum gas education and safety board, **21:1B–12 et seq.**
Monopolies and unfair trade exemptions, **56:9–5**
Motor Vehicle Commission, generally, this index
Municipalities, this index
Nonresident Violator Compact, motor vehicles, board of compact administrators, **39:5F–15 et seq.**
Oaths and Affirmations, generally, this index
Reflectorized license plate selection commission, **39:3–33.9**
Schools and School Districts, this index
Street Railways, this index
Transportation. Transportation Department, generally, this index
Unsatisfied claim and judgment fund board, abolishment, transfer of powers and duties, property liability insurance guaranty association, **39:6–64c**

BOARDWALKS
Bicycles, operation, helmets, **39:4–10.1**

BOATS AND BOATING
See, also, Vessels, generally, this index
Federal boating safety laws, state police, powers and duties, **53:2–1**
State police, powers and duties, **53:2–1**
Theft, **2C:20–2**
Unlawful taking, **2C:20–10**
Vessels, generally, this index
Visual distress signaling devices, **2C:39–6, 2C:58–3, 2C:58–10**
Weapons, visual distress signaling devices, **2C:39–6, 2C:58–3, 2C:58–10**

BODIES
Dead Bodies, generally, this index

BODILY FLUIDS
Definitions, aggravated assault by inmates, throwing bodily fluids, **2C:12–12**

BODILY INJURY
Assault, **2C:12–1**
Burglary, threat to inflict bodily injury, **2C:18–2**
Coercion, **2C:13–5**
Consent of victim, **2C:2–10**

BODILY INJURY—Cont'd
Crime resulting in bodily injury, conviction, assessment, victims of crime compensation board, **2C:43–3.1**
Criminal coercion, threat to inflict bodily injury, **2C:13–5**
Definitions,
Crimes and offenses, endangering injured victim, **2C:12–1.2**
Homicide, **2C:11–1**
Extortion, threat of bodily injury, **2C:20–5**
Firearms and other explosive devices, reports, **2C:58–8**
Force, use to prevent, **2C:3–7**
Kidnapping, **2C:13–1**
Rape, **2C:14–1**
Reasonable fear of, course of conduct creating, stalking, **2C:12–10**
Robbery, **2C:15–1**
Serious bodily injury,
Definitions, justification, **2C:3–11**
Rape, **2C:14–1**
Robbery, **2C:15–1**
Sexual assault, **2C:14–2**
Sodomy, **2C:14–2**
Stalking, reasonable fear, course of conduct creating, **2C:12–10**
Use of force to prevent, **2C:3–7**

BODY ARMOR
Body Armor Replacement fund, fines and penalties, deposits, **39:5–41**
Crimes and offenses, **2C:39–13**

BODY ARMOR PENETRATING BULLETS
Person convicted of crime involving, possession of any weapon prohibited, **2C:39–7**
Possession, **2C:39–3**

BODY CAVITY SEARCH
Generally, **2A:161A–1 et seq.**
Definitions, **2A:161A–3**

BODY PIERCING
Children and minors, consent, **2C:40–21**

BODY REPAIR FACILITIES
Motor vehicles, **39:13–1 et seq.**

BOMBS
Explosives, generally, this index

BONA FIDE PURCHASERS
Stock transfer. Shares and Shareholders, generally, this index

BONDED WAREHOUSES
Alcoholic Beverage Tax, this index

BONDS
Foreclosure actions, pleadings, copies annexed to complaints, **Rule 1:4–3**
Turnpikes, this index

BONDS (OFFICERS AND FIDUCIARIES)
Acceptance, approval by court, **Rule 1:13–3**
Alcoholic Beverages, this index
Approval by court, **Rule 1:13–3**
Bail, **Rule 1:13–3**
Cash deposit, **Rule 1:13–3**
Client protection fund treasurer, **Rule 1:28–4**
Enforcement, **Rule 1:13–3**
Fireworks, this index
Flammable fabrics, confiscation proceedings, **2A:123–10**
Forfeited property, release pending determination, **2C:64–3**

BONDS (OFFICERS AND FIDUCIARIES)
—Cont'd
Jurisdiction, **Rule 1:13–3**
Jury trial, waiver, **Rule 1:13–3**
Motor vehicle division director, **39:2–2**
Motor Vehicles, this index
Municipal Courts, this index
Nonresidents, traffic violations, **39:5F–1 et seq.**
Recreational vehicles, off site sales, licenses
    and permits, **39:10–19.3**
State Treasurer, this index
Sufficiency, approval by court, requirement for
    acceptance, **Rule 1:13–3**

BOOBY TRAPS
Controlled substances, property used for manu-
    facture, distribution or possession, crimes
    and offenses, **2C:35–4.1**

BOOKMAKING
Definitions, **2C:37–1**
Fines and penalties, **2C:37–2**

BOOKS AND PAPERS
Captions, pleadings, **Rule 1:4–1**
Clerks of court, **Rule 1:32–2**
Crimes and offenses, discovery, **Rule 3:13–3**
Electronic retention, **Rule 1:32–2**
Filing, **Rule 1:5–6**
Format, **Rule 1:4–9**
Identity theft, personal identifying information,
    2C:21–17.3
Inspection and Inspectors, this index
Libraries, generally, this index
Microfilming, **Rule 1:32–2**
Municipal courts, judges, **Rule 1:32–2**
Searches and seizures, **Rule 3:5–2**
Service, **Rule 1:5–1 et seq.**
Size, **Rule 1:4–9**
Transfer of actions, **Rule 1:13–4**
Weight, **Rule 1:4–9**

BOROUGHS
    See, also, Municipalities, generally, this index
Civil Service, generally, this index
Housing, generally, this index
Officers and employees. Civil Service, general-
    ly, this index
Turnpike authority, power to acquire property,
    27:23–5

BOTTLES
Crimes and offenses, intoxicating liquors,
    33:1–50
Licenses and permits,
    Bonded warehouse, **33:1–10**
    Intoxicating liquors, **33:1–78**

BOUNDARIES
Reputation, hearsay exception, **Evidence Rule
    803**

BOWLING ALLEYS
Intoxicating liquors,
    Additional licenses, Chain Store Liquor Li-
        cense Act, **33:1–12.32**
    License to sell, **33:1–12**

BOXES
Containers, generally, this index

BOY SCOUTS
Motor vehicles, fees for registration, **39:3–27**

BOYCOTT
Coercion, **2C:13–5**

BOYCOTT—Cont'd
Criminal coercion, threat to bring about or
    continue a boycott, **2C:13–5**
Extortion, threat to bring about or continue
    boycotts, **2C:20–5**

BOYS CLUBS OF AMERICA
Motor vehicles, registration fee exemption,
    39:3–27

BRAKES
Motor Vehicles, this index

BRANDS, LABELS AND MARKS
Adulterated commodities, deceptive business
    practices, **2C:21–7**
Alcoholic Beverages, this index
Alteration or removal, shoplifting, **2C:20–11**
Ambulances, removal, sales, **39:10–9.4**
Construction and design, **39:3–33**
Controlled substances, **24:21–16, 24:21–17**
    Offenses and penalties, **24:21–21**
Counterfeiting, **39:3–38**
Crimes and offenses, counterfeiting, **39:3–38**
Curbs and curbing, parking prohibitions,
    39:4–191.2
Deceptive business practices, mislabeled or
    adulterated commodities, **2C:21–7**
Definitions, food and drugs, **24:21–32**
Drugs and Medicine, this index
Emergency vehicles, removal, sales, **39:10–9.4**
Exhibits, verbatim record of proceedings, **Rule
    1:2–3**
Fireworks, packages, **21:2–15, 21:2–36**
Food, this index
Identification marks, display, **39:3–33**
Lanes for passing, movement of traffic regulat-
    ed, **39:4–88**
Location on vehicle, **39:3–33**
Motor Vehicles, this index
Motorcycles, manufacturers and manufactur-
    ing, certificates and certification, safety,
    39:3–76.3a
Omnibus registration, markers, **39:3–19**
Packages, fireworks, **21:2–36**
Portable oil burning heating devices, **2C:40–7,
    2C:40–8**
Requirements, **39:3–33**
Safety glazing material, motor vehicles, manu-
    facturers designation, **39:3–75**
Shoplifting, alteration or removal, **2C:20–11**
Solid Waste, this index
Trademarks and Trade Names, generally, this
    index
Traffic, **39:4–191.1 et seq.**
Visibility, **39:3–33**

BRANDY
Alcoholic Beverages, generally, this index

BRASS KNUCKLES
Person convicted of crime involving, possession
    of any weapon prohibited, **2C:39–7**
Possession, **2C:39–3**

BREACH OF PEACE
Arrest,
    County bridge police, **27:19–36.3**
    Detective associations, **15:4–4**
County bridge police, authority to arrest,
    27:19–36.3
Detective associations, arrest of offenders,
    15:4–4
Force, use to prevent, **2C:3–7**

BREAKING AND ENTERING
Burglary, generally, this index

**BREAKING AND ENTERING WITH INTENT
    TO COMMIT RAPE**
Rape, generally, this index

BREEDING
Animals, generally, this index

BREWERIES
Alcoholic Beverages, this index

BRIBERY AND CORRUPTION
Generally, **2C:27–1 et seq.**
Abuse of office, **2C:30–2 et seq.**
Attorneys, conviction, discipline, **Rule 1:20–13**
Cease and desist orders, racketeering, **2C:41–4**
Commercial bribery, **2C:21–10**
Compensation and salaries, past official behav-
    ior, limitation of criminal prosecutions,
    2C:1–6
Confidential or privileged information, racke-
    teering investigations, **2C:41–5**
Conviction, effect, **2C:51–2**
Debtors and creditors, racketeering, **2C:41–1 et
    seq.**
Defenses, **2C:27–2**
Definitions, **2C:27–1**
    Funds, **2C:27–12**
    Racketeering, **2C:41–1**
    State property, **2C:27–12**
Discovery, racketeering investigations, **2C:41–5**
Disqualification, public office, **2C:51–2**
Elections, **2C:27–2**
Evidence, public resources, **2C:27–12**
Examinations and examiners, racketeering,
    2C:41–5
Fines and penalties,
    Profits, **2C:30–8**
    Public office, **2C:51–2**
    Racketeering, **2C:41–1 et seq.**
Forfeitures, proceeds, **2C:64–1**
    Public office, **2C:51–2**
    Racketeering, **2C:41–3 et seq.**
Fraud, public resources, **2C:27–12**
Funds, **2C:27–12**
Good cause, profiteering penalty, payment,
    2C:30–8
Indebtedness, racketeering, **2C:41–1 et seq.**
Inspections and inspectors, racketeering inves-
    tigations, **2C:41–5**
Interrogatories, racketeering, investigations,
    2C:41–5
Investigations and investigators, racketeering,
    2C:41–5
Investments, racketeering, **2C:41–1 et seq.**
Judgments and decrees, racketeering, **2C:41–4**
Judicial notice, profits, **2C:30–8**
Jury, **2C:29–8**
Licenses and permits, racketeering, revocation
    or suspension, **2C:41–4**
Limitation of criminal prosecutions, **2C:1–6**
Misconduct in office, **2C:30–2 et seq.**
Motor vehicles, body repair facilities, bribery of
    adjusters or appraisers, fine or license re-
    fusal, revocation, or suspension, **39:13–4**
Official and political matters, **2C:27–2**
Official matters, **2C:27–2, 2C:27–3, 2C:30–2**
    Limitation of criminal prosecutions, **2C:1–6**
Past official behavior, compensation, limitation
    of criminal prosecutions, **2C:1–6**
Political matters, **2C:27–2, 2C:27–3**
    Limitation of criminal prosecutions, **2C:1–6**
Presumptions, public resources, **2C:27–12**
Process, racketeering, **2C:41–5**
Production of books and papers, racketeering,
    2C:41–5
Profits, fines and penalties, **2C:30–8**

BRIBERY AND CORRUPTION—Cont'd
Public resources, 2C:27–12
Public servants,
Assisting private interests, limitation of prosecutions, 2C:1–6
Gifts, limitation of prosecutions, 2C:1–6
Racketeering, 2C:41–1 et seq., 2C:41–4
Records and recordation, racketeering, investigations, 2C:41–5
Restitution, racketeering, 2C:41–4
Retaliation for past official actions, 2C:27–5
Securities, racketeering, 2C:41–1 et seq.
State property, 2C:27–12
Threats, official and political matters, 2C:27–3
Witnesses and informants, tampering, 2C:28–5

BRIDGE TENDERS
County bridges and viaducts, police powers, 27:19–13

BRIDGES AND VIADUCTS
Counties,
Bridge tenders, police powers, 27:19–13
Police, appointment and powers, 27:19–36.3
County bridge commission, police, appointment, 27:19–36.3
Damages,
Overweight vehicles injuring, 39:4–75, 39:4–76
Posting bridge for less weight limits than those set forth in law, 39:3–84.4
Fines and penalties, overweight vehicles, interstate bridges, 39:4–76
Interstate bridges and tunnels, driving overweight vehicles on, penalty and damages, 39:4–76
Loads and Loading, this index
Movable span bridge, care required of motorist when gate or barrier is closed, 39:4–127.2
Moving heavy machinery, damages, 39:4–27
Municipalities, overweight vehicles, liability for driving over municipally owned bridge, 39:4–75
Obstruction, willful interference with other vehicles, 39:4–56.1 et seq.
Overweight vehicles driven over, penalty and liability for damages, intrastate bridge, 39:4–75, 39:4–76
Parking prohibited, 39:4–138
Police, appointment, county bridge commission, 27:19–36.3
Weight of vehicles, interstate bridges, fines and penalties, 39:4–76

BRIDLE PATHS
Motor vehicle and traffic laws, application, 39:5A–1 et seq.

BRIEFS
Amicus curiae, Rule 1:13–9
Answering brief, service and filing, Rule 1:6–5
Appeal and review,
Amicus curiae, Rule 1:13–9
Attorney disciplinary proceedings, review, Rules 1:20–15, 1:20–16
Professional ethics, advisory committee on, petition for review, Rule 1:19–8
Unauthorized practice of law decisions, Rule 1:22–3A
Appeals in criminal prosecutions, Rule 3:23–8
Limited criminal jurisdiction, courts of, appeals from orders, Rule 3:24
Crimes and offenses,
Limited criminal jurisdiction, courts of, orders, appeals, Rule 3:24
Service, Rule 1:5–1 et seq.

BRIEFS—Cont'd
Date of signature, Rule 1:4–5
Failure to comply with requirements, sanctions, Rule 1:2–4
Format, Rule 1:4–9
Leave of court, submitting after expiration of time, Rule 1:6–5
Limited criminal jurisdiction, courts of, appeals, Rule 3:23–8
Motions, failure to comply with requirements, Rule 1:2–4
Place of filing, Rule 1:6–5
Process, Rules 1:5–1 et seq., 1:6–5
Professional ethics, advisory committee, inquiries, Rule 1:19–3
Reading in advance of hearing, judges, Rule 1:6–7
Respondents brief, unauthorized practice of law, appeal of decisions, Rule 1:22–3A
Sanctions, failure to comply with requirements, Rule 1:2–4
Searches and seizures, motions, suppression of evidence and return of property, Rule 3:5–7
Signatures, Rule 1:4–5
Effect of signature, Rule 1:4–8
Names typed or stamped beneath, Rule 1:4–6
Suppression of evidence, municipal courts, Rule 7:5–2
Time,
Answering brief, service and filing, Rule 1:6–5
Service and filing, Rule 1:6–5

BROADCASTING
Radio and Radio Stations, generally, this index
Television, generally, this index

BROKEN GLASS
State highways, prohibition against placing on highways, penalties, 27:7–44

BROKEN SUCCESSION OF TITLE
Definitions, theft, 2C:20–1

BUDGETS
Motor Vehicle Commission, this index
State budget, coastal protection trust fund, request for appropriation, 39:3–27.52
Turnpike authority, report, 27:23–3.2

BUFOTEMINE
Controlled substances, 24:21–1 et seq.

BUILDING CODE
Omissions, criminal liability, 2C:2–1

BUILDING INSPECTORS
Liquefied petroleum gas, 21:1B–3

BUILDINGS
Alarms, false alarms, 2C:33–3 et seq.
Alcoholic Beverages, this index
Arson, 2C:17–1
Bombs, false or facsimile, 2C:33–3 et seq.
Burglary, generally, this index
Collapse,
Causing or risking widespread injury or damage, 2C:17–2
Criminal mischief, 2C:17–3
Controlled substances,
Crimes and offenses, 2C:35–7.1
Nuisances, 24:21–35
Crimes and offenses, controlled dangerous substances, 2C:35–7.1
Criminal trespass, 2C:18–3

BUILDINGS—Cont'd
Definitions,
Controlled substances, crimes and offenses, 2C:35–7.1
Intoxicating liquor law, 33:1–1
Explosives, distances and quantity, manufacturing and storage, 21:1A–135
False public alarms, 2C:33–3 et seq.
Fireworks, 21:2–7
Garages, generally, this index
Housing, generally, this index
Keys, state buildings, distribution and possession, 2C:5–7
Libraries, generally, this index
Liquefied petroleum gas, inspections, 21:1B–3
Nuisance, this index
Places of worship, desecration, 2C:33–9
Religious Corporations and Associations, this index
Sale, radon gas test results, providing purchaser, 26:2D–73
School Buildings and Grounds, generally, this index
Smoking, 2C:33–13
Terroristic threats, 2C:12–3

BULK PLANTS
Definition, liquefied petroleum gas, 21:1B–1

BULLETPROOF VESTS
Unlawful use, 2C:39–13

BULLETS
Ammunition, generally, this index

BUNDLES
Throwing or dropping from vehicle on highway prohibited, 39:4–64

BURDEN OF PROOF
See, also, Presumptions, generally, this index
Attorneys, this index
Belief of defendant that conduct did not constitute an offense, 2C:2–4
Civil actions under Criminal Code, 2C:1–13
Conspiracy, renunciation of purpose, 2C:5–2
Controlled substances,
Dealers, liability, 2C:35B–12
Exemptions, 24:21–37
Crimes and Offenses, this index
Defendants statements, preliminary hearing on admissibility, Evidence Rule 104
Drugs and medicine, controlled substances, exemptions or exceptions, 24:21–37
Entrapment, 2C:2–12
Gambling records, possession, 2C:37–3
Insanity defense, 2C:4–1
Mentally deficient and mentally ill persons, insanity defense, acquittal, continued commitment, 2C:4–1
Preponderance of evidence, civil actions under Criminal Code, 2C:1–13
Renunciation of criminal purpose, 2C:5–1
Termination of complicity by renunciation, 2C:2–6

BUREAU OF ALCOHOL, TOBACCO AND FIREARMS (UNITED STATES)
Arrests, violations of state law, special agents, 2A:154–5

BUREAU OF IDENTIFICATION
Identification Bureau, generally, this index

BURGLARS TOOLS
Generally, 2C:5–5

BURGLARY
Generally, 2C:18–1 et seq., 2C:18–2
Aggravated criminal sexual contact, 2C:14–3
Aggravated sexual assault, 2C:14–2
Arrest,
Force or violence, grand jury, instructions to jury, 2B:22–9
Use of deadly force, 2C:3–7
Warrants, issuance, **Rule 3:3–1**
Without warrant, release, **Rule 3:4–1**
Attempts, body vests, 2C:39–13
Body vests, 2C:39–13
Burglars tools, 2C:5–5
Criminal coercion, threat to expose damaging material, 2C:13–5
Definitions, 2C:18–1, 2C:18–2
Extended term of imprisonment, 2C:43–7, 2C:43–7.1
Force or violence, arrest, grand jury, instructions to jury, 2B:22–9
Homicide, felony murder, sentence and punishment, 2C:11–3
Jurors, peremptory challenges, **Rule 1:8–3**
Jury, number of peremptory challenges, 2B:23–13
Murder, felony murder, sentence and punishment, 2C:11–3
Reward for apprehension and conviction of burglar, 2A:153–1, 2A:153–2, 2A:153–4
Search warrants, alcoholic beverages, execution, 33:1–58
Terrorism, 2C:38–2
Weapons, possession,
Convictions, 2C:39–7
Mandatory sentence, 2C:43–6

BURNING
Arson and Other Burnings, generally, this index
Fires and Fire Protection, generally, this index

BURNS
Injuries, reports by physicians, 2C:58–8

BUSES
Aggravated assault, drivers, 2C:12–1
Air pollution, contaminants, 39:3–70.1, 39:3–70.2
Arrest, driver for traffic laws violated in presence of officer, 39:5–25
Certified copies, resolutions, stops or stations, 39:4–8
Classified licensing, 39:3–10
Counties, resolutions, stops or stations, 39:4–8
Definitions, 39:1–1
Dimensions, maximum width and length, 39:3–84
Doors to be closed, 39:4–68
Drivers, aggravated assault, 2C:12–1
Drivers licenses, 39:3–10.1
Classified licensing, 39:3–10
Emergency warning devices, portable, 39:3–64
Examination permits, 39:3–13
Fees,
Drivers licenses, 39:3–10
Registration, reduced fees, 39:3–22a
Fines and penalties,
Air pollution, 39:3–70.2
Hours of service violation, 39:9–4
Operators, certificates of public convenience or necessity, failure to have, 39:3–79.22 et seq.
Registration, failure to obtain, 39:3–19.1
Flaps, mud flaps, 39:3–79.1 et seq.
Flares or other emergency warning light equipment, 39:3–64

BUSES—Cont'd
Funds, omnibus safety enforcement fund,
Motor vehicle commission, 39:3–79.24
Treasury department, 39:3–79.23
Group charter buses, smoking in public, 2C:33–13
Highjack lights, 39:3–54
Hotels and Motels, this index
Hours of duty of drivers, 39:9–2 et seq.
Interference, 2C:33–14
Jitneys, 2C:33–14
Interstate buses,
Drivers licenses, 39:3–10.1
Operators, drivers licenses, 39:3–10.1
Length of omnibuses, maximum, 39:3–84
Licenses and permits,
Automobile licensed by omnibus operator as owner, 39:3–19
Certificates, 39:3–4.1
Classified licensing, 39:3–10
Fees for drivers, 39:3–10
Omnibuses, 39:3–19
Reduced registration fees, 39:3–22a
Lights, requirement, 39:3–61
Liquid burning flares, emergency warning devices, 39:3–64
Mud flaps, 39:3–79.1 et seq.
Municipalities, resolutions, stops or stations, 39:4–8
Operators,
Certificates of public convenience or necessity, fines and penalties, failure to have, 39:3–79.22 et seq.
Drivers licenses, 39:3–10.1
Permits. Licenses and permits, generally, ante
Portable emergency warning devices, 39:3–64
Railroads, crossings, stopping, 39:4–128
Rear reflectors, 39:3–61
Registration. Licenses and permits, generally, ante
Resolutions, stops or stations, 39:4–8
Right of way, yielding, 39:4–87.1
Road tests, scheduling, 39:3–13
Rules and regulations, length and width, 39:3–84
School Buses, generally, this index
Smoking, 2C:33–13
Stops or stations,
Designation by municipality, 39:4–197
Resolutions, 39:4–8
Summer Camps, this index
Traffic rules and regulations, right of way, yielding, 39:4–87.1
Waiver,
Examination permit, fees, drivers license endorsements, 39:3–13
Fees,
Drivers license endorsements, 39:3–10
Examination permits, 39:3–13
Weight, rules and regulations, 39:3–84
Yielding, right of way, 39:4–87.1

BUSINESS ADVISORY COUNCIL
Motor vehicle commission, 39:2A–26

BUSINESS AND COMMERCE
Actions and proceedings, racketeering, 2C:41–4
Cease and desist orders, racketeering, 2C:41–4
Confidential or privileged information, racketeering investigations, 2C:41–5
Controlled substances, entry on property, injunctions, 2C:35–5.7, 2C:35–5.10
Corporations, generally, this index
Crimes and offenses,
Deceptive business practices, 2C:21–7
Racketeering, 2C:41–1 et seq.

BUSINESS AND COMMERCE—Cont'd
Debtors and creditors, racketeering, 2C:41–1 et seq.
Definitions, racketeering, 2C:41–1
Discovery, racketeering investigations, 2C:41–5
Electronic Transactions, generally, this index
Examinations and examiners, racketeering, 2C:41–5
Fines and penalties, racketeering, 2C:41–1 et seq.
Forfeitures, racketeering, 2C:41–3 et seq.
Indebtedness, racketeering, 2C:41–1 et seq.
Inspections and inspectors, racketeering investigations, 2C:41–5
Interrogatories, racketeering, investigations, 2C:41–5
Investigations and investigators, racketeering, 2C:41–5
Investments, racketeering, 2C:41–1 et seq.
Judgments and decrees, racketeering, 2C:41–4
Libel and slander, coercion, exposing secrets which tend to impair, 2C:13–5
Licenses and permits, racketeering, revocation or suspension, 2C:41–4
Monopolies, generally, this index
Names. Trademarks and Trade Names, generally, this index
Nonprofit Corporations and Associations, generally, this index
Partnerships, generally, this index
Process, racketeering, 2C:41–5
Production of books and papers, racketeering, 2C:41–5
Racketeering, 2C:41–1 et seq.
Records and recordation,
Electronic Transactions, generally, this index
Racketeering, investigations, 2C:41–5
Reputation, libel and slander, coercion, exposing secrets which tend to impair, 2C:13–5
Restitution, racketeering, 2C:41–4
Securities, racketeering, 2C:41–1 et seq.
Sexually oriented businesses, 2C:33–12.2
Zoning and planning, 2C:34–7
Shoplifting, 2C:20–11

BUSINESS ASSOCIATIONS
Partnerships, generally, this index

BUSINESS CORPORATION ACT
Corporations, generally, this index

BUSINESS CORPORATIONS
Corporations, generally, this index

BUSINESS DISTRICTS
Definitions, Motor Vehicle Law, 39:1–1

BUSINESS ENTITIES
Appearance, **Rule 1:21–1**

BUSINESS PLACES
Unlawful possession of weapons, exemption, 2C:39–6

BUSINESS RECORDS
Nonpublic records, evidence, **Rule 1:7–6**

BUTANE
Liquefied Petroleum Gas, generally, this index

BUTYLENE
Liquefied Petroleum Gas, generally, this index

BYLAWS
Board of compact administrators, Nonresident Violator Compact, motor vehicles, 39:5F–18

CABLE TELEVISION
Assault and battery, officers and employees, 2C:12–1
Crimes and offenses, theft of services, 2C:20–8
Theft of services, crimes and offenses, 2C:20–8

CADAVERS
Dead Bodies, generally, this index

CADMIUM
Solid Waste, generally, this index

CAFES AND CAFETERIAS
Restaurants, generally, this index

CALENDARS
Call,
  Failure to appear, sanctions, **Rule 1:2–4**
  Law graduates and students, appearance, **Rule 1:21–3**
  Verbatim records, **Rule 1:2–2**
Military list, inability to prosecute or defend action, **Rule 1:13–6**
Motions, **Rule 1:6–2**
Municipal courts, **Rules 7:12–2, 7:14–3**

CAMERAS
See, also, Photographs, generally, this index
Police and police departments, motor vehicles, tampering, 2C:28–7
Traffic signs and signals, monitoring, intersections, 39:4–8.12 et seq.

CAMPERS AND CAMPING
Alcoholic beverage license and fee exemption, retail sale, 33:1–27
Sleeping bags, flammable fabrics, 2A:123–16 et seq.
Summer Camps, generally, this index
Tents, flammable fabrics, sales, 2A:123–16 et seq.

CAMPUS POLICE OFFICERS
Weapons, unlawful possession, exemptions, 2C:39–6

CANADA
Credit cards, notice of revocation, 2C:21–6
Handicapped persons, special parking privileges, 39:4–207.5

CANAL ZONE
Credit cards, notice of revocation, 2C:21–6

CANALS
Agricultural lands, trespass, damages, 2C:18–4 et seq.

CANCER
Conquer cancer license plates, 39:3–27.90
Licenses and permits, conquer cancer plates, 39:3–27.90

CANDIDATES
Judges and other court related personnel, limitations or prohibitions, **Rule 1:17–1 et seq.**

CANDY
Poison candy, 2C:12–2

CANINES
Dogs, generally, this index

CANNABIS
Marijuana, generally, this index

CANNONS
Antique cannons, rules and regulations, 2C:39–1 et seq.

CAPABILITY
Presumptions, sexual offenses, 2C:14–5

CAPIAS AD RESPONDENDUM
Bail, generally, this index

CAPITAL PUNISHMENT
Additional discovery, **Rule 3:13–4**
Bail, this index
Benefit of clergy, abolition, 2A:152–2
Discovery, additional, **Rule 3:13–4**
Exemptions, resentencing, life imprisonment, 2C:11–3b
Extradition, bail of accused, 2A:160–24
Illegal sentence, correction, petition, limitation of actions, **Rule 3:22–12**
Indictment, information or presentment,
  Aggravating factors, specification, **Rule 3:7–3**
  Crime punishable by death, **Rule 3:7–2**
Judgments and decrees, **Rule 3:21–5**
Jury and jurors,
  Examination of jurors, **Rule 1:8–3**
  List of general panel, availability, **Rule 1:8–5**
  Sentencing proceedings, waiver, **Rule 1:8–1**
Limitation of criminal prosecutions postconviction relief, **Rule 3:22–12**
Postconviction relief, limitations, **Rule 3:22–12**
Presentence investigation, report, **Rule 3:21–2**
Resentencing, life imprisonment, 2C:11–3b
Sentencing proceedings, waiver of jury, **Rule 1:8–1**

CAPITAL STOCK
Shares and Shareholders, generally, this index

CAPS
Fireworks, generally, this index

CAPTION
Affidavits, **Rule 1:4–4**
Complaints, **Rule 1:4–1**
Domicile and residence, parties, first pleading, **Rule 1:4–1**
Pleadings and other papers, **Rule 1:4–1**

CARBOLIC ACID
Turnpike project, transportation regulations, 27:23–31

CARCINOGENIC SUBSTANCES
Hazardous Substances and Waste, generally, this index

CARD GAMES
Casinos, generally, this index

CARDHOLDER
Definitions, credit card offenses, 2C:21–6

CARDIOVASCULAR CONDITIONS OR DISEASES
Deborah heart and lung center, motor vehicles, special plates, 39:3–27.107 et seq.

CARDS
Credit Cards, generally, this index
Identification Cards, generally, this index
Insurance identification cards, possession by motor vehicle driver, 39:3–29, 39:3–29.1
Law enforcement officers organization or association, issuance, bona fide members, 2A:170–20.1

CARE
Persons with special responsibility for care of others, use of force, 2C:3–8

CARJACKING
Generally, 2C:15–2
Definitions, 2C:15–2
Felony murder, 2C:11–3
Homicide, 2C:11–3
Juvenile delinquents and dependents, jurisdiction, 2A:4A–26

CARNAL ABUSE
Rape, generally, this index
Sex Offenses, generally, this index

CARPOOL
Definitions, 39:1–1

CARRIERS
Autobuses. Buses, generally, this index
Buses, generally, this index
Drugs and medicine, controlled dangerous substances, registration exemption, 24:21–10
Empty vehicles, registration plates, 39:3–20.1, 39:3–20.2
Explosives, transportation, 21:1A–137
Fees, registration plates, 39:3–20
Hazardous Substances and Waste, this index
Motor Carriers, generally, this index
Passengers, generally, this index
Railroads, generally, this index
Red flags and red lights, overhanging loads, 39:3–61.4
Registration fees, 39:3–20
Registration plates, empty vehicles, 39:3–20.1, 39:3–20.2
Sales, intoxicating liquors, place of sale, delivery accompanied by transportation, 33:1–69
Street Railways, generally, this index
Terrorism, 2C:38–2
Terroristic threats, 2C:12–3
Vessels, generally, this index
Weight of vehicles, registration statement, 39:3–20

CARS
Motor Vehicles, generally, this index
Railroads, this index

CARTONS
Containers, generally, this index

CARTRIDGES
Weapons, generally, this index

CASE COORDINATOR
Generally, **Rule 1:33–5**

CASE INFORMATION STATEMENT
Confidential or privileged information, **Rule 1:38–3**
Filing pleadings with, **Rule 1:5–6**

CASE MANAGEMENT
Conferences, orders, **Rule 1:2–6**
Orders, **Rule 1:2–6**

CASH
Alcoholic Beverages, this index
Money Laundering and Illegal Investments, generally, this index
Reports, transactions, money laundering and illegal investments, 2C:21–25

CASH BAIL
Director of division of motor vehicles, payment of forfeited deposit to, **39:5–9**

CASH DEPOSIT
Alcoholic beverages, condition precedent to issuance of license, **33:1–33**
Lieu of bail, affidavit, **2A:162–9**

CASH REGISTERS
Under ring, definitions, shoplifting, **2C:20–11**

CASINOS
Antique slot machines, possession, offense under, **2C:37–7**
Applicability of gambling statutes, **2C:37–9**
Attorneys, limitation on practice, industry related activities, **Rule 1:15–4**
Cash, reports, **2C:21–25**
Currency transactions, reports, **2C:21–25**
Electronic surveillance, **2A:156A–1 et seq.**
Money laundering and illegal investments, currency transactions, reports, **2C:21–25**
Municipal court judges, conflict of interest, industry activities, **Rule 1:15–1**
Reports, currency transactions, money laundering and illegal investments, **2C:21–25**
Wiretapping, **2A:156A–1 et seq.**

CATASTROPHES
Emergencies, generally, this index

CATS
Crimes and offenses, sales,
Fur or hair, **4:22–25.3**
Meat and meat products, **4:22–25.4**
Cruelty to animals, **4:22–20**
Destruction, neuromuscular blocking agents, **4:22–19.3, 4:22–19.4**
Fur or hair, sales, crimes and offenses, **4:22–25.3**
Meat and meat products, sales, crimes and offenses, **4:22–25.4**
Reports, motorist hitting or injuring, **4:22–25.1**
Spaying and neutering, animal population control program, animal welfare license plates, **39:3–27.55 et seq.**

CATTLE
Animals, generally, this index

CAUSAL RELATIONSHIP
Conduct and result, criminal offenses, **2C:2–3**

CAUSES OF ACTION
Actions and Proceedings, generally, this index

CEASE AND DESIST ORDERS
Racketeering, **2C:41–4**

CELEBRATIONS
Motor vehicles, special registrations, **39:3–27.2**

CELLULAR TELECOMMUNICATIONS
Motor vehicles, hands free telephones, **39:4–97.3 et seq.**

CEMETERIES
Criminal mischief, **2C:17–3**
Desecration, **2C:33–9, 2C:33–11**
Flags, theft, **2C:20–2.3**
Prepaid funeral agreements. Funerals, this index
Theft, tombstones, flags, **2C:20–2.3**

CENTRAL AUTOMATED BAIL SYSTEM
Bail, **Rule 3:26–4**

CENTRAL MUNICIPAL COURT
Municipal Courts, this index

CENTRAL REGISTRY
Juvenile delinquents and dependents, **2A:4A–60**
Rules and regulations, **2A:4A–60.1**

CERTIFICATE NUMBERS
Definitions, radioactive materials, transportation, **39:5B–18**

CERTIFICATES AND CERTIFICATION
Abuse of children, business records, evidence, **9:6–8.46**
Alcoholic Beverages, this index
Attestation, alcoholic beverage control division director, municipal boards, **33:1–48**
Attorneys, this index
Birth Certificates, generally, this index
Controlled Substances, this index
Conviction of crime, disabilities, labor and employment, revocation or suspension, **2A:168A–7 et seq.**
Dirt bikes, fees, **39:3C–3**
Drivers Licenses, this index
Drugs and Medicine, this index
Engineers, municipalities, traffic regulations, **39:4–8**
Firearms, applications, false statements, **2C:39–10**
Ignition interlock devices, **39:4–50.20**
Jury lists, random selection, **2B:20–5**
Motor carriers, intermodal transportation, chassis, **39:3–79.11, 39:3–79.18**
Motor Vehicles, this index
Motorcycles,
Manufacturers and manufacturing, brands, marks and labels, safety, **39:3–76.3a**
Safety instructors, **39:12–5 et seq.**
Motorized Bicycles, this index
Municipal prosecutors, training, **2B:25–10**
Nurses, this index
Parking, restricted spaces, **39:4–197.5**
Photosensitivity, tinted windshields, **39:3–75.1 et seq.**
Police and Police Departments, this index
Portable oil burning heating devices, testing, **2C:40–7**
Rockets, **21:1C–3**
Salvage certificates of title, damaged or stolen vehicles, **39:10–31**
Seals and sealing, municipal boards, intoxicating liquors, **33:1–48**
Snowmobiles, this index
Transportation Department, this index
Windshields, photosensitivity, tinted windshields, **39:3–75.1 et seq.**

CERTIFICATES OF AUTHORITY
Convicted offenders, rehabilitated, **2A:168A–1 et seq.**
Rehabilitated convicted offenders, **2A:168A–1 et seq.**

CERTIFICATES OF HANDLING
Definitions, radioactive materials, transportation, **39:5B–18**

CERTIFICATES OF LIMITED ADMISSION
Attorneys, appearance, **Rule 1:21–1**

CERTIFICATES OF OWNERSHIP
Manufactured Homes, this index
Mobile Homes and Mobile Home Parks, this index
Motor Vehicles, this index

CERTIFICATES OF TITLE
Motor vehicle commission, motor vehicles, improvements, chief administrator, **39:2A–29**
Salvage certificates of title, motor vehicles, **39:10–31 et seq.**

CERTIFICATION APPEALS
Attorney of record, **Rule 1:11–3**

CERTIFICATION OF SERVICE
Proof of service, **Rule 1:5–3**

CERTIFIED COPIES
Autobusses, resolutions, stops or stations, **39:4–8**
County Clerks, this index
Evidence, this index
Ordinances, this index

CERTIFIED OR REGISTERED MAIL
Mail and Mailing, this index

CESSPOOLS
Abandoned cesspools, hazards, **2C:40–1**

CESTUS
Weapons, generally, this index

CHAIN STORE LIQUOR LICENSES
Club licenses, membership in organization holding, **33:1–12.34**
Corporate licenses, **33:1–12.36**
Fines and penalties, **33:1–12.37**
Inheritance, **33:1–12.33**
Licensees right to hold, use or renew, **33:1–12.35**
Number, limitation, **33:1–12.31**
Exceptions, **33:1–12.32**

CHALLENGES
Jurors, **Rule 1:8–3**

CHAMBERS
Facilities disputes, arbitration, **Rule 1:33–9**
Location, **Rule 1:31–1**
Settlement conferences, **Rule 1:2–1**

CHAMBERS OF COURT
Municipal courts, **2B:12–15**

CHANCERY DIVISION
Superior Court, this index

CHANCROID
Sexual penetration, diseased persons, **2C:34–5**

CHANGE OF NAME
Attorneys, **Rules 1:29–2, 1:29–3**

CHANGE OF VENUE
Venue, this index

CHARACTER AND REPUTATION
Attorneys,
Admission to practice, **Rules 1:25, 1:27–1**
Committees, **Rule 1:25**
Funding, **Rule 1:23–4**
Immunity from liability, **Rule 1:23–3**
Requirement for admission, **Rules 1:25, 1:27–1**
Bail, obligor, hearings, sufficiency, **2A:162–13**
Coercion, exposing secrets which would tend to impair, **2C:13–5**
Evidence, **Evidence Rule 404**
Explosives, permits, qualifications, **21:1A–134**
Extortion, threat to expose or publicize damaging material, **2C:20–5**
Hearsay, **Evidence Rule 803**

CHARACTER AND REPUTATION—Cont'd
Methods of proving, **Evidence Rule 405**

CHARGE CARDS
Credit Cards, generally, this index

CHARGE TO JURY
Jury and Jurors, this index

CHARITABLE ORGANIZATIONS AND AS-SOCIATIONS
Counties, this index
Crimes and offenses, terrorism, material support or resources, 2C:38–5
Definitions, terrorism, 2C:38–5
Fraud, solicitation, deception, 2C:20–4
Highways and roads, solicitation, 39:4–60
Monopolies and unfair trade, exemptions, 56:9–5
Municipalities, solicitation on roadways, 39:4–60
Terrorism, material support or resources, 2C:38–5

CHARITABLE TRUSTS
Actions and proceedings, racketeering, 2C:41–4
Cease and desist orders, racketeering, 2C:41–4
Confidential or privileged information, racketeering investigations, 2C:41–5
Crimes and offenses, racketeering, 2C:41–1 et seq.
Debtors and creditors, racketeering, 2C:41–1 et seq.
Definitions, racketeering, 2C:41–1
Discovery, racketeering investigations, 2C:41–5
Examinations and examiners, racketeering, 2C:41–5
Fines and penalties, racketeering, 2C:41–1 et seq.
Forfeitures, racketeering, 2C:41–3 et seq.
Indebtedness, racketeering, 2C:41–1 et seq.
Inspections and inspectors, racketeering investigations, 2C:41–5
Interrogatories, racketeering, investigations, 2C:41–5
Investigations and investigators, racketeering, 2C:41–5
Investments, racketeering, 2C:41–1 et seq.
Judgments and decrees, racketeering, 2C:41–4
Licenses and permits, racketeering, revocation or suspension, 2C:41–4
Process, racketeering, 2C:41–5
Production of books and papers, racketeering, 2C:41–5
Racketeering, 2C:41–1 et seq.
Records and recordation, racketeering, investigations, 2C:41–5
Restitution, racketeering, 2C:41–4
Securities, racketeering, 2C:41–1 et seq.

CHATTEL MORTGAGES
Motor Vehicles, this index

CHAUFFEURS
Service of process on nonresident owner of motor vehicle, 39:7–8

CHEATING
Fraud, generally, this index

CHECK CASHING BUSINESS
Money laundering and illegal investments, reports, 2C:21–25
Reports, money laundering and illegal investments, 2C:21–25

CHECKS
Negotiable Instruments, this index
Sales, this index

CHEMICAL ANALYSIS
Motor vehicle drivers breath, 39:4–50.3

CHEMICAL AND BIOLOGICAL WARFARE AND WEAPONS
Terrorism, 2C:38–2, 2C:38–3

CHEMICAL DEPENDENCY
Alcoholics and Alcoholism, generally, this index

CHEMICAL REPELLENT
Weapons, lawful possession, 2C:39–6

CHEMICAL TESTS
Drivers license, blood analysis test refusal, suspension or revocation, 39:4–50.4a

CHEMICALS, CHEMISTRY AND CHEMISTS
Alcoholic beverages, certification of findings by chemist, 33:1–37
Controlled Substances, generally, this index
Crimes and offenses, trespass, unlicensed entry of structure, 2C:18–3
Debris from auto accident, towing service failure to remove debris, penalty exemption, 39:4–56.8
Definitions, industrial chemicals, distributors, 2C:35–29
Distributors, industrial chemicals, 2C:35–29
Evidence, industrial chemicals, 2C:35–29
Hazardous Substances and Waste, generally, this index
Industrial chemicals, distributors, 2C:35–29
Manufacturers and manufacturing, industrial chemicals, 2C:35–29
Possession, industrial chemicals, 2C:35–29
Presumptions, industrial chemicals, 2C:35–29
Terrorism, weapons, 2C:38–2, 2C:38–3
Trespass, unlicensed entry of structure, facilities, crimes and offenses, 2C:18–3
Unlicensed entry of structure, crimes and offenses, 2C:18–3
Weapons, terrorism, 2C:38–2, 2C:38–3

CHIEF JUSTICE
Supreme Court, this index

CHILD ABUSE
See, also,
Dependent or Neglected Children, generally, this index
Domestic Violence, generally, this index
Generally, 2C:24–4, 9:6–1 et seq., 9:6–8.8 et seq., 9:6–8.21 et seq.
Absence and absentees, parent or guardian, hearings, 9:6–8.42
Actions and proceedings,
Commitment of child abuser to mental health facility, consent, 9:6–8.58
Disposition of adjudication, 9:6–8.51
Exclusive noncriminal jurisdiction of superior court, chancery division, family part, 9:6–8.22, 9:6–8.24
Jurisdiction, superior court, chancery division, family part, 9:6–8.22, 9:6–8.24
Medically necessary treatment, 9:6–8.86
Persons who may originate proceedings, 9:6–8.34
Rules of court, 9:6–8.26
Suspended judgments, 9:6–8.52
Failure to comply with terms and conditions, 9:6–8.66

CHILD ABUSE—Cont'd
Actions and proceedings—Cont'd
Venue, 9:6–8.26
Adjournment, hearings, 9:6–8.48, 9:6–8.49
Administrative law and procedure, records and recordation, identification check, conviction of crime, sole caretaker, presentence investigations, 9:6–8.10d
Adoption, this index
Agents and agencies, records and recordation, access, 9:6–8.10a
Alcoholics and alcoholism,
Alcoholic parents, juvenile family crisis, 2A:4A–85
Juvenile family crisis, 2A:4A–85
Appeal and review, 9:6–8.70
Juvenile family crisis, long term out of home placement, 2A:4A–90
Sexual abuse, record, closed circuit testimony, 2A:84A–32.4
Application of law, 9:6–1.1
Appropriations, 9:6–8.71
Arrest, 9:6–8
Child committed to society for prevention of cruelty, failure to pay support, 9:6–3
Warrants, 9:6–8.39
Attorneys,
Adjournment, 9:6–8.49
Appointment, out of home placement hearings, juvenile family crisis, 2A:4A–89
Custody, 9:6–8.19a
Records, access, 9:6–8.10a
Reports, access, 9:6–8.10a
Reuniting with parent, 9:6–8.32
Right to counsel, 9:6–8.23
Child, 9:6–8.23, 9:6–8.43
Parent and guardian, 9:6–8.43
Chemically dependent persons, juvenile family crisis, 2A:4A–85
Child fatality and near fatality review board, 9:6–8.88 et seq.
Child protection services,
Citizen review panels, 9:6–8.97
Records, access, 9:6–8.10a
Records, access, 9:6–8.10a
Citizen review panels, child protection services, 9:6–8.97
Records, access, 9:6–8.10a
Closed circuit testimony,
Motions, 2A:84A–32.4
Sexual abuse, 2A:84A–32.4
Colored photographs, evidence, 9:6–8.31
Commitment of child, society for prevention of cruelty, 9:6–3
Complaints, 9:6–8.25 et seq.
Amendment, 9:6–8.50
Copies, forwarding to county prosecutor, 9:6–8.25
Criminal complaint, 9:6–8.25
Dismissal, 9:6–8.50
Originating proceedings, 9:6–8.33
Persons who may prefer, 9:6–5
Lack, 9:6–1
Reports, 9:6–8.25
Physicians and hospitals, 9:6–8.18
Service required, 9:6–8.41
Summary determination, 9:6–4
Comprehensive Child Abuse Prevention and Treatment Act, 9:6–8.83 et seq.
Confidential or privileged information,
Child fatality and near fatality review board, 9:6–8.92
Subpoenas, 9:6–8.93
Disclosures, exceptions, 9:6–8.10a
Records and reports, release, 9:6–8.10a

CHILD ABUSE—Cont'd
Confidential or privileged information—Cont'd
Reports, probation or youth and family ser-
    vices reports, disclosure at dispositional
    hearing, **9:6–8.47**
Conviction of crime, sole caretaker, presen-
    tence investigations, records and recorda-
    tion, identification check, **9:6–8.10c**
Copies, records and recordation, fees, **9:6–8.40**
County institutions and agencies, information,
    disclosure, **9:6–8.10a**
County prosecutors,
    Notice, child fatality and near fatality review
        board, records, **9:6–8.93**
    Originating proceedings, **9:6–8.34**
    Referral from superior court, chancery divi-
        sion, family part, **9:6–8.24**
    Regulations, development, **9:6–8.36a**
    Reports, complaints received, **9:6–8.25**
Crimes and offenses, **2C:24–4**
    Referral of case to county prosecutor,
        9:6–8.25
Custody, **9:6–8.65**
    Abandoned child, **9:6–8.57**
    Change of custody, **9:6–8.65**
    Division of youth and family services,
        9:6–8.65
    Mediation, **Rule 1:40–5**
    Petitions,
        Release of responsibilities, return to custo-
            dy of court, **9:6–8.69**
        Terminate placement, **9:6–8.60 et seq.**
    Protective custody, **9:6–8.16 et seq.**
        Child abuse, **9:6–8.16 et seq.**
    Release to parent or guardian, **9:6–8.53**
    Runaways, **9:6–8.68**
    Safety, **9:6–8.8**
    Short term custody, juvenile family crisis,
        notice, **2A:4A–80**
Death,
    Child fatality and near fatality review board,
        9:6–8.88 et seq.
    Information, disclosure, **9:6–8.10a**
Definitions, **9:6–1, 9:6–8.21**
    Abused child, **9:6–8.9**
    Child advocacy centers, **9:6–8.104**
    Dispositional hearing, **9:6–8.45**
    Facilities, **9:6–8.30**
    Fact finding hearing, **9:6–8.44**
Discharge, placement, **9:6–8.63**
Disclosure,
    Medical records, **9:6–8.30**
    Records and recordation, **9:6–8.10b**
    Privileges and immunities, **9:6–8.40**
Due process, institutions, officers and employ-
    ees, **9:6–3.1**
Emergencies,
    Medical or surgical procedures, **9:6–8.28,
        9:6–8.31**
        Adjournment of fact finding hearing,
            9:6–8.48
    Removal,
        Child other than abused or neglected
            child, **9:6–8.33**
        Notice, **9:6–8.30**
        Without court order, **9:6–8.29**
    Telephone service, **9:6–8.12**
Endangerment, records and recordation, dis-
    closure, **9:6–8.10a**
Evidence, **9:6–8.46**
    Admissibility of statements made in prelimi-
        nary conference, **9:6–8.36**
    Prior statements of child, **9:6–8.46**
    Sexual abuse, closed circuit testimony,
        2A:84A–32.4

CHILD ABUSE—Cont'd
Examinations, petition to terminate placement,
    9:6–8.62
Exclusive noncriminal jurisdiction, **9:6–8.22 et
    seq.**
Failure to report, **9:6–8.14**
Fees, records and recordation, copies, **9:6–8.40**
Fines and penalties, **9:6–6**
    Permitting or encouraging release of records,
        9:6–8.10b
    Support, society for prevention of cruelty to
        children, **9:6–3**
Grand jury, records and recordation, access,
    9:6–8.10a
Grants, prevention, **9:6–8.75**
Guardian Ad Litem, this index
Hearings,
    Absence of parent or guardian, **9:6–8.42**
    Adjournment, **9:6–8.48**
    Certification of business records, **9:6–8.46**
    Closed hearings, **9:6–8.43**
    Dispositional hearing,
        Definitions, **9:6–8.45**
        Evidence, **9:6–8.46**
        Reports, probation or use in family ser-
            vices reports, disclosure of confiden-
            tial information, **9:6–8.47**
        Suspension, **9:6–8.50**
    Evidence, **9:6–8.46**
    Fact finding hearings,
        Adjournment, **9:6–8.48**
        Definitions, **9:6–8.44**
        Evidence, **9:6–8.46**
    Juvenile family crisis, **2A:4A–86**
    Notice requirements, **9:6–8.41**
    Out of door sales, juvenile family crisis,
        2A:4A–89
    Petition to terminate placement, **9:6–8.62**
    Priority of proceedings, **9:6–8.49**
    Records, photographs, memoranda, evi-
        dence, **9:6–8.46**
    Removal of child without court order,
        9:6–8.31
    Return of child to parent or guardian,
        9:6–8.32
    Right to counsel,
        Children, law guardians, **9:6–8.23, 9:6–8.43**
        Parents and guardians, **9:6–8.43**
    Sequence of hearing, **9:6–8.47**
Hospitals,
    Emergency medical or surgical procedures,
        9:6–8.28, 9:6–8.31
    Evidence, **9:6–8.46**
Identification check, conviction of crime, sole
    caretaker, presentence investigations,
    9:6–8.10c
Information, requests, juvenile family crisis,
    2A:4A–77
Investigations, **9:6–8.49**
    Priority to those involving imminent or actu-
        al physical harm, **9:6–8.49**
    Reports of physician and hospital, **9:6–8.18**
    Warrant to enter for, **9:6–8**
Judgments and decrees, suspended judgments,
    9:6–8.52
    Failure to comply with conditions, **9:6–8.66**
Jurisdiction, **9:6–4, 9:6–8.22 et seq.**
    Age, **9:6–8.24**
Juvenile delinquents and dependents, short
    term custody, **Rule 5:16–1**
Juvenile family crisis, **2A:4A–76 et seq.**
Medical care and treatment,
    Auditory or vision problems, juvenile family
        crisis, **2A:4A–85**
    Lack, **9:6–1**

CHILD ABUSE—Cont'd
Medical care and treatment—Cont'd
    Prior emergency removal from home,
        9:6–8.30
    Records and recordation, child fatality and
        near fatality review board, subpoena,
        9:6–8.93
    Regional diagnostic and treatment center,
        9:6–8.101 et seq.
    Withholding treatment, **9:6–8.86**
        Reports, **9:6–8.85**
Medical screening, temporary removal,
    9:6–8.30
Mental health facilities, commitment, **9:6–8.58**
Motions, closed circuit testimony, sexual abuse,
    2A:84A–32.4
Notice,
    County prosecutor, child fatality and near
        fatality review board, records, **9:6–8.93**
    Custody, actions and proceedings, **9:6–8.19a**
    Emergencies, removal, **9:6–8.30**
    Hearing, **9:6–8.41**
    Juvenile family crisis, **2A:4A–86, 2A:4A–89**
        Short term custody, **2A:4A–80**
    Preliminary conferences, **9:6–8.35**
Orders,
    Protection, **9:6–8.51, 9:6–8.55**
    Stay, **9:6–8.59**
    Vacating or setting aside, **9:6–8.59**
Orders of protection, visitation, **9:6–8.19,
    9:6–8.55**
Permanency plans. Dependent or Neglected
    Children, this index
Petitions, termination of placement, **9:6–8.60 et
    seq.**
Photographs,
    Color photographs, physical examination,
        9:6–8.31
    Evidence, **9:6–8.46**
Physical examinations,
    Auditory or vision problems, juvenile family
        crisis, **2A:4A–85**
    Court order, **9:6–8.31**
    Temporary removal, **9:6–8.30**
Physicians and surgeons,
    Court ordered medical or surgical proce-
        dures, physical examinations, **9:6–8.31**
    Emergency medical or surgical procedures,
        9:6–8.28
    Emergency removal of child without court
        order, **9:6–8.29**
    Records, access, **9:6–8.10a**
    Regional diagnostic and treatment center,
        9:6–8.100
Placement, age, consent, **9:6–8.54**
Police and police departments,
    Complaints, **9:6–5**
    Emergency removal of child without court
        order, **9:6–8.29**
    Officers, agents of societies for prevention of
        cruelty, **9:6–7**
    Originating proceedings, **9:6–8.34**
    Records, access, **9:6–8.10a**
    Reports, complaints received, **9:6–8.25**
Preliminary conferences, **9:6–8.35**
    Admissibility of statements made in confer-
        ence, **9:6–8.36**
Preliminary court orders,
    Preliminary hearings not held, **9:6–8.28**
    Protection of child pending criminal actions,
        9:6–8.24
Preliminary hearings, prior preliminary orders,
    9:6–8.28
Presentence investigations, sole caretaker, con-
    viction of crime, records and recordation,
    identification check, **9:6–8.10c**

CHILD ABUSE—Cont'd
Privileges and immunities,
  Child fatality and near fatality review board,
    members, **9:6–8.94**
  Citizen review panels, child protection ser-
    vices, **9:6–8.97**
  Emergency removal of child without court
    order, immunity from civil or criminal
    liability, **9:6–8.29**
  Medical examinations, **9:6–8.30**
  Records and recordation, release, **9:6–8.40**
  Release of records, immunity from civil or
    criminal liability, **9:6–8.40**
    Medical records, **9:6–8.30**
  Reports, **9:6–8.13**
Probation and probation officers, **9:6–3,**
  9:6–8.51
  Court supervision, **9:6–8.56**
  Failure to comply with terms and conditions,
    9:6–8.67
Protective custody, **9:6–8.16 et seq.**
  Parents, notice, **9:6–8.19**
Public defenders, law guardians, **9:6–8.21,**
  9:6–8.43
Public policy, **9:6–8.8**
Radiological examination, **9:6–8.31**
Records and recordation, **9:6–8.40**
  Child fatality and near fatality review board,
    9:6–8.92
  Subpoenas, **9:6–8.93**
  Confidential information, release, **9:6–8.10a**
  Custody of child, release to parent or guard-
    ian, **9:6–8.53**
  Evidence, **9:6–8.46**
  Identification check, conviction of crime,
    sole caretaker, presentence investiga-
    tions, **9:6–8.10c**
  Release, **9:6–8.40**
    Confidential information, **9:6–8.10a**
    Privileges and immunities, **9:6–8.40**
    Unfounded allegations, expunging record,
      9:6–8.40a
Referral, courts,
  Continuing juvenile family crisis, **2A:4A–83 et**
    seq.
  Juvenile family crisis, **2A:4A–80, 2A:4A–81**
Regional diagnostic and treatment center,
  9:6–8.99
Release, **9:6–8.53**
  Responsibilities, custodian of child, **9:6–8.69**
Religion, criterion, orders of protection,
  9:6–8.55
Reports, **9:6–8.10 et seq., 9:6–8.36a**
  Child fatality and near fatality review board,
    9:6–8.92
  Citizen review panels, child protection ser-
    vices, **9:6–8.97**
  Complaints, **9:6–8.25**
  Complaints received, **9:6–8.25**
  Confidential information, release, **9:6–8.10a**
  Criminal courts, complaints received,
    9:6–8.25
  Division, termination of services, referred
    cases, **9:6–8.25**
  Failure to report, **9:6–8.14**
  Immunity of reporter, **9:6–8.13**
  Police officers, complaints received, **9:6–8.25**
  Probation or use in family services reports,
    disclosure at dispositional hearing,
    9:6–8.47
  Protective custody, **9:6–8.17**
  Release, confidential information, **9:6–8.10a**
  Warrants, failure to execute, **9:6–8.39**
  Withholding medical treatment, **9:6–8.85**

CHILD ABUSE—Cont'd
Residential child care facilities, criminal history
  record information, background checks,
  53:1–20.9d
Reuniting with parent. Children and Minors,
  this index
Right to counsel, **9:6–8.23, 9:6–8.43**
Rules and regulations,
  Commissioner of the department of edu-
    cation, **9:6–8.72a**
  County prosecutors, **9:6–8.36a**
  Division of youth and family services,
    9:6–8.72
  Reports, **9:6–8.15**
Rules of court,
  Service, petition to terminate placement,
    9:6–8.61
  Summons, **9:6–8.38**
  Venue, **9:6–8.26**
Safety, **9:6–8.8, 9:6–8.11**
  Temporary removal, **9:6–8.27, 9:6–8.28**
Schools and School Districts, this index
Sexual abuse,
  Definitions, **9:6–8.9**
    Comprehensive Child Abuse Prevention
      and Treatment Act, **9:6–8.84**
  Testimony, closed circuit, **2A:84A–32.4**
Society for prevention of cruelty to children,
  Agents and agency, **9:6–7**
  Commitment, **9:6–3**
  Motor vehicles, registration, **39:3–27**
  Support of persons, fines and penalties,
    9:6–3
Sole caretaker, conviction of crime, presen-
  tence investigations, records and recorda-
  tion, identification check, **9:6–8.10c**
Standing, **9:6–8.34**
Stay, orders, **9:6–8.59**
Subpoenas, child fatality and near fatality re-
  view board, **9:6–8.93**
Summary actions, **9:6–4**
Summons, **9:6–8.37**
  Service of summons, **9:6–8.38**
Suspended judgment, **9:6–8.52**
  Failure to comply with conditions, **9:6–8.66**
Task forces. Child Abuse and Neglect Task
  Force, generally, this index
Telecommunications, emergencies, **9:6–8.12**
Temporary care or custody, society for preven-
  tion of cruelty, **9:6–3**
Temporary removal of child,
  Court ordered removal, **9:6–8.28, 9:6–8.50**
  Emergencies, removal without court order,
    9:6–8.29
    Child other than abused or neglected,
      9:6–8.33
    Hearing, **9:6–8.31**
    Informing parent or guardian, **9:6–8.30**
  Parental consent, **9:6–8.27**
  Physical examinations, **9:6–8.30**
  Return of child to parent or guardian,
    Application and hearing, **9:6–8.32**
    Substance abuse, assessment and treat-
      ment, **9:6–8.58a, 9:6–8.58b**
  Safety of child, imminent danger, **9:6–8.28**
Therapeutic services, child abusers, **9:6–8.51,**
  9:6–8.58
Unfounded allegations, expunging record,
  9:6–8.40a
Unified child care agencies, reports, confiden-
  tial information, release, **9:6–8.10a**
Venue, **9:6–8.26**
Visitation, orders of protection, **9:6–8.19,**
  9:6–8.55
Warrants,
  Appearance of parent or guardian, **9:6–8.39**

CHILD ABUSE—Cont'd
Warrants—Cont'd
  Investigations and investigators, **9:6–8**
Witnesses,
  Anatomically correct dolls or models, sex
    offenses, **2A:84A–16.1**
  Closed circuit, sexual abuse, **2A:84A–32.4**
  Closed circuit testimony, sexual abuse,
    2A:84A–32.4
  Regional diagnostic and treatment center,
    9:6–8.102
  Videotaped testimony, sexual abuse,
    2A:84A–32.4
Youth and family services division, referral,
  9:6–8.50

**CHILD ABUSE AND NEGLECT TASK
FORCE**
  Generally, **9:6–8.74 et seq.**
Establishment, **9:6–8.75**
Expenses, **9:6–8.79**
Funds, **9:6–8.81**
Grants, prevention, **9:6–8.75**
Hearings, **9:6–8.80**
Meetings, **9:6–8.80**
Membership,
  Composition, **9:6–8.76**
  Vacancies, **9:6–8.77**
Powers and functions, **9:6–8.79**
Professional and clerical staff provided by chil-
  dren and families department, **9:6–8.78**
Report, findings and recommendations,
  9:6–8.82
Vacancies in membership, **9:6–8.77**

CHILD ABUSE REGISTRY
Guardian and ward, investigations and investigators, professional guardians, **9:6–8.10e**

CHILD CARE
Centers. Child Care Centers, generally, this
  index

CHILD CARE CENTERS
Criminal history record information, notice,
  53:1–20.9b
Fingerprints and fingerprinting, criminal histo-
  ry record information, **53:1–20.9b**
Notice, criminal history record information,
  53:1–20.9b
Officers and employees,
  Criminal history record information, notice,
    53:1–20.9b
  Disqualification, criminal history record in-
    formation, notice, **53:1–20.9b**
Privileges and immunities, criminal history rec-
  ord information, **53:1–20.9b**
Sexually oriented businesses, zoning and plan-
  ning, **2C:34–7**
Zoning and planning, sexually oriented busi-
  nesses, **2C:34–7**

**CHILD FATALITY AND NEAR FATALITY
REVIEW BOARD**
Generally, **9:6–8.88 et seq.**

CHILD SUPPORT
Support of Persons, generally, this index

CHILD SUPPORT HEARING OFFICERS
Generally, **Rule 5:25–3**

CHILDREN AND FAMILIES DEPARTMENT
Abuse or neglect, custody, **9:6–8.8 et seq.**
Fingerprints and fingerprinting, officers and
  employees, **53:1–20.9f**

CHILDREN AND FAMILIES DEPARTMENT
—Cont'd
New Jersey task force on child abuse and
neglect, provision of professional and cler-
ical staff, **9:6–8.78**
Officers and employees,
Aggravated assault, **2C:12–1**
Fingerprints and fingerprinting, **53:1–20.9f**

CHILDREN AND MINORS
Absence of parents. Guardian and Ward, gen-
erally, this index
Abuse. Child Abuse, generally, this index
Actions and proceedings,
Child Abuse, this index
Court appointed special advocate, **2A:4A–92**
Legal representation, public defender,
2A:158A–24
Financial circumstances, **2A:158A–25**
Adjournment, abuse or neglect, **9:6–8.49**
Adoption, generally, this index
Affirmative defenses, custody, kidnapping,
2C:13–1
Age,
Consent, placement, **9:6–8.54**
Custody, consent, **9:6–8.54**
Passenger restraint systems, **39:3–76.2a**
Aggravated criminal sexual contact, **2C:14–3**
Alcoholic Beverages, this index
All terrain vehicles, operation, **39:3C–16**
Ammunition, transfers, **2C:58–3.3**
Anatomically correct dolls or models, sex of-
fense witnesses, **2A:84A–16.1**
Appeal and review, sexual abuse, record, closed
circuit testimony, **2A:84A–32.4**
Athletics, sex offenders, participation, **2C:7–22,
2C:7–23**
Attorneys, contingent fees, **Rule 1:21–7**
Auto theft, employing a juvenile to commit,
2C:20–17
Bail, conditions, contact, **Rule 3:26–1**
Bicycles, helmet requirements, **39:4–10.1 et seq.**
Birth Certificates, generally, this index
Boarding schools. Child Care Centers, gener-
ally, this index
Body piercing, consent, **2C:40–21**
Car seats, child passenger restraint system,
39:3–76.2a et seq.
Care centers. Child Care Centers, generally,
this index
Certificates and certification. Birth Certifi-
cates, generally, this index
Child Care Centers, generally, this index
Child fatality and near fatality review board,
9:6–8.88 et seq.
Cigarettes and Cigars, this index
Closed circuit testimony, sexual abuse,
2A:84A–32.4
Color photograph, initial drivers license,
39:3–10f
Complaints, abandonment, abuse, cruelty and
neglect,
Jurisdiction, **9:6–4**
Persons who may prefer, **9:6–5**
Computers, child engaging in prohibited sexual
acts, crimes and offenses, **2C:24–4**
Confidential or privileged information,
Child fatality and near fatality review board,
9:6–8.92
Records and recordation, **Rule 1:38–3**
Consent,
Affirmative defenses, custody, kidnapping,
2C:13–1
Body piercing, **2C:40–21**
Custody, age, **9:6–8.54**
Tattoos and tattooing, **2C:40–21**

CHILDREN AND MINORS—Cont'd
Consent—Cont'd
Victim of crime, **2C:2–10**
Containers,
Abandonment, hazards, **2C:40–1**
Hazards, **2C:40–1**
Continuing juvenile family crisis, referral to
court, **2A:4A–83 et seq.**
Controlled Substances, this index
Correctional Institutions, this index
Court appointed special advocate, actions and
proceedings, **2A:4A–92**
Crimes and offenses,
Abandonment, containers, **2C:40–1**
Abuse or neglect, **2C:24–4**
Affirmative defenses, custody, kidnapping,
2C:13–1
Child pornography,
Endangering welfare of children, **2C:24–4**
Racketeering, **2C:41–1**
Containers, abandonment, **2C:40–1**
Custody, kidnapping, **2C:13–1**
Desertion, venue, **Rule 3:14–1**
Employing child to commit crime, **2C:24–9**
Endangering welfare, **2C:24–4**
Prosecution, limitation, **2C:1–6**
Expungement, records, **2C:52–2**
Family court, transfer of proceedings to,
2C:4–11
Firearms, sale or transfer, **2C:39–10**
Handcuffs, sale to, **2C:39–9.2**
Immaturity excluding criminal conviction,
2C:4–11
Interference with custody, **2C:13–4**
Internet, luring and enticing, **2C:13–6**
Juvenile Delinquents, generally, this index
Knives, sales to, **2C:39–9.1**
Lewdness and obscenity, presentation,
2C:34–3
Luring and enticing, **2C:13–6**
Paging devices, **2C:33–19 et seq.**
Racketeering, child pornography, **2C:24–1**
Records, expungement, **2C:52–4.1, 2C:52–5**
Sexual offenses, **2C:24–4**
Anatomically correct dolls, **2A:84A–16.1**
Support, willful nonsupport, **2C:24–5**
Victims of crime, speedy trial, **2A:163–4,
2A:163–5**
Witnesses, sex offenses, anatomically correct
dolls, **2A:84A–16.1**
Criminal Neglect Act, **9:6–1 et seq.**
Criminal restraint, **2C:13–2**
Custodian, definitions, **9:6–2**
Custody,
Affirmative defenses, kidnapping, **2C:13–1**
Age, consent, **9:6–8.54**
Child Abuse, this index
Consent, age, **9:6–8.54**
Domestic violence actions, orders, **2C:25–29**
Guardian and Ward, generally, this index
Interference with, **2C:13–4**
Juvenile Delinquents, this index
Kidnapping, **2C:13–1**
Mediation, complementary dispute resolu-
tion programs, **Rule 1:40–5**
Placement,
Consent, age, **9:6–8.54**
Public assistance, reduction, **9:6–8.54**
Relatives, **9:6–8.54**
Probation officers powers and duties,
2A:168–13
Protective custody, child abuse, **9:6–8.16 et
seq.**
Reuniting with parent, generally, post
Witnesses, juvenile justice, jurisdiction,
2A:4A–24

CHILDREN AND MINORS—Cont'd
Day nurseries. Child Care Centers, generally,
this index
Death, child fatality and near fatality review
board, **9:6–8.88 et seq.**
Definitions,
Abuse or neglect, **9:6–8.9, 9:6–8.21**
Comprehensive Child Abuse Prevention and
Treatment Act, **9:6–8.84**
Crimes and offenses, luring and enticing,
2C:13–6
Endangering welfare of children, **2C:24–4**
Luring and enticing, crimes and offenses,
2C:13–6
Victims of crime, speedy trial, **2A:163–4**
Delinquent children. Juvenile Delinquents,
generally, this index
Dependent or Neglected Children, generally,
this index
Derivative actions, contingent attorney fees,
Rule 1:21–7
Dirt bikes, operation, **39:3C–16**
Diseases, medical care and treatment, religion,
9:6–1.1
Disorderly Persons, this index
Dolls, anatomically correct dolls, sex offense
witnesses, **2A:84A–16.1**
Domestic Violence, generally, this index
Drivers Licenses, this index
Drugs and Medicine, this index
Education. Schools and School Districts, gen-
erally, this index
Emergencies,
Abuse or neglect, telephone service, **9:6–8.12**
Medical care and treatment, alcoholic bever-
ages, consumption, privileges and immu-
nities, **2C:33–15**
Employing a juvenile to commit auto theft,
2C:20–17
Endangering Welfare of Children, generally,
this index
Evidence, closed circuit testimony, sexual
abuse, **2A:84A–32.4**
Expungement of record, young drug offenders,
2C:52–5
False imprisonment, **2C:13–3**
False representations, defense to sale of alco-
holic beverages, **33:1–77**
Fines and penalties,
Abuse, abandonment, cruelty and neglect,
disposition, **9:6–6**
Bicycle and pedestrian violations, **39:4–203.3,
39:4–203.4**
Nonsupport of child committed to society for
prevention of cruelty, **9:6–3**
Flares, signaling devices, **2C:58–3**
Gifts, this index
Good faith defense to sale of alcoholic bever-
ages, **33:1–77**
Guardian and Ward, generally, this index
Handcuffs, sale to, **2C:39–9.2**
Handguns, sales, **2C:58–3**
Hazardous containers, **2C:40–1**
Homicide, trial as an adult, sentencing,
2C:11–3
Illness, treatment in accordance with religious
tenets of church, **9:6–1.1**
Immaturity excluding criminal conviction,
2C:4–11
Incest, **2C:24–4**
Indigent Persons, this index
Injunctions, stalking, **2C:12–10.2**
Interference with custody, **2C:13–4**
Internet, luring and enticing, crimes and of-
fenses, **2C:13–6**
Investigations, reports of abuse, **9:6–8.18**

CHILDREN AND MINORS—Cont'd
Junkyards, hazards, **2C:40–1**
Jurisdiction, custody, witnesses, juvenile justice, **2A:4A–24**
Juvenile and Domestic Relations Courts, generally, this index
Juvenile Delinquents, generally, this index
Juvenile family crisis, **2A:4A–76 et seq.**
  Alcoholics and alcoholism, alcoholic parents, **2A:4A–85**
  Alternate living arrangements, **2A:4A–87**
  Appeal and review, long term out of home placement, **2A:4A–90**
  Continuance, **2A:4A–86**
  Continuing crisis, referral to court, **2A:4A–83 et seq.**
  Drugs and medicine, drug dependent parents, **2A:4A–85**
  Forms, information requests, **2A:4A–77**
  Hearings, **2A:4A–86**
    Out of door sales, **2A:4A–89**
  Information requests, **2A:4A–77**
  Interviews, **2A:4A–78**
    Stabilized crisis, **2A:4A–82**
  Law enforcement referral, **2A:4A–80**
  Notice, **2A:4A–86**
    Out of door sales, petition, **2A:4A–89**
    Short term custody, **2A:4A–80**
  Orders,
    Disposition, **2A:4A–86**
    Long term out of home placement, family service plans, **2A:4A–90**
    Out of door sales, **2A:4A–89**
  Plans and specifications, orders, long term out of home placement, family service plans, **2A:4A–90**
  Referrals, **2A:4A–80, 2A:4A–81**
    To court, **2A:4A–83 et seq.**
  Response, **2A:4A–78**
  Stabilization, interviews, **2A:4A–82**
  Temporary out of home placement, **2A:4A–87 et seq.**
  Twenty four hour on call service, **2A:4A–77**
Kidnapping, **2C:13–1**
  Adult diagnostic and treatment center, referral of offenders, **2C:47–1 et seq.**
  Community notification. Sex Offenses, this index
  Parole supervision for life, special sentence, Violent Predator Incapacitation Act of 1994, **2C:43–6.4**
  Sex offenders, registration. Sex Offenses, this index
Knives, sales to, **2C:39–9.1**
Law enforcement referral, juvenile family crisis, **2A:4A–80**
Lewdness and Obscenity, this index
Licenses, firearms, **2C:58–6.1**
Mediation, custody, **Rule 1:40–5**
Medical care and treatment,
  Emergencies, alcoholic beverages, consumption, privileges and immunities, **2C:33–15**
  Religious tenets of church, treatment in accordance with, **9:6–1.1**
Motions, closed circuit testimony, sexual abuse, **2A:84A–32.4**
Motor vehicles,
  Extended term of imprisonment, **2C:43–7, 2C:43–7.1**
  Intoxication of driver,
    Parent, fines and penalties, **39:4–50.15**
    Passengers, parent, **39:4–50.15**
  Luring and enticing, **2C:13–6**
  Operation under the influence of alcohol, **39:4–50.14**

CHILDREN AND MINORS—Cont'd
Motor vehicles—Cont'd
  Passenger restraint systems, **39:3–76.2a et seq.**
  Seat belts, **39:3–76.2f**
  Title vesting in deceased owners child, transfer of registration, **39:3–30**
Motorized bicycles,
  Age of operator, **39:4–14.3, 39:4–14.3d**
  Suspension, operating privilege, **39:4–14.3h**
Moving pictures, sexual acts, **2C:24–4**
Murder, trial as an adult, sentencing, **2C:11–3**
Neglected children. Dependent or Neglected Children, generally, this index
Notice,
  Child abuse hearings, **9:6–8.41**
  Child support hearing officers, hearings, **Rule 5:25–3**
  Juvenile family crisis, ante
  Protective custody, child abuse, **9:6–8.19**
Offenses. Crimes and offenses, generally, ante
Orders,
  Domestic violence prevention, custody and support, **2C:25–29**
  Juvenile family crisis, ante
Paging devices, **2C:33–19 et seq.**
Pedestrian and bicycle violations, fines and penalties, **39:4–203.3, 39:4–203.4**
Permanency plans. Dependent or Neglected Children, this index
Person having the care, custody and control of any child, definitions, **9:6–2**
Petitions, juvenile family crisis,
  Dismissal, **2A:4A–86**
  Referral to court, **2A:4A–83 et seq.**
Photographs, this index
Physical appearance, defense to sale of alcoholic beverages, **33:1–77**
Physicians and Surgeons, this index
Placement, **9:6–8.63**
  Adoption, this index
  Confidential or privileged information, **Rule 1:38–3**
  Custody, ante
  Juvenile family crisis, **2A:4A–87 et seq.**
  Plans and specifications, juvenile family crisis,
    Long term out of home placement, family service plans, **2A:4A–90**
    Out of door sales, **2A:4A–89**
  Priorities and preferences, **9:6–8.8**
  Temporary placement, juvenile family crisis, **2A:4A–87 et seq.**
  Termination,
    Petitions, **9:6–8.61**
    Successive petitions, **9:6–8.64**
Plans and specifications. Placement, ante
Poisons, food, candy, giving to or enticing to accept, **2C:12–2**
Possession, weapons, **2C:58–6.1**
Private child care centers. Child Care Centers, generally, this index
Privileges and immunities, alcoholic beverages, consumption, emergencies, medical care and treatment, **2C:33–15**
Prostitution, **2C:34–1**
Protective custody, abused children, **9:6–8.16 et seq.**
Rape, **2C:14–1 et seq.**
Records and recordation, confidential or privileged information, **Rule 1:38–3**
Recreation and recreational facilities, sex offenders, participation, **2C:7–22, 2C:7–23**
Reports, abuse, **9:6–8.10 et seq.**
Reuniting with parent,
  Actions and proceedings, **9:6–8.32**

CHILDREN AND MINORS—Cont'd
Reuniting with parent—Cont'd
  Exceptions, imminent danger, **9:6–8.29, 9:6–8.31**
  Safety, **9:6–8.8**
  Substance abuse, assessment and treatment, **9:6–8.58a, 9:6–8.58b**
Roller skates, helmets, **39:4–10.5 et seq.**
Safety, hazards, **2C:40–1**
Sales,
  Firearms, **2C:39–10**
  Handcuffs, **2C:39–9.2**
  Knives, **2C:39–9.1**
School zones, speed limits, **39:4–98**
Schools and School Districts, generally, this index
Seat belts, motor vehicles, **39:3–76.2f**
Sentencing, juvenile tried as an adult, **2C:11–3**
Serving organizations, sex offenders, participation, **2C:7–22, 2C:7–23**
Sex offenders, registration. Sex Offenses, this index
Sex Offenses, this index
Sexual abuse,
  Child Abuse, this index
  Custody, mediation, **Rule 1:40–5**
Sexual activity, statements concerning, hearsay exception, **Evidence Rule 803**
Sexual assault, **2C:14–1 et seq.**
  Limitation of criminal prosecution, **2C:1–6**
Sexual conduct, crimes and offenses, **2C:24–4**
Sexual offenses, hearsay statements, **Evidence Rule 803**
Skateboards, helmets, **39:4–10.5 et seq.**
Snowmobiles, operation, **39:3C–16**
Sodomy, **2C:14–1 et seq.**
Speedy trial, victims of crime, **2A:163–4, 2A:163–5**
Stalking, injunctions, **2C:12–10.2**
Summary determination, abandonment, abuse, cruelty and neglect, **9:6–4**
Superior Court, this index
Support of Persons, generally, this index
Tattoos and tattooing, consent, **2C:40–21**
Television and radio, hazards, **2C:40–1**
Temporary placement. Placement, ante
Tender years hearsay exception, **Evidence Rule 803**
Testimony, closed circuit, sexual abuse, **2A:84A–32.4**
Treatment of child in accordance with religious tenets, **9:6–1.1**
Victims of crime, **2C:44–1**
  Murder, sentence, **2C:11–3**
  Presentence reports, **2C:44–6**
  Sexual abuse, closed circuit testimony motions, **2A:84A–32.4**
  Speedy trial, **2A:163–4, 2A:163–5**
Video games, child engaging in prohibited sexual acts, crimes and offenses, **2C:24–4**
Videotapes, this index
Visitation,
  Abuse or neglect, parent or guardian, **9:6–8.55**
  Complementary dispute resolution programs, **Rule 1:40–5**
  Juvenile delinquents and dependents, temporary out of home placement, **Rule 5:18–2**
  Mediation, complementary dispute resolution programs, **Rule 1:40–5**
Visual distress signaling devices, **2C:58–3**
Weapons, this index
Wells, hazards, abandonment, **2C:40–1**
Willful nonsupport, **2C:24–5**

CHILDREN AND MINORS—Cont'd
Witnesses,
  Closed circuit testimony, sexual abuse,
    2A:84A–32.4
  Custody, juvenile justice, jurisdiction,
    2A:4A–24
  Offense against child, **2A:84A–17**
  Sex offenses, anatomically correct dolls,
    2A:84A–16.1

CHILDRENS GUARDIANS
Guardian and Ward, generally, this index

CHIROPODY AND CHIROPODISTS
Podiatrists and Podiatry, generally, this index

CHIROPRACTORS
Automobile insurance, no fault insurance, ap-
  plication of law, **39:6A–1 et seq.**
Controversies or disputes with patients, review
  committees, immunity from liability,
  2A:84A–22.10
Crimes and offenses,
  Health care claims fraud, **2C:21–4.2,**
    2C:21–4.3
    Licenses and permits, suspension or revo-
      cation, **2C:51–5**
      Rehabilitation, order of debarment, re-
        scission, **2C:27–1**
  Solicitation, disasters or accidents, **2C:40A–4**
Fees, controversies or disputes with patients,
  review committees, immunity from liabili-
  ty, **2A:84A–22.10**
Fines and penalties, health care claims fraud,
  2C:21–4.2, 2C:21–4.3
  Licenses and permits, suspension or revoca-
    tion, **2C:51–5**
    Rehabilitation, order of debarment, rescis-
      sion, **2C:27–1**
Forfeitures, licenses and permits, health care
  claims fraud, **2C:51–5**
Health care claims fraud, **2C:21–4.2, 2C:21–4.3**
  Licenses and permits, suspension or revoca-
    tion, **2C:51–5**
    Rehabilitation, order of debarment, rescis-
      sion, **2C:27–1**
Licenses and permits, health care claims fraud,
  suspension or revocation, **2C:51–5**
  Rehabilitation, order of debarment, rescis-
    sion, **2C:27–1**
No fault insurance, application of law, **39:6A–1**
  et seq.
Solicitation, disasters or accidents, crimes and
  offenses, **2C:40A–4**
Time, solicitation, disasters or accidents,
  2C:40A–4

CHLORAL BETAMINE
Controlled substances, **24:21–1 et seq.**

CHLORAL HYDRATE
Controlled substances, **24:21–1 et seq.**

CHLORHEXADOL
Controlled substances, **24:21–1 et seq.**

CHOICE OF LAW
Presumptions, **Evidence Rule 302**

CHOP SHOPS
Operation or maintenance, second degree
  crime, **2C:20–16**

CHOSEN FREEHOLDERS
Bridges and Viaducts, generally, this index
Compensation and salaries,
  Assistant county prosecutors, **2A:158–15.3**

CHOSEN FREEHOLDERS—Cont'd
Compensation and salaries—Cont'd
  Permits for moving heavy machinery, high-
    ways, **39:4–26**
County Roads, generally, this index
Fines and penalties, return on reversal of con-
  viction, **2A:166–13**
Forms, records of disposition of complaints,
  motor vehicle and traffic laws, **39:5–44**
Motor vehicles, special plates, **39:3–27.29 et**
  seq.
Moving heavy machinery, regulation, **39:4–26**
Probation officers,
  Account as subject to audit of, **2A:168–10**
  Employees, salaries fixed by, **2A:168–8**
Reward, authority to offer, criminal procedure,
  2A:153–2, 2A:153–3
Rules and regulations, permits for moving
  heavy machinery, highways, **39:4–26**
Traffic prohibition by municipality, consent,
  39:4–197.1
Zoning and Planning, generally, this index

CHRONIC DISEASE HOSPITALS
Institutionalized elderly persons, assault,
  2C:12–1

CHURCHES
Religious Corporations and Associations, generally, this index

CIGARETTES AND CIGARS
Advertisements, promotional gifts, children and
  minors, crimes and offenses, **2A:170–51.4**
Children and minors,
  Crimes and offenses,
    Defenses, **2A:170–51.4, 2C:33–13.1**
    Gifts, **2A:170–51.4**
    Sales, **2A:170–51.4**
  Sales, fines and penalties, disorderly persons,
    2C:33–13.1
Crimes and offenses. Children and minors,
  ante
Defenses, this index
Definitions, flavored cigarettes, **2A:170–51.6**
Disorderly persons, children and minors, sales,
  2A:170–51.1, 2C:33–13.1
Electronic smoking devices, children and mi-
  nors,
  Crimes and offenses, **2A:170–51.4**
  Fines and penalties, sales, disorderly persons,
    2C:33–13.1
Explosives, regulations, **21:1A–132**
Fines and penalties,
  Children and minors, sales, disorderly per-
    sons, **2C:33–13.1**
  Flavored cigarettes, sales, **2A:170–51.6**
  Sales, children and minors, **2A:170–51.1 et**
    seq.
Flavored cigarettes, **2A:170–51.5, 2A:170–51.6**
Forfeitures, tax evasion, **2C:64–1**
Gifts, children and minors, crimes and offenses,
  2A:170–51.4
Intoxicating liquor licensee, Sales, **33:1–12**
Licenses and permits, revocation or suspension,
  flavored cigarettes, sales, **2A:170–51.6**
Promotional gifts, children and minors, crimes
  and offenses, **2A:170–51.4**
Public places, **2C:33–13**
  Smoking, **2C:33–13**
Revocation or suspension, licenses and permits,
  flavored cigarettes, sales, **2A:170–51.6**
Sales,
  Children and minors, fines and penalties,
    2A:170–51.1 et seq.
  Disorderly persons, **2C:33–13.1**

CIGARETTES AND CIGARS—Cont'd
Sales—Cont'd
  Flavored cigarettes, **2A:170–51.6**
Throwing or dropping from vehicle on highway,
  39:4–64

CITATION
Court rules, **Rule 1:1–3**
Definitions, Nonresident Violator Compact,
  39:5F–4
Evidence rules, **Evidence Rule 1103**
Motor carriers, intermodal transportation,
  chassis, inspectors and inspection,
  39:3–79.19
Nonresident Violator Compact, motor vehicles,
  39:5F–1 et seq.
Unpublished opinions, **Rule 1:36–3**

CITIES
Municipalities, generally, this index

CITIES OF FIRST CLASS
See, also, Municipalities, generally, this index
Alcoholic beverages, restrictions, **33:1–40.3**
Criminal courts. Municipal Courts, generally,
  this index
Municipal Courts, generally, this index

CITIES OF FOURTH CLASS
Municipal Courts, generally, this index

CITIES OF SECOND CLASS
Municipal Courts, generally, this index

CITIES OF THIRD CLASS
Municipal Courts, generally, this index

CITIZENS AND CITIZENSHIP
See, also, Aliens, generally, this index
Complaints by, **Rule 7:2–2**
Immigration and Naturalization, generally, this
  index
Jurors, grounds for challenge,
  Grand jurors, **2B:21–4**
  Petit jurors, **2B:23–11**
Naturalization. Immigration and Naturaliza-
  tion, generally, this index

CITY COURTS
Municipal Courts, generally, this index

CITY JAILS
Jails, generally, this index

CIVIC ORGANIZATIONS
Intoxicating liquors, temporary permits fees,
  33:1–74

CIVIL AIR PATROL
Motor vehicles owned by New Jersey wing, free
  registration, **39:3–27**

CIVIL COMMITMENT
Records and recordation, confidential or privileged information, **Rule 1:38–3**

CIVIL DEFENSE
Terrorism, generally, this index

CIVIL DISORDERS
Emergencies, generally, this index

CIVIL DIVISION, SUPERIOR COURT
Generally, **Rule 1:33–2**

CIVIL FAMILY ACTIONS
Family Actions, generally, this index

CIVIL RIGHTS
See, also, Discrimination, generally, this index
Conviction of crime, **2C:51–1**
Law enforcement officers, crimes and offenses, racial profiling, **2C:30–5 et seq.**
Police and police departments, crimes and offenses, racial profiling, **2C:30–5 et seq.**

CIVIL SERVICE
County Detectives and Investigators, this index
County investigators, **2A:157–23**
  Civil service law inapplicable to, **2A:157–10**
Motor Vehicle Commission, this index
Motor vehicles division, inspectors, **39:2–9.1, 39:2–9.2**
Nonattorneys, representing parties at proceedings, **Rule 1:21–1**
Probation officers, **2A:168–5**
State Police, this index
Turnpike authority, officers and employees, **27:23–5**

CIVIL UNIONS
Construction of rules, **Rule 1:1–2**
Discrimination, generally, this index

CLAIM OF RIGHT
Theft, defenses, **2C:20–2**

CLASS A LICENSES
Alcoholic Beverages, this index

CLASS ACTIONS
Contingent attorney fees, **Rule 1:21–7**

CLASS B LICENSES
Alcoholic Beverages, this index

CLASS C LICENSES
Alcoholic Beverages, this index

CLASS D LICENSES
Alcoholic Beverages, this index

CLASS E LICENSES
Alcoholic Beverages, this index

CLASS LOAN PROGRAM
Colleges and Universities, generally, this index

CLASSES OF OFFENSES
Grade and degree of offenses. Crimes and Offenses, this index

CLEAR ROAD BEAM
Definitions, **39:3–46**

CLEARANCE LAMPS
Motor vehicles, visibility, **39:3–48**
Mounting, **39:3–61.1**
Regulations, motor vehicles division director, **39:3–63**
Trucks, **39:3–61**

CLEMENCY
Executive clemency. Pardons, generally, this index

CLERGY
Abolishment, benefit of clergy, **2A:152–2**
Cleric, definitions, **2A:84A–23**
Confidential communications, disclosure, **2A:84A–23**
Domestic violence, prevention and treatment course, **2C:25–20**
Police, appointment as chaplain, privilege, **2A:84A–23**

CLERGY—Cont'd
Witness, confidential communications, **2A:84A–23**

CLERICAL MISTAKES
Correction, **Rule 1:13–1**

CLERKS
Clerks of Court, generally, this index
Grand Jury, this index

CLERKS OF COURT
  Generally, **Rule 1:34–2**
Agents and agencies, service of process, bonds (officers and fiduciaries), **Rule 1:13–3**
Applications, issuance of process and entry of default, granting, **Rule 1:6–8**
Assignment clerks, political activities or holding public office, **Rule 1:17–1**
Bail, bond, acceptance, **Rule 1:13–3**
Books, **Rule 1:32–2**
Business hours, **Rule 1:30–4**
Candidates, public office, **Rule 1:17–1 et seq.**
Deputy clerks,
  Practice of law, **Rule 1:15–2**
  Writs, issuance, **Rule 1:34–2**
Electronic retention, books and papers, **Rule 1:32–2**
Fees and charges, liability of attorney of record, **Rule 1:5–6**
Filing, generally, this index
Holding public office or position, **Rule 1:17–1 et seq.**
Hours office open to public, **Rule 1:30–4**
Identification Bureau, this index
Inadequate facilities, **Rule 1:31–1**
Judicial conference, membership, **Rule 1:35–1**
Judicial supervision, **Rule 1:34–2**
Jury and Jurors, this index
Location of offices, **Rule 1:31–1**
Microfilming, books and records, **Rule 1:32–2**
Motions, issuance of process and entry of judgment, granting, **Rule 1:6–8**
Motor vehicle accidents, certified copy of judgment in action for forwarded to director, **39:6–35**
Municipal Courts, this index
Narcotic offenses, reports to state bureau of identification, **53:1–18.2**
Notice, motion to dismiss inactive cases, **Rule 1:13–7**
Offices,
  Hours, **Rule 1:30–4**
  Location, **Rule 1:31–1**
Opinions, filing, **Rule 1:36–1**
Political activities, limitation, **Rule 1:17–1 et seq.**
Practice of law, **Rule 1:15–2**
Process, nonresidents, filing papers relating to service of, **39:7–3**
Records, **Rule 1:32–2**
Removal for failure to report disposition of indictable offense to bureau of identification, **53:1–20**
Reports, **Rule 1:32–1**
  License to operator of motor vehicle convicted of stealing produce of farm, **39:5–46**
Seal of courts, custody, **Rule 1:37–2**
State bureau of identification,
  Punishment for failure to report disposition of indictable offense to, **53:1–20**
  Report,
    Disposition of criminal charges or disorderly persons offenses to, **53:1–18**
    Prosecuted offenses, narcotics or dangerous drugs, **53:1–18.2**

CLERKS OF COURT—Cont'd
Subpoenas, issuance, **Rule 1:9–1**
Superior Court, this index
Supreme court, political activity or public office, **Rule 1:17–1**

CLIENT PROTECTION FUND
Attorneys, **Rule 1:28–1 et seq.**

CLINICS
Study of mental and physical conditions of convicted persons before sentence, **2A:164–1**

CLINTON
Correctional Institutions, this index

CLONING
Human beings, crimes and offenses, **2C:11A–1**

CLONITAZENE
Controlled substances, **24:21–1 et seq.**

CLOSE CORPORATIONS
Nonattorneys, representing at proceedings, **Rule 1:21–1**

CLOSE PURSUIT ACT
Fresh Pursuit Law, generally, this index

CLOSED CIRCUIT TESTIMONY
Children and minors, sexual abuse, **2A:84A–32.4**

CLOSING STATEMENTS
Trial, **Rule 1:7–1**

CLOTHING
Generally, **2A:123–3 et seq.**
Indigent, neglected or abandoned children, definition, **9:6–1**
Manufacturers and manufacturing, sale, **2A:123–3 et seq.**
Sales, manufacturer, **2A:123–3 et seq.**

CLUBS
Alcoholic beverages,
  Applications for licenses, requirements, **33:1–25**
  Licenses and permits, **33:1–12, 33:1–45.1, 33:1–46.1, 33:1 App.**
    Application for, requirements, **33:1–25**
    Issuing authority, member of, **33:1–20**
    Law enforcement officers, **33:1–25.1, 33:1–25.2**
    Membership in organization holding, Chain Store Liquor License Act, **33:1–12.34**
    Interest in retail license, Chain Store Liquor License Act, **33:1–12.34**
    Municipalities rejecting referendum, **33:1–46.1**
    Renewal or transfer, waiver of protection, **33:1–76.1**
    Sales within 200 feet of church or school, **33:1–76**
    Waiver of protection, **33:1–76.1**
    Special permits, **33:1–46.2**
Intoxicating liquors. Alcoholic beverages, generally, ante
Rifle or pistol club,
  Membership, condition of registration of assault firearm, **2C:58–12**
  Unlawful possession of weapons, exemption, **2C:39–6**

COAST GUARD
Alcoholic beverage license and fee exemption, retail sale, 33:1–27

COASTAL PROTECTION LICENSE PLATE PROGRAM
Generally, 39:3–27.47 et seq.

COASTAL PROTECTION TRUST FUND
Generally, 39:3–27.50 et seq.
Appropriations, 39:3–27.52
Coastal protection license plate program, reimbursement of costs, 39:3–27.51

COASTAL WATERS
Coastal protection license plate program, 39:3–27.47 et seq.

COASTAL WETLANDS
Adopt a beach program. Beaches and Beach Fronts, this index
Coastal protection license plate program, 39:3–27.47 et seq.

COATED IMITATION FROZEN DESERT
Frozen Desserts and Dietary Foods, generally, this index

COCA LEAVES
Controlled substances, 24:21–1 et seq.

COCAINE
Generally, 24:21–1 et seq.

CODE ENFORCEMENT OFFICERS
Complaints, Rule 7:2–2

CODE OF CONDUCT FOR JUDICIARY EMPLOYEES
Interpretation, Rule 1:17A–2

CODE OF JUDICIAL CONDUCT
Generally, Rule 1:14
Judges, duty to enforce, Rule 1:18

CODE OF JUVENILE JUSTICE
Generally, 2A:4A–20 et seq.

CODE OF PROFESSIONAL CONDUCT
Interpreters, transliterators, and translators, Rule 1:14

CODEINE
Controlled substances, 24:21–1 et seq.

CODEINE METHYLBROMIDE
Controlled substances, 24:21–1 et seq.

CODEINE N OXIDE
Controlled substances, 24:21–1 et seq.

COERCION
Duress or Coercion, generally, this index

COHABITATION
Domestic Violence, generally, this index

COLLATERAL
Definitions, Nonresident Violator Compact, 39:5F–4

COLLATERAL ESTOPPEL
Unpublished opinions, Rule 1:36–3

COLLECTIONS
Automobile insurance risk exchange, 39:6A–22
Courts, comprehensive enforcement program, 2B:19–1 et seq.

COLLECTIONS—Cont'd
Municipal courts, comprehensive enforcement program, 2B:19–1 et seq.
Racketeering, unlawful debt, 2C:41–2
Restitution, default in payment, summary proceedings, 2C:46–2
Summary proceedings, default in payment of restitution, 2C:46–2
Superior court, comprehensive enforcement program, 2B:19–1 et seq.
Tax court, comprehensive enforcement program, 2B:19–6
Unlawful collection practices, criminal usury, 2C:21–19

COLLECTORS OF FIREARMS OR AMMUNITION
Bullets or defaced firearms, possession, 2C:39–9
Possession of prohibited weapons, 2C:39–3

COLLEGES AND UNIVERSITIES
Aggravated hazing, 2C:40–3
Campus police officers, weapons, unlawful possession, exemption, 2C:39–6
Cannons, antique cannons, possession, 2C:39–6
Consent, hazing, 2C:40–4
Crimes and offenses,
   Hazing, 2C:40–3 et seq.
   Weapons, possession on premises, 2C:39–5
Culinary arts or hotel management programs, intoxicating liquors, possession, children and minors, 2C:33–15
Defenses, hazing, consent, 2C:40–4
Fines and penalties, hazing, 2C:40–3 et seq.
Fraternities, hazing, 2C:40–3 et seq.
Initiation, hazing, 2C:40–3 et seq.
Library materials, purchases, state colleges, contract without bids, theft, civil action, 2C:20–12 et seq.
Out of state institutions, sex offenses, registration, 2C:7–2
Private schools, sex offenses, registration, foreign states, 2C:7–2
Registration, sex offenses, foreign states, 2C:7–2
Sex offenses, registration, foreign states, 2C:7–2
Sororities, hazing, 2C:40–3 et seq.
Student organizations, hazing, 2C:40–3 et seq.
Vocational Education, generally, this index
Weapons, possession, crimes and offenses, 2C:39–5

COLLISION
Traffic Accidents, generally, this index

COLLUSION
Judgments in motor vehicle accident cases, payment of collusive judgments out of unsatisfied claim and judgment fund, 39:6–76

COLOR PHOTOGRAPHS
Drivers Licenses, this index

COLORS AND COLORING
Flashing signals, 39:4–119
Lights and Lighting, generally, this index
School buses, van type vehicles, 39:3B–8, 39:3B–9
Traffic signals, color system, 39:4–105

COMBINATION OF VEHICLES
Definitions, motor vehicles, dimensional and weight limitations, 39:3–84
Dimensional and weight limitations, motor vehicles, 39:3–84

COMBINATIONS
Labor Unions, generally, this index
Monopolies, generally, this index

COMBUSTIBLE MATERIALS
See, also, Fires and Fire Protection, generally, this index
Explosives, generally, this index
Fireworks, generally, this index
Turnpike project, transportation regulations, 27:23–31

COMITY
Reciprocity, generally, this index

COMMENCEMENT OF PROSECUTIONS
Definitions, Code of Criminal Justice, 2C:1–6

COMMERCE AND NAVIGATION
Lights and Lighting, generally, this index
Vessels, generally, this index

COMMERCIAL BANKS
Banks and Banking, generally, this index

COMMERCIAL BRIBERY
Generally, 2C:21–10

COMMERCIAL CODE
Electronic Transactions, generally, this index
Negotiable Instruments, generally, this index
Sales, generally, this index

COMMERCIAL DRIVERS LICENSES
Generally, 39:3–10.9 et seq.
Accidents, fatalities, suspension or revocation, 39:3–10.20
Consent,
   Intoxication of driver, 39:3–10.24
   Taking samples of breath,
      Chemical analyses, performed under methods approved by attorney general, 39:3–10.25
      Chemical tests, alcohol concentration, 39:3–10.24
      Record of, 39:3–10.24
      Refusal, 39:3–10.24
Construction, liberal, 39:3–10.10
Criminal history record information, applications, 39:3–10.17
Death, accidents, suspension or revocation, 39:3–10.20
Definitions, 39:3–10.11
Directors,
   Commercial motor vehicles, contracts, authority, 39:3–10.28
   Knowledge and skills test, administration, 39:3–10.21
   Provide for processing, required persons, obtain commercial drivers license, 39:3–10.23
   Refusal to grant commercial driver license, 39:3–10.16
   Rules and regulations,
      Driving privileges, 39:3–10.27
      Suspension, commercial motor vehicle driving privileges, 39:3–10.20
   Suspension or revocation of commercial motor vehicle license, 39:3–10.16
Driver improvement programs, suspension or revocation, reinstatement, 39:5–30
Examination permits, 39:3–13
Examinations, fees, 39:3–10.30
Exemptions, 39:3–10j et seq.
Expiration, 39:3–10.30
Fees,
   Examinations, 39:3–10.30

COMMERCIAL DRIVERS LICENSES
—Cont'd
Fees—Cont'd
Learners permit, **39:3–10.30**
Providing driving record information,
39:3–10.14
Fines and penalties,
Applying for driving privilege after suspen-
sion, revocation, or disqualification,
39:3–34
Consent, taking samples of breath, refusal,
39:3–10.24
Labor and employment, **39:3–10.18**
Operation of commercial motor vehicle, not
in possession of a valid commercial li-
cense, **39:3–10.18**
Operator not to have more than one license,
39:3–10.26
Out of service orders, **39:3–10.18**
Suspension, commercial motor vehicle driv-
ing privilege, **39:3–10.20**
Fingerprints and fingerprinting, applications,
39:3–10.17
Hazardous substances and waste,
Criminal history record information, applica-
tions, **39:3–10.17**
Suspension or revocation, **39:3–10.20**
Intoxication of driver, out of service orders,
39:3–10.20
Issuance, license, operation of commercial mo-
tor vehicle and is domiciled in state,
39:3–10.17
Knowledge and skills test,
Any person or agency to administer,
39:3–10.21
Commercial motor vehicle, operation,
39:3–10.12
Renewal, commercial drivers license,
39:3–10.12
Labor and employment, fines and penalties,
39:3–10.18
Learners permit, fees, **39:3–10.30**
Notice,
Commercial driver license information sys-
tem, issuance of license, **39:3–10.14**
Conviction, suspension or disqualification,
commercial drivers license, **39:3–10.15**
Criminal history record information, applica-
tions, **39:3–10.17**
Suspension, revocation or cancellation, com-
mercial motor vehicle driving privilege,
39:3–10.20
Waiver, any portion of law, **39:3–10.29**
Operation, commercial motor vehicles,
Alcohol concentration, prohibited,
39:3–10.13
Is domiciled in state, license, issuance,
39:3–10.17
Knowledge and skills test, **39:3–10.12**
Operator not to have more than one license,
39:3–10.26
Possession of valid commercial driver li-
cense, **39:3–10.18**
Public roads, consent, **39:3–10.24**
Under influence of controlled substance,
prohibited, **39:3–10.13**
Waiver, commercial driver license require-
ments, **39:3–10.19**
Out of service orders,
Fines and penalties, **39:3–10.18**
Suspension or revocation, **39:3–10.20**
Penalties. Fines and penalties, generally, ante
Public policy, **39:3–10.10**
Reinstatement, suspension or revocation, driv-
er improvement programs, **39:5–30**
School buses, **39:3–10.12**

COMMERCIAL DRIVERS LICENSES
—Cont'd
Second and subsequent offenses, suspension or
revocation, **39:3–10.20**
Skills test, waiver, **39:3–10.22**
Suspension or revocation,
Accidents, fatalities, **39:3–10.20**
Application for driving privileges during pe-
riod, prohibited, **39:3–34**
Traffic accidents, **39:5–30**
Tank vehicles, criminal history record informa-
tion, applications, **39:3–10.17**
Waiver,
Any portion of law, **39:3–10.29**
Skills test, **39:3–10.22**

COMMERCIAL EXPLOSIVES
Definitions, Explosives Act, **21:1A–129**

COMMERCIAL MOTOR VEHICLES
Motor Carriers, generally, this index

COMMERCIAL PAPER
Negotiable Instruments, generally, this index

COMMERCIAL PUBLICATIONS
Hearsay exception, **Evidence Rule 803**

COMMERCIAL VEHICLES
Buses, generally, this index
Definitions, registration, reciprocity, **39:3–6.1**

COMMISSIONERS
Boards and Commissions, generally, this index

COMMISSIONS
Boards and Commissions, generally, this index

COMMIT
Definitions, juvenile justice, **2A:4A–22**

**COMMITMENT AND ADMISSION TO IN-
STITUTIONS**
Generally, **2C:43–10**
Abuse of children, child abuser, consent,
9:6–8.58
Adult Diagnostic and Treatment Center, gen-
erally, this index
Arrest by officer of another state in fresh
pursuit, **2A:155–4, 2A:155–5**
Attorneys, disability inactive status, **Rule
1:20–12**
Child abuser, consent, **9:6–8.58**
Contempt, terms of release, **Rule 1:10–3**
Criminal defendants, **2C:4–6 et seq.**
Examination, psychiatric hospitals, **2C:4–5**
Custody, interference with, **2C:13–4**
Diagnostic center, sex offenders, **2A:169–3**
Fugitive from justice to jail to await requisition,
2A:160–23
Indigent Persons, this index
Insanity defense, notice, **Rule 3:12–1**
Juvenile Delinquents, this index
Mental defectives, privileged communications
between patient and physician,
2A:84A–22.3
Patient and physician privilege, **Evidence Rule
506**
Presentence investigation and report, disclo-
sure, **2C:44–6**
Records, expungement, **2C:52–1 et seq.**
Release, mentally ill defendants, **2C:4–9**
Transfers,
Continued commitment, defendant acquitted
by reason of insanity, **2C:4–8**
Correctional Institutions, generally, this in-
dex

**COMMITMENT AND ADMISSION TO IN-
STITUTIONS**—Cont'd
Transfers—Cont'd
Prisons and prisoners.   Correctional Institu-
tions, generally, this index

COMMITTEES
Attorneys, this index
Bar admission advisory committee, **Rules
1:27A–1, 1:27A–2**
Disciplinary oversight committee, **Rule 1:20B–1
et seq.**
Attorneys, **Rule 1:20**
Establishment, **Rule 1:20–1**
District ethics committees, attorneys, **Rules
1:20–1, 1:20–3**
District fee arbitration committees, attorneys,
Rules 1:20–1, 1:20A–1 et seq.
Judicial performance committee, **Rule 1:35A–1
et seq.**
Juvenile conference committees, **Rules 5:25–1,
5:25–2**
Court intake services, **2A:4A–75**
Opinions, committees, **Rule 1:36–2**
Peer review committee, medical professions,
immunity from liability, **2A:84A–22.10**
Professional ethics, advisory committee, **Rule
1:19–1 et seq.**

COMMODITIES
Appraisers, commercial bribery and breach of
duty, **2C:21–10**

COMMON CARRIERS
Buses, generally, this index
Carriers, generally, this index
Motor Carriers, generally, this index
Passengers, generally, this index
Railroads, generally, this index
Street Railways, generally, this index

COMMON INFORMERS
Identity, disclosure by witness, privilege,
2A:84A–28

COMMON LAW CRIMES
Abolition, **2C:1–5**

COMMON NUISANCES
Nuisance, generally, this index

COMMON STOCK
Shares and Shareholders, generally, this index

COMMUNICATIONS
Confidential or Privileged Information, gener-
ally, this index
Electronic surveillance, **2A:156A–1 et seq.**
Harassment, **2C:33–4**
Obscene material, public communication,
2C:34–4
Radio and Radio Stations, generally, this index
Television, generally, this index
Wiretapping and electronic surveillance,
2A:156A–1 et seq.

COMMUNICATIONS COMMON CARRIER
Definitions, wiretapping and electronic surveillance, **2A:156A–2**

COMMUNITY AFFAIRS DEPARTMENT
Appropriations, county prosecutors, compensation and salaries, payments to counties,
2A:158–10

COMMUNITY AFFAIRS DEPARTMENT
—Cont'd
Local government services division,
Director, county chief financial officer.
County Officers and Employees, gener-
ally, this index
School Buildings and Grounds, generally,
this index

COMMUNITY RELATED SERVICE
Probation, condition, **Rules 3:21–7, 7:9–1**
Sentence and punishment, authorized disposi-
tion, **2C:43–2**

COMMUNITY RESIDENCES
Crimes and offenses, **2C:43–2**

COMMUNITY SERVICE
Crimes and Offenses, this index

COMMUNITY STANDARDS
Obscene material, adults, **2C:34–2**

COMMUTATION
Pardons, this index

COMMUTER VANS
Generally, **39:3–27.19 et seq.**
Definitions, **39:1–1**
Doors, special exits, merchandising or exhibi-
tion vans or trailers, **39:3–77.2**
Fines and penalties, **39:3–27.22**
Handicapped persons, licenses and permits,
fees, **39:3–8, 39:3–8.1**
Licenses and permits, **39:3–27.19**
Fees, **39:3–8**
Nonresidents, **39:3–19.6**
Plates or markers, **39:3–27.19 et seq.**
Rear view mirrors, **39:3–71.1**
Rules and regulations, **39:3–27.23**
School buses, identification and warning lights,
39:3B–8, 39:3B–9

COMPACT ADMINISTRATORS
Definitions, adult offender supervision, interstate compacts, **2A:168–27**

COMPACTING STATES
Definitions, adult offender supervision, interstate compacts, **2A:168–27**

COMPACTS
Interstate Compacts, generally, this index

COMPANY
Corporations, generally, this index

COMPARATIVE NEGLIGENCE
Controlled substances, dealers, liability,
2C:35B–10

**COMPELLING ATTENDANCE OF WIT-
NESSES**
Witnesses, this index

COMPENSATION AND SALARIES
Alcoholic Beverage Control Division, generally,
this index
Alcoholic Beverages, this index
Arbitrators, motor vehicles, tort claims,
39:6A–28
Automobile insurance risk exchange members,
39:6A–21
Chosen Freeholders, this index
County Detectives and Investigators, this index
County Officers and Employees, this index
County Prosecutors, this index
Definitions, no fault insurance, **39:6A–2**

COMPENSATION AND SALARIES—Cont'd
Disorderly persons, nonpayment, **2C:40A–2**
Juvenile delinquents and dependents, commu-
nity service, **2A:4A–43**
Mediation, **Rule 1:40–4**
Motor Vehicle Commission, this index
Motor Vehicle Insurance, this index
Motor vehicles, arbitrators, tort claims,
39:6A–28
Municipal board of alcoholic beverage control,
33:1–5
Municipal court judges, **2B:12–7**
Municipal Courts, this index
Municipal Officers and Employees, this index
Nonpayment, disorderly persons, **2C:40A–2**
Police and Police Departments, this index
State Officers and Employees, this index
State Police, this index
Victims of Crime, this index

COMPETENCY OF WITNESSES
Generally, **Evidence Rule 601**

COMPETITION
Monopolies, generally, this index

COMPLAINING WITNESS
Definitions, rape, **2A:84A–32.3**

COMPLAINTS
Alcoholic Beverages, this index
Arrest without warrant, preparation, **Rule
3:4–1**
Attorneys, this index
Caption designating, **Rule 1:4–1**
Case information statement, filing with, **Rule
1:5–6**
Child Abuse, this index
Children and Minors, this index
County detectives and investigators,
2A:157–10.1 et seq.
Crimes and Offenses, this index
Denial, record expungement, **2C:52–14**
Disclosure, expungement order, **2C:52–30**
Dismissal and nonsuit, failure to appear, **Rule
1:2–4**
Diversion programs, record expungement,
2C:52–20
Domestic Violence, this index
Exemptions, record expungement, **2C:52–2**
Explosives, **21:1A–130**
Expungement, records, **2C:52–1 et seq.**
Fees, record expungement, **2C:52–29**
Forfeitures, **2C:64–3**
Hearings, record expungement, **2C:52–9 et seq.**
Indictable offenses, record expungement,
2C:52–2
Indictment, Information or Presentment, gen-
erally, this index
Inspection and inspectors, records, expunge-
ment, **2C:52–19**
Juvenile and Domestic Relations Courts, this
index
Juvenile Delinquents, this index
Motor carriers, intermodal transportation,
chassis, drivers, **39:3–79.16**
Motor Vehicles, this index
Municipal Courts, this index
Notice of violation of laws to mayor or chief of
police as authority to make complaint,
2A:152–13
Orders of court, record expungement,
2C:52–11 et seq., 2C:52–26
Petitions, record expungement, **2C:52–7 et seq.**
Presentence report, record expungement,
2C:52–21

COMPLAINTS—Cont'd
Process,
Attorney disciplinary proceedings, **Rule
1:20–4**
Criminal proceedings, **Rule 3:2**
Record expungement, **2C:52–10**
Records, expungement, **2C:52–1 et seq.**
Release, record expungement, **2C:52–19**
Removal, records, **2C:52–15**
Report of physician or hospital, child abuse,
9:6–8.18
Sealing, record expungement, **2C:52–26**
Speed, **39:4–99**
State Police, this index
Statements, record expungement petition,
2C:52–8
Summons, procedure after arrest, **Rule 3:4–1**
Supervisory treatment programs, record ex-
pungement, **2C:52–20**
Traffic offenses, record expungement,
2C:52–28
Traffic Rules and Regulations, this index
Unauthorized practice of law, **Rule 1:22–5**
Warrants, procedure after arrest, **Rule 3:4–1**

**COMPLEMENTARY DISPUTE RESOLU-
TION**
Generally, **Rule 1:33–1 et seq.**

COMPLICITY
Criminal offenses, **2C:2–6**

COMPOUNDING
Generally, **2C:29–4**

COMPOUNDS
Seizure of compound for use in manufacture of
alcoholic beverages, **33:1–66**

**COMPREHENSIVE DRUG REFORM ACT
OF 1986**
Generally, **2C:35–1 et seq.**

**COMPREHENSIVE ENFORCEMENT PRO-
GRAM FUND ACT**
Generally, **2B:19–1 et seq.**

COMPRESSED GAS
Turnpike project, transportation regulations,
27:23–31

COMPROMISE AND SETTLEMENT
Air pollution, fines and penalties, **26:2C–19**
Complementary dispute resolution programs,
Rule 1:40–1 et seq.
Conferences,
Chambers, **Rule 1:2–1**
Failure to appear, sanctions, **Rule 1:2–4**
Verbatim records, **Rule 1:2–2**
Contingent attorney fees, **Rule 1:21–7**
Crimes and offenses,
Motion, consent, **Rule 3:1–4**
Plea discussions, **Rule 3:9–3**
Explosives, fines and penalties, **21:1A–140**
Intoxicating liquors, suspension of license,
33:1–31
Liquefied petroleum gas, fines and penalties,
21:1B–5
Motor vehicle accident,
Claim payable from unsatisfied claim and
judgment fund, **39:6–72**
Settlement of hit and run cases against insur-
ance commissioner under unsatisfied
claim and judgment fund, **39:6–82**
News organizations, searches and seizures, suits
against government, **2A:84A–21.11**
Notice to court, **Rule 1:6–7**

COMPROMISE AND SETTLEMENT—Cont'd

Offers and negotiations, **Evidence Rule 408**

Public defendant, claims, **2A:158A–20**

Solid waste, penalty claims, **13:1E–9**

COMPUTER EQUIPMENT

Definitions, computer related offenses, **2C:20–23**

COMPUTER NETWORK

Definitions, computer related offenses, **2C:20–23**

COMPUTER PROGRAM

Definitions, computer related offenses, **2C:20–23**

COMPUTER SYSTEMS

Definitions, computer related offenses, **2C:20–23**

COMPUTERS

Access, crimes and offenses, unauthorized, **2C:20–25**

Access devices,
  Alteration or defacement, **2C:20–1.1**
  Forgery, **2C:21–1**
  Theft, **2C:20–2**
    Definitions, **2C:20–1**
    Services, **2C:20–8**

Children and Minors, this index

Copies, software, crimes and offenses, **2C:20–33**

Crimes and offenses, **2C:20–23 et seq.**
  Access, unauthorized, **2C:20–25**
  Children and minors, prohibited sexual acts, **2C:24–4**
  Computer criminal activity, **2C:20–2**
  Copies, software, **2C:20–33**
  Data bases, destruction, **2C:20–25**
  Disclosure,
    Data from wrongful access, **2C:20–31**
    Personal information, **2C:20–25**
  Electricity and electric companies, interference, **2C:20–25**
  Gas companies, interference, **2C:20–25**
  Juvenile delinquents and dependents,
    Jurisdiction, waiver, **2A:4A–26**
    Referral to other courts without juveniles consent, **Rule 5:22–2**
  Mass transportation, interference, **2C:20–25**
  Personal information, disclosure, **2C:20–25**
  Public utilities, interference, **2C:20–25**
  Software, copies, **2C:20–33**
  Telecommunications, interference, **2C:20–25**
  Theft, **2C:20–2**
    Data, **2C:20–25**
  Water supply plants and systems, interference, **2C:20–25**

Data bases, destruction, crimes and offenses, **2C:20–25**

Definitions, computer related offenses, **2C:20–23**

Disclosure, crimes and offenses, personal information, **2C:20–25**

DNA Database and Databank, generally, this index

Electricity and Electric Companies, this index

Electronic Transactions, generally, this index

Fines and penalties, **2C:43–3.8**
  Collection, **2C:46–4**

Gas Companies, this index

Identity theft, personal identifying information, **2C:21–17.3**

Information, theft, crimes and offenses, **2C:20–25**

Internet, generally, this index

COMPUTERS—Cont'd

Juvenile delinquents and dependents, crimes and offenses, jurisdiction, waiver, **2A:4A–26**

Mass transportation, crimes and offenses, interference, **2C:20–25**

Offenses. Crimes and offenses, generally, ante

Personal information, crimes and offenses, disclosure, **2C:20–25**

Petit jurors, selection, **2B:23–2**

Programs, children and minors, sexual offenses, **2C:24–4**

Public utilities, crimes and offenses, interference, **2C:20–25**

Records and recordation. Electronic Transactions, generally, this index

Remote computing services, wiretapping and electronic surveillance, **2A:156A–12**

Repairs, value of property or services, computer related offenses, **2C:20–24**

Security, confidential or privileged information, **Rule 1:38–5**

Software,
  Copies, crimes and offenses, **2C:20–33**
  Definitions, computer related offenses, **2C:20–23**
  Theft of services, telecommunications, **2C:20–8**

Telecommunications, interference, crimes and offenses, **2C:20–25**

Theft, **2C:20–2, 2C:20–8, 2C:20–25**
  Data, crimes and offenses, **2C:20–25**
  Situs of offense, **2C:20–34**

Value of property or services, computer related offenses, **2C:20–24**

Water supply plants and systems, interference, crimes and offenses, **2C:20–25**

Wiretapping and electronic surveillance,
  Remote computing services, **2A:156A–12**
  Trespass, **2A:156A–4.1**

World wide web. Internet, generally, this index

CONCEAL

Definitions, shoplifting, **2C:20–11**

CONCEALMENT

Hindering apprehension or prosecution of accused, **2C:29–3**

Recordable instruments, fraud, **2C:21–3**

Records, **2C:21–4**

Secured transactions, defrauding secured creditors, **2C:21–12**

Terrorism, **2C:38–4**

CONCURRENT JURISDICTION

Magistrate of municipality and county traffic court for violation of motor vehicle and traffic laws, **39:5–3**

CONCURRENT SENTENCES

Generally, **2C:44–5**

CONDITIONAL LICENSE

Drivers license, **39:3–11**

CONDITIONAL PLEAS

Municipal courts, **Rule 7:6–2**

CONDITIONAL SALES

Motor Vehicles, this index

CONDUCT

Crimes and offenses, causal relationship between conduct and result, **2C:2–3**

CONDUCT OF PROCEEDING

Generally, **Rule 1:2–1 et seq.**

CONFERENCES

Attorney discipline, prehearing conference, **Rule 1:20–5**

Case Management, this index

Compromise and Settlement, this index

Court intake services, juvenile delinquents and dependents, **2A:4A–74**

Crimes and Offenses, this index

Judicial conferences, **Rules 1:35–1, 1:35–2**

Jury and Jurors, this index

Juvenile delinquents and dependents,
  Court intake services, **2A:4A–74**
  Predispositional conferences, **2A:4A–42**

Motor vehicles, special registration, **39:3–27.2**

Open court proceedings, **Rule 1:2–1**

Pretrial Conferences, generally, this index

Records and recordation, verbatim records, **Rule 1:2–2**

Settlement conferences. Compromise and Settlement, this index

CONFESSIONS

Crimes and Offenses, this index

CONFIDENTIAL COMMUNICATIONS

Confidential or Privileged Information, generally, this index

CONFIDENTIAL OR PRIVILEGED INFORMATION

Administrative records, **Rule 1:38–5**

AIDS (Acquired Immune Deficiency Syndrome), records and recordation, **Rule 1:38–3**

Attorney client privilege, **2A:84A–20**

Attorneys, this index

Bar examiners board files and records, **Rule 1:23–3**

Child Abuse, this index

Child fatality and near fatality review board, **9:6–8.92**

Children and Minors, this index

Clergy, **2A:84A–23**

Complementary dispute resolution, **Rule 1:38–5**

Counselors and counseling, victims of crime, **2A:84A–22.13 et seq.**

Court intake services conference, juvenile delinquents and dependents, **2A:4A–74**

Court records, **Rule 1:38–3**

Crimes and Offenses, this index

Damages, hospital utilization review committee, **2A:84A–22.9**

Definitions, victims of crime, counselors, **2A:84A–22.14**

Developmental disabilities, appeal and review, records and recordation, **Rule 1:38–3**

Diagnostic center report, presentence investigation, sex offenses, **Rule 3:21–3**

Discovery, matters obtained from prosecutor, **Rule 1:38–3**

DNA database and databank,
  Crimes and offenses, motions, **2A:84A–32a**
  Profiles and samples, **53:1–20.27**

Domestic Violence, this index

Epilepsy and similar conditions, motor vehicle division, report filed with, **39:3–10.7**

Family court, records, juvenile delinquents and dependents, **2A:4A–60 et seq.**

Firearms permits, institutional confinement, waiver of confidentiality, **2C:58–3**

Hiv (human immunodeficiency virus), records and recordation, **Rule 1:38–3**

Hospitals, this index

**CONFIDENTIAL OR PRIVILEGED INFOR-
MATION**—Cont'd
Hotlines, law enforcement officers, crisis inter-
vention services, funding, **2C:64–6, 39:5–41**
Identity and Identification, this index
Impounded records, **Rule 1:38–3**
Information disclosure privilege, newspersons,
criminal proceedings, **2A:84A–21.1 et seq.**
Intergovernmental exchanges, records, **Rule
1:38–6**
IOLTA fund, **Rule 1:28A–5**
Judges and Justices, this index
Judicial conduct advisory committee, **Rule
1:38–5**
Jury questionnaires, **Rule 1:38–5**
Juvenile conference committees, **2A:4A–75;
Rule 5:25–1**
Juvenile Delinquents, this index
Juvenile family crisis, hearings, **Rule 5:17–4**
Law enforcement agencies, records, **2A:4A–60
et seq.**
Law enforcement officers, crisis intervention
services, hotlines, funding, **2C:64–6,
39:5–41**
Lie detector tests, employees of drug manufac-
turers, **2C:40A–1**
Mediation, complementary dispute resolution
programs, **Rule 1:40–4**
Newspersons information disclosure privilege,
criminal proceedings, **2A:84A–21.1 et seq.**
Personal identifiers, **Rule 1:38–7**
Personnel records, **Rule 1:38–5**
Physicians and Surgeons, this index
Press associations, news personnel, **2A:84A–21,
2A:84A–21a**
Pretrial intervention programs, **Rule 1:38–3**
Priest penitent privilege, **2A:84A–23**
Privileges and Immunities, generally, this index
Probation records, **Rule 1:38–5**
Psychiatric examinations, statements of defen-
dant, **2C:4–10**
Public defenders, **2A:158A–12**
Public officers and employees, official actions
or information, **2C:30–3**
Racketeering, investigative interrogatories,
2C:41–5
Radio news personnel, **2A:84A–21, 2A:84A–21a**
Radon gas testing, buildings, **26:2D–73**
Search warrants, **Rule 3:5–4**
Filed documents, **Rule 7:5–1**
Sex Offenses, this index
Spouses, **2A:84A–22**
Support proceedings, **2C:62–1**
Tampering with witnesses and informants,
2C:28–5
Television, news personnel, **2A:84A–21,
2A:84A–21a**
Traffic accident, law enforcement officers re-
port, **39:4–131**
Unauthorized practice of law, committees,
Rule 1:22–1
Victims of crime, counselors, **2A:84A–22.13 et
seq.**
Wire services, news personnel, **2A:84A–21,
2A:84A–21a**
Witnesses, **2A:84A–19**

CONFINEMENT
Correctional Institutions, generally, this index
Kidnapping, generally, this index

CONFISCATION
Alcoholic Beverage Law, unlawful property,
33:1–55
Electronic surveillance equipment, **2A:156A–7**

CONFISCATION—Cont'd
Flammable fabrics, sleeping bags and tents,
sales, **2A:123–20**
Motor vehicles, component parts, serial numbers, **39:10B–3**

CONFLAGRATIONS
Fires and Fire Protection, generally, this index

CONFLICT OF INTEREST
Adverse or Pecuniary Interest, generally, this
index

CONFLICT OF LAWS
Driver license compact, **39:5D–6**
Explosives,
Fireworks, **21:3–7**
Jurisdiction, **21:1A–139**
Fireworks, explosives, **21:3–7**
Interstate compact for adult offender supervi-
sion, **2A:168–39**
Liquefied petroleum gas, local ordinances or
regulations, **21:1B–7**

CONFUSING EVIDENCE
Exclusion, **Evidence Rule 403**

**CONGRESSIONAL MEDAL OF HONOR
HOLDERS**
Motor vehicle registration, fee, **39:3–27.1**

CONIINE
Poisons, generally, this index

CONSECUTIVE SENTENCES
Correctional Institutions, this index

CONSENT
Agreements, mediation, complementary dis-
pute resolution programs, **Rule 1:40–4**
AIDS (Acquired Immune Deficiency Syn-
drome), this index
Attorneys, withdrawal or substitution, **Rule
1:11–2**
Children and Minors, this index
Commercial Drivers Licenses, this index
Criminal practice and procedure, settlement,
Rule 3:1–4
Dependent or Neglected Children, this index
Enlargement of time, **Rule 1:3–4**
Hazing and aggravated hazing, defense,
2C:40–4
Medical Care and Treatment, this index
Monopolies and unfair trade, hearings or in-
quiries, specific evidence, **56:9–9**
Motor Vehicles, this index
Photographs, nudity, sexual intercourse, inva-
sion of privacy, **2C:14–9**
Public Lands, this index
Solid waste, roll off dumpsters or containers,
placement along highways or public prop-
erty, **27:51–1**
Victim of crime, **2C:2–10**
Privileged communications, waiver, counsel-
ors, **2A:84A–22.15**
Wiretapping and electronic surveillance,
2A:156A–4

CONSENT JUDGMENTS
Monopolies and unfair trade, failure to comply,
56:9–7
Motor vehicle accident cases, payment out of
unsatisfied claim and judgment fund,
39:6–74

CONSERVATION
Environmental Protection, generally, this index

CONSERVATION—Cont'd
Hackensack Meadowlands, this index
Parks and Parkways, generally, this index
Recycling. Solid Waste, this index

**CONSERVATION AND DEVELOPMENT DE-
PARTMENT**
Environmental Protection Department, gener-
ally, this index

**CONSERVATION AND ECONOMIC DEVEL-
OPMENT DEPARTMENT**
Commissioner. Environmental Protection De-
partment, this index
Environmental Protection Department, gener-
ally, this index

CONSERVATION DEPARTMENT
Environmental Protection Department, generally, this index

CONSERVATORS OF THE PEACE
Law Enforcement Officers, generally, this index

CONSIDERATION
Contracts, generally, this index

CONSOLIDATION OF ACTIONS
Juvenile delinquents and dependents, change
of venue, **Rule 5:19–1**
Complaint, **Rule 5:20–1**
Municipal courts, **Rule 7:8–4**

CONSPIRACY
Generally, **2C:2–6, 2C:5–2, 2C:5–4**
Arrest warrant, issuance, **Rule 3:3–1**
Arrest without warrant, release, **Rule 3:4–1**
Attorneys, conviction, discipline, **Rule 1:20–13**
Automobile no fault insurance, fines and pen-
alties, **39:6A–15**
Bias intimidation, **2C:16–1**
Capacity, **2C:5–3**
Children and minors, using child to commit
crime, **2C:24–9**
Conduct of another, criminal liability, **2C:2–6**
Controlled Substances, this index
Defenses, notice, **Rule 3:12–1**
Definitions, Code of Criminal Justice, **2C:5–2**
Employing child to commit crime, **2C:24–9**
Fines and penalties, **2C:5–4**
Grade and degree of offense, **2C:5–4**
Homicide, **2C:11–3**
Incapacity, irresponsibility or immunity of party
to conspiracy, **2C:5–3**
Included offenses, **2C:1–8**
Juvenile delinquents and dependents,
Jurisdiction, waiver, **2A:4A–26**
Referral to other courts without juveniles
consent, **Rule 5:22–2**
Limitation of criminal prosecutions, **2C:1–6**
Monopolies, generally, this index
Multiple prosecutions, offenses, **2C:1–8**
Murder, **2C:11–3**
Narcotics, conviction, license revocation,
24:21–12
Places of worship, targets of crime, grade and
degree of offense, **2C:5–4**
Territorial applicability of code of criminal jus-
tice, **2C:1–3**
Terrorism, **2C:5–4, 2C:38–2**

CONSTABLES
Associations and societies, intoxicating liquors,
club licenses, **33:1–25.1, 33:1–25.2**
Club licenses, intoxicating liquors, nonprofit
organizations, **33:1–25.1, 33:1–25.2**

CONSTABLES—Cont'd

Cruelty to children, societies for prevention, agents, **9:6–7**

Detective association pursuers, powers of constables, **15:4–1**

Escapes, generally, this index

Fees or other remuneration,
Acquittals, **2A:166–8**
Criminal causes, not to be demanded from parties applying for services, **2A:166–18**

Fraternal societies, intoxicating liquors, club licenses, **33:1–25.1, 33:1–25.2**

Intoxicating liquors, nonprofit organizations, club licenses, **33:1–25.1, 33:1–25.2**

Licenses and permits, intoxicating liquors, nonprofit organizations, **33:1–25.1, 33:1–25.2**

Motor vehicle master keys or devices, **2C:5–6**

Nonprofit organizations, intoxicating liquors, club licenses, **33:1–25.1, 33:1–25.2**

Qualifications, **2A:154–2**

Railroad crossings, enforcement of regulations as to stopping of motor vehicles or school busses, **39:5–1**

Religious societies, intoxicating liquors, club licenses, **33:1–25.1, 33:1–25.2**

Societies, intoxicating liquors, club licenses, **33:1–25.1, 33:1–25.2**

State police to have authority, **53:2–1**

Veterans organizations, intoxicating liquors, club licenses, **33:1–25.1, 33:1–25.2**

CONSTITUTION OF NEW JERSEY

Attorney disciplinary proceedings, appeal and review, preservation, **Rule 1:20–15**

Municipalities, ordinances, unconstitutionality, **2B:12–32**

Ordinances, unconstitutionality, **2B:12–32**

Postconviction relief, grounds, **Rule 3:22–2**

State police, violations, complaints, limitation of actions, **53:1–33**

CONSTITUTION OF THE UNITED STATES

Ordinances, unconstitutionality, **2B:12–32**

CONSTRUCTION

Crimes and offenses, criminal law, **2C:98–1**

Highways and Roads, this index

Laws. Construction of Laws, generally, this index

Portable, oil burning heating device, **2C:40–10**

Statutes. Construction of Laws, generally, this index

CONSTRUCTION OF LAWS

Code of Criminal Justice, **2C:1–1, 2C:1–2**

Criminal Justice Code, **2C:1–1, 2C:1–2, 2C:98–1**

Nonresident Violator Compact, motor vehicles, **39:5F–29**

CONSTRUCTION OF RULES

Generally, **Evidence Rule 102; Rule 1:1–2**

CONSULS AND CONSULAR AGENTS

Traffic rules and regulations, privileges and immunities, records and recordation, **39:5–53 et seq.**

CONSULS GENERAL

Attorneys, **Rule 1:21–4**

CONSULTANTS

Foreign legal consultants, **Rule 1:21–9**

CONSUMER CREDIT

Credit Cards, generally, this index

CONSUMER CREDIT—Cont'd

Identity theft, orders of court, corrections, **2C:21–17.5**

Notice, reports, identity theft, orders of court, corrections, **2C:21–17.5**

CONSUMER PROTECTION

Interchangeable drug products. Drugs and Medicine, this index

Liquefied petroleum gas education and safety board, **21:1B–12 et seq.**

CONSUMER REPORTING AGENCY

Identity theft, orders of court, corrections, **2C:21–17.5**

CONSUMPTION

Alcoholic Beverages, this index

CONTACT LENSES

Definitions, dispensing, **2C:40–25**

Ophthalmic Dispensers and Technicians, this index

CONTAINERS

See, also, Packages, generally, this index

Alcoholic Beverages, this index

Controlled substances, **24:21–16 et seq.**

Definitions,
Food and drugs, **24:21–32**
Intoxicating liquor law, **33:1–1**

Drugs and Medicine, this index

Fireworks, matches, manufacturers, **21:2–20**

Hazardous Substances and Waste, this index

Liquefied Petroleum Gas, this index

Motor carriers, intermodal transportation,
Axle weight limitations, **39:3–84.1**
Chassis, **39:3–79.10 et seq.**

Sales, this index

CONTAMINATION

Water Pollution, generally, this index

CONTEMPT

Generally, **2C:29–9; Rule 1:10–1 et seq.**

Allegations, domestic violence prevention, **2C:25–32**

Arrest, institution of proceedings, **Rule 1:10–2**

Attorney fees, **Rule 1:10–3**

Attorney general, prosecution, **Rule 1:10–2**

Attorneys, this index

Bail,
Jumping, **2C:29–7**
Person charged with contempt, **Rule 1:10–2**

Certificate by judge, presence of court, **Rule 1:10–1**

Child support hearing officers, **Rule 5:25–3**

Client protection fund, noncompliance with subpoena, **Rule 1:28–6**

Commitment, terms of release, **Rule 1:10–3**

Consent, hearing by offended judge, **Rule 1:10–2**

Corporations, fines, nonpayment, **2C:46–2**

County prosecutors, execution, **Rule 1:10–2**

Crimes and offenses, **2C:1–5, 2C:29–9**
Supervisory treatment program, **2C:43–13**

Disqualification of judge, **Rule 1:10–3**

Domestic Violence, this index

Fines and penalties, **2C:1–5**
Corporations, nonpayment, **2C:46–2**

Institution of proceedings, **Rule 1:10–2**

Judicial order, **2C:29–9**

Jumping bail, **2C:29–7**

Juror failing to appear or serve, **2B:20–14**

Jury list, persons refusing to answer questionnaires, **2B:20–14**

Jury trial, **Rule 1:10–2**

CONTEMPT—Cont'd

Juvenile delinquents and dependents, detention facilities, **2A:4A–37**

Notice, summary proceeding on notice, **Rule 1:10–2**

Orders, **2C:29–9; Rule 1:10–1**
Institution of proceedings, show cause or arrest order, **Rule 1:10–2**

Pending hearings, bail, **Rule 1:10–2**

Power to punish, **2C:1–5**

Presence of court, **Rule 1:10–1**

Probable cause, arrests, domestic violence prevention, **2C:25–31**

Prosecution, **Rule 1:10–2**

Relief to litigant, **Rule 1:10–3**

Restraining orders, domestic violence, foreign states, **2C:29–9**

Search warrants, disclosure of information, **Rule 3:5–4**

Subpoenas,
Failure to obey, **Rule 1:9–5**
Public officers or agencies, enforcement, **Rule 1:9–6**

Summary contempt,
Presence of court, adjudication, **Rule 1:10–1**
Proceedings on show cause or arrest order, **Rule 1:10–2**

Support of Persons, this index

Trial, **Rule 1:10–2**

Witnesses, protection orders, **2C:29–9**

CONTENTS

Definitions, wiretapping and electronic surveillance, **2A:156A–2**

CONTEST OF CHANCE

Definitions, **2C:37–1**

Gambling, generally, this index

CONTINGENT FEES

Attorney fees, **Rule 1:21–7**

CONTINUANCE

Briefs, failure to comply with requirements, sanctions, **Rule 1:2–4**

Criminal prosecutions, convicts, interstate agreement on detainers, **2A:159A–3**

Grand jury term, **Rule 3:6–10**

Indigent, neglected or abandoned children, juvenile family crisis, hearings, **2A:4A–86**

Juvenile delinquents and dependents,
Adjudicatory hearing, **Rule 5:21–7**
Juvenile family crisis, hearings, **2A:4A–86**

Juvenile family crisis, hearings, **2A:4A–86; Rule 5:17–2**

CONTRABAND

Forfeitures, **2C:64–1 et seq.**

Prisons and prisoners, **2C:29–6**

CONTRACTS

Arbitration and Award, generally, this index

Bribery and corruption, effect of conviction, **2C:51–2**

County juvenile detention facilities, juvenile justice commission, placement of juveniles in custody of, **2A:4A–44.1**

Courts, collections, **2B:19–6**

Definitions, Motor Vehicle Certificate of Ownership Law, **39:10–2**

Government contracts, conviction of crime, **2C:51–2**

Homicide, murder for hire, **2C:11–3**

Interstate compact for adult offender supervision, **2A:168–39**

CONTRACTS—Cont'd
Juvenile justice commission, placement of juveniles in custody, county juvenile detention facilities, **2A:4A-44.1**
Juveniles, county detention facilities, juvenile justice commission, placements, **2A:4A-44.1**
Leases, generally, this index
Liquidated damages. Damages, generally, this index
Motor vehicle commission,
　Ancillary services, **39:2A-33**
　Powers and duties, **39:2A-13**
Municipal courts, collections, **2B:19-6**
Murder for hire, **2C:11-3**
Nonresident violator compacts, **39:5F-20**
Plea agreements, municipal prosecutors, **2B:25-11**
Political Subdivisions, this index
Prepaid funeral agreements. Funerals, this index
Privileged communications, physician and patients, **2A:84A-22.4**
Public defenders, legal services, **2A:158A-10**
Superior court, collections, **2B:19-6**
Supervisory treatment programs, first offenders, **2C:43-13**
Tax court, collections, **2B:19-6**
Transportation Trust Fund Authority, this index
Turnpike Authority, this index
Turnpikes, this index

CONTRIBUTIONS
Automobile no fault insurance, **39:6A-11**
Soliciting, standing in roadway for purpose prohibited, **39:4-60**

CONTRIBUTORY NEGLIGENCE
Controlled substances, dealers, liability, **2C:35B-11**
Motor vehicles, child passenger restraint system not warned, **39:3-76.2a**

CONTROLLED DANGEROUS SUBSTANCES
Controlled Substances, this index

CONTROLLED PREMISES
Definitions, controlled dangerous substances, administrative inspection warrants, **24:21-32**

CONTROLLED SUBSTANCE ANALOG
Definitions, **2C:35-2**

CONTROLLED SUBSTANCES
Generally, **2C:35-1 et seq., 2C:35B-1 et seq., 53:1-18.1 et seq.**
Abatement of proceedings, effect of repeal law, **24:21-40**
Actions and proceedings, dealers, liability, **2C:35B-1 et seq.**
Addicts. Drug Abuse, generally, this index
Additional penalties, **24:21-26**
Administration of law, **24:21-3, 24:21-31**
Administrative inspection warrants, **24:21-32**
　Controlled dangerous substances, **24:21-31**
Administrative orders, **24:21-31**
Affirmative defenses, distribution or possession with intent, **2C:35-7.1**
Agents, **24:21-2**
Analogs, precursors, possession, crimes and offenses, **2C:35-28**
Appeal and review,
　Controlled dangerous substances, **24:21-38**
　Fines and penalties, **2C:35-7a**

CONTROLLED SUBSTANCES—Cont'd
Arrest,
　Warrants, **24:21-31**
　　Issuance, **Rule 3:3-1**
　　Without warrant, release, **Rule 3:4-1**
Attachment, ex parte proceedings, dealers, liability, **2C:35B-13**
Attempts to commit offense, **24:21-24**
Attorneys, conviction of crime, automatic temporary suspension, **Rule 1:20-13**
Attorneys fees, dealers, liability, **2C:35B-5, 2C:35B-6**
Bail, revocation, injunctions, **2C:35-5.8**
Body cavity searches, **2A:161A-1 et seq.**
Booby traps,
　Crimes and offenses, property used for manufacture, distribution or possession, **2C:35-4.1**
　Property used for manufacture, distribution or possession, **2C:35-4.1**
Brands, labels and marks, **24:21-16 et seq.**
　Alteration or removal, **24:21-17**
　Scheduled substances, **24:21-4**
Buffer zones, entry on property, injunctions, **2C:35-5.7**
Burden of proof. Evidence, post
Bureau of narcotics and dangerous drugs, definitions, **24:21-2**
Business and commerce, entry on property, injunctions, **2C:35-5.7, 2C:35-5.10**
Carriers, registration requirements, **24:21-10**
Certificates and certification, entry on property, injunctions, **2C:35-5.9**
Chemical names, schedules, **24:21-4 et seq.**
Children and minors,
　Distribution to minors, **2C:35-8**
　Employing in distribution scheme, **2C:35-6**
　Fines and penalties, **2C:35-15**
　Paraphernalia, delivery to minors, **2C:36-5**
Classification, controlled substances, **24:21-5 et seq.**
Coca leaves, **24:21-2**
Commitment, drug dependent persons, **2C:35-14**
Common carriers, controlled substances, registration exemption, **24:21-10**
Common names, controlled substances, schedules, **24:21-4 et seq.**
Comparative negligence, dealers, liability, **2C:35B-10**
Comprehensive study and review, penalties, marihuana use and possession, **24:21-44**
Conditional discharge, first offenders, disorderly persons, **2C:36A-1**
Conspiracy, **24:21-24**
　Conviction, license revocation, **24:21-12**
　Distribution or possession with intent to distribute, overt acts, **2C:5-2**
　Narcotics trafficking networks, **2C:35-3**
Construction of statute, **2C:35-1.2**
Container, **24:21-16 et seq.**
Contributory negligence, dealers, liability, **2C:35B-11**
Controlled dangerous substances, **24:21-1 et seq.**
Controlled premises, definitions, administrative inspection warrants, **24:21-32**
Conviction of Crime, this index
Cooperation with federal and other state agencies, **24:21-34**
Costs, dealers, liability, **2C:35B-5, 2C:35B-6**
Counterfeit substance, definitions, **24:21-2**
Crimes and offenses,
　Affirmative defenses,
　　Burden of proof, **2C:35-18**

CONTROLLED SUBSTANCES—Cont'd
Crimes and offenses—Cont'd
　Affirmative defenses—Cont'd
　　Distribution or possession with intent, children and minors, **2C:35-7.1**
　Attempts, **24:21-24**
　Conditional discharge, first offenders, disorderly persons, **2C:36A-1**
　Conspiracy, **24:21-24**
　Date rape drugs, post
　Deaths from drugs, **2C:35-9**
　Defenses, notice, **Rule 3:12-1**
　Disorderly persons, generally, post
　Distribution, generally, post
　Employment of minors, transportation, **2C:35-6**
　Fingerprinting and photographing persons arrested, **53:1-18.1**
　Food, adulteration, **2C:12-2**
　Imitation controlled dangerous substances, **2C:35-11**
　Manufacturing, **2C:35-5**
　Maps and plats, distribution or possession with intent, location, **2C:35-7.1**
　Narcotics trafficking leaders, **2C:35-3**
　Paraphernalia, controlled substances, **2C:36-1 et seq.**
　Parks and parkways, **2C:35-7.1**
　Possession of, **2C:35-10**
　Precursors, possession, **2C:35-28**
　Presumption of nonimprisonment, application, **2C:35-8**
　Production facility, **2C:35-4**
　Public buildings, **2C:35-7.1**
　Public housing, **2C:35-7.1**
　Report of sentence or other disposition, **53:1-18.2**
　Second or subsequent offenses, **24:21-29**
　Use, **2C:35-10**
　Weapons, crimes and offenses, consecutive sentences, **2C:39-4.1**
Damages, dealers, liability, **2C:35B-1 et seq.**
Date rape drugs, crimes and offenses,
　Distribution, **2C:35-5.3**
　Facilitation, **2C:14-1**
　Flunitrazepam,
　　Manufacture, distribution or dispensation, **2C:35-5.3**
　　Possession, **2C:35-10.3**
　Gamma hydroxybutyrate,
　　Manufacture, distribution or dispensation, **2C:35-5.2**
　　Possession, **2C:35-10.2**
　Manufacture, **2C:35-5.3**
　　Facilities, **2C:35-4**
　Possession, **2C:35-10.3**
　Trafficking, **2C:35-3**
Dealers, liability, actions and proceedings, **2C:35B-1 et seq.**
Declaration of policy, Comprehensive Drug Reform Act of 1986, **2C:35-1.1**
Decocainized coca leaves or extracts of coca leaves, **24:21-2**
Definitions, **2C:35-2, 2C:35B-3, 24:21-2**
Delivery, **24:21-2**
Denial, revocation or suspension of registration, **24:21-12**
Dependent or neglected children, juvenile family crisis, drug dependent parents, **2A:4A-85**
Dependent persons, rehabilitation programs, **2C:35-14**
Depressant or stimulant drugs, **53:1-18.1 et seq.**
Designation, **24:21-3**

CONTROLLED SUBSTANCES—Cont'd

Disorderly persons, 24:21–23
  Conditional discharge, first offenders,
    2C:36A–1
  Drug paraphernalia, use or possession,
    2C:36–2
  Fingerprinting and photographing, 53:1–15
  Hypodermic syringe or needle, possession or
    distribution, 2C:36–6
  Inhalants, 2C:35–10.4
  Loitering, use, possession or sale, 2C:33–2.1
  Prescriptions, 2C:35–24
Distribution, 2C:35–5, 24:21–9 et seq.
  Actions and proceedings, dealers, liability,
    2C:35B–1 et seq.
  Area surrounding school property or bus,
    2C:35–7
  Children and minors, 2C:35–8
  Maintenance of premises, nuisance, 24:21–35
  Nuisances, 24:21–35
  Paraphernalia, 2C:36–3
  Parks, public housing or public buildings,
    2C:35–7.1
  Registration, 24:21–11
Drivers license examinations, effect on driving,
  39:3–10
Drug Abuse, generally, this index
Drug abuse education fund. Drug Abuse, this
  index
Drug addicts. Drug Abuse, generally, this in-
  dex
Drug enforcement and demand reduction fund,
  penalties funding, 2C:35–15
  Payment, 2C:46–1
    Transaction fee, 2C:46–1 et seq.
Drug paraphernalia, 2C:36–1 et seq.
Enforcement, 24:21–31
Entry on land or waters,
  Administrative inspections and warrants,
    24:21–32
  Injunctions, 2C:35–5.7, 2C:35–5.9,
    2C:35–5.10
Evidence,
  Burden of proof, 24:21–37
    Dealers, liability, 2C:35B–12
    Exemption from criminal liability,
      2C:35–18
  Conviction of crime, prima facie evidence,
    dealers, liability, 2C:35B–12
  Imitation controlled dangerous substances,
    2C:35–11
  Laboratory certificates, 2C:35–19
  Maps and plats, distribution or possession,
    location, 2C:35–7.1
Ex parte proceedings, attachment, dealers, lia-
  bility, 2C:35B–13
Exemptions, crimes and offenses,
  Burden of proof, 2C:35–18
  Forfeitures, driving privileges, 2C:35–16
Explosives, handling while under the influence,
  21:1A–132
Expunging record, 2C:52–2
  Young drug offenders, 2C:52–5
Extended sentences, controlled dangerous sub-
  stance violations, 2C:43–6
False statements or representations, registered
  manufacturers or distributors, 24:21–22
Federal designation, control, state, 24:21–3
Fees,
  Conditional discharge application, 2C:36A–1
  Forensic laboratories, 2C:35–20
    Payment, 2C:46–1
    Transaction fee, 2C:46–1 et seq.
Fines and penalties,
  Additional penalties, 24:21–25
  Appeal and review, 2C:35–7a

CONTROLLED SUBSTANCES—Cont'd

Fines and penalties—Cont'd
  Being under influence, 2C:35–10
  Children and minors, distribution, 2C:35–8
  Comprehensive study and review, use and
    possession of marihuana, 24:21–44
  Conditional discharge, first offenders,
    2C:36A–1
  Controlled dangerous substances, additional
    penalties, 24:21–25
  Dealers, liability, 2C:35B–1 et seq.
  Death from drugs, 2C:35–9
  Dispensing, 2C:35–5
    Area surrounding school property or bus,
      2C:35–7
  Distributing, 2C:35–5
    Area surrounding school property or bus,
      2C:35–7
  Drivers under influence, victims of crime
    compensation board, 2C:43–3.1
  Driving privileges, forfeiture or postpone-
    ment, 2C:35–16, 39:5–30.12 et seq.
  Drug enforcement and demand reduction
    fund, additional penalty, 2C:35–15
    Payment, 2C:46–1
      Transaction fee, 2C:46–1 et seq.
  Employing juveniles in distribution schemes,
    2C:35–6
  Enhanced punishment, distributing con-
    trolled dangerous substances to minors,
    2C:35–8
  Extended sentences, 2C:43–6
  Failure to make lawful disposition, 2C:35–10
  Food, adulteration, 2C:12–2
  Fraud or misrepresentation,
    Controlled dangerous substances, 24:21–22
    Obtaining, 2C:35–13
  Hallucinogenic drugs, intoxication of driver,
    39:4–50
  Imitation controlled dangerous substances,
    2C:35–11
  Injunctions, 2C:35–5.8
  Intoxication of driver, 39:4–50
  Knowingly possessing while operating motor
    vehicle, 39:4–49.1
  Mandatory terms, waiver, 2C:35–12
  Manufacturing, 2C:35–5
  Narcotics trafficking leaders, 2C:35–3
  Paraphernalia, controlled substances,
    2C:36–1 et seq.
  Possession, 2C:35–10
  Production facilities, 2C:35–4
  Profits, 2C:35A–1 et seq.
    Mandatory sentence, 2C:35–12
  Reduction, defendant entering rehabilitation
    program, 2C:35–15
  Reformative services, reduction, 2C:35–15
  Rehabilitation or treatment instead of sen-
    tence, 2C:35–14
  Street value, used to determine fine, 2C:44–2
  Use, 2C:35–10
First offenders, conditional discharge, disorder-
  ly persons, 2C:36A–1
Flunitrazepam. Date rape drugs, generally,
  ante
Food, adulteration, crimes and offenses,
  2C:12–2
Forensic laboratories, 2C:35–19, 2C:35–20
  Fees, payment, 2C:46–1
    Transaction fee, 2C:46–1 et seq.
Forfeitures, 2C:35–21, 2C:64–1
  Driving privileges, crimes and offenses,
    2C:35–16
  Effect of repeal law, 24:21–40
  Notice, 24:21–12

CONTROLLED SUBSTANCES—Cont'd

Forms,
  Label, 24:21–17
  Order forms, 24:21–14
Fortifications,
  Crimes and offenses, property used for man-
    ufacture, distribution or possession,
    2C:35–4.1
  Property used for manufacture, distribution
    or possession, 2C:35–4.1
Fraud,
  Controlled dangerous substances, 24:21–22
  Obtaining, 2C:35–13
  Registered manufacturers or distributors,
    24:21–22
Gamma hydroxybutyrate. Date rape drugs,
  generally, ante
Hardship, entry on property, injunctions,
  2C:35–5.7, 2C:35–5.10
Hearings, administrative orders, 24:21–31
Homicide, trafficking, 2C:11–3
Hypodermic Needles or Syringes, generally,
  this index
Imitation controlled dangerous substances,
  2C:35–11
Immediate precursor,
  Definitions, 24:21–2
  Designation of substance, 24:21–3
Inhalants, 2C:35–10.4
  Intoxication of driver, 39:4–50
Injunctions, 24:21–33
  Administrative orders, 24:21–31
  Entry on property, 2C:35–5.7, 2C:35–5.9,
    2C:35–5.10
  Trafficking, 2C:35–5.4 et seq.
Intoxication, basis for criminal liability, 2C:2–8
Intoxication of driver. Motor Vehicles, this
  index
Inventories, 24:21–13
  Administrative inspection warrants, 24:21–32
Investigations, stay, dealers, liability,
  2C:35B–15
Joinder of parties, dealers, liability, 2C:35B–9
Judgments and decrees, dealers, liability,
  2C:35B–16
Judicial review, 24:21–38
Juvenile Delinquents, this index
Laboratories, forensic laboratories, 2C:35–19,
  2C:35–20
  Transaction fee, 2C:46–1 et seq.
Landlord and tenant, notice of conviction, of-
  fenses committed on premises, 2C:35–16.1
Leader of narcotics trafficking network,
  2C:35–3
Leases, notice of conviction, offenses commit-
  ted on premises, 2C:35–16.1
Liability,
  Dealers, actions and proceedings, 2C:35B–1
    et seq.
  Drug induced deaths, 2C:35–9
Limitation of actions, dealers, liability,
  2C:35B–14
Loitering to illegally use, possess or sell,
  2C:33–2.1
Mandatory prison terms, waiver, 2C:35–12
Manufacturers and manufacturing, 2C:35–5,
  24:21–1 et seq.
  Brands, marks and labels, 24:21–16
  Controlled dangerous substances, registra-
    tion, 24:21–9 et seq.
  Convictions, controlled substance violations,
    reports, 24:21–36
  Employees, lie detector tests, 2C:40A–1
  Maintenance of buildings or premises for
    unlawful manufacturer, nuisance,
    24:21–35

CONTROLLED SUBSTANCES—Cont'd

Manufacturers and manufacturing—Cont'd
Registration, controlled dangerous substances, 24:21–11
Revocation, 24:21–9 et seq.
Maps and plats, distribution or possession, location, evidence, 2C:35–7.1
Marijuana, generally, this index
Mass transportation, entry on property, injunctions, 2C:35–5.10
Merger of offense, narcotics trafficking network leaders, 2C:35–3
Minimum sentences, 2C:43–6
Misdemeanors. Crimes and offenses, generally, ante
Motor vehicles, entry on property, injunctions, 2C:35–5.10
Narcotics trafficking network, leaders, 2C:35–3
Nitrous oxide, 2C:35–10.4
Nonnarcotic substance, exclusion from schedules, 24:21–3
Notice,
Driving privilege forfeiture or postponement, controlled substance offenses, consequences of driving during, 2C:35–16
Entry on property, injunctions, 2C:35–5.7
Forfeiture action, orders suspending or revoking registration, 24:21–12
Laboratory certificates, introduction as evidence, 2C:35–19
Order suspending or revoking registration, 24:21–12
Nuisances, 24:21–35
Offenses. Crimes and offenses, generally, ante
Order forms, 24:21–14
Controlled dangerous substances, 24:21–14, 24:21–21
Order to show cause, denial, revocation or suspension of registration, 24:21–12
Orders, attachment, ex parte proceedings, dealers, liability, 2C:35B–13
Paraphernalia, controlled substances, 2C:36–1 et seq.
Seizure, 24:21–52
Parks and parkways, crimes and offenses, 2C:35–7.1
Parole,
Area surrounding school property or bus, 2C:35–7
Revocation, injunctions, 2C:35–5.8
Penalties. Fines and penalties, generally, ante
Pending actions, 2C:35–23, 24:21–40
Pethidine, 24:21–6
Pharmacists, this index
Photographs, convicted persons, 2A:169–3
Physicians and Surgeons, this index
Possession, 2C:35–10
Paraphernalia, 2C:36–2, 2C:36–3
Precursors, crimes and offenses, 2C:35–28
Postponement, driving privileges, controlled dangerous substances offenses, 2C:35–16
Precursors, crimes and offenses, possession, 2C:35–28
Prescriptions, generally, this index
Presumptions, registration, 24:21–36
Priorities and preferences, satisfaction of claims, fines and penalties, 2C:46–4.1
Probation and probation officers,
Rehabilitation or treatment in place of sentence, 2C:35–14
Revocation, injunctions, 2C:35–5.8
Production facility, 2C:35–4
Profits, 2C:35A–1 et seq.
Mandatory sentence, 2C:35–12
Satisfaction of claims, priorities and preferences, 2C:46–4.1

CONTROLLED SUBSTANCES—Cont'd

Public buildings, crimes and offenses, 2C:35–7.1
Public housing, crimes and offenses, 2C:35–7.1
Public policy,
Comprehensive Drug Reform Act of 1986, 2C:35–1.1
Trafficking, injunctions, 2C:35–5.5
Rape. Date rape drugs, generally, ante
Records and recordation,
Crimes and offenses, 24:21–21
Manufacturers and distributors, 24:21–21
Registrants, 24:21–13
Reformative services, fines and penalties, reduction, 2C:35–15
Registration, 24:21–9 et seq.
Presumptions, 24:21–37
Rehabilitation of convicted offenders, drug addiction, 2A:168A–4
Rehabilitation programs, drug dependent persons, 2C:35–14
Reports,
Conviction of manufacturers and practitioners, 24:21–36
Drug dependent persons, 24:21–39
Research, registration, 24:21–10, 24:21–11
Residence and residents, injunctions, 2C:35–5.4 et seq.
Residential treatment facilities, commitment of drug dependent persons, 2C:35–14
Revocation,
Parole based on treatment or rehabilitation, 2C:35–14
Registration, 24:21–12
Rules and regulations, controlled dangerous substances, 24:21–9 et seq., 24:21–31
Satisfaction of claims, fines and penalties, priorities and preferences, 2C:46–4.1
Scheduled substances, 24:21–1 et seq.
Schedule I substances, 24:21–5
Schedule II substances, 24:21–6
Schedule III substances, 24:21–7
Schedule IV substances, 24:21–8
Schedule V substances, 24:21–8.1
Standards, 24:21–3 et seq.
Schools and School Districts, this index
Search warrants, 24:21–31
Searches and seizures, 2C:35–21, 24:21–31
Paraphernalia, 2C:36–7, 24:21–52
Pending actions and proceedings, application of law, 24:21–40
Strip searches, 2A:161A–1 et seq.
Second or subsequent offenses, 24:21–29
Sentence and punishment, appeal and review, 2C:35–7a
Severability, controlled substances provisions, 24:21–43
Sexual assault. Date rape drugs, generally, ante
Standards,
Controlled dangerous substances, 24:21–3 et seq.
Scheduled substances, 24:21–3 et seq.
Stay, dealers, liability, 2C:35B–15
Street value, determination of fine, 2C:44–2
Strict liability, drug inducted deaths, 2C:35–9
Strip searches, 2A:161A–1 et seq.
Study of penalties relating to use or possession of marijuana, 24:21–44
Subpoenas, 24:21–31
Summonses, controlled dangerous substances, 24:21–31
Supervisory treatment, conditional discharge of first offenders, 2C:36A–1
Surcharges, intoxication of driver, 39:4–50
Suspension, registration, 24:21–12

CONTROLLED SUBSTANCES—Cont'd

Tests,
Schedule I controlled substances, 24:21–5
Schedule II controlled substances, 24:21–6
Schedule III controlled substances, 24:21–7
Schedule IV dangerous substances, 24:21–8
Schedule V controlled substances, 24:21–8.1
Theft, 2C:20–2
Time, conditional discharge for first offenses, suspension of driving privileges, 2C:36A–1
Trafficking,
Injunctions, 2C:35–5.4 et seq.
Murder, 2C:11–3
Network,
Leader, murder, 2C:11–3
Narcotics, leader, 2C:35–3
Uniform interpretation, controlled substances provisions, 24:21–42
Use,
Controlled dangerous substances, 2C:35–10
Paraphernalia, 2C:36–2
Veterinarians, this index
Waiver, mandatory prison terms, 2C:35–12
Warehouses, registration requirements, 24:21–10
Warrants, 24:21–32
Administrative inspection warrants, 24:21–31, 24:21–32
Weapons,
Crimes and offenses, consecutive sentences, 2C:39–4.1
Persons convicted of sales, possession, 2C:39–7

CONVALESCENT HOMES
Nursing Homes or Hospitals, generally, this index

CONVENTION HALLS
Casinos, generally, this index

CONVENTIONS
Casinos, generally, this index
Motor vehicles, special registrations, 39:3–27.2

CONVERSION
Embezzlement, generally, this index
Theft, generally, this index
Venue, trial, **Rule 3:14–1**

CONVERTER DOLLY
Definitions, 39:3–61, 39:4–54
Semitrailer, rear lamps, 39:3–61

CONVICTION OF CRIME
Generally, 2C:51–1 et seq.
Alcoholic Beverages, this index
Aliens, weapons violation, 2C:58–9
Appeals In Criminal Prosecutions, generally, this index
Assessment, victims of crime compensation board, 2C:43–3.1
Violent crime, transaction fee, 2C:46–1 et seq.
Certificates and certification, disabilities, labor and employment, revocation or suspension, 2A:168A–7 et seq.
Character evidence, **Evidence Rule 405**
Children and minors, presentence investigations, sole caretakers, placement, 2C:44–6.2 et seq.
Civil rights, 2C:51–1
Controlled substances,
Dealer, liability, prima facie evidence, 2C:35B–12
Denial, revocation or suspension of registration, 24:21–12

CONVICTION OF CRIME—Cont'd
Controlled substances—Cont'd
  Entry on property, injunctions, **2C:35–5.7, 2C:35–5.9, 2C:35–5.10**
  Manufacturers and practitioners, **24:21–36**
  Merger, exceptions, **2C:35–7.1**
  Prima facie evidence, dealers, liability, **2C:35B–12**
  Registration, **24:21–11**
    Denial, revocation or suspension, **24:21–12**
    Manufacturing or distribution, **24:21–11**
  Rehabilitation of offenders, drug addiction, **2A:168A–4**
  Residence and residents, injunctions, **2C:35–5.4 et seq.**
Disabilities, revocation or suspension, **2A:168A–7 et seq.**
DNA database and databank, motions, **2A:84A–32a, 2A:84A–32b**
Educational programs, rehabilitated offenders return to profession or occupation, **2A:168A–5**
Elections, **2C:51–3**
Employment, rehabilitated offenders, **2A:168A–1 et seq.**
Evidence, this index
Expungement, records, **2C:52–1 et seq.**
Fines, return, reversal of guilty adjudication on appeal, **2A:166–13**
Forfeitures, this index
Handguns, purchase permit, **2C:58–3**
Hearsay exception, **Evidence Rule 803**
Hit and run drivers, merger, **2C:11–5.1, 2C:12–1.1**
Impeachment of witness, **Evidence Rule 609**
Juvenile delinquents and dependents, orders sealing records, notification, **2A:4A–62**
Labor and employment, **2A:168A–1 et seq.**
Law enforcement, agencies, personnel qualifications, **2A:168A–6**
Licenses and permits,
  Professional and occupational, rehabilitated offenders, **2A:168A–6**
  Rehabilitation, **2A:168A–1 et seq.**
Loss of rights, **2C:51–1 et seq.**
Merger and consolidation,
  Bias intimidation, **2C:16–1**
  Controlled substances, exceptions, **2C:35–7.1**
  Hit and run drivers, **2C:11–5.1, 2C:12–1.1**
  Money laundering and illegal investments, **2C:21–27**
  Street gangs, **2C:33–28**
Motor Vehicles, this index
Multiple offenses, limitations, **2C:1–8**
Narcotics and dangerous substances, manufacturers and practitioners, controlled dangerous substances, **24:21–36**
Presentence investigations, children and minors, sole caretakers, placement, **2C:44–6.2 et seq.**
Prior convictions, **2C:44–4**
Privileges and immunities, **2C:51–1**
Probation and Probation Officers, generally, this index
Professions and occupations, licenses and permits, **2A:168A–1 et seq.**
Records and recordation, expungement, **2C:52–1 et seq.**
Regulated employment, rehabilitated offenders, **2A:168A–5**
Rehabilitated alcoholics and addicts, professional and occupational licenses, disqualification, **2A:168A–1**
Rehabilitated convicted offenders, **2A:168A–1 et seq.**

CONVICTION OF CRIME—Cont'd
Reports,
  Certificates and certification, disabilities, removal, **2A:168A–13, 2A:168A–14**
  Motor vehicles, offense involving use, **39:5–42**
Restoration, rights, **2C:51–1 et seq.**
Reversal on appeal, return of fine, **2A:166–13**
Rights, loss or restoration, **2C:51–1 et seq.**
Sexual offenses, **2C:14–6**
Stalking, **2C:12–10.1**
Violent crime, victims of crime compensation board, **2C:43–3.1**
Vocational programs, rehabilitated offenders, return to profession or occupation, **2A:168A–5**

CONVICTS
Correctional Institutions, generally, this index

CONVULSIVE SEIZURES
Drivers licenses, applicant, **39:3–10.4 et seq.**

COOPERATIVES
Business relocation assistance. Business and Commerce, generally, this index

COORDINATORS
Complementary dispute resolution programs, **Rule 1:40–3**

COPARTNERSHIP
Partnerships, generally, this index

CORPORATIONS
Actions and proceedings, racketeering, **2C:41–4**
Alcoholic beverages. Licenses and permits, post
Appearance, **Rule 1:21–1**
Application by corporations for licenses, alcoholic beverage licenses, **33:1–25**
Attorneys, this index
Banks and Banking, generally, this index
Bribery and corruption, effect of conviction, **2C:51–2**
Buses, generally, this index
Capital. Shares and Shareholders, generally, this index
Capital stock. Shares and Shareholders, generally, this index
Cease and desist orders, racketeering, **2C:41–4**
Charitable Organizations and Associations, generally, this index
Close corporations, nonattorneys, representing, **Rule 1:21–1**
Common stock. Shares and Shareholders, generally, this index
Confidential or privileged information, racketeering investigations, **2C:41–5**
Contempt, fines, nonpayment, **2C:46–2**
Crimes and offenses, **2C:43–4**
  Misconduct, **2C:21–9**
  Racketeering, **2C:41–1 et seq.**
  Summons, **Rule 3:3–1**
    Indictment, accusation, service, execution, **Rule 3:7–10**
Criminal liability, **2C:2–7**
Definitions,
  Code of Criminal Justice, **2C:2–7**
  Racketeering, **2C:41–1**
Directors,
  Alcoholic beverage license, automatic suspension, **33:1–31.1**
  Fraud, **2C:21–9**
  Misconduct, **2C:21–9**
Discovery, racketeering investigations, **2C:41–5**

CORPORATIONS—Cont'd
Electricity and Electric Companies, generally, this index
Examinations and examiners, racketeering, **2C:41–5**
Financial Corporations and Institutions, generally, this index
Fines and penalties, **2C:43–4**
  Nonpayment, contempt, **2C:46–2**
  Payment, **2C:46–2**
  Racketeering, **2C:41–1 et seq.**
Forfeitures,
  Racketeering, **2C:41–3 et seq.**
  Revocation of corporate charters or certificates, **2C:43–4**
Fraud, officers and employees, **2C:21–9**
Government contracts, conviction of crime, **2C:51–2**
Health and Accident Insurance, generally, this index
Indebtedness, racketeering, **2C:41–1 et seq.**
Inspections, racketeering investigations, **2C:41–5**
Insurance companies. Insurance, generally, this index
Interest, usury, **2C:21–19**
Interrogatories, racketeering, investigations, **2C:41–5**
Investigations and investigators, racketeering, **2C:41–5**
Investments, racketeering, **2C:41–1 et seq.**
Judgments and decrees,
  Municipal courts, **Rule 7:9–2**
  Racketeering, **2C:41–4**
Licenses and permits,
  Alcoholic beverages,
    Applications by corporations, **33:1–25**
    Automatic suspension on conviction of officer, **33:1–31.1**
    Club license, **33:1–12**
    Loans or furnishing of fixtures, retail licensee, officer of brewery, **33:1–43.1**
    Manufacture, sale, poisoned liquors, **33:3–9, 33:3–10**
    Member of issuing authority interested, **33:1–20**
    Notice of changes in stockholdings, **33:1–34**
    Person under law relating to, **33:1–1**
    Poisoned liquors, **33:3–9, 33:3–10**
    Retailing of intoxicating liquors by officer or director of corporation interested in brewery, **33:1–43**
    Transfer of interest from parents or grandparents, Chain Store Liquor License Act, **33:1–12.36**
  Racketeering, revocation or suspension, **2C:41–4**
Mentally retarded persons, transport vehicles, identification, **39:4–207.2 et seq.**
Monopolies, this index
Municipal courts, traffic tickets, service, **Rule 7:2–4**
News corporations, searches and seizures, **2A:84A–21.9 et seq.**
Nonprofit Corporations and Associations, generally, this index
Notice in lieu of subpoena, **Rule 1:9–1**
Officers and employees,
  Alcoholic beverage license, automatic suspension, **33:1–31.1**
  Criminal liability, **2C:2–7**
  Fraud, **2C:21–9**
  Misconduct, **2C:21–9**
  Motor vehicles, signature to application for registration, **39:3–4**

CORPORATIONS—Cont'd

Permits. Licenses and permits, generally, ante

Pleas, criminal causes, **Rule 7:6–2**

Private Schools, generally, this index

Process, racketeering, **2C:41–5**

Production of books and papers, racketeering, **2C:41–5**

Production of evidence, **2A:84A–19**

Professional corporations. Attorneys, this index

Railroads, generally, this index

Records and recordation, racketeering, investigations, **2C:41–5**

Religious Corporations and Associations, generally, this index

Restitution, racketeering, **2C:41–4**

Searches and seizures, news corporations, **2A:84A–21.9 et seq.**

Securities. Shares and Shareholders, generally, this index

Shares and Shareholders, generally, this index

Small claims, appearances, **Rule 1:21–1**

Stock and stockholders. Shares and Shareholders, generally, this index

Street Railways, generally, this index

Subsidiaries, motor vehicle insurance, self insurers, **39:6–52**

Summons,
Crimes and offenses, **Rule 3:3–1**
Municipal court issuance, **Rule 7:2–2**

Traction companies. Street Railways, generally, this index

Trust companies. Banks and Banking, generally, this index

Usury, **2C:21–19**

CORPORATIONS AND ASSOCIATIONS NOT FOR PROFIT

Nonprofit Corporations and Associations, generally, this index

CORPSE

Dead Bodies, generally, this index

CORRECTIONAL CENTERS FOR JUVENILE OFFENDERS

Officers and employees, aggravated assault, throwing bodily fluids, **2C:12–13**

CORRECTIONAL FACILITIES

Correctional Institutions, generally, this index

CORRECTIONAL INSTITUTIONS

Administrative law and procedure, records and recordation, identification check, conviction of crime, sole caretaker, presentence investigations, **9:6–8.10d**

Aggravated assault,
Officers and employees, weapons, **2C:12–1**
Throwing bodily fluids, **2C:12–12, 2C:12–13**

Assault and battery, officers and employees, Aggravated assault, weapons, **2C:12–1**

Consecutive sentences, **2C:44–5**

Bail, extended term of imprisonment, **2C:44–5.1**

Beginning sentences, **2C:43–10**

Children and minors, presentence investigations, sole caretakers, placement, **2C:44–6.2 et seq.**

Clinton, young adult offenders, sentence and punishment, **2C:43–5**

Commitment and Admission to Institutions, generally, this index

Concurrent sentence, interstate agreement on detainers, **2A:159A–3**

CORRECTIONAL INSTITUTIONS—Cont'd

Consecutive sentences, **2C:44–5**
Determining place of imprisonment, **2C:43–10**
Hit and run drivers, **2C:11–5.1, 2C:12–1.1**

Contraband, escape implements, **2C:29–6**

Correction officers. Officers and employees, generally, post

Corrections Department, generally, this index

Credits,
Good behavior, sex offenders, restrictions, **2C:47–3**
Adult diagnosis and treatment center, **2C:47–4.1, 2C:47–8**
Parole violations, effect, **2C:47–5.1**
Time served, discretion of court, **2A:164–24**

Definitions,
Aggravated assault by inmates, throwing bodily fluids, **2C:12–12**
Telecommunications, **2C:29–10**

Denial, record expungement, **2C:52–14**

Detainers, generally, this index

Disclosure, expungement order, **2C:52–30**

Diversion programs, record expungement, **2C:52–20**

Domicile and residence, registration, sex offenses, release, **2C:7–2.1**

Drug tests, officers and employees, fraud, **2C:36–10**

Earnings of prisoner, fines and penalties, deductions, victims of crime compensation board, **2C:43–3.1**

Electronic orders, entry, **Rule 3:1–4**

Escapes, generally, this index

Exemptions, record expungement, **2C:52–2**

Expungement, records, **2C:52–1 et seq.**

Extradition, escaped prisoner, **2A:160–31 et seq.**

Fees, record expungement, **2C:52–29**

Fines and penalties, payment, deduction from earnings of employed prisoners, deduction from earnings of employed prisoners, victims of crime compensation board, **2C:43–3.1**

Fingerprints, photographs, persons confined, filing by bureau of identification, **53:1–14**

Fraud, officers and employees, drug tests, **2C:36–10**

Good behavior. Credits, ante

Guards,
Escape, knowingly or recklessly permitting, **2C:29–5**
Weapons, unlawful possession, exemption, **2C:39–6**

Hearings, record expungement, **2C:52–9 et seq.**

Implements for escape, **2C:29–6**

Incarceration of parolee or probationer in receiving state, **2A:168–18 et seq.**

Indictable offenses, record expungement, **2C:52–2**

Inmates,
Aggravated assault, throwing bodily fluids, officers and employees, **2C:12–12, 2C:12–13**
Fines and penalties, deduction from income, victims of crime compensation board, **2C:43–3.1**
Transaction fee, **2C:46–1 et seq.**
Harassment, **2C:33–4**
Stalking, **2C:12–10**

Inspection and inspectors, records, expungement, **2C:52–19**

Intensive supervision program, restrictions, **2C:43–11**

Interference, **2C:13–4**

Interstate agreement on detainers, **2A:159A–12**

CORRECTIONAL INSTITUTIONS—Cont'd

Jails, generally, this index

Juvenile delinquents, **2A:4A–43, 2A:4A–44, 2A:4A–60**
County juvenile detention facilities, agreements, juvenile justice commission, placement of children in custody of, **2A:4A–44.1**
Detention, **Rule 5:21–4**
Officers and employees, aggravated assault, throwing bodily fluids, **2C:12–13**

License to be at large,
Retaking and detention, **2A:167–9**
Return to place of punishment, **2A:167–8**
Revocation,
Governor, **2A:167–10**
Investigation by state parole board prior to, **2A:167–11**
Order, **2A:167–12**

Life imprisonment without parole,
Persistent Offenders Accountability Act, **2C:43–7.1**
Psychological examination, exception, **2C:47–1**

Sex offenders,
Adult diagnostic and treatment center, Restrictions, **2C:47–3**
Transfers, **2C:47–4.1**
Psychological examination, exception, **2C:47–1**

Mentally Deficient and Mentally Ill Persons, this index

Minimum sentence, **2C:43–7.2**

Newspapers, searches and seizures, **2A:84A–21.13**

No Early Release Act, **2C:43–7.2**

Notice, release of inmates,
Bureaus of identification, **53:1–20.3**
Head of police department originally arresting, **53:1–20.4**

Officers and employees,
Aggravated assault by inmates, throwing bodily fluids, **2C:12–12, 2C:12–13**
Assault and battery,
Aggravated assault, weapons, **2C:12–1**
Consecutive sentences, **2C:44–5**
Counties, police powers, **2A:154–3**
Disarming firearm or weapon from, criminal offense, **2C:12–11**
Drug tests, fraud, **2C:36–10**
Fraud, drug tests, **2C:36–10**
Investigators, police powers, **2A:154–4**
Parole officers, police powers, **2A:154–4**
Police powers, **2A:154–4**
Telecommunications, **2C:29–10**
Victims of crime, **2C:44–1**
Weapons, unlawful possession, exemption, **2C:39–6**

Orders of court, record expungement, **2C:52–11 et seq., 2C:52–26**

Parole, generally, this index

Petitions, record expungement, **2C:52–7 et seq.**

Photograph of prisoners prior to release, **53:1–20.3**

Places, imprisonment, **2C:43–10**

Presentence investigations, children and minors, sole caretakers, placement, **2C:44–6.2 et seq.**

Presentence report, record expungement, **2C:52–21**

Prison officers. Officers and employees, generally, ante

Prisoners. Inmates, generally, ante

Probationer in receiving state, **2A:168–18 et seq.**

Process, record expungement, **2C:52–10**

CORRECTIONAL INSTITUTIONS—Cont'd

Records and recordation, expungement, **2C:52–1 et seq.**

Registration, sex offenses, release, domicile and residence, **2C:7–2.1**

Rehabilitated convicted offenders, **2A:168A–1 et seq.**

Release,

Minimum sentence, **2C:43–7.2**

Record expungement, **2C:52–19**

Sex offenders, registration. Sex Offenses, this index

Removal of prisoner, records, **2C:52–15**

Repeat violent offenders, extended term of imprisonment, **2C:43–7.1**

Sealing, record expungement, **2C:52–26**

Searches and seizures, inmate newspapers, public information offices, **2A:84A–21.13**

Sex offenders,

Community notification. Sex Offenses, this index

Registration. Sex Offenses, this index

Sexual assault of prisoner, **2C:14–2**

Sheriffs, generally, this index

Sole caretakers, children and minors, presentence investigations, placement, **2C:44–6.2 et seq.**

Statements, record expungement petition, **2C:52–8**

Supervisory treatment programs, record expungement, **2C:52–20**

Telecommunications, **2C:29–10**

Traffic offenses, record expungement, **2C:52–28**

Trial on other charges, interstate agreements on detainers, **2A:159A–1, 2A:159A–3**

Victims of crime, officers and employees, consecutive sentences, **2C:44–5**

Work release program,

Crimes and offenses, **2C:43–2**

Fines and penalties, deductions from wages, **2C:43–3.1**

Workhouses, generally, this index

Young adult offenders, **2C:43–5**

CORRECTIONS DEPARTMENT

Commissioner,

Detainers from other states, duties, **2A:159A–3 et seq.**

Notice, prisoner enrolled in health insurance plan, **2C:44–6**

Rules and regulations, promulgation, criminal fines and restitution, **2C:44–6**

Corrections computerized collection fund, **2C:46–1.1**

Definitions, aggravated assault by inmates, throwing bodily fluids, **2C:12–12**

Expunged records, use, **2C:52–23**

Fines and penalties, collection, **2C:46–4**

Law enforcement officers training and equipment fund, **2C:43–3.3**

Officers and employees,

Disarming firearm or weapon from, criminal offense, **2C:12–11**

Weapons, possession, exemption, **2C:39–6**

Sex offenders,

Amenability to treatment, examination, **2C:47–1 et seq.**

Registration and notification procedures, **2C:7–2 et seq.**

CORROBORATION

Perjury, **2C:28–1**

CORROSIVE SUBSTANCES

Golf balls, **2C:12–2**

CORRUPTION

Bribery and Corruption, generally, this index

CORRUPTION OF BLOOD

Conviction not to work, **2A:152–2**

COSMETIC MEDICAL PROCEDURES

Drivers licenses, color photographs, update, **39:3–10f**

COSMETICS

See, also, Drugs and Medicine, generally, this index

Crimes and offenses, packages, writings, **2C:40–19**

Definitions, food and drugs, **24:21–32**

Packages, writings, crimes and offenses, **2C:40–19**

Tampering with, **2C:40–16, 2C:40–17**

COSTS

Abatement and survival. Nuisance, this index

Acquittals, payment of fees,

Clerk and sheriff, **2A:166–9**

Witnesses and constables, **2A:166–8**

Adult diagnostic and treatment center, maintenance, **2C:47–7**

Alcoholic Beverages, this index

Appeal and review, deposits, unauthorized practice of law decisions, **Rule 1:22–3A**

Appearance, failure to appear, sanctions, **Rule 1:2–4**

Controlled substances, dealers, liability, **2C:35B–5, 2C:35B–6**

Counties, this index

County Prosecutors, this index

Crimes and Offenses, this index

Default in payment, confinement, traffic violations, **39:5–36**

Definitions, motor vehicles, trial de novo, arbitrated tort claims, **39:6A–34**

Deposits, professional ethics, advisory committee on, review of opinions, **Rule 1:19–8**

Director of division of motor vehicles, costs in court conducted by, **39:5–2**

DNA database and databank, crimes and offenses, motions, **2A:84A–32a**

Drugs and Medicine, this index

Executions, this index

Exemption,

Disciplinary review board, **Rule 1:20–15**

Office of attorney ethics, **Rule 1:20–2**

Failure to appear, sanctions, **Rule 1:2–4**

Frivolous litigation, **Rule 1:4–8**

Information disclosure, proceedings, improperly sought, **2A:84A–21.8**

Interstate compact for adult offender supervision, default, **2A:168–37**

Judge receiving salary, costs not payable to, **2A:166–17**

Mediation, **Rule 1:40–4**

Money laundering and illegal investments, **2C:21–28**

Monopolies and unfair trade, proceedings, **56:9–10**

Motor Vehicle Commission, this index

Motor Vehicles, this index

Motorized bicycles, possession and display, operators, drivers license, insurance identification card, and registration certificate, **39:4–14.3**

Municipal Courts, this index

Newspersons privilege, enforcing subpoena against, **Evidence Rule 508**

Officers, receiving salary, costs not payable to, **2A:166–17**

COSTS—Cont'd

Payment, judge or officer in criminal case reserving salary, costs not payable to, **2A:166–17**

Record expungement, **2C:52–29**

Return of seized stills, distilling apparatus, **33:2–7**

Security, motor vehicles, bond for costs as prerequisite to issuance of warrant under, **39:5–5**

Service,

Commissioner of motor vehicles as attorney for nonresidents, **39:3–7**

Nonresident owner, motor vehicle, **39:7–5**

Solid Waste, this index

State grand jury, payment by state, **2B:22–8**

Tires, projections on tires and locking of wheels of motor vehicles, proceedings for violation of law relating to, **39:3–81**

Traffic Rules and Regulations, this index

Traffic violations, default, term of commitment, **39:5–36**

Waiver, motor vehicles, trial de novo, arbitrated tort claims, **39:6A–34**

Wheels, projections on tires, and locking of wheels of motor vehicles, proceedings for violation of law relating to, **39:3–81**

COUNCILS

Adult offender supervision interstate council, **2A:168–29**

Advisory Councils, generally, this index

Definitions, food and drugs, **24:21–32**

COUNSEL

Attorneys, generally, this index

COUNSELORS AND COUNSELING

Bias intimidation, **2C:16–1**

Confidential or Privileged Information, this index

Domestic violence,

Hearings, **2C:25–29**

Orders, **2C:25–29**

Prevention, sentencing conditions, **2C:25–20, 2C:25–27**

Posttrauma disorders, crisis intervention services, hotlines, funding, **2C:64–6, 39:5–41**

Privileged communications, victims of crime, **2A:84A–22.13 et seq.**

Victims of Crime, this index

COUNSELORS AT LAW

Attorneys, generally, this index

COUNTERCLAIMS

Dismissal and nonsuit, failure to appear, **Rule 1:2–4**

Service, numerous defendants, **Rule 1:5–5**

COUNTERFEIT MARK

Definitions, **2C:21–32**

COUNTERFEIT SUBSTANCE

Definitions,

Controlled dangerous substances, **2C:35–2, 24:21–2**

Controlled substances, **24:21–2**

COUNTERFEITING

Brands, labels and marks, **39:3–38**

Motor vehicle insurance, identification cards, **2C:21–2.3**

Motor vehicles, plates or markers, **39:3–38**

Parking permits, state owned grounds, **39:4–209**

Trademarks and Trade Names, this index

COUNTERTERRORISM
Generally, **2C:38–1 et seq.**
Terrorism, generally, this index

COUNTIES
Actions and proceedings, jurors, challenge to array or poll on grounds of interest, **2B:23–12**
Administration, law or governmental functions, obstruction, **2C:29–1 et seq.**
Adult diagnostic and treatment center inmates, expenses, payment, **2C:47–7**
Agents and agency. County Officers and Employees, generally, this index
Alcoholic beverages, prosecution for sale of beverage in which delivery is accompanied by transportation, **33:1–69**
All terrain vehicles, registration, exemptions, **39:3C–6**
Appropriations, juvenile delinquents and dependents, detention or shelter care facilities, payments, **2A:4A–37**
Autobusses, resolutions, stops or stations, **39:4–8**
Boards and commissions. Chosen Freeholders, generally, this index
Bribery and Corruption, generally, this index
Bridges and Viaducts, this index
Cannons, antique cannons, possession, **2C:39–6**
Charitable organizations and associations, solicitation on roadways, **39:4–60**
Chosen Freeholders, generally, this index
Civil Service, generally, this index
Clinics to study mental and physical conditions of convicted persons before sentence, **2A:164–1**
Compensation and salaries. County Officers and Employees, this index
Constables, generally, this index
Corrupt influence. Bribery and Corruption, generally, this index
Costs,
    Fees of clerk and sheriff payable on acquittals, **2A:166–9**
    Prosecution, trial, state grand jury indictments, **2B:22–8**
County Roads, generally, this index
Crimes and offenses,
    Application of law, **2A:152–4**
    Venue, **Rule 3:14–1 et seq.**
Crosswalks, pedestrians, right of way, traffic signs and signals, **39:4–8**
Detectives. County Detectives and Investigators, generally, this index
Drivers licenses, verification, electronic readers, **39:3–10f1**
Electric personal assistive mobility devices, operation, ordinances, **39:4–14.10**
Electronic readers, drivers licenses, verification, **39:3–10f1**
Emergency management, volunteers, motor vehicles, warning lights, applications, **39:3–54.22**
Employees. County Officers and Employees, generally, this index
Expenses and expenditures, criminal prosecutions, reimbursement, **2A:166A–1 et seq.**
Facilities disputes, arbitration, **Rule 1:33–9**
Family Court, generally, this index
Fines and penalties, display of name of owner of commercial vehicle, disposition, **39:4–47**
Force and violence, obstructing administration of law or governmental functions, **2C:29–1 et seq.**
Fugitives from justice, liability, return, **2A:160–2**

COUNTIES—Cont'd
General Assembly, generally, this index
Governing body. Chosen Freeholders, generally, this index
Grand Jury, generally, this index
Health and Senior Services Department, this index
Highways and roads. County Roads, generally, this index
Indigent Persons, generally, this index
Intimidation, obstructing administration of law or governmental functions, **2C:29–1 et seq.**
Investigators. County Detectives and Investigators, generally, this index
Jails, generally, this index
Jurors, challenge to array or poll on grounds of interest in action by or against county, **2B:23–12**
Juvenile and Domestic Relations Courts, generally, this index
Juvenile Delinquents, this index
Juvenile family crisis intervention units, **2A:4A–76 et seq.**
    Training, **2A:4A–79**
Mentally retarded persons, transport vehicles, identification, **39:4–207.2 et seq.**
Motor vehicles,
    Drivers license, **39:3–14**
    Free registration, **39:3–27**
    Improvement authorities, registration fees, exemption, **39:3–27**
    Sale of abandoned vehicles, **39:10A–1 et seq.**
Municipal Courts, this index
Obstruction, administration of law or governmental function, **2C:29–1 et seq.**
Officers and employees. County Officers and Employees, generally, this index
Ordinances, generally, this index
Pedestrians, right of way, crosswalks, traffic signs and signals, **39:4–8**
Penitentiaries. Jails, generally, this index
Planning. Zoning and Planning, generally, this index
Police and Police Departments, this index
Privileges and immunities, traffic signs and signals, pedestrians, crosswalks, right of way, **39:4–8**
Prosecutors. County Prosecutors, generally, this index
Public assistance. Indigent Persons, generally, this index
Publications, notice, intention to apply for alcoholic beverage license, **33:1–25**
Reimbursement,
    Criminal prosecution expenses, **2A:166A–1 et seq.**
    Prosecution and trial of state grand jury indictments, **2B:22–8**
Right of way, pedestrians, crosswalks, traffic signs and signals, **39:4–8**
Roads. County Roads, generally, this index
Sidewalks, generally, this index
Snowmobiles, registration, exemptions, **39:3C–6**
Special trust funds, use of funds, **39:5–41**
Streets. County Roads, generally, this index
Traffic laws applicable to vehicles owned or operated, **39:4–1**
Traffic lights, application for installation at dangerous intersections, **39:4–121.1**
Traffic rules and regulations, **39:4–8, 39:4–201**
Traffic signs and signals, right of way, pedestrians, crosswalks, **39:4–8**
Treasurer. County Treasurer, generally, this index

COUNTIES—Cont'd
Turnpike authority,
    Appropriations, nonhighway projects, **27:23–44**
    Lease or conveyance of property by county to, **27:23–14**
    Power to acquire property, **27:23–5**
Veterans, detective, appointment, **2A:157–2**
Violence, obstructing administration of law or governmental functions, **2C:29–1 et seq.**
Welfare. Indigent Persons, generally, this index
Workhouses, generally, this index
Zoning and Planning, generally, this index

COUNTIES OF FIRST CLASS
Alcoholic beverage control boards in cities of 15,000, **33:1–5**
County Detectives and Investigators, this index
Prosecutor, full time service, **2A:158–1.1**

COUNTIES OF SECOND CLASS
Prosecutor, full time service, **2A:158–1.1**

COUNTIES OF THIRD CLASS
County Detectives and Investigators, this index
Lieutenant of county detectives, population less than 75,000, **2A:157–6**
Prosecutor, fulltime service, certain counties, **2A:158–1.1**

COUNTIES OF FIFTH CLASS
Prosecutor, fulltime service, **2A:158–1.1**

COUNTIES OF SIXTH CLASS
Alcoholic beverage license, issuance to one permitting lapse while in military service, **33:1–12.22b**
County detectives, **2A:157–9**
Investigators, **2A:157–16**
Prosecutor, fulltime service, **2A:158–1.1**

COUNTY BOARDS OF CHOSEN FREE-HOLDERS
Chosen Freeholders, generally, this index

COUNTY BRIDGE COMMISSION
Bridges and Viaducts, this index

COUNTY BUREAU OF IDENTIFICATION
Criminal records, **53:1–20.1**
Definitions, **53:1–20.2**
Notice of release of prisoner,
    To head of police department, originally arresting, **53:1–20.4**
    Wardens, **53:1–20.3**

COUNTY CHIEF FINANCIAL OFFICERS
County Officers and Employees, generally, this index

COUNTY CLERKS
Ballots, this index
Certified copies, delivery to clerk, resolution for referendum respecting alcoholic beverages, **33:1–45**
Criminal records, forwarding information, **53:1–20.2**
Deputy clerk of superior court, **Rule 1:34–2**
Filing of papers, criminal cases, **Rule 1:5–6**
Jury lists, posting in office of, qualifications and selection, **2B:20–5**
Motor vehicles, special plates, **39:3–27.29 et seq.**
Political activities, **Rule 1:17–2**
Writs, authority to issue, **Rule 1:34–2**

COUNTY CONTRACTS
Crimes and offenses, fraud, 2C:21–34
Fraud, 2C:21–34

COUNTY COUNSEL
Solid waste facilities, counselors to health department, compliance with regulations, 13:1E–9

COUNTY DETECTIVES AND INVESTIGATORS
Generally, 2A:157–1 et seq.
Appeal and review,
  Convictions, 2A:157–10.7
  Law relating to saved from repeal, 2A:157–20
Appointments, 2A:157–2
  Detectives, 2A:157–2
    Fifth class counties, 2A:157–8
    First class counties, 2A:157–3
    Second class counties, 2A:157–4
  Investigators, 2A:157–10
    Fifth class counties, 2A:157–15
    First class counties, 2A:157–11
    Second class counties, 2A:157–12
    Third class counties, 2A:157–13
Arrest, powers, 2A:157–2.1
Captain of detectives, 2A:157–3
  Counties of sixth class, 2A:157–9
Chief of county detectives, 2A:157–3 et seq.
Civil service, 2A:157–2, 2A:157–23
  Applicable to county detectives, 2A:157–2
  Inapplicable to county investigators, 2A:157–10
  Status, 2A:157–23
Compensation and salaries, 2A:157–2, 2A:157–10
  Approval, 2A:157–22
  Fifth class counties, 2A:157–8, 2A:157–15
  First class counties, 2A:157–3, 2A:157–11
  Fixing, 2A:157–18
  Lieutenant of detectives, counties of third class less than 75,000, 2A:157–6
  Payment, 2A:157–18
  Revocation or suspension, illegal, back pay, 2A:157–10.6
  Second class counties, 2A:157–4, 2A:157–12
  Sixth class counties, 2A:157–9, 2A:157–16
  Third class counties, 2A:157–5, 2A:157–6, 2A:157–13
Complaints, 2A:157–10.1 et seq.
Construction of law, 2A:157–23
Counties of first class,
  Detectives, 2A:157–3
    Veterans, 2A:157–2
  Investigators, 2A:157–11
  Less than 800,000, approval of new appointments, 2A:157–22
Counties of second class,
  Detectives, 2A:157–4
  Investigators, 2A:157–12
Counties of third class,
  Detectives, 2A:157–5, 2A:157–6
  Investigators, 2A:157–13
Counties of fifth class,
  Detectives, 2A:157–8
  Investigators, 2A:157–15
Counties of sixth class,
  Detectives, 2A:157–9
  Investigators, 2A:157–16
Crimes and offenses, removal from office, 2A:157–10.4 et seq.
Defenses, crimes and offenses, 2A:157–10.8
Deputy chiefs of county detectives, 2A:157–3
  Second class counties, 2A:157–4
Duty and powers of county detectives, 2A:157–2

COUNTY DETECTIVES AND INVESTIGATORS—Cont'd
Fees for service of process, 2A:157–17
Information concerning offenses, forwarding to bureau of identification, 53:1–20.2
Laws relating to salaries, pension rights, civil service standings, not affected by law, 2A:157–21
Lieutenants of detectives, 2A:157–3
  Third class counties of less than 75,000, 2A:157–6
Number of detectives, 2A:157–2
  Approval of number by board of chosen freeholders, 2A:157–22
  Fifth class counties, 2A:157–8
  First class counties, 2A:157–3
  Second class counties, 2A:157–4
  Sixth class counties, 2A:157–9
  Third class counties, 2A:157–5, 2A:157–6
Number of investigators, 2A:157–10
  Approval of number by board of chosen freeholders, 2A:157–22
  Fifth class counties, 2A:157–15
  First class counties, 2A:157–11
  Second class counties, 2A:157–12
  Sixth class counties, 2A:157–16
  Third class counties, 2A:157–13
Police training courses, prosecutor, power to fix salaries, 2A:157–18
Powers and duties, 2A:157–10
Reinstatement, crimes and offenses, revocation or suspension, 2A:157–10.5
Removal from office, 2A:157–10.1 et seq.
Retirement and pensions, salaries, pension rights, civil service standings, not affected by law relating to county detectives and county investigators, 2A:157–21
Revocation or suspension, hearings, complaints, 2A:157–10.3
Salaries. Compensation and salaries, generally, ante
Secretaries, 2A:158–19, 2A:158–20
Service of process, 2A:157–17
Stenographers, 2A:158–19, 2A:158–20
Subpoenas, complaints, 2A:157–10.2

COUNTY FREEHOLDERS
Chosen Freeholders, generally, this index

COUNTY FUNDS
Motor vehicle violations, fines, disposition, 39:5–41

COUNTY HIGHWAYS
County Roads, generally, this index

COUNTY HOSPITALS FOR TUBERCULOSIS AND OTHER COMMUNICABLE DISEASES
Complaints for violation of motor vehicle and traffic laws, 39:5–3

COUNTY IMPROVEMENT AUTHORITIES
Motor vehicles, fees for registration, exemption, 39:3–27

COUNTY INSTITUTIONS AND AGENCIES
Abuse of children, information, disclosure, 9:6–8.10a
Correctional Institutions, generally, this index
Retention of property seized under Alcoholic Beverage Law for use of, 33:1–66, 33:2–5

COUNTY INVESTIGATORS
County Detectives and Investigators, generally, this index

COUNTY JAILS OR PENITENTIARIES
Jails, generally, this index

COUNTY MEDICAL EXAMINER
Automobile accidents, report of deaths resulting from, 39:4–134
Intoxication of driver, supervised visitation, 39:4–50
Motor vehicle accidents, death resulting from, reports, 39:4–134
Report, death resulting from motor vehicle accident, 39:4–134
Supervised visitation, intoxication of driver, 39:4–50

COUNTY OFFICERS AND EMPLOYEES
Adverse or pecuniary interest, 2C:27–9
Appropriations, spending or incurring obligations in excess of, 2C:30–4
Boards of chosen freeholders. Chosen Freeholders, generally, this index
Bribery and Corruption, generally, this index
Chosen Freeholders, generally, this index
Civil Service, generally, this index
Compensation and salaries, jury duty, 2B:20–16
Correction officers,
  Police powers, 2A:154–3
  Weapons, possession, 2C:39–6
County Prosecutors, generally, this index
Crimes and offenses, spending or incurring obligations in excess of appropriations, 2C:30–4
Detectives. County Detectives and Investigators, generally, this index
Electric personal assistive mobility devices, operation, 39:4–14.10
Excused from employment, jury duty, 2B:20–16
Freeholders. Chosen Freeholders, generally, this index
Investigators and investigations. County Detectives and Investigators, generally, this index
Jurors, challenge to array or poll on grounds of interest, actions by or against, 2B:23–12
Jury duty, excused from employment, 2B:20–16
Juvenile family crisis intervention units, qualifications, 2A:4A–79
Motor vehicles, special plates, 39:3–27.29 et seq.
Motorized scooters, traffic rules and regulations, 39:4–14.14
Obligations, incurring in excess of appropriations, 2C:30–4
Peace officers. Sheriffs, generally, this index
Prosecutors. County Prosecutors, generally, this index
Sheriffs, generally, this index
Spending in excess of appropriations, 2C:30–4
Treasurer. County Treasurer, generally, this index

COUNTY PARKS
Motor vehicles, sale of abandoned and unclaimed vehicles, 39:10A–1 et seq.
Police and police departments, weapons, possession, exemption, 2C:39–6

COUNTY PENITENTIARIES
Generally, 2C:43–10

COUNTY PROBATION OFFICERS
Counties not less than 800,000, 2A:168–6
Member of clinic to study mental and physical conditions of convicted persons before sentence, 2A:164–1
Motor vehicle and traffic laws, supervision of defendant, 39:5–7

COUNTY PROSECUTORS
Generally, **2A:158–1 et seq.**
Abuse of children, closed circuit testimony, motions, **2A:84A–32.4**
Acting county prosecutors, compensation and salaries, **2A:158–10**
Appointments, **2A:158–1**
Assistant prosecutors, **2A:158–15 et seq.**
Counties of first class not exceeding 800,000, **2A:158–18.1, 2A:158–18.2**
Temporary prosecutors, **2A:158–9**
Arson investigation unit, weapons unlawful possession, exemption, **2C:39–6**
Assistant prosecutors,
Compensation and salaries, **2A:158–15.3**
Outside employment, **2A:158–15.1b**
Part time service, **2A:158–15.1b**
Child Abuse, this index
Compensation and salaries, **2A:158–10 et seq.**
Assistant prosecutors, **2A:158–15.3**
Temporary prosecutor, **2A:158–9**
Consent, wiretapping and electronic surveillance, **2A:156A–4**
Contempt, prosecuting, **Rule 1:10–2**
Conviction of Crime, generally, this index
Costs,
Payment of costs into county treasury, **2A:158–13**
Salaries in lieu of costs, **2A:158–13**
Counties of first class, legal assistant, **2A:158–18.1**
County Detectives and Investigators, generally, this index
Criminal business of state, **2A:158–4**
Criminal records, forwarding information for, **53:1–20.2**
Definitions, **2A:158–2**
Criminal procedure, **2A:152–1**
Municipal prosecutors, **2B:25–2**
Searches and seizures, news organizations, **2A:84A–21.12**
Delegates and alternates, national conventions, political parties, **2A:158–21**
Elections,
Political activities, prohibition, **2A:158–21**
To devote full time to office, **2A:158–1.1**
Employment of temporary prosecutor, **2A:158–9**
Enjoining nuisances under federal law, expenses for, **2A:158–8**
Expenses and expenditures,
Detection, arrest, indictment and conviction of offenders, **2A:157–19**
Enforcement of laws, **2A:158–7**
Enjoining nuisances under federal law, **2A:158–8**
Extradition,
Expenses, **2A:160–2 et seq.**
Investigation of demand for fugitive in New Jersey, **2A:160–12**
Fees, **2A:158–6, 2A:158–13**
Payment into county treasury, **2A:158–13**
Salaries in lieu of, **2A:158–13**
Fifth class counties, full time service, **2A:158–1.1**
Fines and penalties, **2A:158–5**
Full time service, certain counties, **2A:158–1.1**
Grand jurors, challenges to qualifications, **2B:21–2**
Identification bureau, report, crime conditions, **53:1–18a**
Jurisdiction over criminal business, **2A:158–4**
Legal assistant in counties of first class not exceeding 800,000, **2A:158–18.1, 2A:158–18.2**
Liabilities, **2A:158–5**

COUNTY PROSECUTORS—Cont'd
Monopolies and unfair trade, proceedings against violators, **56:9–6**
Motor vehicle and traffic law violation, prosecutor to represent complainant on appeal, **39:5–20**
Municipal prosecutors, **2B:25–1 et seq.**
Notice, municipal court, discharge of person charged, **2B:12–19**
Number, assistant prosecutors, **2A:158–15**
Oaths and affirmations, **2A:158–3**
Assistant prosecutors, **2A:158–15**
Temporary prosecutors, **2A:158–9**
Political activities, **Rule 1:17–2**
Prohibition, **2A:158–21**
Powers and duties, **2A:158–1, 2A:158–5**
Assistant prosecutors, **2A:158–18**
Criminal business of state, **2A:158–4**
Temporary prosecutor, **2A:158–9**
Practice of law, **Rule 1:15–3**
Reports, death resulting from motor vehicle accident, **39:4–134**
Searches and seizures, warrants, execution, **Rule 3:5–5**
Secretarial and stenographic positions in office of, **2A:158–19, 2A:158–20**
Special officers, discontinued, **2A:157–23**
Substituted for prosecutor of the pleas, **2A:158–2**
Temporary prosecutor, **2A:158–9**
Term of office, **2A:158–1**
Assistant prosecutors, **2A:158–15**
Terrorism, wiretapping and electronic surveillance, applications, **2A:156A–8**
Victims of crime, consultation, plea bargains, sex offenses, **2C:14–2.1**
Wiretapping and electronic surveillance,
Application for order, **2A:156A–8**
Consent, **2A:156A–4**

COUNTY ROADS
Emergencies, traffic congestion, authority for moving, **39:4–213 et seq.**
Fines and penalties, violation of traffic regulations, **39:4–201**
Maintenance and repair, bail bonds in traffic violation prosecutions, proceeds of forfeited bonds used to repair, **39:5–9**
Motor vehicle violations, fines, disposition, **39:5–41**
One way traffic, regulation by county authorities, **39:4–85.1**
Resolutions, traffic signs and signals, pedestrians, crosswalks, right of way, **39:4–8**
Traffic ordinances or resolutions, **39:4–201**
Pedestrians, crosswalks, right of way, **39:4–8**
Traffic Signs and Signals, this index
Transportation, department of, traffic regulations, proposed orders, copies, **39:4–8.4**

COUNTY SCHOOLS
Vocational Education, this index

COUNTY SUMMER CAMPS FOR CHILDREN
Busses, motorist stopping for loading and unloading busses, **39:4–128.1**

COUNTY SUPERINTENDENTS OF SCHOOLS
Aggravated assault, **2C:12–1**

COUNTY TREASURER
Accuseds counsel assigned in murder case, compensation paid out of treasury, **2A:163–1**

COUNTY TREASURER—Cont'd
Amercement award, after collection or receipt, paid to, **2A:162–7**
Appeal by indigent, payment of transcript, **2A:152–17, 2A:152–18**
Bail, return of amount paid on forfeited recognizance, **2A:162–7**
Extradition expenses, advance of money by treasurer for expenses of, **2A:160–3**
Fines and penalties, conviction of crime, disposition, **2C:46–4**
Inspection of records of disposition of complaints under motor vehicle and traffic laws, **39:5–44**
Probation officers salaries paid by, **2A:168–8**
Transcript on appeal by indigent, payment, **2A:152–17, 2A:152–18**

COUNTY VOCATIONAL SCHOOLS
County schools. Vocational Education, this index

COUNTY WELFARE AGENCIES
Nonattorneys, representation, **Rule 1:21–1**

COUNTY WORKHOUSES
Workhouses, generally, this index

COURIERS
Service, **Rule 1:5–4**

COURT
Courts, generally, this index

COURT ATTENDANTS
Constables, generally, this index
Law enforcement officers, **2A:154–3**
Peace officers, **2A:154–3**

COURT CALENDAR
Calendars, generally, this index

COURT CLERKS
Clerks of Court, generally, this index

COURT COSTS
Costs, generally, this index

COURT CRIERS
Political activities or holding public office, **Rule 1:17–1**

COURT INTAKE SERVICES CONFERENCE
Juvenile delinquents and dependents, **2A:4A–74**

COURT OF COMPETENT JURISDICTION
Definitions, wiretapping and electronic surveillance, **2A:156A–2**

COURT OF PARDONS
Parole, generally, this index

COURT OFFICERS AND EMPLOYEES
Clerks of Court, generally, this index

COURT ORDERS
Orders, generally, this index
Records of Court, generally, this index

COURT REPORTERS
Generally, **Rule 1:34–5**
Appointment, **Rule 1:34–5**
County detectives, **2A:158–19, 2A:158–20**
County prosecutors, **2A:158–19, 2A:158–20**
Grand jury, transcripts, **2B:21–8**
Reports, **Rule 1:32–1**
Verbatim records, **Rule 1:2–2**

COURTESY LAMP
Motor vehicles, color, **39:3–50**

COURTROOMS
Facilities disputes, arbitration, **Rule 1:33–9**
Inadequate facilities, **Rule 1:31–2**
Location, **Rule 1:31–1**
Municipal courts, **2B:12–15**
Proceedings to be conducted in open court, **Rule 1:2–1**

COURTS
See, also, specific courts
Abbreviations, **Rule 1:37–3**
Administrative Director of the Courts, generally, this index
Administrative Office of the Courts, generally, this index
Administrative responsibility, **Rule 1:33–1 et seq.**
Appeal and Review, generally, this index
Appointments, court appointed special advocate, children and minors, **2A:4A–92**
Assessments, generally, this index
Child abuse reports, access to, **9:6–8.10a**
Children and minors, court appointed special advocate, **2A:4A–92**
Clerks of Court, generally, this index
Collections, comprehensive enforcement program, **2B:19–1 et seq.**
Comprehensive enforcement program, **2B:19–1 et seq.**
Confidentiality, records, **Rule 1:38–3**
Contempt, generally, this index
Contracts, collections, **2B:19–6**
Copies, records and recordation, **Rule 1:38–10**
Fees, **Rule 1:38–9**
Costs, generally, this index
Court appointed special advocate, children and minors, **2A:4A–92**
Days of court, **Rule 1:30–3**
Definitions,
    Juvenile justice, **2A:4A–22**
    Nonresident Violator Compact, **39:5F–4**
Denial, record expungement, **2C:52–14**
Director, division of motor vehicles, power to hold court, **39:5–2**
Disclosure, expungement order, **2C:52–30**
Diversion programs, record expungement, **2C:52–20**
Dockets, generally, this index
Employees. Officers and employees, generally, post
Family Court, generally, this index
Fees,
    Costs, generally, this index
    Payment, **Rule 1:13–10**
    Records and recordation, copies, **Rule 1:38–9**
Fines and penalties, payment, **Rule 1:13–10**
Funds, comprehensive enforcement program, **2B:19–3 et seq.**
Geographical division, **Rule 1:33–2**
Hearings, generally, record expungement, **2C:52–9 et seq.**
Hours of court, **Rule 1:30–3**
Improper submission, records, removal, **Rule 1:38–8**
Inadequate facilities, **Rule 1:31–1**
Indictable offenses, record expungement, **2C:52–2**
Inspection and inspectors, records and recordation, **Rule 1:38–10**
    Expungement, **2C:52–19**
Intergovernmental exchanges, records, **Rule 1:38–6**
Judges and Justices, generally, this index

COURTS—Cont'd
Judicial employees. Officers and employees, generally, post
Judicial performance program, **Rule 1:35A–1 et seq.**
Jurisdiction, generally, this index
Jury and Jurors, generally, this index
Juvenile and Domestic Relations Courts, generally, this index
Labor assistance program, comprehensive enforcement program, alternative sentencing option, **2B:19–5**
Location of facilities, **Rule 1:31–1**
Motion days, **Rule 1:30–3**
Municipal Courts, generally, this index
Office hours, **Rule 1:30–1**
Officers and employees,
    Administrative Director of the Courts, generally, this index
    Appointments, appraisers, receivers, guardians, **Rule 1:17–3**
    Clerks of Court, generally, this index
    Gratuities, attorneys or parties, **Rule 1:16–2**
    Holding public office or pursuing gainful activity, **Rule 1:17–1 et seq.**
    Outside activities, advisory committee on, **Rule 1:17A–1 et seq.**
    Private employment, **Rule 1:17–4**
    Supporting personnel, **Rule 1:34–2 et seq.**
    Vacations, **Rule 1:30–5**
Opinions of Court, generally, this index
Orders, generally, this index
Payment, fees, fines and penalties, **Rule 1:13–10**
Performance program, **Rule 1:35A–1 et seq.**
Petitions, record expungement, **2C:52–7 et seq.**
Presentence report, record expungement, **2C:52–21**
Probation and Probation Officers, generally, this index
Process, record expungement, **2C:52–10**
Public policy, comprehensive enforcement program, **2B:19–2**
Recess, **Rule 1:30–3**
Records and recordation,
    Definitions, **Rule 1:38–2**
    Public access, **Rule 1:38–1 et seq.**
    Retention, **Rule 1:32–2**
Records of Court, generally, this index
Release, record expungement, **2C:52–19**
Removal, records, **2C:52–15**
Schedules, **Rule 1:30–1 et seq.**
Sealing, record expungement, **2C:52–26**
Seals and Sealing, this index
Secretaries, political activities or holding public office, **Rule 1:17–1**
Security, confidential or privileged information, **Rule 1:38–5**
Sergeants at arms, political activities or holding public office, **Rule 1:17–1**
Session of court,
    Designating session person excused from jury service must serve, **2B:20–11**
    Service of jurors extending beyond session, **2B:23–8**
Sessions, **Rule 1:30–2**
Sittings of courts, **Rule 1:30–3**
Special sittings, **Rule 1:30–3**
Statements, record expungement petition, **2C:52–8**
Superior Court, generally, this index
Supervisory treatment programs, record expungement, **2C:52–20**
Supporting personnel, **Rule 1:34–2 et seq.**
Supreme Court, generally, this index
Tax Court, generally, this index

COURTS—Cont'd
Terms of court, **Rule 1:30–2**
Title of courts, **Rule 1:37–1**
Traffic offenses, record expungement, **2C:52–28**
Transfer of actions, **Rule 1:13–4**
Vacations, **Rule 1:30–5**
Vicinages, **Rule 1:33–2**

COURTS OF LIMITED CRIMINAL JURISDICTION
Appeals from, **Rule 3:22–1 et seq.**

COVER
Motor vehicles, marks or numbers, crimes and offenses, **2C:17–6**

COWL LAMPS
Color of light, **39:3–52**

COWS
Animals, generally, this index

CRANBERRY BOGS
Trespass, damage to land or crops, **2C:18–4 et seq.**

CRAPS
Casinos, generally, this index

CRATES
Containers, generally, this index

CREDIBILITY OF WITNESSES
Generally, **Evidence Rule 607**
Hearsay statements, admission in evidence, attacking and supporting credibility of declarant, **Evidence Rule 806**

CREDIT
Actions and proceedings, racketeering, **2C:41–4**
Attorney fees, history, identity theft, **2C:21–17.4**
Cease and desist orders, racketeering, **2C:41–4**
Coercion, exposing secrets which would tend to impair, **2C:13–5**
Confidential or privileged information, racketeering investigations, **2C:41–5**
Crimes and offenses,
    Confinement pending sentence, **Rules 3:21–8, 7:9–3**
    Plea agreements, estimated real time served, **Rule 3:9–3**
    Racketeering, **2C:41–1 et seq.**
Criminal coercion, threat to expose material tending to damage credit, **2C:13–5**
Criminal usury, false statements, **2C:21–19**
Debt adjusters, **2C:21–19**
Deceptive business practices, **2C:21–7**
Definitions, racketeering, **2C:41–1**
Discovery, racketeering investigations, **2C:41–5**
Examinations and examiners, racketeering, **2C:41–5**
Extortion, threat to expose or publicize damaging material, **2C:20–5**
False financial statements, **2C:21–4**
Fines and penalties, racketeering, **2C:41–1 et seq.**
Fraud, **2C:21–6**
History, identity theft, damages, **2C:21–17.4**
Identity theft, history, damages, **2C:21–17.4**
Indebtedness, racketeering, **2C:41–1 et seq.**
Inspections and inspectors, racketeering investigations, **2C:41–5**
Interrogatories, racketeering, investigations, **2C:41–5**

CREDIT—Cont'd

Investigations and investigators, racketeering, 2C:41–5

Investments, racketeering, 2C:41–1 et seq.

Judgments and decrees, racketeering, 2C:41–4

Licenses and permits, racketeering, revocation or suspension, 2C:41–4

Process, racketeering, 2C:41–5

Production of books and papers, racketeering, 2C:41–5

Racketeering, 2C:41–1 et seq.

Records and recordation, racketeering, investigations, 2C:41–5

Restitution, racketeering, 2C:41–4

Securities, racketeering, 2C:41–1 et seq.

Wrongful credit practices, 2C:21–19

CREDIT CARDS

Crimes and offenses, 2C:21–6
   Fraud, scanning, 2C:21–6.1

Definitions, 2C:21–6

Fraud, scanning, 2C:21–6.1

Motor vehicle commission, payment, 39:2A–20

Records and recordation, fraud, scanning, 2C:21–6.1

Reencoders, fraud, 2C:21–6.1

Scanning, fraud, 2C:21–6.1

CREDIT UNIONS

Teller machines, security measures. Electronic Fund Transfers, generally, this index

CREDITORS

Debtors and Creditors, generally, this index

CREDITS

Correctional Institutions, this index

CREED

Discrimination, generally, this index

CREEKS

Water Pollution, generally, this index

CRIMES AND OFFENSES

See, also, Fines and Penalties, generally, this index
   Generally, 2C:1–1 et seq.; Rule 3:1–1 et seq.

Abandonment, effort to commit crime, 2C:5–1

Abetting. Accomplices and Accessories, generally, this index

Abolition, common law crimes, 2C:1–5

Absconding from parole, 2C:29–5

Absence of defendant, voluntary, Rule 3:16

Accessories. Accomplices and Accessories, generally, this index

Accidents, health care professionals, solicitation, 2C:40A–4

Accomplices and Accessories, generally, this index

Accountability for conduct of another, criminal liability, 2C:2–6

Act, definitions, 2C:1–14

Act of graffiti, definitions, Criminal mischief, 2C:17–3
   Riot, disorderly conduct and related offenses, 2C:33–24

Acted, definitions, 2C:1–14

Action, definitions, 2C:1–14

Actor, definitions, 2C:1–14

Addresses, discovery, Rule 3:13–3

Administrative dismissal, complaint, Rule 3:25–1

Admissions,
   Joinder of defendants, use, notice, Rule 3:15–2
   Pretrial conferences, evidence, Rule 3:9–1

CRIMES AND OFFENSES—Cont'd

Adoption, this index

Adult Diagnostic and Treatment Center, generally, this index

Adverse or pecuniary interest, 2C:44–1, 2C:44–2

Advertisements, this index

Affidavits,
   Investigative detention, applications, Rule 3:5A–2
   Sentence reduction, change, support, Rule 3:21–10

Affirmative defenses. Defenses, this index

Age,
   Sentence criteria, 2C:44–1
   Verification, false documents, 2C:21–2.1
   Witnesses, depositions, admissibility, Rule 3:13–2

Aged Persons, this index

Agents of corporations, criminal liability, 2C:2–7

Aggravated Assault, generally, this index

Aggravated Criminal Sexual Contact, generally, this index

Aggravated manslaughter, 2C:11–4

Aggravated Sexual Assault, generally, this index

Aggravating circumstances, 2C:44–1 et seq.

Aggravating factors, capital cases, discovery, Rule 3:13–4

Agreements, pleas, Rule 3:9–3

Aiding and abetting. Accomplices and Accessories, generally, this index

AIDS (Acquired Immune Deficiency Syndrome), this index

Air pollution, 26:2C–19

Airports and landing fields, criminal mischief, damage or interference with facilities or equipment, 2C:17–3.1

Alcoholic Beverages, this index

Alcoholics and Alcoholism, this index

Alibi defense, notice, Rule 3:12–2

Alleviation of conduct, defense, 2C:2–5

Ambulances, sales, removal, brands, marks and labels, 39:10–9.4

Amendment, pleadings, postconviction relief, Rule 3:22–9

Ammunition, transfers, 2C:58–3.3

Amount involved, definitions, 2C:1–14

Anatomical gifts, human body parts, purchases, sales, 2C:22–2

Animals, this index

Antishoplifting or inventory control device countermeasure, possession or use, 2C:20–11

Appeals In Criminal Prosecutions, generally, this index

Appearance,
   Assigned counsel, Rule 3:4–2
   Postconviction relief, Rule 3:22–6A
   Corporations, Rule 3:16
   Filing, Rule 3:8–1
   First appearance, Rules 3:3–1, 3:4–2
   Prosecuting attorneys, courts of limited jurisdiction, appeals, Rule 3:23–8
   Public defenders, Rule 3:8–3

Appendices, service, Rule 1:5–1 et seq.

Application of law, 2C:98–1 et seq.

Applications,
   Disposition,
      Consolidated, Rule 3:25A–1
      Reasons, statement, Rule 3:29
   Investigative detention, orders, Rules 3:5A–2, 3:5A–6
   Pretrial intervention programs, Rule 3:28
   Reasons, disposition, statement, Rule 3:29

CRIMES AND OFFENSES—Cont'd

Applications—Cont'd
   Statements, reasons, disposition, Rule 3:29

Apprehension, hindering, 2C:29–3

Arraignment, generally, this index

Arrest, generally, this index

Arson and Other Burnings, generally, this index

Assault and Battery, generally, this index

Assembling, weapons, explosives, or destructive devices, 2C:39–14

Assignment of judges, pretrial intervention programs, Rule 3:28

Atomic energy, release, radiation, 2C:17–7 et seq.

ATP cards, 2C:20–36
   Definitions, food stamps, illegal use, 2C:20–35

Attempts, generally, this index

Attorneys, this index

Audiovisual works, piracy, 2C:21–21

Authorized dispositions, 2C:43–2

Bad checks, 2C:21–5

Bail, generally, this index

Banks and Banking, this index

Bar, postconviction relief,
   Grounds expressly adjudicated, Rule 3:22–5
   Grounds not raised in prior proceedings, Rule 3:22–4

Battery. Assault and Battery, generally, this index

Beginning sentence, 2C:43–10

Benefit card, definitions, food stamps, illegal use, 2C:20–35

Benefits cards, Work First New Jersey, 2C:20–36

Bias intimidation, 2C:16–1

Bigamy, 2C:24–1

Bill of particulars, Rule 3:7–5
   Alibi defense, Rule 3:12–2

Birds, shooting at, 4:22–23

Birth certificates, false certificates, 2C:21–2.1, 2C:21–17.2

Birthdates, discovery, Rule 3:13–3

Blood samples, investigative detention, Rule 3:5A–1 et seq.

Bodily harm, consent of victim to, 2C:2–10

Body vests, 2C:39–13

Bombs, explosives, unlawful purpose, 21:1A–142

Booby traps, controlled dangerous substances, property used for manufacture, distribution or possession, 2C:35–4.1

Books and papers,
   Discovery, Rule 3:13–3
   Filing, Rule 1:5–6

Bribery and Corruption, generally, this index

Briefs,
   Limited criminal jurisdiction, courts of, appeals, Rules 3:23–8, 3:24
   Service, Rule 1:5–1 et seq.

Bullet proof vests, 2C:39–13

Burden of proof, 2C:1–13
   Defense of ignorance or mistake, 2C:2–4
   Termination of complicity by renunciation, affirmative defense, 2C:2–6

Bureau of identification. Identification Bureau, generally, this index

Burglary, generally, this index

Cable Television, this index

Candy, poison candy, 2C:12–2

Capital Punishment, generally, this index

Care, persons with special responsibility for care, force, use, 2C:3–8

Cash deposit, transmittal, limited criminal jurisdiction, courts of, appeals, Rule 3:23–6

CRIMES AND OFFENSES—Cont'd

Cats, this index

Causal relationship between conduct and result, 2C:2–3

Cause a reasonable person to fear, definitions, stalking, 2C:12–10

Causing or risking widespread injury or damage, 2C:17–2

Change of sentence, **Rule 3:21–10**

Character evidence, **Evidence Rule 404**

Methods of proving, **Evidence Rule 405**

Charges. Indictment, Information or Presentment, generally, this index

Charitable Organizations and Associations, this index

Charitable trusts, racketeering, 2C:41–1 et seq.

Cheats. Fraud, generally, this index

Child pornography,

Endangering welfare of children, fourth degree crime, 2C:24–4

Racketeering, 2C:41–1

Children and Minors, this index

Chiropractors, this index

Chop shops, 2C:20–16

Cloning, human beings, 2C:11A–1

Code of Criminal Justice, 2C:1–1 et seq.

Coercion. Duress or Coercion, generally, this index

Coin currency or credit card activated machine, slugs, 2C:21–18

Collateral attack, postconviction relief, grounds, **Rule 3:22–2**

Colleges and Universities, this index

Commercial bribery and breach of duty, 2C:21–10

Commitment and Admission to Institutions, generally, this index

Committing judge, proceedings before, **Rule 3:4–1 et seq.**

Common law crimes, abolition, 2C:1–5

Community related services, requiring performance of, authorized disposition, 2C:43–2

Community residential facilities, 2C:43–2

Community service,

Default in payment of restitution, 2C:46–2

Driving without insurance, 39:6B–2

Graffiti, 2C:33–10, 2C:33–11

Juvenile delinquent, commission by, 2A:4A–43.2

Railroads, signals and signaling, 2C:33–14.1

Mitigating circumstances, 2C:44–1

Motor vehicle operation while under influence, minors, 39:4–50.14

Motor vehicles or vessel, homicide, sentence, 2C:11–5

Pedestrians, stopping, 39:4–36

Suspension, sentence or probation, 2C:45–1

Theft, flags, tombstones, cemeteries, 2C:20–2.3

Commutation. Pardons, this index

Complaints,

Administrative dismissal, **Rule 3:25–1**

Contents, **Rule 3:2–1**

Copy to defendant, **Rule 3:4–2**

Dismissal and nonsuit, **Rule 3:25–1 et seq.**

Disposition of motion, reasons, statement, **Rule 3:29**

Pretrial intervention programs, **Rule 3:28**

Probable cause, **Rule 3:3–1**

Forwarding of indictable complaints, **Rule 3:2–1**

Person arrested without, **Rule 3:4–1**

Probable cause, review of initial finding, **Rule 3:3–1**

Procedure after filing, **Rule 3:4–2**

CRIMES AND OFFENSES—Cont'd

Complaints—Cont'd

Statement, reasons, motion to dismiss, disposition, **Rule 3:29**

Summons, upon complaint, **Rule 3:3–1**

Warrant, upon complaint, **Rule 3:3–1**

Complicity, 2C:2–6

Compounding, 2C:29–4

Witness protection orders, 2C:28–5.1 et seq.

Computers, this index

Conclusions of law, postconviction relief petition, determination, **Rule 3:22–11**

Concurrent sentences, 2C:44–5

Condition of probation, sentence, **Rule 3:21–7**

Conditions of release or detention, witnesses, **Rule 3:26–3**

Conduct and result, causal relationship, 2C:2–3

Conduct of another, criminal liability, 2C:2–6

Conferences,

Arraignment status, **Rule 3:9–1**

Jury and jurors, charge conferences, **Rule 1:8–7**

Verbatim records, **Rule 1:2–2**

Prearraignment, **Rule 3:9–1**

Pretrial, **Rule 3:9–1**

Confessions,

Discovery, **Rule 3:13–3**

Joinder of defendants, use, notice, **Rule 3:15–2**

Confidential or privileged information,

Diagnostic center report, presentence, **Rule 3:21–3**

DNA database and databank, motions, 2A:84A–32a

Expungement, 2C:52–1 et seq.

Newspersons information disclosure privilege, 2A:84A–21.1 et seq.

Physician and patients, 2A:84A–22.6

Records and recordation, expungement, 2C:52–1 et seq.

Confinement pending sentence, credit for, **Rule 3:21–8**

Consecutive sentences, 2C:44–5

Consent, settlement, **Rule 3:1–4**

Consent of victim, 2C:2–10

Consolidated disposition, **Rule 3:25A**

Conspiracy, generally, this index

Constitutional rights, denial, postconviction relief, **Rule 3:22–2**

Construction, this index

Construction of law, Criminal Justice Code, 2C:1–2

Contact lenses, dispensing, licenses and permits, 2C:40–25

Contemplated result and actual result, diversions, 2C:2–3

Contempt, this index

Continuance, discovery, failure to comply, **Rule 3:13–3**

Continuing offenses, theft of services, 2C:20–8

Contraband, furnishing, detention facilities, 2C:29–6

Controlled Substances, this index

Controlled substances near or on school property, defense, notice, **Rule 3:12–1**

Conversion, venue, **Rule 3:14–1**

Conviction of Crime, generally, this index

Cooperation, mitigating circumstances, 2C:44–1

Corporate liability, 2C:2–7

Corporate officials, misconduct, 2C:21–9

Corporations, this index

Correction of sentence, motion, enlargement of time, **Rule 1:3–4**

Correctional Institutions, generally, this index

Corruption. Bribery and Corruption, generally, this index

CRIMES AND OFFENSES—Cont'd

Costs,

Change of venue, trial costs, **Rule 3:14–4**

Courts, traffic violations, 39:5–36

DNA database and databank, motions, 2A:84A–32a

Trial, change of venue, **Rule 3:14–4**

Counties,

Prosecutions, reimbursement, 2A:166A–1 et seq.

Venue, trial, **Rule 3:14–1 et seq.**

County contracts, fraud, 2C:21–34

County detectives and investigators, removal from office, 2A:157–10.4 et seq.

County officers and employees, appropriations, spending or incurring obligations in excess of, 2C:30–4

County penitentiaries, 2C:43–10

County Prosecutors, generally, this index

County reimbursement, prosecution and trial of state grand jury indictments, 2B:22–8

County workhouses, 2C:43–10

Course of conduct, definitions, stalking, 2C:12–10

Credit,

Confinement pending sentence, **Rules 3:21–8, 7:9–3**

Plea agreements, estimated real time served, **Rule 3:9–3**

Racketeering, 2C:41–1 et seq.

Wrongful credit practices, 2C:21–19

Credit cards, 2C:21–6

Fraud, scanning, 2C:21–6.1

Criminal coercion, 2C:13–5

Criminal Justice Code, 2C:1–1 et seq.

Criminal mischief, 2C:17–3

Graffiti, rewards, detection and apprehension, 2A:153–4.1

Criminal restraint, 2C:13–2

Defense, notice, **Rule 3:12–1**

Criminal sexual contact, 2C:14–3

Criminal simulation, 2C:21–2

Criminal trespass, 2C:18–3

Cruelty, sentence criteria, 2C:44–1

Cruelty to Animals, generally, this index

Culpability, general requirements, 2C:2–2

Custodial interrogations, electronic recordation, **Rule 3:17**

Custody, interference, children and minors, 2C:13–4

Data processing, 2C:20–23 et seq.

De minimis infractions, 2C:2–11

De novo hearing, limited criminal jurisdiction, courts of, appeals, **Rule 3:23–1 et seq.**

Dead bodies, 2C:22–1

Deadly Force, generally, this index

Deadly weapons. Weapons, generally, this index

Death,

Assessment, victims of crime compensation board, 2C:43–3.1

Crime causing, venue, **Rule 3:14–1**

Venue, **Rule 3:14–1**

Witnesses, deposition, admissibility, **Rule 3:13–2**

Death by auto or vessel, 2C:11–5

Death penalty. Capital Punishment, generally, this index

Debt adjusters, usury, 2C:21–19

Deception, consent of victim, 2C:2–10

Deceptive business practices, 2C:21–7

Declarations against penal interest, discovery, **Rule 3:13–3**

Decrees. Judgments and decrees, generally, post

CRIMES AND OFFENSES—Cont'd
Defect in institution of prosecution, raising before trial, **Rule 3:10–2**
Defendant,
   Adjudicated guilty, reversal on appeal, return of fine, **2A:166–13**
   Presence, **Rule 3:16**
     Sentencing, **Rule 3:21–4**
Defenses, this index
Definitions, **2C:1–4, 2C:1–14**
   Controlled dangerous substances, trafficking, injunctions, **2C:35–5.6**
   Justification, **2C:3–11**
Defrauding. Fraud, generally, this index
Delay,
   Dismissal, **Rule 3:25–3**
   Imposition of sentence, **Rule 3:21–4**
Delinquent children. Juvenile Delinquents, generally, this index
Demonstrations, funerals, **2C:33–8.1**
Denial, record expungement, **2C:52–14**
Dentists and Dentistry, this index
Department, definitions, food stamps, illegal use, **2C:20–35**
Deposit, bail, form, place, **Rule 3:26–4**
Depositions, **Rule 3:13–2**
   Possibly unavailable witnesses, **Rule 3:26–3**
Depravity, sentence criteria, **2C:44–1**
Desecration of venerated objects, **2C:33–9**
Desertion, venue, **Rule 3:14–1**
Designed result and actual result, diversions, **2C:2–3**
Destruction, records, **2C:21–4**
Detainers, generally, this index
Detective association pursuers, acting without appointment, **15:4–1**
Detention of defendant, probation or suspended sentence, **Rule 3:21–7**
Determination,
   Culpability, **2C:2–2**
   Forgery and fraud, **2C:21–8.1**
Deterrence, aggravating circumstances, **2C:44–1**
Diagnostic center report, presentence investigation, **Rule 3:21–3**
Different offenses, double jeopardy, **2C:1–10**
Differentiating between serious and minor, **2C:1–2**
Disability, **2C:44–1**
   Sentence criteria, **2C:44–1**
   Victims, presentence reports, **2C:44–6**
Disabled veterans, special motor vehicle plates, **39:3–27.18**
Disarming a law enforcement or corrections officer, **2C:12–11**
Disasters, health care professionals, solicitation, **2C:40A–4**
Discharge,
   Defendant, **2C:45–2**
   Fresh pursuit, unlawful arrest, **Rule 3:4–4**
   Judgment, entry, **Rule 3:21–5**
Discipline, persons with special responsibility for discipline, force, use, **2C:3–8**
Disclosure, this index
Discovery, this index
Discrimination, this index
Dismissal and nonsuit, **Rule 3:25–1 et seq.**
   Complaints, ante
   Delay, **Rule 3:25–3**
   Pretrial intervention programs, **Rule 3:28**
Dismissal of prosecution, de minimis infractions, **2C:2–11**
Disorderly Persons, generally, this index
Disreputable persons or places, suspended sentence, **2C:45–1**
Disrupting meetings and processions, **2C:33–8**

CRIMES AND OFFENSES—Cont'd
Diversion programs, record expungement, **2C:52–20**
DNA Database and Databank, generally, this index
Documents, discovery, **Rule 3:13–3**
Dogs, this index
Domestic Violence, generally, this index
Domicile and residence, suspended sentence, condition, **2C:45–1**
Double Jeopardy, generally, this index
Drivers Licenses, this index
Drivers privacy protection, **39:2–3.5**
Drivers schools, seat belts, failure to use, **39:12–15**
Drug tests, **2C:36–10**
Drugs and Medicine, this index
Drunk Driving Victims Bill of Rights, **39:4–50.9 et seq.**
Due process, first appearance, indictment, **Rule 3:4–2**
Duress or Coercion, generally, this index
Educational programs, **2C:43–2**
   Suspended sentence, **2C:45–1**
Effective consent of victim, **2C:2–10**
Electrical contractors, unlicensed persons, **2C:21–33**
Electricity and Electric Companies, this index
Electronic data processing, **2C:20–23 et seq.**
Electronic fund transfers, fraud, payment cards, scanning, **2C:21–6.1**
Electronic recordation, interrogations, **Rule 3:17**
Electronic surveillance, **2A:156A–1 et seq.**
Element of an offense, definitions, **2C:1–14**
Embezzlement, generally, this index
Emergency vehicles, sales, removal, brands, marks and labels, **39:10–9.4**
Emotional distress, definitions, stalking, **2C:12–10**
Employing a juvenile to commit auto theft, **2C:20–17**
Employing child to commit crime, **2C:24–9**
Endangering injured victim, **2C:12–1.2**
Endangering welfare of children, **2C:24–4**
Enhanced sentence. Extended terms of imprisonment, generally, post
Entrapment, **2C:2–12**
   Defense, notice, **Rule 3:12–1**
Entry, orders, **Rule 3:1–4**
Escapes, generally, this index
Evaluation, supervisory treatment program, **2C:43–21**
Eviction, disorderly persons, **2C:33–11.1**
Evidence, generally, this index
Examinations and examiners,
   Adult Diagnostic and Treatment Center, generally, this index
   Presentence investigation reports, **2C:44–6**
Exclusive remedy, postconviction relief, **Rule 3:22–3**
Excuse of conduct,
   Defense, **2C:2–5**
   Mitigating circumstances, **2C:44–1**
Exemptions,
   Custodial interrogations, electronic recordation, **Rule 3:17**
   Record expungement, **2C:52–2**
Exigent circumstances, search warrants, **Rule 3:5–3**
Experiments, discovery, **Rule 3:13–3**
Expert witnesses, discovery, **Rule 3:13–3**
Explosives, this index
Expunging Record, generally, this index

CRIMES AND OFFENSES—Cont'd
Extended terms of imprisonment, **2C:44–3, 2C:44–6, 2C:44–7; Rule 3:21–4**
   Drugs and medicine, **2C:43–6**
   Notice, **2C:44–6**
   Nuclear facilities, release, radiation, **2C:17–7**
Extortion, theft, defense, notice, **Rule 3:12–1**
Extradition, generally, this index
Fabricating physical evidence, **2C:28–6**
Facilitating crime, radio, interception of police, fire or emergency medical communication, **2C:33–21 et seq.**
False financial statements, **2C:21–4**
False imprisonment, **2C:13–3**
False or facsimile bombs, **2C:33–3**
False personation, **2C:21–17**
False public alarms, **2C:33–3**
False reports, law enforcement authorities, **2C:28–4**
False statements, unsworn falsifications, **2C:28–3**
False swearing, **2C:28–2**
   Retraction, defense, notice, **Rule 3:12–1**
Fees,
   Criminal records checks, user fees, **53:1–20.5 et seq.**
   Expunged records, **Rule 3:30**
   Postconviction relief petitions, waiver, **Rule 3:22–6**
   Record expungement, **2C:52–29**
   Supervisory treatment application, drugs and medicine, **2C:43–13**
Felony, definitions, Commercial Driver License Act, **39:3–10.11**
Felony murder, defense, notice, **Rule 3:12–1**
Fences, invisible fences, **2C:40–20**
Fiduciaries,
   Aggravating circumstances, **2C:44–1**
   Misapplication of entrusted property and property of government or financial institution, **2C:21–15**
Filing,
   Attorneys, appearance, **Rule 3:8–1**
   Complaints, procedure after, **Rule 3:4–2**
   Consolidated disposition, order of, **Rule 3:25A–2**
   Fees, postconviction relief, indigent defendant, **Rule 3:22–6**
   Papers, **Rule 1:5–6**
   Postconviction relief petitions, **Rule 3:22–1**
   Search warrants, **Rule 3:5–6**
Financial institutions, receiving deposits, failing institutions, **2C:21–14**
Financial statements and reports, false statements, **2C:21–4**
Findings,
   Nonjury trial, **Rule 1:7–4**
   Postconviction relief petition, determination, **Rule 3:22–11**
Fines and Penalties, generally, this index
Fingernail scrapings, investigative detention, **Rule 3:5A–1 et seq.**
Fingerprints and Fingerprinting, generally, this index
Firearms. Weapons, generally, this index
Fireworks,
   Manufacture, storage and transportation, **21:2–35**
   Possession and sale, **21:3–8**
First appearance, **Rules 3:3–1, 3:4–1, 3:4–2**
   Municipal courts, **Rules 7:3–1, 7:3–2**
First degree crimes, **2C:1–4**
   Sentencing, **2C:43–1**
First offenders,
   Sentence criteria, **2C:44–1**

CRIMES AND OFFENSES—Cont'd

First offenders—Cont'd
    Supervisory treatment programs, **2C:43–12 et seq.**
Food, this index
Food Stamps, this index
Footprints, investigative detention, **Rule 3:5A–1 et seq.**
Force or Violence, generally, this index
Forcible entry and detainer, disorderly persons, **2C:33–11.1**
Foreign,
    Prior conviction, **2C:44–4**
    States. Extradition, generally, this index
Foreign jury, **Rules 3:14–2, 3:14–3**
Foreign states,
    Fresh pursuit, arrest, hearing, **Rule 3:4–4**
    Person dying within jurisdiction, venue, **Rule 3:14–1**
Forests, prevention and control, state forests, **13:9–44.10**
Forfeitures, bail, **Rules 3:26–4, 3:26–6**
Forgery, generally, this index
Form, order, **Rule 3:1–4**
Formal charge, definitions, AIDS or HIV testing for sex offenders, **2C:43–2.2**
Former prosecutions. Double Jeopardy, generally, this index
Fortifications, property used for manufacture, distribution or possession of controlled dangerous substances, **2C:35–4.1**
Fourth degree crimes, **2C:1–4**
    Sentencing, **2C:43–1**
Fraud, generally, this index
Fresh Pursuit Law, generally, this index
Funerals,
    Demonstrations, disruption, **2C:33–8.1**
    Disruption, **2C:33–8.1**
Gambling, **2C:37–2 et seq.**
Gambling devices, possession, **2C:37–7**
Gambling records, possession, **2C:37–3**
Gambling resorts, maintenance, **2C:37–4**
Gangs. Street Gangs, generally, this index
Golf balls, sale or manufacture of balls containing acid or corrosive substance, **2C:12–2**
Grade and degree of offenses, **2C:1–4, 2C:43–1 et seq., 2C:44–1 et seq.**
    Bias intimidation, **2C:16–1**
Graffiti, generally, this index
Grand Jury, this index
Grounds, postconviction relief, **Rule 3:22–2**
Guilty pleas,
    Admissibility of evidence, **Evidence Rule 410**
    Arrest of judgment, **Rule 3:21–9**
    Capital punishment, basis for plea, **Rule 3:9–2**
    Conditional pleas, **Rule 3:9–3**
    Criteria for acceptance, **Rule 3:9–2**
    Death by auto or vessel, admissibility, civil proceeding, **2C:11–5**
    Entry of plea agreement, **Rule 3:9–3**
    Evidence in civil proceeding, **Rule 3:9–2**
    Juvenile delinquents and dependents, form, **Rule 5:21A**
    Municipal courts, **Rule 7:6–2**
    Municipal prosecutors, **2B:25–11**
    Payment, violations bureau, **Rule 7:12–4**
    Pretrial intervention program, application, rejection, review, **Rule 3:28**
    Refusal to accept, **Rule 3:9–2**
    Stipulations, writings, evidence in civil proceeding, **Rule 3:9–2**
    Withdrawal, **Rules 3:9–3, 3:21–1**
Guns. Weapons, generally, this index
Habeas corpus. Postconviction relief, generally, post

CRIMES AND OFFENSES—Cont'd

Habitual criminals. Second or Subsequent Offenses, generally, this index
Hair samples, investigative detention, **Rule 3:5A–1 et seq.**
Halfway houses, **2C:43–2**
Handicapped Persons, this index
Handwriting samples, investigative detention, **Rule 3:5A–1 et seq.**
Hazardous Substances and Waste, this index
Hazards, creation, **2C:40–1**
He, definitions, **2C:1–14**
Health and sanitation, laws protecting public health, **2C:40–18**
Health Care Claims Fraud, generally, this index
Health care professionals, solicitation, disasters or accidents, **2C:40A–4**
Hearings,
    DNA database and databank, motions, **2A:84A–32a**
    Fresh pursuit, **Rule 3:4–4**
    Murder, sentencing hearing, **Rule 3:21–4A**
    Postconviction relief, **Rule 3:22–10**
    Pretrial, **Rule 3:9–1**
        Intervention programs, **Rule 3:28**
    Probable Cause, this index
    Record expungement, **2C:52–9 et seq.**
    Sentence, reduction, change, **Rule 3:21–10**
Heinous, **2C:44–1**
    Sentence criteria, **2C:44–1**
Hindering apprehension or prosecution, **2C:29–3**
    Witness protection orders, **2C:28–5.1 et seq.**
Hit and Run Drivers, generally, this index
Homes,
    Defense, use of force, **2C:3–4, 2C:3–6**
    Protection of third persons, use of force, **2C:3–5**
Homicide, generally, this index
Hostages. Kidnapping, generally, this index
Housing,
    Defense, use of force, **2C:3–6**
    Protection of third persons, use of force, **2C:3–5**
Human body parts, purchases, sales, **2C:22–2**
Human trafficking, **2C:13–8**
Husband and wife,
    Confidential or privileged information, **Evidence Rule 501**
    Desertion, venue, **Rule 3:14–1**
Hypodermic Needles or Syringes, this index
Identification Bureau, generally, this index
Identification cards, public utilities, **2C:21–35**
Identity and identification,
    DNA database and databank, motions, **2A:84A–32a, 2A:84A–32b**
    Municipal court offenses, **Rule 7:2–2**
    Nontestimonial, investigative detention, **Rule 3:5A–1 et seq.**
    Pretrial hearings, **Rule 3:9–1**
    Summons, procedure after arrest, **Rule 3:4–1**
    Theft of identity, **2C:21–17**
    Verification, false documents, **2C:21–2.1**
Ignition keys, motor vehicles, production, proof of ownership, **2C:40–23**
Ignorance, defense, **2C:2–4**
    Notice, defense, **Rule 3:12–1**
Illegal investments. Money Laundering and Illegal Investments, generally, this index
Illegal sentence, correction, **Rule 3:22–2**
    Time, **Rule 3:21–10**
Illegality of conduct, culpability, **2C:2–2**
Imitation firearms, possession, **2C:39–4**
Immediate detention warrant, witnesses, **Rule 3:26–3**

CRIMES AND OFFENSES—Cont'd

Immigration and naturalization, unauthorized practice, **2C:21–31**
Immunity from criminal prosecutions, child abuse reports, **9:6–8.13**
Impeachment, conviction of crime, **2C:51–1**
Incapacity, physicians and surgeons, privileges and immunities, **2A:84A–22.3**
Included offenses,
    Definitions, **2C:1–8**
    Former prosecution as bar to subsequent prosecution, **2C:1–9**
Incompetent persons, endangering welfare, **2C:24–7**
Inconsistent provisions, effect, Criminal Justice Code, **2C:1–1**
Incrimination, definition, **Evidence Rule 502**
Indeterminate sentences, young adult offenders, **2C:43–5**
Index, supervisory treatment program, **2C:43–21**
Index cards, expungement, **2C:52–1 et seq.**
Indictable offenses, record expungement, **2C:52–2**
Indictment, Information or Presentment, generally, this index
Indigent defendants,
    Right to appeal, notification, **Rule 3:21–4**
    Subpoenas, fees, **Rules 1:9–1, 1:9–3**
    Waiver of fees, **Rule 1:13–2**
Inducement, **2C:2–12**
Information. Indictment, Information or Presentment, generally, this index
Informing of rights, first appearance, **Rule 3:4–2**
Infractions, de minimis infractions, **2C:2–11**
Innocence presumption, **2C:1–13**
Insanity Defense, generally, this index
Inspection and inspectors, records, expungement, **2C:52–19**
Insufficient fund checks, **2C:21–5**
Insurance, this index
Intensive supervision program,
    Restrictions, **2C:43–11**
    Sentence change, **Rule 3:21–10**
Intent, explosives, unlawful purpose, **21:1A–142**
Interference with custody of children or committed persons, **2C:13–4**
Interference with transportation, **2C:33–14**
Internet, this index
Interrogations, electronic recordation, **Rule 3:17**
Interstate Agreement on Detainers Act, **2A:159A–1 et seq.**
Interstate compacts, **53:1–32**
Intervention, pretrial intervention, **2C:43–12**
Intimidation, generally, this index
Intoxication,
    Consent of victim, **2C:2–10**
    Criminal liability, **2C:2–8**
    Notice, defense, **Rule 3:12–1**
Intoxication of driver. Motor Vehicles, this index
Invasion of privacy, observation, nudity, sexual intercourse, **2C:14–9**
Investigations, this index
Investigative detention. Arrest, this index
Jewelry, presumptions, records and recordation, **2C:21–38**
Joinder,
    Defendants, **Rules 3:15–1, 3:15–2**
    Indictment, accusation, **Rule 3:7–7**
    Verdict, **Rule 3:19–1**
    Indictments, accusation, **Rule 3:15–1**
    Lesser related infractions with criminal offenses, **Rule 3:15–3**

CRIMES AND OFFENSES—Cont'd
Joinder—Cont'd
Offenses, indictment, accusation, **Rule 3:7–6**
Joint offenses, complicity, **2C:2–6**
Joint resolution, supervisory treatment programs, rules, **2C:43–17 et seq.**
Judgments and decrees, **Rule 3:21–1 et seq.**
Arrest of judgment, **Rule 3:21–9**
Complaints, dismissal, appeals, **Rule 3:24**
Corporations, convictions, **Rule 3:21–6**
Default, bail, forfeiture, execution, **Rule 3:26–6**
Discharge, entry, **Rule 3:21–5**
Insanity, acquittal by reason of, **Rule 3:19–2**
Limitation of actions, postconviction relief, **Rule 3:22–12**
Limited criminal jurisdiction, courts of, appeals, **Rule 3:23–1 et seq.**
Disposition, **Rule 3:23–8**
New trial, **Rule 3:20–1**
Postconviction relief, **Rule 3:22–1 et seq.**
Petition, determination, **Rule 3:22–11**
Posttrial, limited criminal jurisdiction, courts of, appeals, **Rule 3:24**
Pretrial intervention program, **Rule 3:28**
Sentence and punishment, generally, post
Signing, entering, **Rule 3:21–5**
Judicial conference, supervisory treatment program, **2C:43–15, 2C:43–19**
Jumping bail, **2C:29–7**
Jurisdiction, **2C:1–3**
Former persecution in another, bar, **2C:1–11**
Indictment or accusation, use, **Rule 3:7–2**
Lack,
Limited criminal jurisdiction, courts of, appeals, raising, **Rule 3:23–8**
Postconviction relief, petition, **Rule 3:22–2**
Raising defense, **Rule 3:10–2**
Multiple offenses, separate trials, **2C:1–8**
Prior convictions, **2C:44–4**
Prosecution before court lacking jurisdiction, reprosecution, **2C:1–12**
Venue, **Rule 3:14–1 et seq.**
Writs, processes, **Rule 3:1–2**
Jury and Jurors, this index
Justification,
Affirmative defense, **2C:3–1 et seq.**
General principles, of, defense, notice, **Rule 3:12–1**
Juvenile Delinquents, generally, this index
Kennels, destruction of animals, **4:22–19**
Kerosene burning heating devices, **2C:40–15**
Keys, ignition keys, motor vehicles, production, proof of ownership, **2C:40–23**
Kidnapping, generally, this index
Kinds of culpability, **2C:2–2**
Knives. Weapons, generally, this index
Labor and Employment, this index
Labor assistance program, comprehensive enforcement program, alternative sentencing option, **2B:19–5**
Labor Unions, this index
Lack of jurisdiction, defense, **Rule 3:10–2**
Landlord and Tenant, this index
Law, unauthorized practice, **2C:21–22**
Leader of a firearms trafficking network, **2C:39–16**
Leader of auto theft trafficking network, **2C:20–18**
Lesser related infractions, joinder for trial with criminal offenses, **Rule 3:15–3**
Lewdness and Obscenity, generally, this index
Liability of conduct of another, **2C:2–6**
Libel, venue, **Rule 3:14–1**
Libraries, this index
Library theft, **2C:20–12 et seq.**

CRIMES AND OFFENSES—Cont'd
Licenses and permits, suspension or cancellation, **2C:43–2**
Lie detector tests, employer requiring, **2C:40A–1**
Life imprisonment, **2C:11–3 et seq.**
Limitation of Criminal Prosecutions, generally, this index
Limited criminal jurisdiction, courts of, appeals from judgments, **Rule 3:23–1 et seq.**
Lineups, investigative detention, **Rule 3:5A–1 et seq.**
Local laws, code of criminal justice preemption, **2C:1–5**
Location, imprisonment, **2C:43–10**
Loss, conviction of crime, rights, **2C:51–1 et seq.**
Lotteries, generally, this index
Mandatory joinder, indictments, accusations, **Rule 3:15–1**
Mandatory sentence, **2C:43–6**
Review, **2C:43–6.1, 2C:43–6.3**
Manslaughter, generally, this index
Marriage, this index
Material element of an offense, definitions, **2C:1–14**
Material witness hearing, **Rule 3:26–3**
Means of conveyance, unlawful taking, **2C:20–10**
Medicaid, this index
Medical care and treatment, cloning, **2C:11A–1**
Medical records, destruction, alteration, falsification, **2C:21–4.1**
Medical treatment,
Adult Diagnostic and Treatment Center, generally, this index
Suspended sentences, **2C:45–1**
Medicare, this index
Memoranda, service, **Rule 1:5–1 et seq.**
Mental examinations,
Discovery, **Rule 3:13–3**
Presentence, **Rule 3:21–2**
Presentence investigations, reports, **2C:44–6**
Mental state,
Constitute offense, **2C:1–2**
Culpable mental state, construction of law, Code of Criminal Justice, **2C:2–2**
Ignorance, **2C:2–4**
Intoxication, criminal liability, **2C:2–8**
Mistake, criminal prosecutions, **2C:2–4**
Mentally Deficient and Mentally Ill Persons, this index
Merger and consolidation. Conviction of Crime, this index
Minimum requirements of culpability, **2C:2–2**
Minimum sentences,
Drugs and medicine, controlled dangerous substances, **2C:43–6**
Sexual offenses, **2C:14–6**
Weapons, possession, **2C:43–6**
Misappropriation, venue, **Rule 3:14–1**
Mischief, **2C:17–3**
Graffiti, rewards, detection and apprehension, **2A:153–4.1**
Misconduct by corporate official, **2C:21–9**
Misconduct in office, **2C:30–2**
Misdemeanor, definitions, **2C:1–4**
Misrepresentation. Fraud, generally, this index
Mistake, defense, **2C:2–4**
Notice, **Rule 3:12–1**
Mistake of law, force, use, **2C:3–9**
Mitigating circumstances, **2C:44–1**
Capital cases, additional discovery, **Rule 3:13–4**

CRIMES AND OFFENSES—Cont'd
Modification,
Appeal and review, **2C:44–7**
Suspended sentence, **2C:45–2**
Hearing, **2C:45–4**
Money Laundering and Illegal Investments, generally, this index
Monopolies, this index
Motion pictures, nudity, sexual intercourse, invasion of privacy, **2C:14–9**
Motions, **Rule 3:10–1 et seq.**
Acquittal, judgment of, **Rules 3:18–1, 3:18–2**
Arrest of judgment, **Rule 3:21–9**
Attorneys, joint representation, **Rule 3:8–2**
Bill of particulars, **Rule 3:7–5**
Date for hearing, setting, **Rule 3:9–1**
Defenses, objections raised before trial, **Rule 3:10–2**
Depositions, **Rule 3:13–2**
Determination, effect of, **Rule 3:10–7**
Dismissal, **Rule 3:25–1**
Delay, **Rule 3:25–3**
Extended term of imprisonment, **Rule 3:21–4**
Foreign jury, **Rule 3:14–2**
Homicide, capital punishment, life imprisonment, **2C:11–3b**
Joinder, relief, **Rule 3:15–2**
New trial, **Rule 3:20–2**
Postconviction relief petition as substitute, **Rule 3:22–3**
Reasons, disposition, statement, **Rule 3:29**
Reduction or change of sentence, **Rule 3:21–10**
Searches and seizures, suppression of evidence, return of property, **Rule 3:5–7**
Sentence, reduction, change, **Rule 3:21–10**
Separate trials, **Rule 3:15–2**
Service, **Rule 1:5–1 et seq.**
Settlement, **Rule 3:1–4**
Statement, reasons, disposition, **Rule 3:29**
Venue, change, **Rule 3:14–2**
Withdrawal of plea, **Rule 3:21–1**
Motor bicycles, marks or numbers, change or destruction, **2C:17–6**
Motor carriers, marks or numbers, change or destruction, **2C:17–6**
Motor Vehicle Insurance, this index
Motor Vehicles, this index
Motorcycles, marks or numbers, change or destruction, **2C:17–6**
Motorized Bicycles, this index
Multiple counts, verdict, **Rule 3:19–1**
Multiple defendants, verdict, **Rule 3:19–1**
Multiple offenses,
Conspiracy, **2C:5–2**
Conviction of crime, limitation, **2C:1–8**
Former prosecutions, **2C:1–10**
Bar, **2C:1–9**
Limitation on conviction, **2C:1–8**
Method of prosecution, **2C:1–8**
Sentences, **2C:44–5**
Separate trials, **2C:1–8**
Multiple prosecutions. Double Jeopardy, generally, this index
Municipal contracts, fraud, **2C:21–34**
Municipal Courts, generally, this index
Municipal officers and employees, appropriations, spending or incurring obligations in excess of, **2C:30–4**
Murder. Homicide, generally, this index
Names,
Discovery, **Rule 3:13–3**
Expungement, **2C:52–1 et seq.**
Narcotic drugs, pretrial intervention programs, **Rule 3:28**

CRIMES AND OFFENSES—Cont'd

Naturalization, unauthorized practice, 2C:21–31

Necessity, defense, **2C:3–2**

Negligent homicide, motor vehicle or vessel, 2C:11–5

Negligent use of force, **2C:3–9**

Negligently, definitions, **2C:2–2**

New trial, **Rules 3:20–1, 3:20–2**

DNA database and databank, motions, **2A:84A–32a, 2A:84A–32b**

Newly discovered evidence, new trial, motion, **Rule 3:20–2**

News organizations, searches and seizures, **2A:84A–21.9 et seq.**

Non vult, plea of,

Arrest of judgment, **Rule 3:21–9**

Withdrawal, **Rule 3:21–1**

Noncustodial sentences, **2C:44–1**

Nonjury trials, findings, **Rule 1:7–4**

Nonsufficient fund checks, **2C:21–5**

Nontestimonial identification procedures, investigative detention, **Rule 3:5A–1 et seq.**

Not guilty pleas,

Insanity, verdict, **Rule 3:19–2**

Municipal courts, **Rules 7:6–1, 7:6–2**

Refusal to plead, **Rule 3:9–2**

Notice,

Alibi defense, **Rule 3:12–2**

Appeals, sentences, right to, **Rule 3:21–4**

Assignment of counsel, postconviction relief, **Rule 3:22–6A**

Attorneys charged with crimes, **Rule 1:20–13**

Consolidation for plea or sentencing, motion, **Rule 3:25A–1**

Defenses, specific criminal code defenses, **Rule 3:12–1**

Depositions, **Rule 3:13–2**

Discovery, additional material, **Rule 3:13–3**

Dismissal of de minimis infractions, **2C:2–11**

DNA database and databank, motions, **2A:84A–32a**

Extended term of imprisonment, **2C:44–6**

Imposition of sentence, **Rule 3:21–4**

Insanity defense, **Rule 3:12–1**

Investigative detention, applications, **Rule 3:5A–3**

Joint defendants, statements, confession, admission, **Rule 3:15–2**

Limited criminal jurisdiction, courts of, appeals, **Rules 3:23–2, 3:23–3**

Probable cause hearing, **Rule 3:4–3**

Settlement, **Rule 3:1–4**

Suspended sentence, revocation or modification, **2C:45–4**

Nuclear Facilities, this index

Nudity, observation, invasion of privacy, 2C:14–9

Nurses, this index

Oaths and affirmations, complaint, **Rule 3:2**

Objections and exceptions, **Rule 3:10–1 et seq.**

Determination of motion, effect, **Rule 3:10–7**

Hearing on motion, **Rule 3:10–2**

Motion, time, manner of making, **Rule 3:10–2**

Raising before trial, **Rule 3:10–2**

Obscenity. Lewdness and Obscenity, generally, this index

Obstructing highways and other public passages, **2C:33–7**

Obstruction of administration of law, or other governmental functions, **2C:29–1**

Offering false instrument for filing, **2C:21–3**

Officers and Employees, this index

Official misconduct, **2C:30–2**

CRIMES AND OFFENSES—Cont'd

Omissions,

Basis of criminal liability, **2C:2–1**

Definitions, **2C:1–14**

Omitted to act, definitions, **2C:1–14**

Opinion evidence, discovery, **Rule 3:13–3**

Optometrists, this index

Orders,

Acquittal, judgment of, **Rules 3:18–1, 3:18–2**

Bail, **Rule 3:26–1 et seq.**

Change of venue, **Rule 3:14–4**

Consolidated disposition, **Rule 3:25A–2**

Discovery, protective orders, **Rule 3:13–3**

Foreign jury, **Rule 3:14–3**

Form, entry, **Rule 3:1–4**

Investigative detention, **Rule 3:5A–1 et seq.**

Limited criminal jurisdiction, courts of, appeals, **Rule 3:24**

Postconviction relief petition, determination, **Rule 3:22–11**

Pretrial intervention program, **Rule 3:28**

Probation, **Rule 3:21–7**

Protective orders, discovery, **Rule 3:13–3**

Record expungement, **2C:52–11 et seq.**

Sentence and punishment, generally, post

Suspended sentence, **Rule 3:21–7**

Trial, order for, **Rule 3:25–2**

Venue, order for change, **Rule 3:14–4**

Witnesses, appearance, **Rule 3:26–3**

Ordinances, code of criminal justice preemption, **2C:1–5**

Organized Crime, generally, this index

Organized retail theft enterprise, **2C:20–11.2**

Other crimes, wrongs or acts, admissibility, **Evidence Rule 404**

Paging devices,

Children and minors, possession, **2C:33–19 et seq.**

Use in crime, **2C:33–20**

Palm prints, investigative detention, **Rule 3:5A–1 et seq.**

Pardons, generally, this index

Parking, this index

Parole, generally, this index

Pathological intoxication, criminal liability, 2C:2–8

Peering into dwellings, **2C:18–3**

Penalties. Fines and Penalties, generally, this index

Pending prosecutions, Code of Criminal Justice, application of law, **2C:1–1**

Perjury, generally, this index

Permissible joinder, indictments, accusations, **Rule 3:15–1**

Persistent offenders, notice to impose sentence, **Rule 3:21–4**

Persistent Offenders Accountability Act, **2C:43–7, 2C:43–7.1**

Person, definitions, **2C:1–14**

Pet shops, destruction of animals, **4:22–19**

Petit jurors, number, **2B:23–1**

Petitions,

Postconviction relief, **Rule 3:22–1 et seq.**

Fees, waiver, **Rule 3:22–6**

Record expungement, **2C:52–7 et seq.**

Propriety, **2C:52–24**

Service, **Rule 1:5–1 et seq.**

Petty disorderly persons, **2C:1–4; Rule 3:1–6**

Pharmacists, this index

Photographs,

Expungement, **2C:52–1 et seq.**

Investigative detention, **Rule 3:5A–1 et seq.**

Nudity, sexual intercourse, invasion of privacy, **2C:14–9**

Physical characteristics, obtaining evidence, investigative detention, **Rule 3:5A–1 et seq.**

CRIMES AND OFFENSES—Cont'd

Physical examinations,

Adult Diagnostic and Treatment Center, generally, this index

Discovery, **Rule 3:13–3**

Presentence reports, **2C:44–6; Rule 3:21–2**

Privileges and immunities, **Evidence Rule 501**

Physical measurements, investigative detention, **Rule 3:5A–1 et seq.**

Physical Therapists, this index

Physicians and Surgeons, this index

Pistols. Weapons, generally, this index

Place of imprisonment, **2C:43–10**

Places of worship,

Arson, **2C:17–1**

Targets of conspiracy, grade and degree of offense, **2C:5–4**

Pleadings, **Rule 3:10–1**

Postconviction relief, amendment, **Rule 3:22–9**

Pleas, **Rule 3:9–2**

Acceptance, **Rule 3:9–3**

Admissibility of evidence, **Evidence Rule 410**

Agreements, **Rule 3:9–3**

Bargaining, **Rule 3:9–3**

Extended or enhanced term of imprisonment, service of motion, **Rule 3:21–4**

Conditional pleas, **Rule 3:9–3**

Discussions, **Rule 3:9–3**

Offer, **Rule 3:9–1**

Guilty pleas, generally, ante

Municipal courts, **Rules 7:6–1, 7:6–2**

Refusal to plead, **Rule 3:9–2**

Withdrawal, **Rules 3:9–3, 3:21–1**

Podiatrists and Podiatry, this index

Poison food or candy, **2C:12–2**

Police and Police Departments, this index

Police report, discovery, **Rule 3:13–3**

Political subdivisions, contracts, fraud, 2C:21–34

Pornography. Lewdness and Obscenity, generally, this index

Portable kerosene burning heating devices, 2C:40–15

Possession, definitions, **2C:2–1**

Postconviction relief, **Rule 3:22–1 et seq.**

Answer, **Rule 3:22–9**

Assignment,

Counsel, **Rules 3:22–6, 3:22–6A**

Petition, disposition, **Rule 3:22–7**

Attorneys, indigents, **Rule 3:22–6**

Bar,

Ground expressly adjudicated, **Rule 3:22–5**

Ground not raised in prior proceedings, **Rule 3:22–4**

Conclusions, findings, **Rule 3:22–11**

Contents, petition, **Rule 3:22–8**

Determination, **Rule 3:22–11**

Docketing, petition, **Rule 3:22–7**

Enlargement of time, **Rule 1:3–4**

Exclusiveness of remedy, **Rule 3:22–3**

Findings, conclusions, **Rule 3:22–11**

Good cause, assignment of counsel, **Rule 3:22–6**

Grounds, **Rule 3:22–2**

Expressly adjudicated, bar, **Rule 3:22–5**

Not raised in prior proceeding, bar, **Rule 3:22–4**

Hearings, **Rule 3:22–10**

Indigents, waiver of fees, **Rule 3:22–6**

Ineffective counsel, grounds, **Rule 3:22–4**

Judgments, **Rule 3:22–11**

Limitations, **Rule 3:22–12**

Motion, **Rule 3:22–9**

Municipal courts, **Rule 7:10–2**

Petitions, **Rule 3:22–1**

CRIMES AND OFFENSES—Cont'd
Postconviction relief—Cont'd
  Petitions—Cont'd
    Contents, **Rule 3:22–8**
  Pleadings, amendment, **Rule 3:22–9**
  Presence of defendant at hearing, **Rules 3:16, 3:22–10**
  Service, petition, **Rule 3:22–7**
  Substitution, assigned counsel, **Rule 3:22–6**
  Supplementary orders, **Rule 3:22–11**
  Transcript, grant, indigents, **Rule 3:22–6**
  Verification, petition, **Rule 3:22–8**
  Withdrawal, assigned counsel, **Rule 3:22–6**
Postponement, proceedings, pretrial intervention program, **Rule 3:28**
Pounds, destruction of animals, **4:22–19**
Prearraignment conferences, **Rule 3:9–1**
Precursors, drugs and medicine, possession, **2C:35–28**
Prejudicial joinder, relief, **Rule 3:15–2**
Preliminary hearing, admissibility of defendants statements, **Evidence Rule 104**
Preliminary proceedings, **Rule 3:1–1 et seq.**
Premises, defense, use of force, **2C:3–6**
Preponderance of evidence, **2C:1–13**
Prescriptions, this index
Presence of defendant, **Rule 3:16**
  Postconviction relief hearing, **Rule 3:22–10**
  Sentencing, **Rule 3:21–4**
Presentence investigations, **2C:44–6**
  Expungement, **2C:52–21**
Presentence procedure, **Rule 3:21–2**
Presentment. Indictment, Information or Presentment, generally, this index
Presumptions, **2C:1–13; Evidence Rule 303**
  Bad checks, **2C:21–5**
  Child pornography, age of persons depicted, **2C:24–4**
  Credit cards, knowledge, **2C:21–6**
  Definitions, **2C:1–13**
  Gambling offenses, proof of occurrence of sporting events, **2C:37–5**
  Husband coercing wife, **2C:2–9**
  Imprisonment, **2C:44–1**
  Innocence of defendant, **2C:1–13**
  Jewelry, records and recordation, **2C:21–38**
  Licenses and permits, firearms and weapons, **2C:39–2**
  Mentally deficient and mentally ill persons, disease or defect, **2C:4–1**
  Obscene material,
    Knowledge and age of patrons, **2C:34–3**
    Public communication, **2C:34–4**
  Prostitutes, persons supported by, **2C:34–1**
  Receiving stolen property, **2C:20–7**
  Sexual offenses,
    Capability, **2C:14–5**
    Evidence of prior sexual conduct of victim, **2C:14–7**
  Shoplifting, **2C:20–11**
  Theft,
    Failure to make required disposition of property received, **2C:20–9**
    Services, **2C:20–8**
  Weapons, **2C:39–2**
Pretrial conferences, hearings, **Rule 3:9–1**
Pretrial intervention, **2C:43–12**
  Applications, **Rule 3:28**
  Guidelines, **Rule 3:28**
  Informing defendant, **Rule 3:4–2**
  Motion for, statement of reasons for disposition, **Rule 3:29**
  Records, confidentiality, **Rule 1:38–3**
  Registers and registries, **Rule 3:28**
Pretrial procedure, **Rule 3:9–1 et seq.**

CRIMES AND OFFENSES—Cont'd
Pretrial proceedings, presence of defendant, **Rule 3:16**
Principals of criminal liability, **2C:2–1 et seq.**
Prior convictions, **2C:44–4**
  Discovery, **Rule 3:13–3**
Prior offenses code of criminal justice, application of law, **2C:1–1**
Privileges and immunities,
  Conspiracy, immunity of party to conspiracy, **2C:5–3**
  Conviction of crime, **2C:51–1**
  Domestic violence prevention, arrest, **2C:25–22**
  Prosecution, accomplice conviction, **2C:2–6**
  Shoplifting, custody, arrest, **2C:20–11**
  Weapons, voluntary surrender, **2C:39–12**
Probable Cause, generally, this index
Probation and Probation Officers, generally, this index
Process. Service of process, generally, post
Production of documents and things, **Rule 3:13–2**
Professional criminals, extended terms, **2C:44–3**
Promoting prostitution, **2C:34–1**
Property crimes, justification defense, **2C:3–10**
Prosecution,
  Before court lacking jurisdiction, **2C:1–12**
  Hindering, **2C:29–3**
  Multiple offenses, **2C:1–8**
Prostitution, generally, this index
Protection of other persons, **2C:3–5**
Protection of public, **2C:44–1**
Provocation, mitigating circumstances, **2C:44–1**
Psychiatric examinations,
  Adult Diagnostic and Treatment Center, generally, this index
  Reports, **2C:44–6**
Psychiatric Hospitals, this index
Psychiatrists, suspended sentence, treatment, **2C:45–1**
Psychological examinations. Adult Diagnostic and Treatment Center, generally, this index
Psychologists and Psychology, this index
Public communications, obscene material, **2C:34–4**
Public Defenders, generally, this index
Public officers and employees,
  Retaliation for past official actions, **2C:27–5**
  Speculating or wagering on official action or information, **2C:30–3**
Public Utilities, this index
Punishment. Sentence and punishment, generally, post
Purposes of law, **2C:1–2**
Racial profiling, law enforcement officers, **2C:30–5 et seq.**
Racketeers and Racketeering, generally, this index
Radiation protection, **26:2D–22**
Radio and Radio Stations, this index
Radioactive substances, terrorism, **2C:38–2, 2C:38–3**
Radon gas contamination testing, **26:2D–77**
Railroads, this index
Rap sheets, expungement, **2C:52–1 et seq.**
Rape, generally, this index
Real estate,
  Bail location, **Rule 3:26–4**
  Defending, use of force, **2C:3–4**
Reasonable belief, definitions, **2C:1–14**
Reasonable doubt, standard of proof, **2C:1–13**
Reasonably believes, definitions, **2C:1–14**

CRIMES AND OFFENSES—Cont'd
Reasons, statements, disposition of motion or application, **Rule 3:29**
Receiving Stolen Property, generally, this index
Recidivists. Second or Subsequent Offenses, generally, this index
Reckless driving. Motor Vehicles, this index
Reckless use of force, **2C:3–9**
Recklessly, definitions, **2C:2–2**
Recklessly endangering another person, **2C:12–2**
Recognizances, generally, this index
Recordable instruments, fraud, **2C:21–3**
Records and recordation,
  Aggravating circumstances, **2C:44–1**
  Checks, user fees, **53:1–20.5 et seq.**
  Defect, limited criminal jurisdiction, courts of, appeals, **Rule 3:23–8**
  Discovery, **Rule 3:13–3**
  Electronic recordation, interrogations, **Rule 3:17**
  Expunging Record, generally, this index
  Extended terms of imprisonment, **2C:44–3**
  Falsifying or tampering, **2C:21–4**
  Fees,
    Criminal records checks, **53:1–20.5 et seq.**
    Expungement, **2C:52–29**
  Imposing sentence, reasons, **2C:43–2**
  Limited criminal jurisdiction, courts of, appeal of conviction, **Rules 3:23–3, 3:23–4, 3:23–8**
  Mitigating factors, **2C:44–1**
  Plea agreement, **Rule 3:9–3**
  Pretrial intervention registry, **Rule 3:28**
  Prior conviction, **2C:44–4**
  Prisoner delivery, **2C:43–10**
  Recognizance, **Rule 3:26–4**
  User fees, criminal records checks, **53:1–20.5 et seq.**
Reduction of sentence,
  Enlargement of time, **Rule 1:3–4**
  Motion, **Rule 3:21–10**
Registry, pretrial intervention, **Rule 3:28**
Rehabilitation,
  Code of Criminal Justice, purpose, **2C:1–2**
  Rehabilitated convicted offenders, **2A:168A–1 et seq.**
  Supervisory treatment programs, **2C:43–12 et seq.**
  Suspended sentence, **2C:45–1**
Reimbursement, counties, prosecutions, **2A:166A–1 et seq.**
Release, **2C:43–9**
  Arrest without warrant, summons, **Rule 3:4–1**
  Recognizance, **Rule 3:26–1**
  Record expungement, **2C:52–19**
Release from custody, delay in trial, **Rule 3:25–2**
Religious Corporations and Associations, this index
Removal, records, **2C:52–15**
Removal from office, **2C:43–2**
Renunciation of criminal purpose, **2C:5–1**
  Defense, notice, **Rule 3:12–1**
Repealed laws, application, **2C:98–2, 2C:98–3**
Repeatedly, definitions, stalking, **2C:12–10**
Reports,
  Administrative dismissal, complaint, **Rule 3:25–1**
  Diagnostic center reports, presentence investigation, **Rule 3:21–3**
  Discovery, **Rule 3:13–3**
  Presentence investigations, **2C:44–6; Rule 3:21–2**
Refraining from reporting crime, **2C:29–4**

CRIMES

CRIMES AND OFFENSES—Cont'd
Reports—Cont'd
  Refraining from reporting crime—Cont'd
    Witness protection orders, **2C:28–5.1**
  Supervisory treatment program, **2C:43–21**
  Suspended sentences, **2C:45–1**
Request for discovery, **Rule 3:13–3**
Res judicata, postconviction relief, grounds expressly adjudicated, **Rule 3:22–5**
Research facility,
  Burglary, **2C:18–2**
  Damage, destruction, criminal mischief, **2C:17–3**
  Definitions, **2C:1–14**
  Theft, **2C:20–2**
  Unlicensed entry of structure, **2C:18–3**
Resisting arrest, **2C:29–2**
Responsibility, **2C:4–1 et seq.**
Restitution, generally, this index
Restoration, conviction of crime, rights, **2C:51–1 et seq.**
Result and conduct, causal relationship, **2C:2–3**
Retaliation,
  Past official actions, **2C:27–5**
  Witnesses, informants, **2C:28–5**
Retraction,
  False swearing, defense, notice, **Rule 3:12–1**
  Perjury, defense, notice, **Rule 3:12–1**
Revocation,
  Parole, **2C:43–9**
  Probation, suspension of sentence, **Rule 3:21–7**
  Suspended sentences, **2C:45–3**
    Hearing, **2C:45–4**
Rewards, apprehension of persons accused of crime, **2A:153–1 et seq.**
Rigging publicly exhibited contests, **2C:21–11**
Right to bail before conviction, **Rule 3:26–1**
Right to counsel. Attorneys, this index
Risked result and actual result, diversions, **2C:2–3**
Robbery, generally, this index
Rules of court, supervisory treatment program, **2C:43–14 et seq.**
Safety,
  Laws protecting public safety, **2C:40–18**
  Persons with special responsibilities for safety of others, force, use, **2C:3–8**
Sales, this index
Saliva samples, investigative detention, **Rule 3:5A–1 et seq.**
Same offense, double jeopardy, **2C:1–9**
School buses, drivers, cellular phones, **39:3B–25**
Schools and School Districts, this index
Scientific tests, discovery, **Rule 3:13–3**
Scope of rules, **Rule 3:1–1**
Sealing, record expungement, **2C:52–26**
Search Warrants, generally, this index
Searches and Seizures, generally, this index
Second degree crimes, **2C:1–4**
  Aiding escape, **2C:29–6**
  Chop shops, operation or maintenance, **2C:20–16**
  Dead bodies, **2C:22–1**
  Employing a juvenile to commit auto theft, **2C:20–17**
  Endangering welfare of children, **2C:24–4**
  Extended terms of imprisonment, **2C:44–3**
  Firearms, possession, **2C:39–7**
  Leader of auto theft trafficking network, **2C:20–18**
  Motor vehicle homicide, **2C:11–5**
  Nuclear power plants, **2C:17–9**
  Sentencing, **2C:43–1**
  Vessel, homicide by, **2C:11–5**

CRIMES AND OFFENSES—Cont'd
Second degree crimes—Cont'd
  Weapons, teaching, demonstrating or assembling, **2C:39–14**
Second or Subsequent Offenses, generally, this index
Secured creditors, defrauding, **2C:21–12**
Securing execution of documents by deception, **2C:21–16**
Seizures. Searches and Seizures, generally, this index
Self defense, **2C:3–4**
Self induced intoxication, criminal liability, **2C:2–8**
Sentence and punishment, **Rule 3:21–1 et seq.**
  Access, postconviction relief, petition, **Rule 3:22–2**
  Aged persons, sentence, reduction, change, **Rule 3:21–10**
  Alcohol abuse, treatment, rehabilitation, change of sentence, **Rule 3:21–10**
  Appeal, right to, notification, **Rule 3:21–4**
  Bail, crimes committed during release on, notice to impose sentence, **Rule 3:21–4**
  Change, motion, **Rule 3:21–10**
    Statement of reasons for disposition, **Rule 3:29**
  Community related service, probation, condition, **Rule 3:21–7**
  Corporations, conviction, **Rule 3:21–6**
  Correction, **Rules 3:21–10, 3:22–2**
  Credit, confinement pending sentence, **Rule 3:21–8**
  Deduction of sentence, **Rule 3:21–10**
  Diversion, motion for, statement of reasons for disposition, **Rule 3:29**
  Drug abuse, treatment, rehabilitation, change of sentence, **Rule 3:21–10**
  Estimated real time, statement, **Rule 3:21–4**
  Extended or enhanced term of imprisonment, **Rule 3:21–4**
  Extradition, application of law, **Rule 3:21–4**
  Finality, **Rule 3:21–4**
  Good cause, reduction, change, **Rule 3:21–10**
  Hearing, capital cases, aggravating factors, additional discovery, **Rule 3:13–4**
  Illegal sentence, correction, **Rule 3:22–2**
    Petition, limitation of actions, **Rules 3:21–10, 3:22–12**
  Imposition, presence of defendant, **Rule 3:16**
  Intensive supervision program, changing custodial sentence, **Rule 3:21–10**
  Investigation, presentence, **Rule 3:21–2**
  Judgment, entry, **Rule 3:21–5**
  Juvenile delinquents, **Rule 5:24–4**
    Modification, **Rule 5:24–6**
  Limitation of actions, postconviction relief, **Rule 3:22–12**
  Limited criminal jurisdiction, courts of, appeals, **Rule 3:23–1 et seq.**
  Murder, sentencing hearing, **Rule 3:21–4A**
  Notice, **Rule 3:21–4**
  Persistent offenders, notice to impose sentence, **Rule 3:21–4**
  Postconviction relief, **Rule 3:22–1 et seq.**
    Petition, determination, **Rule 3:22–11**
  Presence of defendant, **Rule 3:21–4**
  Presentence procedure, **Rule 3:21–2**
  Pretrial intervention program, **Rule 3:28**
  Probation, **Rule 3:21–7**
  Reason for sentence, statement, **Rule 3:21–4**
    Judgment, entry, **Rule 3:21–5**
  Reduction, motion, **Rule 3:21–10**
    Statement of reasons for disposition, **Rule 3:29**

CRIMES AND OFFENSES—Cont'd
Sentence and punishment—Cont'd
  Release on bail, crimes committed during, notice to impose sentence, **Rule 3:21–4**
  Relief pending appeal, **Rule 3:23–5**
  Reports,
    Physical, mental examination, presentence, **Rule 3:21–2**
    Presentence investigation, **Rule 3:21–2**
    Statement of defendant, **Rule 3:21–4**
  Suspended sentence, **Rule 3:21–7**
    Appeals, **Rule 3:23–1 et seq.**
  Treatment, rehabilitation programs, drug, alcohol abuse, change of sentence, **Rule 3:21–10**
  Unauthorized by law, postconviction relief, **Rule 3:22–2**
  Unreasonable delay, **Rule 3:21–4**
  Violent offenders, notice to impose sentence, **Rule 3:21–4**
Separate trials, **Rules 3:15–1, 3:15–2**
  Multiple offenses, **2C:1–8**
Service of process, **Rule 1:5–1 et seq.**
  Investigative detention, orders, **Rule 3:5A–7**
  Notice of appeal, limited criminal jurisdiction, courts of, **Rule 3:23–2**
  Postconviction relief, petition, **Rule 3:22–7**
  Record expungement, **2C:52–10**
  Sentence and punishment, **Rule 3:21–4**
  Summons, **Rule 3:3–3**
  Territorial limits, **Rule 3:1–2**
  Warrants, summons, **Rule 3:7–10**
Settlement, motion, consent, **Rule 3:1–4**
Severance, indictment, accusation, **Rule 3:15–1**
Sex Offenses, generally, this index
Sexual intercourse, observation, invasion of privacy, **2C:14–9**
Sexual penetration, diseased persons, venereal diseases, **2C:34–5**
Sexually oriented businesses, **2C:33–12.2**
  Zoning and planning, **2C:34–7**
Shelters, destruction of animals, **4:22–19**
Shipboard gambling, **2C:37–4.1**
Sickness, witnesses, depositions, use, **Rule 3:13–2**
Slugs, coin, currency or credit card activated machine, **2C:21–18**
Smoking in public, **2C:33–13**
Sole caretakers, presentence investigations, children and minors, placement, **2C:44–6.2 et seq.**
Soliciting, generally, this index
Solid Waste, this index
Sound recordings,
  Admissibility, pretrial hearings, **Rule 3:9–1**
  Piracy, **2C:21–21**
Specific instances of conduct, character evidence, **Evidence Rule 405**
Speculating or wagering on official action or information, **2C:30–3**
Speed, generally, this index
Spouses, this index
Spray paint,
  Definitions,
    Criminal mischief, **2C:17–3**
    Riot, disorderly conduct and related offenses, **2C:33–24**
  Sale, required posting of warning sign, **2C:33–25**
Stalking, generally, this index
Standard of proof, **2C:1–13**
State bureau of identification. Identification Bureau, generally, this index
State contracts, fraud, **2C:21–34**
State documents, discovery, **Rule 3:13–3**
State Officers and Employees, this index

CRIMES AND OFFENSES—Cont'd

Statements,
  Accused,
    Admissibility, pretrial hearings, **Rule 3:9–1**
    Pretrial intervention programs, returning to prosecution, use, **Rule 3:28**
  Discovery, **Rule 3:13–3**
  Joinder of defendants, use, notice, **Rule 3:15–2**
  Probation, agreement, **Rule 3:21–7**
  Reasons,
    Disposition of motion or application, **Rule 3:29**
    Sentence, **Rule 3:21–4**
  Record expungement petition, **2C:52–8**
Statute of limitations. Limitation of Criminal Prosecutions, generally, this index
Statutes,
  Definitions, **2C:1–14**
  Instruction, **2C:98–1**
Statutory construction, culpability requirements, **2C:2–2**
Stay, generally, this index
Stills and Distilling Apparatus, this index
Storage, fees, **27:23–6.2**
Street Gangs, generally, this index
Structure, definitions, luring and enticing, children and minors, **2C:13–6**
Subpoenas, this index
Subsequent offenses. Second or Subsequent Offenses, generally, this index
Substitute for appeal, postconviction relief, **Rule 3:22–3**
Suicide, aiding suicide, **2C:11–6**
Summons,
  Accusation, indictment, issuance, **Rules 3:7–8, 3:7–9**
  Additional summons, **Rule 3:3–1**
  Amendment, defect, **Rule 3:3–4**
  Arrest, **Rule 3:3–1 et seq.**
    Failure to appear, **Rule 3:3–1**
    Without warrant, issuance, **Rule 3:4–1**
  Corporations, service, **Rule 3:7–10**
  Defective, **Rule 3:3–4**
  Execution, service, **Rule 3:7–10**
  Failure to appear, **Rule 3:3–1**
  Form, **Rule 3:2–2**
    Indictment, accusation, **Rule 3:7–9**
  Identification procedures, issuance, **Rule 3:3–1**
  Indictment, accusation, issuance, **Rules 3:7–8, 3:7–9**
  Issuance, **Rule 3:3–1**
    Indictment, accusation, **Rules 3:7–8, 3:7–9**
  New summons issued, defect, **Rule 3:3–4**
  Procedure after arrest, **Rule 3:4–1**
  Publication, service by, corporations, **Rule 3:7–10**
  Service, **Rules 3:3–3, 3:7–10**
Superior court, **Rule 3:1–1 et seq.**
  Trials, nonindictables, **Rule 3:1–6**
Supervisory treatment,
  First offenders, **2C:43–12 et seq.**
  Record expungement, **2C:52–20**
Supplemental indictments, aggravating factors, capital cases, discovery, **Rule 3:13–4**
Supplementary food stamp program, **2C:20–35**
Support, willful nonsupport, **2C:24–5**
Support of Persons, this index
Sureties, justification, **Rule 3:26–5**
Suspended sentences, **Rule 3:21–7**
  Appeal, **Rule 3:23–1 et seq.**
  Arrest, **2C:45–3**
  Attorneys, representation, **2C:45–4**
  Conditions, **2C:45–1**
  Discharge, **2C:45–2**

CRIMES AND OFFENSES—Cont'd

Suspended sentences—Cont'd
  Evidence, revocation or modification, **2C:45–4**
  Hearings, revocation or modification, **2C:45–4**
  Modification, **2C:45–2**
    Hearings, **2C:45–4**
  Multiple periods, **2C:44–5**
  Notice, revocation or modification, **2C:45–4**
  Obligations, satisfaction, **2C:45–2**
  Revocation, **2C:45–3**
    Hearings, **2C:45–4**
  Satisfaction, obligation, **2C:45–2**
  Summons, **2C:45–3**
  Time, **2C:45–2**
Tampering, generally, this index
Taxation, this index
Telecommunications, this index
Television newspersons, information disclosure privilege, **2A:84A–21.1 et seq.**
Temporary detention, investigations, **Rule 3:5A–1 et seq.**
Terms of imprisonment, **2C:43–6, 2C:43–7, 2C:43–7.1, 2C:44–1**
  Review, **2C:43–6.1, 2C:43–6.3**
Territorial applicability of code of criminal justice, **2C:1–3**
Territorial limits, writs, processes, **Rule 3:1–2**
Terrorism, generally, this index
Theft, generally, this index
Third degree crimes, **2C:1–4**
  Agricultural land, vandalism, **2C:18–6**
  Aiding escape with weapons, **2C:29–6**
  Dead bodies, **2C:22–1**
  Dentists and dentistry, practice,
    Under false or assumed name, **2C:21–30**
    Without license, **2C:21–30**
  Destructive devices, possession, **2C:39–3**
  Endangering welfare of children, **2C:24–4**
  Extended terms of imprisonment, **2C:44–3**
  Firearms, sale or transfer of firearm to minors, **2C:39–10**
  Nuclear power plants, **2C:17–7**
  Sentencing, **2C:43–1**
  Wiretapping and electronic surveillance, **2A:156A–3**
Third offenses. Second or Subsequent Offenses, generally, this index
Third persons, protection, use of force, **2C:3–5**
Threats, generally, this index
Time,
  Effective date, **2C:98–4**
  First appearance, **Rules 3:3–1, 3:4–2**
  Limitation of Criminal Prosecutions, generally, this index
  Supervisory treatment program, **2C:43–17 et seq.**
Tow Trucks and Towing Companies, this index
Toxic packaging reduction, **13:1E–99.54**
Tractors, marks or numbers, change, destruction, **2C:17–6**
Trademarks and Trade Names, this index
Traffic accidents, jurisdiction, serious bodily injury, **2B:12–17.2**
Traffic control preemption devices, interference with transportation, use, **2C:33–14**
Traffic offenses, record expungement, **2C:52–28**
Training, authorized disposition, **2C:43–2**
Transcript, postconviction relief, indigents, grant, **Rule 3:22–6**
Transfer of actions, **Rules 3:1–5, 3:1–6**
Transfers, prisoners, county institutions, **2C:43–10**

CRIMES AND OFFENSES—Cont'd

Transportation,
  State prison, **2C:43–10**
  Terrorism, **2C:38–2**
Treason, venue, **Rule 3:14–1**
Trespass, criminal trespass, **2C:18–3**
Trial,
  Acquittal, judgment of, motion for, **Rules 3:18–1, 3:18–2**
  Defendant, presence, **Rule 3:16**
  Depositions, use, evidence, **Rule 3:13–2**
  Dismissal, indictment, accusation, complaint, **Rule 3:25–1 et seq.**
  Joinder,
    Defendants, **Rule 3:15–2**
    Indictments, accusations, **Rule 3:15–1**
  Jury and Jurors, generally, this index
  Lesser related infractions, joinder with criminal offenses, **Rule 3:15–3**
  Limited criminal jurisdiction, courts of, appeals, de novo, **Rule 3:23–8**
  Multiple offenses, **2C:1–8**
  New trial, **Rules 3:20–1, 3:20–2**
  Order for, **Rule 3:25–2**
  Presence of defendant, **Rule 3:16**
  Verdict, generally, post
Trucks,
  Marks or numbers, change, destruction, **2C:17–6**
  Solid waste, use for transportation of food without sanitization, **48:13A–12.2**
Trusts and Trustees, this index
Turnpike authority, officers and employees, adverse or pecuniary interest, **27:23–14**
Turnpikes, this index
Unconstitutional provisions, enforcement, Criminal Justice Code, **2C:1–1**
Underage person driving motor vehicle under influence, **39:4–50.14**
Uniform Fresh Pursuit Law, **2A:155–1 et seq.**
Unlawful taking of a motor vehicle, definitions, **2C:1–14**
Urine samples, investigative detention, **Rule 3:5A–1 et seq.**
User fees, criminal records checks, **53:1–20.5 et seq.**
Usury, **2C:21–19**
Vending machines, slugs, **2C:21–18**
Venue, generally, this index
Verdict, **Rules 3:19–1, 3:19–2**
  Acquittal,
    Judgment, motion for, **Rule 3:18–2**
    Reason of insanity, **Rule 3:19–2**
  Arrest of judgment, motion, **Rule 3:21–9**
  Return, presence of defendant, **Rule 3:16**
  Several defendants, counts, **Rule 3:19–1**
  Written verdict sheets, **Rule 3:19–1**
Verification, postconviction relief petition, **Rule 3:22–8**
Vessels, this index
Veterans, disabled veterans, special motor vehicles plates, **39:3–27.18**
Victim and witness advocacy fund, victims of crime compensation board, **2C:43–3.1**
Victimless crimes, supervisory treatment program, **2C:43–12 et seq.**
Victims of Crime, generally, this index
Videotapes,
  Depositions, **Rule 3:13–2**
  Nudity, sexual intercourse, invasion of privacy, **2C:14–9**
Violence. Force or Violence, generally, this index
Violent criminal apprehension program. Identification Bureau, this index

CRIMES AND OFFENSES—Cont'd

Violent offenders, notice to impose sentence, **Rule 3:21–4**
Vocational training, suspended sentence, **2C:45–1**
Voice exemplars, investigative detention, **Rule 3:5A–1 et seq.**
Voluntary absence, defendant, **Rule 3:16**
Voluntary acts, basis of criminal liability, **2C:2–1**
Voluntary renunciation of complicity, **2C:2–6**
Voting machines, **2A:149–1**
Waiver,
  Indictment, trial by jury, **Rule 3:4–2**
  Jury trial, **Rule 1:8–1**
  Presence of defendant at trial, **Rule 3:16**
  Raising before trial, defenses, objections, **Rule 3:10–2**
Warrants,
  Arrest, this index
  Search Warrants, generally, this index
Water Pollution, this index
Weapons, generally, this index
Weights and Measures, this index
Window peeping, **2C:18–3**
Wiretapping and Electronic Surveillance, generally, this index
Withdrawal,
  Attorney, pending proceedings, **Rule 1:11–2**
  Plea, **Rules 3:9–3, 3:21–1**
Witnesses, this index
Work First New Jersey, this index
Work product, attorneys, discovery, **Rule 3:13–3**
Work release, **2C:43–2**
Workhouses, county workhouses, **2C:43–10**
Worthless checks, **2C:21–5**
Writs, territorial limits, **Rule 3:1–2**
Written verdict sheets, **Rule 3:19–1**
Young adult offenders, **2C:43–5**
Zoning and planning, sexually oriented businesses, **2C:34–7**

CRIMINAL COURTS

Municipal Courts, generally, this index

CRIMINAL DISPOSITION AND REVENUE COLLECTION FUND

Generally, **2C:43–3.1**

CRIMINAL DIVISION, SUPERIOR COURT

Generally, **Rule 1:33–2**

CRIMINAL ESCAPE

Escapes, generally, this index

CRIMINAL ESTOPPEL

Double Jeopardy, generally, this index

CRIMINAL EXPOSURE

Generally, **2C:14–4**

CRIMINAL HISTORY RECORD INFORMATION

Adoption, this index
Aged Persons, this index
Assisted living facilities, **53:1–20.9c**
Child Care Centers, this index
Commercial drivers licenses, applications, **39:3–10.17**
Court appointed special advocate, **2A:4A–92**
Drivers schools, licenses and permits, **39:12–2**
  Instructors, **39:12–5**
Expunging of records, **2C:52–1 et seq.**
Fingerprints and Fingerprinting, generally, this index

CRIMINAL HISTORY RECORD INFORMATION—Cont'd

Guardian and ward, professional guardians, **53:1–20.9e**
Health care service firms, homemaker home health aides, certificates, **53:1–20.9a**
Homemaker home health aides, certificates, **53:1–20.9a**
Identification Bureau, this index
Interstate compacts, **53:1–32**
Intoxicating liquors,
  Conviction of crime, removal of disqualification to hold license, **33:1–31.2**
  Licenses and permits, **33:1–25, 33:1–26**
Limousine or livery service, drivers, **39:5G–2**
Mentally Deficient and Mentally Ill Persons, this index
Mentally Retarded and Developmentally Disabled Persons, this index
Motor vehicle commission, officers and employees, **39:2A–32**
Motor vehicles, certificates of ownership, dealers, license, **39:10–19**
Nurses, this index
Nurses aides, certificates, **53:1–20.9a**
Nursing Homes or Hospitals, this index
Personal assistance services, certificates, **53:1–20.9a**
Public adjusters, licenses, **53:1–20.16**
Residential child care facilities, child abuse, **53:1–20.9d**
Residential Health Care Facilities, this index

CRIMINAL HISTORY RECORD INFORMATION FUND

Generally, **53:1–20.7**

CRIMINAL JUDICIAL DISTRICT COURTS

Fines and Penalties, generally, this index
Penalties. Fines and Penalties, generally, this index

CRIMINAL JUSTICE DIVISION

Directors, written request for impaneling state grand juries, **2B:22–1**
Domestic violence, aged persons, training course development and approval, **2C:25–20**
State grand juries, reimbursement of expenses, **2B:22–8**

CRIMINAL MISCHIEF

Generally, **2C:17–3**
Force, use in defense of property, **2C:3–6**

CRIMINAL NEGLECT ACT

Generally, **9:6–1 et seq.**

CRIMINAL RESTRAINT

Generally, **2C:13–2**
Terrorism, **2C:38–2**

CRIMINAL SENTENCING AND DISPOSITION COMMISSION

Generally, **2C:48A–1 et seq.**

CRIMINAL SEXUAL CONTACT

Generally, **2C:14–3**
Aggravated Criminal Sexual Contact, generally, this index
Closed circuit testimony, sexual abuse, children, **2A:84A–32.4**
Evidence, previous sexual conduct of victim, **2C:14–7**
Expungement, record, **2C:52–2**
Extended term of imprisonment, **2C:43–7, 2C:43–7.1**

CRIMINAL SEXUAL CONTACT—Cont'd

Fines and penalties, surcharges, **2C:43–3.7**
Limitation of criminal prosecutions, **2C:1–6**
Parole supervision for life, special sentence, Violent Predator Incapacitation Act of 1994, **2C:43–6.4**
Records and recordation, expungement, **2C:52–2**
Surcharges, **2C:43–3.7**

CRIMINAL SIMULATION

Generally, **2C:21–2**

CRIMINAL STREET GANGS

Street Gangs, generally, this index

CRIMINAL TRESPASS

Generally, **2C:18–3**

CRIMINAL VICTIMS

Victims of Crime, generally, this index

CRIPPLED PERSONS

Handicapped Persons, generally, this index

CRISIS INTERVENTION RESPONSE

Definitions, juvenile family crisis, **2A:4A–78**

CROPS

Agricultural Products, generally, this index

CROSS CLAIMS

Dismissal and nonsuit, failure to appear, **Rule 1:2–4**
Notice, filing on service of pleadings, **Rule 1:5–5**
Service, numerous defendants, **Rule 1:5–5**

CROSS EXAMINATION

Depositions, criminal proceedings, **Rule 3:13–2**
Excluded evidence, **Rule 1:7–3**
Motions, affidavits, **Rule 1:6–6**
Preliminary hearing, admissibility of defendants statements, **Evidence Rule 104**
Scope, **Evidence Rule 611**
Writings used to refresh memory, **Evidence Rule 612**

CROSS MOTIONS

Motions, this index

CROSSINGS

Railroad Crossings, generally, this index
School Buildings and Grounds, this index
Street Railways, this index

CROSSWALKS

See, also, Pedestrians, generally, this index
Generally, **39:4–33 et seq.**
Definitions, traffic regulations, **39:1–1**
Highways with medial barriers, **39:4–34**
Horses, tie ropes, obstructing, **39:4–19**
Older and walking impaired persons crossing, designation of areas and erection of signs, **39:4–183.1b**
Ordinances or resolutions, **39:4–8**
Parking, permissible parking distances, **39:4–138**
  Municipalities, **39:4–138.6**
Right half to be used by pedestrians, **39:4–33**
Right of way, pedestrians, **39:4–34 et seq.**
Safety, **39:4–36.3, 39:4–36.4**
Street cars, obstruction by prohibited, **39:4–45**
Traffic signals obstructing, **39:4–114**

CRUELTY

Crimes and offenses, **2C:44–1**

CRUELTY TO ANIMALS
Acts permitted, **4:22–16**
Animal, definitions, **4:22–15**
Baiting animals, **4:22–24**
Beating horses, **39:4–23**
Birds, use as targets, **4:22–23**
Cats, **4:22–20**
Confined animals, offenses, **4:22–19**
Counties, impoundment facilities, destruction of animals, **4:22–19**
Creature, definitions, **4:22–15**
Destruction, **4:22–19**
Disabled animals. Abandonment, this index
Diseases, refusal to euthanize animals, **4:22–22**
Dogs, **4:22–20**
Domestic livestock, **4:22–16.1**
Euthanasia, offenses, **4:22–19**
Exceptions, **4:22–16**
Fighting animals, **4:22–24**
Fines and penalties,
   Destruction, **4:22–19**
   Disorderly persons offense, **4:22–17**
Fish and game, laws not affected, **4:22–16**
Horses, **39:4–23, 39:4–24**
Impounded animals, failure to care for, **4:22–19, 4:22–24**
Motor vehicles,
   Registration, associations and societies, **39:3–27**
   Unattended animals, **4:22–17**
Motorist hitting domestic animal, **4:22–25.1, 4:22–25.2**
Motorists, injury to animal, reports, society for prevention of cruelty, **4:22–25.1**
Municipalities, impoundment facilities, destruction, **4:22–19**
Mutilation, **4:22–17**
Notice, animal control officers, convictions, disqualification, **2B:12–17.1**
Offenses, **4:22–17 et seq.**
Owner, definitions, **4:22–15**
Person,
   As including corporation, **4:22–15**
   Definitions, **4:22–15**
Registration, anticruelty societies, free registration, **39:3–27**
Sale of horses unfit for work, **4:22–21**
Scientific experiments permitted, when, **4:22–16**
Society for the prevention of cruelty to animals, officers and employees, unlawful possession of weapons, exemption, **2C:39–6**
Transporting in cruel manner, **4:22–18**

CRUELTY TO CHILDREN
Child Abuse, generally, this index

CULPABILITY
Criminal offenses, **2C:2–2**
Liability for conduct of another, **2C:2–6**

CUNNILINGUS
Generally, **2C:14–1 et seq.**
Children and minors, second degree crime, **2C:24–4**

CURBS AND CURBING
Backing vehicle against curb to load or unload, **39:4–79**
Bulbouts,
   Construction, **39:4–8.21**
   Parking, **39:4–138**
Extensions,
   Construction, **39:4–8.21**
   Parking, **39:4–138**

CURBS AND CURBING—Cont'd
Giving place to vehicle about to take on or let off passengers, duty of vehicle at curb, **39:4–62**
Markings, parking prohibitions, **39:4–191.2**
Parking, generally, this index
Stopping vehicle to let off or take on persons, curb as proper place, **39:4–65**

CURRICULUM
Schools and School Districts, this index

CURVES
Speed in traversing, reducing, **39:4–98**
Turning vehicle around on curve prohibited, **39:4–125**
Vehicle disablement, emergency warning devices, **39:3–64**
Warning required from motor vehicle approaching curve, **39:4–55**

CUSTARD ICE CREAM
Frozen Desserts and Dietary Foods, generally, this index

CUSTODIAL INTERROGATIONS
Crimes and offenses, electronic recordation, **Rule 3:17**

CUSTODIANS
Definitions, abandonment, abuse, cruelty and neglect of children, **9:6–2**

CUSTODY
Children and Minors, this index
Correctional Institutions, generally, this index
Crimes and offenses, interference, **2C:13–4**
Guardian and Ward, generally, this index
Interference with custody, **2C:13–4**
Juvenile Delinquents, this index
Prisons and prisoners. Correctional Institutions, generally, this index
Service of process on nonresident owner by service on person in custody of motor vehicle, **39:7–8**
Shoplifting, powers, **2C:20–11**
Stolen property, disposition, **2C:65–1 et seq.**

CUSTOMER SERVICE ADVISORY COUNCIL
Motor vehicle commission, **39:2A–26**

CUTTING SUBSTANCES
Placing on highway, fine imposed, **39:4–63**

CYPRENORPHINE
Controlled substances, **24:21–1 et seq.**

DAGGERS
Weapons, generally, this index

DAIRIES AND DAIRY PRODUCTS
Farm products, inclusion, **39:3–25**
Frozen Desserts and Dietary Foods, generally, this index
Ice cream and other frozen products. Frozen Desserts and Dietary Foods, generally, this index

DAMAGES
Agricultural land, trespass, **2C:18–4 et seq.**
Archaeology and archaeologists, transportation, state property, archaeological findings, alteration, **27:5J–1**
Attorneys, client protection fund, **Rule 1:28–1 et seq.**

DAMAGES—Cont'd
Automobile no fault insurance,
   Admissibility of evidence, **39:6A–12**
   Limitations, **39:6A–8**
Bridges and Viaducts, this index
Calculation, closing statement, **Rule 1:7–1**
Chiropractors, review committees, immunity from liability, **2A:84A–22.10**
Contingent attorney fees, **Rule 1:21–7**
Credit, history, identity theft, **2C:21–17.4**
Dentists and dentistry, review committees, immunity from liability, **2A:84A–22.10**
Dietitians, review committees, immunity from liability, **2A:84A–22.10**
Domestic violence actions, **2C:25–29**
Drivers privacy protection, **39:2–3.6**
Force, use to prevent, **2C:3–6, 2C:3–7**
Grand jury, injurious disclosure of information, actions, **2B:21–10**
Horticultural land, trespass, **2C:18–4 et seq.**
Hospitals, this index
Identity theft, **2C:21–17.4**
Incapacitated persons, conduct, physician patient privilege, **2A:84A–22.3**
Jury room, taking list into, **Rule 1:8–8**
Justification, **2C:3–10**
Leases, generally, this index
Licensed administrators, health facilities, review committees, **2A:84A–22.10**
Low speed vehicles, waiver, **39:4–31.4**
Money laundering and illegal investments, **2C:21–28**
Motor vehicle commission, privileges and immunities, board, **39:2A–23**
Motor Vehicle Insurance, this index
Motor Vehicles, this index
News organizations, searches and seizures, suits against government, **2A:84A–21.11**
Nuclear power plants, crimes and offenses, **2C:17–7 et seq.**
Nurses, this index
Optometrists, review committees, immunity from liability, **2A:84A–22.10**
Pharmacists, review committees, immunity from liability, **2A:84A–22.10**
Physicians and Surgeons, this index
Psychologists and psychology, review committees, immunity from liability, **2A:84A–22.10**
Punitive damages, drivers privacy protection, **39:2–3.6**
Real Estate, this index
Searches and seizures, news organizations, **2A:84A–21.11**
Solid Waste, this index
Stolen property, persons receiving, actions against, **2C:20–20**
Veterinarians, review committees, immunity from liability, **2A:84A–22.10**

DAMS AND RESERVOIRS
Agricultural land, trespass, damages, **2C:18–4 et seq.**

DANGEROUS DRUGS
Controlled Substances, generally, this index

DANGEROUS FIREWORKS
Definitions, **21:2–3**

DANGEROUS SUBSTANCES
Generally, **24:21–1 et seq.**

DANGEROUS WEAPONS
Weapons, generally, this index

DATA PROCESSING
Computers, generally, this index

DATA PROCESSING—Cont'd
Electronic Transactions, generally, this index

DATE
Time, generally, this index

DATE RAPE
Date rape drugs. Controlled Substances, this index

DAY CARE
Child Care Centers, generally, this index

DAY SCHOOL
Definitions, children and minors, abuse or neglect, 9:6–8.21

DE MINIMIS INFRACTIONS
Generally, 2C:2–11

DEAD ANIMALS
Fines and penalties, 4:22–19

DEAD BODIES
Anatomical Gifts, generally, this index
Application of law, crimes and offenses, 2C:22–1
Crimes and offenses, 2C:22–1
Criminal mischief, 2C:17–3
Desecration, 2C:22–1
Criminal mischief, 2C:17–3
Disposal, crimes and offenses, 2C:22–1
Gifts. Anatomical Gifts, generally, this index
Sex offenses, 2C:22–1
Theft, 2C:20–2, 2C:22–1
Criminal mischief, 2C:17–3

DEADLY FORCE
See, also, Assault and Battery, generally, this index
Generally, 2C:12–1
Defense of other persons, 2C:3–5
Defense of premises or personal property, 2C:3–6
Definitions, justification, 2C:3–11
Execution of public duty, 2C:3–3
Law enforcement officers,
Grand jury, instructions to jury, 2B:22–9
Use of force, 2C:3–7
Mistake of law, use of force, 2C:3–9
Persons with special responsibility for care, discipline or safety of others, use by, 2C:3–8
Self defense, 2C:3–4

DEADLY POISONS
Poisons, generally, this index

DEADLY WEAPONS
Weapons, generally, this index

DEAF AND HEARING IMPAIRED PERSONS
Alcohol and drug abuse, drug enforcement and demand reduction fund, 2C:35–15
Drivers Licenses, this index

DEALERS
Definitions,
Motor vehicles, 39:1–1
Theft, 2C:20–1
Firearms, retail sales, licenses, 2C:58–2
Food, generally, this index
Handguns, licenses and permits, 2C:58–3
Motor Vehicles, this index
Motorized bicycles, licenses and permits, planning or zoning restrictions or regulations, 39:4–14.3r
Snowmobiles, registration, exemptions, 39:3C–6

DEALERS—Cont'd
Weapons, this index

DEALING IN STOLEN PROPERTY
Receiving Stolen Property, generally, this index

DEATH
Alcoholic beverages, manufacture, sale, poisoned liquors, 33:3–9, 33:3–10
Alcoholic liquor licensee, extension of license to executor or administrator, 33:1–22
Attorneys, this index
Automobile, death by, guilty plea, admissibility in civil proceeding, 2C:11–5
Belief of impending death, statements under, hearsay exception, **Evidence Rule 804**
Bigamy, defense, 2C:24–1
Children and Minors, this index
Commercial drivers licenses, accidents, suspension or revocation, 39:3–10.20
Crimes and Offenses, this index
Drunk Driving Victims Bill of Rights, 39:4–50.9 et seq.
Funerals, generally, this index
Grand juror, filling vacancy, 2B:21–4
Jury and jurors, substitution of alternate jurors, **Rule 1:8–2**
Law Enforcement Officers, this index
Motor Vehicles, this index
Nuclear power plants, vandalism, 2C:17–8
Probate Proceedings, generally, this index
Reasonable fear, stalking, 2C:12–10
Reports, motor vehicle accidents, 39:4–134
Spouses, this index
Stalking, reasonable fear, course of conduct creating, 2C:12–10
Terrorism, 2C:38–2
Threats, grade and degree of offense, 2C:12–3
Time, homicide, assault and death of victim, bar to prosecution, 2C:11–2.1
Traffic Accidents, this index
Trustworthy statements, deceased declarants, **Evidence Rule 804**
Unregistered vehicles, permits to cross public highways, Motor Vehicle Security Responsibility Law, 39:3–26.5
Vessel, death by, guilty plea, admissibility in civil proceedings, 2C:11–5
Witnesses, criminal proceedings, deposition, **Rule 3:13–2**

DEATH BY AUTO OR VESSEL
Generally, 2C:11–5

DEATH PENALTY
Capital Punishment, generally, this index

DEBIT CARD
Electronic Fund Transfers, generally, this index

DEBT
Debtors and Creditors, generally, this index

DEBT ADJUSTERS
Criminal usury, 2C:21–19

DEBTORS AND CREDITORS
Actions and proceedings, racketeering, 2C:41–4
Attachment, generally, this index
Cease and desist orders, racketeering, 2C:41–4
Collections, generally, this index
Confidential or privileged information, racketeering investigations, 2C:41–5
Credit Cards, generally, this index
Crimes and offenses,
Racketeering, 2C:41–1 et seq.
Usury, 2C:21–19

DEBTORS AND CREDITORS—Cont'd
Definitions,
Motor vehicles, 39:10–2
Racketeering, 2C:41–1
Discovery, racketeering investigations, 2C:41–5
Examinations and examiners, racketeering, 2C:41–5
Executions, generally, this index
Fines and penalties, racketeering, 2C:41–1 et seq.
Inspectors and inspections, racketeering investigations, 2C:41–5
Interrogatories, racketeering investigations, 2C:41–5
Investigations and investigators, racketeering, 2C:41–5
Investments, racketeering, 2C:41–1 et seq.
Licenses and permits, racketeering, revocation or suspension, 2C:41–4
Motor vehicles, spouses, vesting of title on either, 39:3–30.1, 39:3–30.2
Partnerships, this index
Process, racketeering, 2C:41–5
Production of books and papers, racketeering, 2C:41–5
Racketeering, 2C:41–1 et seq., 2C:41–4
Records and recordation, racketeering, investigations, 2C:41–5
Restitution, racketeering, 2C:41–4
Secured creditors, defrauding secured creditors, 2C:21–12
Securities, racketeering, 2C:41–1 et seq.
Unlawful debt, definitions, racketeering, 2C:41–1

DECALS
Drivers Licenses, this index
Motor Vehicles, this index

DECEDENTS ESTATES
Probate Proceedings, generally, this index

DECEIVE
Definitions, theft, 2C:20–4

DECEPTION
Fraud, generally, this index

DECEPTIVE TRADE PRACTICES
Generally, 2C:21–7

DECLARATION AGAINST PENAL INTEREST
Crimes and offenses, discovery, **Rule 3:13–3**

DECLARATION OF TAKING
Eminent Domain, this index

DECREES
Judgments and Decrees, generally, this index

DEDICATION
Private road application of Motor Vehicle Law to, 39:5A–3
Semipublic road application of Motor Vehicle Law to, 39:5A–3

DEEDS AND CONVEYANCES
Forgery, 2C:21–1

DEER
Fish and Game, this index

DEFACE
Definitions, firearms, 2C:39–1

DEFACEMENT
Motor vehicles, marks or numbers, crimes and offenses, 2C:17–6
Weapons, 2C:39–9
Possession, 2C:39–3
Prior conviction, 2C:39–7

DEFAULT
Collection proceedings, default in payment of restitution, 2C:46–2
Fines or restitution,
Municipal courts, community service performance, 2B:12–23
Payments, 2C:46–1, 2C:46–2
Mandatory assessments, 2C:46–1
Penalty assessments, 2C:46–1
Student loans, attorneys, **Rule 1:20–11B**
Summary collection proceedings, default in payment of restitution, 2C:46–2

DEFAULT JUDGMENT
Attorneys, fee arbitration, **Rule 1:20A–3**
Bonds (officers and fiduciaries), affidavits, nonmilitary service, **Rule 1:5–7**
Calendar call, failure to appear, sanctions, **Rule 1:2–4**
Child support hearing officers, **Rule 5:25–3**
Entry, clerk of court, granting of motion or application, **Rule 1:6–8**
Fee arbitration, attorneys, **Rule 1:20A–3**
Motion, entering, granting by clerk of court, **Rule 1:6–8**
Motor vehicle accidents, payment of default judgment out of unsatisfied claim and judgment fund, 39:6–74
Nonmilitary service affidavit, **Rule 1:5–7**

DEFENDANTS
Parties, generally, this index

DEFENSE OF OTHER PERSONS
Generally, 2C:3–5

DEFENSE OF PROPERTY
Generally, 2C:3–6

DEFENSES
Absconding from parole, criminal prosecutions, 2C:29–5
Affirmative defenses, 2C:1–13
Controlled substances, distribution or possession with intent, 2C:35–7.1
Custody, kidnapping, 2C:13–1
Duress or coercion, 2C:2–9
Endangering injured victim, 2C:12–1.2
Felony murder, 2C:11–3
Human trafficking, 2C:13–8
Intoxication, 2C:2–8
Justification, 2C:3–1 et seq.
Prostitution, human trafficking, 2C:34–1
Termination of criminal complicity by renunciation, 2C:2–6
Alcoholic beverages sold to persons under legal age, 33:1–77
Arrest, use of force, 2C:3–7
Attorney disciplinary proceedings, setting forth in answer, **Rule 1:20–4**
Bail jumping, 2C:29–7
Belief of defendant that conduct did not constitute an offense, 2C:2–4
Bigamy, 2C:24–1
Bribery, official and political matters, 2C:27–2
Cigarettes and cigars, children and minors, 2A:170–51.4, 2C:33–13.1
Coercion, 2C:13–5
Compounding, 2C:29–4
Consent of crime victim, 2C:2–10

DEFENSES—Cont'd
Conspiracy, 2C:5–2
County detectives and investigators, crimes and offenses, 2A:157–10.8
Crimes and offenses, 2C:1–13, 2C:2–5; **Rule 3:10–1 et seq.**
Absconding from parole, 2C:29–5
Accomplices, notice, **Rule 3:12–1**
Affirmative defenses, generally, ante
Alibi defense, notice, **Rule 3:12–2**
Alleviation of conduct, 2C:2–5
Arrest, use of force, 2C:3–7
Attempt, renunciation of purpose, **Rule 3:12–1**
Bail jumping, 2C:29–7
Bigamy, 2C:24–1
Bribery, official and political matters, 2C:27–2
Clear and convincing evidence, 2C:2–4
Coercion, 2C:13–5
Compounding, 2C:29–4
Consent, victims, 2C:2–10
Conspiracy, 2C:2–5
Renunciation of purpose, **Rule 3:12–1**
Controlled dangerous substances near or on school property, **Rule 3:12–1**
Criminal restraint, notice, **Rule 3:12–1**
Custody, interference with, 2C:13–4
De minimis infractions, 2C:2–11
Deceptive business practices, 2C:21–7
Determination of motion, effect, **Rule 3:10–7**
Duress, 2C:2–9
Notice, **Rule 3:12–1**
Entrapment, 2C:2–12
Notice, **Rule 3:12–1**
Escape, 2C:29–5
Estate, notice, **Rule 3:12–1**
Excuse of conduct, 2C:2–5
Execution of public duty, 2C:3–3
Extortion, 2C:20–5
Theft, notice, **Rule 3:12–1**
False imprisonment, children and minors, 2C:13–3
False swearing, retraction, **Rule 3:12–1**
Felony murder, notice, **Rule 3:12–1**
Fencing, 2C:20–7.1
Gambling, 2C:37–2
Records, possession, 2C:37–3
Hearing on motion, **Rule 3:10–2**
Ignorance, 2C:2–4
Notice, **Rule 3:12–1**
Inducement, 2C:2–12
Insanity, 2C:4–1 et seq.
Notice, **Rule 3:12–1**
Intoxication, 2C:2–8
Notice, **Rule 3:12–1**
Jurisdiction, lack, **Rule 3:10–2**
Justification, 2C:3–1
Law enforcement, use of force, 2C:3–7
Limited criminal jurisdiction, courts of, appeals, raising before trial, **Rule 3:23–8**
Lottery offenses, 2C:37–6
Means of conveyance, unlawful taking, 2C:20–10
Mental disease or defect, 2C:4–1 et seq.
Mistake, 2C:2–4
Endangering welfare of child, age, exception, 2C:24–4
Mistake of law, use of force or legality of arrest, 2C:3–9
Mitigating factors, capital cases, additional discovery, **Rule 3:13–4**
Motions, time, manner of making, **Rule 3:10–2**
Murder, 2C:11–3
Affirmative defenses, notice, **Rule 3:12–1**

DEFENSES—Cont'd
Crimes and offenses—Cont'd
Necessity, 2C:3–2
Negligent use of force, 2C:3–9
Obscene material, children and minors, 2C:34–3
Perjury, 2C:28–1
Retraction, **Rule 3:12–1**
Persons with special responsibility for care, discipline or safety of others, force, use, 2C:3–8
Premises or personal property, defense of, 2C:3–6
Property crimes, justification defense, 2C:3–10
Protection of other persons, 2C:3–5
Public duty, execution, 2C:3–3
Raising before or after trial, **Rule 3:10–2**
Receiving stolen property, 2C:20–7
Reckless use of force, 2C:3–9
Renunciation of purpose, 2C:5–1; **Rule 3:12–1**
Retraction, perjury, false swearing, **Rule 3:12–1**
Self defense, 2C:3–4
Sexual offenses, mistake as to age, 2C:14–5
Specific criminal code defenses, notice, **Rule 3:12–1**
Spouses, duress, 2C:2–9
Termination of criminal complicity by renunciation, affirmative defense, 2C:2–6
Theft, 2C:20–2
Extortion, notice, **Rule 3:12–1**
Trespass, 2C:18–3
Unlawful restraint, children and minors, 2C:13–2
Custody, interference, criminal prosecutions, 2C:13–4
Deceptive business practices, criminal prosecutions, 2C:21–7
Defense of others, 2C:3–5
Duress, criminal prosecutions, 2C:2–9
Entrapment, 2C:2–12
Escape, criminal prosecutions, 2C:29–5
Extortion, criminal prosecutions, 2C:20–5
False imprisonment, children, criminal prosecutions, 2C:13–3
Fencing, criminal prosecutions, 2C:20–7.1
Force,
Reckless or negligent use, 2C:3–9
Use by law enforcement authorities, 2C:3–7
Gambling, criminal prosecutions, 2C:37–2
Records, possession, 2C:37–3
Handicapped persons, parking, 39:4–198
Homicide, 2C:11–3
Housing,
Defending, self defense, 2C:3–4
Use of self defense, 2C:3–6
Human trafficking, 2C:13–8
Ignorance or mistake, criminal prosecutions, 2C:2–4
Inducement, 2C:2–12
Insanity Defense, generally, this index
Intoxication, criminal prosecutions, 2C:2–8
Invasion of privacy, crimes and offenses, observation, nudity, sexual intercourse, 2C:14–9
Jury and jurors, lists, taking into jury room, **Rule 1:8–8**
Justification, criminal prosecutions, 2C:3–1
Juvenile delinquents and dependents, 2A:4A–40
Kosher food, misbranding or sale of nonkosher food, 2C:21–7.3
Law enforcement, use of force, 2C:3–7
Lotteries, criminal prosecutions, 2C:37–6
Mental disease or defect, 2C:4–1 et seq.
Mistake, criminal prosecutions, 2C:2–4

DEFENSES—Cont'd
Mistake of law, criminal prosecutions, use of force, **2C:3–9**
Motor vehicle offenses, number of penalty points, **39:5–30.11**
Murder, **2C:11–3**
Necessity, criminal prosecutions, **2C:3–2**
Numbered paragraphs, **Rule 1:4–2**
Obscene material, children, criminal prosecutions, **2C:34–3**
Perjury, criminal prosecutions, **2C:28–1**
Persons with special responsibilities, use of force, criminal prosecutions, **2C:3–8**
Property,
   Defense property, criminal prosecutions, **2C:3–6**
   Justification, **2C:3–10**
Prostitution, human trafficking, **2C:34–1**
Public Defenders, generally, this index
Receiving stolen property, criminal prosecutions, **2C:20–7**
Reckless or negligent use of force, **2C:3–9**
Renunciation, criminal intent, **2C:5–1**
Restraint, children, criminal prosecutions, **2C:13–2**
Self defense, **2C:3–4**
Separate statements, **Rule 1:4–2**
Service, numerous parties, **Rule 1:5–5**
Sex offenses, age, mistake, **2C:14–5**
Spouses, duress, criminal prosecutions, **2C:2–9**
Theft, **2C:20–2**
Trespass, criminal prosecutions, **2C:18–3**
Unlawful restraint, children, criminal prosecutions, **2C:13–2**

DEFILEMENT
Kidnapping, generally, this index
Rape, generally, this index

DEFINITIONS
Words and Phrases, generally, this index

DEFLECTORS
Stickers, not to be placed on motor vehicles, **39:3–74**
Windshields, motor vehicles, **39:3–75**

DEFRAUD
Fraud, generally, this index

DEGREE OF OFFENSE
   Generally, **2C:1–4**
Grade and degree of offense. Crimes and Offenses, generally, this index

DELAY
Construction of rules, **Rule 1:1–2**
Crimes and offenses, dismissal, **Rule 3:25–3**
Pleadings, interposing for delay, **Rule 1:4–8**

DELEGATES AND ALTERNATES
National conventions, county prosecutor, **2A:158–21**

DELICATESSEN STORES
Intoxicating liquors,
   Limited retail distribution license, **33:1–12**
   Packaged merchandise, sale, **33:1–12**

DELINQUENCY
Definitions, juvenile justice, **2A:4A–23**

DELINQUENT CHILDREN
Juvenile Delinquents, generally, this index

DEMAND FOR JURY TRIAL
Generally, **Rule 1:8–1**

DEMONSTRATIONS
Registration of motor vehicles operated for purpose of, **39:3–18**

DENATURED ALCOHOL
Sale, **33:1–30**

DENTISTS AND DENTISTRY
Automobile insurance, no fault insurance, application of law, **39:6A–1 et seq.**
Controversies or disputes with patients, review committees, immunity from liability, **2A:84A–22.10**
Crimes and offenses,
   False or assumed name, practicing under, **2C:21–30**
   Health care claims fraud, **2C:21–4.2, 2C:21–4.3**
      Licenses and permits, suspension or revocation, **2C:51–5**
         Rehabilitation, order of debarment, rescission, **2C:27–1**
   Practice without license, under false or assumed name, third degree crimes, **2C:21–30**
Definitions, controlled substances, **2C:35–2, 24:21–2**
False or assumed name, practicing under, third degree crime, **2C:21–30**
Fees, controversies or disputes with patients, review committees, immunity from liability, **2A:84A–22.10**
Fines and penalties, health care claims fraud, **2C:21–4.2, 2C:21–4.3**
   Licenses and permits, suspension or revocation, **2C:51–5**
      Rehabilitation, order of debarment, rescission, **2C:27–1**
Forfeitures, licenses and permits, health care claims fraud, **2C:51–5**
Fraud, **2C:21–30**
Health care claims fraud, **2C:21–4.2, 2C:21–4.3**
   Licenses and permits, suspension or revocation, **2C:51–5**
      Rehabilitation, order of debarment, rescission, **2C:27–1**
Licenses and permits,
   Health care claims fraud, suspension or revocation, **2C:51–5**
      Rehabilitation, order of debarment, rescission, **2C:27–1**
   Revocation or suspension, practicing dentistry with suspended or revoked license, crimes and offenses, **2C:21–30**
Names, false or assumed name, practicing under, third degree crime, **2C:21–30**
No fault insurance, application of law, **39:6A–1 et seq.**
Practicing dentistry, false or assumed name, third degree crime, **2C:21–30**
Qualifications, peer review committee, immunity from liability, **2A:84A–22.10**
Revocation or suspension. Licenses and permits, ante

DEPARTMENTS
Definitions,
   Flammable fabrics, **2A:123–3**
   Food and drugs, **24:21–32**
   Hazardous material, **39:5B–25**
   Historic preservation license plates, **39:3–27.72**
   Liberty State Park plates, **39:3–27.91**
   Liquefied petroleum gas education and safety board, **21:1B–1**

DEPARTMENTS—Cont'd
Definitions—Cont'd
   Motor carriers, intermodal transportation, chassis, **39:3–79.10**
   Snowmobiles, all terrain vehicles, **39:3C–1**
   Speed bumps, municipalities, highways and roads, **39:4–8.9**
   Traffic rules and regulations, **39:4–8.9**
   Water pollution control, **58:10A–3**

DEPENDENT OR NEGLECTED CHILDREN
See, also,
   Child Abuse, generally, this index
   Juvenile Delinquents, generally, this index
Advocates, court appointed special advocate, **2A:4A–92**
Alcoholics and alcoholism, juvenile family crisis, **2A:4A–85**
Consent, medical care or treatment after emergency removal from home, **9:6–8.30**
Court appointed special advocate, **2A:4A–92**
Delinquent children. Juvenile Delinquents, generally, this index
Food, **9:6–1**
Guardian and Ward, generally, this index
Juvenile family crisis, **2A:4A–76 et seq.**
Medical care, attendance and treatment, medical neglect, withholding treatment, **9:6–8.86**
   Reports, **9:6–8.85**
Permanency plans, **9:6–8.8**
   Actions and proceedings, **9:6–8.24, 9:6–8.54**
Placement. Children and Minors, this index
Reuniting with parent. Children and Minors, this index
Runaways, court ordered placement, **9:6–8.68**
Youth and family services division, custody, **9:6–8.8 et seq.**

DEPENDENTS
See, also, Children and Minors, generally, this index
Endangering welfare of child, **2C:24–4**
Willful nonsupport, **2C:24–5**

DEPOSITIONS
Crimes and offenses, **Rule 3:13–2**
   Possibly unavailable witnesses, **Rule 3:26–3**
Cross examination, criminal proceedings, **Rule 3:13–2**
Determining admissibility of evidence, criminal proceedings, **Rule 3:13–2**
Director of division of motor vehicles, power to take depositions, **39:10–20**
Foreign jurisdictions, criminal proceedings, **Rule 3:13–2**
Foreign practitioners, attorneys, taking deposition not deemed making appearance, **Rule 1:21–1**
Instructions to jury, criminal prosecutions, inferences from use, **Rule 3:13–2**
Material witness, **2C:104–8**
Money laundering and illegal investments, **2C:21–29**
Motions, **Rule 1:6–2**
   Affidavits, **Rule 1:6–6**
Motor vehicle dealers license, proceedings to suspend or revoke, **39:10–20**
Municipal courts, **Rule 7:7–6**
Perjury, generally, this index
Records and recordation, videotaped depositions, **Rule 7:7–6**
Search warrant under alcoholic beverage law, prerequisite to issuance, **33:1–57**
Use of depositions, **Rule 3:13–2**

DEPOSITIONS—Cont'd
Videotapes, criminal proceedings, **Rules 3**:13–2, 7:7–6

DEPOSITORIES
Turnpike authority, revenues not pledged to pay indebtedness, 27:23–9

DEPOSITS
Attorneys, **Rule 1**:21–6
Bail, this index
Cash deposit in lieu of bond, **Rule 1**:13–3
Costs, professional ethics, advisory committee on, review of opinions, **Rule 1**:19–8
Fee with alcoholic beverage license application, 33:1–25
Motor Vehicle Security Responsibility Law, this index
Savings and Loan Associations, this index
Stolen money, disposition procedure, 2C:65–3
Trust funds, unidentifiable or unclaimed funds held by attorneys, **Rule 1**:21–6

DEPRAVITY
Crimes and offenses, 2C:44–1

DEPRESSANT OR STIMULANT DRUGS
Controlled Substances, this index
Drugs and Medicine, this index

DEPRIVE
Definitions, theft, 2C:20–1

DEPUTY CHIEF ADMINISTRATORS
Definitions, motor vehicles, 39:1–1

DEPUTY DIRECTOR
Definitions, motor vehicles, 39:1–1

DEPUTY FOREPERSON
Grand jury, **Rule 3**:6–4

DEPUTY SHERIFFS
Sheriffs, this index

DESECRATE
Definitions, venerated objects, 2C:33–9

DESECRATION
Property used for religious, educational, purposes, criminal offense, 2C:33–11
Venerated objects, 2C:33–9

DESERTION
Bigamy, defense, 2C:24–1
Defense, bigamy, 2C:24–1
Support, 2C:62–1
Venue, trial, **Rule 3**:14–1

DESIGN
Portable, oil burning heating device, 2C:40–11

DESOMORPHINE
Controlled dangerous substance, 24:21–1 et seq.

DESSERTS
Frozen Desserts and Dietary Foods, generally, this index

DESTITUTE PERSONS
Indigent Persons, generally, this index

DESTRUCTIVE DEVICES
Assembling, crimes and offenses, 2C:39–14
Definitions, 2C:39–1
Demonstrating, crimes and offenses, 2C:39–14

DESTRUCTIVE DEVICES—Cont'd
Person convicted of crime involving, possession of any weapon prohibited, 2C:39–7
Possession, 2C:39–3, 2C:58–7
    Unlawful purposes, 2C:39–4
        Person convicted of crime involving, possession of any weapon prohibited, 2C:39–7
Teaching, demonstrating or assembling, crimes and offenses, 2C:39–14

DETAINERS
    Generally, 2A:159A–1 et seq.
Administrator, 2A:159A–14
Appropriate court, definitions, 2A:159A–10
Construction of statute, 2A:159A–9
Copies of statute, transmission to officials, 2A:159A–15
Custody of inmates person, 2A:159A–12
Custody of prisoner for trial, 2A:159A–4, 2A:159A–5
Definitions, 2A:159A–2
    Appropriate court, 2A:159A–10
Enforcement, 2A:159A–11
Escape from custody under detainer, 2A:159A–13
Inability to stand trial, effect, 2A:159A–6
Information agent, 2A:159A–14
Mentally ill persons, applicability, 2A:159A–6
Partial invalidity, 2A:159A–9
Policy of statute, 2A:159A–1
Receiving state, definitions, 2A:159A–2
Rules and regulations, 2A:159A–7, 2A:159A–14
Sending state, definitions, 2A:159A–2
Severability of clauses, 2A:159A–9
Speedy trial, 2A:159A–3, 2A:159A–4
State, definitions, 2A:159A–2
Withdrawal of state from agreement, 2A:159A–8

DETECTIVES
Associations and societies, 15:4–1 et seq.
    Compensation, pursuers, 15:4–2
    Fees and rewards for services as pursuers, 15:4–2
    Insurance of members against losses by robbery, burglary, larceny, 15:4–3
    Members, arrest without warrant, power to, 15:4–4
    New Jersey detective agency, establishment, 15:4–4
    Pursuers, 15:4–1
        Compensation, 15:4–2
    Rewards, 15:4–2
Community security services, motor vehicle identification lights, 39:3–54.14
Compensation, pursuers, association of detectives, 15:4–2
County Detectives and Investigators, generally, this index
Fees, pursuers, association of detectives, 15:4–2
Licensed private businesses, community security services, motor vehicle identification lights, 39:3–54.14
Licenses and permits, community security services, motor vehicle identification lights, 39:3–54.14
Motor vehicle identification lights, community security services, 39:3–54.14
Nonprofit corporations and associations. Associations and societies, generally, ante
Pursuers, detective associations, 15:4–1, 15:4–2
Rewards, pursuers, association of detectives, 15:4–2

DETENTION
Correctional Institutions, generally, this index
Definitions, juvenile justice, 2A:4A–22
Denial, record expungement, 2C:52–14
Disclosure, expungement order, 2C:52–30
Diversion programs, record expungement, 2C:52–20
Exemptions, record expungement, 2C:52–2
Expungement, record, 2C:52–1 et seq.
Fees, record expungement, 2C:52–29
Hearings, record expungement, 2C:52–9 et seq.
Indictable offenses, record expungement, 2C:52–2
Inspection of places of detention, records, expungement, 2C:52–19
Investigative detention. Arrest, this index
Juvenile Delinquents, this index
Library theft, suspects, 2C:20–14
Orders of court, record expungement, 2C:52–11 et seq., 2C:52–26
Petitions, record expungement, 2C:52–7 et seq.
Presentence report, record expungement, 2C:52–21
Prisons and prisoners. Correctional Institutions, generally, this index
Process, record expungement, 2C:52–10
Records, expungement, 2C:52–1 et seq.
Release, record expungement, 2C:52–19
Removal, records, 2C:52–15
Sealing, record expungement, 2C:52–26
Shoplifting, detention by law enforcement officer, 2C:20–11
Statements, record expungement petition, 2C:52–8
Supervisory treatment programs, record expungement, 2C:52–20
Traffic offenses, record expungement, 2C:52–28
Witnesses, criminal cases, **Rule 3**:26–3

DEVELOPMENTALLY DISABLED PERSONS
Mentally Retarded and Developmentally Disabled Persons, generally, this index

DEVISES AND DEVISEES
Probate Proceedings, generally, this index

DEXTROMORAMIDE
Controlled dangerous substance, 24:21–1 et seq.

DEXTRORPHAN
Controlled dangerous substance, 24:21–1 et seq.

DIAGNOSIS
Physicians and Surgeons, generally, this index

DIAGNOSTIC CENTER
Records and recordation, confidential or privileged information, **Rule 1**:38–3
Sex offenses, presentence investigation, report, **Rule 3**:21–3

DIAMPROMIDE
Controlled dangerous substance, 24:21–1 et seq.

DIESEL FUEL
Emissions. Motor Vehicles, this index

DIETARY FOODS
Frozen Desserts and Dietary Foods, generally, this index

DIETHYLTHIAMBUTENE
Controlled dangerous substance, **24:21–1 et seq.**

DIETHYLTRYPTAMINE
Controlled dangerous substance, **24:21–1 et seq.**

DIETITIANS
Fees, controversies or disputes with patients, review committees, immunity from liability, **2A:84A–22.10**

DIHYDROCODEINE
Controlled dangerous substance, **24:21–1 et seq.**

DIHYDROCODEINONE
Controlled dangerous substance, **24:21–1 et seq.**

DIMENOXADOL
Controlled dangerous substance, **24:21–1 et seq.**

DIMEPHEPTANOL
Controlled dangerous substance, **24:21–1 et seq.**

DIMETHYLTHIAMBUTENE
Controlled dangerous substance, **24:21–1 et seq.**

DIMETHYLTRYPTAMINE
Controlled dangerous substance, **24:21–1 et seq.**

DIOXAPHETYL BUTYRATE
Controlled dangerous substance, **24:21–1 et seq.**

DIPHENOXYLATE
Controlled dangerous substance, **24:21–1 et seq.**

DIPIPANONE
Controlled dangerous substance, **24:21–1 et seq.**

DIPLOMATIC OFFICERS
Traffic rules and regulations, privileges and immunities, records and recordation, **39:5–53 et seq.**

DIRECTORS
Administrative Office of the Courts, this index
Alcoholic Beverage Control Division, this index
Automobile insurance risk exchange, **39:6A–21**
Colleges and Universities, generally, this index
Commercial Drivers Licenses, this index
Definitions,
 Auto body repair facilities, **39:13–1**
 Drivers privacy protection, **39:2–3.3**
 Flammable sleeping bags and tents, **2A:123–16**
 Historic motor vehicles, **39:3–27.3**
 Historic preservation license plates, **39:3–27.72**
 Liberty State Park plates, **39:3–27.91**
 Motor Vehicle Law, **39:1–1**
 Motor Vehicle Security Responsibility Law, **39:6–24**
 Parking offenses, **39:4–139.3**
 Registration and regulation of snowmobiles and all terrain vehicles, **39:3C–1**
 School buses, in terminal inspections, **39:3B–20**
 Tow trucks and towing companies, **39:3–84.6**

DIRECTORS—Cont'd
Misconduct, corporate directors, **2C:21–9**
Monopolies, subpoena information, **56:9–9**

DIRKS
Weapons, generally, this index

DIRT BIKES
Generally, **39:3C–1 et seq.**

DISABILITY INACTIVE STATUS
Attorneys, this index

DISABLED PERSONS
Handicapped Persons, generally, this index

DISABLED VEHICLES
Parking, **39:4–136**

DISABLED VETERANS
Veterans, this index

DISASTERS
Attorneys, solicitation, crimes and offenses, **2C:40A–5**
Control, commercial drivers licenses, exemption, **39:3–10j, 39:3–10k**
Crimes and offenses, health care professionals, solicitation, **2C:40A–4**
Health care professionals, solicitation, crimes and offenses, **2C:40A–4**
Terrorism, generally, this index

DISBARMENT
Attorneys, this index

DISCHARGE
Bail, this index
Jury and Jurors, this index

DISCHARGE OF INMATES OF INSTITUTIONS
Parole, generally, this index

DISCIPLINARY OVERSIGHT COMMITTEE
Generally, **Rule 1:20B–1 et seq.**
Establishment, **Rule 1:20–1**

DISCIPLINARY REVIEW BOARD
Attorneys, **Rules 1:20–1, 1:20–15**

DISCIPLINE
Attorneys, this index
Juvenile conference committees, **Rule 5:25–1**
Persons with special responsibility for discipline of others, use of force, **2C:3–8**
Police and Police Departments, this index
State Police, this index

DISCLOSURE
See, also, Confidential or Privileged Information, generally, this index
Attorneys, this index
Child Abuse, this index
Court appointed special advocate, records, juvenile delinquents and dependents, **2A:4A–60 et seq.**
Crimes and offenses,
 Expungement order, **2C:52–30**
 Presentence investigation reports and examinations, **2C:44–6**
Domestic violence, registry, injunctions, **2C:25–34**
Drivers privacy protection, **39:2–3.3 et seq.**
Elections, this index
Family court, records, juvenile delinquents and dependents, **2A:4A–60 et seq.**

DISCLOSURE—Cont'd
Grand jury, injurious information, crime, **2B:21–10**
Hospitals, this index
Identification, juvenile delinquents and dependents, **2A:4A–60**
Judges and justices, financial statements and reports, **Rule 1:18B–3**
Juvenile delinquents and dependents, records, **2A:4A–60 et seq.**
Law enforcement agencies, records, **2A:4A–60 et seq.**
Monopolies and unfair trade, inquiries, **56:9–9**
Motor Vehicles, this index
Newspapermans privilege, rules of evidence, **2A:84A–21**
Radon gas test results, buildings, **26:2D–73**
Search warrants, application or issuance, punishable as contempt, **Rule 3:5–4**
Unauthorized practice of law, committees, confidential records, **Rule 1:21–1**
Wiretapping and electronic surveillance, Results of tap, **2A:156A–17 et seq.**
 Wire, electronic or oral communication, contents of, disclosure of, crimes and offenses, **2A:156A–3**

DISCOUNTS
Alcoholic beverages, sales to retailers, **33:1–90, 33:1–93**

DISCOVERY
Attorney disciplinary proceedings, **Rule 1:20–5**
Crimes and offenses, **Rule 3:13–2 et seq.**
 Attorney work product, **Rule 3:13–3**
 Capital cases, additional discovery, **Rule 3:13–4**
 Continuing duty to disclose, **Rules 3:13–3, 7:7–7**
 Documents not subject to, **Rule 3:13–3**
 Materials obtained from prosecutor, confidentiality, **Rule 1:38–3**
 Protective orders, **Rule 3:13–3**
 Specific criminal code defenses, **Rule 3:12–1**
Depositions, generally, this index
Driving while intoxicated, second or subsequent offenses, **39:4–50**
Failure to comply, admissibility, **Rule 3:13–3**
Mediation, confidential or privileged information, **Evidence Rule 519**
Money laundering and illegal investments, **2C:21–29**
Motions, **Rule 1:6–2**
Municipal courts, **Rule 7:7–7**
Municipal prosecutors, **2B:25–5**
Offenses. Crimes and offenses, generally, ante
Pretrial Conferences, generally, this index
Protective orders, **Rule 7:7–7**
Racketeering, investigative interrogatories, **2C:41–5**
Time, attorney disciplinary proceedings, **Rule 1:20–5**
Traffic control signal monitoring system, **39:4–8.15**
Unsatisfied claim and judgment fund, discovery as condition to recover from fund, **39:6–70**

DISCRIMINATION
Assault, intimidation based on bias, **2C:43–7**
Bias intimidation, crimes and offenses, **2C:16–1**
Crimes and offenses,
 Bias crimes, intimidation, **2C:16–1**
 Intimidation based on bias, fourth degree crime, extended term of imprisonment, **2C:43–7, 2C:43–7.1**

DISCRIMINATION—Cont'd

Handicapped persons, bias crimes, intimidation, **2C:16–1**

Harassment, intimidation based on bias, fourth degree crime, extended term of imprisonment, **2C:43–7, 2C:43–7.1**

Intimidation based on bias, extended term of imprisonment, **2C:43–7, 2C:43–7.1**

Law enforcement officers, racial profiling, crimes and offenses, **2C:30–5 et seq.**

Police and police departments, racial profiling, crimes and offenses, **2C:30–5 et seq.**

Religious Corporations and Associations, this index

State police, complaints, limitation of actions, **53:1–33**

DISEASES

Alcoholics and Alcoholism, generally, this index

Animals, this index

Children and minors, medical care and treatment, religion, **9:6–1.1**

Discrimination, generally, this index

Grand juror, filling vacancy, **2B:21–4**

Hazardous Substances and Waste, generally, this index

Health and Accident Insurance, generally, this index

Health Maintenance Organizations, generally, this index

Medical Care and Treatment, generally, this index

Photosensitivity, tinted windshields, **39:3–75.1 et seq.**

Sexual penetration, venereal diseases, **2C:34–5**

Windshields, photosensitivity, tinted windshields, **39:3–75.1 et seq.**

DISHONOR

Negotiable Instruments, this index

DISINHERSION

Conviction of crime not to work, **2A:152–2**

DISMISSAL AND NONSUIT

Affidavit, inactive cases, **Rule 1:13–7**

Answers, filing, **Rule 1:13–7**

Appeals in criminal prosecutions, **Rule 3:23–7**

  Attorney fee arbitration, **Rule 1:20A–3**

  Timely appeals, failure to comply, **Rule 3:23–2**

Attorney disciplinary proceedings, **Rule 1:20–3**

  Motions, **Rule 1:20–5**

Complaints, failure to appear, **Rule 1:2–4**

Consent orders, reinstatement, **Rule 1:13–7**

Counterclaims, failure to appear, **Rule 1:2–4**

Courts of limited criminal jurisdiction, enlargement of time, **Rule 1:3–4**

Crimes and Offenses, this index

Cross claims, failure to appear, **Rule 1:2–4**

De minimis infractions, **2C:2–11**

Default, entry, **Rule 1:13–7**

Default judgments, entry, **Rule 1:13–7**

Drunk Driving Victims Bill of Rights, **39:4–50.12**

Expungement, record, **2C:52–6**

Failure to appear, **Rule 1:2–4**

Failure to prosecute, **Rule 1:13–7**

Inactive cases, **Rule 1:13–7**

Indictment, Information or Presentment, this index

Indigent, neglected or abandoned children, juvenile family crisis, petitions, **2A:4A–86**

Juvenile delinquents and dependents, juvenile family crisis, petitions, **2A:4A–86**

DISMISSAL AND NONSUIT—Cont'd

Juvenile family crisis, petitions, **2A:4A–86**

Mentally ill defendant, **2C:4–6**

Motions,

  Attorney disciplinary proceedings, **Rule 1:20–5**

  Failure to comply with requirements, **Rule 1:2–4**

  Inactive cases, **Rule 1:13–7**

Municipal courts, **Rules 7:7–1, 7:8–5**

Parking offenses, **Rule 7:8–9**

Prior offense no longer an offense, **2C:1–1**

Records and recordation, expungement, **2C:52–6**

Reinstatement, inactive cases, **Rule 1:13–7**

Service,

  Evidence, **Rule 1:13–7**

  Time, failure, **Rule 1:13–7**

Special civil part, law division, Superior court, **Rule 1:13–7**

Supervisory treatment programs, first offenders, **2C:43–13**

DISOBEDIENCE

Contempt, generally, this index

DISORDERLY CONDUCT

Disorderly Persons, generally, this index

DISORDERLY HOUSES

Prostitution, generally, this index

DISORDERLY PERSONS

  See, also, Petty Disorderly Persons, generally, this index

Generally, **2C:1–4, 2C:33–2**

Abuse of children, failure to report, **9:6–8.14**

Advertisements, machine guns or semiautomatic rifles, **2C:39–15**

AIDS (Acquired Immune Deficiency Syndrome), tests and testing, **2A:4A–43.4, 2C:43–2.3**

Alcoholic beverages,

  Misrepresenting age, sales, children and minors, **33:1–81**

  Possession, persons under legal age, **2C:33–15**

  Restaurants, unlicensed premises, **2C:33–27**

  Sales, persons under legal age, **33:1–77**

  Serving or making available to minors, **2C:33–17**

Alcoholics and Alcoholism, generally, this index

Animal decompression or gas chambers, removal, **4:22–19.2**

Animals, this index

Appeal, bail or recognizances, **2A:162–11**

Arrest without process, **2A:169–3**

Assault, **2C:12–1**

Assault firearms, advertisements, **2C:39–15**

Bad checks, **2C:21–5**

Badges, emblems and insignia, law enforcement officers, unauthorized transfer, **2C:21–2.2**

Bail, **2C:6–1**

  Appeal, **2A:162–11**

  Jumping, **2C:29–7**

Bias intimidation, grade and degree of offenses, **2C:16–1**

Bigamy, **2C:24–1**

Body piercing, children and minors, consent, **2C:40–21**

Burglars tools, **2C:5–5**

Cable television, theft of services, **2C:20–8**

Certificates and certification, conviction of crime, rehabilitation, **2A:168A–11**

DISORDERLY PERSONS—Cont'd

Children and minors,

  Abuse or neglect, failure to report, **9:6–8.14**

  Body piercing, consent, **2C:40–21**

  Cigarettes and cigars, sales, **2A:170–51.1, 2C:33–13.1**

  Definitions, access to loaded firearm, **2C:58–15**

  Intoxicating liquors, sales to persons under legal age, **33:1–77**

  Paging devices, **2C:33–19**

  Tattoos and tattooing, consent, **2C:40–21**

Cigarettes and cigars, children and minors, sales, **2A:170–51.1, 2C:33–13.1**

Compensation and salaries, nonpayment, **2C:40A–2**

Constable, arrest without process, **2A:169–3**

Controlled Substances, this index

County bridge police, authority to arrest, **27:19–36.3**

Credit terms, false statements, **2C:21–19**

Criminal mischief, **2C:17–3**

Criminal trespass, **2C:18–3**

Deceptive business practices, **2C:21–7**

Demonstrations, funerals, **2C:33–8.1**

Desecration, venerated objects, **2C:33–9**

Detective associations, arrest of offenders, **15:4–4**

Disrupting meetings and processions, **2C:33–8**

Disruption, funerals, **2C:33–8.1**

DNA database and databank, disclosure of information, **53:1–20.26**

Dogs, owned or used by law enforcement officers, killing or harming, **2C:29–3.1**

Drugs and medicine,

  Prescription legend drugs, **2C:35–10.5**

  Stramonium, **2C:35–10.5**

Expungement of records, **2C:52–3, 2C:52–4**

  Disclosure, **2C:52–30**

False imprisonment, **2C:13–3**

False personation, **2C:21–17**

False reports, law enforcement authorities, **2C:28–4**

False statements, unsworn falsifications, **2C:28–3**

Fines and penalties, **2C:43–3, 2C:43–3.1, 2C:43–8**

  Payment and collection, **2C:46–4**

  Law enforcement officers training and equipment fund, **2C:43–3.3**

Seasonally leased premises, right to occupy or visit, termination, **2C:43–8.1**

Fingerprinting, drug addicts, **53:1–15**

Firearms, leaving loaded firearm within easy reach of a minor, **2C:58–15**

Food stamps, illegal use, **2C:20–37**

Funerals, disruption, **2C:33–8.1**

Gambling devices, possession, **2C:37–7**

Gambling records, possession, **2C:37–3**

Handcuffs,

  Possession, **2C:39–3**

  Sale to children and minors, **2C:39–9.2**

Harassment, **2C:33–4**

Hazardous substances and waste, inhalants, **2C:35–10.4**

Hazards, creation, **2C:40–1**

Hazing, **2C:40–3 et seq.**

Hindering apprehension or prosecution of accused, **2C:29–3**

HIV testing, **2A:4A–43.4, 2C:43–2.3**

Horses,

  Cruelty, **39:4–23**

  Law enforcement officers animal, killed, maimed or inflicted with harm, **2C:29–3.1**

  Sales, unfit horse, **4:22–21**

DISORDERLY PERSONS—Cont'd

Hypodermic needles or syringes, discarding or abandoning, 2C:36–6.1

Impersonating public servant, 2C:28–8

Imprisonment, 2C:43–8

Incompetent persons, endangering welfare, 2C:24–7

Interference with transportation, 2C:33–14

Jumping bail, 2C:29–7

Jury duty, employment protection, employer violations, 2B:20–17

Juvenile delinquents and dependents, disclosure, designated records, 2A:4A–60

Kosher food, misbranding, 2C:21–7.4

Labor and employment,
Lie detector tests, requirement, 2C:40A–1
Wrongful discharge, 2C:40A–3

Law, unauthorized practice, 2C:21–22

Law enforcement officers, unauthorized transfer of badges, 2C:21–2.2

Law enforcement officers organization or association,
Animals owned or used by, killing or inflicting harm, 2C:29–3.1
Honorary membership cards, 2A:170–20.1

Legal representation, public defender, 2A:158A–5.2

Lewdness, 2C:14–4

Limitation of prosecutions, 2C:1–6

Loitering, illegal use, possession or sale of controlled dangerous substances, 2C:33–2.1

Loitering for the purpose of engaging in prostitution, 2C:34–1.1

Machine guns, advertisements, 2C:39–15

Means of conveyance, theft, 2C:20–10

Minors. Children and minors, generally, ante

Misdemeanor designated as disorderly persons offense, 2C:1–4

Motor Vehicles, this index

Municipal Courts, this index

Obscene materials, adults, 2C:34–2

Obstructing administration of law or other governmental function, 2C:29–1

Obstruction, funerals, 2C:33–8.1

Offering false instrument for filing, 2C:21–3

Own recognizance, appeal, 2A:162–11

Penalties. Fines and penalties, generally, ante

Petty Disorderly Persons, generally, this index

Prescriptions, this index

Privileged communications, physician and patients, 2A:84A–22.1 et seq.

Probation, prison term as condition, 2C:45–1

Prostitution, 2C:34–1

Racing on public highway, 39:5C–1

Recognizance or bail, appeal, 2A:162–11

Resisting arrest, 2C:29–2

Restaurants, intoxicating liquors, unlicensed premises, 2C:33–27

Rigging publicly exhibited contests, 2C:21–11

Riots, 2C:33–1

Rules and regulations by director of alcoholic beverage control, 33:1–39

Sales, motor vehicles, Sunday, 2C:33–26

Seasonally leased premises, definitions, termination of right to occupy or visit, 2C:43–8.1

Semiautomatic rifles, advertisements, 2C:39–15

Sentence and punishment, 2C:43–8

Shoplifting, 2C:20–11

Slugs or fraudulent devices, coin currency, or credit card activated machine, 2C:21–18

Stramonium, drugs and medicine, 2C:35–10.5

Sunday, motor vehicles, sales, 2C:33–26

Tampering with public records or information, 2C:28–7

DISORDERLY PERSONS—Cont'd

Tattoos and tattooing, children and minors, consent, 2C:40–21

Telegraphs and telephones, harassment, 2C:33–4

Telephone party line, refusing to yield, emergency, 2C:40–2

Theft, 2C:20–2

Theft of services, 2C:20–8

Tobacco, sale to minors, 2A:170–51.1

Traffic signs and signals, damaging or removing sign or signal, criminal mischief, 2C:17–3.1

Trial, **Rule 3:1–6**

Unauthorized practice of law, 2C:21–22

Usury, 2C:21–19

Weapons, generally, this index

Wrongful discharge, 2C:40A–3

DISPENSARIES

Health Maintenance Organizations, generally, this index

DISPENSERS

Definitions,
Controlled dangerous substances, 24:21–2
Controlled substances, 24:21–2

DISPLAYS

Motor carriers, placards, radioactive materials, 39:5B–18

Outdoor Advertising, generally, this index

Roadside advertising. Outdoor Advertising, generally, this index

DISPOSAL

Dead Bodies, this index

Hazardous Substances and Waste, this index

Solid Waste, this index

DISPOSITION OF CASES

Juvenile Delinquents, this index

DISPUTE RESOLUTION

Arbitration and Award, generally, this index

Complementary dispute resolution, **Rule 1:33–1 et seq.**

DISREPUTABLE PERSONS OR PLACES

Probation or suspended sentences, conditions, 2C:45–1

DISRUPTING MEETINGS AND PROCESSIONS

Generally, 2C:33–8

DISTANCES

Explosives, quantity, manufacturing and storage, 21:1A–135

DISTILLING APPARATUS

Stills and Distilling Apparatus, generally, this index

DISTRIBUTE

Definitions, controlled substances, 2C:35–2, 24:21–2

DISTRIBUTION

Controlled Substances, this index

DISTRIBUTORS

Agricultural Products, generally, this index

Chemicals, chemistry and chemists, industrial chemicals, 2C:35–29

Definitions,
Chemicals, chemistry and chemists, industrial chemicals, 2C:35–29
Controlled substances, 2C:35–2

DISTRIBUTORS—Cont'd

Definitions—Cont'd
Industrial chemicals, 2C:35–29

Industrial chemicals, 2C:35–29

Motor vehicles, master keys or devices, 2C:5–6

Nuisances, controlled dangerous substances, 24:21–35

DISTRICT ETHICS COMMITTEES

Attorneys, **Rules 1:20–1, 1:20–3**

DISTRICT FEE ARBITRATION COMMITTEES

Attorneys, **Rules 1:20–1, 1:20A–1 et seq.**

DISTRICT WATER SUPPLY COMMISSION

North Jersey district water supply commission, motor vehicles, exemption from payment of registration fee, 39:3–27

DIVERSION

Juvenile Delinquents, this index

DIVERSION PROGRAMS

Crimes and offenses, records, expungement, 2C:52–20

DIVIDENDS

Misconduct, corporate officials, 2C:21–9

DIVISION MANAGERS

Generally, **Rule 1:33–7**

DIVISIONS

Alcoholic Beverage Control Division, generally, this index

Definitions,
Abuse of children, 9:6–8.21
Children and minors, abuse or neglect, 9:6–8.21
Comprehensive Child Abuse Prevention and Treatment Act, 9:6–8.84
Drivers privacy protection, 39:2–3.3
Frozen dessert trucks, traffic rules and regulations, 39:4–128.3
Historic preservation license plates, 39:3–27.72
Liberty State Park plates, 39:3–27.91
Motor vehicles, 39:1–1
Parking offenses, 39:4–139.3
School buses, in terminal inspections, 39:3B–20
Tow trucks and towing companies, 39:3–84.6

Fish and wildlife division. Environmental Protection Department, this index

Human Services Department, this index

Motor vehicles division. Motor Vehicle Commission, generally, this index

Parks and forestry division. Environmental Protection Department, this index

State police division. State Police, generally, this index

DIVORCE

Complementary dispute resolution programs, **Rule 1:40–1 et seq.**

Domestic violence actions, evidence, 2C:25–25

Economic aspects, complementary dispute resolution programs, **Rule 1:40–5**

Family Actions, generally, this index

Privileged communications, effect, 2A:84A–22

Probation officers, supervision of persons required to pay for support, 2A:168–11

Visitation. Children and Minors, this index

DNA

DNA Database and Databank, generally, this
index

DNA DATABASE AND DATABANK

Generally, **53:1–20.17 et seq.**
Attorneys, right to counsel, motions,
2A:84A–32a
CODIS, definitions, **53:1–20.19**
Confidential or privileged information, crimes
and offenses, motions, **2A:84A–32a**
Confidentiality of profiles and samples,
53:1–20.27
Conviction of crime, motions, **2A:84A–32a,**
2A:84A–32b
Costs, tests, liens, **53:1–20.29 et seq.**
Creation of separate population database after
removal of personal identification,
53:1–20.24
Definitions, **53:1–20.19**
Disclosure of information, guilty of disorderly
persons offense, **53:1–20.26**
Division, definitions, **53:1–20.19**
DNA record, definitions, **53:1–20.19**
DNA sample, definitions, **53:1–20.19**
Expungement from DNA databank, overruling
of conviction, **53:1–20.25**
FBI, definitions, **53:1–20.19**
Funds obtained through seizure, forfeiture, use
by attorney general for implementation of
provisions, **53:1–20.28**
Genetic Privacy Act. Discrimination, general-
ly, this index
Hearings, crimes and offenses, motions,
2A:84A–32a
Juvenile delinquents and dependents,
53:1–20.20, 53:1–20.22, 53:1–20.25
Legislative findings and declaration, **53:1–20.18**
Liability for drawing blood, **53:1–20.22**
Liens and incumbrances, tests, costs, **53:1–20.29**
et seq.
Mentally deficient and mentally ill persons,
53:1–20.20
People qualified to draw sample, **53:1–20.22**
Place where DNA sample to be drawn,
53:1–20.22
Retaining information, **53:1–20.37**
Rules and regulations, samples, identification
and submission, **53:1–20.23**
State DNA databank, definitions, **53:1–20.19**
State DNA database, definitions, **53:1–20.19**
State police division, duty to store, analyze,
DNA record of identification characteristic
profiles, **53:1–20.24**
Tests on blood samples,
Costs, liens, **53:1–20.29 et seq.**
Use of results, **53:1–20.21**

DOCKETS

Caption, docket number, **Rule 1:4–1**
Denial, record expungement, **2C:52–14**
Disclosure, expungement order, **2C:52–30**
Diversion programs, record expungement,
2C:52–20
Exemptions, record expungement, **2C:52–2**
Expungement, records, **2C:52–1 et seq.**
Fees, record expungement, **2C:52–29**
Hearings, record expungement, **2C:52–9 et seq.**
Indictable offenses, record expungement,
2C:52–2
Inspection and inspectors, records, expunge-
ment, **2C:52–19**
Limited criminal jurisdiction, courts of, ap-
peals, **Rule 3:23–4**
Municipal courts, **Rule 7:14–4**
Orders, record expungement, **2C:52–11 et seq.**

DOCKETS—Cont'd

Petitions, record expungement, **2C:52–7 et seq.**
Presentence report, record expungement,
2C:52–21
Process, record expungement, **2C:52–10**
Records, expungement, **2C:52–1 et seq.**
Release, record expungement, **2C:52–19**
Removal, records, **2C:52–15**
Sealing, record expungement, **2C:52–26**
Statements, record expungement petition,
2C:52–8
Superior court, municipal court judgments,
2B:12–26
Supervisory treatment programs, record ex-
pungement, **2C:52–20**
Traffic offenses, record expungement,
2C:52–28

DOCTOR PATIENT PRIVILEGE

Attorneys, waiver, application for restoration
from disability inactive status, **Rule
1:20–12**

DOCTORS

Chiropractors, generally, this index
Dentists and Dentistry, generally, this index
Optometrists, generally, this index
Physicians and Surgeons, generally, this index
Podiatrists and Podiatry, generally, this index
Psychologists and Psychology, generally, this
index
Veterinarians, generally, this index

DOCUMENTARY EXHIBITS

Disposition, **2C:65–4**

DOCUMENTS

Crimes and offenses, discovery, **Rule 3:13–3**
Searches and seizures, warrants, **Rule 3:5–2**
Subpoena, production, **Rule 1:9–2**

DOGS

Animal population control program, animal
welfare license plates, **39:3–27.55 et seq.**
Control facilities, controlled substances, regis-
tration, **24:21–11**
Controlled substances, control facilities, regis-
tration, **24:21–11**
Crimes and offenses,
Sales,
Fur or hair, **4:22–25.3**
Meat and meat products, **4:22–25.4**
Search and rescue dogs, **2C:29–3.1**
Cruelty to animals, **4:22–20**
Destruction, neuromuscular blocking agents,
4:22–19.3, 4:22–19.4
Disorderly persons, law enforcement officers
animal, killed, maimed or inflicted with
harm, **2C:29–3.1**
Fighting animals, cruelty to animals, **4:22–24**
Fur or hair, sales, crimes and offenses,
4:22–25.3
Guide dogs. Blind Persons, this index
Harmed, law enforcement officers animal, dis-
orderly persons, **2C:29–3.1**
Killed, law enforcement officer animal, disor-
derly persons, **2C:29–3.1**
Law enforcement officers, owned or used by,
killing or harming, disorderly persons,
2C:29–3.1
Maimed, law enforcement officers animal, dis-
orderly persons, **2C:29–3.1**
Meat and meat products, sales, crimes and
offenses, **4:22–25.4**
Motorists duty to stop and report injury to dog,
4:22–25.1, 4:22–25.2
Sales. Crimes and offenses, ante

DOGS—Cont'd

Search and rescue dogs, crimes and offenses,
2C:29–3.1
Sodium pentobarbital, registration and certification, **24:21–11**
Spaying and neutering, animal population control program, animal welfare license
plates, **39:3–27.55 et seq.**

DOLLS

Anatomically correct dolls, sex offenses, children as witnesses, **2A:84A–16.1**

DOLLY

Semitrailer, rear lamps of converter dolly not
permanently attached to semitrailer,
39:3–61

DOMESTIC ANIMALS

Animals, generally, this index

DOMESTIC COMPANION ANIMAL

Definitions, theft, **2C:20–1**
Theft, **2C:20–2**

DOMESTIC PARTNERSHIPS

Construction of rules, **Rule 1:1–2**

DOMESTIC RELATIONS ACTIONS

Family Actions, generally, this index

DOMESTIC RELATIONS COURT

Juvenile and Domestic Relations Courts, generally, this index

DOMESTIC VIOLENCE

Generally, **2C:25–17 et seq.**
Actions and proceedings, return of weapons,
2C:25–21
Administrative law and procedure, weapons,
2C:25–21.1
Appeal and review, weapons seizure, **2C:25–21**
Arrest,
Contempt, **2C:25–31**
Probable cause, **2C:25–21**
Bail, release conditions, **2C:25–26**
Burden of proof, hearings, **2C:25–29**
Complaints, **2C:25–28**
Confidential or privileged information,
2C:25–25
Contempt, **2C:25–32**
Electronic signatures, **Rule 1:4–4**
Confidential or privileged information, **Rule
1:38–3**
Registry, injunctions, **2C:25–34**
Victims, location, **2C:25–26**
Contempt,
Allegations, **2C:25–32**
Arrest, procedures, **2C:25–31**
Foreign states, restraining orders, **2C:29–9**
Proceedings, **2C:25–30**
Violation of orders, **2C:25–30**
Convictions, sentencing conditions, **2C:25–27**
Counselors and Counseling, this index
Crisis teams, law enforcement officers,
2C:25–20
Custody, release, **2C:25–26**
Notice to victim, **2C:25–26.1**
Definitions, **2C:25–19**
Disclosure, registry, injunctions, **2C:25–34**
Dismissal of charges, **2C:25–25**
Divorce, evidence, **2C:25–25**
Domestic violence offense reports, **2C:25–24**
Emancipated minor, definitions, **2C:25–19**
Emergency relief, **2C:25–29**
Ex parte, **2C:25–28**
Evidence, **2C:25–29**

DOMESTIC VIOLENCE—Cont'd
Fines and penalties, 2C:25–29.1, 2C:25–29.2
  Surcharges, 2C:25–29.4
Fingerprints and fingerprinting, 53:1–15
Foreign states, contempt, restraining orders, 2C:29–9
Hearing officers, **Rule 5:25–4**
Hearings, 2C:25–29
  Weapons seizure, 2C:25–21
Injunctions, 2C:25–34
  Bail, 2C:25–26
  Contempt, 2C:25–31
    Foreign states, 2C:29–9
  Counselors and counseling, 2C:25–27, 2C:25–29
  Ex parte proceedings, 2C:25–28
  Issuance, 2C:25–28
  Notice, 2C:25–23
  Release conditions, 2C:25–26
  Weapons, possession, 2C:25–29
Judges and justices, education, 2C:25–20
Jurisdiction, 2C:25–28
  Contempt proceedings, 2C:25–30
Law enforcement officers, privileges and immunities, weapons, seizure, 2C:25–21
Legislative findings and declarations, 2C:25–18
Mediation, exceptions, **Rule 7:8–1**
Notice,
  Released offenders, notification to victim, 2C:25–26.1
  Rights of victim, 2C:25–23
Orders for relief, 2C:25–29
  Violation, 2C:25–30
Person convicted of crime involving, possession of any weapon prohibited, 2C:39–7
Personal recognizance, release conditions, 2C:25–26
Privileges and immunities,
  Arrest, 2C:25–22
  Law enforcement officers, 2C:25–22
    Weapons, seizure, 2C:25–21
  Weapons seizure, 2C:25–21
Probable cause, arrest, 2C:25–21
Proceedings, return of weapons, 2C:25–21
Records and recordation,
  Relief applications, 2C:25–33
  Rules and regulations, 2C:25–35
Release from custody, 2C:25–26
  Notification to victim, 2C:25–26.1
Relief, 2C:25–29
  Records, 2C:25–33
Reports, 2C:25–24, 2C:25–33
Restraining orders. Injunctions, generally, ante
Review, weapons seizure, 2C:25–21
Rights, notice, 2C:25–23
Rules and regulations, records and recordation, 2C:25–35
Seizures, weapons, 2C:25–21, 2C:25–26, 2C:25–28, 2C:25–29
Sentence and punishment, 2C:25–27
Service of process, 2C:25–28
Summons and complaint, forms, availability, 2C:25–28
Surcharges, 2C:25–29.4
Temporary restraining orders. Injunctions, generally, ante
Training course, domestic violence and abuse and neglect prevention and treatment, 2C:25–20
Victims of crime,
  Confidentiality of location, 2C:25–26
  Notice, released offender, 2C:25–26.1
  Rights, notice, 2C:25–23

DOMESTIC VIOLENCE—Cont'd
Victims of crime—Cont'd
  Victims of crime compensation board, reimbursement by defendant, compensation paid to victim, 2C:25–29
Violation of orders, 2C:25–30
Weapons,
  Administrative law and procedure, 2C:25–21.1
  Injunctions, possession, 2C:25–29
  Licenses and permits, 2C:58–3
  Seizure, 2C:25–21, 2C:25–26, 2C:25–28, 2C:25–29

DOMICILE
Residence and Residents, generally, this index

DONATE LIFE NJ REGISTRY
Anatomical gifts, 39:3–12.3 et seq.

DONATIONS
Gifts, generally, this index

DONOR
Anatomical Gifts, this index

DOORS
Autobus or street car not to be operated with door open, 39:4–68
Breaking and entry in execution of search warrant under alcoholic beverage law, 33:1–58
Special exit door, motor vehicles used for merchandising or exhibition purposes, 39:3–77.2

DOUBLE JEOPARDY
  Generally, 2C:1–9
Bar to prosecution,
  Different offense, 2C:1–10
  Same offense, 2C:1–9
Concurrent jurisdiction, state and United States, United States prosecution, 2C:1–11
Different offenses, bar to prosecution, 2C:1–10
Dismissal, **Rule 3:25–1**
Former persecution in other jurisdiction, bar, 2C:1–11
Fraudulent procurement by defendant, 2C:1–12
Lack of jurisdiction of former court, 2C:1–12
Lesser related infractions, avoiding joinder, **Rule 3:15–3**
Limited criminal jurisdiction, courts of, appeals, raising, **Rule 3:23–8**
Mandatory joinder, indictment, accusation, **Rule 3:15–1**
Multiple offenses, 2C:1–10
Other jurisdictions, 2C:1–11
Postconviction relief, grounds expressly adjudicated, **Rule 3:22–5**
Raising before trial, **Rule 3:10–2**
Same offense, 2C:1–9
United States district court prosecution, concurrent state and United States jurisdiction, 2C:1–11

DOWER
Conviction of crime not to cause loss of, 2A:152–2

DRAINAGE AND RECLAMATION OF LANDS
Agricultural land, trespass, damages, 2C:18–4 et seq.

DRAWINGS
Jury and Jurors, this index

DRIVER IMPROVEMENT PROGRAMS
Commercial drivers licenses, suspension or revocation, reinstatement, 39:5–30

DRIVERS
Definitions, 39:1–1
  Motor vehicles, 39:1–1
School Buses, this index

DRIVERS LICENSES
Accidents,
  Death, revocation or suspension, 2C:40–22
  Leaving scene of accident, suspension or revocation, 39:5–30
  Reexamination, two or more accidents, 39:3–10e
Age,
  Applicant for license, 39:3–10
  Color photograph, 39:3–10f
  Persons under 17 and over 16, agricultural pursuits, 39:3–11.1 et seq.
  Probationary licenses, 39:3–13.4
Aged persons, color photographs, exceptions, 39:3–10f
Agricultural pursuits, persons under age 17 and over 16, 39:3–11.1 et seq.
Alcoholic beverages,
  Examination permits, 39:3–13
  Examinations, effect on driving, 39:3–10
  Identity theft, personal identifying information, obtaining, 2C:21–17.2
  Implied consent, blood analysis, 39:4–50.2 et seq.
  Probationary licenses, 39:3–13.4
  Special learners permits, 39:3–13.2a
  Suspension or revocation, 39:4–50
    Death or serious bodily injury of another, 39:5–30
    Extension, 39:3–40
    Persons under legal age, 33:1–81
    Possession, person under legal age, 2C:33–15
Aliens, authorized presence in U.S., 39:3–10
  Examination permits, 39:3–13
Anatomical gifts, donors, 39:3–10, 39:3–12.2, 39:3–12.4
Applications,
  Epilepsy and similar conditions, 39:3–10.5
  False statements, 39:3–37
  Indexing, 39:3–28
  Street address, 39:3–9b
Armed forces, temporary licenses, 39:3–10n
Articulated vehicle endorsements, 39:3–10
Bar codes, information, 39:3–10h
Basic drivers license, 39:3–10
Behind the wheel instruction, special learners permits, 39:3–13.1
Bicycles, this index
Blood analysis,
  Chemical test, refusal, suspension or revocation, 39:4–50.4a
  Implied consent, intoxication of driver, 39:4–50.2 et seq.
Buses, this index
Card designating anatomical gift donor, 39:3–12.2
Certificates and certification,
  Data processing, 39:2–3.8
  Licensing drivers of state, county, or city owned vehicles, 39:3–14
  Vision test, 39:3–10c
Change of address of licensee, notice, 39:3–36
Chauffeurs, endorsements, 39:5G–2
Chemical tests,
  Blood analysis, refusal, suspension or revocation, 39:4–50.4a

DRIVERS LICENSES—Cont'd
Chemical tests—Cont'd
  Implied consent, intoxication of driver, 39:4–50.4a
Children and minors, 39:3–10
  Agricultural pursuits, 39:3–11.1 et seq.
  Color photographs, 39:3–10f
  Distinctiveness, 39:3–10f
  Examination permits, 39:3–10, 39:3–13
  Examinations, 39:3–13 et seq.
  Identity or age verification, false documents, crimes and offenses, 2C:21–2.1
  Initial photo license, 39:3–10f
  New drivers, monitoring, 39:3–13.6
  Probationary licenses, 39:3–13.4
  Records and recordation, inspection, 39:3–13b
  Special permits, 39:3–13.1 et seq.
  Supervision, examination permit, 39:3–13
City owned vehicles operated exclusively for use of city, 39:3–14
Classification, 39:3–10
Classified licensing, 39:3–10
Color photographs, 39:3–10f
  Disclosure, 39:3–10f2
  Identification cards, 39:3–29.4
  Integrity, 39:3–10h
Commercial Drivers Licenses, generally, this index
Compact, 39:5D–1 et seq.
  Nonresident Violator Compact, 39:5F–1 et seq.
Compliance with law relating to, sufficiency, 39:3–42
Conditional license, physically defective applicant, 39:3–11
Conflict of laws, compact, 39:5D–6
Cosmetic or reconstructive surgery, color photographs, update, 39:3–10f
Counties,
  County owned vehicles, exclusive use, 39:3–14
  Verification, electronic readers, 39:3–10f1
Crimes and offenses,
  Compact, 39:5D–4
  False documents, identity or age verification, 2C:21–2.1
  Probationary licenses, 39:3–13.4
  Revocation or suspension, 2C:43–2
  Special learners permits, 39:3–13.2a
  Suspension or revocation, 2C:40–26, 39:3–40
  Theft of identity, exceptions, 2C:21–17
  Use, loan, 39:3–37.1
Crossings, school buildings and grounds, suspension or revocation, extension, 39:3–40
Data processing, 39:2–3.8
Deaf and hearing impaired persons, 39:3–11a, 39:3–11b
  Certifying condition of vehicle sold, 39:11–9
  Definitions, 39:1–1
  Reassignment certificates, 39:10–11
  Registration certificates and plates, temporary, 39:3–4c
  Registration of motor vehicles owned by dealer, 39:3–18
  Sabbath Day Law violation, suspension or revocation of license, 39:10–20
  Temporary registration certificates and plates, issuance, 39:3–4c
Death of another, suspension or revocation of license, 2C:40–22, 39:5–30
Decals,
  Examination permits, 39:3–13
  Probationary licenses, 39:3–13.4
  Special learners permits, 39:3–13.2a

DRIVERS LICENSES—Cont'd
Definitions,
  Compact, 39:5D–2
  Nonresident Violator Compact, 39:5F–4
Digitized color pictures, 39:3–10f
Display by nonresident, 39:3–17
Donor, anatomical gifts, designation, 39:3–10, 39:3–12.2
Drivers privacy protection, 39:2–3.3 et seq.
Drivers Schools, generally, this index
Drug related convictions, suspension or revocation, 39:5–30.12 et seq.
Drugs and medicine, effect on driving, examinations, 39:3–10
Duplicate license on loss or destruction of original, 39:3–31
Electric personal assistive mobility devices, 39:4–14.10
Electronic readers, verification, law enforcement agencies, 39:3–10f1
Emergencies,
  Examination permits, 39:3–13
  Probationary licenses, 39:3–13.4
Endorsements, 39:3–10
  Chauffeurs, 39:5G–2
Epilepsy, person subject to, applicants, 39:3–10.4 et seq.
Examination permits, 39:3–10, 39:3–13
  Fines and penalties, 39:3–13.8
  Motorcycles, 39:3–10b
Examinations and examiners,
  Ability as operator, 39:3–10, 39:3–10.1
  Agricultural pursuits, persons under age 17 and over 16, 39:3–11.1
  Alcoholic beverages and drug effect on driving, 39:3–10
  Anatomical gifts, inclusion of question regarding, 39:3–10
  Authorized presence in U.S., proof, requirement, 39:3–10
  Children and minors, 39:3–10
  Drivers manual, availability of copies, 39:3–41
  Drugs and alcoholic beverages, effect on driving, 39:3–10
  Examination permit as prerequisite for, 39:3–13
  Identity and identification, 39:3–10
  Motor vehicles division director, 39:3–10
  Necessity of applicants taking license examination, 39:3–12
  Reexamination,
    Notice, confirmation, 39:3–10.33
    Two or more accidents, 39:3–10, 39:3–10e
  Renewal, 39:3–10c, 39:3–10d
  Special learners permit holder entitled to examination, 39:3–13.4
  Vision, 39:3–10
Exemptions, commercial drivers licenses, 39:3–10j et seq.
Exhibition on request, 39:3–29
  Injured person, duty of driver of vehicle involved in accident, 39:4–129
  Magistrate hearing complaint against driver arrested for violating motor vehicle or traffic laws, 39:5–27
Expenses and expenditures, compact administrator, 39:5D–11
Expiration, 39:3–10
  Color photographs, effect, 39:3–10f
False documents, identity or age verification, crimes and offenses, 2C:21–2.1
Fees, 39:3–10
  Agents, 39:3–3
  Agricultural pursuits, persons under age 17 and over 16, 39:3–11.1

DRIVERS LICENSES—Cont'd
Fees—Cont'd
  Credit to state highway fund, 39:5–40
  Digitized color pictures, 39:3–10f
  Duplicate license, 39:3–31
  Examination permits, 39:3–13
  Maximum, limitations, 39:3–3
  Military or naval service, 39:3–11.5
  Motorized bicycles, 39:4–14.3
  Official drivers, license without charge, 39:3–14
  Omnibus endorsement, waiver, 39:3–10
    Examination permits, 39:3–13
  Renewal, 39:3–10f
  Restoration, suspended, revoked license, 39:3–10a
  Special learners permits, 39:3–13.1
Fines and penalties, 39:3–10
  Applying for license after suspension or revocation of former license, 39:3–34
  Blood analysis test, refusal, suspension or revocation, 39:4–50.4a
  Compact, 39:5D–4
  Decals, 39:3–13.8
  Endorsements, failure to make, 39:3–9a
  Epilepsy and similar conditions, failure to report, 39:3–10.8
  Examination permits, 39:3–13, 39:3–13.8
  Failure,
    Have or exhibit license, 39:3–29
    Notice of change of address of licensed operator, 39:3–36
    Produce license on demand of magistrate hearing complaint, 39:5–27
    Return license, suspended or revoked, 39:5–35
    Take license examination, 39:3–12
  False statements, 39:3–37
  Forfeiture of right to operate motor vehicle,
    Drug related convictions, 39:5–30.12 et seq.
    Drunken driving, 39:4–50
    Failure to have liability insurance, 39:6B–2
  Illegal securing, 39:3–12
  Implied consent,
    Blood analysis test refusal, suspension or revocation, 39:4–50.4a
    Chemical test, refusal, 39:4–50.4a
  Interstate compact, 39:5D–1 et seq.
  Minors driving under influence of alcohol, 39:4–50.14
  Motorized bicycle, 39:4–14.3
  Name changes, 39:3–9a
  Operating vehicle after refusal, suspension, or revocation of license, 2C:40–26, 39:3–40
  Points, 39:5–30.5 et seq.
  Possession by operator of motor vehicle required, 39:3–29
  Probationary licenses, 39:3–13.4, 39:3–13.8
  Second and subsequent offenses, 39:3–40
  Special learners permits, 39:3–13.2a, 39:3–13.8
  Surrender of foreign licenses, 39:3–10
  Suspension or revocation, generally, post
    Turnpike Law violation, 27:23–38
  Use, loan, 39:3–37.1
  Violations of conditions or restrictions, 39:3–11
Foreign countries, surrender, 39:3–10
Foreign states,
  Intoxication of driver, implied consent, prior convictions, effect, 39:4–50.4a
  Surrender, 39:3–10
Forfeitures,
  Hit and run, 39:4–129

DRIVERS LICENSES—Cont'd

Forfeitures—Cont'd

Right to operate motor vehicle, trucks used for transportation of solid waste, use for transportation of food, **48:13A–12.2**

Right to operate vehicle, littering, **39:4–63**

Fraud,

Children and minors, signatures,

Examination permit, **39:3–13**

Special learners permit, **39:3–13.3**

Identity or age verification, false documents, **2C:21–2.1**

Funds, driver education fund, reports, **39:3–13.6**

Graduated drivers license program, **39:3–10 et seq.**

Habitual offenders, **39:5–30a, 39:5–30b**

Handicapped persons, examination permits, **39:3–13**

Hearings,

Penalty points, suspension, **39:5–30.5 et seq.**

Suspension or revocation, **39:5–30**

Hit and run, license forfeiture, **39:4–129**

Homicide, compact, **39:5D–4**

Identification cards,

Anatomical gifts, donors, **39:3–12.2**

Nondrivers, **39:3–29.2 et seq.**

Identity and identification,

Examinations and examiners, **39:3–10**

Furnishing for misleading license application, **39:3–37**

Probationary licenses, **39:3–13.4**

Identity theft, **2C:21–17.2**

Intoxicating liquors, personal identifying information, obtaining, **2C:21–17.2**

Illegal securing, **39:3–12**

Imitations, crimes and offenses, **2C:21–2.1**

Immigration and naturalization, expiration, **39:3–10**

Indexing, applications for registration and drivers license, **39:3–28**

Indigent persons, traffic offenses, failure to pay fine on installment basis, **39:4–203.2**

Information, data processing, **39:2–3.8**

Initial licenses, color photographs, **39:3–10f**

Inspection and inspectors,

Complaint for violation of, Drivers School Law on information and belief, **39:12–13**

Exhibition on request, **39:3–17, 39:3–29**

Magistrate hearing complaint against driver under arrest, **39:5–27**

Physician stopped for speeding, **39:4–102**

Integrity, preservation, **39:3–10h**

Intentional misstatement of material fact in application, **39:3–37**

Interstate compact, **39:5D–1 et seq.**

Nonresident Violator Compact, **39:5F–1 et seq.**

Intoxicating liquors. Alcoholic beverages, generally, ante

Intoxication of driver. Motor Vehicles, this index

Joint and several liability, examination permits, **39:3–13**

Jury lists, preparation, **2B:20–2**

Juvenile delinquents, suspension or revocation,

False alarms, **2C:33–3.1**

Graffiti, **2A:4A–43.3**

Imitation license, **2C:21–2.1**

Postponement, **2A:4A–43**

Larceny, duplicates issued, **39:3–31**

Learners permit, **39:3–13 et seq.**

Children and minors, records and recordation, inspection, **39:3–13b**

Drivers manual, availability of copies, **39:3–41**

DRIVERS LICENSES—Cont'd

Learners permit—Cont'd

Examination permits, **39:3–10, 39:3–13**

Special learners permits, **39:3–13.1 et seq.**

Liability, examination permits, **39:3–13**

Littering, forfeiture of right to operate motor vehicle, **39:4–63**

Loan, use, crimes and offenses, **39:3–37.1**

Low speed vehicles, operation, **39:4–31.3**

Mail and mailing, probationary licenses, **39:3–13.4**

Manslaughter, compact, **39:5D–4**

Medical review, notice, confirmation, **39:3–10.33**

Military or naval service fee, **39:3–11.5**

Minors. Children and minors, generally, ante

Misrepresentation, imitation license, crimes and offenses, **2C:21–2.1**

Mobile phones,

Examination permits, **39:3–13**

Probationary licenses, **39:3–13.4**

Special learners permits, **39:3–13.2a**

Monitoring, new drivers, **39:3–13.6**

Motor Vehicle Security Responsibility Law, this index

Motorized bicycles, juvenile delinquents and dependents, suspension or revocation, false alarms, **2C:33–3.1**

Municipalities,

Motor vehicles owned by, **39:3–14**

Verification, electronic readers, **39:3–10f1**

New drivers, monitoring, **39:3–13.6**

New state residents, **39:3–17.1**

Nonalterable construction, **39:3–10h**

Nondrivers, identification cards, **39:3–29.2 et seq.**

Nonresidents,

Compact, **39:5F–1 et seq.**

New state residents, **39:3–17.1**

Temporary licenses, **39:3–10n**

Notice,

Proposed final suspension or revocation, **39:5–30**

Suspension hearings, penalty points, **39:5–30.5 et seq.**

Offenses. Crimes and offenses, generally, ante

Official drivers, **39:3–14**

Parking, suspension or revocation, fines and penalties, **39:3–40**

Passengers for hire, **39:3–10.1**

Penalties. Fines and penalties, generally, ante

Penalty points, **39:5–30.5 et seq.**

Personal information, data processing, **39:2–3.8**

Photo licenses, **39:3–10f**

Renewal license, option, **39:3–10f**

Photographic or micrographic copies of applications for evidence, **39:3–28**

Physical condition as ground for conditional or restricted license, **39:3–11**

Plastic surgery, color photographs, update, **39:3–10f**

Points, penalty points, **39:5–30.5 et seq.**

Possession by operator of motor vehicle required, **39:3–29**

Postponement, juvenile delinquents and dependents, **2A:4A–43**

Preliminary hearing, revocation or suspension, **39:5–30**

Preliminary suspension, license certificate or nonresident reciprocity privileges, **39:5–30**

Private driveways, definitions, **39:1–1**

Probationary licenses, **39:3–13.4**

Fines and penalties, **39:3–13.8**

Records and recordation, inspection, **39:3–13b**

Road test, **39:3–10**

DRIVERS LICENSES—Cont'd

Prostitution, suspension, **2C:34–1**

Reading deficiencies, written examinations, **39:3–13a**

Reciprocity, **39:3–17**

Penalty points, suspension or revocation of license, **39:5–30**

Suspension or revocation, **39:5–30, 39:5–30.1**

Penalty for subsequent operation, **39:3–40**

Reckless driving, suspension or revocation of license, death or serious bodily injury of another, **39:5–30**

Records and recordation, children and minors, inspection, **39:3–13b**

Reexamination,

Notice, confirmation, **39:3–10.33**

Two or more motor vehicle accidents, **39:3–10e**

Refusal of blood analysis test, suspension or revocation, **39:4–50.4a**

Refusal of license, **39:3–10, 39:3–40**

Registration of voters, applications, **39:2–3.2, 39:3–10m**

Remedial training,

Examination permits, **39:3–13**

Special learners permits, **39:3–13.2a**

Renewal,

Examination, **39:3–10c, 39:3–10d**

Optional photo license, **39:3–10f**

Reports,

Compact, **39:5D–13**

Epilepsy and similar conditions, **39:3–10.7**

Graduated drivers license program, **39:3–13.6**

Interstate compact, **39:5D–3**

Juvenile delinquents and dependents, revocation or suspension, imitation license, **2C:21–2.1**

Requirement for, **39:3–10**

Restoration,

Operation of motor vehicle without liability insurance, **39:6B–2**

Pending appeal, **39:5–22**

Restricted license, **39:3–11**

Revenues, motor vehicle commission, **39:3–10f5**

Revocation. Suspension or revocation, generally, post

Road test,

Probationary licenses, **39:3–10**

Scheduling, **39:3–13**

Rules and regulations, **39:3–10f3**

Graduated drivers license program, **39:3–13.7**

Sales, false documents, identity and identification, age, crimes and offenses, **2C:21–2.1**

School Buildings and Grounds, this index

School Buses, this index

Schools and school districts, driver education, special learners permit, **39:3–13.1**

Seat belts. Motor Vehicles, this index

Second or subsequent offenses,

Operating vehicle without license, fines and penalties, **2C:40–26, 39:3–40**

Penalty points, suspension, **39:5–30.10**

Serious bodily injury, suspension or revocation of license, **39:5–30**

Signatures, **39:3–9a**

Children and minors,

Examination permit, **39:3–13**

Special learners permits, **39:3–13.3**

Special control devices, conditions on issuance of drivers license, **39:3–11**

Special learners permits, **39:3–13.1**

Children and minors, parent or guardian, signature, **39:3–13.3**

DRIVERS LICENSES—Cont'd
Special learners permits—Cont'd
  Decals, **39:3–13.2a**
  Duration, **39:3–13.2a**
  Fines and penalties, **39:3–13.8**
Speeding, death or serious bodily injury of
  another, **39:5–30**
State owned vehicles operated exclusively for
  use of state, **39:3–14**
Supervision, special learners permits,
  39:3–13.2a
Surcharges, forfeiture of right to operate motor
  vehicle, drunken driving, **39:4–50**
Surrender,
  Foreign licenses, **39:3–10**
  Special certificates of official drivers, **39:3–14**
Suspension or revocation, **39:5–30**
  Abandonment of motor vehicle, **39:4–56.5**
  Alcoholic beverages, ante
  Application for another license during peri-
    od of prohibited, **39:3–34**
  Blood analysis, chemical test, refusal,
    39:4–50.4a
  Challenge of suspension, penalty points,
    39:5–30.8
  Chemical test, blood analysis, refusal,
    39:4–50.4a
  Compact, **39:5D–4**
  Controlled substances, **2C:35–16**
    Supervisory treatment, **2C:36A–1**
  Conviction, definitions, drug related convic-
    tions, **39:5–30.12**
  Crosswalks, yielding, **39:4–36**
  Death or serious bodily injury of another,
    2C:40–22
    Resulting from violation, **39:5–30**
  Driver improvement school, attendance, in
    lieu of, **39:5–30.2**
  Drivers schools, fees, failure to pay,
    39:5–30.4
  Drug offense, definitions, drug related con-
    victions, **39:5–30.12**
  Drug related convictions, **39:5–30.12 et seq.**
  Examination permits, **39:3–13**
  Extension, **39:3–40**
  False statements, **39:3–37**
  Fleeing law enforcement officers, **2C:29–2**
  Hearing, **39:5–30**
  Hours of Service Law violation, **39:9–4**
  Ignition interlock devices, **39:4–50.19**
    Reinstatement, **39:4–50.18**
  Implied consent,
    Blood analysis test refusal, **39:4–50.4a**
    Chemical test, refusal, **39:4–50.4a**
  Indigent persons, traffic offenses, failure to
    pay fines on installment basis,
    39:4–203.2
  Insolvency or bankruptcy of insurer, license
    of judgment debtor, **39:6–37**
  Insurance fraud, **39:6A–15**
  Interstate compact, **39:5D–1 et seq.**
  Intoxicating liquors, purchase or consump-
    tion by persons under legal age, **33:1–81**
  Intoxication of driver, **39:4–50**
    Extension, **39:3–40**
  Judgment for damages, failure to pay as
    ground, **39:6–35**
  Juvenile delinquents, ante
  Law regarding stopping when school bus
    stops for children, **39:4–128.1**
  Leaving scene of accident, death or serious
    bodily injury of another, **39:5–30**
  Magistrate, **39:5–31**
  Mail and mailing, notice, drug related con-
    victions, **39:5–30.14**

DRIVERS LICENSES—Cont'd
Suspension or revocation—Cont'd
  Minors,
    Drug related convictions, **39:5–30.13**
    Intoxication, **39:4–50**
  Motor Vehicle Security Responsibility Law
    violations, **39:6–55**
  Motor vehicles division director, **39:5–31**
  Motor vehicles security responsibility law,
    agreement to reimburse the unsatisfied
    claim and judgment fund, **39:6–25**
  Municipal courts, **Rule 7:8–9**
  New license, **39:5–33**
    After revocation, power to grant, **39:5–32**
  Notice,
    Drug related convictions, **39:5–30.14**
    Habitual offenders, **39:5–30b**
    Hearings, penalty points, **39:5–30.5 et seq.**
  Operation of vehicle,
    By holder of suspended or revoked license,
      appeal of conviction, representation
      of prosecution, **39:5–20**
    Fines and penalties, **2C:40–26**
    Prohibition, **39:3–40**
    Without liability insurance, **39:6B–2**
  Parking offenses, **39:4–139.10**
    Fees, **39:4–139.12**
    Restoration, **39:4–139.11**
  Penalty points, **39:5–30.5 et seq.**
  Person, definitions, drug related convictions,
    39:5–30.12
  Preliminary hearing, **39:5–30**
  Probationary licenses, **39:3–13.4**
  Prostitution, **2C:34–1**
  Reckless driving, death or serious bodily in-
    jury of another, **39:5–30**
  Reexamination, failure, **39:3–10e**
  Refusal of blood analysis test, **39:4–50.4a**
  Reinstatement, ignition interlock devices,
    39:4–50.18
  Report,
    Drug related convictions, **39:5–30.15**
    Resisting arrest or fleeing or eluding po-
      lice officers, **2C:29–2**
  Report on accident, violation of statute re-
    quiring, **39:4–130**
  Residents license after suspension or revoca-
    tion of reciprocity privilege in another
    state, **39:5–30.1**
  Residents privilege after suspension or revo-
    cation of reciprocity privilege in another
    state, **39:5–30.1**
  Resisting arrest, **2C:29–2**
  Restoration,
    Fee, **39:3–10a**
    Pending appeal, **39:5–22**
  Return of license on suspension, fine im-
    posed for nonperformance of duty,
    39:5–35
  Rules and regulations, drug related convic-
    tions, **39:5–30.16**
  Special learners permits, **39:3–13.2a**
  Speeding, death or serious bodily injury of
    another, **39:5–30**
  Validation of revoked license, **39:5–32**
  Vehicle used in crime, **2C:43–2**
  Vehicular homicide, **2C:11–5**
  Violation of motor vehicle or traffic laws,
    revocation by director or magistrate,
    39:5–31
  Willful violation of law as ground, **39:5–31**
Temporary licenses, **39:3–10n**
Temporary orders, license prohibition, **39:5–30**
Termination, official drivers, **39:3–14**
Tests. Examinations and examiners, generally,
  ante

DRIVERS LICENSES—Cont'd
Theft of identity, exceptions, **2C:21–17**
Three wheeled vehicles, **39:3–10**
Time,
  Examination permits, **39:3–13**
  Probationary licenses, **39:3–13.4**
  Special learners permits, **39:3–13.2a**
Trackless trolley, **39:3–10.1**
Uniform Anatomical Gift Act, designation as
  donor, **39:3–10, 39:3–12.2**
Unregistered vehicles, permits to cross public
  highways, operation of vehicle with license,
  39:3–26.3
Use, loan, crimes and offenses, **39:3–37.1**
Valid without photo license, **39:3–10f**
Validation,
  Examination permits, **39:3–19**
  Special learners permits, **39:3–13.2a**
Vehicular homicide, suspension or revocation,
  2C:11–5
Verification, electronic readers, law enforce-
  ment agencies, **39:3–10f1**
Victims of crime, mailing address, **39:3–4,**
  39:3–9c
Vision test, **39:3–10**
  Certification, **39:3–10c**
Waiver,
  Examination permits, **39:3–13**
  Examinations and examiners, nonresidents
    holding licenses, **39:3–10**
  Fees, examination permits, omnibus endorse-
    ments, **39:3–13**
  Omnibus or school bus endorsement,
    39:3–10
Withdrawal, compact, **39:5D–8**
Written examinations, reading deficiencies,
  39:3–13a

DRIVERS MANUAL
Anatomical Gift Act, information explaining
  provisions, **39:3–10**
Distribution, **39:3–41**

DRIVERS SCHOOLS
  Generally, **39:12–1 et seq.**
Attendance in lieu of suspension or revocation
  of license, **39:5–30.2**
Complaint on information and belief by motor
  vehicle inspector or member of state po-
  lice, **39:12–13**
Conviction of crime as ground for refusal to
  issue license, **39:12–3**
Crimes and offenses, **39:12–12**
  Seat belts, failure to use, **39:12–15**
Criminal history record information,
  Instructors, licenses and permits, background
    check, **39:12–5**
  Licenses and permits, background check,
    39:12–2
Definitions, **39:12–1**
Duplicate license, **39:12–2**
Effective date of act, **39:12–14**
Enforcement of act in accordance with Penalty
  Enforcement Law, **39:12–13**
False statements,
  Application for instructors license as grounds
    for denial, **39:12–6**
  Ground for denial of license, **39:12–3**
Fees, **39:5–30.4**
Fines and penalties,
  Enforcement in accordance with Penalty En-
    forcement Law, **39:12–13**
  Inspectors and inspection, **39:12–4.1**
  Seat belts, failure to use, **39:12–15**
  Violations, **39:12–12**

DRIVERS SCHOOLS—Cont'd
Inspectors and inspection, **39:12–4.1**
Records and recordation, **39:12–11**
Instructors, licenses and permits, **39:12–2,
39:12–5**
Criminal history record information, background check, **39:12–5**
Fee, **39:12–5**
Fraud as ground for revocation, **39:12–8**
Grounds for denial, **39:12–6, 39:12–8**
Licenses, motorcycle safety education program, **39:12–5**
Requirements, behind the wheel instruction, school teachers, **39:12–2.1**
Revocation or suspension, grounds, **39:12–8**
Insurance, licenses and permits, **39:12–2**
Insurance to meet damage claims, revocation or suspension of license for failure to maintain, **39:12–7**
Licenses and permits, **39:12–2**
Application, **39:12–2**
Accompanied by copy of standard liability policy, **39:12–3**
Denial, grounds, **39:12–3**
Conviction of crime as ground for, Refusal to issue, **39:12–3**
Revocation or suspension, **39:12–7**
Criminal history record information, background check, **39:12–2**
False statement, revocation or suspension, grounds, **39:12–7**
Hearing before denial or revocation, **39:12–10**
Instructors, ante
Insurance, **39:12–2**
Lists, **39:12–2.2**
Records, **39:12–11**
Renewal,
Fee, **39:12–2**
Revocation or suspension of renewed license, **39:12–9**
Revocation or suspension, **39:12–4.1**
Grounds, **39:12–7**
Hearing, **39:12–10**
Renewal, **39:12–9**
Lists, **39:12–2.2**
Municipal courts jurisdiction of proceedings for violations of act, **39:12–13**
Permits. Licenses and permits, generally, ante
Records required to be kept, **39:12–11**
Revocation or suspension. Licenses and permits, ante
Seat belts, use required, **39:12–15**
Special learners permit, **39:3–13.1**
Standard liability policy to accompany application for license, **39:12–3**
Standards, **39:12–4.1**
Violations of act, penalty, **39:12–12**

DRIVES AND DRIVEWAYS
Application of motor vehicle and traffic laws, **39:5A–1 et seq.**
Fire stations, parking within certain distance of driveway entrance prohibited, **39:4–138**
Motor vehicles and traffic laws applicable to driveways in parks, **39:5A–4**
Private driveways,
Application of motor vehicle and traffic laws, **39:5A–1 et seq.**
Definitions, **39:1–1**
Parking, **39:4–138.3 et seq.**
Parking in front prohibited, **39:4–138**
Right of way to pedestrian on sidewalk, **39:4–66.1**
Sidewalk in front of alley or passageway, driving vehicle or horse across, **39:4–71**

DRIVES AND DRIVEWAYS—Cont'd
Stopping vehicle emerging from, **39:4–66**

DRIVING UNDER THE INFLUENCE
Intoxication of driver. Motor Vehicles, this index

DRIVING WHILE INTOXICATED
Intoxication of driver. Motor Vehicles, this index

DROPPING
Bundle, object, from vehicle on highway, **39:4–64**

DRUG ABUSE
Attorneys, disability inactive status, **Rule 1:20–12**
Child abuse or neglect, regional diagnostic and treatment center, **9:6–8.102**
Convicted offenders, professional and occupational licenses, disqualification, **2A:168A–4**
Crimes and offenses,
Drug enforcement and demand reduction fund, **2C:35–15**
Sentence, change, **Rule 3:21–10**
Driving under influence, homicide, sentence and punishment, **2C:11–5**
Drug abuse education fund, fines and penalties,
Collection, **2C:46–4**
Deposits, **2C:43–3.5**
Nonpayment, **2C:46–2**
Payment, **2C:46–1**
Satisfaction, **2C:46–4.1**
Fines and penalties,
Drug abuse education fund, ante
Drug enforcement and demand reduction fund, **2C:35–15**
Treatment, probation and probation officers, **2C:35–14**
Fingerprinting addicts, **53:1–15**
Handguns, purchase permits, **2C:58–3**
Judicial notice, treatment, probation and probation officers, **2C:35–14**
Narcotic and drug abuse treatment centers, probation and probation officers, **2C:35–14**
Partnership for drug free New Jersey, funding, **2C:35–15**
Penalties. Fines and penalties, generally, ante
Photographing addicts, **53:1–15**
Prevention and control, drug enforcement and demand reduction fund, **2C:35–15**
Probation and probation officers, narcotic and drug abuse treatment centers, **2C:35–14**
Rehabilitated convicted offenders, professional and occupational licenses, disqualification, **2A:168A–4**
Rehabilitation programs, **2C:35–14**
Reports,
Controlled substances, **24:21–39**
Drug dependent persons, **24:21–39**
Treatment, abused or neglected children, reuniting with parent, **9:6–8.58a, 9:6–8.58b**
Vessel, operating under influence, homicide, sentence and punishment, **2C:11–5**

DRUG ABUSE EDUCATION FUND
Drug Abuse, this index

DRUG ADDICTS
Drug Abuse, generally, this index

DRUG DEALER LIABILITY ACT
Generally, **2C:35B–1 et seq.**

DRUG DEPENDENT PERSONS
Definitions, controlled dangerous substances, **24:21–2**
Drug Abuse, generally, this index

DRUG ENFORCEMENT ADMINISTRATION (UNITED STATES)
Arrests, violation of state laws, special agents, **2A:154–5**

DRUG ENFORCEMENT AND DEMAND REDUCTION FUND
Generally, **2C:35–15**
Payment of penalty, **2C:46–1**
Transaction fee, **2C:46–1 et seq.**

DRUG INSPECTORS
Administrative inspection warrants, **24:21–31, 24:21–32**
Controlled substances, **24:21–32**

DRUG OR ALCOHOL DEPENDENT PERSONS
Definitions, controlled dangerous substances, **2C:35–2**

DRUG STORES
Pharmacists, generally, this index

DRUGGISTS
Pharmacists, generally, this index

DRUGS AND MEDICINE
Abuse of drugs. Drug Abuse, generally, this index
Addicts. Drug Abuse, generally, this index
Advertisements, paraphernalia, **2C:36–4**
Alcohol in preparations unfit for beverage purposes, **33:1–30**
Alcoholic beverages, use by druggists and hospitals, **33:1–29**
Amphetamine, phenylalanine, possession, manufacturing, **2C:35–28**
Anhydrous ammonia,
Possession, methamphetamine, manufacturing, **2C:35–28**
Theft, methamphetamine, manufacturing, **2C:20–2**
Appeals, controlled substances, **24:21–38**
Being under influence of controlled dangerous substances, **2C:35–10**
Brands, labels and marks,
Alteration or removal, **24:21–17**
Removal, alteration, offenses, **24:21–21**
Certificates and certification, laboratories, controlled dangerous substances, **2C:35–19, 2C:35–20**
Chemical names, controlled substances, schedules, **24:21–4 et seq.**
Children and minors, forensic laboratory fees, **2C:35–20**
Classification, controlled substances, **24:21–5 et seq.**
Containers, controlled substances, **24:21–16 et seq.**
Controlled Substances, generally, this index
Costs, rehabilitation or treatment programs, drug dependent persons, **2C:35–14**
Crimes and offenses,
Ephedrine, pseudoephedrine, phenylpropanolamine, **2C:35–25**
Packages, writings, **2C:40–19**
Precursors, possession, **2C:35–28**
Tampering with, **2C:40–16, 2C:40–17**
Unlawful practice, **2C:21–21**
Definitions, **24:21–32**
Controlled substances, **2C:35–2, 24:21–2**

DRUGS AND MEDICINE—Cont'd

Definitions—Cont'd

Dangerous drugs, substances or compounds, Controlled Dangerous Substances Registry Act of 1970, **53:1–18.5**

Ephedrine, pseudoephedrine, phenylpropanolamine, **2C:35–25**

Profits, **2C:35A–3**

Delivery vehicles, commercial motor vehicles, license plates, exceptions, **39:4–46**

Dependent or neglected children, drug dependent parent, juvenile family crisis, **2A:4A–85**

Depressant or stimulant drugs, **53:1–18.1 et seq.**

Destruction, controlled substances, **2C:35–21**

Devices, **24:21–32**

Disorderly persons,

Prescription legend drugs, **2C:35–10.5**

Stramonium, **2C:35–10.5**

Distribution. Controlled Substances, this index

Drug Abuse, generally, this index

Drug addicts. Drug Abuse, generally, this index

Enforcement of law, controlled substances, **24:21–31**

Evidence, ephedrine, pseudoephedrine, phenylpropanolamine, **2C:35–27**

Explosives, handling while under the influence, **21:1A–132**

Failure to make lawful disposition, **2C:35–10**

Fines and penalties,

Drivers under influence,

Hallucinogenic drugs, **39:4–50**

Victims of crime compensation board, **2C:43–3.1**

Intoxication of driver, **39:4–50**

Knowingly possessing while operating motor vehicle, **39:4–49.1**

Fireworks, manufacturers and manufacturing, entry, **21:2–17**

Forms,

Label, controlled dangerous substances, **24:21–17**

Order forms, controlled dangerous substances, **24:21–14**

Hypodermic Needles or Syringes, generally, this index

Interchangeable drug products, controlled substances, labels, **24:21–17**

Intoxication, basis for criminal liability, **2C:2–8**

Intoxication of driver. Motor Vehicles, this index

Labor and employment, lie detector tests, **2C:40A–1**

Laboratories, this index

Manufacturers and manufacturing, definitions, controlled substances, **24:21–2**

Misdemeanors. Crimes and offenses, generally, ante

Motor Vehicles, this index

Nonnarcotic substance, exclusion from schedules, **24:21–3**

Offenses. Crimes and offenses, generally, ante

Packages, writings, crimes and offenses, **2C:40–19**

Pharmacists, generally, this index

Phenylalanine, methamphetamine, possession, manufacturing, **2C:35–28**

Physicians and Surgeons, this index

Poisons, generally, this index

Possession,

Ephedrine, pseudoephedrine, phenylpropanolamine, **2C:35–27**

Precursors, crimes and offenses, **2C:35–28**

DRUGS AND MEDICINE—Cont'd

Precursors, crimes and offenses, possession, **2C:35–28**

Prescriptions, generally, this index

Sales,

Ephedrine, limitations, **2C:35–25**

Phenylpropanolamine, limitations, **2C:35–25**

Prescriptions, generally, this index

Pseudoephedrine, limitations, **2C:35–25**

Scheduled substances, **24:21–1 et seq.**

Tampering with, **2C:40–16, 2C:40–17**

Trademarks and trade names, scheduled substances, **24:21–4**

Trafficking network, leadership, indictment, **Rule 3:7–3**

DRUNK DRIVING ENFORCEMENT FUND

Generally, **39:4–50.8**

DRUNK DRIVING VICTIMS BILL OF RIGHTS

Generally, **39:4–50.9 et seq.**

DRUNKARDS AND DRUNKENNESS

Alcoholics and Alcoholism, generally, this index

DUE PROCESS

Child abuse or neglect, institutional employees, **9:6–3.1**

First appearance, indictment, **Rule 3:4–2**

DUM DUM BULLETS

Person convicted of crime involving, possession of any weapon prohibited, **2C:39–7**

Prohibited weapons, **2C:39–3**

DUMP TRUCK TRAILERS AND SEMI-TRAILERS

Axle weight limitations, **39:3–84.1**

Lamps and reflectors, **39:3–61**

DUMPS

Solid Waste, generally, this index

DUPLICATES

Motor vehicle registration certificate, **39:3–31.1**

Motorized bicycles, registration certificates, **39:3–31, 39:3–31.1**

DURESS OR COERCION

See, also, Intimidation, generally, this index

Generally, **2C:2–9, 2C:13–5**

Bias intimidation, crimes and offenses, **2C:16–1**

Consent, victim of crime, **2C:2–10**

Criminal liability, **2C:2–9**

Criminal sexual contact, **2C:14–3**

Defenses, notice, **Rule 3:12–1**

Definitions, sexual offenses, **2C:14–1**

Human trafficking, **2C:13–8**

Kidnapping, generally, this index

Sexual assault, **2C:14–2**

Street gangs, soliciting, **2C:33–28**

DWELLINGS

Housing, generally, this index

DYNAMITE

Explosives, generally, this index

EARNINGS

Compensation and Salaries, generally, this index

Definitions, wrongful discharge, **2C:40A–3**

EATING PLACES

Restaurants, generally, this index

EAVESDROPPING

Search warrant based on wiretap, filing, **Rule 3:5–6**

Wiretapping and electronic surveillance, **2A:156A–1 et seq.**

ECOLOGY

Environmental Protection, generally, this index

ECONOMIC LOSS

Definitions, no fault insurance, **39:6A–2**

EDUCATION

Alcoholic Beverages, this index

Anatomical gifts, organ and tissue donor awareness education fund, **39:3–12.3**

Attorneys, advertising, **Rule 1:19A–2**

Behind the wheel automobile driving, special learners permits, **39:3–13.1 et seq.**

Colleges and Universities, generally, this index

Convicted offenders, rehabilitation, return to profession or occupation, **2A:168A–5**

Crimes and offenses, **2C:43–2**

Suspended sentence, **2C:45–1**

Drug abuse education fund. Drug Abuse, this index

Juvenile delinquents and dependents, out of door sales, **Rule 5:18–3**

Libraries, generally, this index

Liquefied petroleum gas education and safety board, **21:1B–12 et seq.**

Organ and tissue donor awareness education fund, **39:3–12.3**

Private Schools, generally, this index

Probation, conditions, **2C:45–1**

Rehabilitated convicted offenders, return to profession or occupation, **2A:168A–5**

Schools and School Districts, generally, this index

Vocational Education, generally, this index

EDUCATION DEPARTMENT

Colleges and Universities, generally, this index

Commissioner. School Buildings and Grounds, generally, this index

EDUCATIONAL CORPORATIONS AND AS-SOCIATIONS

See, also, Colleges and Universities, generally, this index

Intoxicating liquors, temporary permits, fees, **33:1–74**

Private Schools, generally, this index

ELDERLY PERSONS

Aged Persons, generally, this index

ELECTIONS

Bribery and Corruption, this index

Candidates, judges and other court personnel, limitations or prohibitions, **Rule 1:17–1**

Conviction of crime, **2C:51–3**

County Prosecutors, this index

Disclosure, vote, **2A:84A–25**

Electronic voting system, legislative, public bodies, **2A:149–1**

Hearsay exception, voter statements, **Evidence Rule 804**

Judges and other court personnel, **Rule 1:17–1**

Libraries, generally, this index

Motor vehicle commission, vice chair, board, **39:2A–14**

Restoration of rights by governor, **2A:167–5**

State police, assignment of troopers to enforce election laws, **53:2–1**

Threats, **2C:27–3**

Vacancies In Office, generally, this index

ELECTIONS—Cont'd
Witnesses,
Compelling disclosure of vote, **2A:84A–25**
Privilege, **Evidence Rule 513**

ELECTRIC PERSONAL ASSISTIVE MOBILITY DEVICES
Generally, **39:4–14.10**
Fines and penalties, **39:4–14.11**
Notice, warnings, **39:4–10.8**

ELECTRIC PLANTS
Electricity and Electric Companies, generally, this index

ELECTRIC RAILROADS
Street Railways, generally, this index

ELECTRIC SIGNS
Signs, generally, this index

ELECTRIC WIRES
Change or repair, movement of heavy machinery, highway, **39:4–28**
Turnpike authority, use of right of way, **27:23–9**

ELECTRICAL CONTRACTORS
Crimes and offenses, unlicensed persons, **2C:21–33**
Licenses and permits, crimes and offenses, unlicensed persons, **2C:21–33**

ELECTRICITY AND ELECTRIC COMPANIES
Burglary, facilities, **2C:18–2**
Computers, interference, crimes and offenses, **2C:20–25**
Crimes and offenses,
Criminal mischief, **2C:17–3**
Facilities, burglary, **2C:18–2**
Unlicensed entry of structure, generation, facilities, **2C:18–3**
Explosives, magazines, **21:1A–136**
Facilities, burglary, **2C:18–2**
Generation, facilities, unlicensed entry of structure, crimes and offenses, **2C:18–3**
Monopolies, exemptions, **56:9–5**
Nuclear electricity generating facility,
Radiation Protection, generally, this index
Security guards, weapons, possession, **2C:39–6**
Unlicensed entry of structure, crimes and offenses, **2C:18–3**
Vandalism, crimes and offenses, **2C:17–7 et seq.**
Weapons, security guards, possession, **2C:39–6**
Nuclear power plants. Radiation Protection, generally, this index
Radiation Protection, generally, this index
Railroads. Street Railways, generally, this index
Street Railways, generally, this index
Theft of services, **2C:20–8**
Trespass, unlicensed entry of structure, facilities, crimes and offenses, **2C:18–3**
Turnpike authority, use of right of way, **27:23–9**
Unlicensed entry of structure, facilities, crimes and offenses, **2C:18–3**

ELECTRONIC, MECHANICAL OR OTHER DEVICE
Definitions, wiretapping and electronic surveillance, **2A:156A–2**

ELECTRONIC COMMUNICATIONS
Electronic Transactions, generally, this index

ELECTRONIC DATA PROCESSING
Electronic Transactions, generally, this index

ELECTRONIC DEVICES
Jurors, public and random selection, qualifications and selection, **2B:20–4**
Petit jurors, selection, **2B:23–2**
Theft of services, **2C:20–8**

ELECTRONIC FILING
Electronic Transactions, generally, this index
Filing, this index

ELECTRONIC FUND TRANSFERS
Crimes and offenses, fraud, payment cards, scanning, **2C:21–6.1**
Fraud, payment cards, scanning, **2C:21–6.1**
Motor vehicle commission, payment, **39:2A–20**
Municipal courts, court fees and financial obligations, **Rule 7:14–4**
Records and recordation, payment cards, fraud, scanning, **2C:21–6.1**
Reencoders, payment cards, fraud, **2C:21–6.1**
Scanning, payment cards, fraud, **2C:21–6.1**

ELECTRONIC RETENTION
Court records, **Rule 1:32–2**

ELECTRONIC STORAGE
Definitions, wiretapping and electronic surveillance, **2A:156A–2**

ELECTRONIC SURVEILLANCE
Generally, **2A:156A–1 et seq.**

ELECTRONIC TRANSACTIONS
Computer programs,
Copies, crimes and offenses, **2C:20–33**
Jurors, random and public selection, **2B:20–4**
Computer related offenses, **2C:20–25**
Corrections computerized collection fund, **2C:46–1.1**
Courts computerized collection fund, **2C:46–1.1**
Crimes and offenses, **2C:20–23 et seq.**
Definitions, wiretapping and electronic surveillance, **2A:156A–2**
Destruction, **2C:20–23 et seq.**
Drivers licenses, **39:2–3.8**
Electronic Fund Transfers, generally, this index
Funds transfers. Electronic Fund Transfers, generally, this index
Interception of data, **2C:20–23 et seq.**
Motor vehicle commission, payment, **39:2A–20**
Motor vehicles,
Devices, **39:4–97.3 et seq.**
Licenses and permits, **39:2–3.8**
Software, copies, crimes and offenses, **2C:20–33**
Theft, **2C:20–23 et seq.**
Value of property or services, computer related offenses, **2C:20–24**

ELECTRONIC TRANSMISSIONS
Electronic Transactions, generally, this index

ELECTRONIC VOTING SYSTEMS
Legislative or public bodies, **2A:149–1**

ELEEMOSYNARY INSTITUTIONS
Charitable Organizations and Associations, generally, this index

ELEMENTARY SCHOOLS
Schools and School Districts, generally, this index

ELIGIBLE
Definitions, intoxicating liquor law, **33:1–1**

ELIGIBLE HANDICAPPED PERSON
Definitions, handicapped parking, **39:4–207.6**

ELLIS ISLAND
Park police, power to arrest, **2A:154–6**

EMBEZZLEMENT
Generally, **2C:20–2**
Attorneys,
Conviction, discipline, **Rule 1:20–13**
Lawyers fund for client protection, **Rule 1:28–1 et seq.**
Prepaid funeral agreements, advance funeral payments, **2A:102–13 et seq.**
Definitions, **2A:102–18**
Exceptions, cemetery lots or graves, **2A:102–17**
Insurance policies funding prepaid funeral agreements, inapplicability of provisions, **2A:102–17**
Invalid agreements, **2A:102–15**
Irrevocable prepaid funeral trusts,
Beneficiary or grantor, **2A:102–16.1**
Solicitation or overcharge, **2A:102–16.2**
Presumptions, knowledge of obligations, **2A:102–16**
Repayment on demand, **2A:102–14**
Solicitation, misrepresentation, **2A:102–16.2**
Violations, theft, **2A:102–16**
Venue, trial, **Rule 3:14–1**

EMBLEMS
Badges, Emblems and Insignia, generally, this index

EMBRACERY
Expungement of record, **2C:52–2**

EMERGENCIES
Alarms, false alarms, **2C:33–3 et seq.**
Attorneys, temporary practice of law, foreign states, **Rule 1:21–10**
Child Abuse, this index
Children and Minors, this index
Crimes and offenses, threats, aggravating factors, **2C:12–3**
Declarations of emergency, threats, aggravating factors, **2C:12–3**
Definitions, **39:3–11.5**
False public alarms, **2C:33–3 et seq.**
Hours of duty of certain drivers, extension, **39:9–2**
Motor vehicle, dimensional and weight limitations, exceptions, **39:3–84**
Municipalities, this index
Physicians and Surgeons, this index
Rescue Squads, generally, this index
School buses, drivers, cellular phones, **39:3B–25**
State of emergency, threats, aggravating factors, **2C:12–3**
Telecommunications, this index
Telephone party line, failure to relinquish in case of emergency, **2C:40–2**
Telephone service, child abuse reports, **9:6–8.12**
Terrorism, generally, this index
Threats, aggravating factors, **2C:12–3**
Traffic congestion, authority for moving traffic, **39:4–213 et seq.**
Turnpike authority, contracts, bids, **27:23–6.1**
Volunteers, motor vehicles, warning lights, **39:3–54.7**
Applications, **39:3–54.22, 39:3–54.23**

EMERGENCY CALLS
Definitions, telephone party line, refusal to yield, **2C:40–2**

EMERGENCY MEDICAL SERVICES
Assault on emergency personnel, 2C:12–1
Motor vehicles, radio, interception of police,
    fire or emergency medical communication,
    used to commit crime, 2C:33–21 et seq.
Radio and radio stations,
    Definition of police, fire or emergency medi-
        cal communication system excluding ra-
        dar, 2C:33–23
    Interception of message, crimes and of-
        fenses, 2C:33–21 et seq.
    Possession of radio receiving police, message
        during commission of crime, fourth de-
        gree crime, 2C:33–22

**EMERGENCY MEDICAL TECHNICIAN
    TRAINING FUND**
Court cost assessments, motor vehicle, traffic
    violations, deposit, 2B:12–31
Deposits, 2B:12–31
Traffic fines, collection, payment into Fund,
    39:5–41

EMERGENCY SERVICES
Definitions, false alarms, fines and penalties,
    2C:33–3.2

EMERGENCY SERVICES PERSONNEL
Aggravated assault, 2C:12–1
Assault, 2C:12–1
Definitions, aggravated assault, 2C:12–1

EMERGENCY SQUADS
Motor vehicles, registration fees, exemption,
    39:3–27

EMERGENCY STOPPING SYSTEM
Motor carriers, 39:3–68.1 et seq.

EMERGENCY VEHICLES
Ambulances, generally, this index
Approaching, stationary vehicles, 39:4–92.2
Brands, marks and labels, removal, sales,
    39:10–9.4
Cellular telephones, operators, hands free tele-
    phones, application of law, motor vehicles,
    39:4–97.4
Clearance for, 39:4–92
Commercial drivers licenses, exemption,
    39:3–10j
Crimes and offenses, sales, removal, brands,
    marks and labels, 39:10–9.4
Definition, authorized emergency vehicles,
    39:1–1
Destruction of agricultural or recreational
    property by operation of vehicle, excep-
    tion, 39:4–97a
Drivers, privileges and immunities, 39:4–91
Exemption, commercial drivers license require-
    ment, 39:3–10j
Fire Engines, Apparatus and Equipment, gen-
    erally, this index
Flashing lights, volunteers, 39:3–54.7 et seq.
Following emergency vehicles, 39:4–92
Hands free telephones, operators, application
    of law, 39:4–97.4
Lights and lighting,
    Color, 39:3–50
    Flashing lights, volunteers, 39:3–54.7 et seq.
    Identification cards, permits for use and dis-
        play, 39:3–54.11
Operators, hands free telephones, application
    of law, 39:4–97.4
Privileges and immunities, drivers, 39:4–91
Processions, 39:4–93
Removal, brands, marks and labels, sales,
    39:10–9.4

EMERGENCY VEHICLES—Cont'd
Rescue Squads, generally, this index
Right of way, 39:4–91
    Procession, 39:4–93
Sales, removal, brands, marks and labels,
    39:10–9.4
Sirens, whistles, or bells, 39:3–69
Stationary vehicles, approaching, 39:4–92.2
Telecommunications, hands free telephones,
    operators, application of law, 39:4–97.4
Traffic Rules and Regulations, this index
Turnpikes, tolls, 27:23–40
Warning lights,
    Equipment, commercial motor vehicles,
        39:3–64
    Volunteers, 39:3–54.7 et seq.
Wireless telephones, operators, hands free tele-
    phones, application of law, motor vehicles,
    39:4–97.4

EMINENT DOMAIN
Declaration of taking, turnpike authority, filing,
    27:23–5
Intoxicating liquor distributors license, renewal,
    33:1–11.6
Transportation Department, this index
Turnpike authority, power to exercise, 27:23–5
Turnpikes, 27:23–5

EMISSIONS
Motor Vehicles, this index

EMOTIONAL CONDITION
Hearsay exception, then existing condition, Evi-
    dence Rule 803

EMPLOYEE WELFARE TRUST FUNDS
Officers and employees, commercial bribery
    and breach of duty, 2C:21–10

EMPLOYEES
Labor and Employment, generally, this index
Officers and Employees, generally, this index

EMPLOYERS
Labor and Employment, generally, this index

EMPLOYMENT
Labor and Employment, generally, this index

ENCODED MESSAGES
Wiretapping and electronic surveillance,
    2A:156A–12

ENCUMBRANCES
Liens and Incumbrances, generally, this index

ENDANGERING WELFARE OF CHILDREN
    Generally, 2C:24–4
Community notification. Sex Offenses, this in-
    dex
Crimes and offenses, wiretapping and electron-
    ic surveillance, orders permitting,
    2A:156A–8
Evidence, previous sexual conduct of victim,
    2C:14–7
Extended term of imprisonment, 2C:43–7
Limitation of prosecution, 2C:1–6
Offenders, registration. Sex Offenses, this in-
    dex
Parole supervision for life, special sentence,
    Violent Predator Incapacitation Act of
    1994, 2C:43–6.4
Persons convicted of, possession of weapons,
    prohibition, 2C:39–7
Records and recordation, expungement,
    2C:52–2

ENDANGERING WELFARE OF CHILDREN
    —Cont'd
Sexual assault, limitation of criminal prosecu-
    tion, 2C:1–6

ENERGY
Electricity and Electric Companies, generally,
    this index

ENGINEERS
Solid waste, design of facilities, compliance
    with regulations, 13:1E–9
Traffic regulations, counties or municipalities,
    39:4–8

ENGINES
Motor Vehicles, this index

ENGLISH LANGUAGE
Jurors, ability to read and understand, qualifi-
    cations and selection, 2B:20–1
Publication, notice of intention to apply for
    alcoholic beverage license, 33:1–25

ENTERPRISE
Definitions,
    Racketeering, 2C:41–1
    Theft, 2C:20–1

ENTERTAINMENT
Definitions, intoxicating liquor law, 33:1–1
Intoxicating liquor law, 33:1–12
Jury, corrupting or influencing, 2C:29–8
Lewdness and Obscenity, generally, this index
Restaurants, generally, this index

ENTITLING PROCEEDINGS
Name of state with director, inspector, prosecu-
    tor, 39:5–5

ENTRAPMENT
    Generally, 2C:2–12
Crimes and offenses, defenses, notice, Rule
    3:12–1

ENTRY ON LAND OR WATERS
Controlled Substances, this index
Limousine or livery service, inspection and in-
    spectors, 39:5G–1
Narcotics and dangerous substances, controlled
    dangerous substances, 24:21–32
Unlicensed entry of structures, 2C:18–3

ENVIRONMENTAL IMPACT STATEMENTS
Impact statements. Environmental Protection,
    this index

ENVIRONMENTAL PROTECTION
Adopt a beach program. Beaches and Beach
    Fronts, this index
Air Pollution, generally, this index
All terrain vehicles, rules and regulations,
    39:3C–14
Coastal protection license plate program,
    39:3–27.47 et seq.
Dirt bikes, 39:3C–14
Hazardous Substances and Waste, generally,
    this index
Impact statements, New Jersey turnpike exten-
    sion, 27:23–23.3 et seq.
Liberty State Park license plate fund,
    39:3–27.94
Liquefied petroleum gas education and safety
    board, 21:1B–12 et seq.
New Jersey turnpike extension, impact state-
    ments, 27:23–23.3 et seq.

ENVIRONMENTAL PROTECTION—Cont'd
Nuclear energy. Radiation Protection, generally, this index
Radiation Protection, generally, this index
Snowmobiles, rules and regulations, **39:3C–14**
Water Pollution, generally, this index

ENVIRONMENTAL PROTECTION DEPARTMENT
Air Pollution, generally, this index
Appropriations, coastal protection license plate program, **39:3–27.52**
Coastal protection license plate program, **39:3–27.47 et seq.**
Commissioner, guidelines, environmental impact, New Jersey turnpike extension, **27:23–23.5**
Environmental Protection, generally, this index
Fish and wildlife division, wildlife conservation fund, establishment, monies from wildlife conservation license plate fees, **39:3–33.10**
Marine mammal stranding center fund, establishment, **39:3–33.11**
Funds, shade tree and community forest preservation license plate fund, establishment, deposits into, uses, **39:3–27.81**
Hazardous Substances and Waste, generally, this index
Injunction, air pollution code, rule or regulation, violation, air pollution control, **26:2C–19**
Interagency memorandum of agreement, coastal protection license plate program, **39:3–27.54**
Motor Vehicles, generally, this index
Parks and forestry division, shade tree and community forest preservation license plate fund, administration of fund, **39:3–27.81**
Rules and regulations, trucks used for transportation of solid waste, use for transportation of food, cleansing and sanitizing, **48:13A–12.1**
Solid Waste, generally, this index
Turnpike authority, roadside areas and facilities, **27:23–45, 27:23–46**
Water Pollution, generally, this index

ENVIRONMENTAL RIGHTS ACT
Environmental Protection, generally, this index

EPHEDRINE
Losses, reports, **2C:35–26**
Possession,
Evidence, **2C:35–27**
Precursors, **2C:35–28**
Sales, limitations, **2C:35–25**

EPILEPSY
Discrimination, generally, this index
Drivers licenses, applicant, **39:3–10.4 et seq.**

EQUESTRIANS
Horses, generally, this index

EQUINE
Horses, generally, this index

EQUIPMENT
Machinery and Equipment, generally, this index

ERRORS AND OMISSIONS
Clerical mistakes, correction, **Rule 1:13–1**
Crimes and offenses, defenses, notice, **Rule 3:12–1**

ERRORS AND OMISSIONS—Cont'd
Privileges and immunities, overruling of claim, **Evidence Rule 533**
Trial, notice, **Rule 1:7–5**

ESCAPES
Generally, **2C:29–5**
Accomplices and accessories, sentence and punishment, **2C:29–6**
Aggravated criminal sexual contact, **2C:14–3**
Aggravated sexual assault, **2C:14–2**
Aiding escape, **2C:29–3**
Attempts, body vests, **2C:39–13**
Body vests, **2C:39–13**
Custody under interstate agreement on detainers, **2A:159A–5**
Defenses, **2C:29–5**
Detainers,
Escape from custody under, **2A:159A–13**
Interstate agreement on, effect of escape, **2A:159A–4**
Escape implements, third person furnishing, **2C:29–6**
Extradition, generally, this index
Force or violence,
Grand jury, instructions to jury, **2B:22–9**
Use to prevent, **2C:3–7**
Fresh Pursuit Law, generally, this index
Implements, third person furnishing, **2C:29–6**
Knowingly or recklessly permitting, **2C:29–5**
Murder, **2C:11–3**
Recklessly permitting, **2C:29–5**
Reward for apprehension of escaped county prisoners, **2A:153–3**
Weapons, **2C:29–6**
Mandatory sentence, **2C:43–6**
Persons convicted of, possession, **2C:39–7**
Wiretapping and electronic surveillance, **2A:156A–1 et seq.**

ESSENTIAL SERVICES
Definitions, no fault insurance, **39:6A–2**

ESTATES
Decedents estates. Probate Proceedings, generally, this index
Forfeiture on conviction of crime, **2A:152–2**
Probate Proceedings, generally, this index

ESTATES OF DECEDENTS
Probate Proceedings, generally, this index

ESTIMATES
Motor vehicles, body repair facilities, fines or license refusal, revocation or suspension, **39:13–4**

ESTOPPEL
Theft, final judgments, **2C:20–22**

ETHCHLOROVYNOL
Controlled substances, **24:21–1 et seq.**

ETHER
Poisons, this index

ETHICS
Attorneys, this index
Confidential or privileged information, **Rule 1:38–5**
Judges, duty to enforce, **Rule 1:18**

ETHINAMATE
Controlled dangerous substance, **24:21–1 et seq.**

ETHNICITY
Discrimination, generally, this index

ETHYLMETHYLTHIAMBUTENE
Controlled dangerous substance, **24:21–1 et seq.**

ETHYLMORPHINE
Controlled dangerous substance, **24:21–1 et seq.**
Poisons, generally, this index

ETONITAZENE
Controlled dangerous substance, **24:21–1 et seq.**

ETORPHINE
Controlled dangerous substance, **24:21–1 et seq.**

ETOXERIDINE
Controlled substances, **24:21–1 et seq.**

EUTHANASIA
Cruelty to animals, offenses, **4:22–19**

EVALUATION
Supervisory treatment programs, first offenders, **2C:43–21**

EVASION
Revocation of alcoholic beverage license on ground of, **33:1–25**

EVICTION
Crimes and offenses, disorderly persons, **2C:33–11.1**
Criminal mischief, **2C:17–3**
Disorderly persons, crimes and offenses, **2C:33–11.1**
Fines and penalties, criminal mischief, **2C:17–3**

EVIDENCE
See, also, Witnesses, generally, this index
Generally, **Evidence Rule 101 et seq.**
Accomplice conviction, **2C:2–6**
Accomplices, **2C:2–6**
Administrative Law and Procedure, generally, this index
Admissibility, **2A:84A–32 et seq., 2A:84A–44; Evidence Rule 104**
Admissions. Rules of evidence, post
Aggravated criminal sexual contact, children and minors, closed circuit testimony, **2A:84A–32.4**
Aggravated sexual assault, children and minors, closed circuit testimony, **2A:84A–32.4**
Alcoholic Beverages, this index
Appeal and review,
Abuse of children, closed circuit testimony, **2A:84A–32.4**
Pending direct appeal and proceedings on certification, preservation of evidence, **Rule 1:2–3**
Wiretapping and electronic surveillance, computers, trespass, **2A:156A–4.1**
Application of law, **Evidence Rule 101**
Attorney client privilege, **2A:84A–20**
Authentication, **Evidence Rule 901**
Copies of, documents executed or filed by director of motor vehicles division, **39:2–10**
Subscribing witness testimony, **Evidence Rule 903**
Bail, jumping, **2C:29–7**
Best evidence, original writings, **Evidence Rule 1001 et seq.**

EVIDENCE—Cont'd

Bias intimidation, **2C:16–1**
   Crimes and offenses, **2C:16–1**
Body cavity search, obtained by, **2A:161A–10**
Bribery and corruption, public resources, **2C:27–12**
Burden of Proof, generally, this index
Business records, copies, **Rule 1:7–6**
Certificates of rehabilitation, employing rehabilitated convicted offenders, **2A:168A–3**
Certified copies, drivers licenses, applications, **39:3–28**
Character for truthfulness or untruthfulness, witnesses, **Evidence Rule 608**
Character of party, **Evidence Rule 404**
   Methods of proving, **Evidence Rule 405**
Chemicals, chemistry and chemists, industrial chemicals, **2C:35–29**
Child Abuse, this index
Child support hearing officers, **Rule 5:25–3**
Children and minors,
   Sexual abuse, closed circuit testimony, **2A:84A–32.4**
   Sexual offenses, hearsay statements, **Evidence Rule 803**
Choice of law, presumptions, **Evidence Rule 302**
Cleric penitent privilege, **2A:84A–23**
Closed circuit testimony, abuse of children, **2A:84A–32.4**
Coercion, providing or withholding evidence, **2C:13–5**
Competency of witnesses, **Evidence Rule 601**
Compromise and settlement, offers and negotiations, **Evidence Rule 408**
Confessions, joint defendants, notice of use, **Rule 3:15–2**
Confidential or Privileged Information, generally, this index
Confusing, exclusion, **Evidence Rule 403**
Conspiracy, **2C:5–2**
Construction, **Evidence Rule 102**
Controlled Substances, this index
Convicted offenders, rehabilitation, **2A:168A–3**
Conviction of crime, **2C:51–1**
   Character evidence, **Evidence Rule 405**
   Impeaching credibility of witness, **Evidence Rule 609**
   Rehabilitation, **2A:168A–9**
Copies of records, **Evidence Rule 68**
   Nonpublic business records, **Rule 1:7–6**
Court records, electronic or photographic copies, **Rule 1:32–2**
Criminal prosecutions, **2C:1–13**
Criminal sexual contact, children and minors, closed circuit testimony, **2A:84A–32.4**
Cross examination, scope, **Evidence Rule 611**
Custody of children, interference with, age, **2C:13–4**
Defendants statements, preliminary hearing on admissibility, **Evidence Rule 104**
Defense, clear and convincing, **2C:2–4**
Depositions, generally, this index
Destruction,
   Documentary exhibits, notice, **2C:65–4**
   Hindering apprehension or prosecution, **2C:29–3**
Director of division of motor vehicles, power to take testimony on suspension or revocation of license, **39:10–20**
Disclosure, wrongfully compelled, **2A:84A–30**
Discovery, generally, this index
DNA database and databank, motions, **2A:84A–32a, 2A:84A–32b**
Dockets, generally, this index
Documentary exhibits, disposition, **2C:65–4**

EVIDENCE—Cont'd

Domestic violence,
   Burden of proof, **2C:25–29**
   Dissolution of marriage, **2C:25–25**
Drugs and Medicine, this index
Duplicates, admissibility, **Evidence Rule 1003**
Effect of presumption, **Evidence Rule 301**
Effective date, Evidence Act, **2A:84A–36**
Electronic Surveillance Control Act, **2A:156A–1 et seq.**
Entrapment, **2C:2–12**
Ephedrine, pseudoephedrine, phenylpropanolamine, **2C:35–27**
Exclusion, record, **Rule 1:7–3**
Exhibits, generally, this index
Expert or opinion testimony, mental condition of defendant, **2C:4–6**
Expunging of criminal conviction, employing rehabilitated convicted offenders, **2A:168A–3**
Extended terms, **2C:44–6**
Extortion, threat to withhold or provide evidence, **2C:20–5**
Fabricating physical evidence, **2C:28–6**
False accusations, prior false accusations, character for truthfulness or untruthfulness, **Evidence Rule 608**
Fencing, **2C:20–7.1**
Forfeited property, **2C:64–1 et seq.**
Gambling, this index
Guilty plea, use in civil proceeding, **Rule 3:9–2**
Habits, **Evidence Rule 406**
Harmless error, **Rule 1:7–5**
Hearsay Evidence, generally, this index
Hindering apprehension or prosecution of accused, **2C:29–3**
Homicide, this index
Hospitals,
   Privileged communications, utilization, review committee, **2A:84A–22.8, 2A:84A–22.9**
   Professional standards review organizations, peer review committees, **2A:84A–22.10**
Identification, **Evidence Rule 901**
Identity theft, actions and proceedings, **2C:21–17.4**
Incapacitated persons, physician patient privilege, exceptions, **2A:84A–22.3**
Included offenses, **2C:1–8**
Indigent, neglected or abandoned children, sexual abuse, closed circuit testimony, **2A:84A–32.4**
Industrial chemicals, **2C:35–29**
Information disclosure privilege, newsperson, criminal proceedings, **2A:84A–21.1 et seq.**
Informers, identity, disclosure, **2A:84A–28**
Insurance coverage, relevancy, **Evidence Rule 411**
Interpreters, **Evidence Rule 604**
Interrogation, mode and order, **Evidence Rule 611**
Intoxication, clear and convincing evidence, criminal liability, **2C:2–8**
Joint defendants, statements, confessions and admissions, notice of use, **Rule 3:15–2**
Judges and justices,
   Calling and interrogation of witnesses, **Evidence Rule 614**
   Determining sufficiency of proof, contents of writings or photographs, **Evidence Rule 1008**
   Witnesses, **Evidence Rule 605**
Judicial notice of foreign law act. Judicial Notice, generally, this index
Jumping bail, **2C:29–7**

EVIDENCE—Cont'd

Jury,
   Determining sufficiency of proof, contents of writing or photograph, **Evidence Rule 1008**
   Taking into jury room, **Rule 1:8–7**
Juvenile Delinquents, this index
Juvenile family crisis, **Rule 5:17–2**
Lawyer client privilege, **2A:84A–20**
Leading questions, **Evidence Rule 611**
Lesser related infractions, trial with criminal offenses, **Rule 3:15–3**
Life expectancy and mortality tables, **Rule 1:13–5**
Limited admissibility, **Evidence Rule 105**
Limited criminal jurisdiction, courts of, Appeals, **Rule 3:23–8**
   De novo appeals, **Rule 3:23–8**
Marital privilege, confidential communications, **2A:84A–22**
Mediation, privileges and immunities, **Evidence Rule 519**
Medical expenses, payment, **Evidence Rule 409**
Mental disease or defect, **2C:4–2**
Mental incompetence, validity of wills, nonprivileged communications, **2A:84A–22.3**
Mentally Deficient and Mentally Ill Persons, this index
Military list, inability to prosecute or defend action, **Rule 1:13–6**
Monopolies and unfair trade, hearings and inquiries, **56:9–9**
Mortality and life expectancy tables, **Rule 1:13–5**
Motions, abuse of children, closed circuit testimony, **2A:84A–32.4**
Motor Vehicle Security Responsibility Law, this index
Motor Vehicles, this index
Neutralization, testimony of witnesses, **Evidence Rule 607**
Newly discovered evidence, new trial, **Rule 3:20–2**
Newsperson information disclosure privilege, **2A:84A–21.1 et seq.**
Nonpublic business records, copies, **Rule 1:7–6**
Oaths and affirmations, **Evidence Rule 603**
Objections, depositions, **Rule 3:13–2**
Official information, disclosure, state or United States, **2A:84A–27**
Order, interrogation and presentation, **Evidence Rule 611**
Original writing or photograph, Requirement, **Evidence Rule 1002**
   Unavailable, admissibility of other evidence, **Evidence Rule 1004**
Other crimes or civil wrongs, **Evidence Rule 404**
Overruling claim of privilege, effect of error, **2A:84A–32**
Pardon, employing rehabilitated convicted offenders, **2A:168A–3**
Parole, this index
Party, testimony or written admission of, contents of writings or photographs, **Evidence Rule 1007**
Perjury, generally, this index
Personal knowledge, witnesses, **Evidence Rule 602**
Photographic or micrographic copies of applications for registration and drivers licenses, **39:3–28**
Photographs,
   Contents, **Evidence Rule 1001 et seq.**
   Victims of crime, homicide, **2C:11–3**

EVIDENCE—Cont'd
Photographs—Cont'd
  Victims of crime, homicide—Cont'd
    Sentence and punishment, rules and regulations, 2C:11–3a
Physician and patients, privileged communications, 2A:84A–22.1
  Nonprivileged communications, obtaining physician for commission of crime or tort, 2A:84A–22.6
Pleas and plea discussions, **Evidence Rule 410**
Political vote, compelling disclosure, 2A:84A–25
Prejudicial, exclusion, **Evidence Rule 403**
Preliminary hearing, admissibility of defendants statements, **Evidence Rule 104**
Preliminary questions, **Evidence Rule 104**
Presentation, mode and order, **Evidence Rule 611**
Presumptions, generally, this index
Pretrial conferences, admissions, **Rule 3:9–1**
Prima facie evidence,
  Contraband, **2C:64–1**
  Newsperson information disclosure privilege, 2A:84A–21.1 et seq.
  Shoplifting, 2C:20–11
  Unlawful for driver to exceed statutory speed limitations, 39:4–99
Prior convictions, 2C:44–4
Prior false accusations, character for truthfulness or untruthfulness, **Evidence Rule 608**
Prior statements of witnesses, **Evidence Rules 607, 613**
Privileges and Immunities, generally, this index
Probation, revocation or modification of conditions, hearings, 2C:45–4
Production of Books and Papers, generally, this index
Psychiatric examinations, admissibility of statements by defendant, 2C:4–10
Purpose, **Evidence Rule 102**
Qualifications of witnesses, **Evidence Rule 104**
Rape, previous sexual conduct of complainant, admissibility, 2A:84A–32.1 et seq.
Records and recordation, child abuse proceedings, 9:6–8.46
Refreshing memory, writings, **Evidence Rule 612**
Rehabilitation of convicted offenders, 2A:168A–3
  Employment, 2A:168A–3
Related writings or statements, **Evidence Rule 106**
Relevancy, **Evidence Rule 401 et seq.**
  Character evidence, **Evidence Rule 404**
    Methods of proving, **Evidence Rule 405**
  Compromise and settlement, offers and negotiations, **Evidence Rule 408**
  Conditioned on fact, **Evidence Rule 104**
  Exclusion due to prejudice, confusion or waste of time, **Evidence Rule 403**
  General admissibility, **Evidence Rule 402**
  Habit, **Evidence Rule 406**
  Insurance coverage, **Evidence Rule 411**
  Medical and similar expenses, payment, **Evidence Rule 409**
  Pleas and plea discussions, **Evidence Rule 410**
  Routine practice, **Evidence Rule 406**
  Subsequent remedial measures, **Evidence Rule 407**
Religious belief,
  Compelling disclosure, 2A:84A–24
  Impeaching credibility of witness, **Evidence Rule 610**
Remainder, admitted writing or statement, **Evidence Rule 106**

EVIDENCE—Cont'd
Reports, traffic accidents, inadmissibility, 39:4–131
Reputation of party, **Evidence Rule 405**
Return following conclusion of trial, **Rule 1:2–3**
Routine practice, **Evidence Rule 406**
Rules of evidence,
  Accused, privilege, 2A:84A–17
  Admissibility, disclosure, wrongfully compelled, 2A:84A–30
  Admissions, psychiatric examinations, admissibility of statements of defendant, 2C:4–10
  Agents, production of evidence, 2A:84A–19
  Amendments, 2A:84A–37
  Cleric penitent privilege, 2A:84A–23
  Client, definitions, lawyer client privilege, 2A:84A–20
  Comments on exercise of privileges by witness, 2A:84A–31
  Crimes and offenses, voluntary testimony by accused, subsequent privilege, 2A:84A–19
  Definitions,
    Client, lawyer client privilege, 2A:84A–20
    Incrimination, 2A:84A–18
    Lawyer client privilege, 2A:84A–20
  Effective date of rules, 2A:84A–36
  Employees, production of evidence, 2A:84A–19
  Exercise of privileges by witnesses, comment on, 2A:84A–31
  Existing rights or remedies, effect, 2A:84A–42
  Hospitals, professional standard review organizations, peer review committees, 2A:84A–22.10
  Inconsistent prior laws, 2A:84A–40
  Incrimination, definitions, 2A:84A–18
  Informers identity, disclosure, 2A:84A–28
  Judicial conference, 2A:84A–34
  Jury trial, abridging or modifying right, 2A:84A–41
  Lawyer, definitions, lawyer client privilege, 2A:84A–20
  Lawyer client privilege, 2A:84A–20
  Marital privilege, confidential communications, 2A:84A–22
  Mental incompetence, validity of wills, nonprivileged communications, 2A:84A–22.3
  Newspapermans privilege, 2A:84A–21
  Nonprivileged communications, obtaining physician for commission of crime or tort, 2A:84A–22.6
  Officers, production of evidence, 2A:84A–19
  Official information, state or United States, disclosure, 2A:84A–27
  Overruling claim of privilege, effect of error, 2A:84A–32
  Patient and physician privilege, 2A:84A–22.2
  Pending proceedings, effect, 2A:84A–42
  Political vote, compelling disclosure, 2A:84A–25
  Previous sexual conduct of complainant, admissibility, 2A:84A–32.1 et seq.
  Privileges and Immunities, generally, this index
  Production of evidence, 2A:84A–19
  Religious belief, compelling disclosure, 2A:84A–24
  Self incrimination, 2A:84A–19
  Spouses, witnesses, 2A:84A–17
  Supreme court, adoption of rules, 2A:84A–33
  Trade secrets, disclosure, 2A:84A–26
  United States, official information, disclosure, 2A:84A–27

EVIDENCE—Cont'd
Rules of evidence—Cont'd
  Voluntary testimony by party or accused, subsequent privilege, 2A:84A–19
  Waiver, witnesses, privilege, 2A:84A–29
Seized property, 2C:64–4
Self authentication, **Evidence Rule 902**
Sequestration of witnesses, **Evidence Rule 615**
Sexual offenses, 2C:14–5
  Children and minors, closed circuit testimony, 2A:84A–32.4
  Previous sexual conduct of victim, 2C:14–7
Shoplifting, 2C:20–11
Specific instances of conduct, **Evidence Rule 608**
  Character evidence, **Evidence Rule 405**
  Statements, joint defendants, use, notice, **Rule 3:15–2**
Standard of Proof, generally, this index
State grand juries, presentation by attorney general, 2B:22–6
State Police, this index
Stolen property, photographic records in lieu of property, 2C:65–1
Strip search, evidence obtained by, 2A:161A–1
Subpoenas, generally, this index
Subscribing witness, testimony unnecessary for authentication, **Evidence Rule 903**
Subsequent remedial conduct, **Evidence Rule 407**
Summaries of writings or photographs, **Evidence Rule 1006**
Supervisory treatment programs, 2C:43–13
  First offenders, statements or other disclosures, 2C:43–13
Support of persons, willful nonsupport, proof of marriage, 2C:62–1
Suppression,
  Appeal of order, **Rule 3:24**
  Hindering apprehension or prosecution, 2C:29–3
  Motion, searches and seizures, **Rule 3:5–7**
  Municipal courts, **Rule 7:5–2**
  Wiretapping and electronic surveillance, 2A:156A–21
Supreme court, proposed rules, 2A:84A–35
Suspended sentences, revocation or modification, 2C:45–4
Tables of mortality and life expectancy, **Rule 1:13–5**
Tampering, 2C:28–6
  Hindering apprehension or prosecution, 2C:29–3
  Physical evidence, 2C:28–6
  Terrorism, 2C:38–4
  Wiretapping and electronic surveillance, 2A:156A–21
Tender years hearsay exception, **Evidence Rule 803**
Termination of complicity by renunciation, 2C:2–6
Terrorism, 2C:38–2
  Tampering, 2C:38–4
Theft, 2C:20–2
Trade secrets, disclosure, 2A:84A–26
Traffic control signal monitoring system, 39:4–8.15
Truthful character of witness, **Evidence Rule 608**
Untruthful character of witness, **Evidence Rule 608**
Utilization review committees, hospitals, extended care facilities, privileged communications, 2A:84A–22.8, 2A:84A–22.9
Victims of Crime, this index

EVIDENCE—Cont'd
Videotaped testimony, abuse of children,
　2A:84A–32.4
View, presentation of evidence to jury,
　2B:23–16
Voters and voting, compelling disclosure,
　2A:84A–25
Waiver, witnesses, privilege, **2A:84A–29**
Waste of time, exclusion, **Evidence Rule 403**
Weapons, possession, mandatory sentence,
　2C:43–6
Weight or credibility of evidence, **Evidence
　Rule 104**
Wiretapping and Electronic Surveillance Control Act, **2A:156A–1 et seq.**
Witnesses, generally, this index
Writings,
　Contents, **Evidence Rule 1001 et seq.**
　Use to refresh memory, **Evidence Rule 612**

EVIDENCE OF INDEBTEDNESS
Forgery, **2C:21–1**

EX PARTE PROCEEDINGS
Affidavits, taking outside state, **Rule 1:4–4**
Controlled substances, attachment, dealers, liability, **2C:35B–13**
Domestic violence, emergency relief, **2C:25–28**
Evidence, application of law, **Evidence Rule
　101**
Motions,
　Time for service and filing, **Rule 1:6–3**
　Verbatim records, **Rule 1:2–2**
Pleadings, verification, **Rule 1:4–7**
Probate proceedings, enlargement of time,
　Rule 1:3–4
Subpoenas, request by public officer or agency,
　Rule 1:9–6
Verbatim records, **Rule 1:2–2**
Verification of pleadings, **Rule 1:4–7**
Wiretapping and electronic surveillance, orders,
　Entry by judge, **2A:156A–10**
　Grounds, **2A:156A–10**

EXAMINATION PERMITS
Drivers licenses, **39:3–10, 39:3–13**

EXCAVATIONS
Parking near street excavation prohibited,
　39:4–138

EXCEPTIONS
Controlled substances, **24:21–7**
Explosives, blasting operations, **21:1A–138**
Fireworks, application of law, **21:2–4, 21:3–7**
Objections and Exceptions, generally, this index
Speedway from speed law if not crossing railroad, **39:4–101**
Traction engine from law, **39:3–1**

EXCISE TAX
Suspension or revocation of alcoholic beverage
　license for nonpayment, **33:1–31**

EXCITED UTTERANCES
Hearsay exceptions, **Evidence Rule 803**

EXECUTIONS
Alcoholic beverages, order by director on appeal, **33:1–38**
Costs, execution against municipality for costs
　returned unsatisfied, **2A:166–12**
Exemptions, motor vehicle insurance, no fault
　benefits, **39:6A–4**

EXECUTIONS—Cont'd
Final process, issuance, motions and applications, **Rule 1:6–8**
Fines and penalties,
　Execution against municipality for fines returned unsatisfied, **2A:166–12**
　Municipalities, fines returned unsatisfied,
　　2A:166–12
　Nonpayment, **2C:46–2**
Forgery, **2C:21–1**
Funeral expense benefits, motor vehicle insurance, exemptions, **39:6A–4**
Motions, granting by clerk of court, **Rule 1:6–8**
Motor vehicle insurance, no fault benefits, exemptions, **39:6A–4**
Motor vehicles, surrender of title papers,
　39:10–15
Municipal Courts, this index
Municipalities, execution against municipality
　for fines and costs returned and satisfied,
　2A:166–12
Restitution, nonpayment, **2C:46–2**
Securing execution of documents by deception,
　2C:21–16
Unsatisfied claim and judgment fund, return of
　execution unsatisfied as condition to recovery from fund, **39:6–70**

EXECUTIVE AUTHORITY
Definitions, Uniform Criminal Extradition Act,
　2A:160–6

EXECUTIVE BRANCH OR DEPARTMENT
Attorney General, generally, this index
Governor, generally, this index
Public defender, **2A:158A–1 et seq.**
State Treasurer, generally, this index

EXECUTIVE CLEMENCY
Pardons, generally, this index

EXECUTIVE HEAD
Definitions, drivers licenses, **39:5D–12**

EXECUTORS AND ADMINISTRATORS
Attorneys,
　Bank accounts, **Rule 1:21–6**
　Disciplined attorneys, future activities, **Rule
　　1:20–20**
Judicial employees, appointment, **Rule 1:17–3**

EXEMPLARY DAMAGES
Punitive damages. Damages, this index

EXEMPTIONS
Alcoholic Beverage Tax, this index
Assessments, this index
Attachment, motor vehicle insurance, no fault
　benefits, **39:6A–4**
Automobile no fault insurance, **39:6A–7**
　Torts, **39:6A–8**
Commercial motor vehicle operators, **39:3–10j
　et seq.**
Crimes and offenses, custodial interrogations,
　electronic recordation, **Rule 3:17**
Executions, this index
Explosives, application of law, **21:1A–141**
Grade crossings, stopping regulations, **39:4–128**
Highways, length of vehicles, **39:3–84**
Hypodermic needles or syringes, possession,
　bloodborne disease harm reduction,
　2C:36–6a
Labor and Employment, this index
Motor Vehicles, this index
Process, this index
Public Utilities, this index
Snowmobiles, registration, **39:3C–6**

EXEMPTIONS—Cont'd
Taxation, this index
Weapons,
　Possession, **2C:39–6**
　Sales, delivery, limitations, **2C:58–2, 2C:58–3**

EXHAUST SYSTEM
Motor Vehicles, this index

EXHIBITIONS
Rigging publicly exhibited contests, **2C:21–11**

EXHIBITS
Audiotapes, **Rule 1:2–2**
Copies of documents, exhibits to pleading, **Rule
　1:4–3**
Documentary exhibits, disposition, **2C:65–4**
Jury and jurors, taking into jury room, **Rule
　1:8–8**
Obscene material, **2C:34–4**
Pleadings, adoption by reference, **Rule 1:4–3**
Record of proceedings, **Rule 1:2–3**
Verdict sheets, **Rule 3:19–1**
Videotapes, **Rule 1:2–2**

EXITS
Special exit door, motor vehicles used for merchandising or exhibition purposes,
　39:3–77.2

EXPERIMENTS
Crimes and offenses, discovery, **Rule 3:13–3**

EXPERT WITNESSES
Witnesses, this index

EXPERTS
Fees. Witnesses, this index
Mental condition of defendant, **2C:4–6**

EXPIRED CREDIT CARD
Definitions, **2C:21–6**

EXPLOSIVES
　Generally, **21:1A–128 et seq., 21:1A–140**
Act, definitions, **21:1A–129**
Age,
　Blasting operations, **21:1A–138**
　Permits, qualifications, **21:1A–134**
Alarms, false alarms, **2C:33–3 et seq.**
Alcoholic beverages, handling explosives while
　under influence, **21:1A–132**
Amateur rocket experimentation, permits, exceptions, **21:1A–134**
Appeal and review, orders, **21:1A–130**
Application of law, **21:1A–141**
Armed forces, application of law, **21:1A–141**
Arson, **2C:17–1**
　Investigations, permit applications,
　　21:1A–134
Artificial barricade, definitions, **21:1A–129**
Assembling, crimes and offenses, **2C:39–14**
Barricaded, definitions, **21:1A–129**
Blasting operations, **21:1A–138**
Bodily injury, reports, **2C:58–8**
Buildings, distances and quantity, manufacturing and storage, **21:1A–135**
Burglary, **2C:18–2**
Carriers, transportation, **21:1A–137**
Causing or risking widespread injury or damage, **2C:17–2**
Character and reputation, permit qualifications, **21:1A–134**
Commercial explosives, definitions, **21:1A–129**
Commissioner, definitions, **21:1A–129**
Complaint, **21:1A–130**

EXPLOSIVES—Cont'd

Compromise and settlement, fines and penalties, 21:1A–140
Conflicts of law,
  Fireworks, 21:3–7
  Jurisdiction, 21:1A–139
Crimes and offenses, 21:1A–140
  Permits, qualifications, 21:1A–134
  Unlawful purpose, 21:1A–142
Criminal mischief, 2C:17–3
Definitions, 2C:39–1, 21:1A–129
  Motor vehicles, 39:1–1
Demonstrating, crimes and offenses, 2C:39–14
Deteriorated explosives, disposal, 21:1A–132
Distances, manufacturing and storage, quantity, 21:1A–135
Drugs and medicine, handling explosives while under influence, 21:1A–132
Electricity, magazines, 21:1A–136
Enforcement of law, 21:1A–130
Examinations, 21:1A–134
Exceptions, blasting operations, 21:1A–138
Exemptions, application of law, 21:1A–141
Experience, permits, qualifications, 21:1A–134
False or facsimile devices, 2C:33–3 et seq.
False public alarms, 2C:33–3 et seq.
Fees, permits, 21:1A–134
Fines and penalties, 21:1A–140
Firefighters and fire departments, application of law, 21:1A–141
Fires, prohibited acts, 21:1A–132
Fireworks, generally, this index
Foreign commerce, application of law, 21:1A–141
Garbage and refuse, magazines, 21:1A–136
Handling,
  Permits, 21:1A–133
  Prohibited acts, 21:1A–132
Hazardous Substances and Waste, generally, this index
Hearings,
  Orders, 21:1A–130
  Permits, revocation, 21:1A–140
  Rules and regulations, promulgation, 21:1A–131
Highways and roads, distances and quantity, manufacturing and storage, 21:1A–135
Inhabited building, definitions, 21:1A–129
Injunction, hazards, 21:1A–130
Inspection and inspectors,
  Authority, 21:1A–130
  Manufacturing establishment plan, 21:1A–135
  Records, 21:1A–132
Intent, unlawful purpose, 21:1A–142
Interstate commerce, application of law, 21:1A–141
Intoxicating liquors, handling explosives while under influence, 21:1A–132
Intraexplosives plant quantity and distance table, 21:1A–135
Jurisdiction, 21:1A–139
Law and public safety department, transportation, powers, 21:1A–130
Leaking explosives, disposal, 21:1A–132
Licenses and permits. Permits, generally, post
Location, distances and quantity, manufacturing and storage, 21:1A–135
Magazines, 21:1A–136
  Definitions, 21:1A–129
  Distances and quantity, 21:1A–135
  Limitations, quantity, 21:1A–136
  Permit, 21:1A–133
  Supervision, 21:1A–136
Manufacturers and manufacturing,
  Building, definitions, 21:1A–129

EXPLOSIVES—Cont'd

Manufacturers and manufacturing—Cont'd
  Distances and quantity, 21:1A–135
  Permits, 21:1A–133
  Plans and specifications, 21:1A–135
  Prohibited acts, 21:1A–132
Mines and minerals, blasting, licenses and permits, 21:1A–138
Misdemeanors, bombs, 21:1A–142
Model rockets. Rockets, generally, this index
Motor carriers, transportation, 21:1A–137
Narcotics, handling explosives while under influence, 21:1A–132
Natural barricade, definitions, 21:1A–129
Nitro carbo nitrate, definitions, 21:1A–129
Notice,
  Hearing, rules and regulations, promulgation, 21:1A–131
  Possession, 2C:58–7
  Rules and regulations, proposed promulgation, 21:1A–131
Open lights or fire or flame producing devices, 21:1A–132
Orders, 21:1A–130
  Violations, 21:1A–140
Permits, 21:1A–133 et seq.
  Blasting operations, 21:1A–138
  Contents, 21:1A–133
  Examinations, 21:1A–134
  Expiration, 21:1A–134
  Fees, 21:1A–134
  Inspection, 21:1A–133
  Investigations, 21:1A–134
  Possession, 21:1A–132
  Qualifications, 21:1A–134
  Revocation, 21:1A–140
  Without permits, crimes and offenses, 21:1A–142
Person, definitions, 21:1A–129
Personal injuries, reports, 2C:58–8
Plans and specifications,
  Magazines, 21:1A–136
  Manufacturers, 21:1A–135
Police and police departments, application of law, 21:1A–141
Possession, 2C:58–7
  Bombs, 21:1A–142
  Notice, 2C:58–7
  Regulatory provisions, violations, 2C:39–10
  Unlawful purposes, 2C:39–4
    Person convicted of crime involving, possession of any weapon prohibited, 2C:39–7
Prohibited acts, 21:1A–132
Propellants, definitions, 21:1A–129
Prosecutions of law violations, 21:1A–130
Public conveyance, definitions, 21:1A–129
Qualifications, permits, 21:1A–134
Railroads, distances and quantity, manufacturing and storage, 21:1A–135
Railway, definitions, 21:1A–129
Records, 21:1A–132
  Transportation, 21:1A–137
Repeals of statutes, 21:1A–144
Reports,
  Sales, 21:1A–132
  Theft, 21:1A–132
  Wounds, 2C:58–8
Rockets, amateur experimentation, permits, exception, 21:1A–138
Rules and regulations, 21:1A–131
Sales,
  Permits, 21:1A–133
  Prohibited acts, 21:1A–132
  Reports, 21:1A–132
Searches and seizures, 2C:58–7

EXPLOSIVES—Cont'd

Sentence and punishment, unlawful purpose, 21:1A–142
Severable provisions, 21:1A–143
Small arms ammunition, smokeless powder for hand loading, 21:1A–133
Smokeless powder, small arms, necessity of permit, 21:1A–133
Smoking regulations, 21:1A–132
State police division, transportation, powers, 21:1A–130
Stay, regulatory order enforcement, 21:1A–130
Storage,
  Distances and quantity, 21:1A–135
  Permits, 21:1A–133
  Prohibited acts, 21:1A–132
Teaching, demonstrating or assembling, crimes and offenses, 2C:39–14
Theft, reports, 21:1A–132
Time, permits, expiration, 21:1A–134
Trailers and semitrailers, transportation, 21:1A–137
Transportation, 21:1A–137
  Permit, 21:1A–133
  Prohibited acts, 21:1A–132
Turnpike project, transportation regulation, 27:23–31
United States, application of law, 21:1A–141
Unlawful purpose, 21:1A–142
Use permit, 21:1A–133
Ventilation, magazines, 21:1A–136
Wounds, reports, 2C:58–8

EXPOSURE
Criminal exposure, 2C:14–4

EXPUNGING RECORD
  Generally, 2C:52–1 et seq.
Agencies, use by, pending petition, 2C:52–17
Confidential or privileged information, **Rule 1:38–3**
Construction, 2C:52–32
Controlled substances, 2C:52–2
  Young drug offenders, 2C:52–5
Corrections department, use by, 2C:52–23
County prosecutors obligation to ascertain propriety of petition, 2C:52–24
Definitions, 2C:52–1
Disclosure, 2C:52–30
Diversion programs, use in setting, 2C:52–20
Effect, 2C:52–27
Fees, 2C:52–29; **Rule 3:30**
Health care claims fraud, rehabilitation, 2C:27–1
Limitation, 2C:52–31
Parole board, use by, 2C:52–22
Records, 2C:52–1 et seq.
Rehabilitated convicted offenders, evidence, employment, 2A:168A–3
Retroactive application, 2C:52–25
Sentencing, use in setting, 2C:52–21
Supervisory treatment, use in setting, 2C:52–20
Violent crimes compensation board, supplying information, 2C:52–18

EXTENDED CARE FACILITIES
Institutionalized elderly persons, assault, 2C:12–1
Utilization review committees, privileges and immunities, **Evidence Rule 507**

EXTENDED TERMS OF IMPRISONMENT
Crimes and Offenses, this index

EXTORTION
  Generally, 2C:20–2, 2C:20–5
Attorneys, conviction, discipline, **Rule 1:20–13**

EXTORTION—Cont'd
Defenses, notice, **Rule 3:12–1**
Forfeiture, proceeds, 2C:64–1
Threat to expose or publicize damaging material, 2C:20–5
Weapons, possession, persons convicted of, 2C:39–7

EXTRADITION
Generally, 2A:160–1 et seq.
Accounting, expenses advanced by county treasurer, 2A:160–4
Advance of money to prosecutor for expenses, 2A:160–3
Affidavits,
Accompanying demand for fugitive, 2A:160–11, 2A:160–32
Arrest of fugitive before requisition made, 2A:160–21
Extradition of fugitive, 2A:160–11, 2A:160–32
Agreement by governor of New Jersey to return person from state extradited, 2A:160–33
Aiding and abetting taking persons out of state to answer criminal charge, 2A:160–1
Arrest, 2A:160–10
Assistance of officer making arrest, 2A:160–17
Authority of officer making arrest, 2A:160–16, 2A:160–17
Bail,
Admission, **Rule 3:26–1**
Arrest of fugitive forfeiting bail, 2A:160–26
Requisition, arrest before requisition made, 2A:160–21 et seq.
Right of person arrested, 2A:160–18
Warrants, 2A:160–10, 2A:160–15, 2A:160–16
Alias warrant, 2A:160–29
Before requisition made, 2A:160–21
Execution, 2A:160–16
Issuance, 2A:160–15
Recall, 2A:160–29
Recitals, 2A:160–15
Without warrant of fugitive,
Before requisition made, 2A:160–22
Forfeiting bail, 2A:160–26
Bail, **Rule 3:26–1**
Admission to, **Rule 3:26–1**
Authority to admit to, **Rule 3:26–2**
Capital offenses, 2A:160–24
Fugitive arrested before requisition made and confined to jail awaiting requisition, 2A:160–24 et seq.
Fugitive breaking bail before requisition made, 2A:160–21 et seq.
New bail for appearance, 2A:160–25
Bond, action on bond or forfeiture of bail, 2A:160–26
Collection, 2C:46–4
Commitment to jail of fugitive arrested before requisition made to await requisition, 2A:160–23
Complaint to accompany application to governor for requisition, 2A:160–32
Consent of fugitive to return to demanding state, 2A:160–1, 2A:160–30
Construction of uniform criminal extradition laws, 2A:160–7
Correctional institutions, escaped prisoners, 2A:160–31 et seq.
Costs, restitution, 2C:43–3.4
Countys liability for expenses of returning fugitive, 2A:160–2
Criminal prosecution while in New Jersey against person extradited, 2A:160–35
Death offense, bail of accused, 2A:160–24

EXTRADITION—Cont'd
Definition of terms used in Uniform Extradition Law, 2A:160–6
Delivery of fugitive to demanding state, 2A:160–10
Without complying with law as offense, 2A:160–19
Demand, fugitive found in New Jersey, 2A:160–11, 2A:160–31
Statement of executive authority of demanding state accompanying, 2A:160–11
Discharge of fugitive arrested before requisition made, 2A:160–25
Escaped prisoners, 2A:160–31 et seq.
Executive authority, definitions, 2A:160–6
Exemption of extradited person,
Other criminal prosecutions while in New Jersey, 2A:160–35
Service of process in civil actions, 2A:160–34
Expenses and expenditures, returning fugitive from justice, 2A:160–2
Accounting of expenditures, 2A:160–4
Advance of money to prosecutor, 2A:160–3
Return of excess advancement to county treasurer, 2A:160–4
Superior court judges approval, 2A:160–2 et seq.
Extension of time, commitment of accused, 2A:160–25
Extradited person confined in county or municipal jail temporarily, 2A:160–20
Foreign state, from another state by New Jersey, 2A:160–31 et seq.
Forfeiture of bail of fugitive arrested before requisition made, 2A:160–26
Guilt of accused, inquiry by governor into, 2A:160–28
Habeas corpus, 2A:160–30
Informing person of right to writ, 2A:160–30
Validity of arrest, 2A:160–18
Hearings,
Habeas corpus to test validity of arrest of fugitive, 2A:160–18
Person arrested,
Before delivery to demanding state, 2A:160–18
Without warrant before requisition made, 2A:160–22, 2A:160–23
Imprisoned persons in another state, extradition of, 2A:160–33
Indictment, information or presentment,
Application to governor for requisition, 2A:160–32
Demand for fugitive, 2A:160–11
Informing person arrested before extradition made of rights, 2A:160–30
Innocence of fugitive, inquiry into by governor, 2A:160–28
Investigation of demand for extradition of fugitive in New Jersey, 2A:160–12
Involuntarily leaving state demanding extradition, 2A:160–13
Judgment of conviction to accompany demand for extradition of fugitive in New Jersey, 2A:160–11
Life imprisonment, offense, bail of accused, 2A:160–24
Misdemeanors, noncompliance with act, 2A:160–19
Murder,
Person charged with in demanding state and imprisoned in New Jersey for term less than life, 2A:160–10

EXTRADITION—Cont'd
Murder—Cont'd
Return of person imprisoned in another state if acquitted or found guilty of offense not punishable by death or life imprisonment, 2A:160–5
New Jersey into another state, 2A:160–10 et seq.
Notice of hearing on habeas corpus to test validity of arrest, 2A:160–18
Parole, 2A:160–21 et seq.
Arrest before requisition made, 2A:160–30
New Jersey extradition by, 2A:160–31 et seq.
Pendency of criminal prosecution,
Another state, extradition of person by New Jersey pending prosecution, 2A:160–33
New Jersey, extradition of fugitive pending outcome of, 2A:160–27
Presence in demanding state at time of commission of crime, extradition of person not present, 2A:160–14
Procedure, violation of statute regulating as offense, 2A:160–1
Process in civil actions, exemption of person extradited, 2A:160–34
Prosecuting attorneys application to governor for requisition, 2A:160–32
Recall of warrant of arrest, 2A:160–22
Recommitment, fugitive arrest before requisition made, 2A:160–25
Requisitions,
Application by prosecuting attorney to governor for requisition, 2A:160–32
Arrest of fugitive before requisition made, 2A:160–21 et seq.
Return of person,
Charged with murder extradited from and imprisoned in another state to such state, 2A:160–5
Imprisoned in New Jersey for term less than life on acquittal in demanding state, 2A:160–10
Rights, powers and privileges of state unaffected by uniform extradition law, 2A:160–8
Satisfaction, 2C:46–4.1
Secretary of state, copy of application to governor for requisition filed with, 2A:160–32
Sentence and punishment, application of law, **Rule 3:21–4**
Service of process in civil actions, persons extradited from another state, 2A:160–34
State, definitions, 2A:160–6
Superior court judges approval, expenses of extradition, 2A:160–2 et seq.
Temporary confinement of person arrested in county or municipal jail, 2A:160–20
Territorial applicability code of criminal justice, 2C:1–3
Transportation of fugitive through state to demanding state, confinement temporarily in jails in New Jersey, 2A:160–20
Treason, 2A:160–10
Uniform Criminal Extradition Law, 2A:160–6 et seq.
Uniform Fresh Pursuit Law, commitment pending, **Rule 3:4–4**
Verification of application to governor for requisition, 2A:160–32
Voluntary return of fugitive to demanding state, 2A:160–30
Waiver, 2A:160–1
By requests for final disposition, interstate agreement on detainers, 2A:159A–3
Fugitive arrested before requisition made, 2A:160–30
State, right, 2A:160–8

EXTRADITION—Cont'd
Warrants,
Arrest, ante
Commanding agent to receive fugitive in another state, **2A:160–31**
Commitment of person arrested before requisition made, **2A:160–23**
Governor as authority to surrender person to demanding state, **2A:160–10**

EXTRAJUDICIAL ACTIVITIES ADVISORY COMMITTEE
Generally, **Rule 1:18A–1 et seq.**

EYES AND EYESIGHT
Anatomical Gifts, generally, this index
Optometrists, generally, this index

EZ PASS SYSTEM
Turnpikes, finances, plans and specifications, **27:23–41**

FACSIMILES
Municipal courts, arrest warrants, complaints, service, **Rule 7:2–6**
Signatures,
Affidavits, **Rule 1:4–4**
Certificates of approval of motor vehicles, **39:8–2**
Mortgages, foreclosure, **Rules 1:4–4, 1:4–5**

FACTORIES
Manufacturers and Manufacturing, generally, this index

FAIR AUTOMOBILE INSURANCE REFORM ACT
Motor Vehicle Insurance, generally, this index

FAIR EMPLOYMENT PRACTICES
Discrimination, generally, this index

FAIR SALES ACT
Monopolies and unfair trade, exemptions, **56:9–5**

FAITH HEALERS
Automobile insurance, no fault insurance, application of law, **39:6A–1 et seq.**

FALSE ALARMS
Generally, **2C:33–3**
Drivers licenses, suspension or revocation, juvenile delinquents and dependents, **2C:33–3.1**
Fines and penalties, **2C:33–3.2**
Juvenile delinquents and dependents, drivers licenses, suspension or revocation, **2C:33–3.1**

FALSE FINANCIAL STATEMENTS
Generally, **2C:21–4**

FALSE IMPRISONMENT
Generally, **2C:13–3**
Human trafficking, **2C:13–8**

FALSE INSTRUMENTS
Filing, fraud, **2C:21–3**

FALSE PERSONATION
Generally, **2C:21–17**

FALSE PROMISES
Fraud, generally, this index

FALSE REPORTS
Law enforcement authorities, **2C:28–4**

FALSE STATEMENTS OR REPRESENTATIONS
Fraud, generally, this index

FALSE SWEARING
Perjury, generally, this index

FALSE TESTIMONY
Perjury, generally, this index

FALSIFYING RECORDS
Crimes and offenses, **2C:21–4**

FAMILY
Bigamy, **2C:24–1**
Crimes and offenses, **2C:24–1 et seq.**
Domestic Violence, generally, this index
Discrimination, generally, this index
Domestic Violence, generally, this index
Nonsupport. Support of Persons, generally, this index
Spouses, generally, this index
Support of Persons, generally, this index

FAMILY ACTIONS
Affidavits, complaint, nonconforming papers, **Rule 1:5–6**
Case information statement, confidential or privileged information, **Rule 1:38–3**
Confidential litigant information sheets, public access, **Rule 1:38–3**
Confidential or privileged information, records, **Rule 1:38–3**
Custody. Children and Minors, this index
Juvenile Delinquents, generally, this index
Records, confidential or privileged information, **Rule 1:38–3**
Subpoenas, inspection of objects designated in subpoena, **Rule 1:9–2**
Support of Persons, generally, this index
Visitation. Children and Minors, this index

FAMILY COURT
Confidential or privileged information, records, juvenile delinquents and dependents, **2A:4A–60 et seq.**
Disclosure, records, juvenile delinquents and dependents, **2A:4A–60 et seq.**
Employees, juvenile family crisis intervention units, qualifications, **2A:4A–79**
Indigent, neglected or abandoned children, juvenile family crisis, referral to court, **2A:4A–83 et seq.**
Intake service, juvenile family crisis,
Intervention units, **2A:4A–76**
Training and skills, **2A:4A–79**
Referral to court, **2A:4A–83 et seq.**
Jurisdiction, **2A:4A–24**
Retention of jurisdiction, **2A:4A–45**
Waiver, **2A:4A–26**
Juvenile Delinquents, generally, this index
Juvenile family crisis intervention units,
Intake service, **2A:4A–76**
Training and skills, **2A:4A–79**
Referral to court, **2A:4A–83 et seq.**
Records and recordation, confidentiality, **2A:4A–60 et seq.**
Sealing of records, **2A:4A–62**
Referral to court, juvenile family crisis, **2A:4A–83 et seq.**
Superior Court, generally, this index

FAMILY CRISIS INTERVENTION
Juvenile delinquents and dependents,
Out of door sales, petitions, **Rule 5:18–1**
Unit, short term custody, **Rule 5:16–2**

FAMILY DAY CARE HOMES
Family day care sponsoring organization, child abuse reports, access to, **9:6–8.10a**

FAMILY HISTORY
Hearsay exception, **Evidence Rule 804**
Reputation, **Evidence Rule 803**

FAMILY RECORDS
Hearsay exception, **Evidence Rule 803**

FAMILY SERVICE PLAN
Juvenile delinquents and dependents, temporary out of home placement, **Rule 5:18–2**

FARM MACHINERY
Agricultural Machinery and Equipment, generally, this index

FARM PRODUCTS
Agricultural Products, generally, this index

FARM SUPPLIES
Definitions, license plates, **39:3–25**

FARM TRACTORS
Agricultural Machinery and Equipment, generally, this index
Definitions, Motor Vehicle Law, **39:1–1**

FARM WINERY LICENSES
Generally, **33:1–10, 33:1 App.**

FARMERS
Agriculture, generally, this index

FARMS AND FARMING
Agriculture, generally, this index

FEDERAL ACT
Definitions,
Food and drugs, **24:21–32**
Water pollution control, **58:10A–3**

FEDERAL AGENCIES
Attorneys, limitation on practice, **Rule 1:15–5**

FEDERAL AID
Highways, width of vehicles disqualifying state from receiving federal highway funds, **39:3–84**
Medicaid, generally, this index

FEDERAL AID ROADS
Funds, width of vehicle disqualifying state from receiving funds, **39:3–84**

FEDERAL BUREAU OF INVESTIGATION
Arrest powers, violation of state laws, **2A:154–5**
DNA Database and Databank, generally, this index
Fingerprints, information, exchanges, **53:1–20.9d**
Violent criminal apprehension program. Identification Bureau, this index

FEDERAL CLEAN AIR MANDATE COMPLIANCE ACT
Generally, **39:8–41 et seq.**

FEDERAL CORPORATIONS AND AGENCIES
See, also, United States, generally, this index
Abuse of children, information, disclosure, **9:6–8.10a**
Controlled substances, cooperation with state agencies, **24:21–34**

FEDERAL COURTS
Attorneys, limitation on practice, **Rule 1:15–5**

FEDERAL GOVERNMENT
United States, generally, this index

FEDERAL OFFICERS AND EMPLOYEES
Officers and employees. United States, this
index

FEE SIMPLE
Turnpike authority, power to acquire property,
27:23–5

FEED IMPREGNATING MACHINES
Licenses, 39:3–26

FEEDER ROADS
Turnpikes, this index

FEES
Alcoholic Beverages, this index
Attorney Fees, generally, this index
Buses, this index
Carriers, this index
Commercial Drivers Licenses, this index
Complaints, this index
Costs, generally, this index
County health departments, sanitary landfills,
13:1E–9
County Prosecutors, this index
Crimes and Offenses, this index
Dentists and Dentistry, this index
Detective businesses, community security ser-
vices, motor vehicle identification lights,
permits, 39:3–54.14
Disabled veterans, motor vehicles, plates or
markers, 39:3–27.16
Drivers Licenses, this index
Explosives, permits, 21:1A–134
Farm tractors, highway operations, 39:3–24
Fireworks, agricultural use, permits, 21:2–29.1
Hazardous Substances and Waste, this index
Identification lights, motor vehicles, private de-
tective business community security ser-
vices, 39:3–54.14
Intoxicated driver resource centers, 39:4–50
Intoxicated driving programs, 39:4–50
Judges and Justices, this index
Jury and Jurors, this index
Limousine or livery service, plates or markers,
39:3–19.5
Mentally retarded persons, transportation,
county vehicles, 39:4–207.2 et seq.
Motor Carriers, this index
Motor Vehicle Commission, this index
Motor Vehicles, this index
Motorcycles, licenses and permits, 39:3–10
Motorized bicycles,
D plates, 39:3–18
Duplicate registration certificates, 39:3–31
Operators licenses, 39:4–14.3
Registration, 39:4–14.3i, 39:4–14.3j,
39:4–14.3l, 39:4–14.3w
Municipal Courts, this index
Municipalities, this index
National guard, motor vehicles, special regis-
tration plates, 39:3–27.13
Nonprofit Corporations and Associations, this
index
Nurses, this index
Officer receiving salary, fees not payable to,
2A:166–17
Optometrists, this index
Pharmacists, this index
Physicians and Surgeons, this index
Police and Police Departments, this index

FEES—Cont'd
Private detective businesses, community securi-
ty services, motor vehicle identification
lights, permits, 39:3–54.14
Process, this index
Psychologists and Psychology, this index
Registration, commercial motor vehicles,
39:3–20
Sanitary landfills, county health departments,
13:1E–9
School Buses, this index
Service of process, county detectives and inves-
tigators, 2A:157–17
Solid Waste, this index
State Treasurer, this index
Subpoenas, this index
Tow Trucks and Towing Companies, this index
Unregistered vehicles, permits to cross public
highways, 39:3–26.2, 39:3–26.4
Veterans, motor vehicle plates or markers, dis-
abled veterans, 39:3–27.16
Weapons, licenses and permits, 2C:58–3
Wildlife conservation license plates, 39:3–33.10
Annual renewal fees, uses, 39:3–33.11
Witnesses, this index

FEET
Podiatrists and Podiatry, generally, this index

FELLATIO
Generally, 2C:14–1 et seq.
Children and minors, second degree crime,
2C:24–4

FELONIES
Crimes and Offenses, generally, this index

FELONY MURDER
Aggravating factors, life imprisonment,
2C:11–3
Defenses, notice, **Rule 3:12–1**

FENCES
Crimes and offenses, invisible fences, 2C:40–20
Fireworks plants, 21:2–10
Invisible fences, 2C:40–20
Markers, invisible fences, 2C:40–20
Trespass, damages, 2C:18–4 et seq.

FENCING
Alterations, possession of altered property,
2C:20–7.1
Actions and proceedings, civil actions
against, damages, 2C:20–20
Stolen property, 2C:20–7.1
Actions and proceedings, civil actions
against, damages, 2C:20–20
Injunctive relief, 2C:20–21

FENTANYL
Controlled dangerous substance, 24:21–1 et
seq.

FERMENTED LIQUORS
Alcoholic Beverages, this index

FIDUCIARIES
Alcoholic beverages, more than one license in
different capacities, 33:1–40
Attorneys,
Accounts, record keeping, **Rule 1:21–6**
Disciplined attorneys, future activities, **Rule
1:20–20**
Bonds (Officers and Fiduciaries), generally,
this index
Commercial bribery and breach of duty,
2C:21–10

FIDUCIARIES—Cont'd
Crimes and offenses, aggravating circum-
stances, 2C:44–1
Definitions,
Misapplication of entrusted property,
2C:21–15
Theft, 2C:20–1
Guardian and Ward, generally, this index
Intoxicating liquors, holding more than one
license in different capacities, 33:1–40
Investments, turnpike authority bonds,
27:23–13
Misapplication, entrusted property and proper-
ty of government or financial institution,
2C:21–15
Misconduct, corporate official, 2C:21–9
Personal representatives. Probate Proceed-
ings, this index
Theft, 2C:20–2, 2C:20–4, 2C:20–9
Failure to make required disposition of
property received, 2C:20–9
Trusts and Trustees, generally, this index

FIGHTING
Disorderly conduct, 2C:33–2

FIGHTING ANIMALS
Cruelty to animals, 4:22–24

FILING
See, also, specific index headings
Generally, **Rule 1:5–6**
Appeals In Criminal Prosecutions, this index
Books and papers, **Rule 1:5–6**
Briefs, generally, this index
Caption appearing on papers, **Rule 1:4–1**
Case information statement, filing pleadings
with, **Rule 1:5–6**
Copies, **Rule 1:5–6**
Court schedules, **Rule 1:30–1**
Crimes and Offenses, this index
Electronic filing, **Rule 1:4–9**
Pleadings, signatures, **Rule 1:4–5**
Signatures,
Affidavits, **Rule 1:4–4**
Pleadings, **Rule 1:4–5**
Proof of service, **Rule 1:5–3**
Fees,
Presented for filing without payment, **Rule
1:5–6**
Waiver, petitions for review, judiciary em-
ployees, **Rule 1:17A–8**
Income Tax—State, this index
Indigent persons, applications, waiver of fees,
Rule 1:13–2
Insurance, coverage, affidavits, **Rule 1:5–6**
Investigative detention, orders, applications,
Rule 3:5A–8
Judicial opinions, **Rule 1:36–1**
Letter opinions, **Rule 1:36–1**
Memorandum decisions, **Rule 1:36–1**
Motions, this index
Nonconforming papers, **Rule 1:5–6**
Nonmilitary service affidavit, entry of default
judgment, **Rule 1:5–7**
Notice, nonconforming papers, **Rule 1:5–6**
Office hours of courts, **Rule 1:30–1**
Opinions, **Rule 1:36–1**
Schedules of courts, **Rule 1:30–1**
Search warrants, **Rule 7:5–1**
Affidavits, transcripts, summary of oral testi-
mony, **Rule 3:5–6**
Signatures, date on which signed, **Rule 1:4–5**
Size of filed papers, **Rule 1:4–9**
Time, **Rule 1:5–6**
Title search, certification, **Rule 1:5–6**

FILING—Cont'd
Trial court, **Rule 1:5–6**
Typewritten names, **Rule 1:4–6**
Unauthorized practice of law, appeal of decisions, **Rule 1:22–3A**
Weight of filed papers, **Rule 1:4–9**

FILLING STATIONS
See, also, Motor Fuels, generally, this index
Title papers for vehicle in possession of, compliance with statute, **39:10–6**
Turnpike authority, use of right of way, **27:23–9**

FILOMENAS LAW
Intoxication of driver. School Buildings and Grounds, this index

FINAL ADJUDICATION, JUDGMENTS AND DECREES
Judgments and Decrees, generally, this index

FINANCE
State Highways, generally, this index

FINANCE COMPANIES
Registration of motor vehicles owned or controlled by, **39:3–18**

FINANCIAL ASSISTANCE
Colleges and Universities, generally, this index
Terrorism, **2C:38–5**

FINANCIAL CORPORATIONS AND INSTITUTIONS
Accounts and accounting, terrorism, freezing, **2C:66–1 et seq.**
Application of law, forfeiture, terrorism, funds, freezing, **2C:66–11**
Attorney IOLTA trust accounts, **Rule 1:28A–2**
Attorney trust accounts, **Rule 1:21–6**
Banks and Banking, generally, this index
Contests, hearings, terrorism, funds, freezing, **2C:66–5**
Crimes and offenses, tear gas, **2C:39–6**
Definitions,
  Terrorism, funds, freezing, **2C:66–1**
  Theft, **2C:20–1**
Electronic Fund Transfers, generally, this index
Fiduciaries, misapplication of property, **2C:21–15**
Forfeiture, state, terrorism, funds, freezing, **2C:66–6**
Freezing, terrorism, funds, **2C:66–1 et seq.**
Funds, freezing, terrorism, **2C:66–1 et seq.**
Health and Accident Insurance, generally, this index
Hearings, contests, terrorism, funds, freezing, **2C:66–5**
Insurance, generally, this index
Interest on lawyers trust accounts, **Rule 1:28A–2**
Limitation, time, terrorism, funds, freezing, **2C:66–7**
Notice, terrorism, funds, freezing, **2C:66–8**
Orders of court, terrorism, funds, freezing, **2C:66–3**
Privileges and immunities, terrorism, funds, freezing, **2C:66–10**
State, forfeiture, terrorism, funds, freezing, **2C:66–6**
Tear gas, unlawful possession, exemption, **2C:39–6**
Teller machines. Electronic Fund Transfers, generally, this index
Terrorism, freezing, funds, **2C:66–1 et seq.**
Theft by failure to make required disposition of property received, **2C:20–9**

FINANCIAL CORPORATIONS AND INSTITUTIONS—Cont'd
Time, limitation, terrorism, funds, freezing, **2C:66–7**
Trust companies. Banks and Banking, generally, this index
Weapons, security guards, possession, **2C:39–6**

FINANCIAL INSTITUTIONS
Financial Corporations and Institutions, generally, this index

FINANCIAL INSTRUMENT
Definitions, computer related offenses, **2C:20–23**

FINANCIAL RESPONSIBILITY
Generally, **39:6–23 et seq.**
Electric personal assistive mobility devices, **39:4–14.10**
Motor Vehicles, this index

FINANCIAL STATEMENTS OR REPORTS
Crimes and offenses, false statements, **2C:21–4**
False statements, **2C:21–4**
Judges and justices, **Rule 1:18B–1 et seq.**
Motor vehicle commission, **39:2A–22**
Turnpike authority, **27:23–3.2, 27:23–14**

FINDINGS
Generally, **Rule 1:7–4**
Amended or additional findings, **Rule 1:7–4**
Motion, enlargement of time, **Rule 1:3–4**
Attorney discipline, hearings involving misconduct, **Rule 1:20–6**

FINES AND PENALTIES
See, also,
  Crimes and Offenses, generally, this index
  Forfeitures, generally, this index
Generally, **2C:1–4, 2C:43–1 et seq., 2C:44–2, 2C:46–2**
Abandonment, motor vehicle, **39:4–56.5**
Abolition, common law crimes, **2C:1–5**
Adult Diagnostic and Treatment Center, generally, this index
Aggravated manslaughter, **2C:11–4**
Aggravated sexual assault, surcharges, **2C:43–3.7**
Aggravating circumstances, **2C:44–1**
Agricultural lands, vandalism, **2C:18–6**
Air Pollution, this index
Alcoholic Beverages, this index
Alcoholics and alcoholism, treatment, probation and probation officers, **2C:35–14**
All Terrain Vehicles, this index
Animals, this index
Archaeology and archaeologists, transportation, state property, archaeological findings, alteration, **27:5J–1**
Arrest, nonpayment, **2C:46–2**
Arson, **2C:17–1**
Assessments, conviction of crime, victims of crime compensation board, **2C:43–3.1**
  Transaction fee, **2C:46–1 et seq.**
Attempts, **2C:5–4**
Attorneys, this index
Authorized dispositions, **2C:43–2**
Automobile no fault insurance, **39:6A–15**
Automobile theft, **2C:20–2.1**
Bail, double fines, **2C:44–5.1**
Bias intimidation, **2C:16–1**
Bicycles, this index
Biological warfare and weapons, terrorism, **2C:38–3**

FINES AND PENALTIES—Cont'd
Blood analysis, implied consent, intoxication of driver, **39:4–51**
Bribery and Corruption, this index
Bridges, interstate bridges, overweight vehicles, **39:4–76**
Buses, this index
Chemical and biological warfare and weapons, terrorism, **2C:38–3**
Child Abuse, this index
Child passenger restraint systems, **39:3–76.2d**
Children and Minors, this index
Chiropractors, this index
Chop shops, operation or maintenance, **2C:20–16**
Cigarettes and Cigars, this index
Classification of offenses, **2C:1–4**
Colleges and Universities, this index
Commercial Drivers Licenses, this index
Common law crimes, abolition, **2C:1–5**
Commuter vans, **39:3–27.22**
Comprehensive enforcement program, definitions, nonpayment of fines or restitution, **2C:46–2**
Computers, this index
Conspiracy, **2C:5–4**
Construction of criminal justice code, **2C:1–2**
Contact lenses, dispensing, licenses and permits, **2C:40–25**
Contempt, this index
Controlled Substances, this index
Corporations, this index
Correction of sentence, motion enlargement of time, **Rule 1:3–2**
Correctional Institutions, this index
Counties, this index
Court imposed financial obligation, default on payments, punishment, **2C:46–2**
Credit card fraud, **2C:21–6**
Criminal sexual contact, surcharges, **2C:43–3.7**
Criminal usury, **2C:21–19**
Criteria, **2C:44–2**
Cruelty to Animals, this index
Cruelty to children, disposition, **9:6–6**
Death penalty. Capital Punishment, generally, this index
Default in payments, **2C:46–1, 2C:46–2**
  Traffic violations, **39:5–36**
Defendants adjudicated guilty, reversal on appeal, return of fine, **2A:166–13**
Definitions, municipal courts, **2B:12–23.1**
Dentists and Dentistry, this index
Detective businesses, community security services, motor vehicle identification lights, **39:3–54.14**
Dirt bikes, **39:3C–28**
  Races, **39:3C–22**
Disorderly Persons, this index
Dispositions authorized, **2C:43–2**
Domestic animals, destruction, use of neuromuscular blocking agents, **4:22–19.4**
Domestic violence, **2C:25–29.1, 2C:25–29.2**
Drivers Licenses, this index
Drivers Schools, this index
Drug Abuse, this index
Drugs and Medicine, this index
Drunken driving, sentence to county jail or workhouse, **39:4–50, 39:4–51**
Electric personal assistive mobility devices, **39:4–14.11**
Electronic surveillance, **2A:156A–3, 2A:156A–5**
Emergency warning lights, volunteer fire company or rescue squad members, wrongful operation, **39:3–54.13**
Employing a juvenile to commit auto theft, **2C:20–17**

FINES AND PENALTIES—Cont'd

Enforced community service, definitions, non-payment of fines or restitution, **2C:46–2**

Eviction, criminal mischief, **2C:17–3**

Evidence, application of rules, **Evidence Rule 101**

Executions, this index

Explosives, this index

Expungement orders, disclosure, **2C:52–30**

Extended or enhanced term of imprisonment, **Rule 3:21–4**

Failure to appear, **Rule 1:2–4**

False alarms, **2C:33–3.2**

False public alarms, **2C:33–3.2**

Fines and penalties. Taxation, this index

First degree crimes, **2C:1–4**

Flammable fabrics, **2A:123–11, 2A:123–12**
  Sleeping bags and tents, sales, **2A:123–21**

Food, this index

Forest fire service, criminal penalties, civil administrative remedy, **13:9–44.10**

Forests, fire prevention and control, state forests, **13:9–44.10**

Forgery, personal identifying information, **2C:21–17.1**

Fourth degree crimes, **2C:1–4**

Fraud, this index

Frivolous litigation, **Rule 1:4–8**

Frozen dessert trucks, traffic rules and regulations, **39:4–128.10**

Gambling, this index

Good behavior, remission of sentence, **2A:164–24**

Grade Crossings, this index

Graffiti, this index

Grand juries, injurious disclosure of information, **2B:21–10**

Guilty pleas, payment, violations bureau, **Rule 7:12–4**

Guns. Weapons, generally, this index

Habitual criminals. Second or Subsequent Offenses, generally, this index

Hazardous Substances and Waste, this index

Health and Accident Insurance, this index

Health Maintenance Organizations, this index

Helmets, bicycle helmets, **39:4–10.2**

Highways and Roads, this index

Hit and run drivers, multiple sentences, **2C:11–5.1, 2C:12–1.1**

Homicide, multiple victims, attempts, conspiracy, **2C:5–4**

Horses, owned or used by law enforcement officers, injuries, **2C:29–3.1**

Identification lights, motor vehicles, private detective businesses, community security services, **39:3–54.14**

Implied consent, blood analysis, intoxication of driver, **39:4–51**

Inmates, failure to pay, deduction from income, victims of crime compensation board, **2C:43–3.1**

Installment payments, **2C:46–1**
  Transaction fee, **2C:46–1 et seq.**

Intensive supervision program, restrictions, **2C:43–11**

Intermunicipal courts, **2C:46–4**

Interstate bridges, overweight vehicles, **39:4–76**

Interstate compact for adult offender supervision, default, **2A:168–37**

Intervention, pretrial intervention, **2C:43–12**

Intoxication of driver. Motor Vehicles, this index

Jails, this index

Judgments and decrees, nonpayment, **2C:46–2**

Jury and Jurors, this index

Juvenile Delinquents, this index

FINES AND PENALTIES—Cont'd

Juvenile family crisis hearing, **Rule 5:17–2**

Kennels, destruction of animals, **4:22–19**

Kidnapping, **2C:13–1**

Labor and Employment, this index

Labor assistance program, definitions, nonpayment of fines or restitution, **2C:46–2**

Labor Unions, this index

Law enforcement officers, animals, injuries, **2C:29–3.1**

Leader of auto theft trafficking network, **2C:20–18**

Lights and Lighting, this index

Limited criminal jurisdiction, courts of, appeals, relief pending, **Rule 3:23–5**

Limousine or livery service, **39:5G–1**

Liquefied Petroleum Gas, this index

Littering, this index

Loads and Loading, this index

Luring and enticing, **2C:13–7**
  Children and minors, **2C:13–6**

Mandatory assessments, **2C:46–1**
  Transaction fee, **2C:46–1 et seq.**

Medicaid, this index

Medicare, this index

Minimum sentence, **2C:43–7.2**

Mitigation,
  Attempts or conspiracy, **2C:5–4**
  Circumstances, **2C:44–1**

Money Laundering and Illegal Investments, this index

Monopolies and unfair trade, **56:9–11**

Motor Carriers, this index

Motor Fuels, this index

Motor vehicle dealers, misrepresentation of vehicle mileage, **2C:21–8**

Motor Vehicle Inspection Law, violations, **39:8–9**

Motor Vehicle Insurance, this index

Motor Vehicle Junk Yard Law, violations, **39:11–11**

Motor Vehicle Security Responsibility Law, **39:6–55**

Motor Vehicles, this index

Motorcycles, passengers, helmets, **39:3–76.5**

Motorized Bicycles, this index

Motorized scooters, **39:4–14.13**

Municipal Courts, this index

Municipalities, this index

Murder, **2C:11–3**

Names, changes, drivers licenses, **39:3–9a**

Noncustodial sentences, **2C:44–1**

Nonpayment, **2C:44–2, 2C:46–2**
  Motor vehicles, **39:5–36**

Nonresident reciprocity privilege, suspension or revocation, failure to pay fines and penalties, victims of crime compensation board, **2C:43–3.1**

Nuclear or radiological devices, terrorism, **2C:38–3**

Nuclear power plants, vandalism, **2C:17–7 et seq.**

Nurses, this index

Office, bribery and corruption, **2C:51–2**

Optometrists, this index

Ordinances, this index

Organized retail theft enterprise, **2C:20–11.2**

Outdoor advertising, **27:5–16**

Pardons, generally, this index

Parking, this index

Partnerships, this index

Payment, this index

Pedestrians, this index

Pending prosecutions, **2C:1–1**

FINES AND PENALTIES—Cont'd

Persons convicted of crimes, **2C:46–4**
  Law enforcement officers training and equipment fund, **2C:43–3.3**
  Victims of crime compensation board, **2C:43–3.1**

Pet shops, destruction of animals, **4:22–19**

Pharmacists, this index

Photosensitivity, tinted windshields, **39:3–75.3**

Physical Therapists, this index

Physicians and Surgeons, this index

Piracy, sound recordings, audiovisual works, **2C:21–21**

Plea agreements, estimated real time served, **Rule 3:9–3**

Poisoning food or gifts, **2C:12–2**

Poor,
  Parking, installments, **39:4–139.10**
  Traffic rules and regulations, installments, **39:4–203.1**

Pounds, destruction of animals, **4:22–19**

Presentence investigations and reports, **2C:44–6**

Pretrial intervention, **2C:43–12**

Prior offenses, **2C:1–1**

Private detective businesses, community security services, motor vehicle identification lights, **39:3–54.14**

Probation and Probation Officers, generally, this index

Psychologists and Psychology, this index

Public private intersections, **39:4–120.10**

Public smoking, **2C:33–13**

Public Utilities, this index

Racketeers and racketeering, **2C:41–3, 2C:41–4**

Radiation Protection, this index

Radioactive Substances, this index

Records and recordation, aggravating or mitigating factors, **2C:44–1**

Reduction of sentence, motion, enlargement of time, **Rule 1:3–4**

Refunds, unconstitutionality, **2B:12–32**

Relief pending appeal, **Rule 3:23–5**

Revocation, **2C:46–3**

Rockets, **21:1C–5**

Roller skates, helmets, **39:4–10.6, 39:4–10.9**

Sales, this index

School Buildings and Grounds, this index

School Buses, this index

Second degree crimes, **2C:1–4**

Second or Subsequent Offenses, generally, this index

Sex Offenses, this index

Sexual assault, surcharges, **2C:43–3.7**

Sexual offenses, **2C:14–6**

Shelters, destruction of animals, **4:22–19**

Shoplifting, **2C:20–11, 2C:20–11.1**

Sirens, unlawful use, volunteer fire companies, **39:3–54.20**

Skateboards, helmets, **39:4–10.6, 39:4–10.9**

Sleeping bags, flammable fabric, sales, **2A:123–21**

Snowmobiles, this index

Soliciting, sales, highways and roads, **39:4–60**

Solid Waste, this index

Speed, this index

Spill compensation, petroleum, pollution of waters, **58:10–23.11u**

State bureau of identification, report of sentence imposed sent to, **53:1–18**

State Highways, this index

State owned grounds, parking permits, altering, counterfeiting or misuse of permits, **39:4–209**

State Treasurer, this index

Statements on the record by court at imposition of sentence, **2C:43–2**

FINES

FINES AND PENALTIES—Cont'd
Storage, fees, **27:23–6.2**
Street gangs, antidrug profiteering, **2C:35A–3**
Street Railways, this index
Streets and Alleys, this index
Subsequent offenses. Second or Subsequent Offenses, generally, this index
Summary proceedings, collection and enforcement, **2C:46–2**
Summons, collection, nonpayment, **2C:46–2**
Sunday, sales, motor vehicles, **2C:33–26**
Sunday law violations. Sunday, generally, this index
Superior Court, this index
Supervisory treatment, pretrial intervention, **2C:43–12**
Support of Persons, this index
Taxation, this index
Telecommunications, this index
Tents, flammable fabrics, sales, **2A:123–21**
Terrorism, this index
Theft, this index
Third degree crimes, **2C:1–4**
Time, payment, **2C:46–1**
Tires, this index
Tobacco or cigarettes, sales to minors, **2A:170–51.1 et seq.**
Toll Collection Monitoring System, this index
Tow Trucks and Towing Companies, this index
Toxic packaging reduction, **13:1E–99.54**
Trademarks and trade names, counterfeiting, **2C:21–32**
Traffic Accidents, this index
Traffic control preemption devices, possession, **2C:40–24**
Traffic Rules and Regulations, this index
Traffic Signs and Signals, this index
Unconstitutionality, **2B:12–32**
Underage person driving motor vehicle under influence of alcohol, **39:4–50.14**
Unlawful taking of a motor vehicle, **2C:20–2.1**
Veterinarians, this index
Victims of crime compensation board, **2C:43–3.1**
Violent crime, conviction, victims of crime compensation board, **2C:43–3.1**
Volunteer firemen, flashing lights, **39:3–54.7**
Warning lights, volunteer fire company or rescue squad members,
Wrongful display, chief or first assistant chief, **39:3–54.20**
Wrongful operation, **39:3–54.13**
Water Pollution, this index
Weapons, this index
Weight of vehicles, excess, registration in another state, **39:3–84.3**
Weights and Measures, this index
Windshields, photosensitivity, tinted windshields, **39:3–75.3**
Wiretapping and electronic surveillance, **2A:156A–3, 2A:156A–5**
Young adult offenders, **2C:43–5**

FINGERNAIL SCRAPINGS
Investigative detention, **Rule 3:5A–1 et seq.**

FINGERPRINTS AND FINGERPRINTING
Arrested persons, indictable offense, **53:1–15**
Assisted living facilities, criminal history record information, **53:1–20.9c**
Bar examinations, applicants, **Rule 1:24–1**
Child care centers, criminal history record information, **53:1–20.9b**
Children and families department, officers and employees, **53:1–20.9f**

FINGERPRINTS AND FINGERPRINTING—Cont'd
Commercial drivers licenses, applications, **39:3–10.17**
Complaints, persons charged with indictable offense, **53:1–15**
Dangerous drugs, persons arrested, **53:1–18.1 et seq.**
Domestic violence, **53:1–15**
Drug addicts, **53:1–15**
Federal Bureau of Investigation, information, exchanges, **53:1–20.9d**
Fees, criminal records checks, user fees, **53:1–20.5 et seq.**
Guardian and ward, criminal history record information, professional guardians, **53:1–20.9e**
Habitual criminals, **53:1–15**
Identification Bureau, generally, this index
Identity in question, **53:1–15**
Investigative detention, **Rule 3:5A–1 et seq.**
Juvenile delinquents and dependents, **2A:4A–61**
Limousine or livery service, drivers, **39:5G–2**
Motor vehicle commission, officers and employees, **39:2A–32**
Narcotic drug violations, persons arrested, **53:1–18.1**
Persons confined in penal institutions, filing by bureau of identification, **53:1–14**
Prior conviction, evidence, **2C:44–4**
Prostitution, **53:1–15**
Records and recordation,
Criminal records checks, user fees, **53:1–20.5 et seq.**
Expungement, **2C:52–1 et seq.**
Shoplifters, **53:1–15**
State bureau of identification. Identification Bureau, generally, this index
State Police, this index
Street gangs, arrest, **53:1–15.1**
User fees, criminal records checks, **53:1–20.5 et seq.**
Weapons, handguns, purchases, **2C:58–3**

FIRE ALARMS AND FIRE ALARM SYSTEMS
False alarms, **2C:33–3 et seq.**

FIRE COMPANIES
Firefighters and Fire Departments, generally, this index
Volunteer Firefighters and Fire Companies, generally, this index

FIRE ENGINE HOUSES
Traffic lights in vicinity of, installation on state roads in suburban districts, **39:4–121**

FIRE ENGINES, APPARATUS AND EQUIPMENT
Authorized emergency vehicles, status, **39:1–1**
Destruction of agricultural or recreational property by operation of vehicle, exception, **39:4–97a**
Exception from motor vehicle laws, **39:3–1**
Flashing red lights, use, returning to fire station, **39:4–92.1**
Following by other vehicles,
Certain distance prohibited, **39:4–92**
Returning to fire station, **39:4–92.1**
Parking other vehicles within certain distance prohibited, **39:4–92**
Police whistle indicating approach of, **39:4–122**
Returning to fire station, following by other vehicles, **39:4–92.1**
Turnpikes, tolls, **27:23–40**

FIRE ENGINES, APPARATUS AND EQUIPMENT—Cont'd
Volunteer fire departments, free registration of motor vehicles owned by, **39:3–27**

FIRE PROTECTION AND PREVENTION
Fires and Fire Protection, generally, this index

FIRE STATIONS
Parking within certain distance from driveway entrance prohibited, **39:4–138**

FIREARM SILENCERS
Definitions, **2C:39–1**
Manufacture, transport, disposition and defacement, **2C:39–9**
Person convicted of crime involving, possession of any weapon prohibited, **2C:39–7**
Prohibited weapons, **2C:39–3**

FIREARMS
Weapons, generally, this index

FIREARMS TRAINING COURSE
Definitions, unlawful possession, exemption, **2C:39–6**

FIRECRACKERS
Fireworks, generally, this index

FIREFIGHTERS AND FIRE DEPARTMENTS
Apparatus. Fire Engines, Apparatus and Equipment, generally, this index
Application of law, motor vehicles, hands free telephones, **39:4–97.4**
Arson investigation units, weapons possession, exemption, **2C:39–6**
Assault, **2C:12–1**
Cellular telephones, hands free telephones, application of law, motor vehicles, **39:4–97.4**
Commercial drivers licenses, exemption, **39:3–10j et seq.**
Drug tests, fraud, **2C:36–10**
Engines. Fire Engines, Apparatus and Equipment, generally, this index
Equipment. Fire Engines, Apparatus and Equipment, generally, this index
Explosives, application of law, **21:1A–141**
Fraud, drug tests, **2C:36–10**
Hands free telephones, motor vehicles, application of law, **39:4–97.4**
Machinery and equipment. Fire Engines, Apparatus and Equipment, generally, this index
Motor vehicles,
Hands free telephones, application of law, **39:4–97.4**
Radio, interception of police, fire or emergency medical communication, used to commit crime, **2C:33–21 et seq.**
Special license plates, **39:3–27.8 et seq.**
Nonprofit Corporations and Associations, generally, this index
Radio and radio stations,
Definition of police, fire or emergency medical communication system excluding radar, **2C:33–23**
Interception of message, crimes and offenses, **2C:33–21 et seq.**
Possession of radio receiving police, message during commission of crime, fourth degree crime, **2C:33–22**
Telecommunications, hands free telephones, operators, application of law, **39:4–97.4**
Tests, drug tests, fraud, **2C:36–10**
Turnpikes, fire fighting equipment, tolls, **27:23–40**

FIREFIGHTERS AND FIRE DEPARTMENTS
—Cont'd
Vehicles. Fire Engines, Apparatus and Equipment, generally, this index
Victims of crime, **2C:44–1**
Volunteer Firefighters and Fire Companies, generally, this index
Wireless telephones, hands free telephones, application of law, motor vehicles, **39:4–97.4**

FIRES AND FIRE PROTECTION
Arson and Other Burnings, generally, this index
Criminal mischief, **2C:17–3**
Explosives, prohibited acts, **21:1A–132**
Extinguishers, limousine or livery service, fines and penalties, **39:5G–1**
False alarms, **2C:33–3 et seq.**
Firefighters and Fire Departments, generally, this index
Fireworks, manufacturers, fire protection, **21:2–11, 21:2–12**
Flammable Fabrics Act, **2A:123–3 et seq.**
Hazardous Substances and Waste, generally, this index
Intoxicating liquor distributors license, renewal, **33:1–11.6**
Kerosene burning heating devices, **2C:40–6 et seq.**
Liquefied petroleum gas education and safety board, **21:1B–12 et seq.**
Oil burning heating devices, **2C:40–6 et seq.**
Portable oil burning heating devices, **2C:40–6 et seq.**
Turnpikes, tolls, **27:23–40**

FIREWORKS
Generally, **21:2–1 et seq.**
Agriculture, this index
Airports and landing fields, exceptions, application of law, **21:2–4**
Application, public displays, permits, contents, **21:3–4**
Application of law, **21:2–4**
Armed forces, exceptions, application of law, **21:2–4**
Bonds (officers and fiduciaries),
Manufacturers, **21:2–27, 21:2–28**
Public displays, **21:3–5**
Brands, marks and labels, packages, **21:2–15, 21:2–36**
Buildings, **21:2–7**
Certificates of registration. Manufacturers and manufacturing, post
Conflicts of laws, explosives, **21:3–7**
Containers, matches, manufacturers, **21:2–20**
Copies, public display, permits and applications, **21:3–6**
Crimes and offenses,
Manufacture, storage and transportation, **21:2–35**
Possession and sale, **21:3–8**
Definitions, **21:2–2**
Dangerous fireworks, **21:2–3**
Distribution. Sales, generally, post
Drugs and medicine, manufacturers and manufacturing, entry, **21:2–17**
Enforcement, **21:3–9**
Exceptions, application of law, **21:2–4, 21:3–7**
Factories. Manufacturers and manufacturing, generally, post
Fees, licenses and permits, agricultural use, **21:2–29.1**
Fences, fireworks plants, **21:2–10**
Fires and fire protection, manufacturers, **21:2–11, 21:2–12**

FIREWORKS—Cont'd
Foreign commerce, exceptions, application of law, **21:2–4**
Gates, fireworks plants, **21:2–10**
Indemnity, manufacturers, bonds, **21:2–27, 21:2–28**
Inspection and inspectors, manufacturers, **21:2–21**
Insurance, public displays, **21:3–5**
Interstate commerce, exceptions, application of law, **21:2–4**
Intoxicating liquors, manufacturers and manufacturing, entry, **21:2–17**
Labels, brands and marks, packages, **21:2–15, 21:2–36**
Licenses and permits,
Agricultural use, **21:2–29.1**
Public displays, **21:3–3**
Applications, contents, **21:3–4**
Copies, **21:3–6**
Purchase, possession, and public display of fireworks, **21:3–3**
Requirements, delivery of fireworks, **21:2–36**
Location,
Buildings, storage, **21:2–9**
Manufacturers and manufacturing, buildings, **21:2–8**
Public display, **21:3–3**
Storage, buildings, **21:2–9**
Manufacturers and manufacturing, **21:2–8 et seq.**
Bonds (officers and fiduciaries), **21:2–27, 21:2–28**
Certificates of registration, **21:2–22 et seq.**
Denial, **21:2–23**
Posting, **21:2–22**
Records, revocation, **21:2–26**
Revocation, **21:2–24**
Statement of reasons, revocation, **21:2–25**
Drugs and medicine, entry, **21:2–17**
Fences and gates, **21:2–10**
Fires and fire protection, **21:2–11, 21:2–12**
Inspection and inspectors, **21:2–21**
Intoxicating liquors, entry, **21:2–17**
Location, buildings, **21:2–8**
Matches,
Entry, **21:2–17**
Possession, **21:2–18**
Safety containers, **21:2–20**
Prohibition, **21:2–18**
Smoking, **21:2–18**
Storage, buildings, location, **21:2–9, 21:2–13**
Types permitted, **21:2–14**
Uniforms, employees, **21:2–16**
Warning signs, **21:2–19**
Watchmen, **21:2–10**
Marks, brands and labels, packages, **21:2–15, 21:2–36**
Matches. Manufacturers and manufacturing, ante
Model rockets. Rockets, generally, this index
Municipalities,
Enforcement, **21:3–9**
Public displays, permits, **21:3–3**
Purchase, possession and public display of fireworks, licenses and permits, **21:3–3**
Registration, legally operated commercial enterprise involving manufacture, distribution, fireworks, **21:2–37**
Office of Safety Compliance, department of labor, duplicate copy, permits and applications, **21:3–6**
Permits. Licenses and permits, generally, ante
Pest control bombs, storage or sale, **21:2–29.1**
Pesticides, agricultural use, permits, **21:2–29.1**

FIREWORKS—Cont'd
Posting, certificate of registration, fireworks plants, **21:2–22**
Prohibitions, **21:2–6**
Possession and sales, **21:3–2**
Showers, buildings, **21:2–7**
Public displays. Licenses and permits, ante
Public halls, fireworks showers, prohibition, **21:2–7**
Public policy, possession and sale, declaration, **21:3–1**
Railroads, exceptions, application of law, **21:2–4**
Records and recordation, manufacturers and manufacturing, certificates of registration, revocation, **21:2–26**
Registration, certificates of registration. Manufacturers and manufacturing, generally, ante
Registration with municipality, legally operated commercial enterprise involving manufacture, distribution, fireworks, **21:2–37**
Repeals of statutes, **21:2–5**
Rockets, generally, this index
Sales,
Agricultural use, permits, **21:2–29.1**
Authorized purchasers, **21:3–2**
Crimes and offenses, **21:3–8**
License requirements, delivery of fireworks, **21:2–36**
Prohibited places, **21:2–29**
Prohibitions, **21:2–6, 21:3–2**
Public policy, declaration, **21:3–1**
Smoking, prohibition, **21:2–30**
Showers of fireworks, buildings, prohibition, **21:2–7**
Signals and signaling, exceptions, application of law, **21:2–4**
Smoking,
Manufacturers and manufacturing, **21:2–18**
Warning signs, **21:2–19**
Places of sale, **21:2–30**
Plants, **21:2–18**
Warning signs, **21:2–19**
Storage, **21:2–9**
Agricultural purposes, **21:2–29.1**
Prohibited places, **21:2–13, 21:2–29**
Public displays, approval, **21:3–4**
Theaters, showers, prohibition, **21:2–7**
Toy guns or devices, caps, possession and sales, prohibitions, **21:3–2**
Transportation,
License and permit requirements, persons to whom fireworks delivered, **21:2–36**
Prohibition, **21:2–6**
Types permitted, manufacturing, **21:2–14**
Turnpike project, transportation regulations, **27:23–31**
Types, manufacturing, **21:2–14**
Uniforms, employees in plants, **21:2–16**
Warning signs,
Fireworks plants, **21:2–19**
Packages, **21:2–15**
Places of sale, smoking, **21:2–30**
Watchmen, fireworks plants, **21:2–10**

FIREWORKS REGULATION LAW
Generally, **21:2–1 et seq.**

FIRST AID
Limousine or livery service, fines and penalties, **39:5G–1**
Nonprofit Corporations and Associations, generally, this index

FIRST AID SQUADS
Flashing lights, volunteers, **39:3–54.7 et seq.**
License plates, special, **39:3–27.8 et seq.**
Registration fees, exemption, **39:3–27**
Special license plates, **39:3–27.8 et seq.**
Turnpikes, tolls, **27:23–40**

FIRST APPEARANCE
Municipal courts, **Rules 7:3–1, 7:3–2**

FIRST DEGREE CRIMES
Generally, **2C:1–4**
Crimes and Offenses, this index

FIRST OFFENDERS
Supervisory treatment programs, **2C:43–12 et seq.**

FISH AND GAME
All terrain vehicles, harassment, **39:3C–19**
Cruelty to animals, fish and game laws not affected by act relating to, **4:22–16**
Deer,
Licenses and permits, managers and management, **2C:39–3**
Managers and management,
Firearm silencers, **2C:39–3**
Licenses and permits, **2C:39–3**
Dirt bikes, harassment, **39:3C–19**
Division, fish and wildlife division. Environmental Protection Department, this index
Fish and wildlife division. Environmental Protection Department, this index
Fur bearing animals,
Cats, sales, crimes and offenses, **4:22–25.3**
Dogs, sales, crimes and offenses, **4:22–25.3**
License plates, applications, fees, **39:3–33.10, 39:3–33.11**
Licenses and permits. Deer, ante
Shooting, birds, crimes and offenses, **4:22–23**
Snowmobiles, harassment, **39:3C–19**
State police, powers and duties, **53:2–1**
Trapping, **39:1–1 et seq.**
Unlawful possession of weapons, hunting or fishing, exemption, **2C:39–6**
Violation of laws, jurisdiction, **2B:12–17**
Weapons,
Deer, managers and management, firearm silencers, **2C:39–3**
Firearm silencers, deer, managers and management, **2C:39–3**
Temporary transfer and possession, **2C:58–3.1**
Unlawful possession, hunting or fishing, exemption, **2C:39–6**

FISH AND GAME WARDENS
State Police, this index
Weapons, authority to carry, nonlethal weapons, **2C:39–6**

FISH AND WILDLIFE DIVISION
Environmental Protection Department, this index

FITTING ROOMS
Invasion of privacy, defenses, crimes and offenses, observation, nudity, **2C:14–9**

FIXTURES
Intoxicating liquors,
Fixtures as subject to seizure, forfeiture, **33:1–66**
Furnishing, repair or replacement by brewer for retail licensee, **33:1–43.1**

FLAGS
Definitions, theft, **2C:20–2.3**
Red flags,
Motor vehicles, overhanging loads, **39:3–61.4**
Overhanging loads on motor vehicles, **39:3–84**
Theft, cemeteries, **2C:20–2.3**

FLAMMABLE FABRICS
Generally, **2A:123–3 et seq.**
Sleeping bags, sales, **2A:123–16 et seq.**
Tents, sales, **2A:123–16 et seq.**

FLAMMABLE FABRICS ACT
Generally, **2A:123–4**

FLAMMABLE LIQUIDS
Definitions, Motor Vehicle Law, **39:1–1**

FLAMMABLES
Hazardous Substances and Waste, generally, this index

FLAPS
Motor vehicles, mud flaps, **39:3–79.1 et seq.**

FLARES
Commercial motor vehicles, carrying and placing of flares or other emergency warning light equipment, **39:3–64**

FLASHING LIGHTS
Emergency vehicles, volunteers, **39:3–54.7 et seq.**
Fines and penalties, wrongful operation, **39:3–54.13**
Identification cards, emergency vehicles, permit for use and display, **39:3–54.11**
Omnibuses, highjack lights, **39:3–54**
Outdoor advertising, use on signs prohibited, **27:5–9**
Traffic control signals, **39:4–119**
Use on motor vehicles prohibited except to indicate turn, **39:3–54**
Volunteer fire companies, vehicles, **39:3–54.7 et seq.**

FLASHING SIGNALS
Traffic Signs and Signals, this index

FLAVORED CIGARETTES
Sales, **2A:170–51.6**

FLAVORING EXTRACTS
Alcohol in extracts unfit for beverage purposes, **33:1–30**

FLIGHT
Body vests, **2C:39–13**
Homicide, **2C:11–3**
Limitation of criminal prosecutions, **2C:1–6**
Motor vehicles, vessels, fleeing or attempting to elude law enforcement officers, **2C:29–2**
Murder, committing during flight, **2C:11–3**

FLOODS AND FLOOD CONTROL
Causing or risking widespread injury or damage, **2C:17–2**
Criminal mischief, **2C:17–3**

FLORENCES LAW
Motor vehicles, intoxication of driver, **39:4–50**

FLUNITRAZEPAM
Date rape drugs. Controlled Substances, this index

FOG
Lights, animal drawn vehicles, **39:4–25**

FOOD
Adulteration, controlled dangerous substances, crimes and offenses, **2C:12–2**
Advertisements, kosher food, **2C:21–7.2 et seq.**
Alcohol in food products unfit for beverage purposes, **33:1–30**
Brands, labels and marks, kosher food, **2C:21–7.2 et seq.**
Controlled dangerous substances, adulteration, crimes and offenses, **2C:12–2**
Crimes and offenses,
Controlled dangerous substances, adulteration, **2C:12–2**
Packages, writings, **2C:40–19**
Culinary arts or hotel management programs, intoxicating liquors, possession, children and minors, **33:3–15**
Definitions, food and drugs, **24:21–32**
Devices, **24:21–32**
Fines and penalties, poisoning, **2C:12–2**
Frozen Desserts and Dietary Foods, generally, this index
Ice cream and other frozen products. Frozen Desserts and Dietary Foods, generally, this index
Indigent, neglected or abandoned children, definition, **9:6–1**
Intoxicating liquors, licensee, sale, **33:1–12**
Misbranding, kosher food, **2C:21–7.2 et seq.**
Motor vehicle commission, concessions, contracts, **39:2A–33**
Packages, this index
Poison food, **2C:12–2**
Restaurants, generally, this index
Tampering with, **2C:40–16, 2C:40–17**
Truck used for transportation of solid waste, use for transportation of food,
Cleansing and sanitization required, **48:13A–12.1**
Crime of third degree, penalties, **48:13A–12.2**

FOOD ESTABLISHMENTS
Restaurants, generally, this index

FOOD STAMP COUPON
Definitions, food stamps, crimes and offenses, **2C:20–35**

FOOD STAMPS
Crimes and offenses, **2C:20–36**
Definitions, illegal use, **2C:20–35**
Illegal use, **2C:20–35 et seq.**
Prohibited transactions involving food stamp coupons or ATP card, less than $150, **2C:20–37**

FOOTPRINTS
Investigative detention, **Rule 3:5A–1 et seq.**

FORCE OR VIOLENCE
Actions and proceedings, racketeering, **2C:41–4**
Arrest, use of force, **2C:3–7**
Bias intimidation, **2C:16–1**
Bodily violence, fear of, placement of graffiti on property in attempt to instill, **2C:33–10**
Cease and desist orders, racketeering, **2C:41–4**
Confidential and privileged information, racketeering investigations, **2C:41–5**
Consent of victim, **2C:2–10**
Criminal sexual contact, **2C:14–3**
Deadly Force, generally, this index
Debtors and creditors, racketeering, **2C:41–1 et seq.**

FORCE OR VIOLENCE—Cont'd
Defense of premises or personal property,
  2C:3–6
Definitions,
  Justification, **2C:3–11**
  Racketeering, **2C:41–1**
Discovery, racketeering investigations, **2C:41–5**
Disorderly conduct, **2C:33–2**
Domestic Violence, generally, this index
Duress, **2C:2–9**
Examinations and examiners, racketeering,
  2C:41–5
Fines and penalties, racketeering, **2C:41–1 et
  seq.**
Hostages. Kidnapping, generally, this index
Indebtedness, racketeering, **2C:41–1 et seq.**
Inspections and inspectors, racketeering inves-
  tigations, **2C:41–5**
Interrogatories, racketeering, investigations,
  2C:41–5
Investigations and investigators, racketeering,
  2C:41–5
Investments, racketeering, **2C:41–1 et seq.**
Judgments and decrees, racketeering, **2C:41–4**
Justification, **2C:3–4**
  Criminal prosecution defense, **2C:3–3**
Kidnapping, generally, this index
Law enforcement, use of force, **2C:3–7**
Licenses and permits, racketeering, revocation
  or suspension, **2C:41–4**
Mistake of law, use of force, **2C:3–9**
Obstructing administration of law or other gov-
  ernmental functions, **2C:29–1**
Process, racketeering, **2C:41–5**
Production of books and papers, racketeering,
  2C:41–5
Protection of third persons, **2C:3–5, 2C:3–8**
Racketeering, **2C:41–1 et seq.**
Records and recordation, racketeering, investi-
  gations, **2C:41–5**
Restitution, racketeering, **2C:41–4**
Securities, racketeering, **2C:41–1 et seq.**
Sexual assault, **2C:14–2**
State police, complaints, limitation of actions,
  53:1–33
Use of force, self protection, **2C:3–4**

FORCIBLE ENTRY AND DETAINER
Crimes and offenses, disorderly persons,
  2C:33–11.1
Disorderly persons, crimes and offenses,
  2C:33–11.1

FORCIBLE SODOMY
Expungement of record, **2C:52–2**

FORECLOSURE
Exhibits, copies, **Rule 1:4–3**
Mortgages, this index
Tax foreclosure actions, filing of papers, **Rule
  1:5–6**

FORECLOSURE OFFICE
Generally, **Rule 1:34–6**

FOREIGN BORN
Aliens, generally, this index

FOREIGN COMMERCE
Explosives, application of law, **21:1A–141**
Fireworks, exceptions, application of law,
  21:2–4

FOREIGN CORPORATIONS
Certificate to do business, revocation, **2C:43–4**
Certificates of authority, revocation, **2C:43–4**

FOREIGN CORPORATIONS—Cont'd
Crimes and offenses, certificate, revocation,
  2C:43–4
Monopolies and unfair trade, violations, suspension of privilege of conducting business, **56:9–8**

FOREIGN COUNTRIES
Consuls, attorneys, **Rule 1:21–4**
Conviction of crime, aggravating circumstances,
  2C:44–4
Definitions, lotteries, **2C:37–6.1**
Drivers licenses, surrender, **39:3–10**
Human trafficking, **2C:13–8**
Immigration and Naturalization, generally, this
  index
Lotteries, equipment, tickets, sale, transporta-
  tion, **2C:37–6.1**
Motor vehicles,
  Drivers licenses, surrender, **39:3–10**
  Registration in foreign country, operation in
    state, **39:3–4f**
Self authentication, public documents, **Evi-
  dence Rule 902**
Weapons, persons convicted of certain crimes,
  possession, **2C:39–7**

FOREIGN GOVERNMENT
Foreign Countries, generally, this index

FOREIGN JURISDICTIONS
Depositions, this index

FOREIGN JURY
Courts authorized to order trial by, petit jurors,
  2B:23–9
Expenses, petit jurors, **2B:23–9**
Ineligibility, persons whose names do not ap-
  pear on jury lists, **2B:23–11**
Number of jurors, petit jurors, **2B:23–9**
Order for, petit jurors, **2B:23–9**
Peremptory challenges, number, **2B:23–13**
Qualifications, petit jurors, **2B:23–9**
Summoning and returning, petit jurors,
  2B:23–9

FOREIGN LANGUAGES
Wiretapping and electronic surveillance,
  2A:156A–12

FOREIGN LAWS
Judicial Notice, generally, this index

FOREIGN LEGAL CONSULTANTS
Generally, **Rule 1:21–9**

FOREIGN PERSON
Definitions, intoxicating liquors, **33:1–11.2**

FOREIGN STATES
  See, also, Foreign Countries, generally, this
    index
Adult offender supervision interstate compact,
  2A:168–26 et seq.
All terrain vehicles, reciprocity, **39:3C–7**
Attorneys, this index
Conflict of Laws, generally, this index
Conviction of crime, aggravating circumstances,
  2C:44–4
Crimes and offenses, death causing, venue,
  Rule 3:14–1
Domestic violence, contempt, restraining or-
  ders, **2C:29–9**
Drivers Licenses, this index
Ex parte affidavits, **Rule 1:4–4**
Extradition, generally, this index

FOREIGN STATES—Cont'd
Handicapped persons, special parking privilege,
  39:4–207.5
Interstate Compacts, generally, this index
Interstate Highway System, generally, this in-
  dex
Interstate movement, offenders, **2A:168–34**
Intoxication of driver, prior convictions,
  39:4–50
Law enforcement agencies, juvenile delin-
  quents and dependents, records, confiden-
  tiality, **2A:4A–60 et seq.**
Limousine or livery service, licenses and per-
  mits, **39:3–19.6**
Long Arm Act, **39:7–1 et seq.**
Lotteries drawn or conducted in foreign states,
  2C:37–6
  Equipment, tickets, sale, transportation,
    2C:37–6.1
Major disasters, attorneys, temporary practice
  of law, **Rule 1:21–10**
Motor Vehicles, this index
Offenses committed in, territorial applicability
  of code of criminal justice, **2C:1–3**
Parking, special parking privilege, handicapped
  persons, **39:4–207.5**
Reciprocity, generally, this index
Schools and school districts, sex offenses, regis-
  tration, **2C:7–2**
Snowmobiles, reciprocity, **39:3C–7**
Taxicabs, licenses and permits, **39:3–19.6**
Traffic violations, **39:5F–1 et seq.**
Uniform Fresh Pursuit Law, arrest, hearing,
  Rule 3:4–4
Vocational education, sex offenses, registra-
  tion, **2C:7–2**
Weapons, persons convicted of certain crimes,
  possession, **2C:39–7**

FOREIGNERS
Aliens, generally, this index

FORENSIC DNA LABORATORY FUND
Fines and penalties, surcharge, **53:1–20.28a**

FORENSIC LABORATORIES
Drugs and medicine, controlled dangerous substances, **2C:35–19, 2C:35–20**

FORENSIC LABORATORY FUND
Generally, **2C:35–20**

FOREPERSON
Grand jury, **Rule 3:6–4**
Jurors, **Rule 1:8–4**

FOREST FIRE SERVICE
Fines and penalties, criminal penalties, civil
  administrative remedy, **13:9–44.10**

FOREST FIRES
Crimes and offenses, state forests, **13:9–44.10**
Fines and penalties, state forests, **13:9–44.10**

FOREST WARDENS
Police, acting, **53:2–1**

**FORESTRY, GEOLOGY, PARKS AND HIS-
  TORIC SITES DIVISION**
Environmental Protection Department, gener-
  ally, this index

FORESTS AND FORESTRY
Aggravated arson, **2C:17–1**
Crimes and offenses, fire prevention and con-
  trol, state forests, **13:9–44.10**
Definitions, aggravated arson, **2C:17–1**

FORESTS AND FORESTRY—Cont'd

Fines and penalties, fire prevention and control, state forests, **13:9–44.10**

Parks and forestry division. Environmental Protection Department, this index

FORFEITURES

See, also, Fines and Penalties, generally, this index

Generally, **2C:43–2, 2C:64–1 et seq.**

Agents, rights of owner, **2C:64–5**

Alcoholic Beverages, this index

Bail, this index

Banks and Banking, this index

Bribery and Corruption, this index

Contact lenses, dispensing, licenses and permits, **2C:40–25**

Controlled Substances, this index

Conviction of crime,

    Estate on conviction, **2A:152–2**

    Public officers, **2C:51–2**

    Revocation or suspension, **2A:168A–7 et seq.**

Corporations, this index

Court ordered, public officers, conviction of crime, **2C:51–2**

Defenses against, **2C:64–5**

Destruction, **2C:64–6**

Disposal, forfeited property, **2C:64–6**

Drug paraphernalia, **24:21–52**

Electronic surveillance equipment, **2A:156A–7**

Estate on conviction of crime, **2A:152–2**

Evidence, seized property, **2C:64–4**

Hazardous Substances and Waste, this index

Health and Accident Insurance, this index

Interest in seized property, notice, **2C:64–3**

Limitation of actions, claims to seized property, **2C:64–8**

Limited criminal jurisdiction, courts of, appeals, relief pending, **Rule 3:23–5**

Money Laundering and Illegal Investments, generally, this index

Motor Vehicles, this index

Motorized scooters, **39:4–14.13**

Municipal courts, collection and disposition, **Rule 7:14–4**

Notice,

    Interest in seized property, **2C:64–3**

    Property, **2C:64–3**

Nuisances, chattels, liquors, **2C:33–12.1**

Office or position, bribery and corruption, **2C:51–2**

Offroad vehicles, public lands, **39:3C–34**

Owners, rights of owners and others holding interest and property, **2C:64–5**

Piracy, sound recordings, audiovisual works, **2C:21–21**

Prima facie contraband, **2C:64–2**

Proceeds,

    Dividing, **2C:64–6**

    Illegal activities, **2C:64–1**

Property subject, **2C:64–1**

Public officers and employees, conviction of crime, forfeiture of office, **2C:51–2**

Racketeering, **2C:41–3, 2C:41–4**

Recognizances, this index

Release, property pending determination of proceedings, **2C:64–3**

Rights of owners and others holding interest in property, **2C:64–5**

Solid Waste, this index

Summary hearings, **2C:64–3**

Theft of services, **2C:20–8**

Time, **2C:64–3**

Title, vesting, **2C:64–7**

Trademarks and trade names, counterfeiting, **2C:21–32**

FORFEITURES—Cont'd

Use of property in illegal activities, **2C:64–1**

Waiver, public officers and employees, **2C:51–2**

FORGERY

Generally, **2C:21–1 et seq.**

Credit cards, **2C:21–6**

Fines and penalties, personal identifying information, **2C:21–17.1**

Jurors, peremptory challenges, **Rule 1:8–3**

Jury, number of peremptory challenges, **2B:23–13**

Negotiable instruments, **2C:21–1**

Proof of financial responsibility under motor vehicle security responsibility law, **39:6–55**

Venue, **Rule 3:14–1**

Writings or records, false statements or information, **2C:21–4**

FORMA PAUPERIS

Probation officers investigation of financial status of person, **2A:168–13**

Public defenders, **2A:158A–1 et seq.**

FORMALDEHYDE

Turnpike projects, transportation regulation, **27:23–31**

FORMER JEOPARDY

Double Jeopardy, generally, this index

FORMER PROSECUTIONS

Double Jeopardy, generally, this index

FORMS

Advisory opinions, unauthorized practice of law committee, **Rule 1:22–3**

Alcoholic Beverages, this index

Children and minors, juvenile delinquents and dependents, information requests, juvenile family crises, **2A:4A–77**

Controlled substances, ordering, **24:21–14**

Drugs and Medicine, this index

Indigent, neglected or abandoned children, information requests, juvenile family crisis, **2A:4A–77**

Judges weekly report, **Rule 1:32–1**

Juvenile delinquents and dependents, information requests, juvenile family crises, **2A:4A–77**

Juvenile pleas, **Rule 5:21A**

Motor Vehicles, this index

Motorized bicycles, registration,

    Certificates, **39:4–14.3i, 39:4–14.3j**

    Ownership transfers, **39:4–14.3***l*

Nonresident Violator Compact, motor vehicles, **39:5F–21**

Process, **Rule 1:32–3**

Sex offenders, registration, **2C:7–4**

Traffic regulations, Nonresident Violator Compact, **39:5F–21**

FORTIFICATIONS

Controlled substances, property used for manufacture, distribution or possession, crimes and offenses, **2C:35–4.1**

FORTIFIED WINES

Alcoholic Beverages, this index

FORUM

Jurisdiction, generally, this index

FOURTH DEGREE CRIMES

Crimes and Offenses, this index

FRANCHISES

Public Utilities, this index

FRATERNAL BENEFIT SOCIETIES

Club officers, intoxicating liquors, law enforcement personnel, **33:1–25.1, 33:1–25.2**

Constables, intoxicating liquors, licenses and permits, **33:1–25.1, 33:1–25.2**

Intoxicating liquors, club licenses, law enforcement personnel as officers, **33:1–25.1, 33:1–25.2**

Law enforcement officers, intoxicating liquors, licenses and permits, **33:1–25.1, 33:1–25.2**

Licenses and permits, intoxicating liquors, law enforcement personnel as club officers, **33:1–25.1, 33:1–25.2**

Officers and employees, intoxicating liquors, law enforcement personnel, **33:1–25.1, 33:1–25.2**

Police and police departments, intoxicating liquors, licenses and permits, **33:1–25.1, 33:1–25.2**

Sheriffs, intoxicating liquors, licenses and permits, **33:1–25.1, 33:1–25.2**

FRATERNAL ORGANIZATIONS

Alcoholic beverages, sales within 200 feet of church or school, **33:1–76**

Club officers, intoxicating liquors, law enforcement personnel, **33:1–25.1, 33:1–25.2**

Fraternal Benefit Societies, generally, this index

Intoxicating liquors, club licenses, law enforcement personnel as officers, **33:1–25.1, 33:1–25.2**

Law enforcement officers, intoxicating liquors, licenses and permits, **33:1–25.1, 33:1–25.2**

FRATERNITIES

Colleges and Universities, this index

Hazing, crimes and offenses, **2C:40–3 et seq.**

FRAUD

Generally, **2C:21–1 et seq.**

Affidavits, certification in lieu of affidavit, **Rule 1:4–4**

Age,

    Alcoholic beverages, sale to minor, **33:1–81**

    Defense, **33:1–77**

Alcoholic beverages,

    Licenses and permits, revocation, **33:1–25**

    Sales, children and minors, **33:1–81**

Attorneys,

    Client protection fund, **Rule 1:28–1 et seq.**

    Conviction, discipline, **Rule 1:20–13**

Automobile no fault insurance, **39:6A–15**

Bad checks, **2C:21–5**

Bribery and corruption, public resources, **2C:27–12**

Charitable Organizations and Associations, this index

Children and minors, alcoholic beverages, sales, **33:1–81**

Defenses, **33:1–77**

Consent, victim of crime, **2C:2–10**

Controlled Substances, this index

Corporations, this index

Correctional institutions, officers and employees, drug tests, **2C:36–10**

County contracts, **2C:21–34**

Credit cards, **2C:21–6**

    Scanning, **2C:21–6.1**

Criminal simulation, **2C:21–2**

Deceptive business practices, **2C:21–7**

Deeds and conveyances, **2C:21–3**

Dentists and Dentistry, this index

FRAUD—Cont'd
Drivers Licenses, this index
Drivers schools, revocation or suspension of
 license, **39:12–7**
 Instructors license, **39:12–8**
Drug tests, **2C:36–10**
Drugs and medicine, registered manufacturers
 or distributors, **24:21–22**
Electronic fund transfers, payment cards, scan-
 ning, **2C:21–6.1**
Embezzlement, generally, this index
False personation, **2C:21–17**
Fiduciaries, misapplication of property,
 2C:21–15
Financial institutions, receiving deposits,
 2C:21–14
Fines and penalties, personal identifying infor-
 mation, **2C:21–17.1**
Forgery, generally, this index
Former prosecution as bar to subsequent pros-
 ecution, fraudulent procurement by defen-
 dant, **2C:1–12**
Funeral expenses, prepaid monies, **2A:102–16.2**
Hazardous Substances and Waste, this index
Health and Accident Insurance, this index
Health Care Claims Fraud, generally, this index
Health Maintenance Organizations, this index
Hindering apprehension or prosecution,
 2C:29–3
Human body parts, sales, purchases, **2C:22–2**
Identity Theft, generally, this index
Immigration and naturalization, counselors, un-
 authorized practice, **2C:21–31**
Insolvency, **2C:21–13**
Insurance, this index
Judgments and decrees, motor vehicle accident
 case not paid out of unsatisfied claim and
 judgment fund, **39:6–76**
Jury, **2C:29–8**
Kidnapping, **2C:13–1**
Kosher foods, **2C:21–7.2 et seq.**
Labor and Employment, this index
Law enforcement officers, drug tests, labor and
 employment, **2C:36–10**
Medicaid, this index
Medicare, this index
Money Laundering and Illegal Investments,
 generally, this index
Mortgages, this index
Motor Vehicle Insurance, this index
Motor Vehicle Security Responsibility Law,
 protection, identification cards, possession
 by driver, **39:3–29.1**
Motor Vehicles, this index
Motorized bicycles, ownership proof,
 39:4–14.3p
Municipal contracts, **2C:21–34**
Political subdivisions, contracts, **2C:21–34**
Prepaid funeral agreements, **2A:102–16.2**
Public records, **2C:21–3**
Public utilities, identification cards, **2C:21–35**
Receivers, this index
Records and Recordation, this index
Revocation of alcoholic beverage license,
 33:1–25
Rigging public contest, **2C:21–11**
Sales, this index
Secured creditors, defrauding, **2C:21–12**
Securing execution of documents by deception,
 2C:21–16
Securities, this index
Sex offenses, registration, **2C:7–2**
Slugs, coin currency or credit card activated
 machine, **2C:21–18**
Solicitation, charitable contributions, decep-
 tion, **2C:20–4**

FRAUD—Cont'd
State contracts, **2C:21–34**
Theft by deception, **2C:20–4**
Theft of services, **2C:20–8**
Universal product codes, **2C:21–2.4**
Unsworn falsifications, **2C:28–3**
Weapons, sales, **2C:39–10**
Wills, this index
Wrongful impersonating, **2C:21–17**

FRAUDULENT CONVEYANCES
Deed documents, **2C:21–3**
Recordable instruments, **2C:21–3**

**FRAUDULENT REPRESENTATIONS OR
 STATEMENTS**
Fraud, generally, this index

FREE LIBRARIES
Libraries, generally, this index

FREE SCHOOLS
Schools and School Districts, generally, this
 index

FREEHOLDERS
Board of chosen freeholders. Chosen Free-
 holders, generally, this index
Chosen Freeholders, generally, this index

FREEWAYS AND PARKWAYS
Advertisements. Outdoor Advertising, gener-
 ally, this index
All terrain vehicles, operation, **39:3C–17**
Dimensional and weight limitations, **39:3–84**
Dirt bikes, operation, **39:3C–17**
Outdoor Advertising, generally, this index
Snowmobiles, operation, **39:3C–17**

FREIGHT
Cars. Railroads, this index

FRENCH CUSTARD
Frozen Desserts and Dietary Foods, generally,
 this index

FRENCH ICE CREAM
Frozen Desserts and Dietary Foods, generally,
 this index

FRESH FOOD PRODUCTS
Truck used for transportation of solid waste,
 use for transportation of food,
Cleansing and sanitization required,
 48:13A–12.1
Crime of third degree, penalties, **48:13A–12.2**

FRESH MEAT AND POULTRY
Definitions, kosher food, **2C:21–7.4**

FRESH PURSUIT LAW
Generally, **2A:155–1 et seq.**
Arrest, **2A:155–1 et seq.**
Commitment of person arrested by officer of
 another state, **2A:155–5**
Construction and application of Uniform Fresh
 Pursuit Law, **2A:155–3**
Copies of Uniform Fresh Pursuit Law certified
 to executive department of other states,
 2A:155–7
Definitions, **2A:155–2**
 Intrastate fresh pursuit, **2A:156–2**
Discharge of person arrested by officer of an-
 other state, **2A:155–5**
Hearing before magistrate, person arrested by
 officer of other state, **2A:155–5**
Intrastate fresh pursuit, **2A:156–1 et seq.**

FRESH PURSUIT LAW—Cont'd
Lawfulness of arrest, **2A:155–6**
Officers of other states, authority to make ar-
 rests, **2A:155–4**
Peace officer in fresh pursuit within state,
 2A:156–1 et seq.
Uniform Fresh Pursuit Law, **2A:155–1 et seq.**

FRIVOLOUS LITIGATION
Sanctions, **Rule 1:4–8**

FROZEN CUSTARD
Frozen Desserts and Dietary Foods, generally,
 this index

FROZEN DESSERTS AND DIETARY FOODS
Customer safety, frozen dessert trucks,
 39:4–128.3 et seq.
Definitions, trucks, traffic rules and regulations, **39:4–128.3**
Ice cream trucks, traffic rules and regulations,
 39:4–128.3 et seq.
Motor carriers, frozen dessert trucks,
 39:4–128.3 et seq.
Safety of customers, frozen dessert trucks,
 39:4–128.3 et seq.
Traffic rules and regulations, frozen dessert
 trucks, **39:4–128.3 et seq.**
Trucks, traffic rules and regulations, **39:4–128.3
 et seq.**

FUEL
Liquefied Petroleum Gas, generally, this index
Motor Fuels, generally, this index
Oil and Gas, generally, this index

FUGITIVE FROM JUSTICE
Extradition, generally, this index

FULL RETAIL VALUE
Definitions, shoplifting, **2C:20–11**

FUND RAISERS
Charitable Organizations and Associations,
 generally, this index

FUND RAISING ACTIVITIES
Charitable Organizations and Associations,
 generally, this index

FUNDS
See, also, State Treasurer, generally, this in-
 dex
Adult offender supervision fund, **2A:168–35**
Anatomical gifts, organ and tissue donor
 awareness education fund, **39:3–12.3**
Automated traffic system statewide moderniza-
 tion fund, **2B:12–30.1**
Battleship New Jersey Memorial Fund,
 39:3–27.69
Bicycle and skating safety fund, **39:4–10.2**
Bribery and corruption, **2C:27–12**
Coastal protection trust fund, **39:3–27.50 et
 seq.**
Commercial vehicle enforcement fund, estab-
 lishment, **39:8–75**
Comprehensive enforcement program fund.
 Superior Court, generally, this index
Computer crime prevention fund, **2C:43–3.8**
Corrections computerized collection fund, es-
 tablishment, administration, purposes,
 2C:46–1.1
Corruption, **2C:27–12**
Courts, comprehensive enforcement program,
 2B:19–3 et seq.
Courts computerized collection fund, establish-
 ment, administration, purposes, **2C:46–1.1**

FUNDS—Cont'd

Criminal history record information fund, 53:1–20.7

Deborah hospital foundation fund, Deborah heart and lung center, 39:3–27.108 et seq.

Definitions,
Historic preservation license plates, 39:3–27.72
Liberty State Park plates, 39:3–27.91
Motor vehicles, plates or markers, special plates, united we stand, 39:3–27.131
Unsatisfied claim and judgment fund, 39:6–62

Drivers Licenses, this index

Drug abuse education fund. Drug Abuse, this index

Drunk driving enforcement fund, 39:4–50.8

Environmental Protection Department, this index

Forensic DNA laboratory fund, fines and penalties, surcharge, 53:1–20.28a

Garden State games trust fund, 39:3–27.64 et seq.

General Fund of State, generally, this index

Highway safety fund, fines and penalties, nonresident vehicles, weight, 39:3–20.4

Highways and Roads, this index

Historic preservation license plate fund, historic preservation license plates, 39:3–27.75

Interest on lawyers trust accounts fund, **Rule 1:28A–1 et seq.**

Interstate compact adult offender supervision fund, 2A:168–35

Law enforcement officers, law enforcement officers training and equipment fund, criminal assessments, 2C:43–3.3

Law enforcement officers memorial fund, special plates, 39:3–27.125

Lawyers fund for client protection, **Rule 1:28–1 et seq.**

Liberty State Park license plate fund, 39:3–27.94

Marine mammal stranding center fund, moneys from wildlife conservation license plate fees, 39:3–33.11

Motor carriers, highway safety fund, fines and penalties, nonresident vehicles, weight, 39:3–20.4

Motor vehicle commission, powers and duties, 39:2A–13

Motor vehicle snow and ice removal safety fund, 39:4–77.2

Motor Vehicles, this index

Motorized bicycles, educational program, safe operation, 39:4–14.3v

New Jersey emergency medical service helicopter response program fund, motor vehicle registration fees, additional fee deposited into fund, 39:3–8.2

Offroad vehicle recreational fund, 39:3C–3.1

Omnibus safety enforcement fund,
Motor vehicle commission, 39:3–79.24
Treasury department, 39:3–79.23

Organ and tissue donor awareness education fund, 39:3–12.3

Pedestrian safety enforcement and education fund, 39:4–36.2
Deposits, 39:4–36

Revolving funds,
Drug enforcement and demand reduction fund, 2C:35–15
Pedestrian safety enforcement and education fund, 39:4–36.2
Deposits, 39:4–36

Sex crime victim treatment fund, deposits, 2C:14–10

FUNDS—Cont'd

Rewards for justice license plate fund, **39:3–27.134 et seq.**

Sex crime victim treatment fund, deposits, 2C:14–10

Spinal cord, research, fines and penalties, motor vehicles, 39:5–41

Streets and Alleys, this index

Traffic Rules and Regulations, this index

U.S.S. New Jersey educational museum fund, 39:3–27.69

Uninsured motorist prevention fund, 39:6B–3

Victims of Crime, this index

Wildlife conservation fund, establishment, monies from wildlife conservation license plate fees, 39:3–33.10

FUNDS TRANSFERS

Electronic Fund Transfers, generally, this index

Teller machines. Electronic Fund Transfers, generally, this index

FUNERAL EXPENSES

Motor Vehicle Insurance, this index

Prepaid funeral agreements. Funerals, this index

Trust funds, prepaid monies, irrevocable trust, 2A:102–16.1

FUNERALS

Contracts. Prepaid funeral agreements, generally, post

Crimes and offenses, disruption, 2C:33–8.1

Demonstrations, disorderly persons, 2C:33–8.1

Disorderly persons, disruption, 2C:33–8.1

Insurance. Prepaid funeral agreements, post

Obstruction, disorderly persons, 2C:33–8.1

Prepaid funeral agreements,
Assigned funeral insurance policy, definitions, 2A:102–18
Crimes and offenses, solicitation, misrepresentation, 2A:102–16.2
Definitions, 2A:102–18
Delivery, 2A:102–18
Embezzlement, 2A:102–18
Fraud, 2A:102–16.2
Insurance, definitions, 2A:102–18
Intended funeral recipient, definitions, 2A:102–18
Newly issued funeral insurance policy, definitions, 2A:102–18
P.O.D. account, definitions, 2A:102–18
Payable on death account, definitions, 2A:102–18
Pooled trust, definitions, 2A:102–18
Provider, definitions, 2A:102–18
Purchaser, definitions, 2A:102–18
Trusts and trustees, definitions, 2A:102–18

Trusts and trustees. Prepaid funeral agreements, ante

FUR BEARING ANIMALS

Fish and Game, this index

FURETHIDINE

Controlled dangerous substance, 24:21–1 et seq.

GAMBLING

Generally, 2C:37–1 et seq.

Antique slot machines, possession, 2C:37–7

Casinos, generally, this index

Crimes and offenses, 2C:37–2 et seq.

Defenses, 2C:37–2
Records, possession, 2C:37–7

Definitions, 2C:37–1

GAMBLING—Cont'd

Evidence, 2C:37–2
Presumptions, sporting events, publication, 2C:37–5
Records, possession, 2C:37–3

Fines and penalties,
Bookmaking, 2C:37–2
Records, possession, 2C:37–3
Resorts, maintenance, 2C:37–4

Foreign countries, lotteries, 2C:37–6.1

Foreign states, lotteries, 2C:37–6
Equipment, tickets, manufacture, sale, 2C:37–6.1

Jurisdiction, 2C:37–8

Lotteries, generally, this index

Maintenance of gambling resorts, 2C:37–4

Motor vehicle operation on highway for wager, 39:4–52

Official action or information, 2C:30–3

Possession,
Gambling devices, 2C:37–7
Gambling records, 2C:37–3

Presumptions, proof of occurrence of sporting events, 2C:37–5

Promoting gambling, 2C:37–2

Public officers and employees, official actions or information, 2C:30–3

Publication, sporting event, proof of occurrence, 2C:37–5

Records and recordation, possession, 2C:37–3

Resorts, maintenance, 2C:37–4

Rigging publicly exhibited contests, 2C:21–11

Rules and regulations, alcoholic beverage control, 33:1–39

Shipboard gambling, crimes and offenses, 2C:37–4.1

Sporting events, presumption, proof of occurrence, 2C:37–5

Standard of proof, defenses, 2C:37–2

GAMBLING DEVICES

Definitions, 2C:37–1

Forfeitures, 2C:64–1

GAMBLING RESORT

Definitions, 2C:37–1

GAME

Fish and Game, generally, this index

GAMING

Gambling, generally, this index

GAMMA HYDROXYBUTYRATE

Date rape drugs. Controlled Substances, this index

GANGS

Street Gangs, generally, this index

GARAGE KEEPERS LEGAL LIABILITY

Definitions, tow trucks and towing companies, 39:3–84.6

GARAGES

Motor vehicle master keys or devices, 2C:5–6

Reports, motor vehicles, bullet holes or evidence of serious accident, 39:4–132

Right of way to pedestrians on sidewalk, 39:4–66.1

Stopping vehicle emerging from, 39:4–66

Title papers for vehicle in possession of, compliance with statute, 39:10–6

Turnpike authority, use of right of way, 27:23–9

GARBAGE AND REFUSE

Solid Waste, generally, this index

GARDEN PRODUCTS
Agricultural Products, generally, this index

GARDEN STATE
Motor vehicle registration license plates to contain phrase, **39:3–33.2**

GARDEN STATE ARTS CENTER
Turnpike authority, sale, **27:23–5**

GARDEN STATE PARKWAY
Turnpike authority,
   Addition to turnpike, powers and duties, **27:23–23.1**
   Transfer of powers and duties, highway authority, **27:23–43**

GAS
Oil and Gas, generally, this index

GAS COMPANIES
Computers, interference, crimes and offenses, **2C:20–25**
Monopolies, exemptions, **56:9–5**

GATES
Fireworks plants, **21:2–10**
Railroad crossings, unnecessary interference with use of highway, **39:4–94**

GENDER
Discrimination, generally, this index

GENDER IDENTITY OR EXPRESSION
Discrimination, generally, this index

GENERAL ASSEMBLY
   See, also, Senate, generally, this index
Bribery and Corruption, generally, this index
Crimes and offenses, bribes, **2C:27–10, 2C:27–11**
Electronic voting, **2A:149–1**
Former members, motor vehicles, special plates, **39:3–27.115**
Gifts, crimes and offenses, **2C:27–10, 2C:27–11**
Judicial conference, rules of evidence, **2A:84A–34**
Motor vehicle commission,
   Financial statements and reports, **39:2A–22**
   Reports, **39:2A–22**
Motor vehicles, special plates, former members, **39:3–27.115**
Public Policy, generally, this index
Reports,
   Assault firearms, **2C:58–14**
   Domestic violence, **2C:25–24**
   Motor vehicle commission, **39:2A–22**
   Motor vehicles, emission control, diesel vehicles, **39:8–78**
   Narcotic offenses, arrests and disposition, **53:1–18.3**
   New Jersey task force on child abuse and neglect, findings and recommendations, **9:6–8.82**
   Transportation, **39:4–6**
Statutes, generally, this index
Supervisor treatment programs, first offenders, rules, **2C:43–16 et seq.**
Unlawful benefits, crimes and offenses, **2C:27–10, 2C:27–11**
Voting machines, **2A:149–1**

GENERAL CORPORATION LAW
Corporations, generally, this index

GENERAL ELECTIONS
Elections, generally, this index

GENERAL EQUITY DIVISION, SUPERIOR COURT
Generally, **Rule 1:33–2**
Filing of papers, **Rule 1:5–6**
Juvenile delinquents and dependents, proceedings,
   Practice and procedure, **Rule 3:1–1**
   Scope, rules, **Rule 3:1–1**
Motions, **Rule 1:6–2**
   Filing of copy, **Rule 1:6–4**
Municipal court, transfer of action from, **Rule 3:1–6**
Presiding judge, **Rule 1:33–2**
Title of court, **Rule 1:37–1**
Transfer of actions, from municipal court, **Rule 3:1–6**

GENERAL FUND OF STATE
Commercial vehicle enforcement fund, **39:8–75**
Corrections computerized collection fund, establishment in, **2C:46–1.1**
Courts computerized collection fund, establishment in, **2C:46–1.1**
Highway safety fund, fines and penalties, nonresident vehicles, weight, **39:3–20.4**
Unsatisfied claim and judgment fund,
   Excess fees, transfer, **39:6–88**
   Excess medical expense benefits, reimbursement of insurer, **39:6–73.1**

GENERAL PUBLIC ASSISTANCE LAW
Indigent Persons, generally, this index

GENERAL STATE FUND
General Fund of State, generally, this index

GENETIC TESTS
DNA Database and Databank, generally, this index

GEOGRAPHICAL DISTRICTS
Definitions, motor vehicles, **39:3–4d**

GIFTS
   Generally, **Rule 1:16–2**
Alcoholic Beverages, this index
Anatomical Gifts, generally, this index
Board of compact administrators, Nonresident Violator Compact, motor vehicles, **39:5F–19**
Bribery and Corruption, generally, this index
Children and minors, cigarettes and cigars, crimes and offenses, **2A:170–51.4**
Cigarettes and cigars, children and minors, crimes and offenses, **2A:170–51.4**
Dead bodies, Anatomical Gift Act. Anatomical Gifts, generally, this index
Drivers licenses, anatomical gift donor designations, **39:3–10, 39:3–12.2**
General Assembly, this index
Motor vehicles,
   Body repair facilities, **39:13–4**
   Keys, **2C:5–6**
Poisoned liquors, **33:3–9, 33:3–10**
Poisonous gifts, **2C:12–2**
Promotional gifts, cigarettes and cigars, children and minors, crimes and offenses, **2A:170–51.4**
Public servants, gifts to, bribery, limitation of criminal prosecutions, **2C:1–6**
Turnpike authority, gifts to, **27:23–5**

GIN
Alcoholic Beverages, generally, this index

GIRL SCOUTS
Motor vehicles, fee for registration, **39:3–27**

GIRLS CLUBS OF AMERICA
Motor vehicles, registration fee exemption, **39:3–27**

GLASS
Placing on highway, fine imposed, **39:4–63**
Windshields, generally, this index

GLASSES
Examination, condition of drivers license renewal, **39:3–10c**
Optometrists, generally, this index

GLUTETHIMIDE
Controlled dangerous substance, **24:21–1 et seq.**

GOGGLES
Motorcycles, **39:3–76.8, 39:3–76.10**
Threewheeled vehicles, **39:3–76.8**

GOLF BALLS
Manufacture or sale of balls containing acid or corrosive substances, **2C:12–2**

GOLF COURSES
All terrain vehicles, **39:3C–30.1**
Destruction by motor vehicles, **39:4–97a**
   Point system, assessing against driver, **39:5–30.5a**
Intoxicating liquor licenses, **33:1–46.1 et seq.**

GOOD BEHAVIOR
Remission of sentence, county jail or penitentiary, **2A:164–24**

GOOD CAUSE
Bribery and corruption, profiteering penalty, payment, **2C:30–8**
Definitions, malt beverages, **33:1–93.14**
Malt beverages, **33:1–93.14**

GOOD FAITH
Alcoholic beverages,
   Defense, sale to persons under legal age, **33:1–77**
   Return of seized property to claimant, **33:1–66**
Lien or interest in property seized or forfeited under Alcoholic Beverage Law, **33:1–66**

GOODS
Leases, generally, this index
Sales, generally, this index

GOVERNING BODY
Definitions, **2B:25–2**

GOVERNMENT
Commercial paper, issuance,
   Bribery and corrupt influence, **2C:27–1**
   Theft, **2C:20–1**
Fiduciaries, misapplication of government property, **2C:21–15**

GOVERNMENT CONTRACTS
Conviction of crime, **2C:51–2**

GOVERNMENT OFFICERS AND EMPLOYEES
Bribery and Corruption, generally, this index
Municipal Officers and Employees, generally, this index
Officers and Employees, generally, this index

GOVERNMENTAL AGENCIES
State Agencies, generally, this index

GOVERNMENTAL FUNCTIONS

Kidnapping, interference with functions, **2C:13–1**

GOVERNMENTAL UNITS

Definitions, searches and seizures, news organizations, **2A:84A–21.12**

GOVERNOR

Appointments,
Automobile insurance risk exchange directors, **39:6A–21**
Compact administrators, Nonresident Violator Compact, motor vehicles, **39:5F–15**
County prosecutors, **2A:158–1**
Directors, motor vehicles division, **39:2–2**
Judges and justices, joint municipal court, **2B:12–4**
Definitions, Uniform Criminal Extradition Act, **2A:160–6**
Directors. Appointments, ante
Executive clemency. Pardons, generally, this index
Extradition, generally, this index
Financial statements or reports, motor vehicle commission, **39:2A–22**
Interstate compacts, parolee supervision, **2A:168–14 et seq.**
Medical advisory panel, appointments, **39:2–14**
Motor Vehicle Commission, this index
Notice, continued law violations, mayor or chief of police, **2A:152–12, 2A:152–13**
Pardons, generally, this index
Parole, this index
Powers and duties, commutation of sentence, **2A:167–4**
Reports,
Domestic violence, **2C:25–24**
Motor vehicle commission, **39:2A–22**
Motor vehicles, emission control, diesel vehicles, **39:8–78**
Narcotic offenses, arrests and disposition, **53:1–18.3**
New Jersey task force on child abuse and neglect, findings and recommendations, **9:6–8.82**
Public defender, **2A:158A–22**
Statistics on crime conditions, state police annual report, **53:1–18a**
Rewards, authority to offer, **2A:153–1**
State Police, this index
Turnpike Authority, this index
Veto, this index
Warrant for arrest of convict on revocation of license to be at large, **2A:167–12**

GRADE AND DEGREE OF OFFENSES

Crimes and Offenses, this index

GRADE CROSSINGS

Abandonment,
Stopping regulations, **39:4–128**
Warning signs, **39:4–183.21a**
Enforcement, regulations as to stopping of motor vehicles or school busses, **39:5–1**
Exemptions, stopping, **39:4–128**
Fines and penalties, stopping, **39:4–128**
Flagmans signal requiring motor vehicle to stop, **39:4–127.1**
Railroad advance warning signs, **39:4–199.1**
Stopping of vehicle, **39:4–127.1**
Tractors, notice of intention to cross, **39:4–128**
Traffic signs, **39:4–199.1**
Warnings, order for removal, abandoned grade crossings, **39:4–183.21a**

GRADES OF HIGHWAYS AND STREETS

Separations, traffic signs, **39:4–199.1**
Turnpike authority, power to change, **27:23–6**

GRAFFITI

Act of graffiti, definitions, **2C:17–3, 2C:33–24**
Criminal mischief, **2C:17–3**
Rewards, **2A:153–4.1**
Defacement or damage of property, **2C:33–11**
Putting or attempting to put in fear of violence, **2C:33–10**
Juvenile delinquent, commission by, **2A:4A–43.2**
Fines and penalties, defacement or damage of property, **2C:33–11**
Putting or attempting to put in fear of violence, **2C:33–10**
Juvenile delinquent, commission by, **2A:4A–43.2**
Railroads, signals and signaling, **2C:33–14.1**
Rewards, detection and apprehension, **2A:153–4.1**
Spray paint,
Definitions, **2C:17–3, 2C:33–24**
Sale, required posting of warning sign, **2C:33–25**

GRAND JURY

Generally, **Rule 3:6–1 et seq.**
Abuse of children, records, access, **9:6–8.10a**
Adverse or pecuniary interest, **Rule 3:6–3**
Age, grounds for challenge, **2B:21–2**
Appeal and review, presentment, **Rule 3:6–9**
Array, challenging, **Rule 3:6–2**
Assignment judge, designation, **Rule 3:6–11**
Attendance at session, **Rule 3:6–6**
Attorneys,
Assigned to grand jury, practice of law, **Rule 1:15–2**
Interviewing jurors subsequent to trial, **Rule 1:16–1**
Bias, **Rule 3:6–3**
Book contracts, jurors, **2C:29–8.1**
Censure, public officials, presentment, **Rule 3:6–9**
Challenge,
Array, **Rule 3:6–2**
Grounds, **2B:21–2**
Charging, **Rule 3:6–3**
Child abuse reports, access to, **9:6–8.10a**
Clerk, **Rule 3:6–5**
Attendance, **Rule 3:6–6**
Political activity or holding public office, **Rule 1:17–1**
Continuance, term, **Rule 3:6–10**
Contracts, movie, book or entertainment rights, **2C:29–8.1**
County prosecutors, assistant, attend session of grand jury, **2A:158–18**
Crimes and offenses,
Contracts, movie, book or entertainment rights, **2C:29–8.1**
Injurious disclosure of information, **2B:21–10**
Damages, injurious disclosure of information, **2B:21–10**
Death of juror, filling vacancy, **2B:21–4**
Deferrals, voir dire of members, consideration of grounds, **2B:21–2**
Delay, charge, dismissal, **Rule 3:25–3**
Deputy foreperson, **Rule 3:6–4**
Selection, **2B:21–5**
Discharge, **Rule 3:6–10**
Disclosure, injurious information, crime, **2B:21–10**
Discovery, **Rule 3:13–3**
Dismissal, charge, delay, **Rule 3:25–3**

GRAND JURY—Cont'd

Employees, political activities or holding public office, **Rule 1:17–1**
Entertainment contracts, jurors, **2C:29–8.1**
Escape, force or violence, instructions to jury, **2B:22–9**
Evidence, application of law, **Evidence Rule 101**
Excusing, voir dire of members, consideration of grounds, **2B:21–2**
Filing, presentment, **Rule 3:6–9**
Fines and penalties, injurious disclosure of information, crime, **2B:21–10**
Foreperson, **Rule 3:6–4**
Selection, **2B:21–5**
Witnesses, swearing, **2B:21–6**
Former service, grounds for excuse, **2B:21–2**
Indictment, Information or Presentment, generally, this index
Injurious information, disclosure, **2B:21–10**
Instructions to jury, law enforcement officers, force or violence, **2B:22–9**
Interviewing subsequent to trial, **Rule 1:16–1**
Investigation, statements, unindicted suspects and witnesses, **2B:21–9**
Law enforcement officers,
Excuse from service, **2B:21–2**
Instructions to jury, force or violence, **2B:22–9**
Lists. Jury Lists, generally, this index
Material witnesses, bail, **Rule 3:26–3**
Members, number, **Rule 3:6–1**
Movie rights, jurors contract, **2C:29–8.1**
No bill, **Rule 3:6–8**
Number of jurors, **2B:21–1, 2B:21–2; Rule 3:6–1**
Oaths and affirmations,
Administration, **Rule 3:6–4**
County grand jurors, **2B:21–3**
Foreperson, swearing in of witnesses, **2B:21–6**
Secrecy, **Rule 3:6–7**
Objections, **Rule 3:6–2**
Orders,
Continuance, **Rule 3:6–10**
Transcripts, **Rule 3:6–6**
Panel, minimum number, **2B:21–1**
Parties, interviewing jurors subsequent to trial, **Rule 1:16–1**
Police,
Excuse from service, **2B:21–2**
Instructions to jury, force or violence, **2B:22–9**
Potential bias, **Rule 3:6–3**
Presentment, finding, return, **Rule 3:6–9**
Prosecuting attorney, attendance, **Rule 3:6–6**
Publication, presentment, **Rule 3:6–9**
Qualifications, challenges, grounds for disqualification, **2B:21–2**
Records and recordation, **Rule 3:6–5 et seq.**
Clerk, **Rule 3:6–5**
Confidential or privileged information, **Rule 1:38–3**
Discovery, **Rule 3:13–3**
Indictment, required finding, **2B:21–7**
Presentment, examining, **Rule 3:6–9**
Transcripts, **2B:21–8**
Release, no bill, **Rule 3:6–8**
Reports, no bill, **Rule 3:6–8**
Return, presentment, **Rule 3:6–9**
Sealing,
Indictment, **Rule 3:6–8**
Records, **Rule 3:6–6**
Secrecy, **Rule 3:6–6 et seq.**
Selection, public and random manner, **2B:21–2**

GRAND JURY—Cont'd

Service, voir dire, consideration of excusals or deferrals of service, **2B:21–2**

Sheriffs, summoning jurors, state grand jurors, **2B:22–4**

Sickness of grand juror, filling vacancy, **2B:21–4**

Sound recording, **Rule 3:6–6**

State grand jury, **Rule 3:6–1 et seq.**
    Applicability of provisions, **2B:22–2**
    Application of rules, **Rule 3:6–11**
    Assignment judge, designation, **Rule 3:6–11**
    Attorney general, presentation of evidence, **2B:22–6**
    Costs, reimbursement, **2B:22–8**
    Evidence, presentation by attorney general, **2B:22–6**
    Expenses, reimbursement, **2B:22–8**
    Impaneling, written request, **2B:22–1**
    Indictment, information or presentment,
      Return to designated judge, **2B:22–5**
      Venue, **2B:22–7**
    Judicial supervision, **2B:22–5**
    Jurisdiction, **2B:22–2**
    Jury list, selection of jurors, **2B:22–3**
    Powers and duties, **2B:22–2**
    Prosecution and trial, reimbursement, expenses incurred, **2B:22–8**
    Prospective jurors, summoning, **2B:22–4**
    Selection process, random and public, **2B:22–3**
    Summoning prospective jurors, sheriffs, powers and duties, **2B:22–4**
    Venue,
      Indictments, information, **2B:22–7**
      Trial of indictments returned by, **Rule 3:14–1**

Statement of investigation, unindicted suspects and witnesses, **2B:21–9**

Striking presentment, **Rule 3:6–9**

Summoning, **Rule 3:6–1**
    State grand jury, **2B:22–4**

Term, **Rule 3:6–10**

Transcripts, **2B:21–8**
    Proceedings, **Rule 3:6–6**

Typists, secrecy, **Rule 3:6–7**

Unindicted suspects, statement of investigation, **2B:21–9**

Vacancies, **2B:21–4**

Witnesses, this index

GRAND JURY LISTS

Jury Lists, generally, this index

GRANDFATHER RIGHTS

County detectives and investigators, **2A:157–20**

Motorized bicycles, registration, **39:4–14.3u**

GRANDPARENTS

Alcoholic beverages, transfer of interest in corporation, Chain Store Liquor License Act, **33:1–12.36**

GRANTS

Anatomical gifts, registration, **39:3–12.5**

Board of compact administrators, Nonresident Violator Compact, motor vehicles, **39:5F–19**

Child abuse, prevention, **9:6–8.75**

Interest on lawyers trust account fund, **Rule 1:28A–4**

Motor vehicle commission, powers and duties, **39:2A–13**

Municipalities, this index

GRATUITIES

Gifts, generally, this index

GRAVES ACT

Weapons, **2C:43–6**

GRAVITY KNIFE

Definitions, **2C:39–1**

Manufacture, transport, disposition and defacement, **2C:39–9**

Person convicted of crime involving, possession of any weapon prohibited, **2C:39–7**

Prohibited weapons, **2C:39–3**

GREAT SEAL

Affixed to warrant of arrest of extradited person, **2A:160–15**

GRENADES

Weapons, generally, this index

GRIEVANCES

Complaints, generally, this index

GROCERY STORES

Stores, this index

GROSS RECEIPTS TAX

Turnpike authority, exemption from tax, **27:23–12**

GROSS WEIGHT

Definitions, motor vehicles, **39:1–1**

GUARDIAN AD LITEM

Child abuse,
    Appointments, **9:6–8.43**
    Attorneys, **9:6–8.23**
    Definitions, abuse or neglect, **9:6–8.21**

Judicial employees, appointments, **Rule 1:17–3**

Juvenile delinquents and dependents, waiver of rights by incompetent juveniles, appointment of guardian, **2A:4A–39**

GUARDIAN AND WARD

Aggravated criminal sexual contact, **2C:14–3**

Alcoholic beverages,
    Hearing, violation by minor, attendance, **33:1–81.1**
    License in different capacities, **33:1–40**

Appearance, guardian of party, **Rule 1:21–1**

Attorneys, bank accounts, record keeping, **Rule 1:21–6**

Bonds. Investments, post

Child abuse registry, investigations and investigators, professional guardians, **9:6–8.10e**

Closed circuit testimony, abuse of children, motions, **2A:84A–32.4**

Commercial bribery and breach of duty, **2C:21–10**

Confidential or privileged information, **Rule 1:38–3**

Crimes and offenses, support, willful nonsupport, **2C:24–5**

Criminal history record information, professional guardians, **53:1–20.9e**

Criminal restraint, **2C:13–2**

Definitions,
    Abuse of children, **9:6–8.21**
    Juvenile justice, **2A:4A–22**

Endangering welfare of children, **2C:24–4**

Evidence, abuse of children, closed circuit testimony, motions, **2A:84A–32.4**

False imprisonment, **2C:13–3**

Fingerprints and fingerprinting, criminal history record information, professional guardians, **53:1–20.9e**

Illness of child, treatment in accordance with religious tenets of church, **9:6–1.1**

Interference with custody of ward, **2C:13–4**

GUARDIAN AND WARD—Cont'd

Investigations and investigators, child abuse registry, professional guardians, **9:6–8.10e**

Investments, bonds, turnpike authority, **27:23–13**

Juvenile Delinquents, this index

Kidnapping, **2C:13–1**
    Adult diagnostic and treatment center, referral of offenders, **2C:47–1 et seq.**
    Community notification. Sex Offenses, this index
    Parole supervision for life, special sentence, Violent Predator Incapacitation Act of 1994, **2C:43–6.4**

Misapplication, entrusted property, **2C:21–15**

Motions, closed circuit testimony, abuse of children, **2A:84A–32.4**

Names, criminal history record information, professional guardians, **53:1–20.9e**

Notice,
    Child abuse registry, investigations and investigators, professional guardians, **9:6–8.10e**
    Protective custody, child abuse, **9:6–8.19**

Prostitution, **2C:34–1**

Sexual abuse, children and minors, closed circuit testimony motions, **2A:84A–32.4**

Sexual assault, **2C:14–2**

Videotaped testimony, abuse of children, motions, **2A:84A–32.4**

Willful nonsupport, **2C:24–5**

GUARDS

Correctional Institutions, this index

Nightsticks,
    Person convicted of crime involving, possession of any weapon prohibited, **2C:39–7**
    Training requirement, **2C:39–3**

Nuclear electricity generating facilities, weapons, possession, **2C:39–6**

Weapons, unlawful possession, exemptions, **2C:39–6**

GUIDE DOGS

Blind Persons, this index

GUIDE MARKS

Traffic Signs and Signals, generally, this index

GUILTY PLEAS

Crimes and Offenses, this index

Municipal Courts, this index

GUNS

Weapons, generally, this index

HABEAS CORPUS

Drunken driving, statute requiring term of imprisonment to be served, effect, **39:4–51**

Extradition, this index

HABIT FORMING DRUGS

Controlled Substances, generally, this index

HABITS

Evidence, **Evidence Rule 406**

HABITUAL CRIMINALS

Second or Subsequent Offenses, generally, this index

HABITUAL DRUNKARDS

Alcoholics and Alcoholism, generally, this index

HACKENSACK MEADOWLANDS

Conservation,
Motor vehicles, plates or markers,
39:3–27.100 et seq.
Trusts and trustees, motor vehicles, plates or
markers, **39:3–27.105**
Motor vehicles, plates or markers, conservation, **39:3–27.100 et seq.**

HAIR SAMPLES

Investigative detention, **Rule 3:5A–1 et seq.**

HALFWAY HOUSES

Alcoholics and Alcoholism, generally, this index
Crimes and offenses, **2C:43–2**

HALLUCINOGENIC SUBSTANCES

Controlled substances, **24:21–1 et seq.**
Driving under influence, homicide, sentence
and punishment, **2C:11–5**
Motor vehicles, operating under influence,
fines and penalties, **39:4–50**
Vessel, operating under influence, homicide,
sentence and punishment, **2C:11–5**

HALTERS

Unbitted horses, halter required, **39:4–17**

HAND GUNS

Definitions, **2C:39–1**
Weapons, generally, this index

HAND SIGNALS

Traffic Signs and Signals, generally, this index

HANDCUFFS

Definitions, sale to minor, disorderly persons
offense, confiscation, **2C:39–9.2**
Possession, disorderly persons offense, confiscation, **2C:39–3**

HANDICAPPED PERSONS

Abandonment, crimes and offenses, **2C:24–8**
Abuse or neglect, prevention and treatment
training course, law enforcement officers,
2C:25–20
Age, identification cards for disabled persons,
39:3–29.3
Bias intimidation, crimes and offenses, **2C:16–1**
Canadian vehicles, special parking privileges,
39:4–207.5
Crimes and offenses, **2C:44–1**
Bias intimidation, **2C:16–1**
Endangering injured victim, **2C:12–1.2**
Identification cards for disabled persons,
39:3–29.8
Neglect or failure to care for, **2C:24–8**
Presentence reports, **2C:44–6**
Sentence criteria, **2C:44–1**
Crosswalks, older and walking impaired per-
sons crossing, designation of areas and
erection of signs, **39:4–183.1b**
Defenses, parking, **39:4–198**
Definitions, motor vehicle plates and markers,
39:4–204
Depositions, criminal proceedings, **Rule 3:13–2**
Disabled veterans. Veterans, this index
Discrimination, bias crimes, intimidation,
2C:16–1
Disorderly persons, identification cards for dis-
abled persons, **39:3–29.10**
Drivers licenses, examination permits, **39:3–13**
Electric personal assistive mobility devices, op-
eration, **39:4–14.10**
Endangering injured victim, crimes and of-
fenses, **2C:12–1.2**

HANDICAPPED PERSONS—Cont'd

Examination permits, drivers licenses, **39:3–13**
Failure to care for, **2C:24–8**
Fines and penalties. Parking, post
Foreign state vehicles, special parking privi-
leges, **39:4–207.5**
Fraud, identification cards for disabled per-
sons, **39:3–29.8**
Handguns, purchase permits, **2C:58–3**
Handicapped parking enforcement units,
39:4–197.9 et seq.
Identification cards, nondrivers, **39:3–29.3**
Validity for life, **39:3–29.5**
Jurors, physically and mentally disabled per-
sons, qualifications and selection, **2B:20–1**
Loss or destruction, identification cards for
disabled persons, **39:3–29.6**
Medicaid, generally, this index
Medical care and treatment. Medicaid, gener-
ally, this index
Mentally Retarded and Developmentally Dis-
abled Persons, generally, this index
Motor vehicles, **39:4–207.1**
Disabled veterans, plates or markers,
39:3–27.15 et seq.
Identification cards, **39:4–206**
Nondrivers, **39:3–29.3**
Validity for life, **39:3–29.5**
License plates, issuance, national wheelchair
symbol, **39:4–206**
Parking, generally, post
Temporary placards, **39:4–206**
Motorcycles, license plates, issuance, national
wheelchair symbol, **39:4–206**
Motorized scooters, traffic rules and regula-
tions, stickers, **39:4–14.15**
Municipalities,
Handicapped parking enforcement units,
39:4–197.9 et seq.
Restricted parking places, **39:4–197,**
39:4–197.5
Neglect, **2C:24–8**
Noncommercial trucks, licenses and permits,
fees, **39:3–8.1**
Notice, parking, fines and penalties, **39:4–198**
Parking, **39:4–138**
Access, **39:4–207.9**
Canadian vehicles, special parking privilege,
39:4–207.5
Defenses, **39:4–198**
Fines and penalties,
Notice, **39:4–198**
Spaces, access, **39:4–207.9**
Violators, **39:4–197, 39:4–201**
Handicapped parking enforcement units,
39:4–197.9 et seq.
Notice, fines and penalties, **39:4–198**
Nursing home residents, **39:4–207.8**
Overtime parking, **39:4–206, 39:4–207**
Permits, **39:4–197.7**
Restricted zones, **39:4–197.6**
Snow removal, **39:4–207.9**
Spaces, **39:4–138, 39:4–206**
Access, **39:4–207.9**
Facilities to accommodate, inspection,
39:4–8.1
Fines and penalties, **39:4–197**
Access, **39:4–207.9**
Foreign state vehicles, **39:4–207.5**
Handicapped parking enforcement units,
39:4–197.9 et seq.
Nursing home residents, **39:4–207.8**
Removal and storage, unlawfully parked
vehicles, **39:4–207.6, 39:4–207.7**
Snow removal, **39:4–207.9**
Temporary placards, **39:4–206**

HANDICAPPED PERSONS—Cont'd

Parking—Cont'd
Unlawfully parked vehicle, towing and stor-
age, **39:4–207.6, 39:4–207.7**
Violators, fines and penalties, **39:4–201**
Photocopies, identification cards for disabled
persons, crimes and offenses, **39:3–29.8**
Police and Police Departments, this index
Rules and regulations, identification cards,
39:3–29.9
School buses, van type vehicles, identification,
39:3B–9
Schools and School Districts, this index
Special education proceedings, nonattorneys
appearance, **Rule 1:21–1**
Stickers, traffic rules and regulations, motor-
ized scooters, **39:4–14.15**
Traffic Rules and Regulations, this index
Vans, licenses and permits, fees, **39:3–8,**
39:3–8.1
Victims of crime, **2C:44–1**
Endangering injured victim, **2C:12–1.2**
Presentence reports, **2C:44–6**

HANDLEBAR GRIPS

Motorcycles, **39:3–76.3**

HANDLING

Explosives, this index

HANDWRITING

Investigative detention, **Rule 3:5A–1 et seq.**

HARASSMENT

Generally, **2C:33–4**
Domestic Violence, generally, this index
Intimidation based on bias, fourth degree
crime, extended term of imprisonment,
2C:43–7, 2C:43–7.1
Telegraphs and telephones, **2C:33–4**

HARBORING

Hindering apprehension or prosecution of accused, **2C:29–3**

HARM

Crimes and offenses, mitigating or aggravating
circumstances, **2C:44–1**
Definitions, bribery and corrupt influence,
2C:27–1

HARMLESS ERROR

Generally, **Rule 1:7–5**

HASHISH

Definitions, **24:21–2**
Controlled substances, **2C:35–2, 24:21–2**
Expungement of record, **2C:52–2**
Young drug offenders, **2C:52–5**

HAWKERS AND PEDDLERS

Motor vehicles, flashing lights on stopped vehicles, **39:3–64.1 et seq.**

HAZARDOUS CONDITIONS

Disorderly conduct, **2C:33–2**

HAZARDOUS DISCHARGE SITE REMEDIA-
TION

Environmental Opportunity Zone Act. Taxation, generally, this index

HAZARDOUS MATERIAL

Hazardous Substances and Waste, generally,
this index

HAZARDOUS MATERIALS TRANSPORTA-TION COMPLIANCE AND ENFORCE-MENT OFFICE
Generally, **39:5B–27**

HAZARDOUS SUBSTANCES AND WASTE
Cargo seals, breaking, inspection, **39:5B–31**
Carriers, transportation, **39:5B–30 et seq.**
Causing or risking widespread injury or damage, **2C:17–2**
Commercial drivers licenses,
    Criminal history record information, applications, **39:3–10.17**
    Suspension or revocation, **39:3–10.20**
Commercial motor vehicles, commercial drivers licenses, suspension or revocation, **39:3–10.20**
Containers, transportation, **39:5B–30 et seq.**
Conveyances, willful discharge, forfeiture, **13:1E–9**
Crimes and offenses,
    Causing or risking widespread injury or damage, **2C:17–2**
    Terrorism, **2C:38–2, 2C:38–3**
    Trespass, unlicensed entry of structure, **2C:18–3**
Debris from auto accident, towing service failure to remove, penalty exemption, **39:4–56.8**
Definitions,
    Terrorism, **2C:38–3**
    Transportation, **39:5B–25**
Discharge,
    Causing or risking widespread injury or damage, **2C:17–2**
    Conveyances, willful discharge, forfeiture, **13:1E–9**
    Forfeiture, conveyances used in willful discharge, **13:1E–9**
Disorderly persons, inhalants, **2C:35–10.4**
Disposal,
    Fines and penalties, **13:1E–9**
    Unauthorized transportation, fines and penalties, **13:1E–9**
Fees, transportation by railroad freight car, **39:5B–31.1**
Fines and penalties,
    Causing or risking widespread injury or damage, **2C:17–2**
    False or misleading statements, **13:1E–9**
    Terrorism, **2C:38–3**
    Transportation, **39:5B–29**
Forfeitures, **13:1E–9**
    Willful discharge, **13:1E–9**
Fraud,
    Disposal applications, **13:1E–9**
    Fines and penalties, **13:1E–9**
Hazardous materials transportation compliance and enforcement office, **39:5B–27**
Hours of duty, motor carriers, **39:9–2 et seq.**
Inspectors and inspections, vehicles used for transportation, **39:5B–31**
Interstate commerce, motor carriers, rules and regulations, qualifications, **39:5B–30 et seq.**
Intoxication,
    Inhalants, **2C:35–10.4**
    Nitrous oxide, **2C:35–10.4**
Limitation of actions, handling or disposal, violations, **13:1E–9**
Motor carriers,
    Commercial drivers licenses, suspension or revocation, **39:3–10.20**
    Rules and regulations, qualifications, **39:5B–30 et seq.**
Nitrous oxide, intoxication, **2C:35–10.4**

HAZARDOUS SUBSTANCES AND WASTE
  —Cont'd
Portable, oil burning heating device, carbon monoxide, **2C:40–12**
Radiation Protection, generally, this index
Radioactive Substances, generally, this index
Repairs, transportation, fines and penalties, reductions, **39:5B–29**
Reports, transportation, **39:5B–28**
    Railroad freight cars, number, **39:5B–31.1**
Rules and regulations,
    Carriers, qualifications, **39:5B–32**
    Transportation, **39:5B–25 et seq.**
Second and subsequent offenses, fines and penalties, transportation, **39:5B–29**
Storage, causing or risking widespread injury or damage, **2C:17–2**
Terrorism, this index
Transportation, **39:5B–25 et seq.**
    Nonresident Violator Compact, application of law, **39:5F–25**
    Railroad freight cars, fee, report, **39:5B–31.1**
Trespass, unlicensed entry of structure, crimes and offenses, **2C:18–3**
Unlicensed entry of structure, trespass, crimes and offenses, **2C:18–3**

HAZARDS
Public safety, **2C:40–1**

HAZING
Generally, **2C:40–3**
Consent, **2C:40–4**
Defense, **2C:40–4**
Prosecution, **2C:40–5**

HEALING BY PRAYER
Prayers, this index

HEALTH AND ACCIDENT INSURANCE
Appeal and review, runners, probation and probation officers, **2C:21–22.1**
Fines and penalties,
    Health care claims fraud, **2C:21–4.2, 2C:21–4.3**
        Licenses and permits, suspension or revocation, **2C:51–5**
        Rehabilitation, order of debarment, rescission, **2C:27–1**
    Runners, **2C:21–22.1**
Forfeitures, fraud, licenses and permits, **2C:51–5**
Fraud, **2C:21–4.2, 2C:21–4.3**
    Licenses and permits, suspension or revocation, **2C:51–5**
        Rehabilitation, order of debarment, rescission, **2C:27–1**
    Runners, **2C:21–22.1**
Health Maintenance Organizations, generally, this index
Indigent persons. Medicaid, generally, this index
Licenses and permits, health care claims fraud, suspension or revocation, **2C:51–5**
    Rehabilitation, order of debarment, rescission, **2C:27–1**
Medicaid, generally, this index
Motor Vehicle Insurance, generally, this index
Presentence investigation and report, psychological evaluation, cost, **2C:44–6.1**
Probation and probation officers, runners, **2C:21–22.1**
Runners, fraud, **2C:21–22.1**
Soliciting, fraud, runners, **2C:21–22.1**

HEALTH AND ACCIDENT INSURANCE
  —Cont'd
Utilization review committees established by certified hospitals, privileged communications, **2A:84A–22.8**

HEALTH AND SANITATION
Accident insurance. Health and Accident Insurance, generally, this index
Alcoholic beverages, sale, poisoned liquors, **33:3–9, 33:3–10**
Crimes and offenses, laws protecting public health, **2C:40–18**
Department. Health and Senior Services Department, generally, this index
Dwellings unfit for habitation. Buildings, generally, this index
Environmental Protection, generally, this index
Fireworks, sale, use, distribution, declared against public health, **21:3–1**
Food, generally, this index
Hazardous Substances and Waste, generally, this index
Indigent Persons, generally, this index
Insurance. Health and Accident Insurance, generally, this index
Juvenile delinquents and dependents,
    Out of door sales, **Rule 5:18–3**
    Short term custody, **Rule 5:16–1**
Medicaid, generally, this index
Motor vehicles, license plates, location, **39:3–33**
Radiation Protection, generally, this index
Rules and regulations, alcoholic beverages, **33:1–39**
Solid Waste, generally, this index
State department of health and senior services. Health and Senior Services Department, generally, this index

HEALTH AND SENIOR SERVICES DEPART-MENT
Air Pollution, generally, this index
Alcoholics and Alcoholism, generally, this index
Animal welfare license plates,
    Cooperation with motor vehicles division, **39:3–27.58**
    Notice, posters and signs supplied to motor vehicles division, **39:3–27.57**
Controlled substances, **24:21–1 et seq.**
Counties,
    Actions and proceedings, solid waste facilities, notice, **13:1E–9**
    Sanitary landfills, fees, **13:1E–9**
    Solid waste facilities, compliance with regulations, **13:1E–9**
Dead Bodies, generally, this index
Definitions, food and drugs, **24:21–32**
Frozen Desserts and Dietary Foods, generally, this index
Nursing Homes or Hospitals, generally, this index
Radiation Protection, generally, this index
Water Pollution, generally, this index

HEALTH BENEFITS PLANS
Health and Accident Insurance, generally, this index

HEALTH CARE
Medical Care and Treatment, generally, this index

HEALTH CARE CLAIMS FRAUD
Generally, **2C:21–4.2, 2C:21–4.3**
Definitions, **2C:21–4.2**

HEALTH CARE CLAIMS FRAUD—Cont'd
Expunging record, professions and occupations, licenses and permits, forfeitures, rescission, **2C:52–27.1**
Forfeitures, licenses and permits, **2C:51–5**
Rescission, expunging record, **2C:52–27.1**
Licenses and permits, suspension or revocation, **2C:51–5**
Rehabilitation, order of debarment, rescission, **2C:27–1**
Rescission, licenses and permits, forfeitures, expunging record, **2C:52–27.1**

HEALTH CARE FACILITIES
Aggravated arson, fines and penalties, **2C:17–1**
AIDS (Acquired Immune Deficiency Syndrome), generally, this index
Criminal history record information, assisted living facilities, **53:1–20.9c**
Definitions, arson, **2C:17–1**
Hospitals, generally, this index
Long term health care facility committee, utilization review plan, immunity from liability, **2A:84A–22.10**
Nursing Homes or Hospitals, generally, this index
Supervised visitation, **39:4–50**

HEALTH CARE PROFESSIONALS
See, also, Counselors and Counseling, generally, this index
Claims, fraud, **2C:21–4.2, 2C:21–4.3**
Licenses and permits, suspension or revocation, **2C:51–5**
Rehabilitation, order of debarment, rescission, **2C:27–1**
Crimes and offenses, solicitation, disasters or accidents, **2C:40A–4**
Drugs and medicine, tampering, **2C:40–17**
Forfeitures, licenses and permits, health care claims fraud, **2C:51–5**
Licenses and permits, health care claims fraud, suspension or revocation, **2C:51–5**
Rehabilitation, order of debarment, rescission, **2C:27–1**
Nurses, generally, this index
Physicians and Surgeons, generally, this index
Solicitation, disasters or accidents, crimes and offenses, **2C:40A–4**
Time, solicitation, disasters or accidents, **2C:40A–4**

HEALTH CARE PROVIDERS
Health Care Professionals, generally, this index
Health Maintenance Organizations, generally, this index

HEALTH CARE SERVICE FIRMS
Homemaker home health aides, criminal history record information, certificates, **53:1–20.9a**

HEALTH CARE SERVICES
Medical Care and Treatment, generally, this index

HEALTH COMMISSIONER
Anatomical Gifts, generally, this index
Animal welfare license plates, design of notices, posters and signs, **39:3–27.57**
Controlled substances, **24:21–1 et seq.**
Health Maintenance Organizations, generally, this index
Organ donation. Anatomical Gifts, generally, this index

HEALTH DEPARTMENT
Health and Senior Services Department, generally, this index

HEALTH INSURANCE
Health and Accident Insurance, generally, this index

HEALTH MAINTENANCE ORGANIZA-TIONS
Fines and penalties, health care claims fraud, **2C:21–4.2, 2C:21–4.3**
Licenses and permits, suspension or revocation, **2C:51–5**
Rehabilitation, order of debarment, rescission, **2C:27–1**
Forfeitures, licenses and permits, health care claims fraud, **2C:51–5**
Fraud, **2C:21–4.2, 2C:21–4.3**
Licenses and permits, suspension or revocation, **2C:51–5**
Rehabilitation, order of debarment, rescission, **2C:27–1**
Health Care Claims Fraud, generally, this index
Licenses and permits, health care claims fraud, suspension or revocation, **2C:51–5**
Rehabilitation, order of debarment, rescission, **2C:27–1**
Motor Vehicle Insurance, generally, this index
No fault insurance. Motor Vehicle Insurance, this index
Oversight committees, privileges and immunities, **2A:84A–22.10**

HEARINGS
Administrative Law and Procedure, this index
AIDS (Acquired Immune Deficiency Syndrome), generally, this index
Air Pollution, this index
Alcoholic Beverages, this index
Correctional Institutions, this index
De minimis infractions, dismissal, **2C:2–11**
Domestic violence, weapons seizure, **2C:25–21**
Evidence, sexual offenses, previous sexual conduct of victim, **2C:14–7**
Explosives, this index
Extradition, this index
Information disclosure privilege, newspersons, criminal proceedings, **2A:84A–21.5**
Juvenile Delinquents, this index
Material witness, **2C:104–6**
Monopoly or unfair trade, **56:9–9**
Motor vehicle dealers, license revocation, mileage misrepresentation, **2C:21–8**
Motor Vehicles, this index
Municipal prosecutors, removal from office, **2B:25–9**
Notice. Mail and Mailing, this index
Parking, drivers licenses, suspension or revocation, **39:4–139.10**
Police and Police Departments, this index
Stills and Distilling Apparatus, this index
Toxic packaging reduction, **13:1E–99.54**
Turnpikes, this index
Weapons, possession, mandatory sentence, **2C:43–6**

HEARSAY EVIDENCE
Generally, **Evidence Rule 801 et seq.**
Admissibility, **Evidence Rule 802**
Credibility of declarant, attacking and supporting, **Evidence Rule 806**
Definitions, **Evidence Rule 801**
Exceptions,
Declarant unavailable, **Evidence Rule 804**

HEARSAY EVIDENCE—Cont'd
Exceptions—Cont'd
Exclusion, discretion of judge, **Evidence Rule 807**
Expert opinion included in statement, **Evidence Rule 808**
Hearsay within hearsay, **Evidence Rule 805**
Not dependent on declarants unavailability, **Evidence Rule 803**

HEAT
Machinery and equipment, portable, oil burning, **2C:40–6 et seq.**
Oil burning heating devices, **2C:40–6 et seq.**

HEAVY EQUIPMENT
Moving Heavy Machinery, generally, this index

HEIGHT
Heavy machinery, being moved on highway, change or repair of overhead wires, **39:4–28**
Maximum height of,
Motor vehicles, **39:3–84**
Private utility or house type semitrailers and trailers, **39:3–8**
Traffic signals, **39:4–110**

HEINOUS OFFENSES
Crimes and offenses, **2C:44–1**
Rewards for detection and apprehension, **2A:153–4**

HEIRS AND DEVISEES
Probate Proceedings, generally, this index

HELMETS
Bicycles, **39:4–10.1 et seq.**
Statement promoting use, **39:4–14.4a, 39:4–14.7a**
Electric personal assistive mobility devices, operation, **39:4–14.10**
Motorcycles, **39:3–76.7, 39:3–76.10**
Passengers, **39:3–76.5**
Motorized bicycles, **39:4–14.3q**
Roller skates, **39:4–10.5 et seq.**
Skateboards, **39:4–10.5 et seq.**
Threewheeled vehicles, **39:3–76.7**

HEMOGLOBIN C TRAIT
Discrimination, generally, this index

HERD
Animals, generally, this index

HERO ACT
Anatomical gifts, **39:2–3.4, 39:3–12.2 et seq.**

HEROIN
Controlled dangerous substance, **24:21–1 et seq.**

HERPES VIRUS
Sexual activity, diseased persons, **2C:34–5**

HIGH MISDEMEANOR
Definitions, Code of Criminal Justice, **2C:1–4**
Prostitution, generally, this index
Restitution, **2A:93–5.1**
Sale, poisoned liquors, serious injury or death, **33:3–10**
Turnpike projects, violation of law regulation, **27:23–33**
Weapons, generally, this index

HIGH SCHOOLS
Schools and School Districts, this index

HIGHER EDUCATION
Colleges and Universities, generally, this index

HIGHWAY AUTHORITY
Abolishment, **27:23–41**
Transfer of powers and duties, turnpike authority, **27:23–41 et seq., 27:23–42**
Turnpike Authority, generally, this index

HIGHWAY COMMISSIONER
Transportation Department, generally, this index

HIGHWAY DEPARTMENT
Transportation Department, generally, this index

HIGHWAY SAFETY FUND
Motor carriers, fines and penalties, nonresident vehicles, weight, **39:3–20.4**

HIGHWAY WEIGHT LIMITATION ACT
Generally, **39:3–84 et seq.**

HIGHWAYS AND ROADS
See, also,
   State Highways, generally, this index
   Streets and Alleys, generally, this index
Advertisements. Outdoor Advertising, generally, this index
Agricultural products, sales, **27:23–48**
All terrain vehicles, **39:3C–1 et seq.**
   Crossing, **39:3C–17**
Authority. Turnpike Authority, generally, this index
Bicycles, operation, **39:4–14.2**
   Helmets, **39:4–10.1**
Brands, marks and labels, garbage dumpsters or container, placement along highway, **27:5I–1**
Bridges and Viaducts, generally, this index
Carriers. Motor Carriers, generally, this index
Charitable organizations, solicitation, **39:4–60**
Closed roads, sign mutilation, fines and penalties, **39:4–94.2**
Closing highway for horse racing, **39:4–21**
Commercial vehicles,
   Route 94 in Sussex and Warren counties, **39:4–197.8**
   Width, **39:3–84**
Common carriers. Motor Carriers, generally, this index
Consent, roll off dumpsters or containers for garbage, placement along highway, **27:5I–1**
Construction, traffic offenses in construction or repair areas, fines, **39:4–203.5**
Continuously controlled highway, traffic signals required at every intersection in order to constitute, **39:4–113**
Controlled highways, traffic signals required at every intersection in order to constitute continuously controlled highway, **39:4–113**
County Roads, generally, this index
Curbs and Curbing, generally, this index
Definitions,
   Explosives Act, **21:1A–129**
   Motor Vehicle Law, **39:1–1**
   Traffic rules and regulations, **39:1–1, 39:4–203.5**
   Within Fireworks Regulation Law, **21:2–2**
Dirt bikes,
   Application of law, **39:3C–30**
   Operation, **39:3C–17**
Disorderly person, racing, **39:5C–1**
Dividing space, vehicles to be driven upon right hand roadway, **39:4–82.1**
Drives and Driveways, generally, this index

HIGHWAYS AND ROADS—Cont'd
Electric personal assistive mobility devices, operation, **39:4–14.10**
Entering or leaving at entrances and exits established by public authority, **39:4–90.1**
Exemptions, length of vehicles, **39:3–84**
Explosives, distances and quantity, manufacturing and storage, **21:1A–135**
Express highways. Turnpikes, generally, this index
Farm tractors and traction equipment,
   Maximum width and length, **39:3–84**
   Registration, operation on highways, **39:3–24**
Farm trucks, width, **39:3–84**
Fines and penalties,
   Closed roads, sign mutilation, **39:4–94.2**
   Display of name of owner of commercial vehicle, fund for repair of roads, **39:4–47**
   Garbage and refuse, roll off dumpsters or containers, placement along road, **27:5I–1**
   Glass or other injurious substance placed on highway, **39:4–63**
   Moving heavy machinery, highway, violation of law, **39:4–31**
   Soliciting sales, **39:4–60**
Funds,
   Disposition of fines for violating law relating to projections on tires and locking of wheels of motor vehicles, **39:3–81**
   Fines for violations of law relating to display of name of owner of commercial vehicle, fund for repair of roads, **39:4–47**
Garbage and refuse, dumpsters or roll off containers, placement along, **27:5I–1**
Glass or other injurious substance placed on highway, fine imposed, **39:4–63**
Grade Crossings, generally, this index
Intersections, generally, this index
Interstate bridges and tunnels. Bridges and Viaducts, this index
Interstate Highway System, generally, this index
Junk yards. Motor Vehicle Junk Yards, generally, this index
Law of road. Traffic Rules and Regulations, generally, this index
Licenses and permits,
   Movement of heavy machinery, highway, **39:4–26**
   Unregistered vehicles, permits to cross public highways, **39:3–26.1 et seq.**
   Width of commercial vehicles, **39:3–84**
Lights and Lighting, this index
Limited access highways,
   Abandoned and unclaimed vehicles, **39:4–56.5**
   Definitions, motor vehicles, **39:1–1**
Limiting use to certain class of vehicles, power of municipality, **39:4–197**
Littering, signs, **39:4–64.1**
Location, turnpike authority, power to change, **27:23–6**
Low speed vehicles, operation, **39:4–31.1**
Maintenance and repair,
   Motor vehicles, approaching, **39:4–92.2**
   Reduction of speed limit, **39:4–98.2**
   Traffic offenses in construction or repair areas, fines, **39:4–203.5**
Markings, **39:4–191.1 et seq.**
Medial barriers, pedestrians, crossing, **39:4–34**
Motor Carriers, generally, this index
Motor Vehicle Junk Yards, generally, this index
Motor Vehicles, generally, this index

HIGHWAYS AND ROADS—Cont'd
Mountain highways, motor vehicle to be kept on right side and under control, **39:4–55**
Moving heavy machinery,
   Damages, **39:4–27**
   Regulation, **39:4–26**
Municipalities,
   Speed bumps, **39:4–8.9 et seq.**
   Transportation, department of, traffic regulations, proposed orders, copies, **39:4–8.4**
Mutilation of signs, closed roads, fines and penalties, **39:4–94.2**
No passing zones, **39:4–86**
Nuisance, rotating or flashing lights on or near highways, **39:4–60.1 et seq.**
Obscene material, public communication, **2C:34–4**
Obstruction and obstructions, **2C:33–7**
   Crimes and offenses, **2C:33–7**
   State highways, permission required for construction of safety zones, guide posts, or other structures, **39:4–199**
   Willful interference with other vehicles, **39:4–56.1 et seq.**
Outdoor Advertising, generally, this index
Overtaking and passing vehicles. Traffic Rules and Regulations, this index
Parking, generally, this index
Pedestrians, crosswalks, right of way, **39:4–34 et seq.**
Penalties. Fines and penalties, generally, ante
Pornographic material, public communication, **2C:34–4**
Private Roads, generally, this index
Public nuisance, rotating or flashing lights on or near highways, **39:4–60.1 et seq.**
Racing, disorderly person, **39:5C–1**
Railroad Crossings, generally, this index
Railroads,
   Crossings. Railroad Crossings, generally, this index
   Grade Crossings, generally, this index
   Interference, use of highway by operation of locomotive, train or crossing gate prohibited, **39:4–94**
Registration, farm machinery and implements, operation on highways, **39:3–24**
Relocation, public roads affected by construction of Turnpike project, **27:23–6**
Roll off dumpsters or containers, garbage, placement along highway, **27:5I–1**
Roller skates, **39:4–10.10, 39:4–10.11**
Route 94, Sussex and Warren counties, commercial vehicles, **39:4–197.8**
Self propelled vehicles, unregistered, permits to cross public highways, **39:3–26.1 et seq.**
Signs and signals. Traffic Signs and Signals, generally, this index
Skateboards, **39:4–10.10, 39:4–10.11**
Slippery condition, tire chains permitted, **39:3–73**
Snowmobiles, **39:3C–1 et seq.**
   Application of law, **39:3C–30**
   Crossing, **39:3C–17**
Soliciting sales, fines and penalties, **39:4–60**
Solid waste, roll off dumpsters or containers, placement along, **27:5I–1**
Speed, generally, this index
Speed bumps, municipalities, **39:4–8.9 et seq.**
State highway department. Transportation Department, generally, this index
State Institutions, this index
Stop signs. Traffic Signs and Signals, this index
Throwing or dropping articles from vehicle on highway, **39:4–64**

HIGHWAYS AND ROADS—Cont'd

Tractors crossing at grade, notice of intention to cross, **39:4–128**

Traffic Rules and Regulations, generally, this index

Traffic Signs and Signals, generally, this index

Trailers and semitrailers, width, **39:3–84**

Transportation, department of, traffic regulations, **39:4–8.2 et seq.**

Trucks. Motor Carriers, generally, this index

Turnpike Authority, generally, this index

Turnpikes, generally, this index

Unregistered vehicles, permits to cross the public highways, **39:3–26.1 et seq.**

Vacation of public highway affected by construction of turnpike project, **27:23–6**

Vehicles loaded, spilling of contents, prohibited, **39:4–77**

Viaducts. Bridges and Viaducts, generally, this index

Width,
    Commercial vehicles, **39:3–84**
    Farm trucks, **39:3–84**
    Trailers and semitrailers, **39:3–84**

Workmen engaged in work on surface of highway, traffic laws inapplicable, **39:4–1**

HILLS AND GRADES

Coasting with gears of motor vehicle in neutral prohibited, **39:4–55**

Control of vehicle on steep grade required, **39:4–55**

Parking on grade, turning wheels of vehicle to curb or side of highway, **39:4–137**

Right side, motor vehicle on steep grade, **39:4–55**

Turning vehicle around near crest of grade prohibited, **39:4–125**

HINDERING

Crimes and offenses, apprehension or prosecution, **2C:29–3**

Terrorism, **2C:38–4**

HISPANIC PERSONS

Discrimination, generally, this index

HISTORIC MOTOR VEHICLES

Generally, **39:3–27.3, 39:3–27.4**

Definitions, **39:3–27.3**

Inspection, **39:8–1**

HISTORICAL SITES AND PROPERTY

Hotels and motels, intoxicating liquors, licenses and permits, **33:1–12.20**

Intoxicating liquors, licenses and permits, hotels and motels, **33:1–12.20**

National register, hotels and motels, intoxicating liquors, licenses and permits, **33:1–12.20**

HISTORY

Reputation, hearsay exception, **Evidence Rule 803**

HIT AND RUN DRIVERS

Generally, **39:4–129**

Conviction of crime, merger, **2C:11–5.1, 2C:12–1.1**

Death, crimes and offenses, **2C:11–5.1**

Jurisdiction, actions and proceedings, property liability insurance guaranty association, **39:6–78**

Knowledge, **2C:11–5.1, 2C:12–1.1**

Personal injuries, crimes and offenses, **2C:12–1.1**

HIT AND RUN DRIVERS—Cont'd

Property liability insurance guaranty association, actions and proceedings, unsatisfied claim and judgment fund, **39:6–78 et seq.**

HITCH HIKING

Standing in roadway while soliciting ride, **39:4–59**

HITCHING ON VEHICLES

Person on bicycle, skates, **39:4–14**

HIV (HUMAN IMMUNODEFICIENCY VIRUS)

AIDS (Acquired Immune Deficiency Syndrome), generally, this index

Records and recordation, confidential or privileged information, **Rule 1:38–3**

HIV INFECTION

AIDS (Acquired Immune Deficiency Syndrome), generally, this index

HOBS

Motor vehicle tire projections, **39:3–81**

HOLDER

Negotiable Instruments, generally, this index

HOLIDAYS

Computation of time, **Rule 1:3–1**

Court recesses, **Rule 1:30–3**

Process, service for violation of law relating to turnpike projects, **27:23–34**

Sunday, generally, this index

HOME HEALTH CARE SERVICES

Agents and agencies,
    Criminal history record information, nurses aides or personal care assistants, certificates, **53:1–20.9a**
    Nurses aides or personal care assistants, criminal history record checks, certificates, **53:1–20.9a**

Homemaker home health aides. Nurses, this index

HOME STATE

Definitions, drivers licenses, **39:5D–2**

HOMEMAKER HOME HEALTH AIDES

Nurses, this index

HOMEOWNERS

Housing, generally, this index

HOMES

Housing, generally, this index

HOMES FOR BOYS AND GIRLS

Parking on roadway, **39:4–208**

Traffic regulation on grounds, **39:4–208**

HOMESTEADS

Taxation, this index

HOMICIDE

Generally, **2C:11–1 et seq., 2C:44–1**

Affirmative defenses, felony murder, **2C:11–3**

Aggravated criminal sexual contact, **2C:14–3**

Aggravated manslaughter. Manslaughter, this index

Aggravated sexual assault, **2C:14–2**

Aggravating factors, sentence and punishment, **2C:11–3**

Arrest, force or violence, **2C:3–7**
    Grand jury, instructions to jury, **2B:22–9**

HOMICIDE—Cont'd

Arrest warrant,
    Issuance, **Rule 3:3–1**
    Release, **Rule 3:4–1**

Attempts,
    Body vests, unlawful use, **2C:39–13**
    Multiple victims, fines and penalties, **2C:5–4**

Bail,
    Authority to admit to, **Rule 3:26–2**
    Cash, crime with bail restrictions, **2A:162–12**

Bodily injury, definitions, **2C:11–1**

Carjacking, **2C:11–3**

Children and minors, sentencing, **2C:11–3**

Commutation, life imprisonment, **2C:11–3**

Conspiracy, **2C:11–3**
    Multiple victims, fines and penalties, **2C:5–4**

Contracts, murder for hire, **2C:11–3**

Deadly weapon, definitions, **2C:11–1**

Death by auto or vessel, **2C:11–5**

Defenses, notice, **Rule 3:12–1**

Definitions, **2C:11–1 et seq., 2C:11–3**

DNA database and databank, conviction, **53:1–20.20**

Domestic Violence, generally, this index

Duress, defense, **2C:2–9**

Evidence,
    Aggravating and mitigating factors, **2C:11–3**
    Photographs,
        Rules and regulations, **2C:11–3a**
        Victims of crime, **2C:11–3**
    Sentence proceeding, **2C:11–3 et seq.**

Expungement of records, **2C:52–2**

Extended term of imprisonment, **2C:43–7, 2C:43–7.1**

Extradition of person,
    Charged with murder in demanding state and imprisoned in New Jersey for term less than life, **2A:160–10**
    Imprisoned in another state on acquittal of murder, **2A:160–5**

Felony murder, **2C:11–3**

Flight, **2C:11–3**

Force or violence, arrest, grand jury, instructions to jury, **2B:22–9**

Hit and run drivers, vehicular homicide, **2C:11–5, 2C:11–5.1**

Homicidal act, definitions, **2C:11–3**

Indictment, contents, **Rule 3:7–3**

Jury and jurors, peremptory challenges, **2B:23–13; Rule 1:8–3**

Juvenile delinquents,
    Jurisdiction, waiver, **2A:4A–26**
    Referral to other courts without juveniles consent, **Rule 5:22–2**
    Sentence and punishment, **2C:11–3**
    Transfer of causes, **Rule 5:22–1 et seq.**
        Election by juvenile under certain age, **2A:4A–27**

Life imprisonment, parole, **2C:11–3**

Limitation of criminal prosecutions, **2C:1–6**
    Time between assault and death of victim, **2C:11–2.1**

Manslaughter, generally, this index

Mitigating factors, sentence and punishment, **2C:11–3**

Motions, capital punishment, life imprisonment, **2C:11–3b**

Motor Vehicles, this index

Multiple victims, fines and penalties, attempts, conspiracy, **2C:5–4**

Murder for hire, **2C:11–3**

Nuclear power plants, vandalism, **2C:17–8**

Parole, life imprisonment, **2C:11–3, 2C:11–3b**

Photographs, victims of crime, sentence and punishment, **2C:11–3**

Rules and regulations, **2C:11–3a**

HOMICIDE—Cont'd

Presentence investigation and report, disclosure, 2C:44–6

Cost of evaluation, 2C:44–6.1

Prosecution, bar, time between assault, death of victim, 2C:11–2.1

Records and recordation, expungement, 2C:52–2

Restitution, 2C:11–3c

Reward for apprehension and conviction of murderer, 2A:153–1, 2A:153–2, 2A:153–4

Robbery, 2C:15–1

Sentence and punishment, 2C:11–3 et seq.

Jurors, peremptory challenges, **Rule 1:8–3**

Separate sentencing hearing, **Rule 3:21–4A**

Waiver of jury, **Rule 1:8–1**

Serious bodily injury, definitions, 2C:11–1

Significant bodily injury, definitions, 2C:11–1

Special verdict, sentence and punishment, 2C:11–3

Territorial applicability of criminal justice, 2C:1–3

Terrorism, 2C:11–3, 2C:38–2

Vehicular homicide, 2C:11–5, 2C:11–5.1

Verdicts, sentencing, 2C:11–3

Vessels, death by, 2C:11–5

Victims of crime,

Photographs, ante

Restitution, 2C:11–3c

Weapons,

Mandatory sentence, 2C:43–6

Possession, 2C:39–7

HOMOSEXUALS

Discrimination, generally, this index

Sex offenses, 2C:14–1 et seq.

HONORARY MEMBERSHIP CARDS

Law enforcement officers organization or association, unlawful to issue, 2A:170–20.1

HORNS

Motor Vehicles, this index

HORSE DRAWN VEHICLES

Generally, 39:4–15 et seq.

Backing against curb to load or unload vehicles, horse to stand parallel to curb and face traffic, 39:4–79

Fastening wheels of vehicle on leaving horse unattended in highway, 39:4–16

Lights, 39:4–25

Rights and duties of drivers, 39:4–25.1

Unhitching of horses, prerequisite to removing part of vehicle or harness, 39:4–18

HORSE RACING

Exemptions, highways, 39:4–21

Highway prohibited, 39:4–21

HORSEBACK RIDING

Agricultural lands, damages, 2C:18–5

HORSES

See, also, Horse Drawn Vehicles, generally, this index

Backing horse drawn vehicle against curb, horse to stand parallel to curb and facing traffic, 39:4–79

Cruelty to animals, 39:4–23, 39:4–24

Definitions, 39:1–1

Directions of police or other officers, duty of driver to comply, 39:4–57

Disorderly Persons, this index

Fines and penalties, 39:4–203

Halter, unbitted horses, 39:4–17

HORSES—Cont'd

Hitching to pole, tree, or hydrant, prohibited, 39:4–20

Ill treatment prohibited, 39:4–23

Law enforcement officers, police animals, injuries, 2C:29–3.1

Motor vehicles, operation near, 39:4–72

Obstructing sidewalk or crosswalk with tie ropes, prohibited, 39:4–19

Offenses, sale of horse unfit for work, 4:22–21

Penalties, 39:4–203

Poles, hitching to, 39:4–20

Reins to be held in hands, 39:4–22

Sales, unfit horse, 4:22–21

Sidewalks,

Driving or backing across prohibited, when, 39:4–71

Maximum speed in crossing, 39:4–100

Obstructions, prohibition, 39:4–19

Sleigh bells required on horse attached to sleigh or sled, 39:4–15

Theft, 2C:20–2

Traffic rules and regulations, operation near, 39:4–72

Treatment, 39:4–23, 39:4–24

Trees, hitching to, 39:4–20

Unattended in highway, fastening required, 39:4–16

Unbitted horses, halter required, 39:4–17

Unhitching of horse as prerequisite to removal of part of vehicle or harness, 39:4–18

Unlawful taking, means of conveyance, 2C:20–10

Water hydrants, hitching to, 39:4–20

Whips, use of, 39:4–23, 39:4–24

HOSPITAL AMBULANCES

Ambulances, generally, this index

HOSPITAL SERVICE CORPORATIONS

Utilization review committees established by certified hospitals, privileged communications, 2A:84A–22.8

HOSPITALIZATION INSURANCE

Health and Accident Insurance, generally, this index

HOSPITALS

Actions and proceedings, review committees, immunity from liability, 2A:84A–22.10

Acute care, intoxication of driver, supervised visitation, 39:4–50

Aged persons, assault of institutionalized elderly persons, 2C:12–1

Alcoholic beverages, regulation of use, 33:1–29

Alcoholics and alcoholism, intoxication of driver, supervised visitation, 39:4–50

Anatomical Gifts, generally, this index

Automobile insurance, no fault insurance, application of law, 39:6A–1 et seq.

Burns, injuries, reports, 2C:58–8

Carrying injured person to, duty of driver of vehicle involved in accident, 39:4–129

Child Abuse, this index

Committees, privileged information, utilization review committees, 2A:84A–22.8, 2A:84A–22.9

Confidential or privileged information,

Child abuse, reports, 9:6–8.20

Disclosure, utilization review committees, 2A:84A–22.8, 2A:84A–22.9

Criminal history record information, nurses aides, certificates, **53:1–20.9a**

HOSPITALS—Cont'd

Damages,

Directors, reports of child abuse, immunity, **9:6–8.20**

Disclosure of privileged communications, 2A:84A–22.9

Deborah heart and lung center, motor vehicles, special plates, 39:3–27.107 et seq.

Definitions, controlled substances, 2C:35–2, 24:21–2

Disclosure, privileged communications, utilization review committees, 2A:84A–22.8, 2A:84A–22.9

Emergency services, intoxication of driver, supervised visitation, 39:4–50

Evaluations, quality of care, medical staff, immunity from liability, 2A:84A–22.10

Expenses and expenditures, definitions, no fault insurance, 39:6A–2

Health Maintenance Organizations, generally, this index

Institutionalized elderly persons, assault, 2C:12–1

Intoxicating liquor, regulation of use by hospitals, 33:1–29

Intoxication of driver, supervised visitation, 39:4–50

Medical staff committees, immunity from liability, 2A:84A–22.10

Motor vehicles owned by, free registration, 39:3–27

No fault insurance, application of law, 39:6A–1 et seq.

Nurses aides, criminal history record checks, certificates, 53:1–20.9a

Nursing Homes or Hospitals, generally, this index

Parking vehicle near entrance for purpose of taking on or letting off passengers, time limited, 39:4–139

Peer review committee, immunity from liability, 2A:84A–22.10

Protective custody, abused children, 9:6–8.16

Reports, protective custody, abused child, 9:6–8.17

Retention,

Property seized under Alcoholic Beverage Law for use of, 33:1–66

Seized stills, distilling apparatus, use of, 33:2–5

Sexual assault, inmate, 2C:14–2

Sexually oriented businesses, zoning and planning, 2C:34–7

Surgeons. Physicians and Surgeons, generally, this index

Trauma centers, intoxication of driver, supervised visitation, 39:4–50

Utilization review committees, privileges and immunities, **Evidence Rule 507**

Victims of crime, intoxication of driver, supervised visitation, 39:4–50

Zoning and planning, sexually oriented businesses, 2C:34–7

HOSTAGES

Kidnapping, generally, this index

HOTELS AND MOTELS

Alcoholic beverages. Intoxicating liquors, generally, post

Burglary, generally, this index

Buses, registration, licensing, certificates, 39:3–4.1

Definitions, intoxicating liquors, 33:1–43

Historical sites and property, intoxicating liquors, licenses and permits, 33:1–12.20

HOTELS

I-116

HOTELS AND MOTELS—Cont'd
Hotel management programs, intoxicating liquors, possession, children and minors, 2C:33–15
Intoxicating liquors,
Guests, sale and delivery, 33:1–12.25
Hotel management programs, possession, children and minors, 2C:33–15
Licenses and permits, 33:1–12.20
Additional retail license, Chain Store Liquor License Act, 33:1–12.32
Contingent on completion of construction, 33:1–12.20a
Limitations, 33:1–12.20
Sales within 200 feet of church or school, 33:1–76
Ownership, manufacturing or wholesaling facilities, 33:1–43
Sale and delivery to guests, 33:1–12.25
Licenses and permits. Intoxicating liquors, ante
Liquor. Intoxicating liquors, generally, ante
Parking vehicle near entrance for purpose of taking on or letting off passengers, time limited, 39:4–139
Theft of services, 2C:20–8
Turnpike authority, use of right of way, 27:23–9

HOURS OF SALE
Alcoholic Beverages, this index

HOUSE OF ASSEMBLY
General Assembly, generally, this index

HOUSE OF PROSTITUTION
Prostitution, generally, this index

HOUSE TYPE SEMITRAILERS AND TRAILERS
Registration, size, 39:3–8

HOUSEHOLD ARTS SCHOOLS
Vocational Education, generally, this index

HOUSES
Housing, generally, this index

HOUSES OF GAMBLING
Gambling, generally, this index

HOUSES OF PROSTITUTION OR ILL FAME
Prostitution, generally, this index

HOUSING
Arson and Other Burnings, generally, this index
Burglary, generally, this index
Criminal trespass, 2C:18–3
Force, use in defense of dwelling, 2C:3–6
Hotels and Motels, generally, this index
Inspection and inspectors, liquefied petroleum gas, 21:1B–3
Landlord and Tenant, generally, this index
Liquefied petroleum gas, inspection, 21:1B–3
Manufactured Homes, generally, this index
Mobile Homes and Mobile Home Parks, generally, this index
Peering into dwellings, crimes and offenses, 2C:18–3
Protection, third persons, 2C:3–5
Public housing,
Crimes and offenses, controlled dangerous substances, 2C:35–7.1
Definitions, controlled dangerous substances, crimes and offenses, 2C:35–7.1

HOUSING—Cont'd
Sales, radon gas test results, providing to purchaser, 26:2D–73
Search Warrants, generally, this index
Self defense, 2C:3–4, 2C:3–6
Unlawful possession of weapons, exemption, 2C:39–6
Window peeping, crimes and offenses, 2C:18–3
Wines, home manufacture, special permits, 33:1–75

HULLS
Boats and Boating, generally, this index

HUMAN BEINGS
Cloning, crimes and offenses, 2C:11A–1

HUMAN BODY PARTS
Crimes and offenses, purchases, sales, 2C:22–2
Theft, 2C:20–2

HUMAN IMMUNODEFICIENCY VIRUS
AIDS (Acquired Immune Deficiency Syndrome), generally, this index

HUMAN SERVICES DEPARTMENT
Commitment and Admission to Institutions, generally, this index
Definitions, abuse of children, 9:6–8.21
Divisions, parole, supervision of convicts at large, 2A:167–8
Family development division. Support of Persons, generally, this index
Medicaid, generally, this index
Mentally Deficient and Mentally Ill Persons, generally, this index
Motor vehicle and traffic laws, application to roads, streets, public or semipublic institutions, 39:5A–1 et seq.
Parole, generally, this index
Placement. Children and Minors, this index
Police officers, weapons possession, exemption, 2C:39–6
Records and recordation, abuse or neglect, unfounded allegations, expunging record, 9:6–8.40a
Released prisoners, registration and notification procedures, 2C:7–2 et seq.
Sex offenses, released offenders, registration and notification procedures, 2C:7–2 et seq.

HUMAN TRAFFICKING
Crimes and offenses, 2C:13–8
Expungement of record, 2C:52–2

HUMAN TRANSPLANTS
Anatomical Gifts, generally, this index

HUMANE SOCIETIES
Controlled substances, registration, 24:21–11
Motor vehicles owned by, free registration, 39:3–27
Officers and employees, weapons, possession, 2C:39–6

HUNTING
Fish and Game, generally, this index

HUSBAND AND WIFE
Spouses, generally, this index

HYDRANTS
Horse not to be hitched to, 39:4–20
Parking within certain distance of prohibited, 39:4–138

HYDROCHLORIC ACID
Turnpike projects, transportation regulation, 27:23–31

HYDROMORPHINOL
Controlled dangerous substance, 24:21–1 et seq.

HYDROXYPETHIDINE
Controlled dangerous substance, 24:21–1 et seq.

HYPODERMIC NEEDLES OR SYRINGES
Bloodborne disease harm reduction, possession, exemptions, 2C:36–6a
Crimes and offenses,
Discarding or abandoning, 2C:36–6.1
Possession, sale or distribution, 2C:36–6
Discarding or abandoning, 2C:36–6.1
Disorderly persons, discarding or abandoning, 2C:36–6.1
Exemptions, possession, bloodborne disease harm reduction, 2C:36–6a
Possession,
Bloodborne disease harm reduction, exemptions, 2C:36–6a
Sale or distribution, 2C:36–6
Prescriptions, 2C:36–6

HYPOXIA
Animals, chambers or devices to induce hypoxia, dismantling, 4:22–19.1

IBOGAINE
Controlled dangerous substance, 24:21–1 et seq.

ICE
Intoxicating liquors, licensee, sale, 33:1–12
Motor vehicles, dislodging from moving vehicle, fines and penalties, 39:4–77.1

ICE CREAM AND OTHER FROZEN PRODUCTS
Frozen Desserts and Dietary Foods, generally, this index

ICE MILK
Frozen Desserts and Dietary Foods, generally, this index

IDENTIFICATION
Identity and Identification, generally, this index

IDENTIFICATION BUREAU
Arrested person,
Comparison of records with record on file, 53:1–16
Copies sent to bureau, 53:1–15
Clerks of court,
Punishment for failure to report disposition of indictable offense, 53:1–20
Report to bureau on disposition of criminal charge or disorderly person offenses, 53:1–18
Collection, violent criminal apprehension program (VICAP, 53:1–20.13
Comparison of records received with records on file with bureau, 53:1–16
Cooperation,
Local police, 53:1–17
National bureau and other agencies, 53:1–19
Coordination, violent criminal apprehension program (VICAP, state and local enforcement agencies, participation, 53:1–20.11
Criminal history record information,
Employees, 53:1–20.8

IDENTIFICATION BUREAU—Cont'd
Criminal history record information—Cont'd
Public adjusters license, applicants and sublicensees, 53:1–20.16
User fees, 53:1–20.5 et seq.
Criminal history record information fund, establishment, deposits, 53:1–20.7
Criminal records, 53:1–20.1
Definitions, 53:1–20.5
Habitual criminals,
Fingerprints and photographs sent by arresting officer to bureau, 53:1–15
Procuring and filing fingerprints, photographs and information concerning, 53:1–13
Information,
Furnished by keepers of penal institutions, 53:1–14
Procured by supervisor, 53:1–13
Violent criminal apprehension program, post
Instruction of local police, 53:1–17
International or interstate systems of identification, duty to develop and carry on, 53:1–19
Local systems of procuring, cooperation of bureau in establishing, 53:1–17
Narcotic offenses,
Fingerprints, photographs and descriptions of persons arrested, 53:1–18.1
Report of sentence or other disposition of case, 53:1–18.2, 53:1–18.3 et seq.
National bureau, cooperation with, 53:1–19
Noncriminal matter, definitions, criminal history record information, 53:1–20.5
Notice of release of prisoner to be given bureau by wardens, 53:1–20.3
Offense by officer failing or neglecting to perform duties, 53:1–20
Penal institutions, procuring and filing fingerprints or photographs, inmates, 53:1–14
Processing criminal history record background checks, definitions, 53:1–20.5
Prosecutors, reports, crime conditions, 53:1–18a
Record of fingerprints, photographs, persons confined in penal institutions, 53:1–14
Removal of officer failing or neglecting to perform duties, 53:1–20
Reports,
Crime conditions, 53:1–18a
Disposition of criminal charge or disorderly person offenses, 53:1–18
Punishment of officer failing to make, 53:1–20
Violent criminal apprehension program (VICAP, 53:1–20.13
Rules and regulations, criminal history record background checks, user fees, 53:1–20.6
Sentence on trial of criminal charge or disorderly person offense reported to bureau, 53:1–18
State institutions to furnish information, 53:1–13
Superintendent of state police, request by superintendent for information from state institutions, 53:1–13
Supervisor,
Comparison of records received with records on file, 53:1–16
Cooperation,
Local police, 53:1–17
National bureau and other agencies, 53:1–19
Filing fingerprints, photographs, measurements, 53:1–13
Persons confined in penal institutions, 53:1–14

IDENTIFICATION BUREAU—Cont'd
Unknown dead, fingerprints sent to bureau, 53:1–15
User fees, criminal history record background checks, 53:1–20.5 et seq.
Violent criminal apprehension program,
Coordination, state and local enforcement agencies, participation, 53:1–20.11
Equipment, supplies or services, purchases, 53:1–20.14
Information,
Collection and reporting, 53:1–20.13
Format, 53:1–20.12
Legislative findings and declarations, 53:1–20.10
Rules and regulations, 53:1–20.15
Statewide central registry, 53:1–20.11

IDENTIFICATION CARDS
Aliens, authorized presence in U.S., proof, requirement, 39:3–29.3
Anatomical gifts, donors, 39:3–12.2, 39:3–12.4
Color photographs, 39:3–29.4
Crimes and offenses,
False documents, 2C:21–2.1
Public utilities, 2C:21–35
Drivers license replacement, nondrivers, 39:3–29.2 et seq.
Emergency vehicles, permit to display warning lights, 39:3–54.11
Fees, 39:3–29.7
Firearms purchasers, applications, false statements, 2C:39–10
Fraud, public utilities, 2C:21–35
Insurance identification cards, possession by motor vehicle driver, 39:3–29
Motor Vehicle Insurance, this index
Motor Vehicle Security Responsibility Law, possession by driver, 39:3–29, 39:3–29.1
Motor vehicles, 39:3–29.2 et seq.
Nondrivers, 39:3–29.2 et seq.
Period of validity, 39:3–29.5
Public utilities, crimes and offenses, 2C:21–35
Retired law enforcement officers, weapons, 2C:39–6, 2C:39–6.1
Weapons, this index

IDENTIFICATION CARDS FOR NONDRIVERS ACT
Generally, 39:3–29.2 et seq.

IDENTIFICATION LAMPS
Motor Vehicles, this index
Truck tractors, 39:3–61

IDENTITY AND IDENTIFICATION
Cards. Identification Cards, generally, this index
Confidential or privileged information, juvenile delinquents and dependents, 2A:4A–60
Crimes and Offenses, this index
Disclosure, juvenile delinquents and dependents, 2A:4A–60
DNA Database and Databank, generally, this index
Drivers Licenses, this index
Evidence, **Evidence Rule 901**
False personation, 2C:28–8
Fingerprints and Fingerprinting, generally, this index
Intoxicating liquors, purchasing, identification card, 33:1–81.2 et seq.
Jewelry, secondhand dealers, sales, 2C:21–36
Low speed vehicles, numbers and numbering, 39:4–31.2

IDENTITY AND IDENTIFICATION—Cont'd
Mentally retarded persons, transportation, county vehicles, 39:4–207.2 et seq.
Motor Vehicles, this index
Personalized handguns, 2C:58–2.2 et seq.
School busses, van type vehicles, 39:3B–8, 39:3B–9
State bureau of identification. Identification Bureau, generally, this index
Stolen property, release, disposition procedure, 2C:65–2
Stopping to give assistance and identification. Traffic Accidents, this index
Theft. Identity Theft, generally, this index
Traffic Accidents, this index
Verification, false documents, crimes and offenses, 2C:21–2.1
Victims of crime,
Confidential or privileged information, **Rule 1:38–3**
Privileged communications, counselors, 2A:84A–22.15
Volunteer fire company chief and first assistant chief vehicles, red warning lights and sirens, permits to display, 39:3–54.18
Weapons, personalized handguns, 2C:58–2.2 et seq.

IDENTITY THEFT
Generally, 2C:21–17
Actions and proceedings, 2C:21–17.4
Attorney fees, 2C:21–17.4
Books and papers, personal identifying information, 2C:21–17.3
Computers, personal identifying information, 2C:21–17.3
Consumer credit reports, orders of court, corrections, 2C:21–17.5
Costs, 2C:21–17.4
Credit, history, damages, 2C:21–17.4
Damages, 2C:21–17.4
Definitions, personal identifying information, 2C:21–17.3
Documents, personal identifying information, 2C:21–17.3
Drivers licenses, 2C:21–17.2
Intoxicating liquors, personal identifying information, obtaining, 2C:21–17.2
Evidence, actions and proceedings, 2C:21–17.4
Fines and penalties, 2C:44–1
Intoxicating liquors, personal identifying information, obtaining, 2C:21–17.2
Law enforcement officers, reports, 2C:21–17.6
Manufacturers and manufacturing, personal identifying information, 2C:21–17.3
Orders of court, consumer credit reports, corrections, 2C:21–17.5
Personal identifying information, possession, 2C:21–17.3
Possession, personal identifying information, 2C:21–17.3
Reports, law enforcement officers, 2C:21–17.6
Restitution, 2C:21–17.4
Treble damages, 2C:21–17.4

IGNITION INTERLOCK DEVICES
Motor vehicles, intoxication of driver, 39:4–50.16 et seq.

IGNITION KEYS
Motor vehicles, production, proof of ownership, 2C:40–23

IGNORANCE
Crimes and offenses,
Defenses, notice, **Rule 3:12–1**

IGNORANCE—Cont'd
Crimes and offenses—Cont'd
Liability, **2C:2–4**

ILLEGITIMATE CHILDREN
Child support hearing officers, **Rule 5:25–3**

ILLNESS
Attorneys, disability inactive status, **Rule 1:20–12**
Crimes and offenses, sentence, reduction, change, **Rule 3:21–10**
Jury and jurors, alternate jurors, substitution, **Rule 1:8–2**
Juvenile delinquents and dependents,
Out of door sales, **Rule 5:18–3**
Short term custody, **Rule 5:16–2**

ILLUMINATION
Lights and Lighting, generally, this index

IMITATION FIREARMS
Weapons, this index

IMITATION FROZEN DESSERTS
Frozen Desserts and Dietary Foods, generally, this index

IMMIGRATION AND NATURALIZATION
Arrests, violation of State law, special agents, **2A:154–5**
Crimes and offenses, human trafficking, **2C:13–8**
Documents, improper retention, crimes and offenses, **2C:21–31**
Drivers licenses, expiration, **39:3–10**
Human trafficking, **2C:13–8**
Identification cards, expiration, **39:3–29.5**
Unauthorized practice, **2C:21–31**

IMMIGRATION CONSULTANT
Definitions, unauthorized practice, **2C:21–31**
Unauthorized practice, **2C:21–31**

IMMIGRATION OR NATURALIZATION MATTER
Definitions, unauthorized practice, **2C:21–31**

IMMIGRATION RELATED DOCUMENT
Definitions, unauthorized practice, **2C:21–31**

IMMOVABLE PROPERTY
Theft, transfer of interest, **2C:20–3**

IMMUNITY
Privileges and Immunities, generally, this index

IMPACT STATEMENTS
Environmental Protection, this index

IMPANELING JURY
Jury and Jurors, generally, this index

IMPEACHMENT
Witnesses, this index

IMPERSONATION
Generally, **2C:21–17**
Public servants, **2C:28–8**

IMPLEMENTS
Stills and Distilling Apparatus, generally, this index

IMPLICATION
Presumptions, generally, this index

IMPORTS AND EXPORTS
Alcoholic Beverages, this index
Stolen property, bringing into state, **2C:20–7**

IMPOTENCY
Sexual offenses, capability, presumption, **2C:14–5**

IMPOUNDING
Agricultural land, trespass, damages, **2C:18–4 et seq.**
Electric personal assistive mobility devices, **39:4–14.11**
Flammable fabrics, sleeping bags and tents, sales, **2A:123–20**
Motor Vehicles, this index
Offroad vehicles, public lands, **39:3C–34**
Sleeping bags, flammable fabrics, sales, **2A:123–20**
Tents, flammable fabrics, sales, **2A:123–20**

IMPRISONMENT
Correctional Institutions, generally, this index
Crimes and Offenses, generally, this index

IMPROPER INFLUENCE
Bribery and Corruption, generally, this index

IMPROVEMENTS
Assessments, generally, this index
County Roads, generally, this index

IN CAMERA HEARINGS
Sexual offenses, evidence of previous sexual conduct of victim, **2C:14–7**

IN CAMERA PROCEEDINGS
Newspersons privilege, judicial inspection, **Evidence Rule 508**

IN LOCO PARENTIS
Sexual assault, **2C:14–2**

IN PROGRESS TRACE
Definitions, wiretapping and electronic surveillance, **2A:156A–2**
Wiretapping and electronic surveillance, **2A:156A–1 et seq.**

IN TERMINAL INSPECTION
Definitions, school buses, **39:3B–20**

IN THE COURSE OF COMMITTING
Definitions, burglary, **2C:18–2**

IN TIME OF EMERGENCY
Definitions, **39:3–11.5**

INACTIVE CASES
Dismissal, **Rule 1:13–7**

INCARCERATION
Correctional Institutions, generally, this index

INCENDIARY AMMUNITION
Discharge, **2C:58–10**

INCEST
Generally, **2C:14–2**
Children and minors, **2C:24–4**

INCLUDED OFFENSES
Former prosecution as bar to subsequent prosecution, **2C:1–9**
Prosecutions for multiple offenses, **2C:1–8**

INCOME
Compensation and Salaries, generally, this index

INCOME PRODUCER
Definitions, no fault insurance, **39:6A–2**

INCOME TAX—STATE
Filing, jury list preparation, qualifications and selection, **2B:20–2**

INCOMPETENT PERSONS
Attorneys, this index
Mediation, exceptions, **Rule 7:8–1**

INCONSISTENT LAWS
Conflict of Laws, generally, this index

INCORPORATED TOWNS
Chosen Freeholders, generally, this index

INCRIMINATION
Definitions, rules of evidence, **2A:84A–18**

INCUMBRANCES
Liens and Incumbrances, generally, this index

INDEBTEDNESS
See, also, Debtors and Creditors, generally, this index
Corporations, this index
Misconduct, corporate official, **2C:21–9**
Turnpike authority, highway authority, transfer of powers and duties, **27:23–42**

INDECENCY
Lewdness and Obscenity, generally, this index

INDEMNITY
Adult offender supervision interstate commission, **2A:168–31**
Attorneys, professional corporations, **Rule 1:21–1A**
Compounding, **2C:29–4**
Fireworks, manufacturers, bonds, **21:2–27, 21:2–28**
Judgment against person entitled to indemnity, hearsay, **Evidence Rule 803**

INDETERMINATE SENTENCES
Young adult offenders, **2C:43–5**

INDEX
Applications for motor vehicle registration and drivers license, **39:3–28**
Copying and destruction, applications for motor vehicle registration and drivers licenses, **39:3–28**
Motor vehicles, application for registration and drivers license, **39:3–28**
Supervisory treatment programs, first offenders, **2C:43–21**

INDEX CARDS
Crimes and offenses, expungement, **2C:52–1 et seq.**

INDICTMENT, INFORMATION OR PRESENTMENT
Generally, **Rule 3:7–1 et seq.**
Aggravating factors, capital offenses, specification, **Rule 3:7–3**
Alcoholic Beverages, this index
Amendments, **Rule 3:7–4**
Municipal prosecutors, **2B:25–11**
Application, bill of particulars, **Rule 3:7–5**
Arraignment, copy of, **Rule 3:9–1**

INDICTMENT, INFORMATION OR PRES-ENTMENT—Cont'd

Arrest, warrant,
Execution, **Rule 3:7–10**
Summons,
Form, **Rule 3:7–9**
Issuance, **Rule 3:7–8**
Assignment of counsel, indigent persons, **Rule 3:4–2**
Attorneys,
Indigent persons, assignment, **Rule 3:4–2**
Multidefendant indictment, representation, **Rule 3:8–2**
Bill of particulars, **Rule 3:7–5**
Capital offenses, aggravating factors, specification, **Rule 3:7–3**
Capital punishment, failure to indict, admitting to bail, **Rule 3:26–1**
Commencement of prosecution, 2C:1–6
Confidential or privileged information, **Rule 1:38–3**
Contents, nature, **Rule 3:7–3**
Counts, allegations, **Rule 3:7–3**
Criminal coercion, threat to accuse anyone of an offense, 2C:13–5
Defendants, joinder, **Rule 3:7–7**
Defenses,
Defects, objections before trial, **Rule 3:10–2**
Failure to charge offense, charged based on invalid statute, **Rule 3:10–2**
Definitions, indictment, 2A:152–1
Dismissal and nonsuit, **Rule 3:25–1 et seq.**
Appeal by state, delay, **Rule 3:25–3**
Defenses, objections, **Rules 3:10–2, 3:10–7**
Delay, **Rule 3:25–3**
Disposition, reasons, statement, **Rule 3:29**
Pretrial intervention programs, **Rule 3:28**
Disorderly persons offenses, 2C:1–4
Disposition, motion for dismissal, reasons, statement, **Rule 3:29**
Downgrading of offense to nonindictable offense, 2C:1–6
Drug trafficking network leaders, murder, **Rule 3:7–3**
Endorsement, **Rule 3:7–3**
Grand jury, **Rule 3:6–4**
Execution, service, **Rule 3:7–10**
Extortion, threat of accusation or prosecution, 2C:20–5
Extradition, this index
Failure,
Bail, admitting to, **Rule 3:26–1**
Death penalty, crimes punishable by, admission to bail, **Rule 3:26–1**
Failure to charge offense, defense, **Rules 3:10–2, 3:10–3**
Failure to move, **Rule 3:26–1**
Finding, return, **Rule 3:6–8**
Form, warrant, summons, **Rule 3:7–9**
Indigent persons, assignment of counsel, **Rule 3:4–2**
Informing defendant of right, **Rule 3:4–2**
Invalid statute or regulation, defense, **Rule 3:10–2**
Joinder, **Rule 3:15–1**
Defendants, **Rule 3:7–7**
Offense, **Rule 3:7–6**
Juvenile delinquents and dependents, 2A:4A–40, 2C:4–11
Limitation of criminal prosecutions, 2C:1–6
Motor Vehicle Hours of Service Law, proceedings for violation of, 39:9–4
Motor Vehicle Inspection Law, violation of, 39:8–9
Motor Vehicle Junk Yard Law, violation of, 39:11–11

INDICTMENT, INFORMATION OR PRES-ENTMENT—Cont'd

Motor Vehicle Security Responsibility Law, complaints in proceedings for violation of, 39:6–55
Multiple counts, verdict, **Rule 3:19–1**
Municipal courts, jurisdiction, indictment and trial by jury waived, 2B:12–18
Murder, contents, **Rule 3:7–3**
Nature, contents, **Rule 3:7–3**
No bill, **Rule 3:6–8**
Offenses, joinder, **Rule 3:7–6**
Petty disorderly persons offenses, 2C:1–4
Preparation, **Rule 3:7–2**
Pretrial intervention programs, dismissal, **Rule 3:28**
Reading, arraignment, **Rule 3:9–1**
Required finding, 2B:21–7
Return, **Rule 3:6–8**
Execution of service, warrant, **Rule 3:7–10**
Rights, waiver, **Rule 3:4–2**
Sealing, **Rule 3:6–8**
Secrecy, **Rule 3:6–8**
Separate defendants, **Rule 3:7–7**
Separate offenses, **Rule 3:7–6**
Service, execution, **Rule 3:7–10**
Several defendants, verdict, **Rule 3:19–1**
Severance, **Rule 3:15–1**
Specification, aggravating factors, capital offenses, **Rule 3:7–3**
State grand jury, 2B:22–5
Return to designated judge, 2B:22–5
Venue, 2B:22–7
Venue, 2B:22–7
Statement of reasons, disposition, motion to dismiss, **Rule 3:29**
Summons, warrant,
Form, **Rule 3:7–9**
Issuance, **Rule 3:7–8**
Superior court, **Rule 3:1–5**
Supplemental indictments, time, **Rule 3:7–3**
Time, supplemental indictments, **Rule 3:7–3**
Transfer, **Rule 3:1–5**
Verdict, several defendants, counts, **Rule 3:19–1**
Waiver, **Rules 3:4–2, 3:7–2**
Reading, arraignment, **Rule 3:9–1**
Warrants,
Execution, **Rule 3:7–10**
Summons,
Form, **Rule 3:7–9**
Issuance, **Rule 3:7–8**
When information will not lie, 2A:152–3
Writing, waiver, **Rule 3:7–2**

INDIGENT DEFENDANT
Definitions, public defenders, 2A:158A–2
Public Defenders, generally, this index

INDIGENT PERSONS
Appeal and review, transcripts, 2A:152–17, 2A:152–18
Appeals In Criminal Prosecutions, this index
Attorneys, this index
Charitable Organizations and Associations, generally, this index
Children and minors, placement, reduction, 9:6–8.54
Commitment and admission to institutions, change of status or classification of patient, reopening of case, 39:4–71
Crimes and Offenses, this index
Defendants, public defender, 2A:158A–1 et seq.
Fees, waiver, **Rule 1:13–2**

INDIGENT PERSONS—Cont'd
Fines and penalties,
Parking, installments, 39:4–139.10, 39:4–203.1
Traffic rules and regulations, installments, 39:4–203.1
Ignition interlock devices, 39:4–50.21
Juvenile delinquents and dependents,
Right to counsel, appointment of counsel, **Rule 5:20–2**
Temporary out of home placement, right to counsel, **Rule 5:18–2**
Medicaid, generally, this index
Medical assistance. Medicaid, generally, this index
Motor vehicle insurance, special policies, 39:6A–3.3
Motor vehicles,
Ignition interlock devices, 39:4–50.21
Fees, 39:4–50.17a
Traffic regulations, fines and penalties, installment payments, 39:4–203.1, 39:4–203.2
Paralegals or legal assistants, assisting in representation, **Rule 1:21–1**
Parking, fines and penalties, installments, 39:4–139.10, 39:4–203.1
Public Defenders, generally, this index
Right to counsel. Attorneys, this index
Supervisory treatment programs, first offenders, 2C:43–12 et seq.
Traffic rules and regulations, fines and penalties, installments, 39:4–203.1

INDISPENSABLE PARTIES
Transfer of actions, **Rule 1:13–4**

INDOOR POOR
Indigent Persons, generally, this index

INDUCTION COILS
Wiretapping and electronic surveillance, 2A:156A–1 et seq.

INDUSTRIAL ALCOHOL
Investigating sale, purchase, 33:1–30

INDUSTRIAL CHEMICALS
Distributors, 2C:35–29

INDUSTRIAL POLLUTION CONTROL FINANCING LAW
Environmental Protection, generally, this index

INDUSTRIAL SCHOOLS
Vocational Education, generally, this index

INDUSTRIAL WASTES
Solid Waste, generally, this index

INDUSTRIES
Manufacturers and Manufacturing, generally, this index

INEBRIATION
Alcoholics and Alcoholism, generally, this index

INFANTS
Children and Minors, generally, this index

INFERIOR COURTS
Municipal Courts, generally, this index

INFLAMMABLES
Explosives, generally, this index

INFLUENCE
Corrupt influence. Bribery and Corruption, generally, this index

INFORMATION
Colleges and Universities, generally, this index
Electronic Transactions, generally, this index
Grand jury, injurious disclosure, crime, **2B:21–10**
Indictment, Information or Presentment, generally, this index
Indigent, neglected or abandoned children, juvenile family crisis, **2A:4A–77**
Tampering with public information, **2C:28–7**

INFORMATION OR PRESENTMENT
Indictment, Information or Presentment, generally, this index

INFORMED CONSENT
Consent, generally, this index

INFORMERS
Identity, privilege, **Evidence Rule 516**
Suppression or tampering, hindering apprehension or prosecution, **2C:29–3**
Tampering with, **2C:28–5**

INFRACTIONS
De minimis infractions, criminal prosecution dismissal, **2C:2–11**
Joinder, trial with criminal offenses, **Rule 3:15–3**

INHABITED BUILDING
Definitions, Explosives Act, **21:1A–129**

INHALANTS
Controlled substances, **2C:35–10.4**
Intoxication of driver, **39:4–50**

INHERITANCE
Probate Proceedings, generally, this index

INITIATION
Hazing, student or fraternal organization, **2C:40–3 et seq.**

INJUNCTIONS
Air pollution, **26:2C–19**
Attorneys, practice of law, disbarment, **Rule 1:20–16**
Children and Minors, this index
Controlled Substances, this index
County prosecutors expenses in enjoining nuisances under federal law, **2A:158–8**
Developmentally disabled persons, stalking, **2C:12–10.2**
Domestic Violence, this index
Explosives, hazards, **21:1A–130**
Flammable fabrics, **2A:123–10**
Sleeping bags and tents, sales, **2A:123–20**
Liquefied petroleum gas, violation of law, **21:1B–6**
Monopolies and unfair trade, **56:9–10**
Nuisance, this index
Racketeers and racketeering, **2C:41–3**
Sleeping bags, flammable fabrics, sales, **2A:123–20**
Solid Waste, this index
Stalking, **2C:12–10.1, 2C:12–10.2**
Stolen property, **2C:20–21**
Tents, flammable fabrics, sales, **2A:123–20**
Theft, **2C:20–21**
Toxic packaging reduction, **13:1E–99.54**
Water Pollution, this index

INJURIES
Damages, generally, this index
Personal Injuries, generally, this index
Vandalism, generally, this index

INJUSTICE
Relaxation of rules to prevent, **Rule 1:1–2**

INLETS
Adopt a beach program. Beaches and Beach Fronts, this index

INMATES
Correctional Institutions, this index

INNOCENCE OF DEFENDANT
Presumption, **2C:1–13**

INNS AND INNKEEPERS
Hotels and Motels, generally, this index

INSANE ASYLUMS OR HOSPITALS
Mentally Deficient and Mentally Ill Persons, generally, this index

INSANE PERSONS
Mentally Deficient and Mentally Ill Persons, generally, this index

INSANITY DEFENSE
Generally, **2C:4–1 et seq.**
Acquittal,
Civil commitment, **2C:4–8**
Disclosure, presentence investigation and report, **2C:44–6**
Verdict, **Rule 3:19–2**
Acquittal by reason of, verdict, **Rule 3:19–2**
Criminal prosecutions, **2C:4–1 et seq.**
DNA database and databank, **53:1–20.20**
Sexual assault, **53:1–20.20**
Fitness to proceed, determination, **2C:4–6**
Notice, **2C:4–3; Rules 3:12–1, 7:7–4**

INSIDE LANE
Definitions, **39:1–1**

INSIGNIA
See, also, Badges, Emblems and Insignia, generally, this index
Alcoholic Beverages, this index
Mentally retarded persons, transportation, county vehicles, **39:4–207.2 et seq.**
Motor vehicles, license plates for handicapped persons, wheelchairs, **39:4–206**
Transportation vehicles, mentally retarded persons, **39:4–207.3**

INSOLVENCY
Fraud in insolvency, **2C:21–13**
Motor Vehicle Insurance, this index

INSPECTION AND INSPECTORS
Alcoholic beverage control division, inspector as officer, **33:1–1**
Alcoholic Beverage Control Enforcement Bureau, this index
Alcoholic Beverages, this index
All terrain vehicles, equipment, **39:3C–25**
Books and papers, disposition of complaints under motor vehicle and traffic laws, inspection by county treasurer, **39:5–44**
Buildings, liquefied petroleum gas, **21:1B–3**
Controlled substances,
Administrative inspection warrants, **24:21–31, 24:21–32**
Establishment of registrant, **24:21–10**
Correctional Institutions, this index

INSPECTION AND INSPECTORS—Cont'd
Crimes and offenses, records, expungement, **2C:52–19**
Dirt bikes, equipment, **39:3C–25**
Drivers Licenses, this index
Drivers schools, **39:12–4.1**
Records and recordation, **39:12–11**
Explosives, this index
Fireworks plants, labor commissioner, **21:2–21**
Flammable fabrics, **2A:123–9**
Sleeping bags and tents, places of sale, **2A:123–19**
Frozen dessert trucks, **39:4–128.7**
Handicapped parking spaces, **39:4–8.1**
Housing, this index
Juvenile Delinquents, this index
Liquefied petroleum gas, residential buildings, **21:1B–3**
Motor carriers,
Intermodal transportation, chassis, **39:3–79.10 et seq.**
Radiation, **39:5B–23**
Motor Vehicles, this index
Police reports, motor vehicle accidents, **39:4–131**
Racketeering, investigative interrogatories, **2C:41–5**
Radiation Protection, generally, this index
Railroad crossings, enforcement of regulations as to stopping of motor vehicles or school busses, **39:5–1**
Records and recordation, **Rule 1:38–10**
Reports, traffic accidents, public inspection forbidden, **39:4–131**
School Buses, this index
Search warrants and supporting documents, defendants, **Rule 7:5–1**
Sleeping bags, flammable fabrics, places of sale, **2A:123–19**
Snowmobiles, equipment, **39:3C–25**
Solid Waste, this index
Subpoenas, objects designated in subpoena, **Rule 1:9–2**
Tents, flammable fabrics, places of sale, **2A:123–19**
Tires, inspection by law enforcement officers, **39:3–72**
Traffic control signal monitoring system, **39:4–8.14**

INSPECTION STATIONS
Motor Vehicles, this index

INSTALLMENTS
Fines and penalties, **2C:46–1**
Transaction fee, **2C:46–1 et seq.**
Judgment against motorist for damages installment payment affecting restoration of license and registration, **39:6–39**
Leases, generally, this index
Mandatory assessments, **2C:46–1**
Transaction fee, **2C:46–1 et seq.**
Restitution, **2C:46–1**
Transaction fee, **2C:46–1 et seq.**
Traffic rules and regulations, fines and penalties, indigent persons, **39:4–203.1, 39:4–203.2**

INSTITUTION OF HIGHER EDUCATION
Colleges and Universities, generally, this index

INSTITUTIONS AND AGENCIES
Correctional Institutions, generally, this index

INSTITUTIONS FOR THE INSANE
Mentally Deficient and Mentally Ill Persons, generally, this index

INSTITUTIONS OF LEARNING
Colleges and Universities, generally, this index
Private Schools, generally, this index
Schools and School Districts, generally, this index

INSTRUCTIONAL WINEMAKING FACILITIES
Alcoholic beverages, licenses and permits, 33:1–10, 33:1–75

INSTRUCTIONS
Burglar tools, manufacture, publication, 2C:5–5
Portable, oil burning heating device, accompaniment, 2C:40–9

INSTRUCTIONS TO JURY
Jury and Jurors, this index

INSTRUCTORS
Drivers Schools, this index

INSTRUMENTS
Weapons, generally, this index

INSUFFICIENT FUND CHECKS
Generally, 2C:21–5

INSURANCE
Accident insurance. Health and Accident Insurance, generally, this index
Affidavits, family actions, nonconforming papers, Rule 1:5–6
All terrain vehicles, 39:3C–20
Arson, 2C:17–1
Automobiles,
　Motor Vehicle Insurance, generally, this index
　Motor Vehicle Security Responsibility Law, generally, this index
Bail, generally, this index
Coverage, affidavit, filing, Rule 1:5–6
Crimes and offenses, insurance fraud prosecutor, hindering apprehension or prosecution, 2C:29–3
Definitions,
　Motor vehicle unsatisfied claim and judgment fund, 39:6–62
　Unsatisfied claims, 39:6–62
Detectives, robbery losses, 15:4–3
Dirt bikes, 39:3C–20
Drivers schools, licenses and permits, 39:12–2
Evidence, liability insurance, Evidence Rule 411
Family actions, affidavits, nonconforming papers, Rule 1:5–6
Fireworks, public displays, 21:3–5
Fraud, insurance fraud prosecutor, hindering apprehension or prosecution, 2C:29–3
Health and Accident Insurance, generally, this index
Insurance fraud prosecutor, hindering apprehension or prosecution, 2C:29–3
Investments, turnpike authority bonds, 27:23–13
Licenses and permits. Public Adjusters, this index
Life expectancy tables, evidence, Rule 1:13–5
Medicare, generally, this index
Monopolies, joint underwriting regulated by insurance commissioner, exemption, 56:9–5
Mortality tables, evidence, Rule 1:13–5
Motor Vehicle Insurance, generally, this index
Motor Vehicle Security Responsibility Law, generally, this index

INSURANCE—Cont'd
Policies,
　Assigned funeral insurance policy, prepaid funeral agreements, embezzlement, 2A:102–18
　Newly issued funeral insurance policy, prepaid funeral agreements, embezzlement, 2A:102–18
Privileged communications, physician and patients, 2A:84A–22.4
Registry, bail, Rule 1:13–3
Snowmobiles, 39:3C–20
Theft insurance, registration of motor vehicles by insurer obtaining ownership or control under theft policy, 39:3–18
Vehicles. Motor Vehicle Insurance, generally, this index

INSURANCE COMPANIES
Insurance, generally, this index

INSURANCE FRAUD PROSECUTOR
Crimes and offenses, hindering apprehension or prosecution, 2C:29–3
Hindering apprehension or prosecution, 2C:29–3

INSURRECTION OR SEDITION
Speed law inapplicable to military vehicles used in time of insurrection or invasion, 39:4–103

INTENSIVE SUPERVISION PROGRAM
Crimes and offenses, sentence reduction, change, Rule 3:21–10

INTERCEPT
Definitions, wiretapping and electronic surveillance, 2A:156A–2

INTERCEPTION OF COMMUNICATIONS
Search warrant based on wiretap, filing, Rule 3:5–6

INTEREST
Alcoholic Beverages, this index
Corporations, this index
Criminal usury, 2C:21–19
No fault insurance, payments, motor vehicle insurance, 39:6A–5
Protection of individual or public interests, 2C:1–2
Turnpikes, this index
Usury,
　Crimes and offenses, 2C:21–19
　Debt adjusters, crimes and offenses, 2C:21–19
　Limited liability companies, maximum rates, 2C:21–19
　Limited liability partnerships, maximum rates, 2C:21–19

INTEREST ON LAWYERS TRUST ACCOUNTS FUND
Generally, Rules 1:21–6, 1:28A–1 et seq.

INTERFERENCE WITH ADMINISTRATION OF JUSTICE
Attorneys, conviction, discipline, Rule 1:20–13

INTERLOCUTORY JUDGMENTS OR DECREES
Judgments and Decrees, generally, this index

INTERMEDIATE CARE FACILITIES
Institutionalized elderly persons, assault, 2C:12–1

INTERMODAL TRANSPORTATION
Motor Carriers, this index

INTERMUNICIPAL COURTS
Fines and costs, 2C:46–4

INTERNAL REVENUE SERVICE (UNITED STATES)
Arrests, violations of state laws, special agents, 2A:154–5

INTERNET
Anatomical gifts, registration, donors, 39:3–12.3 et seq.
Children and minors, luring and enticing, crimes and offenses, 2C:13–6
Crimes and offenses, luring and enticing, 2C:13–7
　Children and minors, 2C:13–6
Definitions,
　Computer related offenses, 2C:20–23
　Endangering welfare of child, pornography, 2C:24–4
Electronic Transactions, generally, this index
Luring and enticing, 2C:13–7
　Crimes and offenses, children and minors, 2C:13–6
Sex Offenses, this index

INTERPRETERS
Generally, Rule 1:34–7
Code of professional conduct, Rule 1:14
Rule relating to witnesses, Evidence Rule 604

INTERROGATIONS
Crimes and offenses, electronic recordation, Rule 3:17

INTERROGATORIES
Money laundering and illegal investments, 2C:21–29
Monopolies and unfair trade, hearings and inquiries, 56:9–9
Racketeering, investigative interrogatories, 2C:41–5

INTERSECTIONS
Generally, 39:4–83
Clearance by motor vehicle or streetcar, restriction, 39:4–67
Clearing intersection before stopping on approach of emergency vehicles, 39:4–92
Definitions, Motor Vehicle Law, 39:1–1
Entering where unable to clear, 39:4–67
Highway construction or repair, certain vehicular offenses, double fines, 39:4–203.5
Local authorities, turning of vehicles at intersections, determining method, 39:4–124
Low speed vehicles, operation, 39:4–31.1
Parking, permissible parking distances, 39:4–138
　Municipalities, 39:4–138.6
Pedestrians, this index
Private road open to the public, definitions, public private intersections, 39:4–120.5
Public private intersections,
　Definitions, 39:4–120.5
　Fines and penalties, 39:4–120.10
　Rules and regulations, 39:4–120.11
　Traffic control devices,
　　Acquisition, installation and maintenance, 39:4–120.8
　　Approval, 39:4–120.7
　　Erection, 39:4–120.6
　　Obeyance, 39:4–120.9
Regulations governing congested street corners, power of municipality, 39:4–197

INTERSECTIONS—Cont'd
Right of way, **39:4–90**
Right side, keeping on required, **39:4–83**
Right Turns, this index
Speed at, **39:4–98**
Stop intersections, designation, marking, **39:4–140, 39:4–197**
Stopping distance determined as regards right to proceed through intersection on amber light, **39:4–105**
Street Railways, this index
Through streets,
Intersecting through streets, **39:4–143**
Stopping before entering, **39:4–144**
Traffic Signs and Signals, this index
Yield intersections, designation, marking, **39:4–140**

INTERSTATE BRIDGES AND TUNNELS
Fines and penalties, overweight vehicles, **39:4–76**
Overweight vehicles driven over bridge, penalty and liability for damages, **39:4–76**

INTERSTATE BUSES
Buses, this index

INTERSTATE COMMERCE
Explosives, application of law, **21:1A–141**
Fireworks, exceptions, application of law, **21:2–4**

INTERSTATE COMMISSIONS
Definitions, adult offender supervision, interstate compacts, **2A:168–27**

INTERSTATE COMPACTS
Adult offender supervision, **2A:168–26 et seq.**
Crimes and offenses, **53:1–32**
Criminal history record information, **53:1–32**
Definitions, crimes and offenses, **53:1–32**
Driver license compact, **39:5D–1 et seq.**
Governor, this index
Nonresident Violator Compact, motor vehicles, **39:5F–1 et seq.**

INTERSTATE HIGHWAY SYSTEM
Advertisements. Outdoor Advertising, generally, this index
Commercial activity, rest areas or rights of way, **39:4–216**
Dimensional and weight limitations, **39:3–84**
Motorized bicycles, **39:4–14.3d**
Outdoor Advertising, generally, this index
Rest areas, commercial activity, **39:4–216**
Rights of way, commercial activity, **39:4–216**
Violation of weight limitations, **39:3–84.3**

INTERVENTION
Attorney general, municipal prosecutors, **2B:25–7**
Criminal proceedings, newspersons, information disclosure privilege exercise hearing, **2A:84A–21.7**
Health department, notice, solid waste facilities, compliance with regulations, **13:1E–9**
Pretrial intervention, **2C:43–12**

INTESTATE SUCCESSION
See, also, Probate Proceedings, generally, this index
Intoxicating liquors,
Retail license, transfer of interest, Chain Store Liquor License Act, **33:1–12.32, 33:1–12.33**
Transfer of interest, **33:1–26**

INTESTATE SUCCESSION—Cont'd
Motor vehicles, title vesting in registered owners surviving spouse or child, transfer of registration, **39:3–30**
Personal representatives. Probate Proceedings, this index
Privileged communications, physician, patients, **2A:84A–22.3**
Probate Proceedings, generally, this index

INTIMATE PARTS
Definitions, sexual offenses, **2C:14–1**

INTIMIDATION
See, also, Duress or Coercion, generally, this index
Assault, intimidation based on bias, fourth degree crime, extended term of imprisonment, **2C:43–7, 2C:43–7.1**
Bias intimidation, crimes and offenses, **2C:16–1**
Harassment, intimidation based on bias, fourth degree crime, extended term of imprisonment, **2C:43–7, 2C:43–7.1**
Human trafficking, **2C:13–8**
Obstructing administration of law or other governmental function, **2C:29–1**
Witnesses, protection orders, **2C:28–5.1 et seq.**

INTOXICATED DRIVER RESOURCE CENTERS
Generally, **39:4–50**

INTOXICATED DRIVING PROGRAMS
Generally, **39:4–50**

INTOXICATED PERSONS
Alcoholics and Alcoholism, generally, this index

INTOXICATING LIQUORS
Alcoholic Beverages, generally, this index

INTOXICATION
Alcoholics and Alcoholism, generally, this index

INTRAEXPLOSIVES PLANT QUANTITY AND DISTANCE TABLE
Generally, **21:1A–135**

INTRASTATE FRESH PURSUIT ACT
Fresh Pursuit Law, generally, this index

INTRUSION ON PROPERTY
Justification, **2C:3–10**

INVASION OF PRIVACY
Crimes and offenses,
Observation, nudity, sexual intercourse, **2C:14–9**
Window peeping, **2C:18–3**
Defenses, crimes and offenses, observation, nudity, sexual intercourse, **2C:14–9**
Fitting rooms, defenses, crimes and offenses, observation, nudity, **2C:14–9**
Law enforcement officers, privileges and immunities, observation, nudity, sexual intercourse, **2C:14–9**
Notice, fitting rooms, defenses, crimes and offenses, observation, nudity, **2C:14–9**

INVENTORIES
Alcoholic Beverage Law, property seized under search warrant, **33:1–61**
Attorneys, appointment of attorney trustee, protection of clients interest, suspension, disbarment, death, **Rule 1:20–19**

INVENTORIES—Cont'd
Controlled substances, **24:21–13**
Administrative inspection warrants, **24:21–32**
Intoxicating liquors, property seized under warrant, **33:1–61**
Searches and seizures, warrants, execution, **Rule 3:5–5**

INVESTIGATION COMMISSION
Weapons, possession, exemption, **2C:39–6**

INVESTIGATIONS
Alcoholic Beverages, this index
Arson and other burnings, weapons possession, exemption, **2C:39–6**
Attorneys, this index
Child Abuse, this index
Children and Minors, this index
Controlled substances, stay, dealers, liability, **2C:35B–15**
Corrections department investigators, police powers, **2A:154–4**
County detectives and county investigators, **2A:157–1 et seq.**
Crimes and offenses,
Presentence investigation, **Rule 3:21–2**
Weapons, criminal justice division, exemption, **2C:39–6**
Criminal justice division, weapons, unlawful possession, exemption, **2C:39–6**
Detectives, generally, this index
Explosives, permit applications, **21:1A–134**
Grand Jury, generally, this index
Housing, generally, this index
Investigative detention. Arrest, this index
Medical care and treatment, review committee, immunity from liability, **2A:84A–22.10**
Money laundering and illegal investments, **2C:21–29**
Liability for costs, **2C:21–28**
Monopolies and unfair trade, hearings or inquiries, **56:9–9**
Motor vehicles,
Body repair facilities, statutory violations, **39:13–3**
Expenses, trial de novo, arbitrated tort claims, **39:6A–34**
Parole officers, police powers, **2A:154–4**
Peer review committees, medical or dental treatment, immunity from liability, **2A:84A–22.10**
Preliminary investigations, unauthorized practice of law, **Rule 1:22–4**
Presentence investigation, report, **2C:44–6**
Production of Books and Papers, generally, this index
Public Defenders, this index
Racketeering, investigative interrogatories, **2C:41–5**
Stills and Distilling Apparatus, this index
Subpoenas, medical records, **Rule 7:7–8**
Traffic accidents, death, investigation, time, **39:5–30**
Unauthorized practice of law, committees, **Rule 1:22–2**

INVESTIGATIVE DETENTION
Arrest, this index

INVESTIGATIVE OR LAW ENFORCEMENT OFFICER
Definitions, wiretapping and electronic surveillance, **2A:156A–2**

INVESTMENT COMPANIES
Investments, turnpike authority bonds, **27:23–13**

INVESTMENTS
Banks and Banking, this index
Fiduciaries, this index
Guardian and Ward, this index
Insurance, this index
Investment Companies, this index
Money Laundering and Illegal Investments,
    generally, this index
Racketeering, **2C:41–1 et seq.**
Savings and Loan Associations, this index
Savings Banks, this index
State, turnpike authority bonds, **27:23–13**
Trusts and Trustees, this index
Turnpike authority bonds, eligibility for invest-
    ment, **27:23–13**
Unsatisfied claim and judgment fund, **39:6–88**

INVOLUNTARY COMMITMENT
Attorneys, disability inactive status, **Rule
    1:20–12**

INVOLUNTARY SERVITUDE
Criminal restraint, **2C:13–2**

IOLTA ACCOUNTS
    Generally, **Rule 1:21–6**
Attorneys, this index

IOLTA FUND
    Generally, **Rule 1:28A–1 et seq.**
Certifying compliance, attorney registration,
    Rule 1:20–1

IRON CLAWS
Weapons, generally, this index

ISOBUTANE
Liquefied Petroleum Gas, generally, this index

ISOMETHADONE
Controlled dangerous substance, **24:21–1 et
    seq.**

ISSUER
Definitions, credit card offenses, **2C:21–6**

JAILS
    See, also,
        Correctional Institutions, generally, this in-
            dex
        Workhouses, generally, this index
Boards of chosen freeholders, remission of sen-
    tence for good conduct, **2A:164–24**
Crimes and offenses, credit, confinement pend-
    ing sentence, **Rule 3:21–8**
Domicile and residence, sex offenses, release,
    registration, **2C:7–2.1**
Escapes, generally, this index
Extradited persons, confinement, **2A:160–20**
Fines and penalties, violation of motor vehicle
    laws, imprisonment in default of payment,
    39:5–36
Fingerprints, photographs, persons confined,
    filing by bureau of identification, **53:1–14**
Good behavior, remission of sentence,
    2A:164–24
Inmate advocacy office. Public Defenders,
    generally, this index
Juvenile delinquents,
    Age, **2A:4A–37**
    Detention, **Rule 5:21–4**
    Short term custody, **2A:4A–32**
Keepers,
    Notice to county and state bureaus of identi-
        fication of release of prisoner, **53:1–20.3**
    State police, **53:2–1**

JAILS—Cont'd
Motor vehicles, operation of motor vehicle
    while under influence of liquor or drug,
    Sentence to jail or workhouse, **39:4–50,
        39:4–51**
    Temporary detention of person arrested
        without warrant, **39:5–25**
Notice, release of prisoner, **53:1–20.3**
Officers and employees, aggravated assault,
    throwing bodily fluids, **2C:12–13**
Registration, sex offenses, release, domicile
    and residence, **2C:7–2.1**
Release, sex offenses, registration, domicile
    and residence, **2C:7–2.1**
Serving sentences in jails, **2C:43–10**
Sex offenses, registration, release, domicile and
    residence, **2C:7–2.1**
Traffic violations, **39:5–36**

JAY WALKING
Pedestrians, **39:4–33, 39:4–34**

JERSEY FRESH
Agricultural products, sales, **27:23–48**

JEWELRY
Sales, secondhand dealers, **2C:21–36 et seq.**

JOINDER
Attorney fees, arbitration proceedings, third
    party attorneys or law firms, **Rule 1:20A–3**
Crimes and Offenses, this index
Indictment, Information or Presentment, this
    index
Separate offenses, indictment, accusation, **Rule
    3:7–6**

JOINDER OF PARTIES
Controlled substances, dealers, liability,
    2C:35B–9

JOINT AND SEVERAL LIABILITY
Drivers licenses, examination permits, **39:3–13**
Juvenile delinquents and dependents, restitu-
    tion, **2A:4A–43**
Money laundering and illegal investments,
    2C:21–28
Traffic rules and regulations, traffic control
    signal monitoring system, **39:4–8.15**

JOINT LIBRARIES
Libraries, generally, this index

JOINT MUNICIPAL COURTS
Municipal Courts, generally, this index

JOINT RESOLUTIONS
Supervisory treatment programs, first offend-
    ers, rules, **2C:43–17 et seq.**

JOINT TENANCY
Motor vehicles, joint registration with spouse,
    39:3–30

JUDGES AND JUSTICES
Abbreviations, **Rule 1:37–3**
Acceptance of papers for filing, **Rule 1:5–6**
Acting judge, substitution, disqualification or
    inability to hear matter, **Rule 1:12–3**
Adverse or pecuniary interest,
    Disqualification, **Rule 1:12–1 et seq.**
    Practicing law, **Rule 1:15–1**
Advisory committees, judicial financial report-
    ing, **Rule 1:18B–2**
Aged persons, abuse or neglect, education,
    2C:25–20
Aggravated assault, **2C:12–1**

JUDGES AND JUSTICES—Cont'd
Alcoholic beverages, licenses, **33:1–40**
Bail, generally, this index
Bribery and Corruption, generally, this index
Candidates, public office, **Rule 1:17–1 et seq.**
Code of judicial conduct, **Rule 1:14**
    Duty to enforce, **Rule 1:18**
Confidential or privileged information,
    Judicial evaluations, **Rule 1:35A–3**
    Judicial performance records, **Rule 1:38–5**
Conflict of interest, disqualification, **Rule
    1:12–1 et seq.**
    Practicing law, **Rule 1:15–1**
Definitions, wiretapping and electronic surveil-
    lance, **2A:156A–2**
Disclosure, financial statements and reports,
    Rule 1:18B–3
Disqualification, **Rule 1:12–1 et seq.**
    Contempt hearings, **Rules 1:10–4, 1:10–5**
    Municipal courts, **Rule 7:8–2**
Domestic violence, education, **2C:25–20**
Ethics, **Rule 1:14**
Evaluation, judicial performance program,
    Rule 1:35A–2
Evidence, this index
Extrajudicial activities, advisory committee,
    Rule 1:18A–1 et seq.
Family members, disqualification, **Rule 1:12–1**
Fees, not payable to judge receiving salary,
    2A:166–17
Financial statements and reports, **Rule 1:18B–1
    et seq.**
Grand jury, assignment judge, **Rule 3:6–11**
Hearsay evidence, exclusion under exceptions,
    discretion, **Evidence Rule 807**
Inability to hear pending manner, substituted
    judges, **Rule 1:12–3**
Inadequate facilities, **Rule 1:31–1**
Judicial conduct code, **Rule 1:14**
Judicial conferences, **Rules 1:35–1, 1:35–2**
Judicial performance program, **Rule 1:35A–1 et
    seq.**
Jurors, examination supervised and controlled,
    2B:23–10
Marriage, relationship to parties or attorneys,
    disqualification, **Rule 1:12–1**
Motions, disqualification, **Rule 1:12–2**
Motor vehicles, reports to director, violations
    and convictions, **39:5–42**
Municipal Courts, this index
Officers and employees. Courts, this index
Opinions of Court, generally, this index
Pending proceedings, disqualification or inabili-
    ty to hear matter, substituted judges, **Rule
    1:12–3**
Performance program, **Rule 1:35A–1 et seq.**
Political activity, limitation, **Rule 1:17–1 et seq.**
Practice of law, **Rule 1:15–1**
    Employees or attorneys assigned to judges,
        Rule 1:15–2
Professional conduct rules, duties, **Rule 1:18**
Public office, holding, **Rule 1:17–1 et seq.**
Relationship to parties, disqualification, **Rule
    1:12–1**
Reports,
    Financial statements and reports, **Rule
        1:18B–1 et seq.**
    Weekly report, **Rule 1:32–1**
Retirement and pensions,
    Assignment, title, **Rule 1:37–3**
    Attorneys, misconduct, hearings, **Rule 1:20–6**
Robes, open court, **Rule 1:2–1**
Substituted judge, disqualification or inability
    to hear pending matters, **Rule 1:12–3**
Superior Court Judges, generally, this index
Supervising judges, **Rule 1:33–6A**

JUDGES AND JUSTICES—Cont'd
Supreme Court, this index
Tax Court, this index
Temporary assignment, title, **Rule 1:37–3**
Terrorism, wiretapping and electronic surveillance, orders, **2A:156A–8**
Vacations, **Rule 1:30–5**
Weekly report, **Rule 1:32–1**
Wiretapping and electronic surveillance, orders permitting, **2A:156A–8 et seq.**
   Content and limitations, **2A:156A–12**
Witnesses, **Evidence Rule 605**
Writing of motions and briefs in advance, **Rule 1:6–7**
Writings or photographs, proof of contents, determining sufficiency, **Evidence Rule 1008**

JUDGMENT DEBTORS AND CREDITORS
Debtors and Creditors, generally, this index

JUDGMENT DOCKETS
Municipal court judgments, docketed in superior court, **2B:12–26**
Revival. Judgments and Decrees, this index
Superior court, municipal court judgments, **2B:12–26**

JUDGMENT NOTWITHSTANDING VERDICT
Motion, enlargement of time, **Rule 1:3–4**

JUDGMENTS AND DECREES
Abbreviations, **Rule 1:37–3**
Abuse of children, suspended judgments, **9:6–8.52**
   Failure to comply with conditions, **9:6–8.66**
Acquittal, insanity defense, grounds, **2C:4–3**
Alteration, motion, enlargement of time, **Rule 1:3–4**
Amendments, motion, enlargement of time, **Rule 1:3–4**
Appeal and Review, generally, this index
Assignments, motor vehicle accident cases, state treasurer, **39:6–77**
Associations and Societies, this index
Bail, forfeitures, municipal courts, **Rule 7:4–5**
Clerical mistakes, correction, **Rule 1:13–1**
Consent, judgments, motor vehicle accident cases, **39:6–74**
Controlled substances, dealers, liability, **2C:35B–16**
Corporations, this index
Costs, generally, this index
Creditors. Debtors and Creditors, generally, this index
Crimes and Offenses, this index
Debtors and Creditors, generally, this index
Default Judgment, generally, this index
Dismissal and Nonsuit, generally, this index
Enforcement, **2C:1–5**
   Final process, issuance, motions and applications, **Rule 1:6–8**
Entry,
   Court schedules, **Rule 1:30–1**
   Nonjury trials, **Rule 1:7–4**
   Uncontested foreclosure matters, office of foreclosure recommending, **Rule 1:34–6**
Errors, correction, **Rule 1:13–1**
Estoppel, theft, final judgment, **2C:20–22**
Fines, nonpayment, **2C:46–2**
Foreclosure, uncontested foreclosures, office of foreclosure recommending entry, **Rule 1:34–6**
Fraud, this index
Imposition of civil penalty, **2C:43–2**

JUDGMENTS AND DECREES—Cont'd
Justification defense, criminal prosecution, **2C:3–3**
Juvenile family crisis hearing disposition, **Rule 5:17–3**
Limitation of actions, revival, **2A:162–6**
Money laundering and illegal investments, **2C:21–28**
Motions, acquittal after discharge of jury, enlargement of time, **Rule 1:3–4**
Motor Vehicle Security Responsibility Law, this index
Motor Vehicles, this index
Municipal Courts, this index
Nonsuit. Dismissal and Nonsuit, generally, this index
Partnerships, this index
Reconsideration, motion, **Rule 1:7–4**
Relief, motion, enlargement of time, **Rule 1:3–4**
Renewal of motion, enlargement of time, **Rule 1:3–4**
Restitution, nonpayment, **2C:46–2**
Review. Appeal and Review, generally, this index
Revival,
   Forfeited recognizance, **2A:162–6**
   Limitation of actions, **2A:162–6**
Service, **Rule 1:5–1 et seq.**
Temporary out of home placement, **Rule 5:18–2**
Unsatisfied claim and judgment fund. Motor Vehicles, this index

JUDICIAL BRANCH
Courts, generally, this index

JUDICIAL CONDUCT ADVISORY COMMITTEE
Confidential or privileged information, **Rule 1:38–5**

JUDICIAL CONDUCT CODE
   Generally, **Rule 1:14**
Duties of judges, **Rule 1:18**

JUDICIAL CONFERENCE
   Generally, **Rules 1:35–1, 1:35–2**
Rules of evidence, **2A:84A–34**
Supervisory treatment programs, first offenders, presentation of proposed rules, **2C:43–15, 2C:43–19**

JUDICIAL EVALUATION COMMISSION
Generally, **Rule 1:35A–4**

JUDICIAL NOTICE
   Generally, **Evidence Rules 201, 202**
Alcoholics and alcoholism, treatment, probation and probation officers, **2C:35–14**
Bribery and corruption, profits, **2C:30–8**
Drug abuse, treatment, probation and probation officers, **2C:35–14**
Forfeitures, motor vehicles, vehicular homicide, **2C:11–5**
Motor vehicles, forfeitures, vehicular homicide, **2C:11–5**
Vehicular homicide, motor vehicles, forfeitures, **2C:11–5**

JUDICIAL OFFICERS
Judges and Justices, generally, this index

JUDICIAL PERFORMANCE COMMITTEE
Generally, **Rule 1:35A–1 et seq.**

JUDICIAL PERFORMANCE PROGRAM
Generally, **Rule 1:35A–1 et seq.**

JUDICIAL REVIEW
Appeal and Review, generally, this index

JUDICIARY
Courts, generally, this index

JUDICIARY EMPLOYEES, CODE OF CONDUCT FOR
Interpretation, **Rule 1:17A–2**

JUMPING BAIL
Generally, **2C:29–7**

JUNK AND JUNK DEALERS
Hazards, **2C:40–1**
Motor Vehicle Junk Yards, generally, this index

JURISDICTION
Child Abuse, this index
Children and minors, custody, witnesses, juvenile justice, **2A:4A–24**
County prosecutors, **2A:158–4**
Crimes and Offenses, this index
Domestic violence prevention, **2C:25–28 et seq.**
Explosives, **21:1A–139**
Family Court, this index
Forfeiture, property, **2C:64–1**
Former prosecutions, **2C:1–11, 2C:1–12**
Gambling offenses, **2C:37–8**
Juvenile and Domestic Relations Courts, this index
Juvenile Delinquents, this index
Long Arm Act, **39:7–1 et seq.**
Motor Vehicles, this index
Multiple offenses, separate trials, **2C:1–8**
Municipal Courts, this index
Municipal housing courts, **2B:12–20**
State grand jury, **2B:22–2**
Support of Persons, this index
Toxic packaging reduction, **13:1E–99.54**
Traffic accidents, serious bodily injury, crimes and offenses, **2B:12–17.2**

JURY AND JURORS
   Generally, **Rule 1:8–1 et seq.**
Additional panel, drawing, qualifications and selection, **2B:20–4**
Age,
   Challenge, grounds,
      Grand juror, **2B:21–2**
      Petit jurors, **2B:23–11**
   Persons 18 and older, qualifications and selection, **2B:20–1**
   Persons 75 and older, grounds for excuse, **2B:20–10**
Aggravated assault, peremptory challenges, **Rule 1:8–3**
Alternate jurors, **Rule 1:8–2**
   Petit juries, **2B:23–3**
   Selection as forepersons, **Rule 1:8–4**
Array,
   Challenges, **Rule 1:8–3**
   Interest, county or municipality action, challenge, **2B:23–12**
   Trial of challenges, **2B:23–14**
Arson, peremptory challenges, **Rule 1:8–3**
Book contracts, **2C:29–8.1**
Bribery and corrupt influence, **2C:29–8**
Burglary, peremptory challenges, **Rule 1:8–3**
Capital Punishment, this index
Cause, challenges, **Rule 1:8–3**
Challenges, **2B:23–10 et seq.; Rule 1:8–3**
   Examinations, **2B:23–10**

JURY AND JURORS—Cont'd
Challenges—Cont'd
Interest, action by or against county, **2B:23–12**
Peremptory, **2B:23–13**
Qualifications, petit jurors, **2B:23–11**
Time, **2B:23–15**
Trial, **2B:23–14**
Charge to jury. Instructions to jury, generally, post
Citizenship,
Challenge, grounds, petit jurors, **2B:23–11**
U.S. citizenship required, qualifications and selection, **2B:20–1**
Civil action,
Economic damages, employment protection for jury service, employer violations, **2B:20–17**
Petit jurors, number, **2B:23–1**
Claims, list, taking into jury room, **Rule 1:8–8**
Clerks of court,
Names replaced in jury box, **2B:23–5**
Oath of officer attending, **2B:23–7**
Petit jurors, additional members, **2B:23–3**
Conferences,
Charge conference, **Rule 1:8–7**
Verbatim records, **Rule 1:2–2**
Voir dire examination, **Rule 1:8–3**
Contempt,
Failing to appear or serve, **2B:20–14**
Jury trial, **Rule 1:10–2**
Continuance of service beyond period, **2B:23–8**
Contracts, movie, book or entertainment rights, **2C:29–8.1**
Conviction of crime, **2C:51–3**
Corrupting or influencing, **2C:29–8**
County officers and employees, **2B:20–16**
Crimes and offenses, **Rule 1:8–1**
Alternate jurors, **Rule 1:8–2**
Charge conference, **Rule 1:8–7**
Verbatim records, **Rule 1:2–2**
Contracts, movie, book or entertainment rights, **2C:29–8.1**
Corrupting or influencing, **2C:29–8**
Discharge, acquittal, judgment of, motion for, **Rule 3:18–2**
Employment protection, employer violations, **2B:20–17**
Failure to appear or serve, **2B:20–14**
Family part, transfer to law division, **Rule 3:1–5**
Foreign jury, motion for, **Rules 3:14–2, 3:14–3**
Impaneling, presence of defendant, **Rule 3:16**
Informing defendant of right, **Rule 3:4–2**
Joinder, trials of criminal offenses and lesser related infractions, **Rule 3:15–3**
New trial, **Rules 3:20–1, 3:20–2**
Number of jurors, **Rule 1:8–2**
Order, selection, foreign jury, **Rule 3:14–3**
Peremptory challenges, **Rule 1:8–3**
Petit jurors, number, **2B:23–1**
Right to jury trial, informing defendant, **Rule 3:4–2**
Sequestration, **Rule 1:8–6**
Unanimous verdict, **Rule 1:8–9**
Written verdict sheets, **Rule 3:19–1**
Death, substitution of alternate jurors, **Rule 1:8–2**
Defaulting jurors, failure to pay fine, personal property, **2B:20–15**
Defenses, lists, taking into jury room, **Rule 1:8–8**

JURY AND JURORS—Cont'd
Deferrals, **2B:20–9**
Designating session person excused must serve, **2B:20–11**
Deliberations, sequestration, **Rule 1:8–6**
Demand for jury trial, **Rule 1:8–1**
Disagreement, new trial, **2B:23–18**
Discharge,
Foreperson, **Rule 1:8–4**
Number greater than necessary, **2B:20–13**
Polling of jury, **Rule 1:8–10**
Substitution of alternate jurors, **Rule 1:8–2**
Disorderly persons offenses, jury trial right, **2C:1–4**
Drawings,
Additional panels, qualifications and selection, **2B:20–4**
Names drawn for jury trial replaced in box, **2B:23–5**
Number greater than necessary, **2B:20–13**
Part of session of court, petit juries, **2B:20–6**
Petit jurors, **2B:23–2**
Alternate jurors, **2B:23–3**
Separate panels, qualifications and selection, **2B:20–4**
Sheriffs, post
Use of electronic devices, qualifications and selection, **2B:20–4**
Employees,
Employment protection, crimes and offenses, **2B:20–17**
Excuse from employment for jury duty, **2B:20–16**
English language, ability to read and understand, qualifications and selection, **2B:20–1**
Entertainment,
Contracts, **2C:29–8.1**
Corrupting or influencing, **2C:29–8**
Entreaties, corrupting or influencing, **2C:29–8**
Evidence, taking into jury room, **Rule 1:8–8**
Examination, **2B:23–10**; **Rule 1:8–3**
Excluded evidence, record, **Rule 1:7–3**
Excusing jurors, **2B:20–9**
Alternate petit jurors, **2B:23–3**; **Rule 1:8–2**
Grounds, **2B:20–10**
Exhibits, taking into jury room, **Rule 1:8–8**
Expenses, jury view, **2B:23–16**
Fees, public officers and employees, **2B:20–16**
Fines and penalties,
Defaulting jurors, **2B:20–15**
Failure to answer or serve, **2B:20–14**
Foreign Jury, generally, this index
Foreperson, **Rule 1:8–4**
Forgery, peremptory challenges, **Rule 1:8–3**
Former service, challenge on grounds, petit jurors, **2B:23–11**
Fraud, **2C:29–8**
Further deliberations, polling of jury, **Rule 1:8–10**
General panel, lists, availability, **Rule 1:8–5**
Grand Jury, generally, this index
Homicide, this index
Illness, alternate jurors, substitution, **Rule 1:8–2**
Impanelling, **Rule 1:8–2**
Ineligibility, persons whose names do not appear on list, **2B:23–11**
Instructions to jury,
Alternate juror substituted, supplemental instructions, **Rule 1:8–2**
Charge conference, criminal cases, **Rule 1:8–7**
Verbatim records, **Rule 1:2–2**
Copies,
Requests, **Rule 1:8–7**
Taking into jury room, **Rule 1:8–8**

JURY AND JURORS—Cont'd
Instructions to jury—Cont'd
Corrupting or influencing, **2C:29–8**
Depositions, criminal proceedings, drawing inferences from use, **Rule 3:13–2**
Dispersal of jury, **Rule 1:8–6**
Included offenses, **2C:1–8**
Judicial notice, effect, **Evidence Rule 201**
Limited admissibility of evidence, **Evidence Rule 105**
No fault insurance, damages, **39:6A–12**
Objections, **Rules 1:7–2, 1:8–7**
Presumptions against accused, criminal cases, **Evidence Rule 303**
Privileges and immunities, exercise, **Evidence Rule 532**
Records and recordation, charge conferences, **Rule 1:8–7**
Verbatim records, **Rule 1:2–2**
Requests, **Rule 1:8–7**
Reserving questions for review, objections, **Rule 1:7–2**
Sequestration, **Rule 1:8–6**
Supplemental instructions, alternate juror substituted, **Rule 1:8–2**
Taking into jury room, **Rule 1:8–8**
Time, submission of request, **Rule 1:8–7**
Intermissions in deliberations, dispersal, **Rule 1:8–6**
Interrogation, witnesses, **Rule 1:8–8**
Interviewing subsequent to trial, attorneys or parties, **Rule 1:16–1**
Investigations and investigators, attorneys or parties, interviewing jurors subsequent to trial, **Rule 1:16–1**
Items of damage, lists, taking into jury room, **Rule 1:8–8**
Jury box, deposit of names, **2B:23–2**
Jury Lists, generally, this index
Juvenile delinquents and dependents, **2A:4A–40, 2C:4–11**
Kidnapping, peremptory challenges, **Rule 1:8–3**
Letters, corrupting or influencing, **2C:29–8**
List of claims, taking into jury room, **Rule 1:8–8**
List of general panel, availability, **Rule 1:8–5**
Lists. Jury Lists, generally, this index
Mail and mailing, service of summons, **2B:20–8**
Manslaughter, peremptory challenges, **Rule 1:8–3**
Meals, dispersal, **Rule 1:8–6**
Mental and physical disabilities, qualifications and selection, **2B:20–1**
Motor Vehicles, this index
Movie contracts, **2C:29–8.1**
Municipal courts, jurisdiction on waiver, **2B:12–18**
Municipal officers and employees, **2B:20–16**
Municipalities, challenge, interest, action by or against, **2B:23–12**
Murder, peremptory challenges, **2B:23–13**; **Rule 1:8–3**
Names,
Petit jurors, selected for trial, **2B:23–4**
Replaced in box, **2B:23–5**
New trial, disagreement, **2B:23–18**
Note taking by jurors, **Rule 1:8–8**
Notice,
Sheriff to defaulting jurors, **2B:20–15**
Summons, **2B:20–8**
Waiver of jury trial, criminal cases, **Rule 1:8–1**
Numbers and numbering,
Foreign jurors, **2B:23–9**
Greater than necessary for service, discharge, **2B:20–13**

JURY AND JURORS—Cont'd
Numbers and numbering—Cont'd
  Peremptory challenges, **Rule 1:8–3**
  Petit jurors, **Rule 1:8–2**
    Civil actions, criminal cases, **2B:23–1**
    Impaneling, **2B:23–3**
Oaths and affirmations, **2B:23–6**
  Officer attending, **2B:23–7**
  Petit jurors, **2B:20–18**
Objections,
  Instructions to jury, **Rule 1:8–7**
  Want of view, **2B:23–16**
Offenses. Crimes and offenses, generally, ante
Officer attending, oath, **2B:23–7**
Orders,
  Service beyond period for which drawn, **2B:23–8**
  Summoning, qualifications and selection, **2B:20–7**
  View, evidence, **2B:23–16**
Panel, petit jurors,
  Designation to serve for part of term, **2B:20–6**
  Division into separate panels, **2B:23–2**
    Qualifications and selection, **2B:20–4**
  Number, civil and criminal cases, **2B:23–1**
  Selection, **2B:23–2**
Parties, availability of list of general panel, **Rule 1:8–5**
Peremptory challenges, **2B:23–13; Rule 1:8–3**
Persuasion, corrupting or influencing, **2C:29–8**
Petty disorderly persons offenses, jury trial right, **2C:1–4**
Polling, **Rule 1:8–10**
  Trial of challenges, **2B:23–14**
Presumptions, criminal cases, submission to jury, **Evidence Rule 303**
Process, defaulting jurors, collection of fines, **2B:20–15**
Promises, corrupting or influencing, **2C:29–8**
Property, view by jury, **2B:23–16**
Prospective jurors, examination, **Rule 1:8–3**
Qualifications,
  Challenge, grounds, petit jurors, **2B:23–11**
  Petit jurors, **2B:23–11**
Questionnaires,
  Confidentiality of records, **Rule 1:38–5**
  Qualifications and selection, **2B:20–3**
Questions, witnesses, **Rule 1:8–8**
Records and recordation,
  Petit jurors selected for trial, names, public record, **2B:23–4**
  Retention, excuses, deferrals, questionnaires, **2B:20–12**
Reduction in size of jury, excusing of jurors, **Rule 1:8–2**
Requests, instructions to jury, **Rule 1:8–7**
Residency, county in which summoned, qualifications and selection, **2B:20–1**
Return of verdict, **Rule 1:8–9**
Returns, names of persons summoned, **2B:20–7**
Robbery, peremptory challenges, **Rule 1:8–3**
Rules of evidence, modifying or eliminating right of jury trial, **2A:84A–41**
Selections,
  Directions, qualifications and selection, **2B:20–4**
  Foreign Jury, generally, this index
  Names, petit jurors selected for trial, **2B:23–4**
  Petit jurors, **2B:23–2**
Sentencing proceedings, homicide, **Rule 1:8–1**
Separate panels, division of general panel, Qualifications and selection, **2B:20–4**
Summons, **2B:20–8**

JURY AND JURORS—Cont'd
Sequestration, **Rule 1:8–6**
  Alternate jurors, **Rule 1:8–2**
Service, prior service, grounds for excuse, **2B:20–10**
Session of court,
  Designating panel to serve for part, petit juries, **2B:20–6**
  Designating session person excused must serve, **2B:20–11**
  Service of jurors extended, **2B:23–8**
Severe hardship, grounds for excuse, **2B:20–10**
Sexual assault, peremptory challenges, **Rule 1:8–3**
Sheriffs,
  Notice, defaulting jurors, **2B:20–15**
  Summoning, qualifications and selection, **2B:20–7**
  View, powers and duties, **2B:23–16**
Six member jury, civil actions, **Rule 1:8–2**
State officers and employees, **2B:20–16**
Stipulations,
  Less than unanimous verdict, **Rule 1:8–2**
  Number of jurors, criminal cases, **Rule 1:8–2**
Substitutions, alternate jurors, **Rule 1:8–2**
Summary Proceedings, generally, this index
Summoning,
  Defaulting jurors, service, notice, considered, **2B:20–15**
  Form, **2B:20–8**
  Qualifications and selection, **2B:20–7**
  Service, **2B:20–8**
  Sheriff, qualifications and selection, **2B:20–7**
Threats, **2C:29–8**
Time, list of general panel, availability, **Rule 1:8–5**
Trial by jury, **Rule 1:8–1**
Verdicts, this index
View, **2B:23–16**
Voir dire examination, **2B:23–10; Rule 1:8–3**
Volunteer fire department or fire patrol, members, grounds for excuse, **2B:20–10**
Volunteer first aid or rescue squad, members, grounds for excuse, **2B:20–10**
Waiver, **Rule 1:8–1**
  Bonds (officers and fiduciaries), **Rule 1:13–3**
  Capital punishment, sentencing proceedings, **Rule 1:8–1**
  Criminal cases, **Rule 1:8–1**
    Transfer from law division to family part, **Rule 3:1–5**
  Municipal courts, jurisdiction, **2B:12–18**
  Notice to prosecutor, **Rule 1:8–1**
Witnesses, **Evidence Rule 606**
  Questions, **Rule 1:8–8**
Writings and photographs, determining contents, sufficiency of proof, **Evidence Rule 1008**

JURY COMMISSIONERS
Practice of law, attorneys regularly assigned to, **Rule 1:15–2**

JURY LISTS
Certified copies for county clerks and assignment judges, **2B:20–5**
Compilation, qualifications and selection, **2B:20–2**
County Clerks, this index
Expansion, qualifications and selection, **2B:20–2**
Ineligibility, persons whose names do not appear on list, **2B:23–11**
Names, eligible persons, qualifications and selection, **2B:20–2**

JURY LISTS—Cont'd
Posting copy in clerks office, qualifications and selection, **2B:20–5**
Preparation, qualifications and selection, **2B:20–2**
Questionnaires, qualifications and selection, **2B:20–3**
State grand jury, selection of jurors, **2B:22–3**

JURY TRIAL
Jury and Jurors, generally, this index

JUSTICES
Judges and Justices, generally, this index

JUSTICES DOCKETS
Dockets, generally, this index

JUSTIFICATION
Criminal prosecutions defense, **2C:3–1 et seq.**

JUVENILE AND DOMESTIC RELATIONS COURTS
Complaints, **2A:4A–70 et seq.**
  Diversion, court intake services, **2A:4A–73**
  Review and recommendation, **2A:4A–71**
Conferences, court intake services, **2A:4A–74**
Confidential or privileged,
  Court intake services conferences, **2A:4A–74**
  Juvenile conference committees, **2A:4A–75**
Court intake services conference, **2A:4A–74**
Detention or shelter care facilities, intake services, **2A:4A–70**
Diversion,
  Complaints, court intake services, **2A:4A–73**
  Intake services, recommendations, **2A:4A–72**
Family Court, generally, this index
Family crisis referrals, intake services, screening, **2A:4A–70**
Intake services, **2A:4A–70 et seq.**
Jurisdiction,
  Intake services, **2A:4A–71**
  Transfer of proceedings, **2C:4–11**
Juvenile conference committee, **2A:4A–75**
Legal representation, public defender, **2A:158A–24**
  Financial circumstances, **2A:158A–25**
Referrals, complaints and juvenile family crisis, **2A:4A–70**
Review and recommendation, complaints, **2A:4A–71**
Screening, intake services, **2A:4A–70**
Superior Court, generally, this index
Support of Persons, generally, this index

JUVENILE CONFERENCE COMMITTEES
Generally, **Rules 5:25–1, 5:25–2**
Court intake services, **2A:4A–75**

JUVENILE COURTS
Family Court, generally, this index
Juvenile and Domestic Relations Courts, generally, this index

JUVENILE DELINQUENTS
See, also, Dependent or Neglected Children, generally, this index
Generally, **2A:4A–20 et seq.; Rule 5:19–1 et seq.**
Absence and absentees, detention hearings, **2A:4A–38**
Adjournment, disposition of case, formal entry, **2A:4A–43**
Adjudication,
  Expungements, **2C:52–4.1**
  Fines and penalties, victims of crime compensation board, **2C:43–3.1**

JUVENILE DELINQUENTS—Cont'd
Adjudication—Cont'd
Notification of order sealing record,
2A:4A–62
Age, 2A:4A–22
Detention, 2A:4A–34
Jurisdiction waiver cases, 2A:4A–36
Standards, **Rule 5:21–5**
Disposition of cases, 2A:4A–43
Orders, termination, 2A:4A–47
Fingerprints, 2A:4A–61
Incarceration, mitigating circumstances,
2A:4A–44
Jails, 2A:4A–37
Jurisdiction, waiver, 2A:4A–26
Photographs, 2A:4A–61
Referral to other courts without juveniles
consent, **Rule 5:22–2**
Release on own recognizance, 2A:4A–35
Aggravation, incarceration, 2A:4A–44
AIDS or HIV testing,
Disorderly persons, 2A:4A–43.4
Sex offenders, 2A:4A–43.1, 2C:43–2.2
Alcoholic beverages,
Emergencies, consumption, privileges and
immunities, 2C:33–15
Privileges and immunities, consumption,
emergencies, 2C:33–15
Alcoholics and alcoholism,
Alcoholic parents, juvenile family crisis,
2A:4A–85
Juvenile family crisis, alcoholic parents,
2A:4A–85
Treatment, probation and probation officers,
2C:35–14
Alternate living arrangements, juvenile family
crisis, 2A:4A–87
Appeal and review,
Detention, 2A:4A–38
Juvenile family crisis, long term out of home
placement, 2A:4A–90
Armed forces, enlistment, sealing of records,
2A:4A–62
Arrest, this index
Attorneys,
Appointment of counsel, juvenile family cri-
sis, out of home placement hearings,
2A:4A–89
Critical stages in proceedings, 2A:4A–39
Detention hearings, 2A:4A–38
Auditory problems, juvenile family crisis,
2A:4A–85
Auto theft, jurisdiction, waiver, 2A:4A–26
Bail, 2A:4A–40
Central registry, 2A:4A–60
Rules and regulations, 2A:4A–60.1
Commitment and admission to institutions,
County juvenile detention facility, agree-
ments, juvenile justice commission,
placement of juveniles in custody of,
2A:4A–44.1
Juvenile family crisis, 2A:4A–46
Orders of court, **Rule 5:24–4**
State facilities, 2A:4A–44
Treatment, 2A:4A–43
Community services,
Exhaustion, juvenile family crisis, **Rules
5:15–1, 5:17–2**
Performance,
Acts of graffiti, 2A:4A–43.2
Orders, 2A:4A–43
Compensation and salaries, community service,
2A:4A–43
Complaints, 2A:4A–30; **Rule 5:20–1**
Amendment, **Rule 5:20–1**
Court intake services, 2A:4A–70 et seq.

JUVENILE DELINQUENTS—Cont'd
Complaints—Cont'd
Custody, filing complaint following taking
into custody, 2A:4A–38
Diversion, court intake services, 2A:4A–73
Intake services, review and recommenda-
tions, 2A:4A–71
Postcomplaint detention, **Rule 5:21–6**
Taking into custody without process, **Rule
5:21–1**
Transfer of causes from other courts, **Rule
5:23–2**
Computers, crimes and offenses, jurisdiction,
waiver, 2A:4A–26
Conferences,
Court intake services, 2A:4A–74
Predispositional conferences, 2A:4A–42
Confidential or privileged information, **Rule
1:38–3**
Court intake services conferences, 2A:4A–74
Hearings, **Rule 5:19–2**
Juvenile conference committees, 2A:4A–75
Records, 2A:4A–60 et seq.
Sealing of records, 2A:4A–62
Screening, suicide, mentally deficient and
mentally ill persons, 2A:4A–60.2,
2A:4A–60.3
Continuance, juvenile family crisis, hearings,
2A:4A–86
Continuing juvenile family crisis, referral to
court, 2A:4A–83 et seq.
Controlled substances,
Controlled dangerous substances, jurisdic-
tion, waiver, 2A:4A–26
Drug dependent parents, juvenile family cri-
sis, 2A:4A–85
Entry on property, injunctions, 2C:35–5.7
Jurisdiction, waiver, 2A:4A–26
Juvenile family crisis, drug dependent par-
ents, 2A:4A–85
Referral to other courts without juveniles
consent, **Rule 5:22–2**
Conviction of crime, orders sealing records,
notification, 2A:4A–62
Correctional Institutions, this index
Counties, detention, 2A:4A–43
Admissions cessation orders, appropriations,
2A:4A–37
Agreements, juvenile justice commission,
placement of juveniles in custody of,
2A:4A–44.1
Incarceration, 2A:4A–43
County facilities, agreements, juvenile justice
commission, placement of children in cus-
tody of, 2A:4A–44.1
Court appointed special advocate, 2A:4A–92
Records, confidentiality, 2A:4A–60 et seq.
Court intake services, 2A:4A–70 et seq.
Referrals, **Rule 5:20–1**
Court ordered shelter care, credit for time
served, **Rule 5:21–3**
Credit for time served, pretrial detention, **Rule
5:21–3**
Criminal mischief, 2C:17–3.1
Crisis intervention response, definitions,
2A:4A–78
Custody, 2A:4A–31 et seq., 2A:4A–32
Filing complaint after taking into custody,
2A:4A–38
Grounds, taking into custody, 2A:4A–31
Interference with, 2C:13–4
Jails, 2A:4A–32
Juvenile family crisis, notice, 2A:4A–80
Notice, 2A:4A–33
Short term custody, **Rule 5:16–1**
Notice to parents, **Rule 5:16–2**

JUVENILE DELINQUENTS—Cont'd
Custody—Cont'd
Taking into custody without process, **Rule
5:21–1**
Transfers, orders of court, 2A:4A–43
Witnesses, jurisdiction, 2A:4A–24
Defenses, 2A:4A–40
Definitions, juvenile justice, 2A:4A–22,
2A:4A–23
Detention, 2A:4A–34
Counties, ante
Court intake services, 2A:4A–70
Hearings, 2A:4A–38; **Rules 5:21–3, 5:22–3**
Jurisdiction waiver cases, 2A:4A–36
Location, 2A:4A–37
Notice, hearing, 2A:4A–38
Officers and employees, aggravated assault,
throwing bodily fluids, 2C:12–13
Place of detention or shelter care, **Rule
5:21–4**
Postcomplaint detention, **Rule 5:21–6**
Presence at hearings, 2A:4A–38
Review hearing, **Rule 5:21–3**
Short term custody, 2A:4A–32
Standards, **Rule 5:21–5**
Supervision, **Rule 5:21–2**
Disabilities, civil disabilities, disposition of
cases, 2A:4A–48
Disclosure, records, 2A:4A–60 et seq.
Disorderly persons,
Disclosure, information concerning particu-
lar juveniles from designated records,
2A:4A–60
HIV or AIDS testing, 2A:4A–43.4
Disposition of cases, 2A:4A–48
Civil disabilities and criminal status,
2A:4A–48
Factors to consider, 2A:4A–43
Juvenile family crisis, 2A:4A–46, 2A:4A–86
Orders, 2A:4A–43
Termination, 2A:4A–47
Dispositional hearings, 2A:4A–41
Diversion,
Complaints, court intake services, 2A:4A–73
Court intake services, recommendations,
2A:4A–72
DNA database and databank, sexual assault,
53:1–20.20, 53:1–20.22, 53:1–20.25
Drivers Licenses, this index
Emergencies, medical care and treatment, alco-
holic beverages, consumption, privileges
and immunities, 2C:33–15
Evaluation, predispositional evaluation,
2A:4A–42
Evidence,
Application of law, **Evidence Rule 101**
Disposition of cases, 2A:4A–48
Juveniles testimony at case referral hearing,
2A:4A–29
Transfer of causes, **Rule 5:22–2**
Examination and examiners, predispositional
examination, 2A:4A–42
Expenses, commitment proceedings, **Rule
5:24–4**
Expungement of records,
Adjudications, 2C:52–4.1
Young drug offenders, 2C:52–5
Family crisis referrals, court intake services,
screening, 2A:4A–70
Family service plan, temporary out of home
placement, **Rule 5:18–2**
Findings, nonjury trials, **Rule 1:7–4**
Fines and penalties, 2A:4A–43
Adjudications of delinquents, victims of
crime compensation board, 2C:43–3.1
Criminal mischief, 2A:4A–43.2, 2C:17–3.1

JUVENILE DELINQUENTS—Cont'd
Fines and penalties—Cont'd
Graffiti, acts of, **2A:4A–43.2**
Suspension of driving privileges,
2A:4A–43.3
Fingerprints, **2A:4A–61**
Firearms, possession, **2C:58–6.1**
Forms, information requests, juvenile family
crisis, **2A:4A–77**
Guardian ad litem, appointment, waiver of
rights by incompetent juveniles, **2A:4A–39**
Guardian and ward,
Commitment expenses, assignment, **Rule
5:24–4**
Necessary parties, **Rule 5:20–4**
Notice of detention, **Rule 5:21–1**
Short term custody, notice, **Rule 5:16–2**
Guilty pleas, form, **Rule 5:21A**
Hearings, **Rule 5:19–2**
Court hearing, **Rule 5:21–7**
Court intake services, **2A:4A–72**
Detention, **2A:4A–38; Rules 5:21–3, 5:22–3**
Dispositional hearings, **2A:4A–41; Rule
5:24–1**
Time, **Rule 5:24–1**
Individual hearings, **Rule 5:19–3**
Juvenile family crisis, **2A:4A–86**
Out of door sales, juvenile family crisis,
2A:4A–89
Homicide, this index
Identity and identification, disclosure,
2A:4A–60
Indictment and information, **2A:4A–40**
Information requests, juvenile family crisis,
2A:4A–77
Inspection and inspectors,
Files and records, sealing, **2A:4A–62**
Records, **2A:4A–60; Rule 5:19–2**
Sealing of records, **2A:4A–62**
Interviews, juvenile family crisis, **2A:4A–78**
Stabilized crisis, **2A:4A–82**
Jails, this index
Joint and several liability, restitution, **2A:4A–43**
Jurisdiction, **2A:4A–24**
Discretionary retention of jurisdiction, **Rule
5:24–5**
Family court, **2A:4A–24**
Retention, **2A:4A–45**
Sex offenses, juveniles in need of supervi-
sion, **2C:14–8**
Waiver, **2A:4A–26**
Evidence at probable cause hearing, **Rule
5:21–3**
Family court, **2A:4A–26**
Jury, **2A:4A–40**
Juvenile conference committees, court intake
services, **2A:4A–75**
Juvenile family crisis, **2A:4A–76 et seq.; Rule
5:15–1 et seq.**
Alcoholics and alcoholism, alcoholic parents,
2A:4A–85
Alternate living arrangements, **2A:4A–87**
Appeal and review, long term out of home
placement, **2A:4A–90**
Commitment, **2A:4A–46**
Continuance, **2A:4A–86**
Continuing crisis, referral to court, **2A:4A–83
et seq.**
Disposition, orders, **2A:4A–46**
Drugs and medicine, drug dependent par-
ents, **2A:4A–85**
Forms, information requests, **2A:4A–77**
Hearings, **2A:4A–86**
Out of door sales, **2A:4A–89**
Information requests, **2A:4A–77**
Interviews, **2A:4A–78**

JUVENILE DELINQUENTS—Cont'd
Juvenile family crisis—Cont'd
Interviews—Cont'd
Stabilized crisis, **2A:4A–82**
Law enforcement referral, **2A:4A–80**
Notice, **2A:4A–80, 2A:4A–86**
Out of door sales, petition, **2A:4A–89**
Orders,
Disposition, **2A:4A–86**
Long term out of home placement, family
service plans, **2A:4A–90**
Out of door sales, **2A:4A–89**
Petitions, **2A:4A–30**
Dismissal, **2A:4A–86**
Referral to court, **2A:4A–83 et seq.**
Plans and specifications, orders, placement,
2A:4A–90
Referral to court, **2A:4A–83 et seq.**
Referrals, **2A:4A–80, 2A:4A–81, 2A:4A–83 et
seq.**
Response, **2A:4A–78**
Stabilization, interviews, **2A:4A–82**
Temporary out of home placement,
2A:4A–87 et seq.
Twenty four hour on call service, **2A:4A–77**
Law enforcement agencies, records, confiden-
tiality, **2A:4A–60 et seq.**
Law enforcement officers, privileges and immu-
nities, release of juvenile to nonparent,
2A:4A–32
Law enforcement referral, juvenile family crisis,
2A:4A–80
Legal representation, public defender,
2A:158A–24
Financial circumstances, **2A:158A–25**
Location, detention, **2A:4A–37**
Long term placement out of home, **Rule 5:18–3**
Material witness, detention, **Rule 5:21–8**
Medical care and treatment,
Confidential records, **Rule 5:19–2**
Emergencies, alcoholic beverages, consump-
tion, privileges and immunities,
2C:33–15
Out of door sales, **Rule 5:18–3**
Short term custody, **Rule 5:16–2**
Medical examinations, auditory or vision prob-
lems, juvenile family crisis, **2A:4A–85**
Mentally deficient and mentally ill persons,
Incarceration, state correctional facilities,
2A:4A–44
Screening, confidential or privileged infor-
mation, **2A:4A–60.2, 2A:4A–60.3**
Mitigation, incarceration, **2A:4A–44**
Motions,
Return from correctional institution before
parole, **2A:4A–44**
Sealing of records, **2A:4A–62**
Motor vehicles,
Drivers licenses and registration certificates,
postponement, suspension, or revoca-
tion, **2A:4A–43**
Theft, orders of incarceration or community
service, **2A:4A–43**
Motorized bicycles, drivers licenses, suspension
or revocation, false alarms, **2C:33–3.1**
Necessary parties, **Rule 5:20–4**
Nonjury trial, findings, **Rule 1:7–4**
Notice,
Conferences, diversion to juvenile confer-
ence committee, **2A:4A–75**
Controlled substances, entry on property, in-
junctions, **2C:35–5.7**
Court intake service conferences, **2A:4A–74**
Custody, **2A:4A–33**
Detention, hearing, **2A:4A–38**

JUVENILE DELINQUENTS—Cont'd
Notice—Cont'd
Dispositional hearings, **2A:4A–41; Rule
5:24–1**
Motions, sealing of records, **2A:4A–62**
Short term custody, **2A:4A–32**
Orders, **Rule 5:24–4**
Community service, performance, stolen ve-
hicles, **2A:4A–43**
Incarceration, stolen vehicles, **2A:4A–43**
Juvenile family crisis, ante
Sealing of records, **2A:4A–62**
Out of door sales,
Juvenile family crisis, **2A:4A–87 et seq.**
Long term placement, **Rule 5:18–3**
Temporary placement, hearings, **Rule 5:18–2**
Parents,
Commitment expenses, assignment, **Rule
5:24–4**
Necessary parties, **Rule 5:20–4**
Notice of detention, **Rule 5:21–1**
Short term custody, notice, **Rule 5:16–2**
Parole, release from incarceration, **2A:4A–44**
Parties, **Rule 5:20–4**
Penalties. Fines and penalties, generally, ante
Pendency, release, disposition of case,
2A:4A–34
Per diem allowance or compensation, detention
or shelter care facilities receiving juveniles,
2A:4A–37
Petitions,
Juvenile family crisis, ante
Out of door sales, **Rule 5:18–1**
Sealing of records, armed forces enlistees,
2A:4A–62
Transfer of causes, **Rule 5:22–1**
Photographs, **2A:4A–61**
Physical examinations, auditory or vision prob-
lems, juvenile family crisis, **2A:4A–85**
Placement, temporary, **2A:4A–88**
Plans and specifications,
Juvenile family crisis,
Long term out of home placement, family
service plans, **2A:4A–90**
Out of door sales, **2A:4A–89**
Service plans, **2A:4A–43**
Plea forms, **Rule 5:21A**
Postdisposition relief, **Rule 5:24–6**
Predisposition evaluation, **Rule 5:24–2**
Presence, detention hearings, **2A:4A–38**
Privileged communications, physician and pa-
tients, **2A:84A–22.1 et seq.**
Privileged information. Confidential or privi-
leged information, generally, ante
Privileges and immunities, alcoholic beverages,
consumption, emergencies, medical care
and treatment, **2C:33–15**
Probable cause, detention, **2A:4A–38**
Probable cause hearings, **Rule 5:21–3**
Referral to other courts, **Rule 5:22–2**
Probation and Probation Officers, this index
Public attendance during proceedings,
2A:4A–60
Public hearings, **Rule 5:19–2**
Recognizances, release on own recognizance,
2A:4A–35
Records and recordation,
Confidential or privileged information,
2A:4A–60 et seq.
Confidential records, **Rules 1:38–3, 5:19–2**
Detention hearings, **Rule 5:21–3**
Expungements, adjudications, **2C:52–4.1**
Inspection, **2A:4A–60**
Sealing of records, **2A:4A–62**

JUVENILE DELINQUENTS—Cont'd
Referrals,
    Complaints and juvenile family crisis, court intake services, **2A:4A–70**
    Courts, **Rule 5:22–1 et seq.**
    Juvenile family crisis, **2A:4A–80 et seq.**
Registry, **2A:4A–60**
    Rules and regulations, **2A:4A–60.1**
Rehabilitation, orders of court, **2A:4A–43**
Release, **Rule 5:21–2**
    Detention found unnecessary or unrequired, **2A:4A–38**
    Disposition of case, **2A:4A–43**
    Incarceration, parole, **2A:4A–44**
    Initial detention hearing, **Rule 5:21–3**
    On own recognizance, **2A:4A–35**
    Orders, detention found unnecessary or unrequired, **2A:4A–38**
    Parole, **2A:4A–44**
    Pendency, disposition of case, **2A:4A–34**
    Prehearing release, **Rule 5:21–2**
    Recognizance, release on own recognizance, **2A:4A–35; Rule 5:21–2**
Reports, predispositional reports, **Rule 5:24–2**
Restitution, this index
Retention, jurisdiction, **2A:4A–45**
Right to counsel,
    Commitment, **Rule 5:24–2**
    Temporary out of home placement, **Rule 5:18–2**
    Trial, **Rule 5:20–2**
Rules and regulations, detention or shelter care facilities, **2A:4A–37**
Schools and School Districts, this index
Scope of rules, **Rule 3:1–1**
Screening,
    Court intake services, **2A:4A–70**
    Suicide, mentally deficient and mentally ill persons, confidential or privileged information, **2A:4A–60.2, 2A:4A–60.3**
Sealing of records, **2A:4A–62**
Sentence and punishment, **Rule 5:24–4**
    Extended term, incarceration, **2A:4A–44**
    Modification, **Rule 5:24–6**
Service,
    Complaint, contents, **Rule 5:20–1**
    Juvenile family crisis, notice of hearing, **Rule 5:15–3**
Service plans, **2A:4A–43**
Sex Offenses, this index
Shelters,
    Court intake services, **2A:4A–70**
    Location, **2A:4A–37**
    Placement in lieu of detention, **2A:4A–34**
    Short term custody, **2A:4A–32**
Subpoenas, inspection of objects designated in subpoena, **Rule 1:9–2**
Suicide, screening, confidential or privileged information, **2A:4A–60.2, 2A:4A–60.3**
Summons, **Rule 5:20–2**
Supervision, parole, **2A:4A–44**
Temporary out of home placement, juvenile family crisis, **2A:4A–87 et seq.**
Temporary placement, prior to hearing, **2A:4A–88**
Termination of parental rights, temporary out of home placement, **Rule 5:18–2**
Theft, auto theft, jurisdiction, waiver, **2A:4A–26**
Time,
    Disposition of cases, orders, termination, **2A:4A–47**
    Dispositional hearings, **2A:4A–41**
    Incarceration, **2A:4A–44**
    Term, **2A:4A–43**
    Jurisdiction, waiver motions, **2A:4A–26**

JUVENILE DELINQUENTS—Cont'd
Time—Cont'd
    Juvenile family crisis, twenty four hour on call service, **2A:4A–77**
    Short term custody, **2A:4A–32**
Transfer of actions, **2A:4A–25, 2A:4A–28; Rule 5:22–1 et seq.**
    Consent of juvenile, **Rule 5:22–2**
    Detention hearing after transfer, **Rule 5:22–3**
    Election by juvenile charged with delinquency, **2A:4A–27**
    Proceedings after transfer, **Rule 5:22–4**
    Transfers from other courts, **Rule 5:23–1 et seq.**
    Proceedings after transfer, **Rule 5:23–2**
Transfers, jails, age, **2A:4A–37**
Transportation, detention or shelter care facilities, admissions cessation orders, **2A:4A–37**
Treatment, commitment, **2A:4A–43**
Trial, time, **Rule 5:21–7**
Twenty four hour on call service, juvenile family crisis, **2A:4A–77**
Venue, **Rule 5:19–1**
Verification, petitions sealing of records, armed forces enlistees, **2A:4A–62**
Victims or relatives of victims, statement for predispositional report, **2A:4A–42**
Vision problems, juvenile family crisis, **2A:4A–85**
Waiver,
    Court proceedings, rights afforded juveniles, **2A:4A–39**
    Jurisdiction,
        Family court, **2A:4A–26**
        Transfer of causes, **Rule 5:22–2**
Warrant for arrest, issuance, **Rule 5:20–3**
Weapons,
    Jurisdiction, **2C:58–6.1**
        Waiver, **2A:4A–26**
    Licenses and permits, **2C:58–3**
        Records and recordation, **2A:4A–60**
Witnesses,
    Custody, jurisdiction, **2A:4A–24**
    Hearings, **Rule 5:20–2**
    Material witnesses, detention, **Rule 5:21–8**
Work programs, **2A:4A–43**
Young drug offenders, expungement of record, **2C:52–5**

JUVENILE FAMILY CRISIS
    Generally, **Rule 5:15–1 et seq.**
Children and Minors, this index
Juvenile Delinquents, this index

JUVENILE FAMILY CRISIS INTERVENTION UNITS
Counties, this index
Family Court, this index

JUVENILE JUSTICE CODE
Generally, **2A:4A–20 et seq.**

JUVENILE JUSTICE COMMISSION
Corrections officer, weapons, unlawful possession, exemption, **2C:39–6**
Counties, juvenile detention facility, agreement, placement of juveniles in custody of, **2A:4A–44.1**
Custody, county juvenile detention facilities, agreements, **2A:4A–44.1**
Registration and notification procedures, sex offender, **2C:7–2 et seq.**
Sex offenders, registration and notification procedures, **2C:7–2 et seq.**

JUVENILE OFFENDER REHABILITATION ACT
Disposition of cases, **2A:4A–43**

JUVENILES
Children and Minors, generally, this index

KEEPERS
Jails, this index

KEEPSAFE PROGRAM
Trigger locks, rebates, **2C:58–17**
    Reports, **2C:58–18**

KEGS
Intoxicating liquors, distributors licenses, **33:1–11**

KENNELS
Crimes and offenses, destruction of animals, **4:22–19**
Destruction of animals, **4:22–19, 4:22–19.2**

KEROSENE
Turnpike project transportation regulations, **27:23–31**

KEROSENE BURNING HEATING DEVICES
Generally, **2C:40–6 et seq.**

KETOBEMIDONE
Controlled dangerous substance, **24:21–1 et seq.**

KEYS
Motor vehicles,
    Ignition keys, evidence, **2C:40–23**
    Master keys, **2C:5–6**
State Property, this index

KIDNAPPING
    Generally, **2C:13–1 et seq., 2C:44–1**
    Aggravated sexual assault, **2C:14–2, 2C:14–3**
    Arrest, force or violence, **2C:3–7**
        Grand jury, instructions to jury, **2B:22–9**
    Arrest warrant, issuance, **Rule 3:3–1**
    Arrest without warrant, release, **Rule 3:4–1**
    Attempts, body vests, **2C:39–13**
    Bail,
        Authority to admit to, **Rule 3:26–2**
        Cash, crime with bail restrictions, **2A:162–12**
    Body vests, **2C:39–13**
    Children and Minors, this index
    DNA database and databank, **53:1–20.20**
    Domestic Violence, generally, this index
    Expungement, record, **2C:52–2**
    Extended term of imprisonment, **2C:43–7, 2C:43–7.1**
    Guardian and Ward, this index
    Human trafficking, **2C:13–8**
    Jury,
        Number of peremptory challenges, **2B:23–13**
        Peremptory challenges, **Rule 1:8–3**
    Juvenile delinquents and dependents, Jurisdiction, waiver, **2A:4A–26**
        Referral to other courts without juveniles consent, **Rule 5:22–2**
    Murder, sentence and punishment, **2C:11–3**
    Parole, supervision for life, special sentence, Violent Predator Incapacitation Act of 1994, **2C:43–6.4**
    Presentence investigation and report, disclosure, **2C:44–6**
        Cost of evaluation, **2C:44–6.1**
    Rape, **2C:14–2**
    Records and recordation, expungement, **2C:52–2**

KIDNAPPING—Cont'd

Reward, apprehension and conviction, 2A:153–1, 2A:153–2, 2A:153–4

Sodomy, 2C:14–2

Terrorism, 2C:38–2

Weapons, possession, 2C:39–7
Mandatory sentence, 2C:43–6

KNIVES

Weapons, generally, this index

KNOWINGLY

Definitions,
Code of Criminal Justice, 2C:2–2
Crimes and offenses, 2C:2–2
Obscene material, children and minors, 2C:34–3

KNOWLEDGE

Hit and run drivers, 2C:11–5.1, 2C:12–1.1

KOSHER FOOD

Deceptive business practices, 2C:21–7.2 et seq.

KYLEIGHS LAW

Generally, 39:3–13, 39:3–13.2a, 39:3–13.4, 39:3–13.8

LABELS

Brands, Labels and Marks, generally, this index

LABOR AND EMPLOYMENT

Adoption, agencies, criminal history record information, 53:1–20.9d

Alcoholic beverages, licenses and permits, 33:1 App.

Application of law, certificates and certification, conviction of crime, disabilities, removal, 2A:168A–12

Compensation and Salaries, generally, this index

Controlled substances, lie detector tests, 2C:40A–1

Convicted offenders, 2A:168A–1 et seq.

Crimes and offenses,
Drug tests, 2C:36–10
Human trafficking, 2C:13–8
Jury service, employment protection, employer violations, 2B:20–17
Lie detector tests, 2C:40A–1
Suspended sentence, 2C:45–1

Discharge, wrongful discharge, 2C:40A–3

Disorderly Persons, this index

Drug manufacturers, lie detector tests, 2C:40A–1

Drug tests, crimes and offenses, 2C:36–10

Employment protection, jury duty, 2B:20–17

Evidence, requiring employee to produce evidence, 2A:84A–19

Exemptions, lie detector test, 2C:40A–1

Fines and penalties, lie detector test, 2C:40A–1

Fraud,
Drug tests, 2C:36–10
Public contracts, 2C:21–34

Human trafficking, crimes and offenses, 2C:13–8

Jury and jurors, 2B:20–17

Labor Unions, generally, this index

Law Enforcement Officers, this index

Lie detector tests, requirement, 2C:40A–1

Poisoned liquors, manufacture or sale, 33:3–9, 33:3–10

Probation, conditions, 2C:45–1

Rehabilitated convicted offenders, 2A:168A–1 et seq.

Reinstatement, jury service, employment protection, employer violations, 2B:20–17

LABOR AND EMPLOYMENT—Cont'd

Retaliation, public officers and employees, past official action, 2C:27–5

Suspended sentences, 2C:45–1

Test,
Drug tests, crimes and offenses, 2C:36–10
Lie detector test, 2C:40A–1

Theft of services, 2C:20–8

Trade secrets, compelling disclosure, 2A:84A–26

Unions. Labor Unions, generally, this index

Wages. Compensation and Salaries, generally, this index

Wrongful discharge. Discharge, ante

LABOR AND WORKFORCE DEVELOPMENT DEPARTMENT

Explosives, generally, this index

Labor and Employment, generally, this index

LABOR COMMISSIONER

Fires and Fire Protection, generally, this index

Fireworks, generally, this index

Labor and Employment, generally, this index

Rules and regulations, liquefied petroleum gas, handling, 21:1B–2

LABOR DISPUTES

See, also, Labor Unions, generally, this index

Coercion, 2C:13–5

Criminal coercion, threat to bring about or continue a strike, 2C:13–5

Extortion, threat to bring about or continue strike, 2C:20–5

LABOR ORGANIZATIONS

Labor Unions, generally, this index

LABOR UNIONS

Actions and proceedings, racketeering, 2C:41–4

Cease and desist orders, racketeering, 2C:41–4

Confidential or privileged information, racketeering investigations, 2C:41–5

Crimes and offenses, racketeering, 2C:41–1 et seq.

Debtors and creditors, racketeering, 2C:41–1 et seq.

Definitions, racketeering, 2C:41–1

Discovery, racketeering investigations, 2C:41–5

Examinations and examiners, racketeering, 2C:41–5

Fines and penalties, racketeering, 2C:41–1 et seq.

Indebtedness, racketeering, 2C:41–1 et seq.

Inspections and inspectors, racketeering investigations, 2C:41–5

Interrogatories, racketeering, investigations, 2C:41–5

Investigations and investigators, racketeering, 2C:41–5

Investments, racketeering, 2C:41–1 et seq.

Judgments and decrees, racketeering, 2C:41–4

Licenses and permits, racketeering, revocation or suspension, 2C:41–4

Monopolies and unfair trade, exemptions, 56:9–5

Officers and employees, commercial bribery and breach of duty, 2C:21–10

Process, racketeering, 2C:41–5

Production of books and papers, racketeering, 2C:41–5

Racketeering, 2C:41–1 et seq.

Records and recordation, racketeering, investigations, 2C:41–5

Restitution, racketeering, 2C:41–4

Securities, racketeering, 2C:41–1 et seq.

LABORATORIES

Certificates, controlled dangerous substances, 2C:35–19, 2C:35–20

Definitions,
Controlled dangerous substances, 2C:35–2, 24:21–2
Controlled substances, 24:21–2

Drugs and medicine, forensic laboratories, 2C:35–19, 2C:35–20

Fees, payment, 2C:46–1
Transaction fee, 2C:46–1 et seq.

Health Maintenance Organizations, generally, this index

LAKES AND PONDS

Water Pollution, generally, this index

LAMP POSTS

Horse hitching, 39:4–20

LAND

Real Estate, generally, this index

LAND USE PLANNING

Zoning and Planning, generally, this index

LANDING FIELDS

Airports and Landing Fields, generally, this index

LANDLORD AND TENANT

See, also, Leases, generally, this index

Alcoholic beverages, violation of law, leased premises, 33:1–54

Crimes and offenses, alcoholic beverages, violation on leased premises, 33:1–54

Criminal mischief, 2C:17–3

Mediation, complementary dispute resolution programs, Rules 1:40–6, 1:40–7

Mobile homes and mobile home parks, abandonment, disposition, certificates of ownership, 39:10–15.1

Notice,
Drug offenses on premises, conviction, 2C:35–16.1
Exercise of option, violation on leased premises, 33:1–54

Possession, reversion to lessor, violation of alcoholic beverage law, 33:1–54

LANDS

Real Estate, generally, this index

LANES

Definitions, 39:1–1

LANGUAGE

Offensive language, disorderly conduct, 2C:33–2

LAPSE

Uninsured motorist prevention fund, nonlapsing, revolving fund, 39:6B–3

LARCENY

Theft, generally, this index

LARGE CAPACITY AMMUNITION MAGAZINE

Definitions, 2C:39–1

Manufacture, sale, unlawful purpose,
Fourth degree crime, 2C:39–9
Person convicted of crime involving, possession of any weapon prohibited, 2C:39–7

LASCIVIOUSNESS

Lewdness and Obscenity, generally, this index

LASER LIGHTING DEVICES
Transportation, interference, **2C:33–14**

LASER SIGHTING SYSTEM DEVICES
Aggravated assault, **2C:12–1**

LAW AND PUBLIC SAFETY DEPARTMENT
Alcoholic Beverage Control Division, generally, this index
Attorney General, generally, this index
Divisions. State Police, generally, this index
DNA Database and Databank, generally, this index
Explosives, transportation, concurrent enforcement power, **21:1A–130**
Fund, deposits, criminal assessments, law enforcement officers training and equipment fund, **2C:43–3.3**
Safe and secure communities program, fund, deposits, criminal assessments, **2C:46–4, 2C:46–4.1**
State Police, generally, this index
Vessels, generally, this index

LAW DIVISION
Attorney General, generally, this index
Deputy attorney general. Attorney General, generally, this index

LAW DIVISION, SUPERIOR COURT
Crimes and offenses, prosecution in, **Rule 3:1–5**
Filing of papers, **Rule 1:5–6**
Limited criminal jurisdiction, courts of, orders, appeals, **Rule 3:24**
Sessions, **Rule 1:30–2**
Special civil part,
  Filing of papers, **Rule 1:5–6**
  Inactive cases, dismissal, **Rule 1:13–7**
  Supervising judges, **Rule 1:33–6A**
Title of court, **Rule 1:37–1**
Transfer from other courts, crimes and offenses, **Rule 3:1–5**

LAW ENFORCEMENT AGENCIES
Combating theft of motor vehicles, records of registered owners, availability, **39:3–85.8**
Convicted offenders, hiring, **2A:168A–6**
DNA Database and Databank, generally, this index
Juvenile delinquents and dependents, records, confidentiality, **2A:4A–60 et seq.**
Officers and employees. Law Enforcement Officers, generally, this index
Records, expungement, **2C:52–1 et seq.**
Service of petition and documents, **2C:52–10**

LAW ENFORCEMENT OFFICERS
Actions and proceedings, stolen property, **2C:65–3**
Aged persons, abuse or neglect, treatment and prevention training course, **2C:25–20**
Aggravated assault, **2C:12–1**
  Throwing bodily fluids, **2C:12–13**
  Weapons, **2C:12–1**
Animals owned or used by officers, killing or harming, **2C:29–3.1**
Application of law, motor vehicles, hands free telephones, **39:4–97.4**
Arrest, generally, this index
Assault and battery, aggravated assault, weapons, **2C:12–1**
Associations and societies, intoxicating liquors, club licenses, **33:1–25.1, 33:1–25.2**
Badges, unauthorized transfer, **2C:21–2.2**
Bicycles, **39:4–14.1**
Cellular telephones, hands free telephones, application of law, motor vehicles, **39:4–97.4**

LAW ENFORCEMENT OFFICERS—Cont'd
Child abuse reports, access, **9:6–8.10a**
Civil rights, crimes and offenses, racial profiling, **2C:30–5 et seq.**
Club licenses, intoxicating liquors, nonprofit organizations, **33:1–25.1, 33:1–25.2**
Combating theft of motor vehicles, chief, municipality, informed consent forms, fees, **39:3–85.9**
Complaint, **Rule 7:2–2**
  Domestic violence prevention, temporary restraining order, service with, **2C:25–28**
Constables, generally, this index
Controlled substances, exception from registration, **24:21–10**
Convicted offenders, rehabilitation, application of law, **2A:168A–6**
County correction officers, police powers, **2A:154–3**
County Detectives and Investigators, generally, this index
Court attendants, **2A:154–3**
Crimes and offenses, racial profiling, **2C:30–5 et seq.**
Crisis intervention services, hotline, funding, **2C:64–6, 39:5–41**
Custody, stolen property, **2C:65–1 et seq.**
Deadly force, grand jury, instructions to jury, **2B:22–9**
Death, line of duty, memorial plates, **39:3–27.123 et seq.**
Detectives, generally, this index
Disabled officers, firearms, possession, **2C:39–6, 2C:39–6.1**
Disarming, criminal offense, **2C:12–11**
Disciplinary action, strip or body cavity searches, **2A:161A–6**
Discrimination, racial profiling, crimes and offenses, **2C:30–5 et seq.**
Disorderly Persons, this index
Dogs, owned or used by officers, killing or harming, **2C:29–3.1**
Domestic Violence, this index
Drug tests, labor and employment, fraud, **2C:36–10**
Evidence, stolen property, **2C:65–1**
False reports, **2C:28–4**
Fingerprinting, arrested persons, **53:1–15**
Firearms, disarming, criminal offense, **2C:12–11**
Force or violence, grand jury, instructions to jury, **2B:22–9**
Fraternal societies, intoxicating liquors, club licenses, **33:1–25.1, 33:1–25.2**
Fraud, drug tests, labor and employment, **2C:36–10**
Funds,
  Law enforcement officers memorial fund, special plates, **39:3–27.125**
  Law enforcement officers training and equipment fund, criminal assessments, **2C:43–3.3**
Grand jury, instructions to jury, force or violence, **2B:22–9**
Handicapped persons, abuse or neglect, treatment and prevention course, programs, **2C:25–20**
Hands free telephones, motor vehicles, application of law, **39:4–97.4**
Homicide, victims of crime, sentence, **2C:11–3**
Horses, owned or used by officers, killing or harming, **2C:29–3.1**
Identity theft, reports, **2C:21–17.6**
Impersonation, crimes and offenses, **2C:28–8**
Intoxicating liquors, nonprofit organizations, club licenses, **33:1–25.1, 33:1–25.2**

LAW ENFORCEMENT OFFICERS—Cont'd
Intrastate fresh pursuit, **2A:156–1**
Judges and magistrates, **2A:154–1**
Jury duty, grand jury service, grounds for excuse, **2B:21–2**
Justifiable force, grand jury, instructions to jury, **2B:22–9**
Juvenile delinquents and dependents, release to nonparent, privileges and immunities, **2A:4A–32**
Labor and employment, drug tests, fraud, **2C:36–10**
Laser sighting system device, aggravated assault, **2C:12–1**
Licenses and permits, intoxicating liquors, nonprofit organizations, **33:1–25.1, 33:1–25.2**
Memorials and monuments, special plates, **39:3–27.123 et seq.**
Mistake, force or violence, grand jury, instructions to jury, **2B:22–9**
Murder, victims of crime, sentence, **2C:11–3**
Negligence, force or violence, grand jury, instructions to jury, **2B:22–9**
Nonprofit organizations, intoxicating liquors, club licenses, **33:1–25.1, 33:1–25.2**
Notice,
  Domestic violence prevention, **2C:25–23**
  Stolen property, disposition, **2C:65–2**
Numbers and numbering, stolen property, **2C:65–1**
Orders of court, stolen property disposition, **2C:65–3**
Outdoor advertising, duties, **27:5–23**
Personalized handguns, **2C:58–2.5**
Photographs and photography,
  Arrested persons, **53:1–15**
  Stolen property, **2C:65–1**
Police and Police Departments, generally, this index
Powers and duties, **2A:154–1**
Privileges and immunities,
  Domestic violence,
    Arrest, **2C:25–22**
    Weapons, seizure, **2C:25–21**
  Invasion of privacy, observation, nudity, sexual intercourse, **2C:14–9**
  Juvenile delinquents and dependents, release to nonparent, **2A:4A–32**
Property, stolen property, **2C:65–1 et seq.**
Qualifications, **2A:154–2**
Racial profiling, crimes and offenses, **2C:30–5 et seq.**
Recklessness, force or violence, grand jury, instructions to jury, **2B:22–9**
Records and recordation, stolen property, **2C:65–1**
Rehabilitated convicted offenders, application of law, **2A:168A–6**
Release, stolen property, **2C:65–2**
Religious societies, intoxicating liquors, club licenses, **33:1–25.1, 33:1–25.2**
Retirement and pensions, retired officers, firearms, possession, **2C:39–6, 2C:39–6.1**
Sales, stolen property, **2C:65–3**
Search Warrants, generally, this index
Searches and Seizures, generally, this index
Service of petition and documents, **2C:52–10**
Sex offenders, community notification. Sex Offenses, this index
Sheriffs, generally, this index
Shoplifters, taking into custody, **2C:20–11**
Societies, intoxicating liquors, club licenses, **33:1–25.1, 33:1–25.2**
State Police, generally, this index
Stolen property, disposition, **2C:65–1 et seq.**

LAW ENFORCEMENT OFFICERS—Cont'd
Telecommunications, hands free telephones, operators, application of law, **39:4–97.4**
Training,
Aged or handicapped persons, abuse or neglect, prevention and treatment, **2C:25–20**
Domestic violence prevention, **2C:25–20**
Transfers, badges, **2C:21–2.2**
Unclaimed property, sales, **2C:65–3**
Unlawful to issue, offer, cards except to bona fide members, **2A:170–20.1**
Use of force, **2C:3–7**
Veterans organizations, intoxicating liquors, club licenses, **33:1–25.1, 33:1–25.2**
Victims of crime, murder, sentence, **2C:11–3**
Weapons,
Disarming, criminal offense, **2C:12–11**
Personalized handguns, **2C:58–2.5**
Retired officers, **2C:39–6, 2C:39–6.1**
Unlawful possession, exemptions, **2C:39–6**
Wireless telecommunications, hands free telephones, application of law, motor vehicles, **39:4–97.4**
Wiretapping and electronic surveillance, **2A:156A–1 et seq.**

LAW ENFORCEMENT OFFICERS MEMORIAL SCHOLARSHIP ACT
Generally, **39:3–27.123 et seq.**

LAW OF ROAD
Traffic Rules and Regulations, generally, this index

LAW SCHOOLS
Deans, judicial conference, membership, **Rule 1:35–1**
Students, appearance, **Rule 1:21–3**
Teachers, admission to practice, **Rule 1:27–3**

LAWS
Statutes, generally, this index

LAWSUITS
Actions and Proceedings, generally, this index

LAWYERS
Attorneys, generally, this index

LAWYERS FUND FOR CLIENT PROTECTION
Generally, **Rule 1:28–1 et seq.**

LEAD
Solid Waste, generally, this index

LEADING QUESTIONS
Generally, **Evidence Rule 611**

LEARNED TREATISES
Hearsay exceptions, **Evidence Rule 803**

LEARNERS PERMIT
Drivers Licenses, this index

LEASES
Commercial motor vehicle, weights and measurements, fines, **39:3–84.3**
Crimes and offenses, alcoholic beverage law violations, **33:1–54**
Landlord and Tenant, generally, this index
Motor vehicle commission, property needed to carry out law relating to inspection, **39:8–2**
Motor Vehicles, this index
Notice, drug offenses committed on premises, notice, **2C:35–16.1**

LEASES—Cont'd
Option of lessor to terminate lease for violation of alcoholic beverage law, **33:1–54**
Prostitution, **2C:34–1**
Seasonally leased premises, disorderly persons, termination of right to occupy or visit, **2C:43–8.1**
Turnpike authority, **27:23–14**

LEAVE OF COURT
Appeal and review, attorney disciplinary proceedings, constitutional issues, **Rule 1:20–16**
Attorneys, withdrawal or substitution, **Rule 1:11–2**
Interviewing jurors subsequent to trial, parties or attorneys, **Rule 1:16–1**

LEFT TURNING ACT
Generally, **39:4–123**

LEFT TURNS
Flashing lights on vehicle to indicate turn permitted, **39:3–54**
Intersections, right of way, **39:4–90**
Intersections controlled by traffic signals or officers, **39:4–115**
Green arrow as authorizing turn, **39:4–116**
Method of turning at intersections, **39:4–123**
Local authorities may determine, **39:4–124**
Passing on right of vehicle making left turn permitted, **39:4–85**
Right of way at intersection, **39:4–90**
Signal, continuous, **39:4–126**
Traffic signals or officers, intersections controlled by, **39:4–115**

LEGAL ADVERTISEMENTS
Advertisements, generally, this index

LEGAL AID SOCIETIES
Law students or graduates, appearance, **Rule 1:21–3**

LEGAL ASSISTANCE
Attorneys, generally, this index
Public Defenders, generally, this index

LEGAL ASSISTANTS
Indigent persons, representation, assisting, **Rule 1:21–1**

LEGAL HOLIDAYS
Computation of time, **Rule 1:3–1**

LEGAL SERVICES CORPORATIONS
Grants, interest on lawyers trust accounts fund, **Rule 1:28A–4**
Practice of law, **Rule 1:21–1**

LEGAL SERVICES SOCIETIES
Indigent persons, waiver of fees, **Rule 1:13–2**

LEGISLATION
Statutes, generally, this index

LEGISLATIVE COMMITTEES
Child abuse reports, access, **9:6–8.10a**

LEGISLATIVE DEPARTMENT
General Assembly, generally, this index
Senate, generally, this index

LEGISLATIVE FINDINGS
Public Policy, generally, this index

LEGISLATIVE INTENT
Criminal prosecutions, exclusion, defenses, **2C:2–5**

LEGISLATURE
General Assembly, generally, this index
Judicial conference, membership, **Rule 1:35–1**

LESSEES
Definitions, toll collection monitoring system, turnpike authority, **27:23–34.1**
Leases, generally, this index

LESSER INCLUDED OFFENSES
Juvenile delinquents and dependents, complaint, amendment, **Rule 5:20–1**

LESSER OFFENSES
Infractions, trial with criminal offenses, **Rule 3:15–3**

LESSORS
Definitions, toll collection monitoring system, turnpike authority, **27:23–34.1**
Leases, generally, this index

LETTER OPINIONS
Filing, **Rule 1:36–1**

LETTERING
Noncommercial trucks, **39:3–8.1**

LETTERS
Jury, corrupting or influencing, **2C:29–8**

LEVOMETHORPHAN
Controlled dangerous substance, **24:21–1 et seq.**

LEVOMORAMIDE
Controlled dangerous substance, **24:21–1 et seq.**

LEVOPHENACYLMORPHAN
Controlled dangerous substance, **24:21–1 et seq.**

LEVORPHANOL
Controlled dangerous substance, **24:21–1 et seq.**

LEVY
Attachment, generally, this index
Executions, generally, this index
Taxation, generally, this index

LEWDNESS AND OBSCENITY
Generally, **2C:14–4, 2C:34–1 et seq.**
Adult diagnostic and treatment centers, inmates, possession, distribution or exhibition, **2C:47–10**
Adults, **2C:34–2**
Children and minors,
Adult diagnostic and treatment centers, inmates, sanctions, **2C:47–10**
Endangering welfare of children, **2C:24–4**
Exposure, **2C:14–4**
Fines and penalties, **2C:43–3.8**
Presentation, **2C:34–3**
Prohibited sexual acts, photographs or films, **2C:24–4**
Racketeering, **2C:41–1**
Definitions,
Adults, **2C:34–2**
Children and minors, **2C:34–3**
Evidence, victims previous sexual conduct, **2C:14–7**
Language, offensive language, **2C:33–2**

LEWDNESS AND OBSCENITY—Cont'd
Nuisance, 2C:33–12
Public communications, 2C:34–4
Retailers, display, 2C:34–3.1, 2C:34–3.2
Sexually oriented businesses, 2C:33–12.2
Signs, 2C:34–7
Zoning and planning, 2C:34–7
Signs, sexually oriented businesses, 2C:34–7
Zoning and planning, sexually oriented businesses, 2C:34–7

LEWISITE
Turnpike project, transportation regulation, 27:23–31

LIABILITY
Damages, generally, this index

LIABILITY INSURANCE
See, also,
Insurance, generally, this index
Motor Vehicle Insurance, generally, this index
Arbitration and award, representation, **Rule 1:21–1**
Attorneys, this index
Automobile insurance. Motor Vehicle Insurance, generally, this index
Electric personal assistive mobility devices, 39:4–14.10
Evidence, **Evidence Rule 411**
Motor Vehicle Insurance, generally, this index

LIBEL AND SLANDER
Newspapers, generally, this index
Venue, trial, **Rule 3:14–1**

LIBERTY STATE PARK
Park police, power to arrest, 2A:154–6

LIBERTY STATE PARK LICENSE PLATE FUND
Generally, 39:3–27.94

LIBRARIES
Controlled substances, crimes and offenses, 2C:35–7.1
Crimes and offenses,
Controlled substances, 2C:35–7.1
Theft, 2C:20–12 et seq.
Museums, theft of library materials, 2C:20–12 et seq.
Schools and School Districts, this index
Signs, theft prevention, 2C:20–15
Theft of library material, 2C:20–12 et seq.

LIBRARY FACILITIES
Definitions, theft of library materials, 2C:20–12

LIBRARY MATERIAL
Definitions, theft, 2C:20–12
Purposeful concealment, 2C:20–13

LICENSE PLATES
Plates or markers. Motor Vehicles, this index

LICENSED ADMINISTRATORS
Medical professions, fees, controversies or disputes with patients, review committees, immunity from liability, 2A:84A–22.10

LICENSED BUILDING
Definitions, intoxicating liquor law, 33:1–1

LICENSED REAL ESTATE BROKER
Definitions, mobile or manufactured home dealers, 39:10–19

LICENSES AND PERMITS
Agricultural Machinery and Equipment, this index
Alcoholic Beverages, this index
Assault Firearms, this index
Attorneys, this index
Auto body repair facilities, 39:13–1 et seq.
Body repair facilities, vehicles, 39:13–1 et seq.
Buses, this index
Chiropractors, this index
Collectors of weapons,
Defaced firearms, 2C:39–9
Possession of prohibited weapons, 2C:39–3
Commuter Vans, this index
Contact lenses, dispensing, 2C:40–25
Conviction of Crime, this index
Corporations, this index
Counties of sixth class issuance to one permitting lapse of license while in armed forces, 33:1–12.22b
Definitions,
Financial responsibility, 39:6–24
Water pollution control, 58:10A–3
Dentists and Dentistry, this index
Detectives, this index
Driver License Compact Act, 39:5D–1 et seq.
Drivers Licenses, generally, this index
Drivers Schools, this index
Electrical contractors, crimes and offenses, unlicensed persons, 2C:21–33
Fireworks, this index
Fish and Game, this index
Fraternal Benefit Societies, this index
Health and Accident Insurance, this index
Health Care Professionals, this index
Health Maintenance Organizations, this index
Highways and Roads, this index
Identification lights, motor vehicles, private detective businesses, community security services, 39:3–54.14
Limousine or Livery Service, this index
Machine guns, 2C:58–5
Marriage, this index
Motor Carriers, this index
Motor Vehicle Commission, this index
Motor Vehicle Junk Yards, this index
Motor Vehicles, this index
Motorcycles, this index
Municipalities, this index
Music Licensing Practices Act. Trademarks and Trade Names, generally, this index
Nurses, this index
Ophthalmic Dispensers and Technicians, this index
Optometrists, this index
Outdoor Advertising, this index
Parking, private driveways, 39:4–138.3 et seq.
Partnerships, this index
Pharmacists, this index
Physical Therapists, this index
Physicians and Surgeons, this index
Podiatrists and Podiatry, this index
Police and Police Departments, this index
Private detective businesses, community security services, motor vehicle identification lights, 39:3–54.14
Psychologists and Psychology, this index
Public Adjusters, this index
Radio and radio stations, transmissions, 2C:33–23.1
Crimes and offenses, 2C:33–23.2
Recreational vehicles, off site sales, 39:10–19.1 et seq.
Rehabilitated convicted offenders, 2A:168A–1 et seq.

LICENSES AND PERMITS—Cont'd
Religious Corporations and Associations, this index
Restaurants, intoxicating liquors, consumption on premises, Chain Store Liquor License Act, 33:1–12.32
Retired law enforcement officers, firearms, possession, 2C:39–6, 2C:39–6.1
Rockets, 21:1C–4
School Buses, this index
Taxicabs, this index
Veterans Associations and Organizations, this index
Weapons, this index

LICENSING AUTHORITY
Definitions, drivers licenses, 39:5D–10

LIE DETECTOR TESTS
Drug manufacturers, employees, 2C:40A–1
Employer requiring, 2C:40A–1

LIENS AND INCUMBRANCES
Alcoholic beverages, licenses and permits, 33:1–26
Assessments, generally, this index
Discharge, sex offenders, DNA database and databank, tests, costs, 53:1–20.35, 53:1–20.36
DNA database and databank, tests, costs, 53:1–20.29 et seq.
Intoxicating liquor license, 33:1–26
Leases, generally, this index
Manufactured homes, sales, certificates of ownership, 39:10–15.1
Mobile homes and mobile home parks, sales, certificates of ownership, 39:10–15.1
Mortgages, generally, this index
Motor Vehicles, this index
Priorities, **Rule 1:13–8**
Property, seized or forfeited under alcoholic beverage law, 33:1–66
Public Defenders, this index
Recognizances, this index
Sex offenders, DNA database and databank, tests, costs, 53:1–20.29 et seq.
Superior court clerk, public defenders, services, 2A:158A–18

LIFE EXPECTANCY TABLES
Evidence, **Rule 1:13–5**

LIGHT MEDIUM DUTY
Definitions, tow trucks and towing companies, 39:3–84.6

LIGHTS AND LIGHTING
All terrain vehicles, 39:3C–19
Equipment, 39:3C–24
Exemptions, special events, 39:3C–23
Animal drawn vehicles, 39:4–25
Automated teller machine locations, security measures. Electronic Fund Transfers, generally, this index
Automobiles. Motor vehicles, generally, post
Bicycles, 39:4–10, 39:4–14.4
Dirt bikes, 39:3C–19, 39:3C–24
Exemptions, special events, 39:3C–23
Driving lamps. Motor vehicles, generally, post
Electric light plants. Electricity and Electric Companies, generally, this index
Emergency Vehicles, this index
False lights, loss or destruction of vessels, 2C:12–2
Fines and penalties, animal drawn vehicles, violation of law requiring lights, 39:4–25
Flashing Lights, generally, this index

LIGHTS AND LIGHTING—Cont'd

Headlamps. Motor vehicles, post

Highways and roads, rotating or flashing lights, **39:4–60.1 et seq.**

Hijack lights, omnibuses, **39:3–54**

Laser lighting devices, transportation, interference, **2C:33–14**

Laser sighting system devices, aggravated assault, **2C:12–1**

Motor vehicles,

Agricultural machinery or implements, **39:3–65**

Applicability of law relating to lights, **39:3–45**

Amber lamp, **39:3–61.4**

Amber parking lights, approval, **39:3–62**

Amber warning lights, public utilities, **39:3–54.24, 39:3–54.25**

Approval by director, **39:3–61**

Approved, definitions, **39:3–46**

Auxiliary driving lamps, **39:3–51**

Color, **39:3–50**

Definitions, **39:3–46**

Back up lamps, **39:3–52**

Color, **39:3–50**

Visibility, **39:3–48**

Beam indicator lights, **39:3–59**

Buses, **39:3–61**

Class A reflector, visibility, **39:3–48**

Class B reflector, visibility, **39:3–48**

Clear road beam, definitions, **39:3–46**

Clearance lamps,

Combining with tail or identification lamps, **39:3–61.2**

Regulations, **39:3–63**

Visibility, **39:3–48**

Color, **39:3–50**

Combining into one shell or housing, **39:3–61.2**

Compliance with statute and conditions of approval required, **39:3–47**

Construction and location, regulations by director, **39:3–63**

Courtesy lamp, color, **39:3–50**

Cowl lamps, color of light, **39:3–52**

Dazzling lights, spot lamps, use, **39:3–53**

Dimming of lights, parked vehicles, **39:3–62**

Director, rules and regulations, **39:3–63**

Display, when required, **39:3–61**

Distance of illumination of certain lamps, **39:3–54**

Driving lights, number required or permitted, **39:3–56**

Emergency motor vehicles, color, **39:3–50**

Emergency warning light equipment, **39:3–64**

Farm tractors, **39:3–65**

Applicability of law relating to lights, **39:3–45**

Fender lamps, **39:3–52**

Color, **39:3–50**

Fines and penalties, **39:3–66.2**

Flashing lights, **39:3–54**

Flat bed vehicles, mounting, **39:3–61.1**

Headlamps, **39:3–48, 39:3–49, 39:3–61**

Alternate equipment, **39:3–55**

Approved headlamps not required, **39:3–55**

Asymmetric headlamps, definitions, **39:3–46**

Color of light, **39:3–50**

Motorcycle equipped with side car, **39:3–49**

Unapproved lamps, **39:3–55**

Definitions, **39:3–46**

Failure to use when required, fines and penalties, **39:3–47**

LIGHTS AND LIGHTING—Cont'd

Motor vehicles—Cont'd

Headlamps—Cont'd

Multiple beam headlamps, **39:3–58**

Definitions, **39:3–46**

Use, **39:3–60**

Single beam headlamps, **39:3–57**

Definitions, **39:3–46**

Use, requirement, **39:3–46**

Height, tail lights, **39:3–61.1**

Hijack lights, omnibuses, **39:3–54**

Identification lamps,

Mounting, **39:3–61.1**

Visibility, **39:3–48**

Intensity of light or beam of headlamps, **39:3–58**

Interior lights, law enforcement stops, **39:4–57.1**

License plate, **39:3–48, 39:3–61**

Color, **39:3–50**

Lower beam, definitions, **39:3–46**

Maintenance and mounting, **39:3–66**

Meeting beam, definitions, **39:3–46**

Mounting, **39:3–61.1**

Omnibuses, hijack lights, **39:3–54**

Operation without required lights, prohibition, **39:3–47**

Overhang, **39:3–61.4**

Parked vehicles, **39:3–62**

Parking lights, **39:3–61**

Visability, **39:3–48**

Permit for using certain color lights, **39:3–50**

Projecting loads,

Color, **39:3–50**

Marker lamps, **39:3–61.4**

Rear lights, **39:3–61**

Combining with clearance lamp, **39:3–61.2**

Parked vehicles, **39:3–62**

Requirements as to all vehicles, **39:3–65**

Visibility, **39:3–48**

Rear registration marker, **39:3–61**

Red lights,

Carrying red electric lanterns and placing on highways, **39:3–64**

Overhanging loads, **39:3–61.4**

Commercial or motor drawn vehicles, **39:3–84**

Rear lamps, **39:3–61**

Traffic signals, duty to stop, **39:4–105, 39:4–119**

Volunteer fire company chief or first assistant chief, **39:3–54.15 et seq.**

Reflectors,

Carrying red reflector emergency warning devices and placing on highways, **39:3–64**

Combining into one shell or housing, **39:3–61.2**

Definitions, **39:3–46**

License plates, **39:3–33**

Maintenance and mounting, **39:3–66**

Mounting, **39:3–61.1**

Overhanging loads, **39:3–48, 39:3–61.4**

Rear reflectors, **39:3–61**

Regulations by director, **39:3–63**

Trucks, **39:3–61**

Requirements, applicability to all vehicles, **39:3–65**

Retroreflective surface on vehicle, regulation by director, **39:3–63**

Road machinery and rollers, **39:3–65**

Applicability of law relating to lights, **39:3–45**

Rotating or flashing lights on or near highways, **39:4–60.1 et seq.**

Running board, color, **39:3–50**

LIGHTS AND LIGHTING—Cont'd

Motor vehicles—Cont'd

Running board lamps, **39:3–52**

School buses, color, **39:3–50**

Side marker lamps, **39:3–63**

Mounting, **39:3–61.1**

Side reflectors, **39:3–48**

Special permit, **39:3–50**

Spot lamps, **39:3–53**

Color, **39:3–50**

Stop lights, **39:3–61**

Combination with turn signal prohibited, **39:3–61.2**

Indicating application of brakes, **39:3–61.3**

Visibility, **39:3–48**

Tail lights, **39:3–61.1**

Traction engines, **39:3–65**

Applicability of law relating to lights, **39:3–45**

Traffic hazard warning signals, **39:3–64**

Turn signals,

Color, **39:3–50**

Flashing simultaneously as hazard warning, **39:3–64**

Not to be combined with head lamp or other lighting device, **39:3–61.2**

Regulations by director, **39:3–63**

Required, **39:3–61**

Visibility, **39:3–48**

Unregistered vehicles, permits to cross public highways, **39:3–26.2**

Visibility,

Lights required on all vehicles, **39:3–65**

Rear reflectors, **39:3–61**

Requirements applicable, when, **39:3–48**

When lights are required, **39:3–46**

Volunteer fire companies,

Flashing lights, **39:3–54.7 et seq.**

Red lights, **39:3–54.15 et seq.**

Warning lights, **39:3–54**

Hijack lights, omnibuses, **39:3–54**

When lighted lamps are required, definitions, **39:3–46**

White light to illuminate rear registration marker, **39:3–61**

Omnibuses, hijack lights, **39:3–54**

Outdoor advertising, **27:5–9**

Rear lights,

Animal drawn vehicles, **39:4–25**

Bicycles, **39:4–10**

Motor vehicles, ante

Red lights,

Motor vehicles, ante

Traffic control signals, **39:4–119**

Reflectors,

Bicycles, **39:4–14.4**

Buttons or panels, **39:4–191.2**

Motor vehicles, ante

Portable red emergency reflectors, **39:3–64**

Traffic markings, **39:4–191.6**

Road rollers, **39:3–65**

Applicability of law relating to lights, **39:3–45**

School Buses, this index

Snowmobiles, **39:3C–19**

Exemptions, special events, **39:3C–23**

Stop lights. Rear lights, generally, ante

Traffic markings, **39:4–191.6**

Traffic rules and regulations. Motor vehicles, generally, ante

Traffic Signs and Signals, generally, this index

Turn signals. Motor vehicles, ante

Vehicles. Motor vehicles, generally, ante

Volunteer firemen,

Chief or first assistant chief, red lights on vehicles, **39:3–54.15 et seq.**

Flashing lights, vehicles, **39:3–54.7 et seq.**

LIMITATION OF ACTIONS
See, also, Limitation of Criminal Prosecutions, generally, this index
Capital offenses, postconviction relief, petitions, **Rule 3:22–12**
Civil actions, based on code of criminal justice, 2C:1–6
Code of Criminal Justice, basis for civil actions, 2C:1–6
Contraband, seized property, claims, 2C:64–8
Controlled substances, dealers, liability, 2C:35B–14
Crimes and offenses, postconviction relief, petitions, **Rule 3:22–12**
Criminal prosecution. Limitation of Criminal Prosecutions, generally, this index
Judgments and Decrees, this index
Monopolies and unfair trade, suspension of statute, 56:9–15
Motor vehicles, tort claims, arbitration and award, tolling, limitation, 39:6A–26
No fault insurance, motor vehicles, 39:6A–13.1
Parking, crimes and offenses, 39:4–139.10a
Recognizances, this index
State police, complaints, 53:1–33
Torts, motor vehicles, arbitration and award, tolling of limitation, 39:6A–26
Toxic packaging reduction, 13:1E–99.54

LIMITATION OF CRIMINAL PROSECUTIONS
See, also, Limitation of Actions, generally, this index
Generally, 2C:1–6
Homicide, time between assault and death of victim, 2C:11–2.1
Monopolies and unfair trade, suspension of statute, 56:9–15
Postconviction relief, **Rule 3:22–12**
Terrorism, 2C:1–6
Traffic law violation, 39:5–3
Appeal as waiving limitations, 39:5–11

LIMITED ACCESS HIGHWAYS
Definitions, Motor Vehicle Law, 39:1–1
Highways and Roads, this index

LIMITED ADMISSIBILITY
Generally, **Evidence Rule 105**

LIMITED CERTIFICATION
Attorneys, **Rule 1:21–3**

LIMITED LIABILITY COMPANIES
Limited liability partnerships. Partnerships, this index
Usury, maximum rates, 2C:21–19

LIMITED LIABILITY ENTITIES
Attorneys, this index

LIMITED LIABILITY PARTNERSHIPS
Partnerships, this index

LIMITED PARTNERSHIP
Limited liability partnerships. Partnerships, this index

LIMITED PARTNERSHIP ASSOCIATIONS
Limited liability partnerships. Partnerships, this index

LIMOUSINE OR LIVERY SERVICE
Applications, drivers, 39:5G–2
Criminal history record information, drivers, 39:5G–2
Drivers, 39:5G–2

LIMOUSINE OR LIVERY SERVICE—Cont'd
Fees, plates or markers, 39:3–19.5
Fines and penalties, 39:5G–1
Licenses and permits, 39:5G–2
Fingerprints and fingerprinting, drivers, 39:5G–2
Fires and fire protection, extinguishers, fines and penalties, 39:5G–1
First aid, fines and penalties, 39:5G–1
Foreign states, licenses and permits, 39:3–19.6
Intoxicating liquors,
Passengers, 39:4–51a
Plenary retail transit license, 33:1–12
Licenses and permits,
Fines and penalties, 39:5G–1
Nonresidents, 39:3–19.6
Limousine, definitions, intoxicating liquor law, 33:1–1
Nonresidents, licenses and permits, 39:3–19.6
Passengers, intoxicating liquors, 39:4–51a
Plates or markers, 39:3–19.5
Fines and penalties, 39:5G–1
Safety, fines and penalties, 39:5G–1
Sideboards, fines and penalties, 39:5G–1
Smoking in public, 2C:33–13
Telecommunications, fines and penalties, 39:5G–1

LINEUPS
Investigative detention, **Rule 3:5A–1 et seq.**

LIQUEFIED PETROLEUM GAS
Generally, **21:1B–1 et seq.**
Abatement, violations, 21:1B–6
Actions and proceedings, violations, 21:1B–6
Boards and commissions, liquefied petroleum gas education and safety board, 21:1B–12 et seq.
Buildings, inspections, 21:1B–3
Compromise and settlement, fines and penalties, 21:1B–5
Conflicts of law, local ordinances or regulations, 21:1B–7
Consumer protection, education and safety board, 21:1B–12 et seq.
Containers, distribution, restrictions, 21:1B–4
Declaration of necessity, 21:1B–8
Definitions,
Education and safety board, 21:1B–1
School buses, 39:3B–13
Distribution, containers and receptacles, restrictions, 21:1B–4
Education, liquefied petroleum gas education and safety board, 21:1B–12 et seq.
Fines and penalties, 21:1B–5
Funds, education and safety board, 21:1B–15
Hearings, rules and regulations, 21:1B–2
Housing, inspection, 21:1B–3
Injunction, violations, 21:1B–6
Inspectors and inspections, 21:1B–3
Installations, inspection, 21:1B–3
Labor and industry commissioner,
Rules and regulations, 21:1B–2
Transfer of powers and duties, state police, 21:1B–9 et seq.
Liquefied petroleum gas education and safety board, 21:1B–12 et seq.
Local regulations, conflicts of law, 21:1B–7
Municipalities, conflicts of law, 21:1B–7
Notice,
Correct violation of law, rule or regulation, 21:1B–6
Orders, violations, 21:1B–6
Orders, violations, 21:1B–6
Ordinances, conflicts of law, 21:1B–7
Predominately residential, definitions, 21:1B–3

LIQUEFIED PETROLEUM GAS—Cont'd
Receptacles, distribution, restrictions, 21:1B–4
Reports, education and safety board, 21:1B–13
Residential buildings, inspections, 21:1B–3
Rules and regulations, 21:1B–2
Safety, liquefied petroleum gas education and safety board, 21:1B–12 et seq.
Sales, containers and receptacles, restrictions, 21:1B–4
School buses, 39:3B–13 et seq.
State police, transfer of powers and duties, 21:1B–9 et seq.
Transfer of powers and duties, state police, labor and industry commissioner, 21:1B–9 et seq.
Violations, prosecution, 21:1B–6

LIQUIDATED DAMAGES
Damages, generally, this index

LIQUIDS
Alcoholic Beverages, generally, this index
Shellac, turnpike project, transportation regulation, 27:23–31

LIQUORS
Alcoholic Beverages, generally, this index

LISTS
Bicycle helmets that meet legal standards, 39:4–10.1
Drivers schools, 39:12–2.2
Jury Lists, generally, this index
Motorized bicycles, approved bicycles, 39:4–14.3n

LITTERING
Adopt a beach program. Beaches and Beach Fronts, this index
Fines and penalties, motor vehicles, 39:4–64
Motor vehicles, 39:4–63 et seq.
Rebuttable presumptions, drivers or owners responsibility, motor vehicles, 39:4–64
Traffic rules and regulations, 39:4–63 et seq.

LIVE ASHES
Throwing or dropping from vehicle on highway, 39:4–64

LIVESTOCK
Domestic, humane treatment, 4:22–16.1
Domestic livestock, definitions, 4:22–16.1

LOADING ISLANDS
Safety zones, 39:4–196.2

LOADS AND LOADING
Axle weight limitations, 39:3–84, 39:3–84.1
Backing to curb to load or unload, prohibition, 39:4–79
Bridges and viaducts, driving overweight vehicles on,
Interstate bridge, 39:4–76
Intrastate bridge, 39:4–75
Constructor,
Application of limitations as to weight of vehicle and load, 39:3–84.1
License plates, 39:3–20
Damages from violation of weight limitations, liability, 39:3–84.4
Delay in traffic because of condition or loading of vehicle to be avoided, 39:4–56
Exceeding provision of registration certificate, 39:3–20
Fines and penalties,
Distributing load according to tire width, 39:3–82

LOADS AND LOADING—Cont'd
Fines and penalties—Cont'd
Flat bed motor vehicles or motor drawn vehicles, **39:4–77**
Refusal to stop and submit to measurement or weighing, **39:3–84.3**
Flat bed motor vehicles or motor drawn vehicles, **39:4–77**
Gross wheel loads, **39:3–84**
Information plate on certain vehicles to show allowable load, **39:3–82**
Iron, precautions against noise required, **39:4–78**
License and registration of vehicles, fees, **39:3–20**
Lights, **39:3–61.4**
Maximum weight of motor vehicle and load, **39:3–84, 39:3–84.1**
Maximum width and length of motor vehicle and load, **39:3–84**
Motor vehicle inspector, stopping vehicle to submit to measurement or weighing, **39:3–84.3**
Parking for purpose of loading or unloading passengers or materials, time permitted, **39:4–139**
Partial invalidity of act, **39:3–84.5**
Red flag or light required, overhanging loads, **39:3–84**
Registration certificate, unlawful to operate vehicle in excess of weight provided on certificate, **39:3–20**
Signal for turn or stop obscured, mechanical signal required, **39:4–126**
Solid waste, application of limitations as to weight of vehicle and load, **39:3–84.1**
Spilling of contents by vehicles prohibited, **39:4–77**
State police, stopping vehicle to submit to measurement or weighing, **39:3–84.3**
Tire width, distribution of load as governed by, **39:3–82**

LOANS
See, also, Credit, generally, this index
Brewer to retail licensee, **33:1–43.1**
Criminal usury, **2C:21–19**
Motor Vehicles, this index
Usury. Interest, this index
Veterans, this index
Weapons, security for loans, **2C:39–11**

LOCAL AGENCIES
Definitions, water pollution control, **58:10A–3**

LOCAL AUTHORITIES
Definitions, traffic regulations, **39:1–1**

LOCAL BOARD
Definitions, food and drugs, **24:21–32**

LOCAL BOARD OF HEALTH
Definitions, food and drugs, **24:21–32**

LOCAL GOVERNMENT
Political Subdivisions, generally, this index

LOCAL HEALTH BOARDS
Actions and proceedings, solid waste facilities, notice, **13:1E–9**
Dead Bodies, generally, this index
Emergency fuel oil delivery. Landlord and Tenant, generally, this index
Fuel oil delivery, emergency. Landlord and Tenant, generally, this index
Rules and regulations. Dead Bodies, generally, this index

LOCAL HEALTH BOARDS—Cont'd
Solid waste facilities, compliance with regulations, **13:1E–9**

LOCAL LAWS
Conflict with or preemption by code of criminal justice, **2C:1–5**
Ordinances, generally, this index

LOCAL OPTION ACT (INTOXICATING LIQUORS)
Generally, **33:1–44 et seq.**

LOCAL REGISTRARS OF VITAL STATISTICS
Birth Certificates, generally, this index

LOCAL UNITS
Counties, generally, this index
Municipalities, generally, this index

LOCATION
Explosives, distances and quantity, manufacturing and storage, **21:1A–135**
Juvenile delinquents and dependents, detention, **2A:4A–37**
Outdoor advertising, **27:5–9**

LOCKS
Motor vehicles,
Ignition interlock devices, intoxication of driver, **39:4–50.16 et seq.**
Master keys or devices, **2C:5–6**
Trigger locks. Weapons, this index
Weapons, handguns, **2C:58–2**

LOCKUPS
Jails, generally, this index

LOITERING
Illegal use, possession or sale of controlled dangerous substances, public places, **2C:33–2.1**
Prostitution, **2C:34–1.1**
Public place, definitions, **2C:33–2.1**

LOITERING FOR THE PURPOSE OF ENGAGING IN PROSTITUTION
Generally, **2C:34–1.1**

LONG ARM ACT
Generally, **39:7–1 et seq.**

LONG TERM CARE FACILITIES
Nursing Homes or Hospitals, generally, this index

LOSSES
Definitions, fines and penalties, **2C:43–3**

LOST PROPERTY
Theft, **2C:20–6**
Weapons, reports, **2C:58–19**

LOTS
Parking Lots and Facilities, generally, this index

LOTTERIES
Generally, **2C:37–6, 2C:37–6.1**
Defenses, **2C:37–6**
Definitions, **2C:37–1**
Foreign countries, **2C:37–6.1**
Foreign states, **2C:37–6**
Manufacturers and manufacturing, tickets, **2C:37–6.1**
Possession, tickets, **2C:37–6.1**
Sales, tickets, **2C:37–6.1**

LOTTERIES—Cont'd
Tickets, manufacturing, **2C:37–6.1**

LOW INCOME PERSONS
Indigent Persons, generally, this index

LOW SPEED VEHICLES
Generally, **39:4–31.1 et seq.**
Definitions, traffic rules and regulations, **39:1–1**

LOWER BEAM
Definitions, **39:3–46**

LP GAS
Liquefied Petroleum Gas, generally, this index

LUNGS
Deborah heart and lung center, motor vehicles, special plates, **39:3–27.107 et seq.**

LURING AND ENTICING
Generally, **2C:13–7**
Children and minors, **2C:13–6**

LYSERGIC ACID
Controlled dangerous substance, **24:21–1 et seq.**

LYSERGIC ACID AMIDE
Controlled dangerous substance, **24:21–1 et seq.**

LYSERGIC ACID DIETHYLAMIDE
Controlled dangerous substance, **24:21–1 et seq.**

MACHINE GUNS
See, also, Assault Firearms, generally, this index
Conviction, crime involving use of,
Extended term of imprisonment,
Criteria for sentence of, **2C:44–3**
Eligibility for parole, **2C:43–7**
Term of imprisonment, **2C:43–6**
Definitions, **2C:39–1**
Disorderly persons, advertisements, **2C:39–15**
Licenses, **2C:58–5**
Manufacture, transport, disposition and defacement, **2C:39–9**
Person convicted of crime involving, possession of any weapon prohibited, **2C:39–7**
Previous conviction, crime involving use of, term of imprisonment, **2C:43–6**
Unlawful possession, **2C:39–5**

MACHINERY AND EQUIPMENT
Agricultural Machinery and Equipment, generally, this index
Dirt bikes, **39:3C–24**
Electric personal assistive mobility devices, safety, operation, **39:4–14.10**
Fire Engines, Apparatus and Equipment, generally, this index
Heat, this index
Helmets, generally, this index
Motor Carriers, this index
Moving Heavy Machinery, generally, this index
Municipal courts, **2B:12–15**
Nuclear power plants, tampering, crimes and offenses, **2C:17–7 et seq.**
Public utilities, motor vehicles, special mobile equipment, length of vehicles, **39:3–84**
Tractors and Traction Engines, this index
Turnpike authority, hiring, bids, **27:23–6.1**
Violent criminal apprehension program (VICAP, purchase, **53:1–20.14**

MAGAZINES
Explosives, this index

MAGISTRATES COURTS
Municipal Courts, generally, this index

MAGNESIUM
Turnpike projects, transportation of powdered
    metallic magnesium, regulation, **27:23–31**

MAIL AND MAILING
Certified or registered mail,
    Alcoholic beverage license, notice,
        Refusal to issue license, **33:1–22**
        Suspension or revocation, **33:1–31**
    Notice, motor vehicles, abandoned or un-
        claimed, sale, **39:10A–1**
    Process,
        Enlargement of time for response, **Rule
            1:3–3**
        Nonresidents, **39:7–3**
        Motorist, **39:3–7**
        Notice,
            Application for correction,
                Motor vehicle title papers, **39:10–16**
                Of motor vehicle title papers,
                    39:10–16
            Hearing on, suspension or revocation of
                license, motor vehicle dealers li-
                cense, **39:10–20**
            Proceeding to revoke motor vehicle regis-
                tration or drivers license, **39:5–30**
    Service, **Rules 1:5–2, 1:5–4**
        Proof of service, **Rule 1:5–3**
    Drivers licenses, probationary licenses,
        39:3–13.4
    Electric personal assistive mobility devices, offi-
        cers and employees, operation, **39:4–14.10**
    Habitual offenders, motor vehicles, license sus-
        pensions, **39:5–30b**
    Jurors, service of summons, **2B:20–8**
    Motor Vehicles, this index
    Municipal courts, guilty plea, nontraffic of-
        fenses, **Rule 7:6–3**
    Notice,
        Certified or registered mail, ante
        Habitual offenders, motor vehicles, license
            suspensions, **39:5–30b**
        Hearings,
            Alcoholic beverage control division di-
                rector after seizure of stills, **33:2–4**
            Forfeiture, property seized under Alcohol-
                ic Beverage Law, **33:1–66**
        License suspensions, motor vehicles, habitual
            offenders, **39:5–30b**
        Motor vehicles, habitual offenders, license
            suspensions, **39:5–30b**
        Refusal of issuing authority,
            Grant refund of alcoholic beverage license
                fee, **33:1–31**
            Revoke or suspend alcoholic beverage li-
                cense, **33:1–31**
    Officers and employees, electric personal assis-
        tive mobility devices, operation, **39:4–14.10**
    Process. Certified or registered mail, ante
    Registered mail. Certified or registered mail,
        generally, ante
    Right of way, processions, **39:4–93**
    Rural mail routes, vehicles used on not com-
        mercial cars, **39:3–2**
    Service, **Rule 1:5–2 et seq.**
    Vehicles, right of way, processions, **39:4–93**

MAINTENANCE OF PERSONS
Support of Persons, generally, this index

MAJOR DISASTERS
Attorneys, temporary practice of law, foreign
    states, **Rule 1:21–10**

MAJOR FACILITIES
Definitions, water pollution control, **58:10A–3**

MALFEASANCE IN OFFICE
Mandatory sentence, **2C:43–6.5**

MALPRACTICE
Professional corporations, insurance, **Rule
    1:21–1A**

**MALT ALCOHOLIC BEVERAGE PRAC-
TICES ACT**
Generally, **33:1–93.12 et seq.**

MALT BEVERAGES
Alcoholic Beverages, this index

MAMMALS
Animals, generally, this index
Fish and Game, generally, this index

MANAGED CARE PLANS
Health Maintenance Organizations, generally,
    this index

MANAGERS AND MANAGEMENT
Person under Alcoholic Beverage Law, **33:1–1**

MANDATORY SENTENCE
Generally, **2C:43–6**
Sex offenders, treatment, **2C:47–3**

MANSLAUGHTER
Generally, **2C:11–2, 2C:11–4**
Aggravated manslaughter, **2C:11–4**
    Hit and run drivers, **2C:11–5.1**
        Fleeing from law enforcement officers,
            2C:11–4
Arrest warrant,
    Issuance, **Rule 3:3–1**
    Release, **Rule 3:4–1**
Attempts, body vests, **2C:39–13**
Bail, authority to admit to, **Rule 3:26–2**
Body vests, **2C:39–13**
Duress, defense, **2C:2–9**
Extended term of imprisonment, **2C:43–7,
    2C:43–7.1**
Jurors, peremptory challenges, **2B:23–13; Rule
    1:8–3**
Juvenile delinquents and dependents, referral
    to other courts without juveniles consent,
    Rule 5:22–2
Limitation of criminal prosecutions, **2C:1–6**
Strict liability, fleeing, law enforcement,
    2C:11–4
Weapons, possession, mandatory sentence,
    2C:43–6

MANUAL TRAINING
Vocational Education, generally, this index

MANUFACTURE
Definitions,
    Controlled dangerous substances, **24:21–2**
    Controlled substances, **24:21–2**

MANUFACTURED HOMES
    See, also, Mobile Homes and Mobile Home
        Parks, generally, this index
Certificates of ownership,
    Application of law, **39:10–2**
    Relocation, **39:10–11.1**
    Sales, **39:10–15.1**
Dealers, licensed real estate brokers, **39:10–19**

MANUFACTURED HOMES—Cont'd
Delivery, registration plates, **39:3–20.1**
House type semitrailer, special permits, **39:3–8**
Landlord and tenant, abandonment, disposi-
    tion, certificates of ownership, **39:10–15.1**
Licenses and permits, house type semitrailer,
    transportation, **39:3–8**
Liens and incumbrances, sales, certificates of
    ownership, **39:10–15.1**
Notice, relocation, certificates of ownership,
    39:10–11.1
Real estate brokers, dealers, **39:10–19**
Registration plates, transportation, **39:3–20.1**
Sales,
    Certificates of ownership, **39:10–15.1**
    Real estate brokers, **39:10–19**
Transportation, house type semitrailer, special
    permits, **39:3–8**

**MANUFACTURERS AND MANUFACTUR-
ING**
Alcoholic Beverages, this index
Burglar tools, plans or instructions, publishing,
    2C:5–5
Chemicals, chemistry and chemists, industrial
    chemicals, **2C:35–29**
Clothing, sale, **2A:123–3 et seq.**
Controlled Substances, this index
Definitions,
    Certificate of Motor Vehicle Ownership
        Law, **39:10–2**
    Chemicals, chemistry and chemists, industrial
        chemicals, **2C:35–29**
    Controlled substances, **2C:35–2**
    Firearms, **2C:39–1**
    Industrial chemicals, **2C:35–29**
    Intoxicating liquor law, **33:1–1**
    Motor vehicles, **39:1–1**
Drugs and Medicine, this index
Electronic surveillance equipment, **2A:156A–5**
Explosives, this index
Firearms, registration, **2C:58–1**
Fireworks, this index
Flammable fabrics, **2A:123–3 et seq.**
Frozen Desserts and Dietary Foods, generally,
    this index
Homes. Manufactured Homes, generally, this
    index
Identity theft, personal identifying information,
    2C:21–17.3
Industrial chemicals, **2C:35–29**
Lottery tickets, **2C:37–6.1**
Monopolies, generally, this index
Motor Vehicles, this index
Motorcycles, brands, marks and labels, safety,
    certificates and certification, **39:3–76.3a**
Nuisances, controlled dangerous substances,
    24:21–35
Number, required on motor vehicles, **39:10–7**
Personalized handguns, **2C:58–2.4, 2C:58–2.5**
Poisoned liquors, **33:3–9**
Registration of motor vehicles owned or con-
    trolled by, **39:3–18**
Weapons, this index
Wiretapping or electronic surveillance equip-
    ment, **2A:156A–5**

MAPS AND PLATS
Controlled substances, distribution or posses-
    sion, location, evidence, **2C:35–7.1**
Drugs and medicine, criminal prosecutions, de-
    piction of area surrounding schools,
    2C:35–7
School Buildings and Grounds, this index
Zoning and Planning, generally, this index

MARIJUANA

See, also, Drugs and Medicine, generally, this index
Generally, **24:21–1 et seq.**
Definitions, 24:21–2
Controlled substances, 2C:35–2, 24:21–2
Expungement, record, 2C:52–2
Young drug offenders, 2C:52–5
Fines and penalties, comprehensive study, **24:21–44**
Records and recordation, expungement, 2C:52–2
Wiretapping and electronic surveillance, 2A:156A–1 et seq.

MARINE CORPS

Armed Forces, generally, this index
Veterans, generally, this index

MARINE EQUIPMENT

Boats and Boating, generally, this index

MARINE PATROL

Weapons, unlawful possession, exemption, 2C:39–6

MARITAL STATUS

Marriage, generally, this index

MARKERS

See, also, Brands, Labels and Marks, generally, this index
Definitions, tow trucks and towing companies, 39:3–84.6
Fences, invisible fences, 2C:40–20
Method of turning vehicles at intersections indicated by, 39:4–124

MARKETING AND DISTRIBUTION OF AGRICULTURAL AND OTHER PRODUCTS

Agricultural Products, generally, this index

MARKETS AND MARKETING

Agricultural Products, generally, this index
Reports, hearsay exception, **Evidence Rule 803**

MARKS AND MARKING

Brands, Labels and Marks, generally, this index
Exhibits, verbatim records of proceedings, **Rule 1:2–3**
Trademarks and Trade Names, generally, this index

MARRIAGE

See, also, Spouses, generally, this index
Accomplices and accessories, bigamy, 2C:24–1
Certificates and certification, hearsay exception, **Evidence Rule 803**
Construction of rules, **Rule 1:1–2**
Crimes and offenses, support, willful nonsupport, 2C:24–5
Custody. Children and Minors, this index
Death, bigamy, defense, 2C:24–1
Domestic Violence, generally, this index
Judges, parties or attorneys, relationship, disqualification, **Rule 1:12–1**
Judgments and decrees, bigamy, defense, 2C:24–1
Licenses and permits, immigration and naturalization, improper retention, crimes and offenses, 2C:21–31
Sexual offenses, 2C:14–5
Support of Persons, generally, this index

MARRIAGE COUNSELORS

Privileges and immunities, **Evidence Rule 510**

MARRIED WOMEN

Spouses, generally, this index

MARSHALS

Qualifications, 2A:154–2

MASOCHISM

Children and minors, crimes, films and pictures, 2C:24–4

MASS TRANSPORTATION

Computers, interference, crimes and offenses, 2C:20–25
Controlled substances, entry on property, injunctions, 2C:35–5.10

MASTER AND SERVANT

Labor and Employment, generally, this index

MASTER KEYS

Motor vehicles, 2C:5–6

MASTURBATION

Children and minors, crimes, films and pictures, 2C:24–4

MATCHES

Throwing or dropping from vehicle on highway, 39:4–64

MATERIAL WITNESS

Witnesses, this index

MATRIMONIAL ACTIONS OR SUITS

Family Actions, generally, this index

MAYHEM

Wiretapping and electronic surveillance, 2A:156A–1 et seq.

MAYORS

Appointments by mayor, municipal court judges, 2B:12–4
Motor vehicles, special plates, 39:3–27.42
Former mayors, 39:3–27.114
Notice, violation of criminal law, 2A:152–12, 2A:152–13
Prevention, violation of criminal laws, duty after notice, 2A:152–12, 2A:152–13

MEALS

Jury, dispersal, **Rule 1:8–6**

MEANS OF CONVEYANCE

Definitions, theft, 2C:20–10

MEAT AND MEAT PRODUCTS

Truck used for transportation of solid waste, use for transportation of,
Cleansing and sanitization required, 48:13A–12.1
Crime of third degree, penalties, 48:13A–12.2

MEAT MARKETS

Intoxicating liquors, limited retail distribution license, 33:1–12

MECHANICAL PRODUCTS

Alcohol in products unfit for beverage purposes, 33:1–30

MECHANISM

Machinery and Equipment, generally, this index

MEDALS

Congressional medal of honor, motor vehicle fee registration, holders, 39:3–27.1

MEDIA

Television, generally, this index

MEDIAL BARRIERS

Highways, pedestrians, crossing, **39:4–34**

MEDIATION

Generally, **Rule 1:40–4**
Children and minors, custody, **Rule 1:40–5**
Complementary dispute resolution programs, **Rules 1:40–1 et seq., 1:40–6, 1:40–7**
Confidential or privileged information, **Rule 1:38–3**
Domestic violence, exceptions, **Rule 7:8–1**
Exceptions, **Rule 7:8–1**
Minor disputes, **Rule 1:40–8**
Municipal courts, **Rule 7:8–1**
Privileges and immunities, **Evidence Rule 519**
Qualifications and training, mediators, **Rule 1:40–12**
Relaxation of guidelines, **Rule 1:40–10**
Small claims and landlord tenant disputes, complementary dispute resolution programs, **Rules 1:40–6, 1:40–7**
Training, mediators, **Rule 1:40–12**

MEDICAID

Crimes and offenses, health care claims fraud, 2C:21–4.2, 2C:21–4.3
Licenses and permits, suspension or revocation, 2C:51–5
Rehabilitation, order of debarment, rescission, 2C:27–1
Fines and penalties, health care claims fraud, 2C:21–4.2, 2C:21–4.3
Licenses and permits, suspension or revocation, 2C:51–5
Rehabilitation, order of debarment, rescission, 2C:27–1
Forfeitures, licenses and permits, health care claims fraud, 2C:51–5
Fraud, health care claims fraud, 2C:21–4.2, 2C:21–4.3
Licenses and permits, suspension or revocation, 2C:51–5
Rehabilitation, order of debarment, rescission, 2C:27–1

MEDICAL ADVISORY PANEL

Generally, **39:2–13 et seq.**

MEDICAL AND SURGICAL INSURANCE

Health and Accident Insurance, generally, this index

MEDICAL ASSISTANCE

Medicaid, generally, this index

MEDICAL ASSISTANCE AND HEALTH SERVICES ACT

Medicaid, generally, this index

MEDICAL ASSOCIATIONS

Review committees, immunity from liability, 2A:84A–22.10

MEDICAL CARE AND TREATMENT

Abuse or neglect of children, prior emergency removal from home, 9:6–8.30
Adult Diagnostic and Treatment Center, generally, this index
Alcoholics and Alcoholism, generally, this index
Automobile insurance, no fault insurance, application of law, 39:6A–1 et seq.
Child Abuse, this index
Children and Minors, this index

MEDICAL CARE AND TREATMENT
—Cont'd
Cloning, crimes and offenses, **2C:11A–1**
Consent, children and minors, abuse or neglect
of children, treatment after emergency re-
moval from home, **9:6–8.30**
Crimes and offenses,
Cloning, **2C:11A–1**
Suspended sentence, **2C:45–1**
Diagnosis or treatment statements, hearsay ex-
ception, **Evidence Rule 803**
Discrimination, generally, this index
Drugs and Medicine, generally, this index
Drunk driving victims rights, **39:4–50.11**
Fetal alcohol syndrome, drinking during preg-
nancy, warning notices, posting require-
ments, alcoholic beverages, **33:1–12a**
Health and Accident Insurance, generally, this
index
Health Maintenance Organizations, generally,
this index
Insurance. Health and Accident Insurance,
generally, this index
Juvenile Delinquents, this index
Medicaid, generally, this index
Medicare, generally, this index
No fault insurance, application of law, **39:6A–1
et seq.**
Payment of expenses, **Evidence Rule 409**
Privileges and immunities, emergency removal
of children from home, abuse or neglect,
9:6–8.30
Probation, conditions, **2C:45–1**

MEDICAL EXAMINATIONS
Physical Examinations, generally, this index

MEDICAL EXPENSES
Definitions, no fault insurance, **39:6A–2**

MEDICAL INSTITUTIONS
Hospitals, generally, this index

MEDICAL MALPRACTICE
Motions, dismissal and nonsuit, affidavits, non-
involvement, **Rule 1:6–2**

MEDICAL SCHOOLS
Anatomical Gifts, generally, this index

MEDICAL SERVICE
Medical Care and Treatment, generally, this
index

MEDICAL SERVICE CORPORATIONS
Utilization review committees established by
certified hospitals, privileged communications, **2A:84A–22.8**

MEDICAL WASTE
Legislative findings, **13:1E–48.2**

MEDICALLY NECESSARY
Definitions, no fault insurance, **39:6A–2**

MEDICARE
Crimes and offenses, health care claims fraud,
2C:21–4.2, 2C:21–4.3
Licenses and permits, suspension or revocation, **2C:51–5**
Rehabilitation, order of debarment, rescission, **2C:27–1**
Fines and penalties, health care claims fraud,
2C:21–4.2, 2C:21–4.3
Licenses and permits, suspension or revocation, **2C:51–5**

MEDICARE—Cont'd
Fines and penalties, health care claims fraud
—Cont'd
Licenses and permits, suspension or revoca-
tion—Cont'd
Rehabilitation, order of debarment, rescis-
sion, **2C:27–1**
Forfeitures, licenses and permits, health care
claims fraud, **2C:51–5**
Fraud, health care claims fraud, **2C:21–4.2,
2C:21–4.3**
Licenses and permits, suspension or revoca-
tion, **2C:51–5**
Rehabilitation, order of debarment, rescis-
sion, **2C:27–1**

MEDICINE AND SURGERY
Drugs and Medicine, generally, this index
Medical Care and Treatment, generally, this
index
Physicians and Surgeons, generally, this index
Radiation Protection, generally, this index

MEGANS LAW
Generally, **2C:7–1 et seq.**

MELLORINE FROZEN DESSERTS
Frozen Desserts and Dietary Foods, generally,
this index

MEMORANDUM
Abbreviations, **Rule 1:37–3**
Crimes and offenses, service, **Rule 1:5–1 et seq.**
Format, **Rule 1:4–9**
Professional ethics, advisory committee on, in-
quiries, **Rule 1:19–3**

MEMORANDUM DECISIONS
Filing, **Rule 1:36–1**
Trial, **Rule 1:7–4**

MEMORIALS AND MONUMENTS
Desecration, **2C:33–9**
Law Enforcement Officers, this index

MEN WORKING SIGNS
Authority to erect, **39:4–183.1**

MENS REA
Mental state. Crimes and Offenses, this index

MENTAL CONDITION OR CAPACITY
Mentally Deficient and Mentally Ill Persons,
generally, this index
Mentally Retarded and Developmentally Disabled Persons, generally, this index

MENTAL EXAMINATIONS
Adult Diagnostic and Treatment Center, gen-
erally, this index
Crimes and Offenses, this index
Privilege, refusal to submit to, **2A:84A–19**

MENTAL HEALTH
Mentally Deficient and Mentally Ill Persons,
generally, this index

MENTAL ILLNESS
Mentally Deficient and Mentally Ill Persons,
generally, this index

MENTAL RETARDATION
Mentally Retarded and Developmentally Disabled Persons, generally, this index

MENTAL STATE
Crimes and Offenses, this index

MENTALLY DEFECTIVE
Definitions, sexual offenses, **2C:14–1**

**MENTALLY DEFICIENT AND MENTALLY
ILL PERSONS**
See, also, Mentally Retarded and Devel-
opmentally Disabled Persons, general-
ly, this index
Generally, **2C:4–1 et seq.**
Acquittal by reason of insanity, **2C:4–7 et seq.**
Adult Diagnostic and Treatment Center, gen-
erally, this index
Aged persons, institutionalized elderly persons,
assault, **2C:12–1**
Alcoholic Beverages, this index
Attorneys, this index
Burden of proof, insanity defense, acquittal,
continued commitment, **2C:4–1**
Commitment and Admission to Institutions,
generally, this index
Competency,
Establishing, privileged communications be-
tween patient and physician,
2A:84A–22.3
To stand trial, **2C:4–4, 2C:4–6**
Consent, victim of crime, **2C:2–10**
Correctional institutions, treatment, **2C:4–6**
Crime victims, **2C:44–1**
Presentence investigations and reports,
2C:44–6
Crimes and offenses,
Dismissal of charges, **2C:4–6**
Endangering injured victim, **2C:12–1.2**
Endangering welfare, **2C:24–7**
Evidence, generally, post
Fitness to proceed, **2C:4–6**
Insanity Defense, generally, this index
Psychiatric examinations, **2C:4–5**
Acquittal of defendant by reason of insani-
ty, **2C:4–8**
Admissibility of statements of defendant,
2C:4–10
Release, persons committed by reason of
insanity, crimes and offenses, **2C:4–9**
Regaining fitness to proceed, **2C:4–6**
Release, persons committed by reason of
insanity, **2C:4–9**
Responsibility, **2C:4–1 et seq.**
Sexual assault, **2C:14–2, 2C:14–4**
DNA database and databank, **53:1–20.20**
Sodomy, **2C:14–2**
Suspension of proceedings against defen-
dants, **2C:4–6**
Treatment, correctional institutions, **2C:4–6**
Criminal history record information,
Homemaker home health aides, certificates,
53:1–20.9a
Nurses aides or personal care assistants, cer-
tificates, **53:1–20.9a**
Criminal sexual contact, **2C:14–3**
Criminally insane. Crimes and offenses, gen-
erally, ante
Custody and control, interference, **2C:13–4**
Damages, conduct of patient, privileged com-
munications between patient and physi-
cian, **2A:84A–22.3**
Defenses. Crimes and offenses, generally, ante
Definitions, **2C:4–1**
Competency to stand trial, **2C:4–4**
Crimes and offenses, endangering injured
victim, **2C:12–1.2**
Sexual offenses, **2C:14–1**
Depositions, criminal proceedings, **Rule 3:13–2**
Detainers, interstate agreement on, applicabili-
ty to mentally ill persons, **2A:159A–6**

MENTALLY DEFICIENT AND MENTALLY ILL PERSONS—Cont'd

Determination of defendants fitness to proceed, 2C:4–6

Dismissal of charges, 2C:4–6

Endangering injured victim, crimes and offenses, 2C:12–1.2

Endangering welfare of incompetent persons, 2C:24–7

Evidence,
Acquittal of defendant by reason of insanity, civil commitment, 2C:4–8
Burden of proof, insanity defense, acquittal, continued commitment, 2C:4–1
Defendants fitness to proceed, 2C:4–6
Mental disease or defect, 2C:4–2, 2C:4–3
Psychiatric examinations, statements by defendant, 2C:4–10

Fitness to proceed, crimes and offenses, 2C:4–6

Handguns, purchase permits, 2C:58–3

Hearings, defendants fitness to proceed, 2C:4–6

Hearsay exception, then existing condition, **Evidence Rule 803**

Homemaker home health aides, criminal history record checks, certificates, 53:1–20.9a

Homicide, sentence and punishment, mitigating factors, 2C:11–3

Incapacity, trial, 2C:4–4

Insanity Defense, generally, this index

Institutionalized elderly persons. Aged persons, ante

Juvenile Delinquents, this index

Law enforcement officers. Post trauma disorders, post

Lewdness, exposure in presence of, fourth degree crime, 2C:14–4

Mediation, exceptions, **Rule 7:8–1**

Nonprofit corporations and associations, care and treatment, transport vehicles, identification, 39:4–207.2 et seq.

Notice, insanity defense, 2C:4–3

Nurses aides, criminal history record checks, certificates, 53:1–20.9a

Offenses. Crimes and offenses, generally, ante

Parking permits, 39:4–207.2, 39:4–207.3

Personal care assistants, criminal history record checks, certificates, 53:1–20.9a

Physicians and surgeons, privileges and immunities, 2A:84A–22.3

Post trauma disorders, law enforcement officers, crisis intervention services, hotlines, funding, 2C:64–6, 39:5–41

Presentence investigation and report, evaluation, disclosure, 2C:44–6
Cost of evaluation, 2C:44–6.1

Presumptions of incompetence, 2C:4–1

Proof. Evidence, generally, ante

Rape, 2C:14–1

Regaining fitness to proceed, criminal proceedings, 2C:4–6

Release, persons committed by reason of insanity, 2C:4–9

Reports,
Application for release, committed criminal defendants, 2C:4–9
Psychiatric or psychological examinations, criminal defendants, 2C:4–5

Responsibility, crimes and offenses, 2C:4–1 et seq.

Sexual assault, 2C:14–1 et seq.
DNA database and databank, 53:1–20.20

Sodomy, crimes and offenses, 2C:14–2

Suspension of proceedings against criminal defendant, 2C:4–6

MENTALLY DEFICIENT AND MENTALLY ILL PERSONS—Cont'd

Transportation, parking permits, 39:4–207.2, 39:4–207.3

Treatment, correctional institutions, 2C:4–6

Victims of crime, endangering injured victim, 2C:12–1.2

Weapons,
Firearms, permits to persons confined for mental disorder, 2C:58–3
Possession, 2C:39–7

MENTALLY INCOMPETENT PERSONS

Mentally Deficient and Mentally Ill Persons, generally, this index

MENTALLY RETARDED AND DEVELOP-MENTALLY DISABLED PERSONS

See, also, Mentally Deficient and Mentally Ill Persons, generally, this index

Appeal and review, records and recordation, confidential or privileged information, **Rule 1:38–3**

Criminal history record information,
Homemaker home health aides, certificates, 53:1–20.9a
Nurses aides or personal care assistants, certificates, 53:1–20.9a

Definitions, handicapped parking permits, 39:4–207.2

Hearsay exception, then existing condition, **Evidence Rule 803**

Homemaker home health aides, criminal history record checks, certificates, 53:1–20.9a

Injunctions, stalking, 2C:12–10.2

Motor vehicles, county transportation, 39:4–207.2 et seq.

Nurses aides, criminal history record checks, certificates, 53:1–20.9a

Personal care assistants, criminal history record checks, certificates, 53:1–20.9a

Stalking, injunctions, 2C:12–10.2

MEPROBAMATE

Controlled substances, 24:21–1 et seq.

MERCANTILE ESTABLISHMENTS

Intoxicating liquors, packaged merchandise, sale, 33:1–12

MERCHANDISE

Definitions, shoplifting, 2C:20–11

MERCHANTS

Deceptive business practices, 2C:21–7

Definitions, shoplifting, 2C:20–11

Firearms, retail dealers, unlawful possession, exemption, 2C:39–6

Leases, generally, this index

Sales, generally, this index

Shoplifting, 2C:20–11

MERGER AND CONSOLIDATION

Conviction of Crime, this index

MERIT RATING PLAN

Motor vehicle insurance, plan implementation expenses, unsatisfied claimant judgment fund, 39:6–88

MERIT SERVICE

Civil Service, generally, this index

MERITORIOUS PUBLIC SERVICE

Definitions, disorderly persons enumerated, 2A:170–20.1

MESCALINE

Controlled substances, 24:21–1 et seq.

MESNE PROCESS

Issuance by clerk of court, motions and applications, **Rule 1:6–8**

METAL KNUCKLES

Weapons, generally, this index

METAL TIRE

Definitions, 39:1–1

METALS

Noise when loaded on vehicle to be avoided, 39:4–78

METAZOCINE

Controlled substances, 24:21–1 et seq.

METERS

Theft of services, 2C:20–8

METHADONE

Controlled substances, 24:21–1 et seq.

METHAMPHETAMINE

Generally, 24:21–1 et seq.

Anhydrous ammonia,
Possession, manufacturing, 2C:35–28
Theft, manufacturing, 2C:20–2

Phenylalanine, possession, manufacturing, 2C:35–28

METHOHEXITAL

Controlled substances, 24:21–1 et seq.

METHYLDERSORPHINE

Controlled substances, 24:21–1 et seq.

METHYLHYDROMORPHINE

Controlled substances, 24:21–1 et seq.

METHYLPHENIDATE

Controlled substances, 24:21–1 et seq.

METHYLPHENOBARBITAL

Controlled substances, 24:21–1 et seq.

METHYLPRYLON

Controlled substances, 24:21–1 et seq.

MICHAELS LAW

Motor vehicles, intoxication of driver, 39:4–50

MICROFILM AND MICROPHOTOGRAPHING

Clerks of court, books and records, **Rule 1:32–2**

Drivers licenses, records and alphabetical indices, 39:3–28

Indices of motor vehicle registration or drivers license applications, 39:3–28

Motor vehicles,
Applications for registration and drivers licenses, evidence, 39:3–28
Registration, records of registration and alphabetical indices, 39:3–28

MIDDLESEX COUNTY

See, also, Counties, generally, this index

High speed limited access superhighway, project, 27:23–23.8

MILEAGE

Witnesses, this index

MILITARY FORCES

Armed Forces, generally, this index

MILITARY SERVICE
Armed Forces, generally, this index

MILITARY VEHICLES
Speed law inapplicable, when, **39:4–103**

MINES AND MINERALS
Blasting operations, **21:1A–138**
Explosives, this index

MINIMUM SENTENCES
Weapons, possession, **2C:43–6**

MINISTERS
Clergy, generally, this index

MINOR DISPUTES
Municipal courts, notice in lieu of complaint,
 Rule 7:8–1

MINOR UNETHICAL CONDUCT
Attorneys, determination, **Rule 1:20–3**

MINORITIES
Discrimination, generally, this index

MINORS
Children and Minors, generally, this index

MINUTES
Municipal authorities issuing alcoholic beverage licenses, **33:1–24**
Turnpike authority, delivery to governor,
 27:23–3

MISAPPROPRIATION
Embezzlement, generally, this index

MISBEHAVIOR
Contempt, generally, this index

MISBRANDING
Food, this index

MISCHIEF
Criminal mischief, **2C:17–3**

MISCONDUCT
Corporate official, **2C:21–9**

MISDEMEANORS
Crimes and Offenses, generally, this index

MISFEASANCE
Limitation of criminal prosecutions, **2C:1–6**

MISLABELED
Definitions, deceptive business practices,
 2C:21–7

MISLAID PROPERTY
Theft, **2C:20–6**

MISLEADING STATEMENTS
Revocation of alcoholic beverage license,
 33:1–25

MISREPRESENTATION
Fraud, generally, this index

MISSING PERSONS
Trust funds, possession or control by attorney,
 duties, **Rule 1:21–6**

MITIGATION
Attempt or conspiracy, grade and degree of
 offense, **2C:5–4**
Crimes and offenses, **2C:44–1**

MIXTURES
Alcoholic beverage as misdemeanor, **33:1–50**

**MOBILE HOMES AND MOBILE HOME
 PARKS**
 See, also, Manufactured Homes, generally,
  this index
Certificates of ownership,
 Application of law, **39:10–2**
 Relocation, **39:10–11.1**
 Sales, **39:10–15.1**
Dealers, licensed real estate brokers, **39:10–19**
Delivery, registration plates, **39:3–20.1**
Landlord and Tenant, this index
Liens and incumbrances, sales, certificates of
 ownership, **39:10–15.1**
Notice, relocation, certificate of ownership,
 39:10–11.1
Real estate brokers, dealers, **39:10–19**
Registration plates, transportation, **39:3–20.1**
Sales,
 Certificates of ownership, **39:10–15.1**
 Real estate brokers, **39:10–19**
Transportation, registration plates, **39:3–20.1**

MOBILE TELECOMMUNICATIONS
Telecommunications, this index

MODELS
Anatomically correct models, sex offenses, chil-
 dren as witnesses, **2A:84A–16.1**
Model rockets.   Rockets, generally, this index

MONEY
Bail, source, hearings, sufficiency, **2A:162–13**
Contraband, illegal gambling enterprises,
 2C:64–1 et seq.
Illegal investments.   Money Laundering and
 Illegal Investments, generally,   this index

**MONEY LAUNDERING AND ILLEGAL IN-
 VESTMENTS**
 Generally, **2C:21–23 et seq., 2C:21–27**
Allocation of monies, **2C:21–28**
Attorney general,
 Definitions, **2C:21–24**
 Powers and duties, **2C:21–28 et seq.**
Casinos, currency transactions, reports,
 2C:21–25
Civil action, **2C:21–28**
Conspiracy, grade and degree of offense,
 2C:5–4
Conviction of crime, merger and consolidation,
 2C:21–27
Costs, **2C:21–28**
Damages, **2C:21–28**
Definitions, **2C:21–24**
Depositions, **2C:21–29**
Derived from, definitions, **2C:21–24**
Discovery, **2C:21–29**
Elements of offense, **2C:21–25**
Engagement in transaction involving property
 known to be derived from criminal activity,
 element of offense, **2C:21–25**
Fines and penalties, **2C:21–27 et seq.**
 Satisfaction of claims, **2C:46–4.1**
Grade and degree of offense, **2C:21–27**
Interrogatories, **2C:21–29**
Investigations, **2C:21–29**
Joint and several liability, **2C:21–28**
Judgments and decrees, **2C:21–28**
Liability, **2C:21–28**
Person, definitions, **2C:21–24**
Possession of property known to be derived
 from criminal activity, element of offense,
 2C:21–25
Production of books and papers, **2C:21–29**

**MONEY LAUNDERING AND ILLEGAL IN-
 VESTMENTS**—Cont'd
Property, definitions, **2C:21–24**
Public policy, **2C:21–23**
Remedies, **2C:21–28**
Reports, currency transactions, **2C:21–25**
Requisite knowledge, **2C:21–26**
Satisfaction of claims, fines and penalties,
 2C:46–4.1
Sentence and punishment, **2C:21–27**
 Additional, **2C:21–28**
Service of process, interrogatories, **2C:21–29**
Standard of proof, **2C:21–28**
Subpoenas, **2C:21–29**
Time, fines and penalties, payment schedule,
 2C:21–27.4
Transportation of property known to be de-
 rived from criminal activity, element of
 offense, **2C:21–25**
Treble damages, **2C:21–28**

MONEY TRANSMITTERS
Money laundering and illegal investments, currency transactions, reports, **2C:21–25**
Reports, currency transactions, money laundering and illegal investments, **2C:21–25**

MONOPOLIES
Actions and proceedings, **56:9–13**
 Hearings or inquiries, **56:9–9**
Agricultural or horticultural cooperatives, ex-
 empted, **56:9–5**
Alcoholic beverages, **33:1–23.1**
Assets of corporations, acquisition to lessen
 competition, **56:9–4**
Associations, societies or boards, recommend-
 ing fees, exemptions, **56:9–5**
Attempt to monopolize, combine or conspire,
 56:9–4
Attorney general, investigations and proceed-
 ings, **56:9–9**
Attorneys, hearings and inquiries, right to at-
 torney, **56:9–9**
Attorneys fees, **56:9–10**
Banking institutions, exemptions, **56:9–5**
Capital, acquisition, **56:9–4**
Charitable organizations and associations, ex-
 emptions, **56:9–5**
Civil penalties, **56:9–12**
Consent,
 Hearings and inquiries, specific evidence,
  56:9–9
 Judgments, failure to comply, **56:9–7**
Contracts, combinations or conspiracies in re-
 straint of trade, **56:9–3**
Cooperative societies, exemptions, **56:9–5**
Corporations, dissolutions, **56:9–7**
Costs, **56:9–10**
County prosecutors, proceedings against viola-
 tors, **56:9–6**
Crimes and offenses,
 Actions and proceedings, **56:9–13**
 Fines and penalties, **56:9–11**
 Hearings and inquiries, **56:9–9**
 Judgment evidence in civil suit for damages,
  56:9–13
Damages, **56:9–12**
Definitions, **56:9–2**
Disclosures, subpoena information, **56:9–9**
Electricity and Electric Companies, this index
Evidence, hearings and inquiries, **56:9–9**
Exemptions, **56:9–5**
Fair sales, activities, exemptions, **56:9–5**
Fines and penalties, **56:9–11**
Foreign corporations, violations, **56:9–8**
Hearings, **56:9–9**

MONOPOLIES—Cont'd
Horticultural or agricultural cooperatives, exempted, **56:9–5**
Injunctions, **56:9–10**
Insurance, this index
Interrogatories, hearings and inquiries, **56:9–9**
Intoxicating liquor, **33:1–23.1**
Investigations,
    Attorney general, **56:9–6**
    Hearings or inquiries, **56:9–9**
Investments, stock purchases, exemptions, **56:9–4**
Judgments and decrees, evidence, **56:9–13**
Labor organizations, exempted, **56:9–5**
Limitation of actions and prosecutions, **56:9–15**
Liquor, **33:1–23.1**
Prior transactions, **56:9–4**
Production of books and papers, hearings or inquiries, **56:9–9**
Public utilities, exempted, **56:9–5**
Religious corporations and associations, exemptions, **56:9–5**
Restraining orders, **56:9–10**
Savings and loan associations, exemptions, **56:9–5**
Security dealers, issuers or agents, licensed by state, exemptions, **56:9–5**
Service, subpoena, **56:9–9**
State, actions initiated by, **56:9–15**
Statute of limitations, suspension, **56:9–15**
Subsidiary corporations, exemptions, **56:9–4**
Summary proceedings, **56:9–10**
Suspension, privilege of doing business, **56:9–7**
Trade and professional organizations, exempted, **56:9–5**
Vested rights, **56:9–4**
Violations of act, bar to future business activities, **56:9–7**

MOONSHINE
Stills and Distilling Apparatus, generally, this index

MOPEDS
Motorized Bicycles, generally, this index

MORACYMETHADOL
Controlled substances, **24:21–1 et seq.**

MORAL TURPITUDE
Alcoholic beverage license, issuance of as affected by conviction of crime, **33:1–25**
Intoxicating liquor licenses, employment affected by conviction of crime, **33:1–26**

MORALS
Controlled substances, **24:21–1 et seq.**

MORGUES AND MORGUE KEEPERS
Intoxication of driver, supervised visitation, **39:4–50**
Supervised visitation, intoxication of driver, **39:4–50**

MORPHERIDINE
Controlled substances, **24:21–1 et seq.**

MORPHINE
Controlled substances, **24:21–1 et seq.**

MORPHINE METHYLBROMIDE
Controlled substances, **24:21–1 et seq.**

MORPHINE METHYLSULFONATE
Controlled substances, **24:21–1 et seq.**

MORPHINE N OXIDE
Controlled substances, **24:21–1 et seq.**

MORTALITY TABLES
Evidence, **Rule 1:13–5**

MORTGAGES
Firearms as security, **2C:39–11**
Foreclosure,
    Affidavits, facsimile signatures, **Rule 1:4–4**
    Case management, electronic filing, **Rule 1:5–6**
    Certificates and certification, facsimile signatures, **Rule 1:4–4**
    Copies annexed to complaints, **Rule 1:4–3**
    Courts, records and recordation, **Rule 1:32–2**
    Electronic filing, **Rule 1:4–9**
    Filing of papers, **Rule 1:5–6**
    Frivolous litigation, facsimile signatures, **Rule 1:4–8**
    Judges, facsimile signatures, **Rule 1:34–6**
    Motions, electronic filing, **Rule 1:6–2**
    Nonconforming papers, electronic filing, **Rule 1:5–6**
    Personal service, **Rule 1:5–2**
    Pleadings, facsimile signatures, **Rule 1:4–5**
    Proof of service, **Rule 1:5–3**
    Seals, **Rule 1:37–2**
    Transfer of actions, records and recordation, **Rule 1:13–4**
Fraud, **2C:21–3**
    Mortgage instruments, **2C:21–3**
Theft by failure to make required disposition of property received, **2C:20–9**
Turnpikes, **27:23–8**

MORTUARY SCIENCE
Drivers licenses, motor vehicles, medical examinations, **39:3–10.11a**
Medical examinations, motor vehicles, drivers licenses, **39:3–10.11a**
Motor vehicles, drivers licenses, medical examinations, **39:3–10.11a**
Trust funds, money paid to funeral director, burial services, **2A:102–13**

MOSQUES
Religious Corporations and Associations, generally, this index

MOTELS
Hotels and Motels, generally, this index

MOTION DAYS
Generally, **Rule 1:30–3**

MOTIONS
Generally, **Rule 1:6–1 et seq.**
Acquittal after discharge of jury, enlargement of time, **Rule 1:3–4**
Affidavits, this index
Alteration of judgment or order, enlargement of time, **Rule 1:3–4**
Amendments,
    Findings, **Rule 1:7–4**
        Enlargement of time, **Rule 1:3–4**
    Judgment or order, enlargement of time, **Rule 1:3–4**
Amicus curiae, application for leave to appear, **Rule 1:13–9**
Answer, opposing affidavits and cross motions, service and filing, **Rule 1:6–3**
Appeals in criminal prosecutions, defenses raised before trial, **Rule 3:23–8**
Appearance, failure to appear, sanctions, **Rule 1:2–4**
Application, court order, **Rule 1:6–2**

MOTIONS—Cont'd
Application of rules, **Rule 1:6–1**
Arrest of judgment, enlargement of time, **Rule 1:3–4**
Bail, this index
Bonds (officers and fiduciaries), enforcement of liability, **Rule 1:13–3**
Calendar motions, **Rule 1:6–2**
Certifications, service and filing, **Rule 1:6–3**
Chancery division, superior court, **Rules 1:6–2, 1:6–4**
Clerical mistakes, judgments, orders or other parts of record, correction, **Rule 1:13–1**
Contents, **Rule 1:6–2**
Copies, filing, **Rule 1:6–4**
Correction of clerical mistakes, judgments, orders or other parts of the record, **Rule 1:13–1**
Correction of sentence, enlargement of time, **Rule 1:3–4**
Court schedules, **Rule 1:30–1**
Crimes and Offenses, this index
Cross examination, affidavits, **Rule 1:6–6**
Cross motions,
    Manner of filing, **Rule 1:6–4**
    Service and filing, **Rule 1:6–3**
Date of signature, **Rule 1:4–5**
Days, **Rule 1:30–3**
Default, entry, granting by clerk of court, **Rule 1:6–8**
Depositions, this index
Discovery, **Rule 1:6–2**
Dismissal and Nonsuit, this index
Disposition, papers, **Rule 1:6–2**
Disqualification of judges, **Rule 1:12–2**
Enlargement of time, **Rule 1:3–4**
Ex Parte Proceedings, this index
Failure to appear, sanctions, **Rule 1:2–4**
Family court, chancery division of superior court, discovery and calendar motions, **Rule 1:6–2**
Filing, **Rule 1:5–6**
    Copies, **Rule 1:6–4**
    Failure to comply with requirements, sanctions, **Rule 1:2–4**
    Signatures, date on which signed, **Rule 1:4–5**
    Time, **Rule 1:6–3**
Forms, **Rule 1:6–2**
Grant by clerk of court, **Rule 1:6–8**
Hearings,
    Open court proceedings, **Rule 1:2–1**
    Sanctions, failure to appear or comply with requirements, **Rule 1:2–4**
Homicide, capital punishment, life imprisonment, **2C:11–3b**
Inactive cases, dismissal, **Rule 1:13–7**
Judges,
    Disqualification, **Rule 1:12–2**
    Subsequent motions, hearing by same judge, **Rule 1:6–2**
Judgments, acquittal after discharge of jury, enlargement of time, **Rule 1:3–4**
Medical malpractice, dismissal, affidavits, non-involvement, **Rule 1:6–2**
Municipal courts, **Rule 7:7–2**
New Trial, this index
Newsperson information disclosure privilege, criminal proceedings, **2A:84A–21.1 et seq.**
Notice, **Rule 1:6–2**
    Filing, **Rule 1:6–3**
    Oral arguments, discovery and calendar motion, **Rule 1:6–2**
    Service, **Rule 1:6–3**
    Time, service and filing, **Rule 1:6–3**
Objections, **Rule 1:7–2**
    Service and filing, **Rule 1:6–3**

MOTIONS—Cont'd

Open court proceedings, **Rule 1:2–1**

Opposing affidavits,
    Manner of filing, **Rule 1:6–4**
    Service and filing, **Rule 1:6–3**

Oral arguments, discovery or calendar motions, **Rule 1:6–2**

Oral motions, **Rule 1:6–2**

Place for filing, superior court, **Rule 1:6–4**

Pretrial conferences, discovery and calendar motions, setting forth date, **Rule 1:6–2**

Pro hac vice appearances, application for admission, **Rule 1:21–2**

Process, **Rule 1:5–1 et seq.**
    Issuance,
        Grant by clerk of court, **Rule 1:6–8**
        Granting by clerk of court, **Rule 1:6–8**
    Time, **Rule 1:6–3**

Reading in advance of hearing, judges, **Rule 1:6–7**

Record, telephone arguments, **Rule 1:6–2**

Relief from judgment or order, enlargement of time, **Rule 1:3–4**

Renewal of motion or judgment, enlargement of time, **Rule 1:3–4**

Responsive papers, **Rule 1:6–2**
    Opposing and cross motions, service and filing, **Rule 1:6–3**

Return, failure to appear, **Rule 1:2–4**

Sanctions, frivolous litigation, **Rule 1:4–8**

Schedules of courts, **Rule 1:30–1**

Searches and seizures, suppression of evidence and return of property, **Rule 3:5–7**

Signatures, **Rule 1:4–5**
    Effect of signature, **Rule 1:4–8**
    Name typed or stamped beneath, **Rule 1:4–6**

Specially assigned cases, **Rule 1:6–2**

Subpoenas, this index

Subsequent motions, hearing judge, **Rule 1:6–2**

Superior court, filing, **Rule 1:6–4**

Suppression of evidence,
    Municipal courts, **Rule 7:5–2**
    Wiretapping and electronic surveillance, **2A:156A–21**

Telephone conference, argument of motions, **Rule 1:6–2**

Time, service and filing, **Rule 1:6–3**

Transfer of actions, **Rule 1:13–4**

Uncontested motions, **Rule 1:6–2**

Withdrawals, **Rule 1:6–2**

MOTOR BUS CARRIERS

Buses, generally, this index

MOTOR CARRIERS

Abstract, definitions, **39:10–2**

Advertising, noncommercial trucks, **39:3–8.1**

Agreements, registration, reciprocity, **39:3–6.1 et seq.**

Agricultural Machinery and Equipment, generally, this index

Air brakes, emergency system, **39:3–68.1 et seq.**

Air contaminants, **39:3–70.1, 39:3–70.2**

Attachable auxiliary motor vehicle axle, **39:4–54**

Audits and auditors,
    Intermodal transportation, chassis, facilities, **39:3–79.18**
    Operational accounts, **39:3–6.18**

Autobuses. Buses, generally, this index

Axle weight limitations, **39:3–84, 39:3–84.1**

Bailee, weights and measurements, fine, **39:3–84.3**

Blasting caps, transportation, **21:1A–137**

Brakes, **39:3–67**
    Emergency braking systems, **39:3–68.1 et seq.**

MOTOR CARRIERS—Cont'd

Bridges, liability for damages to bridges posted for weight limits, **39:3–84.4**

Bumpers rear end protection device, **39:3–84**

Buses, generally, this index

Certificates and certification, intermodal transportation, chassis, **39:3–79.11, 39:3–79.18**

Chaining, **39:4–54**

Chassis, intermodal transportation, **39:3–79.10 et seq.**

Citation, intermodal transportation, chassis, inspectors and inspection, **39:3–79.19**

Clearance lamps, **39:3–61**
    Mounting, **39:3–61.1**

Combination vehicles,
    Dimensional and weight limitations, **39:3–84**
    Drawn vehicles, **39:4–54**
    Name plates, **39:4–46**
    Weights and measures, **39:3–84.3**

Commercial drivers licenses, **39:3–10.9 et seq.**
    Exemption, **39:3–10j et seq.**

Commercial vehicle enforcement fund, establishment, **39:8–75**

Complaints,
    Intermodal transportation, chassis, drivers, **39:3–79.16**
    Traffic rules and regulations, notice, **39:5–25.1**

Constructor vehicles, **39:3–20**
    Registration plates, **39:3–20**
    Speed limitations, **39:3–20**
    Weight limitations, exemptions, **39:3–84.1**

Containers, intermodal transportation,
    Axle weight limitations, **39:3–84.1**
    Chassis, **39:3–79.10 et seq.**

Converter dolly or auxiliary axle, **39:4–54**
    Attached to, rear lamps, **39:3–61**

Crimes and offenses, marks or numbers, change or destruction, **2C:17–6**

Damages, liability for damages from exceeding weight limitations, **39:3–84.4**

Definitions, **39:1–1**
    Gross weight, **39:3–20**
    Registration, reciprocity, **39:3–6.1**
    Registration year, **39:3–20**
    Semitrailers, traffic regulations, **39:1–1**

Diesel fuel, emissions. Motor Vehicles, this index

Director, motor vehicles division,
    Fines and penalties, display of name of owner of commercial vehicle, disposition, **39:4–47**
    Registration fees, paid to for commercial vehicles, **39:3–20**

Disabled vehicles, gross weight, registration fee of drawing vehicle, **39:3–20**

Disposition, **39:4–47**

Display,
    Name plates, **39:4–46**
    Placards, radioactive materials, **39:5B–18**

Division, definitions, **39:3–6.1**

Doors, special exits, merchandising or exhibition vans or trailers, **39:3–77.2**

Dump trucks, axle weight limitations, **39:3–84.1**

Electronic rear backup monitoring devices, **39:3–71.1**

Emergency brake systems, **39:3–68.1 et seq.**

Emergency warning devices, portable, **39:3–64**

Emissions. Motor Vehicles, this index

Empty vehicles, registration plates, **39:3–20.1, 39:3–20.2**

Explosives, transportation, **21:1A–137**

Federal registration, enforcement, **39:5B–32**

Fees, registration, reduced registration fees, **39:3–22a**

Financial responsibility, enforcement, **39:5B–32**

MOTOR CARRIERS—Cont'd

Fines and penalties,
    Air pollution, **39:3–70.2**
    Driving privileges, suspensions, **39:3–10.20**
    Exceeding weight limitations, **39:3–20**
    Excess weight, **39:3–84.3**
    Flatbed vehicles, loading, **39:4–77**
    Hours of service, **39:9–4**
    Intermodal transportation, post
    Labor and employment, **39:3–10.18**
    Loads, distribution according to tire width, **39:3–82, 39:3–84**
    Name, failure to display, **39:4–47**
    Nonresident vehicles, **39:3–15**
        Weight, **39:3–20.3**
    Number and fastening of trailers, **39:4–54**
    Offenses in construction or repair areas, conditions, **39:4–203.5**
    Operation, not in possession of valid commercial license, **39:3–10.18**
    Out of service orders, **39:3–10.18**
    Overweight vehicles driven over bridges, **39:4–75, 39:4–76**
    Radioactive materials, **39:5B–24**
    Rubber tires, required, **39:3–80**
    Taking samples of breath, consent, refused, **39:3–10.24**
    Tires, lack of rubber tires, **39:3–80**
    Weights and measures,
        State highways, **39:4–197.21**
        Violations, **39:3–84.3**

Flares or other emergency warning light equipment, **39:3–64**

Fleet, definitions, **39:3–6.1**

Fleet operations, name plates, **39:4–46**

Following another truck, **39:4–89**

Frozen dessert trucks, traffic rules and regulations, **39:4–128.3 et seq.**

Fuels. Motor Fuels, generally, this index

Funds, highway safety fund, fines and penalties, nonresident vehicles, weight, **39:3–20.4**

Garages, generally, this index

Goods, wares and merchandise, noncommercial trucks, **39:1–1, 39:3–8, 39:3–8.1**

Hazardous Substances and Waste, this index

Heavy equipment. Moving Heavy Machinery, generally, this index

Height, **39:3–84**
    Maximum, **39:3–84**
    Private utility or house type semitrailers and trailers, **39:3–8**

Highway Route 94 in Sussex and Warren counties, rules and regulations, **39:4–197.8**

Highway safety fund, fines and penalties, nonresident vehicles, weight, **39:3–20.4**

Hours of duty, **39:9–2 et seq.**

Ice and snow, removal, **27:23–49**

Ice cream trucks, traffic rules and regulations, **39:4–128.3 et seq.**

Identification marks, **39:3–33**

Inflammable liquids, portable emergency warning devices, **39:3–64**

Information plates, **39:3–82**

Inspectors and inspection,
    Intermodal transportation, chassis, **39:3–79.10 et seq.**
    Radiation, **39:5B–23**

Interference, intermodal transportation, chassis, inspectors and inspection, **39:3–79.20**

Interior and exterior mirrors, **39:3–71**

Intermodal transportation,
    Axle weight limitations, **39:3–84.1**
    Chassis, **39:3–79.10 et seq.**
    Fines and penalties, chassis, **39:3–79.16, 39:3–79.18, 39:3–79.20**
    Inspectors and inspection, **39:3–79.11**

MOTOR CARRIERS—Cont'd

Intoxication of driver, prevention, programs, **39:5B–32**

Jurisdiction, definitions, registration and reciprocity, **39:3–6.1**

Labor and employment, fines and penalties, **39:3–10.18**

Lamps and reflectors, **39:3–61**

Length, **39:3–84**
  Private utility or house type semitrailers and trailers, **39:3–8**

Lessee, weights and measurements, **39:3–84.3**

Lettering,
  Noncommercial trucks, **39:3–8.1**
  Size, **39:4–46**

License plate elimination, **39:3–61**

Licenses and permits,
  Fees, **39:3–20**
  Limitations as to width or length, exceeding, **39:3–84**
  Moving heavy machinery, **39:4–26**
  Noncommercial trucks, **39:1–1, 39:3–8, 39:3–8.1**
  Nonresidents vehicles, **39:3–15**
  Plates, farmers trucks, **39:3–25**
  Special permit to operate private utility or house type semitrailer or trailer, **39:3–8**

Limousine or Livery Service, generally, this index

Liquefied petroleum gas, rules and regulations, **21:1B–2**

Liquid burning flares, emergency warning devices, **39:3–64**

Loads and Loading, generally, this index

Machinery and equipment,
  Frozen dessert trucks, **39:4–128.5**
  Ice and snow, removal, **27:23–49**
  Intermodal transportation, chassis, **39:3–79.10 et seq.**

Maintenance, intermodal transportation, chassis, **39:3–79.12**

Maximum width and length, **39:3–84**

Mirrors,
  Interior and exterior, **39:3–71**
  Rear view mirrors, **39:3–71.1**

Motor drawn vehicles, registration, **39:3–20, 39:3–22a**

Motor vehicle inspector, stopping vehicle for measurement or weighing, **39:3–84.3**

Moving Heavy Machinery, generally, this index

Mud flaps, **39:3–79.1 et seq.**

Name,
  Display, **39:4–46**
  Noncommercial trucks, **39:3–8.1**

Noncommercial trucks, licenses, **39:1–1, 39:3–8, 39:3–8.1**

Nonresident vehicles, fines and penalties, **39:3–15**
  Weight, **39:3–20.3**

Numbers, **39:4–54**
  Change or destruction, crimes and offenses, **2C:17–6**

Out of service,
  Federal registration, enforcement, **39:5B–32**
  Fines and penalties, **39:3–10.18**
  Intermodal transportation, chassis, tags and tagging, **39:3–79.13**

Overhanging loads, red flags, **39:3–61.4**

Overweight vehicles, shipper liability, **39:3–84.3**

Penalties. Fines and penalties, generally, ante

Permits. Licenses and permits, generally, ante

Pharmacists, license plates, exceptions, **39:4–46**

Placards, posting, radioactive materials, **39:5B–18**

Portable emergency warning devices, **39:3–64**

MOTOR CARRIERS—Cont'd

Posting, placards, radioactive materials, **39:5B–18**

Proportional registration, reciprocity, **39:3–6.1 et seq.**

Public utility owners, display of municipality name, **39:4–46**

Qualifications, intermodal transportation, chassis, inspectors and inspection, **39:3–79.15**

Radioactive substances, **39:5B–18 et seq.**

Railroad crossings, approaching, **39:4–128.11**

Rear crossview mirrors, **39:3–71.1**

Rear end protection device, requirements, **39:3–84**

Rear lamps, **39:3–61**

Rear reflectors, **39:3–61**

Rear view mirrors, **39:3–71.1**

Rear wheels, preventing wheels from throwing debris, **39:3–79.1 et seq.**

Reciprocity, registration, **39:3–6.1 et seq.**

Records and recordation, intermodal transportation, chassis, **39:3–79.17**

Red flags, overhanging loads, **39:3–61.4**

Registration, **39:3–20**
  Federal, enforcement, **39:5B–32**
  Fees, **39:3–20**
    Reduced registration fees, **39:3–22a**
  Intermodal transportation, chassis, providers, **39:3–79.18**
  Motor drawn commercial vehicles, **39:3–20**
  Plates, empty vehicles, **39:3–20.1, 39:3–20.2**
  Private utility and house type semitrailers and trailers, **39:3–8**
  Reciprocity, **39:3–6.1 et seq.**
  Rubber tires as prerequisite, **39:3–23**
  Semitrailers, heavy machinery, **39:4–26**
  Solid waste vehicles, **39:3–20**

Rental, noncommercial trucks, **39:3–8, 39:3–8.1**
  Fees, **39:3–20**

Repairs, intermodal transportation, chassis, **39:3–79.16**

Replacement, intermodal transportation, chassis, **39:3–79.16**

Rules and regulations,
  Intermodal transportation, chassis, **39:3–79.21**
  Length and width, **39:3–84**

Rural mail routes, **39:3–2**

Second and subsequent offenses, radioactive materials, fines and penalties, **39:5B–24**

Side marker lamps, **39:3–61**

Signs, noncommercial trucks, **39:3–8.1**

Solid Waste, this index

Speed,
  Limitations, constructor vehicles, **39:3–20**
  Lower maximum limits, **39:4–98.1**
  Railroad crossings, approaching, **39:4–128.11**

Stopping vehicle for measurement or weighing, **39:3–84.3**

Summons, traffic rules and regulations, notice, **39:5–25.1**

Tags and tagging, intermodal transportation, chassis, out of service, **39:3–79.13**

Taillamps, **39:3–61**

Tandem axle, **39:4–54**

Theft alarm signal device permitted, **39:3–69**

Time, intermodal transportation, chassis, inspectors and inspection, **39:3–79.14**

Tires,
  Pneumatic tires, information plate required on chassis, **39:3–82**
  Prerequisite to registration, **39:3–23**
  Requirements, penalty, **39:3–80**
  Safety requirements, **39:3–72**
  Size and development of load, **39:3–82**

MOTOR CARRIERS—Cont'd

Tow Trucks and Towing Companies, generally, this index

Traffic hazard warning signals, **39:3–64**

Traffic Rules and Regulations, generally, this index

Turn signals, **39:3–61**

Weights and measures, **39:3–20, 39:3–84.3**
  Dump trucks, axle weight limitations, **39:3–84.1**
  Maximum weight, **39:3–84**
  Nonresident vehicles, fines and penalties, **39:3–20.3**
  Registration, **39:3–20**
  Solid waste vehicles, **39:3–84.1**
  State highways, **39:4–197.16 et seq.**

Width,
  Maximum width, **39:3–84**
  Private utility or house type semitrailer or trailer, **39:3–8**

MOTOR FUEL TAX

Diesel fuel, untaxed special fuel as including, **2C:64–1**

Kerosene, untaxed special fuel as including, **2C:64–1**

No. 2 fuel oil, untaxed special fuel as including, **2C:64–1**

Special fuels, untaxed special fuel, definitions, subject to forfeiture, **2C:64–1**

MOTOR FUELS

Compressed gaseous fuels, vehicle labels, **39:3–79.4 et seq.**

Crimes and offenses, vehicles powered by compressed or liquified gaseous fuel, **39:3–79.4 et seq.**

Fines and penalties, compressed or liquified gaseous fuel users, **39:3–79.7, 39:3–79.8**

Identification, vehicles using compressed or liquified gaseous fuel, **39:3–79.4 et seq.**

Liquified gaseous fuels, vehicle labels, **39:3–79.4 et seq.**

School buses, liquefied petroleum gas, **39:3B–13 et seq.**

Turnpike projects, transportation regulation, **27:23–31**

MOTOR HOTELS

Hotels and Motels, generally, this index

MOTOR VEHICLE COMMISSION

Generally, **39:2–1 et seq., 39:2A–1 et seq.**

Actions and proceedings, chief administrator, powers and duties, **39:2A–28**

Administrative law and procedure, **39:2A–21**

Adverse or pecuniary interest, board, application of law, **39:2A–18**

Advisory councils, **39:2A–26**

Agency facilities, studies, **39:2A–27**

Ancillary services, contracts, **39:2A–33**

Application of law, **39:2A–4**
  Board, adverse or pecuniary interest, **39:2A–18**
  Reorganization, **39:2A–34**

Appointments,
  Board, members and membership, **39:2A–12**
  Chief administrator, powers and duties, **39:2A–11**

Attorney general, board, members and membership, **39:2A–12**

Attorneys, legal representation, **39:2A–25**

Audits and auditors, **39:2A–22**

Beverages, concessions, contracts, **39:2A–33**

Bids and bidding, ancillary services, contracts, **39:2A–33**

MOTOR VEHICLE COMMISSION—Cont'd
Board, **39:2A–12 et seq.**
Budgets, **39:2A–4**
  Officers and employees, chief administrator, powers and duties, **39:2A–28**
  Powers and duties, **39:2A–13**
Business advisory council, **39:2A–26**
Certificates of title, motor vehicles, improvements, chief administrator, **39:2A–29**
Chief administrator, **39:2–2**
  Appointments, powers and duties, **39:2A–11**
  Battleship U.S.S. New Jersey license plates, issuance, **39:3–27.67**
  Definitions, **39:1–1**
  Deputy chief administrator, **39:2A–10**
    Definitions, **39:1–1**
    Powers and duties, **39:2–4**
  Powers and duties, **39:2A–28**
    Historic preservation license plates, **39:3–27.72 et seq.**
  Qualifications, appointment and removal, **39:2–2**
  Record of official acts, **39:2–10**
  Registration, motor vehicles, improvements, **39:2A–29**
Civil service,
  Private motor vehicle agency, transfers, **39:2A–6 et seq.**
  Transfers,
    Motor vehicles division, **39:2A–5**
    Private motor vehicle agency, **39:2A–6 et seq.**
Commercial bus unit, transportation department, transfer of powers and duties, **39:2A–35**
Commissioner,
  Defined as meaning director of division, **39:1–1**
  Deputy commissioner,
    Acting commissioner, **39:2–15**
    Defined as meaning deputy director, **39:1–1**
Compensation and salaries,
  Board, members and membership, **39:2A–15**
  Officers and employees, chief administrator, powers and duties, **39:2A–28**
  Private motor vehicle agency, officers and employees, transfers, **39:2A–8**
Concessions, beverages, food, contracts, **39:2A–33**
Construction of law, **39:2A–40, 39:2A–41**
Continued, **39:2–1**
Contracts,
  Ancillary services, **39:2A–33**
  Powers and duties, **39:2A–13**
Costs,
  Animal welfare license plates, reimbursement, **39:3–27.56**
  Battleship U.S.S. New Jersey license plates, reimbursement, **39:3–27.70**
  Coastal protection license plate program, reimbursement, **39:3–27.51**
Creation, **39:2A–4**
Credit cards, payment, **39:2A–20**
Criminal history record information, officers and employees, **39:2A–32**
Customer service advisory council, **39:2A–26**
Damages, privileges and immunities, board, **39:2A–23**
Defined as meaning division, **39:1–1**
Deputy chief administrator. Chief administrator, ante
Digitalized picture fee, revenues, **39:2A–37**
Elections, board, vice chair, **39:2A–14**
Electronic funds transfers, payment, **39:2A–20**
Electronic transactions, payment, **39:2A–20**

MOTOR VEHICLE COMMISSION—Cont'd
Employees. Officers and employees, generally, post
Expenses and expenditures, board, members and membership, reimbursement, **39:2A–15**
Fees,
  Dishonored check, **39:5–36.1**
  Increases, **39:2A–36.1**
  Revenues, **39:2A–37**
  Service charges, **39:2A–36**
Financial statements and reports, **39:2A–22**
  General assembly, **39:2A–22**
Fingerprints and fingerprinting, officers and employees, **39:2A–32**
Food, concessions, contracts, **39:2A–33**
Funds,
  Omnibus safety enforcement fund, **39:3–79.24**
  Powers and duties, **39:2A–13**
General assembly,
  Financial statements and reports, **39:2A–22**
  Reports, **39:2A–22**
Governor,
  Financial statements and reports, **39:2A–22**
  Minutes, meetings, board, approval, **39:2A–17**
  Reports, **39:2A–22**
Grants, powers and duties, **39:2A–13**
Hearings, removal from office, board, **39:2A–19**
Improvements, registration, motor vehicles, chief administrator, **39:2A–29**
Incentives, payment, surcharges, **39:2A–42**
Inspectors, abolition, **39:2–9.2**
Interagency memorandum of agreement, coastal protection license plate program, **39:3–27.54**
Leases, property needed to carry out law relating to inspection, **39:8–2**
Legal representation, attorneys, **39:2A–25**
Licenses and permits,
  Agents, officers and employees, **39:3–3**
  Motor vehicles, improvements, chief administrator, **39:2A–29**
  Revocation or suspension, motor vehicle affordability and fairness task force, **39:2A–30**
Meetings, board, **39:2A–16**
Members and membership,
  Board, **39:2A–12**
  Compensation and salaries, board, **39:2A–15**
  Expenses and expenditures, reimbursement, board, **39:2A–15**
  Motor vehicle affordability and fairness task force, **39:2A–30**
Minutes, meetings, board, governor, approval, **39:2A–17**
Motor vehicle affordability and fairness task force, **39:2A–30**
Municipal courts, suspension of driving privileges, notice, **2B:12–31**
Notice, meetings, board, **39:2A–16**
Oaths and affirmations,
  Deputy director, **39:2–4**
  Director of, **39:2–2**
  Members and membership, board, **39:2A–19**
Officers and employees,
  Chief administrator, powers and duties, **39:2A–28**
  Criminal history record information, **39:2A–32**
  Fingerprints and fingerprinting, **39:2A–32**
  Licenses and permits, agents, **39:3–3**
  Organization, chief administrator, **39:2A–28**
  Private motor vehicle agency, transfers, **39:2A–6 et seq.**

MOTOR VEHICLE COMMISSION—Cont'd
Officers and employees—Cont'd
  Transfers,
    Motor vehicles division, **39:2A–5**
    Private motor vehicle agency, **39:2A–6 et seq.**
Omnibus safety enforcement fund, funds, **39:3–79.24**
Open public meetings, board, **39:2A–16**
Organization, chief administrator, **39:2A–28**
Payment,
  Electronic transactions, **39:2A–20**
  Incentives, surcharges, **39:2A–42**
  Revenues, proportional revenues, **39:2A–39**
Plans and specifications,
  Motor vehicle affordability and fairness task force, **39:2A–30**
  Officers and employees, chief administrator, powers and duties, **39:2A–28**
  Powers and duties, **39:2A–13**
Powers and duties, **39:2–3, 39:2A–13**
  Chief administrator, **39:2A–28**
Private motor vehicle agency, transfers, officers and employees, **39:2A–6 et seq.**
Privileges and immunities,
  Damages, board, **39:2A–23**
  Torts, board, **39:2A–24**
Probationary period, officers and employees, private motor vehicle agency, transfers, **39:2A–7**
Promotional payment incentives, surcharges, **39:2A–42**
Provisional employees, private motor vehicle agency, civil service, transfers, **39:2A–9**
Public policy, **39:2A–2**
Quorum, meetings, board, **39:2A–16**
Registration,
  Fees, security surcharges, **39:2A–38**
  Motor vehicles, chief administrator, improvements, **39:2A–29**
Reimbursement, board, members and membership, expenses and expenditures, **39:2A–15**
Removal from office, board, **39:2A–19**
Reorganization, application of law, **39:2A–34**
Reports, **39:2A–22**
Revenues, fees, **39:2A–37**
Security surcharges, motor vehicles, registration, fees, **39:2A–38**
Service charges, fees, **39:2A–36**
Severability, construction of law, **39:2A–41**
State treasurer, board, members and membership, **39:2A–12**
Studies, agency facilities, **39:2A–27**
Surcharges,
  Increases, **39:2A–36.1**
  Promotional payment incentives, **39:2A–42**
Task forces, motor vehicle affordability and fairness task force, **39:2A–30**
Taxation, exemptions, **39:2A–31**
Technology advisory council, **39:2A–26**
Terms of office, board, members and membership, **39:2A–12**
Torts, privileges and immunities, **39:2A–24**
Transfer of powers and duties, **39:2A–4**
  Commercial bus unit, transportation department, **39:2A–35**
Transfers. Officers and employees, ante
Vacancies in office, board, members and membership, **39:2A–12**
Vetoes, governor, minutes, meetings, board, **39:2A–17**
Vice chair, board, elections, **39:2A–14**

MOTOR VEHICLE INSPECTION LAW
Generally, **39:8–1 et seq.**

MOTOR VEHICLE INSURANCE
All terrain vehicles, 39:3C–20
Arbitration and award, no fault insurance, **39:6A–24 et seq.**
 Personal injury protection benefits paid, **39:6A–9.1**
Assignments, no fault insurance, personal injuries, **39:6A–4**
 Medical expense benefits, **39:6A–3.1**
Attachment, funeral expense benefits, exemption, **39:6A–4**
Automobile full insurance underwriting association, automobile insurance risk exchange membership, **39:6A–21**
Automobile Insurance Cost Reduction Act, **39:6A–1.1 et seq.**
Automobile insurance risk exchange, **39:6A–21, 39:6A–22**
 Investments, **39:6A–22.1**
 Premium differential, transfers by member insurers, **39:6A–22**
Automobile Reparation Reform Act. No fault insurance, generally, post
Binders, policy issued under security responsibility law, **39:6–48**
Compensation and salaries,
 Dispute resolution, no fault insurance, medical expense benefits, **39:6A–5.1**
 Dispute resolution professionals, no fault insurance, medical expense benefits, **39:6A–5.1**
Compliance, mandatory insurance, low income persons, special policies, **39:6A–3.3**
Compulsory insurance, **39:6A–3 et seq.**
 Liability insurance, **39:6B–1**
 Uninsured motorists prevention fund, **39:6B–3**
Conflict of interest, dispute resolution, no fault insurance, medical expense benefits, **39:6A–5.1**
Costs, Automobile Insurance Cost Reduction Act, **39:6A–1.1 et seq.**
Counterfeiting, identification cards, **2C:21–2.3**
Coverage,
 Alternative coverage, **39:6A–3.1**
 Selection form, **39:6A–23**
Crimes and offenses,
 Identification cards, counterfeiting, **2C:21–2.3**
 No fault insurance,
  Exclusions, **39:6A–7**
  Tort options, false statements or fraud, **39:6A–8**
Damages, unsatisfied claim and judgment fund, **39:6–70**
Death benefits,
 No fault insurance, **39:6A–4**
 Payment, no fault insurance, **39:6A–4**
 Special policies, low income persons, **39:6A–3.3**
Definitions,
 Automobile Insurance Cost Reduction Act, **39:6A–2**
 Immediate family members, no fault insurance, election of tort option, **39:6A–8.1**
Dirt bikes, **39:3C–20**
Dispute resolution, no fault insurance,
 Medical expense benefits, **39:6A–5.1**
 Personal injury coverage, **39:6A–5.1**
Drivers licenses, suspension or revocation, fraud, **39:6A–15**
Driving while intoxicated, loss recovery, exceptions, **39:6A–4.5**
Election, compulsory coverage, alternative coverage, Automobile Insurance Cost Reduction Act, **39:6A–3.2**

MOTOR VEHICLE INSURANCE—Cont'd
Electric personal assistive mobility devices, **39:4–14.10**
Essential services benefits, no fault insurance, **39:6A–4**
Execution,
 Exemption of no fault benefits, **39:6A–4**
 Funeral expense benefits, exemption, **39:6A–4**
Exemptions. No fault insurance, post
Fines and penalties,
 Liability insurance, operation of motor vehicle without, **39:6B–2**
 Operation of vehicle after suspension of license for failure to carry insurance, **39:3–40**
 Tort options, false statements or fraud, **39:6A–8**
Fraud,
 Drivers licenses, suspension or revocation, **39:6A–15**
 No fault insurance, tort options, **39:6A–8**
Funeral expense benefits, exemption from execution of attachment, **39:6A–4**
Funeral expenses, no fault insurance, **39:6A–4**
Identification cards,
 Counterfeiting, **2C:21–2.3**
 Low speed vehicles, **39:4–31.3**
 Possession by driver, **39:3–29**
Impounding,
 Identification cards, possession, **39:3–29, 39:3–29.1a**
 Release, **39:3–40.6**
Income continuation benefits, no fault insurance, **39:6A–4**
Information, insurers disclosure, **39:3–4e**
Insolvency, license or registration, **39:6–37**
Investments, automobile insurance risk exchange, **39:6A–22**
Levy,
 Exemption of no fault benefits, **39:6A–4**
 Funeral expense benefits, exemption, **39:6A–4**
Limitation of actions, no fault insurance, **39:6A–13.1**
 Options, **39:6A–8**
Low income persons, special policies, **39:6A–3.3**
Medical expense benefits. No fault insurance, post
Medical review organizations, **39:6A–5.2**
 Disputed tests or treatment, **39:6A–5.1**
Merit rating plan,
 Comprehensive enforcement program, surcharges, **2B:19–6, 2B:19–10**
 Implementation expenses, unsatisfied claimant judgment fund, **39:6–88**
 Superior court, comprehensive enforcement program, surcharges, **2B:19–6, 2B:19–10**
Motorized bicycles, **39:4–14.3e**
No fault insurance, **39:6A–1 et seq.**
 Actions and proceedings, **39:6A–8**
 Additional coverage, **39:6A–4**
 Admissibility of evidence, **39:6A–12**
 Agreement between insurer paying personal injury protection benefits and tortfeasors insurer, reimbursement, **39:6A–9.1**
 Application of law, **39:6A–4.4, 39:6A–17**
 Applications, notice, available coverage and rate credits, deductibles, exclusions, **39:6A–23**
 Arbitration and award, **39:6A–24 et seq.**
  Insurer against insured tortfeasor, personal injury protection benefits paid, **39:6A–9.1**
 Arrest, resisting arrest, exemptions, **39:6A–7**
 Assignments, personal injuries, **39:6A–4**

MOTOR VEHICLE INSURANCE—Cont'd
No fault insurance—Cont'd
 Assignments, personal injuries—Cont'd
  Medical expense benefits, **39:6A–3.1**
 Automobile Insurance Cost Reduction Act, **39:6A–1.1 et seq.**
  Compulsory coverage, alternative coverage, **39:6A–3.1**
  Election, **39:6A–3.2**
  Compulsory insurance, alternative coverage, **39:6A–3.1**
 Automobile insurance risk exchange, **39:6A–21, 39:6A–22**
  Investments, **39:6A–22**
  Premium differential, transfer by member insurers, **39:6A–22**
 Base territorial rates, reductions, options, **39:6A–4.3**
 Buyers guides, policy coverages,
  Benefit limits and coverage options, **39:6A–23**
  Written in plain English, **39:6A–23**
 Cancellation, **39:6A–3**
 Certificates and certification, medical review organizations, **39:6A–5.2**
 Collateral sources, **39:6A–6**
 Compulsory insurance, **39:6A–3 et seq.**
  Automobile Insurance Cost Reduction Act, election, **39:6A–3.2**
 Compulsory uninsured motorist protection, **39:6A–14**
 Conflict of interest, dispute resolution, medical expense benefits, **39:6A–5.1**
 Conspiracy, fines and penalties, **39:6A–15**
 Construction of act, **39:6A–16**
 Contribution, **39:6A–11**
 Crimes and offenses, exemptions, **39:6A–7**
 Damages,
  Admissibility of evidence, **39:6A–12**
  Limitations, **39:6A–8**
  Noneconomic loss, tort options, **39:6A–8**
 Death benefits, **39:6A–4**
  Income continuation, coverage, **39:6A–10**
 Deductibles, medical expense benefits, **39:6A–4**
 Deductions, **39:6A–6**
 Definitions, **39:6A–2**
  Personal injury coverage, **39:6A–4**
 Discovery, **39:6A–13**
 Dispute resolution,
  Medical expense benefits, **39:6A–5.1**
  Personal injury coverage, **39:6A–5.1**
  Referrals, **39:6A–5.2**
 Driver benefits, **39:6A–4**
 Drugs, operating under influence, exemptions, **39:6A–7**
 Drunken driving, exemptions, **39:6A–7**
 Election,
  Alternative coverage, **39:6A–3.1**
  Compulsory coverage, alternative coverage, Automobile Insurance Cost Reduction Act, **39:6A–3.2**
 Essential services benefits, **39:6A–4**
 Evidence,
  Coverage selection form, **39:6A–23**
  Damages, admissibility, **39:6A–12**
 Exemptions, **39:6A–7**
  Levy and attachment, **39:6A–4**
  Torts, **39:6A–8**
 Fee schedule, medical expense benefits, **39:6A–4.6**
 Fines and penalties, **39:6A–15**
 Form, additional coverage, **39:6A–10**
 Fraud, **39:6A–15**
 Funeral expense benefits, **39:6A–4**

MOTOR VEHICLE INSURANCE—Cont'd
No fault insurance—Cont'd
  Funeral expense benefits—Cont'd
    Exemption from levy and attachment,
    39:6A–4
  Income continuation benefits, **39:6A–4**
  Income continuation coverage, additional
    coverage, **39:6A–10**
  Instructions to jury, damages, **39:6A–12**
  Limitation of actions, **39:6A–13.1**
  Loss recovery, exceptions, **39:6A–4.5**
  Medical expense benefits, **39:6A–4**
    Alternative coverage, **39:6A–3.1**
    Automobile Insurance Cost Reduction
      Act, **39:6A–3.1**
    Collateral sources, **39:6A–6**
    Crimes and offenses, exclusions, **39:6A–7**
    Deductible or copayment, **39:6A–4**
    Dispute resolution, **39:6A–5.1**
      Referrals, **39:6A–5.2**
    Evidence, admissibility, **39:6A–12**
    Exclusions, **39:6A–7**
    Fee schedule, **39:6A–4.6**
    Medical review organizations, **39:6A–5.2**
      Disputed tests or treatment, **39:6A–5.1**
    Medicare, **39:6A–6**
    Military benefits, **39:6A–6**
    Options, **39:6A–4.3**
    Payment, collateral sources, **39:6A–6**
    Temporary disability payments, **39:6A–6**
    Tortfeasors, reimbursement, **39:6A–9.1**
    Workers compensation, **39:6A–6**
  Medical review organizations, disputed tests
    or treatment, **39:6A–5.1**
  Medical tests or treatment, valid diagnostic
    tests, lists, **39:6A–4.7**
  Medicare, **39:6A–6**
  Military benefits, **39:6A–6**
  Multiple policies, exemption, **39:6A–7**
  Notice,
    Available coverages and rate credits, de-
      ductibles, exclusions, **39:6A–23**
    Toll free telephone number, **39:6A–23**
    Tort options available, **39:6A–8.1**
  Options,
    Medical expense benefits, **39:6A–4.3**
    Personal injury coverage, **39:6A–4.3**
  Other policies, exemption, **39:6A–7**
  Payment, **39:6A–5**, **39:6A–6**
    Interest, **39:6A–5**
  Pedestrian coverage, **39:6A–4**
  Personal injuries, **39:6A–4**
    Alternative coverage, **39:6A–3.1**
    Benefits, payment, time, **39:6A–5**
    Dispute resolution, **39:6A–5.1**
    Notice, payment, **39:6A–5**
    Options, **39:6A–4.3**
    Payment, **39:6A–5**
    Primacy of coverages, **39:6A–4.2**
  Physical or mental examination, discovery,
    39:6A–13
  Premium differentials, transfers to automo-
    bile insurance risk exchange by member
    insurers, **39:6A–22**
  Primacy of coverages, personal injuries,
    39:6A–4.2
  Rates and charges, **39:6A–18**
  Reduced personal injury protection premi-
    um, **39:6A–4.1**
  Reimbursement, insurer paying personal in-
    jury protection benefits by tortfeasors
    insurer, agreement or arbitration,
    39:6A–9.1
  Reimbursement to insurer, **39:6A–6**

MOTOR VEHICLE INSURANCE—Cont'd
No fault insurance—Cont'd
  Reports, compulsory coverage, alternative
    coverage, Automobile Insurance Cost
    Reduction Act, **39:6A–3.2**
  Rules and regulations, personal injury cover-
    age, **39:6A–4.3**
  Setoff, medical expense benefits coverage,
    failure to maintain, **39:6A–4.5**
  Stacking of coverages, personal injuries,
    39:6A–4.2
  Standards, notice and buyers guide, available
    coverages and rate credits, **39:6A–23**
  Subrogation, elected deductibles, **39:6A–4.3**
  Survivor benefits, **39:6A–4**
  Temporary disability benefits, **39:6A–6**
  Title of act, **39:6A–1**
  Toll free telephone number, **39:6A–23**
  Torts,
    Election of option, **39:6A–8.1**
    Exemptions, **39:6A–8**
    Intentional acts, loss recovery, exceptions,
      39:6A–4.5
    Noneconomic loss, tort options, **39:6A–8**
  Two or more automobiles, reduced personal
    injury protection premium, **39:6A–4.1**
  Uninsured motorist coverage, **39:6A–14**
  Unsatisfied claim and judgment fund, discov-
    ery, **39:6A–13**
  Valid diagnostic tests, lists, **39:6A–4.7**
  Willful and wanton injuries, exemptions,
    39:6A–7
  Workers compensation, **39:6A–6**
Notice. No fault insurance, ante
Personal injuries,
  Application of law, **39:6A–4.4**
  Automobile Insurance Cost Reduction Act,
    compulsory insurance, alternative cover-
    age, **39:6A–3.1**
  Medical tests and treatment, standards, Au-
    tomobile Insurance Cost Reduction Act,
    39:6A–3.1
  No fault insurance, ante
  Noncompliance, loss recovery, exceptions,
    39:6A–4.5
  Special policies, low income persons,
    39:6A–3.3
Points, traffic control signal monitoring system,
    39:4–8.15
Possession, identification cards, counterfeiting,
    2C:21–2.3
Premiums,
  Differentials, transfer to automobile insur-
    ance risk exchange by member insurers,
    39:6A–22
  Sample comparison, publication, **39:6A–23.1**
Publication, sample premium comparison,
    39:6A–23.1
Rates and charges, low income persons, special
    policies, **39:6A–3.3**
Registration, insurer obtaining ownership or
    control under theft policy, **39:3–18**
Reimbursement, no fault insurer paying per-
    sonal injury protection benefits by tortfea-
    sors insurer, agreement or arbitration,
    39:6A–9.1
Renewal,
  Automobile Insurance Cost Reduction Act,
    39:6A–3.2
    Refusal, **39:6A–3.1**
  Refusal, Automobile Insurance Cost Reduc-
    tion Act, **39:6A–3.1**
Repair of vehicles, proof to lien holders or
    lessors, **39:13–8**

MOTOR VEHICLE INSURANCE—Cont'd
Reports,
  Automobile insurance risk exchange, invest-
    ments, **39:6A–22**
  No fault insurance, compulsory coverage, al-
    ternative coverage, Automobile Insur-
    ance Cost Reduction Act, **39:6A–3.2**
Rules and regulations, no fault insurance, per-
    sonal injury coverages, **39:6A–4.3**
Income continuation, **39:6A–10**
Sample comparison of premiums, publication,
    39:6A–23.1
Satisfaction of debts, exemption, no fault bene-
    fits, **39:6A–4**
Snowmobiles, **39:3C–20**
Special policies, low income persons, **39:6A–3.3**
Territorial rating plans, no fault insurance, re-
    ductions, options, **39:6A–4.3**
Toll free telephone number, no fault insurance,
    notices, **39:6A–23**
Torts. No fault insurance, ante
Tow trucks and towing companies, registration,
    39:3–84.8
Uninsured motorist prevention fund, identifica-
    tion cards, possession by driver, fines and
    penalties, deposits, **39:3–29**
Uninsured motorists,
  Losses, recovery, exceptions, **39:6A–4.5**
  No fault insurance, compulsory protection,
    39:6A–14
  Prevention fund, **39:6B–3**
Unsatisfied claim and judgment fund, **39:6–61**
    et seq.
  Excess medical expense benefits, reimburse-
    ment of insurers, **39:6–73.1**
  Automobile Insurance Cost Reduction
    Act, **39:6A–3.1**
  Fraud, **39:6A–15**
  No fault insurance, discovery, **39:6A–13**

MOTOR VEHICLE JUNK YARDS
Generally, **39:11–1 et seq.**
Abandoned and unclaimed property, certifi-
    cates, **39:10A–3**
Appeal from municipal governing body, zoning
    commission or director of division of mo-
    tor vehicles, **39:11–10**
Certifying condition of vehicle sold, **39:11–9**
Complaint in proceeding for violating Junk
    Yard Law, **39:11–11**
Definitions, **39:11–2**
Disposition of fines for violation of law,
    39:11–11
Fees,
  Examination of proposed location, **39:11–8**
  Hearing on application for municipal permit,
    39:11–6
Fines and penalties, **39:11–11**
Form, application for license, **39:11–7**
Jurisdiction of proceedings for violating Junk
    Yard Law, **39:11–11**
Jury, hearing without jury in proceeding for
    violation of Junk Yard Law, **39:11–11**
Licenses and permits,
  Director of motor vehicles division, **39:11–7**
  Examination of proposed location, **39:11–7**
  Fees, **39:11–8**
  Term of license, **39:11–8**
  Fees, **39:11–5**, **39:11–6**
  Findings, **39:11–5**
  Hearings, application, **39:11–5**, **39:11–6**
  Necessity, **39:11–4**
  Recommendations, **39:11–6**
  Revocation for violation of law, **39:11–11**
Motor vehicle junk business, definitions,
    39:11–2

MOTOR VEHICLE JUNK YARDS—Cont'd
Notice, hearing on application for permit for motor vehicle junk yard, **39:11–5, 39:11–6**
Permits. Licenses and permits, generally, ante
Process in proceeding for violating Junk Yard Law, **39:11–11**
Revocation, junk yard license for violation of law, **39:11–11**
Surrender, title papers, **39:10–23**
Title papers, surrender, **39:10–23**
Warrant in proceedings for violating, **39:11–11**

MOTOR VEHICLE RACES AND EXHIBITIONS
Fines and penalties, **39:4–52**
Public highway, disorderly person, **39:5C–1**

MOTOR VEHICLE RECORD
Definitions, drivers privacy protection, **39:2–3.3**

MOTOR VEHICLE SECURITY AND CUSTOMER SERVICE ACT
Generally, **39:2A–1 et seq.**

MOTOR VEHICLE SECURITY RESPONSIBILITY LAW
See, also, Motor Vehicle Insurance, generally, this index
Generally, **39:6–23 et seq.**
Action, failure to bring action within one year affecting suspension or renewal of license, registration or nonresidents operating privilege, **39:6–27**
Administration, **39:6–50**
Amount of security, **39:6–25**
Limits, **39:6–29**
Application of law, liability insurance, **39:6–25**
Application of security deposited, **39:6–30**
Apportionment, amount certified among liability insurers, **39:6–59**
Audits and auditors, self insurers, **39:6–52**
Bond,
Application of law when operator or owner is covered by bond, **39:6–25**
Operating record of motorist furnished to surety, **39:6–42**
Cancellation of certificate of self insurance, **39:6–52**
Certificate of Ownership Law, nonconventional type of motor vehicles,
Definitions, **39:10–2**
Manufacturers identification number, **39:10–7**
Certificate of self insurance, **39:6–52**
Certified copy, nonresidents operating privilege, **39:6–28**
Citation of law, **39:6–23**
Complaint in proceeding for violation, **39:6–55**
Compulsory liability coverage, **39:6B–1**
Consent of owner to operation, law inapplicable to vehicle operated without consent, **39:6–26**
Damages. Judgments and decrees, post
Definitions, **39:6–24**
Deposits,
Accident report considered in determining whether law is inapplicable, **39:4–131**
Evidence of negligence, security filed, **39:6–53**
Reinstatement or renewal of suspended license or registration conditioned on, **39:6–27**
Residents license suspended until deposit of security in another state, **39:6–28**
Transfer of registration of vehicle involved in accident, **39:6–49**

MOTOR VEHICLE SECURITY RESPONSIBILITY LAW—Cont'd
Director, definitions, **39:6–24**
Drivers licenses,
Informing persons holding license of contents of law, **39:6–51**
Refusal to issue to nonresidents for failure to pay judgment for damages, **39:6–36**
Reinstatement of revoked license after payment from unsatisfied claim and judgment fund, **39:6–87**
Revocation or suspension for nonpayment or judgment for damages, **39:6–35**
Enforcement, **39:6–55**
Evidence, **39:6–48**
Application for registration of motor vehicle, **39:3–4**
Forgery, **39:6–55**
Installment payments, proof of financial responsibility of person paying, **39:6–39**
Negligence, **39:6–53**
Operating record of insureds furnished to insurance company, **39:6–42**
Examinations, self insurers, **39:6–52**
Exemptions, **39:6–26, 39:6–54**
Expenses in administering, **39:6–58**
Extension of time, judgment, payment, **39:3–65**
Fee, certificate of operating record, **39:6–42**
Filing fee, self insurers certificate application, **39:6–52**
Findings, evidence, negligence, **39:6–53**
Fines and penalties, **39:6–55**
Foreign insurance company, nonresident motorist insured by, service of process on insured, **39:6–25**
Form of security, **39:6–29**
Fraud, protection, identification cards, possession by driver, **39:3–29.1**
Hearing in proceeding for violation, **39:6–55**
Identification cards, possession by driver, **39:3–29, 39:3–29.1**
Imprisonment, **39:6–55**
Information, **39:3–4e**
Correction of, **39:6–25**
Insolvency, insurer, license and registration suspension, **39:6–37**
Installment payment of damages, default, **39:6–27**
Judgments and decrees,
Application of security deposited to payment of judgments against person causing injuries, **39:6–30**
Damages,
Cancellation of certificate of self insurance for failure to pay judgment, **39:6–52**
Certified copy or transcript forwarded to director, **39:6–35**
Deposited security, **39:6–30**
Extension of time for payment by director, **39:6–35**
Failure to pay as ground for suspension or revocation of license or registration, **39:6–35**
Installment payment of judgment, **39:6–39**
Nonresidents operating privilege withdrawn on failure to pay judgment, **39:6–36**
Notice given to director in respect of satisfaction or discharge, **39:6–35**
Part payment as satisfaction of judgment, **39:6–38**
Renewal or issuance of another license affected by nonpayment of judgment, **39:6–35**
Satisfaction, **39:6–38**

MOTOR VEHICLE SECURITY RESPONSIBILITY LAW—Cont'd
Jurisdiction of proceedings to enforce law, **39:6–55**
Jury, hearing without proceeding for violation of law, **39:6–55**
Licenses and registration, **39:3–4**
Compliance with law as condition to issuance, **39:6–28**
Definition, **39:6–24**
Informing person holding registration certificate of contents of act, **39:6–51**
Insurance carriers, name on application for registration of motor vehicle, **39:3–4**
Insurance coverage, required personal injury protection benefit coverage, **39:6–25**
Nonresident, refusal of registration for failure to pay judgment for damages, **39:6–36**
Removal, suspension, evidence of coverage or personal injury protection benefit, **39:6–27**
Resident whose nonresident operating privilege was suspended in other state, **39:6–28**
Return of registration, failure to return as offense, **39:6–55**
Security deposits, return, **39:6–30**
Suspension or revocation,
Agreement to reimburse, unsatisfied claim and judgment fund, **39:6–25**
Duration of suspension, **39:6–27**
Exemption from suspension, **39:6–26**
Insolvency or bankruptcy of insurer affecting suspension, **39:6–37**
Installment payment of judgment for damages, default in payment as ground for suspension, **39:6–39**
Judgment, failure to pay as ground, **39:6–35**
Insolvent insurer, personal injury protection coverage, **39:6–37**
Noncompliance with law, **39:6–25 et seq.**
Renewal of suspended license, **39:6–27, 39:6–35**
Restoration of license or registration,
After payment out of unsatisfied claim and judgment fund, **39:6–87**
Person paying judgment in installments, **39:6–39**
Transfer of vehicle in violation of law as ground for, **39:6–49**
Unregistered vehicles, permits to cross public highways, death, bodily injury or property damage, **39:3–26.5**
Violation of law as ground, **39:6–55**
Transfer of registration of vehicle involved in accident, **39:6–49**
Written agreement to pay unsatisfied claim and judgment fund, **39:6–26**
Manufacturers identification number, nonconventional type motor vehicles, **39:10–7**
Motor vehicles which constitute inventory held for sale, definitions, **39:10–2**
Negligence, evidence, **39:6–53**
Nonconventional type motor vehicles, **39:10–2**
Manufacturers identification number, **39:10–7**
Nonresidents,
Judgment against nonresident in action for injuries transmitted to state of residence, **39:6–35**
Operating privilege,
Certified copy of record of suspension transmitted to state issuing license and registration, **39:6–28**

**MOTOR VEHICLE SECURITY RESPONSI-
BILITY LAW**—Cont'd
Nonresidents—Cont'd
Operating privilege—Cont'd
Compliance with law as condition to issu-
ance, **39:6–28**
Definitions, **39:6–24**
Reinstatement of,
Effect of nonpayment of judgment for
damages, **39:6–36**
Suspended privilege, **39:6–27**
Renewal of suspended privilege, **39:6–27**
Suspension, **39:6–28**
After accident for noncompliance of
law, **39:6–25**
Duration of, **39:6–27**
Exemption, **39:6–26**
Withdrawal, nonpayment of judgment for
damages, **39:6–36**
Service of process on director of division of
motor vehicles in action against, **39:6–25**
Offenses, **39:6–55**
Operating record, **39:6–42**
Parked vehicle, law inapplicable to vehicle
parked at time of accident, **39:6–26**
Payment over of fines for violation, **39:6–55**
Personal injury protection coverage, **39:6–27**
Persons on whose behalf deposit is made,
39:6–29
Procedure for enforcement of law and recovery
of penalty, **39:6–55**
Process, **39:6–55**
Nonresident, **39:6–25**
Reduction of amount of security, **39:6–29**
Registration. Licenses and registration, gener-
ally, ante
Release from liability,
Effect on right to reinstatement or renewal
of suspended license or nonresidents op-
erating privilege, **39:6–27**
Return of security deposited on filing re-
lease, **39:6–30**
Renewal, **39:6B–2**
Retention of security deposited, **39:6–30**
Return of security deposited, **39:6–30**
Review of orders or acts of director, **39:6–50**
Rules and regulations for administration of act,
39:6–50
Satisfaction of judgment for damages, **39:6–38**
Self insurers, **39:6–25**
Certificate, **39:6–52**
Service of process on foreign insurer covering
liability of nonresident motorist, **39:6–25**
State, definitions, **39:6–24**
Suspension or revocation. Licenses and regis-
tration, ante
Time law becomes effective, **39:6–57**
Tires, designing construction, **39:3–81**
Transfer of registration of vehicle involved in
accident, **39:6–49**
Warrants, proceeding for violation of law,
39:6–55

MOTOR VEHICLES
See, also, Traffic Rules and Regulations,
generally, this index
Generally, **39:1–1 et seq., 39:4–1 et seq.**
Abandoned or unclaimed property, **39:4–56.5,
39:10A–1 et seq.**
Certificate of ownership, public sales,
39:10A–4
Junk title certificates, **39:10A–3, 39:10A–9 et
seq.**
Liens, notice of sale, **39:10A–11 et seq.**
Notice, removal and storage, **39:10A–10**

MOTOR VEHICLES—Cont'd
Abandoned or unclaimed property—Cont'd
Obstructing passage on highways, **39:4–56.1
et seq.**
Reclaiming possession, **39:10A–2**
Repair facilities, **39:10A–8 et seq.**
Rules and regulations, **39:10A–6**
Sales, **39:10A–1 et seq.**
Security interest, notice of sale, **39:10A–11 et
seq.**
Storage, notice to owner, **39:10A–10**
Abstract, definitions, **39:10–2**
Accidents. Traffic Accidents, generally, this
index
Actions and proceedings,
Arbitration and award, tort claims, **39:6A–24
et seq.**
Complaints, generally, post
Damages, exceeding weight limitations,
39:3–84.4
Death of owner or operator pending pro-
ceeding, continuance against executor or
administrator, **39:7–2.1**
Emissions, control, civil penalties, **39:8–72**
Evidence, generally, post
Fines and penalties, body repair facilities,
39:13–6
Service of process, generally, post
Administrative law and procedure, penalty
points, **39:5–30.5**
Advertisements,
Identification, compressed or liquefied gas-
eous fuel users, **39:3–79.9**
License plates, **39:3–33**
Noncommercial trucks exterior, **39:3–8.1**
Affidavits, husband and wife registrants, death,
39:3–30.1a
Age,
Child passenger restraint systems, **39:3–76.2a**
Identification cards for nondrivers, **39:3–29.3**
Validity for life, **39:3–29.5**
Registration, **39:3–4**
Agricultural land,
Destruction by operation of vehicle, **39:4–97a**
Point system, assessment against drivers
license, **39:5–30.5a**
Trespass, **2C:18–5**
Agricultural Machinery and Equipment, gener-
ally, this index
Agricultural products,
License plates, trucks, **39:3–25**
Theft, reports, **39:5–46**
Air pollution. Emissions, generally, post
Alcoholic beverages,
Consumption while vehicle being operated,
39:4–51a
Delivery by licensees without transportation
license, **33:1–28**
Intoxication of driver, generally, post
Return of seized vehicle to carrier, **33:1–66**
Searches and seizures, **33:1–58**
Contraband, **33:1–66**
Warrants, **33:1–56, 33:1–57**
Without warrant, **33:1–65**
Unlawful property, **33:1–55**
Alley, definitions, **39:1–1**
Alteration,
Approved equipment to defeat purpose of
inspection, **39:3–47**
Marks or numbers, crimes and offenses,
2C:17–6
Alumni organizations, nonprofit, special plates,
39:3–27.35 et seq.
Amateur radio licensees, registration plates,
39:3–27.5
Ambulances, generally, this index

MOTOR VEHICLES—Cont'd
Amendment of complaint on appeal, **39:5–11**
Anchorage units,
Child passenger restraint systems, **39:3–76.2a
et seq.**
Seat safety belts, **39:3–76.2**
Animals,
Traffic accidents, **4:22–25.1, 4:22–25.2**
Unattended animals, crimes and offenses,
4:22–17
Appeal and review, **39:5–11**
Revocation or suspension of license,
39:10–20
Applicability of traffic laws, **39:4–1**
Application of law, arbitration and award, tort
claims, **39:6A–25**
Applications. Licenses and permits, post
Apportioned vehicle,
Definitions, registration, **39:3–6.11**
Fines and penalties, **39:3–6.17**
International Registration Plan, **39:3–6.12**
Registration, **39:3–6.13**
Definitions, **39:3–6.11**
Fees, **39:3–6.14**
Records, preservation, **39:3–6.15**
Supersedure, **39:3–6.19**
Temporary registration, **39:3–6.16**
Appraisals and appraisers, body repair facili-
ties, fine or license refusal, revocation, or
suspension, **39:13–4**
Approval, traffic ordinances or resolutions,
39:4–8
Arbitration and award, tort claims, **39:6A–24 et
seq.**
Armed forces,
Commercial drivers licenses, exemption,
39:3–10j, 39:3–10k
Plates or markers,
Battleship U.S.S. New Jersey plates,
39:3–27.67 et seq.
Combat infantryman badge recipients,
39:3–27.46
Military reserve units, **39:3–27.33,
39:3–27.34**
National guard, special plates, **39:3–27.13,
39:3–27.14**
Reserves, **39:3–27.33, 39:3–27.34**
Special plates, purple heart, recipients,
39:3–27.43 et seq.
Surviving spouses, **39:3–27.41**
Refund on registration fee to person enter-
ing service, **39:3–22.1**
Payment, **39:3–22.2**
Veterans, generally, post
Arraignment, power of clerk or deputy clerk,
39:5–6
Arrest,
Bond for costs, **39:5–5**
Component parts, serial numbers, **39:10B–3**
Hours of Service Law, **39:9–4**
Inspection Law, **39:8–9**
Junk Yard Law, **39:11–11**
Refusal to stop to submit to measurement or
weighing, **39:3–84.3**
Resisting arrest, no fault insurance, exemp-
tions, **39:6A–7**
Service of summons, in lieu of arrest for
violation in presence of officer, **39:5–25**
Service of warrant in another county,
39:5–28
Violation in presence of officer, **39:5–25**
Articles, throwing or dropping from vehicle on
highway, **39:4–64**
Assault by auto or vessel, **2C:12–1**
Mandatory sentence, **2C:43–6**
Assignments. Certificates of ownership, post

MOTOR VEHICLES—Cont'd

Attachable auxiliary motor vehicle axle, definitions, **39:4–54**
Attorney fees,
　Arbitration, tort claims, **39:6A–28**
　Trial de novo, arbitrated tort claims, **39:6A–34**
Attorney general, representation of complainant on appeal from conviction, **39:5–20**
Auctions and auctioneers,
　Abandoned and unclaimed vehicles, **39:10A–1 et seq.**
　Impounded or immobilized vehicles, parking offenses, **39:4–139.13**
　Licenses and permits, new state residents, **39:3–17.1**
　Wholesale automobile auction block, **39:3–18**
Audits, motor carriers, operational accounts, **39:3–6.19**
Authorized emergency vehicles, definitions, **39:1–1**
Autism medical research and treatment fund, fines and penalties, surcharge, **39:5–41**
Autobuses. Buses, generally, this index
Automobile, definitions, **39:1–1**
Automobile insurance. Motor Vehicle Insurance, generally, this index
Backing vehicles. Traffic Rules and Regulations, this index
Banks and banking, impounding, release, **39:3–40.6**
Base jurisdiction, definitions, apportioned vehicles, registration, **39:3–6.11**
Beam indicator, **39:3–59**
Berm, definitions, **39:1–1**
Bicycles. Motorized Bicycles, generally, this index
Bill of Sale Law, name changed to Certificate of Ownership Law, **39:10–1**
Blind persons,
　Identification cards for nondrivers, **39:3–29.3**
　Validity for life, **39:3–29.5**
　Right of way, **39:4–37.1**
Blood alcohol percentage, tests, refusal, fines and penalties, **2C:40–26**
Blood analysis, intoxication, implied consent, **39:4–50.2 et seq.**
Boards and commissions. Motor Vehicle Commission, generally, this index
Body repair facilities, **39:13–1 et seq.**
Bona fide converter, registration and registration plates, **39:3–18**
Bonds (officers and fiduciaries),
　Issuance of warrant, **39:5–5**
　Off site sales, licenses and permits, **39:10–19.3**
Booklets, safety seat belt systems, preparation, **39:3–76.2k**
Boys Clubs of America, registration fee exemption, **39:3–27**
Brain injury research fund, fines and penalties, surcharge, **39:5–41**
Brakes,
　Bicycles, **39:4–11.1**
　Illuminated lights to indicate application of brakes on motor vehicle, **39:3–61**
　Leaving vehicle with engine running, failure to set hand brake, fine, **39:4–53**
　Lights, indicating application of brakes, **39:3–61**
　Low speed vehicles, **39:4–31.2**
　Motor carriers, emergency system, **39:3–68.1 et seq.**
　Parked or stationary vehicles, **39:4–137**
　Proper and safe condition, certificate of approval, **39:8–3**

MOTOR VEHICLES—Cont'd

Brakes—Cont'd
　Requirements, **39:3–67, 39:3–68**
　Three axle truck tractors, **39:3–67**
　Trailers, rolling backward on hill, adequate preventive device, **39:4–54**
Brands, labels and marks,
　Change or destruction, crimes and offenses, **2C:17–6**
　Compressed or liquefied gaseous fuel users, **39:3–79.4 et seq.**
　Plates or markers, generally, post
　Regulate traffic, **39:4–191.1 et seq.**
　Safety glass material, **39:3–75**
　Vehicles powered by compressed or liquified gaseous fuel, **39:3–79.4 et seq.**
Bribery and corrupt influence, adjusters or appraisers by body repair facilities, fine or license refusal, revocation, or suspension, **39:13–4**
Bulbouts, definitions, **39:1–1**
Bundle, throwing or dropping from vehicle on highway, **39:4–64**
Buses, generally, this index
Business district,
　Definitions, **39:1–1**
　Speed, **39:4–98**
Car seats, child passenger restraint systems, **39:3–76.2a et seq.**
Careless driving, **39:4–97**
Carjacking, **2C:15–2**
Carriers. Motor Carriers, generally, this index
Cats, hitting or injuring, **4:22–25.1**
Cellular telephones,
　Accidents, reports, **39:4–131**
　Hands free telephones, **39:4–97.3 et seq.**
Certificates and certification,
　Certificates of approval. Inspection and inspectors, post
　Certificates of origin, endorsement of security interest at time of sale, **39:10–8**
　Certificates of ownership, generally, post
　Certificates of registration. Licenses and permits, post
　Crimes and offenses, certificates of conviction, nonresident, transmission to nonresidents state, **39:4–9.1**
　Ignition interlock devices, **39:4–50.20**
　Salvage certificates of title, **39:10–31**
Certificates of origin, low speed vehicles, **39:4–31.4**
Certificates of ownership, **39:10–1 et seq.**
　Additional fees, luxury cars, **39:3–8.4**
　Amendment, registration with spouse, **39:3–30**
　Assignments,
　　Certificate of origin, **39:10–8**
　　Certificate of ownership or bill of sale, **39:10–9**
　Certificate of registration, refusal to grant, **39:10–18**
　Certified copies of instrument showing lien, **39:10–14**
　Citation of Act, **39:10–1**
　Commissioner, definitions, **39:10–2**
　Conditional sales,
　　Certificate showing status of contract, **39:10–14**
　　Copy of certificate of ownership delivered to purchaser, **39:10–11**
　Contract, **39:10–2**
　　Notation of satisfaction, **39:10–10**
　Criminal history record information, background check, dealers, license, **39:10–19**
　Dealers, **39:10–2**
　　Evidence of purchase, **39:10–11**

MOTOR VEHICLES—Cont'd

Certificates of ownership—Cont'd
　Dealers—Cont'd
　　License, **39:10–19**
　　Possession, production of title papers, **39:10–6**
　　Reassignment certificates, **39:10–11**
　　Vehicles in possession, certificate of origin, **39:10–21**
　Definitions, **39:10–2**
　Delivery, security interest, **39:10–11**
　Evidence, purchase required to be submitted by purchaser, **39:10–11**
　Expenses of administering law, **39:10–25**
　Fees,
　　Additional fees, luxury cars, **39:3–8.3, 39:3–8.4**
　　Agent issuing and filing certificate of ownership, **39:10–25**
　　Certificate showing status of condition of sale or instrument, **39:10–14**
　　Correction of defect in certificate of ownership or title papers, **39:10–16**
　　Disposition, **39:10–25**
　　Duplicate certificate of ownership, **39:10–11**
　　License of dealer, **39:10–19**
　Fines and penalties, **39:10–11, 39:10–24**
　Forms prescribed by director, **39:10–22**
　Fuel efficient cars, luxury cars, additional fees, exemptions, **39:3–8.4**
　Garage keeper, title papers to vehicle in possession, **39:10–6**
　Junk title, **39:10A–3**
　License dealer, **39:10–19**
　Loss of certificate of ownership or title papers, **39:10–12**
　Luxury cars, additional fees, **39:3–8.4**
　Manufactured homes,
　　Application of law, **39:10–2**
　　Relocation, **39:10–11.1**
　Manufacturer, **39:10–2**
　Manufacturers numbers, certificate of origin to state, **39:10–8**
　New motor vehicle, definitions, **39:10–2**
　Number plates, refusal to grant without certificate of ownership, **39:10–18**
　Penalty for false statement of loss, **39:10–12**
　Production of title papers to vehicle in possession, **39:10–6**
　Public sales of abandoned and unclaimed vehicles, **39:10A–4**
　Records,
　　Contract as to registered vehicle, **39:10–14**
　　Purchase, **39:10–11**
　Registration plates of another state, necessity of documents of title or right of possession, **39:10–6**
　Return for warranty nonconformity, **39:10–9.3**
　Sales,
　　Evidence of purchase, **39:10–11**
　　Judicial process, delivery of application for certificate to purchaser, **39:10–15**
　　Other than absolute, **39:10–11**
　　Scrap or junk, **39:10–23**
　　Used vehicles, **39:10–26 et seq.**
　Salvage certificates of title, **39:10–31 et seq.**
　Security interest, endorsement on sale of used car, **39:10–9**
　Seller, definitions, **39:10–2**
　Standards, used vehicles, sales, **39:10–26 et seq.**
　Title to property, **39:10–2**
　　Dealer to require to have title papers, **39:10–21**

MOTOR VEHICLES—Cont'd
Certificates of ownership—Cont'd
  Title to property—Cont'd
    Defective or improper, **39:10–16, 39:10–21**
    Purchasing or receiving vehicle in violation of law, **39:10–24**
    Refusal to grant registration certificate without papers, **39:10–18**
  Used motor vehicle,
    Definitions, **39:10–2**
    Sales, **39:10–26 et seq.**
Certificates of registration. Licenses and permits, post
Chains for tires, **39:3–73**
Changes, marks or numbers, crimes and offenses, **2C:17–6**
Changing design or performance of equipment required to be approved, **39:3–77**
Chattel mortgages,
  Evidence of satisfaction, **39:10–14**
  Notation of performance of condition in contract, **39:10–14**
  Recording, **39:10–11**
Checks, dishonored, fees, **39:5–36.1**
Chemical analysis of blood, intoxication, implied consent, **39:4–50.2 et seq.**
Children and Minors, this index
Cigarettes or cigar, throwing or dropping from vehicle on highway, **39:4–64**
Citations, definitions, Nonresident Violator Compact, **39:5F–4**
Claims. Unsatisfied claim and judgment fund, generally, post
Clean Air Act. Emissions, generally, post
Clearance of intersection, restriction, **39:4–67**
Coasting. Traffic Rules and Regulations, this index
Collateral, definitions, Nonresident Violator Compact, **39:5F–4**
Collection of fine and costs,
  Duty to give receipt, **39:5–45**
  Suppliers of compressed or liquefied gaseous fuel, **39:3–79.8**
Collectors items, historic motor vehicles, **39:3–27.3, 39:3–27.4**
Combination of vehicles, dimensional and weight limitations, **39:3–84**
Commercial Drivers Licenses, generally, this index
Commercial vehicle enforcement fund, establishment, **39:8–75**
Commissioner,
  Definitions, coastal protection license plate program, **39:3–27.47**
  Transportation Department, this index
Common carriers. Motor Carriers, generally, this index
Community organizations, nonprofit, special plates, **39:3–27.35 et seq.**
Community service,
  Driving without insurance, second and subsequent offenses, **39:6B–2**
  Homicide, drunken driving, **2C:11–5**
Commuter Vans, generally, this index
Compacts, Nonresident Violator Compact, **39:5F–1 et seq.**
Compensation and salaries,
  Arbitrators, tort claims, **39:6A–28**
  Inspections, **39:8–10**
Complaints, **39:5–3**
  Amendment on appeal to superior court, **39:5–11**
  Detention of persons arrested without warrant until making of complaint, **39:5–25**
  Drunken driving, charge of previous offense, punishment as second offender, **39:4–50**

MOTOR VEHICLES—Cont'd
Complaints—Cont'd
  Hours of service law violations, **39:9–4**
  Inspection law violations, **39:8–9**
  Junk Yard Law violations, **39:11–11**
  Records and record, **39:5–44**
  Taking of by clerk or deputy clerk authorized, **39:5–6**
Compliance, definitions, Nonresident Violator Compact, **39:5F–4**
Component parts, serial numbers, **39:10B–1 et seq.**
Compressed gaseous fuel, identification of vehicles using, **39:3–79.4 et seq.**
Conclusions of law, arbitrators, tort claims, **39:6A–30**
Conditional sales,
  Copy of certificate of ownership recording delivered to purchaser, **39:10–11**
  Registration of repossessed motor vehicles, **39:3–18**
Confidential or privileged information, drivers privacy protection, **39:2–3.3 et seq.**
Confirmation, arbitration decisions, tort claims, **39:6A–31**
Confiscation, component parts, serial numbers, **39:10B–2**
Congressional medal of honor holder, fee registration, **39:3–27.1**
Consent,
  Implied consent, blood analysis, intoxication, **39:4–50.2 et seq.**
  Owner to operation,
    Fine and imprisonment, **39:4–48, 39:4–49**
    Security responsibility law inapplicable to vehicle operated without consent, **39:6–26**
  Riding on rear end of vehicle, **39:4–61**
Constructor, license plates, **39:3–20**
Contributory negligence, child passenger restraint system not warned, **39:3–76.2a**
Controlled substances,
  Entry on property, injunctions, **2C:35–5.10**
  Knowingly possessing while operating, **39:4–49.1**
Conventions, special registration, **39:3–27.2**
Converter, registration and registration plates, **39:3–18**
Converter dolly, definitions, **39:4–54**
Conviction of crime,
  Reports by judge or magistrate, **39:5–42**
  Suspension or revocation of license, **39:10–20**
    Reciprocity privileges, **39:5–30.1**
Cost bond, issuance of warrant, **39:5–5**
Costs,
  Collection of fine and costs, receipt, **39:5–45**
  Impounding, identification cards, possession by driver, failure, **39:3–29.1a**
  Physicians fee in drunken driving cases, **39:5–39**
  Possession and display, operators, drivers license, insurance identification card, and registration certificate, **39:4–14.3**
  Trial de novo, arbitrated tort claims, **39:6A–34**
Counterfeiting, plates or markers, **39:3–38**
Counties, this index
County officers and employees, special plates, **39:3–27.29 et seq.**
Course on improvement of driving, penalty point reduction credits, **39:5–30.9**
Courts, definitions, Nonresident Violator Compact, **39:5F–4**
Cowls, serial number, **39:10B–1 et seq.**
Crimes and offenses,
  Arrest, generally, ante

MOTOR VEHICLES—Cont'd
Crimes and offenses—Cont'd
  Assault by auto, **2C:12–1**
    Mandatory sentence, **2C:43–6**
  Carjacking, **2C:15–2**
  Certificates of conviction, nonresident, transmission to nonresidents state, **39:4–9.1**
  Chop shops, operation or maintenance, **2C:20–16**
  Complaints, generally, ante
  Courtesy plates, restrictions, **39:3–33.5a**
  Cruelty to animals, **4:22–17**
  Death by auto, **2C:11–5**
  Destruction by operation of vehicle, point system, assessment against drivers license, **39:5–30.5a**
  Disorderly persons, generally, post
  Drivers licenses, revocation or suspension, **2C:43–2, 39:3–40**
  Employing a juvenile to commit auto theft, **2C:20–17**
  Expungement, records, **2C:52–28**
  Fines and penalties, generally, post
  Flight, law enforcement officers, **2C:29–2**
  Fourth degree crimes,
    Component parts, serial numbers, **39:10B–4**
    Unlawful taking of means of conveyance, **2C:20–10**
  Fraud, generally, post
  Hit and Run Drivers, generally, this index
  Identification cards for disabled persons, **39:3–29.8**
  Ignition interlock devices, **39:4–50.19**
  Ignition keys, proof of ownership, **2C:40–23**
  Inspection Law violation, private inspection, **39:8–18**
  Insurance, operation without insurance, **39:6B–2**
  Intoxicating liquors,
    Search without warrant, **33:1–65**
    Unlawful property, **33:1–55**
  Intoxication of driver, generally, post
  Jurisdiction, traffic accidents, serious bodily injury, **2B:12–17.2**
  Larceny, generally, post
  Leader of auto theft trafficking network, **2C:20–18**
  Licenses and permits, theft of identity, exceptions, **2C:21–17**
  Littering, **39:4–63 et seq.**
  Luring and enticing, **2C:13–7**
  Marks or numbers, change, destruction, **2C:17–6**
  Master keys or devices, **2C:5–6**
  Mileage misrepresentation, **2C:21–8**
  Motor vehicle, definitions, Code of Criminal Justice, **2C:1–14**
  No fault insurance, exemptions, **39:6A–7**
  Penalty points, **39:5–30.5 et seq.**
  Plates or markers, disabled veterans, **39:3–27.18**
  Points, penalty points, **39:5–30.5 et seq.**
  Probable cause, suspending or revoking license certificate, **39:5–30**
  Reckless driving, generally, post
  Revocation or suspension, drivers licenses, **2C:43–2, 39:3–40**
  Searches and seizures, generally, post
  Second or subsequent offenses, generally, post
  Special plates, restrictions, **39:3–33.5**
  Tampering, **39:4–49**
  Third degree crime,
    Abandoned vehicles, sales, **39:10A–18**

MOTOR VEHICLES—Cont'd
Crimes and offenses—Cont'd
Third degree crime—Cont'd
Component parts, serial numbers,
39:10B–4
Unlawful taking of means of conveyance,
2C:20–10
Unattended animals, **4:22–17**
Unattended vehicles, private property,
39:4–56.6, 39:4–56.7
Unlawful taking of means of conveyance,
2C:20–10
Unlawful taking of motor vehicle, definitions, **2C:1–14**
Unsafe driving, **39:4–97.2**
Vehicles powered by compressed or liquified gaseous fuel, labels, **39:3–79.4 et seq.**
Criminal history record information, certificates of ownership, dealers, license,
39:10–19
Crossing, no passing line, **39:4–86**
Crosswalks, generally, this index
Cruelty to animals, unattended animals,
4:22–17
Curb extensions, definitions, **39:1–1**
Curb markings, parking prohibitions,
39:4–191.2
Damages,
Intoxication of driver, supervised visitation,
39:4–50
Theft of vehicle, sentence, **2C:43–2.1**
Unsatisfied claim and judgment fund,
39:6–70
Data processing, licenses and permits, **39:2–3.8**
Deaf and hearing impaired persons. Drivers Licenses, this index
Dealers,
Body repair facilities, sublet license,
39:13–2.2
Certificates of ownership, ante
Leases, post
Licensed real estate brokers, mobile and manufactured homes, **39:10–19**
Licenses and permits, **39:10–18 et seq.**
Body repair facilities, sublet license,
39:13–2.2
Exemption, real estate brokers, **39:10–19**
Suspension or revocation,
Misrepresentation of vehicle mileage,
2C:21–8
Sunday sales, **2C:33–26**
Used motor vehicles, post
Death, **2C:11–5**
Actions and proceedings, executors and administrators, **39:7–2.1**
Drivers licenses, revocation or suspension,
2C:40–22
Juveniles, referral to other courts without juveniles consent, **Rule 5:22–2**
Vesting of title in husband or wife, **39:3–30.1**
Victims of crime, notice of prosecution status, **39:5–51, 39:5–52**
Debris, throwing or dropping from vehicle on highway, **39:4–64**
Debtors and creditors,
Definitions, **39:10–2**
Husband and wife, vesting of title, **39:3–30.2**
Decals,
Examination permits, **39:3–13**
Fines and penalties, **39:3–13.8**
Probationary licenses, **39:3–13.4**
Special learners permits, **39:3–13.2a**
Decreasing speed, signal, **39:4–126**
Deductions. Unsatisfied claim and judgment fund, post

MOTOR VEHICLES—Cont'd
Defacement, marks or numbers, crimes and offenses, **2C:17–6**
Defective vehicles, used vehicles, sales, dealer liability, **39:10–26 et seq.**
Defenses. Unsatisfied claim and judgment fund, post
Definitions, **39:1–1**
Body repair facilities, licenses and permits,
39:13–1
Coastal protection license plate program,
39:3–27.47
Commercial Driver License Act, **39:3–10.11**
Converter dolly, **39:3–61**
Dimensional and weight limitations, **39:3–84**
Handicapped persons, **39:4–204**
Liberty State Park plates, **39:3–27.91**
Luxury cars, certificates of ownership, additional fees, **39:3–8.3**
Marks or numbers, change or destruction, crimes and offenses, **2C:17–6**
No fault insurance, **39:6A–2**
Olympic license plates, **39:3–27.61**
Salvage certificates of title, **39:10–31**
Toll collection monitoring system, turnpike authority, **27:23–34.1**
Traffic rules, **39:1–1**
Department. Motor Vehicle Commission, generally, this index
Deputy clerk, power of, **39:5–6**
Destruction,
Marks or numbers, crimes and offenses,
2C:17–6
Scrapping or junking, surrender of certificate of ownership to commissioner, **39:10–23**
Destruction of agricultural or recreational property by operation of vehicle, **39:4–97a**
Point system, assessment against drivers license, **39:5–30.5a**
Detective businesses, community security services, identification lights, **39:3–54.14**
Detention of persons arrested without warrant,
39:5–25
Diesel powered motor vehicles,
Definitions, emissions inspection, **39:8–60**
Emissions, generally, post
Dimensions, maximum dimensions of vehicles and loads, **39:3–84**
Director,
Definitions,
Coastal protection license plate program,
39:3–27.47
Olympic license plates, **39:3–27.61**
Revocation of vehicle registration, **39:3–40.5**
Disabled, emergency warning devices, **39:3–64**
Disclosure, drivers privacy protection, **39:2–3.3 et seq.**
Disorderly persons,
Identification cards for disabled persons,
39:3–29.10
Ignition interlock devices, **39:4–50.19**
Interference with transportation, **2C:33–14**
Intoxication of driver, parent, children and minors, passengers, **39:4–50.15**
Marks or numbers on vehicle or parts, change or destruction, **2C:17–6**
Mileage misrepresentation, **2C:21–8**
Private inspection center, discontinuance of operation, failure to return unused stickers, records, **39:8–20**
Sales, **39:10–30**
Sunday, **2C:33–26**
Display, handicapped persons, identification cards, **39:4–206**
Distance between vehicles. Traffic Rules and Regulations, this index

MOTOR VEHICLES—Cont'd
Divided highways, keeping to right, **39:4–82.1**
Division, definitions,
Coastal protection license plate program,
39:3–27.47
Olympic license plates, **39:3–27.61**
Division of motor vehicles. Motor Vehicle Commission, generally, this index
Documents, data processing, **39:2–3.8**
Doors,
Serial numbers, **39:10B–1 et seq.**
Special exits, merchandising or exhibition vehicles, **39:3–77.2**
Double saddle mount, number permitted to be drawn, **39:4–54**
Drawing double saddle mount operation,
39:4–54
Drivers Licenses, generally, this index
Drivers Schools, generally, this index
Drives and Driveways, generally, this index
Driving privileges,
Forfeiture or postponement, controlled dangerous substances offenses, **2C:35–16**
Suspension, defendants failure to comply with court order, notice, **2B:12–31**
Driving under the influence. Intoxication of driver, generally, post
Dropping objects from vehicle, highways,
39:4–64
Drugs and medicine,
Intoxication of driver, generally, post
Knowingly possessing while operating,
39:4–49.1
Drunken driving. Intoxication of driver, generally, post
Electric personal assistive mobility devices,
39:4–14.10, 39:4–14.11
Electronic rear backup monitoring devices, commercial motor vehicles, **39:3–71.1**
Electronic transactions,
Devices, **39:4–97.3 et seq.**
Licenses and permits, **39:2–3.8**
Emergency Vehicles, generally, this index
Emissions, **39:8–59 et seq.**
Actions and proceedings, civil penalties,
39:8–72
Administrative out of service order against vehicle, **39:8–73**
Apportioned vehicle, generally, ante
Certificate of approval,
Definitions, **39:8–43**
Private inspection facility, provision by director, **39:8–47**
Commercial vehicle enforcement fund,
39:8–75
Dangerous gases, **39:3–76**
Definitions, **39:8–43, 39:8–60**
Disbursements, **39:8–74**
Dispute resolution, contract compliance, official inspection facility, **39:8–44**
Division, definitions, **39:8–43**
Emission related repairs, **39:8–56**
Facilities, registration, **39:8–53**
Expenses and expenditures,
Disbursements, **39:8–74**
Receivable account, **39:8–76**
Federal Clean Air Act,
Compliance, **39:8–41 et seq.**
Definitions, **39:8–43**
Fees, **39:8–74**
Emissions control provisions, disbursements, **39:8–74**
Fines and penalties, **39:3–70.2, 39:8–63, 39:8–68, 39:8–70**
Actions to recover, **39:8–72**

MOTOR VEHICLES—Cont'd
Emissions—Cont'd
Fines and penalties—Cont'd
Certificate of approval or rejection sticker, private inspection facility owners, **39:8–47**
Collection, municipal court proceedings, **39:8–73**
Gross weight, definitions, **39:8–43**
Idling, fines and penalties, **39:3–70.2**
Inspection and inspectors, **39:3–70.1, 39:8–64**
Diesel fuel, operation, **39:8–62**
Fraud, **39:8–54**
Inspection stations, generally, post
Licenses and permits, **39:8–52**
Periodic inspection program, procedures, **39:8–66**
Roadside enforcement programs, diesel vehicles, law enforcement officers, **39:8–67**
School buses, **39:3B–21**
Legislative findings and declarations, **39:8–42, 39:8–59**
Liability insurance, requirement, private inspection facility, **39:8–45**
Licenses and permits,
Denial, suspension or revocation, private inspection facility, **39:8–49**
Emissions inspectors, **39:8–52**
Expiration, **39:8–51**
Private inspection facilities,
Denial, suspension or revocation, director, **39:8–49**
Revocation or suspension, **39:8–69**
Powers, duties, licensing,
Emissions inspectors, fees, standards, establishment, **39:8–52**
Official inspection facility, **39:8–44**
Private inspection facility, licensing, **39:8–45**
Receivable account, establishment, **39:8–76**
Registration, suspension, **39:8–73**
Rejection stickers, private inspection facility, **39:8–47**
Reports, diesel vehicles, **39:8–78**
Roadside enforcement programs, diesel vehicles, **39:8–64, 39:8–65**
Law enforcement officers, **39:8–67**
Procedures, **39:8–66**
Rules and regulations, **39:8–77**
Adoption, **39:8–57**
Exhaust emission standards and test methods, **39:8–61, 39:8–66**
Schedule of charges, posting requirements, private inspection facility, **39:8–46**
School buses, inspectors and inspection, **39:3B–21**
State treasurer, powers and duties, **39:8–44**
Tests and testing, equipment,
Certificates and certification, requirements, **39:8–50**
Private inspection centers, **39:8–38**
Tickets, **39:8–71**
Violations, **39:8–63**
Proceedings, **39:8–71**
Engines,
Running, **39:4–53**
Serial numbers, **39:10B–1 et seq.**
Entering or leaving prohibited, **39:4–65**
Entitling proceedings under motor vehicle and traffic laws, **39:5–5**
Environmental protection. Emissions, generally, ante
EPA, definitions, emissions inspection, **39:8–60**
Equipment, **39:3–43 et seq.**
Anchorage units, seat safety belts, **39:3–76.2**

MOTOR VEHICLES—Cont'd
Equipment—Cont'd
Child passenger restraint systems, **39:3–76.2a et seq.**
Construction of statute, **39:3–78**
Inspection and safe condition required, **39:8–1, 39:8–3**
Intermodal transportation, chassis, **39:3–79.10 et seq.**
Low speed vehicles, **39:4–31.2**
Restraining devices, **39:3–76.2**
Seat safety belts and anchorage units, **39:3–76.2**
Separate exit door, merchandising or exhibition vehicles, **39:3–77.2**
Trademark or name to be visible, **39:3–77**
Estimates, body repair facilities, fines or license refusal, revocation, or suspension, **39:13–4**
Evidence,
Abandoned and unclaimed vehicle, **39:4–56.5**
Application for motor vehicle registration or drivers license, **39:3–28**
Child passenger restraint system not warned, **39:3–76.2a**
Expenses, trial de novo, arbitrated tort claims, **39:6A–34**
Homicide, reckless driving, presumptions, **2C:11–5**
Repair of vehicles, proof to lien holder or lessor, **39:13–8**
Trial de novo, arbitrated tort claims, **39:6A–33**
Examiners. Inspection and inspectors, generally, post
Executors and administrators, service of process, resident operator becoming nonresident, **39:7–2.1**
Exemptions,
Application of law, **39:3–1**
Certificates of ownership, fuel efficient cars, luxury cars, additional fees, **39:3–8.4**
Dealer licenses, real estate brokers, **39:10–19**
Driving privileges, forfeiture or postponement, controlled dangerous substances offenses, **2C:35–16**
Drugs and medicine, possession, **39:4–49.2, 39:4–49.3**
Length limitation on highways, **39:3–84**
Length regulations, **39:3–84**
Registration fee, certain disabled veterans, **39:3–27.1**
Weights and measures, post
Exhaust emission standards and test methods, rules and regulations, **39:8–61, 39:8–66**
Exhaust system,
Dangerous gases, **39:3–76**
Devices emitting sounds, **39:3–69**
Mufflers required, **39:3–70**
Exit doors, merchandising or exhibition vehicles, **39:3–77.2**
Expenses and expenditures,
Emissions, ante
Investigation and evidence, trial de novo, arbitrated tort claims, **39:6A–34**
Owner due to theft, restitution, **2C:43–2.1**
Removing and storing unregistered vehicle on highway, **39:3–4**
Unsatisfied claim and judgment fund, **39:6–67**
Explosives, definitions, **39:1–1**
Extension of period of revocation or suspension, vehicle operation after revocation or suspension, **39:3–40**
Exterior mirror on drivers side, **39:3–71**
Failure to meet standards, used motor vehicles, **39:10–27**

MOTOR VEHICLES—Cont'd
False statements or representations, title, **2C:21–4.8**
Federal Clean Air Act. Emissions, post
Federal heavy vehicle use tax, proof of payment, registration of vehicle, **39:3–5.1**
Fees,
Apportioned vehicles, registration, administrative fees, **39:3–6.14**
Arbitrators, tort claims, trial de novo petitions, **39:6A–32**
Certificates of ownership, ante
Checks,
Dishonor, **39:5–36.1**
Dishonored, **39:5–36.1**
Combating theft of, chief of municipality, informed consent forms, **39:3–85.9**
Disabled veterans, plates or markers, **39:3–27.16**
Emissions, ante
Identification cards for nondrivers, **39:3–29.7**
Identification cards, private detective businesses, security services, **39:3–54.14**
Ignition interlock devices, **39:4–50.17a**
Increases, **39:2A–36.1**
Inspections, **39:3–8, 39:8–10**
Certificate of ownership issuance after larceny or damage rendering repairs economically impractical, **39:10–35**
International Registration Program Agreement, disbursements, **39:3–6.20**
Labels, compressed or liquefied gaseous fuel users, **39:3–79.4**
Leases, post
Licenses and permits, post
Noncommercial trucks, **39:3–8, 39:3–8.1**
Off site sales, licenses and permits, **39:10–19.3**
Photo licenses, **39:3–10**
Plates or markers, post
Reduced registration fees, **39:3–22a**
Registration, security surcharges, **39:2A–38**
Service charges, **39:2A–36**
Service of process on person resident when accident or collision occurred and later becoming nonresident, **39:7–2.2**
Street rods, special license plates, **39:3–27.27, 39:3–27.28**
Transportation of mentally retarded persons, identification cards, **39:4–207.2 et seq.**
Unregistered vehicles, permits to cross public highways, **39:3–26.2, 39:3–26.4**
Unsatisfied claim and judgment fund, post
Fences, destruction by operation of vehicle, **39:4–97a**
Fender lamps, color of light, **39:3–52**
Fenders, serial number, **39:10B–1 et seq.**
Fields, destruction by operation of vehicle, **39:4–97a**
Point system, assessment against drivers license, **39:5–30.5a**
Financial responsibility,
Electric personal assistive mobility devices, **39:4–14.10**
Motor Vehicle Security Responsibility Law, generally, this index
Findings, arbitrators, tort claims, **39:6A–30**
Fines and penalties,
Air pollution, **39:3–70.2**
Apportioned vehicles, registration, **39:3–6.17**
Autism medical research and treatment fund, surcharge, **39:5–41**
Auto theft, **2C:20–2.1**
Body repair facilities, **39:13–4, 39:13–6**
Brain injury research fund, surcharge, **39:5–41**

MOTOR VEHICLES—Cont'd
Fines and penalties—Cont'd
Child passenger restraint systems, **39:3–76.2d**
Collection of fines,
Account, **39:5–43**
Receipt, **39:5–45**
Community services, driving while intoxicated, second or subsequent offenses, **39:4–50**
Commuter vans, **39:3–27.22**
Component parts, serial numbers, **39:10B–2**
Compressed gaseous fuel users, identification, **39:3–79.7, 39:3–79.8**
Consent of owner, using motor vehicle without, **39:4–48**
Credit to state highway fund, **39:5–40**
Disposition and use of, **39:5–41**
Drivers licenses, **39:3–40 et seq.**
Revocation and suspension,
Hit and run, **39:4–129**
Vehicle used in crime, **2C:43–2**
Driving on unauthorized property, traffic sign or signal avoidance, **39:4–66.2**
Drug related convictions, **39:5–30.12 et seq.**
Drunken driving, **39:4–50, 39:4–51**
Surcharges, drunk driving enforcement fund, **39:4–50.8**
Emissions, ante
Equipment of motor vehicles, **39:3–79**
Exceeding weight limitations, **39:3–20**
Forensic DNA laboratory fund, surcharge, **53:1–20.28a**
General penalty, **39:3–86, 39:4–203**
Hitting or injuring domestic animal, failure to stop and report, **4:22–25.2**
Hours of Service Law, violation, **39:9–4**
Ice and snow,
Dislodging from moving vehicle, **39:4–77.1**
Removal, **39:4–77.1**
Information plates, failure to attach, **39:3–82**
Inspection Law violation, **39:8–9**
Private inspection, **39:8–18**
Interior lights, law enforcement stops, **39:4–57.1**
Intoxication of driver, post
Junk Law violation, **39:11–11**
Leaving motor vehicle with engine running, **39:4–53**
Licenses and permits, post
Lights and lighting, **39:3–66.2**
Liquefied gaseous fuel users, **39:3–79.7, 39:3–79.8**
Littering, **39:4–64**
Locking of wheels of motor vehicle, **39:3–81**
Low speed vehicles, equipment, **39:4–31.2**
Mirror requirement violation, **39:3–71**
Narcotic or habit producing drugs, operation of vehicle while under influence of, **39:4–50, 39:4–51**
Nonpayment of fines, imprisonment authorized, **39:5–36**
Nonresident chauffeur or driver, reciprocity provisions, **39:3–17**
Offenses in construction or repair areas, conditions, **39:4–203.5**
Omnibuses, operators, certificates of public convenience or necessity, failure to have, **39:3–79.22 et seq.**
Operation of a vehicle after suspension of license for failure to carry insurance, **39:3–40**
Operation without liability insurance, **39:6B–2**
Pedestrians, violation of law relating to, **39:4–203**
Penalty points, **39:5–30.5 et seq.**

MOTOR VEHICLES—Cont'd
Fines and penalties—Cont'd
Plates or markers, forgery or counterfeiting, **39:3–38**
Points, penalty points, **39:5–30.5 et seq.**
Police cars, sale of used police cars, **39:10–9.2**
Projections on tires and locking of wheels, **39:3–81**
Racing on highways, **39:5C–1**
Reckless driving, **39:4–96**
Registration or drivers license, operation of vehicle after revocation, **2C:40–26, 39:3–40**
Registration plates for empty trucks, **39:3–20.2**
Revocation of registration certificate and registration plates, **39:3–40.1**
Seat belts, failure to use, **39:3–76.2j, 39:3–76.2n**
Second and subsequent offenses, **39:3–40**
Body repair facilities, **39:13–6**
Special license plates, firemen, unauthorized use, **39:3–27.12**
Stopping to give assistance and identification, violation of duty, **39:4–129**
Street rods, special license plates, **39:3–27.27**
Summons, failure to obey, **39:5–30**
Suspension, **39:5–7**
Child passenger restraint systems, **39:3–76.2d**
Operating privileges of foreign vehicle or nonresident, **39:3–16**
Tampering with motor vehicle, **39:4–49**
Traffic signs or signals,
Avoidance, driving on unauthorized property, **39:4–66.2**
Failure to equip vehicle with, **39:3–66.2**
Unlawful taking, **2C:20–2.1**
Unsafe driving, **39:4–97.2**
Used motor vehicles, sales, **39:10–30**
Vehicles powered by compressed or liquified gaseous fuel, labels, **39:3–79.4 et seq.**
Weight of vehicles and loads, **39:3–82, 39:3–84, 39:3–84.3**
Wheelchairs, securing, **39:3–76.2m**
Fire Engines, Apparatus and Equipment, generally, this index
Firefighters and Fire Departments, this index
Flammable liquid, definitions, **39:1–1**
Flaps, mud flaps, **39:3–79.1 et seq.**
Flashing warning lights, **39:3–54**
Fleeing,
Assault, **2C:12–1**
Mandatory sentence, **2C:43–6**
Law enforcement officer, **2C:29–2**
Manslaughter, **2C:11–4**
Fleet, definitions, apportioned vehicles, registration, **39:3–6.11**
Florences Law, intoxication of driver, **39:4–50**
Foreign country registration, operation in state, **39:3–4f**
Foreign states,
Acquisition and temporary registration of vehicle by state resident, **39:3–4a**
Drivers licenses, surrender, **39:3–10**
Handicapped persons, parking, **39:4–207.5**
Intoxication of driver, **39:4–50**
Prior convictions, chemical tests, implied consent, effect, **39:4–50.4a**
Reciprocity, generally, post
Forensic DNA laboratory fund, fines and penalties, surcharge, **53:1–20.28a**
Forfeitures,
Driving privilege, drugs and medicine, **2C:35–16, 39:4–49.1**

MOTOR VEHICLES—Cont'd
Forfeitures—Cont'd
Judicial notice, vehicular homicide, **2C:11–5**
Knowingly possessing narcotics while operating, **39:4–49.1**
Vehicular homicide, **2C:11–5**
Forgery, title, **2C:21–4.8**
Former prisoners of war, registration plates, **39:3–27.24**
Forms,
Affidavits, husband and wife registrants, survivors, **39:3–30.1a**
Licenses and permits, post
Registration plate applications, amateur radio licensees, **39:3–27.6**
Frame, serial number, **39:10B–1 et seq.**
Fraud,
Body repair facilities, fines or license refusal, suspension, or revocation, **39:13–4**
Certificate of approval, **39:8–9**
Emissions, inspectors and inspection, **39:8–54**
Identification cards for disabled persons, **39:3–29.8**
Mileage misrepresentation, **2C:21–8**
Suspension or revocation of license, **39:10–20**
Title, **2C:21–4.8**
Freeholders, special license plates, **39:3–27.29 et seq.**
Front end assembly, serial numbers, **39:10B–1 et seq.**
Fuel efficient cars, luxury cars, certificates of ownership, additional fees, exemptions, **39:3–8.3, 39:3–8.4**
Fuels. Motor Fuels, generally, this index
Funds,
Definitions,
Coastal protection license plate program, **39:3–27.47**
Olympic license plates, **39:3–27.61**
Garden State games trust fund, olympic license plates. Plates or markers, post
Proportional registration distributive fund, **39:3–6.20**
Rewards for justice license plate fund, **39:3–27.134 et seq.**
Unsatisfied claim and judgment fund, generally, post
Garages, generally, this index
Gifts, body repair facilities to adjusters or appraisers, fine or license refusal, revocation, or suspension, **39:13–4**
Girls clubs of America, registration fee exemption, **39:3–27**
Gross vehicle weight rating, definitions, **39:10–2**
Emissions inspection, **39:8–60**
Gross weight, definitions, **39:1–1**
Guest, evidence on application for payment of judgment from unsatisfied claim and judgment fund, **39:6–70**
GVWR, definitions, emissions inspection, **39:8–60**
Habitual offenders, **39:5–30a, 39:5–30b**
Hallucinogenic drugs. Intoxication of driver, generally, post
Handicapped Persons, this index
Hands free telephones, **39:4–97.3 et seq.**
Hawkers and peddlers, flashing lights on stopped vehicles, **39:3–64.1 et seq.**
Hazardous substances, transportation, **39:5B–30 et seq.**
Hearings,
Body repair facilities, license refusal, revocation, or suspension, **39:13–5**
License suspension or revocation, **39:5–30**

MOTOR VEHICLES—Cont'd
Hearings—Cont'd
Penalty points, license suspension, **39:5–30.5 et seq.**
Suspension or revocation, license or registration, **39:5–30**
Heavy duty diesel truck, definitions, emissions inspection, **39:8–60**
Heavy equipment. Moving Heavy Machinery, generally, this index
Heavy vehicle use tax, proof of payment, registration of vehicle, **39:3–5.1**
High occupancy vehicle, definitions, **39:1–1**
Highjack lights, omnibuses, **39:3–54**
Hit and Run Drivers, generally, this index
Holder, license plates, obscuring numbers, **39:3–33**
Home jurisdiction, definitions, Nonresident Violator Compact, **39:5F–4**
Homicide, **2C:11–2, 2C:11–5**
Hit and run drivers, vehicular homicide, **2C:11–5.1**
Terrorism, **2C:38–2**
Horns, **39:3–69**
Curves, approaching, **39:4–55**
Overtaking and passing vehicles, **39:4–85**
Horse Drawn Vehicles, generally, this index
Horses, **39:4–72**
Horticultural land, trespass, **2C:18–5**
Hours of duty for operators, **39:9–1 et seq.**
Citation of law, **39:9–1**
Hours of inspection stations, **39:8–2.2**
HOV, definitions, **39:1–1**
Husband and wife. Spouses, generally, post
Ice and snow, dislodging from moving vehicle, fines and penalties, **39:4–77.1**
Identification cards,
Disabled persons, **39:4–205, 39:4–206**
Nondrivers, **39:3–29.2 et seq.**
Identification lamps,
Mounting, **39:3–61.1**
Private detective businesses, community security services, **39:3–54.14**
Visibility, **39:3–48**
Identity and identification,
Change or destruction, crimes and offenses, **2C:17–6**
Compressed or liquefied gaseous fuel users, **39:3–79.4 et seq.**
Low speed vehicles, numbers and numbering, **39:4–31.2**
Marks or numbers, change, destruction, crimes and offenses, **2C:17–6**
Mentally retarded persons, transportation vehicles, identification, **39:4–207.2 et seq.**
Parts, **39:10B–1 et seq.**
Registration and drivers licenses, misleading applications, furnishing identification for, **39:3–37**
Vehicles using compressed or liquefied gaseous fuel, **39:3–79.4 et seq.**
Idling, emissions, fines and penalties, **39:3–70.2**
Ignition interlock devices,
Blood analysis test refusal, **39:4–50.4a**
Intoxication of driver, **39:4–50.16 et seq.**
Second or subsequent offenses, **39:4–50**
Ignition keys,
Production, proof of ownership, **2C:40–23**
Proof of ownership, **2C:40–23**
Impeding traffic, slow speed, **39:4–97.1**
Implied consent. Intoxication of driver, post
Impounding,
Identification cards, possession by driver, failure, **39:3–29.1a**
Intoxication of driver, **39:4–50.23**

MOTOR VEHICLES—Cont'd
Impounding—Cont'd
Licenses and permits,
New state residents, **39:3–17.1**
Omnibus registration, **39:3–19.1**
Operation of vehicle by unlicensed driver, invalid registration or plates, **39:3–40.3**
Parking offenses, public auction, **39:4–139.13**
Release, **39:3–40.6**
Improperly equipped vehicles, operation, **39:3–44**
Improvement course, point reduction credits, **39:5–30.9**
In jurisdiction miles, definitions, apportioned vehicles, registration, **39:3–6.11**
Index, applications for registration and drivers licenses, destruction, **39:3–28**
Indigent Persons, this index
Inflammable liquid seeping or leaking from container, warning devices, **39:3–64**
Inside lane, definitions, **39:1–1**
Inspection and inspectors, **39:8–1 et seq.**
Air contaminants, **39:3–70.1**
Alteration of equipment to defeat purpose of inspection, **39:3–47**
Arrest, power, **39:5–25**
Certificates of approval, **39:8–2**
Obtaining fraudulently or refusing to display, **39:8–9**
Previously rejected vehicles, **39:8–12**
Private inspection approval stickers, **39:8–11 et seq.**
Registration of vehicle, **39:8–8**
Compensation and salaries, **39:8–10**
Complaints, **39:5–44**
Damage rendering repairs economically impractical, certificate of ownership issuance, **39:10–34**
Diesel vehicles, emissions control, **39:8–64**
Procedures, **39:8–66**
Directions, drivers required to comply, **39:4–57**
Emissions, ante
Fees, **39:3–8, 39:8–2, 39:8–10**
Certificate of ownership issuance after larceny report or damage rendering repairs economically impractical, **39:10–35**
Fines and penalties, **39:8–9**
Private inspection, **39:8–18**
Hazardous waste transportation, **39:5B–31**
Historic vehicles, **39:8–1**
Initial inspections, **39:8–14**
Inspection stations, generally, ante
Labels, compressed or liquefied gaseous fuel users, **39:3–79.6**
Larceny, certificate of ownership issuance after certificate surrendered, **39:10–33**
Necessity, **39:8–1**
Process for motor vehicle or traffic law violations directed to, **39:5–3**
Production of certificate of ownership on demand, **39:10–6**
Records, component parts, serial numbers, **39:10B–2**
Reinspection, licenses and permits, **39:8–11 et seq.**
Reinspection centers, redesignation as private inspection centers, **39:8–37**
Removal of unregistered vehicle from highway, **39:3–4**
Repairs or necessary adjustments to be made, **39:8–4**
Private inspection centers, **39:8–13**
Reports, **39:8–5**
State police may act as inspectors, **53:2–1**

MOTOR VEHICLES—Cont'd
Inspection and inspectors—Cont'd
Stopping vehicles to submit to measurement or weighing, **39:3–84.3**
Title papers, **39:10–6, 39:10–21, 39:10–22**
Vehicles powered by compressed or liquified gaseous fuel, **39:3–79.4 et seq.**
Inspection stations,
Hours opened, **39:8–2.2**
Official inspection facilities, **39:8–44**
Definitions, **39:8–43**
Emissions testing equipment, certification by environmental protection department, requirements, **39:8–50**
Private inspection facilities,
Definitions, **39:8–43**
Emissions testing equipment, certification by environmental protection department, requirements, **39:8–50**
Liability, certificates of approval or rejection stickers, **39:8–47**
Licenses and permits,
Denial, suspension or revocation, director, **39:8–49**
Director, powers and duties, **39:8–44**
Operation, licensing, director, **39:8–43**
Uniforms for employees, **39:8–2.1**
Insurance,
Motor Vehicle Insurance, generally, this index
Motor Vehicle Security Responsibility Law, generally, this index
Unsatisfied claim and judgment fund, generally, post
Intentional misstatement of material fact, registration application, **39:3–37**
Interference with transportation, **2C:33–14**
Interior lights, law enforcement stops, **39:4–57.1**
Interior mirror, **39:3–71**
International Registration Plan,
Apportioned vehicle, registration, **39:3–6.12**
Definitions, apportioned vehicles, registration, **39:3–6.11**
Supersedure, **39:3–6.19**
Intersections, generally, this index
Interstate compacts, Nonresident Violator Compact, **39:5F–1 et seq.**
Interstate operations, definitions, apportioned vehicles, registration, **39:3–6.11**
Intoxication of driver, **39:4–50, 39:4–51**
Appeal of conviction, representation of prosecution, **39:5–20**
Arrest without warrant, **39:5–25**
Assault by auto or vessel, **2C:12–1**
Blood alcohol levels, Florences Law, **39:4–50**
Chemical analyses of arrested persons breath, **39:4–50.3**
Children and minors,
Fines and penalties, **39:4–50.14**
Passengers, parent, **39:4–50.15**
Community service, performance, second or subsequent offenses, **39:4–50**
Courtesy plates, crimes and offenses, restrictions, **39:3–33.5a**
Damages, supervised visitation, **39:4–50**
Death, sentence and punishment, **2C:11–5**
Death of another, license suspension or revocation, **39:5–30**
Discovery rights, second or subsequent offenses, **39:4–50**
Disorderly persons, parent, children and minors, passengers, **39:4–50.15**
Drunk Driving Victims Bill of Rights, **39:4–50.9 et seq.**

MOTOR VEHICLES—Cont'd

Intoxication of driver—Cont'd

Fees,
Intoxicated driver resource centers, **39:4–50**
Intoxicated driving programs, **39:4–50**
Fines and penalties, **39:3–40 et seq., 39:4–50**
Implied consent, blood analysis, **39:4–51**
Parent, children and minors, passengers, **39:4–50.15**
Second and subsequent offenses, municipal prosecutors, additional penalties, **2B:25–5.1**
Surcharges, drunk driving enforcement fund, **39:4–50.8**
Victims of crime compensation board, **2C:43–3.1**
Florences Law, **39:4–50**
Hallucinogenics, **39:4–50**
Homicide, sentence and punishment, **2C:11–5**
Hospitals, supervised visitation, **39:4–50**
Ignition interlock devices, **39:4–50.16 et seq.**
Second or subsequent offenses, **39:4–50**
Implied consent,
Blood analysis, **39:4–50.2 et seq.**
Chemical test, **39:4–50.4a**
Fines and penalties, **39:4–51**
Impounding, **39:4–50.23**
Imprisonment, term, **39:4–50**
Intoxicated driver resource centers, **39:4–50**
Intoxicated driving programs, **39:4–50**
Michaels Law, **39:4–50**
Minors, penalties, **39:4–50.14**
Morgues and morgue keepers, supervised visitation, **39:4–50**
Motor carriers, prevention, programs, **39:5B–32**
Motor vehicle insurance, loss recovery, exceptions, **39:6A–4.5**
Motorized bicycles, **39:4–14.3g**
Municipalities, second and subsequent offenses, fines and penalties, additional penalties, **2B:25–5.1**
No fault insurance, exemptions, **39:6A–7**
Notice, intoxicated driving programs, failure to report, **39:4–50**
Parent, children and minors, passengers, **39:4–50.15**
Period of detainment, **39:4–50**
Physicians fee taxed as costs in proceedings under statute, **39:5–39**
Public policy, ignition interlock devices, **39:4–50.16**
Revoked license not restored pending appeal, **39:5–22**
School Buildings and Grounds, this index
Second and subsequent offenses, **39:4–50**
Fines and penalties, municipal prosecutors, additional penalties, **2B:25–5.1**
Second degree crimes, homicide, **2C:11–5**
Sentence and punishment, homicide, **2C:11–5**
Serious bodily injury of another, license suspension or revocation, **39:5–30**
Special plates, restrictions, **39:3–33.5**
Surcharges, **39:4–50**
Suspension or revocation, drivers licenses, **39:4–50**
Death or serious bodily injury of another, **39:5–30**
Extension, **39:3–40**
Fines and penalties, **2C:40–26**
Third and subsequent offenses, **39:4–50**
Third parties, liability, **39:4–50.22**
Turnpike project, **27:23–26**

MOTOR VEHICLES—Cont'd

Intoxication of driver—Cont'd

Victims, Drunk Driving Victims Bill of Rights, **39:4–50.9 et seq.**
Investigations,
Body repair facilities, statutory violations, **39:13–3**
Expenses, trial de novo, arbitrated tort claims, **39:6A–34**
Invoices, sale of vehicles, contents of invoice, **39:10B–3**
Irrevocable agreements, director of motor vehicles appointed as agent for service of process, **39:7–2.1**
Issuing jurisdiction, definitions, Nonresident Violator Compact, **39:5F–4**
Itinerant vendors, flashing lights, stopped vehicles, **39:3–64.1 et seq.**
Joint registration with spouse, **39:3–30**
Judgments and decrees,
Damages. Unsatisfied claim and judgment fund, generally, post
Offers of judgment before arbitration, rules of court, **39:6A–28**
Unsatisfied claim and judgment fund, generally, post
Judicial notice, forfeitures, vehicular homicide, **2C:11–5**
Junk yards. Motor Vehicle Junk Yards, generally, this index
Jurisdiction,
Crimes and offenses, traffic accidents, serious bodily injury, **2B:12–17.2**
Definitions,
Apportioned vehicles, registration, **39:3–6.11**
Nonresident Violator Compact, **39:5F–4**
Jury and jurors,
Hours of Service Law, **39:9–4**
Inspection Law, **39:8–9**
Juvenile delinquents and dependents, drivers licenses and registration certificates, postponement, revocation, or suspension, **2A:4A–43**
Keys, ignition keys, production, proof of ownership, **2C:40–23**
Labels, compressed or liquefied gaseous fuel users, **39:3–79.4 et seq.**
Larceny, **2C:20–2**
Combating theft of, **39:3–85.5**
Component parts, serial numbers, **39:10B–1 et seq.**
Criteria for sentencing of imprisonment, **2C:44–1**
Damages, payment as part of sentence, **2C:43–2.1**
Extended terms of imprisonment, **2C:44–3**
Identity, licenses and permits, exceptions, **2C:21–17**
Informed consent agreement, **39:3–85.5**
Juveniles,
Orders of incarceration or community service, **2A:4A–43**
Referral to other courts without juveniles consent, **Rule 5:22–2**
Notice, **39:3–85.1**
Reports, **39:3–85.1, 39:3–85.2**
Salvage certificates of title, **39:10–31 et seq.**
Seizure and sale of stolen vehicles, **39:5–47**
Theft alarm signal devices, **39:3–69**
Unlawful taking of means of conveyance, **2C:20–10**
Unsatisfied claim and judgment fund, **39:6–70**
Law enforcement officers. Peace officers, generally, post

MOTOR VEHICLES—Cont'd

Leases,
Courtesy plates, fees, **39:3–33a**
Dealers, license, **39:10–19**
Suspension or revocation, **39:10–20**
Definitions, **39:1–1**
Fees, license fee, leasing dealers, **39:10–19**
Fraud, **39:10–20**
Licenses and permits, leasing dealers, **39:10–19**
Suspension or revocation, **39:10–20**
Misrepresentation, **39:10–20**
Noncommercial trucks, **39:3–8, 39:3–8.1**
Parking violations, lessors liability, **39:4–139.5**
Personalized plates, fees, **39:3–33a**
Plates or markers, special plates, **39:3–33a**
Proof of repair to lessor, **39:13–8**
Registration, **39:3–4**
Revocation of leasing dealers license, **39:10–20**
Special plates, fees, **39:3–33a**
Suspension of leasing dealers license, **39:10–20**
TRAC clauses, **39:10–5.1**
Traffic accidents, presumptions, involvement, **39:4–129, 39:4–130**
Leasing or renting companies, temporary registration, **39:3–18**
Leaving engine running, fine imposed, **39:4–53**
Left Turns, generally, this index
Length and width, public utility vehicles, **39:3–84**
Lettering, exterior of noncommercial trucks, **39:3–8.1**
Levy on, surrender of title papers, **39:10–15**
Liability insurance. Motor Vehicle Insurance, generally, this index
License cards or plates. Plates or markers, generally, post
Licenses and permits, **39:10–20**
Age of owner, specification on application, **39:3–4**
Agents,
Deposits of moneys received by, **39:3–3**
Motor vehicle commission, officers and employees, **39:3–3**
Another vehicle, registration by original owner, **39:3–30**
Applications, **39:3–4**
False statements, **39:3–37**
Indexing, **39:3–28**
Noncommercial trucks, **39:3–8, 39:3–8.1**
Renewal, **39:3–12.1**
Apportioned vehicle, generally, ante
Attachable auxiliary axle, **39:4–54**
Auctions and auctioneers, new state residents, **39:3–17.1**
Auxiliary axle or converter dolly, **39:4–54**
Battleship U.S.S. New Jersey license plate renewal, **39:3–27.68**
Body repair facilities, **39:13–1 et seq.**
Boy and girl scouts of United States, **39:3–27**
Boys Clubs of America, fees, exemption, **39:3–27**
Certificates of approval after inspection, prerequisite for obtaining registration, **39:8–8**
Certificates of registration,
Amendment, joint registration with spouse, **39:3–30**
Commuter vans, **39:3–27.19**
Death of husband or wife, **39:3–30.1, 39:3–30.2**
Display by nonresident operators, **39:3–17**

MOTOR VEHICLES—Cont'd
Licenses and permits—Cont'd
  Certificates of registration—Cont'd
    Duplicate certificate on loss or destruction of original, **39:3–31**
    Exhibiting to injured person, **39:4–129**
    Exhibition on request, **39:3–29**
    Juvenile delinquents and dependents, postponement, revocation, or suspension, **2A:4A–43**
    Loan, **39:3–35**
    Necessity, **39:10–6**
    New certificate on loss or defacement, **39:3–32**
    Omnibus license, **39:3–19**
    Photographic or micrographic copies of applications for as evidence, **39:3–28**
    Possession by operator, **39:3–29**
    Production on demand, **39:10–6**
    Suspension or revocation,
      Application for certificate during period of suspension or revocation, **39:3–34**
      Hours of Service Law violation, **39:9–4**
      Inspection Law violation, **39:8–9**
      Motor Vehicle Security Responsibility Law violations, **39:6–55**
      Return or surrender of certificate, **39:5–35**
  Change of address of registered owner, **39:3–36**
  Combating theft of, request driver to produce a valid, **39:3–85.6**
  Commercial vehicles, empty trucks, **39:3–20.1, 39:3–20.2**
  Commuter vans, **39:3–27.19**
  Compliance with law relating to, sufficiency, **39:3–42**
  Congressional medal of honor holder, fee registration, **39:3–27.1**
  Construction and equipment, **39:3–43**
  Convention, **39:3–27.2**
  Converter, **39:3–18**
  Crossing public highways, unregistered and self propelled vehicles, **39:3–26.1 et seq.**
  Data processing, **39:2–3.8**
  Dealers, ante
  Death,
    Husband or wife, certificate to survivor, **39:3–30.1, 39:3–30.2**
    Registered owner, operation by surviving spouse or member of family, **39:3–30.3**
  Definitions, off site sales, **39:10–19.1 et seq.**
  Demonstration, vehicles operated for purpose of, **39:3–18**
  Destruction of vehicle, expiration of registration, **39:3–30**
  Dimensional and weight limitations,
    Operation of vehicle in excess of, **39:3–84**
    Special written permits, **39:3–84**
  Disabled veterans as exempt from registration fee, **39:3–27.1**
  Drivers Licenses, generally, this index
  Drivers privacy protection, **39:2–3.3 et seq.**
  Duplicate certificates for family members, **39:3–31.1**
  Electric personal assistive mobility devices, **39:4–14.10**
  Emissions, ante
  Evidence, death of husband or wife, **39:3–30.1a**
  Expiration, **39:3–4**
  Farm machinery or farm implements, operation on highways, **39:3–24**
  Farmers truck, **39:3–25**

MOTOR VEHICLES—Cont'd
Licenses and permits—Cont'd
  Federal heavy vehicle use tax, proof of payment, **39:3–5.1**
  Fees, **39:6–63, 39:6–63.1**
    Additional,
      New Jersey emergency medical service helicopter response program fund, **39:3–8.2**
      State police trooper classes, **39:3–8.2**
      Traumatic brain injury fund, **39:3–8.2**
    Agents, **39:3–3**
    Ambulances, exemption, **39:3–27**
    Animal welfare license plate renewal, **39:3–27.55**
    Body repair facilities, **39:13–2**
    Boys Clubs of America, exemption, **39:3–37**
    Coastal protection license plate renewal, **39:3–27.49**
    Commercial vehicles, **39:3–20**
    Commuter vans, **39:3–27.19**
    County improvement authority, exemption, **39:3–27**
    Credit to state highway fund, **39:5–40**
    Dealer, **39:10–19**
    Duplicate certificate for family members, **39:3–31.1**
    Duplicate certificate of registration, **39:3–31**
    Emergency squads, exemption, **39:3–27**
    Exemption, **39:3–27, 39:3–27.1**
    Farm tractors and traction equipment license, **39:3–24, 39:3–25**
    Girls clubs of America, exemption, **39:3–27**
    Historic motor vehicles, **39:3–27.4**
    Joint registration with spouse, **39:3–30**
    Motorcycles, **39:3–18, 39:3–21**
    New motor vehicles, **39:3–8**
    New registration plates on loss or defacement, **39:3–32**
    Noncommercial trucks, **39:3–8, 39:3–8.1**
    Nonprofit organizations, exemption, **39:3–27**
    Nonresidents, agricultural employee, **39:3–15**
    Omnibuses, **39:3–19**
    Passenger vehicles, **39:3–8**
    Police Athletic League, exemption, **39:3–27**
    Police auxiliary or reserve, exemption, **39:3–27**
    Private utility and house type semitrailers and trailers, **39:3–8**
    Reduced registration fees, **39:3–22a**
    Regional school districts, exemption, **39:3–27**
    Rescue squads, exemption, **39:3–27**
    Restoration, suspended or revoked license, **39:3–10a**
    Schools and school districts, exemption, **39:3–27**
    Security surcharges, **39:2A–38**
    Semitrailers, **39:3–20**
    Special registration, **39:3–27.30, 39:3–27.32**
    Specially marked plates, **39:3–33.4**
    State police trooper classes, **39:3–8.2**
    State treasurer, payment to agent, **39:3–3**
    Transfer of registration, **39:3–30**
    Traumatic brain injury fund, **39:3–8.2**
    Uninsured vehicle, **39:6–63, 39:6–63.1**
    Vocational schools, exemption, **39:3–27**
  Finance companies, owned or controlled by, **39:3–18**
  Fines and penalties, **39:3–33, 39:10–20**

MOTOR VEHICLES—Cont'd
Licenses and permits—Cont'd
  Fines and penalties—Cont'd
    Certificate of registration, failure to possess or exhibit, **39:3–29**
    Change of address, failure to notify, **39:3–36**
    Counterfeiting or using other number plates or markers, **39:3–38**
    Dealers, violation of law relating to, **39:3–18**
    False statements, **39:3–37**
    New state residents, **39:3–17.1**
    Omnibus registration, failure to obtain, **39:3–19.1**
    Operation after revocation, **39:3–40 et seq.**
    Suspended or revoked certificates, failure to return or surrender, **39:5–35**
  Fire department, free registration, **39:3–27**
  Flashing lights, **39:3–50**
  Foreign country registration, operation in state, **39:3–4f**
  Foreign state, acquisition and temporary registration of vehicle by state resident, **39:3–4a**
  Former prisoners of war, **39:3–27.24 et seq.**
  Forms, **39:3–4**
    Applications, noncommercial trucks, **39:3–8, 39:3–8.1**
    Nonresident, **39:3–15.1**
  Free registration, **39:3–27**
    Disabled veterans, **39:3–27.1**
  General registration by manufacturers, dealers, finance companies, **39:3–18**
  Geographical district, definitions, **39:3–4d**
  Girls clubs of America, fees, exemption, **39:3–27**
  Historic motor vehicles, **39:3–27.4**
  Hospitals, free registration, **39:3–27**
  Identification, furnishing for misleading purpose, **39:3–37**
  Identification card for nondrivers, **39:3–29.2 et seq.**
  Impounding,
    New state residents, **39:3–17.1**
    Omnibus registration, **39:3–19.1**
  Inspections, certification, **39:8–14**
  Insurance, **39:3–4**
    Compulsory liability coverage, **39:6B–1**
  Insurance companies, vehicles owned or controlled by under theft policy, **39:3–18**
  Intentional misstatement of material fact, registration application, **39:3–37**
  International Registration Program Agreement, fees, disbursements, **39:3–6.20**
  Joint registration with spouse, **39:3–30**
  Juvenile delinquents and dependents, postponement, revocation, or suspension, **2A:4A–43**
  Liens and incumbrances, auctions and auctioneers, notice, **39:3–17.1**
  Lights and lighting, flashing lights, **39:3–50**
  Loss or destruction, identification cards for disabled persons, **39:3–29.6**
  Low speed vehicles, **39:4–31.3**
  Manufacturers vehicles, **39:3–18**
  Mentally retarded persons, vehicles, insignia, **39:4–207.3**
  New motor vehicles, **39:3–4**
  New state residents, **39:3–17.1**
  Noncommercial trucks, **39:1–1, 39:3–8, 39:3–8.1**
  Noncompliance with laws, **39:3–5**
  Nondrivers, identification cards, **39:3–29.2 et seq.**

MOTOR VEHICLES—Cont'd
Licenses and permits—Cont'd
Nonresidents,
New state residents, **39:3–17.1**
Temporary registration, **39:3–4b**
Notice,
Auctions and auctioneers, new state residents, **39:3–17.1**
Body repair facilities, suspension or revocation, **39:13–5**
New state residents, auctions and auctioneers, **39:3–17.1**
Penalty points, **39:5–30.5 et seq.**
Suspension or revocation, **39:5–30**
Penalty points, **39:5–30.5 et seq.**
Number plates. Plates or markers, generally, post
Off site sales, **39:10–19.1 et seq.**
Official vehicles, free registration, **39:3–27**
Omnibuses, **39:3–19**
Operation by surviving spouse or member of family of registered owner, **39:3–30.3**
Penalty points, suspension of license, **39:5–30.5 et seq.**
Plates or markers, generally, post
Police Athletic League, fees, exemption, **39:3–27**
Postponement, juvenile delinquents and dependents, **2A:4A–43**
Prisoners of war, **39:3–27.24 et seq.**
Private inspection facilities, **39:8–69, 39:8–90**
Private utility and house type semitrailers and trailers, **39:3–8**
Proportional registration distributive fund, **39:3–6.20**
Receipts for licenses, annual apportionment, **39:3–87**
Reciprocity privileges, **39:3–15, 39:3–16**
Red Cross, free registration, **39:3–27**
Refund to persons entering military service, payment of, **39:3–22.1, 39:3–22.2**
Reinspection centers, **39:8–11 et seq.**
Renewal,
Body repair facilities, **39:13–2**
Identification cards for nondrivers, **39:3–29.5**
Ridesharing, **39:3–4.1**
Rubber tires as prerequisite to registration, **39:3–23**
Serial numbers on component parts, **39:10B–4**
Signature to application for registration, **39:3–4**
Societies for prevention of cruelty, free registration, **39:3–27**
Special registration,
Conventions, **39:3–27.2**
Fees, **39:3–27.30, 39:3–27.32**
Historic vehicles, **39:3–27.4**
State owned vehicles, certificates and special number plates, **39:3–27**
Surrender, **39:3–27.31**
Spouses, **39:3–30.1, 39:3–30.2**
Statement noncommercial trucks, use, **39:3–8, 39:3–8.1**
Street rods, special license plates, **39:3–27.27**
Surplus property of United States, temporary identification marker, **39:3–33.1**
Surrender, special registration, **39:3–27.31**
Suspension or revocation, **39:5–30, 39:10–20**
Auto theft, **2C:20–2.1**
Body repair facilities, **39:13–4**
Death of another, **2C:40–22, 39:5–30**
Defendants failure to appear, pay fine, **2B:12–31**

MOTOR VEHICLES—Cont'd
Licenses and permits—Cont'd
Suspension or revocation—Cont'd
Discoloration or other defective condition of safety glazing material, **39:3–75**
Driver improvement school attendance in lieu of, **39:5–30.2**
Emissions control, diesel vehicles, **39:8–70, 39:8–73**
Failure to display certificate of approval, **39:8–7**
False statements, **39:3–37**
Habitual offenders, **39:5–30a, 39:5–30b**
Hours of Service Law violation, **39:9–4**
Inspection disclosing inability to place vehicle in safe condition, **39:8–7**
Junk yard license for violation of law, **39:11–11**
Juvenile delinquents and dependents, **2A:4A–43**
Municipal courts, **Rule 7:8–9**
New registration, **39:5–34**
Notice, habitual offenders, **39:5–30b**
Parking offenses, **39:4–139.10**
Restoration, **39:4–139.11**
Penalty points, **39:5–30.5 et seq.**
Plates for empty trucks, **39:3–20.2**
Private inspection facilities, **39:8–69**
Reciprocity privileges, **39:5–30**
Residents license after suspension or revocation of reciprocity driving privilege, **39:5–30.1**
Restoration, fees, **39:3–10a**
Rules and regulations, **39:3–40.5**
School bus, failure to stop when bus stops, **39:4–128.1**
Temporary registration, **39:3–40.2**
Sale or transfer, **39:3–40.4**
Unlawful taking of a motor vehicle, **2C:20–2.1**
Willful obstruction of passage of other vehicles, **39:4–56.1 et seq.**
Temporary registration,
Foreign states, registration in foreign state by state resident, **39:3–4a**
Leasing or renting companies, **39:3–18**
Nonresident, **39:3–4b**
Theft of identity, exceptions, **2C:21–17**
Title papers as prerequisite, **39:10–18**
Transfer of ownership,
Expiration of registration, **39:3–30**
Person engaged in business of, **39:3–18**
Uninsured motor vehicles, **39:3–4**
Unsatisfied claim and judgment fund, post
Veterans organizations, **39:3–27**
Victims of crime, mailing address, **39:3–4, 39:3–9c**
Weight, excess of limitation permitted by registration, **39:3–84.3**
Liens and incumbrances,
Licenses and permits, auctions and auctioneers, notice, **39:3–17.1**
Repair of vehicle, proof to lien holder, **39:13–8**
Lights and Lighting, this index
Limitation of actions, arbitration and award, tort claims, tolling of limitation, **39:6A–26**
Limitations, arbitration awards, tort claims, **39:6A–30**
Limited access highway,
Definitions, **39:1–1**
Entrances and exits established by public authority, **39:4–90.1**
Limousine or Livery Service, generally, this index

MOTOR VEHICLES—Cont'd
Liquefied gaseous fuel, identification of vehicles using, **39:3–79.4 et seq.**
Liquors. Alcoholic beverages, generally, ante
Live ashes, throwing or dropping from vehicle on highway, **39:4–64**
Loads and Loading, generally, this index
Loans,
Disabled veterans, special plates, **39:3–27.17**
Master keys or devices, **2C:5–6**
Registration of motor vehicles owned or controlled by persons lending money thereon, **39:3–18**
Local authorities,
Definitions, **39:1–1**
Lanes for traffic, designation, **39:4–88**
Through streets designation, **39:4–140**
Loss or destruction, identification cards for disabled persons, **39:3–29.6**
Low speed vehicles, **39:4–31.1 et seq.**
Definitions, **39:1–1**
Luring and enticing, crimes and offenses, **2C:13–7**
Luxury cars, certificates of ownership, additional fees, **39:3–8.4**
Machinery and equipment. Equipment, generally, ante
Magistrate, definitions, **39:1–1**
Mail and mailing,
Right of way through processions, **39:4–93**
Rural mail routes, commercial cars, **39:3–2**
Maintenance and repairs,
Body repair facilities, **39:13–1 et seq.**
Damage rendering repair economically impractical, salvage certificates of title, **39:10–31 et seq.**
Dealers, sale of defective motor vehicles, **39:10–26 et seq.**
Joint payment insurance check, **39:13–8**
Lien priority, **39:13–8**
Low speed vehicles, **39:4–31.2**
Proof to lessor or lien holder, **39:13–8**
Time, certificate of approval, **39:8–4**
Manslaughter, **2C:11–4**
Manufactured homes, dealers, licensed real estate brokers, **39:10–19**
Manufacturers and manufacturing,
Certificate of origin, delivery, **39:10–8**
Definitions, **39:1–1**
Delivery, certificate of origin on delivery of vehicle in state, **39:10–8**
Master keys or devices, **2C:5–6**
Numbers and numbering, **39:10–7**
Parts, serial numbers, **39:10B–1 et seq.**
Warranty nonconformity, returns, **39:10–9.3**
Master keys or devices, **2C:5–6**
Match, throwing or dropping from vehicle on highway, **39:4–64**
Medical expenses. Unsatisfied claim and judgment fund, post
Member jurisdiction, definitions, apportioned vehicles, registration, **39:3–6.11**
Mentally retarded persons, transportation, county vehicles, **39:4–207.2 et seq.**
Metal tire, definitions, **39:1–1**
Michaels Law, intoxication of driver, **39:4–50**
Military reserve units, license plates, **39:3–27.33, 39:3–27.34**
Minuteman emblem, special national guard registration plates, **39:3–27.13, 39:3–27.14**
Mirrors, **39:3–71**
Misrepresentation of mileage, **2C:21–8**
Mobile homes, dealers, licensed real estate brokers, **39:10–19**
Modification, marks or numbers, crimes and offenses, **2C:17–6**

MOTOR VEHICLES—Cont'd
Motor Carriers, generally, this index
Motor drawn vehicle, definitions, **39:1–1**
Motor Fuels, generally, this index
Motor Vehicle Commission, generally, this index
Motor Vehicle Insurance, generally, this index
Motorcycles, generally, this index
Motorists, definitions, Nonresident Violator Compact, **39:5F–4**
Motorized Bicycles, generally, this index
Motorized Scooters, generally, this index
Mountain highways, control, **39:4–55**
Movable span of bridge, gate or barrier, care required when being closed, **39:4–127.2**
Moving Heavy Machinery, generally, this index
Mud flaps, **39:3–79.1 et seq.**
Mufflers, **39:3–70**
Municipal Courts, this index
Municipalities,
　Free registration of motor vehicles, **39:3–27**
　Handicapped parking enforcement units, **39:4–197.9 et seq.**
　Parking offenses, impoundment or immobilization of vehicles, **39:4–139.13**
　Sale of abandoned and unclaimed vehicles, **39:10A–1 et seq.**
　Sidewalks, driving on, sidewalk maintenance or cleaning purposes, **39:4–71**
　Special traffic regulation, **39:4–197.3**
Name and address,
　Arbitrators, tort claims, stipulation to names of arbitrators, **39:6A–27**
　Noncommercial trucks, **39:3–8.1**
National guard special registration plates, **39:3–27.13, 39:3–27.14**
Negotiable title, definitions, apportioned vehicles, registration, **39:3–6.11**
New motor vehicles,
　Certificate of origin, security interest, **39:10–8**
　Licenses and permits, **39:3–4**
　　Fees, **39:3–8**
　Security interest, **39:10–8**
New state residents, licenses and permits, **39:3–17.1**
Newspaper reporters, limitation on use of press identification, **39:3–76.1**
No passing zones, **39:4–86**
Noncommercial trucks, **39:1–1, 39:3–8, 39:3–8.1**
Nonprofit community, alumni or service organizations, special plates, **39:3–27.35 et seq.**
Nonprofit corporations and associations, registration fees, exemption, **39:3–27**
Nonresidents,
　Age, minimum, **39:3–17**
　Agent for acceptance of process, **39:7–2, 39:7–2.1**
　Certificate of conviction transmitted to nonresidents state, **39:4–9.1**
　Continuance of action against, **39:7–4**
　Licenses and permits,
　　New state residents, **39:3–17.1**
　　Temporary registration, **39:3–4b**
　New state residents, licenses and permits, **39:3–17.1**
　Reciprocity, generally, post
　Service of process, post
　Substituted service, service of process, **39:7–3**
　Violator compact, **39:5F–1 et seq.**
Nonrubber tires, **39:3–23.1**
North Jersey district water supply commission, exemption from payment of registration fee, **39:3–27**

MOTOR VEHICLES—Cont'd
Notice,
　Abandoned and unclaimed vehicles, sale, **39:10A–1**
　Animal welfare license plates, availability, **39:3–27.57**
　Battleship U.S.S. New Jersey license plates, availability, **39:3–27.71**
　Body repair facilities, license refusal, revocation, or suspension, **39:13–5**
　Change of address of registered owner or licensed operator, **39:3–36**
　Child passenger restraint systems, types meaning federal safety standards, **39:3–76.2c**
　Coastal protection license plates, availability, **39:3–27.53**
　Driving privilege forfeiture or postponement, controlled substance offenses, consequences of driving during, **2C:35–16**
　Habitual offenders, license suspensions, **39:5–30b**
　Hearing on revocation or suspension of license, **39:10–20**
　Licenses and permits, ante
　Nonresidents, **39:7–2.2**
　Olympic license plates, availability, **39:3–27.66**
　Penalty, driving while license suspended, driving under influence, **39:4–50**
　Penalty points, license suspension hearings, **39:5–30.5 et seq.**
　Plates or markers, post
　Repairs, certificate of approval, **39:8–4**
　Sale of motor vehicles, name and address of buyer, **39:3–30**
　Service of process, executors and administrators of operator or owner, **39:7–2.1**
　Special plates, anatomical gifts, **39:3–27.129**
　Special traffic regulation adopted by municipality, **39:4–197.3**
　Unsatisfied claim and judgment fund, post
　Wildlife conservation license plates, **39:3–33.10**
Nuisance, rotating or flashing lights on or near highways, **39:4–60.1 et seq.**
Number plates. Plates or markers, generally, post
Numbers,
　Arbitrators, stipulation to number of arbitrators, tort claims, **39:6A–27**
　Change or destruction, crimes and offenses, **2C:17–6**
　Title, forgery, **2C:21–4.8**
Objects, throwing or dropping from vehicle on highway, **39:4–64**
Obliteration, marks or numbers, crimes and offenses, **2C:17–6**
Obstructed view,
　Condition or load of vehicle obstructing view, **39:4–58**
　Equipment or load of motor vehicle, **39:3–74**
　Rear or side view, **39:4–58**
　Turning of vehicle, **39:4–125**
Odometers,
　Low speed vehicles, **39:4–31.2**
　Misrepresentation, **2C:21–8**
Off site sales, licenses and permits, **39:10–19.1 et seq.**
Offenses. Crimes and offenses, generally, ante
Offers of judgment before arbitration, rules of court, **39:6A–28**
Official inspection stations, uniforms for employees, **39:8–2.1**
Official traffic control devices,
　Definitions, **39:1–1**

MOTOR VEHICLES—Cont'd
Official traffic control devices—Cont'd
　Traffic Signs and Signals, generally, this index
Older and walking impaired persons crossing, designation of areas and erection of signs, **39:4–183.1b**
Olympic license plates. Plates or markers, post
Omnibuses. Buses, generally, this index
Operating privileges, mandatory forfeiture or postponement, controlled dangerous substances offenses, **2C:35–16**
Operating without permission of owner, unsatisfied claim and judgment fund, **39:6–70**
Operators, definitions, **39:1–1**
Optional records, definitions, apportioned vehicles, registration, **39:3–6.11**
Orders,
　Emissions control, administrative out of service order against vehicle, **39:8–73**
　Unsatisfied claim and judgment fund, post
Out of State Motorist Act, **39:7–1 et seq.**
Outside lane, definitions, **39:1–1**
Overtaking and passing vehicles. Traffic Rules and Regulations, this index
Owners and ownership, definitions, apportioned vehicles, registration, **39:3–6.11**
Ownership. Title to property, generally, post
Parades, special registration, **39:3–27.2**
Park roads, drives, bridle paths, application of motor vehicle and traffic laws to, **39:5A–4**
Parking, generally, this index
Parks and Parkways, this index
Passaic valley sewerage commissioner, exemption from payment of registration fee, **39:3–27**
Passenger automobile, definitions, **39:1–1**
Passengers,
　Children and minors, restraint systems, **39:3–76.2a et seq.**
　Intoxicating liquors, consumption, **39:4–51a**
　Moving vehicles, **39:4–65**
　Seat belt, **39:3–76.2e et seq.**
Peace officers,
　Combating theft of, **39:3–85.6**
　Directions to drivers, compliance required, **39:4–57**
　Fleeing or attempting to elude law enforcement officers, **2C:29–2**
　Hands free telephones, application of law, **39:4–97.4**
　Hours of Service Law, **39:9–4**
　Impoundment, operation of vehicle by unlicensed driver, invalid registration or plates, **39:3–40.3**
　Inspection Law, **39:8–9**
　Interior lights, stops, **39:4–57.1**
　Junk Yard Law, **39:11–11**
　Railroad crossings, enforcement of regulation, **39:5–1**
　Special plates, law enforcement officers memorial plates, **39:3–27.123 et seq.**
Pedestrians, generally, this index
Penalties. Fines and penalties, generally, ante
Penalty points, **39:5–30.5 et seq.**
Periodic inspection, definitions, emissions inspection, **39:8–60**
Periodic inspection program, definitions, emissions inspection, **39:8–60**
Person, definitions, emissions inspection, **39:8–60**
Personal injuries,
　Ice and snow, dislodging from moving vehicle, fines and penalties, **39:4–77.1**

MOTOR VEHICLES—Cont'd
Personal injuries—Cont'd
Towing service failure to pick up debris, fines and penalties, **39:4–56.8**
Victims of crime, notice of prosecution status, **39:5–51, 39:5–52**
Personal recognizances, definitions, Nonresident Violator Compact, **39:5F–4**
Photocopy, identification cards for disabled persons, crimes and offenses, **39:3–29.8**
Photographs, repaired vehicle, evidence to lien holder or lessor, **39:13–8**
Physicians and Surgeons, this index
Placards, handicapped persons, temporary placards, **39:4–206**
Plates or markers,
Advertising plates, **39:3–33**
Amateur radio licensees, **39:3–27.5 et seq.**
Animal welfare plates, **39:3–27.55**
Cooperation with health department, **39:3–27.58**
Costs, reimbursement, **39:3–27.56**
Armed forces, ante
Barnegat Bay Decoy and Baymens Museum, **39:3–27.86 et seq.**
Battleship U.S.S. New Jersey plates, **39:3–27.67 et seq.**
Canadian vehicles, handicapped parking privileges, **39:4–207.5**
Certificates and certification, costs, anatomical gifts, special plates, **39:3–27.130**
Coastal protection plates, **39:3–27.47 et seq.**
Combat infantryman badge recipients, **39:3–27.46**
Commercial plates, **39:3–20**
Issuance, **39:3–20.1, 39:3–20.2**
Commuter vans, **39:3–27.19 et seq.**
Conquer cancer plates, **39:3–27.90**
Construction and design, **39:3–33**
Constructors, **39:3–20**
Converter, **39:3–18**
Costs, anatomical gifts, special plates, **39:3–27.130**
Counterfeiting or using other markers, **39:3–38**
County officers and employees, special identification plates, **39:3–27.29 et seq.**
Courtesy plates,
Crimes and offenses, restrictions, **39:3–33.5a**
Fees, **39:3–33.4**
Reissuance, **39:3–33a**
Subsequent sets, **39:3–33b**
D plates, **39:3–18**
Deborah heart and lung center, **39:3–27.107 et seq.**
Destruction, fee for new plates, **39:3–30**
Display, motorized bicycles, **39:4–14.3m**
Duplicate plates, amateur radio licensees, **39:3–27.5**
Emergency medical technician ambulance, **39:3–27.59, 39:3–27.60**
Special plates, issuance, **39:3–27.59, 39:3–27.60**
Farmer plates, **39:3–25**
Fees, **39:3–32**
Animal welfare plates, **39:3–27.55**
Battleship U.S.S. New Jersey license plates, **39:3–27.68**
Coastal protection license plates, **39:3–27.49**
Combat infantryman badge recipients, **39:3–27.46**
County officers and employees, special plates, **39:3–27.29 et seq.**
Courtesy plates, reissuance, **39:3–33a**

MOTOR VEHICLES—Cont'd
Plates or markers—Cont'd
Fees—Cont'd
Deborah heart and lung center, **39:3–27.108, 39:3–27.111**
Emergency medical technician ambulance, **39:3–27.59, 39:3–27.60**
Former mayors, **39:3–27.114**
General assembly, former members, **39:3–27.115**
Historic preservation license plates, **39:3–27.74**
Liberty State Park plates, **39:3–27.93, 39:3–27.95**
National guard members and former members, special plates, **39:3–27.13**
Olympic license plates, **39:3–27.63**
Personalized plates, reissuance, **39:3–33a**
Pinelands preservation license plates, **39:3–27.85**
Promote agriculture plates, **39:3–27.117 et seq.**
Reflectorized plates, **39:3–33.9**
Senate, former members, **39:3–27.115**
Special plates, **39:3–33a**
Law enforcement officers memorial plates, **39:3–27.123**
Specially marked plates, **39:3–33.4**
Subsequent sets, **39:3–33b**
Temporary placards, handicapped persons, **39:4–206**
Transfers, special plates, **39:3–33a**
United we stand, special plates, **39:3–27.133**
Wildlife conservation license plates, **39:3–33.10, 39:3–33.11**
Fictitious numbers, **39:3–33**
Firefighters or first aid rescue squads, **39:3–27.8 et seq.**
Firemen, special plates, **39:3–27.8 et seq.**
First aid squad, special plates, **39:3–27.8 et seq.**
Foreign state or country,
Handicapped persons parking, **39:4–207.5**
Necessity of title, **39:10–6**
Forgery or counterfeiting, penalties, **39:3–38**
Former prisoners of war, **39:3–27.24 et seq.**
Frame obscuring license plate, **39:3–33**
Funds, rewards for justice license plate fund, **39:3–27.134 et seq.**
Garbage trucks, **39:3–33**
Garden State to appear on plates, **39:3–33.2**
General assembly, former members, **39:3–27.115**
Hackensack Meadowlands, conservation, **39:3–27.100 et seq.**
Handicapped persons, **39:4–206**
Foreign state vehicles, **39:4–207.5**
Historic preservation license plates, **39:3–27.72 et seq.**
Historic vehicles, **39:3–27.4**
Holder obscuring plate, **39:3–33**
Illuminated markers, **39:3–61**
Illumination, **39:3–61**
Information plate on certain vehicles to include, **39:3–82**
Inserts, issuance, **39:3–33**
Insignia for license plates of vehicles of amputee, **39:4–206**
Lending, **39:3–35**
Liberty State Park plates, **39:3–27.91 et seq.**
Limousine or livery service, **39:3–19.5**
Fines and penalties, **39:5G–1**
Location on vehicle, **39:3–33**
Lost or defaced plates replaced, **39:3–32**
Mayors, **39:3–27.42**

MOTOR VEHICLES—Cont'd
Plates or markers—Cont'd
Mayors—Cont'd
Former mayors, **39:3–27.114**
Military reserve members, **39:3–27.34**
Military reserve units, **39:3–27.33, 39:3–27.34**
Motorized bicycles, **39:4–14.3j et seq.**
National guard, **39:3–27.13, 39:3–27.14**
Special plates, **39:3–27.13, 39:3–27.14**
Nonconventional type vehicles, **39:3–18**
Nonprofit community, alumni or service organizations, **39:3–27.35 et seq.**
Notice,
Deborah heart and lung center, **39:3–27.112**
Olympic license plates, **39:3–27.66**
Special plates, anatomical gifts, **39:3–27.129**
Wildlife conservation license plates, **39:3–33.10**
O plates or markers, **39:3–19**
Olympic license plates,
Application, **39:3–27.63**
Authorization, **39:3–27.62**
Definitions, **39:3–27.61**
Fees, **39:3–27.63**
Garden State games trust fund,
Allocation of funds, **39:3–27.65**
Creation, **39:3–27.64**
Notice, availability, **39:3–27.66**
Permanent nature, design, **39:3–33**
Phase in, reflectorized plates, **39:3–33.9**
Pinelands preservation license plates, **39:3–27.85**
Prisoners of war, **39:3–27.24 et seq.**
Surviving spouse, **39:3–27.41**
Promote agriculture plates, **39:3–27.116 et seq.**
Records and recordation, stolen, **39:3–85.3**
Reflectorized material, **39:3–33**
Phase in, **39:3–33.9**
Refusal to grant without certificate of ownership, **39:10–18**
Removal on sale of vehicle, **39:3–30**
Return or surrender, suspension or revocation of certificate of registration, **39:5–35**
Revocation,
Rules and regulations, **39:3–40.5**
Suspended license, **39:3–40.1**
Temporary certificate, **39:3–40.2**
Sale or transfer, **39:3–40.4**
Rewards for justice license plate fund, **39:3–27.134 et seq.**
Road building machinery, **39:4–30**
Sanitation vehicles, **39:3–33**
Security, **39:3–18**
Senate, former members, **39:3–27.115**
Shade tree and community forest preservation license plates, **39:3–27.79 et seq.**
Special identifying marks, **39:3–33.3 et seq.**
Special plates, **39:3–27.2 et seq.**
Anatomical gifts, **39:3–27.127 et seq.**
Crimes and offenses, restrictions, **39:3–33.5**
Fees, **39:3–33a, 39:3–33.4**
Law enforcement officers memorial plates, **39:3–27.123 et seq.**
Leases, reissuance, **39:3–33a**
Navy Cross, **39:3–27.106**
Organ donor, **39:3–27.127 et seq.**
Reissuance, fees, **39:3–33a**
Restrictions, **39:3–33.5**
Subsequent sets, **39:3–33b**
Transfers, **39:3–33a**
United we stand, **39:3–27.131 et seq.**

MOTOR VEHICLES—Cont'd
Plates or markers—Cont'd
Street rods, **39:3–27.27, 39:3–27.28**
Special license plates, **39:3–27.27, 39:3–27.28**
Submarine veterans, **39:3–27.98, 39:3–27.99**
Subsequent sets, fees, **39:3–33b**
Surplus property of United States, temporary marker for purchaser, **39:3–33.1**
Surviving spouses,
Prisoners of war or purple heart recipients, **39:3–27.41**
Silver star medal recipients, **39:3–27.45**
T plates, **39:3–20**
Temporary plates, **39:3–18**
Handicapped persons, **39:4–206**
Leasing or renting companies, **39:3–18**
Wholesale auction block, **39:3–18**
Theft, notice, **39:3–85.1**
Tow Trucks and Towing Companies, this index
Traction engines, **39:4–30**
Transfers, special plates, **39:3–33a**
United we stand, special plates, **39:3–27.131 et seq.**
Use for another vehicle, **39:3–35**
Veterans, post
Visibility, **39:3–33**
Wheelchairs, **39:4–206**
Wholesale auction block, **39:3–18**
Wildlife conservation plates, **39:3–33.10, 39:3–33.11**
Wrong numbers, **39:3–33**
X plates, **39:3–20**
Z plates, **39:3–20**
Points,
Motorcycle operators, failure to wear protective helmet, **39:3–76.7**
Penalty points, **39:5–30.5 et seq.**
Reduction, defensive driving course, against licensee, **39:5–30.9**
Pole trailer, definitions, **39:1–1**
Police and Police Departments, this index
Police Athletic League, registration fee exemption, **39:3–27**
Police officers, definitions, Nonresident Violator Compact, **39:5F–4**
Possession, marks or numbers on vehicle or parts, change or destruction, crimes and offenses, **2C:17–6**
Posting,
Copy of process served on nonresident owners, **39:7–8**
Limitation on use of word press by newspaper reporters, **39:3–76.1**
Notice, special plates, anatomical gifts, **39:3–27.129**
Notice of sale of motor vehicle, seized on suspicion of having been stolen, **39:5–47**
Postponement, driving privileges, controlled dangerous substances offenses, **2C:35–16**
Power of attorney, nonresidents, accidents or collisions, **39:7–7**
Preceding year, definitions, apportioned vehicles, registration, **39:3–6.11**
Present roads of corporations or institutions, application of motor vehicle laws to, **39:5A–1 et seq.**
Press, reporters, limitation on use of stickers, **39:3–76.1**
Presumptions,
Abandoned and unclaimed vehicles, **39:4–56.5**
Insurance, **39:6B–2**
Intoxicating liquors, consumption by driver or passenger, **39:4–51a**

MOTOR VEHICLES—Cont'd
Presumptions—Cont'd
Spouses, title vesting in both, **39:3–30.1**
Printing, child passenger restraint systems, meaning federal safety standards, information, **39:3–76.2c**
Priorities and preferences, repair of vehicle, lien, **39:13–8**
Prisoners of war, registration plates, **39:3–27.24**
Private detective businesses, community security services, identification lights, **39:3–54.14**
Private inspection centers. Inspection and inspectors, generally, ante
Private property,
Operation on, traffic sign or signal avoidance, prohibition, **39:4–66.2**
Unattended vehicles, **39:4–56.6, 39:4–56.7**
Private road or driveway, definitions, **39:1–1**
Privileges and immunities, low speed vehicles, liability, waiver, **39:4–31.4**
Probation, placing defendant on, **39:5–7**
Process. Service of process, generally, post
Production of books and papers, **39:4–7**
Tort claim arbitrations, **39:6A–29**
Proof of ownership, ignition keys, production, **2C:40–23**
Proportional registration distributive fund, **39:3–6.20**
Public nuisance, lights, rotating or flashing lights on or near highways, **39:4–60.1 et seq.**
Public policy, intoxication of driver, ignition interlock devices, **39:4–50.16**
Public property, operation on, traffic sign or signal avoidance, prohibition, **39:4–66.2**
Public Utilities, this index
Publications,
Identification, compressed or liquefied gaseous fuel users, statutory provisions, **39:3–79.9**
Notice of application for correction, title papers, **39:10–16**
Notice of sale of motor vehicle, seized on suspicion of having been stolen, **39:5–47**
Racing on public highway, disorderly persons, **39:5C–1**
Railroad crossings, stopping of vehicles, **39:4–128**
Railroad train, definitions, **39:1–1**
Real estate brokers, mobile or manufactured home dealers, **39:10–19**
Rear end assembly, serial numbers, **39:10B–1 et seq.**
Rear reflectors, **39:3–61**
Rear view mirrors, **39:3–71**
Commercial motor vehicles, **39:3–71.1**
Crossview mirrors, **39:3–71.1**
Necessity of device showing road to rear and side, **39:4–58**
Rear wheels, equipment preventing wheels from throwing material, **39:3–79.1 et seq.**
Reassignment certificates, dealers, **39:10–11**
Rebuttable presumptions, littering, drivers or owners responsibility, **39:4–64**
Reciprocity, **39:3–15 et seq.**
Commercial vehicles, **39:3–6.21**
Definitions, apportioned vehicles, registration, **39:3–6.11**
License suspension or revocation, **39:5–30**
Penalty, **39:3–40**
Reciprocal exchange, **39:4–9.1**
Residents privilege after suspension, **39:5–30.1**
Reckless driving, **39:4–96**
Assault by auto, **2C:12–1**
Courtesy plates, restrictions, **39:3–33.5a**

MOTOR VEHICLES—Cont'd
Reckless driving—Cont'd
Death or serious bodily injury of another, license suspension or revocation, **39:5–30**
Homicide, evidence, presumptions, **2C:11–5**
Special plates, restrictions, **39:3–33.5**
Reclaiming abandoned vehicles, **39:10A–2**
Records and recordation,
Apportioned vehicle, registration, **39:3–6.15**
Chattel mortgage on vehicle, **39:10–11**
Complaints, **39:5–44**
Component parts, serial numbers, **39:10B–2**
Dealers, **39:10–22**
Penalty points, **39:5–30.6**
Security interest, **39:10–14**
Service of process, **39:7–6**
Stolen motor vehicles, registration plates, **39:3–85.3**
Recovery, impounding, identification cards, **39:3–29.1a**
Recreational property, destruction by operation of vehicle, **39:4–97a**
Point system, assessment against drivers license, **39:5–30.5a**
Recreational Vehicles, generally, this index
Recycling. Motor Vehicle Junk Yards, generally, this index
Red flags, overhanging loads, **39:3–61.4**
Referees and reference, arbitration and award, tort claims, **39:6A–24 et seq.**
Regional air pollution control agency, registration fees exemption, **39:3–27**
Registrant, definitions, apportioned vehicles, registration, **39:3–6.11**
Registration. Licenses and permits, generally, ante
Registration plates. Plates or markers, generally, ante
Registration year, definitions, apportioned vehicles, registration, **39:3–6.11**
Reinspection, licenses and permits, **39:8–11 et seq.**
Removal,
Ice and snow, **39:4–77.1**
Marks or numbers, crimes and offenses, **2C:17–6**
Unattended vehicles, private property, **39:4–56.6, 39:4–56.7**
Unregistered vehicle from public highway, **39:3–4**
Renewal,
Body repair facility licenses, **39:13–2**
Identification cards for nondrivers, **39:3–29.5**
Rent. Leases, generally, ante
Repairs. Maintenance and repairs, generally, ante
Reporters, limitation on use of press identification, **39:3–76.1**
Reports,
Emissions, diesel vehicles, **39:8–78**
Theft, **39:3–85.1, 39:5–46**
Traffic Accidents, this index
Rescue Squads, this index
Residence and residents,
Nonresident violator compacts, **39:5F–1 et seq.**
Process on one resident when accident or collision occurred and later becoming nonresident, **39:7–2.1, 39:7–2.2**
Residence district,
Definitions, **39:1–1**
Speed, **39:4–98**
Restitution,
Auto theft, **2C:20–2.2**

MOTOR VEHICLES—Cont'd

Restitution—Cont'd
Damages incurred by owner, from theft, **2C:43–2.1**
Restraining devices, **39:3–76.2**
Children and minors, **39:3–76.2a et seq.**
Restricted plate, definitions, apportioned vehicles, registration, **39:3–6.11**
Retroactivity, arbitration and award, tort claims, **39:6A–25**
Retroreflective surface, regulation by director, **39:3–63**
Revocation,
Plates or markers, ante
Suspension or revocation. Licenses and permits, ante
Riding on part not intended for passengers, **39:4–69**
Rear end of vehicle, **39:4–61**
Right of Way, generally, this index
Right Turns, generally, this index
Roadside enforcement programs. Emissions, ante
Roadway, definitions, **39:1–1**
Robbery, carjacking, **2C:15–2**
Rules and regulations,
Body repair facilities, **39:13–7**
Court, arbitration and award, tort claims, **39:6A–35**
Emissions, ante
Exhaust emission standards and test methods, **39:8–61, 39:8–66**
Fees, labels identifying compressed or liquefied gaseous fuel users, **39:3–79.4**
Handicapped persons, **39:4–207.1**
Identification cards for disabled persons, **39:3–29.9**
Ignition interlock devices, **39:4–50.21**
Labels, compressed or liquefied gaseous fuel users, placement and appearance of labels, **39:3–79.5**
Length and width, **39:3–84**
Penalty points, **39:5–30.5 et seq.**
Prisoners of war, registration plates, **39:3–27.25**
Repairs, **39:8–4.1**
Salvage certificates of title, **39:10–37**
Silver star medal recipient special registration plates, issuance, **39:3–27.45**
Temporary plates and registration certificates, **39:3–4c**
Traffic Rules and Regulations, generally, this index
Safety belts. Seat belts, generally, post
Safety Zones, generally, this index
Sales, **39:10–1 et seq.**
Abandoned or unclaimed property, **39:10A–1 et seq.**
Certificate of origin, endorsement of security interest, **39:10–8**
Certificates of ownership, ante
Certifying condition of vehicle sold, **39:11–9**
Component parts, serial numbers, **39:10B–3**
Filing evidence of satisfaction of contract, **39:10–10**
Impounding, identification cards, possession by driver, failure, **39:3–29.1a**
Low speed vehicles, **39:4–31.4**
Manufactured homes, dealers, licensed real estate brokers, **39:10–19**
Mobile homes, dealers, licensed real estate brokers, **39:10–19**
Notice, name and address of buyer, **39:3–30**
Odometers, misrepresentation of mileage of motor vehicle, **2C:21–8**

MOTOR VEHICLES—Cont'd

Sales—Cont'd
Off site sales, licenses and permits, **39:10–19.1 et seq.**
Police cars, used police cars, **39:10–9.1, 39:10–9.2**
Public agencies, **39:10A–1 et seq.**
Registration plates, removal, **39:3–30**
Returns to manufacturer, requirements, **39:10–9.3**
Security interest, generally, post
Stolen vehicles, **39:5–47**
Sunday, **2C:33–26**
Suspension or revocation of registration certificate or plates, **39:3–40.4**
Title to property, generally, post
Unapproved devices or equipment, **39:3–77**
Used motor vehicles, post
Wholesale auction block, **39:3–18**
Salvage,
Certificates of title, **39:10–31 et seq.**
Impounded vehicles, **39:3–40.6**
Motor Vehicle Junk Yards, generally, this index
Parts, records, **39:10B–2**
Processors, component parts, serial numbers, **39:10B–5**
Size and weight limit exemptions, **39:3–84**
Satisfaction of security interest, **39:10–10**
Fees, **39:10–11**
Savings and loan associations, impounding, release, **39:3–40.6**
Savings banks, impounding, release, **39:3–40.6**
School Buildings and Grounds, this index
School Buses, generally, this index
Schools and School Districts, this index
Searches and seizures,
Certificate of ownership, **39:10–22**
Dealer in possession without certificate of ownership, **39:10–21**
Failure to have or produce title papers, **39:10–6, 39:10–21**
Notice,
Sale on seizure from dealer without proper certificate, **39:10–21**
Seizure of vehicle filed with commissioner, **39:10–15**
Stolen vehicles, **39:5–47**
Surrender of title papers, **39:10–15**
Seat belts, **39:3–76.2e et seq.**
Child passenger restraint systems, **39:3–76.2a et seq.**
Drivers licenses,
Examination permits, **39:3–13**
Probationary licenses, **39:3–13.4**
Special learners permits, **39:3–13.2a**
Drivers schools, use required, **39:12–15**
Fines and penalties, failure to use, **39:3–76.2n**
Passenger automobiles, **39:3–76.2, 39:3–76.2e et seq.**
Traffic accident report forms, **39:4–131**
Second or subsequent offenses,
Abandonment, **39:4–56.5**
Body repair facilities, penalties, **39:13–6**
Compressed or liquefied gaseous fuel suppliers, **39:3–79.8**
Driving under influence, **39:4–50**
Driving without insurance, **39:6B–2**
Luring and enticing, children and minors, **2C:13–6**
Penalty points, license suspension, **39:5–30.10**
Radioactive materials, fines, **39:5B–24**
Sale of used police cars, **39:10–9.2**
Sales, Sunday, **2C:33–26**
Unsafe driving, **39:4–97.2**

MOTOR VEHICLES—Cont'd

Secured party, definitions, **39:10–2**
Secured transactions, master keys, or devices, **2C:5–6**
Security, surcharges, registration, fees, **39:2A–38**
Security interest, **39:10–1 et seq.**
Definitions, **39:10–2**
Endorsement on certificate of origin at time of sale, **39:10–8**
Filing requirements, **39:10–11**
Low speed vehicles, **39:4–31.4**
Used cars, endorsement on certificate of ownership, **39:10–9**
Security Responsibility Law. Motor Vehicle Security Responsibility Law, generally, this index
Seizures. Searches and seizures, generally, ante
Self propelled vehicles, unregistered permits to cross public highways, **39:3–26.1 et seq.**
Semipublic roads of corporations or institutions, application of motor vehicle laws to, **39:5A–1 et seq.**
Semitrailers. Motor Carriers, generally, this index
Sentence and punishment,
Crimes and offenses, generally, ante
Fines and penalties, generally, ante
Separate exit door, merchandising or exhibition vehicle, **39:3–77.2**
Serial numbers, change or destruction, crimes and offenses, **2C:17–6**
Serious bodily injury, definitions, implied consent, **39:4–50.2**
Service charges, fees, **39:2A–36**
Service of process,
Arrest of persons violating laws relating to, **39:5–25**
Inspection Law, **39:8–9**
Issuance, **39:5–6**
Lieu of arrest for violation in presence of officer, **39:5–25**
Motor Vehicle Security Responsibility Law, **39:6–55**
Nonresidents,
Director of division of motor vehicles as agent for acceptance of service, **39:7–2, 39:7–2.1**
Insurance in foreign company, **39:6–25**
Manner of service of process, **39:7–2.2**
Motor vehicles division, **39:6–25**
Other county, **39:5–28**
Person resident when accident or collision occurred and later becoming nonresident, **39:7–2.1, 39:7–2.2**
Unattended vehicles, private property, **39:4–56.7**
Valid throughout state, **39:5–28**
Service organizations, nonprofit, special plates, **39:3–27.35 et seq.**
Sheriffs, special plates, **39:3–27.29 et seq.**
Shipper, definitions, **39:1–1**
Shoulder, definitions, **39:1–1**
Sidewalks,
Definitions, **39:1–1**
Driving on, municipal sidewalk maintenance or cleaning purposes, **39:4–71**
Signs and signals. Traffic Signs and Signals, generally, this index
Sirens, **39:3–69**
Slow moving vehicles,
Definitions, **39:1–1**
Impeding traffic prohibited, **39:4–97.1**
Right hand lanes designated for, **39:4–88**
Snowmobiles, generally, this index

MOTOR VEHICLES—Cont'd
Solid waste, axle weight limitations, **39:3–84.1**
Special plates. Plates or markers, ante
Special registration. Licenses and permits, ante
Special traffic regulation by municipality, **39:4–197.3**
Special written permits, exceeding dimensional and weight limitations, **39:3–84**
Speed, generally, this index
Speedometers, low speed vehicles, **39:4–31.2**
Spouses,
    Disabled veterans, free joint registration, **39:3–27.1**
    Joint registration, **39:3–30**
    Operation by surviving spouse of registered owner, **39:3–30.3**
    Registration, **39:3–30.1, 39:3–30.2**
    Title, vesting in registered owners surviving spouse, transfer of registration, **39:3–30**
State, this index
State owned grounds, regulation of parking and traffic, **39:4–208 et seq.**
State Police, this index
State Treasurer, this index
Statement of repair, evidence to lien holder or lessor, **39:13–8**
Stolen vehicles. Larceny, generally, ante
Stop signs. Traffic Signs and Signals, this index
Stopping,
    Brakes, performance of, **39:3–68**
    Distance for safe stopping determined as regards right to proceed through intersection on amber light, **39:4–105**
    Emerging from alley, driveway or garage, **39:4–66**
    Injuring animal, stopping after, **4:22–25.1, 4:22–25.2**
    Pedestrians, **39:4–32**
    Persons to be let off or taken on, stopping at curb, **39:4–65**
    Railroad grade crossings, **39:4–127.1**
    School busses, **39:4–128.1**
    Street car receiving or discharging passengers, overtaking vehicle to stop, **39:4–40**
    Through streets, **39:4–144**
Storage,
    Abandoned and unclaimed vehicles, **39:10A–2**
    Costs, abandoned and unclaimed vehicles, **39:10A–1**
    Removal, handicapped parking spaces, **39:4–207.6, 39:4–207.7**
    Unattended vehicles, private property, **39:4–56.6, 39:4–56.7**
    Unregistered vehicle removed from public highway, **39:3–4**
Street, definitions, **39:1–1**
Street rod, special license plates, **39:3–27.27**
Streetcar, definitions, **39:1–1**
Submarine veterans, plates or markers, **39:3–27.98, 39:3–27.99**
Subpoenas, **39:4–7**
    Arbitration, tort claims, **39:6A–29**
Substituted Service Act, **39:7–2**
Suburban business or residential district, definitions, **39:1–1**
Summary proceeding, body repair facilities, penalties, **39:13–6**
Summons. Service of process, generally, ante
Sunday, this index
Surcharges,
    Increases, **39:2A–36.1**
    Intoxication of driver, **39:4–50**

MOTOR VEHICLES—Cont'd
Surcharges—Cont'd
    Intoxication of driver—Cont'd
        Drunk driving enforcement fund, **39:4–50.8**
    Unsafe driving, fines and penalties, **39:4–97.2**
Surplus property of United States, temporary identification marker for purchaser, **39:3–33.1**
Surrender, certificates of ownership, vehicle larceny or damage rendering repair economically impractical, **39:10–32**
Suspension or revocation. Licenses and permits, ante
Tampering, **39:4–49**
Television sets, **39:3A–1, 39:3A–2**
Temporary placards, handicapped persons, **39:4–206**
Temporary plates. Plates or markers, ante
Temporary registration, **39:3–40.2**
    Nonresident, **39:3–4b**
Terminal rental adjustment clauses, definitions, leases, **39:10–5.1**
Terms of citations, definitions, Nonresident Violator Compact, **39:5F–4**
Terrorism, vehicular homicide, **2C:38–2**
Tests and testing. Emissions, ante
Theft. Larceny, generally, ante
Third or subsequent offenses, driving under influence, **39:4–50**
Third parties, intoxication of driver, liability, **39:4–50.22**
Three wheeled vehicles,
    Drivers licenses, **39:3–10**
    Goggles and face shields, **39:3–76.8**
    Protective helmets, **39:3–76.7**
Throwing objects from vehicle, highways, **39:4–64**
Tickets, emissions control violations, **39:8–71**
Tires, generally, this index
Title to property,
    Certificates of ownership, ante
    Defective or improper papers, correction, **39:10–16**
    Delivery to buyer, **39:10–10**
    Destruction or junking, vehicle, **39:10–23**
    Drivers licenses, operation of vehicle after revocation, allowance, **39:3–40**
    Drivers privacy protection, **39:2–3.3 et seq.**
    Filing fee, **39:10–11**
    Forgery, **2C:21–4.8**
    Fraud, **2C:21–4.8**
    Lost papers, certified copies issued, **39:10–12**
    Necessity, **39:10–6, 39:10–18**
    Production on demand, **39:10–6**
    Registration in husband and wife, **39:3–30.1, 39:3–30.2**
    Sale of vehicle, **39:10–8**
    Second or subsequent sale, **39:10–9**
    Time limitations on submission of, receipt of papers out of time, **39:10–16**
    Traffic accidents, presumptions, involvement, **39:4–129, 39:4–130**
Torts, arbitration and award, **39:6A–24 et seq.**
Total miles, definitions, apportioned vehicles, registration, **39:3–6.11**
Tow Trucks and Towing Companies, generally, this index
TRAC leases, **39:10–5.1**
Tractors and Traction Engines, generally, this index
Trademark or name,
    Change or destruction, crimes and offenses, **2C:17–6**
    Visibility of mark or name under which equipment was approved, **39:3–77**

MOTOR VEHICLES—Cont'd
Traffic, definitions, **39:1–1**
Traffic Accidents, generally, this index
Traffic calming devices, municipalities, powers and duties, **39:4–8.10**
Traffic fines. Fines and penalties, generally, ante
Traffic hazard warning signals, **39:3–64**
Traffic Rules and Regulations, generally, this index
Traffic Signs and Signals, generally, this index
Trailers and semitrailers. Motor Carriers, generally, this index
Training. Drivers Schools, generally, this index
Transfers,
    Salvage certificate of title, **39:10–31 et seq.**
    Suspension or revocation of registration certificate or plates, **39:3–40.4**
Transmission, serial number, **39:10B–1 et seq.**
Transportation Department, generally, this index
Transportation of vehicles without serial numbers on component parts, **39:10B–4**
Trial de novo, arbitrated tort claims, fee, **39:6A–32 et seq.**
Trucks. Motor Carriers, generally, this index
Turnpike authority, hiring, bids, **27:23–6.1**
Turnpikes, this index
Unapproved devices or equipment, sale, **39:3–77**
Unattended animals, crimes and offenses, **4:22–17**
Unattended vehicles, private property, **39:4–56.6, 39:4–56.7**
Unclaimed vehicles. Abandoned or unclaimed property, generally, ante
Under age drivers, implied consent, blood analysis test, **39:4–50.4a**
United States, this index
United we stand, special plates, **39:3–27.131 et seq.**
Unlawful taking,
    Carjacking, **2C:15–2**
    Fines and penalties, **2C:20–2.1**
Unregistered vehicles, permits to cross public highways, **39:3–26.1 et seq.**
Unsafe vehicles, operation, **39:3–44**
Unsatisfied claim and judgment fund, **39:6–61 et seq.**
    Actions and proceedings, **39:6–78 et seq.**
    Agreements, reimbursement of fund, **39:6–77**
    Amounts payable from fund, **39:6–73**
    Application, payment, **39:6–69, 39:6–86.5**
    Approval, settlement of actions, **39:6–72**
    Assessment of estimated deficiency against insurers for contribution to fund, **39:6–63**
    Assignments, judgment to state treasurer, **39:6–77**
    Bankruptcy discharge, **39:6–87**
    Board,
        Abolishment, transfer of powers and duties, property liability insurance guaranty association, **39:6–64c**
        Consent to settlement, **39:6–72**
    Collusive judgment not paid out of fund, **39:6–76**
    Commissioner, definitions, **39:6–62**
    Condition precedent to fees, **39:6–70**
    Consent judgment, payment out of fund, **39:6–74**
    Court approval, settlement of actions, **39:6–72**
    Death benefits, payments, **39:6–86.1**
    Death or injury, unidentifiable operator or owner, **39:6–86.4**

MOTOR VEHICLES—Cont'd
Unsatisfied claim and judgment fund—Cont'd
Deductions,
Amount due on judgment, **39:6–71**
Hit and run cases, judgments and decrees, **39:6–83**
Maximum amounts payable from fund, **39:6–73**
Medical expense benefits, **39:6–86.1**
Default judgments, payment out of fund, **39:6–74**
Defenses,
Action against motorist, **39:6–67, 39:6–68**
Hit and run cases, **39:6–81**
Deficiency, assessment against insurers for contribution to fund, **39:6–63**
Definitions, **39:6–62**
Denial, payments, **39:6–86.3**
Essential services benefits, payment, **39:6–86.1**
Estimate of damages to accompany notice of intention to file claim, **39:6–65**
Evidence in hearing on application for payment of unsatisfied judgment, **39:6–70**
Execution return unsatisfied as condition to recovery from fund, **39:6–70**
Exemptions, payments, **39:6–86.1**
Expenses and expenditures, defending action by insurers and motorist, **39:6–67**
False statements, penalty for, **39:6–90**
Fees,
Paid on registering vehicle, **39:6–63**
Remitted to treasurer, **39:6–88**
Uninsured motor vehicle, **39:6–63.1**
Fraudulent judgment not paid out of fund, **39:6–76**
Funeral expenses, payments, **39:6–86.1**
Hearing on application for payment of unsatisfied judgment, **39:6–70**
Hit and run cases, **39:6–78 et seq.**
Hospital, medical or dental benefit plan, benefits and payments, **39:6–86.2**
Impleading, hit and run cases, **39:6–80**
Income continuation benefits, payment, **39:6–86.1**
Insurers, payment of percentage of net direct written premiums, **39:6–63**
Investment and reinvestment, **39:6–88**
Licenses and permits,
Reinstatement of revoked or suspended license or registration, **39:6–87**
Removal of suspension, evidence of coverage, personal injury protection benefit, **39:6–27**
Required personal injury protection benefits insurance coverage, **39:6–25**
Security deposits,
Reimbursement of fund, personal injury protection benefits coverage, **39:6–30**
Return of security, personal injury protection benefits coverage, **39:6–30**
Suspension or revocation, agreement to reimburse fund, **39:6–25**
Liens, subordination, reimbursement of fund, **39:6–77**
Limitation on amounts payable from fund, **39:6–73**
Loans, powers and duties, **39:6–64.1**
Lump sum payments, reimbursement of fund, **39:6–77**
Maximum payments, increases, **39:6–84.1**
Medical expenses,
Payments, **39:6–86.1**
Reimbursement, excess, time, limitations, **39:6–73.1**

MOTOR VEHICLES—Cont'd
Unsatisfied claim and judgment fund—Cont'd
Net direct written premiums, definitions, **39:6–62**
No fault insurance, **39:6A–13**
Notice,
False notice, **39:6–90**
Intention,
Enter default judgment and file claim thereof, **39:6–74**
File claim, **39:6–65**
Payment, claims, **39:6–86.2**
Orders,
Approving settlement, **39:6–72**
Hit and run cases, **39:6–82**
Damages, payment, **39:6–84**
Property liability insurance guaranty association, **39:6–78**
Partial invalidity of law, **39:6–90.1**
Payments,
Benefits, **39:6–86.1 et seq.**
Unsatisfied judgment from fund, **39:6–69, 39:6–71**
Pedestrians, **39:6–86.1**
Application of law, **39:6–86.7**
Petition for settlement, **39:6–72**
Hit and run cases, **39:6–82**
Plans and specifications, operation, **39:6–64.1**
Qualified person, definitions, **39:6–62**
Registration license year, definitions, **39:6–62**
Reimbursements,
Fund, **39:6–77, 39:6–86.6**
Medical expenses, excess, time, limitations, **39:6–73.1**
Review of action defended by insurers, **39:6–67**
Settlement of actions, **39:6–72**
Hit and run cases, **39:6–82**
Stolen vehicles, **39:6–70**
Subrogation, **39:6–85**
Survivor benefits, payments, **39:6–86.1**
Trust, fund held in, **39:6–88**
Unidentifiable operator or owner, death or injury, **39:6–86.4**
Uninsured motor vehicle, definitions, **39:6–62**
Workers compensation, **39:6–78, 39:6–79**
Evidence person is not covered under law on application for payment from fund, **39:6–70**
Used motor vehicles,
Condition of vehicle, **39:10–26 et seq.**
Dealers,
Licenses and permits, suspension or revocation, **39:10–20**
Sales, Sunday, **2C:33–26**
Sales, Sunday, **2C:33–26**
Definitions, Certificate of Motor Vehicle Ownership Law, **39:10–2**
Disorderly persons, sales, Sunday, **2C:33–26**
Mileage misrepresentation, **2C:21–8**
Motor Vehicle Junk Yards, generally, this index
Parts, component parts, serial numbers, **39:10B–2**
Police cars, sales, **39:10–9.1, 39:10–9.2**
Sales,
Condition of vehicles, **39:10–26 et seq.**
Police cars, **39:10–9.1, 39:10–9.2**
Security interest,
Certificate of ownership, **39:10–9**
Indorsement on certificate of ownership, **39:10–9**
Sunday, **2C:33–26**
Security interest, certificate of ownership, **39:10–9**

MOTOR VEHICLES—Cont'd
Used motor vehicles—Cont'd
Serial numbers, component parts, **39:10B–2**
Sunday, sales, **2C:33–26**
Warranties, **39:10–26 et seq.**
Vandalism, component parts, serial numbers, **39:10B–3**
Vanpooling, definitions, **39:1–1**
Vehicle, definitions, TRAC leases, **39:10–5.1**
Veterans,
Free registration to disabled veterans filing jointly with wives, **39:3–27.1**
Plates or markers,
Disabled veterans, **39:3–27.15 et seq.**
Loans, disabled veterans, **39:3–27.17**
Special plates,
Combat infantryman badge recipients, **39:3–27.46**
Disabled veterans, **39:3–27.15 et seq.**
Navy Cross, **39:3–27.106**
Prisoners of war, **39:3–27.24 et seq.**
Purple heart, recipients, **39:3–27.43 et seq.**
Surviving spouses, **39:3–27.41**
Silver star medal recipients and surviving spouses, **39:3–27.45**
Submarine veterans, **39:3–27.98, 39:3–27.99**
Registration, **39:3–27.1**
Fees, disabled veterans, **39:3–27.1**
Surplus property of United States, temporary identification markers, **39:3–33.1**
Victims of crime, death or personal injury, notice to victim of prosecution status, **39:5–51, 39:5–52**
Vocational schools, registration fee exemption, **39:3–27**
Volunteer Firefighters and Fire Companies, this index
Waiver,
Low speed vehicles, liability, **39:4–31.4**
Used motor vehicles, obligations, **39:10–29**
Walking impaired persons crossing, designation of areas and erection of signs, **39:4–183.1b**
Warnings, volunteer fire company or rescue squad members, warning lights, **39:3–54.7 et seq.**
Warranties,
Nonconformity, return indicated on certificate of ownership, **39:10–9.3**
Used motor vehicles, ante
Weapons,
Presumption of possession, **2C:39–2**
Transportation, **2C:39–6**
Weights and measures, **39:3–84.3 et seq.**
Allowance as to statutory and registered weight limitations, **39:3–20**
Bridges, penalty and liability for damages caused by driving over,
Interstate bridge, **39:4–76**
Intrastate bridge, **39:4–75**
Commercial vehicles, **39:3–20, 39:3–84**
Constructor registration plates, vehicle or combination vehicle, restriction, **39:3–20**
Converter dolly, **39:4–54**
Damages, **39:3–84.4**
Disabled vehicles, exemption, **39:3–84**
Dump trucks, **39:3–84.1**
Exceeding provisions of registration certificate, **39:3–20**
Exemptions, **39:4–197.18**
Construction vehicles, **39:3–84.1**
Solid waste vehicles, **39:3–84.1**
Fines and penalties, **39:3–84.3**
Gross weight, definitions, **39:1–1**

MOTOR VEHICLES—Cont'd
Weights and measures—Cont'd
Heavy machinery, distribution of weight according to tire width, moving along or across highway, **39:4–27**
Information plate on certain vehicles to show weight, **39:3–82**
Intermodal ocean containers, **39:3–84.1**
Intrastate bridges, **39:4–75, 39:4–76**
Nonresident Violator Compact, application of law, **39:5F–25**
Private utility or house type semitrailers and trailers, **39:3–8**
Redistribution of weight to prevent axle weight limitation, **39:3–84.3**
Registration fees based on, **39:3–20**
Solid waste vehicles, **39:3–84.1**
State highways, **39:4–197.16 et seq.**
Tandem three axle solid waste vehicles, **39:3–84.1**
Unregistered vehicles, permits to cross public highways, fees based on weight, **39:3–26.4**
Wheelchairs,
Plates or markers, handicapped persons, **39:4–206**
Securing, **39:3–76.2l, 39:3–76.2m**
Wheels,
Locking, **39:3–81**
Single axle limitation, dimensional and weight limitations, **39:3–84**
Turning wheels of parked vehicles toward side of highway, **39:4–137**
Whistles, **39:3–69**
Width, commercial motor vehicles, **39:3–84**
Wife. Spouses, generally, ante
Wildlife conservation license plates, application, fees, **39:3–33.10**
Willful and wanton injuries, no fault insurance, exemptions, **39:6A–7**
Windshields, generally, this index
Wireless telephones, hands free telephones, **39:4–97.3 et seq.**
Witnesses, this index
Workers compensation. Unsatisfied claim and judgment fund, ante
Yielding right of way to traffic on through street, **39:4–144**

MOTOR VEHICLES CARRYING PASSENGERS FOR HIRE
Buses, generally, this index
Licensing of driver, **39:3–10.1**

MOTOR VEHICLES DIVISION
Motor Vehicle Commission, generally, this index

MOTOR VEHICLES WHICH CONSTITUTE INVENTORY HELD FOR SALE
Definitions, Certificate of Ownership Law, **39:10–2**

MOTORBUSES
Buses, generally, this index

MOTORCYCLES
See, also, Motorized Bicycles, generally, this index
Brakes, **39:3–67**
Brands, marks and labels, manufacturers and manufacturing, certificates and certification, safety, **39:3–76.3a**
Certificates and certification, manufacturers and manufacturing, brands, marks and labels, safety, **39:3–76.3a**

MOTORCYCLES—Cont'd
Crimes and offenses, marks or numbers, change or destruction, **2C:17–6**
Definitions, Motor Vehicles Law, **39:1–1**
Drivers Schools, generally, this index
Equipment, **39:3–76.6, 39:3–76.10**
Examination permits, **39:3–13**
Fees, licenses and permits, **39:3–10**
Fines and penalties, passengers, helmets, **39:3–76.5**
Forfeitures, public lands, **39:3C–34**
Goggles and face shield, **39:3–76.8, 39:3–76.10**
Handicapped persons, license plates, issuance, national wheelchair symbol, **39:4–206**
Handlebar grips, **39:3–76.3**
Headlamps, **39:3–49**
Helmet, **39:3–76.7, 39:3–76.10**
Passengers, **39:3–76.5**
Identification marks, **39:3–33**
Impounding, public lands, **39:3C–34**
Inspection, time, **39:3–4**
Lamp required on side car, **39:3–49**
License plates,
Illumination, **39:3–61**
Issuance, national wheelchair symbol, handicapped persons, **39:4–206**
Licenses and permits, **39:3–10**
Examination permits, **39:3–10b**
Fees, **39:3–10**
Road tests, waiver, safety education program, **39:3–10.31**
Lights, **39:3–61**
Manufacturers and manufacturing, brands, marks and labels, safety, certificates and certification, **39:3–76.3a**
Motorized Scooters, generally, this index
Mufflers, **39:3–76.4**
Passengers, **39:3–76.5**
Permanent seat, **39:3–76.5**
Photo licenses, **39:3–10f**
Public lands, operation, **39:3C–32 et seq.**
Registration,
Fees, **39:3–21**
Renewal, **39:3–4**
Riding position, **39:3–76.5**
Road tests,
Scheduling, **39:3–13**
Waiver, safety education program, **39:3–10.31**
Safety instructors, certification, **39:12–5 et seq.**
Side car or other extension, lamps, **39:3–61**
Stop lights, **39:3–61**
Vision test, **39:3–10**
Waiver, road tests, safety education program, **39:3–10.31**
Wheelchair symbol, license plates, handicapped persons, **39:4–206**
Windshield, **39:3–76.9**

MOTORIZED BICYCLES
See, also,
Motorcycles, generally, this index
Motorized Scooters, generally, this index
Generally, **39:1–1 et seq.**
Accident reports, **39:4–14.3f**
Affidavits, ownership proof, bicycles purchased before registration statute effective, **39:4–14.3p**
Age of operator, **39:4–14.3, 39:4–14.3d**
Alleys, entering or leaving, fines and penalties, **39:4–14.3x**
Certificates and certification,
Make and model numbers, **39:4–14.3n**
Registration, **39:4–14.3i et seq.**
D plates, **39:3–18**

MOTORIZED BICYCLES—Cont'd
Certificates and certification—Cont'd
Registration—Cont'd
Duplicate registration certificates, **39:3–31, 39:3–31.1**
Possession, operator, **39:4–14.3**
Costs, possession and display, operators, drivers license, insurance identification card, and registration certificate, **39:4–14.3**
Crimes and offenses, **39:4–14.3, 39:4–14.3t**
False proof of ownership, **39:4–14.3p**
Fraud, ownership evidence, **39:4–14.3p**
Marks or numbers, change or destruction, **2C:17–6**
Dealers, licenses and permits, planning or zoning restrictions or regulations, **39:4–14.3r**
Death of another, license suspension or revocation, **39:5–30**
Definitions, traffic rules, **39:1–1**
Destruction, notice, **39:4–14.3l**
Drivers licenses, **39:4–14.3**
Juvenile delinquents and dependents, suspension or revocation, false alarms, **2C:33–3.1**
Surrender of foreign licenses, **39:3–10**
Driveways, entering or leaving, fines and penalties, **39:4–14.3x**
Driving while intoxicated, **39:4–14.3g**
Duplicates, registration certificates, **39:3–31, 39:3–31.1**
Educational programs, safe operation, funds, **39:4–14.3v1**
Fees,
D plates, **39:3–18**
Duplicate registration certificates, **39:3–31**
Fines and penalties, **39:4–14.3b, 39:4–14.3t**
Alleys, driveways, garages or private roads, entering or leaving, **39:4–14.3x**
Driving while intoxicated, **39:4–14.3g**
Penalty points, **39:5–30.5**
Possession and display, drivers license, insurance registration card, and registration certificate, operators, **39:4–14.3**
Residence changes, notices, owners, **39:3–36**
Forfeiture of operating privilege, controlled substance offenses, **2C:35–16**
Funds, educational programs, safe operation, **39:4–14.3v**
Garages, entering or leaving, fines and penalties, **39:4–14.3x**
Grandfather rights, registration, **39:4–14.3u**
Helmets, **39:4–14.3q**
Insurance, **39:4–14.3e**
Identification card, operator, possession, **39:4–14.3**
Interstate highways, **39:4–14.3, 39:4–14.3d**
Intoxication of driver, **39:4–14.3g**
Juvenile delinquents and dependents, drivers licenses, suspension or revocation, false alarms, **2C:33–3.1**
License plates, **39:4–14.3j et seq.**
D plates, **39:3–18**
Lists, approved bicycles, **39:4–14.3n**
Motor vehicle insurance, **39:4–14.3e**
Nonresident owners, registration, application of law, **39:4–14.3o**
Notice,
Removal from state, theft, destruction, or discontinuance of use, **39:4–14.3l**
Residence changes, owners, **39:3–36**
Operation after ownership transfer, time, **39:4–14.3l**
Penalty points, **39:5–30.5**
Plates or markers, **39:4–14.3j et seq.**

MOTORIZED BICYCLES—Cont'd

Possession, drivers license, insurance identification card, and registration certificate, **39:4–14.3**

Postponement of operating privileges, controlled substance offenses, **2C:35–16**

Private roads or driveways, entering or leaving, fines and penalties, **39:4–14.3x**

Railroads, right of ways, **39:4–14.3**

Records and recordation, registration certificates, **39:4–14.3i**

Registration, **39:4–14.3i et seq.**

Certificates,

Duplicates, **39:3–31.1**

Possession, operator, **39:4–14.3**

D plates, **39:3–18**

Removal from state, notice, **39:4–14.3l**

Rentals, liability insurance, **39:4–14.3d**

Reports, accident reports, **39:4–14.3f**

Rules and regulations, **39:4–14.3s**

Certification of make and model numbers, **39:4–14.3n**

Make and model number certification, **39:4–14.3n**

Penalty points, **39:5–30.5**

Promulgation, **39:4–14.3c**

Temporary plates and registration certificates, **39:3–4c**

Sales, rules and regulations, **39:4–14.3a**

Serious bodily injury of another, license suspension or revocation, **39:5–30**

State funds, educational program, safe operation, **39:4–14.3v**

Suspension, privilege to operate, minors, **39:4–14.3h**

Temporary registration,

Certificates, **39:4–14.3j**

Plates, **39:3–18**

Theft, notice, **39:4–14.3l**

Title, **39:4–14.3i et seq.**

Traffic regulations, **39:4–14.3d**

Suspension of privileges, violations, minors, **39:4–14.3h**

Transfer of ownership, registration certificate already issued, **39:4–14.3l**

MOTORIZED SCOOTERS

See, also, Motorized Bicycles, generally, this index

Counties, traffic rules and regulations, **39:4–14.14**

Definitions,

Handicapped persons, traffic rules and regulations, stickers, **39:4–14.15**

Traffic rules and regulations, **39:1–1**

Fines and penalties, **39:4–14.13**

Forfeitures, **39:4–14.13**

Handicapped persons, traffic rules and regulations, **39:4–14.12**

Stickers, **39:4–14.15**

Ordinances, **39:4–14.14**

Searches and seizures, **39:4–14.13**

Traffic rules and regulations, **39:4–14.12 et seq.**

MOTORMAN

Arrest for violation of motor vehicle and traffic law, **39:5–25**

MOUNTAIN HIGHWAYS

Motor vehicle to be kept on right side and under control, **39:4–55**

MOVABLE PROPERTY

Definitions, theft, **2C:20–1**

MOVABLE SPAN BRIDGE

Motorist approaching bridge while gate or barrier is closed, care required, **39:4–127.2**

MOVING HEAVY MACHINERY

Generally, **39:4–26 et seq.**

Brakes, **39:3–68**

Damages, **39:4–27**

Equipment, applicability of statute, **39:3–45**

Exceptions, application of law, **39:4–30**

Motor Vehicle Laws, **39:3–1**

Fee for registration plate, **39:4–30**

Fines and penalties, violation of statute, **39:4–31**

Height as affecting overhead wires, **39:4–28**

Lights, **39:3–65**

Applicability of statute, **39:3–45**

Loading trailer or semitrailer to prevent injuries to highway, **39:4–27**

Registration plates, **39:4–30**

Time for moving along street railway tracks, **39:4–29**

Trailers, use and registration, **39:4–26**

Weight, distribution according to tire width, **39:4–27**

MOVING PICTURES

Children, prohibited sexual acts, **2C:24–4**

Consent, nudity, sexual intercourse, invasion of privacy, **2C:14–9**

Lewdness and Obscenity, generally, this index

Nudity, crimes and offenses, invasion of privacy, **2C:14–9**

Obscenity. Lewdness and Obscenity, generally, this index

Pornography. Lewdness and Obscenity, generally, this index

Possession, showing child engaging in prohibited sexual act, fourth degree crime, **2C:24–4**

Viewing, child engaging in prohibited sexual act, fourth degree crime, **2C:24–4**

MUD FLAPS

Motor vehicles, **39:3–79.1 et seq.**

MUFFLERS

All terrain vehicles, **39:3C–19, 39:3C–24**

Inspection, **39:3C–25**

Dirt bikes, **39:3C–19, 39:3C–24**

Inspection, **39:3C–25**

Motor vehicles, requirement, **39:3–70**

Motorcycles, **39:3–76.4**

MULTIPLE DWELLINGS

Hotels and Motels, generally, this index

MULTIPLE OFFENSES

Crimes and Offenses, this index

MULTIPLE PARTY ACTIONS

Contingent attorney fees, **Rule 1:21–7**

Peremptory challenges to jurors, additional challenges, representation by different attorneys, **Rule 1:8–3**

MULTIPLE PROSECUTIONS

Double Jeopardy, generally, this index

MULTIPLE SENTENCES

Crimes and offenses, **2C:44–5**

MUNICIPAL ATTORNEYS, COUNSELORS AND SOLICITORS

Municipal Courts, generally, this index

Municipal judges, practicing as municipal attorney, **Rule 1:15–1**

MUNICIPAL ATTORNEYS, COUNSELORS AND SOLICITORS—Cont'd

Practice of law, **Rule 1:15–3**

Prosecuting attorneys, limitation on practice, **Rules 1:15–3, 1:15–4**

Solid waste facilities, counselor to health department, compliance with regulations, **13:1E–9**

Traffic law regulations, representation of complainant on appeal from conviction, **39:5–20**

MUNICIPAL BONDS

Warrants, generally, this index

MUNICIPAL CLERKS

Summons for service on persons violating motor vehicle or traffic laws in presence of officer, **39:5–25**

MUNICIPAL CONTRACTS

Autonomous computer system, operation, review, audit, **2B:12–30**

Crimes and offenses, fraud, **2C:21–34**

Fraud, **2C:21–34**

Parking offenses, processing services, **39:4–139.14**

Processing services, parking offenses, **39:4–139.14**

MUNICIPAL CORPORATIONS

Municipalities, generally, this index

MUNICIPAL COURTS

Generally, **2B:12–1 et seq.**

Accounts and accounting, **Rule 7:14–4**

Acquittal of defendant, costs charged to complainant, **2B:12–24**

Acting judges,

Practicing, **Rule 1:15–1**

Substitution where previous judge disqualified or unable to hear manner, **Rule 1:12–3**

Additional arrest warrants or summonses, **Rule 7:2–2**

Additional judges, **2B:12–5**

Adjournment, **Rule 7:8–3**

Administrator, **2B:12–10**

Authorization to take oaths, issue warrants, **2B:12–21**

Bonds (officers and fiduciaries), required coverage, **2B:12–12**

Certification Board, establishment, qualifications, duties, **2B:12–11**

Insurance, required coverage, **2B:12–12**

Issuance of oaths, warrants, summonses, authorization, **2B:12–21**

Powers, **2B:12–13**

Signature on orders, warrants, **2B:12–13**

Aggravated assault, judges, **2C:12–1**

Alibi defense, crimes and offenses, notice, **Rule 7:7–3**

Amendments,

Defective warrant or summons, **Rule 7:2–5**

Process or pleading, **Rule 7:14–2**

Appeal and review, **Rule 7:13–1**

Disorderly persons, bail or recognizances, **2A:162–11**

Notice of right, **Rule 7:14–1**

Reversal of judgment, remission of penalties and costs, **Rule 7:13–3**

Stay pending appeal, **Rule 7:13–2**

Appearance, **Rules 7:7–9, 7:8–7, 7:14–3**

Failure to appear, suspension of driving privileges, **2B:12–31**

Applicability of rules, **Rule 1:1–1**

MUNICIPAL COURTS—Cont'd
Appointments,
　Certification, municipal court administrator,
　　requirements, **2B:12–11**
　Judges, **2B:12–4**
　　Additional or temporary judges, **2B:12–5**
Arraignment, **Rule 7:6–1**
Arrest, non custody arrests, **Rule 7:3–1**
Arrest warrants, **Rule 7:2–1 et seq.**
　Contents, **Rule 7:2–1**
　Defective warrants, amendment, **Rule 7:2–5**
　Execution and service, **Rule 7:2–3**
　Facsimiles, service, **Rule 7:2–6**
　Issuance, **Rule 7:2–2**
　Parking, **Rule 7:8–9**
　Telecommunications, **Rule 7:2–1**
　Traffic tickets, **Rule 7:8–9**
Arrest without warrant, procedure after, **Rule
　7:3–1**
Associations and societies, traffic tickets, ser-
　vice, **Rule 7:2–4**
Attorneys,
　Appointment as acting judge, **2B:12–6**
　Prosecutors, employment, **2B:12–27**
　Qualifications of judges, **2B:12–7**
Bail, **Rules 7:3–1, 7:4–1 et seq.**
　Disorderly persons, appeal, **2A:162–11**
　Forfeitures, disposition, **2C:46–4**
Boating, jurisdiction of specified offenses,
　2B:12–17
Bonds (officers and fiduciaries), judges, admin-
　istrators, **2B:12–12**
Calendar, **Rule 7:14–3**
Calendar parts, traffic offenses, **Rule 7:12–2**
Cash deposits, bail, **Rule 7:4–3**
Casino industry activities, judges, conflicts of
　interest, **Rule 1:15–1**
Central municipal court,
　Courtrooms and equipment, **2B:12–15**
　Establishment, **2B:12–1**
　Fines, assessments and restitution, collection,
　　2C:46–4
　Judges, appointment, **2B:12–4**
　Motor vehicles, fines, penalties and forfei-
　　tures, powers and duties, **39:5–41**
　Name, **2B:12–2**
　Prosecutors, **2B:12–27**
　Territorial jurisdiction, **2B:12–16**
Certification, municipal court administrator, re-
　quirements, **2B:12–11**
Chambers, **2B:12–15**
Change or reduction of sentence, **Rule 7:9–4**
Charges, amendments, prosecutors, **2B:25–11**
Chief judge, designation, **2B:12–8**
Children, abuse, abandonment, cruelty and ne-
　glect, jurisdiction, **9:6–4**
　Warrant to enter and arrest, **9:6–8**
Citizen complaints, **Rule 7:2–2**
Clerks,
　Office hours, **Rule 1:30–4**
　Political activities or holding public office,
　　Rule 1:17–1
　Violations bureau, **Rule 7:12–4**
Clerks of court, jurisdiction, Ministerial Acts,
　Motor Vehicle and Traffic Law, **39:5–6**
Code enforcement officers, complaints, **Rule
　7:2–2**
Collections, comprehensive enforcement pro-
　gram, **2B:19–1 et seq.**
Community related service, condition of proba-
　tion, **Rule 7:9–1**
Community service,
　Noncompliance by offender, transfer to com-
　　prehensive enforcement program,
　　2B:19–7

MUNICIPAL COURTS—Cont'd
Community service—Cont'd
　Performance, default, payment of fines,
　　2B:12–23
Compensation and salaries,
　Acting administrator, **2B:12–10**
　Administrator, personnel, **2B:12–10**
　Judges, **2B:12–7**
　Presiding judge, **2B:12–9**
Complaints, **Rules 7:2–1, 7:2–2**
　Contents, **Rule 7:2–1**
　Dismissal, costs charged to complainant,
　　2B:12–24
　Facsimiles, service, **Rule 7:2–6**
　Issuance, **Rule 7:2–2**
　Motor vehicle and traffic laws, violations,
　　39:5–3
　Persons authorized to take, **2B:12–21**
Complementary dispute resolution programs,
　Rule 1:40–1 et seq.
Comprehensive enforcement program, **2B:19–1
　et seq.**
Conditional pleas, **Rule 7:6–2**
Confidential or privileged information, records
　and recordation, **Rule 1:38–3**
Conflict of interest, judges, **Rule 1:15–1**
Consolidation, actions, **Rule 7:8–4**
Continuing education, certification, municipal
　court administrator, requirements,
　2B:12–11
Contracts, collections, **2B:19–6**
Corporations, traffic tickets, service, **Rule 7:2–4**
Costs, appeals, reversal, **Rule 7:13–3**
Counties,
　Additional municipal judges, **2B:12–5**
　Central municipal court, generally, ante
　Chief judges, designation, **2B:12–8**
　Community service, powers and duties,
　　2B:12–23
　Judges, **2B:12–4**
　Jurisdiction of specific offenses, **2B:12–17**
　Municipal court administrator and person-
　　nel, powers and duties, **2B:12–10**
　Prosecutors, employment, **2B:12–27**
County bridge police, conducting arrested per-
　son to, **27:19–36.3**
Courtrooms, **2B:12–15**
　Sessions, place, **2B:12–3**
Credit for confinement pending sentence, **Rule
　7:9–3**
Custody, non custody arrests, **Rule 7:3–1**
Days of court, **Rule 1:30–3**
Defective warrant or summons, **Rule 7:2–5**
Defense of traffic offenses, mail and mailing,
　Rule 7:12–3
Definitions,
　Establishment, **2B:12–1**
　Intoxicating liquor law, **33:1–1**
　Magistrate, **33:1–1, 39:1–1**
　Motor Vehicle Law, **39:1–1**
　Municipal prosecutors, **2B:25–2**
Deposit of bail, **Rule 7:4–3**
Depositions, **Rule 7:7–6**
Deputy clerk, jurisdiction, motor vehicle and
　traffic law proceedings, **39:5–6**
Designation,
　Acting judges, **2B:12–6**
　Chief judge, **2B:12–8**
Detective associations, arrest of disorderly per-
　sons, **15:4–4**
Discovery, **Rule 7:7–7**
Dismissal, **Rules 7:7–1, 7:8–5**
　Costs charged to complainant, **2B:12–24**
Disorderly persons,
　Appeals, bail or recognizances, **2A:162–11**

MUNICIPAL COURTS—Cont'd
Disorderly persons—Cont'd
　Failure to appear, suspension of driving priv-
　　ileges, **2B:12–31**
　Offenses, jurisdiction, **2B:12–17**
Dockets and docketing, **Rule 7:14–4**
　Judgments and decrees, superior court,
　　2B:12–26
Drivers schools, jurisdiction of proceedings for
　violations, **39:12–13**
Driving privileges, suspension, **Rule 7:8–9**
Electronic payment, court fees and financial
　obligations, **Rule 7:14–4**
Enhanced sentence, appeals in criminal prose-
　cutions, **Rule 7:10–2**
Equipment, **2B:12–15**
Establishment, **2B:12–1**
Evidence, suppression, **Rule 7:5–2**
Examination, certification, municipal court ad-
　ministrators, **2B:12–11**
Exclusion of public, **Rule 7:8–7**
Executions,
　Arrest warrants, **Rule 7:2–3**
　Officers, **2B:12–14**
　Summons, **Rule 7:2–4**
Exoneration of bail, **Rule 7:4–6**
Facsimiles, arrest warrants, complaints, service,
　Rule 7:2–6
Failure to appear, **Rule 7:8–9**
　After summons, **Rule 7:2–2**
False charge, costs charged to complainant,
　2B:12–24
Fees,
　Certification, municipal court administrators,
　　2B:12–11
　Charged to complainant, certain cases,
　　2B:12–24
　Crimes and offenses, **2C:46–4**
　Parties applying for services, **2A:166–18**
　Defendant with suspended driving privileges,
　　2B:12–31
Fines and penalties, **2C:46–4**
　Appeals, reversal, **Rule 7:13–3**
　Collection, **Rule 7:14–4**
　　Jurisdiction, **2B:12–17**
　Complaints and summons, penalty proceed-
　　ings, **Rule 7:2–1**
　Default in payment, community service,
　　2B:12–23
　Defendant with suspended driving privileges,
　　2B:12–31
　Failure to pay, suspension of driving privi-
　　leges, **2B:12–31**
　Guilty pleas, payment, violations bureau,
　　Rule 7:12–4
　Installments, **2B:12–23.1**
　Mediation, minor disputes, **Rule 7:8–1**
　Stay pending appeal, **Rule 7:13–2**
　Violations bureau, **Rule 7:12–4**
First appearance, **Rules 7:3–1, 7:3–2**
Forfeitures, collection and disposition, **Rule
　7:14–4**
Good faith, complaint not made in, costs
　charged to complainant, **2B:12–24**
Grandfather rights, certification, municipal
　court administrator, requirements,
　2B:12–11
Guilty pleas, **Rule 7:6–2**
　Fines and penalties, payment, violations bu-
　　reau, **Rule 7:12–4**
Mail and mailing,
　Nontraffic offenses, **Rule 7:6–3**
　Traffic offenses, parking, **Rule 7:12–3**
　Traffic offenses, notice of consequences,
　　Rule 7:14–1
Hearing on first appearance, **Rule 7:3–2**

MUNICIPAL COURTS—Cont'd
Hours of court, **Rule 1:30–3**
Housing courts, jurisdiction, **2B:12–20**
Identity and identification, offenders, **Rule 7:2–2**
Indictable offenses, trial, **Rule 3:4–2**
Insanity defense, notice, **Rule 7:7–4**
Insurance, judges, administrators, required coverage, **2B:12–12**
Joint municipal court,
  Establishment, ordinance, **2B:12–1**
  Name, **2B:12–2**
  Territorial jurisdiction, **2B:12–16**
Joint representation, criminal defendants, **Rule 7:7–10**
Judges and justices,
  Acting administrator, designation, compensation, **2B:12–10**
  Acting judge, appointment to serve temporarily, **2B:12–6**
  Additional, **2B:12–5**
  Appointment, **2B:12–4**
  Arrest, citizen appointed by judge to make, **2A:161–1**
  Authority, conduct of proceedings prior to indictment, **2B:12–19**
  Bonds (officers and fiduciaries), required coverage, **2B:12–12**
  Chief judge, designation, **2B:12–8**
  Compensation, **2B:12–7**
  Disqualification, **Rule 7:8–2**
  Inability to sit, **2B:12–6**
  Insurance, required coverage, **2B:12–12**
  Limitation on practice, **Rule 1:15–4**
  Oath of office, **Rule 7:14–5**
  Opening statements, **Rule 7:14–1**
  Powers and duties, **2A:154–1**
  Practicing law, **Rule 1:15–1**
  Presiding judge, powers, compensation, **2B:12–9**
  Qualifications, **2B:12–7**
  Records and books, **Rule 1:32–2**
  Substituted judge, disqualification or inability of judge to hear manner, **Rule 1:12–3**
  Temporary, appointment, **2B:12–5**
  Term of office, **2B:12–4**
  Vacations, **Rule 1:30–5**
  Weekly reports, **Rule 1:32–1**
Judgments and decrees, **Rule 7:9–2**
  Docketing in superior court, **2B:12–26**
  Service, execution, return, officers empowered, **2B:12–14**
  Signature of judge, administrator, **2B:12–13**
  Traffic offenses, **Rule 7:12–3**
Judicial conference, rules of evidence, judges as members, **2A:84A–34**
Jurisdiction, certain offenses, **2B:12–17,** **2B:12–18**
Jury trial, waiver, jurisdiction of offenses, **2B:12–18**
Justification, sureties, **Rule 7:4–4**
Law enforcement officer complaints, **Rule 7:2–2**
Mail and mailing,
  Guilty plea, nontraffic offenses, **Rule 7:6–3**
  Pleas, traffic offenses, parking, **Rule 7:12–3**
Mediation, minor disputes, **Rule 7:8–1**
Mitigation of traffic offenses, statements, **Rule 7:12–3**
Motions, **Rule 7:7–2**
Motor vehicles,
  Central municipal court, fines, penalties and forfeitures, powers and duties, **39:5–41**
  Drivers license and registration certificate, exhibition on request, **39:3–29**

MUNICIPAL COURTS—Cont'd
Motor vehicles—Cont'd
  Driving privileges, suspension, defendants failure to comply with court order, **2B:12–31**
  Emissions control, penalties, collection, **39:8–73**
  Hours of Service Law, jurisdiction of violations, **39:9–4**
  Inspection Law, jurisdiction of violations, **39:8–9**
  Junk Yard Law, jurisdiction of violations, **39:11–11**
  Security Responsibility Law, jurisdiction to enforce and recover penalty, **39:6–55**
  Violations, jurisdiction, **2B:12–17**
Municipal attorneys, practicing, **Rule 1:15–3**
Name of court, **2B:12–2**
New trial, **Rule 7:10–1**
Non custody arrests, **Rule 7:3–1**
Noncourt dispute resolution, **Rule 1:40–11**
Nonindictable offenses, transfer, **Rule 3:1–6**
Not guilty pleas, **Rules 7:6–1, 7:6–2**
  Mail and mailing, traffic offenses, parking, **Rule 7:12–3**
Notice,
  County prosecutor, discharge of person charged, **2B:12–19**
  Defendant, suspension of driving privileges, failure to appear, **2B:12–31**
Oaths and affirmations,
  Judges, **Rule 7:14–5**
  Persons authorized to take, **2B:12–21**
Officers and employees, execution of process, **2B:12–14**
Offices, **2B:12–15**
Officials authorized to act for court, **2B:12–21**
Opening statement by judge, **Rule 7:14–1**
Orders,
  Service, execution, return, officers empowered, **2B:12–14**
  Signature of judge, administrator, **2B:12–13**
  Unresolved matters, transfer to comprehensive enforcement program, **2B:19–6**
Ordinances,
  Establishment, **2B:12–1**
  Violation,
    Failure to appear, suspension of driving privileges, **2B:12–31**
    Jurisdiction, **2B:12–17**
Parking,
  Mail and mailing, pleas, **Rule 7:12–3**
  Offenses, appearance, **Rule 7:8–9**
  Summons, execution, service, **Rule 7:2–4**
Partnerships, traffic tickets, service, **Rule 7:2–4**
Penalties. Fines and penalties, generally, ante
Periodic service of imprisonment, **2B:12–22**
Personnel, **2B:12–10**
Place of court, **2B:12–3**
Place of deposit, bail, **Rule 7:4–7**
Plea agreements, municipal prosecutors, **2B:25–11**
Plea bargaining, **Rule 7:6–2**
Pleadings, **Rule 7:7–1**
  Amendment, **Rule 7:14–2**
Pleas, **Rules 7:6–1, 7:6–2**
  Mail and mailing, traffic offenses, parking, **Rule 7:12–3**
Police officers, authorization to take oaths, issue summons, **2B:12–21**
Postconviction bail, **Rule 7:4–8**
Postconviction relief, **Rule 7:10–2**
Presence of defendant, **Rule 7:8–7**
Presiding judge, powers, compensation, **2B:12–9**
Pretrial procedure, **Rule 7:7–1 et seq.**

MUNICIPAL COURTS—Cont'd
Probable cause finding, **Rule 7:3–1**
Probation, **Rule 7:9–1**
Process, **Rule 7:2–1 et seq.**
  Amendment, **Rule 7:14–2**
  Execution, service, **Rule 7:2–4**
  Service, execution, return, officers empowered, **2B:12–14**
  Signature of judge, administrator, **2B:12–13**
Prosecutors,
  Appearance, **Rule 7:8–7**
  Discovery, **Rule 7:7–7**
  Employment, **2B:12–27**
  Limitation on practice, **Rule 1:15–4**
  Municipal prosecutors, **2B:25–1 et seq.**
  Practice of law, **Rule 1:15–3**
Protective orders, discovery, **Rule 7:7–7**
Public Defenders, generally, this index
Qualifications,
  Administrator Certification Board, member, **2B:12–11**
  Judges, **2B:12–7**
Recognizances, disorderly persons, appeal, **2A:162–11**
Records and recordation, **Rules 7:2–1, 7:8–8**
  Bail, **Rule 7:4–3**
  Confidential or privileged information, **Rule 1:38–3**
  Funds, **Rule 7:14–4**
  Judges, **Rule 1:32–2**
  Maintenance, **2B:12–25**
Reduction or change of sentence, **Rule 7:9–4**
Removal of mediators, **Rule 1:40–8**
Reopening cases, **Rule 7:8–9**
Reports, **Rule 7:2–1**
  Filing, **2B:12–25**
  Motor vehicles division, failure to appear, **Rule 7:8–9**
Return,
  Arrest warrants, **Rule 7:2–3**
  Property illegally seized, Alcoholic Beverage Law, **33:1–62**
  Search warrant under alcoholic beverage law, **33:1–61**
  Summons, **Rule 7:2–4**
Revision of bail, **Rule 7:4–2**
Revocation, drivers license or registration certificate for violation of,
  Hours of Service Law, **39:9–4**
  Junk Yard Law, **39:11–11**
  Motor Vehicle Inspection Law, **39:8–9**
  Motor Vehicle Security Responsibility Law, **39:6–55**
  Municipal court administrator certificate, **2B:12–11**
Right to appeal, notice, **Rule 7:14–1**
Right to counsel,
  First appearance, **Rule 7:3–2**
  Waiver, **Rule 7:8–10**
Schedule of penalties, violations bureau, **Rule 7:12–4**
Seal, **Rule 1:37–2**
Search and seizure without warrant, **Rule 7:5–3**
Search warrants,
  Alcoholic Beverage Law, issuance, **33:1–56,** **33:1–57**
  Filing, **Rule 7:5–1**
Sentence and punishment, **Rule 7:9–1**
  Enhanced sentence, appeals in criminal prosecutions, **Rule 7:10–2**
  Mitigation of traffic offenses, statements, **Rule 7:12–3**
  Reduction or change, **Rule 7:9–4**
Service, **Rule 7:2–1 et seq.**
  Amendment, **Rule 7:14–2**
  Arrest warrants, **Rule 7:2–3**

MUNICIPAL COURTS—Cont'd
Service—Cont'd
  Facsimiles, arrest warrants, complaints, **Rule 7:2–6**
  Summons, **Rules 7:2–2, 7:2–4**
Sessions, traffic offenses, **Rule 7:12–2**
Signatures, summons and complaints, **Rule 7:2–1**
Special forms, complaints and summons, **Rule 7:2–1**
Standards, facilities and staff, promulgation by supreme court, **2B:12–25**
State owned grounds, motor vehicle and traffic regulations, jurisdiction of violations, **39:4–210**
Stay of sentence pending appeal, **Rule 7:13–2**
Subpoenas, **Rule 7:7–8**
  Issuance, **Rule 1:9–1**
Substituted judges, disqualification or inability of judge to hear pending manner, **Rule 1:12–3**
Summons, **Rule 7:2–1 et seq.**
  Arrest without warrant, **Rule 7:3–1**
  Contents, **Rule 7:2–1**
  Defective summons, amendment, **Rule 7:2–5**
  Execution and service, **Rule 7:2–4**
  Issuance, **Rule 7:2–2**
  Persons authorized to issue, **2B:12–21**
Superior court, judgments docketed in, **2B:12–26**
Supplies, **2B:12–15**
Suppression of evidence, **Rule 7:5–2**
Telecommunications, arrest warrants, **Rule 7:2–1**
Term of office, judges, **2B:12–4**
Territorial jurisdiction, **2B:12–16**
Time, certification, municipal court administrator, requirements, **2B:12–11**
Title of court, **Rule 1:37–1**
Traffic rules and regulations, **Rules 7:8–9, 7:12–1 et seq.**
  Complaints, **Rule 7:2–1**
  Jurisdiction, **2B:12–17**
  Summons, execution, service, **Rule 7:2–4**
Transcript of record, **Rule 7:8–8**
Transfer of causes, **Rule 7:8–6**
Trial, **Rule 7:8–1 et seq.**
  Adjournment, **Rule 7:8–3**
  Traffic offenses, **Rule 7:12–1**
Turnpike projects, jurisdiction of violation, **27:23–34**
Vacancy in office, appointment for unexpired term, **2B:12–4**
Venue, **Rule 7:8–2**
Violations bureau, **Rule 7:12–4**
Waiver, indictment and jury trial, jurisdiction, **2B:12–18**
Warrantless search and seizure, **Rule 7:5–3**
Warrants,
  Persons authorized to issue, **2B:12–21**
  Service, execution, return, officers empowered, **2B:12–14**
  Signature of judge, administrator, **2B:12–13**
Withdrawal of pleas, **Rule 7:6–2**

MUNICIPAL ENGINEER
Handicapped parking spaces, inspection, **39:4–8.1**

MUNICIPAL MAGISTRATES
Municipal Courts, generally, this index

MUNICIPAL OFFICERS AND EMPLOYEES
Adverse or pecuniary interest, **2C:27–9**
Appropriations, spending or incurring obligations in excess of, **2C:30–4**

MUNICIPAL OFFICERS AND EMPLOYEES —Cont'd
Bribery and Corruption, generally, this index
Compensation and salaries, jury duty, **2B:20–16**
Constables, generally, this index
Crimes and offenses, appropriations, spending or incurring obligations in excess of, **2C:30–4**
Electric personal assistive mobility devices, operation, **39:4–14.10**
Excuse from employment, jury service, **2B:20–16**
Executive officer. Mayors, generally, this index
Firefighters and Fire Departments, generally, this index
Jurors, challenge to array or poll on grounds of interest, actions by or against, **2B:23–12**
Jury duty, excuse from employment, **2B:20–16**
Mayors, generally, this index
Municipal courts, administrator, designation, **2B:12–10**
Obligations, incurring in excess of appropriations, **2C:30–4**
Police and Police Departments, generally, this index
Prosecutors, **2B:25–1 et seq.**
Spending in excess of appropriations, **2C:30–4**

MUNICIPAL PROSECUTORS
Generally, **2B:25–1 et seq.**

MUNICIPAL PUBLIC DEFENDERS
Public Defenders, generally, this index

MUNICIPAL TREASURER
Motor Vehicle Junk Law, payment of fees and expenses, **39:11–5**
Payment, fees and expenses under motor vehicle junk law, **39:11–5**

MUNICIPAL TREATMENT WORKS
Definitions, water pollution, **58:10A–3**

MUNICIPALITIES
Administration, law or governmental functions, obstruction, **2C:29–1 et seq.**
Alcoholic Beverages, this index
All terrain vehicles, registration, exemptions, **39:3C–6**
Animals, impoundment, destruction, **4:22–19**
Appropriations, handicapped parking enforcement units, **39:4–197.14**
Automated traffic system, interconnection with, autonomous computer system, approval, **2B:12–30**
Autonomous computer system, use, automated operations, interconnection with automated traffic system, **2B:12–30**
Boards and commissions, definitions, intoxicating liquors, **33:1–1**
Boats and Boating, generally, this index
Bribery and Corruption, generally, this index
Bridges and Viaducts, this index
Buses, this index
Cannons, antique cannons, possession, **2C:39–6**
Charitable organizations and associations, solicitation on roadways, **39:4–60**
Civil Service, generally, this index
Compensation and salaries. Municipal Officers and Employees, generally, this index
Constables, generally, this index
Courts. Municipal Courts, generally, this index
Crimes and offenses, notice to municipal authorities, **2A:152–12**

MUNICIPALITIES—Cont'd
Criminal courts. Municipal Courts, generally, this index
Criminal practice, scope of rules, summons, service, execution, **Rule 3:7–10**
Crosswalks, generally, this index
Cruelty to animals, impoundment facilities, destruction, **4:22–19**
Curbs and Curbing, generally, this index
Definitions, intoxicating liquor laws, **33:1–1**
Dogs, generally, this index
Drivers Licenses, this index
Electric personal assistive mobility devices, operation, ordinances, **39:4–14.10**
Emergencies, motor vehicles, warning lights, applications, **39:3–54.23**
Employees. Municipal Officers and Employees, generally, this index
Executions, this index
Fees, permit to move heavy machinery, **39:4–26**
Fines and penalties, execution against, returned unsatisfied, **2A:166–12**
Fireworks, this index
Force and violence, obstructing administration of law or governmental functions, **2C:29–1 et seq.**
Free libraries. Libraries, generally, this index
Governing body, appointment, municipal court judge, **2B:12–4**
Grants, drunk driving, enforcement, **39:4–50.8**
Handicapped Persons, this index
Highways and Roads, this index
Horse Drawn Vehicles, generally, this index
Housing, generally, this index
Intimidation, obstructing administration of law or governmental functions, **2C:29–1 et seq.**
Jails, generally, this index
Junk yards. Motor Vehicle Junk Yards, generally, this index
Jurors, challenge to array or polls, ground of interest in action by or against municipality, **2B:23–12**
Libraries, generally, this index
Licenses and permits, motor vehicle identification lights, private detective businesses, **39:3–54.14**
Lights and Lighting, generally, this index
Liquefied petroleum gas, conflicts of law, **21:1B–7**
Mayors, generally, this index
Mentally deficient and mentally ill persons, transport vehicles, identification, **39:4–207.2 et seq.**
Motor drawn vehicles, number permitted to be used in collecting garbage, **39:4–54**
Motor Vehicle Junk Yards, generally, this index
Motor Vehicles, this index
Moving heavy machinery, resolution regulating, **39:4–26**
Municipal Courts, generally, this index
Municipal Officers and Employees, generally, this index
Obstruction, administration of law or governmental function, **2C:29–1 et seq.**
Officers. Municipal Officers and Employees, generally, this index
Ordinances, generally, this index
Parking, this index
Pilot programs, traffic signs and signals, monitoring, intersections, **39:4–8.12 et seq.**
Poles, horse not to be hitched to pole carrying wires, **39:4–20**
Police and Police Departments, generally, this index

MUNICIPALITIES—Cont'd

Privileges and immunities, traffic signs and signals, pedestrians, crosswalks, right of way, **39:4–8**

Prosecutors, **2B:25–1**

Resolutions,
Autobusses, stops or stations, **39:4–8**
Parking, restricted spaces, **39:4–197, 39:4–197.5**

Retention of property, seized under Alcoholic Beverage Law, **33:1–66, 33:2–5**

Rewards, criminal detection and apprehension, **2A:153–4**

Roller skates, rules and regulations, **39:4–10.10a**

Security services, private detective businesses, permits, motor vehicle identification lights, **39:3–54.14**

Sex offenders, community notification. Sex Offenses, this index

Skateboards, rules and regulations, **39:4–10.10a**

Snowmobiles, registration, exemptions, **39:3C–6**

Streets and Alleys, generally, this index

Traffic calming devices, powers and duties, **39:4–8.10**

Traffic control device, regulation, **39:4–120.2 et seq.**

Traffic lights, application to state highway commissioner for installation at dangerous intersections, **39:4–121.1**

Traffic on county or state highways, consent of chosen freeholders or highway commissioner, **39:4–197.1**

Traffic Rules and Regulations, this index

Traffic Signs and Signals, this index

Trucks. Motor Carriers, generally, this index

Turnpike authority,
Appropriations, nonhighway projects, **27:23–44**
Lease or conveyance of property, **27:23–14**
Power to acquire property, **27:23–5**

Violence, obstructing administration of law or governmental functions, **2C:29–1 et seq.**

Water Supply Plants and Systems, generally, this index

Zoning and Planning, generally, this index

MURDER
Homicide, generally, this index

MUSEUMS
Cannons, antique cannons, possession, **2C:39–6**

Controlled substances, crimes and offenses, **2C:35–7.1**

Crimes and offenses, controlled dangerous substances, **2C:35–7.1**

Libraries, this index

MUTILATION
Motor vehicles, marks or numbers, crimes and offenses, **2C:17–6**

MYROPHINE
Controlled substances, **24:21–1 et seq.**

NALORPHINE
Drugs and Medicine, generally, this index

NAMED INSURED
Definitions, no fault insurance, **39:6A–2**

NAMES
Alcoholic beverage licenses, statement in application, **33:1–25**

Attorneys, this index

Crimes and offenses,
Discovery, **Rule 3:13–3**

NAMES—Cont'd

Crimes and offenses—Cont'd
Expungement, **2C:52–1 et seq.**

Dentists and Dentistry, this index

Guardian and ward, criminal history record information, professional guardians, **53:1–20.9e**

Juvenile delinquents and dependents, complaint, contents, **Rule 5:20–1**

Juvenile family crisis, petition, contents, **Rule 5:15–2**

Municipal court, **2B:12–2**

Noncommercial trucks, exterior, **39:3–8.1**

Outdoor advertising, permit holders name displayed upon sign, **27:5–9**

Pleadings, typed or stamped names, **Rule 1:4–6**

Professional corporations, **Rule 1:21–1A**

Trademarks and Trade Names, generally, this index

NARCOTIC ADDICTS
Drug Abuse, generally, this index

NARCOTIC AND DRUG ABUSE TREATMENT CENTERS
Probation and probation officers, **2C:35–14**

NARCOTICS
Controlled Substances, generally, this index

NARCOTICS AND DRUG ABUSE CONTROL DIVISION
Definitions, controlled dangerous substances, **24:21–2**

NATIONAL CONVENTIONS
Delegates and Alternates, this index

NATIONAL CRIME PREVENTION AND PRIVACY COMPACT
Generally, **53:1–32**

NATIONAL GUARD
Commercial drivers licenses, exemption, **39:3–10j et seq.**

Exemptions, commercial drivers licenses, **39:3–10j et seq.**

Fees, motor vehicles, special registration plates, **39:3–27.13**

Minuteman emblem, special registration plates, **39:3–27.13, 39:3–27.14**

Motor vehicles,
Commercial drivers licenses, exemption, **39:3–10j et seq.**
Special registration plates, **39:3–27.13, 39:3–27.14**

Museum, forfeited weapons, donation, **2C:64–9**

Prohibited weapons, exceptions, **2C:39–3**

Weapons, unlawful possession, exemptions, **2C:39–6**

NATIONAL OFFENSES
Termination of complicity, **2C:2–6**

NATIONAL ORIGIN
Discrimination, generally, this index

NATIONAL POLLUTANT DISCHARGE ELIMINATION SYSTEM
Definitions, water pollution control, **58:10A–3**

NATIONAL RESOURCES
Oil and Gas, generally, this index

NATIONAL SECURITIES EXCHANGE
Intoxicating liquors retail licensee, acquiring shares of corporation traded on exchange, Chain Store Liquor License Act, **33:1–12.36**

NATIONAL SYSTEM OF INTERSTATE AND DEFENSE HIGHWAYS
Width of vehicles, receiving federal funds, **39:3–84**

NATIONALITY
Discrimination, generally, this index

NATURAL BARRICADE
Definitions, Explosives Act, **21:1A–129**

NATURAL RESOURCES
Environmental Protection, generally, this index

Fish and Game, generally, this index

Oil and Gas, generally, this index

NATURALIZATION
Immigration and Naturalization, generally, this index

NAVAL MILITIA
See, also, National Guard, generally, this index

Battleship U.S.S. New Jersey license plates, **39:3–27.67 et seq.**

NAVIGATION
Vessels, generally, this index

NAVIGATION DIVISION
Vessels, generally, this index

NAVY
Armed Forces, generally, this index

NEAR FATALITY
Definitions, Comprehensive Child Abuse Prevention and Treatment Act, **9:6–8.84**

NECESSARY PARTIES
Transfer of actions, **Rule 1:13–4**

NECESSITY
Criminal prosecutions, defense, **2C:3–2**

NEEDLES
Hypodermic Needles or Syringes, generally, this index

NEEDY PERSONS
Indigent Persons, generally, this index

NEGLECTED CHILDREN
Dependent or Neglected Children, generally, this index

NEGLIGENCE
Attorneys, client protection fund, **Rule 1:28–1 et seq.**

Contingent attorney fees, **Rule 1:21–7**

Damages, generally, this index

Definitions, Code of Criminal Justice, **2C:2–2**

Duress, criminal liability, **2C:2–9**

Homicide, death by auto or vessel, **2C:11–5**

Law enforcement officers, force or violence, grand jury, instructions to jury, **2B:22–9**

Use of force, **2C:3–9**

Vessel, death by operation of, **2C:11–5**

NEGLIGENTLY
Definitions, Code of Criminal Justice, **2C:2–2**

NEGOTIABLE INSTRUMENTS
Bad checks, **2C:21–5**
Checks,
  Bad checks, **2C:21–5**
  Forgery, **2C:21–1**
  Fraud, sales, **2C:21–2.4**
  Insufficient funds checks, **2C:21–5**
  Motor vehicles division, dishonored checks,
    fees, **39:5–36.1**
  Worthless checks, **2C:21–5**
Crimes and offenses, insufficient fund checks,
    2C:21–5
Criminal usury, **2C:21–19**
Dishonor,
  Attorney fee arbitration, administrative filing
    fee, **Rule 1:20A–3**
  Failure to make required disposition of
    property, evidence, **2C:20–9**
Forgery, **2C:21–1**
Insufficient funds checks. Checks, ante
Misconduct, corporate officials, **2C:21–9**
Motor vehicles, security interests,
  Endorsement on certificate of origin and
    certificate of ownership, **39:10–8,**
    39:10–9
  Filing requirements, **39:10–11**
Nonsufficient fund checks, **2C:21–5**
Sales, generally, this index
Self authentication, **Evidence Rule 902**
Turnpike authority, issuance, **27:23–7.1**
Worthless checks, **2C:21–5**

NEGOTIATION
Sales, generally, this index

NEPOTISM
Adverse or Pecuniary Interest, generally, this
index

NET DIRECT WRITTEN PREMIUMS
Definitions, unsatisfied claim and judgment
  fund board, **39:6–62**

NEUROMUSCULAR BLOCKING AGENTS
Domestic animals, destruction, **4:22–19.3,**
  4:22–19.4

NEW DRUGS
Definitions, food and drugs, **24:21–32**

NEW JERSEY REGISTER
Air pollution control, odors, investigation procedure, publication, **26:2C–19**

NEW TRIAL
Crimes and offenses, **Rules 3:20–1, 3:20–2**
Disagreement of jurors, **2B:23–18**
DNA database and databank, motions,
  2A:84A–32a, 2A:84A–32b
Motions,
  Amendment, findings, motion, **Rule 1:7–4**
  Enlargement of time, **Rule 1:3–4**
Motor vehicles, arbitrated tort claims, **39:6A–32**
  et seq.
Municipal courts, **Rule 7:10–1**
Substituted judge, previous judge disqualified
  or unable to hear manner, **Rule 1:12–3**
Time, rejection, **Rule 1:5–6**

NEWS
Definitions, privileged communications,
  2A:84A–21a

NEWS AGENCY
Definitions, privileged communications,
  2A:84A–21a

NEWS MEDIA
Definitions, privileged communications,
  2A:84A–21a
Newspapers, generally, this index
Privileges and immunities, **2A:84A–21 et seq.**
Radio and Radio Stations, generally, this index
Reporters, stickers, motor vehicles, **39:3–76.1**
Searches and seizures, news organizations,
  2A:84A–21.9 et seq.
Television, generally, this index

NEWSPAPERMANS PRIVILEGE ACT
Generally, **2A:84A–21**

NEWSPAPERS
Correctional institutions, searches and seizures,
  2A:84A–21.13
Criminal proceedings, newsperson information
  disclosure privilege, **2A:84A–21.1 et seq.**
Definitions,
  News personnel privilege, **2A:84A–21a**
  Privileged communications, **2A:84A–21a**
Information disclosure privilege, newspersons,
  criminal proceedings, **2A:84A–21.1 et seq.**
Motor vehicles, reporters, stickers, **39:3–76.1**
Privileged communications, **2A:84A–21**
  Criminal proceedings, newsperson informa-
    tion disclosure privilege, **2A:84A–21.1 et**
    seq.
Reporters, press designation, limitation,
  39:3–76.1
Searches and seizures, **2A:84A–21.9 et seq.**

NEWSPERSONS
Privileges and immunities, **Evidence Rule 508**

NEXT OF KIN
Children and Minors, generally, this index

NICOCODEINE
Controlled substances, **24:21–1 et seq.**

NICOLE'S LAW
Sex offenses, **2C:14–11, 2C:14–12, 2C:44–8,**
  2C:45–1, 2C:45–2

NICOMORPHINE
Controlled substances, **24:21–1 et seq.**

NIGHTTIME
Bicycles, lights and reflectors, **39:4–10**
Service of search warrant under alcoholic bev-
  erage law, **33:1–59**
Snowmobiles, operation, **39:3C–19**

NITRO CARBO NITRATE
Definitions, Explosives Act, **21:1A–129**

NITRO CELLULOSE FILMS
Turnpike project, transportation regulations,
  27:23–31

NITROGLYCERINE
Turnpike project, transportation regulation,
  27:23–31

NO EARLY RELEASE ACT
Generally, **2C:43–7.2**

NO FAULT INSURANCE
Motor Vehicle Insurance, this index

NOISE
Iron loaded on vehicle, precautions against
  noise, **39:4–78**
Mufflers required on motor vehicles, **39:3–70**
Target Ranges, generally, this index

NON VULT, PLEA OF
Crimes and Offenses, this index

NONCOMMERCIAL MOTOR VEHICLES
Definitions, Commercial Driver License Act,
  39:3–10.11

NONCOMMERCIAL TRUCKS
Definitions, **39:1–1**
Handicapped persons, licenses and permits,
  fees, **39:3–8.1**
Licenses and registration, **39:1–1, 39:3–8,**
  39:3–8.1

NONCOMPACTING STATE
Definitions, adult offender supervision, interstate compacts, **2A:168–27**

**NONCONVENTIONAL TYPE MOTOR VEHI-
CLE**
Definitions, **39:10–2**

NONCOURT DISPUTE RESOLUTIONS
Generally, **Rule 1:40–11**

NONECONOMIC LOSS
Definitions, no fault insurance, **39:6A–2**

NONMILITARY SERVICE AFFIDAVIT
Default judgment, **Rule 1:5–7**

**NONPROFIT CORPORATIONS AND ASSO-
CIATIONS**
Alcoholic Beverages, this index
Auctions and auctioneers, intoxicating liquors,
  licenses and permits, **33:1–97**
Charitable Organizations and Associations,
  generally, this index
Club officers, intoxicating liquors, law enforce-
  ment personnel, **33:1–25.1, 33:1–25.2**
Fees, special organization vehicle registration
  plates, **39:3–27.36**
Fire companies. Volunteer Firefighters and
  Fire Companies, generally, this index
Fraternal Benefit Societies, generally, this in-
  dex
Intoxicating liquors,
  Auctions and auctioneers, licenses and per-
    mits, **33:1–97**
  Club licenses, law enforcement personnel as
    officers, **33:1–25.1, 33:1–25.2**
  Plenary retail consumption license, musical
    or theatrical performances, **33:1–19.7**
License plates, special organization plates,
  39:3–27.35 et seq.
Licenses and permits, intoxicating liquors, auc-
  tions and auctioneers, **33:1–97**
Mentally Deficient and Mentally Ill Persons,
  this index
Motor vehicles,
  Registration fees, exemption, **39:3–27**
  Special organization vehicle registration
    plates, **39:3–27.35 et seq.**
Musical performances, intoxicating liquors, ple-
  nary retail consumption license, **33:1–19.7**
Private Schools, generally, this index
Sheriffs, intoxicating liquors, licenses and per-
  mits, **33:1–25.1, 33:1–25.2**
Special organization vehicle registration plates,
  39:3–27.35 et seq.
Theatrical performances, intoxicating liquors,
  plenary retail consumption license,
  33:1–19.7
Volunteer Firefighters and Fire Companies,
  generally, this index

NONPROFIT ORGANIZATION
Nonprofit Corporations and Associations, generally, this index

NONPUBLIC SCHOOLS
Private Schools, generally, this index

NONRESIDENT VIOLATOR COMPACT
Motor vehicles, 39:5F–1 et seq.

NONRESIDENTS
See, also, Residence and Residents, generally, this index
Commuter vans, licenses and permits, 39:3–19.6
Drivers Licenses, this index
Foreign States, generally, this index
Limousine or livery service, licenses and permits, 39:3–19.6
Motor Vehicles, this index
Motorized bicycle owners, registration, application of law, 39:4–14.3o
Nonresident Violator Compact, motor vehicles, 39:5F–1 et seq.
Pro hac vice appearances, Rules 1:21–1, 1:21–2
Taxicabs, licenses and permits, 39:3–19.6
Traffic regulations, Nonresident Violator Compact, 39:5F–1 et seq.

NONRESIDENTS OPERATING PRIVILEGE
Definitions, financial responsibility, 39:6–24

NONSUFFICIENT FUND CHECKS
Generally, 2C:21–5

NONSUIT
Dismissal and Nonsuit, generally, this index

NONSUPPORT
Support of Persons, generally, this index

NONTESTAMENTARY TRUSTEES
Trusts and Trustees, generally, this index

NONTESTIMONIAL EVIDENCE
Investigative detention, Rule 3:5A–1 et seq.

NORLEVORPHANOL
Controlled substances, 24:21–1 et seq.

NORMETHADONE
Controlled substances, 24:21–1 et seq.

NORMORPHINE
Controlled substances, 24:21–1 et seq.

NORTH JERSEY DISTRICT WATER SUPPLY COMMISSION
District Water Supply Commission, this index

NOT GUILTY PLEAS
Crimes and Offenses, this index

NOTE TAKING
Jurors, Rule 1:8–8

NOTICE
Adult offender supervision interstate commission, meetings, 2A:168–32
Advertisements, generally, this index
Air Pollution, this index
Alcoholic Beverages, this index
Alibi defense, crimes and offenses, Rules 3:12–2, 7:7–3
Appeal and Review, this index
Appeals In Criminal Prosecutions, this index
Appearance, entry by new attorney, Rule 1:11–3

NOTICE—Cont'd
Arrest, records and recordation, expungement, 2B:12–32
Attorney General, this index
Attorneys, this index
Bail, this index
Banks and Banking, this index
Child Abuse, this index
Child Care Centers, this index
Children and Minors, this index
Clerical mistakes, correction, Rule 1:13–1
Commercial Drivers Licenses, this index
Complementary dispute resolution, alternatives, affidavits, filing, Rule 1:5–6
Consumer Credit, this index
Contempt, summary proceeding on notice, Rule 1:10–2
Controlled Substances, this index
Correctional Institutions, this index
Credit care revocation, 2C:21–6
Crimes and Offenses, this index
Cross claims, filing on service of pleadings, Rule 1:5–5
Cruelty to animals, animal control officers, convictions, disqualification, 2B:12–17.1
De minimis infractions, dismissal, 2C:2–11
Destructive devices, possession, 2C:58–7
Documentary exhibits, disposition, 2C:65–4
Domestic Violence, this index
Drivers licenses, name changes, 39:3–9a
Drunk Driving Victims Bill of Rights, 39:4–50.11
Electric personal assistive mobility devices, warnings, 39:4–10.8
Explosives, this index
Fee arbitration hearings, attorneys, Rule 1:20A–3
Filing, nonconforming papers, Rule 1:5–6
Financial Corporations and Institutions, this index
Fitting rooms, invasion of privacy, defenses, crimes and offenses, observation, nudity, 2C:14–9
Forfeitures, this index
Guardian and Ward, this index
Habeas corpus, hearings, 2A:160–18
Handicapped Persons, this index
Insanity defense, acquittal, 2C:4–3
Jails, this index
Judicial Notice, generally, this index
Jury and Jurors, this index
Juvenile custody, short term, Rule 5:16–2
Juvenile Delinquents, this index
Juvenile family crisis, hearings, Rule 5:15–3
Landlord and Tenant, this index
Law Enforcement Officers, this index
Leases, this index
Liquefied Petroleum Gas, this index
Mail and Mailing, this index
Mediation of disputes, Rule 1:40–8
Mentally Deficient and Mentally Ill Persons, this index
Mobile Homes and Mobile Home Parks, this index
Motions, this index
Motor vehicle commission, board, meetings, 39:2A–16
Motor Vehicles, this index
Motorized Bicycles, this index
Name changes, drivers licenses, 39:3–9a
Nonresident Violator Compact, motor vehicles, personal recognizances, 39:5F–1 et seq.
Parking, drivers licenses, suspension or revocation, 39:4–139.10
Physicians and Surgeons, this index
Podiatrists and Podiatry, this index

NOTICE—Cont'd
Police and Police Departments, this index
Portable oil burning heating devices, multiple dwellings, use, 2C:40–13
Preliminary conferences, abuse of children, 9:6–8.35
Professional ethics, advisory committee on, opinions, appeals, Rule 1:19–8
Public defenders, liens for services, 2A:158A–17
Publications, generally, this index
Roller skates,
Helmets, posting signs, 39:4–10.9
Sales, warning, protective gear, 39:4–10.8
Sanctions, frivolous litigation, motions, Rule 1:4–8
Service,
Lieu of subpoena, client protection fund, Rule 1:28–6
Mail, additional time for response, Rule 1:3–3
Sex offenders, community notification. Sex Offenses, this index
Sheriffs, this index
Skateboards,
Helmets, posting signs, 39:4–10.9
Sales, warning, protective gear, 39:4–10.8
Solid Waste, this index
State Police, this index
Stills and Distilling Apparatus, this index
Stolen property, disposition procedure, 2C:65–2
Storage, fees, 27:23–6.2
Street Railways, this index
Subpoena, notice in lieu of, Rule 1:9–1
Production of documentary evidence, Rule 1:9–2
Temporary out of home placement, Rule 5:18–2
Theft, scrap metal, 2C:20–7.2
Tow trucks and towing companies, fees, 27:23–6.2
Turnpike authority, public hearings, tolls, 27:23–5.11
Turnpikes, this index
Victims of Crime, this index
Voluntary surrender of weapons, 2C:39–12
Warning notices, harmful effects, drinking during pregnancy,
Posting requirements, class C license holders, alcoholic beverages, 33:1–12a
Fines and penalties, 33:1–12b
Preparation of warning notice by health department, 33:1–12a
Weapons, this index
Withdrawal from nonresident violator compact, motor vehicles, 39:5F–24

NOTICE IN LIEU OF SUBPOENA
Generally, Rule 1:9–1
Client protection fund investigations, Rule 1:28–6
Production of documentary evidence, Rule 1:9–2

NSF CHECKS
Generally, 2C:21–5

NUCLEAR ELECTRICITY GENERATING FACILITY
Electricity and Electric Companies, this index

NUCLEAR FACILITIES
Crimes and offenses,
Release, radiation, 2C:17–7 et seq.
Terrorism, 2C:38–2, 2C:38–3
Trespass, unlicensed entry of structure, 2C:18–3

NUCLEAR FACILITIES—Cont'd
Crimes and offenses—Cont'd
    Vandalism, **2C:17–8**
Radiation Protection, generally, this index
Terrorism, **2C:38–2**
Trespass, unlicensed entry of structure, crimes and offenses, **2C:18–3**
Unlicensed entry of structure, crimes and offenses, **2C:18–3**

NUCLEAR MATERIALS
Radioactive Substances, generally, this index

NUCLEAR OR RADIOLOGICAL DEVICES
Terrorism, **2C:17–2, 2C:38–2, 2C:38–3**

NUDITY
Children and minors, second degree crime, **2C:24–4**
Crimes and offenses, observation, invasion of privacy, **2C:14–9**

NUISANCE
    Generally, **2C:33–12**
Abatement and survival, **2C:33–12.1**
Buildings, **2C:33–12**
    Closing, **2C:33–12.1**
    Controlled substances, **24:21–35**
Controlled substances, **24:21–35**
Highways and Roads, this index
Injunctions, federal law, expenses of county prosecutor in enjoining, **2A:158–8**
Lewdness and obscenity, **2C:33–12**
Lights, rotating or flashing lights on or near highways, **39:4–60.1 et seq.**
Motor vehicles, rotating or flashing lights on or near highways, **39:4–60.1 et seq.**
Narcotics and dangerous substances, controlled dangerous substances, **24:21–35**
Outdoor advertising, **27:5–9**
Person, definitions, sexually oriented business, **2C:33–12.2**
Prostitution, **2C:33–12**
Sexually oriented businesses, **2C:33–12.2**
Specified anatomical area, definitions, sexually oriented business, **2C:33–12.2**
Specified sexual activity, definitions, sexually oriented business, **2C:33–12.2**
Stills and distilling apparatus, unregistered stills, **33:2–11**
Traffic sign, unauthorized sign, **39:4–183.4**

NULLITY OF MARRIAGE
Bigamy, defense, **2C:24–1**

NUMBERS AND NUMBERING
Alcoholic Beverages, this index
Arbitration and award, number of arbitrators, motor vehicles, tort claims, **39:6A–27**
Grand juries, minimum number, **2B:21–1**
Jury and Jurors, this index
Motor vehicles,
    Arbitrators, stipulation to number, tort claims, **39:6A–27**
    Change or destruction, crimes and offenses, **2C:17–6**
Riots and mobs, participants, **2C:33–1**
Stolen property, procedure in disposition, **2C:65–1**
Weapons, generally, this index

NUMBERS GAME
Definitions, **2C:37–1**

NURSE PRACTITIONER/CLINICAL NURSE SPECIALIST CERTIFICATION ACT
Nurses, generally, this index

NURSERIES AND NURSERYMEN
Agricultural land, trespass, damages, **2C:18–4 et seq.**

NURSERY SCHOOLS
Child Care Centers, generally, this index

NURSES
Aides, criminal history record checks, certificates, **53:1–20.9a**
Automobile insurance, no fault insurance, application of law, **39:6A–1 et seq.**
Certificates and certification, aides, criminal history record checks, **53:1–20.9a**
Controversies or disputes with patients, review committees, immunity from liability, **2A:84A–22.10**
Crimes and offenses, health care claims fraud, **2C:21–4.2, 2C:21–4.3**
    Licenses and permits, suspension or revocation, **2C:51–5**
        Rehabilitation, order of debarment, rescission, **2C:27–1**
Criminal history record information, aides, certificates, **53:1–20.9a**
Damages, review committees, immunity from liability, **2A:84A–22.10**
Fees, controversies or disputes with patients, immunity from liability, **2A:84A–22.10**
Fines and penalties, health care claims fraud, **2C:21–4.2, 2C:21–4.3**
    Licenses and permits, suspension or revocation, **2C:51–5**
        Rehabilitation, order of debarment, rescission, **2C:27–1**
Forfeitures, licenses and permits, health care claims fraud, **2C:51–5**
Health care claims fraud, **2C:21–4.2, 2C:21–4.3**
    Licenses and permits, suspension or revocation, **2C:51–5**
        Rehabilitation, order of debarment, rescission, **2C:27–1**
Homemaker home health aides, criminal history record information, certificates, **53:1–20.9a**
Licenses and permits, health care claims fraud, suspension or revocation, **2C:51–5**
    Rehabilitation, order of debarment, rescission, **2C:27–1**

NURSING BOARD
Licenses and permits. Nurses, this index
Nurse practitioner/clinical nurse specialist. Nurses, generally, this index

NURSING HOMES OR HOSPITALS
Assault, institutionalized elderly persons, **2C:12–1**
Criminal history record information,
    Assisted living facilities, **53:1–20.9c**
    Nurses aides, certificates, **53:1–20.9a**
Health Maintenance Organizations, generally, this index
Identification cards for residents, parking, **39:4–207.8**
Institutionalized elderly persons, assault, **2C:12–1 et seq.**
Motor vehicles, parking in handicapped space, **39:4–207.8**
Nurses aides, criminal history record information, certificates, **53:1–20.9a**
Skilled nursing homes, institutionalized elderly persons, assault, **2C:12–1**
Windshield placards, residents, handicapped parking spaces, **39:4–207.8**

OATHS AND AFFIRMATIONS
Affidavits, generally, this index
Alcoholic Beverages, this index
Allegiance, petit jurors, **2B:20–18**
Assistant county prosecutors, **2A:158–15**
Attorneys, this index
County Prosecutors, this index
Deputies, director of division of motor vehicles, **39:2–4**
False financial statements, **2C:21–4**
Forfeitures, claim against seized property, **2C:64–3**
Grand Jury, this index
Handguns, permits to carry, **2C:58–4**
Jury and Jurors, this index
Motor Vehicle Commission, this index
Municipal Courts, this index
Perjury, generally, this index
Public defenders, **2A:158A–23**
Stolen property, release, sworn declaration of ownership, **2C:65–2**
Temporary county prosecutors, **2A:158–9**
Turnpike authority members, **27:23–3**
Witnesses, this index

OBJECTIONS AND EXCEPTIONS
Crimes and Offenses, this index
Instructions to jury, **Rules 1:7–2, 1:8–7**
Motions, **Rule 1:7–2**
    Service and filing, **Rule 1:6–3**
Orders, **Rule 1:7–2**
Reserving questions for review, **Rule 1:7–2**
Trial, **Rule 1:7–2**
    Record of excluded evidence, **Rule 1:7–3**
Waiver, evidence admission, **Rule 7:5–2**

OBLITERATION
Motor vehicles, marks or numbers, crimes and offenses, **2C:17–6**

OBSCENE FILM
Definitions, children and minors, **2C:34–3**

OBSCENITY
Lewdness and Obscenity, generally, this index

OBSTRUCTED VIEW
Motor Vehicles, this index

OBSTRUCTING GOVERNMENT OPERATIONS
Compounding, limitation of criminal prosecution, **2C:1–6**

OBSTRUCTING JUSTICE
    Generally, **2C:29–1 et seq.**
Intoxicating liquors, search warrant service or execution, **33:1–63**
Terrorism, **2C:38–4**

OBSTRUCTION AND OBSTRUCTIONS
Highways and Roads, this index
Streets and Alleys, this index
Traffic, this index

OBSTRUCTS
Definitions, obstructing highways and other public passages, **2C:33–7**

OBTAIN
Definitions, theft, **2C:20–1**

OCCUPIED STRUCTURES
Criminal trespass, **2C:18–3**

ODOMETERS
Low speed vehicles, **39:4–31.2**

ODOMETERS—Cont'd
Misrepresentation of mileage, motor vehicles, **2C:21–8**

ODORS
Air pollution control, investigation, publication of procedure, **26:2C–19**

OFFENSES
Crimes and Offenses, generally, this index

OFFENSIVE LANGUAGE
Disorderly conduct, **2C:33–2**
Harassment, **2C:33–4**

OFFICE
Bribery and corruption, forfeiture, **2C:51–2**
Elections, generally, this index
Public defender, **2A:158A–7**

OFFICE HOURS
Clerks of court, **Rule 1:30–4**
Courts, **Rules 1:30–1, 1:30–3**

OFFICE OF ATTORNEY ETHICS
Generally, **Rules 1:20–1, 1:20–2**

OFFICERS AND EMPLOYEES
Abuse of office, **2C:30–2 et seq.**
Administration, law or governmental functions, obstruction, **2C:29–1 et seq.**
Adverse or Pecuniary Interest, generally, this index
Aggravated assault, throwing bodily fluids, **2C:12–13**
Alcoholic Beverages, this index
Appropriations, spending or incurring obligations in excess of, **2C:30–4**
Bonds (Officers and Fiduciaries), generally, this index
Bribery and Corruption, generally, this index
Chosen Freeholders, generally, this index
Civil Service, generally, this index
Coercion, criminal coercion, threat to take or withhold official action, **2C:13–5**
Commercial bribery and breach of duty, **2C:21–10**
Compensation and Salaries, generally, this index
Confidential or privileged information, official actions or information, **2C:30–3**
Conflict of interest. Adverse or Pecuniary Interest, generally, this index
Conviction of crime, forfeiture of office, **2C:51–2**
Corporations, this index
Correctional Institutions, this index
County Detectives and Investigators, generally, this index
County Officers and Employees, generally, this index
County Prosecutors, generally, this index
Courts, this index
Crimes and offenses,
    Abuse of office, **2C:30–2, 2C:30–3**
    Appropriations, spending or incurring obligations in excess of, **2C:30–4**
    Malfeasance, mandatory sentence, **2C:43–6.5**
    Records, expungement, **2C:52–2**
Criminal coercion, threat to take or withhold official action, **2C:13–5**
Criminal history record information, background checks, **53:1–20.8**
Definitions, intoxicating liquor law, **33:1–1**
Disqualification, bribery and corruption, **2C:51–2**
Escapes, generally, this index

OFFICERS AND EMPLOYEES—Cont'd
Evidence, requiring officer to produce evidence, **2A:84A–19**
Excess spending or incurring of obligations over appropriations, **2C:30–4**
Extortion, threats to take or withhold official action, **2C:20–5**
Financial institutions,
    Receiving deposits in failing institutions, **2C:21–14**
    Theft by failure to make required disposition of property received, **2C:20–9**
Force and violence, obstructing administration of law or governmental functions, **2C:29–1 et seq.**
Forfeitures, bribery and corruption, **2C:51–2**
Fraternal Benefit Societies, this index
Gambling, official actions or information, **2C:30–3**
Gifts or gratuities, attorneys or parties, **Rule 1:16–2**
Grand jury,
    Injurious disclosure of information, crime, **2B:21–10**
    Presentment, censure, **Rule 3:6–9**
Homicide, aggravating factors, sentence and punishment, **2C:11–3**
Impersonating a public servant, **2C:28–8**
Intimidation, obstructing administration of law or governmental functions, **2C:29–1 et seq.**
Judicial officers. Judges and Justices, generally, this index
Labor Unions, this index
Mandatory sentence, crimes and offenses, malfeasance, **2C:43–6.5**
Misconduct in office, **2C:30–2 et seq.**
    Limitation of criminal prosecutions, **2C:1–6**
Municipal Officers and Employees, generally, this index
Murder, aggravating factors, sentence and punishment, **2C:11–3**
Nonattorneys, appearance, administrative agencies, **Rule 1:21–1**
Obstruction, administration of law or governmental function, **2C:29–1 et seq.**
Official misconduct, **2C:30–2**
Past official action, retaliation, **2C:27–5**
Police and Police Departments, generally, this index
Probation and Probation Officers, generally, this index
Public Utilities, this index
Railroads, this index
Religious Corporations and Associations, this index
Removal from office, conduct giving rise to conviction, **2C:51–2**
Retaliation. Labor and Employment, this index
Sheriffs, this index
Speculating or wagering on official action or information, **2C:30–3**
State Officers and Employees, generally, this index
State Police, this index
Subpoenas, enforcement, **Rule 1:9–6**
Theft by failure to make required disposition of property received, **2C:20–9**
Threats and other improper influence, **2C:27–3**
Threats to take or withhold official action, **2C:20–5**
Turnpike Authority, this index
Unions, appearances by nonattorneys, **Rule 1:21–1**
United States, this index
Vacancies In Office, generally, this index

OFFICERS AND EMPLOYEES—Cont'd
Victims of crime, **2C:44–1**
Violence, obstructing administration of law or governmental functions, **2C:29–1 et seq.**
Wagering, official actions or information, **2C:30–3**

OFFICIAL ACTS
Criminal coercion, threat to take or withhold official action, **2C:13–5**
Extortion, threat to take or withhold official action, **2C:20–5**

OFFICIAL ADVERTISING
Advertisements, generally, this index

OFFICIAL BONDS
Bonds (Officers and Fiduciaries), generally, this index

OFFICIAL COMPENDIUM
Definitions, food and drugs, **24:21–32**

OFFICIAL DETENTION
Definitions, escape, **2C:29–5**

OFFICIAL MISCONDUCT
Generally, **2C:30–2**

OFFICIAL NOTICE
Notice, generally, this index

OFFICIAL OATHS
Oaths and Affirmations, generally, this index

OFFICIAL PROCEEDINGS
Definitions, bribery and corrupt influence, **2C:27–1**

OFFICIAL REPORTS
Reports, generally, this index

OFFICIAL TRAFFIC CONTROL DEVICES
Definitions, Motor Vehicle Law, **39:1–1**

OFFICIAL WRITTEN ORDER
Definitions,
    Controlled dangerous substances, **24:21–2**
    Controlled substances, **24:21–2**

OFFICIALS
Officers and Employees, generally, this index

OFFROAD VEHICLE RECREATIONAL FUND
Generally, **39:3C–3.1**

OIL AND GAS
Criminal mischief, **2C:17–3**
Debris after auto accident, towing vehicle failure to remove, penalty exemption, **39:4–56.8**
Definitions, portable oil burning heating devices, **2C:40–6**
Exhaust gases from motor vehicle, injury to be prevented, **39:3–76**
Hazardous Substances and Waste, generally, this index
Liquefied Petroleum Gas, generally, this index
Motor Fuels, generally, this index
Portable heating devices, **2C:40–6 et seq.**
Theft of services, **2C:20–8**
Water Pollution, generally, this index

OIL BURNING HEATING DEVICES
Generally, **2C:40–6 et seq.**

OLD AGE
Aged Persons, generally, this index

OLD PERSONS
Aged Persons, generally, this index

OLYMPIC ATHLETIC COMPETITIONS
Counterfeiting, trademarks and trade names, 2C:21–32
Trademarks and trade names, counterfeiting, 2C:21–32

OMNIBUS SAFETY ENFORCEMENT FUND
Motor vehicle commission, funds, 39:3–79.24
Treasury department, 39:3–79.23

OMNIBUSES
Buses, generally, this index

ONE WAY STREETS
Streets and Alleys, this index

OPEN COURT PROCEEDINGS
Generally, **Rule 1:2–1**

OPEN PUBLIC MEETINGS
Motor vehicle commission, board, 39:2A–16

OPENING STATEMENTS
Trial, **Rule 1:7–1**

OPHTHALMIC DISPENSERS AND TECHNI-CIANS
Contact lenses, licenses and permits, dispensing, 2C:40–25
Licenses and permits, contact lenses, dispensing, 2C:40–25

OPIATE
Definitions, controlled substances, 2C:35–2, 24:21–2

OPINION OR EXPERT TESTIMONY
Witnesses, this index

OPINIONS COMMITTEE
Generally, **Rule 1:36–2**

OPINIONS OF COURT
Generally, **Rule 1:36–1 et seq.**
Abbreviations, **Rule 1:37–3**
Advisory opinions, unauthorized practice of law, committees, **Rules 1:22–2, 1:22–3**
Finding of facts and statement of conclusions, **Rule 1:7–4**
Professional ethics, advisory committee on, **Rule 1:19–4 et seq.**
Publication, **Rule 1:36–2**
Unpublished opinions, **Rule 1:36–3**

OPIUM
Generally, **24:21–1 et seq.**
Definitions, controlled dangerous substances, 2C:35–2

OPIUM POPPY
Definitions,
Controlled dangerous substances, **2C:35–2**
Controlled substances, **24:21–2**

OPTOMETRISTS
Contact lenses, licenses and permits, dispensing, 2C:40–25
Controversies or disputes with patients, review committees, immunity from liability, 2A:84A–22.10

OPTOMETRISTS—Cont'd
Crimes and offenses, health care claims fraud, 2C:21–4.2, 2C:21–4.3
Licenses and permits, suspension or revocation, 2C:51–5
Rehabilitation, order of debarment, rescission, 2C:27–1
Fees, controversies or disputes with patients, review committees, immunity from liability, 2A:84A–22.10
Fines and penalties, health care claims fraud, 2C:21–4.2, 2C:21–4.3
Licenses and permits, suspension or revocation, 2C:51–5
Rehabilitation, order of debarment, rescission, 2C:27–1
Forfeitures, licenses and permits, health care claims fraud, 2C:51–5
Health care claims fraud, 2C:21–4.2, 2C:21–4.3
Licenses and permits, suspension or revocation, 2C:51–5
Rehabilitation, order of debarment, rescission, 2C:27–1
Licenses and permits,
Contact lenses, dispensing, 2C:40–25
Health care claims fraud, suspension or revocation, 2C:51–5
Rehabilitation, order of debarment, rescission, 2C:27–1
Medical advisory panel, 39:2–13 et seq.
Motor vehicles division, medical advisory panel, liability for reports, 39:2–16
Reports, medical advisory panel, motor vehicles division, 39:2–16

ORAL ARGUMENT
Appeal and review, attorney disciplinary proceedings, **Rules 1:20–15, 1:20–16**
Attorneys, this index
Motions, discovery and calendar motions, **Rule 1:6–2**

ORAL COMMUNICATIONS
Definitions, wiretapping and electronic surveillance, 2A:156A–2

ORAL MOTIONS
Generally, **Rule 1:6–2**

ORCHARDS
Agricultural land, trespass, damages, 2C:18–4 et seq.

ORDER FORMS
Controlled substances, 24:21–14
Offenses and penalties, 24:21–21

ORDER TO SHOW CAUSE
Alcoholic Beverages, this index
Application, court order, **Rule 1:6–2**
Contempt, institution of proceedings, **Rule 1:10–2**
Copies, filing, **Rule 1:6–4**
Place for filing, superior court, **Rule 1:6–4**
Subpoenas, application of public officer or agency, **Rule 1:9–6**

ORDERS
Abbreviations, **Rule 1:37–3**
Administrative Law and Procedure, this index
Air Pollution, this index
Alcoholic Beverages, this index
Amicus curiae, leave to appear, **Rule 1:13–9**
Appearance, failure to appear, sanctions, **Rule 1:2–4**
Caption designating, **Rule 1:4–1**
Case management order, **Rule 1:2–6**

ORDERS—Cont'd
Child Abuse, this index
Child support hearing officers, **Rule 5:25–3**
Children and Minors, this index
Clerical mistakes, correction, **Rule 1:13–1**
Compromise and Settlement, generally, this index
Contempt, this index
Controlled substances, attachment, ex parte proceedings, dealers, liability, 2C:35B–13
Copies, **Rule 1:6–4**
Court schedules, **Rule 1:30–1**
Crimes and Offenses, this index
Enforcement, 2C:1–5
Enlargement of time, **Rule 1:3–4**
Entry, court schedules, **Rule 1:30–1**
Errors, clerical mistakes, correction, **Rule 1:13–1**
Explosives, 21:1A–130
Violations, 21:1A–140
Expungement, records, 2C:52–11 et seq.
Failure to appear, sanctions, **Rule 1:2–4**
Financial corporations and institutions, terrorism, funds, freezing, 2C:66–3
Foreclosure matters, uncontested orders, office of foreclosure recommending entry, **Rule 1:34–6**
Foreign legal consultants, **Rule 1:21–9**
Forfeited property, 2C:64–3
Frivolous litigation, **Rule 1:4–8**
Hindering, contempt, 2C:29–9
Identity theft, consumer credit reports, corrections, 2C:21–17.5
Imposition of civil penalty, 2C:43–2
Impoundment records, confidentiality, **Rule 1:38–3**
Investigative detention, **Rule 3:5A–1 et seq.**
Jury and Jurors, this index
Justification, criminal prosecution defense, 2C:3–3
Juvenile Delinquents, this index
Liquefied petroleum gas, violations, 21:1B–6
Material witness. Witnesses, this index
Motor Vehicles, this index
Municipal Courts, this index
Notice, settlement of form of order, **Rule 3:1–4**
Objections, reserving questions for review, **Rule 1:7–2**
Obstruction, contempt, 2C:29–9
Place for filing, superior court, **Rule 1:6–4**
Pleadings, service, numerous defendants, **Rule 1:5–5**
Police and Police Departments, this index
Pro hac vice admission, **Rule 1:21–2**
Racketeering, 2C:41–4
Reconsideration, motion, **Rule 1:7–4**
Rehearing, motion, **Rule 1:7–4**
Relief, motion, enlargement of time, **Rule 1:3–4**
Sequestration, **Rule 1:8–6**
Service, **Rule 1:5–1 et seq.**
Solid Waste, this index
Stalking, violation of existing order prohibiting, third degree crime, 2C:12–10
Stills and Distilling Apparatus, this index
Stolen property, disposition, 2C:65–3
Superior court, unresolved matters, transfer to comprehensive enforcement program, 2B:19–6
Suppression of evidence, municipal courts, **Rule 7:5–2**
Theft, injunctive relief, 2C:20–21
Vacation, expungement of record, 2C:52–26
Wiretapping and Electronic Surveillance, this index

ORDINANCES

Alcoholic Beverages, this index

Amendments, alcoholic beverages, possession or sale, prevention, **33:1–40**

Angle parking, approval, **39:4–197.4**

Appeal and review, traffic signs and signals, pedestrians,
Crosswalks, right of way, **39:4–8**
Right of way, crosswalks, **39:4–8.19**

Approval, traffic ordinances, **39:4–8**

Arrest, unconstitutionality, **2B:12–32**

Certified copies, traffic signs and signals, pedestrians, right of way, crosswalks, **39:4–8**

Compromise and settlement, unconstitutionality, **2B:12–32**

Conflict with or preemption by code of criminal justice, **2C:1–5**

Constitution of New Jersey, unconstitutionality, **2B:12–32**

Crimes and offenses, expungement of records, **2C:52–4**

Crosswalks, pedestrians, right of way, traffic signs and signals, **39:4–8**

Electric personal assistive mobility devices, operation, **39:4–14.10**

Expungement, record, **2C:52–1 et seq.**

Fines and penalties, unconstitutionality, **2B:12–32**

Handicapped parking enforcement units, **39:4–197.9**

Liquefied petroleum gas, not to conflict with provisions of law regulating, **21:1B–7**

Motor vehicles, parking offenses, impoundment or immobilization, **39:4–139.13**

Motorized scooters, **39:4–14.14**

Municipal Courts, this index

Obscene material, adults, **2C:34–2**

Parking, this index

Pedestrians, crosswalks, right of way, traffic signs and signals, **39:4–8**

Preemption by code of criminal justice, **2C:1–5**

Records and recordation, arrest, unconstitutionality, **2B:12–32**

Refunds, fines and penalties, unconstitutionality, **2B:12–32**

Right of way, crosswalks, pedestrians, traffic signs and signals, **39:4–8**

Traffic, turnpike projects not governed by resolution or ordinance, **27:23–37**

Traffic control devices, **39:4–120.2 et seq.**

Traffic Rules and Regulations, this index

Traffic Signs and Signals, this index

Unconstitutionality, **2B:12–32**

ORGAN DONOR

Anatomical Gifts, generally, this index

ORGAN TRANSPLANTS

Anatomical Gifts, generally, this index

ORGANIZED CRIME

See, also, Racketeers and Racketeering, generally, this index

Emergency situation involving conspiratorial activities of, wiretapping and electronic surveillance, interception of wire, electronic or oral communications, order, **2A:156A–13**

Human trafficking, **2C:13–8**

Intensive supervision program, restrictions, **2C:43–11**

Leader of organized crime, **2C:5–2**
Grade and degree of offense, **2C:5–4**

Legislative findings, policy, **2C:41–1.1**

Money Laundering and Illegal Investments, generally, this index

ORGANIZED CRIME—Cont'd

Racketeering, **2C:41–1 et seq.**

Street Gangs, generally, this index

Weapons, possession, presumptions, **2C:39–5**

Wiretapping and electronic surveillance, **2A:156A–1 et seq.**

ORGANIZED RETAIL THEFT ENTERPRISE

Shoplifting, **2C:20–11.2**

ORIGINAL CONTAINERS

Definitions, intoxicating liquor law, **33:1–1**

OTHER STATES

Foreign States, generally, this index

OUT OF STATE INCARCERATION LAW

Generally, **2A:168–18 et seq.**

OUT OF STATE MOTORIST ACT

Generally, **39:7–1 et seq.**

OUT OF STATE PAROLEE SUPERVISION

Generally, **2A:168–17**

OUTBOARD MOTORS

Boats and Boating, generally, this index

OUTDOOR ADVERTISING

Enforcement of act, **27:5–23**

Engagement in the business of outdoor advertising, licenses and permits, **27:5–8**

Erection, use or maintenance of signs, licenses and permits, **27:5–8**

Fines and penalties, **27:5–16**

Flashing, moving or intermittent lights, prohibition, **27:5–9**

Hazardous signs, **27:5–9**

Hearings, new licenses, **27:5–8**

Illumination, **27:5–9**

Imitation traffic signs, prohibition, **27:5–9**

Licenses and permits, **27:5–8 et seq.**
Conditions, **27:5–9**
Engagement in the business of outdoor advertising, **27:5–8**
Erection, use or maintenance of signs, **27:5–8**
Hearings, new licenses, **27:5–8**
Right of ways, **27:5–10**

Lights and lighting, **27:5–9**
Rotating or flashing lights on or near highways, **39:4–60.1 et seq.**

Locations, **27:5–9**

Maintenance of signs, **27:5–9**

Names, permit holders name displayed upon signs, **27:5–9**

Natural features, placing signs upon, **27:5–9**

Nuisance, rotating or flashing lights on or near highways, **39:4–60.1 et seq.**

Obstruction of view, **27:5–9**

Permits. Licenses and permits, generally, ante

Police, duties, **27:5–23**

Public utility poles, placing signs upon, **27:5–9**

Reflectorized materials, prohibition, **27:5–9**

Right of way,
Erection or maintenance of signs prohibited, exceptions, **27:5–10**
Zoning and planning, **27:5–9.1**

Rocks, placing signs upon, **27:5–9**

Rotating or flashing lights on or near highways, **39:4–60.1 et seq.**

Rules and regulations, enforcement, **27:5–23**

State police, duties, **27:5–23**

Trees, placing signs upon, **27:5–9**

Visibility, obstruction, **27:5–9**

Zoning and planning, **27:5–9.1**

OUTSIDE ACTIVITIES OF JUDICIARY EMPLOYEES ADVISORY COMMITTEE

Generally, **Rule 1:17A–1 et seq.**

OUTSIDE LANE

Definitions, **39:1–1**

OUTSTANDING PUBLIC SERVICE

Definitions, disorderly persons, enumerated, **2A:170–20.1**

OVERHEAD PEDESTRIAN CROSSING

Right of way of vehicles upon roadway, **39:4–36, 39:4–36.1**

OVERT ACTS

Conspiracy, **2C:5–2**

OVERTAKING AND PASSING VEHICLES

Traffic Rules and Regulations, this index

PACKAGE SALES

Intoxicating liquors, distillers, brewers and vintners packaged merchandise, **33:1–12**

PACKAGES

See, also, Containers, generally, this index

Advertisements, consumer products, crimes and offenses, **2C:40–19**

Consumer products, writings, crimes and offenses, **2C:40–19**

Cosmetics, writings, crimes and offenses, **2C:40–19**

Definitions, food and drugs, **24:21–32**

Drugs and Medicine, this index

Food, writings, crimes and offenses, **2C:40–19**

Writings, consumer products, crimes and offenses, **2C:40–19**

PADLOCKING

Building or premises by director of alcoholic beverage control division, **33:2–5**
Violation of order as misdemeanor, **33:2–9**

PAGING DEVICES

Crimes and offenses, **2C:33–20**
Children and minors, possession, **2C:33–19 et seq.**

PALM PRINTS

Investigative detention, **Rule 3:5A–1 et seq.**

PANDERING

Prostitution, **2C:34–1**

PANEL

Definitions, Comprehensive Child Abuse Prevention and Treatment Act, **9:6–8.84**

Jury and Jurors, this index

PAPER

Books and Papers, generally, this index

Negotiable Instruments, generally, this index

Newspapers, generally, this index

Recycling. Solid Waste, this index

PARADES

Interruption for passage of traffic, **39:4–93**

Motor vehicles, special registrations, **39:3–27.2**

Right of way through, emergency vehicles entitled to, **39:4–93**

Traffic prohibition by municipality, necessity of consent of chosen freeholders or highway commissioner, **39:4–197.1**

PARALDEHYDE

See, also, Drugs and Medicine, generally, this index

PARALDEHYDE—Cont'd
Controlled substances, 24:21–1 et seq.

PARALEGALS
Indigents, assisting, **Rule 1:21–1**

PARAPHERNALIA
Stills and Distilling Apparatus, generally, this
index

PARDONS
Commutation, sentence and punishment,
2A:167–4 et seq.
Application, forms, 2A:167–6
Arrest by parole officer, belief person is
about to resume criminal conduct,
2A:167–9
Confinement on revocation of parole,
2A:167–12
Form of order, 2A:167–4
Imprisonment, 2A:167–4
Legal custody of persons at liberty, 2A:167–8
Order, form, 2A:167–4
Order revoking order for commutation,
2A:167–12
Report, 2A:167–3.1
Retaking and detention of person at liberty,
2A:167–9
Return of person at large to place of punish-
ment, 2A:167–8
Return to place of confinement on revoca-
tion of order, 2A:167–12
Revocation, 2A:167–10
Investigation by state board of parole,
2A:167–11
Order, 2A:167–12
Time of confinement, 2A:167–12
Security, terms, conditions and limitations
subject to, 2A:167–8
Subject to security, terms and limitations,
2A:167–8
Warrant for arrest on order for revocation,
2A:167–12
Evidence, employing rehabilitated convicted of-
fenders, 2A:168A–3
Forms of application for commutation of sen-
tences, 2A:167–6
Investigation by state board of parole,
2A:167–7
Report, 2A:167–3.1
Restoration of rights, 2A:167–5
Suffrage rights, restoration, 2A:167–5

PARENT AND CHILD
Children and Minors, generally, this index

PARENT OR GUARDIAN
Definitions, Comprehensive Child Abuse Prevention and Treatment Act, 9:6–8.84

PARENTAL RIGHTS
Temporary out of home placement, **Rule
5:18–2**

PARENTING TIME
Visitation. Children and Minors, this index

PARENTS
Definitions, 9:6–2
Abuse of children, 9:6–8.21
Custody, interference, 2C:13–4
Kidnapping, 2C:13–1
Juvenile Delinquents, this index

PARK POLICE
Power to arrest, United States, 2A:154–6

PARKING
Generally, 39:4–135 et seq., 39:5A–1 et seq.
Angle parking, 39:4–135
Notice of ordinance or regulation, 39:4–198
Ordinances, approval, 39:4–197.4
Permitted on streets marked or signed,
39:4–135
Arrest warrants, offenses, **Rule 7:8–9**
Backing against curb to load or unload vehicles
prohibited, when, 39:4–79
Brakes to be set and motor stopped, 39:4–137
Counties, ordinances or resolutions, 39:4–8
Crimes and offenses,
Appearance, municipal courts, **Rule 7:8–9**
Contracts for processing services,
39:4–139.14
Default judgments, 39:4–139.8
Drivers licenses,
Restoration of suspended license,
39:4–139.11
Suspension, 39:4–139.10
Fees, suspended drivers licenses, 39:4–139.12
Fines and penalties, 39:4–139.9
Hearings, 39:4–139.8
Impound or immobilization of vehicles,
39:4–139.13
Joint liability, owner and operator of vehicle,
39:4–139.5
Lessors liability, 39:4–139.5
Limitation of actions, 39:4–139.10a
Tickets, 39:4–139.4
Curb markings prohibiting parking, 39:4–191.2
Definitions, Motor Vehicle Law, 39:1–1
Disabled vehicles, parking, 39:4–136
Dismissal of offenses, **Rule 7:8–9**
Distances, permissible parking distances,
39:4–138
Municipalities, 39:4–138.6
Drivers licenses, suspension or revocation,
39:3–40
Emergency vehicles, 39:4–92
Facilities. Parking Lots and Facilities, general-
ly, this index
Fines and penalties, 39:4–139.9
Drivers licenses, suspension or revocation,
39:3–40
Handicapped spaces, violations, 39:4–197,
39:4–201
Hearings, drivers licenses, suspension or rev-
ocation, 39:4–139.10
Installments, poor, 39:4–139.10, 39:4–203.1
Parking permits, state owned grounds, alter-
ing, counterfeiting or misuse of permits,
39:4–209
Fire apparatus, parking near prohibited,
39:4–92
Flares or other warning lights, 39:3–64
Giving place to vehicle about to take on or let
off passengers, duty of vehicle waiting at
curb, 39:4–62
Handicapped Persons, this index
Hearings, drivers licenses, suspension or revo-
cation, 39:4–139.10
Identification cards, restricted spaces,
39:4–197.5
Improperly parked vehicles, 39:4–136
Institution grounds and roadways, regulation,
39:4–208
Investigations, 39:4–6
Leaving engine running, fine imposed, 39:4–53
Lights, 39:3–62
Limitation of actions, 39:4–139.10a
Loading or unloading of passengers or materi-
als, time permitted, 39:4–139
Lots. Parking Lots and Facilities, generally,
this index

PARKING—Cont'd
Motor vehicle security responsibility act inap-
plicable to parked vehicle, 39:6–26
Moving vehicle improperly parked, 39:4–136
Municipal Courts, this index
Municipalities,
Authority to regulate, county roads,
39:4–197.2
Contracts, processing of parking offenses,
39:4–139.14
Distances, permissible parking distances,
39:4–138.6
Handicapped persons,
Handicapped parking enforcement units,
39:4–197.9 et seq.
Restricted parking spaces, 39:4–197,
39:4–197.5
Notice of ordinance or regulation, 39:4–198
Offenses, impoundment or immobilization of
vehicles, 39:4–139.13
Ordinances or resolutions, 39:4–8
Power to regulate parking of vehicles,
39:4–197
Private driveways, 39:4–138.3 et seq.
No parking zones on state highways, 39:4–138.1
Nonresident Violator Compact, application of
law, 39:5F–25
Notice, drivers licenses, suspension or revoca-
tion, 39:4–139.10
Nursing home residents, handicapped parking
places, 39:4–207.8
Offenses. Crimes and offenses, generally, ante
One way streets, 39:4–135
Ordinances, 39:4–8, 39:4–197
Impoundment or immobilization of vehicles,
39:4–139.13
Notice, 39:4–198
Private driveways, 39:4–138.3 et seq.
Overtime parking, handicapped persons,
39:4–207
Park unlawfully, definitions, handicapped park-
ing, 39:4–207.6
Passageway required, minimum width, 39:4–136
Peace officers, moving vehicle improperly
parked, 39:4–136
Penalties. Fines and penalties, generally, ante
Permits,
Private driveways, 39:4–138.3 et seq.
State owned grounds, altering, counterfeiting
or misuse of permits, 39:4–209
Poor, fines and penalties, installments,
39:4–139.10, 39:4–203.1
Private driveways, 39:4–138.3 et seq.
Private parking areas, application of law,
39:5A–1 et seq.
Prohibited, places specified, 39:4–138
Public parking lots. Parking Lots and Facili-
ties, generally, this index
Regulations, power of municipality, 39:4–197
Resolutions, municipalities, 39:4–8
Restricted spaces, identification cards,
39:4–197.5
Semipublic parking areas, application of law,
39:5A–1 et seq.
Spaces, 39:4–138
State institutions, jurisdiction to hear and de-
termine violations, 39:4–210
State owned grounds, 39:4–208 et seq.
Street excavation or obstruction, parking near
prohibited, 39:4–138
Tickets, 39:4–139.4
Turning wheels to curb or side of highway,
39:4–137
Unregistered motor vehicle on public highway,
39:3–4
Visibility, minimum distance, 39:4–136

PARKING AREAS
Parking Lots and Facilities, generally, this index

PARKING LOTS AND FACILITIES
Mentally retarded persons, transportation vehicles, identification, **39:4–207.4**
Municipalitys power to regulate parking of vehicles, **39:4–197**
  Notice of ordinance or regulation, **39:4–198**
Notice of ordinance or regulation, **39:4–198**
Regulation of parking, municipalities power, **39:4–197**
Workmen engaged in work on surface of highway, traffic laws inapplicable, **39:4–1**

PARKING METERS
Installation, counties or municipalities, **39:4–8**

PARKING OFFENSES
Definitions, **39:4–139.3**

PARKING TICKET
Definitions, **39:4–139.3**

PARKS AND FORESTRY DIVISION
Environmental Protection Department, this index

PARKS AND PARKWAYS
All terrain vehicles, **39:3C–1 et seq.**
Application, motor vehicle and traffic laws, **39:5A–1 et seq.**
Billboards, visible from. Outdoor Advertising, generally, this index
Controlled substances, crimes and offenses, **2C:35–7.1**
Crimes and offenses, controlled dangerous substances, **2C:35–7.1**
Definitions, controlled substances, crimes and offenses, **2C:35–7.1**
Destruction by motor vehicles, **39:4–97a**
  Point system, assessment against drivers license, **39:5–30.5a**
Liberty State Park license plate fund, **39:3–27.94**
Mobile Homes and Mobile Home Parks, generally, this index
Motor vehicles,
  Destruction of recreational property, **39:4–97a**
  Point system, assessing against drivers license, **39:5–30.5a**
  Traffic laws, application, **39:5A–1 et seq.**
Parks and forestry division. Environmental Protection Department, this index
Snowmobiles, **39:3C–1 et seq.**
Traffic rules and regulations, **39:5A–4**
Turnpike authority, power to acquire property, **27:23–5**

PARKWAY
Parks and Parkways, generally, this index

PAROCHIAL SCHOOLS
Private Schools, generally, this index

PAROLE
See, also, Probation and Probation Officers, generally, this index
Absconding from parole, criminal prosecutions, **2C:29–5**
Adult offender supervision, interstate compacts, **2A:168–26 et seq.**
Bail, cash, **2A:162–12**
Compact between states, persons convicted of crime on probation or parole, **2A:168–14**

PAROLE—Cont'd
Compact institution, interstate compact, **2A:168–20**
Confidential or privileged information, reports, sexually violent predators, exception, **2C:47–5**
Controlled dangerous substances,
  Area surrounding school property or bus, **2C:35–7**
  Revocation, injunctions, **2C:35–5.8**
Costs, interstate compact, **2A:168–23**
Default, interstate compact for adult offender supervision, **2A:168–37**
Definitions,
  Adult offender supervision, interstate compacts, **2A:168–27**
  Escape, **2C:29–5**
  Receiving state, **2A:168–19**
Eligibility,
  Life imprisonment, exceptions, **2C:11–3, 2C:11–3b**
  Presentence investigation and report, waiver, period of ineligibility, **2C:44–6**
  Weapons, possession, **2C:39–5**
Enforcement, interstate compact for adult offender supervision, **2A:168–37**
Escape, **2C:29–5**
Evidence, employing rehabilitated convicted offenders, **2A:168A–3**
Expenses, interstate compact, **2A:168–23**
Explanation during sentencing, **2C:43–2**
Extended sentences, **2C:43–7, 2C:43–7.1**
Extradition, this index
Governor,
  Revocation, **2A:167–10**
  Signature to order revoking license to be at large or commutation of sentence, **2A:167–12**
Harassment, **2C:33–4**
Homicide, eligibility, exceptions, **2C:11–3, 2C:11–3b**
Humane treatment, interstate compact, **2A:168–22**
Imprisonment, condition of probation, application of law, **2C:45–1**
Incarceration of parolee in receiving state, **2A:168–18 et seq.**
Intensive supervision program,
  Restrictions, **2C:43–11**
  Weapons, possession, **2C:39–5**
Interstate compacts,
  Adult offender supervision, **2A:168–26 et seq.**
  Persons convicted of crime on probation or parole, **2A:168–14 et seq.**
Investigation, state parole board, **2A:167–11**
Jurisdiction, sending state, interstate compact, **2A:168–21**
Juvenile Delinquents, this index
Kidnapping, supervision for life, special sentence, Violent Predator Incapacitation Act of 1994, **2C:43–6.4**
License to convicts to be at large, **2A:167–8**
Life imprisonment, eligibility, exceptions, **2C:11–3, 2C:11–3b**
Motor vehicle homicide, drunken driving, **2C:11–5**
No Early Release Act, **2C:43–7.2**
Order revoking license to be at large or commutation of sentence, **2A:167–12**
Plea agreements, estimated real time served, **Rule 3:9–3**
Psychological evaluations, presentence investigation and report, waiver, period of ineligibility, **2C:44–6**
Records of court, explanation of parole laws during sentencing, **2C:43–2**

PAROLE—Cont'd
Rehabilitated convicted offenders, employment, evidence, **2A:168A–3**
Reincarceration of parolee in receiving state, **2A:168–18 et seq.**
Reinstatement, interstate compact for adult offender supervision, **2A:168–37**
Release, No Early Release Act, status, **2C:43–7.2**
Retaking and detention of person on liberty, **2A:167–9**
Return of person at large to punishment to which originally sentenced, **2A:167–8**
Rules and regulations, interstate compact, **2A:168–24**
Security, terms, conditions and limitations, subject to, **2A:167–9**
Sex offenses,
  Eligibility, violations, effect, **2C:47–5.1**
  Registration. Sex Offenses, this index
  Restrictions, **2C:47–3**
  Revocation, **2C:47–5.1**
Sexually violent predators,
  Referral, **2C:47–5**
  Special classification review board, recommendation, **2C:47–5**
Stalking, **2C:12–10**
Statements on the record by court at imposition of sentence, **2C:43–2**
Supervision,
  Incarceration as probation condition, **2C:45–1**
  Life, special sentence, **2C:43–6.4**
  Suspension or revocation, **2A:167–10, 2C:43–9**
  Computation of time of confinement, **2A:167–12**
Termination, interstate compact for adult offender supervision, **2A:168–37**
Terms and conditions, **2C:43–6**
  Explanation on record during sentencing, **2C:43–2**
  Extended sentences, **2C:43–7, 2C:43–7.1**
Terrorism, minimum sentence, **2C:43–7.2**
Time, **2C:45–2**
  Interstate compact, **2A:168–25**
Uniform act for out of state supervision, **2A:168–14 et seq.**
Vessel, death by operation of, intoxication or drug use, **2C:11–5**
Warrants,
  Apprehension of convict at large on license, **2A:167–9**
  Arrest, convict whose license to be at large was revoked, **2A:167–12**
Withdrawal, interstate compact for adult offender supervision, **2A:168–37**

PAROLE AGENTS OR OFFICERS
Appointment as probation officers in counties of not less than 800,000, **2A:168–6**
Internet, access, enforcement, training, **2C:43–6.7**
Police powers, **2A:154–4**
Weapons possession, exemption, **2C:39–6**

PAROLE BOARD
See, also, Parole, generally, this index
Governors order commuting sentence to be kept in office of, **2A:167–4**
Investigations,
  Application for commutation of sentence, **2A:167–7**
  Revocation of parole, **2A:167–11**
Order of revocation of convicts license to be at large to be filed with, **2A:167–12**

PART PAYMENT
Installments, generally, this index

PARTICULARS
Indictments, accusations, **Rule 3:7–5**

PARTIES
Adjudication of guilt, reversal on appeal, return of fine, **2A:166–13**
Amicus curiae, **Rule 1:13–9**
Appearance, real party in interest, **Rule 1:21–1**
Complaints, names included in title of action, **Rule 1:4–1**
Consent, enlargement of time, **Rule 1:3–4**
Depositions, generally, this index
Enlargement of time, consent in writing, **Rule 1:3–4**
Exhibits, record of proceedings, **Rule 1:2–3**
Failure to appear, sanctions, **Rule 1:2–4**
Fines and penalties, return, reversal of guilty adjudication, **2A:166–13**
Interviewing jurors subsequent to trial, **Rule 1:16–1**
Jurors, interviewing subsequent to trial, **Rule 1:16–1**
Juvenile delinquents and dependents, **Rule 5:20–4**
Liens and encumbrances, priorities, **Rule 1:13–8**
Military list, inability to prosecute or defend action, **Rule 1:13–6**
Names, generally, this index
Necessary parties, juvenile delinquency, **Rule 5:20–4**
Numerous defendants, service of papers, **Rule 1:5–5**
Public defenders, **2A:158A–1 et seq.**
Representatives for receipt of service, numerous defendants, **Rule 1:5–5**
Service, **Rule 1:5–1 et seq.**
Statements by party opponents, hearsay exception, **Evidence Rule 803**
Subpoenas, issuance in name of clerk of court, **Rule 1:9–1**
Third Parties, generally, this index
Writings or photographs, proving contents, testimony or admissions of parties, **Evidence Rule 1007**

PARTNERSHIPS
Actions and proceedings, racketeering, **2C:41–4**
Alcoholic beverages,
    Application for license, **33:1–25**
    Automatic suspension of license on conviction of member, **33:1–31.1**
    Person, partnership as person within Alcoholic Beverage Law, **33:1–1**
Attorneys, this index
Bribery and corruption, effect of conviction, **2C:51–2**
Cease and desist orders, racketeering, **2C:41–4**
Commercial bribery and breach of duty, **2C:21–10**
Confidential or privileged information, racketeering investigations, **2C:41–5**
Death of partner, racketeering, **2C:41–1 et seq.**
Debtors and creditors, racketeering, **2C:41–1 et seq.**
Definitions, racketeering, **2C:41–1**
Discovery, racketeering investigations, **2C:41–5**
Drivers Schools, generally, this index
Examinations and examiners, racketeering, **2C:41–5**
Fines and penalties, racketeering, **2C:41–1 et seq.**
Indebtedness, racketeering, **2C:41–1 et seq.**

PARTNERSHIPS—Cont'd
Inspectors and inspection, racketeering investigations, **2C:41–5**
Interrogatories, racketeering, investigations, **2C:41–5**
Investigations and investigators, racketeering, **2C:41–5**
Investments, racketeering, **2C:41–1 et seq.**
Judgments and decrees, racketeering, **2C:41–4**
Licenses and permits, racketeering, revocation or suspension, **2C:41–4**
Limited liability partnerships,
    Practice of law, **Rules 1:21–1, 1:21–1C**
    Usury, maximum rates, **2C:21–19**
Municipal courts, traffic tickets, service, **Rule 7:2–4**
News partnerships, searches and seizures, **2A:84A–21.9 et seq.**
Person, definitions, Alcoholic Beverage Law, **33:1–1**
Pleas, criminal causes, **Rule 7:6–2**
Process, racketeering, **2C:41–5**
Production of books and papers, racketeering, **2C:41–5**
Racketeering, **2C:41–1 et seq.**
Records and recordation, racketeering, investigations, **2C:41–5**
Restitution, racketeering, **2C:41–4**
Searches and seizures, news partnerships, **2A:84A–21.9**
Summons, municipal court issuance, **Rule 7:2–2**

PARTY LINE
Definitions, telephones, refusing to yield, emergency, **2C:40–2**

PARTY OFFICIAL
Definitions, bribery and corrupt influence, **2C:27–1**

PASSAGEWAYS
Drives and Driveways, generally, this index

PASSAIC VALLEY SEWERAGE COMMISSIONERS
Motor vehicles, exemption from payment of registration fee, **39:3–27**

PASSENGER AUTOMOBILE
Definitions,
    Seat belts, **39:3–76.2f**
    Traffic rules, **39:1–1**

PASSENGER AUTOMOBILE SEAT BELT USAGE ACT
Generally, **39:3–76.2e et seq.**

PASSENGERS
All terrain vehicles, helmets, **39:3C–19**
Dirt bikes, helmets, **39:3C–19**
Giving place to vehicle about to take on or let off passengers, duty of vehicle waiting at curb, **39:4–62**
Motor Vehicles, this index
Parking vehicle for purpose of taking on or letting off, time limited, **39:4–139**
Snowmobiles, helmets, **39:3C–19**
Stopping vehicle to let off or take on prohibited except at curb or side of road, **39:4–65**

PASSPORTS
Human trafficking, **2C:13–8**

PATENTS
Preparations, alcohol in patent preparations unfit for beverage purposes, **33:1–30**

PATERNITY
Child support hearing officers, **Rule 5:25–3**
Confidential or privileged information, **Rule 1:38–3**

PATHOLOGICAL INTOXICATION
Definitions, Code of Criminal Justice, **2C:2–8**

PATIENT PHYSICIAN PRIVILEGE
Generally, **Evidence Rule 506**

PATRIOTIC ORGANIZATIONS AND SOCIETIES
Charitable Organizations and Associations, generally, this index

PATROLS
Police and Police Departments, generally, this index

PATTERN OF RACKETEERING ACTIVITY
Definitions, **2C:41–1**

PAVEMENT MARKINGS
Notice of ordinances in lieu of addition to signs, **39:4–198**
Types, **39:4–191.2**

PAVING
Sidewalks, generally, this index
Turnpikes, reuse, reclaimed asphalt pavement, **27:23–14.1**

PAWNBROKERS
Selling or accepting weapons as security, **2C:39–11**

PAY
Compensation and Salaries, generally, this index

PAYMENT
Costs, this index
Fines and penalties, transaction fee, **2C:46–1 et seq.**
Installments, generally, this index
Mandatory assessments, **2C:46–1**
    Transaction fee, **2C:46–1 et seq.**
Motor Vehicle Commission, this index
Municipal Treasurer, this index
Restitution, this index
Student loans, attorneys, suspension from practice, **Rule 1:20–11B**

PAYROLLS
Compensation and Salaries, generally, this index

PEACE CORPS
Attorneys, client protection fund, exemption from payment, **Rule 1:28–2**

PEACE OFFICERS
Law Enforcement Officers, generally, this index
Police and Police Departments, generally, this index

PECUNIARY BENEFIT
Definitions, bribery and corrupt influence, **2C:27–1**

PECUNIARY INTEREST
Adverse or Pecuniary Interest, generally, this index

PEDESTRIAN SAFETY ENFORCEMENT AND EDUCATION FUND
Generally, **39:4–36.2**

PEDESTRIAN SAFETY ENFORCEMENT AND EDUCATION FUND—Cont'd
Deposits, 39:4–36

PEDESTRIANS
See, also, Crosswalks, generally, this index
Generally, 39:4–32 et seq.
Blind persons, right of way, crossing highway or intersection, 39:4–37.1
Children and minors, bicycle violations, fines and penalties, 39:4–203.3, 39:4–203.4
Crossing roadway, 39:4–32
Definitions,
  Motor Vehicle Law, 39:1–1
  No fault insurance, 39:6A–2
Fines and penalties,
  Crosswalks, yielding, 39:4–36
    Deposits, 39:4–36.2
  Violation of law relating to pedestrians, 39:4–203
Funds, pedestrian safety enforcement and education fund, 39:4–36.2
  Deposits, 39:4–36
Intersections,
  Controlled by traffic signals or officers,
    Crossing against stop signal prohibited unless otherwise directed, 39:4–32
    Crosswalk required to be used, 39:4–33
    Ordinances regulating crossing at intersections controlled by signals, 39:4–37
    Special pedestrian interval in operation of signals, 39:4–117
  Safety, 39:4–36.3, 39:4–36.4
  Uncontrolled intersection, crossing at right angles to roadway, 39:4–34
Intervals, 39:4–117
Investigations, 39:4–6
Jaywalking, 39:4–33, 39:4–34
Medial barriers separating roadways, crossing, 39:4–34
Official traffic control devices, duty to obey instructions of, 39:4–81
Overhead pedestrian crossing, right of way of vehicles upon roadway, 39:4–36.1
Pedestrian safety enforcement and education fund, 39:4–36.2
  Deposits, 39:4–36
Right of way, 39:4–34 et seq.
  Blind persons, crossing highway or intersection, 39:4–37.1
  Crossing at point other than designated crosswalk, 39:4–34
  Crosswalks, 39:4–34 et seq.
  Marked crosswalks or unmarked sidewalks at end of blocks, 39:4–36
  Motor vehicle entering or leaving private road or driveway, 39:4–66.1
  Older and walking impaired persons crossing, designation of areas and erection of signs, 39:4–183.1b
  Pedestrian starting across on go signal, 39:4–32
Right turns, intersections, safety, 39:4–36.4
Safety, intersections, 39:4–36.3, 39:4–36.4
Safety Zones, generally, this index
Sentence and punishment, crosswalks, yielding, 39:4–36
Signals, crossing roadways, 39:4–32
Stopping, motor vehicles, 39:4–32, 39:4–144
Traffic Accidents, generally, this index
Tunnels, right of way of vehicles, 39:4–36, 39:4–36.1
Walking on left side of highway required, 39:4–34
Yield signs, safety, 39:4–183.31

PEDESTRIANS—Cont'd
Yielding, 39:4–144
  Crosswalks, 39:4–36

PENAL INSTITUTIONS
Correctional Institutions, generally, this index

PENALTIES
Fines and Penalties, generally, this index

PENDING ACTIONS AND PROCEEDINGS
Attorneys, counsellors and solicitors,
  Death, disbarment, notice to appoint another attorney, Rule 1:11–1
  Disciplinary actions and proceedings, Rule 1:20–3
  Withdrawal or substitution, Rule 1:11–2
Contempt, bail, Rule 1:10–2
Dismissal, inactive cases, Rule 1:13–7
Dispensing with rules, Rule 1:1–2
Judges, disqualification or inability to hear manner, substitution, Rule 1:12–3
Military list, inability to prosecute or defend action, Rule 1:13–6
Professional ethics, advisory committee on, consideration of inquiries involving, Rule 1:19–2
Relaxing or dispensing with rules, Rule 1:1–2
Rules of evidence, adoption, effect, 2A:84A–42

PENDING PROSECUTIONS
Code of Criminal Justice, application of law, 2C:1–1

PENITENTIARIES
Correctional Institutions, generally, this index

PER DIEM ALLOWANCE OR COMPENSATION
Intoxicated driving programs, fees, 39:4–50

PEREMPTORY CHALLENGES
Jury, Rule 1:8–3

PERIODICALS
Definitions, privileged communications, 2A:84A–21a
News personnel privilege, 2A:84A–21, 2A:84A–21a

PERJURY
Generally, 2C:28–1, 2C:28–2
Affirmative defense, retraction, 2C:28–1
Attorneys, conviction, discipline, Rule 1:20–13
Corroboration, 2C:28–1
Defenses, 2C:28–1
  Notice, Rule 3:12–1
Expungement of record, 2C:52–2
Irregularity, oaths and affirmations, 2C:28–1
Jury, number of peremptory challenges, 2B:23–13
Pleas and plea discussions, admissibility, Evidence Rule 410
Question of law, 2C:28–1
Records and recordation, expungement, 2C:52–2
Retraction, 2C:28–1
  Defense, Rule 3:12–1
Standard of proof, 2C:28–1
Unsworn falsifications, 2C:28–3

PERMITS
Licenses and Permits, generally, this index

PEROXIDES
Turnpike projects, transportation regulations, 27:23–31

PERSISTENT OFFENDERS
Definitions, crimes, 2C:44–3
Notice to impose sentence, Rule 3:21–4
Second or Subsequent Offenses, generally, this index

PERSON
Definitions,
  Adult offender supervision, interstate compacts, 2A:168–27
  Alcoholic beverages, 33:1–1
  Certificate of Motor Vehicle Ownership Law, 39:10–2
  Controlled dangerous substances, trafficking, injunctions, 2C:35–5.6
  Controlled substances, 2C:35–2, 24:21–2
  Drivers privacy protection, 39:2–3.3
  Drivers schools, 39:12–1
  Electronic surveillance, 2A:156A–2
  Explosives Act, 21:1A–129
  Motor Vehicle Law, 39:1–1
  Motor vehicle unsatisfied claim and judgment fund, 39:6–62
  Prevention of cruelty to animals, 4:22–15
  Racketeering activity, 2C:41–1
  Shoplifting, 2C:20–11
  Theft, 2C:20–1
  Unsatisfied Claim and Judgment Fund Law, 39:6–62
  Water pollution control, 58:10A–3
  Wire tapping and electronic surveillance, 2A:156A–2

PERSONAL ASSISTANCE SERVICES
Certificates and certification, criminal history record checks, 53:1–20.9a
Criminal history record information, certificates, 53:1–20.9a

PERSONAL IDENTIFIERS
Confidential or privileged information, Rule 1:38–7
Definitions, theft of identity, 2C:21–17
Theft, telecommunications, 2C:20–2
  Definitions, 2C:20–1

PERSONAL INFORMATION
Definitions, drivers privacy protection, 39:2–3.3

PERSONAL INJURIES
Arbitration and award, representation, insurance companies, Rule 1:21–1
Assault and Battery, generally, this index
Crimes and offenses, endangering injured victim, 2C:12–1.2
Damages, generally, this index
Drunk Driving Victims Bill of Rights, 39:4–50.9 et seq.
Endangering injured victim, crimes and offenses, 2C:12–1.2
Motor Vehicle Insurance, this index
Motor Vehicles, this index
Negligence, generally, this index
Notice of prosecution status, victims of motor vehicle or traffic offenders, 39:5–51, 39:5–52
Nuclear power plants, vandalism, 2C:17–9
Torts, generally, this index

PERSONAL INJURY PROTECTION COVERAGE
Definitions,
  Motor vehicle insurance, 39:6A–3.1
  No fault insurance, 39:6A–4

PERSONAL PROPERTY
Attachment, generally, this index

PERSONAL PROPERTY—Cont'd
Executions, generally, this index
Force, defense of personal property, **2C:3–6**
Forfeitures, generally, this index
Nuisances, seizure, forfeiture, **2C:33–12.1**
Sales, generally, this index
Search warrants, execution, motion for return, **Rule 3:5–7**
Theft, generally, this index

PERSONAL RECOGNIZANCES
Definitions, Nonresident Violator Compact, **39:5F–4**

PERSONAL REPRESENTATIVES
Probate Proceedings, this index

PERSONALIZED HANDGUNS
Weapons, this index

PESTICIDES
Fireworks, agricultural use, permits, **21:2–29.1**

PET SHOPS
Crimes and offenses, destruction of animals, **4:22–19**
Destruction of animals, **4:22–19**
Removal of decompression or gas chambers, **4:22–19.2**

PETHIDINE
Controlled substances, **24:21–1 et seq.**

PETIT JURY
Jury and Jurors, generally, this index

PETIT JURY LIST
Jury Lists, generally, this index

PETITIONS
Appeal and Review, this index
Children and Minors, this index
Crimes and Offenses, this index
Juvenile Delinquents, this index
Juvenile family crisis, **Rule 5:15–2**
Service, **Rule 1:5–1 et seq.**
Verification, juvenile delinquents and dependents, sealing of records, armed forces enlistees, **2A:4A–62**

PETRICHLORAL
Controlled substances, **24:21–1 et seq.**

PETROLEUM
Oil and Gas, generally, this index

PETS
Cats, generally, this index
Dogs, generally, this index

PETTY CASH FUND
Alcoholic beverage control division director, **33:1–23**

PETTY DISORDERLY PERSONS
Generally, **2C:1–4, 2C:33–2**
Bail, **2C:6–1**
Contraband, furnishing, detention facilities, **2C:29–6**
Criminal trespass, **2C:18–3**
Expungement of record, **2C:52–3, 2C:52–4**
Fines and penalties, victims of crime compensation board, **2C:43–3.1**
Seasonally leased premises, termination of right to occupy or visit, **2C:43–8.1**
Firearms, warning concerning loaded firearms and minors, failure to deliver or post, **2C:58–16**

PETTY DISORDERLY PERSONS—Cont'd
Fireworks, possession or use, **21:3–8**
Harassment, **2C:33–4**
Jumping bail, **2C:29–7**
Obstructing highways and other public passages, **2C:33–7**
Portable, oil burning heating device, sale, **2C:40–15**
Prostitution, **2C:34–1**
Seasonally leased premises, termination of right to occupy or visit, **2C:43–8.1**
Sentence of imprisonment, **2C:43–8**
Sexual penetration, venereal diseases, diseased persons, **2C:34–5**
Smoking in public, **2C:33–13**

PETTY OFFENSES
Petty Disorderly Persons, generally, this index

PEYOTE
See, also, Drugs and Medicine, generally, this index
Controlled substances, **24:21–1 et seq.**

PHARMACEUTICAL ASSOCIATION
Review committees, immunity from liability, **2A:84A–22.10**

PHARMACEUTICAL PREPARATIONS
Alcohol in preparations unfit for beverage purposes, **33:1–30**

PHARMACIES
Pharmacists, generally, this index

PHARMACISTS
Alcohol, act relating to sale or possession of inapplicable, **33:1–87**
Alcoholic beverages, **33:1–29**
Associations and societies, review committees, immunity from liability, **2A:84A–22.10**
Commercial motor vehicles, license plates, exceptions, **39:4–46**
Controlled substances, **24:21–1 et seq.**
Dispensing, registration, **24:21–9 et seq.**
Controversies or disputes with patients, review committees, immunity from liability, **2A:84A–22.10**
Crimes and offenses, health care claims fraud, **2C:21–4.2, 2C:21–4.3**
Licenses and permits, suspension or revocation, **2C:51–5**
Rehabilitation, order of debarment, rescission, **2C:27–1**
Defined, controlled substances, **24:21–2**
Definitions,
Controlled dangerous substances, **24:21–2**
Controlled substances, **24:21–2**
Delivery vehicles, commercial motor vehicles, license plates, exceptions, **39:4–46**
Ephedrine, losses, reports, **2C:35–26**
Fees, controversies or disputes with patients, review committees, immunity from liability, **2A:84A–22.10**
Fines and penalties, health care claims fraud, **2C:21–4.2, 2C:21–4.3**
Licenses and permits, suspension or revocation, **2C:51–5**
Rehabilitation, order of debarment, rescission, **2C:27–1**
Forfeitures, licenses and permits, health care claims fraud, **2C:51–5**
Health care claims fraud, **2C:21–4.2, 2C:21–4.3**
Licenses and permits, suspension or revocation, **2C:51–5**
Rehabilitation, order of debarment, rescission, **2C:27–1**

PHARMACISTS—Cont'd
Intoxicating liquors, **33:1–29**
Packaged merchandise, sale, **33:1–12**
Labels,
Altering or removing, **24:21–17**
Form of labels, **24:21–17**
Licenses and permits, health care claims fraud, suspension or revocation, **2C:51–5**
Rehabilitation, order of debarment, rescission, **2C:27–1**
Order forms, sale of controlled substances, **24:21–14**
Phenylpropanolamine, losses, reports, **2C:35–26**
Pseudoephedrine, losses, reports, **2C:35–26**
Registration, controlled substances, dispensing, **24:21–9 et seq.**

PHENADOXONE
Controlled substances, **24:21–1 et seq.**

PHENAMPROMIDE
Controlled substances, **24:21–1 et seq.**

PHENAZOCINE
Controlled substances, **24:21–1 et seq.**

PHENCYCLIDINE
Controlled substances, **24:21–1 et seq.**

PHENMETRAZINE
Controlled substances, **24:21–1 et seq.**

PHENOBARBITAL
Controlled substances, **24:21–1 et seq.**

PHENOMORPHAN
Controlled substances, **24:21–1 et seq.**

PHENOPERIDINE
Controlled substances, **24:21–1 et seq.**

PHENYLALANINE
Amphetamine, methamphetamine, possession, manufacturing, **2C:35–28**

PHENYLPROPANOLAMINE
Losses, reports, **2C:35–26**
Possession,
Evidence, **2C:35–27**
Precursors, **2C:35–28**
Sales, limitations, **2C:35–25**

PHILANTHROPIC ORGANIZATIONS
Charitable Organizations and Associations, generally, this index

PHOCLODINE
Controlled substances, **24:21–1**

PHOSGENE
Turnpike project, transportation regulations, **27:23–31**

PHOTOGRAPHS
Arrested persons, indictable offense, **53:1–15**
Child Abuse, this index
Children and minors,
Abuse or neglect,
Color photographs, physical examinations, **9:6–8.31**
Evidence, **9:6–8.46**
Prohibited sexual acts, **2C:24–4**
Consent, nudity, sexual intercourse, invasion of privacy, **2C:14–9**
Contents, **Evidence Rule 1001**
Crimes and Offenses, this index
Drug addicts, **53:1–15**
Evidence, this index

PHOTOGRAPHS—Cont'd
Habitual criminals, 53:1–15
Homicide, victims of crime, 2C:11–3
  Sentence and punishment, rules and regulations, 2C:11–3a
Identification Bureau, generally, this index
Identification cards, intoxicating liquors, purchase, 33:1–81.2
Initial drivers license, color photograph, **39:3–10f**
Intoxicating liquors, identification card, **33:1–81.2**
Investigative detention, **Rule 3:5A–1 et seq.**
Juvenile delinquents and dependents, 2A:4A–61
Lewdness and Obscenity, generally, this index
Narcotic drug offenses, persons arrested, **53:1–18.1**
Nudity, crimes and offenses, invasion of privacy, 2C:14–9
Possession, showing child engaging in prohibited sexual act, fourth degree crime, **2C:24–4**
Prisoners, prior to release, **53:1–20.3**
Registration of persons convicted of offenses relating to narcotics, 2A:169–3
Sexual intercourse, crimes and offenses, invasion of privacy, 2C:14–9
Stolen property, procedure for disposition, **2C:65–1**
Summary of contents, admissibility, **Evidence Rule 1006**
Traffic signs and signals, monitoring, intersections, **39:4–8.12 et seq.**
Victims of crime. Homicide, ante
Viewing, child engaging in prohibited sexual act, fourth degree crime, **2C:24–4**

PHOTOSTATIC COPIES
Alcoholic beverage license application, 33:1–25

PHRASES
Words and Phrases, generally, this index

PHYSICAL CHARACTERISTICS
Investigative detention, crimes and offenses, **Rule 3:5A–1 et seq.**

PHYSICAL CONDITION
Hearsay exception, then existing condition, **Evidence Rule 803**

PHYSICAL EXAMINATIONS
Abuse of children,
  Court order, **9:6–8.31**
  Temporary removal, **9:6–8.30**
Adult Diagnostic and Treatment Center, generally, this index
Crimes and Offenses, this index
Indigent, neglected or abandoned children, auditory or vision problems, juvenile family crisis, 2A:4A–85
Juvenile delinquents and dependents, auditory or vision problems, juvenile family crisis, 2A:4A–85
Privileges and immunities, **Evidence Rules 501, 503**
Radiological examinations, abuse of children, **9:6–8.31**
Refusal, privilege, **2A:84A–19**

PHYSICAL FORCE
Force or Violence, generally, this index

PHYSICAL MEASUREMENTS
Investigative detention, **Rule 3:5A–1 et seq.**

PHYSICAL THERAPISTS
Crimes and offenses, health care claims fraud, **2C:21–4.2, 2C:21–4.3**
  Licenses and permits, suspension or revocation, **2C:51–5**
    Rehabilitation, order of debarment, rescission, **2C:27–1**
Fines and penalties, health care claims fraud, **2C:21–4.2, 2C:21–4.3**
  Licenses and permits, suspension or revocation, **2C:51–5**
    Rehabilitation, order of debarment, rescission, **2C:27–1**
Forfeitures, licenses and permits, health care claims fraud, **2C:51–5**
Health care claims fraud, 2C:21–4.2, 2C:21–4.3
  Licenses and permits, suspension or revocation, **2C:51–5**
    Rehabilitation, order of debarment, rescission, **2C:27–1**
Licenses and permits, health care claims fraud, suspension or revocation, **2C:51–5**
  Rehabilitation, order of debarment, rescission, **2C:27–1**

PHYSICAL THERAPISTS LICENSING ACT OF 1983
Physical Therapists, generally, this index

PHYSICALLY HANDICAPPED PERSONS
Handicapped Persons, generally, this index

PHYSICIANS AND SURGEONS
Actions and proceedings,
  Privileged communications, **2A:84A–22.1 et seq.**
  Review committees, immunity from liability, **2A:84A–22.10**
Aggravated arson, offices, fines and penalties, **2C:17–1**
Attorneys, waiver of doctor patient privilege, application for transfer to disability inactive status, **Rule 1:20–12**
Automobile insurance, no fault insurance, application of law, **39:6A–1 et seq.**
Burns, injuries, reports, 2C:58–8
Carrying injured person to, duty of driver of vehicle involved in accident, 39:4–129
Child Abuse, this index
Children and minors, reports of physical abuse, **9:6–8.10, 9:6–8.16 et seq.**
Commercial bribery and breach of duty, **2C:21–10**
Confidential or privileged information, **2A:84A–22.1 et seq.**
Controlled substances, 24:21–1 et seq.
Controversies or disputes with patients, review committees, immunity from liability, **2A:84A–22.10**
Crimes and offenses,
  Expungement of records, notice of petition, **2C:52–2**
  Health care claims fraud, 2C:21–4.2, 2C:21–4.3
    Licenses and permits, suspension or revocation, **2C:51–5**
      Rehabilitation, order of debarment, rescission, **2C:27–1**
  Records, destruction, **2C:21–4.1**
  Solicitation, disasters or accidents, **2C:40A–4**
  Unlicensed practice, **2C:21–20**
Damages,
  Reports of child abuse, immunity, **9:6–8.20**
  Review committees, immunity from liability, **2A:84A–22.10**

PHYSICIANS AND SURGEONS—Cont'd
Definitions, controlled substances, 2C:35–2, 24:21–2
Dentists and Dentistry, generally, this index
Drug dependent persons, reports, 24:21–39
Drugs and medicine, definitions, controlled dangerous substances, 24:21–2
Emergencies, epilepsy and similar conditions, reports to motor vehicle division, **39:3–10.4**
Fees,
  Controversies or disputes with patients, review committees, immunity from liability, **2A:84A–22.1**
  Drunken driving prosecutions, fee for testifying in, 39:5–39
Fines and penalties,
  Epilepsy and similar conditions, failure to report to motor vehicle division, **39:3–10.8**
  Health care claims fraud, 2C:21–4.2, **2C:21–4.3**
    Licenses and permits, suspension or revocation, **2C:51–5**
      Rehabilitation, order of debarment, rescission, **2C:27–1**
Forfeitures, licenses and permits, fraud, **2C:51–5**
Health care claims fraud, 2C:21–4.2, 2C:21–4.3
  Licenses and permits, suspension or revocation, **2C:51–5**
    Rehabilitation, order of debarment, rescission, **2C:27–1**
Hospitals, generally, this index
Licenses and permits,
  Health care claims fraud, suspension or revocation, **2C:51–5**
    Rehabilitation, order of debarment, rescission, **2C:27–1**
  Unlicensed practice, 2C:21–20
Medical advisory panel, **39:2–13 et seq.**
  Motor vehicles division, liability for reports, **39:2–16**
Medical Care and Treatment, generally, this index
Member of clinic to study mental and physical conditions before sentence of convicted persons, 2A:164–1
Motor vehicle division, medical advisory panel, liability for reports, **39:2–16**
Motor vehicles,
  Drivers duty to take injured person to physician, 39:4–129
  Fee for testifying in drunken driving prosecutions, 39:5–39
  Right of way, 39:4–93
  Speed on emergency call, 39:4–102
Narcotics, reports, drug dependent persons, **24:21–39**
No fault insurance, application of law, **39:6A–1 et seq.**
Notice, supervisory treatment programs, enrollment, 2C:43–12
Optometrists, generally, this index
Physical Examinations, generally, this index
Podiatrists and Podiatry, generally, this index
Prescriptions, controlled substances, 24:21–15
Privileges and immunities, **Evidence Rule 506**
  Controlled substances, attempt to obtain, exception to privilege, 2C:35–17
  Exceptions, incapacitated persons, **2A:84A–22.3**
  Report of child abuse, 9:6–8.20
  Review committees, immunity from liability, **2A:84A–22.10**
Protective custody, abused children, 9:6–8.16

PHYSICIANS AND SURGEONS—Cont'd
Psychologists and Psychology, generally, this
index
Qualifications, peer review committee, immuni-
ty from liability, **2A:84A–22.10**
Records and recordation,
Destruction, **2C:21–4.1**
Privileged communications, **2A:84A–22.5**
Registration, controlled substances, dispensa-
tion, **24:21–9 et seq.**
Reports,
Children, physical abuse, **9:6–8.10, 9:6–8.16
et seq.**
Drug dependent persons, **24:21–39**
Epilepsy and similar conditions, reports to
division of motor vehicles, **39:3–10.4**
Medical advisory panel, motor vehicles divi-
sion, immunity, **39:2–16**
Protective custody, abused child, **9:6–8.17**
Public officials, privileged communications,
2A:84A–22.5
Right of way of vehicles operated by, through
processions, **39:4–93**
Solicitation, disasters or accidents, crimes and
offenses, **2C:40A–4**
Speed of physicians motor vehicle on emergen-
cy call, **39:4–102**
Supervisory treatment programs, notice of en-
rollment, **2C:43–12**
Time, solicitation, disasters or accidents,
2C:40A–4
Unlicensed practice, **2C:21–20**
Vehicles, right of way through procession,
39:4–93
Veterinarians, generally, this index

PICTURES
Photographs, generally, this index

PILOT PROGRAMS
Traffic signs and signals, monitoring, intersections, **39:4–8.12 et seq.**

PIMINODINE
Controlled substances, **24:21–1 et seq.**

PIMPS
Generally, **2C:34–1**

PINELANDS AREAS
Outdoor advertising, zoning and planning,
27:5–9.1
Zoning and planning, outdoor advertising,
27:5–9.1

PIPES AND PIPELINES
Brewers cleaning and repairing of pipes for
retail licensee, **33:1–43.1**
Theft of services, **2C:20–8**

PIRACY
New Jersey Antipiracy Act, **2C:21–21**

PIRITRAMIDE
Controlled substances, **24:21–1 et seq.**

PISTOL CLUBS
Unlawful possession of weapons, exemption,
2C:39–6

PISTOL GRIP
Definitions, **2C:39–1**

PISTOLS
Weapons, generally, this index

PLACARDS
Motor carriers, radioactive materials, posting
placards, **39:5B–18**

PLACE OF ABODE
Residence and Residents, generally, this index

PLACE OF BUSINESS
Definitions, driving schools, **39:12–1**

PLACE OF IMPRISONMENT
Generally, **2C:43–10**

PLACEMENT
Children and Minors, this index

PLAINTIFF
Parties, generally, this index

PLANK ROADS AND BRIDGES
Turnpikes, generally, this index

PLANNING
Zoning and Planning, generally, this index

PLANS AND SPECIFICATIONS
Burglar tools, publishing, **2C:5–5**
Explosives,
Magazines, **21:1A–136**
Manufacturers, **21:1A–135**
Juvenile Delinquents, this index
Motor Vehicle Commission, this index
Publishing, burglar tools, **2C:5–5**
Zoning and Planning, generally, this index

PLANTS
Definitions, controlled substances, **2C:35–2**

PLASTIC SURGERY
Drivers licenses, color photographs, update,
39:3–10f

PLATES OR MARKERS
Motor Vehicles, this index

PLAYER
Definitions, gambling, **2C:37–1**

**PLAYGROUNDS AND RECREATION
PLACES**
Intersections, stop intersections, designation,
marking, **39:4–197**
Parks and Parkways, generally, this index
Sexually oriented businesses, zoning and plan-
ning, **2C:34–7**
Stop intersections, designation, marking,
39:4–197
Turnpike authority, power to acquire property,
27:23–5
Zoning and planning, sexually oriented busi-
nesses, **2C:34–7**

PLEA AGREEMENTS
Crimes and offenses, **Rule 3:9–3**
Municipal courts, **Rule 7:6–2**
Municipal prosecutors, **2B:25–11**

PLEADINGS
Address of parties, **Rule 1:4–1**
Adoption by reference, statements and exhibits,
Rule 1:4–3
Affidavits, format, **Rule 1:4–4**
Amendments, municipal courts, **Rule 7:14–2**
Assignments, copies, annexation to complaints,
foreclosure actions, **Rule 1:4–3**
Attorneys, this index
Bonds, copies, annexation to complaints, fore-
closure actions, **Rule 1:4–3**

PLEADINGS—Cont'd
Briefs, generally, this index
Caption, **Rule 1:4–1**
Case information statement, filing with, **Rule
1:5–6**
Complaints, generally, this index
Copies of documents, exhibits, **Rule 1:4–3**
Crimes and Offenses, this index
Date of signature, **Rule 1:4–5**
Delay, interposing for delay, **Rule 1:4–8**
Domicile and residence, caption, **Rule 1:4–1**
Ex parte relief, verification of pleadings, **Rule
1:4–7**
Exhibits, adoption by reference, **Rule 1:4–3**
Filing, signatures, date on which signed, **Rule
1:4–5**
Foreclosure, exhibits, copies, **Rule 1:4–3**
Forfeitures, interest in seized property, **2C:64–3**
Format, **Rule 1:4–1 et seq.**
Incorporation by reference, verification, **Rule
1:4–7**
Interposing for delay, **Rule 1:4–8**
Malice, captions, **Rule 1:4–1**
Mortgages, copies, annexation to complaints,
foreclosure actions, **Rule 1:4–3**
Motions, generally, this index
Motor vehicle and traffic laws, taking of plea
by clerk or deputy clerk authorized, **39:5–6**
Municipal courts, **Rule 7:7–1**
Amendment, **Rule 7:14–2**
Names, typed or stamped names, **Rule 1:4–6**
Numbered paragraphs, **Rule 1:4–2**
Paragraphs, **Rule 1:4–2**
Professional corporations, corporate name,
Rule 1:21–1A
Separate counts, **Rule 1:4–2**
Service, **Rule 1:5–1 et seq.**
Numerous defendants, **Rule 1:5–5**
Signatures, **Rule 1:4–5**
Effect of signature, **Rule 1:4–8**
Name typed or stamped beneath, **Rule 1:4–6**
Size of filed papers, **Rule 1:4–9**
Statements, adoption by reference, **Rule 1:4–3**
Striking, frivolous litigation, **Rule 1:4–8**
Tax sale certificates, copies, annexation to com-
plaints, foreclosure actions, **Rule 1:4–3**
Verification, **Rule 1:4–7**
Weight of filed papers, **Rule 1:4–9**

PLEAS
Crimes and Offenses, this index
Guilty pleas. Crimes and Offenses, this index
Municipal Courts, this index

PLEDGES
Alcoholic beverage licenses, **33:1–26**
Intoxicating liquor licenses, **33:1–26**
Turnpike projects tolls or revenues, **27:23–8,
27:23–16**

PNEUMATIC TIRE
Definitions, Motor Vehicle Law, **39:1–1**

PODIATRISTS AND PODIATRY
Controversies or disputes with patients, review
committees, immunity from liability,
2A:84A–22.10
Crimes and offenses,
Expungement of records, notice of petition,
2C:52–2
Records, destruction, **2C:21–4.1**
Unlicensed practice, **2C:21–20**
Licenses and permits, unlicensed practice,
2C:21–20
Notice, supervisory treatment programs, enroll-
ment, **2C:43–12**

PODIATRISTS AND PODIATRY—Cont'd
Records and recordation, destruction, 2C:21–4.1
Supervisory treatment programs, notice of enrollment, 2C:43–12
Unlicensed practice, 2C:21–20

POINT OF INTERCEPTION
Definitions, wiretapping and electronic surveillance, 2A:156A–2

POISON BAIT
Poisons, generally, this index

POISONED LIQUORS
Manufacture, transportation, sale, 33:3–9, 33:3–10

POISONS
Arsenic, turnpike project, transportation regulations, 27:23–31
Children and Minors, this index
Ether, turnpike project, transportation regulation, 27:23–31
Food or candy, 2C:12–2
Gas,
  Causing or risking widespread injury or damage, 2C:17–2
  Criminal mischief, 2C:17–3
Hazardous Substances and Waste, generally, this index
Liquors, manufacture, transportation or sale, 33:3–9, 33:3–10
Potassium cyanide, turnpike project, transportation regulations, 27:23–31
Prussic acid, turnpike project, transportation regulations, 27:23–31
Terrorism, 2C:17–2, 2C:38–3

POLE TRAILER
Definitions, Motor Vehicle Law, 39:1–1
Rear lamps, 39:3–61
Traffic hazard warning signals, 39:3–64

POLES
Municipalities, this index
Public Utilities, this index

POLICE AND FIREMENS RETIREMENT SYSTEM
Motor vehicles division, inspectors, transfer, 39:2–9.5

POLICE AND POLICE DEPARTMENTS
Actions and proceedings, stolen property, 2C:65–3
Administration, law or governmental functions, obstruction, 2C:29–1 et seq.
Aged persons, abuse or neglect, treatment and prevention training course, 2C:25–20
Aggravated assault, 2C:12–1
Alarms, false alarms, 2C:33–3 et seq.
All terrain vehicles, furnishing identification, 39:3C–9
Animals, owned or used by officers, killing or harming, 2C:29–3.1
Arrest, generally, this index
Assault, 2C:12–1
Associations and societies, intoxicating liquors, club licenses, 33:1–25.1, 33:1–25.2
Bridge police, county bridge commission appointees, 27:19–36.3
Burns, injuries, reports, 2C:58–8
Cameras, motor vehicles, tampering, 2C:28–7
Certificates and certification,
  Approval of motor vehicle to be displayed on request, 39:8–6

POLICE AND POLICE DEPARTMENTS —Cont'd
Certificates and certification—Cont'd
  Motor vehicle registration, surrender, suspended or revoked certificates, 39:5–35
Chief of police,
  Chemical analyses forms, arrested motorists, breath, 39:4–50.3
  Fingerprints and fingerprinting,
    Arrested persons, 53:1–15
    Weapons, licenses and permits, 2C:58–3
  Narcotic offenses, fingerprinting and photographing persons arrested, 53:1–18.1
  Notice, continued violation of criminal laws, 2A:152–12, 2A:152–13
  Photographs, arrested persons, 53:1–15
  Service of subpoenas, alcoholic beverage control division, 33:1–36
  Weapons, licenses and permits, 2C:58–3
Child Abuse, this index
Civil rights, crimes and offenses, racial profiling, 2C:30–5 et seq.
Club licenses, intoxicating liquors, nonprofit organizations, 33:1–25.1, 33:1–25.2
Compensation and salaries, society for prevention of cruelty to children, acting agents, 9:6–7
Complaints, domestic violence prevention, temporary restraining orders, service with, 2C:25–28
Convicted offenders,
  Hiring, 2A:168A–6
  Rehabilitation and employment, application of law, 2A:168A–6
Counties,
  Complaints,
    Junk yards, 39:11–11
    Motor vehicle security responsibility, 39:6–55
  Enforcement, motor vehicle inspections, 39:8–9
  Intoxicating liquors, employment, 33:1–26.1
County bridge commission, 27:19–36.3
County Detectives and Investigators, generally, this index
Crimes and offenses, racial profiling, 2C:30–5 et seq.
Custody, stolen property, 2C:65–1 et seq.
Deadly force, grand jury, instructions to jury, 2B:22–9
Definitions, Nonresident Violator Compact, 39:5F–4
Denial, record expungement, 2C:52–14
Diligence in detection of violations of alcoholic beverage law, 33:1–71
Disability, retired officers, weapons, possession, exceptions, 2C:39–6
Discipline, strip or body cavity searches, 2A:161A–6
Disclosure, expungement order, 2C:52–30
Discrimination, racial profiling, crimes and offenses, 2C:30–5 et seq.
Disorderly persons, arrest without process, 2A:169–3
Diversion programs, record expungement, 2C:52–20
Dogs, owned or used by officers, killing or harming, 2C:29–3.1
Electronic devices, motor vehicles, tampering, 2C:28–7
Entrapment, 2C:2–12
Escape, knowingly or recklessly permitting, 2C:29–5
Evidence, stolen property, 2C:65–1
Exemption, record expungement, 2C:52–2
Explosives, application of law, 21:1A–141

POLICE AND POLICE DEPARTMENTS —Cont'd
Expungement, records, 2C:52–1 et seq.
False public alarms, 2C:33–3 et seq.
False reports, 2C:28–4
Fees, record expungement, 2C:52–29
Fictitious reports, 2C:28–4
Fingerprinting, certain arrested persons, 53:1–15
Force or violence,
  Grand jury, instructions to jury, 2B:22–9
  Obstructing administration of law or governmental functions, 2C:29–1 et seq.
Fraternal societies, intoxicating liquors, club licenses, 33:1–25.1, 33:1–25.2
Fresh Pursuit Law, generally, this index
Grand jury, instructions to jury, force or violence, 2B:22–9
Handicapped persons, abuse or neglect, treatment and prevention training course, 2C:25–20
Hearings, record expungement, 2C:52–9 et seq.
Hindering apprehension or prosecution, 2C:29–3
Human Services Department, generally, this index
Indictable offenses, record expungement, 2C:52–2
Information concerning offenses, forwarding to bureau of identification, 53:1–20.2
Inspectors and inspections, records, expungement, 2C:52–19
Intimidation, obstructing administration of law or governmental functions, 2C:29–1 et seq.
Intoxicating liquors,
  Employment, 33:1–26.1
  Nonprofit organizations, club licenses, 33:1–25.1, 33:1–25.2
Jury service, grand jury, grounds for excuse, 2B:21–2
Justifiable force, grand jury, instructions to jury, 2B:22–9
Juvenile delinquents, detention at police station, **Rule 5:21–4**
Laser sighting system device, aggravated assault, 2C:12–1
Licenses and permits, intoxicating liquors, nonprofit organizations, 33:1–25.1, 33:1–25.2
Mistake, force or violence, grand jury, instructions to jury, 2B:22–9
Motor vehicle commission, communication with police, 39:2–3
Motor vehicles,
  Accidents,
    Notice, 39:4–130
    Reports, 39:4–131
  Authorized emergency vehicles, status, 39:1–1
  Electronic devices, tampering, 2C:28–7
  Fleeing or attempting to elude police officers, 2C:29–2
  Master keys or devices, 2C:5–6
  Motor vehicle security responsibility, 39:6–55
  Notice, accident involving injury or death, 39:4–130
  Radio, interception of police, fire or emergency medical communication, used to commit crime, 2C:33–21 et seq.
  Removal of unregistered vehicle from public highway, 39:3–4
  Sale of used police cars, 39:10–9.1, 39:10–9.2
  Speed law, exemption, 39:4–103
  Tampering, electronic devices, 2C:28–7
  Weights and measurements, roadside examinations, 39:3–84.3
Municipal Courts, generally, this index

POLICE AND POLICE DEPARTMENTS —Cont'd

Negligence, force or violence, grand jury, instructions to jury, **2B:22–9**

Nonprofit organizations, intoxicating liquors, club licenses, **33:1–25.1, 33:1–25.2**

Notice,
Application for correction, motor vehicle title papers, **39:10–16**
Domestic violence prevention, **2C:25–23**
Release of prisoner, to department originally arresting, **53:1–20.4**
Stolen property, disposition, **2C:65–2**
Vehicle or street car accidents, **39:4–130**

Numbers and numbering, stolen property, **2C:65–1**

Obstruction, administration of law or governmental function, **2C:29–1 et seq.**

Orders,
Record expungement, **2C:52–11, 2C:52–26 et seq.**
Stolen property disposition, **2C:65–3**

Outdoor advertising, duties, **27:5–23**

Outside employment, intoxicating liquors, **33:1–26.1**

Part time employment, intoxicating liquors, **33:1–26.1**

Personalized handguns, **2C:58–2.5**

Petitions, record expungement, **2C:52–7 et seq.**

Privileges and immunities, domestic violence prevention, arrest, **2C:25–22**

Process, record expungement, **2C:52–10**

Racial profiling, crimes and offenses, **2C:30–5 et seq.**

Radar device to monitor car speed, police, fire or emergency medical communication system defined to exclude, **2C:33–23**

Radio,
Definition of police, fire or emergency medical communication system excluding radar, **2C:33–23**
Interception of message, crimes and offenses, **2C:33–21 et seq.**
Possession of radio receiving police, message during commission of crime, fourth degree crime, **2C:33–22**

Railroad crossings, enforcement of regulation as to stopping of motor vehicles or school buses, **39:5–1**

Recklessness, force or violence, grand jury, instructions to jury, **2B:22–9**

Records and recordation,
Expungement, **2C:52–1 et seq.**
Stolen property, **2C:65–1**

Refraining to submit reports, **2C:29–4**

Rehabilitated convicted offenders,
Employment, application of law, **2A:168A–6**
Hiring, **2A:168A–6**

Release,
Record expungement, **2C:52–19**
Stolen property, **2C:65–2**

Religious societies, intoxicating liquors, club licenses, **33:1–25.1, 33:1–25.2**

Reports,
Abuse of children, **9:6–8.25**
Confidential or privileged information, **Rule 1:38–3**
Crimes and offenses, discovery, **Rule 3:13–3**
Domestic violence prevention, **2C:25–24**
False reports, **2C:28–4**
Motor vehicle accidents, **39:4–131**
Duty of garageman or repairman, **39:4–132**
Refraining, pecuniary gain, **2C:29–4**

Resisting arrest, **2C:29–2**

POLICE AND POLICE DEPARTMENTS —Cont'd

Retirement and pensions, firearms, possession, **2C:39–6**

Sales, stolen property, **2C:65–3**

Search Warrants, generally, this index

Searches and Seizures, generally, this index

Shoplifting, arrest, custody, powers, **2C:20–11**

Snowmobiles, furnishing identification, **39:3C–9**

State Parks and Parkways, this index

State Police, generally, this index

Statements, expungement petitions, **2C:52–8**

Stolen property, disposition, **2C:65–1 et seq.**

Street gangs, arrest, fingerprints and fingerprinting, **53:1–15.1**

Street Railways, this index

Supervisory treatment programs, record expungement, **2C:52–20**

Tampering, motor vehicles, electronic devices, **2C:28–7**

Teams, domestic violence prevention, **2C:25–20**

Traffic Rules and Regulations, generally, this index

Training,
Aged and handicapped persons, abuse or neglect treatment and prevention, **2C:25–20**
Domestic violence prevention, **2C:25–20**

Turnpikes, tolls for use of road, **27:23–40**

Unclaimed property, disposition, **2C:65–3**

Use of force, **2C:3–7**

Used police cars, sales, **39:10–9.1, 39:10–9.2**

Vehicles. Motor vehicles, generally, ante

Vessels, fleeing or attempting to elude police officers, **2C:29–2**

Veterans organizations, intoxicating liquors, club licenses, **33:1–25.1, 33:1–25.2**

Videotapes, motor vehicles, tampering, **2C:28–7**

Violence, obstructing administration of law or governmental functions, **2C:29–1 et seq.**

Violent criminal apprehension program. Identification Bureau, this index

Weapons,
Personalized handguns, **2C:58–2.5**
Retired officers, **2C:39–6**
Unlawful possession, exemptions, **2C:39–6**

Whistles, stopping vehicles on signal, **39:4–122**

POLICE ATHLETIC LEAGUE, INC.

Motor vehicles, registration fee exemption, **39:3–27**

POLICE COURTS AND MAGISTRATES

Municipal Courts, generally, this index

POLICE POWER

Bridge tenders, county bridges and viaducts, **27:19–13**

Correction officers, **2A:154–4**

County correction officers, **2A:154–3**

Parole officers, **2A:154–4**

Sheriffs officers, **2A:154–3**

POLICE TRAINING COMMISSION

Firearms, training course, unlawful possession, exemption, **2C:39–6**

POLICIES

Definitions, gambling, **2C:37–1**

Insurance, this index

POLITICAL ACTIVITIES

Elections, generally, this index

POLITICAL PARTIES

Bribery and Corruption, generally, this index

POLITICAL PARTIES—Cont'd

Corrupt influence. Bribery and Corruption, generally, this index

County prosecutors, prohibition, **2A:158–21**

Threats and other improper influence, **2C:27–3**

POLITICAL SUBDIVISIONS

See, also,
Counties, generally, this index
Municipalities, generally, this index

Administration, law or governmental functions, obstruction, **2C:29–1 et seq.**

All terrain vehicles, registration, exemptions, **39:3C–6**

Bribery and Corruption, generally, this index

Cannons, antique cannons, possession, **2C:39–6**

Civil Service, generally, this index

Contracts, crimes and offenses, fraud, **2C:21–34**

Corrupt influence. Bribery and Corruption, generally, this index

Counties, generally, this index

Crimes and offenses, contracts, fraud, **2C:21–34**

Force and violence, obstructing administration of law or governmental functions, **2C:29–1 et seq.**

Intimidation, obstructing administration of law or governmental functions, **2C:29–1 et seq.**

Motor vehicles, exemption from motor vehicle security responsibility law, **39:6–54**

Municipalities, generally, this index

Obstruction, administration of law or governmental function, **2C:29–1 et seq.**

Schools and School Districts, generally, this index

Snowmobiles, registration, exemptions, **39:3C–6**

Tow trucks and towing companies, taxation, **39:3–84.12**

Traffic Rules and Regulations, generally, this index

Violence, obstructing administration of law or governmental functions, **2C:29–1 et seq.**

POLLING OF JURY

Generally, **Rule 1:8–10**

POLLUTION

Adopt a beach program. Beaches and Beach Fronts, this index

Air Pollution, generally, this index

Environmental Protection, generally, this index

Solid Waste, generally, this index

Water Pollution, generally, this index

PONIES

Horses, generally, this index

POOR

Indigent Persons, generally, this index

POOR PERSON

Indigent Persons, generally, this index

POPPY STRAW

See, also, Drugs and Medicine, generally, this index

Controlled substances, **24:21–1 et seq.**

Definitions,
Controlled dangerous substances, **2C:35–2, 24:21–2**
Controlled substances, **24:21–2**

POPULAR NAME LAWS

Alcoholic Beverage Control Act, **33:1–1 et seq.**

AntiDrug Profiteering Act, **2C:35A–1 et seq.**

Antipiracy Act, **2C:21–21**

Antitrust Act, **56:9–1 et seq.**

POPULAR NAME LAWS—Cont'd

Automobile Insurance Cost Reduction Act, **39:6A–1.1 et seq.**

Automobile Reparation Reform Act, **39:6A–1 et seq.**

Automobiles,
Motor Vehicle Certificate of Ownership Law, **39:10–1 et seq.**
Passenger Automobile Seat Belt Usage Act, **39:3–76.2e et seq.**

Code of Criminal Justice, **2C:1–1 et seq.**

Code of Juvenile Justice, **2A:4A–20 et seq.**

Commercial Driver License Act, **39:3–10.9 et seq.**

Comprehensive Drug Reform Act, **2C:35–1 et seq.**

Comprehensive Enforcement Program Fund Act, **2B:19–1 et seq.**

Controlled Dangerous Substances Act, **24:21–1 et seq.**

County Detectives and County Investigators Act, **2A:157–1 et seq.**

Criminal Justice Code, **2C:1–1 et seq.**

Criminal procedure, **2A:152–1 et seq.**

Detainers, interstate agreement on detainers, **2A:159A–1 et seq.**

DNA Database and Databank Act, **53:1–20.17 et seq.**

Driver License Compact Act, **39:5D–1 et seq.**

Drug Dealer Liability Act, **2C:35B–1 et seq.**

Drunk Driving Victims Bill of Rights, **39:4–50.9 et seq.**

Explosives Act, **21:1A–128 et seq.**

Extradition, Uniform Criminal Extradition Law, **2A:160–6 et seq.**

Federal Clean Air Mandate Compliance Act, **39:8–41 et seq.**

Financial Responsibility Act (Motor Vehicles), **39:6–23 et seq.**

Fireworks Regulation Law, **21:2–1 et seq.**

Flammable Fabrics Act, **2A:123–4**

Florences Law, **39:4–50**

Fresh pursuit,
Uniform Act on Intrastate Fresh Pursuit, **2A:156–1 et seq.**
Uniform Law on Fresh Pursuit, **2A:155–1 et seq.**

Graves Act, weapons, **2C:43–6**

Hero Act, anatomical gifts, **39:2–3.4, 39:3–12.2 et seq.**

Highway Weight Limitation Act, **39:3–84 et seq.**

Hit and Run Statute, **39:4–129**

Identification Cards for Nondrivers Act, **39:3–29.2 et seq.**

Insurance,
Automobile Reparation Reform Act, **39:6A–1 et seq.**
No fault insurance, New Jersey Automobile Reparation Reform Act, **39:6A–1 et seq.**

Interstate agreement on detainers, **2A:159A–1 et seq.**

Juvenile Justice Code, **2A:4A–20 et seq.**

Kyleighs Law, **39:3–13, 39:3–13.2a, 39:3–13.4, 39:3–13.8**

Law Enforcement Officers Memorial Scholarship Act, **39:3–27.123 et seq.**

Law Enforcement Officers Protection Act, **2A:4A–43.4, 2C:11–3, 2C:43–2.3, 2C:43–3.3**

Left Turning Act, **39:4–123 et seq.**

Local Option Act (alcoholic beverages), **33:1–44 et seq.**

Long Arm Act, **39:7–1 et seq.**

Malt Alcoholic Beverage Practices Act, **33:1–93.12 et seq.**

Megans Law, **2C:7–1 et seq.**

POPULAR NAME LAWS—Cont'd

Michaels Law, **39:4–50**

Motor Vehicle Certificate of Ownership Law, **39:10–1 et seq.**

Motor Vehicle Inspection Law, **39:8–1 et seq.**

Motor vehicle insurance, Automobile Reparation Reform Act, **39:6A–1 et seq.**

Motor Vehicle Junk Law, **39:11–1 et seq.**

Motor Vehicle Security and Customer Service Act, **39:2A–1 et seq.**

Motor Vehicle Security Responsibility Law, **39:6–23 et seq.**

Motor vehicles, **39:4–1 et seq.**
Nonresident Violator Compact, **39:5F–1 et seq.**
Passenger Automobile Seat Belt Usage Act, **39:3–76.2e et seq.**

National Crime Prevention and Privacy Compact, **53:1–32**

Newspapermans Privilege Act (Disclosure), **2A:84A–21**

Nicole's Law, sex offenses, **2C:14–11, 2C:14–12, 2C:44–8, 2C:45–1, 2C:45–2**

No Early Release Act, **2C:43–7.2**

No fault insurance, Automobile Reparation Reform Act, **39:6A–1 et seq.**

Nonresident Motorist Service Act, **39:7–1 et seq.**

Nonresident Violator Compact, motor vehicles, **39:5F–1 et seq.**

Out of State Motorist Act, **39:7–1 et seq.**

Out of state parolee supervision, **2A:168–17**

Parking Offenses Adjudication Act, **39:4–139.2 et seq.**

Parolee supervision, Uniform Act for Out of State Parolee Supervision, **2A:168–17**

Passenger Automobile Seat Belt Usage Act, **39:3–76.2e et seq.**

Persistent Offenders Accountability Act, **2C:43–7, 2C:43–7.1**

PIP (Personal Injury Protection Automobile), **39:6A–4**

Prevention of Domestic Violence Act, **2C:25–17 et seq.**

Public Corruption Profiteering Penalty Act, **2C:30–8**

Right and Left Hand Turns, **39:4–123**

School Bus Enhanced Safety Inspection Act, **39:3B–18 et seq.**

Seat belts, Passenger Automobile Seat Belt Usage Act, **39:3–76.2e et seq.**

Security Responsibility Law (Motor Vehicles), **39:6–23 et seq.**

September 11th, 2001 Antiterrorism Act, **2C:38–1 et seq.**

Sixty Five MPH Speed Limit Implementation Act, **39:4–98.3 et seq.**

Skinners and Michelles Law, **2C:11–5.1, 2C:12–1.1, 2C:44–1**

Substituted Service Act, **39:7–1 et seq.**

Task Force on Child Abuse and Neglect Act, **9:6–8.74 et seq.**

Traffic rules and regulations, Nonresident Violator Compact, **39:5F–1 et seq.**

Turnpike Authority Act, **27:23–1 et seq.**

Uniform Act for Out of State Parolee Supervision, **2A:168–17**

Uniform Act on Intrastate Fresh Pursuit, **2A:156–1 et seq.**

Uniform Criminal Extradition Law, **2A:160–6 et seq.**

Uniform Law on Fresh Pursuit, **2A:155–1 et seq.**

Unsatisfied Claim and Judgment Fund Law, **39:6–61 et seq.**

Violent Predator Incapacitation Act, **2C:43–6.4**

POPULAR NAME LAWS—Cont'd

Weight Limitation Act, **39:3–84 et seq.**

Wiretapping and Electronic Surveillance Control Act, **2A:156A–1 et seq.**

PORNOGRAPHY

Lewdness and Obscenity, generally, this index

PORTABLE EMERGENCY WARNING DEVICES

Commercial motor vehicles and buses, **39:3–64**

PORTABLE OIL BURNING HEATING DEVICES

Generally, **2C:40–6 et seq.**

PORTERS

Presumption, fitness for beverage purposes and alcoholic content, **33:1–1.1**

POSSE

State police, use as posse prohibited, **53:2–1**

POSSESSION

Alcoholic Beverages, this index

Antique slot machines, **2C:37–7**

Chemicals, chemistry and chemists, industrial chemicals, **2C:35–29**

Child pornography, photograph, film, videotape, fourth degree crime, **2C:24–4**

Contraband, forfeiture, **2C:64–1 et seq.**

Controlled Substances, this index

Definitions, Code of Criminal Justice, **2C:2–1**

Drugs and Medicine, this index

Electronic, mechanical or other device, interception of wire, electronic or oral communication, crimes and offenses, **2A:156A–5**

Explosives, this index

Forgery devices, **2C:21–1**

Identity theft, personal identifying information, **2C:21–17.3**

Industrial chemicals, **2C:35–29**

Landlord and Tenant, this index

Lottery tickets, **2C:37–6.1**

Motor vehicles or parts, marks or numbers, changed or destroyed, crimes and offenses, **2C:17–6**

Motorized bicycles, operators, drivers license, insurance identification card, and registration certificate, **39:4–14.3**

Third degree crimes, wiretapping and electronic surveillance, **2A:156A–5**

Traffic control preemption devices, **2C:40–24**

Weapons, this index

POST OFFICE

Mail and Mailing, generally, this index

POSTCONSUMER WASTE

Recycling. Solid Waste, this index

POSTCONVICTION RELIEF

Appeals In Criminal Prosecutions, this index

Crimes and Offenses, this index

POSTING

Alcoholic beverage control division director, notice of hearing after seizure of stills, **33:2–4**

Fireworks, manufacturers and manufacturing, certificate of registration, **21:2–22**

Motor carriers, placards, radioactive materials, **39:5B–18**

Motor Vehicles, this index

Trespass, generally, this index

POSTING—Cont'd
Warning notices, harmful effects, drinking during pregnancy, class C license holders, alcoholic beverages, **33:1–12a**
　Violation of provisions, fines and penalties, **33:1–12b**

POSTS
Alcoholic beverage license and fee exemption, retail sale, **33:1–27**
State highway, permission required for guide posts in, **39:4–199**

POTABLE WATERS
Water Supply Plants and Systems, generally, this index

POTASSIUM CYANIDE
Poisons, this index

POULTRY
Farm products as including, **39:3–25**
Transportation, truck used for transportation of solid waste,
　Cleansing and sanitization required, **48:13A–12.1**
　Crime of third degree, penalties, **48:13A–12.2**

POUNDS
Crimes and offenses, destruction of animals, **4:22–19**
Cruelty to animals, offenses, **4:22–19**
Destruction of animals, **4:22–19, 4:22–19.2**

POVERTY
Indigent Persons, generally, this index

POWDER
Explosives, generally, this index
Fireworks, generally, this index

POWER
Electricity and Electric Companies, generally, this index
Public Utilities, generally, this index

POWER BOATS
Vessels, generally, this index

POWER PLANTS
Public Utilities, generally, this index

PRACTICAL NURSING
Nurses, generally, this index

PRACTICE OF LAW
Attorneys, this index

PRACTICING PSYCHOLOGY LICENSING ACT
Psychologists and Psychology, generally, this index

PRACTITIONERS
Definitions, controlled substances, **2C:35–2, 24:21–2**

PRAYERS
Healing by prayer, automobile insurance, no fault insurance, application of law, **39:6A–1 et seq.**

PRECEDENT
Unpublished opinions, **Rule 1:36–3**

PREDATORY ANIMALS
Fish and Game, generally, this index

PREDISPOSITIONAL EVALUATIONS
Juvenile delinquents and dependents, **2A:4A–42**

PREDOMINATELY RESIDENTIAL
Definitions, liquefied petroleum gas, **21:1B–3**

PREEMPTION
Local laws or regulations, preemption by code criminal justice, **2C:1–5**

PREGNANCY
AIDS (Acquired Immune Deficiency Syndrome), generally, this index
Alcoholic beverages, warning notices, pregnant women, harmful effects, class C licenses, **33:1–12a**
　Fines, **33:1–12b**
Birth defects, drinking during pregnancy, dangers of, warning notices, posting requirements, alcoholic beverages, **33:1–12a**
Cloning, crimes and offenses, **2C:11A–1**
Crimes and offenses, cloning, **2C:11A–1**
Fetal alcohol syndrome, warning notice, posting, alcoholic beverages, **33:1–12a**

PREJUDICE
Discrimination, generally, this index

PREJUDICIAL EVIDENCE
Exclusion, **Evidence Rule 403**

PRELIMINARY HEARINGS
Drivers license or motor vehicle registration, suspension or revocation, **39:5–30**

PREMISES
Definitions, intoxicating liquor law, **33:1–1**
Force, defense of premises, **2C:3–6**
Nuisance, **2C:33–12**

PREMISES OF A STORE OR RETAIL MERCANTILE ESTABLISHMENT
Definitions, shoplifting, **2C:20–11**

PREMIUMS
Motor Vehicle Insurance, this index

PRENATAL AND POSTNATAL CARE
Drinking during pregnancy, harmful effects, warning notices, posting requirements, class C license holders, alcoholic beverages, **33:1–12a**
Fetal alcohol syndrome, harmful effects, drinking during pregnancy, warning notices, posting requirements, class C license holders, alcoholic beverages, **33:1–12a**

PREPONDERANCE OF EVIDENCE
Civil actions under Criminal Code, burden of proof, **2C:1–13**
Insanity defense, **2C:4–1**

PREROGATIVE COURT
Superior Court, generally, this index

PREROGATIVE WRITS
Actions in lieu of, enlargement of time, **Rule 1:3–4**
Motor Vehicles Junk Yard Law, orders, **39:11–10**

PRESCRIPTION
Limitation of Actions, generally, this index

PRESCRIPTIONS
Generally, **24:21–15**
Alcoholic beverages, use by druggists and hospitals, **33:1–29**

PRESCRIPTIONS—Cont'd
Blanks,
　Forgery, **2C:21–1**
　Theft, **2C:20–2**
Crimes and offenses, prescription legend drugs, **2C:35–10.5**
Disorderly persons, **2C:35–24**
　Controlled dangerous substances, **2C:35–24**
　Prescription legend drugs, **2C:35–10.5**
Hypodermic needles or syringes, **2C:36–6**
Interchangeable drug products. Drugs and Medicine, this index
Legend drugs,
　Crimes and offenses, **2C:35–10.5**
　Definitions, **2C:35–2**
Motor vehicles, knowingly possessing while operating, exemption, **39:4–49.1**
Name, generic or brand name, **24:21–17**
Physicians and Surgeons, this index
Possession, **2C:35–24**
Veterinarians, this index

PRESENT SENSE IMPRESSION
Hearsay exception, **Evidence Rule 803**

PRESENTENCE INVESTIGATIONS
Generally, **2C:44–6; Rules 3:21–2, 3:21–3**
Expunged records, use in preparing, **2C:52–21**

PRESENTMENT
Grand jury, finding, return, **Rule 3:6–9**
Indictment, Information or Presentment, generally, this index

PRESIDING JUDGES
Generally, **Rule 1:33–6**

PRESS
Newspapers, generally, this index
Television, generally, this index

PRESS ASSOCIATIONS
Definitions, privileged communications, **2A:84A–21a**
Newspersons privilege, **Evidence Rule 508**

PRESUMPTIONS
　See, also,
　　Burden of Proof, generally, this index
　　Standard of Proof, generally, this index
Generally, **Evidence Rule 301 et seq.**
Accidents, knowledge of involvement, duty to stop and assist injury victims, **39:4–129**
Alcoholic content of liquors, **33:1–1.1**
Attorney and client, communications, privilege, **2A:84A–20**
Bribery and corruption, public resources, **2C:27–12**
Chemicals, chemistry and chemists, industrial chemicals, **2C:35–29**
Choice of law, **Evidence Rule 302**
Controlled substances, manufacture or distribute, registration, **24:21–36**
Crimes and Offenses, this index
Deadly force, justification, **2C:3–6**
Effect, **Evidence Rule 301**
Exercise of privileges by witnesses, **2A:84A–31**
Fencing, **2C:20–7.1**
Fitness of liquors for beverage purposes, **33:1–1**
Industrial chemicals, **2C:35–29**
Intoxicating liquors, consumption by driver or passenger, **39:4–51a**
Kosher food, possession of nonkosher food in same establishment, **2C:21–7.3**
Lawyer client communications, **2A:84A–20**
Library theft, concealment of materials on premises, **2C:20–13**

PRESUMPTIONS—Cont'd

Littering, rebuttable presumptions, drivers or owners responsibility, 39:4–64

Motor Vehicles, this index

Notice, involvement in traffic accident causing injury or death, 39:4–129

Prepaid funeral agreements, recipient of moneys under, knowledge of obligations, 2A:102–16

Rape, previous sexual conduct of complainant, admissibility, 2A:84A–32.2

Rebuttal,
Endangering welfare of child, pornography, age, 2C:24–4
School bus traffic rule violation, 39:4–128.1

School bus traffic rule violation, rebuttable, 39:4–128.1

Sexual offenses, age, impotency or marriage to victim, 2C:14–5

Shoplifting, 2C:20–11.1

Signatures or documents, statutory presumption, **Evidence Rule 902**

Theft of services, 2C:20–8

Witness,
Exercise of privileges, 2A:84A–31
Rape, previous sexual conduct of complainant, admissibility, 2A:84A–32.2

PRETRIAL CONFERENCES

Attorneys, withdrawal, **Rule 1:11–2**

Crimes and offenses, hearings, **Rule 3:9–1**

Date, setting forth in discovery and calendar motions, **Rule 1:6–2**

Failure to appear, sanctions, **Rule 1:2–4**

Municipal courts, **Rule 7:7–5**

Open court proceedings, **Rule 1:2–1**

Records, verbatim records, **Rule 1:2–2**

Verbatim records, **Rule 1:2–2**

Withdrawal of attorney, **Rule 1:11–2**

PRETRIAL DISCOVERY

Discovery, generally, this index

PRETRIAL INTERVENTION

Crimes and Offenses, this index

PRETRIAL PROCEDURE

Crimes and offenses, **Rule 3:9–1 et seq.**
Presence of defendant, **Rule 3:16**

Municipal courts, **Rule 7:7–1 et seq.**

PRETRIAL RELEASE

Conditions, form of warrant and summons, **Rule 3:7–9**

Probable cause hearing, continuation, **Rule 3:4–3**

PREVENTION OF CRUELTY

Cruelty to Animals, generally, this index

PREVENTION OF DOMESTIC VIOLENCE ACT OF 1990

Domestic Violence, generally, this index

PREVENTION OF DOMESTIC VIOLENCE ACT OF 1991

Domestic Violence, generally, this index

PRICE TAGS

Alteration or removal, shoplifting, 2C:20–11

PRIESTS

Benefit of clergy, abolition, 2A:152–2

Privileges and immunities, priest and penitent, **Evidence Rule 511**

PRIMA FACIE EVIDENCE

Evidence, this index

PRINCIPAL AND AGENT

Agents and Agencies, generally, this index

PRINCIPAL AND SURETY

Bail, generally, this index

Fiduciaries, generally, this index

PRIOR CONVICTIONS

Crimes and offenses, discovery, **Rule 3:13–3**

Definitions, crimes and offenses, 2C:44–4

PRIOR OFFENSES

Code of Criminal Justice, application of law, 2C:1–1

PRIORITIES AND PREFERENCES

Attorneys, discipline, **Rule 1:20–8**

Children and minors, abuse or neglect, placement, 9:6–8.8

Handicapped parking enforcement units, 39:4–197.11

Liens and incumbrances, **Rule 1:13–8**

Property seized or forfeited under alcoholic beverage law, claims and liens, 33:1–66

PRISONERS OF WAR

Motor vehicles, registration plates, 39:3–27.24 et seq.

PRISONS AND PRISONERS

Correctional Institutions, generally, this index

PRIVACY

Crimes and offenses, invasion, observation, nudity, sexual intercourse, 2C:14–9

Invasion of Privacy, generally, this index

Search Warrants, generally, this index

PRIVATE CHILD CARE CENTERS

Child Care Centers, generally, this index

PRIVATE CORPORATIONS

Corporations, generally, this index

PRIVATE CROSSING

Railroad Crossings, generally, this index

PRIVATE DETECTIVES

Detectives, generally, this index

PRIVATE DRIVEWAYS

Drives and Driveways, this index

PRIVATE DWELLINGS

Housing, generally, this index

PRIVATE FOUNDATION TRUSTS

Charitable Trusts, generally, this index

PRIVATE INSTITUTIONS AND AGENCIES

Hospitals, generally, this index

Nursing Homes or Hospitals, generally, this index

PRIVATE NURSING HOMES OR HOSPITALS

Nursing Homes or Hospitals, generally, this index

PRIVATE ROADS

Application of motor vehicle laws, 39:5A–1 et seq.

Definitions, 39:1–1
Speed bumps, municipalities, 39:4–8.9

PRIVATE ROADS—Cont'd

Right of way to pedestrians on sidewalk, 39:4–66.1

Speed bumps, municipalities, 39:4–8.9 et seq.

Stopping vehicle emerging from, 39:4–66

PRIVATE SCHOOLS

Aggravated assault, officers and employees, 2C:12–1

Assault and battery, aggravated assault, officers and employees, 2C:12–1

Busses, operator licenses, 39:3–10, 39:3–10.1, 39:3–10.1a

Child Care Centers, generally, this index

Colleges and Universities, this index

Drivers school, exemption from license for conducting, 39:12–2

Officers and employees, aggravated assault, 2C:12–1

School buses,
Crossing control arms, 39:3B–1.1 et seq.
Operators, licenses and permits, 39:3–10, 39:3–10.1, 39:3–10.1a

Traffic signs and signals, installation, 39:4–183.1a

PRIVILEGED COMMUNICATIONS

Confidential or Privileged Information, generally, this index

PRIVILEGED INFORMATION

Confidential or Privileged Information, generally, this index

PRIVILEGES AND IMMUNITIES

See, also, Confidential or Privileged Information, generally, this index

Generally, 2A:84A–17

Accused, 2A:84A–17; **Evidence Rule 501**

Adult offender supervision interstate commission, 2A:168–31

Ambassadors, traffic rules and regulations, records and recordation, 39:5–53 et seq.

Application of law, **Evidence Rule 101**

Attorneys, this index

Banks and Banking, this index

Burn injuries, reports by physician, 2C:58–8

Child Abuse, this index

Child Care Centers, this index

Children and Minors, this index

Comment on exercise of, **Evidence Rule 532**

Consuls and consular agents, traffic rules and regulations, records and recordation, 39:5–53 et seq.

Contract, waiver of privilege, **Evidence Rule 530**

Court appointed special advocate, 2A:4A–92

Crimes and Offenses, this index

Diplomatic immunity, traffic rules and regulations, records and recordation, 39:5–53 et seq.

Domestic Violence, this index

Emergency vehicle, drivers, 39:4–91

Error, overruling claim of privilege, **Evidence Rule 533**

Existence, **Evidence Rule 104**

Husband and wife, **Evidence Rules 501, 509**

Incrimination, definition, **Evidence Rule 502**

Informers identity, **Evidence Rule 516**

Jewelry, stolen goods, secondhand, reports, 2C:21–40

Law Enforcement Officers, this index

Low speed vehicles, liability, waiver, 39:4–31.4

Marital privilege, **Evidence Rule 509**

Marriage counselors, **Evidence Rule 510**

Mediation, **Evidence Rule 519**

PRIVILEGES AND IMMUNITIES—Cont'd
Medical advisory panel, liability, **39:2–16**
Medical care, attendance and treatment, emergency removal of children from home, abuse or neglect, **9:6–8.30**
Medical records, release, abused children, **9:6–8.30**
Motor vehicle commission,
    Damages, board, **39:2A–23**
    Torts, **39:2A–24**
Motor vehicle division, liability, **39:2–16**
Motor Vehicles, this index
News organizations, searches and seizures, **2A:84A–21.9 et seq.**
Newspersons privilege, **Evidence Rule 508**
Official information, **Evidence Rule 515**
Overruling claim, effect of error, **Evidence Rule 533**
Patient physician privilege, **Evidence Rule 506**
    Attorneys, waiver, application for restoration from disability inactive status, **Rule 1:20–12**
Peer review committees, medical and dental care and treatment, immunity from liability, **2A:84A–22.10**
Physical examinations, abused children, **9:6–8.30**
Physicians and Surgeons, this index
Police and Police Departments, this index
Political vote, **Evidence Rule 513**
Previous disclosure, waiver of privilege, **Evidence Rule 530**
Priest penitent privilege, **Evidence Rule 511**
Psychologists, **Evidence Rule 505**
Reference to exercise, **Evidence Rule 532**
Religious belief, **Evidence Rule 512**
Reports, jewelry, stolen goods, secondhand, **2C:21–40**
Roller skates, **39:4–10.8, 39:4–10.9**
Searches and seizures, news organizations, state immunity, **2A:84A–21.11**
Sex offenses, registration, **2C:7–15**
    Released records, **2C:7–5**
Skateboards, **39:4–10.8, 39:4–10.9**
State Officers and Employees, this index
Stolen goods, jewelry, secondhand, reports, **2C:21–40**
Trade secrets, **Evidence Rule 514**
Traffic rules and regulations, diplomatic immunity, records and recordation, **39:5–53 et seq.**
Utilization review committees, hospitals or extended care facilities, **Evidence Rule 507**
Victim and counselor privilege, **Evidence Rule 517**
Waiver, **2A:84A–29; Evidence Rule 530**
    Mediation, **Evidence Rule 519**
Witnesses, this index
Wrongfully compelled disclosure, admissibility, **Evidence Rule 531**

PRIZES
Rewards, generally, this index

PRO HAC VICE
Attorneys, payment, client protection fund, **Rule 1:28–2**

PRO HAC VICE APPEARANCE
Generally, **Rules 1:21–1, 1:21–2**

PROBABLE CAUSE
Complaint, dismissal, **Rule 3:3–1**
Definitions,
    Controlled dangerous substances, administrative inspection warrants, **24:21–32**

PROBABLE CAUSE—Cont'd
Definitions—Cont'd
    Controlled substances, **24:21–32**
Determination, arrest without warrant, **Rule 3:4–1**
Domestic violence, arrest, **2C:25–21**
Hearings,
    Discharge from custody, **Rule 3:4–3**
    Evidence, application of law, **Evidence Rule 101**
    Juvenile delinquents and dependents, referral to other courts, **Rule 5:22–2**
    Material witnesses, detention, **Rule 3:26–3**
    Municipal courts, **Rule 7:3–1**
    Right to, informing defendant, **Rule 3:4–2**
    Technical insufficiency, irregularity, release, **Rule 3:4–5**
    Waiver, **Rule 3:4–3**
Juvenile delinquents and dependents, detention, **2A:4A–38**
News organizations, searches and seizures, **2A:84A–21.9**
Shoplifting, arrest, **2C:20–11**

PROBATE PROCEEDINGS
Appeal and review, ex parte actions, enlargement of time, **Rule 1:3–4**
Enlargement of time, review of ex parte actions, **Rule 1:3–4**
Filing of papers, **Rule 1:5–6**
Firearms passing to heirs or legatees, **2C:58–3**
Mediation, **Rule 1:40–6**
Personal representatives,
    Alcoholic beverages, licenses and permits,
        Extension of license to executor or administrator, **33:1–22**
        More than one license in different capacities, **33:1–40**
    Commercial bribery and breach of duty, **2C:21–10**
    Investments, turnpike authority bonds, **27:23–13**
    Misapplication, entrusted property, **2C:21–15**
    Motor vehicles, resident operator becoming nonresident, service of process, **39:7–2.1**
Surrogates, practice of law, **Rule 1:15–1**
Time, enlargement of time, review of ex parte actions, **Rule 1:3–4**

PROBATION AND PROBATION OFFICERS
Generally, **2A:168–5 et seq., 2C:44–1, 2C:45–1 et seq.; Rules 1:34–4, 3:21–7**
Accounts, **2A:168–10**
    Record to be kept by officers, **2A:168–11**
Adult offender supervision, interstate compacts, **2A:168–26 et seq.**
Aggravated assault,
    Throwing bodily fluids, **2C:12–13**
    Weapons, **2C:12–1**
Alcoholics and alcoholism, treatment, commitment and admission to institutions, **2C:35–14**
Appointment, **Rule 1:34–4**
    Temporary officers, **2A:168–9**
Arrest, **2C:45–3**
Assault and battery, aggravated assault, weapons, **2C:12–1**
Assessments,
    Condition of probation, **2C:46–1**
    Transaction fee, **2C:46–1 et seq.**
Attorneys, representation, **2C:45–4**
Audit of account of officers, **2A:168–10**
Bonds, **2A:168–10**
Chief probation officer,
    Investigations for superior court, **2A:168–13**
    Powers and duties, **2A:168–7**

PROBATION AND PROBATION OFFICERS—Cont'd
Chief probation officer—Cont'd
    Vicinages, **Rule 1:33–8**
Child Abuse, this index
Civil service, appointments, **2A:168–5**
Community related services, performance, condition of probation, **2C:45–1**
Community service supervision fund, fees deposited into, use, **2C:45–1**
Compact institution, interstate compact, **2A:168–20**
Compensation and salaries, **2A:168–8**
    Temporary officers, **2A:168–9**
Concurrent sentences, **2C:44–5**
Conditions,
    Assessments, **2C:46–1**
    Authorized dispositions, **2C:43–2**
    Fines or restitution, payment, **2C:46–1**
    Mandatory assessments, **2C:46–1**
    Suspension, **2C:45–1**
Confidential or privileged information, records, **Rule 1:38–3**
Consecutive sentences, **2C:44–5**
Controlled dangerous substances, revocation, injunctions, **2C:35–5.8**
Costs, interstate compact, **2A:168–23**
County probation departments, records, confidentiality, **Rule 1:38–3**
Court ordered financial obligations, transaction fee, **2C:46–1**
Criminal records, forwarding information for, **53:1–20.2**
Definitions,
    Adult offender supervision, interstate compacts, **2A:168–27**
    Receiving state, **2A:168–19**
Denial, record expungement, **2C:52–14**
Department, attorneys, practice of law, **Rule 1:15–2**
Discharge, **2C:45–2**
Disclosure, expungement order, **2C:52–30**
Diversion programs, record expungement, **2C:52–20**
Divorce, supervision of person to require to pay for support, **2A:168–11**
Drug dependent persons, rehabilitation or treatment in place of sentence, **2C:35–14**
Education, suspended sentence, **2C:45–1**
Employees,
    Appointment by chief probation officer, **2A:168–7**
    Salaries and expenses, **2A:168–8**
Enforcement, interstate compact for adult offender supervision, **2A:168–37**
Escape, **2C:29–5**
Evidence, revocation or modification hearing, **2C:45–4**
Exemptions, record expungement, **2C:52–2**
Expenses, **2A:168–8**
    Interstate compact, **2A:168–23**
Expungement, record, **2C:52–1 et seq.**
    Use, **2C:52–22**
Extension, **2C:45–2**
Extradition, generally, this index
Fees,
    Collection, expenditures, community service supervision fund, **2C:45–1**
    Record expungement, **2C:52–29**
Fines or restitution, **2C:44–2**
    Condition of probation, **2C:46–1**
    Conviction of crime, collection, **2C:46–4**
    Transaction fee, **2C:46–1 et seq.**
Food, poisoning, **2C:12–2**
Health and accident insurance, runners, **2C:21–22.1**

PROBATION AND PROBATION OFFICERS
—Cont'd

Hearings,
   Record expungement, **2C:52–9 et seq.**
   Revocation or modification, **2C:45–4**
Humane treatment, interstate compact,
   2A:168–22
Imprisonment, condition of probation,
   2C:43–2, 2C:45–1
Incarceration of probationer in receiving state,
   2A:168–18 et seq.
Indictable offenses, record expungement,
   2C:52–2
Inspection and inspectors, records, expunge-
   ment, **2C:52–19**
Interstate compacts,
   Adult offender supervision, **2A:168–26 et seq.**
   Persons convicted of crime on probation or
     parole, **2A:168–14 et seq.**
Investigations, **2A:168–11**
   Financial status of persons seeking relief in
     forma pauperis, **2A:168–13**
   Jurisdiction of sending state, interstate com-
     pact, **2A:168–21**
Juvenile delinquents, **2A:4A–43**
   Alcoholics and alcoholism, treatment,
     2C:35–14
   Disposition of case, **2A:4A–43**
   Drug abuse, treatment, **2C:35–14**
   Orders of court, **Rule 5:24–4**
Labor and employment, suspension, **2C:45–1**
Mandatory assessments,
   Condition of probation, **2C:46–1**
   Transaction fee, **2C:46–1 et seq.**
Medical treatment, suspended sentence,
   2C:45–1
Modification, **2C:45–2**
Monthly probation fee, nonpayment, **2C:46–2**
Motor Vehicle or Traffic Laws, violation,
   39:5–7
Multiple periods, **2C:44–5**
Municipal courts, **Rule 7:9–1**
Notice, sentence and punishment, **Rule 3:21–4**
Oath, **2A:168–10**
Offense committed while on probation,
   2C:44–5
Orders appointing officers, **2A:168–5**
Orders of court, record expungement,
   2C:52–11 et seq., 2C:52–26
Parole officers, appointed as officers, **2A:168–6**
Petitions, record expungement, **2C:52–7 et seq.**
Poisoning of food, **2C:12–2**
Political activities, **Rule 1:17–1**
Powers and duties, **2A:168–11**
   Chief probation officer, **2A:168–7**
   Transferred probationers, **2A:168–12**
Presentence report, record expungement,
   2C:52–21
Prior offenses, application of code of criminal
   justice, **2C:1–1**
Process, record expungement, **2C:52–10**
Public office, holding, **Rule 1:17–1**
Qualifications, officers, **2A:168–5**
Records and recordation,
   Confidentiality, **Rule 1:38–3**
   Expungement, **2C:52–1 et seq.**
   Work to be kept, **2A:168–11**
Rehabilitation, suspended sentence, **2C:45–1**
Reinstatement, interstate compact for adult of-
   fender supervision, **2A:168–37**
Release, **2C:43–9**
   Record expungement, **2C:52–19**
Relief pending appeal, **Rule 3:23–5**
Removal, records, **2C:52–15**

PROBATION AND PROBATION OFFICERS
—Cont'd

Reports, **2A:168–11**
   Alcoholics and alcoholism, treatment,
     2C:35–14
   Conditions, **2C:45–1**
   Drug abuse, treatment, **2C:35–14**
   Revocation or suspension, **2C:45–3**
   Alcoholics and alcoholism, treatment,
     2C:35–14
   Conditions, **2C:45–1**
   Drug abuse, treatment, **2C:35–14**
   Multiple sentences, **2C:44–5**
Rules and regulations,
   Conduct of officers, **2A:168–7**
   Interstate compact, **2A:168–24**
Runners, health and accident insurance,
   2C:21–22.1
Satisfaction, probation obligation, **2C:45–2**
Sealing, record expungement, **2C:52–26**
Sentence, **Rule 3:21–7**
Sex Offenses, this index
Sexual assault of probationer or parolee,
   2C:14–2
Social work conferences, expenses, **2A:168–8**
Statements,
   Conditions of probation furnished by offi-
     cers, **2A:168–11**
   Record expungement petition, **2C:52–8**
Summons, **2C:45–3**
Superior court, investigations for by probation
   officers, **2A:168–13**
Supervision, incarceration as condition of pro-
   bation, **2C:45–1**
Supervisory treatment programs,
   First offenders, **2C:43–12 et seq.**
   Record expungement, **2C:52–20**
Support of persons,
   Suspended sentence, **2C:45–1**
   Willful nonsupport, **2C:62–1**
Temporary officers, **2A:168–9**
Term of imprisonment in addition to proba-
   tion, **2C:45–1**
Termination, interstate compact for adult of-
   fender supervision, **2A:168–37**
Time effective, interstate compact, **2A:168–25**
Traffic offenses, record expungement,
   2C:52–28
Training, community safety units, **2C:39–6**
Transfer of probationers to jurisdiction of an-
   other officer, **2A:168–12**
Uniform Act for Out of State Parolee Supervi-
   sion, **2A:168–14 et seq.**
Vicinage chief probation officers, **Rule 1:33–8**
Volunteers in probation, **Rule 1:34–4**
Weapons offenses, reduction of sentence,
   2C:43–6.2, 2C:43–6.3
Withdrawal, interstate compact for adult of-
   fender supervision, **2A:168–37**
Writing, orders appointing officers, **2A:168–5**

PROBATION DIVISION
Probation and Probation Officers, generally,
this index

PROCEEDINGS
Actions and Proceedings, generally, this index

PROCESS
Generally, **Rule 1:5–1 et seq.**
Acknowledgments, proof of service, **Rule 1:5–3**
Advertising committee, grievances, **Rule 1:19A–4**
Agents for service of process,
   Nonresident attorneys, **Rule 1:21–1**
   Pro hac vice appearances, **Rule 1:21–2**

PROCESS—Cont'd

Agents for service of process—Cont'd
   Surety and bail bonds, **Rule 1:13–3**
Amendment, municipal courts, **Rule 7:14–2**
Answer, forfeiture claim, **2C:64–1 et seq.**
Appeal and Review, this index
Appeals In Criminal Prosecutions, this index
Appendices, service, **Rule 1:5–1 et seq.**
Associations and Societies, this index
Attorney of record, **Rule 1:11–3**
Bail, agent for service, **Rule 1:13–3**
Briefs, this index
Certification of service, **Rule 1:5–3**
Clerks of courts, nonresidents, filing papers,
   relating to service, **39:7–3**
Client protection fund, subpoenas, **Rule 1:28–6**
Commencement of prosecution, **2C:1–6**
Complaints, this index
Corporations, this index
Counterclaims, numerous defendants, **Rule 1:5–5**
County detectives and investigators, service by,
   2A:157–17
Courier, **Rule 1:5–4**
Court schedules, **Rule 1:30–1**
Crimes and Offenses, this index
Cross claims, numerous defendants, **Rule 1:5–5**
Definitions, theft of services, **2C:20–8**
Domestic violence, complaint, temporary re-
   straining orders, **2C:25–28**
Executions, generally, this index
Exemptions, extradited person, **2A:160–34**
Fee arbitration, **Rule 1:20A–3**
Fees,
   Person resident when motor vehicle accident
     or collision occurred and later becoming
     nonresident, **39:7–2.2**
   Service by county detectives and investiga-
     tors, **2A:157–17**
Forfeiture, property, **2C:64–1**
Forms, **Rule 1:32–3**
Inability to serve parties, transfer of actions,
   Rule 1:13–4
Indictment, Information or Presentment, gen-
   erally, this index
Indigent defendants, waiver of fees, **Rule 1:13–2**
Injunctions, generally, this index
Issuance, motions and applications, **Rule 1:6–8**
Judgments, **Rule 1:5–1 et seq.**
Jury, **2B:20–15**
Justification, execution of process, criminal
   prosecution defense, **2C:3–3**
Juvenile Delinquents, this index
Limitation of criminal prosecutions, process is-
   suance, **2C:1–6**
Manner of serving process, **Rule 1:5–2**
Money laundering and illegal investments,
   2C:21–29
Motions, this index
Motor Vehicle Security Responsibility Law,
   proceedings for violation, **39:6–55**
Municipal Courts, this index
Notice, this index
Numerous defendants, **Rule 1:5–5**
Order of suspension, conviction of crime, **Rule 1:20–13**
Orders, **Rule 1:5–1 et seq.**
Out of State Motorist Act, **39:7–1 et seq.**
Parents, child abuse, protective custody,
   9:6–8.19
Parties, **Rule 1:5–1 et seq.**
Partnerships, this index
Personal service, **Rule 1:5–2**
Petition for review, unauthorized practice of
   law, **Rule 1:22–3A**

PROCESS—Cont'd
Petitions, **Rule 1:5–1 et seq.**
Pleadings, this index
Police and Police Departments, this index
Proof of service, **Rule 1:5–3**
Racketeering, service of investigative interrogatories, **2C:41–5**
Record expungement, **2C:52–10**
Representatives for receipt of service, numerous defendants, **Rule 1:5–5**
Residence and Residents, this index
Return of process, court schedules, **Rule 1:30–1**
Subpoenas, generally, this index
Substituted service,
    Nonresidents, motor vehicles, **39:7–2**
    Manner of service, **39:7–2.2**
    Notice, motor vehicles, nonresidents, **39:7–2.2**
Summons, generally, this index
Sunday, this index
Territorial limits, **Rule 3:1–2**
Time, **Rule 1:5–1**
    Service by mail, additional time for response, **Rule 1:3–3**
Waiver of fees, indigent persons, **Rule 1:13–2**
Warrants, generally, this index

PROCESSIONS
Disrupting processions, **2C:33–8**

PROCESSORS OF GOODS
Alcoholic beverage processing as misdemeanor, **33:1–50**
Crimes and offenses, alcoholic beverages, **33:1–50**

PROCURERS
Prostitution, **2C:34–1**

PRODUCTION
Definitions,
    Controlled dangerous substances, **2C:35–2, 24:21–2**
    Controlled substances, **24:21–2**

PRODUCTION OF BOOKS AND PAPERS
    See, also, Subpoenas, generally, this index
Generally, **Rule 1:9–2**
Arbitration and award, motor vehicle tort claims, **39:6A–29**
Attorneys, this index
Criminal proceedings, **Rule 3:13–2**
    Newspersons information disclosure privilege, **2A:84A–21.1 et seq.**
DNA database and databank, motions, **2A:84A–32a**
Money laundering and illegal investments, **2C:21–29**
Monopolies and unfair trade, hearings or inquiries, **56:9–9**
Motor vehicles, arbitration, tort claims, **39:6A–29**
Newspersons information disclosure privilege, criminal proceedings, **2A:84A–21.1 et seq.**
Racketeering, investigative interrogatories, **2C:41–5**
Radioactive materials, certificates of handling or certificate numbers, transportation, **39:5B–18**
Searches and seizures, news organizations, **2A:84A–21.9 et seq.**
Subpoenas, municipal courts, **Rule 7:7–8**

PRODUCTS LIABILITY
Contingent fees, **Rule 1:21–7**

PROFESSIONAL CONDUCT RULES
Generally, **Rule 1:14**
Interpreters, transliterators, and translators, **Rule 1:14**
Judges duty to enforce, **Rule 1:18**

PROFESSIONAL CORPORATIONS
Attorneys, this index

PROFESSIONAL CRIMINALS
Crimes and offenses, imprisonment, extended terms, **2C:44–3**

PROFESSIONAL EMPLOYMENT
Definitions, health care professionals, solicitation, disasters or accidents, **2C:40A–4**

PROFESSIONAL ETHICS ADVISORY COMMITTEE
Generally, **Rule 1:19–1 et seq.**

PROFESSIONAL NURSING
Nurses, generally, this index

PROFESSIONAL SERVICES
Turnpike authority, contracts, bids, **27:23–6.1**

PROFESSIONS AND OCCUPATIONS
Attorneys, generally, this index
Chiropody and chiropodists. Podiatrists and Podiatry, generally, this index
Chiropractors, generally, this index
Clergy, generally, this index
Commercial bribery and breach of duty, **2C:21–10**
Conviction of crime, licenses and permits, **2A:168A–1 et seq.**
Counselors and Counseling, generally, this index
Dentists and Dentistry, generally, this index
Detectives, generally, this index
Druggists. Pharmacists, generally, this index
Firefighters and Fire Departments, generally, this index
Nurse practitioner/clinical nurse specialist. Nurses, generally, this index
Nurses, generally, this index
Optometrists, generally, this index
Pharmacists, generally, this index
Physical Therapists, generally, this index
Physicians and Surgeons, generally, this index
Podiatrists and Podiatry, generally, this index
Police and Police Departments, generally, this index
Private detectives. Detectives, generally, this index
Probation and Probation Officers, generally, this index
Psychologists and Psychology, generally, this index
Rehabilitated convicted offenders, licenses, **2A:168A–1 et seq.**
Surgeons. Physicians and Surgeons, generally, this index
Theft of services, **2C:20–8**
Veterinarians, generally, this index

PROFITS
Bribery and corruption, fines and penalties, **2C:30–8**
Controlled Substances, this index

PROHEPTAZINE
Controlled substances, **24:21–1 et seq.**

PROHIBITED SEXUAL ACT
Definitions, endangering welfare of children, **2C:24–4**

PROJECTIONS
Motor vehicle tires, **39:3–81**

PROMISES
Jury, corrupting or influencing, **2C:29–8**

PROMOTING GAMBLING
Definitions, **2C:37–2**

PROMOTING PROSTITUTION
Definitions, **2C:34–1**

PROMOTIONS
Advertisements, generally, this index

PROOF
Evidence, generally, this index

PROOF OF SERVICE
Generally, **Rule 1:5–3**

PROPANE
Liquefied Petroleum Gas, generally, this index

PROPELLANTS
Definitions, Explosives Act, **21:1A–129**

PROPER ITEMIZED COMPUTER GENERATED RECEIPT
Definitions, motor vehicles, fines and penalties, **39:5–45**

PROPER ITEMIZED MANUAL RECEIPT
Definitions, motor vehicles, fines and penalties, **39:5–45**

PROPERIDINE
Controlled substances, **24:21–1 et seq.**

PROPERTY
    See, also, Real Estate, generally, this index
Damage to property,
    Motor vehicle accidents, towing service failure to remove, fines and penalties, **39:4–56.8**
    Placement of symbol, object or graffiti, **2C:33–11**
        Putting or attempting to put in fear of bodily violence, **2C:33–10**
Defense of property, use of force, **2C:3–4**
Definitions,
    Computer related offenses, **2C:20–1**
    Criminal procedure, **2A:152–1**
    Theft, **2C:20–1**
Force, use to prevent damage to or loss of property, **2C:3–7**
Immovable or movable property, theft, **2C:20–3**
Liens and Incumbrances, this index
Records, hearsay exception, **Evidence Rule 803**
State Police, this index
Theft, generally, this index

PROPERTY LIABILITY INSURANCE GUARANTY ASSOCIATION
Assessments, unsatisfied claim and judgment fund, **39:6–63**
Motor vehicles, unsatisfied claim and judgment fund, fees and additional charges remitted to treasurer, **39:6–88**
Unsatisfied claim and judgment fund board, abolishment, transfer of powers and duties, **39:6–64c**

PROPERTY OF ANOTHER
Definitions, theft, **2C:20–1**

PROPERTY OFFENSES
Generally, **2C:17–1 et seq.**
Justification, **2C:3–10**

PROPERTY TAX
Taxation, generally, this index

PROPRIETARY PREPARATIONS
Alcohol in preparations unfit for beverage purposes, **33:1–30**

PROPYLENE
Liquefied Petroleum Gas, generally, this index

PRORATION
Fee, intoxicating liquors, **33:1–31**

PROSECUTING ATTORNEYS
County Prosecutors, generally, this index
Defined, limited criminal jurisdiction, courts of, appeals, **Rule 3:23–9**
Discovery, **Rule 7:7–7**
Grand jury, attendance, **Rule 3:6–6**
Municipal Courts, this index

PROSTHETIC APPLIANCES
Automobile insurance, no fault insurance, application of law, **39:6A–1 et seq.**

PROSTITUTION
Generally, **2C:34–1**
Evidence, former crimes, nuisance, proceeds, **2C:64–1**
Fingerprints, **53:1–15**
Human trafficking, **2C:13–8**
Identity and identification, offenders, **Rule 7:2–2**
Loitering for the purpose of engaging in prostitution, **2C:34–1.1**
Nuisances, **2C:33–12**
Rules and regulations, alcoholic beverage control, **33:1–39**

PROTECTIVE ORDERS
Confidential or privileged information, **Rule 1:38–3**

PROVIDER
Definitions,
Health and accident insurance, runners, **2C:21–22.1**
No fault insurance, **39:6A–2**
Prepaid funeral agreements, **2A:102–18**

PROVOCATION
Crimes and offenses, mitigating circumstances, **2C:44–1**

PRUSSIC ACID
Poisons, this index

PSEUDOEPHEDRINE
Losses, reports, **2C:35–26**
Possession,
Evidence, **2C:35–27**
Precursors, **2C:35–28**
Sales, limitations, **2C:35–25**

PSILOCYBIN
Controlled substances, **24:21–1 et seq.**

PSILOCYN
Controlled substances, **24:21–1 et seq.**

PSYCHIATRIC HOSPITALS
Adult Diagnostic and Treatment Center, generally, this index
Commitment and Admission to Institutions, generally, this index
Crimes and offenses, defendants, examination, **2C:4–5**
Institutionalized elderly persons, assault, **2C:12–1**
Trenton psychiatric hospital, parking and traffic regulation on roadways, **39:4–208**

PSYCHIATRISTS AND PSYCHIATRY
Crimes and offenses, suspended sentences, treatment, **2C:45–1**
Examinations,
Admissibility of statements of defendant, **2C:4–10**
Mentally deficient or mentally ill defendants, **2C:4–5**
Mentally Deficient and Mentally Ill Persons, generally, this index
Probation, treatment, conditions, **2C:45–1**

PSYCHOLOGICAL EXAMINERS BOARD
Licenses and permits. Psychologists and Psychology, this index

PSYCHOLOGISTS AND PSYCHOLOGY
Adult Diagnostic and Treatment Center, generally, this index
Automobile insurance, no fault insurance, application of law, **39:6A–1 et seq.**
Crimes and offenses,
Defendants, examinations, **2C:4–5**
Health care claims fraud, **2C:21–4.2,** **2C:21–4.3**
Licenses and permits, suspension or revocation, **2C:51–5**
Rehabilitation, order of debarment, rescission, **2C:27–1**
Defendants, examinations, **2C:4–5**
Examinations, criminal defendants, **2C:4–5**
Statements, admissibility, **2C:4–10**
Fees, controversies or disputes with patients, review committees, immunity from liability, **2A:84A–22.10**
Fines and penalties, health care claims fraud, **2C:21–4.2, 2C:21–4.3**
Licenses and permits, suspension or revocation, **2C:51–5**
Rehabilitation, order of debarment, rescission, **2C:27–1**
Forfeitures, licenses and permits, health care claims fraud, **2C:51–5**
Health care claims fraud, **2C:21–4.2, 2C:21–4.3**
Licenses and permits, suspension or revocation, **2C:51–5**
Rehabilitation, order of debarment, rescission, **2C:27–1**
Licenses and permits, health care claims fraud, suspension or revocation, **2C:51–5**
Rehabilitation, order of debarment, rescission, **2C:27–1**
Member of clinic to study mental and physical conditions before sentence of convicted persons, **2A:164–1**
Presentence investigation and report, evaluation, disclosure, **2C:44–6**
Cost of evaluation, **2C:44–6.1**
Privileges and immunities, **Evidence Rule 505**

PUBLIC
Definitions, disorderly conduct, **2C:33–2**

PUBLIC ACCOMMODATIONS
Discrimination, generally, this index

PUBLIC ACCOMMODATIONS—Cont'd
Hotels and Motels, generally, this index
Smoking, **2C:33–13**
Theft of services, **2C:20–8**

PUBLIC ADJUSTERS
Criminal history record background check, license applicants, **53:1–20.16**
Licenses and permits, criminal history record background check, **53:1–20.16**

PUBLIC ADVOCATE RESTRUCTURING ACT OF 1994
Public Defenders, generally, this index

PUBLIC AGENCIES
Appearance, nonattorneys, **Rule 1:21–1**
Attorneys, practice of law, **Rule 1:15–3 et seq.**
Subpoenas, enforcement, **Rule 1:9–6**

PUBLIC ASSEMBLIES
Motor vehicle junk yard, location, **39:11–5**
Obstructing highways and other public passages, **2C:33–7**
Parking vehicle near entrance, taking on or letting off passengers, time limited, **39:4–139**
Terroristic threats, **2C:12–3**

PUBLIC ASSISTANCE
Indigent Persons, generally, this index

PUBLIC BUILDINGS
Buildings, generally, this index

PUBLIC BUILDINGS CONSTRUCTION BOND ACT OF 1963
Turnpike authority,
Operation and maintenance of toll roads after payment of bonds, **27:23–16**
Revenues and funds, payment of indebtedness, **27:23–9**

PUBLIC CHARGES
Indigent Persons, generally, this index

PUBLIC COLLEGES
Colleges and Universities, generally, this index

PUBLIC COMMUNICATIONS
Criminal mischief, **2C:17–3**
Obscene material, **2C:34–4**

PUBLIC CONVEYANCES
Buses, generally, this index
Carriers, generally, this index
Definitions, Explosives Act, **21:1A–129**

PUBLIC CORRUPTION PROFITEERING PENALTY ACT
Generally, **2C:30–8**

PUBLIC DEFENDERS
Generally, **2A:158A–1 et seq.**
Allocation to department of public advocate, **2A:158A–3**
Appeals in criminal prosecutions, assignment, **Rule 3:8–3**
Appearance, **Rule 3:8–3**
Appointment, **2A:158A–4**
Eligibility, **2A:158A–14 et seq.**
Assignments, indigent persons, **Rule 3:4–2**
Charges, services, **2A:158A–7**
Claims, compromise and settlement, **2A:158A–20**
Collection,
Liens and incumbrances, comprehensive enforcement program, **2B:19–6, 2B:19–11**

PUBLIC DEFENDERS—Cont'd
Collection—Cont'd
Money, **2A:158A–19**
Communications, privilege, **2A:158A–12**
Compromise and settlement, claims,
2A:158A–20
Confidential or privileged information,
2A:158A–12
Contesting value of services rendered,
2A:158A–19
Contracts, legal services, **2A:158A–10**
Deputies,
Appointment, **2A:158A–6**
Compensation and salaries, **2A:158A–6**
Oaths and affirmations, **2A:158A–23**
Salaries, **2A:158A–6**
Selection, **2A:158A–8**
Determination, eligibility, **2A:158A–14 et seq.**
Duties, **2A:158A–11**
Eligibility, determination, **2A:158A–14 et seq.**
Fees, **2A:158A–7**
Waiver, **Rule 1:13–2**
Grants and donations, authority to solicit,
2A:158A–7
Independent office, **2A:158A–3**
Investigations, **2A:158A–7**
Oaths and affirmations, **2A:158A–23**
Juvenile delinquents and dependents,
2A:158A–24; Rule 5:21–3
Financial circumstances, **2A:158A–25**
Legal representation, **2A:158A–5.2**
Liens and incumbrances,
Comprehensive enforcement program,
2B:19–6, 2B:19–11
Services, **2A:158A–17**
Recordation, **2A:158A–18**
Notice, liens for services, **2A:158A–17**
Oaths and affirmations, **2A:158A–23**
Office, **2A:158A–7**
Established, **2A:158A–3**
Officers and employees, **2A:158A–7**
Payment, cost for services, **2A:158A–16**
Records, **2A:158A–7**
Referrals, **Rule 3:4–2**
Report, legislature, governor and supreme
court, **2A:158A–22**
Representation, **Rule 3:8–3**
Rules and regulations, **2A:158A–7**
Service charges, **2A:158A–7**
Standards, performance, **2A:158A–13**
State department, public defender, office, es-
tablishment within, **2A:158A–3**
Voluntary workers or consultants, **2A:158A–7**
Workload division, **2A:158A–9**

PUBLIC EMPLOYEES
County Officers and Employees, generally, this
index
Municipal Officers and Employees, generally,
this index
Officers and Employees, generally, this index
State Officers and Employees, generally, this
index

**PUBLIC EMPLOYEES RETIREMENT SYS-
TEM**
Motor vehicles division, inspectors, transfer of
pension contributions, reserves, **39:2–9.5**

PUBLIC EMPLOYMENT
County Officers and Employees, generally, this
index
Officers and Employees, generally, this index
State Officers and Employees, generally, this
index

PUBLIC FUNDS
Funds, generally, this index

PUBLIC HALLS
Fireworks, showers, prohibition, **21:2–7**

PUBLIC HEALTH
Health and Sanitation, generally, this index

PUBLIC HEALTH SERVICE
Health and Sanitation, generally, this index

PUBLIC HIGHER EDUCATION
Colleges and Universities, generally, this index

PUBLIC HIGHWAYS
Definitions, traffic regulations, commissioner
of transportation, **39:4–8.2**
Highways and Roads, generally, this index

PUBLIC HOSPITALS
Hospitals, generally, this index

PUBLIC HOUSING
Housing, this index

PUBLIC HOUSING FACILITY
Definitions, controlled dangerous substances,
crimes and offenses, **2C:35–7.1**

PUBLIC IMPROVEMENTS
Curbs and Curbing, generally, this index
Highways and Roads, generally, this index
Parks and Parkways, generally, this index
Sidewalks, generally, this index
Streets and Alleys, generally, this index

PUBLIC INCONVENIENCE
Terroristic threats, **2C:12–3**

PUBLIC INDECENCY
Lewdness and Obscenity, generally, this index

PUBLIC INSTRUCTION
Schools and School Districts, generally, this
index

PUBLIC LANDS
All terrain vehicles, operation, **39:3C–32 et seq.**
Brands, labels and marks, garbage dumpsters
or containers, placement, **27:5I–1**
Consent, garbage and refuse, roll off dumpsters
or containers, placement, **27:5I–1**
Definitions,
Offroad vehicles, **39:3C–32**
Snowmobiles, all terrain vehicles, **39:3C–1**
Dirt bikes, operation, **39:3C–32 et seq.**
Dumpsters, placement on, **27:5I–1**
Fines and penalties, garbage and refuse, roll off
dumpsters or containers, placement,
27:5I–1
Garbage and refuse, roll off dumpsters or con-
tainers, placement on, **27:5I–1**
Motorcycles, operation, **39:3C–32 et seq.**
Parks and Parkways, generally, this index
Roll off container or dumpster, garbage and
refuse, placement, **27:5I–1**
Snowmobiles, operation, **39:3C–32 et seq.**
Solid waste, roll off dumpsters or containers,
placement on, **27:5I–1**
Turnpike authority, power to acquire, **27:23–5**

PUBLIC LAWS
Statutes, generally, this index

PUBLIC LIBRARIES
Libraries, generally, this index

PUBLIC MEDIA
Definitions, health and accident insurance, runners, **2C:21–22.1**

PUBLIC MONEYS
State Treasurer, generally, this index

PUBLIC NEW TRADED STOCKS
Shares and Shareholders, generally, this index

PUBLIC NOTICE
Notice, generally, this index

PUBLIC NUISANCE
Nuisance, generally, this index

PUBLIC OFFICERS AND EMPLOYEES
Bribery and Corruption, generally, this index
Civil Service, generally, this index
County Officers and Employees, generally, this
index
Crimes and Offenses, this index
Municipal Officers and Employees, generally,
this index
Officers and Employees, generally, this index
State Officers and Employees, generally, this
index

PUBLIC PARKS
Definitions, controlled dangerous substances,
crimes and offenses, **2C:35–7.1**
Parks and Parkways, generally, this index

PUBLIC PLACES
Cigarettes and Cigars, this index
Definitions, loitering for the purpose of engag-
ing in prostitution, **2C:34–1.1**
Obscene material, public communication,
2C:34–4

PUBLIC POLICY
Abuse of children, **9:6–8.8**
Child Abuse, this index
Controlled dangerous substances,
Profits, **2C:35A–2**
Trafficking, injunctions, **2C:35–5.5**
Courts, comprehensive enforcement program,
2B:19–2
Fireworks, possession and sale, declaration,
21:3–1
Juvenile Justice Code, **2A:4A–21**
Money laundering and illegal investments,
2C:21–23
Motor vehicle commission, **39:2A–2**
Motor Vehicles, this index
Municipal prosecutors, **2B:25–1**
New Jersey Medical Assistance and Health
Services Act. Medicaid, generally, this in-
dex
Nonresidents, traffic violators, **39:5F–2**
School buses, in terminal inspections, **39:3B–19**
Sex offenses, registration, studies, application
of law, **2C:7–20**

PUBLIC PRIVATE INTERSECTIONS
Intersections, this index

PUBLIC PROPERTY
Public Lands, generally, this index

PUBLIC RECORDS
Records and Recordation, generally, this index

PUBLIC RESOURCES
Bribery and corruption, **2C:27–12**

PUBLIC ROADS
Highways and Roads, generally, this index

PUBLIC ROADS AND HIGHWAYS BOND ACT OF 1963
Turnpike authority,
    Operation and maintenance of toll roads after payment of bonds, 27:23–16
    Revenues and funds, payment of indebtedness, 27:23–9

PUBLIC SALE
Sales, generally, this index

PUBLIC SCHOOLS
Schools and School Districts, generally, this index

PUBLIC SERVANT
Definitions, bribery and corrupt influence, 2C:27–1

PUBLIC SERVICE
Civil Service, generally, this index
Officers and Employees, generally, this index
Public Utilities, generally, this index

PUBLIC SERVICE COMMISSION
Public Utilities, generally, this index

PUBLIC TRANSPORTATION
Buses, generally, this index
Crimes and offenses, terrorism, 2C:38–2
False public alarm, 2C:33–3
Terrorism, 2C:38–2

PUBLIC UTILITIES
Assault and battery, officers and employees, 2C:12–1
Autobuses. Buses, generally, this index
Boards and commissions. Street Railways, this index
Broadcasting stations. Radio and Radio Stations, generally, this index
Burglary, facilities, 2C:18–2
Buses, generally, this index
Commercial motor vehicles, display of municipality names, 39:4–46
Computers, interference, crimes and offenses, 2C:20–25
Corporations, officers and employees, unlawful possession of weapons, exemption, 2C:39–6
Crimes and offenses,
    Computers, interference, 2C:20–25
    Facilities, burglary, 2C:18–2
    Identification cards, 2C:21–35
    Unlicensed entry of structure, 2C:18–3
Criminal mischief, 2C:17–3
Electricity and Electric Companies, generally, this index
Exemptions, vehicles, lettering or name plates, 39:4–46
Facilities, burglary, 2C:18–2
Fines and penalties, motor vehicles, amber warning lights, magnetic signs, 39:3–54.26
Franchises, vehicle lettering or name plates, exemption, 39:4–46
Fraud, identification cards, 2C:21–35
Identification cards, crimes and offenses, 2C:21–35
Monopolies and unfair trade, exempted, 56:9–5
Motor vehicles,
    Amber warning lights, 39:3–54.24
        Fines and penalties, 39:3–54.26
    Length of vehicle, 39:3–84
    Lettering or name plates, exemption, 39:4–46
    Magnetic signs, 39:3–54.25
        Fines and penalties, 39:3–54.26

PUBLIC UTILITIES—Cont'd
Nuclear generating plants. Radiation Protection, generally, this index
Officers and employees,
    Assault and battery, 2C:12–1
    Motor vehicles, generally, ante
    Weapons, exemption, 2C:39–6
Omnibus, maximum length, prescribing, 39:3–84
Pole trailers, lamp requirements, 39:3–61
Poles, outdoor advertising, signs, 27:5–9
Radiation Protection, generally, this index
Radio and Radio Stations, generally, this index
Railroads, generally, this index
Steam railroads. Railroads, generally, this index
Street Railways, generally, this index
Telecommunications, generally, this index
Theft of services, 2C:20–8
Turnpikes, this index
Unlicensed entry of structure, crimes and offenses, 2C:18–3
Water Supply Plants and Systems, generally, this index

PUBLIC UTILITY COMMISSIONERS
Public Utilities, generally, this index

PUBLIC WATER SUPPLY
Water Supply Plants and Systems, generally, this index

PUBLIC WELFARE
Indigent Persons, generally, this index

PUBLICATIONS
See, also,
    Advertisements, generally, this index
    Newspapers, generally, this index
Alcoholic Beverages, this index
Attorneys, disciplinary proceedings, **Rule 1:20–15**
Burglar tools, plans or instructions, 2C:5–5
Counties, this index
Crimes and offenses, summons, service by, **Rule 3:7–10**
Filing, proof of publication of notice, **Rule 1:5–6**
Forgery, generally, this index
Gambling, proof of occurrence of sporting events, presumption, 2C:37–5
Lewdness and Obscenity, generally, this index
Motor vehicle junk yard, notice of hearing on application for permit, 39:11–5, 39:11–6
Motor Vehicles, this index
Newspapers, generally, this index
Obscene materials. Lewdness and Obscenity, generally, this index
Opinions, **Rule 1:36–1 et seq.**
Rules of evidence, 2A:84A–43
Sales, this index
Searches and seizures, 2A:84A–21.9 et seq.
Turnpike authority, hearings, tolls, 27:23–5.11

PUBLICITY
Advertisements, generally, this index

PUERTO RICO
Credit cards, notice of revocation, 2C:21–6

PUNISHMENT
Crimes and Offenses, this index
Fines and Penalties, generally, this index

PUNITIVE DAMAGES
Damages, this index

PUPILS
Schools and School Districts, generally, this index

PURCHASERS
Definitions,
    Certificate of Motor Vehicle Ownership Law, 39:10–2
    Prepaid funeral agreements, 2A:102–18

PURCHASES
See, also, Sales, generally, this index
Alcoholic Beverages, this index
Definitions, Certificate of Motor Vehicle Ownership Law, 39:10–2
Human body parts, crimes and offenses, 2C:22–2
Jewelry, records and recordation, secondhand dealers, 2C:21–37
Sales, generally, this index

PURPLE HEART, MILITARY ORDER OF
Emblems for license plates, 39:3–27.43 et seq

PURPOSELY
Definitions,
    Code of Criminal Justice, 2C:2–2
    Crimes and offenses, 2C:2–2

PURSUIT
Fresh Pursuit Law, generally, this index

QUALIFIED PERSONS
Definitions, unsatisfied claim and judgment fund board, 39:6–62

QUALIFIED POSTSECONDARY NONDE-GREE INSTITUTION OF HIGHER EDUCATION LOCATED OUTSIDE THE STATE
Findings, nonjury trials, **Rule 1:7–4**

QUASHING
Subpoena, unreasonable requests, **Rule 1:9–2**

QUESTIONNAIRES
Jurors, qualifications and selection, 2B:20–3

QUESTIONS OF LAW AND FACT
Solicitation of sales or contributions as sole question in determining violation of statute, 39:4–60

QUIESCENTLY FROZEN CONFECTION
Frozen Desserts and Dietary Foods, generally, this index

QUORUM
Attorney certification,
    Board, **Rule 1:39–1**
    Committees, **Rule 1:39–1A**
Attorney discipline,
    Hearing panels, **Rule 1:20–6**
    Review Board, **Rule 1:20–15**
Fee arbitration hearings, attorneys, **Rule 1:20A–3**
Unauthorized practice of law, committees, **Rule 1:22–1A**

RABBIS
Clergy, generally, this index

RACE
Discrimination, generally, this index

RACEMETHORPHAN
See, also, Drugs and Medicine, generally, this index

RACEMETHORPHAN—Cont'd
Controlled substances, **24:21–1 et seq.**

RACEMORAMIDE
See, also, Drugs and Medicine, generally, this index
Controlled substances, **24:21–1 et seq.**

RACEMORPHAN
See, also, Drugs and Medicine, generally, this index
Controlled substances, **24:21–1 et seq.**

RACIAL DISCRIMINATION
Discrimination, generally, this index

RACIAL PROFILING
Law enforcement officers, crimes and offenses, **2C:30–5 et seq.**

RACING
All terrain vehicles, **39:3C–22**
Dirt bikes, **39:3C–22**
Gambling, generally, this index
Snowmobiles, **39:3C–1 et seq.**

RACISM
Discrimination, generally, this index

RACKETEERING ACTIVITY
Definitions, **2C:41–1**

RACKETEERS AND RACKETEERING
See, also, Organized Crime, generally, this index
Generally, **2C:41–1 et seq.**
Fines and penalties, **2C:41–3, 2C:41–4**
Minimum sentence, **2C:43–7.2**
Money Laundering and Illegal Investments, generally, this index
Terrorism, **2C:38–2, 2C:41–1 et seq.**
Weapons, **2C:41–1 et seq.**
Wiretapping and electronic surveillance, **2A:156A–1 et seq.**

RADIATION PROTECTION
Certificates, radioactive substances, handling, **26:2D–18**
Information submission, issuance, **26:2D–19**
Crimes and offenses, **26:2D–22**
Nuclear facilities, release, radiation, **2C:17–7 et seq.**
Definitions, certificates of handling, transportation, **39:5B–18**
Fines and penalties, **26:2D–22**
Nuclear facilities, release, radiation, **2C:17–7 et seq.**
Motor carriers, **39:5B–18 et seq.**
Nuclear electric generating facilities, crimes and offenses, release, **2C:17–7 et seq.**
Production of books and papers, certificates of handling or certificate numbers, transportation, **39:5B–18**
Radioactive Substances, generally, this index
Storage, radioactive substances, **26:2D–18 et seq.**
Transportation, **39:5B–18 et seq.**
Radioactive substances, **26:2D–18**
Vandalism causing release of radiation, crimes and offenses, **2C:17–7 et seq.**

RADIO AND RADIO STATIONS
See, also, Television, generally, this index
Amateur radio licensees, motor vehicle registration plates, **39:3–27.5**

RADIO AND RADIO STATIONS—Cont'd
Crimes and offenses,
Interception of police, fire or emergency medical communications, crimes and offenses, **2C:33–21 et seq.**
Possession of radio receiving police, fire or emergency medical communications during commission of crime, **2C:33–22**
Transmissions, licenses and permits, **2C:33–23.2**
Wiretapping and electronic surveillance, exceptions, **2A:156A–4**
Criminal proceedings, newsperson information disclosure privilege, **2A:84A–21.1 et seq.**
Emergency Medical Services, this index
Firefighters and Fire Departments, this index
Interception of police, fire or emergency medical communication, used to commit crime, **2C:33–21 et seq.**
Licenses and permits, transmissions, **2C:33–23.1**
Crimes and offenses, **2C:33–23.2**
Motor vehicle registration plates, amateur radio licensees, **39:3–27.5 et seq.**
News personnel privilege, **2A:84A–21, 2A:84A–21a**
Newsperson information disclosure privilege, criminal proceedings, **2A:84A–21.1 et seq.**
Privileged communications, newspersons information disclosure privilege, criminal proceedings, **2A:84A–21.1 et seq.**
Searches and seizures, **2A:84A–21.9 et seq.**
Transmissions, licenses and permits, **2C:33–23.1**
Crimes and offenses, **2C:33–23.2**
Wiretapping and electronic surveillance, crimes and offenses, exceptions, **2A:156A–4**

RADIOACTIVE SUBSTANCES
See, also, Radiation Protection, generally, this index
Causing or risking widespread injury or damage, **2C:17–2**
Certificates, handling, **26:2D–18**
Information submission, issuance, **26:2D–19**
Crimes and offenses,
Causing or risking widespread injury or damage, **2C:17–2**
Terrorism, **2C:38–2, 2C:38–3**
Criminal mischief, **2C:17–3**
Fines and penalties,
Causing or risking widespread injury or damage, **2C:17–2**
Terrorism, **2C:38–3**
Storage, **26:2D–18 et seq.**
Terrorism, **2C:17–2, 2C:38–2, 2C:38–3**
Transportation, **26:2D–18, 39:5B–18 et seq.**
Turnpike project, transportation regulation, **27:23–31**

RAFFLES
Rigging publicly exhibited contests, **2C:21–11**

RAFTS
Unlawful taking, **2C:20–10**

RAILROAD CROSSINGS
Blocking of highway by railroad prohibited, **39:4–94**
Busses, stopping, **39:4–128**
Commercial motor vehicles, approaching, **39:4–128.11**
Exemptions, motor vehicle stopping requirements, **39:4–128**
Explosives, trucks carrying explosives, stopping, **39:4–128**
Gates, this index

RAILROAD CROSSINGS—Cont'd
Grade Crossings, generally, this index
Motor carriers, approaching, **39:4–128.11**
Motor vehicles and school busses required to stop, **39:4–128**
Rates of speed, **39:4–98**
Moving heavy machinery, damages, **39:4–27**
Parking within certain distance prohibited, **39:4–138**
Police or peace officers, enforcement of regulations, stopping of motor vehicles, **39:5–1**
Regulations not to relieve operator of motor vehicles from state law, **39:4–128**
Right side of highway, keeping on required, **39:4–83**
School busses, stopping, **39:4–128**
Speedway excepted from Speed Law if not crossing railroad, **39:4–101**
Tractors, stopping before crossing, **39:4–128**
Traffic Rules and Regulations, this index

RAILROAD STATIONS
Street cars, regulation of stopping or starting at, power of municipality, **39:4–197**

RAILROAD TRAINS
Railroads, generally, this index

RAILROAD TRANSPORTATION DIVISION
Transportation Department, generally, this index

RAILROADS
Aggravated assault, officers and employees, **2C:12–1**
Alcoholic beverages,
Municipal referendum on retail sales, **33:1–46**
Place of sale where delivery is accompanied by transportation, **33:1–69**
Plenary retail transit license, **33:1–12**
All terrain vehicles, trespass, **39:3C–19**
Buses, this index
Cars, smoking cars, **2C:33–13**
Credit card offenses, tickets, **2C:21–6**
Crimes and offenses, crossing warning signals, vandalism, **2C:33–14.1**
Crossings. Railroad Crossings, generally, this index
Definitions,
Explosives Act, **21:1A–129**
Fireworks Regulation Law, **21:2–2**
Motor Vehicle Law, **39:1–1**
Dirt bikes, trespass, **39:3C–19**
Explosives, distances and quantity, manufacturing and storage, **21:1A–135**
Fireworks, exceptions, application of law, **21:2–4**
Grade Crossings, generally, this index
Graffiti, signals and signaling, **2C:33–14.1**
Hazardous materials, transportation, **39:5B–30 et seq.**
Highways and Roads, this index
Interference with transportation, **2C:33–14**
Intermodal transportation,
Axle weight limitations, **39:3–84.1**
Chassis, **39:3–79.10 et seq.**
Motorized bicycles, use of right of way, **39:4–14.3d**
Officers and employees, aggravated assault, **2C:12–1**
Reports, transportation of hazardous material, number of placarded freight cars, **39:5B–31.1**
Signals and signaling,
Graffiti, **2C:33–14.1**

RAILROADS—Cont'd

Signals and signaling—Cont'd
Vandalism, **2C:33–14.1**
Signs, removal of advanced warning signs, **39:4–183.21a**
Smoking cars, **2C:33–13**
Snowmobiles, trespass, **39:3C–19**
Street Railways, generally, this index
Suburban passenger service. Passengers, generally, this index
Tracks, turnpikes, use of right of way, **27:23–9**
Traction companies. Street Railways, generally, this index
Turnpike, use by railroad, **27:23–9**
Turnpike authority, relocation of facilities, **27:23–6**
Unlawful taking, **2C:20–10**

RAILWAY EXPRESS COMPANIES

Guards, weapons, unlawful possession, exemption, **2C:39–6**

RAILWAY POLICEMEN

Weapons, unlawful possession, exemption, **2C:39–6**

RANDOM AUDIT COMPLIANCE PROGRAM

Office of attorney ethics, **Rule 1:20–2**

RANSOM

Kidnapping, generally, this index

RAP SHEETS

Crimes and offenses, expungement, **2C:52–1 et seq.**

RAPE

Generally, **2C:14–1 et seq.**
Arrests, use of deadly force, **2C:3–7**
Attempts, body vest, **2C:39–13**
Body vests, **2C:39–13**
Date rape drugs. Controlled Substances, this index
Definitions, **2C:14–1**
Evidence, previous sexual conduct of complainant, admissibility, **2A:84A–32.1 et seq.**
Expungement of record, **2C:52–2**
Juvenile delinquents and dependents, jurisdiction, waiver, **2A:4A–26**
Murder, **2C:11–3**
Records and recordation, expungement, **2C:52–2**
Victims of crime, consultation, plea bargains, prosecutors, **2C:14–2.1**

RAZOR BLADES

Blades imbedded in wood,
Person convicted of crime involving, possession of any weapon prohibited, **2C:39–7**
Prohibited weapons, **2C:39–3**

READILY ACCESSIBLE TO THE GENERAL PUBLIC

Definitions, wiretapping and electronic surveillance, **2A:156A–2**

REAL ESTATE

Alcoholic beverages, consumption on, person making available, disorderly persons offense, exception, **2C:33–17**
Alimony, payment to probation officers, **2A:168–13**
Attachment, generally, this index
Availability for consumption of alcoholic beverages, persons guilty of offense, **2C:33–17**
Bail, criminal proceedings,
Location, **Rule 3:26–4**

REAL ESTATE—Cont'd

Bail, criminal proceedings—Cont'd
Municipal courts, **Rule 7:4–3**
Damages, unregistered vehicles, permits to cross public highways, Motor Vehicle Security, Responsibility Law, **39:3–26.5**
Defending, use of force, **2C:3–4**
Exemptions. Taxation, this index
Housing, generally, this index
Landlord and Tenant, generally, this index
Leases, generally, this index
Liens and Incumbrances, generally, this index
Mortgages, generally, this index
Parks and Parkways, generally, this index
Public Lands, generally, this index
School Buildings and Grounds, generally, this index
Taxation, generally, this index
Yards, alcoholic beverages, stills and distilling apparatus, **33:2–2**
Seizure, **33:2–3**
Zoning and Planning, generally, this index

REAL ESTATE APPRAISAL AND APPRAISERS

Commercial bribery and breach of duty, **2C:21–10**

REAL ESTATE BROKERS AND SALESPERSONS

Manufactured homes, dealers, **39:10–19**
Mobile homes, dealers, **39:10–19**

REAL PROPERTY

Real Estate, generally, this index

REAR LIGHTS

Lights and Lighting, this index

REAR VIEW MIRRORS

Motor Vehicles, this index

REASONABLE DOUBT

Juvenile delinquents and dependents, evidence, **Rule 5:24–3**
Standard of proof, criminal prosecutions, **2C:1–13**

REASONABLE EFFORTS

Definitions, abuse of children, **9:6–8.84**

REASONABLE SEARCHES AND SEIZURES

Search Warrants, generally, this index

REBATES

Alcoholic beverages, sales to retailers, **33:1–93**
Trigger locks, weapons, **2C:58–17**
Weapons, trigger locks, **2C:58–17**

RECEIPTS

Alcoholic beverages,
Receipt for property seized under warrant, **33:1–61**
Sale of receipts given on storage, **33:1–72**
Collection of fine under Motor Vehicle or Traffic Laws, **39:5–45**
Motor vehicle title papers, surrender on junking, vehicle, **39:10–23**
Property seized under search warrant, Alcoholic Beverage Law, **33:1–61**
Sales, this index
Searches and seizures, warrants, execution, **Rule 3:5–5**

RECEIVERS

See, also, Fiduciaries, generally, this index

RECEIVERS—Cont'd

Alcoholic beverages, more than one license in different capacities, **33:1–40**
Attorneys,
Bank accounts, recordkeeping, **Rule 1:21–6**
Client protection fund, **Rule 1:28–8**
Attorney misconduct, **Rule 1:28–6**
Court employees, appointment, **Rule 1:17–3**
Fraud, insolvency, **2C:21–13**
Judicial employees, appointment, **Rule 1:17–3**
Misapplication, entrusted property, **2C:21–15**
Solid Waste Management Act, **13:1E–9**

RECEIVING

Definitions,
Credit card offenses, **2C:21–6**
Receiving stolen property, **2C:20–7**

RECEIVING STATE

Definitions, probation or parole, **2A:168–19**

RECEIVING STOLEN PROPERTY

Generally, **2C:20–7**
Actions and proceedings, persons receiving stolen property, damages, **2C:20–20**
Credit cards, **2C:21–6**
Fencing, **2C:20–7.1**
Damages, **2C:20–20**
Injunctions, **2C:20–21**

RECEPTACLES

Containers, generally, this index
Packages, generally, this index

RECESSES

Courts, **Rule 1:30–3**

RECIDIVISTS

Second or Subsequent Offenses, generally, this index

RECIPE

Seizure of recipe for use in manufacture of alcoholic beverages, **33:1–66**

RECIPROCITY

All terrain vehicles, registration, **39:3C–7**
Attorneys, discipline, **Rule 1:20–14**
Commercial motor vehicles, registration, **39:3–6.1 et seq.**
Dirt bikes, registration, **39:3C–7**
Drivers Licenses, this index
Information between states concerning Traffic Law violations, **39:4–9.1**
Intoxicating liquors, **33:1–39.1**
Intoxication of driver, prior convictions, **39:4–50**
Motor Vehicles, this index
Nonresident traffic violators, **39:5F–3**
Registration, commercial vehicles, **39:3–6.1 et seq.**
Snowmobiles, **39:3C–7**
Trailers and semitrailers, registration, **39:3–6.1 et seq.**
Trucks, registration, **39:3–6.1 et seq.**

RECKLESS DRIVING

Motor Vehicles, this index

RECKLESSLY

Definitions, Code of Criminal Justice, **2C:2–2**

RECKLESSLY ENDANGERING ANOTHER PERSON

Generally, **2C:12–2**

RECKLESSNESS

Criminal mischief, **2C:17–3**

Intoxication, self induced, criminal liability, **2C:2–8**

Law enforcement officers, force or violence, grand jury, instructions to jury, **2B:22–9**

Obstructing highways and other public passages, **2C:33–7**

Use of force, **2C:3–9**

RECOGNIZANCES

See, also, Bail, generally, this index

Bail, record of, **Rule 3:26–4**

Disorderly persons, appeal, **2A:162–11**

Forfeitures,

Duration of lien of forfeited recognizance not prosecuted to judgment, **2A:162–5**

Money collected on forfeited recognizances paid to county treasurer, **2A:162–7**

Return by county treasurer of amount paid on, **2A:162–8**

Revival of judgment on forfeited recognizance, **2A:162–6**

Willful nonsupport, **2C:62–1**

Juvenile delinquents and dependents, release on own recognizance, **2A:4A–35**

Liens and incumbrances,

Forfeited recognizance not prosecuted to judgment, **2A:162–5**

Real estate in county other than where recognizance taken, **2A:162–1**

Time for enforcement against personal property, **2A:162–5**

Limitation of actions,

Bail, return of amount paid on forfeiture, **2A:162–8**

Return of money paid on forfeited recognizance, **2A:162–8**

Revival of judgment on forfeited recognizance, **2A:162–6**

Nonresident Violator Compact, motor vehicles, personal recognizances, **39:5F–1 et seq.**

Own recognizance, disorderly persons, appeal, **2A:162–11**

Personal property, time for enforcement of claim, lien or charge against, **2A:162–5**

Records, counties other than where taken, **2A:162–1**

Release of defendant, crime with bail restrictions, court determination, **2A:162–12**

Return of amount paid on forfeited recognizance, **2A:162–8**

Revival of judgment on forfeited recognizance, **2A:162–6**

Support, willful nonsupport, **2C:62–1**

Transmittal, limited criminal jurisdiction, courts of, appeals, **Rule 3:23–6**

RECOMMENDATIONS

Supervisory treatment programs, first offenders, referrals, **2C:43–12**

RECONSIDERATION

Material witness orders, **Rule 3:26–3**

RECONSTRUCTIVE SURGERY

Drivers licenses, color photographs, update, **39:3–10f**

RECORD ON APPEAL

Appeal and review, professional ethics, advisory committee on, opinion, **Rule 1:19–8**

RECORDED RECOLLECTIONS

Hearsay exception, **Evidence Rule 803**

RECORDERS AND RECORDERS COURTS

Municipal Courts, generally, this index

RECORDS AND RECORDATION

Alcoholic Beverages, this index

Anatomical gifts, disclosure, **39:2–3.4, 39:3–12.2**

Appeals In Criminal Prosecutions, this index

Arrest, this index

Attorneys, this index

Business and Commerce, this index

Certificate of lack of record, self authentication, **Evidence Rule 902**

Charge conferences, instructions to jury, **Rule 1:8–7**

Verbatim records, **Rule 1:2–2**

Child Abuse, this index

Child fatality and near fatality review board, **9:6–8.92**

Subpoenas, **9:6–8.93**

Child support hearing officers, **Rule 5:25–3**

Clerical mistakes, correction, **Rule 1:13–1**

Clerks of court, **Rule 1:32–2**

Controlled Substances, this index

Copies, public records, **Evidence Rule 1005**

Corporations, racketeering, investigations, **2C:41–5**

Correction of mistakes and errors, **Rule 1:13–1**

Correctional Institutions, this index

Corrections, theft of identity, **2C:21–17**

Court appointed special advocate, **2A:4A–92**

Court records. Records of Court, generally, this index

Courts, this index

Credit cards, fraud, scanning, **2C:21–6.1**

Crimes and Offenses, this index

Criminal History Record Information, generally, this index

Criminal usury, loan records, **2C:21–19**

Depositions, this index

Destruction or disposition, recordable instruments, fraud, **2C:21–3**

DNA Database and Databank, generally, this index

Domestic Violence, this index

Electronic fund transfers, fraud, payment cards, scanning, **2C:21–6.1**

Electronic retention, **Rule 1:32–2**

Electronic Transactions, generally, this index

Errors, clerical mistakes, correction, **Rule 1:13–1**

Evidence, this index

Excluded evidence, **Rule 1:7–3**

Explosives, **21:1A–132**

Transportation, **21:1A–137**

Expunging Record, generally, this index

Falsifying or tampering, **2C:21–4**

Family Court, this index

Family records, hearsay exception, **Evidence Rule 803**

Fingerprints and Fingerprinting, this index

Fireworks, manufacturers and manufacturing, certificates of registration, revocation, **21:2–26**

Forgery, **2C:21–1**

Fraud, **2C:21–3, 2C:21–13**

Gambling records, possession, **2C:37–3**

Grand Jury, this index

Hearsay exception, **Evidence Rule 803**

Human Services Department, this index

Impounded records, confidentiality, **Rule 1:38–3**

Jewelry, secondhand dealers, sales, **2C:21–36**

Jurors and juries, excuses, deferrals and questionnaires, retention, **2B:20–12**

Jury lists, public record, qualifications and selection, **2B:20–5**

RECORDS AND RECORDATION—Cont'd

Juvenile Delinquents, this index

Juvenile family crisis, hearings, **Rule 5:17–4**

Medical advisory panel,

Liability, immunity, **39:2–16**

Motor vehicles division, liability for disclosure, **39:2–16**

Motions, telephone arguments, **Rule 1:6–2**

Motor carriers, intermodal transportation, chassis, **39:3–79.17**

Motor Vehicles, this index

Motor vehicles division, liability, immunity, **39:2–16**

Motorized bicycles, registration certificates, **39:4–14.3i**

Municipal Courts, this index

Nonresident Violator Compact, motor vehicles, personal recognizances, **39:5F–1 et seq.**

Offering false instruments for filing, **2C:21–3**

Open court proceedings, sealing of records, **Rule 1:2–1**

Ordinances, this index

Partnerships, this index

Petit jurors, names, selection for trial, public record, **2B:23–4**

Physicians and Surgeons, this index

Podiatrists and Podiatry, this index

Pretrial intervention programs, confidentiality, **Rule 1:38–3**

Probation and Probation Officers, this index

Production of Books and Papers, generally, this index

Public defenders, **2A:158A–7**

Racketeering, investigative interrogatories, **2C:41–5**

Radio stations, broadcasts, news personnel privilege, **2A:84A–21**

Recognizance of bail,

Counties other than where taken, **2A:162–1**

Criminal proceedings, **Rule 3:26–4**

Regularly conducted activities, hearsay exception, **Evidence Rule 803**

Release, this index

Schedule of retention, **Rule 1:32–2**

School buses, inspectors and inspection, **39:3B–21**

Self authentication, public documents, **Evidence Rule 902**

Sex offenders, registration, **2C:7–5**

Sheriffs, this index

State Police, this index

Stolen property, photographic records, law enforcement agencies, **2C:65–1**

Summaries, admissibility, **Evidence Rule 1006**

Tampering, **2C:21–4, 2C:28–7**

Television, telecasts, news personnel privilege, **2A:84A–21**

Theft, **2C:20–2**

Identity and identification, corrections, **2C:21–17**

Transcripts, generally, this index

Transfer of actions, **Rule 1:13–4**

Transportation Department, this index

Trial, this index

Unauthorized practice of law,

Appeal of decisions, **Rule 1:22–3A**

Committees, **Rule 1:22–1**

Verbatim records, **Rule 1:2–2**

Exhibits, **Rule 1:2–3**

Weapons, this index

Wiretapping and electronic surveillance, **2A:156A–14**

RECORDS OF COURT

Aggravating factors, sentences, **2C:44–1**

Expungement, **2C:52–1 et seq.**

RECORDS OF COURT—Cont'd
Mitigating factors, sentences, 2C:44–1
Sentence and punishment,
    Aggravating or mitigating factors, 2C:44–1
    Parole laws, 2C:43–2
    Reasons for imposing sentence, 2C:43–2

**RECREATION AND RECREATIONAL FA-
CILITIES**
All terrain vehicles, 39:3C–1 et seq.
Bowling alleys, intoxicating liquors, license to
    sell, 33:1–12
Children and Minors, this index
Parks and Parkways, generally, this index
Sexually oriented businesses, zoning and plan-
    ning, 2C:34–7
Snowmobiles, 39:3C–1 et seq.
Summer Camps, generally, this index
Zoning and planning, sexually oriented busi-
    nesses, 2C:34–7

RECREATIONAL PROPERTY
Definitions, destruction by operation of motor
    vehicle, 39:4–97a
Penalty points system, 39:5–30.5a

RECREATIONAL VEHICLES
Definitions,
    Commercial Driver License Act, 39:3–10.11
    Traffic laws, 39:1–1
Length and width, 39:3–84
Off site sales, licenses and permits, 39:10–19.1
    et seq.
Sales, off site sales, licenses and permits,
    39:10–19.1 et seq.
Sunday, sales, deposits, 2C:33–26

RECTIFYING AND BLENDING PLANTS
Alcoholic beverage as misdemeanor, 33:1–50
License, 33:1–10
    Bottling without, 33:1–78
Persons interested in retailing, 33:1–43

RECYCLING
Solid Waste, this index

RECYCLING VEHICLES
Definitions, vehicle size and weight limits,
    39:3–84

RED CROSS
Motor vehicles, free registration, 39:3–27

RED ELECTRIC LANTERNS
Carrying and placing on highways by motor
    vehicles, 39:3–64

RED FLAGS
Flags, this index

RED LIGHTS
Lights and Lighting, this index

REFEREES AND REFERENCE
Commercial bribery and breach of duty,
    2C:21–10
Juvenile delinquents, Rule 5:25–2
    Complaints, family crisis, 2A:4A–70
Mediation, Rules 1:40–5, 1:40–6
Motor vehicles, arbitration and award, tort
    claims, 39:6A–24 et seq.

**REFLECTORIZED LICENSE PLATE SELEC-
TION COMMISSION**
Generally, 39:3–33.9

REFLECTORS
Bicycles, 39:4–10, 39:4–14.4

REFLECTORS—Cont'd
Definitions, 39:3–46
Lights and Lighting, this index
Motor vehicles. Lights and Lighting, this index
Outdoor advertising, use on signs, 27:5–9

REFORMATORIES
Correctional Institutions, generally, this index

REFRESHING MEMORY
Writings, use to refresh memory, Evidence
    Rule 612

REFUGE ISLANDS
Safety zones, 39:4–196.2

REFUNDING BONDS
Turnpike authority, 27:23–5, 27:23–7, 27:23–15

REFUNDS
Alcoholic Beverage Tax, this index
Fines and penalties, unconstitutionality,
    2B:12–32
Ordinances, unconstitutionality, fines and pen-
    alties, 2B:12–32

REFUSE
Solid Waste, generally, this index

REGIMENTAL EXCHANGE
Alcoholic beverage license and fee exemption,
    retail sale, 33:1–27

**REGIONAL AIR POLLUTION CONTROL
AGENCY**
Motor vehicles, registration fee exemption,
    39:3–27

**REGIONAL DIAGNOSTIC AND TREAT-
MENT CENTER**
Child abuse or neglect, 9:6–8.99
Indigent, neglected or abandoned children,
    9:6–8.99

REGIONAL SCHOOL DISTRICTS
Schools and School Districts, this index

REGISTERED MAIL
Certified or registered mail. Mail and Mailing,
    this index

REGISTERED NURSES
Nurses, generally, this index

REGISTERED PHARMACISTS
Pharmacists, generally, this index

REGISTERS
Domestic violence, injunctions, 2C:25–34
Juvenile delinquents and dependents, 2A:4A–60
    Rules and regulations, 2A:4A–60.1
Violent criminal apprehension program (VI-
    CAP, 53:1–20.11
Weapons, sales, 2C:58–2

REGISTRARS OF VITAL STATISTICS
Marriage licenses and certificates. Marriage,
    generally, this index

REGISTRATION
All Terrain Vehicles, this index
Dirt bikes, 39:3C–4 et seq.
    Exemptions, special events, 39:3C–23
    Fees, disposition, 39:3C–29
Electric personal assistive mobility devices,
    39:4–14.10
Firearms, manufacturers and wholesale dealers,
    2C:58–1

REGISTRATION—Cont'd
Motor Carriers, this index
Motor vehicle commission, motor vehicles, im-
    provements, chief administrator, 39:2A–2
Motorized Bicycles, this index
New Jersey turnpike authority, towing vehicle
    27:23–6.2
Pharmacists, this index
Physicians and Surgeons, this index
Sex Offenses, this index
Snowmobiles, this index
Stills and Distilling Apparatus, this index
Storage, New Jersey turnpike authority,
    27:23–6.2
Support of persons, suspension or revocation,
    child support enforcement. Support of
    Persons, generally, this index
Tow Trucks and Towing Companies, this inde
Turnpikes, towing vehicles, 27:23–6.2
Weapons, 2C:39–9

REGISTRATION OF VOTERS
Jury list, eligible county residents, qualification
    and selection, 2B:20–2
Motor vehicles, drivers licenses, application,
    Distribution of forms, 39:3–10m
    Simultaneous applications, 39:2–3.2

REGISTRY
Bail, insurers, Rule 1:13–3
Pretrial intervention registry, criminal proce-
    dure, Rule 3:28

REGULARLY CONDUCTED ACTIVITIES
Records, hearsay exemption, Evidence Rule
    803

REGULATED EMPLOYMENT
Rehabilitated convicted offenders, 2A:168A–5

REGULATIONS
Rules and Regulations, generally, this index

REGULATORY COMMISSIONERS
Public Utilities, generally, this index

**REHABILITATED CONVICTED OFFEND-
ERS**
Generally, 2A:168A–1 et seq.

REHABILITATION
Aged Persons, this index
Centers, institutionalized elderly persons, as-
    sault, 2C:12–1
Code of Criminal Justice, 2C:1–2
Crimes and Offenses, this index
Juvenile Delinquents, this index
Probation, conditions, 2C:45–1
Supervisory treatment programs, first offend-
    ers, 2C:43–12 et seq.

REHEARINGS
Findings by court, nonjury trials, Rule 1:7–4

REIMPRISONMENT
Parolee in receiving state, 2A:168–18 et seq.

RELATIVES
Aggravated sexual assault, 2C:14–2
Aggravated sexual contact, 2C:14–3
Criminal restraint, 2C:13–2
False imprisonment, 2C:13–3
Judges, disqualification, Rule 1:12–1

RELAXATION OF RULES
Generally, Rule 1:1–2

RELEASE
Correctional Institutions, this index
Criminal defendant, delay in trial, **Rule 3:25–2**
Domestic violence, defendant, release before trial, bail, **2C:25–26**
Juvenile Delinquents, this index
Medical records, abused children, **9:6–8.30**
Mentally deficient and mentally ill persons, persons committed by reason of insanity, crimes and offenses, **2C:4–9**
Motorist from liability affecting suspension or renewal of license or nonresidents operating privilege, **39:6–27**
Records and recordation, child abuse or neglect, **9:6–8.40**
Stolen property, delivery prior to proceedings, **2C:65–2**
Witnesses in criminal cases, conditions, **Rule 3:26–3**

RELEVANCY
Evidence, this index

RELIEF
Indigent Persons, generally, this index

RELIGION
Abuse of children, protection orders, **9:6–8.55**
Child, treatment of ill in accordance with religious tenets of church, **9:6–1.1**
Cleric penitent privilege, **2A:84A–23**
Discrimination, generally, this index
Medical treatment, children, accordance with religious tenets of church, **9:6–1.1**
Records of organizations, hearsay exception, **Evidence Rule 803**
Witnesses,
  Barring from testifying, religious belief or lack, **Evidence Rule 603**
  Compelling disclosure, **2A:84A–24**
  Impeaching credibility, **Evidence Rule 610**
  Priest penitent privilege, **Evidence Rule 511**
  Privileged communications, **Evidence Rule 512**

RELIGIOUS CORPORATIONS AND ASSOCIATIONS
Benefit of clergy, abolition, **2A:152–2**
Bias intimidation, crimes and offenses, **2C:16–1**
Buildings,
  Desecration, **2C:33–9**
  Targets of crime, conspiracy, grade and degree of offense, **2C:5–4**
Clergy, generally, this index
Cleric penitent privilege, **2A:84A–23**
Club officers, intoxicating liquors, law enforcement personnel, **33:1–25.1, 33:1–25.2**
Constables, intoxicating liquors, licenses and permits, **33:1–25.1, 33:1–25.2**
Crimes and offenses,
  Bias intimidation, **2C:16–1**
  Places of worship,
    Arson, **2C:17–1**
    Targets of conspiracy, grade and degree of offense, **2C:5–4**
Desecration, **2C:33–9**
Discrimination, bias intimidation, crimes and offenses, **2C:16–1**
Evidence, cleric penitent privilege, **2A:84A–23**
Intoxicating liquors,
  Club licenses, law enforcement personnel as officers, **33:1–25.1, 33:1–25.2**
  Temporary permit, fees, **33:1–74**
Law enforcement officers, intoxicating liquors, licenses and permits, **33:1–25.1, 33:1–25.2**

RELIGIOUS CORPORATIONS AND ASSOCIATIONS—Cont'd
Licenses and permits, intoxicating liquors, law enforcement personnel as club officers, **33:1–25.1, 33:1–25.2**
Ministers. Clergy, generally, this index
Monopolies and unfair trade, exemptions, **56:9–5**
Motor vehicle junk yard, proximity of churches to be considered on application for permit, **39:11–5**
Officers and employees, intoxicating liquors, law enforcement personnel, **33:1–25.1, 33:1–25.2**
Parking vehicle near entrance to church for purpose of taking on or letting off passengers, time limited, **39:4–139**
Parochial schools. Private Schools, generally, this index
Places of worship,
  Arson, **2C:17–1**
  Targets of conspiracy, grade and degree of offense, **2C:5–4**
Police and police departments, intoxicating liquors, licenses and permits, **33:1–25.1, 33:1–25.2**
Priests. Clergy, generally, this index
Rabbis. Clergy, generally, this index
Sales, alcoholic beverages within 200 feet of church, **33:1–76**
  Waiver of protection, **33:1–76.1, 33:1–76.2**
Schools. Private Schools, generally, this index
Sexually oriented businesses, zoning and planning, **2C:34–7**
Sheriffs, intoxicating liquors, licenses and permits, **33:1–25.1, 33:1–25.2**
Target of crime,
  Arson, **2C:17–1**
  Conspiracy, grade and degree of offense, **2C:5–4**
Zoning and planning, sexually oriented businesses, **2C:34–7**

RELIGIOUS DISCRIMINATION
Discrimination, generally, this index

RELIGIOUS ORGANIZATIONS
Religious Corporations and Associations, generally, this index

RELIGIOUS SERVICES
Religious Corporations and Associations, generally, this index

RELOCATION
Highways and Roads, this index

REMOTE COMPUTING SERVICE
Definitions, wiretapping and electronic surveillance, **2A:156A–2**

REMUNERATION
Compensation and Salaries, generally, this index

RENT
See, also,
  Landlord and Tenant, generally, this index
  Leases, generally, this index
Noncommercial trucks, license requirements, **39:3–8, 39:3–8.1**
Nursing Homes or Hospitals, generally, this index

RENUNCIATION OF CRIMINAL PURPOSE
Generally, **2C:5–1**
Accomplices, **2C:2–6**

RENUNCIATION OF CRIMINAL PURPOSE—Cont'd
Conspiracy, defense, **2C:5–2**

REPAYMENT
Restitution, generally, this index

REPEALS
Crimes and offenses, **2C:98–2**
  Law saved from repeal, **2C:98–3**
Criminal laws, statutes saved from repeal, **2C:98–3**

REPETITIVE DISORDERLY PERSONS OFFENSES
Definitions, juvenile justice, **2A:4A–22**

REPORTERS
Motor vehicles, limitation on use of signs, posters and stickers with word press, **39:3–76.1**

REPORTS
Accidents, this index
Administrative director of the courts, trial judges, **Rule 1:32–1**
Administrative office of the courts, motor vehicles, tort claims arbitration, **39:6A–35**
Adult diagnostic and treatment center, examinations, sex offenders, **2C:47–5**
Agricultural Products, this index
Alarms, false alarms, **2C:33–3 et seq.**
Alcoholic Beverages, this index
Aliens, weapons violations, convictions, **2C:58–9**
All terrain vehicles, accidents, **39:3C–21**
Animals, this index
Attorney certification board, **Rule 1:39–1**
Attorney General, this index
Attorneys, this index
Banks and Banking, this index
Casinos, this index
Chemical analysis, arrested motorists breath, **39:4–50.3**
Child Abuse, this index
Children and minors, abuse, **9:6–8.10 et seq.**
Clerks of Court, this index
Controlled Substances, this index
Conviction of Crime, this index
County Prosecutors, this index
Crimes and Offenses, this index
Criminal sentencing and disposition commission, **2C:48A–4**
Death, motor vehicle accidents, **39:4–134**
Dirt bikes, accidents, **39:3C–21**
Domestic violence, **2C:25–24**
  Prevention, **2C:25–33**
Drivers Licenses, this index
Drug Abuse, this index
Epilepsy and similar conditions, drivers licenses, **39:3–10.8**
Evidence, this index
False public alarms, **2C:33–3 et seq.**
Fires and fire protection, failure to report, arson, **2C:17–1**
General Assembly, this index
Governor, this index
Hazardous Substances and Waste, this index
Hospitals, this index
Identification Bureau, this index
Identity theft, law enforcement officers, **2C:21–17.6**
Inspection and Inspectors, this index
Jewelry, stolen goods, secondhand, **2C:21–39**
  Privileges and immunities, **2C:21–40**
Judges and Justices, this index
Juvenile delinquents and dependents, predispositional reports, **Rule 5:24–2**

REPORTS—Cont'd

Law enforcement authorities, false reports,
2C:28–4

Medical advisory panel, liability, immunity,
39:2–16

Mentally Deficient and Mentally Ill Persons,
this index

Money laundering and illegal investments, currency transactions, 2C:21–25

Money Transmitters, this index

Motor vehicle commission, 39:2A–22

Motor Vehicle Insurance, this index

Motor Vehicles, this index

Motorized bicycles, accident reports, 39:4–14.3f

Municipal courts, **Rule 7:2–1**

Narcotics and dangerous substances, conviction
of manufacturers and practitioners, controlled dangerous substances, 24:21–36

New Jersey task force on child abuse and
neglect, findings and recommendations,
9:6–8.82

Nonresident Violator Compact, motor vehicles,
personal recognizances, **39:5F–1 et seq.**

Optometrists, this index

Physicians and Surgeons, this index

Police and Police Departments, this index

Presentence investigations and reports, 2C:44–6
Expunged records, use in preparing,
2C:52–21

Privileges and immunities, jewelry, stolen
goods, secondhand, 2C:21–40

Probation and Probation Officers, this index

Psychiatric examinations, mentally deficient or
mentally ill defendants, 2C:4–5

Public defenders, 2A:158A–22

Radon gas test results, environmental protection department, 26:2D–74

Railroads, this index

Rigging publicly exhibited contests, 2C:21–11

Searches and seizures, strip or body cavity
searches, 2A:161A–4

Sex Offenses, this index

Snowmobiles, accidents, 39:3C–21

Speed, sixty five mph, 39:4–98.7

State Police, this index

Stolen goods, jewelry, secondhand, 2C:21–39
Privileges and immunities, 2C:21–40

Supervisory treatment programs, first offenders, 2C:43–21

Traffic Accidents, this index

Traffic control signal monitoring system,
39:4–8.17

Traffic offenses, municipal courts, **Rule 7:8–9**

Transportation Department, this index

Victim and witness advocacy fund, victims of
crime compensation board, 2C:43–3.1

Weapons, this index

Wiretapping and electronic surveillance,
2A:156A–20, 2A:156A–22, 2A:156A–23

Wounds, firearms and other explosive devices,
2C:58–8

REPRESENTATIONS

Fraud, generally, this index

REPRESENTATIVES

General Assembly, generally, this index

REPRIEVES

Reports, 2A:167–3.1

REPRIMAND

Attorneys, **Rule 1:20–15A**
Private reprimand, **Rule 1:20–2**

REPRODUCTION

Definitions, endangering welfare of child, pornography, 2C:24–4

REPTILES

Marine reptiles, conservation, marine mammal
stranding center fund, wildlife conservation license plate renewal fees, 39:3–33.11

REPUTATION

Character and Reputation, generally, this index

REQUESTS FOR PUBLICATION

Opinions, **Rule 1:36–2**

REQUISITIONS

Extradition, this index

Purchase of supplies, alcoholic beverage control division director, 33:1–23

RES JUDICATA

Crimes and offenses. Double Jeopardy, generally, this index

Unpublished opinions, **Rule 1:36–3**

RESALE

Sales, this index

RESCUE SQUADS

Commercial drivers licenses, exemption,
39:3–10j, 39:3–10k

Exemption, commercial drivers license requirement, 39:3–10j

Motor vehicles,
Emergency warning lights, volunteers,
39:3–54.7 et seq.
Registration fees, exemption, 39:3–27
Special license plates, 39:3–27.8 et seq.

Warning lights, volunteers, 39:3–54.7 et seq.

RESEARCH

Attorneys, ethics, advertising and solicitation,
telephone research service, **Rule 1:19–9**

Colleges and Universities, generally, this index

Controlled substances, registration, 24:21–10,
24:21–11

Facilities,
Burglary, 2C:18–2
Criminal mischief, 2C:17–3
Criminal trespass, 2C:18–3
Theft, 2C:20–2
Unlicensed entry of structures, 2C:18–3

Spinal cord, funds, fines and penalties, motor
vehicles, 39:5–41

RESEARCH AND DEVELOPMENT LABORATORIES

Burglary, 2C:18–2

Criminal trespass, 2C:18–3

RESEARCH AND TRAINING CENTERS

Burglary, 2C:18–2

Criminal trespass, 2C:18–3

RESERVATIONS

Turnpike authority, power to acquire property,
27:23–5

RESERVE FUND

Interest on lawyers trust account fund, **Rule
1:28A–4**

RESERVES

Armed Forces, this index

RESIDENCE AND RESIDENTS

See, also, Nonresidents, generally, this index

All terrain vehicles, registration fees, 39:3C–3

RESIDENCE AND RESIDENTS—Cont'd

Assessments, generally, this index

Commercial motor vehicles, agreements, registration, reciprocity, 39:3–6.1 et seq.

Controlled dangerous substances, injunctions,
2C:35–5.4 et seq.

Crimes and offenses, suspended sentences,
conditions, 2C:45–1

Definitions, Commercial Driver License Act,
39:3–10.11

Foreign States, generally, this index

Jails, sex offenses, release, registration,
2C:7–2.1

Jurors, county in which summoned, 2B:20–1

Long Arm Act, 39:7–1 et seq.

Motor vehicles, Nonresident Violator Compact
39:5F–1 et seq.

Out of State Motorist Act, 39:7–1 et seq.

Pleadings, caption, **Rule 1:4–1**

Probation, conditions, 2C:45–1

Process,
Cost of service, nonresidents, 39:7–3
Taxed in successful plaintiffs costs, 39:7–5
Custody, service on nonresident owner by
serving person in custody of motor vehicle, 39:7–8

Registration, sex offenses, release, 2C:7–2.1

Snowmobiles, registration fees, 39:3C–3

Speed of motor vehicles, 39:4–98

Support proceedings, 2C:62–1

Traffic regulations, Nonresident Violator Compact, **39:5F–1 et seq.**

Witnesses, generally, this index

RESIDENCE DISTRICTS

Definitions, 39:1–1

RESIDENT PERSON

Definitions, intoxicating liquors, 33:1–11.2

RESIDENTIAL HEALTH CARE FACILITIES

Criminal history record information,
Assisted living facilities, 53:1–20.9c
Nurses aides, certificates, 53:1–20.9a

Institutionalized elderly persons, assault,
2C:12–1

Nurses aides, criminal history record checks,
certificates, 53:1–20.9a

RESIDENTIAL TREATMENT CENTERS

Definitions, controlled dangerous substances,
2C:35–2

RESIGNATION

Attorneys, this index

RESISTANCE

Sexual offenses, proof of resistance, 2C:14–5

RESISTING ARREST

Generally, 2C:29–2

Unlawful arrest, use of force, 2C:3–4

RESOLUTIONS

See, also, Ordinances, generally, this index

Alcoholic Beverages, this index

Autobusses, stops or stations, 39:4–8

County Roads, this index

Handicapped parking enforcement units,
39:4–197.9

Municipalities, this index

Nonresident Violator Compact, motor vehicle
39:5F–23

Turnpike authority, emergencies, 27:23–6.1

RESORTS

Casinos, generally, this index

ESORTS—Cont'd
isorderly persons, termination of right to occupy or visit, **2C:43–8.1**
ambling resorts, maintenance, **2C:37–4**
uisances, **2C:33–12**

ESOURCE FAMILY CARE
ggravated criminal sexual contact, **2C:14–3**
x offenses,
Aggravated criminal sexual contact, **2C:14–3**
Sexual assault, **2C:14–2**

ESPONDENTS BRIEF
riefs, this index

EST AREAS
ights of way, commercial activity, **39:4–216**
ate and interstate highways, commercial activities, **39:4–216**

EST HOMES
ursing Homes or Hospitals, generally, this index

ESTAURANTS
efinitions,
Intoxicating liquor law, **33:1–1**
Intoxicating liquors, **33:1–1**
iscrimination, generally, this index
isorderly persons, intoxicating liquors, unlicensed premises, **2C:33–27**
toxicating liquors,
Disorderly persons, unlicensed premises, **2C:33–27**
Licenses and permits, **33:1–12.32**
Unlicensed premises, consumption, **2C:33–27**
icenses and permits, intoxicating liquors, consumption on premises, Chain Store Liquor License Act, **33:1–12.32**
noking, **2C:33–13**
heft of services, **2C:20–8**
urnpike authority, use of right of way, **27:23–9**

ESTITUTION
Generally, **2C:43–3, 2C:43–3.2, 2C:44–1, 2C:46–1, 2C:46–2**
gricultural land, vandalism, **2C:18–6**
rchaeology and archaeologists, transportation, state property, archaeological findings, alteration, **27:5J–1**
uto theft, **2C:20–2.2**
ias intimidation, **2C:16–1**
ollection proceedings,
Default in payment of restitution, **2C:46–2**
Persons convicted of crime, **2C:46–4**
ompounding, **2C:29–4**
omprehensive enforcement program, definitions, nonpayment of fines or restitution, **2C:46–2**
orporations, **2C:43–4**
riminal convictions, assessments, **2C:43–3.1, 2C:46–4**
Law enforcement officers training and equipment fund, **2C:43–3.3**
Transaction fee, **2C:46–1 et seq.**
efault, punishment, **2C:46–2**
nforced community service, definitions, nonpayment of fines or restitution, **2C:46–2**
raffiti,
Conviction of, defacement or damage of property, **2C:33–10, 2C:33–11**
Defacement or damage of property, juvenile delinquents and dependents, **2A:4A–43.2**
igh misdemeanors, **2A:93–5.1**
omicide, **2C:11–3c**
uman trafficking, **2C:13–8**
lentity theft, **2C:21–17.4**

RESTITUTION—Cont'd
Juvenile delinquents, **2A:4A–43**
Graffiti, **2A:4A–43.2**
Incarceration, mitigating circumstances, **2A:4A–44**
Labor assistance program, definitions, nonpayment of fines or restitution, **2C:46–2**
Mitigating circumstances, **2C:44–1**
Murder, **2C:11–3c**
Nonpayment, **2C:44–2**
Payment, **2C:46–1, 2C:46–2**
Transaction fee, **2C:46–1 et seq.**
Racketeering, **2C:41–4**
Satisfaction of claims, **2C:46–4.1**
Summary collection proceedings, default in payment, **2C:46–2**
Superior court, chancery division, family part, **2C:46–5**
Suspended sentences, conditions, **2C:43–2, 2C:45–1**
Theft of services, **2C:20–8**
Victims of crime,
Code of Criminal Justice, **2C:1–2**
Criteria, **2C:44–2**
Definitions, fines and penalties, **2C:43–3**

RESTRAINING DEVICES
Motor vehicles,
Children and minors, **39:3–76.2a et seq.**
Passenger automobiles, **39:3–76.2**

RESTRAINING ORDERS
Injunctions, generally, this index

RESTRAINT
Criminal restraint, **2C:13–2**
Human trafficking, **2C:13–8**

RESTRAINT OF TRADE
Monopolies, generally, this index

RESTRICTED PARKING SPACE
Definitions, handicapped parking, **39:4–207.6**

RESTRICTED PARKING ZONE
Definitions, handicapped parking, **39:4–207.6**

RETAIL DEALERS
Definitions, firearms, **2C:39–1**

RETAIL MERCANTILE ESTABLISHMENTS
Definitions, ephedrine, pseudoephedrine, phenylpropanolamine, **2C:35–26**

RETAIL SALES
Sales, generally, this index

RETAIL STORES
Stores, generally, this index

RETAIL VALUE
Definitions, counterfeiting, trademarks and trade names, **2C:21–32**

RETAILERS
Alcoholic Beverages, this index
Definitions,
Intoxicating liquor law, **33:1–1**
Obscene materials, display, **2C:34–3.1**
Obscene materials, display, **2C:34–3.1, 2C:34–3.2**

RETALIATION
Labor and Employment, this index
Public officers and employees, past official actions, **2C:27–5**
Witnesses and informants, **2C:28–5**

RETIRED JUDGES
Assignments, title, **Rule 1:37–3**

RETIREMENT AND PENSIONS
County Detectives and Investigators, this index
Judges and Justices, this index
Law Enforcement Officers, this index
Police and Police Departments, this index

RETRACTION
Perjury, **2C:28–1**

RETROACTIVITY
Motor vehicles, arbitration and award, tort claims, **39:6A–25**

RETURNS
Arrest warrant, **Rule 3:3–3**
Jury and Jurors, this index
Summons, crimes and offenses, **Rule 3:3–3**

REVENUE
Taxation, generally, this index
Turnpikes, this index

REVERSAL
Appeal and review, return of fine to defendant, **2A:166–13**

REVERSIONS
Leases, possession to lessor for violation of Alcoholic Beverage Law, **33:1–54**

REVIEW
Appeal and Review, generally, this index

REVISED UNIFORM ANATOMICAL GIFT ACT
Anatomical Gifts, generally, this index

REVOLVERS
Weapons, generally, this index

REVOLVING FUNDS
Funds, this index

REWARDS
Generally, **2A:153–1 et seq.**
Amount, **2A:153–1 et seq.**
Associations of detectives, pursuers, services, **15:4–2**
Bribery and Corruption, generally, this index
Chosen freeholders authority to offer, criminal procedure, **2A:153–2**
Escaped county prisoners, reward for apprehension, **2A:153–3**
Governors authority to offer, **2A:153–1**
Graffiti, detection and apprehension, **2A:153–4.1**
Kidnapping, **2C:13–1**
Municipalities, criminal detection and apprehension, **2A:153–4**

REWARDS FOR JUSTICE LICENSE PLATE FUND
Generally, **39:3–27.134 et seq.**

RIDESHARING
Definitions, motor vehicles, **39:1–1**
Licenses and registration, **39:3–4.1**

RIFLES
Weapons, generally, this index

RIGGING PUBLICLY EXHIBITED CONTESTS
Generally, **2C:21–11**

RIGHT OF WAY
Autobuses, yielding, **39:4–87.1**
Blind persons, **39:4–37.1**
Crosswalks, pedestrians, **39:4–34 et seq.**
Definitions, Motor Vehicle Law, **39:1–1**
Electric personal assistive mobility devices, **39:4–14.10**
Emergency vehicles, **39:4–91**
Intersections, **39:4–90**
Mail vehicles, **39:4–93**
Outdoor advertising,
  Erection or maintenance of signs prohibited, exceptions, **27:5–10**
  Zoning and planning, **27:5–9.1**
Pedestrians, this index
Processions, **39:4–93**
School buses, yielding, **39:4–87.1**
State or interstate highway system, commercial activities, **39:4–216**
Streetcars, vehicle required to give way to streetcar, **39:4–38**
Through streets, line of vehicles entering after stopping, **39:4–144**
Yield,
  Location, **39:4–141**
  Regulations, municipalities, **39:4–8**
  Signs, **39:4–140**
Zoning and planning, outdoor advertising, **27:5–9.1**

RIGHT TO COUNSEL
Attorneys, this index

RIGHT TURNS
Flashing lights on vehicle to indicate turn permitted, **39:3–54**
Intersections,
  Controlled by traffic signals or officers, **39:4–115**
  Green arrow as authorizing turn, **39:4–116**
  Method of turning, **39:4–123**
    Local authorities may determine, **39:4–124**
Signal, continuous, **39:4–126**
Traffic lights, **39:4–115**

RIOTS AND MOBS
  Generally, **2C:33–1**
Numbers and numbering, participants, **2C:33–1**
Speed law inapplicable to military vehicles used in time of riot, **39:4–103**
Weapons, **2C:33–1**

ROAD BUILDING EQUIPMENT
Moving Heavy Machinery, generally, this index

ROAD FUND
Disposition of fines for violating law relating to projections on tires and locking of wheels of motor vehicles, **39:3–81**
Fines for violations of law relating to display of name of owner of commercial vehicle, fund for repair of roads, **39:4–47**

ROAD ROLLERS
Moving Heavy Machinery, generally, this index

ROAD TESTS
Motorcycles, this index

ROAD TRACTOR
Definitions, Motor Vehicle Law, **39:1–1**

ROADS
County Roads, generally, this index
Highways and Roads, generally, this index
State Highways, generally, this index

ROADSIDE AREAS AND FACILITIES
Turnpike authority, **27:23–46**

ROADWAYS
Definitions, **39:1–1**

ROBBERY
  See, also, Theft, generally, this index
  Generally, **2C:15–1**
Aggravated offenses,
  Criminal sexual contact, **2C:14–3**
  Sexual assault, **2C:14–2**
Arrest, force or violence, **2C:3–7**
  Grand jury, instructions to jury, **2B:22–9**
Arrest warrants,
  Issuance, **Rule 3:3–1**
  Release, **Rule 3:4–1**
Associations of detective, insurance of members against loss, **15:4–3**
Attempts, body vests, **2C:39–13**
Body vests, **2C:39–13**
Burglary, generally, this index
Carjacking, **2C:15–2**
Definitions, **2C:15–1**
Expungement of record, **2C:52–2**
Felony murder, sentence and punishment, **2C:11–3**
Force or violence,
  Arrest, grand jury, instructions to jury, **2B:22–9**
  Use in defense of property, **2C:3–6**
Jurors, peremptory challenges, **Rule 1:8–3**
Jury, number of peremptory challenges, **2B:23–13**
Juvenile delinquents,
  Jurisdiction, waiver, **2A:4A–26**
  Referral to other courts without juveniles consent, **Rule 5:22–2**
Murder, **2C:11–3**
Receiving Stolen Property, generally, this index
Records and recordation, expungement, **2C:52–2**
Reward for apprehension and detection, **2A:153–4**
Terrorism, **2C:38–2**
Weapons, possession, **2C:39–7**
  Mandatory sentence, **2C:43–6**

ROCKETS
Age, purchase and use, **21:1C–4**
Amateur rocket experimentation, supervision, **21:1A–138**
Certificates and certification, **21:1C–3**
Definitions, **21:1C–1**
Examinations, **21:1C–2**
Fines and penalties, **21:1C–5**
Licenses and permits, **21:1C–4**
Model rocket, **21:1C–1 et seq.**
  Definitions, **21:1C–1**
Rocket motor, definitions, **21:1C–1**
Rules and regulations, **21:1C–6**
Tests, **21:1C–2**

ROLL OFF CONTAINERS
Solid waste, placement along highways or public property, consent and markers, **27:5I–1**

ROLLER SKATES
Children and minors, helmets, **39:4–10.5 et seq.**
Definitions,
  Helmets, **39:4–10.5**
  Municipalities, rules and regulations, **39:4–10.10a**
Fines and penalties, helmets, **39:4–10.6, 39:4–10.9**
Funds, bicycle and skating safety fund, **39:4–10.2**

ROLLER SKATES—Cont'd
Helmets, **39:4–10.5 et seq.**
Highways and roads, **39:4–10.10, 39:4–10.11**
  Municipalities, rules and regulations, **39:4–10.10a**
Hitching on to vehicles by person on roller skates prohibited, **39:4–14**
Municipalities, rules and regulations, **39:4–10.10a**
Notices,
  Helmets, posting signs, **39:4–10.9**
  Sales, warning, protective gear, **39:4–10.8**
Privileges and immunities, **39:4–10.8, 39:4–1**
Safety,
  Bicycle and skating safety fund, **39:4–10.2**
  Helmets, **39:4–10.5 et seq.**
  Hitching on to vehicles, **39:4–14**
Transportation commissioner, powers and duties, exceptions, **39:4–10.10b**

ROLLER SKATING RINK SAFETY AND FAIR LIABILITY ACT
Safety. Roller Skates, this index

ROLLERS
Moving Heavy Machinery, generally, this ind

ROMAN CANDLES
Fireworks, generally, this index

ROULETTE
Casinos, generally, this index

ROUTINE PRACTICE
Evidence, **Evidence Rule 406**

ROYALTIES
Trademarks and Trade Names, generally, this index

RUBBER TIRES
Tires, generally, this index

RUBBISH
Solid Waste, generally, this index

RULES AND REGULATIONS
  See, also, Administrative Law and Procedure, generally, this index
Alcoholic Beverages, this index
All Terrain Vehicles, this index
Autobusses, length and width, **39:3–84**
Automobile insurance risk exchange, **39:6A–2**
Bicycles,
  Helmet requirements, **39:4–10.4**
  Motorized bicycles, **39:4–14.3c**
Chosen Freeholders, this index
Commercial motor vehicles,
  Driving privileges, **39:3–10.27**
    Suspension, **39:3–10.20**
  Length and width, **39:3–84**
Commuter vans, **39:3–27.23**
Definitions, intoxicating liquor law, **33:1–1**
Dirt bikes, **39:3C–2**
Domestic violence, records and recordation, **2C:25–35**
Drivers licenses, **39:3–10f3**
  Graduated drivers license program, **39:3–13.7**
Environmental Protection Department, this dex
Explosives, **21:1A–131**
Flammable fabrics, sleeping bags and tents, sales, **2A:123–20**
Handicapped Persons, this index
Hazardous Substances and Waste, this index
Ignition interlock devices, **39:4–50.21**

RULES AND REGULATIONS—Cont'd
Intoxicated driving programs, **39:4–50**
Jewelry, secondhand, sales, **2C:21–41**
Juvenile delinquents and dependents, detention or shelter care facilities, **2A:4A–37**
Labor Commissioner, this index
Liquefied Petroleum Gas, this index
Motor carriers,
    Intermodal transportation, chassis, **39:3–79.21**
    Length and width, **39:3–84**
Motor Vehicle Insurance, this index
Motor Vehicles, this index
Motorized Bicycles, this index
Portable oil burning heating devices, **2C:40–14**
Public private intersections, **39:4–120.11**
Rockets, **21:1C–6**
School buses, **39:3B–1 et seq.**
Sleeping bags, flammable fabrics, sales, **2A:123–20**
Snowmobiles, **39:3C–2**
Solid Waste, this index
State police, superintendent, combating theft of motor vehicles, **39:3–85.10**
Tents, flammable fabrics, sales, **2A:123–20**
Tow Trucks and Towing Companies, this index
Transportation Department, this index
Turnpike Authority, this index

RULES OF CONSTRUCTION
Construction of Laws, generally, this index

RULES OF COURT
Arbitrators, compensation, motor vehicle tort claims, **39:6A–28**
Attorneys fees, schedule, motor vehicle tort claim arbitrations, **39:6A–28**
Automated traffic system fund, **2B:12–30**
Domestic violence, fines and penalties, **2C:25–29.3**
Motor vehicles, arbitration and award, tort claims, **39:6A–35**
Supervisory treatment programs, first offenders, **2C:43–14 et seq.**
Supreme Court, this index

RULES OF EVIDENCE
Evidence, this index

RULES OF PROFESSIONAL CONDUCT
Generally, **Rule 1:14**

RUNAWAYS
Juvenile delinquents and dependents, short term custody, **Rule 5:16–1**

RUNNERS
Definitions, health and accident insurance, **2C:21–22.1**
Health and accident insurance, fraud, **2C:21–22.1**

RUNNING BOARD LAMPS
Use on motor vehicles and color of light, **39:3–52**

RURAL FREE DELIVERY
Motor vehicles used on not considered as commercial cars, **39:3–2**

SABBATH
Sunday, generally, this index

SADDLE MOUNT
Towing motor vehicles, **39:4–54**

SADISM
Children and minors, second degree crime, **2C:24–4**

SAFE AND SECURE COMMUNITIES PROGRAM
Law and Public Safety Department, this index

SAFE CORRIDORS
Definitions, traffic regulations, repair or construction areas, **39:4–203.5**
Traffic rules and regulations, traffic control, construction or repair areas, **39:4–203.5**

SAFE NEIGHBORHOODS SERVICES FUND
Deposits, criminal restitution assessments, **2C:43–3.2, 2C:46–4, 2C:46–4.1**

SAFETY
Generally, **2C:40–1**
Aircraft, this index
Airports and Landing Fields, this index
Bicycles, helmets, **39:4–10.1 et seq.**
Children and Minors, this index
Crimes and offenses, laws protecting public safety, **2C:40–18**
Crosswalks, **39:4–36.3, 39:4–36.4**
Dirt bikes, **39:3C–15**
Electric personal assistive mobility devices, operation, **39:4–14.10**
Explosives, generally, this index
Helmets, generally, this index
Limousine or Livery Service, this index
Liquefied petroleum gas education and safety board, **21:1B–12 et seq.**
Motor vehicles, dimensional and weight limitations, **39:3–84**
Pedestrians, intersections, **39:4–36.3, 39:4–36.4**
Persons with special responsibility for safety of others, use of force, **2C:3–8**
Portable oil burning heating devices, **2C:40–6 et seq.**
Radiation Protection, generally, this index
Roller skates, helmets, **39:4–10.5 et seq.**
School Buses, this index
Skateboards, helmets, **39:4–10.5 et seq.**
Snowmobiles, generally, this index
State police, powers and duties, **53:2–1**
Traffic, willful obstruction of highways, **39:4–56.1 et seq.**
Traffic regulations, **39:4–8**

SAFETY ADVISORY COUNCIL
Motor vehicle commission, **39:2A–26**

SAFETY APPLIANCES AND DEVICES
Motor vehicles,
    Child passenger restraint systems, **39:3–76.2a et seq.**
    Seat belts, **39:3–76.2**
Restraining devices, motor vehicles, **39:3–76.2**
Unregistered vehicles, permits to cross public highways, **39:3–26.2**

SAFETY GLASS
Definitions, **39:3–75**
Discolored or other defective glass prohibited, **39:3–75**
Marking safety glazing material with manufacturers designation, **39:3–75**
Required on motor vehicles manufactured after certain date, **39:3–75**

SAFETY GLAZING MATERIAL
Motor vehicles, **39:3–75**

SAFETY ISLES
Safety Zones, generally, this index

SAFETY ZONES
Generally, **39:4–196.1 et seq.**
Definitions, Motor Vehicle Law, **39:1–1**
Driving through safety zones prohibited, **39:4–41**
Establishment, **39:4–196.1 et seq.**
Parking near prohibited, **39:4–138**
State highway, permission required for construction in, **39:4–199**
Traffic signals, location on raised safety zones permitted, **39:4–114**
Traffic signs, **39:4–199.1**
Vehicle overtaking streetcar may proceed, **39:4–40**

SAILBOATS
Vessels, generally, this index

SAILORS
Armed Forces, generally, this index

SALARIES
Compensation and Salaries, generally, this index

SALES
Agricultural Products, this index
Alcoholic Beverages, this index
Ambulances, markings, removal, **39:10–9.4**
Anatomical gifts, human body parts, crimes and offenses, **2C:22–2**
Archaeology and archaeologists, transportation, state property, archaeological findings, **27:5J–1**
Bicycles,
    Exemptions, **39:4–14.6**
    Lights, **39:4–14.4**
Carriers, this index
Checks, fraudulent sales, **2C:21–2.4**
Children and Minors, this index
Cigarettes and Cigars, this index
Containers, liquefied petroleum gas, restrictions, **21:1B–4**
Corporate officials, misconduct, **2C:21–9**
Crimes and offenses, identification cards, public utilities, **2C:21–35**
Deceptive business practices, **2C:21–7**
Definitions,
    Certificate of Motor Vehicle Ownership Law, **39:10–2**
    Flammable fabrics, **2A:123–3**
    Intoxicating liquor law, **33:1–1**
Dirt bikes, equipment, **39:3C–26**
Drugs and Medicine, this index
Electronic surveillance equipment, **2A:156A–5**
Explosives, this index
Fencing, stolen property, **2C:20–7.1**
    Actions and proceedings, civil actions against, damages, **2C:20–20**
Fines and penalties, Sunday, motor vehicles, **2C:33–24**
Firearms, licenses, dealers, **2C:58–2**
Fireworks, this index
Flammable fabrics, **2A:123–3 et seq.**
Forgery, receipts, universal product codes, **2C:21–1**
Fraud,
    Checks, **2C:21–2.4**
    Receipts, **2C:21–2.4**
    Universal product codes, **2C:21–2.4**
Gambling device, **2C:37–7**
Handcuffs, children and minors, **2C:39–9.2**
Horses, this index
Housing, this index

SALES—Cont'd

Human body parts, crimes and offenses, **2C:22–2**

Hypodermic Needles or Syringes, generally, this index

Jewelry, secondhand dealers, **2C:21–36 et seq.**

Kerosene burning heating devices, **2C:40–6 et seq.**

Knives, children and minors, **2C:39–9.1**

Lewdness and Obscenity, generally, this index

Liquefied Petroleum Gas, this index

Lottery tickets, **2C:37–6.1**

Manufactured homes,
  Certificates of ownership, **39:10–15.1**
  Real estate brokers, **39:10–19**

Mobile Homes and Mobile Home Parks, this index

Motor Vehicles, this index

Motorized bicycles, **39:4–14.3a**

Oil burning heating devices, **2C:40–6 et seq.**

Portable oil burning heating devices, **2C:40–6 et seq.**

Publications, abandoned and unclaimed motor vehicles, **39:10A–1**

Receipts, forgery, **2C:21–1**

Religious Corporations and Associations, this index

Resale, bottling alcoholic beverages, resale without license, **33:1–78**

Schools and School Districts, this index

Secondhand dealers, jewelry, **2C:21–36 et seq.**

Shoplifting, **2C:20–11**

Sleeping bags, flammable fabrics, **2A:123–16 et seq.**

Soliciting while standing in roadway prohibited, **39:4–60**

Spray paint, required posting of warning sign, **2C:33–25**

State, motor vehicles seized on suspicion of having been stolen, **39:5–47**

State Buildings, this index

State Police, this index

Stills, distilling apparatus, after seizure, **33:2–5**

Stolen property, unclaimed, disposition, **2C:65–3**

Storage, generally, this index

Sunday, this index

Tents, flammable fabrics, **2A:123–16 et seq.**

Tires, fitted with blocks, hobs, studs or other projections, **39:3–81**

Turnpike authority, property to authority, **27:23–14**

Turnpikes, this index

Universal product codes,
  Forgery, **2C:21–1**
  Fraud, **2C:21–2.4**

Weapons, this index

Wiretapping or electronic surveillance equipment, **2A:156A–5**

SALIVA

Investigative detention, **Rule 3:5A–1 et seq.**

SALUTES

Fireworks, generally, this index

SALVAGE

Motor Vehicles, this index

SALVAGE CERTIFICATES OF TITLE

Motor vehicles, **39:10–31 et seq.**

SAMPLES

DNA Database and Databank, generally, this index

SAND CLUBS

Weapons, generally, this index

SANITATION

Health and Sanitation, generally, this index

SATURDAYS

Computation of time, **Rule 1:3–1**

SAVINGS AND LOAN ASSOCIATIONS

Deposits, receiving deposits in failing institutions, **2C:21–14**

Investments, turnpike authority bonds, **27:23–13**

Monopolies and unfair trade, exemptions, **56:9–5**

Motor vehicle insurance, impounded vehicles, release, **39:3–40.6**

Motor vehicles, impounding, release, **39:3–40.6**

Teller machines, security measures. Electronic Fund Transfers, generally, this index

SAVINGS BANKS

See, also, Banks and Banking, generally, this index

Deposits, receiving deposits in failing institutions, **2C:21–14**

Electronic Fund Transfers, generally, this index

Investments, turnpike authority bonds, **27:23–13**

Motor vehicle insurance, impounded vehicles, release, **39:3–40.6**

Motor vehicles, impounding, release, **39:3–40.6**

Teller machines, security measures. Electronic Fund Transfers, generally, this index

SAVINGS INSTITUTIONS

Banks and Banking, generally, this index

Financial Corporations and Institutions, generally, this index

SAWED OFF SHOTGUNS

Weapons, this index

SCHEDULES

Controlled substances, **24:21–3 et seq.**

Drugs and Medicine, generally, this index

SCHOOL BUILDINGS AND GROUNDS

Alcoholic drinks, possession or consumption, **2C:33–16**

Assault by auto or vessel, crossings, **2C:12–1**

Crimes and offenses,
  Notice, **2C:43–5.1**
  Weapons, possession, **2C:39–5**

Criminal trespass, **2C:18–3**

Crossings, **39:1–1**
  Assault by auto or vessel, **2C:12–1**
  Drivers licenses, suspension or revocation, Extension, **39:3–40**
    Intoxication of driver, **39:3–50**
  Fines and penalties, **39:4–80.1**
    Intoxication of driver, **39:3–50**
  Intoxication of driver, implied consent, **39:4–50.4a**
  Vehicular homicide, **2C:11–5**

Drivers licenses, suspension or revocation, Extension, **39:3–40**

Intoxication of driver, **39:3–50**
  Implied consent, **39:4–50.4a**

Fines and penalties,
  Crossings, **39:4–80.1**
    Intoxication of driver, **39:3–50**
  Implied consent, intoxication of driver, **39:4–50.4a**

Intoxication of driver, **39:3–50**
  Implied consent, **39:4–50.4a**

SCHOOL BUILDINGS AND GROUNDS —Cont'd

Implied consent, intoxication of driver, fines and penalties, **39:4–50.4a**

Intersections, stop intersections, designation, marking, **39:4–197**

Intoxicating liquors, possession or consumption, **2C:33–16**

Intoxication of driver, **39:4–50**
  Assault by auto or vessel, **2C:11–5**
  Drivers licenses, suspension or revocation, extension, **39:3–40**
  Fines and penalties, **39:3–50**
    Implied consent, **39:4–50.4a**

Maps and plats, prosecutors,
  Assault by auto or vessel, **2C:11–5**
  Drivers licenses, suspension or revocation, extension, **39:3–40**
  Implied consent, intoxication of driver, **39:4–50.4a**
  Intoxication of driver, **39:3–50**
    Implied consent, **39:4–50.4a**
  Vehicular homicide, **2C:11–5**

Motor vehicles, speed, **39:4–98**

Paging devices, possession by student, **2C:33–1**

Parking, permissible parking distances, municipalities, **39:4–138.6**

Prosecutors. Maps and plats, ante

School crossings. Crossings, generally, ante

Stop intersections, designation, marking, **39:4–197**

Traffic control signals, installation, **39:4–183.1**

Vehicular homicide, **2C:11–5**

Weapons. Schools and School Districts, this index

SCHOOL BUSES

Generally, **39:3B–1 et seq.**

Abandonment, repainting, **39:3–77.1**

Age of bus, date of termination, **39:3B–5.1 et seq.**

Aggravated assault, drivers, **2C:12–1**

Air pollution, **39:3–70.1, 39:3–70.2**

Annual registration fees, **39:3–19.2**

Bodily integrity, safety requirements, retired buses, transportation of children and aged persons, **39:3B–5.4**

Butane, motor fuel, **39:3B–13 et seq.**

Butylene, motor fuel, **39:3B–13 et seq.**

Camps and camping, exemption from license fee, **39:3–19.3**

Cellular phones, drivers, crimes and offenses, **39:3B–25**

Certificates of approval, information, **39:3B–3**

Classified licensing, **39:3–10**

Color, **39:3–77.1 et seq.**
  Van type vehicles, **39:3B–8, 39:3B–9**

Commercial drivers licenses, **39:3–10.12**

Contractors, crossing control arms, requirements, **39:3B–1.1 et seq.**

Convex mirrors, equipment, **39:3B–4**

Crimes and offenses, drivers, cellular phones, **39:3B–25**

Crossing control arms,
  Equipment, requirements, **39:3B–1.1**
  Equipment lists, requirements, **39:3B–1.3**
  Reimbursements, **39:3B–1.2**

Definitions,
  In terminal inspection, **39:3B–20**
  Liquefied petroleum gas, **39:3B–13**
  Motor Vehicle Law, **39:1–1**

Drivers,
  Aggravated assault, **2C:12–1**
  Cellular phones, crimes and offenses, **39:3B–25**
  Drug tests, fraud, **2C:36–10**

CHOOL BUSES—Cont'd
rivers—Cont'd
Records and recordation, inspectors and inspection, **39:3B–21**
Fines and penalties, **39:3B–22**
rivers licenses, 39:3–10
Commercial drivers licenses, **39:3–10.12**
Photo license, **39:3–10f**
rug tests, drivers, fraud, 2C:36–10
mergencies, drivers, cellular phones, 39:3B–25
mergency exits, required equipment, 39:3B–12
missions, inspectors and inspection, 39:3B–21
quipment, 39:3B–1 et seq.
vidence, traffic rule violation by another driver, rebuttable presumptions, 39:4–128.1
xamination permits, 39:3–13
ees,
Drivers licenses, **39:3–10**
Examination permits, **39:3–13**
Inspectors and inspection, **39:8–2**
ines and penalties,
Air pollution, **39:3–70.2**
Drivers, cellular phones, **39:3B–25**
Inspectors and inspection, **39:3B–22**
Schedule, **39:3B–24**
Loading or unloading violations, **39:4–128.1**
lashing red light, 39:4–128.1
raud, drug tests, drivers, 2C:36–10
uel, liquefied petroleum gas, 39:3B–13 et seq.
andicapped persons, van type vehicles, identification, 39:3B–9
ighway, stopping requirements, 39:4–128.1
dentification, warning lamps, 39:3B–1
lling, air pollution, 39:3–70.2
spection and inspectors,
Fees, **39:8–2**
In terminal inspections, **39:3B–18 et seq.**
Specification inspections, **39:8–2**
egislative findings, in terminal inspections, 39:3B–19
ettering, van type vehicles, 39:3B–8, 39:3B–9
icense plates, school vehicle types I and II, 39:3–19.2, 39:3–19.3
icenses and permits,
Classified licensing, **39:3–10**
Fees for drivers, **39:3–10**
Operator licenses, **39:3–10.1a**
Photo licenses, **39:3–10f**
ights and lighting,
Color, **39:3–50**
Van type vehicles, **39:3B–8, 39:3B–9**
Warning lamps, identifications, **39:3B–1**
iquefied petroleum gas, 39:3B–13 et seq.
oading or unloading, flashing red lights, 39:4–128.1
lechanical condition, safety requirements, retired buses, 39:3B–5.4
lirrors, equipment, 39:3B–4
lotor fuels, liquefied petroleum gas, 39:3B–13 et seq.
perator licenses, 39:3–10.1a
assing, parked bus, speed, 39:4–128.1
hoto license, 39:3–10f
rivate Schools, this index
rivileges and immunities, liquefied petroleum gas, 39:3B–16
ropane, motor fuel, 39:3B–13 et seq.
ropylene, motor fuel, 39:3B–13 et seq.
ailroad crossings, stopping before crossing, 39:4–128
ebuttable presumptions, 39:4–128.1
ecords and recordation, inspectors and inspection, 39:3B–21
emoval from service, inspectors and inspection, 39:3B–23

SCHOOL BUSES—Cont'd
Retired buses, safety requirements, transportation of children or aged persons, **39:3B–5.4**
Right of way, yielding, **39:4–87.1**
Road tests, scheduling, **39:3–13**
Rules and regulations,
Equipment, **39:3B–5**
Inspectors and inspection, **39:3B–24**
Safety,
Crossing control arms, **39:3B–1.1 et seq.**
In terminal inspections, **39:3B–18 et seq.**
Retired buses, transportation of children or senior citizens, **39:3B–5.4**
School vehicle type I,
Definitions, **39:1–1**
Exemption, omnibus registration, **39:3–19.3**
License plates, **39:3–19.2, 39:3–19.3**
School vehicle type II,
Definitions, **39:1–1**
Exemption, omnibus registration, **39:3–19.3**
License plates, **39:3–19.2, 39:3–19.3**
Seat belts,
Required equipment, **39:3B–10**
Use, requirement, **39:3B–11**
Seating reference point, definitions, minimum seat back height, **39:3B–10**
Seats, minimum seat back height, **39:3B–10**
Signs displayed, **39:3B–2**
Smoking, **2C:33–13**
Stopping and waiting until children reach place of safety, **39:4–128.1**
Summer day camps, use, **39:3–77.1**
Telecommunications, drivers, crimes and offenses, **39:3B–25**
Termination of bus use, age and date, **39:3B–5.1 et seq.**
Van type vehicles, identification and warning lights, **39:3B–8, 39:3B–9**
Violation of traffic rules by another driver, rebuttable presumptions, **39:4–128.1**
Waiver,
Examination fees, endorsements, drivers licenses, **39:3–19.2, 39:3–19.3**
Fees, drivers licenses, **39:3–10**
Warning lamps, identification, **39:3B–1**
Weapons, possession, **2C:39–5**
Yielding, right of way, **39:4–87.1**

SCHOOL CROSSING GUARDS
Disobedience, fines and penalties, **39:4–80.1**

SCHOOL CROSSINGS
Definitions, traffic regulations, **39:1–1**

SCHOOL NURSES
Aggravated assault, **2C:12–1**
Substitutes, credentials, **39:5B–32**

SCHOOL OFFICERS AND EMPLOYEES
Aggravated assault, **2C:12–1**
Assault and battery, aggravated assault, **2C:12–1**
Civil Service, generally, this index

SCHOOL PRINCIPALS
Aggravated assault, **2C:12–1**
Special learners permit, behind the wheel automobile driving instruction, retention of permit in principals office, **39:3–13.1**

SCHOOL PSYCHOLOGISTS
Aggravated assault, **2C:12–1**

SCHOOL SOCIAL WORKERS
Aggravated assault, **2C:12–1**

SCHOOL TEXTBOOKS AND SUPPLIES
Library materials, theft, **2C:20–12 et seq.**

SCHOOL ZONES
Definitions, Motor Vehicle Law, **39:1–1**
School Buildings and Grounds, generally, this index

SCHOOLHOUSES
School Buildings and Grounds, generally, this index

SCHOOLS AND SCHOOL DISTRICTS
Adults, alcoholic beverages, possession, **2C:33–16**
Aggravated assault, officers and employees, **2C:12–1**
Alcoholic beverages,
Age, possession, **2C:33–16**
Possession, **2C:33–16**
Sales within 200 feet, license renewal, **33:1–76.2**
Waiver of protection, **33:1–76.1, 33:1–76.2**
Assault and battery,
Aggravated assault, **2C:12–1**
Auto or vessel, crossings, **2C:12–1**
Sports, events, **2C:12–1**
Athletics,
Aggravated assault, **2C:12–1**
Events, assault and battery, **2C:12–1**
Boards and commissions, drivers school, exception from license for conducting, **39:12–2**
Boards of education,
License for conducting drivers school, exemption from, **39:12–2**
Parking,
Municipalitys power to regulate on grounds maintained by board, **39:4–197**
Notice of ordinance, **39:4–198**
Buildings. School Buildings and Grounds, generally, this index
Buses. School Buses, generally, this index
Cannons, antique cannons, possession, **2C:39–6**
Child abuse, complaints, **9:6–5**
Controlled substances,
Dispensing, distribution or possession on area surrounding school property or bus, **2C:35–7**
Possession, use or being under influence, school grounds, **2C:35–10**
Crimes and offenses,
Definitions, **2C:1–14**
Trespass, **2C:18–3**
Weapons, possession, **2C:39–5**
Crossings. School Buildings and Grounds, this index
Curriculum, handicapped parking enforcement, **39:4–197.13**
Delinquent children. Juvenile delinquents, post
Drivers licenses. Drivers Schools, generally, this index
Drivers Schools, generally, this index
Foreign states, sex offenses, registration, **2C:7–2**
Grounds. School Buildings and Grounds, generally, this index
Handicapped persons,
Driver education programs, written examinations, **39:3–13a**
School buses, van type vehicles, identification and warning lights, **39:3B–9**
High schools,
Confidential or privileged information, crimes and offenses, notice, **2C:43–5.1**

SCHOOLS AND SCHOOL DISTRICTS
—Cont'd

High schools—Cont'd
Crimes and offenses, students, notice, **2C:43–5.1**
Notice, crimes and offenses, **2C:43–5.1**
Industrial schools. Vocational Education, generally, this index
Intoxication of driver. School Buildings and Grounds, this index
Junk yard for motor vehicles, proximity of school to be considered on application for permit, **39:11–5**
Juvenile delinquents,
Complaints, **9:6–5**
Records and recordation, disclosure, **2A:4A–60**
Land. School Buildings and Grounds, generally, this index
Libraries, theft of materials, **2C:20–12 et seq.**
Motor vehicles,
Drivers education, special learners permits, **39:3–13.1 et seq.**
Junk yard, proximity of school to be considered on application for permit, **39:11–5**
Parking, time limit, **39:4–139**
Registration fee exemption, **39:3–27**
School Buses, generally, this index
Speed when passing school zone, **39:4–98**
Nonpublic schools. Private Schools, generally, this index
Paging devices, minors use on school property, **2C:33–19**
Parking, time limited, **39:4–139**
Parochial schools. Private Schools, generally, this index
Possession, alcoholic beverages, **2C:33–16**
Private Schools, generally, this index
Real estate. School Buildings and Grounds, generally, this index
Regional school districts, motor vehicles, registration fee exemption, **39:3–27**
Registration, sex offenses, foreign states, **2C:7–2**
Sales, alcoholic beverages, proximity, **33:1–76**
Protection, waiver, **33:1–76.1, 33:1–76.2**
School Buildings and Grounds, generally, this index
School Buses, generally, this index
Sex, crimes and offenses, registration, foreign states, **2C:7–2**
Sexually oriented businesses, zoning and planning, **2C:34–7**
Special educational services,
Driver education programs, written examinations, **39:3–13a**
Nonattorneys, appearance at hearings, **Rule 1:21–1**
Speed of motor vehicle when passing school zone, **39:4–98**
Traffic signs and signals, school crossing intersections, **39:4–183.1a**
Trespassers, presentence investigations, report, defendants mental condition, **2C:44–6**
Vocational Education, generally, this index
Weapons, possession, crimes and offenses, **2C:39–5**
Zoning and planning, sexually oriented businesses, **2C:34–7**

SCHOOLS FOR INDUSTRIAL EDUCATION
Vocational Education, generally, this index

SCIENCE
Alcohol in products unfit for beverage purposes, **33:1–30**

SCIENCE—Cont'd
Animals, cruelty, **4:22–16**

SCIENCE AND TECHNOLOGY COMMISSION
Agricultural molecular biology center, satellite field testing facility, establishment, construction, appropriations, **39:4–103.1**

SCIENTIFIC TESTS
Crimes and offenses, discovery, **Rule 3:13–3**

SCOOTERS
Motorized Scooters, generally, this index

SCOWS
Vessels, generally, this index

SCRAP
Motor vehicles, surrender of certificate of ownership on sale for scrap, **39:10–23**

SCRAP METAL
Theft, notice, **2C:20–7.2**

SEALED SCALES
Motor vehicles, weight limitations, violations, **39:3–84.3**

SEALS AND SEALING
Alcoholic beverage control director, **33:1–37**
Certificates and certification, municipal boards, intoxicating liquors, **33:1–48**
Courts, **Rule 1:37–2**
Records, **Rules 1:38–11, 1:38–12**
Open court proceedings, **Rule 1:2–1**
Forgery, **2C:21–1**
Motor vehicle division director, **39:2–10**
Municipalities, certification of municipal boards, intoxicating liquors, **33:1–48**
Turnpike authority, **27:23–5**
Revenue bonds, **27:23–7**

SEAMEN
Armed Forces, generally, this index

SEARCH WARRANTS
See, also, Searches and Seizures, generally, this index
Generally, **Rule 3:5–1 et seq.**
Affidavits,
Alcoholic beverages, prerequisite to issuance, **33:1–57**
Filing, **Rule 3:5–6**
Secrecy, **Rule 3:5–4**
Testimony, issuance, **Rule 3:5–3**
Alcoholic Beverages, this index
Appeal and review, motions, suppressing evidence, returning property, **Rule 3:5–7**
Authority to issue, **Rule 3:5–1**
Bad faith, irregularity, **Rule 3:5–7**
Body cavity searches, **2A:161A–1 et seq.**
Books and papers, documents, **Rule 3:5–2**
Briefs, motions, suppressing evidence, returning property, **Rule 3:5–7**
Confidential or privileged information, **Rules 1:38–3, 3:5–4, 3:5–6**
Contempt, disclosures, **Rule 3:5–4**
Contents, **Rule 3:5–3**
Disclosure, application, issuance, contempt, **Rule 3:5–4**
Distilling apparatus, **33:2–3**
Electronically communicated oral testimony, issuance, **Rule 3:5–3**
Execution, **Rule 3:5–5**
Exigent circumstances, electronic communication, oral testimony, **Rule 3:5–3**

SEARCH WARRANTS—Cont'd
Filing, **Rules 3:5–6, 7:5–1**
Grounds, issuance, **Rule 3:5–2**
Hearings, suppressing evidence, returning property, motions, **Rule 3:5–7**
Inventory, return, **Rule 3:5–5**
Irregularity, effect, **Rule 3:5–7**
Issuance, **Rule 3:5–2 et seq.**
Motions, suppressing evidence, returning property, **Rule 3:5–7**
Municipal Courts, this index
News organizations, searches and seizures, **2A:84A–21.10 et seq.**
Nighttime, service under Alcoholic Beverage Law, **33:1–59**
Notice, motion to suppress evidence, return property, **Rule 3:5–7**
Oaths and affirmations, issuance, **Rule 3:5–3**
Property, return, **Rule 3:5–7**
Radio, oral testimony supporting, **Rule 3:5–3**
Receipts, property taken, **Rule 3:5–5**
Recording testimony, issuance, **Rule 3:5–3**
Return, inventory, **Rule 3:5–5**
Search without warrant as misdemeanor, **33:1–65**
Secrecy, **Rule 3:5–4**
Signatures, transcripts, record, **Rule 3:5–5**
Stenographic record,
Electronic recording, oral testimony, **Rule 3:5–3**
Filing, **Rule 3:5–6**
Stills and distilling apparatus, **33:2–3**
Strip searches, **2A:161A–1 et seq.**
Suppression of evidence, motion, **Rule 3:5–7**
Tape recording, record, **Rule 3:5–3**
Telephone, oral testimony supporting, **Rule 3:5–3**
Testimony, affidavit, issuance, **Rule 3:5–3**
Transcript, record, **Rules 3:5–3, 3:5–5**
Waiver, motions, suppressing evidence, returning property, **Rule 3:5–7**
Wiretap cases, filing, **Rule 3:5–6**
Witnesses, applicants, **Rule 3:5–3**

SEARCHES AND SEIZURES
See, also, Search Warrants, generally, this index
Generally, **Rule 3:5–1 et seq.**
Admissibility of evidence, strip and body searches, **2A:161A–10**
Affidavits. Search Warrants, this index
Alcoholic Beverages, this index
Ammunition, **2C:58–7**
Body cavity searches, **2A:161A–1 et seq.**
Contact lenses, dispensing, licenses and permits, **2C:40–25**
Contraband, **2C:64–1**
Controlled Substances, this index
Correctional institutions, inmate newspapers, public information offices, **2A:84A–21.1**
Electric personal assistive mobility devices, **39:4–14.11**
Electronic surveillance equipment, **2A:156A–7**
Evidence,
Seized property, **2C:64–4**
Strip and body searches, **2A:161A–10**
Explosives, **2C:58–7**
Forfeitures, generally, this index
Immunity from liability, body cavity searches, **2A:161A–5**
Justification, **2C:3–10**
Motor Vehicles, this index
Motorized scooters, **39:4–14.13**
News organizations, **2A:84A–21.9 et seq.**
Nuisances, personal property, seizure, **2C:33–12.1**

RCHES AND SEIZURES—Cont'd
ses, body cavity searches, **2A:161A–5**
ers and ownership, **2C:64–5**
onal searches, **2A:161A–1 et seq.**
sicians and surgeons, body cavity searches,
    2A:161A–5
io and radio stations, **2A:84A–21.9 et seq.**
orts, strip or body cavity searches,
    2A:161A–4
s and distilling apparatus, **33:2–3**
estruction of seized property, **33:2–5**
orfeiture of seized property, **33:2–5**
etention of seized property for use of hos-
    pitals, **33:2–5**
eturn of seized property, **33:2–7**
ale of seized property, **33:2–5**
eizure of unregistered stills, apparatus,
    33:2–3
p searches, **2A:161A–1 et seq.**
evision and television stations, **2A:84A–21.9
et seq.**
rantless searches, legality, **Rules 3:5–8,
7:5–3**
rants for search. Search Warrants, gener-
    ally, this index
apons, strip searches, **2A:161A–1 et seq.**

ASONALLY LEASED PREMISES
inition, criminal justice, **2C:43–8.1**
orderly persons, termination of right to oc-
    cupy or visit, **2C:43–8.1**

T BELTS
or Vehicles, this index

COND DEGREE CRIMES
nes and Offenses, this index

COND OR SUBSEQUENT OFFENSES
ndonment of motor vehicles, **39:4–56.5**
ravating circumstances, **2C:44–1**
pollution, fines and penalties, **26:2C–19**
oholic beverages, conviction of second or
    subsequent offense, **33:1–53**
ault firearm, offense involving, previous
    firearms conviction, **2C:43–6**
eau of identification to procure and file
    fingerprints, photographs and information
    concerning, **53:1–13, 53:1–15**
current sentences, **2C:44–5**
asecutive sentences, **2C:44–5**
trolled substances, **24:21–29**
inition, persistent offenders, **2C:44–3**
cretion of court, requiring service of remit-
    ted time in addition to new sentence,
    2A:164–24
vers license violations, fines and penalties,
    39:3–40 et seq.
uspension, penalty points, **39:5–30.10**
ving while intoxicated, discovery, **39:4–50**
unken driving, complaint need not charge
    previous offense to justify punishment as
    second offender, **39:4–50**
ctric personal assistive mobility devices,
    39:4–14.11
ended terms of imprisonment, **2C:44–3**
gerprinting, **53:1–13, 53:1–15**
eign states, sentence and punishment, ag-
    gravating circumstances, **2C:44–4**
micide, life imprisonment, **2C:11–3 et seq.**
risonment, extended terms, **2C:44–3**
enile delinquents referral to other courts
    without juveniles consent, **Rule 5:22–2**
e imprisonment, homicide, **2C:11–3 et seq.**
ing and enticing, **2C:13–7**
hildren and minors, **2C:13–6**

SECOND OR SUBSEQUENT OFFENSES
—Cont'd
Motor Vehicles, this index
Murder, **2C:11–3**
Narcotics, penalties, **24:21–29**
Photographing, **53:1–13, 53:1–15**
Probationer, **2C:45–3**
Remitted time from previous term, service in
    addition to new sentence, **2A:164–24**
Sales, motor vehicles, Sunday, **2C:33–26**
Sexual offenses, sentence and punishment,
    2C:14–6
Shoplifting, **2C:20–11**
Stalking, act or creditable threat of violence,
    third degree crime, **2C:12–10**
Surcharges, driving while intoxicated, **39:4–50**
Suspended sentence, defendant under, **2C:45–3**
Volunteer firemen, flashing lights, **39:3–54.7**
Weapons, possession, extended terms, **2C:44–3**

SECONDHAND
Used motor vehicles. Motor Vehicles, this
    index

SECONDHAND DEALERS
Jewelry, sales, **2C:21–36 et seq.**
Used motor vehicles. Motor Vehicles, this
    index

SECONDHAND VEHICLES
Used motor vehicles. Motor Vehicles, this
    index

SECRECY
Confidential or Privileged Information, gener-
    ally, this index
Criminal coercion, exposing secrets, **2C:13–5**
Extortion, threats to expose or publicize,
    2C:20–5
Grand jury proceedings, **Rule 3:6–7**
Search warrants, **Rule 3:5–4**

SECRETARY
Courts, political activities or public office, **Rule
1:17–1**
Definitions, historic preservation license plates,
    39:3–27.72

SECRETARY OF STATE
Director of motor vehicle division, oaths, filing
    with, **39:2–2**
Extradition, copy of application to governor for
    requisition filed with, **2A:160–32**
Nonprofit Corporations and Associations, gen-
    erally, this index
Trademarks and Trade Names, generally, this
    index
Uniform Fresh Pursuit Law, certified copies to
    executive department of other states,
    2A:155–7

SECTARIAN SCHOOLS
Private Schools, generally, this index

SECURED PARTY
Definitions, motor vehicles, **39:10–2**

SECURED TRANSACTIONS
Defrauding secured creditors, **2C:21–12**
Destruction, defrauding secured creditors,
    2C:21–12
Fraud, recordable instruments, **2C:21–3**
Motor Vehicles, this index
Security agreements, definitions, motor vehi-
    cles, **39:10–2**
Theft by failure to make required disposition
    of property received, **2C:20–9**

SECURITIES
See, also, Shares and Shareholders, general-
    ly, this index
Deceptive business practices, **2C:21–7**
Fraud,
    Instruments, **2C:21–3**
    Security instruments, **2C:21–3**
Intoxicating liquor wholesalers, **33:1–43a**
Racketeering, **2C:41–1 et seq.**
Stock and stockholders. Shares and Share-
    holders, generally, this index

SECURITY
Costs, this index
Motor Vehicle Security Responsibility Law,
    generally, this index
Motor Vehicles, this index
State police, powers and duties, **53:2–1**
Teller machines, security measures. Electronic
    Fund Transfers, generally, this index

SECURITY AGREEMENTS
Secured Transactions, this index

SECURITY INTEREST
Definitions, motor vehicles, **39:10–2**
Motor Vehicles, this index

SECURITY RESPONSIBILITY ACT
Motor vehicles, **39:6–23 et seq.**

SEDUCTION
Generally, **2C:14–3**

SEGREGATION
Discrimination, generally, this index

SEIZED PROPERTY
Searches and Seizures, generally, this index

SEIZURE
Searches and Seizures, generally, this index

SELF AUTHENTICATION
Evidence, **Evidence Rule 902**

SELF DEFENSE
Generally, **2C:3–4**

SELF INCRIMINATION
Generally, **2A:84A–18, 2A:84A–19**
Rules of evidence, **2A:84A–19; Evidence Rules
502, 503**

SELF INDUCED INTOXICATION
Definitions, Code of Criminal Justice, **2C:2–8**

SELF INSURANCE
Application for certificate, **39:6–52**
Motor Vehicle Security Responsibility Law,
    39:6–25, 39:6–52

SELF PROTECTION
Force, limitation, **2C:3–4**

SELL
Definitions, intoxicating liquor law, **33:1–1**

SELLERS
Definitions, Certificate of Motor Vehicle Own-
    ership Law, **39:10–2**

SEMAPHORES
Regulations, **39:4–108**

SEMIAUTOMATIC
Definitions, assault firearms, **2C:39–1**

SEMIAUTOMATIC RIFLES
Disorderly persons, advertisements, 2C:39–15

SEMIPUBLIC ROADS
Application of motor vehicles and traffic laws,
39:5A–1 et seq.

SEMITRAILERS
Motor Carriers, generally, this index

SENATE
See, also, General Assembly, generally, this
index
Appointments, advice and consent,
County prosecutors, 2A:158–1
Directors, motor vehicle division, 39:2–2
Electronic voting, 2A:149–1
Former members, motor vehicles, special
plates, 39:3–27.115
Judicial conference, rules of evidence,
2A:84A–34
Motor vehicles, special plates, former mem-
bers, 39:3–27.115
Public Policy, generally, this index
Voting machines, 2A:149–1

SENATORS
State senators. Senate, generally, this index

SENIOR CITIZENS
Aged Persons, generally, this index

SENSITIVITY TRAINING
Bias intimidation, 2C:16–1

SENTENCE AND PUNISHMENT
Correctional Institutions, generally, this index
Crimes and Offenses, this index
Fines and Penalties, generally, this index
Jails, generally, this index
Juvenile Delinquents, this index
Municipal Courts, this index
Second or Subsequent Offenses, generally, this
index

SENTENCING CONFERENCES
Open court proceedings, Rule 1:2–1

SEPARATE OFFENSES
Joinder, indictment, accusation, Rule 3:7–6

SEPARATE TRIAL
Multiple offenses, 2C:1–8

SEPARATION
Husband and wife, confidential communications, effect, 2A:84A–22

**SEPTEMBER 11TH, 2001 ANTITERRORISM
ACT**
Generally, 2C:38–1 et seq.

SEQUESTRATION
Juries, Rule 1:8–6
Alternate jurors, Rule 1:8–2
Witnesses, Evidence Rule 615

SERGEANT AT ARMS
Political activities or holding public office, Rule
1:17–1
Superior Court, generally, this index

SERIAL NUMBERS
Motor vehicles,
Change or destruction, crimes and offenses,
2C:17–6
Component parts, 39:10B–1 et seq.

SERIOUS BODILY INJURY
Bodily Injury, this index
Definitions,
Homicide, 2C:11–1
Justification, 2C:3–11
Motor vehicle offenses, 39:5–30

SERVICE
Process, generally, this index

SERVICE MARKS
Trademarks and Trade Names, generally, this
index

SERVICE OF PROCESS
Process, generally, this index

SERVICES
Definitions, computer related offenses,
2C:20–23

SETOFF AND COUNTERCLAIM
Alcoholic beverages, refund of license fee on
surrender of license where setoffs or counterclaims paid, 33:1–31

SETTLEMENT
Compromise and Settlement, generally, this index

SEVERANCE
Accusation, Rule 3:15–1

SEVERE PERSONAL INJURY
Aggravated criminal sexual contact, 2C:14–3
Definitions, sexual offenses, 2C:14–1

SEWERS AND SEWER SYSTEMS
Crimes and offenses, unlicensed entry of struc-
ture, 2C:18–3
Trespass, 2C:18–3
Unlicensed entry of structure, crimes and of-
fenses, 2C:18–3

SEX CRIME VICTIM TREATMENT FUND
Deposits, 2C:14–10

SEX OFFENSES
Generally, 2C:14–1 et seq.
Adult Diagnostic and Treatment Center, gen-
erally, this index
Advisory councils, internet registry, 2C:7–18
Aggravated Criminal Sexual Contact, generally,
this index
Aggravated Sexual Assault, generally, this in-
dex
AIDS or HIV testing for persons charged with,
2A:4A–43.1, 2C:43–2.2
Appeal and review, record, closed circuit testi-
mony of children, 2A:84A–32.4
Arrests,
Repetitive or compulsive sex offenders, re-
cidivism, monitoring, 2C:47–9
Use of deadly force, 2C:3–7
Assault. Sexual Assault, generally, this index
Bail, victims of crime, injunctions, 2C:14–12
Bias intimidation, 2C:16–1
Business and commerce, sexually oriented busi-
nesses, 2C:33–12.2
Zoning and planning, 2C:34–7
Children and minors, 2C:24–4
Abuse or neglect, 9:6–8.21
Anatomically correct dolls, 2A:84A–16.1
Closed circuit testimony, 2A:84A–32.4
Confidential or privileged information, Rule
1:38–3
Defined as abuse of children, 9:6–8.9

SEX OFFENSES—Cont'd
Children and minors—Cont'd
DNA database and databank, 53:1–20.20
Endangering welfare, 2C:24–4
Expungement of record, 2C:52–2
Hearsay statements, admissibility, **Evidence
Rule 803**
Witnesses, anatomically correct dolls or
models, 2A:84A–16.1
Closed circuit testimony, sexual abuse, chil-
dren, 2A:84A–32.4
Colleges and universities, registration, foreign
states, 2C:7–2
Community notification,
Advisory council, establishment, qualificatio
of members, 2C:7–11
Chief law enforcement officer to provide
notification to community, 2C:7–7
Civil or criminal liability for providing or
failing to provide relevant information,
2C:7–9
Guidelines and procedures, 2C:7–8
Identification of factors relevant to risk of
reoffense, 2C:7–8
Immunity from civil and criminal liability fo
providing or failing to provide relevant
information, 2C:7–9
Intent of sex offender released from correc-
tional facility or adjudicated delinquent
to reside in community, 2C:7–6
Notification concerning other dangerous ci
cumstances unaffected by provisions,
2C:7–10
Confidential or privileged information, victims
of crime, location, 2C:14–12
Costs, examination and treatment, 2C:47–7
Criminal Sexual Contact, generally, this index
Dead bodies, 2C:22–1
Definitions, 2C:14–1
Victims of crime, injunctions, 2C:14–11
Diseased persons, 2C:34–5
DNA Database and Databank, generally, this
index
Domestic Violence, generally, this index
Domicile and residence, registration, release,
2C:7–2.1
Endangering welfare of children, 2C:24–4
Evidence,
Closed circuit testimony, children,
2A:84A–32.4
Previous sexual conduct of victim, 2C:14–7
Examination, costs, 2C:47–7
Female offenders, 2C:47–4.2
Fines and penalties, 2C:14–6, 2C:14–10
Sexual assault nurse examiner program fun
2C:43–3.6
Surcharges, 2C:43–3.7
Fraud, registration, 2C:7–2
Funds, sex crime victim treatment fund, depo
its, 2C:14–10
Human trafficking, 2C:13–8
Indigent, neglected or abandoned children,
closed circuit testimony, 2A:84A–32.4
Injunctions. Victims of crime, generally, post
Internet,
Access, 2C:43–6.6
Enforcement, training, 2C:43–6.7
Parole, 2C:43–6.4
Probation, 2C:45–1
Registration, 2C:7–12 et seq.
Jails, domicile and residence, release, registra-
tion, 2C:7–2.1
Juvenile delinquents, 2C:14–8
Assault, jurisdiction, waiver, 2A:4A–26
Referral to other courts without juveniles
consent, Rule 5:22–2

SEX OFFENSES—Cont'd
Juveniles in need of supervision, **2C:14–8**
Limitation of criminal prosecution, **2C:1–6**
Mistake as to age, **2C:14–5**
Motions, closed circuit testimony, children and minors, **2A:84A–32.4**
Murder, **2C:11–3**
Notice. Community notification, generally, ante
Parole, this index
Plea bargains, prosecutors, victims of crime, consultation, **2C:14–2.1**
Presumptions, capability, **2C:14–5**
Privileges and immunities, registration, **2C:7–15**
Probation and probation officers, **2C:47–3**
  Registration, **2C:7–1 et seq.**
  Victims of crime, injunctions, **2C:45–1, 2C:45–2**
Proof of resistance, **2C:14–5**
Prosecutors, victims of crime, consultation, plea bargains, **2C:14–2.1**
Prostitution, generally, this index
Public policy, registration, studies, application of law, **2C:7–20**
Rape, generally, this index
Recidivism, repetitive or compulsive sex offenders, monitoring, **2C:47–9**
Registration, **2C:7–1 et seq.**
  Internet, **2C:7–12 et seq.**
  Studies, application of law, **2C:7–21**
  Public policy, **2C:7–20**
Release, domicile and residence, registration, **2C:7–2.1**
Repetitive or compulsive sex offenders,
  Amenability to treatment, examination, **2C:47–1 et seq.**
  Recidivism, monitoring, **2C:47–9**
Reports,
  Parole, revocation, **2C:47–5.1**
  Repetitive or compulsive sex offenders,
    Amenability to treatment, examination, **2C:47–2, 2C:47–3**
    Recidivism, **2C:47–9**
Resource Family Care, this index
Restraining orders. Victims of crime, generally, post
Schools and school districts, registration, foreign states, **2C:7–2**
Sentence and punishment, **2C:14–6, 2C:47–3**
  Victims of crime, injunctions, **2C:44–8**
Sexual Assault, generally, this index
Sexually oriented businesses, **2C:33–12.2**
  Zoning and planning, **2C:34–7**
Studies,
  Megans Law, application of law, **2C:7–21**
  Public policy, **2C:7–20**
  Repetitive or compulsive sex offenders, recidivism, **2C:47–9**
Surcharges, **2C:43–3.7**
Transcripts, record, closed circuit testimony of children, **2A:84A–32.4**
Treatment, repetitive or compulsive sex offenders,
  Amenability to treatment, examination, **2C:47–1 et seq.**
  Effectiveness, recidivism, **2C:47–9**
Venereal diseases, sexual penetration, **2C:34–5**
Victims of crime,
  Bail, injunctions, **2C:14–12**
  Confidential or privileged information, location, **2C:14–12**
  Definitions, injunctions, **2C:14–11**
  Location, confidential or privileged information, **2C:14–12**
  Probation and probation officers, injunctions, **2C:45–1, 2C:45–2**

SEX OFFENSES—Cont'd
Victims of crime—Cont'd
  Prosecuting attorneys, plea bargains, consultation, **2C:14–2.1**
  Sentence and punishment, injunctions, **2C:44–8**
  Treatment fund, deposits, **2C:14–10**
  Videotaped testimony, children and minors, **2A:84A–32.4**
  Vocational education, registration, foreign states, **2C:7–2**
  Weapons, possession, persons convicted of, **2C:39–7**
  Witnesses, children and minors,
    Anatomically correct dolls, **2A:84A–16.1**
    Closed circuit testimony, **2A:84A–32.4**
  Youth serving organizations, participation, sex offenders, **2C:7–22, 2C:7–23**
  Zoning and planning, sexually oriented businesses, **2C:34–7**

SEXUAL ABUSE
Child Abuse, this index

SEXUAL ACTIVITY
Definitions, prostitution, **2C:34–1**

SEXUAL ASSAULT
Generally, **2C:14–1 et seq.**
Adult Diagnostic and Treatment Center, generally, this index
Aggravated Sexual Assault, generally, this index
Appeal and review, record, closed circuit testimony of children, **2A:84A–32.4**
Arrest warrant,
  Issuance, **Rule 3:3–1**
  Release, **Rule 3:4–1**
Bail,
  Authority to admit to, **Rule 3:26–2**
  Cash, crime with bail restrictions, **2A:162–12**
Body vests, **2C:39–13**
Children and minors, closed circuit testimony, **2A:84A–32.4**
Closed circuit testimony, sexual abuse, children, **2A:84A–32.4**
Community notification. Sex Offenses, this index
Diagnostic center report, presentence investigation, **Rule 3:21–3**
DNA Database and Databank, generally, this index
Domestic Violence, generally, this index
Evidence,
  Closed circuit testimony, children, **2A:84A–32.4**
  Previous sexual conduct of victim, **2C:14–7**
Extended term of imprisonment, **2C:43–7, 2C:43–7.1**
Fines and penalties,
  Sexual assault nurse examiner program fund, **2C:43–3.6**
  Surcharges, **2C:43–3.7**
Indigent, neglected or abandoned children, closed circuit testimony, **2A:84A–32.4**
Jury,
  Number of peremptory challenges, **2B:23–13**
  Peremptory challenges, **Rule 1:8–3**
Limitation of criminal prosecution, **2C:1–6**
Minor, limitation of criminal prosecution, **2C:1–6**
Motions, closed circuit testimony, children and minors, **2A:84A–32.4**
Murder, **2C:11–3**
Offenders, registration. Sex Offenses, this index

SEXUAL ASSAULT—Cont'd
Parole supervision for life, special sentence, Violent Predator Incapacitation Act of 1994, **2C:43–6.4**
Plea bargains, prosecutors, victims of crime, consultation, **2C:14–2.1**
Rape, generally, this index
Surcharges, **2C:43–3.7**
Transcripts, record, closed circuit testimony of children, **2A:84A–32.4**
Victims of crime, consultation, plea bargains, prosecutors, **2C:14–2.1**
Videotaped testimony, children and minors, **2A:84A–32.4**
Weapons, possession, persons convicted of, **2C:39–7**
Witnesses, children and minors, closed circuit testimony, **2A:84A–32.4**

SEXUAL CONDUCT
Definitions, sexual offenses, evidence of previous sexual conduct of victim, **2C:14–7**

SEXUAL CONTACT
Definitions, sexual offenses, **2C:14–1, 2C:14–3**

SEXUAL INTERCOURSE
Children and minors, second degree crime, **2C:24–4**
Crimes and offenses, observation, invasion of privacy, **2C:14–9**
Sexual offenses, **2C:14–1**

SEXUAL PENETRATION
Definitions, sexual offenses, **2C:14–1**

SEXUALLY ORIENTED BUSINESSES
Crimes and offenses, zoning and planning, **2C:34–7**

SEXUALLY ORIENTED MATERIALS
Lewdness and Obscenity, generally, this index

SEXUALLY TRANSMITTED DISEASES
AIDS (Acquired Immune Deficiency Syndrome), generally, this index

SEXUALLY VIOLENT PREDATORS
Parole, this index

SHARES AND SHAREHOLDERS
Alcoholic beverages,
  Application by corporation for licenses, **33:1–25**
  Automatic suspension of corporations license on conviction of stockholder, **33:1–31.1**
  Loans or furnishing of fixtures, to retail licensee by stockholder of brewery, **33:1–43.1**
  Notice by corporate licensees of changes, **33:1–34**
  Retail license holder, acquiring interest in stocks traded on national securities exchange, Chain Store Liquor License Act, **33:1–12.36**
Misconduct, corporate official, **2C:21–9**
Professional corporations, **Rule 1:21–1A**
Racketeering, **2C:41–1 et seq.**

SHARP SUBSTANCES
Placing on highway, fine imposed, **39:4–63**

SHELTER CARE
Definitions, juvenile justice, **2A:4A–22**

SHELTERS

Animal shelters, destruction of animals, 4:22–19

Animals, this index

Crimes and offenses, destruction of animals, 4:22–19

Juvenile Delinquents, this index

SHERBET

Frozen Desserts and Dietary Foods, generally, this index

SHERIFFS

Actions and proceedings, stolen property, 2C:65–3

Aggravated assault,
    Throwing bodily fluids, 2C:12–13
    Weapons, 2C:12–1

Alcoholic beverages,
    Nonprofit organizations, club licenses, 33:1–25.1, 33:1–25.2
    Officer under Alcoholic Beverage Law, 33:1–1

Arrest, powers, 2A:157–2.1

Assault and battery, aggravated assault, weapons, 2C:12–1

Associations and societies, intoxicating liquors, club licenses, 33:1–25.1, 33:1–25.2

Attorneys, practice of law, **Rule 1:15–3**

Club licenses, intoxicating liquors, nonprofit organizations, 33:1–25.1, 33:1–25.2

Crisis intervention services, hotline, funding, 2C:64–6, 39:5–41

Custody, stolen property, 2C:65–1 et seq.

Deputy sheriffs, officer under Alcoholic Beverage Law, 33:1–1

Disclosure, expungement order, 2C:52–30

Diversion programs, record expungement, 2C:52–20

Escapes, generally, this index

Evidence, stolen property, 2C:65–1

Expungement, records, 2C:52–1 et seq.

Extradition, application by sheriff to governor for requisition, 2A:160–32

Fees or other remuneration,
    Payment, on acquittal, 2A:166–9
    Record expungement, 2C:52–29

Fingerprints and photographs of arrested persons or unknown dead sent by sheriff to bureau of identification, 53:1–15

Fraternal societies, intoxicating liquors, club licenses, 33:1–25.1, 33:1–25.2

Grand Jury, this index

Hearings, record expungement, 2C:52–9 et seq.

Indictable offenses, record expungement, 2C:52–2

Information concerning offenses, forwarding to bureau of identification, 53:1–20.2

Inspection and inspectors, records, expungement, 2C:52–1

Jury and Jurors, this index

Licenses and permits, intoxicating liquors, nonprofit organizations, 33:1–25.1, 33:1–25.2

Motor vehicles, special plates, 39:3–27.29 et seq.

Narcotic offenses, fingerprinting and photographing persons arrested, 53:1–18.1

Nonprofit organizations, intoxicating liquors, club licenses, 33:1–25.1, 33:1–25.2

Notice, stolen property, disposition, 2C:65–2

Officers and employees,
    Aggravated assault, throwing bodily fluids, 2C:12–13
    Police powers, 2A:154–3

Orders of court,
    Record expungement, 2C:52–11 et seq.

SHERIFFS—Cont'd

Orders of court—Cont'd
    Stolen property disposition, 2C:65–3

Petitions, record expungement, 2C:52–7 et seq.

Photographing,
    Arrested persons, 53:1–15
    Stolen property, 2C:65–1

Political activities, **Rule 1:17–2**

Practice of law, **Rule 1:15–3**

Presentence report, record expungement, 2C:52–21

Process, generally, this index

Property, stolen property, 2C:65–1 et seq.

Records and recordation,
    Delivery of prisoners to state prison, 2C:43–10
    Expungement, 2C:52–1 et seq.
    Stolen property, 2C:65–1

Release,
    Record expungement, 2C:52–19
    Stolen property, 2C:65–2

Religious societies, intoxicating liquors, club licenses, 33:1–25.1, 33:1–25.2

Removal, records, 2C:52–15

Searches and seizures, warrants, execution, **Rule 3:5–5**

Societies, intoxicating liquors, club licenses, 33:1–25.1, 33:1–25.2

State grand jurors, summoning, 2B:22–4

Stolen property, disposition, 2C:65–1 et seq.

Supervisory treatment programs, record expungement, 2C:52–20

Traffic offenses, record expungement, 2C:52–28

Transportation, prisoners to correctional institutions, 2C:43–10

Veterans organizations, intoxicating liquors, club licenses, 33:1–25.1, 33:1–25.2

View by jury, duties and powers, 2B:23–16

Weapons, unlawful possession, exemption, 2C:39–6

SHERIFFS SALES

Stolen property, 2C:65–3

SHIELDS

Side shields,
    Stickers, not to be placed on motor vehicles, 39:3–74
    Windshield of motor vehicle as including, 39:3–75

SHIPS

Vessels, generally, this index

SHOOTING

Fish and Game, this index

SHOPLIFTING

Generally, 2C:20–11, 2C:20–11.1

Fingerprinting, 53:1–15

Identity and identification, offenders, **Rule 7:2–2**

Organized retail theft enterprise, 2C:20–11.2

SHOPPING CARTS

Definitions, shoplifting, 2C:20–11

SHOPPING CENTERS

Handicapped parking enforcement units, 39:4–197.9

SHOPS

Stores, generally, this index

SHORELINES

Adopt a beach program. Beaches and Beach Fronts, this index

Coastal protection license plate program, 39:3–27.47 et seq.

SHORT TERM CUSTODY

Juvenile delinquents and dependents, 2A:4A–31, 2A:4A–32

SHOTGUNS

See, also, Weapons, generally, this index

Definitions, 2C:39–1

Possession, crimes and offenses, 2C:39–3

Purchase or sale, 2C:58–3

Retail sales, purchase or identification cards, 2C:58–2

Sawed off shotguns, 2C:58–3

Security for loan of money, 2C:39–11

Temporary transfer and possession, 2C:58–3.1

Tracer ammunition, trap or skeet shooting, 2C:58–10

Unlawful possession, 2C:39–5

SHOULDER

Definitions, Motor Vehicle Law, 39:1–1

SHOW

Definitions, lewdness and obscenity, children and minors, 2C:34–3

SHRINES

Desecration, 2C:33–9

SIDE MARKER LAMPS

Regulations, motor vehicles, 39:3–63

Trailers and semitrailers, 39:3–61

Trucks, 39:3–61

SIDE SHIELDS

Stickers, not to be placed on motor vehicles, 39:3–74

Windshield of motor vehicle as including, 39:3–75

SIDEWALKS

Crosswalks, generally, this index

Definitions, 39:1–1

Driving vehicle or horse across prohibited, when, 39:4–71

Electric personal assistive mobility devices, operation, 39:4–14.10

Horses, this index

Motor vehicle entering or leaving private road or driveway, yield right of way to pedestrians, 39:4–66.1

Motor vehicles, driving on, municipal cleaning or maintenance purposes, 39:4–71

Obstructing public passages, 2C:33–7

Parking of vehicle on sidewalk prohibited, 39:4–138

Pedestrians prohibited from walking upon adjacent roadway, 39:4–34

Speed of vehicle or horse in crossing, maximum, 39:4–100

Stopping vehicle emerging from alley, driveway or garage, 39:4–66

SIGNALS AND SIGNALING

See, also, Signs, generally, this index

Crosswalks, older and walking impaired persons crossing, 39:4–183.1b

False public alarms, 2C:33–3 et seq.

Fireworks, exceptions, application of law, 21:2–4

Lights, rotating or flashing lights on or near highways, 39:4–60.1 et seq.

SIGNALS AND SIGNALING—Cont'd
Motor vehicles. Traffic Signs and Signals, generally, this index
Public nuisance, lights, rotating or flashing lights on or near highways, **39:4–60.1 et seq.**
Railroads, this index
Traffic Signs and Signals, generally, this index

SIGNATURES
Arrest warrants, **Rule 3:3–2**
Attorneys, this index
Briefs, this index
Complaints, municipal courts, **Rule 7:2–1**
Domestic violence, complaints, electronic signatures, **Rule 1:4–4**
Drivers Licenses, this index
Facsimiles, this index
Identification card, intoxicating liquor purchasing, **33:1–81.2**
Intoxicating liquors, identification card, **33:1–81.2**
Juvenile delinquents, complaint, contents, **Rule 5:20–1**
Motions, this index
Motor vehicles, application for registration, **39:3–4**
Pleadings, this index
Proof of service, **Rule 1:5–3**
Search warrant under alcoholic beverage law, **33:1–57**
Securing execution of documents by deception, **2C:21–16**
Summons, municipal courts, **Rule 7:2–1**
Weapons, registers, sales, **2C:58–2**

SIGNIFICANT BODILY INJURY
Definitions, Comprehensive Child Abuse Prevention and Treatment Act, **9:6–8.84**

SIGNS
Construction warning, **39:4–183.22a**
Definitions, motor vehicles, **39:1–1**
Erection, use or maintenance, outdoor advertising, **27:5–8**
Highways,
 Littering, **39:4–64.1**
 Outdoor Advertising, generally, this index
Imitation traffic signs, prohibition, **27:5–9**
Lewdness and obscenity, sexually oriented businesses, **2C:34–7**
Noncommercial trucks, **39:3–8.1**
Older and walking impaired persons crossing, **39:4–183.1b**
Outdoor Advertising, generally, this index
Railroads, this index
Reflectors. Lights and Lighting, this index
Roadside advertising. Outdoor Advertising, generally, this index
Sexually oriented businesses, **2C:34–7**
Stop signs. Traffic Signs and Signals, this index
Yield right of way signs, location, **39:4–141**

SIMPLE ASSAULT
Generally, **2C:12–1**
Intimidation based on bias, fourth degree crime, extended term of imprisonment, **2C:43–7**
Vessel, operation of, **2C:12–1**

SIMULATION
Criminal simulation, **2C:21–2**

SINGLE AXLE LIMITATION
Motor vehicles, dimensional and weight limitation, **39:3–84**

SINGLE BEAM HEADLAMPS
Definitions, **39:3–46**

SIRENS
Bicycle not to be equipped with, **39:3–69, 39:4–11**
Use on vehicles other than emergency vehicles prohibited, **39:3–69**
Volunteer fire company chief or first assistant chief, siren on vehicle, **39:3–54.15 et seq.**

SKATEBOARDS
Children and minors, helmets, **39:4–10.5 et seq.**
Fines and penalties, helmets, **39:4–10.6, 39:4–10.9**
Funds, bicycle and skating safety fund, **39:4–10.2**
Helmets, **39:4–10.5 et seq.**
Highways and roads, **39:4–10.10, 39:4–10.11**
 Municipalities, rules and regulations, **39:4–10.10a**
Municipalities, rules and regulations, **39:4–10.10a**
Notices, sales, warning, protective gear, **39:4–10.8**
Privileges and immunities, **39:4–10.8, 39:4–10.9**
Transportation commissioner, powers and duties, exceptions, **39:4–10.10b**

SKATES
Roller Skates, generally, this index

SKILLED NURSING HOMES
Nursing Homes or Hospitals, this index

SKILLS AND METHODS COURSES
Attorneys, practice requirement, **Rule 1:21–1**

SKIMOBILES
Snowmobiles, generally, this index

SKINNERS AND MICHELLES LAW
Generally, **2C:11–5.1, 2C:12–1.1, 2C:44–1**

SLEDS AND SLEDDING
Hitching onto streetcar or vehicle prohibited, **39:4–14**
Sleighbells required on horse attached to sleigh or sled, **39:4–15**

SLEEPING BAGS
Definitions, flammable fabrics, **2A:123–16**
Flammable fabrics, **2A:123–16 et seq.**

SLEIGHBELLS
Horse attached to sleigh or sled, **39:4–15**

SLING SHOTS
Weapons, generally, this index

SLOGANS
Animal welfare license plates, **39:3–27.55**
Coastal protection license plates, **39:3–27.48**

SLOT MACHINES
Definitions, **2C:37–1**
Possession, **2C:37–7**
Rules and regulations by director of alcoholic beverage control, **33:1–39**
Slugs, **2C:21–18**
Theft of services, **2C:20–8**

SLOW MOVING VEHICLES
Motor Vehicles, this index

SLUG
Definitions, coin, currency or credit card activated machine, **2C:21–18**

SMALL CLAIMS
Appearances, corporations, **Rule 1:21–1**
Business entities, appearances, **Rule 1:21–1**
Complementary dispute resolution programs, **Rules 1:40–6, 1:40–7**
Evidence, application of law, **Evidence Rule 101**
Mediation, complementary dispute resolution programs, **Rules 1:40–6, 1:40–7**

SMART GROWTH DEVELOPMENT PROJECTS
Alcoholic beverages, licenses and permits, **33:1–24.1 et seq.**
Definitions, alcoholic beverages, **33:1–24.2**

SMOKE
Motor vehicles, air pollution, **39:3–70.1, 39:3–70.2**

SMOKING
Cigarettes and Cigars, generally, this index

SNOW
Motor vehicles, dislodging from moving vehicle, fines and penalties, **39:4–77.1**
Removal equipment, certain farm machinery or implements under contract with municipality to remove snow upon public highway,
 License plates, **39:3–25**
 Registration, **39:3–24**

SNOWMOBILES
Generally, **39:3C–1 et seq.**
Accidents, reports, **39:3C–21**
Agricultural land, registration, **39:3C–6**
Animals, harassment, **39:3C–19**
Brakes, **39:3C–19**
 Equipment, **39:3C–24**
Certificates and certification,
 Fees, **39:3C–3**
 Registration, generally, post
Children and minors, operation, **39:3C–16**
Crossing highways, **39:3C–17**
 Application of law, **39:3C–30**
Definitions, **39:3C–1**
Enforcement of law, **39:3C–27**
Environmental rules and regulations, **39:3C–14**
Equipment, **39:3C–24**
 Rules and regulations, **39:3C–15**
 Sale, **39:3C–26**
Exemption, registration, **39:3C–6**
Fees, registration, **39:3C–3**
Fines and penalties,
 Crossing highways, **39:3C–30**
 Insurance, **39:3C–20**
 Public lands, **39:3C–33**
 Races, **39:3C–22**
 Rules and regulations, **39:3C–28**
Forfeitures, public lands, **39:3C–34**
Freeways, operation, **39:3C–17**
Helmets, **39:3C–19**
Highways and Roads, this index
Impounding, public lands, **39:3C–34**
Inspection, **39:3C–25**
Insurance, **39:3C–20**
Licenses and permits. Registration, generally, post
Lights and lighting, **39:3C–19**
 Equipment, **39:3C–24**
 Special events, exemptions, **39:3C–23**
Limited access highways, rules and regulations, **39:3C–17**
Mufflers, **39:3C–19, 39:3C–24**
 Inspection, **39:3C–25**
Nighttime, **39:3C–19**
Nonresidents, registration fees, **39:3C–3**

SNOWMOBILES—Cont'd
Passengers, **39:3C–19**
Protective helmets, **39:3C–19**
Public lands, operation, **39:3C–32 et seq.**
Railroads, trespass, **39:3C–19**
Reciprocity, **39:3C–7**
Reckless driving, **39:3C–19**
Registration, **39:3C–3**
   Change of address, **39:3C–10**
   Display of number, **39:3C–8**
   Exclusive registration, **39:3C–13**
   Exemptions, **39:3C–6**
   Fees, disposition of funds, **39:3C–29**
   Issuance, **39:3C–5**
   Permanent number, **39:3C–4**
   Police identification, **39:3C–9**
   Racing, exemptions, **39:3C–23**
   Reciprocity, **39:3C–7**
   Removal from state, **39:3C–12**
   Special events, exemptions, **39:3C–23**
   Transfer of ownership, **39:3C–11**
Removal from state, notification, **39:3C–12**
Rules and regulations, **39:3C–2**
   Environmental protection, **39:3C–14**
   Races, **39:3C–22**
Safety equipment, **39:3C–15**
Sales, equipment, **39:3C–26**
Speed, **39:3C–19**
Temporary registration dealers, **39:3C–6**
Theft, notification, **39:3C–12**
Traffic rules and regulations, **39:3C–19**
Transfer of ownership, registration, **39:3C–5,
   39:3C–11**
Trespass, **39:3C–18**
   Permit, **39:3C–19**
Unlawful taking, **2C:20–10**

SOCIAL CLUBS OR SOCIETIES
Nonprofit Corporations and Associations, generally, this index

SOCIAL SECURITY
Medicaid, generally, this index
Numbers and numbering, confidential or privi-
   leged information, **Rule 1:38–7**

SOCIAL SERVICES
Indigent Persons, generally, this index

SOCIAL WORKERS
Child abuse or neglect, regional diagnostic and
   treatment center, **9:6–8.100**
Conferences, probation officers, expenses,
   2A:168–8
Crisis intervention services, hotlines, referrals,
   funding, **2C:64–6, 39:5–41**
Domestic violence prevention, **2C:25–20**

SOCIETIES AND ORDERS
Associations and Societies, generally, this index
Fraternal Organizations, generally, this index

**SOCIETY FOR PREVENTION OF CRUELTY
   TO CHILDREN**
Child Abuse, this index

**SOCIETY FOR THE PREVENTION OF CRU-
   ELTY TO ANIMALS**
Cruelty to Animals, this index

SODIUM CHLORATE
Turnpike project, transportation regulations,
   27:23–31

SODOMY
Generally, **2C:14–1 et seq., 2C:14–2**

SODOMY—Cont'd
Children and minors, second degree crime,
   2C:24–4
Expungement of record, **2C:52–2**
Records and recordation, expungement,
   2C:52–2

SOFTWARE
Computers, this index

SOLDIERS AND SAILORS
Armed Forces, generally, this index
Veterans, generally, this index

SOLICIT
Definitions, health care professionals, disasters
   or accidents, **2C:40A–4**

SOLICITING
Accomplices, **2C:2–6**
Charitable Organizations and Associations,
   generally, this index
Conspiracy, **2C:5–2**
Contributions, this index
Criminal street gangs, **2C:33–28**
Fraud, runners, health and accident insurance,
   2C:21–22.1
Gangs, **2C:33–28**
Health and accident insurance, runners, fraud,
   2C:21–22.1
Jury question, solicitation of sales as sole ques-
   tion of law and fact in determining viola-
   tion of statute, **39:4–60**
Prostitution, **2C:34–1**
Rigging publicly exhibited contests, **2C:21–11**
Rules and regulations by director of alcoholic
   beverage control, **33:1–39**
Runners, health and accident insurance, fraud,
   2C:21–22.1
Standing in roadway to solicit rides, sales, or
   contributions prohibited, **39:4–59, 39:4–60**
Street gangs, **2C:33–28**

SOLICITORS
Attorneys, generally, this index

SOLID TIRE
Definitions, Motor Vehicle Law, **39:1–1**

SOLID WASTE
Actions and proceedings,
   Enforcement actions, **13:1E–9**
   Toxic packaging reduction, **13:1E–99.54**
Adopt a beach program. Beaches and Beach
   Fronts, this index
Assessments, violators, expenses of removing,
   adverse effects on water and air quality,
   13:1E–9
Brands, labels and marks, roll off dumpsters or
   containers, placement along highways or
   public property, **27:5I–1**
Civil penalties, **13:1E–9**
Compromise and settlement, penalty claims,
   13:1E–9
Consent, roll off dumpsters or containers,
   placement along highways or public prop-
   erty, **27:5I–1**
Constructor vehicles, registration fees, **39:3–20**
Conveyances, willful discharge, forfeiture,
   13:1E–9
Costs, assessment of violators, **13:1E–9**
County health department, fees, **13:1E–9**
Crimes and offenses, **13:1E–9, 48:13A–12**
   Hazardous waste, **13:1E–9**
   Toxic packaging reduction, **13:1E–99.54**
Damages, aquatic life, fish or wildlife, loss or
   destruction, **13:1E–9**

SOLID WASTE—Cont'd
Discharge, conveyances used in willful dis-
   charge, forfeiture, **13:1E–9**
Disposal,
   Fines and penalties, **13:1E–9**
   Unauthorized transportation, fines and pen-
     alties, **13:1E–9**
Dumpsters, placement along highways or pub-
   lic property, **27:5I–1**
   Consent and markers, **27:5I–1**
Enforcement of law, **13:1E–9**
Engineers, this index
Expenses and expenditures, removal, adverse
   effects on water and air quality, **13:1E**
Explosives, magazines, **21:1A–136**
Facilities, health department, compliance wit
   regulations, **13:1E–9**
False or misleading statements, fines and pen-
   alties, **13:1E–9**
Fees, county health departments, **13:1E–9**
Fines and penalties, **13:1E–9, 48:13A–12**
   Recycling, post
   Roll off dumpsters or containers, placemer
     along highways or public property,
     27:5I–1
   Toxic packaging reduction, **13:1E–99.54**
Forfeitures,
   Conveyances used in willful discharge,
     13:1E–9
   Willful discharge, conveyances, **13:1E–9**
Hazardous Substances and Waste, generally,
   this index
Hearings,
   Enforcement of law, **13:1E–9**
   Toxic packaging reduction, **13:1E–99.54**
Highways and roads, roll off dumpsters or cc
   tainers, placement along, **27:5I–1**
Injunctions, **13:1E–9**
   Toxic packaging reduction, **13:1E–99.54**
Inspection and inspectors, disposal facilities,
   13:1E–9
Jurisdiction, toxic packaging reduction,
   13:1E–99.54
Motor carriers,
   Axle weight limitations, **39:3–84.1**
   Food,
     Cleansing and sanitization required,
       48:13A–12.1
     Crime of third degree, penalties,
       48:13A–12.2
   Identification marks, **39:3–33**
   Registration, **39:3–20**
Motor Vehicles, this index
Notice, enforcement of law, **13:1E–9**
Number, motor drawn vehicles used in collec
   tion, **39:4–54**
Orders, rules and regulation enforcement,
   13:1E–9
Public property, roll off dumpsters or contain
   ers,
   Placement along, **27:5I–1**
   Placement on or along, **27:5I–1**
Recycling,
   Fines and penalties, disposition, **39:5–41**
   Motor Vehicle Junk Yards, generally, this
     index
Roll off dumpsters or containers, placement
   along highways or public property, **27:5I**
Rules and regulations, Solid Waste Utility Cc
   trol Act, enforcement, **13:1E–9**
Transportation, manifest, **13:1E–9**
Unauthorized transportation, disposal faciliti
   fines and penalties, **13:1E–9**

SOMETHING OF VALUE
Definitions, gambling, **2C:37–1**

SORORITIES
Hazing, crimes and offenses, **2C:40–3 et seq.**

SOUND RECORDINGS
Crimes and offenses, admissibility, pretrial hearings, **Rule 3:9–1**
Grand jury, record, **Rule 3:6–6**
Lewdness and Obscenity, generally, this index
Piracy, **2C:21–21**
Verbatim records, **Rule 1:2–2**
Wiretapping and electronic surveillance, **2A:156A–14**

SOUTHEAST ASIAN CONFLICT
Drivers licenses, veterans, waiver of fee, **39:3–11.5**

SOVEREIGN IMMUNITY
Searches and seizures, news organizations, **2A:84A–21.11**

SPANISH LANGUAGE
Victims of crime, motor vehicle or traffic offenders, notice of status of prosecution, **39:5–52**

SPARKLERS
Fireworks, generally, this index

SPARKLING WINE
Presumption, fitness for beverage purposes and alcoholic content, **33:1–1.1**
Wholesalers license, **33:1–11**

SPAYING AND NEUTERING
Animals, this index
Cats, this index
Dogs, this index

SPECIAL ASSESSMENTS
Assessments, generally, this index

SPECIAL CIVIL PART
Law Division, Superior Court, this index

SPECIAL EDUCATIONAL SERVICES
Schools and School Districts, this index

SPECIAL EVENTS
Definitions, registration and regulation of snowmobiles and all terrain vehicles, **39:3C–1**

SPECIAL EXECUTION
Executions, generally, this index

SPECIAL FROZEN DIETARY FOOD
Frozen Desserts and Dietary Foods, generally, this index

SPECIAL HOSPITALS
Institutionalized elderly persons, assault, **2C:12–1**

SPECIAL LAWS
Criminal procedure, law relating to not to affect laws relating to any particular counties or localities, **2A:152–4**

SPECIAL OFFICERS
Discontinued in office of county prosecutor, **2A:157–23**
Weapons, unlawful possession, exemption, **2C:39–6**

SPECIAL ORDER
Executions, generally, this index

SPECIAL POLICE
Carrying weapons, **2C:39–6**

SPECIAL SITTINGS
Courts, **Rule 1:30–3**

SPECIAL VERDICT
Homicide, aggravating and mitigating factors, **2C:11–3**

SPECIALLY ASSIGNED CASES
Motions, **Rule 1:6–2**

SPECIFIED ANATOMICAL AREA
Definitions, obscene material, children and minors, **2C:34–3**

SPECIFIED SEXUAL ACTIVITY
Definitions, obscene material, children and minors, **2C:34–3**

SPECTACLES
Optometrists, generally, this index

SPECULATION
Public officers and employees, official actions or information, **2C:30–3**

SPEED
Generally, **39:4–95 et seq.**
Appeal of reckless driving conviction, representation of prosecution, **39:5–20**
Blocking traffic, slow speeds, **39:4–97.1**
Business district, **39:4–98**
Careless driving, **39:4–97**
Complaints, **39:4–99**
Constructor registration plates,
Vehicles carrying, **39:3–20**
Vehicles registered in using, **39:3–20**
Curves, speed in traversing, **39:4–98**
Death of another, license suspension or revocation, **39:5–30**
Definitions, vehicle, **39:4–95**
Electric personal assistive mobility devices, operation, **39:4–14.10**
Emergencies, physicians, **39:4–102**
Evidence, **39:4–99**
Exceeding statutory speed limitations, prima facie unlawful, **39:4–99**
Exemptions from speed law, **39:4–101,
39:4–103**
Fines and penalties,
Offenses in construction or repair areas, conditions, **39:4–203.5**
Racing or attempting to make speed record, **39:4–52**
Reckless driving, **39:4–96**
Sixty five mph, **39:4–98.6**
Violating speed law, **39:4–104**
Headlamps not approved, limitation on speed of vehicle, **39:3–55**
Information plate on certain vehicles to show maximum speed, **39:3–82**
Intersections, **39:4–98**
Lanes marked for traffic, **39:4–88**
Limit periods, **39:4–98.2**
Limits. Rates of speed, generally, post
Low speed vehicles, **39:4–31.1 et seq.**
Military vehicles, exemption, **39:4–103**
Motor Carriers, this index
Municipalities, limits,
Alteration, **39:4–197**
Self contained streets, **39:4–8**
Notice of ordinance, **39:4–198**
Ordinances or resolutions, limits, traffic regulations, **39:4–8**

SPEED—Cont'd
Overtaken vehicles, increase of speed before complete passing by overtaking vehicle, **39:4–87**
Photo radar,
Definitions, motor vehicle speeding laws, **39:4–103.1**
Speeding laws, enforcement, **39:4–103.1**
Physician on emergency call, **39:4–102**
Police vehicles, exemption, **39:4–103**
Punishment, reckless driving, **39:4–96**
Racing on highway or attempting to make speed record, **39:4–52**
Rates of speed, **39:4–98**
Alteration, **39:4–197**
Notice, **39:4–198**
Self contained streets, **39:4–8**
Sidewalks, crossing, **39:4–100**
Sixty five mph, implementation, **39:4–98.3 et seq.**
Trucks, lower maximum speed, **39:4–98.1**
Reckless driving, **39:4–96**
Courtesy plates, **39:3–33.5a**
Special plates, **39:3–33.5**
Reduction, highway repair, **39:4–98.2**
Reports, sixty five mph, **39:4–98.7**
Residence districts, speed, **39:4–98**
Riots, exemptions, **39:4–103**
Safe stopping distance determined, proceeding through intersection on amber light, **39:4–105**
Safety zone, vehicle passing streetcar receiving or discharging passengers, **39:4–40**
Serious bodily injury of another, license suspension or revocation, **39:5–30**
Sidewalks, speed in crossing, **39:4–100**
Sixty five mph, implementation, **39:4–98.3 et seq.**
Slow speed, blocking traffic, **39:4–97.1**
Speedways excepted from speed law, **39:4–101**
Studies, sixty five mph, **39:4–98.7**
Suburban business or residential district, definitions, **39:1–1**
Sudden decrease, **39:4–126**
Summons, **39:4–99**
Trucks, highway commissioner, designation of lower maximum speed limits, **39:4–98.1**
Turnpikes and turnpike companies, **27:23–27**
Sixty five mph, implementation, **39:4–98.3 et seq.**

SPEED BUMPS
Municipalities, highways and roads, **39:4–8.9 et seq.**

SPEEDWAYS
Speed law inapplicable, **39:4–101**

SPEEDY TRIAL
Children and minors, victims of crime, **2A:163–4, 2A:163–5**
Convicts, interstate agreement on detainers, **2A:159A–1, 2A:159A–3, 2A:159A–4**
Delay following indictment, motion for trial date, **Rule 3:25–2**
Juvenile delinquents and dependents, **Rule 5:21–3**

SPINAL CORD
Funds, research, fines and penalties, motor vehicles, **39:5–41**

SPORTS
Athletics, generally, this index

SPORTS AND EXPOSITION AUTHORITY
Alcoholic beverages, entertainment facilities,
33:1–12

SPORTS OFFICIALS
Victims of crime, 2C:44–1

SPOT LAMPS
Use on motor vehicles, 39:3–53

SPOUSAL ABUSE
Domestic Violence, generally, this index

SPOUSES
Accomplices and accessories, bigamy, 2C:24–1
Actions and proceedings, testifying as witness,
2A:84A–17
Competency, privileged communications, dis-
closure, 2A:84A–22
Construction of rules, Rule 1:1–2
Crimes and offenses,
Desertion, venue, Rule 3:14–1
Privileged communications, Evidence Rules
501, 509
Support, willful nonsupport, 2C:24–5
Death,
Bigamy, defense, 2C:24–1
Privileged communications, subsequent dis-
closure, 2A:84A–22
Vesting of motor vehicle title, 39:3–30.1
Derivative actions, contingent attorney fees,
Rule 1:21–7
Domestic Violence, generally, this index
Duress, 2C:2–9
Evidence, privileged communications,
2A:84A–22
Marriage, generally, this index
Marriage counselors, privileges and immuni-
ties, Evidence Rule 510
Motor Vehicles, this index
Nonsupport. Support of Persons, generally,
this index
Pregnancy, generally, this index
Preparation, confidential communications, ef-
fect, 2A:84A–22
Privileges and immunities, 2A:84A–22; Evi-
dence Rules 501, 509
Prostitution, 2C:34–1
Sexual offenses, 2C:14–5
Support of Persons, generally, this index
Theft, 2C:20–2
Veterans, free joint motor vehicle registration,
39:3–27.1
Willful nonsupport, 2C:24–5
Witnesses, privileges and immunities,
2A:84A–17

SPRAY PAINT
Definitions, criminal mischief, 2C:17–3,
2C:17–3.1

STADIUMS
Intoxicating liquor law, entertainment facilities,
33:1–12
Definitions, 33:1–12

STAKES
Gambling, generally, this index

STALKING
Generally, 2C:12–10
Children and minors, injunctions, 2C:12–10.2
Conviction, judgment of, 2C:12–10.1
Conviction of crime, possession of any weapon
prohibited, 2C:39–7
Developmentally disabled persons, injunctions,
2C:12–10.2

STALKING—Cont'd
Injunctions, 2C:12–10.1, 2C:12–10.2
Judgment of conviction, 2C:12–10.1
Presentence investigation and report, disclo-
sure, 2C:44–6
Cost of evaluation, 2C:44–6.1
Restraining orders, 2C:12–10.1

STAMPS
Alcoholic Beverages, this index

**STANDARD AUTOMOBILE INSURANCE
POLICY**
Definitions, no fault insurance, 39:6A–2

STANDARD OF PROOF
See, also, Presumptions, generally, this index
Bail jumping, defenses, 2C:29–7
Criminal prosecutions, 2C:1–13
Gambling, defenses, 2C:37–2
Money laundering and illegal investments,
2C:21–28
Obscene material, children and minors,
2C:34–3
Perjury, 2C:28–1
Renunciation as defense, conspiracy, 2C:5–2
Sexual offenses,
Evidence of previous sexual conduct of vic-
tim, 2C:14–7
Resistance, 2C:14–5

STANDARD POLICY
Health and Accident Insurance, generally, this
index

STANDARDS
Controlled substances, 24:21–3 et seq.
Drivers schools, 39:12–4.1
Motor vehicle insurance, no fault insurance,
notice and buyers guide, available coverag-
es and rate credits, 39:6A–23

STARTING VEHICLES
Duties of driver as to signals, 39:4–126

STATE
Administration, law or governmental functions,
obstruction, 2C:29–1 et seq.
Adult offender supervision interstate compact,
2A:168–26 et seq.
Agencies. State Agencies, generally, this index
All terrain vehicles, registration, exemptions,
39:3C–6
Banks and banking, forfeiture, terrorism, funds,
freezing, 2C:66–6
Boards and Commissions, generally, this index
Bribery and Corruption, generally, this index
Bridges owned or maintained by, liability for
driving overweight vehicles over, 39:4–75,
39:4–76
Bureau of identification. Identification Bu-
reau, generally, this index
Commissions. Boards and Commissions, gen-
erally, this index
Compacts between states, detainers of prison-
ers, 2A:159A–1 et seq.
Correctional Institutions, generally, this index
Corrupt influence. Bribery and Corruption,
generally, this index
Default, interstate compact for adult offender
supervision, 2A:168–37
Definitions,
Adult offender supervision, interstate com-
pacts, 2A:168–27
Code of Criminal Justice, 2C:1–3
Commercial Driver License Act, 39:3–10.11
Controlled substances, 2C:35–2, 24:21–2

STATE—Cont'd
Definitions—Cont'd
Drivers licenses, 39:5D–2
Fresh Pursuit Law, 2A:155–2
Interstate agreement on detainers,
2A:159A–2
Motor Vehicle Security Responsibility Law,
39:6–24
Uniform Criminal Extradition Law, 2A:160–
Employees. State Officers and Employees,
generally, this index
Enforcement, interstate compact for adult of-
fender supervision, 2A:168–37
Finances, adult offender supervision interstate
commission, 2A:168–35
Financial institutions, forfeiture, terrorism,
funds, freezing, 2C:66–6
Fines and penalties,
Default, interstate compact for adult offend-
er supervision, 2A:168–37
Parking permits, state owned grounds, alter-
ing, counterfeiting or misuse of permit,
39:4–209
Force and violence, obstructing administration
of law or governmental functions, 2C:29–
et seq.
Foreign States, generally, this index
Fraud against, aggravating circumstance, crim-
nal sentence, 2C:44–1
General Fund of State, generally, this index
Health and Senior Services Department, gener-
ally, this index
Highways. State Highways, generally, this in-
dex
Identification Bureau, generally, this index
Intimidation, obstructing administration of law
or governmental functions, 2C:29–1 et seq.
Investments, this index
Judicial enforcement, interstate compact for
adult offender supervision, 2A:168–37
Lands. Public Lands, generally, this index
Mentally retarded persons, transport vehicles,
identification, 39:4–207.2 et seq.
Motor vehicles,
Drivers license, 39:3–14
Exempt from Motor Vehicle Security Re-
sponsibility Law, 39:6–54
Free registration, 39:3–27
Sale of abandoned vehicles, 39:10A–1 et se
Obstruction, administration of law or govern-
mental function, 2C:29–1 et seq.
Officers and employees. State Officers and
Employees, generally, this index
Official information, disclosure by witnesses,
2A:84A–27
Parking permits, state owned grounds, altering
counterfeiting or misuse of permits,
39:4–209
Peremptory challenges, jurors, criminal cases,
Rule 1:8–3
Police. State Police, generally, this index
Prisons. Correctional Institutions, generally,
this index
Privileges and immunities, official informatio
Evidence Rule 515
Public Lands, generally, this index
Real estate. Public Lands, generally, this inde
Reinstatement, interstate compact for adult c
fender supervision, 2A:168–37
Roads. State Highways, generally, this index
Sales, motor vehicles seized on suspicion of
having been stolen, 39:5–47
Seal, affixed to warrant of arrest of extradited
person, 2A:160–15
Snowmobiles, registration, exemptions, 39:3C-
State Police, generally, this index

STATE—Cont'd

Support of Persons, generally, this index

Termination, interstate compact for adult offender supervision, **2A:168–37**

Traffic laws applicable to vehicles owned or operated by, **39:4–1**

Treasurer. State Treasurer, generally, this index

Turnpike authority,
Advancement or contributions, **27:23–5.8**
Bonds and interest, credit of state not pledged to pay, **27:23–2**

Violence, obstructing administration of law or governmental functions, **2C:29–1 et seq.**

Withdrawal, interstate compact for adult offender supervision, **2A:168–37**

Witnesses, official information, disclosure, **2A:84A–27**

STATE AGENCIES

Abuse of children, information, disclosure, **9:6–8.10a**

Administration, law or governmental functions, obstruction, **2C:29–1 et seq.**

Administrative Law and Procedure, generally, this index

Bribery and Corruption, generally, this index

Force and violence, obstructing administration of law or governmental functions, **2C:29–1 et seq.**

Fraud, aggravating circumstances, criminal sentence, **2C:44–1**

Intimidation, obstructing administration of law or governmental functions, **2C:29–1 et seq.**

Nonattorneys, representation, **Rule 1:21–1**

Obstruction, administration of law or governmental function, **2C:29–1 et seq.**

Reports, generally, this index

Restitution, offenses against, **2C:43–3**

Violence, obstructing administration of law or governmental functions, **2C:29–1 et seq.**

STATE AID

Medicaid, generally, this index

STATE BANKS

Banks and Banking, generally, this index

STATE BAR FOUNDATION

Grants, interest on lawyers trust account fund, **Rule 1:28A–4**

STATE BOARDS AND COMMISSIONS

Boards and Commissions, generally, this index

STATE BUDGET

Budgets, this index

STATE BUILDINGS

Keys, distribution and possession, **2C:5–7**

Sales, alcoholic beverages in, **33:1–42**

STATE BUREAU OF IDENTIFICATION

Criminal History Record Information, generally, this index

STATE CAPITOL POLICE FORCE

Motor vehicles and traffic regulations on state owned grounds, enforcement, **39:4–211**

State police, powers and duties, **53:2–1**

STATE CHARITABLE INSTITUTIONS

Charitable Organizations and Associations, generally, this index

STATE CIVIL SERVICE

Civil Service, generally, this index

STATE COMMISSIONS

Boards and Commissions, generally, this index

STATE COMPACTS

Interstate Compacts, generally, this index

STATE COMPTROLLER

Turnpike authority bonds, approval, **27:23–3**

STATE CONTRACTS

Crimes and offenses, fraud, **2C:21–34**

Fraud, **2C:21–34**

STATE DEPARTMENT

Public Defenders, this index

STATE DEPARTMENTS

Corrections Department, generally, this index

Definitions, food and drugs, **24:21–32**

Environmental Protection Department, generally, this index

Fraud, aggravating circumstances, criminal sentence, **2C:44–1**

Health and Senior Services Department, generally, this index

Human Services Department, generally, this index

Restitution, offenses against, **2C:43–3**

Transportation Department, generally, this index

STATE FUNDS

Funds, generally, this index

STATE GRAND JURY

Grand Jury, this index

STATE HIGHWAY ENGINEER

Commercial activity rights of way or rest areas, **39:4–216**

Obstruction, willful interference with other vehicles, **39:4–56.1 et seq.**

Rest areas, rights of way commercial activity, **39:4–216**

Rights of way, rest areas, commercial activity, **39:4–216**

STATE HIGHWAY FUND

Traffic lights at dangerous intersections, expenses of installation and maintenance, **39:4–121.2**

STATE HIGHWAYS

See, also, Highways and Roads, generally, this index

Broken glass or other injurious objects or substances, penalties, **27:7–44**

Fines and penalties, injurious substances on highways, **27:7–44**

Injurious substances or objects on highway, **27:7–44**

Intersections, traffic control devices, approval, **39:4–120.7**

Moving heavy machinery,
Damages, **39:4–27**
Regulation, **39:4–26**

No parking zones, authority, **39:4–138.1**

Protection, property along highway, **27:7–44**

State owned lands. Public Lands, generally, this index

Structures in, permission required, **39:4–199**

Traffic Signs and Signals, this index

Turning vehicles around on highway marked with no U turn signs, **39:4–125**

Turnpike Authority, generally, this index

Turnpike projects to become part of on payment of bonds, **27:23–16**

STATE HOSPITALS

Commitment and Admission to Institutions, generally, this index

Crimes and offenses, credit, confinement pending sentence, **Rule 3:21–8**

STATE HOUSE COMMISSION

Motor vehicles division, office facilities and supplies, **39:2–11**

STATE INSTITUTIONS

Correctional Institutions, generally, this index

Highways and roads, parking and traffic regulation, **39:4–208**

Mentally Deficient and Mentally Ill Persons, generally, this index

Notice of release of prisoner to be given bureaus of identification, **53:1–20.3**

Parking regulation on grounds and roadways, **39:4–208**

Traffic regulations, **39:4–208, 39:4–212**

STATE LANDS

Public Lands, generally, this index

STATE OFFICERS AND EMPLOYEES

Adverse or pecuniary interest, **2C:27–9**

Anatomical gifts, education, **39:3–12.2**

Appropriations, spending or incurring obligations in excess of, **2C:30–4**

Attorney General, generally, this index

Bribery and Corruption, generally, this index

Compensation and salaries, jury duty, **2B:20–16**

Crimes and offenses,
Appropriations, spending or incurring obligations in excess of, **2C:30–4**
Bribes, **2C:27–10, 2C:27–11**
Malfeasance, mandatory sentence, **2C:43–6.5**

Electric personal assistive mobility devices, operation, **39:4–14.10**

Excuse from employment, jury duty, **2B:20–16**

General Assembly, generally, this index

Gifts, crimes and offenses, **2C:27–10, 2C:27–11**

Governor, generally, this index

Jury duty, excuse from employment, **2B:20–16**

Malfeasance, crimes and offenses, mandatory sentence, **2C:43–6.5**

Mandatory sentence, crimes and offenses, malfeasance, **2C:43–6.5**

Merit system. Civil Service, generally, this index

Obligations, incurring in excess of appropriations, **2C:30–4**

Privileges and immunities, searches and seizures, news organizations, **2A:84A–21.11**

Spending in excess of appropriations, **2C:30–4**

Superintendents. State Police, this index

Treasurer. State Treasurer, generally, this index

Unlawful benefits, crimes and offenses, **2C:27–10, 2C:27–11**

STATE OFFICES

Hazardous materials transportation compliance and enforcement office, **39:5B–27**

STATE PARKS AND PARKWAYS

Police and police departments, weapons, unlawful possession, exemption, **2C:39–6**

STATE PLANNING BOARD

Environmental Protection Department, generally, this index

STATE POLICE

Actions and proceedings, stolen property, **2C:65–3**

STATE POLICE—Cont'd

Alcoholic Beverage Control Enforcement Bureau, this index

Appeal and review, complaints, **53:1–33**

Arrest, power to execute warrant, **53:2–1**

Boats and boating, powers and duties, **53:2–1**

Bureau of identification. Identification Bureau, generally, this index

Burns, injuries, reports, **2C:58–8**

Civil service, motor vehicles division, inspectors, appointment, **39:2–9.2 et seq.**

Compensation and salaries, motor vehicle division, inspectors, **39:2–9.3**

Complaints,
> Discipline, **53:1–33**
> Motor Vehicle Hours of Service Law, **39:9–4**
> Motor Vehicle Junk Yard Law, **39:11–11**

Constitution of New Jersey, violations, complaints, limitation of actions, **53:1–33**

Cooperation with other authorities, **53:2–1**

Custody, stolen property, **2C:65–1 et seq.**

Dangerous drugs, substances or compounds, report of offenses, **53:1–18.3**

Detectives, generally, this index

Discipline, complaints, **53:1–33**

Discrimination, complaints, limitation of actions, **53:1–33**

DNA Database and Databank, generally, this index

Drivers schools, complaint for violation on information and belief by member of police, **39:12–13**

Elections, assignment of troopers to enforce election laws, **53:2–1**

Evidence,
> Duty to procure, **53:2–1**
> Stolen property, **2C:65–1**

Explosives, transportation, concurrent enforcement power, **21:1A–130**

Expungement, records, **2C:52–1 et seq.**

Federal boating safety laws, powers and duties, **53:2–1**

Fingerprints and fingerprinting, certain arrested persons, **53:1–15**

Fish and game wardens,
> Authority to act, **53:2–1**
> Police, acting, **53:2–1**

Force or violence, complaints, limitation of actions, **53:1–33**

Forest wardens, **53:2–1**

Governor, call to duty, **53:2–1**

Hazardous materials transportation compliance and enforcement office, **39:5B–27**

Hearings, complaints, notice, **53:1–33**

Imitating uniform as offense, **53:3–6**

Information concerning offenses, forwarding to bureau of identification, **53:1–20.2**

Just cause, removal from office, **53:1–33**

Limitation of actions, complaints, **53:1–33**

Liquefied petroleum gas, transfer of powers and duties, **21:1B–9 et seq.**

Motor vehicles,
> Complaint for violation of inspection law, **39:8–9**
> Division of, inspectors, appointment, **39:2–9.2 et seq.**
> Inspectors of vehicles, **53:2–1**
> Power to execute, **53:2–1**
> Roadside enforcement programs, assistance, **39:8–67**
> Stopping vehicles to submit to measurement or weighing, **39:3–84.3**

Narcotic offenses,
> Annual report of arrest and disposition of cases, **53:1–18.3**

STATE POLICE—Cont'd

Narcotic offenses—Cont'd
> Fingerprinting and photographing persons arrested, **53:1–18.1**

Notice,
> Application for correction, motor vehicle title papers, **39:10–16**
> Complaints, **53:1–33**
> Stolen property, disposition, **2C:65–2**
> Vehicle or street car accident given to, **39:4–130**

Numbers and numbering, stolen property, **2C:65–1**

Officers and employees,
> Alcoholic Beverage Law, **33:1–1**
> Motor vehicles division, inspectors, **39:2–9.2 et seq.**
> Removal from office, complaints, **53:1–33**

Orders of court, stolen property disposition, **2C:65–3**

Outdoor advertising, duties, **27:5–23**

Peace officers, **53:2–1**

Personalized handguns, **2C:58–2.5**

Photographing,
> Arrested persons, **53:1–15**
> Stolen property, **2C:65–1**

Politics, removal from office, **53:1–33**

Posse, use as prohibited, **53:2–1**

Powers and duties, **53:2–1**

Private detective associations, pursuers, appointment, approval, **15:4–1**

Property, stolen property, **2C:65–1 et seq.**

Qualifications, motor vehicles division, inspectors, **39:2–9.4**

Rank and grade, motor vehicles division, inspectors, **39:2–9.3**

Records and recordation,
> Domestic violence offense reports, **2C:25–24**
> Expungement, **2C:52–1 et seq.**
> Stolen property, **2C:65–1**

Release, stolen property, **2C:65–2**

Removal, officers and troopers, complaints, **53:1–33**

Reports, domestic violence, **2C:25–24**

Safety, powers and duties, **53:2–1**

Sales, stolen property, **2C:65–3**

Security, powers and duties, **53:2–1**

Sex offenders, registration. Sex Offenses, this index

State Alcoholic Beverage Control Act, powers and duties, **53:2–1**

State bureau of identification. Identification Bureau, generally, this index

State capitol police force, powers and duties, **53:2–1**

State owned grounds, enforcement of motor vehicle and traffic regulations, **39:4–211**

Stolen property, disposition, **2C:65–1 et seq.**

Superintendents,
> Combating theft of motor vehicles,
>> Establishment of program, **39:3–85.5**
>> Informed consent agreement,
>>> Decal, **39:3–85.5**
>>> Manner and form, **39:3–85.7**
>> Recording, registered owners, who participate in program, **39:3–85.8**
>> Rules and regulations, **39:3–85.10**
> Liquefied petroleum gases, compromise of claim, **21:1B–5**
> Private detectives. Detectives, generally, this index
> Request for information from state institutions, **53:1–13**
> Rules and regulations,
>> Combating theft of motor vehicles, **39:3–85.10**

STATE POLICE—Cont'd

Superintendents—Cont'd
> Rules and regulations—Cont'd
>> Criminal history record background checks, user fees, **53:1–20.6**
>> Violent criminal apprehension program (VICAP), **53:1–20.15**

Sex offenders, registration. Sex Offenses, this index

Threats, complaints, limitation of actions, **53:1–33**

Unclaimed property, sales, **2C:65–3**

Uniforms, penalty for wearing or imitating, **53:3–6**

Vehicles. Motor vehicles, generally, ante

Violent criminal apprehension program. Identification Bureau, this index

Waiver, hearings, complaints, **53:1–33**

Wardens, police, **53:2–1**

Waters and watercourses, powers and duties, **53:2–1**

Weapons,
> Personalized handguns, **2C:58–2.5**
> Unlawful possession, exemption, **2C:39–6**

Wearing uniform, penalty for illegal wearing, **53:3–6**

STATE PRISON

See, also, Correctional Institutions, generally, this index

Notice, release of prisoner to be given bureau of identification, **53:1–20.3**

Parole, generally, this index

Photograph of prisoner taken before release, **53:1–20.3**

STATE PROPERTY

Bribery and corruption, **2C:27–12**

Keys, distribution and possession, **2C:5–7**

Real estate. Public Lands, generally, this index

STATE ROADS

State Highways, generally, this index

STATE TREASURER

Bonds. State Officers and Employees, generally, this index

Bonds (officers and fiduciaries), director of division of motor vehicles, filing with, **39:2–2**

Coastal protection trust fund, **39:3–27.50**

Conviction of crime, payment to, law enforcement officers training and equipment fund, **2C:43–3.3**

Fees, inspection of motor vehicles, payment to **39:8–10**

Fines and penalties,
> Conviction of crime, payment to, **2C:46–4**
> Display of name of owner of commercial vehicle, disposition, **39:4–47**
> Motor Vehicle Hours of Service Law violation, **39:9–4**
> Motor Vehicle Inspection Law violation, **39:8–9**
> Motor Vehicle Junk Yard Law violation, **39:11–11**
> Motor Vehicle Security Responsibility Law violations, **39:6–55**
> Overweight vehicle driven on interstate bridge, disposition, **39:4–76**
> Projections on tires and locking of wheels motor vehicles, **39:3–81**
> State Highway Law, **27:7–44**

Forensic laboratory fund, **2C:35–20**

General Fund of State, generally, this index

STATE TREASURER—Cont'd
Motor vehicle commission, board, members and membership, **39:2A–12**
Motor vehicles,
  Bills for disbursement of money under laws, payment, **39:2–3**
  Registration agent, payment of fees to, **39:3–3**
  Unsatisfied Claim and Judgment Fund Law,
    Assignment of judgments to, **39:6–77**
    Creation of fund, **39:6–63**
    Order for payment of judgment, **39:6–71**
    Payment by treasurer from fund, **39:6–71 et seq.**
    Settlement of actions, **39:6–72**
Penalties. Fines and penalties, generally, ante
Powers, functions and duties, marine mammal stranding center fund, moneys from wildlife conservation license plate renewal fees, **39:3–33.11**
Turnpike authority bonds, approval, **27:23–3**
Unsatisfied claim and judgment fund. Motor vehicles, ante

STATEMENTS
Crimes and offenses, records, expungement, **2C:52–8**
Definitions, bribery and corrupt influence, **2C:27–1**
False or inconsistent statements, **2C:28–2**
Grand jury, statements of investigation, unindicted suspects and witnesses, **2B:21–9**
Perjury, **2C:28–1**
Psychiatric examinations, admissibility of statements of defendant, **2C:4–10**
Unsworn falsifications, **2C:28–3**

STATEMENTS AGAINST INTEREST
Hearsay exception, **Evidence Rule 803**

STATEMENTS OF ACCUSED
Pretrial hearing, admissibility, **Rule 3:9–1**

STATIONS
Radio and Radio Stations, generally, this index
Television, generally, this index

STATUTE OF LIMITATIONS
Limitation of Actions, generally, this index
Limitation of Criminal Prosecutions, generally, this index

STATUTES
Application of law,
  Code of Criminal Justice, **2C:1–1**
    Territorial applicability, **2C:1–3**
  Criminal Justice Code, **2C:1–1**
  Explosives, **21:1A–141**
  Fireworks, **21:2–4**
  Labor and Employment, this index
  New Jersey Code of Criminal Justice, **2C:1–1**
Construction of Laws, generally, this index
Crimes and offenses, **2C:98–1**
Culpability, Code of Criminal Justice, **2C:2–2**
Definitions, Explosives Act, **21:1A–129**
Evidence Act, 1960, effective date, **2A:84A–36**
Ignorance, defense, criminal prosecutions, **2C:2–4**
Mistake, defense, criminal prosecutions, **2C:2–4**
Offenses defined by statute, **2C:1–5**
Ordinances, generally, this index

STATUTORY PENALTIES
Fines and Penalties, generally, this index

STAY
Appeal and review,
  Intoxicating liquor license, suspension or revocation pending appeal, **33:1–31**
  Suppression of evidence, municipal courts, **Rule 7:5–2**
Attorney fee arbitration, filing of notice of appeal, **Rule 1:20A–3**
Attorneys, interlocutory review, disciplinary proceedings, constitutional challenge, **Rule 1:20–16**
Controlled substances, dealers, liability, **2C:35B–15**
Explosives, regulatory order enforcement, **21:1A–130**
Fines and penalties,
  Limited criminal jurisdiction, courts of, appeals, relief pending, **Rule 3:23–5**
  Relief pending appeal, **Rule 3:23–5**
Health care claims fraud, licenses and permits, suspension or revocation, **2C:51–5**
Limited criminal jurisdiction, courts of, appeals, relief pending, **Rule 3:23–5**
Mediation, referral, **Rule 1:40–6**
Municipal courts, appeals, stay of fine or sentence pending appeal, **Rule 7:13–2**
Pretrial intervention programs,
  Further proceedings, **Rule 3:28**
  Order enrolling over prosecutors objection, **Rule 3:28**
Probation, limited criminal jurisdiction, courts of, appeals, relief pending, **Rule 3:23–5**
Relief pending appeal, **Rule 3:23–5**
Sentence, limited criminal jurisdiction, courts of, relief pending, **Rule 3:23–5**

STEALING
Burglary, generally, this index
Robbery, generally, this index
Theft, generally, this index

STEAM ROLLERS
Exception of from motor vehicle laws, **39:3–1**
Moving Heavy Machinery, generally, this index

STENOGRAPHERS AND STENOGRAPHIC REPORTERS
Grand jury, attendance, **Rule 3:6–6**

STICKERS
Windshields of motor vehicles not to be obscured by, **39:3–74**

STILETTOS
See, also, Weapons, generally, this index
Manufacture, transport, disposition and defacement, **2C:39–9**
Person convicted of crime involving, possession of any weapon prohibited, **2C:39–7**
Prohibited weapons, **2C:39–3**

STILLS AND DISTILLING APPARATUS
Accounting for moneys, **33:2–8**
Appeal and review, order of director, **33:2–6**
Arrest of offenders, **33:2–3**
Articles,
  Seizure of articles, **33:2–3**
  Unlawful character, unregistered still or apparatus, **33:2–2**
Costs, return of seized property, **33:2–7**
Crimes and offenses, **33:1–50**
  Padlocking order, violation, **33:2–9**
  Registration, **33:2–10**
  Unlawful property, hearing, **33:2–4**
Definitions, **33:2–1**
Destruction,
  Seized property, **33:2–5**

STILLS AND DISTILLING APPARATUS—Cont'd
Destruction—Cont'd
  Unregistered stills, **33:2–11**
Determination, costs on return of seized property, **33:2–7**
Failure to register, **33:2–10**
Forfeitures,
  Return of forfeited property, **33:2–7**
  Seized property, **33:2–5**
Hearings,
  After seizure of property, **33:2–4**
  Destruction of unregistered stills, **33:2–11**
Hospitals, retention of seized property for use of, **33:2–5**
Imprisonment for violation of padlocking order, **33:2–9**
Investigations, **33:2–1**
  Unregistered stills, **33:2–3**
Jurisdiction of seized property, **33:2–3**
Misdemeanor, owning or possessing, alcoholic beverages, **33:1–50**
Notice,
  Destruction of unregistered stills, **33:2–11**
  Hearing after property seized, **33:2–4**
Nuisance, unregistered stills in actual operation, **33:2–11**
Orders,
  Building or premises, occupied or used for certain period, **33:2–5**
    Violation of order as misdemeanor, **33:2–9**
  Form of order, **33:2–6**
  Prerogative writs to review, **33:2–6**
Padlocking premises, **33:2–5**
Personal property declared unlawful property, **33:2–2**
Place of hearing after seizure of property, **33:2–4**
Premises, occupy or use for certain period, **33:2–5**
  Violation of order, **33:2–9**
Punishment,
  Failure to register, **33:2–10**
  Violation of padlocking order, **33:2–9**
Registration, **33:2–1**
  Failure to register still or apparatus, crimes and offenses, **33:2–10**
  Seizure of unregistered stills, **33:2–3**
  Unregistered stills,
    Actual operation declared nuisance, **33:2–11**
    Apparatus, unlawful property, **33:2–2**
Retention of seized property for use of hospitals, **33:2–5**
Return of seized property, **33:2–7**
Rules and regulations, **33:2–1**
Sale of seized property, **33:2–5**
Searches and Seizures, this index
Storage of paraphernalia for manufacture as misdemeanor, **33:1–50**
Time of hearing after seizure of property, **33:2–4**
Unlawful character, unregistered still, **33:2–2**
Unlawful property, **33:2–2**
  Declaration, unregistered stills, **33:2–2**
  Forfeiture and sale, seized property, **33:2–5**
  Hearing as to whether seized property constitutes, **33:2–4**
  Return of seized property not constituting, **33:2–7**
Violation of padlocking order as misdemeanor, **33:2–9**
Warrant for search, **33:2–3**

STIMULANT DRUGS
Depressant or stimulant drugs. Controlled Substances, this index

STIPULATIONS
Arbitration and award,
Attorneys fees, fee arbitration, **Rule 1:20A–3**
Names or number, motor vehicles, tort claims, **39:6A–27**
Attorneys fees, arbitration and award, **Rule 1:20A–3**
Evidence, application of law, **Evidence Rule 101**
Jury and Jurors, this index
Nonpublic business records, admissibility of copies, **Rule 1:7–6**

STOCK AND STOCKHOLDERS
Shares and Shareholders, generally, this index

STOLEN GOODS
Disposition, **2C:65–1 et seq.**
Jewelry, secondhand, reports, **2C:21–39**
Privileges and immunities, **2C:21–40**
Procedure for disposition, **2C:65–1 et seq.**
Receiving Stolen Property, generally, this index

STOP
Definitions, Motor Vehicle Law, **39:1–1**

STOP INTERSECTIONS
Designation, **39:4–140**
Municipalities, regulations, **39:4–8**

STOP SIGNS
Traffic Signs and Signals, this index

STOPPING
Motor Vehicles, this index
Street Railways, this index

STORAGE
Alcoholic Beverages, this index
Crimes and offenses, fees, **27:23–6.2**
Explosives, this index
Fees, fines and penalties, **27:23–6.2**
Fines and penalties, fees, **27:23–6.2**
Fireworks, this index
Garages, generally, this index
Hazardous Substances and Waste, this index
Motor Vehicles, this index
New Jersey turnpike authority, registration, **27:23–6.2**
Notice, fees, **27:23–6.2**
Radioactive Substances, this index
Registration, New Jersey turnpike authority, **27:23–6.2**
Tow Trucks and Towing Companies, this index

STORE OR OTHER RETAIL MERCANTILE ESTABLISHMENT
Definitions, shoplifting, **2C:20–11**

STORES
Definitions, ephedrine, pseudoephedrine, phenylpropanolamine, **2C:35–26**
Fitting rooms, invasion of privacy, defenses, crimes and offenses, observation, nudity, **2C:14–9**
Grocery stores, intoxicating liquors,
Limited retail distribution license, **33:1–12**
Packaged merchandise, sale, **33:1–12**
Invasion of privacy, fitting rooms, defenses, crimes and offenses, observation, nudity, **2C:14–9**
Sales, generally, this index
Shoplifting, **2C:20–11**

STORES—Cont'd
Turnpike authority, use of right of way, **27:23–9**

STRAMONIUM
Definitions, drugs and medicine, **2C:35–2**
Disorderly persons, drugs and medicine, **2C:35–10.5**

STRAMONIUM PLANT
Definitions, drugs and medicine, **2C:35–2**

STRAMONIUM PREPARATION
Definitions, drugs and medicine, **2C:35–2**

STRAY AND TRESPASSING ANIMALS
Pasture lands, damages to fences, **2C:18–4 et seq.**

STREET CARS
Definitions, traffic regulations, **39:1–1**

STREET GANGS
Generally, **2C:33–29, 2C:33–30**
Aggravating circumstances, criminal sentence, **2C:44–1**
Antidrug profiteering, fines and penalties, **2C:33–28, 2C:35A–3**
Arrest, fingerprints and fingerprinting, **53:1–15.1**
Conviction of crime, merger and consolidation, soliciting, **2C:33–28**
Fines and penalties,
Antidrug profiteering, **2C:35A–3**
Solicitation, **2C:33–28**
Fingerprints and fingerprinting, arrest, **53:1–15.1**
Grade and decree of offenses, **2C:33–29, 2C:33–30**
Juvenile delinquents and dependents, jurisdiction, waiver, **2A:4A–26**
Minimum sentence, **2C:43–7.2**
Promotion, **2C:33–30**
Soliciting, **2C:33–28**
Weapons, possession, presumptions, **2C:39–5**

STREET RAILWAYS
Arrest without warrant, motorman not subject to arrest for violation of traffic laws in presence of officer, **39:5–25**
Backing against curb to load or unload vehicle, obstructing passage of street car prohibited, **39:4–79**
Boards and commissions, street car stops, **39:4–44**
Clearing intersection, **39:4–67**
Crossings, signals, **39:4–43**
Crosswalks, obstruction by cars prohibited, **39:4–45**
Delaying or hindering passage of street car prohibited, **39:4–43**
Delaying or obstructing motor cars or vehicles prohibited, **39:4–67**
Directions of police and other officers, compliance required, **39:4–57**
Distance, traveling behind, **39:4–39**
Doors, closing required, **39:4–68**
Entering intersection where unable to clear, **39:4–67**
Fines and penalties, violation of law relating to, **39:4–203**
Following streetcar, distance to be kept by vehicle behind, **39:4–39**
Heavy machinery, hours when movement along tracks permitted, **39:4–29**
Interference with transportation, **2C:33–14**
Intersections,
Car stops, **39:4–44**

STREET RAILWAYS—Cont'd
Intersections—Cont'd
Interference, **39:4–38**
Obstruction of crosswalks by cars prohibited, **39:4–45**
Signal on approach, duty of motorman, **39:4–43**
Notice, street car drivers notice of accident to police department, **39:4–130**
Obstruction, crosswalks, **39:4–45**
Official traffic control device, duty to obey instructions of, **39:4–81**
Overtaking, **39:4–38, 39:4–40**
Passing street car by motor vehicle,
Care required, **39:4–38**
Passing on left prohibited, **39:4–40**
Person on bicycle or skates, hitching onto car, prohibition, **39:4–14**
Personal injuries, stopping, **39:4–42**
Police and police departments, directions of required to be obeyed, **39:4–57**
Riding on part not intended for passengers prohibited, **39:4–69**
Safety Zones, generally, this index
Signs and signals, crossings, **39:4–33**
Speed, generally, this index
Starting of street cars at special places, regulation by municipality, **39:4–197**
Stopping,
Approach of emergency vehicles, **39:4–92**
Before entering through street, **39:4–144**
Giving identification and assistance, duty of motorman, **39:4–42**
Places, **39:4–44**
Receiving or discharging passengers, overtaking motor vehicle to stop, **39:4–4**
Special places, regulation by municipality, **39:4–197**
Street cars, definitions, **39:1–1**
Tractors crossing at grade, notice of intention to cross, **39:4–128**
Traffic regulations, **39:4–38 et seq.**
Traffic signals, stopping during pedestrian interval, **39:4–117**
Trolley buses, drivers license, **39:3–10.1**
Turning at intersections controlled by traffic signals or officers, **39:4–115**
Wires, change or repair necessitated by movement of heavy machinery, highway, **39:4–28**
Yielding right of way to traffic on through street, **39:4–144**

STREET RODS
Special license plates, **39:3–27.27**

STREET SIGNS
Traffic Signs and Signals, generally, this index

STREETS AND ALLEYS
See, also, Highways and Roads, generally, this index
Angle parking, ordinances, approval, **39:4–197.4**
Closing, horse racing, **39:4–21**
Continuously controlled highway, traffic signal required at every intersection to constitute, **39:4–113**
Crosswalks, generally, this index
Curbs and Curbing, generally, this index
Definitions,
Motor Vehicle Law, **39:1–1**
Traffic regulations, **39:1–1**
Drives and Driveways, generally, this index

STREETS AND ALLEYS—Cont'd
Fines and penalties,
  Display name of owner of commercial vehicle, fund for repair of roads, **39:4–47**
  Movement of heavy machinery, highway, disposition, **39:4–31**
Funds, roads, disposition of fines for violating law relating to projections on tires and locking of wheels of motor vehicles, **39:3–81**
Glass or other injurious substance placed on highway, fine imposed, **39:4–63**
Intersections, generally, this index
Low speed vehicles, operation, **39:4–31.1**
Motor drawn vehicles, number permitted to be used in street repair, **39:4–54**
Mountain highways, motor vehicle to be kept on right side and under control, **39:4–55**
Moving heavy machinery,
  Damages, **39:4–27**
  Regulation, **39:4–26**
Obscene material, public communication, **2C:34–4**
Obstruction and obstructions, parking along side of obstruction prohibited, **39:4–138**
One way streets, **39:4–85.1**
  Designation by municipality, **39:4–197**
  Keeping to right not required, **39:4–82**
  Notice of ordinance, **39:4–198**
  Parking on left side of roadway may be permitted, **39:4–135**
  Parking ordinances, notice, **39:4–198**
  Passing street car on left permitted, **39:4–40**
  Right side, keeping on, **39:4–82**, **39:4–83**
Parking, generally, this index
Parks and Parkways, generally, this index
Pedestrians, right of way, **39:4–34**
Penalties. Fines and penalties, ante
Private Roads, generally, this index
Right of way to pedestrians on sidewalk, **39:4–66.1**
Semipublic streets, application of motor vehicle laws, **39:5A–1 et seq.**
Sidewalks, driving vehicle or horse across, **39:4–71**
Signs and signals. Traffic Signs and Signals, generally, this index
Slippery condition, tire chains permitted, **39:3–73**
Speed bumps, **39:4–8.9 et seq.**
Stop signs. Traffic Signs and Signals, this index
Stopping vehicle emerging from, **39:4–66**
Street Railways, generally, this index
Through streets,
  Designation, **39:4–140**
  Intersections, this index
  Notice of designation, **39:4–140**
  Ordinances, designation, **39:4–140**
  Right of way at intersections, **39:4–90**
  Stop signs. Traffic Signs and Signals, this index
  Stopping before entering, **39:4–144**
  Yield right of way signs, **39:4–140**
    Location, **39:4–141**
  Yielding right of way, **39:4–144**
Traffic calming devices, municipalities, powers and duties, **39:4–8.10**
Traffic Rules and Regulations, generally, this index
Traffic Signs and Signals, generally, this index

STRICT LIABILITY
Construction of law, Code of Criminal Justice, **2C:2–2**

STRICT LIABILITY—Cont'd
Manslaughter, fleeing, law enforcement, **2C:11–4**

STRIP SEARCHES
Generally, **2A:161A–1 et seq.**

STROPHANTHUS
Poisons, generally, this index

STRUCTURAL UNITS
Incapable of dismemberment, registering, loading and operating trailer or semitrailer, **39:4–27**

STUDENT
Colleges and Universities, generally, this index
Schools and School Districts, generally, this index

STUDENT LOANS
Attorneys, suspension from practice, default, **Rule 1:20–11B**

STUDENT ORGANIZATIONS
Hazing, **2C:40–3 et seq.**

STUDIES
Megans Law, application of law, **2C:7–20**
Motor vehicle commission, agency facilities, **39:2A–27**
Sex Offenses, this index
Speed, sixty five mph, **39:4–98.7**

STUDS
Motor vehicle tire projections, **39:3–81**

STUN GUN
Definitions, **2C:39–1**
Person convicted of crime involving, possession of any weapon prohibited, **2C:39–7**
Possession, **2C:39–3**

SUBDIVISIONS
Political Subdivisions, generally, this index

SUBORDINATE LODGES
Fraternal Organizations, generally, this index

SUBPOENA DUCES TECUM
Production of Books and Papers, generally, this index

SUBPOENAS
  See, also, Production of Books and Papers, generally, this index
  Generally, **Rule 1:9–1 et seq.**
Advertising, grievance hearings, **Rule 1:19A–4**
Affidavits, public officers or agencies, support motions, **Rule 1:9–6**
Alcoholic beverages,
  Director, attendance of witnesses and production of documents, **33:1–35**
  Service of subpoenas, **33:1–36**
Arbitration and award, motor vehicle tort claims, **39:6A–29**
Attachment, subpoena of public officer or agency, failure to obey, **Rule 1:9–6**
Attendance of witnesses, **Rule 1:9–1**
Attorney disciplinary proceedings, **Rule 1:20–7**
  Investigation, **Rule 1:20–3**
Attorney general, disobedience, suspension or revocation of motor vehicle registration or drivers license, recovery, **39:5–30**
Attorneys, this index
Books and papers, production, **Rule 1:9–2**
Child fatality and near fatality review board, records, **9:6–8.93**

SUBPOENAS—Cont'd
Child support hearing officers, **Rule 5:25–3**
Clerk of court, issuance, **Rule 1:9–1**
Client protection fund, **Rule 1:28–6**
Contempt,
  Failure to obey, **Rule 1:9–5**
  Subpoena of public officer or agency, failure to obey, **Rule 1:9–6**
Contents, **Rule 1:9–1**
Controlled substances, **24:21–31**
Corporations, notice in lieu of subpoena, **Rule 1:9–1**
County detectives and investigators, complaints, **2A:157–10.2**
Crimes and offenses, **Rule 1:9–1**
  Fees, **Rule 1:9–3**
  Privileges and immunities, newspersons, **2A:84A–21.1 et seq.**
Delivery, service, **Rule 1:9–3**
Director of motor vehicles division, power to issue, **39:10–20**
Disciplinary proceedings, **Rule 1:20–7**
Documentary evidence, production, **Rule 1:9–2**
Electronic records, production, **Rule 1:9–2**
Enforcement, subpoenas of public officers or agencies, **Rule 1:9–6**
Ex parte applications, public officers or agencies, **Rule 1:9–6**
Failure to obey,
  Contempt, **Rule 1:9–5**
  Subpoena of public officer or agency, **Rule 1:9–6**
Fees,
  Appearance without prepayment, criminal actions for state or indigent defendants, **Rule 1:9–1**
  Service, alcoholic beverage control director, **33:1–36**
  Tendering, service, **Rule 1:9–3**
Guardian of minor, hearing for violation of Alcoholic Beverage Law, **33:1–81.1**
Hearings, subpoena of public officer or agency, order to show cause, **Rule 1:9–6**
Indigent defendants, **Rule 1:9–1**
  Fees, **Rule 1:9–3**
Inspection of objects designated in subpoena, parties and attorneys, **Rule 1:9–2**
Intoxicating liquors, director, power to issue, **33:1–35**
Issuance, **Rule 1:9–1**
Juvenile proceedings,
  Examination of objects designated in subpoena, **Rule 1:9–2**
  Service, **Rule 5:20–2**
Material witness. Witnesses, this index
Matrimonial actions, examination of objects designated in subpoena, **Rule 1:9–2**
Modification, **Rule 1:9–2**
Money laundering and illegal investments, **2C:21–29**
Motions,
  Public officers or agencies, supported by affidavit, **Rule 1:9–6**
  Quashing or modifying, **Rule 1:9–2**
Motor vehicle dealers license, proceedings to suspend or revoke, **39:10–20**
Motor vehicles,
  Issuance, **39:4–7**
  Tort claim arbitrations, **39:6A–29**
Municipal courts, **Rules 1:9–1, 7:7–8**
Newsperson information disclosure privilege, **Evidence Rule 508**
  Criminal proceedings, **2A:84A–21.1 et seq.**
Notice in lieu of subpoena, **Rule 1:9–1**
  Production of documentary evidence, **Rule 1:9–2**

SUBPOENAS—Cont'd
Oppressive requests, quashing or modifying, **Rule 1:9–2**
Order to show cause, subpoena of public officer or agency, **Rule 1:9–6**
Parent of minor, hearing for violation of Alcoholic Beverage Law, **33:1–81.1**
Parties, **Rule 1:9–1**
Place of service, **Rule 1:9–4**
Prepayment of witness fee, criminal actions for state or indigent defendants, **Rule 1:9–1**
Privileges and immunities, newspersons, **2A:84A–21.1 et seq.**
Production of documentary evidence, **Rule 1:9–2**
Public officers or agencies, enforcement of subpoena, **Rule 1:9–6**
Quashing, **Rule 1:9–2**
Sanctions,
  Notice in lieu of subpoena, failure to respond, **Rule 1:9–1**
  Subpoena of public officer or agency, **Rule 1:9–6**
Service, **Rule 1:9–3**
  Alcoholic beverage control director, **33:1–36**
  Attorney disciplinary proceedings, **Rule 1:20–7**
  Fees, ante
  Motor vehicle tort claim arbitrations, **39:6A–29**
  Notice in lieu of subpoena, **Rule 1:9–1**
  Place, **Rule 1:9–4**
Show cause order, subpoena of public officer or agency, **Rule 1:9–6**
Time,
  Notice in lieu of subpoena, service, **Rule 1:9–1**
  Order to show cause, subpoena of public officer or agency, return, **Rule 1:9–6**

SUBROGATION
Property liability insurance guaranty association, unsatisfied claim and judgment fund, payment, **39:6–85**
State treasurer paying judgment in hit and run case out of unsatisfied claim and judgment fund, **39:6–85**

SUBSEQUENT CONDUCT
Evidence, **Evidence Rule 407**

SUBSEQUENT OFFENSES
Second or Subsequent Offenses, generally, this index

SUBSIDIARIES
Corporations, motor vehicle insurance, self insurers, **39:6–52**

SUBSTANTIAL STEP
Definitions, conduct, **2C:5–1**

SUBSTITUTE TEACHERS
Teachers, this index

SUBSTITUTED FIDUCIARIES
Fiduciaries, generally, this index

SUBSTITUTED SERVICE
Process, this index

SUBURBAN PASSENGER SERVICE
Passengers, generally, this index

SUBWAYS
Interference with transportation, **2C:33–14**

SUDDEN DEATH
Death, generally, this index

SUFFRAGE
Elections, generally, this index

SUICIDE
Aiding suicide, **2C:11–6**
Crimes and offenses, aiding suicide, **2C:11–6**
Force, use to prevent, **2C:3–7**
Juvenile delinquents, screening, confidential or privileged information, **2A:4A–60.2, 2A:4A–60.3**

SUITS
Actions and Proceedings, generally, this index

SULFONDIETHYLMETHANE
See, also, Drugs and Medicine, generally, this index
Controlled dangerous substance, **24:21–1 et seq.**

SULFONETHYLMETHANE
See, also, Drugs and Medicine, generally, this index
Controlled dangerous substance, **24:21–1 et seq.**

SULFONMETHANE
See, also, Drugs and Medicine, generally, this index
Controlled dangerous substance, **24:21–1 et seq.**

SULPHURIC ACID
Turnpike project, transportation regulations, **27:23–31**

SUMMARY ACTIONS
Summary Proceedings, generally, this index

SUMMARY PROCEEDINGS
Attorneys, fee arbitration, **Rule 1:20A–3**
Collection, default in payment of restitution, **2C:46–2**
Contempt, generally, this index
Fines and penalties, collection and enforcement, **2C:46–2**
Monopolies and unfair trade, **56:9–10**
Motor vehicles, body repair facilities, penalties, **39:13–6**
Restitution, collection, **2C:46–2**
Unsatisfied claim and judgment fund, reimbursement, **39:6–86.6**
Witnesses, generally, this index

SUMMER CAMPS
Buses,
  Annual inspection, **39:3–19.4**
  Inspection, insurance and registration requirements, **39:3–19.3, 39:3–19.4**
  Insurance, **39:3–19.4**
  Motorist stopping for loading and unloading busses, **39:4–128.1**
  Operator licenses, **39:3–10.1**
    Application fees, **39:3–19.4**
  Registration fees, **39:3–19.3, 39:3–19.4**

SUMMONS
See, also, Process, generally, this index
Abuse of children, **9:6–8.37**
Service of summons, **9:6–8.38**
Associations and societies, municipal court issuance, **Rule 7:2–2**
Complaint summons, procedure after arrest, **Rule 3:4–1**

SUMMONS—Cont'd
Controlled substances, **24:21–31**
Corporations, this index
County bridge police, service on offenders, **27:19–36.3**
Crimes and Offenses, this index
Definitions, traffic signs and signals, monitoring, **39:4–8.13**
Fines and Penalties, this index
Grand Jury, generally, this index
Indictment, Information or Presentment, this index
Issuance, **Rule 7:2–2**
Jury and Jurors, generally, this index
Juvenile delinquents, **Rule 5:20–2**
  Service, **Rule 5:20–1**
Juvenile family crisis, service, **Rule 5:15–3**
Municipal Courts, this index
Partnerships, this index
Probationer, **2C:45–3**
Restitution, nonpayment, **2C:46–2**
Speed, **39:4–99**
Suspended sentence, defendant under, **2C:45–**
Tires, safety regulation violations, **39:3–72**
Traffic rules and regulations,
  Commercial motor vehicles, notice, **39:5–25.**
  Traffic control signal monitoring system, **39:4–8.15**

SUNDAY
Alcoholic Beverages, this index
Computation of time, **Rule 1:3–1**
Fines and penalties, sales, motor vehicles, **2C:33–26**
Motor vehicle and traffic laws, institution of proceedings and service of process, **39:5–24**
Motor vehicles,
  Dealers, licenses and permits, suspension or revocation, **39:10–20**
  Institution of proceedings under Motor Vehicle and Traffic Laws, **39:5–24**
  Sales, **2C:33–26**
  Service of process on, **39:5–24**
Process, service on for violation of laws relatin to, turnpike projects, **27:23–34**
Recreational vehicles, sales, deposits, **2C:33–2**
Sales, motor vehicles, **2C:33–26**

SUNSET
Lights required after sunset,
  Animal drawn vehicles, **39:4–25**
  Motor vehicles after sunset, **39:3–46**

SUPERHIGHWAYS
Turnpikes, generally, this index

SUPERINTENDENTS
Definitions, firearms, **2C:39–1**
Notice of release of prisoner to be given bureaus of identification by superintendents of state institutions, **53:1–20.3**
State Police, this index

SUPERIOR COURT
Appellate division,
  Clerk, political activity, **Rule 1:17–1**
  Days of court, **Rule 1:30–3**
  Judges,
    Presiding judge, administration, **Rule 1:33–4**
    Vacations, **Rule 1:30–5**
  Judicial conference, rules of evidence, membership, **2A:84A–34**
  Motor licenses, appeal, order revoking or suspending, **39:10–20**
  Title of court, **Rule 1:37–1**

SUPERIOR COURT—Cont'd
Appellate division—Cont'd
Transcript on appeal by indigent, payment, 2A:152–17
Applicability of rules, **Rule 1:1–1**
Caption setting forth name, division and part, papers to be filed, **Rule 1:4–1**
Chancery division, family part, **2C:46–5; Rule 1:33–2**
Abuse or neglect, 9:6–8.21 et seq.
Adoption of children, captioning, **Rule 1:5–6**
Appeal and review, abuse or neglect, permanency plans, 9:6–8.24
Appointment of counsel, law guardians, abuse of children actions, 9:6–8.23
Child support hearing officers, **Rule 5:25–3**
Deputy clerks, supervision, **Rule 1:34–2**
Filing of papers, **Rule 1:5–6**
Fines and penalties, 2C:46–5
Intake services, juvenile family crisis, **Rule 5:15–1 et seq.**
Jurisdiction, abuse or neglect, exclusive noncriminal jurisdiction, 9:6–8.22, 9:6–8.24
Law guardians, appointments, abuse of children actions, 9:6–8.23
Motions, discovery and calendar motions, **Rule 1:6–2**
Preliminary orders, abuse or neglect, 9:6–8.28
Support of Persons, generally, this index
Transfer of causes, **Rule 7:8–6**
Juvenile justice, 2A:4A–25
Children and minors,
Abuse, abandonment, cruelty and neglect, warrant for investigation, 9:6–8
Complaints respecting abandonment, abuse, cruelty and neglect, jurisdiction, 9:6–4
Family part. Chancery division, generally, ante
Civil division, **Rule 1:33–2**
Clerks,
Political activity, **Rule 1:17–1**
Public office, holding, **Rule 1:17–1**
Collections, comprehensive enforcement program, **2B:19–1 et seq.**
Commissioners, abolished title, **Rule 1:21–5**
Community service, noncompliance by offender, transfer to comprehensive enforcement program, **2B:19–7**
Complementary dispute resolution program, **Rule 1:40–1 et seq.**
Comprehensive enforcement program, **2B:19–1 et seq.**
Labor assistance program, **2C:46–2**
Contracts, collections, **2B:19–6**
Criminal division, **Rule 1:33–2**
Dockets, municipal court judgments, **2B:12–26**
Examiners, abolished title, **Rule 1:21–5**
Family part. Chancery division, generally, ante
Financial statements and reports, judges, **Rule 1:18B–1 et seq.**
Fines and penalties,
Chancery division, family part, **2C:46–5**
Imposition, collection, **2C:46–4**
General Equity Division, Superior Court, generally, this index
Geographical divisions, **Rule 1:33–2**
Grand Jury, generally, this index
Hearing officers, comprehensive enforcement program,
Determination of financial hardship of payor, powers and duties, **2B:19–8**
Recommendations, conformity and approval, **2B:19–9**

SUPERIOR COURT—Cont'd
Hearing officers, comprehensive enforcement program—Cont'd
Revocation of work order, failure to report for or perform assigned work, labor assistance or enforced community service programs, 2C:46–2
Indictment, **Rule 3:1–5**
Judges. Superior Court Judges, generally, this index
Judgment Dockets, this index
Jurisdiction, abandonment, abuse, cruelty and neglect of children, 9:6–4
Jury and Jurors, generally, this index
Law Division, Superior Court, generally, this index
Master of superior court, abolished title, **Rule 1:21–5**
Motions, filing, **Rule 1:6–4**
Motor vehicle junk yards, appeal to court from orders concerning, 39:11–10
Motor vehicles, process on person resident when accident or collision occurred and later becoming nonresident, 39:7–2.1
Municipal court judgments, docketing in, 2B:12–26
Municipal prosecutors, practice of law, **Rule 1:15–3**
Noncourt dispute resolution, **Rule 1:40–11**
Orders, unresolved matters, transfer to comprehensive enforcement program, 2B:19–6
Papers, filing, **Rule 1:5–6**
Presiding judges, **Rules 1:33–2, 1:33–6**
Probation officers, investigations, 2A:168–13
Process,
Person resident at time of motor vehicle accident or collision and later becoming nonresident, 39:7–2.1
Writs, territorial limits, **Rule 3:1–2**
Public defenders liens, recordation, 2A:158A–18
Religious Corporations and Associations, generally, this index
Reward, approval of award, criminal procedure, 2A:153–2
Sessions, **Rule 1:30–2**
Special civil part. Law Division, Superior Court, this index
Special master, abolished title, **Rule 1:21–5**
Territorial limits, writs, processes, **Rule 3:1–2**
Title of court, **Rule 1:37–1**
Transfer of actions, **Rule 3:1–5**
Trust funds, attorneys, holding unidentifiable or unclaimed trust funds, deposit in court fund, **Rule 1:21–6**
Turnpike authority, proceedings for acquiring property, 27:23–5
Turnpike projects, jurisdiction of violations, 27:23–34
Units, **Rule 1:33–2**
Verbatim records, **Rule 1:2–2**
Vicinages, **Rule 1:33–2**
Writs,
Issuance, deputy clerks, **Rule 1:34–2**
Territorial limits, **Rule 3:1–2**

SUPERIOR COURT CLERK
Attachment, generally, this index
Liens and incumbrances, public defenders, services, 2A:158A–18

SUPERIOR COURT JUDGES
See, also, Superior Court, generally, this index
Aggravated assault, 2C:12–1

SUPERIOR COURT JUDGES—Cont'd
Arrest, citizen appointed by judge to make, 2A:161–1
Assignment judge,
Appointment, chief probation officer, 2A:168–5
Clinic to study mental and physical conditions of convicted persons, 2A:164–1
Temporary prosecutor, power to appoint, 2A:158–9
Bail, authority, **Rule 3:26–2**
County prosecutors expenses, approval, 2A:158–7
Enjoining nuisance under federal law, 2A:158–8
Financial statements and reports, **Rule 1:18B–1 et seq.**
Judicial conference, rules of evidence, 2A:84A–34
Motor vehicle division,
Deputy director, bond, approval, 39:2–4
Director, bond, approval, 39:2–2
Oath of director, 39:2–2
Peacekeeping, powers and duties, 2A:154–1
Presiding judges, **Rules 1:33–2, 1:33–6**
Superior Court, generally, this index

SUPERSEDEAS
Stay, generally, this index

SUPERVISORY TREATMENT PROGRAMS
Crimes and offenses, records, expungement, 2C:52–20
Disclaimer, 2C:43–22
First offenders, 2C:43–12 et seq.

SUPPLEMENTARY FOOD STAMP PROGRAM
Crimes and offenses, 2C:20–35

SUPPLIES
Municipal courts, 2B:12–15
Violent criminal apprehension program (VICAP, purchase, 53:1–20.14

SUPPORT OF PERSONS
Attorneys, failure to pay, discipline, **Rule 1:20–11A**
Confidential or privileged information, **Rule 1:38–3**
Willful nonsupport, 2C:62–1
Contempt, willful nonsupport, 2C:62–1
Crimes and offenses, 2C:62–1
Suspended sentence, 2C:45–1
Willful nonsupport, 2C:24–5
Custody of children, confidential or privileged information, **Rule 1:38–3**
Domestic violence, relief orders, 2C:25–29
Endangering welfare, 2C:24–4
Enforcement, child support hearing officers, **Rule 5:25–3**
Evidence, willful nonsupport, 2C:62–1
Fines and penalties, society for prevention of cruelty to children, 9:6–3
Forfeitures, willful nonsupport, 2C:62–1
Hearing officers, **Rule 5:25–3**
Incompetent persons, endangering welfare of, 2C:24–7
Jurisdiction, crimes and offenses, willful nonsupport, 2C:62–1
Parole and probation, willful nonsupport, 2C:62–1
Presentence investigations, reports, 2C:44–6
Probation, conditions, 2C:45–1
Probation officers, payments, 2A:168–13
Society for prevention of cruelty, commitment of child, 9:6–3

SUPPORT OF PERSONS—Cont'd
Suspended sentence, 2C:45–1
Temporary orders, 2C:62–1
Willful nonsupport, crimes and offenses,
2C:24–5
Prosecution in chancery division, family part,
Rule 3:1–5
Witnesses, support proceedings, 2C:62–1

SUPPRESSION OF EVIDENCE
Municipal courts, **Rule 7:5–2**

SUPREME COURT
Administrative Office of the Courts, generally,
this index
Appointments,
Bar examiners board, **Rule 1:23–1**
Judicial evaluation commission, **Rule
1:35A–4**
Judicial performance committee, **Rule
1:35A–1**
Outside activities of judiciary employees, ad-
visory committee on, **Rule 1:17A–1**
Attorneys, generally, this index
Chief justice,
Acting chief justice, determination by senior-
ity, **Rule 1:33–1**
Administration of courts, **Rule 1:33–1 et seq.**
Grand jury, assignment judge, appointment,
Rule 3:6–11
State grand juries, judicial supervision,
2B:22–5
Substitution of judges, disqualification or in-
ability to hear matter, **Rule 1:12–3**
Clerks of court, political activities or holding
office, **Rule 1:17–1**
Days of court, **Rule 1:30–3**
Disciplinary review board, appointment, **Rule
1:20–15**
District fee arbitration committees, appoint-
ment, **Rule 1:20A–1**
Evidence Act, effective date, 2A:84A–36
Financial statements and reports, justices, **Rule
1:18B–1 et seq.**
Judicial conference, rules of evidence, member-
ship, 2A:84A–34
Justices,
Aggravated assault, 2C:12–1
Chief justice, generally, ante
Financial statements and reports, **Rule
1:18B–1 et seq.**
Oaths and affirmations, director of motor
vehicle division, 39:2–2
Vacations, **Rule 1:30–5**
Juvenile family crisis intervention units, powers
and duties, rules of court, 2A:4A–79
Lawyers fund for client protection, trustee ap-
pointment, **Rule 1:28–1**
Opinions, filing and publication, **Rules 1:36–1,
1:36–2**
Professional ethics, advisory committee on, in-
quiries, **Rule 1:19–4**
Proposed rules of evidence, announcement,
time, 2A:84A–35
Reports, public defender, 2A:158A–22
Rules of court,
Criminal fines and restitution, 2C:44–6
Evidence Act, effective date, 2A:84A–36
Juvenile family crisis intervention units, pow-
ers and duties, 2A:4A–79
Turnpike project, proceedings for violations,
27:23–34
Rules of evidence, adoption, 2A:84A–33,
2A:84A–38
Seal, **Rule 1:37–2**

SUPREME COURT—Cont'd
State grand juries, promulgation of rules,
2B:22–2
Title of court, **Rule 1:37–1**
Unauthorized practice of law, committees, ap-
pointment, **Rule 1:22–1**

SURCHARGES
Domestic violence, 2C:25–29.4
Driving while intoxicated, 39:4–50
Motor Vehicles, this index
Sex offenses, 2C:43–3.7

SURETIES
Bonds (Officers and Fiduciaries), generally,
this index

SURETY COMPANIES
Bail, generally, this index

SURFBOARDS
Unlawful taking, 2C:20–10

SURGEONS AND SURGERY
Medical Care and Treatment, generally, this
index
Physicians and Surgeons, generally, this index

SURGICAL INSURANCE
Health and Accident Insurance, generally, this
index

SURGICAL TREATMENT
Medical Care and Treatment, generally, this
index

SURPLUS
Motor vehicles, temporary identification marker for purchaser, 39:3–33.1

SURROGATES
Political activities, **Rule 1:17–1**
Practice of law, **Rule 1:15–1**

SURROGATES COURTS
Applicability of rules, **Rule 1:1–1**
Probate proceedings, filing of papers, **Rule
1:5–6**

SURVEILLANCE
Permitted actions, wiretapping and electronic
surveillance, 2A:156A–4
Unlawful acts, exceptions, wiretapping and
electronic surveillance, 2A:156A–4
Wiretapping and electronic surveillance,
2A:156A–1 et seq.
Application for order, 2A:156A–9

SURVIVING SPOUSE
Motor vehicles,
License plates, purple heart veteran or for-
mer prisoner of war, 39:3–27.41
Vesting of title, 39:3–30.1, 39:3–30.2
Prisoner of war, motor vehicle license plate,
39:3–27.41
Purple heart veteran, motor vehicle license
plate, 39:3–27.41

SUSPENDED SENTENCES
Generally, 2C:43–2
Crimes and Offenses, this index

SUSSEX COUNTY
See, also, Counties, generally, this index
Highways and roads, commercial vehicles,
39:4–197.8

SWEARING
Oaths and Affirmations, generally, this index
Perjury, generally, this index

SWITCHBLADE KNIVES
Definitions, 2C:39–1
Manufacture, transport, disposition and deface-
ment, 2C:39–9
Person convicted of crime involving, possession
of any weapon prohibited, 2C:39–7
Prohibited weapons, 2C:39–3

SWORN
Oaths and Affirmations, generally, this index

SYNAGOGUES
See, also, Religious Corporations and Asso-
ciations, generally, this index
Desecration of places of worship, 2C:33–9
Target of crime,
Arson, 2C:17–1
Conspiracy, grade and degree of offense,
2C:5–4

SYPHILIS
Sexual penetration, diseased persons, 2C:34–5

SYRINGES
Hypodermic Needles or Syringes, generally,
this index

SYRUPS
Alcohol in syrups unfit for beverage purposes,
33:1–30

TABLES
Explosives, generally, this index
Intraexplosives plant quantity and distance ta-
ble, 21:1A–135
Mortality and life expectancy, evidence, **Rule
1:13–5**

TABLETS
Seizure of tablet for use in manufacture of
alcoholic beverages, 33:1–66

TAGS AND TAGGING
See, also, Brands, Labels and Marks, generally, this index
Motor carriers, intermodal transportation,
chassis, out of service, 39:3–79.13

TAILBOARDS
Riding on rear end of vehicle, regulation,
39:4–61

TAILLIGHTS
Lights and Lighting, generally, this index

TAKING
Impounding, generally, this index

TALESMEN
Jury and Jurors, generally, this index

TAMPERING
Electronic devices, police and police depart-
ments, motor vehicles, 2C:28–7
Evidence, this index
Food, drugs or cosmetics, 2C:40–16, 2C:40–17
Motor vehicles,
Fine and imprisonment, 39:4–49
Police and police departments, electronic de-
vices, 2C:28–7
Physical evidence, 2C:28–6
Police and police departments, motor vehicles,
electronic devices, 2C:28–7
Public information, 2C:28–7

AMPERING—Cont'd
blic records, 2C:28–7
ecords, 2C:21–4, 2C:28–7
gging publicly exhibited contest, 2C:21–11
itnesses, this index

ANDEM AXLES
efinitions, motor vehicles, dimensional and
weight limitations, 39:3–84
ross weights on highways, 39:3–84

ANK TRUCKS
entification marks, 39:3–33

ANKS
quefied Petroleum Gas, generally, this index

ARGET RANGES
andgun, temporary transfer and possession,
2C:58–3.1
ifle, temporary transfer and possession,
2C:58–3.1
otgun, temporary transfer and possession,
2C:58–3.1
eet shooting, shotgun, temporary transfer
and possession, 2C:58–3.1
apshooting, shotgun, temporary transfer and
possession, 2C:58–3.1
nlawful possession of weapons, exemption,
2C:39–6

ASK FORCES
hild Abuse and Neglect Task Force, generally, this index
otor vehicle commission, motor vehicle affordability and fairness task force,
39:2A–30

ATTOOS AND TATTOOING
hildren and minors, consent, 2C:40–21

AX ASSESSMENTS
ssessments, generally, this index

AX COMMISSIONERS
lcoholic Beverage Tax, generally, this index

AX COURT
dministrator, political activities or running for
office, Rule 1:17–1
ggravated assault, 2C:12–1
ppearance, failure of party to appear, sanctions, Rule 1:2–4
pplicability of rules, Rule 1:1–1
hief justice, assignment of substituted judge,
Rule 1:12–3
ollections, comprehensive enforcement program, 2B:19–6
ontracts, collections, 2B:19–6
ling of papers, Rule 1:5–6
nancial statements and reports, judges, Rule
1:18B–1 et seq.
dges,
Financial statements and reports, Rule
1:18B–1 et seq.
Presiding judge, Rule 1:33–2
Substituted judge, prior judge disqualified or
unable to hear pending matter, Rule
1:12–3
Vacations, Rule 1:30–5
residing judge, Rule 1:33–2
Designation of substituted judge, Rule
1:12–3
ecords, verbatim records, Rule 1:2–2
eal, Rule 1:37–2
itle of court, Rule 1:37–1
erbatim records, Rule 1:2–2

TAX LEVY
Taxation, generally, this index

TAX SALES
Certificates, copies annexed to complaints,
foreclosure actions, Rule 1:4–3

TAXATION
Alcoholic Beverage Tax, generally, this index
Benefit derived, definition, avoidance or eva-
sion of tax, 2C:21–15
Courts. Tax Court, generally, this index
Crimes and offenses, second or subsequent of-
fenses, 2C:43–3
Exemptions,
Alcoholic Beverage Tax, this index
Motor vehicle commission, 39:2A–31
Turnpike authority, 27:23–12
Turnpikes, 27:23–12
Fines and penalties, second or subsequent of-
fenses, 2C:43–3
Homesteads,
Credits, jury list preparation, qualifications
and selection, 2B:20–2
Rebates, jury list preparation, qualifications
and selection, 2B:20–2
Motor vehicle commission, exemptions,
39:2A–31
Rebates. Homesteads, ante
Restitution, 2C:43–3
Second or subsequent offenses, terms of im-
prisonment, 2C:43–6
Special assessments. Assessments, generally,
this index
Terms of imprisonment, third or subsequent
offense, 2C:43–6
Theft, amount unpaid or avoided, 2C:20–2
Tow trucks and towing companies, political
subdivisions, 39:3–84.12
Turnpike authority, 27:23–12

TAXATION DIVISION
Alcoholic Beverage Tax, generally, this index
Outdoor Advertising, generally, this index

TAXICABS
Foreign states, licenses and permits, 39:3–19.6
Licenses and permits,
Certificates, 39:3–4.1
Nonresidents, 39:3–19.6
Nonresidents, licenses and permits, 39:3–19.6
Smoking in public, 2C:33–13

TAXPAYERS
Taxation, generally, this index

TEACHERS
Drivers schools, license requirements, behind
the wheel instruction, 39:12–2.1
Substitute teachers, credentials, 39:5B–32

TEAR GAS
Lawful possession, 2C:39–6
Manufacture, transport and disposition,
2C:39–9
Person convicted of crime involving, possession
of any weapon prohibited, 2C:39–7
Turnpike projects, transportation regulations,
27:23–31
Weapon defined as including, dangerous weap-
ons, 2C:39–1

TECHNOLOGY
Electronic Transactions, generally, this index

TECHNOLOGY ADVISORY COUNCIL
Motor vehicle commission, 39:2A–26

TELECOMMUNICATIONS
Abuse of children, emergency service, 9:6–8.12
Access devices,
Alteration or defacement, 2C:20–1.1
Definitions, 2C:20–1
Forgery, 2C:21–1
Receiving stolen property, 2C:20–7
Theft, 2C:20–2
Services, 2C:20–8
Arrest, witnesses, warrants, Rule 3:2–3
Attorneys, ethics, advertising and solicitation,
telephone research service, Rule 1:19–9
Computers, interference, crimes and offenses,
2C:20–25
Correctional institutions, 2C:29–10
Credit cards. Access devices, generally, ante
Crimes and offenses,
Access devices, generally, ante
Correctional institutions, 2C:29–10
Party lines, refusing to yield, 2C:40–2
School buses, drivers, 39:3B–25
Telephone party line, refusal to yield in
emergency, 2C:40–2
Wiretapping and electronic surveillance,
2A:156A–3, 2A:156A–5
Definitions, correctional institutions, 2C:29–10
Disorderly persons, harassment, 2C:33–4
Electronic surveillance, 2A:156A–1 et seq.
Electronic Transactions, generally, this index
Emergencies,
Child abuse calls, 9:6–8.12
Party lines, refusing to yield, 2C:40–2
Fines and penalties, wiretapping and electronic
surveillance, 2A:156A–3, 2A:156A–5
Harassment, 2C:33–4
Internet. Electronic Transactions, generally,
this index
Limousine or livery service, fines and penalties,
39:5G–1
Mobile telecommunications, school buses, driv-
ers, crimes and offenses, 39:3B–25
Motor vehicles, wireless telephones, hands free
telephones, 39:4–97.3 et seq.
Municipal courts, arrest warrants, Rule 7:2–1
Offenses. Crimes and offenses, generally, ante
Party line, refusing to yield, 2C:40–2
Personal identification numbers,
Access devices, generally, ante
Theft, 2C:20–2
Definitions, 2C:20–1
Receiving stolen property, access devices,
2C:20–7
School buses, drivers, crimes and offenses,
39:3B–25
Search warrants, exigent circumstances, oral
testimony supporting, Rule 3:5–3
Theft of services, 2C:20–8
Turnpike authority, use of right of way, 27:23–9
Wireless telephones,
Motor vehicles, hands free telephones,
39:4–97.3 et seq.
School buses, drivers, crimes and offenses,
39:3B–25
Wiretapping and electronic surveillance,
2A:156A–1 et seq.

TELEGRAPHS AND TELEPHONES
Telecommunications, generally, this index

TELEPHONE COMPANIES
Telecommunications, generally, this index

TELEPHONE CONFERENCE
Motions, argument, Rule 1:6–2

TELEVISION

See, also, Radio and Radio Stations, generally, this index

Arrest, witnesses, warrants, **Rule 3:2–3**

Criminal proceedings, newspersons information disclosure privilege, **2A:84A–21.1 et seq.**

Defendants, presence, video link, **Rule 7:8–7**

Hazards, discarded or abandoned picture tubes, **2C:40–1**

Information disclosure privilege, newspersons, criminal proceedings, **2A:84A–21.1 et seq.**

Motor vehicles, prohibition, **39:3A–1, 39:3A–2**

Newspersons information disclosure privilege, **2A:84A–21, 2A:84A–21a**

Criminal proceedings, **2A:84A–21.1 et seq.**

Picture tubes, discarding or abandoning, place accessible to children, **2C:40–1**

Privileges and immunities, **Evidence Rule 508**

Newspersons, information disclosure privilege, criminal proceedings, **2A:84A–21.1 et seq.**

Search warrants, exigent circumstances, oral testimony supporting, **Rule 3:5–3**

Searches and seizures, **2A:84A–21.9 et seq.**

TELLER MACHINES

Electronic Fund Transfers, generally, this index

TEMPERANCE

Commission on alcoholism and promotion of temperance, **33:4–1**

TEMPLES

Religious Corporations and Associations, generally, this index

TEMPORARY DETENTION

Crimes and offenses, investigation, **Rule 3:5A–1 et seq.**

TEMPORARY LICENSES

Drivers licenses, **39:3–10n**

TEMPORARY RESTRAINING ORDERS

Injunctions, generally, this index

TENANCY

Landlord and Tenant, generally, this index

TENANCY AT WILL

Landlord and Tenant, generally, this index

TENANTS

Landlord and Tenant, generally, this index

TENDER YEARS

Hearsay exception, **Evidence Rule 803**

TENTS

Definitions, flammable fabrics, **2A:123–16**

Flammable fabrics, **2A:123–16 et seq.**

TERM OF OFFICE

Alcoholic Beverages, this index

Automobile insurance risk exchange members, **39:6A–21**

Juvenile conference committees, **Rule 5:25–1**

Liquefied petroleum gas education and safety board, **21:1B–12**

Mediators, **Rule 1:40–8**

Medical advisory panel, **39:2–14**

Municipal board of alcoholic beverage control, **33:1–5**

TERMS OF CITATIONS

Definitions, Nonresident Violator Compact, **39:5F–4**

TERMS OF COURT

Generally, **Rule 1:30–2**

TERMS OF COURT—Cont'd

Expiration, time, computation, **Rule 1:3–2**

TERMS OF IMPRISONMENT

Crimes and Offenses, this index

TERRACES

Motor vehicle and traffic laws, application, **39:5A–1 et seq.**

Terraces in parks, **39:5A–4**

TERROR

Kidnapping, terrorizing victim, **2C:13–1**

TERRORISM

Generally, **2C:38–1 et seq.**

Accomplices and accessories, **2C:38–4**

Homicide, **2C:11–3**

Material support or resources, **2C:38–5**

Arrest, hindering apprehension or prosecution, **2C:38–4**

Attempts, **2C:5–4, 2C:38–2**

Biological warfare and weapons, **2C:38–2, 2C:38–3**

Charitable organizations and associations, material support or resources, **2C:38–5**

Chemical and biological warfare and weapons, **2C:38–2, 2C:38–3**

Concealment, **2C:38–4**

Conspiracy, **2C:5–4, 2C:38–2**

Fines and penalties, **2C:5–4**

Death, **2C:38–2**

Definitions, **2C:38–2**

Chemical and biological warfare and weapons, **2C:38–3**

Evidence, **2C:38–2**

Tampering, **2C:38–4**

Expungement of record, **2C:52–2**

Financial assistance, **2C:38–5**

Financial corporations and institutions, funds, freezing, **2C:66–1 et seq.**

Fines and penalties, **2C:38–2**

Accomplices and accessories, **2C:38–4**

Attempts, **2C:5–4**

Chemical and biological warfare and weapons, **2C:38–3**

Conspiracy, **2C:5–4**

Material support or resources, **2C:38–5**

Minimum sentence, **2C:43–7.2**

Nuclear or radiological devices, **2C:38–3**

Threats, **2C:12–3**

Flight, homicide, **2C:11–3**

Foreign terrorist organizations, material support or resources, **2C:38–5**

Funds, financial corporations and institutions, freezing, **2C:66–1 et seq.**

Hazardous substances and waste, **2C:17–2, 2C:38–2, 2C:38–3**

Hindering, apprehension or prosecution, **2C:38–4**

Homicide, **2C:11–3, 2C:38–2**

Limitation of criminal prosecutions, **2C:1–6**

Minimum sentence, **2C:43–7.2**

Murder, **2C:11–3, 2C:38–2**

Nuclear facilities, **2C:38–2**

Nuclear or Radiological Devices, this index

Obstructing justice, **2C:38–4**

Parole, minimum sentence, **2C:43–7.2**

Poisons, this index

Prosecution,

Hindering apprehension or prosecution, **2C:38–4**

Limitation of criminal prosecutions, **2C:1–6**

TERRORISM—Cont'd

Public transportation, **2C:38–2**

Racketeers and racketeering, **2C:38–2, 2C:41–1**

Radioactive Substances, this index

Sentence and punishment, **2C:38–2**

Terroristic threats, **2C:12–3**

Threats, **2C:12–3, 2C:38–2**

Weapons,

Chemical and biological warfare and weapons, **2C:38–2, 2C:38–3**

Nuclear or radiological devices, **2C:38–2, 2C:38–3**

Wiretapping and electronic surveillance, **2A:156A–8**

TESTAMENTARY TRUSTS AND TRUSTEES

Charitable Trusts, generally, this index

TESTIMONY

Evidence, generally, this index

Witnesses, generally, this index

TESTS

Attorneys, admission to practice, improprieties, **Rule 1:23–5**

Blood analysis test refusal, drivers license, suspension or revocation, **39:4–50.4a**

Controlled Substances, this index

Defects of applicants for drivers license, **39:3–10**

Drivers license, blood analysis test, refusal, suspension or revocation, **39:4–50.4a**

Drug tests, crimes and offenses, **2C:36–10**

Implied consent, blood analysis test refusal, drivers license, suspension or revocation, **39:4–50.4a**

Portable oil burning heating devices, **2C:40–7**

Rockets, **21:1C–2**

TETRAHYDROCANNABINOLS

See, also, Drugs and Medicine, generally, this index

Controlled dangerous substance, **24:21–1 et seq.**

THALASSEMIA TRAIT

Discrimination, generally, this index

THEATERS

Fireworks showers in, forbidden, **21:2–7**

Lewdness and Obscenity, generally, this index

Parking vehicle near entrance for purpose of taking on or letting off passengers, time limited, **39:4–139**

THEBACON

See, also, Drugs and Medicine, generally, this index

Controlled dangerous substance, **24:21–1 et seq.**

THEFT

Generally, **2C:20–1 et seq.**

Actions and proceedings,

Estoppel, final judgment, **2C:20–22**

Injunctive relief, **2C:20–21**

Persons receiving stolen property, damages, **2C:20–20**

All terrain vehicles, notification, **39:3C–12**

Amount, grade and degree of offense, **2C:20–2**

Anhydrous ammonia, methamphetamine, manufacturing, **2C:20–2**

Attorneys, conviction, discipline, **Rule 1:20–13**

Auto theft, **2C:20–2**

Carjacking, **2C:15–2**

Chop shops, operation or maintenance, **2C:20–16**

THEFT—Cont'd
Auto theft—Cont'd
Employing a juvenile to commit, **2C:20–17**
Fines and restitution, **2C:20–2.2**
Juvenile delinquents and dependents, jurisdiction, waiver, **2A:4A–26**
Leader of auto theft trafficking network, **2C:20–18**
Penalties, **2C:20–2.1**
Bad checks, **2C:21–5**
Benefits for persons health care, **2C:20–2**
Bringing stolen property into state, **2C:20–7**
Burglars tools used to commit, offense, **2C:5–5**
Burglary, generally, this index
Cable television, services, **2C:20–8**
Charitable contributions, solicitation, deception, **2C:20–4**
Computers, this index
Consolidation, offenses, **2C:20–2**
Contributions, charities, solicitation, deception, **2C:20–4**
Credit cards, **2C:21–6**
Damages, actions against persons receiving stolen property, **2C:20–20**
Dead bodies, **2C:20–2, 2C:22–1**
Criminal mischief, **2C:17–3**
Dealing in stolen property, **2C:20–7.1**
Actions and proceedings, civil actions against, damages, **2C:20–20**
Deception, **2C:20–4**
Defenses, **2C:20–2**
Notice, **Rule 3:12–1**
Definitions, **2C:20–1**
Dirt bikes, **39:3C–12**
Disposition of stolen property, **2C:65–1 et seq.**
Estoppel, final judgment, **2C:20–22**
Explosives, reports, **21:1A–132**
Extortion, **2C:20–5**
Defenses, notice, **Rule 3:12–1**
Failure to make required disposition of property received, **2C:20–9**
Fencing, **2C:20–7.1**
Actions and proceedings, civil actions against, damages, **2C:20–20**
Injunctive relief, **2C:20–21**
Fines and penalties,
Flags, tombstones, cemeteries, **2C:20–2.3**
Identity, **2C:21–17**
Services, **2C:20–8**
Theft of identity, **2C:44–1**
Flags, cemeteries, **2C:20–2.3**
Force, use in defense of property, **2C:3–6**
Grade or degree of offenses, **2C:20–2**
Identity Theft, generally, this index
Immovable property, transfer of interest, **2C:20–3**
Injunctions, **2C:20–21**
Insurance, registration of motor vehicles by insurer obtaining ownership or control under theft policy, **39:3–18**
Juvenile delinquents and dependents, auto theft, jurisdiction, waiver, **2A:4A–26**
Library materials, **2C:20–12 et seq.**
Lost, mislaid or mistakenly delivered property, **2C:20–6**
Motor vehicles. Auto theft, generally, ante
Motorized bicycles, notice, **39:4–14.3l**
Movable or immovable property, theft by unlawful taking or disposition, **2C:20–3**
Movable property, **2C:20–3**
Notice, scrap metal, **2C:20–7.2**
Prepaid funeral agreements, misappropriation or misapplication of moneys received, **2A:102–16**
Real or personal property, research facility, **2C:20–2**

THEFT—Cont'd
Receiving Stolen Property, generally, this index
Records and recordation, **2C:20–2**
Corrections, theft of identity, **2C:21–17**
Robbery, generally, this index
Scrap metal, notice, **2C:20–7.2**
Services, theft of, **2C:20–8**
Shoplifting, **2C:20–11**
Snowmobiles, notification, **39:3C–12**
Solicitation, charitable contributions, deception, **2C:20–4**
Taxation, avoidance or nonpayment, **2C:20–2**
Tombstones, cemeteries, **2C:20–2.3**
Venue, trial, **Rule 3:14–1**
Weapons, reports, **2C:58–19**

THERAPY
Abuse of children, child abusers, **9:6–8.51, 9:6–8.58**
Physical Therapists, generally, this index

THIRD DEGREE CRIMES
Crimes and Offenses, this index

THIRD OFFENSES
Second or Subsequent Offenses, generally, this index

THIRD PARTIES
Action by third party beneficiaries on bond for return of property seized under Alcoholic Beverage Law, **33:1–66**
Conspiracy, **2C:5–2**
Crimes and offenses, criminal liability for conduct of another, **2C:2–6**
Force, use by persons with special responsibility for care, discipline or safety of others, **2C:3–8**
Forfeitures,
Claims to seized property, **2C:64–8**
Interest in seized property, **2C:64–3, 2C:64–5**
Juvenile delinquents and dependents, short term custody, **Rule 5:16–2**
Motor vehicles, intoxication of driver, liability, **39:4–50.22**
Protection of third persons, use of force, **2C:3–5**
Reckless or negligent use of force, **2C:3–9**

THREATS
Bias intimidation, **2C:16–1**
Death, grade and degree of offense, **2C:12–3**
Disorderly conduct, **2C:33–2**
Duress or Coercion, generally, this index
Emergencies, aggravating factors, **2C:12–3**
Hindering apprehension or prosecution, **2C:29–3**
Human trafficking, **2C:13–8**
Informants, tampering, retaliation, **2C:28–5**
Jury, **2C:29–8**
Kidnapping, generally, this index
Monopolies and unfair trade, threat of loss or damage, injunctive relief, **56:9–10**
Political and other official matters, **2C:27–3**
Stalking, **2C:12–10**
State police, complaints, limitation of actions, **53:1–33**
Terrorism, this index
Terroristic threats, **2C:12–3**
Theft accomplished by, **2C:20–2**
Witnesses, protection orders, **2C:28–5.1 et seq.**

THREE WHEELED VEHICLES
Motor Vehicles, this index

THROUGH HIGHWAYS
Definitions, Motor Vehicle Law, **39:1–1**

THROUGH STREETS
Streets and Alleys, this index

TICKETS
Lotteries, manufacturing, **2C:37–6.1**
Standing in roadway to solicit purchase prohibited, **39:4–60**

TIDEWATERS
Adopt a beach program. Beaches and Beach Fronts, this index

TIME
Generally, **Rule 1:3–1 et seq.**
Alcoholic Beverages, this index
Appeal and Review, this index
Appeals In Criminal Prosecutions, this index
Appearance, crimes and offenses, first appearance, **Rules 3:3–1, 3:4–2**
Attorney certification board, eligibility determinations, **Rule 1:39–4**
Briefs, this index
Chiropractors, solicitation, disasters or accidents, **2C:40A–4**
Computation, **Rule 1:3–1**
Expiration of term of court, **Rule 1:3–2**
Crimes and Offenses, this index
Disclosure, newsperson, actions and proceedings, **2A:84A–21.2**
Discovery, attorney disciplinary proceedings, **Rule 1:20–5**
Drivers Licenses, this index
Driving while intoxicated, subsequent offenses, **39:4–50**
Effective date, Evidence Act, **2A:84A–49**
Eminent domain, enlargement of time, **Rule 1:3–4**
Enlargement of time, **Rule 1:3–4**
Response, service by mail, **Rule 1:3–3**
Expiration of term of court, **Rule 1:3–2**
Explosives, permits, expiration, **21:1A–134**
Filing, **Rule 1:5–6**
Fines and penalties, payment, **2C:46–1**
Forfeitures, claim to seized property, **2C:64–3**
Health care professionals, solicitation, disasters or accidents, **2C:40A–4**
Holidays, computation, **Rule 1:3–1**
Homicide, time between assault, death of victim, bar to prosecution, **2C:11–2.1**
Instructions to jury, submission of written requests, **Rule 1:8–7**
Joint representation of criminal defendants, motion, **Rule 3:8–2**
Jury and jurors, challenges, **2B:23–15**
Juvenile Delinquents, this index
Legal holidays, computation, **Rule 1:3–1**
Limitation of Actions, generally, this index
Limitation of criminal prosecutions, **2C:1–6**
Mandatory assessments, payment, **2C:46–1**
Military list, inability to prosecute or defend action, **Rule 1:13–6**
Motions, this index
Motor vehicles, operation while intoxicated, subsequent offenses, **39:4–50**
New trial, rejection, **Rule 1:5–6**
Parole, this index
Physicians and surgeons, solicitation, disasters or accidents, **2C:40A–4**
Prerogative writs, actions in lieu of, enlargement, **Rule 1:3–4**
Pretrial intervention programs, application, **Rule 3:28**
Probate Proceedings, this index
Process, this index
Proposed rules of evidence, supreme court, announcement, **2A:84A–35**

TIME—Cont'd

Records and recordation, schedule of retention, **Rule 1:32–2**

Restitution, payment, **2C:46–1**

Saturdays, computation, **Rule 1:3–1**

Separate trials, criminal actions, motion, **Rule 3:15–2**

Statute of limitations. Limitation of Actions, generally, this index

Subpoenas, public officers or agencies, enforcement, order to show cause, return, **Rule 1:9–6**

Sundays, computation, **Rule 1:3–1**

Supervisory treatment programs, first offenders, rules, effective date, **2C:43–17 et seq.**

Traffic accidents, death, investigation, **39:5–30**

TIRES

Approval of nonrubber tires, **39:3–23.1**

Chains for, **39:3–73**

Condition, dangerous tires prohibited, **39:3–72**

Determination of size and distribution of load, **39:3–82**

Fines and penalties,
  Dangerous tires, **39:3–72**
  Operation of vehicle without rubber tires, **39:3–80**
  Projections on tires, **39:3–81**
  Solid rubber tires,
    Impairment likely to damage highways, **39:3–80**
    Minimum thickness, **39:3–72**

Metal tire, definitions, Motor Vehicle Law, **39:1–1**

Motor Carriers, this index

Pneumatic tire,
  Definitions, Motor Vehicle Law, **39:1–1**
  Lack of as requiring information plate on commercial vehicles and tractors, **39:3–82**

Projections, blocks, hobs, or studs, prohibition, **39:3–81**

Registration of certain vehicles prohibited unless equipped with rubber tires, **39:3–23**

Rules and regulations,
  Agricultural tractors without rubber tires, operation over highways, **39:3–80**
  Designing construction, **39:3–81**

Size, determination and distribution of load on commercial or motor drawn vehicles, **39:3–82**

Solid rubber tires,
  Impairment likely to damage highways, **39:3–80**
  Minimum thickness, **39:3–72**

Solid tire, definitions, Motor Vehicle Law, **39:1–1**

Tractors,
  Pneumatic tires, lack of as requiring information plates, **39:3–82**
  Rubber tires not required on agricultural tractors operated over highways, **39:3–80**

TITLE TO PROPERTY

Alcoholic Beverages, this index

Dirt bikes, registration, **39:3C–11**

Forfeited property, **2C:64–7**

Motor Vehicles, this index

Motorized bicycles, **39:4–14.3i et seq.**

TOBACCO

Cigarettes and Cigars, generally, this index

TOILET ARTICLES

Alcohol in preparations unfit for beverage purposes, **33:1–30**

TOLL COLLECTION MONITORING SYSTEM

Definitions, turnpike authority, **27:23–34.1**

Fines and penalties, turnpike authority, **27:23–34.2 et seq.**

Turnpike authority, **27:23–34.1 et seq.**

TOLL ROADS

Turnpikes, this index

TOLLS

Turnpikes, this index

TOMBSTONES

Theft, **2C:20–2.3**

TOOLS

Burglars tools, **2C:5–5**

TORTS

Arbitration and award, motor vehicles, **39:6A–24 et seq.**

Attorneys, lawyers fund for client protection, **Rule 1:28–1 et seq.**

Contingent attorney fees, **Rule 1:21–7**

Controlled substances, nuisances, **24:21–35**

Drunk Driving Victims Bill of Rights, **39:4–50.13**

Limitation of actions, motor vehicles, arbitration and award, tolling of limitation, **39:6A–26**

Motor vehicle commission, privileges and immunities, **39:2A–24**

Motor vehicles, arbitration and award, **39:6A–24 et seq.**

Negligence, generally, this index

No fault insurance, exemptions, **39:6A–8**

Nuisances, controlled dangerous substances, **24:21–35**

Privileged communications, physician and patients, **2A:84A–22.6**

Privileges and Immunities, generally, this index

Trespass, generally, this index

TORTURE

Homicide, sentencing, **2C:11–3**

TOURISM

Barnegat Bay Decoy and Baymens Museum, special license plates, **39:3–27.86 et seq.**

Casinos, generally, this index

TOW TRUCKS AND TOWING COMPANIES

Generally, **39:3–84.6 et seq.**

Applications, registration, **39:3–84.8**

Approaching, stationary vehicles, **39:4–92.2**

Backing to curb when loading or unloading, **39:4–79**

Crimes and offenses, fees, **27:23–6.2**

Debris, failure to remove, fines and penalties, **39:4–56.8**

Definitions, **39:3–84.6**

Double saddle mount operation, **39:4–54**

Fees, **27:23–6.2**
  Fines and penalties, **27:23–6.2**
  Licenses and permits, **39:3–84.9**
  Registration, **27:23–6.2, 39:3–84.7**
  Storage, **27:23–6.2**

Fines and penalties,
  Failure to remove debris, **39:4–56.8**
  Fees, **27:23–6.2**
  Plates or markers, **39:3–84.13**

Handicapped parking spaces, unlawfully parked vehicles, **39:4–207.6, 39:4–207.7**

Licenses and permits, **39:3–84.9**

Motor vehicle insurance, registration, **39:3–84.8**

TOW TRUCKS AND TOWING COMPANIES —Cont'd

New Jersey turnpike authority, registration, **27:23–6.2**

Notice, fees, **27:23–6.2**

Plates or markers, **39:3–84.7, 39:3–84.11**
  Fines and penalties, **39:3–84.13**

Political subdivisions, taxation, **39:3–84.12**

Registration, **39:3–84.7**
  Applications, **39:3–84.8**
  New Jersey turnpike authority, **27:23–6.2**
  Suspension or revocation, **39:3–84.10**

Rules and regulations, **39:3–84.14**

Stationary vehicles, approaching, **39:4–92.2**

Stop lamps, **39:3–61.3**

Storage, fees, **27:23–6.2**

Suspension or revocation, registration, **39:3–84.10**

Taxation, political subdivisions, **39:3–84.12**

Turnpikes, registration, **27:23–6.2**

Weights and measures, **39:3–84**

TOWNS

See, also, Municipalities, generally, this index

All terrain vehicles, registration, exemptions, **39:3C–6**

Firefighters and Fire Departments, generally, this index

Housing, generally, this index

Municipality or municipal corporation as including, Alcoholic Beverage Law, **33:1–1**

Sidewalks, generally, this index

Snowmobiles, registration, exemptions, **39:3C–6**

Turnpike authority,
  Lease or conveyance of property by town to authority, **27:23–14**
  Power to acquire property, **27:23–5**

TOWNSHIPS

See, also, Municipalities, generally, this index

All terrain vehicles, registration, exemptions, **39:3C–6**

Housing, generally, this index

Municipality or municipal corporation as including, Alcoholic Beverage Law, **33:1–1**

Snowmobiles, registration, exemptions, **39:3C–6**

Turnpike authority,
  Lease or conveyance of property by township to, **27:23–14**
  Power to acquire property, **27:23–5**

TOXIC CHEMICALS

Definitions, intoxication, inhalants, **2C:35–10.4**

TOXIC POLLUTANT

Definitions, water pollution control, **58:10A–3**

TOXIC SUBSTANCES

Hazardous Substances and Waste, generally, this index

TOXINS

Poisons, generally, this index

TOYS

Fireworks, generally, this index

Vehicles, hitching onto street car or vehicle prohibited, **39:4–14**

TRACER AMMUNITION

Discharge, **2C:58–10**

TRACKING DEVICE

Definitions, wiretapping and electronic surveillance, **2A:156A–2**

TRACKLESS TROLLEYS
Definitions, motor vehicles, **39:1–1**

TRACKS
Railroads, this index

TRACTION COMPANIES
Street Railways, generally, this index

TRACTION ENGINES
Tractors and Traction Engines, generally, this index

TRACTION RAILWAYS
Street Railways, generally, this index

TRACTORS AND TRACTION ENGINES
Brakes, **39:3–68**
Crimes and offenses, marks or numbers, change or destruction, **2C:17–6**
Dimensions, maximum, **39:3–84**
Empty vehicles, registration plates, **39:3–20.1, 39:3–20.2**
Excepted from Motor Vehicle Laws, **39:3–1**
Exemption, registration and registration fees, reciprocity, **39:4–26**
Farm machinery, maximum width and length, **39:3–84**
Fines and penalties,
    Hours of service violation, **39:9–4**
    Rubber tires, requirements, **39:3–80**
Hours of duty of drivers, **39:9–2 et seq.**
Information plates required if not equipped with pneumatic tires, **39:3–82**
Length, limitations, **39:3–84**
Lights, **39:3–65**
    Applicability of statute, **39:3–45**
Loading trailer or semitrailer on which engine is moved, **39:4–27**
Machinery and equipment, applicability of statute, **39:3–45**
Moving Heavy Machinery, generally, this index
Nonresidents vehicles, license and registration, **39:3–15**
Notice of intention to cross at grade, **39:4–128**
Number of trailers or semitrailers permitted to be drawn, **39:4–54**
Registration, **39:3–20**
    Nonresidents vehicles, **39:3–15**
Registration plates, **39:4–30**
    Empty vehicles, **39:3–20.1**
Rubber tires,
    Operation of agricultural tractors over highways permitted without rubber tires, **39:3–80**
    Prerequisite to registration, **39:3–23**
Stopping before crossing railroad tracks, **39:4–128**
Weight,
    Excess of limitation, **39:3–84.3**
    Maximum weight of vehicle and load, **39:3–84**
Well drilling equipment,
    Licensing of, **39:3–26**
    Operation on highways, **39:3–80**

TRADE NAMES
Trademarks and Trade Names, generally, this index

TRADE OR BUSINESS
Business and Commerce, generally, this index
Definitions, racketeering, **2C:41–1**

TRADE SCHOOLS
Vocational Education, generally, this index

TRADE SECRETS
Definitions, theft, **2C:20–1**
Labor and Employment, this index
Privileges and immunities, **Evidence Rule 514**
Witnesses, compelling disclosure, **2A:84A–26**

TRADE UNIONS
Labor Unions, generally, this index

TRADEMARKS AND TRADE NAMES
Counterfeiting, **2C:21–32**
Crimes and offenses, motor vehicles, change or destruction, **2C:17–6**
Definitions, counterfeiting, **2C:21–32**
Drugs and Medicine, this index
Fines and penalties, counterfeiting, **2C:21–32**
Forfeitures, counterfeiting, **2C:21–32**
Motor vehicles,
    Change, destruction, crimes and offenses, **2C:17–6**
    Equipment, visibility of trademark or name under which equipment was approved, **39:3–77**

TRAFFIC
Definitions, **39:1–1**
Fines and penalties, obstructing passage of other vehicles, **39:4–56.2**
Lanes, movement regulated, **39:4–88**
Obstruction and obstructions,
    Abandoning vehicle on highways, **39:4–56.1 et seq.**
    Backing against curb to load or unload vehicle, **39:4–79**
    Condition or loading of vehicle, likelihood of delay to be avoided, **39:4–56**
    Lanes marked for traffic, unnecessarily decreasing speed prohibited, **39:4–88**
    Locomotive, train or crossing gate, unnecessary interference with use of highway prohibited, **39:4–94**
    Passing vehicle in street prohibited if interfering with other vehicles, **39:4–127**
    Prohibited, **39:4–67**
    Standing in roadway to solicit purchases or contributions prohibited, **39:4–60**
    Street cars, delaying of prohibited, **39:4–43**
    Traffic signals,
        Beacon or flashing signals not to be erected within travelable portion of roadway, **39:4–118**
        Paved portion of highway not to be obstructed by, **39:4–114**
    Turning vehicle in street prohibited if interfering with other vehicles, **39:4–127**
Slow speed impeding traffic prohibited, **39:4–97.1**
Traffic Signs and Signals, generally, this index
Willfully causing disability of vehicle, **39:4–56.1 et seq.**

TRAFFIC ACCIDENTS
All terrain vehicles, reports, **39:3C–21**
Animals, **4:22–25.1, 4:22–25.2**
Certified copy, judgment in action forwarded to director of division of motor vehicles, **39:6–35**
Concealment, evidence, fines and penalties, **39:4–129, 39:4–130**
Condition or loading of vehicle likely to cause accident prohibited, **39:4–56**
Confidential information, law enforcement officers report, **39:4–131**
Copies, reports, fees, **39:4–131**
Crimes and offenses, jurisdiction, serious bodily injury, **2B:12–17.2**

TRAFFIC ACCIDENTS—Cont'd
Death,
    Crimes and offenses, **2C:40–22**
    Driving without license, **2C:40–22**
    Investigation, time, **39:5–30**
    License suspension or revocation, **2C:40–22, 39:5–30**
Dirt bikes, **39:3C–21**
Drivers licenses,
    Accident occurring during suspension, **39:3–40**
    Death, **2C:40–22**
    Reexamination, **39:3–10e**
Driving without license, death, **2C:40–22**
Drunk Driving Victims Bill of Rights, **39:4–50.9 et seq.**
Evidence, concealment, fines and penalties, **39:4–129, 39:4–130**
Excessive fees, **39:4–131.1**
Fees, reports,
    Copies, **39:4–131**
    Excessive fees, **39:4–131.1**
Fines and penalties,
    Drivers license suspension, accident occurring while license suspended, **39:3–40**
    Death, **2C:40–22**
    Evidence, concealment, **39:4–129, 39:4–130**
    Reports, **39:4–130**
    Stopping at scene of accident, **39:4–129**
Forfeiture, driving rights, **39:4–129**
Forms for accident reports to be supplied by, **39:4–131**
Hours of duty of certain drivers, extension, **39:9–2**
Identity and identification, concealment, fines and penalties, **39:4–129, 39:4–130**
Insurance identification card, exhibition by driver, **39:4–129**
Investigations, death, time, **39:5–30**
Jurisdiction, serious bodily injury, crimes and offenses, **2B:12–17.2**
Law enforcement officers, reports, **39:4–131**
Leases, presumptions, involvement, **39:4–129, 39:4–130**
Leaving scene, death of another, license suspension or revocation, **39:5–30**
Mobile phones, reports, **39:4–131**
Notice, **39:4–129, 39:4–130**
Obstruction, stopping to give assistance and identification, **39:4–129**
Occupant of vehicle, duty to give notice or make report of accident, **39:4–130**
Penalties. Fines and penalties, generally, ante
Presumptions, knowledge of involvement, injury or death occurring, **39:4–129**
Reports,
    All terrain vehicles and snowmobiles, **39:3C–21**
    Animals, injuries to, **4:22–25.1, 4:22–25.2**
    Copies, fees, **39:4–131**
    Death, report to director of division of motor vehicles, **39:4–134**
    Drunk driving victims, access to reports, **39:4–50.11**
    Evidence, admissibility in, **39:4–131**
    Fees,
        Copies, **39:4–131**
        Excessive fees, **39:4–131.1**
    Fines and penalties, **39:4–130**
    Form furnished by division, **39:4–130, 39:4–131**
    Forwarding report of accident to motor vehicles division, **39:4–130**
    Garageman, duty of, **39:4–132**
    Inspection, reports not open to public inspection, **39:4–131**

TRAFFIC ACCIDENTS—Cont'd
Reports—Cont'd
Law enforcement officers, **39:4–131**
Mobile phones, **39:4–131**
Motorized bicycles, **39:4–14.3f**
Nature and effect of, **39:4–131**
Prepared by law enforcement officers, **39:4–134**
Repairman or garageman, duty of, **39:4–132**
Security deposit determinations, **39:4–130**
Supplemental reports, **39:4–130, 39:4–131**
Revocation, license privilege, notice and report of accident, violation, **39:4–130**
Seat belt use, accident report forms, **39:4–131**
Serious bodily injury,
Jurisdiction, crimes and offenses, **2B:12–17.2**
License suspension or revocation, **39:5–30**
Stopping to give assistance and identification,
Duty of driver of vehicle, **39:4–129**
Obstruction of traffic, **39:4–129**
Penalty for violation of statute requiring, **39:4–129**
Street car motorman, **39:4–42**
Time, investigation, death, **39:5–30**
Title to property, presumptions, involvement, **39:4–129, 39:4–130**
Unattended vehicles, **39:4–129**

TRAFFIC CONTROL PREEMPTION DEVICES
Definitions,
Interference with transportation, use, **2C:33–14**
Possession, **2C:40–24**
Interference with transportation, use, **2C:33–14**
Possession, fines and penalties, **2C:40–24**

TRAFFIC ISLANDS
Safety Zones, generally, this index

TRAFFIC LIGHTS
Traffic Signs and Signals, generally, this index

TRAFFIC MARKINGS
Generally, **39:4–191.1 et seq.**

TRAFFIC RULES AND REGULATIONS
Generally, **39:1–1 et seq.**
Accidents. Traffic Accidents, generally, this index
Administrative law and procedure, penalty points, **39:5–30.5**
Alley,
Definitions, **39:1–1**
Emerging from, **39:4–66**
Application of law, **39:4–1**
Electric personal assistive mobility devices, **39:4–14.10**
Area of highway construction or repair, definitions, **39:4–203.5**
Arrest, records and recordation, expungement, **2C:52–28**
Attachable auxiliary motor vehicle axle, **39:4–54**
Authorized emergency vehicles, definitions, **39:1–1**
Autobuses, right of way, yielding, **39:4–87.1**
Automated traffic system statewide modernization fund, **2B:12–30.1**
Automobile, definitions, **39:1–1**
Backing vehicles, **39:4–79**
Duties of driver, signaling, **39:4–126**
Frozen dessert trucks, **39:4–128.8**
Prohibition, interfering with other vehicles, **39:4–127**
Sidewalks, driving or backing across, **39:4–71**
Bail, this index

TRAFFIC RULES AND REGULATIONS
—Cont'd
Begging, **39:4–59**
Berm, definitions, **39:1–1**
Bicycles, generally, this index
Bridges,
Intrastate bridges, overweight vehicles, **39:4–75, 39:4–76**
Movable span bridge, **39:4–127.2**
Business district, definitions, **39:1–1**
Carrying, metals, **39:4–78**
Charitable organizations and associations, solicitation on roadways, **39:4–60**
Chief administrator, definitions, **39:1–1**
Children and minors, bicycle and pedestrian violations, fines and penalties, **39:4–203.3, 39:4–203.4**
Chosen freeholders, powers of, **39:4–201**
Citations,
Definitions, Nonresident Violator Compact, **39:5F–4**
Nonresident Violator Compact, **39:5F–1 et seq.**
Clearance,
Emergency vehicles, **39:4–92**
Intersections, **39:4–67**
Coasting,
Gears of vehicle in neutral, coasting down grade, **39:4–55**
Hitching on to street car or vehicle, **39:4–14**
Collateral, definitions, Nonresident Violator Compact, **39:5F–4**
Commercial motor vehicles,
Constructor plates, speed limitations, **39:3–20**
Definitions, **39:1–1**
Commission, definitions, **39:1–1**
Commissioner, definitions, **39:1–1**
Community service, indigent persons, **39:4–203.1**
Compacts, Nonresident Violator Compact, **39:5F–1 et seq.**
Complaints, **Rule 7:2–1**
Commercial motor vehicles, notice, **39:5–25.1**
Magistrates, **39:5–3**
Compliance, definitions, Nonresident Violator Compact, **39:5F–4**
Contributions, soliciting, **39:4–60**
Control devices, **39:4–6**
Costs,
Deductions from forfeited bail, **39:5–9**
Default in payment, imprisonment, term, **39:5–36**
Counties, this index
Courts, definitions, Nonresident Violator Compact, **39:5F–4**
Crimes and offenses, **39:4–203**
Crosswalks,
Definitions, **39:1–1**
Pedestrians, right of way, **39:4–34 et seq.**
Curves,
Leaving, **39:4–62**
Mountain highways, **39:4–55**
Dealer, definitions, **39:1–1**
Debris, throwing or dropping, **39:4–64**
Delays, **39:4–56**
Deputy chief administrator, definitions, **39:1–1**
Deputy director, definitions, **39:1–1**
Destruction of recreational or agricultural property, **39:4–97a**
Point system, assessment against drivers license, **39:5–30.5a**
Diplomatic immunity, privileges and immunities, records and recordation, **39:5–53 et seq.**
Director, definitions, **39:1–1**

TRAFFIC RULES AND REGULATIONS
—Cont'd
Dirt bikes, **39:3C–19**
Distance between vehicles,
Fire apparatus, following, **39:4–92**
Reasonableness and prudence as test, **39:4–89**
Trucks outside of business or residence district, **39:4–89**
Divided highways, driving upon, **39:4–82.1**
Division, definitions, **39:1–1**
Driver, definitions, **39:1–1**
Drivers manual, availability of copies, **39:3–41**
Driveways,
Emerging from, **39:4–66**
Highways, entering or leaving, **39:4–66.1**
Driving in left hand lane, trucks, **39:4–88**
Dropping bundles, **39:4–64**
Drunk Driving Victims Bill of Rights, **39:4–50.9 et seq.**
Electric personal assistive mobility devices, **39:4–14.10**
Emergencies,
Peak hours or seasonal congestion, **39:4–213 et seq.**
Right of way, processions, **39:4–93**
Emergency vehicles, **39:4–92**
Duty on approach, **39:4–92**
Right of way, **39:4–91**
Stationary vehicles, approaching, **39:4–92.2**
Emerging, alleys or driveways, **39:4–66**
Explosives, definitions, **39:1–1**
Farm tractor, definitions, **39:1–1**
Fines and penalties, **39:4–203**
Children and minors, bicycle and pedestrian violations, **39:4–203.3, 39:4–203.4**
Crosswalks, yielding, **39:4–36**
Deposits, **39:4–36.2**
Default, imprisonment, term of commitment, **39:5–36**
Double fine amount, certain motor vehicle offenses, **39:4–203.5**
Emergency vehicles, tow trucks and towing companies, approaching, **39:4–92.2**
Frozen dessert trucks, **39:4–128.10**
Handicapped persons, parking spaces, violators, **39:4–201**
Indigent persons, installment payments, **39:4–203.1, 39:4–203.2**
Litter, **39:4–63**
Low speed vehicles, application of law, **39:4–31.1**
Points, penalty points, **39:5–30.5 et seq.**
School crossing guards, **39:4–80.1**
Wheelchairs, securing, **39:3–76.2m**
Flammable liquid, definitions, **39:1–1**
Following, **39:4–89**
Emergency vehicles, **39:4–92**
Forms, Nonresident Violator Compact, **39:5F–21**
Four way stop installations, **39:4–140**
Frozen dessert trucks, **39:4–128.3 et seq.**
Funds,
Automated traffic system statewide modernization fund, **2B:12–30.1**
Pedestrian safety enforcement and education fund, **39:4–36.2**
Deposits, **39:4–36**
Garages, emerging from, **39:4–66**
Gross weight, definitions, **39:1–1**
Handicapped persons, **39:4–207.1**
Motorized scooters, stickers, **39:4–14.15**
Parking, violators, fines and penalties, **39:4–201**
Restricted parking zones, **39:4–197.6**
Permits, **39:4–197.7**

RAFFIC RULES AND REGULATIONS
—Cont'd

awkers and peddlers, flashing lights on
stopped vehicles, **39:3–64.1 et seq.**
elmets, generally, this index
igh occupancy vehicle, definitions, **39:1–1**
it and Run Drivers, generally, this index
itchhiking, **39:4–59**
itching on vehicles, persons on bicycles or
skates, **39:4–14**
ome jurisdiction, definitions, Nonresident Violator Compact, **39:5F–4**
orns, mountain highways, **39:4–55**
orses, operation near, **39:4–72**
OV, definitions, **39:1–1**
e cream trucks, **39:4–128.3 et seq.**
digent persons, fines and penalties, installment payments, **39:4–203.1, 39:4–203.2**
side lane, definitions, **39:1–1**
spection and inspectors, frozen dessert
trucks, **39:4–128.7**
stallment payments, fines and penalties, indigent persons, **39:4–203.1, 39:4–203.2**
tersections, generally, this index
terstate compacts, Nonresident Violator
Compact, **39:5F–1 et seq.**
toxication of driver. Motor Vehicles, this
index
trastate bridges, overweight vehicles, **39:4–75,
39:4–76**
vestigations, **39:4–6**
on, carrying, **39:4–78**
suing jurisdiction, definitions, Nonresident
Violator Compact, **39:5F–4**
inerant vendors, flashing lights, stopped vehicles, **39:3–64.1 et seq.**
int and several liability, traffic control signal
monitoring system, **39:4–8.15**
urisdiction, definitions, Nonresident Violator
Compact, **39:5F–4**
Keeping to right, **39:4–82**
Intersections, **39:4–83**
Meeting vehicles, **39:4–84**
aned roadway,
Definitions, **39:1–1**
Trucks, **39:4–88**
anes marked for traffic, driving in lane nearest right edge of highway normally required, **39:4–88**
eased motor vehicle, definitions, **39:1–1**
eases, traffic control signal monitoring system,
39:4–8.15
Leaving curb, **39:4–62**
Leaving scene of accident, death of another,
license suspension or revocation, **39:5–30**
eft hand lane, trucks, **39:4–88**
eft Turns, generally, this index
Letting off passengers, **39:4–65**
imitation on speed limits, limited periods,
39:4–98.2
Definitions, **39:1–1**
imited access highways, traffic rules and regulations, **39:4–90.1**
ittering, **39:4–63 et seq.**
oading, spilling, **39:4–77**
ocal authorities, definitions, **39:1–1**
ow speed vehicles, **39:4–31.1 et seq.**
Definitions, **39:1–1**
Magistrate, definitions, **39:1–1**
Maintenance of roads, reduction of speed limits, **39:4–98.2**
Manuals, horses, operation near, **39:3–41.1,
39:4–72**
Manufacturer, definitions, **39:1–1**
Meeting vehicles, passing to right, **39:4–84**
Metal tire, definitions, **39:1–1**

TRAFFIC RULES AND REGULATIONS
—Cont'd

Motor drawn vehicle, definitions, **39:1–1**
Motorcycle, definitions, **39:1–1**
Motorists, definitions, Nonresident Violator
Compact, **39:5F–4**
Motorized bicycles, **39:4–14.3d**
Motorized scooters, **39:4–14.12 et seq.**
Handicapped persons, stickers, **39:4–14.15**
Mountain highways, **39:4–55**
Movable span bridge, **39:4–127.2**
Municipal Courts, this index
Municipalities, **39:4–8**
Applicable to vehicles owned or operated by,
39:4–1
Approval, **39:4–202**
County road traffic and parking authority,
39:4–197.2
Handicapped persons, restricted parking
zones, **39:4–197.6**
Permits, **39:4–197.7**
Power of, **39:4–197**
Special regulation, notice, **39:4–197.3**
Traffic calming devices, powers and duties,
39:4–8.10
No passing zones, **39:4–86, 39:4–201.1**
Noise, iron, carrying, **39:4–78**
Nonresident Violator Compact, **39:5F–1 et seq.**
Obstructions, **39:4–67**
Railroads, highways, **39:4–94**
Turning vehicle, **39:4–125**
Official traffic control devices, definitions,
39:1–1
Omnibus, definitions, **39:1–1**
Operator, definitions, **39:1–1**
Ordinances,
Appeal and review, **39:4–8.19**
Approval, **39:4–8**
Turnpike projects not governed by, **27:23–37**
Outside lane, definitions, **39:1–1**
Overtaking and passing vehicles, **39:4–86**
Giving way, **39:4–87**
Keeping to right, **39:4–85**
Left side, **39:4–85**
Driving on left half of highway prohibited
unless obstructed, **39:4–86**
Meeting vehicles, passing to right and giving
half of highway required, **39:4–84**
No passing zones, **39:4–86**
Pedestrians, stopping, **39:4–32**
Right side, passing on, **39:4–85**
School buses, **39:4–128.1**
Signals, audible warning required, **39:4–85**
Speed, increase of speed of overtaken vehi-
cle prohibited until completely passed,
39:4–87
Streetcar, care required, **39:4–38**
Turning vehicles, passing on right side of
vehicle making left turn, **39:4–85**
Owner, definitions, **39:1–1**
Parking, generally, this index
Passenger automobile, definitions, **39:1–1**
Passing vehicles. Overtaking and passing vehi-
cles, generally, ante
Peak hours, **39:4–213 et seq.**
Pedestrians, generally, this index
Penalties. Fines and penalties, generally, ante
Penalty points, **39:5–30.5 et seq.**
Person, definitions, **39:1–1**
Personal recognizances, definitions, Nonresi-
dent Violator Compact, **39:5F–4**
Pneumatic tire, definitions, **39:1–1**
Points, penalty points, **39:5–30.5 et seq.**
Traffic control signal monitoring system,
39:4–8.15
Pole trailer, definitions, **39:1–1**

TRAFFIC RULES AND REGULATIONS
—Cont'd

Police,
Directions to drivers, compliance required,
39:4–57
Nonresident Violator Compact, **39:5F–4**
Record, expungement, **2C:52–28**
Traffic control, **39:4–80**
Construction or repair areas, **39:4–203.5**
Private or semipublic roads of corporations or
institutions, application of traffic laws to,
39:5A–1 et seq.
Private road or driveway,
Definitions, **39:1–1**
Entering or leaving, **39:4–66.1**
Stopping vehicle emerging from, **39:4–66**
Processions, **39:4–93**
Railroad crossings, **39:4–83**
Commercial motor vehicles, approaching,
39:4–128.11
Stopping, **39:4–127.1**
Railroad train, definitions, **39:1–1**
Railroads, highway blocking, **39:4–94**
Rear lights. Lights and Lighting, this index
Rearview mirrors, **39:4–58**
Reckless driving, death or serious bodily injury
of another, license suspension or revoca-
tion, **39:5–30**
Records and recordation,
Diplomatic immunity, privileges and immuni-
ties, **39:5–53 et seq.**
Traffic control signal monitoring system,
39:4–8.15
Red lights. Lights and Lighting, this index
Removal, control devices, **39:4–6**
Repair of roads, reduction of speed limit,
39:4–98.2
Reports, traffic control signal monitoring sys-
tem, **39:4–8.17**
Residence district, definitions, **39:1–1**
Resolutions, approval, **39:4–8**
Riding on part not intended for passengers,
39:4–69
Right half of road, keeping to, **39:4–82**
Right of Way, generally, this index
Right Turns, generally, this index
Road tractor, definitions, **39:1–1**
Roadway, definitions, **39:1–1**
Safe corridors, traffic control, construction or
repair areas, **39:4–203.5**
Safety Zones, generally, this index
School Buses, generally, this index
School crossing guards, fines and penalties,
39:4–80.1
School zone, definitions, **39:1–1**
Seasonal traffic congestion, **39:4–213 et seq.**
Semitrailer, definitions, **39:1–1**
Shipper, definitions, **39:1–1**
Shoulder, definitions, **39:1–1**
Side mirrors, **39:4–58**
Sidewalk,
Definitions, **39:1–1**
Driving on, **39:4–71**
Skates, hitching ride on vehicle, **39:4–14**
Snowmobiles, **39:3C–19**
Soliciting, **39:4–60**
Solid tire, definitions, **39:1–1**
Space, following, **39:4–89**
Speed, generally, this index
Spilling, loading, **39:4–77**
State institutions, jurisdiction to hear and de-
termine violations, **39:4–210**
State owned grounds, **39:4–208 et seq.**
Statements to law enforcement officers, victims
of drunk drivers, **39:4–50.11**

TRAFFIC RULES AND REGULATIONS —Cont'd

Steep grade or mountain highway, motor vehicle on, **39:4–55**

Stickers, motorized scooters, handicapped persons, **39:4–14.15**

Stop, definitions, **39:1–1**

Stopping or standing, definitions, **39:1–1**

Stopping vehicles,
  Commercial motor vehicles, railroad crossings, approaching, **39:4–128.11**
  On approach of emergency vehicles, **39:4–92**
  Passengers, **39:4–65**
  Railroad crossings, **39:4–127.1**
  Solicitation, **39:4–60**
  To let off or take on persons at curb or side of highway, **39:4–65**

Street, definitions, **39:1–1**

Street railways, **39:4–38 et seq.**

Streetcar, definitions, **39:1–1**

Suburban business or residential district, definitions, **39:1–1**

Summons,
  Commercial motor vehicles, notice, **39:5–25.1**
  Traffic control signal monitoring system, **39:4–8.15**

Tailboard, riding on, **39:4–61**

Taking on passengers, **39:4–65**

Televisions, visible to driver, **39:3A–1, 39:3A–2**

Terms of citations, definitions, Nonresident Violator Compact, **39:5F–4**

Through highway, definitions, **39:1–1**

Throwing litter, **39:4–64**

Tickets, soliciting, **39:4–60**

Time,
  Limitation on speed limits, limited period, **39:4–98.2**
  Speed limits, limited periods, **39:4–98.2**

Tires, safety requirements, **39:3–72**

Toll road authority, definitions, **39:4–203.5**

Trackless trolley, definitions, **39:1–1**

Traffic, definitions, **39:1–1**

Traffic calming devices, municipalities, powers and duties, **39:4–8.10**

Traffic control devices, transportation commissioner, jurisdiction, **39:4–8.3**

Traffic control preemption devices,
  Interference with transportation, use, **2C:33–14**
  Possession, fines and penalties, **2C:40–24**

Traffic control signal, definitions, **39:1–1**

Trailers,
  Definitions, **39:1–1**
  Tire requirements, **39:3–72**

Transportation commissioner, **39:4–8.2**

Trial, municipal courts, **Rule 7:12–1**

Truck,
  Definitions, **39:1–1**
  Driving in left hand lane, **39:4–88**

Truck tractor, definitions, **39:1–1**

Turning to right, keeping near right curb or side of roadway, **39:4–123**

Two roadway highways, driving upon, **39:4–82.1**

U turns, **39:4–125**

Vanpooling, definitions, **39:1–1**

Vehicle, definitions, **39:1–1**

Victims of crime, death or personal injury, notice to victim of prosecution status, **39:5–51, 39:5–52**

Violations bureau, municipal courts, **Rule 7:12–4**

Waiver, fines and penalties, indigent persons, **39:4–203.1**

Wheelchairs, securing, motor vehicles, **39:3–76.2l, 39:3–76.2m**

Yielding, right of way, buses, **39:4–87.1**

TRAFFIC SIGNS AND SIGNALS

Generally, **39:4–198**

Action for removal of prohibited signs, **39:4–183.4**

Advertising on signs prohibited, **39:4–183.3**

Approval of, mechanical signal devices, **39:4–126**

Arrangement of lights vertically or horizontally, **39:4–109**

Automated traffic system statewide modernization fund, **2B:12–30.1**

Avoidance, driving on unauthorized property, prohibition, penalties, **39:4–66.2**

Backing of vehicle, duty of driver, **39:4–126**

Blind persons, right of way, **39:4–37.1**

Bridge type signs, **39:4–183.9**
  Maximum weight, overweight vehicles prohibited, **39:4–75, 39:4–76**

Cameras, monitoring, intersections, **39:4–8.12 et seq.**

Closed roads, sign mutilation, fines and penalties, **39:4–94.2**

Color, **39:4–105, 39:4–183.22a**
  Flashing signals, **39:4–119**

Commercial motor vehicles, weight limitations, **39:3–20**

Conformity to provisions of law, **39:4–183.2**

Confusion with other colored lights, discontinuation, **39:4–105**

Construction, materials, **39:4–183.8**

Control devices,
  Municipal regulation, **39:4–120.2 et seq.**
  Public private intersections, **39:4–120.6 et seq.**

Control preemption devices,
  Interference with transportation, use, **2C:33–14**
  Possession, fines and penalties, **2C:40–24**

County roads,
  Installation, **39:4–121.3**
  Pedestrians, crosswalks, right of way, **39:4–8**

Crimes and offenses, emergencies, **39:4–215**

Criminal mischief, damaging or removing sign or signal, **2C:17–3.1**

Curves, motor vehicle approaching, **39:4–55**

Damaging or removing sign or signal, criminal mischief, **2C:17–3.1**

Definitions, **39:1–1**
  Traffic signs and signals, monitoring, **39:4–8.13**

Designs, plans and specifications, **39:4–183.9**

Destroyed signs, removal of, **39:4–183.15**

Devices, signalling devices on motor vehicles, permitted or required, **39:4–126**

Dimensions, **39:4–183.9, 39:4–183.22a**

Display of unauthorized signs, **39:4–183.3**

Duties of drivers on appearance of lights, **39:4–105, 39:4–119**

Emergencies, rotating or flashing lights, **39:4–60.3**

Emergency vehicles,
  Duty of other vehicles to stop as affected by signal, **39:4–92**
  Right of way as dependent on audible signal, **39:4–91**

Entrance to state, speed limits, posting, **39:4–98**

Fines and penalties,
  Avoidance, driving on unauthorized property, **39:4–66.2**
  Closed roads, sign mutilation, **39:4–94.2**
  Emergencies, **39:4–215**
  Traffic control signal monitoring system, **39:4–8.20**

Fire stations, installation near in suburban districts, **39:4–121**

Flashing mechanism, municipalities, **39:4–120.2**

TRAFFIC SIGNS AND SIGNALS—Cont'd

Flashing signals, **39:4–60.1 et seq.**
  Duties of drivers, **39:4–119**
  Obstruction of travelable portion of roadway prohibited, **39:4–118**
  Suspending over intersection or using pedestals or posts, **39:4–118**

Four way stop installations, **39:4–140**

Funds, automated traffic system statewide modernization fund, **2B:12–30.1**

Grade crossings, **39:4–199.1**

Grade separations, **39:4–199.1**

Handicapped persons, special parking spaces, **39:4–198**

Height, **39:4–110**

Highway construction or repair areas, requirements, **39:4–203.5**

Horses, motor vehicles, stopping, **39:4–72**

Imitation of sign, **39:4–183.3, 39:4–183.11**
  Removal of, **39:4–183.4**

Information signs, **39:4–183.24**

Inspection and inspectors, traffic control signal monitoring system, **39:4–8.14**

Installation,
  Approval by director of division of motor vehicles, **39:4–121**
  Counties or municipalities, approval, **39:4–121.3**
  Rules and regulations, **39:4–183.27 et seq.**
  Traffic lights. State highways, post Intersections, **39:4–112**
  Continuously controlled highways, **39:4–113**
  Installation on state highway at dangerous intersections, **39:4–121.1, 39:4–121.2**
  Monitoring, **39:4–8.12 et seq.**
  Public private intersections, **39:4–120.6 et seq.**
  Right turns, **39:4–115**
  Stop intersections, **39:4–141**
  Turning of vehicles, post
  Yield intersections, **39:4–141**

Left Turns, generally, this index

Littering, **39:4–64.1**

Location, **39:4–141, 39:4–183.12 et seq., 39:4–183.24**

Maintenance, **39:4–183.15**

Malfunctioning signals, **39:4–81**

Manual for uniform system, **39:4–183.6**
  Adoption, **39:4–120**

Materials for construction, **39:4–183.8**

Men working signs, authority to erect, **39:4–183.1**

Message, **39:4–183.10**

Monitoring, intersections, **39:4–8.12 et seq.**

Municipalities,
  Engineers, certification, **39:4–8**
  Installation, **39:4–121.3**
  Pedestrians, crosswalks, right of way, **39:4–8**
  Pilot programs, monitoring, intersections, **39:4–8.12 et seq.**
  Power of, **39:4–197**
  Regulation, **39:4–120.2 et seq.**

Mutilation of signs, closed roads, fines and penalties, **39:4–94.2**

No parking zones on state highways, approval of establishment, **39:4–138.1**

Notice,
  Traffic control signal monitoring system, **39:4–8.14**
  Traffic ordinances, **39:4–198**

Nuisance, prohibited signs, **39:4–183.4**

Obedience, duty of drivers, construction or repair areas, fines, **39:4–81**

Obstructing view, **39:4–183.3**

Obstruction of crosswalk or paved portion of highway prohibited, **39:4–114**

TRAFFIC SIGNS AND SIGNALS—Cont'd
ne way traffic, **39:4–85.1**
rdinances,
Effective date, **39:4–120.4**
Pedestrians,
    Crosswalks, right of way, **39:4–8**
    Regulating traffic at intersections con-
        trolled by traffic signals, **39:4–37**
Regulating special conditions in municipali-
    ties, necessity of giving notice by placing
    signs, **39:4–198**
School crossings, installation, **39:4–183.1a**
utdoor advertising, imitation traffic signs pro-
    hibited, **27:5–9**
vertaking and passing vehicles,
Audible warning required, **39:4–85**
Overtaken vehicle to give way to right on
    signal, **39:4–87**
avement markings, **39:4–198**
edestrians, generally, this index
notographs, monitoring, intersections,
    39:4–8.12 et seq.
lot programs, monitoring, intersections,
    39:4–8.12 et seq.
acing, **39:4–141**
    By authority of public body or official having
        jurisdiction, **39:4–120.1**
olice or other officers, drivers of vehicles or
    horses required to comply with directions,
    39:4–57
olice whistle, duties of drivers, **39:4–122**
osition, lenses, **39:4–109**
ower of lights, **39:4–111**
ublic awareness campaign, traffic control sig-
    nal monitoring system, **39:4–8.14**
ublic body authorizing erection, **39:4–183.1**
urpose of erecting, **39:4–183.1**
ailroad advance warning signs, **39:4–199.1**
ed traffic light, **39:4–105, 39:4–119**
eflectors. Lights and Lighting, this index
emoval,
    Criminal mischief, **2C:17–3.1**
    Destroyed or inapplicable signs, **39:4–183.15**
    Prohibited signs, **39:4–183.4**
    Rotating or flashing lights, **39:4–60.2**
    Stop signs, post
epeal, certain statutes repealed, **39:4–183.25**
eplacements to conform with act, **39:4–183.2**
esolutions, effective date, **39:4–120.4**
ight Turns, generally, this index
otating lights, **39:4–60.1 et seq.**
ules and regulations, **39:4–183.27 et seq.**
afety zones, **39:4–199.1**
    Location on raised zones permitted,
        39:4–114
chool zones and school crossings, **39:4–183.1a,
    39:4–197**
emaphores, **39:4–108**
equence of lights, **39:4–106**
hape, **39:4–183.22a**
pecifications, uniform system, **39:4–183.6**
peed bumps, warnings, **39:4–8.11**
peed signs, **39:4–183.6**
tandard construction warning signs,
    39:4–183.22a
tandard location and information signs to
    conform to specifications adopted by,
    39:4–183.24
tate highways,
    Installation of traffic lights,
        Approval of installation, **39:4–121.1**
        Dangerous intersections, **39:4–121.1**
        Expenses paid from state highway fund,
            39:4–121.2
        Fire engine houses in suburban districts,
            39:4–121

TRAFFIC SIGNS AND SIGNALS—Cont'd
State highways—Cont'd
    Permission required for construction in,
        39:4–199
    Suburban districts, approval, **39:4–121**
Stop lights, right turns, **39:4–115**
Stop or yield intersections, erection, **39:4–141**
Stop signs,
    Four way stop installation, **39:4–140**
    Illumination, **39:4–183.11**
    Improperly installed, removal, **39:4–6**
    Investigations, **39:4–6**
    Location, **39:4–141**
    Parking, permissible parking distances,
        39:4–138
    Municipalities, **39:4–138.6**
    Placing, duty of board or body charged with
        maintenance of through streets,
        39:4–140, 39:4–141
    Removal, **39:4–6**
        Withdrawal of designation of through
            streets, **39:4–140**
    Yield right of way sign, **39:4–140**
        Location, **39:4–141**
Stopping vehicle or slowing down, **39:4–126**
Street cars,
    Approaching intersections, duty of motor-
        man, **39:4–43**
    Vehicle required to give way to street car,
        39:4–38
Suspended from mast arms, **39:4–183.9**
Symbols, **39:4–183.10**
Timing of lights, **39:4–106, 39:4–107**
Traffic control preemption devices,
    Interference with transportation, use,
        2C:33–14
    Possession, fines and penalties, **2C:40–24**
Traffic control signal,
    Definitions, **39:1–1**
    Devices, approval, **39:4–120**
Traffic islands, **39:4–199.1**
Turning of vehicles,
    Duty of driver, **39:4–126**
    Intersections, **39:4–115**
        Green arrow as authorizing turn, **39:4–116**
        Method of indicated by, **39:4–124**
    Left Turns, generally, this index
    Right Turns, generally, this index
Turnpike project, **27:23–28**
Uniform system, **39:4–183.6**
Vanes and colors, **39:4–108**
Visibility, **39:4–110 et seq.**
Warnings, speed bumps, **39:4–8.11**
Weight limitations, commercial motor vehicles,
    39:3–20
Whistle, police whistle, **39:4–122**
Yield right of way signs, **39:4–140**
    Location, **39:4–141**

TRAFFIC TICKETS
Municipal courts, **Rule 7:8–9**
    Summons, execution, service, **Rule 7:2–4**

TRAFFICKING
Controlled Substances, this index

TRAILERS AND SEMITRAILERS
Definitions, traffic regulations, **39:1–1**
Motor Carriers, generally, this index
Tractors and Traction Engines, generally, this
    index

TRAILS
Bicycles, operation, helmets, **39:4–10.1**

TRAILS—Cont'd
Motor vehicle and traffic laws, application,
    39:5A–1 et seq.
Trails in parks, **39:5A–4**

TRAINING
Child abuse or neglect, regional diagnostic and
    treatment center, **9:6–8.101**
Crimes and offenses, authorized disposition,
    2C:43–2
Destructive devices, crimes and offenses,
    2C:39–14
Explosives, crimes and offenses, **2C:39–14**
Law Enforcement Officers, this index
Municipal prosecutors, **2B:25–10**
Police and Police Departments, this index
Service or guide dogs, traffic rules and regula-
    tions, **39:4–37.1**
Weapons, this index

TRAINING SCHOOLS
Inmate advocacy office. Public Defenders,
    generally, this index

TRAINS
Passengers, generally, this index
Railroads, generally, this index

TRAMWAYS
Unlawful taking, **2C:20–10**

TRANSACTIONS
Sales, generally, this index

TRANSCRIPTS
Abuse of children, closed circuit testimony,
    2A:84A–32.4
Appeal and review, abuse of children, closed
    circuit testimony, **2A:84A–32.4**
Appeals In Criminal Prosecutions, this index
Attorney disciplinary proceedings, **Rule 1:20–7**
Closed circuit testimony, abuse of children,
    2A:84A–32.4
Grand jury, **2B:21–8; Rule 3:6–6**
Indigents on appeal, payment, **2A:152–17,
    2A:152–18**
Limited criminal jurisdiction, courts of, ap-
    peals, **Rules 3:23–3, 3:23–4, 3:23–8**
Municipal courts, **Rule 7:8–8**
Radio or television broadcasts, news personnel
    privilege, **2A:84A–21**
Sex offenses, children and minors, closed cir-
    cuit testimony, **2A:84A–32.4**
Trial courts, verbatim record, **Rule 1:2–2**
Videotaped testimony, abuse of children,
    2A:84A–32.4

TRANSFER INHERITANCE TAXES
Motor vehicles, husband and wife, title vesting
    in survivor, **39:3–30.1, 39:3–30.2**

TRANSFER OF ACTIONS
Generally, **Rule 1:13–4**
Abuse of children, transfer from family part to
    criminal court, **9:6–8.25**
Attorney disciplinary proceedings, **Rule 1:20–2**
Family part to law division, **Rule 3:1–5**
Juvenile Delinquents, this index
Law division to family part, **Rule 3:1–5**
Municipal courts, **Rule 7:8–6**
Nonindictables, **Rule 3:1–6**

TRANSFER OF INTEREST
Immovable property, theft, **2C:20–3**

TRANSFER OF POWERS AND DUTIES
Colleges and Universities, generally, this index

TRANSFER OF POWERS AND DUTIES
—Cont'd
Highway authority to turnpike authority,
    27:23–41 et seq.
Liquefied petroleum gas, regulation, superin-
    tendent of state police, labor and industry
    commissioner, **21:1B–9 et seq.**
Motor Vehicle Commission, this index
Motor vehicle division, motor vehicle commis-
    sion, **39:2A–4**
Turnpike authority from highway authority,
    27:23–41 et seq.

TRANSFERS
Motor vehicles, salvage certificates of title,
    39:10–31 et seq.
Motorized bicycles, ownership, registration cer-
    tificates already issued, **39:4–14.3l**

TRANSIT INSIGNIA
Alcoholic beverage licensees vehicles, **33:1–28**

TRANSIT POLICE DEPARTMENT
Weapons, unlawful possession, exemption,
    2C:39–6

TRANSLATORS AND TRANSLITERATORS
Generally, **Rule 1:34–7**
Code of professional conduct, **Rule 1:14**

TRANSMITTERS
Radio and Radio Stations, generally, this index
Television, generally, this index

TRANSPLANTS
Anatomical Gifts, generally, this index

TRANSPORTATION
Alarms, false alarms, **2C:33–3 et seq.**
Alcoholic Beverage Tax, generally, this index
Alcoholic Beverages, this index
Archaeology and archaeologists, state property,
    archaeological findings, alteration, **27:5J–1**
Blasting caps, **21:1A–137**
Buses, generally, this index
Carriers, generally, this index
Common carriers. Carriers, generally, this in-
    dex
Crimes and offenses, terrorism, **2C:38–2**
Criminal mischief, **2C:17–3**
Electric personal assistive mobility devices,
    39:4–14.10, 39:4–14.11
Explosives, this index
Fireworks, this index
Hazardous Substances and Waste, this index
Human trafficking, **2C:13–8**
Interference with transportation, **2C:33–14**
Juvenile delinquents and dependents, detention
    or shelter care facilities, admissions cessa-
    tion orders, **2A:4A–37**
Laser lighting devices, interference, **2C:33–14**
Limousine or Livery Service, generally, this
    index
Liquefied Petroleum Gas, generally, this index
Mentally Deficient and Mentally Ill Persons,
    this index
Mentally retarded persons, transportation,
    county vehicles, **39:4–207.2 et seq.**
Motor Carriers, generally, this index
Motor Vehicles, generally, this index
Noncommercial trucks, license, **39:3–8,**
    39:3–8.1
Obscene material, public communications,
    2C:34–4
Passengers, generally, this index
Prostitution, **2C:34–1**
Radiation Protection, this index

TRANSPORTATION—Cont'd
Radioactive Substances, this index
Railroads, generally, this index
Registration of vehicles by persons engaged in
    business of, **39:3–18**
School Buses, generally, this index
Sheriffs, prisoners to correctional institutions,
    2C:43–10
Smoking, **2C:33–13**
Solid Waste, this index
Street Railways, generally, this index
Terrorism, **2C:38–2**
Terroristic threats, **2C:12–3**
Theft of services, **2C:20–8**
    Tickets, credit card offenses, **2C:21–6**
Tickets, credit card offenses, **2C:21–6**
Unlawful taking of means of conveyance,
    2C:20–10
Vessels, generally, this index
Weapons, **2C:39–6, 2C:39–9**

TRANSPORTATION DEPARTMENT
Generally, **39:2–1 et seq.**
Actions and proceedings, penalties, violation of
    law relating to projections on tires and
    locking of wheels of motor vehicles,
    39:3–81
Approval, construction of safety zones, guide
    posts or other structures, state highways,
    39:4–199
Authorities. Turnpike Authority, generally,
    this index
Boards and commissions. Motor Vehicle
    Commission, generally, this index
Bridges and Viaducts, generally, this index
Certificates and certification, licensing, motor
    vehicles for transportation of passengers
    for hire, **39:3–4.1**
Commercial bus unit, transfer of powers and
    duties, motor vehicle commission,
    39:2A–35
Commissioner,
    Exchange of information between states,
        39:4–9.1
    Hearings, **39:4–7**
    Investigations, **39:4–6**
    Motor vehicle commission, board, members
        and membership, **39:2A–12**
    Ordinances, installation of traffic control de-
        vices and signs, submission for review
        and approval, **39:4–183.1a**
    Powers and duties, **39:4–2 et seq.**
    Roller skates and skateboards, powers and
        duties, exceptions, **39:4–10.10b**
    Shade tree and community forest preserva-
        tion license plates, powers and duties,
        39:3–27.79 et seq.
    Traffic regulations, **39:4–8.2**
Cooperative agreements, interstate route 95,
    27:23–23a
Counties, traffic regulations, proposed orders,
    copies, **39:4–8.4**
Division of motor vehicles. Motor Vehicle
    Commission, generally, this index
Eminent domain, **39:8–2.3**
Highways and Roads, generally, this index
Inspection and inspectors, abolition, **39:2–9.1,**
    39:2–9.2
Lanes for traffic, designation, **39:4–88**
Motor Vehicle Commission, generally, this in-
    dex
Motor vehicles commissioner. Commissioner,
    generally, ante
No passing zones, power to establish,
    39:4–201.1
One way traffic, regulation, **39:4–85.1**

TRANSPORTATION DEPARTMENT—Cont'd
Records and recordation, traffic regulations,
    permanent record of orders, **39:4–8.5**
Reimbursement of department for funds ex-
    tended for study of turnpike projects,
    27:23–17
Reports, annual reports, **39:4–6**
Roads on state owned land. Public Lands,
    generally, this index
Rules and regulations,
    Public highways or transportation systems,
        traffic regulations, **39:4–8.2**
    Traffic regulations, public highways or trans-
        portation systems, **39:4–8.2**
Speed of vehicles, powers and duties, **39:4–98**
State Highways, generally, this index
State owned lands. Public Lands, generally,
    this index
Through streets, designation, **39:4–140**
Traffic control devices, jurisdiction, **39:4–8.3**
Traffic lights,
    Installation at dangerous intersections,
        39:4–121.1, 39:4–121.2
    Installation near fire stations in suburban
        districts, **39:4–121**
Traffic prohibition on state highways by munic-
    ipality requiring consent of, **39:4–197.1**
Traffic regulations, **39:4–8, 39:4–8.2**
    Approval, **39:4–202**
Turning at intersections, modification of statu-
    tory method, **39:4–124**
Turnpike Authority, generally, this index
Turnpikes, generally, this index

TRANSPORTATION SYSTEM
Definitions, traffic regulations, commissioner
    of transportation, **39:4–8.2**

**TRANSPORTATION TRUST FUND AU-
THORITY**
Contracts, turnpike authority, **27:23–5.8,**
    27:23–9
Turnpike authority, contracts, **27:23–5.8,**
    27:23–9

TRANSPORTERS
Definitions, tow trucks and towing companies,
    39:3–84.6

TRAPPING
Fish and Game, this index

TRASH
Solid Waste, generally, this index

TRAUMA CENTERS
Intoxication of driver, defendants, supervised
    visitation, **39:4–50**

TREASON
Expungement of record, **2C:52–2**
Extradition of person charged with treason in
    demanding state, **2A:160–10**
Records and recordation, expungement,
    2C:52–2
Venue, trial, **Rule 3:14–1**

TREASURERS
County Treasurer, generally, this index
Definitions,
    Motor vehicle unsatisfied claim and judg-
        ment fund, **39:6–62**
    Unsatisfied claim and judgment fund,
        39:6–62
State Treasurer, generally, this index

TREASURY DEPARTMENT
Coastal protection trust fund, **39:3–27.50**
Funds, omnibus safety enforcement fund, **39:3–79.23**
Interagency memorandum of agreement, coastal protection license plate program, **39:3–27.54**
Omnibus safety enforcement fund, **39:3–79.23**
U.S.S. New Jersey educational museum fund, **39:3–27.69**

TREATING
Crimes and offenses, alcoholic beverages, **33:1–50**

TREATMENT
Alcoholics and Alcoholism, this index
Mentally Deficient and Mentally Ill Persons, this index
Sex offenses, repetitive or compulsive sex offenders, effectiveness, recidivism, **2C:47–9**

TREBLE DAMAGES
Identity theft, **2C:21–17.4**
Money laundering and illegal investments, **2C:21–28**

TREES
Horse not to be hitched to shade tree or in protecting casing, **39:4–20**
Outdoor advertising, placing signs upon, **27:5–9**
Vandalism, **2C:18–5**

TRENTON
See, also, Municipalities, generally, this index
School for the deaf, parking and traffic regulation on roadway, **39:4–208**
State owned grounds, enforcement of motor vehicle and traffic regulations, **39:4–211**

TRENTON PSYCHIATRIC HOSPITAL
Psychiatric Hospitals, this index

TRESPASS
Agricultural land, damages, **2C:18–4 et seq.**
All terrain vehicles, **39:3C–18**
Permits, **39:3C–19**
Computers, wiretapping and electronic surveillance, **2A:156A–4.1**
Criminal trespass, **2C:18–3**
Dirt bikes, **39:3C–18**
Permits, **39:3C–19**
Force, defense of premises, **2C:3–6**
Horticultural lands, damages, **2C:18–4 et seq.**
Justification, **2C:3–10**
Snowmobiles, **39:3C–18**
Permits, **39:3C–19**

TRIAL
Generally, **Rule 1:7–1 et seq.**
Appeal and Review, generally, this index
Attorneys, generally, this index
Bail, generally, this index
Calendars, generally, this index
Clerical mistakes, correction, **Rule 1:13–1**
Closing statement, **Rule 1:7–1**
Contempt, **Rule 1:10–2**
Conviction of Crime, generally, this index
Costs, generally, this index
Court records. Records of Court, generally, this index
Crimes and Offenses, this index
Date, setting forth in discovery and calendar motions, **Rule 1:6–2**
Demand for jury trial, **Rule 1:8–1**
Denial, record expungement, **2C:52–14**
Disclosure, expungement order, **2C:52–30**

TRIAL—Cont'd
Discovery, generally, this index
Discretion of court, excluded evidence, **Rule 1:7–3**
Dismissal and Nonsuit, generally, this index
Disorderly persons, **Rule 3:1–6**
Diversion programs, record expungement, **2C:52–20**
Error, notice, **Rule 1:7–5**
Evidence, generally, this index
Exemptions, record expungement, **2C:52–2**
Exhibits, generally, this index
Expungement, records, **2C:52–1 et seq.**
Failure to appear, sanctions, **Rule 1:2–4**
Informing defendant at arraignment, **Rule 3:9–1**
Fees, record expungement, **2C:52–29**
Findings of fact and conclusions of law, **Rule 1:7–4**
Foreign Jury, generally, this index
Harmless error, **Rule 1:7–5**
Hearings, record expungement, **2C:52–9 et seq.**
Indictable offenses, record expungement, **2C:52–2**
Inspection and inspectors, records, expungement, **2C:52–19**
Instructions to jury. Jury and Jurors, this index
Judgments and Decrees, generally, this index
Jury and Jurors, generally, this index
Law students and graduates, appearance, **Rule 1:21–3**
Memorandum decision, **Rule 1:7–4**
Military list, inability to prosecute or defend action, **Rule 1:13–4**
Municipal Courts, this index
New Trial, generally, this index
Newsperson information disclosure privilege, exercise, criminal proceedings, **2A:84A–21.1 et seq.**
Nonjury trial, findings, **Rule 1:7–4**
Objections,
Record of excluded evidence, **Rule 1:7–3**
Reserving questions for review, **Rule 1:7–2**
Open court, **Rule 1:2–1**
Opening statements, **Rule 1:7–1**
Opinions, findings, **Rule 1:7–4**
Orders of court, record expungement, **2C:52–11 et seq., 2C:52–26**
Petitions, record expungement, **2C:52–7 et seq.**
Presence at, informing defendant of right, **Rule 3:9–1**
Presentence report, record expungement, **2C:52–21**
Pretrial Conferences, generally, this index
Process, record expungement, **2C:52–10**
Proof. Evidence, generally, this index
Recall of witnesses, substituted judge, previous judge disqualified or unable to hear manner, **Rule 1:12–3**
Records and recordation,
Excluded evidence, **Rule 1:7–3**
Transcripts, generally, this index
Verbatim record, **Rule 1:2–2**
Exhibits, **Rule 1:2–3**
Records of Court, generally, this index
Rehearing, findings, nonjury trials, **Rule 1:7–4**
Release, record expungement, **2C:52–19**
Removal, records, **2C:52–15**
Reserving questions for review, rulings, orders or instructions, **Rule 1:7–2**
Sealing, record expungement, **2C:52–26**
Statements, record expungement petition, **2C:52–8**
Supervisory treatment programs, record expungement, **2C:52–20**

TRIAL—Cont'd
Sustained objection, record of excluded evidence, **Rule 1:7–3**
Termination of attorneys responsibility, **Rule 1:11–3**
Testimony. Evidence, generally, this index
Traffic offenses, record expungement, **2C:52–28**
Traffic rules and regulations, municipal courts, **Rule 7:12–1**
Transcripts, generally, this index
Transfer of actions, **Rule 1:13–4**
Verbatim record. Records and recordation, ante
Verdicts, generally, this index
Waiver. Jury and Jurors, this index
Withdrawal of attorney, **Rule 1:11–2**
Witnesses, generally, this index

TRIAL ATTORNEYS
Certification, **Rule 1:39–1 et seq.**

TRIAL COURT ADMINISTRATORS
Generally, **Rule 1:33–5**
Division managers, **Rule 1:33–7**

TRIAL DE NOVO
New Trial, generally, this index

TRIGGER LOCKING DEVICE
Definitions, weapons, **2C:39–1**

TRIGGER LOCKS
Definitions, **2C:39–1**
Weapons, this index

TRIMEPERIDINE
See, also, Drugs and Medicine, generally, this index
Controlled dangerous substance, **24:21–1 et seq.**

TROLLEY BUSES
Street Railways, this index

TRUCK TRACTORS
Definitions, Motor Vehicle Law, **39:1–1**
Motor Carriers, generally, this index

TRUCKS
Motor Carriers, generally, this index

TRUST ACCOUNTS
Attorneys, this index

TRUST COMPANIES
Banks and Banking, generally, this index

TRUST FUNDS
Mortuary Science, this index
Turnpike authority, **27:23–10**

TRUSTS AND TRUSTEES
Alcoholic beverage license, more than one license in different capacities, **33:1–40**
Attorneys, this index
Charitable Trusts, generally, this index
Client protection fund, **Rule 1:28–1 et seq.**
Commercial bribery and breach of duty, **2C:21–10**
Crimes and offenses,
Aggravating circumstances, **2C:44–1**
Fraud, prepaid funeral trust, **2A:102–16.2**
Embezzlement, generally, this index
Funeral expenses, prepaid monies, irrevocable trust, **2A:102–16.1**
Interest on lawyers trust accounts fund, **Rule 1:28A–1 et seq.**

TRUSTS

TRUSTS AND TRUSTEES—Cont'd
Investments, turnpike authority bonds, 27:23–13
IOLTA fund trustees, **Rule 1:28A–1 et seq.**
Misapplication, entrusted property, 2C:21–15
Monopolies, generally, this index
Prepaid funeral expense monies, irrevocable trust, 2A:102–16.1
Turnpike authority, 27:23–10
Remedies, 27:23–11
Unsatisfied claim and judgment fund held in trust, 39:6–88

TUBERCULOSIS
Commitment and admission of tuberculous persons to institutions. Commitment and Admission to Institutions, generally, this index

TUBERCULOSIS HOSPITALS
Health Maintenance Organizations, generally, this index

TUMULT
Disorderly conduct, 2C:33–2

TUNNELS AND TUNNEL COMPANIES
Obstruction, willful interference with other vehicles, 39:4–56.1 et seq.
Parking within highway tunnel prohibited, 39:4–138
Pedestrian tunnel, yield right of way to vehicles upon roadway, 39:4–36, 39:4–36.1

TURN SIGNALS
Motor vehicles. Lights and Lighting, this index

TURNING OF VEHICLES
Duty of driver, 39:4–126
Left Turns, generally, this index
Obstructed view, turning prohibited, 39:4–125
Prohibited if interfering with other vehicles, 39:4–127
Right of way, pedestrian starting across intersection on go signal, 39:4–32
Right Turns, generally, this index
Traffic Signs and Signals, this index

TURNPIKE AUTHORITY
Generally, 27:23–1 et seq.
Actions and proceedings,
Bondholders or trustees, 27:23–11
Power to sue and be sued, 27:23–5
Administrative law and procedure, highway authority, transfer of powers and duties, 27:23–42
Advisory committees, capital project and investment plan, annual, 27:23–3.2
Appointments, members and membership, governor, 27:23–3
Appropriations, nonhighway projects, 27:23–44
Bonds, 27:23–7 et seq.
Highway authority, retirement, 27:23–5
Bonds (officers and fiduciaries), 27:23–3
Capital project and investment plan, annual, 27:23–3.2
Chairperson, 27:23–3
Revenue bonds, signature, 27:23–7
Compensation and salaries,
Members, 27:23–3
Officers and employees, 27:23–5
Congestion, plans and specifications, 27:23–41
Construction of law, highway authority, transfer of powers and duties, 27:23–42
Contracts,
Highway authority, transfer of powers and duties, 27:23–42

TURNPIKE AUTHORITY—Cont'd
Contracts—Cont'd
Partial payments, 27:23–6.3, 27:23–6.4
Counties, appropriations, nonhighway projects, 27:23–44
Crimes and offenses, officers and employees, adverse or pecuniary interest, 27:23–14
Dates, transfer of powers and duties, highway authority, 27:23–42
Definitions, 27:23–4
Environmental protection department, roadside areas and facilities, 27:23–45, 27:23–46
EZ pass system, finances, plans and specifications, 27:23–41
Garden State arts center, sale, 27:23–5
Garden State Parkway, transfer of powers and duties, highway authority, 27:23–43
Governor,
Bonds, approval, 27:23–3
Projects, approval, 27:23–23.4
Turnpike authority, chairperson and vice chairperson, designation, 27:23–3
Improvements, operations, plans and specifications, 27:23–41
Inconsistent general or special laws inapplicable, 27:23–21
Indebtedness, highway authority, transfer of powers and duties, 27:23–42
Members and membership, 27:23–3
Municipalities, this index
Obligations, highway authority, transfer of powers and duties, 27:23–42
Officers and employees, 27:23–5
Adverse or pecuniary interest, 27:23–14
Highway authority, transfers, 27:23–42
Operations, plans and specifications, improvements, 27:23–41
Partial payments, contracts, 27:23–6.3, 27:23–6.4
Plans and specifications, operations, improvements, 27:23–41
Political subdivisions,
Appropriations, nonhighway projects, 27:23–44
Loan of property, 27:23–14
Power to acquire property, 27:23–5
Powers and duties, 27:23–5 et seq.
Additional and alternative powers, 27:23–18
Limitation on, 27:23–5.9
Rules and regulations, amendments, 27:23–29
Reimbursement, state highway department, 27:23–17
Revenue bonds, 27:23–7 et seq.
Roadside areas and facilities, 27:23–45, 27:23–46
Rules and regulations,
Duty to comply with, 27:23–29
Establishment, turnpike authority, 27:23–5
Turnpike authority,
Amendments, 27:23–29
Establishment, 27:23–5
Transfer of powers and duties, highway authority, 27:23–41 et seq., 27:23–42
Trust agreement, issuance of revenue bonds, 27:23–8 et seq.
Vietnam veterans memorial, perpetual maintenance, 27:23–47

TURNPIKES
Generally, 27:23–1 et seq.
Accidents, duty to stop, 27:23–30
Acids, transportation, prohibition, 27:23–31
Addition to highway system, 27:23–23.2

TURNPIKES—Cont'd
Additional projects, refunding bonds issued to pay expenses, 27:23–15
Advancements, federal or state government, 27:23–5.8
Alcohol, transportation prohibited, 27:23–31
Ammonium nitrate, transportation prohibited, 27:23–31
Application of law, 27:23–7a
Laws relating to operation of motor vehicles, 27:23–39
Arsenic, transportation prohibited, 27:23–31
Assessments, exemption from, 27:23–12
Audits and auditors, 27:23–14
Authority. Turnpike Authority, generally, this index
Bids and bidding, contracts, 27:23–6.1
Black powder, transportation prohibited, 27:23–31
Blasting caps, transportation prohibited, 27:23–31
Bonds,
Additional projects, refunding bonds issued to pay expenses, 27:23–15
Authority to issue, 27:23–1
Construction,
Operation and maintenance of toll roads after payment of bonds, 27:23–16
Tolls paying indebtedness, 27:23–9
Credit of state or political subdivision not pledged to pay, 27:23–2
Credit of state or political subdivisions, payment, restrictions, 27:23–2
Interest, post
Interim receipts, 27:23–7
Investment, 27:23–13
State or financial institution, eligibility, 27:23–13
Issuance, 27:23–7
Laws not applicable to issuance, 27:23–18
Payment, 27:23–2
Source, 27:23–1, 27:23–2
Power to issue for corporate purposes, 27:23–5
Preliminary expenses of projects, reimbursement from proceeds of, 27:23–17
Proceeds as trust funds, 27:23–10
Refunding, 27:23–7, 27:23–15
Reports, 27:23–3.2
Tax exemptions, 27:23–12
Tolls, cessation after payment of, 27:23–16
Trust agreement as security, 27:23–8
Combining projects, 27:23–23
Concessions,
Fees, power to fix and collect, 27:23–5
Power to fix and collect, 27:23–9
Congestion, plans and specifications, 27:23–41
Consent to location of projects, 27:23–23
Construction of act, 27:23–19
Construction of turnpike, jurisdiction, 27:23–24
Contracts, 27:23–5
Adverse or pecuniary interest, 27:23–14
Turnpike authority, 27:23–14
Bids and bidding, 27:23–6.1
Reports, 27:23–3.2
Revenues, 27:23–9
Transportation trust fund authority, 27:23–5.8, 27:23–9
Contributions, federal or state government, 27:23–5.8
Cooperative agreements, 27:23–23.7
Funding, 27:23–5.8
Interstate route 95, 27:23–23a
Jurisdiction, 27:23–24a
Coupon bonds, 27:23–7

TURNPIKES—Cont'd
Credit of state or political subdivision not
pledged to pay bonds or interest, **27:23-2**
Crimes and offenses, **27:23-32**
High misdemeanor, **27:23-33**
Jurisdiction, **27:23-34**
Penalty, **27:23-34**
Deeds and conveyances, public roads, **27:23-14**
Definitions, **27:23-4**
Depositories, revenues not pledged to pay in-
debtedness, **27:23-9**
Drivers certificate or license, suspension or
revocation, **27:23-38**
Driving while intoxicated prohibited, **27:23-26**
Dynamite, transportation prohibited, **27:23-31**
Emergencies, contracts, bids, **27:23-6.1**
Eminent domain, **27:23-5**
Entry upon land, **27:23-6**
Equipment, hiring, bids, **27:23-6.1**
Ether, transportation prohibited, **27:23-31**
Exceptions, bids and bidding, **27:23-6.1**
Exemption from taxation and assessment,
27:23-12
Expenses and expenditures,
Carrying out trust agreement, **27:23-8**
Funds for study and survey, **27:23-17**
Grade separation, **27:23-6**
Payment, **27:23-2**
Preliminary studies and surveys, **27:23-17**
Relocation of public utilities and facilities,
27:23-6
Explosives, transportation prohibited, **27:23-31**
EZ pass system, finances, plans and specifica-
tions, **27:23-41**
Federal aid, **27:23-5**
Feeder roads, **27:23-5.2**
Construction, repair and maintenance,
27:23-5.2
Disposition, **27:23-5.6**
Existing roads as, **27:23-5.3**
New alignment, **27:23-5.4**
Return to local authorities, **27:23-5.6**
Fees, power to fix and collect, **27:23-5, 27:23-9**
Financial statement, **27:23-14**
Fines and penalties, **27:23-34**
Suspension or revocation of certificate or
license, **27:23-38**
Fireworks, transportation prohibited, **27:23-31**
Formaldehyde, transportation prohibited,
27:23-31
Funds, investments, **27:23-5**
Garden State Parkway, project authorized,
27:23-23.1
Gas stations, establishment, **27:23-9**
Gasoline, transportation prohibited, **27:23-31**
Grade separations, power to construct, **27:23-6**
Hearings,
Extension to New Jersey turnpike, Middle-
sex, Monmouth and Ocean counties, en-
vironmental impact, **27:23-23.5**
Tolls, **27:23-5.10, 27:23-5.11**
Hydrochloric acid, transportation prohibited,
27:23-31
I 95 extension,
Acquisition, **27:23-23.7**
Cooperative agreements, **27:23-23a**
Funding of repairs, **27:23-5.8**
Jurisdiction, **27:23-24a**
Improvements, operations, plans and specifica-
tions, **27:23-41**
Income tax, exemption from tax, **27:23-12**
Ingress and egress, limitation and control,
27:23-5
Interchange, construction, maintenance and re-
pair authorized, **27:23-23.6**

TURNPIKES—Cont'd
Interest, bonds, **27:23-7**
Cessation of tolls on payment of all interest,
27:23-16
Credit of state or political subdivision not
pledged to pay, **27:23-2**
Refunding bonds to pay, **27:23-15**
Investments, funds, **27:23-5**
Kerosene, transportation prohibited, **27:23-31**
Leases, public roads, **27:23-14**
Lewisite, transportation prohibited, **27:23-31**
Liens and incumbrances, toll or revenue,
pledge, **27:23-8**
Liquid shellac, transportation prohibited,
27:23-31
Locations, **27:23-23**
Project addition, **27:23-23.2**
Public highway, power to change, **27:23-6**
Turnpike, **27:23-5**
Maintenance, **27:23-14**
Minutes of meetings, delivery to governor,
27:23-3
Mortgages, **27:23-8**
Motor vehicles,
Hiring, bids, **27:23-6.1**
Weights and measures,
Limitations, **27:23-5**
Vehicles, compliance, **27:23-29**
Nitro cellulose film, transportation prohibited,
27:23-31
Nitroglycerin, transportation prohibited,
27:23-31
Nonresidents, violations, reciprocity, privileges
suspended or revoked, **27:23-38**
Notes, issuance,
Tolls, **27:23-7.1**
Turnpike authority, **27:23-7.1**
Notice, hearings, tolls, **27:23-5.11**
Operation and maintenance of projects as part
of state highway system, **27:23-16**
Operations, improvements, plans and specifica-
tions, **27:23-41**
Paving, reuse, reclaimed asphalt pavement,
27:23-14.1
Peroxides or oxidizing materials, transportation
prohibited, **27:23-31**
Phosgene, transportation prohibited, **27:23-31**
Plans and specifications, operations, improve-
ments, **27:23-41**
Pledge of toll or revenues, **27:23-8**
Pay bonds issued by another project,
27:23-16
Police, duty to comply with directions, **27:23-28**
Policing project, **27:23-14**
Political subdivisions, real estate, sales,
27:23-14
Potassium cyanide, transportation prohibited,
27:23-31
Powdered metallic magnesium, transportation
prohibited, **27:23-31**
Preliminary expenses, **27:23-17**
Professional services, contracts, bids, **27:23-6.1**
Projects, **27:23-23 et seq.**
Authorization, **27:23-23 et seq.**
Combining, **27:23-23**
Direction, designation by legislature,
27:23-23
Extension to New Jersey turnpike, Middle-
sex, Monmouth and Ocean counties,
27:23-23.3 et seq.
High speed limited access superhighway,
Middlesex County, **27:23-23.8**
Interchange connecting route 295 with New
Jersey turnpike Pennsylvania extension,
Burlington County, **27:23-23.6**

TURNPIKES—Cont'd
Public utilities,
Contract for placing facilities on, **27:23-9**
Powers and duties, installation or repairs of
facilities, **27:23-6**
Products or services, contracts, bids,
27:23-6.1
Use and occupation of projects, fee and
charges, **27:23-9**
Radioactive substances, transportation prohib-
ited, **27:23-31**
Railroads,
Relocation of facilities, **27:23-6**
Use of project by, **27:23-9**
Rates and charges, use of project, **27:23-9**
Real estate, sales, political subdivisions,
27:23-14
Reckless driving prohibited, **27:23-26**
Reclaimed asphalt pavement, paving, reuse,
27:23-14.1
Records and recordation, bonds, resolution or
trust agreement, **27:23-8**
Redemption premium, refunding bonds, issu-
ance, **27:23-15**
Refunding bonds, **27:23-5, 27:23-15**
Maturity, **27:23-15**
Registration,
Storage, **27:23-6.2**
Towing vehicles, **27:23-6.2**
Relocation, public roads, **27:23-6**
Remedies of bondholders and trustees,
27:23-11
Rent,
Power to fix and collect, **27:23-5, 27:23-9**
Use of project, **27:23-9**
Repair of project, **27:23-14**
Repeal of laws restricting acquisition of bridges
or tunnels, **27:23-24.1**
Reports, **27:23-3.2, 27:23-14**
Accident, **27:23-30**
Revenues, **27:23-9**
Resolution, political subdivisions, vehicles on
turnpike project, applicability, **27:23-37**
Reuse, paving, reclaimed asphalt pavement,
27:23-14.1
Revenue, **27:23-8 et seq.**
Payment of bonds or interest from, **27:23-2**
Proceeds as trust funds, **27:23-10**
Sales, political subdivisions, real estate,
27:23-14
Seals and sealing, turnpike authority, **27:23-5**
Affixed to bonds, **27:23-7**
Secretary of state, regulations and amend-
ments, filing, **27:23-29**
Service of process,
Sunday, **27:23-34**
Turnpike authority, Sunday, **27:23-34**
Severability, **27:23-20, 27:23-24.2, 27:23-36**
Sodium chlorate, transportation prohibited,
27:23-31
Speed, **27:23-27**
Sixty five mph, implementation, **39:4-98.3 et
seq.**
State highway department,
Construction, jurisdiction, termination,
27:23-24
Reimbursement, **27:23-17**
Termination of jurisdiction on undertaking
of construction of turnpike project,
27:23-24
State highway system,
Operation and maintenance of projects,
27:23-16
Project to become part of, **27:23-16**
Stopping after accident, **27:23-30**
Storage, registration, **27:23-6.2**

TURNPIKES—Cont'd
Sulfuric acid, transportation prohibited,
27:23–31
Tax exemptions, 27:23–12
Tear gas, transportation prohibited, 27:23–31
Temporary bonds, 27:23–7
Toll roads,
Operation and maintenance, 27:23–16
Tolls, generally, post
Tolls,
Approval of governor and other state officers, 27:23–3
Cessation of, 27:23–16
Collection, monitoring system, 27:23–34.1 et
seq.
Exemptions, 27:23–40
Notice, public hearings, 27:23–5.11
Payment of bonds or interest from, 27:23–2,
27:23–8
Payment of indebtedness, 27:23–9
Penalty for violation, 27:23–34
Pledge of, 27:23–8
Pay bonds of another project, 27:23–16
Power to fix and collect, 27:23–5, 27:23–9
Public hearings, 27:23–5.10, 27:23–5.11
Refusal to pay, 27:23–25
Remedies of bondholders and trustees,
27:23–11
Towing vehicles, registration, 27:23–6.2
Traffic signals, duty to obey, 27:23–28
Transportation of prohibited articles, 27:23–31
Transportation trust fund authority, contracts,
27:23–5.8, 27:23–9
Trust funds, 27:23–10
Trustees, remedies, 27:23–11
Turpentine, transportation prohibited, 27:23–31
Vacation of public road affected by construction of turnpike project, 27:23–6
Weights and measures,
Motor vehicles, limitations, 27:23–5
Vehicles, compliance, 27:23–29
Wet hemp, transportation prohibited, 27:23–31

TURPENTINE
Turnpike project, transportation regulation,
27:23–31

ULTIMATE USER
Definitions,
Controlled dangerous substances, 2C:35–2,
24:21–2
Controlled substances, 24:21–2

**UNAUTHORIZED PRACTICE OF LAW
COMMITTEE**
Generally, **Rule 1:22–1 et seq.**

UNCONSCIOUSNESS
Drivers licenses, persons subject to recurrent
unconsciousness, 39:3–10.4 et seq.

UNDER RING
Definitions, shoplifting, 2C:20–11

UNDER THE JURISDICTION OF THE COMMISSIONER
Definitions, traffic regulations, commissioner
of transportation, 39:4–8.2

UNDERPASSES
Parking prohibited, 39:4–138

UNETHICAL CONDUCT
Attorneys, determination, **Rule 1:20–3**

UNFAIR COMPETITION
See, also, Monopolies, generally, this index

UNFAIR COMPETITION—Cont'd
Alcoholic beverages, 33:1–23.1
Rules and regulations by director, 33:1–39
Intoxicating liquors, 33:1–23.1
Liquor, 33:1–23.1

UNFAIR DISCRIMINATION
Discrimination, generally, this index

UNFOUNDED
Definitions, child abuse or neglect, unfounded
allegations, expunging record, 9:6–8.40a

UNIFIED CHILD CARE AGENCIES
Child abuse, reports, confidential information,
release, 9:6–8.10a

**UNIFORM ACT ON INTRASTATE FRESH
PURSUIT**
Generally, 2A:156–1 et seq.

UNIFORM ANATOMICAL GIFT ACT
Anatomical Gifts, generally, this index

UNIFORM FIRE SAFETY CODE
Omissions, criminal liability, 2C:2–1

UNIFORM FORM
Chemical analyses of arrested motorists breath,
39:4–50.3

UNIFORM FRESH PURSUIT LAW
Arrest, hearing, **Rule 3:4–4**

UNIFORM LAWS
Extradition, 2A:160–6 et seq.
Fresh Pursuit Law, 2A:155–1 et seq.
Intrastate fresh pursuit, 2A:156–1 et seq.
Out of state parolee supervision, 2A:168–17

**UNIFORM NEGOTIABLE INSTRUMENTS
LAW**
Negotiable Instruments, generally, this index

UNIFORMS
Fireworks, manufacturers, employees, 21:2–16
Handicapped parking enforcement units,
39:4–197.15
Military, driving motor vehicle without payment of fee when attired in, 39:3–11.5
Motor vehicle official inspection stations, employees, 39:8–2.1
State Police, this index

UNINCORPORATED ASSOCIATIONS
Associations and Societies, generally, this index

UNINSURED MOTOR VEHICLE
Definitions,
Unsatisfied claim and judgment fund board,
39:6–62
Unsatisfied Claim and Judgment Fund Law,
39:6–62

**UNINSURED MOTORIST PREVENTION
FUND**
Revolving funds, 39:6B–3

UNINSURED MOTORISTS
Motor Vehicle Insurance, this index

UNIONS
Labor Unions, generally, this index

UNITED STATES
All terrain vehicles, registration, exemptions,
39:3C–6
Armed Forces, generally, this index

UNITED STATES—Cont'd
Citizenship, jurors, qualifications and selection,
2B:20–1
Defense department, commercial drivers licenses, exemption, 39:3–10j et seq.
Explosives, application of law, 21:1A–141
Law enforcement officers, arrest for violation
of state laws, 2A:154–5
Mail vehicles, right of way, through procession,
39:4–93
Mentally retarded persons, transport vehicles,
identification, 39:4–207.2 et seq.
Military forces,
Prohibited weapons, exceptions, 2C:39–3
Weapons, unlawful possession, exemptions,
2C:39–6
Motor vehicles,
Exempt from Motor Vehicle Security Responsibility Law, 39:6–54
Free registration, 39:3–27
Traffic regulation, applicability of law, 39:4–1
Navy. Armed Forces, generally, this index
Officers and employees,
Fresh Pursuit Law, generally, this index
Law enforcement officers, arrest for violation of state law, 2A:154–5
Weapons, unlawful possession, exemptions,
2C:39–6
Official information, disclosure by witness,
2A:84A–27
Postal service employees, weapons, 2C:39–6
Registration, free registration of motor vehicles
owned by, 39:3–27
Snowmobiles, registration, exemptions, 39:3C–6
Turnpike authority, advancements or contributions, 27:23–5.8
Witnesses, official information, disclosure,
2A:84A–27

UNITED STATES AGENCIES
Attorneys, practice of law, **Rules 1:15–5, 1:21–1**
Official information, privileges and immunities,
Evidence Rule 515

UNITED STATES CONSTITUTION
Postconviction relief, grounds, **Rule 3:22–2**

UNITED STATES COURTS
Attorneys, limitation on practice, **Rule 1:15–5**
Public defenders, 2A:158A–5

UNITED STATES CUSTOMS SERVICE
Arrests, violation of state laws, special agents,
2A:154–5

UNITED STATES DEPARTMENT OF AGRICULTURE
Arrests, state law violations, special agents,
2A:154–5

UNITED STATES DEPARTMENT OF DEFENSE
Police officers, powers and duties, 2A:154–5

**UNITED STATES DEPARTMENT OF THE
INTERIOR**
Officers and employees, arrest, state law,
2A:154–5

UNITED STATES DISTRICT COURTS
Former prosecutions, bar to subsequent prosecutions, 2C:1–11

UNITED STATES GENERAL SERVICES ADMINISTRATION
Arrests, violation of state laws, special agents,
2A:154–5

UNITED STATES MARSHALS
Arrests, violation of state laws, **2A:154–5**

UNITED STATES POSTAL SERVICE
Employees, weapons, exemption, **2C:39–6**
Inspectors, arrests for violation of state law, **2A:154–5**
Police officers, arrest, state law, **2A:154–5**
Rural route letter carrier, amber warning light on motor vehicle, **39:3–54.21**

UNITED STATES SECRET SERVICE
Arrests, violation of State law, **2A:154–5**

UNITED WE STAND
Special license plates, **39:3–27.131 et seq.**

UNITS OF GOVERNMENT
Political Subdivisions, generally, this index

UNIVERSAL PRODUCT CODES
Sales, this index

UNIVERSITIES
Colleges and Universities, generally, this index

UNKNOWN PERSONS
Fingerprints and description sent to bureau of identification, **53:1–15**

UNLAWFUL
Definitions, gambling, **2C:37–1**

UNLAWFUL DEBT
Definitions, racketeering, **2C:41–1**

UNLAWFUL DISCRIMINATION
Discrimination, generally, this index

UNLAWFUL FORCE
Definitions, justification, **2C:3–11**

UNLAWFULLY
Definitions, contraband or escape implements, detention facilities, **2C:29–6**

UNPUBLISHED OPINIONS
Generally, **Rule 1:36–3**

UNREASONABLE BURDEN
Probation or suspended sentences, conditions, **2C:45–2**

UNSATISFIED CLAIM AND JUDGMENT FUND
Motor Vehicles, this index

UNSATISFIED CLAIM AND JUDGMENT FUND BOARD
Abolishment, transfer of powers and duties, property liability insurance guaranty association, **39:6–64c**
Definitions, **39:6–62**

UNSEALED
Definitions, presumption, liquor consumption by driver or passenger, **39:4–51a**

UNSOUND MIND
Guardian and Ward, generally, this index
Mentally Deficient and Mentally Ill Persons, generally, this index

UNSWORN FALSIFICATIONS
Generally, **2C:28–3**

URBAN ENTERPRISE ZONES
Alcoholic beverages, licenses and permits, smart growth development projects, **33:1–24.3**

URINE
Investigative detention, **Rule 3:5A–1 et seq.**

USED MOTOR VEHICLES
Motor Vehicles, this index

USERS
Definitions, wiretapping and electronic surveillance, **2A:156A–2**

USURY
Interest, this index

UTILITIES
Public Utilities, generally, this index

UTILIZATION REVIEW COMMITTEES
Hospitals or extended care facilities, privileges and immunities, **Evidence Rule 507**

UTTERING
Forgery, generally, this index

VACANCIES IN OFFICE
Automobile insurance risk exchange members, **39:6A–21**
County prosecutors, **2A:158–1**
Grand jurors, filling, **2B:21–4**
Juvenile conference committees, **Rule 5:25–1**
Liquefied petroleum gas education and safety board, **21:1B–12**
Municipal board of alcoholic beverage control, **33:1–5**
Municipal courts, appointment for unexpired term, **2B:12–4**
Municipal prosecutors, **2B:25–6**
    Attorney general, assistants, reimbursement, **2B:25–8**

VACATING OR SETTING ASIDE
Bail, forfeitures, **Rule 3:26–6**

VACATION OF STREETS AND HIGHWAYS
Construction of turnpike project, **27:23–6**

VACATIONS
Courts, judges and other personnel, **Rule 1:30–5**

VALUE AND VALUATION
Assessments, generally, this index
Definitions, turnpike authority, contracts, partial payments, **27:23–6.3**

VANDALISM
Agricultural land, **2C:18–5, 2C:18–6**
Horticultural land, **2C:18–5**
Motor vehicles, serial numbers on component parts, **39:10B–3**
Nuclear power plants, crimes and offenses, **2C:17–7 et seq.**
Railroads, crossing warning signals, **2C:33–14.1**

VANPOOLING
Definitions, motor vehicles, **39:1–1**

VANS
Commuter Vans, generally, this index

VEHICLES
Motor Vehicles, generally, this index

VEHICULAR HOMICIDE
Homicide. Motor Vehicles, this index

VENDING MACHINES
Slugs, **2C:21–18**
Theft of services, **2C:20–8**

VENDOR AND PURCHASER
Sales, generally, this index

VENERATED OBJECTS
Desecration, **2C:33–9**

VENEREAL DISEASES
Sexual penetration, diseased persons, **2C:34–5**

VENIRE
Jury and Jurors, generally, this index
Municipal Courts, generally, this index

VENTILATION
Explosives, magazines, **21:1A–136**

VENUE
Abuse of children, **9:6–8.26**
Change of venue,
    Criminal actions,
        Motion, **Rule 3:14–2**
        Order, **Rule 3:14–4**
    Juvenile actions, **Rule 5:19–1**
Counties, **Rule 3:14–1**
Criminal actions, **Rule 3:14–1 et seq.**
Establishment, juvenile actions, **Rule 5:19–1**
Juvenile delinquents and dependents, actions and proceedings, **Rule 5:19–1**
Multiple offenses, separate trials, **2C:1–8**
Municipal courts, **Rule 7:8–2**
State grand jury indictments, **2B:22–7**

VERBATIM RECORDS
Records and Recordation, this index

VERDICTS
Civil actions, five sixths verdicts, **2B:23–17**
Civil jury trials, five sixths verdicts, **2B:23–17**
Crimes and Offenses, this index
Disagreement of jurors, new trial, **2B:23–18**
Five sixths verdicts, **2B:23–17**
Homicide, aggravating or mitigating factors, **2C:11–3**
Jury and jurors,
    Less than unanimous, civil actions, **Rules 1:8–2, 1:8–9**
    Lists, taking into jury room, **Rule 1:8–8**
    Polling of jury, **Rule 1:8–10**
    Return, **Rule 1:8–9**
Less than unanimous verdict, criminal actions, **Rule 1:8–2**
Six member jury, **Rule 1:8–2**

VERMIN
Killing, animal cruelty laws, exception, **4:22–16**

VESSELS
See, also,
    Boats and Boating, generally, this index
    Carriers, generally, this index
Alcoholic beverages,
    Death while operating under influence of, crime of second degree, **2C:11–5**
    Municipal referendum on retail sales, **33:1–46**
    Plenary retail transit license, **33:1–12**
Assault by operation of, **2C:12–1**
Crimes and offenses,
    Assault by, **2C:12–1**
    Death by, **2C:11–5**

VESSELS—Cont'd

Crimes and offenses—Cont'd
  Flight, law enforcement officers, **2C:29–2**
  Loss or destruction, putting up false light, **2C:12–2**
  Criminal homicide, death by operation of vessel, **2C:11–5**
  Death by operation of, crime of second degree, **2C:11–5**
  Definitions,
    Assault by, **2C:12–1**
    Assault by auto or vessel, **2C:11–5**
  Destruction of vessel, putting up false light, **2C:12–2**
  Federal boating safety laws, state police, powers and duties, **53:2–1**
  Fleeing, law enforcement officer, **2C:29–2**
  Homicide, death by operation of vessel, **2C:11–5**
  Intermodal transportation, axle weight limitations, **39:3–84.1**
  Loss or destruction, false light, **2C:12–2**
  Narcotic drugs, death while operating under influence of, crime of second degree, **2C:11–5**
  Peace officers, fleeing or attempting to elude law enforcement officers, **2C:29–2**
  Reckless and careless operation, assault, **2C:12–1**
  Shipboard gambling, crimes and offenses, **2C:37–4.1**
  Signals, flare type guns, **2C:58–10**
  State police, powers and duties, **53:2–1**
  Theft, **2C:20–2**
  Unlawful taking, **2C:20–10**
  Visual distress signalling device, signal purposes, **2C:58–10**

VESTED RIGHTS

Corporations, antitrust law exemptions, **56:9–4**
Motor vehicles, death of husband or wife, **39:3–30.1, 39:3–30.2**

VETERANS

Alcoholic beverages, licenses and permits, **33:1–12.19**
  Exlicensees entitled to, **33:1–12.19**
  Lapses, counties of sixth class, **33:1–12.22b**
  Transfer to spouse, surrender or expiration, **33:1–12.22a**
Association of war veterans. Veterans Associations and Organizations, generally, this index
Counties, this index
Crimes and offenses, disabled veterans, special motor vehicle plates, **39:3–27.18**
Disabled veterans,
  License plates, **39:3–27.15 et seq.**
  Motor vehicles, plates or markers, **39:3–27.15 et seq.**
Fees, motor vehicles, plates or markers, disabled veterans, **39:3–27.16**
Intoxicating liquors, licenses, **33:1–12.19**
  Sixth class counties, **33:1–12.22b**
  Surrender during service in armed forces, **33:1–12.22a**
License plates,
  Combat infantryman badge recipients, **39:3–27.46**
  Disabled veterans, **39:3–27.15 et seq.**
Licenses and permits. Alcoholic beverages, ante
Loans, special plates, motor vehicles, **39:3–27.17**
Motor Vehicles, this index

VETERANS—Cont'd

Organizations. Veterans Associations and Organizations, generally, this index
Spouses, free joint vehicle registration, **39:3–27.1**
Vietnam Conflict, this index

VETERANS ASSOCIATIONS AND ORGANIZATIONS

Club officers, intoxicating liquors, law enforcement personnel, **33:1–25.1, 33:1–25.2**
Constables, intoxicating liquors, licenses and permits, **33:1–25.1, 33:1–25.2**
Intoxicating liquors,
  Club licenses, law enforcement personnel as officers, **33:1–25.1, 33:1–25.2**
  Temporary permits, fees, **33:1–74**
Licenses and permits, intoxicating liquors, law enforcement personnel as club officers, **33:1–25.1, 33:1–25.2**
Police and police departments, intoxicating liquors, licenses and permits, **33:1–25.1, 33:1–25.2**
Sheriffs, intoxicating liquors, licenses and permits, **33:1–25.1, 33:1–25.2**

VETERANS HOSPITALS

Institutionalized elderly persons, assault, **2C:12–1**

VETERANS OF FOREIGN WARS

Veterans, generally, this index
Veterans Associations and Organizations, generally, this index

VETERINARIANS

Actions and proceedings, review committees, immunity from liability, **2A:84A–22.10**
Controlled substances, **24:21–1 et seq.**
  Prescriptions, **24:21–15**
  Registration, **24:21–11**
Controversies and disputes with patients owners, review committees, immunity from liability, **2A:84A–22.10**
Damages, review committees, immunity from liability, **2A:84A–22.10**
Defined, controlled substances, **24:21–2**
Definitions, controlled substances, **2C:35–2, 24:21–2**
Domestic animals, destruction, use of neuromuscular blocking agents, **4:22–19.3, 4:22–19.4**
Fines and penalties, destruction of domestic animals, use of neuromuscular blocking agents, **4:22–19.4**
Prescriptions, controlled substances, **24:21–15**
Privileges and immunities, review committees, immunity from liability, **2A:84A–22.10**
Qualifications, peer review committee, immunity from liability, **2A:84A–22.10**
Sodium pentobarbital, registration and certification, **24:21–11**

VETERINARY MEDICAL EXAMINERS BOARD

Veterinarians, generally, this index

VETO

Governor,
  Motor vehicle commission, minutes, meetings, board, **39:2A–17**
  Turnpike authority bonds, **27:23–3**

VIADUCTS

Bridges and Viaducts, generally, this index

VICE AND IMMORALITY

Lewdness and Obscenity, generally, this index
Prostitution, generally, this index
Sex Offenses, generally, this index

VICINAGES

Generally, **Rule 1:33–2**
Assignment judges, **Rule 1:33–4**
Chief probation officer, **Rule 1:33–8**
Division managers, **Rule 1:33–7**
Presiding judges, **Rule 1:33–6**
Trial court administrators and case coordinators, **Rule 1:33–5**

VICTIM AND WITNESS ADVOCACY FUND

Generally, **2C:43–3.1**

VICTIM AND WITNESS ADVOCACY OFFICE

AIDS or HIV testing,
  Disorderly person, results, notification to victims, **2A:4A–43.4, 2C:43–2.3**
  Sex offenders, results, notification to victims, **2C:43–2.2**

VICTIMLESS CRIMES

Supervisory treatment programs, first offenders, **2C:43–12 et seq.**

VICTIMS OF CRIME

Abuse of children, closed circuit testimony, motions, **2A:84A–32.4**
Accomplice status, **2C:2–6**
Aged Persons, this index
Aggravating circumstances, **2C:44–1**
Character evidence, **Evidence Rule 404**
  Methods of proving, **Evidence Rule 405**
Children and Minors, this index
Closed circuit testimony, abuse of children, motions, **2A:84A–32.4**
Code of Criminal Justice, **2C:1–2**
Compensation and salaries,
  Accounts and accounting, **2C:43–3.1**
  Assessments, collection and disposition, **2C:43–3.1**
  Attorney general, moneys received and deposited, monthly accounting, **2C:43–3.1**
  Child abuse reports, access to, **9:6–8.10a**
  Claims, satisfaction, funding, **2C:43–3.1**
  Criminal disposition and revenue collection fund, **2C:43–3.1**
  Domestic violence, victims, compensation paid to by board, reimbursement by defendant, **2C:25–29**
  Law and public safety department, criminal justice division, victim and witness advocacy fund, **2C:43–3.1**
  Orders, compensation payment, predispositional evaluation, **2A:4A–42**
  Predispositional evaluation, compensation payments, **2A:4A–42**
  Records and recordation, expungement, supplying information, **2C:52–18**
  Victim and witness advocacy fund, **2C:43–3.1**
  Victims of crime compensation board account, **2C:43–3.1**
Confidential or privileged information, **Rule 1:38–3**
Counselors, **2A:84A–22.13 et seq.**
Consent, **2C:2–10**
  Privileged communications, waiver, counselors, **2A:84A–22.15**
Correctional institutions, officers and employees, consecutive sentences, **2C:44–5**
Counselors and counseling, confidential or privileged information, **2A:84A–22.13 et seq.; Evidence Rule 517**

VICTIMS OF CRIME—Cont'd
Definitions,
Children and minors, speedy trial, **2A:163–4**
Confidential or privileged information, counselors, **2A:84A–22.14**
Drunk Driving Victims Bill of Rights, **39:4–50.10**
Sex offenses, **2C:14–1, 2C:14–11**
Domestic Violence, this index
Drunk Driving Victims Bill of Rights, **39:4–50.9 et seq.**
Endangering injured victim, **2C:12–1.2**
Evidence,
Abuse of children, closed circuit testimony, motions, **2A:84A–32.4**
Closed circuit testimony, abuse of children, motions, **2A:84A–32.4**
Homicide, sentencing proceedings, **2C:11–3**
Funds, victim and witness advocacy fund, victims of crime compensation board account, **2C:43–3.1**
Handicapped Persons, this index
Homicide, this index
Identification, privileged communications, counselors, **2A:84A–22.15**
Incapacitated persons, endangering injured victim, **2C:12–1.2**
Inducement of offense, mitigating circumstances, **2C:44–1**
Motions, closed circuit testimony, abuse of children, **2A:84A–32.4**
Motor vehicle offenses, death or personal injury, notice to victim of prosecution status, **39:5–51, 39:5–52**
Motor vehicles,
Drivers licenses, mailing address, **39:3–9b, 39:3–9c**
License and registration, mailing address, **39:3–4, 39:3–9c**
Notice, status of prosecution, traffic or motor vehicle offenses, **39:5–51, 39:5–52**
Photographs, homicide, sentence and punishment, **2C:11–3**
Rules and regulations, **2C:11–3a**
Plea bargains, sex offenses, prosecuting attorneys, consultation, **2C:14–2.1**
Predisposition report, juvenile delinquents and dependents, statement by victim or relative, **2A:4A–42**
Presentence investigations and reports, **2C:44–6**
Privileged communications,
Counselors, **2A:84A–22.13 et seq.**
Victim and counselor, **Evidence Rule 517**
Prosecuting attorneys, consultation, sex offenses, plea bargains, **2C:14–2.1**
Restitution, this index
Sex Offenses, this index
Sexual abuse, children and minors, closed circuit testimony motions, **2A:84A–32.4**
Statements, application for change in custodial sentence to permit entry into intensive supervision program, **2C:43–11**
Traffic offenses, death or personal injury, notice to victim of prosecution status, **39:5–51, 39:5–52**
Videotaped testimony, abuse of children, motions, **2A:84A–32.4**
Waiver, privileged communications, counselors, **2A:84A–22.15**

VIDEO GAMES
Children and minors, prohibited sexual acts, crimes and offenses, **2C:24–4**
Possession, showing child engaging in prohibited sexual acts, crimes and offenses, **2C:24–4**

VIDEO GAMES—Cont'd
Viewing, child engaging in prohibited sexual acts, crimes and offenses, **2C:24–4**

VIDEOTAPES
Child pornography, prohibited sexual acts, **2A:84A–32.4, 2C:24–4**
Children and minors, sexual abuse, **2A:84A–32.4**
Consent, nudity, sexual intercourse, invasion of privacy, **2C:14–9**
Crimes and offenses, nudity, sexual intercourse, invasion of privacy, **2C:14–9**
Depositions, this index
Nudity, crimes and offenses, invasion of privacy, **2C:14–9**
Police and police departments, motor vehicles, tampering, **2C:28–7**
Sexual intercourse, crimes and offenses, invasion of privacy, **2C:14–9**
Verbatim record, **Rule 1:2–2**

VIETNAM CONFLICT
Veterans,
Drivers license, waiver of fee, **39:3–11.5**
Turnpike authority, perpetual maintenance, **27:23–47**

VIEW
Jury and jurors, **2B:23–16**

VILLAGES
Municipalities, generally, this index

VIOLATIONS BUREAU
Municipal courts, **Rule 7:12–4**

VIOLATIONS CLERK
Clerks of Court, generally, this index

VIOLENCE
Force or Violence, generally, this index

VIOLENT CRIME
Definitions, No Early Release Act, **2C:43–7.2**

VIOLENT OFFENDERS
Notice to impose sentence, **Rule 3:21–4**

VIOLENT PREDATOR INCAPACITATION ACT OF 1994
Generally, **2C:43–6.4**

VIRGIN ISLANDS
Credit cards, notice of revocation, **2C:21–6**

VISIBILITY
Identification marks, motor vehicles, **39:3–33**
Lights and Lighting, generally, this index
Motor vehicle registration markers, rear marker, **39:3–61**
Obstructed view. Motor Vehicles, this index
Outdoor advertising, interference, **27:5–9**
Parked vehicles, minimum distance for obtaining clear view of, **39:4–136**

VISITATION
Children and Minors, this index

VISTA
Attorneys, client protection fund, exemption from payment, **Rule 1:28–2**

VITAL STATISTICS
Birth Certificates, generally, this index
Hearsay exception, records, **Evidence Rule 803**

VOCATIONAL EDUCATION
Convicted offenders, rehabilitation complete, return to profession or occupation, **2A:168A–5**
County schools, motor vehicles, registration fee exemption, **39:3–27**
Culinary arts or hotel management programs, intoxicating liquors, possession, children and minors, **2C:33–15**
Foreign states, sex offenses, registration, **2C:7–2**
Registration, sex offenses, foreign states, **2C:7–2**
Rehabilitated convicted offenders, return to profession or occupation, **2A:168A–5**
Sex offenses, foreign states, registration, **2C:7–2**

VOICE EXEMPLARS
Investigative detention, **Rule 3:5A–1 et seq.**

VOIR DIRE
Grand jurors, **2B:21–2**
Jurors, **2B:23–10; Rule 1:8–3**

VOLUNTARY ACTS
Basis of criminal liability, **2C:2–1**

VOLUNTEER FIREFIGHTERS AND FIRE COMPANIES
Chief, motor vehicles, red warning lights and signals, **39:3–54.15 et seq.**
Commercial drivers licenses, exemption, **39:3–10j et seq.**
Exemption, commercial drivers license requirement, **39:3–10j et seq.**
Flashing lights, motor vehicle members, **39:3–54.7 et seq.**
Identification cards, emergency vehicles,
Permit for flashing lights, **39:3–54.11**
Permits for flashing lights, **39:3–54.11**
Jurors, members, grounds for excuse, **2B:20–10**
Lights on vehicles,
Flashing lights, **39:3–54.7 et seq.**
Red lights, chief or first assistant chief, **39:3–54.15 et seq.**
Members, jurors, grounds for excuse, **2B:20–10**
Motor vehicles,
Chief or first assistant chief, red warning lights and sirens, **39:3–54.15 et seq.**
Emergency vehicles, identification cards, permits for flashing lights, **39:3–54.11**
Flashing lights, **39:3–54.7 et seq.**
Free registration, **39:3–27**
Sirens, private vehicles, chief or first assistant chief, **39:3–54.15 et seq.**
Warning lights, private vehicles, **39:3–54.7 et seq.**
Chief or first assistant chief, **39:3–54.15 et seq.**

VOLUNTEER FIRST AID OR RESCUE SQUADS
Emergency vehicles, identification cards, permit for use and display of flashing lights, **39:3–54.11**
Jurors, members, grounds for excuse, **2B:20–10**

VOLUNTEERS
Adopt a beach program. Beaches and Beach Fronts, this index
Court appointed special advocate, **2A:4A–92**
Emergencies, this index
Fire companies. Volunteer Firefighters and Fire Companies, generally, this index

VOTERS AND VOTING
Elections, generally, this index

WAGERS
Gambling, generally, this index

WAGES
Compensation and Salaries, generally, this index

WAIVER
Buses, this index
Commercial driver applicant, skills test, **39:3–10.22**
Commercial motor vehicles, any portion of law, **39:3–10.29**
Costs, trial de novo, motor vehicle tort claim arbitrations, **39:6A–34**
Crimes and Offenses, this index
Doctor patient privilege, attorneys, application for restoration from disability inactive status, **Rule 1:20–12**
Drivers Licenses, this index
Extradition, this index
Fees, indigent persons, **Rule 1:13–2**
Indigent persons, fees, **Rule 1:13–2**
Jurisdiction, delinquent children, **2A:4A–26**
Jury and jurors. Jury and Jurors, this index
Juvenile Delinquents, this index
Leases, generally, this index
Low speed vehicles, liability, **39:4–31.4**
Motor Vehicles, this index
Motorcycles, road tests, safety education program, **39:3–10.31**
Newspersons, information disclosure privilege, **2A:84A–21.3, 2A:84A–21.4**
Objections, evidence admission, **Rule 7:5–2**
Privileges and immunities, **Evidence Rule 530**
Road tests, motorcycle licenses, safety education program, **39:3–10.31**
School buses,
  Drivers licenses, fees for endorsement, **39:3–10**
  Examination permit fee, drivers license endorsements, **39:3–13**
Victims of crime, privileged communications, counselors, **2A:84A–22.15**
Witnesses, privilege, **2A:84A–29**

WALKS
Crosswalks, generally, this index
Sidewalks, generally, this index

WAR
Drivers license, fee, **39:3–11.5**
Justification defense, criminal prosecutions, **2C:3–3**

WAR ASSETS CORPORATION
Motor vehicles purchased from, temporary identification marker for purchaser, **39:3–33.1**

WAR VETERANS
Veterans, generally, this index

WARDENS
Custody of inmates person, interstate agreement on detainers, **2A:159A–12**
Detainers from other states, duties of warden, **2A:159A–3 et seq.**
Weapons, unlawful possession, exemption, **2C:39–6**

WARDS
Guardian and Ward, generally, this index

WAREHOUSE RECEIPTS
Alcoholic beverages, **33:1–72**

WAREHOUSES
Alcoholic Beverages, this index
Crimes and offenses, alcoholic beverages, **33:1–50**
Drugs, controlled substances, registration requirements, **24:21–10**

WARNINGS
Electric personal assistive mobility devices, **39:4–10.8**
Fireworks, packages, **21:2–15**
Grade Crossings, this index
Motor Vehicles, this index
Volunteer firefighters and fire companies, flashing lights, **39:3–54.7 et seq.**

WARRANTIES
Motor Vehicles, this index

WARRANTS
Arrest, this index
Child support hearing officers, failure of party or witness to appear, **Rule 5:25–3**
Children and minors, abuse, abandonment, **9:6–8**
Commencement of prosecution, **2C:1–6**
Commitment of fugitive arrested before requisition made, **2A:160–23**
Complaint warrant, procedure after arrest, **Rule 3:4–1**
Controlled Substances, this index
Discovery, crimes and offenses, **Rule 3:13–3**
Expungement, records, **2C:52–1 et seq.**
Extradition, this index
Issuance, limitation of criminal prosecutions, **2C:1–6**
Juvenile family crisis hearing appearance, **Rule 5:17–1**
Limitation of criminal prosecutions, warrant issuance, **2C:1–6**
Material witness. Witnesses, this index
Motor Vehicle Security Responsibility Law, proceedings for violation, **39:6–55**
Motor vehicles, impoundment or immobilization, parking offenses, **39:4–139.13**
Municipal Courts, this index
Parole, this index
Records, expungement, **2C:52–1 et seq.**
Search Warrants, generally, this index
State polices power to execute, **53:2–1**

WARREN COUNTY
See, also, Counties, generally, this index
Highways and roads, commercial vehicles, **39:4–197.8**

WASTE OF TIME
Evidence, exclusion, **Evidence Rule 403**

WASTE (REFUSE)
Hazardous Substances and Waste, generally, this index
Solid Waste, generally, this index

WATCHMEN
Fireworks plants, **21:2–10**

WATER DISTRIBUTION OR SUPPLY SYSTEMS
Water Supply Plants and Systems, generally, this index

WATER ICE
Frozen Desserts and Dietary Foods, generally, this index

WATER PLANTS OR WORKS
Water Supply Plants and Systems, generally, this index

WATER POLLUTION
Assessment, violation of Water Pollution Control Act, **58:10A–10 et seq.**
Coastal protection license plate program, **39:3–27.47 et seq.**
Crimes and offenses, Water Pollution Control Act, **58:10A–10**
Fines and penalties,
  Spill compensation, **58:10–23.11u**
  Water Pollution Control Act, **58:10A–10**
Injunctions,
  Spill compensation and control, petroleum, **58:10–23.11u**
  Water Pollution Control Act, **58:10A–10**
Penalty enforcement law, spill compensation, **58:10–23.11u**

WATER PURIFICATION OR TREATMENT PLANTS
Crimes and offenses, unlicensed entry of structure, facilities, **2C:18–3**
Trespass, unlicensed entry of structure, facilities, crimes and offenses, **2C:18–3**
Unlicensed entry of structure, facilities, crimes and offenses, **2C:18–3**

WATER QUALITY
Water Pollution, generally, this index

WATER SUPPLY FACILITIES
Water Supply Plants and Systems, generally, this index

WATER SUPPLY PLANTS AND SYSTEMS
Computers, interference, crimes and offenses, **2C:20–25**
Crimes and offenses, trespass, unlicensed entry of structure, **2C:18–3**
Criminal mischief, **2C:17–3**
Theft of services, **2C:20–8**
Trespass, unlicensed entry of structure, crimes and offenses, **2C:18–3**
Unlicensed entry of structure, crimes and offenses, **2C:18–3**
Water Pollution, generally, this index

WATERCRAFT
Vessels, generally, this index

WATERS AND WATERCOURSES
Adopt a beach program. Beaches and Beach Fronts, this index
All terrain vehicles, **39:3C–1 et seq.**
Boats and Boating, generally, this index
Bridges and Viaducts, generally, this index
Fish and Game, generally, this index
Quality. Water Pollution, generally, this index
Snowmobiles, **39:3C–1 et seq.**
State police, powers and duties, **53:2–1**
Supply. Water Supply Plants and Systems, generally, this index
Supply plants and systems. Water Supply Plants and Systems, generally, this index
Viaducts. Bridges and Viaducts, generally, this index
Water Pollution, generally, this index
Water Supply Plants and Systems, generally, this index

WATERWORKS
Water Supply Plants and Systems, generally, this index

WAYS
Highways and Roads, generally, this index
Streets and Alleys, generally, this index

WEAPONS
Generally, **2A:155–1** et seq., **2C:39–1** et seq., **2C:58–1** et seq.
Advertisements, machine guns or semiautomatic rifles, **2C:39–15**
Agents, wholesale dealers, licenses, **2C:58–1**
Aggravated assault, **2C:12–1**
Persons convicted of, possession, **2C:39–7**
Aggravated criminal sexual contact, **2C:14–3**
Aggravated sexual assault, **2C:14–2**
Aircraft, visual distress signaling devices, **2C:39–6**, **2C:58–3**, **2C:58–10**
Aliens, violations of law, reports, **2C:58–9**
Ammunition, generally, this index
Antique Firearms, generally, this index
Appeal and review,
Handguns, licenses and permits, **2C:58–3**
Registration, **2C:58–1**
Armor piercing ammunition, possession, **2C:39–3**
Arrest warrant, issuance, **Rule 3:3–1**
Arrest without warrant, release, **Rule 3:4–1**
Arson, persons convicted of, possession, **2C:39–7**
Assault, aggravated assault, **2C:12–1**
Assault Firearms, generally, this index
Assembling, crimes and offenses, **2C:39–14**
Atomic energy, power plants, guards, possession, **2C:39–3**, **2C:39–6**
Biological warfare and weapons, terrorism, **2C:38–2**, **2C:38–3**
Boats, visual distress signaling devices, **2C:39–6**, **2C:58–3**, **2C:58–10**
Bodily injury, reports, **2C:58–8**
Body cavity searches, **2A:161A–1** et seq.
Burglary, **2C:18–2**
Persons convicted of, possession, **2C:39–7**
Cannons, antique cannons, **2C:39–1** et seq.
Possession, **2C:39–6**
Chemical and biological warfare and weapons, terrorism, **2C:38–2**, **2C:38–3**
Chemicals, chemistry and chemists, repellent, lawful possession, **2C:39–6**
Children and minors,
Crimes and offenses, illegal sale or transfer to minors, **2C:39–10**
Handcuffs, sale to, **2C:39–9.2**
Knives, sales to, **2C:39–9.1**
Leaving within easy reach, **2C:58–15**
Possession, **2C:58–6.1**
Purchases, **2C:58–3**
Sale or transfer, **2C:39–10**
Collectors, multiple purchases, **2C:58–3.4**
Colleges and universities, possession, **2C:39–5**
Community guns, possession for unlawful purposes, **2C:39–4**
Confidential or privileged information, waiver, **2C:58–3**
Controlled dangerous substances, crimes and offenses, consecutive sentences, **2C:39–4.1**
Conviction of crime, possession of any weapon prohibited, **2C:39–7**
Copies, registers, sales, **2C:58–2**
Corrections officer, disarming, criminal offense, **2C:12–11**
Dealers,
Crimes and offenses, **2C:39–10**
Personalized handguns, **2C:58–2.5**
Licenses and permits, **2C:58–2**, **2C:58–3**
Possession, **2C:39–3**
Records and recordation, **2C:58–2**
Trigger locks, **2C:58–17**

WEAPONS—Cont'd
Dealers—Cont'd
Reimbursement, trigger locks, **2C:58–17**
Sales, generally, post
Trigger locks, **2C:58–2**
Records and recordation, **2C:58–17**
Defaced firearms, crimes and offenses, **2C:39–3**, **2C:39–9**
Defacement, this index
Defenses, knives, sales to children and minors, **2C:39–9.1**
Definitions, **2C:39–1**
Personalized handguns, **2C:39–1**
Delivery, sales, limitations, **2C:58–2**
Demonstrating, crimes and offenses, **2C:39–14**
Destructive devices, possession for unlawful purposes, **2C:39–4**
Disarming a law enforcement or corrections officer, criminal offense, **2C:12–11**
Domestic Violence, this index
Escapes, this index
Exemptions, **2C:39–6**
Multiple purchases, **2C:58–3.4**
Personalized handguns, **2C:58–2.4**, **2C:58–2.5**
Sales, delivery, limitations, **2C:58–2**, **2C:58–3**
Explosives, generally, this index
Extortion, persons convicted of, possession, **2C:39–7**
False statements, sales, **2C:39–10**
Fees,
Licenses and permits, **2C:58–3**
Retail dealers and employees, **2C:58–2**
Registration, **2C:58–1**
Fines and penalties, **2C:39–4.1**
Personalized handguns, sales, **2C:58–2.5**
Reduction of sentence, **2C:43–6.2**, **2C:43–6.3**
Reports, theft, lost property, **2C:58–19**
Fingerprints and fingerprinting, handguns, purchases, **2C:58–3**
Firearms purchaser identification card, **2C:58–3**
Firearms training course,
Arson investigators, lawful possession, **2C:39–6**
Parole officers, lawful possession, **2C:39–6**
Fish and Game, this index
Forfeited weapons, donations, **2C:64–9**
Forfeiture, unlawful use, **2C:64–1**
Forms, registration, **2C:58–1**
Hearings, exemptions, multiple purchases, **2C:58–3.4**
Heirs, probate proceedings, **2C:58–3**
Homicide, persons convicted of, possession, **2C:39–7**
Housing authority police force, cities of first class, **2C:39–6**
Human services department, police officers, lawful possession, **2C:39–6**
Humane law enforcement officers, possession, **2C:39–6**
Identification cards,
False statements, **2C:39–10**
Retail sales, **2C:58–3**
Retired law enforcement officers, **2C:39–6**
Identity and identification, personalized handguns, **2C:58–2.2** et seq.
Illegal sale or transfer to minor,
Crimes and offenses, **2C:39–10**
Possession by certain persons, second degree crime, **2C:39–7**
Probation, **2C:43–6.2**
Imitation firearms,
Definitions, **2C:39–1**
Extended term of imprisonment, **2C:43–7**
Person convicted of crime involving, possession of any weapon prohibited, **2C:39–7**
Possession, **2C:39–4**

WEAPONS—Cont'd
Imitation firearms—Cont'd
Possession—Cont'd
Extended term of imprisonment, **2C:43–7**, **2C:43–7.1**
Inspection and inspectors, sales records, **2C:58–1**
Instructors, temporary transfers, training, **2C:58–3.2**
Interference with transportation, **2C:33–14**
Jurisdiction, juvenile delinquents and dependents, **2C:58–6.1**
Juvenile Delinquents, this index
KeepSafe program, trigger locks, rebates, **2C:58–17**
Reports, **2C:58–18**
Kidnapping, persons convicted of, **2C:39–7**
Large capacity ammunition magazine,
Definitions, **2C:39–1**
Manufacture, sale, unlawful purpose, fourth degree crime, **2C:39–9**
Possession, crime of fourth degree, exception, registered assault firearm, **2C:39–3**
Law Enforcement Officers, this index
Leader of a firearms trafficking network, definition and classification of offense, **2C:39–16**
Legal owner, definitions, temporary transfer and possession, **2C:58–3.1**
Licenses and permits, **2C:39–9**, **2C:58–1** et seq.
Agents, wholesale dealers, **2C:58–1**
Applications, false statements, **2C:39–10**
Children and minors, **2C:58–6.1**
Dealers, **2C:58–2**, **2C:58–3**
Employee of armored car company, **2C:58–4.1**
Identification cards, applications, false statements, **2C:39–10**
Manufacturers, **2C:58–1**
Presumptions, **2C:39–2**
Purchases, **2C:58–3**
Retail dealers and employees, **2C:58–2**
Revocation, **2C:58–1**
Wholesale dealers, **2C:58–1**
Limitations, delivery, sales, **2C:58–2**
Lists, personalized handguns, **2C:58–2.4**
Loans, pawnbrokers, security, **2C:39–11**
Lost property, reports, **2C:58–19**
Machine Guns, generally, this index
Mandatory sentence, possession, **2C:43–6**
Review, **2C:43–6.1**, **2C:43–6.3**
Manufacturers and manufacturing, **2C:39–9**
Personalized handguns, **2C:58–2.4**, **2C:58–2.5**
Regulatory provisions, violations, **2C:39–10**
Transport, disposition and defacement, **2C:39–9**
Violations, **2C:39–10**
Mentally deficient and mentally ill persons,
Firearms, permits to persons confined for mental disorder, **2C:58–3**
Possession, **2C:39–7**
Minors. Children and minors, generally, ante
Motor vehicles,
Possession presumption, **2C:39–2**
Transportation, **2C:39–6**
Multiple purchases, **2C:58–3**, **2C:58–3.4**
National guard militia museum, forfeited weapons, donation, **2C:64–9**
Notice,
Personalized handguns, lists, **2C:58–2.4**
Trigger locks, rebates, **2C:58–17**
Voluntary surrender, **2C:39–12**
Nuclear or radiological devices, terrorism, **2C:38–2**, **2C:38–3**
Pawnbrokers, selling or accepting as security, **2C:39–11**

WEAPONS—Cont'd

Permits. Licenses and permits, generally, ante
Personal injuries, reports, **2C:58–8**
Personalized handguns, **2C:58–2.2 et seq.**
   Definitions, **2C:39–1**
Pistol grip, definitions, **2C:39–1**
Poisons, terrorism, **2C:38–3**
Police and Police Departments, this index
Possession, **2C:39–1 et seq.**
   Certain persons not to have, **2C:39–7**
   Controlled dangerous substances, convic-
     tions, consecutive sentences, **2C:39–4.1**
   Crimes and offenses, **2C:39–3**
   Domestic violence prevention, prohibition,
     release conditions, **2C:25–26**
   Extended term of imprisonment, **2C:43–7,
     2C:43–7.1**
   Juvenile delinquents and dependents, juris-
     diction, waiver, **2A:4A–26**
   Mandatory sentence, **2C:43–6**
   Personalized handguns, **2C:58–2.4, 2C:58–2.5**
   Presumptions, **2C:39–2**
   Second and subsequent offenses, **2C:44–3**
   Sentence and punishment, **2C:39–7, 2C:43–6**
   Temporary transfers, training, **2C:58–3.2**
   Training, temporary transfers, **2C:58–3.2**
   Transfers, training, **2C:58–3.2**
   Unlawful purposes, **2C:39–4, 2C:39–5**
     Person convicted of crime involving, pos-
       session of any weapon prohibited,
       2C:39–7
Posting, trigger locks, rebates, **2C:58–17**
Presumptions, **2C:39–2**
Privileges and immunities, voluntary surrender,
   2C:39–12
Probate proceedings, heirs, **2C:58–3**
   Multiple purchases, **2C:58–3.4**
Probation,
   Conditions, **2C:45–1**
   Firearms, illegal sale or transfer to minors,
     2C:43–6.2
   Reduction of sentence, **2C:43–6.2, 2C:43–6.3**
Probation officers community safety units,
   2C:39–6
Prohibited weapons and devices, **2C:39–3**
   Person convicted of crime involving, posses-
     sion of any weapon prohibited, **2C:39–7**
Purchase, **2C:58–3**
Racketeers and racketeering, **2C:41–1 et seq.**
Radioactive substances, terrorism, **2C:38–2,
   2C:38–3**
Rebates, trigger locks, **2C:58–17**
   Reports, **2C:58–18**
Records and recordation,
   Manufacturers or wholesale dealers, sales,
     2C:58–1
   Retail dealers, **2C:58–2**
   Sales, **2C:58–1, 2C:58–2**
   Trigger locks, **2C:58–17**
Reduction of sentence, crimes committed with,
   2C:43–6.2, 2C:43–6.3
Registers, sales, **2C:58–2**
Registration, **2C:39–9, 2C:58–1**
   Manufacturers or wholesale dealers, **2C:58–1**
Regulatory provisions, violations, **2C:39–10**
Reimbursement, dealers, trigger locks,
   2C:58–17
Reports,
   Aliens, convictions, **2C:58–9**
   Motor vehicles apparently struck by bullet,
     duty of garageman or repairman,
     39:4–132
   Personalized handguns, **2C:58–2.3**
   Theft, lost property, **2C:58–19**
   Trigger locks, rebates, **2C:58–18**
   Wounds, **2C:58–8**

WEAPONS—Cont'd

Rifle, temporary transfer and possession,
   2C:58–3.1
Riots, **2C:33–1**
Robbery,
   Persons convicted of, possession, **2C:39–7**
   Use, **2C:15–1**
Rules and regulations, sales, **2C:58–2.1**
Sales, **2C:58–2**
   Crimes and offenses, **2C:39–10**
   Firearms purchaser identification card,
     2C:58–3
   Handcuffs, children and minors, **2C:39–9.2**
   Knives, children and minors, **2C:39–9.1**
   Personalized handguns, **2C:58–2.4, 2C:58–2.5**
   Records and recordation, **2C:58–2**
     Inspection, **2C:58–1**
   Regulatory provisions, violations, **2C:39–10**
   Unlawful possession, exemption, **2C:39–6**
   Violations, **2C:39–10**
   Warnings concerning loaded firearms and
     minors, failure to deliver or post,
     2C:58–16
Sawed off shotguns,
   Possession, crimes and offenses, **2C:39–3**
   Purchase, **2C:58–3**
Schools and School Districts, this index
Searches and seizures, personal searches,
   2A:161A–1 et seq.
Second and subsequent offenses, possession of
   firearm, **2C:44–3**
Security, pawnbrokers, loans, **2C:39–11**
Semiautomatic, definitions, **2C:39–1**
Semiautomatic rifles, advertisements, **2C:39–15**
Sexual assault, persons convicted of, **2C:39–7**
Signatures, registers, sales, **2C:58–2**
Special police, carrying, **2C:39–6**
State police, personalized handguns, **2C:58–2.5**
Statements, false statements, **2C:39–10**
Strip searches, **2A:161A–1 et seq.**
Surrender, voluntary surrender, **2C:39–12**
Suspended sentences, conditions, **2C:45–1**
Teaching, demonstrating or assembling, crimes
   and offenses, **2C:39–14**
Tear gas, lawful possession, **2C:39–6**
Temporary transfers, **2C:58–3.1**
   Training, **2C:58–3.2**
Terrorism, this index
Tests and testing, personalized handguns,
   2C:58–2.4
Theft, **2C:20–2**
   Reports, **2C:58–19**
Trafficking network, leaders, crimes and of-
   fenses, **2C:39–16**
Training, **2C:39–14**
   Arson investigators, lawful possession,
     2C:39–6
   Racketeers and racketeering, **2C:41–1 et seq.**
   Temporary transfers, **2C:58–3.1, 2C:58–3.2**
Transfers,
   Temporary transfer and possession,
     2C:58–3.1
   Training, **2C:58–3.2**
Transportation, **2C:39–6, 2C:39–9**
Trigger locks,
   Dealers, **2C:58–2**
     Records and recordation, **2C:58–17**
   Handguns, **2C:58–2**
   Rebates, **2C:58–17**
     Reports, **2C:58–18**
Unlawful possession, **2C:39–5**
Visual distress signaling devices, aircraft or
   boats, **2C:39–6, 2C:58–3, 2C:58–10**
Voluntary surrender, **2C:39–12**
Wholesale dealers, registration, **2C:58–1**

WEAPONS—Cont'd

Wholesale sales, warnings concerning loaded
   firearms and minors, failure to deliver or
   post, **2C:58–16**
Wounds, reports, **2C:58–8**

WEIGHT LIMITATION ACT (HIGHWAYS)
Generally, **39:3–84 et seq.**

WEIGHTS AND MEASURES
Crimes and offenses, deceptive business prac-
   tices, **2C:21–7**
Deceptive business practices, **2C:21–7**
Fines and penalties, overweight motor vehicles,
   driving over bridge, **39:4–75, 39:4–76**
Loads and Loading, generally, this index
Motor Carriers, this index
Motor Vehicles, this index
Tow trucks and towing companies, **39:3–84**

WEIGHTS AND MEASURES DEPARTMENT
Superintendents. Liquefied Petroleum Gas,
   generally, this index

WELFARE
Indigent Persons, generally, this index

WELL DRILLERS
Traction or tractor well drilling equipment,
   Licensing of, **39:3–26**
   Operation on highways, **39:3–80**

WELLS
Hazards, abandoned wells or cesspools,
   2C:40–1

WET HEMP
Turnpike project, transportation regulations,
   27:23–31

WETLANDS
Adopt a beach program. Beaches and Beach
   Fronts, this index

WHEELCHAIRS
Motor vehicle license plates, fees, **39:4–206**
Motor vehicles, securing, **39:3–76.2l,
   39:3–76.2m**
National wheelchair symbol, license plates, motor vehicles, motorcycles, handicapped
   person, **39:4–206**

WHEELS
Motor Vehicles, this index

WHIPPED CREAM CONFECTION
Frozen Desserts and Dietary Foods, generally,
   this index

WHIPS
Horses, **39:4–24**

WHISKEY
Alcoholic Beverages, generally, this index

WHISTLES
Bicycle not to be equipped with, **39:3–69,
   39:4–11**
Stopping vehicles on signal by police whistle,
   39:4–122
Use on vehicles other than emergency vehicles
   prohibited, **39:3–69**

WHITE LIGHT
Illumination of rear registration marker on motor vehicle, **39:3–61**

WHOLESALE DEALERS
Definitions, firearms, 2C:39–1
Firearms,
Registration, 2C:58–1
Regulatory provisions, violations, 2C:39–10

WHOLESALERS
Alcoholic Beverages, this index
Definitions, intoxicating liquor law, 33:1–1
Weapons, generally, this index

WIDESPREAD INJURY OR DAMAGE
Definitions, 2C:17–2

WIDTH
Farm tractors, maximum width and length,
39:3–84
Motor Carriers, this index
Motor vehicles, maximum, 39:3–84
Passageway opposite standing vehicle, 39:4–136
Private utility or house type semitrailers and
trailers, 39:3–8

WIFE AND HUSBAND
Spouses, generally, this index

WILD ANIMALS
Fish and Game, generally, this index

WILDLIFE
Fish and Game, generally, this index

WILLS
Fiduciaries, generally, this index
Fraud, will instruments, 2C:21–3
Intoxicating liquors, disposal of retail license by
will, Chain Store Liquor License Act,
33:1–12.32
Motor vehicle, spouse or child, transfer of reg-
istration, 39:3–30
Probate Proceedings, generally, this index

WINDOW PEEPING
Crimes and offenses, 2C:18–3

WINDOWS
Breaking and entry in execution of search warrant under alcoholic beverage law, 33:1–58
Safety glass required on motor vehicles,
39:3–75
Stickers, not to be placed on windows of motor
vehicles, 39:3–74

WINDSHIELDS
Definition, 39:3–75
Fines and penalties, tinted windshields,
39:3–75.3
Motorcycles, 39:3–76.9
Photosensitivity, tinted windshields, 39:3–75.1
et seq.
Stickers or other nontransparent material on
prohibited, 39:3–74
Tinted windshields, photosensitivity, 39:3–75.1
et seq.
Wiper or cleaning device required, 39:3–74

WINE
Blended wine,
Presumption, fitness for beverage purposes
and alcoholic content, 33:1–1.1
Wholesalers license, 33:1–11
Farm winery licenses, 33:1–10, 33:1 App.
Sales, fermented wines and fruit juices,
33:1–10
Fortified wine,
Presumption, fitness for beverage purposes
and alcoholic content, 33:1–1.1

WINE—Cont'd
Fortified wine—Cont'd
Wholesalers license, 33:1–11
Licenses and permits. Wineries, post
Manufacture, sale, poisoned liquors, 33:3–9,
33:3–10
Municipal referendum on retail sales of bever-
ages, 33:1–44
Naturally fermented wine,
Presumption, fitness for beverage purposes
and alcoholic content, 33:1–1.1
Wholesalers license, 33:1–11
On and off premises consumption, sales,
33:1–40.3
Sampling parties, 33:1–12
Special permits, manufacture for personal con-
sumption, 33:1–75
Tasting parties, 33:1–12
Treated wines, presumption, fitness for bever-
age purposes and alcoholic content,
33:1–1.1
Wholesalers license, 33:1–11
Wineries,
Blending licenses, 33:1–10, 33:1 App.
Crimes and offenses,
Interest by wholesaler, 33:1–43a
Persons interested in wholesaling or retail-
ing, 33:1–43
Farm winery licenses, 33:1–10, 33:1 App.
Interest by wholesaler, 33:1–43, 33:1–43a
Licenses and permits, 33:1–10
Bottling without license, 33:1–78
Persons interested in retailing, 33:1–43
Wholesale license, 33:1–11
Wholesaling, interest in, 33:1–43

WINGS
Stickers, not to be placed on motor vehicles,
39:3–74
Windshield of motor vehicle as including,
39:3–75

WIRE COMMUNICATION
Definitions, 2A:156A–2

WIRE SERVICE
Definitions, privileged communications,
2A:84A–21a
News personnel privilege, 2A:84A–21a
Newspersons, information disclosure privilege,
criminal proceedings, 2A:84A–21.1 et seq.
Privileges and immunities, Evidence Rule 508

WIRELESS TELEPHONES
Telecommunications, this index

WIRES
Moving heavy machinery, highway, change or
repair of overhead wires, 39:4–28
Street Railways, this index

**WIRETAPPING AND ELECTRONIC SUR-
VEILLANCE**
Generally, 2A:156A–1 et seq.
Access,
Requirements, 2A:156A–29
Stored communications, crimes and offenses,
2A:156A–27
Actions and proceedings,
Civil actions, 2A:156A–32
Defenses, 2A:156A–33
Attorney general, consent, 2A:156A–4
Backup preservation, 2A:156A–30
Civil actions, 2A:156A–32
Communications relating to other offenses, in-
terception of, disclosure, 2A:156A–18

**WIRETAPPING AND ELECTRONIC SUR-
VEILLANCE**—Cont'd
Computers,
Remote computing services, 2A:156A–12
Trespass, 2A:156A–4.1
Consent, 2A:156A–4
Cost reimbursement, law enforcement agency
obtaining contents of communications,
2A:156A–31
County prosecutors, consent, 2A:156A–4
Definitions, 2A:156A–2
Emergency situations, authority to grant verbal
approval for interception without order,
2A:156A–13
Encoded messages, 2A:156A–12
Evidence, computers, trespass, 2A:156A–4.1
Foreign languages, 2A:156A–12
Intercepted communications, recording,
2A:156A–14
Intercepting devices, possession or sale,
Crimes and offenses, 2A:156A–5
Exceptions, 2A:156A–6
Seizure, 2A:156A–7
Orders, 2A:156A–8 et seq.
Application for order, contents, 2A:156A–7
Contents and limitations, 2A:156A–12
Ex parte order, entry by judge, interception
of wire, electronic or oral communica-
tion, 2A:156A–10
Grounds for entry of order, 2A:156A–10
Unlawful use or disclosure, 2A:156A–19
Verbal approval without order, authority to
grant, emergency situations, 2A:156A–13
Organized crime, 2A:156A–1 et seq.
Parties, consent, 2A:156A–4
Privileged communications, public facilities or
facilities of persons entitled to,
2A:156A–11
Radio and radio stations, crimes and offenses,
exceptions, 2A:156A–4
Records and recording, intercepted communi-
cations, 2A:156A–14
Remedies, exclusivity of remedies, 2A:156A–34
Remote computing services, 2A:156A–12
Sealing of applications, orders and supporting
documents, 2A:156A–15
Search warrants, issuance based on wiretap,
filing, Rule 3:5–6
Stored communication,
Disclosure of contents, 2A:156A–28
Unlawful access, 2A:156A–27
Unlawful access, stored communications,
2A:156A–27
Wire, electronic or oral communications,
Contents of intercepted communications or
derivative evidence,
Disclosure or use, 2A:156A–15
Copy of order and application, service,
2A:156A–20
Motion to suppress, 2A:156A–21
Crimes and offenses,
Disclosure, 2A:156A–3
Exceptions, 2A:156A–4
Interception, 2A:156A–3

**WIRETAPPING AND ELECTRONIC SUR-
VEILLANCE CONTROL ACT**
Generally, 2A:156A–1 et seq.

**WITHHOLDING OF MEDICALLY INDICAT-
ED TREATMENT**
Definitions, Comprehensive Child Abuse Pre-
vention and Treatment Act, 9:6–8.84

WITNESSES

Abuse of children, closed circuit testimony, **2A:84A–32.4**

Aggravated criminal sexual contact, children and minors, closed circuit testimony, **2A:84A–32.4**

Aggravated sexual assault, children and minors, closed circuit testimony, **2A:84A–32.4**

Alcoholic beverages, power to compel attendance, **33:1–35**

Anatomically correct dolls, sex offenses, children and minors, **2A:84A–16.1**

Appeal and review, abuse of children, closed circuit testimony, **2A:84A–32.4**

Attendance of witness, subpoenas, **Rule 1:9–1**

Attorneys, disciplinary hearings, immunity from liability, **Rule 1:20–7**

Bail, **Rule 3:26–3**
  Failure to appear, commitment, deposition, **Rule 3:13–2**

Bribery, tampering with, **2C:28–5**

Calling by judge, **Evidence Rule 614**

Character evidence, **Evidence Rule 404**
  Methods of proving, **Evidence Rule 405**

Character for truthfulness or untruthfulness, **Evidence Rule 608**

Child Abuse, this index

Children and Minors, this index

Clergymen, privileges, **2A:84A–23**

Closed circuit testimony, abuse of children, **2A:84A–32.4**

Compelling attendance of witnesses,
  Alcoholic beverage control director, **33:1–35**
  Motor vehicle tort claim arbitrations, **39:6A–29**
  Subpoenas, generally, this index

Competency, **Evidence Rule 601**

Contempt, protection orders, **2C:29–9**

Convenience, juvenile delinquents and dependents, change of venue, **Rule 5:19–1**

Conviction of crime, impeaching credibility, **Evidence Rule 609**

Crimes and offenses,
  Accused, right not to be called as witness or testify, **2A:84A–17**
  Alibi defense, notice, **Rule 3:12–2**
  Bail, **Rule 3:26–3**
  Conditions of release or detention, **Rule 3:26–3**
  Depositions, **Rule 3:13–2**
    Possibly unavailable witness, **Rule 3:26–3**
  Discovery, **Rule 3:13–3**
  Evidence, deposition, use, **Rule 3:13–2**
  Immediate detention warrants, **Rule 3:26–3**
  Informers identity, disclosure, **2A:84A–28**
  Newspersons, information disclosure privilege, **2A:84A–21.1 et seq.**
  Orders to appear, **Rule 3:26–3**
  Search warrants, applicants, **Rule 3:5–3**
  Specific criminal code defenses, refusing presentation, **Rule 3:12–1**
  Subpoena, failure, deposition, use, **Rule 3:13–2**
  Trial witness hearings, **Rule 3:26–3**

Criminal sexual contact, children and minors, closed circuit testimony, **2A:84A–32.4**

Custody, juvenile justice, jurisdiction, **2A:4A–24**

Death, criminal proceedings, deposition, **Rule 3:13–2**

Depositions, generally, this index

Discovery, generally, this index

Dolls and models, anatomically correct dolls, sex offenses against children, **2A:84A–16.1**

Elections, this index

Examinations, self incrimination, **2A:84A–19**

WITNESSES—Cont'd

Exemptions. Privileges and immunities, generally, post

Exhibiting drivers license and registration certificate of vehicle involved in accident, **39:4–129**

Experts. Opinion or expert testimony, generally, post

False accusations, prior false accusations, character for truthfulness or untruthfulness, **Evidence Rule 608**

Fees,
  Acquittals, **2A:166–8**
  Motor vehicle director, attendance before, **39:5–30**
  Subpoenas, **Rule 1:9–3**
    Criminal actions, witness for state or indigent defendants, **Rule 1:9–1**

Grand jury,
  Statements of investigation, **2B:21–9**
  Swearing of witness by foreperson, **2B:21–6**

Harassment or embarrassment, prevention, **Evidence Rule 611**

Immunity from liability, attorney disciplinary proceedings, **Rule 1:20–7**

Impeachment, conviction of crime, **2C:51–1**

Indigent persons, neglected or abandoned children, sexual abuse, closed circuit testimony, **2A:84A–32.4**

Informers identity, disclosure, **2A:84A–28**

Interrogation,
  By judge, **Evidence Rule 614**
  Jury and jurors, **Rule 1:8–8**
  Mode and order, **Evidence Rule 611**

Intimidation, protection orders, **2C:28–5.1 et seq.**

Judges, **Evidence Rule 605**
  Calling and interrogation of witnesses, **Evidence Rule 614**

Jurisdiction, custody, juvenile justice, **2A:4A–24**

Jury and jurors, **Evidence Rule 606**
  Questions, **Rule 1:8–8**

Juvenile Delinquents, this index

Lawyer client privilege, **2A:84A–20**

Leading questions, **Evidence Rule 611**

Material witness,
  Appeal and review, material witness order, **2C:104–9**
  Arrest,
    With warrant, **2C:104–4**
    Without warrant, **2C:104–5**
  Conditions of release, **2C:104–7**
  Confinement, **2C:104–7**
  Definitions, **2C:104–1**
  Deposition, **2C:104–8**
  Hearing, **2C:104–6**
  Juvenile proceedings, detention, **Rule 5:21–8**
  Material witness order,
    Appealable, **2C:104–9**
    Application, contents, **2C:104–2**
    Definitions, **2C:104–1**
  Order to appear, **2C:104–3**
  Payment, confinement, **2C:104–7**

Mediation, complementary dispute resolution programs, **Rule 1:40–4**

Mileage, motor vehicle director, attendance before, **39:5–30**

Motions, abuse of children, closed circuit testimony, **2A:84A–32.4**

Motor vehicles,
  Compelling attendance, **39:4–7**
    Tort claim arbitrations, **39:6A–29**
  Title papers, **39:10–8**

Neutralization of testimony, **Evidence Rule 607**

WITNESSES—Cont'd

Newspersons,
  Information disclosure privilege, **2A:84A–21.1 et seq.**
  Privileged communications, **2A:84A–21**

Oaths and affirmations, **Evidence Rule 603**
  Alcoholic Beverage Law proceedings, **33:1–35**

Official information, state or United States, disclosure, **2A:84A–27**

Opinion or expert testimony, **Evidence Rule 702 et seq.**
  Basis of opinion, **Evidence Rule 703**
  Character and reputation, **Evidence Rule 608**
    Methods of proving, **Evidence Rule 405**
  Crimes and offenses, discovery, **Rule 3:13–3**
  Disclosure, facts or data underlying opinion, **Evidence Rule 705**
  Hearsay statement, inclusion in, admissibility, **Evidence Rule 808**
  Hypothetical questions, **Evidence Rule 705**
  Lay witnesses, **Evidence Rule 701**
  Mental condition of defendant, **2C:4–6**
  Ultimate issue, **Evidence Rule 704**
  Underlying facts, disclosure, **Evidence Rule 705**

Overruling claim of privilege, effect of error, **2A:84A–32**

Perjury, generally, this index

Personal knowledge and experience, **Evidence Rule 602**

Political vote, compelling disclosure, **2A:84A–25**

Presumption, exercise of privileges, **2A:84A–31**

Prior false accusations, character for truthfulness or untruthfulness, **Evidence Rule 608**

Prior statements, **Evidence Rules 607, 613**
  Hearsay exceptions, **Evidence Rule 803**

Privileges and immunities, **2A:84A–19**
  Accused, **2A:84A–17**
  Admissibility of disclosure wrongfully compelled, **2A:84A–30**
  Clergymen, **2A:84A–23**
  Comments on exercise of privileges, **2A:84A–31**
  Husband and wife, **2A:84A–17**
  Identity of informer, disclosure, **2A:84A–28**
  Lawyer client privilege, **2A:84A–20**
  Magazines, news personnel, **2A:84A–21, 2A:84A–21a**
  Marital privilege, **2A:84A–22**
  Newspaperman, information disclosure privilege, criminal proceedings, **2A:84A–21.1 et seq.**
  Official information of state or United States, disclosure, **2A:84A–27**
  Overruling claim of privilege, effect of error, **2A:84A–32**
  Physician and patients, **2A:84A–22.1 et seq.**
  Political votes, **2A:84A–25**
  Press association, news personnel, **2A:84A–21, 2A:84A–21a**
  Radio news personnel, **2A:84A–21, 2A:84A–21a**
  Religious belief, **2A:84A–24**
  Self incrimination, **2A:84A–18, 2A:84A–19**
  Television, news personnel, **2A:84A–21, 2A:84A–21a**
  Trade secrets, **2A:84A–26**
  Waiver, **2A:84A–29**
  Wire services, news personnel, **2A:84A–21, 2A:84A–21a**

Process. Subpoenas, generally, this index

Qualifications, **Evidence Rule 104**

Radio news personnel, **2A:84A–21, 2A:84A–21a**

Rape, previous sexual conduct of complainant, admissibility, **2A:84A–32.1 et seq.**

WITNESSES—Cont'd

Recall, substituted judge, previous judge disqualified or unable to hear manner, **Rule 1:12–3**

Recognizances, generally, this index

Refreshing memory, use of writings, **Evidence Rule 612**

Religion, this index

Retaliation, tampering with, 2C:28–5

Sequestration, **Evidence Rule 615**

Sex offenses, children and minors,

Anatomically correct dolls or models, 2A:84A–16.1

Closed circuit testimony, 2A:84A–32.4

Specific instances of conduct, character evidence, **Evidence Rule 608**

Spouses, privileges and immunities, 2A:84A–17

States, official information, disclosure, 2A:84A–27

Subpoenas, generally, this index

Summoning, director of motor vehicles, **39:5–30**

Support proceedings, 2C:62–1

Suppression or tampering, hindering apprehension or prosecution, 2C:29–3

Tampering, 2C:28–5

Apprehension or prosecution, 2C:29–3

Protective orders, 2C:28–5.1 et seq.

Television, news personnel, 2A:84A–21, 2A:84A–21a

Threats, protection orders, 2C:28–5.1 et seq.

Trade secrets, disclosure, 2A:84A–26

Truthful character, **Evidence Rule 608**

United States, official information, disclosure, 2A:84A–27

Untruthful character, **Evidence Rule 608**

Victims and witness advocacy fund, 2C:43–3.1

Videotaped testimony, abuse of children, 2A:84A–32.4

Voluntary testimony by accused or party, subsequent privilege, 2A:84A–19

Waiver of privilege, 2A:84A–29

Wire services, news personnel, 2A:84A–21, 2A:84A–21a

Writings, refreshing memory, **Evidence Rule 612**

WOMEN

Alcoholic beverages, warning notices, pregnant women, harmful effects, class C licenses, 33:1–12a

Fines, 33:1–12b

Pregnancy, generally, this index

Prostitution, generally, this index

Rape, generally, this index

Sex offenses, female offenders, 2C:47–4.2

WORDS AND PHRASES

Abandon, vulnerable adults, crimes and offenses, 2C:24–8

Abstract, motor vehicles, 39:10–2

Abused child, 9:6–8.9

Abused or neglected child, 9:6–8.21

Access, computer related offenses, 2C:20–23

Access device, theft, 2C:20–1

Accomplices, Code of Criminal Justice, 2C:2–6

Acquisition, explosives, 21:1A–129

Act,

Code of Criminal Justice, 2C:1–14

Turnpikes, 27:23–4

Act of graffiti, 2A:153–4.1

Criminal mischief, 2C:17–3.1

Criminal offenses, 2C:17–3, 2C:33–24

Railroads, signals and signaling, 2C:33–14.1

WORDS AND PHRASES—Cont'd

Act of violence,

Victim and counselor privilege, **Evidence Rule 517**

Victims, privileged communications, 2A:84A–22.14

Acted, Code of Criminal Justice, 2C:1–14

Action,

Code of Criminal Justice, 2C:1–14

Motor vehicle insurance, valid diagnostic tests, lists, 39:6A–4.7

Actor,

Code of Criminal Justice, 2C:1–14

Manslaughter, 2C:11–4

Sexual offenses, 2C:14–1

Adjudicative processes, complementary dispute resolution, **Rule 1:40–2**

Administer, controlled dangerous substances, 2C:35–2, 24:21–2

Administrative proceeding, bribery and corrupt influence, 2C:27–1

Administrative records, confidential or privileged information, **Rule 1:38–4**

Administrator, water pollution control, 58:10A–3

Adult,

Adult offender supervision, interstate compacts, 2A:168–27

Juvenile justice, 2A:4A–22

Adulterated, deceptive business practices, 2C:21–7

Advertise, kosher food, 2C:21–7.2

Affirmative defenses, 2C:1–13

Agencies, motor vehicle commission, 39:2A–3

Agents,

Code of Criminal Justice, 2C:2–7

Controlled substances, 2C:35–2, 24:21–2

Motor vehicle commission, 39:2A–3

Aggravated assault, 2C:12–1

Aggravated criminal sexual contact, 2C:14–3

Aggravated sexual assault, 2C:14–2

Aggrieved person, wiretapping and electronic surveillance, 2A:156A–2

Agreement in lieu of discipline, attorneys, discipline, **Rule 1:20**

Alcohol, 33:1–1

Alcohol concentration, Commercial Driver License Act, 39:3–10.11

Alcoholic beverages, 33:1–1

All terrain vehicles, registration and regulation of snowmobiles and all terrain vehicles, 39:3C–1

Alley, motor vehicles, 39:1–1

Alter, computer related offenses, 2C:20–23

Amount involved, Code of Criminal Justice, 2C:1–14

Animals, cruelty to animals, 4:22–15

Antique cannon, 2C:39–1

Antique firearm, 2C:39–1

Antique handgun, 2C:39–1

Antique slot machines, 2C:37–7

Antishoplifting or inventory control device countermeasure, shoplifting, 2C:20–11

Any motor vehicle, certificate of ownership, 39:10–2

Anything of value, theft, 2C:20–1

Apportioned vehicle, registration, 39:3–6.11

Appropriate court, detainers, 2A:159A–10

Appropriate identification, handicapped parking, 39:4–207.6

Appropriate victim, motor vehicles, intoxication of driver, 39:4–50

Approved, motor vehicle equipment, 39:3–46

Aquaculture, water pollution, 58:10A–3

Aquatic organism, water pollution, 58:10A–3

WORDS AND PHRASES—Cont'd

Area of highway construction or repair, traffic regulations, 39:4–203.5

Areawide plan, water pollution control, 58:10A–3

Arrest, delinquent children, taking into custody, 2A:4A–31

Articles of wearing apparel, manufacturer, sale, 2A:123–3

Artificial barricade, explosives, 21:1A–129

Assault, 2C:12–1

Assault firearm, 2C:39–1

Assigned funeral insurance policy, embezzlement, prepaid funeral agreements, 2A:102–18

Assignment, motor vehicles, 39:10–2

Association, unsatisfied claim and judgment fund, 39:6–62

Asymmetric headlamps, motor vehicles, 39:3–46

ATP card, crimes and offenses, food stamps, 2C:20–35

Attempt, criminal attempt, 2C:5–1

Attorney,

Abuse of children, 9:6–8.21

Codes of ethics, **Rule 1:14**

Discipline, **Rule 1:20**

Attorney general,

Interstate compacts, crimes and offenses, 53:1–32

Municipal prosecutors, 2B:25–2

Theft, 2C:20–1

Money laundering and illegal investments, 2C:21–24

Racketeering, 2C:41–1

Searches and seizures, news organizations, 2A:84A–21.12

Audiovisual recording function, New Jersey Antipiracy Act, 2C:21–21

Audiovisual work, New Jersey Antipiracy Act, 2C:21–21

Aural transfer, wiretapping and electronic surveillance, 2A:156A–2

Authorities,

Speed, sixty five mph, implementation, 39:4–98.4

Toll collection monitoring system, turnpike authority, 27:23–34.1

Turnpikes, 27:23–4

Authorization, computer related offenses, 2C:20–23

Authorized emergency vehicles, traffic laws, 39:1–1

Auto body repair facilities, 39:13–1

Proof of repair, 39:13–8

Auto or vessel,

Assault by, 2C:12–1

Death by, 2C:11–5

Automobiles,

No fault insurance, 39:6A–2

Traffic laws, 39:1–1

Auxiliary driving lamp, motor vehicles, 39:3–46

Ballistic knife, 2C:39–1

Barricaded, explosives, 21:1A–129

Base jurisdiction, appointed vehicle, registration, 39:3–6.11

Base product, malt beverages, 33:1–93.14

Basic automobile insurance policy, no fault insurance, 39:6A–2

Benefit,

Bribery and corruption, 2C:27–1

Code of Criminal Justice, 2C:1–14

Theft of identity, 2C:21–17

Benefit as consideration, bribery, 2C:27–2

Benefit card, crimes and offenses, food stamps, 2C:20–35

WORDS AND PHRASES—Cont'd
Benefit derived,
Determination of degree of offense,
2C:21–8.1
Taxation, 2C:21–15
Berm, motor vehicles, 39:1–1
Bicycles,
Equipment, 39:4–14.5
Helmet requirements, 39:4–10.1
Biological agents, terrorism, 2C:38–3
Boards,
Comprehensive Child Abuse Prevention and
Treatment Act, 9:6–8.84
Liquefied petroleum gas education and safe-
ty board, 21:1B–1
Motor vehicle commission, 39:2A–3
Unsatisfied claim and judgment fund,
39:6–62
Bodily fluids, aggravated assault by inmates,
throwing bodily fluids, 2C:12–12
Bodily harm, force, justification, 2C:3–11
Bodily injury, crimes and offenses,
Endangering injured victim, 2C:12–1.2
Homicide, 2C:11–1
Body cavity search, 2A:161A–3
Body vests, crimes and offenses, 2C:39–13
Bonds, turnpike, 27:23–4
Booby traps, controlled dangerous substances,
property used for manufacture, distribu-
tion or possession, 2C:35–4.1
Bookmaking, 2C:37–1
Brand extension, malt beverages, 33:1–93.14
Brewer, malt beverages, 33:1–93.14
Bribery and corruption, 2C:27–1
Broken succession of title, theft, 2C:20–1
Building, intoxicating liquor law, 33:1–1
Bulk plants, liquefied petroleum gas, 21:1B–1
Burden of persuasion, evidence, **Evidence Rule
101**
Burden of producing evidence, **Evidence Rule
101**
Burglary, 2C:18–2
Business, hearsay evidence, **Evidence Rule 801**
Business district, motor vehicles, 39:1–1
Buyer, motor vehicles, 39:10–2
Bylaws, adult offender supervision, interstate
compacts, 2A:168–27
Bypass, water pollution control, 58:10A–3
Cardholder, credit card offenses, 2C:21–6
Carjacking, Code of Criminal Justice, 2C:15–2
Carpool, 39:1–1
Cause a reasonable person to fear, stalking,
2C:12–10
CDL, Commercial Driver License Act,
39:3–10.11
CDLIS, Commercial Driver License Act,
39:3–10.11
Certificate numbers, radioactive materials,
transportation, 39:5B–18
Certificate of handling, radioactive materials,
transportation, 39:5B–18
Certificate of ownership, motor vehicles,
39:10–2
Certification date, limousine or livery service,
39:5G–2
Chair, motor vehicle commission, 39:2A–3
Characterizing flavor other than tobacco, clove
or menthol, flavored cigarettes,
2A:170–51.6
Charitable purpose, terrorism, 2C:38–5
Chassis, motor vehicles, intermodal transporta-
tion, 39:3–79.10
Chemical weapon, terrorism, 2C:38–3
Chief administrators,
Motor vehicle commission, 39:2A–3
Motor vehicles, 39:1–1

WORDS AND PHRASES—Cont'd
Chief administrators—Cont'd
Snowmobiles, all terrain vehicles, 39:3C–1
Chief executive officer, abuse of children,
9:6–8.21
Child,
Abuse of children, 9:6–8.21
Comprehensive Child Abuse Prevention and
Treatment Act, 9:6–8.44
Endangering welfare of children, 2C:24–4
Luring and enticing, crimes and offenses,
2C:13–6
Victims of crime, speedy trial, 2A:163–4
Child advocacy center, child abuse, 9:6–8.104
Cigarettes and cigars, flavored cigarettes,
2A:170–51.6
Citation, Nonresident Violator Compact,
39:5F–4
Clear road beam, motor vehicles, 39:3–46
Client, attorney client privilege, **Evidence Rule
504**
Cloning of a human being, crimes and offenses,
2C:11A–1
CMV, Commercial Driver License Act,
39:3–10.11
CODIS, DNA Database and Databank Act of
1994, 53:1–20.19
Coercion, 2C:13–5
Sexual offenses, 2C:14–1
Collateral, Nonresident Violator Compact,
39:5F–4
Collectors, weapons, 2C:58–3.4
Combination of vehicles, motor vehicles, di-
mensional and weight limitations, 39:3–84
Commencement of prosecution, Code of Crim-
inal Justice, 2C:1–6
Commercial driver license, Commercial Driver
License Act, 39:3–10.11
Commercial driver license information system,
Commercial Driver License Act,
39:3–10.11
Commercial explosives, 21:1A–129
Commercial motor vehicle,
Commercial Driver License Act, 39:3–10.11
Traffic laws, 39:1–1
Commercial vehicle, registration, reciprocity,
39:3–6.1
Commission of offenses, Code of Criminal Jus-
tice, 2C:1–6
Commissioners,
Adult offender supervision, interstate com-
pacts, 2A:168–27
Coastal protection license plate program,
39:3–27.47
Comprehensive Child Abuse Prevention and
Treatment Act, 9:6–8.84
Controlled substances, 24:21–2
Explosives, 21:1A–129
Intoxicating liquor law, 33:1–1
Liberty State Park plates, 39:3–27.91
Liquefied petroleum gas education and safe-
ty board, 21:1B–1
Motor vehicle commission, 39:2A–3
Motor vehicles, 39:1–1
Registration and regulation of snowmobiles
and all terrain vehicles, 39:3C–1
Speed, sixty five mph, implementation,
39:4–98.4
Turnpikes, 27:23–4
Unsatisfied claim and judgment fund,
39:6–62
Water pollution control, 58:10A–3
Wearing apparel, 2A:123–3
Commissions,
Juvenile justice, 2A:4A–22
Motor vehicle commission, 39:2A–3

WORDS AND PHRASES—Cont'd
Commissions—Cont'd
Motor vehicles, 39:1–1
Commit, juvenile justice, 2A:4A–22
Committed person, interference with custody,
2C:13–4
Communication, crimes and offenses, 2C:1–14
Communications common carrier, wiretapping
and electronic surveillance, 2A:156A–2
Community guns, possession for unlawful pur-
poses, 2C:39–4
Commuter van, 39:1–1
Compact administrator, adult offender supervi-
sion, interstate compacts, 2A:168–27
Compact officer, interstate compacts, crimes
and offenses, 53:1–32
Compacting state, adult offender supervision,
interstate compacts, 2A:168–27
Competency to stand trial, 2C:4–4
Complaining witness, rape, 2A:84A–32.3
Complaint, attorneys, discipline, **Rule 1:20**
Compliance, Nonresident Violator Compact,
39:5F–4
Component part thereof, flavored cigarettes,
2A:170–51.6
Comprehensive enforcement program, nonpay-
ment of fines or restitution, 2C:46–2
Computer contaminant, computer related of-
fenses, 2C:20–23
Computer equipment, computer related of-
fenses, 2C:20–23
Computer network, computer related offenses,
2C:20–23
Computer program, computer related offenses,
2C:20–23
Computer software, computer related offenses,
2C:20–23
Computer system, computer related offenses,
2C:20–23
Computer trespassers, wiretapping and elec-
tronic surveillance, 2A:156A–4.1
Computers, computer related offenses,
2C:20–23
Conceal, shoplifting, 2C:20–11
Conduct, Code of Criminal Justice, 2C:1–14,
2C:2–3
Confidential communication, victim and coun-
selor privilege, **Evidence Rule 517**
Confidential communication between physician
and patient, privileges and immunities, **Ev-
idence Rule 506**
Confidential communications,
Physician and patient, 2A:84A–22.1
Rape counselors, 2A:84A–22.1
Victims of crime, counselors, 2A:84A–22.14
Confidential personal identifiers, public access,
Rule 1:38–7
Consent matter, attorneys, discipline, **Rule 1:20**
Conspiracy, 2C:5–2
Construction, turnpikes, 27:23–4
Construction of law, Code of Criminal Justice,
2C:1–2
Contact lenses, dispensing, 2C:40–25
Container, intoxicating liquor law, 33:1–1
Contents, wiretapping and electronic surveil-
lance, 2A:156A–2
Contest of chance, 2C:37–1
Contract, motor vehicles, 39:10–2
Controlled premises, controlled dangerous sub-
stances, administrative inspection war-
rants, 24:21–32
Controlled substance analog, 2C:35–2
Commercial Driver License Act, 39:3–10.11
Controlled substances, 2C:35–2, 24:21–2
Commercial drivers licenses, 39:3–10.11
Conventional fuel, school buses, 39:3B–13

WORDS AND PHRASES—Cont'd
Converter dolly, **39:3–61**
Conviction,
  Commercial Driver License Act, **39:3–10.11**
  Drivers licenses, **39:5–30.12, 39:5D–2**
Corporation, Code of Criminal Justice, **2C:2–7**
Corrupt influence, **2C:27–1**
Cosmetic, tampering, **2C:40–16**
Cost,
  Motor vehicles, trial de novo, arbitrated tort claims, **39:6A–34**
  Turnpikes, **27:23–4**
Council, interstate compacts, crimes and offenses, **53:1–32**
Counterfeit mark, trademarks and trade names, **2C:21–32**
Counterfeit substances, controlled dangerous substances, **2C:35–2, 24:21–2**
County correctional facility, telecommunications, **2C:29–10**
County juvenile detention facility, telecommunications, **2C:29–10**
County prosecutor,
  Municipal prosecutors, **2B:25–2**
  Searches and seizures, news organizations, **2A:84A–21.12**
Course of conduct, stalking, **2C:12–10**
Court,
  Juvenile justice, **2A:4A–22**
  Nonresident Violator Compact, **39:5F–4**
Court appointed special advocate, dependent or neglected children, **2A:4A–92**
Court of competent jurisdiction, wiretapping and electronic surveillance, **2A:156A–2**
Court records, public access, **Rule 1:38–2**
Creature, cruelty to animals, **4:22–15**
Credit agreement, turnpikes, **27:23–4**
Credit cards, fraud, **2C:21–6**
Crime, **2C:1–5**
  Code of Criminal Justice, **2C:1–4**
Crime with bail restrictions, certain offenses, bail, **2A:162–12**
Criminal attempt, **2C:5–1**
Criminal history record repository, interstate compacts, **53:1–32**
Criminal history records, interstate compacts, **53:1–32**
Criminal justice, interstate compacts, **53:1–32**
Criminal justice agency, interstate compacts, **53:1–32**
Criminal justice services, interstate compacts, **53:1–32**
Criminal mischief, **2C:17–3**
Criminal offense, controlled dangerous substances, trafficking, injunctions, **2C:35–5.6**
Criminal restraint, **2C:13–2**
Criminal street gangs, crimes and offenses, **2C:33–29**
Criminal trespass, **2C:18–3**
Crisis intervention response, juvenile family crises, **2A:4A–78**
Criterion offense, interstate compacts, **53:1–32**
Crosswalk, traffic rules, **39:1–1**
Culpability, Code of Criminal Justice, **2C:2–2**
Custodian, abuse, abandonment, cruelty and neglect of children, **9:6–2**
Damage, computer related offenses, **2C:20–23**
Dangerous drugs, substances or compounds, **53:1–18.5**
Dangerous fireworks, **21:2–3**
Data, computer related offenses, **2C:20–23**
Data base, computer related offenses, **2C:20–23**
Day school, abuse of children, **9:6–8.21**
Deadly force, justification, **2C:3–11**

WORDS AND PHRASES—Cont'd
Deadly weapon,
  Homicide, **2C:11–1**
  No Early Release Act, **2C:43–7.2**
Dealer, motor vehicles, **39:1–1, 39:10–2**
Dealer in property, theft, **2C:20–1**
Debtor, motor vehicles, **39:10–2**
Deceive, theft, **2C:20–4**
Declarant, hearsay evidence, **Evidence Rule 801**
Deface, firearms, **2C:39–1**
Defaced access device, theft, **2C:20–1**
Defraud the administration of a drug test, crimes and offenses, **2C:36–10**
Delegated local agency, water pollution control, **58:10A–3**
Delinquency, juvenile justice, **2A:4A–23**
Deliver,
  Controlled substances, **24:21–2**
  Embezzlement, prepaid funeral agreements, **2A:102–18**
Delivery,
  Controlled substances, **2C:35–2, 24:21–2**
  Embezzlement, prepaid funeral agreements, **2A:102–18**
Delivery system, biological and chemical agents, **2C:38–3**
Demonstrations, funerals, disorderly persons, **2C:33–8.1**
Dentists, controlled dangerous substances, **2C:35–2, 24:21–2**
Department of Corrections employee, aggravated assault by inmates, throwing bodily fluids, **2C:12–12**
Departments,
  Coastal protection license plate program, **39:3–27.47**
  Crimes and offenses, food stamps, **2C:20–35**
  Flammable fabrics, **2A:123–3**
  Hazardous materials, **39:5B–25**
  Historic preservation license plates, **39:3–27.72**
  Liberty State Park plates, **39:3–27.91**
  Liquefied petroleum gas education and safety board, **21:1B–1**
  Motor carriers, intermodal transportation, chassis, **39:3–79.10**
  Motor vehicle commission, **39:2A–3**
  Snowmobiles, all terrain vehicles, **39:3C–1**
  Speed bumps, municipalities, highways and roads, **39:4–8.9**
  Traffic rules and regulations, **39:4–8.9**
  Turnpikes, **27:23–4**
  Water pollution control, **58:10A–3**
Deprive, theft, **2C:20–1**
Deputy administrator, motor vehicle commission, **39:2A–3**
Deputy chief administrator,
  Motor vehicle commission, **39:2A–3**
  Motor vehicles, **39:1–1**
Derived from, money laundering and illegal investments, **2C:21–24**
Desecrate, venerated objects, **2C:33–9**
Designed, Code of Criminal Justice, **2C:2–2**
Destroy, computer related offenses, **2C:20–23**
Destructive device, **2C:39–1**
Detention, juvenile justice, **2A:4A–22**
Device, ignition interlock devices, intoxication of driver, **39:4–50.17**
Diesel bus, motor vehicle emissions inspection, **39:8–60**
Diesel powered motor vehicle, motor vehicle emissions inspection, **39:8–60**
Direct access, interstate compacts, crimes and offenses, **53:1–32**

WORDS AND PHRASES—Cont'd
Directors,
  Attorneys, discipline, **Rule 1:20**
  Auto body repair facilities, **39:13–1**
  Coastal protection license plate program, **39:3–27.47**
  Controlled substances, **24:21–2**
  Drivers privacy protection, **39:2–3.3**
  Financial responsibility, **39:6–24**
  Flammable tents and sleeping bags, **2A:123–16**
  Historic motor vehicles, **39:3–27.3**
  Historic preservation license plates, **39:3–27.72**
  Intoxicating liquors, educational programs, **33:1–12.41**
  Liberty State Park plates, **39:3–27.91**
  Motor vehicle commission, **39:2A–3**
  Olympic license plates, **39:3–27.61**
  Parking offenses, **39:4–139.3**
  Registration and regulation of snowmobiles and all terrain vehicles, **39:3C–1**
  School buses, in terminal inspections, **39:3B–20**
  Tow trucks and towing companies, **39:3–84.6**
Directory, motor vehicles, **39:10–2**
Dirt bikes, snowmobiles, all terrain vehicles, **39:3C–1**
Discharge, water pollution control, **58:10A–3**
Discipline by consent, attorneys, **Rule 1:20**
Disorderly persons offense, Code of Criminal Justice, **2C:1–4**
Dispense, controlled dangerous substances, **2C:35–2, 24:21–2**
Dispose of, weapons, **2C:39–1**
Dispositional hearing, abuse of children, **9:6–8.45**
Distribute, controlled substances, **2C:35–2, 24:21–2**
Distributee, identity theft, personal identifying information, **2C:21–17.3**
Distributor, controlled substances, **2C:35–2, 24:21–2**
Diversion, attorneys, discipline, **Rule 1:20**
Divisions,
  Abuse of children, **9:6–8.21**
  Coastal protection license plate program, **39:3–27.47**
  Commercial motor vehicles, registration, reciprocity, **39:3–6.1**
  Comprehensive Child Abuse Prevention and Treatment Act, **9:6–8.84**
  Controlled substances, **24:21–2**
  DNA Database and Databank Act of 1994, **53:1–20.19**
  Drivers privacy protection, **39:2–3.3**
  Frozen dessert trucks, traffic rules and regulations, **39:4–128.3**
  Historic preservation license plates, **39:3–27.72**
  Intoxicating liquors, educational programs, **33:1–12.41**
  Liberty State Park plates, **39:3–27.91**
  Motor vehicle commission, **39:2A–3**
  Olympic license plates, **39:3–27.61**
  Parking offenses, **39:4–139.3**
  School buses, in terminal inspections, **39:3B–20**
  Tow trucks and towing companies, **39:3–84.6**
DMV, motor vehicle commission, **39:2A–3**
DNA, DNA Database and Databank Act of 1994, **53:1–20.19**
DNA record, DNA Database and Databank Act of 1994, **53:1–20.19**
DNA sample, DNA Database and Databank Act of 1994, **53:1–20.19**

WORDS AND PHRASES—Cont'd

Documentary material,
Racketeering, **2C:41–1**
Searches and seizures, news organizations,
2A:84A–21.12
Domestic companion animal, theft, **2C:20–1**
Domestic dog or cat, crimes and offenses,
sales,
Fur or hair, **4:22–25.3**
Meat and meat products, **4:22–25.4**
Domestic livestock, **4:22–16.1**
Domestic violence, **2C:25–19**
Double saddle mount, motor vehicle regulation, **39:4–54**
Drivers, motor vehicles, **39:1–1**
Drivers licenses,
Commercial Driver License Act, **39:3–10.11**
Nonresident Violator Compact, **39:5F–4**
Drivers school, motor vehicles, **39:12–1**
Drug,
Controlled substances, **2C:35–2, 24:21–2**
Ephedrine, pseudoephedrine, phenylpropanolamine, **2C:35–25**
Tampering, **2C:40–16**
Drug dependent persons, controlled dangerous substances, **24:21–2**
Drug Enforcement Administration, controlled substances, **24:21–2**
Drug offense, drivers licenses, **39:5–30.12**
Drug or alcohol dependent person, controlled dangerous substances, **2C:35–2**
Drug paraphernalia, controlled substances, **2C:36–1**
Drug profiteer, AntiDrug Profiteering Act, **2C:35A–3**
Duplicate, evidence, **Evidence Rule 1001**
Dwelling, justification, **2C:3–11**
Earnings, wrongful discharge, **2C:40A–3**
Economic loss, no fault insurance, **39:6A–2**
Effluent limitation, water pollution control, **58:10A–3**
Electric personal assistive mobility devices, **39:4–14.10**
Electronic, mechanical or other device, wiretapping and electronic surveillance, **2A:156A–2**
Electronic communication, wiretapping and electronic surveillance, **2A:156A–2**
Electronic communication service, wiretapping and electronic surveillance, **2A:156A–2**
Electronic communication system, wiretapping and electronic surveillance, **2A:156A–2**
Electronic means, luring and enticing, **2C:13–7**
Children and minors, crimes and offenses, **2C:13–6**
Electronic storage, wiretapping and electronic surveillance, **2A:156A–2**
Element of an offense,
Code of Criminal Justice, **2C:1–14**
Presumptions against accused, **Evidence Rule 303**
Eligible, intoxicating liquor law, **33:1–1**
Eligible handicapped person, handicapped parking, **39:4–207.6**
Eligible public highways, speed, sixty five mph, implementation, **39:4–98.4**
Emancipated minor, domestic violence, prevention, **2C:25–19**
Emergency calls, telephone party line, refusal to yield, **2C:40–2**
Emergency services, false alarms, fines and penalties, **2C:33–3.2**
Emergency services personnel, aggravated assault, **2C:12–1**
Emotional distress, stalking, **2C:12–10**

WORDS AND PHRASES—Cont'd

Endorsement, Commercial Driver License Act, **39:3–10.11**
Enforced community service,
Comprehensive enforcement program, alternative sentencing option, **2B:19–5**
Nonpayment of fines or restitution, **2C:46–2**
Enterprise,
Racketeering, **2C:41–1**
Theft, **2C:20–1**
Environmental protection administrative average fuel efficiency rating, motor vehicles, luxury cars, certificates of ownership, additional fees, **39:3–8.3**
EPA, motor vehicle emissions inspection, **39:8–60**
Equipment interchange receipt, motor carriers, intermodal transportation, chassis, **39:3–79.10**
Equipment provider, motor carriers, intermodal transportation, chassis, **39:3–79.10**
Essential services, no fault insurance, **39:6A–2**
Ethics committee, attorneys, discipline, **Rule 1:20**
Ethics counsel, attorneys, discipline, **Rule 1:20**
Evaluative processes, complementary dispute resolution, **Rule 1:40–2**
Every motor vehicle, certificate of ownership, **39:10–2**
Evidence of physical characteristics, investigative detention, **Rule 3:5A–9**
Evidence of previous sexual conduct of victim, **2C:14–7**
Excluded sex offenders, youth serving organizations, **2C:7–22**
Executive authority, uniform extradition, **2A:160–6**
Executive head, drivers licenses, **39:5D–12**
Executive order, interstate compacts, crimes and offenses, **53:1–32**
Exhibit, obscene material, **2C:34–2**
Children and minors, **2C:34–3**
Expired credit card, **2C:21–6**
Explosive, **2C:39–1, 21:1A–129**
Motor vehicles, **39:1–1**
Explosives manufacturing building, **21:1A–129**
Explosives manufacturing establishment, **21:1A–129**
Expungement, **2C:52–1**
Fabric, wearing apparel, **2A:123–3**
Facilitative process, complementary dispute resolution, **Rule 1:40–2**
Facility,
Abuse of children, **9:6–8.30**
New Jersey Antipiracy Act, **2C:21–21**
Fact finding hearing, abuse of children, **9:6–8.44**
Fair market value, malt beverages, **33:1–93.14**
Falsely embosses, credit card offenses, **2C:21–6**
Falsely makes, credit card offenses, **2C:21–6**
Farm supplies, license plates, **39:3–25**
Farm tractor, traffic laws, **39:1–1**
FBI,
DNA Database and Databank Act of 1994, **53:1–20.19**
Interstate compacts, crimes and offenses, **53:1–32**
Federal act, water pollution control, **58:10A–3**
Fee committee, attorneys, discipline, **Rule 1:20**
Feeder road, turnpikes, **27:23–4**
Felony,
Commercial Driver License Act, **39:3–10.11**
Fresh pursuit, **2A:155–2**
Fiduciary,
Misapplication of entrusted property, **2C:21–15**

WORDS AND PHRASES—Cont'd

Fiduciary—Cont'd
Theft, **2C:20–1**
Final judgment, frivolous litigation, **Rule 1:4–8**
Financial institutions,
Terrorism, funds, freezing, **2C:66–1**
Theft, **2C:20–1**
Financial instrument, computer related offenses, **2C:20–23**
Financier,
Narcotics trafficking network, **2C:35–3**
Organized crime, **2C:5–2**
Finished product, industrial chemicals, **2C:35–29**
Firearm, **2C:39–1**
Firearm silencer, **2C:39–1**
Firearms training course, unlawful possession, exemption, **2C:39–6**
Fireworks, **21:2–2**
Fireworks factory buildings, **21:2–2**
Fireworks plant, **21:2–2**
Flags, theft, **2C:20–2.3**
Flame resistant, flammable tents and sleeping bags, **2A:123–16**
Flammable liquids, motor vehicles, **39:1–1**
Fleet,
Apportioned vehicle, registration, **39:3–6.11**
Commercial vehicles, registration, reciprocity, **39:3–6.1**
Food, kosher food, **2C:21–7.2**
Food commodity in packaged form, kosher food, **2C:21–7.2**
Food product, tampering, **2C:40–16**
Food stamp coupon, crimes and offenses, **2C:20–35**
For use as weapon, terrorism, **2C:38–3**
Force, justification, **2C:3–11**
Forcible entry and detainer, disorderly persons, **2C:33–11.1**
Foreign country, lotteries, **2C:37–6.1**
Foreign jurisdiction, Commercial Driver License Act, **39:3–10.11**
Foreign person, intoxicating liquors, **33:1–11.2**
Forest, aggravated arson, **2C:17–1**
Forgery, **2C:21–1**
Formal charge, crimes and offenses, AIDS or HIV testing for sex offenders, **2C:43–2.2**
Former prosecution, bar to subsequent prosecution, **2C:1–9**
Franchise utility, commercial motor vehicles, **39:4–46**
Franchised public utility, vehicle lettering or name plates, **39:4–46**
Fraudulent practices, driving schools, **39:12–1**
Fresh meat and poultry, kosher foods, **2C:21–7.4**
Fresh pursuit, **2A:155–2**
Intrastate, **2A:156–2**
Frozen dessert trucks, traffic rules and regulations, **39:4–128.3**
Full retail value, shoplifting, **2C:20–11**
Funds,
Coastal protection license plate program, **39:3–27.47**
Historic preservation license plates, **39:3–27.72**
Liberty State Park plates, **39:3–27.91**
Motor vehicles, plates or markers, special plates, united we stand, **39:3–27.131**
Olympic license plates, **39:3–27.61**
Unsatisfied claim and judgment fund, **39:6–62**
Funeral, disruption, disorderly persons, **2C:33–8.1**
Funeral insurance policy, embezzlement, prepaid funeral agreements, **2A:102–18**

WORDS AND PHRASES—Cont'd
Gain, fines and penalties, 2C:43–3
Gambling, 2C:37–1
Gambling device, 2C:37–1
Gambling resort, 2C:37–1
Garage keepers legal liability, tow trucks and towing companies, 39:3–84.6
Garden State arts center, turnpikes, 27:23–4
Gender identity or expression, bias intimidation, 2C:16–1
Geographical district, motor vehicles, 39:3–4d
Good cause, malt beverages, 33:1–93.14
Governing board or body, intoxicating liquor law, 33:1–1
Governing body, 2B:25–2
Government,
Bribery and corruption, 2C:27–1
Terrorism, 2C:38–2
Theft, 2C:20–1
Governmental entity, school buses, liquefied petroleum gas, 39:3B–13
Governmental units, searches and seizures, news organizations, 2A:84A–21.12
Governor, uniform extradition, 2A:160–6
Graffiti, act of, 2A:153–4.1
Gravity knife, 2C:39–1
Grievance, attorneys, discipline, **Rule 1:20**
Gross vehicle weight rating,
Commercial Driver License Act, 39:3–10.11
Motor vehicles, 39:10–2
Emissions inspection, 39:8–60
Gross weight,
Commercial motor vehicles, 39:3–20
Motor vehicles, 39:1–1
Guardian,
Abuse of children, 9:6–8.21
Juvenile justice, 2A:4A–22
GVWR,
Commercial Driver License Act, 39:3–10.11
Commercial motor vehicles, 39:4–46
Motor vehicle emissions inspection, 39:8–60
Habitual offender, motor vehicles, 39:5–30a
Half of the roadway, pedestrians, 39:4–32, 39:4–36
Handcuffs, sale to minor, 2C:39–9.2
Handgun, 2C:39–1
Handgun ammunition, transfers, 2C:58–3.3
Handicapped persons, motor vehicle plates and markers, 39:4–204
Harm, bribery and corruption, 2C:27–1
Hashish, controlled dangerous substance, 2C:35–2, 24:21–2
Hazardous material,
Commercial Driver License Act, 39:3–10.11
Transportation, 39:5B–25
Hazardous pollutant, water pollution control, 58:10A–3
He, Code of Criminal Justice, 2C:1–14
Headlamp, motor vehicles, 39:3–46
Health care claims fraud, 2C:21–4.2
Health care facilities, arson, 2C:17–1
Health care providers, no fault insurance, 39:6A–2
Hearsay, **Evidence Rule 801**
Heavy duty, tow trucks and towing companies, 39:3–84.6
Heavy duty diesel truck, motor vehicle emissions inspection, 39:8–60
High managerial agent, Code of Criminal Justice, 2C:2–7
High misdemeanor, Code of Criminal Justice, 2C:1–4
High occupancy vehicle, traffic regulations, 39:1–1
Highway project, turnpikes, 27:23–4

WORDS AND PHRASES—Cont'd
Highways,
Explosives, 21:1A–129
Fireworks, 21:2–2
Stopping requirements, school buses, 39:4–128.1
Traffic regulations, 39:1–1
Repair or construction areas, 39:4–203.5
Historic motor vehicles, 39:3–27.3
Historic resources, historic preservation license plates, 39:3–27.72
Holder of the privilege, patient and physician privilege, **Evidence Rule 506**
Home jurisdiction, Nonresident Violator Compact, 39:5F–4
Home state, drivers license, 39:5D–2
Homicide, 2C:11–1 et seq.
Horse, traffic laws, 39:1–1
Hospital, controlled substances, 2C:35–2, 24:21–2
Hospital expenses, no fault insurance, 39:6A–2
Hotel, intoxicating liquors, 33:1–43
House of prostitution, 2C:34–1
HOV, traffic regulations, 39:1–1
Human remains, dead bodies, crimes and offenses, 2C:22–1
Hybrid process, complementary dispute resolution, **Rule 1:40–2**
Ignition interlock devices, intoxication of driver, 39:4–50.17
Illicit beverage, intoxicating liquor law, 33:1–1
Imitation firearm, 2C:39–1
Immediate family members, no fault insurance, election of tort option, 39:6A–8.1
Immediate precursor, controlled dangerous substances, 2C:35–2, 24:21–2
Immigration consultant, unauthorized practice, 2C:21–31
Immigration or naturalization matter, unauthorized practice, 2C:21–31
Immigration related document, unauthorized practice, 2C:21–31
Importing, intoxicating liquor law, 33:1–1
In any manner, money laundering and illegal investments, 2C:21–25
In fact, false public alarms, 2C:33–3
In house counsel, attorneys, limited licenses, admission to practice, **Rule 1:27–2**
In jurisdiction miles, appointed vehicle, registration, 39:3–6.11
In progress trace, wiretapping and electronic surveillance, 2A:156A–2
In terminal inspection, school buses, 39:3B–20
In the course of committing, burglary, 2C:18–2
In the course of pursuing his professional activities,
News personnel privilege, 2A:84A–21a
Newspersons privilege, **Evidence Rule 508**
Included offenses, 2C:1–8
Income, no fault insurance, 39:6A–2
Income producer, no fault insurance, 39:6A–2
Incrimination, **Evidence Rule 502**
Rules of evidence, 2A:84A–18
Indictment, criminal procedure, 2A:152–1
Indigent defendant, public defender, 2A:158A–2
Individual user of controlled dangerous substance, 2C:35B–3
Industrial distribution, chemicals, chemistry and chemists, 2C:35–29
Industrial product, chemicals, chemistry and chemists, 2C:35–29
Industrial use chemical, 2C:35–29
Industrial use chemical distributor, 2C:35–29
Industrial use chemical manufacturer, 2C:35–29
Information, forgery, 2C:21–1

WORDS AND PHRASES—Cont'd
Inhabited building, explosives, 21:1A–129
Innerlining, wearing apparel, 2A:123–3
Inoperable, assault firearms, 2C:58–13
Inside lane, motor vehicles, 39:1–1
Institution, abuse of children, 9:6–8.21
Insurer, unsatisfied claim and judgment fund, 39:6–62
Intended funeral recipient, embezzlement, prepaid funeral agreements, 2A:102–18
Intercept, wiretapping and electronic surveillance, 2A:156A–2
Interchange receipt, motor carriers, intermodal transportation, chassis, 39:3–79.10
Interest in property which has been stolen, 2C:20–1
Intermodal chassis, motor carriers, 39:3–79.10
Intermodal equipment facility, motor carriers, chassis, 39:3–79.10
Intermodal equipment provider, motor carriers, chassis, 39:3–79.10
International Registration Plan, apportioned vehicle, registration, 39:3–6.11
Internet,
Computer related offenses, 2C:20–23
Endangering welfare of child, pornography, 2C:24–4
Intersection, motor vehicles, 39:1–1
Interstate commission, adult offender supervision, interstate compacts, 2A:168–27
Interstate identification system, interstate compacts, crimes and offenses, 53:1–32
Interstate operations, apportioned vehicle, registration, 39:3–6.11
Intimate parts, sexual offenses, 2C:14–1
Intoxication, Code of Criminal Justice, 2C:2–8
Investigative or law enforcement officer, wiretapping and electronic surveillance, 2A:156A–2
Involving or touching such office, position or employment, bribery and corruption, disqualification, public office, 2C:51–2
Issuer, credit card offenses, 2C:21–6
Issuing jurisdiction, Nonresident Violator Compact, 39:5F–4
Item, identity theft, personal identifying information, 2C:21–17.3
Items bearing a counterfeit mark, forfeitures, 2C:64–1
Itinerant vendors, vehicle, flashing lights, 39:3–64.1 et seq.
Judges, wiretapping and electronic surveillance, 2A:156A–2
Jurisdiction,
Apportioned vehicle, registration, 39:3–6.11
Commercial vehicles, registration, reciprocity, 39:3–6.1
Foreign, Commercial Driver License Act, 39:3–10.11
Nonresident Violator Compact, 39:5F–4
Juvenile family crisis, juvenile justice, 2A:4A–22
Juvenile family crisis intervention units, 2A:4A–32
Juveniles, juvenile justice, 2A:4A–22
Kidnapping, 2C:13–1
Knowingly,
Code of Criminal Justice, 2C:2–2
Obscene material, children and minors, 2C:34–3
Kosher, food, 2C:21–7.2
Labor assistance program,
Comprehensive enforcement program, alternative sentencing option, 2B:19–5
Nonpayment of fines or restitution, 2C:46–2
Laboratory, controlled dangerous substances, 2C:35–2, 24:21–2

WORDS AND PHRASES—Cont'd

Land and improvement, turnpikes, **27:23–4**

Laned roadway, motor vehicles, **39:1–1**

Large capacity ammunition magazine, **2C:39–1**

Laser lighting device, transportation, interference, **2C:33–14**

Laser sighting system device, **2C:12–1**

Law enforcement agency, prevention of domestic violence, **2C:25–19**

Law enforcement officer, prevention of domestic violence, **2C:25–19**

Law guardian, abuse of children, **9:6–8.21**

Lawyer,
  Attorney client privilege, **Evidence Rule 504**
  Rule of conduct, **Rule 1:14**

Leader of a firearms trafficking network, **2C:39–16**

Leader of organized crime, **2C:5–2**

Lease price, motor vehicles, luxury cars, certificates of ownership, additional fees, **39:3–8.3**

Leased limousine, traffic rules and regulations, **39:1–1**

Leased motor vehicle, traffic rules, **39:1–1**

Legal name, drivers licenses, **39:3–9a**

Legal owner, firearms, temporary transfer and possession, **2C:58–3.1**

Less lethal ammunition, justification, law enforcement officers, **2C:3–11**

Lessee, toll collection monitoring system, turnpike authority, **27:23–34.1**

Lessor, toll collection monitoring system, turnpike authority, **27:23–34.1**

Level 1 offense, controlled substances, **2C:35B–3**

Level 2 offense, controlled substances, **2C:35B–3**

Level 3 offense, controlled substances, **2C:35B–3**

Level 4 offense, controlled substances, **2C:35B–3**

Lewd acts, **2C:14–4**

Library facility, theft of library materials, **2C:20–12**

Library material, theft, **2C:20–12**

Licensed building, intoxicating liquor law, **33:1–1**

Licensed premises, intoxicating liquor law, **33:1–1**

Licensed real estate broker, motor vehicle dealers license, **39:10–19**

Licenses, financial responsibility, **39:6–24**

Licensing authority, drivers licenses, **39:5D–10**

Light medium duty, tow trucks and towing companies, **39:3–84.6**

Limited access highway, traffic rules, **39:1–1**

Limousine, intoxicating liquor law, **33:1–1**

Limousine or livery service, criminal history record information, **39:5G–2**

Liquefied petroleum gas, **21:1B–1**
  Education and safety board, **21:1B–1**
  School buses, **39:3B–13**

Local agency, water pollution control, **58:10A–3**

Local authorities, motor vehicles, **39:1–1**

Location information, wiretapping and electronic surveillance, **2A:156A–2**

Loss, fines and penalties, **2C:43–3**

Lottery, **2C:37–1**

Low speed vehicles, traffic rules and regulations, **39:1–1**

Lower beam, motor vehicles, **39:3–46**

Machine gun, **2C:39–1**

Magazine,
  Explosives, **21:1A–129**
  Newspersons privilege, **2A:84A–21a; Evidence Rule 508**

WORDS AND PHRASES—Cont'd

Magazine—Cont'd
  Privileged communications, **2A:84A–21a**

Magistrate,
  Intoxicating liquor law, **33:1–1**
  Motor vehicles, **39:1–1**

Major facility, water pollution control, **58:10A–3**

Manslaughter, **2C:11–4**

Manufacture,
  Controlled substances, **2C:35–2**
  Intoxicating liquors, **33:1–10**

Manufacturer,
  Controlled substances, **2C:35–2**
  Firearms, **2C:39–1**
  Flammable fabrics, **2A:123–3**
  Intoxicating liquor law, **33:1–1**
  Motor vehicles, **39:1–1, 39:10–2**

Manufacturer of an industrial product, chemicals, chemistry and chemists, **2C:35–29**

Manufacturers number, motor vehicles, **39:10–2**

Marijuana, controlled dangerous substances, **2C:35–2, 24:21–2**

Marker, tow trucks and towing companies, **39:3–84.6**

Marketing of controlled dangerous substances, **2C:35B–3**

Material element of an offense, Code of Criminal Justice, **2C:1–14**

Material support or resources, terrorism, **2C:38–5**

Material witness, **2C:104–1**

Material witness order, **2C:104–1**

Means of conveyance, theft, **2C:20–10**

Medical expenses, no fault insurance, **39:6A–2**

Medically necessary, no fault insurance, **39:6A–2**

Meeting beam, motor vehicles, **39:3–46**

Member, adult offender supervision, interstate compacts, **2A:168–27**

Member jurisdiction, apportioned vehicle, registration, **39:3–6.11**

Mental disease or defect, **2C:4–1**

Mentally defective, sexual offenses, **2C:14–1**

Mentally incapacitated,
  Crimes and offenses, endangering injured victim, **2C:12–1.2**
  Sexual offenses, **2C:14–1**

Mentally retarded person, handicapped parking permits, **39:4–207.2**

Merchandise, shoplifting, **2C:20–11**

Merchant,
  Credit cards, fraud, scanning, **2C:21–6.1**
  Shoplifting, **2C:20–11**

Metal tire, motor vehicles, **39:1–1**

Mid block crosswalk, traffic regulations, **39:1–1**

Minor unethical conduct,
  Attorney discipline, **Rule 1:20–3**
  Attorneys, discipline, **Rule 1:20**

Minors, loaded firearms, **2C:58–15**

Misdemeanor, Code of Criminal Justice, **2C:1–4**

Mislabeled, deceptive business practices, **2C:21–7**

Model rocket, **21:1C–1**

Motel, intoxicating liquors, **33:1–43**

Motor carrier audit, apportioned vehicle, registration, **39:3–6.11**

Motor drawn vehicle, traffic regulations, **39:1–1**

Motor vehicle agency, motor vehicle commission, **39:2A–3**

Motor vehicle agent, motor vehicle commission, **39:2A–3**

Motor vehicle junk business, permits, **39:11–2**

Motor vehicle moving violations,
  Drivers licenses, **39:3–40**

WORDS AND PHRASES—Cont'd

Motor vehicle moving violations—Cont'd
  Traffic rules and regulations, privileges and immunities, records and recordation, **39:5–53**

Motor vehicle record, drivers privacy protection, **39:2–3.3**

Motor vehicles,
  Body repair facilities, **39:13–1**
  Code of Criminal Justice, **2C:1–14**
  Commercial, registration, reciprocity, **39:3–6.1**
  Commercial Driver License Act, **39:3–10.11**
  Marks or numbers, change or destruction, crimes and offenses, **2C:17–6**
  No fault insurance, **39:6A–2**
  Traffic regulations, **39:1–1**

Motorcycle, traffic regulations, **39:1–1**

Motorists, Nonresident Violator Compact, **39:5F–4**

Motorized bicycle, traffic rules, **39:1–1**

Motorized scooter, traffic regulations, **39:1–1**

Motorized skateboard, traffic regulations, **39:1–1**

Motorized wheelchair, traffic regulations, **39:1–1**

Movable property, theft, **2C:20–1**

Multiple beam headlamps, motor vehicles, **39:3–46**

Municipal board, intoxicating liquor law, **33:1–1**

Municipal court,
  Establishment, **2B:12–1**
  Municipal prosecutors, **2B:25–2**

Municipal prosecutors, **2B:25–2**

Municipal treatment works, water pollution control, **58:10A–3**

Municipalities, intoxicating liquor law, **33:1–1**

Named insured, no fault insurance, **39:6A–2**

Narcotic, hallucinogenic or habit producing drugs, **39:4–50**
  Motor vehicles, intoxication of driver, **39:4–50**

Narcotic drugs, controlled substances, **2C:35–2, 24:21–2**

National fingerprint file, interstate compacts, criminal history record information, **53:1–32**

National identification index, interstate compacts, criminal history record information, **53:1–32**

National indices, interstate compacts, criminal history record information, **53:1–32**

National pollutant discharge elimination system, water pollution control, **58:10A–3**

Natural barricade, explosives, **21:1A–129**

Natural resources, snowmobiles, all terrain vehicles, **39:3C–1**

Navigable streams, fireworks, **21:2–2**

Near fatality, Comprehensive Child Abuse Prevention and Treatment Act, **9:6–8.84**

Need, weapons, **2C:58–3.4**

Negligence, Code of Criminal Justice, **2C:2–2**

Negligently, Code of Criminal Justice, **2C:2–2**

Negotiable title, apportioned vehicle, registration, **39:3–6.11**

Net direct written premiums,
  Unsatisfied claim and judgment fund, **39:6–62**
  Unsatisfied claim and judgment fund board, **39:6–62**

Neutral, complementary dispute resolution, **Rule 1:40–2**

New Jersey pollutant discharge elimination system, water pollution control, **58:10A–3**

WORDS AND PHRASES—Cont'd

New motor vehicle, certificate of ownership, **39:10–2**

Newly issued funeral insurance policy, embezzlement, prepaid funeral agreements, **2A:102–18**

News, newspersons privilege, **2A:84A–21a; Evidence Rule 508**

News agency, newspersons privilege, **2A:84A–21a; Evidence Rule 508**

News media, newspersons privilege, **2A:84A–21a; Evidence Rule 508**

Newspaper, newspersons privilege, **2A:84A–21a; Evidence Rule 508**

Nitro carbo nitrate, explosives, **21:1A–129**

Noncommercial motor vehicles, Commercial Driver License Act, **39:3–10.11**

Noncommercial truck, traffic regulations, **39:1–1**

Noncompacting state, adult offender supervision, interstate compacts, **2A:168–27**

Nonconventional type motor vehicles, certificate of ownership, **39:10–2**

Noncriminal justice purposes, interstate compacts, criminal history record information, **53:1–32**

Noncriminal matter, criminal records checks, user fees, **53:1–20.5**

Noneconomic loss, no fault insurance, **39:6A–2**

Nonparty state, interstate compacts, crimes and offenses, **53:1–32**

Nonresidents operating privilege, financial responsibility, **39:6–24**

Nuclear or radiological device, terrorism, **2C:38–3**

Numbers game, **2C:37–1**

Obscene film, children and minors, **2C:34–3**

Obscene material,
Adults, **2C:34–2**
Children and minors, **2C:34–3**

Obstructs, highways and other public passages, **2C:33–7**

Obtain, theft, **2C:20–1**

Off site sales, motor vehicles, sales, **39:10–19.1**

Offender, adult offender supervision, interstate compacts, **2A:168–27**

Offense, Code of Criminal Justice, **2C:1–3, 2C:1–4, 2C:1–14**

Office associates, attorneys, limitation on practice, **Rule 1:15–5**

Officers, intoxicating liquor law, **33:1–1**

Official detention, escape, **2C:29–5**

Official proceedings, bribery and corrupt influence, **2C:27–1**

Official traffic control devices, motor vehicles, **39:1–1**

Official written order, controlled dangerous substances, **24:21–2**

Offroad vehicles, **39:3C–32**

Oil, portable oil burning heating devices, **2C:40–6**

Omission, Code of Criminal Justice, **2C:1–14**

Omitted to act, Code of Criminal Justice, **2C:1–14**

Omnibus, motor vehicles, **39:1–1**

Operational records, apportioned vehicle, registration, **39:3–6.11**

Operators,
Motor vehicles, **39:1–1**
School buses, in terminal inspection, **39:3B–20**
Toll collection monitoring system, turnpike authority, **27:23–34.1**

Opiate,
Controlled substances, **2C:35–2, 24:21–2**
Narcotic drugs, **24:21–2**

WORDS AND PHRASES—Cont'd

Opium poppy, controlled dangerous substances, **2C:35–2, 24:21–2**

Oral communication, wiretapping and electronic surveillance, **2A:156A–2**

Organized retail theft enterprise, shoplifting, **2C:20–11**

Original, evidence, **Evidence Rule 1001**

Original container, intoxicating liquor law, **33:1–1**

Other CDR programs, complementary dispute resolution, **Rule 1:40–2**

Out of service order, Commercial Driver License Act, **39:3–10.11**

Outside lane, motor vehicles, **39:1–1**

Owners,
Apportioned vehicle, registration, **39:3–6.11**
Commercial motor vehicles, registration, reciprocity, **39:3–6.1**
Cruelty to animals, **4:22–15**
Motor vehicles, **39:1–1**
New Jersey Antipiracy Act, **2C:21–21**
Toll collection monitoring system, turnpike authority, **27:23–34.1**
Turnpikes, **27:23–4**

P.O.D. account, embezzlement, prepaid funeral agreements, **2A:102–18**

Panel, Comprehensive Child Abuse Prevention and Treatment Act, **9:6–8.84**

Parent,
Abuse of children, **9:6–8.21**
Custody, interference, **2C:13–4**
Indigent, neglected or abandoned children, **9:6–2**
Interference with custody, **2C:13–4**
Kidnapping, **2C:13–1**

Parent or guardian, Comprehensive Child Abuse Prevention and Treatment Act, **9:6–8.84**

Park unlawfully, handicapped parking, **39:4–207.6**

Parking, traffic regulations, **39:1–1**

Parking facility, turnpikes, **27:23–4**

Parking offenses, **39:4–139.3**

Parking ticket, **39:4–139.3**

Parole, escape, **2C:29–5**

Participate in the illegal marketing of controlled dangerous substances, **2C:35B–3**

Partnership, code of ethics, **Rule 1:14**

Party line, telephone, refusal to yield in emergency, **2C:40–2**

Party official, bribery and corrupt influence, **2C:27–1**

Party state, interstate compacts, crimes and offenses, **53:1–32**

Passenger automobile,
Seat belts, **39:3–76.2f**
Traffic regulations, **39:1–1**

Pathological intoxication, Code of Criminal Justice, **2C:2–8**

Patient,
Physician privilege, **2A:84A–22.1**
Privileges and immunities, **Evidence Rule 506**

Pattern of racketeering activity, **2C:41–1**

Payable on death account, embezzlement, prepaid funeral agreements, **2A:102–18**

Payment card, fraud, scanning, **2C:21–6.1**

Pecuniary benefit, bribery and corrupt influence, **2C:27–1**

Pedestrian,
No fault insurance, **39:6A–2**
Traffic regulations, **39:1–1**

Penalties, municipal courts, **2B:12–23.1**

Period of illegal use, controlled substances, **2C:35B–3**

WORDS AND PHRASES—Cont'd

Periodic inspection, motor vehicle emissions inspection, **39:8–60**

Periodic inspection program, motor vehicle emissions inspection, **39:8–60**

Perjury, **2C:28–1**

Permit, water pollution control, **58:10A–3**

Persistent offenders, extended term of imprisonment, **2C:44–3**

Person having the care, custody and control of any child, indigent, neglected or abandoned children, **9:6–2**

Person with diplomatic immunity, traffic rules and regulations, privileges and immunities, records and recordation, **39:5–53**

Personal identifying information,
Computer related offenses, **2C:20–23**
Theft, **2C:20–1**

Personal information, drivers privacy protection, **39:2–3.3**

Personal injury protection coverage,
Motor vehicle insurance, **39:6A–3.1**
No fault insurance, **39:6A–4**

Personal recognizances, Nonresident Violator Compact, **39:5F–4**

Personalized handguns, **2C:39–1**

Persons,
Adult offender supervision, interstate compacts, **2A:168–27**
Code of Criminal Justice, **2C:1–14**
Commercial motor vehicles, registration, reciprocity, **39:3–6.1**
Controlled dangerous substances, trafficking, injunctions, **2C:35–5.6**
Controlled substances, **2C:35–2, 2C:35B–3, 24:21–2**
Cruelty to animals, **4:22–15**
Drivers licenses, **39:5–30.12**
Drivers privacy protection, **39:2–3.3**
Drivers schools, **39:12–1**
Explosives, **21:1A–129**
Intoxicating liquor law, **33:1–1**
Malt beverages, **33:1–93.14**
Money laundering and illegal investments, **2C:21–24**
Motor vehicle emissions inspection, **39:8–60**
Motor vehicles, **39:1–1**
Certificate of ownership, **39:10–2**
Racketeering activity, **2C:41–1**
Sexually oriented business, **2C:33–12.2**
Shoplifting, **2C:20–11**
Theft, **2C:20–1**
Unsatisfied claim and judgment fund, **39:6–62**
Water pollution control, **58:10A–3**
Wiretapping and electronic surveillance, **2A:156A–2**

Petty disorderly persons offenses, Code of Criminal Justice, **2C:1–4**

Pharmacist, controlled dangerous substances, **24:21–2**

Pharmacy owner, controlled dangerous substances, **24:21–2**

Photo radar, speed regulations, motor vehicles, **39:4–103.1**

Photographs, evidence, **Evidence Rule 1001**

Physically helpless, sexual offenses, **2C:14–1**

Physicians,
Controlled substances, **2C:35–2, 24:21–2**
Privilege communications, **2A:84A–22.1**
Privileges and immunities, **Evidence Rule 506**

Pistol grip, assault firearms, **2C:39–1**

Place, controlled dangerous substances, trafficking, injunctions, **2C:35–5.6**

Place of business, driving schools, **39:12–1**

WORDS AND PHRASES—Cont'd

Place of illegal activity, controlled substances, **2C:35B–3**

Place of participation, controlled substances, dealers, liability, **2C:35B–3**

Plant, controlled substances, **2C:35–2**

Player, gambling, **2C:37–1**

Pneumatic tires, motor vehicles, **39:1–1**

Point of interception, wiretapping and electronic surveillance, **2A:156A–2**

Point source, water pollution control, **58:10A–3**

Pole trailer, motor vehicles, **39:1–1**

Police, fire or emergency medical communication system, **2C:33–23**

Police officers, Nonresident Violator Compact, **39:5F–4**

Policy, gambling, **2C:37–1**

Pollutant, water pollution control, **58:10A–3**

Pooled trust, embezzlement, prepaid funeral agreements, **2A:102–18**

Poppy straw, controlled dangerous substances, **2C:35–2, 24:21–2**

Portable oil burning heating device, **2C:40–6**

Positive identification, interstate compacts, criminal history record information, **53:1–32**

Possession, Code of Criminal Justice, **2C:2–1**

Practitioners,
Controlled substances, **2C:35–2**
Health care claims fraud, **2C:21–4.2**
Narcotic drugs, **24:21–2**

Preceding year, apportioned vehicle, registration, **39:3–6.11**

Predominately residential, liquified petroleum gas inspections, **21:1B–3**

Premises, intoxicating liquor law, **33:1–1**

Premises of store or retail mercantile establishment, shoplifting, **2C:20–11**

Preneed funeral arrangements, embezzlement, prepaid funeral agreements, **2A:102–18**

Prepaid funeral agreements, embezzlement, **2A:102–18**

Prepaid funeral goods, embezzlement, prepaid funeral agreements, **2A:102–18**

Prepaid funeral services, embezzlement, prepaid funeral agreements, **2A:102–18**

Prescription legend drug, **2C:35–2**
Controlled dangerous substances, **2C:35–2**

Presenter, attorneys, discipline, **Rule 1:20**

Press association,
News personnel privilege, **2A:84A–21a**
Newspersons privilege, **Evidence Rule 508**
Privileged communications, **2A:84A–21a**

Presumption, **2C:1–13**

Pretreatment standards, water pollution control, **58:10A–3**

Prior conviction, **2C:44–4**

Private road,
Speed bumps, municipalities, highways and roads, **39:4–8.9**
Traffic rules and regulations, **39:4–8.9**

Private road open to the public, public private intersections, **39:4–120.5**

Private road or driveway, traffic regulations, **39:1–1**

Probable cause, controlled dangerous substances, administrative inspection warrants, **24:21–32**

Processing criminal history record background checks, **53:1–20.5**

Product, intoxicating liquors, Class A licenses, **33:1–10**

Production, controlled dangerous substances, **2C:35–2, 24:21–2**

Production models, personalized handguns, **2C:58–2.3**

WORDS AND PHRASES—Cont'd

Professional criminal, extended term of imprisonment, **2C:44–3**

Professional employment, health care professionals, solicitation, disasters or accidents, **2C:40A–4**

Professional fund raisers, terrorism, **2C:38–5**

Prohibited sexual act, endangering welfare of children, **2C:24–4**

Projects, alcoholic beverages, **33:1–24.2**

Promoting gambling, **2C:37–2**

Promoting prostitution, **2C:34–1**

Propellants, explosives, **21:1A–129**

Proper itemized computer generated receipt, motor vehicles, fines and penalties, **39:5–45**

Proper itemized manual receipt, motor vehicles, fines and penalties, **39:5–45**

Properly registered, commercial vehicles, reciprocity, registration, **39:3–6.1**

Property,
Criminal procedure, **2A:152–1**
Money laundering and illegal investments, **2C:21–24**
Theft, **2C:20–1**

Property of another, theft, **2C:20–1**

Prosecuting attorney, limited criminal jurisdiction, courts of, appeals, **Rule 3:23–9**

Prosecutor, criminal procedure, **2A:152–1**

Prostitution, **2C:34–1**

Provider,
Embezzlement, prepaid funeral agreements, **2A:102–18**
Health and accident insurance, runners, **2C:21–22.1**
No fault insurance, **39:6A–2**

Public, disorderly conduct, **2C:33–2**

Public building, controlled substances, crimes and offenses, **2C:35–7.1**

Public conveyance, explosives, **21:1A–129**

Public employment, conviction of crime, disabilities, labor and employment, **2A:168A–7**

Public highway,
Traffic regulations, commissioner of transportation, **39:4–8.2**
Turnpikes, **27:23–4**

Public housing facility, controlled substances, crimes and offenses, **2C:35–7.1**

Public lands,
Offroad vehicles, **39:3C–32**
Snowmobiles, all terrain vehicles, **39:3C–1**

Public media, health and accident insurance, runners, **2C:21–22.1**

Public official, hearsay evidence, **Evidence Rule 801**

Public parks, controlled dangerous substances, crimes and offenses, **2C:35–7.1**

Public place,
Loitering, **2C:33–2.1**
Loitering for the purpose of engaging in prostitution, **2C:34–1.1**

Public private intersection, **39:4–120.5**

Public resource, bribery and corruption, **2C:27–12**

Public servant, bribery and corrupt influence, **2C:27–1**

Publicly communicate, obscene material, **2C:34–4**

Purchase, motor vehicles, **39:10–2**

Purchaser,
Embezzlement, prepaid funeral agreements, **2A:102–18**
Motor vehicles, **39:10–2**

Purging, court records, **Rule 1:32–2**

Purposely, Code of Criminal Justice, **2C:2–2**

WORDS AND PHRASES—Cont'd

Qualified offenders, conviction of crime, disabilities, labor and employment, **2A:168A–7**

Qualified person,
Unsatisfied claim and judgment fund, **39:6–62**
Unsatisfied claim and judgment fund board, **39:6–62**

Qualified supervising instructor, drivers schools, **39:12–2**

Qualifying development project, alcoholic beverages, licenses and permits, **33:1–12.49**

Racketeering activity, **2C:41–1**

Radio transmission of energy, licenses and permits, **2C:33–23.1**

Railroad, fireworks, **21:2–2**

Railroad train, traffic regulations, **39:1–1**

Railway, explosives, **21:1A–129**

Real property, turnpikes, **27:23–4**

Reasonable belief, Code of Criminal Justice, **2C:1–14**

Reasonable efforts, abuse of children, **9:6–8.84**

Reasonably believes, Code of Criminal Justice, **2C:1–14**

Receiving,
Credit card offenses, **2C:21–6**
Receiving stolen property, **2C:20–7**

Receiving states,
Detainers, **2A:159A–2**
Probation and parole, **2A:168–19**

Reciprocity, apportioned vehicle, registration, **39:3–6.11**

Reciprocity agreement, apportioned vehicle, registration, **39:3–6.11**

Recklessly, Code of Criminal Justice, **2C:2–2**

Recklessness, Code of Criminal Justice, **2C:2–2**

Recorded images, traffic signs and signals, monitoring, **39:4–8.13**

Recreation vehicles,
Commercial Driver License Act, **39:3–10.11**
Traffic laws, **39:1–1**

Recreational property, destruction by motor vehicle, penalty points system, **39:5–30.5a**

Recycling vehicle, vehicle size and weight limits, **39:3–84**

Reencoders, credit cards, fraud, **2C:21–6.1**

Reflector, motor vehicles, **39:3–46**

Reformative services, controlled substances, fines and penalties, **2C:35–15**

Registrant, apportioned vehicle, registration, **39:3–6.11**

Registration, commercial motor vehicles, **39:3–20**

Registration year, apportioned vehicle, registration, **39:3–6.11**

Relevant evidence, **Evidence Rule 401**

Remote computing service, wiretapping and electronic surveillance, **2A:156A–2**

Renunciation of criminal purpose, **2C:5–1**

Repeatedly, stalking, **2C:12–10**

Repetitive disorderly persons offenses, juvenile justice, **2A:4A–22**

Representative vehicle, Commercial Driver License Act, **39:3–10.11**

Reproduction, endangering welfare of child, pornography, **2C:24–4**

Research facility, Code of Criminal Justice, **2C:1–14**

Residence district, motor vehicles, **39:1–1**

Resident person, intoxicating liquors, **33:1–11.2**

Residential treatment facility, controlled dangerous substances, **2C:35–2**

Respondent, attorneys, discipline, **Rule 1:20**

Restaurant, intoxicating liquor, **33:1–1**